SUPREME VIGILANCE.

SUPREME VISION.

Dawn. A pilot approaches the confines of one of the world's most sophisticated combat aircraft. He is ready to resume his role in the front line of his country's defence.

He is the watchful eyes of a nation.

A supreme responsibility that demands the supreme vision of Pilkington Optronics – manufacturers of the most advanced head-up display optics, forward looking infra-red and thermal imaging systems for helicopters and fixed wing aircraft.

The far-seeing air forces of tomorrow.

PILKINGTON
OPTRONICS

Pilkington P.E. Limited
Glascoed Road, St. Asaph, Clwyd LL17 0LL. U.K.
Telephone (0745) 588000
Telex: 61430 Pilks G. Fax: (0745) 584258
Barr & Stroud Limited
Caxton Street, Anniesland, Glasgow G13 1HZ. U.K.
Telephone: 041-954 9601
Telex: 778114 Fax: 041-954 2380

AERMACCHI
the technology of ideas

PUBBLIAERMACCHI 91

At the forefront in aircraft design and production, Aermacchi has shown a constant and exceptional ability to interpret contemporary needs through a continual effort aimed at preserving and developing its design capabilities. This traditional competence has originated from a solid research structure allowing Aermacchi to maintain a leading position in the aeronautical field collaborating on the most significant domestic and international military programmes: MB-339, AMX, TORNADO, EFA, PTS 2000 and on those of the civil aviation sector: DO 328 with Dornier; MD 11, Airbus, DC 8 Cargo and ATR 42 through its associate company, Sicamb.

JANE'S
ALL THE WORLD'S
AIRCRAFT

EIGHTY-SECOND YEAR OF ISSUE

EDITOR-IN-CHIEF: Mark Lambert
DEPUTY EDITOR: Kenneth Munson
ASSISTANT EDITOR: Michael J H Taylor

EDITOR EMERITUS: John W R Taylor OBE

1991-92

ISBN 0 7106 0965 5
JANE'S DEFENCE DATA
"Jane's" is a registered trade mark

In the USA and its dependencies
Jane's Information Group Inc, 1340 Braddock Place, Suite 300, Alexandria VA 22314-1651, USA

Printed and bound in Great Britain by Butler & Tanner Ltd, Frome and London.

CONTENTS

This Edition has been compiled by:

Mark Lambert   AIRCRAFT SECTION: GERMANY, ITALY

Kenneth Munson   AIRCRAFT SECTION: ARGENTINA TO FINLAND, GREECE TO ISRAEL, JAPAN TO TURKEY; LIGHTER THAN AIR

Paul Jackson   AIRCRAFT SECTION: FRANCE, UNITED KINGDOM, UNITED STATES OF AMERICA (MILITARY AIRCRAFT), YUGOSLAVIA

John Cook   AIRCRAFT SECTION: FRANCE, UNITED KINGDOM, UNITED STATES OF AMERICA (CIVIL AIRCRAFT)

John Taylor   AIRCRAFT SECTION: UNION OF SOVIET SOCIALIST REPUBLICS

Michael Taylor   SPORT AIRCRAFT; MICROLIGHTS; SAILPLANES; HANG GLIDERS; METRIC CONVERSIONS

Bill Gunston   AERO ENGINES; GLOSSARY

Alphabetical list of advertisers

ALENIA.
WE KNOW THE SECRETS OF FLIGHT.

ALENIA AERONAUTICS. We design and manufacture aircraft, engines and

aeronautical systems. We modify and overhaul defense and commercial

aircraft and participate in the most advanced international cooperation

programs. Alenia is Italy's leading company in aeronautics, electronics

and space technology. Alenia. Sharing with man the secrets of flight.

Because at Alenia, tomorrow's

knowledge is already at work.

G R U P P O   I R I   F I N M E C C A N I C A

Classified list of advertisers

The companies listed advertising in this publication have informed us that they are involved in the fields of manufacture indicated below

Accelerometers and gyroscopes
Allied Signal

Accessories
Armtec Industries

Actuators, electric
Allied Signal
FIAT CIEI - Division Marelli Avio

Actuators, hydraulic
Allied Signal
FIAT CIEI - Division Marelli Avio

Advisory and consultants service
Short Brothers

Aero engine controls and accessories
Allied Signal
FIAT CIEI - Division Marelli Avio

Aero-engine test plant
Central Engineering

Aero-engines
Allied Signal

Aeronautical engineers & consultants
Short Brothers

Airbourne acoustic & magnetic mine
Allied Signal

Airbourne surveillance drone systems
FR Group
Kaman Aerospace

Air compressors (cabin and engine starting)
Allied Signal

Air conditioning equipment
Allied Signal

Air-control equipment for cabins
Allied Signal

Air traffic control equipment
Allied Signal

Aircraft, ambulance
Agusta

Aircraft, combat
AMX
Short Brothers

Aircraft, commercial
Aermacchi
Agusta
Lake Aircraft
Short Brothers

Aircraft, commercial trainers
Agusta
Lake Aircraft

Aircraft, construction
Agusta
Lake Aircraft

Aircraft, executive
Agusta

Aircraft, military
Aermacchi
Agusta
Lake Aircraft
Short Brothers

Aircraft, naval
Agusta
Lake Aircraft

Aircraft, private
Agusta
Lake Aircraft

Aircraft, radio controlled
FR Group

Aircraft, training
Aermacchi
Agusta
Lake Aircraft
Short Brothers

Aircraft, transport
Agusta
Short Brothers

Aircraft, v/stol
Lake Aircraft
Short Brothers

Aircraft construction
Short Brothers

Aircraft developments
Short Brothers

Aircraft field operations and support
Lake Aircraft
Short Brothers

Aircraft modifications
FR Group

Aircraft product support
Aermacchi
Short Brothers

Airframes
Short Brothers

Airport ground handling equipment
Aermacchi
Allied Signal
FR Group

Ailerons
Short Brothers

Airspeed indications
Allied Signal

Air traffic control equipment
Allied Signal
FIAR

Aircraft jewellery
The Clivedon Collection

Aircraft models
The Clivedon Collection

Air traffic control systems, civilian & military
FIAT CIEI - Division Marelli Avio

Alternators
Allied Signal
Fiat C.I.E.I - Divisione Marelli Avio

Amplifiers
Allied Signal

Antennas, aircraft
Allied Signal
FR Group

Antennas
Allied Signal
FR Group

ASW
Allied Signal
Kaman Aerospace

Automatic digital data equipment
Allied Signal
Central Engineering

Automatic pilot
Allied Signal

Automatic voltage and current regulators
Allied Signal
FIAT CIEI - Division Marelli Avio

Auxiliary power plants
Allied Signal

Avionic systems
Agusta
Allied Signal
FIAT CIEI - Division Marelli Avio
FIAR

ONLY GOODYEAR HAS THREE FLIGHTS THAT COVER THE WORLD.

FLIGHT CUSTOM II
General Aviation

FLIGHT EAGLE
Business Jet

FLIGHT LEADER
Commercial Aviation

It makes no difference whether it's North or South America, Europe, Africa, Asia, or Australia. Because anywhere in the world that you'll find aircraft, you'll find Goodyear Aircraft tyres.

Only Goodyear produces aircraft tyres and retreads at 20 plants worldwide. And when you add worldwide availability to Goodyear's outstanding record of prompt supply and service, that's good news. Whether you manufacture airplanes, fly for fun, or fly for a living.

Flight Custom II for general aviation. Flight Eagle for business jets. Flight Leader for commercial aviation. Goodyear's three Flights that cover the world.

And whatever your aircraft, wherever your destination, they're ready whenever you need them.

For more information, please contact: Air Treads, A Division of Goodyear Great Britain Limited.
Tel: 081-759 1922

FIRST IN AIRCRAFT TYRES, RETREADS, WHEEL AND BRAKE SERVICES

Badges
The Clivedon Collection

Brakes for aircraft
Allied Signal

Brakes for aircraft repair & Overhaul
Airtreads

Carbon fibre components
FR Group
Short Brothers

Cabin pressure control systems
Allied Signal

Coating, erosion resistant
Barr & Stroud
Pilkington Optronics
Pilkington P.E.

Combat command & control
Allied Signal

Combustion systems (gas turbine)
Fiat Aviazione

Communications control systems
Allied Signal

Components
Allied Signal
FR Group
Short Brothers

Composite structures
FR Group
Short Brothers

Computers
Allied Signal

Computers, aerodynamic analogue and digital
Allied Signal

Connectors, connector accessories
Allied Signal

Control equipment for aircraft
Allied Signal

Controls, cockpit
Allied Signal

Controls, main engine fuel
Allied Signal

Conversions, aircraft and equipment
FR Group

Corporate gifts
The Clivedon Collection

Couplings
Allied Signal
FR Group

Cryogenic equipment
FR Group

Data links
Allied Signal
Kaman Aerospace
Short Brothers

Data processing equipment
Allied Signal

DC generators
Allied Signal
FIAT CIEI - Division Marelli Avio

DC motors
Allied Signal
FIAT CIEI - Division Marelli Avio

Defence contractors
Allied Signal
FR Group
Kaman Aerospace
Short Brothers

De-icing equipment
Allied Signal

Desktop aluminium model planes
Fomaer

Design services
Kaman Aerospace
Short Brothers

Display systems
Allied Signal
FIAR

Displays in cockpit
Agusta
Allied Signal
FIAR

Drive shafts
Kaman Aerospace

Drones
FR Group
Kaman Aerospace
Short Brothers

Electrical equipment
Agusta
Allied Signal
FIAT CIEI - Division Marelli Avio

Electrical equipment and components
Allied Signal

Electrical solenoids and relays
Allied Signal
FR Group

Electro-optical systems
Allied Signal
Short Brothers

Electronic countermeasures (ECM)
FR Group

Electronic equipment
Allied Signal

Electronic flight controls
Allied Signal
Kaman Aerospace

Electronic fuel control systems
Allied Signal
FR Group

Electronic map systems
Allied Signal

Electronics & guidance
Allied Signal
Short Brothers

Engine design & manufacture
Allied Signal
Fiat Aviazione

Engine parts fabrication
Allied Signal
Fiat Aviazione
Short Brothers

Engine run-up facilities - mobile
Central Engineering

Engine starting equipment
Allied Signal

Engine testing equipment
Allied Signal
Central Engineering

Engines, aircraft
Allied Signal

Engines, auxiliary
Allied Signal

Environmental control systems
Allied Signal

Experimental assemblies
Short Brothers

Fibre optics
Agusta
Allied Signal

Filters, air/liquid
Allied Signal

Filters, electronic
Allied Signal

Filters - fuel and oil
Allied Signal
FR Group

Filters hydraulic
Allied Signal

Fire suppresion systems
Armtec Industries

Flight instrument test sets
Allied Signal

AIRBORNE SELF PROTECTION EW

Success in airborne operations largely depends on the ability to overcome the adversary's offensive capability.
This is why self protection, based on threat warning receivers and deception jammers - internally installed or pod contained - constitute the cost effective ingredient of mission success. ELETTRONICA, with thirty years' experience in airborne EW, produces a full range of Self Protection EW suites meeting present and future operational requirements.

ELETTRONICA - THE EW PEOPLE

ELETTRONICA S.p.A. Via Tiburtina Km 13.700 ROME - ITALY

Flir systems
Barr & Stroud
Pilkington Optronics
Pilkington P.E.

Flow gauges
FR Group

Fuel flow proportioners
FR Group

Fuel pipes
FR Group

Fuel systems
FR Group

Fuel systems and refuelling equipment
FR Group

Fuelling equipment - airborne
FR Group

Fuelling equipment - ground
FR Group

Gas turbine starting systems
Allied Signal
FIAT CIEI - Division Marelli Avio

Gas turbines
Fiat Aviazione

Generators
Aermacchi
Allied Signal
FIAT CIEI - Division Marelli Avio

Ground support equipment
Aermacchi
Allied Signal
Central Engineering

Guided missiles
Short Brothers

Guided weapon control and equipment
Allied Signal
Short Brothers

Helicopter parts and components
Agusta
Allied Signal
Fiat Aviazione
FR Group
Kaman Aerospace

Helicopter stabilisation
Kaman Aerospace

Helicopter surface-to-air refuelling equipment
FR Group

Helicopter support
Kaman Aerospace

Helicopter training and support
Agusta

Helicopter, ambulances
Agusta

Helicopter, commercial-executive
Agusta

Helicopters, military-naval
Agusta
Kaman Aerospace

High pressure couplings
Allied Signal

Hydraulic actuation systems
Allied Signal

Hydraulic control/systems
Allied Signal

Hydraulic equipment
Allied Signal

Hydraulic pressure pumps
Allied Signal

Intertial navigation & cockpit systems
Allied Signal

Infra-red
FR Group

Infra-red equipment
Barr & Stroud
Pilkington Optronics
Pilkington P.E.

Infra-red materials
Barr & Stroud
Pilkington Optronics
Pilkington P.E.

Infra-red systems
FIAR

Instruments, accessories
Allied Signal

Instruments, aircraft
Agusta
Allied Signal
Armtec Industries
FR Group

Instruments, navigational
Agusta
Allied Signal

Instruments - test equipment
Central Engineering

Jet engine parts
Allied Signal

Jet engine test part
Allied Signal

Jet fuel starters
Allied Signal

Jet propulsion engines
Allied Signal

Jet trainer, military
Aermacchi

Kevlat components
Short Brothers

Landing gear
Allied Signal

Lasers
Allied Signal

Linear actuators
FIAT CIEI - Division Marelli Avio

Low light level TV systems
FIAR

Maintenance and overhaul-airframe
Agusta
Allied Signal
Short Brothers

Maintenance and overhaul-avionics
Allied Signal

Maintenance and overhaul-electrical equipment
Agusta
Allied Signal
Fiat Aviazione

Marketing gifts
The Clivedon Collection

Manufacturing services
Short Brothers

Material technology
Short Brothers

Medium lift helicopters
Kaman Aerospace

Military aircraft training
Agusta
Short Brothers

Missile launchers
Short Brothers

Missile optics
Short Brothers
FIAR

Missiles, guided
Short Brothers

Model aircraft
The Clivedon Collection

Model planes in aluminium
Fomaer
The Clivedon Collection

It takes leading-edge innovation to fly.

FiatAvio means aeronautic, marine and space propulsion, and energy production. The most important international aerospace programmes use FiatAvio at every turn – from research to service.

In the defence sector, FiatAvio designs, develops and manufactures mechanical engine components for the latest military aircraft and helicopters. It designs and manufactures auxiliary power units, helicopter transmissions and turbines for marine propulsion which are used by navies throughout the world.

In civil aviation, FiatAvio participates in international programmes to design, develop and manufacture engines for a wide range of commercial aircraft and transmissions for helicopters.

In space propulsion, FiatAvio is designing and manufacturing the turbine-driven liquid oxygen pump that will be used on the Ariane 5 European rocket. It conducts ongoing research on the most sophisticated aspects of the cryogenic and airbreathing engines for the suborbital aircraft of the future.

In energy generators, FiatAvio manufactures gas turbines with outputs ranging from 18 to 130 MW for power generation and other industrial applications, and supplies complete power plants worldwide.

Once its products have been installed, FiatAvio offers the most comprehensive and competitively priced service, from overhauling to technical assistance and logistic support.

FiatAvio S.p.A. - Via Nizza 312 - 10127 Turin
Tel. 011/6931.1 - Fax 011/636385-6931291

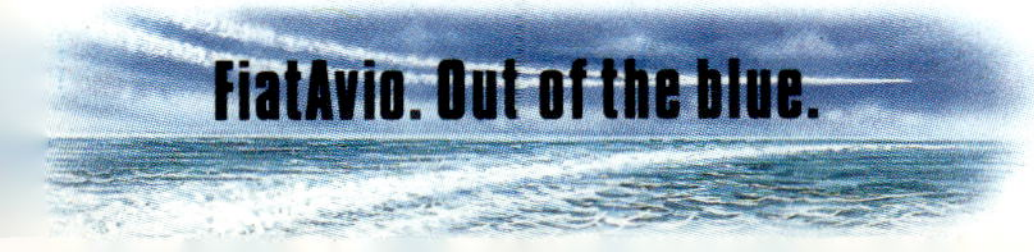

FiatAvio. Out of the blue.

 FiatAvio

Modernisation and conversion, aircraft and equipment modifications
Agusta
FR Group

Motor generators
Allied Signal
FIAT CIEI - Division Marelli Avio

Motors, electric
Allied Signal

Night vision equipment
Allied Signal
Barr & Stroud
Pilkington Optronics
Pilkington P.E.

Oil-hydraulic equipment
Armtec Industries

Optical infared detectors
Armtec Industries

Oxygen breathing apparatus
FR Group

Parts for US built aircraft
Kaman Aerospace
Short Brothers

Patrol aircraft, maritime
Lake Aircraft

Plastic fabrications (reinforced with fibreglass)
FR Group

Pin badges
The Clivedon Collection

Pneumatic actuation systems
Allied Signal

Pneumatic controls
Allied Signal

Pressure regulation valves, fluids and gases
Allied Signal
FR Group

Private planes, civil and military
Lake Aircraft

Pumps, fuel and oil
Allied Signal

Pumps, hydraulic
Allied Signal

Radar processing
FIAR

Radar test sets
FIAR

Radio equipment, ground HF & airbourne HF/VHF
Allied Signal

Radio navigation equipment
Allied Signal

Reconnaissance equipment
Barr & Stroud
Pilkington Optronics
Pilkington P.E.

Reconnaissance, airborne
FR Group
Lake Aircraft

Repair and maintenance of aircraft
Aermacchi
Agusta
Allied Signal
FR Group

Repair and overhaul of aero-engines
Allied Signal

Repair & overhaul of aircraft wheels & brakes
Airtreads

Repair of aircraft instruments
Allied Signal

Rotor parts & components
Kaman Aerospace

RPV electronics
FR Group

RPVs
FR Group
Short Brothers

Satellite navigation
FIAR

Sensors & transducers
Armtec Industries

Sheet metal work
Short Brothers

Simulators
Agusta
Short Brothers

Sonar
Allied Signal
FIAR

Space systems
Kaman Aerospace

Spare parts for US built aircraft
Allied Signal
Kaman Aerospace

Starting systems, airborne
Allied Signal

Storage equipment
FR Group

Support operations
Allied Signal
Short Brothers

Surveillance systems
FR Group
Lake Aircraft

Switches
Allied Signal

Targets, aerial
FR Group
Short Brothers

Target towing winches
FR Group

Test equipment
Aermacchi
Allied Signal
FIAR

Test equipment, aero-engines
Allied Signal
Central Engineering

Test equipment, radar, air data computer, fire control systems, avionics etc
Allied Signal
Armtec Industries

Test equipment airborne radio
Allied Signal

Test facilities
Allied Signal
Central Engineering

Thermal imaging systems
FIAR

Thrust reversers
Allied Signal

Training and simulation
Agusta
FR Group
Short Brothers

Training devices
Agusta
Kaman Aerospace

Troop transport
Short Brothers

Turbofan engines
Allied Signal

Turboprop
Allied Signal
Short Brothers

Tyres for aircraft
Air Treads

Tyres for aircraft new & retreads
Air Treads

A FACE A MOTHER COULD LOVE.

Especially if that mother has been waiting for vital food, medicine and blankets that could save the lives of her earthquake-stricken family.

For over three decades the tough, muscular Hercules airlifter has been taking on every assignment as though that were the one mission for which it was designed.

Besides being a veteran of countless humanitarian missions, the Hercules has proved to be perfect for logistics, country development, maritime patrol, search and rescue, weather reconnaissance, in-flight refueling, even fire fighting.

It may not be the prettiest plane on earth, but to millions, it's the most beautiful.

✈ Lockheed
Aeronautical Systems Company
Giving shape to imagination.

Unmanned aircraft
FR Group
Kaman Aerospace

Valves
Allied Signal

Valves, control hydraulic
Allied Signal

Valves, relief hydraulic
Allied Signal

Voltage and current regulators
Allied Signal

Weapons equipment
Short Brothers

Weapon subsystems
Allied Signal

Wheels for aircraft
Allied Signal
Air Treads

**Wheels for aircraft repair &
overhaul**
Air Treads

Wires & cables, all tyres
Armtec Industries

Goodyear technology.
Air Treads service.

Now under one roof.

To meet the high-tech needs of the 90's, Goodyear Aviation Products proudly announces its merger with Air Treads.

Your Goodyear Aviation Products salesperson is now doing business under the Air Treads name to provide you with a *single* source for commercial aircraft tires, retreads, and wheel and brake service.

With 50 service centers, 5 manufacturing plants and 12 retread plants in 20 cities around the world, our combined strength offers the most complete product and service package available *anywhere.*

It's good business for us.

And good news for you.

A Subsidiary of The Goodyear Tire and Rubber Company

Promote your company with our top-quality miniature scale models and coloured enamel badges — pin badges, tie bars, cufflinks, key rings, desk models. Ideal for advertising gifts, company logos, inflight and shop sales etc. Large range available or made to your designs. Catalogue on request.

Utilisez nos modèles réduits et badges en émail en couleur de haute qualité pour la promotion de votre société — épingles, fixe-cravates, boutons de manchette, porte-clefs, modèles de table. Idéal comme cadeaux de promotion, logo de société, ventes en boutiques et à bord etc. Grade gamme de produits à votre disposition ou fait à vos dessins. Catalogue sur demande.

Werben Sie für Ihre Firma anhanden unserer hochqualitativen maßstabgetreuen Miniaturmodelle und farbigen Emailabzeichen Anstecknadeln, Krawattenclips, Manschettenknöpfe, Schlüsselringe. Schreibtischmodelle. Ideal als Werbegeschen Firmenlogo, An-Bord- und Ladenverkauf. Große Auswahl oder hergestellt nach Ihrem Entwurf. Katalog auf Anfrage.

Witham Friary
Frome, Somerset
BA11 5HH UK
Tel: +44 (0)74 985 728
Fax: +44 (0)74 985 729

THE Clivedon COLLECTION

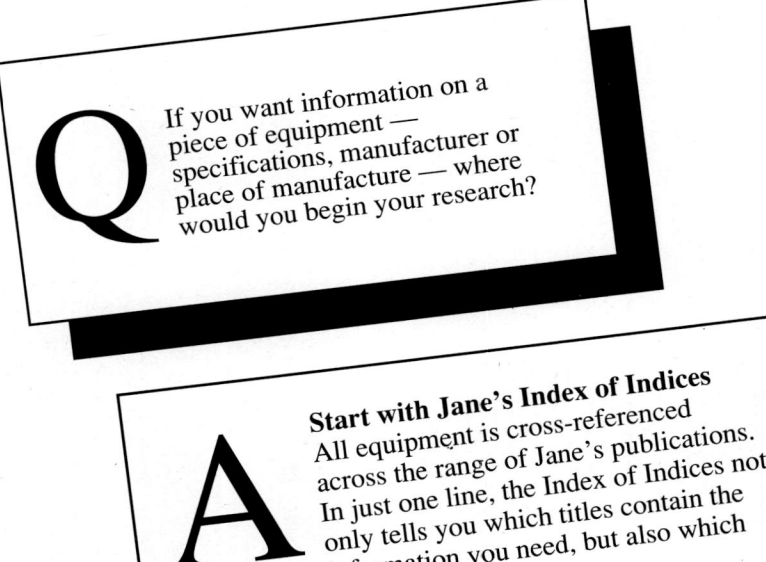

The McDonnell Douglas AH-64 Apache proved to be a potent weapon in the front line and beyond during the Gulf War

Lockheed/Boeing/General Dynamics F-22 will be the first stealthy, supercruising air superiority fighter and establishes Lockheed as one of the future survivors among the US airframe prime contractors

Yakovlev's Yak-141 supersonic VTOL fighter, officially revealed at the 1991 Paris Air Show, already holds several world performance records *(Brian M. Service)*

The MiG-31, seen at the 1991 Paris Air Show, sported a fixed, electronically scanned radar antenna associated with semi-active long-range air-to-air missiles *(Brian M. Service)*

JANE'S ALL THE WORLD'S AIRCRAFT 1991-92

Jane's Information Group, Sentinel House, 163 Brighton Road, Coulsdon, Surrey CR5 2NH, UK
Jane's Information Group Inc, 1340 Braddock Place, Suite 300, Alexandria VA 22314-1651, USA

RETROFIT AND READY FOR ACTION

STANDARD ON THE HAWK 108 & 208 - NOW PROPOSED FOR THE F5E/F UPGRADE

Smiths Industries' retrofit service offers military aircraft a new lease of life with State-of-the-Art Nav/Attack systems.

A whole squadron of current inventory aircraft can now have an enhanced weapon delivery performance for less than the cost of a single new aircraft.

Smiths Industries' retrofit capability goes far beyond simply providing the hardware. By co-ordinating a team of systems engineers, installation specialists, flight test managers and a recertification authority, Smiths Industries provides a complete turnkey service.

Current contracts include up-grades of the F-5E, F-4E and A-4, improving target acquisition, weapon delivery and navigation accuracy, threat warning and survivability, and reconnaissance facilities.

Smiths Industries have earned a reputation for innovation and leadership in many of the World's major advances in systems development. The retrofit service now provides the opportunity to give a new operational life to the aircraft of today with the technology for tomorrow.

Smiths Industries – together we move towards a bigger and better future in Aerospace.

SMITHS INDUSTRIES
Aerospace & Defence Systems

CHELTENHAM, ENGLAND. TEL: 024 267 3333.
GRAND RAPIDS, U.S.A. TEL: (616) 241 7000.

THE LOGICAL CHOICE

FOREWORD: The year of turbulence

BAe Jaguars and a Victor tanker, all in desert camouflage, fly a refuelling exercise during preparations for the Gulf War
(Crown Copyright)

In the last edition of this book, I described the year gone by as one of reorientation. The aerospace world needed to adapt quickly to the new east-west relationship emerging from the decline of Communism. I warned that there was still no common basis on which the various aerospace industries could work together under the pressures of *détente* and the economic downturns that were accompanying them. In that, I proved right. But I did not foresee war in the Gulf and the unexpected conflicts when people wanted their freedom 'now', including virtual civil war in Yugoslavia.

War seems close at hand once again, just when the governments are looking with refreshed determination for a peace dividend. The problem for Europe is that the reduced armed forces will have a greater need than ever for the advanced weapons and systems that we have been frittering away in little mud-holes of government indecision. We will have no alternative but to buy American and, who knows, Soviet.

Yet life in the industry goes on. Boeing, Douglas and Airbus seem to agree that the airliner industry will deliver 9,000 new jet airliners during the next 15 years. The regional airlines look like absorbing 2,100 of the medium-sized regional jets (some of which may overlap the 9,000), all in spite of the present economic problems. It is curious but characteristic that the forecasts turn downwards long after the other indices have signalled trouble ahead. At least civil work seems to be offering the successful manufacturers some refuge from the sharp dip in military business.

One of the most alluring prospects of growth, at least in the medium term, still lies in a new east-west relationship. Here, the picture is clearing and the harmonisation of practices and regulations, which I suggested was an essential preliminary, is now being pursued with increasing energy.

It is strange to see the all-powerful, entrenched Soviet defence industrial complex, which was virtually a state within a state, emerging rather hesitantly into the demand-economy world. Whether in defence or trade, it could continue to be the mainspring of the Soviet economy.

Trading deals are multiplying, but the most positive progress seems to be that the USSR has finally been allowed to acquire western civil engines. The most practical step is that western manufacturers have begun to 'buy labour' in the USSR, supplying approved raw materials from which Soviet factories, seemingly idle, produce complete airframes or major components. Two Soviet airliners and one or two helicopters are to be powered by western engines. The American General GA-7 Cougar light business twin and several different sets of components for Dassault Falcons are to be manufactured in the USSR, still using western raw materials. Similarly, Deutsche Airbus is moving assembly work into the former East German repair centres at Dresden and Ludwigsfelde.

In order to begin to operate as demand-economy enterprises, the Soviet, Polish, Czechoslovak, Romanian and Yugoslav industries have been extensively reorganised and given some control over their capital. News of the final Romanian moves reached us so late that the two new company names are only detailed in the Addenda to this edition. The Soviet engine industry is almost unrecognisable from last year and we had to rearrange it completely at page-proof stage.

At the same time, the expected problems are now really biting. Severe shortage of government or private money and hard currency will put a brake on all east-west dealings for a time. Eastern companies are having trouble launching new programmes and are hardly able to contribute investment as distinct from resources of labour and facilities to east-west programmes.

Aeroflot, the world's largest customer, is short of fuel and aircraft, but even shorter of money. The Romanian plan to build the Kamov Ka-126 is held up because Aeroflot has not exercised an option for 1,000 of them and the Soviet industry is being slow to develop the TV-O-100 turboshaft. Polish developments are held up, because manufacture of the M-14 radial engine was transferred to Romania and has not yet started.

Soviet manufacturers have still to overcome the euphoria of freedom and settle down to a more viable set of programmes. The Sukhoi/Gulfstream Supersonic Business Jet is certainly not going to be as easy as some suggested.

JAWA's new look

Because of these events and other factors JAWA has changed more this year than for many years. I would estimate that some 80 per cent of the book has been rewritten, reordered or expanded, compared with the usual 50 to 60 per cent. Those who used to buy one copy to last two years will have to think again.

Our contributors attended the Paris Air Show in June, operating in various specialised capacities as well as for Jane's, and all the significant aircraft information and pictures from that unmissable event were incorporated in the Addenda at the

What keeps RAF jet pilots out in front?

The flying skills of the Royal Air Force are internationally admired. And these days it's the Shorts Tucano that's propelling our young pilots into the jet class.

With the pedigree of the fastest selling turbo-prop trainer in the world, the tandem seat Shorts Tucano combines jet-like performance with low life-cycle costs from a turbo-prop engine.

In fact, it substantially out-performs the Jet Provost trainer it replaces in virtually every respect. Particularly cost.

Chosen by the RAF from the stiffest competition, the Tucano has been tailored by Shorts to meet the rigorous requirements of the Ministry of Defence.

No other Air Force laid down such tough specifications. The Shorts Tucano meets them all.

More and more, Shorts are developing particular strength in fulfilling military contracts.

18 of our C23 Sherpa freighter aircraft are currently in service with the US Air Force. More are on order for the US Army National Guard.

We are acknowledged experts in the area of close air defence weapon systems and are the country's major exporter of missiles.

Our latest Starstreak missile will shortly be added to Britain's defences. Travelling at many times the speed of sound, Starstreak has an awesome degree of reliability and accuracy, that is matched only by its selling potential.

A high performance, high specification trainer aircraft like the Shorts Tucano provides us with yet another chance to show what we can do. Like the RAF, Shorts believe in setting the pace.

SHORTS

SHORT BROTHERS PLC, PO Box 241, Airport Road, Belfast BT3 9DZ, Northern Ireland.

[24]

The MiG-31 (Foxhound A) revealed its singular landing gear and electronically scanned radar at the 1991 Paris Air Show. A drawing of the newer MiG-31M (Foxhound B) appears in the Addenda *(Air Portraits)*

very last moment. The new engine information from Paris, including changes in the organisation of the Soviet industry, were included in the main pages just before they went to press.

Alongside the reorganisation of companies and the exceptional number of new projects, we have this year begun a new format for the main Aircraft section. Following development of the CD-ROM version of the book, now in its third year and which is encased in an extremely powerful quick access database, we have eliminated the unstructured preamble to each aircraft and placed the whole of each entry under subtitles. All information in each entry can therefore be accessed through a set of standard subtitles. The TYPE heading is now at the top and the chronology of a programme, past and future, appears next under PROGRAMME. There are headings for VARIANTS and CUSTOMERS.

For the first time, we introduce a COSTS heading, when costs or prices are announced, we record them in that year's original currency, without

conversions. Also, we have rearranged the former headings of WINGS, FUSELAGE and TAIL UNITS into DESIGN FEATURES, FLYING CONTROLS and STRUCTURE. The objectives of the design and how they were attained come under DESIGN FEATURES. FLYING CONTROLS combines all the moving surfaces and actuating methods as a whole, including flaps, spoilers, leading-edges and so on. In these days of flaperons, tailerons and leading-edge flaps all automated, that is unavoidable. The STRUCTURE heading gives a coherent home to details which have often obscured the other two concepts.

At the same time as we rearranged the data in these sections, which took several man-years of work, we have adopted a very compact, note-form style of writing, which further speeds-up access to information. By doing this, I feel that we are serving both the needs of the CD-ROM database and the 'manual' reader. The vast amount of information in Jane's will now be easier to extract.

We have saved more than 30 pages in the main Aircraft section despite an increase in several

sections, including International Programmes and the inclusion of much more information. But Sport Aircraft has grown considerably and Microlights is augmented by three pages of pictures. The Sailplane section, now more accessibly presented in tabular form, is accompanied by no fewer than 80 pictures.

Unfortunately, it has not been possible to apply the new format throughout the 530 or so pages of the Aircraft section in one annual edition. We choose to do it first in the USSR, UK and USA sections which are continuous in the book, and in the International section, which already contains the most significant European programmes and will, for example, next year receive the combined Aerospatiale and MBB helicopter activities under the banner of Eurocopter International. As it is, the International section is three pages longer this year and contains nine new programmes. The remainder of the Aircraft section will receive the same treatment for next year's edition.

US industry: all change

A year ago, I wrote in these columns that the US aerospace industry might finally be close to the kind of fundamental rationalisation that was imposed on the leading European aerospace industries 20 or more years ago. Curiously, the process has now begun with a vengeance, but in the form of working associations rather than outright takeovers or mergers.

In Europe, the process was imposed by governments and widely discussed or resisted, but those industries have passed on to another process under the stimulus of the European Common Market. During the past five years, cross-frontier alliances have produced a set of international alliances. Instead of one producer per country, there are now several international groups in each sector to compete for programmes which may themselves be international. Competition has actually been restored.

In the USA, the initial process of contraction is now well under way, but in a very different form. The succession of portentous decisions, including 'down-selections' of ATF and LH, and a succession of programme cancellations, including P-7 and A-12 (ATA). The A-X replacing A-12 will hardly be as big a programme. A very narrow escape for the V-22 and the cropping of potentially big programmes like C-17 and B-2 make it clear that over-capacity is really hurting and that some big names may become modest players. LTV, Grumman and Fairchild have already made their peace with the future.

The remarkable fact is that the major programme decisions of early 1991 were taken, according to the selectors themselves, without considering their effect on the companies and therefore on the balance and viability of the industry. Only the quality and plausibility of the proposals counted.

Uncompromising free enterprise is a hardy flower indeed but is it edible or poisonous? Perhaps we in Britain, after 10 years of Thatcherism, have our own feelings on this point but, when free enterprise is taken to its ultimate limit, caveat vendor.

It would be very surprising if the Pentagon were not fully aware of the process and feeling some kind of preferences for the future shape of the industry. But compared with the noisy public and private struggles in Britain, France, Italy, Germany and even Spain from the late 1950s onwards, the process in the USA is almost another manifestation of stealth technology.

The three major decisions in ATF, LH/RAH-66 Comanche and ATA/A-12A Avenger II look like taking at least one major airframe developer out of the prime contractor business. Others will have to struggle to maintain their size and prestige. For Bell Helicopter, the V-22 Osprey programme continues to hover between life and death and LH slipped away to Boeing and Sikorsky.

How can anyone be sure what Bell Helicopter in Texas will become? The company moved most of its civil helicopters away to Canada over the years to make room for Fort Worth for V-22 assembly and there is not a lot of work left in the OH-58D and AH-1 Cobra. This by no means reduces Bell

The Beriev TASTC at Taganrog has joined with Ilta Trade Finance of Geneva to market the Be-200 civil amphibian and would like to join the DASA/Alenia Advanced Amphibious Aircraft venture *(Brian M. Service)*

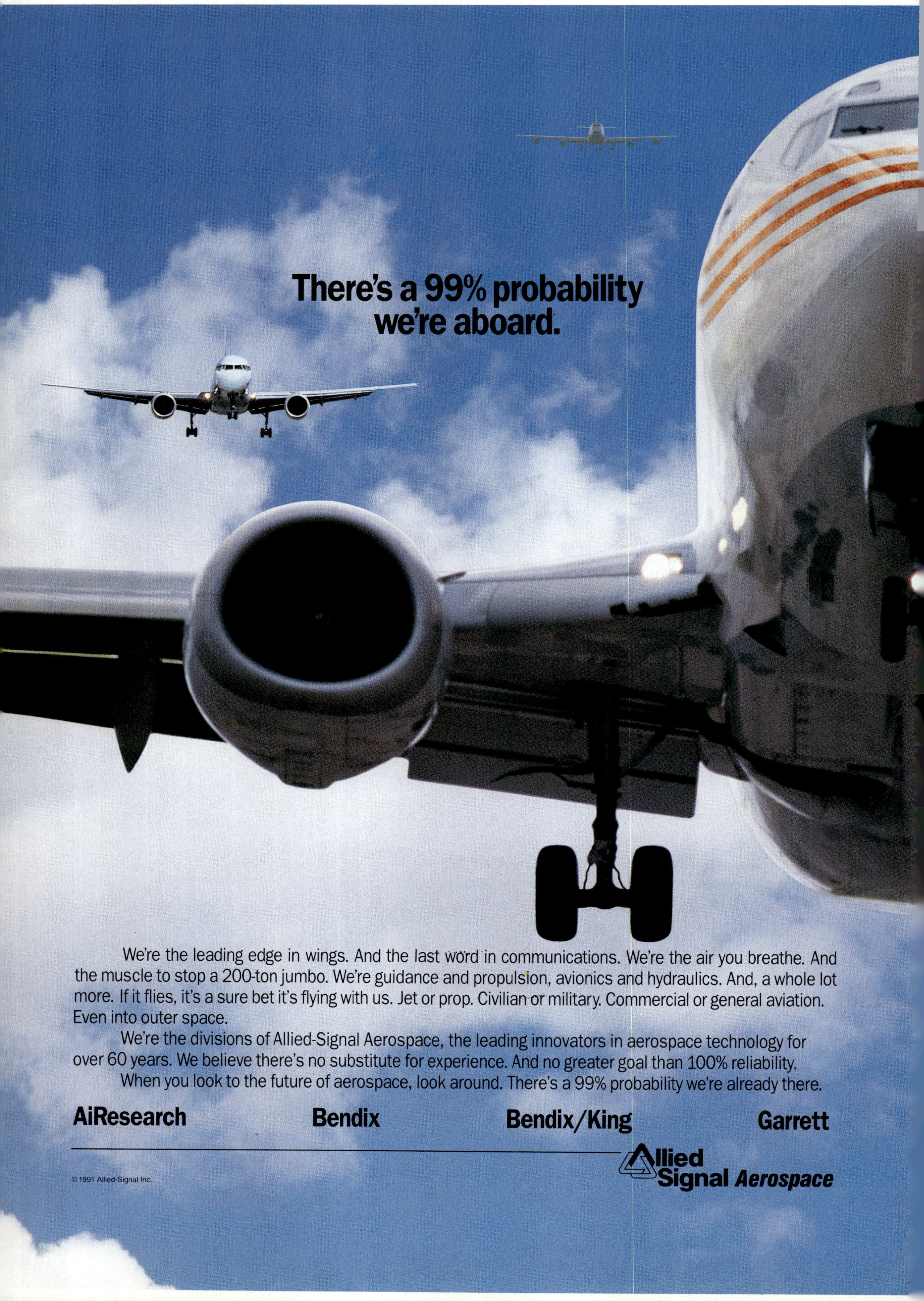

There's a 99% probability we're aboard.

We're the leading edge in wings. And the last word in communications. We're the air you breathe. And the muscle to stop a 200-ton jumbo. We're guidance and propulsion, avionics and hydraulics. And, a whole lot more. If it flies, it's a sure bet it's flying with us. Jet or prop. Civilian or military. Commercial or general aviation. Even into outer space.

We're the divisions of Allied-Signal Aerospace, the leading innovators in aerospace technology for over 60 years. We believe there's no substitute for experience. And no greater goal than 100% reliability.

When you look to the future of aerospace, look around. There's a 99% probability we're already there.

AiResearch   **Bendix**   **Bendix/King**   **Garrett**

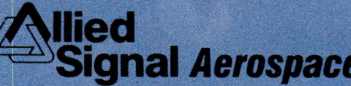

Allied
Signal *Aerospace*

Virtually all the USAF Lockheed F-117 stealth attack aircraft took part in the Gulf War and achieved outstanding results. How long can the stealth aircraft retain its edge?

Helicopter to nothing. The company still manufactures the dynamic components for the Canadian-assembled helicopters and has a large spares business to support thousands of helicopters in service around the world. In addition, the Canadian enterprise is also a member of the parent Textron concern. But will Bell be able to finance a civil tilt-rotor, as it wants to, or an important new civil or military helicopter to start it back on the road to prime contractorship?

McDonnell Douglas Helicopter Company is not so badly placed. The AH-64 has every prospect of continuing as a popular export as well as in its Longbow form for the US Army; and one AH-64 brings in as much revenue as 10 MD 500s. NOTAR is an important practical development for both civil and military helicopters and the eight-seat MDX, first important step towards a family of helicopters such as can save a company's life in hard times, should be able to start earning money before revenue from the AH-64 drops off. The company has done its homework.

MDHC may face the future with some confidence, but what of McDonnell Douglas as a whole? Its survival is not, of course, dependent on aircraft alone, but the situation on the military aircraft side is not bright. The years of total quality upheaval and turmoil at McDonnell Douglas are beginning to subside and revenue flowing from the MD-11 and MD-80/90 lines should give some stability. The C-17 has been downgraded to a realistic performance capability, but still has problems as it moves towards production. Early performance estimates were always extremely optimistic. Loss of ATA and ATF casts a shadow over McDonnell Aircraft, which was already facing the end of both F-15 and F/A-18, unless the F-18E/F replaces the ATA. At least Switzerland has reconfirmed its tiny order for F/A-18s, after Korea switched from F/A-18 to F/16, and Kuwait will take its 40 F/A-18s. Even then, we can probably expect a smaller McDonnell Douglas.

General Dynamics, in which aircraft are not the dominant part of the group, is equally facing the end of the F-16 programme and the loss of the

ATA (in which they were joined with McDonnell Douglas).

In all this, Boeing (airliners, ATF and RAH-66A) and Lockheed (ATF and space/electronics) alone are firmly established as prime aircraft contractors for the future.

The Gulf War
There is a strong feeling that the Gulf War somehow changed the nature of war. But let no-one suppose that the Gulf War was normal enough to be a realistic example for the future. It was brilliantly executed, but it was not new. The only lesson may have been that the advantage has swung towards the attacker.

In the air, a mighty group of air forces crippled a large, but incompetent one. Behind that devastating result lies the fact that Saddam Hussein probably did not value air power very highly. He counted, as he often pronounced, on the mother of battles reserved for his infantry but air power ensured that that never came. That is not new.

The war saw the first use of a fascinating variety of new precision weapons in relatively small numbers. It highlighted the psychological effect of 'junk' weapons like Scud. Medium-sized nations will now spend billions trying to improve the weapon or the counter to it. All that, but not much philosophy. There will be a worldwide hunt for 'naughty' warheads.

We tend to think that never before has air power by itself gone so far towards defeating a large ground army. Yet, I wonder how Desert Storm compares with the bombing campaign, the electronic decoying and the overpowering close air support that preceded and accompanied the Second World War Normandy invasion.

Only seven per cent of the weapons dropped during Desert Storm were 'smart'. Only 300 Tomahawks were launched. Scud B with a conventional warhead is essentially a V-2, of which 2,000 or so failed to reduce London and Antwerp in 1944. A Scud war will never go like this again and Patriot is only the first step on the see-saw progression into the future.

That seven per cent of 'smart' weapons was much nearer 75 per cent than 100 per cent accurate. Dropping laser-guided bombs on target took great skill and co-ordination and might not have been so successful in heavily defended areas. Most of the other 82,000 tons of iron bombs are said to have missed their targets, though the word miss needs to be much more precisely defined to make sense.

The super-precision weapons once again persuaded people that they are potentially an executioner's sword, allowing the forces of justice, whoever they might be at any one time, to exact retribution from one distinct element in a transgressor country. Neither the royal palace nor the republican bunker are safe any longer. But they did not knock out Saddam Hussein's nuclear facilities and there is no reason to suppose that they will in future.

The use of Tomahawk was a daring act of faith that paid off. But it is reported that the tercom guidance was eventually put off by the changes in ground profile caused by destruction of buildings in the target area. Block 3 modifications and the addition of GPS should take care of that.

Very significantly, the attack on two Iraqi radar defence points at the outset of the campaign was made by a force of eight AH-64s and two Chinooks that flew a 15-hour round trip of 950 nm (1,760 km; 1,092 miles) and deployed its own forward area refuelling and rearming point on the way. The US Army (and, in a different war, the USSR) has always made aggressive use of helicopters and other armed forces might finally be encouraged to believe that it is possible. Fresh theories will inevitably be followed by new technical advances. There is plenty of scope for progress in armed helicopters.

AWACS was a central factor in the Gulf War, if only as an air traffic control system to separate the hundreds of military missions under way day and night. Everybody seemed to be asking AWACS for clearance to attack and warning of defences.

The two J-STARS development aircraft did useful work in detecting ground movements. Would they do as well in the face of air

Agustability

EFIM

MEANS AGUSTA'S ABILITY IN THE DEVELOPMENT OF TRAINING SOLUTIONS

SF260, S211 Agusta has defined the essential stages in pilot training. First the SF260, then the S211: two aircraft that best develop the training syllabus and achieve an excellent cost-effectiveness ratio. SF260, fitted with piston or turbine engines for utmost realiability, is the ultimate in primary pilot training, with over 800 units sold all over the world. S211, a turbofan jet-trainer, equipped with pressurized cockpit and 0-0 type ejection seats. Its vanguard avionics systems and exceptional flight performance set this plane as the unrivalled master of basic training. A candidate in the American JPATS program with the Agusta-Grumman joint venture. Besides training aircraft, Agusta develops new solutions that designate it as a leader on the integrated training systems market. Gruppo Agusta: a leading company in the development of its own innovative technologies, participating in the most prestigious international programs, with a global commitment to the service to society.

GRUPPO
AGUSTA

The first EFA airframe is now virtually complete at MBB's flight test centre at Manching. First flight is scheduled for 1992

opposition? Would AWACS? Is the French Orchidée/Horizon approach superior?

Despite all the resources of unmanned air vehicles, satellites and special reconnaissance aircraft, there was a great gap in determining the results of attacks. Some of the laser and TV aiming systems produced their own real-time record, but they were strictly in the minority. After many raids, the attackers had trouble assessing the results.

The United Nations as a world power

One of the very few hopeful aspects of the Gulf War was that the United Nations seemed to have developed the ability to act, to take charge of an international situation and to be deferred to. It would be naive to believe that this was not orchestrated by states with a combination of power, influence and private purpose, but the UN did emerge as a potential world influence. If that resolution and capability continued, it could prove to be the most dramatic move towards true internationalism we have yet seen. Could it be that the UN would both keep the peace and organise international action in disasters and famines? We shall see.

The post-war situation in Iraq and the Yugoslavian war suggest that there is a need for a permanent UN force. If that included air power, what would be its first type of aircraft? Transport, various forms of reconnaissance device or attack aircraft? As long as UN enforcers go into northern Iraq with pistols, we are essentially playing school games.

The quick reaction force out of theatre

Western Europe has realised that it may have to become embroiled in military actions outside the geographical confines of NATO or the EEC. That

is leading to the creation of the out of area quick reaction force and requires a new look at equipment.

The most urgent need in this context is air transport, which is integral with air refuelling. This means long-range heavy transports capable of carrying troops and equipment in large volumes over possibly circuitous routes to virtually anywhere in the world. It should give renewed impulse to the European future large aircraft Euroflag, or adoption of specialised military versions of Airbus airliners or the outright purchase of the McDonnell Douglas C-17, if it lives up to its performance and cost objectives. Could the Guppy Airbus become a military heavy lifter? Is Euroflag more important than the long-range transport?

The next most urgent need is for battle damage assessment and reconnaissance. This requires the leading-edge of technology, a complete spectrum of vehicles from satellites to high-precision battlefield surveillance systems such as J-STARS and small unmanned vehicles. NATO has a powerful fleet of AWACS, should it also have a long-endurance, self-deploying J-STARS? In many of these capabilities, Europe is amazingly deficient, the USA relatively well provided. Britain and France even cancelled or frittered away the projects they had, with the apparent exception of Orchidée/Horizon. Europe is as ever unwilling to spend the necessary money and the US industry is ready to supply and hungry for new markets.

Finally, the intervention force will need mobility over the ground, which means plenty of helicopters for transport of troops and equipment, fire support, evacuation and special forces operations. Europe as a whole has never managed to agree on a common battlefield helicopter. The Eurocopter Tiger is only a narrow-fronted step in the right direction and the French and British armed helicopters in the Gulf hardly made outstanding

contributions. The common transport helicopter, the NH 90, is still vulnerable.

The transport force should be able to airlift most of a brigade in one move and to mount a long-range penetration operation. That means greater speed and longer endurance than the helicopter normally offers, which means tilt-rotor or tilt-wing or some vehicle like the Rutan Advanced Technology Tactical Transport or Sukhoi S-80. Who remembers the Breguet 941 blown-flap transport? Just when the Bell/Boeing V-22 Osprey is being squeezed almost to extinction, Europe may have a vital need for a simpler, more efficient aircraft to do that kind of job.

One is forced to the conclusion that Europe will continue to buy all kinds of military aircraft from the USA. There is only one exception, the Eurofighter, haloed with doubt though it be. That could be the strongest and most bitter message for European aerospace to emerge from the Gulf War.

Commuter airliners

A major new market has been recognised. Naturally, too many contestants have come forward. The Paris Air Show revealed some new surprises. MPC-75 has been merged with the DAA 91/122, but Fokker will persist with its Fokker 80 and 130, as will BAe with the 146 NRA. Boeing is already there with the 737-500 and McDonnell Douglas announced the MD-95 at the Paris Air Show in June 1991. The Airbus A319 seems closer to launch, but cannot be shrunk to carry fewer than 130 passengers. Most surprisingly, CASA launched its own new fast turboprop. Embraer is hit by financial problems and the EMB 145 must be under threat.

The commuter/regional airliner will never catch on completely with the public until it offers the same comfort and cabin noise environment as the

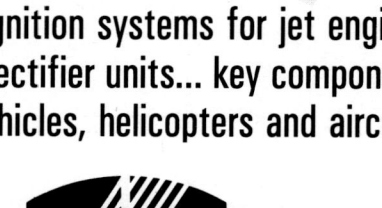
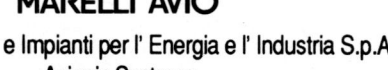
[30]

The DASA/Aerospatiale/Alenia DAA 92/122 projects for 90- and 120-passenger regional airliners replaced the German/Chinese MPC-75 during 1991 and the marketing of all three companies' regional airliners is centralised at Toulouse

A major step for Europe's helicopter industry in 1991 is the formation of Eurocopter SA and Eurocopter International to combine Aerospatiale (here the new AS532 U2 Cougar) and MBB helicopters under common management and marketing companies

formula. ARES, AT³ and Pond Racer are far more practical applications. Voyager was truly epoch-making, though in human rather than aeronautical terms.

Acknowledgements

The compilation of *Jane's All the World's Aircraft* will never be a one-man band, although the editor acts like conductor in aiming at a given result.

Six most experienced compilers collect, collate and present the vast assembly of facts and figures from the widest variety of sources, but always checked against manufacturers' basic information. Deputy Editor Ken Munson compiles the disparate and diverse countries ranging through the alphabet from Argentina to Turkey, and the International section. He also compiles the Lighter than Air section. Assistant Editor Michael Taylor compiles Sport Aircraft, Sailplanes, Microlights and Hang Gliders and applies the thousands of conversions between metric and pound-inch systems. Between them, Ken and Michael handle the immense and critical sub-editing and final page-proof reading load for the whole book.

Paul Jackson is our military aircraft expert and covers the military sections of the USA, UK and France. Mike Jerram, who used to cover the civil sections of those countries, decided to concentrate on other interests and his place has been taken this year by John Cook. My hard-to-follow predecessor, Editor Emeritus John Taylor OBE, continues to contribute his unique knowledge of the USSR and the incomparable Bill Gunston tracks the world's aero engines.

The special three-view drawings, in which we pride ourselves, are still drawn by Dennis Punnett of Pilot Press (Greenborough Associates) and by Mike Keep. They often have to work from minimal references. Maurice Allward compiles our 10-year index so expertly that he is another valued long-stop in the compilation and cross-checking process.

Supporting us all is a network of hawk-eyed contributors of material and pictures, but particularly a group of the kind of aviation observer who pops up everywhere and records what is actually happening. Many of them prefer to stay out of the limelight. Those we are happy to credit in this issue include Andrea Artoni of Volare, the Avio Data team, Peter Bowers, Piotr Butowski, Peter J. Cooper, David Davies of Air Portraits, Artur Demek of Aerosvet, Roland Eichenberger, John Fricker, R. Nelson Fuller, Lutz Freundt, Andrzej Glass, Mike Gradidge, Geoffrey P. Jones, Vaclav Jukl, Howard Levy, Ryszard Jaxa-Malachowski, Jacques Marmain of Aviation International, Peter Selinger, Brian and Margaret Service, Ivo Sturzenegger and Lech Zielaskowski.

All this would come to nothing without the Jane's in-house production team who see the book to press. Queen Bee Ruth Simmance who runs the whole annual production cycle and just happens to admire the A-10A Warthog; Lynn Morse, who organises all the illustrations, reads all the pages and finds misprints we have all missed; Sarah Erskine and Christine Varndell who keyboard and typeset the whole weighty tome with incredible accuracy; Chrissie Richards who is the link-person with the printers and knows what we should all be doing and how at any one time; Jack Brenchley, Keith Biller and Gary Hornett at Method Ltd, who make up the pages and survive in spite of us all. With the right people, life can be fun.

The big white chiefs in all this are Keith Faulkner, who keeps us all on the rails, and Publishing Director Bob Hutchinson, who thumps the table very constructively.

As I said, *Jane's* is not a one-man band.

Coulsdon, July 1991　　　　　**Mark Lambert**

average airliner. That puts the turboprop out of the running for the long-term future – unless the devices now becoming available prove fully practical. Anti-sound and anti-vibration, as shown by Dowty at the Paris Air Show, might make the turboprop feel like a jet. That would radically change the economics of the situation.

Amateurisation of private aviation

How are the mighty fallen. This year's edition records the near-demise of Piper, and lists all the light aircraft that neither Piper, Cessna nor Beech manufacture any longer. At the same time, small new-start enterprises have relaunched manufacture of Taylorcraft, Helio, American General, Rockwell and other types. The market has also passed to the kit manufacturer who can prove that fractionally over 50 per cent of the manufacturing was done by the customer. When will the fateful problem of product liability raise its head here too?

To an extent under the stimulus of Rutan, composites are steadily taking over the light aircraft business. Yet Rutan did the professional aircraft world no great service with the foreplane, tipsail, propeller-in-the-wake and fuel-in-the-middle

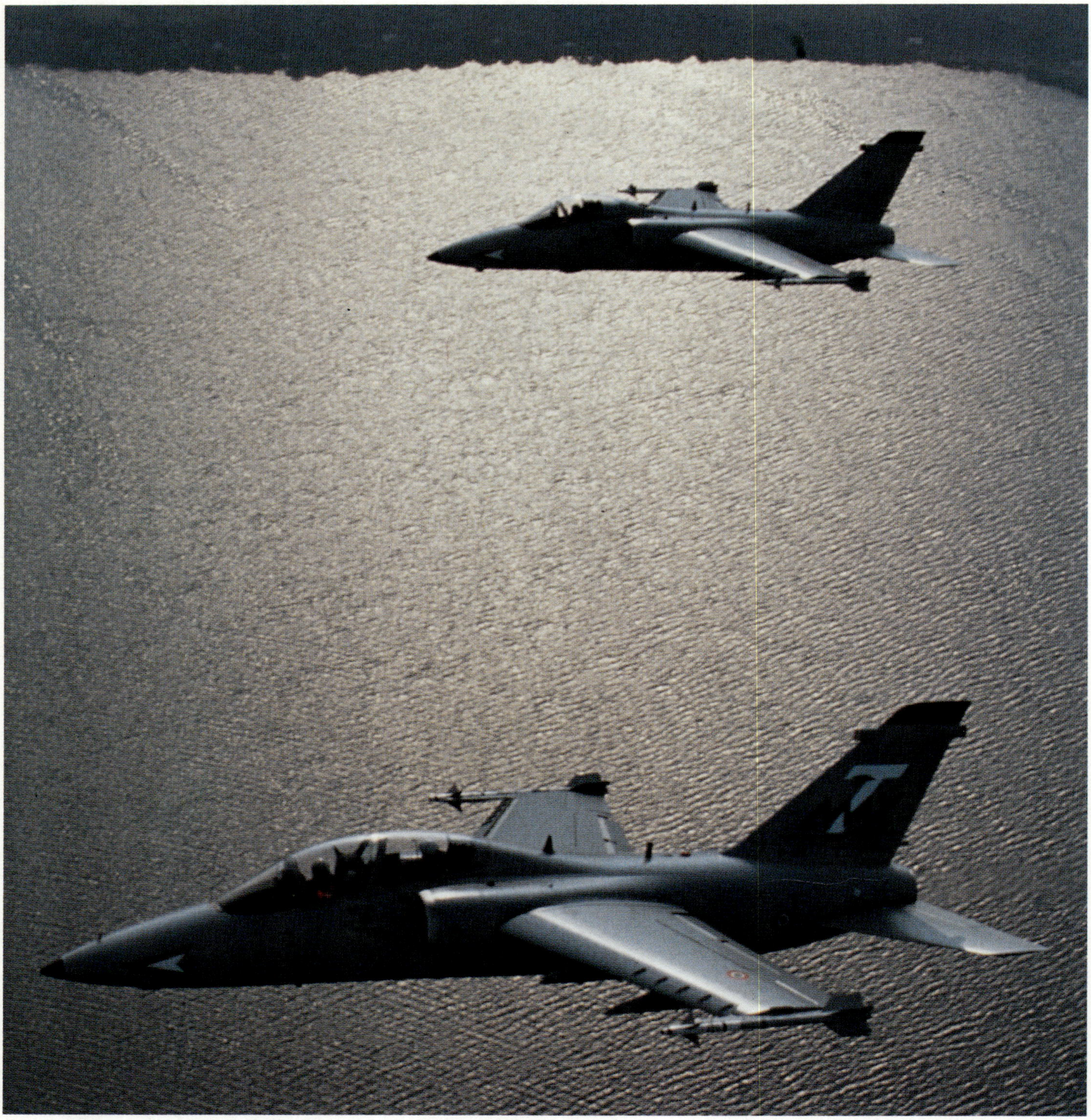

AMX single and two-seater flying over a Philippine volcanic lake.

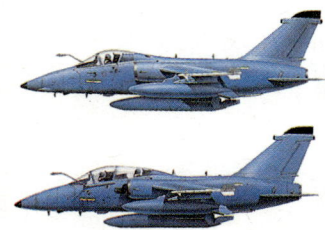

AMX. THE NEW DIMENSION OF COST EFFECTIVENESS.

As the soaring cost of front-line aircraft puts renewed pressure on defence budgets, the AMX is being recognised as the uniquely effective solution.

This dedicated light combat aircraft gives you several aircraft in one incomparably versatile airframe, for it is equally adept at close air support, battlefield interdiction, anti-ship operations, reconnaissance, electronic combat and OCU.

The AMX is a flexible platform for today's and tomorrow's avionics, surveillance and targeting systems. It carries conventional or smart weapons. And it's available in single-seat and two-seat versions, with identical dimensions and combat capability plus high parts commonality.

In squadron service, pilots approve the superb low level manoeuvrability and minimal workload by day or night. Moreover, the very low IR signature, active and passive ECM, multiple systems redundancy and damage tolerant structure set new standards for survivability.

On the ground, simplified maintenance combined with sophisticated BITE systems ensure exceptional rates of mission availability, enabling aircraft inventories to be safely reduced.

With its unparalleled flexibility, performance survivability and availability, the AMX is rewriting the economics of fighter procurement.

And it's ready for export right now.

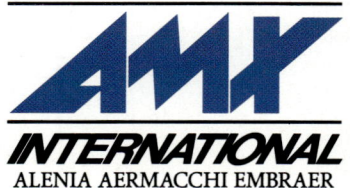

AMX INTERNATIONAL
ALENIA AERMACCHI EMBRAER

First Flights

Some of the first flights made during the period 1 April 1990 to 30 June 1991

APRIL 1990

3   LTV YA-7F Corsair II, second prototype (70-1039, converted A-7D) (USA)

4   Celair Eagle 300 (ZS-WLD) (South Africa)

6   MBB/Kawasaki BK 117, first flight with Arriel 1E engines (F-WMBB) (International)

7   Classic Aircraft Replicas LM-5X homebuilt (USA)

20   PZL Warszawa-Okecie PZL-126 Mrówka (SP-PMA) (Poland)

24   EHI EH 101, pre-production aircraft for Heliliner version (PP8/G-OIOI) (International)

26   McDonnell Douglas MD-11, third aircraft (first with PW engines) (N311MD) (USA)

27   Aero Mercantil EL1 Gavilán (HK-3500-1) (Colombia)

30   Cessna Citation 500, FJ44 engine testbed for Model 525 Citationjet (N501CC) (USA)

MAY 1990

1   McDonnell Douglas MD520N (N520NT) (USA)

2   McDonnell Douglas F-15E, first flight with F100-PW-229 engines (USA)

4   IG JAS 39 Gripen, second prototype (39-2) (Sweden)

9   Bell/Boeing V-22 Osprey, third prototype (fourth to fly) (163913) (USA)

11   Schempp-Hirth Nimbus 4 sailplane (Germany)

24   BAe Sea Harrier FRS. Mk 2 (XZ439), first flight with B model Blue Vixen radar (UK)

30   Piaggio P.180 Avanti, first production (NC1004) (Italy)

JUNE 1990

1   Boeing MH-47E Chinook (88-0267) (USA)

5   McDonnell Douglas MD-11, fourth aircraft (N411MD) (USA)

6   Sikorsky H-76 'Fantail' Eagle, testbed for RAH-66 Comanche tail rotor (N3124G) (USA)

14   Grumman P-16E (S-2E) Tracker, first IMP upgrade for Brazilian Air Force (USA/Canada)

16   BAe 1000 (G-EXLR) (UK)

27   Boeing E-3F, first for French Air Force (EDA 201) (USA)

JULY 1990

2   Dee Howard BAC 1-11 2400 (N650DH) (UK/USA)

16   Alenia/Aermacchi/Embraer AMX-T, second prototype (MM55025) (International)

18   Embraer/FMA CBA-123 Vector (PT-ZVE) (International)

20   Westland Lynx AH. Mk 9, first production (ZG884) (UK)

30   Lockheed NC-141A ARTB (USA)

AUGUST 1990

8   Aerotechnick L-13SL Vivat motor glider (OK-062) (Czechoslovakia)

10   Sikorsky MH-60K (89-26194) (USA)

10   Huahang KF-4 airship (China, People's Republic)

24   TBM 700, first production (International)

27   Northrop YF-23, first prototype (87-0800) (USA)

SEPTEMBER 1990

9   E-Systems/Grob D-500, second prototype (D-FGEO) (International)

21   Shorts S312 Tucano T. Mk 52, first for Kuwait Air Force (ZH506/KAF 101) (UK)

29   Lockheed YF-22, first prototype (N22YF) (USA)

OCTOBER 1990

5   Dassault Super Étendard Modernisé, first upgraded aircraft (France)

11   Rockwell/MBB X-31A (164584) (International)

18   Learjet 55C, proof of concept aircraft for Learjet 60 with one TFE731 engine replaced by PW305 (N60XL) (USA)

19   Northrop B-2, second prototype (82-1067) (USA)

24   Dassault Mirage 2000-5, first flight with RDY radar (France)

26   Northrop YF-23, second prototype (87-0801) (USA)

28   Ruschmeyer R90-230RG (D-EEHE) (Germany)

30   Lockheed YF-22, second prototype (N22YX) (USA)

19 May 1991: Dassault Rafale C 01 later appeared briefly at the Paris Air Show in June

Day after day, under extreme weather and battle conditions, the ALQ-162 Continuous Wave Radar Jammer proved itself in a constantly changing threat environment. On a wide variety of aircraft: AV-8, MH-53, CF-18 and EH-60 Quick-Fix. Stand-alone or compatible with other electronic equipment. Proven reliability. Lightweight. Affordable. Available now. ALQ-162: The Art of Self-Defense.

NORTHROP

People making advanced technology work.

© 1991 Northrop Corporation.   Northrop Electronics Systems Division. 600 Hicks Road, Rolling Meadows, Illinois 60008

NOVEMBER 1990
9   GAIC FT-7P, first for Pakistan Air Force
    (China, People's Republic)
14 Air Tractor AT-802 (N802LS) (USA)
16 General Avia F.22/R Pinguino-Sprint
    (I-GEAE) (Italy)
17 Technical Centre LT-1 Swati (VT-XIV) (India)
21 NAMC/PAC K-8 Karakorum (K8-001)
    (International)
23 SZD-56 sailplane (Poland)
26 XAC Y7-200B (B-528L) (China, People's
    Republic)
26 BAe 1000, second aircraft (G-OPFC) (UK)

DECEMBER 1990
17 SAC (Shaanxi) Y-8C (China, People's Republic)
20 IG JAS Gripen, fourth prototype (third to fly)
    (39-4) (Sweden)
20 Lockheed AC-130U Spectre, first Rockwell
    conversion (87-0128) (USA)
23 Politechnika Warszawska PW-4 motor glider
    (Poland)
26 HAMC Y-11B (China, People's Republic)

JANUARY 1991
3   Seabird SB5 Sentinel, second prototype
    (VH-SBU) (Australia)
11 Swift S-1 sailplane (Poland)
16 EHI EH 101, last pre-production aircraft
    (PP9) (International)
16 NASA high-alpha research F/A-18A Hornet
    (NASA 840/160780), first flight with thrust
    vector system installed (USA)
16 Tridair 206L-3ST Gemini ST, second
    prototype (N700TH) (USA)
16 Terzi T30 Katana homebuilt (I-KTAN) (Italy)
19 Rockwell/MBB X-31A, second aircraft
    (164585) (International)
21 Pacific Aerospace CT4C (New Zealand)

FEBRUARY 1991
6   Mooney EFS/M20T (N222FS) (USA)
12 Volpar Falcon PW300-F20 (c/n 140) (USA)
13 Swearingen SJ30 (N30SJ) (USA)
14 Aerospatiale Panther, MTR 390 engine testbed
    for Eurocopter Tiger (France)
14 Rockwell/MBB X-31A (164584), first flight
    with thrust vectoring paddles installed
    (International)
19 Dassault Mirage 2000D (D01) (France)
25 Robin X4 (F-WKQX) (France)

MARCH 1991
2   BAe 146-300, first flight with Textron
    Lycoming LF 507-1H engines (G-LUXE) (UK)
11 McDonnell Douglas AH-64A Apache, first
    flight with Longbow mockup radome for
    AH-64C (USA)
15 Embraer/FMA CBA-123 Vector, second
    prototype (PT-ZVB) (International)
15 Yakovlev Yak-42E-LL, testbed for D-236
    propfan (SSSR-42525) (USSR)
16 Hoffman LF 2000 Turbo (OE-VPX) (Austria)
22 Scaled Composites Pond Racer PR-01
    (N221BP)
25 IG JAS 39 Gripen, third prototype (fourth to
    fly) (39-3) (Sweden)
27 Socata TB 200 Tobago XL (F-WJXL) (France)

APRIL 1991
4   De Chevigny/Wilson Explorer (International)
7   Aerodis AA200 Orion (USA)
27 Dassault Mirage 2000-5, first single-seat
    prototype (01) (France)
27 Eurocopter Tiger/Tigre (F-ZWWW)
    (International)
29 FFT Eurotrainer 2000A (D-EJDZ) (Germany)
29 Atlas turboprop trainer (South Africa)
29 Cessna Model 525 Citationjet (N525CJ) (USA)

MAY 1991
3   Dassault Mirage F1-CT, first conversion from
    F1-C-200 (France)
10 Canadair Regional Jet (C-FCRJ) (Canada)
19 Dassault Rafale C (C01) (France)
31 Rockwell/MBB X-31A (164584), first flight
    with paddles operative (International)
31 Pilatus PC-12 (HB-FOA) (Switzerland)

JUNE 1991
5   DASA/MBB BO 108, second prototype
    (D-HBEC) (Germany)
11 Bell/Boeing V-22 Osprey, fifth prototype
    (163915) (USA)
13 Learjet 60 prototype (modified Learjet 55C)
    (N60XL) (USA)
14 Northrop CF-5B, first Bristol Aerospace
    upgrade (USA/Canada)
18 Northrop B-2 third prototype (USA)
26 WAI Sentinel 1000 airship (USA)

10 May 1991: Canadair Regional Jet gets airborne from Montreal Dorval

13 February 1991: Swearingen SJ30 small business jet

**5 June 1991: Second prototype of Eurocopter BO 108 powered by Turbomeca Arrius
turboshafts**

GRIFO: airborne multimode radar

R.P. Milano

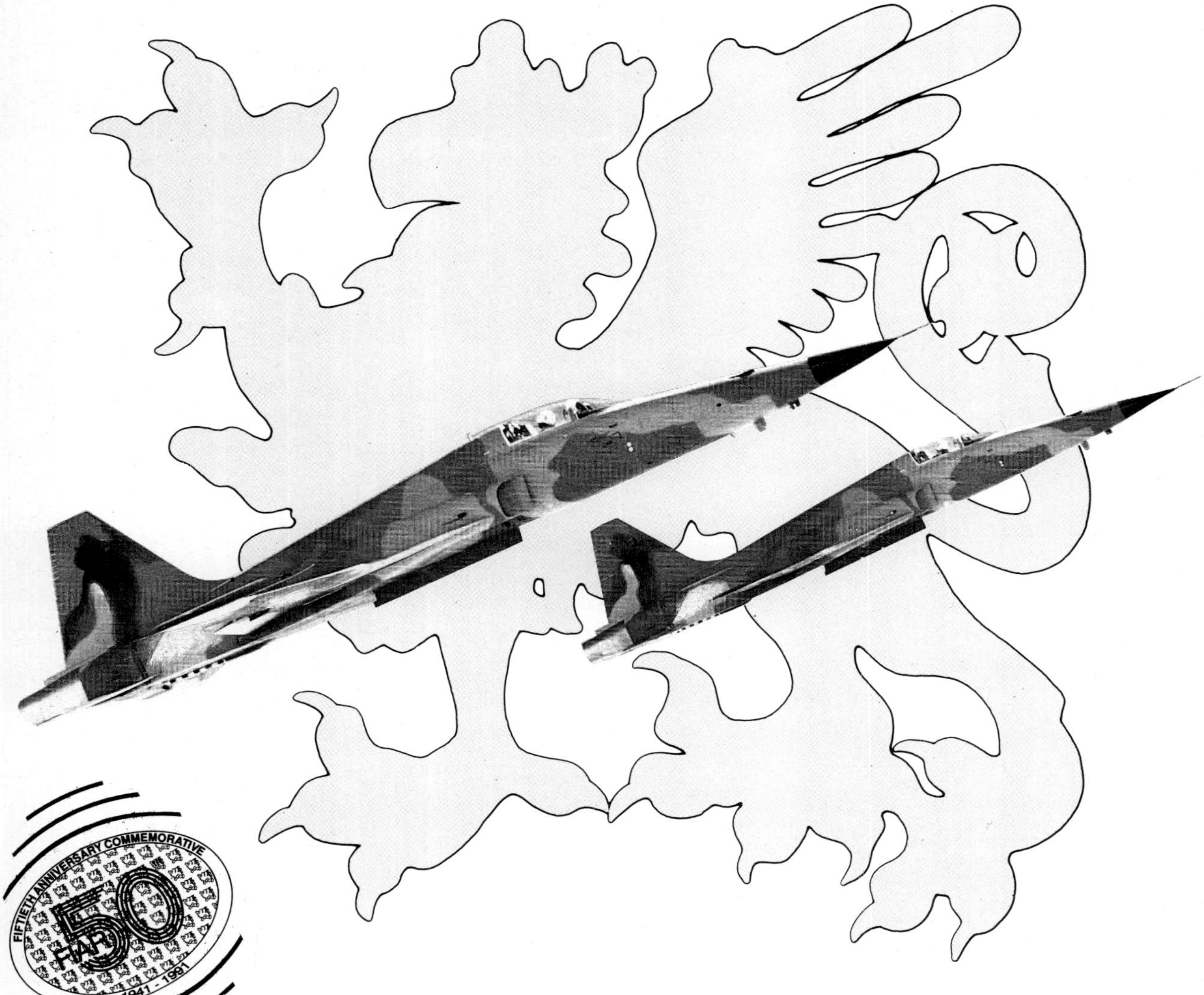

FIFTIETH ANNIVERSARY COMMEMORATIVE
FIAR 50
1941 - 1991

The GRIFO Multimode Pulse Doppler Radar is the key element for enhancing the effectiveness of proven aircraft (such as the Mirage, MIG, A-4, F-5) in today's tactical scenarios.
The comprehensive set of Air-to-Air and Air-to-Surface Search and Track modes, the effective all-altitude, all-aspect, look up-look down target detectability, the low weight coupled with high degree of modularity and low maintenance costs make the GRIFO an attractive choice for new aircraft or for weapon system upgrading.
The GRIFO, FIAR's latest achievement in 30-years of experience in the airborne radars field, is available now for the needs of the 1990's.

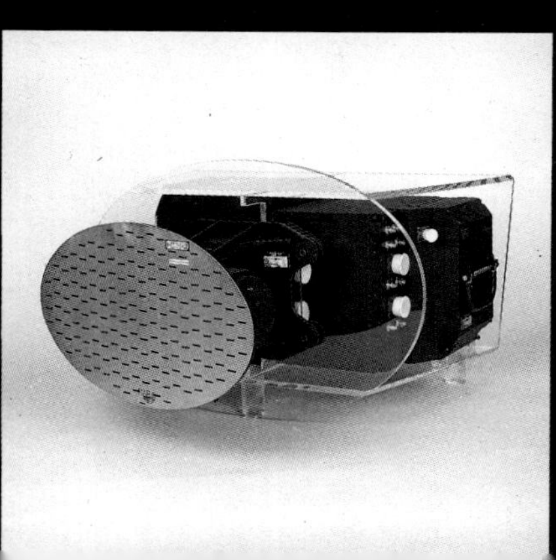

For further information please contact:
Electronic Systems Group Marketing manager
Phone + 39.2.35790537
Telefax + 39.2.3567325
Telex 331265 FIARGR I

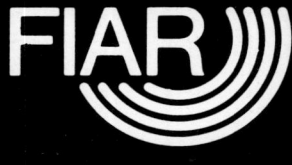

FIAR

HIGHWAY
TO TECHNOLOGY

Future Programme Milestones

Manufacturers' forecasts

Lockheed/Boeing/GD V-22 ATF prototype powered by P&W F119 engines

1991

Date	Aircraft	Milestone
September	Lockheed P-3	Final aircraft delivered as Canadian CP-140A Arcturus
September	Eurocopter/CATIC/SA P120L	Development starts
October	Airbus A340-300	Flies
October	Beechcraft T-1A Jayhawk	First USAF delivery
October	CFMI CFM56-5C (A340)	Certificated
November	Hindustan Advanced Light Helicopter	Flies
November	Sikorsky MH-60K	First aircraft delivered
December	Bell Model 230	Certificated
December	Saab 2000	Roll-out
December	Tridair 206L-3ST Gemini ST	Certificated
Second half	Embraer Tucano H	Flies
Late	Panavia Tornado GR Mk 4	Flies
Late	GE F110-GE-129 turbofan	In service with F-16s
Late	Saab 2000	Roll-out
End	EHI EH 101 UK and Italian Navy versions	Fifth MoU to launch full-scale production
End	Dassault Falcon 900B	CAA certification

1992

Date	Aircraft	Milestone
	BAe Hawk 100/200	First of 16 delivered to Oman
	Boeing 727-100 (Tay 650)	Delivered
	Dassault Falcon 2000	Flies
	Eurocopter/Kawasaki BK 117C-1	Certificated
	General Dynamics F-16	Production by Fokker stops
	Hindustan Light Attack Helicopter	May fly
	Learjet 60	Certificated
	McDonnell Douglas C-17	First delivery
	Piaggio (Duncan) P.180	First aircraft delivered
	Rockwell/MBB Fan Ranger (JPATS)	Flies
	Soko G-4M Super Galeb	Ready for delivery
	Sukhoi S-80	Might fly
January	Bell Model 230	Delivered
January	Cessna Citation VII	Delivered
January	McDonnell Douglas/BAe T-45	First modified aircraft delivered from St Louis
Early	BAe VC10, C. Mk 1 (K)	Redelivered
Early	Fairchild Metro 25	Certificated
Early	McDonnell Douglas Helicopter AH-64C Longbow Apache	Flies
Early	Pilatus PC-9	Last of 67 for Australia delivered
Early	Saab 2000	Flies
March	Boeing E-3D Sentry AEW Mk. 1	Seventh delivered to RAF
March	FFT Eurotrainer 2000	Certificated
March	Tridair 206L-3ST Gemini ST	Delivered
Spring	Boeing 727-100 with RR Spey 650	Certificated for UPS
June	LTV F-8E (FN)	First upgrade redelivered
Summer	Eurofighter EFA	DA1 (RB199s) flies at Manching
July	McDonnell Douglas Helicoper MDX	Flies
September	Grumman A-6E Block 1A update	First FSD aircraft flies
October	Cessna 525 CitationJet	Certificated
Autumn	BAe Jetstream 41	Delivered
October	McDonnell Douglas/BAe Harrier II Plus	Flies
October	Airbus A330	Flies
Late	Dornier 328	JAR certification
End	Rogerson RH-100S Stretch	Flies
End	Swearingen SJ30	Certificated

1993

Date	Aircraft	Milestone
	Northrop B-2	First production deliveries
	Dassault Falcon 2000	Flies
	Eurocopter/CATIC/SA P120L	Flies
	EHI EH 101 Heliliner	Certificated
	Eurofighter EFA	DA4 two-seater flies with ECR-90 radar
	Grumman A-6E Block 1A/IDAP	Update of 110 starts
	Hindustan Advanced Light Helicopter	Delivered
	Ilyushin Il-96-350	Flies
	Ilyushin Il-114	Certificated (USSR)
	McDonnell Douglas/BAe Harrier II Plus	Delivered to USMC
	Mil Mi-38	Flies
	Rockwell/MBB Fan Ranger	Certificated
	Tupolev Tu-334 (turbofan)	Flies
January	Dassault Rafale BO1	Flies with RBE2 radar
Early	Eurofighter EFA	DA3, first with EJ20 engines, flies in Italy
Early	McDonnell Douglas MD-90	Flies
Early	NASA X-30 Aero-Space Plane	Programme go-ahead

DASA/Aerospatiale/Alenia DAA 122 regional airliner could enter service at the end of the decade

First fuselage of the DASA/Dornier 328 in Munich. The 328 will be marketed by the planned joint DASA/Aerospatiale/Alenia sales office being set up in Toulouse

February	Airbus A340-300	In service
March	Airbus A321	Flies
March	Cessna Model 750 Citation X	Flies
Mid	LTV F-8E (FN) upgrades	First 6 delivered
June	McDonnell Douglas F-15E Eagle	Production ends
Second half	Saab 2000	Certificated
August	Boeing 747-400F	Delivered
August	General Dynamics F-111F Pacer Strike update	Kits delivered
September	McDonnell Douglas MDX	Certificated
October	Boeing CH-47D Chinook	Production of 472 complete
December	Airbus A321-100	JAR certification
Late	Airbus A330	JAR certification
Late	Boeing Canada Dash 8-400	Flies
Late	SAAB AJS 37 Viggen	Operational
End	JAS 39 Gripen	Production aircraft delivered

1994

	Antonov An-218	Flies
	BAe 146 NRA	Delivered (or 1995)
	Beriev Be-200	Flies
	CASA AX	Pre-feasibility study ends
	Dassault Falcon 2000	Certificated
	Eurocopter BO 108	Certificated
	Eurofighter EFA	DA7 final development aircraft flies
	International Eurofar	Flies
	Eurocopter NH 90	Flies
	Ishida TW-68	Flies
	Italian Navy EHI 101	Delivered
	McDonnell Douglas MD-12X	Possible first flight
	McDonnell Douglas AH-64C Longbow Apache	Conversions begin
	Tupolev Tu-334 (turbofan)	In service
January	Airbus A321-100	Delivered
May	General Electric GE90	Certificated
June	CFM International CFM56-5C4	Certificated
July	Boeing 777	Flies
July	McDonnell Douglas MD-95	Flies
August	Boeing/Sikorsky RAH-66 Comanche	Dem/val prototype flies
October	Airbus A340-300 Combi	Delivered
Fourth quarter	McDonnell Douglas MD-90-30	Certificated
Late	Boeing Canada Dash 8-400	Delivered
December	LTV F-8E (FN) upgrades	Last of 10 delivered
End	Dassault Falcon 2000	Delivered

1995

	ADA Light Combat Aircraft	Flies
	Advanced Amphibious Aircraft	Flies
	BAe 146 NRA	Delivered (or 1994)
	EHI EH 101 military version	In service
	Eurocopter/CATIC/SA P120L	Certificated
	Lockheed P-3C for Korea	Delivered
	Lockheed/Boeing/GD YF-22	First of 11 EMD prototypes flies
	McDonnell Douglas C-17A	Initial operating capability
March	Cessna Model 750 Citation X	Delivered
First quarter	DAA 92	Flies
First quarter	McDonnell Douglas MD90-10	Certificated
April	IPTN N-250	Flies
May	Boeing 777	Certificated
Second quarter	CASA 3000	Flies
Mid	McDonnell Douglas MD-12X	Possible certification
August	Boeing/Sikorsky RAH-66 Comanche	39-month full-scale development starts
October	McDonnell Douglas MD-95	Delivered
Late	GD F-111C RAAF	Australian avionics update completed

1996

	Airbus A340-300X and A330-300X	Deliveries planned
	EHI EH 101 Merlin (UK Royal Navy)	Delivered
	International Euroflag	Full scale development starts
	IPTN N-250	Certificated
	McDonnell Douglas Helicopter AH-64C Longbow Apache	Delivered
	Mil Mi-38	In production
January	Lockheed/Boeing/GD F-22A	First production contract placed
Mid	DAA 92	In service
July	Dassault Rafale ACM	Delivered
December	Boeing 777	B Model certificated

1997

	Airbus A330-400X	Delivery planned
	Boeing/Grumman E-8 (J-STARS)	Initial operational capability
	Eurofighter EFA	Goes into service
	Ishida TW-68	Delivered
	Taiwan IDF	Up to 256 completed
	Yakovlev Yak-46	Delivered
End	Advanced Amphibious Aircraft	Certificated

1998

	Eurocopter Tiger	Delivered
Late	Dassault Rafale ACM	First 15 delivered
December	Boeing/Sikorsky RAH-66 Comanche	Initial operational capability

1999

	DAA 122	In service
	Eurocopter NH 90	Naval version ready
	Japan FSX	In service

2000

	International Euroflag	Flies
	Eurocopter NH 90	Delivered
	Lockheed/Boeing/GD F-22A	In service

Model of the Eurofighter EFA to be powered by Eurojet EJ200s.

Glossary of aerospace terms in this book

AAM Air-to-air missile.
AATH Automatic approach to hover.
AC Alternating current.
ACE Actuator control electronics.
ACLS (1) Automatic carrier landing system; (2) Air cushion landing system.
ACMI Air combat manoeuvring instrumentation.
ACN Aircraft classification number (ICAO system for aircraft pavements).
ADAC Avion de décollage et atterrissage court (STOL).
ADAV Avion de décollage et atterrissage vertical (VTOL).
ADC (1) US Air Force Aerospace Defense Command (no longer active); (2) air data computer.
ADF Medium frequency automatic direction finding (equipment).
ADG Accessory-drive generator.
ADI Attitude/director indicator.
aeroplane (N America, airplane) Heavier-than-air aircraft with propulsion and a wing that does not rotate in order to generate lift.
AEW Airborne early warning.
AFB Air Force Base (USA).
AFCS Automatic flight control system.
AFRP Aramid fibre reinforced plastics.
afterburning Temporarily augmenting the thrust of a turbofan or turbojet by burning additional fuel in the jetpipe.
AGREE Advisory Group on Reliability in Electronic Equipment.
Ah Ampère-hours.
AHRS Attitude/heading reference system.
AIDS Airborne integrated data system.
aircraft All man-made vehicles for off-surface navigation within the atmosphere, including helicopters and balloons.
airstair Retractable stairway built into aircraft.
AIS Advanced instrumentation subsystem.
ALCM Air-launched cruise missile.
AM Amplitude modulation.
AMAD Airframe mounted accessory drive.
anhedral Downward slope of wing seen from front, in direction from root to tip.
ANVIS Aviator's night vision system.
AP Ammonium perchlorate.
APFD Autopilot flight director.
approach noise Measured 1 nm from downwind end of runway with aircraft passing overhead at 113 m (370 ft).
APS Aircraft prepared for service; a fully equipped and crewed aircraft without usable fuel and payload.
APU Auxiliary power unit (part of aircraft).
ARINC Aeronautical Radio Inc, US company whose electronic box sizes (racking sizes) are the international standard.
ARV Air recreational vehicle.
ASE (1) Automatic stabilisation equipment; (2) Aircraft survivability equipment.
ASI Airspeed indicator.
ASIR Airspeed indicator reading.
ASM Air-to-surface missile.
aspect ratio Measure of wing (or other aerofoil) slenderness seen in plan view, usually defined as the square of the span divided by gross area.
ASPJ Advanced self-protection jammer.
AST Air Staff Target (UK).
ASV (1) Air-to-surface vessel; (2) Anti-surface vessel.
ASW Anti-submarine warfare.
ATA Air Transport Association of America.
ATC Air traffic control.
ATDS Airborne tactical data system.
ATHS Airborne target handover (US, handoff) system.
ATR Airline Transport Radio series of ARINC standard box sizes.
attack, angle of (alpha) Angle at which airstream meets aerofoil (angle between mean chord and free-stream direction). Not to be confused with angle of incidence (which see).
augmented Boosted by afterburning.
autogyro Rotary-wing aircraft propelled by a propeller (or other thrusting device) and lifted by a freely running autorotating rotor.
AUW All-up weight (term meaning total weight of aircraft under defined conditions, or at a specific time during flight). Not to be confused with MTOGW (which see).
avionics Aviation electronics, such as communications radio, radars, navigation systems and computers.
AVLF Airborne very low frequency.
AWACS Airborne warning and control system (aircraft).

bar Non-SI unit of pressure adopted by this yearbook pending wider acceptance of Pa. 1 bar = 10^5Pa, and ISA pressure at S/L is 1013.2 mb. or just over 1 bar.

bare weight Undefined term meaning unequipped empty weight.
basic operating weight MTOGW minus payload (thus, including crew, fuel and oil, bar stocks, cutlery etc).
BCAR British Civil Airworthiness Requirements.
bearingless rotor Rotor in which flapping, lead/lag and pitch change movements are provided by the flexibility of the structural material and not by bearings. No rotor is rigid.
Beta mode Propeller or rotor operating regime in which pilot has direct control of pitch.
BFO Beat-frequency oscillator.
BITE Built-in test equipment.
bladder tank Fuel (or other fluid) tank of flexible material.
bleed air Hot high-pressure air extracted from gas turbine engine compressor or combustor and taken through valves and pipes to perform useful work such as pressurisation, driving machinery or anti-icing by heating surfaces.
blisk Blade plus disc (of turbine engine) fabricated in one piece.
blown flap Flap across which bleed air is discharged at high (often supersonic) speed to prevent flow breakaway.
BOW Basic operating weight (which see).
BPR Bypass ratio.
BRW Brake release weight, maximum permitted weight at start of T-O run.
BTU Non-SI unit of energy (British Thermal Unit) = 0.9478 J.
bulk cargo All cargo not packed in containers or on pallets.
bus Busbar, main terminal in electrical system to which battery or generator power is supplied.
BVR Beyond visual range.
bypass ratio Airflow through fan duct (not passing through core) divided by airflow through core.

C³ Command, control and communications.
C³CM Command, control, communications and countermeasures.
CAA Civil Aviation Authority (UK).
cabin altitude Height above S/L at which ambient pressure is same as inside cabin.
CAD/CAM Computer-assisted design/computer-assisted manufacture.
CAM Cockpit-angle measure (crew field of view).
canards Foreplanes, fixed or controllable aerodynamic surfaces ahead of CG.
CAN 5 Committee on Aircraft Noise (ICAO) rules for new designs of aircraft.
CAR Civil Airworthiness Regulations.
CAS (1) Calibrated airspeed, ASI calibrated to allow for air compressibility according to ISA S/L; (2) close air support; (3) Chief of the Air Staff (also several other aerospace meanings).
CBR California bearing ratio, measure of ability of airfield surface (paved or not) to support aircraft.
CBU Cluster bomb unit.
CCV Control configured vehicle.
CEAM Centre d'Expériences Aériennes Militaires.
CEAT Centre d'Essais Aéronautiques de Toulouse.
CEP Circular error probability (50/50 chance of hit being inside or outside) in bombing, missile attack or gunnery.
CEV Centre d'Essais en Vol.
CFRP Carbonfibre-reinforced plastics.
CG Centre of gravity.
chaff Thin slivers of radar-reflective material cut to length appropriate to wavelengths of hostile radars and scattered in clouds to protect friendly aircraft.
chord Distance from leading-edge to trailing-edge measured parallel to longitudinal axis.
CKD Component knocked down, for assembly elsewhere.
clean (1) In flight configuration with landing gear, flaps, slats etc retracted; (2) Without any optional external stores.
c/n Construction (or constructor's) number.
COINS Computer operated instrument system.
combi Civil aircraft carrying both freight and passengers on main deck.
comint communications intelligence.
composite material Made of two constituents, such as filaments or short whiskers plus adhesive.
CONUS Continental USA (ie, excluding Hawaii, etc).
convertible Transport aircraft able to be equipped to carry passengers or cargo.
core Gas generator portion of turbofan comprising compressor(s), combustion chamber and turbine(s).
C/R Counter-rotating (propellers).
CRT Cathode-ray tube.
CSAS Command and stability augmentation system (part of AFCS).

CSD Constant-speed drive (output shaft speed held steady, no matter how input may vary).
CSRL Common strategic rotary launcher (for ALCMs or SRAMs).

DADC Digital air data computer.
DADS Digital air data system.
daN Decanewtons (Newtons force × 10).
DARPA Defense Advanced Research Projects Agency.
databus Electronic highway for passing digital data between aircraft sensors and system processors, usually MIL-STD-1553B or ARINC 419.
dB Decibel.
DC Direct current.
DECU Digital engine control unit.
derated Engine restricted to power less than potential maximum (usually such engine is flat rated).
design weight Different authorities have different definitions; weight chosen as typical of mission but usually much less than MTOGW.
DF Direction finder, or direction finding.
DGAC Direction Générale à l'Aviation Civile.
dibber bomb Designed to cause maximum damage to concrete runways.
dihedral Upward slope of wing seen from front, in direction from root to tip.
DINS Digital inertial navigation system.
disposable load Sum of masses that can be loaded or unloaded, including payload, crew, usable fuel etc; MTOGW minus OWE.
DLC Direct lift control.
DME UHF distance-measuring equipment; gives slant distance to a beacon; DME element of Tacan.
dog-tooth A step in the leading-edge of a plane resulting from an increase in chord. (See also saw-tooth).
Doppler Short for Doppler radar – radar using fact that received frequency is a function of relative velocity between transmitter or reflecting surface and receiver; used for measuring speed over ground or for detecting aircraft or moving vehicles against static ground or sea.
double-slotted flap One having an auxiliary aerofoil ahead of main surface to increase maximum lift.
dP Maximum design differential pressure between pressurised cabin and ambient (outside atmosphere).
drone Pilotless aircraft, usually winged, following preset programme of manoeuvres.
DS Directionally solidified.

EAA Experimental Aircraft Association (divided into local branches called Chapters).
EAS Equivalent airspeed, RAS minus correction for compressibility.
ECCM Electronic counter-countermeasures.
ECM Electronic countermeasures.
EFIS Electronic flight instrument(ation) system, in which large multifunction CRT displays replace traditional instruments.
EGT Exhaust gas temperature.
ehp Equivalent horsepower, measure of propulsive power of turboprop made up of shp plus addition due to residual thrust from jet.
EICAS Engine indication (and) crew alerting system.
EIS Entry into service.
ekW Equivalent kilowatts, SI measure of propulsive power of turboprop (see ehp).
elevon Wing trailing-edge control surface combining functions of aileron and elevator.
ELF Extreme low frequency.
elint electronics intelligence.
ELT Emergency locator transmitter, to help rescuers home on to a disabled or crashed aircraft.
EMP Electro-magnetic pulse of nuclear or electronic origin.
EO Electro-optical.
EPA Environmental Protection Agency.
EPNdB Effective perceived noise decibel, SI unit of EPNL.
EPNL Effective perceived noise level, measure of noise effect on humans which takes account of sound intensity, frequency, character and duration, and response of human ear.
EPU Emergency power unit (part of aircraft, not used for propulsion).
EROPS Alternative abbreviation (favoured by airlines) for ETOPS.
ERP Effective radiated power.
ESA European Space Agency.
ESM Electronic surveillance (or support) measures; (2) Electronic signal monitoring.
ETOPS Extended-range twin (engine) operations, routing not more than a given flight time (120 min or 180 min) from a usable alternative airfield.
EVA Extra-vehicular activity, ie outside spacecraft.

EW Electronic warfare.
EWSM Early-warning support measures.

FAA Federal Aviation Administration.
factored Multiplied by an agreed number to take account of extreme adverse conditions, errors, design deficiencies or other inaccuracies.
FADEC Full authority digital engine (or electronic) control.
FAI Fédération Aéronautique Internationale.
fail-operational System which continues to function after any single fault has occurred.
fail-safe Structure or system which survives failure (in case of system, may no longer function normally).
FAR Federal Aviation Regulations.
FAR Pt 23 Defines the airworthiness of private and air taxi aeroplanes of 5670 kg (12,500 lb) MTOGW and below.
FAR Pt 25 Defines the airworthiness of public transport aeroplanes exceeding 5670 kg (12,500 lb) MTOGW.
FBW Fly by wire (which see).
FDS Flight director system.
feathering Setting propeller or similar blades at pitch aligned with slipstream to give resultant torque (not tending to turn shaft) and thus minimum drag.
FEBA Forward edge of battle area.
FEL Fibre elastomeric rotor head.
fence A chordwise projection on the surface of a wing, used to modify the distribution of pressure.
fenestron Helicopter tail rotor with many slender blades rotating in short duct.
ferry range Extreme safe range with zero payload.
FFAR Folding-fin (or free-flight) aircraft rocket.
FFVV Fédération Française de Vol à Voile (French gliding authority).
field length Measure of distance needed to land and/or takeoff; many different measures for particular purposes, each precisely defined.
flaperon Wing trailing-edge surface combining functions of flap and aileron.
flat-four Engine having four horizontally opposed cylinders; thus, flat-twin, flat-six etc.
flat rated Propulsion engine capable of giving full thrustor power for take-off to high airfield height and/or high ambient temperature (thus, probably derated at S/L).
FLIR Forward-looking infra-red.
FLOT Forward line of own troops.
fly by light Flight control system in which signals pass between computers and actuators along fibre optic leads.
fly by wire Flight control system with electrical signalling (ie, without mechanical interconnection between cockpit flying controls and control surfaces).
FM Frequency modulation.
FMCS Flight management computer system.
FMS Foreign military sales (US DoD).
FOL Forward operating location.
footprint (1) A precisely delineated boundary on the surface, inside which the perceived noise of an aircraft exceeds a specified level during take-off and/or landing; (2) Dispersion of weapon or submunition impact points.
Fowler flap Moves initially aft to increase wing area and then also deflects down to increase drag.
free turbine Turbine mechanically independent of engine upstream, other than being connected by rotating bearings and the gas stream, and thus able to run at its own speed.
frequency agile (frequency hopping) Making a transmission harder to detect by switching automatically to a succession of frequencies.
FSD Full scale development.
FSW Forward-swept wing.
FY Fiscal year (1 July to 30 June in US government affairs).

g Acceleration due to mean Earth gravity, ie of a body in free fall; or acceleration due to rapid change of direction of flight path.
gallons Non-SI measure; 1 Imp gallon (UK) = 4.546 litres, 1 US gallon = 3.785 litres.
GCI Ground-controlled interception.
GfK Glassfibre-reinforced plastics (German).
GFRP Glassfibre-reinforced plastics.
glide ratio Of a sailplane, distance travelled along track divided by height lost in still air.
glove (1) Fixed portion of wing inboard of variable sweep wing; (2) additional aerofoil profile added around normal wing for test purposes.
GPS Global Positioning System, US military/civil satellite-based precision navaid.
GPU Ground power unit (not part of aircraft).
GPWS Ground-proximity warning system.
green aircraft Aircraft flyable but unpainted, unfurnished and basically equipped.
gross wing area See wing area.
GS Glideslope, of ILS.

GSE Ground support equipment (such as special test gear, steps and servicing platforms).
GTS Gas turbine starter (ie starter is miniature gas turbine).
gunship Helicopter designed for battlefield attack, normally with slim body carrying pilot and weapon operator only.

h Hour(s).
hardened Protected as far as possible against nuclear explosion.
hardpoint Reinforced part of aircraft to which external load can be attached, eg weapon or tank pylon.
helicopter Rotary-wing aircraft both lifted and propelled by one or more power-driven rotors turning about substantially vertical axes.
HF High frequency.
HMD Helmet-mounted display.
hot and high Adverse combination of airfield height and high ambient temperature, which lengthens required TOD.
hovering ceiling Ceiling of helicopter (corresponding to air density at which maximum rate of climb is zero), either IGE or OGE.
HP High pressure (HPC, compressor; HPT, turbine).
hp Horsepower.
HSI Horizontal situation indicator.
HUD Head-up display (bright numbers and symbols projected on pilot's windscreen and focused on infinity so that pilot can simultaneously read display and look ahead).
HVAR High-velocity aircraft rocket.
Hz Hertz, cycles per second.

IAS Indicated airspeed, ASIR corrected for instrument error.
IATA International Air Transport Association.
ICAO International Civil Aviation Organisation.
ICNIA Integrated communications, navigation and identification avionics.
IFF Identification friend or foe.
IFR Instrument flight rules (ie, not VFR).
IGE In ground effect: helicopter performance with theoretical flat horizontal surface just below it.
ILS Instrument landing system.
IMC Instrument meteorological conditions, basically IFR.
IMK Increased manoeuvrability kit.
IMS Integrated multiplex system.
INAS Integrated nav/attack system.
incidence Strictly, the angle at which the wing is set in relation to the fore/aft axis. Wrongly used to mean angle of attack (which see).
inertial navigation Measuring all accelerations imparted to a vehicle and, by integrating these with respect to time, calculating speed at every instant (in all three planes) and by integrating a second time calculating total change of position in relation to starting point.
INEWS Integrated electronic warfare system.
INS Inertial navigation system.
integral construction Machined from solid instead of assembled from separate parts.
integral tank Fuel (or other liquid) tank formed by sealing part of structure.
intercom Wired telephone system for communication within aircraft.
inverter Electric or electronic device for inverting (reversing polarity of) alternate waves in AC power to produce DC.
IOC Initial operational capability.
IP Intermediate pressure.
IR Infra-red.
IRAN Inspect and repair as necessary.
IRLS Infra-red linescan (builds TV-type picture showing cool regions as dark and hot regions as light).
IRS Inertial reference system.
IRST Infra-red search and track.
ISA International Standard Atmosphere.
ISIS (1 Boeing Vertol) Integral spar inspection system; (2 Ferranti) integrated strike and interception sight.
ITE Involute throat and exit (rocket nozzle).
IVSI Instantaneous VSI.

J Joules, SI unit of energy.
JAR Joint Airworthiness Requirements, agreed by all major EC countries (JAR.25 equivalent to FAR.25).
JASDF Japan Air Self-Defence Force.
JATO Jet-assisted take-off (actually means rocket-assisted).
JCAB Japan Civil Airworthiness Board.
JDA Japan Defence Agency.
JGSDF Japan Ground Self-Defence Force.
JMSDF Japan Maritime Self-Defence Force.
joined wing Tandem wing layout in which forward and aft wings are swept so that the outer sections meet.

J-STARS US Air Force/Navy Joint Surveillance Target Attack Radar System in Boeing E-8A.
JTIDS Joint Tactical Information Distribution System.

K One thousand bits of memory.
Kevlar Aramid fibre used as basis of high-strength composite material.
km/h Kilometres per hour.
kN Kilonewtons (the Newton is the SI unit of force; 1 lbf = 4.448 N).
knot 1 nm per hour.
Krueger flap Hinges down and then forward from below the leading-edge.
kVA Kilovolt-amperes.
kW Kilowatt, SI measure of all forms of power (not just electrical).

LABS Low-altitude bombing system designed to throw the bomb up and forward (toss bombing).
LANTIRN Low-altitude navigation and targeting infra-red, night.
LARC Low-altitude ride control.
LBA Luftfahrtbundesamt (German civil aviation authority).
LCD Liquid crystal display, used for showing instrument information.
LCN Load classification number, measure of 'flotation' of aircraft landing gear linking aircraft weight, weight distribution, tyre numbers, pressures and disposition.
LDNS Laser Doppler navigation system.
LED Light-emitting diode.
LGSC Linear glideslope capture.
Lidar Light detection and ranging (laser counterpart of radar).
LITVC Liquid-injection thrust vector control.
LLTV Low-light TV (thus, LLLTV, low-light-level).
load factor (1) percentage of max payload; (2) stress limit.
LOC Localiser (which see).
localiser Element giving steering guidance in ILS.
loiter Flight for maximum endurance, such as supersonic fighter on patrol.
longerons Principal fore-and-aft structural members (eg in fuselage).
Loran Long range navigation; family of hyperbolic navaids based on ground radio emissions, now mainly Loran C.
LOROP Long-range oblique photography.
low observables Materials and structures designed to reduce aircraft signatures of all kinds.
lox Liquid oxygen.
LP Low pressure (LPC, compressor; LPT, turbine).
LRMTS Laser ranger and marked-target seeker.
LRU Line-replaceable unit.

m Metre(s), SI unit of length.
M or Mach number The ratio of the speed of a body to the speed of sound (1116 ft; 340 m/sec in air at 15°C) under the same ambient conditions.
MAC (1) US Air Force Military Airlift Command; (2) mean aerodynamic chord.
MAD Magnetic anomaly detector.
Madar Maintenance analysis, detection and recording.
Madge Microwave aircraft digital guidance equipment.
marker, marker beacon Ground beacon giving position guidance in ILS.
mb Millibars, bar × 10⁻³.
MBR Marker beacon receiver.
MEPU Monofuel emergency power unit.
METO Maximum except take-off.
MF Medium frequency.
MFD Multi-function (electronic) display.
mg Milligrammes, grammes × 10⁻³.
MLS Microwave landing system.
MLW Maximum landing weight.
mm Millimetres, metres × 10⁻³.
MMH Monomethyl hydrazine.
MO Maximum permitted operating Mach number.
MMS Mast-mounted sight.
MNPS Minimum navigation performance specification.
monocoque Structure with strength in outer shell, devoid of internal bracing.
MoU Memorandum of understanding.
MPA Man-powered aircraft.
mph Miles per hour.
MRW Maximum ramp weight.
MSIP US armed forces multi-staged improvement programme.
MTBF Mean time between failures.
MTBR Mean time between removals.
MTI Moving-target indication (radar).
MTOGW Maximum take-off gross weight (MRW minus taxi/run-up fuel).
MTTR Mean time to repair.
MZFW Maximum zero-fuel weight.

NACA US National Advisory Committee for Aeronautics (now NASA).
Nadge NATO air defence ground environment.

NAS US Naval Air Station.
NASA National Aeronautics and Space Administration.
NASC US Naval Air Systems Command (also several other aerospace meanings).
NATC US Naval Air Training Command or Test Center (also several other aerospace meanings).
NBAA US National Business Aircraft Association.
NDB Non-directional beacon.
NDT Non-destructive testing.
NGV Nozzle guide vane.
NH$_4$ClO$_4$ Ammonium perchlorate.
nm nautical mile, 1.8532 km, 1.15152 miles.
NOAA US National Oceanic and Atmospheric Administration.
NOE Nap-of-the-Earth (low flying in military aircraft, using natural cover of hills, trees etc).
NOGS Night observation gunship.
NOS Night observation surveillance.
Ns Newton-second (1 N thrust applied for 1 second.)
NVG Night vision goggles.

OAT Outside air temperature.
OBOGS Onboard oxygen generating system.
OCU Operational Conversion Unit.
OEI One engine inoperative.
offset Workshare granted to a customer nation to offset the cost of an imported system.
OGE Out of ground effect; helicopter hovering, far above nearest surface.
Omega Long-range hyperbolic radio navaid.
OMI Omni-bearing magnetic indicator.
omni Generalised word meaning equal in all directions (as in omni-range, omni-flash beacon).
on condition maintenance According to condition rather than at fixed intervals.
OSTIV Organisation Scientifique et Technique Internationale du Vol à voile (international gliding authority).
OTH Over the horizon.
OTPI On-top position indicator (indicates overhead of submarine in ASW).
OWE Operating weight empty. MTOGW minus payload, usable fuel and oil and other consumables.

PA system Public or passenger address.
pallet (1) for freight, rigid platform for handling by forklift or conveyor; (2) for missile, mounting and electronics box outside aircraft.
payload Disposable load generating revenue (passengers, cargo, mail and other paid items), in military aircraft loosely used to mean total load carried of weapons, cargo or other mission equipment.
PD radar Pulse-Doppler.
penaids Penetration aids, such as jammers, chaff or decoys to help aircraft fly safely through hostile airspace.
PFA Popular Flying Association (UK).
PFCS Primary flight computer system.
phased array Radar in which the screen is swept electronically in one or both axes without moving the antenna.
PHI Position and heading (or homing) indicator.
plane A lifting surface (eg wing, tailplane).
plug door Door larger than its frame in pressurised fuselage, either opening inwards or arranged to retract parts prior to opening outwards.
plume The region of hot air and gas emitted by a helicopter jetpipe.
pneumatic de-icing Covered with flexible surfaces alternately pumped up and deflated to throw off ice.
port Left side, looking forward.
power loading Aircraft weight (usually MTOGW) divided by total propulsive power or thrust at T-O.
prepreg Glassfibre cloth or rovings pre-impregnated with resin to simplify layup.
pressure fuelling Fuelling via a leakproof connection through which fuel passes at high rate under pressure.
pressure ratio In gas turbine engine, compressor delivery pressure divided by ambient pressure (in supersonic aircraft, divided by ram pressure downstream of inlet).
primary flight controls Those used to control trajectory of aircraft (thus, not trimmers, tabs, flaps, slats, airbrakes or lift dumpers etc).
primary flight display Single screen bearing all data for aircraft flight path control.
propfan A family of new technology propellers characterised by multiple scimitar-shaped blades with thin sharp-edged profile. Single and contra-rotating examples promise to extend propeller efficiency up to about Mach 0.8. See also UDF.
pulse-Doppler Radar sending out pulses and measuring frequency-shift to detect returns only from moving target(s) in background clutter.
pylon Structure linking aircraft to external load (engine nacelle, drop tank, bomb etc). Also used in conventional sense in pylon racing.

radius In terms of performance, the distance an aircraft can fly from base and return without intermediate landing.

RAE Royal Aerospace Establishment.
RAI Registro Aeronautico Italiano.
RAM Radar absorbent material.
ram pressure Increased pressure in forward-facing aircraft inlet, generated by converting (relative) kinetic energy to pressure.
ramp weight Maximum weight at start of flight (MTOGW plus taxi/run-up fuel).
range Too many definitions to list, but essentially the distance an aircraft can fly (or is permitted to fly) with specified load and usually whilst making allowance for specified additional manoeuvres (diversions, stand-off, go-around etc).
RANSAC Range surveillance aircraft.
RAS Rectified airspeed, IAS corrected for position error.
raster Generation of large-area display, eg TV screen, by close-spaced horizontal lines scanned either alternately or in sequence.
RAT Ram air turbine.
redundant Provided with spare capacity or data channels and thus made to survive failures.
refanned Gas turbine engine fitted with new fan of higher BPR.
RFP Request(s) for proposals.
rigid rotor (see bearing less rotor).
RLD Rijksluchtvaartdienst. Netherlands civil aviation department.
RMI Radio magnetic indicator; combines compass and navaid bearings.
R/Nav Calculates position, distance and time from groups of airways beacons.
RON Research octane number.
rotor-kite Rotary-wing aircraft with no internal power, lifted by a freely running autorotating rotor and towed by an external vehicle.
roving Multiple strands of fibre, as in a rope (but usually not twisted).
RPV Remotely piloted vehicle (pilot in other aircraft or on ground).
RSA Réseau du Sport de l'Air.
ruddervators Flying control surfaces, usually a V tail, that control both yaw and pitch attitude.
RVR Runway visual range.

s Second(s)
SAC US Air Force Strategic Air Command.
safe-life A term denoting that a component has proved by testing that it can be expected to continue to function safely for a precisely defined period before replacement.
salmon (French saumon) Streamlined fairings, usually at wingtip of sailplane, serving same function as end plate and acting also as tip-skid.
SAR (1) Search and rescue; (2) synthetic aperture radar.
SAS Stability augmentation system.
SATS (1) Small airfield for tactical support; (2) Small Arms Target System.
saw-tooth Same as dog-tooth.
SCAS Stability and control augmentation system.
second-source Production of identical item by second factory or company.
semi-active Homing on to radiation reflected from target illuminated by radar or laser energy beamed from elsewhere.
service ceiling Usually height equivalent to air density at which maximum attainable rate of climb is 100 ft/min.
servo A device which acts as a relay, usually augmenting the pilot's efforts to move a control surface or the like.
SFAR Special Federal Aviation Regulation(s).
sfc Specific fuel consumption.
SGAC Secrétariat Général a l'Aviation Civile (now DGAC).
shaft Connection between gas turbine and compressor or other driven unit. Two-shaft engine has second shaft, rotating at different speed, surrounding the first (thus, HP surrounds inner LP or fanshaft).
Shoran Short range navigation (radio).
shp Shaft horsepower, measure of power transmitted via rotating shaft.
sideline noise EPNdB measure of aircraft landing and taking off, at point 0.25 nm (2- or 3-engined) or 0.35 nm (4-engined) from runway centre line.
sidestick Control column in the form of a short hand-grip beside the pilot.
SIF Selective identification facility.
sigint Signals intelligence.
signature Characteristic 'fingerprint' of all electro-magnetic radiation (radar, IR etc).
single-shaft Gas turbine in which all compressors and turbines are on common shaft rotating together.
S/L Sea level.
SLAR Side-looking airborne radar.
snap-down Air-to-air interception of low-flying aircraft by AAM fired from fighter at a higher altitude.
soft target Not armoured or hardened.

specific fuel consumption Rate at which fuel is consumed divided by power or thrust developed, and thus a measure of engine efficiency. For jet engines (air-breathing, ie not rockets) unit is mg/Ns, milligrams per Newton-second; for shaft engines unit is µg/J, micrograms (millionths of a gram) per Joule (SI unit of work or energy).
specific impulse Measure of rocket engine efficiency; thrust divided by rate of fuel/oxidant consumption per second, the units for mass and force being the same so that the answer is expressed in seconds.
SPILS Stall protection and incidence-limiting system.
spool One complete axial compressor rotor; thus a two-shaft engine may have a fan plus an LP spool.
SSB Single-sideband (radio).
SSR Secondary surveillance radar.
SST Supersonic transport.
st Static thrust.
stabiliser Fin (thus, horizontal stabiliser = tailplane).
stall strips Sharp-edged strips on wing leading-edge to induce stall at that point.
stalling speed Airspeed at which aircraft stalls at 1g, ie wing lift suddenly collapses.
standard day ISA temperature and pressure.
starboard Right side, looking forward.
static inverter Solid-state inverter of alternating wave-form (ie, not rotary machine) to produce DC from AC.
stick-pusher Stall-protection device that forces pilot's control column forward as stalling angle of attack is neared.
stick-shaker Stall-warning device that noisily shakes pilot's control column as stalling angle of attack is neared.
STOL Short take-off and landing. (Several definitions, stipulating allowable horizontal distance to clear screen height of 35 or 50 ft or various SI measures).
store Object carried as part of payload on external attachment (eg bomb, drop tank).
strobe light High-intensity flashing beacon.
substrate The underlying layer on which something (such as a solar cell or integrated circuit) is built up.
supercritical wing Wing of relatively deep, flat-topped profile generating lift right across upper surface instead of concentrated close behind leading-edge.
sweepback Backwards inclination of wing or other aerofoil, seen from above, measured relative to fuselage or other reference axis, usually measured at quarter-chord (25%) or at leading-edge.
synchronous satellite Geostationary.

t Tonne, 1 Megagram, 1000 kg.
tabbed flap Fitted with narrow-chord tab along entire trailing-edge which deflects to greater angle than main surface.
tabs Small auxiliary surfaces hinged to trailing-edge of control surfaces for purposes of trimming, reducing hinge moment (force needed to operate main surface) or in other way assisting pilot.
TAC US Air Force Tactical Air Command.
Tacan Tactical air navigation UHF military navaid giving bearing and distance to ground beacons.
taileron Left and right tailplanes used as primary control surfaces in both pitch and roll.
tailplane Main horizontal tail surface, originally fixed and carrying hinged elevator(s) but today often a single 'slab' serving as control surface.
TANS Tactical air navigation system; Decca Navigator or Doppler-based computer, control and display unit.
TAS True airspeed, EAS corrected for density (often very large factor) appropriate to aircraft height.
TBO Time between overhauls.
t/c ratio Ratio of the thickness (aerodynamic depth) of a wing or other surface to its chord, both measured at the same place parallel to the fore-and-aft axis.
TET Turbine entry temperature (of the gas); also turbine inlet temperature (TIT), inter-turbine temperature (ITT) and turbine gas temperature (TGT).
TFR Terrain-following radar (for low-level attack).
thickness Depth of wing or other aerofoil; maximum perpendicular distance between upper and lower surfaces.
tilt-rotor Aircraft with fixed wing and rotors that tilt up for hovering and forward for fast flight.
T-O Take-off.
T-O noise EPNdB measure of aircraft taking off, at point directly under flight path 3.5 nm from brakes-release (regardless of elevation).
TOD Take-off distance.
TOGW Take-off gross weight (not necessarily MTOGW)
ton Imperial (long) ton = 1.016t (Mg) or 2240 lb. US (short) ton = 0.9072 t or 2000 lb.
track Distance between centres of contact areas of main landing wheels measured left/right across aircraft (with bogies, distance between centres of contact areas of each bogie).
transceiver Radio transmitter/receiver.

transponder Radio transmitter triggered automatically by a particular received signal as in civil secondary surveillance radar (SSR).

TRU Transformer/rectifier unit.

TSFC Thrust specific fuel consumption of jet engine (turbojet, turbofan, ducted propfan or ramjet).

TSO Technical Standard Order (FAA).

turbofan Gas-turbine jet engine generating most thrust by a large-diameter cowled fan, with small part added by jet from core.

turbojet Simplest form of gas turbine comprising compressor, combustion chamber, turbine and propulsive nozzle.

turboprop Gas turbine in which as much energy as possible is taken from gas jet and used to drive reduction gearbox and propeller.

turboshaft Gas turbine in which as much energy as possible is taken from gas jet and used to drive high-speed shaft (which in turn drives external load such as helicopter gearbox).

TVC Thrust vector control (rocket).

TWT Travelling-wave tube.

tyre sizes In simplest form, first figure is rim diameter (in or mm) and second is rim width (in or mm). In more correct three-unit form, first figure is outside diameter, second is max width and third is wheel diameter.

UAV Unmanned air vehicle.

UBE, Ubee Ultra bypass engine, alternative terminology (Boeing) for UDF.

UDF Unducted fan, one form of advanced propulsion system in which gas turbine blading directly drives large fan (propfan) blades mounted around the outside of the engine pod. (GE registered abbreviation).

UHF Ultra-high frequency.

unfactored Performance level expected of average pilot, in average aircraft, without additional safety factors.

upper surface blowing Turbofan exhaust vented over upper surface of wing to increase lift.

usable fuel Total mass of fuel consumable in flight, usually 95-98 per cent of system capacity.

useful load Usable fuel plus payload.

US gallon 0.83267 Imperial gallon; 3.785 litres.

variable geometry Capable of grossly changing shape in flight, especially by varying sweep of wings.

V Maximum permitted diving speed.

VDU Video (or visual) display unit.

vernier Small thruster, usually a rocket, for final precise adjustment of a vehicle's trajectory and velocity.

VFR Visual flight rules.

VHF Very high frequency.

VLF Very low frequency (area-coverage navaid).

V_{MO} Maximum permitted operating flight speed (IAS, EAS or CAS must be specified).

VMS Vehicle management system.

V_{NE} Never-exceed speed (aerodynamic or structural limit).

VOR VHF omni-directional range (VHF radio beacons providing bearing to or from beacon).

vortex generators Small blades attached to wing and tail surfaces to energise local airflow and improve control.

VSI Vertical speed (climb/descent) indicator.

VTOL Vertical take-off and landing.

washout Inbuilt wing twist reducing angle of incidence towards the tip.

WDNS Weapon delivery and navigation system.

wheelbase Minimum distance from nosewheel or tailwheel (centre of contact area) to line joining mainwheels (centres of contact areas).

wing area Total projected area of clean wing (no flaps, slats etc) including all control surfaces and area of fuselage bounded by leading- and trailing-edges projected to centreline (inapplicable to slender-delta aircraft with extremely large leading-edge sweep angle). Described in *Jane's* as gross wing area; net area excludes projected areas of fuselage, nacelles, etc.

wing loading Aircraft weight (usually MTOGW) divided by wing area.

winglet Small auxiliary aerofoil, usually sharply upturned and often sweptback, at tip of wing.

wire guidance Guidance of missile on UAV by signals transmitted through fine wire(s) linking it with operator.

zero-fuel weight MTOGW minus usable fuel and other consumables, in most aircraft imposing severest stress on wing.

zero/zero seat Ejection seat designed for use even at zero speed on ground.

ZFW Zero-fuel weight.

μg Microgrammes, grammes × 10^6.

AIRCRAFT

ARGENTINA

AERO BOERO

AERO BOERO SA
Brasil y Alem, 2421 Morteros, Córdoba
Telephone: 54 (562) 2121 and 2690
PRESIDENT: Hector A. Boero
OTHER WORKS: Av 9 de Julio 1101, 2400 San Francisco, Córdoba
Telephone: 54 (562) 22972 and 24118

Aero Boero has so far produced more than 300 aircraft of various models, including 40 for export to Brazil. A total of 450 AB 115 civil trainers and over 70 AB 180 RVRs have been ordered, and in 1989 an agreement was signed with Indaer-Peru (which see) for the manufacture of both types in that country.

AERO BOERO 115 TRAINER

The original AB 115 was developed from the AB 95 (1969-70 *Jane's*). Thirty had been built by January 1983, including examples of the AB 115 BS ambulance version and the 112 kW (150 hp) AB 115/150, descriptions of which can be found in the 1983-84 edition.

An order for 100 AB 115 Trainers was received from the Brazilian government in 1988, followed by an order for 350 more in the Summer of 1989. Deliveries are due to be completed in mid-1993.

The AB 115 has the same airframe as the AB 180 RVR (which see), except for Dacron fabric covering and no rudder tab. Other differences are as follows:

TYPE: Two/three-seat light aircraft.
POWER PLANT: One 86 kW (115 hp) Textron Lycoming O-235-C2A flat-four engine, driving a Sensenich 72-CK-0-50 two-blade fixed-pitch propeller. Two aluminium fuel tanks in wings, combined capacity 128 litres (33.9 US gallons; 28.2 Imp gallons). Gravity refuelling point in top of each tank.
ACCOMMODATION: Pilot and one or two passengers in fully enclosed, heated and ventilated cabin.
SYSTEMS: 40A alternator and 12V battery.
AVIONICS: Com/nav equipment, blind-flying instrumentation and landing lights optional.
DIMENSIONS, EXTERNAL: As for AB 180, plus:
Propeller diameter   1.93 m (6 ft 4 in)
WEIGHTS AND LOADINGS:
Weight empty   556 kg (1,226 lb)
Max T-O weight   802 kg (1,768 lb)
Max wing loading   45.7 kg/m² (9.36 lb/sq ft)
Max power loading   9.33 kg/kW (15.37 lb/hp)
PERFORMANCE (at max T-O weight):
Never-exceed speed (VNE)
    118 knots (220 km/h; 136 mph)
Max cruising speed   91 knots (169 km/h; 105 mph)
Stalling speed, power off:
   flaps up   41 knots (75 km/h; 47 mph)
   flaps down   35 knots (64 km/h; 40 mph)
Max rate of climb at S/L   204 m (669 ft)/min
T-O run   100 m (330 ft)
T-O to, and landing from, 15 m (50 ft)   250 m (820 ft)
Landing run   80 m (265 ft)
Range with max fuel   664 nm (1,230 km; 765 miles)

AERO BOERO 180 RVR

The Aero Boero 180 is a higher-powered variant of the AB 150 (see 1983-84 *Jane's*). It has been built in four versions, of which the 180 RV, 180 Ag and 180 SP have been described in earlier editions. Production is continuing of the glider-towing AB 180 RVR, for customers in Brazil (seven ordered in 1987, followed by 70 more in 1989, for delivery by mid-1993) and Argentina. This version has a cabin rear window and a towing hook.

TYPE: Single/three-seat light aircraft.
WINGS: Strut braced high-wing monoplane. Streamline section V bracing strut each side. Wing section NACA 23012 (modified). Dihedral 1° 45'. Incidence 3° at root, 1° at tip. Light alloy structure, including skins. Aluminium alloy flaps and ailerons. No tabs.
FUSELAGE: Welded steel tube structure (SAE 4130), covered with Ceconite.
TAIL UNIT: Wire braced welded steel tube structure, covered with Ceconite. Sweptback fin and rudder; non-swept

Aero Boero 115 Trainer two/three-seat training and touring aircraft *(Kenneth Munson)*

Aero Boero 180 RVR glider-towing aircraft

fixed incidence tailplane with elevators. Ground adjustable tab on rudder; trim tab in port elevator.
LANDING GEAR: Non-retractable tailwheel type, with shock absorption by helicoidal springs inside fuselage. Mainwheels carried on faired-in V struts and half-axles. Mainwheels and tyres size 6.00-6; tailwheel tyre size 2.80-2.50. Hydraulic disc brakes on main units; tailwheel steerable and fully castoring.
POWER PLANT: One 134 kW (180 hp) Textron Lycoming O-360-A1A flat-four engine, driving a Sensenich 76-EM8 fixed-pitch or Hartzell HC-92ZK-8D constant-speed two-blade propeller. Fuel capacity (two aluminium wing tanks) 200 litres (53 US gallons; 44 Imp gallons); oil capacity 8 litres (2.1 US gallons; 1.75 Imp gallons).
ACCOMMODATION: Pilot and two passengers in fully enclosed, heated and ventilated cabin. Cockpit rear window.
DIMENSIONS, EXTERNAL:
Wing span   10.90 m (35 ft 9 in)
Wing chord, constant   1.61 m (5 ft 3½ in)
Wing aspect ratio   6.8
Length overall   7.08 m (23 ft 2¾ in)
Height overall   2.10 m (6 ft 10½ in)
Wheel track   2.05 m (6 ft 8¾ in)
Wheelbase   5.10 m (16 ft 8¾ in)
AREAS:
Wings, gross   17.55 m² (188.9 sq ft)
Ailerons (total)   1.84 m² (19.81 sq ft)
Trailing-edge flaps (total)   1.94 m² (20.88 sq ft)

Fin   0.93 m² (10.01 sq ft)
Rudder   0.41 m² (4.41 sq ft)
Tailplane   1.40 m² (15.07 sq ft)
Elevators (total, incl tab)   0.97 m² (10.44 sq ft)
WEIGHTS AND LOADINGS:
Weight empty   602 kg (1,327 lb)
Max T-O weight   890 kg (1,962 lb)
Max wing loading   50.7 kg/m² (10.38 lb/sq ft)
Max power loading   6.64 kg/kW (10.90 lb/hp)
PERFORMANCE (at max T-O weight except where indicated):
Never-exceed speed (VNE)
    132 knots (245 km/h; 152 mph)
Max level speed at S/L   122 knots (225 km/h; 140 mph)
Max cruising speed at S/L
    108 knots (201 km/h; 125 mph)
Stalling speed, flaps down   40 knots (73 km/h; 45 mph)
Max rate of climb at S/L   312 m (1,025 ft)/min
Rate of climb: with single-seat sailplane
    more than 180 m (590 ft)/min
   with two-seat sailplane   120 m (394 ft)/min
Time to 600 m (1,970 ft), 75% power, with Blanik
   two-seat sailplane   3 min 10 s
Service ceiling   more than 7,000 m (22,965 ft)
T-O run   100 m (330 ft)
T-O to 15 m (50 ft), two persons   188 m (615 ft)
Landing from 15 m (50 ft)   160 m (525 ft)
Landing run   60 m (195 ft)
Range with max fuel   636 nm (1,180 km; 733 miles)

CHINCUL

CHINCUL S.A.C.A.I.F.I.
25 de Mayo 489, 6° Piso, 1339 Buenos Aires
Telephone: 54 (1) 312 5671/5
Fax: 54 (1) 311 5742
Telex: 22706 MACUB AR
WORKS: Calle Mendoza entre 6 y 7, 5400 San Juan, Pcia de San Juan; and at Avenida Diaz Velez 1034, 1702 Ciudadela, Buenos Aires
PRESIDENT: José Maria Beraza
SALES DIRECTOR: Juan Pablo Beraza
EXPORT MANAGER: Oscar A. Prieto

This company, a wholly owned subsidiary of La Macarena SA, Piper's Argentine distributor, was formed in December 1971 to assemble a range of Piper aircraft in Argentina with a gradually increasing degree of local manufacture. Some Chincul products have incorporated more than 60 per cent local manufacture. The factory at San Juan has a covered area of 16,500 m² (177,600 sq ft) and a workforce of about 300 people, and had delivered approximately 900 aircraft by January 1990. The Ciudadela plant produces jigs, dies and aircraft parts for production and as spares. All Piper kits delivered to Chincul have for

several years been for Phase 3 completion, involving the assembly and riveting of wings and control surfaces, manufacture of interiors, electrical harness, and other systems installation. Items of Argentine manufacture include batteries, upholstery, fabrics, tyres, engine instruments, fire extinguishers, and glassfibre components. Chincul also assembles a range of Bendix/King avionics for its Piper product line.

Under an agreement signed on 17 May 1989, Chincul and Embraer of Brazil rationalised their licence production and marketing of Piper aircraft and the EMB-201A Ipanema agricultural aircraft to avoid duplication of types. Following this agreement, Chincul no longer produces the Saratoga or Seneca III.

Piper-designed aircraft currently produced by Chincul are the PA-18-115 and PA-18-150 Super Cub, PA-25-235 and PA-25-260 Pawnee, PA-28-161 Warrior II, PA-28-181 Archer II, PA-28-236 Dakota, PA-28RT-201 Arrow IV, PA-28RT-201T Turbo Arrow IV, PA-31-350 Navajo Chieftain, PA-31T Cheyenne I and II, PA-36-375 Pawnee Brave, and PA-42 Cheyenne III and 400. The company has developed its own tandem two-seat conversion of the Pawnee D agricultural aircraft, and a two-seat aerobatic military trainer based on the Cherokee Arrow, as described in the 1983-84 and earlier editions of *Jane's*.

In July 1990 Chincul signed an MoU with Bell Helicopter Textron intended to lead to co-production of the latter's Model 212 and 412 SP helicopters (see Canadian section) by the Argentine company. Initially, Chincul will assemble CKD kits imported from Bell; in the second phase, 20 per cent (by value) of each helicopter will be of Argentine manufacture.

Chincul built example of the Piper PA-25-235/-260 Pawnee *(Kenneth Munson)*

FMA
FÁBRICA MILITAR DE AVIONES SA
Avenida Fuerza Aérea Argentina Km 5½, 5103 Guarnición
   Aérea Córdoba
Telephone: 54 (51) 690364
Fax: 54 (51) 111 1774
Telex: 51965 AMCOR AR
MANAGING DIRECTOR:
   Brigadier Alberto H. Lindow
COMMERCIAL DIRECTOR: Comodoro Roberto Gomez
COMMERCIAL MANAGER: Ing H. Francisco Luciano

The original Fábrica Militar de Aviones (Military Aircraft Factory) came into operation on 10 October 1927 as a central organisation for aeronautical research and production in Argentina. After several changes of name (see 1987-88 and earlier *Jane's*), it reverted to its original title in 1968 as a component of the Area de Material Córdoba (AMC) division of the Argentine Air Force.

In 1988 the Argentine Air Force, Aeritalia (now Alenia) and the national industrial company Techint announced the creation of FAMA (Fábrica Argentina de Materiales Aeroespaciales), which was intended to incorporate FMA facilities as a major capital asset. However, this situation was never achieved, and FMA remained 100 per cent owned by the Argentine Air Force until re-launched in mid-February 1991, as FMA SA, with private capital investment.

Main activities of FMA are aircraft design, manufacture, maintenance and repair. Its facility at Córdoba also accommodates the Centro de Ensayos en Vuelo (Flight Test Centre), a separate division also controlled by the Argentine Air Force, to which all aircraft produced in Argentina are sent for certification tests. The laboratories, factories and other aeronautical division buildings occupy a total covered area of approx 253,000 m² (2,723,265 sq ft); the Area de Material Córdoba employs more than 3,500 persons, of whom about 2,000 are engaged in design and manufacturing.

Major current product is the nationally designed IA 63 Pampa basic and advanced jet trainer. Upgrading of the IA 58 Pucará close support aircraft continues.

EMBRAER/FMA CBA-123 VECTOR
This twin-turboprop regional transport aircraft is described in the International section. FMA is responsible for 33 per cent of its development and manufacture.

FMA IA 58A PUCARÁ
Four versions of this twin-turboprop light attack aircraft were built, of which the IA 58B and IA 66 did not go beyond the prototype stage and the single-seat IA 58C (1989-90 and earlier *Jane's*) has been suspended. Major version was the two-seat IA 58A. A total of 108 was ordered for the Fuerza Aérea Argentina (FAA). Deliveries began in the Spring of 1976, and the last example was completed in 1986. Some early production aircraft were converted to single-seat configuration, with an extra fuselage fuel tank in place of the rear seat; none of these is currently operational, and no further conversions are planned. Six IA 58As were delivered to the Fuerza Aérea Uruguaya, and a further 40 were made available for export in 1986. No details of further sales have been received, but five Pucarás were loaned to the Colombian government in late 1989 for anti-drug traffic operations.

The IA 58A currently equips the III Brigada Aérea, 3rd Attack Group, of the FAA at Reconquista, Santa Fe; others serve with the IX Brigada's 9th Transport Group at Comodoro Rivadavia in Chubut Province. Aircraft still in service are currently receiving a new, autonomous navigation and weapon delivery system known as SINT (Sistema Integrado de Navegación y de Tiro), developed by the FAA at its Río Cuarto base.

A full description of the IA 58A in its final production form can be found in the 1987-88 edition. A shortened version last appeared in the 1990-91 *Jane's*.

IA 63 Pampa tandem-seat jet trainer in Argentine Air Force camouflage *(Ivo Sturzenegger)*

FMA IA 63 PAMPA
The Fuerza Aérea Argentina (FAA) initiated the IA 63 programme in 1979, and the eventual configuration, powered by a single Garrett TFE731 turbofan, was selected from seven possible designs in early 1980. Dornier GmbH of Germany provided technical assistance during development, including manufacture of the wings and tailplanes for the prototypes and ground test airframes, and is continuing to assist in development and marketing. The Pampa airframe incorporates integrated structures for high-load components such as wing spar box and main frames; numerically controlled, mechanically and chemically milled components; and the use of fibre composites.

Two IA 63 airframes were allocated for static and fatigue testing. The first of three flying prototypes (EX-01) flew on 6 October 1984, and the first production aircraft was completed in October 1987. Firm orders have so far been placed for 18 Pampas, of which the first three were delivered to the IV Brigada Aérea at Mendoza in April 1988. Twelve were in service with this Brigada's Escuadron 2 at El Plumerillo Air Base by the end of 1989, and the remaining six were expected to follow in early 1991. Funding for the second batch (of 12) was then awaited.

A version for the Argentine Navy is under development, as is a new autonomous navigation/weapon aiming system. Two prototypes were reported in early 1990 to have been upgraded to ground attack configuration, with an Argentine Air Force developed HUD and other new avionics, prior to this becoming a standard installation for existing and future production Pampas. Certification of the HUD was under way in late 1990.

The designation **Pampa 2000** applies to a version proposed, with LTV as FMA's partner, for the USAF/USN JPATS trainer programme. One aircraft was provided to LTV for modification in 1990, and a second requested for delivery in early 1991.

The following description applies to the production trainer version, except where indicated:
TYPE: Single-engined basic and advanced jet trainer.
WINGS: Cantilever shoulder-wing monoplane. Non-swept tapered wings are of Dornier DoA-7 advanced transonic section, with thickness/chord ratios of 14.5 per cent at root, 12.5 per cent at tip. Dihedral 3°. Two-spar wing box forms integral fuel tank. Hydraulically actuated two-segment single-slotted Fowler trailing-edge flaps inboard of ailerons. Ailerons hydraulically operated by Liebherr tandem servo-actuators. Stick forces simulated by artificial feel. Three-axis trim is operated electromechanically.

FUSELAGE: Conventional semi-monocoque structure. Hydraulically actuated door type airbrake on each side of upper rear fuselage.
TAIL UNIT: Sweptback fin and rudder; non-swept all-moving anhedral tailplane. Control surface actuation as for ailerons.
LANDING GEAR: SHL (Israel) retractable tricycle type, with hydraulic extension/retraction and emergency free-fall extension. Oleo-pneumatic shock absorbers. Single wheel and low-pressure tyre on each unit. Tyre sizes 6.50-10 (10 ply rating) on mainwheels, 380 × 150 mm (4-6 ply rating) on nosewheel. Nosewheel retracts rearward, mainwheels inward into underside of engine air intake trunks. Braking system incorporates an anti-skid device; nosewheel steering is optional. Gear designed for operation from unprepared surfaces.
POWER PLANT: One 15.57 kN (3,500 lb st) Garrett TFE731-2-2N turbofan installed in rear fuselage, with twin lateral air intakes. Standard internal fuel capacity of 968 litres (255 US gallons; 213 Imp gallons) in integral wing tank of 550 litres (145 US gallons; 121 Imp gallons) and 418 litre (110 US gallon; 92 Imp gallon) flexible fuselage tank with a negative *g* chamber permitting up to 10 s of inverted flight. Additional 415 litres (109 US gallons; 91 Imp gallons) can be carried in auxiliary tanks inside outer wing panels, to give a max internal capacity of 1,383 litres (364 US gallons; 304 Imp gallons). Single-point pressure refuelling, plus gravity point in upper surface of each wing. Engine air intakes anti-iced by engine bleed air.
ACCOMMODATION: Instructor and pupil in tandem (instructor at rear, on elevated seat), on UPC (Stencel) S-III-S3IA63 zero/zero ejection seats. Ejection procedure can be pre-selected for separate single ejections, or for both seats to be fired from front or rear cockpit. Dual controls standard. One-piece wraparound windscreen. One-piece canopy, with internal screen, is hinged at rear and opens upward. Entire accommodation pressurised and air-conditioned.
SYSTEMS: AiResearch environmental control system, supplied by high or low pressure engine bleed air, provides a 1,980 m (6,500 ft) cockpit environment up to flight level 5,730 m (18,800 ft) and also provides ram air for negative *g* system and canopy seal. Oxygen system supplied by lox converter. Two independent hydraulic systems, each at pressure of 207 bars (3,000 lb/sq in), each supplied by engine driven pump. Each system incorporates a bootstrap reservoir pressurised at 4 bars (58 lb/sq in). No. 1 system, with flow rate of 16 litres (4.2 US gallons; 3.5 Imp gallons)/min, actuates primary flight controls,

airbrakes, landing gear and wheel brakes; No. 2 system, with flow rate of 8 litres (2.1 US gallons; 1.75 Imp gallons)/min, actuates primary flight controls, wing flaps, emergency and parking brakes, and (if fitted) nosewheel steering. A ram air turbine provides emergency hydraulic power for No. 2 system if engine shuts down in flight and pressure in this system drops below minimum. Electrical system (28V DC) supplied by 400A 11.5kW engine driven starter/generator; secondary supply (115/26V AC power at 400Hz) from two 450VA static inverters and two 27Ah nickel-cadmium batteries. Thirty minute emergency electrical power available in case of in-flight engine shutdown.

AVIONICS: Standard avionics package comprises two redundant VHF com transceivers, intercom system, VOR/ILS with marker beacon receiver, DME, and ADF radio compass. Navigation system allows complete navigation/ landing training under IFR conditions. Attitude and heading information provided by a three-gyro platform, with magnetic flux valve compass for additional heading reference.

ARMAMENT: No built-in weapons. Five attachments for external stores, with max pylon load of 400 kg (882 lb) on each inboard underwing station, 250 kg (551 lb) each on fuselage centreline and outboard underwing pair. With a 30 mm gun pod containing 145 rds on the fuselage station, typical underwing loads can include six Mk 81 bombs, two each Mk 81 and Mk 82 bombs, or one 7.62 mm twin-gun pod and one practice bomb/rocket training container. Gyro-stabilised sighting system in front cockpit (optional in rear cockpit), with recorder and front sight. Weapon management system adequate for several different tactical configurations.

DIMENSIONS, EXTERNAL:	
Wing span	9.686 m (31 ft 9¼ in)
Wing aspect ratio	6.0
Length overall (excl pitot probe)	10.90 m (35 ft 9¼ in)
Height overall	4.29 m (14 ft 1 in)
Tailplane span	4.58 m (15 ft 0⅓ in)
Wheel track	2.66 m (8 ft 8¾ in)
Wheelbase	4.42 m (14 ft 6 in)
AREAS:	
Wings, gross reference	15.63 m² (168.2 sq ft)
Vertical tail surfaces (total)	2.52 m² (27.13 sq ft)
Horizontal tail surfaces (total)	4.35 m² (46.82 sq ft)
WEIGHTS AND LOADINGS:	
Weight empty	2,821 kg (6,219 lb)
Fuel load:	
wings (incl auxiliary tanks)	780 kg (1,719 lb)
fuselage	338 kg (745 lb)
Max underwing load with normal internal fuel	1,160 kg (2,557 lb)
T-O weight, clean configuration:	
968 litres internal fuel	3,700 kg (8,157 lb)
1,383 litres internal fuel	3,800 kg (8,377 lb)

Max T-O weight with external stores	5,000 kg (11,023 lb)
Typical landing weight	3,500 kg (7,716 lb)
Wing loading:	
at clean T-O weight:	
968 litres internal fuel	236.72 kg/m² (48.51 lb/sq ft)
1,383 litres internal fuel	243.12 kg/m² (49.82 lb/sq ft)
at max T-O weight with external stores	319.90 kg/m² (65.55 lb/sq ft)
Power loading:	
at clean T-O weight:	
968 litres internal fuel	237.8 kg/kN (2.33 lb/lb st)
1,383 litres internal fuel	244.2 kg/kN (2.39 lb/lb st)
at max T-O weight with external stores	321.4 kg/kN (3.15 lb/lb st)

PERFORMANCE (ISA, at 3,800 kg; 8,377 lb clean T-O weight with max internal fuel, except where indicated):

Max level speed at S/L	405 knots (750 km/h; 466 mph)
Approach speed at S/L, landing weight of 3,630 kg (8,000 lb)	120 knots (222 km/h; 138 mph)
Stalling speed	92 knots (171 km/h; 106 mph)
Max rate of climb: at S/L	1,560 m (5,120 ft)/min
at 4,575 m (15,000 ft)	1,215 m (3,990 ft)/min

Max rate of roll	150°/s
Service ceiling	12,900 m (42,325 ft)
T-O run at S/L, AUW of 3,700 kg (8,157 lb)	424 m (1,390 ft)
Landing run at landing weight of 3,500 kg (7,716 lb)	461 m (1,512 ft)

Typical mission radius:
air-to-air gunnery (hi-hi), T-O weight of 3,950 kg (8,708 lb) with 250 kg (551 lb) external load, 5 min allowance for dogfight, 30 min reserves
237 nm (440 km; 273 miles)
air-to-ground (hi-lo-hi), T-O weight of 4,860 kg (10,714 lb) with 1,000 kg (2,205 lb) external load, 5 min allowance for weapon delivery, 30 min reserves 194 nm (360 km; 223 miles)

Range at 300 knots (556 km/h; 345 mph) at 4,000 m (13,125 ft):
968 litres internal fuel   540 nm (1,000 km; 621 miles)
1,383 litres internal fuel   809 nm (1,500 km; 932 miles)

Ferry range at 280 knots (519 km/h; 322 mph) at 10,060 m (33,000 ft), max internal/external fuel
1,000 nm (1,853 km; 1,151 miles)

Max endurance at 300 knots (556 km/h; 345 mph) at 4,000 m (13,125 ft), 1,383 litres internal fuel
3 h 48 min
g limits   +6/−3 (+4.5 max sustained)

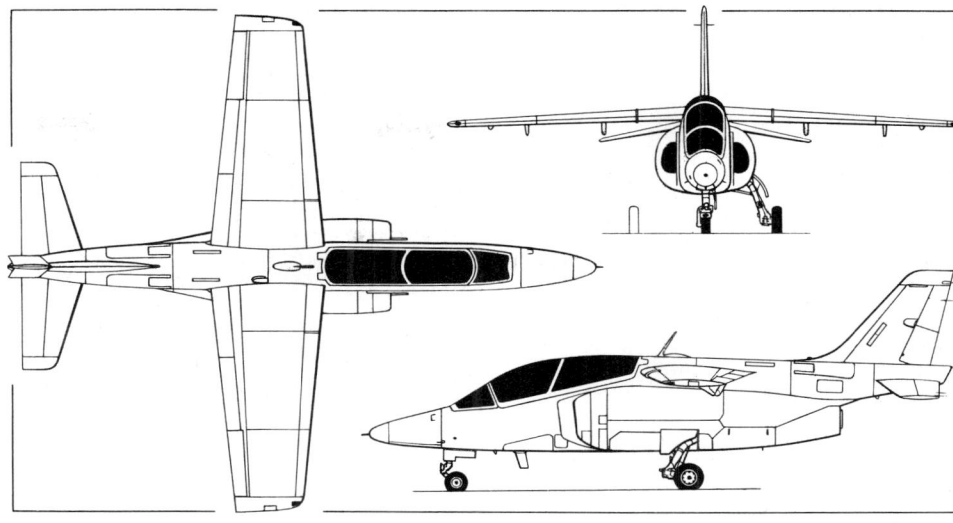

FMA IA 63 Pampa two-seat basic and advanced jet trainer (*Pilot Press*)

AUSTRALIA

AIRCORP
AIRCORP PTY LTD
Suite 11, 261 Given Terrace (PO Box 21), Paddington, Queensland 4064
Telephone: 61 (7) 369 0188
Fax: 61 (7) 369 1120
MANAGING DIRECTOR: H. Anning
PROJECT DIRECTOR, BUSHMASTER: Brian P. Creer

AIRCORP BUSHMASTER

Four years in design and development, the Bushmaster is a two- to four-seat aerobatic light aircraft intended for club training, private flying and rural support. It conforms to FAR Pt 23 standards.

The **B2-N** designation applies to the two-seat prototype (VH-BOI), which first flew on 28 October 1989 powered by a Norton Aerotor rotary engine. Wings of this aircraft were constructed with two metal spars, sheet alloy webs, extruded caps, metal ribs and fabric covering, and were braced by V struts. Fuel was carried in integral tanks within the metal D-nose of each wing leading-edge. The rear fuselage was fabric covered.

Difficulties during test flying, and the absence of expected certification of the Norton engine, obliged Aircorp to abandon its original plan to offer the Bushmaster with a choice of this or Textron Lycoming engines. Airframe changes have also been made to make the aircraft more suitable for series production. Principally, these involve using one-piece extruded spars with the fuel tanks between them, all-metal wing skins, adding three-stage trailing-edge flaps, and bracing each wing by a single I strut.

Production Bushmasters will be marketed in four basic versions, three of them powered by the 86.5 kW (116 hp) Textron Lycoming O-235-N2C flat-four engine and providing two, '2 + 2' and three seats respectively. The three-seat **B3-16** accommodates a single pilot on the centreline, with a bench seat behind for two persons. This rear seat can be removed for the carriage of cargo. The fourth version, a full four-seater with a lengthened fuselage,

Aircorp B2-N Bushmaster two-seat prototype with Norton Aerotor rotary engine

is powered by a 119 or 134 kW (160 or 180 hp) engine (designations **B4-60** and **B4-80** respectively).

The following details apply to the B2 and B3, except where indicated:

TYPE: Two- to four-seat light aircraft.
WINGS: High-wing monoplane, with V strut bracing each side. All-metal constant chord wings, with rounded tips. Three-stage flaps on production version. (Prototype has no flaps.)
FUSELAGE: Welded steel tube structure, with light alloy skin. Prototype has fabric covered rear fuselage.
TAIL UNIT: Conventional structure, with wire braced horizontal surfaces.
LANDING GEAR: Non-retractable tailwheel type. Main units have faired-in side Vs, half-axles, and speed fairings on wheels.
POWER PLANT: One 67.1 kW (90 hp) Norton Aerotor 90 two-chamber rotary engine in prototype. Production aircraft to have an 86.5 kW (116 hp) Textron Lycoming O-235-N2C flat-four. Three-blade propeller. Fuel

capacity 136.4 litres (36 US gallons; 30 Imp gallons) standard.
ACCOMMODATION: To be offered with choice of two, '2 + 2', three or four seats, in fully enclosed cabin with forward opening door on each side. Space for 55 kg (121 lb) of baggage aft of seats.

DIMENSIONS, EXTERNAL:	
Wing span	10.00 m (32 ft 9¾ in)
Length overall	6.40 m (21 ft 0 in)
Wheel track	2.14 m (7 ft 0¼ in)
Wheelbase	4.00 m (13 ft 1½ in)
DIMENSIONS, INTERNAL:	
Cabin: Length	2.70 m (8 ft 10¼ in)
Max width	1.10 m (3 ft 7¼ in)
Max height	1.10 m (3 ft 7¼ in)
AREAS:	
Wings, gross	14.00 m² (150.7 sq ft)
WEIGHTS AND LOADINGS:	
Weight empty: Norton	350 kg (772 lb)
Lycoming	410 kg (904 lb)

Max T-O weight: Utility category	700 kg (1,543 lb)	Max power loading:			PERFORMANCE:	
Normal category	811 kg (1,788 lb)	Utility (Norton)	10.43 kg/kW (17.15 lb/hp)		Max cruising speed	more than 100 knots (185 km/h; 115 mph)
Max wing loading: Utility	50.00 kg/m² (10.24 lb/sq ft)	Utility (Lycoming)	8.16 kg/kW (13.42 lb/hp)		Stalling speed	35 knots (65 km/h; 41 mph)
Normal	57.93 kg/m² (11.86 lb/sq ft)	Normal (Norton)	12.09 kg/kW (19.87 lb/hp)		g limits (Utility category)	+4.4/−2.2
		Normal (Lycoming)	9.46 kg/kW (15.55 lb/hp)			

ASTA
AEROSPACE TECHNOLOGIES OF AUSTRALIA PTY LTD
226 Lorimer Street, Fishermen's Bend, Port Melbourne, Victoria 3207
Telephone: 61 (3) 647 3111
Fax: 61 (3) 646 4381
Telex: AA 34851 ASTAML
MANAGING DIRECTOR: George W. Stuart
MANAGER, CORPORATE AFFAIRS: Andre R. van der Zwan

BUSINESS UNITS:

ASTA Aircraft Services Pty Ltd, Pousties Road, Lara, Victoria 3212
Telephone: 61 (52) 821188
Fax: 61 (52) 823505
GENERAL MANAGER: Graeme Reed

ASTA Military Aircraft Services, Beach Road, Lara, Victoria 3212
Telephone: 61 (52) 822988
Fax: 61 (52) 823345
GENERAL MANAGER: John Jansen

ASTA Systems, 226 Lorimer Street, Fishermen's Bend, Port Melbourne, Victoria 3207
Telephone: 61 (3) 647 3111
Fax: 61 (3) 646 4381
Telex: AA 34851 ASTAML
GENERAL MANAGER: George Watts
ASST GENERAL MANAGER, AND MANAGER UAVs: Les Jones
MANAGER, DEFENCE ELECTRONICS AND SOFTWARE: David Prowse

ASTA Engineering, 226 Lorimer Street, Fishermen's Bend, Port Melbourne, Victoria 3207
Telephone: 61 (3) 647 3111
Fax: 61 (3) 646 4381
Telex: AA 34851 ASTAML
MANAGER, PROJECTS AND BUSINESS DEVELOPMENTS: Noel Jenkinson

AeroSpace Technologies of Australia was established in 1986 as a private enterprise organisation, to succeed the former Government Aircraft Factories (GAF: see earlier editions of *Jane's*). The ASTA group specialises in the design, development, manufacture, assembly, maintenance and modification of aircraft, target drones and guided weapons. The early 1990 workforce totalled about 1,900, located at Fishermen's Bend and Avalon, but ASTA was

reported to be reducing this to just under 1,500 by the end of that year. At Avalon airfield, subassembly of components, final assembly, modification, repair and test flying of jet and other aircraft are undertaken.

ASTA's current aircraft activity includes component manufacture (trailing-edge flaps, flap shrouds, windscreens, canopies and radomes), forward fuselage fitting out, final assembly and flight test of AF/ATF-18A Hornets for the RAAF, and 40 per cent of the Australian production work on the RAAF Pilatus PC-9/A programme. ASTA also produces Krueger flaps for the Boeing 747, in-spar wing ribs and rudders for the 757, rotor blade components for the Sikorsky Black Hawk and Seahawk, fixed shrouds for the Airbus A320, and components for the McDonnell Douglas MD-80 series. An MoU to build rudders for the Boeing 777 was signed in 1990. In addition, ASTA is contracted by Rohr Industries to manufacture CFM56 nacelle components for the McDonnell Douglas MD-11, and is a risk-sharing contractor to Aerospatiale to design, develop and manufacture carbonfibre main and central landing gear doors and floor support panels for the Airbus A330 and A340. ASTA Military Aircraft Services (AMAS) assembles and flight tests the Seahawk helicopter.

AUSTRALIAN AUTOGYRO
THE AUSTRALIAN AUTOGYRO CO
29 Benning Avenue, Turramurra, Sydney, NSW 2074
Telephone: 61 (2) 449 9816
PROPRIETOR: E. R. Minty

AUSTRALIAN AUTOGYRO SKYHOOK
Development history of Mr Ted Minty's Skyhook was recorded in the 1982-83 and earlier *Jane's*. Other specific design features were summarised in the 1989-90 and previous editions. A basic 'open frame' model is designated **Mk I**; also available are a **Mk II** (unpainted, with enclosed body) and a fully customised **Mk III**. Sales by 1 February 1990 included 24 Mk Is and two Mk IIIs, as well as numerous kits and components. These were powered by a 1,835 cc Volkswagen engine, but in 1990 the Rotax 503 dual-ignition engine became available as an alternative power plant. Three Skyhooks (two with VW engines and one with Rotax) were sold during 1990. The aircraft is currently offered with an improved glassfibre body shell and all-composite rotor blades, and the description applies to this version.
TYPE: Single-seat lightweight autogyro.
ROTOR SYSTEM: Two-blade rotor, with low-drag all-composite blades attached directly to a fully adjustable hub bar. Blades are twisted and tapered, with NASA 8H12 aerofoil section inboard and NASA 23012 outboard. Joystick control actuates two nylon encased 6.35 mm (¼ in) stainless steel push/pull cables to operate rotor head and blades.
FUSELAGE: Single keel to which are attached the landing gear, fuselage structure, seat, engine mounting frame, rotor mast and tail unit. Keel and rotor mast are of 5.1 cm (2 in) square section 6061-T6 aluminium alloy with radiused corners. The majority of structural attachments are clamped, rather than bolted or riveted, to reduce to a minimum the number of potential fracture locations in the airframe. Glassfibre fuselage shell on Mks II and III.
TAIL UNIT: Twin rudders, united by a dihedral tailplane attached to the keel. The upper ends of the rudders are braced by double V triangular frames of light alloy and chrome molybdenum steel tube. Rudders manufactured from marine quality aluminium, tailplane from 2024 aluminium sheet. Entire tail assembly operates as a single unit which swivels from side to side to provide directional stability and power-off manoeuvrability.
LANDING GEAR: Non-retractable type with small sprung tailwheel at rear end of keel. Fully sprung steerable nosewheel, linked to rudders. Mainwheels are ultra-lightweight 5 in nylon go-kart rims, each with a 4.00-5 tyre and tube. Disc brakes optional.
POWER PLANT: One 37.25 kW (50 hp) Rotax 503 two-cylinder two-stroke engine, mounted on chrome molybdenum brackets attached to mast and keel, and driving a

Skyhook Mk I single-seat autogyro with Rotax engine and new lightweight open frame

three-blade adjustable-pitch wooden pusher propeller. Also available with 1,835 cc VW engine and two-blade fixed-pitch propeller (see 1990-91 and earlier editions). Fuel contained in pilot's hollow seat, capacity 45.5 litres (12 US gallons; 10 Imp gallons).
ACCOMMODATION: Pilot only, in enclosed cockpit, on rotationally moulded super-strength cross-linked poly-ethylene seat/fuel tank located just forward of mast/keel junction, close to CG. Aircraft can be flown without fuselage shell and Plexiglas windscreen enclosure if desired. Adjustable vents in fuselage nose provide ventilation when the aircraft is flown with the cockpit enclosed.
EQUIPMENT: Standard equipment includes cylinder head high temperature and low fuel warning lights.
DIMENSIONS, EXTERNAL:

Rotor diameter	7.62 m (25 ft 0 in)
Length overall	3.35 m (11 ft 0 in)
Height: to top of rotor head	2.06 m (6 ft 9 in)
to top of cockpit canopy	1.42 m (4 ft 8 in)
Tailplane span (incl rudders)	0.86 m (2 ft 10 in)
Wheel track	1.68 m (5 ft 6 in)
Propeller diameter	1.37 m (4 ft 6 in)

AREAS:

Rotor disc	38.6 m² (415.5 sq ft)

WEIGHTS AND LOADINGS:
Weight empty, excl rotor blades:

Mk I	98 kg (216 lb)
Mk III	147 kg (325 lb)
Max T-O weight	271 kg (597 lb)
Max disc loading	7.03 kg/m² (1.44 lb/sq ft)
Max power loading	7.28 kg/kW (11.94 lb/hp)

PERFORMANCE:

Max level speed	69 knots (129 km/h; 80 mph)
Cruising speed	43 knots (80 km/h; 50 mph)
Max rate of climb at S/L	457 m (1,500 ft)/min
T-O run (depending on headwind)	approx 122 m (400 ft)
Landing run (with disc brakes)	approx 5 m (15 ft)
Range with max fuel	191 nm (354 km; 220 miles)

EAA
EAGLE AIRCRAFT AUSTRALIA LTD
PO Box 586, Fremantle, WA 6160
Telephone: 61 (9) 384 9803
Fax: 61 (9) 384 3460
CHAIRMAN: A. D. B. Graham
MARKETING DIRECTOR: Deryck F. Graham Jr

EAA EAGLE XTS
The Eagle is an all-composites light aircraft intended originally for farming operations, to perform safely in hazardous low-level conditions such as those encountered in aerial cattle mustering. The prototype is built mainly of glassfibre, but production Eagles will utilise Kevlar, carbonfibre, Nomex honeycomb and advanced resins. The design has a 'three flying surface' configuration, with a high-mounted main wing, a low-mounted foreplane and a

tailplane, conceived by US engineer Mr John Roncz, who was chief aerodynamics designer for the round-the-world Voyager aircraft. It is said to be difficult to stall, virtually impossible to spin, and to have good handling characteristics at the point of stall. The production Eagle is designed to conform to ANO 101-55, similar to that of the European JAR 22.

The XTS (for two-seat) prototype, which conforms to current Australian experimental category regulations

(ANO 101-25), first flew in the Spring of 1988, and by October of that year had completed a rigorous 200 hour test programme in which all original design criteria were met. During flight trials, the original 58 kW (78 hp) Aeropower engine was replaced by a 74.5 kW (100 hp) Continental O-200. For the production Eagle, three engines were under test and consideration in early 1991.

Series production was due to begin in 1989, but the absence of promised loan guarantees by the state government led EAA to seek an overseas partner, and a joint venture was formalised on 31 December 1990 with the Malaysian based Assets Accretion, a corporate vehicle for the Malaysian Finance Ministry. Plans are to complete certification in Australia and put the Eagle into production in both countries. Operations were due to restart on 1 March 1991. Meanwhile, EAA has completed its 6,500 m² (69,965 sq ft) facility, and some 85 per cent of production tooling.

DIMENSIONS, EXTERNAL:
Main wing span	6.40 m (21 ft 0 in)

WEIGHTS AND LOADINGS:
Max T-O weight: prototype	659 kg (1,453 lb)
production	450 kg (992 lb)
Max power loading: prototype 8.85 kg/kW (14.53 lb/hp)	

PERFORMANCE (A: prototype with O-200 engine, B: estimated for production aircraft with 67 kW; 90 hp engine):
Max cruising speed: A	121 knots (224 km/h; 139 mph)	
B	130 knots (241 km/h; 149 mph)	
Normal cruising speed:		
A	115 knots (213 km/h; 132 mph)	
B	120 knots (222 km/h; 138 mph)	

Eagle XTS two-seat prototype (74.5 kW; 100 hp Continental O-200 engine)

Min flying speed (no stall, flaps down):		Max rate of climb at S/L: A	244 m (800 ft)/min
A	44 knots (82 km/h; 51 mph)	B	366 m (1,200 ft)/min
B	40 knots (74 km/h; 46 mph)	Endurance, with reserves: B	4 h

HDH

HAWKER DE HAVILLAND LTD (Member company of the Hawker Siddeley Group)

PO Box 30 (361 Milperra Road), Bankstown, NSW 2200
Telephone: 61 (2) 772 8111
Fax: 61 (2) 771 2632
Telex: AA20719
MANAGING DIRECTOR: J. B. Hattersley
TECHNICAL DIRECTOR: R. H. Jeal
COMMERCIAL DIRECTOR: P. A. Smith

Hawker de Havilland is primarily an aerospace and defence company engaged in design, production and support activities for civil and military customers in Australia, the USA, UK and more than 20 nations in Asia, the Pacific and the Middle East. Employment in early 1991 was about 2,800, at 15 locations in Australia, Singapore and the USA.

International airframe subcontracting is the largest single element of HDH's production activity, with sole source contracts for a variety of major subassemblies on Airbus A300, A310, A320 and A330/A340, Boeing 737, 747 and 757, and McDonnell Douglas MD-11 and MD-80 airliners.

HDH is prime contractor to the RAAF for production of PC-9/A turboprop trainers. Earlier, it was a major participant in the RAAF's Hornet programme, part producing and assembling the aircraft's F404 engines, landing gear, weapons/fuel pylons, engine access doors, rear fuselage fairings, electro-hydraulic actuators and accessory drive gearbox. Production of complete F404

engines for the RAAF was completed in mid-1989; F404 upgrade, and manufacture of selected engine items, is continuing for General Electric. HDH also assembled and tested the GE T700 turboshaft engines for the Australian Black Hawk programme.

Engine component production is a major activity at Hawker de Havilland Victoria, Australia's only aero-engine manufacturer. Through its Space Office, HDH is involved in a variety of space related activities, including the production of hardware for Hughes Aussat B satellites.

HDH operates airframe and engine overhaul facilities around Australia, including Bankstown, NSW; Fishermen's Bend and Laverton, Victoria; Perth, WA; and Townsville, Queensland. Customers include the Australian Defence Forces and regional civil and military operators of small/medium-sized fixed-wing aircraft and helicopters. In a new systems integration hangar on Tullamarine International Airport, HDH Victoria is fitting in-flight refuelling equipment to, and updating the avionics of, four RAAF Boeing 707 transports.

HDH's Systems Division at the Defence Research Centre, South Australia, is involved in airborne weapons system development. Its ASTER (advanced staggered triple ejector rack) bomb rack was test flown on an RAAF AF-18 in late 1988. A Harpoon CCWS (captive carriage weapon simulator) is in production for the RAAF.

Under contract to Sikorsky Aircraft, HDH carried out at Bankstown structural modification, assembly, systems integration and testing of RAAF/Army Black Hawk

helicopters. The Australian Black Hawks incorporate a variety of Australian role-specific modifications including a Seahawk AFCS. HDH completed 37 of the 39 Black Hawks ordered by the Australian government, delivering the last one in early 1991.

Under a risk sharing agreement signed on 21 February 1989, HDH will be responsible for final design and production of the airframe for the McDonnell Douglas MDX light helicopter (see United States section), shipping the airframes to the US manufacturer for final assembly installation, including the engine, transmission and other systems.

HDH (PILATUS) PC-9/A

The version of the PC-9 ordered for the RAAF is designated PC-9/A, differing from the standard Swiss built PC-9 (see Pilatus entry) in having Bendix EFIS instrumentation, and PC-7 low pressure tyres with bulged mainwheel doors. Under a joint marketing arrangement with Pilatus, HDH is offering the PC-9/A to potential regional customers.

The first of two Swiss built PC-9/As (A23-001) was delivered to the RAAF in the Summer of 1987, a further 17 were completed from kits supplied by Pilatus, and HDH is now producing the remaining 48 of the total Australian order for 67. The first three HDH assembled PC-9/As were handed over to the RAAF on 19 December 1987, and 25 had been delivered by early 1990, with deliveries then scheduled to increase to two per month.

MAC

MELBOURNE AIRCRAFT CORPORATION PTY LTD
(trading as International Aircraft Corporation Pty Ltd)

Hangar 102, Essendon Airport, Essendon, Victoria 3041
Telephone: 61 (3) 379 7855
Fax: 61 (3) 379 4555
Telex: 31473 MELAIR AA
MANAGING DIRECTOR: Jess Smith
MARKETING MANAGER: Roger James

MAC MAMBA

After two years in conception and design, the prototype of this new light aircraft (VH-JSA) flew for the first time on 25 January 1989. The original 86.5 kW (116 hp) Textron Lycoming O-235 engine was later replaced by the O-320-D1A or IO-320-D1G.

A pre-production Mamba first flew in December 1989. Certification to Australian ANO 101-22/FAR 23 was nearing completion in the third quarter of 1990, and series production has started. Early orders include one from a local flying school, for aerobatic training, and three for the Conservation and Land Management Department of Western Australia. The latter are to be used for forest fire patrol. The Mamba was also being evaluated in late 1990 by the Royal Thai Army as a possible L-19 Bird Dog replacement.

The following details apply to the pre-production aircraft:
TYPE: Two-seat light aircraft.
WINGS: High-wing monoplane, with single bracing strut each side. NACA 4412 constant section; 1° 30′ dihedral from roots. Two tubular metal spars with aluminium alloy skin. Trailing-edges have split flaps and Frise type differentially operating ailerons, latter each fitted with servo tab.

Prototype MAC Mamba two-seat light aircraft

FUSELAGE: 4130 steel tube frame with aluminium alloy skins.
TAIL UNIT: Slightly sweptback vertical and non-swept horizontal surfaces. Variable incidence tailplane (on prototype only). Trim tab in one elevator.
LANDING GEAR: Non-retractable tricycle type. MAC cantilever self-sprung mainwheel legs, each with Cleveland wheel and Dunlop 6.00-6 × 4 tyre. Cleveland tailwheel has 5.00-5 × 4 Dunlop tyre and is steerable ± 30°. MAC mainwheel brakes. Provision to fit Edo floats.
POWER PLANT: One 119 kW (160 hp) Textron Lycoming O-320-D1A or IO-320-D1G flat-four engine, with Hartzell or Hoffmann two-blade propeller. Fuel capacity 327 litres (86 US gallons; 72 Imp gallons). Oil capacity 9.1 litres (2.4 US gallons; 2 Imp gallons).

ACCOMMODATION: Extensively glazed cabin seating two persons in tandem. Door on starboard side. Space for 20 kg (44 lb) of baggage aft of seats. Cabin heated and ventilated.
SYSTEMS: 14V or 28V DC electrical system (50A alternator).
AVIONICS: Duel nav/com radios; glideslope, marker beacon receiver, ADF, PDR encoder and intercom.
ARMAMENT: External attachment under each outer wing (load limit 136 kg; 300 lb per station) for 3 in standard rockets or gun pods of up to 20 mm calibre.
DIMENSIONS, EXTERNAL:
Wing span	8.74 m (28 ft 8 in)
Wing chord, constant	1.12 m (3 ft 8 in)
Wing aspect ratio	7.9

Length overall	6.63 m (21 ft 9 in)	Max wing loading	86.81 kg/m² (17.79 lb/sq ft)	Stalling speed, flaps down, power off	
Height overall	2.67 m (8 ft 9 in)	Max power loading	7.04 kg/kW (11.56 lb/hp)		53 knots (99 km/h; 61 mph) EAS
Propeller diameter	1.83 m (6 ft 0 in)	PERFORMANCE:		Max rate of climb at S/L	464 m (1,524 ft)/min
Propeller ground clearance	0.20 m (8 in)	Max level speed at S/L, ISA		Service ceiling	4,875 m (16,000 ft)
AREAS:			152 knots (281 km/h; 175 mph)	T-O run	152 m (500 ft)
Wings, gross	9.66 m² (104.0 sq ft)	Max cruising speed at S/L, ISA		T-O to 15 m (50 ft)	305 m (1,000 ft)
WEIGHTS AND LOADINGS:			136 knots (252 km/h; 156 mph)	Range: at 75% power	620 nm (1,149 km; 714 miles)
Weight empty	567 kg (1,250 lb)	Econ cruising speed at S/L, ISA		at 60% power	680 nm (1,260 km; 783 miles)
Max T-O and landing weight	839 kg (1,850 lb)		128 knots (237 km/h; 147 mph)		

SEABIRD

SEABIRD AVIATION AUSTRALIA PTY LTD

Hervey Bay Airport, PO Box 618, Pialba, Queensland 4655
Telephone: 61 (71) 25 3144
Fax: 61 (71) 25 3123
MANAGING DIRECTOR: Donald C. Adams
CHIEF DESIGN ENGINEER: C. W. Whitney

SEABIRD SB5 SENTINEL

The SB5 (originally SB-4) Sentinel is intended for certification under FAR Pt 23. Its primary application is for observation and reconnaissance, for which it offers a helicopter-like view from the cockpit and very good low-speed handling. Secondary roles for training or agricultural missions are also foreseen. Design began in January 1985 and prototype construction in January 1988. Two prototypes have flown: VH-SBI (c/n 001) on 1 October 1989 with a Norton NR 642 rotary engine, and c/n 003 (VH-SBU) on 3 January 1991 with an Emdair CF 112 geared engine with fuel injection. Production aircraft will have a designation suffix letter (**SB5N** or **SB5E**) according to the power plant installed. A structural test airframe (c/n 002) has also been completed. Orders for the SB5 totalled 30 by mid-January 1991. A more powerful version, the **SB7L Seeker**, is described separately.

TYPE: Two-seat observation and training light aircraft.
WINGS: Strut braced high-wing monoplane, with NACA 63₂-215 aerofoil section and constant chord except at tips. Dihedral 2° 30′ from roots. Incidence 6°. No sweepback. Aluminium alloy structure, with mechanically actuated slotted ailerons and trailing-edge slotted flaps. Single bracing strut, with jury strut, each side. NASA leading-edge cuffs to improve stall characteristics. Full-chord fence on top of each wing at mid-span.
FUSELAGE: Pod and boom structure, mainly of 4130 chrome molybdenum steel tube with a Kevlar non load-bearing skin. Aluminium alloy semi-monocoque tailboom. Anti-spin strakes on rear fuselage.
TAIL UNIT: Swept fin (with dorsal fin) and horn balanced rudder; non-swept fixed incidence cantilever tailplane with one-piece horn balanced elevator. Mechanically actuated control surfaces. Construction similar to that of wings. Elevator trim tab.
LANDING GEAR: Non-retractable, with Cleveland 6.00-6 mainwheels and fairings on cantilever spring steel legs plus a Maule solid-tyred tailwheel with oil/nitrogen oleo strut. Mainwheel tyre pressure 1.72 bars (25 lb/sq in); Cleveland disc brakes. Alternative float gear to be developed.
POWER PLANT: One 67 kW (90 hp) Norton NR 642 rotary (first prototype) or 65 kW (87 hp) Emdair CF 112 four-stroke engine, pod mounted above and behind cabin and driving an MT two-blade fixed-pitch pusher propeller (wood and composite blades) via a 3:1 reduction gear. (Electric variable-pitch propeller under development.) Fuel in two integral wing tanks, combined usable capacity 114 litres (30 US gallons; 25 Imp gallons) standard, 200 litres (53 US gallons; 44 Imp gallons) optional. Overwing pressure refuelling point for each tank. Oil capacity 4.5 litres (1.2 US gallons; 1 Imp gallon) for Norton engine, 6 litres (1.6 US gallons; 1.32 Imp gallons) for Emdair CF 112.
ACCOMMODATION: Side by side seats, adjustable fore and aft, for pilot and co-pilot or observer/passenger in enclosed

Second (SB5E) prototype of the Seabird Sentinel lightweight observation aircraft

and extensively glazed cabin. Right hand seat is removable, and aircraft can be flown with both forward opening fully glazed doors removed. Space for 22.7 kg (50 lb) of baggage aft of seats.
SYSTEMS: 24V 35A alternator standard in SB5N (24V 60A in SB5E).
AVIONICS: VOR, ADF and dual VHF com.
EQUIPMENT: Wing hardpoints for external stores. Quick-change photo/survey modules, stretcher or 100 litre (26.4 US gallon; 22 Imp gallon) spraytank in place of right hand seat.

DIMENSIONS, EXTERNAL:
Wing span	10.60 m (34 ft 9¼ in)
Wing chord, constant	1.22 m (4 ft 0 in)
Wing aspect ratio	8.8
Length overall	6.70 m (21 ft 11¾ in)
Fuselage: Max width	1.12 m (3 ft 8 in)
Height overall	1.83 m (6 ft 0 in)
Tailplane span	3.05 m (10 ft 0 in)
Wheel track	1.83 m (6 ft 0 in)
Propeller diameter	1.73 m (5 ft 8 in)

DIMENSIONS, INTERNAL:
Cabin: Max length	1.83 m (6 ft 0 in)
Max width	1.09 m (3 ft 7 in)
Max height	1.12 m (3 ft 8 in)
Baggage compartment volume	0.23 m³ (8.0 cu ft)

AREAS:
Wings, gross	12.77 m² (137.46 sq ft)

WEIGHTS AND LOADINGS:
Basic operating weight empty (prototype)	
	405 kg (893 lb)
Max fuel	113 kg (250 lb)
Max T-O weight: Utility	650 kg (1,433 lb)
Normal	750 kg (1,653 lb)
Max wing loading	50.90 kg/m² (10.43 lb/sq ft)
Max power loading	9.70 kg/kW (15.92 lb/hp)

PERFORMANCE (first prototype, NR 642 engine):
Never-exceed speed (VNE)	
	127 knots (235 km/h; 146 mph)

Max level speed at 1,525 m (5,000 ft)	
	104 knots (193 km/h; 120 mph)
Max cruising speed at 1,525 m (5,000 ft)	
	90 knots (166 km/h; 103 mph)
Stalling speed, flaps down, engine idling	
	38 knots (71 km/h; 44 mph)
Max rate of climb at S/L	244 m (800 ft)/min
Service ceiling	4,875 m (16,000 ft)
T-O and landing run	92 m (300 ft)
T-O to 15 m (50 ft)	305 m (1,000 ft)
Landing from 15 m (50 ft)	365 m (1,200 ft)
Min ground turning radius (based on mainwheel)	
	6.40 m (21 ft 0 in)
Range, 45 min reserves:	
standard fuel and max payload	
	380 nm (704 km; 437 miles)
max optional fuel	800 nm (1,480 km; 920 miles)
g limits	+4.4/−2.23 (Utility category)

SEABIRD SB7L SEEKER

The Seeker is a more powerful four-seat version of the Sentinel, the L suffix indicating a Textron Lycoming engine. A prototype (c/n 004) was expected to fly in April 1991. Differences from the SB5 are as follows:

TYPE: Four-seat light aircraft.
FUSELAGE: Lengthened by 300 mm (11¾ in); cabin widened by 51 mm (2 in).
POWER PLANT: One 86.5 kW (116 hp) Textron Lycoming O-235 flat-four engine, driving an Aero Trading constant-speed propeller. Oil capacity 7 litres (1.85 US gallons; 1.54 Imp gallons).
ACCOMMODATION: Removable rear seat capable of carrying two passengers within specified weight limits. Baggage compartment volume 0.45 m³ (16.0 cu ft) with rear seat removed.

WEIGHTS AND LOADINGS:
Weight empty	550 kg (1,212 lb)
Max T-O weight	850 kg (1,874 lb)

SEAIR

SEAIR PACIFIC PTY LTD

PO Box 166, Airlie Beach, Queensland 4802
Telephone: 61 (79) 46 9133
Telex: 46489
MANAGING DIRECTOR: Shane O'Hare

This company reported in late 1988 that, subject to availability of funding, it was committed to building a full size prototype of an eight-passenger commercial seaplane powered by twin pusher engines, built of composite materials, and having a maximum level speed of 150 knots (278 km/h; 173 mph). Initial design work had then been

completed, and it was hoped to fly the prototype by 1991, but no recent news of progress has been received.

TRANSAVIA

TRANSFIELD CONSTRUCTION PTY LTD, TRANSAVIA DIVISION

73 Station Road, Seven Hills, NSW 2147
Telephone: 61 (2) 624 4400
Fax: 61 (2) 624 2548
Telex: AA 170300 TRANSAC
AVIATION SALES MANAGER: Neil McDonald
Transavia, formed in 1964, is a division of Transfield Construction Pty Ltd, one of Australia's largest construction companies.

TRANSAVIA SKYFARMER

The original PL-12 **Airtruk**, designed by Mr Luigi Pellarini for agricultural use and first flown on 22 April 1965, was type certificated on 10 February 1966. A general purpose version, the **PL-12-U** for passenger/cargo/aerial survey/cropspraying, flew in December 1970, and received certification in February 1971. Deliveries of production aircraft began in December 1966, and by early 1991 about 120 of all versions (including 18 assembled by Flight Engineers Ltd in New Zealand) had been sold for use in Australia, New Zealand, China, Denmark, Malaysia, South Africa, Taiwan, Thailand, the USA and Yugoslavia.

The **Skyfarmer T-300** (first flight July 1978) differs chiefly in having a Textron Lycoming IO-540 engine, and was followed in 1981 by an improved **Skyfarmer T-300A**. Significant changes in the latter include a larger upper-fuselage structure (providing a roomier cockpit and larger hopper throat), and new aerodynamically balanced ailerons, horn balanced elevators and electromechanical flaps to reduce pilot workload. This version received FAA certification in 1986. A **PL-12/M300** military utility version, adapted from the T-300, was under development in 1989.

Five Skyfarmers provided to China in 1986 are of a **Skyfarmer T-400** version, powered by a Textron Lycoming IO-720 engine, for which FAA certification was being sought in 1989.

Details of the original PL-12 and PL-12-U can be found in earlier editions of *Jane's*. The following description applies to the Skyfarmer T-300A, except where indicated:

TYPE: Single-engined agricultural aircraft.

WINGS: Strut braced sesquiplane. Wing section NACA 23012. Dihedral 1° 30′ on upper wings. Incidence (upper wings) 3° 30′, stub-wings 4°. Conventional all-metal structure, covered with Aiclad sheet. All-metal trailing-edge flaps and ailerons, covered with ribbed Alclad sheet, and operated manually. Upper-wing fence on each side of each tailboom to ensure full aileron control, even below stalling speeds. Small stub-wings with door at base of fuselage, constructed on a 4130 steel leading-edge D box section welded to the integral hopper frame and braced to the upper wings by a V strut on each side.

FUSELAGE: Pod shaped structure comprising 4130 welded steel frame with stainless steel and 2024 Alclad covering. Hopper is integrally structured. Entire one-piece rear cabin is of glassfibre to eliminate corrosion and withstand hard wear and tear.

TAIL UNIT: Twin units, each comprising a fin, rudder and separate T tailplane with elevator, and each carried on a cantilever tapered tubular Alclad boom extending from the upper wings.

LANDING GEAR: Non-retractable tricycle type. Mainwheels carried on pivoted trailing legs supported by Transavia short stroke, heavy duty oleo-pneumatic shock absorbing suspension units. Port and starboard main units are interchangeable. Nosewheel carried on a heavy duty, long stroke straight oleo-suspension unit. All wheels and tyres same size (8.00-6); tyre pressure 1.72 bars (25 lb/sq in) (nose); 2.07 bars (30 lb/sq in) (main). Cleveland disc brakes with parking lock.

POWER PLANT: One 224 kW (300 hp) Textron Lycoming IO-540-K1A5 flat-six engine, driving a Hartzell three-blade constant-speed metal propeller (298 kW; 400 hp IO-720-D1BD in Skyfarmer 400). Two upper-wing fuel tanks, total capacity 189 litres (50 US gallons; 41.5 Imp gallons). Optional long-range installation of second tank in each upper mainplane (standard in T-400), increasing total usable capacity to 364 litres (96.2 US gallons; 80.1 Imp gallons). Refuelling point above upper wings. Oil capacity 11.4 litres (3 US gallons; 2.5 Imp gallons).

ACCOMMODATION: Single-seat cockpit, with door on starboard side. Two-seat cabin aft of chemical hopper/tank for carriage of ground crew, with door at rear of lower deck. Accommodation heated and ventilated.

SYSTEMS: 24V electrical system standard, 12V optional.

AVIONICS: Optional VHF, HF, ADF, artificial horizon and directional gyro.

EQUIPMENT: Standard hopper aft of cockpit for 907 kg (2,000 lb) of dry chemical or 818 litres (216 US gallons; 180 Imp gallons) of liquid. Optional Powermist spray system, Transavia safety take-off weight (STOW) checking system, wire cutter, seed spreader attachment, and cockpit heater.

DIMENSIONS, EXTERNAL:
Upper wing span: 300A, 400   11.98 m (39 ft 3½ in)

Transavia Skyfarmer T-300A agricultural aircraft (Textron Lycoming IO-540 engine)

Upper wing chord (300A):	
constant portion	1.76 m (5 ft 9¼ in)
at tip	1.27 m (4 ft 2 in)
Stub-wing span	4.93 m (16 ft 2 in)
Length overall: 300A	6.35 m (20 ft 10 in)
400	7.37 m (24 ft 2 in)
Length of fuselage: 300A	4.19 m (13 ft 9 in)
Height overall: 300A	2.79 m (9 ft 2 in)
400	2.87 m (9 ft 5 in)
Fuselage: Max width	0.97 m (3 ft 2 in)
Tailplane span (each)	2.13 m (7 ft 0 in)
Distance between tailplanes:	
300A, 400	3.48 m (11 ft 5 in)
Wheel track	2.44 m (8 ft 0 in)
Wheelbase	1.64 m (5 ft 4½ in)
Propeller diameter: 300A	2.13 m (7 ft 0 in)
400	2.18 m (7 ft 2 in)
Min propeller ground clearance: 300A	0.36 m (1 ft 2 in)
Passenger door: Height	0.97 m (3 ft 2 in)
DIMENSIONS, INTERNAL:	
Rear passenger cabin: Length	1.83 m (6 ft 0 in)
Max width	0.97 m (3 ft 2 in)
Max height	2.03 m (6 ft 8 in)
Floor area	0.37 m² (4 sq ft)
Volume: Passenger cabin	0.85 m³ (30 cu ft)
Hopper: 300A, 400	1.05 m³ (37 cu ft)
AREAS:	
Wings, gross: 300A	24.53 m² (264.0 sq ft)
400	26.76 m² (288.0 sq ft)
Ailerons, total	1.67 m² (18.0 sq ft)
Trailing-edge flaps, total	1.67 m² (18.0 sq ft)
Fins, total	1.30 m² (14.0 sq ft)
Rudders, total	0.56 m² (6.0 sq ft)
Tailplanes, total	2.60 m² (28.0 sq ft)
Elevators, total, incl tabs	1.30 m² (14.0 sq ft)
WEIGHTS AND LOADINGS:	
Typical weight empty: 300A	953 kg (2,101 lb)
400	1,111 kg (2,450 lb)
Max T-O weight (agricultural category):	
300A	1,925 kg (4,244 lb)
400	2,227 kg (4,910 lb)

Max T-O weight (normal category):	
300A	1,724 kg (3,800 lb)
400	1,814 kg (4,000 lb)
Max landing weight: 300A	1,723 kg (3,800 lb)
400	1,814 kg (4,000 lb)
Max wing loading: 300A	78.5 kg/m² (16.1 lb/sq ft)
400	83.2 kg/m² (17.0 lb/sq ft)
Max power loading: 300A	8.6 kg/kW (14.15 lb/hp)
400	7.5 kg/kW (12.28 lb/hp)
PERFORMANCE (at max agricultural T-O weight, ISA at S/L, except where indicated):	
Never-exceed speed (VNE):	
300A and 400	148 knots (274 km/h; 170 mph)
Max level speed:	
300A at 915 m (3,000 ft)	
	106 knots (196 km/h; 122 mph)
400	109 knots (202 km/h; 125 mph)
Max cruising speed (75% power):	
300A	102 knots (188 km/h; 117 mph)
400	103 knots (191 km/h; 118 mph)
Stalling speed, power on (300A and 400):	
flaps up	47 knots (88 km/h; 55 mph)
flaps down	39 knots (73 km/h; 45 mph)
Stalling speed, power off (300A and 400):	
flaps up	52 knots (97 km/h; 60 mph)
flaps down	50 knots (93 km/h; 58 mph)
Max rate of climb at S/L: 300A	156 m (514 ft)/min
400	168 m (550 ft)/min
* Max light-weight rate of climb:	
300A	457 m (1,500 ft)/min
400	488 m (1,600 ft)/min
Service ceiling: 300A and 400	3,810 m (12,500 ft)
* Light-weight service ceiling:	
300A and 400	6,890 m (22,600 ft)
T-O run: 300A	329 m (1,080 ft)
400	275 m (900 ft)
* Light-weight T-O run: 300A	77 m (252 ft)
400	72 m (234 ft)
* Light-weight landing run: 300A	82 m (270 ft)
400	78 m (255 ft)
* *Weight of empty aircraft plus pilot and 50 per cent standard fuel*	

VTOL

VTOL AIRCRAFT PTY LTD

123 Marshall Street, Kotara Heights, NSW 2288
Telephone: 61 (49) 43 5348
CHAIRMAN: Duan A. Phillips

VTOL PHILLICOPTER Mk 1

The prototype Phillicopter, a photograph of which can be found in the 1989-90 *Jane's*, made its first flight in 1971. Its original 74.5 kW (100 hp) O-200-C engine was later replaced by a 108 kW (145 hp) Rolls-Royce Continental O-300. Weight reduction, ground running tests and transmission component monitoring were being conducted with this aircraft in 1991.

Development of a modified pre-production example, begun some years ago, is still in the design stage, and other engine options are being considered.

AUSTRIA

HB

HB-AIRCRAFT INDUSTRIES LUFTFAHRZEUG AG

Postfach 27, Dr Adolf-Schärf-Strasse 42, A-4053 Haid
Telephone: 43 (7) 229 88375/88355
Fax: 43 (7) 229 80118
Telex: 21909
DIRECTORS:
Willy Reinhardt
Heribert Katzenberger
Heino Brditschka

HB-AIRCRAFT HB-23 HOBBYLINER and SCANLINER

The Hobbyliner and Scanliner are registered in Austria as motor gliders, with numerical instead of alphabetical registrations. The manufacturer, however, wishes them to be regarded as light aircraft.

The following versions were in production in 1989:

HB-23/2400 Hobbyliner: Basic side by side two-seat light aircraft; 40 built by January 1989. Certificated in Austria, Germany, Italy, Switzerland and the USA.

HB-23/2400 Scanliner: Version of HB-23 with bubble canopy to provide optimum air to ground forward

view. Suitable for oil and powerline inspection, coastal and border patrol, policing, observation, survey, fish spotting, pollution control, and communications platform roles. Provision for hardpoint under each wing, on which can be carried a miniature FLIR or SLAR pod, LLL TV, searchlight or other stores. Total of 10 built by January 1989. Certificated in Austria, Italy, Spain and the USA. See also entry for Ciskei Aircraft Industries.

TYPE: Two-seat utility light aircraft.

WINGS: Cantilever high-wing monoplane. Wortmann wing sections: FX-61-184 at root, FX-60-126 at tip. Dihedral 2° on outer panels. Incidence 3°. No sweep. Single main box spar of PhBu 7 (laminated beechwood) and plywood, wooden ribs, and overall plywood covering. All-wood ailerons. Spoilers on upper surface.

FUSELAGE: Main fuselage pod has a welded steel tube frame with glassfibre skin; rear fuselage comprises upper and lower tailbooms, covered in plywood except for triangular cutout in area of propeller arc.

TAIL UNIT: Plywood covered wooden structure comprising fin, rudder, fixed incidence T tailplane, and elevators. Trim tab in starboard elevator.

LANDING GEAR: Non-retractable tricycle type. Mainwheels have self-sprung cantilever glassfibre legs, size 5.00-5 or 6.00-6 tyres (pressure 2.5 bars; 36.3 lb/sq in). Steerable nosewheel, with size 3.00-4, 3.50 or 4.00-4 tyre.

POWER PLANT: One 74.2 kW (98 hp) 2,400 cc Porsche modified Volkswagen G/2 four-cylinder motorcar engine, mounted aft of cabin with rubber belt drive to a Mühlbauer MT 172LD 130 2C or Hoffmann HO-14C/172 130LD two-blade fixed-pitch pusher propeller (constant-speed three-blade propeller optional). Single fuel tank in wing centre-section, capacity 76 litres (20 US gallons; 16.7 Imp gallons) in Hobbyliner, 100 litres (26.4 US gallons; 22 Imp gallons) in Scanliner.

ACCOMMODATION: Fully enclosed cabin for two persons, on side by side adjustable seats; 0.23 m³ (8.1 cu ft) of baggage space aft of seats. One-piece fixed canopy forward, aft of which are twin window/doors hinged on centreline and opening upward. VFR instrumentation standard, IFR panel optional.

DIMENSIONS, EXTERNAL:
Wing span	16.40 m (53 ft 9¾ in)
Wing chord: at root	1.538 m (5 ft 0½ in)
at tip	0.60 m (1 ft 11½ in)
Wing aspect ratio	14.1
Width, outer wing panels removed	7.15 m (23 ft 5½ in)
Length overall: Hobbyliner	8.00 m (26 ft 3 in)

HB-Aircraft HB-23/2400 Hobbyliner two-seat utility light aircraft

Scanliner	7.35 m (24 ft 1½ in)
Height overall	2.45 m (8 ft 0½ in)
Wheel track	1.80 m (5 ft 11 in)
Wheelbase	2.46 m (8 ft 1 in)

AREAS:
Wings, gross	19.067 m² (205.2 sq ft)

WEIGHTS AND LOADINGS:
Weight empty, equipped: both versions	560 kg (1,234 lb)
Max T-O weight: Hobbyliner	760 kg (1,676 lb)
Scanliner	850 kg (1,874 lb)
Max wing loading:	
Hobbyliner	39.86 kg/m² (8.16 lb/sq ft)
Scanliner	44.58 kg/m² (9.13 lb/sq ft)
Max power loading:	
Hobbyliner	10.24 kg/kW (17.10 lb/hp)
Scanliner	11.46 kg/kW (19.12 lb/hp)

PERFORMANCE (unpowered):
Best glide ratio at 53 knots (98 km/h; 61 mph):	
Hobbyliner	22
Scanliner	19
Min rate of sink at 50 knots (92 km/h; 57 mph):	
Hobbyliner	1.20 m (3.94 ft)/s
Scanliner	1.40 m (4.59 ft)/s
Stalling speed	41 knots (75 km/h; 47 mph)
g limits (both versions):	
semi-aerobatic, up to T-O weight of 750 kg; 1,653 lb	+5.3/-3
Utility category	+4.4/-3

PERFORMANCE (powered):
Never-exceed speed (VNE):	
both versions	108 knots (200 km/h; 124 mph) IAS
Max cruising speed (75% power):	
both versions	97 knots (180 km/h; 112 mph)
Min patrol speed:	
both versions	54 knots (100 km/h; 62 mph)
Stalling speed:	
both versions	43 knots (80 km/h; 50 mph)
Max rate of climb at S/L:	
Hobbyliner	228 m (748 ft)/min
Scanliner	216 m (709 ft)/min
Service ceiling: both versions	5,000 m (16,400 ft)
T-O to 15 m (50 ft):	
Hobbyliner	160 m (525 ft)
Scanliner	290 m (950 ft)

Landing run: both versions	210 m (689 ft)
Range with max fuel, no reserves:	
Hobbyliner	432 nm (800 km; 497 miles)
Scanliner	693 nm (1,285 km; 798 miles)
Endurance: Hobbyliner	6 h
Scanliner	10 h

HB-AIRCRAFT HB-202

HB-Aircraft Industries has flown the prototype (OE-AHB) of this derivative of the HB-23 series, intended for certification under European JAR VLA (very light aircraft) regulations and to US FAR Pt 23 standards, with a VW-Porsche or Textron Lycoming flat-four engine respectively. The fuselage and landing gear are substantially similar to those on the Hobbyliner/Scanliner, but the HB-202 has a shorter span one-piece wing (with Fowler trailing-edge flaps instead of spoilers) and a shorter, sweptback fin and rudder with low-set tailplane and elevators. Wingtips and parts of the tail unit are of reinforced glassfibre. The JAR VLA version was to be made available also in kit form. Applications for the HB-202 include pilot training, touring and reconnaissance.

POWER PLANT: One 82 kW (110 hp) 2,400 cc Volkswagen-Porsche VW-HB-2400 G/2 or 119 kW (160 hp) Textron Lycoming O-320 flat-four engine, in installation similar to that of HB-23, driving a three-blade constant-speed pusher propeller.

DIMENSIONS, EXTERNAL:
Wing span	10.00 m (32 ft 9¾ in)
Wing aspect ratio	7.78
Length overall	7.40 m (24 ft 3⅓ in)
Height overall	2.60 m (8 ft 6½ in)

AREAS:
Wings, gross	12.86 m² (138.4 sq ft)

WEIGHTS AND LOADINGS:
Max T-O weight	750 kg (1,653 lb)
Max wing loading	58.32 kg/m² (11.94 lb/sq ft)
Max power loading:	
VW-Porsche	9.15 kg/kW (15.03 lb/hp)
Lycoming	6.30 kg/kW (10.33 lb/hp)

PERFORMANCE (estimated. A with VW engine, B with O-320):
Never-exceed speed (VNE):	
A, B	155 knots (288 km/h; 178 mph)
Max cruising speed: A	102 knots (190 km/h; 118 mph)
B	132 knots (245 km/h; 152 mph)
Stalling speed (A and B):	
flaps up	46 knots (85 km/h; 53 mph)
30° flap	37 knots (67 km/h; 42 mph)
Max rate of climb at S/L: A	270 m (886 ft)/min
B	360 m (1,181 ft)/min
T-O run: A	180 m (591 ft)
B	120 m (394 ft)
Range with max fuel: A	701 nm (1,300 km; 808 miles)
B	593 nm (1,100 km; 683 miles)

Prototype of the HB-Aircraft HB-202 general purpose aircraft

BELGIUM

PROMAVIA
PROMAVIA SA

Chaussée de Fleurus 181, B-6200 Gosselies-Aéroport
Telephone: 32 (71) 35 08 29
Fax: 32 (71) 35 79 54
Telex: 51872 SQUAL B
PRESIDENT: André L. Delhamende
VICE-PRESIDENT: Philippe Delhamende
MARKETING MANAGER: Joseph Bernas

Promavia SA was formed by a number of industrialists, investment companies and a bank, with offices and facilities at Charleroi-Gosselies Airport. Following a market survey completed in 1983, the company initiated the Jet Squalus programme, commissioning Dott Ing Stelio Frati to undertake design and prototype construction. Substantial financial backing was obtained from the Belgian government in 1985 to contribute towards prototype research and development. Marketing and support of any production Jet Squalus, including training programmes, would be undertaken by Promavia; production is intended to be undertaken in various countries worldwide, in addition to Belgium.

Promavia has proposed the Jet Squalus to the USAF and US Navy as a potential replacement for, respectively, the Cessna T-37 and Beechcraft T-34C. For this purpose, it has established contacts with US manufacturers to build any examples ordered for the US market. The Jet Squalus has also been offered to the Canadian Forces, and was due to be demonstrated in that country in March/April 1991.

PROMAVIA JET SQUALUS F1300 NGT

The Jet Squalus (Latin for 'shark') was designed to cover all stages of flying training, from ab initio to part of the advanced syllabus, and to be powered by a small, modern, fuel-efficient and quiet turbofan engine. A side by side seating arrangement was chosen for instructor and trainee, and four underwing attachment points enable it also to undertake weapons training or light tactical missions. Composite materials are used for fairings and some non-structural components; otherwise the aircraft is basically of metal construction throughout.

Marketing programmes have been developed to offer the Jet Squalus to airlines and other civilian customers through leasing companies, to establish a new 'jet air academy' concept. The Jet Squalus has also been proposed as an 'air ward system' (AWS), in the following four versions:

AWS-MS/SAR: Maritime surveillance/search and rescue, with SLAR and VHF-FM com radio.

AWS-R: Reconnaissance, with photographic equipment and a VLF/Omega R/Nav system.

AWS-W: For bombing and gunnery training, police and border defence missions.

AWS-TT: For target towing.

In addition, Promavia was marketing internationally in 1990 a proposed military training package which would combine the Jet Squalus NGT with the ATTA 3000 (see following entry) to offer complete primary, basic and full advanced training enabling young trainee pilots to graduate to such advanced combat aircraft as the F-16, F/A-18 and Tornado.

Two prototypes have been built, the first of which made its first flight on 30 April 1987 and is powered by a Garrett TFE109-1 turbofan. The second prototype (OO-JET), for which an uprated TFE109-3 of 7.12 kN (1,600 lb st) was delivered in February 1991, is equipped with air-conditioning and anti-icing systems. Up to that time, this aircraft had not been flown. Static, flutter and other testing of major components has been completed, as have drawings for the production version. A third prototype, which will have a new pressurised cockpit and advanced design features, is under construction.

In June 1989, at which time the first prototype had completed approx 250 hours' flying, an agreement was announced for 100 or more Jet Squalus NGT trainers to be built by OGMA in Portugal, for use by the Portuguese Air Force (approx 30–35) and civilian agencies. No date for the start of this programme had been announced by early 1991, at which time it was under review by the Portuguese government.

The following description applies to the first prototype, except where indicated:

TYPE: Two-seat aircraft for pilot screening, primary, basic and part of advanced jet training.

WINGS: Cantilever low-wing monoplane, with supercritical wing section (thickness/chord ratio 13 per cent, constant). Dihedral 6° from roots. Incidence 1° at root, –1° 45′ at tip. Single-spar structure in light alloy with flush riveted stressed skin. Differentially operated Frise ailerons with servo-tabs, airbrakes, and hydraulically operated trailing-edge flaps.

FUSELAGE: Semi-monocoque structure with press-formed light alloy frames, linked by stringers and stiffeners; flush riveted aluminium alloy skin. Hydraulically operated two-piece light alloy airbrake in lower central part of fuselage, in line with flaps. Avionics and equipment bay in nose. Large quick-disconnect panel in lower rear fuselage permits rapid engine access or removal.

TAIL UNIT: Cantilever structure with flush riveted skin. Sweptback fin and rudder; fixed incidence non-swept tailplane, with elevators. Electrically operated trim tab in port elevator.

LANDING GEAR: Retractable tricycle type, with single wheel and oleo-pneumatic shock absorber on each unit. Mainwheels retract inward, nosewheel rearward. Hydraulic actuation, with built-in emergency system. Main gear of trailing-arm type. Nosewheel steerable ±18°. Mainwheels and tyres size 6.00-6, nosewheel 5.00-5.

POWER PLANT: One Garrett TFE109-1 turbofan mounted in rear fuselage of first prototype, rated initially at 5.92 kN (1,330 lb st); uprated TFE109-3 of 7.12 kN (1,600 lb st) to be installed in second prototype in 1991. Alternative engine under consideration is an 8.01 kN (1,800 lb st) Williams International FJ44 turbofan. Semi-integral metal fuel tank in centre-fuselage, max usable capacity 720 litres (190 US gallons; 158 Imp gallons). Single gravity refuelling point on top of fuselage, aft of canopy. Electric fuel pump for engine starting and emergency use.

ACCOMMODATION: Two persons side by side in air-conditioned cockpit, on Martin-Baker Mk 11 lightweight ejection seats capable of operation at altitudes up to 12,200 m (40,000 ft) and at any speed between 60 and 400 knots (111–741 km/h; 69–461 mph), including ejection through canopy. One-piece framed canopy is hinged at rear and opens upward.

SYSTEMS: Environmental control system for cockpit air-conditioning. Hydraulic system (operating pressure 117 bars; 1,700 lb/sq in) for actuation of airbrake, landing gear and flaps. System incorporates electrically driven oil pump, with two air/oil accumulators (one for normal and one for emergency operation); separate standby system for emergency lowering of landing gear. Electrical system is 28V DC, using an engine driven starter/generator and nickel-cadmium or lead-acid battery. Negretti Aviation oxygen system.

AVIONICS: Include dual Collins Pro Line II EFIS avionics and radio equipment.

ARMAMENT: Four underwing attachment points, each of 150 kg (331 lb) capacity, capable of carrying a variety of weapons or auxiliary fuel tanks.

DIMENSIONS, EXTERNAL:
Wing span	9.04 m (29 ft 8 in)
Wing chord: at root	1.90 m (6 ft 2¾ in)
at tip	1.00 m (3 ft 3¼ in)
mean aerodynamic	1.575 m (5 ft 2 in)
Wing aspect ratio	6.0
Length of fuselage	9.36 m (30 ft 8½ in)
Height overall	3.60 m (11 ft 9¾ in)
Tailplane span	3.80 m (12 ft 5½ in)
Wheel track	3.59 m (11 ft 9¼ in)
Wheelbase	3.58 m (11 ft 9 in)

AREAS:
Wings, gross	13.58 m² (146.17 sq ft)
Ailerons (total)	1.122 m² (12.08 sq ft)
Trailing-edge flaps (total)	1.784 m² (19.20 sq ft)
Fin	1.256 m² (13.52 sq ft)
Rudder	0.782 m² (8.42 sq ft)
Tailplane	2.04 m² (22.00 sq ft)
Elevators (total, incl tab)	1.61 m² (17.33 sq ft)

WEIGHTS AND LOADINGS (A: TFE109-1 engine, B: TFE109-3):
Weight empty: A	1,300 kg (2,866 lb)
B	1,400 kg (3,086 lb)
Max external stores load	600 kg (1,323 lb)
Max T-O weight: A (Aerobatic)	2,000 kg (4,409 lb)
A (Normal), B	2,400 kg (5,291 lb)
Max wing loading:	
A (Aerobatic)	147.27 kg/m² (30.18 lb/sq ft)
A (Normal), B	176.73 kg/m² (36.21 lb/sq ft)
Max power loading:	
A (Aerobatic)	337.75 kg/kN (3.31 lb/lb st)
A (Normal), B	337.21 kg/kN (3.30 lb/lb st)

PERFORMANCE (at max T-O weight, TFE109-1 engine):
Never-exceed speed (V$_{NE}$)	
	Mach 0.70 (345 knots; 638 km/h; 397 mph)
Max level speed at 4,265 m (14,000 ft)	
	280 knots (519 km/h; 322 mph)
Normal operating speed	260 knots (482 km/h; 299 mph)
Max speed for landing gear extension	
	150 knots (278 km/h; 173 mph)
Max speed for flap extension (landing position)	
	130 knots (241 km/h; 150 mph)
Stalling speed, flaps down	67 knots (124 km/h; 77 mph)
Max rate of climb at S/L	762 m (2,500 ft)/min
Service ceiling	11,275 m (37,000 ft)
Max operating ceiling	7,620 m (25,000 ft)
T-O run	335 m (1,100 ft)
T-O to 15 m (50 ft)	396 m (1,300 ft)
Landing from 15 m (50 ft)	427 m (1,400 ft)
Landing run	366 m (1,200 ft)
Ferry range at 6,100 m (20,000 ft), max internal fuel	
	1,000 nm (1,850 km; 1,150 miles)

First prototype of the Promavia Jet Squalus turbofan trainer

g limits	+2.8 sustained, at 3,050 m (10,000 ft)
	+7/–3.5 Aerobatic

PROMAVIA ATTA 3000

The ATTA 3000 (Advanced Trainer/Tactical Aircraft) is a projected tandem two-seater, with stepped zero/zero ejection seats and EFIS instrumentation; like the Jet Squalus, it has been proposed for the US JPATS (Joint Primary Air Training System) requirement. In the weapons training/tactical role, it could be armed with 7.62 mm or 20 mm guns, 70 mm rocket launchers, infra-red air-to-air missiles, or bombs of up to Mk 82 size. Both single- and twin-engined versions have been proposed.

DIMENSIONS, EXTERNAL:
Wing span	9.20 m (30 ft 2¼ in)
Length overall	9.96 m (32 ft 8 in)
Height overall	3.60 m (11 ft 9¾ in)

AREAS:
Wings, gross	13.81 m² (148.65 sq ft)

WEIGHTS AND LOADINGS:
Weight empty, equipped	1,769 kg (3,900 lb)
Max T-O weight	3,265 kg (7,198 lb)
Max landing weight	2,520 kg (5,555 lb)

PERFORMANCE (estimated):
Max level speed	485 knots (899 km/h; 558 mph)
Stalling speed, flaps down	72 knots (134 km/h; 83 mph)
Max rate of climb at S/L	2,165 m (7,100 ft)/min
Service ceiling	12,200 m (40,000 ft)
T-O run	244 m (800 ft)
Landing run	366 m (1,200 ft)
Ferry range	950 nm (1,760 km; 1,094 miles)

PROMAVIA ARA 3600

The ARA 3600 (Attack/Reconnaissance Aircraft) is a single-seat light strike aircraft project, with an intended power plant of two 7.12 kN (1,600 lb st) TFE109-3 turbofans and the same 757 litre (200 US gallon; 166.5 Imp gallon) internal fuel capacity as the ATTA 3000. It would be capable of carrying 1,000 kg (2,205 lb) of external stores including two 20 mm or four 7.62 mm guns, four 7-tube 70 mm rocket launchers, or up to four Mk 82 or smaller bombs. Dimensions and weights are as for the ATTA 3000.

PERFORMANCE (estimated): As for ATTA 3000 except:
Max rate of climb at S/L	2,440 m (8,000 ft)/min
Service ceiling	13,715 m (45,000 ft)

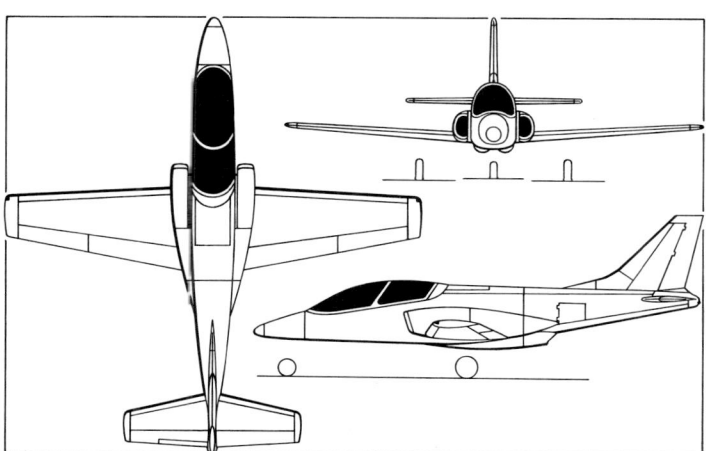
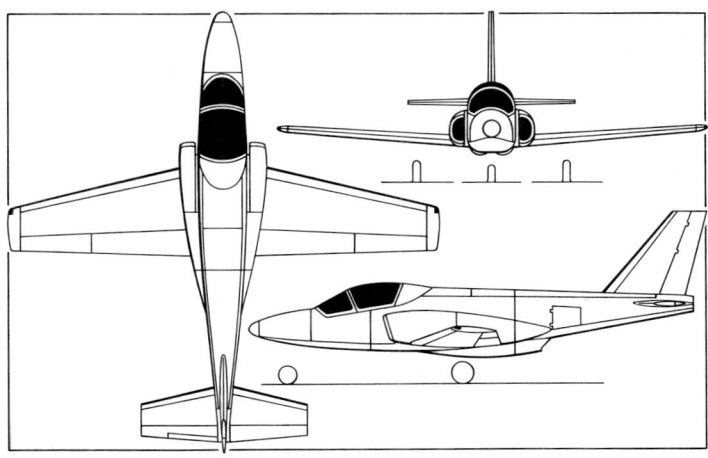

Promavia ATTA 3000 tandem-seat trainer (left) and ARA 3600 single-seat light strike aircraft *(Jane's/Mike Keep)*

SABCA
SOCIÉTÉ ANONYME BELGE DE CONSTRUCTIONS AÉRONAUTIQUES

Chaussée de Haecht 1470, B-1130 Brussels
Telephone: 32 (2) 246 25 11
Fax: 32 (2) 216 15 70
Telex: 21 237 SABCA B
CHAIRMAN: J. Groothaert
DIRECTOR/GENERAL MANAGER: J. Detemmerman
MARKETING MANAGERS:
  J. E. Versmessen (Aerospace)
  P. Johansen (Electronic Defence)
OTHER WORKS: Aéroport de Gosselies-Charleroi, B-6041
  Gosselies
Telephone: 32 (71) 25 42 11
Fax: 32 (71) 34 42 14
Telex: 51 251 SABGO B
Founded in 1920, Sabca is the major aerospace company in Belgium. Since the Second World War, it has participated in various European aircraft programmes. At Haren, Sabca is manufacturing major structures such as wings and nose sections, and other structural components and equipment, for the General Dynamics F-16; Alpha Jet; Mirage III/5/F1 and Atlantic 1/Atlantique 2; Northrop F-5; Airbus A330/340; Fokker 50 and 100; AS 330 Puma; Spacelab; and Ariane launchers. Servo controls are produced for the F-16,

the Ariane launchers and the Hermès European space shuttle.
At Gosselies, Sabca assembles and tests F-16s for Belgium; modifies Belgian Air Force and USAFE F-16s; and is responsible for final assembly of Agusta A 109B helicopters for Belgium, including installing and integrating HeliTOW 2 and all other avionics systems.
Sabca's Electronic Division produces IFF components and aircraft electronic ground equipment, as well as maintaining Doppler equipment.
For many years Sabca has been responsible for the maintenance and overhaul of Belgian and other armed forces' military aircraft, their electronic components and accessories, as well as commercial fixed-wing aircraft and helicopters. It is currently integrating ECM devices in Belgian aircraft.
Sabca is a member of various European industrial consortia; Dassault Aviation (53 per cent) and Fokker (over 40 per cent) have parity holdings in the company. The company's works occupy a total area of approx 82,000 m² (882,640 sq ft) and in early 1991 employed an average of 1,800 people. Dassault Belgique Aviation (DBA) was acquired by Sabca in late 1990.
Construction of a new plant for the Sabca-Limburg NV subsidiary began in 1990. This new factory, due to be operational by mid-1991, will produce components in high

grade composite materials for aircraft and aerospace applications.

MIRAGE SAFETY IMPROVEMENT PROGRAMME

Sabca has been selected as prime contractor for the Belgian Air Force's Mirage Safety Improvement Programme (MIRSIP). In addition to life-extending modifications and maintenance, the aircraft are to be fitted with canard control surfaces and pressure refuelling (both Dassault systems), and a new weapons delivery, navigation and reconnaissance system (Sagem Uliss 92 INS, Sagem Tercor terrain contour matching system with 3D digital map database, Thomson-CSF laser rangefinder, Vinten 3150/2768 colour video recording system and GEC Ferranti HUD) operating via a MIL-STD-1553B databus. (See also Dassault entry in French section.)
The original MIRSIP plan called for upgrading 15 single-seat Mirage 5BAs of No. 8 Squadron and five two-seat Mirage 5BD operational trainers, to be redelivered by the end of 1994. Under changes announced in early 1991, however, No. 8 Squadron was to disband by the end of that year, and the MIRSIP upgrade operator (possibly with fewer aircraft) is now expected to be No. 42 Squadron. First flight by a modified Mirage is expected by late 1992.

SONACA
SOCIÉTÉ NATIONALE DE CONSTRUCTION AEROSPATIALE SA

Parc Industriel, Route Nationale Cinq, B-6041 Gosselies
Telephone: 32 (71) 25 51 11
Fax: 32 (71) 34 40 35
Telex: 51241
GENERAL MANAGER: M. Harmant
MANUFACTURING DIRECTOR: P. Wacquez
SALES AND MARKETING DIRECTOR: Marcel Devresse
PUBLIC RELATIONS: Claude Loriaux

Sonaca SA, formerly Fairey SA (established in 1931), was incorporated on 1 May 1978. Its capital is held 90 per cent by public institutions. Built on 22 ha (54 acres) of ground adjacent to Charleroi Airport, Sonaca's facility covers 87,661 m² (943,574 sq ft). Workforce in early 1991 was 1,380.
Sonaca participates in civil and military aviation manufacturing programmes, co-producing the General Dynamics F-16 (rear fuselage, vertical fin, dorsal fairing and final mating) and components (leading-edge moving surfaces) for the Airbus A310, A320 and A330/340. It supplies parts for various aircraft, including Aerospatiale

and Agusta A 109 helicopters, the Dassault Atlantique 2, Lockheed C-130, Saab 340 and Dassault/Dornier Alpha Jet. The company designed and sells aircraft galley polycarbonate containers.
Sonaca's association in large international military and civil programmes has resulted in a significant increase in its capability to develop and manufacture metallic and composite aerospace structures. R & D resources include an IBM Cadam (2D, 3D) and Catia (3D) computer aided design system. Sonaca is developing structural elements for the Hermès spacecraft.

BRAZIL

EMBRAER
EMPRESA BRASILEIRA DE AERONÁUTICA SA

Av Brig Faria Lima 2170, Caixa Postal 343, 12225 São José
  dos Campos, SP
Telephone: 55 (123) 25 1711
Fax: 55 (123) 21 8466
Telex: (391) 1233589 EBAE BR
RIO OFFICE: Aeroporto Santos-Dumont, Sobreloja, Salão de
  Embarque No. 2, 20021 Rio de Janeiro, RJ
Telephone: 55 (21) 262 6411
CHAIRMAN: Sérgio Xavier Ferolla
CHIEF EXECUTIVE OFFICER: João da Cunha
COMMERCIAL DIRECTOR: Heitor Fernandes Serra
TECHNICAL DIRECTOR: Eng Guido Fontegalante Pessotti
PRESS OFFICER: Mario B. de M. Vinagre
US SUBSIDIARY:
  Embraer Aircraft Corporation, 276 Southwest 34th
  Street, PO Box 21623, Fort Lauderdale, Florida 33315
  Telephone: 1 (305) 524 5755 and 5744
  Telex: (230) 522318 EMBRAER FORT
  LAUDERDALE
PARIS OFFICE:
  Embraer Aviation International, BP 74, Aéroport
  du Bourget, Zone d'Aviation d'Affaires, 93350 Le
  Bourget, France
  Telephone: 33 48 35 94 20
  Telex: 213498F EBAE PAR

Embraer, which celebrated its 20th anniversary and delivered its 4,000th aircraft in 1989, was created on 19 August 1969, and came into operation on 2 January 1970. The Brazilian government owns 63.81 per cent of the voting shares, 36.19 per cent of the subscribed capital being held by private shareholders. Embraer has a factory area of 275,198.55 m² (2,962,210 sq ft), and had built a total of 4,064 aircraft by 1 January 1990.
Since August 1974, Embraer has had an agreement with Piper Aircraft Corporation to manufacture various Piper types under licence. Agreements concluded in 1983-84 with Sikorsky provide for development of Embraer's capability to manufacture aircraft components in composite materials, initially for the S-70C helicopter, the EMB-120 Brasilia and the AMX attack aircraft. A 1987 agreement with McDonnell Douglas provides for the supply of 200 sets of wing flaps, in composites material, for the MD-11 airliner, with a further 100 sets on option. Deliveries began on 29 October 1988 and are continuing.
Embraer has in current production the EMB-120 Brasilia commuter transport, and has begun development of a new regional transport, the EMB-145. The AMX tactical fighter is produced jointly with Alenia and Aermacchi of Italy, and the CBA-123 commuter transport is a joint programme with FMA of Argentina. Manufacture of the EMB-201A

Ipanema agricultural aircraft, and licence produced versions of Piper twin-engined light aircraft, are the responsibility of Neiva (which see), which became a subsidiary of Embraer in March 1980. Neiva production and marketing of these aircraft are co-ordinated with the licence manufacture and sale of single-engined Piper types by Chincul of Argentina (which see).
On 31 October 1990 Embraer announced a major restructuring of the company, including a 4,000 reduction in the workforce, to counter cash flow and other financial problems created by delayed payments from domestic and foreign sources. At that time, programme timetables affected were those for the CBA-123 Vector, EMB-145, MFT/LF, and reactivation of the Tucano production line. By December 1990 the workforce had been reduced from the January figure of 12,507 to 8,472, and in January 1991 the Brazilian government withdrew its financial support for the company, leading to expectations of further cost-cutting measures to follow. As this edition was being prepared, the EMB-145 was being redesigned and production of the Brasilia, AMX and MD-11 flaps was continuing.

AMX
Details of this military aircraft programme with Alenia and Aermacchi are given in the International section.

EMBRAER MFT/LF
This programme (see 1990-91 *Jane's*) is in abeyance for the reasons outlined in the introductory copy.

EMBRAER EMB-110 BANDEIRANTE (PIONEER)
Brazilian Air Force designations: C-95, EC-95, R-95 and SC-95
Bandeirantes have been sold to more than 80 operators in 36 countries worldwide, and by 1 September 1990 the 490 aircraft then delivered had logged more than 5.2 million flying hours. Production ended with the 500th aircraft, a C-95C for the Brazilian Air Force, which was delivered during 1990. With its delivery, that service had received 156 Bandeirantes (60 C-95, 20 C-95A and 28 C-95B transports; 2 EC-95Bs for navaid calibration; 1 XC-95B for artificial rain research; 5 search and rescue SC-95Bs; 6 aerial photogrammetry R-95s; 12 dihedral-tailed, EFIS-equipped C-95Cs) and 22 EMB-111s (see separate entry: 12 P-95s and 10 P-95Bs).
Details of early production models can be found in the 1984-85 and previous editions of *Jane's*. Principal later models (see 1989-90 and earlier editions for details) were:
EMB-110P1A: Updated version of P1 with 10° tailplane dihedral and other detail changes (listed in 1987-88 and earlier editions). Replaced P1 as standard version from c/n 439 onwards.

EMB-110P1K: Military utility, cargo and paradropping version of P1. No tailplane dihedral.
EMB-110P1K SAR: Search and rescue version of P1K, equipped for inland and overwater search, paradropping and aeromedical evacuation. Max T-O weight 6,000 kg (13,230 lb).
EMB-110P2A: Replaced former P2 (1984-85 *Jane's*) as third-level commuter transport version, carrying up to 21 passengers. Incorporates same changes as P1A.
EMB-110P1A/41 and EMB-110P2A/41: Replaced P1/41 and P2/41 from 1983, certificated under SFAR Pt 41 for a max T-O weight of 5,900 kg (13,010 lb). Power plant and dimensions unchanged.
EMB-111: Maritime surveillance version, described separately.

EMBRAER EMB-111
Brazilian Air Force designation: P-95
This land based maritime surveillance aircraft, based on the EMB-110 Bandeirante, was designed to meet specifications issued by the Comando Costeiro, the Brazilian Air Force's Coastal Command. Main external differences are the large nose radome, housing search radar, and the addition of wingtip fuel tanks.
The EMB-111 flew for the first time on 15 August 1977, and 12 were delivered initially, as **P-95s**, to the Brazilian Air Force. Six delivered to the Chilean Navy in 1978 and 1979 have some mission equipment changes, including full de-icing system, and passive ECM antennae under the nose and at the tail. One EMB-111 was delivered in August 1981 to the Gabonese Air Force, and one was ordered in 1986 by the air force of Angola. Delivery date for the Angolan aircraft was still awaiting financial approval in 1991.
In December 1987, the Brazilian Air Force ordered a further 10 EMB-111s, deliveries of which began in October 1989. These new aircraft, designated **P-95B**, are similar to those currently in service, except for structural improvements and updated avionics which include Super Searcher radar and Thomson-CSF DR 2000A Mk II/Dalia 1000A Mk II ESM; Collins EFIS-74 electronic flight instrument system, ADI-84 and APS-65 autopilot; and a Canadian Marconi CMA 771 Mk III Omega navigation system. The earlier P-95s will be brought up to a similar standard. Brazilian Air Force EMB-111s serve with the 1st and 2nd Squadrons of the 7th Aviation Group (GAv 1°/7° and 2°/7°).
A full description of the EMB-111 can be found in the 1985-86 and earlier editions of *Jane's*.
TYPE: Twin-turboprop maritime surveillance aircraft.
POWER PLANT: Two 559 kW (750 shp) Pratt & Whitney Canada PT6A-34 turboprops; Hartzell three-blade reversible-pitch propellers. Total usable fuel capacity (four integral wing tanks and two permanent wingtip tanks) 2,454 litres (648 US gallons; 540 Imp gallons).

Undernose ECM antenna on a Chilean Navy EMB-111 (*Kenneth Munson*)

Embraer EMB-111 (P-95) maritime surveillance aircraft of the Brazilian Air Force with 5 in HVAR rockets underwing

ACCOMMODATION: Two-pilot flight deck; search radar/radio operator, ECM operator, one or two observers, and second radar or ECM operator.

ARMAMENT: Four underwing pylons for eight 5 in HVAR air-to-surface rockets (two per pylon), or four launchers each with seven 2.75 in FFAR rockets.

EQUIPMENT: Aircraft can be flown with armament on three pylons only, plus a 50 million candlepower searchlight on starboard wing leading-edge. Six Brazilian built Mk 6 smoke grenades for target marking (or flares for night marking); chaff dispenser; Motorola SST-121 transponder. Provision for 1.4 kW loudhailer.

DIMENSIONS, EXTERNAL:

Wing span over tip tanks	15.95 m (52 ft 4 in)
Length overall	14.91 m (48 ft 11 in)
Height overall	4.91 m (16 ft 1¼ in)

AREAS:

Wings, gross	29.10 m² (313.23 sq ft)

WEIGHTS AND LOADINGS:

Weight empty, equipped	3,900 kg (8,598 lb)
Max T-O weight	7,000 kg (15,432 lb)
Max wing loading	241.38 kg/m² (49.44 lb/sq ft)
Max power loading	6.26 kg/kW (10.29 lb/shp)

PERFORMANCE (at max T-O weight, ISA +15°C, except where indicated):

Max cruising speed at 3,050 m (10,000 ft)
194 knots (360 km/h; 223 mph)

Econ cruising speed at 3,050 m (10,000 ft)
187 knots (347 km/h; 215 mph)

Stalling speed at 5,450 kg (12,015 lb) max landing weight 73 knots (135 km/h; 84 mph) CAS

Max rate of climb at S/L 362 m (1,190 ft)/min

Service ceiling at AUW of 5,300 kg (11,684 lb)
7,770 m (25,500 ft)

Range at 3,050 m (10,000 ft), max fuel, 45 min reserves 1,590 nm (2,945 km; 1,830 miles)

EMBRAER EMB-120 BRASILIA
Brazilian Air Force designation: VC-97

Design of this twin-turboprop passenger and cargo transport started in September 1979. The first of three flying prototypes (PT-ZBA) made its initial flight on 27 July 1983; Nos. 2 and 5 were static and fatigue test aircraft; No. 6 was a pre-series demonstration aircraft. On 4 January 1989, the first prototype began flight trials as a testbed for the engine installation of the CBA-123 transport (see International section), with a Garrett TPE331-12B turboprop mounted on the port side of its rear fuselage.

Certification of the standard Brasilia by the Brazilian CTA was granted on 10 May 1985, and FAA (FAR Pt 25) type approval on 9 July 1985. Type certification by the British CAA, French DGAC and German LBA was granted in 1986, and by the Australian CAA in April 1990. The first customer, Atlantic Southeast Airlines of the USA, received its first Brasilia in June 1985 and began revenue services in the following October. By 8 February 1991 firm orders totalled 316, with 177 more on option; of these, 214 had been delivered, including four **VC-97** VIP transports for the Brazilian Air Force. The first order for the corporate version was received from United Technologies Corporation (USA) in August 1985. Furnished for 18 passengers, it was delivered in September 1986. Production rate was 4.2 aircraft per month in 1990, with the 200th aircraft delivered on 20 August that year. Brasilias in service had flown one million hours by the end of January 1991.

From Brasilia c/n 120028, delivered in October 1986, composite materials equivalent to 10 per cent of the aircraft's basic empty weight have been used in the airframe, as noted in the following descriptive details:

TYPE: Twin-turboprop general purpose transport.

WINGS: Cantilever low-wing monoplane. Wing section NACA 23018 (modified) at root, NACA 23012 at tip. Dihedral 6° 30' from roots at 66 per cent chord. Incidence 2°. Sweepback 0° at 66 per cent chord. Single continuous fail-safe structure, attached to underside of fuselage on three special frames. Main wing box has three spars (at 15, 28 and 66 per cent chord), ribs, stiffeners and skin. Spar caps machined from 2024 or 7050 aluminium alloy extrusions; skin panels are of 2024 or 7475 laminations, chemically milled. Leading-edges, wingtips and root fairings of Kevlar reinforced glassfibre. Hydraulically actuated electrically controlled double-slotted Fowler trailing-edge flap, of carbonfibre construction, inboard and outboard of each engine nacelle; small plain flap beneath each nacelle. No slats, slots, spoilers or airbrakes. Small fence on each outer wing between outboard flap and aileron. Internally balanced all-metal ailerons. Lateral trimming by tabs (two in starboard aileron, one in port aileron). Ailerons actuated by dual irreversible mechanical actuators operated manually by cable controls. Pneumatic boot de-icing of leading-edges, using engine bleed air.

FUSELAGE: Semi-monocoque pressurised structure, of circular cross-section throughout most of its length. Chemically milled skin, reinforced by extruded stiffeners; C frames attached to skin by shear clips. Entire structure

is of 2024, 7050 and 7475 aluminium alloys, and meets the damage tolerance requirements of FAR Pt 25 (Transport category) up to Amendment 25-54. Nosecone of Kevlar reinforced glassfibre; tailcone also of Kevlar reinforced glassfibre on aircraft without APU. Pressurised area contained within flat bulkhead forward of flight deck and hemispherical rear bulkhead aft of baggage compartment. Twin ventral strakes under rear fuselage.

TAIL UNIT: Cantilever T tail, of three-spar metal construction except for leading-edges and tips, which are of Kevlar reinforced glassfibre. Fixed incidence swept tailplane, with horn balanced elevators. Sweptback fin, with Kevlar reinforced glassfibre dorsal fin. Serially hinged two-segment rudder actuated hydraulically by Bertea CSD unit. Mechanically actuated trim tab in each elevator. Pneumatic boot de-icing of leading-edges, using engine bleed air.

LANDING GEAR: Retractable tricycle type, with Goodrich twin wheels and oleo-pneumatic shock absorber on each unit (main units 12 in, nose unit 8 in). Hydraulic actuation; all units retract forward (main units into engine nacelles). Hydraulically powered nosewheel steering. Goodyear tyres, size 24 × 7.25 in (main), 18 × 5.5 in (nose); pressure 6.90-7.58 bars (100-110 lb/sq in) on main units, 4.14-4.83 bars (60-70 lb/sq in) on nose unit. Goodrich carbon brakes standard (steel optional). Hydro Aire anti-skid system standard; autobrake optional.

POWER PLANT: Two Pratt & Whitney Canada PW118 or PW118A turboprops, each rated at 1,342 kW (1,800 shp) for T-O and max continuous power, and driving a Hamilton Standard 14RF-9 four-blade constant-speed reversible-pitch fully feathering propeller with glassfibre blades containing aluminium spars. Fuel in two-cell 1,670 litre (441 US gallon; 367.2 Imp gallon) integral tank in each wing; total capacity 3,340 litres (882 US gallons; 734.4 Imp gallons), of which 3,312 litres (875 US gallons; 728.6 Imp gallons) are usable. Single-point pressure refuelling (beneath outer starboard wing), plus gravity point in upper surface of each wing. Oil capacity 9 litres (2.4 US gallons; 2 Imp gallons).

ACCOMMODATION: Two-pilot flight deck. Main cabin accommodates cabin attendant and 30 passengers in three-abreast seating at 79 cm (31 in) pitch, with overhead lockable baggage racks, in pressurised and air-conditioned environment. Passenger seats are made of carbonfibre and Kevlar, floor and partitions of carbonfibre and Nomex sandwich, side panels and ceiling of glassfibre/Kevlar/Nomex/carbonfibre sandwich. Provisions for wardrobe, galley and toilet. Downward opening main passenger door, with airstairs, forward of wing on port side. Type II emergency exit on starboard side at rear. Overwing Type III emergency exit on each side. Pressurised baggage compartment aft of passenger cabin, with large door on port side. Also available with all-cargo interior; executive or military transport interior; or in mixed-traffic version with 24 or 26 passengers (toilet omitted in latter case), and 900 kg (1,984 lb) of cargo in enlarged rear baggage compartment.

SYSTEMS: AiResearch air-conditioning/pressurisation system (differential 0.48 bars; 7 lb/sq in), with dual packs of recirculation equipment. Duplicated hydraulic systems (pressure 207 bars; 3,000 lb/sq in), each powered by an engine driven pump, for landing gear, flap, rudder and brake actuation, and nosewheel steering. Emergency standby electric pumps on each system, plus single standby handpump, for landing gear extension. Main electrical power supplied by two 28V 400A DC starter/generators; two 28V 100A DC auxiliary brushless generators for secondary and/or emergency power; one 24V 40Ah nickel-cadmium battery for assisted starting and emergency power. Main and standby 450VA static inverters for 26/115V AC power at 400Hz. Single high-pressure (127.5 bars; 1,850 lb/sq in) oxygen cylinder for crew; individual chemical oxygen generators for passengers. Pneumatic de-icing for wing and tail leading-edges, and engine air intakes; electrically heated windscreens, propellers and pitot tubes; bleed air de-icing of engine air intakes. Optional Garrett GTCP36-150(A)

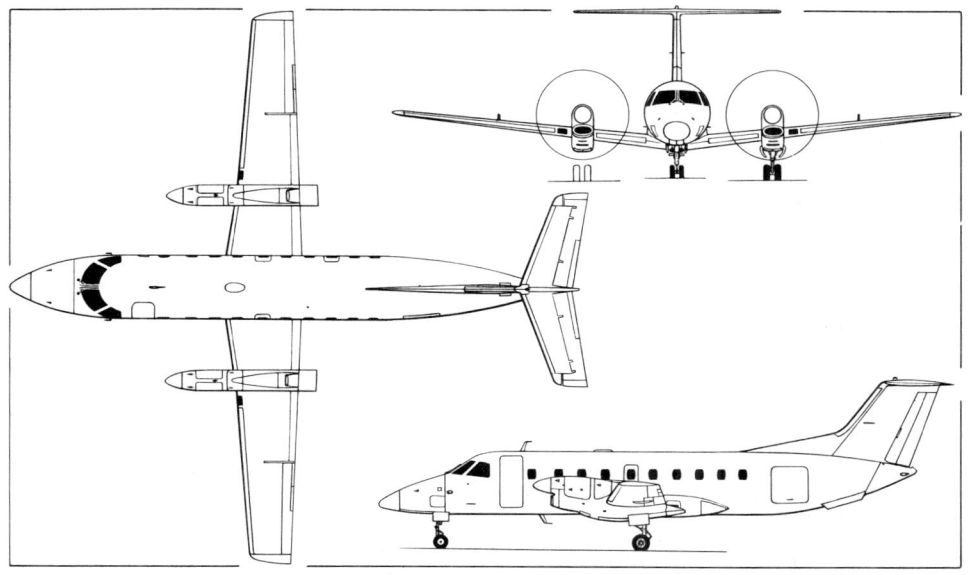

Embraer EMB-120 Brasilia twin-turboprop transport (*Pilot Press*)

Embraer EMB-120 Brasilia twin-turboprop passenger transport in the insignia of Flight West Airlines of Australia

Second EMB-120 operated as a VC-97 VIP transport by the Brazilian Air Force *(Ivo Sturzenegger)*

APU in tailcone, for electrical and pneumatic power supply.

AVIONICS: Collins Pro Line II digital avionics package includes as standard dual VHF-22 com transceivers, dual VIR-32 VHF nav receivers, one ADF-60A, one TDR-90 transponder, CLT-22/32/62/92 control heads, one DME-41, one WXR-270 weather radar, dual AHRS-85 digital strapdown AHRS, dual ADI-84, dual EHSI-74, dual RMI-36, one Dorne & Margolin DMELT-81 emergency locator transmitter, dual Avtech audio/interphones, Avtech PA and cabin interphone, Fairchild voice recorder, and IET standby attitude indicator. Optional avionics include third VHF com, second transponder and DME, WXR-300 weather radar, two EFIS-86 electronic flight instrument systems, one MFD-85 multi-function display, one or two J.E.T. RNS-8000 3D or Racal Avionics RN 5000 nav, one APS-65 digital autopilot, one or two FCS-65 digital flight directors, flight entertainment music, one or two Canadian Marconi CMA-771 Alpha VLF/Omega, one or two ALT-55 radio altimeters, altitude alerter/preselect, MLS, GPWS, flight recorder, and Motorola Selcal. Second (Bendix/King) avionics package is available optionally. Other types of avionics, for special versions of the aircraft, as required for the missions concerned.

DIMENSIONS, EXTERNAL:

Wing span	19.78 m (64 ft 10¾ in)
Wing chord: at root	2.81 m (9 ft 2¾ in)
at tip	1.40 m (4 ft 7 in)
Wing aspect ratio	9.9
Length overall	20.00 m (65 ft 7½ in)
Fuselage: Length	18.73 m (61 ft 5½ in)
Max diameter	2.28 m (7 ft 5¾ in)
Height overall	6.35 m (20 ft 10 in)
Elevator span	6.94 m (22 ft 9¼ in)
Wheel track (c/l of shock struts)	6.58 m (21 ft 7 in)
Wheelbase	6.97 m (22 ft 10½ in)
Propeller diameter	3.20 m (10 ft 6 in)
Propeller ground clearance (min)	0.52 m (1 ft 8½ in)
Passenger door (fwd, port): Height	1.70 m (5 ft 7 in)
Width	0.774 m (2 ft 6½ in)
Height to sill	1.47 m (4 ft 10 in)
Cargo door (rear, port): Height	1.36 m (4 ft 5½ in)
Width	1.30 m (4 ft 3¼ in)
Height to sill	1.67 m (5 ft 5¾ in)

Emergency exit (rear, stbd): Height	1.37 m (4 ft 6 in)
Width	0.51 m (1 ft 8 in)
Height to sill	1.56 m (5 ft 1½ in)
Emergency exits (overwing, each):	
Height	0.91 m (3 ft 0 in)
Width	0.51 m (1 ft 8 in)
Emergency exits (flight deck side windows, each):	
Min height	0.48 m (1 ft 7 in)
Min width	0.51 m (1 ft 8 in)

DIMENSIONS, INTERNAL:

Cabin, excl flight deck and baggage compartment:

Length	9.38 m (30 ft 9¼ in)
Max width	2.10 m (6 ft 10¾ in)
Max height	1.76 m (5 ft 9¼ in)
Floor area	14.97 m² (161.14 sq ft)
Volume	27.40 m³ (967.6 cu ft)

Rear baggage compartment volume:

30-passenger version	6.40 m³ (226 cu ft)
all-cargo version	2.70 m³ (95 cu ft)
passenger/cargo version	11.00 m³ (388 cu ft)

Cabin, incl flight deck and baggage compartment:

Total volume	approx 41.8 m³ (1,476 cu ft)
Max available cabin volume (all-cargo version)	
	31.10 m³ (1,098 cu ft)

AREAS:

Wings, gross	39.43 m² (424.42 sq ft)
Ailerons (total)	2.88 m² (31.00 sq ft)
Trailing-edge flaps (total)	3.23 m² (34.77 sq ft)
Fin, incl dorsal fin	5.74 m² (61.78 sq ft)
Rudder	2.59 m² (27.88 sq ft)
Tailplane	6.10 m² (65.66 sq ft)
Elevator, incl tabs	3.90 m² (41.98 sq ft)

WEIGHTS AND LOADINGS:

* Weight empty, equipped	7,101 kg (15,655 lb)
Operating weight empty	7,465 kg (16,457 lb)
Max usable fuel	2,600 kg (5,732 lb)
* Max payload	3,039 kg (6,700 lb)
Max T-O weight	11,500 kg (25,353 lb)
Max ramp weight	11,580 kg (25,529 lb)
Max landing weight	11,250 kg (24,802 lb)
Max zero-fuel weight	10,500 kg (23,148 lb)
Max wing loading	292 kg/m² (59.8 lb/sq ft)
Max power loading	4.29 kg/kW (7.04 lb/shp)

* 4 kg (8.8 lb) payload increase/empty weight decrease with PW118A engines

PERFORMANCE (at max T-O weight, ISA, except where indicated):

Max operating speed	
	272 knots (504 km/h; 313 mph) EAS
Max level speed at 6,100 m (20,000 ft)	
	328 knots (608 km/h; 378 mph)
Max cruising speed at 7,620 m (25,000 ft):	
PW118	300 knots (555 km/h; 345 mph)
PW118A	310 knots (574 km/h; 357 mph)
Long-range cruising speed at 7,620 m (25,000 ft)	
	260 knots (482 km/h; 299 mph)
Stalling speed, power off:	
flaps up	117 knots (217 km/h; 135 mph) CAS
flaps down	87 knots (162 km/h; 100 mph) CAS
Max rate of climb at S/L	646 m (2,120 ft)/min
Rate of climb at S/L, one engine out	206 m (675 ft)/min
Service ceiling: PW118	9,085 m (29,800 ft)
PW118A	9,750 m (32,000 ft)
Service ceiling, one engine out:	
PW118	5,240 m (17,200 ft)
PW118A	5,790 m (19,000 ft)
FAR Pt 25 T-O field length	1,420 m (4,660 ft)
FAR Pt 135 landing field length, max landing weight at S/L	1,370 m (4,495 ft)
Min ground turning radius	15.76 m (51 ft 8½ in)
Range at 7,620 m (25,000 ft), reserves for 100 nm (185 km; 115 mile) diversion and 45 min hold:	
with max (30) passenger payload (2,721 kg; 6,000 lb):	
PW118	550 nm (1,019 km; 633 miles)
PW118A	500 nm (926 km; 575 miles)
with max fuel and 1,920 kg (4,233 lb) payload (21 passengers)	1,610 nm (2,983 km; 1,854 miles)

OPERATIONAL NOISE LEVELS (FAR Pt 36, BCAR-N and ICAO Annex 16):

T-O	81.2 EPNdB
Approach	92.3 EPNdB
Sideline	83.5 EPNdB

EMBRAER/FMA CBA-123 VECTOR

Details of this twin-turboprop airliner, which is being developed jointly by Embraer and FMA of Argentina, can be found in the International section.

EMBRAER EMB-145

Embraer revealed its plans to develop this new 45/48-seat twin-turbofan regional transport on 12 June 1989. The fuselage is based on that of the EMB-120 Brasilia.

First flight was originally planned for late 1991, and first production deliveries for mid-1993, following international certification to FAR/JAR 25, FAR 121 and FAR 36 (ICAO Annex 16), but the whole EMB-145 programme was delayed in Autumn 1990 as a result of company cutbacks then initiated. In March 1991, a complete redesign of the wing, engine installation and landing gear was completed and new models were put into wind tunnels at Brazil's Centro Tecnico Aeroespacial (CTA) in March and at Boeing in April. First flight is planned for late 1992 and certification in mid or late 1993. Cost is expected to rise from about $11 million to between $12 million and $13 million.

TYPE: Twin-turbofan regional transport.

WINGS: New swept wing of reduced span, area and aspect ratio announced in March 1991; engines underslung and new landing gear. Supercritical section developed by Embraer with 22.3° sweep at quarter-chord and winglets at tips. The leading-edge is fixed and made of metal instead of composites. De-icing by engine bleed air. Structure based on two-spar torsion box with third auxiliary spar. Flying controls include ailerons and in-flight and ground spoilers. Double-slotted inboard and outboard flaps.

FUSELAGE: Stretched EMB-120 Brasilia fuselage with extended nosecone to house lengthened nosewheel leg. Whole passenger cabin in parallel cylindrical section.

TAIL UNIT: Cantilever T tail, with main boxes of semi-monocoque aluminium alloy and leading-edges of composite sandwich construction. Fixed incidence tailplane, with trim tab in each elevator. Serially hinged two-segment rudder, with Bertea duplicated hydraulic actuation.

LANDING GEAR: Twin-wheel main legs retract inward into wing/fuselage fairings. Twin-wheel nose leg retracts forward into nose.

POWER PLANT: Two 30.03 kN (6,750 lb st) Allison GMA 3007 turbofans, one underslung ahead of each wing. Integral fuel tanks in wing torsion boxes hold 4,500 kg (9,920 lb) fuel.

ACCOMMODATION: Flight crew of three, plus a flight observer and a cabin attendant. Standard accommodation for 45 passengers (50 maximum), in three-abreast layout at seat pitch of 79 cm (31 in). Carry-on baggage cabinet and a toilet at front of cabin; galley and main baggage compartment at rear of cabin; overhead bins along starboard side of cabin plus underseat stowage. Alternative location for toilet at rear of cabin. Carry-on baggage capacity 160 kg (352 lb); underseat capacity 405 kg (893 lb); main baggage compartment capacity 1,000 kg (2,204 lb). Outward-opening plug-type door for use with jetways, but hydraulically raised and lowered folding airstair stowed in compartment beside forward passenger door alongside avionics racks. Upward sliding baggage door at rear on port side. Sideways opening service door at rear on starboard side. Inward opening emergency exit above wing on each side. Entire accommodation, including baggage compartments, pressurised and air-conditioned.

DIMENSIONS, EXTERNAL:

Wing span	20.53 m (67 ft 4 in)
Wing aspect ratio	8.97
Length overall	27.96 m (91 ft 9 in)
Fuselage: Length	26.04 m (85 ft 5 in)
Max diameter	2.28 m (7 ft 5¾ in)
Height overall	7.10 m (23 ft 3½ in)
Elevator span	6.94 m (22 ft 9¼ in)
Wheel track	4.60 m (15 ft 1 in)
Wheelbase	11.78 m (38 ft 8 in)
Passenger door (fwd, port):	
Height	1.70 m (5 ft 7 in)
Width	0.77 m (2 ft 6¼ in)
Height to sill (max)	1.57 m (5 ft 1¾ in)
Baggage door (rear, port):	
Height	1.36 m (4 ft 5½ in)
Width	1.30 m (4 ft 3¼ in)
Height to sill (max)	1.89 m (6 ft 2½ in)
Service door (rear, stbd):	
Height	1.38 m (4 ft 6¼ in)
Width	0.67 m (2 ft 2¼ in)
Height to sill (max)	1.76 m (5 ft 9¼ in)
Emergency exits (overwing, each):	
Height	0.92 m (3 ft 0¼ in)
Width	0.51 m (1 ft 8 in)

DIMENSIONS, INTERNAL:

Cabin (excl flight deck, incl galley and toilet):	
Length	15.43 m (50 ft 7½ in)
Max width	2.10 m (6 ft 10¾ in)
Baggage volume:	
rear compartment	8.9 m³ (314.3 cu ft)
front of cabin	0.9 m³ (31.8 cu ft)
overhead bins	1.4 m³ (49.4 cu ft)
underseat	2.0 m³ (70.6 cu ft)

AREAS:

Wings, gross	47.00 m² (505.9 sq ft)
Fin	4.68 m² (50.38 sq ft)
Rudder	2.59 m² (27.88 sq ft)
Tailplane	10.00 m² (107.64 sq ft)
Elevators (total, incl tabs)	3.90 m² (41.98 sq ft)

EMBRAER EMB-312 TUCANO (TOUCAN)
Brazilian Air Force designation: T-27

Design of the Tucano began in January 1978 as part of a programme to develop a new basic trainer for the Brazilian Air Force. On 6 December that year a contract was received from the Departamento de Pesquisas e Desenvolvimento (Department of Research and Development) of the Brazilian Ministry of Aeronautics, for two flying prototypes plus two airframes for static and fatigue testing. The aircraft meets the requirements of FAR Pt 23 Appendix A and MIL and CAA Section K specifications.

The first prototype (Brazilian Air Force serial number 1300) first flew on 16 August 1980, and the second (1301) on 10 December 1980. A third (PP-ZDK), modified to production standard, flew on 16 August 1982.

The EMB-312 is designated **T-27** by the Brazilian Air Force (FAB), to which the 118 Tucanos ordered originally were delivered between September 1983 and September 1986. In January 1990 the FAB ordered a further 10, and has options on 40 more.

The Egyptian government ordered 120 Tucanos in September 1983: 40 for its own air force and 80 for Iraq,

EMB-145 twin-turbofan regional transport in its current configuration

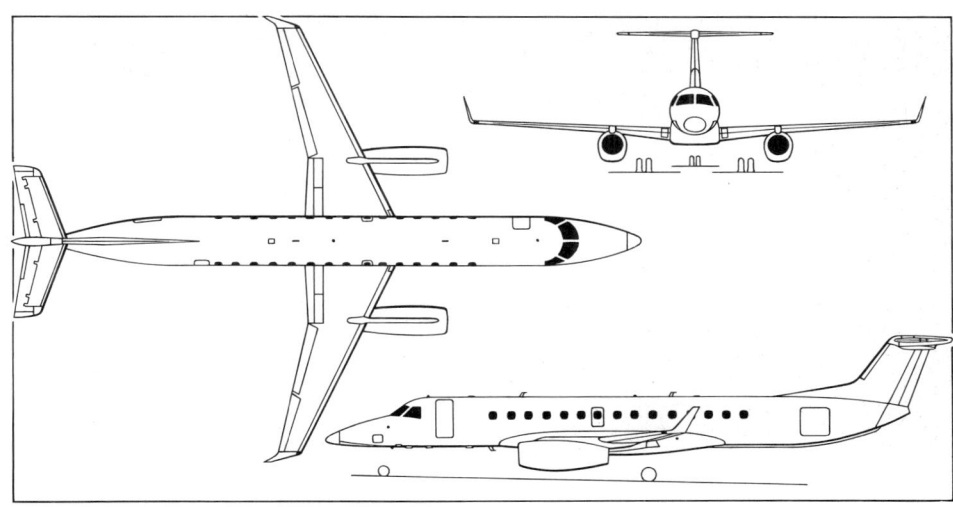

Revised configuration of Embraer EMB-145 with swept wing and underslung engines *(Pilot Press)*

with options on 60 more, of which 20 would be for Iraq. Embraer built the first 10 of these, which were ferried to Egypt from October 1984 in flyaway condition. Kits for the remaining 110 were delivered to AOI in Egypt (which see); all have now been assembled and delivered. Egypt ordered an additional 14 Tucano kits in early 1989. By 1 January 1991 deliveries had also been made to the air forces of Argentina (30), Honduras (12), Iran (five of 15 on order), Paraguay (six), Peru (20) and Venezuela (31). Tucano deliveries then totalled 396 out of 507 firm orders; options were held for a further 115. The French government has announced its intention to order 80 Tucanos; these will have strengthened wings and French avionics.

The version selected for the Royal Air Force, with British equipment and a more powerful 820 kW (1,100 shp) Garrett TPE331 engine, is being built by Short Brothers and is described under that company's entry in the UK section. The Garrett engined prototype, and kits for 25 of the 130 ordered by the RAF, are included in the 396 delivery total in the preceding paragraph.

The following description applies to the standard Embraer version:

TYPE: Tandem two-seat basic trainer.

WINGS: Cantilever low-wing monoplane. Wing section NACA 63₂A-415 at root, NACA 63A-212 at tip. Dihedral 5° 30′ at 30 per cent chord. Incidence 1° 25′. Geometric twist 2° 13′. Sweepback 0° 43′ 26″ at quarter-chord. Aluminium alloy two-spar torsion box structure of 2024-T3511 extrusions and 2024-T3 sheet. Single-slotted electrically actuated trailing-edge flaps of 2024-T3, supported on 4130 steel tracks. Frise constant chord balanced ailerons. Electrically actuated trim tab in, and small geared tab on, each aileron.

FUSELAGE: Conventional semi-monocoque structure of 2024-T3 aluminium alloy.

TAIL UNIT: Cantilever all-metal structure, of similar construction to wings. Non-swept fin, with dorsal fin, and horn balanced rudder. Non-swept fixed incidence tailplane and balanced elevators. Small fillet forward of tailplane root on each side. Electromechanically actuated spring trim in rudder and port elevator.

LANDING GEAR: Hydraulically retractable tricycle type, with single wheel and Piper oleo-pneumatic shock absorber on each unit. Accumulator for emergency extension in the event of hydraulic system failure. Shimmy damper on nose unit. Rearward retracting steerable nose unit; main units retract inward into wings. Parker Hannifin 40-130 mainwheels, Oldi-DI-1.555-02-OL nosewheel. Tyre sizes 6.50-10 (Type III, 8-ply rating) on mainwheels, 5.00-5 (Type III, 6-ply rating) on nosewheel. Tyre pressures (±0.21 bar; 3 lb/sq in each case) are 5.17 bars (75 lb/sq in) on mainwheels, 4.48 bars (65 lb/sq in) on nosewheel. Parker Hannifin 30-95A hydraulic mainwheel brakes.

POWER PLANT: One 559 kW (750 shp) Pratt & Whitney Canada PT6A-25C turboprop, driving a Hartzell HC-B3TN-3C/T10178-8R three-blade constant-speed fully feathering reversible-pitch propeller. Single-lever combined control for engine throttling and propeller pitch adjustment. Two integral fuel tanks in each wing, total capacity 694 litres (183.3 US gallons; 152.7 Imp gallons). Fuel tanks lined with anti-detonation plastics foam. Gravity refuelling point in each wing upper surface. Fuel system allows nominally for up to 30 s of inverted flight. (Aircraft has been test flown inverted for up to 10 min.) Provision for two underwing ferry fuel tanks, total capacity 660 litres (174.4 US gallons; 145 Imp gallons).

ACCOMMODATION: Instructor and pupil in tandem, on Martin-Baker BR8LC lightweight ejection seats, in air-conditioned cockpit. One-piece fully transparent vacuum formed canopy, opening sideways to starboard, with internal and external jettison provisions. Rear seat elevated. Dual controls standard. Baggage compartment in rear fuselage, with access via door on port side. Cockpit heating and canopy demisting by engine bleed air.

SYSTEMS: Freon cycle air-conditioning system, with engine driven compressor. Single hydraulic system, consisting basically of (a) control unit, including reservoir with usable capacity of 1.9 litres (0.5 US gallon; 0.42 Imp gallon); (b) an engine driven pump with nominal pressure of 131 bars (1,900 lb/sq in) and nominal flow rate of 4.6

EMB-312 Tucano tandem two-seat trainer of the Venezuelan Air Force

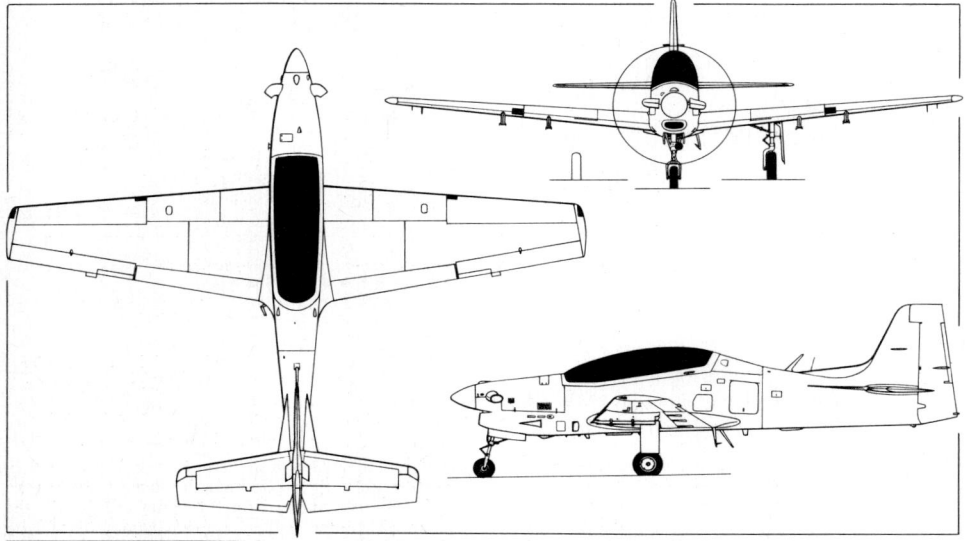

Embraer EMB-312 Tucano basic trainer (Pratt & Whitney Canada PT6A-25C turboprop) *(Pilot Press)*

litres (1.22 US gallons; 1.01 Imp gallons)/min at 3,800 rpm; (c) landing gear and gear door actuators; (d) filter; (e) shutoff valve; and (f) hydraulic fluid to MIL-H-5606. Under normal operation, hydraulic system actuates landing gear extension/retraction and control of gear doors. Landing gear extension can be performed under emergency operation; emergency retraction may also be possible during landing and T-O with engine running. Reservoir and system are suitable for aerobatics. No pneumatic system. 28V DC electrical power provided by a 6kW starter/generator, 26Ah battery and, for 115V and 26V AC power at 400Hz, a 250VA inverter. Diluter-demand oxygen system conforms to MIL-C-5887 and is supplied individually to each occupant by six MS 21227 D2 type cylinders (total capacity approx 1,200 litres; 317 US gallons; 264 Imp gallons) at a pressure of 31 bars (450 lb/sq in).

AVIONICS: Standard avionics include two Collins VHF-20A transceivers; two Collins 387C-4 audio systems, one Embraer radio transferring system; Telephonics audio control panel; one Collins VIR-31A VOR/ILS/marker beacon receiver; one Collins TDR-90 ATC transponder; one Collins DME-40; one Collins PN-101 gyromagnetic compass; and one Collins ADF-60A.

EQUIPMENT: Landing light in each wing leading-edge; taxying lights on nosewheel unit.

ARMAMENT: Two hardpoints under each wing, each stressed for a max load of 250 kg (551 lb). Typical loads, on GB100-20-36B pylons, include two 0.30 in C2 machine-gun pods, each with 500 rds; four 25 lb Mk 76 practice bombs; four 250 lb Mk 81 general purpose bombs; or four LM-37/7A or LM-70/7 launchers, each with seven rockets (Avibras SBAT-37 and SBAT-70 respectively). Fixed reflex-type gunsight.

DIMENSIONS, EXTERNAL:	
Wing span	11.14 m (36 ft 6½ in)
Wing chord: at root	2.30 m (7 ft 6½ in)
at tip	1.07 m (3 ft 6⅛ in)
Wing aspect ratio	6.4
Length overall	9.86 m (32 ft 4¼ in)
Fuselage: Length (excl rudder)	8.53 m (27 ft 11⅞ in)
Max width	1.00 m (3 ft 3¼ in)
Max depth	1.55 m (5 ft 1 in)
Height overall (static)	3.40 m (11 ft 1¾ in)
Tailplane span	4.66 m (15 ft 3½ in)
Wheel track	3.76 m (12 ft 4 in)
Wheelbase	3.16 m (10 ft 4½ in)
Propeller diameter	2.36 m (7 ft 9 in)
Propeller ground clearance (static)	0.33 m (1 ft 1 in)
Baggage compartment door:	
Height	0.60 m (1 ft 11½ in)
Width	0.54 m (1 ft 9¼ in)
Height to sill	1.25 m (4 ft 1¼ in)
DIMENSIONS, INTERNAL:	
Cockpits: Combined length	2.90 m (9 ft 6⅛ in)
Max height	1.55 m (5 ft 1 in)
Max width	0.85 m (2 ft 9½ in)
Baggage compartment volume	0.17 m³ (6.0 cu ft)
AREAS:	
Wings, gross	19.40 m² (208.82 sq ft)
Ailerons (total)	1.97 m² (21.20 sq ft)
Trailing-edge flaps (total)	2.58 m² (27.77 sq ft)
Fin, incl dorsal fin	2.29 m² (24.65 sq ft)
Rudder, incl tab	1.38 m² (14.85 sq ft)
Tailplane, incl fillets	4.77 m² (51.34 sq ft)
Elevators, incl tab	2.00 m² (21.53 sq ft)
WEIGHTS AND LOADINGS:	
Basic weight empty	1,810 kg (3,991 lb)

Max internal fuel load (usable)	529 kg (1,166 lb)
Max external stores load	1,000 kg (2,205 lb)
Max T-O weight: clean	2,550 kg (5,622 lb)
with external stores	3,175 kg (7,000 lb)
Max ramp weight	3,195 kg (7,044 lb)
Max landing weight: clean	2,800 kg (6,173 lb)
Max zero-fuel weight	2,050 kg (4,519 lb)
Max wing loading: clean	131.4 kg/m² (26.92 lb/sq ft)
with external stores	163.7 kg/m² (33.52 lb/sq ft)
Max power loading: clean	4.56 kg/kW (7.50 lb/shp)
with external stores	5.68 kg/kW (9.33 lb/shp)

PERFORMANCE (at max clean T-O weight except where indicated):

Never-exceed speed (VNE)	280 knots (519 km/h; 322 mph) EAS
Max level speed at 3,050 m (10,000 ft)	242 knots (448 km/h; 278 mph)
Max cruising speed at 3,050 m (10,000 ft)	222 knots (411 km/h; 255 mph)
Econ cruising speed at 3,050 m (10,000 ft)	172 knots (319 km/h; 198 mph)
Stalling speed, power off:	
flaps and landing gear up	72 knots (133 km/h; 83 mph) EAS
flaps and landing gear down	67 knots (124 km/h; 77 mph) EAS
Max rate of climb at S/L	680 m (2,231 ft)/min
Service ceiling	9,150 m (30,000 ft)
T-O run	380 m (1,250 ft)
T-O to 15 m (50 ft)	710 m (2,330 ft)
Landing from 15 m (50 ft)	605 m (1,985 ft)
Landing run	370 m (1,214 ft)
Range at 6,100 m (20,000 ft) with max fuel, 30 min reserves	995 nm (1,844 km; 1,145 miles)
Ferry range at 6,100 m (20,000 ft) with underwing tanks	1,797 nm (3,330 km; 2.069 miles)
Endurance on internal fuel at econ cruising speed at 6,100 m (20,000 ft), 30 min reserves	approx 5 h
g limits: fully Aerobatic category, at max clean T-O weight	+6/–3
at max T-O weight with external stores	+4.4/–2.2

EMBRAER EMB-201A IPANEMA

The original version of this agricultural aircraft was designed to Brazilian Ministry of Agriculture specifications, and the EMB-200 prototype (PP-ZIP) made its first flight on 30 July 1970. A type certificate was granted on 14 December 1971.

Details of the EMB-200/200A (73 built), EMB-201 (200 built) and EMB-201R (three built) can be found in the 1977-78 and previous editions of *Jane's*. The current production version, first flown on 10 March 1977, is the EMB-201A, of which 382 had been sold by 1 January 1991, bringing total Ipanema sales (all versions) to 658.

Manufacture of the EMB-201A was transferred to Embraer's Neiva subsidiary during the second half of 1981.

An improved version was launched at the end of 1988 with an enlarged windscreen; redesigned canopy in glassfibre composites, with two overhead windows; doors with built-in side windows, fitted with triple-lock and jettison provisions; an airscoop at the top of the canopy front edge, to improve cockpit ventilation, and one on the fin leading-edge to pressurise the interior of the rear fuselage; an ergonomically improved cockpit and instrument layout; and new engine exhaust mufflers. New optional items include a Hartzell three-blade variable-pitch propeller; ram air pressure generator for use with the liquid spray system; improved lightweight spraybooms; smaller and lighter Micronair AU5000 rotary atomisers; and a trapezoidal spreader with adjustable inlet to improve application of dry chemicals.

TYPE: Single-seat agricultural aircraft.

WINGS: Cantilever low-wing monoplane. Wing section NACA 23015 (modified), with cambered leading-edges. Dihedral 7° from roots. Incidence 3°. All-metal single-spar structure of 2024 aluminium alloy with all-metal Frise ailerons outboard and all-metal slotted flaps on trailing-edge, and detachable cambered leading-edges. No tabs. Cambered wingtips standard.

FUSELAGE: Rectangular section all-metal safe-life structure, of welded 4130 steel tube with removable skin panels of 2024 aluminium alloy and glassfibre. Structure is specially treated against chemical corrosion.

TAIL UNIT: Cantilever two-spar all-metal structure of 2024 aluminium alloy. Slight sweepback on fin and rudder. Fixed incidence tailplane. Trim tab in starboard elevator.

LANDING GEAR: Non-retractable main- and tailwheels, with rubber shock absorbers in main units. Tailwheel has tapered spring shock absorber. Mainwheels and tyres size 8.50-10. Tailwheel diameter 250 mm (10 in). Tyre pressures: main, 2.07-2.41 bars (30-35 lb/sq in); tailwheel, 3.79 bars (55 lb/sq in). Hydraulic disc brakes on mainwheels.

POWER PLANT: One 224 kW (300 hp) Textron Lycoming IO-540-K1J5D flat-six engine, driving a Hartzell two-blade (optionally three-blade) constant-speed metal propeller. Optional engine is Teledyne Continental 224 kW (300 hp) IO-550-E with McCauley two-blade constant-speed propeller. Integral fuel tanks in each wing leading-edge, with total capacity 292 litres (77.1 US gallons; 64.2 Imp gallons). Refuelling point on top of each tank. Oil capacity 12 litres (3.2 US gallons; 2.6 Imp gallons).

ACCOMMODATION: Single horizontally/vertically adjustable seat in fully enclosed cabin with bottom-hinged window/door on each side. Ventilation system in cabin. Inertial shoulder harness standard.

SYSTEMS: 28V DC electrical system supplied by two Cral 18EP 43Ah batteries and a CEN 240074 28V 35A alternator. Power receptacle for external battery (AN-2552-3A type) on port side of forward fuselage.

AVIONICS: Standard VFR avionics include 760-channel Bendix/King KY 96A transceiver and KR 86 ADF.

EQUIPMENT: Hopper for agricultural chemicals, capacity 950 litres (251 US gallons; 209 Imp gallons) liquid or 750 kg (1,653 lb) dry. Dusting system below centre of fuselage. Spraybooms or Micronair atomisers aft of or above wing trailing-edges respectively.

DIMENSIONS, EXTERNAL:

Wing span	11.20 m (36 ft 9 in)
Wing chord, constant	1.71 m (5 ft 7½ in)
Wing aspect ratio	6.3
Length overall (tail up)	7.43 m (24 ft 4½ in)
Height overall (tail down)	2.20 m (7 ft 2½ in)
Fuselage: Max width	0.93 m (3 ft 0½ in)
Tailplane span	3.66 m (12 ft 0 in)
Wheel track	2.20 m (7 ft 2½ in)
Wheelbase	5.20 m (17 ft 7¼ in)
Propeller diameter	2.20 m (7 ft 2½ in)

DIMENSIONS, INTERNAL:

Cockpit: Max length	1.20 m (3 ft 11¼ in)
Max width	0.85 m (2 ft 9½ in)
Max height	1.34 m (4 ft 4¾ in)

AREAS:

Wings, gross	19.94 m² (214.63 sq ft)
Ailerons (total)	1.60 m² (17.22 sq ft)
Trailing-edge flaps (total)	2.30 m² (24.76 sq ft)
Fin	0.58 m² (6.24 sq ft)
Rudder	0.63 m² (6.78 sq ft)
Tailplane	3.17 m² (34.12 sq ft)
Elevators (total, incl tab)	1.50 m² (16.15 sq ft)

WEIGHTS AND LOADINGS (N: Normal, R: Restricted category):

Weight empty: N, R	1,011 kg (2,229 lb)
Max payload: N, R	750 kg (1,653 lb)
Max T-O and landing weight: N	1,550 kg (3,417 lb)
R	1,800 kg (3,968 lb)
Max wing loading: N	77.75 kg/m² (15.92 lb/sq ft)
R	90.29 kg/m² (18.49 lb/sq ft)
Max power loading: N	6.92 kg/kW (11.39 lb/hp)
R	8.03 kg/kW (13.23 lb/hp)

PERFORMANCE (at max T-O weight, clean configuration, ISA):

Never-exceed speed (V_{NE}):	
N	147 knots (272 km/h; 169 mph)
R	113 knots (209 km/h; 130 mph)
Max level speed at S/L:	
N	124 knots (230 km/h; 143 mph)
R	121 knots (225 km/h; 140 mph)
Max cruising speed (75% power) at 1,830 m (6,000 ft):	
N	115 knots (212 km/h; 132 mph)
R	110 knots (204 km/h; 127 mph)
Stalling speed, power off (N):	
flaps up	56 knots (103 km/h; 64 mph)
8° flap	54 knots (100 km/h; 62 mph)
30° flap	50 knots (92 km/h; 57 mph)
Stalling speed, power off (R):	
flaps up	60 knots (110 km/h; 68 mph)
8° flap	58 knots (107 km/h; 66 mph)
30° flap	53 knots (99 km/h; 61 mph)

Embraer Ipanema agricultural aircraft (pre-1989 standard)

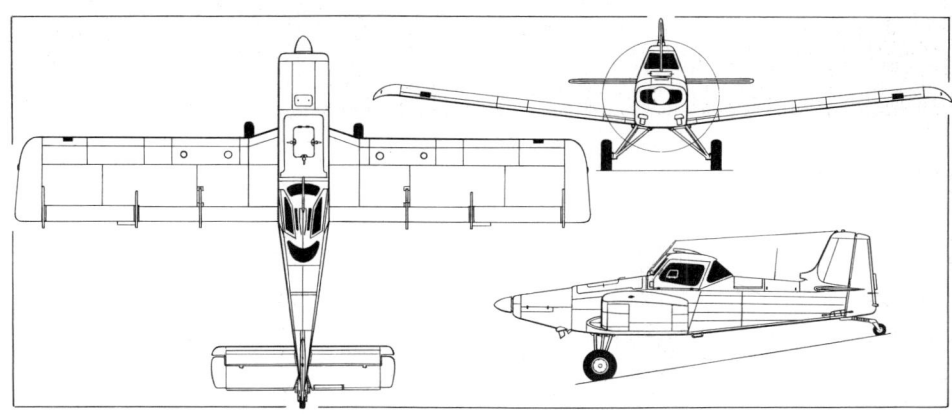

Embraer EMB-201A Ipanema single-seat agricultural aircraft (current version) *(Pilot Press)*

Max rate of climb at S/L, 8° flap:	
N	283 m (930 ft)/min
R	201 m (660 ft)/min
Service ceiling, 8° flap: R	3,470 m (11,385 ft)
T-O run at S/L, 8° flap, asphalt runway:	
N	200 m (656 ft)
R	354 m (1,160 ft)
T-O to 15 m (50 ft), conditions as above:	
N	333 m (1,093 ft)
R	564 m (1,850 ft)
Landing from 15 m (50 ft) at S/L, 30° flap, asphalt runway: N	440 m (1,444 ft)
R	500 m (1,640 ft)
Landing run, conditions as above: N	153 m (502 ft)
R	170 m (558 ft)

Range at 1,830 m (6,000 ft), no reserves:	
N	506 nm (938 km; 583 miles)
R	474 nm (878 km; 545 miles)

EMBRAER-PIPER LIGHT AIRCRAFT PROGRAMME

Detailed descriptions of Piper aircraft built under licence by Embraer can be found in the US section of this and earlier editions of *Jane's*. Manufacture is undertaken by Embraer's subsidiary, Neiva. The following types were in production in 1991:

EMB-720D Minuano: Piper PA-32-301 Saratoga.
EMB-810D Seneca III: Piper PA-34-220T Seneca III. Deliveries include 35 to Brazilian Air Force for liaison duties.

HELIBRAS
HELICÓPTEROS DO BRASIL SA

Rua Projetada Um 200, Distrito Industrial, Caixa Postal 184, 37500 Itajubá, MG
Telephone: 55 (35) 622 3366 and 622 2455
Telex: 31 2602 HLBR BR
PRESIDENT: Fernando Antonio Rainho Thomaz Ribeiro
COMMERCIAL DIRECTOR: Hilton Amaral
PUBLIC RELATIONS: Odilon Martins de Andrade

Formed in 1978 and now owned jointly by Bueninvest of Brazil (30 per cent), Aerospatiale of France (45 per cent) and the state government of Minas Gerais (25 per cent), Helibras is assembling and undertaking partial local manufacture of Aerospatiale SA 315B Lama, AS 350/550 single-engined and AS 355/555 twin-engined Ecureuil/Fennec helicopters, and the AS 565AA (formerly AS 365K) Panther. Of the total assembly hours per helicopter, approx 30 per cent involve the incorporation of locally

manufactured items. The first assembly hall was officially inaugurated on 28 March 1980. The complete facility will extend over an area of 206,650 m² (2,224,360 sq ft), of which 9,747 m² (104,916 sq ft) was covered in 1989, when a total of 320 people was employed.

HELIBRAS HB 315B GAVIÃO

These are the Brazilian name and designation of the SA 315B Lama assembled by Helibras, the first of which

Left: An HB 350B Esquilo of the Paraguayan Air Force. Helibras production also includes the twin-engined HB 355F2 Esquilo, illustrated on the right, which has the FAB designation VH-55

was completed during the latter half of 1979. Production by May 1989 included six for SAR and utility duties with Grupo Aéreo 51 of the Bolivian Air Force and one civil example for a customer in Chile.

HELIBRAS HB 350B, HB 350B1, HB 350L1 and HB 355F2 ESQUILO

All Brazilian models of the Ecureuil and Fennec have the name Esquilo, the HB 350B and B1 being single-engined and the HB 355F2 twin-engined. Deliveries began in 1979, and by early 1991 totalled more than 200. These have included 30 HB 350B/B1s (designations **CH-50** and **TH-50**) and 13 HB 355F2s (11 **CH-55s** and two VIP **VH-55s**) for the Brazilian Air Force; nine HB 350Bs (**UH-12**) and 11 HB 355F2s (**UH-12B**) for the Brazilian

Navy; 16 HB 350L1s (**HA-1**) for the Brazilian Army; and others for the Brazilian police and civilian customers. The Brazilian Navy Esquilos, which serve with the 1° Esquadrão de Helicópteros de Emprego Geral (squadron of general purpose helicopters), are equipped to carry two Avibrás LM-70/7 pods each containing seven SBAT 70 mm rockets, or two FN twin 7.62 mm MAG machine-gun pods, and a door mounted MAG pedestal. Those for the Brazilian Army, delivered to the 1st Aviation Battalion at Taubaté, São Paulo, in 1989, are equipped for tactical support and reconnaissance. Equipment can include a 20 mm gun and 2.75 in unguided rockets, or anti-tank missiles and a HeliTOW sighting system. HB 350Bs have been sold to foreign civil customers in Argentina (three), Bolivia (four), and Venezuela (three), and six HB 350B examples to Paraguay (Air Force four, Navy two).

An aeromedical version of the Esquilo was launched in February 1989. Equipment includes an electrocardiograph, respirator, pacemaker, stretchers, battery operated incubator, oxygen and compressed air cylinders, first aid kit, and a four-way electrical socket for 115V AC (60Hz) and 12V DC power. Apart from the pilot, this version can carry a doctor, nurse and two stretcher patients.

HELIBRAS AS 565 PANTHER

Deliveries of the first 10 Panthers in the present 36-aircraft Brazilian Army contract began at the end of 1989, with a further 16 following in 1990; these 26 aircraft are of Aerospatiale manufacture. Helibras is assembling the final 10 from French built kits. Brazilian Army designation is **HM-1**.

IPE

INDÚSTRIA PARANAENSE DE ESTRUTURAS LTDA

Rua Jeronimo Durski 357 (Caixa Postal 7931), 80430 Curitiba, Paraná
Telephone: 55 (41) 242 2324
MANAGER: Eng J. C. Boscardin

IPE 06 CURUCACA

Developed for the Brazilian market and first flown in January 1990, the Curucaca is a very lightweight tandem two-seat training or general purpose aircraft, powered by a 52.2 kW (70 hp) T2000 (modified VW) engine.

DIMENSIONS, EXTERNAL:

Wing span	9.90 m (32 ft 5¾ in)
Length overall (flying attitude)	6.30 m (20 ft 8 in)
Height overall (flying attitude)	2.30 m (7 ft 6½ in)
Elevator span	2.91 m (9 ft 6½ in)

AREAS:

Wings, gross	13.00 m² (139.9 sq ft)

WEIGHTS AND LOADINGS:

Weight empty	224 kg (494 lb)

Prototype IPE 06 Curucaca two-seat light aircraft

Max T-O weight	444 kg (979 lb)	PERFORMANCE:	
Max wing loading	34.15 kg/m² (6.99 lb/sq ft)	Cruising speed	65 knots (120 km/h; 74 mph)
Max power loading	8.51 kg/kW (13.98 lb/hp)	Stalling speed	27 knots (50 km/h; 31 mph)

NEIVA

INDÚSTRIA AERONÁUTICA NEIVA SA (Subsidiary of Embraer)

Rua Nossa Senhora de Fátima 360, Vila Antártica, Caixa Postal 10, 18600 Botucatu, SP
Telephone: 55 (149) 22 1010
Telex: 142 423 SOAN BR
PRESIDENT: Eng Antonio Garcia da Silveira
ENGINEERING MANAGER: Luíz Carlos Benetti

Neiva, which in January 1991 had a workforce of 519 and factory area of 20,580 m² (221,521 sq ft), was formed in 1954 and became a wholly owned subsidiary of Embraer on 10 March 1980. It designed and built the U-42/L-42 Regente utility/liaison light aircraft and the T-25/AT-25 Universal trainer/light attack aircraft, which continue in

service with the Brazilian Air Force. Currently, Neiva participates in Embraer's general aviation programme, being responsible for all production of the EMB-720D Minuano and EMB-810D Seneca III. It had delivered 1,501 licence-built Piper aircraft of these and other types by January 1991. For many years Neiva has built fuselages for the Embraer Ipanema, and since 1981 has been entirely responsible for Ipanema engineering, manufacture and assembly. The 597th Ipanema, completed in November 1987, was the 2,000th aircraft to be produced at the Neiva facility. The company also produces subassemblies and components for the Embraer Bandeirante (wings, engine nacelles, pilots' seats, hoses and tubing) and Tucano (wing flaps, elevators, tailplanes, fins, rudders, fuselage rear sections and engine exhaust stacks).

NEIVA NE-821 CARAJÁ

Responsibility for the EMB-820C Navajo was transferred to Neiva in mid-1983, and in 1984 (first flight 9 March) four of the last five Embraer assembled examples were converted to Comanchero 500B eight-seat executive configuration (see Schafer entry in US section), in which form they are designated NE-821 Carajá. Deliveries began in November of that year. A total of 39 had been delivered by 1 January 1991. Brazilian certification covers the use of either PT6A-27 or PT6A-34 engines, flat rated in both cases at 410 kW (550 shp) and driving Hartzell three-blade constant-speed propellers. Further details of the Carajá, and a photograph, can be found in the 1989-90 *Jane's*.

SUPER ROTOR

M.M. SUPER ROTOR INDÚSTRIA AERONÁUTICA LTDA

Rua Itapeti 541, Tatuapé, 03324 São Paulo, SP
Telephone: 55 (11) 295 8187
DIRECTOR: José Montalvá Perez

SUPER ROTOR AC-4 ANDORINHA

This all-Brazilian single-seat autogyro was designed in 1970, as a private venture, by Eng Altair Coelho. The prototype first flew in December 1972, being sold subsequently to Sr Francisco Mattos Jr, who introduced a number of modifications before obtaining Brazilian CTA certification in January 1985. It is produced in both ready to fly and kit forms. By early 1990 domestic and foreign orders for the AC-4, including kits, totalled 307.

TYPE: Single-seat autogyro.

ROTOR SYSTEM: Single rotor, with two blades of NACA H-12 (modified) section, each attached to hub by 10 bolts. Aluminium alloy blades (6061-T6 spars and 0.8 mm sheet skins), each with tab inset from tip. No blade folding or rotor brake. Engine power take-off for pre-spinning rotor before T-O.

FUSELAGE: Welded truss structure of SAE 1025 carbon steel tube, with nose fairing and windscreen.

TAIL UNIT: Fin and rudder only, latter with trim tab.

LANDING GEAR: Non-retractable unsprung tricycle type, with belt type mainwheel brakes and steerable nosewheel. Goodyear tyres, size 5.00-5 (main) and 3.50-5 (nose); pressure (all three tyres) 1.38 bars (20 lb/sq in). Streamline fairing on nosewheel.

POWER PLANT: One 63 kW (85 hp) modified VW 1600 motorcar engine, driving a two-blade wooden pusher propeller. Single aluminium fuel tank beneath engine, capacity 40 litres (10.5 US gallons; 8.8 Imp gallons). Oil capacity 3 litres (0.8 US gallon; 0.66 Imp gallon).

ACCOMMODATION: Single open seat for pilot.

EQUIPMENT: 7.5Ah battery.

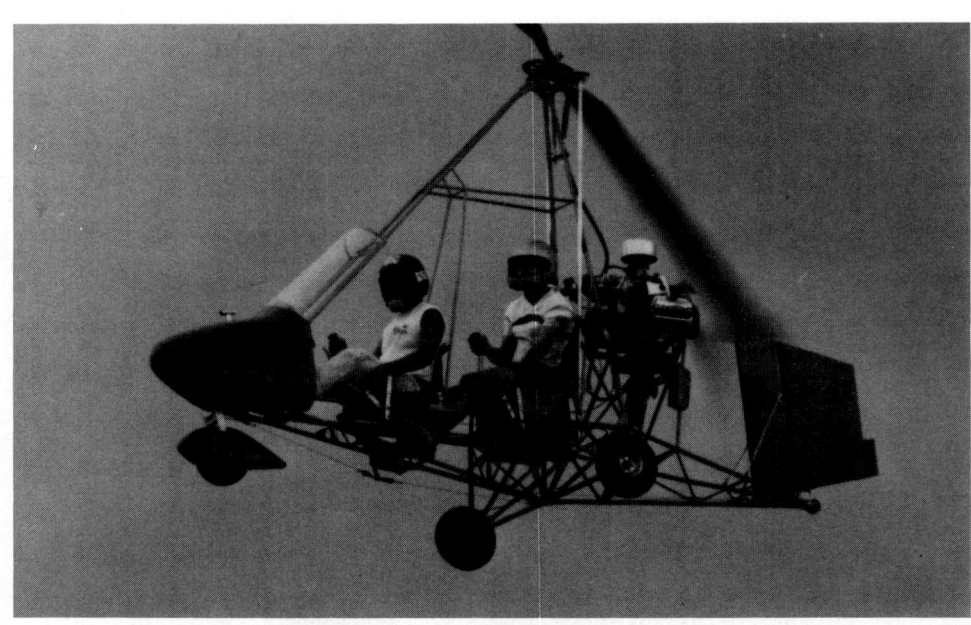

Super Rotor M-1 Montalvá 1 two-seat autogyro

DIMENSIONS, EXTERNAL:		AREAS:	
Main rotor diameter	7.44 m (24 ft 5 in)	Main rotor blades, each	0.63 m² (6.78 sq ft)
Main rotor blade chord	0.185 m (7.3 in)	Main rotor disc	43.47 m² (467.9 sq ft)
Length overall, excl rotors	3.75 m (12 ft 3¾ in)	Fin	0.21 m² (2.26 sq ft)
Height to top of rotor head	2.36 m (7 ft 9 in)	Rudder	0.36 m² (3.88 sq ft)
Width overall, excl main rotor	1.70 m (5 ft 7 in)	WEIGHTS AND LOADINGS:	
Wheel track	1.446 m (4 ft 9 in)	Basic weight empty	190 kg (419 lb)
Propeller diameter	1.51 m (4 ft 11½ in)	Max T-O weight	310 kg (683 lb)

Max disc loading	7.13 kg/m² (1.46 lb/sq ft)
Max power loading	4.92 kg/kW (8.04 lb/hp)

PERFORMANCE (at max T-O weight):

Never-exceed speed (V_{NE})	97 knots (180 km/h; 112 mph)
Max level speed	86 knots (160 km/h; 99 mph)
Max cruising speed	70 knots (130 km/h; 81 mph)
Econ cruising speed	59 knots (110 km/h; 68 mph)
Max rate of climb at S/L	366 m (1,200 ft)/min
Service ceiling	3,660 m (12,000 ft)
T-O run	35 m (115 ft)
T-O to 15 m (50 ft)	100 m (328 ft)
Landing from 15 m (50 ft)	30 m (99 ft)
Landing run	10 m (33 ft)
Range with max fuel	243 nm (450 km; 280 miles)

SUPER ROTOR M-1 MONTALVÁ

Design of this enlarged two-seat development of the AC-4 started in June 1984, and it flew for the first time in March 1985. Production aircraft became available in the Summer of that year, and 75, all to firm orders, had been completed by January 1990. Details are as for the AC-4 except:

TYPE: Tandem two-seat autogyro.

LANDING GEAR: Increased mainwheel tyre pressure of 1.72 bars (25 lb/sq in).

POWER PLANT: One 72 kW (97 hp) modified VW 1600 engine and 27 litre (7 US gallon; 6 Imp gallon) fuel tank.

ACCOMMODATION: Two open seats in tandem.

DIMENSIONS, EXTERNAL:

Main rotor diameter	8.14 m (26 ft 8½ in)
Main rotor blade chord	0.21 m (8¼ in)
Length overall, excl rotors	4.38 m (14 ft 4½ in)
Height to top of rotor head	2.68 m (8 ft 9½ in)
Wheel track	1.90 m (6 ft 3 in)

AREAS:

Main rotor blades, each	0.77 m² (8.29 sq ft)
Main rotor disc	52.04 m² (560.2 sq ft)

WEIGHTS AND LOADINGS:

Basic weight empty	174 kg (383 lb)
Max T-O weight	374 kg (825 lb)
Max disc loading	7.19 kg/m² (1.47 lb/sq ft)
Max power loading	5.19 kg/kW (8.50 lb/hp)

PERFORMANCE (at max T-O weight):

Max level speed	75 knots (140 km/h; 87 mph)
Max cruising speed	65 knots (120 km/h; 75 mph)
Econ cruising speed	54 knots (100 km/h; 62 mph)
Max rate of climb at S/L	213 m (700 ft)/min
T-O run	160 m (525 ft)
T-O to 15 m (50 ft)	250 m (820 ft)
Range with max fuel	118 nm (220 km; 136 miles)

CANADA

AIRTECH

AIRTECH CANADA

Peterborough Municipal Airport, PO Box 415,
Peterborough, Ontario K9J 6Z3

Telephone: 1 (705) 743 9433

Fax: 1 (705) 749 0841

Telex: 06-962912

PRESIDENT: John O'Dwyer

CHIEF ENGINEER: James C. Mewett

PRESS RELATIONS: Alison M. Mewett

Airtech specialises in retrofitting versions of the de Havilland Canada Otter and Beaver with more powerful Polish built engines that offer increased climb rates and considerably greater fuel economy, at lower power settings, than the original engines which they replace. It has also designed, manufactured, tested and installed modifications (in particular, auxiliary fuel tanks and medevac equipment) for various types of aircraft including the Cessna 401, 414 and 421, Piper PA-31 and PA-42, Mitsubishi MU-2 and Fairchild Metro IIB.

There has been no recent news of the DC-3/2000 programme, last described in the 1990-91 *Jane's*.

AIRTECH CANADA DHC-3/1000 OTTER

Airtech Canada refitted eight de Havilland Canada DHC-3 Otters with Polish PZL-3S radial engines. Details of this DHC-3/PZL-3S version can be found in the 1983-84 *Jane's*.

Following the first flight of a prototype on 25 August 1983, the Otter conversion was then offered with a 746 kW (1,000 hp) Polish ASz-62IR engine instead of the 447 kW (600 hp) PZL-3S. Seven of these conversions, designated

Airtech Canada's DHC-3/1000 Otter conversion, powered by a PZL Kalisz ASz-62IR radial engine

DHC-3/1000, were flying in North and South America by February 1989. For further details see the 1990-91 *Jane's*.

AIRTECH CANADA DHC-2/PZL-3S BEAVER

Airtech Canada introduced a conversion of the DHC-2 Beaver with the PZL-3S engine at the request of operators who wanted an increase in power to provide improved performance and safer operation from short airstrips. Four such conversions had been completed by early 1989. Further details were given in the 1990-91 *Jane's*.

BELL

BELL HELICOPTER TEXTRON
(a Division of Textron Canada Ltd)

12800 rue de l'Avenir, St Janvier, Quebec J0N 1L0

Telephone: 1 (514) 437 3400

PRESIDENT: Lloyd Shoppa

EXECUTIVE VICE-PRESIDENT: Jack Cadieux

VICE-PRESIDENT, OPERATIONS: E. H. Barnett

On 7 October 1983 the Canadian government announced the signing of a memorandum of understanding under which Bell had been selected to establish a helicopter industry in Canada, the second largest user of helicopters outside the Soviet bloc. The new 34,560 m² (372,000 sq ft) facility at Mirabel, Quebec, some 32 km (20 miles) from Montreal, opened in late 1985 and employed 805 people in early 1990.

US civil production of the Model 206B JetRanger and 206L LongRanger had been transferred to the Canadian factory by early 1987, followed by the Model 212 in August 1988 and Model 412 in February 1989. Deliveries of these four types from Mirabel totalled 345 by July 1990. About half of each helicopter is now made in Canada and product support for the Model 206 series is based there. The JetRanger and Models 212/412 are produced under licence by Agusta in Italy (which see); production of some cabin components for the 212 now takes place by KBHC in South Korea; Chincul in Argentina is to assemble and later part-build the 212 and 412.

BELL MODEL 206B JETRANGER III

In the Summer of 1977, Bell began delivery of the Model 206B JetRanger III, which subsequently replaced in production the lower-powered JetRanger II, of which 1,619 were delivered. The uprated power plant of the JetRanger III is installed with minimal modification of the original airframe, enabling Bell to offer modification kits to convert JetRanger IIs to JetRanger III standard.

By January 1991, Bell and its licensees had manufactured well over 7,000 helicopters of the Model 206 series,

Bell 206B JetRanger III (Allison 250-C20J turboshaft)

including some 4,200 Model 206Bs and about 2,000 of the military OH-58 series. The Model 206B was transferred to Mirabel in 1986. The first Canadian built example was delivered at the end of 1986 and 120 had been completed at Mirabel by January 1990. Production rate in mid-1990 was six to seven a month.

TYPE: Turbine powered general purpose light helicopter.

ROTOR SYSTEM: Two-blade semi-rigid teetering main rotor, employing pre-coning and underslinging to ensure smooth operation. Blades are of standard Bell 'droop snoot' section. They have a D-shape aluminium spar, bonded aluminium alloy skin, honeycomb core and a trailing-edge extension. Each blade is connected to the head by means of a grip, pitch change bearings and a tension-torsion strap assembly. Two tail rotor blades have bonded aluminium skin but no core. Main rotor blades do not fold, but modification to permit manual folding is possible. Rotor brake available as optional kit.

Rotors driven through tubular steel alloy shafts with spliced couplings. Initial drive from engine through 90° spiral bevel gear to single-stage planetary main gearbox. Transmission rating 236 kW (317 shp). Shaft to tail rotor single-stage bevel gearbox. Freewheeling unit ensures that main rotor continues to drive tail rotor when engine is disengaged. Main rotor/engine rpm ratio 1 : 15; main rotor rpm 374-394. Tail rotor/engine rpm ratio 1 : 2.3.

FUSELAGE: Forward cabin section is made up of two aluminium alloy beams and 25 mm (1 in) bonded aluminium honeycomb sandwich. Rotor, transmission and engine are supported by upper longitudinal beams. Upper and lower structures are interconnected by three fuselage bulkheads and a centrepost to form an integrated structure. Intermediate section is of aluminium alloy semi-monocoque construction. Aluminium monocoque tailboom.

TAIL UNIT: Fixed stabiliser of aluminium monocoque construction, with inverted aerofoil section. Fixed vertical tail fin in sweptback upper and ventral sections, of aluminium honeycomb with aluminium alloy skin.

LANDING GEAR: Aluminium alloy tubular skids bolted to extruded cross-tubes. Tubular steel skid on ventral fin to protect tail rotor in tail-down landing. Special high skid gear (0.25 m; 10 in greater ground clearance) available for use in areas with high brush. Pontoons or stowed floats, capable of in-flight inflation, available as optional kits.

POWER PLANT: One 313 kW (420 shp) Allison 250-C20J turboshaft, flat rated at 236 kW (317 shp). Rupture resistant fuel tank below and behind rear passenger seat, capacity 344 litres (91 US gallons; 75.75 Imp gallons). Refuelling point on starboard side of fuselage, aft of cabin. Oil capacity 5.2 litres (11 US pints; 9 Imp pints).

ACCOMMODATION: Two seats side by side in front and three-seat rear bench. Dual controls optional. Two forward-hinged doors on each side, made of formed aluminium alloy with transparent panels (bulged on rear pair). Baggage compartment aft of rear seats, capacity 113 kg (250 lb), with external door on port side.

SYSTEMS: Hydraulic system, pressure 41.5 bars (600 lb/sq in), for cyclic, collective and directional controls. Maximum flow rate 7.57 litres (2 US gallons; 1.65 Imp gallons)/min. Open reservoir. Electrical supply from 150A starter/generator. One 24V 13Ah nickel-cadmium battery.

AVIONICS: Full range of avionics available in form of optional kits, including VHF communications and omni navigation kit, ADF, DME, R/Nav, transponder and intercom and speaker system.

EQUIPMENT: Standard equipment includes cabin fire extinguisher, first aid kit, door locks, night lighting, and dynamic flapping restraints. Optional items include clock, engine hour meter, turn and slip indicator, custom seating, internal litter kit, cabin heater, environmental control system, camera access door, high intensity night lights, engine fire detection system, and external cargo sling of 680 kg (1,500 lb) capacity.

DIMENSIONS, EXTERNAL:	
Main rotor diameter	10.16 m (33 ft 4 in)
Tail rotor diameter	1.65 m (5 ft 5 in)
Main rotor blade chord	0.33 m (1 ft 1 in)
Distance between rotor centres	5.96 m (19 ft 6½ in)
Length: overall, rotors turning	11.82 m (38 ft 9½ in)
fuselage, incl tailskid	9.50 m (31 ft 2 in)
Height: over tail fin	2.54 m (8 ft 4 in)
overall	2.91 m (9 ft 6½ in)
Stabiliser span	1.97 m (6 ft 5¾ in)
Width over skids	1.92 m (6 ft 3½ in)
DIMENSIONS, INTERNAL:	
Cabin: Length	2.13 m (7 ft 0 in)
Max width	1.27 m (4 ft 2 in)
Max height	1.28 m (4 ft 3 in)
Volume	1.13 m³ (40 cu ft)
Baggage compartment volume	0.45 m³ (16 cu ft)
AREAS:	
Main rotor blades (each)	1.68 m² (18.05 sq ft)
Tail rotor blades (each)	0.11 m² (1.18 sq ft)
Main rotor disc	81.07 m² (872.7 sq ft)
Tail rotor disc	2.14 m² (23.04 sq ft)
Stabiliser	0.90 m² (9.65 sq ft)
WEIGHTS AND LOADINGS:	
Weight empty, standard configuration	742 kg (1,635 lb)
Max payload: internal	635 kg (1,400 lb)
external	680 kg (1,500 lb)
Max T-O weight	1,451 kg (3,200 lb)
Max disc loading	17.92 kg/m² (3.67 lb/sq ft)
Max power loading	6.15 kg/kW (10.09 lb/shp)
PERFORMANCE (at max T-O weight, ISA):	
Never-exceed speed (VNE) at S/L	122 knots (225 km/h; 140 mph)
Max cruising speed:	
at 1,525 m (5,000 ft)	116 knots (216 km/h; 134 mph)
at S/L	115 knots (214 km/h; 133 mph)
Max rate of climb at S/L	384 m (1,260 ft)/min
Vertical rate of climb at S/L	91 m (300 ft)/min
Service ceiling	4,115 m (13,500 ft)
Hovering ceiling: IGE	3,900 m (12,800 ft)
OGE	2,680 m (8,800 ft)
Range with max fuel and max payload:	
at S/L, no reserves	364 nm (674 km; 419 miles)
at 1,525 m (5,000 ft), no reserves	404 nm (748 km; 465 miles)

BELL MODEL 206L-3 LONGRANGER III

Announced on 25 September 1973, Bell's LongRanger was developed to fill the size and performance gap between the five-seat JetRanger II and 15-seat Model 205A-1.

By January 1990 more than 1,100 LongRangers (all versions) had been delivered. They have proved particularly popular in an ambulance role, far outnumbering any other type in the fleet of more than 130 helicopters used by 112 US emergency medical service (EMS) centres at that time. Canadian production of the LongRanger began in January 1987, deliveries beginning in May of that year and totalling 120 by January 1990. Production rate was approx 10 a month in mid-1990.

Bell Model 206L-3 LongRanger III general purpose helicopter of the Pennsylvania State Police

TYPE: Turbine powered general purpose light helicopter.

ROTOR SYSTEM: Bell Noda-Matic cabin suspension system. Detail improvements, first introduced in LongRanger II, include new freewheeling unit, input shaft, forward tail rotor driveshaft, and increased-thrust tail rotor. Transmission rated at 324 kW (435 shp) for take-off, with a continuous rating of 276 kW (370 shp); 340 kW (456 shp) transmission optional. Main rotor rpm 394.

POWER PLANT: One 485 kW (650 shp) Allison 250-C30P turboshaft (max continuous rating 415 kW; 557 shp). Rupture resistant fuel system, capacity 416 litres (110 US gallons; 91 Imp gallons).

ACCOMMODATION: Redesigned rear cabin, with greater volume than that of JetRanger and 5 cm (2 in) more headroom. With a crew of two, standard cabin layout accommodates five passengers in two canted rearward facing seats and three forward facing seats. An optional executive cabin layout has four individual passenger seats. Port forward passenger seat has folding back to allow loading of a 2.44 × 0.91 × 0.30 m (8 × 3 × 1 ft) container, making possible carriage of such items as survey equipment, skis, and long components that cannot be accommodated in any other light helicopter. Double doors on port side of cabin provide opening 1.52 m (5 ft 0 in) wide, for straight-in loading of litter patients or utility cargo; in ambulance or rescue role two litter patients and two ambulatory patients/attendants may be carried.

SYSTEMS: 17Ah battery.

AVIONICS: Standard Collins MicroLine suite includes dual nav/com, ADF, DME, transponder and marker beacon receiver. R/Nav, radio altimeter and encoding altimeter are optional. A Collins AP-107H autopilot can be fitted, to provide single-pilot IFR capability. A Sfena autopilot is also available, featuring automatic heading, altitude navigation, approach and basic stabilisation modes of operation.

EQUIPMENT: Optional kits include emergency flotation gear, 907 kg (2,000 lb) cargo hook, and engine bleed air environmental control system.

DIMENSIONS, EXTERNAL:	
Main rotor diameter	11.28 m (37 ft 0 in)
Tail rotor diameter	1.65 m (5 ft 5 in)
Length: overall, rotors turning	13.02 m (42 ft 8½ in)
fuselage, incl tailskid	10.44 m (34 ft 3 in)
Height: over tail fin	2.90 m (9 ft 6¼ in)
to top of rotor head	3.14 m (10 ft 3¾ in)
Fuselage: Max width	1.32 m (4 ft 4 in)
Stabiliser span	1.98 m (6 ft 6 in)
Width over skids	2.34 m (7 ft 8¼ in)
DIMENSIONS, INTERNAL:	
Cabin volume	2.35 m³ (83 cu ft)
AREAS:	
Main rotor disc	99.89 m² (1,075.2 sq ft)
Tail rotor disc	2.14 m² (23.04 sq ft)
WEIGHTS AND LOADINGS:	
Weight empty, standard	998 kg (2,200 lb)
Max external load	907 kg (2,000 lb)
Max T-O weight: normal	1,882 kg (4,150 lb)
external load	1,927 kg (4,250 lb)
Max disc loading: normal	18.85 kg/m² (3.86 lb/sq ft)
external load	19.29 kg/m² (3.95 lb/sq ft)
Max power loading: transmission for T-O, normal	5.81 kg/kW (9.54 lb/shp)
transmission for T-O, external load	5.95 kg/kW (9.77 lb/shp)
PERFORMANCE (at max normal T-O weight, ISA):	
Never-exceed speed (VNE):	
at S/L	130 knots (241 km/h; 150 mph)
at 1,525 m (5,000 ft)	133 knots (246 km/h; 153 mph)
Max cruising speed at 1,525 m (5,000 ft)	110 knots (203 km/h; 126 mph)
Max rate of climb at S/L	408 m (1,340 ft)/min
Service ceiling at max cruise power	6,100 m (20,000 ft)
Hovering ceiling: IGE	5,030 m (16,500 ft)
OGE	1,645 m (5,400 ft)
Range, no reserves: at S/L	320 nm (592 km; 368 miles)
at 1,525 m (5,000 ft)	360 nm (666 km; 414 miles)

BELL MODEL 212 TWIN TWO-TWELVE

US military designation: UH-1N

Canadian Forces designation: CH-135

Bell announced on 1 May 1968 that the Canadian government had approved development of a twin-engined UH-1 helicopter to be powered by a Pratt & Whitney Canada PT6T-3 power plant. Subsequently, the Canadian government ordered 50 of these aircraft (designated CUH-1N) for the Canadian Forces. Now designated **CH-135**, they were delivered in 1971-72. Simultaneously, the US services ordered 79 **UH-1Ns** for the US Air Force, 40 for the US Navy and 22 for the US Marine Corps. Subsequent orders covered the delivery of 159 more UH-1Ns to the US Navy and Marine Corps in 1973-78. Initial deliveries to USAF began in 1970, when UH-1Ns joined UH-1Ps (modified UH-1Fs) in support of Special Operations Force counter-insurgency activities, psychological warfare and unconventional warfare operations worldwide. Deliveries to the US Navy and US Marine Corps also began during 1971.

Foreign military deliveries have been made to the Argentine Air Force (eight), Bangladesh Air Force (nine), Mexican Air Force (16, with nine more due for delivery in 1990), Panamanian Air Force (two) and Royal Thai Army (nine).

A commercial version, known as the **Twin Two-Twelve**, received FAA type certification with PT6T-3 power plant in October 1970, and FAA Transport Type Category A certification on 30 June 1971. The PT6T-3B engine was introduced in June 1980, offering improved single-engine performance and, consequently, additional safety margins.

The Twin Two-Twelve has been certificated for IFR operations by the FAA, UK's CAA, Norwegian DCA and Canadian DoT. Conversion from VFR to IFR configuration requires a new avionics package, new instrument panel and aircraft stabilisation controls. In June 1977, the Model 212 became the first helicopter FAA certificated for single-pilot IFR operations with fixed floats.

Deliveries of civil Model 212s have included nine to the People's Republic of China in 1979-81 (see 1987-88 and earlier *Jane's* for details) and four to the Japanese Maritime Safety Agency. Five were delivered in 1988 to customers in Australia and Saudi Arabia (one each) and Japan (three).

Production of the Model 212 continues, having been transferred to Bell's Canadian factory in August 1988. More recent orders/deliveries include 18 for Mexico and 23 for Thailand. The production rate was increased from one to two per month in mid-1990.

TYPE: Twin-turbine utility helicopter.

ROTOR SYSTEM: Two-blade all-metal semi-rigid main rotor with interchangeable blades, built up of extruded aluminium spars and laminates. Glassfibre safety straps. Stabilising bar above and at right angles to main rotor blades. Underslung feathering axis head. Two-blade all-metal tail rotor. Main rotor blades do not fold. Rotor brake optional.

FUSELAGE: Conventional all-metal semi-monocoque structure.

TAIL UNIT: Synchronised elevator on rear fuselage.

LANDING GEAR: Tubular skid type. Lock-on ground handling wheels, high skid gear, fixed floats and emergency pop-out nylon float bags optional.

POWER PLANT: Pratt & Whitney Canada PT6T-3B Turbo Twin-Pac, comprising two PT6 turboshafts coupled to a combining gearbox with a single output shaft. Producing 1,342 kW (1,800 shp), the Twin Pac is flat rated at 962 kW (1,290 shp) for T-O and 843 kW (1,130 shp) for continuous operation. In the event of an engine failure, the remaining engine can deliver 764 kW (1,025 shp) for 2½ min, 723 kW (970 shp) for 30 min, or 596 kW (800 shp) continuously. Five interconnected rubber fuel cells,

Bell 212 airdropping food to wildlife stranded by flood waters

total usable capacity 814 litres (215 US gallons; 179 Imp gallons). Two 76 or 341 litre (20 or 90 US gallon; 16.7 or 75 Imp gallon) auxiliary fuel tanks optional, to provide a max possible capacity of 1,495 litres (395 US gallons; 329 Imp gallons). Single-point refuelling on starboard side of cabin. Oil capacity 11.5 litres (3 US gallons; 2.5 Imp gallons) for engines, 8.5 litres (2.25 US gallons; 1.87 Imp gallons) for transmission.

ACCOMMODATION: Pilot and up to 14 passengers. Dual controls optional. In cargo configuration there is a total internal volume of 7.02 m³ (248 cu ft), including baggage space in tailboom, capacity 181 kg (400 lb). Forward opening crew door on each side of fuselage. Two doors on each side of cabin; forward door hinged to open forward, rear door sliding aft. Accommodation heated and ventilated. AiResearch air-cycle environmental control unit optional.

SYSTEMS: Dual hydraulic systems, pressure 69 bars (1,000 lb/sq in) each, max flow rate 22.7 litres (6 US gallons; 5 Imp gallons)/min. Open reservoir. 28V DC electrical system supplied by two completely independent 30V 200A starter/generators. Secondary AC power supplied by two independent 250VA single-phase solid state inverters. A third inverter can acquire automatically the load of a failed inverter. 34Ah nickel-cadmium battery.

AVIONICS: Optional IFR avionics include dual Bendix/King KTR 900A com transceivers, dual KNR 660A VOR/LOC/RMI receivers, KDF 800 ADF, KMD 700A DME, KXP 750A transponder and KGM 690 marker beacon/glideslope receiver; dual Honeywell Tarsyn-444 three-axis gyro units; stability control augmentation system; and an automatic flight control system. Flight director and weather radar also optional.

EQUIPMENT: Optional equipment includes a litter kit, cargo hook, cargo sling and rescue hoist.

DIMENSIONS, EXTERNAL:

Main rotor diameter (with tracking tips)	14.69 m (48 ft 2¼ in)
Tail rotor diameter	2.59 m (8 ft 6 in)
Main rotor blade chord	0.59 m (1 ft 11¼ in)
Tail rotor blade chord	0.292 m (11½ in)
Length:	
overall (main rotor fore and aft)	17.46 m (57 ft 3¼ in)
fuselage	12.92 m (42 ft 4¾ in)
Height: to top of rotor head	3.91 m (12 ft 10 in)
overall	4.53 m (14 ft 10¼ in)
Width: over skids	2.64 m (8 ft 8 in)
overall (main rotor fore and aft)	2.86 m (9 ft 4½ in)
Elevator span	2.86 m (9 ft 4½ in)
Rear sliding doors (each): Height	1.24 m (4 ft 1 in)
Width	1.88 m (6 ft 2 in)
Height to sill	0.76 m (2 ft 6 in)
Baggage compartment door: Height	0.53 m (1 ft 9 in)
Width	1.71 m (2 ft 4 in)
Emergency exits (centre cabin windows, each):	
Height	0.76 m (2 ft 6 in)
Width	0.97 m (3 ft 2 in)

DIMENSIONS, INTERNAL:

Cabin, excl flight deck: Length	2.34 m (7 ft 8 in)
Max width	2.44 m (8 ft 0 in)
Max height	1.24 m (4 ft 1 in)
Volume	6.23 m³ (220 cu ft)
Baggage compartment volume	0.78 m³ (28 cu ft)

AREAS:

Main rotor disc	173.90 m² (1,871.91 sq ft)
Tail rotor disc	5.27 m² (56.74 sq ft)

WEIGHTS AND LOADINGS:

VFR empty weight plus usable oil	2,720 kg (5,997 lb)
Max external load: 212	2,268 kg (5,000 lb)
UH-1N	1,814 kg (4,000 lb)
Max T-O weight and mission weight	5,080 kg (11,200 lb)
Max disc loading	29.20 kg/m² (5.98 lb/sq ft)

PERFORMANCE (at max T-O weight):

Never-exceed speed (V$_{NE}$) and max cruising speed at S/L	100 knots (185 km/h; 115 mph)
Max rate of climb at S/L	402 m (1,320 ft)/min
Service ceiling	3,960 m (13,000 ft)
Max altitude for T-O and landing	1,430 m (4,700 ft)
Hovering ceiling IGE	3,350 m (11,000 ft)
Max range with standard fuel at S/L, no reserves	227 nm (420 km; 261 miles)

BELL MODEL 412SP and 412HP

Launched on 8 September 1978, this derivative of the twin-turbine Model 212 is Bell's first production helicopter with a four-blade main rotor. A pendulum absorber kit, to reduce internal vibration levels, became standard in mid-1984, and is available for retrofit to earlier Model 412s.

Details of the Model 412 development programme have been given in earlier editions of *Jane's*. FAA type approval, in accordance with FAR Pt 29, for VFR operation was received on 9 January 1981, and IFR certification on 13 February 1981. The first (civil) delivery to a customer was made on 18 January 1981. Two military Model 412s are operated by the Venezuelan Air Force, three by the Botswana Defence Force, two by the Public Security Flying Wing of the Bahrain Defence Force, four by Sri Lanka's armed forces and two by the Nigerian Police Air Wing. The Mexican government ordered two for VIP transport duties, and the South Korea Coast Guard one. By the end of September 1990 deliveries totalled 205 (108 Model 412s and 97 Model 412SPs).

The commercial **Model 412SP** (Special Performance) features increased max T-O weight, new interior seating options and a 55 per cent increase in standard fuel capacity. On 29 June 1990 the FAA certificated the **Model 412HP**, with improved transmission and enhanced OGE hover performance at max T-O weight. This version became available from aircraft c/n 36020, delivered in early 1991.

The Indonesian aircraft industry (IPTN) is producing up to 100 Model 412SPs, with progressive increase of manufacturing content. Other orders have been received from the Republic of Honduras (10) and Royal Norwegian Air Force (18). Seventeen of the latter are being assembled by Helikopter Services A/S of Stavanger, using subassemblies and components supplied by Bell. These are to replace Bell UH-1Bs with 339 Squadron at Bardufoss and 720 Squadron at Rygge.

In June 1986 Bell announced the **Military 412SP**, equipped with a 600 rds/min 0.50 in calibre machine gun in a Lucas Aerospace undernose turret, guided by a Honeywell Head Tracker helmet sight system similar to that used in the AH-1S. The installation carries 875 rounds of ammunition, weighs 188 kg (414 lb) including the helmet sight, and can be installed or removed in less than 30 minutes. The turret mounted gun can be fired through a 110° arc in azimuth, at a maximum elevation of 15° and a maximum depression of 45° to the horizontal. With the turret, the 412SP has a max level speed of 120 knots (222 km/h; 138 mph); in addition, it can be equipped with twin dual FN 7.62 mm machine-gun pods, a single FN 0.50 in machine-gun pod, pods of seven or nineteen 2.75 in rockets, M240E1 pintle-mounted door guns, an FN four-round 70 mm rocket launcher and a 0.50 in machine-gun, or two GIAT M621 20 mm cannon pods.

Bell's Italian licensee, Agusta (which see), has developed its own multi-role military version, known as the **Griffon**, capable of performing medical evacuation, armed tactical support, logistic transport, SAR and patrol missions.

Model 412 production was transferred to the Canadian factory in February 1989. The description of the Model 212 applies also to the Model 412SP and/or 412HP, except as follows:

ROTOR SYSTEM: Four-blade flex-beam soft-in-plane main rotor. Each blade spar is of unidirectional glassfibre, with a ±45° wound torque casing of glassfibre cloth. Trailing-edges are also of unidirectional glassfibre, space between them and spars being filled by a Nomex honeycomb core. Entire blade is then bonded together by glassfibre wrapping, with leading-edge protected by a titanium abrasion strip and tip by a replaceable stainless steel cap. Blades are interchangeable and have lightning protection mesh moulded into the structure and provisions for inclusion of de-icing heater elements. New design main rotor head of steel and light alloy, with elastomeric bearings and dampers. Shorter rotor mast than Model 212. Main rotor can be folded. Rotor brake standard. Two-blade all-metal tail rotor. Main rotor rpm 314. Transmission rating 1,044 kW (1,400 shp) for T-O, 846 kW (1,134 shp) max continuous in 412SP; increased to 1,181 kW (1,584 shp) for T-O and 846 kW (1,134 shp) max continuous in 412HP, which also has a rotor mast torque indicator.

LANDING GEAR: High skid, emergency pop-out float, or non-retractable tricycle gear optional.

POWER PLANT: Pratt & Whitney Canada PT6T-3B-1 Turbo Twin-Pac in 412SP, comprising two 671 kW (900 shp) turboshafts, rated to produce a total of 1,044 kW (1,400 shp) for take-off and 843 kW (1,130 shp) for continuous operation. Model 412HP has PT6T-3BE Twin-Pac, rated at 1,342 kW (1,800 shp) for 5 min for T-O and 1,193 kW (1,600 shp) max continuous. In both versions, in the event of engine failure, the remaining engine can deliver up to 764 kW (1,025 shp) for 2½ min, or 723 kW (970 shp) for 30 min. Seven interconnected rupture resistant fuel cells, with automatic shut-off valves (breakaway fittings), have a combined capacity of 1,249 litres (330 US gallons; 275 Imp gallons). Two 76 or 310 litre (20 or 82 US gallon; 16.7 or 68.3 Imp gallon) auxiliary fuel tanks, in any combination, can increase maximum total capacity to 1,870 litres (494 US gallons; 411 Imp gallons). Single-point refuelling on starboard side of cabin.

AVIONICS: Optional IFR avionics include Bendix/King Gold Crown III equipment and dual Honeywell automatic flight control systems.

EQUIPMENT: Optional equipment includes a cargo sling and rescue hoist.

DIMENSIONS, EXTERNAL:

Main rotor diameter	14.02 m (46 ft 0 in)
Tail rotor diameter	2.59 m (8 ft 6 in)
Main rotor blade chord: at root	0.40 m (1 ft 3.9 in)
at tip	0.22 m (8½ in)
Tail rotor blade chord	0.29 m (11½ in)
Length: overall, rotors turning	17.07 m (56 ft 0 in)
fuselage, excl rotors	12.92 m (42 ft 4¾ in)
Height: to top of rotor head	3.29 m (10 ft 9½ in)
overall, tail rotor turning	4.32 m (14 ft 2¼ in)
Stabiliser span	2.86 m (9 ft 4½ in)
Width over skids	2.59 m (8 ft 6 in)
Door sizes	as Model 212

AREAS:

Main rotor disc	154.40 m² (1,661.9 sq ft)
Tail rotor disc	5.27 m² (56.75 sq ft)

WEIGHTS AND LOADINGS (412SP):

Weight empty with utility seating, plus usable oil	2,946 kg (6,495 lb)

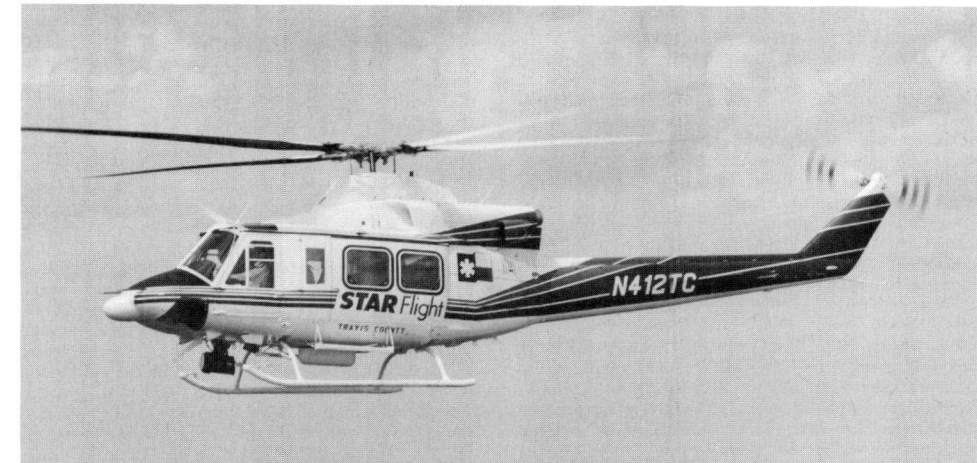

Bell 412SP in EMS (emergency medical service) configuration

Max T-O and landing weight	5,397 kg (11,900 lb)
Max disc loading	34.96 kg/m² (7.16 lb/sq ft)
Max power loading	5.17 kg/kW (8.50 lb/shp)

WEIGHTS AND LOADINGS (412HP):

Weight empty, equipped: VFR	2,950 kg (6,505 lb)
IFR	3,001 kg (6,616 lb)
Max external hook load	2,041 kg (4,500 lb)
Max T-O and landing weight	5,397 kg (11,900 lb)
Max disc loading	34.96 kg/m² (7.16 lb/sq ft)
Max power loading	4.02 kg/kW (6.61 lb/shp)

PERFORMANCE (412SP at max T-O weight except where indicated):

Never-exceed speed (V_NE) at S/L
    140 knots (259 km/h; 161 mph)
Max cruising speed at S/L
    124 knots (230 km/h; 143 mph)

Max rate of climb at S/L	411 m (1,350 ft)/min
Service ceiling	5,030 m (16,500 ft)
Max altitude for T-O and landing	427 m (1,400 ft)
Hovering ceiling: IGE	2,805 m (9,200 ft)
OGE, AUW of 4,762 kg (10,500 lb)	
	2,805 m (9,200 ft)

Range with max payload, standard fuel, at 118 knots (219 km/h; 136 mph) at 3,200 m (10,500 ft), 30 min fuel reserves 375 nm (695 km; 432 miles)
Max range with standard fuel at S/L, no reserves
    354 nm (656 km; 408 miles)

PERFORMANCE (412HP at max T-O weight, ISA):

Max cruising speed:

| at S/L | 122 knots (226 km/h; 140 mph) |
| at 1,525 m (5,000 ft) | 124 knots (230 km/h; 143 mph) |

Service ceiling, one engine out, 30 min power rating
    2,070 m (6,800 ft)

| Hovering ceiling: IGE | 3,110 m (10,200 ft) |
| OGE | 1,585 m (5,200 ft) |

Range at 1,525 m (5,000 ft), long-range cruising speed, standard fuel, no reserves
    402 nm (745 km; 463 miles)

BELL MODEL 230

Announced at the 1989 NBAA convention, the Model 230 is an upgraded derivative of the Model 222 (see US section of the 1990–91 *Jane's*), which it is intended to replace. Two Bell 222s were transferred to Mirabel in 1990 for conversion as Model 230 prototypes, the first of which was expected to fly in mid-1991. Certification is planned for the first quarter of 1992, with first deliveries to follow in

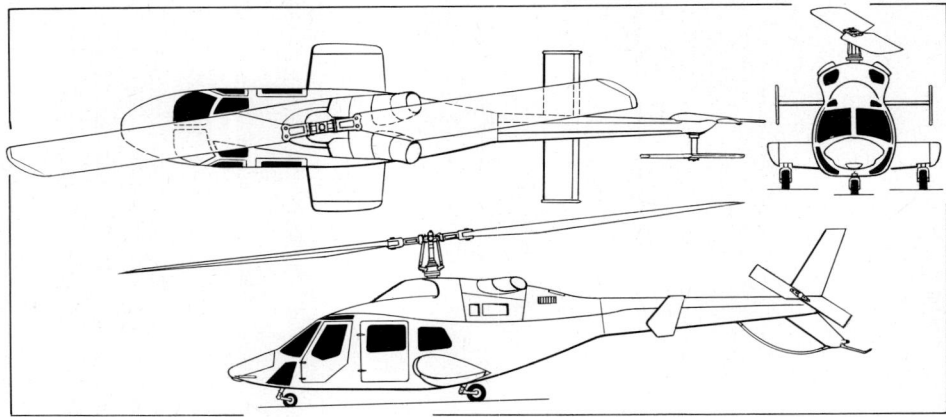

Bell Model 230 twin-turboshaft light helicopter *(Pilot Press)*

August 1992. Bell's Japanese distributor Mitsui & Co, which has ordered 20, will serve as the launch customer. The Canadian government is to provide up to C$15.2 million (repayable) to support development and production.

The following details are provisional:

TYPE: Twin-turboshaft light commercial helicopter.

ROTOR SYSTEM: Two- or four-blade main rotor (Model 680 composites rotor being considered). Aircraft from c/n 15 onwards to have Bell liquid inertia vibration elimination (LIVE) in transmission mounting. Main transmission rated at 690 kW (925 shp) for T-O, 652.5 kW (875 shp) continuous, and 548 kW (735 shp) with one engine inoperative. Two-blade tail rotor.

LANDING GEAR: Wheel or skid type (retractable in former case).

POWER PLANT: First 50 aircraft each to be powered by two 522 kW (700 shp) Allison 250-C30G2 turboshafts; Textron Lycoming LTS 101 optional thereafter.

ACCOMMODATION: Crew of two. Nine passengers or equivalent cargo in utility version, six passengers in executive version.

DIMENSIONS, EXTERNAL: As Model 222 except:

| Length: overall, rotors turning | 15.38 m (50 ft 5½ in) |
| fuselage | 12.97 m (42 ft 6¾ in) |

Height overall, on skids	3.66 m (12 ft 0¼ in)
Width over mainwheel fairings	3.46 m (11 ft 4 in)
Skid track	2.39 m (7 ft 10 in)

DIMENSIONS, INTERNAL:

Cabin (passenger area):

Length	2.21 m (7 ft 3 in)
Max width	1.47 m (4 ft 10 in)
Max height	1.45 m (4 ft 9 in)
Volume, incl crew area	5.53 m³ (195.4 cu ft)
Baggage hold	1.05 m³ (37.2 cu ft)
Baggage access area aft of seats	0.17 m³ (6.0 cu ft)

WEIGHTS AND LOADINGS:

Weight empty (Utility)	2,224 kg (4,903 lb)
Max T-O weight	3,742 kg (8,250 lb)
Max disc loading	29.1 kg/m² (5.95 lb/sq ft)
Max power loading	5.43 kg/kW (8.92 lb/shp)

PERFORMANCE (at max T-O weight, ISA, except where indicated): A: Utility, B: wheeled version):

Max cruising speed: A	136 knots (252 km/h; 157 mph)
B	140 knots (259 km/h; 161 mph)
Service ceiling, one engine out: A	2,285 m (7,500 ft)
B	2,315 m (7,600 ft)
Range, standard fuel: A	421 nm (780 km; 484 miles)
B	329 nm (609 km; 379 miles)

BOEING CANADA

BOEING CANADA, de Havilland Division

Garratt Boulevard, Downsview, Ontario M3K 1Y5
Telephone: 1 (416) 633 7310
Fax: 1 (416) 375 4546
Telex: 0622128
PRESIDENT: W. Daniel Heidt
VICE-PRESIDENT, OPERATIONS: J. Schwalm
VICE-PRESIDENT, ENGINEERING: K. Moan
VICE-PRESIDENT, MARKETING, SALES AND GOVERNMENT AFFAIRS: John Howarth
DIRECTOR, MARKETING: Steven A. Ridolfi
MANAGER, PUBLIC RELATIONS: Colin S. Fisher

The de Havilland Aircraft of Canada Ltd was established in early 1928 as a subsidiary of The de Havilland Aircraft Co Ltd, and both subsequently became a member of the Hawker Siddeley Group. On 26 June 1974 ownership was transferred to the Canadian government, continuing until 31 January 1986 when purchase was completed by The Boeing Company, and de Havilland Canada became a Division of Boeing of Canada Ltd. An agreement was signed on 8 April 1991 for its sale, subject to Canadian government approval, to a European partnership of Aerospatiale (France) and Alenia (Italy).

Approximately 5,000 people were employed by the Division in early 1991.

DHC-8 DASH 8 SERIES 100 and 100A

The first of four flying prototypes of the Dash 8 Series 100 (C-GDNK) made its first flight on 20 June 1983, followed by the second (C-GGMP) on 26 October and the third in November 1983. The fourth aircraft (first with production PW120 engines) was flying by early 1984, followed by the first Dash 8 with production interior in June. Certification by the Canadian DoT, to FAR Pts 25 and 36 and SFAR No. 27, was awarded on 28 September 1984, and FAA type approval before the end of that year. Currently certificated in Australia, Austria, China (People's Republic), Germany, Ireland, Italy, Netherlands, Papua New Guinea, New Zealand, Taiwan and UK. The first customer Dash 8 (c/n 6), one of two Series 100s for NorOntair, was delivered on 23 October 1984 and entered service on 19 December that year.

The **Series 100** is available with PW120A or PW121 engines (as **Model 102** and **Model 103** respectively), and in 1990 became available in **Series 100A** form with restyled cabin interior (6.35 cm; 2.5 in more aisle headroom and redesigned overhead bins); first delivery of a Series 100A, to Pennsylvania Airlines, was made in July 1990. The Series 100/100A Dash 8 is produced in two basic versions:

Commuter: Standard local service version, to which the detailed description mainly applies. With full IFR fuel

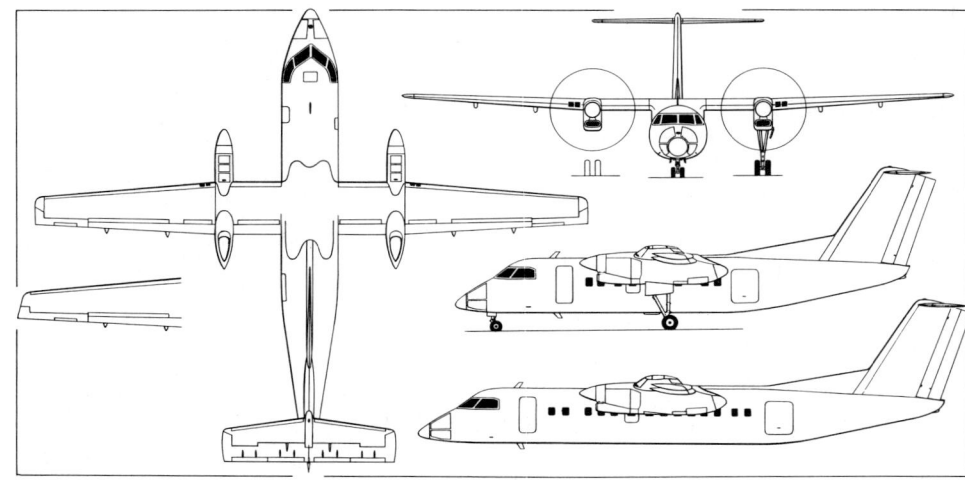

DHC-8 Dash 8 Series 100, with additional side view (bottom) and wingtip of Series 300 *(Pilot Press)*

reserves for a 100 nm (185 km; 115 mile) diversion, plus 45 min at long-range cruising speed at 1,525 m (5,000 ft), this version has enough fuel to fly five 100 nm stages without refuelling, carrying a 3,189 kg (7,030 lb) payload of 37 passengers and their baggage.

Corporate: Marketed in North America exclusively by Innotech Aviation of Montreal, outside North America by Boeing, the corporate version has an extended range capability of up to 2,000 nm (3,706 km; 2,303 miles), plus IFR reserves, with a 544 kg (1,200 lb) payload. In a more typical mission it can carry 17 passengers and their baggage for up to 1,320 nm (2,446 km; 1,520 miles), with reserves, at a max cruising speed of 270 knots (500 km/h; 311 mph). EFIS, long-range fuel and an APU are standard. Alternative layouts can include a single cabin with first class accommodation for about 24 passengers; the standard commuter interior is also available for corporate customers.

By 25 January 1991 a total of 251 firm orders had been received for the Series 100/100A, of which more than 200 had been delivered. Total 1990 Dash 8 sales and deliveries (all versions) were 47 and 62 respectively, and by mid-year those in service had flown more than one million hours.

The military **Dash 8M** and stretched **Dash 8 Series 300 and 400** are described separately. The following description applies to the standard Dash 8 Series 100 and 100A:

TYPE: Twin-turboprop short-range transport.

WINGS: Cantilever high-wing monoplane, with constant chord centre-section and tapered outer panels. Thickness/chord ratio 18 per cent at root, 13 per cent at tip. Sweepback 3° 1′ 48″ at quarter-chord. Dihedral 2° 30′ on outer panels. Drooped inboard leading-edges. Tip to tip torsion box formed by front and rear spars, ribs and skin. Single-slotted Fowler trailing-edge flaps inboard and outboard of engine nacelles. Hydraulically actuated roll control spoilers/lift dumpers forward of each outer flap segment; independent ground spoiler/lift dumper inboard and outboard of each engine nacelle. Mechanically actuated balanced ailerons, with inset tabs. Small stall strip on each wing leading-edge outboard of engine. Pneumatic rubber boot de-icing of leading-edges. Composite materials used for construction of leading-edges, wingtip fairings, flap shrouds, flap trailing-edges and other components.

FUSELAGE: Conventional flush riveted semi-monocoque pressurised structure, of near-circular cross-section. Extensive use of adhesively bonded stringers and cutout reinforcements. Radome, nose bay, wing/fuselage fairings and tailcone of Kevlar and other composites.

TAIL UNIT: Cantilever T tailplane; full span horn balanced elevator, with tabs. Sweptback fin (integral with rear fuselage), large dorsal fin, and two-segment serially

DHC-8 Dash 8 Series 100 twin-turboprop transport in the insignia of Great China Airlines

hinged hydraulically actuated rudder with yaw damper. Composites used in construction of dorsal fin, fin leading-edge, fin/tailplane fairings, tailplane leading-edges and elevator tips. Pneumatic rubber boot de-icing of tailplane and fin leading-edges.

LANDING GEAR: Retractable tricycle type, by Dowty Aerospace, with twin wheels on each unit. Steer by wire nose unit retracts forward, main units rearward into engine nacelles. Goodrich mainwheels and brakes; Hydro-Aire Mk 3 anti-skid system. Standard tyre pressures: main 9.03 bars (131 lb/sq in), nose 5.52 bars (80 lb/sq in). Low pressure tyres optional, pressure 5.31 bars (77 lb/sq in) on main units, 3.31 bars (48 lb/sq in) on nose unit. Wheel doors of Kevlar and other composites.

POWER PLANT: Two 1,491 kW (2,000 shp) Pratt & Whitney Canada PW120A turboprops in Model 102, each driving a Hamilton Standard 14SF-7 four-blade constant-speed fully feathering propeller with reversible pitch. Model 103 has 1,603 kW (2,150 shp) PW121 engines. Propeller blades have a solid aluminium spar, glassfibre outer shell, nickel erosion sheath outboard, electric de-icing, and Beta control. Engine cowlings, produced by British Hovercraft Corporation, have lower panels, air intakes and rear panels of Kevlar/Nomex sandwich, aluminium side panels, and a titanium firewall. Standard usable fuel capacity (in-wing tanks) of 3,160 litres (835 US gallons; 695 Imp gallons); optional auxiliary tank system increases this maximum to 5,700 litres (1,506 US gallons; 1,254 Imp gallons). Pressure refuelling point in rear of starboard engine nacelle; overwing gravity point in each outer wing panel. Oil capacity 21 litres (5.5 US gallons; 4.6 Imp gallons) per engine.

ACCOMMODATION: Crew of two on flight deck, plus one attendant in cabin. Dual controls standard. Standard commuter layout in main cabin provides four-abreast seating, with central aisle, for 37 passengers at 79 cm (31 in) pitch, plus buffet, toilet and large rear baggage compartment. Wardrobe at front of passenger cabin, in addition to overhead lockers and underseat stowage, provides additional carry-on capacity for passengers' baggage. Alternative 39-passenger, mixed passenger/cargo or corporate layouts available at customer's option. Movable bulkhead to facilitate conversion to mixed-traffic or all-cargo configuration. Port side airstair door at front provides access for crew as well as passengers; large inward opening port side door aft of wing for cargo loading. Emergency exit each side, in line with wing leading-edge, and opposite passenger door on starboard side. Entire accommodation pressurised and air-conditioned.

SYSTEMS: Air cycle air-conditioning system provides heating, cooling, ventilation and pressurisation (cabin max differential 0.38 bar; 5.5 lb/sq in). Normal hydraulic installation comprises two independent systems, each having an engine driven variable displacement pump and an electrically driven standby pump; accumulator and handpump for emergency use. Electrical system DC power provided by two starter/generators, two transformer-rectifier units, and two nickel-cadmium batteries. Variable frequency AC power provided by two engine driven AC generators and three static inverters. Ground power receptacles in port side of nose (DC) and rear of starboard nacelle (AC). De-icing system consists of pneumatic system plus electric heating. APU standard in corporate version. Simmonds fuel monitoring system.

AVIONICS: Standard factory installed avionics include Bendix/King Gold Crown III com/nav (KTR 908 VHF com, KNR 634 VHF nav, KDF 806 ADF, KDM 706A DME and KXP 756 transponder), Honeywell SPZ-800

dual-channel digital AFCS with integrated fail-operational flight director/autopilot system, dual digital air data system, electromechanical flight instruments, and Primus 800 colour weather radar; Honeywell electronic flight instrumentation system (EFIS) optional on commuter, standard on corporate version. Avtech audio integrating system. Telephonics PA system.

DIMENSIONS, EXTERNAL:
Wing span	25.91 m (85 ft 0 in)
Wing aspect ratio	12.35
Length overall	22.25 m (73 ft 0 in)
Fuselage: Max diameter	2.69 m (8 ft 10 in)
Height overall	7.49 m (24 ft 7 in)
Elevator span	7.92 m (26 ft 0 in)
Wheel track (c/l of shock struts)	7.87 m (25 ft 10 in)
Wheelbase	7.95 m (26 ft 1 in)
Propeller diameter	3.96 m (13 ft 0 in)
Propeller ground clearance	0.94 m (3 ft 1 in)
Propeller/fuselage clearance	0.76 m (2 ft 6 in)
Passenger/crew door (fwd, port):	
Height	1.65 m (5 ft 5 in)
Width	0.76 m (2 ft 6 in)
Height to sill	1.09 m (3 ft 7 in)
Baggage door (rear, port):	
Height	1.52 m (5 ft 0 in)
Width	1.27 m (4 ft 2 in)
Height to sill	1.09 m (3 ft 7 in)

DIMENSIONS, INTERNAL:
Cabin: Length (incl flight deck)	9.17 m (30 ft 1 in)
Max width	2.49 m (8 ft 2 in)
Width at floor	2.03 m (6 ft 8 in)
Max height	1.94 m (6 ft 4½ in)
Volume	45.3 m³ (1,600 cu ft)
Baggage compartment volume	8.5 m³ (300 cu ft)

AREAS:
Wings, gross	54.35 m² (585.0 sq ft)
Vertical tail surfaces (total)	14.12 m² (152.0 sq ft)
Horizontal tail surfaces (total)	13.94 m² (150.0 sq ft)

WEIGHTS AND LOADINGS:
Operating weight empty	10,251 kg (22,600 lb)
Max usable fuel: standard	2,576 kg (5,678 lb)
optional	4,646 kg (10,244 lb)
Max payload: passengers	3,810 kg (8,400 lb)
cargo	4,241 kg (9,349 lb)
Max ramp weight	15,740 kg (34,700 lb)

Max T-O weight	15,650 kg (34,500 lb)
Max landing weight	15,375 kg (33,900 lb)
Max zero-fuel weight	14,060 kg (31,000 lb)
Max wing loading	287.95 kg/m² (58.97 lb/sq ft)
Max power loading:	
Model 102	5.25 kg/kW (8.62 lb/shp)
Model 103	4.88 kg/kW (8.02 lb/shp)

PERFORMANCE (Model 102 at 95% MTOGW except where indicated):
Max cruising speed	
at 4,575 m (15,000 ft)	265 knots (491 km/h; 305 mph)
at 6,100 m (20,000 ft)	264 knots (489 km/h; 304 mph)
Stalling speed, flaps down	
	72 knots (134 km/h; 83 mph)
Max rate of climb at S/L	475 m (1,560 ft)/min
Rate of climb at S/L, one engine out	137 m (450 ft)/min
Certificated ceiling	7,620 m (25,000 ft)
Service ceiling, one engine out	4,575 m (15,000 ft)
FAR Pt 25 T-O field length at S/L, 15° flap:	
ISA	940 m (3,085 ft)
ISA + 15°C	1,000 m (3,280 ft)
FAR Pt 25 landing field length at S/L, 35° flap, at max landing weight	908 m (2,979 ft)
Range with standard fuel, IFR reserves:	
full passenger load	820 nm (1,519 km; 944 miles)
2,721 kg (6,000 lb) payload	
	1,100 nm (2,038 km; 1,266 miles)

OPERATIONAL NOISE LEVELS (FAR Pt 36 Stage 3 and ICAO Annex 16):
T-O	81 EPNdB
Sideline	86 EPNdB
Approach	95 EPNdB

DHC-8 DASH 8M

Canadian Forces designations: CC-142 and CT-142

US Air Force designation: E-9A

The Dash 8 is adaptable to a wide range of missions, and is currently in service in a number of variants including military transport, flight calibration, missile range control and navigation training. Other potential missions include medevac, surveillance, search and rescue, early warning and ASW/ASV/maritime patrol.

Two Dash 8M-100s are in service with the Canadian Dept of Transport for airways calibration duties. The

Canadian Forces CT-142 navigation trainer version of the DHC-8 Dash 8M

Series 300 stretched version of the Dash 8 in the insignia of Bahamasair

Dash 8M-100 in E-9A configuration as a USAF missile range control aircraft

Canadian Dept of National Defence operates two as **CC-142** passenger/cargo transports and four others configured as **CT-142** navigation trainers with an extended nose housing a mapping radar antenna. These DND aircraft have long-range fuel tanks, rough-field landing gear, high-strength floors and mission-related avionics. Two other Dash 8M-100s, delivered in Spring 1988, were outfitted by Sierra Research in the USA as USAF missile range control aircraft with the designation **E-9A**. They are equipped as flying data links that can relay telemetry, voice communications and drone and fighter control data while simultaneously performing range radar surveillance functions. Equipment includes a large, electronically steerable phased-array antenna in a starboard-side fuselage fairing, an AN/APS-128D surveillance radar in a ventral radome, and extensive internal avionics and electronics. All 10 of these aircraft are included in the order total given for the Dash 8 Series 100.

Other special mission versions of the Dash 8 have been proposed, notably **Triton** maritime patrol versions of the Series 100 and 300 equipped for a variety of roles including fisheries protection. The **Triton ASW** version is based on the Series 300, and would carry equipment including a ventrally mounted maritime surveillance radar, FLIR/IRDS, MAD, ESM, INS, sonobuoy processors, a universal display and control system, and fuselage weapon attachment points. Weapon loads would include ASW torpedoes and mines.

WEIGHTS AND LOADINGS (Triton):
Typical operating weight empty	12,009 kg (26,475 lb)
Max T-O weight	19,504 kg (43,000 lb)
Max zero-fuel weight	17,916 kg (39,500 lb)

PERFORMANCE (Triton ASW, estimated):
Max cruising speed	274 knots (508 km/h; 316 mph)
Service ceiling, one engine out	4,265 m (14,000 ft)

DHC-8 DASH 8 SERIES 300 and 300A

Announced in mid-1985, the Series 300 is a stretched version of the Dash 8 Series 100 with fore and aft plugs totalling 3.43 m (11 ft 3 in) inserted to increase seating capacity to 50 (standard) at a seat pitch of 81 cm (32 in) or 56 passengers (optional) at 73.7 cm (29 in) pitch, plus a second cabin attendant. Other fuselage/cabin changes include enlarging the galley and moving it aft, with a separate galley service door on the starboard side, an additional wardrobe, larger lavatory, dual air-conditioning packs, and an optional Turbomach T-40 APU. Wing span is increased by tip extensions, and the Series 300/300A is powered by 1,775 kW (2,380 shp) PW123 engines driving Hamilton Standard

14SF-15 propellers. Fuel capacity is as for the Series 100. Standard tyre pressures are increased to 6.69 bars (97 lb/sq in) for mainwheels and 4.14 bars (60 lb/sq in) on the nose unit.

The Series 300 prototype (converted from the No. 1 Series 100 aircraft C-GDNK) flew on 15 May 1987. Canadian DoT certification was obtained on 14 February 1989, and deliveries began (with the first of six aircraft for Time Air) on 27 February. FAA type approval followed in June 1989, and German LBA certification was awarded in early 1990. Firm orders for the Series 300/300A totalled 110 by 25 January 1991, of which over 30 had been delivered.

In addition to the standard basic Series 300, two improved payload/range options are available: an intermediate gross weight model and a higher gross weight **Series 300A**. The latter, introduced in 1990, has the same improved interior as the Series 100A plus an option for uprated (1,864 kW; 2,500 shp) PW123B engines. First delivery of a Series 300A, to Contact Air of Germany, was made on 24 August 1990; launch customer for the Series

300A/PW123B combination is Tyrolean Airways, which ordered three in November 1990.

DIMENSIONS, EXTERNAL: As for Series 100/100A except:
Wing span	27.43 m (90 ft 0 in)
Wing aspect ratio	13.39
Length overall	25.68 m (84 ft 3 in)
Wheelbase	10.01 m (32 ft 10 in)

DIMENSIONS, INTERNAL: As for Series 100/100A except:
Cabin: Length (incl flight deck)	15.32 m (50 ft 3 in)
Volume	48.7 m³ (1,720 cu ft)
Baggage compartment volume:	
with 50 passengers	9.06 m³ (320 cu ft)
with 56 passengers	7.93 m³ (280 cu ft)

AREAS:
Wings, gross	56.21 m² (605.0 sq ft)
Tail surfaces	as for Series 100/100A

WEIGHTS AND LOADINGS (A: basic, B: intermediate, C: higher gross weight options):
Operating weight empty: A, B, C	11,657 kg (25,700 lb)
Max usable fuel: A, B, C	as for Series 100/100A
Max payload: A	5,216 kg (11,500 lb)
B	5,806 kg (12,800 lb)
C	6,259 kg (13,800 lb)
Max T-O weight: A	18,642 kg (41,100 lb)
B	18,996 kg (41,880 lb)
C	19,504 kg (43,000 lb)
Max landing weight: A	18,144 kg (40,000 lb)
B	18,597 kg (41,000 lb)
C	19,050 kg (42,000 lb)
Max zero-fuel weight: A	16,873 kg (37,200 lb)
B	17,463 kg (38,500 lb)
C	17,917 kg (39,500 lb)
Max wing loading: A	331.65 kg/m² (67.93 lb/sq ft)
B	337.96 kg/m² (69.22 lb/sq ft)
C	346.99 kg/m² (71.07 lb/sq ft)
Max power loading: A	5.25 kg/kW (8.63 lb/shp)
B	5.35 kg/kW (8.80 lb/shp)
C	5.49 kg/kW (9.03 lb/shp)

PERFORMANCE (at basic max T-O weight except where indicated):
Max cruising speed at 95% of MTOGW:	
at 4,575 m (15,000 ft)	287 knots (532 km/h; 330 mph)
at 6,100 m (20,000 ft)	283 knots (524 km/h; 326 mph)
Stalling speed, flaps down	77 knots (141 km/h; 88 mph)

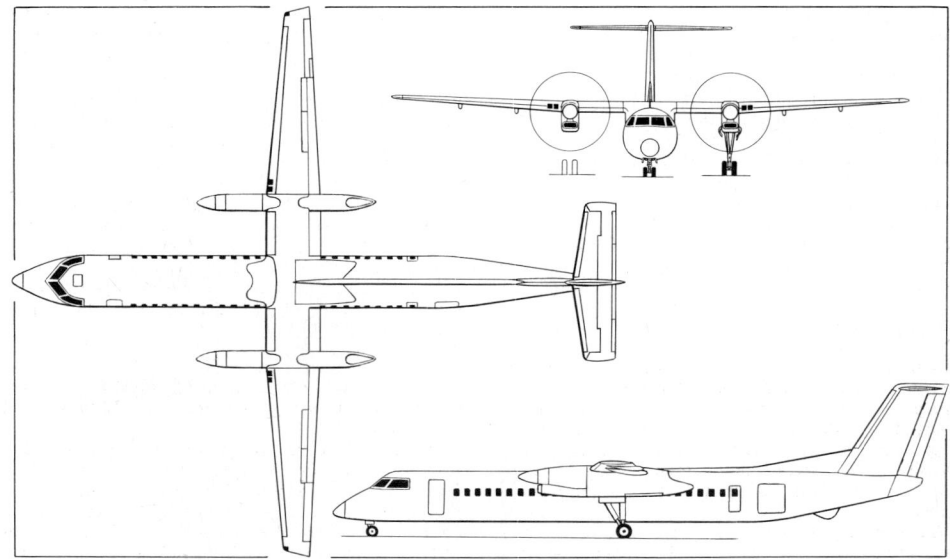

General arrangement of the Dash 8 Series 400 (*Pilot Press*)

Max rate of climb at S/L	549 m (1,800 ft)/min
Rate of climb at S/L, one engine out	137 m (450 ft)/min
Certificated ceiling	7,620 m (25,000 ft)
Service ceiling, one engine out	4,115 m (13,500 ft)
FAR Pt 25 T-O field length at S/L, 15° flap:	
ISA	1,067 m (3,500 ft)
ISA + 15°C	1,160 m (3,800 ft)
FAR Pt 25 landing field length at S/L, 35° flap, at max	
landing weight	1,006 m (3,300 ft)
Range with standard fuel, IFR reserves:	
full passenger load	830 nm (1,538 km; 955 miles)
2,721 kg (6,000 lb) payload	
	870 nm (1,612 km; 1,001 miles)

DHC-8 DASH 8 SERIES 400

The Series 400 represents a further stretch of the Dash 8 with a passenger capacity in the 70-seat range. Power plant selection (candidates are the General Electric/Textron Lycoming GLC38 and Allison GMA 2100, with six-blade propellers) was expected to be made during 1991. First flight is anticipated in late 1993, with certification and first customer delivery about a year later.

The following provisional data for the Series 400 were correct at the beginning of 1991:

DIMENSIONS, EXTERNAL: As for Series 100 except:	
Wing span	27.43 m (90 ft 0 in)
Wing aspect ratio	13.39
Length overall	30.48 m (100 ft 0 in)
Height overall	8.13 m (26 ft 8 in)
Wheelbase	12.57 m (41 ft 3 in)
Baggage compartment door:	
Height to sill	1.45 m (4 ft 9 in)
DIMENSIONS, INTERNAL:	
Cabin: Length (incl flight deck)	19.96 m (65 ft 6 in)
Baggage compartment volume:	
forward	2.12 m³ (75 cu ft)
rear	10.22 m³ (361 cu ft)
AREAS: As for Series 300	
WEIGHTS AND LOADINGS:	
Operating weight empty	14,968 kg (33,000 lb)

Max usable fuel	4,935 kg (10,880 lb)
Max payload (standard passenger aircraft)	
	7,257 kg (16,000 lb)
Max T-O weight	24,993 kg (55,100 lb)
Max landing weight	24,720 kg (54,500 lb)
Max zero-fuel weight	22,225 kg (49,000 lb)
Max wing loading	444.7 kg/m² (91.07 lb/sq ft)
PERFORMANCE (estimated):	
Max cruising speed at 95% of max T-O weight, ISA	
	350 knots (648 km/h; 403 mph)
Service ceiling, one engine out, at 95% of max T-O	
weight, ISA	6,220 m (20,400 ft)
FAR T-O field length at S/L, ISA	1,137 m (3,730 ft)
FAR landing field length at S/L, max landing weight	
	1,180 m (3,870 ft)
Range with 70 passengers and baggage, IFR reserves:	
at max cruising speed	800 nm (1,482 km; 921 miles)
at long-range cruising speed	
	940 nm (1,742 km; 1,082 miles)

BRISTOL AEROSPACE
BRISTOL AEROSPACE LTD

PO Box 874, 660 Berry Street, Winnipeg, Manitoba R3C 2S4
Telephone: 1 (204) 775 8331
Fax: 1 (204) 885 3195
Telex: 0757774
EXECUTIVE VICE-PRESIDENT AND GENERAL MANAGER:
K. F. Burrows

NORTHROP CF-5 UPGRADE PROGRAMME
Canadian Forces designation: CF-116

As the designated support centre for the Canadian Forces' Northrop CF-5, Bristol Aerospace is to upgrade and extend the life of these aircraft into the 21st century. A total of 56 CF-5A fighters and CF-5D fighter/trainers are to be modified for pilot familiarisation and lead-in training for CF-18 Hornets. Significant features of the programme include the repair, overhaul and re-skinning of the wings and vertical fin; replacement of the dorsal longeron, rear fuselage formers and landing gear; total aircraft rewiring and repainting; and a major avionics upgrade which includes a GEC Ferranti HUD, GEC Avionics mission computer/display processor and video camera.

The CF-5 avionics update programme involves two 'prototypes' (under a late 1988 contract) and fleet fitment (C$69.73 million contract awarded November 1990) of 44 of the remaining 54 aircraft. The latter contract includes not only systems procurement but also installation, a new software database, a training simulator, and evaluation equipment. The prototypes were expected to fly in early 1991, with the first of the fleet fitment CF-5s due to re-enter service in the Spring of 1992 with No. 419 Squadron at CFB Cold Lake, Alberta.

Northrop CF-5D fighter/trainer undergoing airframe and avionics upgrade by Bristol Aerospace

---

CANADAIR
CANADAIR GROUP, BOMBARDIER INC

Cartierville Airport, 1800 Laurentien Boulevard, St Laurent, Quebec H4R 1K2
POSTAL ADDRESS: PO Box 6087, Station A, Montreal, Quebec H3C 3G9
Telephone: 1 (514) 744 1511
Fax: 1 (514) 744 6586
Telex: 05-826747
PRESIDENT: Robert E. Brown
PRESIDENT, CHALLENGER DIVISION: Bryan T. Moss
PRESIDENT, REGIONAL JET DIVISION: Robert A. Wohl
VICE-PRESIDENTS/GENERAL MANAGERS:
Trevor F. Young (Amphibious Aircraft Division)
Roland Gagnon (Manufacturing Division)
Walter Niemy (Military Aircraft Division)
William R. Dawes (Surveillance Systems Division)
Keith Garner (Canadair Challenger Inc)
PUBLIC RELATIONS: Catherine Chase

Canadair has manufactured more than 4,100 military and commercial aircraft since 1944. It has also been employed in the research, design, development and production of missile components, pilotless surveillance systems and a variety of non-aerospace products. It currently has three plants in the St Laurent complex at Cartierville Airport, and a fourth has been expanded at Montreal (Dorval) International Airport to accommodate Challenger and Regional Jet assembly. New facilities have opened at Montreal International Airport, Mirabel, to house the CF-18 Hornet programme and other military aircraft services; and in St Laurent to house the Regional Jet Division. Total covered floor space at the beginning of 1991 was 305,000 m² (3,282,990 sq ft). Total workforce at that time was 7,300.

Canadair became a wholly owned Bombardier subsidiary on 23 December 1986. Restructuring into a corporate group and four major business divisions took place in 1987, as detailed in the 1988-89 *Jane's.* On 5 August 1988 Canadair merged with its parent company and is now known as the Canadair Group of Bombardier Inc. The Group comprises six divisions: Challenger, Regional Jet, Amphibious Aircraft, Manufacturing, Military Aircraft, and Surveillance Systems.

The Challenger entered production during 1978, with advanced design of a stretched version starting in 1987, leading to programme go-ahead for the Regional Jet variant in March 1989. Manufacture of the fifth series of CL-215 tanker/utility amphibians (c/n 1081-1125) ended in 1989; certification of the CL-215T turboprop conversion kit was received in March 1991. Major subcontracts concern nose barrel assemblies for the McDonnell Douglas F/A-18 Hornet; six major fuselage components for 600 Airbus A330/A340 aircraft (for Aerospatiale), and inboard wing leading-edge assemblies for these aircraft (for BAe); and rear fuselage sections for the Boeing 767. Engineering support for the CF's CF-18 Hornet fleet is provided under a renewable contract (begun in 1986) by a team comprising Canadair, CAE Electronics (Montreal) and NWI (Edmonton), with Canadair as prime contractor. Production of aircraft spares, and the modification, repair and overhaul of aircraft, are also included in the current work programme.

CANADAIR CHALLENGER
Canadian Forces designations: CC-144 and CE-144A

The first of three pre-production Challengers (C-GCGR-X, c/n 1001) made its first flight on 8 November 1978. The first production Challenger flew on 21 September 1979. Powered by Textron Lycoming ALF 502L-2 turbofans, this version, known as the **Challenger 600**, received Canadian DoT type approval on 11 August 1980, and FAA certification on 7 November of that year. A total of 83 Challenger 600s was delivered, of which 71 had been retrofitted with winglets by 1 January 1991. The Canadian Dept of National Defence received 12 Challenger 600s (seven as CE-144As for electronic support and training, four CC-144s for government transport duties and one for testbed programmes). The Model 600 was described in the 1989-90 and earlier *Jane's.*

The basic Challenger production model since 1982 has been the **Challenger 601**, which has General Electric CF34 series turbofans, increased fuel capacity, and winglets. The prototype flew on 10 April 1982, and the initial basic production model (no longer produced) was the **601-1A**, last described in the 1990-91 edition.

Current variants are as follows:

601-3A: Standard version, with 'glass cockpit' and upgraded engines. First flight 28 September 1986; Canadian and US type certification received on 21 and 30 April 1987 respectively, and Category II certification five months later. Now also has Austrian, German, Indonesian and UK certification, with French and Italian type approval under way in March 1991. Incorporates four main improvements: CF34-3A engines, flat rated to 21°C, for better climb and hot day take-off performance; fully integrated digital flight guidance and flight management system; a power assisted passenger door; and twin landing lights in nose. First delivery 6 May 1987; total of 86 delivered by 25 March 1991.

601-3A/ER: An extended range option, available from 1989 on new production 601-3As and as retrofit for existing 601-1As and 601-3As, increasing range to 3,600 nm (6,667 km; 4,142 miles) with NBAA IFR reserves. First flown 8 November 1988; received Canadian certification 16 March 1989. Option requires replacing existing tail fairing with a conformal tailcone fuel tank and an extended fairing, increasing fuselage length by about 46 cm (18 in) and adding 113 kg (250 lb) to aircraft empty weight. Max ramp weight increased by minor modification of main landing gear. Customers not requiring extended range option can request

Canadair CE-144A (Challenger 600) electronic support and training aircraft of the Canadian Forces

the 907 kg (2,000 lb) increase in gross weight (680 kg; 1,500 lb before October 1990). Total of 43 modification kits delivered by 15 January 1991.

601-S: Launched in June 1989. Designed for transcontinental rather than intercontinental routes, its weight and price are reduced mainly through removal of auxiliary fuselage fuel tanks, deletion of some avionics, and introduction of a new standard 12-passenger interior configuration. None delivered up to mid-February 1991.

Total Challenger deliveries (all versions) had reached 236 by 25 March 1991, of which 23 were delivered during the 1990-91 financial year.

The following description applies to the Challenger 601-3A, except where indicated otherwise:

TYPE: Twin-turbofan business, cargo and commuter transport.

WINGS: Cantilever low-wing monoplane, built in one piece. Advanced technology section, with winglets at tips. Thickness/chord ratio 14 per cent at root, 12 per cent at leading-edge sweep break and 10 per cent at tip. Dihedral 2° 33′. Incidence 3° 30′ at root. Sweepback at quarter-chord 25°. Two-spar structure, primarily of aluminium alloy; spars covered with skin/stringer panels to form rigid torsion box. Two-section double-slotted trailing-edge flaps. Hydraulically powered aluminium plain ailerons. Outboard spoilers for descent control, inboard spoilers for lift dumping. No tabs. Thermal anti-icing of leading-edges by engine bleed air.

FUSELAGE: Aluminium alloy damage-tolerant semi-monocoque pressurised structure of circular cross-section. Chemically milled aluminium alloy skins with riveted frames and stringers, providing optimum strength characteristics while minimising aircraft weight.

TAIL UNIT: Cantilever multi-spar aluminium alloy T tail, with swept vertical and horizontal surfaces. All control surfaces hydraulically powered. Tailplane incidence adjusted by electric trim motor. No tabs.

LANDING GEAR: Hydraulically retractable tricycle type, with twin wheels and Dowty oleo-pneumatic shock absorber on each unit. Mainwheels retract inward into wing centre-section, nose unit forward. Nose unit steerable and self-centring. Mainwheels have Goodyear 25 × 6.75 tyres, pressure 13.17 bars (191 lb/sq in); nosewheels have B. F. Goodrich 18 × 4.4 tyres, pressure 10.0 bars (145 lb/sq in). ABS (Aircraft Braking Systems) hydraulically operated multiple-disc carbon brakes with fully modulated anti-skid system.

POWER PLANT: Two General Electric CF34-3A turbofans, each rated at 40.66 kN (9,140 lb st) with automatic power reserve, or 38.48 kN (8,650 lb st) without APR. One engine is pylon mounted on each side of rear fuselage, fitted with cascade type fan-air thrust reversers. Nacelles and thrust reversers produced by LTV Aircraft Products Group. Integral fuel tank in centre-section (capacity 2,839 litres; 750 US gallons; 624 Imp gallons), one in each wing (each 2,725 litres; 720 US gallons; 600 Imp gallons) and auxiliary tanks (combined capacity 984 litres; 260 US gallons; 216.5 Imp gallons) beneath cabin floor; total capacity 9,278 litres (2,451 US gallons; 2,041 Imp gallons). Optional tank in tailcone (601-3A/ER), capacity 696.5 litres (184 US gallons; 153 Imp gallons). Pressure and gravity fuelling and defuelling. Oil capacity 13.6 litres (3.6 US gallons; 3 Imp gallons).

ACCOMMODATION: Pilot and co-pilot side by side on flight deck with dual controls. Blind-flying instrumentation standard. Cabin interiors (except 601-S) installed to customer's specifications. A maximum of 19 passenger seats is approved. Typical installations include toilet, buffet, bar and wardrobe. Medevac version can carry up to seven stretcher patients, an infant incubator, a full complement of medical staff and comprehensive intensive care equipment. The baggage compartment, with its own loading door, is accessible in flight. Downward opening, power assisted door on port side, forward of wing. Overwing emergency exit on starboard side. Entire accommodation heated, ventilated and air-conditioned.

Extended rear fuselage of Challenger 601-3A/ER, housing additional fuel tank

SYSTEMS: AiResearch pressurisation and air-conditioning systems, max pressure differential 0.62 bar (9.0 lb/sq in). Three independent hydraulic systems, each of 207 bars (3,000 lb/sq in). No. 1 system powers flight controls (via servo-actuators positioned by cables and pushrods); No. 2 system for flight controls and brakes; No. 3 system for flight controls, landing gear extension/retraction, brakes and nosewheel steering. Nos. 1 and 2 systems each powered by an engine driven pump, supplemented by an AC electric pump; No. 3 system by two AC pumps. Two 30kVA engine driven generators supply primary 115/200V three-phase AC electric power at 400Hz. Three transformer-rectifiers to convert AC power to 28V DC; one 43Ah nickel-cadmium battery. Alternative primary power provided by APU and/or an air driven generator, the latter being deployed automatically in flight if the engine driven generators and APU are inoperative. Stall warning system, with stick shakers and stick pusher. Garrett GTCP-100E gas turbine APU for engine start, ground air-conditioning and other services. Electric anti-icing of windscreen, flight deck side windows and

pitot heads; Sundstrand bleed air anti-icing of wings, tailplane, engine intake cowls and guide vanes. Gaseous oxygen system, pressure 127.5 bars (1,850 lb/sq in). Continuous-element fire detectors in each engine nacelle and APU; two-shot extinguishing system for engines, single-shot system for APU.

AVIONICS (601-3A): Honeywell digital avionics include SPZ-8000 five-tube electronic flight instrument system (EFIS) including a single multi-function display (MFD); dual Honeywell laser inertial reference systems (LIRS); dual flight management systems; Lasertrak navigation display unit; digital automatic flight control system, with dual channel fail-operational autopilot and flight director; Mach trim and auto trim; dual digital air data system; Honeywell Primus 650 or 870 four-colour digital weather radar (the latter with turbulence detection); radio altimeter; Collins Pro Line II nav/coms, including dual VHF com; dual VHF nav; dual DME; dual ATC transponders; dual ADF; dual HF com; cockpit voice recorder; standby instruments (artificial horizon, airspeed indicator and altimeter). Systems certificated for Cat. II operations. Space provisions for flight data recorder, ELT, VLF/Omega, GPWS, and full provisions for third LIRS.

AVIONICS (601-S): Generally as listed for 601-3A except for four-tube SPZ-8000, single flight management system, no HF com, and no provision for third LIRS.

EQUIPMENT (Medevac version): Includes a cardio-pulmonary resuscitation unit; a physio control lifepack comprising a heart defibrillator, ECG and cardioscope; an ophthalmoscope; respirators and resuscitators; an infant monitor; X-ray viewer; cardiostimulator; foetal heart monitor; and an anti-shock suit.

DIMENSIONS, EXTERNAL:

Wing span over winglets	19.61 m (64 ft 4 in)
Wing chord: at fuselage c/l	4.89 m (16 ft 0½ in)
at tip	1.27 m (4 ft 1.9 in)
Wing aspect ratio (excl winglets)	8.5
Length overall	20.85 m (68 ft 5 in)
Fuselage: Max diameter	2.69 m (8 ft 10 in)
Height overall	6.30 m (20 ft 8 in)
Tailplane span	6.20 m (20 ft 4 in)
Wheel track (c/l of shock struts)	3.18 m (10 ft 5 in)
Wheelbase	7.99 m (26 ft 2½ in)
Passenger door (port, fwd): Height	1.78 m (5 ft 10 in)
Width	0.91 m (3 ft 0 in)
Height to sill	1.61 m (5 ft 3½ in)
Baggage door (port, rear): Height	0.84 m (2 ft 9 in)
Width	0.71 m (2 ft 4 in)
Height to sill	1.61 m (5 ft 3½ in)
Overwing emergency exit (stbd):	
Height	0.91 m (3 ft 0 in)
Width	0.51 m (1 ft 8 in)

DIMENSIONS, INTERNAL:

Cabin: Length, incl galley, toilet and baggage area, excl	
flight deck	8.61 m (28 ft 3 in)
Max width	2.49 m (8 ft 2 in)
Width at floor level	2.18 m (7 ft 2 in)
Max height	1.85 m (6 ft 1 in)
Floor area	18.77 m² (202 sq ft)
Volume	32.6 m³ (1,150 cu ft)

AREAS:

Wings, gross (excl winglets)	48.31 m² (520.0 sq ft)
Ailerons (total)	1.39 m² (15.0 sq ft)
Trailing-edge flaps (total)	7.80 m² (84.0 sq ft)
Fin	9.18 m² (98.8 sq ft)
Rudder	2.03 m² (21.9 sq ft)

Canadair Challenger 601-3A twin-turbofan business aircraft

Canadair Regional Jet 50/56-passenger transport, first development aircraft

Tailplane	6.45 m² (69.4 sq ft)
Elevators (total)	2.15 m² (23.1 sq ft)

WEIGHTS AND LOADINGS:
Manufacturer's weight empty:

601-3A	9,292 kg (20,485 lb)
601-3A/ER	9,405 kg (20,735 lb)
601-S (incl interior)	10,909 kg (24,050 lb)

Typical operating weight empty:

601-3A	11,197 kg (24,685 lb)
601-3A/ER	11,310 kg (24,935 lb)
601-S	11,371 kg (25,070 lb)
Max fuel: 601-3A	7,559 kg (16,665 lb)
601-3A/ER	8,119 kg (17,900 lb)
601-S	6,740 kg (14,860 lb)
Max payload: 601-3A	2,184 kg (4,815 lb)
601-3A/ER	2,070 kg (4,565 lb)
601-S	2,690 kg (5,930 lb)
Payload with max fuel: 601-3A	862 kg (1,900 lb)
601-3A/ER	868 kg (1,915 lb)
601-S	1,506 kg (3,320 lb)

Max T-O weight:

* 601-3A, 601-S	19,550 kg (43,100 lb)
* 601-3A/ER	20,230 kg (44,600 lb)

Max ramp weight:

**601-3A, 601-S	19,618 kg (43,250 lb)
**601-3A/ER	20,300 kg (44,750 lb)

Max landing weight:

all 601 versions	16,329 kg (36,000 lb)

Max zero-fuel weight:

all 601 versions	13,381 kg (29,500 lb)

Max wing loading:

601-3A, 601-S	404.7 kg/m² (82.88 lb/sq ft)
601-3A/ER	418.8 kg/m² (85.77 lb/sq ft)

Max power loading (without APR):

601-3A, 601-S	254.03 kg/kN (2.49 lb/lb st)
601-3A/ER	262.86 kg/kN (2.58 lb/lb st)

* 20,457 kg (45,100 lb) option available
** 20,525 kg (45,250 lb) option available

PERFORMANCE (at max T-O weight except where indicated):
Max cruising speed:

601-3A, 601-3A/ER, 601-S	
	476 knots (882 km/h; 548 mph)

Normal cruising speed

601-3A, 601-3A/ER, 601-S	
	459 knots (851 km/h; 529 mph)

Long-range cruising speed:

all 601 versions	424 knots (786 km/h; 488 mph)

Time to initial cruise altitude: 601-3A, 601-S 24 min 42 s

601-3A/ER	24 min
Max operating altitude (all)	12,500 m (41,000 ft)
Service ceiling, one engine out (all)	7,315 m (24,000 ft)

Balanced T-O field length (ISA at S/L):

601-3A, 601-S	1,645 m (5,400 ft)
601-3A/ER	1,791 m (5,875 ft)

Landing distance at S/L at max landing weight:

all 601 versions	1,006 m (3,300 ft)

Min ground turning radius:

all 601 versions	20.27 m (66 ft 6 in)

Range with max fuel and five passengers, NBAA IFR reserves (200 nm; 370 km; 230 mile alternate) at long-range cruising speed:

601-3A	3,430 nm (6,356 km; 3,950 miles)
601-3A/ER	3,650 nm (6,764 km; 4,203 miles)
601-3S	3,038 nm (5,630 km; 3,498 miles)
Design g limit: all 601 versions	+2.6

OPERATIONAL NOISE LEVELS (FAR Pt 36):

T-O: 601-3A, 601-S	79.4 EPNdB
601-3A/ER	79.8 EPNdB
Sideline: 601-3A, 601-S	85.9 EPNdB
601-3A/ER	85.7 EPNdB
Approach: all 601 versions	89.4 EPNdB

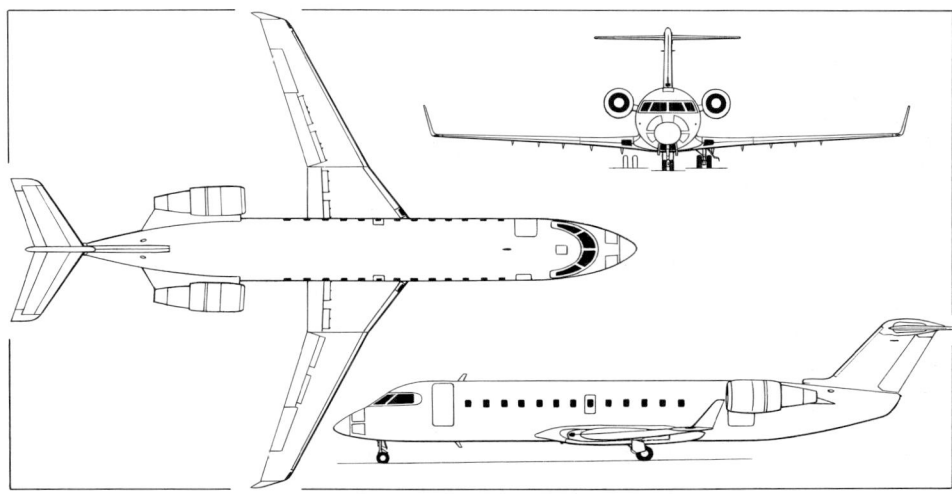

Canadair Regional Jet transport (two General Electric CF34-3A1 turbofans) *(Pilot Press)*

CANADAIR REGIONAL JET

The Regional Jet, or RJ, was designed expressly for the regional airline market. Although inspired by Challenger technology, it is a very different aircraft, optimised to withstand the demands of use in regular airline service. Design studies began in Autumn 1986, and the basic configuration was frozen in June 1988. When programme go-ahead was announced on 31 March 1989 Canadair had received launch commitments for 62 aircraft. By 1 January 1991 orders and options had increased to 139, from nine customers in seven countries.

The RJ has fuselage extensions of 3.25 m (10 ft 8 in) forward of the wings and 2.84 m (9 ft 4 in) aft, which increase passenger capacity while retaining a generous baggage capacity. To meet field length requirements, the wing area has been increased by about 15 per cent, by chordwise and wingtip extension. Short Brothers (see UK section) is manufacturing the fuselage central section, fore and aft fuselage extension plugs, wing flaps, ailerons, spoilerons and inboard spoilers.

Two versions will be available: a **Series 100** as the standard aircraft, and an extended-range **Series 100ER**. The latter, with an optional increase in max T-O weight to 23,133 kg (51,000 lb) and additional fuel capacity, was announced in September 1990 and is intended to offer a range of 1,415 nm (2,623 km; 1,630 miles). Options to be offered include increased design weights for the ER version, additional fuel capacity, a max certificated altitude raised to 12,500 m (41,000 ft), dual flight management systems, dual inertial reference system in lieu of AHRS, Cat. IIIA head-up guidance system, split scan radar, weather radar with turbulence mode, HF transceivers, Selcal, MLS provisions, red strobe lights, logo lights and cargo door lights.

Three development aircraft are being built (c/n 7001-7003), plus a static test airframe (c/n 7991) and a forward fuselage test article (7992). First flight was scheduled for the second quarter of 1991, following a 6 May rollout, and certification is expected in mid-1992.

TYPE: Twin-turbofan regional transport.

WINGS: Of generally similar planform to Challenger 601, but with some design and structural changes including strengthened two-spar box and heavier gauge skins. Supercritical wing sections. Thickness/chord ratios 13.2 per cent at root, 10 per cent at tip. Dihedral 2° 20′.

Incidence 3° 25′ at root. Sweepback at quarter-chord 24° 45′. Double-slotted flaps with dual electric motors. Fly-by-wire spoiler and spoileron system, inner two spoilers each side functioning as ground spoilers, outer two comprising one flight spoiler and one spoileron. Modified outboard leading-edges for high lift, and 0.91 m (3 ft 0 in) wingtip extension each side. Engine bleed air anti-icing of leading-edges.

FUSELAGE: Generally as for Challenger except for increased length, new forward service/emergency door, additional Type III overwing emergency exit, new overhead crew exit hatch, new equipment bay door and enlarged baggage door.

TAIL UNIT: As Challenger except for slightly modified tailplane leading-edges. Tailplane manufactured by Canadian Aircraft Products. Aviac electro-mechanical tailplane actuation.

LANDING GEAR: Hydraulically retractable tricycle type, manufactured by Dowty. Inward retracting main units each have floating piston type shock absorption, and 15 in ABS wheels with 29 × 9-15 Goodyear H type tubeless tyres, pressure (unladen) 11.38 bars (165 lb/sq in). Nose unit has Dowty steer-by-wire steering and unladen tyre pressure of 8.96 bars (130 lb/sq in). ABS steel multi-disc brakes and fully modulated Hydro Aire Mk III anti-skid system.

POWER PLANT: Two General Electric CF34-3A1 turbofans, each rated at 41.0 kN (9,220 lb st) with APR and 38.83 kN (8,729 lb st) without. Nacelles produced by LTV Aircraft Products Group. Intake cowls anti-iced by engine bleed air. Pneumatically actuated cascade type fan-air thrust reversers. Fuel in two integral wing tanks, combined capacity 5,300 litres (1,400 US gallons; 1,166 Imp gallons); increasable to 8,090 litres (2,137 US gallons; 1,780 Imp gallons) with optional centre-wing tank. Pressure refuelling point in starboard leading-edge wingroot; two gravity points on each wing.

ACCOMMODATION: Pilot, co-pilot and one or two cabin attendants. Main cabin seats up to 50 people, four-abreast at 79 cm (31 in) pitch, with centre aisle. High-density seating for 56 passengers at 76 cm (30 in) pitch. Downward opening passenger door at front, port side, with plug type outward opening forward exit/service door opposite on starboard side. Inward opening baggage door on port side at rear. Overwing emergency exit each side. Entire accommodation pressurised, including rear baggage compartment.

SYSTEMS: Primary flight control systems powered by hydraulic servo-actuators with separated cable and pushrod systems. Electrical trim and dual yaw dampers. Three fully independent hydraulic systems, each 207 bars (3,000 lb/sq in). Three-phase 115/200V AC electrical primary power at 400Hz supplied by two 30kVA engine driven generators, with five transformer-rectifiers for conversion to 28V DC. Main (43Ah) and standby (17Ah) nickel-cadmium batteries. Alternative power can be provided by APU and air driven generator. Garrett GTCP 36-150 (RJ) APU and two-pack air-conditioning system in rear of fuselage. Electric anti-icing of windscreen, flight deck windows, pitot heads, air data vanes and sensors.

AVIONICS: Collins Pro Line IV all-digital package, including dual primary flight displays, dual multi-function displays, dual EICAS displays, dual AFCS, dual AHRS, dual nav/com radios, dual air data system and Cat. II capability; digital weather radar; GPWS; windshear detection system; TCAS; Loral/Fairchild F1000 flight data recorder.

DIMENSIONS, EXTERNAL: As for Challenger 601 except:

Wing span over winglets	21.44 m (70 ft 4 in)
Wing chord at fuselage c/l	5.13 m (16 ft 10 in)
Wing aspect ratio (excl winglets)	8.85
Length: overall	26.95 m (88 ft 5 in)
fuselage	24.38 m (80 ft 0 in)
Wheelbase	11.39 m (37 ft 4½ in)
Passenger door (port, fwd):	
Height to sill	1.61 m (5 ft 3½ in)
Service door (stbd, fwd): Height	1.22 m (4 ft 0 in)
Width	0.61 m (2 ft 0 in)
Height to sill	1.61 m (5 ft 3½ in)
Baggage door (port, rear): Width	1.09 m (3 ft 7 in)

DIMENSIONS, INTERNAL:

Cabin (incl baggage compartment, excl flight deck):	
Length	14.76 m (48 ft 5 in)
Max width	2.57 m (8 ft 5 in)
Width at floor	2.18 m (7 ft 2 in)
Max height	1.87 m (6 ft 1½ in)
Floor area	32.14 m² (346.0 sq ft)
Volume	57.06 m³ (2,015 cu ft)
Stowage volume:	
Main (rear) baggage compartment	
	9.17 m³ (324.0 cu ft)
Wardrobes/bins/underseat (total)	
	5.78 m³ (204.0 cu ft)

AREAS:

Wings, gross (excl winglets)	54.54 m² (587.1 sq ft)
Ailerons (total)	1.93 m² (20.8 sq ft)
Trailing-edge flaps (total)	10.60 m² (114.1 sq ft)
Spoilers (total)	2.26 m² (24.3 sq ft)
Winglets (total)	1.38 m² (14.9 sq ft)
Fin	9.18 m² (98.8 sq ft)
Rudder	2.03 m² (21.9 sq ft)
Tailplane	8.59 m² (92.5 sq ft)
Elevators (total)	2.15 m² (23.1 sq ft)

WEIGHTS AND LOADINGS:

Manufacturer's weight empty:	
100, 100ER	13,236 kg (29,180 lb)
Operating weight empty: 100	13,653 kg (30,100 lb)
100ER	13,663 kg (30,122 lb)
Max payload (structural): 100	5,488 kg (12,100 lb)
100ER	6,295 kg (13,878 lb)
Max fuel: 100	4,254 kg (9,380 lb)
100ER	6,504 kg (14,338 lb)
Max T-O weight: 100	21,523 kg (47,450 lb)
100ER	23,133 kg (51,000 lb)
Max ramp weight: 100	21,636 kg (47,700 lb)
100ER	23,246 kg (51,250 lb)
Max zero-fuel weight: 100	19,141 kg (42,200 lb)
100ER	19,958 kg (44,000 lb)
Max landing weight: 100	20,275 kg (44,700 lb)
100ER	21,319 kg (47,000 lb)
Max wing loading: 100	394.6 kg/m² (80.82 lb/sq ft)
100ER	424.14 kg/m² (86.87 lb/sq ft)
Max power loading (APR rating):	
100	262.48 kg/kN (2.57 lb/lb st)
100ER	282.1 kg/kN (2.77 lb/lb st)

PERFORMANCE (estimated, at max T-O weight except where indicated):

Max operating speed above 9,570 m (31,400 ft)	
Mach 0.85 or 335 knots (621 km/h; 386 mph) CAS	
Normal cruising speed at 11,000 m (36,000 ft)	
Mach 0.80 or 459 knots (851 km/h; 529 mph)	
Long-range cruising speed at 11,000 m (36,000 ft)	
Mach 0.74 or 424 knots (786 km/h; 488 mph)	
Stalling speed, 45° flap 100 knots (185 km/h; 115 mph)	
Max rate of climb at S/L: 100	1,067 m (3,500 ft)/min
100ER	975 m (3,200 ft)/min
Max operating altitude	12,500 m (41,000 ft)
FAR T-O field length at S/L, ISA	1,600 m (5,250 ft)
FAR landing field length at S/L, ISA, at 19,050 kg	
(42,000 lb) typical landing weight	1,410 m (4,620 ft)
Min ground turning radius	22.86 m (75 ft 0 in)
Range with max payload at long-range cruising speed,	
FAR Pt 121 reserves:	
100	842 nm (1,561 km; 970 miles)
100ER	1,415 nm (2,623 km; 1,630 miles)

OPERATIONAL NOISE LEVELS (estimated):

T-O	81.0 EPNdB
Approach	91.0 EPNdB
Sideline	87.0 EPNdB

CANADAIR CL-215

A total of 125 piston-engined CL-215s were built, of which 124 were delivered to the governments of France (15); Greece (16); Italy (five); Spain (30); Thailand (two); Venezuela (two); Yugoslavia (five); and eight Canadian provinces and territories (Alberta four, Manitoba five, Newfoundland four, Northwest Territories two, Ontario nine, Quebec 19, Saskatchewan four and Yukon two). The last CL-215, the 16th aircraft for Greece, was delivered on 3 May 1990. A full description of the fifth and final series can be found in the 1989-90 and earlier editions, with amended weight figures in the 1990-91 Jane's.

CANADAIR CL-215T

In August 1986 Canadair announced its intention to develop this turboprop version of the CL-215. Firefighting/aerial spraying are expected to account for some 44 per cent of CL-215T sales, but a larger share of the potential market is envisaged for various maritime, military or paramilitary versions (33 per cent, including surveillance, coastal defence, SAR and customs/immigration patrol), and for civil personnel or utility transport versions (23 per cent).

The CL-215T utilises the well proven basic airframe of the piston engined CL-215, with a number of improvements. These include an upgraded and air-conditioned flight deck, a new fuel system with both pressure and gravity refuelling, increased after-scooping weights, wingtip endplates, auxiliary fins (to offset lateral instability caused by turbulence from slimline nacelles and new propellers), and a larger capacity four-tank drop system for firefighting missions. An extensive list of options will be available for specialised applications. Various military and commercial versions have been defined, including variants equipped with airborne radar for maritime operations.

Two CL-215s were modified as CL-215T prototypes. The first of these (C-FASE) made its initial flight on 8 June 1989, followed on 20 September 1989 by the second, which is fitted with powered ailerons. This aircraft had completed more than 450 hours' flying by 1 November 1990. Restricted category certification (for firefighting) was awarded on 28 March 1991, to be followed shortly thereafter by Utility category approval. Retrofit kits for existing CL-215s became available in 1991; new-build CL-215Ts, to which the detailed description applies, will

enter production when sufficient orders have been obtained. Co-production or licence manufacture agreements are open for negotiation. The government of Quebec is launch customer for the retrofit programme, with an initial contract to convert two of its existing CL-215s. Fifteen conversion kits, including powered ailerons, were ordered by the Spanish government on 3 August 1989 for aircraft operated by No. 43 Squadron of the Spanish Air Force, and the first six converted aircraft were due to be redelivered by the end of 1991.

TYPE: Twin-turboprop multi-purpose amphibian.

WINGS: Cantilever high-wing monoplane. No dihedral. All-metal one-piece fail-safe structure, with front and rear spars at 16 and 49 per cent chord. Spars of conventional construction, with extruded caps and webs stiffened by vertical members. Aluminium alloy skin, with riveted spanwise extruded stringers, is supported at 762 mm (30 in) pitch by interspar ribs. Leading-edge consists of aluminium alloy skin attached to pressed nose-ribs and spanwise stringers. Hydraulically operated all-metal single-slotted flaps, supported by four external hinges on interspar ribs on each wing. Powered ailerons, with Jacottet actuators, standard on new-build aircraft. Trim tab and geared tab in port aileron, rudder/aileron interconnect tab in starboard aileron. Metal endplates, which improve lateral stability and permit use of full engine ratings.

FUSELAGE: All-metal single-step flying-boat hull of conventional fail-safe construction.

TAIL UNIT: Cantilever all-metal fail-safe structure with horizontal surfaces mounted midway up fin. Structure of aluminium alloy sheet, honeycomb panels, extrusions and fittings. 'Arrowhead' auxiliary fin on each half of tailplane. Hydraulically powered elevators and rudder fitted with dynamic balance, trim tab (port elevator only), spring tabs and geared tabs, for manual reversion. Provision for de-icing of leading-edges.

LANDING GEAR: Hydraulically retractable tricycle type. Self-centring twin-wheel nose unit retracts rearward into hull and is fully enclosed by doors. Nosewheel steering standard on fifth series CL-215s and new-build CL-215Ts. Main gear support structures retract into wells in sides of hull. A plate mounted on each main gear assembly encloses bottom of wheel well. Mainwheel tyre pressure 5.31 bars (77 lb/sq in); nosewheel tyre pressure 6.55 bars (95 lb/sq in). Hydraulic disc brakes. Non-retractable stabilising floats are each carried on a pylon cantilevered from wing box structure, with breakaway provision.

Canadair CL-215T prototype, showing wingtip endplates and auxiliary finlets

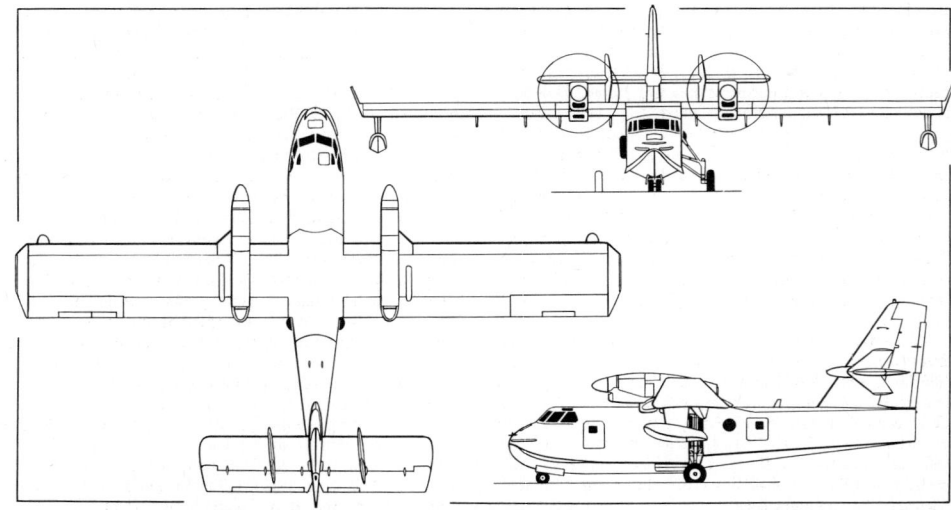

Canadair CL-215T twin-turboprop general purpose amphibian *(Pilot Press)*

POWER PLANT: Two 1,775 kW (2,380 shp) Pratt & Whitney Canada PW123AF turboprops, in damage-tolerant nacelles, each driving a Hamilton Standard 14SF-17 four-blade constant-speed fully-feathering reversible-pitch propeller. Two fuel tanks, each of eight identical flexible cells, in wing spar box, with total usable capacity of 5,796 litres (1,531 US gallons; 1,275 Imp gallons). Single-point pressure refuelling (rear fuselage, starboard side), plus gravity point above each tank. Pneumatic/electric intake de-icing system.

ACCOMMODATION: Normal crew of two side by side on flight deck, with dual controls. Additional stations in maritime patrol/SAR versions for flight engineer, navigator and two observers. For water bomber cabin installation, see under Equipment paragraph. With water tanks removed, transport configurations can include layout for 30 passengers plus toilet, galley and baggage area, with seat pitch of 79 cm (31 in). Combi layout offers cargo at front, full firefighting capability, plus 11 seats at rear. Other quick-change interiors available for medevac (12 stretchers and two medical attendants), utility/paratroop (up to 14 foldup troop-type canvas seats in cabin, in two inward facing rows), all-cargo, or other special missions according to customer's requirements. Flush doors to main cabin on port side of fuselage forward and aft of wings. Emergency exit on starboard side aft of wing trailing-edge. Crew emergency hatch in flight deck roof on starboard side. Mooring hatch in upper surface of nose. Provision for additional cabin windows.

SYSTEMS: Casey vapour cycle air-conditioning system and Janitrol heater. Hydraulic system, pressure 207 bars (3,000 lb/sq in), utilises two engine driven pumps (max flow rate 45.5 litres; 12 US gallons; 10 Imp gallons/min) to actuate nosewheel steering, landing gear, flaps, water drop doors, pickup probes, flight controls and wheel brakes. Unpressurised air/oil reservoir. Electrically driven third pump provides hydraulic power for emergency actuation of landing gear and brakes and closure of water doors. Electrical system includes two 800VA 115V 400Hz static inverters, two 28V 400A DC engine driven starter/generators and two 40Ah nickel-cadmium batteries. Ice protection system optional.

AVIONICS: Standard installation includes dual VHF transceivers, single VHF/FM com, dual VOR/ILS receivers, dual ADF, two marker beacon receivers, ATC transponder and ELT. Optional avionics include autopilot, VLF/Omega nav system, search radar and colour weather radar.

EQUIPMENT (water bomber): Four integral water tanks in main fuselage compartment, near CG (combined capacity 6,132 litres; 1,620 US gallons; 1,350 Imp gallons), plus seven inward facing seats. Hydraulically actuated scoop on each side, aft of hull step, fillable also on ground by hose adapter on each side of fuselage. Four independently openable water drop doors in hull bottom. Improved drop pattern and drop door sequencing compared with CL-215. Optional spray kit can be coupled with firefighting tanks for large scale spraying of oil dispersants and insecticides. In a typical mission profile, with a fire 85 nm (157 km; 98 miles) from the CL-215T's

base, a water source 10 nm (18.5 km; 11.5 miles) from the fire, and 45 min fuel reserves, aircraft could make 26 water scoop and drop circuits before having to return to base to refuel. Water tanks can be scoop-filled completely (on smooth water in ISA conditions) in an on-water distance of only 564 m (1,850 ft); partial water loads can be scooped on smaller bodies of water. Minimum safe water depth for scooping operations is only 1.40 m (4 ft 7 in).

EQUIPMENT (other versions): Stretcher kits, passenger or troop seats, cargo tiedowns, searchlight, and other equipment according to mission and customer requirements. Provision for two underwing pylon attachment points for auxiliary fuel tanks or other stores.

DIMENSIONS, EXTERNAL:

Wing span	28.60 m (93 ft 10 in)
Wing chord (constant)	3.54 m (11 ft 7½ in)
Wing aspect ratio	8.2
Length overall	19.82 m (65 ft 0¼ in)
Beam (max)	2.59 m (8 ft 6 in)
Length/beam ratio	7.5
Height overall: on land	8.98 m (29 ft 5½ in)
on water	6.88 m (22 ft 7 in)
Draught: wheels up	1.12 m (3 ft 8 in)
wheels down	2.03 m (6 ft 8 in)
Tailplane span	10.97 m (36 ft 0 in)
Wheel track	5.28 m (17 ft 4 in)
Wheelbase	7.23 m (23 ft 9 in)
Propeller diameter	3.97 m (13 ft 0¼ in)
Propeller/fuselage clearance	0.59 m (1 ft 11¼ in)
Propeller/water clearance	1.30 m (4 ft 3¼ in)
Propeller/ground clearance	2.77 m (9 ft 1 in)
Forward door: Height*	1.37 m (4 ft 6 in)
Width	1.03 m (3 ft 4 in)
Height to sill	1.68 m (5 ft 6 in)
Rear door: Height	1.12 m (3 ft 8 in)
Width	1.03 m (3 ft 4 in)
Height to sill	1.83 m (6 ft 0 in)
Water drop door: Length	1.60 m (5 ft 3 in)
Width	0.81 m (2 ft 8 in)
Emergency exit: Height	0.91 m (3 ft 0 in)
Width	0.51 m (1 ft 8 in)

* incl 25 cm (10 in) removable sill

DIMENSIONS, INTERNAL:

Cabin, excl flight deck: Length	9.38 m (30 ft 9½ in)
Max width	2.39 m (7 ft 10 in)
Max height	1.90 m (6 ft 3 in)
Floor area	19.69 m² (212 sq ft)
Volume	35.59 m³ (1,257 cu ft)

AREAS:

Wings, gross	100.33 m² (1,080.0 sq ft)
Ailerons (total)	8.05 m² (86.6 sq ft)
Flaps (total)	22.39 m² (241.0 sq ft)
Fin	11.22 m² (120.75 sq ft)
Rudder, incl tabs	6.02 m² (64.75 sq ft)
Tailplane	20.55 m² (221.2 sq ft)
Elevators (total, incl tabs)	7.88 m² (84.8 sq ft)

WEIGHTS AND LOADINGS (A: water bomber, B: utility, land or water based):

Typical operating weight empty:	

A	12,265 kg (27,040 lb)
B	12,000 kg (26,460 lb)
Max internal fuel weight: A, B	4,649 kg (10,250 lb)
Max payload: A (disposable)	6,123 kg (13,500 lb)
B	4,508 kg (9,940 lb)
Max ramp weight: A (land)	19,890 kg (43,850 lb)
A (water), B	17,236 kg (38,000 lb)
Max T-O weight:	
A, production (land)	19,890 kg (43,850 lb)
A (water), B (land and water)	17,100 kg (37,700 lb)
Max touchdown weight for water scooping:	
A	16,420 kg (36,200 lb)
Max flying weight after water scooping:	
A, new production	20,865 kg (46,000 lb)
A, retrofit	20,525 kg (45,250 lb)
Max landing weight:	
A, new production (land)	16,783 kg (37,000 lb)
A, retrofit (land)	15,603 kg (34,400 lb)
A, new production (water), B (water), and retrofit from c/n 1056	16,783 kg (37,000 lb)
A (water), B (water), retrofit c/n 1001-1055	15,603 kg (34,400 lb)
Max zero-fuel weight:	
A, new production	19,051 kg (42,000 lb)
A, retrofit	17,917 kg (39,500 lb)
B	16,511 kg (36,400 lb)
Max wing loading:	
A, production (land)	198.2 kg/m² (40.60 lb/sq ft)
A (water), B (land and water)	170.4 kg/m² (34.91 lb/sq ft)
Max power loading:	
A, production (land)	5.60 kg/kW (9.21 lb/shp)
A (water), B (land and water)	4.82 kg/kW (7.92 lb/shp)

PERFORMANCE (estimated at weights shown):

Max cruising speed at 3,050 m (10,000 ft), AUW of 14,741 kg (32,500 lb) 206 knots (382 km/h; 237 mph)

Long-range cruising speed at 3,050 m (10,000 ft), AUW of 14,741 kg (32,500 lb)
155 knots (287 km/h; 178 mph)

Patrol speed at S/L, AUW of 15,876 kg (35,000 lb)
130 knots (241 km/h; 150 mph)

Stalling speed:
15° flap, AUW of 20,865 kg (46,000 lb)
76 knots (141 km/h; 88 mph) CAS
25° flap, AUW of 16,783 kg (37,000 lb)
65 knots (121 km/h; 75 mph) CAS

Max rate of climb at S/L, AUW of 20,865 kg (46,000 lb)
390 m (1,280 ft)/min

T-O distance at S/L, ISA:
land, AUW of 19,890 kg (43,850 lb) 701 m (2,300 ft)
water, AUW of 17,168 kg (37,850 lb) 677 m (2,220 ft)

Landing distance at S/L, ISA:
land, AUW of 16,783 kg (37,000 lb) 768 m (2,520 ft)
water, AUW of 16,783 kg (37,000 lb) 838 m (2,750 ft)

Scooping distance at S/L, ISA (incl safe clearance heights) 1,189 m (3,900 ft)

Ferry range with 884 kg (1,950 lb) payload
1,125 nm (2,085 km; 1,295 miles)

Design g limits (15° flap) +3.25/−1

CONAIR
CONAIR AVIATION LTD

PO Box 220, Abbotsford, British Columbia V2S 4N9
Telephone: 1 (604) 853 1171
Fax: 1 (604) 853 9017
Telex: 04-363529
PRESIDENT: L. G. (Les) Kerr
VICE-PRESIDENT AND GENERAL MANAGER:
K. B. (Barry) Marsden
MARKETING MANAGER: Robert M. Stitt
MANAGER, CORPORATE COMMUNICATIONS: Lorna Thomassen

Conair operates the largest private fleet of firefighting aircraft in the world, with more than 50 fixed-wing aircraft and 35 helicopters, the latter operated by its subsidiary Frontier Helicopters. The company specialises in aerial control services such as forest fire control, oil spill control, insect control, forest fertilisation, and fish culture. It designs and manufactures many speciality aviation systems such as fire retardant delivery systems, dispersal equipment, and various spray systems. Among these are underbelly retardant tanks for a range of helicopters including the Bell 205 and 212 and Aerospatiale Ecureuil, Lama and Puma, and an 11,365 litre (3,002 US gallon; 2,500 Imp gallon) ventral retardant tank for a firefighting version of the Douglas DC-6B. Since 1978 Conair has undertaken 36 conversions of Grumman or Canadian built S-2 Tracker aircraft to Conair Firecat or Turbo Firecat air tanker configuration.

Orders due for delivery in 1991 included a fifth Turbo Firecat for France, and a follow-on order for four 7,560 litre (1,997 US gallon; 1,663 Imp gallon) modular spray systems for Lockheed C-130s, to be operated by the 356th Tactical Airlift Squadron of USAF. Two such systems had been delivered previously to this operator, the second in late 1989. In addition to the C-130 spray system, Conair produces similar modifications for the Douglas DC-6, Fokker F27 and Alenia G222.

CONAIR FIRECAT

The Firecat is converted from standard Grumman S-2A (S2F-1) or de Havilland Canada CS2F-1/2/3 Tracker aircraft for specialised fire control operation, and the aircraft so converted are part of the Conair fleet as well as being available for export. Conair holds the Canadian type approval for S2F/CS2F, Firecat and Turbo Firecat aircraft. A total of 32 Firecats were to have been delivered by mid-1991.

The Conair conversion includes raising the cabin floor by 20.3 cm (8 in) and installing a 3,296 litre (870 US gallon; 725 Imp gallon) retardant tank in the fuselage; modifying the landing gear by fitting larger wheels with low pressure tyres, for soft field operation; inspecting the wing spar caps for corrosion, and repairing or replacing them as necessary; removing 1,361 kg (3,000 lb) of military equipment; completely rewiring the aircraft; and rebuilding/updating the flight deck instrument panels. Options include a hydraulic or pneumatic system for discharging the retardant, and a microcomputer system to control the drop pattern. The retardant tank has four compartments which can be discharged in a single salvo, two two-door salvos, or any combination of single-door drops. A 173 litre (45.7 US gallon; 38 Imp gallon) foam injection system is available for enhancing water drops.

POWER PLANT: Two 1,100 kW (1,475 hp) Wright 982C9HE2 (R-1820-82) Cyclone nine-cylinder aircooled radial engines, each driving a Hamilton Standard three-blade propeller. Total internal fuel capacity 1,968 litres (520 US gallons; 433 Imp gallons).

ACCOMMODATION: Minimum crew: one pilot.

WEIGHTS AND LOADINGS:

Operating weight empty	6,895 kg (15,200 lb)
Max payload	3,300 kg (7,275 lb)
Max fuel	1,418 kg (3,126 lb)
Max T-O weight	11,793 kg (26,000 lb)
Max landing weight	11,113 kg (24,500 lb)

PERFORMANCE (at max T-O weight):
Never-exceed speed (VNE)
240 knots (444 km/h; 276 mph)
Max level speed at 1,220 m (4,000 ft)
220 knots (408 km/h; 253 mph)
Normal cruising speed 180 knots (333 km/h; 207 mph)
Normal drop speed 120 knots (222 km/h; 138 mph)
Stalling speed, flaps down, power off
82 knots (152 km/h; 95 mph)
Max rate of climb at S/L 366 m (1,200 ft)/min
Rate of climb at S/L, one engine out 107 m (350 ft)/min
Service ceiling 6,100 m (20,000 ft)
T-O to 15 m (50 ft) 915 m (3,000 ft)
Landing from 15 m (50 ft) 762 m (2,500 ft)
Min field length 915 m (3,000 ft)
Endurance with max payload 4 h 30 min

CONAIR TURBO FIRECAT

This turboprop version of the Firecat, which flew for the first time on 7 August 1988, has two P&WC PT6A-67AF turboprops instead of Wright Cyclone piston engines. The turbine engines allow more precise speed control and greater manoeuvrability at the fire site, particularly during steep descents in mountainous terrain.

The Turbo Firecat offers several other improvements over the piston engined Firecat, including turbine reliability, better fuel availability, improved aircraft performance, greater speed for increased productivity, and reduced operating and maintenance costs. It also has a single-point refuelling station on the starboard engine nacelle, and a modern angle of attack and stall warning system.

The four-door, four-compartment retardant tank is 3.25 m (10 ft 8 in) long, 1.27 m (4 ft 2 in) wide and 0.86 m (2 ft 10 in) deep, and has a maximum capacity of 3,455 litres (913 US gallons; 760 Imp gallons). Retardant can be discharged at a max flow rate of 3,955 litres (1,045 US gallons; 870 Imp gallons)/min.

Canadian certification for the Turbo Firecat was granted on 22 December 1989, the first conversion having previously been delivered to the French Sécurité Civile in August 1988. Two more were delivered to France in 1989, a fourth in 1990 and a fifth in 1991. Conair was also completing a sixth Turbo Firecat for use as its own demonstrator in 1991.

POWER PLANT: Two 1,062 kW (1,424 shp) Pratt & Whitney Canada PT6A-67AF turboprops, each driving a Hartzell HC-B5MA-3BXI/M11296SX five-blade propeller. Total fuel capacity of 2,936 litres (775.6 US gallons; 645.8 Imp gallons), consisting of 1,972 litres (521 US gallons; 433.8 Imp gallons) internally and 964 litres (254.7 US gallons; 212 Imp gallons) in two underwing pylon tanks.

ACCOMMODATION: Minimum crew: one pilot.

WEIGHTS AND LOADINGS: As for Firecat except:

Operating weight empty	6,884 kg (15,177 lb)
Max fuel	2,339 kg (5,158 lb)
Max T-O weight	12,473 kg (27,500 lb)

PERFORMANCE (at max T-O weight except where indicated): As for Firecat except:

Normal cruising speed	220 knots (408 km/h; 253 mph)
Rate of climb at S/L, one engine out:	
at max T-O weight	61 m (200 ft)/min
at 9,072 kg (20,000 lb) gross weight	227 m (745 ft)/min
T-O to 15 m (50 ft)	1,220 m (4,000 ft)
* Landing from 15 m (50 ft)	762 m (2,500 ft)
Min field length	1,220 m (4,000 ft)
Endurance with max payload	5 h

* *Without available propeller reversal*

CONAIR F27 FIREFIGHTER

Conair has modified three Fokker F27 Mk 600 commuter transports for firefighting roles, for which it received Canadian DoT type approval on 5 June 1986. It was the world's first turboprop conversion dedicated to forest fire suppression and resource protection. Two F27 Firefighters are currently owned and operated by the French Sécurité Civile.

The modification includes installing a Conair delivery system which can carry 6,364 litres (1,681 US gallons; 1,400 Imp gallons) of long-term retardant. A 455 litre (120 US gallon; 100 Imp gallon) foam injection system is also available. The converted aircraft are readily adaptable to other functions such as transporting cargo and fire crews, infra-red fire detection and mapping, aerial survey, aerial spraying and pararescue operations. Unnecessary internal items such as cabin insulation, bulkheads, pressurisation equipment and galleys are deleted, modern avionics installed, and the eight-compartment retardant delivery system fitted ventrally as an integral part of the fuselage. The tank is blended to the fuselage with Kevlar fairings, and can be loaded at a rate of 1,514 litres (400 US gallons; 333 Imp gallons)/min. Door sequencing is computer controlled, and the entire vent system is integral with the modified fuselage floor so that the aircraft's cargo-carrying capabilities are retained. The aircraft is crewed by two pilots, and seating for 19 support crew members is retained, together with the large forward (port) freight door.

WEIGHTS AND LOADINGS:

Operating weight empty	10,646 kg (23,471 lb)
Max payload	6,731 kg (14,840 lb)
Max fuel	4,152 kg (9,153 lb)
Max T-O weight	20,411 kg (45,000 lb)
Max landing weight	18,143 kg (40,000 lb)

PERFORMANCE (at max T-O weight except where indicated): Never-exceed speed (VNE)

	259 knots (480 km/h; 298 mph)
Max cruising speed	230 knots (426 km/h; 265 mph)
Normal drop speed	125 knots (232 km/h; 144 mph)
Min control speed	80 knots (149 km/h; 92 mph)

Conair Turbo Firecat in action (two P&WC PT6A-67AF turboprops)

Conair 2,355 litre (622 US gallon; 517.5 Imp gallon) helitanker system on a Puma

Stalling speed, flaps down, power off	77 knots (143 km/h; 89 mph)
Max rate of climb at S/L	366 m (1,200 ft)/min
Rate of climb at S/L, one engine out, AUW of 14,060 kg (31,000 lb)	177 m (580 ft)/min
Service ceiling	7,620 m (25,000 ft)
Service ceiling, one engine out, AUW of 14,060 kg (31,000 lb)	5,640 m (18,500 ft)
T-O to 10.7 m (35 ft)	1,600 m (5,250 ft)
Landing from 15 m (50 ft) at max landing weight	987 m (3,240 ft)
Min field length	1,525 m (5,000 ft)
Max endurance	3 h 24 min

CONAIR HELITANKERS

Conair has developed a growing number of helicopter-mounted fire control systems known as helitankers. The semi-monocoque belly-mounted tanks feature individually operated, full-length rigid doors which may be opened in various combinations over a wide range of airspeeds to permit variable retardant line lengths and drop concentrations. A self-loading hover-fill system allows the tank to be filled while the helicopter hovers above a remote water source, and an offload feature allows the water payload to be pumped to a portable ground reservoir for the use of ground-based firefighters. A foam injection system permits the fire suppressing qualities of a water payload to be greatly enhanced. A reversible pump allows single-point loading injection into the tank and single-point offloading.

Helitanker system sales to date have included 24 Bell 205/212s, 12 Aerospatiale AS 350B₁ Ecureuils, 10 SA 315B Lamas and two AS 330 Pumas. System capacities are 1,360 litres (359 US gallons; 299 Imp gallons) for the Bell 205/212; 900 litres (238 US gallons; 198 Imp gallons) for the Lama; 800 litres (211 US gallons; 176 Imp gallons) for the Ecureuil; and 2,355 litres (622 US gallons; 517.5 Imp gallons) for the Puma. The Puma system features an 800 litre (211 US gallon; 176 Imp gallon) two-door belly tank, and a 1,296 litre (342 US gallon; 285 Imp gallon) fuselage main tank with two internal doors for reloading the external tank via a 261 litre (69 US gallon; 57 Imp gallon) chute. Foam tank capacity is 173 litres (46 US gallons; 38 Imp gallons). The Bell 205 and 212 helitankers are available with a rappelling system to deliver firefighters to remote fire sites.

IMP

IMP GROUP LTD (Aerospace Manufacturing Division)

Suite 400, 2651 Dutch Village Road, Halifax, Nova Scotia B3L 4T1
Telephone: 1 (902) 835 4433
Fax: 1 (902) 835 4441
Telex: 1921728

IMP (GRUMMAN) S-2E TRACKER UPGRADE

In 1989 IMP received a contract to re-engine and otherwise upgrade 12 S-2E Tracker ASW aircraft of the Brazilian Air Force (FAB designation **P-16E**). Conversion involved refitting with 1,230 kW (1,650 shp) Pratt & Whitney Canada PT6A-67CF turboprops and Hartzell five-blade propellers, and modifications to the fuel, hydraulic, pneumatic and electrical systems. The prototype conversion made its first flight on 14 June 1990 and was returned to Brazil on 17 December for acceptance trials in the aircraft carrier *Minas Gerais*. Conversion of the other 11 aircraft is taking place in Brazil, using kits supplied by IMP.

IMP (SIKORSKY) SEA KING CONVERSION

Six Canadian Forces' CH-124A Sea King ASW helicopters have been converted for a surface surveillance role in the Gulf, operating from HMCS *Athabaskan* and *Protecteur*. One 'prototype' was completed by IMP and the other five by the Canadian Forces at CFB Shearwater, Nova Scotia, using IMP-provided kits. Changes include the following:

AVIONICS: Tracor SLIPAR (short light pulse alerting receiver) laser warning system, E-Systems AN/APR-39 radar warning receiver, Loral AN/AAR-47 passive missile approach warning system, Sanders AN/ALQ-144 infra-red jammer, Tracor AN/ALE-37 chaff dispenser and M-130 flare dispenser.

ARMAMENT: One C-9 machine-gun mounted in cabin doorway.

KFC

KELOWNA FLIGHTCRAFT AIR CHARTER LTD

Kelowna Airport, RR2, Kelowna, British Columbia V1Y 7R1
Telephone: 1 (604) 765 1481
Fax: 1 (604) 765 1489
Telex: 048 5217

PRESIDENT: Barry Lapointe
OPERATIONS MANAGER: Greg Carter

Kelowna Flightcraft is currently upgrading Canadair CC-109 Cosmopolitan (Canadian built Convair 580) aircraft of the Canadian Forces, in a programme which includes retrofit of a Honeywell SPZ-4500 digital automatic flight control system. The first updated aircraft was redelivered to the CF in December 1989. As an extension of this activity, KFC plans to modify its own fleet of five civil Convair 580s, and to offer a similar retrofit package to other Convairliner operators.

KFC STRETCH 580

This modification includes a 4.34 m (14 ft 3 in) extension of the fuselage, and incorporation of a Honeywell SPZ-4500 digital AFCS, EDZ-803 electronic flight instrumentation system, and Primus II nav/com/ident radio package. These avionics will include dual FZ-450 flight guidance computers, manually switchable into a single control surface servo drive system; a four-tube EFIS; Primus 650 weather radar; a dual VG-14A/C-14A attitude/heading package; and an AA-300 radio altimeter. Thus modified, the Stretch 580 will be a totally refurbished and recon-ditioned aircraft meeting Stage 3 noise and Cat. II landing standards.

A prototype avionics package was due for delivery to KFC in October 1990, and FAA certification of the Stretch 580 was anticipated in April 1991. The modification is applicable to any serviceable Convair 340, 440 or 580 airframe, and is claimed to extend aircraft life by a further 100,000 hours.

MBB
MBB HELICOPTER CANADA LIMITED
(Subsidiary of Messerschmitt-Bölkow-Blohm GmbH)

HEAD OFFICE: PO Box 250, 1100 Gilmore Road, Fort Erie, Ontario L2A 5M9
Telephone: 1 (416) 871 7772
Fax: 1 (416) 871 3320
Telex: 061-5250
VICE-PRESIDENT AND GENERAL MANAGER:
Richard W. Harwood
VICE-PRESIDENT, MARKETING: Donald P. Chambers
GOVERNMENT MARKETING OFFICE: Suite 1202, 60 Queen Street, Ottawa, Ontario K1P 5Y7
Telephone: 1 (613) 232 1557
Fax: 1 (613) 232 5454
Telex: 053-4109
DIRECTOR, GOVERNMENT PROGRAMMES: Ken Edmonds

MBB Helicopter Canada began operations as Canada's first helicopter manufacturer in April 1984 as a result of a contract between MBB of Germany and the Federal and Ontario governments of Canada. In mid-1986, MBB Helicopter Canada opened a 7,897 m² (85,000 sq ft) manufacturing plant in Fort Erie, Ontario.

MBB Helicopter Canada has the world product mandate and design authority to manufacture in Canada the BO 105 LS variant of this helicopter. Production began with the BO 105 LS A-3 version. The first customer delivery was made in February 1987, and 22 of the LS model had been delivered by January 1990, including 11 to the Peruvian Air Force and police.

MBB Helicopter Canada is responsible for sales and completion of all MBB helicopters in Canada, including the BO 105 CBS (see German section) and the larger MBB/Kawasaki BK 117 (see International section).

MBB BO 105 LS

This hot and high version of the BO 105 (L for Lift and S for Stretch) combines the enlarged cabin of the CBS version with more powerful engines and an uprated transmission, permitting operation at a higher gross weight. It was first flown on 23 October 1981. Certification by the German LBA was granted in July 1984, and extended in April 1985 to cover hot and high take-offs and landings at altitudes up to 6,100 m (20,000 ft). It was extended again on 7 July 1986 to cover the A-3 version of the BO 105 LS, with FAA and Canadian DoT certification granted subsequently.

A BO 105 LS B-1 (C-FMCL) was used as a testbed for Pratt & Whitney Canada's PW200 turboshaft engine series, and the first flight test, with two 307 kW (412 shp) PW205B engines, took place on 13 October 1988. Further details of this aircraft, and an illustration, appeared in the 1989-90 *Jane's*. No indication has been given of this programme's subsequent status.

The description of the BO 105 CBS in the German section applies also to the BO 105 LS A-3, except as follows:
ROTOR SYSTEM: Main transmission, type ZF-FS 112, is rated for independent restricted input of 310 kW (416 shp) per engine at T-O power or 294 kW (394 shp) per engine for max continuous operation; or a single-engine restricted input of 368 kW (493 shp) at max continuous power, or 410 kW (550 shp) for 2.5 min at T-O power.
POWER PLANT: Two Allison 250-C28C turboshafts, each rated at 410 kW (550 shp) for 2.5 min, and with 5 min T-O and max continuous power ratings of 373 kW (500 shp) and 368 kW (493 shp) respectively. Fuel capacity as for CB/CBS. Oil capacity 5 litres (1.3 US gallons; 1.1 Imp gallons) per engine.
ACCOMMODATION: Pilot, and co-pilot or passenger, on two front seats; three or four passengers in main cabin. Cargo space behind rear seats, plus additional 20 kg (44 lb) in baggage compartment. Crew door and passengers' sliding door each side; clamshell rear cargo doors, removable for carriage of extra-long cargo. Cabin heating and air-conditioning available optionally.

MBB BO 105 LS five/six-seat helicopter (two Allison 250-C28C turboshafts)

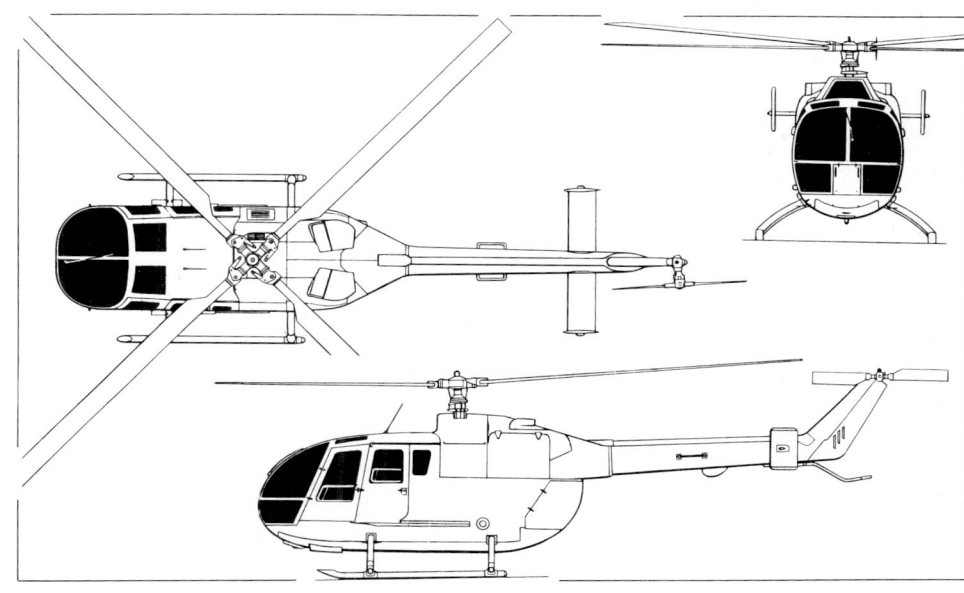

MBB Helicopter Canada Ltd BO 105 LS hot and high helicopter *(Pilot Press)*

SYSTEMS: As for BO 105 CBS, except stability augmentation system is standard, bleed air anti-icing optional.
WEIGHTS AND LOADINGS:
Weight empty, basic	1,430 kg (3,152 lb)
Fuel weight	456 kg (1,005 lb)
Max T-O weight	2,600 kg (5,732 lb)
Max disc loading	34.19 kg/m² (7.00 lb/sq ft)
Max power loading (transmission restricted)	
	4.19 kg/kW (6.89 lb/shp)

PERFORMANCE (at T-O weight of 2,400 kg; 5,291 lb, ISA):
Never-exceed speed (VNE) at S/L
145 knots (270 km/h; 167 mph)
Max cruising speed at S/L
131 knots (243 km/h; 151 mph)
Max rate of climb at S/L 634 m (2,080 ft)/min
Vertical rate of climb at S/L 427 m (1,400 ft)/min
Max operating altitude 6,100 m (20,000 ft)
Service ceiling, one engine out, 30.5 m (100 ft)/min climb reserve 2,590 m (8,500 ft)
Hovering ceiling: IGE 4,265 m (14,000 ft)
OGE 3,385 m (11,100 ft)
Range at S/L, standard fuel, max internal payload, no reserves 281 nm (522 km; 324 miles)

NWI
NORTHWEST INDUSTRIES LIMITED
(a Division of CAE Industries Ltd)

PO Box 9864, Edmonton International Airport, Edmonton, Alberta T5J 2T2
Telephone: 1 (403) 890 6300
Fax: 1 (403) 890 7773
PRESIDENT: L. H. Prokop
VICE-PRESIDENT AND GENERAL MANAGER: F. A. Maybee

NWI is one of Canada's largest aircraft maintenance, repair, overhaul and modification centres for military and commercial aircraft, including the Lockheed C-130 Hercules, Dassault Falcon, Lockheed T-33, Canadair CL-41 (CT-114) and CF-104 Starfighter. In addition to its major in-plant aircraft programmes, mobile repair parties are stationed at CFB Cold Lake in support of CF-5 and CF-18 aircraft of the Canadian Forces. The manufacturing shops produce structural, mechanical and electronic components for its aircraft overhaul and modification programmes, and, under subcontract, for North America's principal aerospace manufacturers.

In 1987 NWI completed a major structural upgrade of the CF fleet of 22 Lockheed C-130E Hercules, as described in the 1989-90 and previous editions of *Jane's*. In addition, two new C-130H-84 and two used C-130H-73 aircraft, purchased by the CF, underwent extensive avionics upgrading, modification, repair and repaint to achieve commonality with the remainder of the fleet. A progressive structural inspection (PSI) programme for CF C-130s, begun in Autumn 1987, will result in the complete fleet being cycled through NWI every three years. Depot level inspection and repair, as well as sampling inspections, will continue to be carried out on CF T-33A Silver Star jet trainers. A prototype rewiring programme on CL-41 (CT-114) Tutor jet trainers was being developed for installation in 1991. This activity, together with a depot level inspection and repair, avionics update, windscreen replacement and operation load monitoring programmes, will be combined into a complete fleet initiative starting in late 1993.

CHILE

CARDOEN
INDUSTRIAS CARDOEN LTDA

HEADQUARTERS: Aeropuerto Los Cerrillos, Los Conquistadores 1700, Piso 28, Santiago
Telephone: 56 (2) 2313420
Fax: 56 (2) 2316366
Telex: 340997 INCAR CK
WORKS: Planta Macul, Exequiel Fernandez 3397, Santiago
Telephone: 56 (2) 5574513 or 5573828
Fax: 56 (2) 5574513
Telex: 241377 INCAR CK
PROJECT MANAGER, CB 206L-III: Rene M. Gonzalez

Cardoen has been well known for many years as a major manufacturer of weapons and other military equipment. It is currently developing a multi-purpose helicopter based on the Bell LongRanger.

CARDOEN CB 206L-III

Development of this modified variant of the Bell LongRanger began in 1988, replacing an earlier abortive proposal to undertake a similar conversion based on the use of an MBB BO 105 airframe. Bell Helicopter Textron, which currently produces the LongRanger at its Canadian facility, has not (apart from a preliminary design study) been involved in the Cardoen programme. Modification, using imported civil Bell 206L-IIIs, began in August 1989, and the first of two converted aircraft made its first flight on 8 December that year.

Changes mainly concern the front fuselage, which has a narrower cross-section with flat-plate cockpit transparencies, an indication of the project's intended potential as a gunship. However, Cardoen says that the stronger cockpit structure and symmetrical field of view should also make the CB 206L-III suited for FLIR training, anti-drug patrol, cropdusting, firefighting, police work, powerline inspection and highway survey work. The first prototype, at least initially, is unarmed, and no details of any proposed armament have been received.

One prototype was despatched in early 1990 to Global Helicopter Technologies in Texas, USA, to undergo trials for civil certification under FAR Pt 27. These trials were completed satisfactorily, but the FAA was reported in early 1991 to have said that it did not plan to issue a type certificate because of possible involvement of Iraq in the programme. Cardoen insists that it has no intention of supplying the CB 206L-III to Iraq and that, even if it did, the absence of a US type certificate would not be a barrier to such a sale.

TYPE: Six-seat multi-purpose light helicopter.
ROTOR SYSTEM: Two-blade all-metal semi-rigid main rotor, bolted to hub, and two-blade tail rotor. No blade or tail folding; no rotor brake. Main rotor/engine rpm ratio 394 : 6,016.
FUSELAGE: Aluminium alloy semi-monocoque fail-safe structure.
LANDING GEAR: Skid type.

Prototype of the Cardoen CB 206L-III multi-purpose helicopter

POWER PLANT: One Allison 250-C30P turboshaft, with max rating of 485 kW (650 shp). Max internal fuel capacity 372.5 litres (98.4 US gallons; 82 Imp gallons).
ACCOMMODATION: Pilot only in cockpit; up to five passengers in main cabin. Forward opening door on each side.
SYSTEMS: Single-pump hydraulic system, operating at pressure of 41.37 bars (600 lb/sq in); capacity 4.7 litres (1.25 US gallons; 1.04 Imp gallons), plus 0.5 litre (1 US pint; 0.8 Imp pint) in reservoir. 28V DC electrical system, with 30V 150A starter/generator and 13Ah nickel-cadmium battery.
AVIONICS: Prototype fitted with Bendix/King VHF com, VOR and ATC transponder. Blind-flying instrumentation standard.

DIMENSIONS, EXTERNAL:
Main rotor diameter	11.28 m (37 ft 0 in)
Tail rotor diameter	1.65 m (5 ft 5 in)
Length: overall, rotors turning	12.95 m (42 ft 6 in)
fuselage, excl rotors	10.49 m (34 ft 5 in)
Height to top of rotor head	3.66 m (12 ft 0 in)
Tailplane span	1.98 m (6 ft 6 in)
Cabin doors (each): Height	0.58 m (1 ft 11 in)
Width	0.94 m (3 ft 1 in)
Baggage door: Height	0.55 m (1 ft 9½ in)
Width	1.07 m (3 ft 6 in)

DIMENSIONS, INTERNAL:
Cabin, excl flight deck: Max width	1.19 m (3 ft 10¾ in)
Max height	1.16 m (3 ft 9½ in)
Floor area	0.98 m² (10.57 sq ft)
Volume	0.82 m³ (29.0 cu ft)

AREAS:
Main rotor disc	99.89 m² (1,075.2 sq ft)
Tail rotor disc	2.14 m² (23.04 sq ft)

WEIGHTS AND LOADINGS:
Weight empty, equipped	1,095 kg (2,414 lb)
Max payload	approx 454 kg (1,000 lb)
Max fuel weight	299 kg (659 lb)
Max T-O weight: normal	1,882 kg (4,150 lb)
with external load	1,928 kg (4,250 lb)
Max disc loading:	
normal max T-O weight	18.85 kg/m² (3.86 lb/sq ft)
with external load	19.29 kg/m² (3.95 lb/sq ft)

PERFORMANCE (at max T-O weight, ISA):
Never-exceed speed (VNE) at S/L	
	130 knots (241 km/h; 149 mph)
Max cruising speed at S/L	
	112 knots (207 km/h; 129 mph)
Max rate of climb at S/L	408 m (1,340 ft)/min
Service ceiling	6,100 m (20,000 ft)
Hovering ceiling: IGE	5,030 m (16,500 ft)
OGE	1,645 m (5,400 ft)
Range at S/L with max fuel	
	322 nm (596 km; 370 miles)
Max loiter endurance	3 h 42 min

ENAER
EMPRESA NACIONAL DE AERONÁUTICA DE CHILE

Avenida José Miguel Carrera 11087, P. 36 ½, Santiago
Telephone: 56 (2) 5282735 and 5282823
Fax: 56 (2) 5282815
Telex: 645115 ENAER CT
PRESIDENT: Caupolicán Boisset
DIRECTOR OF MARKETING: Alejandro Vargas

ENAER is a state owned company which was formed in 1984 from the IndAer industrial organisation set up by the Chilean Air Force in 1980. Aircraft manufacturing started in 1980 with the assembly of 27 Piper PA-28 Dakota light aircraft for Chilean Air Force and flying club use. With a 1989 workforce of about 1,900 people, ENAER's current activities are the design and production of aircraft and electronic warfare equipment.

ENAER's major current programmes are the T-35 Pillán trainer and T-36/A-36 Halcón (CASA C-101) jet trainer/attack aircraft, plus development of Chile's first lightplane of indigenous design, the Namcu (Eaglet). It also undertakes upgrade programmes for the Chilean Air Force which have included conversion of Beechcraft 99s for maritime surveillance (see 1987-88 *Jane's*) and retrofitting FACh Hawker Hunters with a Caiquen II radar warning receiver system. Latest such programme is the Pantera, an airframe/avionics upgrade for the service's Mirage 50s.

ENAER T-35 PILLÁN (DEVIL)
Spanish Air Force designation: E.26 Tamiz

The Pillán tandem two-seat, fully aerobatic aircraft for basic, intermediate and instrument flying training is cleared to FAR Pt 23 (Aerobatic category) and military standards. Design was based on the Piper Cherokee series, utilising in particular many components of the PA-28 Dakota and PA-32 Saratoga.

Two prototypes were developed by Piper, the first of these making its initial flight on 6 March 1981 and the

Prototype of the T-35S single-seat aerobatic version of the Pillán

second at the end of that year. Three kits were then delivered by Piper for assembly by ENAER: the first of these (FACh serial number 101) flew on 30 January 1982 and the third in September of that year. After replacement of the original all-moving tailplane by an electrically trimmable tailplane with a conventional elevator, increasing rudder mass balance and deepening the canopy, series production began in September 1984.

The following versions have been built:

T-35A: Primary trainer version for Chilean Air Force (60 ordered, including the three assembled from Piper kits). First flight 28 December 1984, first delivery (two aircraft)

31 July 1985. All (and all T-35Bs) delivered by Spring 1990. In service with Escuela de Aviación Capitan Avalos at El Bosque, Santiago.

T-35B: Instrument trainer version for Chilean Air Force (20 delivered), with more comprehensive instrumentation.

T-35C: Primary trainer version for Spanish Air Force (40), first flown on 12 May 1986. These have the Spanish designation **E.26 Tamiz**, and were assembled by CASA (which see) from components supplied by ENAER. Kit deliveries to CASA began on 27 December 1985 and were completed in September 1987. One replacement aircraft supplied subsequently. All are now in service.

T-35D: Instrument trainer version for Panamanian Air Force: 10 delivered in 1988-89.

T-35S: Single-seat version, first flown (CC-PZB) on 5 March 1988 with IO-540-K1K5 piston engine; 313 kW (420 shp) Allison 250-B17 turboprop intended for production version. Prototype evaluation continuing in 1990.

T-35T Aucán: Turboprop version, described in 1988-89 *Jane's*. Prototype only (CC-PZC); since modified to have new one-piece canopy, opening sideways to starboard, oxygen system, and some new avionics. Now known as **Turbo Pillán**; being offered in military armed trainer market. Soloy Conversions (see US section) was awarded a 1990 contract to develop a production-ready modification kit for existing T-35s, based on the 313 kW (420 shp) Allison 250-B17D turboprop.

The following description applies to the basic T-35A except where indicated:

TYPE: Two-seat fully aerobatic basic (T-35A/C) and instrument (T-35B/D) military trainer.

WINGS: Cantilever low-wing monoplane. Wing section NACA 65_2-415 on constant chord inboard panels, NACA 65_2-415 (modified) at tips. Dihedral 7°. Incidence 2° at root, −0° 30′ at tip. Single-spar fail-safe structure of light alloy, steel and glassfibre, with components mainly from PA-28-236 Dakota (leading-edges) and PA-32R-301 Saratoga (trailing-edges), modified to shorter span. Slotted aluminium ailerons and electrically operated single-slotted trailing-edge flaps of riveted construction, identical to those of Saratoga. Electrically actuated trim tab in port aileron.

FUSELAGE: Semi-monocoque fail-safe structure of aluminium alloy frames and longerons, with riveted skin. Tailcone assembled from Cherokee components, modified to fit narrower fuselage. Two-piece engine cowling of GFRP.

TAIL UNIT: Cantilever structure of light alloy with sweptback (38° 43′) vertical surfaces, identical to those of Dakota except for heavier gauge skins, minor reinforcement of fin, and increased rudder mass balance. One-piece non-swept variable incidence tailplane, with electric trim and glassfibre tips. Full span mass balanced elevator. Tailplane incorporates some standard PA-28 (Dakota) and PA-31 (Navajo/Cheyenne) components; elevator is of all-new design. No tabs; rudder trimmed electrically.

LANDING GEAR: Hydraulically retractable tricycle type, with single wheel on each unit. Main gear legs and doors identical to those on PA-32R-301; nose gear assembled from PA-32R-301 and PA-28R-200 components. Main units retract inward, steerable nosewheel rearward. Piper oleo-pneumatic shock absorber in each unit. Emergency free-fall extension. Cleveland mainwheels and McCreary tyres size 6.00-6 (8 ply), nosewheel and tyre size 5.00-5 (6 ply). Tyre pressures: 2.62 bars (38 lb/sq in) on mainwheels, 2.41 bars (35 lb/sq in) on nosewheel. Single-disc aircooled hydraulic brake on each mainwheel. Parking brake.

POWER PLANT: One 224 kW (300 hp) Textron Lycoming IO-540-K1K5 flat-six engine, driving a Hartzell HC-C3YR-4BF/FC7663R three-blade constant-speed metal propeller. Fuel contained in two integral aluminium tanks in wing leading-edges, total capacity 291.5 litres (77 US gallons; 64.1 Imp gallons), of which 272.5 litres (72 US gallons; 60 Imp gallons) are usable. Overwing gravity refuelling point on each wing. Oil capacity 11.4 litres (3 US gallons; 2.5 Imp gallons). Fuel and oil systems permit unlimited inverted flight (up to 40 min flight tested).

ACCOMMODATION: Vertically adjustable seats for two persons, with seat belts and shoulder harnesses, in tandem beneath one-piece transparent jettisonable canopy which opens sideways to starboard. One-piece acrylic windscreen, and one-piece window in glassfibre fairing aft of canopy. Rear (instructor's) seat 22 cm (8.7 in) higher than front seat. Dual controls standard. Baggage compartment aft of rear cockpit, with external access on port side. Cockpits ventilated; cockpit heating and canopy demisting are by engine bleed air.

SYSTEMS: Electrically operated hydraulic system, at 124 bars (1,800 lb/sq in) pressure for landing gear retraction and 44.8 bars (650 lb/sq in) for gear extension; separate system at 20.7 bars (300 lb/sq in) for wheel brakes. Electrical system is 24V DC, powered by a 28V 70A engine driven Prestolite alternator and 24V 10Ah battery, with an inverter for AC power at 400Hz to operate RMIs and attitude indicators. External power socket. No oxygen or de-icing provisions.

AVIONICS: (*T-35A*): Two Collins VHF-251 com transceivers, two Collins AMR-350 audio panels, one Clark Isocom, and one each Collins VIR-351 VOR, ADF-650A and TOR-950 IFF. (*T-35C*): One Bendix/King KTR 908, two

ENAER T-35B Pillán instrument trainer of the Chilean Air Force

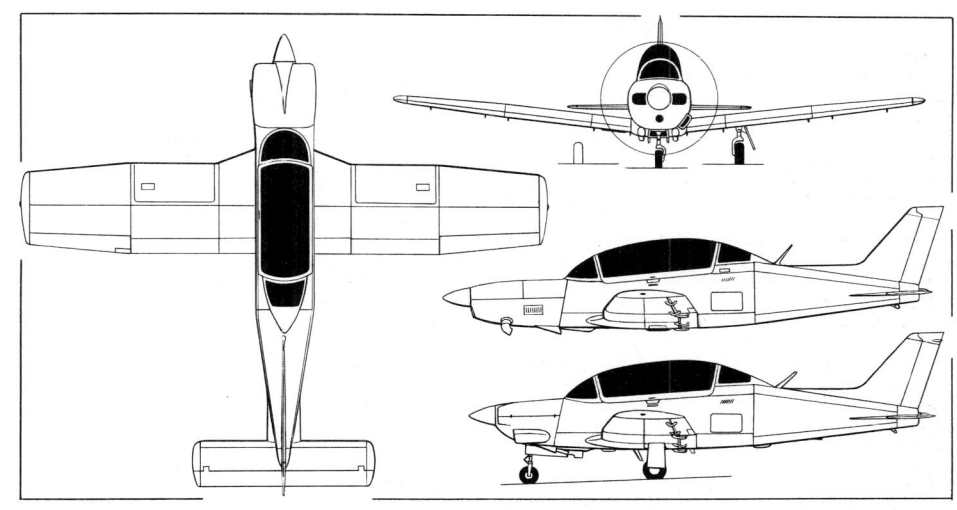

ENAER T-35 Pillán tandem two-seat basic/intermediate trainer with additional side view (centre) of Turbo Pillán (*Pilot Press*)

KFS 598A control units, two KMA 244 audio panels and two KR 87 ADF. Blind-flying instrumentation and full IFR capability in T-35B and D.

DIMENSIONS, EXTERNAL:	
Wing span	8.84 m (29 ft 0 in)
Wing chord: at root	1.88 m (6 ft 2 in)
at tip	1.26 m (4 ft 1½ in)
inboard, constant	1.60 m (5 ft 3 in)
mean aerodynamic	1.55 m (5 ft 1 in)
Wing aspect ratio	5.7
Length overall	8.00 m (26 ft 3 in)
Height overall	2.64 m (8 ft 8 in)
Fuselage: Length	7.66 m (25 ft 1¾ in)
Max width	0.86 m (2 ft 9¾ in)
Max depth	1.56 m (5 ft 1¼ in)
Tailplane span	3.05 m (10 ft 0 in)
Wheel track	3.02 m (9 ft 11 in)
Wheelbase	2.09 m (6 ft 10¼ in)
Propeller diameter	1.93 m (6 ft 4 in)
DIMENSIONS, INTERNAL:	
Cockpit: Length	3.24 m (10 ft 7½ in)
Max width	1.04 m (3 ft 5 in)
Max height	1.48 m (4 ft 10¼ in)
AREAS:	
Wings, gross	13.69 m² (147.34 sq ft)
Ailerons (total)	1.135 m² (12.22 sq ft)
Trailing-edge flaps (total)	1.36 m² (14.64 sq ft)
Fin	0.69 m² (7.43 sq ft)
Rudder	0.38 m² (4.09 sq ft)
Tailplane	1.57 m² (16.90 sq ft)
Elevator	0.77 m² (8.29 sq ft)
WEIGHTS AND LOADINGS:	
Weight empty, equipped	930 kg (2,050 lb)
Fuel	210 kg (462 lb)
Max aerobatic T-O weight	1,315 kg (2,900 lb)
Max T-O and landing weight	1,338 kg (2,950 lb)
Max wing loading	97.73 kg/m² (20.03 lb/sq ft)
Max power loading	5.98 kg/kW (9.83 lb/hp)
PERFORMANCE (at max T-O and landing weight, ISA):	
Never-exceed speed (VNE)	
	241 knots (446 km/h; 277 mph)
Max level speed at S/L	168 knots (311 km/h; 193 mph)
Cruising speed:	
75% power at 2,680 m (8,800 ft)	
	144 knots (266 km/h; 166 mph) IAS

55% power at 5,120 m (16,800 ft)

	138 knots (255 km/h; 159 mph) IAS
Max speed for flap extension	
	118 knots (218 km/h; 136 mph) IAS
Max speed for landing gear extension	
	138 knots (256 km/h; 159 mph) IAS
Approach speed over 15 m (50 ft) obstacle	
	80 knots (148 km/h; 92 mph)
Landing speed	65 knots (120 km/h; 75 mph)
Stalling speed: flaps up	67 knots (125 km/h; 78 mph)
flaps down	62 knots (115 km/h; 72 mph)
Max rate of climb at S/L	465 m (1,525 ft)/min
Time to: 1,830 m (6,000 ft)	4 min 42 s
3,050 m (10,000 ft)	8 min 48 s
Service ceiling	5,840 m (19,160 ft)
Absolute ceiling	6,250 m (20,500 ft)
T-O run	287 m (940 ft)
T-O to 15 m (50 ft)	494 m (1,620 ft)
Landing from 15 m (50 ft)	509 m (1,670 ft)
Landing run	238 m (780 ft)
Min ground turning radius	6.20 m (20 ft 4 in)
Range with 45 min reserves:	
75% power at 2,440 m (8,000 ft)	
	590 nm (1,093 km; 679 miles)
55% power at 3,660 m (12,000 ft)	
	650 nm (1,204 km; 748 miles)
Range, no reserves:	
75% power at 2,440 m (8,000 ft)	
	680 nm (1,260 km; 783 miles)
55% power at 3,660 m (12,000 ft)	
	735 nm (1,362 km; 846 miles)
Endurance at S/L: 75% power	4 h 24 min
55% power	5 h 36 min
g limits	+6/−3

ENAER T-36/A-36 HALCÓN (HAWK)

In 1980 the Chilean Air Force (FACh) ordered 14 C-101 Aviojet trainers from CASA of Spain, the contract including a licence for local manufacture by ENAER in a progressive programme advancing from assembly of CASA built components to partial manufacture of major components in Chile. The first four were built in Spain as C-101BB-02s, then delivered to the FACh to serve as

ENAER A-36 Halcón in Fuerza Aérea de Chile insignia *(Kenneth Munson)*

pattern aircraft in organising the production line. A further 10 of this version were completed by ENAER.

Designated **T-36** Halcón by the FACh, the C-101BB-02 differs from the Spanish Air Force C-101EB in having a more powerful (16.46 kN; 3,700 lb st) Garrett TFE731-3 turbofan instead of the 15.57 kN (3,500 lb st) TFE731-2. Deliveries began in late 1983; they are in service with the Escuela de Aviación Capitan Avalos at El Bosque, Santiago.

During 1982 ENAER and CASA initiated a programme to develop an attack version of the C-101 with a higher thrust turbofan. Designated C-101CC-02 by CASA and **A-36** by the FACh, this flew for the first time in November 1983. Chile ordered 23 of this version, to replace the Cessna A-37 in FACh service. The A-36 is powered by a TFE731-5 of 19.13 kN (4,300 lb st), with a military power reserve (MPR) system which allows the thrust to be increased to 20.91 kN (4,700 lb).

Four of the C-101CC-02s/A-36s from the follow-on order are Spanish built aircraft; the remaining 19, built by ENAER, entered phase 3B (Chilean manufacture of electrical and hydraulic systems and small subassemblies) in the third quarter of 1989 with aircraft serial number 417; final stage for ENAER is phase 4 (manufacture of front fuselage). The A-36 is in service with the 1° Squadron of Brigada Aérea I at Los Cóndores, in northern Chile, and the 12° Squadron of Brigada Aérea IV at Carlos Ibáñez air base in the extreme south.

ENAER PANTERA 50C

With technical assistance from Israel Aircraft Industries, ENAER is to upgrade the Chilean Air Force's 16 Dassault Mirage 50s (eight 50FCs, six 50CHs and two 50DCHs), serving with the 4° Squadron of Brigada Aérea IV at Carlos Ibánez, by fitting them with non-moving canard surfaces, an inertial navigation system, computerised head-up display, modified electrical, hydraulic and armament control systems, ENAER Caiquen III radar warning receiver and Eclipse chaff/flare dispensing system. Flight testing, with foreplanes only, began in 1986. The first fully upgraded aircraft, known as Pantera (Panther) 50C, was rolled out in November 1988. The second Pantera was expected to be completed during 1990.

ENAER ÑAMCU (EAGLET)

Launched in June 1986 under the project name Avión Liviano (light aircraft), the Ñamcu was designed as a small, inexpensive club aircraft, initially for domestic use and later for export. Prototype construction began in February 1987. It has been designed for use also as a trainer, with full capability for aerobatic flying, and conforms to FAR Pt 23 in the Utility category.

The first ENAER aircraft of all-Chilean design, the prototype (CC-PZI) made its initial flight in April 1989. A second, similar prototype (CC-PZJ) was flown in early March 1990. The third, which will be fully aerobatic, may have a more powerful Textron Lycoming engine and variable-pitch propeller. It was hoped to begin series production of the Ñamcu in 1990.

TYPE: Two-seat light aircraft.

WINGS: Cantilever low-wing monoplane. Wing section NACA 63₃-415. Dihedral 5° from roots. Incidence 3° at root, 0° 30′ at tip. Tapered, non-swept all-composites structure (glassfibre/foam sandwich with carbonfibre spar caps). Plain trailing-edge flaps and plain ailerons also of glassfibre/foam sandwich construction.

FUSELAGE: All-composites stressed skin structure of glassfibre/foam sandwich, with four bulkheads.

TAIL UNIT: Conventional assembly, with swept vertical and non-swept horizontal surfaces, of similar construction to wings. Balanced elevators and rudder; trim tab in starboard elevator.

LANDING GEAR: Non-retractable tricycle type. Cantilever spring steel main units; steerable and self-centring nose unit, with oleo-pneumatic shock absorber and shimmy damper. Cleveland wheel and Goodyear 6-ply tyre on each unit; all three tyres size 5.00-5. Cleveland hydraulic mainwheel disc brakes.

POWER PLANT: One 86.5 kW (116 hp) Textron Lycoming O-235-N2C flat-four engine, driving an MT 178 R115-2C two-blade fixed-pitch wooden propeller. Integral fuel tank in each wing leading-edge, combined capacity 100 litres (26.4 US gallons; 22 Imp gallons); overwing gravity fuelling point for each tank.

ACCOMMODATION: Seats for two persons side by side in fully enclosed cockpit, with adjustable headrests and four-piece safety harnesses. Dual controls. Two independent gull wing window/doors, hinged on centreline to open upward. Space for 10 kg (22 lb) of baggage aft of seats. Cockpit heated and ventilated. Electric defrosting of windscreen.

SYSTEMS: Hydraulic system for brakes only. Electrical power supplied by Prestolite 12V 70A alternator and 12V 35Ah lead-acid battery.

AVIONICS: VFR flight and engine instrumentation, Walter Dittel FSG 71M 760-channel VHF com transceiver, and intercom, are standard; IFR instrumentation optional.

DIMENSIONS, EXTERNAL:
Wing span	8.31 m (27 ft 3¼ in)
Wing chord: at root	1.53 m (5 ft 0¼ in)
at tip	0.84 m (2 ft 9 in)
Wing aspect ratio	7.6
Length overall	7.05 m (23 ft 1½ in)
Height overall	2.42 m (7 ft 11¼ in)
Tailplane span	3.00 m (9 ft 10 in)
Wheel track	2.54 m (8 ft 4 in)
Wheelbase	1.50 m (4 ft 11 in)
Propeller diameter	1.78 m (5 ft 10 in)

DIMENSIONS, INTERNAL:
Cockpit: Max width	1.16 m (3 ft 9½ in)

AREAS:
Wings, gross	10.01 m² (107.75 sq ft)
Ailerons (total)	0.44 m² (4.74 sq ft)
Trailing-edge flaps (total)	0.92 m² (9.90 sq ft)
Fin	0.88 m² (9.47 sq ft)
Rudder	0.34 m² (3.66 sq ft)
Tailplane	2.08 m² (22.39 sq ft)
Elevators (total)	0.76 m² (8.18 sq ft)

WEIGHTS AND LOADINGS:
Basic weight empty	546 kg (1,204 lb)
Max fuel	72 kg (159 lb)
Max T-O and landing weight	800 kg (1,763 lb)
Max wing loading	79.92 kg/m² (16.38 lb/sq ft)
Max power loading	9.25 kg/kW (15.20 lb/hp)

PERFORMANCE (at max T-O weight except where indicated):
Never-exceed speed (VNE)	177 knots (328 km/h; 204 mph)
Max level speed at S/L	127 knots (235 km/h; 146 mph)
Max cruising speed, 75% power at 2,440 m (8,000 ft)	103 knots (191 km/h; 119 mph)
Stalling speed, power off:	
flaps up	56 knots (104 km/h; 65 mph)
flaps down	50 knots (93 km/h; 58 mph)
Max rate of climb at S/L	295 m (968 ft)/min
Service ceiling	4,270 m (14,000 ft)
T-O run	304 m (998 ft)
T-O to 15 m (50 ft)	412 m (1,352 ft)
Landing from 15 m (50 ft)	364 m (1,195 ft)
Landing run	177 m (581 ft)
Range at 75% power at 2,440 m (8,000 ft) with max fuel, 10% reserves	500 nm (926 km; 575 miles)
Endurance, conditions as above	3 h 40 min
g limits	+4.4/-2.2

First ENAER Pantera, a modified Mirage 50 with foreplanes and upgraded nav/attack system *(Kenneth Munson)*

Second prototype ENAER Ñamcu two-seat light aircraft *(Kenneth Munson)*

CHINA, PEOPLE'S REPUBLIC

MAS
MINISTRY OF AERO-SPACE INDUSTRY
PO Box 33, Beijing
Telephone: 86 (1) 4013322
Telex: 211244 MAS CN
MINISTER: Lin Zongtang
INTERNATIONAL MARKETING:
CATIC (China National Aero-Technology Import and Export Corporation)
5 Liang Guo Chang Road, East City District (PO Box 647), Beijing
Telephone: 86 (1) 442444
Fax: 86 (1) 4015381
Telex: 22318 AEROT CN
PRESIDENT: Sun Zhaoqing
EXECUTIVE VICE-PRESIDENTS
  Liu Guomin
  Dong Xiao
  Tang Xiaoping
  All Chinese aircraft factories function under the jurisdiction of the Ministry of Aero-Space Industry. There are

design and development centres at Shenyang, Beijing, Harbin and elsewhere. Xian, Chengdu, Shanghai, Shenyang, Harbin and other Chinese factories also carry out subcontract work on the Airbus A300, A310 and A320; ATR 42; BAe 146 and ATP; Boeing 737, 747 and 757; Boeing Canada Dash 8; Canadair CL-215; McDonnell Douglas MD-80 series; and Shorts 360. Total workforce of the aerospace industry was estimated at no fewer than 500,000 in 1990, although most of its factories are engaged also in manufacturing non-aerospace products.

Output of fighters and bombers is now diminishing, with increasing emphasis being placed on the development of new aircraft making use of China's growing technological capability. A reduction of 1 million personnel in China's armed forces manpower released more funds during the seventh Five-Year Plan (1986-90) for the purchase of modern weapons and technology, while at the same time shifting emphasis in the aviation industry towards a target of a 60-40 per cent bias in favour of civil aircraft production.

In addition to continuing with production and new versions of the Y-7, Y-8, Y-11 and Y-12, an international

partner is being sought for a 30/40-passenger commuter airliner programme (existing type or new design). A larger transport, designated MPC 75, is being undertaken by CATIC and Deutsche Airbus of Germany (see MPC 75 entry in the International section). A 150-passenger 'Trunkliner' is being sought, for co-production and service entry in about 1996. Derivatives of the Boeing 737-300 and McDonnell Douglas MD90-30T have been proposed, and a selection was expected during 1991. Up to 150 of the selected type are said to be required.

Increasing attention is also being given to helicopter development. Current programmes include the Changhe Z-8, a Chinese derivative of the Aerospatiale Super Frelon, licence production at Harbin of the same company's Dauphin as the Z-9, and development (see International section) with Aerospatiale and Singapore Aerospace of the P 120L, a small (2,500 kg; 5,500 lb class) type for agricultural and forestry work. The latter could also fulfil a current requirement for a small military helicopter. The PLA is said to need about 50 for anti-tank duties.

CAC
CHENGDU AIRCRAFT CORPORATION
PO Box 800, Chengdu, Sichuan
Telephone: 86 (28) 669629
Fax: 86 (28) 669816
Telex: 60132 CCDAC CN
GENERAL MANAGER: Hou Janwu
DEPUTY GENERAL MANAGER: Li Shaoming
  Founded in 1958, Chengdu Aircraft Corporation is a major centre for the development and production of fighter aircraft. Current activity includes several models of the J-7/F-7 fighter series, and continuing limited batch production of the JJ-5/FT-5 fighter/trainer developed from the Soviet MiG-17. Chengdu is subcontracted by McDonnell Douglas of the USA to manufacture 100 nosecones for MD-80 series airliners, both for the Shanghai MD-82 programme (see SAMF entry in this section) and for the US production line; deliveries were scheduled to start in early 1991 and continue until 1993. The CAC facility occupies a site area of 510 ha (1,260 acres), and had a 1989 workforce of about 20,000. Output includes a number of non-aerospace products.

CAC (MIKOYAN) JJ-5
Chinese name: Jianjiji Jiaolianji-5 (Fighter training aircraft 5) or Jianjiao-5
Westernised designation: FT-5
  This tandem two-seat version of the J-5 (Chinese built MiG-17) was developed at Chengdu in 1965 and flew for the first time on 8 May 1966. In essence, it combines the tandem cockpits and forward fuselage of the MiG-15UTI with the rest of the airframe of the J-5A (Chinese MiG-17PF), though retaining the latter's lipped intake, the small fairing indicating provision for a radar ranging gunsight in the front cockpit. Other changes include use of a non-afterburning Xian (XAE) WP5D turbojet, rated at 26.48 kN (5,952 lb st); and reduction of the armament to a single Type 23-1 (23 mm) gun, carried in a removable belly pack, with the barrel to the starboard side of the nosewheel doors.

Certificated for mass production at the end of 1966, the JJ-5 is still the standard advanced trainer of the Chinese air forces, to which pupil pilots graduate after basic training on the NAMC CJ-6 (which see). A total of 1,061 had been built by the end of 1986, and limited batch production was continuing in 1989-90. More than 100, designated FT-5, have been exported to Bangladesh, Pakistan, Sudan and Tanzania.

WEIGHTS AND LOADINGS:
Weight empty, equipped	4,080 kg (8,995 lb)
Normal T-O weight	5,401 kg (11,907 lb)
Max T-O weight	6,215 kg (13,700 lb)

PERFORMANCE:
Normal operating speed	418 knots (775 km/h; 482 mph)
Max rate of climb at S/L	1,620 m (5,315 ft)/min
Service ceiling	14,300 m (46,900 ft)
T-O run	760 m (2,493 ft)
Landing run	780-830 m (2,559-2,723 ft)
Range with max fuel at 12,000 m (39,370 ft)	664 nm (1,230 km; 764 miles)
Max endurance at 13,700 m (45,000 ft) with two 400 litre (105.5 US gallon; 88 Imp gallon) drop tanks	2 h 38 min

CAC (MIKOYAN) J-7
Chinese name: Jianjiji-7 (Fighter aircraft 7) or Jian-7
Westernised designations: F-7A, F-7B, F-7M, F-7MP, F-7P and F7-3
NATO reporting name: Fishbed
  A Soviet licence to manufacture the MiG-21F-13 fighter and its Tumansky R-11F-300 engine was granted to the Chinese government in 1961, and some pattern aircraft and CKD (component knocked-down) kits for both were

J-7 III Chinese equivalent of the MiG-21MF 'Fishbed-J'

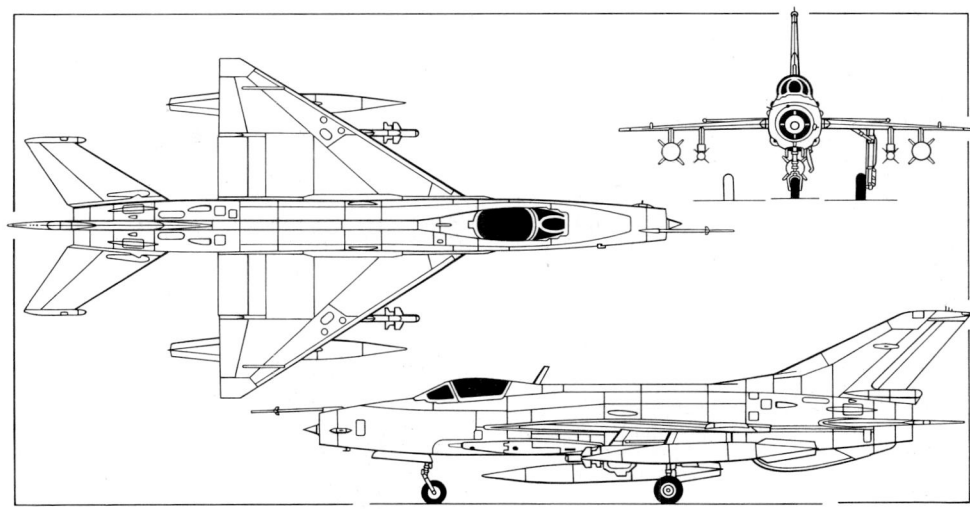

Chengdu F-7M Airguard single-seat fighter and close support aircraft *(Jane's/Mike Keep)*

delivered, but due to the severing of relations between the two countries the necessary technical documentation was not completed. Assembly of the first J-7, at Shenyang, thus did not begin until early 1964, and the first flight of this aircraft eventually took place on 17 January 1966. Static testing had by then been completed (in November 1965), and approval for production was granted in June 1967. Earlier, in 1964-65, it had been planned to make factories at Chengdu and Guizhou the main centres for J-7 airframe and engine production, backed up by Shenyang until the former two locations were fully productive. However, the planned programme was seriously affected by the onset of the cultural revolution, at which time relatively few examples of the original J-7 had been delivered by Shenyang. Some of this version were supplied (as **F-7A**) to Albania and Tanzania.

The following subsequent variants have been developed by Chengdu:

J-7 I: Initial Chengdu production version for PLA Air Force (1967). Not accepted in large numbers, due mainly to unsatisfactory escape system (front-hinged canopy, to which ejection seat was attached).

F-7B: Export counterpart of J-7 I, supplied to Egypt and Iraq.

J-7 II: Much modified and improved development of J-7 I, with WP7B turbojet of increased thrust (43.15 kN; 9,700 lb st dry, 59.82 kN; 13,448 lb st with afterburning); variable intake shock cone; 720 litre (190.2 US gallon; 158.4 Imp gallon) centreline drop tank for increased range; brake-chute relocated at base of rudder to improve landing performance and shorten run; rear-hinged canopy, jettisoned before ejection seat deploys; new Chengdu Type II seat offering ejection at zero height and speeds down to 135 knots (250 km/h; 155 mph); second 30 mm gun; and new Lanzhou compass system. Development began 1975; first flight 30 December 1978. Approved for

Chengdu F-7P strike fighters of No. 19 Squadron of the Pakistan Air Force at Mianwali *(Lindsay Peacock)*

production in September 1979. In service. Small batch production (14 in 1989) is continuing.

F-7M Airguard: Upgraded export version, developed from J-7 II and equipped with GEC Avionics HUDWAC (head-up display and weapon aiming computer); new ranging radar, air data computer, radar altimeter and IFF; more secure com radio; improved electrical power generation system to cater for the new avionics; two additional underwing stores points; an improved WP7B (BM) engine; birdproof windscreen; strengthened landing gear; ability to carry PL-7 air-to-air missiles; and a relocated nose probe. Development began in 1981, and production approval was issued in December 1984. Supplied to Pakistan (60, from 1986), Bangladesh (16), Iran (12-18 or more) and Zimbabwe (48). In production.

F-7P Airguard: Variant of F-7M, embodying 24 modifications to meet specific requirements of Pakistan Air Force, in particular the ability to carry four air-to-air missiles (Sidewinders) underwing instead of two. Martin-Baker Mk 10L ejection seat. Otherwise identical to F-7M. Eighty ordered, of which 75 delivered by February 1991.

F-7MP: Variant of F-7P. Improved cockpit layout and navigation system incorporating Collins AN/ARN-147 VOR/ILS receiver, AN/ARN-149 ADF and Pro Line II digital DME-42.

J-7 III: Chinese equivalent of MiG-21MF, much redesigned from J-7 II with blown flaps and all-weather, day/night capability. Main improvements are more powerful WP13 engine (40.21 kN; 9,039 lb st dry, 64.72 kN; 14,550 lb st with afterburning); additional fuel in deeper dorsal spine; JL-7 (J-band) interception radar, with correspondingly larger nose intake and centrebody radome; sideways opening (to starboard) canopy, with centrally located rearview mirror; improved HTY-4 low-speed/zero height ejection seat; more advanced fire control system; twin-barrel 23 mm gun under fuselage (with HK-03D optical gunsight); broader-chord vertical tail surfaces, incorporating antennae for LJ-2 omnidirectional radar warning receiver; increased weapon/stores capability (four underwing stations), similar to that of F-7M; GT-4 ECM jammer; FJ-1 flight data recorder; Type 605A IFF; angle of attack vane and air data probe similar to those of F-7M; and a Beijing Aeronautical Instruments Factory KJ-11 twin-channel autopilot. Joint development by Chengdu and Guizhou (GAIC); design began in 1981, and first flight was made on 26 April 1984. In production and service. Normal max T-O weight 8,150 kg (17,967 lb); see Armament and Performance headings for further details.

F7-3: Export version of J-7 III.

J-7E: Latest version, with redesigned wing. Reportedly due to fly in April 1990: no other details known at time of going to press.

Super-7: Proposed export development of F-7M; described separately.

JJ-7/FT-7: Tandem two-seat operational trainer, based on J-7 II. Developed at Guizhou and described under GAIC entry.

Total exports of the F-7 (all models) have exceeded 500. Current Soviet versions of the MiG-21 are fully described and illustrated in the USSR section of this edition. The following description applies to the standard Chengdu F-7M except where indicated:

TYPE: Single-seat day fighter and close support aircraft.

WINGS: As for standard MiG-21, with 57° sweepback on leading-edges, 2° anhedral, slotted flaps and balanced ailerons. Blown flap system on J-7 III/F7-3.

FUSELAGE: Generally as MiG-21F except for automatically operated, continuously adjustable shock cone in centre of nose intake. Nose probe relocated above intake, offset to starboard.

TAIL UNIT: All-swept surfaces, with all-moving tailplane, as for MiG-21.

LANDING GEAR: Inward retracting mainwheels, with 660 × 220 tyres and LS-16 disc brakes; forward retracting nosewheel, with 500 × 180 tyre and LS-15 double-acting brake. Tail braking parachute at base of vertical tail.

POWER PLANT: One Chengdu WP7B(BM) turbojet (43.15 kN; 9,700 lb st dry, 59.82 kN; 13,448 lb st with afterburning) in F-7M; WP13 turbojet in J-7 III/F7-3 (see variant paragraph for details). Total internal fuel capacity of 2,385 litres (630 US gallons; 524.5 Imp

gallons), contained in six flexible tanks in fuselage and two integral tanks in each wing. Provision for carrying a 480 or 720 litre (127 or 190.2 US gallon; 105.6 or 158.4 Imp gallon) centreline drop tank, and/or a 480 litre drop tank on each outboard underwing pylon. Max possible internal/external fuel capacity 4,065 litres (1,074 US gallons; 894 Imp gallons).

ACCOMMODATION: Pilot only, on Chengdu Aircraft Corporation zero-height/low-speed ejection seat operable between 70 and 459 knots (130-850 km/h; 81-528 mph) IAS. One-piece canopy, hinged at rear to open upward. J-7 III/F7-3 canopy opens sideways to starboard.

SYSTEMS: Improved electrical system, using three static inverters, to cater for additional avionics. Jianghuai YX-3 oxygen system.

AVIONICS: GEC Avionics suite includes Type 956 HUDWAC, AD 3400 two-band UHF/VHF multi-function com system, Type 226 Skyranger ranging radar with ECCM, and an air data computer. Other avionics include Chinese Type 602 IFF transponder, Type 0101 HR A/2 radar altimeter, WL-7 radio compass, and XS-6A marker beacon receiver. The HUDWAC (head-up display and weapon aiming computer) provides the pilot with displays for instrument flying, with air-to-air and air-to-ground weapon aiming symbols integrated with flight-instrument symbology. It can store 32 weapon parameter functions, allowing for both current and future weapon variants. In air-to-air combat its four modes (missiles, conventional gunnery, snapshoot gunnery, dogfight and standby aiming reticle) allow for all eventualities. The navigation function includes an approach mode.

ARMAMENT (F-7M): Two 30 mm Type 30-1 belt-fed cannon, with 60 rds/gun, in fairings under front fuselage just forward of wingroot leading-edges. Two hardpoints under each wing, of which the outer ones are wet for the carriage of drop tanks only. The centreline pylon is used for a drop tank only. Each inboard pylon is capable of carrying a PL-2, -2A, -5B or -7 missile or, at customer's option, a Matra R.550 Magic; one 18-tube pod of Type 57-2 (57 mm) air-to-air and air-to-ground rockets; one Type 90-1 (90 mm) 7-tube pod of air-to-ground rockets; or a 50, 150, 250 or 500 kg bomb. Each outboard pylon can carry one of the above rocket pods, a 50 or 150 kg bomb, or a 480 litre drop tank.

ARMAMENT (F7-3 and J-7 III): One 23 mm Type 23-3 twin-barrel cannon in ventral pack. Five external stores stations can carry two to four PL-5B air-launched missiles; or four 12-round launchers for Type 57-2 or seven-round pods of Type 90-1 rockets; or two 500 kg, four 250 kg or ten 100 kg bombs, in various combinations with 480 litre (one centreline and/or one under each wing) or 720 litre (underfuselage station only) drop tanks.

DIMENSIONS, EXTERNAL:

Wing span	7.154 m (23 ft 5⅝ in)
Wing aspect ratio	2.2
Length overall: excl nose probe	13.945 m (45 ft 9 in)
incl nose probe	14.885 m (48 ft 10 in)
Height overall	4.103 m (13 ft 5½ in)
Tailplane span	3.74 m (12 ft 3¼ in)

Wheel track	2.692 m (8 ft 10 in)
Wheelbase	4.807 m (15 ft 9¼ in)

AREAS:

Wings, gross	23.00 m² (247.6 sq ft)

WEIGHTS AND LOADINGS:

Weight empty	5,275 kg (11,629 lb)
Normal max T-O weight with two PL-2 or PL-7 air-to-air missiles	7,531 kg (16,603 lb)
Wing loading at normal max T-O weight	327.43 kg/m² (67.10 lb/sq ft)
Power loading at normal max T-O weight	125.5 kg/kN (1.23 lb/lb st)

PERFORMANCE (at normal max T-O weight with two PL-2 or PL-7 air-to-air missiles, except where indicated):

Max level speed between 12,500 and 18,500 m (41,010-60,700 ft)	Mach 2.05 (1,175 knots; 2,175 km/h; 1,350 mph)
Unstick speed	167-178 knots (310-330 km/h; 193-205 mph)
Touchdown speed	162-173 knots (300-320 km/h; 186-199 mph)
Max rate of climb at S/L	10,800 m (35,435 ft)/min
Acceleration from Mach 0.9 to 1.2 at 5,000 m (16,400 ft)	35 s
Max sustained turn rate: Mach 0.7 at S/L	14.7°/s
Mach 0.8 at 5,000 m (16,400 ft)	9.5°/s
Service ceiling	18,200 m (59,710 ft)
Absolute ceiling	18,700 m (61,350 ft)
T-O run	700-950 m (2,297-3,117 ft)
Landing run with brake-chute	600-900 m (1,969-2,953 ft)

Typical mission profiles:
combat air patrol at 11,000 m (36,000 ft) with two air-to-air missiles and three 480 litre drop tanks, incl 5 min combat 45 min
long-range interception at 11,000 m (36,000 ft) at 351 nm (650 km; 404 miles) from base, incl Mach 1.5 dash and 5 min combat, stores as above
hi-lo-hi interdiction radius, out and back at 11,000 m (36,000 ft), with three 480 litre drop tanks and two 150 kg bombs 324 nm (600 km; 373 miles)
lo-lo-lo close air support radius with four rocket pods, no external tanks 200 nm (370 km; 230 miles)
Range: two PL-7 missiles and three 480 litre drop tanks 939 nm (1,740 km; 1,081 miles)
self-ferry with one 720 litre and two 480 litre drop tanks, no missiles 1,203 nm (2,230 km; 1,385 miles)

g limit	+8

PERFORMANCE (F7-3/J-7 III at normal max T-O weight of 8,150 kg; 17,967 lb):

Max operating Mach number	2.1
Unstick speed (with afterburning)	173 knots (320 km/h; 199 mph)
Touchdown speed (with flap blowing)	135-146 knots (250-270 km/h; 155-168 mph)
Min level flight speed	140 knots (260 km/h; 162 mph)
Max rate of climb at S/L	9,000 m (29,525 ft)/min
Service ceiling	18,000 m (59,050 ft)
Acceleration from Mach 1.2 to 1.9 at 13,000 m (42,650 ft)	3 min 27 s
Air turning radius at 5,000 m (16,400 ft) at Mach 1.2	5,093 m (16,710 ft)
T-O run (with afterburning)	800 m (2,625 ft)
Landing run (with flap blowing, drag-chute and brakes deployed)	550 m (1,805 ft)
Range: internal fuel only	518 nm (960 km; 596 miles)
with 720 litre belly tank	701 nm (1,300 km; 807 miles)
with 720 litre belly tank and two 480 litre underwing tanks	898 nm (1,664 km; 1,034 miles)
g limits: up to Mach 0.8	+8.5
above Mach 0.8	+7

CAC SUPER-7

An agreement signed on 21 October 1988 between CATIC and Grumman (USA), to produce a developed export version of the F-7M known as the Super-7, covered a preliminary design phase, which was completed by early 1990. The US government suspended Grumman

Model of the proposed Super-7 advanced development of the Chengdu F-7M *(Kenneth Munson)*

participation in mid-1989, but CATIC is understood to wish to continue the programme if a new partner can be found.

As proposed, the Super-7 would have lateral air intakes for a more powerful engine and a 'solid' ogival nosecone for a modern fire control radar, but other changes would be more extensive. The wings would be enlarged in span and area, fitted with leading-edge slats, and equipped with an additional pair of inboard hardpoints for air-to-air missiles. The fuselage would incorporate an enlarged dorsal spine to house additional fuel, single-point pressure refuelling, an easier-access engine compartment, an arrester hook and a

revised ventral fin. Strengthened main landing gear, with larger tyres, would be combined with a new straight-leg steerable nosewheel unit. The F-7M's two internal 30 mm cannon would be replaced by a belly mounted twin-barrel 23 mm gun. A new cockpit would incorporate a head-up display and a new ejection seat, and a revised environmental control system would cool the avionics. Phase 2 would involve the completion of three prototypes. Wind tunnel testing has been completed.

DIMENSIONS, EXTERNAL:

Wing span	7.92 m (26 ft 0 in)
Length overall	15.04 m (49 ft 4 in)

AREAS:

Wings, gross	approx 24.62 m² (265.0 sq ft)

WEIGHTS AND LOADINGS (estimated):

Design gross weight	8,800 kg (19,400 lb)
Max T-O weight	10,800 kg (23,810 lb)
Max wing loading	approx 438.7 kg/m² (89.85 lb/sq ft)

PERFORMANCE (estimated):

Max level speed	above Mach 1.8
Service ceiling	18,000 m (59,050 ft)

CAF
CHANGHE AIRCRAFT FACTORY

PO Box 109, Jingdezhen, Jiangxi
Telephone: 442019
Telex: 95027 CHAF CN
DIRECTOR: Li Wanxin

Changhe Aircraft Factory, built on a 234 ha (578 acre) site at Jingdezhen, began producing coaches and commercial road vehicles in 1974. These and other automotive products still account for most of its output, but since being placed under MAS jurisdiction it has developed a capability for batch production of helicopters and is one of three members (the others being Harbin Aircraft Manufacturing Co and the Helicopter Design and Research Institute) which form the China Helicopter Industry Corporation. CAF had a 1990 workforce of 5,700, of whom nearly 800 are engineers and technicians.

CAF Z-8
Chinese name: Zhishengji-8 (Vertical take-off aircraft 8) or Zhi-8

Design work on this Chinese equivalent of the Aerospatiale Super Frelon (see 1982-83 *Jane's*) began as long ago as 1975, but development was suspended between 1979 and mid-1984 and the first prototype did not make its initial flight until 11 December 1985. A second prototype was flown in October 1987. Domestic type approval of the Z-8 was granted on 8 April 1989, and on 5 August that year the first Z-8 was handed over to the PLA Naval Air Force for service trials. Initial production has been approved. Eventual applications are expected to include troop transport, ASW/ASV, search and rescue, minelaying/sweeping, aerial survey and firefighting.

TYPE: Multi-role military and civil helicopter.

ROTOR SYSTEM: Six-blade main rotor and five-blade tail rotor. Main rotor head consists basically of two six-armed star plates carrying the drag and flapping hinges for each blade. The root of each main rotor blade carries a fitting for pitch control, and each blade has an individual hydraulic drag damper. Gearboxes are manufactured by Zhongnan Transmission Machinery Factory.

FUSELAGE: Boat-hull fuselage of conventional semi-monocoque construction, with riveted watertight compartments inside planing bottom. Stabilising float attached to small stub-wing at rear on each side.

TAIL UNIT: Small, strut braced fixed horizontal stabiliser on starboard side of tail rotor pylon.

LANDING GEAR: Non-retractable tricycle type, with twin wheels and low-pressure oleo-pneumatic shock absorber on each unit. Small tripod tailskid under rear of tailboom. Boat hull and side floats permit emergency water landings and take-offs.

POWER PLANT: Three Changzhou (CLXMW) WZ6 turboshafts, each having a max emergency rating of 1,156 kW (1,550 shp) and 20 per cent power reserve at S/L, ISA. Two engines side by side in front of main rotor shaft and one aft of shaft. Fuel in flexible tanks under floor of centre fuselage. Auxiliary fuel tanks can be carried inside cabin for extended range or self-ferry missions.

Second prototype of the Changhe Z-8 three-turboshaft helicopter

ACCOMMODATION: Crew of two or three on flight deck. Fully redundant flight control system. Dong Fang KJ-8 autopilot. Accommodation in main cabin for up to 27 fully armed troops, or 39 without equipment; up to 15 stretchers and a medical attendant in ambulance configuration; a BJ-212 jeep and its crew; or other configurations according to mission. Entire accommodation heated, ventilated, soundproofed and vibration-proofed. Forward opening crew door on each side of flight deck. Rearward sliding door at front of cabin on starboard side. Hydraulically actuated rear loading ramp/door.

EQUIPMENT: Equipment for SAR role can include a 275 kg (606 lb) capacity hydraulic rescue hoist and two five-person liferafts. Can also be equipped with sonar, sonobuoys and torpedoes for ASW; with search radar and air-to-surface missiles for anti-shipping missions; with gear for minelaying (eight 250 kg mines) or minesweeping; or with appropriate equipment for oceanography, geological survey and forest firefighting.

DIMENSIONS, EXTERNAL:

Main rotor diameter	18.90 m (62 ft 0 in)
Tail rotor diameter	4.00 m (13 ft 1½ in)
Length overall, rotors turning	23.035 m (75 ft 7 in)
Height overall, rotors turning	6.66 m (21 ft 10¼ in)
Width over main gear sponsons	5.20 m (17 ft 0¾ in)

AREAS:

Main rotor disc	280.48 m² (3,019.1 sq ft)
Tail rotor disc	12.57 m² (135.3 sq ft)

WEIGHTS AND LOADINGS:

Max cargo payload	5,000 kg (11,023 lb)
Max hovering weight OGE at S/L	12,480 kg (27,513 lb)
Max T-O weight	13,000 kg (28,660 lb)
Max disc loading	46.35 kg/m² (9.49 lb/sq ft)

PERFORMANCE (A at T-O weight of 9,000 kg; 19,841 lb, B at 11,000 kg; 24,251 lb, C at 13,000 kg; 28,660 lb):

Never-exceed speed (VNE):

A	170 knots (315 km/h; 195 mph)
B	159 knots (296 km/h; 183 mph)
C	148 knots (275 km/h; 170 mph)
Max cruising speed: A	143 knots (266 km/h; 165 mph)
B	140 knots (260 km/h; 161 mph)
C	134 knots (248 km/h; 154 mph)
Econ cruising speed: A	137 knots (255 km/h; 158 mph)
B	132 knots (246 km/h; 153 mph)
C	125 knots (232 km/h; 144 mph)

Rate of climb at S/L (15° 30′ collective pitch, one engine out): A 690 m (2,263 ft)/min

B	552 m (1,811 ft)/min
C	396 m (1,299 ft)/min
Service ceiling: A	6,000 m (19,685 ft)
B	4,900 m (16,075 ft)
C	3,050 m (10,000 ft)
Hovering ceiling IGE: A	5,500 m (18,045 ft)
B	3,600 m (11,810 ft)
C	1,900 m (6,235 ft)
Hovering ceiling OGE: A	4,400 m (14,435 ft)
B	2,300 m (7,545 ft)

Range with max standard fuel, one engine out, no reserves: A 232 nm (430 km; 267 miles)

B	442 nm (820 km; 509 miles)
C	431 nm (800 km; 497 miles)

Ferry range with auxiliary fuel tanks, one engine out, no reserves: C 755 nm (1,400 km; 870 miles)

Endurance with max standard fuel, one engine out, no reserves: A 2 h 31 min

B	4 h 43 min
C	4 h 10 min

GAIC
GUIZHOU AVIATION INDUSTRY CORPORATION

PO Box 38, Anshun, Guizhou
Telephone: 86 (34) 551027; or 86/Anshun 22228
Telex: 66018 AIMGA CN
GENERAL MANAGER: Sun Ruisheng

GAIC incorporates a number of enterprises, factories and institutes which between them are engaged in many aerospace and non-aerospace activities. The former include the JJ-7/FT-7 fighter/trainer described in this entry, two series of turbojet engines, air-to-air missiles and rocket launchers. It also participates in production of the single-seat J-7/F-7 described under the Chengdu (CAC) heading. GAIC has an aerospace workforce of about 6,000.

GAIGC JJ-7
Chinese name: Jianjiji Jiaolianji-7 or Jianjiao-7 (Fighter training aircraft 7)
Westernised designation: FT-7

First flown on 5 July 1985, the JJ-7 or FT-7 is a tandem two-seat trainer version of the Chengdu J-7 II, outwardly

GAIC JJ-7/FT-7 two-seat trainer version of the CAC J-7/F-7

similar to its Soviet counterpart, the MiG-21U (NATO 'Mongol-A'), and is capable of providing most of the training necessary for the Shenyang J-8 fighter as well as the full syllabus for all versions of the J-7/F-7. Avionics and power plant are generally as described for the single-seat version under the CAC heading. Pakistan has ordered 15 **FT-7P** trainers, the first flight of which was made on 9 November 1990; four had been delivered by February 1991.

Differences from the single-seat J-7 and MiG-21U include sideways opening (to starboard) twin canopies, the rear one fitted with a retractable periscope, twin ventral strakes of modified shape, and a removable saddleback fuel tank aft of the second cockpit. A 480 or 720 litre (127 or 190.2 US gallon; 105.5 or 158.4 Imp gallon) drop tank can be carried under the centre-fuselage, and there is a single underwing pylon each side for such stores as PL-2 or -2B

air-to-air missiles, an HF-5A 18-round launcher for 57 mm rockets, or bombs of up to 250 kg size. The JJ-7 can also be fitted with a Type 23-3 twin-barrel 23 mm gun in an underbelly pack.

DIMENSIONS, EXTERNAL: As J-7 except:
Length overall, incl probe   14.874 m (48 ft 9½ in)

WEIGHTS AND LOADINGS:
Weight empty	5,330 kg (11,750 lb)
Internal fuel	1,891 kg (4,169 lb)
Normal max T-O weight with two PL-2 air-to-air missiles	7,590 kg (16,733 lb)
Max T-O weight with two PL-2 missiles and one 800 litre drop tank	8,600 kg (18,960 lb)

PERFORMANCE:
Max level speed   as for J-7/F-7

Unstick speed	170-181 knots (315-335 km/h; 196-208 mph)
Touchdown speed	165-175 knots (305-325 km/h; 190-202 mph)
Service ceiling	17,300 m (56,760 ft)
Absolute ceiling	17,700 m (58,070 ft)
T-O run	900-1,100 m (2,953-3,609 ft)
Landing run with brake-chute and wheel braking	850-1,100 m (2,789-3,609 ft)

Range at 11,000 m (36,000 ft):
internal fuel only   545 nm (1,010 km; 627 miles)
with 720 litre drop tank   787 nm (1,459 km; 906 miles)
g limit with two PL-2B missiles   +7

GOHL
GUANGZHOU ORLANDO HELICOPTERS LTD

Hoben, Jiahe, Guangzhou, Guangdong
Telephone: 86 (20) 628201
Fax: 86 (20) 342203
Telex: 44526 EECCG CN
GENERAL MANAGER: Kelly Robinson
VICE-GENERAL MANAGER: Zhao Shuxin

GUANGZHOU (ORLANDO) PANDA
Orlando Helicopter Airways (see US section) initiated a

venture in 1985 in which its OHA-S-55 Bearcat is being assembled, and will later be part-built, in China, by a jointly owned company known as Guangzhou Orlando Helicopters Ltd. A 2,323 m² (25,000 sq ft) factory was built for the purpose at an airfield near the city of Guangzhou.

The 20-year contract, signed on 27 October 1985, provides for the initial assembly in China, from Orlando kits, of ten aircraft. Kits for five of these had been shipped to China by early 1989, first flight took place in Spring 1987, and Chinese type certification has been granted. Crop and forestry spraying trials were conducted in 1988, and the

OHA-S-55 is expected to replace some Y-5 (Chinese An-2) biplanes for these duties. Second and third stage batches of 20 and 30 aircraft respectively will include a proportion of OHA-S-55T Challenger and/or Phoenix turbine powered versions, with 671 kW (900 shp) Pratt & Whitney Canada PT6T engines. Chinese built OHA-S-55s are to be marketed, under the name Panda, by Orlando Helicopter Far East Ltd, based in Hong Kong. The contract also contains options for co-production of the Orlando modified S-58T Viking. The Sikorsky S-76 has been deleted from the original programme.

HAMC
HARBIN AIRCRAFT MANUFACTURING COMPANY

PO Box 201, Harbin, Heilongjiang 150066
Telephone: 86 (451) 62951
Fax: 86 (451) 227491
Telex: 87082 HAF CN
GENERAL MANAGER: Yang Shouwen

Harbin had its origin in the plant of the Manshu Aeroplane Manufacturing Company, one of several aircraft and aero engine factories established in Manchukuo (Manchuria) by the Japanese in 1938. After the Communist regime came to power in mainland China in 1949 it was re-established in 1952 and re-equipped with Soviet assistance, and since then has been responsible for production of the H-5 twin-jet light bomber, a reverse engineered version of the Soviet Ilyushin Il-28, and the nationally designed SH-5 amphibian and Y-11 and Y-12 agricultural and utility light twins. Details of the H-5 and original Y-11 can be found in earlier editions of *Jane's*. A new version of the Y-11, designated Y-11B, is currently under development. Landing gear doors for the British Aerospace 146 are produced under a 1981 agreement with BAe, and doors and wing components for the Shorts 360.

Harbin is also the chief centre for helicopter production, which began with the Mil Mi-4 (Chinese Z-5, first flown on 14 December 1958; total of 545 built. Described in 1985-86 and earlier *Jane's*). It is currently responsible for the Aerospatiale Dauphin 2 (Z-9A) manufacturing and assembly programme, and is producing components for China's Mil Mi-8s. The workforce numbers about 15,000.

HAMC SH-5
Chinese name: Shuishang Hongzhaji 5 (Maritime bomber 5) or Shuihong-5
Westernised designation: PS-5

Design of this four-turboprop flying-boat amphibian was undertaken jointly by HAMC and the Seaplane Design Institute, but its development became one of many victims of the cultural revolution. Detail design was completed in February 1970, but static testing of the first complete airframe was not achieved until August 1974, nearly three

Water-bomber version of the HAMC SH-5 in action *(Brian M. Service)*

years after its completion. The first flying prototype, completed in December 1973, underwent water taxi trials totalling some 30 hours, between May 1975 and March 1976, before achieving its first flight on 3 April 1976.

Four more SH-5s were completed and flown in 1984-85, subsequently being handed over to the PLA Naval Air Force on 3 September 1986, for service at Tuandao naval air station, Qingdao.

The SH-5 is intended for a wide range of maritime duties including anti-submarine and anti-surface vessel warfare, patrol and surveillance, minelaying, search and rescue, and the carriage of bulk cargo. A firefighting water-bomber version has already been evaluated.

The Chinese are reportedly seeking an ASW and avionics upgrade for the SH-5.

TYPE: Maritime patrol and anti-submarine bomber, surveillance, SAR and transport amphibian.

WINGS: All-metal cantilever high-wing monoplane. Constant chord centre-section; outer panels tapered, with anhedral outboard of outer engine nacelles. Non-retractable stabilising float, on N struts with twin I struts inboard, beneath each wing near tip. Spoiler forward of each outer flap segment. Trim tab in each aileron.
FUSELAGE: Unpressurised all-metal semi-monocoque hull, with high length/beam ratio and single-step planing bottom. Curved spray suppression strakes along sides of nose; spray suppression slots in lower sides, aft of inboard propeller plane. Small water rudder at rear of hull. Thimble radome on nose; MAD in extended tail sting.
TAIL UNIT: High mounted dihedral tailplane, with oval endplate fins and rudders, mounted on fairing above rear fuselage. Trim tabs in each rudder and each elevator.
LANDING GEAR: Retractable tricycle type, with single mainwheels and twin-wheel nose unit. Oleo-pneumatic

HAMC SH-5 (PS-5) patrol and anti-submarine bomber amphibian, in service with the Chinese PLA Naval Air Force

shock absorbers. Main units retract upward and rearward into wells in hull sides; nose unit retracts rearward.

POWER PLANT: Four 2,349 kW (3,150 ehp) Dongan (DEMC) WJ5A turboprops, each driving a Baoding four-blade propeller. Max fuel capacity approx 21,000 litres (5,548 US gallons; 4,620 Imp gallons).

ACCOMMODATION: Standard eight-person crew includes a flight crew of five (pilot, co-pilot, navigator, flight engineer and radio operator), plus systems/equipment operators according to mission. Three freight compartments in front portion of hull. Mission crew cabin amidships, aft of which are two further compartments, one for communications and other electronic equipment and the rear one for specialised mission equipment. All compartments connected by corridor, with watertight doors aft of flight deck and between each compartment.

AVIONICS: Include inertial navigation system, air data computer, radio altimeter and radio compass. Doppler search radar in thimble radome forward of nose transparencies. Magnetic anomaly detector (MAD) in extended tail sting.

ARMAMENT: Two-gun dorsal turret. Four underwing hardpoints for C-101 sea skimming supersonic anti-shipping or other missiles (one on each inboard pylon), lightweight torpedoes (up to three on each outer pylon), or other stores. Depth charges, mines, bombs, sonobuoys, SAR gear or other mission equipment and stores in rear of hull, as required.

DIMENSIONS, EXTERNAL:
Wing span	36.00 m (118 ft 1¼ in)
Wing aspect ratio	9.0
Length overall	38.90 m (127 ft 7½ in)
Height overall	9.79 m (32 ft 1½ in)
* Span over tail-fins	11.40 m (37 ft 4¾ in)
* Wheel track	3.70 m (12 ft 1¾ in)
* Wheelbase	10.50 m (34 ft 5½ in)
* Propeller diameter	3.80 m (12 ft 5½ in)
* estimated	

AREAS:
Wings, gross	144.0 m² (1,550.0 sq ft)

WEIGHTS AND LOADINGS:
Weight empty, equipped:	
SAR and transport	less than 25,000 kg (55,115 lb)
ASW	26,500 kg (58,422 lb)
Fuel load (max)	16,500 kg (36,376 lb)
Max internal weapons load	6,000 kg (13,228 lb)
Max payload (bulk cargo)	10,000 kg (22,045 lb)
Normal T-O weight	36,000 kg (79,366 lb)
Max T-O weight	45,000 kg (99,208 lb)
Wing loading:	
at normal T-O weight	250.0 kg/m² (51.2 lb/sq ft)
at max T-O weight	312.5 kg/m² (64.0 lb/sq ft)
Power loading:	
at normal T-O weight	3.31 kg/kW (5.44 lb/ehp)
at max T-O weight	4.14 kg/kW (6.80 lb/ehp)

PERFORMANCE:
Max level speed	299 knots (555 km/h; 345 mph)
Max cruising speed	243 knots (450 km/h; 280 mph)
Min patrol speed	124 knots (230 km/h; 143 mph)
T-O speed (water)	87 knots (160 km/h; 100 mph)
Landing speed (water)	92 knots (170 km/h; 106 mph)
Service ceiling	7,000 m (22,965 ft)
T-O run (water)	548 m (1,798 ft)
Landing run (water)	240 m (788 ft)
Range with max fuel	2,563 nm (4,750 km; 2,951 miles)
Endurance (2 engines)	12 to 15 h

HAMC Y-11B
Chinese name: Yunshuji-11B (Transport aircraft 11B) or Yun-11B

A description of the nine/ten-seat original Y-11 can be found in the 1986-87 and earlier editions of *Jane's*. More than 40 are currently in service, including 17 with Flying Dragon Air Service, 10 with the Xinjiang Agricultural Air Service, and 16 with China Feilong Airlines.

The Y-11B, flown for the first time on 26 December 1990, differs mainly in having two 261 kW (350 hp) Teledyne Continental TSIO-550-A1B flat-six engines (instead of the original 212.5 kW; 285 hp Chinese radials) and fully feathering Hartzell propellers. The VFR/IFR panel includes Bendix/King VHF/UHF com radios, marker beacon receiver and radio compass. The Y-11B is intended for both the domestic and international market. Certification was anticipated during 1991, with first deliveries in 1992. Other known details are:

DIMENSIONS, EXTERNAL:
Wing span	17.08 m (56 ft 0½ in)
Length overall	12.00 m (39 ft 4½ in)
Height overall	5.365 m (17 ft 7½ in)

DIMENSIONS, INTERNAL:
Cabin: Length	3.58 m (11 ft 9 in)
Max width	1.27 m (4 ft 2 in)
Max height	1.48 m (4 ft 10¼ in)

WEIGHTS AND LOADINGS:
Weight empty	2,350 kg (5,180 lb)
Max fuel weight	450 kg (992 lb)
Max payload: Normal	900 kg (1,984 lb)
Restricted	1,200 kg (2,645 lb)

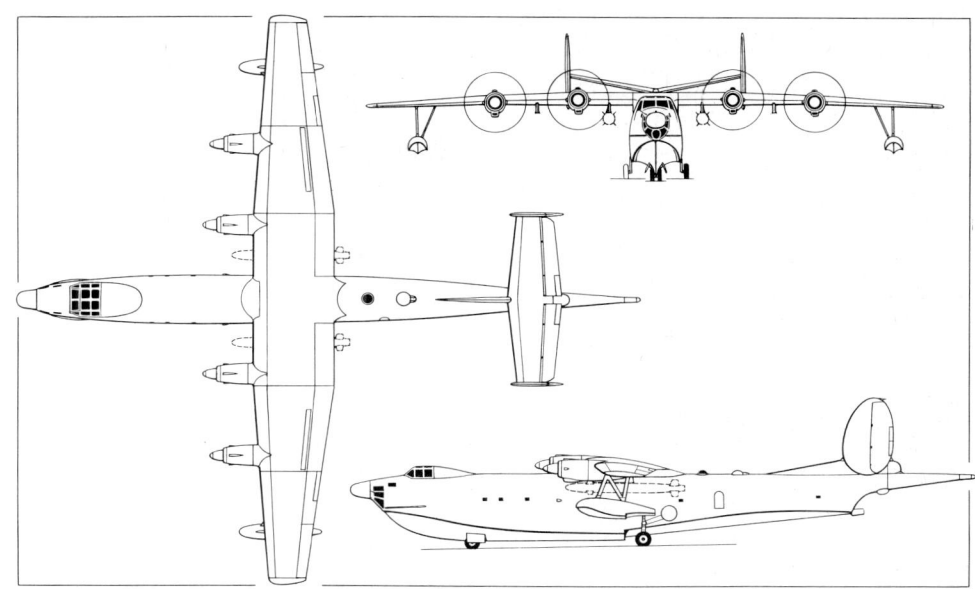

HAMC SH-5 (four Dongan WJ5A turboprops) *(Pilot Press)*

Max T-O weight: Normal	3,500 kg (7,716 lb)
Restricted	3,900 kg (8,598 lb)
Max landing weight	3,500 kg (7,716 lb)

PERFORMANCE (at max Normal T-O weight):
Max level speed	127 knots (235 km/h; 146 mph)
Max cruising speed at 3,000 m (9,840 ft)	
	108 knots (200 km/h; 124 mph)
Stalling speed, 30° flap	57 knots (104 km/h; 65 mph)
Max rate of climb at S/L	336 m (1,100 ft)/min
Rate of climb at 1,500 m (4,920 ft), one engine out	
	41 m (135 ft)/min
Service ceiling	6,000 m (19,685 ft)
T-O run	200 m (657 ft)
Landing run	275 m (903 ft)
Range with max fuel	582 nm (1,080 km; 671 miles)

HAMC Y-12 II
Chinese name: Yunshuji-12 (Transport aircraft 12) or Yun-12

This STOL general purpose transport was developed in order to improve upon the modest payload/range capabilities of the original piston engined Harbin Y-11. Design and construction are to FAR Pt 23 and Pt 135 (Appendix A) standards. Three prototype **Y-12 I**s and about 30 production examples of this PT6A-11 engined version were built, the first flight taking place on 14 July 1982. Details of this version can be found in the 1987-88 and earlier *Jane's*.

Current version is the **Y-12 II**, which has higher rated PT6A-27 engines and no leading-edge slats. First flight of a Y-12 II took place on 16 August 1984. Domestic certification was received in December 1985, and 43 had been ordered by September 1990, of which 30 were then in service. Exports have been made since 1986 to the Sri Lanka Air Force (six, with three more ordered in July 1990) and Lao Aviation (four). Chinese operators include Flying Dragon Air Service, China Feilong Airlines and Southwest China Airlines. Some aircraft, used for mineral detection, have Doppler navigation, a satellite navigation responder, and a long, kinked sensor tailboom.

UK certification to BCAR Section K was awarded on 20 June 1990, and FAA type approval is being sought. China is developing its own turboprop, the 507 kW (680 shp) WJ9,

as a power plant for the Y-12 and other aircraft. There is a domestic requirement for more than 200 Y-12s. Future plans include a stretched version and one with a pressurised cabin.

The description applies to the current production version:

TYPE: Twin-turboprop STOL general purpose transport.

WINGS: Braced high-wing monoplane, with constant chord from root to tip. Wing section LS(1)-0417, with thickness/chord ratio of 17 per cent. Anhedral 1° 41'. Incidence 4°. No sweep. Two-spar fail-safe structure, with aluminium alloy skin; Ziqiang-2 resin bonding on 70 per cent of structure and integral fuel tankage in wing spar box. All-metal drooping ailerons and electrically actuated two-section double-slotted flaps along full span of trailing-edges. Trim tab in starboard aileron. Goodrich Type 29S-7D 5178 anti-icing of leading-edges. Small stub-wings at cabin floor level support the main landing gear units; bracing strut from each stub-wing out to approx one-third span.

FUSELAGE: Conventional semi-monocoque all-metal fail-safe structure of basically rectangular cross-section, swept upward at rear. Ziqiang-2 resin bonding on 40 per cent of structure.

TAIL UNIT: Cantilever non-swept metal structure, with low-set constant chord tailplane and large dorsal fin. Horn balanced rudder and elevators. Trim tab in rudder and each elevator. Ventral fin under tailcone. Goodrich Type 29S-7D 5178 anti-icing of leading-edges.

LANDING GEAR: Non-retractable tricycle type, with oleo-pneumatic shock absorber in each unit. Single-wheel main units, attached to underside of stub-wings. Single steerable nosewheel. Mainwheel tyres size 640 × 230 mm, pressure 5.5 bars (80 lb/sq in); nosewheel tyre size 480 × 200 mm, pressure 3.5 bars (51 lb/sq in). Pneumatic brakes.

POWER PLANT: Two Chinese assembled Pratt & Whitney Canada PT6A-27 turboprops, each flat rated at 507 kW (680 shp) and driving a Hartzell HC-B3TN-3B/T10173B-3 three-blade constant-speed reversible-pitch propeller. All fuel in tanks in wing spar box, total capacity 1,616 litres (427 US gallons; 355.5 Imp gallons), with overwing gravity filling point each side.

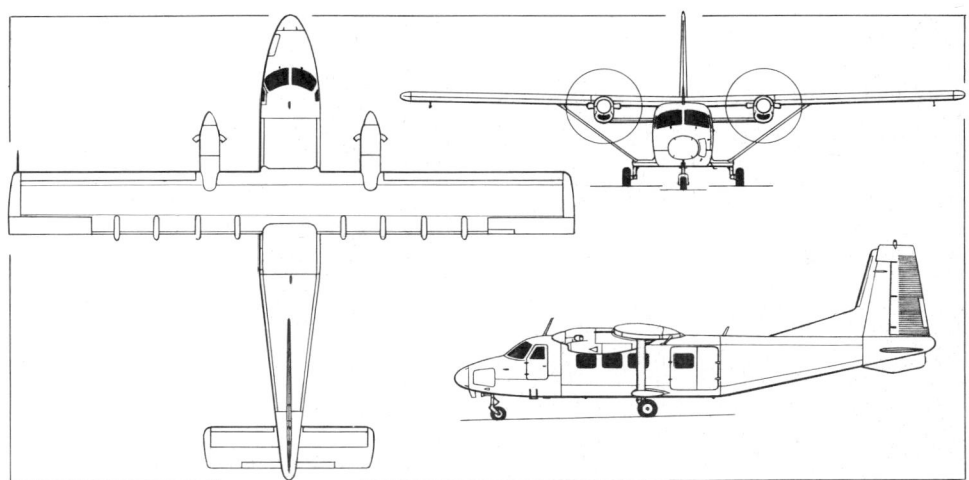

HAMC Y-12 II twin-turboprop STOL general purpose transport *(Pilot Press)*

Harbin Y-12 II of Flying Dragon Air Service equipped for geological survey

ACCOMMODATION: Crew of two on flight deck, access to which is via a forward opening door on the port side. Four-way adjustable crew seats. Dual controls. Main cabin can accommodate up to 17 passengers in commuter configuration, in three-abreast layout (with aisle), at seat pitch of 79 cm (31 in). Alternative layouts for up to 16 parachutists, or an all-cargo configuration with 11 tiedown rings. Passenger/cargo double door on port side at rear, the rear half of which opens outward and the forward half inward; foldout steps in passenger entrance. Emergency exits on each side at front of cabin and opposite passenger door on starboard side at rear. Baggage compartments in nose and at rear of passenger cabin, for 100 kg (220 lb) and 260 kg (573 lb) respectively.

SYSTEMS: Hamilton Standard R70-3WG environmental control system.

AVIONICS: VHF-251 and HF-230 com radio, AUD-251H, ADF-650A radio compass, VIR-351 and Bendix/King 1400C weather radar. Standard instrumentation includes BK-450 airspeed indicator, BDP-1 artificial horizon, BG10-1A altimeter, ZGW-3G altitude indicator, ZHZ-4A radio magnetic heading indicator, BC10 rate of climb indicator, ZWH-1 outside air temperature indicator, and ZEY-1 flap position indicator; dual engine torquemeters, interturbine temperature indicators, gas generator tachometers, oil temperature and pressure indicators, and fuel pressure and quantity indicators; HSZ-2 clock; and XDH-10B warning light box.

EQUIPMENT: Hopper for 1,200 litres (317 US gallons; 264 Imp gallons) of dry or liquid chemical in agricultural version. Appropriate specialised equipment for fire-fighting, geophysical survey and other missions.

DIMENSIONS, EXTERNAL:
Wing span	17.235 m (56 ft 6½ in)
Wing chord, constant	2.00 m (6 ft 6¾ in)
Wing aspect ratio	8.7
Length overall	14.86 m (48 ft 9 in)
Height overall	5.575 m (18 ft 3½ in)
Elevator span	5.365 m (17 ft 7¼ in)
Wheel track	3.60 m (11 ft 9¾ in)
Wheelbase	4.698 m (15 ft 5 in)
Propeller diameter	2.49 m (8 ft 2 in)
Distance between propeller centres	
	4.937 m (16 ft 2⅜ in)
Fuselage/ground clearance	0.65 m (2 ft 1½ in)
Crew door: Height	1.35 m (4 ft 5¼ in)
Width	0.65 m (2 ft 1½ in)
Passenger/cargo door: Height	1.38 m (4 ft 6¼ in)
Width (passenger door only)	0.65 m (2 ft 1½ in)
Width (double door)	1.45 m (4 ft 9 in)
Emergency exits (three, each):	
Height	0.68 m (2 ft 2¾ in)
Width	0.68 m (2 ft 2¾ in)
Baggage door (nose, port):	
Max height	0.56 m (1 ft 10 in)
Width	0.75 m (2 ft 5½ in)

DIMENSIONS, INTERNAL:
Cabin, excl flight deck and rear baggage compartment:	
Length	4.82 m (15 ft 9¾ in)
Max width	1.46 m (4 ft 9½ in)
Max height	1.70 m (5 ft 7 in)
Volume	12.9 m³ (455.5 cu ft)
Baggage compartment volume:	
nose	0.77 m³ (27.20 cu ft)
rear	1.89 m³ (66.75 cu ft)

AREAS:
Wings, gross	34.27 m² (368.88 sq ft)
Vertical tail surfaces (total)	5.064 m² (54.51 sq ft)
Horizontal tail surfaces (total)	7.024 m² (75.61 sq ft)

WEIGHTS AND LOADINGS:
Weight empty, equipped	2,840 kg (6,261 lb)
Operating weight empty	3,000 kg (6,614 lb)
Max fuel load	1,233 kg (2,718 lb)
Max payload	1,700 kg (3,748 lb)

T-O weight for agricultural operation	
	4,500 kg (9,921 lb)
Max T-O and landing weight	5,300 kg (11,684 lb)
Max ramp weight	5,330 kg (11,750 lb)
Max zero-fuel weight	4,700 kg (10,362 lb)
Max cabin floor loading (cargo)	
	750 kg/m² (153.7 lb/sq ft)
Max wing loading	145.9 kg/m² (29.90 lb/sq ft)
Max power loading	5.23 kg/kW (8.59 lb/shp)

PERFORMANCE (at max T-O weight, ISA):
Never-exceed speed (VNE) at 3,000 m (9,840 ft)	
	177 knots (328 km/h; 204 mph)
Max cruising speed at 3,000 m (9,840 ft)	
	157 knots (292 km/h; 181 mph)
Econ cruising speed at 3,000 m (9,840 ft)	
	135 knots (250 km/h; 155 mph)
Max rate of climb at S/L	504 m (1,655 ft)/min
Rate of climb at S/L, one engine out	
	101 m (331 ft)/min
Service ceiling	7,000 m (22,960 ft)
Service ceiling, one engine out, 15 m (50 ft)/min rate of climb, max continuous power	3,000 m (9,840 ft)
T-O run, 15° flap	340 m (1,115 ft)
T-O to 15 m (50 ft), 15° flap	425 m (1,395 ft)
Landing from 15 m (50 ft), with braking and propeller reversal	500 m (1,640 ft)
Landing run with braking and propeller reversal	
	200 m (656 ft)
Min ground turning radius	16.75 m (54 ft 11½ in)
Range at 135 knots (250 km/h; 155 mph) at 3,000 m (9,840 ft) with max fuel, 45 min reserves	
	723 nm (1,340 km; 832 miles)
Endurance, conditions as above	5 h 12 min

HAMC (AEROSPATIALE) Z-9 HAITUN (DOLPHIN)
Chinese name: Zhishengji-9 (Vertical take-off aircraft 9) or Zhi-9

A licence agreement was signed on 2 July 1980 between Aerospatiale and CATIC for the former's AS 365N Dauphin 2 twin-turboshaft helicopter (which see) to be manufactured in China. The first (French built) example for China made its initial acceptance flight in the Beijing area on 6 February 1982. Current examples, designated **Z-9A**, are to the upgraded standard of the AS 365N₁ French version, and have a substantial proportion of locally manufactured components.

The agreement is for an initial batch of 50, of which about 45 had been completed by the end of 1990 and delivered to all three Chinese armed services as well as CAAC. Helicopter units flying Z-9s were established with two PLA group armies in January (Beijing Military Region) and February 1988 (Shenyang Military Region), and others may have been formed subsequently. Some Z-9s are allocated to the PLA Naval Air Force, some to offshore oil rig support work, and some are configured as air ambulances accommodating four stretchers and two seats or two stretchers and five seats. The transmission system is manufactured by the Dongan Engine Manufacturing Company at Harbin, while the aircraft's Arriel 1C and 1C1 turboshafts are produced by SMPMC at Zhuzhou, as the WZ8 and WZ8A; the Baoding Propeller Factory manufactures the hubs and tail rotor blades. Fuel capacity is 1,140 litres (301 US gallons; 251 Imp gallons).

It has been reported that China is seeking a magnetic anomaly detector for installation on naval versions of the Z-9. The first anti-tank version (which carries Norinco 'Red Arrow 8' missiles) made its initial flight in late 1988 or early 1989.

China has an option to continue producing the Dauphin 2 on a licence basis after completion of the original 50, and negotiations for a further 20 were under discussion in late 1990/early 1991.

The following Chinese figures have been published for the Z-9 and Z-9A:

WEIGHTS AND LOADINGS:
Weight empty, equipped: Z-9	1,975 kg (4,354 lb)
Z-9A	2,050 kg (4,519 lb)
Max payload: Z-9	1,863 kg (4,107 lb)
Z-9A	2,038 kg (4,493 lb)
Max load on cargo sling: Z-9, Z-9A	1,600 kg (3,527 lb)
Max T-O weight, internal or external load:	
Z-9	3,850 kg (8,488 lb)
Z-9A	4,100 kg (9,039 lb)

PERFORMANCE (at max T-O weight):
Max cruising speed at S/L:	
Z-9	158 knots (293 km/h; 182 mph)
Z-9A	154 knots (285 km/h; 177 mph)
Max vertical rate of climb at S/L:	
Z-9	252 m (827 ft)/min
Z-9A	246 m (805 ft)/min
Max forward rate of climb at S/L:	
Z-9	462 m (1,515 ft)/min
Z-9A	456 m (1,495 ft)/min
Service ceiling: Z-9	4,500 m (14,765 ft)
Z-9A	6,000 m (19,685 ft)
Hovering ceiling IGE: Z-9	1,950 m (6,400 ft)
Z-9A	2,600 m (8,530 ft)
Hovering ceiling OGE: Z-9	1,020 m (3,350 ft)
Z-9A	1,600 m (5,250 ft)
Max range at 140 knots (260 km/h; 161 mph) normal cruising speed, no reserves:	
standard tanks: Z-9	491 nm (910 km; 565 miles)
Z-9A	464 nm (860 km; 534 miles)
with 180 litre (47.5 US gallon; 39.6 Imp gallon) auxiliary tank:	
Z-9	572 nm (1,060 km; 658 miles)
Z-9A	539 nm (1,000 km; 621 miles)

HAMC Z-9A Haitun twin-turbine light helicopter

NAMC
NANCHANG AIRCRAFT MANUFACTURING COMPANY

PO Box 5001-506, Nanchang, Jiangxi
Telephone: 86 (791) 251833
Fax: 86 (791) 251833-2272
Telex: 95068 NAMC CN
GENERAL MANAGER: Wu Mingwang
INFORMATION: Feng Jinghua

Created in 1951, Nanchang was responsible for licence production of the Soviet Yak-18 trainer, of which it built 379 (as the CJ-5) between 1954 and 1958, and continues to manufacture its own CJ-6A development of that aircraft. In the 1960s it shared in the large production programme for the J-6 fighter (Chinese development of the MiG-19), from which it subsequently developed the Q-5/A-5 attack aircraft series. In 1957-68, NAMC produced 727 examples of the Y-5 (Chinese An-2) biplane, now described under the SAP heading in this section, including 114 as local service transports and 229 for agricultural use. Its latest design, the N-5A, is a dedicated agricultural aircraft which made its first flight at the end of 1989. An upgrade programme for the A-5 is under way, and the K-8 jet trainer is being developed jointly with Pakistan. NAMC occupies a 500 ha (1,235 acre) site, with 10,000 m² (107,639 sq ft) of covered space, and had a 1989 workforce of more than 20,000. About 80 per cent of its activities are non-aerospace.

NAMC Q-5
Chinese name: Qiangjiji-5 (Attack aircraft 5) or Qiang-5
Westernised designation: A-5
NATO reporting name: Fantan

Development of this twin-jet attack aircraft, derived from the J-6/MiG-19 produced in China, began with a design proposal submitted by Shenyang in August 1958. Responsibility for the programme was assigned to Nanchang, but the prototype programme was cancelled in 1961. It was, however, kept alive by a small team of enthusiasts, and was officially resumed two years later, the first prototype eventually making its initial flight on 4 June 1965. On receipt of a preliminary design certificate, a pre-production batch was authorised at the end of that year, but further modifications, to the fuel, armament, hydraulic and other systems, were found necessary, leading to the flight testing of two much modified prototypes beginning in October 1969. Series production of the Q-5 was approved at the end of that year, and deliveries began in 1970. A number of these initial production aircraft were adapted for nuclear weapon delivery tests in the early 1970s.

Details of the adaptation of the J-6 airframe can be found in the 1989-90 and earlier editions of *Jane's*. Major variants of the Q-5 are as follows:

Q-5: Initial production version, with internal fuselage bay approx 4.00 m (13 ft 1½ in) long for two 250 kg or 500 kg bombs, two underfuselage attachments adjacent to bay for two similar bombs, and two stores pylons beneath each wing; Series 6 WP6 turbojets; brake-chute in tailcone, between upper and lower 'pen-nib' fairings.

Q-5 I: Extended payload/range version, first proposed in 1976; flight tested in late 1980 and certificated for production on 20 October 1981. Internal bomb bay blanked off; space used to enlarge main fuselage fuel tank and add a flexible tank, and underfuselage stores points increased to four; improved series WP6 engines; modified landing gear; brake-chute relocated under base of rudder; improved Type I rocket ejection seat; HF/SSB transceiver added. Some Q-5 Is adapted for PLA Naval Air Force to carry two underfuselage torpedoes; these reportedly have Doppler type nose radar and 20 m (66 ft) sea-skimming capability with C-801 anti-shipping missiles.

Q-5 IA/Q-5 II: Improved Q-5 I, certificated as Q-5 IA in January 1985 with additional underwing hardpoint each side (increasing stores load by 500 kg; 1,102 lb), new gun/bomb sighting systems, pressure refuelling, and added

Nanchang A-5Cs of the Pakistan Air Force's No. 16 ('Panther') Squadron *(Lindsay Peacock)*

Q-5 II with ECM pods on its centre underwing stations

warning/countermeasures systems. Forty Q-5 IAs exported to North Korea. Current production version designated Q-5 II.

Q-5K Kong Yun: Upgraded version proposed for Chinese armed forces. Described in 1990-91 *Jane's*; development abandoned in 1990.

A-5C: Export version for Pakistan Air Force, involving 32 modifications from Q-5 I, notably upgraded avionics, Martin-Baker PKD10 zero/zero ejection seats, and adaptation of hardpoints for 356 mm (14 in) lugs compatible with PAF weapons, including Sidewinder missiles. Three prototypes built. Original order for 54, placed in April 1981, delivered between January 1983 and January 1984, equipping Nos. 7, 16 and 26 Squadrons of PAF. Bangladesh has reportedly ordered 20.

A-5M: Upgraded export version of Q-5 II, under development. Described separately.

Including some 200 for export, nearly 1,000 Q-5s (all versions) have been built to date. A design study was carried out in the mid-1980s by FRL in the UK to equip the Q-5 as a receiver for in-flight refuelling, with a Xian H-6 bomber adapted to act as the tanker aircraft. Go-ahead for such a modification had not been given up to the Spring of 1991.

The following description applies to the Q-5 II and A-5C, except where otherwise indicated:

TYPE: Single-seat close air support and ground attack aircraft, with capability also for air-to-air combat.

WINGS: Cantilever all-metal mid-wing monoplane, of low aspect ratio, with 4° anhedral from roots. Sweepback at quarter-chord 52° 30'. Multi-spar basic structure with ribs and stressed skin, with three-point attachment to fuselage. Deep, full chord boundary layer fence on each upper surface at mid span. Inboard of each fence is a hydraulically actuated Gouge flap, the inner end of which is angled to give a trailing-edge at right angles to side of fuselage. Hydraulically actuated (by irreversible servo) internally balanced aileron outboard of each fence. Electrically operated inset trim tab at inboard end of port aileron.

FUSELAGE: Conventional all-metal structure of longerons, stringers and stressed skin, built in forward and rear portions which are detachable aft of wing trailing-edge to provide access to engines. Air intake on each side of fuselage, abreast of cockpit; twin jetpipes side by side at rear. Top and bottom 'pen nib' fairings aft of nozzles. Centre-fuselage is 'waisted' in accordance with area rule. Dorsal spine fairing between rear of cockpit and leading-edge of fin. Forward hinged, hydraulically actuated door type airbrake under centre of fuselage, forward of bomb attachment points. Shallow ventral strake under each jetpipe.

TAIL UNIT: Cantilever all-metal stressed skin structure, with sweepback on all surfaces. Mechanically actuated mass balanced rudder, with electrically operated inset trim tab. One-piece hydraulically actuated (by irreversible servo) all-moving tailplane, with 6° 30' anhedral and anti-flutter weight projecting forward from each tip. Tail warning antenna in tip of fin.

LANDING GEAR: Hydraulically retractable wide-track tricycle type, with single wheel and oleo-pneumatic shock absorber on each unit. Main units retract inward into wings, non-steerable nosewheel forward into fuselage, rotating through 87° to lie flat in gear bay. Mainwheels have size 830 × 205 mm tubeless tyres, and disc brakes. Tail braking parachute, deployed when aircraft is 1 m (3.3 ft) above the ground, in bullet fairing at root of vertical tail trailing-edge beneath rudder.

POWER PLANT: Two Shenyang WP6 turbojets, each rated at 25.50 kN (5,732 lb st) dry and 31.87 kN (7,165 lb st) with afterburning, mounted side by side in rear of fuselage. Improved WP6A engines (see A-5M entry for details) available optionally. Lateral air intake, with small splitter plate, for each engine. Hydraulically actuated nozzles. Internal fuel in three forward and two rear fuselage tanks with combined capacity of 3,648 litres (964 US gallons; 802.5 Imp gallons). Provision for carrying a 760 litre (201 US gallon; 167 Imp gallon) drop tank on each centre underwing pylon, to give max internal/external fuel capacity of 5,168 litres (1,366 US gallons; 1,136.5 Imp gallons). When centre wing stations are occupied by bombs, a 400 litre (105.7 US gallon; 88 Imp gallon) drop tank can be carried instead on each outboard underwing pylon.

ACCOMMODATION: Pilot only, under one-piece jettisonable canopy which is hinged at rear and opens upward. Downward view over nose, in level flight, is 13° 30'. Low-speed seat allows for safe ejection within speed

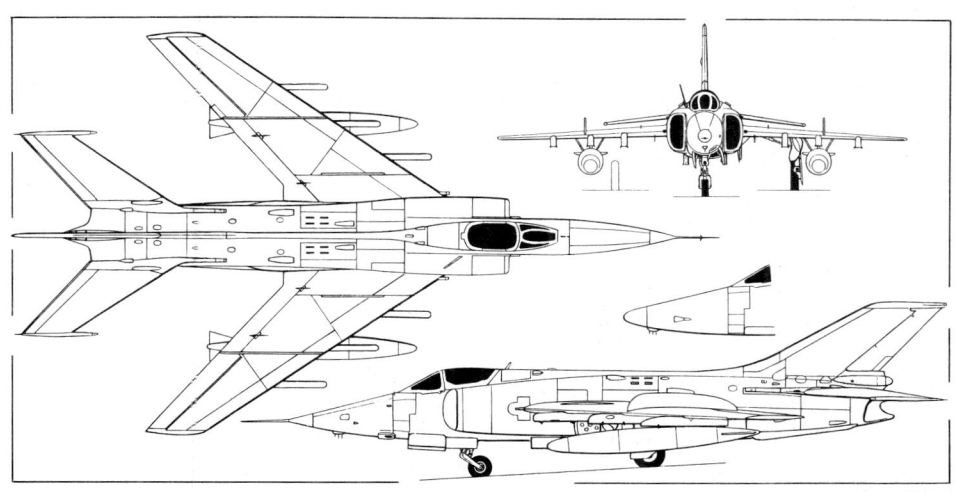

NAMC A-5C 'Fantan' single-seat twin-jet combat aircraft, with scrap view showing nose configuration of A-5M *(Pilot Press)*

range of 135-458 knots (250-850 km/h; 155-528 mph) at zero height or above. Aircraft in Pakistan service have been refitted with Martin-Baker PKD10 zero/zero seats. Armour plating in some areas of cockpit to protect pilot from anti-aircraft gunfire. Cockpit pressurised and air-conditioned.

SYSTEMS: Dual air-conditioning systems, one for cockpit environment and one for avionics cooling. Two independent hydraulic systems, each operating at pressure of 207 bars (3,000 lb/sq in). Primary system actuates landing gear extension and retraction, flaps, airbrake and afterburner nozzles; auxiliary system supplies power for aileron and all-moving tailplane boosters. Emergency system, operating pressure 108 bars (1,570 lb/sq in), for actuation of main landing gear. Electrical system (28V DC) powered by two 6kW engine driven starter/generators, with two inverters for 115V single-phase and 36V three-phase AC power at 400Hz.

AVIONICS: Include CT-3 VHF com transceiver, WL-7 radio compass, WG-4 low altitude radio altimeter, LTC-2 horizon gyro, YD-3 IFF, Type 930 radar warning receiver and XS-6 marker beacon receiver. Combat camera in small 'teardrop' fairing on starboard side of nose (not on export models). 'Odd Rods' type IFF aerials under nose on Q-5 variants, replaced on A-5C by a single blade antenna. Space provision in nose and centre-fuselage for additional or updated avionics, including an attack radar.

EQUIPMENT: Landing light under fuselage, forward of nosewheel bay and offset to port; taxying light on nosewheel leg.

ARMAMENT: Internal armament consists of one 23 mm cannon (Norinco Type 23-2K), with 100 rds, in each wingroot. Ten attachment points normally for external stores: two pairs in tandem under centre of fuselage, and three under each wing (one inboard and two outboard of mainwheel leg). Fuselage stations can each carry a 250 kg bomb (Chinese 250-2 or 250-3, US Mk 82 or Snakeye, French Durandal, or similar). Inboard wing stations can carry 6 kg or 25 lb practice bombs, or a pod containing eight Chinese 57-2 (57 mm), seven 68 mm, or seven Norinco 90-1 (90 mm) or four 130-1 (130 mm) rockets. Centre wing stations can carry a 500 kg or 750 lb bomb, a BL755 600 lb cluster bomb, a Chinese 250-2 or -3 bomb, US Mk 82 or Snakeye, French Durandal, or similar, or a C-801 anti-shipping missile. Normal bomb carrying capacity is 1,000 kg (2,205 lb), max capacity 2,000 kg (4,410 lb). Instead of bombs, the centre wing stations can each carry a 760 litre drop tank (see Power Plant paragraph) or an ECM pod. The outboard wing stations can each be occupied by a 400 litre drop tank (when the larger tank is not carried on the centre wing station) or by air-to-air missiles such as the Chinese PL-2, PL-2B, PL-7, AIM-9 Sidewinder and Matra R.550 Magic. Within the overall max T-O weight, all stores mentioned can be carried provided that CG shift remains within the allowable operating range of 31 to 39 per cent of mean aerodynamic chord, and more than 22 external stores configurations are possible. The aircraft carries an SH-1J or ABS1A optical sight for level and dive bombing, or for air-to-ground rocket launching. Some aircraft in Chinese service can carry a single 5-20 kT nuclear bomb.

DIMENSIONS, EXTERNAL (Q-5 II):
- Wing span 9.70 m (31 ft 10 in)
- Wing chord (mean aerodynamic) 3.097 m (10 ft 2 in)
- Wing aspect ratio 3.37
- Length overall: incl nose probe 16.255 m (53 ft 4 in)
  - excl nose probe 15.415 m (50 ft 7 in)
- Height overall 4.516 m (14 ft 9¾ in)
- Wheel track 4.40 m (14 ft 5¼ in)
- Wheelbase 4.01 m (13 ft 2 in)

AREAS:
- Wings, gross 27.95 m² (300.85 sq ft)
- Vertical tail surfaces (total) 4.64 m² (49.94 sq ft)
- Horizontal tail surfaces:
  - movable 5.00 m² (53.82 sq ft)
  - total, incl projected fuselage area 8.62 m² (92.78 sq ft)

WEIGHTS AND LOADINGS:
- Weight empty 6,494 kg (14,317 lb)
- Fuel: max internal 2,827 kg (6,232 lb)
  - two 400 litre drop tanks 620 kg (1,367 lb)
  - two 760 litre drop tanks 1,178 kg (2,597 lb)
  - max internal/external 4,005 kg (8,829 lb)
- Max external stores load 2,000 kg (4,410 lb)
- Max T-O weight: clean 9,530 kg (21,010 lb)
  - with max external stores 12,000 kg (26,455 lb)
- Max wing loading: clean 341 kg/m² (69.9 lb/sq ft)
  - with max external stores 429 kg/m² (87.9 lb/sq ft)
- Max power loading: clean 149.5 kg/kN (1.47 lb/lb st)
  - with max external stores 188.3 kg/kN (1.85 lb/lb st)

PERFORMANCE (at max clean T-O weight, with afterburning, except where indicated):
- Max limiting Mach number 1.5
- Max level speed:
  - at 11,000 m (36,000 ft) Mach 1.12 (643 knots; 1,190 km/h; 740 mph)
  - at S/L 653 knots (1,210 km/h; 752 mph)
- T-O speed:
  - clean, 15° flap 162 knots (300 km/h; 186 mph)
  - with max external stores, 25° flap 178 knots (330 km/h; 205 mph)
- * Landing speed:
  - 25° flap, brake-chute deployed 150-165 knots (278-307 km/h; 172-191 mph)
- * Max rate of climb at 5,000 m (16,400 ft) 4,980-6,180 m (16,340-20,275 ft)/min
- Service ceiling 15,850 m (52,000 ft)
- T-O run:
  - *clean, 15° flap 700-750 m (2,300-2,460 ft)
  - with max external stores, 25° flap 1,250 m (4,100 ft)
- Landing run:
  - 25° flap, brake-chute deployed 1,060 m (3,480 ft)
- Combat radius with max external stores, afterburners off:
  - lo-lo-lo (500 m; 1,640 ft) 216 nm (400 km; 248 miles)
  - hi-lo-hi (8,000/500/8,000 m; 26,250/1,640/26,250 ft) 324 nm (600 km; 373 miles)
- Range at 11,000 m (36,000 ft) with max internal and external fuel, afterburners off nearly 1,080 nm (2,000 km; 1,243 miles)
- *g* limits:
  - with full load of bombs and/or drop tanks 5
  - with drop tanks empty 6.5
  - clean 7.5

* *depending upon airfield elevation and temperature*

Prototype A-5M improved-capability attack aircraft, with new nav/attack system and digital avionics

NAMC Q-5K KONG YUN (CLOUD)

In a programme similar to that of the A-5M (see next entry), initiated in June 1987, a French team led by Thomson-CSF carried out prototype upgrading of the Q-5 with a new avionics suite as described in the 1990-91 *Jane's*. This programme was intended to fulfil a PLA Air Force requirement, but was abandoned in 1990.

NAMC A-5M

This improved version of the Q-5 II, intended for export, is the subject of a programme started on 1 August 1986 between CATIC and Alenia to upgrade the aircraft's avionics by incorporating a new all-weather nav/attack system similar to that used in the AMX aircraft. The M (for Modified) version also has improved WP6A turbojets with dry and afterburning ratings of 29.42 kN (6,614 lb st) and 36.78 kN (8,267 lb st) respectively.

Two A-5M prototypes were ordered, and the first of these (converted from Q-5 IIs) made its initial flight on 30 August 1988, but was lost in a crash on 17 October 1988. The second prototype flew on 8 March 1989, and a replacement for the first was subsequently completed. On 19 February 1991 it was announced that development and flight testing had been successfully completed, and that an agreement was being negotiated to initiate production to meet potential orders.

The nav/attack system is designed around two Singer central digital computers and a dual-redundant MIL-STD-1553B databus with plenty of growth potential. Other new sensors and equipment include a Pointer 2500 ranging radar, Litton LN-39A inertial navigation system, Alenia HUD-35 head-up display, air data computer, three-axis gyro package, RW-30 radar warning receiver, chaff/flare dispenser, HSI, AG-5 attitude indicator, static inverters, mode controls, and an interface unit linking these with the aircraft's existing AR-3201 VHF com radio, radio altimeter, radio compass, marker beacon receiver, IFF and armament system.

The number of external stores stations is increased to 12 by adding a fourth pylon beneath each outer wing, with some redistribution of the weapons carried on each wing station, and the PL-5B is added to the range of air-to-air missiles. External stores configurations are otherwise essentially the same as for the Q-5 II/A-5C, except that the underwing drop tanks can be of 1,140 litre (301 US gallon; 251 Imp gallon) capacity. The max external stores load of 2,000 kg (4,410 lb) remains unchanged.

DIMENSIONS, EXTERNAL: As for Q-5 II/A-5C except:
- Length overall 15.366 m (50 ft 5 in)
- Height overall 4.53 m (14 ft 10¼ in)

WEIGHTS AND LOADINGS:
- Weight empty 6,728 kg (14,833 lb)
- Max T-O weight: clean 9,769 kg (21,537 lb)
  - with max external stores 12,200 kg (26,869 lb)
- Max wing loading: clean 349.5 kg/m² (71.58 lb/sq ft)
  - with max external stores 436.5 kg/m² (89.40 lb/sq ft)
- Max power loading: clean 132.8 kg/kN (1.30 lb/lb st)
  - with max external stores 165.8 kg/kN (1.63 lb/lb st)

PERFORMANCE (estimated):
- Max level speed at S/L at clean T-O weight 658 knots (1,220 km/h; 758 mph)
- Max level flight Mach number at 11,000 m (36,000 ft) at clean T-O weight 1.205
- Unstick speed, with afterburning:
  - no external stores, 15° flap 162 knots (300 km/h; 187 mph)
  - full external stores, 25° flap 174 knots (322 km/h; 200 mph)
- Landing speed, 25° flap, brakes on and brake-chute deployed (depending upon AUW) 150-166 knots (278-307 km/h; 173-191 mph)
- Max vertical rate of climb at 5,000 m (16,400 ft) at clean T-O weight, with afterburning 6,900 m (22,638 ft)/min
- Service ceiling at clean T-O weight 16,000 m (52,500 ft)
- T-O run, with afterburning:
  - no external stores, 15° flap 911 m (2,989 ft)
  - full external stores, 25° flap 1,250 m (4,101 ft)
- Landing run, 25° flap, brakes on and brake-chute deployed 1,060 m (3,478 ft)
- Combat radius with full external stores:
  - out at 8,000 m (26,250 ft), combat at 500 m (1,640 ft) and back at 11,000 m (36,000 ft) 280 nm (518 km; 322 miles)
  - out, combat and back all at 500 m (1,640 ft) 174 nm (322 km; 200 miles)
- Range at 11,000 m (36,000 ft) with two 760 litre (200 US gallon; 167 Imp gallon) drop tanks 1,080 nm (2,000 km; 1,243 miles)

NAMC K-8 KARAKORUM 8

This tandem two-seat jet trainer (originally L-8) is the subject of a collaborative programme between NAMC and the Pakistan Aeronautical Complex, and is described under the NAMC/PAC heading in the International section.

NAMC N-5A

Chinese name: Nongye Feiji 5 (Agricultural aircraft 5) or Nong-5

First details of this specialised farming and forestry aircraft, design of which began in November 1987, were revealed at the Farnborough International air show in September 1988. The N-5A, of which three prototypes have been built, is designed to meet Chinese (CCAR) and US (FAR) Pt 23 airworthiness requirements (Normal category), and is expected to be offered eventually for export. A domestic market for more than 300, as a Y-5 replacement, has been estimated. It first flew on 26 December 1989, and certification was anticipated in 1991.

TYPE: Single-/two-seat agricultural aircraft.

WINGS: All-metal low-wing monoplane. Non-swept two-spar thin-wall structure, of mainly constant chord (wing section LS(1)-0417 Mod, thickness/chord ratio 17 per cent, throughout span). Root portions sweptforward 18°. Dihedral 4° 30′ from roots. Incidence 2°. Electrically actuated single-slotted trailing-edge flaps. Differential ailerons, actuated mechanically; ground adjustable tab on each aileron.

FUSELAGE: Forward fuselage is a crash-resistant structure of welded alloy steel tube with quickly removable side panels; rear fuselage is of riveted duralumin; lower skin panels, of stainless steel, are non-removable. Entire structure anodised before assembly and has external finish of polyurethane enamel.

TAIL UNIT: Cantilever non-swept structure of aluminium alloy. Fin and tailplane are two-spar box structures, latter having inverted aerofoil section. Electrically actuated trim tab in starboard elevator; ground adjustable tab on rudder.

LANDING GEAR: Non-retractable tricycle type, with single wheel and oleo-pneumatic shock absorber on each unit. Nose unit has a telescopic strut, a size 400 × 150 mm tyre, pressure 2.5 bars (36.3 lb/sq in), and is fitted with a shimmy damper and wire cutter. Main gear legs are of trailing-link type, with wheel tyres size 500 × 200 mm, pressure 3.0 bars (43.5 lb/sq in). Hydraulic mainwheel disc brakes and parking brake.

POWER PLANT: One 298 kW (400 hp) Textron Lycoming IO-720-D1B flat-eight engine, driving a Hartzell HC-C3YR-1RF/F8475R three-blade constant-speed metal propeller. All fuel in wing tanks with combined capacity of 329 litres (87 US gallons; 72.4 Imp gallons). Gravity fuelling point in upper surface of each wing at root.

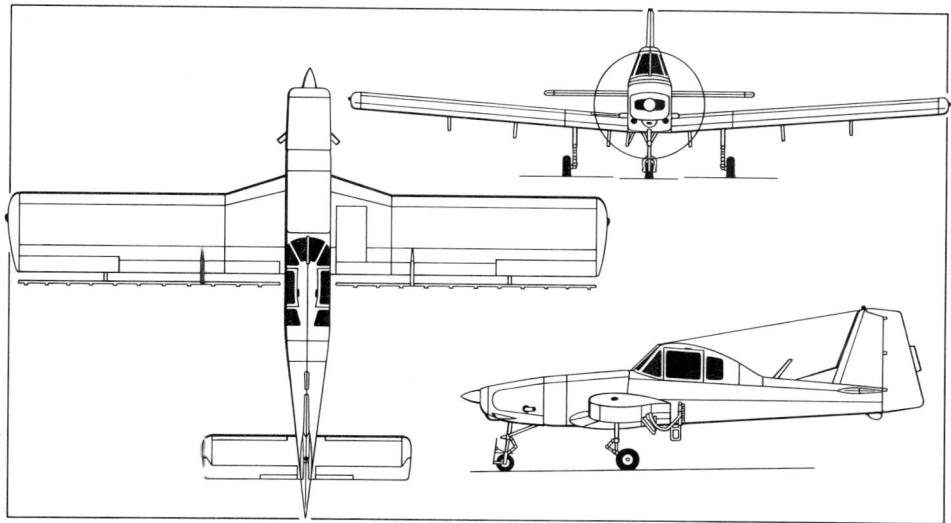

First prototype Nanchang N-5A (Textron Lycoming IO-720 flat-eight engine)

Nanchang N-5A agricultural monoplane *(Jane's/Mike Keep)*

ACCOMMODATION: Tandem seats and inertia reel safety harnesses for pilot and, when required, a loader/mechanic, under hard-top framed canopy with all-round field of view. Downward opening window/door on each side. Cockpit semi-sealed with ram air ventilation, slightly pressurised to prevent chemical ingress. Cockpit heating optional. Windscreen washer, wiper and demister standard. Deflector cable from top of windscreen cable cutter to tip of fin.

SYSTEMS: Hydraulic system for brakes only. No pneumatic system. Electrical system powered by Prestolite 28V 100A AC generator and 30Ah battery.

AVIONICS: Bendix/King KY 96A VHF com transceiver and stall warning system standard; KHF 950 HF/SSB com transceiver optional. Other options include Type 263 radio altimeter; LC-2 magnetic compass; WL-7A radio compass; and XS-6B marker beacon receiver.

EQUIPMENT: Glassfibre honeycomb hopper, for liquid or dry chemicals, forward of cockpit, with quick-dump system permitting release of all contents within 5 s. Solid or spray dispersal system, as appropriate. Dispersal of liquids, powered by fan driven pump, is via Y-type filter and 60-nozzle spraybars and is suitable for high, medium or low volume application. Wire cutters on main landing gear and in front of cockpit canopy.

DIMENSIONS, EXTERNAL:
Wing span	13.418 m (44 ft 0¼ in)
Wing chord: at root	2.319 m (7 ft 7½ in)
at tip	1.877 m (6 ft 2 in)
Wing aspect ratio	6.80
Length overall	10.487 m (34 ft 4⅞ in)
Height overall	3.733 m (12 ft 3 in)
Fuselage: Max width	1.01 m (3 ft 3¾ in)
Max depth	1.735 m (5 ft 8¼ in)
Tailplane span	4.59 m (15 ft 0¾ in)
Wheel track	3.528 m (11 ft 7 in)
Wheelbase	2.713 m (8 ft 10¾ in)
Propeller diameter	2.184 m (7 ft 2 in)

DIMENSIONS, INTERNAL:
Cockpit: Length	2.29 m (7 ft 6¼ in)
Max width	1.00 m (3 ft 3¼ in)
Max height	1.26 m (4 ft 1½ in)
Hopper volume	1.20 m³ (42.38 cu ft)

AREAS:
Wings, gross	26.0 m² (279.86 sq ft)
Ailerons (total)	2.08 m² (22.39 sq ft)
Trailing-edge flaps (total)	4.06 m² (43.70 sq ft)
Fin	2.28 m² (24.54 sq ft)
Rudder, incl tab	1.57 m² (16.90 sq ft)
Tailplane	4.68 m² (50.38 sq ft)
Elevators (total, incl tabs)	2.20 m² (23.68 sq ft)

WEIGHTS AND LOADINGS:
Weight empty	1,328 kg (2,928 lb)
Fuel weight: normal	85 kg (187 lb)
max	233 kg (513 lb)
Payload: normal	763 kg (1,682 lb)
max	963 kg (2,123 lb)
Max T-O weight: normal	2,250 kg (4,960 lb)
overload	2,450 kg (5,401 lb)
Max wing loading: normal	86.54 kg/m² (17.72 lb/sq ft)
overload	94.23 kg/m² (19.30 lb/sq ft)
Max power loading: normal	7.55 kg/kW (12.40 lb/hp)
overload	8.22 kg/kW (13.50 lb/hp)

PERFORMANCE (A: with, B: without dispersal equipment):
Max level speed: A		111 knots (205 km/h; 127 mph)
B		118 knots (220 km/h; 136 mph)
Normal operating speed:		
A, B		92 knots (170 km/h; 105 mph)
Stalling speed, A and B:		
flaps up		57 knots (105 km/h; 66 mph)
flaps down		47 knots (86 km/h; 54 mph)
Max rate of climb at S/L: A		257 m (845 ft)/min
B		281 m (922 ft)/min
Service ceiling: A		3,750 m (12,300 ft)
B		4,280 m (14,040 ft)
T-O run: A		303 m (995 ft)
B		296 m (971 ft)
T-O to 15 m (50 ft): A		569 m (1,867 ft)
B		553 m (1,814 ft)
Landing from 15 m (50 ft): A		373 m (1,225 ft)
B		379 m (1,243 ft)

Landing run: A	246 m (807 ft)
B	252 m (827 ft)
Min banking turn radius: A	145 m (476 ft)
B	140 m (459 ft)
Normal range with standard fuel:	
A	135 nm (250 km; 155 miles)
B	152 nm (282 km; 175 miles)
Endurance with standard fuel: A	1 h 48 min
B	1 h 56 min
Ferry range with max fuel:	
A	528 nm (979 km; 608 miles)
Endurance (self-ferry) with max fuel	5 h 45 min

NAMC CJ-6A
Chinese name: Chuji Jiaolianji-6A (Basic training aircraft 6A) or Chujiao-6A
Westernised designation: PT-6A

The CJ-6's predecessor, the CJ-5, one of the first aircraft to be mass produced in post-1949 China, was a licence built version of the Soviet Yak-18 basic trainer. It first flew on 3 July 1954, and 379 were built at Nanchang between 1954 and 1958, for Air Force, Navy and CAAC use.

Design of the CJ-6, as a Chinese engineered successor to the CJ-5, was initiated at Shenyang in the Autumn of 1956, a prototype powered by a 108 kW (145 hp) Mikulin M-11ER radial engine flying for the first time on 27 August 1958. Flight trials with this power plant proving disappointing, a modified version was tested (first flight 18 July 1960) with a 194 kW (260 hp) Ivchenko AI-14R engine. Responsibility for the CJ-6 was subsequently transferred to Nanchang, where further redesign preceded the first flight of a production-standard prototype on 15 October 1961. Production go-ahead was given in 1962 for the aircraft (in January) and the Chinese HS6 version of the AI-14R engine (in June), and a total of 1,796 CJ-6s (all versions) had been built by the end of 1986, including exports to Albania, Bangladesh, Cambodia, Korea, Tanzania and Zambia.

Standard version since December 1965 has been the **CJ-6A**, signifying introduction of the uprated HS6A engine. Ten examples were built in 1964-66 of an armed version, designated **CJ-6B**. The prototype of a civil agricultural version known as the **Haiyan** (see following entry) has been developed, and a six-seat utility version has been proposed. The details which follow apply to the standard CJ-6A basic trainer:

DESIGN FEATURES: All-metal cantilever low-wing monoplane. Two-spar wings, with detachable, tapered and dihedralled outer panels. Retractable tricycle landing gear, with low-pressure mainwheel tyres, suitable for operation from grass strips.

POWER PLANT: One 213 kW (285 hp) Zhuzhou (SMPMC) HS6A nine-cylinder air-cooled radial engine, driving a Baoding J9-G1 two-blade constant-speed propeller. Fuel capacity (two tanks) 100 litres (26.4 US gallons; 22 Imp gallons).

DIMENSIONS, EXTERNAL:
Wing span	10.18 m (33 ft 4¾ in)
Length overall	8.46 m (27 ft 9 in)
Height overall	3.25 m (10 ft 8 in)

WEIGHTS AND LOADINGS:
Weight empty	1,172 kg (2,584 lb)
Max fuel	110 kg (243 lb)
Max T-O weight	1,419 kg (3,128 lb)

PERFORMANCE:
Max level speed	155 knots (286 km/h; 178 mph)
Landing speed	62 knots (115 km/h; 72 mph)
Max rate of climb at S/L	380 m (1,248 ft)/min
Service ceiling	5,080 m (16,665 ft)
T-O run	280 m (920 ft)
Landing run	350 m (1,150 ft)
Endurance	3 h 36 min

NAMC HAIYAN (PETREL)

To meet a national requirement for a multi-purpose agricultural and forestry aircraft, NAMC began work on a conversion of its CJ-6 basic trainer (see preceding entry) in April 1985, this **Haiyan A** prototype flying for the first time on 17 August that year. It was fitted with a more powerful (257 kW; 345 hp) HS6E engine and a new-design propeller. Removal of the rear seat allowed a 400 kg (882 lb) insecticide tank to be installed, and another 200 kg (441 lb) of chemical was accommodated in the leading-edge of the wing centre-section.

Further details of the Haiyan A and of two proposed production versions (Haiyan B and C) can be found in the 1989-90 and earlier *Jane's*. This programme may now have been superseded by the N-5A.

SAC
SHAANXI AIRCRAFT COMPANY
PO Box 34, Chenggu, Shaanxi 723213
Telephone: 86/Hanzhong 2974 ext 2061
Telex: 70141 SAC CN
GENERAL MANAGER: Yan Guangming
MARKETING MANAGER: Li Yousen

Founded in the late 1970s, SAC is responsible for the Y-8 transport aircraft programme; non-aerospace products include 36-seat coaches and small trucks. The company occupies a 204 ha (504 acre) site and had a 1990 workforce of about 10,000 people; its covered area includes the largest final assembly building in China.

SAC Y-8 YUNSHUJI-8
NATO reporting name: Cub
The Shaanxi Aircraft Company is building a Chinese development of the Antonov An-12B four-turboprop civil/military transport aircraft. Redesign of this version was carried out at Xian, beginning in March 1969; the first Y-8 made its initial flight on 25 December 1974, followed by a second (the first built by SAC) on 29 December 1975.

Outwardly, the Y-8 can be distinguished from the An-12 by its more pointed nose transparencies. The engines, derived from the Ivchenko AI-20M, are produced at Zhuzhou; landing gear and all hydraulic components are

Shaanxi Y-8A four-turboprop multi-purpose medium-range transport of the PLA Air Force

Black Hawk helicopter being unloaded from a Y-8A

manufactured by Shaanxi Aero-Hydraulic Component Factory (SAHCF).

The decision to put the Y-8 into production was taken in January 1980, and 31 had been completed for CAAC and the PLA Air Force by February 1989.

Variants of the Y-8 are designated as follows:

Y-8: Prototype.

Y-8A: Helicopter carrier. Main cabin height increased by 120 mm (4.72 in) by deleting internal gantry; downward opening rear ramp/door. First delivered 1987.

Y-8B: Civil transport. Military equipment deleted; weight reduced by 1,720 kg (3,792 lb); some avionics differ. First delivered 1986.

Y-8C: Fully pressurised version, developed with Lockheed collaboration. Pressurised volume increased from 31 m³ (1,095 cu ft) to 212 m³ (7,487 cu ft); effective length of cargo hold extended by 2.00 m (6 ft 6¾ in). Other changes include redesigned cargo loading door and main landing gear; improved air-conditioning and oxygen systems; additional emergency exits. First flight 17 December 1990; service entry anticipated in 1992, for various civil and military applications.

Y-8D: Export version, with main avionics supplied by Collins and Litton. Delivered 1987 to Sri Lanka Air Force (two).

Y-8E: Drone carrier version. Forward pressure cabin accommodates drone controller's console; carrier/launch trapeze for one drone under each outer wing panel. Delivered 1989.

Y-8F: Livestock (sheep) carrier, with cages to hold up to 350 animals. Delivered early 1990.

Y-8X: Maritime patrol version, previously referred to in *Jane's* as Y-8MPA. Western nav/com, radar, surveillance and search equipment. Larger chin radome. Received type approval September 1984, but not yet in production. May be used for both ASW patrol and civilian offshore duties such as fishery patrol, pollution monitoring, and support for oil exploration industry.

Other variants under development include one for AEW (with assistance from GEC-Marconi). An in-flight refuelling tanker study for the Y-8 was made by Flight Refuelling of the UK in the mid-1980s. Alternative power plants, including the General Electric CT7, are also under consideration.

The following description applies to the standard Y-8A transport, unless otherwise indicated:

TYPE: Four-turboprop transport aircraft.

WINGS: Cantilever high-wing monoplane. All-metal two-spar box structure in five panels, comprising centre-section, intermediate portions and tip sections. Wing sections C-5-18 at root, C-3-16 at rib 15 and C-3-14 at tip, with respective thickness/chord ratios of 18, 16 and 14 per cent. Anhedral 1° on intermediate panels, 4° on outboard sections. Incidence 4°. Sweepback 6° 50′ at quarter-chord. Mechanically actuated, aerodynamically balanced aluminium ailerons, capable of differential operation and fitted with trim tabs. All-metal double-slotted Fowler flaps, actuated hydraulically, in two segments on each trailing-edge. Comb-shaped all-metal spoilers forward of flaps. Hot-air de-icing of leading-edges.

FUSELAGE: All-metal semi-monocoque circular-section structure of frames and stringers. Forward section and tail turret pressurised.

TAIL UNIT: Cantilever all-metal two-spar box structure, with fixed incidence tailplane. Elevators and rudder are manually operated and aerodynamically balanced. Trim tabs in rudder and each elevator. Electric de-icing of fin and tailplane leading-edges.

LANDING GEAR: Hydraulically retractable tricycle type, with Shaanxi (SAHCF) nitrogen/oil shock struts on all units. Four-wheel main bogie on each side retracts inward and upward into blister on side of fuselage. Twin-wheel nose unit, hydraulically steerable to ±35°, retracts rearward. Mainwheel tyres size 1,050 × 300 mm, pressure 28.4 bars

(412 lb/sq in); nosewheel tyres size 900 × 300 mm, pressure 16.7 bars (242 lb/sq in). Hydraulic disc brakes and Xingping inertial anti-skid sensor.

POWER PLANT: Four 3,169 kW (4,250 ehp) Zhuzhou (SMPMC) WJ6 turboprops, each driving a Baoding four-blade J17-G13 constant-speed propeller. All fuel in two integral tanks and 29 bag-type tanks in wings (20,102 litres; 5,310.5 US gallons; 4,422 Imp gallons) and fuselage (10,075 litres; 2,661.5 US gallons; 2,216 Imp gallons), giving total capacity of 30,177 litres (7,972 US gallons; 6,638 Imp gallons). Refuelling points in starboard side of fuselage (between frames 14 and 15), mainwheel fairing, and in wing upper surface.

ACCOMMODATION: Flight crew of five (pilot, co-pilot, navigator, engineer and radio operator). Forward portion of fuselage (up to frame 13) is pressurised, and can accommodate up to 14 passengers in addition to crew. Cargo compartment (between frames 13 and 43) is unpressurised. Max accommodation for up to 96 troops; or 58 paratroops; or 60 severe casualties plus 20 slightly wounded, with three medical attendants; or two 'Liberation' army trucks. Crew door and two emergency exits in forward fuselage. Three additional emergency exits in cargo compartment, access to which is via a large rear-loading ramp/door in underside of rear fuselage. Entire accommodation heated and ventilated.

SYSTEMS: Forward fuselage pressurised to maintain a differential of 0.20 bar (2.84 lb/sq in) at altitudes above 4,300 m (14,100 ft). Two independent hydraulic systems, with operating pressures of 152 bars (2,200 lb/sq in) (port) and 147 bars (2,130 lb/sq in) (starboard), plus hand and electrical standby pumps, for actuation of landing gear extension/retraction, nosewheel steering, flaps, brakes and rear ramp/door. Electrical DC power (28.5V) supplied by eight 12kW generators, an 18kW (24 hp) Xian Aero Engine Co APU (mainly for engine starting) and four 28Ah batteries. Four 12kVA alternators provide 115V AC power at 400Hz. Gaseous oxygen system for crew. Electric de-icing of windscreen, propellers and fin/tailplane leading-edges; hot air de-icing for wing leading-edges.

AVIONICS (Y-8X): Collins VHF, dual HF (DF-2 and DS-3) and HF/SSB radios; Litton Canada AN/APS-504(V)3 search radar; Litton Canada LTN-72 INS and LTN-211 Omega navigation system; Collins ADF, DME-42, TDR-90 ATC transponder, VOR-32, HSI-85, ADI-85A, 520-3337 RMI, IFF and autopilot. Optical and infra-red cameras, IR submarine detection system and sonobuoys.

Enlarged radome of maritime Y-8X

DIMENSIONS, EXTERNAL:
Wing span	38.00 m (124 ft 8 in)
Wing chord: at root	4.73 m (15 ft 6¼ in)
at tip	1.69 m (5 ft 6½ in)
Wing aspect ratio	11.85
Length overall	34.022 m (111 ft 7½ in)
Fuselage: Max diameter of circular section	
	4.10 m (13 ft 5½ in)
Height overall	11.16 m (36 ft 7½ in)
Tailplane span	12.196 m (40 ft 0¼ in)
Wheel track (c/l of shock struts)	4.92 m (16 ft 1¾ in)
Wheelbase (c/l of main bogie)	9.576 m (31 ft 5 in)
Propeller diameter	4.50 m (14 ft 9¼ in)
Propeller ground clearance	1.89 m (6 ft 2½ in)
Crew door: Height	1.455 m (4 ft 9¼ in)
Width	0.80 m (2 ft 7½ in)
Rear loading hatch: Length	7.67 m (25 ft 2 in)
Width: min	2.16 m (7 ft 1 in)
max	3.10 m (10 ft 2 in)
Emergency exits (each): Height	0.55 m (1 ft 9¾ in)
Width	0.60 m (1 ft 11½ in)

DIMENSIONS, INTERNAL:
Cabin (incl flight deck, galley and toilet):	
Length	13.50 m (44 ft 3½ in)
Width: min	3.00 m (9 ft 10 in)
max	3.50 m (11 ft 5¾ in)

Model of the Shaanxi Y-8E with two WZ-5 high-altitude reconnaissance UAVs under the wings

Height: min	2.40 m (7 ft 10½ in)	Max T-O weight	61,000 kg (134,480 lb)	Service ceiling, AUW of 51,000 kg (112,435 lb)	
max	2.60 m (8 ft 6½ in)	Max taxi weight	61,500 kg (135,585 lb)		10,400 m (34,120 ft)
Floor area	55.0 m² (592.0 sq ft)	Max landing weight	58,000 kg (127,870 lb)	Service ceiling, one engine out, AUW of 51,000 kg	
Volume	123.3 m³ (4,354.3 cu ft)	Max zero-fuel weight	36,266 kg (79,955 lb)	(112,435 lb)	8,100 m (26,575 ft)

AREAS:

Wings, gross	121.86 m² (1,311.7 sq ft)	Max wing loading	500.6 kg/m² (102.5 lb/sq ft)	T-O run	1,270 m (4,167 ft)
Ailerons (total)	7.84 m² (84.39 sq ft)	Max power loading	4.81 kg/kW (7.91 lb/ehp)	T-O to 15 m (50 ft)	3,007 m (9,866 ft)
Trailing-edge flaps (total)	26.91 m² (289.66 sq ft)			Landing from 15 m (50 ft)	2,174 m (7,133 ft)
Rudder	6.537 m² (70.36 sq ft)			Landing run	1,050 m (3,445 ft)
Tailplane	27.05 m² (291.16 sq ft)			Range: with max payload	687 nm (1,273 km; 791 miles)
Elevators (total)	7.101 m² (76.43 sq ft)			with max fuel	3,030 nm (5,615 km; 3,490 miles)

PERFORMANCE (at max T-O weight except where indicated):

Max level speed at 7,000 m (22,965 ft) 357 knots (662 km/h; 411 mph)

Max cruising speed at 8,000 m (26,250 ft) 297 knots (550 km/h; 342 mph)

WEIGHTS AND LOADINGS:

Weight empty, equipped	35,488 kg (78,237 lb)	Econ cruising speed at 8,000 m (26,250 ft)		Max endurance 11 h 7 min
Max fuel load	22,909 kg (50,505 lb)		286 knots (530 km/h; 329 mph)	
Max payload: containerised	16,000 kg (35,275 lb)	Max rate of climb at S/L	473 m (1,552 ft)/min	
bulk cargo	20,000 kg (44,090 lb)	Rate of climb at S/L, one engine out	231 m (758 ft)/min	

SAC

SHENYANG AIRCRAFT CORPORATION

PO Box 328, Shenyang, Liaoning
Telephone: 86 (24) 462680
Telex: 80018 SAMC CN
GENERAL MANAGER: Tang Qiansan
DEPUTY MANAGER: Xu Guosheng

One of the pioneer centres of fighter design in China, Shenyang now occupies a site area of more than 800 ha (1,976 acres) and has a workforce of over 20,000 people. Between 1956 and 1959 it produced 767 examples of the J-5 (licence MiG-17F), and from 1963 was the major producer (others were produced at Nanchang) of the J-6 series (Chinese versions of the MiG-19), including 634 tandem two-seat JJ-6 fighter/trainers. Initial development and production of the J-7 series (see Chengdu Aircraft Corporation entry) began at Shenyang, and SAC's principal current programme concerns the J-8 air superiority fighter. Aerospace products account for about 30 per cent of SAC's present activities, and include subcontract manufacture of cargo doors for the Boeing 757 and Boeing Canada Dash 8; rudders for the British Aerospace ATP; wing ribs and emergency exit hatches for the Airbus A320; tailcone, landing gear door and pylon components for the Lockheed C-130 Hercules; and other machined parts for BAe, Boeing, Deutsche Airbus and Saab-Scania.

SAC J-?

A new fighter, for entry into service by the year 2000, is in the design definition stage at Shenyang. Although various alternative configurations are under consideration, studies are understood to have favoured a single-seater with swept wings, close-coupled canards, single or twin engines, and a gross weight in the 10-15 tonne (22,045-33,070 lb) class. Other objectives include extensive use of composites, a fly-by-wire flight control system, and foreign co-operation in developing the power plant and/or avionics.

SAC J-8

Chinese name: Jianjiji-8 (Fighter aircraft 8) or Jian-8
Westernised designation: F-8
NATO reporting name: Finback

Development of the J-8 began at Shenyang in 1964, the first of two original prototypes making its first flight on 5 July 1969. Although all other J-8 activity was suspended during the cultural revolution, flight trials were allowed to continue, and these prototypes accumulated 663 hours of flying, in 1,025 flights, before production was eventually authorised in 1979. The following versions have since been produced:

J-8 ('Finback-A'): Initial clear-weather day fighter, powered by two Liyang (LMC) WP7B turbojets (each 43.15 kN; 9,700 lb st dry and 59.82 kN; 13,448 lb st with

Fourth prototype of the J-8 II single-seat multi-role fighter *(Paul Jackson)*

afterburning) and armed with single twin-barrel 23 mm cannon and four wing-mounted PL-2B air-to-air missiles. Single intake in nose, with conical centrebody. Approved for production in 1979, but built in small numbers only. Retrofitted from 1984 with Sichuan SR-4 fire control radar in intake centrebody. In service.

J-8 I ('Finback-A'): Improved version of J-8, with same power plant and armament but fitted from outset with Sichuan SR-4 radar in intake centrebody. Three prototypes built, one being lost before flight testing; first flight, by second aircraft, made on 24 April 1981. Initial batch production authorised in July 1985. Described in 1985-86 *Jane's.* More than 100 now in service, including upgraded J-8s, by early 1990, but gradually being supplanted by J-8 II.

J-8 II ('Finback-B'): All-weather dual-role version (high altitude interceptor and ground attack), embodying some 70 per cent redesign compared with J-8 I. Main configuration change is to 'solid' nose and twin lateral air intakes, to provide nose space for fire control radar and other avionics, and increased airflow for more powerful WP13A II turbojets. Four prototypes built (first flight 12 June 1984), plus two for static/fatigue testing. In production and service: 'several dozen' built by early 1990, but being manufactured in small economic batches rather than at a steady monthly rate.

Two J-8 IIs were delivered to Grumman Aerospace Corporation for prototype avionics upgrading under a joint Chinese/US programme known as Peace Pearl (see 1990-91 *Jane's* for details), but this programme was embargoed by the US government in mid-1989 and cancelled by the Chinese government in 1990.

The following description applies to the J-8 II:

TYPE: Single-seat twin-engined air superiority fighter, with secondary ground attack capability.

WINGS: Cantilever mid-wing monoplane. Thin-section delta wings, with slight anhedral and 60° sweepback on leading-edges. Small fence on each upper surface near tip. Two-segment single-slotted trailing-edge flaps on each wing inboard of aileron. Main wing structure is of aluminium alloy and high tensile steel. Control surfaces, which have hydraulically boosted actuation, are of aluminium honeycomb with skins of sheet aluminium.

FUSELAGE: Conventional semi-monocoque structure, 'waisted' between air intakes and tail section in accordance with area rule. Construction is mainly of aluminium alloy, with high tensile steel for main load-bearing members and titanium in high-temperature areas. Dielectric nosecone. Rear fuselage detachable for access to engines. Four door-type underfuselage airbrakes, one under each engine air intake trunk and one immediately aft of each mainwheel well. Spine fairing along top of fuselage from cockpit to fin, with small airscoop at foot of fin leading-edge. Additional airscoop at top of rear fuselage on each side, above tailplane.

TAIL UNIT: Cantilever sweptback all-metal surfaces, comprising broad chord fin and rudder and low-set all-moving tailplane; 60° sweepback on tailplane leading-edges. Ventral fin similar to that of MiG-23, with main portion folding sideways to starboard during take-off and landing, to provide additional directional stability. Rudder and rear part of tailplane are of aluminium honeycomb, with sheet aluminium skins; actuation is hydraulically boosted. Dielectric panels at tip of main fin (radar warning receiver antenna) and on non-folding portion of ventral fin leading-edge.

LANDING GEAR: Hydraulically retractable tricycle type, with single wheel and oleo-pneumatic shock absorber on each unit. Nose unit (which is steerable) retracts forward, main units inward into centre-fuselage; mainwheels turn to stow vertically inside fuselage, resulting in a slight overwing bulge. Brake-chute in bullet fairing at base of rudder.

POWER PLANT: Two Liyang (Guizhou Engine Co) WP13A II turbojets, each rated at 42.7 kN (9,590 lb st) dry and 65.9 kN (14,815 lb st) with afterburning, mounted side by side in rear fuselage with 'pen nib' fairing above and between exhaust nozzles. Lateral, non-swept air intakes, with automatically regulated ramp angle and large splitter plates similar in shape to those of MiG-23. Internal fuel capacity (four integral wing tanks plus fuselage tanks) approx 5,400 litres (1,426 US gallons; 1,188 Imp gallons). Single-point pressure refuelling. Provision for auxiliary fuel tanks on fuselage centreline and each outboard underwing pylon.

ACCOMMODATION: Pilot only, on ejection seat under one-piece canopy hinged at rear and opening upward. Cockpit pressurised, heated and air-conditioned. Heated windscreen.

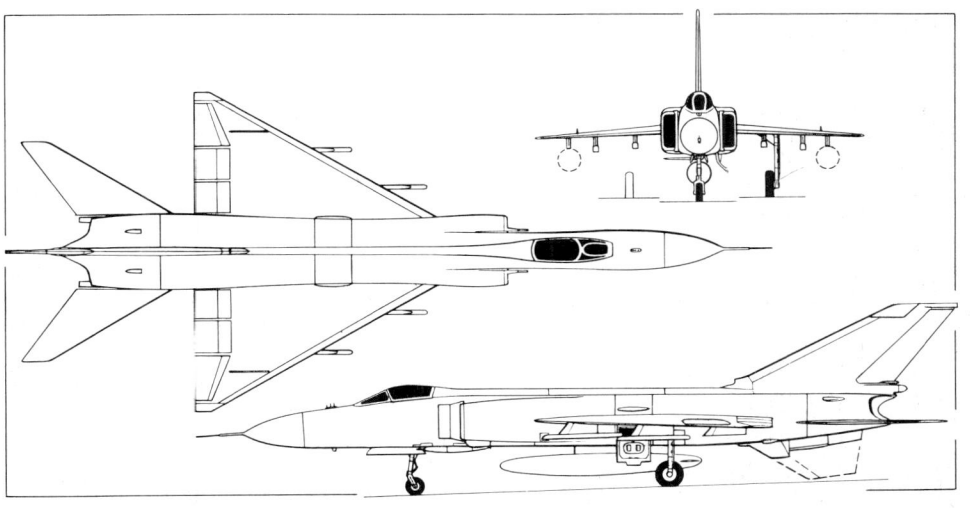
J-8 II version of the 'Finback' twin-jet fighter *(Pilot Press)*

Line-up of early J-8 ('Finback-A') day fighters

SYSTEMS: Two simple air-cycle environmental control systems, one for cockpit heating and air-conditioning and one for radar cooling; cooling air bled from engine compressor. Two 207 bar (3,000 lb/sq in) independent hydraulic systems (main utility system plus one for flight control surfaces boost), powered by engine driven pumps. 28.5V DC primary electrical power from two 12kW engine driven starter/generators, with two 6kVA alternators for 115/200V three-phase AC at 400Hz. Pneumatic bottles for emergency landing gear extension. Pop-out ram air emergency turbine under fuselage.

AVIONICS: VHF/UHF and HF/SSB com radio, Tacan, radio compass, radar altimeter, ILS, marker beacon receiver,

'Odd Rods' type IFF, radar warning receiver and ECM. Autopilot for attitude and heading hold, altitude hold and stability augmentation. Existing fire control system comprises a monopulse radar, optical gyro gunsight and gun camera. Enlarged avionics bays in nose and fuselage provide room for modernised fire control system and other upgraded avionics. Chaff/flare dispensers in tailcone.

ARMAMENT: One 23 mm Type 23-3 twin-barrel cannon, with 200 rds, in underfuselage pack immediately aft of nosewheel doors. Seven external stations (one under fuselage and three under each wing) for a variety of stores which can include PL-2B infra-red air-to-air missiles,

PL-7 medium-range semi-active radar homing air-to-air missiles, 18-round pods of 57 mm Type 57-2 unguided air-to-air rockets, launchers for 90 mm air-to-surface rockets, bombs, or (centreline and outboard underwing stations only) auxiliary fuel tanks.

DIMENSIONS, EXTERNAL:

Wing span	9.344 m (30 ft 7⅞ in)
Wing aspect ratio	2.1
Length overall, incl nose probe	21.59 m (70 ft 10 in)
Height overall	5.41 m (17 ft 9 in)
Wheel track	approx 3.80 m (12 ft 7 in)
Wheelbase	approx 7.25 m (23 ft 9½ in)

AREAS:

Wings, gross	42.2 m² (454.2 sq ft)

WEIGHTS AND LOADINGS:

Weight empty	9,820 kg (21,649 lb)
Normal T-O weight	14,300 kg (31,526 lb)
Max T-O weight	17,800 kg (39,242 lb)
Wing loading:	
at normal T-O weight	338.9 kg/m² (69.4 lb/sq ft)
at max T-O weight	421.8 kg/m² (86.4 lb/sq ft)
Power loading:	
at normal T-O weight	110.5 kg/kN (1.08 lb/lb st)
at max T-O weight	137.5 kg/kN (1.35 lb/lb st)

PERFORMANCE:

Design max operating Mach number	2.2
Design max level speed	701 knots (1,300 km/h; 808 mph) IAS
Unstick speed	175 knots (325 km/h; 202 mph)
Landing speed	156 knots (290 km/h; 180 mph)
Max rate of climb at S/L	12,000 m (39,370 ft)/min
Acceleration from Mach 0.6 to 1.25 at 5,000 m	
(16,400 ft)	54 s
Service ceiling	20,000 m (65,620 ft)
T-O run, with afterburning	670 m (2,198 ft)
Landing run, brake-chute deployed	1,000 m (3,280 ft)
Combat radius	432 nm (800 km; 497 miles)
Max range	1,187 nm (2,200 km; 1,367 miles)
g limit in sustained turn at Mach 0.9 at 5,000 m	
(16,400 ft)	+4.83

SAMF
SHANGHAI AIRCRAFT MANUFACTURING FACTORY (Subsidiary of Shanghai Aviation Industrial Corporation)

PO Box 232-007, Shanghai 200232
Telephone: 86 (21) 4383311
Fax: 86 (21) 6658103
Telex: 33136 SHAIR CN
PRESIDENT: Wu Zuo-Quan

SAMF occupies a site area of 135 ha (333.5 acres) and has a total workforce of about 7,000, of whom some 3,000 are engaged in the present MD-82 programme. The factory has produced main and nose landing gear doors for the McDonnell Douglas MD-80 series since 1979, and had delivered 1,799 sets by the end of 1990. Other MD-80 components now produced include cargo and service doors, avionics bay doors and tailplanes.

Shanghai-assembled McDonnell Douglas MD-82 of China Eastern Airlines

SAMF (MCDONNELL DOUGLAS) MD-82

McDonnell Douglas Corporation announced on 11 January 1984 the signing of a letter of intent with SAMF on a co-production programme for MD-82 jet transports. Details of this new programme were confirmed in an April 1985 announcement of the sale of 26 MD-82s to China, of which 25 are being assembled in Shanghai, all for Chinese airlines.

One Douglas built aircraft was delivered in October 1985, and assembly at Shanghai began in April 1986. Complete major subassemblies were supplied by Douglas for the first

three MD-82s to be assembled at Shanghai; since then, the Chinese industry has taken a gradually increasing share in manufacturing the remaining 22, producing its own landing gear doors, cargo and service doors and aileron supports from aircraft No. 9. Starting with the 23rd aircraft, SAMF has produced tailplanes for both its own and Douglas-built MD-82s.

Rollout of the first Chinese assembled MD-82 took place on 8 June 1987, with first flight following on 2 July. Delivery

to the Shenyang branch of CAAC was made on the last day of that month, and the aircraft entered service with China Northeast Airlines on 4 August. By 1 January 1991, deliveries totalled 20 to CAAC (Shenyang branch) and China Eastern Airlines based at Shanghai. Delivery of the 25th was due in August 1991. Extension of the programme into 1993 with 10 more aircraft (five MD-82s and five MD-83s) received approval in 1990. The MD-83s will be bought back by McDonnell Douglas.

SAP
SHIJIAZHUANG AIRCRAFT PLANT

PO Box 164, Shijiazhuang, Hebei 050062
Telephone: 86/Shijiazhuang 744251
Telex: 26236 HBJXC CN
DIRECTOR: Zhou Enqing

This factory began producing the An-2 transport aircraft in 1970, and had a 1990 workforce of more than 4,000, including some 570 engineers and technicians. Its principal aircraft products are the Y-5 transport/agricultural biplane and the W-5 and W-6 microlight series.

SAP (ANTONOV) Y-5
Chinese name: Yunshuji-5 (Transport aircraft 5) or Yun-5
NATO reporting name: Colt

The Antonov An-2 general purpose biplane was supplied to, and since 1957 has been built under licence in, China in considerable numbers (nearly 1,000). The Y-5 was manufactured initially at Nanchang, which built 727 between 1957-68 (first flight 7 December 1957). A further 225 or more had been built by SAP by the end of 1990. The Y-5 continues to be used extensively by the PLA Air Force, which has about 300, and in a civil capacity for agricultural

and general transport work. Nanchang production included 229 Y-5s for agricultural duties and 114 for regional transport use.

A description of the basic An-2 can be found under the WSK-PZL Mielec heading in the Polish section of this edition. The standard Chinese civil version is designated **Y-5N**, but a more recent development is a specialised agricultural and forestry version known as the **Y-5B**, which first flew on 2 June 1989. It has been certificated to the Chinese equivalent of FAR Pt 23, and is now in production.

The Y-5B retains the airframe, power plant and multi-purpose adaptability of the basic aircraft, but has a corrosion resistant structure and specially developed role equipment. This comprises a large hopper/tank with emergency jettison of contents; a high flow rate wind-driven pump; and spraybars with various nozzle sizes depending on the spray volume required. Cabin has a new environmental control system, the cabin doors are sealed against ingress of chemical, and some electrical and instrument installations are also improved. The Y-5B can be crewed by one or two persons.

The following details apply to the Y-5B:

POWER PLANT: One 735.5 kW (986 hp) PZL Kalisz ASz-62IR-16 or Zhuzhou (SMPMC) HS5 nine-cylinder radial engine, driving an AW-2 or J12-G15 four-blade

propeller (diameters 3.60 m; 11 ft 9¾ in and 3.40 m; 11 ft 2 in respectively).

AVIONICS: Include Bendix/King KHF 950 HF and KY 196 VHF com radios, KR 87 ADF and KMA 24 audio control panel.

WEIGHTS AND LOADINGS (A: with dry chemical spreader, B: with liquid spray system):

Max payload: A, B	1,367 kg (3,013 lb)
Max T-O weight: A, B	5,250 kg (11,574 lb)

PERFORMANCE (A and B as for Weights):

Max level speed at S/L:	
A	110 knots (205 km/h; 127 mph)
B	108 knots (200 km/h; 124 mph)
Max level speed at 1,700 m (5,575 ft):	
A	119 knots (220 km/h; 137 mph)
B	116 knots (215 km/h; 133 mph)
Operating speed: A, B	86 knots (160 km/h; 99 mph)
Stalling speed: A, B	52 knots (95 km/h; 59 mph)
Max rate of climb at S/L: A	120 m (394 ft)/min
B	114 m (374 ft)/min
Rate of climb at 1,600 m (5,250 ft):	
A	133 m (436 ft)/min
B	123 m (404 ft)/min
Service ceiling: A	3,460 m (11,350 ft)
B	3,250 m (10,660 ft)

Air turning radius: A, B	350 m (1,150 ft)
T-O run: A	170 m (558 ft)
B	180 m (591 ft)
Landing run: A	160 m (525 ft)
B	157 m (515 ft)
Range at S/L with fuel load of 670 litres (177 US gallons;	
147 Imp gallons): A, B	456 nm (845 km; 525 miles)
Endurance, conditions as above: A, B	5 h 39 min
Swath width	20-50 m (66-165 ft)

Y-5B agricultural biplane produced by Shijiazhuang Aircraft Plant

XAC
XIAN AIRCRAFT MANUFACTURING COMPANY
PO Box 140, Xian, Shaanxi 710000
Telephone: 86 (29) 61971
Fax: 86 (29) 717859
Telex: 70101 XAC CN
GENERAL MANAGER: Shao Guobin
SALES MANAGER: Fei Yu

Established in 1958, the Xian aircraft factory has a covered area of some 850,000 m² (9,149,315 sq ft). The 1989 workforce numbered about 15,000, of whom about 10,000 were engaged in aircraft production. Aircraft built at Xian include Chinese versions of the Soviet Tupolev Tu-16 bomber (Chinese designation H-6) and Antonov An-24 (Y7-100) and An-26 (Y7H-500) transports. It is also developing a new two-seat supersonic strike aircraft, the H-7, powered by two large turbofan engines.

Since 1980 XAC has manufactured glassfibre header tanks, water float pylons, ailerons and various doors for the Canadair CL-215 amphibian; other subcontract work has included various components for the Airbus A300, Boeing 737 and 747, and ATR 42. It is expected to be the main Chinese centre for the MPC 75 airliner (see International section).

XAC (TUPOLEV) H-6
Chinese name: Hongzhaji-6 (Bomber aircraft 6) or Hong-6
Westernised designation: B-6
NATO reporting name: Badger

A Soviet licence to produce the Tupolev Tu-16 twin-jet bomber in China was granted in September 1957, two pattern aircraft (one disassembled, one in component knocked-down form) being delivered in 1959 and the former of these making its first flight in China on 27 September 1959. It was originally intended that both Harbin (HAMC) and Xian would be involved in the production programme, but in 1961 all work on the H-6, as the Chinese version was designated, was transferred to XAC. The first entirely Chinese built **H-6A** made its initial flight on 24 December 1968.

Production has been relatively slow, but it is continuing at a low rate (three or four per year), and the number in service with the PLA Air Force and Navy is now believed to be about 120, the current version being designated **B-6D**. Development of this version began in 1975, although its first flight did not take place until 29 August 1981. China has

supplied spares for the Tu-16 bombers of the Egyptian Air Force, and the sale of four B-6Ds to Iraq was reported in mid-1987. Those in PLA Air Force service are reportedly being updated with more modern bombing and navigation systems, and the possibility remains that ECM, reconnaissance or other variants may be developed in the future. A probe and drogue aerial tanker design study for the H-6 has been carried out by FRL of the UK, followed by a memorandum of understanding in September 1986 for FRL to assist CATIC in converting a number of H-6s to the tanker role. This version, which had not received a go-ahead up to early 1991, would serve primarily as a refuelling tanker for the Q-5 attack aircraft; there are no plans for a receiver version of the H-6.

As with other Chinese developments of original Soviet designs, some local modifications have been noted: some B-6Ds carrying C-601 missiles, for example, have a bigger and cylindrical chin fairing, housing a Chinese radar associated with cruise missile guidance; other H-6/B-6s have no chin radome at all.

TYPE: Twin-jet strategic bomber, tactical or maritime strike and reconnaissance aircraft.
POWER PLANT: Two 93.17 kN (20,944 lb st) Xian (XAE) WP8 turbojets. WQJ-1 starter motor. Fuel in total of 27 tanks in wings and fuselage, combined capacity approx 43,000 litres (11,360 US gallons; 9,460 Imp gallons).
ACCOMMODATION: Crew of six, including pilot and co-pilot. Ejection seats for all crew members.
AVIONICS: 20-channel VHF//UHF communications system. Automatic navigation system, based on Doppler radar, INS and AHRS, linked to autopilot.
ARMAMENT: Defensive armament of six or seven guns in nose (not on B-6D), dorsal, ventral and tail positions. Conventional or nuclear bombs in internal bay. Two underwing C-601 anti-shipping missiles on B-6D. Chute for flares and marine markers aft of bomb bay.

DIMENSIONS, EXTERNAL:
Wing span	34.189 m (112 ft 2 in)
Length overall	34.800 m (114 ft 2 in)
Height overall	10.355 m (33 ft 11¾ in)
Wheel track	9.755 m (32 ft 0 in)
Wheelbase	10.913 m (35 ft 9¾ in)

AREAS:
Wings, gross: H-6A	164.65 m² (1,772.3 sq ft)
B-6D	167.55 m² (1,803.5 sq ft)

WEIGHTS AND LOADINGS (A: H-6A, B: B-6D):
Weight empty: A	37,729 kg (83,178 lb)
B	38,530 kg (84,944 lb)

Max fuel load: A, B	approx 33,000 kg (72,752 lb)
Normal bomb load: A, B	3,000 kg (6,614 lb)
Max bomb load: B	9,000 kg (19,841 lb)
Two C-601 missiles: B	4,880 kg (10,758 lb)
Normal T-O weight: B	72,000 kg (158,733 lb)
Max T-O weight: A	72,000 kg (158,733 lb)
B	75,800 kg (167,110 lb)
Max landing weight: A, B	55,000 kg (121,254 lb)
Normal landing weight: B	48,000 kg (105,822 lb)
Max wing loading: A	437.3 kg/m² (89.57 lb/sq ft)
B	452.4 kg/m² (92.66 lb/sq ft)
Max power loading: A	386.4 kg/kN (3.79 lb/lb st)
B	406.8 kg/kN (3.99 lb/lb st)

PERFORMANCE (B-6D with two underwing C-601 anti-shipping missiles):
Max cruising speed	424 knots (786 km/h; 488 mph)
T-O speed with full load	163 knots (302 km/h; 188 mph)
Normal landing speed	126 knots (233 km/h; 145 mph)
Max rate of climb at S/L	1,140 m (3,740 ft)/min
Service ceiling	12,000 m (39,370 ft)
T-O run with full load	2,100 m (6,890 ft)
Normal landing run	1,540 m (5,050 ft)
Combat radius	971 nm (1,800 km; 1,118 miles)
Max range	2,320 nm (4,300 km; 2,672 miles)
Max endurance	5 h 41 min

XAC H-7
Chinese name: Hongzhaji-7 (Bomber aircraft 7) or Hong-7
Westernised designation: B-7

This new Chinese multi-role combat aircraft was first shown in model form in September 1988 at the Farnborough Air Show. In the same class as the Soviet Su-24 'Fencer', the H-7 is being developed as an all-weather interdictor/strike aircraft for the PLA Air Force and in maritime attack form for the Naval Air Force. The first of two prototypes was rolled out in August 1988 and made its first flight in late 1988 or early 1989. Static testing has been undertaken.

In 1988 the prototypes were said to be powered by twin 91.2 kN (20,515 lb st) Rolls-Royce Spey Mk 202 augmented turbofans (Xian WS9), but in October 1989 a senior PLA Air Force official was quoted as saying that the aircraft had "a more powerful version of the WP7 Chinese built engine" (presumably a reference to the WP13A II that currently powers the J-8 II fighter); another Chinese source has suggested that US engines are or were envisaged, but have since been embargoed. The eventual intention is believed to be to power production H-7s with the Liming (LEMC)

Xian B-6D maritime strike bomber, showing underwing C-601 missile carriage

XAC Y-7 (Chinese development of the Antonov An-24) after modification by HAECO of Hong Kong as the prototype Y7-100

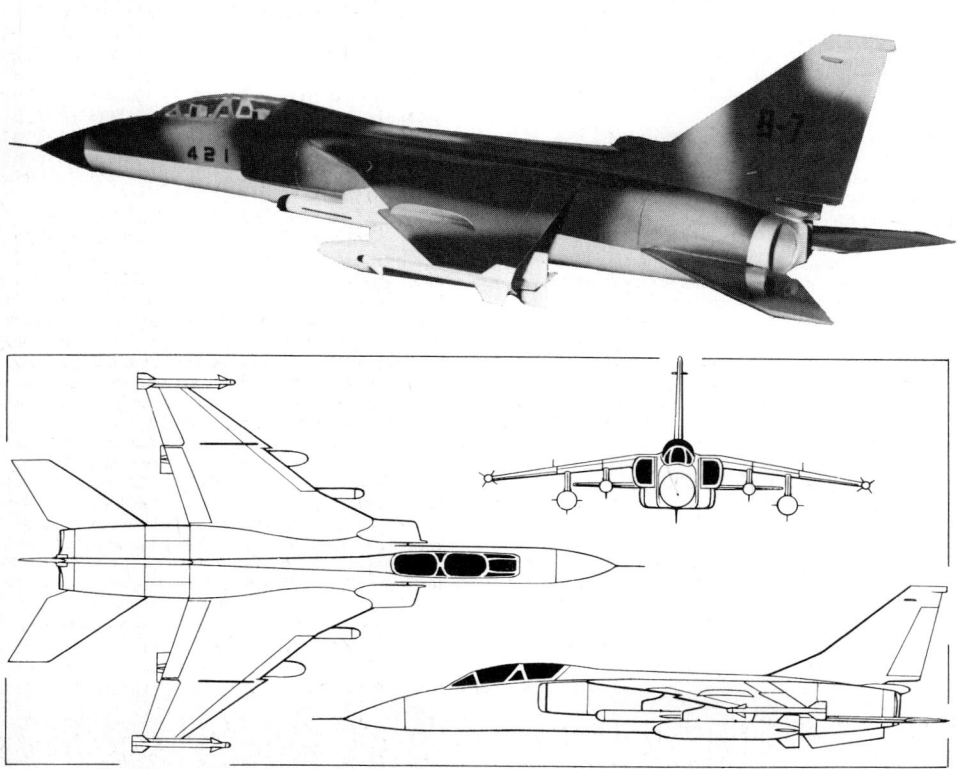

Provisional three-view *(Pilot Press)* **and model of XAC H-7 in maritime attack form**

WS6A turbofan (71.3 kN; 16,027 lb st dry, 138.3 kN; 31,085 lb st with afterburning) of Chinese design.

The general appearance of the H-7 is shown in the accompanying illustrations. It has compound-sweep wings, dog-tooth leading-edges, all-moving tailplane, lateral engine air intakes, and tandem seating for the crew of two on HTY-4 ejection seats operable at speeds from zero to 540 knots (1,000 km/h; 621 mph) and heights from sea level to 20,000 m (65,600 ft). The wings are fitted with leading-edge slats. The large fin is supplemented by a single ventral fin. On the model, the four underwing stores pylons were shown with two C-801 sea-skimming anti-shipping missiles inboard and auxiliary fuel tanks outboard. A 23 mm twin-barrel gun in the nose, and close-range air-to-air missile on each wingtip are claimed to give the H-7 a secondary air-to-air capability. Terrain following radar and avionics on the prototypes are claimed to be of Chinese design and manufacture. Entry into service was originally scheduled for 1992-93, but may have been delayed.

DIMENSIONS, EXTERNAL (estimated):

Wing span	12.65 m (41 ft 6 in)
Length overall, incl probe	18.60 m (61 ft 0 in)

WEIGHTS AND LOADINGS (estimated):

Max T-O weight	27,500 kg (60,627 lb)

PERFORMANCE (estimated):

Max level speed at altitude	Mach 1.8

XAC (ANTONOV) Y7-100

Chinese name: Yunshuji-7 (Transport aircraft 7) or Yun-7

NATO reporting name: Coke

Civil and military examples of the Antonov An-24 twin-turboprop transport aircraft (40 of which were purchased from the USSR) have been in service with CAAC and the PLA Air Force since about 1970. The Y-7, a reverse engineered version of this 48/52-passenger aircraft, received its Chinese certificate of airworthiness in 1980, following the completion of three prototypes (first flight 25 December 1970) plus two additional airframes for static and fatigue testing. Public debut by a pre-production Y-7 took place on 17 April 1982, and production started later that year.

Variants of the Y-7 are as follows:

Y-7: Initial production version: first flight announced

1 February 1984. Deliveries to CAAC began shortly afterwards; scheduled passenger services began 29 April 1986. Twenty built, including at least two for PLA Naval Air Force. Full description in 1988-89 *Jane's*. Being retrofitted with winglet modification of Y7-100.

Y7-100: Improved version, developed in 1985 by conversion of one Y-7 (B-3499) by Hong Kong Aircraft Engineering Company (HAECO). Winglets added; new three-person flight deck layout, all-new cabin interior with 52 reclining seats, windscreen de-icing, new HF/VHF communications, new navigation equipment, and installation of oxygen, air data and environmental control systems. Meets BCAR standards. First production Y7-100 flown in late 1985; certification awarded 23 January 1986. Total of approx 45 delivered by December 1990; production continuing.

Y7-200A: Improved Y7-100, with Pratt & Whitney Canada PW124B turboprops and Collins EFIS 85/86 avionics. First flight expected in mid-1992.

Y7-200B: Improved Y7-100 for domestic market, with Dongan WJ5E turboprops and new three-blade propellers, more advanced avionics (Collins EFIS 85/86), higher max lift coefficient, improved stall characteristics, lower fuel consumption. Overall length increased by 0.74 m (2 ft 5¼ in); empty weight reduced by 500 kg (1,102 lb). First flight 26 November 1990; deliveries scheduled to begin in 1992. Expected performance improvements include reduction of stalling speed from 92 knots (170 km/h; 106 mph) to 76 knots (140 km/h; 87 mph); a 300 m (985 ft) reduction in field length; a range increase (with max payload) of 162 nm (300 km; 186 miles); and Cat. II landing capability.

Y7H-500: Military and civil cargo version, derived from Antonov An-26; described separately.

The following description applies to the Y7-100, except where indicated:

TYPE: Twin-turboprop short/medium-range transport.

WINGS: Cantilever high-wing monoplane, with 2° 12′ 2″ anhedral on outer panels. Incidence 3°. Sweepback at quarter-chord on outer panels 6° 50′. All-metal two-spar structure, built in five sections: constant chord centre-section, two tapered inner wings and two tapered outer panels. Mass balanced servo-compensated ailerons, with large glassfibre trim tabs. Hydraulically operated Fowler flaps along entire wing trailing-edges inboard of unpowered ailerons; single-slotted flaps on centre-section, double-slotted outboard of nacelles. Servo tab and trim tab in each aileron. Winglet at each tip (being retrofitted also on Y-7).

FUSELAGE: All-metal semi-monocoque structure in front, centre and rear portions, of bonded/welded construction.

TAIL UNIT: Cantilever all-metal structure, with single ventral fin. Tailplane dihedral 9°. All controls operated manually. Balance tab in each elevator, trim tab and spring tab in rudder.

LANDING GEAR: Retractable tricycle type (An-24RV) with twin wheels on all units. Hydraulic actuation, with emergency gravity extension. All units retract forward. Mainwheels are size 900 × 300 mm, tyre pressure 5.39-5.88 bars (78.2-85.3 lb/sq in); nosewheels size 700 × 250 mm, tyre pressure 3.92 bars (56.8 lb/sq in). (Mainwheel tyre pressures variable to cater for different

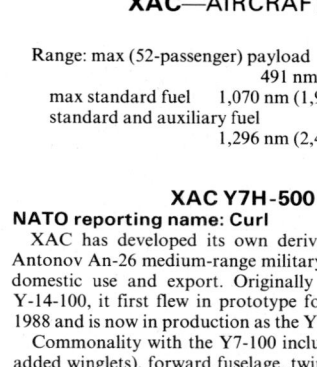

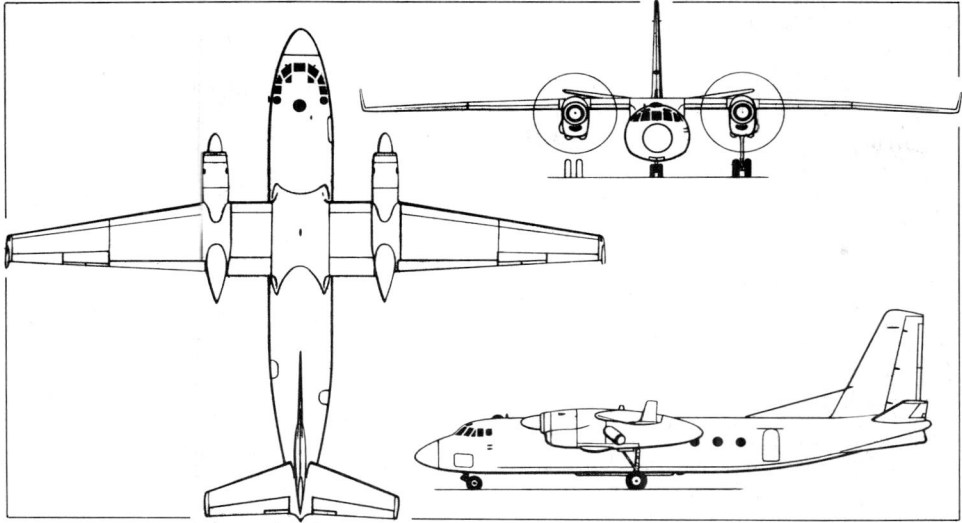

XAC Y7-100 current production version of Y-7 twin-turboprop transport aircraft *(Pilot Press)*

types of runway.) Disc brakes on mainwheels; steerable and castoring nosewheel unit.

POWER PLANT: Two Dongan (DEMC) WJ5A I turboprops, each rated at 2,080 kW (2,790 shp) for T-O and 1,976 kW (2,650 shp) at ISA + 23°C; Baoding four-blade constant-speed fully feathering propellers. Fuel in integral wing tanks immediately outboard of nacelles, and four bag-type tanks in centre-section, total capacity 5,550 litres (1,466 US gallons; 1,220 Imp gallons). Provision for four additional tanks in centre-section. Pressure refuelling point in starboard engine nacelle; gravity fuelling point above each tank. One 8.83 kN (1,985 lb st) Type RU 19A-300 auxiliary turbojet in starboard engine nacelle for engine starting, to improve take-off and in-flight performance, and to reduce stability and handling problems if one turboprop engine fails in flight.

ACCOMMODATION: Crew of three on flight deck, plus one or two cabin attendants. Standard layout has four-abreast seating, with centre aisle, for 52 passengers in air-conditioned, soundproofed (by Tracor) and pressurised cabin. Galley (by Lermer) and toilet at rear on starboard side. Baggage compartments forward and aft of passenger cabin, plus overhead stowage bins in cabin. Passenger door on port side, at rear of cabin, is of airstair type. Doors to forward and rear baggage compartments on starboard side. All doors open inward. Electric windscreen de-icing.

SYSTEMS: Hamilton Standard environmental control system (cabin pressure differential in An-24RV is 0.29 bar; 4.27 lb/sq in). Puritan-Bennett passenger oxygen system optional. Main and emergency hydraulic systems, pressure 152 bars (2,200 lb/sq in), for landing gear actuation, nosewheel steering, flaps, brakes, windscreen wipers and propeller feathering. Electrical system in An-24RV includes two 27V DC starter/generators, two alternators to provide 115V 400Hz AC supply, and two inverters for 36V 400Hz three-phase AC.

AVIONICS: Standard communications equipment comprises Collins 618M-3 dual VHF, Collins 628T-3 single HF, Becker audio selection and intercom, and Sundstrand AV-557C cockpit voice recorder. Standard navigation equipment comprises dual ADI-84A, dual EHSI-74 electronic HSI, dual RMI-36, FGS-65 flight guidance system, dual 51RV-4B VOR/ILS, dual DME-42, dual DF-206 ADF, 860F-4 radio altimeter, 621A-6A ATC transponder, 51Z-4 marker beacon receiver and CWC-80 instrument warning system, all by Collins; Litton LTN-211 VLF/Omega navigation system; Honeywell MHRS dual compass system, dual attitude reference and Primus 90 colour weather radar; IDC air data system; Sundstrand UFDR flight data recorder; and KJ-6A autopilot. Gables control units. Other instrumentation by Gould, IDC, Sfena and Smiths.

DIMENSIONS, EXTERNAL:
Wing span (over winglets)	29.637 m (97 ft 2¾ i
Wing chord: at root	3.50 m (11 ft 5¾ in)
at tip	1.095 m (3 ft 7 in)
Wing aspect ratio	11.7
Length overall	23.708 m (77 ft 9½ in)
Height overall	8.553 m (28 ft 0¾ in)
Fuselage: Max width	2.90 m (9 ft 6¼ in)
Max depth	2.50 m (8 ft 2½ in)
Tailplane span	9.08 m (29 ft 9½ in)
Wheel track (c/l of shock struts)	7.90 m (25 ft 11 in)
Wheelbase	7.90 m (25 ft 11 in)
Passenger door (port, rear):	
Height	1.40 m (4 ft 7 in)
Width	0.75 m (2 ft 5½ in)
Height to sill	1.40 m (4 ft 7 in)
Baggage compartment door (starboard, fwd):	
Height	1.10 m (3 ft 7¼ in)

Width	1.20 m (3 ft 11¼ in)
Height to sill	1.30 m (4 ft 3 in)
Baggage compartment door (starboard, rear):	
Height	1.41 m (4 ft 7½ in)
Width	0.75 m (2 ft 5½ in)

DIMENSIONS, INTERNAL:
Cabin:	
Length, incl flight deck	10.50 m (34 ft 5½ in)
Max width	2.80 m (9 ft 2¼ in)
Max height	1.90 m (6 ft 2¾ in)
Volume	56.0 m³ (1,978 cu ft)
Baggage compartment volume:	
fwd	4.50 m³ (159 cu ft)
rear	6.70 m³ (237 cu ft)

AREAS:
Wings, gross	74.98 m² (807.1 sq ft)
Vertical tail surfaces (total)	13.38 m² (144.0 sq ft)
Horizontal tail surfaces (total)	17.23 m² (185.5 sq ft)

WEIGHTS AND LOADINGS:
Operating weight empty	14,900 kg (32,849 lb)
Max fuel	4,790 kg (10,560 lb)
Max payload	5,500 kg (12,125 lb)
Max T-O and landing weight	21,800 kg (48,060 lb)
Max zero-fuel weight	19,655 kg (43,332 lb)
Max wing loading	290.7 kg/m² (59.6 lb/sq ft)
Max power loading	5.24 kg/kW (8.61 lb/shp)

PERFORMANCE (at max T-O weight except where indicated):
Max level speed	271 knots (503 km/h; 313 mph)
Max cruising speed at 4,000 m (13,125 ft)	
	262 knots (486 km/h; 302 mph)
Econ cruising speed at 6,000 m (19,685 ft)	
	233 knots (432 km/h; 268 mph)
Max rate of climb at S/L, AUW of 21,000 kg (46,297 lb)	
	458 m (1,504 ft)/min
Service ceiling, AUW of 21,000 kg (46,297 lb)	
	8,750 m (28,700 ft)
Service ceiling, one engine out, AUW of 19,000 kg (41,887 lb)	3,850 m (12,630 ft)
T-O run at S/L, FAR Pt 25, AUW of 21,000 kg (46,297 lb): ISA	546 m (1,792 ft)
ISA + 20°C	1,398 m (4,590 ft)
Landing run, AUW of 21,000 kg (46,297 lb)	
	620 m (2,035 ft)

Range: max (52-passenger) payload
491 nm (910 km; 565 miles)
max standard fuel   1,070 nm (1,983 km; 1,232 miles)
standard and auxiliary fuel
1,296 nm (2,403 km; 1,493 miles)

XAC Y7H-500
NATO reporting name: Curl

XAC has developed its own derivative of the Soviet Antonov An-26 medium-range military transport for both domestic use and export. Originally referred to as the Y-14-100, it first flew in prototype form on 8 December 1988 and is now in production as the Y7H-500.

Commonality with the Y7-100 includes the wings (with added winglets), forward fuselage, twin 2,162.5 kW (2,900 shp) WJ5A I turboprops (each driving a Baoding J16-G10 four-blade constant-speed metal propeller), and a turbojet APU for take-off assistance in hot and high conditions. It carries a crew of three (pilot, co-pilot and flight engineer) and has accommodation for up to 38 fully equipped troops or 39 paratroops, or 24 stretcher cases and one medical attendant in a medevac role. Up to 2,000 kg (4,409 lb) of external stores, such as weapons or supply containers, can be carried on fuselage attachment points. The fuselage, like that of the An-26, has a rear-loading ramp/door in the underside. Other features include a nose-mounted weather radar, rough-field landing gear, enlarged flight deck windows, and modern avionics comprising navaids, an AHRS and autopilot.

DIMENSIONS, EXTERNAL:
Wing span	29.20 m (95 ft 9½ in)
Length overall	24.31 m (79 ft 9 in)
Height overall	8.89 m (29 ft 2 in)
Wheel track	7.90 m (25 ft 11 in)
Wheelbase	8.356 m (27 ft 5 in)
Crew door: Height	1.40 m (4 ft 7 in)
Width	0.60 m (1 ft 11½ in)
Rear ramp/door: Max width	2.40 m (7 ft 10½ in)
Max length	3.05 m (10 ft 0 in)
Height to sill	1.74 m (5 ft 8½ in)

DIMENSIONS, INTERNAL:
Cargo hold: Length	11.10 m (36 ft 5 in)
Width	2.78 m (9 ft 1½ in)
Height	1.91 m (6 ft 3¾ in)

AREAS:
Wings, gross	74.98 m² (807.08 sq ft)

WEIGHTS AND LOADINGS:
Operating weight empty	15,400 kg (33,950 lb)
Max fuel weight	5,500 kg (12,125 lb)
Max payload	5,500 kg (12,125 lb)
Max ramp weight	24,230 kg (53,420 lb)
Max T-O and landing weight	24,000 kg (52,910 lb)
Max wing loading	320.08 kg/m² (65.56 lb/sq ft)
Max power loading	5.55 kg/kW (9.12 lb/shp)

PERFORMANCE (at max T-O weight except where indicated):
Max level speed at 6,000 m (19,685 ft) at AUW of 22,500 kg (49,600 lb)	240 knots (445 km/h; 276 mph)
Max cruising speed at 6,000 m (19,685 ft)	
	236 knots (438 km/h; 272 mph)
Max rate of climb at S/L	480 m (1,575 ft)/min
Rate of climb at S/L, one engine out	144 m (472 ft)/min
Service ceiling	8,200 m (26,900 ft)
Service ceiling, one engine out	3,800 m (12,465 ft)
T-O run	857 m (2,812 ft)
Landing run	634 m (2,080 ft)
Range at 236 knots (438 km/h; 272 mph) at 6,000 m (19,685 ft):	
with max payload	560 nm (1,038 km; 645 miles)
with 3,300 kg (7,275 lb) payload	
	1,187 nm (2,200 km; 1,367 miles)
Max endurance	5 h 23 min

Model of XAC Y7H-500 medium-range military transport *(Kenneth Munson)*

CISKEI

CAI
CISKEI AIRCRAFT INDUSTRIES (PTY) LTD
PO Box 1, Kidds Beach, Bisho 5264
Telephone: (04323) 69402 or (011) 8024342
In a newly built factory at Bisho's Bulembu Airport, CAI is producing under licence the Austrian **HB-Aircraft**

Hobbyliner and Scanliner (which see), manufacture having started at the end of 1987 following initial orders from the Wonderboom Flying School in Pretoria, South Africa.

The first aircraft completed by CAI, a Hobbyliner, first flew in December 1988, when 16 other HB-23 series aircraft

were in various stages of fabrication. Certification by the South African Division of Aviation was under way in early 1989. Orders then received by CAI included one from Taiwan, for four aircraft with an option for 16.

COLOMBIA

AERO MERCANTIL
AERO MERCANTIL SA
Carrera 3 No. 56-19, Apartado Aéreo 6781, Bogotá
Telephone: 57 (1) 211 8100
Fax: 57 (1) 212 8952
Telex: 44 581 LAVE CO
PRESIDENT: James G. Leaver
PROJECTS MANAGER: Eric C. Leaver
Aero Mercantil has been associated with Piper Aircraft Corporation since 1952, first as a dealer and then as a distributor. Currently, it markets the aircraft produced by AICSA (see later entry) and provides the quality assurance at the latter's assembly plant. It is currently developing and flight testing a prototype utility aircraft of its own design, known as the Gavilán.

AERO MERCANTIL EL1 GAVILÁN (SPARROWHAWK)
Design and construction of the Gavilán prototype (HK-3500-Z) began in the first half of 1987, and first flight was made on 27 April 1990. After a 50-hour development test flight programme, the fuselage was lengthened by 0.305 m (1 ft 0 in) forward of the wing and max T-O weight was increased by 136 kg (300 lb). The lengthened Gavilán first flew on 7 November 1990, and domestic (Pt 9) certification was expected in December 1991, to be followed by US FAR Pt 23 type approval in mid-1992.

Aero Mercantil planned to begin series production of the Gavilán in the third quarter of 1991. The standard civil aircraft is priced at US$230,000.

TYPE: Eight-seat utility light transport.
WINGS: Braced high-wing monoplane. Wing section NACA 4412. Dihedral 2°. Incidence 1° 30′. Unswept, two-spar structure of 2024-T3 aluminium alloy, with constant chord and single-strut bracing each side. Piano hinged, mechanically actuated ailerons and offset hinged single-slotted trailing-edge flaps also of 2024-T3. No tabs.
FUSELAGE: Mainframe of 4130N steel tube, with 2024-T3 aluminium alloy skin.
TAIL UNIT: Two-spar fin and fixed incidence tailplane. Mechanically actuated elevators and rudder; trim tab in starboard elevator. Entire structure of 2024-T3 aluminium alloy.
LANDING GEAR: Non-retractable tricycle type, with elastomeric shock absorption and single wheel on each unit. Tyre sizes 700 × 6-6 (main) and 600 × 6-6 (nose). Cleveland mainwheel brakes. Float/ski options to be offered later.
POWER PLANT: One 261 kW (350 hp) Textron Lycoming TIO-540-W2A flat-six engine, driving a three-blade constant-speed Hartzell propeller. Fuel tank in each wing, combined capacity 378.5 litres (100 US gallons; 83.3 Imp gallons). Refuelling point in each tank. Oil capacity 11.4 litres (3 US gallons; 2.5 Imp gallons).
ACCOMMODATION: Pilot and co-pilot or one passenger at front. Two rows of three seats to rear of these; middle row faces aft. Door at front on each side, plus larger cargo double door at rear on port side.
SYSTEMS: Pneumatic system, vacuum pump driven at 0.37 bar (5.5 lb/sq in). 12V 70A battery. Gaseous oxygen system optional.
AVIONICS: Bendix/King KX 155 VHF/VOR and KR 87 ADF, and blind-flying instrumentation, are standard.

Aero Mercantil EL1 Gavilán eight-seat utility light transport prototype

DIMENSIONS, EXTERNAL:	
Wing span	12.19 m (40 ft 0 in)
Wing chord, constant	1.55 m (5 ft 1 in)
Wing aspect ratio	7.84
Length overall	9.53 m (31 ft 3 in)
Fuselage: Max width	1.42 m (4 ft 8 in)
Height overall	3.35 m (11 ft 0 in)
Tailplane span	3.10 m (10 ft 2 in)
Wheel track	3.35 m (11 ft 0 in)
Wheelbase	3.35 m (11 ft 0 in)
Propeller diameter	2.13 m (7 ft 0 in)
Propeller ground clearance	0.36 m (1 ft 2 in)
Pilot's door: Height	1.17 m (3 ft 10 in)
Max width	0.74 m (2 ft 5 in)
Height to sill	1.02 m (3 ft 4 in)
Co-pilot's door: Height	0.91 m (3 ft 0 in)
Max width	0.97 m (3 ft 2 in)
Height to sill	1.02 m (3 ft 4 in)
Cargo double door: Height	1.22 m (4 ft 0 in)
Width	1.24 m (4 ft 1 in)
Height to sill	1.02 m (3 ft 4 in)
DIMENSIONS, INTERNAL:	
Cabin: Length	3.40 m (11 ft 2 in)
Max width	1.37 m (4 ft 6 in)
Max height	1.37 m (4 ft 6 in)
Floor area	4.09 m² (44.0 sq ft)
Volume	5.38 m³ (190.0 cu ft)
AREAS:	
Wings, gross	18.95 m² (204.0 sq ft)
Ailerons (total)	0.97 m² (10.4 sq ft)

Trailing-edge flaps (total)	1.12 m² (12.0 sq ft)
Fin	2.16 m² (23.3 sq ft)
Tailplane	1.51 m² (16.3 sq ft)
Elevators (total, incl tab)	0.90 m² (9.7 sq ft)
WEIGHTS AND LOADINGS:	
Weight empty, equipped	1,225 kg (2,700 lb)
Max fuel	272 kg (600 lb)
Max T-O and landing weight	2,041 kg (4,500 lb)
Max wing loading	107.65 kg/m² (22.06 lb/sq ft)
Max power loading	7.82 kg/kW (12.86 lb/hp)
PERFORMANCE (at max T-O weight):	
Never-exceed speed (VNE)	
	204 knots (378 km/h; 235 mph)
Max level speed at 4,570 m (15,000 ft)	
	140 knots (259 km/h; 161 mph)
Max cruising speed at 4,575 m (15,000 ft)	
	135 knots (250 km/h; 155 mph)
Econ cruising speed at 4,575 m (15,000 ft)	
	128 knots (237 km/h; 147 mph)
Stalling speed, 40° flap, engine idling	
	58 knots (108 km/h; 67 mph)
Max rate of climb at S/L	274 m (900 ft)/min
Service ceiling	7,010 m (23,000 ft)
T-O run	275 m (900 ft)
T-O to 15 m (50 ft)	457 m (1,500 ft)
Landing from 15 m (50 ft)	366 m (1,200 ft)
Landing run	183 m (600 ft)
Range, no reserves:	
with max payload	550 nm (1,019 km; 633 miles)
with max fuel	750 nm (1,390 km; 863 miles)

AGRO-COPTEROS
AGRO-COPTEROS LTDA
Calle 20 N 8A-18, Apartado Aéreo 1789, Cali
Telephone: 57 (3) 825110, 833519
Telex: 51138 DIEGO CO
PRESIDENT: Maximo Tedesco Kappler
This company assembles various North American light

aircraft and rotorcraft kits, notably those suitable for agricultural work. Details of its sprayplane version of the Aerosport Scamp B can be found in the 1984-85 *Jane's*.

AGRO-COPTEROS (ZENAIR) STOL CH 701
This is an agricultural version of the Zenair STOL CH

701 side by side two-seat all-metal Experimental category aircraft of which details and an illustration can be found in the Canadian part of the Sport Aircraft section. It is powered by a 47.7 kW (64 hp) Rotax 532 engine and has a Micro AG dispersal system.

AICSA
AERO INDUSTRIAL COLOMBIANA SA
Aeropuerto Guaymaral, Bogotá
GENERAL MANAGER: Pedro Alberto Gil

AICSA has been assembling Piper aircraft since 1968, when the Colombian Air Force permitted these aircraft to be imported in kit form, enabling some locally produced

materials and skilled local labour to be used in their completion. AICSA was created to assemble Pipers not only for Colombia but also for member countries of the Andean Pact, although in the event exports of Colombian assembled aircraft have been limited to Bolivia, Chile and Ecuador. Currently, through another subsidiary, the Colombian Air Force owns 51 per cent of AICSA; the other major shareholder is the Instituto de Fomento Industrial

(IFI), whose 48 per cent holding was due to be placed on the open stock market during 1990.

From 1968 to the end of 1985, AICSA assembled 492 Piper aircraft (275 single-engined and 217 twin-engined), as listed in the 1987-88 *Jane's*. No aircraft were built in 1986, but production was resumed in 1987 with 12 Seneca IIIs, one Cheyenne 400 and a Turbo Saratoga. Three Seneca IIIs and a Cheyenne 400 were assembled during 1989.

In mid-1989, AICSA entered into an agreement with Pezetel of Poland for the PZL Mielec (Antonov) An-2 (which see) to be assembled in Colombia. Two An-2s were completed during that year.

Piper Cheyenne 400 assembled under licence by AICSA

AVIONES DE COLOMBIA
AVIONES DE COLOMBIA SA
Eldorado International Airport, Entrance No 1, PO Box 6876, Bogotá
Telephone: 57 (1) 413 8300, 9857 and 9223
Fax: 57 (1) 413 8075
Telex: 45 220
WORKS: Aeropuerto Guaymaral, Apartado Aéreo 6876, Bogotá
Telephone: 57 (1) 676 0478, 0101 and 0326
Fax: 57 (1) 676 0458
COMMERCIAL MANAGER: Rafael Urdaneta

This company, established in the 1950s and known formerly as Urdaneta y Galvez Ltda, has been a South American distributor for Cessna aircraft since 1961. In 1969 it began assembling and partly building selected Cessna types under licence (see 1981-82 and earlier editions of *Jane's*), and now manufactures complete airframes. Facilities include a 1,330 m² (14,316 sq ft) fixed base operation at Eldorado International Airport; and 13,935 m² (150,000 sq ft) of assembly plant and a maintenance service station, approved by the US FAA, at Guaymaral general aviation airport in Bogotá. On 31 January 1990 the company had a workforce of 170 persons, and had assembled 1,047 Cessna aircraft.

AVIONES DE COLOMBIA/CESSNA AGTRAINER
Illustrated in the accompanying photograph, the AgTrainer is modified by Aviones de Colombia from the Cessna Model 188 Ag Truck (see US section of the 1984-85 *Jane's*). The cabin is widened to accommodate two persons side by side, increasing the empty weight by approx 91 kg (200 lb). Flight characteristics remain unchanged. Two prototypes were flown (the first of them on 16 September 1976), and the first prototype has since been operated by Aeroandes, a local cropspraying flying school.

Eight AgTrainers had been produced by early 1990, of which four were operating in Colombia, three in Central America and one in Ecuador.

TYPE: Two-seat agricultural monoplane.
WINGS: Braced low-wing monoplane, with single streamline section bracing strut each side. Wing section NACA 2412, modified. Dihedral 9°. Incidence 1° 30′ at root, −1° 30′ at tip. All-metal structure with NACA all-metal single-slotted flaps inboard of Frise all-metal ailerons. Aileron leading-edge gaps sealed. Wing fences immediately outboard of bracing strut attachments.
FUSELAGE: Rectangular section welded steel tube structure with removable metal skin panels forward of cabin. All-metal semi-monocoque rear fuselage.
TAIL UNIT: Cantilever all-metal structure. Fixed incidence tailplane. Trim tab in starboard elevator. Tailplane abrasion boots standard.
LANDING GEAR: Non-retractable tailwheel type. Land-O-Matic cantilever main legs of heavy duty spring

Aviones de Colombia AgTrainer two-seat agricultural aircraft

steel. Tapered tubular tailwheel spring shock absorber. Mainwheel tyres size 22 × 8.00-8, 6-ply rating, pressure 2.41 bars (35 lb/sq in). Oversize tyres optional, size 8.50-10, 6-ply rating, pressure 1.72 bars (25 lb/sq in). Tailwheel tyre size 3.50-10, 4-ply rating, pressure 3.45-4.14 bars (50-60 lb/sq in). Steerable tailwheel. Hydraulic disc brakes and parking brake.
POWER PLANT: One 224 kW (300 hp) Teledyne Continental IO-520-D flat-six engine, driving a McCauley three-blade constant-speed propeller. Fuel capacity 204 litres (54 US gallons; 45 Imp gallons). Oil capacity 11.4 litres (3 US gallons; 2.5 Imp gallons).
ACCOMMODATION: Side by side seats for two persons, in enclosed cabin with steel overturn structure. Combined window and door on each side, hinged at bottom. Ventilation standard. Air-conditioning, heating and windscreen defrosting optional.
SYSTEMS: Electrical system powered by a 28V 60A alternator and 24V 12.75Ah battery as standard. 28V 95A alternator and 24V 15.5Ah heavy duty battery optional.
EQUIPMENT: Standard equipment includes a 1,060 litre (280 US gallon; 233 Imp gallon) hopper with shatter-resistant window, engine driven hydraulic spray system and manually controlled spray valve and gearbox without agitator, hopper side loading system on port side, pilot's four-way adjustable seat, control stick lock, wire cutters, cable deflector, navigation lights, tailcone lift handles, quick drain oil valve, remote fuel strainer drain control, and auxiliary fuel pump.

DIMENSIONS, EXTERNAL:
Wing span	12.70 m (41 ft 8 in)
Length overall	8.00 m (26 ft 3 in)
Height overall	2.44 m (8 ft 0 in)
Propeller diameter	2.03 m (6 ft 8 in)

DIMENSIONS, INTERNAL:
Cabin: Max width	1.09 m (3 ft 7 in)
Hopper volume	0.85 m³ (30.0 cu ft)

AREAS:
Wings, gross	19.05 m² (205.0 sq ft)

WEIGHTS AND LOADINGS:
Weight empty:	
without dispersal equipment	1,017 kg (2,242 lb)
with dispersal equipment	1,099 kg (2,424 lb)
Max T-O weight:	
Normal category	1,497 kg (3,300 lb)
Restricted category	1,905 kg (4,200 lb)
Max landing weight	1,497 kg (3,300 lb)
Max wing loading: Normal	78.55 kg/m² (16.10 lb/sq ft)
Restricted	99.98 kg/m² (20.49 lb/sq ft)
Max power loading: Normal	6.69 kg/kW (11.0 lb/hp)
Restricted	8.52 kg/kW (14.0 lb/hp)

PERFORMANCE (at max T-O weight):
Max level speed at S/L	105 knots (195 km/h; 121 mph)
Max cruising speed (75% power) at 1,980 m (6,500 ft)	
	98 knots (182 km/h; 113 mph)
Stalling speed, power off:	
flaps up	53 knots (98 km/h; 61 mph) IAS
flaps down	50 knots (92 km/h; 57 mph) IAS
Max rate of climb at S/L	210 m (690 ft)/min
Service ceiling	3,385 m (11,100 ft)
T-O run	207 m (680 ft)
T-O to 15 m (50 ft)	332 m (1,090 ft)
Landing from 15 m (50 ft)	386 m (1,265 ft)
Landing run	128 m (420 ft)
Range, reserves for start, taxi, T-O and 45 min at 45%	
power	256 nm (474 km; 295 miles)
Endurance, conditions as above	2 h 36 min

CZECHOSLOVAKIA

The Czechoslovak aircraft industry is centrally controlled by the Aero Concern of the Aeronautical Industry, Prague-Letnany, whose General Director is Zdeněk Hořčík.

About 29,000 people are employed by the Czechoslovak aircraft industry. Principal factories concerned with aircraft manufacture are Aero, Let and Zlin, whose current products appear under the appropriate headings in this section. Other Czechoslovak factories engaged in the production of aero engines and sailplanes are listed in the relevant sections of this edition.

Sales of all aircraft products outside Czechoslovakia are handled by the Omnipol Foreign Trade Corporation.

OMNIPOL
FOREIGN TRADE CORPORATION
Nekázanka 11, 112 21 Prague 1
Telephone: 42 (2) 214011
Fax: 42 (2) 226792

Telex: 121297 and 121299
GENERAL DIRECTOR: Ing František Háva
COMMERCIAL DIRECTOR: Ing Josef Stibor
PUBLICITY MANAGER: Ing Eduard Dopita

This concern handles the sales of products of the Czechoslovak aircraft industry outside Czechoslovakia and furnishes all information requested by customers with regard to export goods.

AERO

AERO VODOCHODY AKCIOVÁ SPOLEČNOST
(Aero Vodochody Company Ltd)

250 70 Odolena Voda
Telephone: 42 (2) 843641
Fax: 42 (2) 823172
Telex: 121169 AERO C
MANAGING DIRECTOR: Ing Zdeněk Chalupník
CHIEF DESIGNERS:
Ing Vlastimil Havelka (training aircraft)
Ing Jan Mikula (passenger aircraft)
This factory was established on 1 July 1953. Aero produced about 3,600 L-29 Delfin jet trainers between 1963 and 1974 and has produced more than 2,000 L-39s since 1972.

AERO L-39 ALBATROS

The L-39 basic and advanced jet trainer first flew on 4 November 1968. The prototypes (see earlier *Jane's*) were followed by ten pre-production aircraft from 1971, and series production started in late 1972, following official selection of the L-39 to succeed the L-29 Delfin (1974-75 *Jane's*) as the standard jet trainer for the air forces of the Soviet Union, Czechoslovakia and East Germany. Service trials took place in 1973 in Czechoslovakia and the USSR, and by the Spring of 1974 the L-39 had begun to enter service with the Czechoslovak Air Force. Other recipients now include Afghanistan (18), Algeria (16), Bulgaria (18), Cuba (30), Ethiopia (12), Iraq (80), Libya (170), Nigeria (10), Romania (35), Syria (100) and Vietnam (25).

Production totalled more than 2,350 by 1 January 1989, and was expected to continue for at least five more years, at the rate of 200 a year. The Albatros is used in Czechoslovakia for all pilot training, including that of helicopter pilots. On average, pupils solo after approx 14 hours' dual instruction on the L-39 C.

The following variants have been produced:

L-39 C: Basic version, for basic and advanced flying training, to which the detailed description chiefly applies. Two underwing stations only. In service with the air forces of Afghanistan, Cuba, Czechoslovakia, Germany and USSR. In production.

L-39 V: As basic L-39 C, but modified as single-seater for target towing (see 1987-88 and earlier editions). Two delivered to East Germany.

L-39 Z0: Jet trainer with four underwing weapon stations (Z = Zbrojní: armed) and reinforced wings. Prototype (X-09) first flown 25 August 1975. Customers include the air forces of Germany (52), Iraq (80), Libya (170) and Syria (100). Some Libyan aircraft reportedly transferred to Egypt. In production.

L-39 ZA: Ground attack and reconnaissance version of L-39 Z0, with underfuselage gun pod and four underwing weapon stations; reinforced wings and landing gear. Prototypes (X-10 and X-11) first flown 1975-76. In service with the air forces of Bulgaria (18), Czechoslovakia and Romania (35). In production.

L-39 MS: New advanced training version with improved airframe, more powerful engine and upgraded avionics; described separately.

The following description applies to the current production L-39 C basic version, except where indicated:

TYPE: Two-seat basic and advanced jet trainer; L-39 ZA also has ground attack and reconnaissance capability.

WINGS: Cantilever low-wing monoplane, with 2° 30′ dihedral from roots. Wing section NACA 64A012 mod.5. Incidence 2°. Sweepback 6° 26′ on leading-edges, 1°45′ at quarter-chord. One-piece all-metal stressed skin structure, with main spar and auxiliary spar; four-point attachment to fuselage. All-metal double-slotted trailing-edge flaps, operated by push/pull rods actuated by a single hydraulic jack. Flaps retract automatically when airspeed reaches 167 knots (310 km/h; 193 mph). Mass balanced ailerons, each with electrically operated servo tab; port tab, used also for trim, is operated by electromechanical actuator. Non-jettisonable wingtip fuel tanks, incorporating landing/taxi-ing lights.

FUSELAGE: Metal semi-monocoque structure, built in two portions. Front portion consists of three sections, the first housing avionics, antennae, battery, compressed air and oxygen bottles and the nose landing gear. Next comes the pressurised compartment for the crew. The third section incorporates the fuel tanks, air intakes and the engine bay. The rear fuselage, carrying the tail unit, is attached by five bolts and can be removed quickly to provide access for engine installation and removal. Two airbrakes side by side under fuselage, just forward of wing leading-edge, actuated by single hydraulic jack; these are lowered automatically as airspeed nears a maximum of Mach 0.8.

TAIL UNIT: Conventional all-metal cantilever structure, with sweepback on vertical surfaces. Control surfaces actuated by pushrods. Electrically operated trim tab in each elevator; servo tab in rudder. Elevators deflect 30° up, 20° down; rudder ±30°.

LANDING GEAR: Retractable tricycle type, with single wheel and oleo-pneumatic shock absorber on each unit. Gear is designed for a touchdown sink rate of 3.4 m (11.15 ft)/s at AUW of 4,600 kg (10,141 lb). Retraction/extension is operated hydraulically, with electrical control. All wheel

Aero L-39 V single-seat target tug of the former East German Air Force *(Ivo Sturzenegger)*

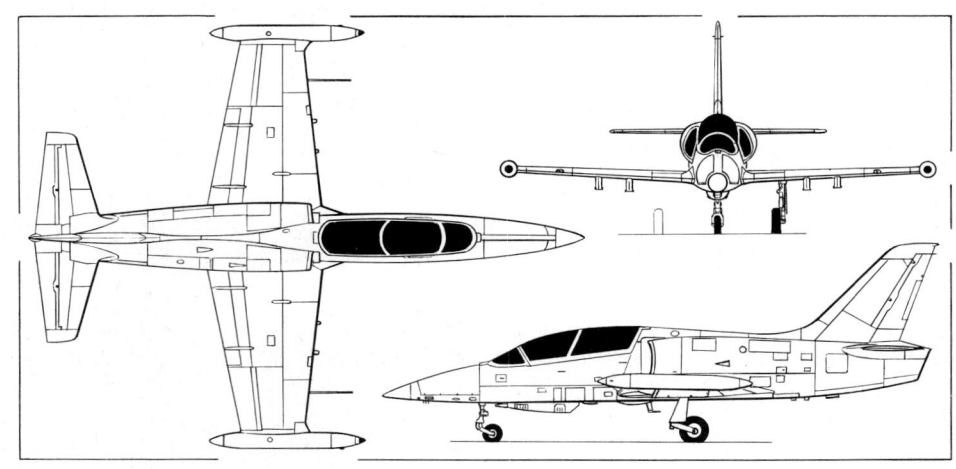

Aero L-39 MS Albatros two-seat basic and advanced jet trainer *(Pilot Press)*

well doors close automatically after wheels are lowered, to prevent ingress of dirt and debris. Mainwheels retract inward into wings (with automatic braking during retraction), nosewheel forward into fuselage. L-39 C and Z0 have K24 mainwheels, with Barum tubeless tyres size 610 × 185 mm, and K25 castoring and self-centring nosewheel, with Barum tubeless tyre size 430 × 150 mm. L-39 ZA has K28 mainwheels with 610 × 215 mm tyres and K27 nosewheel with 450 × 165 mm tyre. Hydraulic disc brakes and anti-skid units on mainwheels; shimmy damper on nosewheel leg. The L-39 is capable of operation from grass strips with a bearing strength of 7 kg/cm² (99 lb/sq in) at up to 4,600 kg (10,141 lb) T-O weight, or from unprepared runways. Landing gear of L-39 ZA reinforced to cater for higher operating weights; at same T-O weight, this version can operate from grass strips with bearing strength of 6 kg/cm² (85 lb/sq in).

POWER PLANT: One 16.87 kN (3,792 lb st) Ivchenko AI-25 TL turbofan mounted in rear fuselage, with semi-circular lateral air intake, fitted with splitter plate, on each side of fuselage above wing centre-section. Fuel in five rubber main bag tanks aft of cockpits, with combined capacity of 1,055 litres (279 US gallons; 232 Imp gallons), and two 100 litre (26.5 US gallon; 22 Imp gallon) non-jettisonable wingtip tanks. Total internal fuel capacity 1,255 litres (332 US gallons; 276 Imp gallons). Gravity refuelling points on top of fuselage and on each tip tank. Provision for two 350 litre (92.5 US gallon; 77 Imp gallon) drop tanks on inboard underwing pylons, increasing total overall fuel capacity to a maximum of 1,955 litres (517 US gallons; 430 Imp gallons). Fuel system permits up to 20 s of inverted flight.

ACCOMMODATION: Crew of two in tandem, on Czechoslovak VS-1-BRI rocket assisted ejection seats, operable at zero height and at speeds down to 81 knots (150 km/h; 94 mph), beneath individual transparent canopies which hinge sideways to starboard and are jettisonable. Rear seat elevated. One-piece windscreen hinges forward to provide access to front instrument panel. Internal transparency between cockpits. Dual controls standard.

SYSTEMS: Cabin pressurised (standard pressure differential 0.227 bar; 3.29 lb/sq in, max overpressure 0.29 bar; 4.20 lb/sq in) and air-conditioned, using engine bleed air and cooling unit. Air-conditioning system provides automatic temperature control from 10° to 25°C at ambient air temperatures from −55°C to +45°C. Main and standby interconnected hydraulic systems, the main system having a variable flow pump with an operating pressure of 147 bars (2,133 lb/sq in) for actuation of landing gear, flaps, airbrakes, ram air turbine and (at 34.3 bars; 500 lb/sq in pressure) wheel brakes. Emergency system, for all of above except airbrakes, incorporates three accumulators. Pneumatic canopy seals supplied by

a 2 litre compressed air bottle in nose (pressure 147 bars; 2,133 lb/sq in). Electrical system (27V DC) is powered by a 7.5kVA engine driven generator. If primary generator fails, a V 910 ram air turbine is extended automatically into the airstream and generates up to 3kVA of emergency power for essential services. 12V 28Ah SAM 28 lead-acid battery for standby power and for APU starting. Two 800VA static inverters (the first for radio equipment, ice warning lights, engine vibration measurement and air-conditioning, the second for navigation and landing systems, IFF and air-to-air missiles) provide 115V single-phase AC power at 400Hz. A second circuit incorporates a 500VA rotary inverter and 40VA static inverter to provide 36V three-phase AC power, also at 400Hz. Saphir 5 APU and SV-25 turbine for engine starting. Air intakes and windscreen anti-iced by engine bleed air; normally, anti-icing is sensor-activated automatically, but a manual standby system is also provided. Six-bottle oxygen system for crew, pressure 147 bars (2,133 lb/sq in).

AVIONICS: Standard avionics include R-832 M two-band com radio (VHF 118-140MHz, UHF 220-389MHz); SPU-9 crew intercom; RKL-41 ADF (150-1,800kHz); RV-5 radar altimeter; MRP-56 P/S marker beacon receiver; SRO-2M IFF; and RSBN-5S navigation and landing system. VOR/ILS system available at customer's option.

ARMAMENT (L-39 Z0 and ZA): Underfuselage pod on ZA only, below front cockpit, housing a single 23 mm Soviet GSh-23 two-barrelled cannon; ammunition for this gun (max 150 rds) is housed in fuselage, above gun pod. Gun/rocket firing and weapon release controls, including electrically controlled ASP-3 NMU-39 Z gyroscopic gunsight and FKP-2-2 gun camera, in front cockpit only (no FKP-2-2 in L-39 V). Z0 and ZA have four underwing hardpoints, the inboard pair each stressed for loads of up to 500 kg (1,102 lb) and the outer pair for loads of up to 250 kg (551 lb) each; max underwing stores load 1,100 kg (2,425 lb). Non-jettisonable pylons, each comprising a D3-57D stores rack. Typical underwing stores can include various combinations of bombs (two 500 kg, four 250 kg or six 100 kg); four UB-16-57 M pods each containing sixteen S-5 57 mm air-to-surface rockets; infra-red air-to-air missiles (outer pylons only); a five-camera day reconnaissance pod (port inboard pylon only); or (on inboard stations only) two 350 litre (92.5 US gallon; 77 Imp gallon) drop tanks.

DIMENSIONS, EXTERNAL:
Wing span, incl tip tanks 9.46 m (31 ft 0½ in)
Wing chord (mean) 2.15 m (7 ft 0½ in)
Wing aspect ratio: geometric 4.4
  incl tip tanks 5.2
Length overall 12.13 m (39 ft 9½ in)

Height overall	4.77 m (15 ft 7¾ in)
Tailplane span	4.40 m (14 ft 5 in)
Wheel track	2.44 m (8 ft 0 in)
Wheelbase	4.39 m (14 ft 4¾ in)

AREAS:

Wings, gross	18.80 m² (202.36 sq ft)
Ailerons (total)	1.23 m² (13.26 sq ft)
Trailing-edge flaps (total)	2.68 m² (28.89 sq ft)
Airbrakes (total)	0.50 m² (5.38 sq ft)
Fin	2.60 m² (27.99 sq ft)
Rudder, incl tab	0.91 m² (9.80 sq ft)
Tailplane	3.93 m² (42.30 sq ft)
Elevators, incl tabs	1.14 m² (12.27 sq ft)

WEIGHTS AND LOADINGS:

Weight empty, equipped: C	3,455 kg (7,617 lb)
Z0	3,480 kg (7,672 lb)
ZA	3,565 kg (7,859 lb)
Fuel load: fuselage tanks	824 kg (1,816 lb)
wingtip tanks	156 kg (344 lb)
Max external stores load: C	284 kg (626 lb)
Z0	1,150 kg (2,535 lb)
ZA	1,290 kg (2,844 lb)
T-O weight clean: C	4,525 kg (9,976 lb)
Z0	4,550 kg (10,031 lb)
ZA	4,635 kg (10,218 lb)
Max T-O weight: C	4,700 kg (10,362 lb)
Z0 and ZA	5,600 kg (12,346 lb)
Max wing loading: C	250.0 kg/m² (51.23 lb/sq ft)
Z0 and ZA	297.9 kg/m² (61.01 lb/sq ft)
Max power loading: C	278.6 kg/kN (2.73 lb/lb st)
Z0 and ZA	332.0 kg/kN (3.25 lb/lb st)

PERFORMANCE (C at clean T-O weight of 4,500 kg; 9,921 lb, Z0 and ZA at max T-O weight):

Max limiting Mach number	0.80
Max level speed at S/L:	
C	378 knots (700 km/h; 435 mph)
Z0 and ZA	329 knots (610 km/h; 379 mph)
Max level speed at 5,000 m (16,400 ft):	
C	405 knots (750 km/h; 466 mph)
Z0 and ZA	340 knots (630 km/h; 391 mph)
Stalling speed: C	90 knots (165 km/h; 103 mph)
Z0 and ZA	103 knots (190 km/h; 118 mph)
Max rate of climb at S/L: C	1,260 m (4,130 ft)/min
Z0 and ZA	810 m (2,657 ft)/min
Time to 5,000 m (16,400 ft): C	5 min
Z0 and ZA	10 min
Service ceiling: C	11,000 m (36,100 ft)
Z0 and ZA	7,500 m (24,600 ft)
T-O run (concrete): C	530 m (1,740 ft)
Z0 and ZA	970 m (3,182 ft)
Landing run (concrete): C	650 m (2,135 ft)
Z0 and ZA	800 m (2,625 ft)

Range at 7,000 m (22,975 ft):

C, 980 kg (2,160 lb) max internal fuel
593 nm (1,100 km; 683 miles)
C, 1,524 kg (3,360 lb) max internal and external fuel
944 nm (1,750 km; 1,087 miles)

Endurance at 7,000 m (22,975 ft):

C, max internal fuel as above	2 h 30 min
C, max internal/external fuel as above	3 h 50 min

g limits:

operational: at 4,200 kg (9,259 lb) AUW	+8/-4
at 5,500 kg (12,125 lb) AUW	+5.2/-2.6
ultimate, at 4,200 kg (9,259 lb) AUW	+12

AERO L-39 MS

The L-39 MS first prototype X22 (OK-184) first flew on 30 September 1986. Two further prototypes, designated X24 and X25, flew on 26 June and 6 October 1987, and the first production L-39 MS flew on 1 October 1989.

Major changes concern the wings, power plant and avionics.

TYPE: Two-seat advanced jet trainer.

WINGS: Similar in planform and construction to L-39 C. Ailerons and trailing-edge flaps are of light alloy/

Third prototype L-39 MS on landing approach (*Air Portraits*)

sandwich construction, ailerons having a Czechoslovak designed irreversible power control system and no tabs.

FUSELAGE: Generally as described for L-39 C, but with more pointed nose section.

TAIL UNIT: Similar to that of L-39 C, but irreversible power control system for elevators.

LANDING GEAR: Czechoslovak design gas/oil shock absorption; K36 mainwheels (610 × 215 mm) and K37 nosewheel (460 × 180 mm). Mainwheel tyre pressures 6.0 bars (87 lb/sq in) on training version, 8.0 bars (116 lb/sq in) on combat version; corresponding nosewheel tyre pressures are 3.5 bars (51 lb/sq in) and 4.5 bars (65 lb/sq in) respectively. Six-piston, aircooled hydraulic disc brakes on mainwheels, plus electronic anti-skid units. Otherwise generally as described for L-39 C.

POWER PLANT: One 21.57 kN (4,850 lb st) Lotarev/ZVL DV-2 turbofan. Internal fuel in fuselage tanks (total 1,077 litres; 284.5 US gallons; 237 Imp gallons) and two 230 litre (60.8 US gallon; 50.6 Imp gallon) non-jettisonable wingtip tanks. Provision for two underwing (inboard) 150 or 350 litre (39.6 or 92.5 US gallon; 33 or 77 Imp gallon) drop tanks.

ACCOMMODATION: Crew of two in tandem, on Czechoslovak VS-2 zero/zero ejection seats. One-piece canopy, hinged at rear and opening upward.

SYSTEMS: Air-conditioning and pressurisation as described for L-39 C. Main and standby interconnected hydraulic systems (two pumps), operating pressure 150 bars (2,175 lb/sq in). Main and standby generators for electrical power, plus DC battery. Gaseous oxygen system for crew. Saphir 5M APU for engine starting and standby drive of hydraulic pump and generator.

AVIONICS: Include LPR-80 two-band com radio, LUN-3524 standby radio, KL-52 ADF, RSBN radio navigation and landing system, RV-5 radar altimeter, MRP-80 marker beacon receiver, SRO-2M IFF and head-up/head-down display.

ARMAMENT: As described for L-39 Z0 and ZA.

DIMENSIONS, EXTERNAL: As for L-39 C except:

Wing span, incl tip tanks	9.54 m (31 ft 3½ in)
Wing chord: at root	2.80 m (9 ft 2¼ in)
at tip	1.40 m (4 ft 7 in)
Length overall	12.20 m (40 ft 0¼ in)

AREAS: As for L-39 C except:

Ailerons (total)	1.686 m² (18.15 sq ft)
Tailplane	4.15 m² (44.64 sq ft)

WEIGHTS AND LOADINGS:

Weight empty: trainer	4,150 kg (9,149 lb)
Max fuel weight:	
internal, incl wingtip tanks	1,200 kg (2,645 lb)
external (two 350 litre drop tanks)	544 kg (1,199 lb)
Max T-O weight: trainer, clean	5,510 kg (12,147 lb)
with external stores (from grass)	5,700 kg (12,566 lb)
Max landing weight (on concrete)	6,000 kg (13,228 lb)
Max wing loading:	
trainer, clean	293.1 kg/m² (60.06 lb/sq ft)
at 5,700 kg (12,566 lb) MTOGW	303.2 kg/m² (62.13 lb/sq ft)
Max power loading:	
trainer clean	255.45 kg/kN (2.50 lb/lb st)
at 5,700 kg (12,566 lb) MTOGW	264.26 kg/kN (2.59 lb/lb st)

PERFORMANCE (at max T-O weight):

Max limiting Mach number	0.82
Max level speed at 5,000 m (16,400 ft)	473 knots (876 km/h; 544 mph)
Stalling speed: flaps up	111 knots (205 km/h; 128 mph)
flaps down	92 knots (170 km/h; 106 mph)
Max rate of climb at S/L	1,560 m (5,120 ft)/min
Service ceiling	11,730 m (38,500 ft)
Min ground turning radius (from nosewheel)	2.50 m (8 ft 2 in)
T-O run	620 m (2,035 ft)
Landing run	650 m (2,135 ft)
Range at 9,000 m (29,530 ft) with max internal and external fuel	809 nm (1,500 km; 932 miles)

AERO L-270

Development of this single-turboprop utility aircraft was announced by Aero in early 1990, and brief details of the concept, with an illustration, appeared in the Addenda to the 1990-91 *Jane's*. However, the programme is still in the preliminary design stage, with the configuration not yet finalised, and revised details had not been released at the time of going to press.

LET

LET KONCERNOVÝ PODNIK (Let Concern Enterprise)

Uherské Hradiste-Kunovice
Telephone: 42 (5) 411111
Telex: 060387 and 060388
MANAGING DIRECTOR: Ing Stanislav Boura
TECHNICAL DIRECTOR: Ing Antonín Zelinka
CHIEF DESIGNER: Ing Marian Mečiar

The Let plant at Kunovice was established in 1950, its early activities including licence production of the Soviet Yak-11 trainer under the Czechoslovak designation C-11. It is currently responsible for the L-410UVP-E light transport aircraft and development of the larger L-610. The factory also produces equipment for radar and computer technology.

LET L-410UVP-E

Details of the prototypes and initial production versions of the Turbolet can be found in the 1980-81 and earlier editions of *Jane's*.

The L-410UVP, first flown on 1 November 1977, introduced a number of major changes (see previous editions for details), becoming in 1980 the first non-USSR aircraft to receive a type certificate under Soviet NLGS-2 airworthiness regulations. Stringent Aeroflot requirements included the ability to operate in temperatures ranging from -50°C to +45°C; systems were required to be survivable in temperatures as low as -60°C. Production of the UVP, in four models, ended in late 1985 and totalled 495.

A prototype of the improved L-410UVP-E (OK-120) was flown on 30 December 1984 and went into production in 1985, replacing the UVP. It received NLGS-2 Soviet certification in March 1986. Suffix numbers (eg -E10, -E20) are given to aircraft modified to individual customer's requirements. In the L-410UVP-E the rear fuselage has the baggage and toilet compartments further aft, creating space for four additional seats without increasing overall length. The wings are reinforced to support two optional streamlined wingtip tanks, enabling range to be increased by more than 40 per cent. Maximum flap deflection is increased compared with the UVP, and the spoilers have two fixed deflection angles: 25° (for use in

flight) and 72°. Power plant associated changes include a vacuum sintered oil cooler of new design, an oil-to-fuel heat exchanger on each engine firewall to avoid the need for fuel additives at low ambient temperatures, relocation of the engine fire extinguishing bottles under the port rear wing/fuselage fairing and, on the instrument panel, separate speed indicators for each engine and propeller. Cabin improvements include installation of portable oxygen equipment and an improved PA system; a fire extinguishing system is installed in the nose baggage compartment. The aircraft can be operated in temperatures ranging from -50°C to +50°C. Its design life is 20,000 flying hours or 20,000 landings.

By 1 January 1990 Let had delivered 358 L-410UVP-Es (318 to the USSR, 12 to operators in Czechoslovakia and 28 to customers in Bulgaria, Denmark, Hungary and Poland). Total L-410 production at that time (all versions) amounted to 1,011. The 1,000th aircraft was the 369th L-410 delivered to the USSR.

TYPE: Twin-turboprop general purpose light transport.

WINGS: Cantilever high-wing monoplane. Wing section NACA 63A418 at root, NACA 63A412 at tip. Dihedral

L-410UVP-E20 twin-turboprop transport, prior to delivery to a Swedish customer

1° 45′. Incidence 2° at root, –0° 30′ at tip. No sweepback at front spar. Conventional all-metal two-spar torsion box structure, attached to fuselage by four-point mountings. Chemically machined skin with longitudinal reinforcement. Hydraulically actuated two-section double-slotted metal flaps. Spoiler forward of each flap. All-metal ailerons, forward of which are pop-up bank control surfaces that come into operation automatically during single-engine operation and decrease the lift on the side of the running engine. Tab in port aileron. Kléber-Colombes pneumatic de-icing of leading-edges.

FUSELAGE: Conventional all-metal semi-monocoque spot welded and riveted structure, built in three main portions.

TAIL UNIT: Conventional cantilever structure, of all-metal construction except for elevators and rudder, which are fabric covered. Vertical tail surfaces sweptback 35°; shallow dorsal fin and deeper ventral fin. One-piece tailplane, with 7° dihedral from roots, mounted part-way up fin. Balance tab in rudder and each elevator. Kléber-Colombes pneumatic de-icing of leading-edges.

LANDING GEAR: Retractable tricycle type, with single wheel on each unit. Hydraulic retraction, nosewheel forward, mainwheels inward to lie flat in fairing on each side of fuselage. Technometra Radotin oleo-pneumatic shock absorbers. Non-braking nosewheel, with servo-assisted steering, fitted with 548 × 221 mm (9.00-6) tubeless tyre, pressure 4.5 bars (65 lb/sq in). Nosewheel is also steerable by rudder pedals. Mainwheels fitted with 718 × 306 mm (12.50-10) tubeless tyres, pressure 4.5 bars (65 lb/sq in). All wheels manufactured by Moravan Otrokovice, tyres by Rudy Rijen, Gottwaldow. Moravan Otrokovice K38-3200.00 hydraulic disc brakes, parking brake and anti-skid units on mainwheels. Metal ski landing gear, with plastics undersurface, optional.

POWER PLANT: Two 559 kW (750 shp) Motorlet Walter M 601 E turboprops, each driving an Avia V 510 five-blade constant-speed reversible-pitch metal propeller with manual and automatic feathering and Beta control. At higher ambient temperatures, engine power can be increased to 603 kW (809 ehp) for short periods by water injection into compressor. De-icing for propeller blades (electrical) and lower intakes (bleed air); anti-icing flaps inside each nacelle. Eight bag fuel tanks in wings, total capacity 1,290 litres (341 US gallons; 284 Imp gallons), plus additional optional 200 litres (52.8 US gallons; 44 Imp gallons) of fuel in each wingtip tank. Fuel system operable after failure of electrical system. Total oil capacity (incl oil in cooler) 22 litres (5.8 US gallons; 4.8 Imp gallons). Water tank capacity (for injection into compressor) 11 litres (2.9 US gallons; 2.4 Imp gallons).

ACCOMMODATION: Crew of one or two on flight deck, with dual controls. Electric de-icing for windscreen. Standard accommodation in main cabin for 19 passengers, with pairs of adjustable seats on starboard side of aisle and single seats opposite, all at 76 cm (30 in) pitch. Baggage compartment (at rear, accessible from cabin), toilet and wardrobe standard. Cabin heated by engine bleed air. Alternative layouts include all-cargo; ambulance, accommodating six stretchers, five sitting patients and a medical attendant; accommodation for 18 parachutists and a dispatcher/instructor; firefighting configuration, carrying 16 firefighters and a pilot/observer. All-cargo version has protective floor covering, crash nets on each side of cabin, and tiedown provisions; floor is at truckbed height. Aircraft can also be equipped for aerial photography or for calibration of ground navigation aids. Double upward opening doors aft on port side, with stowable steps; right hand door serves as passenger entrance and exit. Both doors open for cargo loading, and can be removed for paratroop training missions. Rearward opening door, forward on starboard side, serves as emergency exit.

SYSTEMS: No APU, air-conditioning or pressurisation systems. Duplicated hydraulic systems, No. 1 system actuating landing gear, flaps, spoilers, automatic pitch trim surfaces, mainwheel brakes, nosewheel steering and windscreen wipers. No. 2 system for emergency landing gear extension, flap actuation and parking brake. 28V DC electrical system supplied by two 5.6kW starter/generators, connected for autonomous starting, plus two 25V 25Ah batteries for emergency power. Two input systems for AC power (three-phase 200V/115Hz, variable frequency), incorporating two 3.7kW alternators with alternator control unit. Port alternator provides for windscreen heating, starboard one for propeller blade de-icing. Two static inverters provide three-phase 36V/400Hz AC. Two 115V/400Hz inverters. One three-phase 36V/400Hz static inverter for standby horizon. Two portable oxygen breathing sets on flight deck and two in passenger cabin. Fire extinguishing system for engines and nose baggage compartment.

AVIONICS: Standard instrumentation provides for flight in IMC conditions, with all basic instruments duplicated and three artificial horizons. Communications include two VHF transceivers with a range of 65 nm (120 km; 75 miles) at 1,000 m (3,280 ft) altitude, passenger address system and crew intercom. Standard instruments include LUN 1205 horizon gyros, rate of climb indicators, LUN 1215 turn and bank indicator, RMIs, gyro compasses, ILS/SP-50A instrument landing system with marker beacon receiver, dual ARK-22 ADF, A-037 radio altimeter, SO-69 SSR transponder with encoding altimeter, ASI with stall warning, magnetic compass, GMK-1GE VOR, and BUR-1-2G flight data recorder. Weather radar and VZLU autopilot optional.

EQUIPMENT: Cockpit, instrument and passenger cabin lights, navigation lights, three landing lights in nose (each with two levels of light intensity), crew and cabin fire extinguishers, windscreen wipers, and alcohol spray for windscreen and wiper de-icing, are standard.

DIMENSIONS, EXTERNAL:

Wing span: over tip tanks	19.98 m (65 ft 6½ in)
excl tip tanks	19.48 m (63 ft 11 in)
Wing chord at root	2.534 m (8 ft 3¾ in)
Length overall	14.424 m (47 ft 4 in)
Fuselage: Max width	2.08 m (6 ft 10 in)
Max depth	2.10 m (6 ft 10¾ in)
Height overall	5.83 m (19 ft 1½ in)
Tailplane span	6.74 m (22 ft 1¼ in)
Wheel track	3.65 m (11 ft 11½ in)
Wheelbase	3.67 m (12 ft 0¼ in)
Propeller diameter	2.30 m (7 ft 6½ in)
Propeller ground clearance	1.26 m (4 ft 1½ in)
Distance between propeller centres	4.82 m (15 ft 9½ in)
Passenger/cargo door (port, rear):	
Height	1.46 m (4 ft 9½ in)
Width overall	1.25 m (4 ft 1¼ in)
Width (passenger door only)	0.80 m (2 ft 7½ in)
Height to sill	0.70 m (2 ft 3½ in)
Emergency exit door (stbd, fwd):	
Height	0.97 m (3 ft 2¼ in)
Width	0.66 m (2 ft 2 in)
Height to sill	0.80 m (2 ft 7½ in)

DIMENSIONS, INTERNAL:

Cabin, excl flight deck:	
Length	6.345 m (20 ft 9¾ in)
Max width	1.95 m (6 ft 4¾ in)
Max height	1.66 m (5 ft 5¼ in)
Aisle width at 0.4 m (1 ft 3¾ in) above cabin floor	
	0.34 m (1 ft 1½ in)
Floor area	10.0 m² (107.6 sq ft)
Volume	17.9 m³ (632.1 cu ft)
Baggage compartment volume:	
nose	0.60 m³ (21.19 cu ft)
rear	0.77 m³ (27.19 cu ft)

AREAS:

Wings, gross	35.18 m² (378.67 sq ft)
Ailerons (total)	2.89 m² (31.11 sq ft)
Automatic bank control flaps (total)	
	0.49 m² (5.27 sq ft)
Trailing-edge flaps (total)	5.92 m² (63.72 sq ft)
Spoilers (total)	0.87 m² (9.36 sq ft)
Fin	4.49 m² (48.33 sq ft)
Rudder, incl tab	2.81 m² (30.25 sq ft)
Tailplane	6.41 m² (69.00 sq ft)
Elevators, incl tabs	3.15 m² (33.91 sq ft)

Yellow-painted extremities identify this Czechoslovak Air Force L-410UVP-E as a VIP and special duty version *(Ivo Sturzenegger)*

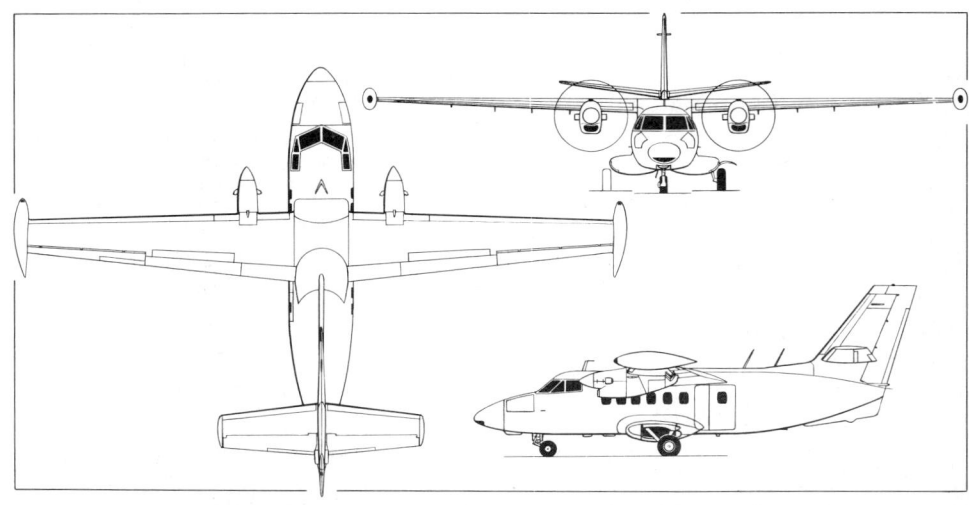

Let L-410UVP-E twin-turboprop 19-passenger light transport *(Pilot Press)*

Fifth (third flying) prototype of the Let L-610 (two Motorlet M 602 turboprops). Deliveries were expected to begin during 1991

WEIGHTS AND LOADINGS:

Weight empty	3,985 kg (8,785 lb)
Operating weight empty, equipped	4,160 kg (9,171 lb)
Max fuel	1,300 kg (2,866 lb)
Max payload	1,615 kg (3,560 lb)
Max ramp weight	6,420 kg (14,154 lb)
Max T-O weight	6,400 kg (14,110 lb)
Max zero-fuel weight	5,775 kg (12,732 lb)
Max landing weight	6,200 kg (13,668 lb)
Max wing loading	181.9 kg/m² (37.26 lb/sq ft)
Max power loading	5.38 kg/kW (8.93 lb/ehp)

PERFORMANCE (at max T-O weight):

Never-exceed speed (V_{NE})	192 knots (357 km/h; 222 mph) EAS
Max level speed at 4,200 m (13,780 ft)	168 knots (311 km/h; 193 mph) EAS
Max cruising speed at 4,200 m (13,780 ft)	205 knots (380 km/h; 236 mph)
Econ cruising speed at 4,200 m (13,780 ft)	197 knots (365 km/h; 227 mph)
Stalling speed:	
flaps up	84 knots (155 km/h; 97 mph) EAS
flaps down	66 knots (121 km/h; 76 mph) EAS
Max rate of climb at S/L	444 m (1,455 ft)/min
Rate of climb at S/L, one engine out	108 m (354 ft)/min
Service ceiling: practical	6,320 m (20,725 ft)
theoretical	7,050 m (23,125 ft)
Service ceiling, one engine out:	
practical	2,700 m (8,860 ft)
theoretical	3,980 m (13,050 ft)
T-O run	445 m (1,460 ft)
T-O to 10.7 m (35 ft)	685 m (2,250 ft)
Landing from 9 m (30 ft)	480 m (1,575 ft)
Landing run	240 m (787 ft)
Min ground turning radius	13.40 m (43 ft 11½ in)

Range at 4,200 m (13,780 ft), max cruising speed, 30 min reserves:

with max payload	294 nm (546 km; 339 miles)
with max fuel and 885 kg (1,951 lb) payload	744 nm (1,380 km; 857 miles)

LET L-610

Intended for certification under Soviet ENLG-S civil airworthiness requirements, the L-610 is designed for short-haul operations over stage lengths of 216-324 nm (400-600 km; 248-373 miles). The first prototype (OK-130) flew on 28 December 1988. Five development aircraft have been built: the first, third and fifth for flight trials, the second for static test and the fourth for fatigue testing. Deliveries (initially to Aeroflot) were expected to begin in 1991. There is said to be a Soviet requirement for 600 L-610s, to replace Aeroflot Yak-40s and An-24s.

Under a contract signed on 18 January 1981, General Electric is supplying its CT7-9 turboprop to power an alternative version of the L-610, which will also have Western avionics. The first two CT7s were shipped to Let in early 1991, and a re-engined prototype was due to fly before the end of the year. Certification of this version to FAR/JAR Pt 25 is expected in 1992.

TYPE: Twin-turboprop transport aircraft.

WINGS: Cantilever high-wing monoplane. Wing sections MS(1)-0318D at root, MS(1)-0312 at tip, with respective thickness/chord ratios of 18.29 and 12 per cent. Dihedral 2°. Incidence 3° 8′ 38″ at root, 0° at tip. Sweepback 1° at quarter-chord. All-metal fail-safe stressed skin structure, built of high grade aluminium alloys and high strength steel and incorporating sandwich panels. All-metal horn balanced ailerons and single-slotted Fowler trailing-edge flaps. Spoiler, of sandwich construction, forward of each outer flap segment. Electro-mechanically actuated trim tab in port aileron. Pneumatic boot de-icing of leading-edges.

FUSELAGE: Pressurised all-metal semi-monocoque structure (except for nose and tailcones), incorporating fail-safe principles. Central portion has a constant circular cross-section.

TAIL UNIT: All-metal structure, with sweptback fin and rudder and long dorsal fin. Non-swept tailplane and elevators mounted near top of fin. Trim tab and spring balance tab in rudder, trim tab and geared tab in each elevator. Pneumatic boot de-icing of fin and tailplane leading-edges.

LANDING GEAR: Retractable tricycle type, with single wheel on each unit. Hydraulic actuation, mainwheels retracting inward to lie flat in fairing each side of fuselage, nosewheel retracting forward. Oleo-pneumatic shock absorber in each unit. Mainwheels are type XK 34-3000.00, with 1,050 × 390 × 480 mm tyres; type XR 25-1000.00 nosewheel has a 720 × 310 × 254 mm tyre. Hydraulic disc brakes and electronically controlled anti-skid units.

POWER PLANT: Two 1,358 kW (1,822 shp) Motorlet M 602 turboprops, each driving an Avia V 518 five-blade fully feathering metal propeller with reversible pitch. Fuel in two integral wing tanks, combined usable capacity 3,500 litres (925 US gallons; 770 Imp gallons). Pressure refuelling point in fuselage, gravity points in wings. Oil capacity 30 litres (7.9 US gallons; 6.6 Imp gallons).

ACCOMMODATION: Crew of two on flight deck, plus one cabin attendant. Standard accommodation for 40 passengers, four-abreast at seat pitch of 75 cm (29.5 in). Aisle width 51 cm (20 in). Galley, two wardrobes, toilet, freight and baggage compartment, all located at rear of cabin. Alternative mixed (passenger/cargo) and all-cargo layouts available. Passenger door at rear of fuselage, freight door at front, both opening outward on port side. Outward opening service door on starboard side, opposite passenger door, serving also as emergency exit; outward opening emergency exit beneath wing on each side. Entire accommodation pressurised and air-conditioned.

SYSTEMS: Bootstrap type air-conditioning system. Max operating cabin pressure differential 0.3 bar (4.35 lb/sq in). Duplicated hydraulic systems (one main and one standby), operating at pressure of 210 bars (3,045 lb/sq in). APU in tailcone, for engine starting and auxiliary on-ground and in-flight power. Electrical system powered by two 115/200V 25kVA variable frequency AC generators, plus a third 8kVA 115/200V three-phase AC generator driven by APU. System also includes two 115V 400Hz inverters (each 1.5kVA), two 27V DC transformer-rectifiers (each 4.5kW), and a 25Ah nickel-cadmium battery for APU starting and auxiliary power supply. Portable oxygen equipment for crew and 10 per cent of passengers. Pneumatic de-icing of wing and tail unit leading-edges, engine inlets and oil cooler; electric de-icing of propeller blade roots, windscreen, pitot static system and horn balances.

AVIONICS: Equipped with dual 760-channel VHF com, single HF com (optional), intercom, cabin address system, weather radar, blind-flying instrumentation, dual ILS with two LOC/glideslope receivers and two marker beacon receivers, single or dual ADF, Doppler radar, navigation computer, dual compasses, single or dual radio altimeters, transponder, autopilot, voice recorder, flight recorder, and Cat. II approach aids.

DIMENSIONS, EXTERNAL:

Wing span	25.60 m (84 ft 0 in)
Wing chord: at root	2.917 m (9 ft 6⅞ in)
at tip	1.458 m (4 ft 9½ in)
Wing aspect ratio	11.7
Length overall	21.419 m (70 ft 3¼ in)
Fuselage: Length	20.533 m (67 ft 4⅜ in)
Max diameter	2.70 m (8 ft 10¼ in)
Distance between propeller centres	7.00 m (22 ft 11½ in)
Height overall	7.608 m (24 ft 11½ in)
Tailplane span	7.908 m (25 ft 11⅓ in)
Wheel track	4.59 m (15 ft 0¾ in)
Wheelbase	6.596 m (21 ft 7¾ in)

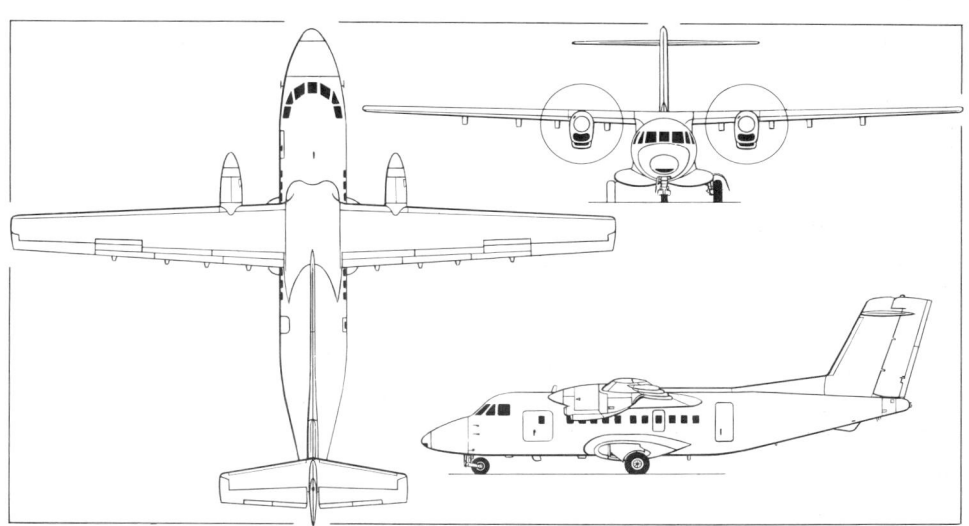

Let L-610 twin-turboprop 40-seat commuter transport (*Pilot Press*)

Propeller diameter	3.50 m (11 ft 5¾ in)
Propeller/fuselage clearance	0.59 m (1 ft 11¼ in)
Propeller ground clearance	1.64 m (5 ft 4½ in)
Passenger door: Height	1.625 m (5 ft 4 in)
Width	0.76 m (2 ft 6 in)
Height to sill	1.448 m (4 ft 9 in)
Freight door: Height	1.30 m (4 ft 3¼ in)
Width	1.25 m (4 ft 1¼ in)
Height to sill	1.448 m (4 ft 9 in)
Service door: Height	1.286 m (4 ft 2⅔ in)
Width	0.61 m (2 ft 0 in)
Emergency exits (underwing, each):	
Height	0.915 m (3 ft 0 in)
Width	0.515 m (1 ft 8¼ in)

DIMENSIONS, INTERNAL:

Cabin (excl flight deck): Length	11.10 m (36 ft 5 in)
Max width	2.54 m (8 ft 4 in)
Width at floor	2.02 m (6 ft 7½ in)
Max height	1.825 m (5 ft 11⅞ in)
Floor area	22.4 m² (241.1 sq ft)
Volume	44.1 m³ (1,557.4 cu ft)
Wardrobe volume (total)	1.0 m³ (35.3 cu ft)
Baggage/freight hold volume (total)	
	4.3 m³ (151.8 cu ft)

AREAS:

Wings, gross	56.0 m² (602.8 sq ft)

Ailerons (total)	3.27 m² (35.20 sq ft)
Trailing-edge flaps (total)	11.29 m² (121.52 sq ft)
Spoilers (total)	3.54 m² (38.10 sq ft)
Fin	8.30 m² (89.34 sq ft)
Rudder, incl tabs	5.54 m² (59.63 sq ft)
Tailplane	7.68 m² (82.67 sq ft)
Elevators (total, incl tabs)	5.82 m² (62.65 sq ft)

WEIGHTS AND LOADINGS:

Weight empty, equipped	8,730 kg (19,246 lb)
Operating weight empty	9,000 kg (19,841 lb)
Max fuel	2,650 kg (5,842 lb)
Max payload	3,800 kg (8,377 lb)
Max ramp weight	14,040 kg (30,953 lb)
Max T-O weight	14,000 kg (30,865 lb)
Max zero-fuel weight	12,800 kg (28,219 lb)
Max landing weight	13,500 kg (29,762 lb)
Max wing loading	250 kg/m² (51.2 lb/sq ft)
Max power loading	5.147 kg/kW (8.47 lb/shp)

PERFORMANCE (at max T-O weight):

Never-exceed speed (VNE)	
	216 knots (400 km/h; 248 mph) EAS
Max level and max cruising speed at 7,200 m (23,620 ft)	
	264 knots (490 km/h; 304 mph)
Long-range cruising speed at 7,200 m (23,620 ft)	
	220 knots (408 km/h; 253 mph)
Approach speed	92 knots (170 km/h; 106 mph)

Stalling speed:	
flaps up	93 knots (172 km/h; 107 mph) EAS
flaps down	75 knots (139 km/h; 87 mph) EAS
Max rate of climb at S/L	570 m (1,870 ft)/min
Rate of climb at S/L, one engine out	
	150 m (492 ft)/min
Service ceiling:	
theoretical	10,750 m (35,270 ft)
practical	10,250 m (33,630 ft)
Service ceiling, one engine out (30.5 m; 100 ft/min rate of climb):	
theoretical	4,750 m (15,585 ft)
practical	3,980 m (13,060 ft)
Min ground turning radius	18.33 m (60 ft 1¾ in)
T-O run	370 m (1,214 ft)
T-O to 10.7 m (35 ft)	613 m (2,011 ft)
Balanced T-O distance	752 m (2,467 ft)
Balanced T-O field length:	
hard runway	875 m (2,870 ft)
unpaved surface	1,030 m (3,380 ft)
Landing from 9 m (30 ft)	545 m (1,788 ft)
Landing run	340 m (1,115 ft)
Range, reserves for 45 min hold:	
with max payload	469 nm (870 km; 540 miles)
with max fuel	1,298 nm (2,406 km; 1,495 miles)

ZLIN
MORAVAN NÁRODNÍ PODNIK (Zlin Aircraft Moravan National Corporation)

76581 Otrokovice
Telephone: 42/Gottwaldov 92 2041/44
Telex: Gottwaldov 067 240
MANAGING DIRECTOR: Ing Josef Panáček
CHIEF DESIGNER: Ing Vojtěch Vraj
VICE-DIRECTOR, SALES: František Mužný

The Moravan company was formed on 18 September 1934 as Zlinská Letecká Akciová Spolecnost (Zlin Aviation Joint Stock Co) in Zlin, although manufacture of Zlin aircraft was actually started in 1933 by the Masarykova Letecká Liga (Masaryk League of Aviation). The factory was renamed Moravan after the Second World War. Moravan also manufactures items of aircraft equipment.

ZLIN 142

The Zlin 142 is employed for basic and advanced flying training, aerobatic flying and the training of aerobatic pilots, glider towing, and (when equipped with appropriate instrumentation) for night and IFR flying training. It is a progressive development of the Zlin 42 M (1980-81 *Jane's*), and first flew on 29 December 1978. In 1980 it received FAR Pt 23 certification in the Aerobatic, Utility and Normal categories, and production began in 1981. A total of 269 had been built by 1 January 1989. Exports have been made to Algeria (32), Bulgaria, Cuba, Germany, Hungary, Poland and Romania. Licence production in Algeria began in 1989.

TYPE: Two-seat fully aerobatic (A), light training (U) and touring (N) aircraft.

WINGS: Cantilever low-wing monoplane. Wing section NACA 63₂416.5. Dihedral 6° from roots. Sweepforward 4° 20′ at quarter-chord. All-metal structure with single main spar and auxiliary spar; skins (fluted on control surfaces) of aluminium plated duralumin sheet. All-metal slotted ailerons and flaps all have same dimensions. Mass balanced flaps and ailerons, operated mechanically by control rods. Ground adjustable tab on each aileron.

FUSELAGE: Engine cowlings of sheet metal. Centre-fuselage of welded steel tube truss construction, covered with laminated glassfibre panels. Rear fuselage is all-metal semi-monocoque structure.

TAIL UNIT: Cantilever all-metal structure with skins (fluted on control surfaces) of duralumin sheet. Control surfaces have partial mass and aerodynamic balance. Trim tabs on elevator and rudder. Rudder actuated by control cables, elevator by control rods.

LANDING GEAR: Non-retractable tricycle type, with nosewheel offset to port. Oleo-pneumatic nosewheel shock absorber. Mainwheels carried on flat spring steel legs. Nosewheel steered by rudder pedals. Mainwheels and Barum tyres size 420 × 150, pressure 1.90 bars (27.6 lb/sq in); nosewheel and Barum tyre size 350 × 135, pressure 2.50 bars (36.3 lb/sq in). Hydraulic disc brakes on mainwheels can be operated from either seat. Parking brake standard.

POWER PLANT: One 156.5 kW (210 hp) Avia M 337 AK inverted six-cylinder aircooled inline engine, with supercharger and low-pressure injection pump, driving a two-blade Avia V 500 A constant-speed metal propeller. Fuel tanks in each wing leading-edge, with combined capacity of 125 litres (33 US gallons; 27.5 Imp gallons). Normal category version has auxiliary 50 litre (13.2 US gallon; 11 Imp gallon) tank at each wingtip, increasing total fuel capacity to 225 litres (59.4 US gallons; 49.5 Imp gallons). Fuel and oil systems permit inverted flying for up to 3 min. Oil capacity 12 litres (3.2 US gallons; 2.6 Imp gallons).

Polish-registered Zlin 142 two-seat light aircraft (*R. J. Malachowski*)

ACCOMMODATION: Individual side by side seats for two persons, the instructor's seat being to port. Both seats are adjustable and permit the use of back type parachutes. Baggage space aft of seats. Cabin and windscreen heating and ventilation standard. Forward sliding cockpit canopy. Dual controls standard.

SYSTEMS: Electrical system includes a 600W 27V engine driven generator and 24V 25Ah Teledyne battery. External power source can be used for starting the engine.

AVIONICS: VHF radio with IC (Mesit LUN 3524.20) and IFR instrumentation optional.

EQUIPMENT: Standard equipment includes cockpit, instrument and cabin lights; navigation lights; landing and taxying lights; and anti-collision light. Towing gear, for gliders of up to 500 kg (1,102 lb) weight, optional.

DIMENSIONS, EXTERNAL:

Wing span	9.16 m (30 ft 0½ in)
Wing aspect ratio	6.4
Wing chord, constant portion	1.42 m (4 ft 8 in)
Length overall	7.33 m (24 ft 0½ in)
Height overall	2.75 m (9 ft 0¼ in)
Elevator span	2.904 m (9 ft 6⅓ in)
Wheel track	2.33 m (7 ft 7¾ in)
Wheelbase	1.66 m (5 ft 5¼ in)
Propeller diameter	2.00 m (6 ft 6¾ in)
Propeller ground clearance	0.40 m (1 ft 3¾ in)

DIMENSIONS, INTERNAL:

Cabin: Length	1.80 m (5 ft 10¾ in)
Max width	1.12 m (3 ft 8 in)
Max height	1.20 m (3 ft 11¼ in)
Baggage space	0.2 m³ (7.1 cu ft)

AREAS:

Wings, gross	13.15 m² (141.5 sq ft)
Ailerons (total)	1.408 m² (15.16 sq ft)
Trailing-edge flaps (total)	1.408 m² (15.16 sq ft)
Fin	0.54 m² (5.81 sq ft)
Rudder, incl tab	0.81 m² (8.72 sq ft)
Tailplane	1.23 m² (13.24 sq ft)
Elevator, incl tabs	1.36 m² (14.64 sq ft)

WEIGHTS AND LOADINGS (A: Aerobatic, U: Utility, N: Normal category):

Basic weight empty (all versions)	730 kg (1,609 lb)
Max T-O weight: A	970 kg (2,138 lb)
U	1,020 kg (2,248 lb)
N	1,090 kg (2,403 lb)
Max landing weight: A	970 kg (2,138 lb)
U	1,020 kg (2,248 lb)
N	1,050 kg (2,315 lb)
Max wing loading: A	73.76 kg/m² (15.11 lb/sq ft)
U	77.57 kg/m² (15.89 lb/sq ft)
N	82.89 kg/m² (16.98 lb/sq ft)
Max power loading: A	6.19 kg/kW (10.17 lb/hp)
U	6.51 kg/kW (10.69 lb/hp)
N	6.96 kg/kW (11.43 lb/hp)

PERFORMANCE (at max T-O weight):

Never-exceed speed (VNE) (all versions)	
	179 knots (333 km/h; 206 mph) IAS
Max level speed at 500 m (1,640 ft):	
A, U	125 knots (231 km/h; 143 mph)
N	122 knots (227 km/h; 141 mph)
Max cruising speed at 500 m (1,640 ft):	
A, U	106 knots (197 km/h; 122 mph)
N	102 knots (190 km/h; 118 mph)
Econ cruising speed at 500 m (1,640 ft):	
A	97 knots (180 km/h; 112 mph)
Stalling speed, flaps up:	
A	56 knots (103 km/h; 64 mph) IAS
U	58 knots (107 km/h; 67 mph) IAS
N	60 knots (110 km/h; 69 mph) IAS
Stalling speed, T-O flap setting:	
A	54 knots (99 km/h; 62 mph) IAS
U	56 knots (102 km/h; 64 mph) IAS
N	57 knots (105 km/h; 66 mph) IAS
Stalling speed, flaps down:	
A	48 knots (88 km/h; 55 mph) IAS
U	50 knots (91 km/h; 57 mph) IAS
N	52 knots (95 km/h; 60 mph) IAS
Max rate of climb at S/L, ISA:	
A	330 m (1,082 ft)/min
U	306 m (1,004 ft)/min
N	264 m (866 ft)/min
Service ceiling: A	5,000 m (16,400 ft)
U	4,700 m (15,425 ft)
N	4,300 m (14,100 ft)
T-O run: A	220 m (722 ft)
T-O to 15 m (50 ft): A	440 m (1,444 ft)
U	475 m (1,560 ft)
N	540 m (1,772 ft)
Landing from 15 m (50 ft): A	400 m (1,313 ft)
U	425 m (1,395 ft)
N	460 m (1,510 ft)
Landing run: A	190 m (624 ft)
Range at max cruising speed:	
A, U	283 nm (525 km; 326 miles)
N	513 nm (950 km; 590 miles)
Max range: N	566 nm (1,050 km; 652 miles)

g limits: A	+6/–3.5
U	+5/–3
N	+3.8/–1.5

ZLIN 242 L

Introduced in 1990, the Zlin 242 L is a modified version of the Z 142 aimed at the North American market, subject to obtaining certification under FAR Pt 35. It is powered by a 149 kW (200 hp) Textron Lycoming AEIO-360-A1B6 flat-six engine, resulting in a shorter nose and non-sweptforward wings to offset the resultant shift in CG. A Hartzell two-blade propeller is fitted, and total fuel capacity is 220 litres (58 US gallons; 48.4 Imp gallons). Other known data include:

WEIGHTS AND LOADINGS (Aerobatic category):
| Weight empty | 710 kg (1,565 lb) |
| Max T-O weight | 1,090 kg (2,403 lb) |

PERFORMANCE (Aerobatic category):
Max level speed at 500 m (1,640 ft)
	113 knots (209 km/h; 130 mph)
Service ceiling	4,785 m (15,700 ft)
Range with max fuel	581 nm (1,077 km; 669 miles)
g limits	+6/–3.5

ZLIN Z 50 L

Full details of the original Z 50 L, with 194 kW (260 hp) Textron Lycoming AEIO-540-D4B5 engine, can be found in the 1982-83 Jane's. Later variants are the more powerful Z 50 LS, and the Z 50 LA, a modified L with propeller pitch control and a propeller speed governor. The LS was flown for the first time on 29 June 1981, and in the following year received FAR Pt 23 certification in the Aerobatic and Normal categories. It won the European Aerobatic Championships in 1983 and the World Championships in 1984 and 1986; in 1985 it came 1st and 2nd in the European Championships, and won nine of the first 22 places. A total of 57 Z 50 L, LA and LS had been delivered by 1 June 1989. Exports have been made to Bulgaria, Germany, Hungary, Italy, Poland, Romania and Spain.

The following description applies to the Z 50 LS:

TYPE: Single-seat aerobatic aircraft.

WINGS: Cantilever low-wing monoplane. Wing section NACA 0018 at root, NACA 0012 at tip. Dihedral 1° 7' 24". All-metal structure, with single continuous main spar, rear auxiliary spar, and aluminium-clad duralumin skin. All-metal mass balanced ailerons, actuated by pushrods, occupy most of each trailing-edge. Ground adjustable tab on port outer aileron; automatic trim tab on each inboard aileron. No flaps. Provision for fitting wingtip fuel tanks for cross-country flights.

FUSELAGE: All-metal semi-monocoque structure with stressed duralumin skin.

TAIL UNIT: Conventional metal structure. Braced tailplane and fin duralumin covered, elevators and rudder fabric covered. One mechanically adjustable balance tab and one automatic trim tab on elevators; automatic balance tab on rudder. Elevators actuated by pushrods, rudder by cables.

LANDING GEAR: Non-retractable tailwheel type. Mainwheels carried on flat-spring titanium cantilever legs. Mechanical mainwheel brakes actuated by rudder pedals. Fully castoring tailwheel, with flat-spring shock absorption, has automatic locking device to maintain aircraft on a straight track during taxying, take-off and landing. Mainwheel tyres size 350 × 135 mm, pressure 2.5 bars (36 lb/sq in); tailwheel tyre size 200 × 80 mm, pressure 1.0 bar (14.5 lb/sq in). Mainwheel fairings optional.

POWER PLANT: One 224 kW (300 hp) Textron Lycoming AEIO-540-L1B5D flat-six engine, driving a Hoffmann HO-V123K-V/200AH three-blade constant-speed wooden propeller. Single main fuel tank in fuselage, aft of firewall, capacity 60 litres (15.9 US gallons; 13.2 Imp gallons). Auxiliary 50 litre (13.2 US gallon; 11 Imp gallon) tank can be attached to each wingtip for cross-country flights only. Fuel and oil systems designed for full aerobatic manoeuvres, including inverted flight. Oil capacity 12 litres (3.2 US gallons; 2.6 Imp gallons).

ACCOMMODATION: Single seat under fully transparent sideways opening (to starboard) bubble canopy, which can be jettisoned in an emergency. Seat and backrest are adjustable, and permit the use of a back type parachute. Cockpit ventilated by sliding panel in canopy.

SYSTEMS: Electrical system includes a 24V LUN 2111 alternator as main power source and two 12Ah batteries. External power socket in fuselage side for engine starting.

AVIONICS: VHF radio optional.

DIMENSIONS, EXTERNAL:
Wing span	8.58 m (28 ft 1¾ in)
Wing span over tip tanks	9.03 m (29 ft 7½ in)
Wing chord: at root	1.73 m (5 ft 8¼ in)
at tip	1.21 m (3 ft 11¾ in)
Wing aspect ratio	5.9
Length overall (tail up)	6.62 m (21 ft 8¾ in)
Height over tail (static)	2.075 m (6 ft 9¾ in)
Elevator span	3.44 m (11 ft 3½ in)
Wheel track	1.90 m (6 ft 2¾ in)
Wheelbase	5.05 m (16 ft 7 in)
Propeller diameter	2.00 m (6 ft 6¾ in)
Propeller ground clearance (tail up)	0.31 m (1 ft 0¼ in)

Zlin Z 50 M single-seat aerobatic aircraft (Avia M 137 AZ inline engine) *(Vaclav Jukl/Letectvi + Kosmonautika)*

AREAS:
Wings, gross	12.50 m² (134.55 sq ft)
Ailerons (total)	2.80 m² (30.14 sq ft)
Fin	0.59 m² (6.35 sq ft)
Rudder, incl tab	0.81 m² (8.72 sq ft)
Tailplane	1.66 m² (17.87 sq ft)
Elevators (total, incl tabs)	1.20 m² (12.92 sq ft)

WEIGHTS AND LOADINGS (A: Aerobatic, N: Normal category):
Weight empty: A	600 kg (1,322 lb)
N	610 kg (1,345 lb)
Max T-O weight: A	760 kg (1,675 lb)
N	840 kg (1,852 lb)
Max wing loading: A	60.8 kg/m² (12.45 lb/sq ft)
N	67.2 kg/m² (13.76 lb/sq ft)
Max power loading: A	3.40 kg/kW (5.58 lb/hp)
N	3.75 kg/kW (6.17 lb/hp)

PERFORMANCE (at max Aerobatic T-O weight):
Never-exceed speed (V_{NE})
| | 181 knots (337 km/h; 209 mph) CAS |
Max level speed at 500 m (1,640 ft), ISA
| | 166 knots (308 km/h; 191 mph) |
Max cruising speed at 500 m (1,640 ft), ISA
| | 148 knots (275 km/h; 171 mph) |
Stalling speed, engine idling
	56 knots (103 km/h; 81 mph) CAS
Max rate of climb at S/L, ISA	840 m (2,755 ft)/min
Service ceiling, ISA	8,175 m (26,820 ft)
T-O run	150 m (492 ft)
T-O to 15 m (50 ft)	300 m (985 ft)
Landing from 15 m (50 ft)	530 m (1,740 ft)
Landing run	300 m (985 ft)
g limits: A	+8/–6
N	+3.8/–1.5

ZLIN Z 50 M

Intended as a successor to the Z 526AFS Akrobat (1975-76 Jane's), the Z 50 M has a longer and slimmer nose than the L series, accommodating a 134 kW (180 hp) Avia M 137 AZ six-cylinder inline engine driving an Avia V 503 A two-blade constant-speed propeller. First flight was made on 25 April 1988. One prototype (OK-080) and two production examples (of 15 ordered) had been built by 1 January 1989. Certification (Aerobatic and Normal categories) was granted in February 1989.

The description of the Z 50 LS applies also to the Z 50 M, except as follows:

DIMENSIONS, EXTERNAL:
| Length overall | 6.96 m (22 ft 10 in) |

AREAS:
| Tailplane | 2.24 m² (24.1 sq ft) |

WEIGHTS AND LOADINGS (A: Aerobatic, N: Normal category):
Weight empty: A	540 kg (1,190 lb)
N	550 kg (1,212 lb)
Max T-O and landing weight: A	700 kg (1,543 lb)
N	780 kg (1,719 lb)
Max wing loading: A	56.0 kg/m² (11.48 lb/sq ft)
N	62.4 kg/m² (12.78 lb/sq ft)
Max power loading: A	5.22 kg/kW (8.57 lb/hp)
N	5.81 kg/kW (9.55 lb/hp)

PERFORMANCE (at max Aerobatic T-O weight):
Never-exceed speed (V_{NE})
| | 170 knots (315 km/h; 195 mph) CAS |
Max level speed at S/L
| | 136 knots (252 km/h; 156 mph) |
Max cruising speed at 1,000 m (3,280 ft)
	114 knots (211 km/h; 131 mph)
Stalling speed	54 knots (100 km/h; 63 mph)
Max rate of climb at S/L	450 m (1,476 ft)/min
Service ceiling	5,200 m (17,060 ft)
T-O run	200 m (656 ft)
T-O to 15 m (50 ft)	360 m (1,181 ft)
Landing from 15 m (50 ft)	640 m (2,100 ft)
Landing run	360 m (1,181 ft)
Ferry range with wingtip tanks
	372 nm (690 km; 429 miles)
g limits	+7/–4.5

ZLIN Z 37T and Z 137T AGRO TURBO

The piston engined Z-37A Cmelák (Bumble-bee) agricultural aircraft, of which more than 700 were built by Let (651 plus 26 two-seaters) and Moravan, was last described in the 1976-77 Jane's. Let then built an XZ-37T prototype (OK-146) of a turboprop version, powered by a 515 kW (691 shp) Walter M 601 B engine, which flew for the first time on 6 September 1981. Brief details of this prototype appeared in the 1982-83 Jane's.

In 1982 Moravan began the design and construction of a lower powered turbine engined version known as the Z 37T. Two prototypes (OK-072 and OK-074) made their first flights on 12 July and 29 December 1983; a third was completed in 1985. Certification under BCAR Section K was received in 1984, followed by the start of series production in 1985. First delivery of a production aircraft, to Slov-Air for operational trials, was made in 1985, and 24 had been delivered to this operator by 1 January 1989.

A two-seat Z 37T-2, for training agricultural pilots, was certificated in 1986. Two had been built by 1 January 1989.

Zlin Z 37T Agro Turbo fitted with underwing fuel tanks

Tandem cockpits distinguish the two-seat Z 37T-2 agricultural pilot trainer
(Vaclav Jukl/Letectvi + Kosmonautika)

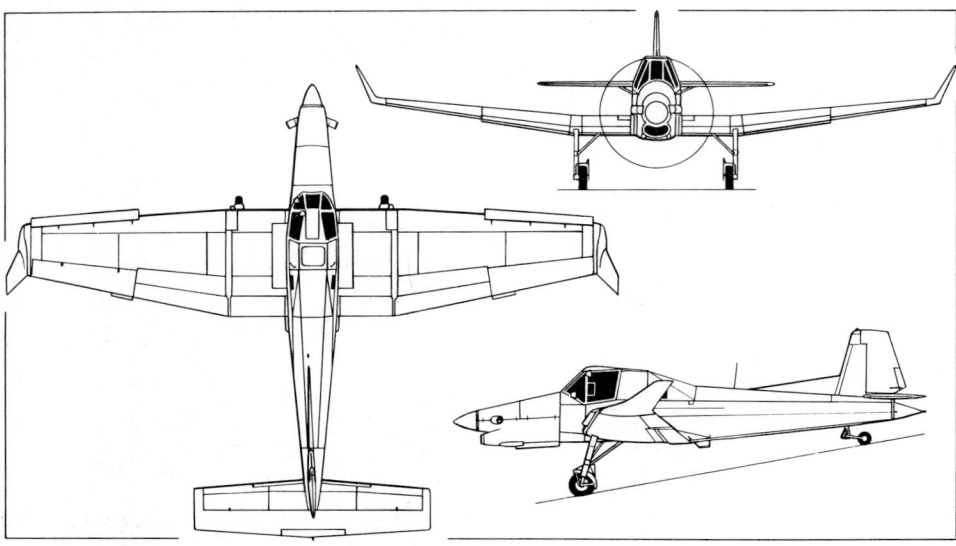

Zlin Z 37T Agro Turbo agricultural aircraft (Motorlet M 601 Z turboprop) *(Pilot Press)*

Current production models are designated **Z 137T**. In the absence of any information from Zlin for this year's edition, it is not possible to indicate how this may differ from the earlier Z 37T model, to which the following description applies:

TYPE: Single/two-seat agricultural aircraft.

WINGS: Cantilever low-wing monoplane. Wing section NACA 33015 at root, NACA 44012A at tip. Dihedral 7° on outer panels only. Incidence 3° at root, 0° at tip. All-metal single-spar structure, with auxiliary rear spar, comprising centre-section, built integrally with fuselage, and two outer panels. Linen covered duralumin ailerons, each with ground adjustable tab. All-metal duralumin skinned double-slotted trailing-edge flaps. Leading-edge fixed slats. Outward canted winglet at each tip.

FUSELAGE: Welded steel tube structure, with part-metal, part-linen covering.

TAIL UNIT: Cantilever all-metal two-spar structure, with fabric covering on control surfaces. Elevator aerody-

namically and mass balanced. Trim tabs in rudder and centre of elevator.

LANDING GEAR: Non-retractable tailwheel type, with Technometra oleo-pneumatic mainwheel shock absorbers, Moravan light alloy wheels and Barum tyres. Steerable tailwheel. Mainwheel tyres size 556 × 163 × 254 mm, tailwheel tyre size 290 × 110 mm; pressure 3.45 bars (50 lb/sq in) on all units. Moravan hydraulic drum brakes on mainwheels.

POWER PLANT: One 365 kW (490 shp) Motorlet Walter M 601 Z turboprop, driving an Avia VJ7-508Z three-blade constant-speed propeller. Two metal fuel tanks in wing centre-section, combined capacity 350 litres (92.5 US gallons; 77 Imp gallons). Fuel can be transported to distant airstrips in four auxiliary tanks with a combined capacity of 500 litres (132 US gallons; 110 Imp gallons). Gravity refuelling point in top of each wing. Oil capacity 7 litres (1.8 US gallons; 1.5 Imp gallons). Air intake filter.

ACCOMMODATION: Pilot in enclosed cockpit, on contoured seat with headrest. Forward opening window/door, on starboard side, can be jettisoned in emergency. Auxiliary seat to rear for mechanic or loader. Cockpit heated, and provided with filtered fresh air intake. Two-seat training version available.

SYSTEMS: Pneumatic system of 50 bars (725 lb/sq in) pressure, reduced to 30 bars (435 lb/sq in) for agricultural equipment and flaps. Electrical power supplied by 28V 5.6kW DC starter/generator.

AVIONICS: LUN 3524 VHF radio standard.

EQUIPMENT: Hopper/tank capacity (max) 1,000 litres (264 US gallons; 220 Imp gallons) of liquid or 900 kg (1,984 lb) of dry chemical. Distribution system for both liquid and dry chemicals is operated pneumatically. Chemicals can be jettisoned in 5 s in emergency. Steel cable cutter on windscreen and each mainwheel leg; steel deflector cable runs from tip of windscreen cable cutter to tip of fin. Windscreen washer and wiper standard. Other equipment includes gyro compass, clock, rearview mirror, second (mechanic's) seat, cockpit air-conditioning, ventilation and heating, and anti-collision light. Can be modified for firefighting role.

DIMENSIONS, EXTERNAL:

Wing span	13.63 m (44 ft 8½ in)
Wing chord: at root	2.39 m (7 ft 10 in)
at tip	1.224 m (4 ft 0¼ in)
Wing aspect ratio	7.0
Length overall (flying attitude)	10.46 m (34 ft 4 in)
Fuselage: Max width	1.70 m (5 ft 7 in)
Height overall	3.505 m (11 ft 6 in)
Elevator span	5.294 m (17 ft 4½ in)
Wheel track	3.30 m (10 ft 10 in)
Wheelbase	6.375 m (20 ft 11 in)
Propeller diameter	2:50 m (8 ft 2½ in)
Propeller ground clearance (min)	0.45 m (1 ft 5¾ in)

AREAS:

Wings, gross	26.69 m² (287.3 sq ft)
Ailerons (total)	2.428 m² (26.13 sq ft)
Trailing-edge flaps (total)	4.37 m² (47.04 sq ft)
Fin	1.185 m² (12.76 sq ft)
Rudder, incl tab	1.054 m² (11.35 sq ft)
Tailplane	2.776 m² (29.88 sq ft)
Elevator, incl tab	3.008 m² (32.38 sq ft)

WEIGHTS AND LOADINGS:

Weight empty with basic agricultural equipment	1,250 kg (2,756 lb)
Max payload	900 kg (1,984 lb)
Max fuel	280 kg (617 lb)
Max T-O weight: ferry flights	2,260 kg (4,982 lb)
agricultural, forestry and waterways work	2,525 kg (5,566 lb)
Max wing loading	89.9 kg/m² (18.41 lb/sq ft)
Max power loading	6.67 kg/kW (10.95 lb/shp)

PERFORMANCE (at 2,525 kg; 5,566 lb max T-O weight):

Never-exceed speed (VNE)	153 knots (285 km/h; 177 mph)
Max level speed at 500 m (1,640 ft)	118 knots (218 km/h; 135 mph)
Max cruising speed at 500 m (1,640 ft)	103 knots (190 km/h; 118 mph)
Working speed 78-89 knots (145-165 km/h; 90-103 mph)	
Stalling speed:	
flaps up	48 knots (88 km/h; 55 mph)
flaps down	42 knots (77 km/h; 48 mph)
Max rate of climb at S/L	252 m (827 ft)/min
T-O run	265 m (870 ft)
T-O to 15 m (50 ft)	580 m (1,905 ft)
Landing from 15 m (50 ft)	720 m (2,365 ft)
Landing run	300 m (985 ft)
Range with max internal fuel 188 nm (350 km; 217 miles)	
Swath width: granules	30 m (98 ft)
liquid	40 m (131 ft)
g limits	+3.2/−1.8

EGYPT

AOI
ARAB ORGANISATION FOR INDUSTRIALISATION
2D Abbassiya Square, PO Box 770, Cairo
Telephone: 20 (2) 932822/823377
Fax: 20 (2) 826010
Telex: 92090/92014 AOI UN
CHAIRMAN: Lt General Ibrahim Al Orabi
MANAGING DIRECTOR: Dr Mohamed Nour Youssef
OPERATIONS AND MARKETING DIRECTOR: Eng Ahmed El Sayed
Aircraft Factory, PO Box 11722, Helwan
Telephone: 20 (2) 782516
Fax: 20 (2) 782408
Telex: 92191 NASR UN
CHAIRMAN: Eng Mostafa Riad

Engine Factory, PO Box 12, Helwan
CHAIRMAN: Dr Mohamed El Semery

Kader Factory, PO Box 287, Heliopolis
SAKR Factory, PO Box 33, Heliopolis
Electronics Factory, PO Box 84, Heliopolis

SUBSIDIARIES:
Arab American Vehicle Co (AAVCo)
Arab British Dynamics Co (ABDCo)
Arab British Engine Co (ABECo)
Arab British Helicopter Co (ABHCo)

The AOI was set up in November 1975 by Egypt, Saudi Arabia, Qatar and the United Arab Emirates, to provide the basis for an Arab military industry. It is organised into five divisions, which between them have a workforce of about 20,000 people, including approximately 3,000 employed in its four subsidiaries. Rockets, missiles and other weapons are produced by the SAKR Factory (except for the Swingfire programme, which is managed by ABDCo).

The main AOI centre is at Helwan, south of Cairo. Helwan also accommodates the Arab British Helicopter Company and Arab British Engine Company. By reverse engineering, ABECo has manufactured components for, and overhauled, Soviet TV2-117A turboshaft engines for Egypt's Mil Mi-8 helicopter fleet.

AOI's major current aircraft programme concerns licence assembly of 134 Embraer EMB-312 Tucano military trainers for the air forces of Egypt (54) and Iraq (80), under contracts placed in 1983 (for 120) and 1989 (for 14). All 134 kits have been delivered by Embraer, and deliveries of Egyptian assembled Tucanos began in November 1985. Five AOI factories (Aircraft, Engine, Kader, Electronics and ABHCo) are involved in the Tucano programme.

Details of similar recent assembly programmes for the Gazelle helicopter and Alpha Jet can be found in the 1986-87 *Jane's*. Other AOI work includes component manufacture for the Aerospatiale Super Puma and the Dassault Mirage 2000 and Falcon 50.

ETHIOPIA

EAL

ETHIOPIAN AIRLINES S.C.

PO Box 1755, Addis Ababa
Telephone: 251 (1) 612222
Fax: 251 (1) 611474
Telex: 21012 ETHAIR ADDIS
GENERAL MANAGER: Capt Mohammed Ahmed
DIRECTOR, AGRO AIRCRAFT MANUFACTURING:
Col Taddele Mekuria
    Under licence from Schweizer Aircraft Corporation in the USA (which see), Ethiopian Airlines is assembling and part-building for domestic use and eventual export the former's Ag-Cat Super B Turbine agricultural aircraft under the Ethiopian name **Eshet**. The first example (ET-AIY) was rolled out on 20 December 1986. Ethiopian Eshets are powered by a 559 kW (750 shp) PT6A-34AG turboprop with a 2.69 m (8 ft 10 in) Hartzell HC-B3TN-3D three-blade propeller, have an optional max fuel load of 435 litres (115 US gallons; 95.75 Imp gallons), and an oil capacity of 10.6 litres (2.8 US gallons; 2.3 Imp gallons). The 507 kW (680 shp) PT6A-15AG is available optionally. Mainwheels are as for the US built version, but with a higher tyre pressure of 3.83 bars (55.58 lb/sq in). Empty equipped weight is 1,500 kg (3,307 lb).
    EAL has the sole rights to build, market and service this aircraft throughout the African continent with the exceptions of Algeria, Tunisia and South Africa. The Eshet programme was launched with assembly of CKD kits supplied by Schweizer, but the amount of local manufacture is being gradually increased. EAL had completed 12 Eshets by the end of 1990, with a further five then in production.

Ethiopian Airlines Eshet licence built version of the Schweizer Ag-Cat Super B Turbine *(Hormuz P. Mama)*

FINLAND

VALMET

VALMET AVIATION INDUSTRIES

Kuninkaankatu 30 (PO Box 11), 33201 Tampere
Telephone: 358 (31) 239444
Fax: 358 (31) 239543
CORPORATE VICE-PRESIDENT AND CHIEF EXECUTIVE OFFICER:
Markku Valtonen
DIRECTORS:
Arto Tonteri (Co-production)
Juhani Mäkinen (Training Aircraft)
Pertti Korhonen (Maintenance)
    Since 1922, Valmet Aviation Industries and its predecessors have built 30 different types of aircraft, of which 18 have been of Finnish design.
    Current activities include production of the L-90 TP Redigo; aircraft and aero engine parts manufacture; maintenance/overhaul/repair/modification of aircraft and accessories; maintenance/overhaul/repair of aero engines and accessories and of marine diesel engines, accessories and gears; and foundry products. Production facilities are located in Kuorevesi, Linnavuori and Tampere; total workforce is approx 890.
    The latest aircraft of Finnish design to be built by Valmet is the L-90 TP Redigo turboprop primary and basic trainer. Valmet is to manufacture the fin, rudder, tailplane and elevators for the Saab 2000 regional transport, under a 1989 contract from Saab-Scania of Sweden.

VALMET L-90 TP REDIGO

    The L-90 TP is developed from, and is slightly larger than, the L-70 (1986-87 *Jane's*), from which it differs primarily in having a turboprop power plant, new wings and retractable landing gear. Design began in 1983, and the Allison engined first prototype (OH-VTP) made its initial flight on 1 July 1986. The second prototype (OH-VTM), which first flew in early December 1987, was powered by a 373 kW (500 shp) Turboméca TP 319 turboprop, derated to 313 kW (420 shp), but was lost in a flying accident on 28 August 1988.
    Suitable for primary and basic flying training, aerobatic training, night and instrument flight training, tactical training, observation and liaison missions, the Redigo is designed to fit a training system that can produce combat-ready pilots within minimum time and cost levels, pupils proceeding directly from the L-90 TP to a demanding advanced trainer such as the BAe Hawk used by the Finnish Air Force. It was designed to the airworthiness requirements of FAR Pt 23 and BCAR Section K. Minimum requirements were a fatigue life of 10,000 flight hours (fatigue spectrum MIL-A-8866B), and 30,000 landings in heavy military use. Additional roles can include search and rescue, weapons training, photographic reconnaissance and target towing.
    The Finnish Air Force placed a contract for 10 of the Allison engined version on 6 January 1989. These are now in production and will be delivered in 1991-92.
TYPE: Two/four-seat multi-purpose military primary and basic training aircraft.
WINGS: Cantilever low-wing monoplane of tapered planform, with forward-swept inboard leading-edges. Wing

First prototype of the Valmet L-90 TP Redigo two/four-seat military trainer, modified to production standard

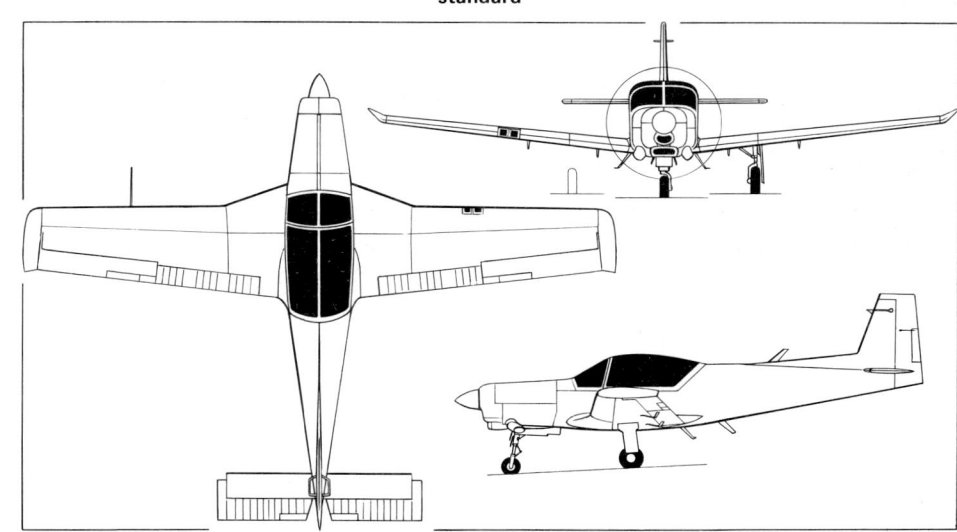

Valmet L-90 TP Redigo turboprop powered multi-stage trainer *(Pilot Press)*

section NACA 63-218 (mod B3) at root, NACA 63-412 (mod B3) at tip. Dihedral 6° from roots. Incidence 3° at root; −3° washout at tip. Fail-safe structure comprising main spar, auxiliary spar, ribs and stringers, bolted to fuselage. Construction mainly of aluminium alloy, with riveted skin (fluted on flaps). In-wing fuel tanks are of Valmet load bearing sandwich construction. Wingroot fairings are of CFRP, upturned wingtips of glassfibre. All-metal single-slotted trailing-edge flaps, actuated electrically by screwjack. Ailerons, also all-metal, are of modified Frise type, mass balanced, and actuated by cables. Geared tab and spring tab in each aileron; starboard geared tab can be operated also as a trim tab.

FUSELAGE: Conventional aluminium alloy semi-monocoque fail-safe structure of frames and longerons, with riveted skin; CFRP and glassfibre used in tailcone and engine cowling panels.
TAIL UNIT: Cantilever non-swept aluminium alloy structure, with riveted skin (fluted on elevators). CFRP dorsal fin. Elevators and rudder horn balanced and cable operated. Geared tab in rudder and each elevator, all three operable also as trim tabs.
LANDING GEAR: AP Precision Hydraulics electro-hydraulically retractable tricycle type, with single wheel and oleo-pneumatic shock absorber on each unit. Nosewheel, which is centred by a spring, is steerable

±25° and retracts rearward; main units retract inward into wings. Spring assisted lowering of all units in event of emergency. Mainwheel tyres size 17.5 × 6.3-6.0 in, pressure 3.79 bars (55 lb/sq in); nosewheel tyre size 14.2 × 4.95-5.0 in, pressure 3.45 bars (50 lb/sq in). Differential brakes on mainwheels. Parking brake.

POWER PLANT: One Allison 250-B17F turboprop (max power 373 kW; 500 shp), flat rated at 313 kW (420 shp), driving a Hartzell HC-B3TF-7A/T10173-15 three-blade constant-speed reversible-pitch propeller. Fuel in four wing tanks and a fuselage collector tank, total usable capacity 378 litres (100 US gallons; 83.2 Imp gallons). Collector tank of 9 litres (2.4 US gallons; 2 Imp gallons) can be used for up to 30 s of inverted flight. Gravity refuelling point in top of each wing tank. Oil capacity 9 litres (2.4 US gallons; 2 Imp gallons). Anti-icing for engine air intake, spinner and propeller blades.

ACCOMMODATION: Instructor and pupil, side by side, beneath one-piece rearward sliding jettisonable canopy with steel tube turnover windscreen frame. Canopy can be locked in partially open position if required. Zero/zero rocket assisted escape system optional. Dual controls standard, but instructor's or pupil's control column can be removed if desired. Both front seats are adjustable longitudinally and for rake, and are fitted with five-point seat belts and inertia reel shoulder harnesses. Provision for two more seats at rear, with four-point harnesses, which can be removed to make room for up to 200 kg (440 lb) of baggage. As ambulance, can accommodate one stretcher patient, and a medical attendant or sitting patient, in addition to pilot. Accommodation heated by bleed air heater. Windscreen heated and ventilated by heat exchanger, fresh air intake and mixer unit. Auxiliary fresh air intake in fin leading-edge. Air-conditioning system optional.

SYSTEMS: No hydraulic or pneumatic systems. Electrical system is 28V DC, powered by a 200A engine driven starter/generator, with a 23Ah nickel-cadmium battery for emergency supply and engine starting. Ground power receptacle. Emergency battery for main artificial horizon. Oxygen system available to customer's requirements.

EQUIPMENT: Dual controls and instrumentation for day and night VFR and IFR operation, including VHF com radios (two), ADF, DME, transponder, RMI, HSI, marker beacon receiver, standby compass, airspeed indicator, attitude indicator, altimeter, turn and bank indicator, vertical speed indicator, outside air temperature gauge, and clock.

Six underwing attachments, each inner point stressed for 250 kg (551 lb) and the other four for 150 kg (331 lb) each; max external stores load 800 kg (1,764 lb). When flown solo, can carry up to four photographic, TV, radar or reconnaissance pods plus two flares. As two-seater, typical loads can include five liferafts or emergency packs and one searchlight pod; and photo and TV pods. Provision for target towing with winch and hit counters. Twin landing lights in starboard wing leading-edge.

DIMENSIONS, EXTERNAL:

Wing span	10.60 m (34 ft 9¼ in)
Wing chord: at root	1.827 m (6 ft 0 in)
mean aerodynamic	1.497 m (4 ft 11 in)
at tip	1.109 m (3 ft 7⅔ in)
Wing aspect ratio	7.62
Length overall	8.53 m (27 ft 11¾ in)
Fuselage: Max width	1.22 m (4 ft 0 in)
Height overall	3.20 m (10 ft 6 in)
Elevator span	3.684 m (12 ft 1 in)
Wheel track	3.367 m (11 ft 0½ in)
Wheelbase	2.112 m (6 ft 11¼ in)
Propeller diameter	2.194 m (7 ft 2½ in)
Propeller ground clearance	0.283 m (11¼ in)

DIMENSIONS, INTERNAL:

Cockpit: Length	2.00 m (6 ft 6¾ in)
Max width	1.14 m (3 ft 9 in)
Height (seat cushion to canopy)	1.02 m (3 ft 4¼ in)

AREAS:

Wings, gross	14.748 m^2 (158.75 sq ft)
Ailerons (total, incl tabs)	1.996 m^2 (21.48 sq ft)
Trailing-edge flaps (total)	1.766 m^2 (19.01 sq ft)
Fin	0.718 m^2 (7.73 sq ft)
Rudder, incl tab	0.70 m^2 (7.53 sq ft)
Tailplane	1.609 m^2 (17.32 sq ft)
Elevators (total, incl tabs)	1.421 m^2 (15.30 sq ft)

WEIGHTS AND LOADINGS (A: Aerobatic category, U: Utility, N: Normal category):

Weight empty, equipped	950 kg (2,094 lb)
Max fuel	303 kg (668 lb)
External stores: max	800 kg (1,764 lb)
with max fuel	600 kg (1,323 lb)
Max T-O weight: A	1,350 kg (2,976 lb)
U	1,470 kg (3,241 lb)
U (with external stores)	1,900 kg (4,189 lb)
N	1,600 kg (3,527 lb)
Max landing weight	1,530 kg (3,373 lb)
Max wing loading: A	91.54 kg/m^2 (18.75 lb/sq ft)
U	99.67 kg/m^2 (20.41 lb/sq ft)
U (with external stores)	128.83 kg/m^2 (26.39 lb/sq ft)
N	108.49 kg/m^2 (22.22 lb/sq ft)
Max power loading: A	4.31 kg/kW (7.08 lb/shp)
U	4.69 kg/kW (7.70 lb/shp)
U (with external stores)	6.07 kg/kW (9.97 lb/shp)
N	5.11 kg/kW (8.40 lb/shp)

PERFORMANCE (at max T-O weight, ISA):

Never-exceed speed (VNE)	251 knots (465 km/h; 289 mph) CAS
Max level speed	224 knots (415 km/h; 258 mph) CAS
Max cruising speed at 2,400 m (7,875 ft)	190 knots (352 km/h; 219 mph)
Cruising speed (75% max continuous power) at 2,400 m (7,875 ft)	168 knots (312 km/h; 194 mph)
Stalling speed, engine idling: flaps up	65 knots (120 km/h; 75 mph)
15° flap	60 knots (111 km/h; 70 mph)
35° flap	55 knots (101 km/h; 63 mph)
Max rate of climb at S/L	540 m (1,771 ft)/min
Time to height: 3,000 m (9,845 ft)	5 min
5,000 m (16,400 ft)	11 min
Service ceiling (engine limited)	7,620 m (25,000 ft)
T-O run	240 m (788 ft)
T-O to 15 m (50 ft)	340 m (1,116 ft)
Landing from 15 m (50 ft)	410 m (1,345 ft)
Landing run (without propeller reversal)	240 m (788 ft)
Min ground turning radius	5.00 m (16 ft 4¾ in)
Range at 6,000 m (19,685 ft) with max internal fuel, 30 min reserves	755 nm (1,400 km; 870 miles)
Endurance, conditions as above	6 h 20 min
g limits	+7/−3.5 aerobatic
	+2.8 max sustained

FRANCE

AEROSPATIALE

AEROSPATIALE SNI

37 boulevard de Montmorency, 75781 Paris Cédex 16
Telephone: 33 (1) 42 24 24 24
Telex: AISPA 620059 F

PRESIDENT AND CHIEF EXECUTIVE OFFICER:
Henri Martre

DIRECTOR OF INFORMATION AND COMMUNICATIONS:
Patrice Kreis

AIRCRAFT DIVISION

DIVISION MANAGER: Jacques Plenier
AIRBUS PROGRAMME DIRECTOR: Alain Bruneau
ATR 42 PROGRAMME DIRECTOR: Jean-Paul Perrais
HYPERSONIC PROGRAMMES DIRECTOR: Jean-Marc Thomas
COMMERCIAL DIRECTOR: Henri Paul Puel

WORKS AND FACILITIES:
Toulouse. PLANT MANAGER: Jean-Marie Mir
Nantes-Bouguenais. PLANT MANAGER: Christian Beugnet
Saint-Nazaire.
PLANT MANAGER: Jean-Claude Chaussonnet
Méaulte. PLANT MANAGER: Jacques Crusson

HELICOPTER DIVISION

DIVISION MANAGER: Jean François Bigay

DIRECTOR OF RESEARCH AND DEVELOPMENT:
René Mouille

COMMERCIAL DIRECTOR: Lucien Lordereau

WORKS AND FACILITIES:
Marignane and La Courneuve.
FACTORY DIRECTOR: Paul Chandez

European Commission approval was given in March 1991 for the helicopter divisions of Aerospatiale and DASA/MBB of Germany to be merged under the title of Eurocopter International GIE. Further details can be found under that heading in the International section.

SUBSIDIARIES
SOGERMA-SOCEA
Société de Construction d'Avions de Tourisme et d'Affaires (SOCATA)
Société d'Exploitation et de Constructions Aéronautiques (SECA)
Sextant Avionique (50:50 with Thomson-CSF)
Unilaser
Aerospatiale Helicopter Corporation (USA)

Aerospatiale was formed on 1 January 1970, by decision of the French government, as a result of the merger of the former Sud-Aviation, Nord-Aviation and SEREB companies. It had a registered capital of 3,747,070,000 francs, facilities extending over a total covered area of 1,802,253 m^2 (19,399,271 sq ft; gross area not available) and a staff (including subsidiary companies) of 32,800 persons on 1 January 1990.

In addition to the programmes of which details follow, Aerospatiale is a partner in the European Airbus programmes (see International section), and participates financially in Helibras (Brazil), Samaero (Singapore) and Maroc Aviation (Morocco). In 1989 Aerospatiale and Lockheed agreed to a joint venture for identification, development and execution of R&D, licensing and/or production projects in several areas of technology, including missiles and space.

Most Aerospatiale helicopter designations were amended in January 1990, the changes being applied retrospectively. The prefix AS (for Aerospatiale) now replaces SA (referring to the former Sud-Aviation) in most cases. Additionally, military versions add 200 to their former numerical designation and adopt a standardised role suffix (except for the Gazelle): A – Armed, land-based; C – anti-tank; M – maritime, non-combatant; S – maritime, armed; and U – utility. Some helicopters were re-named, military versions of Super Puma, Ecureuil and Dauphin becoming Cougar, Fennec and Panther respectively. By December 1990 Aerospatiale had sold approx 8,500 helicopters in 115 countries. Sales during 1990 totalled 289 (206 Ecureuil/Fennec, 32 Dauphin/Panther and 51 Super Puma/Cougar); deliveries in 1990 totalled 259 (86 military, and 173 to civilian operators and government agencies).

AEROSPATIALE AS 100

This 1988 study of a propfan-powered 96/124-passenger medium-range airliner is now merged in the German/French/Italian 80/130-passenger airliner programme being co-ordinated for Deutsche Aerospace by Deutsche Airbus.

AEROSPATIALE/ALENIA ATR 42/72

Details of the ATR 42/72 programme can be found in the International section.

AEROSPATIALE ATSF

Although Aerospatiale has been continuing its future supersonic transport (ATSF) studies, they are associated with Britain's advanced supersonic transport (AST) work within a joint programme called Project Alliance. France also joined the outline agreement concluded in 1990 with Boeing and Douglas and Germany and has periodic contacts with Japan and Tupolev in the Soviet Union (see under SCTICSG in the International section).

HERMÈS AEROSPACECRAFT

Details of Hermès can now be found under the Eurohermespace heading in the International section.

AEROSPATIALE/MBB HAP/PAH-2/HAC TIGER/TIGRE

Details of this Franco-German anti-tank helicopter programme can be found under the Eurocopter GmbH heading in the International section.

AEROSPATIALE P 120L

Details of this demonstrator for a future light helicopter, to be developed jointly with the People's Republic of China and Singapore, may be found in the International section of this edition.

AEROSPATIALE SA 315B LAMA

Manufacture of the Lama continues by HAL in India (which see).

AEROSPATIALE AS 330 PUMA

Sole source of Puma production is now IAR in Romania (which see). See also Westland entry in UK section.

AEROSPATIALE AS 332 SUPER PUMA and AS 532 COUGAR

Brazilian Air Force designation: CH-34
Spanish Air Force designations: HD.21/HT.21
Swedish Air Force designation: Hkp 10

The early history of the Super Puma, a list of its improved features compared with the original AS 330 Puma, and details of earlier versions, can be found in the 1985-86 edition of *Jane's*. The prototype AS 332 Super Puma (F-WZJA) flew on 13 September 1978, military versions being re-named AS 532 Cougar in 1990. Super Puma/Cougar designations also include a suffix letter indicating whether they have a short (C for Court) or long (L for Longue) fuselage. The current versions introduced in 1986, with uprated Turbomeca Makila 1A1 engines, are as follows:

AS 532UC Cougar: Military utility short version; unarmed. Seating for up to 21 troops and two crew. Cabin floor reinforced for loads of 1,500 kg/m^2 (307 lb/sq ft).

AS 532UL Cougar: Military utility stretched version; unarmed. Cabin lengthened by 0.76 m (2 ft 6 in); additional fuel capacity and two additional windows. Up to 25 troops and two crew.

AS 532AC Cougar: Armed AS 532UC.

AS 532AL Cougar: Armed AS 532UL.

AS 532SC Cougar: Naval short version with armament and ASW/ASV equipment. Folding tail rotor pylon and deck landing assistance device.

AS 332L_1 Super Puma: Civil stretched version. As AS 532UL, but 24 passengers.

Super Puma Mk II: This improved version is described separately.

The air component of the French Army (ALAT) has started to replace its current AS 330B Pumas with AS 532L Cougars. An initial 22 AS 532Ls have been received by the Army's Force d'Action Rapide, comprising six ordered in 1987 and eight funded in each of the two years 1988-89. The first was handed over on 13 December 1988 and became operational on 1 July 1989 with 5e Escadrille of 4e RHCM at Phalsbourg. Deliveries were completed in 1991.

All Super Puma variants are certificated for IFR category A and B operation, to FAR Pt 29 standards. The first Super Puma (an AS 332L) equipped for operation to IFR Cat II standards was certificated by the DGAC on 7 July 1983 and delivered to Lufttransport of Norway in September 1983. Certification of this version for flight into known icing conditions was granted on 29 June 1983. Corresponding FAA certifications cover Cat II automatic approach, using a SFIM CDV 85 P4 four-axis flight director coupler, and flight into known icing conditions under FAR Pt 25 Appendix C.

Orders for 350 Super Pumas and Cougars (including 255 military, but excluding six prototypes), for service in 34 countries, had been received by January 1990. They include five for operation by the French Air Force in support of nuclear test facilities in the Pacific (three) and for VIP transport (two); and others for Abu Dhabi (eight including two VIP), Argentina (24, Army), Brazil (16 including six AS 532SCs), Cameroun (one), Chile (two, Army; four AS 532SCs), China (six), Ecuador (eight, including six Army), Finland (two, border police), Gabon (one, Presidential Guard), Germany (three, border police), Indonesia (built under licence), Iraq (six AS 532SCs), Japan (three, Army/VIP), Jordan (eight), South Korea (three, Army/VIP), Mexico (two VIP), Nepal (two, Royal Flight), Nigeria (two), Oman (two, Royal Flight), Panama (one VIP), Saudi Arabia (12 AS 532SCs), Singapore (22), Spain (10 SAR HD.21s, two VIP HT.21s and 18 Army tactical transport HT.21s), Sweden (10 SAR), Switzerland (15), Togo (one), Venezuela (eight) and Zaïre (one VIP). A further 31 AS 332Ls were ordered by Bristow Helicopters, whose 19-passenger aircraft, serving offshore oil platforms, are known as **Tigers**. Special equipment on the Tigers includes foldable seats, large rear baggage compartment, in-flight music, public address system, automatic emergency door jettison, and large capacity liferafts. By 1989, 60 Super Pumas were in service with petroleum support operators.

Aerospatiale AS 532UL Cougar VIP helicopter of the Japanese Army's Special Transport Squadron at Kisarazu *(Ivo Sturzenegger)*

Deliveries of the Super Puma from French production began in mid-1981. IPTN of Indonesia (which see) is manufacturing several versions under licence, and 12 of the Spanish tactical transports are being assembled in Spain by CASA.

TYPE: Twin-turbine multi-role helicopter.

ROTOR SYSTEM: Four-blade main rotor, with a fully articulated hub and integral rotor brake. Each drag hinge is fitted with an elastomeric frequency adaptor. Blade pitch is controlled by twin-cylinder hydraulic powered control units. Each of the moulded blades is made up of a glassfibre roving spar and a composite glassfibre and carbonfibre fabric skin, with Moltoprene filler. The leading-edge is covered with a titanium protective section. The tips are swept. Attachment of each blade to its sleeve by means of two quick-disconnect pins enables the blades to be folded back quickly by hand. The five-blade tail rotor has flapping hinges only, and is located on the starboard side of the tailboom. Optional de-icing system, with heating mat on leading-edge of each main and tail rotor blade.

Mechanical shaft and gear drive. Modular main gearbox is fitted with two torquemeters and has two separate lubrication circuits. It is mounted on top of the cabin behind the engines, has two separate inputs from the engines and five reduction stages. The first stage drives, from each engine, an intermediate shaft directly driving the alternator and indirectly driving the two hydraulic pumps, with a further shaft drive to the ventilation fan. At the second stage the action of the two units becomes synchronised on a single main driveshaft by means of freewheeling spur gears. If one or both engines are stopped, this enables the drive gears to be rotated by the remaining turbine or the autorotating rotor, thus maintaining drive to the ancillary systems when the engines are stopped. Drive to the tail rotor is via shafting and an intermediate angle gearbox, terminating at a right-angle tail rotor gearbox. Turbine output 23,840 rpm; main rotor shaft 265 rpm, tail rotor shaft 1,278 rpm. The hydraulically controlled rotor brake, installed on the main gearbox, permits stopping of the rotor 15 s after engine shutdown.

FUSELAGE: Conventional all-metal semi-monocoque structure, embodying anti-crash features. Local use of titanium alloy under engine installation, which is outside the main fuselage shell. Monocoque tailboom supports the tail rotor on the starboard side and a horizontal stabiliser with fixed leading-edge slat (and optional pneumatic de-icing) on the port side. Large ventral fin. Optional folding tailboom for naval versions.

LANDING GEAR: Retractable tricycle type, of Messier-Bugatti high energy absorbing design. All units retract rearward hydraulically, mainwheels into sponsons on sides of fuselage. Dual-chamber oleo-pneumatic shock absorbers. Optional 'kneeling' capability for main units. Twin-wheel self-centring nose unit, tyre size 466×176, pressure 7.0 bars (102 lb/sq in). Single wheel on each main unit with tyre size 615×225-10 or 640×230-10, pressure 9.0 bars (130 lb/sq in). Hydraulic differential disc brakes, controlled by foot pedals. Lever operated parking brake. Emergency pop-out flotation units can be mounted on main landing gear fairings and forward fuselage.

POWER PLANT: Two Turbomeca Makila 1A1 turboshafts, each with max contingency rating of 1,400 kW (1,877 shp) and max continuous rating of 1,184 kW (1,588 shp). Air intakes protected by a grille against ingestion of ice, snow and foreign objects; but Centrisep multi-purpose intake is necessary for flight into sandy areas. AS 532UC/AC have five flexible fuel tanks under cabin floor, with total usable capacity of 1,497 litres (395 US gallons; 329 Imp gallons). AS 532SC has total basic capacity of 2,141 litres (565 US gallons; 471 Imp gallons). AS 332L₁/532UL/532AL have a basic fuel system of six flexible tanks with total capacity of 2,020 litres (533 US gallons; 444 Imp gallons) in the 332; 2,003 litres (529 US gallons; 440 Imp gallons) in the 532. Provision for additional 1,900 litres (502 US gallons; 418 Imp gallons) in four auxiliary ferry tanks installed in cabin. Two external auxiliary tanks with total capacity of 650 litres (172 US gallons; 143 Imp gallons) are standard on the AS 532SC, optional on other versions. For long range missions (mainly offshore), a special internal auxiliary tank can be fitted in cargo sling well, in addition to the two external tanks, to raise the total usable fuel capacity to 2,994 litres (791 US gallons; 658 Imp gallons) in AS 332L₁. Refuelling point on starboard side of cabin. Fuel system is designed to avoid leakage following a crash. Self-sealing tanks are standard on military versions, optional on other versions. Other options include a fuel dumping system and pressure refuelling.

ACCOMMODATION: One pilot (VFR) or two pilots side by side (IFR) on flight deck, with jump seat for third crew member or paratroop dispatcher. Provision for composite light alloy/Kevlar armour for crew protection on military models. Door on each side of flight deck and internal doorway connecting flight deck to cabin. Dual

AS 532L Cougar of the École d'Application, French Army Aviation *(Ivo Sturzenegger)*

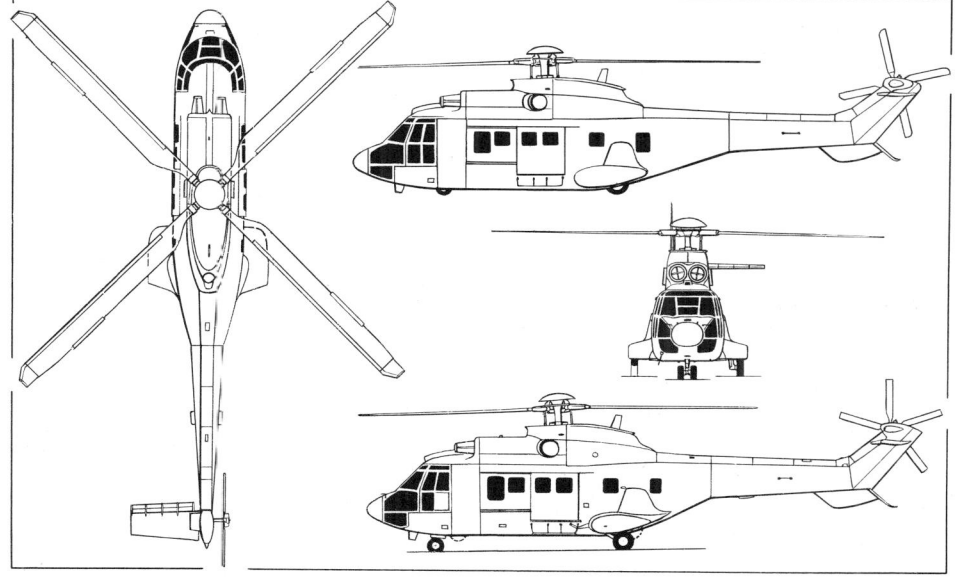

Aerospatiale AS 532UC Cougar (formerly AS 332B₁ Super Puma), with side view (top) of AS 332L₂/AS 532U₂ *(Pilot Press)*

Aerospatiale Hkp 10 Cougar of Helikoptergrupp/F21, Swedish Air Force *(Ivo Sturzenegger)*

Orchidée battlefield radar in Puma testbed as used experimentally in the simplified Horizon (or Horus) system in the Gulf War in early 1991 *(Paul Jackson)*

controls, co-pilot instrumentation and crashworthy flight deck and cabin floors. Max accommodation for 21 passengers in AS 532UC, 24 in AS 332L₁ and 25 in AS 532UL. Variety of interiors available for VIP use, or for air ambulance duty carrying six stretchers and eleven seated casualties/attendants, or nine stretchers and three seated. Strengthened floor for cargo carrying, with lashing points. Jettisonable sliding door on each side of main cabin; or port side door with built-in steps and starboard side double door in VIP or airline configurations. Removable panel on underside of fuselage, at rear of main cabin, permits longer loads to be accommodated, and also serves as emergency exit. Removable door with integral steps for access to baggage racks optional. A hatch in the floor below the centreline of the main rotor is provided for carrying loads of up to 4,500 kg (9,920 lb) on an internally mounted cargo sling. Cabin and flight deck are heated, ventilated and soundproofed. Demisting, de-icing, washers and wipers for pilots' windscreens.

SYSTEMS: Two independent hydraulic systems, supplied by self-regulating pumps driven by the main gearbox. Each system supplies one set of servo unit chambers, the left-hand system supplying in addition the autopilot, landing gear, rotor brake and wheel brakes. Freewheels in main gearbox ensure that both systems remain in operation, for supplying the servo controls, if the engines are stopped in flight. Other hydraulically actuated systems can be operated on the ground from the main gearbox (when a special disconnect system is installed to permit running of port engine with rotors stationary), or by external power through the ground power receptacle.

Independent auxiliary system, fed through a handpump, can be used in an emergency to lower the landing gear. Three-phase 200V AC electrical power supplied by two 20kVA 400Hz alternators, driven by the port side intermediate shaft from the main gearbox and available on the ground under the same conditions as the hydraulic ancillary systems. 28.5V DC power provided from the AC system by two transformer-rectifiers. Main battery used for self starting and emergency power in flight.

AVIONICS: Optional communications equipment includes VHF, UHF, tactical HF and HF/SSB radio installations and intercom system. Navigational equipment includes radio compass, radio altimeter, VLF Omega, Decca navigator and flight log, Doppler, and VOR/ILS with glidepath. SFIM 155 autopilot, with provision for coupling to self contained navigation and microwave landing systems. Full IFR instrumentation available optionally. Offshore models have nose-mounted radar. The search and rescue version has nose-mounted Bendix/King RDR 1400 or Honeywell Primus 500 search radar, Doppler, and Sextant Avionique Nadir or Decca self-contained navigation system, including navigation computer with SAR patterns, polar indicator, roller map display, hover indicator, route mileage indicator and ground speed and drift indicator. Nadir Mk 2 in French Army version. A SFIM CDV 155 autopilot coupler makes possible automatic nav track including search patterns, transitions and hover. A multi-function video display shows radar and route images, SAR patterns and hover indication. For naval ASW and ASV missions, aircraft can be fitted with nose mounted Thomson-CSF Varan radar, linked to a tactical table in the cabin, and an

Alcatel/Thomson-Sintra HS 312 sonar station at the rear of the cabin. Swedish Hkp 10s have Bendix/King 1500 radar with integrated FLIR, Racal RAMS flight management system including GEC Ferranti AHRS, Decca Doppler and GPS.

EQUIPMENT: A fixed or retractable rescue hoist (capacity 275 kg; 606 lb) can be mounted externally on the starboard side of the fuselage. Equipment for naval missions can include sonar, MAD and sonobuoys.

ARMAMENT (optional): Typical alternatives for army/air force missions are one 20 mm gun, two 7.62 mm machine guns, or two pods each containing twenty-two 68 mm rockets or nineteen 2.75 in rockets. Armament for naval missions includes two AM 39 Exocet missiles, or two lightweight torpedoes.

DIMENSIONS, EXTERNAL:	
Main rotor diameter	15.60 m (51 ft 2¼ in)
Tail rotor diameter	3.05 m (10 ft 0 in)
Main rotor blade chord	0.60 m (1 ft 11½ in)
Length: overall, rotors turning	18.70 m (61 ft 4¼ in)
fuselage, incl tail rotor:	
AS 532UC/AC/SC	15.53 m (50 ft 11½ in)
AS 332L₁/532AL/UL	16.29 m (53 ft 5½ in)
Width, blades folded:	
AS 532UC/AC/AL/UL/332L₁	3.79 m (12 ft 5¼ in)
AS 532SC	4.04 m (13 ft 3 in)
Height: overall	4.92 m (16 ft 1¾ in)
blades and tail pylon folded:	
AS 532UC/AC	4.80 m (15 ft 9 in)
to top of rotor head	4.60 m (15 ft 1¼ in)
Width overall, blades folded	3.79 m (12 ft 5¼ in)
Wheel track	3.00 m (9 ft 10 in)
Wheelbase: AS 532UC/AC/SC	4.49 m (14 ft 8¾ in)
AS 332L₁/532AL/UL	5.28 m (17 ft 4 in)
Passenger cabin doors, each:	
Height	1.35 m (4 ft 5 in)
Width	1.30 m (4 ft 3¼ in)
Floor hatch, rear of cabin:	
Length	0.98 m (3 ft 2¾ in)
Width	0.70 m (2 ft 3½ in)
DIMENSIONS, INTERNAL:	
Cabin: Length: AS 532UC/AC/SC	6.05 m (19 ft 10½ in)
AS 332L₁/532AL/UL	6.81 m (22 ft 4 in)
Max width	1.80 m (5 ft 11 in)
Max height	1.55 m (5 ft 1 in)
Floor area: AS 532UC/AC/SC	7.80 m² (84 sq ft)
AS 332L₁/532AL/UL	9.18 m² (98.8 sq ft)
Usable volume: AS 532UC/AC/SC	11.40 m³ (403 cu ft)
AS 332L₁/532AL/UL	13.30 m³ (469.5 cu ft)
AREAS:	
Main rotor disc	191.1 m² (2,057.4 sq ft)
Tail rotor disc	7.31 m² (78.64 sq ft)
WEIGHTS AND LOADINGS:	
Weight empty (standard aircraft):	
AS 532UC/AC	4,330 kg (9,546 lb)
AS 532SC	4,500 kg (9,920 lb)
AS 332L₁/532AL/UL	4,460 kg (9,832 lb)
Max T-O weight:	
AS 532UC/AC/AL/UL/SC, internal load	9,000 kg (19,841 lb)
AS 332L₁, internal load	8,600 kg (18,960 lb)
all versions, with slung load	9,350 kg (20,615 lb)
PERFORMANCE (at max T-O weight):	
Never-exceed speed (VNE)	150 knots (278 km/h; 172 mph)
Cruising speed at S/L:	
AS 532UC/AC/AL/UL	141 knots (262 km/h; 163 mph)
AS 532SC	130 knots (240 km/h; 149 mph)
AS 332L₁	144 knots (266 km/h; 165 mph)
Max rate of climb at S/L:	
AS 532UC/AC/AL/UL	420 m (1,378 ft)/min
AS 532SC	372 m (1,220 ft)/min
AS 332L₁	486 m (1,594 ft)/min
Service ceiling: AS 332L₁	4,600 m (15,090 ft)
AS 532UC/AC/SC/AL/UL	4,100 m (13,450 ft)
Hovering ceiling IGE:	
AS 532AC/UC/SC	2,700 m (8,860 ft)
AS 532AL/UL	2,800 m (9,185 ft)
AS 332L₁	3,100 m (10,170 ft)
Hovering ceiling OGE:	
AS 532AC/UC/SC	1,600 m (5,250 ft)
AS 532AL/UL	1,650 m (5,415 ft)
AS 332L₁	2,300 m (7,545 ft)
Range at S/L, standard tanks, no reserves:	
AS 532UC/AC	334 nm (618 km; 384 miles)
AS 532SC/332L₁	470 nm (870 km; 540 miles)
AS 532AL/UL	455 nm (842 km; 523 miles)
Range at S/L with external (2 × 338 litre) and auxiliary (320 litre) tanks, no reserves:	
AS 532AL/UL	672 nm (1,245 km; 773 miles)

AEROSPATIALE AS 332 SUPER PUMA Mk II and AS 532 COUGAR Mk II

This developed version introduces new main and tail rotors which offer improved performance and economy without changes to the standard power plant of two Makila turboshafts, although the main transmission is upgraded to transmit increased power. Slightly longer main rotor blades with parabolic tips are fitted to a Spheriflex head, which is lighter and simpler than the current type. The rear fuselage

Aerospatiale Super Puma Mk II development aircraft

is lengthened by 0.45 m (1 ft 5¾ in), to provide adequate clearance between the new main rotor and the tail rotor. Similarly, the tail rotor is increased in size, the main change being to four blades, instead of five, and use of a Spheriflex head. Compared with the Mk I, the new variant offers a 300 kg (661 lb) increase in useful load; high speed cruise increased by 6-27 knots (8-50 km/h; 5-31 mph), according to altitude and weight; and a hovering performance improved by 500 kg (1,102 lb) at the same altitude, or 500 m (1,640 ft) at the same weight.

There are no short-fuselage versions of the Mk II. Those proposed are:

AS 532U₂ Cougar: Military utility version.
AS 532A₂ Cougar: Armed version.
AS 332L₂ Super Puma: Civil version.

Internally, the Mk II has the rear cabin bulkhead moved rearwards by 0.55 m (1 ft 9⅝ in), increasing troop capacity from 25 to 29. Medical evacuation capacity is six stretchers, six seated patients and three attendants. In the civil version, maximum passenger capacity is 23 plus a flight attendant. Luggage storage space is increased by 15 per cent.

Following testing of the Spheriflex head on a Puma, a Super Puma Mk II development vehicle flew for the first time on 6 February 1987. Bristow Helicopters, a major Super Puma operator, ordered 20 Mk IIs in June 1989 for delivery between April 1992 and 1995, representing the first commercial contract.

The Mk II was intended as the carrier vehicle for the Orchidée radar system, for which trials began with a smaller Orphée II antenna beneath an AS 330B Puma (No. 1052/F-ZKCQ) in 1986. By 1989, the helicopter had received a Super Puma rotor head and nose-mounted Omera ORB 37 radar and was undertaking trials at the CEV as F-ZVLH. French Army Aviation (ALAT) had a requirement for 20 Orchidée-equipped Super Puma Mk IIs to be delivered from 1996 onwards. A definitive prototype of the AS 532/Orchidée system flew at Marignane in June 1990, but in August the French government abandoned the programme on cost grounds, despite the major portion of its capability having been demonstrated. But the prototype was sent to Saudi Arabia in early 1991, for field trials with French forces in the Gulf in a simplified form known variously as Horus and Horizon (Hélicoptère d'Observation Radar et d'Investigation sur Zone) without its data link. This might be ordered in perhaps 10 Mk I Super Pumas, with existing ECM, and slightly reduced radar capability.

Data generally as for AS 332/532, except:

FUSELAGE: New multi-purpose sponsons with liferaft, luggage space or extra fuel tank, air-conditioning system and emergency floats.

POWER PLANT: Two Turbomeca Makila 1A2 turboshafts, each with continuous rating of 1,374 kW (1,843 shp) and max contingency 1,236 kW (1,658 shp). Emergency ratings are 2 min at 1,461 kW (1,959 shp) and 30 s 'super emergency' at 1,569 kW (2,104 shp).

ACCOMMODATION: Up to 29 commandos; or six stretchers, six sitting wounded and three attendants. Civilian version, 23 passengers.

SYSTEMS: Electrical system simplified.

AVIONICS: Integrated flight data system including two AHRS primary references, a digital dual duplex four-axis autopilot and new control panel with four 15.25 cm (6 in) square screens.

DIMENSIONS, EXTERNAL:

Main rotor diameter	16.20 m (53 ft 1¾ in)
Tail rotor diameter	3.15 m (10 ft 4 in)
Length: overall, rotors turning	19.50 m (63 ft 11¾ in)
fuselage, incl tail rotor	16.79 m (55 ft 1 in)
Height overall	4.97 m (16 ft 3⅝ in)
Width overall, blades folded	3.86 m (12 ft 8 in)

WEIGHTS AND LOADINGS:

Weight empty	4,650 kg (10,251 lb)
Max T-O weight: military	9,500 kg (20,944 lb)
civil	9,070 kg (19,996 lb)
with external load	10,000 kg (22,046 lb)
Max underslung load	4,500 kg (9,921 lb)

PERFORMANCE (at max T-O weight):

Never-exceed speed (VNE)

170 knots (315 km/h; 196 mph)

Cruising speed at S/L	149 knots (276 km/h; 172 mph)
Max rate of climb at S/L	390 m (1,279 ft)/min
Service ceiling	4,000 m (13,125 ft)
Hovering ceiling: IGE	2,500 m (8,200 ft)
OGE	1,585 m (5,200 ft)
Range: at S/L	449 nm (832 km; 517 miles)
with 23 passengers and full reserves	
	up to 200 nm (371 km; 230 miles)
with 19 passengers and full reserves	
	350 nm (649 km; 403 miles)

AEROSPATIALE SA 342 GAZELLE

The first prototype of the Gazelle (designated SA 340) made its first flight on 7 April 1967, powered by an Astazou III engine. Details of early versions of the helicopter can be found in the 1979-80 and 1984-85 *Jane's*. Versions currently available are as follows:

SA 342L₁: Current basic military version, with higher max T-O weight than earlier models. Powered by Astazou XIVM turboshaft with max rating of 640 kW (858 shp) and max continuous rating of 441 kW (592 shp). In 1988, 12 Egyptian SA 342Ls were fitted with SFIM Osloh I laser designation systems for artillery co-operation.

SA 342M: For ALAT (French Army Light Aviation Corps). Differs from SA 342L₁ in having an ALAT instrument panel. Optional equipment specified as standard by ALAT includes SFIM PA 85G autopilot, Sextant Avionique Nadir self-contained navigation system, Decca 80 Doppler and night flying equipment. An exhaust deflector remains optional. Max T-O weight initially 1,900 kg (4,188 lb), the current limit for SA 341F. By February 1989, French orders totalled 188 SA 342Ms, each armed with four HOT missiles and gyro-stabilised sight for anti-tank warfare. This satisfied the original requirement, but procurement has continued. Deliveries to the ALAT trials unit (GALSTA) began on 1 February 1980, and to an operational unit on 9 June 1980.

Two new SA 342M versions have been developed: an escort helicopter with a turret-mounted 20 mm cannon, Sextant Avionique HUD and rate gyro unit; and an anti-helicopter conversion with four Matra Mistral missiles. ALAT will acquire 67 cannon and 30 Mistral Gazelles. Pending availability of the Eurocopter Tigre, France plans retrofit of SA 342Ms with improved Viviane all-weather sights for HOT missiles.

A two-stretcher ambulance configuration has received FAA supplemental type certification. No major modification is necessary to convert the aircraft to carry two patients longitudinally on the port side of the cabin, one above the other, leaving room for the pilot and a medical attendant in tandem on the starboard side. The dual spineboard arrangement weighs 27 kg (60 lb) and stows into the baggage compartment when not in use.

Under an Anglo-French agreement signed in 1967, Gazelles are produced jointly with Westland Helicopters Ltd; they have been assembled in Egypt, and built under licence in Yugoslavia. A total of 1,253 had been ordered from Aerospatiale and Westland for civil and military operation in 41 countries by 1 January 1990, of which 1,242 had been delivered, plus 220 built in Yugoslavia. Westland manufacture of complete Gazelles ended in March 1984 with the 294th example, of which 12 were for civilian use.

Military customers for the Gazelle include Abu Dhabi (12), Angola (seven), Burundi (three), Cameroun (four), Chad (one), China (eight), Cyprus (six), Egypt (90 including local assembly of 30), Ecuador (over 33), France (over 357), Gabon (five), Guinea Republic (one), Iraq (81), Ireland (two), Kenya (two), Kuwait (30), Lebanon (seven), Morocco (30), Qatar (16), Rwanda (four), Senegal (one), Syria (65), Trinidad and Tobago (two), United Kingdom (282) and Yugoslavia (21 French-built). Civilian sales total some 170.

TYPE: Five-seat light utility helicopter.

ROTOR SYSTEM: Three-blade semi-articulated main rotor and 13-blade shrouded fan anti-torque tail rotor (known as a fenestron or fan-in-fin). Rotor head and mast form a single unit. Main rotor blades are NACA 0012 section, attached to NAT hub by flapping hinges. No drag hinges. Each blade has a single leading-edge spar of GFRP, a laminated glass-fabric skin and honeycomb filler. Tail rotor blades of die-forged light alloy, with articulation for pitch change only. Main rotor blades can be folded manually for stowage. Rotor brake standard.

Main reduction gearbox forward of engine, which is mounted above the rear cabin. Intermediate gearbox beneath engine, rear gearbox supporting the tail rotor. Main rotor/engine rpm ratio 387 : 6,334. Tail rotor/engine rpm ratio 5,918 : 6,334.

FUSELAGE: Cockpit structure is based on a welded light alloy frame which carries the windows and doors. This is mounted on a conventional semi-monocoque lower structure consisting of two longitudinal box sections connected by frames and bulkheads. Central section, which encloses the baggage hold and main fuel tank and supports the main reduction gearbox, is constructed of light alloy honeycomb sandwich panels. Rear section, which supports the engine and tailboom, is of similar construction. Honeycomb sandwich panels are also used for the cabin floors and transmission platform. Tailboom is of conventional sheet metal construction, as are the horizontal tail surfaces and the tail fin.

TAIL UNIT: Small horizontal stabiliser on tailboom, ahead of tail rotor fin.

LANDING GEAR: Steel tube skid type. Wheel can be fitted at rear of each skid for ground handling. Provision for alternative float or ski landing gear.

POWER PLANT: One Turbomeca Astazou XIVM turboshaft, installed above fuselage aft of cabin and rated at 640 kW (858 shp). Two standard fuel tanks in fuselage (one beneath baggage compartment) with total usable capacity of 545 litres (144 US gallons; 120 Imp gallons). Provision for 200 litre (53 US gallon; 44 Imp gallon) ferry tank inside rear cabin. Total possible usable fuel capacity 745 litres (197 US gallons; 164 Imp gallons). Refuelling point on starboard side of cabin. Oil capacity 14.6 litres (4 US gallons; 3.2 Imp gallons) for engine, 3.5 litres (0.9 US gallon; 0.77 Imp gallon) for gearbox.

ACCOMMODATION: Crew of one or two side by side, with bench seat to the rear for a further three persons. Bench can be folded into floor wells to leave a completely flat

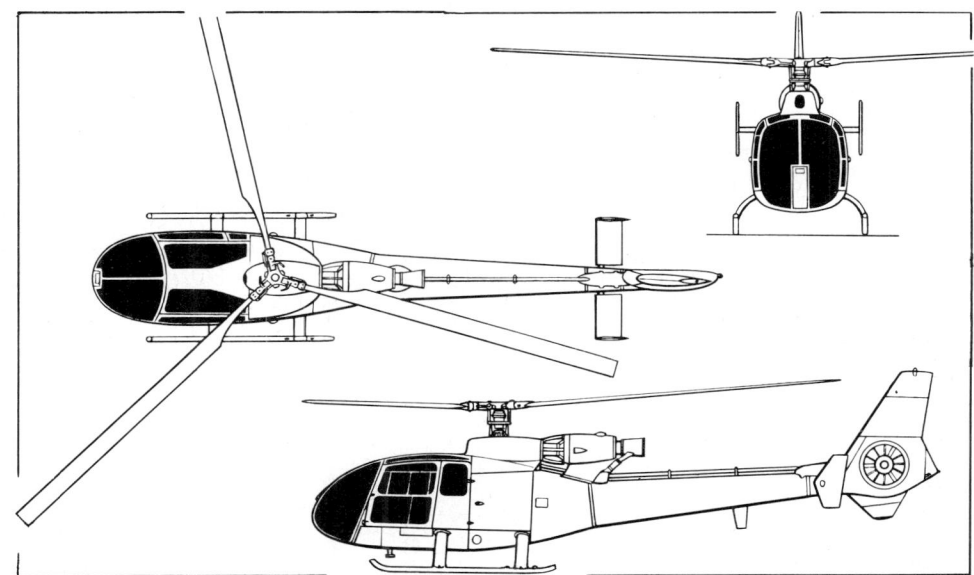

Aerospatiale Gazelle five-seat light utility helicopter (*Pilot Press*)

Trial installation of an SA 342M Gazelle equipped with a Viviane all-weather sight for Euromissile HOT anti-tank missiles

cargo floor. Access to baggage compartment via rear cabin bulkhead, or via optional starboard door. Cargo tiedown points in cabin floor. Forward opening car type door on each side of cabin, immediately behind which are rearward opening auxiliary cargo loading doors. Baggage compartment at rear of cabin. Ventilation standard. Dual controls optional.

SYSTEMS: Hydraulic system, pressure 40 bars (570 lb/sq in), serves three pitch change jacks for main rotor head and one for tail rotor. 28V DC electrical system supplied by 4kW engine driven generator and 40Ah battery. Optional 26V AC system, supplied by 0.5kVA alternator at 115/200V 400Hz.

AVIONICS: Optional communications equipment includes UHF, VHF, HF, intercom systems and homing aids. Optional navigation equipment includes radio compass, radio altimeter and VOR. Blind-flying instrumentation and autopilot optional. APX M397 gyro-stabilised sight for HOT missiles on SA 342M to be replaced by Viviane all-weather sight. Optional Sextant Avionique HUD for 20 mm turreted cannon. During late 1980s, Gazelles of UK Army Air Corps and Royal Marines retrofitted with Ferranti AF 532 magnifying roof sights for unarmed scout duties. Some French Army Gazelles were simultaneously equipped with similar Athos scouting sight. British Army Gazelles being retrofitted with GEC Ferranti AWARE-3 radar warning receivers and Ferranti International laser designators.

EQUIPMENT: A variety of operational equipment can be fitted, according to role, including a 700 kg (1,540 lb) cargo sling, 135 kg (300 lb) hoist, one or two stretchers (internally), or photographic and survey equipment.

ARMAMENT: Military loads can include two pods of Brandt 68 mm or FZ 2.75 in rockets, four or six HOT wire guided missiles, two forward firing 7.62 mm machine guns, or one 20 mm GIAT M.621 cannon on starboard side. Turreted 20 mm cannon under development. Yugoslav SA 342Ls are fitted with dual-role carriers for a total of four AT-3 'Sagger' ATMs and two SA-7 'Grail' AAMs.

DIMENSIONS, EXTERNAL:

Main rotor diameter	10.50 m (34 ft 5½ in)
Tail rotor diameter	0.695 m (2 ft 3⅜ in)
Distance between rotor centres	5.85 m (19 ft 2¼ in)
Main rotor blade chord, constant	0.30 m (11.8 in)
Length:	
overall, main rotor turning	11.97 m (39 ft 3 5/16 in)
fuselage, incl tail rotor	9.53 m (31 ft 3 3/16 in)
Width, rotors folded	2.04 m (6 ft 8½ in)
Height: to top of rotor head	2.72 m (8 ft 11⅛ in)
overall	3.19 m (10 ft 5½ in)
Skid track	2.015 m (6 ft 7 5/16 in)
Main cabin doors, each: Height	1.05 m (3 ft 4 9/16 in)
Width	1.00 m (3 ft 3¼ in)
Height to sill	0.63 m (2 ft 0¾ in)
Auxiliary cabin doors, each: Height	1.05 m (3 ft 4 9/16 in)
Width	0.48 m (1 ft 6¾ in)
Height to sill	0.63 m (2 ft 0¾ in)

DIMENSIONS, INTERNAL:

Cabin: Length	2.20 m (7 ft 2 9/16 in)
Max width	1.32 m (4 ft 4 in)
Max height	1.21 m (3 ft 11⅝ in)
Floor area	1.50 m^2 (16.1 sq ft)
Volume	1.80 m^3 (63.7 cu ft)
Baggage hold volume	0.45 m^3 (15.9 cu ft)

AREAS:

Main rotor blades, each	1.57 m^2 (16.9 sq ft)
Tail rotor blades, each	0.007 m^2 (0.075 sq ft)
Main rotor disc	86.59 m^2 (932.05 sq ft)
Tail rotor disc	0.37 m^2 (3.98 sq ft)
Fin	0.45 m^2 (4.84 sq ft)
Tailplane	1.80 m^2 (19.4 sq ft)

WEIGHTS AND LOADINGS:

Weight empty: $342L_1$	999 kg (2,202 lb)
Max underslung load	700 kg (1,543 lb)
Max T-O and landing weight:	
$342L_1$	2,000 kg (4,410 lb)
342M	2,100 kg (4,630 lb)
Max disc loading: $342L_1$	23.1 kg/m^2 (4.73 lb/sq ft)
342M	21.94 kg/m^2 (4.49 lb/sq ft)

PERFORMANCE (SA $342L_1$ at max T-O weight):

Never-exceed speed (VNE) at S/L	151 knots (280 km/h; 174 mph)
Max cruising speed at S/L	140 knots (260 km/h; 161 mph)
Max rate of climb at S/L	468 m (1,535 ft)/min
Service ceiling	4,100 m (13,450 ft)
Hovering ceiling: IGE	3,040 m (9,975 ft)
OGE	2,370 m (7,775 ft)
Range at S/L with standard fuel	383 nm (710 km; 440 miles)

AEROSPATIALE AS 350 ECUREUIL/ASTAR and AS 550 FENNEC

Brazilian Air Force designations: CH-50 and TH-50 Esquilo
Brazilian Army designation: HA-1 Esquilo
Brazilian Navy designation: UH-12 Esquilo

Developed as a successor to the Alouette, the AS 350 Ecureuil (Squirrel) embodies Aerospatiale's Starflex type of main rotor hub, made of glassfibre, with elastomeric spherical stops and visco-elastic frequency adaptors. The first prototype (F-WVKH) flew on 27 June 1974, powered by a Textron Lycoming LTS 101 turboshaft. It was followed on 14 February 1975 by a second prototype (F-WVKI) with a Turbomeca Arriel turboshaft.

The Textron Lycoming powered version is marketed only in North America, as the **AStar**; and the Arriel powered **Ecureuil** is marketed throughout the rest of the world. Initial production of the latter included the basic AS 350B, with 478 kW (641 shp) Arriel 1B, for which French certification was received on 27 October 1977. Current production versions are as follows:

AS 350B_2 Ecureuil: With 546 kW (732 shp) Arriel 1D1 turboshaft; uprated transmission, with gearbox able to absorb max input of 440 kW (590 shp); and wide-chord, new section main and tail rotor blades developed originally for the Ecureuil 2/TwinStar. French certification granted 26 April 1989. Known as **SuperStar** in North America.

AS 350D AStar: Current AStar Mk III has 459 kW (615 shp) Textron Lycoming LTS 101-600A-3 turboshaft. Otherwise as AS 350B_2.

AS 550 Fennec: (Previously AS 350L_2.) Military version of AS 350B_2, with Arriel 1D1 turboshaft rated at 546 kW (732 shp). Standard features include a taller landing gear, sliding doors, extended instrument panel and airframe reinforcement for axial armament. Provision for armoured seats. Individual versions are utility **AS 550U_2**; armed **AS 550A_2**; missile-armed **AS 550C_2**; unarmed naval **AS 550M_2**; and armed naval **AS 550S_2**.

Deliveries of the basic AS 350B began in March 1978. FAA certification of the original AS 350C AStar was obtained on 21 December 1977 and the first production delivery was made in April 1978. The AS 350C was superseded in 1978 by the AS 350D. By 1 January 1991 a total of 1,560 AS 350 Ecureuils and AStars had been ordered for service in 53 countries; 1,405 had been delivered. Military customers include the Singapore armed forces (six) and the Australian government with 18 AS 350Bs for RAAF pilot training, liaison, search and rescue, and six more for survey and utility duties with the Royal Australian Navy. In mid-1987, the Danish Army ordered 12 AS 550Cs, equipped with the Saab/Emerson Electric HeliTOW anti-tank missile system, for delivery in 1990. Ecureuils are also produced under licence by Helibras of Brazil, with the name Esquilo, 16 being ordered in 1988 as initial equipment of the newly formed army aviation branch, following 30 ordered for the air force and nine for the navy. The French Army has a requirement for up to 100 AS 550s to replace its Alouette IIs.

During 1986, an AS 350B_1 Ecureuil with taller landing gear was fitted with a firefighting kit purchased from Conair of Canada (which see), to test its effectiveness in dealing with forest fires in Southern France. The kit consists of a streamlined tank which can be refilled in 30 s through a snout while the helicopter hovers over a stretch of water.

Under a French government contract, Aerospatiale flew in 1986 an AS 350 fitted with a fenestron shrouded tail rotor, but this is not expected to become a feature of production Ecureuils of the current series.

Aerospatiale AS 350B_2 Ecureuil

A further variant of the AS 350B is currently under development as the **AS 350B₃/L₃** for certification in 1994. Features include an Arriel 2 engine, AS 355 type tail rotor, avionics derived from those planned for the P 120L, and an improved cabin for possibly seven persons.

Aerospatiale has teamed with Hughes Training Systems to offer the aircraft for the US Army's New Training Helicopter (NTH) programme.

TYPE: Five/six-seat light general purpose helicopter.

ROTOR SYSTEM: Three-blade main rotor, with Starflex glassfibre hub in which the three conventional hinges for each blade are replaced by a single balljoint of rubber/steel sandwich construction, requiring no maintenance. Glassfibre blades, with stainless steel leading-edge sheath, produced by an entirely mechanised process. Symmetrical blade section on AS 350B; OA 209 section on wider-chord blades of AS 350B₂ and 550. Two-blade tail rotor; each blade comprises a sheet metal skin around a glassfibre spar, the flexibility of which obviates the need for hinges. Simplified transmission, with single epicyclic main gear train. Tail rotor driveshaft coupling on engine.

FUSELAGE: Basic structure of light alloy pressings, with skin mainly of thermoformed plastics, including baggage compartment doors.

TAIL UNIT: Horizontal stabiliser, of inverted aerofoil section, mid-mounted on tailboom. Sweptback fin, in two sections above and below tailboom.

LANDING GEAR: Steel tube skid type. Taller version standard on military aircraft. Emergency flotation gear optional.

POWER PLANT: One turboshaft (for type see individual model listings) mounted above fuselage to rear of cabin. Plastics fuel tank (self sealing on AS 550) with capacity of 540 litres (142.6 US gallons; 119 Imp gallons).

ACCOMMODATION: Two individual bucket seats at front of cabin and two two-place bench seats are standard. In the alternative layout the two benches are replaced by three armchair seats. Optional ambulance layout. Large forward hinged door on each side of versions for civil use. Optional sliding door at rear of cabin on port side. (Sliding doors standard on military version.) Baggage compartment aft of cabin, with full-width upward hinged door on starboard side. Top of baggage compartment reinforced to provide platform on each side for inspecting and servicing rotor head.

SYSTEMS: Hydraulic system includes four single-body servo units, operating at 40 bars (570 lb/sq in) pressure, and accumulators to protect against a hydraulic power supply failure. Electrical system includes a 4.5kW engine driven starter/generator, a 24V 16Ah nickel-cadmium battery and a ground power receptacle connected to the busbar which distributes power to the electrical equipment. Cabin air-conditioning system optional.

AVIONICS: Optional com/nav radio equipment includes VHF/AM, ICS, VOR/LOC/glideslope, marker beacon indicator, radio compass, HF/SSB, transponder and DME.

EQUIPMENT: Includes a SFIM PA 85T31, Honeywell HelCis or Collins APS-841H autopilot, a 907 kg (2,000 lb) cargo sling (1,160 kg; 2,557 lb for B₂ and 550 versions), a 135 kg (297 lb) electric hoist, a TV camera for aerial filming, and a 735 litre (194 US gallon; 161 Imp gallon) Simplex agricultural spraytank and boom system.

ARMAMENT (AS 550): Provision for wide range of weapons, including 20 mm GIAT M621 gun, FN Herstal TMP twin 7.62 mm machine-gun pods, Thomson-Brandt 68.12 launchers for twelve 68 mm rockets, Forges de Zeebrugge launchers for seven 2.75 in rockets, and Saab/Emerson Electric HeliTOW anti-tank missile systems.

DIMENSIONS, EXTERNAL:
Main rotor diameter	10.69 m (35 ft 0¾ in)
Main rotor blade chord: AS 350B/D	0.30 m (11.8 in)
AS 350B₂/550	0.35 m (13.8 in)
Tail rotor diameter	1.86 m (6 ft 1¼ in)
Tail rotor blade chord: AS 350B/D	0.185 m (7.28 in)
AS 350B₂/550	0.205 m (8.07 in)
Length: overall, rotors turning	12.94 m (42 ft 5½ in)
fuselage	10.93 m (35 ft 10½ in)
Width: fuselage	1.80 m (5 ft 10¾ in)
overall, blades folded (ie. horizontal stabiliser span)	
	2.53 m (8 ft 3¾ in)
Height overall: AS 350B/B₂/D	3.14 m (10 ft 3½ in)
AS 550	3.34 m (10 ft 11½ in)
Skid track: AS 350B/B₂/D	2.17 m (7 ft 1½ in)
AS 550	2.28 m (7 ft 5¾ in)
Cabin doors (civil versions, standard, each):	
Height	1.15 m (3 ft 9¼ in)
Width	1.10 m (3 ft 7¼ in)

DIMENSIONS, INTERNAL:
Cabin: Length	2.42 m (7 ft 11¼ in)
Width at rear	1.65 m (5 ft 5 in)
Height	1.35 m (4 ft 5 in)
Baggage compartment volume	1.00 m³ (35.31 cu ft)

AREAS:
Main rotor disc	89.75 m² (966.1 sq ft)
Tail rotor disc	2.72 m² (29.25 sq ft)

WEIGHTS AND LOADINGS:
Weight empty: 350B	1,102 kg (2,430 lb)
350B₂	1,134 kg (2,500 lb)
350D	1,070 kg (2,359 lb)
550	1,193 kg (2,630 lb)

AS 550C₂ Ecureuil in anti-tank configuration, with HeliTOW system

Max T-O weight: normal: 350B/D	1,950 kg (4,300 lb)
350B₂/550	2,250 kg (4,960 lb)
with max slung load: 350B/D	2,100 kg (4,630 lb)
350B₂/550	2,500 kg (5,511 lb)
in anti-tank configuration: 550C₂	2,350 kg (5,181 lb)

PERFORMANCE (B/D at normal max T-O weight, B₂/550 at 2,200 kg; 4,850 lb):
Never-exceed speed (VNE) at S/L:	
350B/D	147 knots (272 km/h; 169 mph)
350B₂/550	155 knots (287 km/h; 178 mph)
Max cruising speed at S/L:	
350B	125 knots (232 km/h; 144 mph)
350B₂	133 knots (246 km/h; 153 mph)
350D	124 knots (230 km/h; 143 mph)
550	134 knots (248 km/h; 154 mph)
Max rate of climb at S/L:	
350B/D	475 m (1,558 ft)/min
350B₂/550	607 m (1,990 ft)/min
Service ceiling: 350B/D	4,750 m (15,600 ft)
350B₂/550	5,600 m (18,375 ft)
Hovering ceiling IGE: 350B	2,950 m (9,675 ft)
350B₂/550	4,055 m (13,300 ft)
350D	2,500 m (8,200 ft)
Hovering ceiling OGE: 350B	2,250 m (7,380 ft)
350B₂/550	3,415 m (11,200 ft)
350D	1,800 m (5,900 ft)
Range with max fuel at S/L, at econ cruising speed, no reserves:	
350B	389 nm (720 km; 447 miles)
350D	410 nm (760 km; 472 miles)
350B₂/550	370 nm (686 km; 426 miles)

AEROSPATIALE AS 355 ECUREUIL 2/TWINSTAR and AS 555 FENNEC
Brazilian Air Force designations: CH-55 and VH-55 Esquilo
Brazilian Navy designation: UH-12B Esquilo

The AS 355 and 555 are twin-engined versions of the AS 350 Ecureuil/AStar family. Many components, such as the main rotor mast and head, tail rotor hub, servo units, cabin and landing gear, are identical to those of the AS 350. The main and tail rotor blades are also identical to those of the current AS 350B₂/550 versions. Major changes apply to the power plant, transmission, fuel system and fuselage structure.

The first of two prototypes (F-WZLA) flew on 28 September 1979. Details of the AS 355E/F initial production versions, with Allison engines, can be found in the 1984-85 and earlier editions of *Jane's*.

From January 1984, the AS 355F was superseded by the **AS 355F₁**: incorporating three significant modifications. Addition of a laminated tab increased the tail rotor blade chord. The max power transmitted to the main gearbox was increased, by setting the torque limiter to 2 × 78 per cent instead of 2 × 73 per cent. Addition of a rotor overspeed alarm set to 410 rpm represented a complementary function of the normal alarm system. These changes permitted increased max T-O weight and payload.

A further increase in max T-O weight is offered by the **AS 355F₂**: which received DGAC certification on 10 December 1985. This version introduced a load compensator in the yaw channel and an extension of the CG limits.

The AS 355F₂ is intended primarily for the civil market, in particular for use by companies working in the oil industry. It received French civil certification in the Summer of 1989. McAlpine Helicopters of the United Kingdom has developed a dedicated law enforcement version of the AS 355F₂ known as the **Police Twin Squirrel**. It is equipped with a nose-mounted GEC thermal imaging camera, with cabin monitor screen and real-time transmission capability; 30 million candlepower SX 16 Night Sun searchlight mounted in a fully articulated pod aft of the cabin; and Skyshout public address speakers mounted on the landing gear skids, which are taller than standard to provide ground clearance for camera and searchlight. The Police Twin Squirrel is fitted with non-standard sliding cabin doors to facilitate air-to-ground observation and photography, and for fast entry and exit. Several Police Twin Squirrels are in service with police forces in the UK.

AS 355N: Powered by two Turbomeca Arrius; certificated in 1989 and to be delivered from early 1992.

Aerospatiale AS 355AN of the 67 Escadre d'Hélicoptères *(Ivo Sturzenegger)*

Naval AS 555SR with nose radar, homing torpedoes and pop-out floats

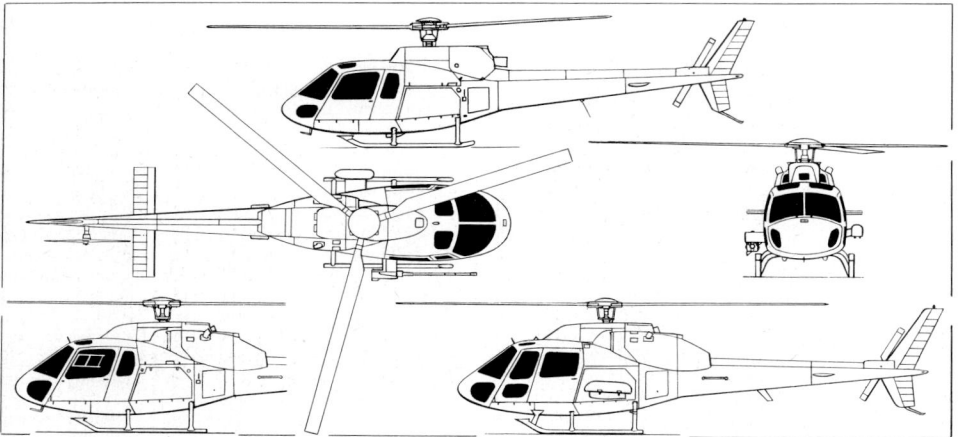

Aerospatiale AS 555AR Ecureuil 2, with additional side elevation (top) of single-engined AS 350 and scrap view of AS 355F₂ *(Pilot Press)*

Since January 1990, military Ecureuil 2s (formerly known as AS 355Ms) have been designated AS 555 Fennec, as follows:

AS 555UN: Utility version.
AS 555AN: Armed export and French Air Force version (formerly AS 355N).
AS 555MN: Naval utility version.
AS 555SN: Naval armed version.

The AS 555SN is intended for operation from small vessels (600 t and above) in the anti-submarine and over-horizon targeting roles. Operational equipment includes a 360° Bendix/King 1500 radar beneath the nose; Sextant Avionique Mk 3 MAD beneath the tailboom; Sextant Nadir Mk 10 navigation system (including Dassault Electronique RDN 85 Doppler and auto-hold); and SFIM 85 T31 three-axis autopilot. Armament comprises two homing torpedoes (Mk 44, Mk 46 or Murène), or the cannon, missiles and rockets of land-based versions. The Brazilian Air Force has 13 AS 555s, of which 11 with armament are designated **CH-55** and two VIP transports are designated **VH-55**. A further 11 are being acquired as **UH-12Bs** by the Brazilian Navy. Brazilian Esquilos are assembled by Helibras (which see).

The French Air Force is currently taking delivery of 52 AS 555s, including eight built as Allison engined AS 355F₁s, used for communications by all six escadrons of the 67e Escadre d'Hélicoptères at Villacoublay and in the security role with a starboard-side GIAT M621 20 mm cannon by ETOM 68 in French Guyana. The remaining 44, of which the first was delivered to training school, Centre d'Instruction des Equipages d'Hélicoptères 341 at Chambéry on 19 January 1990, are powered by Turboméca TM 319 1M Arrius turboshafts and designated AS 555AN. From the 24th onwards, provision is made for a centrally mounted 20 mm cannon and T-100 sight, plus Matra Mistral missiles for anti-helicopter roles. Four Arrius engined AS 555UNs have been ordered by the French Army to provide IFR training for ALAT pilots; a further six options are held.

By 1 January 1991, a total of 484 AS 355/555s had been ordered for service in 32 countries; 432 had been delivered. The version for the North American market is known as the **TwinStar**; aircraft marketed elsewhere are named **Ecureuil 2**.

The following details apply to the AS 355F₂, 355N and 555 versions:

TYPE: Twin-turbine light general purpose helicopter.
ROTOR SYSTEM: Single main gearbox, made up of three modules (coupling gearbox with freewheel, angle gearing with spiral bevel gears, and epicyclic gear train including five oscillating planetary gears). Power take-offs for the accessories and tail rotor. Otherwise as for AS 350B₂/550.
FUSELAGE: Light alloy centre fuselage structure, with deep drawn sheet metal forms of simple geometric design. Cabin skin of thermoformed plastics. Tapered tailboom of light alloy sheet wrapped and riveted around deep drawn sheet metal cylindrical frames.
TAIL UNIT: As for AS 350B₂/550.
LANDING GEAR: As for AS 350B₂/550.
POWER PLANT: Two Allison 250-C20F turboshafts, each rated at 313 kW (420 shp) for take-off and 276 kW (370 shp) max continuous, mounted above fuselage to rear of cabin. AS 355/555N has two Turboméca TM 3191M Arrius turboshafts, each rated at 340 kW (456 shp) for take-off and 295 kW (395 shp) max continuous with full authority digital engine control (FADEC). Two structural fuel tanks, with total usable capacity of 730 litres (193 US gallons; 160 Imp gallons), in body structure.
ACCOMMODATION: As for AS 350B₂, except sliding doors are optional on both sides (standard on military aircraft), and there are three baggage holds with external doors.
SYSTEMS: As for AS 350B₂/550, except that twin-body servo command units and a second electrical generator are standard.
AVIONICS: Options include a second VHF/AM and radio

altimeter. Provisions for IFR instrumentation, and SFIM 85 T31 three-axis autopilot and CDV 85 T3 nav coupler.
EQUIPMENT: Casualty installations optional. See also variant descriptions.
ARMAMENT (AS 555): Optional alternative weapons include Thomson-Brandt or Forges de Zeebrugge rocket packs, Matra or FN machine-gun pods, a 20 mm GIAT M621 gun, and HOT or TOW anti-tank missiles. Naval version carries two homing torpedoes in ASW role, or SAR winch.
DIMENSIONS, EXTERNAL: As for AS 350B₂/550 except:
Height: 355F₂/355N   3.14 m (10 ft 4 in)
 555N   3.34 m (10 ft 11½ in)
DIMENSIONS, INTERNAL: As for AS 350B₂/550
WEIGHTS AND LOADINGS:
Weight empty: 355F₂   1,318 kg (2,906 lb)
 355N   1,382 kg (3,046 lb)
Max sling load: 355F₂/555N   1,134 kg (2,500 lb)
Max T-O weight:
 355F₂/555N, internal load   2,540 kg (5,600 lb)
 355F₂/555N, max sling load   2,600 kg (5,732 lb)
PERFORMANCE (AS 355F₂/555N at max T-O weight, ISA):
Never-exceed speed (structural limitation)
                          150 knots (278 km/h; 172 mph)
Max cruising speed at S/L
                          121 knots (225 km/h; 140 mph)
Max rate of climb at S/L   408 m (1,340 ft)/min
Service ceiling: 555N   4,000 m (13,120 ft)
Hovering ceiling: IGE (555N) 2,600 m (8,530 ft)
 OGE (555N)   1,550 m (5,085 ft)
Radius, SAR, two survivors 70 nm (129 km; 80.5 miles)
Range with max fuel at S/L, no reserves AS 555N
                          389 nm (722 km; 448 miles)
Endurance, AS 555, no reserves:
 two torpedoes   1 h
 one torpedo, or cannon or rocket pods   2 h 20 min
 cannon plus rockets   1 h 50 min

AEROSPATIALE AS 565 PANTHER (NAVY)

Formerly known as the AS 565F, the naval versions of this Dauphin derivative were redesignated in January 1990 as the unarmed **AS 565MA** and the armed **AS 565SA**. The army/air force versions are described separately.

On 13 October 1980, the government of Saudi Arabia placed in France orders for four frigates and associated naval equipment including 24 AS 365F Dauphin 2 helicopters, based on the AS 365N. The first four of these are equipped with an Omera ORB 32 radar for search and rescue duties. The remaining 20 are anti-ship helicopters, equipped with Thomson-CSF Agrion 15 radar, Aerospatiale AS.15TT all-weather air-to-surface missiles and Sextant Avionique MAD, for operation from both shore bases and frigates. Subsequent orders include five for Ireland, equipped with Bendix RDR 1500 search radar, SFIM 155 autopilot, CDV 155 four-axis flight director/coupler, Sextant Nadir Mk II nav computer, Dassault Electronique Cina B Doppler, Sextant Avionique ONS 200A long-distance nav system and five-screen EFIS instrumentation, for fishery surveillance and SAR from ship and shore bases. Irish Dauphins have no AS.15 capability, but may be fitted with other forms of light armament. Three AS 365Fs, ordered by the French Navy in 1988 for detached plane guard duties in the carriers *Clémenceau* and *Foch*, are now in service with 23 Escadrille de Servitude at St Mandrier, near Toulon, and plans call for delivery of a further 15 AS 565MAs against an anticipated total requirement for 40. Four AS 565SAs have been ordered for the Chilean Navy, to have Thomson-CSF TRWR (tactical radar and warning receiver), Varan radar, and to carry AM 39 Exocet and/or Murène homing torpedo.

An AS 365N (c/n 5100) was modified to flight test the equipment and weapon systems of the AS 365F, and made its first flight in the new configuration on 22 February 1982. It was followed by the first production AS 365F (c/n 6014) on 2 July 1982, equipped as a search and rescue helicopter with arrester hook, search radar, searchlight, self-contained

Aerospatiale AS 355F₂ Ecureuil 2 equipped with Wescam gyro-stabilised camera *(Paul Jackson)*

navigation system, automatic hover/transition coupler and rescue winch.

The SA 565MA Panther is intended principally for search and rescue and sea surveillance. In anti-shipping and anti-submarine configuration the AS 565SA is equipped with the Agrion Plan Position radar on a roll-stabilised pivot mounting under its nose to ensure a 360° field of sweep, a total of four AS.15TT radar-guided missiles in pairs on an outrigger on each side of the fuselage, and the MAD bird on the port side of the rear fuselage. Range of the AS.15TT missile is greater than 8 nm (15 km; 9.3 miles). In addition to locating and attacking hostile warships, the AS 565SA/AS.15TT can be used for coastal surveillance and ship escort duties, and to provide over-the-horizon target designation for long-range anti-ship missiles launched from ship or shore. The anti-submarine version is equipped with MAD, Thomson-Sintra ASM HS12 sonar and two homing torpedoes. The sea surveillance/SAR 565MA is equipped with a rescue hoist, sea search radar, self-contained navigation system and automatic hover-transition coupler. All versions can be equipped with the harpoon securing system to help them to operate from the decks of small ships.

The AS 565MA carries a normal crew of two, has provision for 10 passengers and is powered by two Turbomeca Arriel 1M1 turboshafts, each rated at 558 kW (749 shp) for take-off and with a max continuous rating of 487 kW (653 shp). Standard fuel capacity of 1,135 litres (300 US gallons; 250 Imp gallons) can be augmented by a 180 litre (47.5 US gallon; 39.6 Imp gallon) auxiliary tank. Like the current AS 365N₂, it has a larger, carbonfibre 11-blade fenestron to improve hovering performance, particularly in the most severe condition of hovering with the wind from three-quarters aft.

DIMENSIONS, EXTERNAL: As for AS 365N₂, except:

Length: overall, rotor turning	13.68 m (44 ft 10½ in)
fuselage	12.11 m (39 ft 8¾ in)
Height overall	3.99 m (13 ft 1 in)
Width over missiles (565SA)	4.20 m (13 ft 9½ in)

WEIGHTS AND LOADINGS:

Weight empty	2,240 kg (4,938 lb)
Max sling load	1,600 kg (3,527 lb)
Max T-O weight, internal or external load	
	4,250 kg (9,370 lb)

PERFORMANCE (at average mission weight of 4,000 kg; 8,819 lb):

Never-exceed speed (VNE)	
	160 knots (296 km/h; 184 mph)
Max cruising speed at S/L	
	148 knots (274 km/h; 170 mph)
Max rate of climb at S/L	420 m (1,380 ft)/min
Hovering ceiling: IGE	2,600 m (8,530 ft)
OGE	1,860 m (6,100 ft)
Range with max standard fuel at S/L	
	472 nm (875 km; 544 miles)
Radius of action: anti-shipping, with four missiles, 120 knots cruising speed at 3,000 ft, ISA −20°C, 30 min reserves	135 nm (250 km; 155 miles)
with two missiles	150 nm (278 km; 173 miles)
SAR, ISA +20°C, 30 min reserves, carrying six survivors	130 nm (241 km; 150 miles)

AEROSPATIALE AS 365N₂ DAUPHIN 2

The AS 365N₂ is the current production version of the civil Dauphin. Compared with the AS 365N, described in previous editions of *Jane's*, it has improved engines and a larger carbonfibre fenestron tail rotor with 11 blades.

Orders for all versions of AS 365/366 totalled 536 for civil and military use in 43 countries by 1 January 1991, when about 450 had been delivered. The totals included production in China (as the Harbin Z-9, the original order for 50 to be supplemented by a further 20 being negotiated in early 1991), as well as AS 366Gs for the US Coast Guard and AS 565SA/AS.15TTs with special equipment for search and rescue, and for attacking surface ships. These last two variants are described separately.

A special aeromedical version of the AS 365N₂, with a flight crew of two, is available in two forms. An intensive care layout is arranged to carry two patients, one on each side of the cabin on a standard NATO stretcher, with space between for the doctor's seat and medical equipment. One of the stretchers can be replaced by seats for two patients, if required. The alternative ambulance configuration provides space for two stretchers on each side of the cabin, one above the other, plus room for the doctor; or a single pair of stretchers, with room for four seated persons on the other side, and a doctor. Stretchers are loaded through rear doors, with 180° opening, on both models. Those in the ambulance layout are fixed to the sides of the cabin, and the patients are carried to them on special mattresses. Six ambulance versions of the earlier AS 365N₁ were delivered to the State of Maryland in 1989, bringing to 22 the total of Dauphin 2s then in US EMS (emergency medical service) use.

The AS 365N₂ received French certification for VFR and IFR operations in November 1989. It features uprated Arriel 1C2 turboshafts, improved gearbox, a 150 kg (331 lb) increase in max T-O weight, redesigned cabin doors, interior improvements, and optional EFIS instruments. Orders totalled 67 by late 1990 when the first was delivered

Aerospatiale AS 365N₂ for Bond Helicopters is 500th of Dauphin series

Aerospatiale AS 565MA for French Navy carrier plane guard duties *(Ivo Sturzenegger)*

to Bond Helicopters of the United Kingdom, which had ordered 12 for offshore support operations in the North Sea. The second aircraft (G-NTOO), handed over at Marignane early in November, was the 500th example of the Dauphin series, for which Aerospatiale had received orders from 138 customers in 44 countries.

In 1993 Aerospatiale plans to certify the AS 365N₃, which will have the Arriel 2 engine, a five-blade Spheriflex rotor and EFIS.

The following structural description refers to the standard AS 365N₂, but is generally applicable to all versions:

TYPE: Twin-turbine commercial general purpose helicopter.

ROTOR SYSTEM: Four-blade main rotor. Blades attached by quick disconnect pins to Starflex glassfibre/carbonfibre hub, in which the three conventional hinges for each blade are replaced by a single main elastomeric bearing and inboard locator bearing, requiring no maintenance. Blades of new OA 2 section, developed in collaboration with Onera: varying from OA 212 (thickness/chord ratio 12 per cent) at root to OA 207 (7 per cent) at tip, with 10° twist from root to tip. Each blade comprises two Z section carbonfibre spars and carbonfibre skin, a solid glassfibre-resin leading-edge covered with a stainless steel sheath, and Nomex honeycomb filling. Leading-edge of carbonfibre tip is swept back at 45°. Ground adjustable tab on trailing-edge of each blade towards tip. Blade chord extended outboard of tab to align with tab trailing-edge. Rotor brake standard. Eleven-blade fenestron carbonfibre ducted fan anti-torque tail rotor.

Mechanical shaft and gear drive. Transmission shaft from each engine extends forward, through freewheel, to helical and epicyclic reduction stages of main gearbox. Shaft to fenestron driven off bottom of main rotor shaft. Main rotor rpm 350. Fenestron rpm 3,665.

FUSELAGE: Semi-monocoque structure. Bottom structure and framework of front fuselage, primary machined frames fore and aft of the main gearbox platform and at the rear of the centre fuselage, floors under main gearbox and engines, cabin doors and fin are all of light alloy (AU4G). Nose and power plant fairings and fin tip of glassfibre/Nomex sandwich. Centre and rear fuselage assemblies, flight deck floor, roof, walls and bottom skins of fuel tanks of light alloy/Nomex sandwich.

TAIL UNIT: Horizontal stabiliser mid-set on rear fuselage, forward of fenestron; swept endplate fins offset 10° to port. Construction of carbonfibre and Nomex/Rohacell sandwich.

LANDING GEAR: Hydraulically retractable tricycle type. Twin-wheel steerable and self-centring nose unit retracts rearward. Single wheel on each rearward retracting main unit. All three units embody oleo-pneumatic shock

absorber. Mainwheel tyres size 15 × 6.00, pressure 8.6 bars (125 lb/sq in); nosewheel tyres size 5.00-4, pressure 5.5 bars (80 lb/sq in). Hydraulic disc brakes.

POWER PLANT: Two Turbomeca Arriel 1C2 turboshafts, each rated at 551 kW (739 shp) for T-O and 471 kW (631 shp)

POWER PLANT: Two Turbomeca Arriel 1C2 turboshafts, each rated at 547 kW (733 shp) for T-O and 471 kW (631 shp) max continuous, side by side aft of main rotor driveshaft, with stainless steel firewall between them. Standard fuel in four tanks under cabin floor and a fifth tank in the bottom of the centre-fuselage; total capacity 1,135 litres (300 US gallons; 249.5 Imp gallons). Provision for auxiliary tank in baggage compartment, with capacity of 180 litres (47.5 US gallons; 39.5 Imp gallons); or ferry tank in place of rear seats in cabin, capacity 475 litres (125.5 US gallons; 104.5 Imp gallons). Refuelling point above landing gear door on port side. Oil capacity 14 litres (3.7 US gallons; 3 Imp gallons).

ACCOMMODATION: Standard accommodation for pilot and co-pilot or passenger in front, and two rows of four seats to rear. High density seating for one pilot and 13 passengers. VIP configurations for four to six persons in addition to pilot. Three forward opening doors on each side. Freight hold aft of cabin rear bulkhead, with door on starboard side. Cabin heated and ventilated.

SYSTEMS: Air-conditioning system optional. Duplicated hydraulic system, pressure 60 bars (870 lb/sq in). Electrical system includes two 4.8kW starter/generators, one 24V 27Ah battery and two 250VA 115V 400Hz inverters.

AVIONICS: Two-pilot IFR instrument panel and SFIM 155 duplex autopilot standard. Optional avionics include EFIS, VHF and HF com/nav, VOR, ILS, ADF, transponder, DME, radar and self-contained nav system.

EQUIPMENT: Includes a SFIM CDV 85 nav coupler, a 1,600 kg (3,525 lb) capacity cargo sling, and 275 kg (606 lb) capacity hoist with 90 m (295 ft) cable length.

DIMENSIONS, EXTERNAL:

Main rotor diameter	11.94 m (39 ft 2 in)
Diameter of fenestron	1.10 m (3 ft 7⁵⁄₁₆ in)
Main rotor blade chord: basic	0.385 m (1 ft 3¼ in)
outboard of tab	0.405 m (1 ft 4 in)
Length: overall, rotor turning	13.68 m (44 ft 10⅝ in)
fuselage	11.63 m (38 ft 1⅞ in)
Width, rotor blades folded	3.21 m (10 ft 6½ in)
Height: to top of rotor head	3.52 m (11 ft 6½ in)
overall (tip of fin)	3.98 m (13 ft 0¾ in)
Wheel track	1.90 m (6 ft 2¾ in)
Wheelbase	3.61 m (11 ft 10¼ in)
Main cabin door (fwd, each side):	
Height	1.16 m (3 ft 9½ in)
Width	1.14 m (3 ft 9 in)

Main cabin door (rear, each side):
Height	1.16 m (3 ft 9½ in)
Width	0.87 m (2 ft 10¼ in)

Baggage compartment door (stbd):
Height	0.51 m (1 ft 8 in)
Width	0.73 m (2 ft 4¾ in)

DIMENSIONS, INTERNAL:
Cabin: Length	2.30 m (7 ft 6½ in)
Max width	1.92 m (6 ft 3½ in)
Max height	1.40 m (4 ft 7 in)
Floor area	4.20 m² (45.20 sq ft)
Volume	5.00 m³ (176 cu ft)
Baggage compartment volume	1.00 m³ (35.3 cu ft)

AREAS:
Main rotor disc	111.9 m² (1,204.5 sq ft)
Fenestron disc	0.95 m² (10.23 sq ft)

WEIGHTS AND LOADINGS:
Weight empty, equipped	2,239 kg (4,936 lb)
Max T-O weight:	
internal or external load	4,250 kg (9,370 lb)

PERFORMANCE (at max T-O weight):
Never-exceed speed (VNE) at S/L	
	160 knots (296 km/h; 184 mph)
Max cruising speed at S/L	
	154 knots (285 km/h; 177 mph)
Econ cruising speed at S/L	
	140 knots (260 km/h; 161 mph)
Max rate of climb at S/L	420 m (1,379 ft)/min
Service ceiling	4,300 m (14,100 ft)
Hovering ceiling: IGE	2,550 m (8,365 ft)
OGE	1,800 m (5,905 ft)
Max range with standard fuel at S/L	
	484 nm (897 km; 557 miles)
Endurance with standard fuel	4 h

AEROSPATIALE AS 366 DAUPHIN 2
US Coast Guard designation: HH-65A Dolphin

At the 1979 Paris Air Show, Aerospatiale announced that it had won with this aircraft the competition for a helicopter to perform SRR (Short Range Recovery) duties from 18 shore bases, and from icebreakers and cutters, of the US Coast Guard. Current orders for the Coast Guard are for a total of 99 AS 366Gs, basically similar to the AS 365N but with engines and equipment of US manufacture accounting for about 60 per cent of the total cost of each aircraft.

The AS 366G (known to the Coast Guard as the HH-65A Dolphin) is powered by two Textron Lycoming LTS 101-750A-1 turboshafts, each rated at 507 kW (680 shp) and fitted with a Lucas SDS 300 full authority digital electronic control system. It normally carries a crew of three (pilot, co-pilot and aircrewman/hoist operator). Rockwell Collins is prime contractor for the advanced communications, navigation and all-weather search equipment. The communications package includes dual UHF/VHF transceivers and single UHF/FM and HF systems, plus a data link for automatic transmission of data, such as aircraft position, flight path, ground speed, wind and fuel state, to ship or shore base. A nose-mounted Northrop See Hawk forward looking infra-red sensor aids rescue operations in bad weather, darkness or high seas. Important design features include the passive failure characteristics of the Dolphin's automatic flight control system, and an omnidirectional airspeed system able to provide information while the aircraft is hovering. Inflatable flotation bags are effective up to sea state 5. Under a 1988 contract, three HH-65As are being fitted by Grumman with a prototype Fairey Hydraulics Talon lightweight decklock system.

In February 1990 the USCG signed a contract with the Light Helicopter Turbine Engine Company for flight testing an HH-65A with an 895 kW (1,200 shp) T800 turboshaft, with a view to replacing the standard LTS 101s. Two engines for the programme were delivered to the US Army in Autumn 1990 and the first flight was planned for the second quarter of 1991. In April 1991 the Coast Guard decided not to take the T800 trial beyond the end of the first phase in November. The performance and reliability of the Textron Lycoming LTS 101 had been significantly improved. Alternative plans to fit the Dauphin's standard Arriels were also dropped.

The first AS 366G flew for the first time at Marignane on 23 July 1980. It was later shipped to Aerospatiale Helicopter Corporation in Texas for installation of avionics, and flight testing for FAA certification. DGAC certification was received on 20 July 1982. As on the AS 365/565, the size of the tail fin and carbonfibre fenestron is increased on the operational Coast Guard aircraft, designated **AS 366G-1**. Deliveries began on 19 November 1984, and were completed on 24 April 1989. The first life-saving medevac mission was completed on 20 September 1985. In 1985, the Israel Defence Force purchased two ex-USCG trials AS 366s for an 18-month evaluation. This was completed successfully in 1987. A contract with Aerospatiale Helicopter Corporation for 20 more to HH-65A standards, bought with FMS funds, did not materialise. Duties were to have included fire control, ASW and SAR duties from 'Sa'ar' missile boats.

WEIGHTS AND LOADINGS:
Weight empty, incl mission equipment	
	2,718 kg (5,992 lb)
Max T-O weight	4,050 kg (8,928 lb)

PERFORMANCE (at max T-O weight):
Never-exceed speed	150 knots (278 km/h; 172 mph)
Max cruising speed	139 knots (257 km/h; 160 mph)
Hovering ceiling: IGE	2,290 m (7,510 ft)
OGE	1,627 m (5,340 ft)
Range: SRR	166 nm (307 km; 191 miles)
with max passenger load	216 nm (400 km; 248 miles)
with max fuel	410 nm (760 km; 471 miles)
Endurance with max fuel	4 h

AEROSPATIALE AS 565 PANTHER (ARMY/AIR FORCE)
Brazilian Army designation: HM-1

This army/air force development of the Dauphin 2 was first flown in prototype form (AS 365M F-WZJV) on 29 February 1984. It has since undergone considerable refinement, and was first shown in production form, as the Panther, on 30 April 1986. Armament integration and firing trials were completed successfully in late 1986, and a second, improved prototype (F-ZVLO) was flown in April 1987.

Originally designated SA 365K, the Panther has been known since January 1990 as the AS 565:

AS 565AA. Armed version.
AS 565UA. Utility version.
AS 565CA. Anti-tank version.

Initial orders include 36 AAs, delivered from 1989 onwards, for Brazil's 1 BAvEx (Army Aviation Battalion) at Taubaté.

The airframe is basically similar to that of the Naval Panther, but with greater emphasis on survivability in combat areas. Composite materials are used exclusively for the dynamic components and for an increased (15 per cent) proportion of the fuselage structure. The crew seats are armoured, and similar protection is extended to the flying control servos and engine controls of production Panthers. Other features include a cable cutter, self-sealing fuel tanks and redundant hydraulic circuits. Further development is expected to permit continued operation of the main transmission after total loss of lubricating oil. Similar attention has been paid to crashworthiness. The crew seats will tolerate 20g. The entire basic airframe is designed to withstand an impact at a vertical speed of 7 m (23 ft)/s at

Aerospatiale AS 565UA of the Angolan Air Force *(Ivo Sturzenegger)*

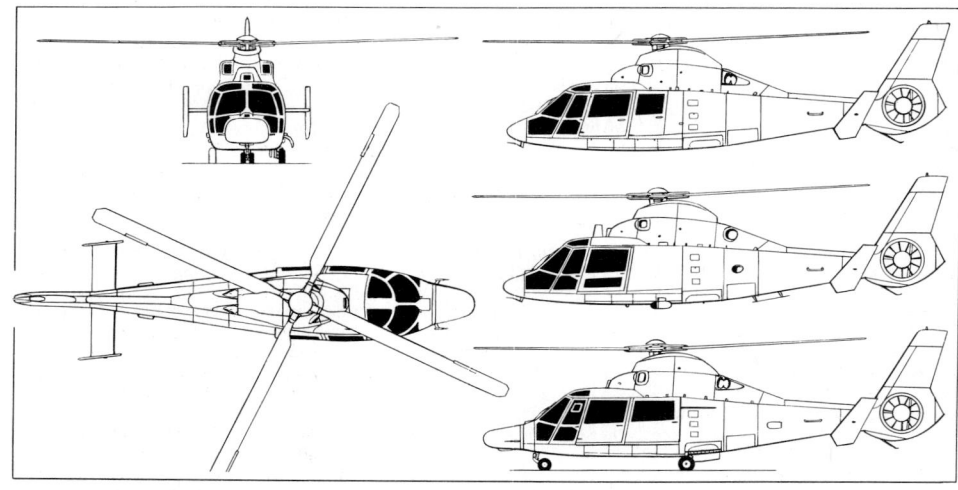

Aerospatiale AS 565AA Panther, with added side views of HH-65A Dolphin (AS 366G-1) for US Coast Guard (centre) and AS 365N₂ Dauphin 2 (top) *(Pilot Press)*

Aerospatiale AS 565AA Panther, armed with two 20 mm gun pods

max T-O weight; the fuel system is capable of withstanding a 14 m (46 ft)/s crash.

The AS 565 Panther is powered by two Turbomeca Arriel 1M1 turboshafts, each rated at 558 kW (748 shp) for take-off with a contingency rating of 584 kW (783 shp) and max continuous rating of 487 kW (653 shp). Full FADEC control gives automatic engine-start sequencing and automatic limiting of power according to a variety of preselected limits. The SFIM 155 autopilot has special tactical fly-through modes. The larger, more powerful carbonfibre fenestron is fitted. The airframe is finished in low IR reflecting paint. Noise level is low, and radar signature is minimised by the aircraft's composite structure and special paints. The cockpit is adapted for night vision goggles. Equipment can include a Thomson-CSF TMV 011 Sherloc radar warning receiver, IR jammer and chaff dispenser.

Two international helicopter records were established by the prototype Panther on 15 September 1987 when, at a weight of 2,774 kg (6,116 lb), it achieved an altitude of 3,000 m in 2 min 54 s and 6,000 m in 6 min 14 s. It is also cleared for aerobatics.

As a high speed assault transport, the Panther will carry a crew of two and eight to ten troops over a radius of action of 215 nm (400 km; 248 miles), or 60 troops per hour over 11 nm (20 km; 12 miles). For close support missions of three-hour duration, the fuselage-side outriggers can each carry a pack of 22 Thomson-Brandt 68 mm rockets, a launcher for 19 Forges de Zeebrugge 2.75 in rockets or a 20 mm GIAT M621 gun pod with 180 rounds. Operations against fixed-wing aircraft or other helicopters are envisaged, using either 20 mm guns or four two-round packs of Matra Mistral infra-red homing air-to-air missiles. Secondary roles could include armed or unarmed reconnaissance, electronic warfare, target designation, aerial command post, search and rescue, casualty evacuation (four stretchers) and transport of up to 1,600 kg (3,525 lb) of external freight.

Light Helicopter Turbine Engine Company, with Aerospatiale Helicopter Corporation, IBM and LTV Aircraft Products, was offering a **Panther 800** derivative of the AS 565 to the US Army.
DIMENSIONS, EXTERNAL: As for AS 565SA
WEIGHTS AND LOADINGS:
Weight empty 2,193 kg (4,835 lb)
Max sling load 1,600 kg (3,527 lb)
Max T-O weight, internal or external load 4,250 kg (9,369 lb)
PERFORMANCE (at average mission weight of 4,000 kg; 8,818 lb):

Dauphin X 380DTP flying testbed for the Spheriflex five-blade rotor hub/mast unit *(Michel Isaac/GIFAS)*

Never-exceed speed (VNE)
160 knots (296 km/h; 184 mph)
Max cruising speed at S/L
150 knots (278 km/h; 173 mph)
Max rate of climb at S/L 420 m (1,378 ft)/min
Hovering ceiling: IGE 2,600 m (8,531 ft)
OGE 1,850 m (6,070 ft)
Range with max standard fuel at S/L
472 nm (875 km; 544 miles)

AEROSPATIALE DAUPHIN X 380, DGV and FBW

On 20 March 1989, Aerospatiale flew a modified Dauphin (F-WDFK) designated X 380DTP (indicating Probationary Technical Development) fitted with a five-blade Spheriflex rotor head in place of the standard production Starflex assembly. Combining the advantages of higher flight speeds with a reduced quantity of components, Spheriflex is an integrated hub/mast unit constructed of filament-wound carbonfibre, coated with a Kevlar safety layer. The hub allows for blade attachment and movement through an elastomeric thrust bearing, so that reduced drag may be achieved by mounting blades close to the rotor axis. Inter-blade dampers replace the conventional drag dampers. Connection of the hub/mast to the transmission unit is via a single large diameter bearing (replacing two normally used). Blades of the X 380 have turned-down tips with leading-edge taper. The whole rotor hub is faired and integrated with a high-speed fairing for transmission and engines.

On the power of two Arriel 1C1 turboshaft engines, the X 380 was flown throughout the flight envelope of the AS 365N₁, and cruised up to 15 knots (27 km/h; 17 mph) faster. The Dauphin Grande Vitesse (DGV) fitted with two Arriel 1X power plants, each developing 660 kW (884 shp) was to fly in March 1991. It has an uprated transmission, a reinforced structure, small fenestron, aerodynamic rudder and new servo-controls and should reach 200 knots (371 km/h; 230 mph).

The Dauphin FBW (Fly By Wire) is a conversion of prototype No. 6001/F-WZJJ, which first flew in this new guise on 6 April 1989 and completed an initial series of tests in October. These were to be followed by an evaluation of more complex attitude control laws, initially using conventional cockpit controls, and with a sidestick controller from April 1990. Traditional controls have been retained for a safety pilot on the left.

CAGNY
RAYMOND DE CAGNY
5 square des Bégonias, 91370 Verrières le Buisson
Telephone: 33 (1) 60 11 98 02

CAGNY PERFORMANCE 2000
No recent news has been received of progress on the Performance 2000. A full description and photograph may be found in the 1989-90 and earlier editions of *Jane's*.

DASSAULT
DASSAULT AVIATION
9 Rond-Point des Champs-Elysées, 75008 Paris
Telephone: 33 (1) 47 95 85 85
Fax: 33 (1) 47 41 67 89
Telex: 203944 AMADAS
PRESS INFORMATION OFFICE: 27, rue du Professor Pauchet, 92420 Vaucresson
Telephone: 33 (1) 47 95 85 85
Fax: 33 (1) 47 95 86 80/47 41 84 53
WORKS: 92214 Saint-Cloud, 95100 Argenteuil, 78140 Vélizy-Villacoublay, 33610 Martignas, 33700 Bordeaux-Mérignac, 91120 Brétigny, 33630 Cazaux, 64600 Biarritz-Anglet, 64200 Biarritz-Parme, 13800 Istres, 74390 Argonay, 59113 Lille-Seclin, 86000 Poitiers
CHAIRMAN AND CHIEF EXECUTIVE OFFICER: Serge Dassault
VICE-PRESIDENT, RESEARCH: Bruno Revellin-Falcoz
VICE-PRESIDENT, MILITARY EXPORTS: Paul-Emile Jaillard
VICE-PRESIDENT, CIVIL AIRCRAFT: Bernard Latreille
DIRECTOR, COMMUNICATIONS: Pierre Pacalon

Avions Marcel Dassault-Breguet Aviation resulted from the merger in December 1971 of Avions Marcel Dassault with Breguet Aviation. In January 1979, 20 per cent of its stock was assigned to the French State, and in November 1981 the State shareholding was raised to 46 per cent. Due to a double voting right of some of its shares, the French State holds a majority control of the company. The name was changed to Dassault Aviation in April 1990. Employees total 13,000. Business in 1990 was devoted 55 per cent to military aircraft, 35 per cent to executive aircraft and 10 per cent to space.

Dassault is engaged in the development and production of military and civil aircraft, flight control system components, maintenance and support equipment, and CAD/CAM software. Series production of its aircraft is undertaken under a widespread subcontracting programme, with final assembly and flight testing handled by the company.

Dassault has established close links with the industries of other countries. The programme for the Atlantique maritime patrol aircraft associates manufacturers in Belgium, France, Germany and Italy under the overall responsibility of their respective governments. In the same way the British and French governments are associated in the SEPECAT concern, formed to control the Dassault/BAe Jaguar programme; and the German and French governments are associated in the Dassault/Dornier Alpha Jet programme. The A.C.E. International consortium formed by Dassault, SNECMA, Thomson-CSF and Dassault Electronique as the nucleus of an international Rafale programme is still in existence, but no foreign partner has materialised. Purchase of Mirage fighters by Belgium and Spain led to Belgian and Spanish participation in production of Dassault aircraft. Similarly, purchase of Mirage 2000 fighters by Greece and Egypt has led to co-production of components for this aircraft by Hellenic Aerospace Industry and AOI. Dassault's Biarritz-Parme factory manufactures fuselages for Fokker. Since 1945, Dassault has produced more than 6,500 aircraft, including 92 prototypes and 78 pre-series.

DASSAULT/DORNIER ALPHA JET
Details of the Alpha Jet programme can be found in the International section of this edition. Some Alpha Jets released by the Luftwaffe might be equipped for carrier operations to replace the existing French Navy Fouga Zéphyrs.

DASSAULT/BAe JAGUAR
Details of the Anglo-French Jaguar programme can be found under SEPECAT in the International section of this edition. Production continues in India (see HAL entry).

HERMÈS AEROSPACECRAFT
Dassault Aviation is responsible for all work required to achieve successful re-entry atmospheric flight by the Hermès aerospacecraft, of which brief details can be found under the Eurohermespace entry in the International section.

MIRAGE ADVANCED TECHNOLOGY UPDATE PROGRAMMES
Although the first-generation Mirage (types III, 5 and 50) remains available to special order, series production has now ended. At the beginning of 1990, orders totalled 1,422, of which 1,415 had been delivered, including 949 exported. Many of these remain in service, or are in storage awaiting re-sale.

Since 1977, Dassault has been involved in programmes to update the navigation and attack systems, flight aids, radio com/nav, power plant and other features of in-service Mirage III/5/50 aircraft. In particular, several air forces have awarded Dassault contracts to install an inertial platform, digital computer, CRT head-up display, air-to-ground laser rangefinder and other equipment for improved navigational accuracy, easier target acquisition, and high bombing precision in the various CCIP (continuous computation of the impact point) or CCRP (continuous computation of the release point) modes, including standoff capability through the introduction of CCRP with initial point. Combat efficiency in the air-to-air gunnery mode is improved considerably by display of a highly accurate hot-line on the HUD.

Another major improvement available for the Mirage III/5/50 series is a flight refuelling kit able to offer an increase of 30 to more than 100 per cent in radius of action. Already ordered by several air forces for their Mirage 5s, this system was demonstrated in flight before becoming generally available to Mirage operators in 1986. It involves lengthening the nose of the aircraft by 90 mm (3½ in) to accommodate system changes associated with a non-retractable probe on the starboard side, forward of the windscreen, and a single-point pressure refuelling port for both internal and external tanks. With the addition of a pressure refuelling system, time for refuelling on the ground is reduced from 15 to three minutes.

Over half the air forces operating Mirage III/5/50s have now opted for update programmes, some of which are undertaken at least partly by local organisations and are of sufficient complexity to warrant mention in other national sections in this book. Brief details are as follows:

Dassault Mirage F1-CR-200 reconnaissance aircraft of the French Air Force *(Paul Jackson)*

Argentina: From 1982 onwards, up to 26 IAI Daggers (Israeli-built Mirage 5s) underwent three-phase 'Finger Ia', 'IIa' and 'IIIa' upgrade programme, eventually receiving a laser rangefinder, INS, HUD, ECM equipment and refuelling probe. Nine ex-Peruvian Mirage 5Ps similarly modified to 'Mara' standard.

Belgium: A Mirage Safety Improvement Programme will be applied to up to 15 Mirage 5BAs and five two-seat 5BDs which will serve with No. 42 Squadron until 2005. A further 36 aircraft, including 5BR reconnaissance versions, will be withdrawn by 1993. Additions, incorporated by Sabca as main contractor, include a GEC Ferranti HUD, Thomson-CSF TMV 630 laser-ranger, Sagem nav/attack avionics (Uliss 92 INS and UTR 90 computer), fixed canard foreplanes, single-point pressure refuelling, pilot's liquid oxygen system, strobe anti-collision lights and complete re-wiring. Martin-Baker Mk 10L ejection seats are being installed under a separate contract. An unspecified reconnaissance pod will be acquired for some aircraft.

Brazil: First of seven ex-French Mirage IIIEs (including two converted to tandem-seat trainers) handed over by Dassault on 30 September 1988 following a complete overhaul and addition of foreplanes; 10 existing Mirage IIIEBRs and two IIIDBRs being modified in Brazil from December 1989.

Chile: Mirage 50C update with foreplanes and Israeli avionics in progress (see ENAER Pantera).

Colombia: In 1988, two Mirage 5COD trainers received Kfir C7-type avionics and half-size Kfir canards. Base Arsenal at Madrid converting 10 Mirage 5COAs and two CORs to similar standards (but with 75 per cent canards) as Mirage 5M (=Modification). First aircraft flown in January 1989.

Egypt: Improvement programme for some Mirages has been completed.

Pakistan: Update programme completed on original aircraft. Fifty ex-Australian Mirage IIIOs acquired in 1990 for re-work at the Mirage Rebuild Factory, Kamra, with some export sales in prospect.

Peru: Some 12 Mirage 5P/P3s and three 5DP/DP3s fitted with refuelling probe, laser-ranger and other improvements, as 5P4 and 5DP4.

South Africa: Mirage IIIs being fitted with foreplanes and Israeli avionics as Atlas Cheetah (which see). Mirage IIICZ withdrawn from service October 1990.

Spain: CESELSA, with CASA as subcontractor, will install Emerson Electric AN/APQ-159 radar, Honeywell AN/AYK-14 mission computer, a HUD, radar warning receiver, HOTAS controls, radar altimeter, Tacan, AN/ALE-40 chaff/flare dispenser and multi-function displays, plus pressure refuelling and in-flight refuelling probes. Re-work involves 18 Mirage IIIEEs and five two-seat IIIBEs — the latter with provision for buddy refuelling pods.

Switzerland: Foreplanes and avionics improvements being installed locally in Mirage IIIS/RS fleet by F + W (which see).

Venezuela: Six single-seat and two two-seat aircraft to receive Atar 9K-50 power plants and improved avionics, under designations Mirage 50EV and 50DV respectively, deliveries beginning on 22 October 1990. Venezuelan aircraft have canards, a Uliss 81 INS, Cyrano IVM3 radar and an in-flight refuelling probe. Armament options will include Magic 2 AAMs and AM 39 Exocet anti-ship missiles. These aircraft are being supplemented by six new Mirage 50EVs, one new Mirage 50DV and three refurbished second-hand Mirage 50EVs.

No modification programmes have been announced for Abu Dhabi, Gabon, Libya or Zaïre. The type has been withdrawn from use in Australia, Israel and Lebanon.

Several standards of equipment for modified or new airframes have been offered by Dassault in recent years, including the Mirage 3NG and Mirage 50M, last described in the 1989-90 *Jane's*. Most recent of these, the **Mirage IIIEX**, was revealed in 1989 as a modified IIIE (being

replaced in French service) with a longer, Mirage F1-type nose; underfuselage strakes (as on Mirage 5D series); an in-flight refuelling probe, offset to port, ahead of the cockpit; and fixed canards. The Doppler fairing below the forward fuselage is deleted. No purchases had been recorded at the time of going to press.

Israel Aircraft Industries (which see), seeking to export surplus Kfirs to nations not authorised to receive the GE J79 turbojet, is undertaking trial installation of a SNECMA Atar 9K-50, thereby 're-inventing' the Mirage 50.

DASSAULT MIRAGE F1
Spanish Air Force designation: C.14

Details of the early history of the Mirage F1 can be found in the 1977-78 *Jane's*. The prototype flew for the first time on 23 December 1966 and was followed by three pre-series aircraft.

The primary role of the single-seat Mirage **F1-C** production version, to which the detailed description applies, is that of all-weather interception at any altitude. It is equally suitable for visual ground attack missions, carrying a variety of external loads beneath the wings and fuselage. Other versions include the **F1-B** two-seat version of F1-C, the first of which made its first flight on 26 May 1976; the **F1-D** two-seat version of F1-E; the single-seat

F1-E multi-role air superiority/ground attack/ reconnaissance version for export customers, with an inertial navigation system, nav/attack central computer, CRT head-up display, and a large inventory of external stores; and the single-seat **F1-R** (French Air Force **F1-CR**) day and night reconnaissance variant. Production of the F1-A ground attack version, with reduced equipment, a retractable flight refuelling probe and increased fuel, has been completed.

Many F1-Cs of the French Air Force were delivered or modified to **F1-C-200** standard by installation of an 8 cm (3.15 in) fuselage plug for a removable flight refuelling probe. Export customers who have F1s equipped with refuelling probes include Iraq, Libya, Morocco, South Africa and Spain.

By January 1990, a total of 731 Mirage F1s had been ordered and deliveries made to: France (251 including five prototypes), Ecuador (two F1-JE and 16 JA, equivalent to F1-B and E), Greece (40 F1-CG), Iraq (98 F1-EQs and 15 BQs), Jordan (two F1-BJ, 17 CJ — to be upgraded to EJ — and 17 EJ), Kuwait (six F1-BK and 27 CK), Libya (six F1-BD, 16 AD and 16 ED), Morocco (30 F1-CH and 20 EH), Qatar (two F1-DDA and 13 EDA), South Africa (32 F1-AZ and 16 CZ) and Spain (six F1-BE, 45 CE and 22 EE). Production ended in 1990 with the last of a follow-on batch of 15 for Iraq, but these, plus five from an earlier order, have been embargoed. Deliveries by January 1991 were 721, reportedly including some (embargoed Iraqi) aircraft to the Kuwait Air Force in exile.

The first production F1 flew on 15 February 1973 and was delivered officially to the French Air Force on 14 March 1973. The first unit to receive the F1 was the 30e Escadre at Reims, which became operational in early 1974. This now has two and a half squadrons of F1-Cs (the half detached to Djibouti) and an OCU squadron of F1-Bs, whilst the 12e Escadre de Chasse at Cambrai has three squadrons of F1-Cs. F1-C-200s made surplus by conversion of units to Mirage 2000Cs are to be issued to 13e Escadre at Colmar in the tactical attack role. Designated **Mirage F1-CT**, they will receive a radar upgrade to Cyrano IVMR standard, INS and navigation computer, as described for the Mirage F1-CR below, plus Martin-Baker F10M ejection seats, radar warning receivers, chaff/flare dispensers, secure radio, laser rangefinder and air-to-ground ordnance. The 1990 defence budget included funding for the first 19 conversions, plus authorisation for a further 22, deliveries being due from late 1991. A prototype conversion was begun at Biarritz-Parme in 1989 and was to begin trials at Istres in 1991. Remaining aircraft will be re-worked at the Atelier Industriel de l'Air at Clermont-Ferrand. Authorisation for a further 14 conversions was deleted from the 1991 budget.

Dassault Mirage IIIEX upgraded version of the basic Mirage IIIE

Updated Mirage III of the Brazilian Air Force

Deliveries of the F1-C series to the French Air Force totalled 162, made up of 83 F-1Cs and 79 F1-C-200s. Twenty tandem-seat F-1Bs were delivered to an OCU squadron, initially at Orange, from June 1980; each aircraft is equipped with the same radar, weapon system and air-to-air missiles as the F1-C, but has no internal guns. Fuel capacity is reduced by 450 litres (119 US gallons; 99 Imp gallons); empty weight increased by 200 kg (441 lb); and the forward fuselage extended by 30 cm (11¾ in).

The French Air Force also purchased F1-CRs to re-equip the three squadrons of the 33e Escadre de Reconnaissance, at Strasbourg. These aircraft are designated **F1-CR-200** (having a fixed in-flight refuelling probe) and differ from the F1-C in being fitted with the IVMR model of Cyrano radar (with additional ground mapping, contour mapping, air-ground ranging and blind let-down modes), a Sagem Uliss 47 inertial platform and Dassault Electronique 182 navigation computer. An SAT SCM2400 Super Cyclope infra-red linescan reconnaissance system replaces the starboard gun, and an undernose bay houses either a 75 mm Thomson-TRT 40 panoramic camera or a 150 mm Thomson-TRT 33 vertical camera. French aircraft have a secondary ground attack role and may also carry a centreline podded sensor in the form of a Thomson-CSF Raphaël TH SLAR or a Thomson-CSF Astac electronic reconnaissance system for detection of ground radars. Ongoing modification is making French F1-CRs compatible with a FLIR pod and a TV reconnaissance pod. Several types of sensor pod are available for fitment to export Mirage F1-Es. The first of two F1-CR-200 prototypes flew on 20 November 1981. Sixty-four (including the prototypes) were ordered for the French Air Force. The first production F1-CR-200 flew on 10 November 1982, and the first squadron (2/33) became operational in July 1983. Deliveries were completed in 1987 and the third and last squadron of 33e Escadre converted from Mirage IIIRs in 1988.

Export F1-Cs have a radar similar to Cyrano IV or IVM. Export F1-Es have radar similar to Cyrano IVMR but repackaged to save space. Mirage F1-EQ5s and EQ6s of the Iraqi Air Force are equipped to carry Exocet anti-ship missiles and laser guided weapons such as the AS.30L missile and Matra 400 kg laser guided bomb. They have Thomson-CSF Agave radar.

The Mirage F1 was produced by Dassault Aviation in co-operation with the Belgian company Sabca, in which Dassault Aviation has a parity interest, and CASA of Spain, which built fuselage sections for all Mirage F1s ordered. Dassault Aviation also has a technical and industrial co-operation agreement with the Armaments Development and Production Corporation of South Africa Ltd (Armscor), whereby the latter company has rights to build the Mirage F1 under licence. Mirage F1 flying hours passed 1,000,000 in June 1989.

The following abbreviated description applies to the F1-C-200 production version for the French Air Force, except where indicated:

TYPE: Single-seat multi-mission fighter and attack aircraft.

WINGS: All-metal two-spar torsion box structure. Trailing-edge control surfaces of honeycomb sandwich construction, with carbonfibre aileron skin. Entire leading-edge can be drooped hydraulically (manually for T-O and landing, automatic in combat). Two differentially operating double-slotted flaps and one aileron on each trailing-edge. Two spoilers on each wing, ahead of flaps.

FUSELAGE: Conventional all-metal semi-monocoque structure. Titanium alloy is used for landing gear trunnions, engine firewall and certain other major structures. High tensile steel wing attachment points. Large hydraulically actuated door type airbrake in forward underside of each intake trunk.

TAIL UNIT: Single-spar fin. All-moving tailplane mid-set on fuselage, and actuated hydraulically by electric or manual control.

LANDING GEAR: Retractable tricycle type, by Messier-Bugatti. Hydraulic retraction, nose unit rearward, main units upward into rear of intake trunk fairings. Twin wheels on each unit. Messier-Bugatti brakes and anti-skid units. Brake parachute in bullet fairing at base of rudder.

POWER PLANT: One SNECMA Atar 9K-50 turbojet, rated at 70.6 kN (15,873 lb st) with afterburning. Fuel in integral tanks in wings (combined capacity 375 litres; 99 US gallons; 82.5 Imp gallons), and three main tanks and one inverted-flight supply tank (combined capacity 3,925 litres; 1,037 US gallons; 863.5 Imp gallons) in fuselage. Total internal fuel capacity 4,300 litres (1,136 US gallons; 946 Imp gallons). Provision for two jettisonable auxiliary fuel tanks (each 1,200 litres; 317 US gallons; 264 Imp gallons) to be carried on inboard wing pylons, plus a single tank of 2,200 litres (581 US gallons; 484 Imp gallons) capacity on the underfuselage station. Non-retractable, but removable, optional flight refuelling probe on starboard side of nose.

ACCOMMODATION: SEM Martin-Baker F1RM4 ejection seat for pilot, under rearward hinged canopy (SEM Martin-Baker F10M rocket seat in latest F1-E and in F1-E and F1-CR. Two Mk 10 seats with inter-seat sequence system in F1-B). No-delay through-the-canopy escape system.

SYSTEMS: Two independent hydraulic systems, pressure 207 bars (3,000 lb/sq in) each, for landing gear actuation,

Dassault Mirage F1-EQ5 of the Iraqi Air Force (*Ivo Sturzenegger*)

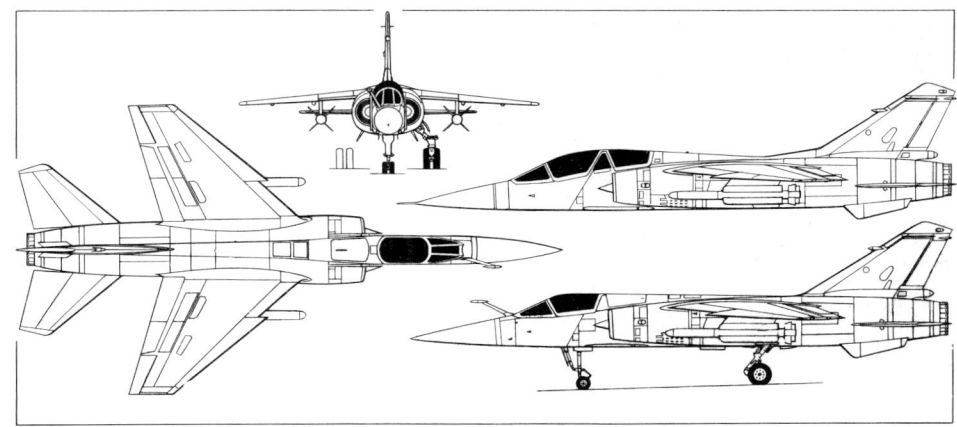

Dassault Mirage F1-C-200, with additional side view (upper) of Mirage F1-B (*Pilot Press*)

flaps and flying controls. Electrical system includes two Auxilec 15kVA variable speed alternators. DC power provided by two transformer-rectifiers operating in conjunction with battery.

AVIONICS: Thomson-CSF Cyrano IV fire control radar in nose. LMT Tacan, LMT NR-AI-4-A IFF, remote setting interception system, three-axis generator, central air data computer, SFIM spherical indicator with ILS pointers, Sextant Avionique Type 63 navigation indicator, SFENA 505 autopilot and CSF head-up display, with wide field-of-view double-converter. (Standard equipment on F-1E includes Sagem Uliss 47 INS. Dassault Electronique 182 central digital computer for nav/attack computations, TH C8F VE-120C CRT head-up display, Sextant Avionique air data computer and digital armament/nav control panels.) Available sensor pods include a Thomson-CSF Raphaël SLAR, a Thomson-TRT/Dassault Harold long-range oblique photographic unit (1,700 mm Thomson-TRT 38), a Thomson-TRT/Dassault COR2 multi-purpose pod (visual spectrum and IR linescan), a Thomson-CSF TMV 018 Syrel real-time electro-optical reconnaissance pod, a Dassault Nora real-time video pod and a Thomson-CSF Astac ground radar detector unit. A Thomson-CSF BF radar warning receiver is standard, and a range of jamming (Barracuda, Barem, Barrax) and chaff/flare (Phimat, Sycomor) pods may be fitted. Some Moroccan F1-EHs and Spanish F1-CEs have chaff/flare dispensers scabbed to each side of rear fuselage.

ARMAMENT: Standard installed armament of two 30 mm DEFA 553 cannon, with 135 rds/gun, mounted in lower central fuselage. Max theoretical external combat load 6,300 kg (13,890 lb), comprising 2,100 kg (4,630 lb) on centreline pylon; 1,300 kg (2,866 lb) on each inner wing pylon; 550 kg (1,213 lb) on each outer wing pylon; 150 kg (331 lb) on each wingtip AAM rail (Matra 550 Magic or AIM-9 Sidewinder) and 100 kg (220 lb) of chaff/flare dispensers on each fuselage shoulder position. Practical max operational load is 4,000 kg (8,818 lb). Externally mounted weapons for interception role include Matra Super 530 air-to-air missiles under inboard wing pylons. For ground attack, typical loads may include one Armat anti-radar missile, or one AM 39 Exocet anti-ship missile, or up to fourteen 250 kg bombs, 30 anti-runway bombs or 144 Thomson-Brandt rockets. Other possible external loads include auxiliary fuel tanks, a Thomson-CSF Atlis laser designator pod with AS.30L missiles or 400 kg laser guided bombs, air-to-surface missiles, and sensor pods.

DIMENSIONS, EXTERNAL (F1-C):

Wing span: without missiles	8.40 m (27 ft 6¾ in)
over Magic missiles	approx 9.32 m (30 ft 6¾ in)
Length overall: F1-C	15.23 m (49 ft 11¾ in)
F1-C-200	15.30 m (50 ft 2½ in)
F1-B	15.53 m (50 ft 11½ in)
Height overall	4.50 m (14 ft 9 in)

AREAS:

Wings, gross	25.00 m² (269.1 sq ft)

WEIGHTS AND LOADINGS (F1-C):

Weight empty	7,400 kg (16,314 lb)
T-O weight, clean	10,900 kg (24,030 lb)
Max T-O weight	16,200 kg (35,715 lb)

PERFORMANCE (F1-C):

Max level speed: high altitude	Mach 2.2
low altitude	Mach 1.2
(800 knots; 1,480 km/h; 920 mph EAS)	
Max rate of climb at S/L (with afterburning)	
	12,780 m (41,930 ft)/min
Service ceiling	20,000 m (65,600 ft)
Stabilised supersonic ceiling	16,000 m (52,500 ft)
T-O run (AUW of 11,500 kg; 25,355 lb)	
	600 m (1,970 ft)
Landing run (AUW of 8,500 kg; 18,740 lb)	
	670 m (2,200 ft)

Combat radius:
hi-lo-hi at Mach 0.75/0.88, with fourteen 250 kg bombs and max internal fuel, with reserves
230 nm (425 km; 265 miles)
lo-lo with one Exocet and two external tanks, with reserves and including missile flight path
378 nm (700 km; 435 miles)
Combat air patrol endurance, with two Super 530 missiles and underbelly tank, with reserves, incl one attack at ceiling 2 h 15 min

DASSAULT MIRAGE 2000
Indian Air Force name: Vajra

The Mirage 2000 was selected on 18 December 1975 as the primary combat aircraft of the French Air Force from the mid-1980s. Under French government contract, it was developed initially as an interceptor and air superiority fighter, powered by a single SNECMA M53 turbofan and with Thomson-CSF RDM multi-mode Doppler radar. The Mirage 2000 is equally suitable for reconnaissance, close support, and low altitude attack missions in areas to the rear of a battlefield. Its early history has been outlined in previous editions of *Jane's*. On the basis of structural testing, the Mirage 2000 airframe was approved for a load factor of +9g and rate of roll of 270°/s in subsonic and supersonic flight, clean or with four air-to-air missiles.

A SNECMA M53-2 turbofan, rated at 83.4 kN (18,740 lb st), was fitted for early prototype testing, and was replaced in 1980 by the uprated M53-5 which also powers early production aircraft. Export aircraft have the more powerful M53-P2, which was introduced on French Air Force Mirage 2000Cs from No. 38 onwards (and 2000Bs from c/n 516 — the sixteenth) in 1987 in conjunction with Thomson-CSF RDI pulse Doppler radar. These aircraft are sometimes referred to as **2000 RDIs**. Nos. 38-48 were built as 2000C-S4 and upgraded in service to S4-1 standard, matching Nos. 49-63. No. 64 and upwards delivered from mid-1990 in S4-2 avionics configuration.

The first production **Mirage 2000C** flew on 20 November 1982 and deliveries began in 1983. The first production **Mirage 2000B** two-seat trainer flew on

Dassault Mirage 2000C of Escadron de Chasse 1/5 above Mt Ventoux *(SIRPA 'AIR')*

7 October 1983. Escadron de Chasse (EC) 1/2 'Cigognes' was the first French Air Force unit to become operational, at Dijon on 2 July 1984. EC 3/2 'Alsace' followed in 1986 and Escadron de Chasse et de Transformation (ECT) 2/2 'Côte d'Or', the OCU with Mirage 2000Bs and three 2000Cs, in early 1987. Eventually, Mirage 2000Cs will equip four wings (escadres), each with three interceptor squadrons. Deliveries of 2000Cs with RDI radar and M53-P2 engines began on 20 July 1988 to EC 1/5 'Vendée' at Orange, the squadron being declared operational on 1 April 1989. The second component of 5e Escadre de Chasse (EC 2/5 'Ile de France') followed on 1 April 1990, and EC 3/5 'Comtat Venaissin' received its first 2000C in September 1990. The designation **'2000DA'** (Défense Aérienne) is used loosely in collective reference to Mirage 2000Bs and Cs.

Following a mid-1979 go-ahead, the first of two prototypes of the **Mirage 2000N** two-seat low-altitude penetration version made its first flight on 3 February 1983; the second flew on 21 September 1983. Strengthened for flight at a typical 600 knots (1,110 km/h; 690 mph) at 60 m (200 ft) above the terrain, this version was intended basically as a vehicle for the ASMP medium-range air-to-surface nuclear missile, and has Antilope 5 terrain-following radar, two Sagem inertial platforms, improved TRT AHV-12 radio altimeter, Thomson-CSF colour CRT, an Omera vertical camera, special ECM and two Magic air-to-air missiles for self-defence. Currently the 2000N is cleared for automatic terrain-following at 91 m (300 ft). A reduction to the design altitude is expected after further trials. Production deliveries began on 19 February 1987, and EC 1/4 'Dauphiné' at Luxeuil received its first on 30 March 1988, being declared operational on 1 July 1988. EC 2/4 'La Fayette' followed on 1 July 1989. Third squadron is EC 3/4 'Limousin', which was detached to Istres on 1 July 1990. First 31 aircraft (Nos. 301-331) are 2000N-K1 with only ASMP capability; from No. 332 in mid-1990, 2000N-K2 added full conventional ordnance and was first issued to re-equip EC 1/4.

Excluding seven prototypes, France plans to fund 372 Mirage 2000s by 1994, taking delivery of the last 2000C in 1998 and the final **2000D** in 2000. The latter — known until 1990 as the 2000N' (N Prime) — is a two-seat version not equipped to carry ASMP. A 1989 government decision to reduce nuclear delivery systems resulted in a change of emphasis between the N and D variants, the Armée de l'Air targets now being 23 2000Bs, 169 2000Cs, 75 2000Ns and 105 2000Ds, of which 23, 146, 75 and 57, respectively, were on firm order at 1 January 1991. A further six 2000C and 18 D aircraft were due to be funded in 1991. Production of the N will be completed in 1992 before D deliveries begin to

replace Mirage IIIEs with EC 3 at Nancy in 1992, although the first 2000D flew on 19 February 1991. Wings are manufactured at Martignas, fuselages at Argenteuil; final assembly and flight testing take place at Mérignac. Origin of contents, by value, of a Mirage 2000C include SNECMA 27 per cent, Dassault Aviation 26 per cent, Thomson-CSF 12 per cent, Aerospatiale 5 per cent and Dassault Electronique 5 per cent. By January 1991, 303 Mirage 2000s (including 146 for export) had been delivered from 470 on firm order.

Export customers for 169 Mirage 2000s comprise Abu Dhabi, Egypt, India, Jordan, Peru and Greece, some of which have chosen the multi-role **Mirage 2000E**. Egypt placed an initial firm contract for 20 (16 2000EM and 4 BM, all with M53-P2 engines) in January 1982. The first was delivered on 30 June 1986. India placed an initial order for 40 in October 1982 (36 2000H and 4 TH), the last of which were delivered in 1986. The four THs and 26 of the Hs had M53-5 engines temporarily; the final 10 Hs were powered from the start by the M53-P2. First flight by a 2000H (KF-101) was made on 21 September 1984, followed in early 1985 by the first TH (KT-201). The first of two Indian squadrons (No. 7 'Battle Axe') was formed at Gwalior AB on 29 June 1985, when the Mirage 2000 received the Indian name **Vajra** (Divine Thunder). A follow-on order for nine aircraft (six Hs and three THs) was signed in March 1986 and executed by late 1988 to complete No.1 'Tigers' Squadron. Peru ordered 26 aircraft in December 1982 (24 2000P and 2 DP), but reduced the total subsequently to 12 (10 2000P and 2 DP). The first 2000DP was handed over on 7 June 1985 to begin pilot training in France and is now with Escuadrón 412 of Grupo Aéreo de Caza 4 at La Joya. Abu Dhabi has ordered 36 (22 2000EAD, eight RAD and six DAD); deliveries were due to begin in 1986 but were delayed for fitment of additional equipment, including provision for carrying US weapons, such as Sidewinder AAMs. Deliveries to Maqatra/Al Dhafra began on 7 November 1989 and were completed 12 months later. The RAD reconnaissance version for this customer is fitted with a COR2 multi-camera pod, but may alternatively carry SLAR 2000 (Raphaël type) or Harold pods. The second 18 for Abu Dhabi are fitted with Elettronica ELT/158 threat-warning receivers and ELT/558 self-protection jammers. Greece ordered 40 (36 2000EGM and four 2000BGM) in July 1985, and received the first on 21 March 1988. They serve 331 and 332 Mire within 114 Pterix at Tanagra. Jordan ordered 10 2000EJs and two DJs in April 1988 and was due to take delivery from early 1991 onwards.

A two-stage private venture update programme announced by Dassault in 1987 includes the **2000-3** with Rafale-type cockpit multifunction displays, flown in 1988. Addition of Thomson-CSF RDY radar and a new central

processing unit to the 2000-3 produces the **2000-5** air defence variant or APSI (advanced pilot-system interface) Mirage, which also features a Thomson-CSF VEH 3020 holographic HUD and compatibility with Matra Mica air-to-air missiles. A prototype of the -3 (BX1 ex-No. 501) flew on 10 March 1988, and the RDY radar flew in a Mirage 2000 (BY1 ex-No. B01) for the first time in May 1988. The definitive -5 prototype flew on 24 October 1990. Associated options include an M88-P20 power plant uprated by four per cent to 98.06 kN (22,046 lb st). The 2000-5 is intended for export, as is the **2000S** (strike), a conventional attack version of the 2000D announced in April 1989. Both versions will become available in 1993.

The following description applies to the single-seat Mirage 2000C, except where indicated:

TYPE: Single-seat interceptor, air superiority and multi-role fighter.

WINGS: Cantilever multi-spar low-wing monoplane of delta planform, with cambered profile. Leading-edge sweepback 58°; trailing-edge sweepforward 3° 30′. Large radius root fairings. Full span two-segment automatic leading-edge slats provide variable camber in combat, but are retracted during all phases of acceleration and low altitude cruise, to reduce drag. Slat downward depression, 17° 30′ for inboard section; 30° outboard. Two-section elevons, forming entire trailing-edge of each wing, have carbonfibre skin, with AG5 light alloy honeycomb core. Elevon movement range −16° to +25°. Fly by wire control system for elevons and slats, with surfaces actuated by hydraulic servo units. No tabs. Retractable airbrake above and below each wing.

FUSELAGE: Conventional semi-monocoque structure, waisted in accordance with area rule; of conventional all-metal construction except for glassfibre radome and carbonfibre/light alloy honeycomb panel over avionics compartment, immediately aft of canopy. Small fixed strake, with marked dihedral, near leading-edge of each air intake trunk.

TAIL UNIT: Cantilever, twin-spar fin and inset rudder only; latter actuated by fly by wire control system via hydraulic servo units. Much of fin skin and all rudder skin of boron/epoxy/carbon composites with a light alloy structure for the fin and light alloy honeycomb core for the rudder. Sweepback on fin leading-edge 53°; trailing-edge 17°. No tab.

LANDING GEAR: Retractable tricycle type by Messier-Bugatti, with twin nosewheels; single wheel on each main unit. Hydraulic retraction, nosewheels rearward, main units inward. Oleo-pneumatic shock absorbers. Electro-hydraulic nosewheel steering (±45°). Manual disconnect permits nosewheel unit to castor through 360° for ground towing. Light alloy wheels and tubeless tyres, size 360 × 135-6, pressure 8.0 bars (116 lb/sq in) on nosewheels, size 750 × 230-15, pressure 15.0 bars (217 lb/sq in) on mainwheels. Messier-Bugatti hydraulically actuated polycrystalline graphite disc brakes on mainwheels, with anti-skid units. Runway arrester gear standard. Brake-chute in canister above jet nozzle.

POWER PLANT: One SNECMA M53-P2 turbofan, rated at 64.3 kN (14,462 lb st) dry and 95.1 kN (21,385 lb st) with afterburning. Movable half-cone centrebody in each air intake. Internal fuel capacity 4,000 litres (1,057 US gallons; 880 Imp gallons) in 2000C, 3,920 litres (1,035 US gallons; 862 Imp gallons) in 2000B. Provision for one jettisonable 1,300 litre (343 US gallon; 286 Imp gallon) fuel tank under centre of fuselage, and a 1,700 litre (449 US gallon; 374 Imp gallon) drop tank under each wing. Total internal/external fuel capacity 8,700 litres (2,298 US gallons; 1,914 Imp gallons) in 2000C, 8,620 litres (2,276 US gallons; 1,896 Imp gallons) in 2000B. Detachable flight refuelling probe forward of cockpit on starboard side. Drop tanks of 2,000 litres (528 gallons; 440 Imp gallons) are available for the 2000N.

ACCOMMODATION: Pilot only in 2000C, on SEMB licence-built Martin-Baker F10Q zero/zero ejection seat, under transparent canopy, in air-conditioned and pressurised cockpit. Canopy hinged at rear to open upward.

SYSTEMS: ABG-Semca air-conditioning and pressurisation system. Two independent hydraulic systems, pressure 280 bars (4,000 lb/sq in) each, to actuate flying control servo units, landing gear and brakes. Hydraulic flow rate 110 litres (29 US gallons; 24 Imp gallons)/min. Electrical system includes two Auxilec 20110 aircooled 20kVA 400Hz constant frequency alternators, two Bronzavia DC transformers, a SAFT 40Ah battery and ATEI static inverter. Fly-by-wire flight control system. Eros oxygen system.

AVIONICS: Thomson-CSF RDM multi-mode radar or Dassault Electronique/Thomson-CSF RDI pulse Doppler radar, each with operating range of 54 nm (100 km; 62 miles). (Mirage 2000N has Dassault Electronique/Thomson-CSF Antilope 5 terrain-following and ground mapping radar.) Sagem Uliss 52 inertial platform, Dassault Electronique Type 2084 central digital computer and Digibus digital data bus, Thomson-CSF TMV-980 data display system (VE-130 head-up and VMC-180 head-down) (two head-down in 2000N), Sfena 605 autopilot, Thomson-CSF/Dassault Electronique ECM with VCM-65 display (jammers on leading-edge of fin and in bullet fairing at base of rudder; chaff/flare dispenser under fuselage at wing trailing-edge), Matra

Dassault Mirage 2000C with Matra Armat anti-radiation missiles on inboard wing pylons
(SIRPA AIR/Matra)

Spirale passive countermeasures, LMT Deltac Tacan, LMT NRAI-7A IFF transponder, Socrat 8900 solid-state VOR/ILS and IO-300-A marker beacon receiver, TRT radio altimeter (AHV-6 in 2000B and C, AHV-9 in export aircraft, AHV-12 in 2000N), TRT ERA 7000 V/UHF com transceiver, TRT ERA 7200 UHF or EAS secure voice com, Thomson-CSF Serval radar warning receiver (antennae at each wingtip and on trailing-edge of fin, near tip), Sextant Avionique type 90 air data computer, and Thomson-CSF Atlis laser designator and marked target seeker (in pod on forward starboard underfuselage station). Omera vertical camera in 2000N. Other sensors can include a Dassault COR2 multi-camera pod or Dassault AA-3-38 Harold long-range oblique photographic (Lorop) pod; a Dassault/TRT/Intertechnique FLIR pod; a Thomson-CSF Atlis laser designator/ marked target seeker pod; two Thomson-CSF DB 3141/3163 self-defence ECM pods; one Thomson-CSF Caiman offensive or intelligence ECM pod; or an Intertechnique 231-300 buddy type in-flight refuelling pod. Fuselage centreline and inboard underwing stations are wet for carriage of fuel drop tanks (see Power Plant paragraph for details).

ARMAMENT: Two 30 mm DEFA 554 guns in 2000C and 2000E (not fitted in B, D, N or S), with 125 rds/gun. Nine attachments for external stores, five under fuselage and two under each wing. Fuselage centreline and inboard wing stations each stressed for 1,800 kg (3,968 lb) loads; other four fuselage points for 400 kg (882 lb) each, and outboard wing points for 300 kg (661 lb) each. Typical interception weapons comprise two Matra Super 530D or (with RDM radar) 530F missiles (inboard) and two Matra 550 Magic or Magic 2 missiles (outboard) under wings. Alternatively, each of the four underwing hardpoints can carry a Magic. Primary weapon for 2000N is ASMP tactical nuclear missile. In an air-to-surface role, the Mirage 2000 can carry up to 6,300 kg (13,890 lb) of external stores, including eighteen Matra 250 kg retarded bombs or Thomson-Brandt BAP 100 anti-runway bombs; sixteen Matra Durandal penetration bombs; one or two Matra BGL 1,000 kg laser guided bombs; five or six Matra Belouga cluster bombs or Thomson-Brandt BM 400 400 kg modular bombs; one Rafaut F2 practice bomb launcher; two Aerospatiale AS.30L, Matra Armat anti-radar, or Aerospatiale AM 39 Exocet anti-ship, air-to-surface missiles; four Matra LR F4 rocket launchers, each with eighteen 68 mm rockets; two packs of 100 mm rockets; or a Dassault CC 630 gun pod, containing two 30 mm guns and ammunition. For air defence weapon training, a Cubic Corporation AIS (airborne instrumentation subsystem) pod, externally resembling a Magic missile, can replace the Magic on its launch rail, enabling pilot to simulate a firing without carrying the actual missile.

DIMENSIONS, EXTERNAL:
Wing span	9.13 m (29 ft 11½ in)
Wing aspect ratio	2.03
Length overall: 2000C	14.36 m (47 ft 1¼ in)
2000B, N	14.55 m (47 ft 9 in)
Height overall: 2000C	5.20 m (17 ft 0¾ in)
2000B, N	5.15 m (16 ft 10¾ in)
Wheel track	3.40 m (11 ft 1¾ in)
Wheelbase	5.00 m (16 ft 4¾ in)

AREAS:
Wings, gross	41.0 m² (441.3 sq ft)

WEIGHTS AND LOADINGS:
Weight empty: 2000C	7,500 kg (16,534 lb)
2000B	7,600 kg (16,755 lb)
Max internal fuel: 2000C	3,160 kg (6,967 lb)
2000B	3,095 kg (6,823 lb)
Max external fuel: 2000C	3,720 kg (8,201 lb)
2000B	3,715 kg (8,190 lb)
Max external stores load	6,300 kg (13,890 lb)

Dassault Mirage 2000N of Escadron de Chasse 3/4 'Limousin' *(Ivo Sturzenegger)*

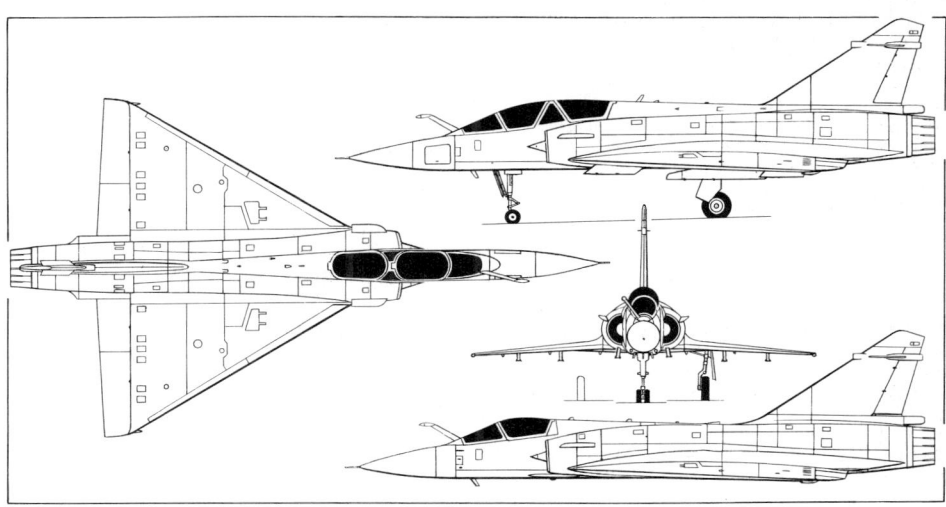

Dassault Mirage 2000N, with added side view (bottom) of Mirage 2000C *(Pilot Press)*

T-O weight clean: 2000C	10,860 kg (23,940 lb)	
2000B	10,960 kg (24,165 lb)	
Max T-O weight: 2000C and B	17,000 kg (37,480 lb)	
Max wing loading:		
2000C and B	414.63 kg/m² (84.97 lb/sq ft)	

PERFORMANCE (Mirage 2000C):
Max level speed	over Mach 2.2
Max continuous speed	Mach 2.2
	(800 knots; 1,482 km/h; 921 mph IAS)

Max speed at low altitude without afterburning, carrying eight 250 kg bombs and two Magic missiles
over 600 knots (1,110 km/h; 690 mph)
Min speed in stable flight
100 knots (185 km/h; 115 mph)
Max rate of climb at S/L 17,060 m (56,000 ft)/min
Time to 15,000 m (49,200 ft) and Mach 2 4 min
Time from brake release to intercept target flying at Mach 3 at 24,400 m (80,000 ft) less than 5 min
Service ceiling 18,000 m (59,000 ft)
Range: with four 250 kg bombs
more than 800 nm (1,480 km; 920 miles)
with two 1,700 litre drop tanks
more than 1,000 nm (1,850 km; 1,150 miles)

with one 1,300 litre and two 1,700 litre drop tanks
1,800 nm (3,335 km; 2,073 miles)
g limits: +9 normal
+13.5 ultimate

DASSAULT RAFALE

The Rafale (Squall) satisfies two French requirements: ACT (Avion de Combat Tactique) to replace air force Jaguars in the strike/attack role and ACM (Avion de Combat Marine), supplanting the navy's Crusaders and Super Étendards. An experimental prototype, the Rafale A, flew on 4 July 1986 and, following replacement of the port GE F404 afterburning turbofan by a SNECMA M88, returned to the air on 27 February 1990. It continues development flying — having completed over 500 sorties by the end of 1990 — and was last described in the 1990-91 edition.

Dassault foresees a market for 800 to 1,200 Rafales, of which 250 are required by the French Air Force and 86 by the French Navy. The ACE International (Avion de Combat Européen) GIE was set up in 1987 (see 1990-91 and earlier *Jane's*) by Dassault Aviation, SNECMA, Thomson-CSF and Dassault Electronique, partly to seek international partners for the development and production phases, although none had come forward by early 1991. Programme costs are estimated as FFr130 billion, including FFr40 billion for R&D and production tooling.

The definitive Rafale C is slightly smaller than the A demonstrator, with radar-suppressant modifications including profile changes at the rear fuselage/wing junction. Canards are larger and use of new constructional materials has been increased from 35 to 50 per cent by weight — half comprising carbon composites. A curved strake from the wingroot to the outer intake wall on the starboard side is above the outlet for a 30 mm cannon, re-positioned from port. The fin shape is revised and includes housing for a radar warning receiver. A new nosewheel leg has two wheels instead of one, whilst the cockpit canopy no longer has a fixed rear section. Ejection seat angle is reduced from 32° to 29°, the pilot having an improved view for carrier landings because of a 1° 30′ lower nose-line.

Five prototypes are planned of the three production versions. The air force is to receive both single and two-seat trainer forms which, following Mirage precedent, will be the **Rafale C** and **B** sub-types, respectively. Both are sometimes referred to loosely as the Rafale D (for Discret, meaning stealthy). Naval aviation is assigned the monoplace **Rafale M** (Marine). The first prototype, single-seat C01, was ordered on 21 April 1988 and was unveiled at St Cloud on 29 October 1990. It was then dismantled and transported to Istres for its first flight in April 1991, undertaken on two

Dassault Mirage 2000-5 development aircraft with Matra Mica AAMs under fuselage *(Aviaplans)*

Dassault Rafale C at rollout ceremony

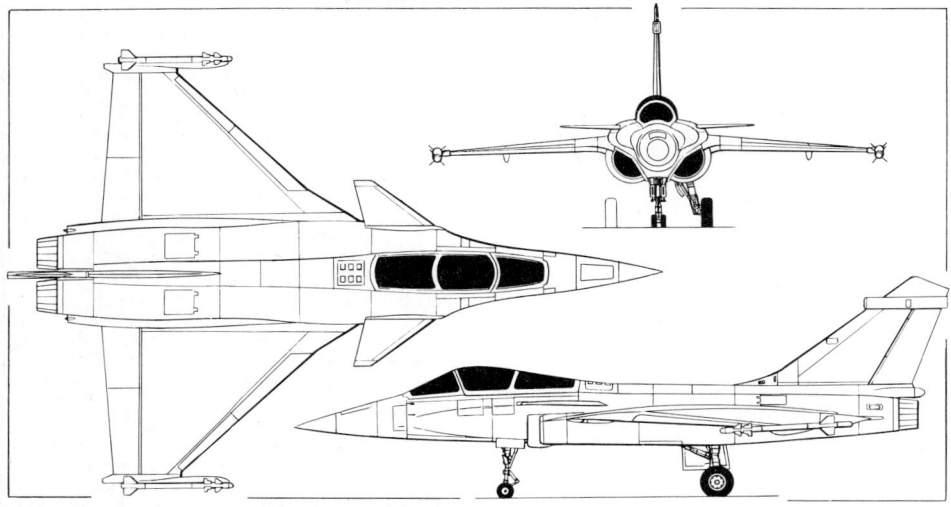

Dassault Rafale C production tactical combat aircraft (*Pilot Press*)

M88 power plants. Second prototype M01, ordered December 1988, was to follow soon afterwards, and both these aircraft will have basic avionics only. A third prototype was ordered on 12 July 1989 as two-seat B01, and will be the first with RBG radar fitted when it flies in January 1993. Aircraft M02 was ordered in 1990, and funding is awaited for C02 to complete the programme. The five prototypes are intended to contribute a total of 5,000 hours to the flight test programme by 1998. A static airframe (CEM) will be delivered to CEAT at Toulouse in October 1991 for fatigue testing.

First production orders will be placed in the 1992 budget, and between 1995 and 2007 it is intended to order 28 Rafales per year against a current requirement for 336: 225 Cs and 25 Bs for the air force and 86 Ms for the navy. Further aircraft will be required if the Rafale is selected to replace the Mirage F1-CR in reconnaissance roles and supplant Mirage IVPs as strategic nuclear strike aircraft. In order to accelerate service entry — particularly to the navy for urgent replacement of LTV Crusader interceptors — the first 20 Rafales for each service will be to the interim S01 standard, lacking ASMP, automatic terrain-following, automatic defensive subsystems, helmet-mounted sight, forward sector electro-optics and voice-commanded controls. Subsequent deliveries will be in definitive S02 configuration, although an avionics upgrade may be introduced in 2005.

Production deliveries are due to begin on 1 July 1996, the Aéronavale receiving 20 in 1996-99 for re-equipment of 12 Flottille. Initially deployed aboard the current-generation aircraft carrier *Foch*, the aircraft will be limited by catapult restrictions to a take-off weight of 16,500 kg (36,376 lb), pending availability of the new *Charles de Gaulle*. After gaining one Rafale in 1996, the Armée de l'Air will receive 41 in 1997-99 to convert the 30ème Escadre de Chasse at Reims. Production will then continue at 28 per year until 2009, with the navy sharing output between 2005 and the end of production for its balance of 66. Rafale Ms suffer a weight penalty of 760 kg (1,675 lb) for naval features including a strengthened main landing gear to absorb sink rates of up to 6.5 m (21 ft)/s; nose gear launch mechanism; and hydraulic arrester hook. Carbonfibre construction will not permit wings to be hinged for folding aboard ship.

Rafale radar will be the two-axis electronic scanning Thomson-CSF/Dassault Electronique RBE2 (Radar à Balayage Electronique Deux Plans) for which a develop-

ment contract was awarded in November 1989. Parameters include a 54 nm (100 km; 62 mile) air-to-air detection range. RBE2 was due to fly in a Mystère 20 testbed in Spring 1991.

TYPE: Single-seat interceptor and multi-role fighter.

WINGS: Cantilever multi-spar mid-wing monoplane of compound delta planform. Most of wing components made from carbonfibre, including two-segment (three on Rafale A) full span elevons on each trailing-edge. Wing spar/fuselage attachment fittings of aluminium-lithium alloy. Elevons can be deflected simultaneously or differentially. Full span two-segment leading-edge slats of SPF-DB titanium on each wing operate automatically with the elevons to alter wing camber and provide high lift. Slats made from titanium. Wingroot and tip fairings of Kevlar. All movable surfaces actuated by fly-by-wire control system, via hydraulic actuators. Shoulder-mounted active foreplanes of sweptback planform, actuated hydraulically by fly-by-wire control system. Made primarily of superplastic-formed diffusion-bonded titanium. Foreplanes automatically raised to 20° on selection of landing gear down, to provide additional lift.

FUSELAGE: Conventional semi-monocoque structure; 50 per cent carbonfibre. Forward fuselage primarily of conventional alloys (apart from air intakes); rear fuselage of carbonfibre. Side-fuselage skin panels of aluminium-lithium alloy. Kevlar fibre nosecone and jetpipe fairings. Wheel doors and engine doors of carbonfibre. Dorsal spine fairing from rear of canopy to jet nozzles. Forward hinged door type airbrake above engine duct on each side of fin leading-edge.

TAIL UNIT: Fin and inset rudder only, of sweptback form, made primarily of carbonfibre, with honeycomb core in rudder. Aramid fibre fin tip. Rudder actuated hydraulically by fly-by-wire control system. No tabs.

LANDING GEAR: Hydraulically retractable tricycle type supplied by Messier-Bugatti, with single mainwheels and twin, hydraulically steerable, nosewheels. All wheels retract forward. Designed for impact at vertical speed of 4 m (13 ft)/s, without flare-out. Michelin radial tyres. Mainwheel tyres size 810 × 275-15, pressure 16.0 bars (232 lb/sq in). Nosewheel tyre size 550 × 200-10. Carbon brakes on all three units, controlled by fly-by-wire system. Brake-chute for emergency use in cylindrical container at base of rudder. Rafale M has 'jump strut' nosewheel leg which releases energy stored in the shock absorber at the end of the deck take-off run, changing the aircraft's attitude for climbout without need for a ski-jump ramp. Dowty Aerospace Yakima holdback fitting. Hydraulic (Rafale M) or tension-stored (Rafale B/C) arrester hook.

POWER PLANT: Two SNECMA M88-2 augmented turbofans, each rated at 48.7 kN (10,950 lb st) dry and 72.9 kN (16,400 lb st) with afterburning. M88-3 of 87 kN (19,558 lb st) max rating in production aircraft. Kidney shape plain air intakes, with splitter plates, mounted low on centre-fuselage. Internal tanks for more than 5,325 litres (1,406 US gallons; 1,171 Imp gallons) of fuel. One 1,700 litre (449 US gallon; 374 Imp gallon) drop tank on centreline; 2,000 litre (528 US gallon; 440 Imp gallon) drop tank on each inboard underwing pylon; and/or 1,300 litre (343 US gallon; 286 Imp gallon) tank on each centre underwing pylon. Max external fuel 6,600 litres (1,742 US gallons; 1,452 Imp gallons). Fixed (detachable) in-flight refuelling probe on Rafale B/C; retractable probe on Rafale M.

ACCOMMODATION: Pilot only, on SEMMB licence-built Martin-Baker Mk 15 zero/zero ejection seat, reclined at angle of 29°. One-piece blister windscreen/canopy, hinged to open sideways to starboard. Canopy gold-coated for radar deflection. HOTAS (hands on throttle and stick) controls, with sidestick controller on starboard console and small-travel throttle lever.

SYSTEMS: Bootstrap cockpit air-conditioning system. Dual hydraulic circuits, pressure 280 bars (4,000 lb/sq in), each with two Messier-Bugatti pumps. Variable frequency electrical system, with two 30/40kVA Auxilec alternators. Triplex digital plus one dual analog fly-by-wire flight control system, integrated with engine controls and linked with weapons system. Eros oxygen system.

AVIONICS: Provision for more than 780 kg (1,720 lb) of avionics equipment and racks, including Thomson-CSF/Dassault Electronique RBE2 lookdown/shootdown radar, able to track up to eight targets simultaneously, with automatic threat assessment and allocation of priority. Sagem Uliss 52X INS. Digital CRT display of fuel, engine, hydraulic, electrical, oxygen and other systems information. Wide-angle diffractive optics HUD, collimated eye-level display and lateral multi-function colour displays by Thomson-CSF/Sfena. TRT com. Socrat VOR/ILS. Sextant Avionique voice activated radio controls and voice alarm warning system. LMT SC25 Mk XII IFF. Spectra radar warning and ECM suite by Thomson-CSF, Dassault Electronique and Matra; Sextant Avionique Navstar/GPS; EAS V/UHF and TRT Saturn UHF radios; Microturbo APU; Thomson-CSF helmet sight; TRT radio altimeter. Communications via SINTAC/JTIDS. Various reconnaissance/ECM pods.

ARMAMENT: One 30 mm GIAT M791B cannon in side of port engine duct. Fourteen external stores attachments: two on fuselage centreline, two beneath engine intakes, two astride rear fuselage, six under wings and two at wingtips. Forward centreline position deleted on Rafale M. Normal external load 6,000 kg (13,228 lb); max

Model of the Rafale M naval version showing 'jump strut' nosewheel with launch bar (*Paul Jackson*)

permissible, 8,000 kg (17,637 lb). In strike role, one Aerospatiale ASMP stand-off nuclear weapon. In interception role, up to eight Matra Mica AAMs (with IR or active homing) and two underwing fuel tanks; or six Micas and 5,700 litres (1,505 US gallons; 1,254 Imp gallons) of external fuel. In air-to-ground role, typically sixteen 227 kg (500 lb) bombs, two Micas and two 1,300 litre (343 US gallon; 286 Imp gallon) tanks; or two Apache stand-off weapon dispensers, two Micas and 5,700 litres of external fuel; or FLIR pod, Atlis laser designator pod, two 1,000 kg (2,205 lb) laser guided bombs, two AS.30L laser ASMs, four Micas and single 1,700 litre (449 US gallon; 374 Imp gallon) tank. In anti-ship role, two sea-skimming missiles, four Micas and 4,300 litres (1,135 US gallons; 946 Imp gallons) of external fuel.

DIMENSIONS, EXTERNAL:
Wing span, incl wingtip missiles 10.90 m (35 ft 9⅛ in)
Length overall 15.30 m (50 ft 2⅜ in)
Height overall (Rafale D) 5.34 m (17 ft 6¼ in)

AREAS:
Wings, gross 46.00 m² (495.1 sq ft)

WEIGHTS AND LOADINGS (estimated):
Basic weight empty, equipped:
Rafale D 9,060 kg (19,973 lb)
Rafale M 9,800 kg (21,605 lb)
Max external load 6,000 kg (13,228 lb)
Max ramp weight: initial version 19,500 kg (42,990 lb)
developed version 21,500 kg (47,399 lb)

PERFORMANCE (estimated):
Max level speed: at altitude Mach 2
at low level 750 knots (1,390 km/h; 864 mph)
Approach speed 115 knots (213 km/h; 132 mph)
T-O distance: air defence 400 m (1,312 ft)
attack 600 m (1,969 ft)
Radius of action: low-level penetration with twelve 250 kg (551 lb) bombs, four Mica AAMs and 4,300 litres (1,135 US gallons; 946 Imp gallons) of external fuel in three tanks 590 nm (1,093 km; 679 miles)
air-to-air, long-range with eight Mica AAMs and 6,600 litres (1,742 US gallons; 1,452 Imp gallons) of external fuel in four tanks, 12,200 m (40,000 ft) transit 1,000 nm (1,853 km; 1,152 miles)
g limits +9.0/−3.6

DASSAULT ATLANTIQUE 2 (ATL2)

The Atlantique 2, or ATL2 (formerly ANG: Atlantique Nouvelle Génération), is a twin-turboprop maritime patrol aircraft derived directly from the earlier Atlantic that was produced in 1964-73 for operation by the armed services of France (40, of which three were sold subsequently to Pakistan), the German Federal Republic (20, including five special-purpose elint/sigint aircraft), Italy (18) and the Netherlands (nine, of which five survivors transferred to French Navy and one sold back to Dassault for transfer to Pakistan in October 1988). Comprehensive avionics update programmes have been undertaken on 14 Atlantics of the German Navy by Dornier in 1979-84 and on Italian aircraft by Aeronavali (see under Alenia heading).

Design definition of the ATL2 was initiated by the French government in July 1977, with the aim of providing a replacement for the first generation Atlantic (now known retrospectively as the Atlantic 1) during the period from 1988 to 1996. This led to launch of the development phase of the ATL2 programme in September 1978.

Two ATL2 prototypes were produced by modification of Atlantic 1 airframes. Work started in January 1979, and the first prototype flew for the first time in its new form on 8 May 1981, followed by the second on 26 March 1982. Series production was authorised on 24 May 1984 and the first production aircraft flew on 19 October 1988. This was formally accepted by the French Navy two days later, at the start of a 100-hour flight trials programme. The aircraft, No. 1, was delivered to Lann-Bihoué for acceptance by 23 Flottille on 26 October 1989, and this unit was declared operational with three Atlantiques on 1 February 1991. Also at Lann, 24 F will equip with eight Atlantiques from 1992 onwards, followed by 21 F and 22 F at Nîmes-Garons, on the Mediterranean seaboard, from 1994 and 1998.

The French Navy requirement is for 42 aircraft, of which two were funded in 1985, followed by three, five, six, five, three and three in 1986-91. Of these, 22 were on firm order by January 1991. Economies have forced a future ceiling of three aircraft per year after 1993, delaying the final delivery until 2001. The work is being shared by most members of the European SECBAT (Société d'Étude et de Construction du Breguet Atlantic) consortium that was responsible for the earlier programme, with some modification of the work-split to reflect varying national interests in the ATL2 aircraft. Companies involved, under Dassault Aviation direction, are Sabca and Sonaca of Belgium, MBB and Dornier of Germany, Alenia of Italy and Aerospatiale of France. The Tyne engines are being produced by SNECMA of France, Rolls-Royce of the UK, FN of Belgium and MTU of Germany; and propellers by Ratier of France and British Aerospace. Production Atlantique No. 2 flew on 20 December 1989. Subsequent aircraft are being built at Bordeaux, following closure of the Toulouse-Colomiers plant.

Structural changes by comparison with the Atlantic 1 include use of a refined bonding technique, improved anti-corrosion protection, better sealing between skin panels, and design improvements offering longer fatigue life and more economical maintenance. These are intended to ensure increased serviceability, with at least 75 per cent of squadron aircraft permanently available for operations; readiness to take off within 30 minutes of an order to go; and an aircraft life of 30 years.

First production Dassault Atlantique 2 (ATL2) maritime patrol aircraft

The basic mission performance requirements envisaged for the ATL2 are similar to those of the Atlantic 1: a high cruising speed to the operational area, quick descent from cruising altitude to patrol height, lengthy patrol endurance at low altitude, and a high degree of manoeuvrability at sea level. It is able to carry a wide variety of weapons and equipment for finding and attacking both submarines and surface targets in all weathers. In particular, its Thomson-CSF Iguane search radar can detect large ships at a range of 150-200 nm (275-370 km; 170-230 miles), and small targets such as submarine schnorkels over 'several dozen nautical miles' in rough seas.

Like the original Atlantic, the ATL2 is able to perform minelaying, logistic support, and passenger and freight transport missions. It could be adapted for advanced AEW duties, and is suitable for civilian tasks such as air/sea rescue and patrol of offshore fishing and oil interests.

During 1988, Dassault announced that it is considering an Atlantique 3 development programme. Following cancellation in 1990 of the Lockheed P-7, which had been ordered by Germany, Dassault sought to promote a European maritime patrol aircraft programme, provisionally named Europatrol. This would 'not necessarily' be based on the Atlantique 2.

TYPE: Twin-turboprop maritime patrol aircraft.

WINGS: Cantilever mid-wing monoplane, with streamlined ESM pods on tips. Wing section NACA 64 series. Dihedral 6° on outer panels only. Incidence 3°. Tapered planform, with 9° sweepback on leading-edge. All-metal three-spar fail-safe structure, with bonded light alloy honeycomb skin panels on torsion box and on main landing gear doors. Two conventional all-metal ailerons on each wing, actuated by SAMM twin-cylinder jacks. All-metal slotted flaps, with bonded light alloy honeycomb filling, in three segments on each wing, over 75 per cent of span. Three hinged spoilers on upper surface of each outer wing, forward of flaps. Metal airbrake above and below each wing. No trim tabs. Air Equipement/Kléber-Colombes pneumatic de-icing system on leading-edges.

FUSELAGE: All-metal double-bubble fail-safe structure, with bonded honeycomb sandwich skin on pressurised central section of upper lobe, upward sliding weapons bay doors and nosewheel door. Large air intake and duct for air-conditioning system on each side of nose.

TAIL UNIT: Cantilever all-metal structure, with bonded honeycomb sandwich skin panels on torsion boxes. Slightly bulged housing for ESM antennae at top of fin leading-edge. Fixed incidence tailplane, with dihedral. Control surfaces operated through SAMM twin-cylinder jacks. No trim tabs. Air Equipement/Kléber-Colombes pneumatic de-icing system on leading-edges.

LANDING GEAR: Retractable tricycle type, supplied by Messier-Bugatti, with twin wheels on each unit. Hydraulic retraction, nosewheels rearward, main units forward into engine nacelles. Kléber-Colombes or Dunlop tyres; size 39 × 13-20 on mainwheels, pressure 12 bars (170 lb/sq in), 26 × 7.75-13 on nosewheels, pressure 6.5 bars (94 lb/sq in). New Messier-Bugatti disc brakes with higher braking energy, and Modistop anti-skid units.

POWER PLANT: Two 4,549 kW (6,100 ehp) Rolls-Royce Tyne RTy.20 Mk 21 turboprops, each driving a four-blade Ratier/British Aerospace constant-speed metal propeller type PD 249/476/3 on prototypes. Four pressure-refuelled integral fuel tanks in wings, with total capacity of 23,120 litres (6,108 US gallons; 5,085 Imp gallons). Updated gauging system. Oil capacity 100 litres (26.5 US gallons; 22 Imp gallons).

ACCOMMODATION: Normal flight crew of 10-12, comprising observer in glazed nose; pilot, co-pilot and flight engineer on flight deck; a radio-navigator, ESM-ECM-MAD operator, radar-IFF operator, tactical co-ordinator and two acoustic sensor operators at stations on the starboard side of the tactical compartment; and two optional observers in beam positions at the rear. Rest/relief crew compartment in centre of fuselage. Primary access via extending airstair door in bottom of rear fuselage. Emergency exits above and below flight deck and on each side, above wing trailing-edge.

SYSTEMS: Air-conditioning system supplied by two compressors driven by gearboxes. Heat exchangers and bootstrap system for cabin temperature control. Duplicated hydraulic system, pressure 186 bars (2,700 lb/sq in), to operate flying controls, landing gear, flaps, weapons bay doors and retractable radome. Hydraulic flow rate 17.85 litres (4.7 US gallons; 3.9 Imp gallons)/min. Three basic electrical systems: variable frequency three-phase 115/200V AC system, with two 60/80kVA Auxilec alternators and modernised control and protection equipment; fixed frequency three-phase 115/200V 400Hz AC system, with four 15kVA Auxilec Auxivar generators, two on each engine; 28V DC system, with four 6kW transformer-rectifiers supplied from the variable frequency AC system, and one 40Ah battery. One 60kVA emergency AC generator, driven at constant speed by APU. Individual oxygen bottles for emergency use. Electric anti-icing for engine air intake lips, propeller blades and spinners. Turbomeca/ABG/SEMCA Astadyne gas turbine APU for engine starting, emergency electrical supply, and air-conditioning on ground.

AVIONICS: SAT/TRT Tango forward-looking infra-red sensor in turret under nose. Thomson-CSF Iguane retractable radar immediately forward of weapons bay, with integrated LMT IFF interrogator and SECRE decoder. Thomson-TRT 35 cameras in starboard side of nose and in bottom of rear fuselage. Sextant Avionique MAD in lengthened tail sting. Thomson-CSF Arar 13A radar detector for ESM. Thomson-CSF Sadang system for processing active and passive acoustic detection data. A distributed data processing system around a databus, with a CIMSA Mitra 125X tactical computer (512K words memory), two Dassault Electronique bus computers, two Sagem magnetic bubble mass memories and Thomson-CSF display subsystem. Other equipment includes IFF transponder and HF com by LMT, UHF AM/FM by Sintra, Tacan and DME by Thomson-CSF, VHF AM/FM com by Socrat, VOR/ILS by EAS, TRT radio altimeter, Collins MF radio compass, ADF, HSI and autopilot/flight director by SFENA, dual Sagem Uliss 53 inertial navigation systems coupled to a GPS/Navstar receiver, Sagem high-speed printer and terminal display, Sextant Avionique navigation table and air data computer.

ARMAMENT: Main weapons bay, 2.1 m x 9.0 m x 1.0 m (6 ft 10¾ in x 29 ft 6¼ in x 3 ft 3¼ in) in unpressurised lower fuselage can accommodate all NATO standard bombs, depth charges, up to eight Mk 46 homing torpedoes, seven French Murène advanced torpedoes or two air-to-surface missiles (typical load comprises three torpedoes and one AM 39 Exocet or AS 37 Martel missile). Max internal weapons load 2,500 kg (5,511 lb). Four underwing attachments for up to 3,500 kg (7,716 lb) of stores, including future air-to-surface and air-to-air missiles or pods.

EQUIPMENT: More than 100 sonobuoys, with Alkan pneumatic launcher, in compartment aft of weapons bay, where whole of upper and lower fuselage provides storage for sonobuoys and 160 smoke markers and flares.

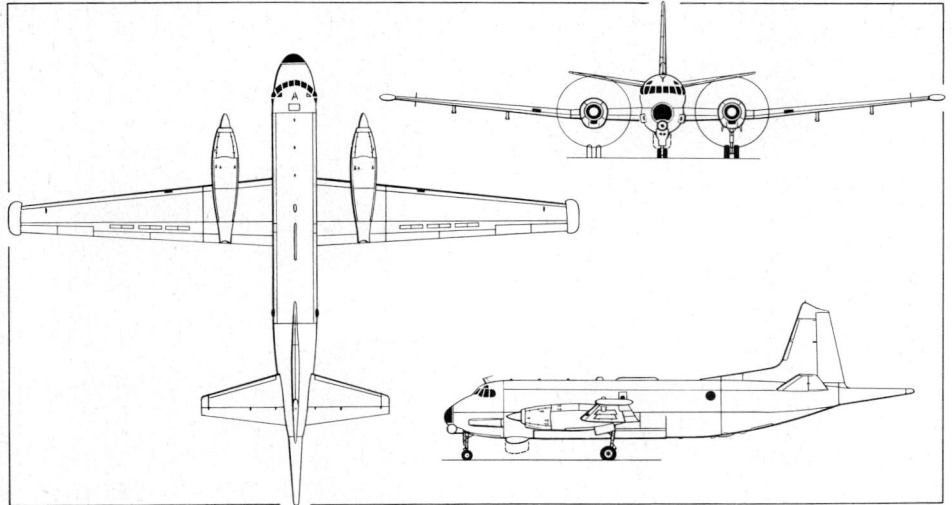

Dassault Atlantique 2 (ATL2) twin-turboprop maritime patrol aircraft (*Pilot Press*)

DIMENSIONS, EXTERNAL:
Wing span, incl wingtip pods	37.42 m (122 ft 9¼ in)
Wing aspect ratio	10.9
Length overall	33.63 m (110 ft 4 in)
Height overall	10.89 m (35 ft 8¾ in)
Fuselage: Max depth	4.00 m (13 ft 1½ in)
Tailplane span	12.31 m (40 ft 4½ in)
Wheel track (c/l of shock struts)	9.00 m (29 ft 6¼ in)
Wheelbase	9.40 m (30 ft 10 in)
Propeller diameter	4.88 m (16 ft 0 in)
Distance between propeller centres	
	9.00 m (29 ft 6¼ in)
Main weapons bay: Length	9.00 m (29 ft 6¼ in)
Width	2.10 m (6 ft 10¾ in)

DIMENSIONS, INTERNAL:
Cabin, incl rest compartment, galley, toilet, aft observers' stations: Length	18.50 m (60 ft 8½ in)
Max width	3.60 m (11 ft 9½ in)
Max height	2.00 m (6 ft 6¾ in)
Floor area	155.0 m² (1,668 sq ft)
Volume	92.0 m³ (3,250 cu ft)

AREAS:
Wings, gross	120.34 m² (1,295.3 sq ft)
Ailerons (total)	5.26 m² (56.62 sq ft)
Flaps (total)	26.42 m² (284.38 sq ft)
Spoilers (total)	1.66 m² (17.87 sq ft)
Vertical tail surfaces (total)	16.64 m² (179.11 sq ft)
Rudder	5.96 m² (64.15 sq ft)
Horizontal tail surfaces (total)	32.50 m² (349.83 sq ft)
Elevators	8.30 m² (89.34 sq ft)

WEIGHTS AND LOADINGS:
Weight empty, equipped, standard mission	
	25,600 kg (56,438 lb)
Military load:	
ASW or ASSW mission	3,000 kg (6,600 lb)
Max fuel	18,500 kg (40,785 lb)
Standard mission T-O weight:	
ASW or ASSW mission	44,200 kg (97,440 lb)
combined ASW/ASSW mission	
	45,000 kg (99,200 lb)
Max T-O weight	46,200 kg (101,850 lb)
Normal design landing weight	36,000 kg (79,365 lb)
Max landing weight	46,000 kg (101,400 lb)
Max zero-fuel weight	32,500 kg (71,650 lb)
Max wing loading	385 kg/m² (78.96 lb/sq ft)
Max power loading	5.07 kg/kW (8.34 lb/ehp)

PERFORMANCE (with metal propellers, at T-O weight of 45,000 kg; 99,200 lb except where indicated):
Max Mach number	0.73
Max level speed at optimum height	
	350 knots (648 km/h; 402 mph)
Max level speed at S/L	320 knots (592 km/h; 368 mph)
Max cruising speed at 7,620 m (25,000 ft)	
	300 knots (555 km/h; 345 mph)
Normal patrol speed, S/L to 1,525 m (5,000 ft)	
	170 knots (315 km/h; 195 mph)
Stalling speed, flaps down	
	90 knots (167 km/h; 104 mph)
Max rate of climb at S/L:	
AUW of 30,000 kg (66,140 lb)	884 m (2,900 ft)/min
AUW of 40,000 kg (88,185 lb)	610 m (2,000 ft)/min
Rate of climb at S/L, one engine out:	
AUW of 30,000 kg (66,140 lb)	365 m (1,200 ft)/min
AUW of 40,000 kg (88,185 lb)	213 m (700 ft)/min
Service ceiling	9,145 m (30,000 ft)
Runway LCN at max T-O weight	60
T-O to 10.7 m (35 ft)	1,840 m (6,037 ft)
Landing from 15 m (50 ft)	1,500 m (4,922 ft)
170 knot turning radius at AUW of 40,000 kg (88,185 lb)	
at: 30° bank	1,380 m (4,530 ft)
45° bank	800 m (2,625 ft)
60° bank	460 m (1,510 ft)

Typical mission profiles, with reserves of 5% total fuel, 5% of fuel consumed and 20 min hold-off:

anti-ship mission: T-O with max fuel and one AM 39 missile; fly 1,800 nm (3,333 km; 2,071 miles) to target area; descend for two-hour search and attack at 90 m (300 ft); return to base

anti-submarine mission: T-O at 44,300 kg (97,665 lb) AUW with 15,225 kg (33,565 lb) of fuel, four Mk 46 torpedoes, 78 sonobuoys, and a full load of markers and flares; cruise to search area at 290 knots (537 km/h; 333 mph) at 7,620 m (25,000 ft); descend for 8 h low altitude patrol at 600 nm (1,110 km; 690 miles) from base, or 5 h patrol at 1,000 nm (1,850 km; 1,150 miles) from base; return to base at 9,145 m (30,000 ft). Total mission time 12 h 31 min

Ferry range with max fuel	
	4,900 nm (9,075 km; 5,635 miles)
Max endurance	18 h

DASSAULT SUPER ÉTENDARD

Production of the original, carrier-based, version of this single-seat transonic strike fighter for the navies of France (71 aircraft) and Argentina (14 aircraft) ended in 1983. However, in late 1986 the French Navy signed a contract to initiate study of a weapon system modernisation, including replacement of the existing Agave radar by the Dassault Electronique Anémone, having twice the detection range against surface targets; a new Sagem INS and UAT 90 computer; a Thomson-CSF wide-angle HUD with TV or IR overlay; and cockpit modernisation, including an electronic warfare display screen, HOTAS controls and provision for pilot's night vision goggles. An additional fuselage stores pylon will be added. Minimal structural changes are required for the aircraft to achieve an extended life of 6,500 hours by 2005, when replacement by Rafale Ms is to begin.

A prototype conversion flew at Dassault's Istres plant on 5 October 1990. The first two of an eventual 56 re-worked aircraft will be delivered by Dassault in late 1992, the remainder being modified by the navy's Atelier d'Aviation at Cuers. Initial conversions will temporarily retain Agave radar, as Anémone will not be available until mid-1994. Thomson-CSF TMV 011 Sherloc radar warning receivers will also be a later retrofit. Funding for the first 10 conversions was included in the 1991 defence budget.

Offers by Dassault to re-launch Super Étendard production for land-based operations, and to transfer production to IPTN of Indonesia, have not been taken up. A full description appeared in the 1982-83 edition of *Jane's*, and expanded weapon options for the land-based version in 1989-90.

DASSAULT (BREGUET) ALIZÉ

In the early 1980s, 28 Aéronavale Alizé shipboard maritime patrol aircraft were modernised, as last described in the 1985-86 *Jane's*. A further, less extensive re-work for 24 of these was begun at the Cuers naval workshops in 1990, involving addition of a Sagem MTP16 micro-computer integrated with a system of tactical data processing and transmission, improved decoy systems and INS data links. The Alizé will be retained in land- and sea-based service until early in the next century.

CRUSADER

Originally due to have been retired on 30 June 1993, the French Navy's Vought F-8E(FN) Crusader carrier-based interceptors will be updated for up to five more years of service before their operating squadron, 12 Flottille at Landivisiau, has completed conversion to Rafale Ms. In 1989, Dassault was contracted to determine the required changes, although work will be performed by the navy's own workshops at Atelier d'Aviation de Cuers, on 17 of the

19 Crusaders remaining from 42 delivered. Apart from a radar warning receiver, modifications are expected to concentrate on alleviation of airframe fatigue, replacement of wiring and ejection seats, and a navigation equipment update. Re-deliveries will begin in June 1992 and should be completed by December 1994.

DASSAULT MYSTÈRE-FALCON 20 and 200
US Coast Guard designation: HU-25 Guardian

The Mystère-Falcon 200 twin-turbofan light transport was based on the Mystère 20 design, first flown in prototype form on 4 May 1963. Manufacture of the Mystère-Falcon 200 began with aircraft c/n 401, first flown on 30 April 1980, concurrent with the production rundown of the earlier Mystère-Falcon 20F series, the last of which (c/n 486) came off the assembly line in late 1983. The model 200 had been introduced, originally as the Mystère-Falcon 20H, at the 1981 Paris Air Show, with Garrett turbofans in place of the F's General Electric CF700s, larger integral fuel tankage in the rear fuselage, redesigned wingroot fairings, automatic slat extension, and many important systems changes. Certification was achieved on 21 June 1981.

One aircraft was built in 1988, completing production of 473 Mystère-Falcon 20s and 35 Mystère-Falcon 200s. Several have been, and are being, converted for specific duties, as listed below, while Mystère-Falcon 20s are eligible for re-engining to 20-5 standard (described separately under the Garrett entry in USA section).

Calibration: Ten Mystère-Falcons, in several different variants, have been delivered to the French DGAC, French Air Force, and authorities in Spain (designation TM.11), Indonesia and Iran, for navaid calibration. Most are equipped with Dassault-designed high/low level navigation facility calibration systems, some in the form of a removable console.

Airline crew training: Mystère-Falcon 20s have been used by Air France to train pilots for its jet airliners, with up to five aircraft being used simultaneously. Japan Air Lines also used three of this version.

Quick-change and cargo: A quick-change kit, consisting of an assembly of nets and supports keeps the centre aisle free and allows direct access to nine freight compartments. Total usable volume of these compartments is 6.65 m³ (235 cu ft), and transformation from executive configuration to cargo configuration, or vice versa, takes less than one hour. A different specific cargo conversion was performed on 33 aircraft in the USA. For both versions the maximum zero-fuel weight of 9,980 kg (22,000 lb) allows a payload of up to 3,000 kg (6,615 lb).

Target towing: A Mystère-Falcon 20 is used by the French Air Force for target towing. It carries a Secapem target on an inboard hardpoint under each wing and a pod containing a winch and cable on each of two outboard hardpoints. Missions of up to 2 h duration can be flown, cruising at up to 300 knots (555 km/h; 345 mph) at 450 m (1,475 ft) or 270 knots (500 km/h; 310 mph) at 4,500 m (14,750 ft). The hardpoints (650 kg; 1,433 lb inboard, 750 kg; 1,650 lb outboard) can be used to carry alternative stores if required. Sixteen former Federal Express cargo aircraft operated by Flight Refuelling Ltd of the UK provide Royal Navy target facilities with equipment including an RM30A target winch, AN/ALQ-167 radar jammer, BOZ-3 chaff dispenser, AN/ALE-43 chaff/flare dispenser and ATRS-5 radar simulator, all mounted under the wings. Late in 1990 FR acquired five Falcon 20s from the Canadian armed forces for conversion and subsequent operation under anticipated French and NATO contracts.

Aerial photography: This version has two ventral camera bays fitted with optical glass windows. It is operated for high altitude photography, survey and scientific research in several countries. The camera installation can be supplemented by a multispectral scanner and other scientific loads.

Systems trainer: Five aircraft fitted with the combat radar and navigation systems of various Mirage types are in service with the French Air Force for training pilots. These comprise two Mystère **20SNA**s (Système de Navigation-Attaque — equivalent to the Mirage IIIE); and single examples of the **20SNR** (Système de Navigation-Reconnaissance — Mirage F1-CR) and versions equivalent to the Mirage 2000N and Mirage IV-P.

Ambulance: Up to three stretchers can be accommodated, together with a large supply of oxygen and equipment for intensive care and monitoring of patients. Cabinets near the door are removed to facilitate the loading of stretchers.

Electronic warfare: Norway, Canada and Morocco have been followed by several other nations, including Pakistan and Spain, in operating Mystère-Falcon 20 aircraft modified for ECM duties such as radar and communications intelligence and jamming.

Remote sensing: In 1988, a Falcon 20 owned by Innotech was fitted with infra-red mapping equipment supplied by the Canada Centre for Remote Sensing and used for fire-spotting by the forestry authorities in Idaho, USA.

Versions of the Falcon 20 supplied to the US Coast Guard have the following designations:

HU-25A Guardian: Basic version delivered in 1982-83 for search and rescue and offshore surveillance (described fully in 1985-86 *Jane's*). Total of 41 includes modified HU-25Bs and Cs.

HU-25B: Retrospective designation for variant tasked with location of sea pollution and identification of vessels responsible. Equipment comprises one of the six Aerojet Aireye detection systems ordered for the Guardian in the form of a Motorola AN/APS-131 SLAR pod under the forward fuselage, offset, starboard; a Texas Instruments RS-18C linescan unit in a starboard underwing pod; and a laser illuminated TV under the port wing.

HU-25C: Designation of eight Guardians converted to identify and track air or seaborne drug smugglers by means of a fighter type Westinghouse AN/APG-66 radar in the nose, and turret-mounted Texas Instruments WF-360 FLIR. Also fitted with secure HF/UHF/VHF-FM radio communications. Entered service 30 May 1988.

Two used Falcon 200s acquired by the Chilean Navy are being fitted with Thomson-CSF TRES (Tactical Radar and ESM System), including Varan radar, and will be capable of firing AM 39 Exocet.

Full data on the Mystère-Falcon 200 appeared in the 1988-89 and previous editions of *Jane's*. An abbreviated specification follows:

TYPE: Twin-turbofan executive transport.

WINGS: Cantilever low-wing monoplane. Thickness/chord ratio varies from 10.5 to 8 per cent. Dihedral 2°. Incidence 1° 30′. Sweepback at quarter-chord 30°. All-metal (copper bearing alloys) fail-safe torsion box structure with machined stressed skin. Hydraulically actuated airbrakes forward of the hydraulically actuated two-section, single-slotted flaps. Leading-edges anti-iced by engine bleed air.

FUSELAGE: All-metal semi-monocoque structure of circular cross-section, built on fail-safe principles.

TAIL UNIT: Cantilever all-metal structure, with variable-incidence tailplane mounted halfway up fin. No trim tabs.

LANDING GEAR: Retractable tricycle type, by Messier-Bugatti, with twin wheels on all three units. Hydraulic retraction. Max steering angle of nosewheel ±50° for taxying, ±180° for towing.

POWER PLANT: Two Garrett ATF 3-6A-4C turbofans (each rated at 23.13 kN; 5,200 lb st). Optional thrust reversers are produced by Hurel-Dubois. Fuel in two integral tanks in wings and large integral tank in rear fuselage, with total capacity of 6,000 litres (1,585 US gallons; 1,320 Imp gallons).

ACCOMMODATION: Flight deck for crew of two, with airline type instrumentation. Airstair door, with handrail, on port side. Main cabin normally seats nine passengers. Alternative arrangement provides 12 compact seats at a pitch of 76 cm (30 in).

SYSTEMS: Duplicated air-conditioning and pressurisation system. Two independent hydraulic systems. Electrical system includes a 9kW 28V DC starter/generator on each engine, three 750VA inverters and two 36Ah batteries. Solar T40 APU optional. Wing leading-edges and engine air inlets anti-iced with LP compressor bleed air.

AVIONICS: Collins FCS-80 flight control system standard, with dual Collins EFIS-86C electronic flight instrument system using colour CRTs. Standard avionics include duplicated VHF, VOR, ADF, DME and ATC transponder, one weather radar and one radio altimeter.

DIMENSIONS, EXTERNAL:
Wing span	16.32 m (53 ft 6½ in)
Wing aspect ratio	6.5
Length: overall	17.15 m (56 ft 3 in)
fuselage	15.55 m (51 ft 0 in)
Height overall	5.32 m (17 ft 5 in)
Wheel track	3.34 m (10 ft 11½ in)
Wheelbase	5.74 m (18 ft 10 in)
Passenger door: Height	1.52 m (5 ft 0 in)
Width	0.80 m (2 ft 7½ in)
Height to sill	1.09 m (3 ft 7 in)

DIMENSIONS, INTERNAL:
Cabin, incl fwd baggage space and rear toilet:
Length	7.26 m (23 ft 10 in)
Max width	1.79 m (5 ft 10½ in)
Max height	1.70 m (5 ft 7 in)
Volume	20.0 m³ (706 cu ft)
Baggage space (cabin)	0.65 m³ (23 cu ft)
Baggage compartment (rear fuselage)	
	0.80 m³ (28.2 cu ft)

AREAS:
Wings, gross	41.00 m² (441.3 sq ft)

WEIGHTS AND LOADINGS:
Weight empty, equipped	8,250 kg (18,190 lb)
Payload with max fuel	1,265 kg (2,790 lb)
Max fuel	4,845 kg (10,680 lb)
Max T-O and ramp weight	14,515 kg (32,000 lb)
Max zero-fuel weight	10,200 kg (22,500 lb)
Max landing weight	13,100 kg (28,800 lb)
Max wing loading	354.0 kg/m² (72.5 lb/sq ft)
Max power loading	313.8 kg/kN (3.08 lb/lb st)

PERFORMANCE:
Max operating Mach No.	0.865
Max operating speed:	
at S/L	350 knots (648 km/h; 402 mph) IAS
at 6,100 m (20,000 ft)	
	380 knots (704 km/h; 438 mph) IAS

Mystère-Falcon 20 modified by Flight Refuelling Ltd with underwing ECM training pods

Dassault Mystère-Falcon 20 converted to a radar testbed for CEV, France *(AGPPA)*

Max cruising speed at 9,150 m (30,000 ft) at AUW of
11,340 kg (25,000 lb)   470 knots (870 km/h; 541 mph)
Econ cruising speed at 12,500 m (41,000 ft)
    420 knots (780 km/h; 485 mph)
Stalling speed   84 knots (156 km/h; 97 mph)
Service ceiling   13,715 m (45,000 ft)
Min ground turning radius about nosewheel
    12.80 m (42 ft 0 in)
FAR 25 balanced T-O field length with 8 passengers and
 full fuel   1,420 m (4,660 ft)
FAR 121 landing distance with 8 passengers, FAR 121
reserves   1,130 m (3,710 ft)
Range with max fuel and 8 passengers at long-range
cruising speed, 45 min reserves
    2,510 nm (4,650 km; 2,890 miles)

DASSAULT GARDIAN 2

The Gardian 2 is a Falcon 200 fitted with a Thomson-CSF Varan radar for maritime detection, a Sextant Avionique Omega navigation system and four underwing hardpoints. With additional equipment, it can perform the following missions:

Target designation: This includes over-the-horizon targeting for maritime forces or coastal missile batteries; missile midcourse retargeting; control of surface operations; and strike guidance against surface ships or land objectives. Equipment includes a navigation table, UHF modem to transmit data, V/UHF DF, and IFF interrogator. Options include ESM, search windows, inertial platform, VHF/FM, HF and track-while-scan radar system.

AM 39 Exocet attack: As well as two Exocet sea-skimming air-to-surface missiles, this requires an inertial platform, Omega/INS interface, AM 39 interface and controls, and IFF interrogator. Options are track-while-scan, navigation table and ESM.

Electronic surveillance and countermeasures: This requires either Thomson-CSF DR 2000 ESM and navigation table, or an integrated system including a Thomson-CSF DR 4000 ESM, a computer, the Varan radar, an inertial platform and tactical visualisation elements from the Atlantique 2 system. Options include an IFF interrogator, AM 39 installation, track-while-scan, countermeasures or decoy pods, elint equipment, HF/VHF/UHF comint equipment and V/UHF DF.

Target towing: As for Falcon 200.

In all cases, the cabin can be arranged to permit secondary transport missions.

DASSAULT MYSTÈRE-FALCON 100

The 226th and last production Falcon 100 was delivered to Mexican charter operator Aeropersonal in September 1990. Full details appeared in the 1990-91 *Jane's*.

DASSAULT MYSTÈRE-FALCON 50

The Mystère-Falcon 50 three-turbofan executive transport has the same external fuselage cross-section as the Mystère-Falcon 200, but is an entirely new design, featuring area ruling and advanced wing aerodynamics. Normal layout is for a crew of two and eight or nine passengers, with provision for up to 12 passengers.

The original prototype (F-WAMD) flew for the first time on 7 November 1976, followed by a second prototype (F-WINR) on 18 February 1978 and the third (and sole pre-production) aircraft on 13 June 1978. DGAC certification was received on 27 February 1979, followed by FAA type approval on 7 March. Falcon 50 c/n 4, flown on 2 March 1979, was the first built on Dassault's Mérignac assembly line and became Falcon Jet's US demonstrator. Deliveries began in July 1979 and totalled 212 aircraft, registered to customers in 30 countries, by 31 December 1990. Since delivery of the fifth aircraft to the Armée de l'Air's GLAM (Groupe de Liaisons Aériennes Ministérielles) in early 1980, for use by the President of the French Republic, Mystère-Falcon 50s have been purchased for state VIP transportation in Djibouti, Iraq, Jordan, Libya, Morocco, Portugal, South Africa, Spain (designation T.16) and Yugoslavia. Three supplied to the Italian Air Force are equipped for both VIP and air ambulance duties.

Fuselages for the Mystère-Falcon 50 are produced at Aerospatiale's Saint-Nazaire works, tail units by Aerospatiale at Méaulte, and cowlings by Hurel-Dubois at Vélizy-Villacoublay.

TYPE: Three-turbofan executive transport.

WINGS: Cantilever low-wing monoplane, with compound leading-edge sweepback and optimised section. Each wing is attached to the central box structure by multiple bolts and forms an integral fuel tank. Full span leading-edge slats, of which the outboard sections are slotted. Double-slotted trailing-edge flaps and ailerons, latter with carbonfibre skin. Three-section two-position airbrakes on top surface of each wing.

FUSELAGE: All-metal semi-monocoque structure of circular cross-section, with aft baggage compartment included in pressure cell.

TAIL UNIT: Cantilever all-metal structure. Horizontal surfaces, with anhedral, mounted partway up fin. Tailplane incidence adjustable by screwjack, driven by two electric motors controlled by normal and emergency controls located respectively on the control wheels and pedestal.

LANDING GEAR: Retractable tricycle type by Messier-Bugatti, with twin wheels on each unit. Hydraulic retraction, main units inward, nosewheels forward. Nosewheel steerable ±60° for taxying, ±180° for towing. Mainwheel tyres size 26 × 6.6-14 in, pressure 14.34 bars (208 lb/sq in).

Dassault Mystère-Falcon 50 of the Italian Air Force

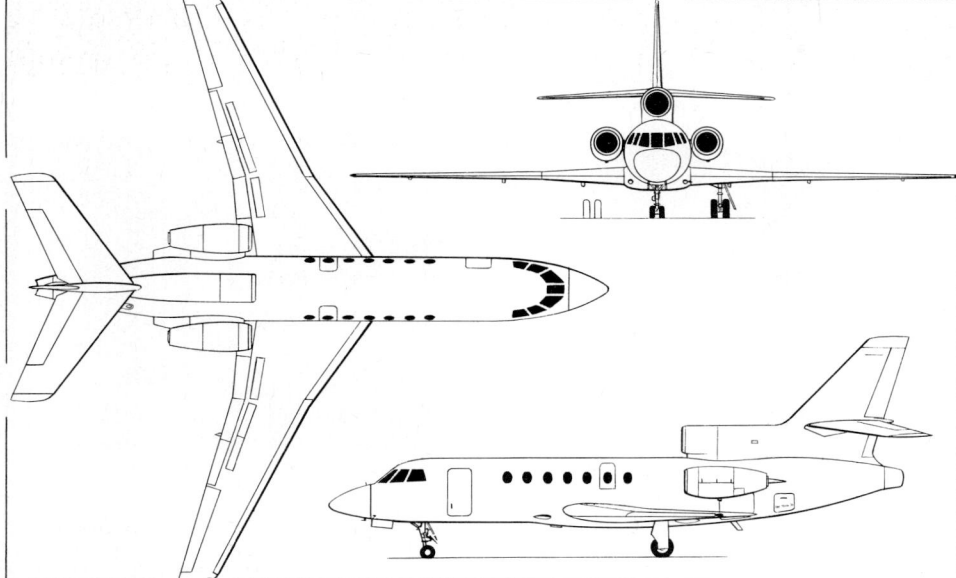

Dassault Mystère-Falcon 50 long-range three-turbofan executive transport *(Pilot Press)*

Nosewheel tyres size 14.5 × 5.5-6 in, pressure 8.96 bars (130 lb/sq in). Four-disc brakes designed for 400 landings with normal energy braking.

POWER PLANT: Three Garrett TFE731-3 turbofans, each rated at 16.5 kN (3,700 lb st) for take-off. Two engines pod mounted on sides of rear fuselage, the third attached by two top mounts. Thrust reverser on centre engine. Fuel in integral tanks, with capacity of 5,787 litres (1,529 US gallons; 1,273 Imp gallons) in wings and 2,976 litres (786 US gallons; 655 Imp gallons) in fuselage tanks. Total fuel capacity 8,763 litres (2,315 US gallons; 1,928 Imp gallons). Single point pressure fuelling.

ACCOMMODATION: Crew of two side by side on flight deck, with full dual controls and airline type instrumentation. Third seat to rear of co-pilot. Various cabin configurations available, based on two alternative toilet locations. An aft cabin toilet allows an eight/nine-passenger arrangement, with four chairs in forward cabin, facing each other in pairs, and a three-place sofa and two facing chairs in the rear cabin. A wardrobe, galley and crew toilet are located forward, in the entrance area. Alternatively, a forward toilet, facing the door, makes possible a lounge in the rear cabin, furnished with a four/five-place angle sofa and a chair. This rear lounge is separated from the forward cabin by either a wardrobe and refreshment/recreation console, or by two additional seats, raising the cabin accommodation to 12 persons. After removing forward cabin equipment (wardrobe and galley) and seats, the cabin will accommodate up to three stretchers, two doctors and medical equipment, or freight. The rear baggage compartment is pressurised and air-conditioned, and has a capacity of 1,000 kg (2,200 lb). Access is by a separate door on the port side.

SYSTEMS: Air-conditioning system utilises bleed air from all three engines. Max pressure differential 0.61 bars (8.8 lb/sq in). Pressurisation maintains a max cabin altitude of 2,440 m (8,000 ft) to a flight altitude of 13,700 m (45,000 ft). Two independent hydraulic systems, pressure 207 bars (3,000 lb/sq in), with three engine driven pumps and one emergency electric pump, actuate primary flying controls, flaps, slats, landing gear, wheel brakes, airbrakes and nosewheel steering. Plain reservoir, pressurised by bleed air at 1.47 bars (21 lb/sq in). 28V DC electrical system, with a 9kW 28V DC starter/generator on each engine and two 23Ah batteries. Automatic emergency oxygen system. Optional 9kW Garrett APU.

AVIONICS: Standard fit provides Collins FCS 80F autopilot in conjunction with dual five-CRT EFIS-85 system, ADC 80 air data computer, dual VHF, VOR, DME, ADF, transponders, radar altimeter and Honeywell Primus 400 weather radar. Main options provide for advanced symbology EFIS-86C, digital radio controllers used in conjunction with autotune FMS (Global GNS 1000 or UNS 1), Honeywell laser inertial systems, which may also replace gyro reference systems, and Omega. Installation of Collins digital avionics including APS-85 autopilot, EFIS-86, ADS-82, AHRS-85 AHRS and Pro Line II com/nav/pulse makes possible certificated Cat II operation.

DIMENSIONS, EXTERNAL:
Wing span	18.86 m (61 ft 10½ in)
Wing chord (mean)	2.84 m (9 ft 3¾ in)
Wing aspect ratio	7.6
Length: overall	18.52 m (60 ft 9¼ in)
fuselage	17.66 m (57 ft 11 in)
Height overall	6.97 m (22 ft 10½ in)
Tailplane span	7.74 m (25 ft 4¾ in)
Wheel track	3.98 m (13 ft 0¾ in)
Wheelbase	7.24 m (23 ft 9 in)
Passenger door: Height	1.52 m (4 ft 11¾ in)
Width	0.80 m (2 ft 7½ in)
Height to sill	1.30 m (4 ft 3¼ in)
Emergency exits (each side, over wing):	
Height	0.92 m (3 ft 0¼ in)
Width	0.51 m (1 ft 8 in)

DIMENSIONS, INTERNAL:
Cabin, incl forward baggage space and rear toilet:
Length	7.16 m (23 ft 6 in)
Max width	1.86 m (6 ft 1¼ in)
Max height	1.79 m (5 ft 10½ in)
Volume	20.15 m³ (711.6 cu ft)
Baggage space	0.75 m³ (26.5 cu ft)
Baggage compartment (rear)	2.55 m³ (90 cu ft)

AREAS:
Wings, gross	46.83 m² (504.1 sq ft)
Horizontal tail surfaces (total)	13.35 m² (143.7 sq ft)
Vertical tail surfaces (total)	9.82 m² (105.7 sq ft)

WEIGHTS AND LOADINGS:
Weight empty, equipped	9,150 kg (20,170 lb)
Max payload: normal	1,570 kg (3,461 lb)
optional	2,170 kg (4,784 lb)
with max fuel	1,130 kg (2,491 lb)

Max fuel	7,040 kg (15,520 lb)
Max T-O and ramp weight:	
standard	17,600 kg (38,800 lb)
optional	18,500 kg (40,780 lb)
Max zero-fuel weight: standard	11,000 kg (24,250 lb)
optional	11,600 kg (25,570 lb)
Max landing weight	16,200 kg (35,715 lb)
Max wing loading: standard	375.8 kg/m² (76.97 lb/sq ft)
optional	395.0 kg/m² (80.90 lb/sq ft)
Max power loading: standard	356.7 kg/kN (3.49 lb/lb st)
optional	374.9 kg/kN (3.67 lb/lb st)

PERFORMANCE:
Max operating Mach No.	0.86
Max operating speed:	
at S/L	350 knots (648 km/h; 402 mph) IAS
at 7,225 m (23,700 ft)	
	370 knots (685 km/h; 425 mph) IAS
Max cruising speed	
	Mach 0.82 or 475 knots (880 km/h; 546 mph)
Long-range cruising speed at 10,670 m (35,000 ft)	
	Mach 0.75 (430 knots; 797 km/h; 495 mph)
Max operating altitude	13,715 m (45,000 ft)
Min ground turning radius about nosewheels	
	13.54 m (44 ft 5 in)
FAR 25 balanced field length with 8 passengers and fuel	
for 3,500 nm (6,480 km; 4,025 miles)	
	1,365 m (4,480 ft)
FAR 121 landing distance with 8 passengers and 45 min	
LR reserves	1,080 m (3,545 ft)
Approach speed, as above	
	99.5 knots (184 km/h; 115 mph)
Range at Mach 0.75 with 8 passengers and 45 min LR	
reserves	3,500 nm (6,480 km; 4,025 miles)

DASSAULT GARDIAN 50

A maritime surveillance and environmental protection version of the Falcon 50 is offered by the manufacturer, equipped with Thomson-CSF Varan sea search radar, Sextant Omega and a Sagem INS. Crew of three includes a radar operator located in the rear of the cabin, although the aircraft is otherwise able to undertake transport and air ambulance missions. Extras include a navigation table, search windows and a dropping hatch, and additional reconnaissance and electronic surveillance roles may be undertaken by fitment of appropriate external pods.

Data as Mystère-Falcon 50 except:

WEIGHTS AND LOADINGS:
Weight empty, equipped	11,640 kg (25,662 lb)

PERFORMANCE:
Balanced field length at max T-O weight	
	1,600 m (5,250 ft)
FAR 25 landing distance with 3 crew	1,050 m (3,445 ft)
Range at sea level with 3 crew and 5% +30 min fuel	
reserves	3,448 nm (6,390 km; 3,970 miles)
Endurance at 7,620 m (25,000 ft), no reserves	10 h

DASSAULT MYSTÈRE-FALCON 900
Spanish military designation: T.18

On 27 May 1983, at the Paris Air Show, Dassault announced a programme to develop an intercontinental three-turbofan executive transport to be known as the Mystère-Falcon 900. The prototype (F-GIDE *Spirit of Lafayette*) made its first flight on 21 September 1984. The second development aircraft (F-GFJC) flew on 30 August 1985. In the following month it made a nonstop flight of 4,305 nm (7,973 km; 4,954 miles) from Paris to Little Rock, Arkansas, USA, for demonstration at the NBAA Convention and at 30 other locations. The return trans-Atlantic flight from Teterboro, New Jersey, to Istres, France, was made at Mach 0.84.

DGAC certification was received on 14 March 1986, and FAA type approval on 21 March. Deliveries began in December 1986. By 31 December 1990, 90 aircraft had been delivered to customers in 20 countries. Outfitting for American customers is undertaken by Falcon Jet Corporation at Little Rock, Arkansas, to customers' requirements. Government/VIP aircraft are operated in Australia, France, Malaysia, Nigeria and Spain. An example registered F-WWFJ, which left the production line on 17 June 1988, was the 1,000th aircraft in the Mystère-Falcon series. Five Falcon 900s are in VIP service with the Royal Australian Air Force.

As can be seen in the accompanying illustrations, the Mystère-Falcon 900 is similar in configuration to the Mystère-Falcon 50, but with increased overall dimensions, notably a larger fuselage. Design and manufacturing programmes are computer assisted, and extensive use is made of carbonfibre and aramid composite (Kevlar) materials. Certification is to FAR Pt 25 and 55 requirements, including qualification of the entire airframe to damage tolerance standards. A secondary pressure bulkhead, while allowing in-flight access to the large baggage compartment at the rear, isolates the latter in the event of pressure loss. In a belly landing, the bottom fuselage fuel tanks would be protected by ventral skids and energy absorbing honeycomb pads which form an integral part of the fuselage structure.

The first two examples of a long-range maritime surveillance Falcon 900 were ordered by the Japan Maritime Safety Agency in September 1987, and entered service on 27 September 1989. These aircraft have

Dassault Mystère-Falcon 900 three-turbofan executive transport of United Arab Emirates *(Ivo Sturzenegger)*

observation windows and observers' seats of the kind fitted on US Coast Guard HU-25As, a drop hatch for sonobuoys, markers and flares, an operations control station with a US search radar and special communications equipment.

Production aircraft from c/n 107 will be designated **Mystère-Falcon 900B** and powered by three Garrett TFE 731-5B turbofans, each rated at 21.13 kN (4,750 lb st) at ISA+8°C, an increase of 1.1 kN (250 lb st). The additional 5.5 per cent power per engine confers performance improvements, including the ability to climb fully loaded to 11,885 m (39,000 ft) initial cruising altitude; take-off from high temperature runways (ISA+18°C), with maximum payload, reduced by nearly 200 m (656 ft); fully loaded range, with NBAA IFR reserves, increased by 100 nm (185 km; 115 miles); and a quoted range example claims that, with four passengers and full reserves, a Mystère-Falcon 900B taking off from a high-altitude airfield such as St Moritz in Switzerland could fly 3,812 nm (7,065 km; 4,390 miles), an increase of 415 nm (770 km; 478 miles), to bring Montreal within operating radius (comparable range for Falcon 900 is given as 3,397 nm; 6,295 km; 3,911 miles). French certification will be followed by UK CAA approval by end of 1991; a retrofit programme is to be offered.

TYPE: Three-turbofan executive transport.

WINGS: Cantilever low-wing monoplane, with profile optimised for Mach 0.84 cruise. Dihedral 0° 30′. Sweepback at quarter-chord 29° inboard, 24° 30′ on outer panels. Constructional details as for Falcon 50, apart from three-position airbrakes.

FUSELAGE: All-metal semi-monocoque damage tolerant structure, with less riveting than in Falcon 50. Kevlar nosecone over radar. Kevlar fairing on each side of fuselage in area of wingroots. Twelve windows each side standard; further six optional.

TAIL UNIT: Cantilever structure, with horizontal surfaces mounted partway up fin at anhedral of 8°. All surfaces swept. Tailplane incidence adjustable by screwjack, driven by two electric motors controlled by normal and emergency controls located respectively on the pilots' control wheels and pedestal. All-metal construction, except for rear portion of fin below rudder, and tailcone, which are of Kevlar. Rudder and elevators operated hydraulically.

LANDING GEAR: Retractable tricycle type by Messier-Bugatti, with twin wheels on each unit. Hydraulic retraction, main units inward, nosewheels forward. Oleo-pneumatic shock absorbers. Mainwheels fitted with Michelin radial tyres size 29 × 7.7-15, pressure 13.0 bars (189 lb/sq in). Nosewheel tyres size 17.5 × 5.75-8, pressure 10.0 bars (145 lb/sq in). Hydraulic nosewheel steering (±60° for taxying, ±180° for towing). Messier-Bugatti triple-disc carbon brakes and anti-skid system. Nosewheel doors of Kevlar; mainwheel doors of carbonfibre.

POWER PLANT: Three Garrett TFE731-5AR-1C turbofans, each rated at 20 kN (4,500 lb st). Thrust reverser on centre engine. Fuel in two integral tanks in wings, centre-section tank, and two tanks under floor of forward and rear fuselage. Total fuel capacity 10,735 litres (2,835 US gallons; 2,361 Imp gallons). Kevlar air intake trunk for centre engine, and rear cowling for side engines. Carbonfibre central cowling around all three engines.

ACCOMMODATION: A Type III emergency exit on the starboard side of the cabin permits a wide range of layouts for up to 19 passengers. Flight deck for two pilots, with a central jumpseat. The flight deck is separated from the cabin by a door, with a crew wardrobe and baggage locker on either side. At the front of the main cabin, on the starboard side opposite the main cabin door, is a galley. The passenger area is divided into three lounges. The forward zone has four armchairs in facing pairs with

tables. The centre zone contains a four-place sofa on the port side, facing a longitudinal table. On the starboard side, a bar cabinet contains a foldaway longitudinal bench, allowing five to six persons to be seated around the table for dinner, while leaving the emergency exit clear. In the rear zone, an inward facing settee on the starboard side converts into a bed. On the port side, two armchairs are separated by a table. At the rear of the cabin, a door leads to the toilet compartment, on the starboard side, and a second structural plug door to the large rear baggage area. The baggage door is electrically actuated. Other interior configurations include Dreyfuss human engineered designs in the USA and IDEI travel ergonomics concepts in France. The Dreyfuss interior features patented seating and galley innovations. It includes a crew lavatory forward, a transverse table with four chairs and two stowable lateral seats in a central conference area, a sofa bed on the port side and an executive work station opposite. An alternative eight-passenger configuration has a bedroom at the rear and three personnel seats in the forward zone. A 15-passenger layout divides a VIP area at the rear from six (three-abreast) chairs forward. The 18-passenger scheme has four rows of three-abreast airline type seats forward, and a VIP lounge with two chairs and a settee aft. Many optional items, including stereo, video and hot running water, are available. Windscreens anti-iced electrically.

SYSTEMS: Air-conditioning system uses engine bleed air or air from Garrett GTCP36-150 APU installed in rear fuselage. Softair pressurisation system, with max differential of 0.64 bars (9.3 lb/sq in), maintains sea level cabin environment to a height of 7,620 m (25,000 ft), and a cabin equivalent of 2,440 m (8,000 ft) at 15,550 m (51,000 ft). Cold air supply is by a single oversize air cycle unit. Two independent hydraulic systems, pressure 207 bars (3,000 lb/sq in), with three engine driven pumps and one emergency electric pump, actuate primary flying controls, flaps, slats, landing gear retraction, wheel brakes, airbrakes, nosewheel steering and thrust reverser.

Bootstrap hydraulic reservoirs. DC electrical system supplied by three 9kW 28V Auxilec starter/generators and two 23Ah batteries. Eros (SFIM/Intertechnique) oxygen system.

AVIONICS: Dual bi-directional Honeywell ASCB digital databus operating in conjunction with dual SPZ 800 flight director/autopilot and EFIS. Dual Honeywell FMZ 605 flight management system, associated with two AZ 810 air data computers and Honeywell laser gyro inertial platforms. Collins Pro Line II ARINC 429 series com/nav receivers. Honeywell Primus 800 colour radar.

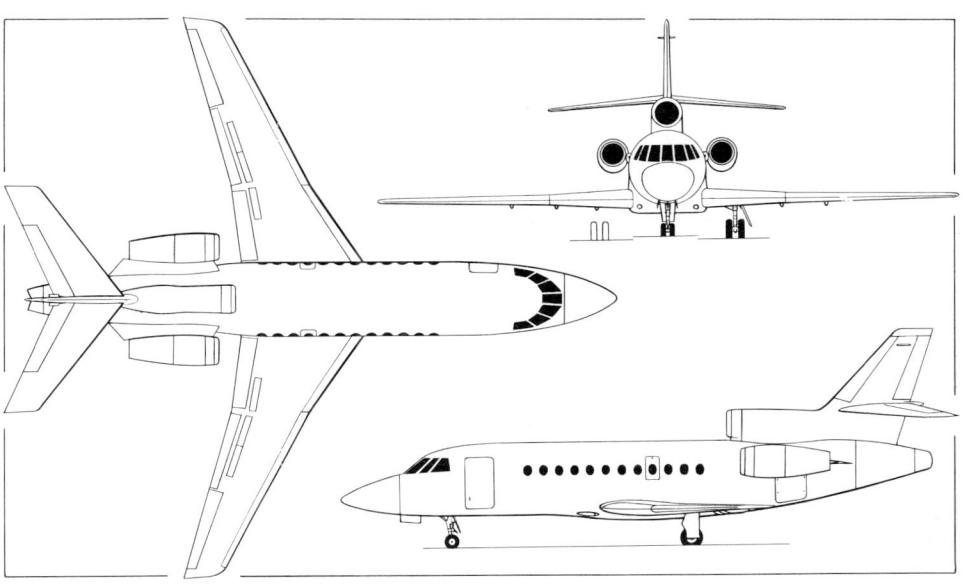

Dassault Mystère-Falcon 900 (three Garrett TFE731-5AR-1C turbofans) *(Pilot Press)*

DIMENSIONS, EXTERNAL:

Wing span	19.33 m (63 ft 5 in)
Wing chord: at root	4.08 m (13 ft 4¾ in)
at tip	1.12 m (3 ft 8 in)
Wing aspect ratio	7.6
Length overall	20.21 m (66 ft 3¾ in)
Fuselage: Max diameter	2.50 m (8 ft 2½ in)
Height overall	7.55 m (24 ft 9¼ in)
Tailplane span	7.74 m (25 ft 4¾ in)
Wheel track	4.45 m (14 ft 7¼ in)
Wheelbase	7.93 m (26 ft 0¼ in)
Passenger door: Height	1.72 m (5 ft 7¾ in)
Width	0.80 m (2 ft 7½ in)
Height to sill	1.79 m (5 ft 10½ in)
Emergency exit (overwing, stbd):	
Height	0.91 m (2 ft 11¾ in)
Width	0.53 m (1 ft 8¾ in)

DIMENSIONS, INTERNAL:

Cabin, excl flight deck, incl toilet and baggage compartments:	
Length	11.90 m (39 ft 0½ in)
Max width	2.34 m (7 ft 8 in)
Width at floor	1.86 m (6 ft 1¼ in)
Max height	1.87 m (6 ft 1½ in)
Volume	35.79 m³ (1,264 cu ft)
Rear baggage compartment volume	3.60 m³ (127 cu ft)
Flight deck volume	3.75 m³ (132 cu ft)

AREAS:

Wings, gross	49.03 m² (527.75 sq ft)

Vertical tail surfaces (total)	9.82 m² (105.7 sq ft)
Horizontal tail surfaces (total)	13.35 m² (143.7 sq ft)

WEIGHTS AND LOADINGS:

Weight empty, equipped (typical)	10,240 kg (22,575 lb)
Operating weight empty	10,545 kg (23,248 lb)
Max payload	1,815 kg (4,000 lb)
Payload with max fuel	1,405 kg (3,097 lb)
Max fuel	8,620 kg (19,004 lb)
Max T-O weight	20,640 kg (45,500 lb)
Max landing weight	19,050 kg (42,000 lb)
Normal landing weight	12,250 kg (27,000 lb)
Max zero-fuel weight: standard	12,430 kg (27,400 lb)
optional	14,000 kg (30,865 lb)
Max wing loading	420.9 kg/m² (86.21 lb/sq ft)
Max power loading: 900	343.9 kg/kN (3.37 lb/lb st)
900B	325.5 kg/kN (3.19 lb/lb st)

PERFORMANCE (at AUW of 12,250 kg; 27,000 lb, except where indicated):

Max operating speed:	
at S/L Mach 0.87 (350 knots; 648 km/h; 402 mph IAS)	
between 3,050-7,620 m (10,000-25,000 ft)	
	Mach 0.84 (370 knots; 685 km/h; 425 mph IAS)
Max cruising speed at 8,230 m (27,000 ft)	
	500 knots (927 km/h; 575 mph)
Econ cruising speed	Mach 0.75
Stalling speed: clean	101 knots (188 km/h; 117 mph)
landing configuration	79 knots (147 km/h; 91 mph)
Approach speed, eight passengers and fuel reserves	
	103 knots (191 km/h; 119 mph)
Max cruising height	15,550 m (51,000 ft)
Min ground turning radius about nosewheels	
	13.54 m (44 ft 5 in)
Balanced T-O field length with full tanks, 8 passengers and baggage	1,515 m (4,970 ft)
FAR 91 landing field length at AUW of 12,250 kg (27,000 lb)	700 m (2,300 ft)
Range with max payload, NBAA IFR reserves	
	3,460 nm (6,412 km; 3,984 miles)
Range at Mach 0.75 with max fuel and NBAA IFR reserves:	
15 passengers	3,760 nm (6,968 km; 4,329 miles)
8 passengers	3,900 nm (7,227 km; 4,491 miles)

DASSAULT MYSTÈRE-FALCON 2000

At the 1989 Paris Air Show, Dassault revealed preliminary details and a full-scale cabin mockup of a new business twin-jet intended to replace the Mystère-Falcon 20/200 series, then known provisionally as the Falcon X, but later designated Falcon 2000. Based substantially on the Falcon 900, and retaining the same cabin cross-section, the prototype is expected to fly in 1992, with French and US certification scheduled for 1994.

Dassault announced the launch of the Falcon 2000 programme on 4 October 1990, having received orders for five from Aeroleasing (Switzerland) and one from Euralair. Sales of 300 aircraft are anticipated, over a nine-year period. Alenia (previously Aeritalia) has joined the programme as a risk-sharing partner and will be responsible for rear fuselage sections and nacelles for the GE/Garrett CFE738 turbofan engines, the selection of which was announced on 2 April 1990. The aircraft has been initially priced at US$13.7 million for 1995 delivery. First flight is scheduled for Spring 1993 and certification in late 1994.

The description of the Falcon 900 applies also to the Falcon 2000 except as follows:

TYPE: Twin-turbofan executive transport.

WINGS: As Falcon 50/900, except for removal of inboard slats and modification of leading-edges.

FUSELAGE: As Falcon 900, but reduced in length by 1.98 m (6 ft 6 in) and redesigned at the rear for two turbofan engines.

POWER PLANT: Two GE/Garrett CFE738 turbofan engines, each rated at 26.7 kN (6,000 lb st).

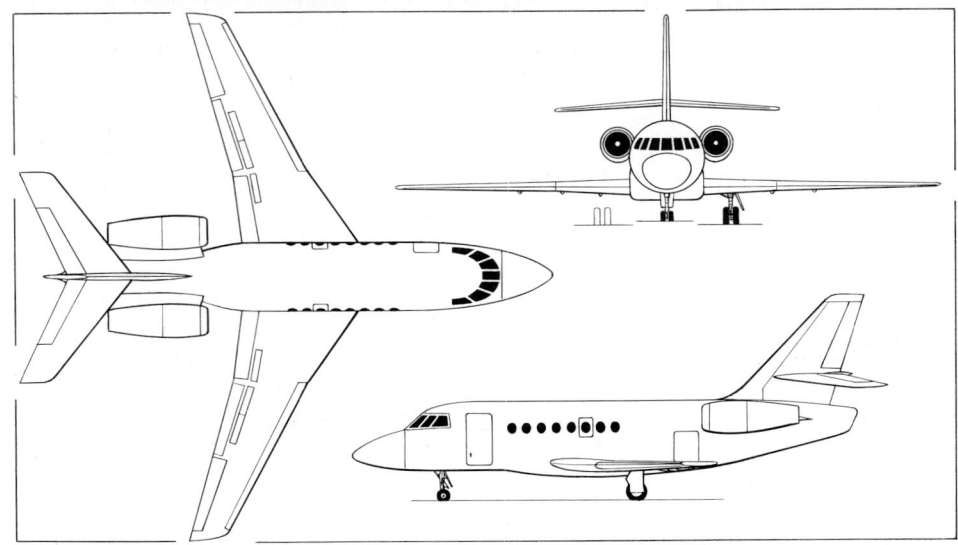

Cabin mockup and three-view drawing *(Pilot Press)* **of Dassault Mystère-Falcon 2000 twin-engined business jet**

ACCOMMODATION: Up to 12 passengers and two flight crew.

AVIONICS: Includes Collins Pro Line 4 four-tube EFIS, Cat. II autopilot and digital flight director also by Collins; Sextant Avionique EICAS (engine indication and crew alerting system); Honeywell FMS.

DIMENSIONS, EXTERNAL:

Length overall	19.23 m (63 ft 1 in)
Height overall	6.98 m (22 ft 10¾ in)

DIMENSIONS, INTERNAL:

Cabin: Length	7.98 m (26 ft 2¼ in)
Max width	2.34 m (7 ft 8¼ in)
Height	1.97 m (6 ft 5½ in)
Volume	28.00 m³ (989.6 cu ft)
Baggage volume	4.00 m³ (141.3 cu ft)

AREAS:

Wings, gross	49.02 m² (527.65 sq ft)

WEIGHTS AND LOADINGS (estimated):

Weight empty, equipped	8,250 kg (18,188 lb)
Max payload	1,390 kg (3,064 lb)
Max fuel weight	5,513 kg (12,154 lb)
Max T-O weight	15,875 kg (35,000 lb)
Max landing weight	14,970 kg (33,000 lb)
Max wing loading	323.8 kg/m² (66.33 lb/sq ft)
Max power loading	297.6 kg/kN (2.92 lb/lb st)

PERFORMANCE (estimated, at max T-O weight, ISA, except where indicated):

Max operating speed	Mach 0.85
Max cruising speed at 11,890 m (39,000 ft)	
	Mach 0.83-0.85
Certificated ceiling	12,500 m (41,000 ft)
T-O run	1,615 m (5,300 ft)
Landing run	1,550 m (5,085 ft)
Range with max fuel, 8 passengers and NBAA IFR reserves	
	2,995 nm (5,550 km; 3,448 miles)

MICROJET

MICROJET SA (Member company of Groupe Creuzet)

Aérodrome de Marmande-Virazeil, 47200 Marmande
Telephone: 33 53 64 53 50

Fax: 33 53 64 54 55
Telex: 550 777 F
CHAIRMAN: Robert Creuzet
INFORMATION OFFICER: Jérôme Creuzet

MICROJET 200 B

The last of three pre-production Microjets flew in 1986, no further aircraft having been produced. A full description appeared in the 1990-91 *Jane's.*

MUDRY

AVIONS MUDRY et CIE

Aérodrome de Bernay, BP 214, 27300 Bernay
Telephone: 33 32 43 47 34
Fax: 33 32 43 47 90
Telex: MUDRY 180 587 F
DIRECTORS GENERAL: A. Mudry (President) and D. Baron
CHIEF DESIGNER: Jean Marie Klinka

Mudry Aviation Ltd

Dutchess County Airport, Wappingers Falls, NY 12590, USA
Telephone: 1 (914) 462 5009
Fax: 1 (914) 462 0258
PRESIDENT: Daniel Heligoin

M Auguste Mudry established this company in 1958 in the works of the former Société Aéronautique Normande at

Bernay, and operated it in parallel with his other aircraft manufacturing company, C.A.A.R.P. of Beynes (see 1977-78 *Jane's*). All activities of C.A.A.R.P. were subsequently combined with those of Avions A. Mudry at Bernay, where some 50 persons are employed, divided between the Courcelles design office and the manufacturing plant at Bernay Aerodrome.

Arising from a visit to the Soviet Union in November 1990, Mudry is collaborating with Sukhoi by undertaking to obtain French FAR 23 certification of the Su-26MX, and in January 1991 Mudry signed an agreement with Sukhoi for the Soviet manufacturer to build airframes for the CAP X4. The first Su-26MX arrived in France on 8 February on board an Il-76T transport, which returned to the USSR a day or two later carrying a CAP X prototype. DGAC certification of the Su-26MX was initiated immediately.

MUDRY CAP 10 B

Developed from the Piel Emeraude two-seat light aircraft (see Sport Aircraft section), via the prototype C.P. 100 aerobatic version built by C.A.A.R.P., the CAP 10 is designed for use as a training, touring or aerobatic aeroplane. The prototype was flown for the first time in August 1968, and certification of the CAP 10 was granted on 4 September 1970. Later production aircraft, with ventral fin and enlarged rudder, are designated **CAP 10 B**. Construction is to French AIR 2052 (CAR 3) Category A standards for aerobatic flying. FAA certification for day and night VFR operation was received in 1974.

A total of 252 CAP 10/10 Bs had been delivered to customers in 24 countries by January 1991, including 56 for the French Air Force and eight for the French Navy. The Air Force aircraft are operated currently by EFIPN 307

Mudry CAP 10 B two-seat aerobatic light aircraft *(Mike Jerram)*

(École de Formation Iniiale du Personnel Navigant) at Avord and the École de l'Air at Salon de Provence. The Navy CAP 10s serve with 51 Escadrille de Servitude at Rochefort/Soubise. Overseas operators include the Mexican Air Force's flying training school, whose 20 aircraft are equipped almost to IFR standard.

To extend the potential market for the CAP 10, Mudry produced the prototype of a version equipped for glider towing, under the designation **CAP 10 R** (for remorqueur). In 1988, however, it was decided to delay marketing of this model.

TYPE: Two-seat aerobatic light aircraft.

WINGS: Cantilever low-wing monoplane. Wing section NACA 23012. Dihedral 5° from roots. Incidence 0°. No sweepback. All-spruce single-spar torsion box structure, with trellis ribs, rear auxiliary spar and okoumé plywood covering, with outer skin of polyester fabric. Inner section of each wing is rectangular in plan, outer section semi-elliptical. Wooden trailing-edge plain flaps and slotted ailerons.

FUSELAGE: Conventional spruce girder structure, built in two halves and joined by three main frames. Of basically rectangular section with rounded top decking. Polyester fabric covering. Forward section also has an inner plywood skin for added strength. Engine cowling panels of non-flammable laminated plastics.

TAIL UNIT: Conventional cantilever structure. All-wood single-spar fin, integral with fuselage, and tailplane. All surfaces covered with both plywood and polyester fabric. Tailplane incidence adjustable on ground. Trim tab in each elevator. Automatic rudder trim. Small ventral fin.

LANDING GEAR: Non-retractable tailwheel type. Mainwheel legs of light alloy, with ERAM type 9 270 C oleo-pneumatic shock absorbers. Single wheel on each main unit, tyre size 380 × 150. Solid tailwheel tyre, size 6 × 200. Tailwheel is steerable by rudder linkage but can be disengaged for ground manoeuvring. Hydraulically actuated mainwheel disc brakes (controllable from port seat) and parking brake. Streamline fairings on mainwheels and legs.

POWER PLANT: One 134 kW (180 hp) Textron Lycoming AEIO-360-B2F flat-four engine, driving a Hoffmann two-blade fixed-pitch wooden propeller. Standard fuel tank aft of engine fireproof bulkhead, capacity 72 litres (19 US gallons; 16 Imp gallons). Optional auxiliary tank, capacity 75 litres (20 US gallons; 16.5 Imp gallons), beneath baggage compartment. Inverted fuel and oil (Aviat/Christen) systems permit continuous inverted flight.

ACCOMMODATION: Side by side adjustable seats for two persons, with provision for back parachutes, under rearward sliding and jettisonable moulded transparent canopy. Special aerobatic shoulder harness standard. Space for 20 kg (44 lb) of baggage aft of seats in training and touring models.

SYSTEMS: Electrical system includes Delco-Rémy 40A engine driven alternator and STECO ET24 nickel-cadmium battery.

AVIONICS: Bendix/King avionics standard.

DIMENSIONS, EXTERNAL:

Wing span	8.06 m (26 ft 5¼ in)
Wing aspect ratio	6.0
Length overall	7.16 m (23 ft 6 in)
Height overall	2.55 m (8 ft 4½ in)
Tailplane span	2.90 m (9 ft 6 in)
Wheel track	2.06 m (6 ft 9 in)

DIMENSIONS, INTERNAL:

Cockpit: Max width	1.054 m (3 ft 5½ in)

AREAS:

Wings, gross	10.85 m² (116.79 sq ft)
Ailerons (total)	0.79 m² (8.50 sq ft)
Vertical tail surfaces (total)	1.32 m² (14.25 sq ft)
Horizontal tail surfaces (total)	1.86 m² (20.0 sq ft)

WEIGHTS AND LOADINGS (A: Aerobatic, U: Utility):

Weight empty, equipped: A, U		550 kg (1,213 lb)
Fuel load: A		54 kg (119 lb)
U		108 kg (238 lb)
Max T-O weight: A		760 kg (1,675 lb)
U		830 kg (1,829 lb)
Max wing loading: A		70.05 kg/m² (14.35 lb/sq ft)
U		76.50 kg/m² (15.67 lb/sq ft)
Max power loading: A		5.66 kg/kW (9.31 lb/hp)
U		6.19 kg/kW (10.16 lb/hp)

PERFORMANCE (at max T-O weight):

Never-exceed speed (VNE)	183 knots (340 km/h; 211 mph)
Max level speed at S/L	146 knots (270 km/h; 168 mph)
Max cruising speed (75% power)	135 knots (250 km/h; 155 mph)
Stalling speed: flaps up	52 knots (95 km/h; 59 mph) IAS
flaps down	43 knots (80 km/h; 50 mph) IAS
Max rate of climb at S/L	480 m (1,575 ft)/min
Service ceiling	5,000 m (16,400 ft)
T-O run	350 m (1,149 ft)
T-O to 15 m (50 ft)	450 m (1,477 ft)
Landing from 15 m (50 ft)	600 m (1,968 ft)
Landing run	360 m (1,182 ft)
Range with max fuel	539 nm (1,000 km; 621 miles)
g limits	+6/-4.5

MUDRY CAP 21

Production has ceased. Full details and an illustration appeared in the 1990-91 Jane's.

MUDRY CAP 230

The 10th and last CAP 230 was delivered to the Aéro Club de L'Herault at Montpellier, outstanding orders being converted into contracts for the improved CAP 231 (which see). CAP 230s can be converted to CAP 231s and three aircraft have been upgraded to the higher standard (c/n 02, 03 and 05). Full details of the CAP 230 and an illustration appeared in the 1990-91 Jane's.

MUDRY CAP 231

The CAP 231 retains the 224 kW (300 hp) Textron Lycoming AEIO-540-L1-B5D engine of the CAP 230 but the standard Hartzell two-blade propeller can now be replaced by an optional Muhlbauer three-blade unit. Aerodynamic improvements include leading-edge wingroot extensions and an elevator servo tab. The first CAP 231 (F-WZCI, c/n 11), which has since been delivered to Tony Bianchi in the United Kingdom, first flew in April 1990 and production began in the following month; DGAC certification was received on 25 July 1990. Seven aircraft had been completed by the end of December 1990 and a further nine were under construction. CAP 231s were flown by 10 pilots in the 1990 World Aerobatic Championships at Yverdon in Switzerland, including Claude Bessière and Patrick Paris of France who won the individual gold and silver medals. Morocco's Marche Verte aerobatic display team is having its four CAP 230s converted to 231s, and purchasing three new-build 231s.

TYPE: Single-seat aerobatic competition aircraft.

WINGS: Cantilever low-wing monoplane. Wing section V16F. Thickness/chord ratio 16 per cent. Dihedral 1° 30'. No twist. All-wood single-spar structure. Assister tabs in outer ailerons to reduce stick forces. Ailerons extend over three-quarters of span.

FUSELAGE: Conventional all-wood structure, of basically triangular section with rounded top decking. Wood covering except for laminated plastics engine cowling.

TAIL UNIT: Cantilever all-wood structure. Trim tab in each elevator, one also a servo tab.

LANDING GEAR: Non-retractable tailwheel type. Cantilever glassfibre main legs, with wheel fairings. Cleveland disc brakes.

POWER PLANT: One 224 kW (300 hp) Textron Lycoming AEIO-540-L1B5D flat-six engine, driving a two-blade Hartzell HC-C2YR-4CF constant-speed propeller or a three-blade Muhlbauer MTV-9BC 200-15. Fuel capacity 65 litres (17.2 US gallons; 14.3 Imp gallons). Aviat/Christen inverted oil system.

ACCOMMODATION: Single glassfibre seat under sideways opening canopy, hinged to starboard. Space for 35 kg (72 lb) baggage behind pilot. Special aerobatic shoulder harness.

DIMENSIONS, EXTERNAL:

Wing span	8.08 m (26 ft 6 in)
Length overall	6.75 m (22 ft 1¾ in)
Height overall	1.90 m (6 ft 2¾ in)
Tailplane span	2.82 m (9 ft 3 in)
Wheel track	2.40 m (7 ft 10½ in)

AREAS:

Wings, gross	9.86 m² (106.13 sq ft)
Ailerons (total)	0.92 m² (9.90 sq ft)
Horizontal tail surfaces (total)	3.89 m² (41.87 sq ft)

WEIGHTS AND LOADINGS (A: Aerobatic, N: Normal):

Weight empty		630 kg (1,389 lb)
Max T-O weight: A		730 kg (1,609 lb)
N		820 kg (1,807 lb)
Max wing loading: A		74.04 kg/m² (15.16 lb/sq ft)
N		83.16 kg/m² (17.03 lb/sq ft)
Max power loading: A		3.26 kg/kW (5.36 lb/hp)
N		3.67 kg/kW (6.03 lb/hp)

PERFORMANCE:

Never-exceed speed (VNE)	216 knots (400 km/h; 248 mph)
Max level speed at S/L	178 knots (330 km/h; 205 mph)
Max cruising speed (75% power)	162 knots (300 km/h; 186 mph)
Stalling speed	49 knots (90 km/h; 56 mph)
Max rate of climb at S/L	1,020 m (3,350 ft)/min
T-O run	150 m (490 ft)
T-O to 15 m (50 ft)	200 m (656 ft)
Landing from 15 m (50 ft)	450 m (1,476 ft)
Landing run	400 m (1,312 ft)
Range with max fuel	194 km (360 km; 223 miles)
g limit	+10

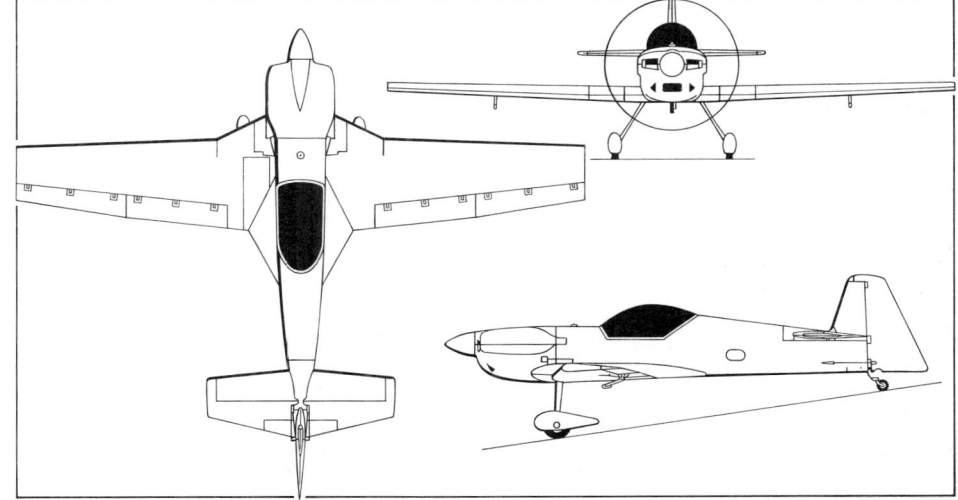

Mudry CAP 231 single-seat aerobatic aircraft as flown in the 1990 World Championships
(Jane's/Mike Keep)

MUDRY CAP X4

Having postponed indefinitely production of the CAP X tricycle lightplane (see 1987-88 *Jane's*), Mudry resuscitated the aircraft as a tailwheel design in response to interest expressed by three French civilian pilot training schools. The classical landing gear, and an increase in engine power from the original 59 kW (80 hp) Mudry-Buchoux MB-4-80 to an 86.5 kW (116 hp) Textron Lycoming O-235-N2A, meet the need for students to perform basic aerobatics in a demanding tailwheel aircraft before beginning airline training.

CAP X1 and X2 are retrospective designations applied to the two nosewheel prototypes, of which X2 has been adapted for ground demonstration of X4 aspects. These aircraft were due to be joined by a CAP X3 featuring a redesigned airframe with wing attachment points farther forward and 70 per cent span ailerons. Depending on market response, this was to be followed by the definitive CAP X4, which would have a fuselage widened and modified for increased field of view; and improved comfort and soundproofing.

TYPE: Two-seat trainer and aerobatic aircraft.

WINGS: Cantilever low-wing single-spar monoplane of wood construction. Wing section ONERA OAAG04. Dihedral 5° from roots; incidence 1° 52'. Wing attached to fuselage at four points. 70 per cent span ailerons.

FUSELAGE: Conventional wooden structure based upon two trellis longerons.

TAIL UNIT: Cantilever wooden structure. Single-spar tailplane with elevators; single-spar vertical fin.

LANDING GEAR: Non-retractable tailwheel type. Disc brakes on mainwheels. Parking brake.

POWER PLANT: One 86.5 kW (116 hp) Textron Lycoming O-235-N2A flat-four engine, driving a two-blade fixed-pitch propeller. Two fuselage fuel tanks with total capacity of 144 litres (38 US gallons; 31.7 Imp gallons).

ACCOMMODATION: Two persons side by side under one-piece canopy.

DIMENSIONS, EXTERNAL:
Wing span	8.41 m (27 ft 7⅛ in)
Wing aspect ratio	7.524
Length overall	6.10 m (20 ft 0¼ in)
Height overall	1.55 m (5 ft 1 in)
Tailplane span	2.84 m (9 ft 3¾ in)
Wheel track	2.60 m (8 ft 6⅜ in)
Wheelbase	4.05 m (13 ft 3½ in)

DIMENSIONS, INTERNAL:
Cabin: Width	1.17 m (3 ft 10 in)
Length	1.38 m (4 ft 6⅜ in)

AREAS:
Wings, gross	9.40 m² (101.2 sq ft)
Fin	1.18 m² (12.7 sq ft)
Horizontal tail surfaces (total)	2.06 m² (22.2 sq ft)

WEIGHTS AND LOADINGS (estimated. A: Aerobatic, U: Utility):
Weight empty	415 kg (914 lb)
Max T-O weight: A	660 kg (1,455 lb)
U	695 kg (1,532 lb)
Max wing loading: A	70.21 kg/m² (14.38 lb/sq ft)
U	73.94 kg/m² (15.14 lb/sq ft)
Max power loading: A	7.63 kg/kW (12.54 lb/hp)
U	8.04 kg/kW (13.21 lb/hp)

PERFORMANCE (estimated):
Never-exceed speed (VNE):		
A		170 knots (315 km/h; 195 mph)
U		156 knots (290 km/h; 180 mph)
Design manoeuvring speed:		
A		127 knots (235 km/h; 146 mph)
U		113 knots (210 km/h; 130 mph)
Cruising speed: A		138 knots (255 km/h; 158 mph)
U		130 knots (240 km/h; 149 mph)
Max rate of climb at S/L		213 m (700 ft)/min
Service ceiling		4,575 m (15,000 ft)
T-O run		240 m (787 ft)
T-O to 15 m (50 ft)		340 m (1,225 ft)
Landing from 15 m (50 ft)		330 m (1,083 ft)
Landing run		180 m (591 ft)
Range		691 nm (1,280 km; 795 miles)
g limits: A		+6/−4.5
U		+4.4/−2

MUDRY CAP '92'

This is the provisional designation of an aerobatic aircraft commissioned from Mudry by the French Air Force for its entry in the 1992 World Aerobatic Championships. Partners in the venture include Socata, the Air Force, a technical school and an engine manufacturer. In early 1991, the last-mentioned had yet to be selected, two firms having been requested to submit proposals for developing a 298 kW (400 hp) piston engine to be installed in the CAP '92'. Mudry continues to research further improvements to the CAP 231 as part of this programme.

REIMS AVIATION

REIMS AVIATION SA

Aérodrome de Reims-Prunay, BP 2745, 51062 Reims Cédex
Telephone: 33 26 48 46 46
Fax: 33 26 49 13 60
Telex: REMAVIA 830754
PRESIDENT DIRECTOR-GENERAL AND PRODUCTION
  DIRECTOR: Jean Pichon
EXTERNAL RELATIONS: Christian Jousset

Reims Aviation is the successor to the former Société Nouvelle des Avions Max Holste, which had been founded in 1956. It has the right to manufacture under licence Cessna designs for sale in Europe, Africa and Asia; but the suspension of Cessna production of piston engined aircraft applies also to Reims Aviation. By 1 January 1991 Reims had completed a total of 6,330 aircraft of all types, including 2,518 Reims-Cessna F150/152s and 2,496 F172s.

As an extension of its collaboration with Cessna, Reims Aviation developed and is manufacturing a twin-turboprop light transport aircraft known as the Reims-Cessna F 406 Caravan II. Manufacture of this aircraft continues, but Cessna sold its former 49 per cent interest in Reims Aviation to Compagnie Française Chaufour Investissement (CFCI) of Paris in early 1989.

Reims Aviation is a subcontractor to Dassault Aviation in the Mystère-Falcon programmes; and a subcontractor to Aerospatiale in the ATR 42/72 and Airbus A300/A310/A320/A330/A340 programmes and for miscellaneous parts. It had 515 employees in 1990. Its offices and factory at Reims-Prunay Airport have an area of 28,488 m² (306,211 sq ft).

REIMS-CESSNA F 406 CARAVAN II

It was announced in mid-1982 that, with financial support from the French government, Reims Aviation and Cessna were collaborating in the development of an unpressurised twin-turboprop transport known as the F 406 Caravan II. Intended for business and utility use, it is a variant of Cessna's 400 series of light twins. A prototype (F-WZLT), constructed by Reims Aviation, was exhibited at the Paris Air Show prior to its first flight on 22 September 1983. Certification was achieved on 21 December 1984, and the F 406 is now being manufactured and marketed exclusively by Reims, using wings supplied by Cessna. By January 1991, 58 aircraft had been ordered from the initial production batch of 85, of which 47 had been delivered.

The first production F 406 to fly was c/n 4 (F-ZBEO) on 20 April 1985, this being one of four F 406s for the French Customs Service, with full Bendix/King Gold Crown IFR avionics, Gemini navigation system (including Sextant Avionique Nadir computer) and a Bendix/King 1500 radar with 360° scan in an underbelly radome. Next to fly, on 3 May, was c/n 1 (N406CE), which was used as Cessna's demonstrator following FAA certification. Two others are operated by No. 3 GHL of the French Army at Rennes as target tugs, with underbelly tow equipment, the first delivered on 18 May 1987. Largest fleet is that of Aviation Lease Holland BV, which has acquired 28 for use primarily as cargo transports throughout Europe.

In 1987, flight testing began of a coastal surveillance and pollution detection version of the F 406. Primary sensors housed in a long underfuselage fairing are a Terma side-looking airborne radar (SLAR) and a SAT infra-red linescan. These are claimed to detect ships over a range of 40 nm (74 km; 46 miles) and oil spills up to about half that distance.

Reims-Cessna F 406 Caravan II with ventral cargo pod

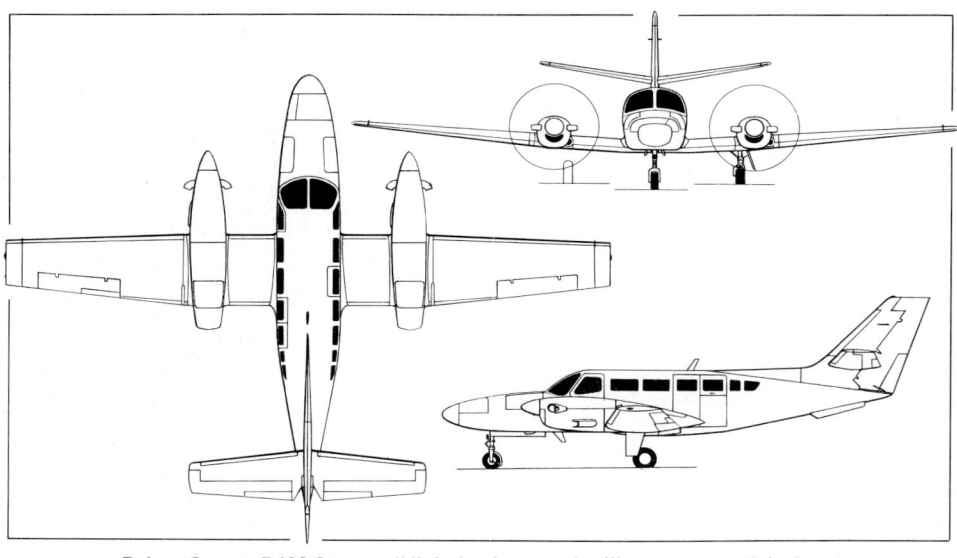

Reims-Cessna F 406 Caravan II light business and utility transport *(Pilot Press)*

A ventral cargo pod has recently been developed for the Caravan II, expanding baggage volume to 3.52 m³ (124.25 cu ft).

TYPE: Twin-turboprop light business and utility transport.

WINGS: Cantilever low-wing monoplane. Wing section NACA 23018 at root, NACA 23012 at tip. Dihedral 3° 30' on wing centre-section, 4° 55' on outer panels. Incidence 2° at root, −1° at construction tip. All-metal three-spar centre-section structure to meet SFAR 41C fail-safe requirements: two-spar structure for outer wing panels. Hydraulically operated Fowler trailing-edge flaps of light alloy construction. Plain ailerons of light alloy construction. Trim tab in port aileron. Goodrich pneumatic de-icing system optional.

FUSELAGE: All-metal semi-monocoque structure of light alloy.

TAIL UNIT: Cantilever all-metal two-spar structure, with horizontal surfaces mounted on sweptback fin. Fin offset 1° to port to counter torque of non-handed engines. Tailplane dihedral 9°. Goodrich pneumatic de-icing of leading-edges optional.

LANDING GEAR: Hydraulically retractable tricycle type with single wheel on each unit. Main units retract inward into wing, nosewheel rearward. Emergency extension by means of a 138 bar (2,000 lb/sq in) rechargeable nitrogen bottle. Cessna oleo-pneumatic shock absorbers. Main units of articulated (trailing link) type. Single-disc hydraulic brakes. Parking brake.

POWER PLANT: Two Pratt & Whitney Canada PT6A-112 turboprops (each 373 kW; 500 shp), each driving a McCauley 9910535-2 three-blade reversible-pitch and automatically feathering metal propeller. Fuel capacity 1,823 litres (481 US gallons; 401 Imp gallons).

ACCOMMODATION: Crew of two and up to 12 passengers, in pairs, facing forward, with centre aisle, except at rear of cabin in 12/14-seat versions. Alternative basic configurations for six VIP passengers in reclining seats in executive version, and for operation in mixed passenger/freight role. Executive version has a partition between cabin and flight deck, and toilet on starboard side at rear. Split main door immediately aft of wing, on port side, with built-in airstair in downward hinged lower portion. Optional cargo door forward of this door to provide single large opening. Overwing emergency exit on each side. Passenger seats removable for cargo carrying, or for conversion to ambulance, air photography, maritime surveillance and other specialised roles. Baggage compartments in nose, with three doors, at rear of cabin and in rear of each engine nacelle. Ventral cargo pod optional. Electric windscreen de-icing optional.

SYSTEMS: Freon air-conditioning system of 17,500 BTU capacity, plus engine bleed air and electric boost heating. Electrical system includes a 28V 250A starter/generator on each engine and a 39Ah nickel-cadmium battery. Hydraulic system, pressure 120 bars (1,750 lb/sq in), for operation of landing gear. Separate hydraulic system for brakes.

AVIONICS: Standard avionics comprise Bendix/King Silver Crown equipment consisting of dual nav/com, ADF and marker beacon receiver. Bendix/King Gold Crown avionics and autopilot optional. Provision for equipment to FAR Pt 135A standards, including dual controls and instrumentation for co-pilot, IFR com/nav, Bendix RDS 82 weather radar and additional emergency exit.

EQUIPMENT: Optional cargo interior includes heavy duty sidewalls, utility floorboards, cabin floodlighting and cargo restraint nets.

Reims-Cessna F 406 Caravan II target tug of the French Army

DIMENSIONS, EXTERNAL:

Wing span	15.08 m (49 ft 5½ in)
Wing aspect ratio	9.7
Length overall	11.89 m (39 ft 0¼ in)
Height overall	4.01 m (13 ft 2 in)
Tailplane span	5.87 m (19 ft 3 in)
Wheel track	4.28 m (14 ft 0½ in)
Wheelbase	3.81 m (12 ft 5⅞ in)
Propeller diameter	2.36 m (7 ft 9 in)
Cabin door: Height	1.27 m (4 ft 2 in)
Width	0.58 m (1 ft 10¾ in)
Cargo double door (optional):	
Total width	1.24 m (4 ft 1 in)

DIMENSIONS, INTERNAL:

Cabin (incl flight deck): Length	5.71 m (18 ft 8¾ in)
Max width	1.42 m (4 ft 8 in)
Max height	1.31 m (4 ft 3¼ in)
Min height (at rear)	1.21 m (3 ft 11½ in)
Width of aisle	0.29 m (11½ in)
Volume	8.64 m³ (305 cu ft)

Baggage compartment (nose):	
Length	2.00 m (6 ft 6¾ in)
Volume	0.74 m³ (26.0 cu ft)
Nacelle lockers:	
Length	1.55 m (5 ft 1¼ in)
Width	0.73 m (2 ft 4¾ in)
Baggage volume: total, internal	2.22 m³ (78.5 cu ft)
incl cargo pod	3.52 m³ (124.3 cu ft)

AREAS:

Wings, gross	23.48 m² (252.75 sq ft)
Ailerons (total)	1.36 m² (14.64 sq ft)
Trailing-edge flaps	3.98 m² (42.84 sq ft)
Fin	4.05 m² (43.59 sq ft)
Rudder, incl tab	1.50 m² (16.15 sq ft)
Tailplane	5.81 m² (62.54 sq ft)
Elevators, incl tabs	1.66 m² (17.87 sq ft)

WEIGHTS AND LOADINGS:

Weight empty, equipped	2,460 kg (5,423 lb)
Max payload	1,563 kg (3,446 lb)
Max fuel	1,444 kg (3,183 lb)
Max ramp weight	4,502 kg (9,925 lb)
Max T-O and landing weight	4,468 kg (9,850 lb)

Max zero-fuel weight	3,856 kg (8,500 lb)
Max wing loading	190.3 kg/m² (38.97 lb/sq ft)
Max power loading	5.99 kg/kW (9.85 lb/shp)

PERFORMANCE:

Max operating Mach No.	0.52
Max operating speed	229 knots (424 km/h; 263 mph) IAS
Max cruising speed	246 knots (455 km/h; 283 mph)
Econ cruising speed	200 knots (370 km/h; 230 mph)
Stalling speed: clean	94 knots (174 km/h; 108 mph) IAS
wheels and flaps down	81 knots (150 km/h; 93 mph) IAS
Max rate of climb at S/L	564 m (1,850 ft)/min
Rate of climb at S/L, one engine out	121 m (397 ft)/min
Service ceiling	9,145 m (30,000 ft)
Service ceiling, one engine out	4,935 m (16,200 ft)
T-O run	526 m (1,725 ft)
T-O to 15 m (50 ft)	803 m (2,635 ft)
Landing from 15 m (50 ft), without reverse pitch	674 m (2,212 ft)
Range with max fuel, at max cruising speed, 45 min reserves	1,153 nm (2,135 km; 1,327 miles)

ROBIN
AVIONS PIERRE ROBIN

BP 87, Aérodrome de Dijon Val-Suzon, Darois, 21121 Fontaine-les-Dijon Cédex
Telephone: 33 80 35 61 01
Fax: 33 80 35 60 80
Telex: 350 818 Robin F
PRESIDENT DIRECTOR GENERAL: Georges Megrelis
DOMESTIC SALES MANAGER: Michel Pelletier
PUBLIC RELATIONS: Jacques Bigenwald

This company was formed in October 1957 as Centre Est Aéronautique. In 1969 the company name was changed to Avions Pierre Robin. In July 1988, it was acquired by Compagnie Francaise Chaufour Investissement (CFCI) and incorporated into its Groupe Aéronautique with Reims Aviation and SN Centre Air. Pierre Robin subsequently left the company. Robin SA continues as an independent after-sales support company based at Dijon Val-Suzon.

Since 1973, Avions Pierre Robin has manufactured the DR 400 series of wooden light aircraft, which represents highly refined developments of the company's earlier Jodel designs. A new variant, the Cadet, was introduced in 1987. Production of DR aircraft of all designations and models totalled more than 3,000 by January 1991.

A total of 90 aircraft was delivered in 1990, comprising 76 DR 400s, eight R 3000s and six ATLs. The company's works cover an area of about 11,500 m² (123,785 sq ft) and employed 160 people in 1990.

ROBIN DR 400/100 CADET

Deliveries began in 1987 of a two-seat DR 400 based on the series 120 Dauphin, but with rear seating removed and max weight reduced by 100 kg (220 lb). The 1988 refinements to the Dauphin (revised instrument panel and toe-operated brakes) are included in the current Cadet. A total of 10 Cadets had been delivered by January 1991.

Data as DR 400/120, except:

TYPE: Two-seat training and touring aircraft.

WEIGHTS AND LOADINGS:

Useful load (incl baggage)	270 kg (595 lb)
Max T-O and landing weight	800 kg (1,764 lb)
Max wing loading	58.8 kg/m² (12.04 lb/sq ft)
Max power loading	9.58 kg/kW (15.75 lb/hp)

PERFORMANCE (at max T-O weight):

Max level speed at S/L	129 knots (239 km/h; 149 mph)
Max rate of climb at S/L	249 m (817 ft)/min
Service ceiling	5,030 m (16,500 ft)

Robin DR 400/100 Cadet two-seat light training aircraft *(Mike Jerram)*

T-O run	190 m (623 ft)
T-O to, and landing from, 15 m (50 ft)	425 m (1,395 ft)
Landing run	180 m (591 ft)
Range with standard fuel at 1,830 m (6,000 ft) and 116 knots (215 km/h; 133 mph) max cruising speed, no reserves	510 nm (945 km; 587 miles)

ROBIN DR 400 DAUPHIN

The prototype of this DR 400 series aircraft first flew on 15 May 1972 and received French and British certification that year. The original version had a 93 kW (125 hp) engine and was manufactured as the DR 400/125 Petit Prince. It was superseded in 1975 by the DR 400/120 Petit Prince, with 88 kW (118 hp) engine, as described in the 1979-80 *Jane's*. The current version has a fine-pitch propeller, and entered production in 1979 as the Dauphin. A redesigned instrument panel, toe brakes, an enlarged baggage compartment and additional windows were introduced in 1988. Twenty-one of this **DR400/120 Dauphin 2+2** version (implying two adults and two children) were built in 1990.

Also in 1990, Robin delivered 14 examples of the **DR400/140B Dauphin 4**, a genuine four-seat variant

possessing additional power sufficient to transport four adults.

TYPE: Three/four-seat light training and touring aircraft.

WINGS: Cantilever low-wing monoplane. Wing section NACA 23013.5 (modified). Centre-section has constant chord and no dihedral; outer wings have a dihedral of 14°. All-wood one-piece structure, with single box spar. Leading-edge plywood covered; Dacron covering overall. Wooden ailerons, covered with Dacron. Aluminium alloy flaps. Ailerons and flaps interchangeable port and starboard. Manually operated airbrake under spar outboard of landing gear on each side. Picketing ring under each wingtip.

FUSELAGE: Wooden semi-monocoque structure of basic rectangular section, plywood covered.

TAIL UNIT: Cantilever all-wood structure, covered with Dacron. Sweptback fin and rudder. All-moving one-piece horizontal surface, with tab.

LANDING GEAR: Non-retractable tricycle type, with oleo-pneumatic shock absorbers and hydraulically actuated disc brakes. All three wheels and tyres are size 380 × 150, pressure 1.57 bars (22.8 lb/sq in) on nose unit, 1.77 bars (25.6 lb/sq in) on main units. Nosewheel steerable via rudder bar. Fairings over all three legs and wheels. Tailskid with damper. Toe brakes and parking brake.

POWER PLANT: *Dauphin 2+2:* One 83.5 kW (112 hp) Textron Lycoming O-235-L2A flat-four engine, driving a Sensenich 72 CKS 6-0-56 two-blade fixed-pitch metal propeller, or Hoffmann two-blade fixed-pitch wooden propeller. *Dauphin 4:* One Textron Lycoming O-320-D flat-four engine developing 104.4 kW (140 hp) at 2,300 rpm and 119 kW (160 hp) at 2,700 rpm. Fuel tank in fuselage, usable capacity 100 litres (26.4 US gallons; 22 Imp gallons); optional 50 litre (13.2 US gallon; 11 Imp gallon) auxiliary tank. Oil capacity 5.7 litres (1.5 US gallons; 1.25 Imp gallons).

ACCOMMODATION: Enclosed cabin, with seats for three or four persons. Max weight of 154 kg (340 lb) on front pair and 136 kg (300 lb), including baggage, at rear in Dauphin 2+2. Additional 55 kg (121 lb) of disposable load in Dauphin 4. Access via forward sliding jettisonable transparent canopy. Dual controls standard. Cabin heated and ventilated. Baggage compartment with internal access.

EQUIPMENT: Standard equipment includes a 12V 50A alternator, 12V 32Ah battery, push-button starter, audible stall warning, and windscreen de-icing. Radio, blind-flying equipment, and navigation, landing and anti-collision lights, to customer's requirements.

DIMENSIONS, EXTERNAL:
Wing span	8.72 m (28 ft 7¼ in)
Wing chord:	
centre-section, constant	1.71 m (5 ft 7½ in)
at tip	0.90 m (3 ft 0 in)
Wing aspect ratio	5.6
Length overall	6.96 m (22 ft 10 in)
Height overall	2.23 m (7 ft 3¾ in)
Tailplane span	3.20 m (10 ft 6 in)
Wheel track	2.60 m (8 ft 6¼ in)
Wheelbase	5.20 m (17 ft 0¾ in)
Propeller diameter	1.78 m (5 ft 10 in)

DIMENSIONS, INTERNAL:
Cabin: Length	1.62 m (5 ft 3¾ in)
Max width	1.10 m (3 ft 7¼ in)
Max height	1.23 m (4 ft 0½ in)
Baggage volume	0.39 m³ (13.75 cu ft)

AREAS:
Wings, gross	13.60 m² (146.39 sq ft)
Ailerons, total	1.15 m² (12.38 sq ft)
Flaps, total	0.70 m² (7.53 sq ft)
Fin	0.61 m² (6.57 sq ft)
Rudder	0.63 m² (6.78 sq ft)
Horizontal tail surfaces, total	2.88 m² (31.00 sq ft)

WEIGHTS AND LOADINGS (A: Dauphin 2+2, B: Dauphin 4):
Weight empty, equipped: A	535 kg (1,179 lb)
B	580 kg (1,279 lb)
Max baggage: A, B	40 kg (88 lb)
Max T-O and landing weight: A	900 kg (1,984 lb)
B	1,000 kg (2,205 lb)
Max wing loading: A	66.2 kg/m² (13.56 lb/sq ft)
B	73.5 kg/m² (15.05 lb/sq ft)
Max power loading: A	10.78 kg/kW (17.71 lb/hp)
B	8.38 kg/kW (13.78 lb/hp)

PERFORMANCE (at max T-O weight):
Never-exceed speed (V_NE):	
A, B	166 knots (308 km/h; 191 mph)
Max level speed at S/L:	
A	130 knots (241 km/h; 150 mph)
B	143 knots (265 km/h; 165 mph)
Max cruising speed: A	116 knots (215 km/h; 133 mph)
B	117 knots (216 km/h; 134 mph)
Stalling speed, flaps down:	
A	45 knots (82 km/h; 51 mph)
B	47 knots (87 km/h; 54 mph)
Max rate of climb at S/L: A	183 m (600 ft)/min
B	264 m (865 ft)/min
Service ceiling: A	3,660 m (12,000 ft)
B	4,265 m (14,000 ft)
T-O run: A	235 m (771 ft)
B	245 m (804 ft)
T-O to 15 m (50 ft): A	535 m (1,755 ft)
B	485 m (1,591 ft)
Landing from 15 m (50 ft): A	460 m (1,510 ft)
B	470 m (1,542 ft)
Landing run: A	200 m (656 ft)
B	220 m (722 ft)
Range with standard fuel at max cruising speed, no reserves: A, B	464 nm (860 km; 534 miles)

ROBIN DR 400/160 MAJOR

The first DR 400/160 flew on 29 June 1972. It was certificated in France and Britain in 1972 and was manufactured as the Chevalier (see 1979-80 *Jane's*). The current version, with wingroot fuel tanks, a baggage hold door and a propeller of finer pitch, has been in production since 1980 as the Major. A total of 115 had been built by January 1991, including one delivered during 1990. Airframe description is generally as for the DR 400/120, but with external baggage door aft of cabin, on port side. Differences are as follows:

TYPE: Four-seat light aircraft.

POWER PLANT: One 119 kW (160 hp) Textron Lycoming O-320-D flat-four engine, driving a Sensenich two-blade metal fixed-pitch propeller. Fuel tank in fuselage, capacity 110 litres (29 US gallons; 24 Imp gallons), and

two tanks in wingroot leading-edges, giving total capacity of 190 litres (50 US gallons; 41.75 Imp gallons), of which 182 litres (48 US gallons; 40 Imp gallons) are usable. Provision for auxiliary tank, raising total capacity to 250 litres (66 US gallons; 55 Imp gallons). Oil capacity 7.5 litres (2 US gallons; 1.6 Imp gallons).

ACCOMMODATION: Seating for four persons, on adjustable front seats (max load 154 kg; 340 lb total) and rear bench seat (max load 154 kg; 340 lb total). Forward sliding transparent canopy. Up to 40 kg (88 lb) of baggage can be stowed aft of rear seats when four occupants are carried.

DIMENSIONS, EXTERNAL:
Propeller diameter	1.83 m (6 ft 0 in)
Baggage door: Height	0.47 m (1 ft 6½ in)
Width	0.55 m (1 ft 9½ in)

AREAS:
Wings, gross	14.20 m² (152.8 sq ft)

WEIGHTS AND LOADINGS:
Weight empty, equipped	570 kg (1,257 lb)
Max T-O and landing weight	1,050 kg (2,315 lb)
Max wing loading	74.2 kg/m² (15.20 lb/sq ft)
Max power loading	8.82 kg/kW (14.47 lb/hp)

PERFORMANCE (at max T-O weight):
Never-exceed speed (V_NE)	166 knots (308 km/h; 191 mph)
Max level speed at S/L	146 knots (271 km/h; 168 mph)
Max cruising speed (75% power) at 2,440 m (8,000 ft)	132 knots (245 km/h; 152 mph)
Econ cruising speed (65% power) at 3,200 m (10,500 ft)	130 knots (241 km/h; 150 mph)
Stalling speed: flaps up	56 knots (103 km/h; 64 mph)
flaps down	50 knots (93 km/h; 58 mph)
Max rate of climb at S/L	255 m (836 ft)/min
Service ceiling	4,115 m (13,500 ft)
T-O run	295 m (968 ft)
T-O to 15 m (50 ft)	590 m (1,936 ft)
Landing from 15 m (50 ft)	545 m (1,788 ft)
Landing run	250 m (820 ft)
Range with standard fuel at econ cruising speed, no reserves	825 nm (1,530 km; 950 miles)

ROBIN DR 400/180 RÉGENT

First flown on 27 March 1972, this most powerful, four/five-seat member of the wooden DR 400 series received DGAC certification on 10 May 1972, and CAA certification in December 1972. A total of 248 had been built by January 1991, including 26 delivered in 1990.

At the 1989 Paris Air Show Robin exhibited a prototype (F-WGXT) **DR 400NGL Régent III** which featured a wider fuselage with cabin width increased by 10 cm (4 in); cabin height at the rear seat positions increased by 5 cm (2 in); new ergonomically designed control columns; raised engine mounting to increase propeller ground clearance; and max T-O weight increased to 1,150 kg (2,535 lb). This variant has not been produced.

The DR 400/180 is generally similar to the DR 400/160 Major, except in the following details:

POWER PLANT: One 134 kW (180 hp) Textron Lycoming O-360-A flat-four engine. Fuel tankage as for DR 400/160.

ACCOMMODATION: Basically as for DR 400/160, but optional seating for three persons on rear bench seat. Baggage capacity 60 kg (132 lb).

DIMENSIONS, EXTERNAL:
Propeller diameter	1.93 m (6 ft 4 in)

WEIGHTS AND LOADINGS:
Weight empty, equipped	600 kg (1,322 lb)
Max T-O and landing weight	1,100 kg (2,425 lb)
Max wing loading	77.7 kg/m² (15.91 lb/sq ft)
Max power loading	8.21 kg/kW (13.47 lb/hp)

PERFORMANCE (at max T-O weight):
Never-exceed speed (V_NE)	166 knots (308 km/h; 191 mph)
Max level speed at S/L	150 knots (278 km/h; 173 mph)
Max cruising speed (75% power) at 2,285 m (7,500 ft)	140 knots (260 km/h; 162 mph)

Econ cruising speed (60% power) at 3,660 m (12,000 ft)	132 knots (245 km/h; 152 mph)
Stalling speed: flaps up	57 knots (105 km/h; 65 mph)
flaps down	52 knots (95 km/h; 59 mph)
Max rate of climb at S/L	252 m (825 ft)/min
Service ceiling	4,720 m (15,475 ft)
T-O run	315 m (1,035 ft)
T-O to 15 m (50 ft)	610 m (2,000 ft)
Landing from 15 m (50 ft)	530 m (1,740 ft)
Landing run	249 m (817 ft)
Range with standard fuel at 65% power, no reserves	783 nm (1,450 km; 900 miles)

ROBIN DR 400 REMORQUEUR

A glider-towing version of the DR 400 first flew and was certificated in France in 1972. Designated **DR 400/180R** (now abbreviated to **Remo 180**) it is powered by a Textron Lycoming flat-four engine and may also be used as a normal four-seat tourer.

In 1985, a prototype was flown of a variant fitted with a Porsche PFM 3200 flat-six engine. Known at first as the DR 400/180RP, it is now designated **DR 400RP** or **Remo 212**. The Remo 212 was delivered from 1987 and was the first aircraft with a Porsche engine to receive German certification. Porsche engine production stopped in 1990.

Remorqueur production totalled 274 by January 1991, including 14 Remo 180s delivered in 1990.

Specification details of the standard Remorqueur are the same as the DR 400/180 Régent except for the following items:

FUSELAGE: No external baggage door. The baggage compartment is covered with transparent Plexiglas as an extension of the canopy, allowing optimum rearward view.

POWER PLANT: *Remo 180:* One 134 kW (180 hp) Textron Lycoming O-360-A flat-four engine, driving (for glider towing) a Sensenich 76 EM 8S5 058 or Hoffmann HO-27-HM-180/138 two-blade propeller. For touring, a Sensenich 76 EM 8S5 064 propeller of the same diameter is fitted. Fuel capacity 110 litres (29 US gallons; 24.2 Imp gallons); optional 60 litre (15.9 US gallon; 13.2 Imp gallon) auxiliary tank. *Remo 212:* One 158 kW (212 hp) Porsche PFM 3200 flat-six engine with forced-fan cooling driving a Hoffman three-blade constant-speed propeller. Fuel capacity 115 litres (30.4 US gallons; 25.3 Imp gallons); optional 50 litre (13.2 US gallon; 11 Imp gallon) auxiliary tank.

DIMENSIONS, EXTERNAL:
Length overall: 212	7.45 m (24 ft 5¼ in)
Propeller diameter	1.83 m (6 ft 0 in)

WEIGHTS AND LOADINGS:
Weight empty, equipped: 180	560 kg (1,234 lb)
212	680 kg (1,499 lb)
Max T-O and landing weight: 180	1,000 kg (2,205 lb)
212	1,100 kg (2,425 lb)
Max wing loading: 180	73.5 kg/m² (15.05 lb/sq ft)
212	80.9 kg/m² (16.57 lb/sq ft)
Max power loading: 180	7.46 kg/kW (12.25 lb/hp)
212	6.96 kg/kW (11.44 lb/hp)

PERFORMANCE (glider tug, at max T-O weight):
Never-exceed speed (V_NE):	
180, 212	166 knots (308 km/h; 191 mph)
Max level speed: 180	146 knots (270 km/h; 168 mph)
212	158 knots (292 km/h; 181 mph)
Cruising speed at 2,440 m (8,000 ft):	
180 (70% power)	124 knots (230 km/h; 143 mph)
212 (75% power)	146 knots (270 km/h; 168 mph)
Stalling speed, flaps down:	
180	47 knots (87 km/h; 54 mph)
212	48 knots (88 km/h; 55 mph)
Max rate of climb at S/L: 180	336 m (1,100 ft)/min
212	420 m (1,380 ft)/min
Max rate of climb at S/L, towing two-seat sailplane:	
180, 212	210 m (690 ft)/min
Service ceiling: 180	6,100 m (20,000 ft)
212	5,335 m (17,500 ft)

Robin DR 400RP Remo 212 powered by the discontinued Porsche PFM 3200 *(Roland Eichenberger)*

T-O to 15 m (50 ft), towing single-seat sailplane:

180	375 m (1,230 ft)
212	330 m (1,083 ft)
Landing from 15 m (50 ft): 180	470 m (1,542 ft)
212	447 m (1,467 ft)

Range at econ cruising speed, with auxiliary fuel, no reserves:

180	647 nm (1,200 km; 745 miles)
212	785 nm (1,455 km; 904 miles)

ROBIN R 3000 SERIES

Development of this series of all-metal light aircraft began in 1978, to replace types then in production. Two prototypes with the designation R 3140 flew in 1980 and 1981, the second having the compound-taper wing.

Marketing of R 3000s was assigned to the Socata division of Aerospatiale from 1 September 1983 until 1 February 1988, when Robin resumed responsibility. Deliveries totalled 49 by 1 January 1991. The basic **series 140** (formerly R 3140E and certificated by DGAC on 13 October 1983) remains in production, but manufacture of the **series 120** ended in 1987, being replaced by the **series 160**. A further seven projected versions, listed in the 1983-84 *Jane's*, have not been built to date.

Robin is investigating the practicability of replacing the present engines of the R 3000 series with engines based on the more modern and fuel-efficient PRV six-cylinder engines built in France for Peugeot, Renault and Volvo motorcars. First aircraft to be fitted with a PRV engine, an R 3140, first flew in 1983. Robin has had engineering assistance from Renault. The power plant currently being evaluated is a three-litre PRV on which the belted reduction drive has been replaced by a gearbox, reduction ratio 0.442:1. The engine features dual electronic ignition and electronic fuel injection and is rated at 134 kW (180 hp). Flight tests are now in progress with the engine installed in an R 3000 airframe. A new company, France Aéromoteur (see Engines section), has been established to produce an aviation certificated PRV engine.

At the 1989 Paris Air Show Robin exhibited an R 3000 equipped with an Aerospatiale ATAL underwing surveillance pod containing black-and-white, colour or LLTV video camera. The camera is steered with a joystick and the picture viewed in the cockpit. The system, which weighs 8.6 kg (19 lb), permits real-time transmission of video images to mobile or fixed ground stations at ranges of 2.7-27 nm (5-50 km; 3.1-31 miles) and 64.75-97 nm (120-180 km; 74.6-112 miles) respectively.

The following details apply to the R 3000/140 except where indicated:
TYPE: Four-seat light aircraft.
WINGS: Cantilever low-wing monoplane, with upturned tips. Wing section NACA 43013.5 on constant chord inner wings, NACA 43010.5 at tip of each tapered outer panel. Dihedral 6° from roots. Incidence 3°. Conventional single-spar aluminium alloy structure. Entire trailing-edge of each constant chord panel comprises an electrically controlled slotted flap. Ailerons and flaps of aluminium alloy.
FUSELAGE: Conventional aluminium alloy semi-monocoque structure, except for glassfibre engine cowling.
TAIL UNIT: Cantilever T tail of aluminium alloy construction, with dorsal fin. Elevator trim with anti-tabs.
LANDING GEAR: Non-retractable tricycle type. Nosewheel, steerable via rudder pedals, is self-centring and locks automatically after take-off. Robin long-stroke low pressure oleo-pneumatic shock absorbers. Mainwheel tyres size 380 × 150-6. Nosewheel tyre size 5.00-5. Cleveland disc brakes. Streamline polyester fairings on all three legs and wheels. Hydraulic disc brakes. Parking brake.
POWER PLANT: *Srs 140:* One 119.3 kW (160 hp) Textron Lycoming O-320-D2A flat-four engine, driving a Sensenich 74DMS5-2-64 two-blade fixed-pitch metal propeller. Two integral fuel tanks in wing leading-edges, with total capacity of 160 litres (42.25 US gallons; 35.2 Imp gallons) standard, or 200 litres (52.8 US gallons; 44 Imp gallons) optional. Oil capacity 7.5 litres (2 US gallons; 1.6 Imp gallons). *Srs 160:* One 134 kW (180 hp) Textron Lycoming O-320-A flat-four engine. Standard fuel capacity 225 litres (59.4 US gallons; 49.5 Imp gallons).
ACCOMMODATION: Four seats in pairs in enclosed cabin, with dual controls and brakes. Adjustable front seats, with inertia reel safety belts. Removable rear seats, with belts. Carpeted floor. Forward sliding jettisonable and tinted transparent canopy, with safety lock, accessible from both sides. Automatically retracting step on each side. Baggage capacity 40 kg (88 lb). Cabin heated and ventilated. Windscreen demister.
SYSTEMS: Electrical system includes 12V 60A alternator and 12V 32Ah battery.
AVIONICS: Three standards of optional avionics and equipment available. Series I includes horizon and directional gyros with vacuum pump, type 9100 electric turn co-ordinator, rate of climb indicator, C 2400 magnetic compass (exchange for standard C 2300), position lights and two beacons, anti-collision light and instrument panel lighting. Series II adds to Series I either Becker AR 2009/25 720-channel VHF, with NR 2029 VOR/LOC receiver and indicator; or Bendix/King KX

155/08 nav/com with audio and KI 203 VOR indicator. Series III adds to Series II either a Becker ATC 2000 transponder and type 2079 ADF; or Bendix/King KT 76A transponder and KR 87 digital ADF.
EQUIPMENT: Optional mission equipment includes agricultural spraygear with underwing spraybars and chemical tank, capacity 350 litres (92.5 US gallons; 77 Imp gallons). Equipment forming part of avionics packages can be found under Avionics.

DIMENSIONS, EXTERNAL:

Wing span	9.81 m (32 ft 2¼ in)
Wing chord: at root	1.72 m (5 ft 7¾ in)
at tip	0.655 m (2 ft 1¾ in)
Wing aspect ratio	6.6
Length overall	7.51 m (24 ft 7¾ in)
Height overall	2.66 m (8 ft 8¾ in)
Tailplane span	3.20 m (10 ft 6 in)
Wheel track	2.64 m (8 ft 8 in)
Wheelbase	1.74 m (5 ft 8½ in)
Propeller diameter	1.83 m (6 ft 0 in)
Propeller ground clearance	0.30 m (11¾ in)

DIMENSIONS, INTERNAL:

Cabin: Length	2.70 m (8 ft 10¼ in)
Max width	1.14 m (3 ft 8¾ in)
Max height	1.20 m (3 ft 11¼ in)
Floor area	2.60 m² (28.0 sq ft)
Volume (incl baggage space)	2.4 m³ (84.75 cu ft)
Baggage space	0.43 m³ (15.2 cu ft)

AREAS:

Wings, gross	14.47 m² (155.75 sq ft)
Ailerons (total)	1.32 m² (14.21 sq ft)
Trailing-edge flaps (total)	2.02 m² (21.74 sq ft)
Vertical tail surfaces (total)	1.30 m² (14.00 sq ft)
Horizontal tail surfaces (total)	2.44 m² (26.26 sq ft)

WEIGHTS AND LOADINGS:

Weight empty: 140	600 kg (1,323 lb)
160	650 kg (1,433 lb)
Max T-O and landing weight: 140	1,050 kg (2,315 lb)
160	1,150 kg (2,535 lb)
Max wing loading: 140	72.6 kg/m² (14.86 lb/sq ft)
160	79.5 kg/m² (16.28 lb/sq ft)
Max power loading: 140	10.10 kg/kW (16.54 lb/hp)
160	8.58 kg/kW (14.08 lb/hp)

PERFORMANCE (at max T-O weight):

Max level speed at S/L:	
140	135 knots (250 km/h; 155 mph)
160	146 knots (270 km/h; 168 mph)
Max cruising speed (75% power) at optimum altitude:	
140	130 knots (240 km/h; 149 mph)
160	138 knots (255 km/h; 158 mph)
Econ cruising speed (65% power):	
140	119 knots (220 km/h; 136 mph)
160	128 knots (238 km/h; 148 mph)

Stalling speed, flaps down:

140	47 knots (87 km/h; 54 mph)
160	49 knots (91 km/h; 57 mph)
Max rate of climb at S/L: 140	258 m (846 ft)/min
160	267 m (875 ft)/min
Service ceiling: 140	4,265 m (14,000 ft)
160	4,570 m (15,000 ft)
T-O run: 140	280 m (920 ft)
160	310 m (1,017 ft)
T-O to 15 m (50 ft): 140	525 m (1,725 ft)
160	565 m (1,854 ft)
Landing from 15 m (50 ft): 140	490 m (1,610 ft)
160	540 m (1,772 ft)
Landing run: 140	190 m (625 ft)
160	210 m (690 ft)

Range with max standard fuel, no reserves:

75% power: 140	605 nm (1,120 km; 696 miles)
160	804 nm (1,490 km; 925 miles)
65% power: 140	640 nm (1,185 km; 736 miles)
160	868 nm (1,610 km; 1,000 miles)

Range with max optional fuel, no reserves:

75% power: 140	756 nm (1,400 km; 870 miles)
65% power: 140	799 nm (1,480 km; 919 miles)

ROBIN ATL

Avions Pierre Robin began design of the ATL (avion très léger) in 1981 to meet the requirement of French flying clubs for a very lightweight two-seat monoplane that would, in the tradition of the veteran Jodel D.112, be economical to buy and to operate. The prototype (F-WFNA) flew initially, on 17 June 1983, with a 35 kW (47 hp) JPX PAL 1,300 three-cylinder aircooled radial two-stroke engine. To speed certification, it was re-engined subsequently with a 41.5 kW (56 hp) JPX converted 1,835 cc Volkswagen motorcar engine, and a 2,050 cc version of this engine was the standard power plant of production ATLs up to the end of 1988. The increased power plant weight necessitated sweeping the wings forward to maintain an acceptable CG.

A first order, for 30, was placed by the French National Aeronautical Federation (FNA) on 28 November 1983. A second ATL flew for the first time on 7 December 1984. Deliveries began on 27 April 1985, when the Coulommiers Aero Club received a production ATL (F-WFNC). Twenty-five more were delivered (one to Australia) with a DGAC 'laissez-passer' before certification was received on 15 January 1986. All of these aircraft were called back to Dijon for modification to full certification standards.

The initial production model, to which the detailed description applies, is known as **ATL Club** in France and **Bijou** in the UK. The **ATL Club Model 88** had a new propeller of smaller diameter (1.50 m; 4 ft 11 in), to increase ground clearance, improvements to the cabin, equipment

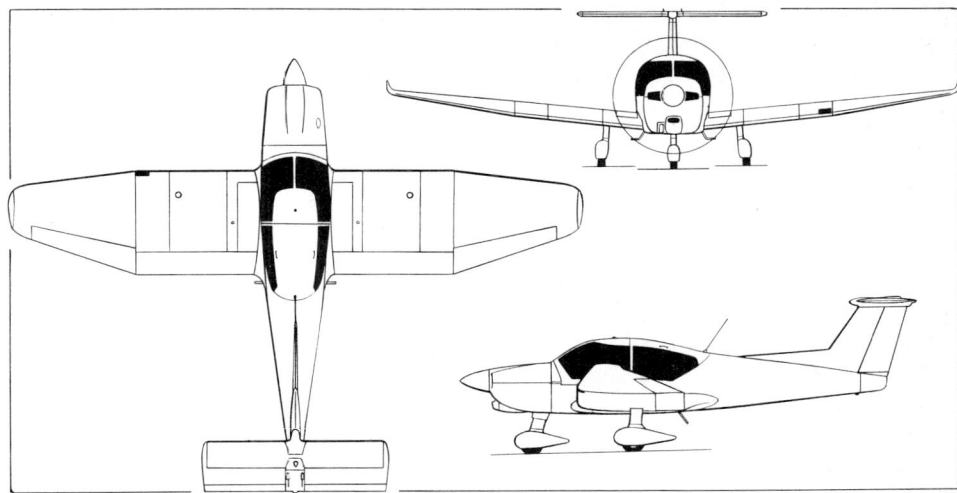

Photograph and three-view drawing *(Pilot Press)* **of Robin R 3000/140 four-seat light aircraft (Textron Lycoming O-320-D2A engine)**

Robin ATL Club very light two-seat personal and club aircraft

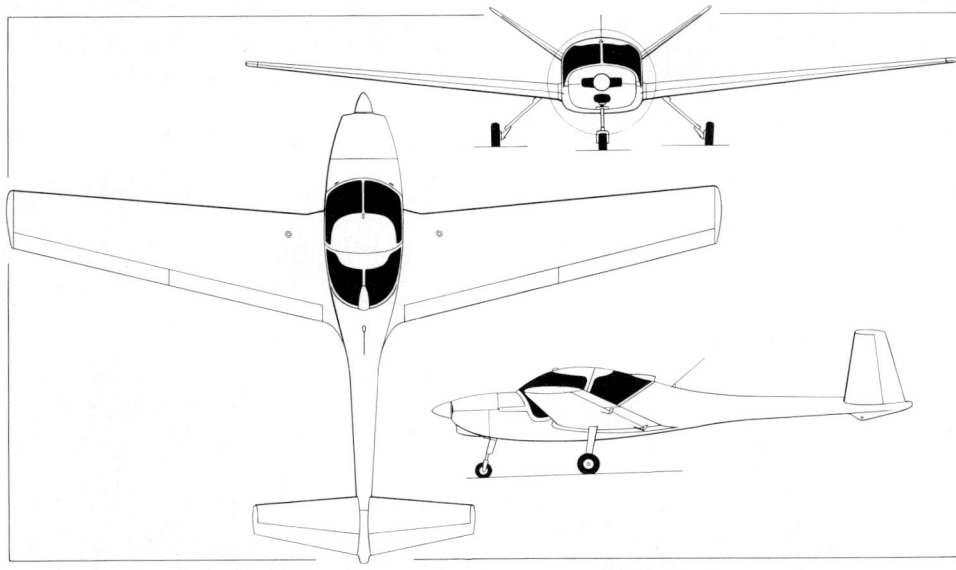

Robin ATL Club Model 88 (JPX 4T 60A) and Model 89 (Limbach) *(Pilot Press)*

steerable via rudder pedals. Mainwheel tyres size 300-130, pressure 2.2 bars (32 lb/sq in); nosewheel tyre size 270-100, pressure 1.6 bars (23 lb/sq in). Hydraulic disc brakes on mainwheels. Parking brake. Wheel fairings optional.

POWER PLANT: One JPX 4T 60A (converted 2,050 cc Volkswagen) aircooled flat-four engine, rated at 48 kW (65 hp) and driving an EVRA two-blade wooden propeller. Current Model 89 powered by 52 kW (70 hp) Limbach four-cylinder engine, with Muhlbauer MT two-blade fixed-pitch propeller. Fuel tank in each wingroot; total capacity 70 litres (18.5 US gallons; 15.4 Imp gallons).

ACCOMMODATION: Two glassfibre seats side by side under large canopy which hinges upward and forward. Dual controls, with adjustable rudder pedals, cabin heating and ventilation standard. All-transparent canopy optional. Baggage shelf behind seats, capacity 10 kg (22 lb).

SYSTEMS: Electrical system includes 12V alternator and 12V 15Ah battery. Anti-collision, navigation, cabin and instrument lights optional.

AVIONICS: Optional avionics include 720 channel VHF transceiver, VOR, ADF and transponder.

EQUIPMENT: Includes basic instruments, inertia reel safety belts and tiedown rings. Optional items include horizon and directional gyros, rate of climb indicator, turn co-ordinator, outside air temperature gauge, hourmeter, exhaust gas temperature gauge, four-strap safety harness, tinted canopy, leather furnishing, faired main landing gear legs and canopy cover.

DIMENSIONS, EXTERNAL:

Wing span	10.25 m (33 ft 7½ in)
Wing mean aerodynamic chord	1.25 m (4 ft 1¼ in)
Wing aspect ratio	8.65
Length overall	6.72 m (22 ft 0½ in)
Height: to tip of tail unit	2.00 m (6 ft 6¾ in)
cockpit canopy open	2.45 m (8 ft 0½ in)
Tailplane span	3.82 m (12 ft 6½ in)
Wheel track	3.00 m (9 ft 10 in)

AREAS:

Wings, gross	12.15 m² (130.8 sq ft)
Ailerons (total)	0.49 m² (5.27 sq ft)
Trailing-edge flaps	0.49 m² (5.27 sq ft)
Fixed V-tail surfaces	2.60 m² (27.99 sq ft)
Elevons (total)	0.96 m² (10.33 sq ft)

WEIGHTS AND LOADINGS (JPX 4T 60A engine):

Weight empty	360 kg (794 lb)
Max T-O weight	580 kg (1,278 lb)
Max wing loading	47.7 kg/m² (9.77 lb/sq ft)
Max power loading	12.1 kg/kW (19.7 lb/hp)

PERFORMANCE (Model 89 with Limbach engine, at max T-O weight):

Max level speed at S/L	105 knots (195 km/h; 121 mph)
Max cruising speed (70% power) at 1,675 m (5,500 ft)	90 knots (167 km/h; 104 mph)
Econ cruising speed (60% power) at 2,590 m (8,500 ft)	90 knots (167 km/h; 104 mph)
Stalling speed, flaps down	41 knots (75 km/h; 47 mph)
Max rate of climb at S/L	183 m (600 ft)/min
Service ceiling	4,265 m (14,000 ft)
T-O run	200 m (656 ft)
T-O to 15 m (50 ft)	405 m (1,330 ft)
Landing from 15 m (50 ft)	475 m (1,560 ft)
Landing run	170 m (558 ft)
Range with max fuel at econ cruising speed, no reserves	542 nm (1,004 km; 624 miles)

ROBIN X4

Robin has developed a four-seat light aircraft based on the ATL airframe and powered by an 88 kW (118 hp) Textron Lycoming O-235 engine. The prototype was scheduled to fly in February 1991.

and systems, and increased fuel capacity, giving a max range of 594 nm (1,100 km; 683 miles). Deliveries began in 1987.

A version of the ATL was developed, initially for the German market, with a 52.2 kW (70 hp) Limbach four-cylinder engine, achieving German certification in January 1989. The Limbach is now the standard engine on all ATLs, beginning with the **ATL Club Model 89**, which received French certification on 6 June 1989.

By January 1991, a total of 132 ATLs had been delivered, 122 with the JPX engine and 10 Limbach-powered. The JPX engines in a further 13 had been replaced by Limbach engines, 11 of these in 1990, during which year six new Limbach ATLs were built.

The following data apply to the initial version of the ATL Club, except where indicated:

TYPE: Two-seat very light personal and club aircraft.

WINGS: Cantilever mid-wing monoplane. Wing section NACA 43015 modified. Dihedral 6° from roots. Incidence 3° at root, −1° at tip. Sweepforward at front spar 7° 30′. Conventional wood single-spar structure in two halves, with plywood covered leading-edge torsion box, light auxiliary rear spar, girder ribs and Dacron covering. Frise ailerons, actuated by cables, and electrically actuated flaps of light alloy along entire trailing-edges. No tabs.

FUSELAGE: Pod and boom configuration, made of glassfibre/ Nomex honeycomb/epoxy sandwich.

TAIL UNIT: Cantilever V structure, with fixed surfaces of Dacron covered wood, and rod actuated light alloy control surfaces. Spring trim in elevator control.

LANDING GEAR: Non-retractable tricycle type. Cantilever main legs. Nosewheel has rubber shock absorption and is

---

SECA
SOCIÉTÉ D'EXPLOITATION ET DE CONSTRUCTIONS AÉRONAUTIQUES
(Subsidiary of Aerospatiale)
Aéroport du Bourget, 93350 Le Bourget
Telephone: 33 (1) 48 35 99 77
Fax: 33 (1) 48 35 96 27
Telex: SECAVIA BRGET 235710 F

SECA/FOKKER F27 FRIENDSHIP ARAT

SECA, the aircraft overhaul and modification centre at Paris Le Bourget, has converted a Friendship Mk 100 to a flying laboratory for the Institut Géographique National. Known as the F27 ARAT (Avion de Recherche Atmosphérique et de Télédétection), it differs substantially from standard in the following ways: addition of Thomson-CSF Varan radar in a ventral radome; a removable nose-probe; two survey camera windows in the lower fuselage; a laser window in the upper starboard rear fuselage; a 30kVA APU for the operation of scientific equipment during flight; four attachments for various small sensor pods around the forward fuselage; underwing pylons; and three multi-purpose equipment panels above (two) and below the forward fuselage.

Friendship Mk 100 F-W(B)YAO converted by SECA as a flying laboratory for the French National Geographic Institute *(Paul Jackson)*

SELLET-PELLETIER
SELLET-PELLETIER HÉLICOPTÈRE
c/o Lange SA, Technopolis 50, 193 Rue J-J Rousseau,
93138 Issy-les-Moulineaux
Telephone: 33 (1) 47 36 25 25
Fax: 33 (1) 47 36 77 37
Telex: 631099

M Christian Sellet and M Jacques Pelletier, engineers, are responsible for a small helicopter known as the Grillon 120, which was designed and built by M Sellet. His partner is handling the administrative, commercial and public relations aspects of the project.

SELLET-PELLETIER GRILLON 120
Although still designated Grillon 120, the helicopter has been completely redesigned, preserving only the rotors and engine, although the engine is now mounted low behind the cabin instead of high above it. No flight test results have been reported. This aircraft is in fact the third Grillon to be completed.

Design of the Grillon began in August 1984; construction of the prototype started three months later. It was almost complete when exhibited at the 1985 Paris Air Show, and flew for the first time on 8 September 1986. In early 1989 it was converted to two-seat configuration.

TYPE: Third prototype light helicopter.
ROTOR SYSTEM: Three-blade fully articulated main rotor and three-blade tail rotor. Boeing Helicopters Vertol VR7 blade section, twist 12° and thickness/chord ratio 12 per cent. NACA 0012 tail rotor blade section. Each main rotor blade has carbonfibre reinforced plastics skin (three laminations at 45°), polyurethane foam filler, and steel weight adjustment bar in leading-edge. Carbonfibre tail rotor blades. Main rotor rpm 780; tail rotor rpm 3,100.
FUSELAGE: Extensively glazed cabin pod, with aluminium alloy structure and skin. Tail rotor carried on aluminium alloy tube supported by mast structure at rear of cabin.
LANDING GEAR: Non-retractable tubular skid type.
POWER PLANT: One 89.5 kW (120 hp) Mazda twin-rotor engine, mounted behind the cabin. Two fuel tanks under

Sellet-Pelletier Grillon 120 light helicopter with revised fuselage and engine location

seats, total capacity 90 litres (23.7 US gallons; 19.7 Imp gallons) on prototype. Oil capacity 5 litres (1.3 US gallons; 1.1 Imp gallons) for engine; 2 litres (0.53 US gallon; 0.44 Imp gallon) for transmission.
ACCOMMODATION: Two pilots side by side with conventional dual controls.
DIMENSIONS, EXTERNAL:

Main rotor diameter	5.18 m (17 ft 0 in)
Main rotor blade chord	0.18 m (7 in)
Tail rotor diameter	1.08 m (3 ft 6½ in)

AREAS:

Main rotor blades (each)	0.32 m² (3.44 sq ft)
Tail rotor blades (each)	0.034 m² (0.366 sq ft)
Main rotor disc	21.07 m² (226.8 sq ft)
Tail rotor disc	0.968 m² (10.42 sq ft)

WEIGHTS AND LOADINGS (single-seat):

Weight empty	270 kg (595 lb)
Max T-O weight	510 kg (1,124 lb)
Max disc loading	24.20 kg/m² (4.96 lb/sq ft)

SOCATA
SOCIÉTÉ DE CONSTRUCTION D'AVIONS DE TOURISME ET D'AFFAIRES
(Subsidiary of Aerospatiale)
12 rue Pasteur, 92150 Surèsnes
Telephone: 33 (1) 45 06 37 60
Fax: 33 (1) 40 99 35 90
Telex: SOCATAS 614 549 F
WORKS AND AFTER-SALES SERVICE: Aérodrome de Tarbes-Ossun-Lourdes, BP 38, 65001 Tarbes Cédex
Telephone: 33 62 41 73 00
Telex: SOCATA 520 828 F
PRESIDENT AND DIRECTOR GENERAL: Etienne Lefort
TECHNICAL DIRECTOR: Jean-Louis Rabilloud
COMMERCIAL DIRECTOR: A. Aubry
MANAGER, PROMOTION AND COMMUNICATION:
Gérard Maoui

This company, formed in 1966, is a subsidiary of Aerospatiale, responsible for producing all of the group's piston engined light aircraft, as well as the Epsilon primary/basic trainer. By 31 January 1991 sales of the TB series of light aircraft, including the international TBM 700, totalled 1,220.

Socata also produces components for the Airbus A300, A320, A330/340, Lockheed C-130, ATR 42, Mystère-Falcon 100, 200 and 50 business aircraft, and Super Puma, Dauphin and Ecureuil helicopters. It is responsible for overhaul and repair of MS 760 Paris light jet aircraft.

Socata's works cover an area of 56,000 m² (602,775 sq ft).

SOCATA TB 30 EPSILON
Production of the Epsilon is believed to have been terminated. Full details and an illustration appeared in the 1990-91 *Jane's*.

SOCATA TB 31 OMÉGA
The Oméga turboprop development of the Epsilon primary/basic trainer is a Socata private venture based on the Turbomeca TP 319. The prototype (F-WOMG) first flew on 30 April 1989 as a conversion of the TP 319 testbed Epsilon (see 1987-88 *Jane's*), itself the original No. 01 prototype. Additional features include optional lightweight Martin-Baker Mk 15FC ejection seats beneath a revised two-piece canopy. There is 60 per cent similarity in components between Epsilon and Oméga, which has a wider manoeuvre envelope and greater fatigue tolerance.

Details of the Epsilon appeared in the 1990-91 *Jane's*; the Oméga is similar except:
WINGS: Local strengthening; four weapons hardpoints standard. Hardpoints stressed for same weapon loads as Epsilon.
FUSELAGE: Revised nose contours, resulting in transfer of landing lights to main landing gear legs. Airframe anti-corrosion protection to MIL-C-81773 and 83286 standards.

Socata Oméga trainer (Turbomeca TP 319 Arrius turboprop)

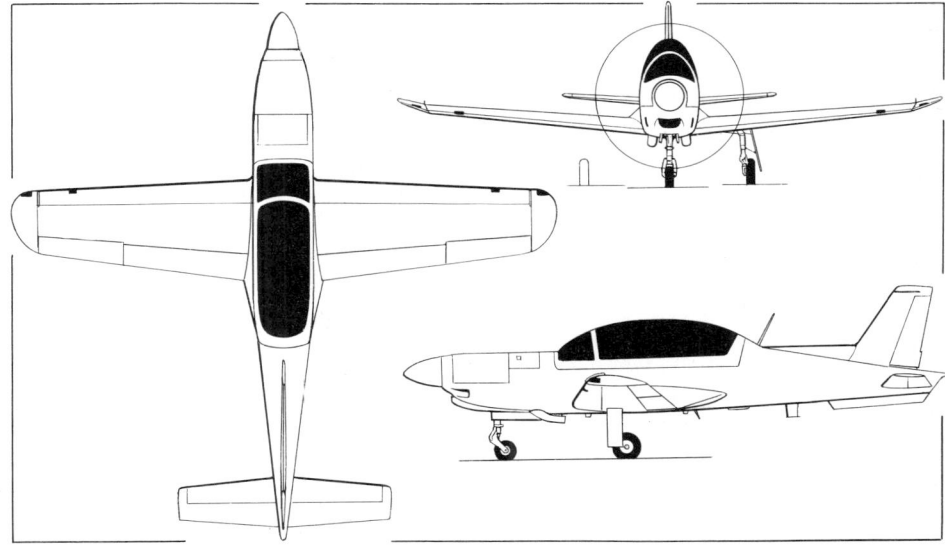

Socata Oméga trainer (Turbomeca TP 319 turboprop) *(Pilot Press)*

POWER PLANT: One 364 kW (488 shp) Turbomeca TP 319 1A2 Arrius turboprop, derated to 268 kW (360 shp) and fitted with a hydromechanical Hartzell propeller turning at 2,377 rpm. Fuel capacity in wing leading-edges of 278 litres (73.3 US gallons; 61.2 Imp gallons). Provision for two minutes of inverted flying.

ACCOMMODATION: Two-piece single-unit canopy of Poly 76, hinged to starboard and including transparent separator between cockpits. MDC at junction of canopy frame for manual emergency evacuation. Martin-Baker 15FC through-canopy ejection seats with zero altitude, 60 knot (111 km/h; 69 mph) capability.

AVIONICS: CRT display of radio/navigation data (as on Portuguese Epsilons).

EQUIPMENT: Alkan E105-E200 armament selection indicator and E105-C02 control panel in front cockpit.

DIMENSIONS, EXTERNAL:

Wing span	7.92 m (25 ft 11¾ in)
Length overall	7.81 m (25 ft 7½ in)
Height overall	2.68 m (8 ft 9½ in)
Wheel track	2.30 m (7 ft 6½ in)
Wheelbase	1.80 m (5 ft 10¾ in)

AREAS:

Wings, gross	9.00 m² (96.9 sq ft)

WEIGHTS AND LOADINGS (approximate):

Weight empty, equipped	860 kg (1,896 lb)
Fuel weight	222 kg (489 lb)
Max T-O and landing weight	1,400 kg (3,086 lb)
Max wing loading	155.5 kg/m² (31.86 lb/sq ft)
Max power loading	5.22 kg/kW (8.57 lb/shp)

PERFORMANCE (calculated):

Never-exceed speed (V_{NE})
  321 knots (595 km/h; 370 mph) CAS
Max level speed at S/L
  280 knots (519 km/h; 322 mph) CAS
Max cruising speed at 3,050 m (10,000 ft)
  234 knots (434 km/h; 269 mph)
Econ cruising speed (75% power)
  191 knots (354 km/h; 220 mph)
Stalling speed, power off, 25° flap, landing gear up or down
  64 knots (119 km/h; 74 mph)
Max rate of climb at S/L
  640 m (2,100 ft)/min
Service ceiling
  9,145 m (30,000 ft)
T-O to 15 m (50 ft)
  570 m (1,870 ft)
Range at 75% power, 20 min reserves
  706 nm (1,308 km; 813 miles)
g limits
  +7/−3.5

SOCATA TB 9 TAMPICO and TB 10 TOBAGO

The prototype for this series of all-metal light aircraft was the original TB 10 (F-WZJP), of which design was initiated by Socata's Research and Development Department in February 1975. Construction began in February 1976, and it made its first flight at Tarbes on 23 February 1977, powered by a 119 kW (160 hp) Textron Lycoming O-320-D2A engine. The second prototype was fitted with a 134 kW (180 hp) Lycoming engine.

Current production versions are as follows:

TB 9 Tampico Club. From 1989, this single model has superseded the Tampico FP (to which it is similar) and Tampico CS (Hartzell constant-speed propeller) of which details can be found in the 1988-89 *Jane's*. It is a four-seater, with 119 kW (160 hp) Textron Lycoming O-320-D2A engine, Sensenich 74 DM6 S8-0-54 fixed-pitch propeller, fuel capacity of 158 litres (41.75 US gallons; 34.75 Imp gallons), and non-retractable landing gear. First flown on 9 March 1979 and received DGAC certification on 27 September 1979.

In January 1991 Socata commenced delivery of 47 Tampico Clubs ordered by the Aero Club of Italy, an umbrella organisation which embraces some 90 separate flying clubs and which also took options on a further 63 aircraft. Socata had received orders for 140 Tampico Clubs by 31 January 1991, of which it had delivered 88.

TB 10 Tobago. Four/five-seater, with 134 kW (180 hp) engine and non-retractable landing gear. DGAC certification received on 26 April 1979, followed by FAA approval on 27 November 1985. Eight are used by SFACT to provide flying training for French air traffic control officers.

By 31 January 1991 Socata had received orders for 475 Tobagos, of which 465 had been delivered.

The more powerful **TB 20/21 Trinidad**, with retractable landing gear, is described separately.

The following description applies specifically to the TB 10 Tobago, but the Tampico is generally similar in basic construction.

Socata TB 9 Tampico Club training aircraft (Textron Lycoming O-320 engine)

TYPE: Four/five-seat all-metal light aircraft.

WINGS: Cantilever low-wing monoplane. Wing section RA 16.3C3. Thickness/chord ratio 16 per cent. Dihedral 4° 30′ from roots. No incidence at root. No sweep. Conventional light alloy single-spar structure of constant chord, with glassfibre tips. Balanced ailerons and electrically actuated slotted flaps, of light alloy. Ground adjustable tabs.

FUSELAGE: Light alloy semi-monocoque structure. Shallow strake under each side of fuselage immediately aft of wing root fillet. Glassfibre engine cowlings.

TAIL UNIT: Cantilever all-metal type, with sweptback vertical surfaces and constant chord all-moving horizontal surfaces mounted at extreme tail, aft of rudder. Ground adjustable tab at top of rudder. Anti-tab in horizontal surfaces.

LANDING GEAR: Non-retractable tricycle type, with steerable nosewheel. Oleo-pneumatic shock absorber in all three units. Mainwheel tyres size 6.00-6, 6-ply rating, pressure 2.3 bars (33 lb/sq in). Glassfibre wheel fairings on all three units. Hydraulic disc brakes. Parking brake.

POWER PLANT: One 134 kW (180 hp) Textron Lycoming O-360-A1AD flat-four engine, driving a Hartzell two-blade constant-speed propeller. Two integral fuel tanks in wing leading-edges; total capacity 210 litres (55.5 US gallons; 46 Imp gallons), of which 204 litres (54 US gallons; 45 Imp gallons) are usable. Oil capacity 7.5 litres (2 US gallons; 1.6 Imp gallons).

ACCOMMODATION: Four/five seats in enclosed cabin, with dual controls. Adjustable front seats with inertia reel seat belts. Removable rear bench seat with safety belts. Sharply inclined low-drag windscreen. Access via upward hinged window/doors of glassfibre. Baggage compartment aft of cabin, with external door on port side. Cabin carpeted, soundproofed, heated and ventilated. Windscreen defrosting standard.

SYSTEMS: Electrical system includes 12V 60A alternator and 12V 32A battery. Hydraulic system for wheel brakes only.

AVIONICS: Bendix/King Silver Crown avionics to customer's specification. Current aircraft are equipped without extra charge with a basic nav pack that includes a rate of climb indicator, electric turn and bank indicator, horizontal and directional gyro, true airspeed indicator, EGT and outside air temperature indicator.

EQUIPMENT: Includes armrests for all seats, map pockets, anti-glare visors, stall warning indicator, tiedown fittings and towbar, landing and navigation lights, four individual cabin lights and instrument panel lighting.

DIMENSIONS, EXTERNAL (Tampico Club and Tobago):

Wing span	9.76 m (32 ft 0¼ in)
Wing chord, constant	1.22 m (4 ft 0 in)
Wing aspect ratio	8.0
Length overall	7.63 m (25 ft 0½ in)
Height overall	3.20 m (10 ft 6 in)
Tailplane span	3.20 m (10 ft 6 in)
Wheelbase	1.96 m (6 ft 5 in)
Propeller diameter	1.88 m (6 ft 2 in)
Propeller ground clearance	0.10 m (4 in)
Cabin doors (each): Width	0.90 m (2 ft 11½ in)
Height	0.76 m (2 ft 6 in)
Baggage door: Width	0.64 m (2 ft 1¼ in)
Max height	0.44 m (1 ft 5¼ in)

DIMENSIONS, INTERNAL (Tampico Club and Tobago):

Cabin: Length:

firewall to rear bulkhead	2.53 m (8 ft 3½ in)
panel to rear bulkhead	2.00 m (6 ft 6¾ in)
Max width: at rear seats	1.28 m (4 ft 2¼ in)
at front seats	1.15 m (3 ft 9¼ in)
Max height, floor to roof	1.12 m (3 ft 8 in)

AREAS (Tampico Club and Tobago):

Wings, gross	11.90 m² (128.1 sq ft)
Ailerons (total)	0.91 m² (9.80 sq ft)
Trailing-edge flaps (total)	3.72 m² (40.04 sq ft)
Fin	0.88 m² (9.47 sq ft)
Rudder	0.63 m² (6.78 sq ft)
Horizontal tail surfaces (total)	2.56 m² (27.56 sq ft)

WEIGHTS AND LOADINGS (A: Tampico Club, B: Tobago):

Weight empty, with unusable fuel and oil:

A	655 kg (1,444 lb)
B	700 kg (1,543 lb)
Baggage: B	45 kg (100 lb)
Max T-O weight: A	1,058 kg (2,332 lb)
B	1,150 kg (2,535 lb)
Max wing loading: A	88.91 kg/m² (18.21 lb/sq ft)
B	96.64 kg/m² (19.79 lb/sq ft)
Max power loading: A	8.87 kg/kW (14.58 lb/hp)
B	8.57 kg/kW (14.08 lb/hp)

PERFORMANCE (at max T-O weight, A and B as above):

Max level speed: A		122 knots (226 km/h; 140 mph)
B		133 knots (247 km/h; 153 mph)
Max cruising speed (75% power):		
A		107 knots (198 km/h; 123 mph)
B		127 knots (235 km/h; 146 mph)
Econ cruising speed (65% power):		
A		100 knots (185 km/h; 115 mph)
B		117 knots (217 km/h; 135 mph)
Stalling speed:		
flaps up: A		58 knots (107 km/h; 67 mph)
B		61 knots (112 km/h; 70 mph)
flaps down: A		48 knots (89 km/h; 56 mph)
B		52 knots (97 km/h; 60 mph)
Max rate of climb at S/L: A		229 m (750 ft)/min
B		240 m (790 ft)/min
Service ceiling: A		3,810 m (12,500 ft)
B		3,960 m (13,000 ft)
T-O run: A		340 m (1,115 ft)
B		325 m (1,066 ft)
T-O to 15 m (50 ft): A		520 m (1,705 ft)
B		505 m (1,657 ft)
Landing from 15 m (50 ft): A		420 m (1,378 ft)
B		425 m (1,395 ft)
Landing run: A		195 m (640 ft)
B		190 m (623 ft)

Range with max standard fuel, allowances for T-O, climb, econ power cruise and descent, 45 min reserves:

A	450 nm (834 km; 518 miles)
B	653 nm (1,210 km; 752 miles)

SOCATA TB 20/21 TRINIDAD

The Trinidad is a four/five-seat touring and IFR training aircraft, basically similar to the TB 10 Tobago (which see) but with a more powerful engine and retractable landing gear. The prototype (F-WDBA) flew for the first time, at Tarbes, on 14 November 1980. French certification was received on 18 December 1981, and the first production

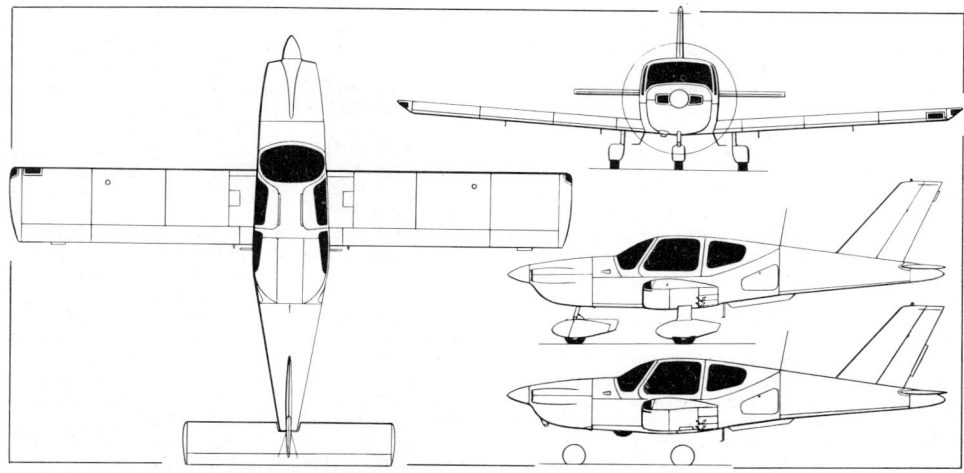

Socata Tobago, with additional side view (bottom) of Trinidad *(Pilot Press)*

Socata TB 21 Trinidad TC, the 1000th TB series production aircraft

Trinidad (F-WDBB) was delivered on 23 March 1982. FAA type approval was obtained on 27 January 1984. A significant number of TB 20/21s has been delivered to civilian pilot training organisations SFACT (42 aircraft), IAAG and CIPRA in France; and equivalents in Australia, China (28 aircraft, deliveries completed in October 1989), India and Tunisia.

There are two current versions of the Trinidad, as follows:

TB 20 Trinidad. Basic version with 186 kW (250 hp) Textron Lycoming IO-540-C4D5D engine.

TB 21 Trinidad TC. Turbocharged version, first flown on 24 August 1984, with 186 kW (250 hp) Textron Lycoming TIO-540-AB1AD engine and oxygen system. DGAC certification received on 23 May 1985, followed by FAA type approval on 5 March 1986. The first production Trinidad TC (F-GENI), displayed at the 1985 Paris Air Show, was the 500th aircraft of the TB 9/10/20/21 series produced by Socata. The 1,000th aircraft of the series was also a Trinidad TC (N21XL), delivered in March 1990. By 31 January 1991, 428 TB 20s and 48 TB 21s had been ordered, when 401 TB 20s and all 48 TB 21s had been delivered.

The description of the Tobago applies also to both versions of the Trinidad, except as follows:

WINGS: Dihedral 6° 30′ from roots. Flap preselector standard.

TAIL UNIT: Span and chord of horizontal tail surfaces increased. Mechanical rudder trim standard.

LANDING GEAR: Hydraulically retractable tricycle type, with single wheel on each unit. Free fall emergency extension. Steerable nosewheel retracts rearward. Main units retract inward into fuselage. Hydraulic disc brakes. Parking brake.

POWER PLANT: One Textron Lycoming flat-six engine, as described in variant listings, driving a Hartzell HC-C2YK-1BF/F8477-4 two-blade metal propeller. Fuel tanks in wings, total usable capacity 326 litres (86 US gallons; 71.75 Imp gallons). Oil capacity 12.6 litres (3.3 US gallons; 2.8 Imp gallons).

SYSTEMS: Self-contained electro-hydraulic system for landing gear actuation. Eros oxygen system is standard in TB 21.

EQUIPMENT: In addition to basic nav pack described in the Tampico/Tobago entry, current aircraft have as standard equipment a heated pitot, emergency static vent, cylinder head temperature gauge, emergency lighting systems, tinted windows and a storm window.

DIMENSIONS, EXTERNAL:

As for Tobago, except:

Length overall	7.71 m (25 ft 3½ in)
Height overall	2.85 m (9 ft 4¼ in)
Tailplane span	3.64 m (11 ft 11¼ in)
Wheelbase	1.91 m (6 ft 3¼ in)
Propeller diameter	2.03 m (6 ft 8 in)

AREAS:

As for Tobago, except:

Horizontal tail surfaces (total)	3.06 m² (32.94 sq ft)

WEIGHTS AND LOADINGS (A: TB 20, B: TB 21):

Weight empty: A	800 kg (1,763 lb)
B	844 kg (1,861 lb)
Max baggage: A, B	65 kg (143 lb)
Max T-O weight: A, B	1,400 kg (3,086 lb)
Max wing loading: A, B	117.6 kg/m² (24.10 lb/sq ft)
Max power loading: A, B	7.51 kg/kW (12.35 lb/hp)

PERFORMANCE (at max T-O weight, A and B as above):

Max level speed: A	167 knots (310 km/h; 192 mph)
B at 4,575 m (15,000 ft)	200 knots (370 km/h; 230 mph)
Max cruising speed (75% power) at 2,440 m (8,000 ft):	
A	164 knots (303 km/h; 188 mph)
Best power cruising speed (75% power) at 7,620 m (25,000 ft): B	190 knots (352 km/h; 219 mph)
Econ cruising speed (65% power):	
A at 3,660 m (12,000 ft)	160 knots (296 km/h; 184 mph)
B at 7,620 m (25,000 ft)	170 knots (315 km/h; 195 mph)
Stalling speed: flaps up:	
A	64 knots (118 km/h; 74 mph)
B	66 knots (121 km/h; 75 mph)
flaps and wheels down:	
A	54 knots (99 km/h; 62 mph)
B	55 knots (101 km/h; 63 mph)
Rate of climb: A at S/L	384 m (1,260 ft)/min
B at 610 m (2,000 ft)	332 m (1,090 ft)/min
B at 5,180 m (17,000 ft)	244 m (800 ft)/min
Service ceiling: A	6,100 m (20,000 ft)
Certification ceiling: B	7,620 m (25,000 ft)
T-O run: A	295 m (968 ft)
B	330 m (1,083 ft)
T-O to 15 m (50 ft): A	479 m (1,572 ft)
B	540 m (1,772 ft)
Landing from 15 m (50 ft): A	530 m (1,739 ft)
B	540 m (1,772 ft)
Landing run: A	230 m (755 ft)

Range with max fuel, allowances for T-O, climb, cruise at best econ setting and descent, 45 min reserves:

A at 75% power at 2,135 m (7,000 ft)	885 nm (1,640 km; 1,019 miles)
A at 65% power at 3,050 m (10,000 ft)	963 nm (1,785 km; 1,109 miles)

Range with max fuel, no reserves:

B at 75% power at 7,620 m (25,000 ft)	890 nm (1,648 km; 1,024 miles)
B at 65% power at 7,620 m (25,000 ft)	1,030 nm (1,907 km; 1,185 miles)

Max ferry range at 6,100 m (20,000 ft):

A	1,158 nm (2,145 km; 1,332 miles)

TBM 700

This Socata/Mooney single-turboprop business aircraft is described under TBM SA in the International section.

GERMANY

DASA

DEUTSCHE AEROSPACE AG

Leopoldstrasse 175, 8000 Munich 40
Telephone: 49 (89) 3 81 99-0
Fax: 49 (89) 3 81 99-890
Telex: 528 576 DASAM D

CHAIRMAN - DEUTSCHE AEROSPACE SUPERVISORY BOARD:
Edzard Reuter

CHAIRMAN OF THE BOARD OF MANAGEMENT:
Jürgen E. Schrempp

DEPUTY CHAIRMAN OF THE BOARD OF MANAGEMENT:
Dr Johann Schäffler (Chairman of Aircraft Division: President of MBB)

MEMBERS OF THE BOARD OF MANAGEMENT:
Dr Manfred Bischoff (Finance and Control)
Karl J. Dersch (Marketing)
Hubert Dunkler (Chairman of Propulsion Systems Division and MTU)
Dr Gerhard Jäger (Chairman of Defence Systems Division and Telefunken Systemtechnik)
Dr Hartwig Knitter (Personnel)
Dr-Ing Helmut Ulke (Chairman of Space Systems Division and Dornier GmbH)

Deutsche Aerospace AG (DASA) was founded on 19 May 1989 to oversee the future aerospace activities of the Daimler-Benz group, which simultaneously assumed a 57.5 per cent shareholding in Dornier GmbH and a 100 per cent shareholding of MTU (Motoren und Turbinen-Union). MTU produces aero engines and diesel engines. At that time Deutsche Aerospace corporations employed a total workforce of about 38,000.

Deutsche Aerospace capital was thereafter raised to acquire all shares in TST (Telefunken Systemtechnik GmbH), and in September 1989 the West German Economics Minister, Helmut Haussmann, authorised DASA's take-over of MBB, in which it now has a 50.24 per cent shareholding. Conditions imposed by the German

government when allowing the integration of MBB into DASA included a commitment by MBB to take over the 20 per cent shareholding of the Kreditanstalt für Wideraufbau bank in Deutsche Airbus by 1996; that DASA should terminate its naval business activities (involving work by MBB and TST); and that MBB should discontinue production of UAVs and armoured vehicle work. MBB subsidiary Rhein Flugzeugbau was sold to the ABS International consortium of Troisdorf. RFB had 245 employees and an expected 1990 turnover of DM43 million ($28.41 million). Headquarters are at Mönchen-Gladbach; the Lübeck and Hamburg production facilities were expected to join Deutsche Airbus.

The combined DASA workforce now stands at over 80,000 people, although the four main companies still operate under individual identities. DASA classifies its activities in four groups, namely Aircraft, Space Systems, Defence Systems and Propulsion Systems.

Deutsche Airbus has acquired the former East German Elbe Flugzeugwerke, which will now manufacture Fokker 100 components. MTU has acquired the other East German concern, Flugzeugwerke Ludwig Felde.

In November 1990, DASA acquired the federal state of Bremen's 12.7 per cent share in MBB for DM230 million ($147.7 million). Bremen had already converted this 12.7 per cent MBB holding into a seven per cent holding in DASA. This gives DASA a 64.89 per cent holding in MBB and leaves Bavaria as the last federal state to have a holding, namely 17 per cent.

The organisation of Deutsche Aerospace was still evolving in early 1991. A group of product-oriented divisions, including the Aircraft Division and Propulsion Systems Division (covered in this book) and the Space Systems, Defence Systems and other activities (covered in other *Jane's* yearbooks) was superimposed on the existing traditional companies MBB, Dornier and Deutsche Airbus. The MBB helicopter activity was transferred to Eurocopter International in May 1991. Progressive redistribution of

the many and inter-diverse units should lead to a comprehensible nomenclature in due course.

In the meantime, the traditional companies continued to operate, but a series of Strategic Business Units were superimposed on them with operational managements, as detailed here:

Strategic Business Unit Military Aircraft: Headed by O. Friedrich; about 7,800 employees; based on MBB, 8000 Munich 80. Covers military combat and training aircraft including guidance, reconnaissance, support and, for the time being, some activities no longer related. Companies brought into this unit include Flugzeug-Union Süd GmbH, Eurofighter Jagdflugzeug GmbH, Panavia Aircraft GmbH, CCI Competence Centre Informatik and ACMA Gesellschaft für Flugzeuggestützte Trag- und Startanlagen mbH.

Strategic Business Unit Regional Aircraft: Headed by Dr H. Blume; about 4,500 employees; based on Dornier Luftfahrt, 8031 Wessling. Covers regional transport aircraft from the existing Dornier 228 to the 328 now under development. This unit also handles participation in the Bell/Boeing V-22 Osprey (in association with the Helicopters SBU) and residual activities in space, avionics and training. Includes Dornier Aviation (North America) Inc.

Strategic Business Unit Helicopters: Headed by H. Plückthun; about 4,600 employees; based on MBB, 8000 Munich 80. Covers helicopter activities, including their special role equipment, the DASA component of the international Eurofar tilt-rotor programme, training and support, and some unrelated activities. Represents the German share in Eurocopter GmbH and the Tiger combat helicopter, Eurocopter International GIE (registered in France) which is the focus of the joint Aerospatiale/MBB helicopter activity, the NATO NH 90 helicopter, and the German/Indian Advanced Light Helicopter (ALH). This unit absorbed Henschel Flugzeug-Werke GmbH.

DEUTSCHE AIRBUS GmbH

PO Box 950109, Kreetslag 10, 2103 Hamburg 95
Telephone: 49 (40) 7437 0
Fax: 49 (40) 743 4422
Telex: 21950-0 DA D
WORKS: Hamburg-Finkenwerder, Bremen, Einswarden, Varel, Lemwerder, Dresden and Stade
PRESIDENT OF THE BOARD: Hans Jakob Kruse
MANAGING DIRECTOR: Hartmut Mehdorn
DIRECTORS:
   Prof Dr Uwe Ganzer
   Dr Hans Ulrich Haensel
   Ulrich Heider
   Hansjörg Kränzle
DIRECTOR, PUBLIC RELATIONS: Josef Grendel

Deutsche Airbus, formerly the MBB Transport Aircraft Group, represents Germany's 37.9 per cent share in Airbus Industrie and covers other airliner projects, such as the 80/130-passenger airliner and the German part of MPC 75, if these two programmes are not merged, and the Advanced Amphibious Aircraft (see below). The company will also run the German share of large military transports such as Euroflag.

In its factories in the Hamburg and Bremen areas, Deutsche Airbus produces most of the fuselage and the vertical tails of the A300/A310/A320 and, now, the A340 and is the main cabin furnishing centre for these aircraft and fits all movable wing parts to the wing torsion boxes produced by British Aerospace.

The A321, the stretched version of the A320, is to be assembled by Deutsche Airbus, the first large airliner to be built in Germany in the last 50 years.

Deutsche Airbus also manufactures (at Dresden from May 1991) large fuselage and tail sections for the Fokker 100.

DASA 80/130-PASSENGER AIRLINER

DASA has been taking the initiative in launching a family of airliners for 80 to 130 passengers in association with Aerospatiale and Alenia/Aeritalia. A memorandum of understanding to avoid competition with the ATR and Airbus series was being prepared in late 1990. Further details are in the International section.

ADVANCED AMPHIBIOUS AIRCRAFT

Alenia/Aeritalia and Dornier have proposed a twin-turboprop amphibian, which is to figure in the EEC Eureka technology programme. It is likely that the German part of this work will be overseen by Deutsche Airbus. For details, see International section.

DASA MPC 75

MBB, Dornier and Deutsche Airbus are all involved in this programme and a definitive industrial organisation has not yet emerged from the Deutsche Aerospace reorganisation. The MPC 75 may yet merge with the 80/130-passenger project above. Details at present appear under the MPC heading in the International section.

EUROFLAG

Deutsche Airbus is responsible for the German share of this future large military transport/tanker aircraft, details of which are given in the International section.

DORNIER LUFTFAHRT GmbH (Subsidiary of Dornier GmbH – part of Deutsche Aerospace AG)

HEADQUARTERS: Dornier Airfield, 8031 Wessling
Telephone: 49 (8153) 300
Fax: 49 (8153) 302901
Telex: 526412 DORW D
EXECUTIVE BOARD:
   Hans-Dieter Abt
   Guntram Bartscherer
   Dr Hans Blume
   Klaus Neuhaus
   Dr Bernd Sträter
CHAIRMAN OF DORNIER GMBH: Dr-Ing Helmut Ulke
PRESS AND INFORMATION: Andrea Schuster
PO Box 3, 8031 Wessling
Telephone: 49 (8153) 302330
Fax: 49 (8153) 302770
Telex: 526412 DORW D

Dornier GmbH, formerly Dornier-Metallbauten, was formed in 1922 by the late Professor Claude Dornier. It has operated as a GmbH since 22 December 1972. Daimler-Benz AG acquired a majority holding (65.5 per cent) in Dornier GmbH in 1985, but had reduced this to 57.55 per cent by 1 January 1989, when a new three-group Dornier company structure came into being with Silvius Dornier (21.22 per cent) and the Claudius Dornier heirs (21.22 per cent) as the other shareholders. The Daimler-Benz shareholding has since been assumed by Deutsche Aerospace AG (which see).

The former Dornier System GmbH no longer exists, its activities having been transferred to the parent Dornier GmbH, which is based at Friedrichshafen. All of Dornier's aviation activities are undertaken by Dornier Luftfahrt GmbH (formerly Dornier Reparaturwerft GmbH) at Oberpfaffenhofen, which is a wholly owned subsidiary of Dornier GmbH. Dornier Medizintechnik GmbH of Munich is also a wholly owned subsidiary of Dornier GmbH. Reorganisation within the Deutsche Aerospace group was continuing during 1991.

Dornier Luftfahrt developed the Alpha Jet training/light attack aircraft, described in the International section, in partnership with Dassault-Breguet, now Dassault Aviation, of France. It is responsible for industrial support of Luftwaffe Alpha Jets and is to modernise the fleet. Dornier is in the multi-nation Eurofighter EFA (see International section), and is a subcontractor to Deutsche Airbus GmbH. It was responsible for integrating the operational avionics in the 18 NATO Boeing E-3A Sentry AWACS and now conducts depot-level maintenance of these aircraft under NATO contract, although this work may be transferred to the MBB base at Manching. Dornier was prime contractor for the NATO Trainer/Cargo Aircraft (TCA) programme (see 1989-90 *Jane's*). It also assisted in the design of the Argentine IA 63 Pampa trainer. In April 1989 Dornier signed a memorandum of understanding with Aermacchi of Italy for the joint definition of a future integrated military Pilot Training System (PTS-2000). MBB joined this consortium early in 1991. The company's latest activities include a new transonic laminar flow wing, Eureka research studies (with Alenia/Aeritalia) on an advanced amphibious aircraft, and hypersonic aircraft technologies.

Dornier Luftfahrt undertakes technical and logistic servicing of the German Navy Breguet Br 1150 Atlantic 1 and contributes to the Atlantique 2. It also became prime contractor for modernisation of the German Atlantics, which are expected to continue in service until replaced around 1997.

Dornier is applying life extension modifications to 168 Bell UH-1D utility helicopters and supplying 30 complete modification kits and 80 tailboom modification kits under a DM253 million German MoD contract. The company built the helicopters under licence in 1968-72 and more than 300 are still in service with the German Air Force, Army and Border Patrol. Modifications include replacing honeycomb floor, gearbox side panels, rear cabin bulkhead and engine support structure with numerically milled parts; replacing underfloor fuel tank panels with new honeycomb components; replacing supports, jacking points and hardpoints with magnesium castings; replacing the tail pylon front spar, upper skin and 90° gearbox support.

STRATEGIC BUSINESS UNIT REGIONAL AIRCRAFT

PO Box 3, 8031 Wessling
Telephone: 49 (8153) 30-0
HEAD OF STRATEGIC BUSINESS UNIT: Dr Hans Blume

DORNIER 228

The design of the Dornier 228 complies with US FAR Pt 23 requirements, including Amendment 23, and Appendix A of FAR Pt 135. One prototype of each initial version was built; the first of these, the Dornier 228-100 (D-IFNS) made its first flight on 28 March 1981. The 228-200 (D-ICDO) flew for the first time on 9 May 1981. A static test airframe of the 228-200 was also completed. Service life is for 62,500 flights without major structural repair.

British CAA and American FAA certification were granted on 17 April and 11 May 1984 respectively, followed by Australian certification on 11 October 1985; in addition, LBA certification has been accepted by the licensing authorities of Bhutan, Canada, India, Japan, Malaysia, Nigeria, Norway, Sweden and Taiwan.

Excluding Indian licence production (see below), firm orders for the Dornier 228 (all versions) totalled 189 by December 1990 from 70 customers in 35 countries; deliveries at that time had reached 178.

The Dornier 228 has been produced in the following versions:

228-100: Basic version with standard accommodation for 15 passengers; out of production.

228-101: Identical to 228-100 except for reinforced fuselage and different mainwheel tyres, to permit higher operating weights; fire extinguishing system added to conform to SFAR Pt 41b. Introduced in 1984. Now out of production.

228-200: Lengthened fuselage, providing standard accommodation for 19 passengers at 76 cm (30 in) seat pitch and a larger rear baggage compartment; otherwise similar to 228-100. Certificated by German LBA on 6 September 1982. Now out of production.

228-201: Introduced in 1984. Identical to 228-200 except for changes noted under 228-101. Accommodation for 19 passengers with two pilots. Now out of production.

228-202: Designed to offer increases in payload/range performance compared with 228-201, with only a slight

Dornier 228-212 of Air Calédonie

difference in empty weight. Certificated by LBA and FAA in August and September 1986. Now out of production.

228-212: Generally as 228-201, but with max T-O weight of 6,400 kg (14,109 lb) and max landing weight of 6,100 kg (13,448 lb) allowing increased payload on short route segments. Reduced empty weight. Max fuel weight 1,885 kg (4,155 lb). Engine T-O rating increased to 579 kW (776 shp) at S/L in ISA. Strengthened landing gear (with modified anti-skid system and carbon brakes), wing boxes and fuselage; two underfuselage strakes to improve STOL and low-speed flying; max flaps extended speed (VFE) increased from 150 to 160 knots (278-297 km/h; 173-189 mph) IAS; elevator and rudder control (electrically actuated rudder trim) modified; battery relocated from the nose to the landing gear bay. Modernised avionics and equipment. Certificated by the LBA in April 1989, FAA and French DGCA in June 1990. The Dornier 228-212 has replaced all preceding 228 models.

228 Troop, Paratroop and Ambulance: Based on the 228-212, Troop accommodates 17, 20 or 22 fully equipped troops with seats along sides and carbon boxes, roller door, military nav/com and loadmaster intercom. Paratroop accommodates 16, 19 or 21 persons, plus jumpmaster. Similar equipment to Troop, but no toilet.

Ambulance also has a roller door and accommodates six stretchers in pairs and nine sitting casualties/attendants. Optional small galley, toilet, refrigerator, oxygen system and cabin intercom.

228 Cargo: For round-the-clock freight operations. The standard 228-212 has been lightened by removal of all equipment superfluous to cargo operations and structurally modified to comply with Federal Aviation Regulations: the cabin is partitioned into five sections. Six cargo nets, spaced approximately 140 cm (55 in) apart, can be installed and secured to aluminium frames and to the seat rails. Fittings include reinforced glassfibre panels on the side walls of the cabin, reinforced cabin floor, smoke detection system and large double door. The 228 Cargo has a max payload of 2,340 kg (5,159 lb) and cargo volume of 16.34 m³ (577 cu ft).

On 29 November 1983 contracts were signed covering the transfer of technology in a progressive programme to manufacture versions of the Dornier 228 under licence in India, by Hindustan Aeronautics Ltd (which see). A production run of about 150 aircraft is envisaged, for various Indian organisations and customers, and was prefaced by the delivery of five 228-201s to Vayudoot, the Indian regional airline, in 1984-85, and three 228-101s to the Indian Coast Guard in 1986-87. Meanwhile, Dornier began delivery of complete sets of aircraft assemblies to India in early 1985, and the first flight of an HAL assembled 228 was made on 31 January 1986. Further details of this licence programme can be found in the HAL entry in the Indian section.

Further details of the -100/101/200/201/202 variants are in the 1990-91 and earlier *Jane's*. The description below applies to the 228-212:

TYPE: Twin-turboprop STOL light transport.

WINGS: Cantilever high-wing monoplane, comprising two-spar rectangular centre-section and two tapered outer panels ending in raked tips. Dornier Do A-5 supercritical wing section. No dihedral or anhedral. Sweepback on leading-edge of outer panels 8°. Wingtips of CFRP; Kevlar used in construction of wing rib webs, wingroot fairings and ailerons. Remainder of wing of light alloy construction. Fowler single-slotted trailing-edge flaps and ailerons of carbonfibre composites. Ailerons can be drooped symmetrically to augment trailing-edge flaps.

FUSELAGE: Conventional stressed skin unpressurised structure of light alloy, built in five sections. GFRP nosecone and Kevlar landing gear fairings.

TAIL UNIT: Cantilever structure, with rudder and horizontal surfaces Eonnex covered. CFRP used for tips of tailplane and elevators; GFRP used for tips of rudder and fin, and hybrid composites used for fin leading-edges. Variable incidence tailplane, with horn balanced elevators. Trim tab in rudder. UK certification requires automatic link between flaps and tailplane angle.

LANDING GEAR: Retractable tricycle type, with single mainwheels and twin-wheel nose unit. Main units retract inward into fairings built on to the lower fuselage. Hydraulically steerable nosewheels retract forward. Goodyear wheels and tyres, size 8.50-10 on mainwheels (12 ply rating on 228-100, 10 ply rating on 228-200); size 6.00-6, 6 ply rating, on nosewheels. Low pressure tyres optional. Goodyear brakes on mainwheels.

POWER PLANT: Two 578.7 kW (776 shp) Garrett TPE331-5-252D turboprops, each driving a Hartzell HC-B4TN-5ML/LT10574 four-blade constant-speed fully feathering reversible-pitch metal propeller. Primary wing box forms an integral fuel tank with a total usable capacity of 2,386 litres (630 US gallons; 525 Imp gallons). Oil capacity per engine 5.9 litres (1.56 US gallons; 1.30 Imp gallons).

ACCOMMODATION: Crew of one or two. Pilots' seats adjustable fore and aft. Individual seats down each side of the cabin with a central aisle. Flight deck door on port side. Combined two-section passenger and freight door, with integral steps, on port side of cabin at rear. One emergency exit on port side of cabin, two on starboard side. Baggage compartment at rear of cabin, accessible externally and from cabin; capacity 210 kg (463 lb). Enlarged baggage door optional. Additional baggage space in fuselage nose, with separate access; capacity 120 kg (265 lb). Modular units using seat rails for rapid changes of role. In air ambulance configuration, six stretchers carried in three double units plus nine seated patients/medical attendants.

SYSTEMS: Entire accommodation heated and ventilated. Air-conditioning system optional. Heating by engine bleed air. Hydraulic system, pressure 207 bars (3,000 lb/sq in), for landing gear, brakes and nosewheel steering. Handpump for emergency landing gear extension. Primary 28V DC electrical system, supplied by two 28V 250A engine driven starter/generators and two 24V 25Ah nickel-cadmium batteries. Two 350VA inverters supply 115/26V 400Hz AC system. APU optional. Air intake anti-icing standard. De-icing system optional for wing and tail unit leading-edges, windscreen and propellers.

AVIONICS: Instrumentation for IFR flight standard. Autopilot optional, to permit single-pilot IFR operation. Standard avionics include dual Bendix/King KY 196 VHF com, dual KN 53 VOR/ILS and KN 72 VOR/LOC converters; KMR 675 marker beacon receiver, dual or single KR 87 ADF and KT 76A transponder; dual or single Aeronetics 7137 RMI; dual or single DME; two Honeywell GH14B gyro horizons; two Bendix/King KPI 552 HSIs; dual ASIs; dual altimeters; dual ADIs; dual VSIs; Becker audio selector and intercom. Weather radar optional.

EQUIPMENT: Standard equipment includes complete internal and external lighting, hand fire extinguisher, first aid kit, gust control locks and tiedown kit. For geophysical role, equipment includes VLF magnetometer in nose probe, VLF or protomagnetometer in port wing fairing, gamma ray detector, camera in rear of cabin with the operator's position in forward section of cabin, navigation telescope, emergency equipment, and magnetometer in tail sting; operator's position for magnetometers on port side of cabin.

DIMENSIONS, EXTERNAL:

Wing span	16.97 m (55 ft 8 in)
Wing aspect ratio	9.0
Length overall	16.56 m (54 ft 4 in)
Height overall	4.86 m (15 ft 11½ in)
Tailplane span	6.45 m (21 ft 2 in)
Wheel track	3.30 m (10 ft 10 in)
Wheelbase	6.29 m (20 ft 7½ in)
Propeller diameter	2.73 m (8 ft 11½ in)
Propeller ground clearance	1.08 m (3 ft 6½ in)
Passenger door (port, rear):	
Height	1.34 m (4 ft 4¾ in)

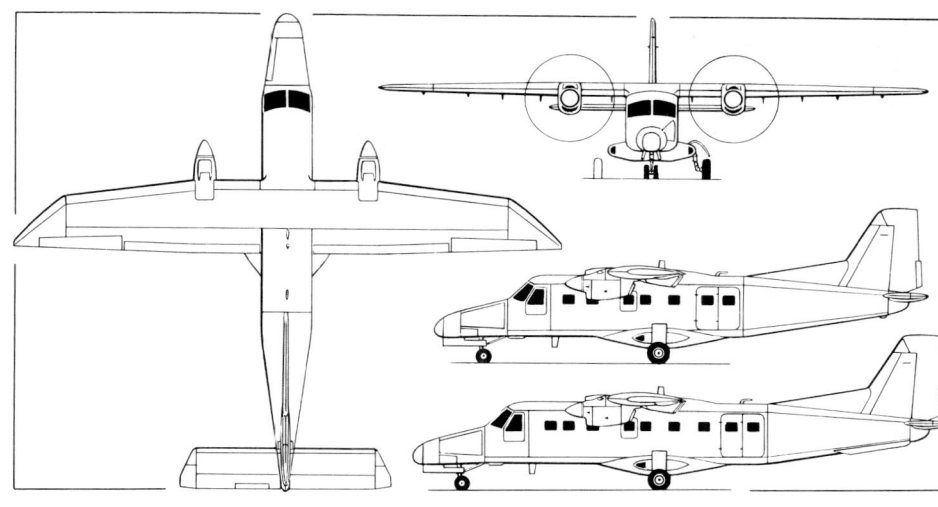

Dornier 228-100 light transport, with additional side view (bottom) of 228-212 *(Pilot Press)*

Width	0.64 m (2 ft 1¼ in)
Height to sill	0.60 m (1 ft 11½ in)
Freight door (port, rear):	
Height	1.34 m (4 ft 4¾ in)
Width, incl passenger door	1.28 m (4 ft 2½ in)
Emergency exits (each): Height	0.66 m (2 ft 2 in)
Width	0.48 m (1 ft 7 in)
Baggage door (nose): Height	0.50 m (1 ft 7½ in)
Width	1.20 m (3 ft 11¼ in)
Standard baggage door (rear):	
Height	0.90 m (2 ft 11½ in)
Width	0.53 m (1 ft 9 in)

DIMENSIONS, INTERNAL:
Cabin, excl flight deck and rear baggage compartment:

Length	7.08 m (23 ft 2¾ in)
Max width	1.346 m (4 ft 5 in)
Max height	1.55 m (5 ft 1 in)
Floor area	9.56 m² (102.9 sq ft)
Volume	14.70 m³ (519.1 cu ft)
Rear baggage compartment volume	2.60 m³ (91.8 cu ft)
Nose baggage compartment volume	0.89 m³ (31.4 cu ft)

AREAS:

Wings, gross	32.00 m² (344.3 sq ft)
Ailerons (total)	2.708 m² (29.15 sq ft)
Trailing-edge flaps (total)	5.872 m² (63.21 sq ft)
Fin, incl dorsal fin	4.50 m² (48.44 sq ft)
Rudder, incl tab	1.50 m² (16.15 sq ft)
Horizontal tail surfaces (total)	8.33 m² (89.66 sq ft)

WEIGHTS AND LOADINGS:

Weight empty, standard	3,258 kg (7,183 lb)
Operating weight empty	3,739 kg (8,243 lb)
Max payload	2,201 kg (4,852 lb)
Max ramp weight	6,430 kg (14,175 lb)
Max T-O weight*	6,400 kg (14,110 lb)
Max landing weight	6,100 kg (13,448 lb)
Max wing loading	200.0 kg/m² (40.96 lb/sq ft)
Max power loading	5.53 kg/kW (9.09 lb/shp)

Increasable to 6,600 kg (14,550 lb) in special cases

PERFORMANCE (at max T-O weight, S/L, ISA, except where indicated):

Never-exceed speed (VNE)	
	255 knots (472 km/h; 293 mph) IAS
Max operating speed (VMO)	
	223 knots (413 km/h; 256 mph) IAS
Max cruising speed at 3,050 m (10,000 ft)	
	234 knots (434 km/h; 269 mph)
Cruising speed at 4,575 m (15,000 ft), average cruise weight of 5,300 kg (11,684 lb)	
	220 knots (408 km/h; 253 mph)
Max cruising speed at S/L	
	199 knots (370 km/h; 230 mph)
Econ cruising speed	180 knots (333 km/h; 207 mph)
Stalling speed, flaps up	
	73 knots (136 km/h; 84 mph) IAS
Stalling speed, flaps down	
	69 knots (128 km/h; 80 mph) IAS
Max rate of climb at S/L	
	570 m (1,870 ft)/min
Rate of climb at S/L, one engine out	
	134 m (440 ft)/min
Service ceiling, 30.5 m (100 ft)/min rate of climb	
	8,535 m (28,000 ft)
Service ceiling, one engine out, 30.5 m (100 ft)/min rate of climb: 100, 200	4,265 m (14,000 ft)
	4,115 m (13,500 ft)
Service ceiling, one engine out, 15 m (50 ft)/min rate of climb	3,960 m (13,000 ft)
T-O run	671 m (2,200 ft)
T-O to 15 m (50 ft)	686 m (2,250 ft)
Landing from 15 m (50 ft) at max landing weight	
	402 m (1,320 ft)
Range at 3,050 m (10,000 ft) with max passenger payload, max cruising speed	
	560 nm (1,037 km; 645 miles)

Range at 3,050 m (10,000 ft) with 19 passengers, reserves for 50 nm (93 km; 57 mile) diversion, 45 min hold and 5% fuel remaining:
at max cruising speed
560 nm (1,038 km; 645 miles)
at max range speed   630 nm (1,167 km; 725 miles)
Range with 775 kg (1,708 lb) payload, conditions as above:
at max cruising speed
1,160 nm (2,150 km; 1,335 miles)
at max range speed
1,320 nm (2,446 km; 1,520 miles)

DORNIER 228 MARITIME PATROL

For the Indian Coast Guard and several other foreign countries, Dornier has developed versions of the 228 equipped for maritime and fisheries patrol, border patrol and oil/chemical pollution patrol (see below).

Modifications to the standard 228 to adapt it to maritime patrol configuration include major corrosion protection and radome beneath fuselage, four wing hardpoints for searchlight, Micronair spraypod and other equipment. Other fittings include roller door for dropping survival equipment and chute in rear cabin for dropping smoke markers and flares.

POWER PLANT: As for standard 228, with optional auxiliary fuel tanks to increase fuel capacity to 2,886 litres (762 US gallons; 635 Imp gallons).

ACCOMMODATION: Pilot and co-pilot with full dual controls and instruments as standard. Co-pilot controls optional searchlight. Two bubble observation windows in front of cabin (180° view) and photography window on port side which can be opened in flight. Console for radar operator on port side of cabin incorporating radar display, digital navigation display and intercom controls. Rest area located on starboard side of rear cabin with optional folding table, galley or refrigerator and toilet.

AVIONICS: Standard items as detailed in introductory description. Optional exchange of standard avionics to Collins Pro Line II. Com/nav equipment comprises Collins AN/ARC-182 VHF/UHF transceiver, Collins DF-301E VHF/UHF direction finder, Collins radio altimeter ALT-55B, low altitude warning system, weather radar, Global/Wulfsberg GNS-500-5 nav system with search pattern mode, and optional GPS and Loran C. Bendix/King RDR-1500B maritime surveillance radar with 360° scan in underfuselage radome. Optional Litton AN/APS-504(V)5, MEL Super Searcher and Eaton AN/APS-128. Day/night mission equipment includes Honeywell forward-looking infra-red system (FLIR), stabilised long range observation system (SLOS), night vision goggles, Spectrolab 80 million candlepower searchlight, markers and flares, loudhailer and Nikon hand-held camera with data annotation.

DORNIER 228 MARITIME POLLUTION CONTROL

The German government (among others) has undertaken airborne surveillance of North Sea and Baltic Sea oil/chemical pollution since 1984. Original equipment was two specially equipped Do 28-2s, but one has been replaced by a Dornier 228 with a state-of-the-art surveillance system to provide increased performance. It entered service with the Bundesmarine (MFG.5 at Kiel-Hottenau) on 10 April 1991.

Modifications to the standard 228 for pollution control are as for the Maritime Patrol version, but with large floor cut-out to carry laser fluorescent sensor (LFS), one black and white and one colour video camera in the lower nose section and various antennae on the fuselage and tail.

POWER PLANT: As for Maritime Patrol version.

ACCOMMODATION: Crew as for Maritime Patrol version. Central operator workstation on port side of mid-cabin incorporates colour monitors, keyboard, trackball for the side-looking radar, infra-red/ultra-violet scanner, laser fluorescent sensor, microwave radiometer, intercom controls and digital navigation display. A 48 cm (19 in) equipment rack on starboard side for SLAR signal processor, IR/UV scanner control, MWR processor unit and central processor. Folding chart table located behind operator station on port side. Toilet in rear cabin optional.

AVIONICS: As for Maritime Patrol version but with additional image data downlink (DDL).

EQUIPMENT: Primary surveillance sensors from Swedish Space Corporation. Equipment includes Ericsson side-looking airborne radar (SLAR) with underfuselage antenna, Daedalus AADS 1221 infra-red/ultra-violet scanner and a microwave radiometer, equipment for data storage, and microwave data downlink for transmitting full quality radar images to ground stations. To secure evidence of pollution, 228 equipped with colour video camera and highly sensitive black and white video camera. For photographic documentation, Nikon hand-held camera interfaces with navigation system. New laser fluorescent sensor will be installed after intensive testing in German government aircraft, enabling registration and measurement of thickness of oil-film layers. Oil quantities drifting under surface of the water, certain chemicals, algae and other turbid substances of natural origin can also be tracked and differentiated from each other.

DORNIER 228 PHOTOGRAMMETRY/GEO-SURVEY

The 228 can accommodate the specific sensor packages needed to gather comprehensive, up-to-date information needed for successful performance of remote sensing missions, which are cost-effective for a wide range of scientific and, in particular, applications-oriented survey projects. Besides being used in a purely photogrammetric version, the 228 can serve a wide variety of users as a working platform in the earth sciences field. The 228 allows good access to the sensors and other equipment both in flight and for maintenance.

Modifications to the standard 228 are as for the Maritime Patrol version, but production model includes large sliding hatch in cabin floor for sensor installation. Wing hardpoints support different sensors, and various antennae are mounted on fuselage and tail.

POWER PLANT: As for Maritime Patrol version.

ACCOMMODATION: Crew dependent on mission, but basically as described for Maritime Patrol version.

AVIONICS: As for Maritime Patrol version.

OPTIONAL EQUIPMENT: Photogrammetry version has aerial survey cameras installed in floor cutout, Wild or Zeiss navigation telescope, operator station, flight track camera, intercom system, toilet modified as darkroom, rest area with folding table, and small galley or refrigerator.

Geo-survey version has VLF electromagnetometer mounted in nose thimble, magnetometer in tail sting, VLF or proton magnetometer installed in wingtips, electromagnetic reflection system mounted on wing hardpoints, and gamma-ray detector in lower fuselage. An aerial survey camera is installed in floor cutout in rear fuselage.

DORNIER 328

On 3 August 1988, the partners of Dornier GmbH took the decision to resume full development of the Dornier 328 twin-turboprop pressurised regional transport, this phase starting that December. The 328 is intended to offer take-off, climb and landing characteristics comparable to those of the company's earlier utility and commuter aircraft, including the capability to operate from STOL-ports and rough unprepared airstrips. Other criteria include a 78 dBA noise level for 75 per cent of the passengers, stand-up cabin height, and a seat width per passenger better than that in the average Boeing 727 or 737. It is expected to replace 19-seat aircraft on routes with growing traffic, and supersede uneconomical 40/50-seat aircraft on steady traffic routes by making more departures.

The basic TNT wing profile of the Dornier 228 is retained, with a new flap system. Ground and flight spoilers are optional. This is combined with a new near-circular-section fuselage giving maximum floor width and headroom, developed using data from the German Ministry of Research and Technology's NRT (Neue Rumpf Technologien: new fuselage technologies) programme, and a new T tail.

First flight was scheduled for Summer 1991, with 13-nation JAR 25 certification set for late 1992 and FAA certification to FAR 25 following three months later in early 1993. Customers include Sunshine Aviation of Switzerland, Contact Air of Germany, Afrimex and Cayenne. Largest order by early 1991 had come from Midway Airlines, for 33, with another 40 on option. Dornier sees a potential market for up to 400 by the year 2006.

Model of Dornier 328 as ordered by lead customer Midway Airlines

Dornier stretched 328 S for 48 to 50 passengers

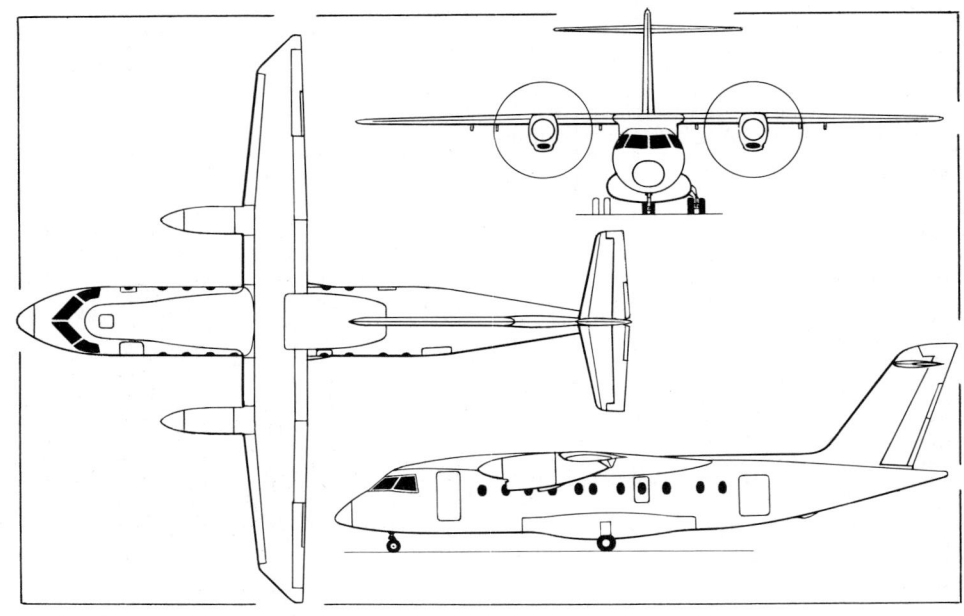

Dornier 328 (two P&WC PW119 turboprops) 30/33-passenger airliner *(Pilot Press)*

Daewoo Heavy Industries of the Republic of Korea will manufacture fuselage shells for the Dornier 328. These will be assembled by Aermacchi of Italy (a risk sharing partner in the 328), which will also be involved in structural testing, engineering and manufacturing. The Daewoo share represents about 20 per cent of the total manufacturing time.

TYPE: Twin-turboprop pressurised regional transport.

WINGS: Cantilever high-wing monoplane. Flight spoiler (outboard) and two optional ground spoilers added forward of trailing-edge flaps on each wing. Wing skins mainly of aluminium-lithium alloy, with Kevlar-CFRP sandwich trailing-edges. Stringers and precision forgings of aluminium-lithium alloy. Flaps, ailerons and wingtips of CFRP.

FUSELAGE: Near-circular-section semi-monocoque pressurised structure, with conical nosecone and tailcone. Primary structure is of aluminium alloy, with aluminium-lithium used for longerons, stringers, window frames and skin panels. Rear fuselage of CFRP, tailcone of Kevlar/CFRP sandwich; nosecone of CFRP sandwich. Doors of superplastic formed aluminium alloy. Long Kevlar/CFRP wing/fuselage fairing, offering space for systems installation outside main pressure shell.

TAIL UNIT: Cantilever T tail, comprising sweptback fin and rudder and tapered, non-swept horizontal surfaces. Entire structure of CFRP except for dorsal fin (Kevlar/CFRP sandwich) and tailplane leading-edge (aluminium alloy). Trim tab in rudder and each elevator.

LANDING GEAR: ERAM/SHL retractable tricycle type, with twin Bendix wheels on each unit. Nose unit retracts forward, main units into long Kevlar/CFRP sandwich unpressurised fairings on fuselage sides. Tyre pressures 3.72 bars (54 lb/sq in) on nose unit, 6.55 bars (95 lb/sq in) on main units. Bendix brakes.

POWER PLANT: Two Pratt & Whitney Canada PW119 turboprops, each rated at 1,353 kW (1,815 shp) for normal take-off and 1,625 kW (2,180 shp) for short-field take-off, each driving a Hartzell six-blade composites propeller with electronic synchrophasing. Improved Performance Kit optional. Nacelles of superplastic formed titanium and carbon composite. All fuel in wing tanks, total capacity 4,045 litres (1,068.5 US gallons; 890 Imp gallons).

ACCOMMODATION: Flight crew and cabin attendant(s). Main cabin seats 30-33 passengers, three-abreast at 79 cm (31 in) or 76 cm (30 in) pitch, with single aisle. Galley to rear of passenger seats; toilet at rear of cabin. Large baggage hold between passenger cabin and rear pressure bulkhead, with external access via baggage door in port side. Additional overhead and underseat baggage stowage in main cabin. Crew/passenger airstair door at front on port side, with Type III emergency exit opposite; Type III emergency exit on port side at rear of cabin, with service door Type II exit at rear on starboard side. Cargo restraint nets and pallet/container system for freight carrying.

SYSTEMS: Air-conditioning and pressurisation systems standard (max differential 0.45 bar; 6.55 lb/sq in). Hydraulic and two independent AC/DC electrical systems housed in main landing gear fairings. APU optional.

AVIONICS: Standard fit comprises Honeywell SPZ-8800 'glass cockpit' with integrated EFIS, AFCS and EICAS (electronic flight instrument system, automatic flight control system, and electronic indication, caution and advisory system); digital air data computer; AHRS with advanced fibre-optic laser gyros; radar altimeter; Primus 650 weather radar; and Primus II digital radio system. Standard options include Honeywell flight management system (FMS), traffic alert and collision avoidance system (TCAS), GPS, MLS, and laser inertial reference system.

DIMENSIONS, EXTERNAL:

Wing span	20.98 m (68 ft 10 in)
Length overall	21.22 m (69 ft 7½ in)
Fuselage: Length	20.92 m (68 ft 7¾ in)
Max width	2.415 m (7 ft 11 in)
Max depth	2.426 m (7 ft 11½ in)
Height overall	7.199 m (23 ft 7½ in)
Elevator span	6.389 m (20 ft 11½ in)

Wheel track (c/l of shock struts)	3.22 m (10 ft 6¾ in)
Wheelbase	7.422 m (24 ft 4¼ in)
Propeller diameter	3.50 m (11 ft 5¾ in)
Propeller/fuselage clearance	0.785 m (2 ft 7 in)
Passenger door (fwd, port): Height	1.70 m (5 ft 7 in)
Width	0.70 m (2 ft 3½ in)
Service door (rear, stbd): Height	1.25 m (4 ft 1¼ in)
Width	0.51 m (1 ft 8 in)
Baggage door (rear, port): Height	1.40 m (4 ft 7 in)
Width	0.92 m (3 ft 0¼ in)

DIMENSIONS, INTERNAL:
Cabin, excl flight deck:

Length	10.35 m (33 ft 11½ in)
Max width	2.18 m (7 ft 2 in)
Width at floor	1.83 m (6 ft 0 in)
Max height	1.89 m (6 ft 2½ in)
Baggage hold volume	6.40 m³ (226.0 cu ft)

WEIGHTS AND LOADINGS:

Max payload	3,450 kg (7,605 lb)
Max baggage load	750 kg (1,653 lb)
Max T-O weight	12,500 kg (27,557 lb)
Max zero-fuel weight	11,625 kg (25,629 lb)
Max landing weight	12,250 kg (27,006 lb)

PERFORMANCE (estimated):

Max cruising speed	345 knots (639 km/h; 397 mph)
Max rate of climb at S/L	740 m (2,430 ft)/min
Design cruising altitude: normal	7,620 m (25,000 ft)
with optional improved performance kit	9,450 m (31,000 ft)
Required runway length:	
normal	1,006 m (3,300 ft)
with improved performance kit	823 m (2,700 ft)

Range at max cruising speed with 30 passengers, with allowance for 100 nm (185 km; 115 mile) diversion and 45 min hold:

at 7,620 m (25,000 ft)	700 nm (1,297 km; 806 miles)
at 9,450 m (31,000 ft)	840 nm (1,556 km; 967 miles)

DORNIER STRETCHED 328 S

A follow-on stretched version of the 328 for 48 to 50 passengers, designated 328 S, was under study in 1990 and early 1991. No details have been released other than the accompanying illustration of a model, and a launch decision was not expected before the first flight of the existing 328.

MESSERSCHMITT-BÖLKOW-BLOHM GmbH (part of Deutsche Aerospace AG)

Postfach 801109, 8000 Munich 80
Telephone: 49 (89) 6070
Telex: 5287-310 MBB D

In May 1969 the former Messerschmitt-Bölkow GmbH and Hamburger Flugzeugbau GmbH (see 1968-69 *Jane's*) merged to form a new group known as Messerschmitt-Bölkow-Blohm GmbH. MBB acquired all shares of VFW on 1 January 1981. In 1989 Daimler-Benz AG, through

Deutsche Aerospace AG, acquired a 50.24 per cent share-holding in MBB and had increased this to 64.89 per cent by November 1990. The last federal state to have a holding in MBB was then Bavaria, with 17.44 per cent.

STRATEGIC BUSINESS UNIT HELICOPTERS

PO Box 801140, 8000 Munich 80
Telephone: 49 (89) 607-0
Fax: 49 (89) 607-24915
Telex: 5287-027 MBB D
HEAD OF STRATEGIC BUSINESS UNIT: H. Plückthun

In April 1990, MBB and Aerospatiale agreed to merge their helicopter activities into a joint venture known as Eurocopter, which will be the second largest helicopter producer after Sikorsky outside the USSR. MBB will have a 40 per cent share in the company. Actual formation was delayed through 1990 by the need to divest the MBB helicopter division of extraneous activities, but took place in May 1991. The existing Eurocopter GIE was renamed Eurocopter International and converted into a French limited company. Eurocopter GmbH is a separate German company running the Tiger programme (see International section). The first function of Eurocopter International is to take over the joint marketing activity of both companies with the exception of North America. Further details in International section.

MBB has been taking part in the ALH programme in co-operation with Hindustan Aeronautics Ltd (see Indian section) since July 1984. The company also overhauls and repairs Sikorsky CH-53G, Westland Sea King Mk 41 and Westland naval Lynx helicopters in service with the German armed forces. The Speyer factory is currently upgrading 22 German Navy Sea Kings of Marinefliegergeschwader 5 with Ferranti Seaspray Mk 3 radar for target acquisition, a Ferranti Link II target data transformer, TST AN/ALR-68 radar warning receiver, Tracor M130 chaff/flare dispenser and four BAe Sea Skua missiles.

212 BO 105 P (PAH-1) military versions for the Federal German Army ended in 1984, and details of these versions can be found in the 1985-86 edition. For details of the Phase I upgrade and BSH escort helicopter, see next entry.

BO 105s have been used by MBB to flight test a TST (formerly AEG) mast mounted radar system, and a Lucas Aerospace bolt-on undernose turret to permit off-axis firing of Stinger air-to-air missiles, controlled by a GEC Ferranti helmet pointing system. This latter helicopter has joined one German Army BO 105 M and two Army BO 105 Ps (PAH-1s) being flown at test and operational training centres to evaluate the weapon and sighting systems needed

for the BSH-1 escort helicopter (which see). A BO 105 has been flown to test the OPST-1 DLR-MBB-Liebherr full-authority, intelligent triplex, optically signalled yaw control that relieves the pilot of the task of yaw/collective axis co-ordination.

By January 1991 more than 1,300 BO 105s of all models had been delivered to 37 countries in five continents. All BO 105 helicopters for the world market are manufactured and assembled at the company's Donauwörth facility, with the exceptions of those for the Spanish market which are assembled in Spain by CASA, those for the Indonesian market which are manufactured and assembled in that

MBB/KAWASAKI BK 117

MBB is building in conjunction with Kawasaki of Japan the 8/11-seat BK 117 multi-purpose helicopter (see International section). Details of the all-German military BK 117 M were given in this section of the 1990-91 *Jane's*. None of these have yet been sold.

EUROCOPTER TIGER

The programme for this Franco-German common anti-tank helicopter, also known in its three versions as PAH-2/HAC/HAP, is described under the Eurocopter GmbH heading in the International section.

NH 90

This four-nation programme (NATO helicopter for the 1990s) is described under the NH 90 heading in the International section.

EUROFAR

This multi-nation European tilt-rotor programme, in which MBB is responsible for the German share, is described under Eurofar in the International section.

MBB BO 105

The first prototype of the BO 105 with hingeless titanium rotor hub and composite rotor blades first flew on 16 February 1967.

Details of prototypes, early BO 105C and D production helicopters and special variants can be found in previous editions of *Jane's*. Production of 100 BO 105 M (VBH) and

CBS version of the BO 105, with searchlight and pop-out floats, operated by New York City Police

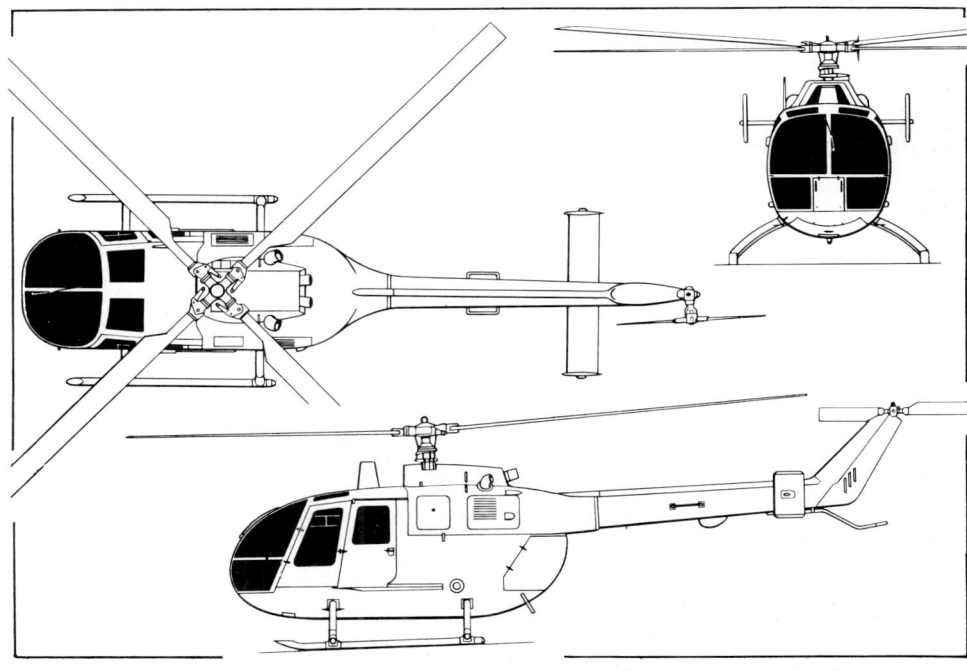

BO 105 CB five-seat light helicopter (two Allison 250-C20B turboshafts) *(Pilot Press)*

Upgraded version of the PAH-1 fires a HOT 2 missile using its lightweight launcher and digital controls

country by IPTN, and BO 105 LS helicopters produced at MBB's Fort Erie facility in Ontario, Canada. Current models are as follows:

BO 105 CB: Standard production version since 1975, with two Allison 250-C20B engines, operable in air temperatures ranging from −45° to +54°C. LBA certification received in November 1976. Details of specially equipped versions for the Mexican Navy (12) and Swedish Army (20, delivered by September 1988) were given in the 1987-88 *Jane's*. In Spain, CASA assembled 57 of an initial 60 for the Spanish Army for armed reconnaissance (18), observation (14) and anti-tank missions (28), and has continued assembly.

BO 105 CBS: Version with increased rear-seat leg room in a cabin extended by a 0.25 m (10 in) plug. Available in five-seat executive or six-seat high density configurations. Identified by small additional window aft of rear door on each side. Marketed in the USA by MBB Helicopter Corporation under the name **Twin Jet II**. Certificated in early 1983 by FAA for IFR operation in accordance with SFAR Pt 29-4, requiring two pilots, radar, Loran C and a separate battery, but not a stability augmentation system, though SAS is available as an option. The Swedish Air Force has four BO 105 CBSs, equipped for IFR search and rescue.

BO 105 LS: Re-engined high altitude version of CBS produced exclusively in Canada and described separately under MBB entry in Canadian section. Five pre-production models produced in Germany during 1984.

The description which follows applies to the BO 105 CBS except where indicated:

TYPE: Five/six-seat light helicopter.

ROTOR SYSTEM: Four-blade main rotor, comprising rigid titanium head and GFRP blades, with titanium anti-erosion strip and pendulous vibration damper on each blade. NACA 23012 lifting aerofoil with drooped leading-edge and reflexed trailing-edge. Roller bearings for pitch change. Main rotor brake standard. Folding of two main rotor blades optional. Two-blade semi-rigid tail rotor; blades of GFRP, with stainless steel anti-erosion strip. Main rotor rpm 424. Tail rotor rpm 2,220.

Main transmission utilises two bevel gear input stages with freewheeling clutches and a spur collector gear stage. Planetary reduction gear; three auxiliary drives for accessories. Main transmission rated for twin-engine input of 257 kW (345 shp) per engine, or a single-engine input of 283 kW (380 shp). Tail rotor gearbox on fin.

FUSELAGE: Conventional light alloy semi-monocoque structure of pod and boom type. Glassfibre reinforced cowling over power plant. Titanium sheet engine deck.

TAIL UNIT: Horizontal stabiliser of conventional light alloy construction with small endplate fins.

LANDING GEAR: Skid type, with cross-tubes designed for energy absorption by plastic deformation in the event of a heavy landing. Inflatable emergency floats can be attached to skids.

POWER PLANT: Two 313 kW (420 shp) Allison 250-C20B turboshafts, each with a max continuous rating of 298 kW (400 shp). Bladder fuel tanks under cabin floor, capacity 580 litres (153.2 US gallons; 127.5 Imp gallons), of which 570 litres (150.6 US gallons; 125.3 Imp gallons) are usable. Fuelling point on port side of cabin. Auxiliary tanks in freight compartment available optionally. Oil capacity: engine 12 litres (3.2 US gallons; 2.6 Imp gallons), gearbox 11.6 litres (3.06 US gallons; 2.55 Imp gallons).

ACCOMMODATION: Pilot and co-pilot or passenger on individual longitudinally adjustable front seats with safety belts and automatic locking shoulder harnesses. Optional dual controls. Bench seat at rear for three persons, removable for cargo and stretcher carrying. A full EMS version is available. Both cabin and cargo compartment have panelling, sound insulation and floor covering. Entire rear fuselage aft of seats and under power plant available as freight and baggage space, with access through two clamshell doors at rear. Two standard stretchers can be accommodated side by side in ambulance role. One forward opening hinged and

jettisonable door and one sliding door on each side of cabin. Ram air and electrical ventilation system. Heating system optional.

SYSTEMS: Tandem fully redundant hydraulic system, pressure 103.5 bars (1,500 lb/sq in), for powered main rotor controls. System flow rate 6.2 litres (1.64 US gallons; 1.36 Imp gallons)/min. Bootstrap/oil reservoir, pressurised at 1.7 bars (25 lb/sq in). Electrical system powered by two 150A 28V DC starter/generators and a 24V 25Ah nickel-cadmium battery; external power socket.

AVIONICS: Wide variety of avionics available including weather radar, Doppler navigation, SAS and autopilot.

EQUIPMENT: Standard equipment includes basic flight instruments, engine instruments, heated pitot, tiedown rings in cargo compartment, cabin and cargo compartment dome lights, position lights and collision warning lights. Options include dual controls, heating system, windscreen wiper, rescue winch, landing light, searchlight, externally mounted loudspeaker, fuel dump valve, external load hook, settling protectors, snow skids, and manual main rotor blade folding.

DIMENSIONS, EXTERNAL:

Main rotor diameter	9.84 m (32 ft 3½ in)
Tail rotor diameter	1.90 m (6 ft 2¾ in)
Main rotor blade chord	0.27 m (10⅝ in)
Tail rotor blade chord	0.18 m (7 in)
Distance between rotor centres	5.95 m (19 ft 6¼ in)
Length: incl main and tail rotors	11.86 m (38 ft 11 in)
excl rotors: CB	8.56 m (28 ft 1 in)
CBS	8.81 m (28 ft 11 in)
fuselage pod: CB	4.30 m (14 ft 1 in)
CBS	4.55 m (14 ft 11 in)
Height to top of main rotor head	3.02 m (9 ft 11 in)
Width over skids: unladen	2.53 m (8 ft 3½ in)
laden	2.58 m (8 ft 5½ in)
Rear loading doors: Height	0.64 m (2 ft 1 in)
Width	1.40 m (4 ft 7 in)

DIMENSIONS, INTERNAL:

Cabin, incl cargo compartment:	
Max width	1.40 m (4 ft 7 in)
Max height	1.25 m (4 ft 1 in)

Volume	4.80 m³ (169 cu ft)
Cargo compartment: Length	1.85 m (6 ft 0¾ in)
Max width	1.20 m (3 ft 11¼ in)
Max height	0.57 m (1 ft 10½ in)
Floor area	2.25 m² (24.2 sq ft)
Volume	1.30 m³ (45.9 cu ft)

AREAS:

Main rotor disc	76.05 m² (818.6 sq ft)
Tail rotor disc	2.835 m² (30.5 sq ft)

WEIGHTS AND LOADINGS:

Weight empty, basic: CB	1,277 kg (2,815 lb)
CBS	1,301 kg (2,868 lb)
Standard fuel (usable)	456 kg (1,005 lb)
Max fuel, incl auxiliary tanks	776 kg (1,710 lb)
Max T-O weight	2,500 kg (5,511 lb)
Max disc loading	32.9 kg/m² (6.74 lb/sq ft)

PERFORMANCE (at max T-O weight):

Never-exceed speed (V~NE~) at S/L	
	131 knots (242 km/h; 150 mph)
Max cruising speed at S/L	
	131 knots (242 km/h; 150 mph)
Best range speed at S/L	110 knots (204 km/h; 127 mph)
Max rate of climb at S/L, max continuous power	
	444 m (1,457 ft)/min
Vertical rate of climb at S/L, T-O power	
	90 m (295 ft)/min
Max operating altitude	3,050 m (10,000 ft)
Hovering ceiling, T-O power: IGE	1,525 m (5,000 ft)
OGE	457 m (1,500 ft)
Range with standard fuel and max payload, no reserves:	
at S/L	300 nm (555 km; 345 miles)
at 1,525 m (5,000 ft)	321 nm (596 km; 370 miles)
Ferry range with auxiliary tanks, no reserves:	
at S/L	519 nm (961 km; 597 miles)
at 1,525 m (5,000 ft)	550 nm (1,020 km; 634 miles)
Endurance with standard fuel and max payload, no reserves: at S/L	3 h 24 min

MBB BO 105/PAH-1/VBH/BSH-1

Production of 100 BO 105 M/VBH scout and 212 BO 105 P/PAH-1 anti-tank helicopters was completed in 1984 (see 1985-86 *Jane's*). The German Parliament approved a DM278 million programme in September 1990 to fit new main rotor blades and improved oil cooling and engine intakes to all 209 remaining PAH-1s. Of these, 155 PAH-1s will also have the HOT 2 missile with digital electronics and lightweight launchers and the other 54 will be converted to BSH-1 escort helicopters and each armed with four air-to-air Stingers. The Lucas turret was not selected.

The new rotor blades allow an increase in max T-O weight to 2,500 kg (5,511 lb). This and the lighter HOT system raise useful load by 180 kg (397 lb). VBH stands for Verbindungs und Beobachtungs Hubschrauber; PAH, Panzer Abwehr Hubschrauber; BSH, Begleitschutz Hubschrauber.

The upgraded Phase I PAH-1 cannot fire at night, has no laser ranger or designator and is not fitted to carry the gun turret. These and a mast-mounted night sight might form a Phase II upgrade.

Data for the upgraded PAH-1 are substantially as for the BO 105 CB, including max T-O weight of 2,500 kg (5,511 lb). Empty weight without fuel, missiles or crew is 1,688 kg (3,721 lb); take-off weight for German Army helicopters on

The six-seat cabin layout of the Turbomeca Arrius-powered second prototype of the MBB BO 108

an anti-tank mission is 2,380 kg (5,247 lb); transmission ratings are 648 kW (869 shp) on two engines and 368 kW (493 shp) with one engine inoperative; and hover ceiling OGE at mission weight is 2,100 m (6,890 ft).

MBB BO 108

The BO 108 was formally confirmed as the successor to the BO 105 at the HAI Heli-Expo in January 1991. Certification is planned for 1994, with first deliveries in 1995. Initial power plant will be two Turbomeca digitally controlled Arrius 1Bs (TM 319-1B), but the P&WC PW206B will be offered as an alternative. The Arrius may be finished in Turbomeca's factory in Texas and shipped to the MBB factory at Fort Erie, Canada, for installation in BO 108 airframes made in Germany. The BO 108 is designed to FAR Pt 29 Category A.

The BO 108 main rotor system has been adopted by Sikorsky and Boeing Helicopters for their US Army AH-66 Comanche, making MBB a partner in the programme. Two prototypes were funded, the first of which (D-HBOX) flew initially on 15 October 1988 powered by two Allison 250-C20Rs. The BO 108 demonstrator programme is being financed by MBB and various equipment manufacturers, with support from the German Federal Ministry of Economics and the German Ministry of Research and Technology.

New features include completely hingeless main rotor, shallow transmission with special vibration absorbers, low-drag aerodynamics, composite structures, and advanced IFR electrical and avionics systems, EFIS instruments and engine integration. One aim is to achieve single-pilot IFR with a cost-effective stability augmentation system. Other objectives are to develop the means to improve handling and simplify maintenance procedures (including provision of a diagnostic system if economical) and reduce the direct operating costs (25 per cent lower than those of the BO 105) and life cycle costs for future helicopters while increasing productivity (by improving the payload/empty weight ratio). Improvements in direct operating costs are achieved partly by better aerodynamics; wind tunnel tests revealed that the fuselage of the BO 108 has almost 30 per cent less drag than that of the BO 105. This is achieved by a 5° rotor installation angle (keeping the fuselage level in cruising flight), optimised nose and tail configurations, and increased usable volume without enlargement of the frontal area (increased interior height, width and cargo volume, plus increased internal fuel capacity and equipment space). All essential dynamically loaded components are to be qualified to 3,000 h MTBR or 'on condition'.

The initial basic flight test programme using the first BO 108 prototype was completed by the end of March 1989. It was followed by flight envelope extension and testing of a new all-composite bearingless tail rotor until the end of 1990. A second prototype was expected to fly in Spring 1991 powered by two Turbomeca Arrius 1Bs and having a single-pilot EFIS-based IFR system. The fuselage is stretched 15 cm (5.9 in) and cabin interior width increased by 10 cm (3.9 in). Max T-O weight is increased to 2,500 kg (5,511 lb).

TYPE: Four/five-seat experimental light helicopter.

ROTOR SYSTEM: Four-blade FVW hingeless main rotor, with rigid cuffs to transmit pitch-change commands from hub to main blade section. Blades of glassfibre construction, with foam core; new DM-H3 and -H4 aerofoil sections, non-linear twist, and tapered transonic tips. Two-blade hingeless tail rotor with FEL (fibre-elastomeric bearings in hub) and composite blades, mounted on port side of tail pylon. Lightweight rotor drive train. Transmission system of new flat design, with two-stage reduction gearing. ARIS (anti-resonance isolation system) provides dynamic separation of rotor and transmission from airframe structure.

FUSELAGE: Constructed mainly of Kevlar/carbonfibre sandwich composites, except for aluminium alloy sidewalls,

Allison-powered first prototype of the MBB BO 108, which will replace the BO 105 in 1995

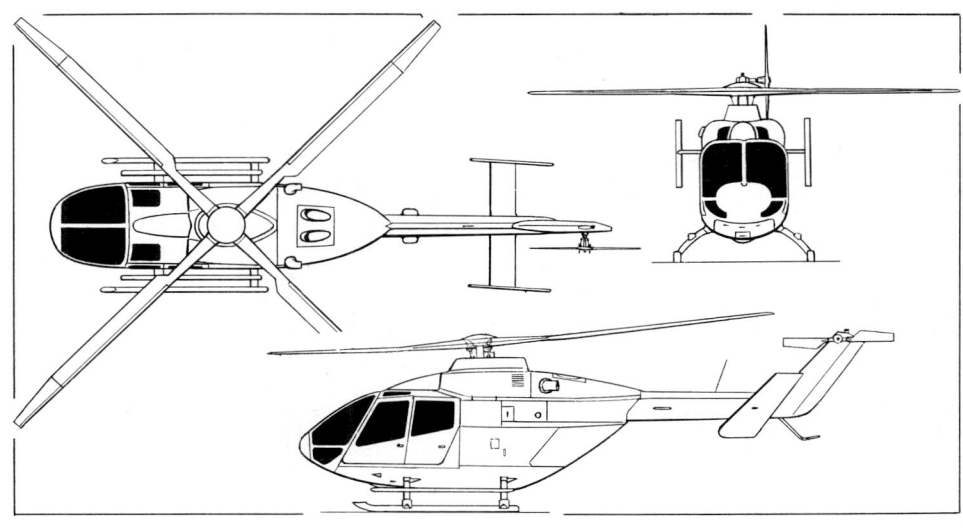

General arrangement of the BO 108 (two Allison 250-C20R-3 turboshafts) *(Pilot Press)*

pod lower module and cabin floor, tailboom and around cargo area, and some titanium components in region of engine bay. Composites tailplane with endplate fins.

LANDING GEAR: Skid type, inclined rearward by 1°.

POWER PLANT: First prototype has two 335.5 kW (450 shp) class Allison 250-C20R-3 turboshafts, mounted side by side aft of the main rotor. Second prototype has two 360 kW (480 shp) Turbomeca Arrius 1B (TM 319-1B) with full authority digital control. Alternative engines will be Pratt & Whitney Canada PW206Bs. Two separate fan powered oil cooling systems. Fuel in underfloor tanks.

ACCOMMODATION: Pilot, plus four or six passengers on crashproof seats. Forward hinged doors for crew. Sliding doors for passengers. Rear of pod clamshell doors for bulky items/cargo; flights permissible with clamshell doors removed. Unobstructed cabin interior. Rear loading cargo volume 1.60 m³ (56.50 cu ft). Total cabin volume 5.00 m³ (176.57 cu ft).

SYSTEMS: Redundant electrical supply systems to FAR Pt 29 standards. Fully redundant dual hydraulic powered flying control system mounted on main rotor transmission with integrated electrical SAS input.

AVIONICS: IFR capability. Provisions for integrated weather radar. Radio/nav systems. Future developments can include liquid-crystal flat panel displays replacing flight instruments, centralised data system and GPS.

DIMENSIONS, EXTERNAL:
Main rotor diameter	10.00 m (32 ft 9¾ in)
Tail rotor diameter	1.90 m (6 ft 2¾ in)
Distance between rotor centres	6.148 m (20 ft 2½ in)
Length:	
incl main and tail rotors	10.637 m (34 ft 10½ in)
fuselage	9.675 m (31 ft 9 in)
fuselage pod	5.966 m (19 ft 7 in)
Height to top of main rotor head	3.062 m (10 ft 0¾ in)
Width of fuselage	1.50 m (4 ft 11 in)
Tailplane span	2.347 m (7 ft 8½ in)
Width over skids	2.20 m (7 ft 2¾ in)

WEIGHTS AND LOADINGS:
Weight empty	1,225 kg (2,700 lb)
Max T-O weight	2,500 kg (5,511 lb)

PERFORMANCE (at max T-O weight, at 1,500 m; 4,920 ft altitude):
Max cruising speed	approx 146 knots (270 km/h; 168 mph)
Econ cruising speed	129 knots (240 km/h; 149 mph)
Max rate of climb	552 m (1,810 ft)/min
Hovering ceiling: IGE	3,850-5,000 m (12,630-16,400 ft)
OGE	3,350 m (11,000 ft)
OGE, ISA +20°C	2,500 m (8,200 ft)
Range with max fuel	431 nm (800 km; 497 miles)
Max endurance, no reserves	4 h 45 min

STRATEGIC BUSINESS UNIT MILITARY AIRCRAFT

PO Box 801160, 8000 Munich 80
Telephone: 49 (89) 607-0
HEAD OF STRATEGIC BUSINESS UNIT: O. Friedrich

Major military aircraft activities of the Group include aircraft armament (Vertical Ballistic Weapon) and airborne reconnaissance systems, disarmament verification systems (LAPAS I and II, PRISMA and BICES), simulation and training systems, and research into advanced aircraft systems, materials and manufacturing technologies. MBB also makes Airbus subassemblies.

PANAVIA TORNADO

MBB is the prime contractor for the German share of the Tornado and assembled the German Air Force and Navy aircraft. Full details are in the International section.

EUROFIGHTER EFA

MBB is prime contractor for the German share of the development of the European Fighter Aircraft, with

Dornier as co-contractor. Full details are in the International section.

ROCKWELL INTERNATIONAL/MBB X-31A

MBB shared the development and manufacture of the two NASA X-31A research aircraft and continues to share the research flying programme. Full details are in the International section.

PTS-2000

This Italo-German military pilot training system is briefly described under Aermacchi/DASA in the International section.

MBB F-4F ICE PROGRAMME

Under a German Defence Ministry programme known as ICE (improved combat effectiveness), 110 Luftwaffe F-4F Phantom IIs, primarily those of fighter wings JG 71 and JG 74, are to be upgraded to give them a lookdown/shootdown capability against multiple targets. The programme, for which MBB is the prime contractor, was initiated in late 1983 and reached the end of the definition phase some two

years later. It entered the full scale development phase in December 1986, and two development aircraft, one with an AN/APG-65 radar and the other equipped to launch AMRAAM, were flying in 1991.

Features include replacement of the existing Westinghouse AN/APQ-120 radar with the all-digital multi-mode Hughes AN/APG-65, built under licence in Germany by Telefunken Systemtechnik, fitting up to four Hughes AIM-120 (AMRAAM) air-to-air missiles, a new TST radar control console, optimisation (by Hughes) of the cockpit display, installation of a new Litef digital fire control computer, Honeywell H-423 laser inertial platform, GEC Avionics CPU-143/A digital air data computer, new IFF system, a Frazer-Nash AMRAAM launcher, a MIL-1553B digital databus with advanced operational software, and improved resistance to electronic jamming and other countermeasures.

A further 40 Luftwaffe F-4Fs, serving in the fighter-bomber role with JBGs 35 and 36, were to undergo partial update (databus, INS and ADC only, initially), with the option of a full ICE installation later.

ROCKWELL/MBB FAN RANGER

Rockwell International and MBB have jointly entered a turbofan powered version of the RFB Fantrainer in the USAF/USN JPATS trainer competition (see International section). RFB is to build and certificate the two aircraft (see RFB Rhein-Flugzeugbau in this section).

German Air Force F-4F with AN/APG-65 radar in nose during development flight testing

SPACE SYSTEMS DIVISION, DEUTSCHE AEROSPACE
Strategic Business Unit
Space Transportation and Propulsion Systems

c/o Deutsche Aerospace, PO Box 440320, 8000 Munich 44
Telephone: 49 (89) 3 81 99-862
Fax: 49 (89) 3 81 99-866
WORKS: Bremen and Ottobrunn

Besides producing major airframe and propulsion assemblies for Ariane 4 and 5, this division is developing structure, propulsion, attitude and orbital control systems for the Hermès manned space vehicle (see International section).

HYTEX/SÄNGER/HORUS

The Sänger two-stage completely reusable hypersonic vehicle, with a manned upper stage called Horus, is Germany's proposal for a space system able to take off and land at normal airports.

Hytex is an intermediate manned Mach 6 technology development vehicle needed to prove key elements of Sänger aerothermodynamics and operation of the propulsion system consisting of kerosene-fuelled turbojets within the atmosphere and hydrogen-fuelled ramjets in near space. First-stage studies should be completed in 1992 and the development programme should run from 1993 to 1999, with a first flight in 1998.

The Sänger fully reusable space vehicle being developed by the Space Systems Division of Deutsche Aerospace

Hytex is not yet funded and Germany is looking for foreign partners. Sweden joined the Hytex programme in Autumn 1990 and Italy was expected to follow.

Hytex has a wing span of 9.30 m (30 ft 6 in), length of 23.01 m (75 ft 6 in), and weight of about 20,000 kg (44,100 lb). Under the German Hypersonic Technology Programme, the first liquid hydrogen ramjet for Sänger was tested on 7 June 1990. A second test was run on 4 July and a third was expected in September.

DORNIER COMPOSITE
DORNIER COMPOSITE AIRCRAFT GmbH & Co KG
Geschäftsbereich Seastar

Flugplatz Oberpfaffenhofen, 8031 Wessling
Telephone: 49 (8153) 401-0
Fax: 49 (8153) 3636
Telex: 5 270 288 DCA D
MANAGING DIRECTOR: Conrado Dornier
TECHNICAL DIRECTOR: Albert H. Halder
DIRECTOR OF FINANCE AND ADMINISTRATION:
Erhard Seeger
PUBLIC RELATIONS: Evelyn Karcher

This company was founded by the late Prof Dipl Ing Claudius Dornier Jr to produce the Seastar utility amphibian, of which design was initiated in January 1982. The VT 01 first prototype (D-ICDS), assembled by Lufthansa and described in the 1984-85 *Jane's*, made its first flight in July 1984, but in mid-1985 was retired after being damaged. In October 1985 the company moved to Oberpfaffenhofen where, with an initial development team of 10 people, work began on an improved version known as the CD2.

Funding for production came originally from the German government, Daimler-Benz (20 per cent shareholder), banks and the Dornier family. The use of about 100,000 m² (1,076,390 sq ft) of the Dornier airfield at Oberpfaffenhofen, plus a hangar for final assembly of the Seastar, resulted from an agreement between Daimler-Benz/Dornier GmbH and the Dornier family. However, on 3 November 1989 the company filed for bankruptcy, while continuing to operate and work towards certification by the German LBA and FAA type approval under FAR Pt 23. The 1991 workforce of 200 was expected to increase.

Seastar production had begun in October 1989 and delivery of the first of 38 aircraft then held on option was expected in December 1990. In January 1990 two rival offers were made to the receiver, one from Conrado Dornier and the Dresdner Bank, and the other from Claudio Dornier who had the support of a West German aerospace company and Albert Blum. In February Claudius Dornier Seastar was finally purchased by Dornier Composite Aircraft, owned by Conrado Dornier. The Dresdner Bank has a 40 per cent shareholding.

Other interest has come from Japan. World Import Mart Co Ltd and Japan Airlines System Trading Inc are Seastar agents in Japan.

DORNIER COMPOSITE SEASTAR CD2

Seastar VT 01 (D-ICDS), with metal wing of Dornier Do 28 and glassfibre fuselage, first flew in Hamburg on 17 August 1984. It was damaged in a wheels-down water landing on Lake Constance on 24 July 1985. D-ICDS was rebuilt as a CD2 with the first all-composites wing and first flew from land on 24 April 1987.

Hull design was improved by a flatter planing bottom, enlarged cockpit, reprofiled nose and extended sponsons, and the original PT6A-11 turboprops were replaced by 373 kW (500 shp) PT6A-112s driving four-blade instead of three-blade propellers. Seaworthiness trials in the Baltic, off Kiel, and on Lake Constance were completed successfully,

and a second pre-production aircraft (D-ICKS) joined the certification flight test programme in October 1988. It differs from D-ICDS only in having larger cabin windows and a fully furnished interior, a max T-O weight increased to 4,600 kg (10,141 lb), and the use of production type PT6A-135A turboprop engines.

The CD2 Seastar was certificated by the LBA on 30 October 1990 and meets US FAR Pt 23 Amendment 34 for commuter aircraft. The two pre-production aircraft had then flown more than 750 hours and made 200 water operations. The all-composites structure and manufacturing methods have been formally defined and structurally tested and a fatigue life of 30,000 hours agreed.

A market for 250 Seastars is expected and options and letters of intent for 50 had been submitted by the end of 1990. The first production Seastar should be delivered at the end of 1991 and rate of production should reach 25 a year

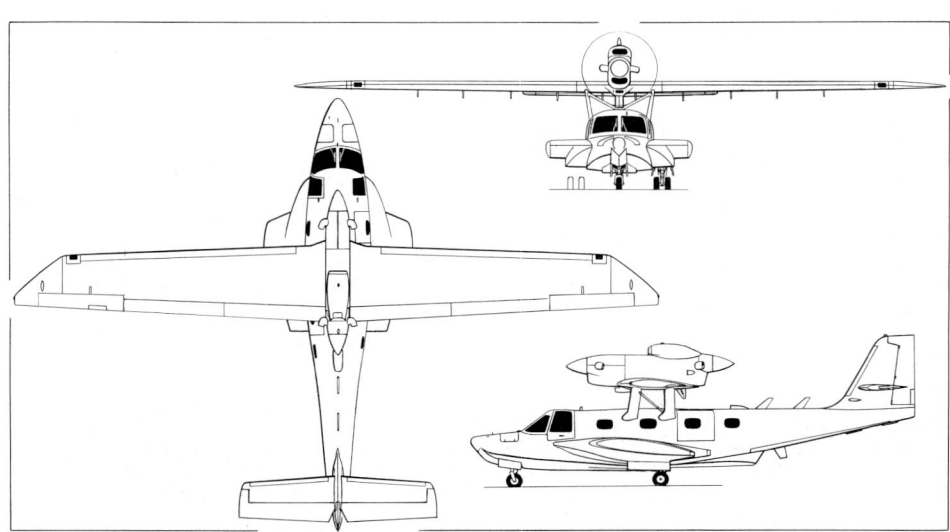

Dornier Composite Aircraft Seastar CD2 in its production form *(Pilot Press)*

in three years. Total development, certification and production preparation cost is reported to have been DM120 million.

The Seastar is suitable for a variety of missions, including feeder transport from water bases to airports; missions for which helicopters would be restricted by range, economics or safety factors; all-cargo transport with flat floor in main cabin; search and rescue; law enforcement; air ambulance with six stretchers; maritime patrol; EEZ surveillance; and civil or military special missions, accommodating four people over a range of 1,000 nm (1,850 km; 1,150 miles). Its ability to operate from land, water, snow or ice enables it to perform such other roles as sightseeing and hunting tours, fire control and firefighting. A typical maritime patrol or law enforcement mission could involve an outward flight to a distance of 80 nm (148 km; 92 miles) taking 30 min; a search pattern lasting 2 h 45 min at a speed of 120 knots (222 km/h; 138 mph), altitude of 610 m (2,000 ft) and taking the aircraft to a distance of 330 nm (612 km; 380 miles); a sea landing and 4 h surveillance of ships with power off and loading of 500 kg (1,102 lb) of seized cargo; and flight back to base with an intermediate stop to unload the cargo, taking 1 h. Total mission time 8 h 15 min. The Seastar can operate in wave heights of up to 1.0 m (3.3 ft), in sea state 1-2.

The following description applies to the second pre-production CD2 and planned production model:

TYPE: Twin-turboprop STOL utility amphibian.

WINGS: Cantilever parasol monoplane, with modified NACA 23015 aerofoil section. Aspect ratio 10.35; taper ratio 0.691; dihedral 0°; mean aerodynamic chord 1.825 m (6 ft 0 in). The high-lift wing has drooped outboard leading-edges. Three-spar fail-safe structure constructed of GFRP with a foam core, with carbonfibre reinforcement of the front and rear spars. Low pressure cured (LPC) composites with subassemblies cured in mould at medium heat and large assemblies cured outside moulds. Special machines apply epoxy and hardener and hold material for lay-up in moulds. Single-slotted electrically actuated trailing-edge flaps and horn balanced ailerons. Flotation compartments are embodied. Leading-edge de-icing.

FUSELAGE: Conventional unpressurised flying-boat hull, constructed almost entirely of glassfibre. Large chined sponson on each side contains fuel and main landing gear. Flotation compartments are embodied. No wingtip floats.

TAIL UNIT: Conventional unit, constructed of glassfibre and incorporating an electrically actuated variable incidence tailplane. Leading-edge de-icing. Horn balanced elevators and rudder, each with trim tab. Shallow dorsal fin on maritime patrol version.

LANDING GEAR: Hydraulically retractable tricycle type, with twin wheels on each main unit and single fully swivelling nosewheel. All wheels size 6.25-7.5. Main units retract forward into hull sponsons, nose unit forward into bow. Goodrich tyres; hydraulic double disc brakes.

POWER PLANT: Two Pratt & Whitney Canada PT6A-135A turboprops, each flat rated at 485 kW (650 shp), mounted in tandem above wing in continuous nacelle and driving one tractor and one pusher propeller at 1,900 rpm. Each is a four-blade McCauley C-760 series constant-speed reversible metal propeller. Front propeller has electric de-icing. Fuel tank in each sponson, combined max usable capacity 1,734 litres (458 US gallons; 381 Imp gallons). Gravity refuelling through top of sponson. Oil capacity 13.25 litres (3.5 US gallons; 2.9 Imp gallons).

ACCOMMODATION: Max accommodation for two pilots and 12 passengers in four rows of three in wide body cabin, at 81 cm (32 in) seat pitch, with single aisle. Dual controls standard. Aircraft approved for single-pilot crew. Alternative layouts for six executives in VIP seating, with a lavatory at rear of cabin and galley in part of baggage compartment; or nine passengers, with lavatory. By utilising entire baggage compartment space, aircraft can

Second pre-production Seastar CD2 amphibian (two P&WC PT6A-135A turboprops)

accommodate six stretchers plus two attendants and medical equipment; or can be configured for all-cargo use with front and rear loading access, providing 10.00 m³ (353.1 cu ft) of space able to transport items up to 5.50 m (18 ft 0½ in) in length. Crew door on port side, plus roof hatch to observe water manoeuvres. Passenger escape door opening upward at front of cabin on starboard side and upward opening main door at rear on port side; latter has an optional airstair incorporated in the adjacent sponson structure. Baggage compartment at rear of cabin, with optional external door on starboard side, capacity 180 kg (397 lb). All accommodation heated and ventilated; air-conditioning optional. Crew of three and 450 kg (992 lb) of mission equipment in maritime patrol role.

SYSTEMS: Hydraulic system for landing gear actuation electrically pressurised to 207 bars (3,000 lb/sq in). Flow rate 11 litres (2.9 US gallons; 2.4 Imp gallons)/min. Two 28V DC 200A starter/generators, two 28V DC to 26V/115V AC static inverters, one 40Ah Nicad battery. Pneumatic de-icing for wing and tail leading-edges and engine intakes, optional on wing struts.

AVIONICS: Complete single-pilot IFR Collins Pro Line II with EHSI-74 standard; optional Collins HF radio, EFIS-84, FCS-65 autopilot, CVR, Fairchild FDR, GPS, Loran C, Omega, Collins WXR 270 or 840 weather radar. For maritime roles, can carry nose-mounted Bendix/King RDR 1400 weather radar and Swedish Space Corporation SLAR.

ARMAMENT: Four underwing stations available for loads of 250 kg (551 lb) each.

DIMENSIONS, EXTERNAL:

Wing span	17.74 m (58 ft 2½ in)
Width over sponsons	4.22 m (13 ft 10¼ in)
Length overall	12.7 m (41 ft 8 in)
Fuselage: Max width	1.90 m (6 ft 2¾ in)
Height overall (on land)	4.83 m (15 ft 10¼ in)
Tailplane span	5.56 m (18 ft 3 in)
Wheel track	2.50 m (8 ft 2½ in)
Propeller diameter: front	2.40 m (7 ft 10½ in)
rear	2.35 m (7 ft 8½ in)
Crew door: Height	0.85 m (2 ft 9½ in)
Width	0.70 m (2 ft 3½ in)
Escape door (fwd, stbd): Height	0.94 m (3 ft 1 in)
Width	1.12 m (3 ft 8 in)
Passenger door (rear, port): Height	0.94 m (3 ft 1 in)
Width	1.12 m (3 ft 8 in)
Height to sill	1.28 m (4 ft 2½ in)
Baggage compartment door: Height	0.50 m (1 ft 7¾ in)
Width	0.75 m (2 ft 5½ in)
Height to sill	1.39 m (4 ft 6¾ in)

DIMENSIONS, INTERNAL:
Cabin, excl flight deck:

Length: excl baggage compartment	
	4.00 m (13 ft 1½ in)
incl baggage compartment	5.50 m (18 ft 0½ in)
Max width	1.65 m (5 ft 5 in)
Max height	1.40 m (4 ft 7 in)
Floor area:	
excl baggage compartment	5.50 m² (59.2 sq ft)
Volume:	
excl baggage compartment	8.23 m³ (290.6 cu ft)
incl baggage compartment	9.86 m³ (348.2 cu ft)
Rear baggage compartment volume	1.63 m³ (57.56 cu ft)

AREAS:

Wings, gross	30.60 m² (329.38 sq ft)
Vertical tail surfaces (total)	3.15 m² (33.9 sq ft)
Horizontal tail surfaces (total)	6.32 m² (68.0 sq ft)

WEIGHTS AND LOADINGS:

Weight empty, equipped (standard)	2,800 kg (6,173 lb)
Max payload	1,116 kg (2,460 lb)
Max usable fuel	1,396 kg (3,077 lb)
Max T-O weight	4,600 kg (10,141 lb)
Max ramp weight	4,650 kg (10,250 lb)
Max landing weight	4,500 kg (9,921 lb)
Max wing loading	150.3 kg/m² (30.79 lb/sq ft)
Max power loading	4.74 kg/kW (7.80 lb/shp)

PERFORMANCE (preliminary, PT6A-135A engines, at max T-O weight):

Max cruising speed at 3,050 m (10,000 ft)	
	180 knots (334 km/h; 207 mph)
Econ cruising speed at 305 m (1,000 ft)	
	173 knots (321 km/h; 199 mph)
Surveillance speed	
	81-180 knots (150-334 km/h; 93-207 mph)
Stalling speed at S/L	65 knots (120 km/h; 75 mph)
Max rate of climb at S/L	396 m (1,300 ft)/min
Rate of climb at S/L, one engine out	149 m (490 ft)/min
Service ceiling	9,150 m (30,000 ft)
Service ceiling, one engine out	6,890 m (22,600 ft)
T-O run (land)	430 m (1,410 ft)
T-O to 11 m (35 ft)	686 m (2,250 ft)
Landing from 15 m (50 ft)	686 m (2,250 ft)
Landing run (land)	366 m (1,200 ft)
Range:	
with 12 passengers at max cruising speed, at 3,050 m (10,000 ft), 45 min reserves	
	212 nm (393 km; 244 miles)
with max fuel, 45 min reserves	
	938 nm (1,738 km; 1,080 miles)

OPERATIONAL NOISE LEVELS: Certificated to German LSL standard VI/X and FAR Part 36 Amendment 36-16.

EXTRA

EXTRA-FLUGZEUGBAU GmbH

Flugplatz Dinslaken, 4224 Hünxe
Telephone: 49 (2858) 6851
MANAGING DIRECTOR: Walter Extra

Production is concentrated on the Extra 300 with carbonfibre wing and tail and steel tube fuselage. The wooden-winged Extra 230 was discontinued more than a year ago, because of the difficulty in obtaining appropriate wood.

EXTRA 260

A batch of three Extra 260s was made to special order and the last was delivered in January 1991. They are not fully certificated and are operated under permits to fly.

The 260 is a scaled-down 300 with a single-seat cockpit and powered by a 194 kW (260 hp) Textron Lycoming IO-540.

EXTRA 300

The latest aerobatic aircraft from Walter Extra is the tandem two-seat Extra 300, the design of which started in

January 1987. Construction of a prototype began that August, and this aircraft (D-EAEW) was first flown on 6 May 1988. Although the general configuration remains similar to the Extra 230 (1990-91 *Jane's*), the new and larger aircraft contains no wood. Still using the familiar steel tube fuselage structure with aluminium alloy and fabric covering, the wings use carbonfibre for the box spars, caps, webs and honeycomb sandwich skins. The tail surfaces are mostly glassfibre, with carbonfibre spar caps and elevators. Trim tab on starboard elevator. Mainwheels size 5.00-5, on glassfibre legs. Parker hydraulic disc brakes. Power is provided by a 224 kW (300 hp) Textron Lycoming AEIO-540-L1B5D engine, driving a Mühlbauer MTU-9-B-C/C200-15 three-blade constant-speed propeller with large spinner. Fuel capacity is 120 litres (31.7 US gallons; 26.4 Imp gallons) in wing tanks plus a 40 litre (10.6 US gallon; 8.8 Imp gallon) fuselage tank. Standard equipment includes a Becker AR 3201 com.

Series production began in July 1988. From November 1989 to early 1990, the Chilean Air Force received six Extra 300s purchased to replace Pitts Specials of the Halcónes

High Aerobatics Team. Deliveries had reached 21 by December 1990. A one-off 300 with engine tuned to give 261 kW (350 hp) has been called Extra 350 and is operating in the UK.

Known technical details follow:

TYPE: Tandem two-seat aerobatic aircraft.

DIMENSIONS, EXTERNAL:

Wing span	8.00 m (26 ft 3 in)
Wing chord: at root	1.25 m (4 ft 1¼ in)
at tip	0.83 m (2 ft 8¾ in)
Wing aspect ratio	6
Length overall	7.28 m (23 ft 10½ in)
Height overall	2.62 m (8 ft 7¼ in)
Tailplane span	3.20 m (10 ft 6 in)
Wheelbase	1.80 m (5 ft 11 in)
Propeller ground clearance	2.00 m (6 ft 6¾ in)

AREAS:

Wings, gross	10.72 m² (115.4 sq ft)

WEIGHTS AND LOADINGS:

Weight empty	630 kg (1,389 lb)
Max T-O weight: Aerobatic	820 kg (1,808 lb)

Normal	905 kg (1,995 lb)
Max wing loading	84.4 kg/m² (17.29 lb/sq ft)
Max power loading	4.04 kg/kW (6.65 lb/hp)

PERFORMANCE:

Never-exceed speed (V_{NE})	
	220 knots (407 km/h; 253 mph)
Max level speed	185 knots (343 km/h; 213 mph)
Max cruising speed	170 knots (315 km/h; 196 mph)
Stalling speed	58 knots (108 km/h; 67 mph)
Max rate of climb at S/L	1,005 m (3,300 ft)/min
T-O to 15 m (50 ft)	approx 250 m (820 ft)
Landing from 15 m (50 ft)	approx 450 m (1,476 ft)
g limits	± 10 Aerobatic

Extra 300 two-seat aerobatic aircraft powered by 224 kW (300 hp) Textron Lycoming AEIO-540
(Peter March)

FFT

FFT GESELLSCHAFT FÜR FLUGZEUG- UND FASERVERBUND-TECHNOLOGIE mbH

PO Box 85, Flugplatz, 7947 Mengen
Telephone: 49 (7572) 6050
Fax: 49 (7572) 605400
Telex: 732 543 SCAV D
PRESIDENT: Dipl-Ing Justus Dornier
MANAGING DIRECTOR: Joachim Rechtsteiner

Dipl-Ing Peter Krauss and Herr Jörg Elzenbeck built, and in April 1977 flew for the first time, the first Rutan VariEze two-seat homebuilt aircraft to be completed in Europe (D-EEEZ). They decided to develop, manufacture and market a similar aircraft, known as the Speed Canard, as a ready to fly, certificated production aircraft that would conform to the requirements of FAR Pt 23. In August 1978, with Dipl-Ing Wolfgang Schiller, they formed Gyroflug, renamed FFT in 1989. At the end of 1984 the company became a member of the Justus Dornier Group. In September 1987 Gyroflug moved to its present location in Mengen, where a new factory complex was built. The 100 person workforce moved into its new production quarters in May 1988.

An agreement with TRW-ESL (USA) and Dornier Luftfahrt GmbH (Germany), signed in 1989, covers the integration of a comint payload in an unmanned SC 01 B-160 platform, named Light Aircraft Surveillance System (LASS). One prototype system, including ground station, has been tested. A second, piloted example, designated Advanced Tactical Surveillance System (ATSS), was tested with FLIR, TV and other sensors in association with Litton Applied Technology Inc, but has been discontinued.

In 1989 all design and development of the FFA-2000 (Switzerland), as described in the 1989-90 *Jane's*, was transferred to FFT and renamed Eurotrainer 2000.

FFT SC 01 B SPEED CANARD

As well as being slightly larger overall than the Rutan VariEze, the Speed Canard differs in a number of important details, as noted in the 1987-88 *Jane's*. Wings and other GFRP/CFRP components, manufactured initially by Glaser-Dirks, are now produced by FFT.

Construction of the first prototype (D-EEEX, c/n A-1) began in late 1978, and this aircraft first flew on 2 December 1980. Initial test flights revealed the need for a number of design changes before it could be approved for series production. Of these, the principal one was the adoption of a new Eppler aerofoil section and 5.9° anhedral on the outer wing sections. A new 'first' flight with this modified wing was made by D-EEEX on 10 July 1981. A second airframe was completed for static testing, followed by a second flying prototype (D-EEEW, c/n A-3), which made its initial flight on 17 April 1983 and enabled the Speed Canard to receive German LBA type certification on 30 September that year.

Series production began with the fourth aircraft (D-EELZ, c/n S-4), and 20 examples of this initial version were built by September 1985 for customers in Germany (17), Switzerland (2), and Belgium (1). As built with the standard O-235 engine, they are designated **SC-01**; some examples have been retrofitted with the more powerful O-320 engine, in which form they are known as the **SC 01-160** and were described in *Jane's* 1987-88.

Beginning with c/n S-24, current production models are designated **SC 01 B** (O-235 engine) and **SC 01 B-160** (O-320 engine). These versions, which first flew in the Summer of 1985 and received LBA certification on 26 March 1986, have winglets of increased area, plus other minor improvements. A number of earlier Speed Canards have also been modified to the current B/B-160 standard. A **GT** version of the SC 01 B-160 was introduced in 1987; this has VFR avionics as standard.

The Speed Canard is certificated in France, Germany, Japan, Switzerland, Scandinavia, UK, USA and the Benelux countries. More than 50 B/B-160s have been ordered.

TYPE: Two-seat sporting and surveillance aircraft.
WINGS: Cantilever mid-wing monoplane. Short-span centre-

FFT SC 01 B-160 Speed Canard

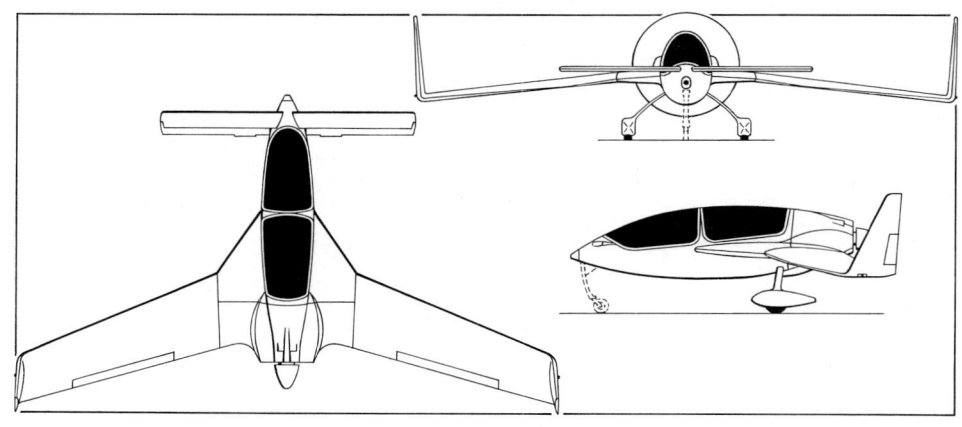

FFT SC 01 B Speed Canard (86.5 kW; 116 hp Textron Lycoming O-235)

section strakes, sweptback approx 60° on leading-edges, without anhedral or dihedral. Main wings have an Eppler E793 aerofoil section, with 15.6 per cent thickness/chord ratio, anhedral angle of 5° 54', and 22° sweepback at quarter-chord. Single-spar structure of GFRP and CFRP, without ribs. Each wingtip is upswept at nearly 90° to form a slightly outward canted NASA type winglet with inset rudder. Centrally located aileron in each wing trailing-edge. No flaps. No aileron or rudder tabs. Main wings are detachable for transportation and storage. Narrow-chord cantilever foreplane, of Eppler E1231 aerofoil section, is mounted high on nose and has a balanced elevator, with fixed tab near inboard end, on each trailing-edge. Construction (GFRP and CFRP) similar to that of wings.
FUSELAGE: Non-pressurised oval-section nacelle type, of GFRP composites construction.
LANDING GEAR: Tricycle type, with fixed main units and electrically retractable nosewheel which is carried on a carbon/Kevlar strut moulded to conform to the outside contour of the fuselage, eliminating need for a fairing door. Main units, carried on cantilever self-sprung carbon/Kevlar struts, are fitted with Cleveland wheels (tyre size 5.00-5), Cleveland disc brakes, and speed fairings. The Scott nosewheel, which retracts rearward, is fitted with a size 10 × 3.5-4 tyre. Nosewheel strut is hinged to allow aircraft to be parked in a kneeling position with only the wheel exposed.

POWER PLANT (SC 01 B): One 86.5 kW (116 hp) Textron Lycoming O-235-P2A flat-four engine, mounted in the rear fuselage and driving a Hoffmann HO-V113B-L/LD 150 + 2A three (composites)-blade constant-speed pusher propeller. Fuel in two integral tanks (one in each wing centre-section strake) with combined capacity of 160 litres (42.3 US gallons; 35.2 Imp gallons). Oil capacity 6 litres (1.58 US gallons; 1.32 Imp gallons).

POWER PLANT (SC 01 B-160): One 119 kW (160 hp) Textron Lycoming O-320-D1A flat-four engine, driving an MT-Propeller (Mühlbauer) MTV-6-C/LD 152-07 three-blade constant-speed propeller. Fuel capacity as for lower powered version. Oil capacity 8 litres (2.11 US gallons; 1.76 Imp gallons).

ACCOMMODATION: Pilot and passenger in tandem, on semi-reclining seats in individual cockpits. Side-stick controls. Separate one-piece moulded canopies, both opening sideways to starboard. Space for 15 kg (33 lb) of baggage aft of rear seat. Both cockpits heated and ventilated.

SYSTEMS: Alternator to provide power for nosewheel extension/retraction.

AVIONICS: To customer's requirements except for GT, which has VFR instrumentation as standard. Can be equipped to full IFR standard, including autopilot, two com/nav, ILS, ADF, artificial horizon, turn and bank indicator and heading gyro.

DIMENSIONS, EXTERNAL:

Wing span	7.77 m (25 ft 6 in)
Foreplane span	3.60 m (11 ft 9¾ in)
Foreplane chord, constant	0.34 m (1 ft 1¾ in)
Wing aspect ratio	7.7
Foreplane aspect ratio	10.6
Length overall	4.70 m (15 ft 5 in)
Fuselage: Length	4.40 m (14 ft 5¼ in)
Max width	0.74 m (2 ft 5 in)
Max depth	1.06 m (3 ft 5¾ in)
Height overall	1.81 m (5 ft 11¼ in)
Wheel track	1.66 m (5 ft 5¼ in)
Wheelbase	2.47 m (8 ft 1¼ in)
Propeller diameter	1.52 m (5 ft 0 in)
Propeller ground clearance	0.31 m (1 ft 0¼ in)

DIMENSIONS, INTERNAL:

Cockpits: Max combined length	2.80 m (9 ft 2¼ in)
Max width	0.64 m (2 ft 1¼ in)
Max height	0.99 m (3 ft 3 in)

AREAS:

Wings, gross	7.84 m² (84.39 sq ft)
Foreplane, gross	1.22 m² (13.13 sq ft)
Ailerons (total)	0.376 m² (4.05 sq ft)
Winglets (total)	2.20 m² (23.68 sq ft)
Rudders (total)	0.168 m² (1.81 sq ft)
Elevators (total, incl tabs)	0.33 m² (3.55 sq ft)

WEIGHTS AND LOADINGS (A: with O-235, B: with O-320 engine):

Weight empty: A	420 kg (926 lb)
B	440 kg (970 lb)
Max fuel: A, B	115 kg (253 lb)
Max payload with 100 litres (26.4 US gallons; 22 Imp gallons) fuel: A	188 kg (414.5 lb)
B	204 kg (450 lb)
Max T-O weight: A	680 kg (1,499 lb)
B	715 kg (1,576 lb)
Max landing weight: A, B	680 kg (1,499 lb)
Max wing loading: A	75.05 kg/m² (15.38 lb/sq ft)
B	75.68 kg/m² (15.5 lb/sq ft)
Max power loading: A	7.86 kg/kW (12.92 lb/hp)
B	6.01 kg/kW (9.85 lb/hp)

PERFORMANCE (at max T-O weight, A and B as above):

Never-exceed speed (V_NE):	
A, B	197 knots (365 km/h; 226 mph) IAS
Max level speed at S/L:	
A	146 knots (270 km/h; 168 mph)
B	159 knots (295 km/h; 183 mph)
Max cruising speed, 75% power:	
A at 1,830 m (6,000 ft)	143 knots (265 km/h; 165 mph)
B at 2,135 m (7,000 ft)	154 knots (285 km/h; 177 mph) IAS
Econ cruising speed, 65% power:	
A at 3,050 m (10,000 ft)	138 knots (257 km/h; 160 mph)
B at 3,350 m (11,000 ft)	148 knots (275 km/h; 171 mph)
Stalling speed: A, B	57 knots (105 km/h; 66 mph) IAS
Max rate of climb at S/L: A	300 m (985 ft)/min
B	396 m (1,300 ft)/min
Service ceiling: A	4,420 m (14,500 ft)
B	5,640 m (18,500 ft)
T-O run: A	450 m (1,475 ft)
B	350 m (1,150 ft)
T-O to 15 m (50 ft): A	700 m (2,300 ft)
B	540 m (1,770 ft)
Landing from 15 m (50 ft): A, B	700 m (2,300 ft)
Landing run: A, B	300 m (985 ft)
Range with max fuel, no reserves:	
55% power: A	1,025 nm (1,900 km; 1,180 miles)
B	890 nm (1,650 km; 1,025 miles)
Range at S/L with max fuel, 45 min reserves:	
75% power: A	728 nm (1,350 km; 839 miles)
B	553 nm (1,025 km; 637 miles)
45% power: A	1,011 nm (1,875 km; 1,165 miles)
B	715 nm (1,325 km; 823 miles)
g limits: A	+4.4/−2.2
B	+3.8/−2.2

FFT EUROTRAINER 2000

On 25 April 1988 FFA of Switzerland announced the receipt of a contract from Swissair for eight trainers of advanced design, designated FFA-2000 (now Eurotrainer 2000), to replace the Piaggio P.149s of the airline's flying school, which had been in service for 25 years. The airline has an option on a further four of these trainers. Development began in 1987, with design assistance from the Swiss ALR group (see 1987-88 Jane's). Development has been taken over by FFT, and the first flight was scheduled for April 1991. Certification is expected in March 1992 and delivery of the first aircraft to Swissair shortly afterwards.

Following discontinuation of the Porsche engines, the prototypes and the eight aircraft for Swissair's civil aviation flying school (SLS) will be powered by the Textron Lycoming AEIO-540 flat rated to 200 kW (268 hp) to meet German noise regulations. The aircraft will sustain +6/−3 g and high-stress parts of the glassfibre airframe are reinforced with carbonfibre. A Christen-type fuel and oil system will permit negative-g manoeuvres.

TYPE: Two/four-seat training and touring aircraft, capable of limited aerobatics.

Model of the FFT Eurotrainer 2000 (Textron Lycoming AEIO-540 flat-rated to meet German noise limits)

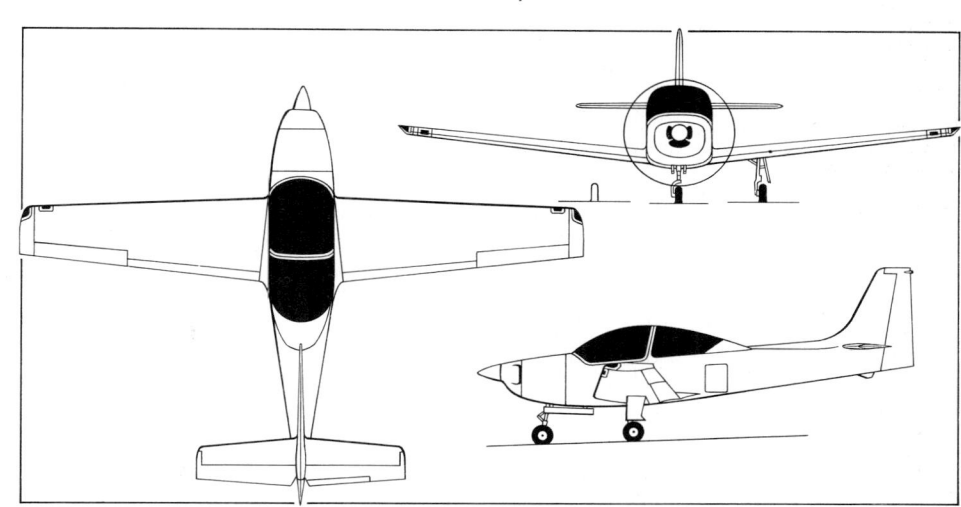

FFT Eurotrainer 2000 (Jane's/Mike Keep)

WINGS: Cantilever low-wing monoplane. Horstmann-Quast advanced laminar wing section, with thickness/chord ratio of 16 per cent. Dihedral 6° 30′ from roots. Fail-safe structure of composites (mainly glassfibre), including ailerons and Fowler trailing-edge flaps. No tabs.

FUSELAGE: Conventional structure, of same materials as wings.

TAIL UNIT: Conventional structure, built in same way as wings. Fixed incidence tailplane. Trim tab in rudder and each elevator.

LANDING GEAR: Hydraulically retractable tricycle type, with single wheel on each unit. Mainwheels retract inward, nosewheel rearward.

POWER PLANT: One Textron Lycoming AEIO-540-L1B5 flat-six engine, flat rated at 200 kW (268 hp). Christen kit for inverted flying. Fuel capacity 260 litres (68.7 US gallons; 57.2 Imp gallons).

ACCOMMODATION: Seats for two or four persons, in pairs, under one-piece forward-hinged canopy. Dual controls and pedal brakes standard. Baggage space aft of seats. Cockpit heated and ventilated.

AVIONICS: From simple VFR to dual control IFR, according to customer's requirements.

DIMENSIONS, EXTERNAL:

Wing span	10.38 m (34 ft 0¾ in)
Wing aspect ratio	7.7
Length overall	8.14 m (26 ft 8½ in)
Height overall	3.20 m (10 ft 6 in)
Elevator span	3.87 m (12 ft 8½ in)
Propeller diameter	2.10 m (6 ft 10¾ in)

AREAS:

Wings, gross	14.00 m² (150.7 sq ft)

WEIGHTS AND LOADINGS:

Basic weight empty	920 kg (2,028 lb)
Max T-O weight	1,480 kg (3,262 lb)
Max aerobatic T-O weight	1,300 kg (2,866 lb)
Max wing loading	105.7 kg/m² (21.6 lb/sq ft)
Max power loading	7.4 kg/kW (12.17 lb/hp)

PERFORMANCE (estimated, at two-seat trainer T-O weight):

Never-exceed speed (V_NE)	224 knots (416 km/h; 258 mph)
Max level speed at S/L	more than 175 knots (324 km/h; 201 mph)
Econ cruising speed (65% power) at S/L	157 knots (291 km/h; 181 mph)
Stalling speed, flaps down	52 knots (96 km/h; 60 mph)
Max rate of climb at S/L	408 m (1,340 ft)/min
Service ceiling	6,100 m (20,000 ft)
T-O to 15 m (50 ft) at 600 m (1,970 ft)	500 m (1,640 ft)
Landing from 15 m (50 ft)	490 m (1,610 ft)
Endurance, 45 min reserves	4 h
g limits:	+5.0/−3.0 (utility)
	+6.0/−3.5 (aerobatic)

GROB

BURKHART GROB LUFT- UND RAUMFAHRT GmbH & Co KG
(Division of Grob-Werke GmbH & Co KG)

Postfach 1257, 8948 Mindelheim
Telephone: 49 (8268) 9980
Fax: 49 (8268) 998-14 or 998-24
Telex: 5 39 623
CHAIRMAN: Dr hc Dipl-Ing Burkhart Grob
DEPUTY CHAIRMAN: Dipl-Ing Klaus Harald Fischer
MARKETING MANAGER: Konrad Lewald

Grob was founded in 1972, employs about 180 people, and has built about 3,500 aircraft.

The name of the company was changed from Burkhart Grob Flugzeugbau to Burkhart Grob Luft- und Raumfahrt GmbH, with the aviation activities divided into light and heavy aircraft sections. In addition to the G 115, G 116 and GF 200 programmes, further batches of gliders were put in hand (see Sailplanes section). The G 116 has been discontinued. The G 109 motor glider was ordered by the British RAF for cadet training (54) and 80 were produced during 1990.

Grob's 'heavy aircraft' section is also concerned with development of the Egrett, described in the International section. The company co-operates with the Weltraum-Institut Berlin space institute on programmes concerned with microgravity and other space research.

Grob G 115-A two-seat light aircraft *(Peter F. Selinger)*

GROB G 115

The first prototype of this light aircraft made its initial flight in November 1985, powered by an O-235 engine with fixed-pitch propeller. The second prototype, which flew in the Spring of 1986, was similarly powered, but had a constant-speed propeller, a taller fin and rudder and relocated tailplane. The latter version entered production as the **G 115-A**. The third prototype, first flown in 1986, represented the **G 115-B**, having an uprated (O-320) engine. The version with an O-320-E2A engine is known as the **G 115-C**. Deliveries of 105 production aircraft began in mid-1987.

The G 115-A was certificated to FAR Pt 23 standards by the LBA on 31 March 1987 and by the British CAA in May 1988. The G 115 later gained full public transport certification and then LBA spinning approval. Production was stopped in 1991 for a major redesign to compete for the USAF Enhanced Flight Screening aircraft order. New name 115T and due to fly by end of 1991 for delivery in 1992-93; powered by 149 to 194 kW (200 to 260 hp) engines and optional retractable landing gear.

TYPE: Two-seat light aircraft.
WINGS: Cantilever low-wing monoplane. Wing section Eppler E 696. Dihedral 5°. Incidence 2°. Ailerons and flaps; anti-servo tab on port aileron deleted from current models. GFRP construction.
FUSELAGE: Conventional GFRP structure.
TAIL UNIT: Conventional GFRP structure, with tailplane, elevators (trim tab on port elevator), fin and horn balanced rudder.
LANDING GEAR: Non-retractable tricycle type, with wheel fairings. Steerable nosewheel, size 5.00-5. Mainwheels size 6.00-5. Cantilever spring suspension. Hydraulic toe-operated brakes. Parking brake.
POWER PLANT: One 85.8 kW (115 hp) Textron Lycoming O-235-H2C flat-four engine in G 115-A, driving a Hoffmann HO 14-175 120 two-blade fixed-pitch propeller; 86.5 kW (116 hp) O-235-P1 and constant-speed propeller optional. One 112 kW (150 hp) Textron Lycoming O-320-E2A with constant-speed propeller in G 115-C. Fuel capacity 100 litres (26.4 US gallons; 22 Imp gallons). Oil capacity for O-235 engine 5.7 litres (1.5 US gallons; 1.25 Imp gallons).
ACCOMMODATION: Two seats side by side under one-piece rearward sliding framed canopy, with dual controls. Baggage space behind seats, with restraining net. Heating.
SYSTEMS: Electrical, with 14V battery. Hydraulic system for brakes only.
AVIONICS: To customer's requirements. Instrument panel will accommodate full IFR instrumentation. Optional avionics include VOR nav system, ADF 2079 with indicator and ATC 2000 transponder.

DIMENSIONS, EXTERNAL:
Wing span	10.00 m (32 ft 9½ in)
Wing aspect ratio	8.19
Length overall	7.36 m (24 ft 1¾ in)
Height overall: A	2.75 m (9 ft 0¼ in)
C	2.82 m (9 ft 3 in)
Wheel track: A, C	1.61 m (5 ft 3½ in)
Wheelbase: A, C	2.50 m (8 ft 2½ in)

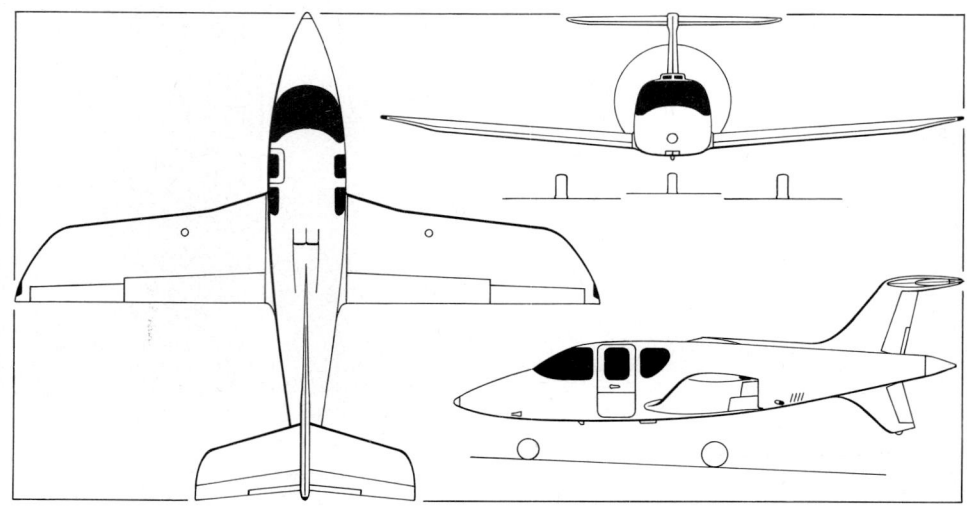

Grob GF 200 all-composites four-seat light aircraft *(Jane's/Mike Keep)*

AREAS:
Wings, gross	12.21 m² (131.43 sq ft)

WEIGHTS AND LOADINGS (Normal category):
Basic weight empty: A	590 kg (1,301 lb)
C	620 kg (1,367 lb)
Fuel weight: A, C	72 kg (159 lb)
Max T-O and landing weight: A, C	850 kg (1,874 lb)
Max wing loading: A, C	69.61 kg/m² (14.26 lb/sq ft)
Max power loading:	
A (115 hp)	9.91 kg/kW (16.30 lb/hp)
A (116 hp)	9.83 kg/kW (16.15 lb/hp)
C	8.04 kg/kW (13.23 lb/hp)

PERFORMANCE (at max T-O weight):
Max level speed: A	119 knots (220 km/h; 137 mph)
C	135 knots (250 km/h; 155 mph)
Cruising speed, 75% power:	
A	110 knots (205 km/h; 127 mph)
C	120 knots (222 km/h; 138 mph)
Stalling speed: A	45 knots (83 km/h; 52 mph)
C	47 knots (87 km/h; 54 mph)
Max rate of climb at S/L: A	210 m (690 ft)/min
C	305 m (1,000 ft)/min
T-O run: A	250 m (820 ft)
C	210 m (690 ft)
T-O to 15 m (50 ft): A	420 m (1,378 ft)
C	390 m (1,280 ft)
Range with max fuel (approx):	
A	540 nm (1,000 km; 621 miles)
C	394 nm (730 km; 453 miles)
g limits:	+3.8/−1.52 (Normal)
	+4.4/−1.76 (Utility)

GROB GF 200

Grob announced this new four-seat all-composites high-performance aircraft in early 1988, displaying a full size mockup that May at the Hanover Air Show. An unpressurised prototype was to fly in May 1991, but the production aircraft will have a pressurised cabin. Following discontinuation of Porsche engines, it is now powered by a 201 kW (270 hp) Textron Lycoming TIO-540-AF1A driving a Mühlbauer three-blade constant-speed propeller. Standard fuel capacity is 250 litres (66 US gallons; 55 Imp gallons) in integral wing tanks. Optional long-range tanks (combined capacity 340 litres; 90 US gallons; 74.8 Imp gallons) will be available.

General appearance of the GF 200 is shown in the accompanying three-view drawing.

DIMENSIONS, EXTERNAL:
Wing span	11.00 m (36 ft 0 in)
Length overall	8.50 m (27 ft 11 in)
Height overall	3.20 m (10 ft 6 in)
Cabin door: Height	1.20 m (3 ft 11¼ in)
Width	0.60 m (1 ft 11½ in)

AREAS:
Wings, gross	12.50 m² (134.0 sq ft)

WEIGHTS AND LOADINGS:
Payload	520 kg (1,146 lb)
Max fuel weight	252 kg (555 lb)
Max T-O weight	1,470 kg (3,240 lb)
Max wing loading	116 kg/m² (23.76 lb/sq ft)
Max power loading	7.3 kg/kW (11.8 lb/hp)

PERFORMANCE:
Max cruising speed at 7,600 m (25,000 ft)	
	229 knots (425 km/h; 264 mph)
Econ cruising speed at 5,790 m (19,000 ft)	
	207 knots (385 km/h; 249 mph)
Max rate of climb at S/L	390 m (1,279 ft)/min
Service ceiling	7,620 m (25,000 ft)
T-O run	296 m (971 ft)
T-O to 15 m (50 ft)	602 m (1,975 ft)
Landing from 15 m (50 ft)	449 m (1,473 ft)
Landing run	234 m (767 ft)
Range at 5,485 m (18,000 ft), 75% power, with 340 litres of fuel	1,052 nm (1,950 km; 1,211 miles)

GYROFLUG — *see FFT*

HOFFMANN
WOLF HOFFMANN FLUGZEUGBAU KG
Sportflugplatz, D-8870 Günzburg/Ulm
Telephone: 49 (8221) 1417
Fax: 49 (8221) 32034
Telex: 531625 HOFBG D
DIRECTOR: Dipl-Ing Wolf D. Hoffmann

HOFFMANN H 40
Design of the H 40 began in January 1986 and construction started in August 1987. The first of two prototypes (D-EIOF) was exhibited at the Hanover Air Show in May 1988 and flew for the first time on 28 August 1988. The H 40 was then modified to meet FAR Pt 23 requirements (Normal category), first flying in this form on 8 February 1990. Details and performance were listed in 1990-91 *Jane's*.

Prototype Hoffmann H 40 (Textron Lycoming O-235-P2A engine)

RFB
RHEIN-FLUGZEUGBAU GmbH
(Owned by ABS International)
Flugplatz (Postfach 408). 4050 Mönchengladbach 1
Telephone: 49 (2161) 6820
Fax: 49 (2161) 682200
Telex: 852 506
PRESIDENT: Albert Blum
COMMERCIAL DIRECTOR: Dipl Betriebsw Norbert Frentzen
CHIEF DESIGNER: Christoph Fischer
MARKETING MANAGER: Hans-Jörg Brandt
RFB was sold by MBB to ABS International in 1990. Workforce is about 245 and expected revenue for 1990 was DM43 million ($28.41 million).

RFB specialises in the development and manufacture of airframe structural components, especially wings and fuselages made entirely of glassfibre reinforced plastics. Recent production has also included components and assemblies of light alloy. steel and GFRP for aircraft in quantity production by other German companies, as well as spare parts and ground equipment.

Under contract to the German government, RFB services military aircraft, and provides target towing flights and other services with special aircraft. It has Luftfahrt-Bundesamt (LBA) approval as an organisation for aircraft development, manufacture, maintenance and overhaul. It also operates a factory certificated service centre for Piper and Mitsubishi aircraft, as well as for Bendix/King and Becker avionics. General servicing of other types of all-metal aircraft is undertaken.

The company continues to work on specialist ground effect vehicles on the lines of its earlier Lippisch-type X113 and X114.

RFB has been engaged for many years in developing specialised applications for ducted propellers, one of which led to the Fantrainer.

RFB FANTRAINER SERIES
RFB continues to market the Fantrainer 400 and 600, but no new sales were reported in 1990 or the first half of 1991. A new, more powerful version is being considered.

Early development history of the Fantrainer was given in the 1987-88 and previous editions of *Jane's*. There are two versions: the **Fantrainer 400**, powered by an Allison 250-C20B turboshaft, and the **Fantrainer 600**, which has an Allison 250-C30. About 92 per cent of the airframe is common to the 400 and the 600. Details and performance were listed in 1990-91 *Jane's*.

The first German built production Fantrainer, a 600, flew for the first time on 12 August 1984. This aircraft and one prototype were allocated to the certification programme, and LBA approval of the 600 was granted on 23 May 1985. One Fantrainer 400 and two 600s were evaluated by the Luftwaffe in 1985.

In August 1982 RFB received a contract covering the production of 31 Fantrainer 400s and 16 Fantrainer 600s for the Royal Thai Air Force. The first two aircraft were built in Germany and delivered to Thailand in October 1984; the remaining 45 were supplied in CKD form for assembly in Thailand by RTAF (which see), all kits having been delivered by RFB by early 1988. All Fantrainer 600s have light composite wings, the Fantrainer 400s having metal wings designed and manufactured by RTAF. The Fantrainer 600s began regular flight operations in January 1987, and all 16 are in service. Assembly of Fantrainer 400s was to be completed in 1991.

ROCKWELL/MBB FAN RANGER
Late in 1990, Rockwell International and MBB announced that they would produce two demonstrators in 1992 of a turbofan-powered Fantrainer, designated Fan Ranger, to compete for the USAF/USN JPATS programme. RFB will manufacture and certificate the demonstrators. Further details in International section.

RUSCHMEYER
RUSCHMEYER LUFTFAHRTTECHNIK
GmbH
Flugplatz, 4520 Melle 1
Telephone: 49 (5422) 6565
Fax: 4 (5422) 6232
GENERAL MANAGER: Horst Ruschmeyer
Demise of the Porsche engines brought an end to the Ruschmeyer MF-85 series of low-wing single-engined four-seaters, details of which appeared in the 1990-91 *Jane's*. Work is now under way on the new R90-230RG, detailed below, from which a family will follow.

RUSCHMEYER R90-230RG
Replacement of the Porsche engine by a 186.4 kW (250 hp) Textron Lycoming IO-540, flat rated at 171.5 kW (230 hp), is the main difference between this aircraft and its predecessor, the MF-85P-RG, now abandoned (see 1990-91 *Jane's*). The new prototype first flew on 28 October 1990. Certification is expected during the second half of 1991 and first deliveries in 1992.

A Wortmann aerofoil, extremely smooth and accurate finish in composite with special manufacturing techniques and no excrescences (such as antennae), plus small cooling intakes made possible by the derated engine, have produced exceptional performance and economy. Measured fuel consumption at 175 knots (see conditions below) and 120 knots TAS is 49 litres (13 US gallons, 10.8 Imp gallons)/h and 30 litres (8 US gallons; 6.6 Imp gallons)/h respectively.

By fitting a four-blade Mühlbauer propeller and a special exhaust system, and limiting propeller rpm to 2,400, the external noise during a full-power fly-over at 300 m (984 ft) has been measured at only 68.6 dBA.

Future plans include a turbocharged version, and a lower-powered (134 kW; 180 hp) fixed-gear model.

WEIGHTS AND LOADINGS:
Max T-O weight	1,350 kg (2,976 lb)
Max power loading	7.87 kg/kW (12.94 lb/hp)

Lycoming-powered Ruschmeyer R90-230 RG prototype

PERFORMANCE:
Max cruising speed at 171.5 kW (230 hp) at 1,675 m (5,500 ft)	175 knots (324 km/h; 202 mph)
Cruising speed (75% power) at 1,675 m (5,500 ft)	170 knots (315 km/h; 196 mph)
Max rate of climb at S/L	457 m (1,500 ft)/min
Time to 4,575 m (15,000 ft)	18 min
T-O run	230 m (755 ft)
Landing run	250 m (821 ft)

GREECE

HAI
HELLENIC AEROSPACE INDUSTRY LTD
Athens Tower, Messogion 2-4, 115 27 Athens
Telephone: 30 (1) 77 99 678-9
Fax: 30 (1) 77 97 670
Telex: 219528 HAI GR
WORKS: Tanagra, PO Box 23, 320 09 Schimatari
Telephone: 30 (262) 52000
Fax: 30 (262) 88 38 714
Telex: 299372 HAI GR
CHAIRMAN AND MANAGING DIRECTOR:
  Christos Tounis (Air Force General, Retd)
GENERAL PLANT DIRECTOR: Dr Dinos Economides
COMMERCIAL DIRECTOR: Dimitris Sarlis
MANAGER, ADVERTISING AND CUSTOMER RELATIONS:
  Thomas Nestor
  Hellenic Aerospace Industry is owned 87 per cent by the Greek government and 13 per cent by the Hellenic

Industrial Development Bank. Industrial facilities at Tanagra occupy a 180 ha (445 acre) site, including 150,000 m² (1,614,585 sq ft) of covered floor space, and comprise an Aircraft Division, Engine Division, Electronics/Avionics Division and Manufacturing Division.
  HAI offers a wide spectrum of aeronautical services and products in the military and commercial fields, supporting several air forces and aerospace manufacturers spread over 22 countries in the Middle East, Africa, Europe and North America. Repair and overhaul facilities include full support for Mirage F1 aircraft, Atar 9K-50 engines, and Lockheed C-130 depot level maintenance. In addition to the Hellenic armed forces, major customers for indicated services include J79 engine overhaul for the USAFE and RAF; C-130 and Atar 9K-50 engine overhaul for the Royal Jordanian Air Force; and repair of Improved HAWK radars for NATO.

Manufacturing capabilities include aircraft, engine structural components and electronic products. Major manufacturing contracts include co-production of Stinger weapon systems; F-16 rear fuselages and air intakes; Airbus A300 door frames; M53 engine afterburner sections; and assembly and test of M53 engines. Through licensing agreements, HAI is producing and marketing TV transponders, wind energy systems, radio transceivers, and own-design artillery fire control systems and other electronic equipment for commercial and military customers.
  The Directorate of Engineering, Research and Development provides support, maintenance and modification of equipment as well as production of new electronic and aeronautical systems. It is also actively involved in various EC-sponsored programmes.

HUNGARY

GANZAVIA
GANZAVIA GT
Dunyov u. 6, H-1134 Budapest
Telephone: 36 (1) 209 020
Telex: 4 22 7951 H
CHIEF DESIGNER: Eng Gyula Kovács

GANZAVIA GA-K-22 DINO
Displayed in model form at the June 1987 Paris Air Show, the Dino is a small, side by side two-seat biplane designed to FAR Pt 23 standards and suitable for training, aerobatics, aerial photography, glider towing and (as the GA-K-22A with 200 kg; 441 lb of liquid chemicals) light agricultural

duties. It was preceded by a proof-of-concept aircraft (HA-XAD), which was illustrated in the 1987-88 *Jane's*.
  Design started in late 1986, and construction of a full size prototype began in early 1987, but no recent news of progress has been received. A description and illustration of the Dino can be found in the 1990-91 *Jane's*.

INDIA

ADA
AERONAUTICAL DEVELOPMENT AGENCY
PO Box 1718, Vimanapura Post Office, Bangalore 560 017
Telephone: 91 (812) 562060
Fax: 91 (812) 569445
Telex: 0845 8114 ADA IN
LCA PROGRAMME DIRECTOR: Dr K. Harinarayana

LIGHT COMBAT AIRCRAFT (LCA)
Development of the LCA, due to enter service with the Indian Air Force in the late 1990s, was approved by the Indian government in 1983. Project definition, begun in the Spring of 1987, was completed in late 1988, and the basic design was finalised in 1990. Two prototypes have so far been funded, in a Rs15,000 million (S872 million) contract, with first flight expected in 1995. Each of these will be powered by a General Electric F404-GE-F2J3 afterburning turbofan; an indigenous engine, the 83.4 kN (18,740 lb st) class GTX-35VS Kaveri, is being developed to power the production version.
  The airframe is designed for minimum weight, using advanced concepts and state of the art materials such as aluminium-lithium alloys, carbonfibre composites and titanium alloys for primary and secondary structures. Demands of high manoeuvrability, agility, and large variations in external stores, are met by incorporating CCV (control configured vehicle) concepts and a quadruplex digital fly-by-wire control system.
TYPE: All-weather air superiority fighter and light close air support aircraft.
WINGS: Shoulder mounted delta wings, of carbonfibre construction, with compound sweepback on leading-edges. Leading-edge slats (three-segment) and trailing-edge elevons (two-segment) on each wing.
TAIL UNIT: Vertical surfaces only (CFRP fin and inset rudder).
LANDING GEAR: Hydraulically retractable tricycle type. Single mainwheels; twin-wheel nose unit.
POWER PLANT: One 80.5 kN (18,100 lb st) General Electric F404-F2J3 afterburning turbofan in prototypes; Indian

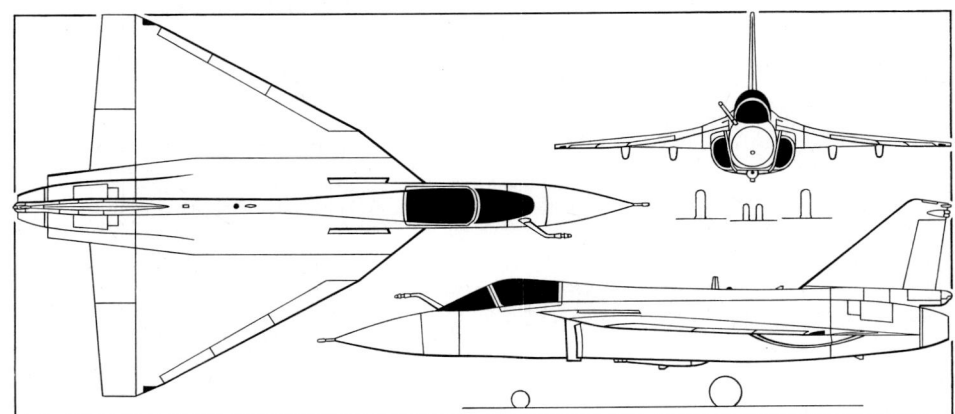

Provisional drawing of the ADA Light Combat Aircraft *(Jane's/Mike Keep)*

GTRE GTX-35VS Kaveri turbofan, with FADEC, under development for production aircraft. In-flight refuelling probe on starboard side of front fuselage. Provision for auxiliary external fuel tanks.
ACCOMMODATION: Pilot only, on zero/zero ejection seat. Development will include two-seat training version.
SYSTEMS: Hydraulic system for brakes and landing gear; electrical system for fly-by-wire and avionics power supply; environmental control system.
AVIONICS: V/UHF and UHF com radios and data link; INS, Tacan and radio altimeter; Hindustan Aeronautics multi-mode radar; IFF transponder/interrogator; FLIR; ECM (radar warning receiver, self-protection jammer and chaff/flare dispenser). Avionics architecture centred round powerful mission computer with three MIL-STD-1553B databuses. Cockpit displays include collimated HUD with holographic combiner, and left and right hand multi-function colour CRTs, and are NVG compatible. HOTAS type real-time controls.

ARMAMENT: Internally mounted GSh-23 twin-barrel 23 mm gun, with 220 rounds. Seven external stores stations (three under each wing and one under fuselage) for wide range of short/medium range missiles and other ordnance.
DIMENSIONS, EXTERNAL:
Wing span	8.20 m (26 ft 10¾ in)
Wing aspect ratio	1.8
Length overall	13.20 m (43 ft 3¾ in)
Height overall	4.40 m (14 ft 5¼ in)
AREAS:
Wings, gross	approx 37.50 m² (403.6 sq ft)
WEIGHTS AND LOADINGS:
Weight empty	approx 5,500 kg (12,125 lb)
Max external stores load	more than 4,000 kg (8,818 lb)
T-O weight (clean)	8,500 kg (18,740 lb)
PERFORMANCE:
Max level speed at altitude	Mach 1.6
Service ceiling	above 15,240 m (50,000 ft)

CIVIL AVIATION DEPARTMENT
TECHNICAL CENTRE, CIVIL AVIATION DEPARTMENT
Opp. Safdarjung Airport, New Delhi 110003
Telephone: 91 (11) 611504
Telex: 31 66407 NAA
DIRECTOR GENERAL: M. R. Sivaraman
DIRECTOR (R&D): Y. P. Bawa

LT-1 SWATI
The prototype (VT-XIV) of this two-seat aircraft (Light Trainer 1) flew for the first time on 17 November 1990. It was designed to meet FAR Pt 23 (Utility and Normal category) airworthiness requirements, and is now being flight tested. The LT-1 is expected to be produced by the Indian aerospace industry to meet domestic flying club trainer requirements.

TYPE: Two-seat light trainer.
WINGS: Cantilever low-wing monoplane, of NASA GA(W)-1 constant section. Dihedral 4° from roots. Incidence 2°. Constant chord structure, comprising a box-type main spar of Himalayan spruce with laminated spruce flanges, plywood covered up to rear spar. Plain ailerons and trailing-edge flaps, all of single-spar spruce construction with ply covered nose cell and remainder fabric covered. Conventional controls (push/pull rods and cables). No aileron tabs.
FUSELAGE: Welded chromoly steel tube structure, fabric covered except for engine cowling and cockpit area (aluminium alloy sheet) and fairings (glassfibre).
TAIL UNIT: Fin and fixed incidence tailplane are two-spar all-metal structures; rudder and elevators similar but single-spar with skins of sheet aluminium alloy. Metal trim tab in starboard elevator. Rudder and elevators actuated mechanically by push/pull rods and cables.

LANDING GEAR: Non-retractable bungee-sprung mainwheels, on side Vs and half-axles, with mechanical brakes. Non-retractable steerable tailwheel.
POWER PLANT: One 97 kW (130 hp) Rolls-Royce Continental O-240-A flat-four engine, driving a Hele Orient IA-135/BRM 7150 two-blade fixed-pitch metal propeller. Fuel capacity 90 litres (23.8 US gallons; 19.8 Imp gallons).
ACCOMMODATION: Two seats, with adjustable safety harnesses, side by side under one-piece cockpit canopy.
AVIONICS: VFR instrumentation standard. Provision for radio.
DIMENSIONS, EXTERNAL:
Wing span	9.20 m (30 ft 2¼ in)
Wing chord, constant	1.30 m (4 ft 3¼ in)
Wing aspect ratio	7.08
Length overall (flying attitude)	7.10 m (23 ft 3½ in)
Height overall (flying attitude)	1.79 m (5 ft 10½ in)
Tailplane span	2.60 m (8 ft 6½ in)

Wheel track	2.00 m (6 ft 6¾ in)
Wheelbase	4.94 m (16 ft 2½ in)
Propeller diameter	1.83 m (6 ft 0 in)

AREAS:

Wings, gross	11.96 m² (128.7 sq ft)
Ailerons (total)	1.10 m² (11.84 sq ft)
Trailing-edge flaps (total)	1.04 m² (11.19 sq ft)
Fin	0.75 m² (8.07 sq ft)
Rudder	0.62 m² (6.67 sq ft)
Tailplane	0.93 m² (10.01 sq ft)
Elevators (total, incl tab)	0.94 m² (10.12 sq ft)

WEIGHTS AND LOADINGS (U: Utility, N: Normal category):

Weight empty, equipped (typical):

U, N	502 kg (1,107 lb)
Max T-O weight: U	700 kg (1,543 lb)
N	750 kg (1,653 lb)
Max wing loading: U	58.53 kg/m² (11.99 lb/sq ft)
N	62.71 kg/m² (12.84 lb/sq ft)
Max power loading: U	7.22 kg/kW (11.87 lb/hp)
N	7.73 kg/kW (12.72 lb/hp)

PERFORMANCE (estimated, at max T-O weight):

Never-exceed speed (V_{NE}):

U, N	134 knots (250 km/h; 155 mph)
Max level speed: U	108 knots (200 km/h; 124 mph)

Cruising speed (75% power):

U	100 knots (185 km/h; 115 mph)

Stalling speed:

flaps up:

U	48 knots (88 km/h; 55 mph)
N	49 knots (91 km/h; 57 mph)

flaps down:

U	42 knots (78 km/h; 49 mph)
N	44 knots (81 km/h; 51 mph)
Max rate of climb at S/L: U	183 m (600 ft)/min
Service ceiling: U	4,575 m (15,000 ft)
T-O run: U	150 m (493 ft)
Landing run: U	170 m (558 ft)
Range with max fuel: U	297 nm (550 km; 342 miles)
Max endurance: U	3 h 30 min
g limits: U	+4.4/−1.76
N	+3.8/−1.52

Prototype of the Technical Centre LT-1 Swati two-seat light trainer

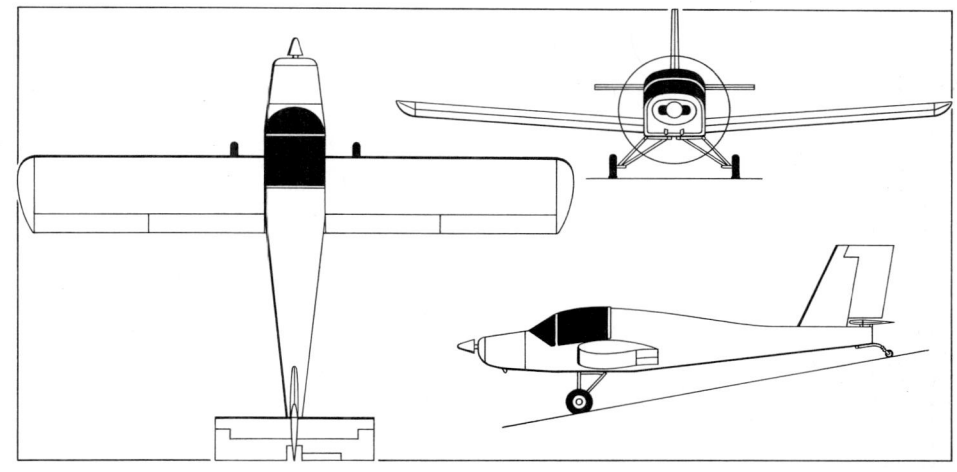

LT-1 two-seat light trainer designed by the Indian Civil Aviation Department's Technical Centre
(Jane's/Mike Keep)

HAL
HINDUSTAN AERONAUTICS LIMITED

CORPORATE OFFICE: PO Box 5150, 15/1 Cubbon Road, Bangalore 560 001

Telephone: 91 (812) 266901

Fax: 91 (812) 268758

Telex: 845 2266 HAL IN

CHAIRMAN: R. N. Sharma

Hindustan Aeronautics Limited (HAL) was formed on 1 October 1964, and has 12 manufacturing divisions at seven locations (Bangalore, Nasik, Koraput, Hyderabad, Kanpur, Lucknow and Korwa), plus a Design Complex. The total workforce is over 40,000.

Kanpur Division is producing the HPT-32 ab initio trainer and assembles, under licence, the Dornier 228. Nasik and Koraput Divisions are manufacturing airframes and engines of the Soviet MiG-27 in collaboration with the USSR. Hyderabad Division manufactures avionics for all aircraft produced by HAL, as well as airport radars. Lucknow Division is producing aircraft accessories under licence from manufacturers in the UK, France and the USSR, and Korwa manufactures inertial navigation systems.

In addition to HAL's manufacturing programmes, major design and development activities include the Advanced Light Helicopter (ALH) programme.

BANGALORE COMPLEX

Post Bag 1785, Bangalore 560 017

Telephone: 91 (812) 565201 and 561020

Telex: 845 2234

MANAGING DIRECTOR: Dr C. G. Krishnadas Nair

Aircraft Division

Post Bag 1788, Bangalore 560 017

Telephone: 91 (812) 565201 and 561020

Fax: 91 (812) 565188

Telex: 845 2234

GENERAL MANAGER: S. N. Sachindran

Helicopter Division

Post Bag 1790, Bangalore 560 017

Telephone: 91 (812) 565201 and 561020

Telex: 845 2764

GENERAL MANAGER: K. N. Murthy

The Bangalore Complex is subdivided into an Aircraft Division, Helicopter Division, Aerospace Division, Engine Division, Overhaul Division, Services Division, Foundry and Forge Division, Flight Operations, and Design Complex. It is engaged in the manufacture of the SEPECAT Jaguar International combat aircraft and its Adour engine. The Complex also undertakes repair and overhaul of airframes, engines, and allied instruments and accessories. A contract to supply up to 150 sets of tailplanes for the British Aerospace ATP transport aircraft was signed in May 1987.

HAL (SEPECAT) JAGUAR INTERNATIONAL
Indian Air Force name: Shamsher (Assault sword)

Deliveries to India of 40 British built Jaguar Internationals with Adour Mk 804 engines were followed by a further 45 (with Mk 811 engines) assembled in India from European built components, and Indian production is continuing with full manufacture of 31 additional aircraft under licence by Hindustan Aeronautics. The first of the latter batch was completed in early 1988, and IAF Jaguar Squadrons include Nos. 5 and 14. Jaguars of No. 6 Squadron assigned to anti-shipping duty have nose mounted Thomson-CSF Agave radar, a Smiths Industries DARIN nav/attack system, and air-to-surface missiles. The first of an initial six aircraft so modified was delivered during January 1986.

SEPECAT Jaguar International single-seat strike aircraft of the Indian Air Force

TYPE: Single-seat tactical support aircraft and two-seat operational or advanced trainer. Airframe details described in International section of 1985-86 and earlier *Jane's*.

POWER PLANT: Two HAL built Rolls-Royce Turbomeca Adour Mk 811 turbofans, each rated at 24.6 kN (5,520 lb st) dry and 37.4 kN (8,400 lb st) with afterburning. Fixed geometry air intake on each side of fuselage aft of cockpit. Fuel in six tanks, one in each wing and four in fuselage. Total internal fuel capacity 4,200 litres (1,110 US gallons; 924 Imp gallons). Armour protection for critical fuel system components. Provision for carrying three auxiliary drop tanks, each of 1,200 litres (317 US gallons; 264 Imp gallons) capacity, on fuselage and inboard wing pylons. Provision for in-flight refuelling, with retractable probe forward of cockpit on starboard side.

ACCOMMODATION (single-seater): Enclosed cockpit for pilot, with rearward hinged canopy and Martin-Baker IN9B zero/zero ejection seat as in two-seaters. Bulletproof windscreen, as in two-seat version.

ACCOMMODATION (trainer): Crew of two in tandem on Martin-Baker IN9B Mk II zero/zero ejection seats. Individual rearward hinged canopies. Rear seat 38 cm (15 in) higher than front seat. Windscreen bulletproof against 7.5 mm rifle fire.

SYSTEMS: As detailed in 1985-86 *Jane's*.

AVIONICS: Include Smiths Industries DARIN (display attack and ranging inertial navigation) nav/attack system, incorporating Sagem Uliss 82 INS, GEC Avionics

HUDWAC (head-up display and weapon aiming computer) and GEC Ferranti COMED 2045 (combined map and electronic display). HAL IFF-400 AM.

ARMAMENT: Two 30 mm Aden cannon in lower fuselage aft of cockpit in single-seater; single Aden gun on port side in two-seater. One stores attachment on fuselage centreline and two under each wing. Centreline and inboard wing points can each carry up to 1,134 kg (2,500 lb) of weapons, outboard underwing points up to 567 kg (1,250 lb) each. Maximum external stores load, including overwing loads, 4,763 kg (10,500 lb). Typical alternative loads include one air-to-surface missile and two 1,200 litre (317 US gallon; 264 Imp gallon) drop tanks; eight 1,000 lb bombs; various combinations of free-fall, laser guided, retarded or cluster bombs; overwing Matra R.550 Magic missiles; air-to-surface rockets; or a reconnaissance camera pack.

DIMENSIONS, EXTERNAL:
Wing span	8.69 m (28 ft 6 in)
Length overall, incl probe:	
single-seat	16.83 m (55 ft 2½ in)
two-seat	17.53 m (57 ft 6¼ in)
Height overall	4.89 m (16 ft 0½ in)
Wheel track	2.41 m (7 ft 11 in)
Wheelbase	5.69 m (18 ft 8 in)

AREAS:
Wings, gross	24.18 m² (260.27 sq ft)

WEIGHTS AND LOADINGS:
Typical weight empty	7,000 kg (15,432 lb)
Normal T-O weight (single-seater, with full internal fuel and ammunition for built-in cannon)	
	10,954 kg (24,149 lb)
Max T-O weight with external stores	
	15,700 kg (34,612 lb)
Max wing loading	649.3 kg/m² (133 lb/sq ft)
Max power loading	209.9 kg/kN (2.06 lb/lb st)

PERFORMANCE:
Max level speed at S/L	
Mach 1.1 (729 knots; 1,350 km/h; 840 mph)	
Max level speed at 11,000 m (36,000 ft)	
Mach 1.6 (917 knots; 1,699 km/h; 1,056 mph)	
Landing speed	115 knots (213 km/h; 132 mph)
T-O run: clean	565 m (1,855 ft)
with four 1,000 lb bombs	880 m (2,890 ft)
with eight 1,000 lb bombs	1,250 m (4,100 ft)
T-O to 15 m (50 ft) with typical tactical load	
	940 m (3,085 ft)
Landing from 15 m (50 ft) with typical tactical load	
	785 m (2,575 ft)
Landing run:	
normal weight, with brake-chute	470 m (1,540 ft)
normal weight, without brake-chute	680 m (2,230 ft)
overload weight, with brake-chute	670 m (2,200 ft)
Typical attack radius, internal fuel only:	
hi-lo-hi	460 nm (852 km; 530 miles)
lo-lo-lo	290 nm (537 km; 334 miles)
Typical attack radius with external fuel:	
hi-lo-hi	760 nm (1,408 km; 875 miles)
lo-lo-lo	495 nm (917 km; 570 miles)
Ferry range with external fuel	
	1,902 nm (3,524 km; 2,190 miles)
g limits	+8.6 (+12 ultimate)

MBB/HAL ADVANCED LIGHT HELICOPTER

In July 1984 the Indian government and MBB signed a contract for the development of an advanced twin-turboshaft light helicopter (ALH), initially for Indian national requirements, which are said to be in the order of 200 for the armed forces and Coast Guard as Chetak/Cheetah replacements. Development of the ALH basic version is by HAL with MBB consultancy. MBB is providing support during design, development and preparations for production of the helicopter in Bangalore.

A full-scale engineering mockup was completed in 1987, and five prototypes are being built. First flight was expected in September 1991; production is expected to start in 1993. A civil version is under consideration.

TYPE: Multi-role light helicopter.

ROTOR SYSTEM: Four-blade hingeless main rotor, with CFRP/GFRP blades of advanced aerofoil section, incorporating sweptback tips. Blades are attached to hub by flexible collars, and are foldable on naval variant. Rotor head is of composites and metal, with elastomeric bearings. Integrated drive system, with direct input to main gearbox from both engines. Four-blade bearingless tail rotor, also with composite blades, mounted on starboard side of main fin.

FUSELAGE: Conventional pod and boom structure, of metal and composites construction (Kevlar, Kevlar/carbonfibre and CFRP/metal sandwich). Tailboom foldable on naval variant.

TAIL UNIT: Single sweptback main fin/tail rotor pylon, plus constant chord tailplane with smaller sweptback endplate fins.

LANDING GEAR: Fully retractable tricycle type on naval variant, with twin nosewheels and single mainwheels, latter retracting into fuselage-side fairings which also house flotation gear and battery; harpoon decklock system. Non-retractable tubular skid gear on other

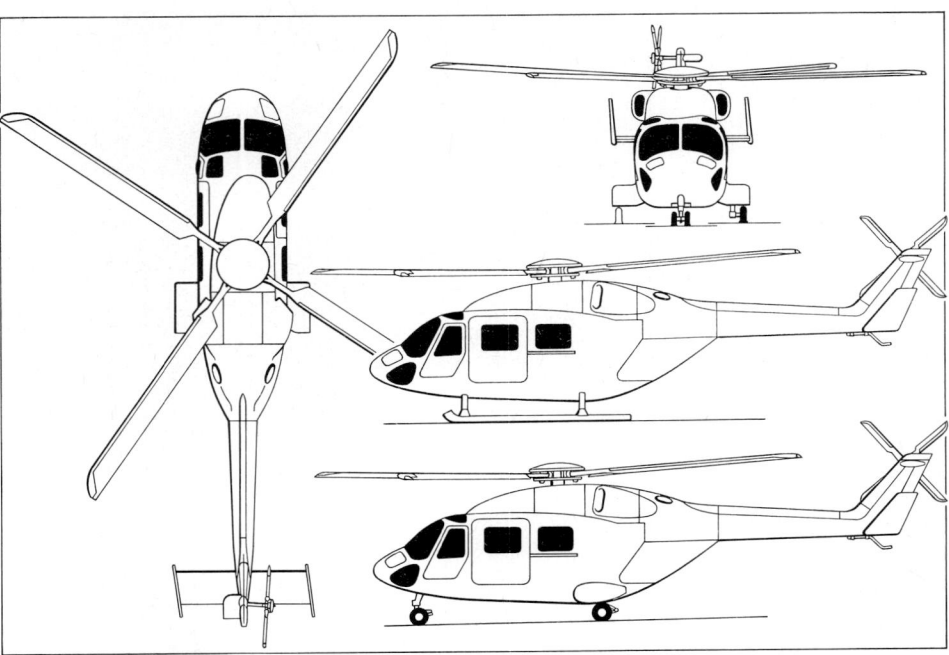

Naval version of the MBB/HAL Advanced Light Helicopter, with additional side view (centre) of air force/army variant *(Jane's/Mike Keep)*

variants. Spring skid under rear of tailboom, to protect tail rotor.

POWER PLANT: Two 746 kW (1,000 shp) Turbomeca TM 333-2B turboshafts, with full authority digital electronic control (FADEC). Pressure refuelling standard.

ACCOMMODATION: Seating capacity for up to 12 persons (14 in high density layout), including a crew of two. Crew door and rearward sliding passenger door on each side; clamshell cargo doors at rear of cabin section.

AVIONICS: V/UHF, HF/SSB and standby UHF com radio, plus intercom. SFIM four-axis AFCS. Doppler navigation system, TAS system, ADF, radio altimeter, heading reference and IFF standard. Oxygen system. Other avionics can include Omega nav system and weather radar.

EQUIPMENT: Depending on mission, can include two stretchers, external hoist and cargo sling.

ARMAMENT: Cabin-side pylons for two torpedoes/depth charges or four anti-ship missiles on naval variant; on army/air force variant, these can be fitted with two anti-tank guided missiles, two pods of 68 mm rockets or two air-to-air missiles. Army/air force variant can also be equipped with ventral 20 mm gun turret or sling for carriage of land mines.

DIMENSIONS, EXTERNAL:
Main rotor diameter	13.20 m (43 ft 3¾ in)
Tail rotor diameter	2.55 m (8 ft 4½ in)
Length:	
overall, both rotors turning	15.87 m (52 ft 0¾ in)
fuselage	12.89 m (42 ft 3¾ in)
Height: overall, tail rotor turning	4.98 m (16 ft 4 in)
to top of rotor head	3.76 m (12 ft 4 in)
Tail unit span (over fins)	3.19 m (10 ft 5½ in)
Wheel track (Naval version)	2.80 m (9 ft 2¼ in)
Skid track (Army/Air Force versions)	
	2.60 m (8 ft 6½ in)

DIMENSIONS, INTERNAL:
Cabin volume	7.33 m³ (258.9 cu ft)
Cargo compartment volume	2.16 m³ (76.28 cu ft)

AREAS:
Main rotor disc	136.85 m² (1,473.0 sq ft)
Tail rotor disc	5.11 m² (55.0 sq ft)

WEIGHTS AND LOADINGS (A: Army/Air Force versions, B: Naval variant):
Weight empty: A, B	2,500 kg (5,511 lb)
Max fuel weight: A, B	1,040 kg (2,293 lb)

Max sling load: A	1,000 kg (2,205 lb)
B	1,500 kg (3,307 lb)
Max T-O weight: A	4,000 kg (8,818 lb)
B	5,000 kg (11,023 lb)
Max disc loading: A	29.23 kg/m² (5.99 lb/sq ft)
B	36.54 kg/m² (7.48 lb/sq ft)

PERFORMANCE (estimated, at S/L, ISA):
Never-exceed speed (VNE)	
	164 knots (305 km/h; 189 mph)
Max level speed	151 knots (280 km/h; 174 mph)
Max cruising speed	132 knots (245 km/h; 152 mph)
Max rate of climb	540 m (1,770 ft)/min
Service ceiling	6,000 m (19,685 ft)
Range with max fuel, 20 min reserves	
	431 nm (800 km; 497 miles)
Endurance, 20 min reserves	3 h 48 min

HAL LIGHT ATTACK HELICOPTER

Hindustan Aeronautics has revealed its intention to develop a tandem two-seat gunship helicopter, based essentially upon the power plant and transmission system of the ALH. The LAH (light attack helicopter) variant, as the accompanying provisional drawing shows, will have stepped cockpits, an undernose gun turret, and stub wings for weapon carriage. According to HAL, no overseas assistance will be sought for the LAH programme.

HAL (AEROSPATIALE) SA 315B LAMA
Indian name: Cheetah

Design of the SA 315B Lama began in late 1968, initially to meet a requirement of the Indian armed forces, and it flew for the first time on 17 March 1969. French certification was granted on 30 September 1970 and FAA type approval on 25 February 1972.

A total of 407 Lamas was delivered by Aerospatiale, by whom production has now ended. Others have been assembled by Helibras in Brazil (which see) under the name Gavião. Indian production, which started in 1972, was continuing in 1990-91, and is now believed to total more than 150.

TYPE: Turbine-driven general purpose helicopter.

ROTOR SYSTEM: Three-blade main and anti-torque rotors. Folding main rotor blades, of NACA 63A section and constant chord, on articulated hinges, with hydraulic drag dampers. Each blade has aluminium alloy spar with

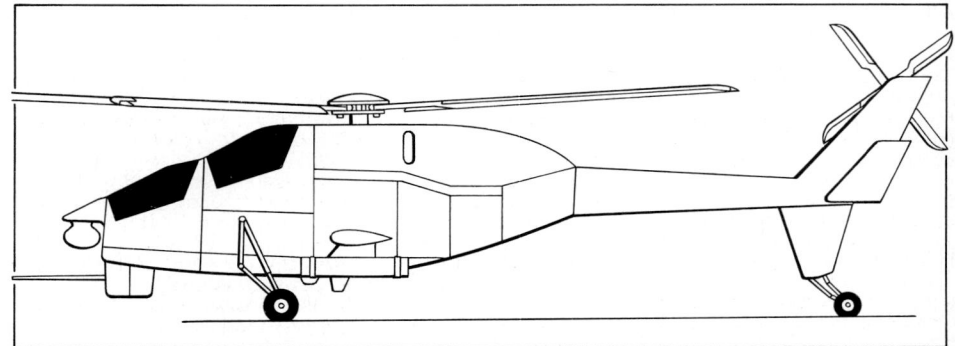

Preliminary drawing of HAL's proposed light attack helicopter *(Jane's/Mike Keep)*

steel cuff, aluminium alloy sheet skin, with stainless steel protective strips, and sandwich type Moltoprene block filling. Rotor brake standard. Tail rotor blades are hollow aluminium alloy aerofoils, with stainless steel leading-edge strip.

Main rotor driven through planetary gearbox, with freewheel for autorotation. Take-off drive for tail rotor at lower end of main gearbox, from where a torque shaft runs to a small gearbox which supports the tail rotor and houses the pitch change mechanism. Steel alloy shafts. Cyclic and collective pitch controls are powered. Main rotor rpm 353. Tail rotor rpm 2,001.

FUSELAGE: Glazed cabin has light metal frame. Centre and rear fuselage have triangulated steel tube framework.

LANDING GEAR: Skid type, with removable wheels for ground manoeuvring. Pneumatic floats for normal operation from water, and emergency flotation gear, inflatable in the air, are available.

POWER PLANT: One 640 kW (858 shp) HAL built Turbomeca Artouste IIIB turboshaft, derated to 404 kW (542 shp). Fuel tank in fuselage centre-section, with capacity of 575 litres (152 US gallons; 126.5 Imp gallons), of which 573 litres (151.5 US gallons; 126 Imp gallons) are usable. Oil capacity 7 litres (1.85 US gallons; 1.55 Imp gallons).

ACCOMMODATION: Glazed cabin seats pilot and co-pilot or passenger side by side in front and three passengers behind. Jettisonable door on each side. Provision for external sling for loads of up to 1,000 kg (2,204 lb). Can be equipped for rescue (hoist capacity 160 kg; 352 lb), liaison, observation, training, agricultural, photographic and other duties. As an ambulance, can accommodate two stretchers and a medical attendant. Cabin heating optional.

SYSTEMS: Single hydraulic system. Electrical system includes engine starter/generator, 36Ah battery and external power socket. Oxygen system optional.

DIMENSIONS, EXTERNAL:
Main rotor diameter	11.02 m (36 ft 1¾ in)
Tail rotor diameter	1.91 m (6 ft 3¼ in)
Distance between rotor centres	6.435 m (21 ft 1½ in)
Main rotor blade chord (constant)	0.35 m (13.8 in)
Length:	
overall, both rotors turning	12.91 m (42 ft 4¼ in)
fuselage	10.23 m (33 ft 6¾ in)
Height overall	3.09 m (10 ft 1¾ in)
Skid track	2.38 m (7 ft 9¾ in)

DIMENSIONS, INTERNAL:
Cabin: Length	2.10 m (6 ft 10½ in)
Max width	1.40 m (4 ft 7 in)
Max height	1.28 m (4 ft 2¼ in)
Volume	3.10 m³ (109.5 cu ft)

AREAS:
Main rotor disc	95.38 m² (1,026.7 sq ft)
Tail rotor disc	2.87 m² (30.84 sq ft)

WEIGHTS AND LOADINGS:
Weight empty	995 kg (2,193 lb)
Max T-O weight: normal	1,750 kg (3,858 lb)
with externally slung cargo	1,850 kg (4,078 lb)
Max disc loading: normal	18.35 kg/m² (3.76 lb/sq ft)
with externally slung cargo	19.40 kg/m² (3.97 lb/sq ft)

PERFORMANCE (at max normal T-O weight at S/L):
Never-exceed speed (V~NE~)	
	113 knots (210 km/h; 130 mph)
Max cruising speed	103 knots (192 km/h; 119 mph)
Max rate of climb	330 m (1,080 ft)/min
Service ceiling	6,400 m (21,000 ft)
Range with max fuel	296 nm (550 km; 341 miles)
Endurance	3 h 30 min

HAL (AEROSPATIALE) SA 316B ALOUETTE III
Indian name: Chetak

The first Alouette III made its initial flight on 28 February 1959, and French production totalled more than

Civil registered HAL Chetak (licence built Alouette III)

1,450. A further 230 were completed by ICA Brasov (now IAR) in Romania. Indian production of the SA 316B, now the only current source of this aircraft, was continuing in 1990-91. HAL production is believed to total at least 300, for both civil and military customers.

TYPE: Turbine driven general purpose helicopter.

ROTOR SYSTEM: Three-blade main and anti-torque rotors. All-metal main rotor blades, of constant chord, on articulated hinges, with hydraulic drag dampers. Main rotor brake and blade folding standard.

Main rotor driven through planetary gearbox, with freewheel for autorotation. Take-off drive for tail rotor at lower end of main gearbox, from where a torque shaft runs to a small gearbox which supports the tail rotor and houses the pitch change mechanism. Cyclic and collective pitch controls are powered.

FUSELAGE: Welded steel tube centre-section, carrying the cabin at the front and a semi-monocoque tailboom.

TAIL UNIT: Cantilever all-metal fixed tailplane, with twin endplate fins, mounted on tailboom.

LANDING GEAR: Non-retractable tricycle type, manufactured under Messier-Bugatti licence. Hydraulic shock absorption. Nosewheel is fully castoring. Provision for skis or emergency pontoon landing gear.

POWER PLANT: One 649 kW (870 shp) HAL built Turbomeca Artouste IIIB turboshaft, derated to 410 kW (550 shp) for max continuous operation. Fuel in single tank in fuselage centre-section, with capacity of 575 litres (152 US gallons; 126.5 Imp gallons), of which 573 litres (151 US gallons; 126 Imp gallons) are usable.

ACCOMMODATION: Normal accommodation for pilot and six persons, with three seats in front and a four-person folding seat at the rear of the cabin. Two baggage holds in centre-section, on each side of the welded structure and enclosed by the centre-section fairings. Provision for carrying two stretchers athwartships at rear of cabin, and two other persons, in addition to pilot. All passenger seats removable to enable aircraft to be used for freight carrying. Can also be adapted for cropspraying or aerial survey roles. Provision for external sling for loads of up to 750 kg (1,650 lb). One forward opening door on each side, immediately in front of two rearward sliding doors. Dual controls and cabin heating optional.

ARMAMENT: In the assault role, the Alouette III can be equipped with a wide range of weapons. A 7.62 mm machine gun (with 1,000 rds) can be mounted

athwartships on a tripod behind the pilot's seat, firing to starboard, either through a small window in the sliding door or through the open doorway with the door locked open. The rear seat is removed to allow the gun mounting to be installed. In this configuration, max accommodation is for pilot, co-pilot, gunner and one passenger, although normally only the pilot and gunner would be carried. Alternatively, a 20 mm cannon (with 480 rds) can be carried on an open turret-type mounting on the port side of the cabin. For this installation all seats except that of the pilot are removed, as is the port side cabin door, and the crew consists of pilot and gunner. Instead of these guns, the Alouette III can be equipped with two or four wire-guided missiles on external jettisonable launching rails, a gyro-stabilised sight, or 68 mm rocket pods.

DIMENSIONS, EXTERNAL:
Main rotor diameter	11.02 m (36 ft 1¾ in)
Main rotor blade chord (each)	0.35 m (13.8 in)
Tail rotor diameter	1.912 m (6 ft 3¼ in)
Spraybar span (agricultural version)	
	10.00 m (32 ft 9¾ in)
Length: overall, rotors turning	12.84 m (42 ft 1½ in)
fuselage, tail rotor turning	10.17 m (33 ft 4½ in)
Width overall, blades folded	2.60 m (8 ft 6¼ in)
Height to top of rotor head	2.97 m (9 ft 9 in)
Wheel track	2.602 m (8 ft 6½ in)

AREAS:
Main rotor disc	95.38 m² (1,026.6 sq ft)
Tail rotor disc	2.87 m² (30.9 sq ft)

WEIGHTS AND LOADINGS:
Weight empty, standard	1,230 kg (2,711 lb)
Max T-O weight	2,200 kg (4,850 lb)
Max disc loading	23.07 kg/m² (4.72 lb/sq ft)

PERFORMANCE (standard version at max T-O weight):
Never-exceed speed (V~NE~) at S/L	
	113 knots (210 km/h; 130 mph)
Max cruising speed at S/L	
	100 knots (185 km/h; 115 mph)
Max rate of climb at S/L	260 m (850 ft)/min
Service ceiling	3,250 m (10,675 ft)
Hovering ceiling: IGE	2,850 m (9,350 ft)
OGE	1,500 m (4,920 ft)
Range with max fuel at S/L	257 nm (477 km; 296 miles)
Endurance	3 h

KANPUR DIVISION
Post Bag 225, Kanpur 208 008
Telephone: 91 (512) 43071 to 43074
Telex: 325 243 HALK IN
GENERAL MANAGER: S. K. Ohri

HAL (HAWKER SIDDELEY) HS 748
Under a programme started in 1985, a number of Kanpur built HS 748s are to be modified to fulfil an ASWAC (airborne surveillance, warning and control) requirement with the Indian Air Force, and an aerodynamic testbed fitted with a 4.80 m (15 ft 9 in) rotodome was flown for the first time on 5 November 1990. The (empty) rotodome was designed and built by MBB under subcontract to HAL, although production units are expected to be manufactured by the latter with technical assistance from the German company. Airframe modification and mounting of the radome was undertaken by Kanpur Division.

The ASWAC programme is managed by India's Defence Research and Development Organisation. Much of the onboard avionics are being designed by the Electronics and Radar Development Establishment, and will be

manufactured by BEL (Bharat Electronics Ltd). Foreign participation is expected in developing the main radar.

HAL (DORNIER) 228
Under a November 1983 contract with Dornier of Germany, HAL is undertaking licence assembly and manufacture of up to 150 Dornier 228 twin-turboprop utility transports in a ten-year technology transfer programme. Kanpur Division is responsible for the airframe, final assembly and flight testing; the Engine Division at Bangalore manufactures the Garrett TPE331-5 turboprops; instrumentation and accessories are supplied by Lucknow Division; and Hyderabad Division provides various items of avionics including the colour weather radar and Omega navigation system.

The 228, in several versions, is used for a wide variety of civil and military duties in India, and while Kanpur Division was preparing for its manufacture a number of Dornier built aircraft were supplied to meet urgent Indian customer needs, as detailed in earlier editions of *Jane's*.

The first Kanpur assembled 228 made its initial flight on 31 January 1986. HAL production is in four basic configurations:

Regional airliner: Five 228-201s for Vayudoot, delivered in March 1986.

Maritime surveillance: Thirty 228-101s for Indian Coast Guard (following three from Germany), first of which were delivered in 1987. In service with No. 750 Squadron at Daman and Madras, they are used for a variety of coastal patrol, environmental control and anti-smuggling missions with equipment that includes a 360° MEL Marec 2 underfuselage search radar, Litton Omega navigation system, a Swedish infra-red/ultra-violet linescanner for pollution detection, search and rescue liferafts, a 1 million candlepower searchlight, side mounted loudhailer, marine markers, and provision for two Micronair underwing spraypods to combat oil spills and chemical pollution. Standard cabin door replaced by sliding door to permit airdropping of 20-man liferaft. Normal crew comprises pilot, co-pilot, radar operator and observer. Marec 2 radar will eventually be replaced in 15 aircraft by Super Marec, ordered in 1987. Armament (optional) can include two 7.62 mm multi-barrel machine-guns and underwing air-to-surface missiles.

For maritime surveillance and anti-shipping tasks, the Indian Navy plans to add 24 specially equipped Dornier 228s to its shore based fixed-wing fleet. These are

HAL-built Dornier 228-101 of the Indian Coast Guard *(John Fricker)*

expected to have anti-ship missile carrying capability and Super Marec radar.

Utility transport: Fifty 228-201s being built for the Indian Air Force. In various utility and logistic support roles they will eventually replace all of the IAF's Otters, Devons and remaining C-47s currently serving with Nos. 41 and 59 Squadrons. Accommodation for up to 22 field-equipped troops on inward facing foldaway seats. Can also be equipped for medevac or other roles. Large roller door at rear on port side.

Executive/Air taxi: Various 228-101 configurations available including six- or 10-seat executive or 15-passenger air taxi layouts, with cabin attendant and galley/wardrobe/toilet facilities. Built-in APU for air-conditioning and lighting in flight or on ground.

One export order for a HAL-built Dornier 228, from Mauritius, was reported in 1990.

HAL HPT-32

The HPT-32 is a fully aerobatic piston engined basic trainer, with side by side seats for instructor and pupil. It can be used for a wide range of ab initio training, including instrument, navigation, night flying and formation flying; for armed patrol; for observation, liaison or sport flying; or for weapon training, light strike duties, supply dropping, search and rescue, reconnaissance, or glider or target towing. The all-metal airframe is designed to FAR Pt 23.

The first prototype (X2157) made its initial flight on 6 January 1977. The third, flown on 31 July 1981, represented the production version, substantially lighter in weight and

with aerodynamic refinements. By 31 March 1987 a total of 40 had been delivered to the Indian Air Force and eight to the Indian Navy. An IAF follow-on order for 30 has been placed, production of which began in late 1987 or early 1988.

TYPE: Two-seat ab initio, aerobatic, night flying, instrument flying and navigation trainer.

WINGS: Cantilever low-wing monoplane. Wing section NACA 64A$_1$-212. Dihedral 5° from roots. Incidence 2° 30′ at root. No sweepback. Light alloy safe-life wings, of tapered planform, with stressed skin. Light alloy plain ailerons and plain trailing-edge flaps. Balance tab in, and ground adjustable tab on, each aileron. Pitot static tube can be heated.

FUSELAGE: Semi-monocoque safe-life structure of light alloy, with stressed skin.

TAIL UNIT: Cantilever light alloy stressed skin structure, with sweptback vertical surfaces. One-piece elevator. Trim tabs in rudder and starboard half of elevator; balance tabs in rudder and port half of elevator.

LANDING GEAR: Non-retractable tricycle type, with HAL oleo-pneumatic shock absorber in each unit. Dunlop UK single mainwheels and nosewheel. Dunlop UK mainwheel tyres, size 446 × 151 × 166 mm, pressure 3.10 bars (45 lb/sq in); Dunlop India nosewheel tyre, size 361 × 126 × 127 mm, pressure 2.41 bars (35 lb/sq in). Dunlop UK aircooled hydraulic disc brakes on mainwheels.

POWER PLANT: One 194 kW (260 hp) Textron Lycoming AEIO-540-D4B5 flat-six engine, driving a Hartzell two-blade constant-speed metal propeller. Total of 220 litres (58.1 US gallons; 48.4 Imp gallons) of fuel in four flexible tanks (two in each wing), plus a 9 litre (2.4 US

gallon; 2 Imp gallon) metal collector tank in fuselage. Total fuel capacity 229 litres (60.5 US gallons; 50.4 Imp gallons). Overwing refuelling points. Oil capacity 13.6 litres (3.6 US gallons; 3 Imp gallons).

ACCOMMODATION: Side by side seats for two persons under rearward sliding jettisonable framed canopy. Seats adjustable in height by 127 mm (5 in). Full dual controls, and adjustable rudder pedals, for instructor and pupil. Cockpit ventilated.

SYSTEMS: Hydraulic system for brakes only. Electrical system (28V DC earth return type) powered by 70A alternator, with SAFT 24V nickel-cadmium standby battery. No air-conditioning, pneumatic, de-icing or oxygen systems.

AVIONICS: HAL (Hyderabad Divn) COM-150 main UHF and COM-104A standby VHF com; directional gyro. No blind-flying instrumentation.

DIMENSIONS, EXTERNAL:
Wing span	9.50 m (31 ft 2 in)
Wing chord: at root	2.24 m (7 ft 4¼ in)
at tip	0.92 m (3 ft 0¼ in)
Wing aspect ratio	6.0
Length overall	7.72 m (25 ft 4 in)
Fuselage: Max width	1.25 m (4 ft 1¼ in)
Height overall	2.88 m (9 ft 5½ in)
Tailplane span	3.60 m (11 ft 9¾ in)
Wheel track	3.45 m (11 ft 4 in)
Wheelbase	2.10 m (6 ft 10¾ in)
Propeller diameter	2.03 m (6 ft 8 in)
Propeller ground clearance (static)	0.23 m (9 in)

AREAS:
Wings, gross	15.00 m² (161.5 sq ft)
Ailerons (total)	1.04 m² (11.19 sq ft)
Trailing-edge flaps (total)	1.82 m² (19.59 sq ft)
Vertical tail surfaces (above fuselage reference line)	2.06 m² (22.17 sq ft)
Rudder (aft of hinge line), incl tabs	0.869 m² (9.35 sq ft)
Tailplane	3.024 m² (32.55 sq ft)
Elevator (aft of hinge line), incl tabs	1.34 m² (14.42 sq ft)

WEIGHTS AND LOADINGS:
Basic weight empty	890 kg (1,962 lb)
Fuel and oil (guaranteed minimum)	164 kg (361 lb)
Max T-O and landing weight	1,250 kg (2,756 lb)
Max wing loading	83.33 kg/m² (17.07 lb/sq ft)
Max power loading	6.44 kg/kW (10.60 lb/hp)

PERFORMANCE (at max T-O weight, ISA):
Never-exceed speed (V$_{NE}$) (structural)	240 knots (445 km/h; 276 mph)
Max level speed at S/L	143 knots (265 km/h; 164 mph) IAS
Max cruising speed at 3,050 m (10,000 ft)	115 knots (213 km/h; 132 mph)
Econ cruising speed	95 knots (176 km/h; 109 mph)
Stalling speed, 20° flap, engine idling	60 knots (110 km/h; 69 mph)
Max rate of climb at S/L	335 m (1,100 ft)/min
Service ceiling	5,500 m (18,045 ft)
T-O run	345 m (1,132 ft)
T-O to 15 m (50 ft)	545 m (1,788 ft)
Landing from 15 m (50 ft)	487 m (1,598 ft)
Landing run	220 m (720 ft)
Min ground turning radius	6.50 m (21 ft 4 in)
Range at 3,050 m (10,000 ft) at econ cruise power	401 nm (744 km; 462 miles)
g limits	+6/−3

HAL HPT-32 two-seat basic training aircraft in Indian Navy insignia

HAL HTT-34

Contrary to the report in the 1990-91 *Jane's*, this turboprop version of the HPT-32 has not been ordered by the Nigerian Air Force or any other customer. One prototype and one pre-production aircraft have been completed.

MiG COMPLEX

Ojhar Township Post Office, Nasik 422 207, Maharashtra
Telephone: 91 (22) 77901
Fax: 91 (22) 77907
Telex: 0752 241 and 0752 256

MANAGING DIRECTOR:
Wg Cdr A. C. Sood (Retd)

GENERAL MANAGER, NASIK DIVISION:
V. M. Akolkar

GENERAL MANAGER, KORAPUT DIVISION:
N. R. Mohanty

The MiG Complex was originally formed with the Nasik, Koraput and Hyderabad Divisions of HAL, which, under an agreement concluded in 1962, built respectively the airframes, power plants and avionics of MiG-21 series fighters under licence from the USSR. Indian production of MiG-21s was phased out in 1986-87, as production of the MiG-27M increased. The Hyderabad Division is now a part of the Accessories Complex.

HAL (MIKOYAN) MiG-27M
Indian Air Force name: Bahadur (Valiant)
NATO reporting name: Flogger-J

Licence assembly of 165 MiG-27Ms (see USSR section) began at HAL in 1984, and the first example assembled by HAL was rolled out in October of that year. These aircraft supplement Soviet built MiG-23s and MiG-27s already supplied to the Indian Air Force, and are the first MiG-27s to be assembled outside the USSR. Since 1988, MiG-27Ms assembled at Nasik are thought to incorporate components manufactured in India. First of five IAF units to receive Bahadurs was No. 32 ('Tiger Sharks') Squadron, the type being formally inducted into IAF service on 11 January 1986.

It was reported in late 1990 that the Indian Air Force planned a mid-life avionics update for its MiG-27Ms, and might also increase the number on order to more than 200, to offset delays in the LCA programme. The avionics

upgrade would include the Smiths/Sagem DARIN nav/attack system currently installed on the IAF's Jaguars.

POWER PLANT: One Tumansky R-29B-300 turbojet, rated at 81.39 kN (18,298 lb st) dry and 112.78 kN (25,353 lb st) with afterburning.

AVIONICS: Include an integrated nav/attack system and active/passive ECM systems.

ARMAMENT: One ventrally mounted six-barrel 30 mm cannon, and seven external hardpoints for up to 3,000 kg (6,614 lb) of stores which can include 500 kg bombs, 57 mm S-24 rockets, two 'Kerry' air-to-surface or four R-60 air-to-air missiles.

WEIGHTS AND LOADINGS:
Max T-O weight	18,000 kg (39,685 lb)

PERFORMANCE:
T-O run at S/L	800 m (2,625 ft)
Combat radius (low level)	210 nm (390 km; 242 miles)
Ferry range	1,349 nm (2,500 km; 1,553 miles)

INDONESIA

IPTN

INDUSTRI PESAWAT TERBANG NUSANTARA (Nusantara Aircraft Industries Ltd)

PO Box 563, Jalan Pajajaran 154, Bandung
Telephone: 62 (22) 611081/2
Fax: 62 (22) 611808
Telex: 28295 IPTN BD IA
HEAD OFFICE: PO Box 3752, 8 Jalan M.H. Thamrin, Jakarta
Telephone: 62 (21) 328169
Telex: 46141 ATP JAKARTA
PRESIDENT DIRECTOR: Prof Dr-Ing B. J. Habibie
DIRECTOR, COMMERCIAL AFFAIRS: Ir S. Paramajuda
CHIEF ENGINEER: Ir Djoko Sartono
PUBLIC RELATIONS MANAGER: Suripto Sugondo

This company was officially inaugurated as PT Industri Pesawat Terbang Nurtanio (Nurtanio Aircraft Industry Ltd) on 23 August 1976, when the government of Indonesia implemented a decision to centralise all existing facilities in the establishment of a single new aircraft industry. The original capital was provided by combining the assets of Pertamina's Advanced Technology and Aeronautical Division with those of the former Nurtanio Aircraft Industry (LIPNUR: see 1977-78 *Jane's*). The present name of the company was adopted in late 1985. A weapons system division, located in Menang Tasikmalaya, West Java, develops and produces the weaponry fitted to aircraft built by the company for military customers. By the end of 1990 the company had contracts for the sale of 270 aircraft, with negotiations then under way for a further 50.

IPTN is jointly responsible with CASA of Spain for development and production of the Airtech CN-235, as well as continuing licence manufacture of the NC-212 Aviocar, NBO-105, NAS-332 Super Puma and NBell-412, as described in the following entries. Studies for the N-442 small helicopter, with DASA (MBB) of Germany, are continuing. Major subcontracting includes the manufacture of components for the Boeing 737 and 767, Fokker 100 and General Dynamics F-16, and for Pratt & Whitney engines. A 1,393 m² (15,000 sq ft) power plant maintenance centre can maintain, overhaul and repair Allison 250, P&WC PT6A, Textron Lycoming LTS 101 and Turbomeca Makila turboshafts and Garrett TPE331 and General Electric CT7 turboprop engines. The company had a workforce of approx 15,500 employees in 1990, and occupies a 69 ha (170.5 acre) site with 365,000 m² (3,928,824 sq ft) of covered accommodation.

AIRTECH (CASA/IPTN) CN-235

Details of this joint transport programme can be found under the Airtech heading in the International section.

IPTN N-250

Indonesia's first entirely indigenously designed transport, the N-250 is a national programme for a 50/54-seat pressurised aircraft powered by twin turboprops in the 2,237 kW (3,000 shp) class, for entry into service in 1996. First flight is planned for mid-1995 and certification in 1996. The N-250's appearance, illustrated in the accompanying three-view drawing, is generally similar to that of the Airtech (CASA/IPTN) CN-235, but it will have a modified fuselage cross-section, longer cabin, and no rear loading ramp. Three flying prototypes are being built.

Indonesian airlines Merpati and Bouraq have signed letters of intent to purchase 127 N-250s (65 and 62 respectively), and FFV Aerotech of Sweden 24. A 60/70-passenger stretched version, provisionally designated **N-270**, is under study.

TYPE: Twin-turboprop regional transport.
WINGS: High-wing monoplane. Fixed-vane double-slotted flaps; spoilers.
LANDING GEAR: Retractable tricycle type, with twin wheels on each unit. Main units retract into fairings on fuselage sides.
POWER PLANT: Two 2,237 kW (3,000 shp) class Allison GMA 2100 turboprops, each driving a six-blade propeller.
ACCOMMODATION: Cabin seating (four-abreast with central aisle) for 50 tourist class passengers at 81 cm (32 in) pitch or 54 passengers at 76 cm (30 in) pitch. One or two cabin attendants. Storage compartments at front of cabin on port side and at rear on starboard side; galley and toilet at rear. Passenger door at front on port side, and service door at rear on starboard side. Type III emergency exits at front (starboard) and rear (port). Large baggage compartment aft of main cabin, with door on port side. Additional bulk storage in underfloor compartment, also with external access.
AVIONICS: State of the art, with six-tube CRT displays.
DIMENSIONS, EXTERNAL:

Wing span	28.00 m (91 ft 10¼ in)
Wing aspect ratio	12.06
Length overall	26.439 m (86 ft 9 in)
Fuselage: Length	25.25 m (82 ft 10 in)
Max diameter	2.90 m (9 ft 6¼ in)
Height overall	8.39 m (27 ft 6¼ in)
Tailplane span	9.40 m (30 ft 10 in)
Propeller diameter	3.81 m (12 ft 6 in)

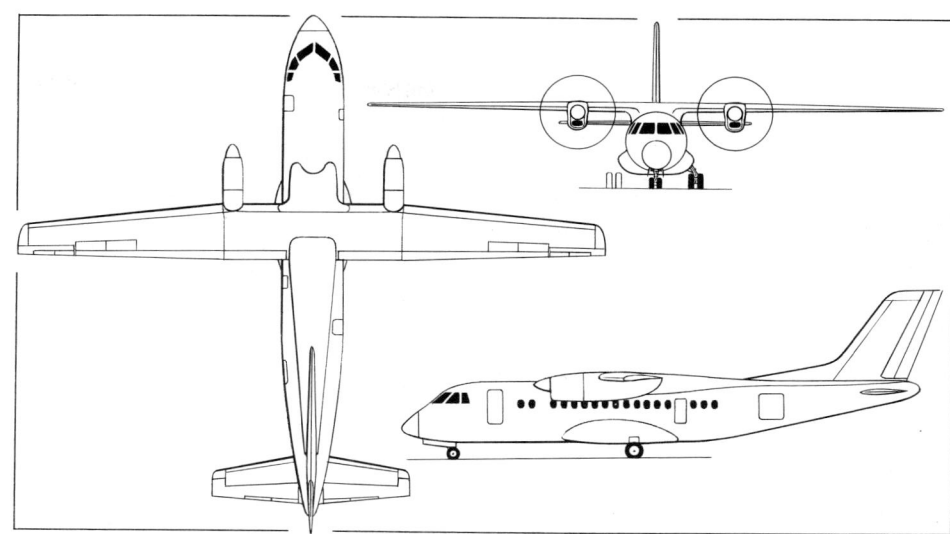

IPTN N-250 twin-turboprop regional transport aircraft *(Pilot Press)*

Passenger door (fwd, port): Height	1.75 m (5 ft 9 in)
Width	0.75 m (2 ft 5½ in)
Service door (rear, stbd): Height	1.75 m (5 ft 9 in)
Width	0.75 m (2 ft 5½ in)
Baggage doors:	
Height: fwd	0.94 m (3 ft 1 in)
rear	1.25 m (4 ft 1¼ in)
Width: fwd	0.85 m (2 ft 9½ in)
rear	1.20 m (3 ft 11¼ in)
DIMENSIONS, INTERNAL:	
Cabin: Length	13.208 m (43 ft 4 in)
Max width	2.70 m (8 ft 10¼ in)
Max height	1.90 m (6 ft 2¾ in)
Main baggage compartment	10.30 m³ (363.7 cu ft)
Underfloor bulk storage	0.60 m³ (21.2 cu ft)
AREAS:	
Wings, gross	65.00 m² (699.7 sq ft)
Vertical tail surfaces (total)	15.52 m² (167.06 sq ft)
Horizontal tail surfaces (total)	17.35 m² (186.75 sq ft)
WEIGHTS AND LOADINGS (design):	
Max payload	6,000 kg (13,227 lb)
Max T-O weight	21,650 kg (47,730 lb)
PERFORMANCE (estimated):	
Max cruising speed at 6,100 m (20,000 ft), ISA	
	320 knots (593 km/h; 368 mph)
T-O to 15 m (50 ft)	1,220 m (4,000 ft)
Landing from 15 m (50 ft)	1,298 m (4,259 ft)
Max range with 50 passengers:	
basic	800 nm (1,482 km; 921 miles)
optional	1,100 nm (2,038 km; 1,266 miles)

IPTN (CASA) NC-212-200 AVIOCAR

The C-212 Aviocar twin-turboprop multi-purpose transport aircraft has been manufactured in Indonesia since 1976, under licence from CASA of Spain (which see). Indonesian built Aviocars have the designation NC-212.

Contracts were placed for 114 NC-212s, and IPTN built 29 NC-212-100 series Aviocars before switching production to the NC-212-200 version, of which 57 had been delivered by January 1991 for duties which include civil passenger and cargo carrying (including a quick-change VIP interior), LAPES airdropping (low altitude parachute extraction system), military transport, search and rescue, maritime patrol, medical evacuation, photographic, survey, and rainmaking. Domestic and foreign sales are 78 and eight respectively. About 20 more are on order, including two for export.

IPTN (MBB) NBO-105

The BO 105 helicopter has been manufactured in Indonesia since 1976, under licence from MBB (see under DASA in German section). Indonesian designation is NBO-105. All airframes and flight controls for the NBO-105 are now of Indonesian manufacture, only the rotors and transmission being supplied from Germany.

By February 1987 a total of 100 NBO-105s had been ordered, and from the 101st aircraft production has continued with the **NBO-105 S**, which has a 25 cm (10 in) longer fuselage and optional radar. An armed version, designated **NBO-105MPDS** (multi-purpose delivery system), can be equipped with unguided rockets (50 mm to 81 mm calibre), machine-gun pods (single or twin 0.30 in or 0.50 in), reconnaissance pods or FLIR pods. Customers for the NBO-105 include the Indonesian Army, Navy (four) and Police (six), Pelita Air Service, the Indonesian Forestry Department, Indonesian Immigration Department, Indonesian Search and Rescue Agency, Gudang Garam, Gunung Madu, and the Indonesian Civil Aviation Training Centre.

IPTN (MBB/KAWASAKI) NBK-117

Under a contract signed with MBB in November 1982, IPTN has rights to build the BK 117 helicopter (see International section) under licence. Indonesian aircraft are designated NBK-117; four had been completed by early 1990, but this programme has been suspended for the time being.

IPTN (AEROSPATIALE) NAS-332 SUPER PUMA

IPTN began assembling the AS 330J Puma in 1981, completing 11 before switching production to the AS 332C and L Super Puma in early 1983.

Rollout of the first IPTN assembled NAS-332 for Pelita Air Service took place on 22 April 1983. Nine had been produced for Indonesian customers by early 1990, including

Indonesian Army NBO-105 helicopter, built by IPTN *(John Fricker)*

four as commando and general purpose transports by the Indonesian Navy. One, for use as a VIP transport, was delivered to the Malaysian Ministry of Finance in November 1988. From the 19th NAS-332, the Super Puma was due to become available from IPTN in its stretched versions, with a 0.765 m (2 ft 6 in) longer cabin.

IPTN (BELL) NBELL-412SP

A licence agreement for IPTN to manufacture the Bell Model 412 (see Canadian section) was signed in November 1982. It covers the partial manufacture and assembly of more than 100 Bell 412s, the first of which was flown for the first time in April 1986. IPTN built aircraft are of approx 40 per cent local manufacture and are designated NBell-412SP. Deliveries totalled 13 by the end of 1990 (Indonesian Army four, Indonesian Navy five, civil operators four). The FN Herstal EMA (external mounting assembly) for 7.62 and 12.7 mm gun and 70 mm rocket pods, already certificated for use on Canadian and Agusta Italian built Bell 412s, was qualified for Indonesian versions in 1990 and has been fitted to a number of NBell-412s in service.

Nusantara-Bell NBell-412SP of Gatari Hutama Airservices, Indonesia

INTERNATIONAL PROGRAMMES

7J7/YXX

PARTICIPATING COMPANIES:
Boeing Commercial Airplane Group: see under USA

Japan Aircraft Development Corporation
Toranomon Daiichi Building, 2-3, Toranomon 2-chome, Minato-ku, Tokyo 105, Japan

Telephone: 81 (3) 503 3225
Fax: 81 (3) 504 0368
Telex: 222 2863
   The agreement between Boeing and the Japanese aircraft industry which has been running since 1984, concerning joint development of a new medium capacity airliner known variously as 7J7 and YXX, was renewed during February

1991 for a further period, though the project is not being very actively pursued.
   JADC was formerly the Civil Transport Development Corporation (CTDC), which co-ordinated the Japanese involvement in the development phase of the Boeing 767. JADC is now doing the same for the sizeable Japanese share of the Boeing 777.

AAA
ADVANCED AMPHIBIOUS AIRCRAFT

PARTICIPATING COMPANIES:
Alenia: see under Italy
DASA: see under Germany
HAI: see under Greece
Per Udsen (Denmark)

AAA

TYPE: Twin-turboprop multi-purpose amphibian; primary roles firefighting, search and rescue, maritime and anti-pollution surveillance, and transport.
PROGRAMME: Definition phase by Alenia and Dornier started 1 April 1988, ended 31 March 1990; now in research and technology phase, led by Alenia, which began 1 June 1990 and continues until 30 September 1992; HAI and Per Udsen became partners, and SOKO (Yugoslavia) an associate, in September 1990; first flight envisaged for April 1995 and certification by end of 1997.
CUSTOMERS: Estimated market for up to 200 such aircraft by year 2000.
COSTS: Funded partly by partner companies and partly from EC's Eureka research programme; 1990 estimate of $650 million for overall project, flyaway cost of $15 million per aircraft.
DESIGN FEATURES: High-lift aerodynamics; low-drag hull; scoop filling of water tanks; rough-sea capability; wing planform based on that of Dornier 228.
FLYING CONTROLS: Mission-tailored flight management system.
STRUCTURE: Extensive use of corrosion-proof composites.
LANDING GEAR: Retractable tricycle type, with twin wheels on each unit; mainwheels retract into large sponsons on fuselage sides.
POWER PLANT: Two 2,013 kW (2,700 shp) class turboprops; six-blade propellers with advanced aerofoil section and composite blades.
DIMENSIONS, EXTERNAL (provisional):
   Wing span   32.833 m (107 ft 8¾ in)

Model of the proposed European Advanced Amphibious Aircraft *(Kenneth Munson)*

Length of fuselage	22.00 m (72 ft 2¼ in)	
Height overall	9.71 m (30 ft 1 in)	
AREAS:		
Wings, gross	98.00 m² (1,054.9 sq ft)	
WEIGHTS AND LOADINGS (estimated):		
Typical operating weight empty	12,200 kg (26,896 lb)	
Max disposable payload	8,000 kg (17,637 lb)	
Max T-O weight: from water	19,400 kg (42,770 lb)	
from land	23,000 kg (50,705 lb)	
PERFORMANCE (estimated, at 23,000 kg; 50,705 lb max T-O weight except where indicated):		

Max cruising speed at 3,050 m (10,000 ft), ISA, at 90% MTOGW
                               220 knots (408 km/h; 253 mph)
Stalling speed, flaps down, AUW of 18,000 kg (39,683 lb)
                               60 knots (112 km/h; 69 mph) EAS
Max rate of climb at S/L, ISA   436 m (1,430 ft)/min
T-O run from land, at S/L, ISA   840 m (2,756 ft)
FAR Pt 25 balanced field length   1,300 m (4,265 ft)
Typical range with 4,000 kg (8,818 lb) payload
                      1,133 nm (2,100 km; 1,305 miles)
Ferry range   2,347 nm (4,350 km; 2,703 miles)

AERMACCHI/DASA

PARTICIPATING COMPANIES:
Aermacchi: see under Italy
DASA: see under Germany

AERMACCHI/DASA PTS-2000

TYPE: Tandem-seat advanced jet trainer.

PROGRAMME: Launched April 1989 by Aermacchi and Dornier, but German involvement now also includes MBB Military Aircraft SBU as result of DASA restructuring; joint studies continue of aircraft, market and complete training system.
VARIANTS: **PTS-2000** is complete Primary Training System; aircraft is designated **AT-2000**.
CUSTOMERS: No firm customer identified by May 1991.

DESIGN FEATURES: No configuration details released by May 1991, but aircraft being used as baseline would be in 5,000-6,000 kg (11,023-13,228 lb) weight range and have 1:1 thrust/weight ratio, full fly-by-wire controls and EFIS cockpits; intended as component of complete military pilot training system including also simulator and computer-based instruction.

AEROSPATIALE/CATIC/SA

PARTICIPATING COMPANIES:
Aerospatiale: see under France

CATIC: see under China

Singapore Aerospace: see under Singapore

P120L

TYPE: Four/five-seat light helicopter.
PROGRAMME: Original agreement included ASTA of Australia, which withdrew late 1989; definition phase launched 15 February 1990 as partnership of Aerospatiale (programme leader, 54 per cent), CATIC (30 per cent) and Singapore Aerospace (16 per cent); detail

design started December 1990; first flight planned for 1993, deliveries for 1996. Aerospatiale responsible for rotor system/transmission/final assembly/flight test/certification, CATIC (through HAMC, which see) for main front fuselage, and SA for upper fuselage, tailboom and fin.

VARIANTS: **Basic** economy version, and more powerful improved performance **hot and high** version, both for civil and military applications.

DESIGN FEATURES: Intended for Lama/Gazelle/JetRanger portion of market; Aerospatiale Spheriflex four-blade main rotor, eight-blade fenestron tail rotor (with stator) and skid landing gear.

STRUCTURE: Composites for main and tail rotor blades and much of fuselage.

POWER PLANT: One Turbomeca Arriel 2 turboshaft derivative of 500 kW (670 shp) in basic version, 746 kW (1,000 shp) in high performance version.

ACCOMMODATION: Pilot and four passengers.

DIMENSIONS, EXTERNAL: Not yet known.

WEIGHTS AND LOADINGS: (A: basic version, B: high performance version):

Max sling load: A	1,000 kg (2,205 lb)
B	1,160 kg (2,557 lb)
Max T-O weight: A	2,000 kg (4,409 lb)
B	2,300 kg (5,070 lb)

PERFORMANCE (estimated, at max T-O weight except where indicated; A and B as under Weights):

Max cruising speed at S/L, ISA:	
A	147 knots (272 km/h; 169 mph)
B	151 knots (280 km/h; 174 mph)
B at 2,000 kg (4,409 lb) AUW	
	157 knots (291 km/h; 181 mph)
Hovering ceiling OGE: A, ISA	3,500 m (11,480 ft)
B, ISA	3,250 m (10,660 ft)
B, ISA, at 2,000 kg (4,409 lb) AUW	
	4,500 m (14,760 ft)

A, ISA +20°C	2,850 m (9,350 ft)
B, ISA +20°C	2,550 m (8,365 ft)
B, ISA +20°C, at 2,000 kg (4,409 lb) AUW	
	3,900 m (12,795 ft)

Range at S/L with 600 litres (158.5 US gallons; 132 Imp gallons) fuel: A	442 nm (820 km; 509 miles)
B	405 nm (750 km; 466 miles)

Model of the P120L light helicopter under development by France, China and Singapore

AIRBUS
AIRBUS INDUSTRIE

1 Rond Point Maurice Bellonte, 31707 Blagnac Cédex, France
Telephone: 33 61 93 33 33
Fax: 33 61 93 37 92
Telex: AIRBU 530526 F
PARIS OFFICE: 12bis avenue Bosquet, 75007 Paris, France
Telephone: 33 (1) 45 51 40 95
MANAGING DIRECTOR: Jean Pierson
CHIEF OPERATING OFFICER: Heribert Flosdorff
SENIOR VICE-PRESIDENT, COMMERCIAL: Stuart Iddles
MANAGER, TECHNICAL PRESS: David Velupillai
AIRFRAME PRIME CONTRACTORS:

Aerospatiale: see under France
Deutsche Airbus: see under Germany
British Aerospace: see under UK
CASA: see under Spain

Airbus Industrie set up December 1970 as Groupement d'Intérêt Economique to manage development, manufacture, marketing and support of A300; this management now extends to A300-600, A310, A320, A321 and A340/A330. Airbus Industrie responsible for all work (total workforce about 30,000) on these programmes by partner companies; Aerospatiale has 37.9 per cent interest in Airbus Industrie, Deutsche Airbus 37.9 per cent, British Aerospace 20 per cent, CASA 4.2 per cent. Fokker is an associate in A300 and A310 and Belairbus in A310, A320 and A330/A340; some Deutsche Airbus work on A300/A310 is subcontracted to Italian aerospace industry, some BAe work to Australian industry; Canadair is an Aerospatiale subcontractor on A330/A340.

In 1990 Airbus Industrie won firm orders for 404 aircraft, (31 A300s, 40 A310s, 183 A320s, 117 A321s, 25 A330s and eight A340s) and delivered 95 (19 A300s, 18 A310s and 58 A320s).

AIRBUS A300-600

TYPE: Large-capacity wide-bodied medium/long-range commercial transport.

PROGRAMME: Launched May 1969; initial variants were A300B1 (first flight 28 October 1972, service entry May 1974: see 1971-72 *Jane's* for details), A300B2 and A300B4 (248 built: see 1984-85 and previous editions); A300-600 go-ahead December 1980, made first flight (F-WZLR) 8 July 1983; certificated (with JT9D-7R4H1 engines) 9 March 1984; first delivery (to Saudia) 26 March 1984. Improved version with CF6-80C2 engines and other changes (see Variants paragraph) made first flight 20 March 1985; French certification for Cat IIIB take-offs and landings 26 March 1985; first delivery of improved version (to Thai Airways) 26 September 1985. Extended range A300-600R (then known as -600ER) made first flight 9 December 1987, receiving European and FAA certification 10 and 28 March 1988 respectively, deliveries (to American Airlines) beginning 21 April 1988.

VARIANTS: **A300-600:** Advanced version of A300B4-200; major production version since early 1984. Passenger and freight capacity increased by using rear fuselage of A310, shorter by two frame pitches in unpressurised section than that of -100/-200 series A300s, with parallel fuselage section extended by three frame pitches to restore tail moment arm; wings have simple Fowler flaps and increased trailing-edge camber; forward facing two-person flight deck with CRT displays; new digital

avionics; new braking control system; new APU; simplified systems; weight saving by use of composites for some secondary structural components; payload/range performance and fuel economy improved by comprehensive drag clean-up. **Improved version** (from 1985), to which detailed description applies, has CF6-80C2 or PW4000 as engine options, carbon brakes, wingtip fences and 'New World' flight deck; basic equipment fit of aircraft delivered from late 1991 will be further improved by incorporating standard options.

A300-600R: Extended range version of A300-600, differing mainly in having fuel trim tank in tailplane and higher MTOGW.

A300-600 Convertible: Convertible passenger/cargo version, described separately.

A300-600 Freighter: Non-passenger version, described separately.

SAT (Super Airbus Transporter): A300-600R conversion as Super Guppy replacement; described separately.

CUSTOMERS: Total of 171 ordered by 31 March 1991 (incl 133 A300-600R and four Convertibles), of which 95 delivered.

DESIGN FEATURES: Mid mounted wings with 10.5 per cent thickness/chord ratio, 28° sweepback at quarter-chord, and (since 1985) tip fences; circular-section pressurised fuselage; many components manufactured from various fibre composites; all-swept tail unit; anti-icing of outer wing leading-edges (but not tail unit).

FLYING CONTROLS: Each wing has three-segment, two-position (T-O/landing) leading-edge slats (no cut-out over engine pylon), Krueger flap at leading-edge wingroot, three cambered tabless flaps on trailing-edge, all-speed aileron between inboard flap and outer pair, and seven spoilers forward of flaps; flaps occupy 84 per cent of trailing-edge, increasing wing chord by 25 per cent when fully extended; ailerons deflect 9° 2' downward automatically when flaps are deployed; all 14 spoilers used as lift dumpers: outboard 10 for roll control and inboard 10 as airbrakes; variable incidence tailplane. Ailerons/elevators/rudder fully powered by hydraulic servos (three per surface), controlled mechanically; secondary surfaces (spoilers/flaps/slats) fully powered hydraulically with electrical control, tailplane by two independent hydraulic motors electrically controlled with additional mechanical input; preselection of spoiler/lift dump lever permits automatic extension of lift dumpers on touchdown; flaps and slats have similar drive mechanisms, each powered by twin motors driving ball screwjacks on each surface with built-in protection against asymmetric operation.

STRUCTURE: Two-spar main wing box, integral with fuselage and incorporating fail-safe principles; third spar across inboard sections; semi-monocoque fuselage (frames and open Z-section stringers), with integrally machined skin panels in high-stress areas; primary structure is of high-strength, damage-tolerant aluminium alloy, with steel or titanium for some critical fuselage components, honeycomb panels or selected glassfibre laminates for secondary structures; metal slats, flaps and ailerons. Composites include AFRP for flap track fairings, rear wing-body fairings, cooling air inlet fairings and radome; GFRP for wing upper surface panels above mainwheel bays, fin leading/trailing-edges, fin-tip, fin-fuselage fairings, tailplane trailing-edges, elevator leading-edges, tailplane and elevator tips and elevator actuator access panel; carbon-reinforced GFRP for elevators and

rudder; CFRP for spoilers, outer flap deflector doors and fin box; all CFRP moving surfaces have aluminium or titanium trailing-edges. Aerospatiale builds nose (incl flight deck), lower centre-fuselage, four inboard spoilers, wing-body fairings and engine pylons; Deutsche Airbus builds forward fuselage (flight deck to wing box), upper centre-fuselage, rear fuselage (incl tailcone), vertical tail, 10 outboard spoilers and some cabin doors, and also equips wings, installs interiors and seats; BAe designed wings and builds wing box; CASA manufactures horizontal tail, port and starboard forward passenger doors and mainwheel nosewheel doors; Fokker produces wingtips, ailerons, flaps, slats and main gear leg fairings; large, fully equipped and inspected airframe sections shipped by Super Guppy to Aerospatiale at Toulouse for final assembly and painting, aircraft then being flown to Hamburg for outfitting and returned to Toulouse for final customer acceptance.

LANDING GEAR: Hydraulically retractable tricycle type, of Messier-Bugatti design, with Messier-Bugatti/Liebherr/Dowty shock absorbers and wheels standard. Twin-wheel nose unit retracts forward, main units inward into fuselage. Free-fall extension. Nosewheel doors and mainwheel leg fairing doors are of CFRP. Nose gear is structurally identical to that of B2/B4/A310; main gear is generally reinforced, with a new-design hinge arm and a new pitch damper hydraulic and electrical installation. Each four-wheel main unit comprises two tandem mounted bogies, interchangeable left with right. Standard bogie size is 927 × 1,397 mm (36½ × 55 in); wider bogie of 978 × 1,524 mm (38½ × 60 in) is optional. Mainwheel tyres size 49 × 17-20 (standard) or 49 × 19-20 (wide bogie), with respective pressures of 12.4 and 11.1 bars (180 and 161 lb/sq in). Nosewheel tyres size 40 × 14-16, pressure 9.4 bars (136 lb/sq in). Steering angles 65°/95°. Messier-Bugatti/Liebherr/Dowty hydraulic disc brakes standard on all mainwheels. Normal braking powered by 'green' hydraulic system, controlled electrically through two master valves and monitored by a brake system control box to provide anti-skid protection. Standby braking (powered automatically by 'yellow' hydraulic system if normal 'green' system supply fails) controlled through a dual metering valve; anti-skid protection is ensured through same box as normal system, with emergency pressure supplied to brakes by accumulators charged from 'yellow' system. Automatic braking system optional. Duplex anti-skid units fitted, with a third standby hydraulic supply for wheel brakes. Bendix or Goodrich wheels and brakes available optionally.

POWER PLANT: Two turbofans in underwing pods. A300-600 was launched with the 249 kN (56,000 lb st) Pratt & Whitney JT9D-7R4H1 and is currently available with the 249 kN (56,000 lb st) Pratt & Whitney PW4156 or 262.4 kN (59,000 lb st) General Electric CF6-80C2A1. A300-600R is offered with the 273.6 kN (61,500 lb st) CF6-80C2A5 or 258 kN (58,000 lb st) PW4158. The CF6-80C2A5 and PW4158 are also available as options on the A300-600. The PW4160 (267 kN; 60,000 lb st) is available as an option on both the A300-600 and A300-600R. Nacelles have CFRP cowling panels and are subcontracted to Rohr (California); pylon fairings are of AFRP. Fuel in two integral tanks in each wing, and fifth integral tank in wing centre-section, giving standard usable capacity of 62,000 litres (16,379 US gallons; 13,638 Imp gallons). Additional 6,150 litre (1,625 US gallon; 1,353 Imp gallon) fuel/trim tank in tailplane (-600R only) increases this total to 68,150 litres (18,004 US gallons;

Airbus A300-600R twin-turbofan extended range transport in the insignia of Egyptair

14,991 Imp gallons). Optional extra fuel cell in aft cargo hold can increase total to 75,350 litres (19,906 US gallons; 16,575 Imp gallons) in -600R. Two standard refuelling points beneath starboard wing; similar pair optional under port wing.

ACCOMMODATION: Crew of two on flight deck, plus two observers' seats. Passenger seating in main cabin in six, seven, eight or nine-abreast layout with two aisles. Typical mixed class layout has 267 seats (26 first class and 241 economy), six/eight abreast at 96/86 cm (38/34 in) seat pitch with two galleys and two toilets forward, one galley and two toilets in mid-cabin, and one galley and two toilets at rear. Typical economy class layout for 289 passengers eight-abreast at 86 cm (34 in) pitch. Max capacity (subject to certification) 375 passengers. Closed overhead baggage lockers on each side (total capacity 10.48 m³; 370 cu ft) and in double-sided central 'super-bin' installation (total capacity 14.50 m³; 512 cu ft), giving 0.03 to 0.09 m³ (1.2 to 3.2 cu ft) per passenger in typical economy layout. Two outward parallel-opening Type A plug type passenger doors ahead of wing on each side, and one on each side at rear. Type I emergency exit on each side aft of wing. Underfloor baggage/cargo holds fore and aft of wings, with doors on starboard side. Forward hold will accommodate twelve LD3 containers, or four 2.24 × 3.17 m (88 × 125 in) or, optionally, 2.43 × 3.17 m (96 × 125 in) pallets, or engine modules. Rear hold will accommodate ten LD3 containers. Additional bulk loading of freight provided for in an extreme rear compartment with usable volume of 17.3 m³ (611 cu ft). Alternatively, the rear hold can be arranged optionally to carry eleven LD3 containers, with bulk cargo capacity reduced to 8.6 m³ (303 cu ft). The bulk cargo compartment can be used for the transport of livestock. Entire accommodation is pressurised, including freight, baggage and avionics compartments.

SYSTEMS: Air supply for air-conditioning system taken from engine bleed and/or APU via two high pressure points. Conditioned air can also be supplied direct to cabin by two low pressure ground connections. Ram air inlet for fresh air ventilation when packs not in use. Pressure control system (max differential 0.574 bar; 8.32 lb/sq in) consists of two identical, independent, automatic systems (one active, one standby). Switchover from one to the other is automatic after each flight and in case of active system failure. In each system, pressure is controlled by two electric outflow valves, its function depending on pre-programmed cabin pressure altitude and rate of change of cabin pressure, aircraft altitude, and pre-selected landing airfield elevation. Automatic pre-pressurisation of cabin before take-off is provided, to prevent noticeable pressure fluctuation during take-off. Hydraulic system comprises three fully independent circuits, operating simultaneously. Each system includes a reservoir of the direct air/fluid contact type, pressurised at 3.5 bars (51 lb/sq in); fluid used is a fire resistant phosphate ester type. Nominal output flow of 136 litres (35.9 US gallons; 30 Imp gallons)/min is delivered at pressure of 207 bars (3,000 lb/sq in). 'Blue' and 'yellow' systems have one pump each, 'green' system has two pumps. The three circuits provide triplex power for primary flying controls; if any circuit fails, full control of the aircraft is retained without any necessity for action by the crew. All three circuits supply the ailerons, rudder and elevators; 'blue' circuit additionally supplies spoiler 7, spoiler/airbrake 4, airbrake 1, yaw damper and slats; 'green' circuit additionally supplies spoiler 6, flaps, Krueger flaps, slats, landing gear, wheel brakes, steering, tailplane trim, artificial feel, and roll/pitch/yaw autopilot;

'yellow' circuit additionally supplies spoiler 5, spoiler/airbrake 3, airbrake 2, flaps, wheel brakes, cargo doors, artificial feel, yaw damper, tailplane trim, and roll/pitch/yaw autopilot. Ram air turbine driven pump provides standby hydraulic power should both engines become inoperative. Main electrical power is supplied under normal flight conditions by two integrated drive generators, one on each engine. A third (auxiliary) generator, driven by the APU, can replace either of the main generators, having the same electromagnetic components but not the constant-speed drive. Each generator is rated at 90kVA, with overload ratings of 112.5kVA for 5 min and 150kVA for 5 s. The APU generator is driven at constant speed through a gearbox. Three unregulated transformer-rectifier units (TRUs) supply 28V DC power. Three 25Ah nickel-cadmium batteries are used for emergency supply and APU starting. Emergency electrical power taken from main aircraft batteries and an emergency static inverter, providing single-phase 115V 400Hz output for flight instruments, navigation, communications and lighting when power is not available from normal sources. Hot air anti-icing of engines, engine air intakes, and outer segments of leading-edge slats. Electrical heating for anti-icing flight deck front windscreens, demisting flight deck side windows, and for sensors, pitot probes and static ports, and waste water drain masts. Garrett GTCP 331-250F APU in tailcone, exhausting upward. The installation incorporates APU noise attenuation. Fire protection system is self-contained, and firewall panels protect main structure from an APU fire. APU provides bleed air to pneumatic system, and drives an auxiliary AC generator during ground and in-flight operation. APU drives a 90kVA oil spray cooled generator, and supplies bleed air for main engine start or air-conditioning system. For current deliveries of A300-600, APU has an improved relight capability, with starting capability throughout the flight envelope. Modular box system provides passenger oxygen to all installation areas. For new A300-600s and -600Rs, two optional modifications are offered for compliance with full extended-range

operations (EROPS) requirements: a hydraulically driven fourth generator and an increased cargo hold fire suppression capability. EROPS kit is qualified for aircraft with CF6-80C2 and JT9D-7R series engines, and since mid-1988 for those with PW4000 series.

AVIONICS: Standard communications avionics include two VHF sets, two HF, one Selcal system, interphone and passenger address systems, groundcrew call system, and voice recorder. Radio navigation avionics include two DME interrogators, two VOR receivers, two ATC transponders, one ADF, two marker beacon receivers, two ILS receivers, weather radar, and two radio altimeters. Full provisions for second weather radar and GPWS; third VHF; structural provision for such future systems as a Mode S ATC transponder. Two Honeywell digital air data computers standard. Most other avionics are to customer's requirements, only those related to the blind landing system (Bendix/King or Collins ILS and Collins or TRT radio altimeter) being selected and supplied by the manufacturer. Six identical and interchangeable CRT electronic displays (four EFIS and two ECAM: electronic flight instrument system and electronic centralised aircraft monitor), plus digitised electromechanical instruments with liquid crystal displays. The basic digital AFCS comprises dual flight control computers (FCC) for flight director and autopilot functions (for Cat III automatic landing), a single thrust control computer (TCC) for speed and thrust control, and two flight augmentation computers (FACs) to provide yaw damping, electric pitch trim, and flight envelope monitoring and protection. Options include second FCC (for Cat III automatic landing); second TCC; two flight management computers (FMCs) and two control display units for full flight management system. Basic aircraft is also fitted with an ARINC 717 data recording system, comprising a digital flight data acquisition unit, digital flight data recorder and three-axis linear accelerometer. An optional additional level of windshear protection is available.

DIMENSIONS, EXTERNAL:

Wing span	44.84 m (147 ft 1 in)
Wing aspect ratio	7.7

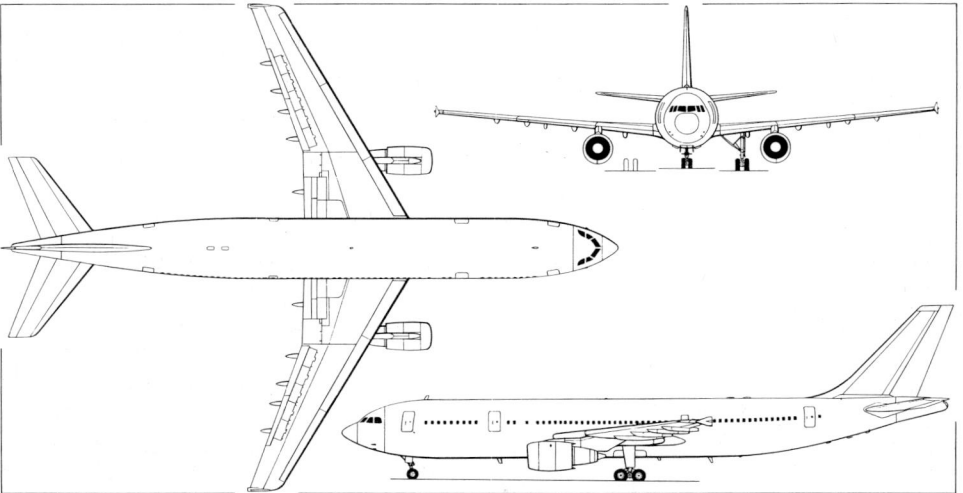

Airbus A300-600R wide-bodied medium-range transport (P&W JT9D turbofans) *(Pilot Press)*

Length overall	54.08 m (177 ft 5 in)
Fuselage: Length	53.30 m (174 ft 10½ in)
Max diameter	5.64 m (18 ft 6 in)
Height overall	16.62 m (54 ft 6½ in)
Tailplane span	16.26 m (53 ft 4 in)
Wheel track	9.60 m (31 ft 6 in)
Wheelbase (c/l of shock absorbers)	18.60 m (61 ft 0 in)
Passengers doors (each): Height	1.93 m (6 ft 4 in)
Width	1.07 m (3 ft 6 in)
Height to sill: fwd	4.60 m (15 ft 1 in)
centre	4.80 m (15 ft 9 in)
rear	5.50 m (18 ft 0½ in)
Emergency exits (each): Height	1.60 m (5 ft 3 in)
Width	0.61 m (2 ft 0 in)
Height to sill	4.87 m (15 ft 10 in)
Underfloor cargo door (fwd):	
Height	1.71 m (5 ft 7½ in)
Width	2.69 m (8 ft 10 in)
Height to sill	3.07 m (10 ft 1 in)
Underfloor cargo door (rear):	
Height	1.71 m (5 ft 7½ in)
Width	1.81 m (5 ft 11¼ in)
Height to sill	3.41 m (11 ft 2¼ in)
Underfloor cargo door (extreme rear):	
Height (projected)	0.95 m (3 ft 1 in)
Width	0.95 m (3 ft 1 in)
Height to sill	3.56 m (11 ft 8 in)

DIMENSIONS, INTERNAL:

Cabin, excl flight deck:	
Length	40.21 m (131 ft 11 in)
Max width	5.28 m (17 ft 4 in)
Max height	2.54 m (8 ft 4 in)
Underfloor cargo hold:	
Length: fwd	10.60 m (34 ft 9¼ in)
rear	7.95 m (26 ft 1 in)
extreme rear	3.40 m (11 ft 2 in)
Max height	1.76 m (5 ft 9 in)
Max width	4.20 m (13 ft 9¼ in)
Underfloor cargo hold volume:	
fwd	75.1 m³ (2,652 cu ft)
rear	55.0 m³ (1,942 cu ft)
extreme rear	17.3 m³ (611 cu ft)

AREAS:

Wings, gross	260.0 m² (2,798.6 sq ft)
Leading-edge slats (total)	30.30 m² (326.15 sq ft)
Krueger flaps (total)	1.115 m² (12.00 sq ft)
Trailing-edge flaps (total)	47.30 m² (509.13 sq ft)
All-speed ailerons (total)	7.06 m² (75.99 sq ft)
Spoilers (total)	5.396 m² (58.08 sq ft)
Airbrakes (total)	12.59 m² (135.52 sq ft)
Fin	45.20 m² (486.53 sq ft)
Rudder	13.57 m² (146.07 sq ft)
Horizontal tail surfaces (total)	64.0 m² (688.89 sq ft)

*WEIGHTS AND LOADINGS (A: CF6-80C2A1/A5 engines, B: PW4156/4158 engines, all in 267-seat configuration):

Manufacturer's weight empty:	
A (600)	79,210 kg (174,628 lb)
A (600R)	79,403 kg (175,053 lb)
B (600)	79,151 kg (174,498 lb)
B (600R)	79,318 kg (174,866 lb)
Operating weight empty:	
A (600)	89,445 kg (197,192 lb)
A (600R)	89,669 kg (197,686 lb)
B (600)	89,397 kg (197,086 lb)
B (600R)	89,595 kg (197,523 lb)
Max payload (structural): A (600)	40,555 kg (89,408 lb)
A (600R)	40,331 kg (88,914 lb)
B (600)	40,603 kg (89,514 lb)
B (600R)	40,405 kg (89,077 lb)
Underfloor cargo capacity (A and B):	
containerised	31,300 kg (69,005 lb)
bulk	2,800 kg (6,173 lb)
Max usable fuel:	
600: standard	49,786 kg (109,760 lb)
600R: standard	54,721 kg (120,640 lb)
with optional cargo hold tank	58,618 kg (129,230 lb)
Max T-O weight (A and B):	
600	165,000 kg (363,765 lb)
600R (standard)	171,400 kg (377,870 lb)
600R (option)	171,700 kg (378,535 lb)
Max ramp weight (A and B):	
600	165,900 kg (365,745 lb)
600R (standard)	170,500 kg (375,885 lb)
600R (option)	172,600 kg (380,520 lb)
Max landing weight (A and B):	
600	138,000 kg (304,240 lb)
600R (standard)	140,000 kg (308,645 lb)
Max zero-fuel weight (A and B):	
600, 600R (standard)	130,000 kg (286,600 lb)
Max wing loading: 600	635 kg/m² (130.0 lb/sq ft)
600R (standard)	656 kg/m² (134.4 lb/sq ft)

*Production aircraft from late 1991 onward. See 1989-90 and previous editions for earlier versions

PERFORMANCE (at max T-O weight except where indicated: A and B as for Weights):

Max operating speed (VMO) from S/L to 8,140 m (26,700 ft)	335 knots (621 km/h; 386 mph) CAS
Max operating Mach number (MMO) above 8,140 m (26,700 ft)	0.82

Max cruising speed at 7,620 m (25,000 ft)	480 knots (890 km/h; 553 mph)
Max cruising speed at 9,150 m (30,000 ft)	Mach 0.82 (484 knots; 897 km/h; 557 mph)
Typical long-range cruising speed at 9,450 m (31,000 ft)	Mach 0.80 (472 knots; 875 km/h; 543 mph)
Approach speed: 600	135 knots (249 km/h; 155 mph)
600R	136 knots (251 km/h; 156 mph)
Max operating altitude	12,200 m (40,000 ft)

Min ground turning radius (effective, aft CG):

wingtips	34.75 m (114 ft 0 in)
nosewheel	22.00 m (72 ft 2¼ in)

Runway ACN for flexible runway, category B:

standard bogie & tyres: 600	56
600R	59
600R (option)	60
optional bogie & tyres: 600	52
600R	55
600R (option)	56

T-O field length at S/L, ISA + 15°C:

600: A	2,384 m (7,820 ft)
B	2,332 m (7,650 ft)
600R: A (C2A5 engines)	2,451 m (8,040 ft)
B (PW4158 engines)	2,500 m (8,200 ft)
Landing field length: 600	1,536 m (5,040 ft)
600R	1,555 m (5,100 ft)

Range (1991 deliveries) at typical airline OWE with 267 passengers and baggage, reserves for 200 nm (370 km; 230 miles):

600: A, B	3,680 nm (6,820 km; 4,240 miles)
600R (standard fuel):	
A	4,050 nm (7,505 km; 4,665 miles)
B	4,070 nm (7,540 km; 4,690 miles)
600R (MTOGW option and additional fuel):	
A	4,210 nm (7,802 km; 4,850 miles)
B	4,230 nm (7,840 km; 4,870 miles)

OPERATIONAL NOISE LEVELS (A300-600R, ICAO Annex 16, Chapter 3):

T-O (flyover): A	91.1 EPNdB (96.3 limit)
B	92.2 EPNdB (96.3 limit)
T-O (sideline): A	98.6 EPNdB (99.9 limit)
B	97.7 EPNdB (99.9 limit)
Approach: A	99.8 EPNdB (103.3 limit)
B	101.7 EPNdB (103.3 limit)

AIRBUS A300-600 CONVERTIBLE and A300-600 FREIGHTER

TYPE: Specialised versions of A300-600.

VARIANTS: **Convertible:** For all-passenger or mixed passenger/cargo configuration. Typical options include accommodation (in mainly eight-abreast seating) for up to 375 passengers (subject to certification) on the upper deck; or 145 passengers (seven/eight abreast) plus six 2.44 × 3.17 m (96 × 125 in) pallets; or 83 passengers plus nine 96 × 125 in pallets; up to twenty 2.24 × 3.17 m (88 × 125 in) pallets; or five 88 × 125 in plus nine 96 × 125 in pallets.

Freighter: For freighting only; no passenger systems provided. Various systems options give airlines ability to adapt basic aircraft to specific freight requirements.

STRUCTURE: Generally similar to A300-600. Main differences are large forward upper deck cargo door, reinforced cabin floor, smoke detection system in main cabin; upper deck cargo door is on opposite side to door of forward underfloor hold, enabling loading or unloading to be carried out simultaneously at all positions.

CUSTOMERS: See under A300-600.

POWER PLANT: Same range of options as for A300-600.

DIMENSIONS, EXTERNAL: As A300-600, plus:

Upper deck cargo door (fwd, port):	
Height (projected)	2.57 m (8 ft 5¼ in)
Width	3.58 m (11 ft 9 in)
Height to sill	4.91 m (16 ft 1 in)

DIMENSIONS, INTERNAL:

Cabin upper deck usable for cargo:	
Length	33.45 m (109 ft 9 in)
Min height	2.01 m (6 ft 7 in)
Max height:	
ceiling trim panels in place	2.22 m (7 ft 3½ in)
without ceiling trim panels	2.44 m (8 ft 0 in)
Volume	192-203 m³ (6,780-7,169 cu ft)

WEIGHTS AND LOADINGS (basic Convertible. A: with CF6-80C2A5 engines, B: with PW4158 engines):

Manufacturer's weight empty:	
A, passenger mode	81,900 kg (180,558 lb)
B, passenger mode	81,820 kg (180,382 lb)
A, freight mode	81,640 kg (179,985 lb)
B, freight mode	81,560 kg (179,809 lb)
Operating weight empty:	
A, passenger mode	92,160 kg (203,178 lb)
B, passenger mode	92,100 kg (203,045 lb)
A, freight mode	83,470 kg (184,020 lb)
B, freight mode	83,410 kg (183,887 lb)
Max payload (structural):	
A, passenger mode	37,840 kg (83,423 lb)
B, passenger mode	37,900 kg (83,555 lb)
A, freight mode	46,530 kg (102,581 lb)
B, freight mode	46,590 kg (102,713 lb)
Max T-O weight: A, B	170,500 kg (375,900 lb)
Max landing weight: A, B	140,000 kg (308,650 lb)
Max zero-fuel weight: A, B	130,000 kg (286,600 lb)

WEIGHTS AND LOADINGS (basic Freighter variant of -600R):

As for Convertible except:

Manufacturer's weight empty:	
A	78,550 kg (173,173 lb)
B	78,470 kg (172,997 lb)
Operating weight empty:	
A	80,120 kg (176,634 lb)
B	80,040 kg (176,458 lb)
Max payload (structural):	
A	49,880 kg (109,966 lb)
B	49,940 kg (110,099 lb)

PERFORMANCE:

Range with max (structural) payload, allowances for 30 min hold at 460 m (1,500 ft) and 200 nm (370 km; 230 mile) diversion:

A, B	2,680 nm (4,960 km; 3,090 miles)

AIRBUS SUPER AIRBUS TRANSPORTER (SAT)

TYPE: Transporter for outsize cargo.

PROGRAMME: Announced December 1990 as likely replacement for four-aircraft Super Guppy transport fleet (average age already 40 years), which will reach end of their useful life by end of 1990s. Decision on go-ahead expected in second quarter 1991, permitting service entry of first aircraft in 1995 with three more SATs following by 1998; Super Guppy capacity meanwhile being supplemented by use of surface transport (except for combined centre/rear fuselage and fin) for carriage of A320 sections; SAT conversion work will be subcontracted; aircraft will be certificated by Airbus Industrie.

DESIGN FEATURES: Based on new A300-600R airframe, with enlarged unpressurised upper fuselage, accessed via new clamshell doors at front above flight deck; new tail unit with endplate auxiliary fins; flight deck located below main deck floor level to permit roll-on/roll-off loading; total payload 45,000-50,000 kg (99,200-110,025 lb).

AIRBUS A310

TYPE: Large-capacity wide-bodied medium/extended-range commercial transport.

PROGRAMME: Launched July 1978; first flight (F-WZLH) 3 April 1982; initial French/German certification 11 March

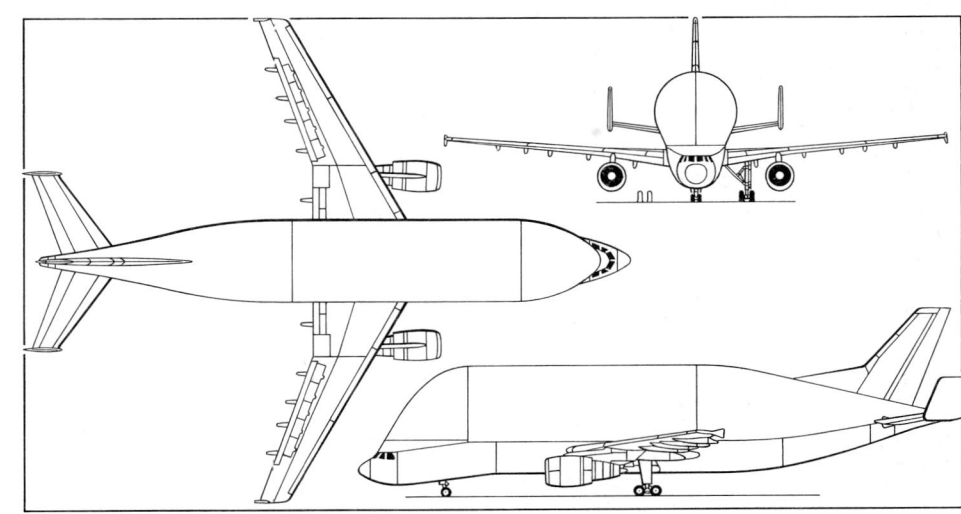

SAT proposed Super Guppy replacement, converted from the A300-600R *(Jane's/Mike Keep)*

Airbus A310-300 extended-range twin-turbofan transport in the livery of Czechoslovak Airlines

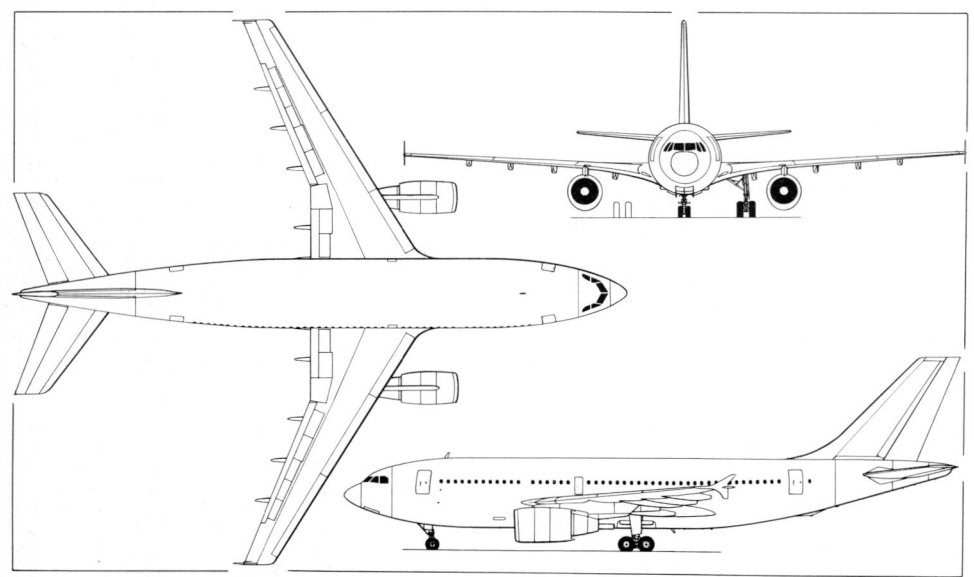

Airbus A310 medium/extended-range transport *(Pilot Press)*

1983; first deliveries (Lufthansa and Swissair) 29 March 1983, entering service 12 and 21 April respectively; JAR Cat IIIA certification (France/Germany) September 1983; UK certification January 1984; JAR Cat IIIB November 1984; FAA type approval early 1985. First flight of extended-range A310-300 8 July 1985 (certificated with JT9D-7R4E engines 5 December 1985, delivered to launch customer Swissair 17 December); wingtip fences introduced as standard on A310-200 from Spring 1986 (first delivery: Thai Airways, 7 May); certification/delivery of A310-300 with CF6-80C2 engines April 1986, with PW4152s June 1987; version with ACTs (additional centre tanks) certificated November 1987 (first customer Wardair of Canada).

VARIANTS: **A310-200:** Basic passenger version, to which detailed description mainly applies.

A310-200C: Convertible version of A310-200; first delivery (Martinair) 29 November 1984.

A310-200F: Freighter version.

A310-300: Extended-range passenger version; second member of Airbus family to introduce delta shaped wingtip fences as standard. Extra range provided by increased basic max T-O weight (150,000 kg; 330,695 lb) and greater fuel capacity (higher max T-O weights optional); standard extra fuel capacity is in tailplane, allowing in-flight CG control for improved fuel efficiency; for extra long range, one or two ACTs (additional centre tanks) can be installed in part of cargo hold.

CUSTOMERS: Total of 252 firm orders (85 A310-200 and 167 A310-300) by 31 March 1991, of which 188 delivered (85 A310-200 and 103 A310-300).

DESIGN FEATURES: Retains same fuselage cross-section as A300, but with cabin 11 frames shorter and overall fuselage 13 frames shorter than A300B2/B4-100 and -200; new advanced-technology wings of reduced span and area; new and smaller horizontal tail surfaces; common pylons able to support all types of GE and PW engines offered; advanced digital two-man cockpit; landing gear modified to cater for size and weight changes. Wings have 28° sweepback at quarter-chord, root incidence 5° 3′, dihedral 11° 8′ (inboard) and 4° 3′

(outboard) at trailing-edge, and thickness/chord ratios of 15.2 (root), 11.8 (at trailing-edge kink), and 10.8 per cent (tip); outer leading-edge slats de-iced by engine bleed air.

FLYING CONTROLS: Wing leading-edge movable surfaces as for A300-600; trailing-edges each have single Fowler flap outboard, vaned Fowler flap inboard, with all-speed aileron between; all 14 spoilers used as lift dumpers, inner eight also as airbrakes; two independent computer systems with different software provide redundancy and operational safety. Tail control surfaces as for A300-600.

STRUCTURE: Mainly of high-strength aluminium alloy except for outer shrouds (structure in place of low-speed ailerons), spoilers, wing leading-edge lower access panels and outer deflector doors, nosewheel doors, mainwheel leg fairing doors, engine cowling panels, elevators and fin box (CFRP); flap track fairings, flap access doors, rear wing/body fairings, pylon fairings, nose radome, cooling air inlet fairings and tailplane trailing-edges (AFRP); wing leading-edge top panels, panel aft of rear spar, upper surface skin panels above mainwheel bays, forward wing/body fairings, glideslope antenna cover, fin leading/trailing-edges, fin and tailplane tips (GFRP); and rudder (CFRP/GFRP). Wing box is two-spar multi-rib metal structure, with top and bottom load-carrying skins. Undertail bumper beneath rear fuselage, to protect structure against excessive nose-up attitude during T-O and landing. Manufacturing breakdown differs in detail from that of A300-600: Aerospatiale builds the nose section (incl flight deck), lower centre-fuselage and wing box, rear wing/body fairings, engine pylons and airbrakes, and is responsible for final assembly; Deutsche Airbus builds forward fuselage, upper centre-fuselage, rear fuselage and associated doors, tailcone, fin and rudder, flaps and spoilers, and is responsible for wing assembly and commercial installation; BAe produces wing fixed structures; CASA's contribution includes horizontal tail surfaces, nose-gear and mainwheel doors, and forward passenger doors; Fokker manufactures main landing gear leg doors, wingtips, all-speed ailerons and flap track fairings; wing leading-edge slats and forward wing/fuselage fairings produced by Belairbus.

LANDING GEAR: Hydraulically retractable tricycle type. Twin-wheel steerable nose unit (steering angle 65°/95°) as for A300. Main gear by Messier-Bugatti, each bogie comprising two tandem mounted twin-wheel units. Retraction as for A300-600. Standard tyre sizes: main, 46 × 16-20, pressure 11.2 bars (163 lb/sq in); nose, 40 × 14-16, pressure 9.0 bars (131 lb/sq in). Two options for low-pressure tyres on main units: (1) size 49 × 17-20, pressure 9.8 bars (143 lb/sq in); (2) size 49 × 19-20, pressure 8.9 bars (129 lb/sq in). Messier-Bugatti brakes and anti-skid units standard; Bendix type optional on A310-200. Carbon brakes standard since 1986.

POWER PLANT: Launched with two 213.5 kN (48,000 lb st) Pratt & Whitney JT9D-7R4D1 or 222.4 kN (50,000 lb st) General Electric CF6-80A3 turbofans; currently available with 238 kN (53,500 lb st) CF6-80C2A2, or 231.2 kN (52,000 lb st) Pratt & Whitney PW4152. To become available from late 1991 with 262.4 kN (59,000 lb st) CF6-80C2A8 or 249.1 kN (56,000 lb st) PW4156A. Total usable fuel capacity 55,000 litres (14,530 US gallons; 12,098 Imp gallons) in A310-200. Increased to 61,100 litres (16,141 US gallons; 13,440 Imp gallons) in A310-300, by additional fuel in tailplane trim tank. Further 7,200 litres (1,902 US gallons; 1,584 Imp gallons) can be carried in each additional centre tank (ACT) in forward part of aft cargo hold. Two refuelling points, one beneath each wing outboard of engine.

ACCOMMODATION: Crew of two on flight deck. Provision for third and fourth crew seats. Cabin, which can be configured with six/seven/eight and nine-abreast seating, normally seats from 210 to 250 passengers, although aircraft is certificated for up to 280. Typical two-class layout is for 218 passengers: 18 first class, six-abreast at 96.5 cm (38 in) seat pitch, plus 200 economy class mainly eight-abreast at 86 cm (34 in) pitch. Max capacity for 280 passengers nine-abreast in high-density configuration at pitch of 76 cm (30 in). Standard layout has two galleys and toilet at forward end of cabin, plus two galleys and four toilets at rear. Depending upon customer requirements, a second toilet can be added forward, and toilets and galleys can be located at the forward end at the class divider position. Overhead baggage stowage as for A300-600, rising to 0.09 m³ (3.2 cu ft) per passenger in typical economy layout. Four passenger doors, one forward and one aft on each side. Oversize Type I emergency exit over wing on each side. Underfloor baggage/cargo holds fore and aft of wings, each with door on starboard side. Forward hold will accommodate eight LD3 containers or three 2.24 × 3.17 m (88 × 125 in) standard or three 2.44 × 3.17 m (96 × 125 in) optional pallets. Rear hold will accommodate six LD3 containers, with an optional seventh LD3 or LD1 position. LD3 containers can be carried two abreast, and/or standard pallets installed crosswise.

SYSTEMS: Garrett GTCP 331-250 APU. Air-conditioning system, powered by compressed air from engines, APU, or a ground supply unit, comprises two separate packs; air is distributed to flight deck, three separate cabin zones, electrical and electronic equipment, avionics bay and bulk cargo compartment. Ventilation of forward cargo compartments optional. Pressurisation system has a max normal differential of 0.57 bar (8.25 lb/sq in). Air supply for wing ice protection, engine starting and thrust reverser system is bled from various stages of the engine compressors, or supplied by the APU or a ground supply unit. Hydraulic system (three fully independent circuits operating at 207 bars; 3,000 lb/sq in: details as described for A300-600). Electrical system, similar to that of A300-600, consists of a three-phase 115/200V 400Hz constant frequency AC system and a 28V DC system. Two 90kVA engine driven brushless generators for normal single-channel operation, with automatic transfer of busbars in the event of a generator failure. Each has an overload rating of 135kVA for 5 min and 180kVA for 5 s. A third (identical) AC generator, directly driven at constant speed by the APU, can be used during ground operations, and also in flight to compensate for the loss of one or both engine driven generators. Current production A310s have APU with improved relight capability, which can be started and operated throughout the flight envelope. Any one generator can provide sufficient power to operate all equipment and systems necessary for an indefinite period of safe flight. DC power is generated via three 150A transformer-rectifiers. Three nickel-cadmium batteries are supplied. Flight crew oxygen system fed from rechargeable pressure bottle of 2,166 litres (76.5 cu ft) capacity. Standard options are a second 76.5 cu ft bottle, a 3,256 litre (115 cu ft) bottle, and an external filling connection. Emergency oxygen sets for passengers and cabin attendants. Anti-icing of outer wing leading-edge slats and engine air intakes by hot air bled from engines; and of pitot probes, static ports and plates, and sensors, by electric heating. For current production A310s, an EROPS (extended-range operations) modification kit, as for the A300-600, is available.

AVIONICS: As described for A300-600.

DIMENSIONS, EXTERNAL:
Wing span	43.89 m (144 ft 0 in)
Wing chord: at root	8.38 m (27 ft 6 in)
at tip	2.18 m (7 ft 1¾ in)
Wing aspect ratio	8.8
Length overall	46.66 m (153 ft 1 in)
Fuselage: Length	45.13 m (148 ft 0¾ in)
Max diameter	5.64 m (18 ft 6 in)
Height overall	15.80 m (51 ft 10 in)
Tailplane span	16.26 m (53 ft 4¼ in)
Wheel track	9.60 m (31 ft 6 in)
Wheelbase (c/l of shock absorbers)	
	15.21 m (49 ft 10¾ in)
Passenger door (fwd, port): Height	1.93 m (6 ft 4 in)
Width	1.07 m (3 ft 6 in)
Height to sill at OWE	4.54 m (14 ft 10¾ in)
Passenger door (rear, port): Height	1.93 m (6 ft 4 in)
Width	1.07 m (3 ft 6 in)
Height to sill at OWE	4.85 m (15 ft 11 in)
Servicing doors (fwd and rear, stbd)	
	as corresponding passenger doors
Upper deck cargo door (A310C/F)	as A300-600
Emergency exits (overwing, port and stbd, each):	
Height	1.39 m (4 ft 6¾ in)
Width	0.67 m (2 ft 2½ in)
Underfloor cargo door (fwd):	
Height	1.71 m (5 ft 7½ in)
Width	2.69 m (8 ft 10 in)
Height to sill at OWE	2.611 m (8 ft 6¾ in)
Underfloor cargo door (rear):	
Height	1.71 m (5 ft 7½ in)
Width	1.81 m (5 ft 11¼ in)
Height to sill at OWE	2.72 m (8 ft 11 in)
Underfloor cargo door (aft bulk hold):	
Height	0.95 m (3 ft 1½ in)
Width	0.95 m (3 ft 1½ in)
Height to sill at OWE	2.751 m (9 ft 0¼ in)

DIMENSIONS, INTERNAL:
Cabin, excl flight deck Length	33.24 m (109 ft 0¾ in)
Max width	5.28 m (17 ft 4 in)
Max height	2.33 m (7 ft 7¾ in)
Volume	210.0 m³ (7,416.1 cu ft)
Fwd cargo hold: Length	7.63 m (25 ft 0½ in)
Max width	4.18 m (13 ft 8½ in)
Height	1.71 m (5 ft 7¼ in)
Volume	50.3 m³ (1,776.3 cu ft)
Rear cargo hold: Length	5.033 m (16 ft 6¼ in)
Max width	4.17 m (13 ft 8¼ in)
Height	1.67 m (5 ft 5¾ in)
Volume	34.5 m³ (1,218.4 cu ft)
Aft bulk hold: Volume	17.3 m³ (610.9 cu ft)
Total overall cargo volume	102.1 m³ (3,605.6 cu ft)

AREAS:
Wings, gross	219 m² (2,357.3 sq ft)
Leading-edge slats (total)	28.54 m² (307.20 sq ft)
Trailing-edge flaps (total)	36.68 m² (394.82 sq ft)
Ailerons (total)	6.86 m² (73.84 sq ft)
Spoilers (total)	7.36 m² (79.22 sq ft)
Airbrakes (total)	6.16 m² (66.31 sq ft)
Fin	45.20 m² (486.53 sq ft)
Rudder	13.57 m² (146.07 sq ft)
Tailplane	44.80 m² (482.22 sq ft)
Elevators (total)	19.20 m² (206.67 sq ft)

WEIGHTS AND LOADINGS (218-seat configuration. A: CF6-80C2A2 engines, B: PW4152s, C: CF6-80C2A8s, D: PW4156As):
Manufacturer's weight empty:
200: A	71,660 kg (157,983 lb)
B	71,601 kg (157,853 lb)
300: A	71,840 kg (158,380 lb)
B	71,781 kg (158,250 lb)
Operating weight empty: 200: A	80,011 kg (176,394 lb)
B	79,963 kg (176,288 lb)
300: A	80,222 kg (176,859 lb)
B	80,174 kg (176,753 lb)
C	80,237 kg (176,892 lb)
D	80,163 kg (176,729 lb)

Max payload: 200: A	33,990 kg (74,935 lb)
B	34,040 kg (75,045 lb)
300: A	33,780 kg (74,472 lb)
B	33,830 kg (74,582 lb)
* Max usable fuel: 200	44,100 kg (97,224 lb)
300	49,039 kg (108,112 lb)
Max T-O weight: 200	142,000 kg (313,055 lb)
300 (basic)	150,000 kg (330,695 lb)
300 (options)	153,000 kg (337,305 lb)
	or 157,000 kg (346,125 lb)
	or 164,000 kg (361,560 lb)
Max landing weight: 200, 300	123,000 kg (271,170 lb)
options (200 and 300)	124,000 kg (273,375 lb)
Max zero-fuel weight: 200, 300	113,000 kg (249,120 lb)
options (200 and 300)	114,000 kg (251,330 lb)

* optional additional tank in aft cargo hold adds 5,779 kg (12,740 lb) of fuel and increases OWE/reduces max payload by 692 kg (1,525 lb). Two additional tanks add 11,560 kg (25,485 lb) of fuel and increase OWE/reduce max payload by 1,320 kg (2,910 lb)

PERFORMANCE (at basic max T-O weight except where indicated; engines as under Weights):
Typical long-range cruising speed at 9,450-12,500 m
(31,000-41,000 ft): A, B, C, D	Mach 0.80

Approach speed at max landing weight:
A, B, C, D	135 knots (250 km/h; 155 mph)

Min ground turning radius (effective, aft CG):
wingtips	33.00 m (108 ft 3¼ in)
nosewheel	18.75 m (61 ft 6 in)

T-O field length at S/L, ISA + 15°C:
200: A	1,860 m (6,100 ft)
B	1,799 m (5,900 ft)
300: A (at 150 tonne MTOGW)	2,408 m (7,900 ft)
B (at 150 tonne MTOGW)	2,225 m (7,300 ft)
C (at 164 tonne MTOGW)	2,560 m (8,400 ft)
D (at 164 tonne MTOGW)	2,400 m (7,875 ft)

Landing field length at S/L, at max landing weight (200 and 300): A
	1,479 m (4,850 ft)
B	1,555 m (5,100 ft)

Runway ACN for flexible runway, category B:
standard tyres: 200	43
300	49
optional tyres: 200	41
300	47

Range (1991 deliveries) at typical airline OWE with 218 passengers and baggage, international reserves for 200 nm (370 km; 230 mile) diversion:
200: A	3,820 nm (7,079 km; 4,399 miles)
B	3,800 nm (7,040 km; 4,375 miles)

300 at basic MTOGW:
A	4,420 nm (8,191 km; 5,090 miles)
B	4,400 nm (8,155 km; 5,065 miles)

300 at 164 tonne MTOGW with ACTs:
C	5,280 nm (9,785 km; 6,080 miles)
D	5,270 nm (9,765 km; 6,070 miles)

OPERATIONAL NOISE LEVELS (ICAO Annex 16, Chapter 3):
T-O (flyover): 200: A	89.6 EPNdB (95.3 limit)
300: A	91.2 EPNdB (95.6 limit)
T-O (sideline): 200: A	96.4 EPNdB (99.2 limit)
300: A	96.3 EPNdB (99.4 limit)
Approach: 200, 300: A	98.6 EPNdB (102.9 limit)

AIRBUS A320

TYPE: Twin-turbofan short/medium-range commercial transport.

PROGRAMME: Launched 2 March 1984; four-aircraft development programme (first flight 22 February 1987 by F-WWAI); JAR (UK/French/German/Dutch) certification of A320-100 with CFM56-5 engines, for two-crew operation, awarded 26 February 1988; first deliveries (Air France and British Airways) 28 and 31 March 1988 respectively; JAR certification of A320-200 with CFM56-5s received 8 November 1988, followed by FAA type approval for both models 15 December 1988; certification with V2500 engines (first flown 28 July 1988) received 20 April (JAR) and 6 July 1989 (FAA), deliveries with this power plant (to Adria Airways) beginning 18 May 1989.

VARIANTS: **A320-100:** Initial version (21 ordered): details in 1987-88 *Jane's*. Superseded by A320-200.

A320-200: Standard version from third quarter 1988; differs from A320-100 in having wingtip fences, wing centre-section fuel tank and higher max T-O weights.

A321-100: Stretched version of A320-200; described separately.

Riblet testbed: Company A320 coated over 75 per cent of airframe with drag-reducing 'riblets' (plastic film with microscopic grooves); first flight 9 November 1989; test programme has confirmed anticipated fuel saving of approx 1.5 per cent; research into other aspects continuing.

CUSTOMERS: Total of 657 firm orders by 23 May 1991, of which 171 delivered.

DESIGN FEATURES: First subsonic commercial aircraft with fly-by-wire control throughout normal flight envelope, side-stick controllers instead of control columns, composites for major primary structures, and centralised maintenance system; advanced technology wings have 25° sweepback at quarter-chord, 5° 6′ 36″ dihedral, and incorporate gust load alleviation system, plus experience from A310 and significant commonality with other Airbus Industrie aircraft where cost-effective; 6° tailplane dihedral.

FLYING CONTROLS: Fly-by-wire electrical control, via hydraulic actuators, of ailerons, elevators, spoilers, flaps and leading-edge slats; rudder movement and tailplane trim connected to FBW system, but also signalled mechanically to provide backup pitch and yaw control; each wing has five-segment leading-edge slats (one inboard, four outboard of engine pylon), two-segment Fowler trailing-edge flaps, and five-segment spoilers forward of outboard flap; all 10 spoilers used as lift dumpers, outer four also for roll and inner six as airbrakes; slat and flap controls by Liebherr and Lucas.

STRUCTURE: Generally similar to that of A310, but with AFRP for fuselage belly fairing skins; GFRP for fin leading-edge and fin/fuselage fairing; CFRP for wing fixed leading/trailing-edge bottom access panels and deflectors, trailing-edge flaps and flap track fairings, spoilers, ailerons, fin (except leading-edge), rudder, tailplane, elevators, nosewheel/mainwheel doors, and main-gear leg fairing doors. Aerospatiale builds entire front fuselage (forward of wing leading-edge), cabin rear doors, nosewheel doors, centre wing box and engine pylons, and is responsible for final assembly; centre and rear fuselage, tailcone, wing flaps, fin, rudder, and commercial furnishing undertaken by Deutsche Airbus; British Aerospace builds main wings, including ailerons, spoilers and wingtips, and main landing gear leg fairings; Belairbus produces leading-edge slats; CASA is responsible for tailplane, elevators, mainwheel doors, and sheet metal work for parts of rear fuselage.

LANDING GEAR: Hydraulically retractable tricycle type, with twin wheels and oleo-pneumatic shock absorber on each unit (four-wheel main-gear bogies, for low-strength runways, optional). Dowty main units retract inward into wing/body fairing; steerable Messier-Bugatti nose unit retracts forward. Nosewheel steering angle ±75° (effective turning angle ±70°). Radial tyres standard, size 45 × 16-R20 on main gear and 30 × 8.8-R15 on nose gear. Optional tyres for main gear are 49 × 17R20 or 49 × 19R20 radials, or 46 × 16-20 or 49 × 19-20 crossplies, and for nose gear 30 × 8.8-15 crossplies. Tyres for

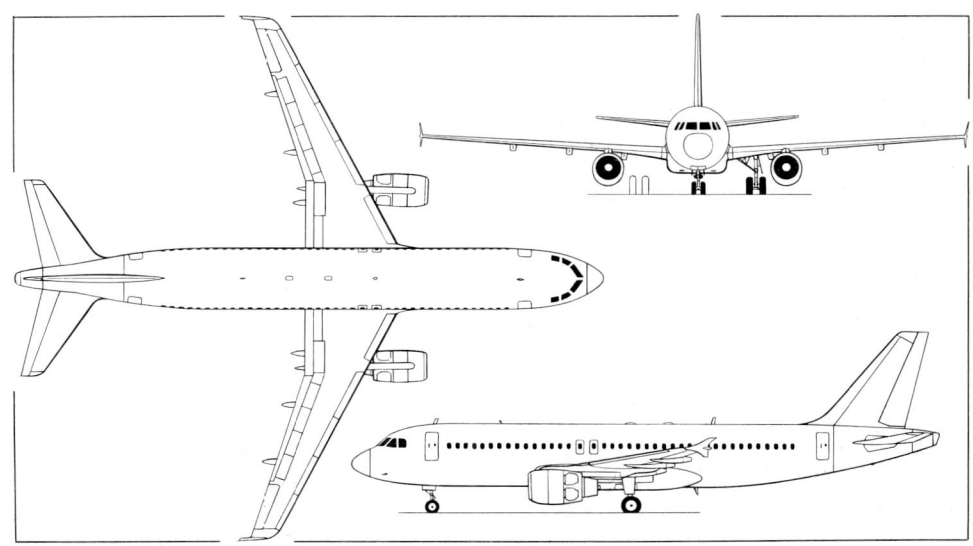

Airbus A320-200 twin-turbofan single-aisle 150/179-seat transport *(Pilot Press)*

America West Airlines, with a firm order for 48, was the second largest airline customer for the A320 in early 1991

main-gear bogie option are either 915 × 300R16 radials or 36 × 11-16 crossplies. Carbon brakes standard.

POWER PLANT: Two 104.5-111.2 kN (23,500-25,000 lb st) class CFM International CFM56-5A1 turbofans for first aircraft delivery in Spring 1988, with 111.2 kN (25,000 lb st) IAE V2500-A1 engines available for aircraft delivered from May 1989. Other available engines are CFM56-5A3 from November 1990 (117.9 kN; 26,500 lb st); and 117.9 kN (26,500 lb st) CFM56-5B4 and 111.2 kN (25,000 lb st) IAE V2525-A5, both from 1994. Nacelles by Rohr Industries; thrust reversers by Hispano-Suiza for CFM56 engines, by IAE for V2500s. Dual-channel FADEC (full authority digital engine control) system standard on each engine. For A320-200, standard fuel capacity in wing and wing centre-section tanks is 23,859 litres (6,303 US gallons; 5,248 Imp gallons); for A320-100, standard fuel capacity without centre-section tank is 15,843 litres (4,185 US gallons; 3,485 Imp gallons).

ACCOMMODATION: Standard crew of two on flight deck, with one (optionally two) forward facing folding seats for additional crew members; seats for four cabin attendants. Single-aisle main cabin has seating for up to 179 passengers, depending upon layout, with locations at front and rear of cabin for galley(s) and toilet(s). Typical two-class layout would have 12 seats four-abreast at 91.5 cm (36 in) pitch in 'super first' and 138 six-abreast at 81 cm (32 in) pitch economy class; or 152 six-abreast seats (84 business + 68 economy) at 86 and 78 cm (34 and 31 in) pitch respectively. Single class economy layout could offer 164 seats at 81 cm (32 in) pitch, or up to 179 in high-density configuration. Compared with existing single-aisle aircraft, fuselage cross-section is significantly increased, permitting use of wider triple seats to provide higher standards of passenger comfort; five-abreast business class seating provides a standard equal to that offered as first class on major competitive aircraft. In addition, wider aisle permits quicker turnrounds. Overhead stowage space superior to that available on existing aircraft of similar capacity, and provides ample carry-on baggage space; best use of underseat space for baggage is provided by improved seat design and optimised positioning of seat rails. Passenger doors at front and rear of cabin on port side, forward one having optional integral airstairs; service door opposite each of these on starboard side. Two overwing emergency exits each side. Fuselage double-bubble cross-section provides increased baggage/cargo hold volume and working height, and ability to carry containers derived from standard interline LD3 type. As base is same as that of LD3, all existing wide-body aircraft and ground handling equipment can accept these containers without modification. Forward and rear underfloor baggage/cargo holds, plus overhead lockers; with 164 seats, overhead stowage space per seat is 0.056 m³ (2.0 cu ft). Mechanised cargo loading system will allow up to seven LD3-46 containers to be carried in freight holds (three forward and four aft).

SYSTEMS: The A320 is the first subsonic commercial aircraft to be equipped for fly-by-wire (FBW) control throughout the entire normal flight regime, and the first to have a side-stick controller (one for each pilot) instead of a control column and hand wheel. The Thomson-CSF/Sfena digital FBW system features five main computers and operates, via hydraulic jacks, all primary and secondary flight controls, except for the rudder and tailplane trim. The pilot's pitch and roll commands are applied through the side-stick controller via two different types of computer. These have a redundant architecture to provide safety levels at least as high as those of the mechanical systems they replace. The system incorporates flight envelope protection features to a degree that cannot be achieved with conventional mechanical control systems, and its computers will not allow the aircraft's structural and aerodynamic limitations to be exceeded: even if the pilot pushes the side-stick fully forward, it is impossible to go beyond the aircraft's maximum design

speed. Similarly, the A320 has angle of attack protection: if the pilot pulls the side-stick fully back, he will just achieve maximum lift from the wing and no more, and therefore cannot stall the aircraft. Nor is it possible to exceed g limits while manoeuvring. Other systems include Liebherr/ABG-Semca air-conditioning, Hamilton Standard/Nord-Micro pressurisation, hydraulic, Sundstrand electrical system, and a new and more efficient Garrett APU. Primary electrical system is powered by two Sundstrand 90kVA constant frequency generators, providing 115/200V three-phase AC at 400Hz. A third generator of the same type, directly driven at constant speed by the APU, can be used during ground operations and, if required, during flight.

AVIONICS: Fully equipped digital avionics fit, to ARINC 700 series specification, including advanced digital automatic flight control and flight management systems. AFCS integrates functions of Sfena autopilot and Honeywell FMS. Each pilot has two Thomson-CSF/VDO electronic flight instrumentation system (EFIS) displays: a primary flight display and a navigation display. Primary flight display is first on an airliner to incorporate speed, altitude and heading. Between these two pairs of displays are two Thomson-CSF/VDO electronic centralised aircraft monitor (ECAM) displays unique to Airbus Industrie and developed from the ECAM systems on the A310 and A300-600. The upper display incorporates engine performance and warnings; the lower display carries warning and system synoptic diagrams. Honeywell air data and inertial reference system.

DIMENSIONS, EXTERNAL:
Wing span	33.91 m (111 ft 3 in)
Wing aspect ratio	9.4
Length overall	37.57 m (123 ft 3 in)
Fuselage: Max width	3.95 m (12 ft 11½ in)
Max depth	4.14 m (13 ft 7 in)
Height overall	11.80 m (38 ft 8½ in)
Tailplane span	12.45 m (40 ft 10 in)
Wheel track (c/l of shock struts)	7.59 m (24 ft 11 in)
Wheelbase	12.63 m (41 ft 5 in)

Passenger doors (port, fwd and rear), each:
Height	1.85 m (6 ft 1 in)
Width	0.81 m (2 ft 8 in)
Height to sill	3.415 m (11 ft 2½ in)

Service doors (stbd, fwd and rear), each
as corresponding passenger doors

Overwing emergency exits (two port and two stbd), each:
Height	1.02 m (3 ft 4¼ in)
Width	0.51 m (1 ft 8 in)

Underfloor baggage/cargo hold doors (stbd, fwd and rear), each:
Height	1.249 m (4 ft 1¼ in)
Width	1.82 m (5 ft 11½ in)

DIMENSIONS, INTERNAL:
Cabin, excl flight deck: Length
Length	27.38 m (89 ft 10 in)
Max width	3.696 m (12 ft 1½ in)
Max height	2.22 m (7 ft 4 in)

Baggage/cargo hold volume:
front	13.28 m³ (469 cu ft)
rear	25.48 m³ (900 cu ft)

AREAS:
Wings, gross	122.4 m² (1,317.5 sq ft)
Leading-edge slats (total)	12.64 m² (136.1 sq ft)
Trailing-edge flaps (total)	21.10 m² (227.1 sq ft)
Ailerons (total)	2.74 m² (29.49 sq ft)
Spoilers (total)	8.64 m² (93.00 sq ft)
Airbrakes (total)	2.35 m² (25.30 sq ft)
Vertical tail surfaces (total)	21.5 m² (231.4 sq ft)
Horizontal tail surfaces (total)	31.0 m² (333.7 sq ft)

WEIGHTS AND LOADINGS (Typical 150-passenger configuration. A: CFM56-5A1 engines, B: V2500-A1s):
Operating weight empty: 100		40,370 kg (89,000 lb)
200: A		41,310 kg (91,073 lb)
B		41,640 kg (91,800 lb)
Max payload: 100		16,630 kg (36,663 lb)
200: A		19,190 kg (42,307 lb)
B		18,860 kg (41,579 lb)

Max fuel: 100	12,722 kg (28,047 lb)
200	19,159 kg (42,238 lb)
Max T-O weight: 100	68,000 kg (149,915 lb)
200	73,500 kg (162,040 lb)
200 (option)	75,500 kg (166,450 lb)
Max landing weight: 100	63,000 kg (138,890 lb)
200	64,500 kg (142,195 lb)
Max zero-fuel weight: 100	57,000 kg (125,665 lb)
200	60,500 kg (133,380 lb)
Max wing loading: 100	555.5 kg/m² (113.8 lb/sq ft)
200	600.5 kg/m² (123.0 lb/sq ft)
200 (option)	616.8 kg/m² (126.3 lb/sq ft)

PERFORMANCE (at max T-O weight except where indicated; engines A and B as for Weights, C: CFM56-5A3):
T-O distance at S/L, ISA + 15°C:
100	1,970 m (6,465 ft)
200: A	2,340 m (7,677 ft)
B	2,300 m (7,546 ft)
C	2,045 m (6,710 ft)

Landing distance at max landing weight:
100	1,500 m (4,920 ft)
200: A, C	1,470 m (4,823 ft)
B	1,442 m (4,730 ft)

Min width of pavement for 180° turn
23.1 m (75 ft 9½ in)

Runway ACN (flexible runway, category B):
twin-wheel, standard 45 × 16R20 tyres:
100	36
200	41

four-wheel bogie option, 36 × 11-16 Type VII or 900 × 300-R16: 200 22

Range with 150 passengers and baggage in two-class layout, typical international reserves and 200 nm (370 km; 230 mile) diversion:
100	1,750 nm (3,243 km; 2,015 miles)
200: A, C	2,870 nm (5,318 km; 3,305 miles)
B	2,895 nm (5,365 km; 3,335 miles)
200 (option): A, C	2,945 nm (5,460 km; 3,390 miles)
B	3,030 nm (5,615 km; 3,490 miles)

OPERATIONAL NOISE LEVELS (ICAO Annex 16, Chapter 3):
T-O (flyover): 100	85.7 EPNdB (90.1 limit)
200: A	88.0 EPNdB (91.5 limit)
B	86.6 EPNdB (91.5 limit)
C	86.5 EPNdB (91.5 limit)
T-O (sideline): 100	94.6 EPNdB (96.5 limit)
200: A	94.4 EPNdB (96.8 limit)
B	92.8 EPNdB (96.8 limit)
C	94.8 EPNdB (96.0 limit)
Approach: 100	96.5 EPNdB (100.2 limit)
200: A	96.2 EPNdB (100.5 limit)
B	96.6 EPNdB (100.5 limit)
C	96.0 EPNdB (100.5 limit)

AIRBUS A321-100

TYPE: Twin-turbofan short/medium-range commercial transport.

PROGRAMME: Announced 22 May and launched 24 November 1989 as stretched version of A320; four development aircraft planned (first flight with lead engine set for March 1993, second aircraft with alternative engine three months later); initial certification planned for December 1993, service entry January 1994, with alternative engine model three months later.

VARIANTS: **A321-100:** Stretched version of A320-200, with 4.27 m (14 ft 0 in) fuselage plug immediately forward of wing and 2.67 m (8 ft 9 in) plug immediately aft; other changes include local structural reinforcement of existing assemblies, modified wing trailing-edge with double-slotted flaps, and uprated landing gear.

CUSTOMERS: Total of 137 firm orders from 10 customers by 7 May 1991.

DESIGN FEATURES: Maximum commonality with A320.

STRUCTURE: As for A320-200 except for airframe changes noted in Variants paragraph; front fuselage plug by

Alenia, rear one by BAe; final assembly and outfitting at Hamburg.

LANDING GEAR: Uprated, with 1,270 × 455R22 mainwheel tyres and increased energy brakes.

POWER PLANT: Offered initially with two CFM56-5B1 or V2530-A5 turbofans, both rated at 133.4 kN (30,000 lb st); not yet decided which will be lead engine, but each type will be flight tested on two development aircraft. CFM56-5B2 engines of 137.9 kN (31,000 lb st) will be available optionally. Fuel capacity 23,700 litres (6,261 US gallons; 5,213 Imp gallons).

ACCOMMODATION: Typically offers 24 per cent more seats and 40 per cent more hold volume than A320-200. Examples are 186 passengers in two-class layout (16 first class at 91 cm; 36 in seat pitch and 170 economy class at 81 cm; 32 in), or 200 passengers in all-economy configuration. Each fuselage plug incorporates one pair of emergency exits, replacing single overwing pair of A320.

DIMENSIONS, EXTERNAL:

Wing span	34.09 m (111 ft 10 in)
Length overall	44.51 m (146 ft 0 in)
Height overall	11.81 m (38 ft 9 in)
Passenger and service doors (port/stbd, fwd and rear)	
	as for A320
Emergency exits (fwd stbd and rear port/stbd, each):	
Height	1.52 m (5 ft 0 in)
Width	0.76 m (2 ft 6 in)
Emergency exit (fwd port, usable also as passenger door):	
Height	1.85 m (6 ft 1 in)
Width	0.76 m (2 ft 6 in)

DIMENSIONS, INTERNAL:

Cabin, excl flight deck: Length	34.39 m (112 ft 10 in)
Baggage/cargo hold volume:	
front	23.02 m³ (813 cu ft)
rear	29.02 m³ (1,025 cu ft)

WEIGHTS AND LOADINGS (Typical 186-passenger layout. A: CFM56-5B1, B:V2530-A5, C: CFM56-5B2):

Operating weight empty: A, C	46,960 kg (103,529 lb)
B	47,070 kg (103,771 lb)
Max payload: A	22,020 kg (48,546 lb)
B	21,950 kg (48,391 lb)
Max fuel: A, B, C	19,025 kg (41,943 lb)
Max T-O weight	82,200 kg (181,220 lb)
Max landing weight	73,000 kg (160,985 lb)
Max zero-fuel weight	69,000 kg (152,120 lb)
Max wing loading	671.6 kg/m² (137.5 lb/sq ft)

PERFORMANCE (estimated):

T-O distance at max T-O weight, S/L, ISA +15°C:

A	2,285 m (7,497 ft)
B	2,280 m (7,481 ft)
C	2,225 m (7,300 ft)

Landing distance at max landing weight:

A, B, C	1,570 m (5,151 ft)

Runway ACN (flexible runway, category B):

standard	48

Range with 186 passengers and baggage at typical airline OWE, FAR domestic reserves and 200 nm (370 km; 230 mile) diversion:

A, C	2,300 nm (4,260 km; 2,648 miles)
B	2,365 nm (4,385 km; 2,723 miles)

OPERATIONAL NOISE LEVELS (ICAO Annex 16, Chapter 3, estimated):

T-O (flyover): A	87.5 EPNdB (92.1 limit)
B	87.8 EPNdB (92.1 limit)
T-O (sideline): A	94.6 EPNdB (97.2 limit)
B	95.2 EPNdB (97.2 limit)
Approach: A	96.2 EPNdB (100.9 limit)
B	96.8 EPNdB (100.9 limit)

AIRBUS A340 and A330

TYPE: Large-capacity wide-bodied medium/long-range commercial transports.

PROGRAMME: Launched as combined programme 5 June 1987, differing mainly in number of engines and in engine-related systems; first six aircraft will be four A340-300s and two -200s; first flight scheduled for October 1991 (A340-300); service entry planned for February 1993 (A340) and late 1993 (A330).

VARIANTS: **A340-300:** Four-engined long-range version, carrying up to 375 passengers (standard) or 440 (optional) and powered initially by CFM56-5C2 turbofans; prototype entered final assembly 15 December 1990; due to fly October 1991 and enter service February 1993.

A340-300 Combi: Passenger/freight version of A340-300; described separately.

A340-200: Longer-range version of A340-300, with same initial power plant and shorter fuselage; exit-limited seating capacities as for A340-300; due to enter service late 1992.

A340-300X: Longer-range version of A340-300, able to carry typical load of 295 passengers over distances of 7,150 nm (13,250 km; 8,235 miles); powered by 151.2 kN (34,000 lb st) CFM56-5C4 turbofans; max T-O weight 267,000 kg (588,635 lb). Under study for 1996 delivery.

A330: Twin-engined, medium/long-range version, with CF6-80E1A1 turbofans initially and seating capacities as for A340-300; alternative power plants will include Rolls-Royce Trent (specified by Cathay Pacific, Garuda

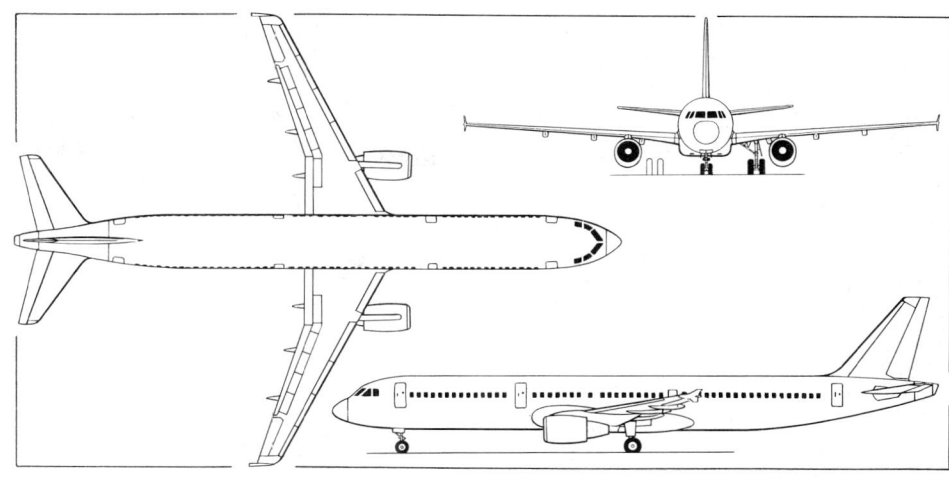

A321-100 stretched development of the Airbus A320-200 (*Pilot Press*)

and TWA) and growth versions of Pratt & Whitney PW4000; due to fly October 1992 and enter service late 1993.

A330-300X: Longer-range version of A330, able to carry typical load of 335 passengers over non-stop distance of 5,300 nm (9,820 km; 6,100 miles); powered by 302.5-320 kN (68,000-72,000 lb) thrust class engines; max T-O weight 223,000 kg (491,630 lb). Under study for 1996 delivery.

A330-400X: Stretched version of A330, with fuselage 12 frame pitches (approx 6.35 m; 20.8 ft) longer than baseline A330, providing typical first/economy seating for 379 passengers on sectors of up to 4,000 nm (7,410 km; 4,605 miles); max T-O weight 223,000 kg (491,630 lb). Under study for 1997 delivery.

CUSTOMERS: Total of 138 firm orders for A330 and 94 for A340 by 31 March 1991.

DESIGN FEATURES: Capitalise on commonality with each other (identical wing/cockpit/tail unit and same basic fuselage) to create aircraft for different markets, and also have much in common (eg, existing Airbus wide-body fuselage cross-sections, A310/A300-600 fin, advanced versions of A320 cockpit and systems) with existing Airbus range; this approach will allow Airbus Industrie to offer common pilot type ratings between A330/A340 and between A330/A320. New design wing (by BAe), approx 40 per cent larger than that of A300-600, has 30° sweepback and is fitted with winglets.

FLYING CONTROLS: Fly-by-wire flight control system similar to that of A320. Seven-segment leading-edge slats, two-segment trailing-edge flaps, two-segment ailerons. Single airbrake (forward of inboard flap) and five-segment spoilers (forward of outboard flap) on each wing; Allied Signal aileron actuators.

STRUCTURE: A330 and A340 wings almost identical except latter is strengthened in area of outboard engine pylon with appropriate modification of leading-edge slats 4 and 5; main three-spar wing box and leading/trailing-edge ribs and fittings of aluminium alloy, with Al-Li under consideration for some secondary structures; steel or titanium slat supports; approx 13 per cent (by weight) of wings is of CFRP, GFRP or AFRP, incl outer flaps and flap track fairings, ailerons, spoilers, leading/trailing-edge fixed surface panels and (possibly) winglets; common

fuselage for all three initial versions, except in overall length (A340-300 and A330 same size and longest, A340-200 eight frames shorter); construction generally similar to that of A310 and A300-600 except centre-section to accept new wing; tail unit (common to all versions) utilises same carbonfibre fin as A300-600 and A310; new tailplane incorporates trim fuel tank and has carbonfibre outer main boxes bridged by aluminium alloy centre-section. Work sharing along lines similar to those for A310 and A300-600, with percentages similar to those held in consortium. Aerospatiale thus responsible for cockpit, engine pylons, part of centre-fuselage, and final assembly and outfitting at Toulouse; British Aerospace (with Textron Aerostructures, USA, as subcontractor) for wings; Deutsche Airbus for most of fuselage, fin and interior; CASA for tailplane; Belairbus for leading-edge slats and slat tracks.

LANDING GEAR: Main (four-wheel bogie) and twin-wheel nose units identical on all versions. A340 has additional twin-wheel auxiliary unit on fuselage centreline amidships. Goodyear tyres on all units.

POWER PLANT (A330): Launched with two 291.4 kN (65,500 lb st) General Electric CF6-80E1A1 turbofans. Alternative engines, using a common pylon and mount, will include developments of the Pratt & Whitney PW4000 and Rolls-Royce Trent series. Fuel capacity 93,500 litres (24,700 US gallons; 20,568 Imp gallons).

POWER PLANT (A340): Four 138.8 kN (31,200 lb st) CFM56-5C2 turbofans initially. Fuel capacity (-200 and -300) 135,000 litres (35,664 US gallons; 29,697 Imp gallons).

ACCOMMODATION: Crew of two on flight deck (all versions). Passenger seating typically six-abreast in first class, seven-abreast in business class and eight-abreast in economy (nine-abreast optional), all with twin aisles. Two-class configurations seat 335 passengers in A330 and A340-300, and 303 passengers in A340-200. More typically, a three-class layout would seat 295 in A340-300 and 262 in the A340-200. Underfloor cargo holds have capacity for up to 32 LD3 containers or 11 standard 2.24 × 3.17 m (88 × 125 in) pallets in A340-300 and A330, and 26 LD3s or 9 pallets in A340-200. Both front and rear cargo holds have doors wide enough to accept 2.44 × 3.17 m (96 × 125 in) pallets. In addition, all models have

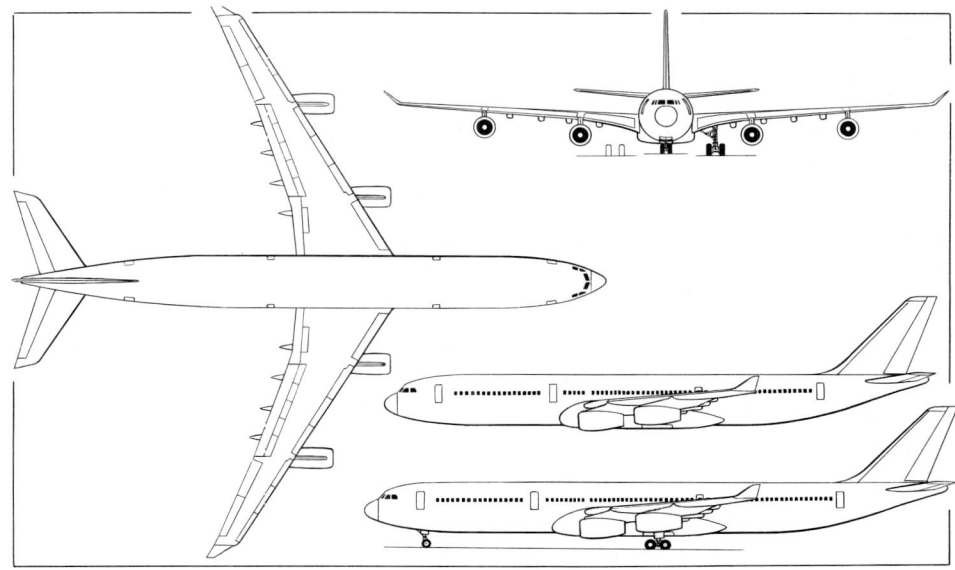

Airbus A340-300 four-turbofan long-range transport, with additional side view (top) of A340-200
(*Pilot Press*)

a 19.68 m³ (695 cu ft) bulk cargo hold aft of the rear cargo hold.

DIMENSIONS, EXTERNAL:

Wing span (all versions)	60.30 m (197 ft 10 in)
Wing aspect ratio (all versions)	10.0
Length overall:	
A340-200	59.39 m (194 ft 10 in)
A330, A340-300	63.65 m (208 ft 10 in)
Fuselage: Max diameter (all versions)	5.64 m (18 ft 6 in)
Height overall (all versions)	16.74 m (54 ft 11 in)
Wheel track (all versions)	10.49 m (34 ft 5 in)

AREAS:

Wings, gross (all versions)	363.1 m² (3,908.4 sq ft)

WEIGHTS AND LOADINGS (engines for A330: A, CF6-80E1; B, PW4164; C, Trent 768. Seating: A330 two-class with 335 passengers, A340 three-class with 262 passengers in -200 and 295 in -300):

Typical airline operating weight empty:

A330: A	118,511 kg (261,272 lb)
B	118,935 kg (262,207 lb)
C	118,234 kg (260,661 lb)
A340-200	122,111 kg (269,209 lb)
A340-300	126,061 kg (277,917 lb)
Max payload: A330: A	45,489 kg (100,286 lb)
B	45,065 kg (99,351 lb)
C	45,766 kg (100,897 lb)
A340-200	46,889 kg (103,372 lb)
A340-300	47,939 kg (105,687 lb)
Max T-O weight: A330	212,000 kg (467,380 lb)
A340-200, -300	253,500 kg (558,870 lb)
Max landing weight: A330	174,000 kg (383,605 lb)
A340-200	181,000 kg (399,040 lb)
A340-300	186,000 kg (410,060 lb)
Max zero-fuel weight: A330	164,000 kg (361,560 lb)
A340-200	169,000 kg (372,580 lb)
A340-300	174,000 kg (383,605 lb)

PERFORMANCE (estimated, definitions as for Weights):

Max operating speed	Mach 0.84 to 0.86
Typical operating speed	Mach 0.82

Range at typical OWE, with allowances for 200 nm (370 km; 230 mile) diversion and international reserves:

A330 with 335 passengers and baggage:

A	4,740 nm (8,785 km; 5,460 miles)
B	4,730 nm (8,765 km; 5,445 miles)
C	4,660 nm (8,635 km; 5,365 miles)
C (from 1996)	4,750 nm (8,800 km; 5,470 miles)

A340-200 with 262 passengers and baggage
7,550 nm (13,990 km; 8,695 miles)

A340-300 with 295 passengers and baggage
6,750 nm (12,510 km; 7,770 miles)

AIRBUS A340-300 COMBI

TYPE: Specialised passenger/cargo version of A340-300.

DESIGN FEATURES: Offered as passenger/cargo version of standard A340-300, with large port-side cargo door in rear fuselage giving clear opening on to main deck flat floor (rear part of this floor slopes slightly upward in standard aircraft). Other layout permutations possible, using optional kits to add one or two extra main deck pallet positions (replacing seats) or to replace all pallet positions by additional seats.

ACCOMMODATION: Able to carry same pallets and containers as other wide-body combis, freighters and convertibles, to allow 'interlining' of freight between different types; typical passenger/cargo configuration would be 221 passengers (in three-class layout) and four 2.44 × 3.17 m (96 × 125 in) freight pallets on main deck; can also accommodate an assembled large turbofan.

DIMENSIONS, EXTERNAL:

Main deck cargo door: Height	2.57 m (8 ft 5 in)
Width	3.58 m (11 ft 9 in)

WEIGHTS AND LOADINGS:

Max T-O weight	267,000 kg (588,600 lb)

The first Airbus A340 being assembled at Toulouse early in 1991 in preparation for a first flight in October

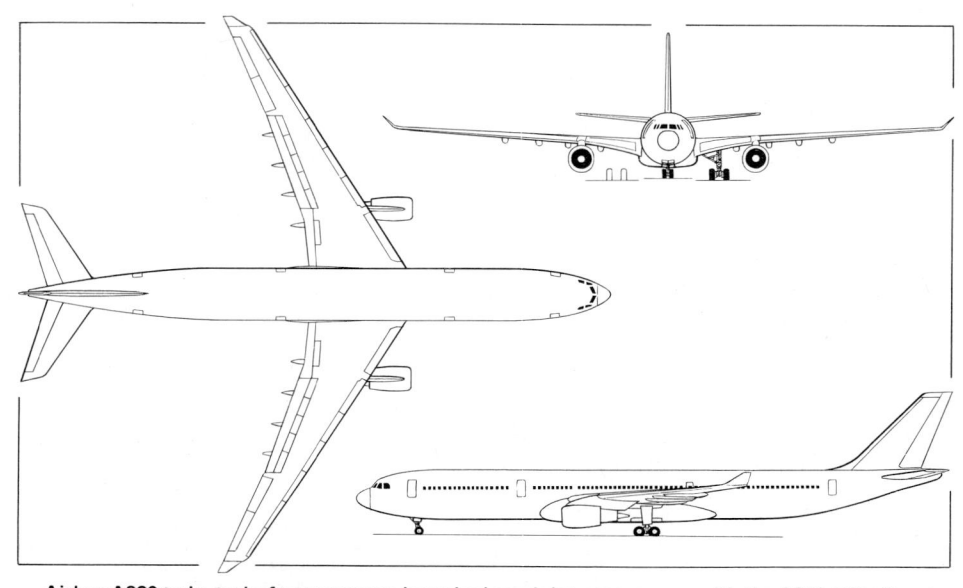

Airbus A330 twin-turbofan transport, launched as a joint programme with the A340 *(Pilot Press)*

Max landing weight	210,000 kg (463,660 lb)
Max zero-fuel weight	197,000 kg (434,300 lb)

PERFORMANCE (estimated):

Range with 221 passengers and a volumetric freight load of 28,300 kg (62,400 lb)
5,250 nm (9,700 km; 6,000 miles)

AIRBUS A350

TYPE: Extra-large capacity commercial transport.

PROGRAMME: Proposed 650/800-seat transport for service entry by end of 1990s; decision on go-ahead expected during 1991.

AIRTECH
AIRCRAFT TECHNOLOGY INDUSTRIES

PRESIDENT: Prof Dr-Ing B. J. Habibie (IPTN)
VICE-PRESIDENT: Javier Alvarez Vara (CASA)
PARTICIPATING COMPANIES:
CASA: see under Spain
IPTN: see under Indonesia

Airtech formed by CASA and IPTN to develop CN-235 twin-turboprop transport; design and production work shared 50-50.

AIRTECH (CASA/IPTN) CN-235 SERIES 100

TYPE: Twin-turboprop civil and military transport.

PROGRAMME: Preliminary design began January 1980, prototype construction May 1981; one prototype completed in each country, with simultaneous rollouts 10 September 1983; first flights 11 November 1983 (by CASA's ECT-100) and 30 December 1983 (IPTN's PK-XNC); Spanish and Indonesian certification 20 June 1986; first flight of production aircraft 19 August 1986; FAA type approval (FAR Pts 25 and 121) 3 December 1986; deliveries began 15 December 1986 from IPTN line and 4 February 1987 from CASA: entered service (with

Merpati Nusantara Airlines) 1 March 1988; licence assembly agreement with TAI (see Turkish section), to lead eventually to local manufacture, announced January 1990.

VARIANTS: **CN-235 Series 10:** Initial production version with CT7-7A turboprops, described in 1986-87 and earlier *Jane's*; 30 built (15 by each company).

CN-235 Series 100: Current version from 1988, with CT7-9C engines in new composite nacelles; replaced Series 10 from 31st production aircraft.

CN-235 M: Military transport version.

CN-235 MP: Maritime patrol version.

CN-235 QC: Quick-change passenger/cargo version.

CUSTOMERS: Total orders 178 (40 civil, 138 military) by 1 May 1991; civil customers include Merpati (15), Pelita (10), Binter Canarias (four), Binter Mediterráneo (five) and other Spanish regional carriers (six); military customers are Botswana (Defence Force two), Brunei (Royal Air Wing three), Chile (Army three), Ecuador (Army one, Navy one), France (Air Force eight), Gabon (Air Force one), Indonesia (Air Force/Navy 24), Ireland (Air Corps one M, two MP), Morocco (Air Force seven), Panama (National Guard one), Saudi Arabia (Air Force four incl two VIP transports), Spain (Air Force 26, incl

two VIP and six MP) and Turkey (Air Force 52); deliveries had reached 23 civil and 28 military by December 1990.

DESIGN FEATURES: Optimised for short-haul operations, enabling it to fly four 100 nm (185 km; 115 mile) stage lengths (with reserves) before refuelling and to operate from paved runways or unprepared strips; high mounted NACA 65_3-218 aerofoil wing with no-dihedral/constant chord centre-section; tapered outer panels have 3° dihedral and 3° 51' 36″ sweepback at quarter-chord; pressurised fuselage (incl baggage compartment) of flattened circular cross-section, with upswept rear end incorporating cargo ramp/door; sweptback fin (with dorsal fin) and rudder; low-set non-swept fixed incidence tailplane and elevators; two small ventral fins; pneumatic boot anti-icing of fin, tailplane and outer wing leading-edges; vortex generators on rudder and elevator leading-edges.

FLYING CONTROLS: Ailerons, elevators and rudder statically and dynamically balanced, with mechanical actuation (duplicated for ailerons); mechanical servo tab and electric trim tab in each aileron, rudder and starboard elevator, trim tab only in port elevator; single-slotted inboard and outboard trailing-edge flaps (each pair

Spanish built Airtech CN-235 in the insignia of Binter Mediterráneo

interchangeable port/starboard), actuated hydraulically by Dowty irreversible jacks.

STRUCTURE: Conventional semi-monocoque, mainly of aluminium alloys with chemically milled skins; composites (mainly glassfibre or glassfibre/Nomex honeycomb sandwich, with some carbonfibre and Kevlar) for leading/trailing edges of wing/tail moving surfaces, wing/fuselage and main landing gear fairings, wing/fin/ tailplane tips, ventral fins and nose radome. CASA builds wing centre-section, inboard flaps, forward and centre fuselage, engine nacelles; IPTN builds outer wings, outboard flaps, ailerons, rear fuselage and tail unit; both manufacturers use numerical control machinery extensively. Final assembly line in each country. TAI (Turkey) to assemble under licence initially, progressing gradually to local manufacture of aircraft for Turkish Air Force.

LANDING GEAR: Messier-Bugatti retractable tricycle type with levered suspension, suitable for operation from semi-prepared runways. Electrically controlled hydraulic extension/retraction, with mechanical backup for emergency extension. Oleo-pneumatic shock absorber in each unit. Each main unit comprises two wheels in tandem, retracting rearward into fairing on side of fuselage. Mainwheels semi-exposed when retracted. Single steerable nosewheel ($\pm 48°$) retracts forward into unpressurised bay under flight deck. Dunlop 28×9.00-12 (12 ply rating) tubeless mainwheel tyres standard, pressure 5.17 bars (75 lb/sq in) on civil version, 5.58 bars (81 lb/sq in) on military version; low pressure mainwheel tyres optional, size 11.00-12/10, pressure 3.45 bars (50 lb/sq in). Dunlop 24×7.7 (10/12 ply rating) tubeless nosewheel tyre, pressure 5.65 bars (82 lb/sq in) on civil version, 6.07 bars (88 lb/sq in) on military version. Dunlop hydraulic differential disc brakes; Dunlop anti-skid units on main gear.

POWER PLANT: Two General Electric CT7-9C turboprops, each flat rated at 1,305 kW (1,750 shp) (S/L, to 41°C) for take-off and 1,394.5 kW (1,870 shp) up to 31°C with automatic power reserve. Hamilton Standard 14-RF21 four-blade constant-speed propellers, with full feathering and reverse-pitch capability. Blades are of glassfibre, with metal spar and urethane foam core. Lightweight low-drag composites nacelles. Fuel in two 1,042 litre (275 US gallon; 229 Imp gallon) integral main tanks in wing centre-section and two 1,592 litre (421 US gallon; 350 Imp gallon) integral outer-wing auxiliary tanks; total fuel capacity 5,264 litres (1,392 US gallons; 1,158 Imp gallons), of which 5,128 litres (1,355 US gallons; 1,128 Imp gallons) are usable. Single pressure refuelling point in starboard main landing gear fairing; gravity filling point in top of each tank. Propeller braking permits No. 2 engine to be used as an on-ground APU. Oil capacity 13.97 litres (3.69 US gallons; 3.07 Imp gallons).

ACCOMMODATION: Crew of two on flight deck, plus cabin attendant (civil version) or third crew member (military version). Accommodation in commuter version for up to 44 passengers in four-abreast seating, at 76 cm (30 in) pitch, with 22 seats each side of central aisle. Toilet, galley and overhead luggage bins standard. Pressurised baggage compartment at rear of cabin, aft of movable bulkhead; additional stowage in rear ramp area and in overhead lockers. Can also be equipped as mixed passenger/cargo combi (eg, 19 passengers and two LD3 containers), or for all-cargo operation, with roller loading system, carrying four standard LD3 containers, five LD2s, or two 2.24 × 3.18 m (88 × 125 in) and one 2.24 × 2.03 m (88 × 80 in) pallets; or for military duties, carrying up to 48 troops or 46 paratroops. Other options include layouts for aeromedical (24 stretchers and four medical attendants),

ASW/maritime patrol (with 360° search radar and Exocet missiles or Mk 46 torpedoes), electronic warfare, geophysical survey or aerial photographic duties. Main passenger door, outward and forward opening with integral stairs, aft of wing on port side, serving also as a Type I emergency exit. Type III emergency exit facing this door on starboard side. Crew/service downward opening door (forward, starboard) has built-in stairs, and serves also as a Type I emergency exit, or as passenger door in combi version; second Type III exit opposite this door on port side. Wide ventral door/cargo ramp in underside of upswept rear fuselage, for loading of bulky cargo. Accommodation fully air-conditioned and pressurised.

SYSTEMS: Hamilton Standard air-conditioning system, using engine compressor bleed air. AiResearch electropneumatic pressurisation system (max differential 0.25 bar; 3.6 lb/sq in) giving cabin environment of 2,440 m (8,000 ft) up to operating altitude of 5,485 m (18,000 ft). Hydraulic system, operating at nominal pressure of 207 bars (3,000 lb/sq in), comprises two engine driven, variable displacement axial electric pumps, a self pressurising standby mechanical pump, and a modular unit incorporating connectors, filters and valves; system is employed for actuation of wing flaps, landing gear extension/retraction, wheel brakes, emergency and parking brakes, nosewheel steering, cargo ramp and door, and propeller braking. Accumulator for backup braking system. 28V DC primary electrical system powered by two 400A Auxilec engine driven starter/ generators, with two 24V 37Ah nickel-cadmium batteries for engine starting and 30 min (minimum) emergency power for essential services. Constant frequency single-phase AC power (115/26V) provided at 400Hz by three 600VA static inverters (two for normal operation plus one standby); two three-phase engine driven alternators for 115/200V variable frequency AC power. Fixed oxygen installation for crew of three (single cylinder at 124 bars; 1,800 lb/sq in pressure); three portable units and individual masks for passengers. Pneumatic boot anti-icing of wing (outboard of engine nacelles), fin and tailplane leading-edges. Electric anti-icing of propellers, engine air intakes, flight deck windscreen, pitot tubes and angle of attack indicators. No APU: starboard engine, with propeller braking, can be used to fulfil this function.

Hand type fire extinguishers on flight deck (one) and in passenger cabin (two); smoke detector in baggage compartment. Engine fire detection and extinguishing system.

AVIONICS: Standard avionics include two Collins VHF-22B com radios, one Avtech DADS crew interphone, one Collins TDR-90 ATC transponder, two Collins VIR-32 VOR/ILS/marker beacon receivers, one Collins DME-42, one Collins ADF-60A, one Collins WXR-300 weather radar, two Collins 332D-11T vertical gyros, two Collins MCS-65 directional gyros, two Collins ADI-85A, two Collins HSI-85, two Collins RMI-36, one Collins APS-65 autopilot/flight director, one Collins ALT-55B radio altimeter, one Fairchild/Teledyne flight data recorder, one Fairchild A-100A cockpit voice recorder, one Avtech PACIS PA system, two Collins 345A-7 rate of turn sensors, one Sfena H-301 APM standby attitude director indicator, one Dorne & Margolin ELT 8-1 emergency locator transmitter, and one Sundstrand Mk II GPWS. Collins EFIS-85 five-tube CRT system optional. Other options include Collins EFIS-85B; second TDR-90, DME-42 and ADF-60A; plus Collins HF-230 com radio, Collins RNS-325 radar nav, Litton LTN-72R inertial nav or Global GNS-500A Omega navigation system.

EQUIPMENT: Navigation lights, anti-collision strobe lights, 600W landing light in front end of each main landing gear fairing, taxi lights, ice inspection lights, emergency door lights, flight deck and flight deck emergency lights, cabin and baggage compartment lights, individual passenger reading lights, and instrument panel white lighting, are all standard.

ARMAMENT (military version): Three attachment points under each wing. Weapons can include McDonnell Douglas Harpoon anti-ship missiles; Indonesian Navy ASW version can be fitted with two AM39 Exocet anti-shipping missiles.

DIMENSIONS, EXTERNAL:

Wing span	25.81 m (84 ft 8 in)
Wing chord: at root	3.00 m (9 ft 10 in)
at tip	1.20 m (3 ft 11¼ in)
Wing aspect ratio	11.3
Length: overall	21.353 m (70 ft 0¾ in)
fuselage	20.90 m (68 ft 7 in)

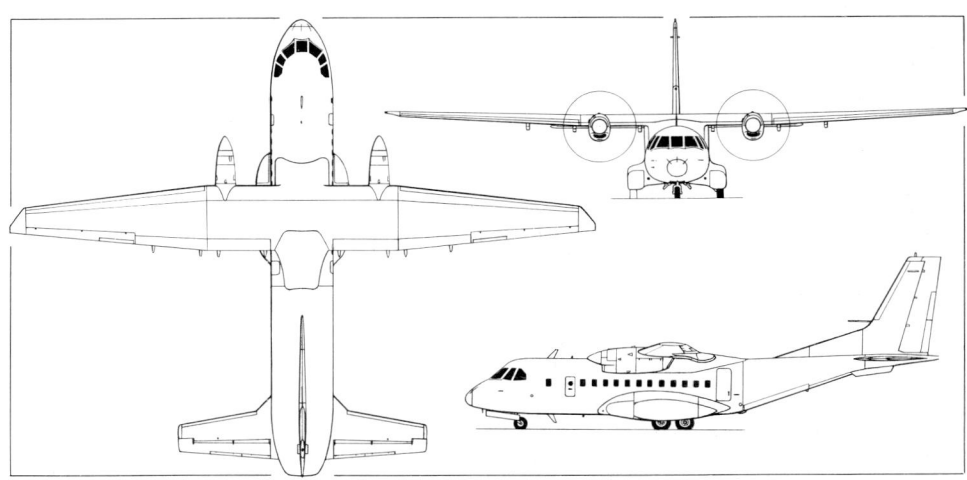

Airtech (CASA/IPTN) CN-235 twin-turboprop military/civil utility transport (*Pilot Press*)

Chilean Air Force CN-235 M, with rear ramp lowered *(Kenneth Munson)*

Fuselage: Max width	2.90 m (9 ft 6 in)
Max depth	2.615 m (8 ft 7 in)
Height overall	8.177 m (26 ft 10 in)
Tailplane span	11.00 m (36 ft 1 in)
Wheel track (c/l of mainwheels)	3.90 m (12 ft 9½ in)
Wheelbase	6.919 m (22 ft 8½ in)
Propeller diameter	3.35 m (11 ft 0 in)
Propeller ground clearance	1.66 m (5 ft 5¼ in)
Distance between propeller centres	
	7.00 m (22 ft 11½ in)
Passenger door (port, rear), paratroop door (stbd, rear)	
and service door (stbd, fwd): Height	1.70 m (5 ft 7 in)
Width	0.73 m (2 ft 4¾ in)
Height to sill	1.22 m (4 ft 0 in)
Ventral upper door (rear): Length	2.366 m (7 ft 9¼ in)
Width	2.349 m (7 ft 8½ in)
Height to sill	1.22 m (4 ft 0 in)
Ventral ramp/door (rear): Length	3.042 m (9 ft 11¾ in)
Width	2.349 m (7 ft 8½ in)
Height to sill	1.22 m (4 ft 0 in)
Type III emergency exits (port, fwd, and stbd, rear):	
Height	0.91 m (3 ft 0 in)
Width	0.51 m (1 ft 8 in)

DIMENSIONS, INTERNAL:
Cabin, excl flight deck: Length	9.65 m (31 ft 8 in)
Max width	2.70 m (8 ft 10½ in)
Width at floor	2.366 m (7 ft 9 in)
Max height	1.88 m (6 ft 2 in)
Floor area	22.822 m² (245.65 sq ft)
Volume	43.24 m³ (1,527.0 cu ft)
Baggage compartment volume:	
ramp	5.30 m³ (187.2 cu ft)
overhead bins	1.68 m³ (59.3 cu ft)

AREAS:
Wings, gross	59.10 m² (636.1 sq ft)
Ailerons (total, incl tabs)	3.07 m² (33.06 sq ft)
Trailing-edge flaps (total)	10.87 m² (117.0 sq ft)
Fin, incl dorsal fin	11.38 m² (122.49 sq ft)
Rudder, incl tabs	3.32 m² (35.74 sq ft)
Tailplane	21.20 m² (228.2 sq ft)
Elevators (total, incl tabs)	6.17 m² (66.41 sq ft)

WEIGHTS AND LOADINGS:
Operating weight empty:	
passenger version	9,800 kg (21,605 lb)
cargo and military versions	8,800 kg (19,400 lb)
Max fuel	4,230 kg (9,325 lb)

Max payload: passenger version	4,000 kg (8,818 lb)
cargo and military versions	6,000 kg (13,227 lb)
Max weapon load (CN-235 M)	3,500 kg (7,716 lb)
Max T-O weight: civil	15,100 kg (33,289 lb)
military	16,500 kg (36,376 lb)
Max landing weight: civil	14,900 kg (32,849 lb)
military	15,500 kg (34,171 lb)
Max zero-fuel weight: civil	14,100 kg (31,085 lb)
military	14,800 kg (32,628 lb)
Cabin floor loading:	
cargo and military versions	
	1,504 kg/m² (308.0 lb/sq ft)
Max wing loading: civil	255.5 kg/m² (52.36 lb/sq ft)
military	279.2 kg/m² (57.18 lb/sq ft)
Max power loading (without APR):	
civil	5.78 kg/kW (9.51 lb/shp)
military	6.32 kg/kW (10.39 lb/shp)

PERFORMANCE (civil versions at max T-O weight, ISA, except where indicated):
Max operating speed at S/L	
	240 knots (445 km/h; 276 mph) IAS
Max cruising speed at 4,575 m (15,000 ft)	
	248 knots (460 km/h; 286 mph)
Stalling speed at S/L:	
flaps up	100 knots (186 km/h; 116 mph) IAS
flaps down	84 knots (156 km/h; 97 mph) IAS
Max rate of climb at S/L	465 m (1,527 ft)/min
Rate of climb at S/L, one engine out	128 m (420 ft)/min
Service ceiling	8,110 m (26,600 ft)
Service ceiling, one engine out	4,800 m (15,750 ft)
T-O run	1,217 m (3,993 ft)
T-O to 10.7 m (35 ft) at S/L (BFL)	1,400 m (4,593 ft)
Landing from 15 m (50 ft) at S/L	1,165 m (3,823 ft)
Min ground turning radius	18.98 m (62 ft 3¼ in)
Range at 5,485 m (18,000 ft), reserves for 87 nm (161 km; 100 mile) diversion and 45 min hold:	
with max payload	450 nm (834 km; 518 miles)
with max fuel	2,110 nm (3,910 km; 2,429 miles)

PERFORMANCE (CN-235 M at max T-O weight, ISA, except where indicated):
As for civil versions except:
Max rate of climb at S/L	579 m (1,900 ft)/min
Rate of climb at S/L, one engine out	156 m (512 ft)/min
Service ceiling	7,620 m (25,000 ft)
Service ceiling, one engine out	4,665 m (15,300 ft)
Min ground turning radius:	
nosewheel	9.50 m (31 ft 2 in)
wingtip	18.98 m (62 ft 3¼ in)
T-O to 15 m (50 ft) (CFL)	1,290 m (4,235 ft)
Landing from 15 m (50 ft)	772 m (2,530 ft)
Landing run, with propeller reversal	398 m (1,306 ft)
Range at 6,100 m (20,000 ft), long-range cruising speed, reserves for 45 min hold:	
with max payload	810 nm (1,501 km; 932 miles)
with 3,600 kg (7,936 lb) payload	
	2,350 nm (4,355 km; 2,706 miles)

OPERATIONAL NOISE LEVELS (civil versions):
T-O	84.0 EPNdB
Approach	87.0 EPNdB
Sideline	86.0 EPNdB

AMX

AMX INTERNATIONAL LTD

PRESIDENT: Dott Ing Giandomenico Cantele (Alenia)
VICE-PRESIDENTS:
Dott Ing Giovanni Gazzaniga (Alenia)
Col Franco Bonazzi (Aermacchi)
Col Rogerio Passos dos Santos (Embraer)
PARTICIPATING COMPANIES:
Alenia: see under Italy
Aermacchi: see under Italy
Embraer: see under Brazil

AMX

Brazilian Air Force designation: A-1

TYPE: Single-seat close air support, battlefield interdiction and reconnaissance aircraft, with secondary capability for offensive counter-air.

PROGRAMME: Resulted from 1977 Italian Air Force specification for small tactical fighter-bomber (see 1987-88 and previous *Jane's* for early background); original Aeritalia/Aermacchi partnership joined by Embraer July 1980; seven single-seat prototypes built (first flight 15 May 1984: further details in 1987-88 and earlier editions); production of first 30 (Italy 21, Brazil nine), and design of two-seater, began mid-1986; first production aircraft rolled out at Turin 29 March 1988, making first flight 11 May; second contract (Italy 59, Brazil 25, incl six and three two-seaters respectively) placed 1988; deliveries to Italian Air Force (six for Reparto Sperimentale di Volo at Pratica di Mare) began April 1989; production A-1 for Brazilian Air Force (s/n 5500) made first flight 12 August 1989, deliveries (two to 1° Esquadrão of 16° Grupo de Aviação at Santa Cruz) following from 17 October 1989; in-flight refuelling test programme completed (by Embraer) August-September 1989; first flight by first (of three) two-seat AMX-Ts 14 March 1990, followed by second on 16 July; series

First production single-seat A-1 for the Brazilian Air Force

production for Italy/Brazil expected to continue until 1994.

VARIANTS: **Single-seater:** Intended to replace G91R/Y and F-104G/S in Italian Air Force (eight squadrons) and EMB-326GB Xavante in Brazilian Air Force for close support/interdiction/reconnaissance, sharing counter-air duties with IDS Tornado (Italy) and F-5E/Mirage III (Brazil); in service with 3° and 51° Stormi (Italy) and 16° Grupo (Brazil); Brazilian Air Force aircraft differ primarily in avionics and weapon delivery systems, and have two 30 mm guns instead of Italian version's single multi-barrel 20 mm weapon.

Two-seater: Second cockpit accommodated by removing forward fuselage fuel tank and relocating environmental control system; dual controls, canopy, integration of rear cockpit GEC Ferranti HUD monitor, and oxygen systems, designed/redesigned by Embraer;

intended both as **AMX-T** operational trainer and, suitably equipped, for such roles as EW and maritime attack; three prototypes (two Italian, one Brazilian) currently in flight test, of which second is equipped with FIAR Grifo I/J-band ASV and maritime search radar to evaluate Exocet-armed anti-ship role; third (Brazilian) prototype has Tecnasa/SMA SCP-01 radar instead of Grifo, and laser rangefinder.

CUSTOMERS: Total of 114 (80 Italy/34 Brazil, incl six and three two-seaters) ordered by end of 1990, of which more than 40 (Italy 30+/Brazil nine+) delivered; eventual requirements are 252 single-seaters (Italy 187/Brazil 65) and 65 two-seaters (Italy 51/Brazil 14). Shortage of funds in Italy may force a cutback to 136 aircraft.

DESIGN FEATURES: Intended for high-subsonic/very low altitude day/night missions, in poor visibility and, if necessary, from poorly equipped or partially damaged runways; wing sweepback 31° on leading-edges, 27° 30′ at quarter-chord; thickness/chord ratio 12 per cent.

FLYING CONTROLS: Hydraulically actuated ailerons and elevators; leading-edge slats and Fowler double-slotted trailing-edge flaps (each two-segment on each wing) actuated electro-hydraulically; pair of hydraulically actuated spoilers forward of each flap pair, deployable separately in inboard and outboard pairs; movement of spoilers, rudder and variable incidence tailplane controlled electronically by Alenia/GEC Avionics flight control computer; ailerons, elevators, rudder have manual reversion for fly-home capability even with both hydraulic systems inoperative; no tabs in primary control surfaces; spoilers serve also as airbrakes/lift dumpers.

STRUCTURE: Mainly aluminium alloy except for carbonfibre fin and elevators; shoulder-mounted wings, each with three-point attachment to fuselage, have three-spar torsion box with integrally stiffened skins; oval-section semi-monocoque fuselage, with rear portion (incl tailplane) detachable for engine access; work split gives programme leader Alenia 46.7 per cent (centre-fuselage, nose radome, tail surfaces, ailerons and spoilers); Aermacchi has 23.6 per cent (forward fuselage incl gun and avionics integration, canopy, tailcone) and Embraer 29.7 per cent (air intakes, wings, leading-edge slats, flaps, wing pylons, external fuel tanks and reconnaissance pallets); single-sourced production, with final assembly lines in Italy and Brazil.

LANDING GEAR: Hydraulically retractable tricycle type, of Messier-Bugatti levered suspension design, built in Italy by Magnaghi (nose unit) and ERAM (main units). Single wheel and oleo-pneumatic shock absorber on each unit. Nose unit retracts forward; main units retract forward and inward, turning through approx 90° to lie almost flat in underside of engine air intake trunks. Nosewheel is hydraulically steerable (60° to left and right), self-centring, and fitted with anti-shimmy device. Main-wheel tyres size 670 × 210-12, pressure 9.65 bars (140 lb/sq in); nosewheel tyre size 18 × 5.5-8, pressure 10.7 bars (155 lb/sq in). Hydraulic brakes and fully modulated anti-skid system. No brake-chute. Runway arrester hook.

POWER PLANT: One 49.1 kN (11,030 lb st) Rolls-Royce Spey Mk 807 non-afterburning turbofan, built under licence in Italy by Fiat, Piaggio and Alfa Romeo Avio, in association with Companhia Eletro-Mecânica (CELMA) in Brazil. Self-sealing, compartmented, rubber fuselage bag tanks and two integral wing tanks with combined capacity of 3,500 litres (924.6 US gallons; 770 Imp gallons). Auxiliary fuel tanks of up to 1,100 litres (290 US gallons; 242 Imp gallons) capacity can be carried on each of the inboard underwing pylons, and up to 580 litres (153 US gallons; 128 Imp gallons) on each of the outboard pylons. Single-point pressure or gravity refuelling of internal and external tanks. In-flight refuelling capability (probe and drogue system) is provided.

ACCOMMODATION: Pilot only, on Martin-Baker Mk 10L zero/zero ejection seat; 18° downward view over nose. One-piece wraparound windscreen; one-piece hinged canopy, opening sideways to starboard. Cockpit pressurised and air-conditioned. Tandem two-seat combat trainer/special missions version also in production.

SYSTEMS: Microtecnica environmental control system (ECS) provides air-conditioning of cockpit, avionics and reconnaissance pallets, cockpit pressurisation, air intake and inlet guide vane anti-icing, windscreen demisting, and anti-g systems. Duplicated redundant hydraulic systems, driven by engine gearbox, operate at pressure of 207 bars (3,000 lb/sq in) for actuation of primary flight control system, flaps, spoilers, landing gear, wheel brakes, anti-skid system, nosewheel steering and gun operation. Primary electrical system AC power (115/200V at fixed frequency of 400Hz) supplied by two 30kVA IDG generators, with two transformer-rectifier units for conversion to 28V DC; 36Ah nickel-cadmium battery for emergency use, to provide power for essential systems in the event of primary and secondary electrical system failure. Aeroeletrônica (Brazil) external power control unit. Fiat FA 150 Argo APU for engine starting. APU driven electrical generator for ground operation. Liquid oxygen system.

AVIONICS: Avionics are divided into six main subsystems: (1) UHF and VHF com, and IFF; (2) navigation (Litton Italia inertial system, with standby AHRS and Tacan, for Italian Air Force; VOR/ILS for Brazil); (3) Alenia computer based weapon aiming and delivery, incorporating an Elta/FIAR range-only radar and Alenia stores management system; (4) digital data displays (OMI/Alenia head-up, Alenia multi-function head-down, and weapons/nav selector); (5) data processing, with Microtecnica air data computer; and (6) Elettronica active and passive ECM, including fin mounted radar warning receiver. The ranging radar in Italian AMXs, known as Pointer, is an I band set modified from the Elta (Israel) EL/M-2001B and built in Italy by FIAR. Brazilian aircraft will have a Technasa/SMA SCP-01 radar. GEC Ferranti MED 2067 video monitor display in rear cockpit of two-seater, for use as HUD monitor by instructor/navigator. Modular design and space provisions within the aircraft permit retrofitting of alternative avionics systems, FLIR and provisions for the

AMX-T two-seat trainer prototype touching down

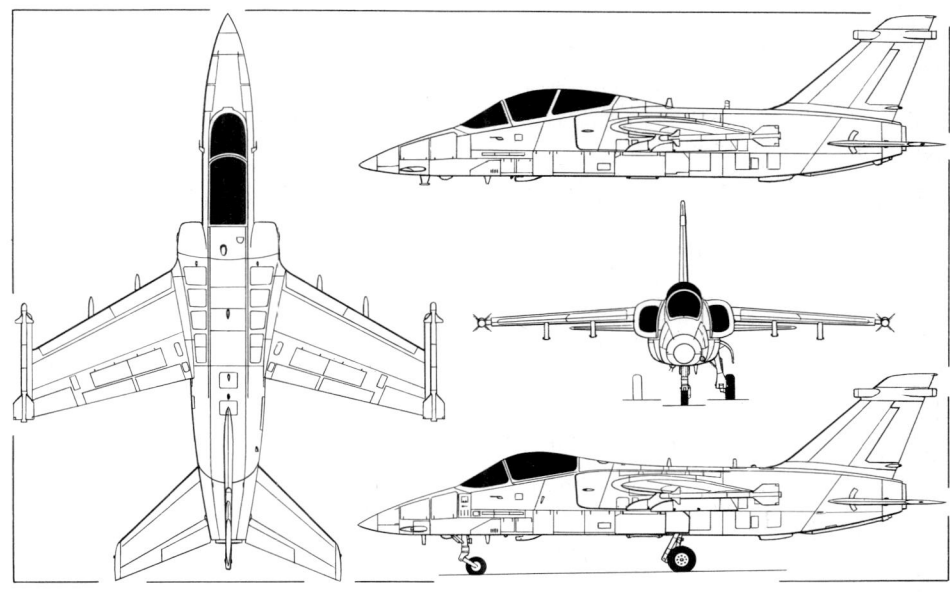
Alenia/Aermacchi/Embraer AMX, in production for the air forces of Italy and Brazil
(Pilot Press)

An AMX prototype during Exocet carriage trials for the anti-ship two-seater

use of night vision goggles if and when required. All avionics/equipment packages are pallet mounted and positioned to allow rapid access.

EQUIPMENT: For reconnaissance missions, any one of three interchangeable Aeroeletrônica (Brazil) pallet mounted photographic systems can be carried, installed internally in forward fuselage; an external infra-red/electro-optical pod can be carried on the centreline pylon. Each of these systems is fully compatible with the aircraft, and will not affect operational capability; the aircraft will therefore be able to carry out reconnaissance missions without effect upon its normal navigation/attack and self defence capabilities. Camera bay is in lower starboard side of fuselage, forward of mainwheel bay.

ARMAMENT: One M61A1 multi-barrel 20 mm cannon, with 350 rds, in port side of lower forward fuselage of aircraft for Italian Air Force (one 30 mm DEFA 554 cannon on each side in aircraft for Brazilian Air Force). Single stores attachment point on fuselage centreline, plus two attachments under each wing, and wingtip rails for two

AIM-9L Sidewinder or similar infra-red air-to-air missiles (MAA-1 Piranha on Brazilian aircraft). Fuselage and inboard underwing points are each stressed for loads of up to 907 kg (2,000 lb); outboard underwing points stressed for 454 kg (1,000 lb) each. Triple carriers can be fitted to inboard underwing pylons, twin carriers to all five stations. Total external stores load 3,800 kg (8,377 lb). Attack weapons can include free-fall or retarded Mk 82/83/84 bombs, laser guided bombs, cluster bombs, air-to-surface missiles (including area denial, anti-radiation and anti-shipping weapons), electro-optical precision guided munitions, and rocket launchers.

DIMENSIONS, EXTERNAL:

Wing span:	
excl wingtip missiles and rails	8.874 m (29 ft 1½ in)
over missiles	9.97 m (32 ft 8½ in)
Wing aspect ratio	3.75
Wing taper ratio	0.5
Length: overall	13.23 m (43 ft 5 in)
fuselage	12.55 m (41 ft 2 in)
Height overall	4.55 m (14 ft 11¼ in)
Tailplane span	5.20 m (17 ft 0¾ in)
Wheel track	2.15 m (7 ft 0¾ in)
Wheelbase	4.70 m (15 ft 5 in)

AREAS:

Wings, gross	21.00 m² (226.04 sq ft)
Ailerons (total)	0.88 m² (9.47 sq ft)
Trailing-edge flaps (total)	3.86 m² (41.55 sq ft)
Leading-edge slats (total)	2.066 m² (22.24 sq ft)
Spoilers (total)	1.30 m² (13.99 sq ft)
Fin (exposed)	4.265 m² (45.91 sq ft)
Rudder	0.833 m² (8.97 sq ft)
Tailplane (total exposed)	5.10 m² (54.90 sq ft)
Elevators (total)	1.00 m² (10.76 sq ft)

WEIGHTS AND LOADINGS (all versions):

Operational weight empty	6,700 kg (14,771 lb)
Max fuel weight: internal	2,762 kg (6,089 lb)
external	1,760 kg (3,880 lb)
Max external stores load	3,800 kg (8,377 lb)
T-O weight clean	9,600 kg (21,164 lb)
Typical mission T-O weight	10,750 kg (23,700 lb)
Max T-O weight	13,000 kg (28,660 lb)
Normal landing weight	7,000 kg (15,432 lb)
Combat wing loading (clean)	457.1 kg/m² (93.62 lb/sq ft)
Max wing loading	619.05 kg/m² (126.79 lb/sq ft)
Max power loading	265.14 kg/kN (2.60 lb/lb st)

PERFORMANCE (A at typical mission weight of 10,750 kg; 23,700 lb with 907 kg; 2,000 lb of external stores, B at max T-O weight with 2,721 kg; 6,000 lb of external stores, ISA in both cases):

Max level speed	Mach 0.86
Max rate of climb at S/L	3,124 m (10,250 ft)/min
Service ceiling	13,000 m (42,650 ft)
T-O run at S/L: A	631 m (2,070 ft)
B	982 m (3,220 ft)
T-O to 15 m (50 ft) at S/L: B	1,442 m (4,730 ft)
Landing from 15 m (50 ft) at S/L: B	753 m (2,470 ft)
Landing run at S/L	464 m (1,520 ft)
Min ground turning radius: A, B	7.53 m (24 ft 8½ in)

Attack radius, allowances for 5 min combat over target and 10% fuel reserves:

lo-lo-lo: A	300 nm (556 km; 345 miles)
B	285 nm (528 km; 328 miles)
hi-lo-hi: A	480 nm (889 km; 553 miles)
B	500 nm (926 km; 576 miles)

Ferry range with two 1,000 litre (264 US gallon; 220 Imp gallon) drop tanks, 10% reserves
1,800 nm (3,336 km; 2,073 miles)

g limits	+7.33/−3

ATR

AVIONS DE TRANSPORT RÉGIONAL

Avenue Pierre Latécoère, 31712 Blagnac Cédex, France
Telephone: 33 61 93 11 11
Fax: 33 61 30 07 40
Telex: 533 984 F/GIE ATR
PRESIDENT AND CHIEF EXECUTIVE OFFICER (alternate):
   Henri-Paul Puel (Aerospatiale)
   Fausto Cereti (Alenia)
EXECUTIVE VICE-PRESIDENT: Gérard Hibon (Aerospatiale)
VICE-PRESIDENT, SALES ENGINEERING: P. Lebouc
COMMUNICATIONS MANAGER: Didier Bertrand
PARTICIPATING COMPANIES:
   Aerospatiale: see under France
   Alenia: see under Italy

This Groupement d'Intérêt Economique (50:50 joint management company) was formally established 5 February 1982 to develop ATR series of transport aircraft (ATR stands for regional transport aircraft in French and Italian, and 42/72 to passenger capacity). Proposed acquisition of Boeing Canada's de Havilland division awaiting approval at press time.

ATR 42

TYPE: Twin-turboprop regional transport.
PROGRAMME: Joint launch by Aerospatiale and Aeritalia (now Alenia) in October 1981, following June 1981 selection of P&WC PW120 turboprop as basic power plant; two prototypes: first flights 16 August 1984 (F-WEGA) and 31 October 1984 (F-WEGB); first flight production aircraft 30 April 1985; simultaneous certification to JAR 25 by France and Italy 24 September 1985, followed by USA (FAR 25) 25 October 1985, Germany 12 February 1988, UK 31 October 1989; deliveries began 3 December 1985 (fourth aircraft, to Air Littoral); into service 9 December 1985; 1991 production rate (incl ATR 72) six per month.
VARIANTS: **ATR 42-300:** Initial production version, with higher MTOGW and better payload/range than prototypes.
   ATR 42-320: Identical to 42-300 except for optional PW121 engines and improved hot/high performance; OWE increased/payload decreased by 5 kg (11 lb).
   ATR 42 F: Commercial freighter with modified interior, reinforced cabin floor, flight-openable port-side cargo/airdrop door; can carry 3,800 kg (8,377 lb) of cargo or 42 passengers over 1,250 nm (2,316 km; 1,439 miles). One delivered to Gabon (Presidential Guard) 1989.
   Petrel: Proposed maritime patrol version (of ATR 42 or 72); details in 1990-91 *Jane's*.
   ATR 72: Stretched ATR 42, described separately.
CUSTOMERS: Total orders 283 by 31 January 1991, of which 187 delivered; options then held for further 49.
DESIGN FEATURES: Designed to JAR 25/FAR 25; wing section Aerospatiale RA-XXX-43 (NACA 43 series derivative); thickness/chord ratio 18 per cent at root, 13 per cent at tip; constant chord, no-dihedral centre-section with 2° incidence at root; outer panels 3° 6′ sweepback at quarter-chord and 2° 30′ dihedral. Fuselage (incl baggage/cargo compartments) pressurised. Sweptback

vertical and non-swept horizontal (T) tail surfaces. Kléber-Colombes pneumatic de-icing of tailplane and outer wing leading-edges.
FLYING CONTROLS: Mechanically actuated controls; lateral control by ailerons and single spoiler surface ahead of each outer flap; ailerons each have electrically actuated automatic trim tab; fixed incidence tailplane; mass balanced rudder and elevators, each with electrically actuated automatic trim tab; two-segment double-slotted single-rotation flaps with Ratier-Figeac hydraulic actuators.
STRUCTURE: Two-spar fail-safe wings, mainly of aluminium alloy, with leading-edges of Kevlar/Nomex sandwich; wing top skin panels aft of rear spar are of Kevlar/Nomex with carbon reinforcement; flaps and ailerons have aluminium frames and spars, with skins of carbonfibre/Nomex and carbon/epoxy respectively; fuselage is fail-safe semi-monocoque, mainly of light alloy except for Kevlar/Nomex nosecone, tailcone, wing/body fairings, nosewheel doors and main landing gear fairings; fin (attached to rearmost fuselage frame) and tailplane mainly of aluminium alloy; carbonfibre/Nomex sandwich rudder and elevators; dorsal fin of Kevlar/Nomex and glassfibre/Nomex sandwich; engine cowlings of carbonfibre/Nomex and Kevlar/Nomex sandwich, reinforced with carbonfibre in nose and underside. Aerospatiale responsible for design and construction of wings, flight deck/cabin layout, installation of power plant/flight controls/electrical and de-icing systems, and final assembly/flight testing of civil passenger versions; Alenia builds fuselage/tail unit, installs landing gear/hydraulic system/air-conditioning/pressurisation systems, and will assemble/flight test any cargo/military variants to have a rear-loading ramp.
LANDING GEAR: Hydraulically retractable tricycle type, of Messier-Bugatti/Magnaghi/Nardi trailing-arm design, with twin wheels and oleo-pneumatic shock absorber on each unit. Nose unit retracts forward, main units inward into fuselage and large underfuselage fairing. Goodyear multi-disc brakes and Hydro-Aire anti-skid units on main gear. No brake cooling. Goodyear mainwheels and tubeless tyres, size 32 × 8.8-10PR, pressure 7.17 bars (104 lb/sq in). Low pressure tyres optional. Goodyear nosewheels and tubeless tyres, size 450 × 190-5TL, pressure 4.14 bars (60 lb/sq in).
POWER PLANT: Two Pratt & Whitney Canada PW120 turboprops in 42-300, each flat rated at 1,342 kW (1,800 shp) and driving a Hamilton Standard 14SF four-blade constant-speed fully feathering and reversible-pitch propeller. Blades have metal spars and glassfibre/polyurethane skins. Two PW121 turboprops, each flat rated at 1,417 kW (1,900 shp), in 42-320. Fuel in two integral tanks formed by wing spar box, total capacity 5,700 litres (1,506 US gallons; 1,254 Imp gallons). Single pressure refuelling point in starboard wing leading-edge. Gravity refuelling points in wing upper surface. Oil capacity 40 litres (10.6 US gallons; 8.8 Imp gallons).
ACCOMMODATION: Crew of two on flight deck, with optional third seat for observer. Seating for 42 passengers at 81 cm (32 in) pitch; or 46, 48 or 50 passengers at 76 cm (30 in) pitch, in four-abreast layout with central aisle. Passenger

door, with integral steps, at rear of cabin on port side. Main baggage/cargo compartment between flight deck and passenger cabin, with access from inside cabin and separate loading door on port side. Toilet, galley, wardrobe, and seat for cabin attendant, at rear of passenger cabin, with service door on starboard side. Rear baggage/cargo compartment aft of passenger cabin. Additional baggage space provided by overhead bins and underseat stowage. Entire accommodation, including flight deck and baggage/cargo compartments, pressurised and air-conditioned. Emergency exit via rear passenger and service doors, and by window exits on each side at front of cabin.
SYSTEMS: AiResearch air-conditioning and Softair pressurisation systems, utilising engine bleed air. Pressurisation system (nominal differential 0.41 bar; 6.0 lb/sq in) provides cabin altitude of 2,000 m (6,560 ft) at flight altitudes of up to 7,620 m (25,000 ft), and a sea level cabin environment at flight levels up to 4,025 m (13,200 ft). Two independent hydraulic systems, each at system pressure of 207 bars (3,000 lb/sq in), driven by an electrically operated Abex pump and separated by an interconnecting valve controlled from the flight deck. System flow rate 7.9 litres (2.09 US gallons; 1.74 Imp gallons)/min. One system actuates wing flaps, spoilers, propeller braking, emergency wheel braking and nosewheel steering; second system for landing gear and normal braking system. Kléber-Colombes pneumatic system for de-icing of outer wing leading-edges, tailplane leading-edges and engine air intakes. Main electrical system is 28V DC, supplied by two Auxilec 12kW engine driven starter/generators and two nickel-cadmium batteries (27Ah and 16Ah) with two solid state static inverters for 115/26V single-phase AC supply, and a third (standby) inverter for 115V only. A 115/200V three-phase supply from two 20kVA frequency-wild engine driven alternators is used for anti-icing of windscreen, flight deck side windows, stall warning and airspeed indicator pitots, pitot tubes, propeller blades and control surface horns. Eros/Puritan oxygen system. No APU.
AVIONICS: Bendix/King Gold Crown III com/nav equipment standard, Collins Pro Line II optional. Other standard avionics include Honeywell DFZ-600 AFCS, Honeywell P-800 weather radar, dual Honeywell AZ-800 digital air data computers and dual AH-600 attitude/heading reference systems with ASCB (avionics standard communication bus), GPWS, radio altimeter, and digital flight deck recorder. EDZ-820 electronic flight instrumentation system (R/Nav, microwave landing system, Omega nav and HF com) optional. Standard avionics package includes two VHF, two VOR/ILS/marker beacon receivers, radio compass, radio altimeter, DME, ATC transponder, cockpit voice recorder, intercom, PA system, and equipment to FAR Pt 121.

DIMENSIONS, EXTERNAL:

Wing span	24.57 m (80 ft 7½ in)
Wing chord: at root	2.57 m (8 ft 5¼ in)
at tip	1.41 m (4 ft 7½ in)
Wing aspect ratio	11.08
Length overall	22.67 m (74 ft 4½ in)
Fuselage: Max width	2.865 m (9 ft 4½ in)
Height overall	7.586 m (24 ft 10¾ in)
Elevator span	7.31 m (23 ft 11¾ in)
Wheel track (c/l of shock struts)	4.10 m (13 ft 5½ in)
Wheelbase	8.78 m (28 ft 9¾ in)
Propeller diameter	3.96 m (13 ft 0 in)
Distance between propeller centres	8.10 m (26 ft 7 in)
Propeller/fuselage clearance	0.82 m (2 ft 8¼ in)
Propeller ground clearance	1.20 m (3 ft 11¼ in)
Passenger door (rear, port): Height	1.75 m (5 ft 9 in)
Width	0.75 m (2 ft 5½ in)
Height to sill (at OWE)	1.375 m (4 ft 6¼ in)
Service door (rear, stbd): Height	1.22 m (4 ft 0 in)
Width	0.61 m (2 ft 0 in)
Height to sill	1.375 m (4 ft 6¼ in)
Cargo/baggage door (fwd, port):	
Height	1.52 m (5 ft 0 in)
Width	1.275 m (4 ft 2¼ in)
Height to sill (at OWE)	1.15 m (3 ft 9¼ in)
Emergency exits (fwd, each): Height	0.91 m (3 ft 0 in)
Width	0.51 m (1 ft 8 in)
Crew emergency hatch (flight deck roof):	
Length	0.51 m (1 ft 8 in)
Width	0.483 m (1 ft 7 in)

DIMENSIONS, INTERNAL:
Cabin:

Length (excl flight deck, incl toilet and baggage compartments)	13.85 m (45 ft 5¼ in)
Max width	2.57 m (8 ft 5¼ in)
Max width at floor	2.263 m (7 ft 5⅛ in)

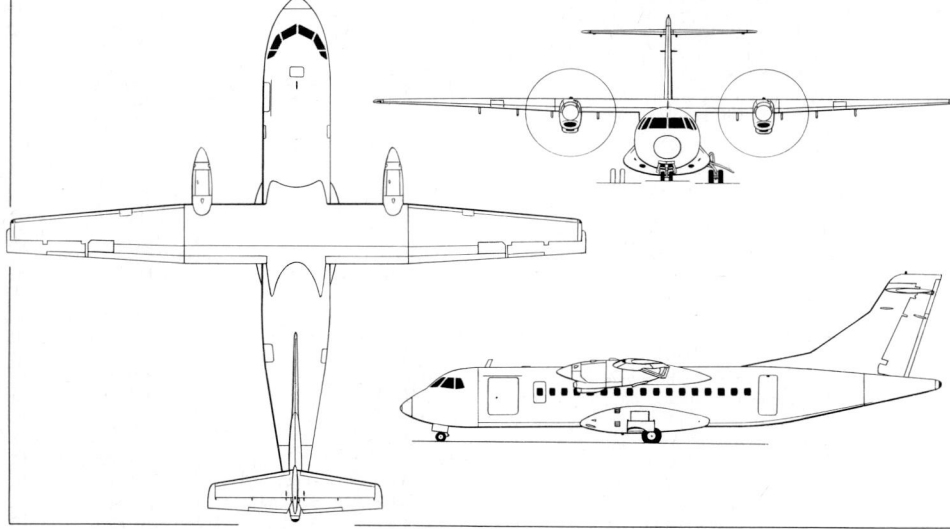

Aerospatiale/Alenia ATR 42 twin-turboprop regional transport *(Pilot Press)*

Aerospatiale/Alenia ATR 42 short-haul transport in the insignia of American Eagle, USA

Max height	1.91 m (6 ft 3¼ in)
Floor area	31.0 m² (333.7 sq ft)
Volume	58.0 m³ (2,048.25 cu ft)

Baggage/cargo compartment volume:
front (42-46 pass)	6.0 m³ (211.9 cu ft)
front (48 pass)	4.8 m³ (169.5 cu ft)
front (50 pass)	3.6 m³ (127.1 cu ft)
rear	4.8 m³ (169.5 cu ft)
overhead bins	1.5 m³ (53.0 cu ft)

AREAS:
Wings, gross	54.50 m² (586.6 sq ft)
Ailerons (total)	3.12 m² (33.58 sq ft)
Flaps (total)	11.00 m² (118.40 sq ft)
Spoilers (total)	1.12 m² (12.06 sq ft)
Fin, excl dorsal fin	8.48 m² (91.28 sq ft)
Rudder, incl tab	4.00 m² (43.05 sq ft)
Tailplane	7.81 m² (84.07 sq ft)
Elevators (total, incl tabs)	3.92 m² (42.19 sq ft)

WEIGHTS AND LOADINGS:
Operating weight empty (incl FAR 121 equipment):
42-300	10,285 kg (22,674 lb)
42-320	10,290 kg (22,685 lb)
Max fuel weight	4,500 kg (9,920 lb)
Max payload: 42-300	4,915 kg (10,835 lb)
42-320	4,910 kg (10,824 lb)
Max T-O weight	16,700 kg (36,817 lb)
Max ramp weight	16,720 kg (36,860 lb)
Max zero-fuel weight	15,200 kg (33,510 lb)
Max landing weight	16,400 kg (36,156 lb)
Max wing loading	306.4 kg/m² (62.79 lb/sq ft)
Max power loading: 42-300	6.22 kg/kW (10.23 lb/shp)
42-320	5.90 kg/kW (9.69 lb/shp)

PERFORMANCE (42-300 at max T-O weight, to FAR Pt 25, incl Amendment 42, ISA, except where indicated):
Never-exceed speed (VNE)
Mach 0.55 (250 knots; 463 km/h; 287 mph CAS)
Max cruising speed at 5,180 m (17,000 ft), AUW of 16,200 kg (35,715 lb)
265 knots (490 km/h; 305 mph)
Econ cruising speed at 7,620 m (25,000 ft)
243 knots (450 km/h; 279 mph)
Stalling speed: flaps up   104 knots (193 km/h; 120 mph)
30° flap   81 knots (151 km/h; 94 mph)
Max rate of climb at S/L, AUW of 15,000 kg (33,069 lb)
640 m (2,100 ft)/min
Rate of climb at S/L, one engine out, AUW as above
191 m (625 ft)/min
Max operating altitude   7,620 m (25,000 ft)
Service ceiling, one engine out, at 97% of max T-O weight, ISA + 10°C
2,315 m (7,595 ft)
T-O balanced field length:
at S/L, ISA   1,090 m (3,576 ft)
at 915 m (3,000 ft), ISA + 10°C   1,300 m (4,265 ft)
Landing field length at S/L at max landing weight
1,030 m (3,380 ft)
Runway LCN at max T-O weight:
rigid pavement, 200 cm radius of relative stiffness:
standard tyres	19
low pressure tyres	16
76 cm flexible pavement, standard tyres	20
83 cm flexible pavement, low pressure tyres	16
Min ground turning radius	17.08 m (56 ft 0½ in)

Max range with 46 passengers, reserves for 87 nm (161 km; 100 mile) diversion and 45 min hold
1,050 nm (1,946 km; 1,209 miles)
Range with max fuel, reserves as above:
max cruising speed   2,420 nm (4,481 km; 2,785 miles)

long-range cruising speed
2,700 nm (5,003 km; 3,109 miles)
PERFORMANCE (42-320, conditions as above): As for 42-300 except:
Max cruising speed at 5,180 m (17,000 ft), AUW of 16,200 kg (35,715 lb)
269 knots (498 km/h; 310 mph)
Service ceiling, one engine out, at 97% of max T-O weight, ISA + 10°C
3,140 m (10,300 ft)
T-O balanced field length:
at S/L, ISA   1,040 m (3,412 ft)
at 915 m (3,000 ft), ISA + 10°C   1,235 m (4,052 ft)
OPERATIONAL NOISE LEVELS:
T-O	83.1 EPNdB
Approach	96.7 EPNdB
Sideline	83.7 EPNdB

PETREL 42/72

No customers have yet been announced for these proposed maritime variants, brief details of which can be found in the 1990-91 *Jane's*.

ATR 72

TYPE: Twin-turboprop regional transport.
PROGRAMME: Go-ahead announced at 1985 Paris Air Show; three development aircraft built: first flights 27 October 1988 (F-WWEY), 20 December 1988 and April 1989; French and US certification 25 September and 15 November 1989 respectively; deliveries, to Kar Air of Finland, began 27 October 1989.
CUSTOMERS: Total orders 121 by 31 January 1991, of which 20 delivered; options then held for further 86.
DESIGN FEATURES: Stretched version of ATR 42 (which see) with more power, more fuel, greater wing span/area, and longer fuselage for up to 74 passengers.

VARIANTS: **ATR 72-210:** Improved hot/high version with 1,849 kW (2,480 shp) PW127 engines and Hamilton Standard 247F propellers; under development for late 1992 certification.
FLYING CONTROLS: As for ATR 42.
STRUCTURE: Generally as for ATR 42, but new wings outboard of engine nacelles have carbonfibre front and rear spars, self-stiffening carbon skin panels and light alloy ribs, resulting in weight saving of 120 kg (265 lb); sweepback on outer panels 2° 18′ at quarter-chord.
LANDING GEAR: Improved main units, with Dunlop wheels (tyres size 34 × 10R-16, pressure 7.86 bars; 114 lb/sq in) and structural carbon brakes; nose gear as ATR 42.
POWER PLANT: Two Pratt & Whitney Canada PW124/2 turboprops, each rated at 1,611 kW (2,160 shp) and driving a Hamilton Standard 14SF-11 four-blade propeller; each new outer wing spar box forms additional 1,500 litre (396 US gallon; 330 Imp gallon) fuel tank; pressure refuelling point in starboard main landing gear fairing.
ACCOMMODATION: As ATR 42 but seating for 64, 66, 70 or (high density) 74 passengers, at respective seat pitches of 81/79/76/76 cm (32/31/30/30 in), plus second cabin attendant's seat. Single baggage compartment at rear of cabin; one or two at front, depending on seating layout and type of port forward door fitted. This can be a passenger or cargo door, with a service door opposite on starboard side. Service door on each side at rear, that on port side replaced by a passenger door when cargo door is fitted at front. Two additional emergency exits (one each side); both rear doors also serve as emergency exits. All doors are of plug type. Increased-capacity air-conditioning system.
AVIONICS: Flight deck equipment and layout generally as for ATR 42. Additions/improvements include engine monitoring mini-aids, and fuel repeater on refuelling panel.

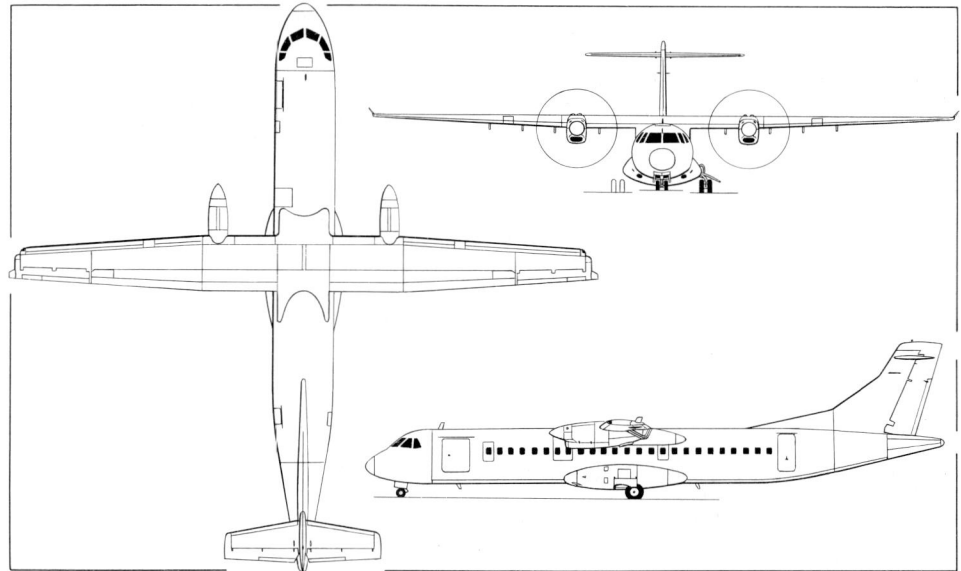

ATR 72 (two Pratt & Whitney Canada PW124/2 turboprops) *(Pilot Press)*

ATR 72 stretched version of this twin-turboprop transport aircraft in the insignia of Kar Air of Finland

DIMENSIONS, EXTERNAL: As ATR 42 except:

Wing span	27.05 m (88 ft 9 in)
Wing chord at tip	1.59 m (5 ft 2½ in)
Wing aspect ratio	12.0
Length overall	27.166 m (89 ft 1½ in)
Height overall	7.65 m (25 ft 1¼ in)
Wheelbase	10.70 m (35 ft 1¼ in)
Passenger door (fwd, port): Height	1.75 m (5 ft 9 in)
Width	0.82 m (2 ft 8¼ in)
Height to sill	1.12 m (3 ft 8 in)
Alternative cargo door (fwd, port):	
Height	1.52 m (5 ft 0 in)
Width	1.275 m (4 ft 2½ in)
Height to sill	1.12 m (3 ft 8 in)

DIMENSIONS, INTERNAL:
Cabin:

Length (excl flight deck, incl toilet and baggage compartments)	19.21 m (63 ft 0¼ in)
Cross-section	as for ATR 42
Floor area	41.7 m² (449 sq ft)
Volume	76.0 m³ (2,684 cu ft)

Baggage/cargo compartment volume (with front passenger door):

front (64-66 passengers)	3.9 m³ (137.7 cu ft)
front (66 passengers)	5.8 m³ (204.8 cu ft)
front (74 passengers)	1.6 m³ (56.5 cu ft)
rear	4.8 m³ (169.5 cu ft)

AREAS: As ATR 42 except:

Wings, gross	61.0 m² (656.6 sq ft)
Ailerons (total)	3.75 m² (40.36 sq ft)
Flaps (total)	12.28 m² (132.18 sq ft)
Spoilers (total)	1.34 m² (14.42 sq ft)

WEIGHTS AND LOADINGS:

Operating weight empty	12,500 kg (27,558 lb)
Max fuel weight	5,000 kg (11,023 lb)
Max payload	7,200 kg (15,873 lb)
Max T-O weight	21,500 kg (47,400 lb)
Max ramp weight	21,530 kg (47,465 lb)
Max zero-fuel weight	19,700 kg (43,430 lb)
Max landing weight	21,350 kg (47,068 lb)
Max wing loading	352.5 kg/m² (72.20 lb/sq ft)
Max power loading	6.01 kg/kW (9.88 lb/shp)

PERFORMANCE (at max T-O weight except where indicated):

Max cruising speed at 7,620 m (25,000 ft)	
	284 knots (526 km/h; 327 mph)
Econ cruising speed at 7,620 m (25,000 ft)	
	248 knots (460 km/h; 286 mph)
Max operating altitude	7,620 m (25,000 ft)
Service ceiling, one engine out, at 97% MTOGW and ISA + 10°C	2,545 m (8,350 ft)
T-O balanced field length:	
at S/L, ISA	1,408 m (4,620 ft)
at 915 m (3,000 ft), ISA + 10°C	1,750 m (5,742 ft)
Landing field length at S/L, ISA	1,210 m (3,970 ft)
Min ground turning radius	19.76 m (64 ft 10 in)
Still air range (ISA), reserves for 87 nm (161 km; 100 mile) diversion and 45 min continued cruise:	
max optional payload	645 nm (1,195 km; 742 miles)
66 passengers	1,440 nm (2,666 km; 1,657 miles)
max fuel and zero payload	2,370 nm (4,389 km; 2,727 miles)

DASA/AEROSPATIALE/ALENIA

PARTICIPATING COMPANIES:
DASA: see under Germany
Aerospatiale: see under France
Alenia: see under Italy
In Spring 1991 a tripartite organisation was being formed to encompass the range of regional transport aircraft (Dornier 228/328, ATR 42/72, and a new 80/130-seat family to be jointly developed) in which these three European manufacturers are currently involved or interested. Deutsche Aerospace (DASA) has a 50 per cent share and Aerospatiale and Alenia (through ATR) the other 50 per cent. A management office was being set up in Munich and the International Commuter System sales office in Toulouse was to market all the regional airliner types, plus possibly the output of Boeing Canada de Havilland acquired by ATR.

DASSAULT/DORNIER

PARTICIPATING COMPANIES:
Dassault: see under France
Dornier: see under Germany

DASSAULT/DORNIER ALPHA JET

TYPE: Tandem-seat jet basic, low-altitude and advanced trainer and close support/battlefield reconnaissance aircraft.

PROGRAMME: Started 1970, initially for air forces of France and Germany; four prototypes (first flight 26 October 1973: see 1978-79 and earlier *Jane's*); production authorised March 1975; has now ended, but any version except Lancier (1989-90 *Jane's*) remains available.

VARIANTS: **Advanced trainer/light attack** (formerly Alpha Jet E) for air forces of France, Belgium, Egypt (designated **MS1**), Ivory Coast, Morocco, Nigeria, Qatar and Togo; further details in 1988-89 and earlier editions.

Close support (formerly Alpha Jet A) for German Luftwaffe: see 1990-91 and earlier editions for further details; original Larzac 04-C6 turbofans replaced by more powerful 04-C20s. Update programme for armament and avionics, to be developed in 1991-93, will include improved instruments, navigation and air data sensors as well as a stall warning indicator; but early 1991 report indicated that Luftwaffe has proposed phasing out of fleet between 1991 and 1993 (decision expected mid-1991), with France and Portugal both said to be interested in acquiring surplus aircraft.

Alternative close support version, with new nav/attack system; ordered by Egypt (designated **MS2**) and Cameroon; further details in 1990-91 edition.

Alpha Jet 2 (formerly NGEA: Nouvelle Génération pour l'École et l'Appui): Improved attack version, incorporating nav/attack system developed for MS2; uprated Larzac 04-C20 engines; capability of carrying Magic 2 air-to-air missiles, plus auxiliary fuel tanks of up to 625 litres (165 US gallons; 137.5 Imp gallons) on inboard underwing stations and 450 litres (119 US gallons; 99 Imp gallons) on inboard or outboard stations. None yet ordered.

Dassault/Dornier Alpha Jet 2, with uprated Larzac engines and Sagem inertial nav/attack system

Alpha Jet 3: Advanced training system version fitted with state of the art cockpit controls, and displays such as CRT raster HUD combined with collimated head-level display, rear cockpit TV monitor, and lateral multi-function displays and multi-function keyboards in each cockpit. Proposed for training in the use of nav/attack systems of future combat aircraft, including training in the operation of such sensors as radar, FLIR, laser and ECM systems. None yet ordered.

Naval version, with reinforced landing gear, proposed by Dassault as Zéphyr replacement for Aéronavale.

CUSTOMERS: Belgium (33), Cameroon (seven), Egypt (30 MS1 and 15 MS2, of which 26 and 11 assembled locally by AOI), France (176), Germany (175, of which 168 remain), Ivory Coast (seven), Morocco (24), Nigeria (24), Qatar (six) and Togo (six); all delivered.

DESIGN FEATURES: Details in 1990-91 and earlier editions.

FLYING CONTROLS: Hydraulically actuated ailerons/rudder/ all-moving tailplane, all with trimmable artificial feel; Fowler slotted flaps and twin rear-fuselage airbrakes, also actuated hydraulically.

STRUCTURE: Details in 1990-91 and earlier editions.

POWER PLANT: Two SNECMA/Turbomeca Larzac 04-C6 turbofans, each rated at 13.24 kN (2,976 lb st), mounted on sides of fuselage; 14.12 kN (3,175 lb st) Larzac 04-C20 turbofans are retrofitted to Luftwaffe aircraft, standard on Alpha Jet 2 and optional for other versions. Internal fuel capacity 1,900 litres (502 US gallons; 418 Imp gallons) or 2,040 litres (539 US gallons; 449 Imp gallons). Provision for 310 or 450 litre (82 or 119 US gallon; 68 or 99 Imp gallon) capacity drop tank on each outer wing pylon, plus (on Alpha Jet 2) a 450 or 625 litre (119 or 165 US gallon; 99 or 137.5 Imp gallon) tank on each inboard wing pylon. Pressure refuelling (point near starboard intake) standard for all tanks, including drop tanks. Gravity system for fuselage tanks and drop tanks. Fuel system permits inverted flying.

ACCOMMODATION: Two persons in tandem, in pressurised cockpit under individual upward opening canopies. Dual controls standard. Zero/zero ejection seats in most aircraft, except French trainer version. Rear seat elevated. Baggage compartment in tailcone, with door on starboard side.

SYSTEMS: See 1990-91 and earlier editions.

AVIONICS: Standard avionics, according to version, include V/UHF and VHF or UHF transceivers, IFF/SIF, VOR/ILS/marker beacon receiver, Tacan, radio compass, gyro platform and intercom. Alpha Jet 2 has Sagem Uliss 81 inertial platform (replacing SFIM 550) and Una 81 nav/attack unit, Thomson-CSF VE 110C head-up display with film or video camera (VEM 130 in Lancier), Thomson-CSF TMV 630 laser rangefinder, TRT AHV 9 radar altimeter and Dassault Electronique Digibus digital multiplexed avionics databus.

ARMAMENT: For armament training and close support, can be equipped with an underfuselage jettisonable pod containing a 30 mm DEFA or 27 mm Mauser cannon with 150 rds; or an underfuselage pylon for one 250 kg bomb, one 400 kg modular bomb, or a target towing system. Provision also for two hardpoints under each wing, with non-jettisonable adaptor pylons. On these can be carried M155 launchers for eighteen 68 mm rockets; HE or retarded bombs of 125, 250 or 400 kg; 625 lb cluster dispensers; 690 or 825 lb special purpose tanks; practice launchers for bombs or rockets; Dassault CC-420 underwing 30 mm gun pods, each with 180 rds; or two drop tanks (see Power Plant paragraph). Provision for air-to-air or air-to-surface missiles such as Sidewinder, Magic or Maverick, or reconnaissance pod. Total load for all five stations more than 2,500 kg (5,510 lb). Dassault CEM-1 (combined external multistore) carriers can be attached to inboard underwing pylons, permitting simultaneous carriage of mixed fuel/bomb/rocket loads, including six rockets and four practice bombs, or 18 rockets with one 500 lb bomb, or six penetration bombs, or grenades or other stores. A special version of the CEM-1 allows carriage of a reconnaissance pod containing four cameras (three Omera 61 cameras and an Omera 40 panoramic camera) and a decoy launcher. Luftwaffe aircraft equipped with ML Aviation twin stores carriers, CBLS 200 practice bomb and rocket launcher carriers, and ejector release units. Fire control system for air-to-air or air-to-ground firing, dive bombing and low-level bombing. Firing by pupil pilot (in front seat) is governed by a safety interlock system controlled by the instructor, which energises the forward station trigger circuit and illuminates a fire clearance indicator in the pupil's cockpit. Thomson-CSF 902 sight and film or video gun camera in French version; Kaiser/VDO KM 808 sight and gun camera in German aircraft.

DIMENSIONS, EXTERNAL:

Wing span	9.11 m (29 ft 10¾ in)
Length overall: trainer	11.75 m (38 ft 6½ in)
close support version, incl probe	13.23 m (43 ft 5 in)
Height overall (at normal T-O weight)	
	4.19 m (13 ft 9 in)
Tailplane span	4.33 m (14 ft 2½ in)
Wheel track	2.71 m (8 ft 10¾ in)
Wheelbase	4.72 m (15 ft 5¾ in)

AREAS:

Wings, gross	17.50 m² (188.4 sq ft)

WEIGHTS AND LOADINGS:

Weight empty, equipped:	
trainer	3,345 kg (7,374 lb)
close support version	3,515 kg (7,749 lb)
Fuel (internal)	1,520 kg (3,351 lb)
	or 1,630 kg (3,593 lb)
Fuel (external)	500 kg (1,102 lb)
	or 720 kg (1,587 lb)
	or 1,440 kg (3,174 lb)
Max external load	more than 2,500 kg (5,510 lb)
Normal T-O weight:	
trainer, clean	5,000 kg (11,023 lb)
Max T-O weight:	
with external stores	8,000 kg (17,637 lb)
Max wing loading: clean	285.7 kg/m² (58.52 lb/sq ft)
with external stores	457.1 kg/m² (93.62 lb/sq ft)
Max power loading:	
04-C6 engines: clean	188.82 kg/kN (1.85 lb/lb st)
with external stores	302.11 kg/kN (2.96 lb/lb st)
04-C20 engines: clean	177.05 kg/kN (1.74 lb/lb st)
with external stores	283.29 kg/kN (2.78 lb/lb st)

PERFORMANCE (at normal clean T-O weight, except where indicated):

Max level speed at 10,000 m (32,800 ft):		
Larzac 04-C6		Mach 0.85
Larzac 04-C20		Mach 0.86
Max level speed at S/L:		
Larzac 04-C6	540 knots (1,000 km/h; 621 mph)	
Larzac 04-C20	560 knots (1,038 km/h; 645 mph)	
Max speed for flap and landing gear extension		
	200 knots (370 km/h; 230 mph)	
Approach speed	110 knots (204 km/h; 127 mph)	
Landing speed at normal landing weight		
	92 knots (170 km/h; 106 mph)	
Stalling speed: flaps and landing gear up		
	116 knots (216 km/h; 134 mph)	
flaps and landing gear down		
	90 knots (167 km/h; 104 mph)	
Max rate of climb at S/L	3,660 m (12,000 ft)/min	
Rate of climb at S/L, one engine out, at 4,782 kg (10,542 lb) AUW, in landing configuration		
	330 m (1,085 ft)/min	
Time to 9,150 m (30,000 ft)	less than 7 min	
Service ceiling	14,630 m (48,000 ft)	
T-O run: Larzac 04-C6	370 m (1,215 ft)	
Larzac 04-C20	320 m (1,050 ft)	
Landing run at usual landing weight		
	approx 500 m (1,640 ft)	
Low altitude radius of action (trainer):		
clean, max internal fuel	291 nm (540 km; 335 miles)	
with external tanks	361 nm (670 km; 416 miles)	
High altitude radius of action (trainer), reserves of 15% internal fuel:		
clean, max internal fuel		
	664 nm (1,230 km; 764 miles)	
with external tanks	782 nm (1,450 km; 901 miles)	
Lo-lo-lo mission radius (close support version), incl combat at max continuous thrust and 54 nm (100 km; 62 mile) dash:		
with belly gun pod and underwing weapons		
	210 nm (390 km; 242 miles)	
with belly gun pod, underwing weapons and external tanks	340 nm (630 km; 391 miles)	
Hi-lo-hi mission radius (close support version), incl combat at max continuous thrust and 54 nm (100 km; 62 mile) dash:		
with belly gun pod and underwing weapons		
	315 nm (583 km; 363 miles)	
with belly gun pod, underwing weapons and external tanks	580 nm (1,075 km; 668 miles)	
Ferry range (internal fuel and four 450 litre external tanks)	more than 2,160 nm (4,000 km; 2,485 miles)	
Endurance (internal fuel only):		
low altitude	more than 2 h 30 min	
high altitude	more than 3 h 30 min	
g limits	+ 12/-6.4 ultimate	

EGRETT

PARTICIPATING COMPANIES:
E-Systems (USA)
Grob: see under Germany
Garrett: see Engines section

Egrett name derived from those of original three companies collaborating in its development; E-Systems claims aircraft could offer opportunities for radio communications spanning huge areas of Earth's surface, including mountainous regions.

EGRETT/D-500

TYPE: Multi-purpose high-altitude surveillance and relay aircraft.

PROGRAMME: Revealed April 1987 as joint programme by E-Systems' Greenville Division (programme leader/ systems integrator), Burkhart Grob (airframe design and construction) and Garrett (turboprop engine); first flights 24 June 1987 (Egrett-1), 20 April 1989 (first D-500) and 9 September 1990 (second D-500); second D-500 was to be fully outfitted for sigint during 1991 (demonstration of imaging radar); new US-German venture Telos GmbH (E-Systems, Grob, MBB and Elekluft) formed June 1990 for in-country logistics and maintenance support for D-500/Egrett-associated programmes.

VARIANTS: **Egrett-1:** Proof-of-concept (POC) aircraft (originally D-FGEI, now N14ES); set time-to-height and two altitude records 1 September 1988 (details in 1990-91 and earlier editions); subsequently continued in use for environmental and other research flying, which included 1989 Stratolab programme (see 1990-91 *Jane's*); total flying time exceeded 250 hours; now back in Germany.

D-500: Modified versions (D-FGEE and D-FGEO), more representative of eventual production version; differ from Egrett-1 in having 5.00 m (16 ft 4¾ in) greater wing span (to house additional antennae), pressurised cockpit, retractable main landing gear (to avoid masking underfuselage DF antenna), modified rear fuselage, and higher speeds and payload weights; total flying time more than 200 hours.

Production Egrett: Equipped to fulfil German EASysLuft (Erfassungs- und Auswertesystem Luft: airborne data gathering and evaluation system) requirement; no firm order up to May 1991.

Two-seat Egrett: Trainer version: to be developed.

Strato 2: Joint Grob/DLR/IABG study for twin-engined version able to carry pilot plus up to four crew members; would have turbocharged engines and ceiling of 18,300 m (60,000 ft) or higher.

The first two E-Systems/Grob/Garrett D-500s

CUSTOMERS: German Luftwaffe expected to acquire up to 15 D-500s for EASysLuft missions, to enter service 1994-97 and probably based at Pferdsfeld.

DESIGN FEATURES: Capacious fuselage and very high aspect ratio wings for HALE (high altitude, long endurance) performance; capable of manned or unmanned operation; bays in rear fuselage can accept various payloads to customer's requirements, in modular packages facilitating installation/servicing/removal; large underfuselage doors provide easy access to payloads.

FLYING CONTROLS: Trim tab in rudder; split flaps on wing inboard trailing-edges.

STRUCTURE: Three-spar mid-mounted wings; airframe built largely of glassfibre, carbonfibre, and Kevlar reinforced composites, for low radio/radar reflectivity.

LANDING GEAR: Tricycle type, with single wheel on each unit. Nose unit retracts rearward; main units non-retractable on Egrett-1, on D-500 retract forward into underwing pods.

POWER PLANT: One Garrett TPE331-14F turboprop, flat rated at approx 596.5 kW (800 shp), driving a Hartzell HC-E4P-5 constant-speed, fully feathering, reversible-pitch propeller with four composite blades and electric de-icing. Integral fuel tank occupying almost the whole of each wing, combined capacity 1,100 litres (290.6 US gallons; 242 Imp gallons). On-station endurance can be extended by installing optional auxiliary internal fuel tanks.

ACCOMMODATION: Egrett-1 has air-conditioned accommodation for pilot only; D-500 has a pressurised cockpit. Large fairing aft of cockpit covers bay for US avionics. Two-seat trainer version to be developed.

SYSTEMS: Electrical DC power provided by 28V 300A generator and 24V 19Ah battery.

AVIONICS: Dual VHF radios, dual VOR/ILS/marker beacon receivers, ADF, magnetic slaved compass system and vertical gyro standard on Egrett-1; Tacan and UHF radio optional. Instrumentation includes vertical gyro indicator, standby attitude indicator, HSI, magnetic standby compass, sensitive altimeter/altitude alerter, ASI, instantaneous VSI, RMI, clock, and engine instruments. Equipment for 1989 Stratolab flights included infra-red scanner, pyranometer (to register thermal radiation) and motorised camera. Hughes Aircraft (USA) teamed late 1989 with three German companies (MBB, Elekluft and Telefunken Systemtechnik) in PRISMA programme (Primary Imaging Systems for Multiple Applications) to develop variety of sensor packages for civil and military applications ranging from environmental monitoring to disarmament verification. Equipped with a microwave relay payload (eg, two computer-pointed antennae, a receiver and a power amplifier, transmitting broadband signals over long distances), Egrett could provide quick response in emergency situations where other long-term communications facilities might become overloaded. One or more Egretts could be deployed carrying payload packages to establish a radio based data communications network over a very large area.

DIMENSIONS, EXTERNAL (A: Egrett-1, B: D-500):

Wing span: A	28.00 m (91 ft 10½ in)
B	33.00 m (108 ft 3¼ in)
Wing aspect ratio: A	20.1
B	27.2
Length overall: A, B	12.00 m (39 ft 4½ in)
Height overall: A, B	6.00 m (19 ft 8¼ in)
* Wheel track: A, B	4.80 m (15 ft 9 in)
* Wheelbase: A, B	3.66 m (12 ft 0 in)
Propeller diameter: A, B	3.05 m (10 ft 0 in)
* *estimated*	

DIMENSIONS, INTERNAL:

Cockpit volume: A, B	2.83 m³ (100 cu ft)
Max payload volume: A	2.83 m³ (100 cu ft)
B	6.40 m³ (226 cu ft)

AREAS (estimated):

Wings, gross: A	39.0 m² (419.8 sq ft)
B	40.5 m² (435.9 sq ft)

WEIGHTS AND LOADINGS:

Max payload: A	more than 408 kg (900 lb)
B	907 kg (2,000 lb)
Max T-O weight: A	more than 3,630 kg (8,000 lb)
B	4,200 kg (9,259 lb)
Max wing loading: B	
	approx 103.7 kg/m² (21.24 lb/sq ft)
Max power loading: B	7.04 kg/kW (11.57 lb/shp)

PERFORMANCE:

Max level speed: A, B	
	more than 190 knots (352 km/h; 219 mph)
Cruising speed: B	162 knots (300 km/h; 186 mph)
Stalling speed: A, B	61 knots (113 km/h; 71 mph)
Max rate of climb at S/L:	
A	more than 457 m (1,500 ft)/min
Optimum operating altitude: B	13,715 m (45,000 ft)
Max operating altitude: B	approx 17,000 m (55,775 ft)
Time to 13,715 m (45,000 ft): B	35 min
T-O distance: A	488-610 m (1,600-2,000 ft)
Endurance, depending on payload, speed and altitude:	
manned	6-9 h
unmanned	more than 15 h
g limits	+5/-3

E-Systems/Grob/Garrett Egrett-1 proof of concept and research aircraft

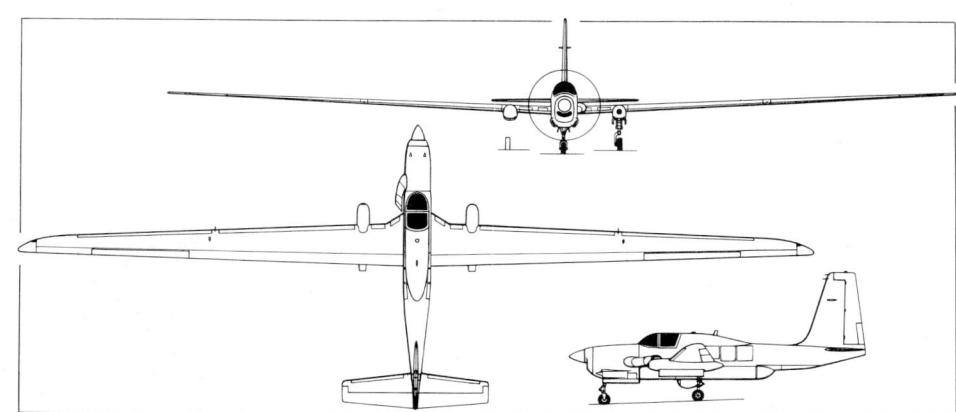

E-Systems/Grob/Garrett D-500 high altitude surveillance aircraft *(Pilot Press)*

EHI

EH INDUSTRIES LIMITED
500 Chiswick High Road, London W4 5RG, UK
Telephone: 44 (81) 995 8221
Telex: 291600 EHILON
CO-CHAIRMEN:
A. Jones
Dott R. D'Alessandro
MANAGING DIRECTOR: G. Bologna
PARTICIPATING COMPANIES:
Agusta: see under Italy
Westland: see under UK

EH Industries formed June 1980 by Westland Helicopters and Agusta (50 per cent each) to undertake joint development of new anti-submarine warfare helicopter for Royal Navy and Italian Navy. Programme handled on behalf of both governments by British Ministry of Defence; Westland has design leadership for commercial version, Agusta for rear loading military/utility version; naval version being developed jointly for UK and Italian navies and export. Two teams (IBM/Westland and GEC/BAe) bidding for management of Royal Navy programme, for which down-selection was due in July 1991; Canadian programme under review in early 1991.

EH INDUSTRIES EH 101
Royal Navy name: Merlin
TYPE: Three-engined multi-role helicopter.
PROGRAMME: Stems from Westland WG 34 (see UK section of 1979-80 *Jane's*), selected by UK MoD as Sea King replacement late Summer 1978; broadly similar requirement by Italian Navy led to 1980 joint venture with Agusta; subsequent market research confirmed compatibility of basic EH 101 design with commercial payload/range and tactical transport/logistics requirements, resulting in decision to develop naval, civil

PP6, the sixth pre-production EH 101, development aircraft for the Italian Navy variant

and military variants based on common airframe. Nine-month project definition phase approved by UK/Italian governments 12 June 1981; full programme go-ahead announced 25 January 1984; development contract signed 7 March 1984; selected by Canadian Navy August 1987; Italian built iron bird ground test airframe followed by nine pre-production aircraft (PP 1, 3, 4, 5 and 8 by Westland; PP 2, 6, 7 and 9 by Agusta) which made their first flights 9 October 1987 (ZF641), 30 September 1988 (G-EHIL), 15 June 1989 (ZF644), 24 October 1989 (ZF649), 24 April 1990 (G-OIOI), 26 November 1987, late April 1989, 18 December 1989 and

16 January 1991 respectively. British and Italian civil certification planned for 1993; service entry for naval version due 1995.

VARIANTS: **Naval variant:** Known as **Merlin** by Royal Navy and provisionally as **NSA** (new shipborne aircraft) by Canadian Navy, for which PP4 (basic), PP5 (RN) and PP6 (Italy) are prototypes; primary roles will be ASW, ASV, anti-ship surveillance/tracking, amphibious operations and SAR, other roles including AEW, vertrep and ECM (deception, jamming and missile seduction); designed for fully autonomous all-weather operation from land bases, large and small vessels (incl merchant ships) and oil rigs, and specifically from a 3,500 tonne frigate, with dimensions tailored to frigate hangar size. Capabilities include frigate launch and recovery in sea states 5-6 with ship on any heading and wind speed (from any direction) up to 50 knots (93 km/h; 57 mph); endurance and carrying capacity needed to meet expanding maritime tactical requirements of 21st century, including ability to operate distantly for up to 5 hours with state of the art equipment and weapons. RN Merlin will operate from Type 23 frigates, 'Invincible' class carriers, RFAs and other ships, and land bases; Italian Navy will place most emphasis on shore-based operation. Canadian specification still being defined under April 1988 contract by EHI, Bell Helicopter Canada, Canadian Marconi, AMTEK Group, IMP Group and Paramax Electronics, under EH Industries (Canada) Inc as overall programme manager; NSA will operate from patrol frigates and destroyers, replacing CH-124A Sea Kings in mid-1990s.

Heliliner: Commercial variant, with detail design tailored to meet civil requirements; main certification programme being flown by PP3, with PP8 as demonstrator; intended to offer 550 nm (1,019 km; 633 mile) range, with full IFR reserves, carrying 30 passengers and baggage; flight crew of two, provision for cabin attendant, stand-up headroom, airline style seating, overhead baggage storage, full environmental control, passenger entertainment, toilet and galley. Category A VTO performance, capable of offshore/oil rig operations or scheduled flights into city centres at high all-up weights under more rigorous future civil operating rules; rear-loading ramp optional.

Military variant: Tactical or logistic transport variant (represented by PP7) with rear-loading ramp; able to airlift six tons or up to 35 combat equipped troops; will also be available in **civil Utility** version (represented by PP9) to commercial operators requiring rear-loading facility.

CUSTOMERS: Royal Navy expected to order 50 of naval variant, Italian Navy 42 and Canadian Navy up to 35; Royal Air Force requires 25 of military variant initially, to provide air mobility for British Army.

DESIGN FEATURES: Three-engine power margin, fail-safe/damage-tolerant airframe and rotating components, high system redundancy, onboard monitoring of engines/transmission/avionics/utility systems; airframe/power plant/rotor and transmission systems/flight controls/utility systems common to all variants; five-blade main rotor with multiple load path hub and elastomeric bearings; blades of advanced aerofoil section with BERP-derived high-speed tips; four-blade tail rotor; transmission has 45 min run-dry capacity; fuselage in four main modules (front and centre ones common to all variants, modified rear fuselage and slimmer tailboom on military/utility variant to accommodate rear-loading ramp); automatic power folding of main rotor blades and tail rotor pylon on naval variant, with emergency manual backup (tail section folds forward/downward, stowing starboard half of tailplane beneath rear fuselage); Lucas Spraymat electric de-icing of main/tail blades standard on naval variant, optional on others; Dunlop electric anti-icing of engine air intakes.

FLYING CONTROLS: Front drive directly into main gearbox from all three engines, with all gears straddle mounted for greater rigidity; dual redundant digital AFCS.

STRUCTURE: Rotor head of composites surrounding a metal core; composite blades; fuselage mainly aluminium alloy, with bonded honeycomb main panels; composites for such complex shapes as forward fuselage, upper cowling panels, tail-fin, tailplane and windscreen. Engine air intakes of Kevlar reinforced with aero-web honeycomb. Westland responsible for front fuselage (incl flight deck and cabin) and main rotor blades, Agusta for rear fuselage, tail assembly, rotor head and transmission, hydraulic system and part of electrical system; single-sourced series production, with final assembly lines in Italy and UK.

LANDING GEAR: Hydraulically retractable tricycle type, with single mainwheels and steerable twin-wheel nose unit, designed and manufactured by AP Precision Hydraulics in association with Officine Meccaniche Aeronautiche. Main units retract into fairings on sides of fuselage. Goodrich wheels, tyres and brakes: main units have size 8.50-10 wheels with 24 × 7.7 tyres, unladen pressure 6.96 bars (101 lb/sq in); nosewheels have size 19.5 × 6.75 tyres, unladen pressure 8.83 bars (128 lb/sq in). A twin-mainwheel gear has been designed for the military and civil variants.

PP8 demonstrator for Heliliner commercial variant of the EH 101

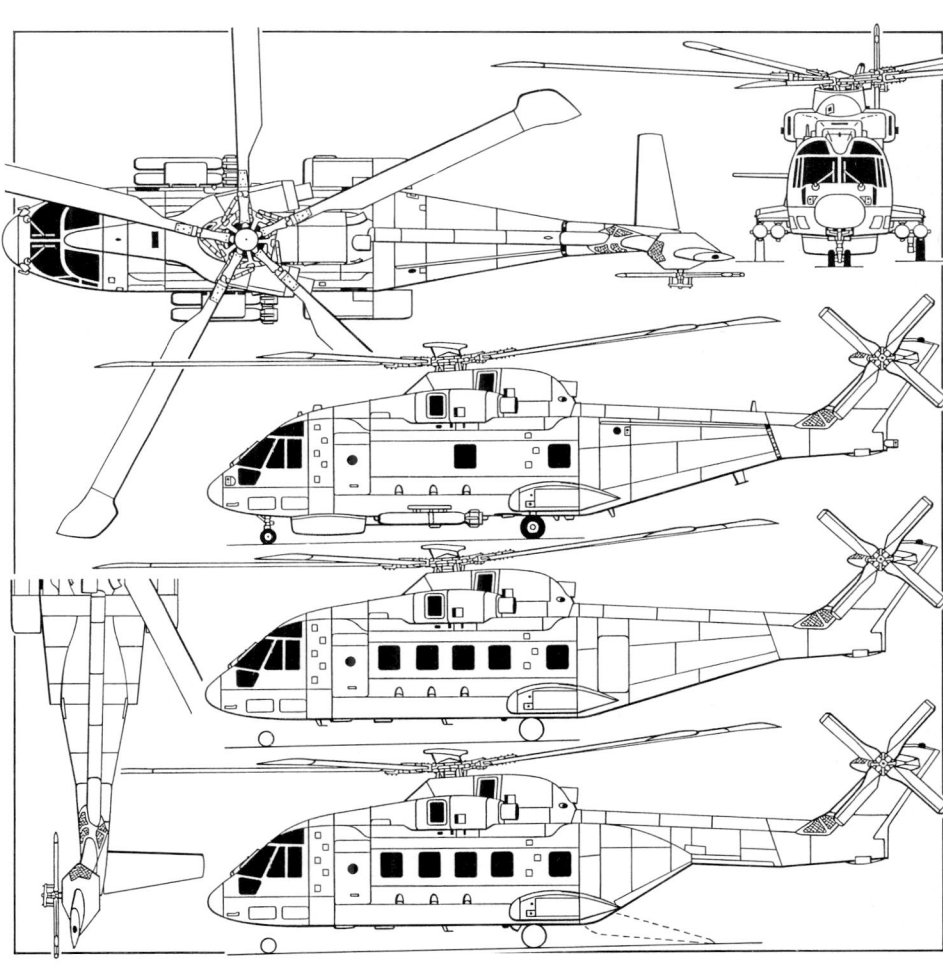

Three-view of the naval EH 101 with additional side views of the Heliliner (centre) and Utility versions (bottom) and scrap top view of the tail of the Utility *(Jane's/Mike Keep)*

POWER PLANT: Three Rolls-Royce Turbomeca RTM 322 turboshafts in Royal Navy Merlin (max contingency and intermediate contingency ratings 1,724 kW; 2,312 shp and 1,566 kW; 2,100 shp respectively); General Electric T700-GE-T6A turboshafts in Italian naval variant, rated at 1,278 kW (1,714 shp) max contingency, 1,254 kW (1,682 shp) intermediate and 1,071 kW (1,437 shp) max continuous at S/L, ISA. Engines for Italian naval variant will be assembled by Alfa Romeo Avio and Fiat. Commercial and military variants powered by three General Electric CT7-6 turboshafts (CT7-6A in PP3) with ratings of 1,432 kW (1,920 shp) max and intermediate contingency, 1,230 kW (1,649 shp) max continuous. Computerised fuel management system. Pressure refuelling point on starboard side; three gravity positions on port side.

ACCOMMODATION: One or two pilots on flight deck (naval version will be capable of single-pilot operation, commercial variant will be certificated for two-pilot operation. ASW version will normally also carry observer and acoustic systems operator. Martin-Baker crew seats in naval version, able to withstand 10.7 m (35 ft)/s impact. Socea or Ipeco crew seats in commercial variant. Commercial version able to accommodate 30 passengers four abreast at approx seat pitch of 76 cm (30 in), plus cabin attendant, with toilet, galley and baggage facilities (including overhead bins). Military variant can accommodate up to 35 combat equipped troops, 16 stretchers plus a medical team, palleted internal loads, or can carry externally slung loads of up to 5,443 kg (12,000 lb). Main passenger door/emergency exit at front on port side with additional emergency exits on starboard side and on each side of cabin at rear, above main landing gear sponson. Large sliding door at mid-cabin position on starboard side, with inset emergency exit. Commercial variant has baggage bay aft of cabin, with external access

PP9, the final pre-production EH 101, will be certificated as the civil Utility version

via door on port side. Cargo loading ramp/door at rear of cabin on military and utility versions. Cabin floor loading 976 kg/m² (200 lb/sq ft) on PP1.

SYSTEMS: Hamilton Standard/Microtecnica environmental control systems. Dual redundant integrated hydraulic system, pressurised by three Vickers pumps each supplying fluid at 207 bars (3,000 lb/sq in) nominal working pressure, with flow rates of 55, 59 and 60 litres (14.5, 15.6 and 15.9 US gallons; 12.1, 13.0 and 13.2 Imp gallons)/min respectively. Hydraulic system reservoirs are of the piston load pressurised type, with a nominal pressure of 0.97 bar (14 lb/sq in). Primary electrical system is 115/200V three-phase AC, powered by two Lucas brushless, oilspray-cooled 45kVA generators (90kVA if Lucas Spraymat blade ice protection system fitted), with one driven by main gearbox and the other by accessory gearbox, plus a third, separately driven standby alternator. APU for main engine air-starting, and to provide electric power, plus air for ECS, without running main engines or using external power supplies. Fire detection and suppression systems by Graviner and Walter Kidde respectively. BAJ Ltd four-float emergency flotation system.

AVIONICS: Integrated avionics systems of naval and military variants based on two MIL-STD-1553B multiplex databuses that link the basic aircraft management, avionics and mission systems. Integrated avionics system of commercial variant based on ARINC 429 data transfer bus. On naval variant, main processing element of the management system is a dual redundant aircraft management computer, which carries out navigation, control and display management, performance computation and health and usage monitoring of the principal systems (engines, drive systems, avionics and utilities); it also controls the basic bus. ASW version will have 360° search radar (GEC Ferranti Blue Kestrel in Merlin) in a chin radome, plus dipping sonar, advanced sonobuoy processing equipment and Racal ESM. GEC Avionics AQS-903 acoustic processing system and NGL mission recorder in UK Merlin. ASST (anti-ship surveillance and tracking) version will carry equipment for tactical surveillance and OTH (over the horizon) targeting, to locate and relay to a co-operating frigate the position of a target vessel, and for midcourse guidance of the frigate's missiles. On missions involving the patrol of an exclusive economic zone it can also, with suitable radar, monitor every hour all surface contacts within an area of 77,700 km² (30,000 sq miles); can patrol an EEZ 400 × 200 nm (740 × 370 km; 460 × 230 miles) twice in one sortie; and can effect boarding and inspection of surface vessels during fishing protection and anti-smuggling missions. On civil variant, a Canadian Marconi CMA-900 flight

management system will include a colour CRT display with graphics and alphanumeric capability; fuel flow, fuel quantity and specific range computations; tuning of nav/com radios; interfaces with electronic instrument systems; two-dimensional multi-sensor navigation; and built-in navigational database with update service. Smiths Industries/OMI SEP 20 dual redundant digital AFCS is standard, providing fail-operational auto-stabilisation and four-axis autopilot modes (auto hover, auto transitions to/from hover standard on naval variants, optional on commercial and military variants). AFCS sensors on naval variant include British Aerospace LINS 300 ring laser gyro inertial reference unit (IRU) and Litton Italia LISA-4000 strapdown AHRS; IRU also provides self-contained navigation, with Racal Doppler 91E velocity sensor; GEC-Plessey GPS receiver selected for Royal Navy variant, Euronav GPS for Italian Navy aircraft. AFCS sensors on commercial variant include two Litton Italia LISA-4000 strapdown AHRS. Advanced flight deck incorporates standard Smiths Industries/OMI electronic instrument system (EIS) providing colour flight instrument, navigation and power systems displays. Other avionics on naval variants include GEC-Plessey/Elettronica PA 5015 I-band radar altimeters, GEC Avionics low airspeed sensing and air data system, MEL pilot's mission display unit, Alenia/Racal cabin mission display unit, and Alenia/GEC Ferranti aircraft management computer. Elmer HF and V/UHF com radios and radio/nav equipment on Italian Navy variant. On commercial variant, standard avionics include Penny and Giles air data system, Racal intercom system, optional Collins or Bendix/King communications and navigation systems, optional Honeywell or Bendix/King weather radar.

EQUIPMENT: ASW variants will have two sonobuoy dispensers, external rescue hoist and Fairey Hydraulics deck lock (UK Merlin).

ARMAMENT (naval and military utility versions): Naval version able to carry up to four homing torpedoes (probably Marconi Sting Ray on UK Merlin) or other weapons. ASV version designed to carry air-to-surface missiles and other weapons, for use as appropriate, from strikes against major units using sea-skimming anti-ship missiles to small-arms deterrence of smugglers. Armament optional on military versions.

DIMENSIONS, EXTERNAL:
Main rotor diameter	18.59 m (61 ft 0 in)
Tail rotor diameter	4.01 m (13 ft 2 in)
Length:	
overall, both rotors turning	22.81 m (74 ft 10 in)
main rotor and tail pylon folded (naval variant)	
	16.00 m (52 ft 6 in)

Width: excl main rotor	4.52 m (14 ft 10 in)
main rotor and tail pylon folded (naval variant)	
	5.49 m (18 ft 0 in)
Height: overall, both rotors turning	6.65 m (21 ft 10 in)
main rotor and tail pylon folded (naval variant)	
	5.21 m (17 ft 1 in)
Passenger door (fwd, port):	
Height	1.70 m (5 ft 7 in)
Width	0.97 m (3 ft 2 in)
Sliding cargo door (mid-cabin, stbd):	
Height	1.63 m (5 ft 4 in)
Width	1.83 m (6 ft 0 in)
Baggage compartment door (rear, port, Heliliner):	
Height	1.63 m (5 ft 4 in)
Width	0.79 m (2 ft 7 in)
Rear-loading ramp/door (rear, military/utility variant):	
Height	1.80 m (5 ft 11 in)
Width	2.11 m (6 ft 11 in)

DIMENSIONS, INTERNAL:
Cabin:	
Length: naval variant	7.09 m (23 ft 3 in)
commercial/utility variant	6.50 m (21 ft 4 in)
Max width	2.49 m (8 ft 2 in)
Width at floor	2.39 m (7 ft 10 in)
Max height	1.83 m (6 ft 0 in)
Volume: naval variant	29.0 m³ (1,024 cu ft)
Heliliner	27.5 m³ (970 cu ft)
Baggage compartment volume (Heliliner)	
	3.82 m³ (135 cu ft)

AREAS:
Main rotor disc	271.51 m² (2,922.5 sq ft)
Tail rotor disc	12.65 m² (136.2 sq ft)

WEIGHTS AND LOADINGS (A: naval variant, B: Heliliner, C: military/utility variant):
Basic weight empty (estimated): A	7,121 kg (15,700 lb)
B	6,967 kg (15,360 lb)
C	7,284 kg (16,060 lb)
Operating weight empty (estimated):	
A	9,298 kg (20,500 lb)
B (IFR, offshore equipped)	8,718 kg (19,220 lb)
C	8,618 kg (19,000 lb)
Max fuel weight (four internal tanks, total):	
A	3,438 kg (7,580 lb)
B, C	3,370 kg (7,430 lb)
Max fuel weight with optional auxiliary tank:	
A	4,298 kg (9,475 lb)
B, C	4,213 kg (9,288 lb)
Disposable load/payload:	
A (four torpedoes)	960 kg (2,116 lb)
B (30 passengers plus baggage)	2,721 kg (6,000 lb)
C (30 combat equipped troops)	4,309 kg (9,500 lb)
Max T-O weight: A	13,000 kg (28,660 lb)
	or 13,530 kg (29,830 lb)
B, C	14,288 kg (31,500 lb)

PERFORMANCE (estimated):
Never-exceed speed (VNE) at S/L, ISA	
	167 knots (309 km/h; 192 mph) IAS
Average cruising speed	160 knots (296 km/h; 184 mph)
Best range cruising speed	
	147 knots (272 km/h; 169 mph)
Best endurance speed	90 knots (167 km/h; 104 mph)
Range (B):	
standard fuel, offshore IFR equipped, with reserves, 30 passengers	550 nm (1,019 km; 633 miles)
auxiliary fuel, offshore IFR equipped, with reserves, 30 passengers	625 nm (1,158 km; 720 miles)
with zero T-O distance (Category A rules)	
	330 nm (611 km; 380 miles)
Ferry range:	
B (standard fuel, IFR equipped, with reserves)	
	630 nm (1,167 km; 725 miles)
B (auxiliary fuel, IFR equipped, with reserves)	
	800 nm (1,482 km; 921 miles)
C (standard fuel plus internal auxiliary tanks)	
	1,130 nm (2,094 km; 1,301 miles)

EMBRAER/FMA

PARTICIPATING COMPANIES:
Embraer: see under Brazil
FMA: see under Argentina

EMBRAER/FMA CBA-123 VECTOR

TYPE: Twin-propfan regional and corporate transport.

PROGRAMME: Begun (as EMB-123) as Embraer private venture mid-1985; first details released April 1986, three months after initial collaboration agreement with FMA (see Addenda to 1986-87 *Jane's*); redesignated CBA-123 (Co-operation Brazil-Argentina) on becoming fully international joint programme (then with 70/30 per cent sharing) 21 May 1987; work sharing defined March 1988; first metal cut March 1989; three flying prototypes (two in Brazil, one in Argentina): first flights 18 July 1990 (PT-ZVE, c/n 801), 15 March 1991 (PT-ZVB, c/n 802) and by Argentine prototype due June 1991 (c/n 803); certification (to Transport Category of FAR/JAR Pt 25 and FAR Pt 36, ICAO Annex 16) expected October

(CTA) and November 1991 (FAA); production start deferred until minimum of 20 firm orders received.

VARIANTS: **Commuter** version standard, **Executive** version optional.

CUSTOMERS: 99 paid options held in early 1991, incl 59 from US/Canadian/French/Finnish regional airlines, 20 from corporate customers in Brazil and 20 by Argentine Air Force.

COSTS: Development programme budgeted at US$300 million in September 1990, incl tooling for series production; unit price then quoted at US$4.8 million, but price reduction programme started in November 1990.

DESIGN FEATURES: Approx 60 per cent commonality with Embraer Brasilia (which see) but with shorter fuselage, new supercritical wing and rear-mounted propfans; low-mounted wing has Embraer aerofoil sections (root EA 160316/tip EA 160313), 3° dihedral, 2° root incidence (tip 0°) and 4° 8′ sweepback at quarter-chord; fuselage waisted at rear; sweptback T tail; undertail bumper to protect propeller blades during T-O rotation; pneumatic boot anti-icing of wing/tailplane/fin leading-edges.

FLYING CONTROLS: Mechanically actuated mass balanced ailerons and horn balanced elevators; hydraulically actuated tandem dual rudders; three-segment double-slotted Fowler flaps, actuated by electrically driven screwjacks; electrically signalled, hydraulically actuated two-segment ground spoilers/lift dumpers forward of each inboard flap; electrical (fly-by-wire) trimming of ailerons, rudders and variable incidence tailplane; single integrated flight director/autopilot AFCS standard, dual AFCS optional; stick pusher/shaker stall warning system.

STRUCTURE: Basic damage-tolerant structure of riveted 7000 series and 2024T-3 aluminium alloys, with extensive use of chemical milling; composites used for nose radome (glassfibre); wing/fin/tailplane leading-edges, wing/tailplane tips, wing/body fairing, dorsal fin, fin/tailplane bullet and engine pylon trailing-edges (Kevlar reinforced glassfibre); ailerons, elevators, rudders, flaps, spoilers, tailcone, landing gear doors, cowlings and engine pylon spars and skin (carbonfibre); and underseat panels (carbonfibre/Nomex); pylons have steel mounts and titanium leading-edges; one-piece, three-spar wing; pressurised fuselage. FMA currently has approx 20 per cent of manufacture, comprising front portion of centre-fuselage, sections 1 and 2 of rear fuselage, tailcone and undertail bumper, tail unit (except rudders) and engine pylons, with Embraer building remainder; assembly line will be set up in each country.

LANDING GEAR: Hydraulically retractable tricycle type, with twin wheels and oleo-pneumatic shock absorber on each unit. Mainwheels retract inward into wing/underfuselage fairing; nose unit retracts forward. Emergency free-fall extension capability. Hydraulically actuated nosewheel steering ($\pm 50°$). Mainwheel tyres size 22 × 6.75-10 (10 ply rating), pressure 7.24 bars (105 lb/sq in); nosewheel tyres size 16 × 4.4 (6 ply rating), pressure 5.17 bars (75 lb/sq in). Hydraulic carbon disc brakes with anti-skid provision. Backup braking system for use if one hydraulic system fails. Mechanical emergency and parking brake systems. High flotation tyres optional.

POWER PLANT: Two Garrett TPF351-20 or -20A propfans, each derated to 969 kW (1,300 shp) and driving a Hartzell HC-E6A-5 contra-rotating, slow-turning constant-speed pusher propeller with reversible pitch, autofeathering, synchrophasing, and six scimitar blades. Engines are pylon mounted in carbonfibre nacelles at rear of fuselage, and have FADEC control and a cruise/climb rating of 746 kW (1,000 shp). Fuel in integral wing tanks and auxiliary wing/body fairing tanks with combined capacity of 2,612 litres (690 US gallons; 574.5 Imp gallons). Single-point underwing pressure fuelling/defuelling, and two overwing gravity points. Oil capacity 9.5 litres (2.5 US gallons; 2.1 Imp gallons) per engine. Pneumatic inflatable de-icing boots on pylon leading-edges and engine air inlets.

ACCOMMODATION: Crew of two on flight deck, with dual controls; optional foldaway seat to rear for observer. Standard commuter cabin layout for 19 passengers, in five rows of three and a final four-seat row, at 79 cm (31 in) pitch, plus wardrobe, toilet, galley and seat for cabin attendant. Underseat and overhead bin stowage for carry-on baggage; main baggage/cargo compartment aft of rear row of seats. Executive interiors, to customer's requirements, available optionally. Hydraulically actuated downward opening plug type airstair door (Type II emergency exit) at front on port side, upward/inward sliding baggage door at rear on port side. Plug type passenger emergency exit above wing on each side; flight deck side windows serve as emergency exits for crew. Entire accommodation pressurised and air-conditioned. Electric anti-icing of windscreens.

SYSTEMS: Dual air-conditioning and pressurisation systems (max differential 0.56 bar; 8.2 lb/sq in), giving a S/L cabin atmosphere up to 6,400 m (21,000 ft) and a 2,440 m (8,000 ft) environment at altitudes up to 12,200 m (40,000 ft). Two independent hydraulic systems (each 207 bars; 3,000 lb/sq in). Primary electrical power supply is 28V DC, provided by two 400A engine driven starter/generators, two 150A brushless auxiliary generators, and two 24V 27Ah nickel-cadmium batteries. Additional 400A starter/generator can be driven by APU. Two 250VA solid state inverters for 115V and 26V single-phase AC power at 400Hz. Digital fly-by-wire system provides electric signalling of flap and rudder actuation. High pressure (127.5 bars; 1,850 lb/sq in) gaseous oxygen system for crew and passengers. Garrett GTCP36-150 (AA) APU for environmental control system and electrical power generation.

AVIONICS: Generally similar to those for EMB-120 Brasilia. Standard basic Collins EFIS-86/EICAS fit will include two Pro Line II VHF com, audio distribution system, two VHF nav (VOR/ILS/marker beacon receiver), DME, WXR-350 colour weather radar, ADF, two ATC transponders with altitude encoders, two EADI, ALI-850 multifunction display system (CRT altimeter/preselector/VSI), two AHS-85 AHRS, two RMI, standby attitude indicator, standby magnetic compass, ELT, PA system, cabin interphone and dual APS-65 autopilots. Options include GPWS, flight data recorder, Selcal, MLS and FMS.

DIMENSIONS, EXTERNAL:

Wing span	17.72 m (58 ft 1½ in)
Wing chord: at root	2.50 m (8 ft 2½ in)
at tip	0.99 m (3 ft 3 in)
Wing aspect ratio	11.5
Length overall	18.09 m (59 ft 4¼ in)
Fuselage: Length	16.90 m (55 ft 5½ in)
Max diameter	2.28 m (7 ft 5¾ in)

First prototype CBA-123 Vector 19-passenger commuter and executive transport

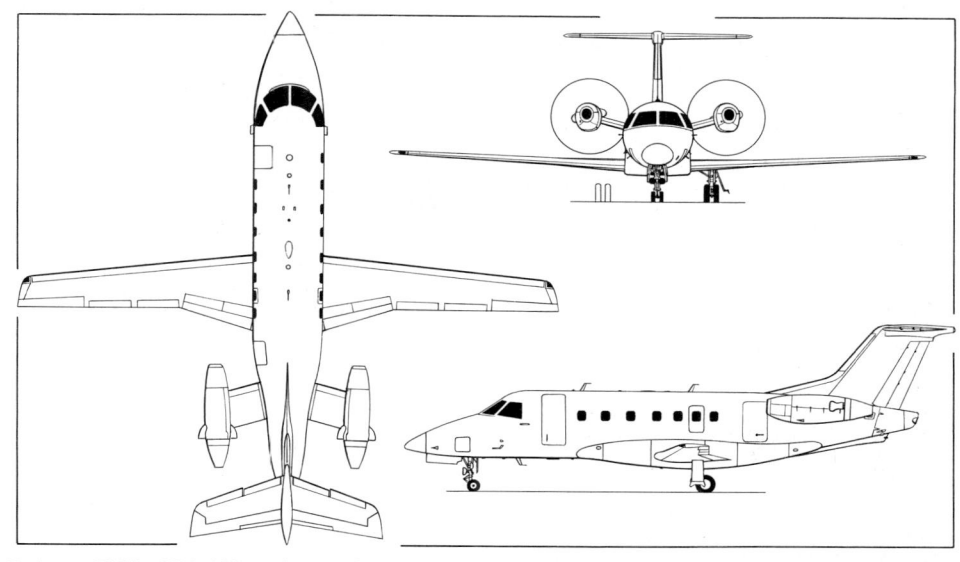

Embraer/FMA CBA-123 twin-propfan transport under development by Brazil and Argentina
(Pilot Press)

Height overall	5.97 m (19 ft 7 in)
Elevator span	6.31 m (20 ft 8½ in)
Wheel track (c/l of shock struts)	3.56 m (11 ft 8¼ in)
Wheelbase	7.53 m (24 ft 8½ in)
Propeller diameter	2.59 m (8 ft 6 in)
Propeller ground clearance: min	1.58 m (5 ft 2¼ in)
max	1.63 m (5 ft 4¼ in)
Distance between propeller centres	4.50 m (14 ft 9¼ in)
Passenger door (fwd, port): Height	1.70 m (5 ft 7 in)
Width	0.77 m (2 ft 6¼ in)
Height to sill	1.52 m (4 ft 11¾ in)
Baggage door (rear, port): Height	1.35 m (4 ft 5¼ in)
Width	0.80 m (2 ft 7½ in)
Height to sill	1.75 m (5 ft 9 in)
Emergency exits (two, each):	
Height	0.92 m (3 ft 0¼ in)
Width	0.51 m (1 ft 8 in)
Height to sill	2.02 m (6 ft 7½ in)
DIMENSIONS, INTERNAL:	
Cabin: Length	6.47 m (21 ft 2¾ in)
Max width	2.10 m (6 ft 10¾ in)
Max height	1.76 m (5 ft 9¼ in)
Baggage compartment volume	4.25 m³ (150 cu ft)
AREAS:	
Wings, gross	27.2 m² (292.8 sq ft)
Ailerons (total)	1.20 m² (12.92 sq ft)
Trailing-edge flaps (total)	4.63 m² (49.84 sq ft)
Spoilers (total)	1.49 m² (16.00 sq ft)
Engine pylons (total)	3.00 m² (32.29 sq ft)
Fin	4.23 m² (45.53 sq ft)
Rudder	1.79 m² (19.27 sq ft)
Tailplane	5.61 m² (60.39 sq ft)
Elevators (total)	2.40 m² (25.83 sq ft)

WEIGHTS AND LOADINGS:	
Basic operating weight empty	6,267 kg (13,816 lb)
Max fuel weight	2,242 kg (4,942 lb)
Max payload	2,233 kg (4,923 lb)
Max T-O weight	9,500 kg (20,944 lb)
Max ramp weight	9,540 kg (21,032 lb)
Max zero-fuel weight	8,500 kg (18,739 lb)
Max landing weight	9,250 kg (20,392 lb)
Max wing loading	349.3 kg/m² (71.54 lb/sq ft)
Max power loading	4.90 kg/kW (8.05 lb/shp)
PERFORMANCE (at max T-O weight):	
Max cruising speed at 7,315 m (24,000 ft)	
	351 knots (650 km/h; 404 mph)
Max rate of climb at S/L	716 m (2,350 ft)/min
Rate of climb at S/L, one engine out	
	158 m (520 ft)/min
Service ceiling	11,000 m (36,000 ft)
Service ceiling, one engine out	5,485 m (18,000 ft)
T-O to 15 m (50 ft):	
FAR 25 at S/L, ISA	1,440 m (4,725 ft)
at 1,525 m (5,000 ft), ISA + 20°C	1,990 m (6,530 ft)
Landing from 15 m (50 ft):	
FAR 135 at S/L, ISA	1,210 m (3,970 ft)
at 1,525 m (5,000 ft), ISA + 20°C	1,390 m (4,560 ft)
Min ground turning radius	10.04 m (32 ft 11 in)
Range at max cruising speed (ISA), reserves for 100 nm	
(185 km; 115 mile) diversion and 45 min hold:	
with 19 passengers	850 nm (1,575 km; 978 miles)
with max fuel	1,860 nm (3,447 km; 2,141 miles)
OPERATIONAL NOISE LEVELS (estimated, ±2 EPNdB):	
T-O	76.1 EPNdB
Sideline	81.0 EPNdB
Approach	91.6 EPNdB

EUROCOPTER INTERNATIONAL
EUROCOPTER INTERNATIONAL GIE

2-20 avenue Marcel Cachin, 93126 La Courneuve Cédex, France

Telephone: 33 (1) 48 38 91 78

Fax: 33 (1) 48 38 91 78

Telex: 212836 F AISPA X

PARTICIPATING COMPANIES:
Aerospatiale: see under France
DASA: see under Germany

Combining of Aerospatiale and MBB helicopter activities announced after signing of MoU in April 1990. Eurocopter

International GIE formed 6 May 1991 to market both groups' helicopters everywhere except North America; company equally owned by Aerospatiale and DASA. By end 1991, a holding company Eurocopter SA will take Eurocopter International as a wholly owned subsidiary; the helicopter divisions will also become subsidiaries; existing Eurocopter GmbH, developing Tiger/Gerfaut, will join Eurocopter SA.

EUROCOPTER GmbH

Gustav Heinemann Ring 135 (Postfach 830356), 8000
 Munich 83, Germany
Telephone: 49 (89) 638250-0
Fax: 49 (89) 638250-50
CHIEF EXECUTIVE OFFICERS:
 Bernard Darrieus
 Ingo Jaschke
PARTICIPATING COMPANIES:
 Aerospatiale: see under France
 DASA: see under Germany

Eurocopter GmbH established 18 September 1985 as wholly owned subsidiary of Eurocopter GIE in Paris, to manage Franco-German battlefield helicopter programme; executive authority for programme is DFHB (Deutsch-Französisches Hubschrauberbüro) in Koblenz; procurement agency is BWB (Bundesamt für Wehrtechnik und Beschaffung).

EUROCOPTER TIGER/TIGRE/GERFAUT

TYPE: Twin-engined anti-tank and ground support helicopter.

PROGRAMME: Original 1984 MoU between French and German defence ministers, to develop common new anti-tank helicopter, was halted mid-1986, after cost escalation, to reappraise requirements and aircraft specifications; re-launched March 1987 on basis of common anti-tank version (PAH-2/HAC) plus HAP escort version for France; MoU amended accordingly 13 November 1987; FSD approved 8 December 1987; main development contract awarded 30 November 1989, when name Tiger (Germany)/Tigre (France) adopted; five development aircraft planned, comprising three unarmed aerodynamic prototypes (PT1, 2 and 3), one (PT4) in HAP configuration and one (PT5) as PAH-2/HAC prototype; PT1 rolled out 4 February 1991; first flight 27 April 1991, with PT2 to fly 1992 followed by rest at approx six-monthly intervals; PT2/3 will be avionics testbeds, later being retrofitted for HAP and PAH-2/HAC weapons trials respectively; joint team at Marignane to flight test basic helicopter, update avionics fit during trials, and test HAP variant; similar team at Ottobrunn to qualify basic avionics, Euromep mission equipment package, and weapons system integration. Aerospatiale responsible for transmission, tail rotor, centre-fuselage (incl engine installation), aerodynamics, fuel and electrical systems, weight control, maintainability, reliability and survivability; MBB for main rotor, flight control and hydraulic systems, front and rear fuselage (incl cockpits), prototype assembly, flight characteristics and performance, stress and vibration testing, and simulation.

VARIANTS: **HAP Gerfaut** (Hélicoptère d'Appui Protection): Escort and fire support version for French Army, for delivery from 1997; armed with 30 mm GIAT AM-30781 automatic cannon in undernose turret, with 150-450 rds ammunition; four Matra Mistral infra-red homing air-to-air missiles and two pods each with twenty-two 68 mm unguided SNEB rockets, mounted on stub-wings, or 12-round rocket pod instead of each pair of Mistrals, making total of 68 rockets; roof mounted TV, FLIR, laser rangefinder and direct-optics sensors.

PAH-2 Tiger (Panzerabwehr-Hubschrauber, 2nd generation): Variant of common anti-tank version for German Army, for delivery from 1998: underwing pylons for up to eight Hot 2 or Trigat long-range anti-tank missiles, or four Hot 2 plus four Trigat (inboard) and four Stinger 2 air-to-air self-defence missiles (outboard); mast mounted TV/FLIR/tracker/laser rangefinder sighting system for gunner; nose mounted FLIR night vision device for piloting.

HAC Tigre (Hélicoptère Anti-Char): Anti-tank variant for French Army, for delivery from 1998; wing pylons for up to eight Hot 2 or Trigat missiles (or four Hot 2 and four Trigat) inboard, four Matra Mistral air-to-air missiles outboard; mast mounted sight and pilot FLIR system similar to that of PAH-2.

CUSTOMERS: Estimated 427 required initially (France 75 HAP and 140 HAC, Germany 212 PAH-2); under consideration by Spain, UK and others.

DESIGN FEATURES: Four-blade semi-rigid main rotor, with two elastomeric bearings per blade; rotor hub comprises two starplates bolted together with titanium spacer, permitting installation of mast mounted sight (MMS); newly developed DMH blade aerofoil sections/geometries, promising performance improvements of about 10 per cent over most existing systems and requisite agility for anti-tank missions; three-blade Aerospatiale Spheriflex tail rotor (OA blade section) on starboard side; main transmission features separate load paths, high run-dry capability (up to 30 min), and compatibility with MMS; low-drag fuselage; stub wings with anhedral on outer panels; sweptback fin/tail rotor pylon and underfin; horizontal stabiliser with sweptback auxiliary fins; ram air infra-red engine exhaust suppressors.

FLYING CONTROLS: Duplex primary hydraulic servo-controls, controlled by autopilot and trim, and duplex main hydraulic servo-controls to generate control loads towards rotors; redundant, four-axis duplex AFCS with

The first Eurocopter Tiger at Ottobrunn before being shipped to Marseille Marignane for its first flight in April 1991

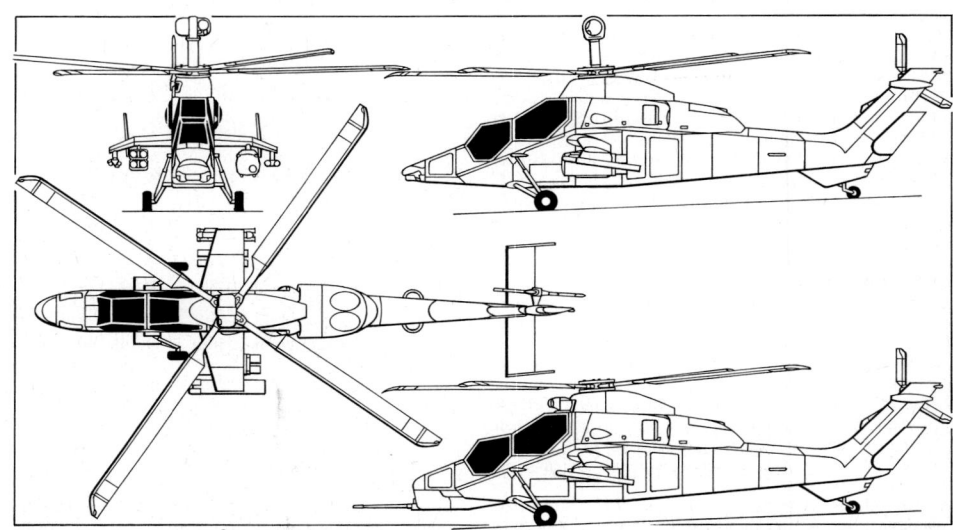

Eurocopter PAH-2 Tiger/HAC Tigre anti-tank helicopter, with additional side view (bottom) of the HAP Gerfaut escort and support version *(Jane's/Mike Keep)*

stabilisation and autopilot functions; SAMM/Liebherr main and tail rotor servo-controls; Labinal/Electrométal servo trim.

STRUCTURE: Extensive use of composites, meeting criteria for safety, crash resistance (to MIL-STD-1290 standards) and damage tolerance (survivable against hits from weapons of up to 23 mm calibre, or 12.7 mm for main transmission); fibre composite blades and starplates; fuselage and wings mainly of carbonfibre, with glassfibre or Kevlar fairings; main features are compact, robust construction, small number of parts, and ease of maintenance.

LANDING GEAR: Non-retractable tailwheel type, with single wheel on each unit. Designed to absorb impacts of up to 6 m (20 ft)/s. Main gear by Messier-Bugatti, tail gear by Liebherr Aerotechnik.

POWER PLANT: Two 958 kW (1,285 shp) MTU/Rolls-Royce/Turbomeca MTR 390 turboshafts, mounted side by side above centre-fuselage. (Engine first flown in Panther testbed 14 February 1991.) Self-sealing crashworthy fuel tanks, with explosion suppression and total capacity of 1,360 litres (359 US gallons; 299 Imp gallons).

ACCOMMODATION: Crew of two in tandem, with pilot in front and weapons system operator at rear. Armoured, impact-absorbing seats. Stepped cockpits, with flat-plate transparencies.

SYSTEMS: Redundant hydraulic, electrical and fuel systems.

AVIONICS: Essential characteristics will be common to both French and German versions, and European in origin.

Systems architecture is based on a MIL-STD-1553B databus. Via two central computers with symbol generation, information for pilot and gunner is shown on multi-function displays in cockpit. Essential flight data for pilot are also displayed by backup conventional instruments. Navigation subsystem consists of two identical strapdown units together with such sensors as ASI, Doppler radar, radar altimeter and magnetic sensor. Subsystem conducts functions of autonomous navigation as well as flight path computation, and supplies data necessary for AFCS and mission equipment packages. A Thomson-CSF/SEL integrated radar/laser threat warning subsystem will be installed to recognise, identify and classify specific threats. Provisions are made for comprehensive additional active ECM. Subcontractors so far announced include Rohde und Schwarz/Sextant Avionique (control and display unit); Teldix GmbH (licence for Canadian Marconi CMA 2012 Doppler velocity sensor); and Dornier/VDO-L (digital map display system). *Anti-tank mission* equipment package, based on a MIL-STD-1553B redundant databus, comprises electro-optical system with mast mounted sight, piloting vision system and gunner's sight, and combined helmet mounted sight and display, plus armament according to variant. Mast mounted sight, controlled by gunner, is a multi-sensor system with TV and infra-red channels and various fields of view. Electro-optical system is stabilised, includes tracker for single and multiple targets, a laser rangefinder, and cockpit display.

Nose mounted IR sensor (piloting vision system, or PVS) image is displayed and steered via helmet sight display; in the event of PVS loss, the gunner's redundant IR image can be used. Mission equipment of HAP *escort/combat support version* is also based on MIL-STD-1553B redundant databus, which interconnects firing control and redundant bus management computer, gunner's sight, HUD, gun turret, rockets, air-to-air missiles, pilot's and gunner's helmet sights, and pilot's and gunner's armament control unit. Between all three versions some equipment (eg com radios, sand filters) will vary according to individual operator's specifications.

ARMAMENT: As listed under Variants.

DIMENSIONS, EXTERNAL:	
Main rotor diameter	13.00 m (42 ft 7¾ in)
Tail rotor diameter	2.70 m (8 ft 10¼ in)
Length of fuselage	14.00 m (45 ft 11¼ in)
Height to top of rotor head	3.81 m (12 ft 6 in)
Wing span	4.32 m (14 ft 2 in)
Wheel track	2.40 m (7 ft 10½ in)
Wheelbase	approx 7.95 m (26 ft 1 in)
AREAS:	
Main rotor disc	132.7 m² (1,428.7 sq ft)
Tail rotor disc	5.72 m² (61.63 sq ft)

WEIGHTS AND LOADINGS:	
Basic weight empty	3,300 kg (7,275 lb)
Mission T-O weight	
	5,300 to 5,800 kg (11,685 to 12,787 lb)
Max overload T-O weight	6,000 kg (13,227 lb)
PERFORMANCE (estimated, at AUW of 5,400 kg; 11,905 lb):	
Cruising speed	
	135-151 knots (250-280 km/h; 155-174 mph)
Max rate of climb at S/L more than 600 m (1,970 ft)/min	
Hovering ceiling OGE	more than 2,000 m (6,560 ft)
Endurance, incl 20 min reserves	2 h 50 min

EUROFAR
EUROPEAN FUTURE ADVANCED ROTORCRAFT

PARTICIPATING COMPANIES:
Aerospatiale: see under France
Agusta: see under Italy
Alenia: see under Italy
CASA: see under Spain
DASA: see under Germany
Westland: see under UK

EUROFAR

TYPE: Twin-turboshaft tilt-rotor transport.

PROGRAMME: Accord signed September 1986 by above six companies to collaborate in three-year preliminary study of a European convertiplane, initially for civil applications, with Agusta leading working group to define specification; first flight (tentative) 1994.

COSTS: Study funded approx 75 per cent from EC Eureka technology programme, which voted £31.5 million in September 1987, and 25 per cent by participating companies (Agusta/Alenia, DASA and Aerospatiale 29 per cent each, CASA and Westland 6.5 per cent each).

POWER PLANT: Two 2,983 kW (4,000 shp) class turboshafts (various alternatives under consideration).

ACCOMMODATION: 30 passengers.

DIMENSIONS, EXTERNAL (provisional):
Rotor diameter (each)
10-11 m (32 ft 10 in - 36 ft 1 in)
Wing span   15.00 m (49 ft 2½ in)

Artist's impression of a possible Eurofar civil tilt-rotor aircraft for the mid-1990s

WEIGHTS AND LOADINGS (provisional):
Max T-O weight   13,000 kg (28,660 lb)

PERFORMANCE (provisional):
Cruising speed   313 knots (580 km/h; 360 mph)
Range   539 nm (1,000 km; 621 miles)

EUROFIGHTER
EUROFIGHTER JAGDFLUGZEUG GmbH

Arabellastrasse 16 (Postfach 860366), 8000 Munich 81, Germany
Telephone: 49 (89) 92803-1
Fax: 49 (89) 92803-443
Telex: 5213908 or 5213744
CHAIRMAN: Dott Ing R. Mannu
MANAGING DIRECTOR: F. G. Willox
MARKETING: A. French
PUBLICITY EXECUTIVE: Ursula Kruse

Eurofighter GmbH formed to manage EFA programme June 1986, followed shortly after by Eurojet Turbo GmbH to manage engine programme; NEFMA (NATO European Fighter Management Agency) supervises EFA programme.

EUROPEAN FIGHTER AIRCRAFT (EFA)

TYPE: Single-seat, highly agile STOL-capable fighter, optimised for air defence/air superiority; secondary capability for ground attack.

PROGRAMME: Outline staff target for common combat aircraft issued December 1983 by air chiefs of staff of France, Germany, Italy, Spain and UK; initial feasibility study launched July 1984; France withdrew July 1985, shareholdings then being readjusted to 33 per cent each to UK and Germany, 21 per cent Italy and 13 per cent Spain; project definition phase completed September 1986; definitive ESR-D (Europèan Staff Requirement - Development) issued September 1987, giving military requirements in greater detail; definition refinement and risk reduction stage completed December 1987; main engine and weapons system development contracts signed 23 November 1988; first flight scheduled for 1992, all seven prototypes by 1994, and first production aircraft 1996-97. Static and fatigue test airframes being built, plus seven flying prototypes (P01-P07), with flight testing in all four countries: P01/06 in Germany (starting 1992), P02/03/05 in UK (starting mid-1992), P04 in Italy and P07 in Spain; P03 (the first with EJ200 engines) and P07 will be two-seaters, P05 (first with ECR 90 radar) and P06 the main avionics testbeds. P01 and P02 entered final assembly in first half of 1991; P03 due to do so in January 1992. BAe responsible for front fuselage, foreplanes, starboard leading-edge slats and flaperons; MBB/Dornier the centre-fuselage, fin and rudder; Alenia the port wing, incl all movable surfaces; Alenia/CASA the rear fuselage; and CASA/BAe the starboard wing; no duplication of tooling; final assembly line at each manufacturer's facility.

Artist's impression of Eurofighter EFA. The first of eight prototypes should fly in 1992

VARIANTS: **Single-seater:** Standard version.
Two-seater: For conversion/operational training.

CUSTOMERS: Approx 700 required by partner nations (Germany 160-200, UK 250, Italy 165, Spain 100, each batch including some two-seaters); export orders also anticipated.

DESIGN FEATURES: Collaborative design by BAe, MBB/Dornier, Alenia and CASA, incorporating some design and technology (incl low detectability) from BAe EAP programme (see UK section of 1990-91 and earlier *Jane's*); low wing, low aspect ratio tail-less delta with 53° leading-edge sweepback; underfuselage box with side by side engine air intakes, each with fixed upper wedge/ramp and vari-cowl (variable position lower cowl lip) with Dowty actuators.

FLYING CONTROLS: Two-segment automatic slats on wing leading-edges, inboard and outboard flaperons on trailing-edges; all-moving nose-mounted foreplanes in line with windscreen; rudder; hydraulically actuated airbrake aft of canopy, forming part of dorsal spine; Liebherr primary flight control actuators. Full-authority four-channel ACT (active control technology) digital fly-by-wire flight control system (team leader MBB), combined with mission adaptive configuring and aircraft's artificial instability in pitch, to provide required

'carefree' handling, gust alleviation and high sustained manoeuvrability throughout flight envelope; pitch and roll control via foreplane/flaperon ACT to provide artificial longitudinal stability; yaw control via rudder; no manual reversion. Quadruplex AFCS will operate through a STANAG 3838 NATO standard databus and will ensure that pilot cannot exceed aircraft's flying limits.

STRUCTURE: Fuselage, wings (incl inboard flaperons), fin and rudder mainly of CFC (carbonfibre composites) except for foreplanes, outboard flaperons and exhaust nozzles (titanium); nose radome and fin-tip (GFRP); leading-edge slats, wingtip pods, fin leading-edge, rudder trailing-edge and major fairings (aluminium-lithium alloy); and canopy surround (magnesium alloy); manufacture, using such advanced techniques as superplastic forming and diffusion bonding, overseen by CASA-led joint structures team.

Most subsystems are being developed by multi-nation teams; in the following description, for clarity, team leaders only are named:

LANDING GEAR: Dowty Aerospace retractable tricycle type. Single-wheel main units retract inward into fuselage, steerable nosewheel unit forward.

POWER PLANT: First two prototypes each powered by two Turbo-Union RB199-122 afterburning turbofans (each more than 71.2 kN; 16,000 lb st). Third and subsequent prototypes, and production aircraft, will have two Eurojet EJ200 advanced technology turbofans (each of approx 60 kN; 13,490 lb st dry and 90 kN; 20,250 lb nominal thrust with afterburning), mounted side by side in rear fuselage with ventral intakes. Dornier digital engine control system. Lucas Aerospace fuel management system. Provision for in-flight refuelling and up to three external fuel tanks.

ACCOMMODATION: Pilot only, on zero/zero ejection seat. Smiths Industries glareshields.

SYSTEMS: Normalair-Garrett environmental control system. Magnaghi hydraulic system. Lucas Aerospace electrical system, with GEC Ferranti-Bendix variable speed constant frequency generator and GEC Ferranti transformer-rectifier units. Alenia-led utilities control system (UCS), controlled by microcomputer. Garrett APU for engine starting, systems running and NBC filtering. Microturbo UK air turbine starter motor.

AVIONICS: BAe has overall team leadership for avionics development and integration. Primary sensor will be GEC Ferranti ECR 90 multi-mode pulse Doppler radar with an interception range of 50-80 nm (92.5-148 km; 57.5-92 miles), able to acquire at least 85 per cent of probable targets (including eight targets simultaneously), and to direct lookdown/shootdown and snap-up weapons against them. Other radar requirements include velocity and single-target search, track-while-scan and range-while-scan, target priority processing, automatic weapons selection, and recommended combat tactics display. In attack mode, it will have capability for ground mapping/ranging and terrain avoidance, but not terrain following. Radar will form part of a comprehensive avionics suite which also includes Rohde & Schwarz Saturn VHF/UHF communications, and a Marconi Defence Systems advanced integrated defensive aids support system (DASS) which includes an ESM/ECM pod at each wingtip. All avionics, flight control and utilities control systems will be integrated through STANAG 3838 NATO standard databus highways with appropriate redundancy levels, using fibre optics and microprocessors. Special attention has been given to reducing pilot workload. New cockpit techniques will simplify flying the aircraft safely and effectively to the limits of the flight envelope while monitoring and managing the aircraft and its operational systems, and detecting/identifying/attacking desired targets while remaining safe from enemy defences. This will be achieved through a high level of system integration and automation, including HOTAS (hands on throttle and stick); a GEC Avionics wide-angle HUD able to display, in addition to other symbology, FLIR pictures from a FIAR Pirate (Passive Infra-Red Airborne Track Equipment) sensor pod-mounted externally to the left of the cockpit; a helmet mounted sight (HMS), with direct voice input (DVI) for appropriate functions; and three Smiths Industries multi-function head-down (MFHD) colour CRT displays. Other cockpit instrumentation includes a Computing Devices video and voice recorder, GEC Ferranti (Elmer) crash survival memory unit, and Teldix cockpit interface unit.

ARMAMENT: Interceptor will have an internally mounted 27 mm Mauser gun on starboard side, plus a mix of medium-range AIM-120 AMRAAM or Aspide and short-range air-to-air missiles carried externally, four of the former being mounted in tandem pairs in a semi-recessed underfuselage installation. The short-range missiles are carried on ML Aviation underwing ejector release units. The EFA will, if necessary, be able to carry a considerable overload of air-to-air weapons. For secondary role air-to-surface weapons, and/or auxiliary fuel tanks, it will have a total of 13 external stores stations: five (incl one wet) on fuselage and four (incl one wet) on each wing.

DIMENSIONS, EXTERNAL:
Wing span   10.50 m (34 ft 5½ in)

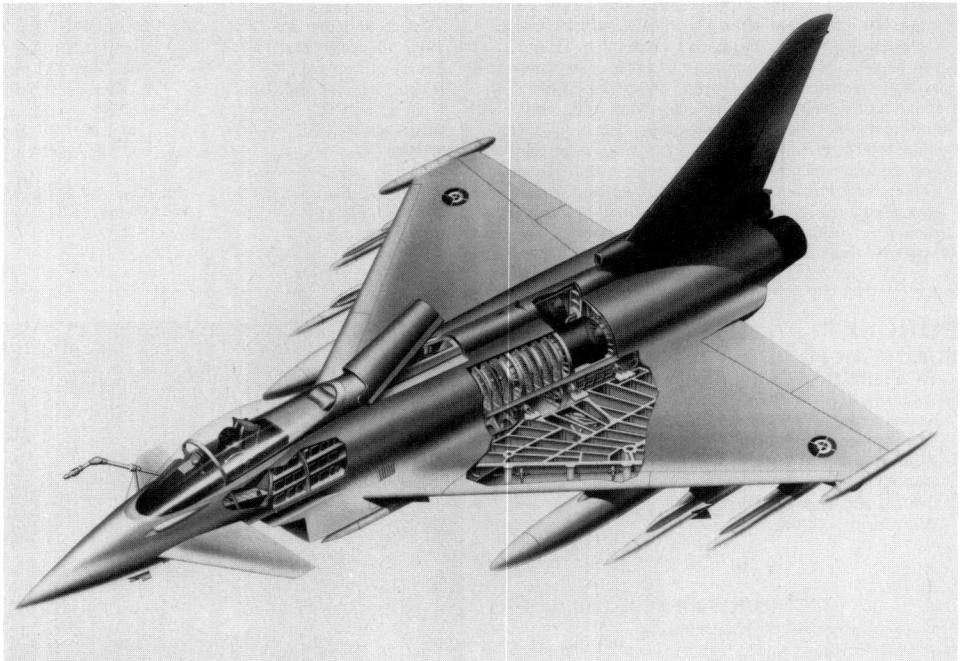

Partly cutaway drawing showing the wing structure, airbrake, avionics bay and refuelling boom of the Eurofighter EFA

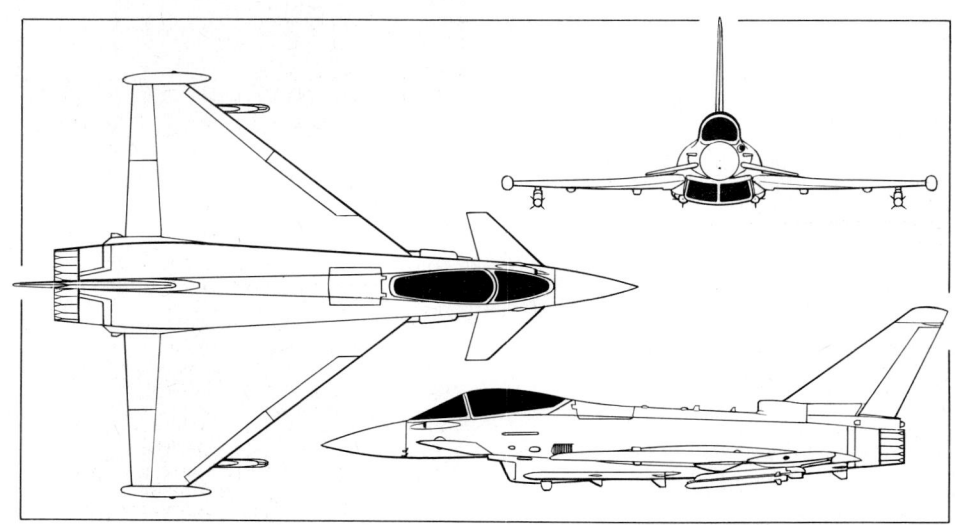

Three-view drawing of Eurofighter EFA (European Fighter Aircraft), under development for four European air forces *(Pilot Press)*

Wing aspect ratio	2.205
Length overall	14.50 m (47 ft 7 in)
AREAS:	
Wings, gross	50.0 m² (538.2 sq ft)
WEIGHTS AND LOADINGS (approx):	
Weight empty	9,750 kg (21,495 lb)
Internal fuel load	4,000 kg (8,818 lb)
External stores load (weapons and/or fuel)	
	6,500 kg (14,330 lb)
Max T-O weight	21,000 kg (46,297 lb)

PERFORMANCE (design):
Max level speed   more than Mach 1.8
T-O and landing distance with full internal fuel and two AMRAAM plus two air-to-air missiles, ISA + 15°C   500 m (1,640 ft)
Combat radius
                   250-300 nm (463-556 km; 288-345 miles)
g limits with full internal fuel and two AMRAAM missiles   +9/-3

EUROFLAG
EUROFLAG srl
TEMPORARY ADDRESS: c/o Alenia, Via Petrolini 2, 00197 Rome, Italy
INFORMATION: A. Felici
PARTICIPATING COMPANIES:
Aerospatiale: see under France
Alenia: see under Italy
British Aerospace: see under UK
CASA: see under Spain
Deutsche Airbus: see under Germany

FUTURE LARGE AIRCRAFT (FLA)
TYPE: Multi-engined military tactical transport.
PROGRAMME: Earlier FIMA programme (see 1989-90 *Jane's*) replaced April 1989 by new five-nation MoU to develop new-technology Lockheed C-130/Transall C-160 replacement, meeting NATO and other European requirements, for service early next century; first flight expected approx 2000, with deliveries beginning two years later, assuming FSD starts 1996; outline European

Artist's impression of the five-nation Euroflag Future Large Aircraft as currently envisaged

staff target (OEST) reportedly frozen by early 1991; formation of Euroflag srl to manage programme expected mid-1991; hopes for pre-feasibility study funding in 1992.

VARIANTS: Primarily for personnel/cargo transport; derivatives may include air-refuelling tanker, surveillance/reconnaissance, long-range maritime patrol and AEW.

CUSTOMERS: Air forces of Belgium, France, Germany, Italy, Spain, Turkey and UK probable, plus possible exports; overall market estimated at 700-1,000 aircraft.

DESIGN FEATURES: Still flexible, but currently seen as high-wing, T-tailed aircraft with rough-field landing gear and much larger cabin/hold floor area and cross-section

than C-130/C-160, permitting high payload factors with low-density cargo, vehicles or mixed passenger/cargo loads and resulting in enhanced payload/range performance plus major savings in fleet operating costs and manpower.

STRUCTURE: Modern design/manufacturing techniques expected to afford major reductions in maintenance man-hour requirements and increases in aircraft availability/survivability.

POWER PLANT: Type and number of engines will be based on availability in mid-1990s of suitably sized new-generation civil or military engines (probably turbofans); all engine configuration options remain under study.

ACCOMMODATION: Probable two-man flight deck.
WEIGHTS AND LOADINGS (provisional):
Design payload
　　　　20,000-25,000 kg (44,090-55,115 lb)
Max T-O weight
　　　　80,000-115,000 kg (176,370-253,530 lb)
PERFORMANCE (provisional):
Econ cruising speed (depending on engine choice)
　　　　Mach 0.65-0.75
Range with design payload
　　2,000-2,500 nm (3,706-4,633 km; 2,303-2,879 miles)

EURO HERMESPACE
EURO HERMESPACE SA
Toulouse, France
PRESIDENT:
　Dr Johann Schäffler (Deutsche Aerospace)
DEPUTY CHIEF EXECUTIVE OFFICER:
　Philippe Couillard (Aerospatiale)
PARTICIPATING COMPANIES:
　Aerospatiale: see under France
　Alenia: see under Italy
　Dassault: see under France
　DASA: see under Germany
Agreement signed 7 November 1990 to create Euro Hermespace in mid-1991 as industrial prime contractor for development/production/operation of Hermès European aerospacecraft under authority of European Space Agency; shareholdings Hermespace France (Aerospatiale 51 per cent/Dassault Aviation 49 per cent) 51.6 per cent, Deutsche Aerospace 33.4 per cent, Alenia 15 per cent; other participating nations include Austria, Belgium, Canada, Denmark, Netherlands, Norway, Spain, Sweden and Switzerland.

HERMÈS
TYPE: Re-usable space shuttle to service Columbus and other space stations.

PROGRAMME: Originated 1978 as French national programme, CNES (Centre National d'Études Spatiales) appointing Aerospatiale as industrial prime contractor on 18 October 1985 to build two vehicles over 10-year period, with Dassault responsible for validating successful flight within the atmosphere; became fully international European programme with signing of November 1990 MoU; Aermacchi currently building new wind tunnel model to final configuration; subsonic test flights originally targeted for 1996, first unmanned flight for 1998 and first manned mission for 1999, but cost-cutting moves in early 1991 seemed likely to result in stretchout of this programme by about two years.

CUSTOMERS: Europe to build two Hermès for own requirements; other sales (eg to NASA) possible.

COSTS: Overall programme estimated at approx US$4.5 billion in 1990.

DESIGN FEATURES: Recoverable delta-wing vehicle (Dassault-led design) with upturned winglets and rudders at tips, plus expendable MRH (Module de Resources

Artist's impression of Hermès aerospacecraft complete with jettisonable resources module

Hermès); pressurised payload compartment linked by airlock tunnel to rear docking port; to save weight, MRH detaches immediately aft of wing just before re-entry.

STRUCTURE: Mainly of aluminium alloy, protected thermally by flexible quartz-fibre mats on upper surfaces and carbon/silica tiles on lower surfaces; nosecone and wing leading-edges of non-oxidising carbon/carbon.

POWER PLANT: To be placed in low Earth orbit (460 km; 286 miles) by Ariane 5 launcher; 20 N (4.5 lb) thrust SEP rocket motors for manoeuvre control in orbit.

ACCOMMODATION: Fully pressurised accommodation for crew of three (commander, pilot and mission specialist) and payload; individual ejection seats for crew, capable of operation during ascent phase (up to 25,000 m; 82,020 ft altitude and Mach 3 velocity) and during re-entry. Modified Mystère-Falcon 900 proposed for crew training.

SYSTEMS: Dornier developing environmental control and life support system (ECLSS).

DIMENSIONS, EXTERNAL (approx):
Wing span (winglet tip to winglet tip)
　　　　9.01 m (29 ft 6¾ in)
Length:
　in orbit (incl MRH)　　18.615 m (61 ft 0⅞ in)
　on re-entry (Hermès only)　12.69 m (41 ft 7⅝ in)
Fuselage: Max depth　　2.953 m (9 ft 8¼ in)
WEIGHTS AND LOADINGS:
Launch weight　　　29,000 kg (63,934 lb)
Orbiting weight　　　23,000 kg (50,705 lb)
Payload:
　outbound (incl. MRH)　　3,000 kg (6,614 lb)
　outbound, useful load　　1,600 kg (3,527 lb)
　Earthbound (incl fixtures)　1,500 kg (3,307 lb)
　Earthbound, useful load　　580 kg (1,279 lb)
Fuel　　　　　　1,500 kg (3,307 lb)
Re-entry weight　　　15,000 kg (33,069 lb)

JEH
JOINT EUROPEAN HELICOPTER
JEH formed November 1986 to manage proposed multi-national programme for multi-role light attack helicopter (LAH) known as Tonal, based on Agusta A 129 Mangusta (see Italian section); this programme cancelled in November 1990 (see 1990-91 edition for brief details).

MBB/KAWASAKI
PARTICIPATING COMPANIES:
　MBB: see under Germany
　Kawasaki: see under Japan

MBB/KAWASAKI BK 117 B-1
TYPE: Twin-turbine multi-purpose helicopter.

PROGRAMME: Developed jointly under agreement of 25 February 1977; four prototypes, first flight 13 June 1979; one pre-production aircraft, first flight 6 March 1981; first flights of production aircraft 24 December 1981 (JQ1001 in Japan) and 23 April 1982 (in Germany); certificated in Germany and Japan 9 and 17 December 1982 respectively, followed by US FAA 29 March 1983 (certification is to FAR Pt 29, Categories A and B, incl Amendments 29-1 to 29-16); deliveries began early 1983. Testbeds include one with all-composites airframe (first flight 27 April 1989) and one with Arriel 1C engines (first flight 6 April 1990).

VARIANTS: **BK 117 A-1:** Initial production model, with max T-O weight of 2,850 kg (6,283 lb): see 1984-85 Jane's.

BK 117 A-3: Max T-O weight increased to 3,200 kg (7,055 lb); enlarged tail rotor with twisted blades; German certification 15 March 1985. Details in 1987-88 Jane's.

BK 117 A-4: Enhanced performance version of A-3, certificated 1986; introduced from January 1987.

Increased transmission limit at T-O power, improved tail rotor head, and (on German built examples) more internal fuel. Details in 1987-88 Jane's.

BK 117 B-1: New (and standard current) series, certificated by LBA and FAA in December 1987 and JCAB in March 1988. Has LTS 101-750B-1 engines, enabling it to hover OGE (ISA) at 427 m (1,400 ft) higher than A-4 with 140 kg (309 lb) more payload; hover IGE with same payload increase at altitudes 457 m (1,500 ft) higher in ISA and 549 m (1,800 ft) higher in ISA + 20°C. To be offered also with Turbomeca Arriel 1E engines.

BK 117 B-1C: Version of B-1 certificated by UK CAA. Basic weight empty 1,762 kg (3,884 lb). Ranges with standard and aux fuel reduced by 11 and 16 nm (20 and 30 km; 12.5 and 18.5 miles) respectively and endurance with standard fuel by 6 min; all other data as for standard B-1.

BK 117 C-1: German version with new cockpit and Turbomeca Arriel 1C engines, for introduction late 1991; first flight (F-WMBB) 6 April 1990; certification expected October 1991.

BK 117 M: Multi-role military version, developed only by MBB and described in German section of 1990-91 Jane's; none yet ordered.

NBK-117: Designation of aircraft built under licence by IPTN (see Indonesian section) under November 1982 agreement with MBB.

All-composites testbed: One aircraft built by

MBB for 3½-year German MoD research programme; 80 per cent of airframe in CFRP and 20 per cent in AFRP (Kevlar). First flight 27 April 1989; flight test programme completed July 1989. Results intended to assist development of such new-generation helicopters as Eurocopter Tiger and NH 90.

CUSTOMERS: Total of 270 delivered by MBB by 1 January 1991; Kawasaki total was 68 by 1 October 1990. Recipients in 1989 included US Customs Service (three for mission support, equipped with FLIR, SX 16 searchlight and NVG cockpit lighting) and Peruvian Ministry of the Interior (two for anti-drug surveillance). Kawasaki agreed 1990 to supply CKD kits (about 30 over five-year period) for local assembly in South Korea by Hyundai Precision Industry; four kits delivered by 1 January 1991, with four to seven more due to follow by year end.

DESIGN FEATURES: System Bölkow four-blade main rotor head, almost identical to that of BO 105; main rotor blades similar to but larger than those of BO 105, with NACA 23012/23010 (modified) section; optional two-blade folding. Two-blade teetering tail rotor with MBB-S102E performance/noise optimised blade section; rotor rpm 383 (main), 2,169 (tail). Kawasaki KB 03 main transmission rated at 736 kW (986 shp) for twin-engine T-O, 632 kW (848 shp) max continuous; for single-engine operation 442 kW (592 shp) for 2½ min, 404 kW (542 shp) for 30 min and 368 kW (493 shp) max continuous. Each

BK 117 B-1 in passenger executive configuration with Arriel engines, to power updated version for introduction in late 1991

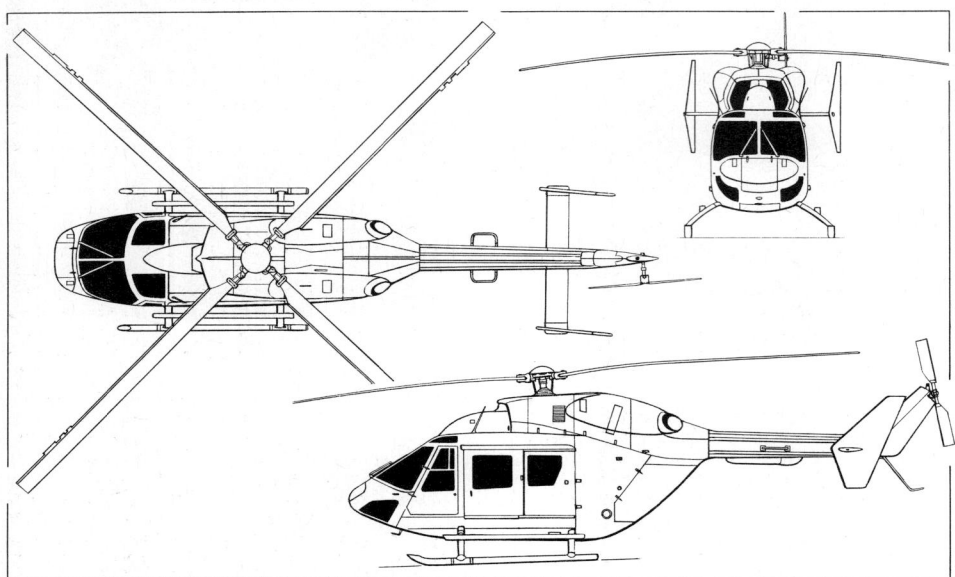

MBB/Kawasaki BK 117 B-1 twin-turboshaft multi-purpose helicopter *(Pilot Press)*

engine has separate drive input into main transmission via single bevel gear and collector; dual redundant lubrication system; auxiliary drive for accessories.

FLYING CONTROLS: Equipped as standard for single-pilot VFR operation, with dual controls and dual VFR instrumentation optional; rotor brake and yaw CSAS standard on German built models, optional on Kawasaki aircraft. Other common options include IFR instrumentation, two-axis (pitch/roll) CSAS and dual digital AFCS.

STRUCTURE: Main rotor has one-piece titanium hub with pitch-change bearings; fail-safe GFRP blades with stainless steel anti-erosion strip. Tail rotor, mounted on port side of central fin, has GFRP blades of high impact resistance. Main fuselage pod and tailboom are aluminium alloy semi-monocoques with single-curvature sheets and (on fuselage) bonded aluminium sandwich panels; secondary fuselage components are compound curvature shells with sandwich panels and Kevlar skins. Level floor throughout cockpit, cabin and cargo compartment. Engine deck, to which tailboom is integrally attached, forms cargo compartment roof and is of titanium adjacent to engine bays. Detachable tailcone carries main fin/tail rotor support, and horizontal stabiliser with offset endplate fins. MBB responsible for rotor systems, tailboom, tail unit, skid landing gear, hydraulic system, engine firewall and cowlings, powered controls and systems integration; Kawasaki for fuselage, transmission (based on that for its earlier KH-7), fuel and electrical systems, and standard equipment. Components single-sourced and exchanged for separate assembly lines at Donauwörth and Gifu; some components and accessories interchangeable with those of MBB BO 105 (see German section), from which hydraulic boost system is also adapted.

LANDING GEAR: Non-retractable tubular skid type, of aluminium construction. Skids are detachable from cross-tubes. Ground handling wheels standard. Emergency flotation gear, settling protectors and snow skids available optionally.

POWER PLANT: Two Textron Lycoming LTS 101-750B-1 turboshafts, each rated at 442 kW (592 shp) for 30 min for take-off and 410 kW (550 shp) max continuous power. Fuel in four flexible bladder tanks (forward and aft main tanks, with two supply tanks between) in compartments

under cabin floor. Two independent fuel feed systems for the engines and a common main fuel tank. Total standard fuel capacity 708 litres (187 US gallons; 155.7 Imp gallons). A 200 litre (53 US gallon; 44 Imp gallon) auxiliary tank is available optionally, raising total capacity to 908 litres (240 US gallons; 199.7 Imp gallons).

ACCOMMODATION: Pilot and up to six (executive version), seven (MBB standard version) or nine passengers (Kawasaki standard version). High-density layouts available for up to 10 passengers in addition to pilot. Provision for two-pilot operation at customer's option. Jettisonable forward hinged door on each side of cockpit, pilot's door having an openable window. Jettisonable rearward sliding passenger door on each side of cabin, lockable in open position. Fixed steps on each side. Two hinged, clamshell doors at rear of cabin, providing access to cargo compartment. Rear cabin window on each side. Aircraft can be equipped, according to mission, for offshore, medical evacuation (one or two stretchers side by side and up to six attendants), firefighting, search and rescue, law enforcement, cargo transport or other operations.

SYSTEMS: Ram air and electrical ventilation system. Fully redundant tandem hydraulic boost system (one operating and one standby), pressure 103.5 bars (1,500 lb/sq in), for flight controls. System flow rate 8.1 litres (2.14 US gallons; 1.78 Imp gallons)/min. Bootstrap/oil reservoir, pressure 1.7 bars (25 lb/sq in). Main DC electrical power from two 150A 28V starter/generators (one on each engine) and a 24V 25Ah nickel-cadmium battery. AC power is provided by an inverter; a second AC inverter is available optionally. Emergency busbar provides direct battery power to essential services in event of a double generator failure. External DC power receptacle.

AVIONICS: Basic instrumentation for single-pilot VFR operation includes airspeed indicator with electrically heated pitot tube and static ports, encoding altimeter, instantaneous vertical speed indicator, 4 in artificial horizon, 3 in standby artificial horizon, gyro magnetic heading system, HSI, magnetic compass, ambient air thermometer, and clock. (The 4 in and 3 in artificial horizons and HSI are optional on Kawasaki built aircraft.) Dual controls and dual VFR instrumentation available optionally. Com/nav and other avionics available to customer's requirements, including VHF-

AM/FM, UHF and HF transceivers, ADF, nav, R/Nav, Loran, Decca, VLF/Omega, LDNS and AHRS systems, radar altimeter, ATC/IFF transponder, encoding altimeter, DME, multi-mode radar, IFR instrumentation packages, pitch/roll command stability augmentation system (CSAS) and Honeywell SPZ-7100 dual digital AFCS.

EQUIPMENT: Standard basic equipment includes rotor brake and yaw CSAS (both optional only on Kawasaki aircraft), annunciator panel, master caution light, rotor rpm/engine fail warning control unit, fuel quantity indicator and low level sensor, outside air temperature indicator, engine and transmission oil pressure and temperature indicators, two exhaust temperature indicators, dual torque indicator, triple tachometer, two NI tachometers, mast moment indicator, instrument panel lights, cockpit/cabin/cargo compartment dome lights, utility lights, emergency exit lights, position lights, anti-collision warning light, retractable landing light, portable flashlight, ground handling wheels, pilot's and co-pilot's windscreen wipers, floor covering, interior panelling and sound insulation, ashtrays, map/document case, tiedown rings in cabin and cargo compartment, engine compartment fire warning indicator, engine fire extinguishing system, portable fire extinguisher, first aid kit, and single colour exterior paint scheme. Optional equipment includes high-density seating arrangement, bleed air heating system, long-range fuel tank, emergency flotation gear, settling protectors, snow skids, main rotor blade folding kit, non-retractable landing light, dual pilot operation kit, stretcher installation, external cargo hook, rescue hoist, SX 16 remotely controlled searchlight, external loudspeaker, and sand filter. Special optional equipment, including special mission kits for rescue, law enforcement and VIP transport, available at customer's request.

DIMENSIONS, EXTERNAL:

Main rotor diameter	11.00 m (36 ft 1 in)
Tail rotor diameter	1.956 m (6 ft 5 in)
Main rotor blade chord	0.32 m (1 ft 0½ in)
Length: overall, both rotors turning	13.00 m (42 ft 8 in)
fuselage, tail rotor blades vertical	9.91 m (32 ft 6¼ in)
Fuselage: Max width	1.60 m (5 ft 3 in)
Height: overall, both rotors turning	3.85 m (12 ft 7½ in)
to top of main rotor head	3.36 m (11 ft 0¼ in)
Tailplane span (over endplate fins)	2.70 m (8 ft 10¼ in)
Tail rotor ground clearance	1.90 m (6 ft 2¾ in)
Width over skids	2.50 m (8 ft 2½ in)

DIMENSIONS, INTERNAL:
Combined cabin and cargo compartment:

Max length	3.02 m (9 ft 11 in)
Width: max	1.49 m (4 ft 10½ in)
min	1.21 m (3 ft 11½ in)
Height: max	1.28 m (4 ft 2½ in)
min	0.99 m (3 ft 3 in)
Useful floor area	3.70 m² (39.83 sq ft)
Volume	5.00 m³ (176.6 cu ft)

AREAS:

Main rotor blades (each)	1.76 m² (18.94 sq ft)
Tail rotor blades (each)	0.0975 m² (1.05 sq ft)
Main rotor disc	95.03 m² (1,022.9 sq ft)
Tail rotor disc	3.00 m² (32.24 sq ft)

WEIGHTS AND LOADINGS:

Basic weight empty	1,727 kg (3,807 lb)
Fuel: standard usable	558 kg (1,230 lb)
incl auxiliary tank	718 kg (1,583 lb)
Max T-O weight, internal and external payload	3,200 kg (7,055 lb)
Max disc loading	33.67 kg/m² (6.90 lb/sq ft)
Max power loading	4.35 kg/kW (7.15 lb/shp)

*PERFORMANCE (ISA; A at gross weight of 2,800 kg; 6,173 lb, B at 3,000 kg; 6,614 lb, C at 3,200 kg; 7,055 lb):

Never-exceed speed (VNE) at S/L:	
A, B, C	150 knots (278 km/h; 172 mph)
Max cruising speed at S/L:	
A	137 knots (254 km/h; 158 mph)
B	135 knots (250 km/h; 155 mph)
C	134 knots (248 km/h; 154 mph)
Max forward rate of climb at S/L:	
A	714 m (2,345 ft)/min
B	660 m (2,165 ft)/min
C	582 m (1,910 ft)/min
Max certificated operating altitude:	
A, B	4,575 m (15,000 ft)
C	3,050 m (10,000 ft)
Service ceiling, one engine out, 46 m (150 ft)/min climb	
reserve: A	3,110 m (10,200 ft)
B	2,440 m (8,000 ft)
C	1,770 m (5,800 ft)
Hovering ceiling IGE (zero wind):	
A	4,205 m (13,800 ft)
B	3,565 m (11,700 ft)
C	2,925 m (9,600 ft)
Hovering ceiling IGE (17 knot; 32 km/h; 20 mph crosswind): A	2,865 m (9,400 ft)
B	2,195 m (7,200 ft)
C	1,495 m (4,900 ft)
Hovering ceiling OGE: A	3,625 m (11,900 ft)
B	2,955 m (9,700 ft)
C	2,285 m (7,500 ft)

Range at S/L with standard fuel, no reserves:
  A   315 nm (585 km; 363 miles)
  B   313 nm (580 km; 360 miles)
  C   307 nm (570 km; 354 miles)
Ferry range at S/L with auxiliary fuel, no reserves:
  A   408 nm (756 km; 469 miles)

  B   404 nm (750 km; 466 miles)
  C   399 nm (740 km; 460 miles)
Endurance at S/L, standard fuel, no reserves:
  A   3 h 15 min
  B   3 h 12 min
  C   3 h 6 min

Data are for German built aircraft: those for Japanese models vary slightly

MCDONNELL DOUGLAS/BAe

PARTICIPATING COMPANIES:
  McDonnell Douglas: see under USA
  British Aerospace: see under UK
VICE-PRESIDENT AND GENERAL MANAGER, AV-8:
  Patrick J. Finneran
VICE-PRESIDENT AND GENERAL MANAGER, T45TS:
  Larry A. Lemke

MCDONNELL DOUGLAS/BRITISH AEROSPACE HARRIER II

US Marine Corps designations: AV-8B and TAV-8B
RAF designations: Harrier GR. Mk 5, 5A and 7, and T. Mk 10
Spanish Navy designation: VA.2 Matador II

TYPE: Single-seat V/STOL close support, night attack and (RAF only) reconnaissance aircraft.

PROGRAMME: Early background given in several previous editions; present collaborative programme began with two YAV-8B (converted AV-8A) aerodynamic prototypes (first flights 9 November 1978 and 19 February 1979); followed by four FSD aircraft (first flight 5 November 1981); first 12 pilot production AV-8Bs ordered FY 1982 (first flight 29 August 1983); deliveries to USMC beginning 12 January 1984; development programme for night attack version announced November 1984; first flights of RAF GR. Mk 5 development aircraft 30 April (ZD318) and 31 July 1985 (ZD319); first USMC AV-8B squadron (VMA-331) achieved IOC August 1985; first flight of two-seat TAV-8B (BuAer No. 162747) 21 October 1986; first flight of night attack AV-8B prototype (BuAer 162966) 26 June 1987; first GR. Mk 5 for RAF (ZD324) handed over 1 July 1987; TAV-8B deliveries (to VMAT-203) began August 1987; EAV-8B deliveries to Spain 1987-88; production contract for new-build GR. Mk 7s placed April 1988; first production night attack AV-8B (BuAer 163853) delivered to VMA-214 on 15 September 1989; first flight of RAF GR. Mk 7 (development aircraft, converted from GR. Mk 5) 29 November 1989; production contract for T. Mk 10 placed February 1990; 24 FY 1991 AV-8Bs for USMC will be to Harrier II Plus standard (announced 4 December 1990).

VARIANTS: **AV-8B Harrier II:** US Marine Corps single-seat close support version, to re-equip three fleet operational AV-8A/C squadrons, one training squadron and five A-4 Skyhawk squadrons. In service with VMA-211/-214/-223/-231/-311/-331/-513/-542 and VMAT-203. Total of 256 ordered by FY 1991, including four FSDs; latest 62 (from 167th USMC aircraft) have night attack capability (see Avionics paragraph), plus (from December 1990 deliveries) uprated 105.87 kN (23,800 lb st) F402-RR-408 (Pegasus 11-61) engine.

AV-8B Harrier II Plus: Radar equipped night attack version (prototype and 24 production aircraft ordered); described separately.

TAV-8B Harrier II: US Marine Corps two-seat operational trainer, with longer forward fuselage and 0.43 m (1 ft 5 in) taller vertical tail than AV-8B; two cockpits in tandem; two underwing stores stations only; BAe major subcontractor for this version; 24 ordered FY 1984-91.

EAV-8B: US designation for Spanish Navy **VA.2 Matador II** single-seat FMS export version, of which 12 delivered 1987-88; in service with No. 9 Squadron, deployed in aircraft carrier *Principe de Asturias*. Existing 11 to be remanufactured to Harrier II Plus standard from mid-1994.

Harrier GR. Mk 5: Royal Air Force single-seat close support and reconnaissance version, of which 60 ordered

McDonnell Douglas/BAe Harrier GR. Mk 5s of the Royal Air Force

for delivery to No. 233 OCU and No. 1 Squadron at Wittering, UK, and No. 3 Squadron at Gütersloh, Germany; 60 scheduled for eventual upgrade to GR. Mk 5A and/or Mk 7 standard (which see). Two additional underwing stations, for Sidewinder missile carriage.

Harrier GR. Mk 5A: Interim upgrade designation for 18 GR. Mk 5s pending eventual upgrade to full GR. Mk 7 standard.

Harrier GR. Mk 7: Royal Air Force single-seat night attack version, based on GR. Mk 5; 27 ordered April 1988 (later increased to 34), preceded by two converted GR. Mk 5 development aircraft (first flight 29 November 1989); first flight of production aircraft (ZG471) May 1990; first delivery (ZG473) to No. 4 Squadron (RAF Germany) 12 September 1990; completion of order concurrent with upgrading 18 GR. Mk 5As (from ZD430), then 42 GR. Mk 5s, to GR. Mk 7 standard.

Harrier T. Mk 10: Royal Air Force operational trainer for GR. Mks 5/5A/7, based on TAV-8B airframe with addition of FLIR and night vision equipment of GR. Mk 7; 14 ordered April 1990.

CUSTOMERS: US Marine Corps (256 AV-8B ordered, incl four FSD and 24 Harrier II Plus, and 24 TAV-8B; 199 AV-8B and 16 TAV-8B delivered by February 1991); Royal Air Force (62 GR. Mk 5, 34 GR. Mk 7 and 14 T. Mk 10 ordered; 67 Mks 5/7 delivered by 28 September 1990); Spanish Navy (12 EAV-8B ordered and delivered); Italy and Spain each expected to order two TAV-8B as Harrier II Plus trainers.

DESIGN FEATURES: Differences compared with Harrier GR. Mk 3/AV-8A (see under BAe in UK section of 1989-90 *Jane's*) include bigger wing and longer fuselage; use of graphite epoxy (carbonfibre) composite materials for wings and parts of fuselage and tail unit; adoption of supercritical wing section; addition of LIDS (lift improvement devices: fuselage mounted or under-gunpod strakes and retractable fence panel forward of pods) to augment lift for vertical take-off; larger wing trailing-edge flaps and drooped ailerons; redesigned forward fuselage and cockpit; redesigned engine air intakes to provide more VTO/STO thrust and more efficient cruise; two additional wing stores stations; wing outriggers relocated at mid-span to provide better ground manoeuvring capability; leading-edge root extensions (LERX) to enhance instantaneous turn rate and air combat capability; landing gear strengthened to cater for higher operating weights and greater external stores loads. Wing span and area increased by approx 20 per

cent and 14.5 per cent respectively compared with GR. Mk 3/AV-8A; leading-edge sweep reduced by 10°; thickness/chord ratios 11.5 per cent (root)/7.5 per cent (tip); marked anhedral on wings and variable incidence tailplane.

FLYING CONTROLS: Hydraulic actuation (by Fairey irreversible jacks) of drooping ailerons and tailplane; rudder actuated mechanically; single-slotted trailing-edge flaps with slot closure doors; additional manoeuvring by thrust vectoring, assisted by jet reaction control valves in nose and tailcone and at each wingtip; LIDS 'box' traps air cushion bounced off ground by engine exhaust in VTOL modes, providing enough extra lift to enable aircraft to take off vertically at a gross weight equal to its max hovering gross weight; large forward hinged airbrake beneath fuselage aft of rear main landing gear bay.

STRUCTURE: One-piece wing (incl main multi-spar torsion box, ribs and skins), ailerons, flaps, LERX, outrigger pods and fairings, forward part of fuselage, LIDS, tailplane and rudder, are manufactured mainly from graphite epoxy (carbonfibre) and other composites; centre and rear fuselage, wing leading-edges (reinforced against bird strikes on RAF aircraft), wingtips, tailplane leading-edges and tips, and fin, are of aluminium alloy; titanium used for front and rear underfuselage heatshields and small area forward of windscreen. McDonnell Douglas/BAe work split is 60/40 for AV-8B and EAV-8B, 50/50 for RAF aircraft. McDonnell Douglas builds entire wing, front and forward centre-fuselage (incl nosecone, air intakes, heatshields, engine access doors and forward fuel tanks) and underfuselage fences/strakes, for all aircraft, plus tailplanes for USMC and Spanish aircraft, and assembles all USMC/Spanish fuselages; BAe builds rear centre and rear fuselage (incl blast and heatshields, centre and rear fuel tanks, dorsal air intakes and tail bullets), fins and rudders, and the complete jet reaction control system, for all aircraft, plus tailplanes for RAF aircraft, and assembles all RAF fuselages; final assembly is by McDonnell Douglas for USMC/Spain, BAe for RAF.

LANDING GEAR: Retractable bicycle type of Dowty design, permitting operation from rough unprepared surfaces of very low CBR (California Bearing Ratio). Hydraulic actuation, with nitrogen bottle for emergency extension. Single steerable nosewheel retracts forward, twin coupled mainwheels rearward, into fuselage. Small outrigger units, at approx mid span between flaps and ailerons, retract rearward into streamline pods. Telescopic oleo-pneumatic main and outrigger gear; levered suspension nosewheel leg. Dunlop wheels, tyres, multi-disc carbon brakes and anti-skid system. Mainwheel tyres (size 26.0 × 7.75-13.00) and nosewheel tyre (size 26.0 × 8.75-11) all have pressure of 8.62 bars (125 lb/sq in). Outrigger tyres are size 13.5 × 6.00-4.00, pressure 10.34 bars (150 lb/sq in). McDonnell Douglas responsible for entire landing gear system.

POWER PLANT: One 95.42 kN (21,450 lb st) Rolls-Royce F402-RR-406A (Pegasus 11-21) vectored thrust turbofan in AV-8B (105.87 kN; 23,800 lb st F402-RR-408/Pegasus 11-61 in aircraft delivered from December 1990); one 96.75 kN (21,750 lb st) Pegasus Mk 105 in Harrier GR. Mk 5; Mk 152-42 in EAV-8B. Up to 25 per cent (by value) of engines for USMC aircraft manufactured by Pratt & Whitney. Redundant digital engine control system (DECS), with mechanical backup, standard from March 1987. Zero-scarf front nozzles. Air intakes have an elliptical lip shape, leading-edges reinforced against bird strikes, and a single row of auxiliary intake doors. Access to engine accessories through top of fuselage,

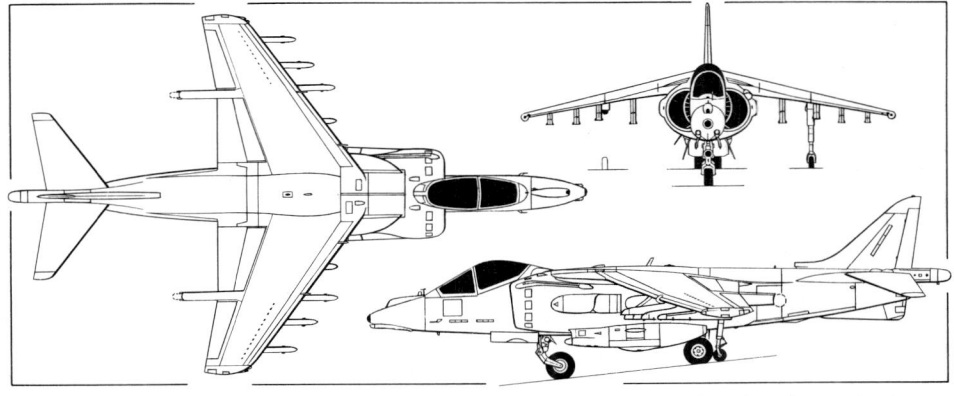

McDonnell Douglas/BAe Harrier GR. Mk 7 V/STOL close support aircraft (*Pilot Press*)

immediately ahead of wing. Integral fuel tanks in wings; total internal fuel capacity (fuselage and wing tanks) 4,319 litres (1,141 US gallons; 950 Imp gallons). Water injection tank with capacity of approx 227 kg (500 lb). Retractable bolt-on in-flight refuelling probe optional. Each of the four inner underwing stations capable of carrying a 1,135 litre (300 US gallon; 250 Imp gallon) auxiliary fuel tank.

ACCOMMODATION: Pilot only, on zero/zero ejection seat (UPC/Stencel for USMC, Martin-Baker for RAF), in pressurised, heated and air-conditioned cockpit. AV-8B cockpit raised approx 30.5 cm (12 in) by comparison with AV-8A/YAV-8B, with redesigned one-piece wraparound windscreen (thicker on RAF aircraft than on those for USMC) and rearward sliding bubble canopy, to improve all-round field of view. Windscreen de-icing. Windscreens and canopies for all aircraft manufactured by McDonnell Douglas.

SYSTEMS: No. 1 hydraulic system has a flow rate of 43 litres (11.4 US gallons; 9.5 Imp gallons)/min; flow rate of No. 2 system is 26.5 litres (7.0 US gallons; 5.8 Imp gallons)/min. Reservoirs are nitrogen pressurised at 2.76-5.52 bars (40-80 lb/sq in). Other systems include Westinghouse variable speed constant frequency (VSCF) solid state electrical system, Lucas Mk 4 gas turbine starter/APU, Clifton Precision onboard oxygen generating system (OBOGS), and Graviner Firewire fire detection system. Dorsal airscoop at base of fin for avionics bay cooling system.

AVIONICS: Include dual Collins RT-1250A/ARC U/VHF com (GEC Avionics AD3500 ECM-resistant U/VHF-AM/FM in GR. Mk 5), R-1379B/ARA-63 all-weather landing receiver (AV-8B only), RT-1159A/ARN-118 Tacan, RT-1015A/APN-194(V) radar altimeter, Honeywell CV-3736/A com/nav/identification data converter, Bendix/King RT-1157/APX-100 IFF (Cossor IFF 4760 transponder in GR. Mk 5), Litton AN/ASN-130A inertial navigation system (being replaced by GEC Ferranti FIN 1075 in GR. Mk 5), AiResearch CP-1471/A digital air data computer, Smiths Industries SU-128/A dual combining glass head-up display and CP-1450/A display computer, IP-1318/A CRT Kaiser digital display indicator, and (GR. Mk 5 only) GEC Ferranti moving map display. Litton AN/ALR-67(V)2 fore/aft looking RWR (AV-8B only), UK MoD AN/ARR-51 FLIR receiver, Goodyear AN/ALE-39 flare/chaff dispenser (upper and lower rear fuselage) (Tracor AN/ALE-40 specified, but not at present fitted, in GR. Mk 5). Primary weapon delivery sensor system for AV-8B and GR. Mk 5 is the Hughes Aircraft AN/ASB-19(V)2 or (V)3 Angle Rate Bombing Set, mounted in the nose and comprising a dual-mode (TV and laser) target seeker/tracker. System functions in conjunction with Control Data Corporation CP-1429/AYK-14(V) mission computer (Computing Devices ACCS 2000 in GR. Mk 5), the Smiths Industries AN/AYQ-13 stores management system, the display computer, the head-up display, and the digital display indicator. Flight controls that interface with the reaction control system are provided by the Honeywell AN/ASW-46(V)2 stability augmentation and attitude hold system, currently being updated to high AOA capable configuration. RAF aircraft have an accident data recorder. Night attack versions equipped with GEC Sensors nose-mounted FLIR, Smiths Industries wide-angle HUD/HDD, digital colour moving map display (Honeywell for USMC, GEC Avionics for RAF) and pilot's NVGs (variant of GEC Ferranti Nite-Op) with compatible cockpit lighting. Provision for Sanders AN/ALQ-164 defensive ECM pod on centreline pylon. GR. Mks 5/7 have a Marconi Defence Systems Zeus internal ECM system comprising an advanced radar warning receiver and a multi-mode jammer with a Northrop RF transmitter; and provision for a nose mounted infra-red reconnaissance sensor. GR. Mk 5 is also to be equipped with a Plessey missile approach warning (MAW) equipment, mounted in the tailboom, which will automatically activate appropriate countermeasures upon detecting approach of enemy missiles.

EQUIPMENT: Backup standby mechanical instrumentation includes ASI altimeter, AOA indicator, attitude indicator, cabin pressure altitude indicator, clock, flap position indicator, HSI, standby compass, turn and slip indicator, and vertical speed indicator. Anti-collision, approach, formation, in-flight refuelling, landing gear position, auxiliary exterior lights, and console, instrument panel and other internal lighting.

ARMAMENT: Two underfuselage packs, mounting on the port side a five-barrel 25 mm cannon based on the General Electric GAU-12/U, and a 300 round container on the starboard side, in the AV-8B; or two 25 mm Royal Ordnance Factories cannon with 100 rds/gun (derived from the 30 mm Aden) in the GR. Mks 5/5A/7. Single 454 kg (1,000 lb) stores mount on fuselage centreline, between gun packs. Three stores stations under each wing on AV-8B, stressed for loads of up to 907 kg (2,000 lb) inboard, 907 kg (2,000 lb) on the intermediate stations, and 281 kg (620 lb) outboard. The four under wing stations are wet, permitting the carriage of auxiliary fuel tanks. GR. Mks 5/5A/7 and night attack AV-8B have an additional underwing station, for a Sidewinder air-to-air missile, ahead of each outrigger wheel fairing. Typical

Prototype of the US night attack version of the AV-8B Harrier II, unladen and with LIDs deployed

Close-up of the nose of a night attack Harrier GR. Mk 7

weapons include two or four AIM-9L Sidewinder, Magic or AGM-65E Maverick missiles, or up to six Sidewinders; up to sixteen 540 lb free-fall or retarded general purpose bombs, 12 BL 755 or similar cluster bombs, 1,000 lb free-fall or retarded bombs, ten Paveway laser guided bombs, eight fire bombs, 10 Matra 155 rocket pods (each with eighteen 68 mm SNEB rockets), or (in addition to the underfuselage gun packs) two underwing gun pods. ML Aviation BRU-36/A bomb release units standard on all versions. TAV-8B can carry six Mk 76 practice bombs or two LAU-68 rocket launchers for weapons training.

DIMENSIONS, EXTERNAL:

Wing span	9.25 m (30 ft 4 in)
Wing aspect ratio	4.0
Length overall (flying attitude):	
AV-8B	14.12 m (46 ft 4 in)
TAV-8B	15.32 m (50 ft 3 in)
Height overall	3.55 m (11 ft 7¾ in)
Tailplane span	4.24 m (13 ft 11 in)
Outrigger wheel track	5.18 m (17 ft 0 in)

AREAS:

Wings, excl LERX, gross	21.37 m² (230.0 sq ft)
LERX (total): up to c/n 198	0.81 m² (8.7 sq ft)
from c/n 199	1.24 m² (13.4 sq ft)
Ailerons (total)	1.15 m² (12.4 sq ft)
Trailing-edge flaps (total)	2.88 m² (31.0 sq ft)
Ventral fixed strakes (total)	0.51 m² (5.5 sq ft)
Ventral retractable fence (LIDs)	0.24 m² (2.6 sq ft)
Ventral airbrake	0.42 m² (4.5 sq ft)
Fin	2.47 m² (26.6 sq ft)
Rudder, excl tab	0.49 m² (5.3 sq ft)
Tailplane	4.51 m² (48.5 sq ft)

WEIGHTS AND LOADINGS (single-seaters, except where indicated):

Operating weight empty (incl pilot and unused fuel):	
AV-8B	6,336 kg (13,968 lb)
GR. Mk 5	6,343 kg (13,984 lb)
TAV-8B	6,451 kg (14,223 lb)
Max fuel: internal only*	3,519 kg (7,759 lb)
internal and external*	7,180 kg (15,829 lb)
Max external stores	6,003 kg (13,235 lb)
Max useful load (incl fuel, stores, weapons, ammunition, and water injection for engine):	
VTO	approx 3,062 kg (6,750 lb)
STO	more than 7,710 kg (17,000 lb)
Basic flight design gross weight for 7g operation	10,410 kg (22,950 lb)
Max T-O weight:	
435 m (1,427 ft) STO	14,061 kg (31,000 lb)
S/L VTO, ISA	9,342 kg (20,595 lb)
S/L VTO, 32°C	8,142 kg (17,950 lb)
Design max landing weight	11,340 kg (25,000 lb)
Max vertical landing weight	9,043 kg (19,937 lb)

205 kg (452 lb) less in TAV-8B

PERFORMANCE:

Max Mach number in level flight:	
at S/L	0.87 (575 knots; 1,065 km/h; 661 mph)
at altitude	0.92
STOL T-O run at max T-O weight:	
ISA	435 m (1,427 ft)
32°C	518 m (1,700 ft)

Operational radius with external loads shown:

short T-O (366 m; 1,200 ft), twelve Mk 82 Snakeye bombs, internal fuel, 1 h loiter
90 nm (167 km; 103 miles)

hi-lo-hi, short T-O (366 m; 1,200 ft), seven Mk 82 Snakeye bombs, two 300 US gallon external fuel tanks, no loiter   594 nm (1,101 km; 684 miles)

deck launch intercept mission, two AIM-9 missiles and two external fuel tanks
627 nm (1,162 km; 722 miles)

Unrefuelled ferry range, with four 300 US gallon external tanks:
tanks retained	1,638 nm (3,035 km; 1,886 miles)
tanks dropped	1,965 nm (3,641 km; 2,263 miles)

Combat air patrol endurance at 100 nm (185 km; 115 miles) from base   3 h
g limits   +8/-3

MCDONNELL DOUGLAS/BRITISH AEROSPACE HARRIER II PLUS

TYPE: Enhanced capability derivative of AV-8B.

PROGRAMME: Intention to develop radar-equipped version of AV-8B announced as McDonnell Douglas/BAe private venture June 1987; radar integration efforts (with Hughes Aircraft) started 1988; tri-national MoU (USA/Italy/Spain) of 28 September 1990 approved joint funding to develop and integrate AN/APG-65 radar; US Navy contract of 3 December 1990 authorised development of prototype and completion to Harrier II Plus standard of 24 AV-8Bs ordered in FYs 1990-91; prototype first flight scheduled for October 1992; deliveries to USMC due to start in second quarter 1993 and finish January 1994.

CUSTOMERS: US Marine Corps (24); orders expected from Italian Navy (16, for operation from carrier *Giuseppe Garibaldi*) and Spanish Navy (18); USMC considering remanufacture of earlier AV-8Bs to Harrier II Plus standard.

DESIGN FEATURES: Generally as for night attack AV-8B with F402-RR-408 engine, plus Hughes Aircraft AN/APG-65 multi-mode pulse Doppler radar, FLIR, and weapon capability extended to include AMRAAM, Sparrow, Sea Eagle and Harpoon; enlarged LERX.

PERFORMANCE: (estimated, with 137 m; 450 ft short T-O deck run, 6.5° ski-jump, 20 knot; 37 km/h; 23 mph wind over deck, air temperature 32°C, optimum cruise conditions, incl reserves for landing):

Anti-shipping combat radius with two Harpoons, two Sidewinders and two 1,136 litre (300 US gallon; 250 Imp gallon) drop tanks
609 nm (1,128 km; 701 miles)

Combat air patrol (incl 2 min combat) with four AMRAAM and two 300 US gallon tanks: time on station:
at 100 nm (185 km; 115 mile) radius	2 h 42 min
at 200 nm (370 km; 230 mile) radius	2 h 6 min

Sea surveillance combat radius (incl 50 nm; 92 km; 57 mile dash at S/L) with two Sidewinders and two 300 US gallon tanks   608 nm (1,127 km; 700 miles)

McDonnell Douglas/BAe T-45A Goshawk derivative of the BAe Hawk

Leading-edge slat, vortex generators and nose tow catapult fittings on development T-45A Goshawk

MCDONNELL DOUGLAS/BRITISH AEROSPACE HARRIER III

McDonnell Douglas and British Aerospace set up in 1990 a joint Harrier III study group to determine the next stage of Harrier development. Although actual definition is still some time away, initial parameters suggest a larger, folding wing of 9.75 m (32 ft) span, made from carbonfibre composites; a longer fuselage and refined aerodynamics; a developed Pegasus 11-61 engine; and EFA-generation avionics, including an advanced radar. The Harrier III would be aimed initially at replacing current Sea Harriers, with increased range and payload and an in-service date of 2000-2005, but could also replace the present generation of AV-8Bs.

MCDONNELL DOUGLAS/BRITISH AEROSPACE T-45A

US Navy designation: T-45A Goshawk

TYPE: Two-seat basic and advanced jet trainer.

PROGRAMME: Selected 18 November 1981 (from five other candidates) as winner of US Navy VTXTS (now T45TS) competition for undergraduate jet pilot trainer to replace T-2C Buckeye and TA-4J Skyhawk; original plan was for initial 54 'dry' (land-based) T-45Bs followed by 253 carrier-capable 'wet' T-45As; B model eliminated in FY 1984 in favour of 300 'all-wet' T-45As; FSD phase began October 1984; construction of two prototypes by Douglas Aircraft Co began February 1986; funding approved 16 May 1986 for first three production lots (incl 60 T-45As and 15 flight simulators during FYs 1988-90); Lot 1 production contract (12 aircraft) awarded 26 January 1988; FSD prototypes made first flights 16 April (BuAer No. 162787) and November 1988 (BuAer 162788); original planned date for first deliveries (October 1989) delayed by further airframe and power plant changes requested by US Navy; announced 19 December 1989 that entire T45TS programme to be transferred to McDonnell Aircraft Co at St Louis; modified FSD prototypes made first flights September and October 1990; two Douglas production aircraft

(BuAer 163599 and '600) delivered to NATC Patuxent River, Maryland, on 10 October and 15 November 1990; main deliveries from St Louis production line expected to start January 1992.

VARIANTS: **T-45A Goshawk:** Based on BAe Hawk 60 series (see UK section), with airframe/power plant/ avionics changes necessary to meet USN specification; scheduled to become operational initially (12 aircraft and associated equipment) at NAS Kingsville, Texas, later also at NAS Chase Field, Texas and NAS Meridian, Mississippi. Introduction expected to meet USN training requirements with 42 per cent fewer aircraft than at present, 25 per cent fewer flight hours, and 46 per cent fewer personnel.

CUSTOMERS: US Navy (two FSD prototypes and 300 production aircraft required, of which 12 so far contracted; next 24 subject to approval at review scheduled for May 1991); complete T45TS programme also involves 32 flight simulators (built by Hughes Flight Systems); 49 computer aided instructional devices, four training integration system mainframes, 200 terminals, plus academic materials and contractor operated logistic support.

DESIGN FEATURES: Generally as for two-seat BAe Hawk, with some redesign and strengthening for carrier operation, incl new main and nose landing gear and provision of nose tow launch bar and arrester hook.

FLYING CONTROLS: Differences from two-seat BAe Hawk include electrically actuated/hydraulically operated full-span wing leading-edge slats (operation limited to landing configuration), aileron/rudder interconnect, two fuselage-side airbrakes instead of single one under fuselage, and addition of 'smurf' (side mounted unit horizontal root tail fin), a small curved surface forward of each tailplane leading-edge root, to eliminate pitch-down during low-speed flaps-down/gear-up manoeuvres; Dowty actuators for slats and airbrakes.

STRUCTURE: Redesigned (incl deeper and longer forward fuselage) and strengthened to accommodate new landing gear and withstand rigours of carrier operation; twin airbrakes of composites material; fin height increased by 15.2 cm (6 in) and single ventral fin added; rudder modified; tailplane span increased by 10.2 cm (4 in); wingtips squared off; underfuselage arrester hook, deployable 20° to each side of longitudinal axis. BAe (as principal subcontractor) builds wings, centre and rear fuselage, fin, tailplane, windscreen, canopy and flying controls.

LANDING GEAR: Wide-track hydraulically retractable tricycle type, stressed for vertical velocities of 7.47 m (24.5 ft)/s. Single wheel and long-stroke oleo (increased from 33 cm; 13 in of standard Hawk to 63.5 cm; 25 in) on each main unit; twin-wheel steerable nose unit with 40.6 cm (16 in) stroke. Articulated main gear, by AP Precision Hydraulics, is of levered suspension (trailing arm) type with a folding side-stay. Cleveland Pneumatic nose gear, with Sterer steering system. Nose gear has catapult launch bar and holdback devices. Main units retract inward into wing, forward of front spar; nose unit retracts forward. All wheel doors are sequenced to close after gear lowering; inboard mainwheel doors are bulged to accommodate larger trailing arm and tyres. Gear emergency lowering by free fall. Goodrich wheels, tyres and brakes. Mainwheel tyres size 24 × 7.7-10; nosewheels have size 19 × 5.25-10 tyres. Tyre pressure (all units) 22.40 bars (325 lb/sq in) for carrier operation; reduced for land operation. Hydraulic multi-disc mainwheel brakes with Dunlop adaptive anti-skid system.

POWER PLANT: FSD aircraft powered by a 24.24 kN (5,450 lb st) Rolls-Royce Turbomeca F405-RR-400L (Adour Mk 861-49) non-afterburning turbofan. Production aircraft to have a 26.00 kN (5,845 lb st) F405-RR-401 (navalised Adour Mk 871) which produces 30 per cent more thrust in low altitude/hot day conditions. Air intakes and engine starting as described for BAe Hawk. Fuel system similar to BAe Hawk, but with revision for carrier operation. Capacities are 840 litres (222 US gallons; 185 Imp gallons) in fuselage bag tank and 860 litres (227 US gallons; 189 Imp gallons) in integral wing tank, giving total internal capacity of 1,700 litres (449 US gallons; 374 Imp gallons). Provision for carrying one 591 litre (156 US gallon; 130 Imp gallon) drop tank on each underwing pylon.

ACCOMMODATION: Similar to BAe Hawk, except that ejection seats are of Martin-Baker Mk 14 NACES (Navy aircrew common ejection seat) zero/zero rocket assisted type.

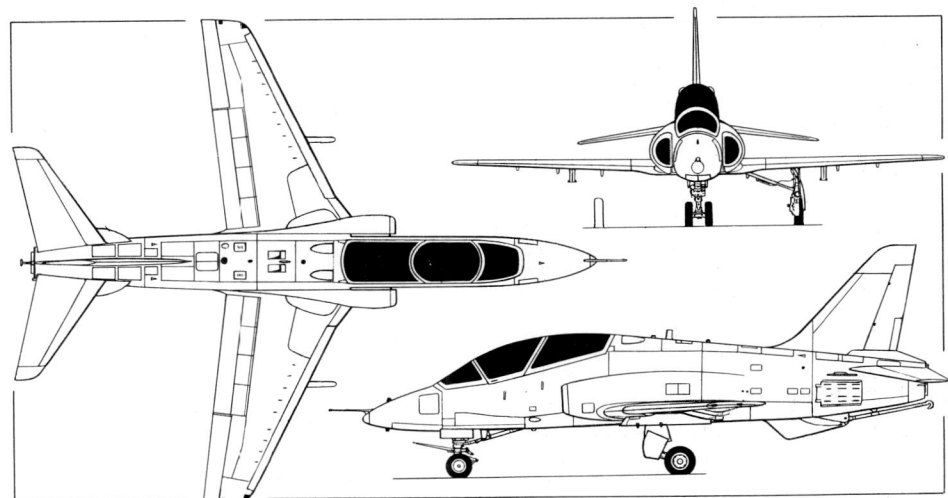

McDonnell Douglas/BAe T-45A Goshawk tandem-seat basic and advanced trainer *(Pilot Press)*

SYSTEMS: Air-conditioning and pressurisation systems, using engine bleed air. Duplicated hydraulic systems, each 207 bars (3,000 lb/sq in), for actuation of control jacks, flaps, airbrakes, landing gear, arrester hook and anti-skid wheel brakes. No. 1 system has a flow rate of 36.4 litres (9.6 US gallons; 8.0 Imp gallons)/min, No. 2 system a rate of 22.7 litres (6.0 US gallons; 5.0 Imp gallons)/min. Reservoirs are nitrogen pressurised at 2.75-5.5 bars (40-80 lb/sq in). Hydraulic accumulator for emergency operation of wheel brakes. Pop-up Dowty Aerospace ram air turbine in upper rear fuselage provides emergency hydraulic power for flying controls in the event of an engine or No. 2 pump failure. No pneumatic system. DC electrical power from single brushless generator, with two static inverters to provide AC power and two batteries for standby power. Onboard oxygen generating system (OBOGS).

AVIONICS: Avionics and cockpit displays optimised for carrier-compatible operations. AN/ARN-182 UHF/VHF com radios and AN/ARN-144 VOR/ILS by Collins, Honeywell AN/APN-194 radio altimeter, Bendix/King APX-100 IFF, Sierra AN/ARN-136A Tacan, US Navy AN/USN-2 standard attitude and heading reference system (SAHRS), Smiths Industries Mini-HUD (front cockpit), Racal Acoustics avionics/com

management system, GEC Avionics yaw damper computer, Electrodynamics airborne data recorder and Teledyne caution/warning system.

ARMAMENT: No built-in armament, but weapons delivery capability for advanced training is incorporated. Single pylon under each wing for carriage of practice multiple bomb rack, rocket pods or auxiliary fuel tank. Provision also for carrying single stores pod on fuselage centreline. CAI Industries gunsight in rear cockpit.

*DIMENSIONS, EXTERNAL:

Wing span	9.39 m (30 ft 9¾ in)
Wing chord: at root	2.65 m (8 ft 8¼ in)
at tip	0.90 m (2 ft 11½ in)
Wing aspect ratio	5.3
Length: overall, incl nose probe	11.97 m (39 ft 3⅛ in)
fuselage	10.89 m (35 ft 9 in)
Height overall	4.09 m (13 ft 5 in)
Tailplane span	4.39 m (14 ft 4¾ in)
Wheel track (c/l of shock struts)	3.90 m (12 ft 9½ in)
Wheelbase	4.29 m (14 ft 1 in)

* before USN modifications

AREAS:

Wings, gross	16.69 m² (179.6 sq ft)
Ailerons (total)	1.05 m² (11.30 sq ft)
Trailing-edge flaps (total)	2.50 m² (26.91 sq ft)

Airbrakes (total)	0.79 m² (8.55 sq ft)
Fin	2.51 m² (27.02 sq ft)
Rudder, incl tab	0.58 m² (6.24 sq ft)
Tailplane	4.33 m² (46.61 sq ft)

WEIGHTS AND LOADINGS:

Weight empty	4,263 kg (9,399 lb)
Internal fuel	1,312 kg (2,893 lb)
Max T-O weight	5,787 kg (12,758 lb)

PERFORMANCE (estimated, at max T-O weight):

Design limit diving speed at 1,000 m (3,280 ft)	
	610 knots (1,130 km/h; 702 mph)
Max true Mach number in dive	1.1
Max level speed at 2,440 m (8,000 ft)	
	538 knots (997 km/h; 620 mph)
Max level Mach number at 9,150 m (30,000 ft)	0.85
Max rate of climb at S/L	2,128 m (6,982 ft)/min
Time to 9,150 m (30,000 ft), clean	7 min 12 s
Service ceiling	12,875 m (42,250 ft)
T-O to 15 m (50 ft)	1,141 m (3,744 ft)
Landing from 15 m (50 ft)	1,189 m (3,900 ft)
Ferry range, internal fuel only	
	1,000 nm (1,850 km; 1,150 miles)
g limits	+7.33/−3

MPC

MPC AIRCRAFT GmbH

Kreetslag 10, Postfach 950109, 2103 Hamburg 95, Germany
Telephone: 49 (40) 74202-0
Fax: 49 (40) 74202-22
Telex: 21950-0 MBB D
DIRECTOR, PUBLIC RELATIONS: Josef Grendel
PARTICIPATING COMPANIES:
  DASA: see under Germany
  CATIC: see under China

MPC 75

TYPE: Twin-turbofan short-haul commercial transport.

PROGRAMME: Began with 3 October 1985 MoU between MBB (now Deutsche Airbus) and CATIC to explore possible development of 60/85-passenger regional transport; Hamburg joint office set up 6 June 1986 tasked with feasibility study and market research, simultaneously with MoU between MBB and GE to consider possibilities of UDF (unducted fan) power plant; further MoU (MBB/Allison) signed May 1988 for similar consideration of T406 propfans; early design (see 1989-90 *Jane's*) had two such engines mounted at rear, but this revised in mid-1989 to present configuration with two underwing turbofans; now in pre-development in basic and stretched versions with programme launch expected mid-1991 (unless merged with DASA 80/130-seater programme, which see); first flight planned for late 1995, with initial certification and service entry expected late 1996; deliveries of stretched -200 to begin three years later.

VARIANTS: **MPC 75-100:** Basic version, with single-class seating for up to 89 passengers.

MPC 75-200: Stretched version (5.10 m; 16 ft 8¾ in longer) for up to 115 passengers in same five-abreast seating as -100.

CUSTOMERS: No firm customers announced up to May 1991.

DESIGN FEATURES: See accompanying illustration.

FLYING CONTROLS: Fully digital fly-by-wire AFCS.

STRUCTURE: Advanced composites for approx 25 per cent of airframe structural weight, incl wing skins, wing/body fairings, wing moving surfaces, pylon leading-edges, cowl fronts, fin, rudder, tailplane, elevators, radome, cabin and landing gear doors, and floor panels; computer controlled fibre layup, superplastic forming and diffusion bonding; remainder built of advanced alloys, possibly including Al-Li.

LANDING GEAR: Retractable tricycle type, with twin wheels on each unit.

POWER PLANT: Two turbofans, with approx ratings of 62.3 kN (14,000 lb st) in MPC 75-100 and 73.4 kN (16,500 lb st) in -200, mounted on underwing pylons. Engine options are Pratt & Whitney/MTU RTF 180, BMW/Rolls-Royce BR 715 and Allison GMA 3014; selected engines will have duplicated FADEC, fully integrated with fly-by-wire AFCS. Fuel in integral wing tanks with combined standard capacity of 9,860 litres (2,605 US gallons; 2,169 Imp gallons); optional additional tank in wing centre-section for both versions, capacity 5,096 litres (1,346 US gallons; 1,121 Imp gallons).

ACCOMMODATION: Fully digital two-person flight deck, with side-stick controllers. Standard five-abreast seating with single aisle. Passenger capacities 82-89 in MPC 75-100 and 107-115 in MPC 75-200, plus one or more cabin attendants. Toilet, galley and wardrobe facilities at front and rear of cabin. Passenger door at front and rear on

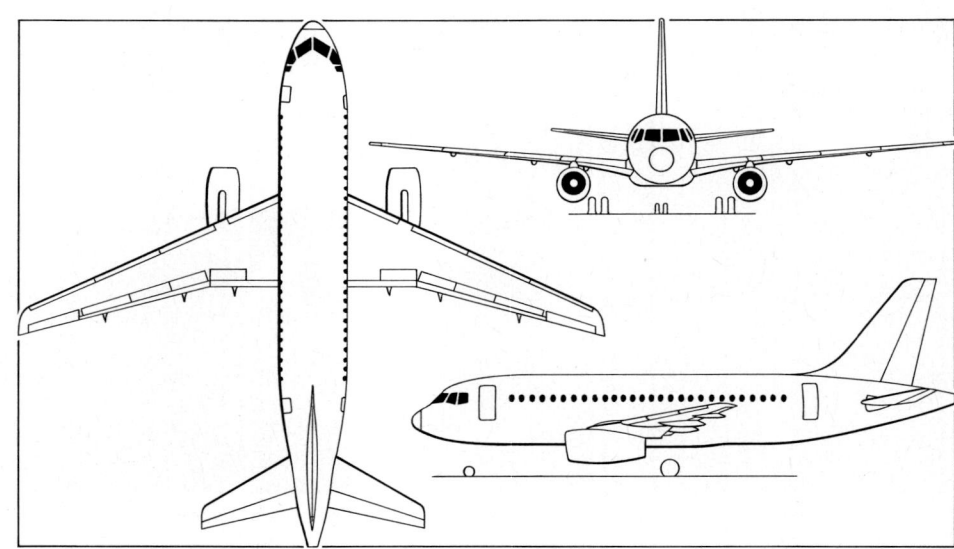

Provisional drawing of the MPC 75-100 twin-turbofan 89-seat transport *(Jane's/Mike Keep)*

port side, each with service door opposite. Overwing emergency exit each side on MPC 75-200. Underfloor baggage/cargo hold, with outward opening door at front and rear on starboard side.

AVIONICS: Com/nav equipment to latest ARINC 700 standards. Options include GPS, GPWS, MLS, Satcom and TCAS.

DIMENSIONS, EXTERNAL:

Wing span: 100, 200	29.70 m (97 ft 5¼ in)
Wing aspect ratio	9.59
Length overall: 100	28.50 m (93 ft 6 in)
200	33.60 m (110 ft 2¾ in)
Height overall: 100, 200	10.20 m (33 ft 5½ in)
Fuselage: Max width: 100, 200	3.45 m (11 ft 3¾ in)
Passenger doors (port):	
Height (both)	1.83 m (6 ft 0 in)
Width: fwd	0.86 m (2 ft 10 in)
rear	0.76 m (2 ft 6 in)
Service doors (stbd, each):	
Height	1.40 m (4 ft 7 in)
Width	0.76 m (2 ft 6 in)
Emergency exits (-200 overwing, each):	
Height	1.22 m (4 ft 0 in)
Width	0.51 m (1 ft 8 in)

DIMENSIONS, INTERNAL:

Cabin: Max width	3.228 m (10 ft 7 in)
Max height	2.075 m (6 ft 9¾ in)
Underfloor hold volume: 100	18.15 m³ (641.0 cu ft)
200	27.55 m³ (973.0 cu ft)

AREAS:

Wings, gross: 100, 200	92.00 m² (990.3 sq ft)

WEIGHTS AND LOADINGS (estimated):

Manufacturer's weight empty: 100	22,600 kg (49,824 lb)
200	24,700 kg (54,454 lb)
Operating weight empty: 100	24,500 kg (54,013 lb)
200	27,000 kg (59,525 lb)
Fuel weight:	
100, 200, standard	7,740 kg (17,064 lb)

100, 200, with centre-section tank

	11,740 kg (25,882 lb)
Max payload: 100	10,850 kg (23,920 lb)
200	14,000 kg (30,865 lb)
Max T-O weight: 100	39,950 kg (88,075 lb)
200	45,100 kg (99,430 lb)
Max landing weight: 100	37,950 kg (83,665 lb)
200	42,850 kg (94,470 lb)
Max zero-fuel weight: 100	35,350 kg (77,935 lb)
200	41,460 kg (91,405 lb)
Max wing loading: 100	434.2 kg/m² (88.93 lb/sq ft)
200	490.2 kg/m² (100.40 lb/sq ft)

PERFORMANCE (estimated, at max T-O weight ISA, except where indicated):

Max operating Mach number	0.82
Econ cruising Mach number	0.77
Max operating speed	330 knots (611 km/h; 380 mph)
Approach speed at max landing weight:	
100	114 knots (211 km/h; 131 mph)
200	120 knots (222 km/h; 138 mph)
Cruising altitude:	
initial (ISA + 10°C)	10,670 m (35,000 ft)
max	11,890 m (39,000 ft)
Service ceiling, one engine out (ISA + 10°C)	
	5,790 m (19,000 ft)
FAR T-O field length	1,675 m (5,500 ft)
Runway ACN, rigid pavement: 100	23
Range with standard fuel and typical international reserves:	
100: with 89 passengers and baggage	
	1,600 nm (2,965 km; 1,842 miles)
with 89 passengers and 2,800 kg (6,173 lb) cargo	
	700 nm (1,297 km; 806 miles)
200: with 115 passengers and baggage	
	1,400 nm (2,595 km; 1,612 miles)
with 115 passengers and 3,600 kg (7,936 lb) cargo	
	450 nm (834 km; 518 miles)

NAMC/PAC

PARTICIPATING COMPANIES:

Nanchang Aircraft Manufacturing Co: see under China

Pakistan Aeronautical Complex: see under Pakistan

NAMC/PAC K-8 KARAKORUM 8

TYPE: Tandem-seat jet basic trainer and light ground attack aircraft.

PROGRAMME: Launched publicly (as L-8) by NAMC at 1987 Paris Air Show as proposed export aircraft to be developed jointly with international partner; with Pakistan as that partner (25 per cent share), detail design began July 1987, with aircraft redesignated K-8 and named after mountain range forming part of China/Pakistan border; five prototypes being built (construction started January 1989); first flight (K8-001) 21 November 1990; initial production batch expected to be 20-25.

CUSTOMERS: Pakistan Air Force (up to 150 reportedly required); PLA Air Force.

DESIGN FEATURES: Tapered, non-swept low wings, with NACA 64A-114 root and NACA 64A-412 tip sections; 2° incidence at root, 3° dihedral from roots; sweptback vertical/non-swept horizontal tail surfaces; intended for full basic flying training plus parts of primary and advanced syllabi, but capable also of light ground attack missions.

FLYING CONTROLS: Mechanically actuated primary control surfaces; variable incidence tailplane; trim tab in rudder and port elevator; Fowler flaps, and split airbrake under each side of rear fuselage, are hydraulically actuated; ailerons have hydraulic boost.

STRUCTURE: All-metal damage-tolerant main structure; ailerons of honeycomb, fin and rudder of composites.

LANDING GEAR: Retractable tricycle type, with single wheel and oleo-pneumatic shock absorber on each unit. Main units retract inward into underside of fuselage; nosewheel, which has hydraulic steering, retracts forward. Mainwheel tyres size 561 × 169 mm, pressure 6.9 bars (100 lb/sq in). Chinese hydraulic disc brakes. Anti-skid units.

POWER PLANT: One 16.01 kN (3,600 lb st) Garrett TFE731-2A-2A turbofan, mounted in rear fuselage, with intake and splitter plate on each side of fuselage. Fuel in two flexible tanks in fuselage and one integral tank in each wing, combined capacity 1,000 litres (264 US gallons; 220 Imp gallons); single refuelling point in fuselage. Provision for carrying one 250 litre (66 US gallon; 55 Imp gallon) drop tank on inboard pylon under each wing.

ACCOMMODATION: Instructor and pupil in tandem, on Martin-Baker CN10LW zero/zero ejection seats; rear seat elevated. One-piece wraparound windscreen; sideways opening bubble canopy. Cockpits pressurised and air-conditioned.

SYSTEMS: AiResearch air-conditioning and pressurisation system, with max differential of 0.27 bar (3.91 lb/sq in). Hydraulic system, pressure 207 bars (3,000 lb/sq in), for operation of landing gear extension/retraction, wing flaps, airbrakes, aileron boost, nosewheel steering and wheel brakes. Flow rate 15 litres (3.96 US gallons; 3.30 Imp gallons)/min, with air pressurised reservoir, plus emergency backup hydraulic system. Abex AP09V-8-01 pump. Electrical systems 28.5V DC (primary) and 24V DC (auxiliary), with 115/26V single-phase AC and 36V three-phase AC available, both at 400Hz. Gaseous oxygen system for occupants. Demisting of cockpit transparencies.

AVIONICS: Bendix/King avionics, including UHF/VHF and Tacan, in first two prototypes. Collins EFIS-86 system selected for first 100 aircraft, incorporating CRT primary flight and navigation displays for each crew member plus dual display processing units and selector panels for

First prototype of the NAMC/PAC K-8, which was undergoing flight test in 1990-91

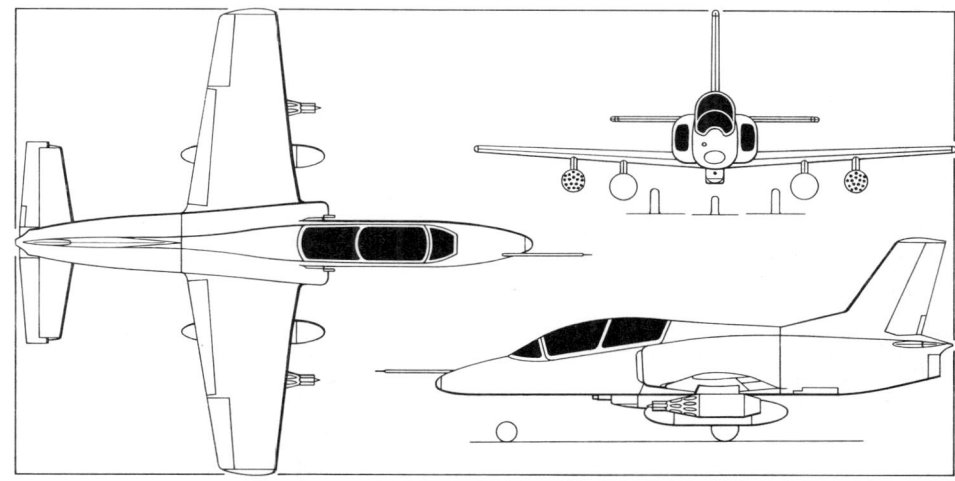

NAMC/PAC K-8 Karakorum 8 jet trainer and light attack aircraft *(Jane's/Mike Keep)*

tandem operation. Collins AN/ARC-186 VHF and Magnavox AN/ARC-164 UHF com radios. Interfaces to the EFIS system include KNR 634A VOR/ILS with marker beacon receiver, ADF, KTU-709 Tacan, Type 265 radio altimeter, WL-7 radio compass, AHRS and air data computer. Standby flight instruments include ASI, rate of climb indicator, barometric altimeter, emergency horizon and standby compass. Blind-flying instrumentation standard.

ARMAMENT: One 23 mm gun pod under centre-fuselage; self-computing optical gunsight in cockpit, plus gun camera. Two external stores points under each wing, capable of carrying gun pods, rocket pods, bombs, missiles, auxiliary fuel tanks (inboard pair only), or a reconnaissance pod.

DIMENSIONS, EXTERNAL:

Wing span	9.63 m (31 ft 7¼ in)
Wing aspect ratio	5.45
Length overall, incl nose pitot	11.60 m (38 ft 0¾ in)
Height overall	4.21 m (13 ft 9¾ in)
Wheel track	2.43 m (7 ft 11¾ in)
Wheelbase	4.38 m (14 ft 4½ in)

AREAS:

Wings, gross	17.05 m² (183.52 sq ft)
Ailerons (total, incl tab)	1.096 m² (11.80 sq ft)
Trailing-edge flaps (total)	2.69 m² (28.95 sq ft)
Fin	1.976 m² (21.27 sq ft)
Rudder, incl tab	1.06 m² (11.41 sq ft)
Tailplane	2.716 m² (29.23 sq ft)
Elevators (total, incl tab)	1.084 m² (11.67 sq ft)

WEIGHTS AND LOADINGS:

Weight empty, equipped	2,557 kg (5,637 lb)
Max fuel: internal	780 kg (1,720 lb)
external (2 drop tanks)	390 kg (860 lb)
T-O weight clean	3,500 kg (7,716 lb)
Max T-O weight with external stores	4,200 kg (9,259 lb)
Max wing loading	246.8 kg/m² (50.57 lb/sq ft)
Max power loading	262.45 kg/kN (2.57 lb/lb st)

PERFORMANCE (at clean T-O weight):

Max level speed at S/L	432 knots (800 km/h; 497 mph)
Touchdown speed	89 knots (165 km/h; 103 mph)
Unstick speed	100 knots (184 km/h; 115 mph)
Max rate of climb at S/L	1,620 m (5,315 ft)/min
Service ceiling	13,290 m (43,600 ft)
T-O run	403 m (1,323 ft)
Landing run	512 m (1,680 ft)
Range:	
max internal fuel	802 nm (1,487 km; 924 miles)
max internal/external fuel	1,214 nm (2,250 km; 1,398 miles)
Endurance: max internal fuel	3 h
max internal/external fuel	4 h 25 min
g limits	+7.33/–3

NH 90

PARTICIPATING COMPANIES:

Aerospatiale: see under France

Agusta: see under Italy

DASA: see under Germany

Fokker: see under Netherlands

PROGRAMME GENERAL CO-ORDINATOR: Gilbert Beziac (Aerospatiale), BP 13, 13725 Marignane Cédex, France

Telephone: 33 42 85 61 95

Telex: AISPA 410975 F

NH 90

TYPE: Multi-role naval (NFH 90) and tactical transport (TTH 90) medium helicopter.

PROGRAMME: September 1985 MoU between defence ministers of France, UK, Germany, Italy and Netherlands led to 14-month feasibility/pre-definition study for new naval/military NH 90 (NATO helicopter for the 1990s); UK withdrew from programme April 1987; German workshare reduced early 1990, Italian participation renegotiated later 1990; common basic configuration for two major versions established by industrial

group of Aerospatiale, MBB, Agusta and Fokker, of which Aerospatiale is general co-ordinator; current percentage workshares are Aerospatiale 43, Agusta 26, MBB 24 and Fokker 7; initial design phase approved December 1986; second MoU in September 1987 led to completion of weapons system definition in 1988; French and German launch decision 26 April 1990; design and development phase to begin 1991; first flight expected late 1994 and initial deliveries late 1998.

VARIANTS: **NFH 90** (NATO Frigate Helicopter): Naval version, primarily for autonomous ASW, ASV and anti-air warfare support missions; additional applications include vertrep, SAR and transport; designed for all-weather/severe ship motion environment.

TTH 90 (Tactical Transport Helicopter): Land-based army/air force version, primarily for tactical transport, airmobile operations, SAR and special (EW) operations; additional applications include tactical support, VIP transport and training; defensive weapons suite; rear-loading ramp/door to be provided for French Army and offered for export.

CUSTOMERS: Estimated total requirements for armed forces of participating countries were 580: 220 NFH 90s and 360 TTH 90s (France 210, Italy 214, Germany 136, Netherlands 20); but French interest reportedly waning.

DESIGN FEATURES: Titanium main rotor hub with elastomeric bearings; four composite blades of advanced aerofoil section and tip planform; bearingless tail rotor with four blades of similar design and construction; automatic folding of main rotor blades and tail pylon in NFH 90; overall design will aim for low vulnerability/detectability, reduced maintenance requirements, and day/night operability within temperature range of –40°C to +50°C.

FLYING CONTROLS: Quadruplex fly-by-wire controls, with higher harmonic blade pitch control to minimise vibration.

STRUCTURE: All-composites fuselage with low radar signature; fail-safe design of structure, rotating parts and systems for high safety levels; automatic health and usage monitoring to maximise survivability, reliability and ease of maintenance.

LANDING GEAR: Retractable crashworthy tricycle gear with twin-wheel nose unit and single-wheel main units.

POWER PLANT: Two 1,599.5 kW (2,145 shp) Rolls-Royce Turbomeca RTM 322-01/02 or 1,558.5 kW (2,090 shp) General Electric CT-7/6 turboshafts.

ACCOMMODATION: Flight crew of two, plus two systems operators (NFH 90) or (in TTH 90) up to 20 equipped troops or a 2 tonne tactical vehicle.

SYSTEMS: Include an APU.

AVIONICS: Will be selected for compatibility with dual MIL-STD-1553B digital databuses, and include multi-function colour displays.

The following data are provisional:

DIMENSIONS, EXTERNAL:
Main rotor diameter	16.00 m (52 ft 6 in)
Tail rotor diameter	3.20 m (10 ft 6 in)
Length: overall, rotors turning	19.38 m (63 ft 7 in)
fuselage, tail rotor turning	16.81 m (55 ft 1¾ in)
folded (NFH)	13.50 m (44 ft 3½ in)
Height: folded (NFH)	4.10 m (13 ft 5½ in)
overall, tail rotor turning	5.422 m (17 ft 9½ in)
Width: over mainwheel fairings	3.69 m (12 ft 1¼ in)
folded	3.84 m (12 ft 7¼ in)
Wheel track	3.20 m (10 ft 6 in)
Wheelbase	6.18 m (20 ft 3¼ in)

DIMENSIONS, INTERNAL:
Cabin: Length, excl rear ramp	4.00 m (13 ft 1½ in)
Max width	2.00 m (6 ft 6¾ in)
Max height	1.58 m (5 ft 2¼ in)
Max volume	18.0 m³ (635.7 cu ft)

AREAS:
Main rotor disc	201.06 m² (2,164.2 sq ft)
Tail rotor disc	8.04 m² (86.57 sq ft)

WEIGHTS AND LOADINGS:
Weight empty, equipped: TTH	5,300 kg (11,684 lb)
NFH	5,700 kg (12,566 lb)
Standard fuel (usable)	1,900 kg (4,189 lb)
Max payload (both)	more than 2,000 kg (4,409 lb)
Max T-O weight: TTH	8,700 kg (19,180 lb)

NFH	9,100 kg (20,062 lb)
Max disc loading: TTH	43.27 kg/m² (8.86 lb/sq ft)
NFH	45.26 kg/m² (9.27 lb/sq ft)

PERFORMANCE (estimated, at appropriate max T-O weight, ISA):
Dash speed at S/L: TTH	162 knots (300 km/h; 186 mph)
Max cruising speed at S/L: TTH	156 knots (290 km/h; 180 mph)
Normal cruising speed at S/L: TTH	135 knots (250 km/h; 155 mph)

Service ceiling: TTH	4,250 m (13,945 ft)
Absolute ceiling: TTH	6,000 m (19,685 ft)
Hovering ceiling: IGE: TTH	3,600 m (11,810 ft)
OGE: TTH	3,000 m (9,850 ft)
Ferry range: TTH	593 nm (1,100 km; 683 miles)

Time on station, 60 nm (111 km; 69 miles) from base, 20 min reserves: NFH   3 h

Max endurance at 75 knots (140 km/h; 87 mph):
NFH   5 h 30 min

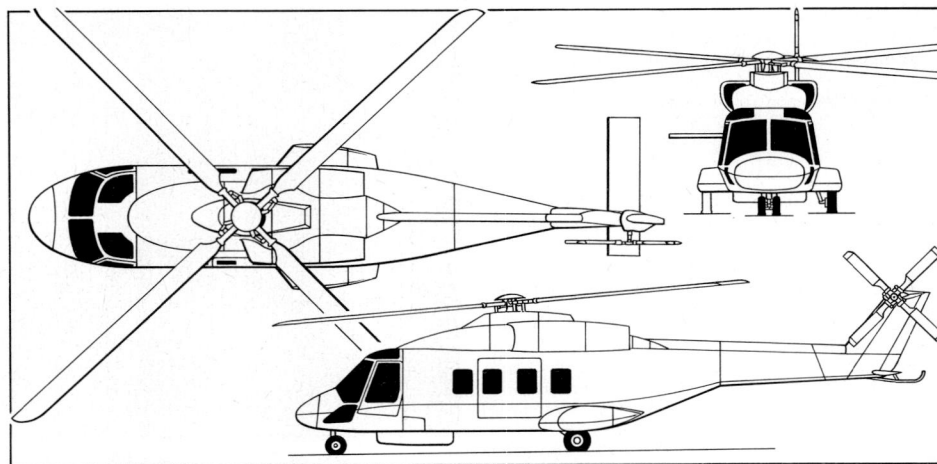

Preliminary three-view of NH 90 NATO helicopter for the 1990s *(Jane's/Mike Keep)*

PANAVIA
PANAVIA AIRCRAFT GmbH

Arabellastrasse 16 (Postfach 860629), 8000 Munich 81, Germany
Telephone: 49 (89) 9217 238/9
Fax: 49 (89) 9217 903
Telex: 05 29 825
PUBLIC RELATIONS: Ralf Wolf
PARTICIPATING COMPANIES:
Alenia: see under Italy
British Aerospace: see under UK
DASA: see under Germany

Panavia formed 26 March 1969 as industrial prime contractor to design, develop and produce an all-weather MRCA (multi-role combat aircraft) for air forces of UK, Germany (incl Navy), Italy and Netherlands; Netherlands withdrew July 1969, shareholdings then readjusted to UK and Germany 42.5 per cent each, Italy 15 per cent. Tornado programme, one of largest European industrial ventures yet undertaken, is guided and monitored on behalf of the three governments by NAMMO (NATO MRCA Management Organisation), whose executive agency NAMMA (formed 15 December 1968) is co-located with Panavia; Tornado production involves three major versions: IDS (interdictor/strike), ECR (electronic combat and reconnaissance) and ADV (air defence variant).

PANAVIA TORNADO IDS
RAF designations: GR. Mks 1, 1A and 4

TYPE: All-weather close air support/battlefield interdiction, interdiction/counter-air strike, naval strike and reconnaissance aircraft.

PROGRAMME: Six-government feasibility study (originally involving Belgium and Canada) initiated 17 July 1968; project definition began 1 May 1969; development phase started 22 July 1970; structural design completed August 1972; first flight 14 August 1974 by first of nine prototypes (P01-09: see 1978-79 *Jane's* for details); Tornado name adopted September 1974; German procurement approved 19 May 1976; production programme initiated 29 July 1976 by three-government MoU for 809 aircraft in six batches (640 IDS, 165 ADV, plus four pre-series aircraft brought up to IDS production standard); first flight 5 February 1977 by first of six pre-series Tornados (PP11-16: see 1980-81 and earlier editions); Italian production began 29 January 1977; first flights by production IDS in UK and Germany 10 and 27 July 1979 respectively; deliveries for operational conversion training (to Tri-national Tornado Training Establishment at RAF Cottesmore) began 1 July 1980; first flight by Italian production aircraft 25 September 1981; operational squadron deliveries began 1982 to RAF (6 January), Germany (Navy, 2 July) and Italy (27 August); first export delivery (to Saudi Arabia) March 1986; batch 7 contract (57 IDS, 35 ECR and 32 ADV) awarded 10 June 1986; contract to develop mid-life update for RAF GR. Mk 1 awarded 16 March 1977; 26 GR. Mk 4 (part of proposed batch 8) cancelled 18 June 1990; completion of IDS/ECR production to batch 7 orders due 1992.

No. IX Squadron Tornado GR. Mk 1 with underfuselage TIALD laser designation pod *(Paul Jackson)*

VARIANTS: **ECR:** Electronic combat and reconnaissance version, utilising IDS airframe; described separately.

German Air Force IDS: Equips nine squadrons: two each with JBGs 31 (Nörvenich), 32 (Lechfeld), 33 (Büchel) and 34 (Memmingen), all NATO-assigned, plus one with weapons training unit JBG 38 (Jever); others at TTTE in UK and WTD 61 at Manching; all German Tornados cleared for in-flight refuelling by USAF KC-10A and KC-135 tankers; mid-life improvement programme under development for German and Italian Tornados, to confer more accurate navigation for blind attacks, improved capability for sortie generation, increased range and target acquisition capability, reduced penetration altitude, improved ESM, better threat suppression and greater reliability/maintainability. Principal weapons MW-1, AIM-9L, AGM-65, AGM-88.

German Navy IDS: Equips four operational squadrons: two (NATO-assigned) with Marinefliegergeschwader 1 (Jagel) and one with MFG 2 (Eggebeck) for strike missions against sea and coastal targets, plus one (1/MFG 2) for reconnaissance using MBB/Alenia multi-sensor pod; mid-life update under development (see preceding paragraph). Principal weapons carried are BL 755, AIM-9L, AGM-88, Kormoran 1 and 2.

Italian Air Force IDS: In service with three operational squadrons: Gruppi 154 (6° Stormo at Brescia-Ghedi), 155 (50° Stormo, Piacenza) and the Kormoran anti-shipping Gruppo 156 (36° Stormo, Gioia del Colle), plus the Reparto Sperimentale di Volo at Pratica di Mare; mid-life update under development (see German Air Force paragraph for details). Principal weapons carried are MW-1, AIM-9L, AGM-65D, AGM-88, Kormoran 2.

Royal Air Force GR. Mk 1: UK IDS version, equipping seven NATO-assigned squadrons with RAF Germany (Nos. IX, 14, 17 and 31 at Brüggen, Nos. XV, 16 and 20 at Laarbruch) and two SACEUR-declared squadrons in UK (Nos. 27 and 617 at Marham), plus UK training units (TTTE at Cottesmore, TWCU at Honington), Strike/Attack Operational Evaluation Unit

(Boscombe Down), A&AEE, and RAE Bedford. Laarbruch Squadrons to be disbanded. Squadron deliveries (to No. IX) began 6 January 1982; modification for tactical nuclear weapon carriage began 1984; first combat use (Gulf War) 17 January 1991; to be redesignated GR. Mk 4 (which see) after receiving mid-life update. Principal weapons carried are JP 233, BL 755, AIM-9L, ALARM, CPU-123.

Royal Air Force GR. Mk 1A: UK day/night all-weather tactical reconnaissance version, equipping No. 2 Squadron (Marham) and No. 13 (Honington); one development aircraft (ZA402, first flight 11 July 1985) followed by 15 others also converted from GR. Mk 1 (delivered from 3 April 1987) and 14 new-production Mk 1As (delivered from 13 October 1989). Retains air-to-surface role except for deletion of guns; identifiable by small underbelly blister fairing (immediately behind laser rangefinder pod) and transparent side panels for BAe SLIR (sideways looking infra-red) system and Vinten Linescan 4000 surveillance system; has Computing Devices Co signal processing and video recording system (first video-based tac/recce system with replay facility) offering capability for future real-time reconnaissance data relay; first operational mission in Gulf War, night of 18/19 January 1991.

Royal Air Force GR. Mk 4: Designation to be applied to GR. Mk 1s after receiving MLU (mid-life update); modifications include new Marconi Defence Systems EW suite; GEC Avionics Spartan TRN/TF (terrain referenced navigation/terrain following), updated weapon control system, advanced video recording system with ground replay facility, and computer loading system; new Ferranti HUD with computer generated symbology, TF display 3-D ground profile, and digital storage/image generating system for moving map display; Smiths colour CRT head-down display. First flight expected late 1991.

Royal Saudi Air Force IDS: Equips two squadrons (Nos. 7 and 66), each including some configured for reconnaissance; deliveries March 1986 to October 1987

(first 20), remainder from May 1989 (continuing in early 1991). Principal weapons carried are JP 233, AIM-9L, ALARM; Sea Eagle on order.

Tornado 2000: Proposed successor to RAF GR. Mk 4; would be single-seat, optimised for low-level/high-speed/long-range penetration and able to carry standoff weapons; longer fuselage than current IDS, containing increased fuel tankage; faceted nose section and pitot intakes to minimise radar signature.

CUSTOMERS: Total of 732 IDS/ECR (plus four refurbished pre-series IDS) ordered for Germany (359: Air Force 157 strike incl two pre-series, 35 ECR and 55 dual control, Navy 100 strike incl 12 dual), Italy (100: Air Force 88 strike incl one pre-series, plus 12 dual), Saudi Arabia (48: Air Force 34 strike or recce plus 14 dual) and UK (229: Air Force 164 strike, 14 recce, and 51 dual incl one pre-series). Total of 664 IDS delivered by 31 December 1990 (Germany Air Force 212/Navy 112, Italy 100, Saudi Arabia 24, UK 216).

DESIGN FEATURES: Continuously variable geometry shoulder wings, with leading-edge sweep angles of 25° (minimum) and 67° (maximum) on movable portions, 60° on fixed inboard portions; modest overall dimensions; high wing loading to minimise low-altitude gust response; swivelling wing pylons to retain stores alignment with fuselage; sweep limited to 63° if 2,250 litre drop tanks carried.

FLYING CONTROLS: Full span double-slotted fixed-vane flaperons (four segments per side), all-moving tailplane (tailerons) and inset rudder, all actuated by electrically controlled tandem hydraulic jacks; full span wing leading-edge slats (three segments each side); two upper-surface spoilers/lift dumpers forward of each central pair of flaperons; tailerons operate together for pitch control and differentially for roll control; spoilers provide augmented roll control at unswept and intermediate wing positions at low speed; Krueger flap on leading-edge of each wing glove box; door type airbrake each side on top of rear fuselage; wing sweep hydraulically powered via ballscrew actuators (aircraft can land safely with wings fully swept if sweep mechanism fails); triple-redundant CSAS (command stability augmentation system), APFD (autopilot/flight director) and TFE (terrain following E-scope), as detailed under Avionics paragraph.

STRUCTURE: Basically all-metal (mostly aluminium alloy with integrally stiffened skins, titanium alloy for wing carry-through box and pivot attachments); FRP for nosecone, dielectric panels and interface between fixed and movable portions of wings; Teflon plated wing pivot bearings; elastic seal between outer wings and fuselage sides; nosecone hinges sideways to starboard for access to radar antennae; slice of fuselage immediately aft of nosecone also hinges to starboard for access to forward avionics bay and rear of radars; passive ECM antenna fairing near top of fin; ram air intake for heat exchanger at base of fin. Alenia builds entire outer wings (incl moving surfaces), with Microtecnica as prime contractor for sweep system; BAe (Warton) builds front and rear fuselage portions (incl engine installation) and entire tail unit; MBB is prime contractor for centre-fuselage (incl engine intake ducts, wing centre-section box, pivot mechanism, and interface with outer wings); radar-transparent nosecone by Telefunken Systemtechnik.

The following details apply to the basic IDS production version; subsystem details are listed by team leader only, for the sake of clarity.

LANDING GEAR: Hydraulically retractable tricycle type, with forward retracting twin-wheel steerable nose unit. Single-wheel main units retract forward and upward into centre section of fuselage. Emergency extension system, using nitrogen gas pressure. Development and manufacture of the complete landing gear and associated hydraulics is headed by Dowty (UK). Dunlop aluminium alloy wheels, hydraulic multi-disc brakes and low-pressure tyres (to permit operation from soft, semi-prepared surfaces) and Goodyear anti-skid units. Mainwheel tyres size 30 × 11.50-14.5, Type VIII (24 or 26 ply); nosewheel tyres size 18 × 5.5, Type VIII (12 ply). Runway arrester hook beneath rear of fuselage.

POWER PLANT: Two Turbo-Union RB199-34R turbofans, fitted with bucket type thrust reversers and installed in rear fuselage with downward opening doors for servicing and engine change. Mk 101 engines of early production aircraft nominally rated at 38.7 kN (8,700 lb st) dry and 66.0 kN (14,840 lb st) with afterburning (uninstalled); RAF aircraft have their engines down-rated to 37.7 kN (8,475 lb st) in squadron service (37.0 kN; 8,320 lb st dry for TTTE) to extend service life. Mk 103 engines, introduced in May 1983 (engine number 761), are dry rated nominally at 40.5 kN (9,100 lb st) uninstalled (38.5 kN; 8,650 lb st for RAF) and provide 71.5 kN (16,075 lb st) with afterburning. RAF ordered 100 modification kits in 1983 to upgrade Mk 101 engined aircraft to Mk 103 standard. All internal fuel in multi-cell Uniroyal self-sealing integral fuselage tanks and/or wing box tanks, all fitted with press-in fuel sampling and water drain plugs, and all refuelled from a single-point NATO connector. Capacity of these tanks totals approx 5,814 litres (1,536 US gallons; 1,279 Imp gallons). Additional 551 litre (145.5 US gallon; 121 Imp gallon) tank in fin (on RAF aircraft only). Detachable and retractable in-flight

Royal Air Force Tornado GR. Mk 1 in 'Pink Panther' camouflage adopted for Operations Desert Shield and Desert Storm, 1990-91 *(Paul Jackson)*

First new-build Tornado GR. Mk 1A reconnaissance variant (ZG705) in the markings of No. 13 Squadron, RAF *(Paul Jackson)*

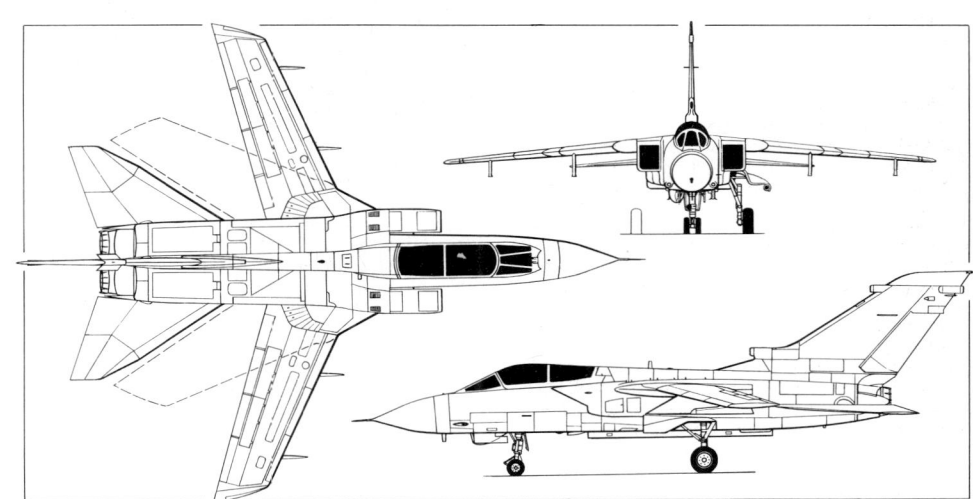
Panavia Tornado IDS multi-role combat aircraft *(Pilot Press)*

refuelling probe can be mounted on starboard side of fuselage, adjacent to cockpit. Provision for one or two drop tanks to be carried beneath fuselage (1,500 litres; 396 US gallons; 330 Imp gallons) and single tanks on the shoulder pylons and inboard underwing pylons (1,500 or 2,250 litres; 396 or 594 US gallons; 330 or 495 Imp gallons). Some German Navy and Italian Air Force aircraft adapted to carry a Sargent-Fletcher Type 28-300 1,135 litre (300 US gallon; 250 Imp gallon) buddy type hose/drogue refuelling pod. Dowty afterburning fuel control system. Telefunken Systemtechnik intake de-icing system.

ACCOMMODATION: Crew of two on tandem Martin-Baker Mk 10A zero/zero ejection seats under Kopperschmidt one-piece canopy, which is hinged at rear and opens upward. Flat centre armoured windscreen panel and curved side panels, built by Lucas Aerospace, incorporate Sierracote electrically conductive heating film for windscreen anti-icing and demisting. Canopy (and windscreen in emergency) demisted by engine bleed air. Windscreen is hinged at front and can be opened forward and upward, allowing access to back of pilot's instrument panel. Seats provide safe escape at zero altitude and at speeds from zero up to 630 knots (1,166 km/h; 725 mph) IAS.

SYSTEMS: Cockpit air-conditioned and pressurised (max differential 0.36 bars; 5.25 lb/sq in) by Normalair-Garrett conventional air cycle system (with bootstrap cold air unit) using engine bleed air with ram air precooler, Marston intercooler, and Teddington temperature

control system. Nordmicro air intake control system, and Dowty engine intake ramp control actuators. Two independent hydraulic systems, each of 276 bars (4,000 lb/sq in pressure), are supplied from two separate, independently driven Vickers pumps, each mounted on an engine accessory gearbox. Each system is supplied from a separate bootstrap type reservoir. Systems provide fully duplicated power for primary flight control system, tailerons, rudder, flaps, slats, wing sweep, pitch Q-feel system, and refuelling probe. Port system also supplies power for Krueger flaps, inboard spoilers, port air intake ramps, canopy, and wheel brakes; starboard system for airbrakes, outboard spoilers, starboard air intake ramps, landing gear, nosewheel steering, and radar stabilisation and scanning. Main system includes Dowty accumulators and Teves power pack. Fairey Hydraulics system for actuation of spoilers, rudder and taileron control. Provision for reversion to single-engine drive of both systems, via a mechanical cross-connection between the two engine auxiliary gearboxes, in the event of a single engine failure. In the event of a double engine flameout, an emergency pump in No. 1 system has sufficient duration for re-entry into the engine cold relight boundary. Flying control circuits are protected from loss of fluid due to leaks in other circuits by isolating valves which shut off the utility circuits if the reservoir contents drop below a predetermined safety limit level. Electrical system consists of a 115/200V AC three-phase 400Hz constant frequency subsystem and a 28V DC subsystem. Power is generated by two Rotax automatically controlled oil-cooled brushless AC generators integrated with a constant speed drive unit and driven by the engines via a KHD accessory gearbox. Normally, each engine drives its own accessory gearbox, but provision is also made for either engine to drive the opposite gearbox through a cross-drive system. In the event of a generator failure, the remaining unit can supply the total aircraft load. Both gearboxes and generators can be driven by APU when aircraft is on ground. The generators supply two main AC busbars and an AC essential busbar. DC power is provided from two fan-cooled transformer/rectifier units (power being derived from the main AC system), these feeding power to two main DC busbars, one essential DC busbar and a battery busbar. Either TRU can supply total aircraft DC load. A fifth DC busbar is provided for maintenance purposes only. Battery is a rechargeable nickel-cadmium type, and provides power for basic flightline servicing and for starting APU. In the event of main electrical system or double TRU failure, it is connected automatically to the essential services busbar to supply essential electrical loads. Normalair-Garrett demand type oxygen system, using a 10 litre (2.6 US gallon; 2.2 Imp gallon) lox converter. Emergency oxygen system installed on each seat. GEC Avionics flow metering system. Eichweber fuel gauging system and Flight Refuelling flexible couplings. Graviner fire detection and extinguishing systems. Rotax contactors. Smiths engine speed and temperature indicators.

AVIONICS: Communications equipment includes GEC-Plessey PTR 1721 (UK and Italy) or Rohde und Schwarz (Germany) UHF/VHF transceiver; Telefunken Systemtechnik UHF/ADF (UK and Germany only); SIT emergency UHF with Rohde and Schwarz switch; BAe HF/SSB aerial tuning unit; Rohde und Schwarz (UK and Germany) or Montedel (Italy) HF/SSB radio; Ultra communications control system; GEC Avionics central suppression unit (CSU); Leigh voice recorder; Chelton UHF communications and landing system aerials.

Primary self-contained nav/attack system includes a European built Texas Instruments multi-mode forward looking, terrain following ground mapping radar; GEC Ferranti FIN 1010 three-axis digital inertial navigation system (DINS) and combined radar and map display; Decca Type 72 Doppler radar system, with Kalman filtering of the Doppler and inertial inputs for extreme navigational accuracy; Microtecnica air data computer; Litef Spirit 3 central digital computer (64K initially, 224K on current production aircraft); Alenia radio/radar altimeter (to be replaced on RAF aircraft by GEC Sensors AD1990 covert radar altimeter); Smiths electronic head-up display with Davall camera; GEC Ferranti nose mounted laser rangefinder and marked target seeker; GEC Avionics TV tabular display; Astronautics (USA) bearing distance and heading indicator and contour map display. Defensive equipment includes Siemens (Germany) or Cossor SSR-3100 (UK and Saudi Arabia) IFF transponder; and Elettronica ARI 23284 radar warning receiver (being replaced in GR. Mk 1 from 1987 by Marconi Defence Systems Hermes RHWR). Production batches 6 and 7 (556th IDS onwards) incorporate a MIL-STD-1553B databus, upgraded radar warning equipment and active ECM, an improved missile control unit, and integration of HARM anti-radar missile.

Flight control system includes a GEC Avionics triplex command stability augmentation system (CSAS), incorporating fly-by-wire and autostabilisation; GEC Avionics autopilot and flight director (APFD), using two self-monitoring digital computers; GEC Avionics triplex transducer unit (TTU), with analog computing and sensor channels; GEC Avionics terrain following E-scope (TFE), Fairey quadruplex electro-hydraulic actuator; and Microtecnica air data set. The APFD provides preselected attitude, heading or barometric height hold, heading and track acquisition, and Mach number or airspeed hold with autothrottle. Flight director operates in parallel with, and can be used as backup for, the autopilot, as a duplex digital system with an extensive range of modes. Automatic approach, terrain following and radio height-holding modes are also available. Other instrumentation includes Smiths HSI, VSI and standby altimeter; Lital standby AHRS; SEL (with Setac) or (in UK aircraft) GEC Avionics AD2770 (without Setac) Tacan; Cossor CILS 75/76 ILS; Bodenseewerk attitude director indicator; Dornier flight data recorder. Marconi Sky Shadow (jamming/deception) and BOZ 101 (Germany), 102 (Italy) or 107 (UK) chaff/flare ECM pods. Telefunken Systemtechnik Cerberus II or III jammer pods on German and Italian aircraft. GEC Ferranti TIALD (thermal imaging airborne laser designator) night/adverse visibility pods for RAF No. IX Squadron Tornados. (Can also carry similar Thomson-CSF CLDP pod.) Various terrain reference navigation systems have also been developed, including BAe Terprom, GEC Spartan, and Ferranti Penetrate, as have night vision systems incorporating FLIR and NVGs.

EQUIPMENT: German Navy and Italian Air Force Tornados can carry an MBB/Alenia multi-sensor reconnaissance pod on the centreline pylon. RAF GR. Mk 1A fitted with infra-red cameras in ammunition bay.

Tornado ECR (electronic combat and reconnaissance) aircraft of the German Luftwaffe, carrying two underfuselage HARM anti-radiation missiles

ARMAMENT: Fixed armament comprises two 27 mm IWKA-Mauser cannon, one in each side of the lower forward fuselage, with 180 rds/gun. Other armament varies according to version, with emphasis on the ability to carry a wide range of advanced weapons. A GEC Avionics stores management system is fitted; Sandall Mace 355 and 762 mm (14 and 30 in) ejector release units standard on UK Tornados; German and Italian aircraft use multiple weapon carriage system (MWCS) ejector release units. ML Aviation CBLS 200 practice bomb carriers are also standard. The battlefield interdiction version is capable of carrying weapons for hard or soft targets. Weapons are carried on seven fuselage and wing hardpoints: one centreline pylon fitted with a single ejection release unit (ERU), two fuselage shoulder pylons each with three ERUs, and, under each wing, one inboard and one outboard pylon each with a single ERU. Among the weapons carried by the IDS Tornado are the Sidewinder air-to-air, and ALARM or HARM anti-radiation missiles; JP 233 low-altitude airfield attack munition dispenser; CPU-123B Paveway laser guided bomb; Maverick, Sea Eagle and Kormoran air-to-surface missiles; napalm; BL755 cluster bombs (277 kg; 611 lb Mk 1 or 264 kg; 582 lb Mk 2); MW-1 munitions dispenser; 1,000 lb bombs; smart or retarded bombs; BLU-1B 750 lb fire bombs; Matra 250 kg ballistic and retarded bombs; Lepus flare bombs; LAU-51A and LR-25 rocket launchers.

DIMENSIONS, EXTERNAL:

Wing span: fully spread	13.91 m (45 ft 7½ in)
fully swept	8.60 m (28 ft 2½ in)
Length overall	16.72 m (54 ft 10¼ in)
Height overall	5.95 m (19 ft 6¼ in)
Tailplane span	6.80 m (22 ft 3½ in)
Wheel track	3.10 m (10 ft 2 in)
Wheelbase	6.20 m (20 ft 4 in)

AREAS:

Wings, gross (to fuselage c/l, 25° sweepback)
$\qquad$ 26.60 m² (286.3 sq ft)

WEIGHTS AND LOADINGS:

Basic weight empty	approx 13,890 kg (30,620 lb)
Weight empty, equipped	14,091 kg (31,065 lb)
Fuel:	
internal: wing/fuselage tanks	4,650 kg (10,251 lb)
fin tank (RAF only)	440 kg (970 lb)
drop tanks (each): 1,500 litre	1,197 kg (2,640 lb)
2,250 litre	1,796 kg (3,960 lb)
Nominal max external stores load	
	more than 9,000 kg (19,840 lb)
Max T-O weight:	
clean, full internal fuel	20,411 kg (45,000 lb)
with external stores	approx 27,950 kg (61,620 lb)

PERFORMANCE:

Max Mach number in level flight at altitude, clean	2.2
Max level speed, clean	
above 800 knots (1,480 km/h; 920 mph) IAS	
Max level speed with external stores	
Mach 0.92 (600 knots; 1,112 km/h; 691 mph)	
Landing speed approx 115 knots (213 km/h; 132 mph)	
Time to 9,150 m (30,000 ft) from brake release	
less than 2 min	
Automatic terrain following down to 61 m (200 ft)	
Required runway length less than 900 m (2,950 ft)	
Landing run 370 m (1,215 ft)	

Max 360° rapid roll clearance with full lateral control
$\qquad$ 4g
Radius of action with heavy weapons load, hi-lo-lo-hi
$\qquad$ 750 nm (1,390 km; 863 miles)
Ferry range $\qquad$ approx 2,100 nm (3,890 km; 2,420 miles)
g limit $\qquad$ +7.5

PANAVIA TORNADO ECR

TYPE: Electronic combat and reconnaissance version of Tornado IDS.

PROGRAMME: Selected by German Luftwaffe to supplement existing in-service tactical reconnaissance aircraft such as Wild Weasel F-4G Phantom; 35 included in batch 7 production contract signed 10 June 1986; two development aircraft (s/n 9803 and 9878) converted from IDS (first flight 18 August 1988); first production aircraft (s/n 4623) made first flight 26 October 1989; deliveries (to 2/JBG 38 initially, later to 3/JBG 32) began 21 May 1990, due for completion July 1991.

VARIANTS: **ECR:** Intended for standoff reconnaissance and border control, reconnaissance via image-forming and electronic means, electronic support, and employment of anti-radar guided missiles.

CUSTOMERS: Germany (Air Force 35, of which 15 delivered by 31 December 1990); Italian intention to acquire about 16 has lapsed.

The description of the IDS Tornado applies generally also to the ECR version except as follows:

POWER PLANT: Mk 105 version of RB199 engine, providing approx 10 per cent more thrust than Mk 103.

AVIONICS: Include Texas Instruments ELS (emitter location system); Honeywell/Sondertechnik infra-red linescan; Zeiss FLIR; onboard processing/storing/transmission systems for reconnaissance data; advanced tactical displays for pilot and weapons officer.

ARMAMENT: Both internal cannon deleted; external load stations can be used for ECR or fighter-bomber missions, or a combination of both; in ECR role will normally be configured to carry two HARM missiles, two AIM-9L Sidewinders, an active ECM pod, chaff/flare dispenser pod, and two 1,500 litre (396 US gallon; 330 Imp gallon) underwing fuel tanks.

PANAVIA TORNADO ADV
RAF designations: Tornado F. Mks 2, 2A and 3

TYPE: All-weather air defence interceptor, air superiority fighter and combat patrol aircraft.

PROGRAMME: Feasibility studies for ADV (air defence variant) for UK, begun in 1968, given impetus by MoD Air Staff Target 395 of 1971 for interceptor with advanced radar and Sky Flash air-to-air missiles; full scale development authorised 4 March 1976; three prototypes (first flight 27 October 1979) included in production batch 1; first flight by F. Mk 2 production aircraft 5 March 1984; last F. Mk 2 delivered 9 October 1985; first flight by F. Mk 3 made 20 November 1985; first export order (by Saudi Arabia) placed 26 September 1985.

VARIANTS: **Royal Air Force F. Mk 2:** Designation of first 18 (batch 4) production ADVs, with RB199 Mk 103 engines (further details in 1989-90 and earlier *Jane's*); currently in store except for one each with A&AEE and

ETPS at Boscombe Down, RAE at Farnborough; scheduled for return to BAe in early 1990s for upgrade to F. Mk 2A (which see).

Royal Air Force F. Mk 2A: Designation to be applied to F. Mk 2s after being upgraded largely to F. Mk 3 standard except for retention of Mk 103 engines.

Royal Air Force F. Mk 3: Current definitive production version (batches 5-7), delivered from 28 July 1986 (to No. 229 OCU/65 Squadron at Coningsby); now equips six UK air defence squadrons (Nos. 5 and 29 at Coningsby, Nos. 11, 23 and 25 at Leeming and Nos. 43 and 111 at Leuchars); primary missions are air defence of UK, protection of NATO's northern and western approaches, and long-range air defence of UK maritime forces; main differences from F. Mk 2 are uprated (Mk 104) engines, automatic wing sweep and manoeuvring systems, and improved avionics (see Flying Controls, Structure, Power Plant and Avionics paragraphs).

Royal Saudi Air Force ADV: Equips Nos. 29 and 34 Squadrons at Dhahran; deliveries began (to No. 29) 20 March 1989.

CUSTOMERS: Total 197 ordered for UK (RAF 173 incl 52 dual control) and Saudi Arabia (Air Force 24 incl six dual); RAF total includes eight dual control aircraft transferred, but not necessarily as trainers, from cancelled Omani order; total of 165 ADVs delivered (UK 141, Saudi Arabia 24) by 31 December 1990.

DESIGN FEATURES: Structural changes reduce drag, especially at supersonic speed, compared with IDS version, and longer fuselage provides more space for avionics and additional 10 per cent internal fuel.

FLYING CONTROLS: Similar to IDS, but with AWS (automatic wing sweep), AMDS (automatic manoeuvre device system) and SPILS (spin prevention and incidence limiting system); AWS allows scheduling of four different sweep angles (25° at speeds up to Mach 0.73, 45° from there up to Mach 0.88, 58° up to Mach 0.95 and 67° above Mach 0.95), enabling specific excess power at transonic speeds and turning capability at subsonic speeds to be maximised; buffet-free handling can be maintained, to limits defined by SPILS, by using AMDS, which schedules with wing incidence to deploy either flaperons and slats at 25° sweep angle or slats-only at 45° (beyond 45°, both flaperons and slats are scheduled in); fly-by-wire CSAS/APFD system modified for increased roll rate and reduced pitch stick forces.

STRUCTURE: Generally as IDS version except: fuselage lengthened forward of front cockpit to accommodate longer radome, and aft of rear cockpit to allow Sky Flash missiles to be carried in two tandem pairs; CG shift compensated by extending fixed inboard portions of wings to increase chord and give 67° leading-edge sweep angle; Krueger flaps deleted; afterburner nozzles extended by 360 mm (14 in) on F. Mk 3, requiring modification to adjacent contours of rudder and tailerons; one internal gun deleted; wing/tailplane/fin leading-edges of 20 F. Mk 3s coated with radar absorbent material (RAM) for early 1991 Gulf operations.

LANDING GEAR: As IDS version, but nosewheel steering augmented to minimise 'wander' on landing.

POWER PLANT: Two Turbo-Union RB199-34R Mk 104 turbofans, each with uninstalled rating of 40.5 kN (9,100 lb st) dry and 73.5 kN (16,520 lb st) with afterburning. Lucas digital engine control. Internal fuel capacity (incl fin tank) 7,114 litres (1,879 US gallons; 1,565 Imp gallons). Internally mounted, fully retractable in-flight refuelling probe in port side of nose, adjacent to cockpit. Provision for drop tanks of 1,500 or 2,250 litres (396 or 594 US gallons; 330 or 495 Imp gallons) capacity to be carried on the shoulder pylons and underwing pylons.

ACCOMMODATION: As for IDS version.

SYSTEMS: Generally as described for IDS version, with the addition of a radar-dedicated cold air unit to cool the Foxhunter radar, and a pop-up ram air turbine to assist recovery in the event of engine flameout at high altitude in a zoom climb.

AVIONICS: Among those in the IDS Tornado which are retained in the ADV are the communications equipment (GEC-Plessey VHF/UHF transceiver, SIT emergency UHF, Rohde und Schwarz HF/SSB, Ultra communications control system and Epsylon cockpit voice recorder); GEC Avionics triplex fly-by-wire CSAS and APFD system; Litef Spirit 3 central digital computer (with capacity increased from 64K to 224K) and data transmission system; Smiths electronic head-up and navigator's head-down display; GEC Ferranti FIN 1010 inertial navigation system (to which is added a second 1010 to monitor the head-up display); GEC Sensors Tacan; Cossor ILS; and Cossor IFF transponder. Those deleted include the Texas Instruments nose radar, Decca 72 Doppler radar with terrain following, GEC Ferranti laser rangefinder and marked target seeker, and Lital standby AHRS.

Nose-mounted Marconi Defence Systems AI Mk 24 Foxhunter multi-mode track-while-scan pulse Doppler radar with FMICW (frequency modulated interrupted continuous wave), with which is integrated a new Cossor IFF-3500 interrogator and a radar signal processor to suppress ground clutter. This system is intended to enable the aircraft to detect targets more than 100 nm (185 km; 115 miles) away, and to track several targets

simultaneously. A ground mapping mode for navigation backup is available. GEC Ferranti is subcontractor for the Foxhunter transmitter and aerial scanning mechanism. New data processor, being introduced during early 1990s, offers final Foxhunter standard considerably more capable than earlier versions of this radar, in particular more automation to improve close combat capability. Modification kits will bring radars already in service up to the new standard. A pilot's head-down display is added, a GEC Ferranti displayed data video recorder (DDVR) replaces the navigator's wet-film display recorder, and a Marconi Defence Systems Hermes modular RHWR is added. Head-up/head-down displays are on front instrument panel only, radar control and data link presentations on rear panel only; both panels have weapon control and RHWR displays. A GEC Ferranti FH 31A AC driven 3 in horizon gyro in the rear cockpit, in addition to providing an attitude display for the navigator, feeds pitch and roll signals to other avionics systems in the aircraft in certain modes. Lucas digital electronic engine control unit (DECU 500). ESM (electronic surveillance measures) and ECCM are standard; a Plessey Electronics ECM-resistant data link system, interoperable with other NATO systems, is under development for installation later. Because of its comprehensive avionics the Tornado ADV can contribute significantly to the transfer of vital information over the entire tactical area and can, if necessary, partially fulfil the roles of both AEW and ground based radar. Smiths Industries/Computing Devices Company missile management system (MMS), which also controls tank jettison, has provision for pilot override, optimised for visual attack. Studies being undertaken for 1553B multiplex digital databus associated with AMRAAM and Sidewinder replacement.

ARMAMENT: Fixed armament of one 27 mm IWKA-Mauser cannon in starboard side of lower forward fuselage. Four BAe Sky Flash semi-active radar homing medium-range air-to-air missiles semi-recessed under the centre-fuselage, carried on internally mounted Frazer-Nash launchers; two European built NWC AIM-9L Sidewinder infra-red homing short-range air-to-air missiles on each inboard underwing station (outboard stations not used on RAF ADVs). The Sky Flash missiles, each fitted with an MSDS monopulse seeker head, can engage targets at high altitude or down to 75 m (250 ft), in the face of heavy ECM, and at standoff ranges of more than 25 nm (46 km; 29 miles). Release system permits the missile to be fired over the Tornado's full flight envelope. For the future, the ADV will be able to carry, instead of Sky Flash and Sidewinder, up to six Hughes AIM-20 AMRAAM or BAe Active Sky Flash medium-range and four new-generation short-range air-to-air missiles.

Royal Air Force 'Desert Eagles' Tornado F. Mk 3 with Stage 1 + modifications *(Paul Jackson)*

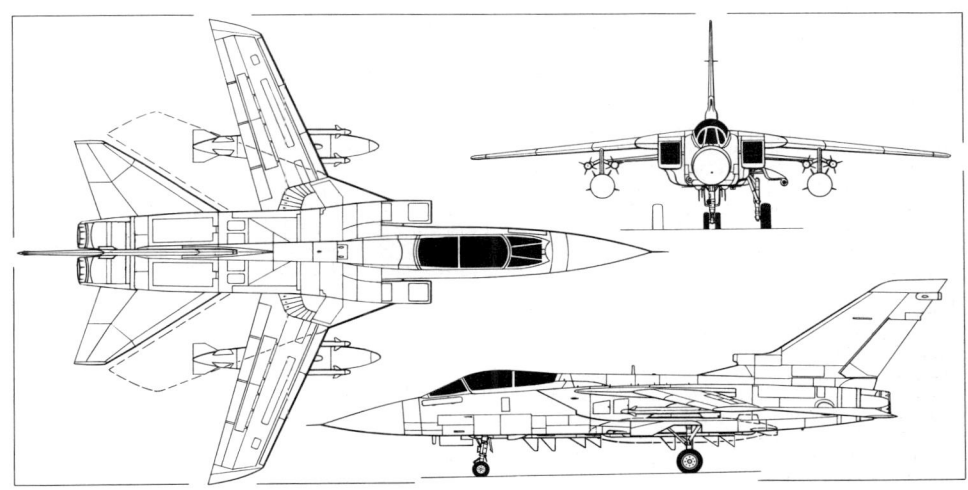

Panavia Tornado F. Mk 3 all-weather air defence interceptor *(Pilot Press)*

DIMENSIONS, EXTERNAL: As for IDS version, except:

Length overall	18.68 m (61 ft 3½ in)

WEIGHTS AND LOADINGS (approx):

Operational weight empty	14,500 kg (31,970 lb)
Fuel:	
internal: wing/fuselage tanks	5,250 kg (11,574 lb)
fin tank	as for IDS version
drop tanks	as for IDS version
Max external fuel	5,806 kg (12,800 lb)
Nominal max external stores load	8,500 kg (18,740 lb)
Max T-O weight	27,986 kg (61,700 lb)

PERFORMANCE:

Max Mach number in level flight at altitude, clean	2.2
Max level speed, clean	800 knots (1,480 km/h; 920 mph) IAS
Rotation speed, depending on AUW	145-160 knots (269-297 km/h; 167-184 mph)
Normal touchdown speed	115 knots (213 km/h; 132 mph)
Demonstrated roll rate at 750 knots (1,390 km/h; 864 mph) and up to 4g	180°/s
Operational ceiling	approx 21,335 m (70,000 ft)
T-O run:	
with normal weapon and fuel load	760 m (2,500 ft)
ferry configuration (four 1,500 litre drop tanks and full weapon load)	approx 1,525 m (5,000 ft)
T-O to 15 m (50 ft)	under 915 m (3,000 ft)
Landing from 15 m (50 ft)	approx 610 m (2,000 ft)
Landing run with thrust reversal	370 m (1,215 ft)

Intercept radius:
supersonic more than 300 nm (556 km; 345 miles)
subsonic more than 1,000 nm (1,853 km; 1,151 miles)
Endurance
2 h combat air patrol at 300-400 nm (555-740 km; 345-460 miles) from base, incl time for interception and 10 min combat

ROCKWELL INTERNATIONAL/MBB

PARTICIPATING COMPANIES:

Rockwell International: see under USA
DASA/MBB: see under Germany

Known also by programme title EFM (Enhanced Fighter Maneuverability), X-31A is first US 'X' series experimental aircraft developed jointly with another country, and was one of first NATO co-operative efforts part-funded under Nunn-Quayle R&D initiative. DARPA, acting through US Naval Air Systems Command, is working with German Ministry of Defence to manage development programme.

The first X-31A fitted with its exhaust deflector paddles

ROCKWELL INTERNATIONAL/MBB X-31A EFM

TYPE: Single-seat combat manoeuvrability research aircraft.

PROGRAMME: Evolved from work begun at MBB 1977; joined by Rockwell 1983; feasibility study began November 1984, followed by US/German MoU May 1986 and start of one-year Phase 2 (vehicle preliminary design) September 1986; two prototypes funded August 1988 and assembled by Rockwell under 22-month Phase 3; first prototype (BuAer No. 164584) rolled out 1 March 1990, making first flight 11 October 1990; first flight of second prototype (164585) 19 January 1991; first aircraft made first flight with thrust vectoring paddles installed 14 February 1991; current Phase 4 is for flight test programme of more than 400 hours, expected to be completed early 1992.

COSTS: Programme costs shared USA 75/Germany 25 per cent.

DESIGN FEATURES: Low mounted 'cranked delta' wings with Rockwell transonic aerofoil section (thickness/chord ratio 5.5 per cent), incorporating camber and twist; no dihedral or anhedral; incidence 0°; sweepback at quarter-chord 48° 6' inboard, 36° 36' outboard; swept-back foreplanes, fin and rudder; no horizontal tail surfaces. Design integrates several technologies to expand manoeuvring flight envelope, including vectored thrust, integrated control systems and aircrew assistance; studies have indicated that enhanced manoeuvrability could yield significant exchange ratio advantages in future close-in fighter combat, and X-31A is intended to break so-called stall barrier by allowing close-in aerial combat beyond normal stall angles of attack; design also expected to enable extremely rapid target acquisition and fuselage pointing for addressing future low-speed, transonic and supersonic engagements; earlier programmes such as Rockwell HiMAT RPV and MBB's TKF-90 contributed much useful data to X-31A design and development. Rockwell primarily responsible for configuration, aerodynamics and construction, MBB for control systems and thrust vectoring design, plus some major components and subassemblies (incl wings).

FLYING CONTROLS: Inboard and outboard trailing-edge flaperons, two-segment leading-edge flaps, all-moving active foreplanes, and rudder; door type airbrake each side of rear fuselage; Allied Signal (Electrodynamics and AiResearch Divisions) fly-by-wire drive system for flight control surfaces; Honeywell flight control computers; Bendix (modified V-22) rudder and foreplane actuators. Pitch and roll stability and control by flaperons, pitch and yaw by thrust vectoring, pitch (up to 70° angle of attack) by foreplanes and engine intake control lip; leading-edge flaps also scheduled for high AOA stability and control, and for conventional performance; three thrust-vectoring paddles attached to rear of nozzles can deflect engine exhaust through approx 10° for yaw control, and can also act as additional airbrakes for rapid deceleration.

STRUCTURE: Wings have aluminium spars and ribs, graphite epoxy (carbonfibre) upper and lower skins; aluminium flaps, fin and rudder, honeycomb ailerons and foreplanes, all with graphite epoxy skins; fuselage mostly has conventional bulkheads and stringers of aluminium; forward panels are honeycomb with graphite epoxy skin, mid-fuselage has aluminium skin, rear 0.76 m (2 ft 6 in) has titanium bulkheads and skin; nose radome is glassfibre.

LANDING GEAR: Menasco hydraulically retractable tricycle type, main units retracting forward into fuselage, nose unit rearward. Entire nose unit, including Goodrich wheel and tyre, is from General Dynamics F-16. Main units, adapted from those of F-16, have Goodrich (Cessna Citation III) wheels and brakes and LTV A-7D tyres (pressure 15.51 bars; 225 lb/sq in). Syndex tail braking parachute.

POWER PLANT: One 71.17 kN (16,000 lb st class with afterburning) General Electric F404-GE-400 turbofan. Single fuel tank in fuselage, with gravity feed post just aft of canopy. Single ventral air intake, with movable lower lip.

ACCOMMODATION: Pilot only, on Martin-Baker SJU-5/6 ejection seat in pressurised, heated and air-conditioned cockpit. Windscreen and rear-hinged, upward opening canopy from McDonnell Douglas F/A-18 Hornet. General Electric's Aerospace Business Group assisted in cockpit development.

SYSTEMS: Include a Sundstrand electrical power generator, Garrett (modified F-16 hydrazine system) emergency

Rockwell/MBB X-31A EFM enhanced fighter manoeuvrability aircraft, showing foreplane and control surfaces deflected

power unit to provide 4½ minutes of electrical hydraulic power, and Garrett (hydrazine powered) emergency air start system from Northrop F-20.

DIMENSIONS, EXTERNAL:

Wing span	7.26 m (23 ft 10 in)
Wing aspect ratio	2.51
Foreplane span	2.64 m (8 ft 8 in)
Length: overall: incl nose probe	14.85 m (48 ft 8½ in)
excl probe	13.21 m (43 ft 4 in)
fuselage, excl probe	12.39 m (40 ft 8 in)
Height overall	4.44 m (14 ft 7 in)
Wheel track	2.29 m (7 ft 6½ in)
Wheelbase	3.51 m (11 ft 6⅓ in)

AREAS:

Wings, gross	21.02 m² (226.3 sq ft)
Foreplanes (total)	2.19 m² (23.60 sq ft)
Ailerons (total)	1.29 m² (13.88 sq ft)
Trailing-edge flaps (total)	1.73 m² (18.66 sq ft)
Leading-edge flaps: inboard (total)	0.60 m² (6.42 sq ft)
outboard (total)	0.77 m² (8.28 sq ft)
Fin, incl dorsal fin	2.68 m² (28.87 sq ft)
Rudder	0.81 m² (8.68 sq ft)

WEIGHTS AND LOADINGS:

Weight empty, equipped	5,175 kg (11,410 lb)
Fuel weight	1,876 kg (4,136 lb)
Normal flying weight	6,622 kg (14,600 lb)
Max T-O weight	7,228 kg (15,935 lb)

PERFORMANCE (estimated, at max T-O weight):

Never-exceed (VNE) and max level speed:

S/L to 8,535 m (28,000 ft)
1,485 knots (2,752 km/h; 1,710 mph)

8,535-12,200 m (28,000-40,000 ft)   Mach 1.3

Max rate of climb at S/L	13,106 m (43,000 ft)/min
Max operating altitude	12,200 m (40,000 ft)
T-O run	457 m (1,500 ft)
T-O to 15 m (50 ft)	823 m (2,700 ft)
Landing from 15 m (50 ft)	1,128 m (3,700 ft)
Landing run	823 m (2,700 ft)
Design g limits	+9/-4

ROCKWELL INTERNATIONAL/MBB FAN RANGER

TYPE: Tandem-seat jet trainer.

PROGRAMME: Teaming agreement announced 16 November 1990 to offer modified version of RFB Fantrainer (see German section) as candidate for USAF/USN JPATS programme; two demonstrators to be built and certificated by MBB; first flight planned for 1992, certification for 1993.

DESIGN FEATURES: Based on Fantrainer, redesigned as necessary to accommodate single turbofan instead of twin-turboshaft/ducted fan power plant.

POWER PLANT: One 11.12 kN (2,500 lb st) Pratt & Whitney JT15D-4 turbofan.

AVIONICS: Cockpit updated with Collins avionics and instrumentation.

DIMENSIONS, EXTERNAL:

Wing span	10.46 m (34 ft 4 in)

WEIGHTS AND LOADINGS:

Design max T-O weight	2,404 kg (5,300 lb)

PERFORMANCE (estimated):

Max level speed	300 knots (556 km/h; 345 mph)

Model of the proposed Rockwell/MBB Fan Ranger turbofan powered trainer

SCTICSG
SUPERSONIC COMMERCIAL TRANSPORT INTERNATIONAL CO-OPERATION STUDY GROUP

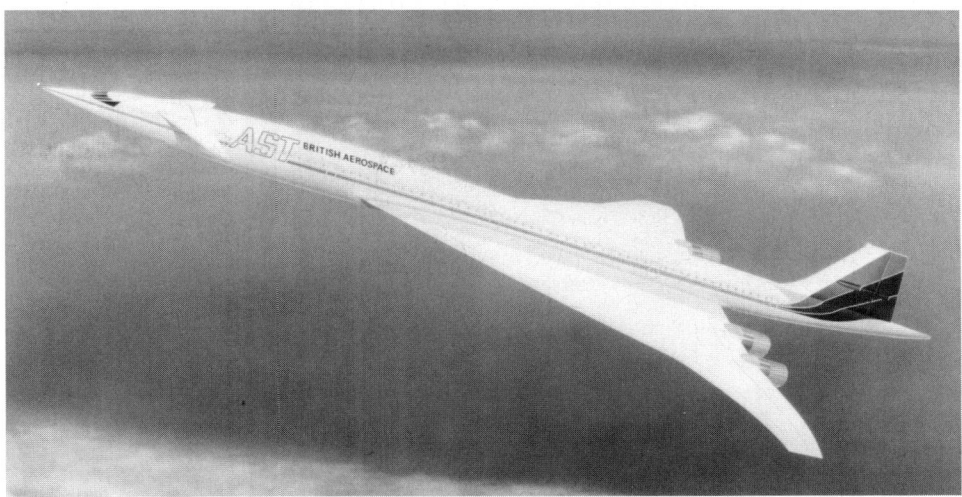

Artist's impression of a possible future Anglo-French successor to the Concorde

FUTURE SST

TYPE: Second generation supersonic commercial transport.

PROGRAMME: Five-year joint study for Concorde successor announced by British Aerospace and Aerospatiale 9 May 1990, combining individual earlier efforts on AST (Advanced Supersonic Transport) and ATSF (Avion de Transport Supersonique Futur) respectively; closely followed on 19 May 1990 by formation of five-company study group (now including Deutsche Airbus, Boeing and McDonnell Douglas) to work for about one year examining environmental implications, market potential, certification basis, and benefits of global co-operation, perhaps eventually contemplating Japanese, Soviet and additional European participation. A five-man Supersonic Transport Development Council was established in 1991 by the Society of Japanese Aerospace Companies to act as liaison committee for possible Japanese participation. In March 1991, Boeing and Deutsche Airbus signed an agreement in principle to pursue their joint studies in selected areas outside the scope of those being examined by the SCTICSG.

DESIGN FEATURES: Aerospatiale/BAe research favours retention of ogival delta wing with leading-edge sweep varying from approx 70° inboard to 50° at tip, optimised for both subsonic (overland) and supersonic cruise; redesigned nose (possibly with larger 'droop-snoot'); four new fuel-efficient variable-cycle engines in separate underwing nacelles; fly-by-wire flight controls; 200-passenger seating capacity; performance parameters to include speed of Mach 2.05-2.4 and max range of 6,475 nm (12,000 km; 7,455 miles).

SEPECAT
SOCIÉTÉ EUROPÉENNE DE PRODUCTION DE L'AVION E.C.A.T.

PARTICIPATING COMPANIES:
British Aerospace: see under UK
Dassault: see under France
PRESIDENT: P. E. Jaillard (Dassault)
PUBLIC RELATIONS: D. Kamiya (BAe)

This Anglo-French company formed May 1966 by Breguet Aviation and British Aircraft Corporation to design and produce Jaguar strike fighter/trainer; production now in India only (see HAL entry).

SEPECAT JAGUAR INTERNATIONAL

TYPE: Single-seat tactical support aircraft and two-seat operational or advanced trainer.

PROGRAMME: Initiated 17 May 1965 by Defence Ministries of UK and France, originally to build 200 **Jaguars** each (with Mk 102 Adour turbofans) for Royal Air Force and Armée de l'Air. Production completed 1982, but RAF aircraft upgraded (1978-84) with more powerful Adour Mk 104s and later with GEC Ferranti FIN 1064 INS (see 1989-90 *Jane's*). One T. Mk 2A fitted for trials with GEC Sensors ATLANTIC (airborne targeting low altitude navigation, thermal imaging and cueing) underwing podded FLIR system; weapons listed for RAF aircraft in 1990-91 *Jane's* now include CBU-87 cluster bombs and 19-round LAU-5003B/A pods of 70 mm CRV7 rockets. Other modifications to RAF Jaguars taking part in early 1991 Gulf War included RWR upgraded to Sky Guardian standard; Vinten LOROP pod fitted; second

RAF Jaguar GR. Mk 1, with overwing Sidewinder rails and visual/IR reconnaissance pod, in 'Pink Panther' desert camouflage after participating in the January/February 1991 Gulf War *(Paul Jackson)*

U/VHF radio (with modified antenna) installed; engine control amplifier modified for increased thrust. French Jaguar units in the Gulf War included aircraft from the 7e and 11e Escadres.

VARIANTS: **Jaguar International:** Export version (first flight 19 August 1976); European production of this ended in 1985, but manufacture of final 31 continues by HAL in India (which see for detailed description).

CUSTOMERS: Total of 403 European built Jaguars produced for RAF (203) and Armée de l'Air (200), plus 139 Jaguar Internationals for air forces of Ecuador (12), India (85, including 45 in CKD form for local assembly), Nigeria (18) and Oman (24).

SOKO/IAv CRAIOVA

PARTICIPATING COMPANIES:
SOKO: see under Yugoslavia
IAv Craiova: see under Romania

SOKO J-22 ORAO (EAGLE) and IAv CRAIOVA IAR-93

TYPE: Single-seat close support, ground attack and tactical reconnaissance aircraft, with secondary capability as low level interceptor. Combat capable two-seat versions used also for advanced flying and weapon training.

PROGRAMME: Joint design by Yugoslav and Romanian engineers, started in 1970 under original project name Yurom, to meet requirements of both air forces; single-seat prototypes started in each country 1972, making simultaneous first flights 31 October 1974; first flight in each country of a two-seat prototype 29 January 1977; each manufacturer then built 15 pre-production aircraft (first flights 1978); series production began in Romania (IAv Craiova) 1979, in Yugoslavia (SOKO) 1980.

VARIANTS: **IAR-93A:** Romanian single- and two-seat versions with non-afterburning Viper Mk 632 turbojets; first flight 1981; production completed.

IAR-93B: Romanian single- and two-seat versions with afterburning Viper Mk 633 turbojets; first flight 1985.

J-22 Orao 1: Yugoslav equivalent of IAR-93A, for tactical reconnaissance (single-seater) and operational

Single-seat interceptor version of the Romanian Air Force's IAR-93B, with underwing air-to-air missiles

conversion training (two-seater); all of latter subsequently converted to Orao 2D standard.

J-22 Orao 2: Yugoslav afterburning version, produced only as single-seat attack aircraft; first flight (s/n 25101) 20 October 1983; increased external stores load; fuel system and capacities differ slightly from other versions. In production.

J-22D Orao 2D: Yugoslav two-seat afterburning operational conversion trainer, with Viper Mk 633-41 engines; wings (with integral fuel tanks) and rear fuselage (with ventral fins and afterburner cooling air inlets) as for Orao 2; first flight 18 July 1986. Continues in production.

CUSTOMERS: Romanian Air Force (26 single-seat and 10 two-seat IAR-93A, all delivered, and 165 IAR-93B); Yugoslav Air Force (Orao 1, 2 and 2D).

SOKO built Orao 2D tandem-seat operational trainer of the Yugoslav Air Force *(Press Office/Sturzenegger)*

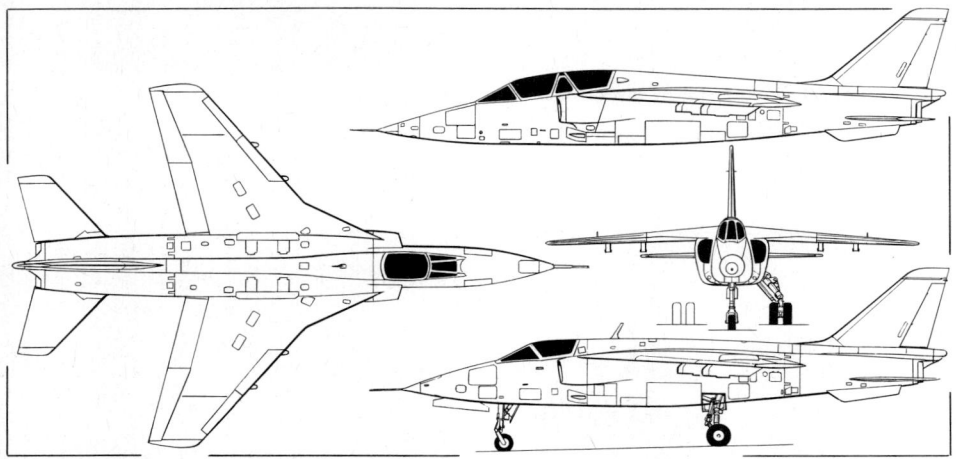

Single-seat Orao 2 close support/ground attack aircraft, with additional side view of two-seat Orao 2D *(Pilot Press)*

DESIGN FEATURES: Wings of NACA 65A-008 (modified) section, shoulder-mounted with 0° incidence and 3° 30′ anhedral from roots; sweepback 35° at quarter-chord and approx 43° on outer leading-edges; inboard leading-edges extended forward (except on prototypes/pre-production) at approx 70° sweepback; small boundary layer fence on upper surface of each outer panel; fuselage has hydraulically actuated door type perforated airbrake underneath on each side forward of mainwheel bay, dorsal spine fairing, pen-nib fairing above exhaust nozzles, and detachable rear portion for access to engine bays; some aircraft (not prototypes or current production Orao 2/2D) have narrow strake each side of nose; all-sweptback tail surfaces, plus (single-seaters and Orao 2D) auxiliary ventral fin beneath rear fuselage each side; anti-flutter weights on tailplane tips of development and early production aircraft.

FLYING CONTROLS: Plain ailerons, semi-Fowler trailing-edge flaps, two-segment leading-edge slats, low-set all-moving tailplane and inset rudder, all hydraulically actuated, with Dowty Aerospace servo-actuators for primary control surfaces; no aileron or rudder tabs.

STRUCTURE: Conventionally built, almost entirely of aluminium alloy except for honeycomb rudder and tailplane on later production aircraft; two-spar wings with ribs, stringers and partially machined skin; wing spar box forms integral fuel tanks on IAR-93B/Orao 2; IAR-93A/Orao 1 have rubber fuel cells, forward of which are sandwich panels.

LANDING GEAR: Hydraulically retractable tricycle type of Messier-Bugatti design, with single-wheel hydraulically steerable nose unit and twin-wheel main units. All units retract forward into fuselage. Two-stage oleo-pneumatic shock absorber in each unit. Mainwheels and tubeless tyres on all versions are size 615 × 225 × 254 mm; pressure is 4.5 bars (65.3 lb/sq in) on Orao 2/2D, 5.2 bars (75.4 lb/sq in) on other versions. Nosewheel and tubeless tyre are size 551 × 250 × 152 mm, pressure 3.1 bars (45.0 lb/sq in), on IAR-93A/Orao 1; and size 451 × 190 × 127 mm, pressure 3.8 bars (55.1 lb/sq in), on all afterburning versions except Orao 2, on which nosewheel tyre pressure is 5.0 bars (72.5 lb/sq in), and Orao 2D, which has a 551 × 250 × 152 mm tyre with pressure of 5.0 bars (72.5 lb/sq in). Hydraulic disc brakes on each mainwheel unit, and electrically operated anti-skid system. Bullet fairing at base of rudder contains a hydraulically deployed 4.2 m (13 ft 9½ in) diameter braking parachute.

POWER PLANT (non-afterburning versions): Two 17.79 kN (4,000 lb st) Turbomecanica/ORAO (licence built Rolls-Royce) Viper Mk 632-41R turbojets, mounted side by side in rear fuselage; air intake on each side of fuselage, below cockpit canopy. Fuel normally in seven fuselage tanks and two collector tanks, with combined capacity of 2,480 litres (655 US gallons; 545.5 Imp gallons), and two 235 litre (62 US gallon; 51.75 Imp gallon) wing tanks, giving total internal fuel capacity of 2,950 litres (779 US gallons; 649 Imp gallons). Provision for carrying three 500 litre (132 US gallon; 110 Imp gallon) auxiliary fuel tanks, one on underfuselage stores attachment and one inboard under each wing. Pressure refuelling point in fuselage; gravity refuelling points in fuselage and each external tank.

POWER PLANT (afterburning versions): Two Turbomecanica/ORAO (licence built Rolls-Royce) Viper Mk 633-41 turbojets, each rated at 17.79 kN (4,000 lb st) dry and 22.24 kN (5,000 lb st) with afterburning. Orao 2 has six fuselage and two collector tanks, with two fuselage and both wing tanks enlarged, giving total internal capacity of 3,100 litres (819 US gallons; 682 Imp gallons). Three 500 litre (132 US gallon; 110 Imp gallon) drop tanks can be carried.

ACCOMMODATION: Single-seat or tandem two-seat cockpit(s), with Martin-Baker zero/zero seat for each occupant (RU10J in IAR-93, YU10J in Orao), capable of ejection through canopy. Canopy of single-seat IAR-93A and Orao 1/2 is hinged at rear and actuated electrically to open upward; single-seat IAR-93B, and all two-seaters, have manually operated canopies opening sideways to starboard. All accommodation pressurised, heated and air-conditioned. Dual controls in two-seat versions.

SYSTEMS: Bootstrap type environmental control system for cockpit pressurisation (max differential 0.214 bar; 3.1 lb/sq in), air-conditioning, and windscreen de-icing/demisting. Two Prva Petoletka independent hydraulic systems, each of 207 bars (3,000 lb/sq in) pressure, for actuation of leading-edge slats, trailing-edge flaps, ailerons, tailplane, rudder, airbrakes, landing gear extension/retraction, mainwheel brakes, nosewheel steering, brake-chute, and afterburner nozzles. No pneumatic system. Main electrical system is 28V DC, supplied by two Lucas BC-0107 9kW engine driven starter/generators through two voltage regulators and a switching system, and a 36Ah battery; two 700VA static inverters (four 300VA in Orao 2/2D) for AC power at 400Hz. High pressure (150 bars; 2,175 lb/sq in) gaseous oxygen system for crew.

AVIONICS: Standard avionics include VHF/UHF air-to-air and air-to-ground com radio (20W transmission power); gyro unit (Honeywell SGP500 twin-gyro platform in Orao), radio altimeter, ADF, radio compass and marker beacon receiver; IFF (Romanian aircraft only); and GEC Avionics three-axis stability augmentation system, incorporating a basic bank/attitude hold autopilot and emergency wings-level facility. Orao 1 and 2 also have Collins VIR-30 VOR/ILS and Collins DME-40; Orao 2 fitted with Iskra SO-1 radar warning receiver. Camera or infra-red reconnaissance pod, or (not yet available for Orao) a night illumination pod, can be carried on underfuselage station. Chaff and IR decoy launch pods (up to three per aircraft) can also be carried.

EQUIPMENT: Landing light under nose, forward of nosewheel bay; taxying light on nosewheel shock strut.

ARMAMENT (IAR-93A/B and Orao 1): Two 23 mm GSh-23L twin-barrel cannon in lower front fuselage, below engine air intakes, with 200 rds/gun. Gun camera and Ferranti D282 gyro gunsight. Five external stores stations, of which the inboard underwing pair and the fuselage centreline station are each stressed for loads up to 500 kg (1,102 lb); outboard underwing stations stressed for up to 300 kg (661 lb) each, giving a max external stores load of 1,500 kg (3,307 lb). Typical weapon loads can include two or three 500 kg bombs; four or five 250 kg bombs; four multiple carriers each with three 100 kg or 50 kg bombs; two such multiple carriers plus two L-57-16MD launchers each with sixteen 57 mm rockets; four L-57-16MD launchers; four launchers each with two 122 mm, one 128 mm or one 240 mm rocket (122 and 240 mm not used on Orao); a GSh-23L cannon pod with four L-57-16MD rocket launchers; four 160 kg KPT-150 or similar munition dispensers; or (Romanian aircraft only) four L-57-32 launchers each with thirty-two 57 mm rockets.

Some IAR-93Bs equipped to carry up to eight air-to-air missiles, on twin launch rails, on the four underwing stations. Centreline and inboard underwing points can carry drop tanks.

ARMAMENT (Orao 2): Guns, gun camera, drop tanks and centreline camera or infra-red reconnaissance pod as for Orao 1. Thomson-CSF VE-120T head-up display. All four wing stations stressed for 500 kg (1,102 lb), and fuselage station for 800 kg (1,763 lb), giving a max external stores capacity of 2,800 kg (6,173 lb). Typical weapon loads include five 50 kg, 100 kg, 250 kg or 500 kg bombs; four multiple carriers for a total of twelve 50 or 100 kg or eight 250 kg bombs; four PLAB-340 napalm bombs (each 360 kg; 794 lb); five BL755 bomblet dispensers, or eight on four multiple carriers; sixteen BRZ-127 5 in HVAR rockets; four pods of L-57-16MD or L-128-04 (4 × 128 mm) rockets, or eight pods on multiple carriers; five 500 kg AM-500 sea mines; or two launch rails for AGM-65B Maverick or Yugoslav developed Grom air-to-surface missiles. The 100 kg and 250 kg bombs can be parachute retarded.

DIMENSIONS, EXTERNAL:

Wing span	9.62 m (31 ft 6¾ in)
Wing chord: at root	4.20 m (13 ft 9⅜ in)
at tip	1.40 m (4 ft 7⅛ in)
Wing aspect ratio	3.6
Length overall, incl probe:	
single-seater	14.90 m (48 ft 10⅝ in)
two-seater	15.38 m (50 ft 5½ in)
Length of fuselage:	
single-seater	13.96 m (45 ft 9⅝ in)
two-seater	14.44 m (47 ft 4½ in)
Fuselage: Max width	1.68 m (5 ft 6⅛ in)
Height overall	4.50 m (14 ft 9¼ in)
Tailplane span	4.72 m (15 ft 5⅞ in)
Wheel track (c/l of shock struts)	2.50 m (8 ft 2½ in)
Wheelbase: single-seater	5.42 m (17 ft 9⅜ in)
two-seater	5.88 m (19 ft 3½ in)

AREAS:

Wings, gross	26.00 m² (279.86 sq ft)
Ailerons (total)	1.92 m² (20.67 sq ft)
Trailing-edge flaps (total)	3.20 m² (34.44 sq ft)
Leading-edge slats (total)	1.56 m² (16.79 sq ft)
Fin	3.55 m² (38.21 sq ft)
Rudder	0.88 m² (9.47 sq ft)
Tailplane	8.20 m² (88.26 sq ft)

WEIGHTS AND LOADINGS (A: IAR-93A, B: IAR-93B, C: Orao 2, D: Orao 2D):

Weight empty, equipped: A	6,150 kg (13,558 lb)
B, C	5,700 kg (12,566 lb)
D	5,975 kg (13,172 lb)
Max internal fuel: A	2,457 kg (5,416 lb)
B, C, D	2,450 kg (5,401 lb)
Max external stores load: A	1,500 kg (3,307 lb)
B, C, D	2,800 kg (6,173 lb)
Normal T-O weight clean: A	8,826 kg (19,458 lb)
B, C	8,400 kg (18,519 lb)
D	8,585 kg (18,926 lb)
Max T-O weight: A	10,326 kg (22,765 lb)
B, C	11,200 kg (24,692 lb)
D	11,520 kg (25,397 lb)
Max landing weight: A	8,826 kg (19,458 lb)
B	9,360 kg (20,635 lb)
C, D	11,000 kg (24,251 lb)
Max wing loading: A	397 kg/m² (81.3 lb/sq ft)
B, C	430.7 kg/m² (88.3 lb/sq ft)
D	443.1 kg/m² (90.75 lb/sq ft)
Max power loading: A	289.8 kg/kN (2.84 lb/lb st)
B, C	251.8 kg/kN (2.47 lb/lb st)
D	259.2 kg/kN (2.54 lb/lb st)

PERFORMANCE (A at max T-O weight; B and C at 8,450 kg; 18,629 lb T-O weight):

Max level speed at S/L:

A	577 knots (1,070 km/h; 665 mph)
B, C	626 knots (1,160 km/h; 721 mph)

Max cruising speed:

A at 7,000 m (22,965 ft)
394 knots (730 km/h; 453 mph)

B at 5,000 m (15,240 ft)
587 knots (1,089 km/h; 676 mph)

Stalling speed at S/L: A	130 knots (241 km/h; 150 mph)	
B, C	148 knots (274 km/h; 171 mph)	
Max rate of climb at S/L: A	2,040 m (6,693 ft)/min	
B, C	4,500 m (14,764 ft)/min	
Service ceiling: A	10,500 m (34,450 ft)	
B, C	13,200 m (43,300 ft)	
Min ground turning radius	7.00 m (22 ft 11½ in)	
T-O run: A	1,500 m (4,921 ft)	
B, C	595 m (1,952 ft)	
T-O to 15 m (50 ft): A	1,600 m (5,249 ft)	
B, C	950 m (3,117 ft)	

Landing from 15 m (50 ft): A	1,650 m (5,413 ft)
B, C	1,520 m (4,987 ft)
Landing run: A	720 m (2,362 ft)
B, C	1,050 m (3,445 ft)
Landing run with brake chute: A, B, C	670 m (2,200 ft)

Mission radius, A, B, C:
lo-lo-lo with four rocket launchers, 5 min over target
140 nm (260 km; 161 miles)
hi-hi-hi patrol with three 500 litre auxiliary fuel tanks, 45 min over target
205 nm (380 km; 236 miles)

lo-lo-hi with two rocket launchers, six 100 kg bombs and one 500 litre auxiliary fuel tank, 10 min over target
243 nm (450 km; 280 miles)
hi-hi-hi with four 250 kg bombs and one 500 litre auxiliary fuel tank, 5 min over target
286 nm (530 km; 329 miles)
Ferry range with three 500 litre auxiliary fuel tanks
1,025 nm (1,900 km; 1,180 miles)
g limits: A, B, C
+8/–4.2

SUKHOI/GULFSTREAM

PARTICIPATING COMPANIES:
Sukhoi: see under USSR
Gulfstream: see under USA

SUKHOI/GULFSTREAM SSBJ (SUPERSONIC BUSINESS JET)

TYPE: Supersonic business aircraft.
PROGRAMME: Separate studies for aircraft of this type started by Sukhoi 1987, Gulfstream 1988; initial MoU to explore feasibility of joint development venture signed 15 June 1989; meetings in September 1989 produced agreements to continue airframe and (by Rolls-Royce and Lyulka) power plant studies, and to set basic size/performance parameters; Gulfstream recommendations released to Sukhoi 15 November 1989; airframe/engine partners' meetings 22-29 June 1990 reviewed performance/operational projections and set schedules for marketing and on-going projects. Sukhoi to be responsible for primary airframe manufacturing, Gulfstream for avionics, interiors and marketing; Soviet designation remains S-21; first flight initially expected 1994, now delayed to late 1990s to await new laminar flow, propulsion and structure techniques.
VARIANTS: **Corporate:** Initial 8/19-passenger version, as described; max T-O weight 45,360 kg (100,000 lb).
Mini-airliner: Longer-term project for 50/60-passenger derivative; max T-O weight 90,720 kg (200,000 lb).
COSTS: Total development cost estimated at up to US$1 billion, unit cost approx $50 million (1989 dollars).
DESIGN FEATURES: Three-engined low/mid-wing aircraft; sweptback wings, with winglets; oval-section fuselage; all-moving foreplanes and low-set tailplane.
FLYING CONTROLS: Digital fly-by-wire AFCS.
LANDING GEAR: Retractable tricycle type with twin wheels on each unit. Main units retract upward into engine air intake trunks, nose unit forward.

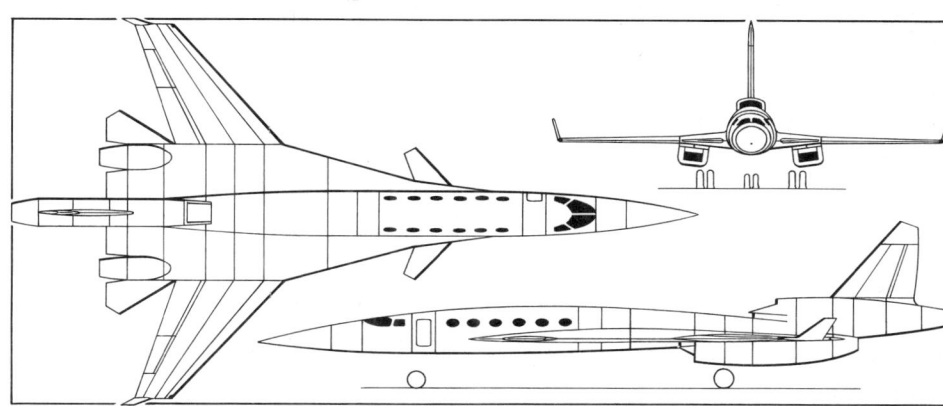

Provisional drawing of Sukhoi/Gulfstream supersonic business jet *(Jane's/Mike Keep)*

POWER PLANT: Prototype(s) may be powered by Lyulka AL-31F augmented turbofans, one under each wing and one on top of rear fuselage. Production aircraft to have two Rolls-Royce/Lyulka engines.
ACCOMMODATION: Crew of two or three and 8-19 passengers. The following data (for the corporate version) are provisional:
DIMENSIONS, EXTERNAL:

Wing span	20.09 m (65 ft 11 in)
Wing aspect ratio	3.1
Length overall	35.88 m (117 ft 8¾ in)
Height overall	8.715 m (28 ft 7⅛ in)

DIMENSIONS, INTERNAL (approx):

Passenger cabin: Length	7.62 m (25 ft 0 in)
Max width	2.10 m (6 ft 10¾ in)
Max height	1.85 m (6 ft 0¾ in)
Volume	23.8 m³ (840 cu ft)

AREAS (approx):

Wings, gross	130.06 m² (1,400 sq ft)

WEIGHTS AND LOADINGS (estimated):

Max T-O weight	45,360 kg (100,000 lb)

PERFORMANCE (estimated):

Max cruising speed	Mach 2.0 to 2.2
Cruising altitude	15,550-18,590 m (51,000-61,000 ft)
T-O distance	1,524 m (5,000 ft)
Landing distance	1,220 m (4,000 ft)
Range, NBAA IFR reserves	4,000 nm (7,410 km; 4,605 miles)

TBM

TBM SA

12 rue Pasteur, 92150 Suresnes, France
Telephone: 33 (1) 47 72 09 34
Fax: 33 (1) 40 99 35 90
Telex: 614549
PRESIDENT: Pierre Gautier
VICE-PRESIDENT, SALES AND MARKETING:
Alain Aubry
US SALES AND MARKETING:
TBM North America Inc, 8901 Wetmore Road, San Antonio, Texas 78216, USA
Telephone: 1 (512) 824 8383
Fax: 1 (512) 824 8393
PRESIDENT: Alex Couvelaire
VICE-PRESIDENT, SALES AND MARKETING:
Brant D. Dahlfors
TBM SA is a joint company formed by Socata of France (70 per cent) and Mooney of USA (30 per cent); dissolution of partnership under discussion in May 1991.

TBM 700

TYPE: Six/seven-passenger pressurised business aircraft.
PROGRAMME: Launched jointly on 12 June 1987 by Socata (France) and Mooney (USA), with one-third of development costs funded by French government loan; three prototypes built: first flights 14 July 1988 (F-WTBM), 3 August 1989 (F-WKPG) and 11 October 1989 (F-WKDL); French certification received 31 January 1990; FAR Pt 23 type approval awarded 28 August 1990; first delivery 21 December 1990; production rate of four per month expected by mid-1991.
CUSTOMERS: Total of 71 production aircraft ordered by 25 April 1991, of which two completed.
COSTS: Standard aircraft US$1.35 million (December 1990).
DESIGN FEATURES: Wing of Aerospatiale RA 16-43 root section with 6° 30' dihedral from roots; twin strakes under rear fuselage; sweptback fin (with dorsal fin) and mass balanced rudder; non-swept tailplane with mass balanced elevators; pneumatic rubber-boot de-icing of wing/tailplane/fin leading-edges.
FLYING CONTROLS: Mechanical (pushrod/cable) controls, with electrically actuated trim tabs in port aileron, rudder and each elevator; scaled-down 'ATR' single-slotted Fowler flaps, also electrically actuated, along 71 per cent of each wing trailing-edge; slotted spoiler

Second prototype TBM 700 six/seven-passenger turboprop pressurised business aircraft

forward of each flap at outer end, linked mechanically to aileron; yaw damper.
STRUCTURE: Mainly of light alloy and steel except for control surfaces, flaps, most of tailplane and fin (all of Nomex honeycomb bonded to metal sheet); wing leading-edges and landing gear doors (carbonfibre/glassfibre); tailcone and wingtips (GFRP); two-spar torsion box forms integral fuel tank in each wing.
LANDING GEAR: Hydraulically retractable tricycle type, with emergency manual operation. Inward retracting main units of trailing-link type; rearward retracting steerable nosewheel (±28°). Parker hydraulic disc brakes.
POWER PLANT: One 522 kW (700 shp) Pratt & Whitney Canada PT6A-64 turboprop, driving a Hartzell four-blade constant-speed fully feathering reversible-pitch metal propeller. Propeller blades anti-iced electrically,

engine inlets by bleed air. Fuel in integral tank in each wing, combined usable capacity 1,080 litres (285 US gallons; 237.5 Imp gallons). Gravity filling point in top of each tank. Oil capacity 12 litres (3.175 US gallons; 2.6 Imp gallons).
ACCOMMODATION: Adjustable seats for one or two pilots at front. Dual controls standard. Four seats in club layout aft of these, with centre aisle, or five seats in high-density layout. Optional toilet at rear of cabin. Upward/downward opening split door on port side aft of wing, with integral airstairs in lower half; overwing emergency exit on starboard side. Individual emergency oxygen mask for each passenger. Pressurised baggage compartment at rear of cabin, with internal access only; additional unpressurised compartment in nose, between engine and firewall, with external access via door on port

side. Electric anti-icing and hot air demisting of windscreen.

SYSTEMS: Engine bleed air pressurisation (to 0.43 bar; 6.2 lb/sq in) and air-cycle (optionally Freon) air-conditioning. Hydraulic system for landing gear only. Electrical system powered by two 28V 200A engine driven starter/generators (one main, one standby) and a 28V 25Ah nickel-cadmium battery.

AVIONICS: Bendix/King Silver Crown digital IFR package, comprising KY 196 VHF com transceiver; KX 165 VHF2/NAV2 with KI 206 indicator; KMA 24H audio panel with interphone; KNS 80 R/Nav with KI 525A indicator; KR 21 marker beacon receiver; KR 87 ADF with KA 44B combined loop/sense antenna and KI 229 RMI; KEA 130A encoding altimeter; KT 79 transponder; and KFC 275 flight director/autopilot with KAS 297 altitude preselect/alerter. Heated pilot and stall warning antennae. Wide range of alternatives to customer's requirements. Options include EFIS, GPS navigation system and weather radar.

DIMENSIONS, EXTERNAL:
Wing span	12.16 m (39 ft 10¾ in)
Wing chord (mean aerodynamic)	1.51 m (4 ft 11½ in)
Wing aspect ratio	8.21

Length overall	10.43 m (34 ft 2½ in)
Height overall	3.99 m (13 ft 1 in)
Elevator span	4.88 m (16 ft 0 in)
Propeller diameter	2.31 m (7 ft 7 in)

DIMENSIONS, INTERNAL:
Cabin: Length (between pressure bulkheads)
	4.56 m (14 ft 11½ in)
Max width	1.24 m (4 ft 0¾ in)
Max height	1.24 m (4 ft 0¾ in)
Volume	6.50 m³ (229.5 cu ft)

Baggage compartment volume:
front	0.25 m³ (8.83 cu ft)
rear	0.90 m³ (31.8 cu ft)

AREAS:
Wings, gross	18.00 m² (193.75 sq ft)
Vertical tail surfaces (total)	2.56 m² (27.55 sq ft)
Horizontal tail surfaces (total)	4.76 m² (51.24 sq ft)

WEIGHTS AND LOADINGS:
Weight empty, equipped	1,826 kg (4,025 lb)
Fuel weight (usable)	866 kg (1,910 lb)
Baggage: front	20 kg (44 lb)
rear	60 kg (132 lb)
Max T-O and landing weight	2,991 kg (6,595 lb)
Max ramp weight	3,003 kg (6,620 lb)

Max wing loading	166.2 kg/m² (34.04 lb/sq ft)
Max power loading	5.73 kg/kW (9.42 lb/shp)

PERFORMANCE (A at AUW of 2,500 kg; 5,511 lb, B at max T-O weight):
Max cruising speed at 7,925 m (26,000 ft):
A	300 knots (555 km/h; 345 mph)

Stalling speed, flaps and landing gear down
	61 knots (113 km/h; 71 mph)
Max rate of climb at S/L: A	702 m (2,303 ft)/min
Certificated ceiling	9,150 m (30,000 ft)

Min ground turning radius (based on nosewheel)
	23.98 m (78 ft 8 in)

Range (B):
with max payload, 45 min reserves:
at max speed	1,001 nm (1,855 km; 1,152 miles)
at long-range cruising speed	
	1,261 nm (2,337 km; 1,452 miles)

with max fuel, no reserves:
at max speed	1,281 nm (2,374 km; 1,475 miles)
at long-range cruising speed	
	1,611 nm (2,985 km; 1,855 miles)
g limits: B	+3.8/−1.5

TRANSALL

Not previously illustrated in *Jane's*, this photograph shows the Gabriel elint version of the Transall C-160 operated by the French Air Force. External features include several blade antennae on top of the fuselage, a large blister fairing each side of the rear fuselage, a retractable ventral radome, and wingtip ECM/ESM pods. The C-160 was last described in the 1989-90 edition
(Ivo Sturzenegger)

IRAN

DORNA
H. F. DORNA CO
4 Satary Street, Mirmotahary Avenue, Seyed Khandan, Tehran 15419
Telephone: 98 (21) 4880120
Fax: 98 (21) 865800 (subs code 176)
MANAGING DIRECTOR: Yaghoub Antesary

This company was established in March 1989 to specialise in aircraft design and development, and in composite materials technology. Design of a lightweight all-composites jet aircraft was under way in late 1990, with prototype construction scheduled to start in 1991.

Plans to acquire the Operation Ability Spur (specially modified Aérodis G802 Orion) from the UK, reported in the 1990-91 *Jane's*, did not come to fruition.

IRGC
ISLAMIC REVOLUTIONARY GUARD CORPS (Air Industries Division)
Tehran

FAJR (DAWN)
The first flight of this side by side two-seat light aircraft was announced in Tehran on 22 February 1988, together with the statement that it "could be used for military purposes" and was to be put into full scale production shortly afterwards. It is assumed that it was intended for primary training and, possibly, in a liaison or reconnaissance role.

Although claimed to be of Iranian design and manufacture, the Fajr appears outwardly identical to the Neico Lancair homebuilt of US origin (see description in Sport Aircraft section). It may embody some local modifications, but no details of the aircraft had been learned at the time of going to press.

Prototype of the Iranian Fajr two-seat light aircraft *(IRNA)*

SEYEDO SHOHADA
DEFENCE INDUSTRIES, SEYEDO SHOHADA PROJECT
Km 5, Qom Road, Kashan
Telephone: 98 (31) 20459 or 23606
DESIGNER/BUILDER: Akbar Akhundzadeh
TEST PILOT: Mahmood Tadayon

ZAFAR 300
The Zafar 300 is a gunship conversion of the Bell 206A JetRanger, design of which was started on 20 March 1987. Construction began on 21 April 1988, and the prototype made its first flight on 31 January 1989. It had completed 100 hours' flying by the end of 1990; further modifications were then under way.

TYPE: Two-seat light attack helicopter; also usable for agricultural operations.

ROTOR SYSTEM: Two-blade main and tail rotors of JetRanger unchanged, but with new controls incorporating mechanical dampers; no rotor brake. Transmission as for JetRanger. Modified collective pitch controls.

FUSELAGE: Modified to low-profile tandem-cockpit configuration; built of locally manufactured aluminium alloy with outer shell of GFRP; sheet metal doors.

LANDING GEAR: Shock-absorbing skid type.

POWER PLANT: One 263.4 kW (317 shp) Allison 250-C18

turboshaft. Fuel capacity (one tank) 270 litres (71.3 US gallons; 59.4 Imp gallons).

ACCOMMODATION: Tandem cockpits for pilot (at rear) and co-pilot/gunner. Cabin doors jettisonable. Underfuselage door at rear for ammunition loading and maintenance access.

SYSTEMS: Hydraulic system as for JetRanger; 24V battery for engine starting; pitot heating and de-icing.

AVIONICS: VFR/VMC instrumentation.

EQUIPMENT: Can be equipped with 250 kg (551 lb) capacity cargo sling and cropspraying kit.

ARMAMENT: Undernose mounted six-barrel gun; attachment on each side of cabin for seven-round rocket launcher.

DIMENSIONS, EXTERNAL:
Main rotor diameter	10.77 m (35 ft 4 in)
Tail rotor diameter	1.575 m (5 ft 2 in)
Length overall, rotors turning	12.075 m (39 ft 7½ in)
Fuselage: Max width	0.775 m (2 ft 6½ in)
Height overall	2.915 m (9 ft 6¾ in)

AREAS:
Main rotor disc	91.10 m² (980.6 sq ft)
Tail rotor disc	4.79 m² (51.58 sq ft)

WEIGHTS AND LOADINGS:
Weight empty	758 kg (1,671 lb)
Max T-O weight	1,300 kg (2,866 lb)
Max disc loading	14.27 kg/m² (2.92 lb/sq ft)

Prototype of the Seyedo Shohada Zafar 300, converted from a Bell JetRanger

PERFORMANCE:
Never-exceed speed (V_{NE}) at S/L
130 knots (240 km/h; 149 mph)
Max endurance, 20 min reserves   3 h

IRAQ

IAF
IRAQI AIR FORCE
Ministry of Defence, Bab Al-Muadam, Baghdad

BAGHDAD and ADNAN
At an exhibition in Baghdad in the Spring of 1989, Iraq displayed an AEW version of one of its Soviet Il-76MD ('Candid-B') standard transports, said to have been modified in-country by the Iraqi Air Force. Named **Baghdad 1**, it had a locally built Thomson-CSF Tigre surveillance radar installed in an inverted position inside a large GFRP blister radome that replaced the standard rear fuselage clamshell doors and upward hinged panel. The Tigre radar is manufactured under licence in Iraq in its basic trailer-mounted form for ground use. Adaptation to airborne use in the Baghdad 1 involved modification of the signal processing to reduce ground clutter, and installation of radio and radar ESM. The navigation system was also modified, and a strake was added at each side of the new

radome. Manned by four operators, the radar is claimed to have much more than 180° scan, and to have been used operationally during the final stages of the Iran-Iraq Gulf War. It could detect, track and identify targets at a maximum range of 189 nm (350 km; 217 miles). The system generator is of Iraqi design. Transmission to the ground is by voice or real-time data link.

At the time of the exhibition, the Iraqi Air Force officer in charge of the programme indicated that plans were under way to upgrade the Baghdad 1 system by installing additional equipment to enable it to control friendly fighter aircraft as well as providing AEW cover. As revealed by a photograph taken later that year, the improved version carries an over-fuselage rotodome installation similar in appearance to that of the 'Mainstay' AEW&C version of the Il-76 described in the Soviet section. On this aircraft, named **Adnan 1** after a former Iraqi defence minister, a long strake is fitted on each side of the rear fuselage to offset instability created by the rotodome installation. The

rotodome is estimated to be about 9 m (29.5 ft) in diameter and mounted about 4 m (13.1 ft) above the fuselage, housing a radar with a detection range reported to be "a few hundred kilometres".

Baghdad television reported the start of testing, on 15 December 1990, of a "new and advanced airborne warning radar", and at the beginning of Operation Desert Storm on 17 January 1991 US and coalition spokesmen stated that Iraq had at least three Adnans. One of these was rendered unflyable during an air strike against Al Taqaddum airfield on 23 January 1991, and two others fled to Iran later that month.

Also shown on Iraqi television, on 20 January 1991, was a flight refuelling tanker variant of the Il-76, with a hose/drogue system deployed from a single centreline refuelling pod mounted at the base of the rear loading ramp.

Close-up of radome under rear fuselage of Baghdad 1 AEW conversion of an Il-76MD of the Iraqi Air Force, showing added strake
(Jane's Defence Weekly/Tony Banks)

Adnan 1 airborne early warning and control aircraft, modified from an Iraqi Air Force Il-76

ISRAEL

IAI
ISRAEL AIRCRAFT INDUSTRIES LTD
Ben-Gurion International Airport, Israel 70100
Telephone: 972 (3) 971 3111
Fax: 972 (3) 971 3131 and 971 2290
Telex: ISRAVIA 381014, 381033 and 381002
PRESIDENT AND CHIEF EXECUTIVE OFFICER: M. Keret
CORPORATE EXECUTIVE VICE-PRESIDENTS:
    A. Ostrinsky
    Dr M. Dvir
VICE-PRESIDENT, MARKETING: D. Onn
DIRECTOR OF CORPORATE COMMUNICATIONS: D. Suslik
FOREIGN PRESS AND CORPORATE ADVERTISING MANAGER:
    F. P. Hermann (Dept 9003).
This company was established in 1953 as Bedek Aviation. The change of name to Israel Aircraft Industries was made on 1 April 1967, and the number of Divisions was reduced in February 1988 from five to four: Aircraft, Electronics, Technologies, and Bedek Aviation. Corporate headquarters provides overall guidance and support of these Divisions, and supports the service and marketing activities of several overseas subsidiaries. IAI covered space totalled 680,000

m² (7.32 million sq ft) at the end of July 1988, when the total workforce numbered 16,500. The company is licensed by the Israel Civil Aviation Administration, US Federal Aviation Administration, British Civil Aviation Authority and the Israeli Air Force, among others, as an approved repair station and maintenance organisation.

In addition to aircraft of its own design (see Aircraft Division subsection), IAI markets a wide range of in-house developed airframe systems and avionics; and service, upgrading and retrofit packages, encompassing civil and military fixed-wing and rotating-wing aircraft. Several of these are described under the Bedek Aviation Division heading, and utilise many electronic and electro-optical equipments (hardware and software) of IAI design and manufacture. Additional corporate activities involve space technology, smart missiles and other ordnance, seaborne and ground equipment, and a wide range of component production and processing capability.

Aircraft Division
    Follows this entry
Bedek Aviation Division
    Follows Aircraft Division entry

Electronics Division
PO Box 105, Yahud Industrial Zone, Israel 56000
Telephone: 972 (3) 717450
Fax: 972 (3) 536 5205
Telex: ISRAVIA 341450
GENERAL MANAGER: M. Ortasse
    The Electronics Division is now IAI's largest Division, with a 1988 workforce of 6,700 housed in 150,000 m² (1,614,585 sq ft) of covered accommodation. Operating plants of the Division are Elta Electronic Industries (a wholly owned subsidiary of IAI), MBT Systems and Space Technology, Tamam Precision Instruments Industries, and MLM System Engineering and Integration. Division capability covers electronic and electro-optical systems and components, space technologies (including those applicable to an SDI environment), and manufacture/marketing of a wide range of military and civil hardware and software products and services.
Technologies Division
    Follows Bedek Aviation Division entry

AIRCRAFT DIVISION

Ben-Gurion International Airport, Israel 70100
Telephone: 972 (3) 9711415
Fax: 972 (3) 971 3131 and 971 2290
Telex: ISRAVIA 381014 and 381033
GENERAL MANAGER: Dr M. Dvir

Established in February 1988, the Aircraft Division consists of five autonomous plants: Lahav, military aircraft; Matan, civil aircraft; Malat, unmanned aerial vehicles (UAVs); Malkam, aeronautical manufacturing; and Tashan, engineering and testing. The military aircraft plant is currently engaged in operating the third prototype Lavi as an advanced combat technology demonstrator; designing and integrating upgrades of the Kfir; and proposals for developing and manufacturing, with overseas partners, customer-specified advanced combat aircraft such as the supersonic multi-mission Nammer. Civil aircraft activity includes production of the Astra business aircraft, product support for the IAI Arava and Westwind, and development of future non-military airframes. The manufacturing plant produces structures and components for domestic and foreign customers. Engineering services include analysis, design, development, integration and testing of platforms and systems for domestic and international military and civil aerospace communities.

IAI SHAHAL (BIBLICAL LION)

The Shahal is an IAI funded conceptual design study for a small, low-cost lightweight fighter with high agility and the capability to carry smart weapons. No other details were known at the time of going to press.

IAI LAVI (YOUNG LION) TECHNOLOGY DEMONSTRATOR

The Lavi multi-role combat aircraft received programme go-ahead in February 1980, and full scale development started in October 1982. First flight of prototype B-1 took place on 31 December 1986, the second (B-2) making its initial flight on 30 March 1987. The programme envisaged production of at least 300 aircraft, including about 60 combat-capable two-seat operational trainers, but was terminated by the Israeli government on 30 August 1987 after 82 flights due to severe budgetary constraints. IAI decided to continue to validate the main tasks of the programme, utilising the B-3 (third prototype) as a Technology Demonstrator (TD). This airframe utilises some components from one of the Lavi prototypes, but is of two-seat configuration, with elevons approximately 15 per cent larger than on the Lavi prototypes. Its prime objective is to serve as a demonstrator of advanced systems and technologies developed and produced by the Israeli industry, and to act as a testbed for future developments. The first flight of the TD was made on 25 September 1989.

Some of the avionics upgrading packages now offered by IAI for various aircraft derive from the TD systems and will have been tested and validated on the TD.

POWER PLANT: One Pratt & Whitney PW1120 afterburning turbojet (military rating approx 55.6 kN; 12,500 lb st dry and 82.7 kN; 18,600 lb st with afterburning). Ventral single-shock intake based on that of General Dynamics F-16. Max fuel capacity 3,330 litres (880 US gallons; 732 Imp gallons) in integral wing tanks, plus 5,095 litres (1,346 US gallons; 1,121 Imp gallons) externally.

ACCOMMODATION: Two Martin-Baker Mk 10 lightweight zero/zero ejection seats, in tandem, under teardrop cockpit canopy.

AVIONICS: Elta electronic warfare self-protection system for rapid threat identification (IFF) and flexible response (ECM). This computer-based, fully automatic system uses active and passive countermeasures, including internal and externally podded power-managed noise and deception jammers. Elbit integrated display system includes a Hughes wide angle holographic HUD (in front cockpit), three multi-function displays (two monochrome and one colour), display computers, and communications controller. Pilot can operate most systems through a single El-Op up-front control. Lear Astronics/MBT quadruple-redundant digital fly-by-wire flight control system, with stability augmentation, MBT control unit and Moog servo-actuators. No mechanical backup. Sundstrand actuation system, with geared rotary actuators, for leading-edge flaps. Cockpit designed to minimise pilot workload in high g and dense threat environment, with full HOTAS (hands on throttle and stick) operation. Elta EL/M-2032 multi-mode pulse Doppler radar (to be installed in TD in 1991), incorporating automatic target acquisition and track-while-scan in the air-to-air mode, and beam-sharpened ground mapping/terrain avoidance and sea search in the air-to-surface mode. The radar's coherent transmitter and stable multi-channel receiver ensure reliable lookup/lookdown performance over a broad band of frequencies, as well as high resolution mapping. Elta programmable signal processor, backed by a network of distributed, embedded computers, provides optimum allocation of computer power and considerable flexibility for algorithm updating and system growth. Advanced versions of Elbit ACE-4 mission computer (128K memory) and SMS-86 stores management systems, both compatible with dual MIL-STD-1553B databuses;

First (B-1) prototype of the IAI Lavi multi-role combat aircraft

SMS-86 capable of managing both conventional and smart weapons and sensors. Elta ARC-740 fully computerised UHF com radio system, Elisra radar warning receiver and Astronautics air data computer. Tamam TINS 1700 advanced inertial navigation system and GPS planned for installation in 1991.

ARMAMENT: Internally mounted 30 mm cannon, with helmet sight. Four underwing hardpoints for air-to-surface missiles, bombs, rockets and other stores; inboard pair wet for carriage of auxiliary fuel tanks. Seven underfuselage stores attachments (three tandem pairs plus one on centreline). Infra-red air-to-air missile at each wingtip.

DIMENSIONS, EXTERNAL:
Wing span	8.78 m (28 ft 9⅔ in)
Length overall	14.57 m (47 ft 9⅔ in)
Height overall	4.78 m (15 ft 8¼ in)
Wheel track	2.31 m (7 ft 7 in)
Wheelbase	3.86 m (12 ft 8 in)

AREAS:
Wings, gross	33.05 m² (355.75 sq ft)

WEIGHTS AND LOADINGS:
Max fuel: internal (usable)	2,624 kg (5,785 lb)
external	4,164 kg (9,180 lb)
Max ordnance (excl air-to-air missiles)	2,721 kg (6,000 lb)
Max external load	7,257 kg (16,000 lb)
T-O weight: basic	9,990 kg (22,024 lb)
max	18,370 kg (40,500 lb)
Max wing loading	555.6 kg/m² (113.8 lb/sq ft)
Combat thrust/weight ratio	1.07

PERFORMANCE (estimated):
Max level speed above 11,000 m (36,000 ft)
Mach 1.85 or 800 knots (1,482 km/h; 921 mph) CAS	
Rotation speed	140 knots (259 km/h; 161 mph)

Low-altitude penetration speed:
two infra-red missiles and eight 750 lb M117 bombs
538 knots (997 km/h; 619 mph)
two infra-red missiles and two 2,000 lb Mk 84 bombs
597 knots (1,106 km/h; 687 mph)

Air turning rate at Mach 0.8 at 4,575 m (15,000 ft):
sustained	13.2°/s
max	24.3°/s
Max rate of roll	300°/s
T-O run	approx 305 m (1,000 ft)

Combat radius:
air-to-ground, lo-lo-lo   600 nm (1,112 km; 691 miles)
air-to-ground, hi-lo-hi with two Mk 84 or six Mk 82 bombs   1,150 nm (2,131 km; 1,324 miles)
air-to-air, combat air patrol
1,000 nm (1,853 km; 1,151 miles)
g limit   +7.2 cleared for TD

IAI KFIR (LION CUB)

US Navy and Marine Corps designation: F-21A

A detailed history of the Kfir has appeared in the 1988-89 and many earlier editions of *Jane's*. A total of 212 was built (27 C1s and 185 C2s/TC2s, most of the latter subsequently being upgraded to C7/TC7). Further details of the C1, C2 and TC2 can be found in the 1983-84 *Jane's*, and of the lease of 25 Kfirs to the US Navy (12) and Marine Corps (13) as **F-21A** 'aggressor' trainers in the 1989-90 and earlier editions.

The following abbreviated description applies to the C7 and TC7, further details of which can be found in the 1987-88 edition:

C7: Upgraded conversion of C2, with 'combat plus' optional increase in engine thrust and improved avionics, delivered to Israeli Air Force from mid-1983. Other features include new HOTAS (hands on throttle and stick) cockpit installation and two additional external stores stations. Colombia ordered 13 in 1988, delivery of which was made in 1989.

TC7: Designation of TC2 when upgraded to C7 standard. Two exported to Colombia with C7s mentioned above. Further details in 1989-90 and earlier *Jane's*.

French government approval was given in the Autumn of 1989 for IAI to purchase five SNECMA Atar 9K-50 turbojet engines for test installation in Kfirs as part of an upgrade and renewed export marketing programme that would be unhampered by US restrictions involving the aircraft's present J79 engines. One is installed in the Nammer prototype (which see).

TYPE: Single-seat strike, ground attack and fighter aircraft.

POWER PLANT: One General Electric J79-J1E turbojet (modified GE-17), with variable area nozzle, rated at 52.89 kN (11,890 lb st) dry and 79.45 kN (17,860 lb st) with afterburning (83.41 kN; 18,750 lb st with 'combat plus' option). Adjustable half-cone centrebody in each air intake. Internal fuel in five fuselage and four integral wing tanks. Total internal capacity 3,243 litres (857 US gallons; 713.4 Imp gallons). Refuelling point on top of fuselage, above forward upper tank. Wet points for the carriage of one drop tank beneath each wing (inboard), and one under fuselage; these tanks may be of 500, 600, 825, 1,300 or 1,700 litres (132, 158.5, 218, 343.5 or 449 US gallons; 110, 132, 181.5, 286 or 374 Imp gallons) capacity; max external fuel capacity 4,700 litres (1,242 US gallons; 1,034 Imp gallons). Provision for boom/receptacle or probe/drogue in-flight refuelling system, and for single-point pressure refuelling.

ACCOMMODATION: Pilot only, on Martin-Baker IL10P zero/zero ejection seat (two tandem seats in TC7), under rearward hinged upward opening canopy. Cockpit pressurised, heated and air-conditioned.

AVIONICS: Compared with C2 (see 1987-88 *Jane's*), C7 differs in having an improved HOTAS (hands on throttle and stick) cockpit installation, WDNS-341 weapons delivery and navigation system, Elbit System 82 computerised stores management and release system, video subsystems, smart weapons delivery capability, and updated electronic warfare systems. The ranging radar is an Elta EL/M-2001B, but the C7 can also mount Elta's EL/M-2021 advanced pulse Doppler fire control radar, with lookup/lookdown capability, Doppler beam-sharpened mapping, terrain avoidance/following and sea search modes.

IAI Kfir-C7 multi-mission combat aircraft, armed with Shafrir air-to-air missiles

ARMAMENT: Fixed armament of one IAI built 30 mm DEFA 552 cannon in underside of each engine air intake (140 rds/gun). Nine hardpoints (five under fuselage and two under each wing) for external weapons, ECM pods or drop tanks. For interception duties, one Sidewinder, Python 3 or Shafrir 2 infra-red homing air-to-air missile can be carried under each outer wing. Ground attack version can carry a 3,000 lb M118 bomb, two 800 or 1,000 lb bombs, up to four 500 lb bombs, or a Shrike, Maverick or GBU-15 air-to-surface weapon under the fuselage, and two 1,000 lb or six 500 lb bombs (conventional, smart or concrete dibber type) under the wings. Alternative weapons can include Mk 82/83/84 and M117/118 bombs; CBU-24/49 and TAL-1/2 cluster bombs; LAU-3A/10A/32A rocket launchers; napalm, flares, chaff, Elta EL-L8202 ECM and other podded systems.

DIMENSIONS, EXTERNAL:
Wing span	8.22 m (26 ft 11½ in)
Foreplane span	3.73 m (12 ft 3 in)
Length overall, incl probe	15.65 m (51 ft 4¼ in)
Height overall	4.55 m (14 ft 11¼ in)
Wheel track	3.20 m (10 ft 6 in)
Wheelbase	4.87 m (15 ft 11¾ in)

AREAS:
Wings, gross	34.8 m² (374.6 sq ft)
Foreplanes (total)	1.66 m² (17.87 sq ft)

WEIGHTS AND LOADINGS:
Weight empty (interceptor, estimated)
7,285 kg (16,060 lb)
Max usable fuel: internal	2,572 kg (5,670 lb)
external	3,727 kg (8,217 lb)
Max external stores	6,085 kg (13,415 lb)

Typical combat weight:
interceptor, 50% internal fuel, two Shafrir missiles
9,390 kg (20,700 lb)
interceptor, two 500 litre drop tanks, two Shafrir missiles
11,603 kg (25,580 lb)
combat air patrol, three 1,300 litre drop tanks, two Shafrir missiles
14,270 kg (31,460 lb)
ground attack, two 1,300 litre drop tanks, seven 500 lb bombs, two Shafrir missiles
14,670 kg (32,340 lb)
Max clean T-O weight	10,415 kg (22,961 lb)
Max T-O weight	16,500 kg (36,376 lb)

Wing/foreplane loading at 9,390 kg (20,700 lb) combat weight
257.5 kg/m² (52.8 lb/sq ft)
Thrust/weight ratio at 9,390 kg (20,700 lb) combat weight
0.91

PERFORMANCE:
Max level speed above 11,000 m (36,000 ft)
over Mach 2.3 (1,317 knots; 2,440 km/h; 1,516 mph)
Max sustained level speed at height, clean   Mach 2.0
Max level speed at S/L. clean
750 knots (1,389 km/h; 863 mph)
Max rate of climb at S/L   14,000 m (45,930 ft)/min
Time to 15,240 m (50,000 ft), full internal fuel, two Shafrir missiles   5 min 10 s
Height attainable in zoom climb   22,860 m (75,000 ft)
Stabilised ceiling (combat configuration)
17,680 m (58,000 ft)
Turn performance at 4,575 m (15,000 ft), combat weight of 9,390 kg (20,700 lb):
turn rate: sustained	9.6°/s
instantaneous	18.9°/s
turn radius: sustained	1,326 m (4,350 ft)
instantaneous	671 m (2,200 ft)

T-O run at max T-O weight   1,450 m (4,750 ft)
Landing from 15 m (50 ft) at 11,566 kg (25,500 lb) landing weight   1,555 m (5,100 ft)
Landing run at 11,566 kg (25,500 lb) landing weight
1,280 m (4,200 ft)
*Combat radius, 20 min fuel reserves:
high-altitude interception, one 825 litre and two 1,300 litre drop tanks, two Shafrir missiles
419 nm (776 km; 482 miles)
combat air patrol, one 1,300 litre and two 1,700 litre drop tanks, two Shafrir missiles, incl 60 min loiter
476 nm (882 km; 548 miles)
ground attack, hi-lo-hi, two 800 lb and two 500 lb bombs, two Shafrir missiles, one 1,300 litre and two 1,700 litre drop tanks
640 nm (1,186 km; 737 miles)
Ferry range:
three 1,300 litre drop tanks
1,614 nm (2,991 km; 1,858 miles)
one 1,300 litre and two 1,700 litre drop tanks
1,744 nm (3,232 km; 2,008 miles)
g limit   +7.5
*Can be increased by 30 per cent with one in-flight refuelling

IAI NAMMER (TIGER)
In addition to the Mirage III/5 upgrade programmes described under the Bedek Aviation Division heading, IAI is developing the Nammer, which made its first flight in the Spring of 1991.
Externally, the Nammer can be identified by a longer nose than the Mirage or single-seat Kfir, fitment of Kfir type canard surfaces on the engine air intake trunks, an additional fuselage plug aft of the cockpit, and a clean fin without the large dorsal airscoop of the Kfir. Like current

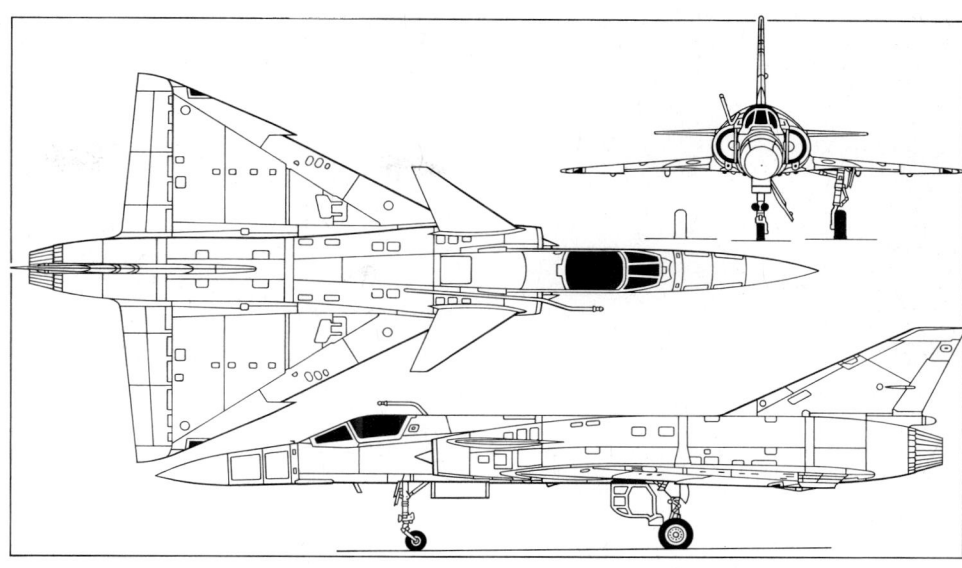
IAI Nammer upgraded version of the Mirage III and 5 (Jane's/Mike Keep)

Kfirs, it is equipped with a contemporary weapon delivery and navigation system, HOTAS cockpit controls, and a related stores management and release system. There are two internally mounted 30 mm cannon, with 140 rds/gun, plus nine external wing and fuselage stations for weapons, drop tanks and other stores (similar to those listed for the Kfir, including capability for launching smart weapons). Elta EL/M-2032 lookup/lookdown pulse Doppler multi-mode fire control radar is standard; a radar warning system with information presented on the tactical display, automatic chaff/flare dispensers, and jamming system, are optional. UHF/VHF com and radio navigation systems are to customer's requirements.

POWER PLANT: One 70.6 kN (15,873 lb st) SNECMA Atar 9K-50 afterburning turbojet in prototype; alternative engines available optionally. (See under Weights and Loadings for fuel load.) In-flight and single-point ground pressure refuelling standard.

DIMENSIONS, EXTERNAL: As for Kfir-C7 except:
Length overall	16.00 m (52 ft 6 in)
Wheel track	3.10 m (10 ft 2 in)

WEIGHTS AND LOADINGS:
Max fuel: internal	3,000 kg (6,614 lb)
external	3,720 kg (8,201 lb)
Max external stores	6,270 kg (13,823 lb)
T-O weight clean	10,250 kg (22,597 lb)
Typical combat weight	9,050 kg (19,952 lb)

Max T-O weight with external stores
15,450 kg (34,061 lb)
PERFORMANCE (estimated, at 9,050 kg; 19,952 lb combat weight except where indicated):
Max level speed:
at S/L	750 knots (1,390 km/h; 863 mph)
at altitude	Mach 2.2
Stabilised ceiling	17,680 m (58,000 ft)

Max instantaneous turn rate at 4,575 m (15,000 ft)   21°/s
Combat radius (tanks dropped when empty):
interceptor, one 1,300 litre tank and four IR air-to-air missiles, out and back at 12,200 m (40,000 ft) at Mach 1.8, incl 2 min combat
250 nm (463 km; 288 miles)
combat air patrol at 9,150 m (30,000 ft) at Mach 0.85,

one 1,300 litre and two 1,700 litre tanks and four IR air-to-air missiles, incl 60 min loiter and 2 min combat   746 nm (1,382 km; 859 miles)
ground attack (hi-lo-hi) at 544 knots (1,008 km/h; 626 mph) attack speed, two 1,700 litre tanks, two Mk 82 bombs and two IR air-to-air missiles
537 nm (995 km; 618 miles)
ground attack (lo-lo-lo-hi) at 535 knots (991 km/h; 616 mph) attack speed, one 1,300 litre and two 1,700 litre tanks, four CBU-58 cluster bombs and two IR air-to-air missiles   573 nm (1,062 km; 660 miles)
g limit   +9

IAI 1125 ASTRA
Known originally as the 1125 Westwind, the Astra is externally similar to its predecessor although, in effect, only the tail unit and engine nacelles remain virtually unchanged from the Westwind airframe. The wings have a new-design aerofoil section, are sweptback, are mounted low on the fuselage, and pass beneath the cabin floor, so avoiding interruption of the available internal space. The Astra has a deeper fuselage profile, with 20.3 cm (8 in) more cabin headroom than the Westwind 2. The cabin is also nearly 0.61 m (2 ft) longer and 5 cm (2 in) wider, but otherwise the fuselage is little changed structurally except for a 50.8 cm (20 in) longer nose providing more space for avionics. Construction makes wider use of composite materials, notably for the control surfaces.

Construction of two flying prototypes began in April 1982. The first of these (4X-WIN, c/n 4001) was the first to fly, on 19 March 1984, being followed by c/n 4002 (4X-WIA) in August 1984. The third airframe was used for static and fatigue testing. First flight by a production Astra (4X-CUA) was made on 20 March 1985, and FAA certification to FAR Pts 25 and 36 was received on 29 August of that year. First delivery, to a US customer, was made on 30 June 1986.

Since January 1988, marketing and product support have been undertaken by IAI subsidiary Astra Jet Corporation in the USA. Atlantic Aviation maintains the principal inventory of Westwind and Astra spare parts for distribution worldwide.

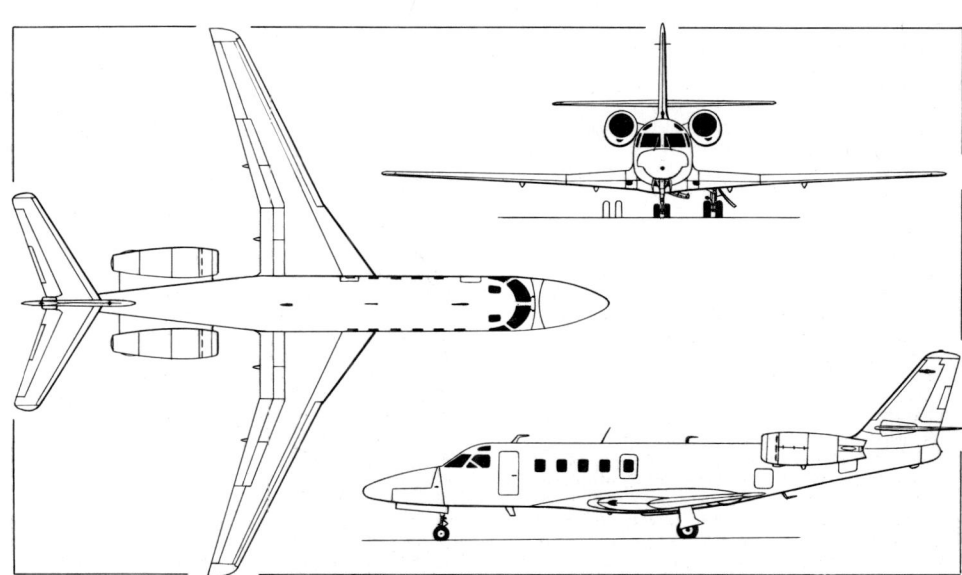
IAI 1125 Astra business transport (two Garrett TFE731-3A-200G turbofans) (Pilot Press)

IAI Astra twin-turbofan business transport

At the NBAA convention in October 1989, IAI and Astra Jet Corporation announced an improved **Astra SP** with redesigned interior, upgraded avionics which include a Collins digital autopilot and EFIS, and aerodynamic refinements which improve high altitude performance and extend range with NBAA IFR reserves by 63 nm (117 km; 72 miles).

The following description applies to the original Astra:

TYPE: Twin-turbofan business transport.

WINGS: Cantilever low-wing monoplane, with sweptback leading-edges (34° inboard, 25° on outer panels) and outboard trailing-edges. Thin, high-efficiency Sigma 2 aerofoil section, of IAI design. One-piece two-spar fail-safe structure, mainly of aluminium alloys, incorporates machined ribs and wing skin panels and is attached to underfuselage by four main and five secondary frames. Wing/fuselage fairings are of Kevlar, wingtips and inboard leading-edges of Kevlar and Nomex. Automatic extending leading-edge slats (outboard), interconnected with trailing-edge flaps; both flaps and slats are actuated electrically. Hydraulically actuated spoilers/lift dumpers forward of flaps. Ailerons, of Kevlar and honeycomb reinforced glassfibre, are hydraulically powered and pushrod operated. Port and starboard aileron control runs can be disconnected if a single aileron jams, allowing control of the aircraft by one aileron only. Pneumatic de-icing of leading-edge slats.

FUSELAGE: Metal semi-monocoque structure, mainly of aluminium alloy frames and chemically milled skins, with steel alloys or titanium in high stress or high temperature areas. Kevlar reinforced upward opening panel over nose avionics bay. Glassfibre tailcone fairing. Heated windscreens are of laminated polycarbonate, with an external layer of glass for scratch resistance.

TAIL UNIT: Cantilever all-sweptback structure, mainly of metal construction, with three-spar fin box and two-spar electrically actuated variable incidence tailplane. Fin and tailplane tips of glassfibre; small glassfibre ram air inlet at base of fin. Elevators and rudder operated manually via pushrods. Electrically driven rudder trim is via interconnected dual actuators. Pitch trim is by variable incidence tailplane. Pitch trim actuator has three separate electric motors, one for normal operation and a second for override operation in case of malfunction. All three motors operate together to provide emergency pitch control in the event of elevator jamming or disconnect. Pneumatic de-icing of tailplane leading-edges.

LANDING GEAR: SHL hydraulically retractable tricycle type, with oleo-pneumatic shock absorber and twin wheels on each unit. Trailing-link main units retract inward, nosewheels forward. Kevlar nosewheel doors. Tyre sizes 23 × 7 in (main), 16 × 4.4 in (nose). Hydraulic extension, retraction and nosewheel steering; hydraulic multi-disc anti-skid mainwheel brakes. Compressed nitrogen cylinder provides additional power source for emergency extension.

POWER PLANT: Two 16.23 kN (3,650 lb st) Garrett TFE731-3A-200G turbofans, with Grumman hydraulically actuated thrust reversers, pod-mounted in Grumman nacelle on each side of rear fuselage. Kevlar reinforced nacelle doors and panels. Thermal anti-icing of intakes. Standard fuel contained in integral tank in wing centre-section, two outer-wing tanks, and upper and lower tanks in centre-fuselage (combined usable capacity 4,910 litres; 1,297 US gallons; 1,080 Imp gallons). Additional fuel can be carried in a 378.5 litre (100 US gallon; 83.3 Imp gallon) removable auxiliary tank in forward area of baggage compartment. Single pressure refuelling point in lower starboard side of fuselage aft of wing, or single gravity point in upper fuselage, allow convenient refuelling of all tanks from one position. Fuel sequencing is automatic, requiring no crew action to maintain safe supply of fuel to the engines and maintenance of correct CG.

ACCOMMODATION: Crew of two on flight deck. Dual controls standard. Sliding door between flight deck and cabin. Standard accommodation in pressurised cabin for six persons, two in forward facing seats at front and four in club layout; galley (port or starboard) at front of cabin, coat closet forward (stbd), toilet at rear. All six seats are individually adjustable fore and aft, laterally, and can be swivelled or reclined; all are fitted with armrests and headrests. Two wall mounted foldaway tables between club seat pairs. Coat closet houses stereo tape deck. Maximum accommodation for nine passengers. Plug type airstair door at front on port side; emergency exit over wing on each side. Heated baggage compartment aft of passenger cabin, with external access. A service compartment in the rear fuselage houses aircraft batteries (or optional APU), electrical relay boxes, inverters and miscellaneous equipment. Cabin soundproofing improved compared with Westwind 2.

SYSTEMS: AiResearch environmental control system, using engine bleed air, with normal pressure differential of 0.615 bar (8.9 lb/sq in). Garrett GTCP36-150(W) APU available optionally. Two independent hydraulic systems, each at pressure of 207 bars (3,000 lb/sq in). Primary system is operated by two engine driven pumps for actuation of brakes, anti-skid, landing gear, nosewheel steering, spoilers/lift dumpers and ailerons. Backup system, operated by electrically driven pump, provides power for emergency/parking brake, ailerons and thrust reversers. Electrical system comprises two 300A 28V DC engine driven starter/generators, with two 1kVA single-phase solid state inverters operating in unison to supply single-phase 115V AC power at 400Hz and 26V AC power for aircraft instruments. Two 24V nickel-cadmium batteries for engine starting and to permit operation of essential flight instruments and emergency equipment. 28V DC external power receptacle standard. Oxygen system for crew (pressure demand) and passengers (drop-down masks) supplied by single 1.35 m^3 (48 cu ft) cylinder. A two-bottle Freon type engine fire extinguishing system is standard.

AVIONICS: Standard avionics suite comprises Collins EFIS-85A(1) five-tube electronic flight instrumentation system, dual FCS-80 flight director systems, dual VHF-22A com, dual VIR-32 nav, APS-80 autopilot, ADS-80 air data system, VNI-80D vertical nav system, provisions for GNS-1000, GNS-X or UNS 1A flight management system, dual DME-42, ADF-60A, dual RMI-36, dual C-14 compass systems, dual TDR-90 transponders, ALT-50A radio altimeter, Baker dual audio systems, and WXT-250A colour weather radar.

EQUIPMENT: Standard equipment includes electric windscreen wipers, electric (warm air) windscreen demisting, cockpit and cabin fire extinguishers, axe, first aid kit, wing ice inspection lights, landing light in each wingroot, taxying light inboard of each mainwheel door, navigation and strobe lights at wingtips and tailcone, rotating beacons under fuselage and on top of fin, and wing/tailplane static wicks.

DIMENSIONS, EXTERNAL:

Wing span	16.05 m (52 ft 8 in)
Wing aspect ratio	8.8
Length overall	16.94 m (55 ft 7 in)
Fuselage: Max width	1.57 m (5 ft 2 in)
Max depth	1.905 m (6 ft 3 in)
Height overall	5.54 m (18 ft 2 in)
Tailplane span	6.40 m (21 ft 0 in)
Wheel track (c/l of shock struts)	2.77 m (9 ft 1 in)
Wheelbase	7.34 m (24 ft 1 in)
Passenger door (fwd, port): Height	1.37 m (4 ft 6 in)
Width	0.66 m (2 ft 2 in)
Overwing emergency exits (each):	
Height	0.69 m (2 ft 3 in)
Width	0.48 m (1 ft 7 in)

DIMENSIONS, INTERNAL:

Cabin: Length: incl flight deck	6.86 m (22 ft 6 in)
excl flight deck	5.23 m (17 ft 2 in)
Max width	1.45 m (4 ft 9 in)
Max height	1.70 m (5 ft 7 in)
Baggage compartment volume	1.56 m^3 (55 cu ft)

AREAS:

Wings, gross	29.40 m^2 (316.6 sq ft)

WEIGHTS AND LOADINGS (A: without, B: with, long-range fuel tanks):

Basic operating weight empty, incl crew (typical):	
A	5,747 kg (12,670 lb)
B	5,801 kg (12,790 lb)
Max usable fuel: A	3,942 kg (8,692 lb)
B	4,248 kg (9,365 lb)
Fuel with max payload: A, B	3,470 kg (7,650 lb)
Max payload: A	1,510 kg (3,330 lb)
B	1,465 kg (3,230 lb)
Payload with max fuel: A	1,080 kg (2,380 lb)
B	730 kg (1,610 lb)
Max ramp weight: A, B	10,727 kg (23,650 lb)
Max T-O weight: A, B	10,659 kg (23,500 lb)
Max landing weight: A, B	9,389 kg (20,700 lb)
Max zero-fuel weight: A, B	7,257 kg (16,000 lb)

PERFORMANCE (at max T-O weight ISA except where indicated):

Max cruising speed at 10,670 m (35,000 ft), AUW of 7,257 kg (16,000 lb)
465 knots (862 km/h; 535 mph)

Max operating speed
Mach 0.855 or 360 knots (667 km/h; 414 mph)

Stalling speed at max landing weight:

flaps and gear up	111 knots (206 km/h; 128 mph)
flaps and gear down	92 knots (171 km/h; 106 mph)
Max rate of climb at S/L	1,112 m (3,650 ft)/min
Rate of climb at S/L, one engine out	335 m (1,100 ft)/min
Max certificated altitude	13,715 m (45,000 ft)
Service ceiling, one engine out	5,790 m (19,000 ft)
FAR 25 T-O balanced field length at S/L at 10,296 kg (22,700 lb) T-O weight	1,518 m (4,980 ft)
FAR 25 landing field length at S/L at max landing weight	806 m (2,645 ft)

Range with long-range tanks and 4 passengers, 45 min reserves:

at Mach 0.80	2,510 nm (4,651 km; 2,890 miles)
at Mach 0.72	3,110 nm (5,763 km; 3,581 miles)

OPERATIONAL NOISE LEVELS (FAR 36 at max T-O weight, estimated):

T-O: normal	89.9 EPNdB
with thrust cutback	84.1 EPNdB
Approach	89.8 EPNdB
Sideline	89.7 EPNdB

BEDEK AVIATION DIVISION

Ben-Gurion International Airport, Israel 70100
Telephone: 972 (3) 9711240
Fax: 972 (3) 971 3131 and 971 2290
Telex: ISRAVIA 381014 and 381033

GENERAL MANAGER: I. Geva (Brig-Gen Retd)

Bedek Aviation Division is internationally approved as a single-site civil and military airframe, power plant, systems and accessory service and upgrading centre. It has four operating plants: Matam, aircraft services and infrastructure; Shaham, aircraft maintenance and upgrading; Masham, engine maintenance; and Mashav, components maintenance; which, with the division headquarters, have a workforce of 3,200 housed in 110,000 m^2 (1,184,030 sq ft) of covered space. Bedek performs most of IAI's military and civil upgrading and retrofit programmes, current examples including the Phantom 2000 and Super Phantom programmes described in this entry and modification of a number of large transport aircraft to passenger/cargo, tanker, EW and reconnaissance mission configurations. Additional ongoing work includes the turnaround inspection, overhaul, repair, retrofit, outfitting and testing of more than 25 types of aircraft. Among these are various models of Boeing 707/727/737/747/767, McDonnell Douglas DC-8/DC-9/DC-10 and Lockheed C-130; combat aircraft that can be handled include the A-4 Skyhawk, F-4 Phantom, F-5, F-15 Eagle, F-16 Fighting Falcon, various MiG fighters and Mirage III/5. Power plants processed encompass 30 types of civil and military piston, turboprop, turbojet and turbofan engine and their components, including the JT3D, JT8D, JT9D, F100, J79, Atar 9C, TFE731, T56, PT6, C-250, T53 and T64. More than 6,000 types of accessories and instruments are serviced. The division provides total technical support to several international operators, and holds warranty and/or approved service centre appointments from domestic and foreign air regulatory agencies, air arms and a large number of leading aerospace manufacturers. Bedek is approved as a repair and overhaul agency by most major civil aviation authorities such as the Israeli CAA, Israeli Air Force, US military, FAA (USA), CAA (UK) and LBA (Germany); these approvals cover aircraft, engine and accessory services.

IAI COMBAT AIRCRAFT UPGRADING

IAI's Bedek Aviation Division is currently offering a number of upgrade possibilities for existing combat aircraft. Modular modernisation packages include new avionics such as a computerised digital weapon delivery and navigation system (WDNS) with multiple weapon delivery in air-to-air and air-to-ground modes and navigation data for up to 40 waypoints; a stores management and release system (SMRS), integrated with the WDNS, for both conventional and smart weapons; various active and passive self-protection (ECM) systems such as podded or internally mounted jammers, radar warning, and flare/chaff dispensers; customised new digital ADI, HSI and ADC systems; and airframe and/or engine modifications and refits.

Typical programmes include the following:

Mirage III/5: Basic airframe modifications consist of the installation of Kfir type foreplanes and landing gear, the former permitting either a substantial reduction (305-457 m; 1,000-1,500 ft) in T-O run or a 907 kg (2,000 lb) increase in T-O gross weight, and the latter an increase in max T-O weight to 16,330 kg (36,000 lb). The foreplanes also offer a marked improvement in air turning radius (from 1,036 m; 3,400 ft to 610 m; 2,000 ft at 4,575 m; 15,000 ft altitude); improved sustained turn, a vastly extended usable angle of attack and low-speed envelope; and much improved handling qualities. By reducing air loads on the wings and fuselage, they extend the fatigue life of the airframe. An additional fuselage fuel tank can be installed aft of the cockpit, and a Kfir type nose provides additional space for avionics such as control and stability augmentation systems. Other avionics include a radar warning system, with omnidirectional threat analysis and cockpit display, and a WDNS-391 fully inertial weapon delivery and navigation system with head-up operation in all air-to-surface and air-to-air modes. Martin-Baker Mk 10 ejection seats are another option, and missiles or ECM pods can be carried on reinforced wingtip stations. Two or four additional external stores stations are provided, and flare/chaff dispensers can be installed under the rear fuselage.

IAI is also offering two other concurrent remanufacturing/upgrading options for Mirage III and 5 airframes:

Option 1 involves replacement of the existing power plant with a General Electric/Flygmotor F404/RM12 turbofan (55.6 kN; 12,500 lb st dry, 80.7 kN; 18,140 lb st with afterburning), permitting a shorter interception reaction time, better air combat performance, enhanced payload/range capability and improved fleet serviceability. In addition to providing some 30 per cent more thrust and up to 20 per cent better sfc, this re-engining saves some 453.5 kg (1,000 lb) in the aircraft's weight and enables it to carry an additional 544 kg (1,200 lb) of internal fuel. Max T-O weight is increased by 2,721 kg (6,000 lb).

Option 2 offers integration of the Elta EL/M-2011 or M-2032 lightweight fire control radar, conferring the following performance benefits: a coherent pulse Doppler radar with low and medium PRFs; lookup/lookdown capability; target tracking by monopulse technique and tracking filter; ability to track low-altitude targets in heavy clutter; full utilisation of the launch envelopes and slaving capability of advanced missiles; all air target information presented on head-up display; improved air-to-ground ranging; extensive built-in testing and calibration; adaptability to other avionics systems; and growth potential through all-software-controlled LRUs and a MIL-STD-1553B interface.

Skyhawk: Major airframe improvements (already applied to Israeli Air Force A-4s) include a life extension overhaul, replacement of all wiring, provision of dual disc brakes on the mainwheels, a steerable nosewheel, addition of wing spoilers, an extra hardpoint under each wing, extension of the tailpipe (to change the heat signature and make the tailpipe more survivable and easier to repair), and addition of a brake-chute in a fairing beneath the rear fuselage. The wingroot cannon are of increased calibre (30 mm instead of 20 mm), and a modern WDNS is installed. Additional space for lighter-weight avionics is made available in an extended nose compartment and in the saddleback hump aft of the cockpit. Flare and chaff dispensers can be installed under the rear fuselage, forward of the brake-chute fairing. Bedek also offers a modification programme to convert single-seat A-4s into two-seat dual control trainers.

Phantom 2000: This programme relates specifically to Israeli Air Force F-4s, the major objectives being to extend service life, enhance mission capability, improve flight safety, and improve reliability and maintainability. These are being achieved by structural modifications, complete rewiring, and upgrading the avionics. A similar programme is available to other F-4 operators.

The Phantom 2000 prototypes were completed by the Israeli Air Force, the first of them flying for the first time on 11 August 1987. Airframe changes to the remainder are being carried out by IAI under IAF contract. The Phantoms are strengthened structurally (reinforced skins and fuel cells in fuselage and wings), to improve flight safety and fatigue life and to extend their service life well into the next century. The aircraft are completely rewired and are equipped with 1553B dual redundant digital databases. Hydraulic lines are selectively replaced and rerouted, built-in test features added, and the number of line-replaceable units reduced. Small strakes above the intake flanks improve stability and manoeuvrability, and cockpit comfort and instrument layout embody the latest human engineering data.

The IAF Phantom 2000s are being given a new, advanced and fully integrated avionics suite, the major items of which are a Norden/UTC multi-mode high-resolution radar, El-Op (Kaiser licence) wide-angle diffractive-optics head-up display, Elbit multi-function CRT displays for both crew

Israeli Air Force Phantoms refuelling from a C-130 Hercules tanker converted by IAI's Bedek Aviation Division

IAI (Bedek) Super Phantom demonstrator, re-engined with PW1120 turbojets

members, a computerised WDNS, HOTAS (hands on throttle and stick) systems selection, Orbit integrated com and com/nav systems, and improved electronic warfare and self-protection (ECM) systems. Elbit Computers Ltd is overall integrator for the avionics refit, the core of which is a data processor derived from the company's ACE-3 currently fitted to all IAF F-16C/Ds. Redelivery of 'production' Phantom 2000 conversions to the Israeli Air Force began on 9 April 1989; first operational use 5 February 1991.

Super Phantom: This programme was launched in 1986, when an IAF F-4E (serial number 334) was refitted with a 60.3 kN (13,550 lb st) Pratt & Whitney PW1120 turbojet (91.7 kN; 20,620 lb st with afterburning) in place of one of its J79s, for use as an engine testbed in the Lavi development programme. It flew for the first time in this form on 30 July 1986, subsequently having the other J79 similarly replaced. Structural changes included modifying the air inlet ducts; new engine attachment points; new or modified engine bay doors; new airframe mounted gearbox with integrated drive generators and automatic throttle system; modified bleed management and air-conditioning ducting system; modified fuel and hydraulic systems; and an engine control/airframe interface.

By mid-1987 flight test results with this Super Phantom demonstrator (all in clean condition and at speeds of Mach 0.98 or below) had indicated significant performance improvements over the J79 powered F-4, as listed in the 1989-90 and earlier *Jane's*.

Super Phantom re-engineering is offered by IAI to F-4 operators worldwide. Options include canards and a conformal underfuselage auxiliary fuel tank.

F-5: Shaham's 'F-5 Plus' upgrade package offers upgraded avionics (incl HOTAS, HUD, two multi-function displays, modern pulse Doppler radar, video camera and recorder), optional helmet-mounted display, improved mission systems (eg, weapons delivery and ECM), introduction of new weapon systems, and maintainability improvements. Other options can include a more modern ejection seat, secure communications, in-flight refuelling capability, and podded or nose-mounted reconnaissance equipment. In early 1990, IAI received a contract to upgrade 12 F-5Es and two F-5Fs of the Chilean Air Force by installing new equipment that includes an Elta EL/M-2032B multi-mode fire control radar, an improved WDNS, El-Op HUD, HOTAS, Astronautics (Israel) modular mission and display processor, and a multiple databus. Nose modifications to accommodate larger radar antenna include deletion of the port M39 20 mm gun and relocation of some subsystems.

F-15: Upgrading effort for the McDonnell Douglas F-15 in which Bedek is involved includes structures, maintainability, and various utility and mission systems.

IAI TRACKER UPGRADING

Shaham offers a number of upgrades to the Grumman S-2 Tracker maritime patrol aircraft. They comprise refitting with modern turboprop engines; installation of modern avionics and flight systems; and introduction of such state of the art mission equipment as search radar, electro-optical systems, and EW, ESM and ECM systems. Upgrading for one unnamed customer, under the designation **S-2UP**, began in 1990 and is due for completion in 1992.

IAI AMIT FOUGA
Israeli Air Force name: Tzukit (Thrush)

The AMIT Fouga (Advanced Multi-mission Improved Trainer) was engineered by the Bedek Aviation Division of IAI to Israeli Air Force requirements, to enable its Fouga Magisters to remain as standard IAF trainers during the 1980s. It is, in effect, completely rebuilt and modernised, and is a dedicated trainer with all armament removed, although it retains capability for patrol and aerial photographic missions. Details of the modifications were given in the 1986-87 *Jane's*. The upgrade programme is available for other operators of this aircraft. The Israeli Air Force was reported in 1990 to be seeking a Tzukit replacement.

IAI LARGE TRANSPORT CONVERSIONS

Bedek Aviation Division has carried out, or can offer, a variety of configuration conversions for large transport aircraft, including the following:

Boeing 707/720: Bedek has refurbished and resold numerous Boeing 707s and 720s, often after conversion from passenger to cargo, sigint, hose or boom refuelling tanker or other configurations, and several of these have been recorded in previous editions of *Jane's*. A **sigint/tanker** conversion with wingtip refuelling pods and Elta EL/L-8300 sigint system was illustrated in the 1987-88 edition. Also under development is an **AEW** version mounting an Elta Electronics Phalcon solid state L-band radar with six conformal phased array antennae: two on each side of the fuselage, one in an enlarged nose and one under the tail. In addition to the radar, the Phalcon system incorporates a sophisticated monopulse IFF, wide-range ESM system and a comint data processing system. A complete Phalcon was to fly in 1991. Phalcon is said to have been sold to Chile.

Modifications involved in the **tanker** conversion include local reinforcement of the outer wings, supports for additional fuel tanks where applicable, and fuselage reinforcement for the boom support point or tail reel hose exit; an additional hydraulic system to power the fuel

Retouched photograph illustrating the Phalcon AEW aircraft based on a Boeing 707 airframe

Max landing weight	265,350 kg (585,000 lb)
Max zero-fuel weight	247,435 kg (545,500 lb)

pumps and boom or tail reel; adaptation of the fuel supply system to the tanker role; electrical system changes to add external illumination, refuelling system controls, boom operator's station with 3-D electro-optical viewing system, and director lights for pilots of receiver aircraft; and avionics to individual customer requirements.

Tanker combis, with a centreline boom and two probe/drogue underwing refuelling pods, have been delivered to the Israeli Air Force, and four similar conversions were produced for the Royal Australian Air Force.

WEIGHTS AND LOADINGS (707-320C tanker, approx):

Operational weight empty	65,770 kg (145,000 lb)
*Internal fuel weight	72,575 kg (160,000 lb)
**Additional fuel weight	up to 13,605 kg (30,000 lb)
Tanker T-O weight	151,950 kg (335,000 lb)

*90,300 litres (23,855 US gallons; 19,863 Imp gallons)
**17,034 litres (4,500 US gallons; 3,747 Imp gallons)

Boeing 747-100 and -200 Freighter: Bedek Aviation converted a Boeing 747-100 to prototype Freighter configuration, for certification in 1990. Changes include installing a 3.05 × 3.40 m (10 ft 0 in × 11 ft 2 in) upward opening main deck cargo door aft of the wing on the port side, with local reinforcement of the fuselage; reinforcing the cabin floor to increase load carrying capacity; installing a fully powered ball mat/roller cargo handling system and restraint system, and a bulkhead between the passenger and cargo compartments; and interior modifications adapted to selected passenger/cargo combinations. Basic configuration options to be offered are (1) all-cargo, with up to 29 main deck standard pallets or containers; (2) Combi, with passengers at front and 7-13 pallets aft; and (3) all-passenger, with interior layout to customer's specification. Versions to accommodate non-standard containers, and similar conversions of the Model 747-200, can be produced.

British lease operator Electra Aviation announced in late 1990 a contract to IAI to convert 10 Boeing 747-100s to all-cargo configuration, with deliveries to begin in mid-1992.

WEIGHTS AND LOADINGS (747-100 Combi, estimated):

Operational weight empty	148,325 kg (327,000 lb)
Max payload	98,883 kg (218,000 lb)
Max T-O weight	334,750 kg (738,000 lb)

Lockheed C-130/L-100 Hercules: Bedek Aviation has already accomplished several successful conversions of C-130 series aircraft to such configurations as in-flight refuelling tanker and sigint platform, with appropriate airframe modifications and avionics refits. Operational configurations currently being offered for any C-130B to C-130H variant, or their L-100 commercial counterparts, include: (1) probe and drogue aerial refuelling tanker, with transfer fuel in an 11,356 litre (3,000 US gallon; 2,498 Imp gallon) cargo compartment tank plus two underwing fuel pods; (2) maritime surface patrol and ASW, with appropriate surveillance, acoustic, MAD, armament and stores management systems, and operator stations; (3) C³I and electronic warfare platform, with comint, elint, communications and EW systems to customer's requirements; (4) search and rescue, with a rescue kit, flare storage/launcher and operator station on a logistic pallet installed on the rear loading ramp; (5) emergency assistance, with an insulated cabin mounted on a logistic pallet for ambulance or flying hospital missions or in a firefighting configuration with up to 11,356 litres (3,000 US gallons; 2,498 Imp gallons) of water and retardant in pallet mounted tanks in the cargo hold; and (6) VIP, 65-seat passenger or passenger/cargo combi transport, with full airliner type seating, galley and toilet facilities, pallet-mounted in an air-conditioned environment.

WEIGHTS AND LOADINGS (C-130H tanker, approx):

Operational weight empty	35,380 kg (78,000 lb)
*Internal fuel weight	29,030 kg (64,000 lb)
**Additional fuel weight	10,885 kg (24,000 lb)
Tanker T-O weight	75,295 kg (166,000 lb)
Max overload T-O weight	79,380 kg (175,000 lb)

*36,643 litres (9,860 US gallons; 8,060 Imp gallons)
**13,627 litres (3,600 US gallons; 2,997 Imp gallons)

Cockpit upgrades: As future development programmes, Bedek Aviation intends to convert existing three-man flight decks of transport aircraft for two-man operation. Conversion will include advanced monitoring and control systems, including engine indicating and crew alerting system (EICAS). Candidate aircraft include the Boeing 727 and McDonnell Douglas DC-10.

TECHNOLOGIES DIVISION

PO Box 190, Lod Industrial Zone 711101
Telephone: 972 (8) 239111
Fax: 972 (8) 222792
Telex: SHLD IL 381520
GENERAL MANAGER: Y. Shapira

This Division is the parent facility to four separate plants: SHL (Servo Hydraulics Lod), Ramta Structures and Systems, MATA Helicopters, and Golan Industries. SHL designs, develops and manufactures hydraulic system components, hydraulic flight control servo-systems, landing gears and brake systems; and produces air actuated chucks, miniature gears, clutches and brakes. Among others, its products equip the Kfir, Arava, Westwind and Astra, and IDF Sikorsky Black Hawk helicopters; manufacturing approvals are held from Boeing, Dornier, General Dynamics and General Electric, among others. Ramta undertakes metal and advanced composites fabrication for the F-4 Phantom, F-16 Fighting Falcon, E-2C Hawkeye, Kfir, Westwind and Astra, as well as manufacturing ground vehicles and patrol boats. MATA repairs, reconfigures and remanufactures helicopter structures and components, and produces equipment and systems for rotating-wing aircraft. Golan designs and manufactures aircraft crew and passenger seats (including designing crashworthy troop seats for the Bell/Boeing V-22 Osprey), aircraft wheels and cockpit controls.

IAI CH-53 2000

Headed by MATA Helicopters, this programme is aimed at upgrading the Israeli Air Force fleet of some 30 Sikorsky CH-53D heavy lift helicopters, with the first example due to be completed in 1993. The CH-53 2000 will embody structural changes to extend service life well into the next century, and improved avionics such as a new mission computer, moving map display, two multi-function displays and a new autopilot system. Other modifications include enternal auxiliary fuel tanks, flight refuelling boom, rescue hoist, crashworthy seats, cockpit armour, improved launching lights, internal batteries, electric pump for reloading APP accumulator and new APP clutch. Elbit is avionics systems integrator for the CH-53 2000.

ITALY

AERITALIA — *see Alenia*

AERONAUTICA MACCHI
AERONAUTICA MACCHI SpA)
Via Don Tornatore 6, 21100 Varese
Telephone: 39 (332) 287700
Telex: 380070

CHAIRMAN: Dott Fabrizio Foresio

AERMACCHI
AERMACCHI SpA (Subsidiary of Aeronautica Macchi SpA)
Via Sanvito Silvestro 80, CP 246, 21100 Varese
Telephone: 39 (332) 254111
Fax: 39 (332) 254555
Telex: 380070 AERMAC I
CHAIRMAN: Dott Fabrizio Foresio
MANAGING DIRECTOR: Dott Ing Giorgio Brazzelli
GROUP GENERAL MANAGER, PLANNING, FINANCE AND CONTROL: Dott Alfonso Romagnoli
GROUP GENERAL MANAGER, STRATEGIES AND PROGRAMMES: Dott Ing Bruno Cussigh
GENERAL MANAGER, OPERATIONS: Dott Ing Romano Antichi
TECHNICAL MANAGER: Dott Ing Massimo Lucchesini
FOREIGN SALES DIRECTOR: Dott Cesare Cozzi
PUBLIC RELATIONS MANAGER: Franca Grandi

Aermacchi, which celebrated its 75th anniversary in 1988, is the aircraft manufacturing company of the Aeronautica Macchi group. Its plants at Venegono airfield occupy a total area of 274,000 m² (2,949,310 sq ft), including 52,000 m² (559,720 sq ft) of covered space; the flight test centre has covered space of 5,100 m² (54,900 sq ft) in a total area of 28,000 m² (301,390 sq ft). Total workforce at the end of 1990 was 2,748.

In addition to its aircraft programmes, Aermacchi is active in the field of aerospace ground equipment, with a complete line of hydraulic, electric and pneumatic ground carts for servicing civil and military aircraft, and also has important roles in the Ariane and EFA programmes.

DORNIER 328
In April 1989, Aermacchi announced the signature of a memorandum for co-operation on the Dornier 328 programme (see German section). Aermacchi has designed and is building the forward fuselage and will assemble the main fuselage by adding barrel sections produced by South Korean Daewoo Heavy Industries.

The original Macchi company was founded in 1913 in Varese, and produced a famous line of high-speed flying boats and seaplanes. On 1 January 1981 the Aeronautica Macchi group reorganised its structure, transforming itself into a holding company and transferring all of its operating activities to a newly formed, wholly owned company known as Aermacchi SpA. The group includes, besides Aermacchi SpA, the subsidiary companies Aero Engineering (aeronautical design), SICAMB (airframe and equipment manufacturing, including licence production of Martin-Baker ejection seats), OMG (precision machining), and Logic (electronics equipment). A 25 per cent holding in Aeronautica Macchi was acquired by Aeritalia (now Alenia) in 1983.

AERMACCHI/DASA PTS-2000
Aermacchi and Dornier signed a memorandum of understanding in April 1989 for a future integrated military pilot training system (PTS-2000) to meet the pilot training requirements of the year 2000. MBB joined the group early in 1991. The PTS-2000 system is described in the International section.

LOCKHEED/AERMACCHI/HUGHES JPATS
In October 1989, Aermacchi, Lockheed and Hughes signed a co-operation agreement to compete in the Joint Primary Aircraft Training System (JPATS) programme for the USAF and US Navy, using the MB-339 in their bid to replace T-37s and T-34Cs. Lockheed would become prime contractor and system integrator for the JPATS programme, holding a manufacturing licence, with Hughes managing the training system and supplying simulators. Rolls-Royce joined the team in September 1990 to develop the RB582 turbojet intended to replace the Viper 680.

AMX

Aermacchi is teamed with Alenia and Embraer in the AMX combat aircraft programme (see International section) for the Italian and Brazilian air forces.

AERMACCHI MB-339A

The first of two MB-339X prototypes (MM588) was flown for the first time on 12 August 1976. The second aircraft (MM589), which made its first flight on 20 May 1977, was built to pre-production standard; the third airframe was used for static and fatigue testing.

The first production MB-339A made its initial flight on 20 July 1978, and the first of an initial series of 51 aircraft for the Italian Air Force was handed over for pre-service trials on 8 August 1979. In addition to MB-339A trainers for the 61° Brigata Aerea at Lecce, this series included a batch of MB-339s originally used as calibration aircraft (radiomisure) with the 8° Gruppo Sorveglianza Elettronica of the 14° Stormo Radiomisure at Pratica di Mare, delivered from 16 February 1981, and a total of 20 **MB-339PAN**s (Pattuglia Acrobatica Nazionale) delivered to the Italian Air Force aerobatic team, the Frecce Tricolori, which began using the type on 27 April 1982. The PAN aircraft have the wingtip tanks deleted (to facilitate formation keeping) and a smoke generating system installed, but are otherwise similar to the standard MB-339A. The last of 101 MB-339As for the Italian Air Force was delivered in 1987, and its pilots now gain their 'wings' after completing all phases of their advanced training on MB-339As. Except for the PAN aircraft, all Italian Air Force MB-339As are camouflaged and all are available for use as an emergency close air support force.

Ten MB-339As were delivered to the Argentine Navy in 1980, 16 to the Peruvian Air Force in 1981-82, 12 to the Royal Malaysian Air Force in 1983-84, two to Dubai in 1984, and 12 to Nigeria in 1985. In 1987 three more were delivered to Dubai and two to the Ghana Air Force. Production of the MB-339A ended in 1987, when about 160 had been produced.

During 1990-91 the Marte Mk 2A anti-ship missile was being integrated with the MB-339A for the Italian Air Force. Two IAF aircraft were being used for qualification.

Details of the MB-339B and single-seat MB-339K, for which no orders have been announced by early 1991, can be found in the 1989-90 *Jane's*. The following description applies to the MB-339A. Full details were given in the 1990-91 *Jane's*.

TYPE: Two-seat basic and advanced trainer and ground attack aircraft.

POWER PLANT: One Italian-made Rolls-Royce Viper Mk 632-43 turbojet, rated at 17.8 kN (4,000 lb st). Fuel in two-cell rubber fuselage tank, capacity 781 litres (206 US gallons; 172 Imp gallons), and two integral wingtip tanks, combined capacity 632 litres (167 US gallons; 139 Imp gallons). Total internal capacity 1,413 litres (373 US gallons; 311 Imp gallons) usable. Single-point pressure refuelling receptacle in port side of fuselage, below wing trailing-edge. Gravity refuelling points on top of fuselage and each tip tank. Provision for two drop tanks, each of 325 litres (86 US gallons; 71.5 Imp gallons) usable capacity, on centre underwing stations. Anti-icing system for engine air intakes.

EQUIPMENT: Provision for towing type A-6B (1.83 × 9.14 m; 6 × 30 ft) aerial banner target; tow attachment point on inner surface of ventral airbrake. External stores can include photographic pod with four 70 mm Vinten cameras; or a single underwing Elettronica ECM pod, combined with a flare/chaff dispenser, onboard RHAW receiver and indicators.

ARMAMENT: Up to 2,040 kg (4,500 lb) of external stores can be carried on six underwing hardpoints, the inner four of which are stressed for loads of up to 454 kg (1,000 lb) each and the outer two for up to 340 kg (750 lb) each. Provisions are made, on the two inner stations, for the installation of two Macchi gun pods, each containing either a 30 mm DEFA 553 cannon with 120 rds, or a 12.7 mm AN/M-3 machine-gun with 350 rds. Other typical loads can include two Matra 550 Magic or AIM-9 Sidewinder air-to-air missiles on the two outer stations; four 1,000 lb or six 750 lb bombs; six SUU-11A/A 7.62 mm Minigun pods with 1,500 rds/pod; six Matra 155 launchers, each for eighteen 68 mm rockets; six Matra F-2 practice launchers, each for six 68 mm rockets; six LAU-68/A or LAU-32G launchers, each for seven 2.75 in rockets; six Aerea AL-25-50 or AL-18-50 launchers, each with twenty-five or eighteen 50 mm rockets respectively; six Aerea AL-12-80 launchers, each with twelve 81 mm rockets; four LAU-10/A launchers, each with four 5 in Zuni rockets; four Thomson-Brandt 100-4 launchers, each with four 100 mm Thomson-Brandt rockets; six Aerea BRD bomb/rocket dispensers; six Aermacchi 11B29-003 bomb/flare dispensers; six Thomson-Brandt 14-3-M2 adaptors, each with six 100 mm anti-runway bombs or 120 mm tactical support bombs. Provision for Aeritalia 8.105.924 fixed reflector sight or Saab RGS 2 gyroscopic gunsight; a gunsight can also be installed in rear cockpit, to enable instructor to evaluate manoeuvres performed by student pilot. All gunsights can be equipped with fully automatic Teledyne TSC 116-2 gun camera.

Italian Air Force Aermacchi MB-339A with underwing tanks (*Paul Jackson*)

DIMENSIONS, EXTERNAL:

Wing span over tip tanks	10.858 m (35 ft 7½ in)
Wing aspect ratio	6.1
Length overall	10.972 m (36 ft 0 in)
Height overall	3.994 m (13 ft 1¼ in)

WEIGHTS AND LOADINGS:

Weight empty, equipped	3,125 kg (6,889 lb)
Fuel load (internal, usable)	1,100 kg (2,425 lb)
T-O weight, clean	4,400 kg (9,700 lb)
Max T-O weight with external stores	5,895 kg (13,000 lb)

PERFORMANCE (at clean T-O weight, ISA):

IAS limit/Mach limit	Mach 0.85 (500 knots; 926 km/h; 575 mph)
Max level speed at S/L	485 knots (898 km/h; 558 mph) IAS
Stalling speed	80 knots (149 km/h; 93 mph)
Max rate of climb at S/L	2,010 m (6,595 ft)/min

AERMACCHI MB-339C

This variant of the MB-339 has a fully integrated digital navigation and attack system, with head-up displays in both cockpits so that the rear crew member can fly a head-up instrument approach and landing as well as air-to-ground weapon delivery and hot-line air-to-air gunnery. However, the system is based on individual avionics units costing less than a purpose-built system. Power plant is the more powerful Rolls-Royce Viper 680.

The MB-339C also has enlarged wingtip tanks and a modified nose shape. It is intended for effective pilot training in modern mission management techniques. Design and development began in 1982-83. The prototype (I-AMDA) flew for the first time on 17 December 1985. An order for 18 MB-339Cs to replace BAe Strikemasters in the Royal New Zealand Air Force was placed in May 1990. The first three were delivered on 19 April 1991; deliveries should be completed in 1993.

The MB-339C's structural design criteria were based on MIL-A-8860A requirements. It has a service life requirement of 10,000 flying hours in the training role.

TYPE: Two-seat advanced and fighter lead-in trainer, with secondary ground attack role.

WINGS: Cantilever low/mid-wing monoplane. Wing section NACA 64A-114 (mod) at centreline; NACA 64A-212 (mod) at tip. Leading-edge sweptback 11° 18′; sweepback at quarter-chord 8° 29′. All-metal stressed skin structure, with single main spar and auxiliary rear spar, built in two portions and bolted to fuselage. Skin stiffened by spanwise stringers, closely spaced ribs and false ribs. Wingtip tanks permanently attached. Single fence on each wing at approx two-thirds span. Servo powered ailerons embody 'Irving' type aerodynamic balance provisions, statically balanced along entire span. Servo tabs facilitate reversion to manual operation in event of hydraulic failure. Hydraulically actuated single-slotted flaps, operated by push/pull rods. Structure is anti-corrosion treated.

FUSELAGE: All-metal semi-monocoque structure, built in two main portions: forward (nose to engine mounting bulkhead) and rear (engine bulkhead to tailcone). Forward portion has C section frame, four C section spars, longitudinal L section stringers, and skin panels. Rear section manufactured entirely from aluminium alloy except for firewall and most of tailcone, which are of stainless steel. Four bolts attach rear section to forward section to facilitate access to engine. Hydraulically actuated, electrically controlled airbrake under centre of fuselage, just forward of CG. Structure is anti-corrosion treated.

TAIL UNIT: Cantilever all-metal structure, of similar construction to wings. Slightly sweptback vertical surfaces. Rudder and elevators are statically balanced, each having electrically actuated dual-purpose balance and trim tab. Two auxiliary fins under rear of fuselage.

LANDING GEAR: Hydraulic retractable tricycle type with oleo-pneumatic shock absorbers, suitable for operation from semi-prepared runways. Hydraulically steerable nosewheel retracts forward; main units retract outward into wings. Low pressure mainwheel tubeless tyres size 545 × 175-10 (14 ply rating); nosewheel tubeless tyre size 380 × 150-4 (6 ply rating). Emergency extension system. Hydraulic disc brakes with anti-skid system.

POWER PLANT: One Rolls-Royce Viper Mk 680-43 turbojet, rated at 19.57 kN (4,400 lb st). Fuel in two-cell rubber fuselage tank, capacity 781 litres (206 US gallons; 172 Imp gallons), and two wingtip tanks with combined capacity of 1,000 litres (264 US gallons; 220 Imp gallons). Total internal usable capacity 1,781 litres (470 US gallons; 392 Imp gallons). Single-point pressure refuelling point in port side of fuselage, below wing trailing-edge. Gravity refuelling points on top of fuselage and each tip tank. Provision for two drop tanks, each of 325 litres (86 US gallons; 71.5 Imp gallons) usable capacity, on centre underwing stations. Anti-icing system for engine air intakes.

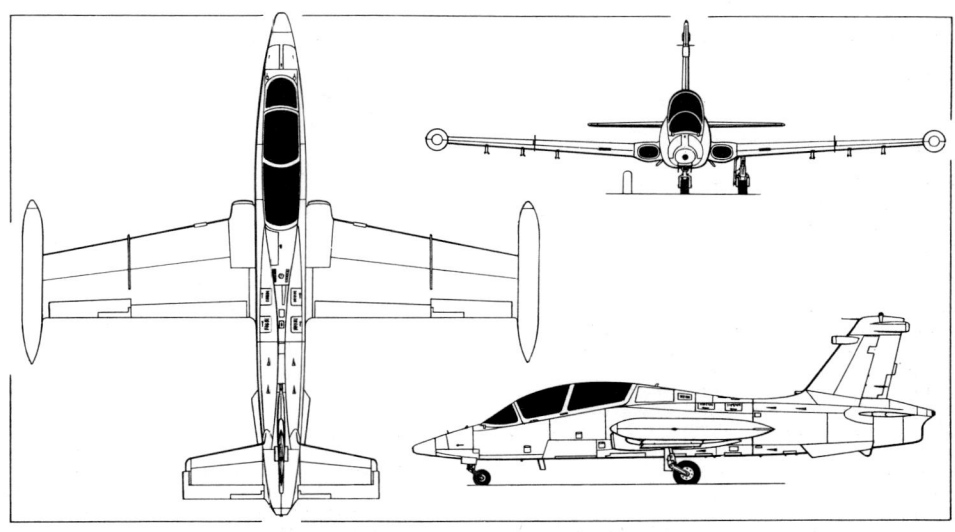

Aermacchi MB-339C, showing revised nose and vertical tail configuration (*Pilot Press*)

Aermacchi MB-339C of the Royal New Zealand Air Force

ACCOMMODATION: Crew of two in tandem, on Martin-Baker IT10LK zero/zero ejection seats in pressurised cockpit. Rear seat elevated 32.5 cm (1 ft 1 in). Rearview mirror for each occupant. Two-piece moulded transparent canopy, opening sideways to starboard.

SYSTEMS: Pressurisation system max differential 0.24 bar (3.5 lb/sq in); cockpit designed for 40,000 pressurisation cycles. Bootstrap type air-conditioning system, also providing air for windscreen and canopy demisting. Hydraulic system, pressure 172.5 bars (2,500 lb/sq in), for actuation of flaps, aileron servos, airbrake, landing gear, wheel brakes and nosewheel steering. Backup system for wheel brakes and emergency extension of landing gear. Main electrical DC power from one 28V 9kW engine driven starter/generator and one 28V 6kW secondary generator. Two 24V 22Ah nickel-cadmium batteries for engine starting. Fixed frequency 115/26V AC power from two 600VA single phase static inverters. External power receptacle. Low pressure demand oxygen system, operating at 28 bars (400 lb/sq in).

AVIONICS: Typical avionics installation includes Collins AN/ARN-118(V), type RT-1159/A Tacan or Bendix/King KDM 706A DME; Collins 51RV-4B VOR/ILS and MKI-3 marker beacon receiver; Collins ADF-60A ADF/L; Collins DF 301E VHF/UHF ADF (optional); GEC Avionics AD-660 Doppler radar integrated with Litton LR-80 inertial platform; GEC Avionics 620K navigation computer; Kaiser Sabre head-up display/weapons aiming computer; Alenia CRT multifunction display; Alenia/Honeywell HG7505 radar altimeter;

FIAR P 0702 laser rangefinder; ELT-156 radar warning system; logic storer management system; Bendix/King AN/APX-100 IFF; Astronautics AN/ARU-50/A attitude director indicator; Astronautics AN/AQU-13 HSI; HOTAS (hands on throttle and stick) controls.

EQUIPMENT: Includes Fairchild Weston video camera; Tracor AN/ALE-40 chaff/flare dispenser; photographic pod with four 70 mm Vinten cameras; or a single underwing Elettronica/ELT-555 ECM pod, combined with a flare/chaff dispenser, onboard RHAW receiver and indicators.

ARMAMENT: Up to 1,815 kg (4,000 lb) of external stores on six underwing hardpoints. Four inner hardpoints each stressed for up to 454 kg (1,000 lb) load, and two outer hardpoints each for up to 340 kg (750 lb) load. Provision on two inner stations for installation of two Macchi gun pods, each containing either a 30 mm DEFA 553 cannon with 120 rounds or a 12.7 mm AN/M-3 machine gun with 350 rounds. Other typical loads can include two Matra 550 Magic or AIM-9 Sidewinder air-to-air missiles on two outer stations; six general purpose or cluster bombs of appropriate weights; six AN/SUU-11A/A 7.62 mm Minigun pods, each with 1,500 rounds; six Matra 155 launchers, each for eighteen 68 mm rockets; six AN/LAU-68/A or AN/LAU-32G launchers, each for seven 2.75 in rockets; six Aerea AL-25-50 or AL-18-50 launchers, each with twenty-five or eighteen 50 mm rockets respectively; six Aerea AL-18-80 launchers, each with twelve 81 mm rockets; four AN/LAU-10/A launchers, each with four 5 in Zuni rockets; four

Thomson-Brandt 100-4 launchers, each with four 100 mm Thomson-Brandt rockets; six Aerea BRD bomb/rocket dispensers; six Aermacchi 11B29-003 bomb/flare dispensers; six Thomson-Brandt 14-3-M2 adapters, each with six BAP 100 anti-runway bombs or BAT 120 tactical support bombs. Nav/attack system makes possible employment of air-to-air infra-red missiles (AIM-9L and Matra Magic), AGM-65 Maverick air-to-ground missiles and Marte Mk II sea-skimming anti-ship missiles.

DIMENSIONS, EXTERNAL:
Wing span over tip tanks	11.22 m (36 ft 9¾ in)
Wing aspect ratio	6.1
Length overall	11.24 m (36 ft 10½ in)
Height overall	3.994 m (13 ft 1¼ in)
Elevator span	4.08 m (13 ft 4½ in)
Wheel track	2.483 m (8 ft 1¾ in)
Wheelbase	4.369 m (14 ft 4 in)

AREAS:
Wings, gross	19.30 m² (207.7 sq ft)
Ailerons (total)	1.328 m² (14.29 sq ft)
Trailing-edge flaps (total)	2.21 m² (23.79 sq ft)
Airbrake	0.68 m² (7.32 sq ft)
Fin	2.37 m² (25.51 sq ft)
Rudder, incl tab	0.61 m² (6.57 sq ft)
Tailplane	3.38 m² (36.38 sq ft)
Elevators (total incl tabs)	0.979 m² (10.54 sq ft)

WEIGHTS AND LOADINGS:
Weight empty, equipped	3,310 kg (7,297 lb)
Fuel load (internal, usable)	1,388 kg (3,060 lb)
T-O weight, clean	4,884 kg (10,767 lb)
Max T-O weight with external stores	6,350 kg (14,000 lb)
Max wing loading	329.0 kg/m² (67.39 lb/sq ft)
Max power loading	324.7 kg/kN (3.18 lb/lb st)

PERFORMANCE (at trainer T-O weight, ISA, except where indicated):
Max level speed at S/L	486 knots (900 km/h; 558 mph)
Max level speed at 9,150 m (30,000 ft)	Mach 0.77 (441 knots; 815 km/h; 508 mph)
Max speed for landing gear extension	175 knots (324 km/h; 202 mph)
T-O speed	100 knots (185 km/h; 115 mph)
Approach speed over 15 m (50 ft) obstacle	98 knots (182 km/h; 113 mph)
Stalling speed	80 knots (149 km/h; 93 mph)
Max rate of climb at S/L	2,160 m (7,085 ft)/min
Time to 9,150 m (30,000 ft)	6.7 min
Service ceiling (30.5 m; 100 ft/min rate of climb)	14,240 m (46,700 ft)
Min ground turning radius	8.45 m (27 ft 9 in)
T-O run at S/L	490 m (1,608 ft)
Landing run at S/L, ISA	455 m (1,493 ft)
Max ferry range with two underwing drop tanks, 10% reserves	1,100 nm (2,038 km; 1,266 miles)
Max endurance with drop tanks	3 h 50 min
g limit, clean	7.33

AGUSTA
AGUSTA SpA
Via Giovanni Agusta 520, 21017 Cascina Costa di Samarate (VA)
Telephone: 39 (331) 229111
Fax: 39 (331) 222595
Telex: 332569 AGUCA I
OFFICES:
Via Caldera 21, 20153 Milan
Telephone: 39 (2) 452751
Fax: 39 (2) 48204701
Telex: 333280 AGUMI I
Via Abruzzi 11, 00187 Rome
Telephone: 39 (6) 49801
Fax: 39 (6) 6799944
Telex: 614398 AGURO I
CHAIRMAN AND CHIEF EXECUTIVE OFFICER:
Dott Roberto D'Alessandro
INTERNATIONAL CO-OPERATION: Ing Luigi Passini
MARKETING AND SALES: Dott Enrico Guerra
CORPORATE COMMUNICATIONS MANAGER:
Ing Francesco Fusco
PLANNING: Dott Roberto Leverone
AERONAUTICAL BUSINESS UNIT:
(temporarily) Dott Roberto D'Alessandro
LOGISTIC BUSINESS UNIT: Ing Michele Ferraioli
RESEARCH AND DEVELOPMENT BUSINESS UNIT:
Ing Bruno Lovera
AEROSPACE SYSTEM BUSINESS UNIT: Ing Mario Barozzi
Formed originally in 1977, the Agusta Group (see 1980-81 *Jane's*) completely reorganised its structure from 1 January 1981 under a new holding company known as Agusta SpA. It became part of the Italian public holding agency EFIM, employing nearly 10,000 people in 12 factories in various parts of Italy.
The various domestic activities of Agusta are grouped under the location of the works. The familiar names of Costruzioni Aeronautiche Giovanni Agusta, SIAI-Marchetti, Caproni Vizzola Costruzioni Aeronautiche and BredaNardi Costruzioni Aeronautiche are no longer in use. In addition, Elicotteri Meridionali is a domestic affiliate

and Agusta has eight international affiliates in addition to its involvement with SAAC Sammi Agusta Aerospace of South Korea (which see). The various works and affiliates are as follows:

DOMESTIC WORKS
Benevento Works
(ex-FOMB – Fonderie e Officine Meccaniche di Benevento SpA)
Contrada Ponte Valentino - S.S. 90 bis, 82100 Benevento
Telephone: 39 (824) 53440/53441/53447
Fax: 39 (824) 53418
Telex: 710667
This works specialises in aircraft co-production and overhaul of helicopters and multi-engined aircraft.

Brindisi Works
(ex-IAM – Industrie Aeronautiche Meridionali SpA)
Contrada Santa Teresa Pinti, 72100 Brindisi
Telephone: 39 (831) 8911
Fax: 39 (831) 452659
Telex: 813360

Cascina Costa Works
(ex-Costruzioni Aeronautiche Giovanni Agusta SpA)
Via Giovanni Agusta 520, 21017 Cascina Costa di Samarate (VA)
Telephone: 39 (331) 229111
Fax: 39 (331) 222595
Telex: 332569 AGUCA I

Monteprandone Works
(ex-BredaNardi Costruzioni Aeronautiche SpA)
Casella Postale 108, San Benedetto del Trento (Ascoli Piceno), Monteprandone (AP)
Telephone: 39 (735) 801721
Fax: 39 (735) 701927
Telex: 560165 BRENAR I

Rome Works
(ex-Ottico Meccanica Italiana SpA)
Via della Vasca Navale 79/81, 00146 Rome
Telephone: 39 (6) 55421
Fax: 39 (6) 5593753
Telex: 610137

Sesto Calende Works
(ex-SIAI-Marchetti SpA)
Via Indipendenza 2, 21018 Sesto Calende (VA)
Telephone: 39 (331) 924421
Fax: 39 (331) 922525
Telex: 332601 SI AIA VI

Somma Lombarda Works
(ex-Caproni Vizzola Costruzioni Aeronautiche SpA)
Via Per Tornavento 15, 21019 Somma Lombardo
Telephone: 39 (331) 230826
Fax: 39 (331) 230622
Telex: 332554 CAVIZ I

Tradate Works
(ex-Agusta Sistemi SpA)
Via Isonzo 33, 21049 Tradate (VA)
Telephone: 39 (331) 815111
Fax: 39 (331) 843910
Telex: 350405

DOMESTIC AFFILIATES
Elicotteri Meridionali SpA
Via G. Agusta 1, Frosinone
S.E.I. - Servizi Elicotteristici Italiani,
Via della Vasca Navale 79/81, 00146 Rome
Telephone: 39 (6) 49801
PRESIDENT: Dott Roberto D'Alessandro
Italcompositi SpA
Via Pomarico, Pisticci, MT

INTERNATIONAL AFFILIATES

Agusta Aerospace Corporation
2655 Interplex Drive, Travose, Philadelphia 19047, USA
Telephone: 1 (215) 281 1400
Fax: 1 (215) 281 0440
Telex: 6851181
CHAIRMAN AND CHIEF EXECUTIVE OFFICER:
Ing Giuseppe Orsi
Agusta Aerospace Services SA
Keiberg Park, Excelsiorlanne 23, Zaventem 1930, Belgium
Telephone: 32 (2) 648585/6485515
Telex: 63349
GENERAL MANAGER: Dott Riccardo Baldini

Agusta Aviation Far East Pte Ltd
11-03 United Square, 101 Thomson Road, 1130 Singapore
Telephone: 65 (273) 3100
Telex: 36126
GENERAL MANAGER: Dott Fulvio Maurogiovanni

EH Industries Ltd
500 Chiswick High Road, London W4 5RG, UK

EH Industries Inc
141 Laurier Avenue West, 6th Floor, Ottawa, Ontario, Canada

Monacair SAM
Héliport de Fontvieille, Principality of Monaco 98000

OMI Corporation of America
1319 Powhatan Street, Alexandria, Virginia 22314, USA
Telephone: 1 (703) 549 9191
Telex: 899141
CHAIRMAN: James F. Byrnes
SAMMI Agusta Aerospace Corporation Ltd
66 Shinchon-Dong-Changwan City, Kyungsangnam, do Korea

CASCINA COSTA WORKS

The original Agusta company, established in 1907 by Giovanni Agusta, built many experimental and production aircraft before the Second World War. In 1952 Agusta acquired a licence to manufacture the Bell Model 47 helicopter, and the first Agusta-built Model 47G made its initial flight on 22 May 1954.

In addition to the A 109A and A 129/139 of its own design, Agusta is currently producing under licence various Bell and Sikorsky helicopters. It developed its own AS-61N1 short-fuselage civil derivative of the Sikorsky H-3 and is collaborating with Westland Helicopters of the UK in developing the EH 101 (see under EHI in the International section).

Other international programmes in which Agusta participates are the Eurofar tilt-rotor project and the NH 90. Details of these also appear in the International section. The Joint European Helicopter LAH Tonal programme is in suspension.

AGUSTA A 109A Mk II (CIVIL VERSIONS)

The first A 109 flew for the first time on 4 August 1971. RAI and FAA certification for VFR operation was announced on 1 June 1975, and deliveries of the original A 109A version started in early 1976. Certification for IFR single-pilot operation was obtained on 20 January 1977. Certification has also been granted in Australia, Brazil, Canada, France, Germany, Japan, Mexico, New Zealand, the Philippines, Sweden, Switzerland, the UK and Venezuela. Approximately 150 of this initial version, described in the 1981-82 *Jane's*, were built.

Deliveries of the uprated **A 109A Mk II** began in September 1981. This has an increase in transmission rating, a new tail rotor driveshaft, increased tail rotor blade life and reliability, new self-damping engine mounts, integral-design oil coolers and blowers, a structurally redesigned tailboom, higher-pressure hydraulic system, improved avionics and instrument layout, and a removable floor in the baggage compartment. It is also available in a utility version with less sophisticated interior and instrumentation. Under a 1983 agreement, Hellenic Aerospace Industries (see Greek section) produced major fuselage components for 77 Mk IIs.

In 1985 Agusta introduced the **Wide Body** version of the Mk II, with a more roomy and comfortable cabin created by modifying the shape of the underfloor fuel tanks and applying bulged fuselage side panels. These changes do not affect either the basic structure or aerodynamic characteristics of the helicopter. The latest **Plus** version features 335.6 kW (450 shp) Allison 250-C20R-1 engines, but with the same transmission ratings as for the C20B engines.

In late 1989 Agusta signed a contract with the Asian Helicopter Corporation of Japan for 65 A 109s, then thought to be the largest civil helicopter contract ever. Another recent order has come from the Turkish Interior Ministry.

Two FAA certificated versions of the A 109 were announced by the company's US subsidiary, Agusta Aerospace Corporation, at the beginning of 1989.

Agusta A 109A Mk II general purpose helicopter in Wide-Body configuration

The **A 109C:** Has 'Plus' type 313/335.6 kW (420/450 shp) Allison 250-C20R-1 turboshafts, transmission rating increased from 552 kW (740 shp) to 589 kW (790 shp), new main rotor blades of composite construction, Wortmann section tail rotor blades, strengthened landing gear, and an increased max T-O weight of 2,720 kg (5,996 lb), permitting a 109 kg (240 lb) increase in payload. Four were ordered in 1989 by the Sultan of Johore, Malaysia.

The **A 109 Max:** Improved medevac variant, with greatly extended upward opening side doors and fairings resulting in a 3.96 m³ (140 cu ft) cabin volume able to accommodate two pilots, two stretcher cases and two sitting casualties or medical attendants. The new cabin layout was engineered by Custom Aircraft Completions of Teterboro, New Jersey.

The following description applies to the standard A 109A Mk II, unless stated otherwise:

TYPE: Twin-engined general purpose helicopter.

ROTOR SYSTEM: Fully articulated four-blade single main rotor and port side two-blade semi-rigid delta-hinged tail rotor. Main rotor blades have an NACA 23011.3/13006 'droop snoot' aerofoil section, with thickness/chord ratios of 11.3 per cent at root and 6 per cent at tip, and are attached to hub by tension/torsion straps. They are of aluminium alloy bonded construction, with a Nomex core, have swept tips, stainless steel tip caps and leading-edge strips, and are protected against corrosion. A manual blade folding capability and rotor brake are optional. Tail rotor blades are of aluminium alloy, bonded at the trailing-edge, with a Nomex honeycomb core and stainless steel leading-edge strip.

Transmission ratings 552 kW (740 shp) for take-off and max continuous twin-engined operation, with max contingency rating of 607 kW (814 shp) for 6 s. Ratings for single-engined operation are 336 kW (450 shp) for take-off (5 min limit) and 313 kW (420 shp) max continuous. Main rotor/engine rpm ratio 1:15.62; tail rotor/engine rpm ratio 1:2.80.

LANDING GEAR: Retractable tricycle type, with oleo-pneumatic shock absorber in each unit. Single main-wheels and castoring (45° each side of centre), self-centring nosewheel. Hydraulic retraction, nosewheel forward, mainwheels upward into fuselage. Hydraulic emergency extension and locking. Magnaghi disc brakes on mainwheels. All tyres are of Kléber-Colombes tubeless type, and of same size (650 × 6) and pressure (5.9 bars; 85 lb/sq in). Tailskid under ventral fin. Emergency pop-out flotation gear and fixed snow skis optional.

POWER PLANT: Two Allison 250-C20B turboshafts (each 313 kW; 420 shp for 5 min for T-O, 298 kW; 400 shp max continuous power, 276 kW; 370 shp max cruise power, derated to 258 kW; 346 shp for twin-engine operation), mounted side by side in upper rear fuselage and separated from passenger cabin and from each other by firewalls. Two bladder fuel tanks in lower rear fuselage, combined capacity 560 litres (148 US gallons; 123 Imp gallons), of which 550 litres (145.3 US gallons; 121 Imp gallons) are usable. Refuelling point in each side of fuselage, near top of each tank. Oil capacity 7.7 litres (2.0 US gallons; 1.7 Imp gallons) for each engine and 12 litres (3.2 US gallons; 2.6 Imp gallons) for transmission. Provision for internal auxiliary tank containing up to 170 litres (44.9 US gallons; 37.4 Imp gallons) of fuel.

DIMENSIONS, EXTERNAL:

Main rotor diameter	11.00 m (36 ft 1 in)
Tail rotor diameter	2.03 m (6 ft 8 in)
Length overall, rotors turning	13.05 m (42 ft 9¾ in)
Fuselage: Length	10.706 m (35 ft 1½ in)
Max width (except wide-body)	1.44 m (4 ft 8½ in)
Height over tail fin	3.30 m (10 ft 10 in)
Elevator span	2.88 m (9 ft 5½ in)
Width over mainwheels	2.45 m (8 ft 0½ in)
Wheelbase	3.535 m (11 ft 7¼ in)
Passenger doors (each): Height	1.06 m (3 ft 5¾ in)
Width	1.15 m (3 ft 9¼ in)
Height to sill	0.65 m (2 ft 1½ in)
Baggage door (port, rear): Height	0.51 m (1 ft 8 in)
Width	1.00 m (3 ft 3¼ in)

DIMENSIONS, INTERNAL:

Cabin, excl flight deck: Length	1.63 m (5 ft 4¼ in)
Max width	1.32 m (4 ft 4 in)
Max height	1.28 m (4 ft 2½ in)
Volume	2.82 m³ (100 cu ft)
Baggage compartment volume	0.52 m³ (18.4 cu ft)

AREAS:

Main rotor blades (each)	1.84 m² (19.8 sq ft)
Tail rotor blades (each)	0.203 m² (2.185 sq ft)
Main rotor disc	95.03 m² (1022.9 sq ft)
Tail rotor disc	3.24 m² (34.87 sq ft)

WEIGHTS AND LOADINGS:

Basic weight empty, equipped:	
standard	1,418 kg (3,126 lb)
standard, 'Plus'	1,432 kg (3,157 lb)
offshore oil support (IFR)	1,604 kg (3,536 lb)
ambulance (IFR)	1,647 kg (3,631 lb)
firefighting	1,596 kg (3,518 lb)
Max external slung load	907 kg (2,000 lb)
Max baggage	150 kg (331 lb)
Typical T-O weight:	
offshore oil support (IFR)	2,596 kg (5,723 lb)
ambulance (IFR)	2,409 kg (5,311 lb)
Max certificated T-O weight	2,600 kg (5,732 lb)
Max disc loading	27.4 kg/m² (5.60 lb/sq ft)
Max power loading:	
A 109A Mk II	4.71 kg/kW (7.75 lb/shp)
A 109C	4.42 kg/kW (7.26 lb/shp)

PERFORMANCE: (S/L, ISA, except where indicated. A: AUW of 2,250 kg; 4,960 lb, B: AUW of 2,450 kg; 5,400 lb, C:

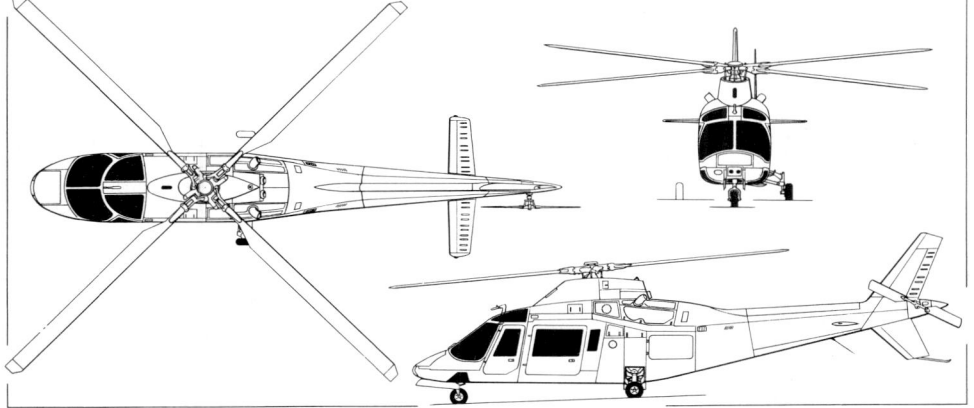
Agusta A 109A Mk II twin-engined general purpose helicopter (*Pilot Press*)

Monaco-registered Agusta A 109C at Helitech '89 *(Kenneth Munson)*

AUW of 2,600 kg; 5,732 lb, D: 'Plus' at AUW of 2,600 kg; 5,732 lb):

Never-exceed speed (VNE):
A, B, C, D 168 knots (311 km/h; 193 mph)
Max cruising speed: A 154 knots (285 km/h; 177 mph)
B, C 150 knots (278 km/h; 172 mph)
D at 1,830 m (6,000 ft) 152 knots (281 km/h; 175 mph)
Econ cruising speed:
A, B, C 126 knots (233 km/h; 145 mph)
Max rate of climb at S/L: A 643 m (2,110 ft)/min
B 555 m (1,820 ft)/min
C 503 m (1,650 ft)/min
D 504 m (1,655 ft)/min
Rate of climb at S/L, one engine out:
A 152 m (500 ft)/min
B 108 m (355 ft)/min
C 78 m (255 ft)/min
D 138 m (455 ft)/min
Service ceiling, 30.5 m (100 ft)/min rate of climb, at max continuous power: A, B, D 4,575 m (15,000 ft)
C 4,450 m (14,600 ft)
Service ceiling, one engine out, 30.5 m (100 ft)/min rate of climb, at max continuous power:
C 1,675 m (5,500 ft)
D 2,530 m (8,300 ft)
Hovering ceiling IGE: A 3,750 m (12,300 ft)
B 2,985 m (9,800 ft)
C 2,410 m (7,900 ft)
D 3,800 m (12,465 ft)
Hovering ceiling OGE: A 2,880 m (9,450 ft)
B 2,072 m (6,800 ft)
C 1,493 m (4,900 ft)
D 2,600 m (8,530 ft)
Range with max standard fuel, no reserves:
A 350 nm (648 km; 402 miles)
B 341 nm (631 km; 392 miles)
C 332 nm (615 km; 382 miles)
D 440 nm (815 km; 506 miles)
Endurance with max fuel, no reserves: A 3 h 12 min
B 3 h 2 min
C 2 h 57 min
D 4 h 35 min

AGUSTA A 109A Mk II (MILITARY, NAVAL and LAW ENFORCEMENT VERSIONS)

Several non-commercial versions of the A 109A have been developed by Agusta. In general, their configuration, structure and power plant are similar to those of the standard civil versions, although specially modified versions are available, including the 'Plus' with 335.6 kW (450 shp) Allison 250-C20R-1 engines.

In late 1988 Belgium ordered 28 in anti-armour and 18 in scout configurations under its Aéromobilité 1 programme to replace existing Aerospatiale Alouette II helicopters. Offset agreements were signed with Belgian manufacturing companies, which include A 109 assembly by Sabca. Deliveries are expected to take place between June 1991 and June 1993. The order includes supply of Saab HeliTOW systems and 500 TOW anti-armour missiles. Collins Government Avionics Division of Rockwell is supplying the avionics management system, Automatic Target Hand-off System, AN/ARN-149 ADF, AN/ARC-186 VHF transceiver and bus interface unit. Collins Defense Communications is supplying HF-9000 transceivers. Agusta also competed for the Canadian Forces' CFLH light helicopter programme and teamed with Grumman to compete for the US Army's 'adversary' helicopter programme.

The principal military, naval and other non-commercial versions were listed in some detail in the 1984-85 *Jane's*. The following is an abbreviated description:

Aerial scout: Can be armed with a flexibly mounted 7.62 mm or 12.7 mm machine-gun, with stabilised sight, plus two XM157 launchers (each with seven 2.75 in rockets). Normal crew of three.

Light attack: Against tanks and other hard point targets. Has been demonstrated with Hughes M65 TOW system incorporating undernose telescopic sight unit, plus four or eight TOW missiles. Normal crew of two. Argentine Army has adapted its A 109As to carry Mathogo anti-tank missiles.

Light attack: Against soft point targets. Various combinations of armament include a pintle mounted 7.62 mm machine-gun in each doorway; a trainable, remotely controlled externally mounted 7.62 mm gun; twin trainable, remotely controlled externally mounted 7.62 mm guns; two external machine-gun pods; or two gun pods and two rocket launchers. Normal crew of two. Suited to escort and area suppression.

Command and control: For target designation and direction of helicopter attack force. Can be armed with combination of rockets and machine guns, as described in preceding paragraph.

Utility: For up to seven troops; two stretcher patients and two medical attendants; externally mounted rescue hoist; or underfuselage hook for slung load.

Mirach: Version carrying two Mirach 100 UAVs for battlefield surveillance, reconnaissance, target acquisition, elint, ECM, attack on ground or naval targets, and enemy defence saturation or decoy.

ESM/ECM: Electronic warfare version, for military and naval use. Available with passive ESM only, plus weapon systems if required; and with passive ESM plus modularised active ECM (jamming), plus any required weapons. Provision for chaff dispenser to be mounted on tailboom.

Naval: Primary naval missions are anti-surface vessel, electronic warfare, standoff missile guidance, reconnaissance, and anti-submarine classification. Secondary capabilities for search and rescue, troop transportation, ambulance, flying crane, coastguard patrol, and inter-ship liaison duties. Configurations for electronic warfare and utility roles generally similar to those described in preceding 'Utility' and 'ESM/ECM' paragraphs. For the ASW role, specialised equipment includes MAD, one or two homing torpedoes and six marine markers. For the ASV role the naval A 109A carries a high performance long-range search radar with high discrimination in rough sea conditions. The surface attack is performed with air-to-surface wire-guided missiles. For the TG-2 (standoff missile guidance) mission, the helicopter is equipped with a special system to control and guide a ship-launched Otomat missile. For armed patrol, the naval A 109A is equipped with a search radar and armament to customer's requirements. The coastguard patrol configuration includes a search radar, a special installation for external high efficiency loudspeakers, and a searchlight.

Law enforcement and other patrol duties: For patrol (including armed patrol) and surveillance, traffic control, search and rescue, firefighting, and similar utility missions. Principal SAR equipment includes search radar, rescue hoist, stretcher/first aid kits, radar altimeter, skis or emergency flotation gear, AFCS, and flare/smoke grenades. For aerial patrol it can include 360° radar, automatic stability control system, external loudspeakers, FLIR, pollution monitoring equipment, system for spraying chemical retardants, and other items depending upon requirements of mission. A specific **coastal patrol** version is in service with the Italian Guardia di Finanza, offering all-weather maritime patrol capability. It has a stretched nose to accommodate the avionics and high-power searchlight, and is also fitted with light emergency floats, survival equipment and a loudspeaker housed in the baggage compartment. The cockpit features a compact instrument panel to improve visibility, with vertical scale engine instruments. Mission equipment includes an Omega LRN 85 navigation system, FIAR (Bendix/King) RDR 1500 360° scan search radar, and a Honeywell SPZ-7300 four-axis automatic flight control system with approach to hovering mode. The fully integrated avionics system enables the helicopter to patrol automatically an area along preset courses and automatically approach radar engaged targets. A cabin-mounted 7.62 mm machine gun can be carried.

ROTOR SYSTEM: As for civil A 109A Mk II, except for twin-engined max contingency transmission rating of 638 kW (856 shp) and 5 min single-engined T-O transmission rating of 313 kW (420 shp).

WEIGHTS AND LOADINGS (military Mk II, typical):
Basic weight empty 1,418 kg (3,126 lb)
Weight empty, equipped: utility 1,560 kg (3,439 lb)
ESM/ECM 1,627 kg (3,587 lb)
ambulance 1,630 kg (3,594 lb)
scout, attack, air defence 1,650 kg (3,638 lb)
anti-tank 1,790 kg (3,946 lb)
Armament/equipment/payload:
ambulance (1 medical attendant) 80 kg (176 lb)
air defence (8 missiles) 150 kg (331 lb)
anti-tank (8 missiles) 196 kg (432 lb)
ESM/ECM (radar warning, deception jammer, noise jammer, ESM equipment) 270 kg (595 lb)
scout (2 podded 12.7 mm and 2 pintle mounted 7.62 mm machine guns) 287 kg (633 lb)
attack (2 podded 12.7 mm machine guns and 14 rockets in pods) 344 kg (758 lb)
utility (7 equipped troops) 630 kg (1,389 lb)
T-O weight: ambulance 2,330 kg (5,136 lb)
air defence 2,500 kg (5,512 lb)
scout, attack, anti-tank, Mirach, ESM/ECM, utility (max T-O weight) 2,600 kg (5,732 lb)
attack ('Plus') (max T-O weight) 2,720 kg (5,995 lb)

PERFORMANCE (S/L, ISA, except where indicated. A: AUW of 2,250 kg; 4,960 lb, B: AUW of 2,450 kg; 5,400 lb, C: AUW of 2,600 kg; 5,732 lb, D: 'Plus' in light attack configuration at 2,720 kg, 5,995 lb AUW): As civil Mk II except:
Max cruising speed: A 155 knots (287 km/h; 178 mph)
B 150 knots (278 km/h; 173 mph)
C 147 knots (272 km/h; 169 mph)
D 136 knots (252 km/h; 157 mph)
Econ cruising speed: A 126 knots (233 km/h; 145 mph)
B 125 knots (232 km/h; 144 mph)
C 124 knots (230 km/h; 143 mph)
Max rate of climb at S/L: A 640 m (2,100 ft)/min
D 516 m (1,690 ft)/min
Service ceiling, 30.5 m (100 ft)/min rate of climb, at max continuous power: A 5,485 m (18,000 ft)
B, D 4,575 m (15,000 ft)
C 4,450 m (14,600 ft)
Range with max standard fuel, no reserves:
A 320 nm (593 km; 368 miles)
B 310 nm (574 km; 357 miles)
C 300 nm (556 km; 345 miles)
Range with max standard fuel, 10 min reserves:
Mirach 360 nm (667 km; 414 miles)
Range: D 360 nm (667 km; 414 miles)
Endurance with max standard fuel, no reserves:
A 3 h 43 min
B 3 h 30 min
C 3 h 15 min
D 3 h 50 min
Endurance with max standard fuel, 10 min reserves:
Mirach 4 h 30 min

AGUSTA A 109 EOA

Twenty-four examples of this light multi-role helicopter (LMH) version of the A 109 were ordered by the Italian Army as EOA (Elicottero d'Osservazione Avanzata) forward observation helicopters. Deliveries were made in 1988 to the Aviazione Leggera dell'Esercito, to take over from fixed-wing SIAI-Marchetti SM 1019s.

The EOA has the lengthened nose and fixed, raised landing gear of the A 109-K (see following entry), but is powered by uprated Allison 250-C20R engines, offering better hot and high performance than the -C20Bs in the standard A 109A Mk II. Other features include sliding cabin doors, crashworthy fuel tanks, a wide range of armament options, and electronic warfare equipment. A description appeared in the 1989-90 *Jane's*.

AGUSTA A 109-K

This multi-role hot and high military variant of the A 109A Mk II is powered by two 538 kW (722 shp) Turbomeca Arriel 1K turboshafts (instead of the A 109's usual 313 kW; 420 shp Allisons). It flew for the first time in April 1983.

Designed for operation by a pilot and gunner in its primary combat role, the A 109-K has an uprated transmission, a new main rotor hub made of composites, elastomeric bearings, composites blades with a hard surface coating that is resistant to abrasion by sand and hard dust, a new tail rotor of Wortmann blade section, a longer nose to house additional avionics, and a taller and non-retractable high shock absorption wheeled landing gear.

The second prototype, which began flying in March 1984, was fully representative of the planned production version. Differences by comparison with the standard A 109A Mk II are as follows:

ROTOR SYSTEM: Composites main rotor blades and hub, with elastomeric bearings, and special blade surface coating, for greater corrosion/abrasion resistance. New tail rotor of slightly reduced diameter, with high-efficiency Wortmann aerofoil section and stainless steel skins. Optional rotor brake. Main transmission uprated to 671 kW (900 shp) for take-off and max continuous twin-engined operation. Ratings for single-engined

Agusta A 109-K multi-role hot and high variant of the A 109A Mk II *(Avio Data)*

operation are 492 kW (660 shp) for 2.5 minutes, and 373 kW (500 shp) max continuous.

FUSELAGE: Nose lengthened by 40 cm (15¾ in) and fitted with an upward hinged door on each side, for access to avionics. Provision for ECM or other sensors on nose.

LANDING GEAR: Non-retractable tricycle type, giving increased clearance between fuselage and ground. Changes restricted to replacement of nose leg actuator by a fixed strut, and replacement of each main leg actuator by a fixed strut and a V support frame.

POWER PLANT: Two Turbomeca Arriel 1K turboshafts, each rated at 540 kW (724 shp) for 2.5 minutes, 522 kW (700 shp) for take-off (5 minutes) and 436 kW (585 shp) max cruise power. Engine particle separator optional. Standard usable fuel capacity 550 litres (145 US gallons; 121 Imp gallons), with optional 150 litre (39.6 US gallon; 33 Imp gallon) auxiliary tanks. Optional closed circuit refuelling system and optional 200 litre (53 US gallon; 44 Imp gallon) ferry tanks in cabin. Self-sealing fuel tanks optional. Independent fuel and oil system for each engine.

AVIONICS: Radar and laser warning systems, FLIR, gyrostabilised sight, night vision goggles, chaff/flare dispenser, are among options.

EQUIPMENT: Options include rescue hoist, searchlight and cargo platform.

ARMAMENT (optional): Total of four stores attachments, two on each side of cabin, on outriggers. Typical loads include two 7.62 mm or 12.7 mm gun pods, 70 mm or 80 mm rocket launchers, or up to eight TOW anti-armour missiles (with roof mounted sight), Stinger air-to-air missiles, UAVs, plus a 7.62 or 12.7 mm side-firing gun in cabin.

DIMENSIONS, EXTERNAL:

Tail rotor diameter	2.00 m (6 ft 6¾ in)
Length of fuselage	11.106 m (36 ft 5¼ in)

AREAS:

Tail rotor disc	3.143 m² (33.83 sq ft)

WEIGHTS AND LOADINGS:

Weight empty	1,592 kg (3,510 lb)
Max T-O weight	2,850 kg (6,283 lb)
Max disc loading	30.0 kg/m² (6.15 lb/sq ft)
Max power loading	4.25 kg/kW (6.98 lb/shp)

PERFORMANCE (at max T-O weight except where indicated):

Never-exceed speed (VNE)

150 knots (278 km/h; 172 mph)

*Max level speed at S/L, clean:

ISA	138 knots (255 km/h; 159 mph)
ISA + 20°C	140 knots (259 km/h; 161 mph)

*Max cruising speed at S/L, at average weight, clean:

ISA	141 knots (261 km/h; 162 mph)
ISA + 20°C	144 knots (266 km/h; 166 mph)

**Econ cruising speed at S/L, at average weight, clean:

ISA	128 knots (237 km/h; 147 mph)
ISA + 20°C	131 knots (243 km/h; 151 mph)
Max rate of climb at S/L: ISA	530 m (1,740 ft)/min
ISA + 20°C	509 m (1,670 ft)/min

Rate of climb at S/L, one engine out:

ISA or ISA + 20°C	167 m (550 ft)/min

Service ceiling:

ISA or ISA + 20°C	6,100 m (20,000 ft)
Service ceiling, one engine out: ISA	2,770 m (9,100 ft)
ISA + 20°C	1,950 m (6,400 ft)

Hovering ceiling IGE at average weight, clean:

ISA	5,640 m (18,500 ft)
ISA + 20°C	4,970 m (16,300 ft)

Hovering ceiling OGE at average weight, clean:

ISA	3,350 m (11,000 ft)
ISA + 20°C	2,680 m (8,800 ft)

Max range at S/L, clean:

ISA	290 nm (537 km; 333 miles)
ISA + 20°C	284 nm (526 km; 326 miles)

*reduced by 9 knots (17 km/h; 11 mph) with two gun pods fitted

**reduced by 6 knots (11 km/h; 7 mph) with two gun pods fitted

AGUSTA A 109-KN

This is a naval variant of the A 109-K, intended for anti-ship, offshore patrol, over the horizon targeting, electronic warfare and vertical replenishment roles.

AGUSTA A 129 MANGUSTA

The Italian Army first made known its requirements for a light anti-armour helicopter in 1972, and the selected A 129 design received Italian Army go-ahead in March 1978, undergoing several changes of configuration before reaching its final form in 1980. Detail design was completed on 30 November 1982. The first A 129 (MM 590/E.I. 901) made its first flight on 11 September 1983; first flights of the second and third took place on 1 July and 5 October 1984; the fourth was flown on 27 May 1985 and the fifth on 1 March 1986.

Initially, the A 129 was intended as a day/night anti-tank and fire support helicopter for the Italian Army. A shipborne anti-ship version was later proposed for export.

The first five of 60 A 129s for two Italian Army Aviation operational squadrons were delivered in October 1990, delayed for well over a year by the decision to fit the SAAB/Emerson HeliTOW system to all the A 129s. Another 10 were to be delivered during 1991 with a slightly higher equipment standard. The Italian Army requires 30 more, some convertible in the field to scouts with

mast-mounted sights, but may have to convert about 20 of the first batch instead.

A plan to equip the Dutch Army with an initial batch of Mangustas (20) was shelved, and no other foreign orders had been received by early 1991.

An A 129 powered by two Allison/Garrett LHTEC T800-LHT-800 turboshafts flew for the first time in October 1988, and was extensively demonstrated in the Gulf region during 1990. The T800 engine gives between 20 and 40 per cent more power than the Gem, according to circumstances, and transmission rating would be raised to 910 kW (1,220 shp). Gross weight would rise to 4,400 kg (9,700 lb). This growth version is being actively marketed for export.

TYPE: Light anti-tank, attack and advanced scout helicopter.

ROTOR SYSTEM: Fully articulated four-blade main rotor and two-blade semi-rigid delta-hinged tail rotor. Each main rotor blade is retained by a single elastomeric bearing and restrained by a hydraulic drag damper and mechanical droop stop. Main rotor blades each consist of a carbonfibre and Kevlar spar, Nomex honeycomb leading- and trailing-edge, stainless steel leading-edge abrasion strip, frangible tip, and skin of composite materials. They are designed to have a ballistic tolerance against hits from 12.7 mm ammunition, but are expected also to have considerable tolerance against 23 mm hits. The hub has the same ballistic tolerance; all mechanical linkages and moving parts are housed inside the rotor mast to eliminate foreign object damage, decrease icing problems, and reduce radar signature. There are no lubricated bearings in the rotor head. Tail rotor blades are also of composite materials, with a stainless steel leading-edge, and have a very wide chord to improve tolerance of 12.7 mm hits.

Transmission rating is 969 kW (1,300 shp) (two engines), 704 kW (944 shp) for single-engined operation, with emergency rating of 759 kW (1,018 shp); power input into transmission is at 27,000 rpm from the Gem and 23,000 rpm in the other direction from the T800. All driveshafts, components and couplings ballistically tolerant to 12.7 mm hits. Main transmission has integral independent oil cooling system; intermediate and tail rotor gearboxes are grease lubricated. Transmission and gearboxes are designed to continue to operate safely for at least 30 min without oil (45 min already demonstrated). Accessory gearbox forward of main transmission. In normal operation, accessories are driven by main gear train, but on ground they can be engaged by a pilot actuated clutch which connects No. 1 engine to the accessory section without engaging the rotors. Rotor brake fitted, to stop rotors quickly while the two engines run at ground idle, one driving the accessories.

WINGS: Cantilever mid-mounted stub wings, built of composite materials, aft of rear cockpit in plane of main rotor mast. Aerofoil and incidence designed to produce minimum lift at cruising speed.

FUSELAGE: Conventional semi-monocoque structure of aluminium alloy longerons and frames. Honeycomb panels in centre-fuselage and fuel tank areas. Composite materials, making up 45 per cent of total fuselage weight (excluding engines) and 16.1 per cent of total empty weight, are used for nosecone, tailboom, tail rotor pylon, engine nacelles, canopy frame and maintenance panels. Total wetted surface area of airframe (excl blades and hub) is 50 m² (538.2 sq ft), of which 35 m² (376.7 sq ft) (70 per cent) are of composite materials. Rollover bulkhead in nose and robust A-shaped reinforced frame extending from lower fuselage to rotor hub, for crew protection; armour protection for vital areas of power plant. Overall infra-red-absorbing paint finish. Airframe has a ballistic tolerance against 12.7 mm armour-piercing ammunition, and meets the crashworthiness standards of MIL-STD-1290 (vertical velocity changes of up to 11.2 m; 36.75 ft/s and longitudinal changes of up to 13.1 m; 43 ft/s).

TAIL UNIT: Sweptback main fin, with tail rotor mounted near top on port side. Small underfin, serving also as mount for tailwheel. Fixed tailplane mounted on tailboom. All tail surfaces built of composite materials.

LANDING GEAR: Non-retractable tailwheel type, with single wheel on each unit. Two-stage hydraulic shock strut in each main unit designed to withstand normal loads and hard landings at descent rates in excess of 10 m (32.8 ft)/s.

POWER PLANT: Two Rolls-Royce Gem 2 Mk 1004D turboshafts, each with a max continuous rating of 615 kW (825 shp) for normal twin-engined operation; intermediate contingency rating of 657 kW (881 shp) for 1 h; max contingency rating of 704 kW (944 shp) for 2½ min; and emergency rating (S/L, ISA) of 759 kW (1,018 shp) for 20 s. Production engines licence built in Italy by Piaggio. Fireproof engine compartment, with engines widely spaced to improve survivability from enemy fire. Two separate fuel systems, with crossfeed capability; interchangeable self-sealing and crash resistant tanks, self-sealing lines, and digital fuel feed control. Tanks can be foam-filled for fire protection. Single-point pressure refuelling. Infra-red exhaust suppression system and low engine noise levels. Separate independent lubrication oil cooling system for each engine. Provision for auxiliary (self-ferry) fuel tanks on inboard underwing stations.

ACCOMMODATION: Pilot and co-pilot/gunner in separate cockpits in tandem. Elevated rear (pilot's) cockpit.

Prototype Agusta A 109 EOA of the Italian Army with roof-mounted sight, grenade launcher pods and antennae for HF, Doppler, signals homing, radar warning and jamming and communications

Prototype Agusta A 129 attack helicopter powered by LHTEC T800s flying over desert during a sales demonstration

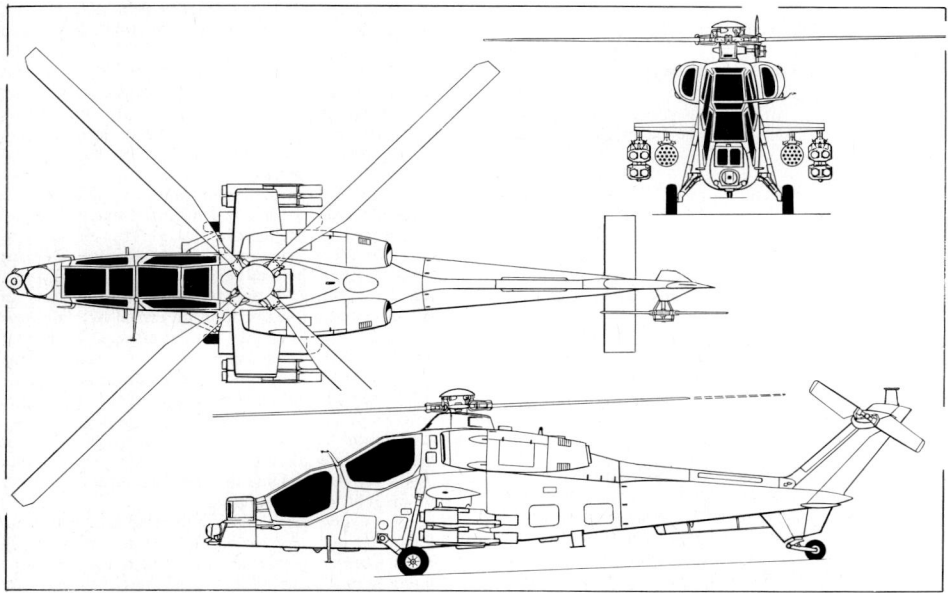

Agusta A 129 light anti-tank, attack and advanced scout helicopter *(Pilot Press)*

External crew field of view exceeds MIL-STD-850B. Each cockpit has a flat plate low-glint canopy with upward hinged door panels on starboard side, blow-out port side panel for exit in emergency, and Martin-Baker crashworthy seat with sliding side panels of composites armour. Landing gear design and crashworthy seats reduce impact from 50*g* to 20*g* in crash. The co-pilot/gunner has a cyclic side arm controller and normal collective and pedals, plus full access to the AFCS.

SYSTEMS: Hydraulic system includes three main circuits dedicated to flight controls and two independent circuits for rotor and wheel braking. Main system operates at pressure of 207 bars (3,000 lb/sq in) and is fed by three independent power groups, two integrated and driven mechanically by the main transmission, the third integrated and driven by the tail rotor gearbox. Tandem actuators are provided for main and tail rotor flight controls. Hydraulic system flow rate 23.6 litres (6.2 US gallons; 5.2 Imp gallons)/min in each main group. Spring type reservoirs, pressurised at 0.39 bar (5.6 lb/sq in). Electrical inputs for AFCS integrated with hydraulic powered control units. Fly-by-wire standby system under development in 1991. Automatic fire extinguishing system.

AVIONICS: All main functions of helicopter are handled and monitored by a fully integrated digital multiplex system (IMS), which controls navigation, flight management, weapon control, autopilot, monitoring of transmission and engine condition, fuel/hydraulic/electrical systems, caution and warning systems. IMS is managed by two Harris central computers, each capable of operating independently. They are backed by two interface units which pick up outputs from sensors and avionic equipment and transfer them, via redundant MIL-1553B databuses, to main computers for real-time processing. Processed information is presented to pilot and co-pilot/gunner on separate graphic/alphanumeric head-down multi-function displays (MFDs) with standard multi-

function keyboards for easy access to information, including area navigation using up to 100 waypoints, weapons status and selection, radio tuning and mode selection, caution and warning, and display of aircraft performance; conventional instruments and dials are provided as backup. IMS computer can store up to 100 pre-set frequencies for HF, VHF and UHF radio management. Navigation is controlled by navigation computer of IMS coupled to a Doppler radar and radar altimeter with the low airspeed indicator normally used for rocket aiming providing back-up velocity data when the Doppler is beyond limits. Synthetic map presentation of waypoints, target areas and dangerous areas is shown on pilot's or co-pilot's MFD. A Litton strapdown inertial reference for both flight control and navigation is being substituted for the present gyro system.

The AFCS provides either three-axis stabilisation or full attitude and heading hold, automatic hover, downward transition to hover or holds for altitude, heading and airspeed or groundspeed and automatic track following.

The A 129 has full day/night operational capability, with equipment designed to give both crew members a view outside helicopter irrespective of light conditions. A pilot's night vision system (HIRNS: helicopter infra-red night system) allows nap-of-the-earth (NOE) flight by night, a picture of world outside being generated by Honeywell mini-FLIR sensor mounted on a Ferranti steerable platform at nose of aircraft and presented to both crewmen through the monocle of the Honeywell integrated helmet and display sighting system (IHADSS), to which it is slaved by helmet position sensors. Symbology containing information required for flight is superimposed onto image, giving a true head-up reference. The HeliTOW sight gives the co-pilot/gunner direct view optics and FLIR, plus a laser for ranging. The A 129 also has provision for a mast mounted sight (MMS). Active and passive self-protection systems

(ECCM and ECM) standard on Italian Army A 129. Passive electronic warfare systems include radar jammer and radar and laser warning receivers, chaff/flare dispensers and IR jammer. The cockpits are coloured to allow use of night vision goggles as a standby night flying aid.

ARMAMENT: Four underwing attachments stressed for loads of up to 300 kg (661 lb) each. All stations incorporate articulation which allows pylon to be elevated 2° and depressed 10° to increase missile launch envelope. They are aligned with the aircraft automatically, with no need for boresighting. Initial armament of up to eight thermal tracking TOW 2 wire guided anti-tank missiles (two, three or four in carriers suspended from each wingtip station), with Saab/Emerson HeliTOW launch system; with these can be carried, on the inboard stations, either two 7.62, 12.7 or 20 mm gun pods, or two launchers each for seven air-to-surface rockets. For general attack missions, rocket launchers can be carried on all four stations (two nineteen-tube plus two seven-tube); Italian Army has specified SNIA-BPD 81 mm and 70 mm rockets. Alternatively, the A 129 can carry six Hellfire anti-tank missiles (three beneath each wingtip); eight HOT missiles; AIM-9L Sidewinder, Matra Mistral, Javelin or Stinger air-to-air missiles for aerial combat; two gun pods plus two nineteen-tube rocket launchers; or grenade launchers.

The Lucas 0.5 in self-contained gun turret was qualified, but is not used by the Italian Army. A 12.7 mm turret has also been fired and 20 mm or 12.7 mm Gatling turrets have been investigated. Optional upgrades offered for export include an auto-tracking sight, a laser designator for Hellfire and a mast-mounted sight for scouting.

DIMENSIONS, EXTERNAL:

Main rotor diameter	11.90 m (39 ft 0½ in)
Tail rotor diameter	2.24 m (7 ft 4¼ in)
Wing span	3.20 m (10 ft 6 in)
Width over TOW pods	3.60 m (11 ft 9¾ in)
Length overall, both rotors turning	
	14.29 m (46 ft 10½ in)
Fuselage: Length	12.275 m (40 ft 3¼ in)
Max width	0.95 m (3 ft 1½ in)
Height:	
over tail fin, tail rotor horizontal	2.65 m (8 ft 8¼ in)
tail rotor turning	3.315 m (10 ft 10½ in)
to top of rotor head	3.35 m (11 ft 0 in)
Tailplane span	3.00 m (9 ft 10 in)
Wheel track	2.20 m (7 ft 3½ in)
Wheelbase	6.955 m (22 ft 9¾ in)

AREAS:

Main rotor disc	111.2 m² (1,196.95 sq ft)
Tail rotor disc	3.94 m² (42.42 sq ft)

WEIGHTS AND LOADINGS:

Weight empty, equipped	2,529 kg (5,575 lb)
Max internal fuel load	750 kg (1,653 lb)
Max external weapons load	1,200 kg (2,645 lb)
Max T-O weight	4,100 kg (9,039 lb)
Max disc loading	33.3 kg/m² (6.8 lb/sq ft)
Max power loading	4.23 kg/kW (6.95 lb/shp)

PERFORMANCE:

At mission T-O weight of 3,700 kg (8,157 lb), at 2,000 m (6,560 ft), ISA + 20°C, except where indicated, the A 129 is designed to meet the following performance requirements:

Dash speed	170 knots (315 km/h; 196 mph)
Max level speed at S/L	140 knots (259 km/h; 161 mph)
Max rate of climb at S/L	655 m (2,150 ft)/min
Hovering ceiling: IGE	3,750 m (12,300 ft)
OGE	3,015 m (9,900 ft)

Basic 2 h 30 min mission profile with 8 TOW and 20 min fuel reserves:
Fly 54 nm (100 km; 62 miles) to battle area, mainly in NOE mode, 90 min loiter (incl 45 min hovering), and return to base

Max endurance, no reserves	3 h
g limits	+3.5/−0.5

AGUSTA A 139 UTILITY

Agusta aims to create a family of new helicopters, with a civil/military utility version combining the dynamics, systems and integrated avionics of the A 129 with a completely new cabin-type fuselage. In its original form, designated Light Battlefield Helicopter, the A 139 could carry weapons and sighting systems or perform many other roles and be able to survive on the battlefield. The consequent long overhaul lives and ease of maintenance would benefit civil operations. The further growth being prepared for the A 129, particularly the more powerful and economical T800 engines, are available for the A 139 Utility. The cabin could accommodate eight to ten passengers or six stretchers and two attendants. Slung loads of 2,000 kg (4,409 lb) could be carried.

Agusta was to complete definition of the Utility during 1991 and was looking for foreign partners to share development. FMA in Argentina and ASTA in Australia, associated with the A 139 (as detailed below), were among the candidates.

On 10 August 1988 a 15-year agreement was signed between Agusta and FMA of Argentina for the joint development and construction of this helicopter, with Agusta responsible for the design, development and production of the drive system and other main systems, while the fuselage is the responsibility of FMA. Subsequently, FMA delegated this work to a consortium in which Agusta has a 49 per cent shareholding, Techint 10 per cent and Tecnologia Aeroespacial SA 41 per cent, which was to assemble and sell the A 139 in Latin America. In 1989 AeroSpace Technologies of Australia (ASTA) negotiated to join Agusta and FMA on the A 139 Utility programme, with the intention of assisting in design, component manufacture and perhaps full assembly in Victoria. A memorandum of understanding was signed between Agusta and ASTA in December 1989. These agreements were reported to be still under negotiation late in 1990.

AGUSTA-BELL 206B JETRANGER III

The JetRanger has been manufactured under licence from Bell since the end of 1967; deliveries began in 1972 of the Agusta-Bell 206B JetRanger II, and of the JetRanger III at the end of 1978. A description of the JetRanger III appears under the Bell entry in the Canadian section. Approx 1,000 JetRangers were built by Agusta.

AGUSTA-BELL 212

The Agusta-Bell 212 is a twin-engined utility transport helicopter generally similar to the Bell Model 212 Twin Two-Twelve described in the Canadian section.

AGUSTA-BELL 212ASW

The AB 212ASW is an extensively modified version of the AB 212, intended primarily for anti-submarine search, classification and attack missions, and for attacks on surface vessels, while operating from the decks of small ships, but suitable also for search and rescue, electronic warfare, fire support, troop transport, liaison and utility roles. More than 100 are in service with the Italian and other navies; customers have included the navies of Greece (12, including some in electronic warfare configuration), Iraq (five), Turkey (12 in both ASW and ASV configurations) and Venezuela (six).

Apart from local strengthening and the provision of deck mooring equipment, the airframe structure remains essentially similar to that of the commercial Model 212 and military UH-1N, described under the Bell entry in the Canadian section. Details appeared in the 1990-91 *Jane's*.

AGUSTA-BELL 412 SP and GRIFFON

The first Bell prototype of the Model 412 was flown for the first time in August 1979, and customer deliveries began in January 1981. Agusta began licence production that year, making the civil 412, mainly for offshore support, and later

Mockup of the A 139 Utility passenger/cargo version of the Mangusta

the Griffon for such applications as direct fire support, area suppression, scouting and reconnaissance, air defence, assault transport, combat equipment transport, and battlefield support.

A version for SAR, maritime surveillance and pollution monitoring has been developed for the Italian forces, equipped with an integrated 360° roof mounted search radar, FLIR, TV, four-axis autopilot and special navigation system.

A prototype of the Griffon was flown for the first time in August 1982. Deliveries began in January 1983. Customers in Italy include the Army (18), Carabinieri (20) and Special Civil Protection fleet (four with more to come), Coast Guard (ultimately 24), national fire service (four) and national forest service (three); others include the Zimbabwe Air Force (10), Ugandan Army, and Finnish coastguard (two). The Griffon, which has a reinforced impact-absorbing landing gear, and armour protection in selected areas, also differs from the standard civil Model 412 SP (see Canadian section) in the following respects:
TYPE: Multi-purpose military helicopter.
POWER PLANT: One 1,342 kW (1,800 shp) Pratt & Whitney Canada PT6T-3B Turbo Twin Pac (single-engine ratings 764 kW; 1,025 shp for 2½ min and 723 kW; 970 shp for 30 min), as in civil Model 412. IR emission reduction devices

optional. Fuel system and capacity as for Model 412 (1,250 litres; 330 US gallons; 275 Imp gallons). Single-point refuelling. Two 76 or 341 litre (20 or 90 US gallon; 16.7 or 75 Imp gallon) auxiliary fuel tanks optional.
ACCOMMODATION: One or two pilots on flight deck, on energy-absorbing, armour protected seats. Fourteen crash-attenuating troop seats in main cabin in personnel transport roles, six patients and two medical attendants in ambulance version, or up to 1,814 kg (4,000 lb) of cargo or other equipment. Space for 181 kg (400 lb) of baggage in tailboom. Total of 51 fittings in cabin floor for attachment of seats, stretchers, internal hoist or other special equipment.
SYSTEMS: Generally as for Bell 212/412.
ARMAMENT: Wide variety of external weapon options for the Griffon includes a swivelling turret for a 12.7 mm gun, two 25 mm Oerlikon cannon, four or eight TOW anti-tank missiles, two launchers each with nineteen 2.75 in SNORA or twelve 81 mm rockets, 12.7 mm machine guns (in pods or door mounted), four air-to-air or air defence suppression missiles, or, for attacking surface vessels, four Sea Skua or similar air-to-surface missiles.
WEIGHTS AND LOADINGS:
Weight empty, equipped (standard configuration)
  2,841 kg (6,263 lb)
Max T-O weight   5,400 kg (11,905 lb)
PERFORMANCE (at max T-O weight, ISA):
Never-exceed speed (VNE) at S/L
  140 knots (259 km/h; 161 mph)
Cruising speed: at S/L   122 knots (226 km/h; 140 mph)
  at 1,500 m (4,920 ft)   125 knots (232 km/h; 144 mph)
  at 3,000 m (9,840 ft)   123 knots (228 km/h; 142 mph)
Max rate of climb at S/L   438 m (1,437 ft)/min
Rate of climb at S/L, one engine out   168 m (551 ft)/min
Service ceiling, 30.5 m (100 ft)/min climb rate
  5,180 m (17,000 ft)
Service ceiling, one engine out, 30.5 m (100 ft)/min climb
  rate   2,320 m (7,610 ft)
Hovering ceiling: IGE   1,250 m (4,100 ft)
  OGE   670 m (2,200 ft)
Range with max standard fuel at appropriate cruising
  speed (see above), no reserves:
  at S/L   354 nm (656 km; 407 miles)
  at 1,500 m (4,920 ft)   402 nm (745 km; 463 miles)
  at 3,000 m (9,840 ft)   434 nm (804 km; 500 miles)
Max endurance: at S/L   3 h 36 min
  at 1,500 m (4,920 ft)   4 h 12 min

AGUSTA-SIKORSKY AS-61 and ASH-3H

Agusta licence manufacture of the Sikorsky S-61S and S-61R in various civil and military forms started in 1967, and deliveries of anti-submarine ASH-3Ds to the Italian Navy began in 1969. Agusta is exclusive repair and overhaul agent for Europe and the Mediterranean basin. Production has ceased, but could be restarted in 36 months. Models most recently in production were the utility **AS-61**, the **SH-3D/TS** (Trasporto Speciale) VIP transport, and the upgraded **SH-3H** multi-role naval version.

AGUSTA-SIKORSKY AS-61R (HH-3F) PELICAN

Agusta began production of this multi-purpose search and rescue helicopter in 1974, and deliveries began in 1976. The production line has been re-opened to make two for the national civil protection service (SNPC) and another 13 rescue helicopters for the Italian Air Force. These will have a new radar, Loran, FLIR and navigation computer, all of which will be retrofitted in the remaining 19 of the original production batch.
TYPE: Twin-engined amphibious helicopter.
ROTOR SYSTEM: Five-blade fully articulated all-metal main rotor. Flanged cuffs on blades bolted to matching flanges

Agusta-Bell 412 Griffon of the Italian Army *(Paul Jackson)*

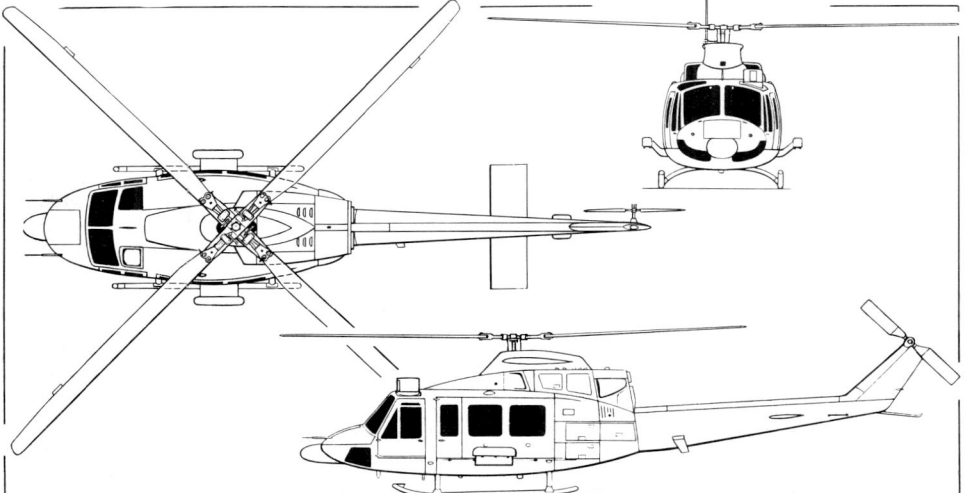
Agusta-Bell Griffon military helicopter, derived from the Bell Model 412 *(Pilot Press)*

Agusta-Sikorsky HH-3F (AS-61R) search and rescue helicopter of the Italian Air Force *(Ivo Sturzenegger)*

on rotor head. Control by rotating and stationary swashplates. Blades do not fold. Rotor brake standard. Conventional tail rotor with five aluminium blades.

Twin turbines drive through freewheeling units and rotor brake to main gearbox. Steel driveshafts. Tail rotor shaft driven through intermediate gearbox and tail gearbox. Main rotor/engine rpm ratio 1 : 93.43. Tail rotor/engine rpm ratio 1 : 16.7.

FUSELAGE: All-metal semi-monocoque structure of pod and boom type. Cabin of basic square section. Rear loading ramp.

TAIL UNIT: Strut braced horizontal stabiliser on starboard side of tail rotor pylon.

LANDING GEAR: Hydraulically retractable tricycle type, with twin wheels on each unit. Mainwheels retract forward into sponsons, each of which provides 2,176 kg (4,797 lb) of buoyancy and, with boat hull, permits amphibious operation. Oleo-pneumatic shock absorbers. All wheels and tyres tubeless Type III rib, size 22.1 × 6.50-10, pressure 6.55 bars (95 lb/sq in). Hydraulic disc brakes.

POWER PLANT: Two 1,118 kW (1,500 shp) General Electric T58-GE-100 turboshafts, mounted side by side above cabin, immediately forward of main transmission. Fuel in four bladder tanks beneath cabin floor, with total capacity of 4,225 litres (1,116 US gallons; 929 Imp gallons), of which 4,183 litres (1,105 US gallons; 920 Imp gallons) are usable. Provisions for removable internal auxiliary fuel tanks. Refuelling point on port side of fuselage. Total oil capacity 26.5 litres (7 US gallons; 5.8 Imp gallons).

ACCOMMODATION: Crew of two side by side on flight deck, with dual controls. Provision for flight engineer or

attendant. Accommodation in SAR configuration for 10 passenger seats and six stretchers; utility version can accommodate up to 26 troops on foldable, safety belt-equipped seats, 15 stretchers plus two medical attendants, or cargo. Jettisonable sliding door on starboard side at front of cabin. Internal door between cabin and flight deck. Hydraulically operated rear loading ramp, in two hinged sections, giving opening with minimum width of 1.73 m (5 ft 8 in) and headroom of up to 2.21 m (7 ft 3 in). Ramp can be operated when helicopter is on the water. Reinforced (41 kg/m²; 200 lb/sq ft loading) cargo floor in utility version.

SYSTEMS: Primary and auxiliary hydraulic systems, pressure 103.5 bars (1,500 lb/sq in), for flying control servos. Utility hydraulic system, pressure 207 bars (3,000 lb/sq in), for landing gear, rear ramp and winches. Pneumatic system, pressure 207 bars (3,000 lb/sq in), for emergency blow-down landing gear extension. Electrical system includes 24V 22Ah battery, two 20kVA 115V AC generators and one 300A DC generator. APU standard.

AVIONICS: SAR version has comprehensive suite for that role (including search/nav radar, Loran, FLIR and nav computer).

EQUIPMENT: SAR version has 272 kg (600 lb) capacity rescue hoist, Nightsun searchlight, detachable rescue platform for use when afloat, auxiliary flotation system, loudhailer set and sea anchor. Equipment for utility missions can include low response external cargo sling.

DIMENSIONS, EXTERNAL:
Main rotor diameter	18.90 m (62 ft 0 in)
Main rotor blade chord	0.46 m (1 ft 6¼ in)
Tail rotor diameter	3.15 m (10 ft 4 in)

Distance between rotor centres	11.22 m (36 ft 10 in)
Length: overall, excl radome	22.25 m (73 ft 0 in)
fuselage	17.45 m (57 ft 3 in)
Width over landing gear	4.82 m (15 ft 10 in)
Height: to top of rotor head	4.90 m (16 ft 1 in)
overall	5.51 m (18 ft 1 in)
Wheel track	4.06 m (13 ft 4 in)
Wheelbase	5.21 m (17 ft 1 in)
Cabin door (fwd, stbd): Height	1.65 m (5 ft 4¾ in)
Width	1.22 m (4 ft 0 in)
Height to sill	1.27 m (4 ft 2 in)
Rear ramp: Length	4.29 m (14 ft 1 in)
Width	1.85 m (6 ft 1 in)

DIMENSIONS, INTERNAL:
Cabin (excl flight deck): Length	7.89 m (25 ft 10½ in)
Max width	1.98 m (6 ft 6 in)
Max height	1.91 m (6 ft 3 in)
Floor area	approx 15.16 m² (168 sq ft)
Volume	approx 29.73 m³ (1,050 cu ft)

AREAS:
Main rotor blades (each)	3.71 m² (39.9 sq ft)
Tail rotor blades (each)	0.22 m² (2.35 sq ft)
Main rotor disc	280.5 m² (3,019 sq ft)
Tail rotor disc	7.80 m² (83.9 sq ft)
Stabiliser	2.51 m² (27.0 sq ft)

WEIGHTS AND LOADINGS:
Weight empty	6,010 kg (13,255 lb)
Max cargo payload: internal	2,270 kg (5,000 lb)
external	3,628 kg (8,000 lb)
Normal T-O weight	9,635 kg (21,247 lb)
Max T-O weight	10,000 kg (22,050 lb)
Max disc loading	35.65 kg/m² (7.30 lb/sq ft)

PERFORMANCE (at normal T-O weight except where indicated):
Max level speed at S/L:	
normal T-O weight	141 knots (261 km/h; 162 mph)
max T-O weight	138 knots (255 km/h; 159 mph)

Cruising speed at S/L, AUW of 9,072 kg (20,000 lb), ISA + 20°C:
for best range	130 knots (241 km/h; 150 mph)
for best endurance	75 knots (139 km/h; 86 mph)
Max rate of climb at S/L	408 m (1,340 ft)/min
Service ceiling: normal T-O weight	3,385 m (11,100 ft)
Hovering ceiling IGE	2,195 m (7,200 ft)
Min ground turning radius	11.29 m (37 ft 0½ in)
Runway LCN at max T-O weight	approx 4.75

Typical mission profiles (ISA + 20°C):
SAR: Loiter for 5 h in search area 50 nm (92 km; 57 miles) from base, hover for 30 min to rescue survivors, return to base and land, 10% fuel remaining
Utility: Fly 240 nm (445 km; 276 miles) from base, pick up 24 fully equipped troops and return to base, landing with 272 kg (600 lb) of fuel remaining

Range with max standard fuel, no reserves
770 nm (1,427 km; 886 miles)
Endurance with max standard fuel, no reserves 8 h

MONTEPRANDONE WORKS

This branch of Agusta, formerly BredaNardi, continues to produce under licence the NH-500E for the Italian government central helicopter pilot training school. It is licensed to manufacture, and to sell in central Europe, the McDonnell Douglas Model 530F. The Group also sells the NH-300C imported from Schweizer. Descriptions of the Model 500/530 series can be found under the McDonnell Douglas Helicopters heading in the US section of this edition, and of the Model 300C under the Schweizer heading.

SESTO CALENDE WORKS

MAIN WORKS: Vergiate (Varese)

AIRFIELD AND WORKS: Sesto Calende (Varese) and Malpensa

Founded in 1915, SIAI-Marchetti produced a wide range of military and civil landplanes and flying-boats up to the end of the Second World War. Now known simply as the Sesto Calende works of Agusta, current products include piston, turboprop and turbofan powered trainers. Since the 1970s it has been engaged in the co-production of licence built Boeing CH-47C, Bell 204/205/212/412, and Sikorsky S-61A, SH-3D/H and HH-3F helicopters.

On 6 October 1988 a memorandum of intent was signed with Grumman Aircraft Systems (a division of Grumman Corporation), to offer a version of the S.211 for the USAF/USN's Joint Primary Aircraft Training System (JPATS) requirement (see US section).

The Sesto Calende works undertakes the overhaul and repair of various types of aircraft (notably the C-130 Hercules, DHC-5 Buffalo and Cessna Citation II). It participates in national or multi-national programmes, producing parts for the Alenia G222, Panavia Tornado, AMX, Airbus A310 and Atlantique 2.

The works at Sesto Calende, Vergiate and Malpensa total 1,370,267 m² (14,749,416 sq ft) in area, of which 119,494 m² (1,286,221 sq ft) are covered.

SIAI-MARCHETTI SF.260

The prototype for the SF.260 series, known as the F.250, was designed by Dott Ing Stelio Frati and built by Aviamilano. Flown for the first time on 15 July 1964, it was powered by a 186.5 kW (250 hp) Textron Lycoming engine and was certificated for aerobatic flying. A description appeared in the 1965-66 *Jane's*.

The version developed initially for civil production was manufactured, at first under licence from Aviamilano, by SIAI-Marchetti, and is designated SF.260. It received FAA type approval on 1 April 1966. Subsequently SIAI-Marchetti became the official holder of the type certificate and of all manufacturing rights in the SF.260.

Descriptions of the civil SF.260A and SF.260B can be found in the 1980-81 and earlier editions of *Jane's*, and of the SF.260C in the 1985-86 edition. Current models are as follows:

SF.260D: Improved and updated civil version, replacing SF.260C, with aerodynamic and structural improvements developed for military SF.260M. Certificated by RAI on 14 December 1985 and by FAA in October 1986.

SF.260M: Two/three-seat military trainer, developed from civil SF.260A and first flown on 10 October 1970. Introduced a number of important structural and aerodynamic improvements, many of which were subsequently applied to later models. Meets requirements for basic flying training; instrument flying; aerobatics, including deliberate spinning; night flying; navigation flying; and formation flying. Detailed customer list in 1984-85 and earlier editions of *Jane's*.

SF.260W Warrior: Trainer/tactical support version of SF.260M, first flown (I-SJAV) in May 1972. Two or four underwing pylons, for up to 300 kg (661 lb) of external stores, and cockpit stores selection panel. Able to undertake a wide variety of roles, including low-level strike; forward air control; forward air support; armed reconnaissance; and liaison. Also meets same requirements as SF.260M for use as a trainer. Customers as listed in 1984-85 and earlier *Jane's*. One aircraft (described in 1980-81 and earlier editions) completed as **SF.260SW Sea Warrior** surveillance/SAR/supply version.

SF.260TP: Turboprop powered development. Described separately.

By early 1991 more than 800 SF.260s of all models had been delivered to civil operators and to 24 air forces worldwide.

Two major new orders for SF.260Ds were announced in March 1990. The Fox 51 Company of Texas is to buy 60, the first seven of which will be used by Doss Aviation for the pre-selection of US military pilots. The Turkish Air Force ordered 40 SF.260Ds for military training with an agreement for co-production by the TAI aerospace manufacturing group.

The following description is generally applicable to all piston engined models unless otherwise stated:

TYPE: Two/three-seat fully aerobatic military light aircraft.

WINGS: All-metal structure. Wing section NACA 64₁-212 (modified) at root, NACA 64₁-210 (modified) at tip. Dihedral 6° 20′ from roots (5° on SF.260D). Incidence 2° 45′ at root, 0° at tip. No sweepback. All-metal light alloy safe-life structure, with single main spar and auxiliary rear spar, built in two portions bolted together at centreline and attached to fuselage by six bolts. Press-formed ribs. Skin butt joined and flush riveted. Differentially operating Frise ailerons, and electrically actuated single-slotted flaps. Flaps operated by torque tube and mechanical linkage, ailerons by pushrods and cables. Servo tab in each aileron.

LANDING GEAR: Electrically retractable tricycle type, with manual emergency actuation. Inward retracting main gear, of trailing arm type, and rearward retracting nose unit, each embodying Magnaghi oleo-pneumatic shock absorber (type 2/22028 in main units). Each welded steel tube main leg is hinged to the main and rear spars. Nose unit is of leg and fork type, with coaxial shock absorber and torque strut. Cleveland P/N 3080A mainwheels, with size 6.00-6 tube and tyre (6-ply rating), pressure 2.45 bars (35.5 lb/sq in). Cleveland P/N 40-77A nosewheel, with size 5.00-5 tube and tyre (6-ply rating), pressure 1.96 bars (28.4 lb/sq in). Cleveland P/N 3000-500 independent hydraulic single-disc brake and parking brake on each mainwheel. Nosewheel steering (±20°) operated directly by rudder pedals, to which it is linked by pushrods.

POWER PLANT: One 194 kW (260 hp) Textron Lycoming O-540-E4A5 flat-six engine, driving a Hartzell HC-C2YK-1BF/8477-8R two-blade constant-speed metal propeller. AEIO-540-D4A5 engine available optionally. Fuel in two light alloy tanks in wings, capacity of each 49.5 litres (13.1 US gallons; 10.9 Imp gallons); and two permanent wingtip tanks, capacity of each 72 litres (19 US gallons; 15.85 Imp gallons). Total internal fuel capacity 243 litres (64.2 US gallons; 53.5 Imp gallons), of which 235 litres (62.1 US gallons; 51.7 Imp gallons) are usable. Individual refuelling point on top of each tank. In addition, SF.260W may be fitted with two 80 litre (21.1 US gallon; 17.5 Imp gallon) auxiliary tanks on underwing pylons. Oil capacity (all models) 11.4 litres (3 US gallons; 2.5 Imp gallons).

ACCOMMODATION (SF.260M; W similar): Side by side front seats (for instructor and pupil in SF.260M), with third seat centrally at rear. Front seats individually adjustable fore and aft, with forward folding backs and provision for back type parachute packs. Dual controls standard. All three seats equipped with lap belts and shoulder harnesses. Baggage compartment aft of rear seat. Upper portion of canopy tinted. Emergency canopy release handle for each front seat occupant. Steel tube windscreen frame for protection in the event of an overturn.

SYSTEMS (SF.260M; other models generally similar): Hydraulic system for mainwheel brakes only. No pneumatic system. 24V DC electrical system of single-conductor negative earth type, including 70A Prestolite engine-mounted alternator/rectifier and 24V 24Ah Varley battery, for engine starting, flap and landing gear actuation, fuel booster pumps, electronics and lighting. Sealed battery compartment in rear of fuselage on port side. Connection of an external power source automatically disconnects the battery. Heating system for carburettor air intake. Emergency electrical system for extending landing gear if normal electrical actuation fails; provision for mechanical extension in the event of total electrical failure. Cabin heating, and windscreen de-icing and demisting, by heat exchanger using engine exhaust air. Additional manually controlled warm air outlets for general cabin heating. Oxygen system optional.

AVIONICS (SF.260M; W generally similar): Basic instrumentation to customer's requirements. Blind-flying instrumentation and communications equipment optional: typical selection includes dual Collins 20B VHF com; Collins VIR-31A VHF nav; Collins ADF-60A; Collins TDR-90 ATC transponder; Collins PN-101 compass; ID-90-000 RMI; and Gemelli AG04-1 intercom. Instrument panel can be slid rearward to provide access to rear of instruments.

EQUIPMENT: Military equipment to customer's requirements. External stores can include one or two reconnaissance pods with two 70 mm automatic cameras, or two supply containers. Landing light in nose, below spinner.

ARMAMENT (SF.260W): Two or four underwing hardpoints, able to carry external stores on NATO standard pylons up to a maximum of 300 kg (661 lb) when flown as a single-seater. Typical alternative loads can include one or two SIAI gun pods, each with one or two 7.62 mm FN machine guns and 500 rds; two Aerea AL-8-70 launchers each with eight 2.75 in rockets; two LAU-32 launchers each with seven 2.75 in rockets; two Aerea AL-18-50 launchers each with eighteen 2 in rockets; two Aerea AL-8-68 launchers each with eight 68 mm rockets; two Aerea AL-6-80 launchers each with six 81 mm rockets; two LUU-2/B parachute flares; two SAMP EU 32 125 kg general purpose bombs or EU 13 120 kg fragmentation bombs; two SAMP EU 70 50 kg general purpose bombs; Mk 76 11 kg practice bombs; two cartridge throwers for 70 mm multi-purpose cartridges, F 725 flares or F 130 smoke cartridges. One or two photo-reconnaissance pods with two 70 mm automatic cameras; two supply containers.

DIMENSIONS, EXTERNAL:
Wing span over tip tanks	8.35 m (27 ft 4¾ in)
Wing chord: at root	1.60 m (5 ft 3 in)
mean aerodynamic	1.325 m (4 ft 4¼ in)
at tip	0.784 m (2 ft 6⅞ in)
Wing aspect ratio (excl tip tanks)	6.3
Wing taper ratio	2.2
Length overall	7.10 m (23 ft 3½ in)
Fuselage: Max width	1.10 m (3 ft 7¼ in)
Max depth	1.042 m (3 ft 5 in)
Height overall	2.41 m (7 ft 11 in)
Elevator span	3.01 m (9 ft 10½ in)
Wheel track	2.274 m (7 ft 5½ in)
Wheelbase	1.66 m (5 ft 5¼ in)
Propeller diameter	1.93 m (6 ft 4 in)
Propeller ground clearance	0.32 m (1 ft 0½ in)

DIMENSIONS, INTERNAL:
Cabin: Length	1.66 m (5 ft 5¼ in)

Agusta (SIAI-Marchetti) SF.260D flown by the *Team America* demonstration team (uprated with 253. 5 kW; 340 hp Textron Lycoming TIO-540 engine) *(John Wegg)*

Max width	1.00 m (3 ft 3¼ in)
Height (seat cushion to canopy)	0.98 m (3 ft 2½ in)
Volume	1.50 m³ (53 cu ft)
Baggage compartment volume	0.18 m³ (6.36 cu ft)

AREAS:
Wings, gross	10.10 m² (108.70 sq ft)
Ailerons (total, incl tabs)	0.762 m² (8.20 sq ft)
Trailing-edge flaps (total)	1.18 m² (12.70 sq ft)
Fin	0.76 m² (8.18 sq ft)
Dorsal fin	0.16 m² (1.72 sq ft)
Rudder, incl tab	0.60 m² (6.46 sq ft)
Tailplane	1.46 m² (15.70 sq ft)
Elevator, incl tab	0.96 m² (10.30 sq ft)

WEIGHTS AND LOADINGS:
Manufacturer's basic weight empty:	
M	755 kg (1,664 lb)
W	770 kg (1,697 lb)
Weight empty, equipped: D	755 kg (1,664 lb)
M	815 kg (1,797 lb)
W	830 kg (1,830 lb)
Fuel:	
in-wing and wingtip tanks (all versions)	169 kg (372.5 lb)
underwing tanks (W only)	114 kg (251.5 lb)
Typical mission weights:	
M, trainer (clean)	1,140 kg (2,513 lb)
W, two 47 kg (103.5 lb) machine-gun pods and full internal fuel	1,163 kg (2,564 lb)
W, one Alkan 500B cartridge thrower, one two-camera reconnaissance pod and full internal fuel	1,182 kg (2,605 lb)
W, trainer with 94 kg (207 lb) external stores	1,249 kg (2,753 lb)
W, self-ferry with two 80 litre (21.1 US gallon; 17.5 Imp gallon) underwing tanks	1,285 kg (2,833 lb)
W, two 125 kg bombs and 150 kg (331 lb) internal fuel	1,300 kg (2,866 lb)
W, two AL-8-70 rocket launchers and 160 kg (353 lb) internal fuel	1,300 kg (2,866 lb)
Max T-O weight: D, M, Aerobatic	1,100 kg (2,425 lb)
D, Utility	1,100 kg (2,425 lb)
M, Utility	1,200 kg (2,645 lb)
W, max permitted	1,300 kg (2,866 lb)
Max wing loading: D	109 kg/m² (22.4 lb/sq ft)
M	119 kg/m² (24.4 lb/sq ft)
W	129 kg/m² (26.4 lb/sq ft)
Max power loading: D	5.68 kg/kW (9.33 lb/hp)
M	6.19 kg/kW (10.17 lb/hp)
W	6.70 kg/kW (11.01 lb/hp)

PERFORMANCE (D at AUW of 1,102 kg; 2,430 lb, M at AUW of 1,200 kg; 2,645 lb, W at 1,300 kg; 2,866 lb, except where indicated):
Never-exceed speed (VNE):	
D, M	235 knots (436 km/h; 271 mph)
Max level speed at S/L:	
D	187 knots (347 km/h; 215 mph)
M	180 knots (333 km/h; 207 mph)
W	165 knots (305 km/h; 190 mph)
Max cruising speed (75% power):	
D at 3,050 m (10,000 ft)	178 knots (330 km/h; 205 mph)
M at 1,500 m (4,925 ft)	162 knots (300 km/h; 186 mph)
W at 1,500 m (4,925 ft)	152 knots (281 km/h; 175 mph)
Stalling speed, flaps and landing gear up:	
M	74 knots (137 km/h; 86 mph)
W	88 knots (163 km/h; 102 mph)
Stalling speed, flaps and landing gear down:	
D	60 knots (111 km/h; 70 mph)
M	68 knots (126 km/h; 79 mph)
W	72 knots (134 km/h; 83 mph)
Max rate of climb at S/L: D	546 m (1,791 ft)/min

M	457 m (1,500 ft)/min
W	381 m (1,250 ft)/min
Time to 1,500 m (4,925 ft): M	4 min
W	6 min 20 s
Time to 2,300 m (7,550 ft): M	6 min 50 s
W	10 min 20 s
Time to 3,000 m (9,850 ft): M	10 min
W	18 min 40 s
Service ceiling: D	5,790 m (19,000 ft)
M	4,665 m (15,300 ft)
W	4,480 m (14,700 ft)
T-O run at S/L: D	480 m (1,575 ft)
M	384 m (1,260 ft)
T-O to 15 m (50 ft) at S/L: M	606 m (1,988 ft)
W	825 m (2,707 ft)
Landing from 15 m (50 ft) at S/L: D	445 m (1,460 ft)
M	539 m (1,768 ft)
W	645 m (2,116 ft)
Landing run at S/L: D, M	345 m (1,132 ft)

Operational radius:
W, 6 h 25 min single-seat armed patrol mission at 1,163 kg (2,564 lb) AUW, incl 5 h 35 min over operating area, 20 kg (44 lb) fuel reserves
50 nm (92 km; 57 miles)

W, 3 h 38 min single-seat strike mission, incl two 5 min loiters over separate en-route target areas, 20 kg (44 lb) fuel reserves 250 nm (463 km; 287 miles)

W, 4 h 54 min single-seat strike mission, incl 5 min over target area, 20 kg (44 lb) fuel reserves
300 nm (556 km; 345 miles)

W, 4 h 30 min single-seat photo-reconnaissance mission at 1,182 kg (2,605 lb) AUW, incl three 1 h loiters over separate en-route operating areas, 20 kg (44 lb) fuel reserves 150 nm (278 km; 172 miles)

W, 6 h 3 min two-seat self-ferry mission with two 80 litre (21.1 US gallon; 17.5 Imp gallon) underwing tanks, at 1,285 kg (2,833 lb) AUW, 30 kg (66 lb) fuel reserves 926 nm (1,716 km; 1,066 miles)

Range with max fuel:
D (two-seat)	805 nm (1,490 km; 925 miles)
M (two-seat)	890 nm (1,650 km; 1,025 miles)

g limits (M):
at max Aerobatic T-O weight	+6/−3
at max Utility T-O weight without external load	+4.4/−2.2

SIAI-MARCHETTI SF.260TP

First flown in July 1980, the SF.260TP is a turboprop powered development of the SF.260M/W, the airframe remaining virtually unchanged aft of the firewall except for inset rudder trim tab and automatic fuel feed system.

More than 60 SF.260TPs have been ordered by military customers. The SF.260M/W description applies also to the TP, except in the following details:

POWER PLANT: One Allison 250-B17D turboprop, flat rated at 261 kW (350 shp) and driving a Hartzell HC-B3TF-7A/T10173-25R three-blade constant-speed fully feathering and reversible-pitch propeller. Fuel capacity as for SF.260M/W; automatic fuel feed system. Oil capacity 7 litres (1.8 US gallons; 1.5 Imp gallons).

DIMENSIONS, EXTERNAL:
Length overall	7.40 m (24 ft 3¼ in)

WEIGHTS AND LOADINGS:
Weight empty, equipped	750 kg (1,654 lb)
Max power loading: trainer	4.60 kg/kW (7.56 lb/shp)
Warrior	4.98 kg/kW (8.19 lb/shp)

PERFORMANCE (at trainer Utility T-O weight of 1,200 kg; 2,645 lb, ISA):
Never-exceed speed (VNE)
236 knots (437 km/h; 271 mph)
Max level speed at 3,050 m (10,000 ft)
228 knots (422 km/h; 262 mph)

Agusta (SIAI-Marchetti) SF.260TP with gun pods *(Avio Data)*

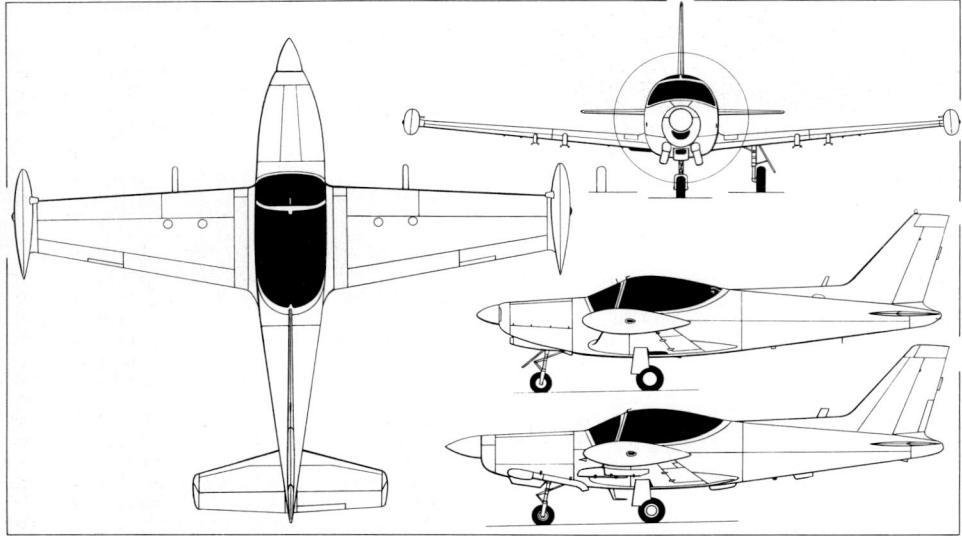

Agusta (SIAI-Marchetti) SF.260TP turboprop trainer, with additional side view (centre) of piston engined SF.260M *(Pilot Press)*

Max cruising speed at 2,440 m (8,000 ft)
216 knots (400 km/h; 248 mph)
Econ cruising speed at 4,575 m (15,000 ft)
170 knots (315 km/h; 195 mph)
Stalling speed at S/L, flaps down, power off
68 knots (126 km/h; 79 mph)
Max rate of climb at S/L   660 m (2,065 ft)/min
Service ceiling   7,500 m (24,600 ft)
T-O run   298 m (978 ft)
T-O to 15 m (50 ft)   467 m (1,532 ft)
Landing from 15 m (50 ft)   533 m (1,749 ft)
Landing run, without reverse pitch   307 m (1,007 ft)
Range at 4,575 m (15,000 ft) with max fuel, 30 min
reserves   512 nm (949 km; 589 miles)

SIAI-MARCHETTI S.211

This lightweight, low-cost basic trainer and light attack aircraft was first revealed in the form of a model at the Paris Air Show in May/June 1977. Two flying prototypes were built initially, and the first of these (I-SITF) made its initial flight on 10 April 1981.

Deliveries of production S.211s began in November 1984. Customers include the air forces of the Philippines (18), Singapore (30) and Haiti (four). The first six S.211s for Singapore were delivered in component knocked-down form for reassembly; subsequent aircraft were built by SAMCO, a subsidiary of Singapore Aerospace (SA, which see). The Philippine order, signed in 1988, also covered an option for a further 18 aircraft, with final assembly of 14 of the initial 18 undertaken by Philippine Aerospace Development Corporation (which see). The first S.211 for the Philippines was delivered in September 1989 and nine had been completed by March 1991. All 18 were expected to be completed during the year. Nine of the aircraft are to be operated by the 100th Training Wing at Fernando Air Base, Lipa City, Laguna. Of the other nine, some will be used by the 5th Fighter Wing at Basa AB, Luzon, for training and the remainder will operate in a ground support role from Mactan AB, Cebu. All four Haitian S.211s were re-sold in the USA.

In partnership with Grumman Aircraft Systems, a version of the S.211 is to be submitted for the USAF/USN's JPATS competition (see introduction).

Features of the S.211 are its safe stalling and spinning characteristics, and the very low airframe weight, made possible by the fact that some 61 per cent of the external surfaces are made from composite materials.

In order to improve the S.211's operational capabilities a special nav/attack version, equipped with an OMI/Litton lightweight head-up display and Omega navigation computer, is under development. Joint development, with SA, of a lengthened version of the S.211 was announced at the Paris Air Show in June 1987 but apparently not pursued. An enhanced version of the S.211 with a 14.2 kN (3,190 lb st) JT15D engine and more fuel is also under development.

The following description applies to the standard production S.211:

TYPE: Two-seat basic trainer and light attack aircraft.
WINGS: Cantilever shoulder-wing monoplane with super-critical section developed. Thickness/chord ratio 15 per cent at root, 13 per cent at tip. Incidence 2° 13′ at root, −1° 17′ at tip. Anhedral 2° from roots. Sweepback 15° 30′ at quarter-chord. Two-spar metal torsion box structure,

forming integral fuel tank; attached to fuselage by four bolts. Upper and lower skins each formed by two one-piece panels joined along centreline and to the spars. Hydraulically actuated ailerons, with electric trim, and large area electrically actuated Fowler flaps, on trailing-edges.

FUSELAGE: Conventional metal and glassfibre semi-monocoque structure. Hydraulically actuated airbrake under centre-fuselage. Equipment bay in nose. Large quick-disconnect panel at rear, for rapid engine access or removal.

TAIL UNIT: Cantilever metal structure. Sweptback fin; horn balanced rudder with electrically operated trim tab; electrically actuated variable incidence tailplane has sweptback leading-edge. Horn balanced elevators, with servo tab.

LANDING GEAR: Hydraulically retractable tricycle type, of Messier-Bugatti/Magnaghi design. Oleo-pneumatic shock absorber in each unit. All units retract forward into fuselage (main units turning through 90° to lie flat in undersides of engine air intake trunks). Nosewheel steerable 18° left and right. Mainwheels size 6.50-8; nosewheel size 5.00-5 with water deflecting tyre. Designed for sink rate of 4 m (13 ft)/s. Wheel brakes actuated hydraulically, independently of main hydraulic system. Provision for emergency free-fall extension.

POWER PLANT: One 11.13 kN (2,500 lb st) Pratt & Whitney Canada JT15D-4C turbofan, with electronic fuel control, mounted in rear of fuselage; lateral intake each side of fuselage, with splitter plate. Fuel in 650 litre (171.5 US gallon; 143 Imp gallon) integral wing tank and 150 litre (39.5 US gallon; 33 Imp gallon) fuselage tank; total capacity 800 litres (211 US gallons; 176 Imp gallons). Single gravity refuelling point in top surface of starboard wing. Electric fuel pump for engine starting and emergency use. Fuel and oil systems permit inverted flight. Provision for two 270 litre (71.3 US gallon; 59.4 Imp gallon) drop tanks on inboard underwing stores points. Oil capacity 10 kg (22 lb).

ACCOMMODATION: Two pilots in tandem stepped up 28 cm (11 in) on Martin-Baker Mk 10 lightweight ejection seats. Blast screen between seats. Pressurised and air-conditioned cockpit under one-piece framed canopy opening sideways to starboard.

SYSTEMS: Environmental control system for cockpit pressurisation and air-conditioning, using engine bleed air for heating, Freon vapour for cooling. Max pressure differential 0.24 bar (3.5 lb/sq in). Hydraulic system, pressure 207 bar (3,000 lb/sq in), for actuation of airbrake, landing gear, Freon compressor and aileron boost, and independent actuation of wheel brakes. Primary electrical system is 28V DC, using an engine driven starter/generator; nickel-cadmium battery; two static inverters supply AC power for instruments and avionics. External power receptacle in port side of lower fuselage aft of wing. Demand type main oxygen system, at 124 bars (1,800 lb/sq in) pressure, sufficient to supply both occupants for 4 hours, plus bottles for emergency oxygen supply.

AVIONICS: Standard avionics fit includes two V/UHF com, ADF, VOR/ILS and DME or Tacan, IFF or ATC, ICS, AHRS, HSI and AI. Provision for dual gyro stabilised gunsight system with miniaturised video recording or film camera. Additional provisions for R/Nav, radar altimeter, Doppler radar, head-up display, radar warning system and ECM.

EQUIPMENT: Inboard wing stations can carry two photo-reconnaissance pods each with four cameras and infra-red linescan.

ARMAMENT: Four underwing hardpoints, stressed for loads of up to 330 kg (727.5 lb) inboard, 165 kg (364 lb) outboard; max external load 660 kg (1,455 lb). Typical loads can include four single- or twin-gun 7.62 mm

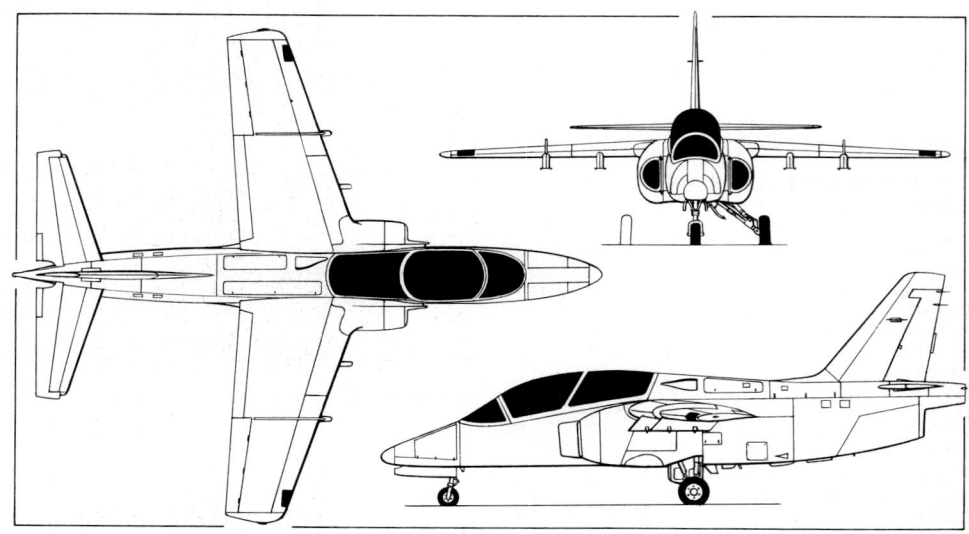

Agusta (SIAI-Marchetti) S.211 basic trainer and light attack aircraft *(Pilot Press)*

Agusta (SIAI-Marchetti) S.211 in the guise of the Grumman-Agusta bid for the USAF/USN JPATS order

machine-gun pods, four 12.7 mm gun pods, or (inboard only) two 20 mm gun pods; four AL-18-50 (18 × 50 mm), Matra F2 (6 × 68 mm), LAU-32 (7 × 2.75 in), or AL-6-80 (6 × 81 mm) rocket launchers, or (inboard only) two Matra 155 (18 × 68 mm), SNORA RWK-020 (12 × 81 mm) or 100 mm rocket launchers; four bombs or practice bombs of up to 150 kg size, or (inboard only) two bombs or napalm containers of up to 300 kg; or four 74 mm cartridge throwers. Ferranti ISIS D-211 optical weapon aiming system optional (fitted in aircraft for Haiti).

DIMENSIONS, EXTERNAL:

Wing span	8.43 m (27 ft 8 in)
Wing chord: at root	2.151 m (7 ft 0¾ in)
mean aerodynamic	1.646 m (5 ft 4¾ in)
at tip	1.00 m (3 ft 3¼ in)
Wing aspect ratio	5.1
Length overall	9.31 m (30 ft 6½ in)
Height overall	3.80 m (12 ft 5½ in)
Tailplane span	3.96 m (13 ft 0 in)
Wheel track	2.29 m (7 ft 6 in)
Wheelbase	4.02 m (13 ft 2¼ in)

AREAS:

Wings, gross	12.60 m² (135.63 sq ft)
Airbrake	0.42 m² (4.52 sq ft)
Vertical tail surfaces (total)	2.01 m² (21.64 sq ft)
Horizontal tail surfaces (total)	3.378 m² (36.36 sq ft)

WEIGHTS AND LOADINGS:

Weight empty, equipped	1,850 kg (4,078 lb)
Max usable fuel: internal	622 kg (1,371 lb)
external	390 kg (860 lb)
Max T-O weight: trainer, clean	2,750 kg (6,063 lb)
armed version	3,150 kg (6,944 lb)
Max wing loading:	
trainer, clean	218.25 kg/m² (44.70 lb/sq ft)
armed version	250.00 kg/m² (51.20 lb/sq ft)
Max power loading:	
trainer, clean	247.4 kg/kN (2.42 lb/lb st)
armed version	283.4 kg/kN (2.78 lb/lb st)

PERFORMANCE (at T-O weight of 2,500 kg; 5,511 lb except where indicated):
Never-exceed speed (VNE)
  Mach 0.80 (400 knots; 740 km/h; 460 mph EAS)
Max cruising speed at 7,620 m (25,000 ft)
  360 knots (667 km/h; 414 mph)
Rotation speed 90 knots (167 km/h; 104 mph)
Stalling speed, flaps down 74 knots (138 km/h; 86 mph)
Max rate of climb at S/L 1,280 m (4,200 ft)/min
Time to 6,100 m (20,000 ft) 6 min 12 s
Service ceiling 12,200 m (40,000 ft)
T-O run (S/L, ISA) 390 m (1,280 ft)
T-O to 15 m (50 ft) 512 m (1,680 ft)
Landing from 15 m (50 ft) 705 m (2,313 ft)
Landing run (S/L, ISA) 361 m (1,185 ft)
Min air turning radius at S/L less than 305 m (1,000 ft)
Typical attack radius with four rocket launchers, AUW of 3,150 kg (6,944 lb):
  hi-lo-hi, out and back at 265 knots (491 km/h; 305 mph) at 9,150 m (30,000 ft), 2 h 50 min mission (incl 5 min over target), 60 kg (132 lb) of fuel remaining 300 nm (556 km; 345 miles)
  lo-lo-lo, out and back at 250 knots (463 km/h; 288 mph) at less than 305 m (1,000 ft), 1 h 5 min mission (incl 5 min over target), 60 kg (132 lb) of fuel remaining 125 nm (231 km; 144 miles)
Max range on internal fuel, 30 min reserves 900 nm (1,668 km; 1,036 miles)
Ferry range (AUW of 3,150 kg; 6,944 lb, max internal and external fuel) at 270 knots (500 km/h; 311 mph) at 9,150 m (30,000 ft), 90 kg (198 lb) of fuel remaining 1,340 nm (2,483 km; 1,543 miles)
Endurance, 30 min reserves 3 h 50 min
Sustained g limit at 4,575 m (15,000 ft) 3.4
g limits: +6/−3 clean
  +5/−2.5 with external stores

SIAI-MARCHETTI SF.600TP CANGURO (KANGAROO)

The prototype F.600 Canguro (I-CANG), built by General Avia and then powered by 261 kW (350 hp) Textron Lycoming TIO-540-J flat-six piston engines, made its first flight on 30 December 1978. This aircraft was described under the General Avia heading in the 1979-80 *Jane's*.

The current standard power plant is two 335 kW (450 shp) Allison 250-B17F engines. The tooling was transferred during 1991 to Sammi Agusta Aerospace Corporation in South Korea (which see) formed by Agusta and Sammi Corporation on 22 May 1989, which may also make and market other Agusta aircraft. Philippine Aerospace Development Corporation (PADC) may also become involved in Canguro production. A description of the Canguro appears under the SAAC heading in the Korean section of this edition.

ELICOTTERI MERIDIONALI SpA

This company was formed with assistance from Agusta and began to operate in October 1967. It remains a separate commercial entity affiliated to Agusta. In 1968 EM (Elicotteri Meridionali SpA) acquired rights to the co-production, marketing and servicing of the Boeing CH-47C Chinook transport helicopter for customers in Italy and certain foreign countries. Italian production of the CH-47C airframe is undertaken by the Sesto Calende works.

EM, whose works occupy a total area of more than 300,000 m² (3,229,170 sq ft), participates in the manufacturing programmes for the Agusta A 109A Mk II and A 129, Agusta-Bell 212/412, and Agusta-Sikorsky ASH-3H helicopters. It has complete facilities for overhaul, repair and field assistance. EM is the designated overhaul organisation for all types of Italian Army helicopter, and is also distributor in Italy for Allison 250 turboshaft engines.

EM (BOEING) CH-47C CHINOOK

Italian manufacture of the CH-47C began in the Spring of 1970, initially to meet an order for the Italian Army Aviation. Later customers are detailed in the 1989-90 *Jane's*.

EM also produced a further 10 aircraft, designated **CH-47C Plus**, for operation by the Italian Army on behalf of the Civil Protection Agency. Simultaneously with this additional production, an upgrading programme was begun, to fit the earlier aircraft with new Textron Lycoming T55-L-712E engines, composite rotor blades and a more advanced transmission system. Max T-O weight is increased to 22,680 kg (50,000 lb).

Agusta developed, jointly with Hosp Ital SpA (a division of Cogefar) of Milan, an **ESFC** (emergency surgery flying centre) version of the Chinook for use as a mobile hospital. Details of the ESFC can be found in the 1983-84 *Jane's*. One was delivered to the Italian Army in 1987.

Italian built Boeing CH-47C Plus with T55-L-712E engines, advanced transmission, composite rotor blades and a 50,000 lb take-off weight *(Avio Data)*

The Italian Army's entire fleet of Chinooks is being overhauled at the rate of three a year by EM, which redelivered the first of 23 then-operational aircraft in March 1986. These aircraft are used for a wide range of duties, one important role being that of firefighting, in which configuration they can be equipped with a 5,000 litre (1,321 US gallon; 1,100 Imp gallon) metal tank for retardant.

ALENIA
(Aeritalia and Selenia)
Via E. Petrolini 2, 00197 Rome
Telephone: 39 (6) 87781
Fax: 39 (6) 872215 or 875184
Telex: 611395 Alenia I
HONORARY PRESIDENT: Amb Umberto La Rocca
CHAIRMAN: Fausto Cereti
DEPUTY CHAIRMAN: Cesare Previti
MANAGING DIRECTOR: Enrico Gimelli
DIRECTORS:
  Raffaele Esposito
  Paolo Micheletta
VICE-PRESIDENT, OPERATIONS: Amedeo Caporaletti
VICE-PRESIDENT, ADMINISTRATION: Antonio Zibellini
SECRETARY GENERAL: Massimo Rizzo
DIRECTOR OF PRESS AND PUBLIC RELATIONS:
  Fabio Danni

Merger of Aeritalia and Selenia, both members of the IRI-Finmeccanica state investment concern, was announced in September 1990 and effected on 20 December 1990. The two businesses were integrated in four sectors, Aeronautics, Space, Defence Systems and Civil Systems, which are listed below.

Alenia has 30,000 employees, 35 factories in Italy and abroad, and had sales of Lire 5,500 billion in 1990.

Aeritalia was formed on 12 November 1969 by an equal shareholding of Fiat and the state-controlled IRI-Finmeccanica to combine Fiat's aerospace activities (except those which concerned aero engines) with those of Aerfer and Salmoiraghi of the Finmeccanica group. It became fully operational under that title on 1 January 1972. On 28 September 1976 IRI-Finmeccanica purchased the Aeritalia stock owned by Fiat, thus acquiring complete control of the company's stock capital. However, in 1990 IRI-Finmeccanica's shareholding stood at 84 per cent, with the remaining shares privately owned. In the Summer of 1981 Aeritalia acquired shareholdings of 100 per cent in Aeronavali Venezia, 60 per cent in Partenavia, and 50 per cent in Meteor. A 25 per cent holding in Aeronautica Macchi was acquired in 1983; in 1988 it acquired a 31 per cent holding in Rinaldo Piaggio (which see), a 44 (since reduced to 22) per cent share in FMA of Argentina, and 60 per cent in Dee Howard (see US section). Meteor came to be 100 per cent owned by Aeritalia.

ALENIA SETTORE AERONAUTICO
Via E. Petrolini 2, 00197 Rome
Telephone: 39 (6) 87781
Fax: 39 (6) 872215/875184
DIRECTOR: Roberto Mannu
ASSISTANT DIRECTORS:
  Nino d'Angelo
  Filippo de Luca
  Mario Pellerei

Includes the former civil and military aircraft groups and Alfa Romeo Avio, Officine Aeronavali Venezia, Partenavia (listed separately in this section), the Dee Howard Company (see USA section) and Sviluppo Aeronautico Meridionale (SVAM).

Main factories are at Naples, Turin, Foggia, Fusoria, Venice and Rome. Activities include AMX, EFA, Tornado, F-104S ASA, Boeing 767/777, ATR 42/72, DASA/ATR 80/130-passenger airliner G222/C-27A, McDonnell Douglas MD-80/90 and MD-11, Airbus A321, AAA amphibian, repairs and conversions and Atlantic modernisation.

ALENIA SPAZIO SpA
Via Saccomuro 24, 00131 Rome
Telephone: 39 (6) 43681
Fax: 39 (6) 4090675/4090773
PRESIDENT: Ernesto Vallerani
GENERAL MANAGER: Andrea Pucci

Includes the space activities of Aeritalia and Selenia, plus Laben, Proel Technologie and Space Software Italia (SSI).

ALENIA SISTEMI DIFESA
Via Tiburtina Km 12,400, 00131 Rome
Telephone: 39 (6) 41971/43601
Fax: 39 (6) 4131133/4131436
DIRECTOR: Nicolas Zalonis
ASSISTANT DIRECTOR: Ing Carlo Scaglia

Includes Elmer, Meteor, Selenia Elsag Sistemi Navali, Vitroselenia.

ALENIA SISTEMI CIVILI
Via Tiburtina Km 12,400, 00131 Rome
Telephone: 39 (6) 41971/43601
Fax: 39 (6) 4131133/4131436
DIRECTOR: Umberto di Nardo
ASSISTANT DIRECTOR: Francesco Zappala

Includes Elecos, Italcad, OTE, Samanta and West.

ADVANCED AMPHIBIOUS AIRCRAFT
Alenia/Aeritalia and Dornier have proposed a twin-turboprop amphibian, now with additional partners, which is to figure in the EEC Eureka technology programme. For details, see under AAA in International section.

AIRBUS A321
Alenia is a risk-sharing contractor. Details can be found in the International section.

AMX
Alenia has the largest share (46.5 per cent) in the AMX. A description and illustration of this programme, also involving Aermacchi and Embraer, can be found in the International section.

ATR 42/72
Alenia is an equal partner with Aerospatiale of France in this regional transport aircraft, descriptions and illustrations of which appear under the ATR heading in the International section. Alenia is also a partner, through ATR, in the DASA-led 80/130-passenger regional airliner development.

DEE HOWARD BAe ONE-ELEVEN
Dee Howard, British Aerospace and Rolls-Royce agreed in 1986 to re-engine One-Elevens with Spey turbofans. Alenia owns 60 per cent of Dee Howard. Certification was expected in early 1991. See under Dee Howard in USA section.

EUROFIGHTER
Alenia has a 21 per cent share in the development of this new generation fighter, details of which can be found in the International section.

NAMC A-5 MODERNISATION
Under a joint programme with CATIC, Alenia has modernised the avionics of the Nanchang A-5C ('Fantan') attack aircraft (see under NAMC in Chinese section). This upgrading encompasses all-weather autonomous and radio-assisted navigation, air and ground communications, IFF, weapon aiming for ground attack and air-to-air self-defence modes, and passive ECM. The avionics system is designed around central computers and a dual redundant MIL-STD-1553B databus. Two equipped aircraft have flown.

TORNADO
Alenia has a 15 per cent participation in the manufacturing programme for the Panavia Tornado (see International section), being responsible for the radomes and the movable wings, including control surfaces. All 100 aircraft for the Italian Air Force have been delivered.

ALENIA G222
US Air Force designation: C-27A
Early history of the Aeritalia (originally Fiat) G222, the first prototype of which made its initial flight on 18 July 1970, can be found in the 1987-88 and previous editions of *Jane's*.

Subcontractors include Aermacchi (outer wings); Piaggio (wing centre-section); Agusta (tail unit); CIRSEA (landing gear); and IAM (miscellaneous airframe components). Wing flaps are contributed by Hellenic Aerospace Industries. Fuselages are built in the Pomigliano d'Arco Works near Naples; final assembly takes place at the Capodichino Works, Naples.

The following versions have been built:

G222: Standard military transport, to which the detailed description mainly applies. The first of 44 G222s for the Italian Air Force (30 standard transports, eight G222SAA, four G222RM and two G222GE) flew on 23 December 1975, and deliveries began on 21 April 1978. Other customers included the Argentine Army (three), Congo (three), Dubai Air Force (one), Guatemala (two), Libyan Air Force (20), Nigerian Air Force (five), Somali Air Force (two), Venezuelan Army (two) and Air Force (six), and Yemen (four). Five were ordered by the Italian Ministry for Civil Defence, to create a rapid-intervention squadron for firefighting, aeromedical evacuation, and airlift of supplies to earthquake and other disaster areas.

G222RM: Flight inspection (Radiomisure) version, detailed in the 1989-90 Jane's.

G222SAA: Firefighting version (Sistema Aeronautico Antincendio), detailed in the 1989-90 Jane's.

G222T: Version with Rolls-Royce Tyne turboprops, larger-diameter propellers and higher operating weights; details in 1986-87 Jane's.

G222VS (Versione Speciale): Electronic warfare version, detailed in the 1989-90 Jane's.

G222GE (Guerra Elettronica): Dimensions, weights and performance similar to those of the standard troop transport.

Italian Air Force Alenia G222 powered by GE T64s made by Fiat *(Peter J. Cooper)*

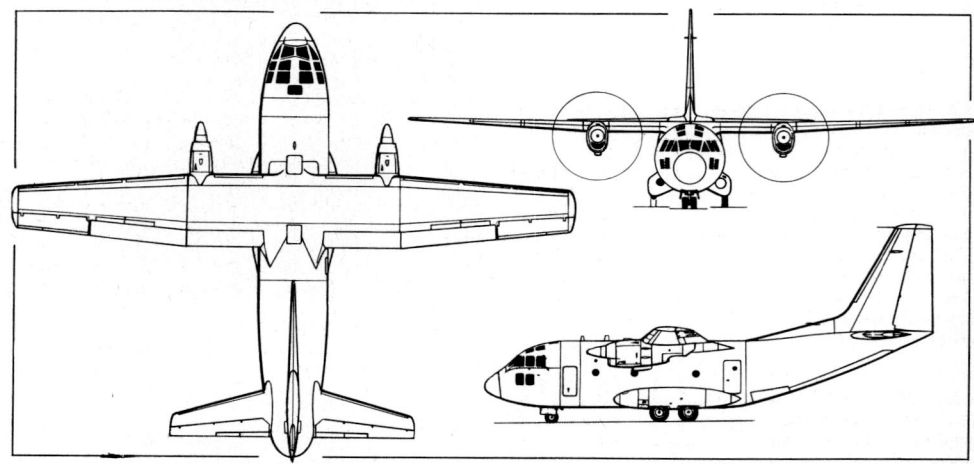

Alenia G222 twin-turboprop general purpose military transport aircraft *(Pilot Press)*

C-27A: Chrysler Technologies and Airborne Systems (CTAS: see US section) won the USAF competition for a mid-range pressurised airlift aircraft with the G222 and will equip them for service in Panama and South America. The first five were ordered for about $80 million. First delivery was scheduled for August 1991 and up to 20 might eventually be ordered.

Total orders for the G222, excluding the C-27, now stand at about 97.

The following abbreviated description applies to the standard G222 transport version. A full description can be found in the 1987-88 and many earlier editions.

TYPE: Twin-turboprop general purpose transport aircraft.

POWER PLANT: Two Fiat built General Electric T64-GE-P4D turboprops, each flat rated at 2,535 kW (3,400 shp) at ISA + 25°C and driving a Hamilton Standard 63E60-27 three-blade variable- and reversible-pitch propeller. Fuel in integral tanks: two in the outer wings, combined capacity 6,800 litres (1,796 US gallons; 1,495 Imp gallons), and two centre-section tanks, combined capacity 5,200 litres (1,374 US gallons; 1,143 Imp gallons), with cross-feed provision to either engine. Total overall fuel capacity 12,000 litres (3,170 US gallons; 2,638 Imp gallons).

ACCOMMODATION: Normal crew of three (two pilots and radio operator/flight engineer) on flight deck. Provision for loadmaster or jumpmaster when required. Standard troop transport version has 32 foldaway sidewall seats and 21 stowable seats for 53 fully equipped troops. Paratroop transport version can carry up to 40 fully equipped paratroops, and is fitted with the 32 sidewall seats, plus eight stowable seats, door jump platforms and static lines. Five-person VIP lounge plus seats for 16 other passengers in VIP transport version. Cargo transport version can accept standard pallets of up to 2.24 m (88 in) wide, and can carry up to 9,000 kg (19,840 lb) of freight. Crew door is forward of cabin on port side. Passenger doors, at front and rear of main cabin on starboard side and at rear on port side, can be used also as emergency exits. Two emergency hatches in cabin roof, forward and aft of wing carry-through structure. Hydraulically operated rear loading ramp and upward opening door in underside of upswept rear fuselage, which can be opened in flight for airdrop operations. In cargo version, five pallets of up to 1,000 kg (2,205 lb) each can be airdropped from rear opening, or a single pallet of up to 5,000 kg (11,023 lb). Paratroop jumps can be made either from this opening or from the rear side doors. Entire accommodation pressurised and air-conditioned.

DIMENSIONS, EXTERNAL:

Wing span	28.70 m (94 ft 2 in)
Wing aspect ratio	10.0
Length overall	22.70 m (74 ft 5½ in)
Height overall	9.80 m (32 ft 1¾ in)
Fuselage: Max diameter	3.55 m (11 ft 7¾ in)
Rear-loading ramp/door: Width	2.45 m (8 ft 0½ in)
Height	2.25 m (7 ft 4½ in)

DIMENSIONS, INTERNAL:

Main cabin: Length	8.58 m (28 ft 1¾ in)
Width	2.45 m (8 ft 0½ in)
Height	2.25 m (7 ft 4½ in)
Floor area: excl ramp	21.00 m² (226.0 sq ft)
incl ramp	25.68 m² (276.4 sq ft)
Volume	58.0 m³ (2,048 cu ft)

WEIGHTS AND LOADINGS:

Weight empty	14,590 kg (32,165 lb)
Weight empty, equipped	15,400 kg (33,950 lb)

Italian Air Force F-104S ASA with outer pylons fitted for Aspide *(Peter J. Cooper)*

Operating weight empty	15,700 kg (34,610 lb)
Max payload (cargo)	9,000 kg (19,840 lb)
Max fuel load	9,400 kg (20,725 lb)
Max T-O weight	28,000 kg (61,730 lb)
Max landing weight	26,500 kg (58,420 lb)
Max zero-fuel weight	24,400 kg (53,790 lb)
Max cargo floor loading	750 kg/m² (155 lb/sq ft)
Max wing loading	341.5 kg/m² (69.9 lb/sq ft)
Max power loading	5.52 kg/kW (9.08 lb/shp)

PERFORMANCE (at max T-O weight except where indicated):

Max level speed at 4,575 m (15,000 ft)	
	291 knots (540 km/h; 336 mph)
Long-range cruising speed at 6,000 m (19,680 ft)	
	237 knots (439 km/h; 273 mph)
Airdrop speed (paratroops or cargo)	
	110-140 knots (204-259 km/h; 127-161 mph) IAS
Drop speed	120 knots (222 km/h; 138 mph)
Stalling speed, flaps and landing gear down	
	84 knots (155 km/h; 97 mph)
Time to 4,500 m (14,760 ft)	8 min 35 s
Max rate of climb at S/L	520 m (1,705 ft)/min
Rate of climb at S/L, one engine out	125 m (410 ft)/min
Service ceiling	7,620 m (25,000 ft)
Service ceiling, one engine out	5,000 m (16,400 ft)
T-O run	662 m (2,172 ft)
Landing run at max landing weight	545 m (1,788 ft)
Accelerate/stop distance	1,200 m (3,937 ft)
Range:	
with max payload, at optimum cruising speed and height	740 nm (1,371 km; 852 miles)
Ferry range with max fuel	
	2,500 nm (4,633 km; 2,879 miles)
g limit	+2.5

ALENIA (LOCKHEED) F-104S ASA

Aeritalia production of the F-104S ended in March 1979 after the manufacture of 246 aircraft, including 40 for the Turkish Air Force. Development was initiated in 1982 of a weapons system updating programme for 150 of the Italian Air Force's F-104Ss. Known as ASA (Aggiornamento Sistema d'Arma), this programme included fitting the FIAR R21G/M1 Setter lookdown/shootdown radar; advanced ECM; improved IFF and altitude reporting system; improved electrical system; improved weapons delivery (armament computer and time delay unit); and a new automatic pitch control computer. Weapons include Aspide 1A medium-range and AIM-9L Sidewinder short-range air-to-air missiles. The 150th and final ASA was to be redelivered in 1991.

ALENIA DC-8 FREIGHTER CONVERSION

Under a US programme launched in 1976, McDonnell Douglas converted 20 DC-8 passenger transports into specialised freighters, as recorded in the 1987-88 and earlier editions of *Jane's*. In 1982 responsibility for the DC-8 freighter conversion programme was taken over by Officine Aeronavali Venezia SpA (a wholly owned subsidiary of Alenia), which delivered its first conversion in February 1986.

ALENIA ATLANTIC 1 MODERNISATION

Some systems of 18 Italian Air Force Breguet Atlantic 1 maritime patrol aircraft are being upgraded. Programme completion is scheduled for October 1992.

AVIOLIGHT
AVIOLIGHT SRL

Via Arangio Ruiz 83, Naples 80522
Telephone: 39 (81) 771 1011
Fax: 39 (81) 771 6763
Telex: 720373
PRESIDENT: Prof Ing Luigi Pascale
GENERAL MANAGER: Raffaele Veneruso

This company was formed on 29 February 1988 by Partenavia (which see), Avio Interiors (Alven) of Latina, and the Naples based company Tecnam owned by the Pascale brothers. All rights to the line of single-engined aircraft developed by Partenavia were transferred to Aviolight in February 1988. Development of the very light P.86 Mosquito was discontinued, but Aviolight has developed a new version of the P.66 called Delta (which see) and it supports the earlier P.66B Oscar and P.66C Charlie. The Delta was not successful in being selected by the Italian national aero club as a trainer, but is being manufactured. Tecnam manufactures the fuselage of the Partenavia P.68, the tailplane of the ATR 42/72 and the wing of the Meteor Mirach 200 UAV.

AVIOLIGHT (PARTENAVIA) P.66D DELTA

Having assumed responsibility for Partenavia's single-engined aircraft, Aviolight is putting into production a new version of the P.66, last described in the 1984-85 edition of *Jane's*. As an initial step, the company fitted a 119 kW (160

hp) Textron Lycoming O-320-D2A piston engine in a P.66B Oscar (I-AVLT), which has also been given P.66T Charlie Trainer type upturned wingtips. In this form, the aircraft was first flown in September 1988.

The production version is designated P.66D Delta and features a full IFR instrument panel. Compared to the previous Oscar model, the Delta has lower fuel consumption, better hot and high performance, and requires less frequent maintenance. Its airframe conforms to FAR Pt 23 requirements.

The following details apply to the prototype:

TYPE: Two/three-seat light monoplane.

WINGS: Braced high-wing monoplane with single streamline section bracing strut each side. Wing section NACA 63A₃-515. Dihedral 1° 30′. Incidence at root 1° 40′. No sweepback. Stressed skin two-spar torsion box structure of aluminium alloy, with one-piece GFRP moulded leading-edges. Ailerons and electrically operated slotted trailing-edge flaps of similar construction to wings. No tabs. Upturned wingtips.

FUSELAGE: Forward portion, to rear of cabin, has a welded steel tube basic structure to which are attached light alloy skin panels. Rear fuselage is of conventional light alloy stressed skin construction.

TAIL UNIT: Cantilever stressed skin metal torsion box structure with sweptback vertical surfaces. All-moving tailplane in two symmetrical halves joined by steel cross-tube. Geared trim tab.

LANDING GEAR: Non-retractable tricycle type, with steerable nosewheel. Cantilever spring steel main legs. Oleo-pneumatic nosewheel shock absorber. Van Sickle wheels (size 40-77B nose, 40-86B main) and McCreary tyres (size

5.00-5 five-ply on nosewheel, 6.00-6 six-ply on main units). Cleveland type 30-18 hydraulic disc brakes.

DIMENSIONS, EXTERNAL:

Wing span	9.99 m (32 ft 9¼ in)
Wing chord, constant	1.36 m (4 ft 5½ in)
Wing aspect ratio	7.43
Length overall	6.98 m (22 ft 10¾ in)
Height overall	2.77 m (9 ft 1 in)
Wheel track	2.10 m (6 ft 10½ in)
Wheelbase	1.51 m (4 ft 11½ in)
Doors (each): Height	0.96 m (3 ft 2 in)
Width	0.62 m (2 ft 0½ in)
Height to sill	0.69 m (2 ft 3 in)

DIMENSIONS, INTERNAL:

Cabin: Max length	2.20 m (7 ft 2½ in)
Max width	0.90 m (2 ft 11½ in)
Max height	1.30 m (4 ft 3 in)
Floor area	2.0 m² (21.53 sq ft)
Volume	2.5 m³ (88.29 cu ft)
Baggage space, aft of seats	0.3 m³ (10.59 cu ft)

AREAS:

Wings, gross	13.40 m² (144.2 sq ft)
Ailerons (total)	0.90 m² (9.69 sq ft)
Trailing-edge flaps (total)	1.00 m² (10.76 sq ft)
Fin	0.70 m² (7.53 sq ft)
Rudder	0.50 m² (5.38 sq ft)
Tailplane, incl tab	2.10 m² (22.60 sq ft)

WEIGHTS AND LOADINGS (prototype):

Weight empty	640 kg (1,411 lb)
Max T-O weight	930 kg (2,050 lb)
Max wing loading	69.40 kg/m² (14.21 lb/sq ft)
Max power loading	**7.80 kg/kW (12.81 lb/hp)**

PERFORMANCE (prototype):

Max level speed at S/L	132 knots (245 km/h; 152 mph)	Stalling speed: flaps up	53 knots (99 km/h; 61 mph)	T-O to 15 m (50 ft)	440 m (1,444 ft)
Max cruising speed (75% power) at 1,800 m (5,900 ft)		flaps down	47 knots (87 km/h; 54 mph)	Landing run	210 m (689 ft)
	124 knots (230 km/h; 143 mph)	Service ceiling	4,500 m (14,765 ft)	Max endurance	more than 5 h
		T-O run	220 m (722 ft)		

GENERAL AVIA
GENERAL AVIA COSTRUZIONI AERONAUTICHE SRL

Via Trieste 22-24, 20096 Pioltello, Milan
Telephone: 39 (2) 92 66 774
Fax: 39 (2) 92 16 03 95
TECHNICAL DIRECTOR: Dott Ing Stelio Frati
TECHNICAL: Dott Ing Giancarlo Monti
PUBLIC RELATIONS: Carla Bielli

Dott Ing Stelio Frati is well known for the many successful light aircraft which, as a freelance designer, he has developed since 1950. These have included the F.8 Falco; F.15 Picchio; the F.250, now manufactured by Agusta as the SF.260; and the F.20 Pegaso, described in the 1981-82 *Jane's*. General Avia developed and built the prototype of the Canguro transport aircraft described under the Agusta heading in this section. In 1983 it developed for SIAI-Marchetti a retractable landing gear version of the Canguro. In the following year it started construction of the F1300 Jet Squalus, which was financed by Promavia of Belgium (which see). Promavia bought out the whole Jet Squalus programme.

In 1988, as a private venture, General Avia began manufacturing the fuselage of a 19-passenger twin-turbofan commuter transport, known as the F.3500 Sparviero, but this has not been continued. Details of the Sparviero appeared in the 1985-86 *Jane's*.

GENERAL AVIA F.20 TP CONDOR

The Condor four-seat turboprop powered prototype (I-GEAC) flew for the first time on 7 May 1983, but was not continued. Full details appear in the 1987-88 *Jane's*.

GENERAL AVIA F.22 PINGUINO (PENGUIN)

On 13 June 1989 the first prototype F.22 Pinguino (I-GEAD) flying club trainer flew for the first time from the airport at Orio al Serio (Bergamo), where work is now based (*Tel:* 39 [35] 31 15 90). A 119 kW (160 hp) Textron Lycoming engine is optional. A batch of nine was being built during 1991; certification was achieved in September 1990.

TYPE: Side by side two-seat primary trainer.
WINGS: All-metal cantilever low-wing monoplane, built in one piece with single spar. Electrically actuated flaps.
FUSELAGE: All-metal semi-monocoque structure.
TAIL UNIT: Cantilever all-metal structure with swept fin and rudder. Trim tab in elevator.
LANDING GEAR: First prototype has non-retractable tricycle type, with steerable nosewheel. Oleo shock absorbers. Faired main legs.
POWER PLANT: One 86.5 kW (116 hp) Textron Lycoming O-235-N2C flat-four engine, driving a two-blade wooden propeller. Optional 119 kW (160 hp) O-320-D2A flown in second prototype. Fuel capacity 135 litres (35.7 US gallons; 29.7 Imp gallons).
ACCOMMODATION: Two seats side by side: sliding canopy.
AVIONICS: Bendix/King Silver Crown nav/com, ADF, audio console and transponder.

DIMENSIONS, EXTERNAL:

Wing span	8.50 m (27 ft 10¾ in)
Wing chord: at root	1.589 m (5 ft 2½ in)
at tip	0.876 m (2 ft 10½ in)
Wing aspect ratio	6.7
Length overall	7.30 m (23 ft 11½ in)
Height overall	2.84 m (9 ft 3¾ in)
Tailplane span	3.00 m (9 ft 10 in)
Wheel track	2.90 m (9 ft 6¼ in)
Wheelbase	1.86 m (6 ft 1¼ in)
Propeller diameter	1.78 m (5 ft 10 in)

AREAS:

Wings, gross	10.82 m² (116.25 sq ft)
Fin	0.738 m² (7.94 sq ft)
Rudder	0.505 m² (5.44 sq ft)
Tailplane	1.24 m² (13.35 sq ft)
Elevator, incl tab	1.02 m² (10.98 sq ft)

WEIGHTS AND LOADINGS (A: 116 hp, B: 160 hp):

Weight empty, equipped: A	520 kg (1,146 lb)
B	550 kg (1,212 lb)
Max T-O weight:	
Aerobatic: A	750 kg (1,653 lb)
B	800 kg (1,763 lb)
Utility: A, B	800 kg (1,764 lb)
Max wing loading:	
Aerobatic: A	69.32 kg/m² (14.20 lb/sq ft)
Utility: A, B	73.94 kg/m² (15.14 lb/sq ft)
Max power loading:	
Aerobatic: A	8.67 kg/kW (14.25 lb/hp)
B	6.3 kg/kW (10.33 lb/hp)
Utility: A	9.25 kg/kW (15.21 lb/hp)
B	6.71 kg/kW (11.02 lb/hp)

PERFORMANCE (86.5 kW; 116 hp engine):

Max level speed at S/L	129 knots (240 km/h; 149 mph)

First General Avia F.22 Pinguino

Cruising speed at 1,830 m (6,000 ft)	
	119 knots (220 km/h; 137 mph)
Stalling speed, flaps down	49 knots (90 km/h; 56 mph)
Max rate of climb at S/L	258 m (845 ft)/min
Service ceiling	4,270 m (14,000 ft)
T-O run	240 m (790 ft)
Landing run	160 m (525 ft)
Max range, no reserves	539 nm (1,000 km; 621 miles)

GENERAL AVIA F.22/R PINGUINO-SPRINT

The F.22/R is a more powerful version of the Pinguino with retractable landing gear, the first (I-GEAE) making its first flight on 16 November 1990. Certification was expected in September 1991. Details are as for the F.22 except for the following:

TYPE: Two-seat club aircraft.
LANDING GEAR: Retractable tricycle type. Mainwheels retract inwards and nosewheel rearwards.
POWER PLANT: One 119 kW (160 hp) Textron Lycoming O-320-D2A flat-four engine. Optional 149 kW (200 hp) Textron Lycoming O-360-A.

DIMENSIONS, EXTERNAL:

Length overall	7.30 m (23 ft 11½ in)

General Avia F.22/R Pinguino-Sprint making first take-off at Orio al Serio, Bergamo

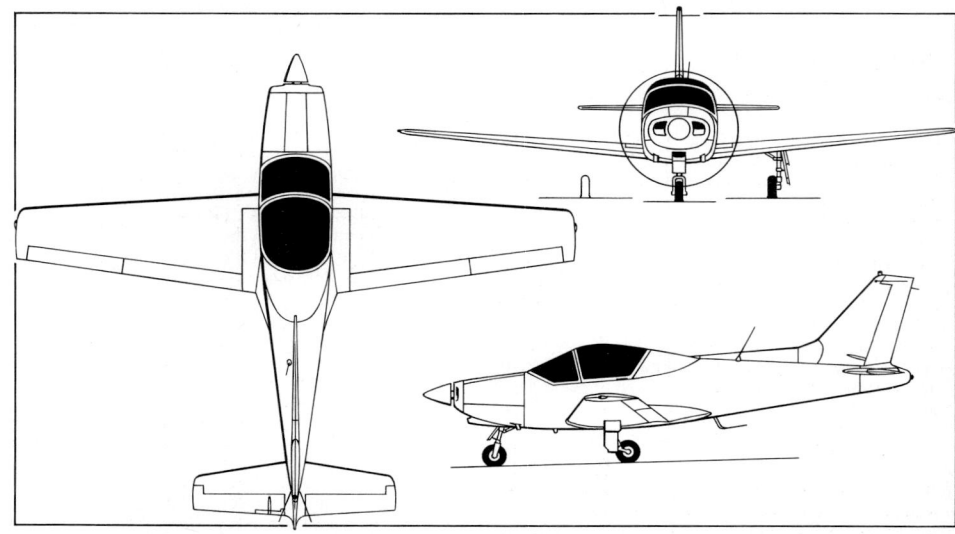

General Avia F.22/R Pinguino-Sprint *(Jane's/Mike Keep)*

WEIGHTS AND LOADINGS (A: 160 hp, B: 200 hp):

Weight empty, incl radio: A		560 kg (1,235 lb)
B		620 kg (1,367 lb)
Max T-O weight:		
Aerobatic: A and B		800 kg (1,764 lb)
Utility: A and B		900 kg (1,984 lb)
Max wing loading:		
Aerobatic: A and B		73.94 kg/m² (15.14 lb/sq ft)
Utility: A and B		83.18 kg/m² (17.04 lb/sq ft)
Max power loading:		
Aerobatic: A		6.71 kg/kW (11.02 lb/hp)

B		5.37 kg/kW (8.82 lb/hp)
Utility: A		7.55 kg/kW (12.40 lb/hp)
B		6.04 kg/kW (9.92 lb/hp)

PERFORMANCE (A: 160 hp, B: 200 hp):

Max level speed at S/L:		
A		165 knots (305 km/h; 190 mph)
B		183 knots (340 km/h; 211 mph)
Cruising speed at 2,440 m (8,000 ft):		
A		146 knots (270 km/h; 168 mph)
B		167 knots (310 km/h; 193 mph)
Stalling speed: A		51 knots (94 km/h; 59 mph)

B		53 knots (98 km/h; 61 mph)
Max rate of climb at S/L: A		390 m (1,280 ft)/min
B		480 m (1,575 ft)/min
Service ceiling: A		5,500 m (18,050 ft)
B		6,200 m (20,350 ft)
T-O run: A		220 m (722 ft)
B		220 m (722 ft)
Landing run: A		170 m (558 ft)
B		200 m (656 ft)
Max range: A		647 nm (1,200 km; 745 miles)
B		809 nm (1,500 km; 932 miles)

PARTENAVIA

PARTENAVIA COSTRUZIONI AERONAUTICHE SpA

Via Giovanni Pascoli 7, 80026 Casoria (Naples)
Telephone: 39 (81) 5502111
Telex: 720199 PARTNA I
PRESIDENT: Gen Fulvio Ristori
GENERAL MANAGER AND EXECUTIVE DIRECTOR:
 Ing Carlo Rosini
TECHNICAL MANAGER: Ing C. A. D'Amato
PRESS RELATIONS: Mrs F. Ridolfi

This company was founded in 1957 and has since built a series of light aircraft designed by its founder, Prof Ing Luigi Pascale. It came under the control of Aeritalia in July 1981 and is now largely owned by Alenia.

Since 1974 Partenavia has occupied a 12,000 m² (129,165 sq ft) facility on Capodichino Airport, Naples, where it is concentrating on production of the P.68C and P.68C-TC twin-engined seven-seat light aircraft, a derivative known as the Observer, and the turboprop powered Viator. All three are being produced to special order. Development and support of its single-engined designs is now the responsibility of Aviolight (which see).

PARTENAVIA P.68

The original P.68, designed by Prof Ing Luigi Pascale in 1968, was described in the 1975-76 *Jane's*. From it was developed the P.68B Victor twin-engined light transport, which entered production in the Spring of 1974. Details of the P.68B, P.68C-R, P.68 floatplane/amphibian and P.68R can be found in the 1980-81 and earlier editions of *Jane's*.

The following versions are available to special order:

P.68C: Improved P.68B with lengthened nose, increased fuel capacity and several internal changes. Detailed description applies primarily to this version (also known formerly as the Victor), which superseded the P.68B in late 1979.

P.68C-TC: Similar to P.68C, but powered by Textron Lycoming TIO-360-A1C6D turbocharged engines with fuel injection. Certificated in June 1980. Available as landplane or with twin amphibious floats. (Latter version first flown from land and water on 26 and 27 June 1985 respectively.)

P.68 Observer: Special observation version, with wide-visibility nose originally produced in Germany by Sportavia-Pützer. **Observer 2** carries 100 litres (26.4 US gallons; 22 Imp gallons) extra fuel in wings and optional Aerospatiale ATAL TV pod in nose. Details in the 1990-91 edition of *Jane's*.

By the beginning of 1990 Partenavia had delivered approx 400 aircraft of the P.68 series, most of them for export to operators in more than 20 countries.

TYPE: Six/seven-seat light transport and trainer.

WINGS: Cantilever high-wing monoplane. Wing section NACA 63-3₁515. Dihedral 1°. Incidence 1° 30'. No sweepback. Stressed skin two-spar torsion box structure of aluminium alloy. All-metal ailerons and electrically operated single-slotted trailing-edge flaps. Hoerner GFRP wingtips. No tabs.

FUSELAGE: Conventional all-metal semi-monocoque structure of frames and longerons, with four main longerons and stressed skin covering. Fuselage/wing intersection mainly of GFRP.

TAIL UNIT: Cantilever stressed skin metal structure. All-moving tailplane, in two symmetrical halves joined by steel cross-tube and of constant chord except for strake at leading-edge roots. Balance/trim tab in tailplane trailing-edge, over 80 per cent of span. Sweptback fin and rudder, with small dorsal fin. Trim tab in rudder.

LANDING GEAR: Non-retractable tricycle type, with steerable nosewheel. Cantilever spring steel main legs. Oleo-pneumatic shock absorber on nosewheel. Cleveland mainwheels, type 40-96, with Pirelli eight-ply tyres size 6.00-6. Goodyear six-ply nosewheel tyre, size 5.00-5. Cleveland type 30-61 hydraulic disc brakes. Parking brake. Streamline wheel fairings standard. C-TC version available optionally with De Vore PK twin-float gear having retractable ground wheels.

POWER PLANT (P.68C): Two 149 kW (200 hp) Textron Lycoming IO-360-A1B6 flat-four engines, each driving a Hartzell HC-C2YK-2C/C-7666A-4 two-blade constant-speed fully feathering propeller. Integral fuel tank in each wing, total capacity 538 litres (142 US gallons; 118 Imp gallons), of which 520 litres (137 US gallons; 114 Imp gallons) are usable. Refuelling point above each wing. Oil capacity 15 litres (4 US gallons; 3.3 Imp gallons).

ACCOMMODATION: Seating for seven persons in cabin, including pilot, in two rows of two seats and a rear bench seat for three persons. A club seating arrangement is available optionally, having the two middle seats facing rearward with a folding table between them and the bench seat. Front seats are of the adjustable sliding type. Access to all seats via large forward opening car type door on port side at front of cabin. Up to 181 kg (400 lb) of baggage can be carried in compartment aft of rear bench seat. Access to baggage compartment from inside cabin, or via large forward hinged door on starboard side at rear, which serves also as emergency exit. Two stretchers or other loads can be carried when all passenger seats are removed. Dual controls, cabin heating, ventilation and soundproofing standard.

SYSTEMS: Electrical power supplied by two 24V 70A alternators and a 24V 17Ah battery. Hydraulic system for brakes only. Goodrich pneumatic de-icing system optional.

AVIONICS (P.68C): Wide range of Collins Micro Line or Bendix/King Silver Crown avionics, and Edo-Aire Mitchell Century III autopilot, to customer's requirements. Provision for SunAir ASB 100 HF radio.

EQUIPMENT: Optional equipment includes Janitrol 45,000 BTU combustion heater, wing and tail pneumatic de-icing system, electrothermal propeller de-icing system, 0.46 × 0.58 m (18 × 23 in) floor panel for photogrammetric camera, including periscope sight hatch, second airspeed indicator, second gyro horizon, chronometer, second altimeter, pilot's and co-pilot's vertically adjustable seats, alcohol windscreen de-icing, heated stall warning indicator, all-leather interior, forced ventilation blower, ice light and second oil cooler.

DIMENSIONS, EXTERNAL:

Wing span	12.00 m (39 ft 4½ in)
Wing chord, constant	1.55 m (5 ft 1 in)
Wing aspect ratio	7.7
Length overall	9.55 m (31 ft 4 in)
Height overall	3.40 m (11 ft 1¾ in)
Tailplane span	3.90 m (12 ft 9½ in)
Wheel track	2.40 m (7 ft 10½ in)
Wheelbase	3.50 m (11 ft 5¾ in)
Propeller diameter	1.88 m (6 ft 2 in)
Distance between propeller centres	4.10 m (13 ft 5½ in)
Baggage door, stbd: Height	0.80 m (2 ft 7½ in)
Width	0.80 m (2 ft 7½ in)

DIMENSIONS, INTERNAL:

Cabin: Length	3.58 m (11 ft 9 in)
Max width	1.16 m (3 ft 9½ in)
Max height	1.20 m (3 ft 11¼ in)
Baggage space	0.56 m³ (20 cu ft)

AREAS:

Wings, gross	18.60 m² (200.2 sq ft)
Ailerons (total)	1.79 m² (19.27 sq ft)
Trailing-edge flaps (total)	2.37 m² (25.51 sq ft)
Fin	1.59 m² (17.11 sq ft)
Rudder, incl tab	0.44 m² (4.74 sq ft)
Tailplane, incl tab	4.41 m² (47.47 sq ft)

WEIGHTS AND LOADINGS:

Weight empty: C	1230 kg (2,711 lb)
C-TC	1,300 kg (2,866 lb)
*Max T-O weight: C, C-TC	1,990 kg (4,387 lb)
Max landing weight: C, C-TC	1,890 kg (4,166 lb)
Max wing loading: C, C-TC	107 kg/m² (21.9 lb/sq ft)
Max power loading: C	6.68 kg/kW (10.97 lb/hp)
C-TC	6.36 kg/kW (10.45 lb/hp)

C-TC amphibian 317 kg (700 lb) heavier

Partenavia P.68C-TC six/seven-seat light aircraft *(Avio Data)*

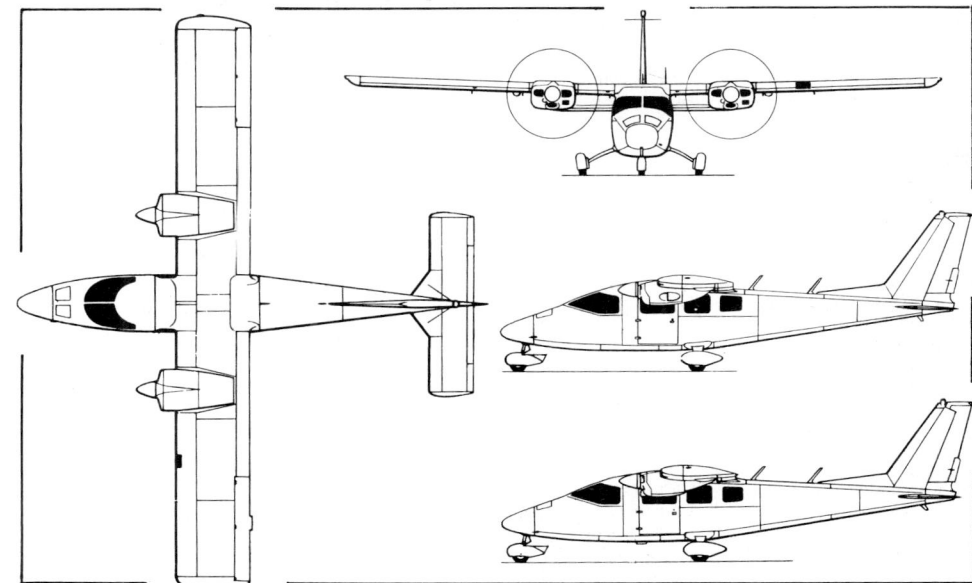

Partenavia P.68C, with additional side view (centre) of P.68C-TC *(Pilot Press)*

PERFORMANCE (at max T-O weight):
Max level speed:
C at S/L 174 knots (322 km/h; 200 mph)
C-TC at 5,335 m (17,500 ft)
  195 knots (361 km/h; 224 mph)
Max cruising speed (75% power):
C at 2,290 m (7,500 ft)
  166 knots (307 km/h; 191 mph)
C-TC at 6,100 m (20,000 ft)
  183 knots (339 km/h; 211 mph)
C-TC at 3,660 m (12,000 ft)
  172 knots (318 km/h; 198 mph)
Cruising speed (65% power):
C at 3,350 m (11,000 ft)
  161 knots (298 km/h; 185 mph)
C-TC at 3,050 m (10,000 ft)
  158 knots (293 km/h; 182 mph)
Cruising speed (55% power):
C at 3,660 m (12,000 ft)
  150 knots (278 km/h; 173 mph)
C-TC at 3,050 m (10,000 ft)
  147 knots (272 km/h; 169 mph)
Stalling speed, flaps up:
C, C-TC 65 knots (120 km/h; 75 mph)
Stalling speed, flaps down:
C, C-TC 58 knots (106 km/h; 66 mph)
Max rate of climb at S/L: C 457 m (1,500 ft)/min
C-TC 472 m (1,550 ft)/min
Rate of climb at S/L, one engine out:
C 82 m (270 ft)/min
C-TC 88 m (290 ft)/min
Service ceiling: C 5,850 m (19,200 ft)
C-TC 7,620 m (25,000 ft)
Service ceiling, one engine out: C 2,100 m (6,900 ft)
C-TC 4,420 m (14,500 ft)
T-O run: C, C-TC 230 m (755 ft)
T-O to 15 m (50 ft): C 396 m (1,300 ft)
C-TC 385 m (1,263 ft)
Landing from 15 m (50 ft): C, C-TC 488 m (1,600 ft)
Landing run: C, C-TC 215 m (705 ft)
Accelerate/stop distance: C 473 m (1,550 ft)
C-TC 510 m (1,673 ft)
Optimum cruising range (C), 45 min reserves:
75% power at 2,290 m (7,500 ft)
  1,050 nm (1,945 km; 1,209 miles)
65% power at 3,350 m (11,000 ft)
  1,140 nm (2,112 km; 1,312 miles)
55% power at 3,660 m (12,000 ft)
  1,210 nm (2,242 km; 1,393 miles)
Optimum cruising range (C-TC) at 3,660 m (12,000 ft), 45
min reserves:
75% power 775 nm (1,436 km; 892 miles)
65% power 940 nm (1,742 km; 1,082 miles)
55% power 1,020 nm (1,890 km; 1,175 miles)
Range with max fuel (C-TC):
65% power at 6,400 m (21,000 ft)
  1,100 nm (2,037 km; 1,266 miles)

PARTENAVIA AP.68TP-600 VIATOR (WAYFARER)

The first retractable landing gear version of the Spartacus (I-RAIZ, c/n 6) made its initial flight in early July 1984. It was followed on 29 March 1985 by a prototype of the Viator (I-RAIL, previously known as the Spartacus 10), which has a longer fuselage than the fixed-gear AP.68TP-300, seating two additional passengers.

Like its piston-engined variants, Viator is being produced to special order.

The description applies to the Viator in early production form, unless stated otherwise:

TYPE: Twin-turboprop general purpose transport.

WINGS: As described for P.68C Victor. Trim tab in starboard aileron. Goodrich pneumatic boot de-icing of leading-edges optional.

FUSELAGE: Similar to P.68C, but slightly longer.

TAIL UNIT: Vertical surfaces similar to P.68C, but of increased chord. Fixed incidence tailplane with separate elevators; geared tab in port elevator. Pneumatic boot de-icing of leading-edges.

LANDING GEAR: Retractable tricycle type, with electrically controlled hydraulic actuation. Oleo-pneumatic shock absorber in each unit. Nosewheel retracts forward, mainwheels inward into fuselage fairing. Cleveland wheels, sizes 40-77B (nose) and 40-163EA (main), with McCreary 8-ply tyres, sizes 6.50-8 (main) and 6.00-6 (nose). Mainwheel tyre pressure 4.83 bars (70 lb/sq in). Cleveland disc brakes. No anti-skid units.

POWER PLANT: Two Allison 250-B17C turboprops, each flat rated at 244.5 kW (328 shp) for T-O and max continuous operation. Hartzell HC-B3TF-7A/T10173B-21R three-blade constant-speed fully feathering reversible-pitch metal propellers with spinners. Fuel in two 380 litre (100.4 US gallon; 83.6 Imp gallon) tanks in wings and a 40 litre (10.6 US gallon; 8.8 Imp gallon) tank in each engine nacelle. Total capacity 840 litres (222 US gallons; 185 Imp gallons). Two 100 litre (26.4 US gallon; 22 Imp gallon) underwing tanks optional. Refuelling point at each wingtip. Oil capacity 11.4 litres (3.0 US gallons; 2.5 Imp gallons) per engine.

ACCOMMODATION: Standard club seating for pilot and nine passengers, in five rows of two seats (second and fourth

Partenavia Viator (two Allison 250-B17C turboprops)

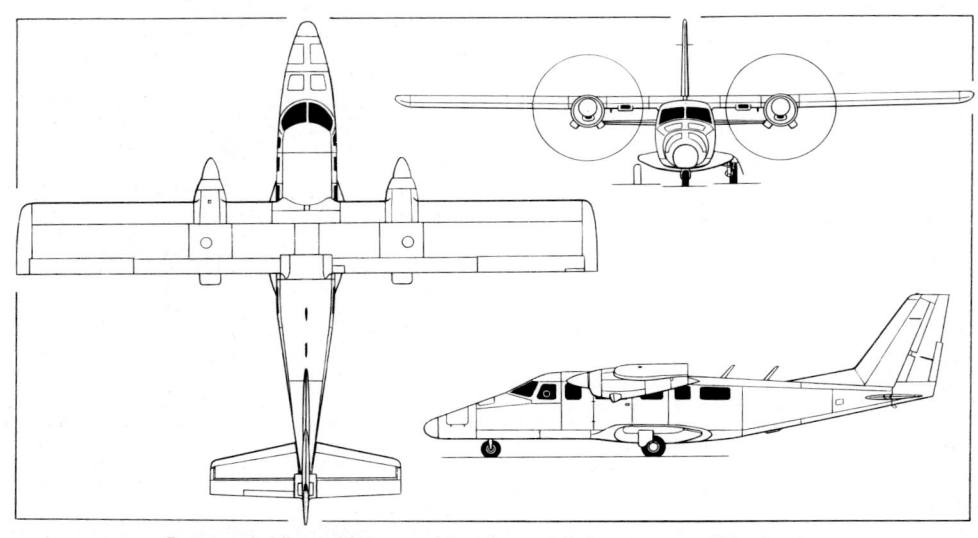

Partenavia Viator 10-seat twin-turboprop light transport *(Pilot Press)*

Partenavia P.68 Observer 2 featuring upturned wingtips to improve low-speed handling characteristics

rows rearward facing). Forward opening door on starboard side of flight deck, and for second/third row passengers on port side at centre of cabin. (Latest examples also have port side flight deck door.) Double door (starboard, rear) provides access for rear seat passengers, and to 181 kg (400 lb) capacity baggage compartment aft of rear seats, and serves also as an emergency exit. With all passenger seats removed and special kits installed, up to 12 parachutists, or two stretcher patients plus two medical attendants, can be carried in cabin. Dual controls, and cabin heating, ventilation and soundproofing, are standard. Hot air for cabin heating and windscreen de-icing is provided by heat exchangers installed on both turbine cases.

SYSTEMS: Primary electrical power supplied by two 150A 28V DC starter/generators and two voltage regulators. In the event of primary electrical failure, power is supplied

by a 24V 29Ah lead-acid battery (self-sufficient for engine starting), and an inverter for 115/26V AC power. Electric de-icing of engine air intakes, propellers, pitot and stall detector; and pneumatic boot de-icing of wing leading-edges, are standard. Oxygen system optional.

AVIONICS: Bendix/King Silver Crown IFR package standard. Typical installations include HF com, DME, weather radar (Honeywell or Bendix/King), autopilot, and Narco ELT.

DIMENSIONS, EXTERNAL:
Wing span 12.00 m (39 ft 4½ in)
Wing chord, constant 1.55 m (5 ft 1 in)
Wing aspect ratio 7.7
Length overall 10.85 m (35 ft 7¼ in)
Fuselage: Length 9.66 m (31 ft 8¼ in)
Max width 1.20 m (3 ft 11¼ in)
Height overall 3.64 m (11 ft 11¼ in)

Tailplane span	4.01 m (13 ft 2 in)
Wheel track	2.167 m (7 ft 1¼ in)
Wheelbase	3.51 m (11 ft 6¼ in)
Propeller diameter	2.03 m (6 ft 8 in)
Propeller ground clearance	0.725 m (2 ft 4½ in)
Distance between propeller centres	
	4.03 m (13 ft 2¾ in)
Passenger door (port): Height	1.03 m (3 ft 4½ in)
Width	0.80 m (2 ft 7½ in)
Height to sill	0.79 m (2 ft 7 in)
Passenger/emergency door (stbd):	
Height (mean)	0.91 m (2 ft 11½ in)
Width	1.10 m (3 ft 7¼ in)
Height to sill	0.79 m (2 ft 7 in)

DIMENSIONS, INTERNAL:
Cabin, excl flight deck and baggage compartment:

Length	3.60 m (11 ft 9¾ in)
Max width	1.12 m (3 ft 8 in)
Max height	1.20 m (3 ft 11¼ in)
Floor area	4.00 m² (43.06 sq ft)
Volume	4.70 m³ (165.98 cu ft)
Baggage compartment volume	0.65 m³ (22.95 cu ft)

AREAS:

Wings, gross	18.60 m² (200.2 sq ft)
Ailerons (total)	1.76 m² (18.94 sq ft)
Trailing-edge flaps (total)	2.42 m² (26.05 sq ft)
Fin	2.90 m² (31.22 sq ft)
Rudder, incl tab	1.64 m² (17.65 sq ft)
Tailplane	3.76 m² (40.47 sq ft)
Elevators (total)	1.30 m² (13.99 sq ft)

WEIGHTS AND LOADINGS:

Basic weight empty	1,640 kg (3,615 lb)
Max fuel load (usable)	680 kg (1,499 lb)
Max payload	910 kg (2,006 lb)
Max T-O and landing weight	2,850 kg (6,283 lb)
Max ramp weight	2,875 kg (6,338 lb)
Max zero-fuel weight	2,550 kg (5,622 lb)
Max wing loading	153.23 kg/m² (31.38 lb/sq ft)
Max power loading	5.83 kg/kW (9.58 lb/shp)

PERFORMANCE (at max T-O weight):
Max operating speed
200 knots (370 km/h; 230 mph) IAS
Max level and max cruising speed at 3,660 m (12,000 ft)
220 knots (408 km/h; 253 mph)

Econ cruising speed at 3,660 m (12,000 ft)	
	170 knots (315 km/h; 196 mph)
Stalling speed, power off:	
flaps up	81 knots (151 km/h; 94 mph)
flaps down	70 knots (130 km/h; 81 mph)
Max rate of climb at S/L	589 m (1,932 ft)/min
Rate of climb at S/L, one engine out	131 m (430 ft)/min
Max operating altitude	7,620 m (25,000 ft)
Service ceiling, one engine out	3,355 m (11,000 ft)
T-O run	275 m (900 ft)
T-O to 15 m (50 ft)	460 m (1,510 ft)
Landing from 15 m (50 ft)	500 m (1,640 ft)
Landing run	250 m (820 ft)
Min ground turning radius	10.36 m (34 ft 0 in)

Range at long-range power, allowances for start, taxi, take-off, descent, and 45 min reserves:

with max payload	445 nm (824 km; 512 miles)
with max fuel	860 nm (1,594 km; 990 miles)

PIAGGIO

INDUSTRIE AERONAUTICHE E MECCANICHE RINALDO PIAGGIO SpA

Via Cibrario 4, 16154 Genova Sestri, Genoa
Telephone: 39 (10) 60041
Fax: 39 (10) 603378
Telex: 270695 AERPIA I
WORKS: Genova Sestri, Finale Ligure (SV), and Wichita, Kansas, USA
BRANCH OFFICE: Via A. Gramsci 34, 00197 Rome
CHAIRMAN AND MANAGING DIRECTOR:
    Dott Rinaldo Piaggio
GENERAL MANAGER: Dott Ing Giulio C. Valdonio
DIRECTOR OF INTERNATIONAL PROGRAMMES:
    Dott Ing Bruno Mori
DIRECTOR, AIRCRAFT DIVISION: Dott Ing Piero Selvaggi
DIRECTOR, ENGINES/SHELTERS DIVISION:
    Dott Ing Roberto Vianson
DIRECTOR, COMMERCIAL: Commander G. B. Pizzinato

The original Piaggio company began the construction of aeroplanes in its Genova Sestri plant in 1916, and later in the Finale Ligure works. The present company was formed on 29 February 1964, and has since operated as an independent concern. It employs about 2,000 people in three production divisions and in Italy has a total covered works area (Genova Sestri and Finale Ligure) of approx 120,000 m² (1,291,670 sq ft). In the USA, Piaggio Aviation Inc at Wichita, Kansas, was founded by Piaggio on 9 September 1987 with head office in Dover, Delaware. The Wichita factory of approximately 10,000 m² (107,640 sq ft) is producing Avanti fuselages. The association with Duncan Aviation is detailed below. In addition to aircraft of its own design, Piaggio is producing components for the Alenia G222, Panavia Tornado and AMX. Aeritalia, now Alenia (which see), acquired a 31 per cent holding in Piaggio in 1988.

The activities of the Aero-Engine Division are described in the appropriate section of this edition.

PIAGGIO P.180 AVANTI

Active development of this new corporate aircraft was started by Piaggio in 1982. Gates Learjet became a partner in 1983, but withdrew for economic reasons on 13 January 1986. All of Gates' P.180 tooling, together with the forward fuselages of the first three development aircraft (two flying prototypes and one for static tests), were transferred to Piaggio.

Construction began in late 1984, and the first Avanti (I-PJAV) made its first flight on 23 September 1986. The second aircraft (I-PJAR) first flew on 14 May 1987. RAI type certification was awarded on 7 March 1990. Piaggio is building two initial production batches of 12 and 18 aircraft, and a third batch of 24 has been launched.

The first P.180 to the full production standard made its first flight on 30 May 1990 and received concurrent RAI and FAA certification on 2 October 1990, two days before being delivered to its US customer, Robert J. Bond. Production from Genoa was at one a month during 1991, expecting to reach two a month in 1992. First European delivery, to a German customer, was expected in June 1991. AMR, the parent organisation of American Airlines, has been marketing the P.180 in the USA.

At its initial max T-O weight of 4,903 kg (10,810 lb), the P.180 could carry three passengers with full fuel. Piaggio decided to increase max T-O weight and these are the figures listed in the weights and performance section of this entry. The structural reinforcement needed to allow the new higher weights are to be retrofitted to earlier aircraft.

Duncan Aviation of New Orleans, USA (which was contracted to fit interiors to the first 11 P.180s sold in North America), formed Duncan Piaggio Aircraft with Piaggio in October 1990 to assemble as well as furnish the aircraft using fuselages from Piaggio Aviation Inc, Wichita, Kansas, wings from Italy, and tails made by Sikorsky and

Piaggio P.180 Avanti in production form

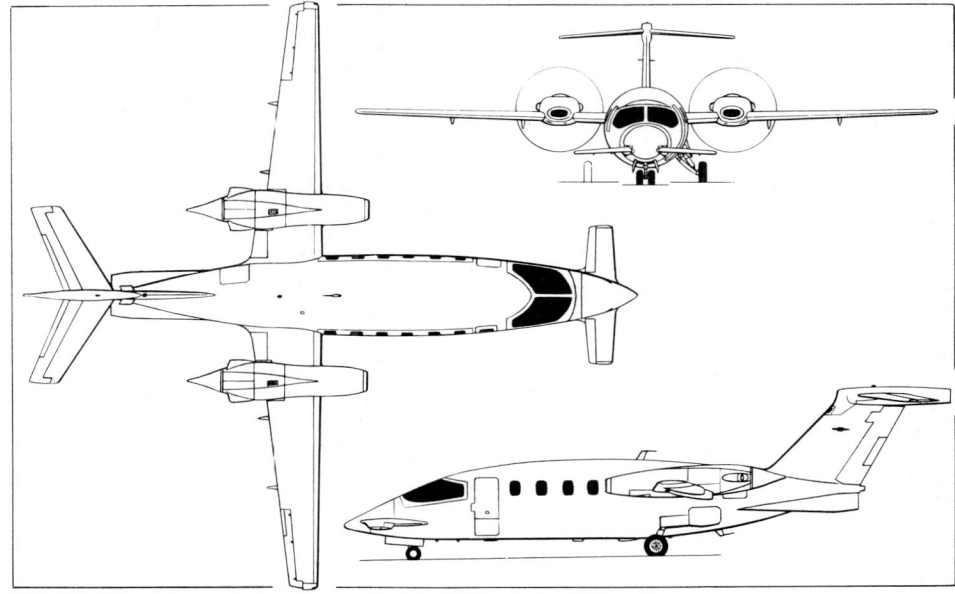

Piaggio P.180 Avanti corporate transport, production configuration *(Pilot Press)*

Edo. The Duncan assembly line will come on stream in 1992.

Major design features are a three surface concept, to reduce cruise drag and fuel consumption, and placement of the engines aft of the rear pressure bulkhead to minimise engine noise levels in the cabin. Primary lifting surface is the main wing, which is situated just above the mid position (to avoid drag-inducing bulges in the circular-section fuselage) and, by virtue of the pusher engine installation, has no propeller induced vortices impinging on the leading-edge. The second lifting surface is the horizontal T tailplane and elevators, which provide orthodox control from a conventional location. The third is the foreplane, which contributes lift to avoid the usual download at the tail and consequent trim drag. Both wing and engines are behind the cabin, which not only reduces noise, but allows full stand-up headroom. The cabin is pressurised to allow sustained cruise at 12,500 m (41,000 ft). In assembly, fuselage skins are stretch-formed in unusually large panels to minimise seams, maintaining precise contour tolerances to ten one-thousandths of an inch. Structural members are then shaped to conform exactly to the skin, rather than the conventional reverse.

While most of the Avanti is of conventional metal

construction, the nosecone, tailcone, tail unit, engine nacelles, foreplanes, wing outboard flaps and landing gear doors are built of composite materials: graphite/epoxy (carbonfibre) in areas of high stress and glassfibre or Kevlar/epoxy elsewhere. These parts of the airframe—48 components in all, representing about 18 per cent of the aircraft's operating weight empty—are manufactured under subcontract (main parts by Sikorsky Aircraft and Edo). The wings and rear fuselage sections are Italian built; front fuselage sections are constructed in the USA.

TYPE: Twin-turboprop corporate transport.

WINGS: Cantilever non-swept mid-wing monoplane, tapered on leading- and trailing-edges. Piaggio PE 1491 G (modified) section at root, PE 1332 G section at tip; thickness/chord ratio 13 per cent. Dihedral 2° from roots. Incidence 0°. Sweep 0° at 15 per cent chord. Integrally machined skins and spars of aluminium alloy; main spar forms an integral fail-safe structural unit with rear pressure bulkhead and main landing gear. Trailing-edge flaps (outboard of engine nacelles) are made in composites. Flaps are actuated electrically, as is trim tab in starboard aileron. Hot air anti-icing of outboard leading-edges.

All-composite fail-safe fixed incidence (+3°) foreplane at tip of nose, with 5° anhedral, fitted with electrically actuated all-composite single-slotted auxiliary trailing-edge flaps. Piaggio PE 1300 GN4 aerofoil section, thickness/chord ratio 13 per cent, and 0° sweep at 50 per cent chord. Electric anti-icing of leading-edges. Auxiliary flaps do not control the aircraft in pitch, but are coupled with the main wing flaps and deflect with them to offset changes in trim.

FUSELAGE: Circular-section pressurised fail-safe structure of mainly metal construction (machined aluminium alloy), with rear pressure bulkhead in line with wing main spar. Nosecone, tailcone, baggage door and landing gear doors are built of composite materials. Two composite ventral fins under tailcone.

TAIL UNIT: All-sweptback, all-composite T tail, with variable incidence, 5° anhedral tailplane and balanced elevators and rudder. Trim tab in rudder and each elevator. No tail unit anti-icing.

LANDING GEAR: Dowty Aerospace hydraulically retractable tricycle type, with single-wheel main units and steerable, twin-wheel nose unit. Main units retract rearward into sides of fuselage; nose unit retracts forward. Dowty hydraulic shock absorbers. Tyre sizes 6.50-10 (main) and 5.00-4 (nose). Multi-disc carbon brakes.

POWER PLANT: Two 1,107 kW (1,485 shp) Pratt & Whitney Canada PT6A-66 turboprops, flat rated at 634 kW (850 shp), each mounted above the wing in an all-composite nacelle and driving a counter-rotating Hartzell five-blade constant-speed fully feathering reversible-pitch pusher propeller. Propeller blades de-iced by engine exhaust. Fuel in two fuselage tanks totalling 680 litres (180 US gallons; 149.5 Imp gallons) and two 460 litre (121.5 US gallon; 101 Imp gallon) wing tanks; total fuel capacity 1,600 litres (423 US gallons; 352 Imp gallons). Optional single pressure refuelling point in lower centre-fuselage. Gravity refuelling point in upper part of fuselage.

ACCOMMODATION: Crew of one or two on flight deck; certificated for single pilot operation. Seating in main cabin for up to nine passengers, with galley, fully enclosed toilet and coat storage area. Club passenger seats are armchair type, which can be reclined, tracked and swivelled, and locked at any angle. Foldaway tables can be extended between facing club seats. Two-piece wraparound windscreen. Rectangular cabin windows, including one emergency exit at front on starboard side. Indirect lighting behind each window ring, plus individual overhead lights. Airstair door at front on port side. Baggage compartment aft of rear pressure bulkhead, with door immediately aft of wing on port side. Entire cabin area pressurised and air-conditioned.

SYSTEMS: AiResearch bleed air environmental control system, with max pressure differential of 0.62 bar (9.0 lb/sq in). Single hydraulic system driven by electric motor, with handpump for emergency backup, for landing gear extension only. Electrical system powered by two starter/generators and a 25V 38Ah nickel-cadmium battery; 0.62 m³ (22 cu ft) oxygen system. Hot air anti-icing of main wing outer leading-edges; electric anti-icing for foreplane and windscreen; rubber boot for engine intakes, with dynamic particle separator.

AVIONICS: Standard Collins EFIS (three CRTs), Collins VHF com/nav equipment, Collins WXR-840 weather radar, Collins dual transponder TDR-90, Collins single DME and ADF system, Collins radio altimeter, Collins primary and secondary compass systems, Aeronetics dual RMI, Collins APS-65A digital autopilot systems, JET dual vertical gyro, and Collins electronic air data system.

DIMENSIONS, EXTERNAL:

Wing span	14.03 m (46 ft 0½ in)
Foreplane span	3.38 m (11 ft 1 in)
Wing chord: at root	1.82 m (5 ft 11¾ in)
at tip	0.62 m (2 ft 0½ in)
Foreplane chord: at root	0.79 m (2 ft 7 in)
at tip	0.55 m (1 ft 9⅔ in)
Wing aspect ratio	12.30
Foreplane aspect ratio	5.05
Length overall	14.41 m (47 ft 3½ in)
Fuselage: Length	12.53 m (41 ft 1¼ in)
Max width	1.95 m (6 ft 4¾ in)
Height overall	3.94 m (12 ft 11 in)
Tailplane span	4.25 m (13 ft 11½ in)
Wheel track	2.84 m (9 ft 4 in)
Wheelbase	5.79 m (19 ft 0 in)
Propeller diameter	2.16 m (7 ft 1 in)
Propeller ground clearance	0.80 m (2 ft 7½ in)
Distance between propeller centres	4.13 m (13 ft 6½ in)
Passenger door (fwd, port): Height	1.35 m (4 ft 5 in)
Width	0.61 m (2 ft 0 in)
Height to sill	0.58 m (1 ft 10¾ in)
Baggage door (rear, port): Height	0.60 m (1 ft 11¾ in)
Width	0.70 m (2 ft 3½ in)
Height to sill	1.38 m (4 ft 6½ in)
Emergency exit (stbd): Height	0.67 m (2 ft 2¼ in)
Width	0.48 m (1 ft 7 in)

Piaggio P.166-DL3SEM used by the Italian Ministry of Merchant Marine

DIMENSIONS, INTERNAL:

Passenger cabin: Length	4.45 m (14 ft 7¼ in)
Max width	1.85 m (6 ft 0¾ in)
Max height	1.75 m (5 ft 9 in)
Volume	10.62 m³ (375.0 cu ft)
Baggage compartment: Floor length	1.70 m (2 ft 3½ in)
Max length	2.10 m (6 ft 10¾ in)
Volume	1.25 m³ (44.14 cu ft)

AREAS:

Wings, gross	16.00 m² (172.22 sq ft)
Ailerons (total, incl tab)	0.66 m² (7.10 sq ft)
Trailing-edge flaps (total)	1.60 m² (17.23 sq ft)
Foreplane	2.25 m² (24.22 sq ft)
Foreplane flaps (total)	0.58 m² (6.30 sq ft)
Fin	4.73 m² (50.91 sq ft)
Rudder, incl tab	1.05 m² (11.30 sq ft)
Tailplane	3.83 m² (41.23 sq ft)
Elevators (total, incl tabs)	1.24 m² (13.35 sq ft)

WEIGHTS AND LOADINGS:

Weight empty, equipped	3,384 kg (7,460 lb)
Operating weight empty, one pilot	3,461 kg (7,630 lb)
Max usable fuel load	1,193 kg (2,630 lb)
Max payload	848 kg (1,870 lb)
Payload with max fuel	440 kg (990 lb)
Max T-O weight	5,080 kg (11,200 lb)
Max ramp weight	5,103 kg (11,250 lb)
Max landing weight	4,805 kg (10,595 lb)
Max zero-fuel weight	4,309 kg (9,500 lb)
Max wing loading	317.5 kg/m² (65.03 lb/sq ft)
Max power loading	4.01 kg/kW (6.59 lb/shp)

PERFORMANCE:

Max operating Mach number 0.67

Max operating speed
260 knots (482 km/h; 299 mph) IAS

Max level speed at 8,625 m (28,300 ft)
395 knots (732 km/h; 455 mph)

Stalling speed at max landing weight:
flaps up 106 knots (197 km/h; 122 mph) IAS
flaps down 91 knots (169 km/h; 105 mph) IAS

Max rate of climb at S/L 875 m (2,870 ft)/min

Rate of climb at S/L, one engine out
247 m (810 ft)/min

Service ceiling 12,500 m (41,000 ft)

Service ceiling, one engine out 7,770 m (25,500 ft)

T-O to 15 m (50 ft) ISA, S/L at max T-O weight
864 m (2,835 ft)

Landing from 15 m (50 ft) ISA, S/L at max landing weight
831 m (2,726 ft)

Range at 11,890 m (39,000 ft):
IFR reserves 1,423 nm (2,637 km; 1,638 miles)
VFR reserves 1,720 nm (3,187 km; 1,980 miles)

PIAGGIO P.166-DL3SEM

The P.166 has been produced in several basic versions, of which the original piston engined P.166 was described in the 1963-64 *Jane's*; the P.166M, P.166B Portofino and P.166C in the 1971-72 *Jane's*; the P.166S in the 1974-75 *Jane's*; and the P.166-DL2 in the 1978-79 *Jane's*.

Current version is the turboprop powered P.166-DL3, which flew for the first time on 3 July 1976 and received FAA and RAI certification in 1978. It can be configured and equipped for a wide variety of duties, including executive transport (EXC); transport and dropping of up to 10 paratroops (PAR); air ambulance for two stretchers and two medical attendants (AMB); multi-engine aircrew training (MTR); light tactical transport (LTT); armed military counter-insurgency, field support, and search and rescue (AML); maritime reconnaissance (MAR); environmental control and geophysical survey (ECS); aerial photogrammetry (APH); and aerial firefighting (AFF). Piaggio completed a batch of 12 P.166-DL3SEM maritime and ecological patrol aircraft for the Italian Ministry of Merchant Marine in mid-1990. They are equipped for a variety of surveillance, reconnaissance and search and rescue duties. Another 10 in virtually the same configuration are being produced for the Italian Guardia di Finanza (Customs Service).

Full details were given in the 1990-91 *Jane's*. Salient points are:

POWER PLANT: Two Textron Lycoming LTP 101-700 turboprops, each flat rated at 447.5 kW (600 shp) and driving a Hartzell HC-B3DL/LT10282-9.5 three-blade constant-speed fully feathering metal pusher propeller. Fuel in two 212 litre (56 US gallon; 46.5 Imp gallon) outer-wing main tanks, two 323 litre (85.3 US gallon; 71 Imp gallon) wingtip tanks, and a 116 litre (30.6 US gallon; 25.5 Imp gallon) fuselage collector tank; total standard internal fuel capacity 1,186 litres (313.3 US gallons; 260.9 Imp gallons). Auxiliary fuel system available optionally, comprising a 232 litre (61.3 US gallon; 51 Imp gallon) fuselage tank, transfer pump and controls; with this installed, total usable fuel capacity is increased to 1,418 litres (374.6 US gallons; 312 Imp gallons). Gravity refuelling points in each main tank and tip tank. Provision for two 177 or 284 litre (46.8 or 75 US gallon; 39 or 62.5 Imp gallon) underwing drop tanks. Air intakes and propeller blades de-iced by engine exhaust.

ACCOMMODATION: Crew of two on raised flight deck, with dual controls. Aft of flight deck, accommodation consists of a passenger cabin, utility compartment and baggage compartment. Access to flight deck is via passenger/cargo double door on port side, forward of wing, or via individual crew door on each side of flight deck. External access to baggage compartment via port side door aft of wing. Passenger cabin extends from rear of flight deck to bulkhead at wing main spar; fitting of passenger carrying, cargo or other interiors is facilitated by two continuous rails on cabin floor, permitting considerable flexibility in standard or customised interior layouts. Standard seating for eight passengers, with individual lighting, ventilation and oxygen controls. Flight deck can be separated from passenger cabin by a screen. Door in bulkhead at rear of cabin provides access to utility compartment, in which can be fitted a toilet, bar, or mission equipment for various roles. Entire accommodation is heated, ventilated and soundproofed. Emergency exit forward of wing on starboard side. Windscreen hot-air demisting standard. Windscreen wipers, washers and methanol spray de-icing optional.

DIMENSIONS, EXTERNAL:

Wing span with tip tanks	14.69 m (48 ft 2½ in)
Length overall	11.88 m (39 ft 0 in)
Height overall	5.00 m (16 ft 5 in)
Cabin door: Height	1.38 m (4 ft 6 in)
Width	1.28 m (4 ft 2 in)

WEIGHTS AND LOADINGS:

Weight empty, equipped	2,688 kg (5,926 lb)
Max fuel	1,036 kg (2,284 lb)
Max payload	1,092 kg (2,407 lb)
Max T-O weight	4,300 kg (9,480 lb)
Max ramp weight	4,320 kg (9,524 lb)
Max zero-fuel weight	3,800 kg (8,377 lb)
Max landing weight	4,085 kg (9,006 lb)
Max wing loading	161.9 kg/m² (33.16 lb/sq ft)
Max power loading	4.81 kg/kW (7.90 lb/shp)

PERFORMANCE (at max T-O weight except where indicated):

Never-exceed speed (V_{NE})
220 knots (407 km/h; 253 mph) CAS

Max level and max cruising speed at 3,050 m (10,000 ft)
215 knots (400 km/h; 248 mph)

Range, VFR:
with max payload 750 nm (1,390 km; 863 miles)
with max fuel 1,150 nm (2,131 km; 1,324 miles)

TERZI

TERZI AERODIN

Via Cesare Battisti 15, 20122 Milan
Telephone: 39 (2) 5518 0268
Fax: 39 (2) 5518 0268

This company has specialised in the construction and repair of glassfibre sailplanes. The new Terzi T30 Katana specialised aerobatic aircraft is described in the Sport Aircraft section.

TERZI T-9 and T-9R STILETTO

Terzi Aerodin designed and made the T-9 Stiletto light aircraft, the prototype of which made its first flight in December 1990 powered by a 55.9 kW (75 hp) Limbach L2000 EBI with a wooden fixed-pitch Hoffmann propeller. The aircraft was being fitted with the Rotax engine noted below, which changes the designation to T-9R, and was expected to resume flight testing during July 1991.

Terzi delegated manufacture to Sivel of Padua in March 1991.

TYPE: Light sporting aircraft.

WINGS: Mid/low-set constant chord wing: Wortmann FX-67-K-150/17 wing section with symmetrical tips. Dihedral 2° 30′, incidence 0°, twist 0°. Metal structure (2024 light alloy) with main spar extending from tip to tip and auxiliary torsion spars spigoted to fuselage frame. Each semi-span has 17 ribs equally spaced at 275 mm (10¾ in). The metal skin panels are riveted. The main spar is simply jointed at the centreline so that the wings can be very easily removed.

FUSELAGE: Steel tube centre fuselage with composite skin. Stressed skin light alloy tailcone.

TAIL UNIT: All-metal structure: fin and rudder have NACA 64A-008 section; all-moving slab tailplane with Wortmann FX-71-L-150/20 section has trimmable anti-balance tab.

LANDING GEAR: Non-retractable tricycle type with cantilever legs mounted on fuselage frame. Hydraulic disc brakes

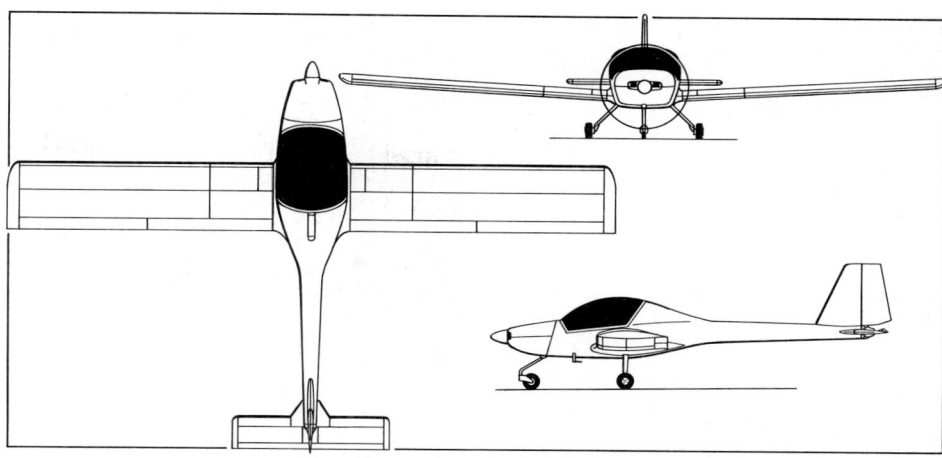

Terzi Aerodin T-9 Stiletto light aircraft *(Jane's/Mike Keep)*

controlled from the rudder pedals. Fully castoring nosewheel.

POWER PLANT: The prototype T-9 is powered by a Limbach L2000, but the definitive T-9R will have a 59 kW (79 hp) Rotax 912 flat-four driving an MT Elcoprop propeller. The 912 is certificated to JAR 22.

DIMENSIONS, EXTERNAL:

Wing span	10.26 m (33 ft 8 in)
Length overall	6.74 m (22 ft 1½ in)

AREAS:

Wings, gross	12.30 m² (132.4 sq ft)

WEIGHTS AND LOADINGS:

Weight empty	400 kg (882 lb)
Max T-O weight	620 kg (1,367 lb)
Max wing loading	50.41 kg/m² (10.32 lb/sq ft)
Max power loading: T-9	11.09 kg/kW (18.22 lb/hp)
T-9R	10.53 kg/kW (17.30 lb/hp)

PERFORMANCE:

Max level speed	108 knots (200 km/h; 124 mph)
Cruising speed at 60% power	87 knots (162 km/h; 100 mph)
Rate of climb	324 m (1,063 ft)/min
T-O run	150 m (492 ft)
T-O to 15 m (50 ft)	300 m (984 ft)
g limits	+3.8/−2.2

JAPAN

CAC

COMMERCIAL AIRPLANE COMPANY

Toranomon Daiichi Building, 2-3, Toranomon 1-chome, Minato-ku, Tokyo 105
Telephone: 81 (3) 3503 3221
Fax: 81 (3) 3508 2418
Telex: 222 2863

PRESIDENT: Masahiko Iwata

The CAC took over Japan's share in the manufacture of the Boeing 767 in July 1982, when the Civil Transport Development Corporation (CTDC) relinquished its 767 development activity following certification of the aircraft.

Kawasaki manufactures the forward main barrel section of the fuselage and the main wing ribs, Mitsubishi the rear main barrel section and Fuji the wingroot fairings. Japan Aircraft Manufacturing Company (Nippi) and Shin Meiwa are subcontractors.

FUJI

FUJI HEAVY INDUSTRIES LTD (Fuji Jukogyo Kabushiki Kaisha)

Subaru Building, 7-2 1-chome, Shinjuku-ku, Tokyo 160
Telephone: 81 (3) 3347 2525
Fax: 81 (3) 3347 2588
Telex: 0 232 2268 FUJI J
PRESIDENT: Toshihiro Tajima
UTSUNOMIYA MANUFACTURING DIVISION: 1-11, Yonan 1-chome, Utsunomiya, Tochigi 320
Telephone: 81 (286) 58 1111

Aircraft Division

GENERAL MANAGERS:
Yasumasa Honda (Managing Director)
Koichiro Shimmen (Commercial Business)
Satoshi Idei (Marketing and Sales, Defence Programmes)

Utsunomiya Manufacturing Division

GENERAL MANAGERS:
Akitoshi Nagao (Managing Director, and General Manager of Aircraft Plant)
Takeshi Makino (Director and General Manager, Aircraft Engineering Division)

Fuji Heavy Industries, established on 15 July 1953, is a successor to the Nakajima aircraft company, which was established in 1917 and built 25,935 aircraft up to the end of the Second World War.

The Utsunomiya Manufacturing Division (Aircraft and Rolling Stock Plants) occupies a site of 599,816 m² (6,456,359 sq ft) including a floor area of 188,490 m² (2,028,887 sq ft) and in April 1991 employed 2,940 people.

Details of Fuji production of the Cessna L-19E Bird Dog, Beechcraft Mentor, and several modified versions of the Mentor designated LM-1 Nikko, LM-2, KM, KM-2, KM-2B and TL-1, have appeared in previous editions of *Jane's*. The KM-2Kai, a turboprop version of the KM-2, is described in this entry.

Fuji is currently producing the Bell Model 205 and AH-1S HueyCobra helicopters, as described in this entry. It is building wing main assemblies for JMSDF Lockheed P-3C Orions (see Kawasaki entry); main landing gear doors and some titanium airframe parts for Japanese built McDonnell Douglas F-15J fighters (see Mitsubishi entry); and wings, tailplanes and canopies for the Kawasaki T-4 jet trainer (which see). Commercial aircraft components are produced for the Boeing 747 (spoilers, inboard and outboard ailerons), Boeing 757 (outboard trailing-edge flaps), Boeing 767 (wing/body fairings and main landing gear doors), McDonnell Douglas MD-11 (outboard ailerons) and Fokker 50 (rudder and elevators).

Fuji and Kawasaki are investigating the configuration of the National Aeronautical Laboratory medium-range fan-lift VTOL airliner (which see). Fuji is also involved in research on the Japanese SST and hypersonic transport and has an important composites department.

FUJI KM-2Kai

JMSDF designation: T-5

In 1984 Fuji refitted a company owned KM-2 with an Allison 250-B17D turboprop in place of the Textron Lycoming IGSO-480 piston engine. Designated KM-2D, it made its first flight on 28 June 1984, and was described in the 1988-89 *Jane's*. JCAB certification (Aerobatic and Utility categories) was gained on 14 February 1985.

In March 1987 Fuji received an initial JMSDF contract to replace the current fleet of 31 KM-2s with a further developed variant of the KM-2D, designated KM-2Kai, which has a sliding canopy and modernised cockpit. Visibility, payload and cockpit volume are all increased. First flight of a production KM-2Kai was made on 27 April 1988, and deliveries began on 30 August 1988 under the JMSDF designation T-5. Fifteen T-5s had been ordered by March 1991, of which eight had been delivered.

The following description applies to the T-5:

TYPE: Two/four-seat primary trainer.

WINGS: Cantilever low-wing monoplane. All-metal light alloy structure. Tapered, non-swept wings of NACA 23016.5 section at root, NACA 23012 at tip. Dihedral 6° from roots. Incidence 4° at root, 1° at tip. Plain ailerons and single-slotted flaps, of light alloy, on trailing-edges. Anti-servo tab in each aileron, port tab being controllable for trim.

FUSELAGE: Conventional light alloy semi-monocoque structure.

TAIL UNIT: Cantilever light alloy structure, with sweptback vertical and non-swept horizontal surfaces. Fixed incidence tailplane; balanced elevators and rudder. Controllable anti-servo tab in each elevator; anti-servo tab in rudder.

LANDING GEAR: Electrically retractable tricycle type, with emergency manual control. Oleo-pneumatic shock absorber in each unit. Main units retract inward into wings, nose unit rearward into fuselage. Single Parker wheel and Goodyear tyre on each main unit, size 6.50-8 (6 ply); Goodyear nosewheel and tyre, size 5.00-5 (4 ply). Nose unit is steerable ±16°. Parker single-disc hydraulic brakes.

POWER PLANT: One Allison 250-B17D turboprop, flat rated at 261 kW (350 shp), driving a Hartzell HC-B3TP-7A/T10173-18 three-blade constant-speed fully feathering propeller. Two bladder type fuel tanks in each wing, one of 94.6 litres (25 US gallons; 20.8 Imp gallons) capacity and one of 87 litres (23 US gallons; 19.2 Imp gallons); total capacity 363 litres (96 US gallons; 80 Imp gallons). Gravity refuelling point in top surface of each wing. Oil capacity 9.5 litres (2.5 US gallons; 2.1 Imp gallons).

ACCOMMODATION: Enclosed cabin seating two persons side by side, with dual controls (Aerobatic version), or four persons in pairs in Utility version. Rearward sliding canopy. Accommodation heated and ventilated.

SYSTEMS: Hydraulic system for brakes only. Electrical system includes a 30V 150A starter/generator, two 160VA static inverters, and a 24Ah battery for engine starting and emergency.

AVIONICS: Standard items include UHF and VHF radio, intercom, ADF, Tacan, SIF, and IFR training hood.

DIMENSIONS, EXTERNAL:

Wing span	10.04 m (32 ft 11¼ in)
Wing chord: at root	2.13 m (6 ft 11¾ in)
at tip	1.07 m (3 ft 6¼ in)
Wing aspect ratio	6.11
Length overall	8.44 m (27 ft 8¼ in)
Height overall	2.96 m (9 ft 8½ in)
Elevator span	3.71 m (12 ft 2 in)
Wheel track	2.92 m (9 ft 7 in)
Wheelbase	2.27 m (7 ft 5½ in)
Propeller diameter	2.12 m (6 ft 11½ in)
Propeller ground clearance	0.37 m (1 ft 2½ in)

DIMENSIONS, INTERNAL:

Cabin: Length	2.90 m (9 ft 6¼ in)
Max width	1.27 m (4 ft 2 in)
Max height	1.33 m (4 ft 4½ in)

AREAS:

Wings, gross	16.50 m² (177.6 sq ft)
Ailerons (total, incl tabs)	1.09 m² (11.73 sq ft)
Trailing-edge flaps (total)	1.98 m² (21.31 sq ft)
Fin, incl dorsal fin	1.28 m² (13.78 sq ft)

First production Fuji KM-2Kai (T-5) for the JMSDF

Rudder, incl tab	0.66 m² (7.10 sq ft)
Tailplane	3.46 m² (37.24 sq ft)
Elevators (total, incl tabs)	1.39 m² (14.96 sq ft)

WEIGHTS AND LOADINGS (A: Aerobatic, U: Utility):

Weight empty: A, U	1,082 kg (2,385 lb)
Max fuel weight: A, U	644 kg (1,420 lb)
Max T-O weight: A	1,585 kg (3.494 lb)
U	1,805 kg (3,979 lb)
Max wing loading: A	96.06 kg/m² (19.67 lb/sq ft)
U	109.39 kg/m² (22.40 lb/sq ft)
Max power loading: A	6.07 kg/kW (9.98 lb/shp)
U	6.92 kg/kW (11.37 lb/shp)

PERFORMANCE (at max Aerobatic T-O weight except where indicated):

Never-exceed speed (Vne)	
	223 knots (413 km/h; 256 mph) EAS
Max level speed at 2,440 m (8,000 ft)	
	193 knots (357 km/h; 222 mph)
Econ cruising speed at 2,440 m (8,000 ft)	
	155 knots (287 km/h; 178 mph)
Stalling speed, flaps and landing gear down, power off	
	56 knots (104 km/h; 65 mph)
Max rate of climb at S/L	518 m (1,700 ft)/min
Service ceiling	7,620 m (25,000 ft)
T-O run	302 m (990 ft)
T-O to 15 m (50 ft)	430 m (1,410 ft)
Landing from 15 m (50 ft)	515 m (1,690 ft)
Landing run	174 m (570 ft)
Min ground turning radius	7.38 m (24 ft 2½ in)
Range with max payload (Utility version), MIL-C-5011A reserves	510 nm (945 km; 587 miles)

FUJI-BELL UH-1H and ADVANCED MODEL 205A-1

Japanese designation: HU-1H

Fuji is manufacturing Bell UH-1H helicopters under sublicence from Mitsui and Co Ltd, Bell's Japanese licensee, following the completion of 34 commercial 204Bs between 1962 and 1973 and 20 of the higher powered Model 204B-2 (1989-90 and earlier *Jane's*) from 1974-87.

Following the delivery of 90 HU-1Bs (Japanese military version of the 204B) to the Japan Ground Self-Defence Force by early 1973, Fuji production continued with the UH-1H (military version of the Bell 205 and known in Japan as the HU-1H), of which the first example flew for the first time on 17 July 1973; 133 had been ordered for the JGSDF by March 1991. One HU-1H out of 13 planned for the FY 1991 budget is reported to have been cancelled to help pay for the Gulf War.

The Fuji-Bell HU-1H has the same airframe and dynamic components as the Bell built UH-1H but has a tractor tail rotor and Kawasaki built Textron Lycoming T53 engine. Fuji is now the sole producer of this helicopter, US production having ended.

The **Advanced Model 205A-1** was a joint Bell-Fuji upgrade of the Bell 205 with UH-1N/212-type tapered rotor blades, Textron Lycoming T53-L-703 engine, 212-type transmission rated at 962 kW (1,290 shp) and LIVE vibration absorber. A prototype (N19AL) first flew in

Texas on 23 April 1988, was demonstrated to the US Army during that year and in Japan, the Far East and Southeast Asia during 1989. None have yet been ordered by Japan.

The following details apply to the standard Fuji-Bell HU-1H:

TYPE: Single-engined general purpose helicopter.
ROTOR SYSTEM: Two-blade teetering main rotor. Interchangeable metal blades now being replaced by new composite blades. Stabilising bar above and at right angles to main rotor blades. Underslung feathering axis head. Two-blade all-metal tail rotor of honeycomb construction. Transmission rating 820 kW (1,100 shp). Main rotor rpm 294-324.
FUSELAGE: Conventional all-metal semi-monocoque structure.
TAIL UNIT: Small synchronised elevator on rear fuselage is connected to the cyclic control to increase allowable CG travel.
LANDING GEAR: Tubular skid type. Lock-on ground handling wheels and inflated nylon float bags available.
POWER PLANT: One 1,044 kW (1,400 shp) Kawasaki built Textron Lycoming T53-K-13B turboshaft, mounted aft of the transmission on top of the fuselage and enclosed in cowlings. Five interconnected rubber fuel cells, total capacity 844 litres (223 US gallons; 186 Imp gallons), of which 799 litres (211 US gallons; 176 Imp gallons) are usable. Overload fuel capacity of 1,935 litres (511 US gallons; 425 Imp gallons) usable, obtained by installation of kit comprising two 568 litre (150 US gallon; 125 Imp gallon) internal auxiliary fuel tanks interconnected with the basic fuel system.
ACCOMMODATION: Pilot and 11-14 troops, or six litters and a medical attendant, or 1,759 kg (3,880 lb) of freight. Crew

doors open forward and are jettisonable. Two doors on each side of cargo compartment; front door is hinged to open forward and is removable, rear door slides aft. Forced air ventilation system.
AVIONICS: FM, UHF, VHF radio, IFF transponder, Gyromatic compass system, direction finder set, VOR receiver and intercom standard.
EQUIPMENT: Standard equipment includes bleed air heater and defroster, comprehensive range of engine and flight instruments, power plant fire detection system, 30V 300A DC starter/generator, navigation, landing and anti-collision lights, controllable searchlight, hydraulically boosted controls. Optional equipment includes external cargo hook, auxiliary fuel tanks, rescue hoist, 150,000 BTU muff heater.

DIMENSIONS, EXTERNAL:

Main rotor diameter	14.63 m (48 ft 0 in)
Tail rotor diameter	2.59 m (8 ft 6 in)
Main rotor blade chord	0.53 m (1 ft 9 in)
Tail rotor blade chord	2.56 m (8 ft 4¾ in)
Length:	
overall (main rotor fore and aft)	17.62 m (57 ft 9⅝ in)
fuselage	12.77 m (41 ft 10¾ in)
Height:	
overall, tail rotor turning (excl fin tip antenna)	4.41 m (14 ft 5½ in)
to top of main rotor head	3.60 m (11 ft 9¾ in)
Tailplane span	2.84 m (9 ft 4 in)
Width over skids	2.91 m (9 ft 6½ in)

DIMENSIONS, INTERNAL:

Cabin: Max width	2.34 m (7 ft 8 in)
Max height	1.25 m (4 ft 1¼ in)
Volume (excl flight deck)	approx 6.23 m³ (220 cu ft)

AREAS:

Main rotor disc	168.11 m² (1,809.56 sq ft)
Tail rotor disc	5.27 m² (56.7 sq ft)

WEIGHTS AND LOADINGS:

Weight empty, equipped	2,390 kg (5,270 lb)
Max T-O and landing weight	4,309 kg (9,500 lb)
Max disc loading	25.63 kg/m² (5.25 lb/sq ft)
Max power loading	5.26 kg/kW (8.64 lb/shp)

PERFORMANCE (at max T-O weight):

Max level and max cruising speed	
	110 knots (204 km/h; 127 mph)
Max rate of climb at S/L	488 m (1,600 ft)/min
Service ceiling	3,840 m (12,600 ft)
Hovering ceiling: IGE	4,145 m (13,600 ft)
OGE	335 m (1,100 ft)
Range at S/L	252 nm (467 km; 290 miles)

FUJI-BELL AH-1S

In FY 1982 Fuji was selected as prime contractor for a licence manufacturing programme for Bell AH-1S HueyCobra anti-armour helicopters for the JGSDF; these correspond to the US Army AH-1F version. Kawasaki is delivering the T53-K-703 engines for these aircraft. The JGSDF had previously purchased two Bell built AH-1Es in 1977 and 1978, later upgraded to Fs, for operational evaluation.

The first Fuji built AH-1S made its initial flight on 2 July 1984. Original JGSDF plans were to purchase 88 AH-1S. These will equip five anti-tank helicopter squadrons, with a surplus for attrition and training. Orders have so far been placed for 71 aircraft, of which 54 were due to be delivered by the end of March 1991. The first squadron is based at Obihiro on Hokkaido, the second at Hachinohe and the third at Metabaru. Two of the eight AH-1Ss to be ordered under the 1991 budget have been cut to offset the cost of Japan's Gulf War contribution.

NEC is to produce 33 Hughes Aircraft C-Nite thermal imaging sight attachments for the AH-1S by 1996 under the FY 1992 budget. AH-1S cockpits will also be adapted for night vision goggles and an integrated com/nav control and display panel.

Fuji-built AH-1S HueyCobra for the JGSDF

ISHIDA
THE ISHIDA CORPORATION

116 Myoken-cho, Showa-ku, Nagoya 466
Telephone: 81 (52) 833 8167
Fax: 81 (52) 834 1546
Texas Technical Centers:
Ishida Aerospace Research Inc, 3908 Sandshell Drive, Fort
   Worth, Texas 76137, USA
Telephone: 1 (817) 847 5502
Fax: 1 (817) 847 5815
PRESIDENT: Dr J. David Kocurek

DMAV Inc, 4056 Sandshell Drive, Fort Worth, Texas
   76137, USA
Telephone: 1 (817) 847 5620
Fax: 1 (817) 847 5627
PRESIDENT: Cecil Haga
Management Company:
TW-68 Industries Inc, 88 Howard Street, Room 1904, San
   Francisco, California 94105, USA
Telephone: 1 (415) 495 3492
Fax: 1 (415) 495 3798

As well as funding and directing the development of the
TW-68 tilt-wing transport in the USA, Ishida is marketing
the Swearingen SJ30 and Jaffe SA-32T in Asia and
Australia. The address of TW-68 Industries Inc, above, is
also that of its parent company T. Ishida USA Inc.

The Ishida Foundation has been sponsoring the TW-68
programme and, in 1990, founded Ishida Aerospace
Research Inc in Texas to carry through engineering design
and prototype fabrication to the beginning of flight testing.
DMAV (Dual Mode Air Vehicle), which has moved to a
location alongside Ishida Aerospace Research on the edge
of the new Alliance Airport north of Fort Worth, remains as
a consultant. Further financing is being arranged to cover
certification and production.

Construction of a 1,858 m² (20,000 sq ft) development
centre on a six-acre site alongside Alliance Airport was
begun on 11 June 1990 and will be occupied in September
1991. A further 3,716 m² (40,000 sq ft) factory and delivery
centre will be begun immediately afterwards. Employment
is expected to rise from 15 at the end of 1990 to 100 during
1992.

ISHIDA TW-68

The TW-68 is being developed near Fort Worth, Texas,
by Ishida Aerospace Research with DMAV as consultant.
Funding estimated at $10 million from the Ishida
Foundation should take the project to first flight in 1994.
Further funds are required to reach certification in 1997.

The tilt-wing system was shown by the final flight tests of
the Canadair CL-84 tilt-wing to be relatively uncritical
without exotic controls and the configuration offers lower
weight and complexity. It also streamlines the wing with the
propeller downwash during hover rather than leaving it
athwart the downwash as in the tilt-rotor, which normally
reduces rotor lift by some 10 per cent.

Ishida plans a first pressurised passenger version with
cabin differential something over 0.34 bar (5 lb/sq in) to
allow cruising at 7,620 m (25,000 ft). Eventual derivatives
might include a stretched 19-passenger commuter and an
unpressurised utility version of the basic TW-68 intended
for such roles as offshore oil support and search and rescue.
The downwash of the propellers, which are smaller than the
rotors of a corresponding tilt-rotor, is more intense, but
there should still be a calm area between the two columns of
air to facilitate picking up loads or survivors.

Ishida signed a memorandum of understanding with
Pratt & Whitney Canada on 3 October 1990 for the supply
of P&WC PT6A engines of unspecified mark for the
TW-68. By March 1991 a tiltable version of the PT6A-67,
which can be rated from 821 to over 1,119 kW (1,100 to over
1,500 shp), had been selected. Ishida had decided to fit four
engines in two pairs which, together with combiner
gearboxes and the cross shafting, would achieve full
Category A performance out of ground effect with one
engine inoperative. The engines would be flat rated and the
combiner gearboxes rated to deliver 1,493 kW (2,000 shp) to
each propeller. This would be a five-blade unit with a
maximum diameter of 5.08 m (16 ft 8 in) turning at less than
800 rpm. There will be no cyclic pitch control, as in
helicopter and tilt-rotor. The propeller supplier had not
been selected by March 1991. The PT6 was chosen in
preference to more advanced but relatively untried engines,
in order to take advantage of its known reliability
and maintainability. Shortly afterwards, Ishida placed a
contract with Lucas Western Inc for preliminary design and
eventual development of the combiner gearbox.

The TW-68 will have plain hydraulic powered controls
without advanced electronic assistance, but with a mechanical mixer box to alter the function of the control surfaces
and devices progressively during the transition. In hover,
the double-slotted flaperons will operate differentially for
yaw control, a hydraulically driven fan in the upper
tailplane will control pitch attitude, and lateral control is by
varying propeller power output. In forward flight, the
flaperons act as ailerons, the elevator on the upper tailplane
replaces the fan, which is stopped, and the normal rudder
becomes effective. The foreplane in the original design has
been eliminated.

Artist's impression of the Ishida TW-68 tilt-wing transport, powered by four P&WC PT6A-67s, in the rescue utility version

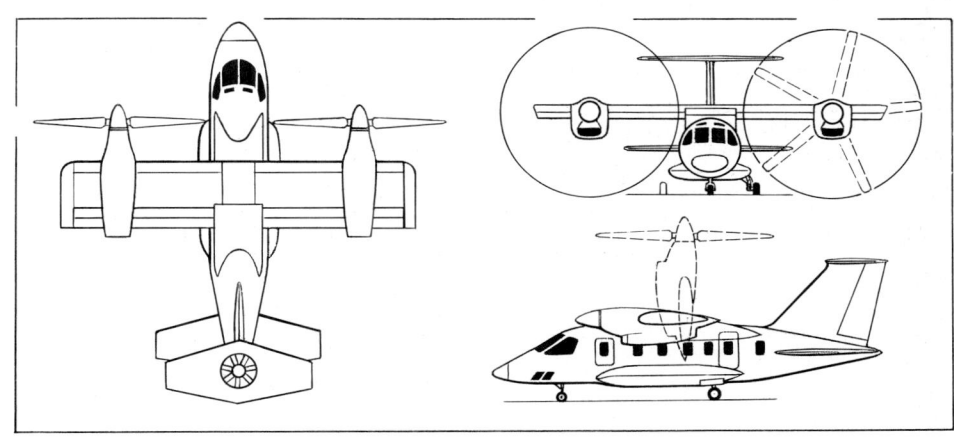

Ishida TW-68 in 14-passenger, four-engined version *(Pilot Press)*

Details below refer to the initial pressurised V/STOL
TW-68:
TYPE: Four-engined tilt-wing light transport.
POWER PLANT: Four P&WC PT6A-67 turboshaft engines,
   adapted for tilting operation and totalling between about
   2,985 kW (4,000 shp) and 4,478 kW (6,000 shp), driving
   two five-blade slow-turning propellers. Capacity and
   layout of the fuel system had not been specified at press
   time.
ACCOMMODATION: Flight crew of one or two. Cabin seating
   for nine (corporate), 14 (commuter) or a maximum of 16
   passengers, or equivalent freight or other payload.

DIMENSIONS, EXTERNAL:

Wing span	10.97 m (36 ft 0 in)
Total span (incl propellers)	12.62 m (41 ft 4¾ in)
Wing chord, constant	2.16 m (7 ft 1 in)
Wing aspect ratio	5.08
Distance between propeller centres	7.53 m (24 ft 8½ in)
Length overall	12.01 m (39 ft 4¾ in)
Fuselage: Length	9.26 m (30 ft 4½ in)
Max width	1.78 m (5 ft 10 in)
Height overall	4.08 m (13 ft 4¾ in)
Propeller diameter	5.08 m (16 ft 8 in)

DIMENSIONS, INTERNAL:

Cabin: Length	4.82 m (15 ft 10 in)
Max width	1.63 m (5 ft 4 in)
Max height	1.60 m (5 ft 3 in)
Volume	9.91 m³ (350 cu ft)
Baggage volume	3.31 m³ (117 cu ft)

AREAS:

Wings, gross	23.69 m² (255.0 sq ft)

WEIGHTS AND LOADINGS (A: VTOL, B: STOL):

Weight empty, equipped	3,810 kg (8,400 lb)
Operating weight empty	3,992 kg (8,800 lb)
Fuel capacity	1,519 kg (3,350 lb)
Payload with max fuel: A	812 kg (1,790 lb)
B	1,982 kg (4,370 lb)
Max T-O weight: A	6,323 kg (13,940 lb)
B	7,493 kg (16,520 lb)

PERFORMANCE (estimated):

Max level speed	350 knots (648 km/h; 403 mph)
Max cruising speed	297 knots (550 km/h; 342 mph)
Best range speed	187 knots (346 km/h; 215 mph)
Best endurance speed	170 knots (315 km/h; 196 mph)
Service ceiling, one engine out	5,485 m (18,000 ft)
Range: max fuel, 30 min reserves	834 nm (1,545 km; 960 miles)
14 passengers: STOL	955 nm (1,770 km; 1,100 miles)
VTOL	616 nm (1,142 km; 710 miles)

JADC

JAPAN AIRCRAFT DEVELOPMENT CORPORATION

Toranomon Daiichi Building, 2-3, Toranomon 1-chome, Minato-ku, Tokyo 105
Telephone: 81 (3) 3503 3225
Fax: 81 (3) 3504 0368
Telex: 222 2863 JADC J
CHAIRMAN: Yotaro Iida

Japan Aircraft Development Corporation is the new name of Civil Transport Development Corporation (CTDC) and is now the co-ordinating body for Japan's 20 per cent share in the Boeing 777. Participation includes design, testing and sales financing as well as manufacturing. The number of Japanese staff assigned to Boeing in Seattle will reach a peak of 200 during 1991.

JADC is also running the Japanese involvement in the YXX/7J7, on which the agreement started in 1984 was renewed in February 1991. Little immediate progress is expected. JADC also co-ordinates work on the YSX 75-passenger airliner for which a Project Office was opened in July 1989. A feasibility study was conducted in FY 1989 and 1990. A new stage was planned for FY 1991.

KAWASAKI

KAWASAKI JUKOGYO KABUSHIKI KAISHA (Kawasaki Heavy Industries Ltd)

1-18 Nakamachi-Dori, 2-chome, Chuo-ku, Kobe
TOKYO AND AEROSPACE GROUP OFFICE: World Trade Center Building, 4-1, Hamamatsu-cho 2-chome, Minato-ku, Tokyo 105
Telephone: 81 (3) 3435 2111
Fax: 81 (3) 3436 3037
Telex: 242-4371 KAWAJU J
PRESIDENT: Hiroshi Ohba
Aerospace Group
EXECUTIVE MANAGING DIRECTOR AND GROUP SENIOR GENERAL MANAGER: Kanji Sonoda
WORKS: Gifu and Akashi

Kawasaki Aircraft Co amalgamated with Kawasaki Dockyard Co and Kawasaki Rolling Stock Mfg Co to form Kawasaki Heavy Industries Ltd on 1 April 1969. The Aerospace Group employs some 5,100 people. Kawasaki has a 25 per cent holding in Nippi (which see).

In addition to extensive overhaul work, Kawasaki has built many US aircraft under licence since 1955, as detailed in earlier *Jane's*. From the Lockheed P2V-7 (P-2H) Neptune it developed the P-2J anti-submarine aircraft (see 1978-79 *Jane's*), two of which were later converted to UP-2J configuration with equipment for target towing, ECM training and drone launch operations, and two others as UP-2J(E) electronic intelligence (elint) aircraft, equipped with HLR-105 and HLR-106 systems.

Kawasaki developed and produced the C-1 transport (see 1988-89 *Jane's*), is extensively involved in satellites and launch vehicles and the HOPE orbiting spaceplane to operate with the NASA Space Station, is a member of the International Aero Engines consortium, produces the Textron Lycoming T53 and T55 under licence (see Aero Engines section) and overhauls aero engines. The company also builds hangars, docks, passenger bridges and similar airport equipment.

Kawasaki is producing, as prime contractor, the T-4 intermediate jet trainer to succeed the Lockheed T-33A and Fuji T-1. The company has developed, jointly with MBB of Germany, the BK 117 twin-engined multi-purpose helicopter described in the International section. Kawasaki has exclusive rights to produce and develop the former Boeing 107 Model II helicopter. McDonnell Douglas MD 500 series light helicopters are being manufactured under a licence agreement concluded in October 1967. By 1 April 1990 a total of 160 KV107 series helicopters had been delivered, and 286 MD 500s to government and commercial operators in Japan. The company is now co-producing Boeing CH-47 Chinooks for the Japanese armed forces.

Kawasaki is a subcontractor to Mitsubishi (which see) for rear fuselages, wings and tail units of the McDonnell Douglas F-15J and DJ Eagles being licence built in Japan; is subcontracted to build forward and mid fuselage sections, and wing ribs, for the Boeing 767 jet transport; and has been nominated by the JASDF as prime contractor for maintenance and support of its Grumman E-2C Hawkeye AEW and Lockheed C-130 Hercules transport aircraft.

Kawasaki is sharing with Mitsubishi configuration studies of the National Aerospace Laboratory (NAL) fan lift medium-range VTOL airliner.

KAWASAKI (LOCKHEED) P-3C ORION

Kawasaki is prime contractor for licence production of the Lockheed P-3C/Update II and III Orion, 110 of which are to be purchased by the JMSDF. Of these, 96 had been ordered up to and including FY 1990; a further two were approved for FY 1991. The first three (US built) P-3Cs were handed over to the JMSDF in April 1981. The next four were assembled by Kawasaki from knocked-down assemblies; the first of these made its initial flight on 17 March 1982, and was delivered on 26 May that year to Fleet Squadron 51 at Atsugi Air Base. The remaining 81 are being built almost entirely in Japan, and 69 had been delivered by 31 March 1991. Two squadrons, each with 10 aircraft, are based at Atsugi. The third and fourth P-3C squadrons, at Hachinohe, were equipped in 1985-86, a fifth at Shimofusa in 1987, a sixth at Kanoya in 1989 and a seventh at Naha in 1990. The Japan Defence Agency plans to introduce Update IV, made under licence in Japan, from 1993. Two aircraft, ordered in FYs 1987 and 1988, are equipped as **EP-3C** electronic surveillance versions. The first of these flew in October 1990 and was delivered in March 1991, with delivery of the second due about a year later. A further three EP-3Cs are planned during FYs 1991-95. NEC and Mitsubishi Electric produced the low and high frequency detector systems. The Japanese Navy is also to procure one

Lockheed P-3C Orion for the JMSDF, assembled by Kawasaki

NP-3C navaid flight checking aircraft and two **UP-3C** ECM trainers in the FY 1991 budget. Kawasaki is responsible for building P-3C centre-fuselages, and for final assembly and flight testing. Participants in the programme include Fuji, Mitsubishi, Nippi and Shin Meiwa for the airframe, and IHI for the Allison T56-IHI-14 engines.

For possible future procurement, Kawasaki has proposed a number of variants to the Japan Defence Agency including an ocean surveillance version, a military transport and a systems testbed.

KAWASAKI T-4

Kawasaki was named by the Japan Defence Agency on 4 September 1981 as the prime contractor to develop a new intermediate trainer to replace Lockheed T-33As and Fuji T-1A/Bs in service with the JASDF. The designation XT-4 was allocated officially to the type during its development.

Current plans call for procurement of about 200 production T-4s, for pilot training, liaison and other duties. Funding was approved in the FY 1983 and 1984 defence budgets to procure four flying prototypes. A total of 91 production aircraft had been ordered by 31 March 1990, of which 56 had been delivered. One T-4 out of 22 planned for the FY 1991 budget is reported to have been dropped to help pay for the Gulf War.

The T-4 is based on Kawasaki's KA-851 design, by an engineering team led by Mr Kohki Isozaki. Mitsubishi (centre fuselage and engine air intakes) and Fuji (rear fuselage, wings and tail unit) each have a 30 per cent share in the production programme. Kawasaki, as prime contractor, builds the forward fuselage, and is responsible for final assembly and flight test.

The T-4 was required to have high subsonic manoeuvrability, and to be able to carry external loads under the wings and fuselage. Basic design studies were completed in October 1982, and prototype construction began in April 1984. The first XT-4 (56-5601) made its first flight on 29 July 1985, and all four prototypes were delivered between December 1985 and July 1986, preceded by static and fatigue test aircraft. Production began in FY 1986, and the first production T-4 made its initial flight on 28 June 1988. Deliveries started on 20 September 1988, and the first 56 aircraft are in service with the Flying Training Squadrons of the JASDF's 1st Air Wing at Hamamatsu, near Tokyo, and of four other Wings in Japan. An enhanced capability version has been proposed to the Japan Defence Agency as a possible replacement for the Mitsubishi T-2.

TYPE: Tandem two-seat intermediate jet trainer and liaison aircraft.

WINGS: Cantilever mid-wing monoplane. Supercritical aerofoil section, with thickness/chord ratios of 10.3 per cent (root) and 7.3 per cent (tip). Anhedral 7° from roots. Incidence 0°. Sweepback at quarter-chord 27° 30′. Extended chord on outer panels, giving a dog-tooth leading-edge. Main structure of aluminium alloy, with slow crack growth characteristics. Double-slotted trailing-edge flaps of aluminium alloy with AFRP trailing-edges. Ailerons of plain hinged type, made of CFRP and fitted with Teijin hydraulically powered actuators. No tabs.

FUSELAGE: Conventional semi-monocoque structure (frames and longerons), mainly of aluminium alloy with minimum use of titanium in critical areas. Slow crack growth characteristics. CFRP airbrake on each side at rear.

TAIL UNIT: Cantilever structure, with sweepback on all surfaces. Fin and rudder are made of CFRP; all-moving anhedral tailplane is of aluminium alloy except for CFRP trailing-edge. Rudder and tailplane powered hydraulically via Mitsubishi servo actuators.

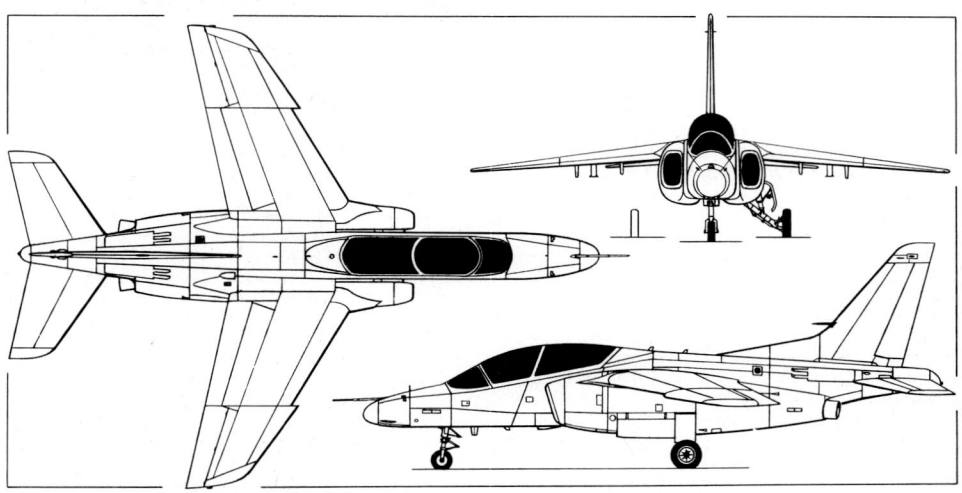

Kawasaki T-4 trainer (two Ishikawajima-Harima F3-IHI-30 turbofans) *(Pilot Press)*

LANDING GEAR: Hydraulically retractable tricycle type, with Sumitomo oleo-pneumatic shock absorber in each unit. Single-wheel main units retract forward and inward; steerable nosewheel retracts forward. Bendix (Kayaba) mainwheels, tyre size 22 × 5.5-13.8, pressure 19.31 bars (280 lb/sq in); Bendix (Kayaba) nosewheel, tyre size 18 × 4.4-11.6, pressure 12.76 bars (185 lb/sq in). Bendix (Kayaba) carbon brakes and Hydro-Aire (Sumitomo) anti-skid units on mainwheels.

POWER PLANT: Two 16.37 kN (3,680 lb st) Ishikawajima-Harima F3-IHI-30 turbofans, mounted side by side in centre-fuselage. Internal fuel in two 401.25 litre (106 US gallon; 88.3 Imp gallon) wing tanks and two Japanese built Goodyear rubber bag tanks in fuselage, one of 776 litres (205 US gallons; 170.7 Imp gallons) and one of 662.5 litres (175 US gallons; 145.7 Imp gallons). Total internal capacity 2,241 litres (592 US gallons; 493 Imp gallons). Single pressure refuelling point in outer wall of port engine air intake. Provision to carry one 450 litre (119 US gallon; 99 Imp gallon) Shin Meiwa drop tank on each underwing pylon. Oil capacity 5 litres (1.3 US gallons; 1.1 Imp gallons).

ACCOMMODATION: Crew of two in tandem in pressurised and air-conditioned cockpit with wraparound windscreen and one-piece sideways (to starboard) opening canopy. Dual controls standard; rear (instructor's) seat elevated 27 cm (10.6 in). UPC (Stencel) SHIS-3J ejection seats and Teledyne McCormick Selph canopy severance system, licence built by Daicel Chemical Industries. Baggage compartment in centre of fuselage, with external access via door on port side.

SYSTEMS: Shimadzu bootstrap type air-conditioning and pressurisation system (max differential 0.28 bar; 4.0 lb/sq in). Two independent hydraulic systems (one each for flight controls and utilities), each operating at 207 bars (3,000 lb/sq in) and each with separate air/fluid reservoir pressurised at 3.45 bars (50 lb/sq in). Flow rate of each hydraulic system 45 litres (12 US gallons; 10 Imp gallons)/min. No pneumatic system. Electrical system powered by two 9kW Shinko engine driven starter/generators. Tokyo Aircraft Instruments onboard oxygen generating system.

AVIONICS: Mitsubishi Electric J/ARC-53 UHF com, Nagano JRC J/AIC-103 intercom, Nippon Electric J/ARN-66 Tacan, Toyo Communication (Teledyne Electronics) J/APX-106 SIF, Japan Aviation Electronics (Honeywell) J/ASN-3 AHRS, Tokyo Keiki (Honeywell) J/ASK-1 air data computer, Shimadzu (Kaiser) J/AVQ-1 HUD, and Tokyo Aircraft Instrument J/ASH-3 VGH recorder.

EQUIPMENT: Two Nippi pylons under each wing for carriage of drop tanks (see Power Plant paragraph); one Nippi pylon under fuselage, on which can be carried target towing equipment, an ECM/chaff dispenser or an air sampling pod.

ARMAMENT: No built-in armament.

DIMENSIONS, EXTERNAL:

Wing span	9.94 m (32 ft 7½ in)
Wing chord: at root	3.11 m (10 ft 2½ in)
at tip	1.12 m (3 ft 8 in)
Wing aspect ratio	4.7
Length: overall	13.00 m (42 ft 8 in)
fuselage	11.96 m (39 ft 3 in)
Height overall	4.60 m (15 ft 1¼ in)
Tailplane span	4.40 m (14 ft 5¼ in)
Wheel track	3.20 m (10 ft 6 in)
Wheelbase	5.10 m (16 ft 9 in)

DIMENSIONS, INTERNAL:

Cockpit: Length	3.20 m (10 ft 6 in)
Max width	0.69 m (2 ft 3 in)
Max height	1.40 m (4 ft 7¼ in)

AREAS:

Wings, gross	21.00 m² (226.05 sq ft)
Ailerons (total)	1.51 m² (16.25 sq ft)
Trailing-edge flaps (total)	2.93 m² (31.54 sq ft)
Fin	3.78 m² (40.69 sq ft)
Rudder	0.91 m² (9.80 sq ft)
Tailplane	6.04 m² (65.02 sq ft)

WEIGHTS AND LOADINGS:

Weight empty	3,700 kg (8,157 lb)
T-O weight, clean	5,500 kg (12,125 lb)
Max design T-O weight	7,500 kg (16,535 lb)
Max wing loading	357.1 kg/m² (73.15 lb/sq ft)
Max power loading	229.2 kg/kN (2.25 lb/lb st)

PERFORMANCE (in clean configuration. A: at weight of 4,700 kg; 10,361 lb with 50% fuel, B: at T-O weight of 5,500 kg; 12,125 lb):

Max level speed: A	Mach 0.9
Max level speed at S/L:	
A	560 knots (1,038 km/h; 645 mph)
Cruising speed: B	Mach 0.75
Stalling speed: A	90 knots (167 km/h; 104 mph)
Max rate of climb at S/L: B	3,050 m (10,000 ft)/min
Service ceiling: B	15,240 m (50,000 ft)
T-O run, 35°C: B	549 m (1,800 ft)
Landing run: A	670 m (2,200 ft)
Min ground turning radius	9.45 m (31 ft 0 in)
Range (B) at Mach 0.75 cruising speed:	
internal fuel only	700 nm (1,297 km; 806 miles)
with two 450 litre drop tanks	900 nm (1,668 km; 1,036 miles)
g limits	+7.33/-3

Kawasaki T-4 twin-turbofan intermediate trainers of the Japan Air Self-Defence Force

Kawasaki built Boeing CH-47J Chinook in JASDF camouflage (*Ivo Sturzenegger*)

Kawasaki (McDonnell Douglas) OH-6D light helicopter of the JGSDF (*Ivo Sturzenegger*)

KAWASAKI KV107IIA

Kawasaki has exclusive rights to manufacture and sell the Boeing 107 Model II helicopter. The first KV107 which it produced under this licence agreement flew for the first time in May 1962, and FAA type approval for this initial version was granted in November 1965. Details of the initial production KV107II models have been given in the 1984-85 and earlier editions of *Jane's*.

The KV107IIA, introduced in 1968, has uprated turboshafts for improved performance during VTOL and in hot and high conditions. Type approval was granted by the JCAB on 26 September 1968 and by the FAA on 15 January 1969. Production of the KV107IIA ended on 16 February 1990, with delivery of the last four A-5s to the JASDF. A total of 160 KV107IIs and IIAs (all versions) had been delivered by that date.

Several versions of the KV107IIA were produced, including the **A-2** (three built), **A-3** (seven for MCM: mine countermeasures duties with the JMSDF), **A-4** (18 as tactical transports for the JGSDF), **A-5** (35 for long-range SAR duties with the JASDF, of which 31 have a Kawasaki/Boeing AFCS), **A-17** (one for Japanese Metropolitan Police), and a series of special missions **A-SM-1/-2/-3/-4** versions (16 in all) for Saudi Arabia. Details of these, which remain available, can be found in the 1990-91 and earlier editions of *Jane's*.

KAWASAKI (BOEING) CH-47 CHINOOK
JASDF/JGSDF designation: CH-47J

The FY 1984 defence budget approved the purchase of three Boeing CH-47 Chinook helicopters: two for the JGSDF and one for the JASDF, which have eventual requirements for 39 and 15 respectively. The first two aircraft, delivered in Spring 1986, were US built, the third was delivered in CKD (component knocked down) form for assembly in Japan. Kawasaki has been granted a licence for local manufacture of Chinooks ordered for the Japanese services; the Japanese version is generally similar to the CH-47D, and is designated CH-47J. The first CH-47Js for the JGSDF and JASDF were delivered in late 1986, and deliveries totalled 18 and 10 respectively by 31 March 1991. The FY 1990 and 1991 budgets provided for nine more for the JGSDF and three for the JASDF. One CH-47J out of a planned four in the FY 1991 budget is reported to have been dropped to help pay for the Gulf War.

KAWASAKI (MCDONNELL DOUGLAS) MODEL 500D
JGSDF/JMSDF designation: OH-6D

The first Model 369D (500D) built by Kawasaki under licence from Hughes (now McDonnell Douglas) Helicopters was flown for the first time on 2 December 1977; JCAB Normal category certification was awarded on 20 April 1978. Nine Model 500Ds had been delivered for civil operation in Japan by March 1990. The JGSDF ordered 111 as OH-6Ds, all of which had been delivered by the end

of March 1991. Two out of a planned 16 OH-6Ds in the FY 1991 budget are reported to have been cancelled to help pay for the Gulf War. The OH-6D was also selected by the JMSDF for the training role. Nine had been delivered by 31 March 1991.

MITSUBISHI
MITSUBISHI JUKOGYO KABUSHIKI KAISHA (Mitsubishi Heavy Industries Ltd)

5-1, Marunouchi 2-chome, Chiyoda-ku, Tokyo 100
Telephone: 81 (3) 3212 3111
Fax: 81 (3) 3212 9852
Telex: J22443
NAGOYA AIRCRAFT WORKS: 10, Oye-cho, Minato-ku, Nagoya 455
PRESIDENT: Kentaro Aikawa
EXECUTIVE VICE-PRESIDENTS:
   Nobuichi Tsuruoka
   Yu Tashiro
   Takaaki Yamada (Managing Director, and General Manager of Aircraft and Special Vehicle Headquarters)
GENERAL MANAGER, AIRCRAFT DEPARTMENT:
   Tatsuji Tamaki

Mitsubishi began the production of aircraft in 1921, and manufactured 18,000 aircraft of approximately 100 different types prior to 1945, as well as 52,000 engines in the 1,000-2,500 hp range. The present Komaki South plant was built in 1952 and, together with the Oye and Komaki North plants, was later consolidated as Nagoya Aircraft Works, with a combined floor area of 552,463 m² (5,946,666 sq ft).

Mitsubishi developed the YS-11, MU-2, MU-3 and the CCV T-2 and is prime contractor for the Japanese F-4E and F-15, and for the FS-X. It was prime contractor for the T-2 supersonic trainer and F-1 close air support aircraft for the JASDF, with Fuji, Nippi and Shin Meiwa as principal subcontractors; and is currently producing forward and rear fuselages for JMSDF Lockheed P-3C Orions, under subcontract to Kawasaki (which see). Other subcontract work includes manufacture of rear passenger cabin sections of the Boeing 767 jet transport. Part of this work is, in turn, subcontracted by Mitsubishi to Shin Meiwa. Mitsubishi also manufactures tailcones for the McDonnell Douglas MD-11.

Mitsubishi's aero engine activities are described in the appropriate section of this edition. The company also produces rocket engines and participates in the H-I and H-II launchers and the Japanese Experimental Module for the US Space Station and for the HOPE orbiting spaceplane.

The Japan Defence Agency has authorised service introduction of the AAM-3 short-range air-to-air missile developed by Mitsubishi with NEC seeker and proximity fuse and Komatsu warhead. AAM-3 will replace the AIM-9 on F-15Js and F-4EJs.

MITSUBISHI F-4EJKai and RF-4EJ

In co-operation with Kawasaki as subcontractor, Mitsubishi was the JDA's prime contractor in producing F-4EJ Phantom tactical fighters for the JASDF, under licence from McDonnell Douglas Corporation. The last of 140 F-4EJs was delivered to the JASDF on 20 May 1981; Mitsubishi is engaged currently in a major programme to update F-4EJ equipment and weapon systems. The prototype F-4EJKai (07-8431) was first flown on 17 July 1984 and delivered on the following 13 December. It has a Westinghouse AN/APG-66J fire control system, advanced avionics which include a Litton LN-39 INS, head-up display and J/APR-4Kai radar warning receiver, lookdown/shootdown capability with AIM-7E/F Sparrows or AIM-9P/L Sidewinders, and can carry two ASM-1 anti-shipping missiles. Current plans are to convert 100 of the JASDF's 125 remaining F-4EJs to F-4EJKai configuration and another 17 to RF-4EJ reconnaissance-fighters. These and 14 existing RF-4EJs are being fitted with Texas Instruments AN/APQ-172 nose radars and digital displays. An initial batch of 45 F-4EJKai conversions is being produced. Some of the upgraded aircraft are now expected to be allocated to close air support rather than interceptor duties.

Mitsubishi Electric is in charge of the RF-4EJ conversion programme, which will utilise a development by its Melco subsidiary of an elint pod derived from the Thomson-CSF Astac system fitted to French Air Force Mirage F1-CRs.

MITSUBISHI (MCDONNELL DOUGLAS) F-15J and F-15DJ EAGLE

The Japan Defence Agency plans to procure a total of 187 McDonnell Douglas F-15 Eagles, including 14 US built aircraft (two single-seat F-15Js and 12 two-seat F-15DJs). The two US built F-15Js were followed by eight assembled in Japan from US supplied knocked-down assemblies. First aircraft of the latter batch flew on 26 August 1981 and was delivered on 11 December that year. A total of 177

Artist's impression of the Mitsubishi FS-X fighter derived from the General Dynamics F-16C

F-15J/DJs had been funded up to FY 1991. Production is due to continue into the late 1990s, but another 15 or 20 may be ordered to fill the gap before deliveries of the first FS-Xs.

First JASDF F-15 squadron was No. 202 (5th Air Wing) at Nyutabaru, which was activated in December 1982 with 20 F-15J/DJs. Other units now equipped are No. 201 and No. 203 Squadrons of the 2nd Air Wing at Chitose, Hokkaido; No. 204 (7th Air Wing, at Hyakuri); and Nos. 205 and 303 (6th Air Wing, Komatsu). Mitsubishi is building the forward and centre-fuselages, and is responsible for final assembly and flight testing. Participants in the programme include Fuji (landing gear doors), Kawasaki (wings and tail assembly), Nippi (pylons and missile launchers), Shin Meiwa (drop tanks), Sumitomo (landing gear), and IHI (engines). The J/ALQ-8 ECM and XJ/APQ-1 radar warning systems of all these aircraft are of Japanese design and manufacture. Starting in FY 1991, the F100-PW-100 engines in Japanese F-15Js will be upgraded to -220 standard, offering an additional 13.34 kN (3,000 lb) of thrust.

MITSUBISHI FS-X

A modified F-16C was selected as Japan's FS-X replacement for the F-1 in October 1987 and Mitsubishi was appointed prime contractor in November 1988. Initial airframe and radar design contracts were awarded by the JDA in March 1990 and the General Electric F110-GE-129 Increased Performance Engine was selected in December 1990. It is rated at 129.0 kN (29,000 lb st) and will be part-manufactured under licence in Japan.

Between 100 and 130 FS-Xs will be required and four prototypes are to be made in the mid-1990s before production deliveries start in 1999. Development has been held up for virtually two years by questions of development sharing with General Dynamics, which is taking a 40 per

cent share in the FS-X programme, and technology transfer to Japan. In May 1991, the Japan Defence Agency reported that the FS-X development cost had risen by some 70 per cent to $2.1 billion. The first of four prototypes should fly in 1995. A production decision is due in 1996. An additional squadron of F-15Js may be ordered to fill the gap in factory workload.

Other Japanese airframe companies involved will include Kawasaki and Fuji. The active phased-array radar, EW (ECM/ESM) mission computer and IRS will be developed using Japanese domestic technology. Japan will be totally responsible for the FS-X programme, including all funding. Selection of subcontractors was due to be completed by June 1991. Those announced by March included Japan Aviation Electronics Industry (flight management computer), Mitsubishi Rayon (windscreen), and Mitsubishi's Nagoya Guidance and Propulsion Systems division (direct drive valve cartridge).

The FS-X will have a new wing, of Japanese design and all-composites co-cured construction, with a greater area than that of the F-16, a lengthened nose to accommodate the additional mission avionics, and a longer rear fuselage than the F-16. Ventral canard surfaces will flank the air intake duct and full fly-by-wire allowing fuselage pointing will be included, based on Mitsubishi's work with the T-2 CCV up to 1986. Armament is expected to include Mitsubishi AAM-3 air-to-air missiles and Mitsubishi XASM-2 air-to-ship missiles.

MITSUBISHI (SIKORSKY) S-61

Mitsubishi holds licence agreements to manufacture the Sikorsky S-61, S-61B (HSS-2/2A/2B) and S-61A helicopters. Between 1 April 1989 and 31 March 1990 Mitsubishi delivered 17 HSS-2Bs (for ASW) to the JMSDF. By mid-1990 it had delivered to the JMSDF, for ASW and

Second prototype Mitsubishi (Sikorsky) XSH-60J anti-submarine helicopter

rescue, 167 helicopters of the HSS-2 series and 18 S-61As, completing the total order for 185 HSS-2/2A/2B/S-61As.

MITSUBISHI (SIKORSKY) SH-60J and UH-60J

Detailed design work on the S-70B-3 version of the Sikorsky SH-60B Seahawk anti-submarine helicopter, to meet the specific requirements of the JMSDF, was funded under the FY 1983 budget. Japanese avionics and equipment, including ring laser gyro AHRS, data link, tactical data processing and automatic flight management systems, are integrated by the Technical Research and Development Institute of the Japan Defence Agency. The first of two prototype XSH-60Js, based on imported airframes, flew for the first time on 31 August 1987. These two aircraft had almost completed evaluation by the 51st Air Unit of the JMSDF at Atsugi at the end of 1990. The JMSDF has a requirement for nearly 100 SH-60Js, the first 12 of which were funded in FY 1989, 11 in FY 1990, 17 in FY 1991 and 16 in FY 1992. The first shipborne deployment was expected early in 1991. Half the force will be land-based.

Mitsubishi is also prime contractor for the licence assembly of 46 Sikorsky UH-60J helicopters to be procured for combat search and rescue duties with the JASDF. The first three UH-60Js (one US built and two CKD kits) were ordered in FY 1988 and were delivered during 1990. Eleven had been funded by March 1991. The JMSDF requirement is for 18, six of which had been funded by March 1991. Equipment includes the ESSU external stores suspension unit, FLIR and nose radar. The UH-60J can fly a one-hour search at 250 nm (463 km; 288 miles) from base.

NAL

NATIONAL AEROSPACE LABORATORY

7-44-1 Jindaijihigashi-machi, Chofu City, Tokyo 182
Telephone: 81 (422) 47 5911
DIRECTOR-GENERAL: Dr Kazuyuki Takeuchi
DEPUTY DIRECTOR-GENERAL: Kazuaki Takashima

The National Aerospace Laboratory (NAL) is a government establishment responsible for research and development in the field of aeronautical and space sciences. Since 1962 it has extended its activity in the field of V/STOL techniques.

NAL ASUKA

The Asuka was an experimental upper surface blowing STOL transport aircraft developed by the NAL. It first flew on 28 October 1985 and completed its test programme during 1989. The aircraft was based upon the airframe of the Kawasaki C-1 tactical transport, with the two Pratt & Whitney JT8D engines replaced by four MITI/NAL FJR710/600S high bypass ratio turbofans, installed above and far ahead of the wing leading-edges in nacelles producing upper surface blowing (USB); wing leading-edge and aileron boundary layer control systems; inboard flaps replaced by USB flaps; structural strengthening of the fuselage and landing gear; and a digital stability and control augmentation system.

A full description of the Asuka, and a three-view drawing, were published in the 1986-87 *Jane's*, and a shortened version in the 1988-89 and 1989-90 editions.

NAL SPACEPLANE STUDIES

The NAL is assisting in the study programme for a possible future Japanese spaceplane, and has tunnel tested a number of alternative configurations since about 1982. In 1988 it received a Dornier 228-200 to be used for simulation of the final approach and landing phases of an eventual spaceplane. This aircraft is equipped with INS, GPS, and a special work station from which its flight characteristics can be changed and controlled by computers. An extensive system study on the single-stage-to-orbit (SSTO) aircraft has been carried out with the aid of computational fluid dynamics on supercomputers. Researches on hypersonic air-breathing engines and lightweight high-temperature structures are also being conducted. Construction of a ramjet/scramjet engine test facility was initiated in April 1989 as a three-year plan, by partly remodelling an existing rocket engine high altitude test facility. Composite structure test facilities are under construction for test and evaluation of advanced materials and structures. The hypersonic wind tunnel test section is being enlarged from 0.50 m (1 ft 7¾ in) to 1.20 m (3 ft 11¼ in) as part of a three-year programme.

Expenditure was about $35 million in 1990, plus funds from Mitsubishi, Kawasaki and Fujitsu, and NAL hoped to increase this to $67 million in 1991 and $133 million in 1992. A test vehicle should fly in five years, leading to an operational vehicle as a Japanese national goal, but with foreign co-operation. A high altitude rocket test facility at Kakuda is being modified to test scramjet engines at between Mach 4 and 8. About half of NAL's research workers are working on aerospace plane technology.

NAL 100-PASSENGER VTOL AIRLINER

Fuji, Kawasaki and Ishikawajima have joined an NAL study of a lift/cruise fan, 100-passenger, medium-range VTOL airliner intended to fly in 2010. Three core engines would drive either six lift fans beside the centre fuselage or two propulsion fans at the tail. Pitch-axis control would be by foreplane and by deflecting the core engine exhausts. Range would be 1,350 nm (2,500 km; 1,550 miles) and cruising speed Mach 0.8.

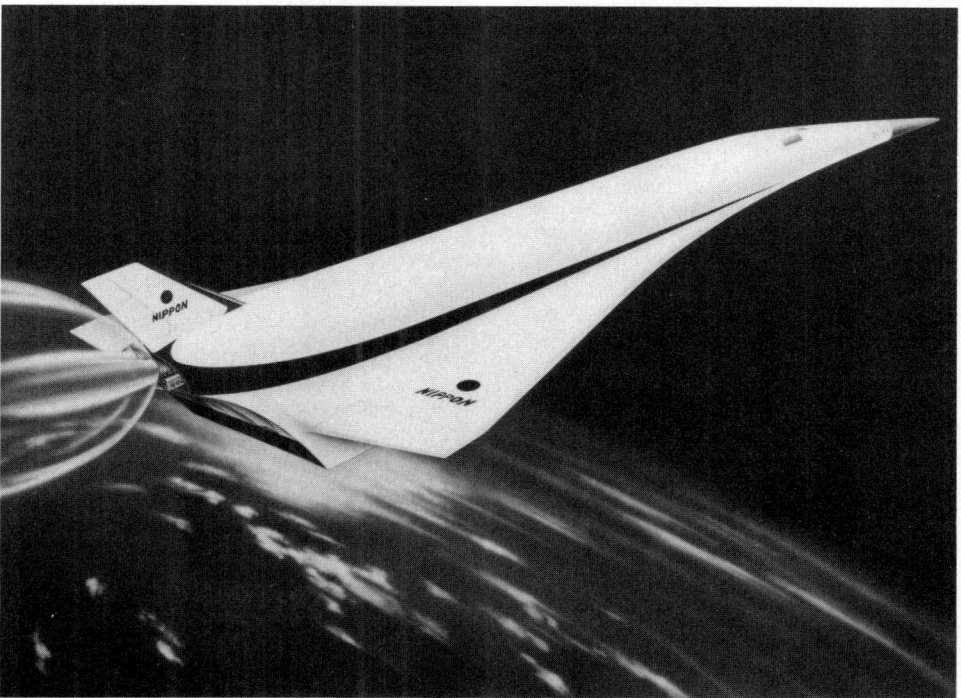

Artist's impression of the NAL spaceplane which it is intended to develop as an international project

Artist's impression of the NAL fan-lift VTOL medium-range airliner

NIPPI

NIHON HIKOKI KABUSHIKI KAISHA (Japan Aircraft Manufacturing Co Ltd)

3175 Showa-machi, Kanazawa-ku, Yokohama 236
Telephone: 81 (45) 773 5111
Fax: 81 (45) 771 1253
Telex: (3822) 267 NIPPI J
OTHER WORKS: Atsugi
PRESIDENT: Teruaki Yamada
EXECUTIVE MANAGING DIRECTOR:
   Atsumasa Kubota (General Affairs and Public Relations)

Nippi's Yokohama plant has a floor area of 58,235 m² (626,836 sq ft) and employs about 1,000 persons. The Atsugi plant, which employs about 650 persons, has a floor area of 40,975 m² (441,051 sq ft). Kawasaki Heavy Industries has a 25 per cent holding in Nippi.

The Yokohama plant manufactures wing in-spar ribs for the Boeing 767; elevators for the Boeing 757; underwing 'Y-barrels' for the McDonnell Douglas MD-11; components and assemblies for the Kawasaki built P-3C (engine nacelles) and T-4 (pylons) and Mitsubishi built F-15J (pylons and launchers); major dynamic components for the Kawasaki CH-47J; V2500 engine ducts; shelters for Mitsubishi built Patriot ground-to-air missiles; body structures for Japanese satellites; tail units for Japanese built rocket vehicles; and targets for the Japan Defence Agency.

The Atsugi plant is engaged chiefly in the overhaul, repair and maintenance of various types of aircraft and helicopters, including those of the Japan Defence Agency and Maritime Safety Agency, and carrier based aircraft of the US Navy.

SHIN MEIWA

SHIN MEIWA INDUSTRY CO LTD

Nippon Building, 6-2, Otemachi 2-chome, Chiyoda-ku,
Tokyo 100
Telephone: 81 (3) 3245 6611
Fax: 81 (3) 3245 6616
Telex: 222 2431 SMIC T J
PRESIDENT: Shinji Tamagawa
HEAD OFFICE: 1-5-25, Kosone-Cho, Nishinomiya-Shi,
Hyogo-Ken 663
Telephone: 81 (798) 47 0331
Telex: 5644493

Aircraft Division

EXECUTIVE MANAGING DIRECTOR AND GENERAL MANAGER:
Yukio Koya
BOARD DIRECTOR AND GENERAL MANAGER:
Isao Tomioka (Konan Plant)
DIRECTOR AND GENERAL MANAGER:
Junpei Matsuo (Sales, Head Office)
GENERAL MANAGER (SALES) AND PUBLIC RELATIONS:
Yushi Tanaka (Tokyo Office)
WORKS: Konan and Tokushima

The former Kawanishi Aircraft Company became Shin
Meiwa Industry Company in 1949 and established itself as a
major overhaul centre for Japanese and US military and
commercial aircraft.

Shin Meiwa's principal current activities concern production of the US-1A medium-range STOL search and
rescue amphibian for the JMSDF, and overhaul work on
flying-boats and amphibians. It manufactures external drop
tanks for Mitsubishi built McDonnell Douglas F-15J
Eagles, and in 1991 modified four Learjet 36As into U-36A
naval fleet training support aircraft for the JMSDF.

Shin Meiwa also produces components for other aircraft,
including drop tanks for the Kawasaki T-4 trainer; nose and
tail cones, ailerons and trailing-edge flaps for the Kawasaki
built Lockheed P-3C; tailplanes for the Mitsubishi built
Sikorsky SH-60J; internal cargo handling system for the
Kawasaki built Boeing CH-47J; wing and tail engine pylons
for the McDonnell Douglas MD-11; thrust reverser doors
for the McDonnell Douglas MD-80, under subcontract to
Rohr Industries Inc; tailplane trailing-edges for the Boeing
757/767, under subcontract to LTV; and other components
for the Boeing 767, under subcontract to Mitsubishi.

Shin Meiwa has been studying and looking for partners
to develop its Amphibious Air Transport System, which is a
30/50-passenger airliner powered by two wing-mounted
turbofans with upper surface blowing. Range would vary
from 500 nm (926 km; 575 miles) with full payload to 1,200
nm (2,224 km; 1,380 miles) with full fuel. Take-off distance
would be 1,000 m (3,280 ft) on water and 800 m (2,624 ft) on
soft ground. Cruising speed would be between 300 and 360
knots (556 and 667 km/h; 345 and 414 mph).

SHIN MEIWA SS-2A
JMSDF designation: US-1A

The US-1 search and rescue amphibian first flew on 16
October 1974, and the first US-1 was delivered on 5 March
1975 as described in the 1985-86 and earlier editions of
Jane's.

Twelve aircraft were ordered and delivered, of which
eight are now in service with No. 71 SAR Squadron of the
JMSDF, at Iwakuni and Atsugi bases. All now have
T64-IHI-10J turboprops, and are designated US-1A.

Following the 1976 modification of a PS-1 to firefighting
configuration, with a 7,348 kg (16,200 lb) capacity water
tank in the centre fuselage aft on the step, a similar
experimental conversion has been made more recently using
a US-1A with a tank capacity increased to more than 13,608
kg (30,000 lb). The water tank system was developed by
Conair of Canada.

To make very low landing and take-off speeds possible,
the US-1A possesses both a boundary layer control system
and extensive flaps for propeller slipstream deflection.
Control and stability in low-speed flight are enhanced by
'blowing' the rudder, flaps and elevators, and by use of an
automatic flight control system controlling the elevators,
rudder and outboard flaps.

The following data apply to the US-1A:

TYPE: Four-turboprop STOL air/sea rescue amphibian.
WINGS: Cantilever high-wing monoplane. Conventional
all-metal two-spar structure with rectangular centre-
section and tapered outer panels. High-lift devices
include outboard leading-edge slats extending over
nearly 17 per cent of the span and large outer and
inner blown trailing-edge flaps deflecting 60° and 80°
respectively. Outboard flaps can be linked with ailerons.
Two spoilers in front of outer flaps on each wing.
Hydraulically powered ailerons, with 'feel' trim. Leading-
edge de-icing boots.
FUSELAGE: All-metal semi-monocoque hull, with high
length/beam ratio. V shaped single-step planing bottom,
with curved spray suppression strakes along sides of nose
and spray suppressor slots in lower fuselage sides aft of
inboard propeller line. Double-deck interior.
TAIL UNIT: Cantilever all-metal T tail. Large dorsal fin.
Tailplane has inverted slats and de-icing boots on
leading-edge. Rudder and elevators are hydraulically
powered, fitted with 'feel' trim, and blown by BLC
system. Tab in each elevator.

Shin Meiwa SS-2A (US-1A) (four Ishikawajima/GE T64-IHI-10J turboprops)

LANDING GEAR: Flying-boat hull, plus hydraulically retractable Sumitomo tricycle landing gear with twin wheels on
all units. Steerable nose unit. Oleo-pneumatic shock
absorbers. Main units, which retract rearward into
fairings on hull sides, have size 40 × 14-22 (type VII)
tyres, pressure 7.79 bars (113 lb/sq in). Nosewheel tyres
size 25 × 6.75-18 (type VII), pressure 20.69 bars (300
lb/sq in). Three-rotor hydraulic disc brakes. No anti-skid
units.
POWER PLANT: Four 2,605 kW (3,493 ehp) Ishikawajima
built General Electric T64-IHI-10J turboprops, each
driving a Sumitomo built Hamilton Standard 63E60-27
three-blade constant-speed reversible-pitch propeller.
Fuel in five wing tanks, with total usable capacity of
11,640 litres (3,075 US gallons; 2,560.5 Imp gallons) and
two fuselage tanks (10,849 litres; 2,866 US gallons;
2,386.5 Imp gallons); total usable capacity 22,489 litres
(5,941 US gallons; 4,947 Imp gallons). Pressure refuelling
point on port side, near bow hatch. Oil capacity 152 litres
(40.2 US gallons; 33.4 Imp gallons). The aircraft can be
refuelled on open sea, either from a surface vessel or from
another US-1A fitted with detachable at-sea refuelling
equipment.
ACCOMMODATION: Crew of three on flight deck (pilot,
co-pilot and flight engineer), plus navigator/radio
operator's seat in main cabin. Latter can accommodate
up to 20 seated survivors or 12 stretchers, one auxiliary
seat and two observers' seats. Sliding rescue door on port
side of fuselage, aft of wing.
SYSTEMS: Cabin air-conditioning system. Two independent
hydraulic systems, each 207 bars (3,000 lb/sq in). No. 1
system actuates ailerons, outboard flaps, spoilers,
elevators, rudder and control surface 'feel'; No.2 system
actuates ailerons, inboard and outboard flaps, wing
leading-edge slats, elevators, rudder, landing gear
extension/retraction and lock/unlock, nosewheel steering, mainwheel brakes and windscreen wipers. Emergency system, also of 207 bars (3,000 lb/sq in), driven by
24V DC motor, for actuation of inboard flaps, landing
gear extension/retraction and lock/unlock, and mainwheel brakes. Oxygen system for all crew and stretcher
stations. Garrett GTCP85-131J APU provides power for
starting main engines and shaft power for 40kVA
emergency AC generator. BLC system includes a
C-2 compressor, driven by a 1,014 kW (1,360 shp)
Ishikawajima built General Electric T58-IHI-10-M2 gas
turbine, housed in the upper centre portion of the
fuselage, which delivers compressed air at 14 kg (30.9
lb)/s and pressure of 1.86 bars (27 lb/sq in) for ducting to
inner and outer flaps, rudder and elevators. Electrical
system includes 115/200V three-phase 400Hz constant
frequency AC and three transformer-rectifiers to provide
28V DC. Two 40kVA AC generators, driven by Nos. 2
and 3 main engines. Emergency 40kVA AC generator
driven by APU. 24V emergency DC power from two
34Ah nickel-cadmium batteries. Anti-icing, air-conditioning, fire detection and extinguishing systems
standard.
AVIONICS: HIC-3 interphone, HRC-107 HF, N-CU-58/HRC
antenna coupler, HGC-102 teletypewriter, HRC-106
radio, HRC-110 radio, HRN-101 ADF, AN/ARA-50
UHF/DF, HRN-105 Tacan, HRN-104 Loran, HRA-4
Loran signal processor, HRN-106 ILS marker beacon
receiver, AN/APN-171 (N2) radio altimeter, HPN-101B
wave height meter, AN/APC-187C Doppler radar,
AN/AYK-2 navigation computer, A/A24G-9 TAS transmitter, N-PT-3 dead reckoning plotting board, N-OA-
35/HSA tactical plotter group, AN/APS-80N search
radar, AN/APA-125N indicator group, AN/APX-68N
IFF transponder, RRC-15 emergency transmitter and
N-ID-66/HRN BDHI.
EQUIPMENT: Marker launcher, 10 marine markers, six green
markers, two droppable message cylinders, 10 float

lights, pyrotechnic pistol, parachute flares, two flare
storage boxes, binoculars, two rescue equipment kits, two
droppable liferaft containers, rescue equipment launcher,
lifeline pistol, lifeline, three lifebuoys, loudspeaker, hoist
unit, rescue platform, lifeboat with outboard motor,
camera, and 12 stretchers. Sea anchor in nose compartment. Stretchers can be replaced by troop seats.

DIMENSIONS, EXTERNAL:

Wing span	33.15 m (108 ft 9 in)
Wing chord: at root	5.00 m (16 ft 4¾ in)
at tip	2.39 m (7 ft 10 in)
Wing aspect ratio	8.1
Length overall	33.46 m (109 ft 9¼ in)
Height overall	9.95 m (32 ft 7¾ in)
Tailplane span	12.36 m (40 ft 8½ in)
Wheel track	3.56 m (11 ft 8¼ in)
Wheelbase	8.33 m (27 ft 4 in)
Propeller diameter	4.42 m (14 ft 6 in)
Rescue hatch (port side, rear fuselage):	
Height	1.58 m (5 ft 2¼ in)
Width	1.46 m (4 ft 9½ in)

AREAS:

Wings, gross	135.82 m² (1,462.0 sq ft)
Ailerons (total)	6.40 m² (68.90 sq ft)
Inner flaps (total)	9.40 m² (101.18 sq ft)
Outer flaps (total)	14.20 m² (152.85 sq ft)
Leading-edge slats (total)	2.64 m² (28.42 sq ft)
Spoilers (total)	2.10 m² (22.60 sq ft)
Fin	17.56 m² (189.0 sq ft)
Dorsal fin	6.32 m² (68.03 sq ft)
Rudder	7.01 m² (75.50 sq ft)
Tailplane	23.04 m² (248.0 sq ft)
Elevators, incl tab	8.78 m² (94.50 sq ft)

WEIGHTS AND LOADINGS (search and rescue):

Manufacturer's weight empty	23,300 kg (51,367 lb)
Weight empty, equipped	25,500 kg (56,218 lb)
Usable fuel: JP-4	17,518 kg (38,620 lb)
JP-5	18,397 kg (40,560 lb)
Max oversea operating weight	36,000 kg (79,365 lb)
Max T-O weight: from water	43,000 kg (94,800 lb)
from land	45,000 kg (99,200 lb)
Max wing loading	331.4 kg/m² (67.9 lb/sq ft)
Max power loading	4.32 kg/kW (7.10 lb/ehp)

PERFORMANCE (search and rescue, at max T-O weight from
land, except where indicated):

Max level speed	276 knots (511 km/h; 318 mph)
Max level speed at 3,050 m (10,000 ft), AUW of 36,000 kg	
(79,365 lb)	282 knots (522 km/h; 325 mph)
Cruising speed at 3,050 m (10,000 ft)	
	230 knots (426 km/h; 265 mph)
Max rate of climb at S/L	488 m (1,600 ft)/min
Max rate of climb at S/L, AUW of 36,000 kg (79,365 lb)	
	713 m (2,340 ft)/min
Service ceiling	7,195 m (23,600 ft)
Service ceiling, AUW of 36,000 kg (79,365 lb)	
	8,655 m (28,400 ft)
T-O to 15 m (50 ft) on land, 30° flap, BLC on (ISA)	
	655 m (2,150 ft)
T-O distance on water, AUW of 43,000 kg (94,800 lb), 40°	
flap, BLC on (ISA)	555 m (1,820 ft)
Landing from 15 m (50 ft) on land, AUW of 36,000 kg	
(79,365 lb), 40° flap, BLC on, with reverse pitch (ISA)	
	810 m (2,655 ft)
Landing distance on water, AUW of 36,000 kg	
(79,365 lb), 60° flap, BLC on (ISA)	220 m (722 ft)
Min ground turning radius:	
self-powered	21.20 m (69 ft 6¾ in)
towed	18.80 m (61 ft 8¼ in)
Runway LCN requirement at AUW of 43,000 kg	
(94,800 lb)	42
Max range at 230 knots (426 km/h; 265 mph) at 3,050 m	
(10,000 ft)	2,060 nm (3,817 km; 2,372 miles)

JORDAN

JA
JORDAN AEROSPACE
c/o Jordan Technology Group, PO Box 5296, Amman
Telephone: 962 (6) 89160/2
Fax: 962 (6) 89161

PUBLIC RELATIONS MANAGER: Ms Rana Abu-Odeh

This company was established in 1989 to manufacture locally the Schweizer 330 helicopter and to market it in the Middle East and Africa. The venture has not progressed.

KOREA, SOUTH

DHI
DAEWOO HEAVY INDUSTRIES CO LTD
6 Mansok-dong, Tong-gu (PO Box 7955), Inchon 160
Telephone: 82 (32) 721011-16
Telex: 23301
MANAGING DIRECTOR, AEROSPACE PRODUCT DIVISION:
Hyo Sang Cho

Daewoo Heavy Industries began manufacturing aircraft components in 1985; current activities include producing components for the BAe Hawk jet trainer. The company

was to manufacture wing assemblies for the Lockheed P-7A, since cancelled, and will produce fuselage panels for the Dornier 328 regional transport.

Daewoo is associated with Samsung Aerospace in producing fuselage and tailboom assemblies for the Bell 212 and 412SP. It is also in the three-company team led by Korean Air to produce the Sikorsky UH-60P under licence and was designated in 1990 as the prime integrator for the Korean scout helicopter, of which between 75 and 100 will be required. Contenders in the scout programme include

the Bell 406 Combat Scout, Agusta A 109C, Aerospatiale AS 355, MBB BO 105 and McDonnell Douglas MD 500.

Daewoo and Sikorsky planned to offer the S-76 for the Korean light utility helicopter programme, but the Korean Government did not approve the initiative.

Daewoo is main subcontractor to Samsung in the co-production of the KF-X fighter, for which the General Dynamics F-16 was selected on 28 March 1991.

KA
KOREAN AIR
KAL Building, CPO Box 864, 41-3 Seosomun-Dong, Chung-Ku, Seoul
Telephone: 82 (2) 751 7114
Telex: KALHO K 27526
CHAIRMAN AND CHIEF EXECUTIVE OFFICER: C. H. Cho
PRESIDENT: C. K. Cho
Aerospace Division
Marine Center Building 18FL, 118-2-ka, Namdaemun-Ro, Chung-Ku, Seoul
Telephone: 82 (2) 771 66
Fax: 82 (2) 756 7929
Telex: KALHO K 27526 (SELDBKE)
SENIOR MANAGING VICE-PRESIDENT: Y. T. Shim
MANAGING VICE-PRESIDENT, MARKETING AND SALES:
J. K. Lee
Korean Institute of Aeronautical Technology (KIAT)
Address/telephone/telex/fax details as for Aerospace Division
RESEARCH ENGINEER: Chang Duk Hwang

Aerospace Division, one of several divisions of Korean Air, was established in 1976 to manufacture and develop aircraft. By early 1989 the Aerospace Division occupied a 64.75 ha (160 acre) site at Kim Hae, including a floor area of 130,065 m² (1.4 million sq ft), and had a workforce of about 1,800 people.

Korean Air is supported by Daewoo and Samsung in producing between 80 and 90 Sikorsky UH-60Ps worth over $500 million under licence in a five-year programme up to 1995. Korean Air will first assemble, paint and flight test seven UH-60Ps, and manufacture the entire airframe by the end of the programme. Dynamic components and rotors will come from the USA. The UH-60P is essentially the current US Army UH-60L with T700-GE-701C engines and 2,535 kW (3,400 shp) transmission, with added avionics. Korean Air will also make parts for and assemble the T700 engines. Eventually, Korean Air might market and manufacture entire UH-60s for other countries in the region and become a supplier to Sikorsky. The first UH-60P was delivered to Korean Air late in 1990.

Since 1978, Korean Air has overhauled Republic of Korea Air Force aircraft. Programmed depot maintenance of US military aircraft in the Pacific area began in 1979, including structural repair of F-4 Phantoms, systems modifications for the F-16 Fighting Falcon, MSIP upgrading of the F-15 Eagle and overhaul of C-130 Hercules transports. KA began deliveries in April 1988 of wingtip extensions and flap track fairings for the Boeing 747 and fuselage components for the McDonnell Douglas MD-11.

As a part of the Korean aircraft industry development programme from 1988, Korean Air developed microlight aircraft (see Sport Aircraft section), the five-seat Chang-Gong 91, and a modified Model 520MK light helicopter, derived from the Model 500, in association with McDonnell Douglas. Also projected is a primary trainer for the Korean Air Force, designated KTX-1.

KA (KIAT) CHANG-GONG 91 (BLUE SKY 91)
The name Chang-Gong has been applied to a number of projects undertaken by the KIAT division of Korean Air, the first two of which (Chang-Gong I and II) were adaptations of foreign microlight designs. Chang-Gong 3, which made its first flight in the Autumn of 1988, was an experimental twin-fuselage two-seat microlight built mainly of composites and powered by two 22.4 kW (30 hp) Italian piston engines.

Following these three projects, and benefiting from the experience gained from them, KIAT is now building a more ambitious design, the five-seat Chang-Gong 91 cabin monoplane illustrated in an accompanying three-view drawing. Construction of the prototype began on 21 June

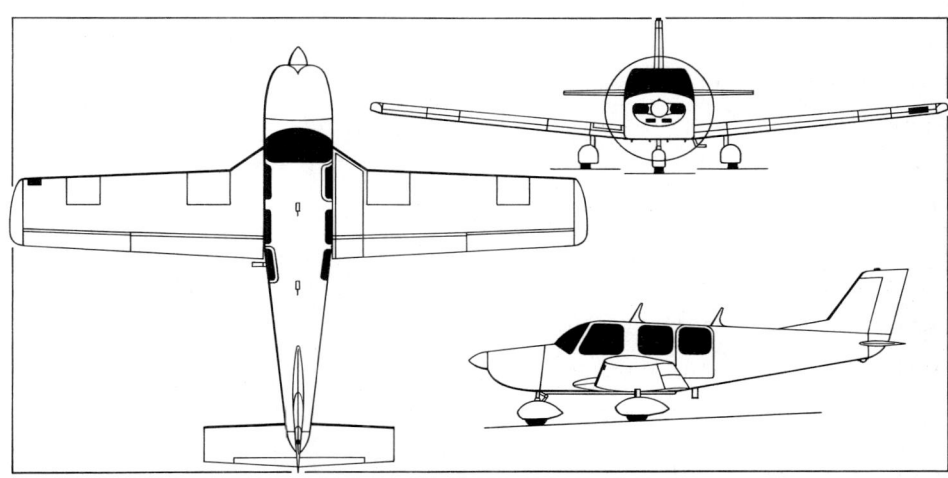

Korean Air Chang-Gong 91 four/five-seat cabin monoplane *(Jane's/Mike Keep)*

1988, and it is scheduled to fly for the first time in February 1992. It was partly funded by Hankook glassfibre and Samsun aluminium companies, and may be put into production. The details of the Chang-Gong 91 below are updated:

TYPE: Four/five-seat light aircraft.
WINGS: Cantilever low-wing monoplane, with constant NACA 63₂-415 section and slightly tapered trailing-edges. Dihedral 6° from roots. Incidence 2°. Sweepback 0° 52' 48" at quarter-chord. All-metal single-spar fail-safe wings, with all-composite Frise ailerons and single-slotted flaps on trailing-edges. Control surfaces actuated mechanically. No tabs.
FUSELAGE: Light alloy semi-monocoque structure, with glassfibre cowling panels and tailcone.
TAIL UNIT: Cantilever all-composites structure, with swept-back vertical and non-swept horizontal surfaces. One-piece all-moving tailplane, with large central servo tab. Balanced rudder, with ground adjustable tab. Control surfaces actuated mechanically.
LANDING GEAR: Non-retractable tricycle type, with single wheel, oleo-pneumatic shock absorber and speed fairing on each unit. Nosewheel steerable ±35°.
POWER PLANT: One 149 kW (200 hp) Textron Lycoming IO-360-A1B6 flat-four engine, driving a two-blade constant-speed propeller. Two integral fuel tanks in wings each holding 112 litres (29.6 US gallons; 24.6 Imp gallons). Total fuel capacity 224 litres (59 US gallons; 49.3 Imp gallons). Refuelling points in wing upper surfaces. Oil capacity 7.6 litres (2 US gallons; 1.7 Imp gallons).
ACCOMMODATION: Side by side seats in front for pilot and one passenger. Second pair of seats behind these, to rear of which is a fifth (child's) seat. Space for 45.4 kg (100 lb) of baggage behind rearmost seat. Front-hinged, outward opening door at front on starboard side, over wing, and at rear (aft of wing) on port side. Entire accommodation ventilated.
SYSTEMS: 14V DC electrical system powered by engine driven alternator. No air-conditioning, oxygen, hydraulic or pneumatic systems.
AVIONICS: Bendix/King KX 155/165 Silver Crown com/nav.

DIMENSIONS, EXTERNAL:

Wing span	10.20 m (33 ft 5½ in)
Wing chord: at root	1.66 m (5 ft 5½ in)
at tip	1.20 m (3 ft 11¼ in)
Wing aspect ratio	7.0
Length: overall	7.70 m (25 ft 3¼ in)
fuselage	7.00 m (22 ft 11½ in)
Height overall	2.70 m (8 ft 10¼ in)
Tailplane span	3.69 m (12 ft 1¼ in)
Wheel track	2.88 m (9 ft 5½ in)
Wheelbase	1.95 m (6 ft 4¾ in)
Propeller diameter	1.88 m (6 ft 2 in)
Passenger door (fwd, stbd):	
Height	0.93 m (3 ft 0½ in)
Width	0.93 m (3 ft 0½ in)
Height to sill	0.92 m (3 ft 0¼ in)
Passenger door (rear, port):	
Height	0.91 m (2 ft 11¾ in)
Width	0.77 m (2 ft 6¼ in)
Height to sill	0.81 m (2 ft 7¾ in)

DIMENSIONS, INTERNAL:

Cabin: Max length	3.05 m (10 ft 0 in)
Max width	1.22 m (4 ft 0 in)
Max height	1.86 m (6 ft 1¼ in)
Floor area	3.41 m² (36.7 sq ft)
Volume	2.24 m³ (79.0 cu ft)
Baggage compartment volume	0.34 m³ (12.0 cu ft)

AREAS:

Wings, gross	14.86 m² (160.0 sq ft)
Ailerons (total)	1.09 m² (11.73 sq ft)
Trailing-edge flaps (total)	2.02 m² (21.74 sq ft)
Fin, incl dorsal fin	1.33 m² (14.32 sq ft)
Rudder, incl tab	0.52 m² (5.60 sq ft)
Tailplane, incl tab	2.64 m² (28.42 sq ft)

WEIGHTS AND LOADINGS:

Basic operating weight empty	680 kg (1,500 lb)
Max fuel weight	159 kg (350 lb)
Max T-O weight	1,225 kg (2,700 lb)
Max wing loading	82.39 kg/m² (16.87 lb/sq ft)
Max power loading	8.22 kg/kW (13.50 lb/hp)

PERFORMANCE (estimated, at max T-O weight):

Max level speed at S/L	130 knots (241 km/h; 150 mph)
Max cruising speed at 1,525 m (5,000 ft)	125 knots (232 km/h; 144 mph)
Econ cruising speed (65% power) at 1,525 m (5,000 ft)	108 knots (200 km/h; 124 mph)
Stalling speed at S/L, 40° flap, power off	51 knots (95 km/h; 59 mph)
Max rate of climb at S/L	270 m (886 ft)/min
Service ceiling	4,420 m (14,500 ft)
T-O run	301 m (988 ft)
T-O to 15 m (50 ft)	501 m (1,644 ft)

Landing from 15 m (50 ft)	381 m (1,250 ft)
Landing run	197 m (647 ft)
Range at 1,525 m (5,000 ft), max fuel, 75% power	
	810 nm (1,500 km; 932 miles)

KA (MCDONNELL DOUGLAS) MODELS 500, 520 and 530

Korean Air has manufactured the McDonnell Douglas (originally Hughes) Models 500D and 500MD under licence from the US manufacturer since 1976, as described in earlier editions of *Jane's*. A total of 307 of these two models had been delivered by 1 January 1989. A new offset agreement was signed in 1984, under which KA has supplied McDonnell Douglas Helicopter Co with major fuselage assemblies for the 500 and 530. KAL is delivering fuselage subassemblies at the rate of about 80 a year and these are made into the specific model required by Intertech in the USA. The agreement runs for two more years and is renewable. Descriptions of the 500E and 530F can be found under McDonnell Douglas Helicopter Company in the US section. A modified version of the Model 520, designated **520MK**, is under development.

KBHC
KOREA BELL HELICOPTER COMPANY
8-10, Hyorim-ri, Sapkyo-eup, Yesan-kun, Chungcheong Nam-do
Telephone: 82 458 37 1991/5
Fax: 82 458 37 1996

REPRESENTATIVE DIRECTOR: Jin W. Song

SEOUL OFFICE: 1460-10 Hanjong Building, Sucho-dong, Sucho-ku, Seoul
Telephone: 82 (2) 585 1881/8
Fax: 82 (2) 587 1881
Telex: K 25622

KBHC is a joint venture corporation between Bell Helicopter Textron (see US section) and Korea Technologies Corporation (KTC), a subsidiary of United Industries International that has represented Bell Helicopter and other US companies in Korea for many years. Since April 1988, KBHC has been licensed to inspect, overhaul and carry out depot level maintenance on Bell helicopters, to train air and ground crews and to manufacture parts for the subassemblies of the Bell 212 and 412SP made by Samsung Aerospace and Daewoo Heavy Industries.

SAAC
SAMMI AGUSTA AEROSPACE CORPORATION LTD
66 Shinchon-Dong-Changwan City, Kyungsangnam, do Korea
PRESIDENT: Sil Dong Kim
SENIOR VICE-PRESIDENT: O. I. Romiti (Agusta)

Inaugurated on 22 May 1989, this Italo-Korean company is a joint venture by the Agusta group and Sammi Corporation, one of the major engineering industrial groups in South Korea, to build the Agusta (SIAI-Marchetti) SF.600TP Canguro twin-engined light transport in Korea and to market it in the Pacific basin area.

A new 400,000 m² (4.3 million sq ft) factory is being built, which will have a workforce of about 400 people, and Canguro tooling has been transferred. SAAC might produce other Agusta types.

SAAC (AGUSTA) SF.600TP CANGURO (KANGAROO)

The prototype F.600 Canguro (I-CANG), built in Italy by General Avia and then powered by 261 kW (350 hp) Textron Lycoming TIO-540-J flat-six piston engines, made its first flight on 30 December 1978. This aircraft was described under the General Avia heading in the 1979-80 *Jane's*.

The basic production aircraft can be adapted for passenger/troop or cargo transport, paratroop transport, air ambulance, maritime surveillance, electronic intelligence, and agricultural duties. The retractable gear version is considered especially suitable for a maritime surveillance role, equipped with an underfuselage radar system, or FLIR and/or SLAR.

Certification by the RAI was received in the Spring of 1987 in accordance with FAR Pt 23. The initial Italian production batch totalled nine aircraft, the first three being delivered in April 1988. The Canguro is now to be produced in South Korea by Sammi Agusta Aerospace. In addition to Canguro production, SAAC is to be responsible for marketing.
TYPE: Twin-turboprop passenger, cargo, ambulance and general utility transport.
WINGS: Cantilever high-wing monoplane. Wing section NASA GAW-1, with 17 per cent thickness/chord ratio. Dihedral 2°. Incidence (constant) 1° 30'. All-metal riveted structure in aluminium alloy, with stressed skin. Centre-section has main spar and two auxiliary spars; outboard of engines, wings have two spars. All-metal ailerons and electrically operated double-slotted flaps. Electrically operated trim tab in port aileron.
FUSELAGE: Aluminium alloy semi-monocoque structure of frames, stringers, bulkheads and stressed skin. Swing-tail rear fuselage available optionally.
TAIL UNIT: Cantilever all-metal stressed skin structure. Trim tabs in rudder (actuated mechanically) and each elevator (electrically/mechanically actuated). Small dorsal fin.
LANDING GEAR: Choice of retractable or non-retractable tricycle gear, of trailing arm type, with oleo-pneumatic shock absorber in each unit. Twin-wheel main units, mounted on small stub-wings attached to fuselage floor; single steerable nose unit. Mainwheels and tyres size 7.00-6, pressure 2.90 bars (42 lb/sq in); nosewheel and tyre size 6.00-6. Hydraulic disc brakes on main units.
POWER PLANT: Two 335 kW (450 shp) Allison 250-B17F turboprops, each driving a Hartzell three-blade constant-speed fully-feathering reversible-pitch propeller. Fuel in four identical outer-wing tanks, total capacity 1,100 litres (290.6 US gallons; 242 Imp gallons). Self-sealing tanks optional on military versions. Provision for underwing tanks, total capacity 600 litres (158.5 US gallons; 132 Imp gallons). Oil capacity 11.4 litres (3.0 US gallons; 2.5 Imp gallons).
ACCOMMODATION: Pilot and co-pilot or passenger on flight deck. Dual controls standard. Cabin accommodates up to nine passengers at 100 cm (40 in) seat pitch (2-2-2-2-1); six passengers in VIP version, with reclining seats, folding tables, bar and toilet; or 10 paratroops on inward facing

Agusta (SIAI-Marchetti) built SF.600TP in standard form with non-retractable landing gear

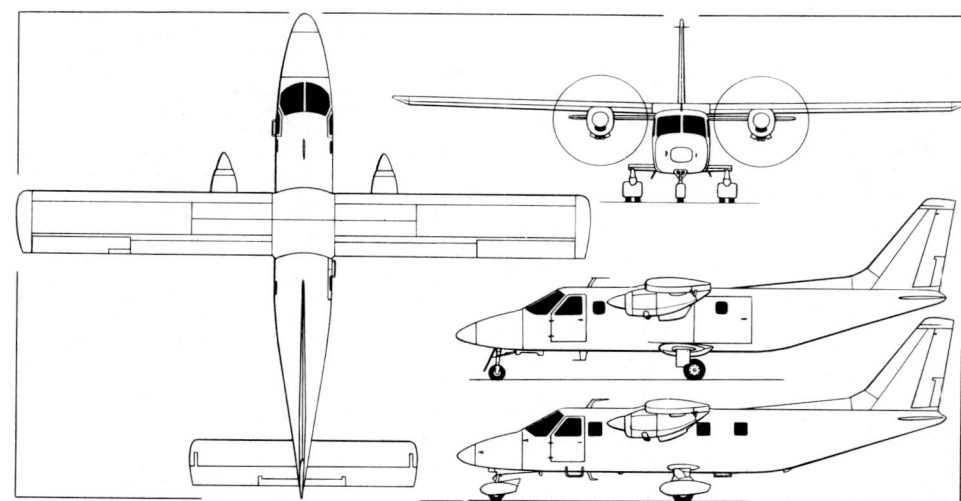

Basic SF.600TP, with additional side view (centre) of retractable landing gear version *(Pilot Press)*

seats; or two stretcher patients and two medical attendants; or freight. Baggage compartment at rear of cabin in standard passenger version; in centre of cabin, opposite toilet, in VIP version; rear compartment used to store folding passenger seats when converted for cargo use. Forward door on port side for crew. Wider, sliding door at rear on port side for passenger and freight loading and paratroop dropping, with smaller emergency door opposite this on starboard side. Cargo version can accept three 1.30 × 1.15 × 1.07 m (51 × 45 × 42 in) containers, or two of size 2.20 × 1.15 × 1.07 m (87 × 45 × 42 in).
SYSTEMS: Standard cabin heating/defrosting system uses engine bleed air; ventilation is provided by ram air; freon air-conditioning system optional. Primary electrical system is 28V DC, powered by two 150A engine driven starter/generators, with a 24V 22Ah nickel-cadmium battery for independent engine starting and emergencies. AC power, 115V at 400Hz, is provided when required by a static inverter. Pneumatic de-icing system for wings and tail unit, and electric de-icing of propellers, are optional.
AVIONICS: Wide range of IFR com/nav avionics available, to customer's requirements. Typical installation includes VHF, UHF and HF com, ADF, VOR/LOC/ILS, DME and ATC transponder. Options include Omega nav system, weather radar, three-axis autopilot and flight director. The maritime surveillance version can be equipped with nose mounted search and navigation radar, underfuselage side/down-looking surveillance radar, belly mounted panoramic camera and forward looking oblique camera, FLIR or low light level TV camera under fuselage and Omega-VLF area navigation.
EQUIPMENT: Can be equipped for target towing, with floor mounted winch, 2,000 m (6,560 ft) of cable, electric power unit (100A/28V DC), and miss-distance indicator system; with undertail hook for towing one or more gliders; with one or two Wild or Zeiss type photogrammetric,

automatic cameras (plus additional avionics at customer's option); with equipment for in-flight inspection and calibration of ground radio/navigation aids; with advanced compass, periscopic sextant, searchlight and observers' bubble windows for maritime surveillance; or with appropriate sensors and radar warning receiver. Other specialised applications include agricultural duties (single underfuselage tank, plus bubble type and additional lower windows in pilot's door, windscreen and nose-gear wire cutters, ceiling mounted airscoop, and anti-corrosion paint finish).

DIMENSIONS, EXTERNAL:

Wing span	15.00 m (49 ft 2½ in)
Wing chord, constant	1.60 m (5 ft 3 in)
Wing aspect ratio	9.4
Length overall	12.15 m (39 ft 10½ in)
Height overall	4.60 m (15 ft 1 in)
Tailplane span	5.89 m (19 ft 4 in)
Wheel track	2.40 m (7 ft 10½ in)
Wheelbase	4.88 m (16 ft 0 in)
Propeller diameter	2.29 m (7 ft 6 in)
Crew door (fwd, port): Height	1.14 m (3 ft 9 in)
Width	0.86 m (2 ft 10 in)

Height to sill	0.90 m (2 ft 11½ in)
Cargo door (rear, port): Height	1.13 m (3 ft 8½ in)
Width	1.49 m (4 ft 10¾ in)
Height to sill	0.90 m (2 ft 11½ in)

DIMENSIONS, INTERNAL:

Cabin, excl flight deck: Length	5.05 m (16 ft 6¾ in)
Width	1.23 m (4 ft 0½ in)
Height	1.27 m (4 ft 2 in)
Floor area	6.0 m² (64.6 sq ft)
Volume	7.90 m³ (279 cu ft)

AREAS:

Wings, gross	24.00 m² (258.3 sq ft)
Fin	1.69 m² (18.19 sq ft)
Rudder	1.35 m² (14.53 sq ft)
Tailplane	3.68 m² (39.61 sq ft)
Elevators (total)	2.76 m² (29.71 sq ft)

WEIGHTS AND LOADINGS:

Weight empty (standard utility version)	1,875 kg (4,133 lb)
Max T-O weight	3,400 kg (7,495 lb)
Max cargo floor loading	400 kg/m² (81.93 lb/sq ft)
Max wing loading	141.7 kg/m² (29.0 lb/sq ft)

Max power loading	5.07 kg/kW (8.33 lb/shp)

PERFORMANCE (at max T-O weight, ISA):

Max cruising speed at 1,525 m (5,000 ft)	165 knots (306 km/h; 190 mph)
Cruising speed (75% power) at 3,050 m (10,000 ft)	155 knots (287 km/h; 178 mph)
Stalling speed, flaps down	59 knots (109 km/h; 68 mph)
Max rate of climb at S/L	451 m (1,480 ft)/min
Rate of climb at S/L, one engine out	152 m (500 ft)/min
Service ceiling	7,315 m (24,000 ft)
Service ceiling, one engine out	3,050 m (10,000 ft)
T-O run	287 m (940 ft)
T-O to 15 m (50 ft)	408 m (1,340 ft)

Landing from 15 m (50 ft):

without propeller reversal	479 m (1,570 ft)
with propeller reversal	396 m (1,300 ft)
Landing run: without propeller reversal	280 m (920 ft)
with propeller reversal	204 m (670 ft)

Range at 3,050 m (10,000 ft), 10% reserves:

with max payload	324 nm (600 km; 372 miles)
with max fuel and 500 kg (1,102 lb) payload	853 nm (1,580 km; 981 miles)

SSA
SAMSUNG AEROSPACE

15/16th Floor, Dongbang Main Building, PO Box 9762, Seoul
Telephone: 82 (2) 751 8850
Telex: 22933

Samsung is prime contractor in licence manufacture of the General Dynamics F-16s selected in March 1991 for the RoKAF (see below). Initial deliveries are scheduled for 1994.

Bell Helicopter Textron and Samsung Aerospace are approved by the Korean Government to produce medium helicopters in Korea. The agreement with Bell calls for SSA to produce major fuselage and tailboom assemblies for the Bell Models 212 and 412SP (see Bell heading in the Canadian section). Initial production began in May 1988 and will continue until 1992. Bell and SSA have facilities to build complete helicopters at SSA's manufacturing centres in Changwon and Sacheon. Plans call for 93 per cent local manufacture by the early 1990s.

SAMSUNG (GENERAL DYNAMICS) F-16

After reconsidering co-production of 120 McDonnell Douglas F/A-18s in October 1990, when the cost had increased to $6.6 billion, the South Korean Government announced on 28 March 1991 that it would co-produce 120 General Dynamics F-16s with improved weapon delivery systems for $5.2 billion. The programme has been known under the designation KF-X. Samsung is the main Korean contractor. The original plan was to acquire 12 aircraft off the shelf, assemble 36 from kits and manufacture the rest. Daewoo and Hanjin are main subcontractors to Samsung.

NETHERLANDS

FOKKER
NV KONINKLIJKE NEDERLANDSE VLIEGTUIGFABRIEK FOKKER

CORPORATE CENTRE: PO Box 12222, 1100 AE Amsterdam-Zuidoost
Telephone: 31 (20) 6056666
Fax: 31 (20) 6057015
Telex: 11526 FMHS NL
CHAIRMAN: Eric J. Nederkoorn
OPERATING COMPANIES:

Fokker Aircraft BV, PO Box 12222, 1100 AE Amsterdam-Zuidoost
Telephone: 31 (20) 6056666
Fax: 31 (20) 6057015
Telex: 11526 FMHS NL
PRESIDENT: M. van der Veen
EXECUTIVE VICE-PRESIDENT, MARKETING AND SALES: C. H. Biersma

Fokker Aircraft Services BV, PO Box 3, 4630 AA Hoogerheide

Fokker Space and Systems BV, PO Box 12222, 1100 AE Amsterdam-Zuidoost

Fokker Special Products BV, PO Box 59, 7900 AB Hoogeveen

Aircraft Financing and Trading BV, PO Box 12222, 1100 AE Amsterdam-Zuidoost

Avio-Diepen BV, PO Box 5952, 2280 HZ Rijswijk

Royal Netherlands Aircraft Factories NV Fokker, founded by Anthony Fokker in 1919, forms the main aircraft industry in the Netherlands, employing some 13,000 people in early 1991. Under a new company structure which became effective on 1 January 1987, Fokker comprises a corporate centre and six operating companies.

Fokker has an important share in the European manufacturing programme for the General Dynamics F-16 fighter, being responsible for component production and assembly of F-16s for the Netherlands (214) and Denmark (12). Seventy-two F-16s for Norway were delivered between January 1980 and June 1984 (see earlier editions of *Jane's*). Deliveries to the RNethAF began in June 1979, following the first flight by a Dutch assembled F-16 (J-259) on 3 May 1979. Deliveries totalled 200 to the RNethAF by 1 January 1991, and 12 to the Royal Danish Air Force. Altogether, Fokker is producing 1,506 centre-fuselages, 1,407 wing moving surfaces, 1,054 main landing gear doors, 526 main landing gear legs, 286 horizontal stabilisers, 688 rudders and 673 fin leading-edges (for Fokker's own assembly line, as well as for a similar line in Belgium and for General Dynamics, which manufactures F-16s for the USAF and for export). Fokker-built F-16s for the RNethAF are being fitted with brake-chute housings in an extended fin root fairing. The first new aircraft so fitted was delivered to No. 315 Squadron on 30 June 1987; older aircraft will be modified later.

Some 6,000 people are employed at the Schiphol plant, Amsterdam, which accommodates the Fokker 50 and 100

and F-16 assembly lines and test flying facilities. Also at Schiphol are the design offices, spare parts stores, research and development department, numerically controlled milling department, metal bonding department, electronics division, space integration and test facilities and scientific and administrative computer facilities.

The Drechtsteden plant, formed by the integrated production facilities at Dordrecht and Papendrecht, employs approx 2,200 people. Most of these are engaged on detail production and component assembly for the Fokker 50 and 100, F-16 and Shorts 330/360/Sherpa.

At Ypenburg the installation of F-16 centre-fuselages is carried out by a workforce of 800 people. Composite material components for the Fokker 50, Fokker 100, Shorts 330/360/Sherpa, and radomes and fairings for the Westland Lynx helicopter, are manufactured at Ypenburg. A new 30,000 m² (322,917 sq ft) composites plant at Ypenburg started operating in May 1990.

Woensdrecht (Fokker Aircraft Services BV), which has a current workforce of about 900, specialises in maintenance, overhaul, repair and modification of civil and military aircraft. Component production for the Patriot missile began in mid-1985. Also at Woensdrecht the ELMO plant (Fokker Aircraft), with a workforce of approx 600, produces electrical and electronic systems and cable harnesses.

Hoogeveen (Fokker Special Products BV) is engaged in all activities relating to industrial products such as licence programmes, shelters, missile launchers, pylons, fuel tanks and thermoplastics components. It employs about 600 people.

FOKKER 50

On 24 November 1983, to mark the 25th anniversary in airline service of the F27 Friendship, Fokker announced follow-on developments of both the F27 and the F28 Fellowship, to be known respectively as the Fokker 50 and Fokker 100. Both aircraft build on successfully proven airframes, but with significant design and structural changes, allied to more efficient (and more fuel-efficient) power plants, increased use of composite materials, greater passenger comfort and convenience, advanced digital avionics, and improved airport handling characteristics. In consequence, more than 80 per cent of the component parts of the Fokker 50 are new or modified by comparison with those of the F27.

The two prototypes utilised modified F27 fuselages rather than the redesigned fuselage of the production aircraft. The first of them (PH-OSO) flew for the first time on 28 December 1985, and the second (PH-OSI) on 30 April 1986; the first production Fokker 50 (PH-DMO) flew on 13 February 1987, and JAR 25 certification was granted by the Dutch RLD on 15 May 1987. FAA type approval (FAR 25) was awarded on 16 February 1989.

Differences from the F27 include new-technology engines, in redesigned nacelles, with six-blade propellers; use of carbon, aramid and glassfibre composites in such

areas as the wings, tailplane, fin, radome, engine nacelles and propellers; passenger door relocated at the front of the aircraft, and the large cargo door deleted; more windows in the passenger cabin; newly designed cabin interior; extensive interior noise reduction; all-new cockpit design; a twin-wheel nose landing gear; latest technology systems; dedicated door concept; pneumatic system replaced by a hydraulic system; and a cruising speed some 12 per cent higher than that of the F27. Seating range is 46-58, with 50 as standard, but the cabin offers considerable flexibility for other layouts, including ample accommodation for baggage and freight. Studies for a stretched 50-200 are continuing. The production programme is shared with Dassault (centre and rear fuselage sections), Fuji (rudder and elevators), Deutsche Airbus (wing trailing-edges/control surfaces, tailcone and dorsal fin), Sabca (outer wing skins and wingtips) and Dowty (propellers and landing gear).

Firm orders for 130 Fokker 50s had been received by 31 March 1991, of which 108 had been delivered, including 37 in 1990. Deliveries (to DLT) began on 7 August 1987. Thirty-four Fokker 50s were scheduled to be built in 1991.

TYPE: Twin-turboprop short-haul transport.

WINGS: Cantilever high-wing monoplane. Wing section NACA 64₄-421 (modified) at root, NACA 64₂-415 (modified) at tip. Outer panels have 2° 30′ dihedral and 2° washout. Incidence 3° 30′. No sweepback. All-metal riveted and metal-bonded two-spar stressed skin primary structure, consisting of centre-section and two detachable outer wings. Detachable AFRP leading-edges with rubber boot de-icers. Trailing-edge skins are of composite material, supported by ribs of composite or metal construction. Single-slotted all-metal trailing-edge flaps (two segments per wing, divided by engine nacelle), operated by spindle/drive-nut. Flaps are actuated hydraulically, with electrical backup system, and are mechanically interconnected. Aileron structure is formed by bonded skin/stringer assemblies riveted to front, centre and rear spars and ribs, with leading-edges of composite material. Ailerons are actuated mechanically via cables. Each has an inboard spring tab and outboard geared/balance tab; starboard balance tab serves also as an electrically operated trim tab. Horn balance, known as Foklet, of metal reinforced composites, at each wingtip to increase lateral stability at low airspeeds.

FUSELAGE: All-metal stressed skin primary structure, built to fail-safe principles, with cylindrical portions metal bonded and conical part riveted. Pressurised between rear bulkhead of nosewheel compartment and circular pressure bulkhead aft of baggage compartment. Nosecone, fairings, nosewheel doors, access doors and cabin floor are of composite materials.

TAIL UNIT: Cantilever fin and fixed incidence tailplane of all-metal primary construction. Leading-edges are made of composites and have integral pneumatic de-icing boots; part of dorsal fin also of composite material. Elevators and rudder (both built by Fuji in Japan) **are cable actuated. Elevators are mechanically**

Fokker 50 twin-turboprop transport (two Pratt & Whitney Canada PW125B engines)

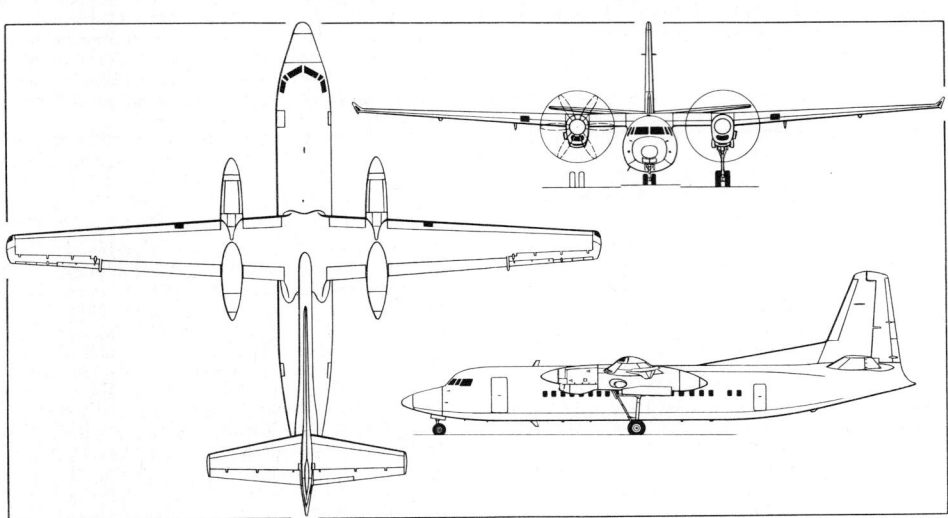

Fokker 50 twin-turboprop short-haul transport *(Pilot Press)*

interconnected, with trim tab in starboard elevator. Rudder is provided with a trim tab, geared balance tab and horn balance.

LANDING GEAR: Retractable tricycle type of Dowty manufacture, with twin wheels on all units. Main units are attached to wings, retracting rearward hydraulically into rear extension of engine nacelle; nosewheels retract forward. Long-stroke oleo-pneumatic shock absorber in each unit (single-stroke on nose unit, double-acting on main units). Goodyear wheels and tyres on all units. Standard main unit tyres are size 34 × 10.75-R16, with pressure of 5.86 bars (85 lb/sq in); size 34 × 10.75-16 tyres, pressure 5.52 bars (80 lb/sq in), are optional. Nosewheel tyres are size 24 × 7.7-10, with pressure of 3.10 bars (45 lb/sq in). Goodyear hydraulic brakes, incorporating anti-skid system. Hydraulic nosewheel steering (±73°); free-castoring angle of ±130° available for towing.

POWER PLANT: Two 1,864 kW (2,500 shp) Pratt & Whitney Canada PW125B turboprops, each driving a Dowty six-blade propeller. Propellers have all-composite blades and Beta control. Lucas Aerospace 8.2 kW (11 hp) electric motor for engine starting. Composite materials used in construction of engine air intakes and nacelle cowlings. Fuel in two integral tanks located between the two spars of the central spar box outboard of the engine nacelle, with total standard capacity of 5,136 litres (1,357 US gallons; 1,130 Imp gallons). Single-point pressure refuelling and overwing gravity points. Engine air intakes, propeller blades and spinners de-iced electrically.

ACCOMMODATION: Crew of two and observer seat on flight deck, plus one cabin attendant. Second attendant seat optional. Two cabin configurations available: basic configuration with four cabin doors (also serving as Type I emergency exits), accommodating 50 passengers at 81 cm (32 in) pitch; or optional configuration with two cabin doors (Type I emergency exits), two Type III emergency exits and a dedicated cargo door, accommodating 54 seats at 81 cm (32 in) pitch. Both configurations have a four-abreast layout with an aisle width of 46 cm (18 in)

and overhead stowage bins. Toilet, stowage area, passenger door with integral airstair (port side) and service door (starboard side) are at front of cabin. Baggage/cargo compartment at rear of cabin, with cargo door on starboard side. Aft cabin wall in optional configuration is movable, to create different baggage/cargo compartment volumes. Basic configuration has a forward baggage/cargo compartment and rear galley with two doors (one service and one cargo). Optional configuration has galley at front of cabin. Both configurations have alternative layouts with seats for up to 58 passengers. Entire accommodation pressurised and air-conditioned. Windscreens anti-iced electrically, flight deck side windows and cabin windows demisted by hot air.

SYSTEMS: Hamilton Standard air-conditioning system. AiResearch digital cabin pressure control system. Max pressure differential 0.38 bar (5.46 lb/sq in). Hydraulic system, operating at 207 bars (3,000 lb/sq in) pressure via two engine driven Abex pumps, for landing gear actuation, brakes, nosewheel steering and flap drive. Pneumatic de-icing of wing, fin and tailplane leading-edges, using engine bleed air. Primary electrical system powered by a Sundstrand 30/40kVA integrated drive generator mounted on propeller gearbox of each engine, supplying 115/200V three-phase AC at 400Hz, with two 300A transformer-rectifiers and two 43Ah nickel-cadmium batteries for 28V DC power. Sundstrand/Turbomach T62T-46C APU optional. Configured for ground use, APU (combined with a Sundstrand 115V 20kVA oil-cooled generator, accessory controls and provisions) provides AC self-sufficiency during turnaround cycles, servicing and maintenance. APU also provides air supply for flight deck and cabin air-conditioning. Unit is fitted to fireproof bulkhead aft of wheel bay in starboard nacelle.

AVIONICS: Flight deck has dual Honeywell EDZ-806 electronic flight instrument system (EFIS) with CRT displays for primary flight and navigation information, and space provisions for a central multifunction display.

Standard avionics include Honeywell SPZ-600 AFCS with Cat. I landing (Cat. II landing optional); Honeywell FZ-500 dual flight director systems; Bendix/King dual Series III VHF com, single Series III ADF and DME (latter including frequency hold facility), and Series III ATC transponder; Honeywell Primus P-650 weather radar with dual presentation on EFIS; dual Bendix/King Series III VHF nav with VOR/ILS/marker beacon receiver; TRT AHV-530A (ARINC 552A) radio altimeter with dual presentation on EFIS; dual Litton LTR 81.01 AHRS; Sundstrand Mk II GPWS (ARINC 549); Honeywell AZ-800 air data computer; Fairchild A100 (ARINC 557) cockpit voice recorder; Collins 346-2B (ARINC 560) PA system; Sundstrand 980-4100 DXUS (ARINC 573) flight data recorder, incl underwater locator beacon; and Teledyne Model 70-275 flight data acquisition unit. Full provisions for Cat. II landing on AFCS, single Collins 628T-2A HF com to ARINC 559A2 and second ADF; space provisions for second DME, second ATC transponder, VLF-Omega/Bendix/King KNS 660 nav system, and Dorne & Margolin ELT.

DIMENSIONS, EXTERNAL:

Wing span	29.00 m (95 ft 1¾ in)
Wing chord: at root	3.464 m (11 ft 4½ in)
at tip	1.40 m (4 ft 7 in)
Wing aspect ratio	12.0
Length overall	25.247 m (82 ft 10 in)
Fuselage: Max width	2.70 m (8 ft 10¼ in)
Height overall (static)	8.317 m (27 ft 3½ in)
Tailplane span	9.746 m (31 ft 11¾ in)
Wheel track	7.20 m (23 ft 7½ in)
Wheelbase	9.70 m (31 ft 10 in)
Propeller diameter	3.66 m (12 ft 0 in)
Propeller ground clearance	1.162 m (3 ft 9¾ in)
Propeller/fuselage clearance	0.593 m (1 ft 11¼ in)
Passenger door (fwd, port): Height	1.78 m (5 ft 10 in)
Width	0.76 m (2 ft 6 in)
Service door (rear, port) and cargo door (fwd, stbd), each:	
Height	1.27 m (4 ft 2 in)
Width	0.61 m (2 ft 0 in)
Cargo door (rear, stbd): Height	1.27 m (4 ft 2 in)
Width	0.86 m (2 ft 9¾ in)

DIMENSIONS, INTERNAL:

Cabin, excl flight deck: Length	15.96 m (52 ft 4 in)
Width at floor	2.11 m (6 ft 11 in)
Max width	2.50 m (8 ft 2½ in)
Max height	1.96 m (6 ft 5¼ in)
Floor area (excl toilet)	30.2 m² (325.0 sq ft)
Baggage/cargo volume (standard commuter version):	
main compartments	7.38 m³ (260.6 cu ft)
wardrobe compartment	0.82 m³ (29.0 cu ft)
overhead bins	2.22 m³ (78.4 cu ft)

AREAS:

Wings, gross	70.0 m² (753.5 sq ft)
Ailerons (total)	3.66 m² (39.40 sq ft)
Trailing-edge flaps (total)	17.15 m² (184.60 sq ft)
Fin, incl dorsal fin	17.60 m² (189.44 sq ft)
Rudder, incl tab	3.17 m² (34.12 sq ft)
Tailplane	16.00 m² (172.22 sq ft)
Elevators (total, incl tab)	3.17 m² (34.12 sq ft)

WEIGHTS AND LOADINGS:

Typical operating weight empty	12,520 kg (27,602 lb)
Max fuel load	4,123 kg (9,090 lb)
Max payload	6,080 kg (13,404 lb)
Max ramp weight: standard	19,990 kg (44,070 lb)
optional	20,820 kg (45,900 lb)
Max T-O weight: standard	19,950 kg (43,982 lb)
optional	20,820 kg (45,900 lb)

Max landing weight: standard 19,500 kg (42,990 lb)
optional 19,730 kg (43,500 lb)
Max zero-fuel weight 18,600 kg (41,000 lb)
Max wing loading: standard 285.0 kg/m² (58.37 lb/sq ft)
optional 297.4 kg/m² (60.92 lb/sq ft)
Max power loading: standard 5.35 kg/kW (8.80 lb/shp)
optional 5.59 kg/kW (9.18 lb/shp)

PERFORMANCE:
Max operating Mach number 0.507
Typical cruising speed 282 knots (522 km/h; 325 mph)
Typical climb speed
200 knots (370 km/h; 230 mph) CAS
Typical descent speed
227 knots (420 km/h; 261 mph) CAS
Max operating altitude 7,620 m (25,000 ft)
Service ceiling, one engine out, AUW of 18,250 kg (40,234 lb), ISA 4,110 m (13,485 ft)
Min ground turning radius 18.07 m (59 ft 3½ in)
Runway LCN (51 cm; 20 in flexible pavement), 34 × 10.75-R16 tyres at 5.86 bars (85 lb/sq in):
AUW of 19,050 kg (42,000 lb) 16.9
AUW of 20,820 kg (45,900 lb) 18.4
T-O field length at S/L, ISA, 15° flap:
standard MTOW 1,200 m (3,937 ft)
optional MTOW 1,355 m (4,450 ft)
Landing field length at S/L, ISA, 35° flap:
standard MLW 1,120 m (3,675 ft)
optional MLW 1,130 m (3,710 ft)
Range with 50 passengers and baggage, reserves for 45 min continued cruise at long-range schedule* and 100 nm (185 km; 115 mile) diversion:
at standard MTOW:
high-speed* procedure
1,109 nm (2,055 km; 1,277 miles)
min fuel procedure 1,216 nm (2,253 km; 1,400 miles)
at optional MTOW:
high speed* procedure
1,523 nm (2,822 km; 1,754 miles)
min fuel procedure
1,665 nm (3,085 km; 1,917 miles)

* *relevant speed and altitude details not supplied*

OPERATIONAL NOISE LEVELS:
T-O 79.4 EPNdB
Approach 96.7 EPNdB
Sideline 85.2 EPNdB

FOKKER 50 HOT and HIGH

The hot and high variant was launched in September 1990 for first delivery early in 1993. The P&WC PW125B engine, which is flat rated to 1,864 kW (2,500 shp) at 30°C ambient at sea level, is replaced by the PW127, which maintains this power at up to 42.5°C.

The first 100 PW127s were ordered when the aircraft was launched. A version of the PW127 giving increased power (2,050 kW; 2,750 shp) rather than a high ambient temperature capability is also available for eventual stretched Fokker 50s.

FOKKER 50 MARITIME and SURVEILLANCE VERSIONS

The following maritime and surveillance variants of the Fokker 50 are available.

Maritime Mk 2. Basic unarmed maritime patrol version, for duties which include coastal surveillance, search and rescue, and environmental control. Airframe heavily treated with anti-corrosive measures. Crew of up to six persons. No orders had been announced at the time of going to press.

Maritime Enforcer Mk 2. Similar to Maritime Mk 2, but equipped for armed surveillance, anti-submarine and anti-shipping warfare, with enhanced avionics and provisions for carrying external stores (armament chosen and installed by operator). Second Fokker 50 being converted as prototype/demonstrator, with US, British and Canadian equipment and Teledyne Systems as risk-sharing partner. First deliveries envisaged for late 1993. Singapore selected a version of the Enforcer Mk 2 for its maritime patrol aircraft in March 1991. The order is believed to be for four, plus an option on another four.

Differences from the standard transport are as follows:

TYPE: Twin-turboprop maritime patrol aircraft.

LANDING GEAR: Mainwheel tyre pressures 5.52 bars (80 lb/sq in) standard, 4.50 bars (65 lb/sq in) for low pressure tyres. Nosewheel tyre pressure increased to 3.80 bars (55 lb/sq in).

POWER PLANT: Additional centre-wing fuel tank of 2,310 litres (610 US gallons; 508 Imp gallons) capacity, and two 938 litre (248 US gallon; 206.5 Imp gallon) tanks on underwing pylons, giving overall total fuel capacity of 9,322 litres (2,463 US gallons; 2,051 Imp gallons). Methyl bromide fire extinguishing system, with flame detectors.

ACCOMMODATION: Crew of two on flight deck, with folding seat for third crew member if required. Main cabin of Maritime Mk 2 fitted out as tactical compartment (for two to four operators), containing advanced avionics, galley, toilet and crew rest area. Enforcer accommodates crew of seven including two pilots; tactical co-ordinator (Tacco) responsible for off-airways navigation and overall efforts of mission crew; acoustic sensor operator (ASO) to handle active and passive sonobuoys, acoustic receivers and processor display system; non-acoustic sensor operator (NASO) controlling search radar and electronic surveillance subsystem; and two observers. Bubble windows for observers at front of main cabin. Rear cabin door is openable in flight.

SYSTEMS: Oxygen system includes individual supply for each tactical crew member.

AVIONICS: Com/nav equipment comprises AN/ARC-190(V) HF transceivers, two Bendix/King VCS-40 VHF transceivers, Elmer SRT-561 VHF/UHF transceiver (three in Enforcer), interphone, crew address system, two Litton LTN-92 inertial navigation systems, Honeywell AZ-800 air data computer, Bendix/King DFS-43 radio compass, two TRT AHV-530 radio altimeters, Collins DF-301E VHF/UHF direction finder, two Bendix/King VNS-41 VOR/ILS/marker beacon receivers, Honeywell EDZ-806 EFIS, Teledyne AN/APX-109 IFF transponder/interrogator, dual Honeywell SPZ-600 AFCS, Honeywell P-650 weather radar, low altitude warning system, and Tacan. Both versions fitted with Litton AN/APS-140(V) 360° search radar in ventral radome. Additional mission equipment in Enforcer includes Teledyne AN/ASN-150(V) central tactical computer and display system, radar detection and display system, on-top position indicator/receiver, and CDC AN/UYS-503 sonobuoy processing system with Honeywell AN/AQH-4(V) acoustic signal recorder and dual Dowty/Resdel AN/ARR-XXX sonobuoy signal receivers. General Instrument AN/ALR-606(V)3 electronic surveillance and monitoring equipment to detect radar transmissions, which can be classified and recorded and their bearings transferred to the tactical display. Honeywell AN/ASH-34 mission recorder. GEC Sensors TICM II infra-red detection system (IRDS). CAE AN/ASQ-504(V) MAD. A Teledyne DTP-11 data link with available ground or shipborne systems can be provided.

EQUIPMENT: NGL and Alkan 8025 active/passive sonobuoy launchers; sonobuoys (up to 40 of SSQ-36, SSQ-41B or SSQ-47B type, up to 120 smaller buoys, or a mixture of both sizes) in rear of cabin. PEAB BOP-300 chaff/flare dispenser.

ARMAMENT (Maritime Enforcer Mk 2): Fokker installs Alkan T930 stores management system and provisions for armament; weapon mix and purchase is up to customer. Two 907 kg (2,000 lb) stores attachments on the fuselage and three under each wing (capacities 295 kg; 650 lb inboard, 680 kg; 1,500 lb in centre, and 113 kg; 250 lb outboard). Typical ASW armament can include two or four Mk 44, Mk 46, Sting Ray or A244/S torpedoes and/or depth bombs. For anti-shipping warfare, two AM39 Exocet, AGM-65F Maverick, AGM-84A Harpoon, Sea Skua, Sea Eagle or similar air-to-surface missiles can be carried. Auxiliary fuel tanks can be carried on the central underwing pylons.

WEIGHTS AND LOADINGS (A: Maritime Mk 2, B: Maritime Enforcer Mk 2):
Operating weight empty: A 13,314 kg (29,352 lb)
B (typical) 14,796 kg (32,620 lb)
Max fuel (incl pylon tanks): A 7,257 kg (16,000 lb)
B 7,511 kg (16,560 lb)
Normal T-O weight: both 20,820 kg (45,900 lb)
Max T-O weight: both 21,545 kg (47,500 lb)
Emergency overload T-O weight:
B 22,680 kg (50,000 lb)
Max landing weight: both 19,730 kg (43,500 lb)
Max zero-fuel weight: both 18,144 kg (40,000 lb)
Max wing loading: both 291.6 kg/m² (59.75 lb/sq ft)
Max power loading: both 6.39 kg/kW (10.5 lb/shp)

PERFORMANCE (at normal T-O weight except where indicated):
Normal cruising speed 259 knots (480 km/h; 298 mph)
Typical search speed at 610 m (2,000 ft)
150 knots (277 km/h; 172 mph)
Service ceiling: both 7,620 m (25,000 ft)
Service ceiling, one engine out: A 3,565 m (11,700 ft)
Runway LCN (42 per cent tyre deflection) at 15,875 kg (35,000 lb) AUW: A:
rigid pavement, L 76.2 cm (30 in) 10.4
flexible pavement, h 25.4 cm (10 in) 11.4
flexible pavement, h 12.7 cm (5 in) 9.0
Runway LCN (42 per cent tyre deflection) at 20,410 kg (45,000 lb) AUW: A:
rigid pavement, L 76.2 cm (30 in) 16.0
flexible pavement, h 25.4 cm (10 in) 14.8
extended pavement, h 12.7 cm (5 in) 12.0
Runway CBR, unpaved soil, h 25.4 cm (10 in), 3,000 passes: A:
AUW of 15,875 kg (35,000 lb) 6.2%
AUW of 20,410 kg (45,000 lb) 7.8%
T-O run at S/L, AUW of 21,320 kg (47,000 lb):
ISA 1,525 m (5,000 ft)
ISA + 20°C 1,700 m (5,575 ft)
Landing distance (unfactored, ISA at S/L), landing weight of 18,990 kg (41,866 lb) 762 m (2,500 ft)
Max radius of action with 1,814 kg (4,000 lb) mission load 1,200 nm (2,224 km; 1,382 miles)
Max range, no reserves
3,680 nm (6,820 km; 4,237 miles)
Max endurance, reserves for 30 min hold, 5% fuel remaining 14 h 42 min

FOKKER 100

Announced simultaneously with the Fokker 50, the Fokker 100 is derived from the F28 Mk 4000, which it superseded on the production line. It has a longer fuselage, extended and redesigned wings, Rolls-Royce Tay turbofans, a completely new CRT flight deck and cabin interior, and extensively modernised systems. The first prototype (PH-MKH) made its initial flight on 30 November 1986, and a second (PH-MKC) joined the flight test and certification programme on 25 February 1987, followed by the first series production aircraft (for the Ivory Coast Government) on 25 September 1987.

The Fokker 100 complies with the Stage 3 noise requirements of FAR Pt 36, and RLD certification to JAR Pt 25 was received on 20 November 1987, followed by Cat. IIIB autoland certification in June 1988. The first aircraft for Swissair made its initial flight on 30 December 1987, and was delivered on 29 February 1988. FAA type approval was granted on 30 May 1989, and certification of a version with uprated Tay Mk 650 engines, flown for the first time on PH-MKH on 8 June 1988, was received on 1 July 1989. First delivery of this version, to USAir, took place on the same day. Other options include intermediate (44,452 kg; 98,000 lb) and high max T-O (45,813 kg; 101,000 lb) weights, the last available in 1993, plus large passenger door, larger cargo doors, upper deck avionics and a polished outer skin.

The Fokker 100 is being produced in collaboration with Deutsche Airbus (large fuselage sections and tail section) and Shorts (wings); Grumman is subcontractor for the engine nacelles and thrust reversers, and Dowty for the landing gear. An agreement for IPTN of Indonesia to supply milled components and wing and tail components was announced in June 1988.

Firm orders totalled 246 by 31 March 1991 (with 128 more on option), of which 70 had been delivered, including 33 in 1990. Thirty-five Fokker 100s were due for completion during 1991, during which year a new assembly hall was being built. Output is planned to rise to 67 a year by early 1993.

TYPE: Twin-turbofan short/medium-haul transport.

WINGS: Cantilever low-wing monoplane. Fokker designed, advanced transonic wing sections, which offer substantially improved aerodynamic efficiency, especially at high speeds. Thickness/chord ratio up to 12.3 per cent on inner panels, 9.6 per cent at tip. Dihedral 2° 30′. Sweepback at quarter-chord 17° 27′. Light alloy torsion box structure, comprising two-spar centre-section (integral with fuselage) and two outer panels with two main spars and

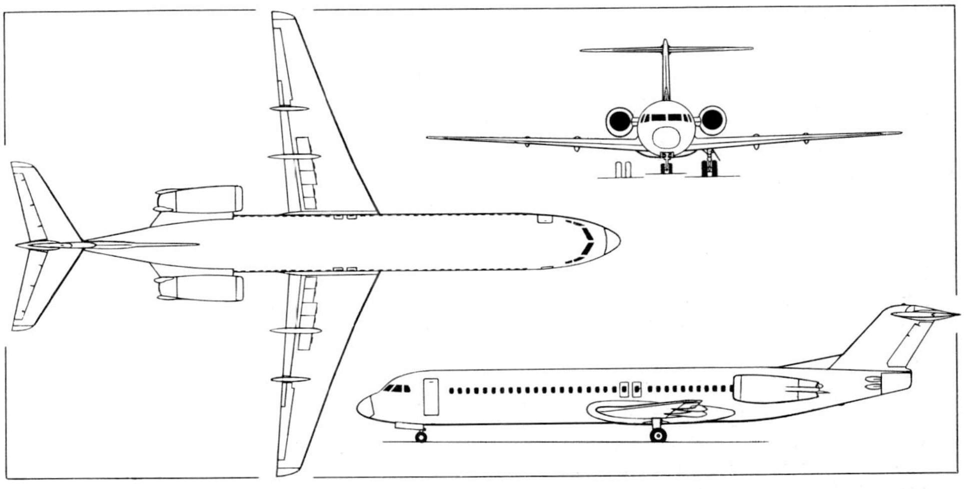

Fokker 100 short/medium-haul transport (two Rolls-Royce Tay turbofans) *(Pilot Press)*

Fokker 100 twin-turbofan short/medium-range transport in the insignia of TAM of Brazil

auxiliary front spar. Fail-safe construction. Lower skin of outer wings made of three planks. Taper rolled top skin. Forged ribs in centre-section, built-up ribs in outer panels. Light alloy leading-edges, with hot air de-icing. Irreversible hydraulically operated ailerons. In the third mode, both ailerons are driven manually via servo tabs. Hydraulically operated double-slotted Fowler flaps with electrical alternative extension. Five-panel, hydraulically operated lift dumpers in front of flaps on each wing. Flaps and ailerons are of carbonfibre, spoilers and aileron servo tabs of aluminium alloy.

FUSELAGE: Circular-section semi-monocoque light alloy fail-safe structure, made up of skin panels with bonded Z-stringers. Bonded double plates at door and window cutouts. Quickly detachable sandwich floor panels (carbonfibre and glassfibre with Nomex core). Hydraulically operated metal airbrakes form rear end of fuselage. AFRP wing/fuselage fairing panels.

TAIL UNIT: Cantilever light alloy T structure, with hydraulically actuated variable incidence tailplane. Third mode is electric operation. Hydraulically boosted elevators, with manual backup. Hydraulically operated rudders, with manual third mode. Fin constructed from honeycomb sandwich skin panels in conjunction with multiple spars; dorsal fin of aramid fibre. Light alloy elevator, carbonfibre rudder. Hot air de-icing of tailplane leading-edge.

LANDING GEAR: Hydraulically retractable tricycle type, with twin wheels on each unit. Main units retract inward into wing/body fairing; nosewheel retracts forward. Dowty shock absorber in each unit. Goodyear tyres, size H40 × 14-19 on main units (pressure 9.38 bars; 136 lb/sq in), size 24 × 7.7-10 (pressure 5.86 bars; 85 lb/sq in) on nose unit. Loral multiple-disc carbon brakes, with anti-skid system. Steerable nose unit (effective angle ±76°).

POWER PLANT: Two 61.6 kN (13,850 lb st) Rolls-Royce Tay Mk 620 turbofans initially, fitted with thrust reversers and pylon mounted on sides of rear fuselage. Nacelles manufactured from composite materials. Option from 1989 of 67.2 kN (15,100 lb st) Tay Mk 650 turbofans. Fuel in 4,840 litre (1,278.5 US gallon; 1,064.5 Imp gallon) main tank in each wing. In 1993, at same time as 101,000 lb max T-O weight option, an integral centre wing tank with a capacity of 3,785 litres (1,000 US gallons; 833 Imp gallons), giving the aircraft a total capacity of 13,465 litres (3,557 US gallons; 2,962 Imp gallons) will become a standard fitting. Refuelling point under starboard wing, near wing/fuselage belly fairing. Oil capacity (two engines) 23 kg (51 lb).

ACCOMMODATION: Crew of two on flight deck; three cabin attendants. Standard accommodation for 107 passengers, in five-abreast seating (3+2) at 81 cm (32 in) pitch. Optional layouts include 12 first class seats (four-abreast) at 91 cm (36 in) pitch plus 85 economy class (five-abreast) at 32 in; 55 business class at 86 cm (34 in) plus 50 economy class, all five-abreast; or 122 tourist class passengers at 74 cm (29 in) pitch. Reduced galley and stowage space in 122 seat layout. Standard layout includes two galleys, two toilets, two wardrobes, two other stowage/wardrobe compartments, and carry-on baggage compartment. Outward opening passenger door at front of cabin on port side, with outward opening service/emergency door opposite on starboard side. Optional auxiliary service door on port side near rear galley. Two overwing emergency exits (inward opening plug type) each side. Two underfloor baggage/cargo holds (one forward of wing, one aft), with three downward opening doors on

starboard side. Option for three identical enlarged, upward opening cargo doors and a moving belt loading system. Entire accommodation air-conditioned.

SYSTEMS: AiResearch air-conditioning and pressurisation system. Two fully independent hydraulic systems for actuation of flight control surfaces, landing gear, brakes and nosewheel steering. AiResearch pneumatic system. Sundstrand integrated drive generator electrical supply system. Oxygen system for flight crew and passengers. AiResearch thermal anti-icing system for wings and tail unit. Electric anti-icing of flight deck windows, pitot tubes, static vents, angle of attack vanes and ice detector probe. Garrett GTCP36-150R APU is standard; GTCP36-150RR is optional.

AVIONICS: Standard avionics include dual VHF com (to ARINC 716), PA system (ARINC 715), audio management system, ATC transponder (ARINC 718), triple AHRS (ARINC 705), dual radio altimeters (ARINC 707), dual VOR with marker beacon receiver (ARINC 711), dual ILS (ARINC 710), dual ADF (ARINC 712), dual DME (ARINC 709), Collins EFIS electronic display systems: primary flight display (PFD) and navigation display (ND) for each pilot, and multi-function display system (MFDS), consisting of two CRTs on centre instrument panel. EFIS and MFDS display units are identical in size. Dual digital air data systems (ARINC 706) with computer driven instruments, weather radar (ARINC 708 on ND), dual advanced flight management systems (AFMS), and Collins digital automatic flight control and augmentation system (AFCAS) for Cat. IIIA automatic landing plus full flight regime autothrottle system. Optional avionics include single or dual HF com (ARINC 719), third VHF com, Selcal (ARINC 714), second ATC, third ILS, third radio altimeter, music reproducer, ACARS, aircraft integrated data system, Cat. IIIB autoland capability (certificated in 1988) and a noise abatement profile (NAP, certificated in November 1990) as an optional addition to the AFCS.

DIMENSIONS, EXTERNAL:

Wing span	28.08 m (92 ft 1½ in)
Wing chord: at root	5.28 m (17 ft 4 in)
at tip	1.26 m (4 ft 1½ in)
Wing aspect ratio	8.4
Length overall	35.53 m (116 ft 6¾ in)
Fuselage: Length	32.50 m (106 ft 7½ in)
Max diameter	3.30 m (10 ft 10 in)
Height overall	8.50 m (27 ft 10½ in)
Tailplane span	10.04 m (32 ft 11¼ in)
Wheel track (c/l of shock struts)	5.04 m (16 ft 6½ in)
Wheelbase	14.01 m (45 ft 11½ in)
Passenger door (fwd, port): Height	2.10 m (6 ft 10½ in)
Width	0.86 m (2 ft 9¾ in)
Service door (fwd, stbd): Height	1.30 m (4 ft 3¼ in)
Width	0.86 m (2 ft 9¾ in)
Cargo compartment doors (fwd and rear, stbd):	
Height (each)	0.95 m (3 ft 1½ in)
Width (each)	0.90 m (2 ft 11½ in)
Height to sill (MTOW):	
fwd door at front	1.31 m (4 ft 3½ in)
fwd door at rear	1.37 m (4 ft 6 in)
rear door	1.46 m (4 ft 9½ in)
Overwing emergency exits (four, each):	
Height	0.91 m (3 ft 0 in)
Width	0.51 m (1 ft 8 in)

DIMENSIONS, INTERNAL:

Cabin, excl flight deck: Length	21.19 m (69 ft 6¼ in)
Max length of seating area	18.80 m (61 ft 8¼ in)

Max width	3.10 m (10 ft 2 in)
Width at floor	2.88 m (9 ft 5½ in)
Max height	2.01 m (6 ft 7¼ in)
Max floor area	58.48 m² (629.5 sq ft)
Max volume	107.58 m³ (3,799 cu ft)
Overhead stowage bins (total)	5.23 m³ (184.7 cu ft)
Additional baggage space (total)	3.17 m³ (112.0 cu ft)
Underfloor compartment volume:	
fwd	9.72 m³ (343.3 cu ft)
rear	7.36 m³ (260 cu ft)

AREAS:

Wings, gross	93.50 m² (1,006.4 sq ft)
Ailerons (total)	3.528 m² (37.98 sq ft)
Trailing-edge flaps (total)	17.00 m² (182.99 sq ft)
Lift dumpers (total)	5.30 m² (57.05 sq ft)
Rudder	2.30 m² (24.76 sq ft)
Elevators (total)	3.96 m² (42.63 sq ft)
Airbrakes (total)	3.62 m² (38.97 sq ft)

WEIGHTS AND LOADINGS (A: basic weights and Tay 620, B: current intermediate weights and Tay 650, C: 1993 high gross weights and Tay 650):

Typical operating weight empty:	
A	24,375 kg (53,738 lb)
B	24,505 kg (54,024 lb)
C	24,512 kg (54,040 lb)
Max payload (weight-limited): A	11,460 kg (25,265 lb)
B	12,235 kg (26,973 lb)
C	12,228 kg (26,958 lb)
Max ramp weight: A	43,320 kg (95,505 lb)
B	44,680 kg (98,500 lb)
C	46,040 kg (101,500 lb)
Max T-O weight: A	43,090 kg (95,000 lb)
B	44,450 kg (98,000 lb)
C	45,810 kg (101,000 lb)
Max landing weight: A	38,780 kg (85,500 lb)
B, C	39,915 kg (88,000 lb)
Max zero-fuel weight: A	35,835 kg (79,000 lb)
B, C	36,740 kg (81,000 lb)
Max wing loading: A	460.8 kg/m² (94.39 lb/sq ft)
B	475.4 kg/m² (97.37 lb/sq ft)
C	489.9 kg/m² (100.35 lb/sq ft)
Max power loading: A	350.0 kg/kN (3.43 lb/lb st)
B	361.2 kg/kN (3.54 lb/lb st)
C	372.4 kg/kN (3.65 lb/lb st)

PERFORMANCE (A, B and C as for Weights):

Max operating Mach number: A, B, C	0.77
Max operating speed at 8,230 m (27,000 ft):	
A	456 knots (845 km/h; 525 mph)
B, C	459 knots (850 km/h; 528 mph)
Approach speed at max landing weight:	
A	128 knots (237 km/h; 147 mph)
B, C	130 knots (241 km/h; 150 mph)
Service ceiling: A, B, C	10,670 m (35,000 ft)
FAR T-O field length at S/L, ISA, at max T-O weight:	
A	1,855 m (6,086 ft)
B	1,720 m (5,643 ft)
C	1,825 m (5,988 ft)
FAR landing field length at S/L, ISA, at max landing weight: A	1,320 m (4,330 ft)
B, C	1,350 m (4,420 ft)
Range with 107 passengers and baggage:	
A	1,350 nm (2,502 km; 1,554 miles)
B	1,610 nm (2,984 km; 1,854 miles)
C	1,710 nm (3,167 km; 1,969 miles)

OPERATIONAL NOISE LEVELS: Comply with FAR Pt 36 Stage 3, ICAO Annex 16 Chapter 3, Washington National night time limits and Orange County (SNA) Class E exempt.

NEW ZEALAND

PAC

PACIFIC AEROSPACE CORPORATION LIMITED

Private Bag HN 3027, Hamilton Airport, Hamilton
Telephone: 64 (71) 436 144
Fax: 64 (71) 436 134
Telex: NZ 21242 PACORP
CHIEF EXECUTIVE: Andrew Hyde
ENGINEERING MANAGER: Ron Guest
SALES MANAGER: Bob Geer

The former New Zealand Aerospace Industries Ltd was reconstituted on 1 July 1982 as Pacific Aerospace Corporation Ltd. PAC maintains full spares support for the Airtrainer CT4A/CT4B, Fletcher FU24-954 series and the Cresco 600. It is continuing to market the Fletcher FU24-954, Cresco 600, and new CT4C/CR variants of the Airtrainer. A new civilian version of the CT4B military trainer is also being marketed. PAC carries out phase servicing of BAC 167 Strikemasters (now being replaced by Aermacchi MB-339Cs) and Bell Iroquois helicopters of the RNZAF, and manufactured installation kits for the RNZAF's Project Kahu A-4K Skyhawk upgrade.

Shareholding in PAC is divided between ASTA of Australia (75.1 per cent, previously held by Agricultural Holdings) and Lockheed Corporation of the USA (24.9 per cent).

PAC FLETCHER FU24-954

The US built FU24 prototype flew in July 1954, followed by the first production aircraft five months later. Type certification was granted on 22 July 1955. All manufacturing and sales rights were transferred to New Zealand in 1964, and by 1990 a total of 292 Fletcher FU24 series aircraft had been completed, including 62 for export to Australia, Bangladesh, Dubai, Iraq, Pakistan, Thailand, Uruguay and the USA. A factory refurbishment/upgrade programme is offered by PAC for earlier FU24 series aircraft.

A full description of the current standard version, the FU24-954, can be found in the 1985-86 *Jane's*. The following is an abbreviated version of that entry:
TYPE: Agricultural and general purpose aircraft.
POWER PLANT: One 298 kW (400 hp) Textron Lycoming IO-720-A1A or A1B flat-eight engine, driving a Hartzell HC-C3YR-1R/847SR three-blade constant-speed metal propeller. Fuel tanks in wing leading-edges; total usable capacity 254 litres (67 US gallons; 55.8 Imp gallons) normal, 481 litres (127 US gallons; 105.75 Imp gallons) with optional long-range tanks.
ACCOMMODATION: Two-seat cockpit with sliding canopy and roll-over protection. Rear compartment, with freight door at rear to port, holds six passengers, equivalent freight or a 1,211 litre (320 US gallon; 266 Imp gallon) liquid or 1,066 kg (2,350 lb) dry hopper. Transland or Micronair application equipment. Options include dual controls, heating, full instruments, radio, dual main-wheels, and wheel/leg fairings.

DIMENSIONS, EXTERNAL:
Wing span	12.81 m (42 ft 0 in)
Length overall	9.70 m (31 ft 10 in)
Height overall	2.84 m (9 ft 4 in)
Wheel track	3.71 m (12 ft 2 in)
Wheelbase	2.28 m (7 ft 6 in)
Propeller diameter	2.18 m (7 ft 2 in)

DIMENSIONS, INTERNAL:
Cabin: Length	3.18 m (10 ft 5 in)
Max width	1.22 m (4 ft 0 in)
Max height	1.27 m (4 ft 2 in)
Floor area	3.87 m² (41.7 sq ft)
Volume aft of hopper	3.37 m³ (119.0 cu ft)
Hopper volume	1.22 m³ (43.0 cu ft)

AREAS:
Wings, gross	27.31 m² (294.0 sq ft)

WEIGHTS AND LOADINGS:
Weight empty, equipped	1,188 kg (2,620 lb)
Max disposable load (Agricultural)	1,275 kg (2,810 lb)
Normal max T-O weight	2,204 kg (4,860 lb)
Max Agricultural T-O weight	2,463 kg (5,430 lb)
Max cabin floor loading	1,884.6 kg/m² (386 lb/sq ft)
Wing loading at Normal max T-O weight	
	80.71 kg/m² (16.53 lb/sq ft)
Power loading at Normal max T-O weight	
	7.39 kg/kW (12.15 lb/hp)

PERFORMANCE (at Normal max T-O weight):
Never-exceed speed (V$_{NE}$)	
	143 knots (265 km/h; 165 mph)
Max level speed at S/L	126 knots (233 km/h; 145 mph)
Max cruising speed (75% power)	
	113 knots (209 km/h; 130 mph)
Operating speed for spraying (75% power)	
	90-115 knots (167-212 km/h; 104-132 mph)
Stalling speed: flaps up	55 knots (102 km/h; 64 mph)
flaps down	49 knots (91 km/h; 57 mph)
Max rate of climb at S/L	280 m (920 ft)/min
Service ceiling	4,875 m (16,000 ft)
T-O run	244 m (800 ft)
T-O to 15 m (50 ft)	372 m (1,220 ft)
Landing from 15 m (50 ft)	390 m (1,280 ft)
Landing run	207 m (680 ft)

Two Pacific Aerospace Corporation turbine powered Cresco 08-600 utility aircraft

Swath width (agricultural models):
oily	23 m (75 ft)
aqueous	21.3-24.4 m (70-80 ft)
dust	7.6-15.2 m (25-50 ft)
Range with max normal fuel, 45 min reserves	
	383 nm (709 km; 441 miles)

PAC CRESCO 08-600

Design of this turboprop development of the FU24 began in 1977, and the prototype (ZK-LTP) first flew on 28 February 1979. The Cresco has many components interchangeable with the FU24-954; its name is Latin for 'I grow'. The first production Cresco was flown in early 1980, and the type entered service in January 1982. Five, all for domestic customers, were completed by April 1986. Production in 1990 included three for Bangladesh, one equipped for agricultural roles and the other two in utility configuration, with passenger conversion kits supplied.

Marketing and support are continuing for the agricultural/utility and counter-insurgency versions, and a variant powered by a P&WC PT6A-27 or -34AG turboprop was offered.

The description of the FU24-954 applies also to the current production Cresco, except in the following respects:
TYPE: Turboprop powered agricultural and general purpose aircraft.
POWER PLANT: One Textron Lycoming LTP 101-700A-1A turboprop, flat rated at 447 kW (599 shp) and driving a Hartzell HC-B3TN-3D/T10282 three-blade constant-speed metal propeller. Four fuel tanks in wing centre-section, total capacity 545.5 litres (144 US gallons; 120 Imp gallons). Oil capacity 5.5 litres (1.4 US gallons; 1.2 Imp gallons). Two refuelling points in upper surface of each wing. Chin mounted engine air intake, fitted with Centrisep filter panel.

DIMENSIONS, EXTERNAL:
Wing span	12.81 m (42 ft 0 in)
Length overall	11.07 m (36 ft 4 in)
Height overall	3.63 m (11 ft 10¾ in)
Wheelbase	2.77 m (9 ft 1¼ in)
Propeller diameter	2.59 m (8 ft 6 in)
Cargo door (port): Height	0.94 m (3 ft 1 in)
Width	0.94 m (3 ft 1 in)
Height to sill	0.91 m (3 ft 0 in)

DIMENSIONS, INTERNAL:
Cargo compartment volume (aft of hopper)	
	3.40 m³ (120.0 cu ft)
Hopper volume	1.77 m³ (62.5 cu ft)

AREAS:
Wings, gross	27.31 m² (294.0 sq ft)

WEIGHTS AND LOADINGS:
Weight empty, equipped	1,270 kg (2,800 lb)
Max disposable load (Agricultural, incl fuel)	
	1,828 kg (4,030 lb)
Max fuel load	435 kg (960 lb)
Max T-O weight: Normal	2,925 kg (6,450 lb)
Agricultural	3,175 kg (7,000 lb)
Max landing weight	2,925 kg (6,450 lb)
Wing loading:	
at Normal max T-O weight	
	107.12 kg/m² (21.94 lb/sq ft)
at Agricultural max T-O weight	
	116.25 kg/m² (23.81 lb/sq ft)
Power loading:	
at Normal max T-O weight	6.55 kg/kW (10.77 lb/shp)
at Agricultural max T-O weight	
	7.11 kg/kW (11.69 lb/shp)

PERFORMANCE (at max Normal T-O weight, ISA, except where indicated):
Never-exceed speed (V$_{NE}$)	
	177 knots (328 km/h; 204 mph)
Max level speed at S/L	148 knots (274 km/h; 170 mph)
Max cruising speed (75% power)	
	133 knots (246 km/h; 153 mph)
Stalling speed at 2,767 kg (6,100 lb) AUW, flaps down, power off	52 knots (97 km/h; 60 mph)
Max rate of climb at S/L	379 m (1,245 ft)/min
Absolute ceiling	5,485 m (18,000 ft)
T-O run	323 m (1,058 ft)
T-O to 15 m (50 ft)	436 m (1,430 ft)
Landing from 15 m (50 ft)	500 m (1,640 ft)
Range at 3,175 kg (7,000 lb) MTOGW with standard fuel, no reserves	460 nm (852 km; 529 miles)

PAC AIRTRAINER CT4B, C and CR

The CT4 Airtrainer was a New Zealand redesign of the Australian Victa Airtourer and first flew in prototype form on 23 February 1972. A total of 96 CT4 series aircraft was built before production ceased in 1977. The Royal Thai Air Force fleet of 18 (of 24 originally acquired) is undergoing fatigue life extension of the wings, carried out by RTAF personnel with assistance from PAC.

PAC is now offering three CT4 variants, as follows:
CT4B: With 157 kW (210 hp) Teledyne Continental IO-360-HB flat-six engine. Production line reopened: 12 civil aircraft to be produced during 1991.
CT4C: With 313 kW (420 shp) Allison 250-B17D turboprop, throttle-limited to 149 kW (200 shp). Non-

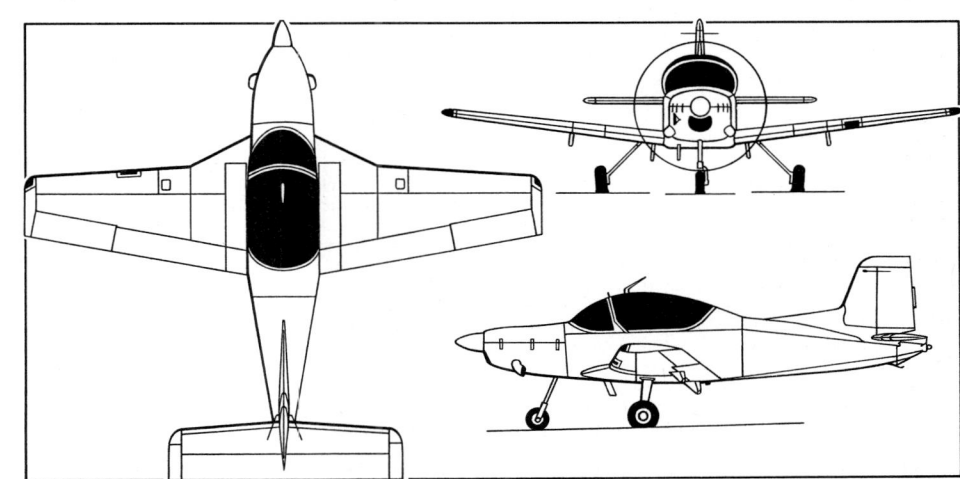

PAC Airtrainer CT4C turboprop conversion of the CT4 *(Jane's/Mike Keep)*

retractable landing gear. Overall length increased. Prototype made first flight on 21 January 1991.

CT4CR: As CT4C, but with retractable landing gear. A prototype should be completed in late 1991 or early 1992.

TYPE: Two/three-seat fully aerobatic light training aircraft.

WINGS: Cantilever low-wing monoplane. Wing section NACA 23012 (modified) at root, NACA 4412 (modified) at tip. Dihedral 6° 45′ at chord line. Incidence 3° at root, 0° at tip. Root chord increased by forward sweep of the inboard leading-edges. Single main spar light alloy stressed skin structure, with glassfibre wingtips that are detachable to permit optional wingtip fuel tanks to be fitted. Single-slotted electrically actuated flap and aerodynamically balanced bottom-hinged aileron on each trailing-edge, of light alloy construction with fluted skins. No tabs.

FUSELAGE: All-metal stressed skin semi-monocoque structure. Glassfibre engine cowling.

TAIL UNIT: Cantilever light alloy structure, with some aerodynamic balance. One-piece elevator, statically balanced. Ground adjustable tab on rudder. Rudder controlled by rod and cable linkage, elevator by rod and mechanical linkage. Electrically actuated trim control for rudder and elevator.

LANDING GEAR: Tricycle type, retractable on CT4CR, non-retractable on CT4B and C. Non-retractable gear has cantilever spring steel main legs, and steerable nosewheel carried on telescopic strut and oleo shock absorber. Main units fitted with Dunlop Australia wheels and tubeless tyres size 6.00-6; nosewheel fitted with tubeless tyre size 5.00-5. Dunlop Australia single-disc toe operated hydraulic brakes, with hand operated parking lock. Landing gear designed to shear before any excess impact loading is transmitted to wing, to minimise structural damage in the event of a crash landing.

POWER PLANT: As given in individual model listings. CT4B has a total standard fuel capacity of 204.5 litres (54 US gallons; 45 Imp gallons). Wingtip tanks, each of 77 litres (20.5 US gallons; 17 Imp gallons) capacity, available optionally.

ACCOMMODATION: Two seats side by side under hinged, fully transparent Perspex canopy. Space to rear for optional third seat or 52 kg (115 lb) of baggage or equipment. Dual controls standard.

DIMENSIONS, EXTERNAL (all versions, except where indicated):

Wing span	7.92 m (26 ft 0 in)
Wing chord: at root	2.17 m (7 ft 1¼ in)
at tip	0.98 m (3 ft 2½ in)
Wing aspect ratio	5.25
Length overall: B	7.06 m (23 ft 2 in)
C, CR	7.14 m (23 ft 5 in)
Height overall	2.59 m (8 ft 6 in)
Fuselage: Max width	1.12 m (3 ft 8 in)
Max depth	1.40 m (4 ft 7¼ in)
Tailplane span	3.61 m (11 ft 10 in)
Wheel track	2.97 m (9 ft 9 in)
Wheelbase	1.71 m (5 ft 7⅜ in)

DIMENSIONS, INTERNAL (all versions):

Cabin: Length	2.74 m (9 ft 0 in)
Max width	1.08 m (3 ft 6½ in)
Max height	1.35 m (4 ft 5 in)

AREAS (all versions):

Wings, gross	11.98 m² (129.0 sq ft)
Ailerons (total)	1.07 m² (11.56 sq ft)
Flaps (total)	2.10 m² (22.60 sq ft)
Fin	0.60 m² (6.43 sq ft)
Rudder, incl tab	0.58 m² (6.26 sq ft)
Tailplane	1.43 m² (15.40 sq ft)
Elevator	1.26 m² (13.60 sq ft)

WEIGHTS AND LOADINGS:

Max T-O weight (all)	1,202 kg (2,650 lb)
Max wing loading (all)	100.3 kg/m² (20.54 lb/sq ft)
Max power loading: B	7.68 kg/kW (12.62 lb/hp)
C, CR	8.06 kg/kW (13.25 lb/shp)

PERFORMANCE (estimated: C and CR at AUW of 1,111 kg; 2,450 lb):

Max level speed at S/L:		
C		205 knots (380 km/h; 236 mph)
CR		234 knots (434 km/h; 269 mph)
Max level speed at 3,050 m (10,000 ft):		
C		208 knots (385 km/h; 239 mph)
CR		240 knots (445 km/h; 276 mph)
Max level speed at 6,100 m (20,000 ft):		
C		195 knots (361 km/h; 224 mph)
CR		228 knots (422 km/h; 262 mph)
Stalling speed at S/L:		
flaps up: C, CR		57 knots (106 km/h; 66 mph)
flaps down: C, CR		44 knots (82 km/h; 51 mph)
Max rate of climb at S/L, ISA:		
C		843 m (2,765 ft)/min
CR		930 m (3,050 ft)/min
Service ceiling: CR		9,900 m (32,500 ft)
Time to 6,100 m (20,000 ft): CR		10 min 9 s
T-O run at S/L, ISA:		
C, CR		117 m (384 ft)
T-O to 15 m (50 ft) at S/L, ISA:		
C, CR		206 m (675 ft)
Landing run: CR		160 m (525 ft)
Range with max fuel (75% power), ISA, no reserves:		
at S/L: C		464 nm (860 km; 534 miles)
CR		529 nm (980 km; 609 miles)
at 3,050 m (10,000 ft): C		624 nm (1,156 km; 718 miles)
CR		724 nm (1,342 km; 834 miles)

RNZAF
ROYAL NEW ZEALAND AIR FORCE

Air Staff, Defence Headquarters, Stout Street, Wellington C1
Telephone: 64 (4) 726 499
Telex: 3513 DEF COM NZ
KAHU PROJECT MANAGER: Gp Capt James Barclay

RNZAF A-4 SKYHAWK UPGRADE

Under the project name Kahu (Maori for 'Hawk'), the remaining 21 of the RNZAF's fleet of 22 A-4 Skyhawks (16 out of 17 A-4s and five TA-4s) have been upgraded and refurbished. Installation kits were made by Pacific Aerospace Corporation and fitted by Safe Air. The first Kahu A-4K was handed over on 6 July 1989 and the last in December 1990. One A-4 was destroyed in an accident before upgrading.

The upgrade included new wing spars and systems for launching; AGM-65 Maverick, AIM-9L Sidewinder and GBU-16 laser guided bomb capability, plus Westinghouse AN/APG-66 (NZ) radar with maritime target tracking; HOTAS controls and provision for FLIR and night vision goggles; MIL-STD-1553B databus; Collins AN/ARC-182 VHF/UHF and AN/ARC-159 UHF standby radios, VIR-130 VOR/ILS with glideslope and AN/ARN-118 Tacan; Smiths AN/APN-194 radar altimeter; Hazeltine AN/APX-72 IFF; General Instrument AN/ALR-66 (VE) radar warning receiver; Garrett digital air data computer; and Goodyear AN/ALE-39 chaff/flare dispenser.

NIGERIA

AIEP
AERONAUTICAL INDUSTRIAL ENGINEERING AND PROJECT MANAGEMENT CO LTD

General Aviation Service Centre, PO Box 5662, Old Kaduna Airport
Telephone: 234 (62) 217573
Fax: 234 (62) 217325
Telex: 71327 AIEP NG
MANAGING DIRECTOR: Klaus Gloege

It was reported in 1990 that the Nigerian Air Force was seeking "a closer relationship" with AIEP, including a possible major shareholding.

AIEP AIR BEETLE

AIEP, in which Dornier GmbH of Germany has a 60 per cent holding, completed about 500 hours' flying in this version of the US Van's RV-6A homebuilt (see Sport Aircraft section) by late 1990. It is powered by a 134 kW (180 hp) Textron Lycoming flat-four engine with a fixed-pitch propeller. The programme continued during 1991 and, after certification, the Air Beetle was expected to enter production to supplement the Nigerian Air Force's BAe Bulldog trainers.

PAKISTAN

PAC
PAKISTAN AERONAUTICAL COMPLEX

Kamra, District Attock
WORKS: F-6 Rebuild Factory; Mirage Rebuild Factory; Kamra Avionics and Radar Factory; Aircraft Manufacturing Factory (all at Kamra)
Telephone: 92 (51) 580260/5
Fax: 92 (51) 584162
Telex: 5601 PAC KAMRA PK
DIRECTOR GENERAL: Air Vice-Marshal S. K. Abbas Zaidi
MANAGING DIRECTORS:
Air Cdre Abdul Wahid (AMF)
Air Cdre Ijaz Rasul (F-6RF)
Air Cdre Abdul Wahid Malik (MRF)
Air Cdre Rafi ul Qadir (KARF)

Located approximately midway between Islamabad and Peshawar, the Pakistan Aeronautical Complex is an organ of the Pakistan Ministry of Defence. It consists of four factories, as follows:

The **Aircraft Manufacturing Factory** (AMF) came into operation in mid-1981, as licence production centre for the Saab Safari/Supporter two/three-seat light aircraft, which has the Pakistani name Mushshak (Urdu for 'proficient'). Initially, 23 aircraft were supplied complete. Another 92 were assembled from completely knocked down kits at Risalpur from 1975 to 1982 and another 25 in the AMF at Kamra from 1983 to 1985. Completely indigenous production followed, and 75 of these had been delivered by mid-February 1991, including most of 25 for the Iranian Pasdaran Revolutionary Guards. Between 1980 and 1991, 42 Mushshaks were overhauled at Kamra. Present production rate is 24 a year. In 1989, a Mushshak with a more powerful 156.6 kW (210 hp) Teledyne Continental TIO-360-MB engine, resulting in a considerable increase in performance, received US certification to FAR Pt 23. Only one prototype (86-5147) had been built by 1991.

Major facilities at the AMF include equipment to manufacture all GFRP components of the Mushshak. Engines, instruments, electrical equipment and radios are imported, but almost all other items are manufactured locally.

The AMF is collaborating with NAMC in China in developing a new jet trainer known as the **Karakorum 8** (see NAMC/PAC heading in the International section) which made its first flight in 1990.

The **Mirage Rebuild Factory** (MRF), which began operating in 1978, can accomplish complete overhaul of Mirage III/5 aircraft, Atar 9C turbojets, and all associated aircraft components and engine accessories. It has a current capacity for overhauling 8-10 aircraft and more than 50 engines per year. It can overhaul and rebuild third country Mirage III/5s, engines, components and accessories. Since 1988 the MRF is also overhauling Mirages of the United Arab Emirates Air Force.

Overhaul of the 43 Dassault/Commonwealth Mirage IIIOAs and seven two-seat IIIDs bought from Australia has been transferred from the PAF Air Logistics Depot at Sharea Faisal to the MRF. The first, IIID A3-111, was received in January 1991.

The facility is being upgraded to undertake improved life core (ILC) modification and overhaul of Pratt & Whitney F100-PW-200/220E turbofans, together with their engine jet fuel starter, and will soon have a limited capability to service and overhaul F-16 aircraft components. The MRF has a site area of more than 810,000 m² (8,715,000 sq ft) and a workforce of nearly 2,000 trained engineers and technicians.

The **F-6 Rebuild Factory**, or F-6RF, was established in 1980 for the primary purpose of overhauling the Pakistan Air Force's Chinese Shenyang F-6 aircraft and their accessories. It is authorised to manufacture about 4,000 spares items for that aircraft, and also produces the 1,140 litre (301 US gallon; 250 Imp gallon) auxiliary fuel tanks fitted to the F-6. Production of 500 and 800 litre (132 and 211 US gallon; 110 and 176 Imp gallon) supersonic drop tanks for the F-7P started in mid-1991.

The F-6RF possesses modern technical facilities for various engineering processes such as surface treatment, heat treatment, forging, casting, non-destructive testing, and other machine tools required to manufacture items from raw materials. It overhauls Pakistan Air Force FT-5s, FT-6s and F-5 IIIs and in due course is expected to assume responsibility for the rebuild of Chinese F/FT-7s in PAF service.

The **Kamra Avionics and Radar Factory** has been recently established to rebuild PAF radars and avionics. It is presently rebuilding Siemens mobile pulse Doppler radar 45-E, rebuilding complex components and modules of MPDR-45 and rebuilding Siemens and associated power generators.

The factory has modern, environmentally controlled electronics workshops and test equipment including an automated Pegamat tester. By early 1991, the factory had rebuilt seven radars, 86 generators and more than 4,000 components. It then employed 18 engineers and 135 technicians. The factory is one of the leading electronics concerns of the country.

KARF intends to rebuild MPDR-60 and MPDR-90 radars and the Siemens Control and Reporting Centre and to assemble line replaceable units of the radars. It is investigating the international market for co-production of avionics, including radar warning receivers and airborne radios.

PAC (AMF) Mushshak at Kamra awaiting delivery to the Iranian Islamic Air Force *(Lindsay Peacock)*

PAC (AMF) MUSHSHAK and SHAHBAAZ

Production rate in 1991 was 24 a year. A Mushshak powered by a turbocharged 156.6 kW (210 hp) Teledyne Continental TIO-360-MB, called Shahbaaz, made its first flight in July 1987 and was certificated to US FAR Pt 23 in 1989. Only one was produced by 1991. Take-off run at 1,402 m (4,600 ft) ASL in +41°C (106°F) was reduced by 25 to 30 per cent to 290 m (590 ft). About 190 Mushshaks had been acquired and produced by 1990, 50 for the PAF and the rest for the Army. Since October 1987, Kamra has been responsible for all MFI-15/17 product support worldwide.

The following description applies to the initial production version with 149 kW (200 hp) power plant; no data were received for the higher powered version.

TYPE: Two/three-seat training and observation light aircraft.
WINGS: Braced shoulder-wing monoplane with single strut each side. Thickness/chord ratio 10 per cent. Dihedral 1° 30′. All-metal structure, sweptforward 5° from roots. Mass balanced all-metal ailerons. Electrically operated all-metal plain sealed flaps. Servo tab in starboard aileron.
FUSELAGE: Metal box structure. Glassfibre tailcone, engine cowling panels and wing strut/landing gear attachment fairings.
TAIL UNIT: Cantilever metal structure comprising swept fin and rudder and one-piece mass balanced horizontal 'stabilator' with large anti-servo and trimming tab. Glassfibre fin tip. Trim tab in rudder.
LANDING GEAR: Non-retractable tricycle type. Cantilever composite spring main legs. Goodyear 6.00-6 mainwheels and 5.00-5 steerable nosewheel. Cleveland disc brakes on main units.
POWER PLANT: One 149 kW (200 hp) Textron Lycoming IO-360-A1B6 flat-four engine initially, driving a Hartzell HC-C2YK-4F/FC7666A-2 two-blade constant-speed metal propeller (see other engine above). Two integral wing fuel tanks, total capacity 190 litres (50.2 US gallons; 41.8 Imp gallons). Oil capacity 7.5 litres (2.0 US gallons;

1.6 Imp gallons). From 10-20 s inverted flight (limited by oil system) permitted.
ACCOMMODATION: Side by side adjustable seats, with provision for back type or seat type parachutes, for two persons beneath fully transparent upward hinged canopy. Dual controls standard. Space aft of seats for 100 kg (220 lb) of baggage (with external access on port side) or, optionally, a rearward facing third seat. Upward hinged door, with window, beneath wing on port side. Cabin heated and ventilated.
SYSTEMS: 28V 50A DC electrical system.
AVIONICS: Provision for full blind-flying instrumentation and radio.
ARMAMENT: Provision for six underwing attachment points, the inner two stressed to carry up to 150 kg (330 lb) each and the outer four up to 100 kg (220 lb) each. Possible armament loads include two 7.62 mm machine-gun pods, two pods each with seven 75 mm air-to-surface rockets, four pods each with seven 68 mm rockets, eighteen 75 mm rockets, or six wire guided anti-tank missiles.

DIMENSIONS, EXTERNAL:
Wing span	8.85 m (29 ft 0½ in)
Wing chord (outer panels, constant)	1.36 m (4 ft 5½ in)
Length overall	7.00 m (22 ft 11½ in)
Height overall	2.60 m (8 ft 6½ in)
Tailplane span	2.80 m (9 ft 2¼ in)
Wheel track	2.30 m (7 ft 6½ in)
Wheelbase	1.59 m (5 ft 2¾ in)
Propeller diameter	1.88 m (6 ft 2 in)
Cabin door (port): Height	0.78 m (2 ft 6¾ in)
Width	0.52 m (1 ft 8½ in)

DIMENSIONS, INTERNAL:
Cabin: Max width	1.10 m (3 ft 7¼ in)
Max height (from seat cushion)	1.00 m (3 ft 3¼ in)

AREAS:
Wings, gross	11.90 m² (128.1 sq ft)
Ailerons (total)	0.98 m² (10.55 sq ft)
Flaps (total)	1.55 m² (16.68 sq ft)
Fin	0.77 m² (8.29 sq ft)
Rudder, incl tab	0.73 m² (7.86 sq ft)
Horizontal tail surfaces (total)	2.10 m² (22.6 sq ft)

WEIGHTS AND LOADINGS:
Weight empty, equipped	646 kg (1,424 lb)
Max T-O weight: Normal	1,200 kg (2,645 lb)
Utility	1,125 kg (2,480 lb)
Aerobatic	900 kg (1,984 lb)

PERFORMANCE (at max T-O weight, Utility category):
Never-exceed speed (V_{NE})	197 knots (365 km/h; 227 mph)
Max level speed at S/L	127 knots (236 km/h; 146 mph)
Cruising speed	112 knots (208 km/h; 129 mph)
Stalling speed, flaps down, power off	58 knots (107 km/h; 67 mph)
Max rate of climb at S/L	246 m (807 ft)/min
Time to 1,830 m (6,000 ft)	9 min 18 s
Service ceiling	4,100 m (13,450 ft)
T-O run	205 m (673 ft)
T-O to 15 m (50 ft)	385 m (1,263 ft)
Landing from 15 m (50 ft)	390 m (1,280 ft)
Landing run	155 m (509 ft)
Max endurance (65% power) at S/L, 10% reserves	5 h 10 min
g limits:	+4.4/−1.76 Utility
	+6/−3 Aerobatic

PERU

INDAER PERU
INDUSTRIA AERONAUTICA DEL PERU SA
Chinchon 1070, Lima 27
Telephone: 51 (14) 42 0355
Fax: 51 (14) 42 4953
Telex: 20125 PE MINAR
PRESIDENT: Alfredo Arrisueno
GENERAL MANAGER: Fernando Carulla

An early entry for Indaer Peru, the nation's sole aircraft manufacturer, appeared in the 1985-86 *Jane's*. At that time, financial constraints had compelled abandonment of plans to assemble, and eventually manufacture, MB-339A jet trainers under licence from Aermacchi of Italy.

After studying the Peruvian civil aircraft inventory and the country's needs for a specific type of aircraft, as well as the potential domestic and external markets, especially in developing countries, it was decided instead to undertake a more modest programme for a general aviation aircraft that would provide an alternative to both microlights and the more expensive light aircraft. This resulted in the Chuspi and Urpi designs described in the following entries.

In addition, Indaer Peru has signed agreements with Aero Boero of Argentina (which see) to produce the AB 115 and AB 180 in Peru, and with Pilatus (see Swiss section) for production of the PC-6 Turbo-Porter.

INDAER PERU IAP-001 CHUSPI (MOSQUITO)

Design of the prototype Chuspi, Indaer Peru's first production aircraft, was based upon those of such popular aircraft as the Avid Aircraft Avid Flyer, Denney Kitfox, HAPI Cygnet and Piper Cub. It began in late 1986, criteria including STOL capability; steep angle of climb; ease of flying and maintenance; ability to operate from unprepared fields, and to adapt to float gear; and an adequate service ceiling for operation over the Andes.

IAP-001 Chuspi demonstrating the use of ULV cropspraying equipment

The prototype was built by Indaer with the collaboration of the Escuela de Oficiales y Suboficiales of the Peruvian Air Force. It was unveiled in July 1987 and made its first flight, in Peruvian Air Force insignia, in the following month. Conceived initially for sport flying, dual control basic training, and (with a Louisiana Agrilites ULV system) cropspraying, the Chuspi was put into production in January 1988, the first production aircraft making its initial flight in September of that year. By the following month, 20 had been ordered: 12 by the Ministry of Transportation and eight, for agricultural use, by private farmers. The first 10 Chuspis had been completed by the end of 1989, and 12 had been delivered by late January 1990.

TYPE: Two-seat sport aircraft.
WINGS: Braced high-wing monoplane, with streamline section V struts each side. Thickness/chord ratio 12 per cent. Dihedral 2° 30′. Incidence 2° 30′ at root, 0° at fifth

rib. Two aluminium spars, I-beam plywood ribs, covered with heat-shrunk Dacron. Glassfibre wingtips. Full span aluminium flaperons, hinged at centre of pressure. Wings can be folded for transportation and storage.
FUSELAGE: Rectangular section welded structure of 4130 chrome molybdenum steel tube, covered with Dacron. Two-piece engine cowling of pre-moulded glassfibre.
TAIL UNIT: Welded structure of 4130 Chromoly steel tube, covered with heat-shrunk Dacron. Sweptback fin, integral with fuselage; wire braced, non-swept fixed incidence tailplane.
LANDING GEAR: Choice of tailwheel or tricycle type, both non-retractable, with 4130 steel tube mainwheel Vs and side axles. Tyre sizes 8.00-6 (main), 5.00-5 (nose); pressure (all three) 1.38 bars (20 lb/sq in). Mainwheel drum brakes. Can be adapted to glassfibre or Edo inflatable floats, or skis.

Two views of the Indaer Peru Chuspi: prototype (left) with tricycle landing gear, and (right) in 'taildragger' configuration with mainwheel speed fairings

POWER PLANT: One 48 kW (64 hp) Rotax 532 LC two-cylinder piston engine, with twin carburettors and electric starter, driving a two-blade fixed-pitch propeller via a 2.58:1 planetary reduction gear. Standard fuel capacity of 45.4 litres (12 US gallons; 10 Imp gallons) in tank in starboard wing; second, optional tank of same capacity in port wing. Gravity refuelling point for each tank in wing upper surface. Oil capacity 0.95 litre (0.25 US gallon; 0.21 Imp gallon).

ACCOMMODATION: Two seats side by side, in fully enclosed cabin protected by rollover cage. Upward opening window/door on each side. Cabin heater optional.

SYSTEMS: Electrical system.

AVIONICS: VHF transceiver optional.

DIMENSIONS, EXTERNAL:

Wing span	9.15 m (30 ft 0¼ in)
Wing chord, constant	1.07 m (3 ft 6 in)
Wing aspect ratio	7.23
Length overall	5.20 m (17 ft 0¾ in)
Fuselage: Max width	3.26 m (10 ft 8¼ in)
Max depth	3.83 m (12 ft 6¾ in)
Width, wings folded	2.40 m (7 ft 10½ in)
Height overall (tail up)	1.75 m (5 ft 9 in)
Tailplane span	2.36 m (7 ft 9 in)
Wheel track	1.53 m (5 ft 0¼ in)
Wheelbase: tricycle version	1.00 m (3 ft 3¼ in)
tailwheel version	3.80 m (12 ft 5½ in)
Propeller diameter	1.83 m (6 ft 0 in)
Propeller ground clearance:	
tricycle version	0.16 m (6⅜ in)
tailwheel version	0.44 m (1 ft 5½ in)

DIMENSIONS, INTERNAL:

Cabin: Length	1.23 m (4 ft 0½ in)
Max width	0.99 m (3 ft 3 in)
Max height	1.17 m (3 ft 10 in)
Floor area	0.41 m² (4.42 sq ft)
Volume	1.42 m³ (50.1 cu ft)

AREAS:

Wings, gross	11.58 m² (124.6 sq ft)
Flaperons (total)	1.40 m² (15.07 sq ft)
Fin	0.507 m² (5.46 sq ft)
Rudder	0.339 m² (3.65 sq ft)
Tailplane	0.893 m² (9.61 sq ft)
Elevators (total)	0.680 m² (7.32 sq ft)

WEIGHTS AND LOADINGS:

Weight empty	214 kg (472 lb)
Max fuel weight: 1 tank	80 kg (176.5 lb)
2 tanks	160 kg (353 lb)
Max T-O weight	409 kg (901 lb)
Max wing loading	35.32 kg/m² (7.23 lb/sq ft)
Max power loading	8.58 kg/kW (14.09 lb/hp)

PERFORMANCE (A: single-seat at 322 kg; 710 lb AUW, B: two-seat at 392 kg; 864 lb):

Never-exceed speed (V$_{NE}$):	
A, B	96 knots (177 km/h; 110 mph)
Max cruising speed: A, B	69 knots (129 km/h; 80 mph)
Stalling speed: A	22 knots (40 km/h; 25 mph)
B	28 knots (51 km/h; 32 mph)
Max rate of climb at S/L: A	427 m (1,400 ft)/min
B	293 m (960 ft)/min
Service ceiling: A	6,700 m (22,000 ft)
B	4,880 m (16,000 ft)
T-O run: A	30 m (99 ft)
B	50 m (164 ft)
T-O to 15 m (50 ft): A	70 m (230 ft)
B	150 m (493 ft)
Landing from 15 m (50 ft): A	110 m (361 ft)
B	180 m (591 ft)
Landing run: A	70 m (230 ft)
B	93 m (305 ft)
Range with max optional fuel:	
A, B	238 nm (441 km; 274 miles)
g limits	+3.8 (+5.8 ultimate)

INDAER PERU IAP-002 AG-CHUSPI

Due to an increasing domestic and foreign demand for an economical cropspraying aircraft, Indaer began to redesign the Chuspi in July 1989 to fulfil such a requirement. A prototype flew in November 1989. The test programme was due to be completed in March 1990, enabling series production to begin in May.

The Ag-Chuspi is equipped with an 18-nozzle ultra-low-volume (ULV) spraybar system (nine nozzles each wing). To reduce drag and improve manoeuvrability for operations in small fields surrounded by trees and mountains, it carries its chemical payload in modified in-wing tanks. The starboard wing contains a 30.3 litre (8 US gallon; 6.7 Imp gallon) fuel tank, sufficient to allow two hours of operation with an adequate reserve, plus a 22.7 litre (6 US gallon; 5 Imp gallon) chemical tank. The port wing has a 53 litre (14 US gallon; 11.7 Imp gallon) chemical tank, giving a total load of 75.7 litres (20 US gallons; 16.7 Imp gallons) of chemical. In addition, the Ag-Chuspi differs in being a single-seater, with cabin width reduced to 0.89 m (2 ft 11 in). With appropriate specialised equipment, the Ag-Chuspi can also be used for seeding or fishery farm feeding.

INDAER PERU IAP-003 URPI (DOVE)

The Urpi is a reinforced and stretched version of the Chuspi, with a 0.51 m (1 ft 8 in) longer fuselage, wider (1.07 m; 3 ft 6 in) and more comfortable two-seat cabin, and a 56 kW (75 hp) Revmaster VW engine. It is intended for basic training, sport and flying club use, and highway/traffic patrol. Design was completed in November 1989, and first flight was expected in March 1990, followed by the start of series production three months later.

PHILIPPINES

ACT
AVIATION COMPOSITE TECHNOLOGY
FJM Hangar, Domestic Airport Road, Pasay City 1300
Telephone: 63 (2) 833 2510
Fax: 63 (2) 833 2509

This company was beginning to manufacture the US Lancair 320 kit-built sport aircraft in the Philippines and had completed one registered RPX-320. The venture was associated with Aerotech of Lugano, Switzerland, and the company literature stated that its US sales office was Neico Aviation Inc, of Santa Paula, California. ACT was developing the Apache 1 military trainer version of the Lancair and the aircraft was to be manufactured by Philippine Aerospace Development Corporation (PADC) (which see). Unfortunately, ACT president Robert Schaeffer was killed during a demonstration at the Philippine air show on 9 March 1991. The effect on the enterprise was not immediately known.

ACT APACHE 1
The plan to produce a military trainer version of the civilian Lancair 320 in the Philippines was announced in September 1990. Advanced Composite Technology was to be supported by Neico Aviation in the USA and the Philippine branch of the Swiss Aerotech Industries. The aircraft was to be manufactured by Philippine Aerospace Development Corporation (which see). PADC had signed a memorandum of agreement with ACT and Aerotech concerning the venture.

The Apache 1 is to be powered by a 134.2 kW (180 hp) Textron Lycoming AEIO-360 with constant-speed propeller and be made of carbon/Kevlar composites cured under vacuum pressure at 250°F. The civilian Lancair 320, powered by a 119.3 kW (160 hp) Textron Lycoming IO-320,

ACT all-composites Apache 1 military trainer based on the ACT/Neico Lancair 320
(Anglo Philippine Aviation)

claims a maximum speed at sea level of 217 knots (402 km/h; 250 mph) and a cruising speed at 2,440 m (8,000 ft) and 75 per cent power of 209 knots (387 km/h; 241 mph). The Apache 1 should have ultimate g limits of +12 and –6,

ballistic recovery system for both the aircraft and pilots, jettisonable canopy, landing gear suitable for grass fields, and capacity for IFR avionics and Global Positioning System.

PACI

PHILIPPINE AIRCRAFT COMPANY INC

RPMCI Hangar, Manila Domestic Airport, PO Box 7633,
Airport Airmail Exchange, Pasay City 1300, Metro
Manila
Telephone: 63 (2) 832 3375 and 832 3380
Fax: 63 (2) 833 0605
Telex: 66621 WPAC PN
PRESIDENT: Rolando P. Moscardon
EXECUTIVE VICE-PRESIDENT AND GENERAL MANAGER:
Col Manuel B. Camacho (Ret'd)

It was announced in November 1987 that PACI had
concluded an agreement with Denney Aerocraft of the USA
(see Sport Aircraft section) to manufacture, market and
support the latter company's Kitfox two-seat single-engined
homebuilt aircraft in the Western Pacific area. PACI also
manufactures some parts and components for other US
companies.

PACI Skyfoxes, powered by Rotax 582 LC engines *(Anglo Philippine Aviation)*

PACI SKYFOX

Local production of the Denney Kitfox, as the PACI
Skyfox, began in early 1988. Three had been completed by
March 1990. A fourth was almost complete and another
three fuselages had been built. Another fuselage with a
cabin 10.1 cm (4 in) wider was being built. The first two were
certificated and had flown more than 140 hours by late
1990, but general certification was still being held up. The
first prototype, with Rotax 532 engine, was fitted with
Louisiana Agrilite spray gear and the second, with Rotax
582, was evaluated by the Philippine Integrated Police
Force. The PIPF has a possible requirement and has
specified dual ignition, venturi-driven artificial horizon,
dual brakes and non-folding wings. An airframe description
of the Kitfox can be found in the Sport Aircraft section; the
following details apply to the PACI Skyfox:
POWER PLANT: One 47.7 kW (64 hp) two-stroke Rotax
Bombardier 582 LC dual-ignition piston engine, with
electric starter, driving a fixed-pitch, three-blade wooden
propeller. Fuel capacity (two wing tanks) 45.5 litres (12
US gallons; 10 Imp gallons). Gravity refuelling.
DIMENSIONS, EXTERNAL:
Wing span   9.55 m (31 ft 4 in)

Wing chord, constant	1.07 m (3 ft 6 in)
Wing aspect ratio	7.65
Length: overall	5.21 m (17 ft 1 in)
wings folded	6.40 m (21 ft 0 in)
Width, wings folded	2.39 m (7 ft 10 in)
Height overall	1.70 m (5 ft 7 in)
Wheel track	1.45 m (4 ft 9 in)
Wheelbase	3.86 m (12 ft 8 in)
Propeller ground clearance	0.56 m (1 ft 10 in)

AREAS:

Wings, gross (incl flaperons)	11.92 m² (128.3 sq ft)
Tailplane	1.46 m² (15.72 sq ft)

WEIGHTS AND LOADINGS:

Weight empty	190.5 kg (420 lb)
Max T-O weight	431 kg (950 lb)
Max zero-fuel weight	398 kg (878 lb)
Max wing loading	36.15 kg/m² (7.40 lb/sq ft)
Max power loading	9.03 kg/kW (14.84 lb/hp)

PERFORMANCE (A: single-seat at 123.5 kg; 600 lb AUW,
B: two-seat at 175 kg; 850 lb):
Max level speed at S/L:

A, B	86 knots (160 km/h; 100 mph)

Max cruising speed (75% power) at S/L:

A	78 knots (145 km/h; 90 mph)
B	74 knots (137 km/h; 85 mph)

Stalling speed, power off, flaps up:

A	28 knots (52 km/h; 32 mph)
B	33 knots (62 km/h; 38 mph)

Stalling speed, power on, flaps down:

A	22 knots (41 km/h; 25 mph)
B	27 knots (49 km/h; 30 mph)
Max rate of climb at S/L: A	488 m (1,600 ft)/min
B	366 m (1,200 ft)/min
Service ceiling (approx): A	6,100 m (20,000 ft)
B	3,660 m (12,000 ft)
T-O run: A	15-23 m (50-75 ft)
B	19-28 m (60-90 ft)
Landing run: A	31-37 m (100-120 ft)
B	37-46 m (120-150 ft)
Range at 65% power: A	252 nm (467 km; 290 miles)
B	221 nm (410 km; 255 miles)

PADC

PHILIPPINE AEROSPACE DEVELOPMENT CORPORATION

PO Box 7395, Domestic Post Office, Lock Box 1300,
Domestic Road, Pasay City, Metro Manila
Telephone: 63 (2) 832 2741/50
Fax: 63 (2) 832 2568
Telex: 66019 PADC PN
PRESIDENT: Angelo Dwight L. Penson
EXECUTIVE VICE-PRESIDENT: Antonio S. Duarte
SUBSIDIARIES:

Philippine Helicopter Services Inc (PHSI)
PRESIDENT: Col Rodolfo A. Cacdac (Ret'd)
Maintenance and overhaul of BO 105 helicopters,
including all inspections from 50 to 1,800 hours; overhaul
and repair of MDHC (Hughes) helicopter rotor blades; and
repair of Zahnradfabrik Friedrichshafen AG products.

Air Philippines Corporation (APC)
Joint air freight business with TNT of Australia.
PADC is a government owned corporation established in
1973 to undertake aerospace projects in the Philippines.
Under licence agreements with MBB of Germany and
Pilatus Britten-Norman of the UK, PADC assembled 44
BO 105s and 67 Islanders (including 22 Islanders for the
Philippine Air Force) and manufactured the GFRP
components for both types of aircraft. This is now
complete.

PADC had reassembled four and assembled five
SIAI-Marchetti S.211s out of the 18 ordered from Agusta
(which see in Italian section) by March 1991. All 18 were to
be completed by mid-1991. PADC is producing components
for the SF.260 and may assemble the SF.600TP Canguro
(see below).

PADC is the appointed area service centre for the
Islander, and for Piper aircraft, Bendix/King com/nav
equipment, and Allison 250 series turboprops. It is also
engaged in the repair and overhaul of Textron Lycoming
and Teledyne Continental piston engines up to 298 kW
(400 shp). PADC was appointed by Allison authorised

Agusta S.211 assembled under licence by PADC *(Anglo Philippine Aviation)*

maintenance and overhaul centre for 250-C30 turboshafts
in Sikorsky helicopters and 250-B17 turboprops and
propellers in Nomads by Hawker Pacific Pty Ltd. Overhaul
and repair of the Textron Lycoming T53 turboshaft for the
Bell UH-1H was transferred to PADC. Other activities
include aircraft hangarage, repair and customising; aircraft
and aero engine related accessories sales; spare parts sales;
and inspection and repair as necessary (IRAN) of Fokker
F27 aircraft.

PADC was to manufacture the Apache 1 military trainer
developed by Aviation Composite Technology Inc in the
Philippines (which see).

During March 1991, PADC President Angelo Dwight

Penson and Mikhail Simonov, head of the Soviet company
Aerokonversiya and Sukhoi design bureau, signed a
memorandum of understanding covering the possible
manufacture in the Philippines of the Sukhoi S-80
tandem-wing twin-boom utility transport. No programme
was stated, and a cost of setting up the production line is
reported to be $36 million.

It is also reported that PADC has agreed with Agusta of
Italy to form a company, 90 per cent owned by PADC, to
build light transport aircraft for the Philippines Air Force.
This seems likely to encompass the SF.600TP Canguro,
referred to above.

UDRD

UNIVERSAL DYNAMICS RESEARCH AND DEVELOPMENT

Penthouse, Zeta II Building, 191 Salcedo Street, Legaspi
Village, Makati, Metro Manila
Telephone: 63 (2) 878 997 and 876 493
Telex: 66497 DEFCO PN or 23708 DEFCON PH
PRESIDENT AND GENERAL MANAGER:
Capt Panfilo V. Villaruel

UDRD DEFIANT 500 and 1000
The Defiant 300 tandem two-seat monoplane powered by
a 224 kW (300 hp) Textron Lycoming IO-540-K1B5 flew
twice in February 1988 but was abandoned because of

problems in obtaining the local hardwood for manufacture.
During 1990, the company decided to produce an
all-metal turboprop powered version designated Defiant
500, but funds for development and production had not
been obtained by April 1991.

The company also proposes the single-seat Defiant 1000
counter-insurgency aircraft powered by a 1,342 kW (1,800
shp) turboprop, but has released no firm details.

This description applies to the Defiant 500 trainer:
TYPE: Tandem two-seat turboprop trainer.
WINGS: Cantilever low wing built in one piece with two
spars; mechanical ailerons and electrically actuated
aileron trim tab; hydraulically actuated airbrake and
flaps.
FUSELAGE: All-metal stressed skin.

TAIL UNIT: Trim tab in starboard elevator and trim/anti-
balance tab in rudder. Tabs electrically actuated. Two
small drag-reducing strakes underneath rear fuselage.
LANDING GEAR: Retractable tricycle type, with main legs
retracting hydraulically inward into wing and nosewheel
rearward. All legs covered by doors when retracted.
Oleo-pneumatic shock absorbers and hydraulic disc
brakes.
POWER PLANT: One 708 kW (950 shp) Pratt & Whitney
Canada PT6A-62 turboprop, driving a Hartzell four-
blade propeller. Two integral fuel tanks in wing and
aerobatic tank in fuselage.
ACCOMMODATION: Student and instructor in tandem.
Martin-Baker Mk CH11A lightweight ejection seats
optional. Cockpit air-conditioned.

DIMENSIONS, EXTERNAL:
Wing span	10.21 m (33 ft 6 in)
Wing chord, mean	1.37 m (4 ft 6 in)
Wing aspect ratio	7.37
Length overall	8.72 m (28 ft 7¼ in)
Height overall	3.00 m (9 ft 10 in)

AREAS:
Wings, gross	14.15 m² (152.3 sq ft)
Horizontal tail surfaces (total)	4.10 m² (44.13 sq ft)

WEIGHTS AND LOADINGS:
Basic weight empty	1,593 kg (3,512 lb)
Max T-O weight	2,451 kg (5,403 lb)
Max wing loading	173.22 kg/m² (35.48 lb/sq ft)
Max power loading	3.46 kg/kW (5.69 lb/shp)

PERFORMANCE:
Max operating speed at S/L	290 knots (537 km/h; 334 mph)
Max cruising speed at 5,485 m (18,000 ft)	348 knots (645 km/h; 401 mph)
Stalling speed:	
flaps and gear down	65 knots (120 km/h; 75 mph)
flaps and gear up	73 knots (135 km/h; 84 mph)
Max rate of climb at S/L	1,228 m (4,029 ft)/min
T-O run at S/L	210 m (689 ft)
Landing run at S/L	249 m (817 ft)
Max range, conditions unstated	1,635 nm (3,030 km; 1,883 miles)
Max endurance, 10% fuel reserve	4 h 24 min
g limits	+7.0/–3.5

Model of Universal Dynamics Defiant 500 trainer *(Anglo Philippine Aviation)*

POLAND

PZL
ZRZESZENIE WYTWÓRCÓW SPRZETU LOTNICZEGO I SILNIKOWEGO PZL (Association of Aircraft and Engine Industry)

ul. Miodowa 5, 00-251 Warsaw
Telephone: 48 (22) 261441
Telex: 814281
PRESIDENT: Tadeusz Ryczaj
DIRECTOR: Ing Jan Stojanowicz, MSc

The manufacture of aircraft in Poland began in 1910. In 1928 an industrial syndicate was established, grouping the existing aircraft factories into the Panstwowe Zaklady Lotnicze (State Aviation Works) to produce aircraft to meet domestic and export needs. Since then the Polish aircraft industry has designed and built nearly 35,000 aircraft, helicopters and gliders of various types, as well as aero engines and equipment.

Until 1981 the aviation industry was organised under control of the ZPLS-PZL (Aircraft and Engine Industry Union). In 1982 (see earlier editions of this annual) its activities came under the control of the Bureau of Ministers Plenipotentiary for the Aircraft and Engine Industry. It is currently organised as the Zrzeszenie Wytwórców Sprzetu

Lotniczego i Silnikowego PZL (Association of Aircraft and Engine Industry), managed by a council representing all factories which are members of the Association. Production plants within the Association are self-dependent.

Other members of the Association include the BTNU (Biuro Techniczne Nowych Uruchomień: Engineering Office for the Implementation of New Projects), and the PPT (Przedsiebiorstwo Projektowo-Technologiczne: Design and Production Methods Enterprise). The Instytut Lotnictwa (which see) is also a member of the Association.

The Polish aviation and diesel engine industry currently comprises 23 factories, scientific and development units, technical and commercial organisations, which between them employ about 90,000 qualified workers. Its work has a broad base which includes research, design, development, manufacture, foreign trade, agricultural aviation services, and technical support for its own products operated by other countries.

Production by the Polish aviation industry relies substantially on aircraft, engines and equipment of its own design, as well as on co-operation and co-production with leading foreign aircraft manufacturers in both the East and the West. These programmes currently include the multi-purpose PZL-104 Wilga, the PZL-106 Kruk, PZL-126

Mrówka and M-18 Dromader agricultural aircraft; component manufacture and assembly for the Soviet Il-86 and Il-96 wide-bodied transports; the PZL-110 Koliber and M-20 Mewa light multi-purpose, training and sporting aircraft; local service transports such as the An-2 and An-28; the Mi-2, Kania, Sokól and SW-4 helicopters; sailplanes (see SZD entry in that section); piston, turbojet and turboprop engines (see PZL entries in the Aero Engines section); and aircraft military equipment, propellers, and ground equipment for agricultural aircraft and helicopters.

The export sales of all Polish aviation products are handled by:

Pezetel Foreign Trade Enterprise Ltd

Aleja Stanów Zjednoczonych 61, PO Box 6, Warsaw 04-028
Telephone: 48 (22) 10 80 01
Fax: 48 (22) 13 49 65
GENERAL MANAGER: Jerzy Krezlewicz, MA
MARKETING MANAGER: WJodzimierz Skrzypiec
MANAGER OF AVIATION DEPARTMENT: Kazimierz Niepsuj
MANAGER OF PUBLICITY DEPARTMENT:
   Ing Wojciech Kowalczyk

IL
INSTYTUT LOTNICTWA (Aviation Institute)

Al. Krakowska 110/114, 02-256 Warsaw-Okecie
Telephone: 48 (22) 460011 and 460993
Fax: 48 (22) 464232
Telex: 813537
GENERAL MANAGER: Roman Czerwiński, MScEng
CHIEF CONSULTANT FOR SCIENTIFIC AND TECHNICAL
   CO-OPERATION: Jerzy Grzegorzewski, MScEng

Founded in 1926, the Instytut Lotnictwa is directly subordinate to the Ministry of Heavy and Machine Building Industry and is responsible for all research and development work in the Polish aviation industry. It conducts scientific research, including the investigation of problems associated with low-speed and high-speed aerodynamics, static and fatigue tests, development and testing of aero engines, flight instruments, space science instrumentation, and other equipment, flight tests, and materials technology. It is also responsible for the construction of aircraft and aero engines, the latest such programme being the I-22 two-seat jet trainer.

PZL I-22 IRYDA (IRIDIUM)

Pictures of this new jet trainer and light attack aircraft appeared in a Polish television programme in October 1986, and it was identified by the designation I-22 a few weeks later, although the first prototype had made its first flight as long ago as 3 March 1985. Four further prototypes (first flights 26 June 1988, 13 May 1989, 22 October 1989 and 1990) have since been completed, and a single-seat **I-22MS** combat version is under development.

The I-22 was designed at the Instytut Lotnictwa by a team led by chief designer Dr Eng Alfred Baron. They were assisted by the Ośrodek Badawczo-Rozwojowy Sprzetu Komunikacyjnego (Communications Equipment Research and Development Centre) at Mielec, where the prototypes were built, and various other Polish aviation industry establishments.

A candidate to succeed the PZL Mielec TS-11 Iskra, the I-22 is designed to cover the full spectrum of pilot, navigation, air combat, reconnaissance and ground attack training, with day/night and bad-weather capability. This versatility, coupled with the ability to operate from unprepared airstrips and carry a useful variety of ordnance, enables the I-22 also to fulfil the role of light close support aircraft. To this end, the airframe is designed to be tolerant of battle damage, capable of quick and inexpensive repair, and is stressed to a standard that will permit later the use of more powerful engines (one designated K-15, rated at 14.7 kN; 3,305 lb st, is under development, as described in the Engines section) and the carriage of a greater weapons load, without jeopardising permissible load factors. Service life of the I-22 has been calculated on the basis of 2,500 flying hours or 10,000 take-offs and landings.

Two I-22s were due for delivery to the Polish Air Force in late 1990/early 1991, reportedly for competitive evaluation against the Aero L-39 Albatros, Aermacchi MB-339, BAe Hawk and Sukhoi Su-28.

TYPE: Two-seat advanced jet trainer, reconnaissance and light close support aircraft.

WINGS: Cantilever high-wing monoplane, with 18° sweep-back on leading-edges, non-swept trailing-edges, and 4° 30' anhedral from roots. Two-spar all-metal stressed skin structure, built as one unit with centre and inboard portions forming integral fuel tanks. Laminar flow aerofoil section, with multi-stage geometric and aerodynamic twist. All-metal mass balanced ailerons, actuated by pushrods with hydraulic boost. All-metal single-slotted trailing-edge flaps deflect hydraulically (20° for take-off, 40° for landing), with auxiliary pneumatic system for emergency deflection in the event of hydraulic failure.

FUSELAGE: Conventional oval-section all-metal semi-monocoque structure of frames and longerons, with aluminium alloy skin. Door type airbrake on each side beneath centre-fuselage, actuated hydraulically.

TAIL UNIT: Conventional all-metal structure, with sweepback on all surfaces. Curved fillet at base of fin. Variable incidence tailplane, mid-mounted on fuselage tailcone, is actuated hydraulically; will have slight anhedral on production version. Mass balanced elevators and rudder, actuated by pushrods. Ground adjustable tab on rudder.

LANDING GEAR: Retractable tricycle type, with single wheel and low pressure tubeless tyre on each unit. Hydraulic extension and retraction: nose unit retracts forward, main units upward into engine nacelles. Auxiliary pneumatic system for lowering gear in an emergency. Oleo-pneumatic shock absorber in each unit. Hydraulic disc brakes on mainwheels; auxiliary mainwheel parking brake serves also as emergency brake. Braking parachute in fuselage tailcone. Small tail bumper under rear of fuselage.

POWER PLANT: Two 10.79 kN (2,425 lb st) PZL Rzeszów SO-3W22 non-afterburning turbojets, pod mounted on lower sides of centre-fuselage. Fuel in three integral wing tanks (combined capacity 1,180 litres; 312 US gallons; 259.5 Imp gallons) and two fuselage tanks (combined capacity 1,360 litres; 359 US gallons; 299 Imp gallons), to give total internal capacity of 2,540 litres (671 US gallons; 558.5 Imp gallons). Provision for one 400 litre (106 US gallon; 88 Imp gallon) auxiliary tank to be carried under each wing. Fuel system permits up to 30 s of inverted flight. Single-point pressure refuelling (at front of port engine nacelle), plus gravity filling point for each tank. Air intakes anti-iced by engine bleed air.

ACCOMMODATION: Pressurised, heated and air-conditioned cockpit, with tandem seating for pupil (in front) and instructor; rear seat elevated 400 mm (15¾ in). For solo flying, pilot occupies front seat. Back-type parachute, oxygen bottle and emergency pack for both occupants. Individual framed canopies, each hinged at rear and opening upward pneumatically. Rearview mirror in front cockpit. VS-1 rocket assisted ejection seats, fitted with canopy breakers, can be operated at zero altitude and at speeds down to 81 knots (150 km/h; 94 mph). Dual controls standard; front cockpit equipped for IFR flying. Windscreen anti-iced by electric heating, supplemented by alcohol spray. Remaining transparencies anti-iced and demisted by hot engine bleed air.

SYSTEMS: Cockpits pressurised and air-conditioned by engine bleed air. Air from air-conditioning system also used to pressurise crew's g suits. Main hydraulic system, nominal pressure 210 bars (3,045 lb/sq in), actuates landing gear extension and retraction, wing flaps, airbrakes, tailplane incidence, brake-chute deployment, differential braking of mainwheels, and parking/emergency brake. Auxiliary hydraulic system for aileron control boost. Pneumatic system comprises three separate circuits, each supplied by a nitrogen bottle pressurised at 150 bars (2,175 lb/sq in): one powers emergency extension of wing flaps for landing, one the emergency extension of the landing gear; the third is for canopy opening, closing and sealing, windscreen fluid de-icing system, and hydraulic reservoir pressurisation. All three bottles charged simultaneously through a common nozzle. Electrical system, powered by two 9kW DC starter/generators, supplies 115V single-phase AC (via two 1kVA static converters) and 36V three-phase AC (via 500VA electro-mechanical converters), both at 400Hz; two 24V batteries provide DC power in the event of a double failure. Each AC voltage is supplied by one main converter and one standby, the latter automatically assuming full load if a main converter fails. Engine fire detection and extinguishing system (two freon bottles in rear fuselage). Electronic control system for gun firing and weapon release.

AVIONICS: Avionics bays in nose and under floor of rear cockpit. Avionics include VHF and UHF multi-channel com radio; ADF; radar altimeter for low level flying; marker beacon receiver; ILS; IFF; and audio-visual radar warning system. Blind-flying instrumentation. Flight data recorder in dorsal fin fillet.

ARMAMENT: One 23 mm GSh-23L twin-barrel cannon in underfuselage pack, with up to 200 rds (50 rds normally carried for training missions), plus gyro gunsight and nose mounted gun camera. Four underwing attachments, each stressed for load of up to 500 kg (1,102 lb), for bombs, guided or unguided rockets, or (inboard stations only) auxiliary fuel tanks.

DIMENSIONS, EXTERNAL:
Wing span	9.60 m (31 ft 6 in)
Wing aspect ratio	4.6
Length overall	13.22 m (43 ft 4½ in)
Height overall	4.30 m (14 ft 1¼ in)
Wheel track	2.71 m (8 ft 10¾ in)
Wheelbase	4.90 m (16 ft 1 in)

AREAS:
Wings, gross	19.92 m² (214.4 sq ft)
Ailerons (total)	1.362 m² (14.66 sq ft)
Trailing-edge flaps (total)	3.36 m² (36.17 sq ft)
Airbrakes (total)	0.60 m² (6.46 sq ft)
Fin	2.72 m² (29.28 sq ft)
Rudder, incl tab	0.957 m² (10.30 sq ft)
Tailplane	3.14 m² (33.80 sq ft)
Elevators (total)	1.694 m² (18.23 sq ft)

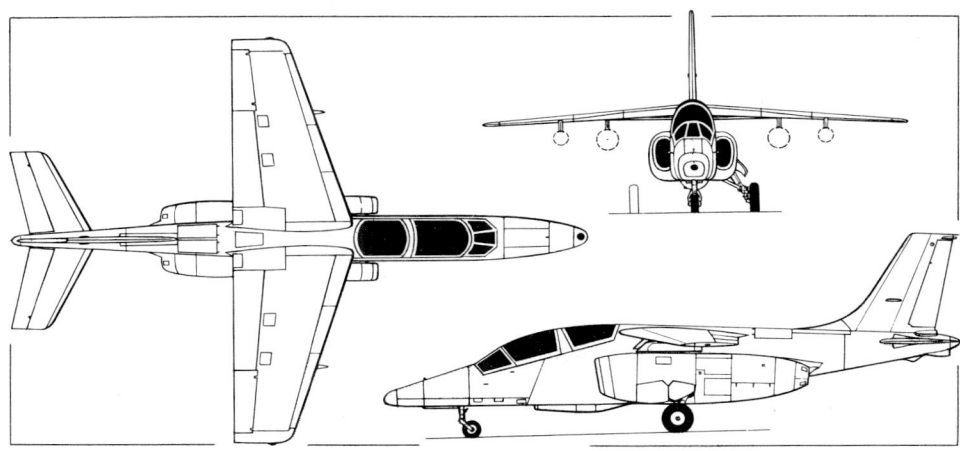

Three-view drawing *(Pilot Press)* **and photograph of the PZL I-22 tandem-seat advanced trainer, reconnaissance and ground attack aircraft. Photo shows fourth flying prototype**

WEIGHTS AND LOADINGS:
Operational weight empty	3,962 kg (8,735 lb)
Max fuel weight: internal	2,120 kg (4,674 lb)
external:	640 kg (1,411 lb)
Max external stores load	1,200 kg (2,645 lb)
Max T-O weight	7,493 kg (16,519 lb)
Max wing loading	376.15 kg/m² (77.08 lb/sq ft)
Max power loading	694.6 kg/kN (6.81 lb/lb st)

PERFORMANCE:
Max Mach number	0.85
Max level speed at S/L, ISA	
	494 knots (915 km/h; 568 mph)
Max cruising speed at altitude	
	499 knots (924 km/h; 574 mph)
Max rate of climb at S/L, ISA	2,220 m (7,283 ft)/min
Service ceiling	12,600 m (41,340 ft)
T-O run	770 m (2,525 ft)
T-O to 15 m (50 ft)	1,020 m (3,350 ft)
Landing from 15 m (50 ft)	950 m (3,115 ft)
Landing run	330 m (1,085 ft)
Range with max internal fuel	
	901 nm (1,670 km; 1,037 miles)
g limits (clean, at 5,865 kg; 12,930 kg AUW)	+8/−4

WSK-PZL MIELEC
WYTWÓRNIA SPRZĘTU KOMUNIKACYJNEGO-PZL MIELEC (Transport Equipment Manufacturing Centre, Mielec)

ul. Ludowego Wojska Polskiego 3, 39-300 Mielec
Telephone: 48 (196) 7010
Telex: 0632293 C WSK PL
GENERAL MANAGER: Ing Mieczysław Szymanski
COMMERCIAL DIRECTOR: Stanisław Markowski, MSc
MARKETING MANAGER: Alex Palej

Largest and best equipped aircraft factory in Poland, the PZL facility at Mielec was founded in 1938, and had produced more than 15,000 aircraft by 1 January 1991. In current production are the An-2 general utility biplane, the An-28 twin-turboprop light general purpose transport, the Dromader series of agricultural aircraft and the twin-engined M-20 Mewa executive and ambulance aircraft. In 1977 Mielec began to manufacture components, including fins, tailplanes, engine pylons, and wing slats and flaps, for the Ilyushin Il-86 Soviet wide-bodied transport. By the end of 1991 Mielec will have made about 110 sets of Il-86 components and 13 sets for the Il-96. Manufacture and subassembly of components for the Socata TB series of light aircraft (see French section) was about to begin in March 1991, with work for three TB 10 Tobagos due for completion by the end of the year. Output is planned to rise to 13 aircraft in 1992 and 30 in 1993.

PZL MIELEC (ANTONOV) An-2 ANTEK
NATO reporting name: Colt

The prototype of the An-2, designed to a specification of the Ministry of Agriculture and Forestry of the USSR, made its first flight on 31 August 1947. In 1948 the aircraft went into production in the USSR as the An-2, with a 746 kW (1,000 hp) ASh-62 engine.

Standard Mielec-built An-2P passenger transport biplane

By 1960, more than 5,000 An-2s had been built in the Soviet Union, as fully described in previous editions of *Jane's*. Licence rights were granted to China, where the first locally produced An-2 was completed in December 1957, as the Yunshuji-5 or Y-5. Limited production continues in China, as described under the SAP heading in that section.

Since 1960, apart from a few dozen Soviet built An-2Ms (1971-72 *Jane's*), continued production of the An-2 has been primarily the responsibility of PZL Mielec, the original licence arrangement providing for two basic versions: the An-2T transport and An-2R agricultural version. The first Polish built An-2 was flown on 23 October 1960. Mielec has since built more than 11,950 An-2s for domestic use and for export to the USSR (10,427), Bulgaria, Czechoslovakia, Egypt, France, the then German Democratic Republic, Hungary, Iraq, North Korea, Mongolia, Netherlands, Nicaragua, Romania, Sudan, Tunisia, Turkey, the UK, Venezuela and Yugoslavia. They include 7,777 An-2Rs. In 1989 AICSA of Colombia (which see) assembled two An-2s from kits supplied from PZL Mielec via Pezetel.

Polish built versions have different designations from those built in the USSR. They include the An-2 Geofiz; An-2LW; An-2P, PK, P-Photo and PR; An-2R; An-2S; An-2T, TD and TP. Further details of these can be found in the 1983-84 and earlier editions of *Jane's*.

The following details apply to the PZL Mielec An-2P:
TYPE: Single-engined general purpose biplane.
WINGS: Unequal span single-bay biplane. Wing section RPS 14 per cent (constant). Dihedral, both wings, approx 2° 48'. All-metal two-spar structure, fabric covered aft of

Antonov An-28, built by PZL Mielec, in Polish Air Force insignia *(Andrzej Glass)*

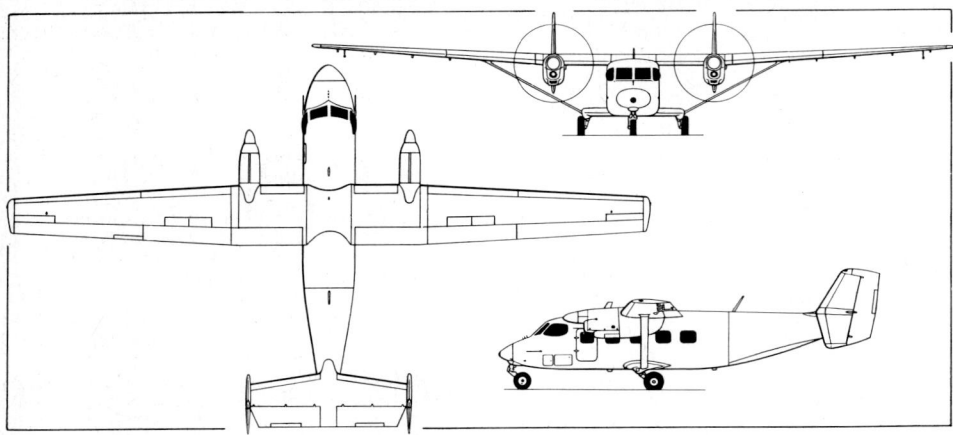

Antonov An-28 short-range passenger transport, produced in Poland by WSK-PZL Mielec *(Pilot Press)*

front spar. I type interplane struts. Differential ailerons and full span automatic leading-edge slots on upper wings, slotted trailing-edge flaps on both upper and lower wings. Flaps operated electrically, ailerons mechanically by cables and push/pull rods. Electrically operated trim tab in port aileron.

FUSELAGE: All-metal stressed skin semi-monocoque structure of circular section forward of cabin, rectangular in the cabin section and oval in the tail section.

TAIL UNIT: Braced metal structure. Fin integral with rear fuselage. Fabric covered tailplane. Elevators and rudder operated mechanically by cables and push/pull rods. Electrically operated trim tab in rudder and port elevator.

LANDING GEAR: Non-retractable split axle type, with long stroke oleo shock absorbers. Mainwheel tyres size 800 × 260 mm, pressure 2.25 bars (32.7 lb/sq in). Pneumatic shoe brakes on main units. Fully castoring and self-centring PZL Krosno tailwheel, size 470 × 210, with electro-pneumatic lock. For rough field operation the oleo-pneumatic shock absorbers can be charged from a compressed air cylinder installed in the rear fuselage. Interchangeable ski landing gear available optionally.

POWER PLANT: One 746 kW (1,000 hp) PZL Kalisz ASz-62IR nine-cylinder radial aircooled engine, driving an AW-2 four-blade variable-pitch metal propeller. Six fuel tanks in upper wings, with total capacity of 1,200 litres (317 US gallons; 264 Imp gallons). Oil capacity 120 litres (31.7 US gallons; 26.4 Imp gallons).

ACCOMMODATION: Crew of two on flight deck, with access via passenger cabin. Standard accommodation for 12 passengers, in four rows of three with centre aisle. Two foldable seats for children in aisle between first and second rows, and infant's cradle at front of cabin on starboard side. Toilet at rear of cabin on starboard side. Overhead racks for up to 160 kg (352 lb) of baggage, with space for coats and additional 40 kg (88 lb) of baggage between rear pair of seats and toilet. Emergency exit on starboard side at rear. Walls of cabin are lined with glass-wool mats and inner facing of plywood to reduce internal noise level. Cabin floor is carpeted. Cabin heating and starboard windscreen de-icing by engine bleed air; port and centre windscreens are electrically de-iced. Cabin ventilation by ram air intakes on underside of top wings.

SYSTEMS: Compressed air cylinder, of 8 litres (0.28 cu ft) capacity, for pneumatic charging of shock absorbers and operation of tailwheel lock at 49 bars (711 lb/sq in) pressure and operation of mainwheel brakes at 9.80 bars (142 lb/sq in). Contents of cylinder are maintained by AK-50 P engine driven compressor, with AD-50 automatic relief device to prevent overpressure. DC electrical system is supplied with basic 27V power (and 36V or 115V where required) by an engine driven generator and a storage battery. CO_2 fire extinguishing system with automatic fire detector.

AVIONICS: Dual controls and blind-flying instrumentation standard. R-842 HF and RS-6102 or Baklan-5 VHF lightweight radio transceivers, RW-UM radio altimeter (A-037 from 1 April 1989), ARK-9 radio compass, MRP-56P marker beacon receiver, GIK-1 gyro compass, GPK-48 gyroscopic direction indicator and SPU-7 intercom.

DIMENSIONS, EXTERNAL:

Wing span: upper	18.18 m (59 ft 7¾ in)
lower	14.24 m (46 ft 8½ in)
Wing chord (constant): upper	2.45 m (8 ft 0½ in)
lower	2.00 m (6 ft 6¾ in)
Wing aspect ratio: upper	7.6
lower	7.1
Wing gap	2.17 m (7 ft 1½ in)
Length overall: tail up	12.74 m (41 ft 9½ in)
tail down	12.40 m (40 ft 8¼ in)
Height overall: tail up	6.10 m (20 ft 0 in)
tail down	4.01 m (13 ft 2 in)
Tailplane span	7.20 m (23 ft 7½ in)
Wheel track	3.36 m (11 ft 0¼ in)
Wheelbase	8.19 m (26 ft 10½ in)
Propeller diameter	3.60 m (11 ft 9¾ in)
Propeller ground clearance	0.69 m (2 ft 3¼ in)
Cargo door (port): Mean height	1.55 m (5 ft 1 in)
Mean width	1.39 m (4 ft 6¾ in)
Emergency exit (stbd, rear): Height	0.65 m (2 ft 1½ in)
Width	0.51 m (1 ft 8 in)

DIMENSIONS, INTERNAL:

Cargo compartment: Length	4.10 m (13 ft 5½ in)
Max width	1.60 m (5 ft 3 in)
Max height	1.80 m (5 ft 11 in)

AREAS:

Wings, gross: upper	43.54 m² (468.7 sq ft)
lower	27.98 m² (301.2 sq ft)
Ailerons (total)	5.90 m² (63.5 sq ft)
Trailing-edge flaps (total)	9.60 m² (103 sq ft)
Fin	3.20 m² (34.4 sq ft)
Rudder, incl tab	2.65 m² (28.52 sq ft)
Tailplane	7.56 m² (81.4 sq ft)
Elevators (total, incl tab)	4.72 m² (50.81 sq ft)

WEIGHTS AND LOADINGS:

Weight empty	3,450 kg (7,605 lb)
Max fuel weight	900 kg (1,984 lb)
Max T-O weight	5,500 kg (12,125 lb)
Max landing weight	5,250 kg (11,574 lb)
Max zero-fuel weight	4,800 kg (10,582 lb)
Max wing loading	76.82 kg/m² (15.7 lb/sq ft)
Max power loading	7.38 kg/kW (12.13 lb/hp)

PERFORMANCE (at AUW of 5,250 kg; 11,574 lb):

Max level speed at 1,750 m (5,740 ft)	
	139 knots (258 km/h; 160 mph)
Econ cruising speed	100 knots (185 km/h; 115 mph)
Min flying speed	49 knots (90 km/h; 56 mph)
T-O speed	43 knots (80 km/h; 50 mph)
Landing speed	46 knots (85 km/h; 53 mph)
Max rate of climb at S/L	210 m (689 ft)/min
Service ceiling	4,400 m (14,425 ft)
Time to 4,400 m (14,425 ft)	30 min
T-O run: hard runway	150 m (492 ft)
grass	170 m (558 ft)
T-O to 15 m (50 ft): hard runway	475 m (1,558 ft)
grass	495 m (1,624 ft)
Landing from 15 m (50 ft): hard runway	427 m (1,401 ft)
grass	432 m (1,417 ft)
Landing run: hard runway	170 m (558 ft)
grass	185 m (607 ft)
Range at 1,000 m (3,280 ft) with 500 kg (1,102 lb) payload	485 nm (900 km; 560 miles)

PZL MIELEC (ANTONOV) An-28
NATO reporting name: Cash

The Antonov bureau developed the An-28 for service on Aeroflot's shortest routes, particularly those operated by An-2s into places relatively inaccessible to other fixed-wing types. It is suitable for carrying passengers, cargo and mail, for scientific expeditions, geological survey, forest fire patrol, air ambulance or rescue operations, and parachute training. The An-28 will not stall, even with the control column held in the extreme rearward position, because of the action of its automatic slots. If an engine fails, the upper surface spoiler forward of the aileron on the opposite wing is opened automatically; as a result, the wing bearing the dead engine drops only 12° in 5 s instead of the 30° that it would drop through loss of lift without the action of the Antonov patented spoiler. The fixed tailplane slat, also patented, improves handling during a high angle of attack climbout. Under icing conditions, if the normal anti-icing system fails, ice collects on the slat rather than the tailplane, to retain controllability.

The early history of this twin-turboprop light general purpose transport has been given in many previous editions of *Jane's*. Official Soviet flight testing was completed in 1972, and the production designation An-28 was allocated during 1973. The first pre-production An-28 (SSSR-19723) originally retained the same engines as the prototype, but in April 1975 (re-registered SSSR-19753) it flew for the first time with 716 kW (960 shp) Glushenkov TVD-10 turboprops (now WSK-PZL Rzeszów TWD-10B). An-28 production was entrusted to PZL Mielec in 1978, and a temporary type certificate, under Soviet NLGS-2 regulations, was awarded on 4 October that year to the second Soviet built pre-production aircraft (originally SSSR-19754, later SSSR-48105).

Polish manufacture began with an initial batch of 15 aircraft, and 163 had been ordered by 1 January 1991. First flight by a Polish built An-28 (SSSR-28800) was made on 22 July 1984, and this version received its full Soviet type certificate on 7 February 1986. Flight trials with PT6A-65B turboprops were due to begin in second half of 1991.

TYPE: Twin-turboprop short-range transport.

WINGS: Braced high-wing monoplane, with single streamline section bracing strut each side. Wing section TsAGI P-II-14 (thickness/chord ratio 14 per cent). Constant chord, non-swept no-dihedral centre-section, set at 4° incidence; tapered outer panels have 2° dihedral, negative incidence and 2° sweepback at quarter-chord. Conventional two-spar all-duralumin torsion box structure, with steel attachment fittings. Duralumin automatic leading-edge slats over full span of outer panels. Entire trailing-edges hinged, the single-slotted mass and aerodynamically balanced ailerons being designed to droop with the large, two-segment double-slotted flaps. Unpowered ailerons and hydraulically actuated flaps are of duralumin, with fabric and CFRP skins respectively; port aileron has a CFRP trim tab. Slab type spoiler, also of CFRP, forward of each aileron and each outer flap segment at 75 per cent chord. Thermal anti-icing of wing leading-edges by engine bleed air. Short stub-wing extends from each side of the lower fuselage, carrying the main landing gear unit and providing lower attachment for the wing bracing strut.

FUSELAGE: Conventional all-metal semi-monocoque non-pressurised structure. Underside of rear fuselage upswept and incorporating clamshell doors for passenger and cargo loading.

TAIL UNIT: Cantilever all-metal structure. Twin fins and rudders, mounted vertically on an inverted-aerofoil, no-dihedral fixed incidence tailplane. Conventional elevators. Fixed leading-edge slat under full span of tailplane leading-edge. Electrically actuated trim tab in each rudder and each elevator; main controls are unpowered. Thermal (engine bleed air) anti-icing of tailplane and fin leading-edges.

LANDING GEAR: Non-retractable tricycle type, with single Soviet built wheel and PZL oleo-pneumatic shock absorber on each unit. Main units have wide tread balloon tyres of Soviet manufacture, size 720 × 320 mm, pressure 3.5 bars (51 lb/sq in), and are mounted on small stub-wings which curve forward and downward at front to serve as mudguards. Steerable (± 50°) and self-centring nosewheel, with size 595 × 185 × 280 mm Stomil (Poland) tyre, pressure 3.5 bars (51 lb/sq in). Soviet multi-disc hydraulic brakes on main units, and Soviet inertial anti-skid units. Ski gear under development.

POWER PLANT: Two 716 kW (960 shp) WSK-PZL Rzeszów TWD-10B turboprops, each driving an AW-24AN three-blade automatic propeller with full feathering and reversible-pitch capability. Two centre-section and two outer-wing integral fuel tanks in wing spar boxes, with total capacity of 1,960 litres (518 US gallons; 431 Imp gallons). Refuelling point on each tank. Oil capacity 16 litres (4.2 US gallons; 3.5 Imp gallons) per engine. Air intakes lined with epoxy laminate and anti-iced by engine bleed air; propellers, spinners and pitot heads anti-iced electrically.

ACCOMMODATION: Pilot and co-pilot on flight deck, which has bulged side windows and electric anti-icing for windscreens, and is separated from main cabin by a bulkhead with connecting door. Dual controls standard. Jettisonable emergency door at front on each side. Standard cabin layout of passenger version has seats for 17 people, with six single seats on port side, one single seat and five double seats on starboard side of aisle, at 72 cm (28 in) pitch. Aisle width 34.5 cm (13.5 in). Five passenger windows in each side of cabin. Seats fold back against walls when aircraft is operated as a freighter or in mixed passenger/cargo role, the seat attachments providing cargo tiedown points. Hoist of 500 kg (1,102 lb) capacity able to deposit cargo in forward part of cabin. Entire cabin heated, ventilated and soundproofed. Outward/downward opening clamshell double door, under upswept rear fuselage, for passenger and cargo loading. Emergency exit at rear of cabin on each side.

SYSTEMS: No air-conditioning, pressurisation or pneumatic systems. Hydraulic system for flap and spoiler actuation. mainwheel brakes and nosewheel steering, with emergency backup system for spoiler extension and mainwheel braking. Primary electrical system is three-phase AC, with two engine driven alternators providing 200/115V power for heating systems, engine vibration monitoring, fuel pump, radio, recorders, and instrument lights. Transformer-rectifiers on this system provide 36V AC power for pressure gauges, artificial horizon, navigation and recording equipment, and 27V DC for control systems and signalling, internal and external lighting, firefightning system, propeller pitch control and feathering, radio, and engine starting and monitoring systems. In emergency, 36V AC can be provided by a static inverter and 27V DC by two 25Ah batteries. Thermal (engine bleed air) anti-icing of outer-wing, fin and tailplane leading-edges. Electric anti-icing of flight deck windscreens, propellers, spinners and pitot heads. Oxygen system (for crew plus two passengers) optional. No APU.

AVIONICS: Standard avionics include Baklan-5 (USSR) VHF com radio, R-855UM (USSR) VHF emergency locator transmitter, ARK-15 radio compass, MRP-66 marker beacon receiver, RW-5 or A-037 radio altimeter, Grebien-1 navigation unit, BUR-1-2A flight recorder, and SGU-6 intercom. Blind-flying instrumentation standard.

DIMENSIONS, EXTERNAL:

Wing span	22.063 m (72 ft 4½ in)
Wing chord: at root	2.20 m (7 ft 2½ in)
mean aerodynamic	1.886 m (6 ft 2¼ in)
at tip	1.10 m (3 ft 7¼ in)
Wing aspect ratio	12.25
Length overall	13.10 m (42 ft 11¾ in)
Fuselage: Length	12.68 m (41 ft 7¼ in)
Max width	1.90 m (6 ft 2¾ in)
Max depth	2.14 m (7 ft 0¼ in)
Height overall	4.90 m (16 ft 1 in)
Tailplane span	5.14 m (16 ft 10¼ in)
Wheel track	3.405 m (11 ft 2 in)
Wheelbase	4.354 m (14 ft 3½ in)
Propeller diameter	2.80 m (9 ft 2¼ in)
Propeller ground clearance	1.25 m (4 ft 1¼ in)
Distance between propeller centres	5.20 m (17 ft 0¾ in)
Rear clamshell doors: Length	2.40 m (7 ft 10½ in)
Total width: at top	1.00 m (3 ft 3¼ in)
at sill	1.40 m (4 ft 7 in)
Emergency exits (rear, each): Height	0.91 m (3 ft 0 in)
Width	0.51 m (1 ft 8 in)

DIMENSIONS, INTERNAL:

Cabin, excl flight deck: Length	5.26 m (17 ft 3 in)
Max width	1.74 m (5 ft 8½ in)
Max height	1.60 m (5 ft 3 in)
Floor area	approx 7.5 m² (80.73 sq ft)
Volume	approx 14.0 m³ (494.4 cu ft)

AREAS:

Wings, gross	39.72 m² (427.5 sq ft)
Ailerons (total)	4.33 m² (46.61 sq ft)
Trailing-edge flaps (total)	7.986 m² (85.96 sq ft)
Spoilers (total)	1.667 m² (17.94 sq ft)
Fins (total)	10.00 m² (107.64 sq ft)
Rudders (total, incl tabs)	4.00 m² (43.06 sq ft)
Tailplane	8.85 m² (95.26 sq ft)
Elevators (total, incl tabs)	2.56 m² (27.56 sq ft)

WEIGHTS AND LOADINGS:

Weight empty, equipped	3,900 kg (8,598 lb)
Max fuel load	1,529 kg (3,371 lb)
Max payload	2,000 kg (4,409 lb)
Max T-O and landing weight	6,500 kg (14,330 lb)
Max zero-fuel weight	5,884 kg (12,972 lb)
Normal wing loading	153.5 kg/m² (31.5 lb/sq ft)
Max power loading	4.64 kg/kW (7.62 lb/shp)

Polish-built Antonov An-28 light general purpose transport (two PZL Rzeszów TVD-10B turboprops)

PERFORMANCE (at max T-O weight):

Never-exceed speed (VNE)	210 knots (390 km/h; 242 mph)
Max level and max cruising speed at 3,000 m (9,850 ft)	189 knots (350 km/h; 217 mph)
Econ cruising speed at 3,000 m (9,850 ft)	181 knots (335 km/h; 208 mph)
Lift-off speed	73 knots (135 km/h; 84 mph)
Approach speed	70 knots (130 km/h; 81 mph)
Landing speed, flaps down	76 knots (140 km/h; 87 mph)
Max rate of climb at S/L	500 m (1,640 ft)/min
Rate of climb at S/L, one engine out	210 m (689 ft)/min
Service ceiling	above 6,000 m (19,685 ft)
Min ground turning radius	16.00 m (52 ft 6 in)
T-O run	260 m (853 ft)
T-O to 10.7 m (35 ft)	360 m (1,180 ft)
Landing from 15 m (50 ft)	315 m (1,035 ft)
Landing run	170 m (558 ft)
Range:	
max payload, no reserves	302 nm (560 km; 348 miles)
max fuel and 1,000 kg (2,205 lb) payload, 30 min reserves	736 nm (1,365 km; 848 miles)
g limit	+3

PZL MIELEC M-18 DROMADER (DROMEDARY)

The Dromader agricultural aircraft was designed to meet the requirements of FAR Pt 23. Particular attention was paid to pilot safety, and all parts of the structure exposed to contact with chemicals are treated with polyurethane or epoxy enamels, or manufactured from stainless steel.

The prototype was first flown on 27 August 1976, and a second prototype flew on 2 October 1976. They were followed by 10 pre-series aircraft, of which eight were used for operating trials. The Dromader has been certificated in Australia, Brazil, Canada, China, Czechoslovakia, France, Germany, Poland, the USA and Yugoslavia. Customers include operators in Australia, Brazil, Bulgaria, Canada, Chile, China, Cuba, Czechoslovakia, Germany, Greece (30 for firefighting), Hungary, Iran, Morocco, Nicaragua, Poland, Portugal, Spain, Swaziland, Trinidad, Turkey, the USA, Venezuela and Yugoslavia.

Series production began in 1979, and the following versions have been produced:

M-18: Initial single-seat agricultural version, last described in 1988-89 *Jane's*. Awarded Polish type certificate on 27 September 1978. Production ended in 1984, but this version remains available to order.

M-18A: Two-seat agricultural version, introduced for operators requiring to transport a ground mechanic/loader to provisional airstrips. Entered production in 1984, following Polish supplementary type certification on 14 February that year. FAA type certificate for M-18 extended to M-18A in September 1987. In production.

M-18AS: Two-seat training version of M-18A, with smaller hopper to create space for instructor's cockpit aft of front seat. This rear cockpit installation is readily interchangeable with that of M-18A. First flight 21 March 1988. In production (five built by 1 January 1991).

T45 Turbine Dromader: Turboprop version, powered by an 895 kW (1,200 shp) Pratt & Whitney Canada PT6A-45AG engine with Hartzell propeller. Under development by James Mills in co-operation with Melex USA Inc and described under Melex heading in US section.

In addition to the above, any M-18 can be converted to a firefighting role, a prototype in this configuration having been flown for the first time on 11 November 1978. An amphibious water bomber floatplane variant is under consideration.

A total of 590 Dromaders (all versions) had been built by 1 January 1991, of which 90 per cent were for export.

The following description applies to the current production M-18A, unless stated otherwise:

TYPE: Two-seat agricultural aircraft.

WINGS: Cantilever all-metal low-wing monoplane, of constant chord, with 1° 25′ dihedral on centre-section and 6° on outer panels. Wing sections NACA 4416 at root, NACA 4412 at end of centre-section, and NACA 4412 on outer panels. Incidence 3°. Single steel capped duralumin spar. All-metal two-section trailing-edge slotted flaps, actuated hydraulically. All-metal slotted ailerons, mass and aerodynamically balanced, actuated by pushrods. Trim tab in each aileron.

FUSELAGE: All-metal structure. Main frame, of helium-arc welded chrome-molybdenum steel tube, oiled internally against corrosion. Duralumin side panels, detachable for airframe inspection and cleaning. Fixed stainless steel bottom covering.

TAIL UNIT: All-metal structure, with braced tailplane. Corrugated skin. Aerodynamically and mass balanced rudder and elevators. Elevator actuated by pushrods, rudder by cables. Trim tab on rudder and each elevator.

LANDING GEAR: Non-retractable tailwheel type. Oleo-pneumatic shock absorber in each unit. Main units have tyres size 800 × 260 mm, and are fitted with hydraulic disc brakes, parking brake and wire cutters. Fully castoring tailwheel, lockable for take-off and landing, with size 380 × 150 mm tyre.

POWER PLANT: One 746 kW (1,000 hp) PZL Kalisz ASz-62IR nine-cylinder radial aircooled supercharged engine, driving a PZL Warszawa AW-2-30 four-blade constant-speed aluminium propeller. Integral fuel tank in each outer wing panel, combined usable capacity 400 or 712 litres (105.7 or 188 US gallons; 88 or 156.6 Imp gallons). Gravity feed header tank in fuselage.

ACCOMMODATION: Single adjustable seat in fully enclosed, sealed and ventilated cockpit which is stressed to withstand 40g impact. Additional cabin located behind cockpit and separated from it by a wall. Latter is equipped with a rigid seat, with protective padding and safety belt, a port-side jettisonable door, windows (port and starboard), fire extinguisher, and ventilation valve. Communication with the pilot is provided via a window in the dividing wall, and by intercom. In M-18AS, standard hopper is replaced by a smaller one, permitting

M-18A two-seat version of the Dromader agricultural aircraft

PZL Mielec M-18AS two-seat dual-control training version of the Dromader

installation of a bolt-on instructor's cabin. Second cockpits of M-18A and M-18AS are quickly interchangeable. Glassfibre cockpit roof and rear fairing, latter with additional small window each side. Rear cockpit of M-18AS has more extensive glazing. Adjustable shoulder type safety harness. Adjustable rudder pedals. Quick-opening door on each side of front cockpit; port door jettisonable.

SYSTEMS: Hydraulic system, pressure 98-137 bars (1,421-1,987 lb/sq in), for flap actuation, disc brakes and dispersal system. Electrical system powered by 28.5V 100A generator, with 24V 25Ah nickel-cadmium battery and overvoltage protection relay.

AVIONICS: RS6102 (Polish built), Bendix/King KX 175B or KY 195B com transceiver, KI 201C nav receiver, VOR-OBS indicator, gyro compass, radio compass and stall warning.

EQUIPMENT: Glassfibre epoxy hopper, with stainless steel tube bracing, forward of cockpit; capacity (M-18A) 2,500 litres (660 US gallons; 550 Imp gallons) of liquid or 1,350 kg (2,976 lb) of dry chemical (1,850 kg; 4,078 lb under CAM 8 conditions). Smaller hopper in M-18AS. Deflector cable from cabin roof to fin. M-18 variants can be fitted optionally with several different types of agricultural and firefighting systems, as follows: spray system with 54/96 nozzles on spraybooms; dusting system with standard, large or extra large spreader; atomising system with six atomisers; water bombing installation; and fire bombing installation with foaming agents. Aerial application roles can include seeding, fertilising, weed or pest control, defoliation, forest and bush firefighting, and patrol flights. Special wingtip lights permit agricultural flights at night, and the aircraft can operate in both temperate and tropical climates. Landing lights, taxi light and night working light optional. Navigation lights, cockpit light, instrument panel lights and two rotating beacons standard. Built-in jacking and tiedown points in wings and rear fuselage; towing lugs on main landing gear. Cockpit fire extinguisher and first aid kit.

DIMENSIONS, EXTERNAL:
Wing span	17.70 m (58 ft 0¾ in)
Wing chord, constant	2.286 m (7 ft 6 in)
Wing aspect ratio	7.8
Length overall	9.47 m (31 ft 1 in)
Height: over tail fin	3.70 m (12 ft 1¾ in)
overall (flying attitude)	4.60 m (15 ft 1 in)
Tailplane span	5.60 m (18 ft 4½ in)
Wheel track	3.48 m (11 ft 5 in)
Propeller diameter	3.30 m (10 ft 10 in)
Propeller ground clearance (tail up)	0.23 m (9 in)

AREAS:
Wings, gross	40.00 m² (430.5 sq ft)
Ailerons (total)	3.84 m² (41.33 sq ft)
Trailing-edge flaps (total)	5.69 m² (61.25 sq ft)
Vertical tail surfaces (total)	2.65 m² (28.5 sq ft)
Horizontal tail surfaces (total)	6.50 m² (70.0 sq ft)

WEIGHTS AND LOADINGS (M-18A):
Basic weight empty	2,690 kg (5,930 lb)
Weight empty, equipped	2,750-2,860 kg (6,063-6,305 lb)
Payload: FAR 23	1,050-1,350 kg (2,315-2,976 lb)
CAM 8	1,550-1,850 kg (3,417-4,078 lb)
Max T-O weight: FAR 23	4,200 kg (9,259 lb)
CAM 8	4,700 kg (10,362 lb)
Max landing weight	4,200 kg (9,259 lb)
Max wing loading (FAR 23)	105.0 kg/m² (21.51 lb/sq ft)
Max power loading (FAR 23)	5.63 kg/kW (9.26 lb/hp)

PERFORMANCE (M-18A at 4,200 kg; 9,259 lb T-O weight, ISA. A: without agricultural equipment, B: with spreader equipment):
Never-exceed speed (VNE):		
A		151 knots (280 km/h; 174 mph)
Max level speed: A		138 knots (256 km/h; 159 mph)
B		128 knots (237 km/h; 147 mph)
Cruising speed at S/L:		
A		110 knots (205 km/h; 127 mph)
B		102 knots (190 km/h; 118 mph)
Normal operating speed:		
A		124 knots (230 km/h; 143 mph)
B		108 knots (200 km/h; 124 mph)

Stalling speed, power off, flaps up:		
A, B		65 knots (119 km/h; 74 mph)
Stalling speed, power off, flaps down:		
A, B		59 knots (109 km/h; 68 mph)
Max rate of climb at S/L: A		414 m (1,360 ft)/min
B		340 m (1,115 ft)/min
Service ceiling: A		6,500 m (21,325 ft)
T-O run: A		180-200 m (590-656 ft)
B		210-245 m (689-805 ft)
Landing run: A, B		260-300 m (853-984 ft)
Max range, no reserves:		
A, 400 litres (105.7 US gallons; 88 Imp gallons) fuel		291 nm (540 km; 335 miles)
A, 712 litres (188 US gallons; 156.6 Imp gallons) fuel		523 nm (970 km; 602 miles)
g limits: FAR 23		+3.4/-1.4
CAM 8		+3/-1.2

PZL MIELEC M-20 MEWA (GULL)

The M-20 Mewa six/seven-seat twin-engined aircraft is the Polish version of the Piper PA-34-200T Seneca II, developed under an agreement made with Piper Aircraft Corporation in 1977. It is designed for passenger transport, training, liaison and ambulance duties, is certificated to FAR Pt 23, and can be operated from concrete runways or grass strips.

Adaptation of the PA-34-200T Seneca II airframe to accept Polish built PZL-F engines occupied the first half of 1978, and the first Polish prototype made its initial flight on 25 July 1979. The Mewa has been produced in three versions, any of which can be configured for passenger carrying or as an air ambulance. Details of the **M-20 00** (four built in 1979-80) and **M-20 01** (five built in 1983-84) can be found in the 1987-88 and earlier *Jane's*. The M-20 02 was not produced.

Current production in 1990-91, for customers in Austria, Germany, India and Turkey, was centred on a batch of 15 **M-20 03** aircraft powered by Teledyne Continental TSIO/LTSIO-360-KB turbocharged engines. A further 15 have reportedly been ordered by South Africa. The following details apply to the M-20 03:

TYPE: Six/seven-seat executive and ambulance aircraft.

WINGS: Cantilever low-wing monoplane. NACA 65₂-415 section constant chord wings, with 7° dihedral from roots and 2° incidence. Leading-edges sweptforward at root. Safe-life stressed skin structure of aluminium alloy, including the Frise ailerons and single-slotted trailing-edge flaps. Optional pneumatic anti-icing of leading-edges.

FUSELAGE: Semi-monocoque safe-life structure of aluminium alloy.

TAIL UNIT: Cantilever type, of similar construction to wings, with sweptback vertical and non-swept horizontal surfaces. Rudder is aerodynamically and mass balanced, and fitted with an anti-servo tab. Slab type all-moving tailplane, with trim tab. Pneumatic anti-icing of fin and tailplane leading-edges optional.

LANDING GEAR: Hydraulically retractable tricycle type, with single wheel and oleo strut on each unit. Mainwheels retract inward into wings, nosewheel forward. Size 6.00-6 wheels on all three units, tyre pressures 3.79 bars (55 lb/sq in) on main units, 2.76 bars (40 lb/sq in) on nose unit.

Emergency gravity extension. PZL Hydral disc brakes; parking brake.

POWER PLANT: Two 164 kW (220 hp) Teledyne Continental TSIO/LTSIO-360-KB turbocharged, counter-rotating flat-six engines, each driving a three-blade constant-speed propeller with optional electric blade de-icing. Two 92.75 litre (24.5 US gallon; 20.4 Imp gallon) fuel tanks in each wing leading-edge; total standard fuel capacity 371 litres (98 US gallons; 81.6 mp gallons). Optional auxiliary tank in each leading-edge can increase this total to 484.5 litres (128 US gallons; 106.6 Imp gallons). Oil capacity 10 litres (2.64 US gallons; 2.2 Imp gallons) per engine.

ACCOMMODATION: Passenger version seats one or two pilots plus five or four passengers, with optional seventh seat. Baggage space aft of rear seats. Ambulance version can carry one stretcher patient, two medical attendants and one other person in addition to the pilot. The stretcher rack replaces the right hand centre seat and, like the seat, can be quickly and easily removed. The rack has special guides which can be connected to the door threshold to facilitate stretcher loading; they can be folded back when the stretcher is on board and locked. There are hooks in the cabin ceiling for suspending a transfusion set, and the aircraft carries an oxygen installation for the patient. The doctor's seat (centre, left) has an earphone and microphone, enabling him to contact the ground for assistance if required, and there is a nurse's seat at the rear. A modified electrical system permits an incubator to be installed.

SYSTEMS: Two independent hydraulic systems, one operating at 154 bars (2,233 lb/sq in) for landing gear extension/retraction and the other at 103.5 bars (1,500 lb/sq in) for wheel braking. Electrical system powered by two 24V 55A alternators and a 24V 25Ah battery. Pneumatic wing and tail anti-icing system optional.

AVIONICS: Multi-channel VOR/LOC radio and blind-flying instrumentation standard. Radio rangefinder, radio marker, radio compass and three-axis autopilot optional. Polish ARL 1601 ADF, CG 121 slaved gyro, RS 6102 VHF com transceiver, MRP-66 marker transceiver and SSA-1 audio control panel.

DIMENSIONS, EXTERNAL:
Wing span	11.86 m (38 ft 11 in)
Wing chord: at root	1.88 m (6 ft 2 in)
at tip	1.60 m (5 ft 3 in)
Wing aspect ratio	7.3
Length overall	8.72 m (28 ft 7¼ in)
Height overall	3.02 m (9 ft 11 in)
Tailplane span	4.13 m (13 ft 6½ in)
Wheel track	3.37 m (11 ft 0¾ in)
Wheelbase	2.13 m (7 ft 0 in)
Propeller diameter	1.93 m (6 ft 4 in)

DIMENSIONS, INTERNAL:
Cabin: Length	3.17 m (10 ft 4¾ in)
Max width	1.24 m (4 ft 0¾ in)
Max height	1.07 m (3 ft 6¼ in)
Volume	5.53 m³ (195.3 cu ft)

AREAS:
Wings, gross	19.18 m² (206.5 sq ft)
Ailerons (total)	1.17 m² (12.59 sq ft)
Trailing-edge flaps (total)	1.94 m² (20.88 sq ft)
Fin	1.96 m² (21.10 sq ft)
Rudder	0.89 m² (9.58 sq ft)
Tailplane, incl tab	3.60 m² (38.75 sq ft)

WEIGHTS AND LOADINGS:
Weight empty (standard)	1,290 kg (2,844 lb)
Max T-O weight	2,070 kg (4,563 lb)
Max landing weight	1,970 kg (4,343 lb)
Max zero-fuel weight	1,810 kg (3,990 lb)
Max wing loading	107.9 kg/m² (22.10 lb/sq ft)
Max power loading	6.86 kg/kW (11.13 lb/hp)

PERFORMANCE (at max T-O weight):
Never-exceed speed (VNE):		
		194 knots (360 km/h; 223 mph)
Max level speed at 4,500 m (14,765 ft)		
		194 knots (360 km/h; 223 mph)
Econ cruising speed at 7,500 m (24,600 ft)		
		168 knots (311 km/h; 193 mph)
Stalling speed, flaps down		61 knots (112 km/h; 70 mph)
Max rate of climb at S/L		456 m (1,496 ft)/min
Service ceiling		7,680 m (25,200 ft)
T-O to 15 m (50 ft)		444 m (1,457 ft)
Landing from 15 m (50 ft)		655 m (2,150 ft)

PZL Mielec M-20 Mewa, a Polish version of the Piper PA-34-200T Seneca II

Range, 45 min reserves:
with max standard fuel   669 nm (1,240 km; 770 miles)
with max standard and auxiliary fuel
989 nm (1,833 km; 1,139 miles)

PZL MIELEC M-21 DROMADER MINI

This reduced capacity version of the Dromader was developed in response to a need expressed by users of the M-18 for a smaller version, with a less powerful engine and reduced chemical load. Details and an illustration of the Dromader Mini can be found in the 1989-90 and earlier editions of *Jane's*. No orders had been placed up to 1 January 1991.

PZL MIELEC M-24 DROMADER SUPER

The Dromader Super is the largest member of the Dromader family, but utilises the same rear fuselage, outer wings, landing gear, power plant and tail unit as the M-18A. Fuel capacity is increased to 1,400 litres (370 US gallons; 308 Imp gallons).

Five prototypes of the M-24 were built, including one for static testing. The first two, which flew for the first time on 14 July 1987 (SP-PFA) and 27 April 1988 (SP-PFB), were each powered by a 746 kW (1,000 hp) ASz-62IR radial engine; the next two, first flown on 14 October and 18 November 1988, each have a K9-AA engine (conversion of the ASz-62IR) rated at 860 kW (1,170 hp). Hopper capacity is increased to 2,700 litres (713 US gallons; 594 Imp gallons) or 1,800 kg (3,968 lb), and other features include increased span wings with a new aerofoil section. Production has not yet begun.

DIMENSIONS, EXTERNAL:
Wing span   19.90 m (65 ft 3½ in)
Wing aspect ratio   8.8
Length overall   10.80 m (35 ft 5¼ in)
Height overall: tail up   4.30 m (14 ft 1¼ in)
tail down   3.78 m (12 ft 4¾ in)
Wheelbase   7.40 m (24 ft 3½ in)
Propeller diameter   3.60 m (11 ft 9¾ in)
AREAS:
Wings, gross   45.00 m² (484.4 sq ft)
WEIGHTS AND LOADINGS:
Weight empty   2,870 kg (6,327 lb)
Max fuel weight   1,010 kg (2,226 lb)
Max T-O and landing weight:
Normal   5,000 kg (11,023 lb)
Max T-O weight: Restricted   5,500 kg (12,125 lb)
Max wing loading:
Normal   111.1 kg/m² (22.75 lb/sq ft)
Restricted   122.2 kg/m² (25.03 lb/sq ft)
Max power loading, 746 kW (1,000 hp) engine:
Normal   6.71 kg/kW (11.02 lb/hp)
Restricted   7.38 kg/kW (12.12 lb/hp)
PERFORMANCE (746 kW; 1,000 hp engine):
Max cruising speed   119 knots (220 km/h; 137 mph)
Stalling speed, flaps down 59 knots (110 km/h; 68 mph)
Max rate of climb at S/L: clean   300 m (984 ft)/min
with agricultural equipment   180 m (590 ft)/min
Service ceiling   4,000 m (13,125 ft)
T-O to 15 m (50 ft)   340 m (1,116 ft)
Landing from 15 m (50 ft)   470 m (1,542 ft)
Range: standard   971 nm (1,800 km; 1,118 miles)
self-ferry   1,888 nm (3,500 km; 2,175 miles)
g limits   +3.5/−1.4

PZL MIELEC M-26 ISKIERKA (LITTLE SPARK)

The Iskierka is a single-piston-engined aircraft, designed to FAR Pt 23 and intended for civil pilot training and pilot selection for military training. Selected parts and assemblies of the M-20 Mewa were used in the design of the wings, tail unit, landing gear, power plant, and electrical and power systems. Chief designer is Mr Krzysztof Piwek.

The Iskierka is being developed with two different engines, as the **M-26 00** with a PZL-F engine and **M-26 01** with a Textron Lycoming AEIO-540. The first prototype (SP-PIA), with a PZL-F, made its initial flight on 15 July 1986; first flight of the Textron Lycoming powered M-26 01 (SP-PIB) took place on 24 June 1987. Flight testing has been completed, and certification was expected by the end of the first quarter of 1991.

TYPE: Tandem two-seat primary training aircraft.
WINGS: Cantilever low-wing monoplane. NACA 65₂-415 section constant chord wings, with 7° dihedral from roots and 2° incidence. Sweptforward leading-edges at root. Safe-life stressed skin structure of aluminium alloy, including the Frise ailerons and single-slotted trailing-edge flaps. No spoilers, airbrakes or tabs.
FUSELAGE: Semi-monocoque safe-life structure of aluminium alloy.
TAIL UNIT: Conventional cantilever type, of similar construction to wings, with sweptback vertical and non-swept horizontal surfaces. Fixed incidence tailplane. Trim tab in starboard elevator.
LANDING GEAR: Retractable tricycle type, actuated hydraulically, with single wheel and oleo strut on each unit. Mainwheels retract inward into wings, nosewheel rearward. Size 6.00-6 wheels on all three units; tyre pressures 3.43 bars (50 lb/sq in) on main units, 2.16 bars (31 lb/sq in) on nose unit. PZL Hydral hydraulic disc brakes on mainwheels. Parking brake.

Second prototype of the PZL Mielec M-24 Dromader Super agricultural aircraft

POWER PLANT (M-26 00): One 153 kW (205 hp) PZL-F 6A-350CA flat-six engine, driving a PZL Warszawa-Okecie US 142 three-blade constant-speed propeller, or a two-blade Hartzell BHC-C2YF-2CKUF constant-speed propeller. One 92 litre (24.3 US gallon; 20.2 Imp gallon) fuel tank in each wing leading-edge, plus a 9 litre (2.4 US gallon; 2.0 Imp gallon) fuselage tank, to give total capacity of 193 litres (51 US gallons; 42.4 Imp gallons). Gravity fuelling point in top of each wing tank. Oil capacity 10 litres (2.6 US gallons; 2.2 Imp gallons).
POWER PLANT (M-26 01): One 224 kW (300 hp) Textron Lycoming AEIO-540-L1B5D flat-six engine, driving a Hoffmann HO-V123K-V/200AH-10 three-blade constant-speed propeller. Second tank in each wing. Total fuel capacity 377 litres (99.6 US gallons; 82.8 Imp gallons). Gravity fuelling point in top of each outer wing tank. Oil capacity 15 litres (4.0 US gallons; 3.3 Imp gallons).
ACCOMMODATION: Tandem seats for pupil (in front) and instructor, under framed canopy which opens sideways to starboard. Rear seat is elevated. Baggage compartment aft of rear seat. Both cockpits heated and ventilated.
SYSTEMS: Two independent hydraulic systems, one operating at 154 bars (2,233 lb/sq in) for landing gear extension/retraction and the other at 103 bars (1,494 lb/sq in) for wheel braking. DC electrical power supplied by a 24V alternator (50A in M-26 00, 100A in M-26 01) and a 25Ah battery.

AVIONICS: Polish made ARL 1601 ADF system, CG 121 slaved gyro system, RS 6102 VHF com transceiver, SSA-1 audio control panel, and ORS-2M marker beacon receiver standard.
EQUIPMENT: Landing light in port wing leading-edge.
DIMENSIONS, EXTERNAL:
Wing span   8.60 m (28 ft 2½ in)
Wing chord: at root   1.88 m (6 ft 2 in)
at tip   1.60 m (5 ft 3 in)
Wing aspect ratio   5.3
Length overall   8.30 m (27 ft 2¾ in)
Height overall   2.96 m (9 ft 8½ in)
Tailplane span   3.80 m (12 ft 5½ in)
Wheel track   2.93 m (9 ft 7¼ in)
Wheelbase   1.93 m (6 ft 4 in)
Propeller diameter   1.90 m (6 ft 2¾ in)
DIMENSIONS, INTERNAL:
Cockpits: Total length   2.91 m (9 ft 6½ in)
Max width   0.88 m (2 ft 10½ in)
Max height   1.30 m (4 ft 3¼ in)
AREAS:
Wings, gross   14.00 m² (150.7 sq ft)
Ailerons (total)   1.17 m² (12.59 sq ft)
Trailing-edge flaps (total)   1.06 m² (11.41 sq ft)
Fin   1.96 m² (21.10 sq ft)
Rudder   0.89 m² (9.58 sq ft)
Tailplane   3.30 m² (35.52 sq ft)
Elevators (total, incl tab)   1.15 m² (12.38 sq ft)

Second prototype PZL Mielec M-26 01 Iskierka (224 kW; 300 hp AE10-540 engine)

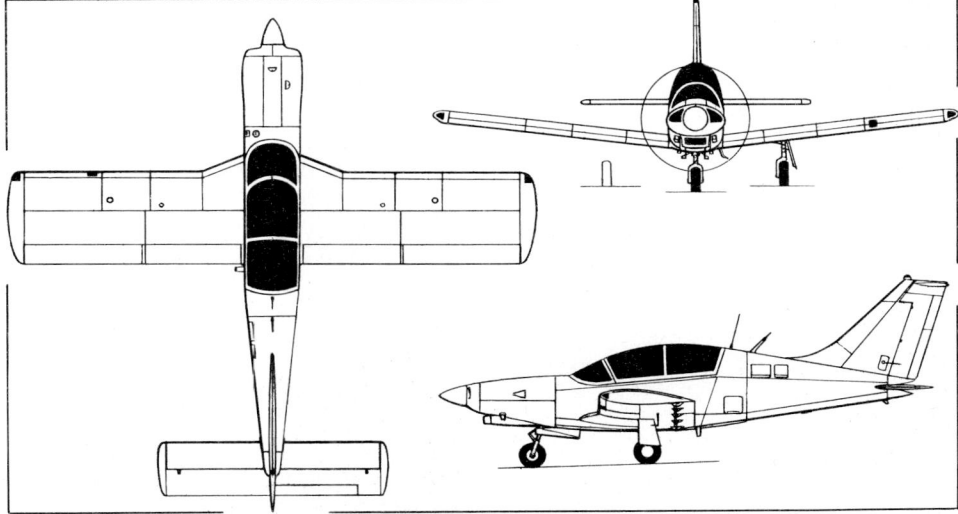

PZL Mielec M-26 Iskierka tandem two-seat primary trainer *(Pilot Press)*

WEIGHTS AND LOADINGS (M-26 01):

Weight empty	940 kg (2,072 lb)
Max fuel weight	271 kg (597 lb)
Max T-O and landing weight	1,400 kg (3,086 lb)
Max wing loading	100.0 kg/m² (20.5 lb/sq ft)
Max power loading	6.26 kg/kW (10.29 lb/hp)

PERFORMANCE (M-26 01 at max T-O weight except where indicated):

Never-exceed speed (V_{NE})	
	202 knots (375 km/h; 233 mph)
Max level speed at S/L	178 knots (330 km/h; 205 mph)
Stalling speed, flaps down	61 knots (112 km/h; 70 mph)
Max rate of climb at S/L	350 m (1,148 ft)/min

T-O to 15 m (50 ft)	625 m (2,051 ft)
Landing from 15 m (50 ft)	685 m (2,248 ft)
Range with max fuel, 30 min reserves	
	761 nm (1,410 km; 876 miles)
g limits	+7/−3.5 at 1,100 kg (2,425 lb) AUW
	+4/−1.72 at max T-O weight

WSK-PZL SWIDNIK
WYTWÓRNIA SPRZETU KOMUNIKACYJNEGO lm. ZYGMUNTA PULAWSKIEGO-PZL SWIDNIK (Zygmunt Pulawski Transport Equipment Manufacturing Centre, Swidnik)

ul. Przodowników Pracy 1, 21-045 Swidnik k/Lublina
Telephone: 48 (81) 12061, 12071, 13061 and 13071
Telex: 0642301 WSK PL
GENERAL MANAGER: Mieczyslaw Majewski
DIRECTOR OF RESEARCH AND DEVELOPMENT, AND CHIEF
 DESIGNER: Stanisław Kaminski, MScEng
SALES MANAGER: Jan Widz, MSc
PRESS RELATIONS: Jerzy Jurak, MSc

The factory at Swidnik was established in 1951 and was engaged initially in manufacturing components for the LiM-1 (MiG-15) jet fighter. In 1955, Swidnik began licence production of the Soviet designed Mi-1 helicopter, some 1,700 of which were built under the designation SM-1, followed by 450 examples of the Swidnik developed SM-2. A design office was formed at the factory to work on variants and developments of the basic SM-1 design and on original projects such as the SM-4 Latka.

In September 1957, the Swidnik works was named after the famous pre-war PZL designer Zygmunt Pulawski, and currently employs about 10,000 people. Production is concentrated at present on various developments of the Soviet designed Mil Mi-2 turbine powered helicopter, and manufacture of wing and tailplane slats for the PZL Mielec (Antonov) An-28.

Swidnik, together with other PZL factories at Mielec and Kalisz, is manufacturing components for the Soviet Ilyushin Il-86 wide-bodied airliner. Manufacture of components for Aerospatiale helicopters was expected to start in late 1990/early 1991.

On 22 February 1991 the Polish government announced its intention to privatise the Swidnik factory, initially as a state-owned limited company.

PZL SWIDNIK (MIL) Mi-2
NATO reporting name: Hoplite

The Mil Mi-2, first flown in September 1961, was designed in the USSR by the Mikhail L. Mil bureau. Development of the two prototypes continued in the USSR until the helicopter had completed its initial State trials programme. Then, in accordance with an agreement signed in January 1964, further development, production and marketing of the Mi-2 were assigned exclusively to the Polish aircraft industry, which flew its own first example of the Mi-2 on 4 November 1965.

Series production began in 1965, and Swidnik has since built more than 5,250 for various civil and military operators; the majority of these have been exported. Among the operators of the Mi-2 are the air forces of Bulgaria, Czechoslovakia, Germany, Hungary, Iraq, North Korea, Libya, Poland (Mi-2CH, Mi-2T, Mi-2URN, Mi-2URP and Mi-2US and other variants), Syria and the USSR, and civil operators in European and various developing countries. Production of the Mi-2B (see separate entry) accounts for "a few per cent" of the overall total.

During the course of production the Mi-2 has undergone continuous improvement and upgrading, with versions for new applications being developed to meet specific customers' requirements. A full list of these can be found in the 1984-85 and earlier *Jane's*; the principal civil versions being produced recently were as follows:

Mi-2URN of the Polish Air Force, armed with a 23 mm cannon and twin pods of 57 mm rockets

(a) Convertible passenger/cargo transport;
(b) Ambulance and rescue versions (Mi-2R);
(c) Agricultural version, for dusting or conventional and ultra-low-volume spraying. In service in Bulgaria, Czechoslovakia, Egypt, Iraq, Poland and USSR;
(d) Freighter version, with external cargo sling and electric hoist;
(e) Training version;
(f) Aerial photography versions, able to carry photographic, photogrammetric, thermal imaging or TV cameras for oblique or vertical pictures.

The following armed military variants have been produced:

Mi-2URN: As Mi-2US, but with four Mars 2 launchers (each with 16 S-5 57 mm unguided rockets) instead of pylon mounted gun pods. PKV gunsight in cockpit for aiming of all weapons. In service since 1973.

Mi-2URP: Anti-tank version, with cabin-side outriggers for four 9M14M Malyutka (AT-3 'Sagger') wire-guided missiles. Four additional missiles carried in cargo compartment. In service since 1976; later version can carry four 9M32 Strela 2 missiles.

Mi-2US: Gunship version, equipped with 23 mm NS-23KM cannon on port side of fuselage, two 7.62 mm gun pods on each side pylon, and two other 7.62 mm PK type movable machine guns in rear cabin.

The following details apply specifically to the basic Mi-2, except where indicated:

TYPE: Twin-turbine general purpose light helicopter.

ROTOR SYSTEM: Three-blade main rotor fitted with hydraulic blade vibration dampers. All-metal blades, of NACA 230-12M section. Flapping, drag and pitch hinges on each blade. Main rotor blades and those of two-blade tail rotor each consist of an extruded duralumin spar with bonded honeycomb trailing-edge pockets. Anti-flutter weights on leading-edges, balancing plates on trailing-edges. Hydraulic boosters for longitudinal, lateral and collective pitch controls. Coil spring counterbalance mechanism in main and tail rotor systems. Pitch change centrifugal loads on tail rotor carried by ribbon type steel torsion elements. Rotors do not fold. Electric blade

de-icing system for main and tail rotors. Rotor brake fitted.

Main rotor shaft driven via gearbox on each engine; three-stage WR-2 main gearbox, intermediate gearbox and tail rotor gearbox. Main rotor/engine rpm ratio 1 : 24.6; tail rotor/engine rpm ratio 1 : 4.16. Main gearbox provides drive for auxiliary systems and take-off for rotor brake. Freewheel units permit disengagement of a failed engine and also autorotation.

FUSELAGE: Conventional semi-monocoque structure of pod and boom type, made up of three main assemblies: the nose (including cockpit), central section, and tailboom. Construction is of sheet duralumin, bonded and spot welded or riveted to longerons and frames. Main load bearing joints are of steel alloy.

TAIL UNIT: Variable incidence horizontal stabiliser controlled by collective pitch lever.

LANDING GEAR: Non-retractable tricycle type, plus tailskid. Twin-wheel nose unit. Single wheel on each main unit. Oleo-pneumatic shock absorbers in all units, including tailskid. Main shock absorbers designed to cope with both normal operating loads and possible ground resonance. Mainwheel tyres size 600 × 180, pressure 4.41 bars (64 lb/sq in). Nosewheel tyres size 400 × 125, pressure 3.45 bars (50 lb/sq in). Pneumatic brakes on mainwheels. Metal ski landing gear optional.

POWER PLANT: Two 298 kW (400 shp) Polish built Isotov GTD-350 turboshafts, mounted side by side above cabin. Fuel in single rubber tank, capacity 600 litres (158.5 US gallons; 131 Imp gallons), under cabin floor. Provision for carrying a 238 litre (63 US gallon; 52.4 Imp gallon) external tank on each side of cabin. Refuelling point in starboard side of fuselage. Oil capacity 25 litres (6.6 US gallons; 5.4 Imp gallons). Engine air intake de-icing by engine bleed air.

ACCOMMODATION: Normal accommodation for one pilot on flight deck (port side). Seats for up to eight passengers in air-conditioned cabin, comprising back to back bench seats for three persons each, with two optional extra starboard side seats at the rear, one behind the other. All passenger seats are removable for carrying up to 700 kg (1,543 lb) of internal freight. Access to cabin via forward hinged doors on each side at front of cabin and aft on port side. Pilot's sliding window jettisonable in emergency. Ambulance version has accommodation for four stretchers and a medical attendant, or two stretchers and two sitting casualties. Side by side seats and dual controls in pilot training version. Cabin heating, ventilation and air-conditioning standard. Electric de-icing of windscreen.

SYSTEMS: Cabin heating, by engine bleed air, and ventilation; heat exchangers warm atmospheric air for ventilation system during cold weather. Hydraulic system, pressure 65 bars (940 lb/sq in), for cyclic and collective pitch control boosters. Hydraulic fluid flow rate 7.5 litres (1.98 US gallons; 1.65 Imp gallons)/min. Vented reservoir, with gravity feed. Pneumatic system, pressure 49 bars (710 lb/sq in), for mainwheel brakes. AC electrical system, with two STG-3 3kW engine driven starter/generators and 208V 16kVA three-phase alternator. 24V DC system, with two 28Ah lead-acid batteries.

AVIONICS: Standard items include two transceivers (MF/HF), gyro compass, radio compass, radio altimeter, intercom system and blind-flying panel. Nose and tail warning radar fitted to some military versions.

EQUIPMENT: Agricultural version carries a hopper on each side of the fuselage (total capacity 1,000 litres; 264 US gallons; 220 Imp gallons of liquid or 750 kg; 1,650 lb of

PZL Swidnik (Mil) Mi-2T helicopter of the Polish Air Force *(Ivo Sturzenegger)*

dry chemical) and either a spraybar to the rear of the cabin on each side or a distributor for dry chemicals under each hopper. Swath width covered by the spraying version is 40-45 m (130-150 ft). As a search and rescue aircraft, an electric hoist, capacity 120 kg (264 lb), is fitted. In the freight role an underfuselage hook can be fitted for suspended loads of up to 800 kg (1,763 lb). Illustrations in the Polish press have shown a version equipped for laying smokescreens. Diesel oil from external tanks on each side of the cabin is injected into large-diameter pipes extending backward and downward from the upper part of the rotor pylon. These pipes do not touch the engine exhausts but are warmed sufficiently to convert the diesel oil into dense white smoke. Electrically operated wiper for pilot's windscreen. Fire extinguishing system, for engine bays and main gearbox compartment, is generally similar to, but simpler than, the Freon system fitted to the Soviet Mil Mi-8, and can be actuated automatically or manually.

ARMAMENT: Mi-2URN combat support and armed reconnaissance version of the Polish Air Force (see model listings) has a 23 mm and two 7.62 mm guns, plus two pylon mounted pods of sixteen 57 mm unguided rockets on each side of the fuselage; a seven-gun variant (one fixed 23 mm on port side, four pylon mounted and two cabin mounted 7.62 mm) is designated Mi-2US. Polish Air Force Mi-2 URPs (see illustration in 1988-89 *Jane's*) can carry two 'Sagger' anti-tank missiles mounted on pylons on each side of the cabin.

DIMENSIONS, EXTERNAL:
Main rotor diameter 14.50 m (47 ft 6⅞ in)
Main rotor blade chord (constant, each) 0.40 m (1 ft 3¾ in)
Tail rotor diameter 2.70 m (8 ft 10¼ in)
Length: overall, rotors turning 17.42 m (57 ft 2 in)
fuselage 11.40 m (37 ft 4¾ in)
Height to top of rotor head 3.75 m (12 ft 3½ in)
Stabiliser span 1.85 m (6 ft 0¾ in)
Wheel track 3.05 m (10 ft 0 in)
Wheelbase 2.71 m (8 ft 10¾ in)
Tail rotor ground clearance 1.59 m (5 ft 2¾ in)
Cabin door (port, rear): Height 1.065 m (3 ft 5¾ in)
Width 1.115 m (3 ft 8 in)
Cabin door (stbd, front): Height 1.11 m (3 ft 7¾ in)
Width 0.75 m (2 ft 5½ in)
Cabin door (port, front): Height 1.11 m (3 ft 7¾ in)
Width 0.78 m (2 ft 6¾ in)

DIMENSIONS, INTERNAL:
Cabin:
Length: incl flight deck 4.07 m (13 ft 4¼ in)
excl flight deck 2.27 m (7 ft 5½ in)
Mean width 1.20 m (3 ft 11¼ in)
Mean height 1.40 m (4 ft 7 in)

AREAS:
Main rotor blades (each) 2.40 m² (25.83 sq ft)
Tail rotor blades (each) 0.22 m² (2.37 sq ft)
Main rotor disc 166.4 m² (1,791.11 sq ft)
Tail rotor disc 5.73 m² (61.68 sq ft)
Horizontal stabiliser 0.70 m² (7.53 sq ft)

WEIGHTS AND LOADINGS:
Weight empty, equipped:
passenger version 2,402 kg (5,295 lb)
cargo version 2,372 kg (5,229 lb)
ambulance version 2,410 kg (5,313 lb)
agricultural version 2,372 kg (5,229 lb)
Basic operating weight empty:
single-pilot versions 2,365 kg (5,213 lb)
dual control version 2,424 kg (5,344 lb)
Max payload, excl pilot, oil and fuel 800 kg (1,763 lb)
Normal T-O weight (and max T-O weight of agricultural version) 3,550 kg (7,826 lb)
Max T-O weight (special versions) 3,700 kg (8,157 lb)
Max disc loading 22.4 kg/m² (4.6 lb/sq ft)

PERFORMANCE (at 3,550 kg; 7,826 lb T-O weight):
Never-exceed speed (VNE) at 500 m (1,640 ft):
agricultural version 84 knots (155 km/h; 96 mph)
other versions 113 knots (210 km/h; 130 mph)
Max cruising speed at 500 m (1,640 ft):
agricultural version (without agricultural equipment) 102 knots (190 km/h; 118 mph)
other versions 108 knots (200 km/h; 124 mph)
Max level speed with agricultural equipment 84 knots (155 km/h; 96 mph)
Econ cruising speed at 500 m (1,640 ft):
for max range 102 knots (190 km/h; 118 mph)
for max endurance 54 knots (100 km/h; 62 mph)
Max rate of climb at S/L 270 m (885 ft)/min
Time to 1,000 m (3,280 ft) 5 min 30 s
Time to 4,000 m (13,125 ft) 26 min
Service ceiling 4,000 m (13,125 ft)
Hovering ceiling: IGE approx 2,000 m (6,560 ft)
OGE approx 1,000 m (3,280 ft)
Min landing area 30 × 30 m (100 × 100 ft)
Range at 500 m (1,640 ft):
max payload, 5% fuel reserves 91 nm (170 km; 105 miles)
max internal fuel, no reserves 237 nm (440 km; 273 miles)
max internal and auxiliary fuel, 30 min reserves 313 nm (580 km; 360 miles)

PZL Swidnik Kania Model 1 twin-turboshaft light helicopter *(Lech Zielaskowski)*

max internal and auxiliary fuel, no reserves 430 nm (797 km; 495 miles)
Endurance at 500 m (1,640 ft), no reserves:
max internal fuel 2 h 45 min
max internal and auxiliary fuel 5 h
Endurance (agricultural version), 5% reserves:
spraying 40 min
dusting 50 min

PZL SWIDNIK Mi-2B

The PZL Mi-2B differs from the Mi-2 in having a different electrical system and more modern navigation aids. It has been manufactured in the same versions (except agricultural) as the Mi-2, and has the same flight performance. Empty equipped weights are 2,300 kg (5,070 lb) for the passenger version and 2,293 kg (5,055 lb) for the cargo version; T-O weight remains unchanged at 3,550 kg (7,826 lb). Rotor blade de-icing is not available on the Mi-2B.

PZL SWIDNIK KANIA/KITTY HAWK

In collaboration with Allison in the USA, PZL Swidnik developed the Kania or Kitty Hawk, powered by two Allison 250-C20B turboshaft engines. Two examples were converted from Mi-2 airframes, and the first of these (SP-PSA) made its initial flight on 3 June 1979.

Polish certification of the Kania was carried out in two stages. The first took place in 1979-81 and resulted, on 1 October 1981, in a supplementary type certificate to that of the Mi-2. The second stage, concerning a considerably improved **Kania Model 1** version, was carried out during 1982-86 under the leadership of Stanisław I. Markisz. Improvements included, among others, redesigned cockpit and cabin layout, engine and flight controls, engine and transmission cowlings. On 21 February 1986 this version of the Kania was granted a separate type certificate as an FAR Pt 29 (Transport Category B) day and night SVFR multi-purpose utility helicopter with Category A engine isolation, but only three had been built by early 1991.

The Kania Model 1 is offered in a number of versions and configurations. These include passenger transport (with standard, executive or customised interiors), cargo transport (internal or slung load), agricultural (LV and ULV spraying, spreading and dusting), medical evacuation, training, rescue, and aerial surveillance.

A full description of the Kania can be found in the 1990-91 and earlier editions of *Jane's*. The following is an abbreviated version:

TYPE: Twin-turboshaft multi-purpose light helicopter.

POWER PLANT: Two Allison 250-C20B turboshafts, mounted side by side above cabin; each rated at 313 kW (420 shp) for T-O, 30 min twin-engine emergency power and one engine out max continuous power, and 276 kW (370 shp) for normal cruise. Automatic and manual torque sharing control systems standard. Two separate fuel boost systems, each with fuel filter bypass switch, fuel pressure gauge and switch, connected by crossfeed. Standard usable fuel capacity of 600 litres (158.5 US gallons; 131 Imp gallons), with provision for additional 423 litres usable (111.75 US gallons; 93 Imp gallons) in optional auxiliary tanks. Fuel quantity gauge and fuel reserve warning. Two separate oil systems, each with oil cooling, temperature and pressure gauges, oil filter bypass pop-up and chip warning. Each engine equipped with starter/generator, engine fuel pump effective for cruise after both boost pumps out, N1 and N2 tacho-generators, TOT gauge and switch, start counter, and 'engine out' warning. Dual engine inlet anti-icing standard. Each engine compartment equipped with fire detection system and with automatic and manual fire extinguishing systems.

ACCOMMODATION: Pilot (port side), and co-pilot or passenger, on adjustable and removable front seats, each fitted with safety belt. Dual controls optional. Accommodation for up to eight more persons, on two three-person bench seats and a single or double seat at rear of cabin, all with safety belts. Seats removable for carriage of cargo (up to 1,200 kg; 2,645 lb), two or four stretchers plus medical attendants, agricultural or other specialised equipment. Access to cabin via jettisonable door on each side at front (port door of sliding type) and larger passenger/cargo door at rear on port side. Pilot's windscreen wiper standard, co-pilot's optional. Cargo and stretcher tiedown points in cabin floor. Cabin soundproofing and ventilation standard; heating, carpets, double pane windows, pilot's heated windscreen, all optional. Baggage compartment at rear of cabin. Cockpit and cabin lighting standard.

EQUIPMENT: According to mission, the Kania can be equipped with an 800 kg (1,763 lb) capacity stabilised cargo sling; 120 kg (265 lb) capacity hoist; stretchers and casualty care equipment; or equipment for a variety of agricultural duties.

DIMENSIONS, EXTERNAL:
Main rotor diameter 14.558 m (47 ft 9¼ in)
Tail rotor diameter 2.70 m (8 ft 10¼ in)
Length: overall, rotors turning 17.47 m (57 ft 3¾ in)
fuselage 12.03 m (39 ft 5½ in)
Height to top of rotor head 3.75 m (12 ft 3½ in)
Stabiliser span 1.84 m (6 ft 0½ in)
Wheel track 3.05 m (10 ft 0 in)
Wheelbase 2.71 m (8 ft 10¾ in)

DIMENSIONS, INTERNAL:
Cabin: Length, incl flight deck 4.07 m (13 ft 4¼ in)
Max width 1.50 m (4 ft 11 in)
Max height 1.62 m (5 ft 3¾ in)
Floor area 5.68 m² (61.1 sq ft)
Volume 7.76 m³ (274.0 cu ft)
Baggage compartment volume 0.45 m³ (15.89 cu ft)

AREAS:
Main rotor disc 166.50 m² (1,792.2 sq ft)
Tail rotor disc 5.725 m² (61.6 sq ft)

WEIGHTS AND LOADINGS:
Basic weight empty 2,000 kg (4,409 lb)
Max load in cabin 1,200 kg (2,645 lb)
Max cargo sling load 800 kg (1,763 lb)
Max agricultural chemical load 1,000 kg (2,205 lb)
Max load in baggage compartment 100 kg (220 lb)
Normal T-O weight 3,350 kg (7,385 lb)
Max T-O weight 3,550 kg (7,826 lb)
Max disc loading 21.32 kg/m² (4.37 lb/sq ft)

PERFORMANCE (clean aircraft at S/L, ISA, zero wind, at normal T-O weight):
Max cruising speed 116 knots (215 km/h; 134 mph)
Econ cruising speed 102 knots (190 km/h; 118 mph)
Max rate of climb (T-O power) 525 m (1,725 ft)/min
Rate of climb, one engine out 61 m (200 ft)/min
Service ceiling 4,000 m (13,125 ft)
Hovering ceiling: IGE 2,500 m (8,200 ft)
OGE 1,375 m (4,510 ft)
Range at econ cruising speed:
standard fuel, 30 min reserves 232 nm (430 km; 267 miles)
standard fuel, no reserves 266 nm (493 km; 306 miles)
max fuel, 30 min reserves 432 nm (800 km; 497 miles)
max fuel, no reserves 466 nm (863 km; 536 miles)

PZL SWIDNIK W-3 SOKÓL (FALCON)

Development of this all-new Polish helicopter took place in the second half of the 1970s, and the first flight was made on 16 November 1979 by one of five prototypes, which subsequently underwent a wide range of tiedown tests. The remaining prototypes were completed embodying changes made as a result of these tests, the manufacturer's flight trials being resumed on 6 May 1982 by the second aircraft (SP-PSB). Certification trials with two other aircraft were carried out in a wide range of operating conditions, including heavy icing conditions and extreme temperatures of −60°C and +50°C. Certification to Soviet NLGW regulations has been completed. Larger than the Mi-2/Kania, the Sokól accommodates a crew of two, and 12

PZL Swidnik W-3 Sokól with AT-6 'Spiral' missiles, tracking sight and command antenna, 80 mm rocket pods and GSh-23 cannon (port side) *(Adam Fiedovow)*

PZL Swidnik W-3 Sokól in Polish Air Force insignia *(Ivo Sturzenegger)*

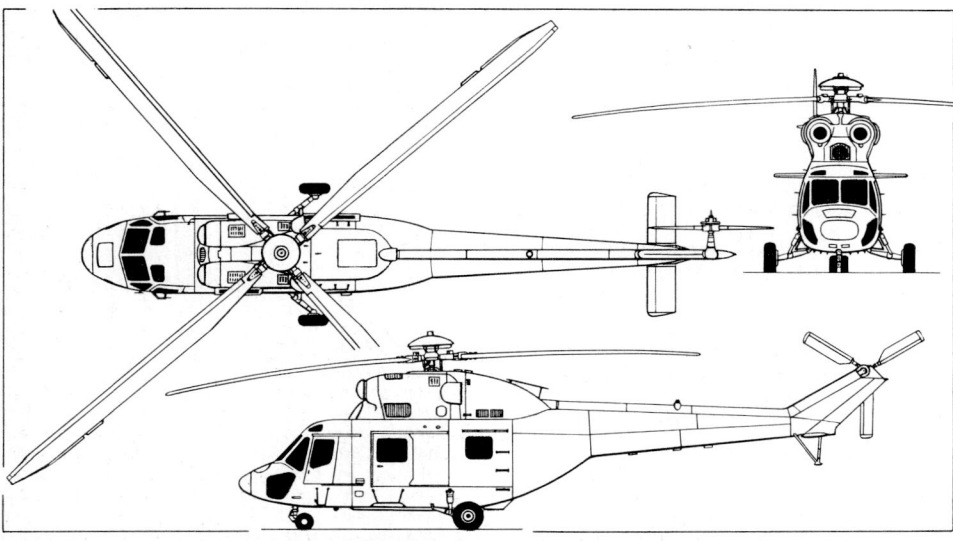

PZL Swidnik W-3 Sokól twin-turboshaft helicopter *(Pilot Press)*

passengers or a maximum 2,100 kg (4,630 lb) of internal cargo.

Thirty-five Sokóls had been built by early 1991, including three for the Polish Air Force and 26 of a Soviet order for 35; a further batch of 20 is now under construction.

TYPE: Twin-turboshaft medium weight multi-purpose helicopter.

ROTOR SYSTEM: Four-blade fully articulated main rotor and three-blade tail rotor. Main rotor has a pendular Salomon type vibration absorber, providing smooth flight and low vibration levels. Blades of both rotors constructed of laminated glassfibre impregnated with epoxy resin. Main rotor blades have tapered tips. Three hydraulic boosters for longitudinal, lateral and collective pitch control of main rotor, and one booster for tail rotor control. Blade anti-icing by electrically heated elements. Rotor brake fitted. Transmission driven via main rotor, intermediate and tail rotor gearboxes. Tail rotor driveshaft of duralumin tube with splined couplings.

FUSELAGE: Light alloy semi-monocoque structure, with circular section semi-monocoque tailboom.

TAIL UNIT: Fin integral with tailboom structure and fitted with glassfibre trailing-edge panels. Horizontal stabiliser, under end of tailboom, has a single continuous spar, is built up of laminated glassfibre impregnated with epoxy resin, and is not interconnected with the main rotor control system.

LANDING GEAR: Non-retractable tricycle type, plus tailskid beneath tailboom. Twin-wheel castoring nose unit; single wheel on each main unit. Oleo-pneumatic shock absorber in each unit. Mainwheel tyres size 500 × 250 mm; nosewheel tyres size 400 × 150 mm. Pneumatic disc brakes on mainwheels. Metal ski landing gear optional.

POWER PLANT: Two WSK-PZL Rzeszów TWD-10W turboshafts (Polish-made Glushenkov TVD-10), each with rating of 662 kW (888 shp) for T-O and 30 min OEI, and emergency ratings of 735 kW (986 shp) and 845.5 kW (1,134 shp) for 8 min and 2½ min OEI respectively. Particle separators on engine intakes, and inlet de-icing, are standard. Power plant is equipped with advanced electronic fuel control system for maintaining rotor speed at pilot-selected value amounting to ±5 per cent of normal rpm, and also for torque sharing as well as for supervising engine limits during start-up and normal or OEI operation. Engines and main rotor gearbox are mounted on a bed frame, eliminating any drive misalignment due to deformations of the fuselage structure. Bladder fuel tanks beneath cabin floor, with combined capacity of 1,700 litres (449 US gallons; 374 Imp gallons). Auxiliary tank, capacity 1,100 litres (290.5 US gallons; 242 Imp gallons), optional.

ACCOMMODATION: Pilot (port side), and co-pilot or flight engineer, side by side on flight deck, on adjustable seats with safety belts. Dual controls and dual flight instrumentation optional. Accommodation for 12 passengers in main cabin. Seats removable for carriage of internal cargo. Ambulance version will carry four stretcher cases and a medical attendant. Baggage space at rear of cabin. Door on each side of flight deck; large sliding door for passenger and/or cargo loading on port side at forward end of cabin; second sliding door at rear of cabin on starboard side. Optically flat windscreens, improving view and enabling wipers to sweep a large area. Accommodation soundproofed, heated (by engine bleed air) and ventilated.

SYSTEMS: Two independent hydraulic systems, working pressure 90 bars (1,300 lb/sq in), for controlling main and tail rotors, unlocking collective pitch control lever, and feeding damper of directional steering system. Flow rate 11 litres (2.9 US gallons; 2.4 Imp gallons)/min in each system. Vented gravity feed reservoir, at atmospheric pressure. Pneumatic system for actuating hydraulic mainwheel brakes. Electrical system providing both AC and DC power. Fire detection/extinguishing system. Air-conditioning and oxygen systems optional. Neutral gas system optional, for inhibiting fuel vapour explosion.

AVIONICS: Standard IFR nav/com avionics permit adverse weather operation by day or night. Weather radar optional. Stability augmentation system standard. Chrom (NATO 'Pin Head') IFF transponder and modified Syrena RWR in military version.

EQUIPMENT: Cargo version equipped with 2,100 kg (4,630 lb) capacity external hook and 150 kg (331 lb) capacity rescue hoist; 300 kg (661 lb) capacity hoist to become available.

ARMAMENT: Polish Air Force aircraft can be fitted with twin-GSh-23 cannon pack on lower port side of fuselage, plus cabin outriggers for AT-6 (NATO 'Spiral') anti-tank missiles and 12-round launchers for 80 mm air-to-surface unguided rockets.

DIMENSIONS, EXTERNAL:
Main rotor diameter	15.70 m (51 ft 6 in)
Tail rotor diameter	3.03 m (9 ft 11¼ in)
Length: overall, rotors turning	18.85 m (61 ft 10⅛ in)
fuselage	14.21 m (46 ft 7½ in)
Height to top of rotor head	4.12 m (13 ft 6¼ in)
Stabiliser span	3.45 m (11 ft 3¾ in)
Wheel track	3.40 m (11 ft 2 in)
Wheelbase	3.55 m (11 ft 7¾ in)
Passenger/cargo doors:	
Height (each):	1.20 m (3 ft 11¼ in)

Width: port	0.95 m (3 ft 1½ in)
starboard	1.25 m (4 ft 1¼ in)
DIMENSIONS, INTERNAL:	
Cabin: Length	3.20 m (10 ft 6 in)
Max width	1.55 m (5 ft 1 in)
Max height	1.40 m (4 ft 7 in)
AREAS:	
Main rotor disc	193.6 m² (2,083.8 sq ft)
Tail rotor disc	7.21 m² (77.6 sq ft)
WEIGHTS AND LOADINGS:	
Minimum basic weight empty	3,300 kg (7,275 lb)
Basic operating weight empty (multi-purpose versions)	
	3,630 kg (8,002 lb)
Max payload, internal or external	2,100 kg (4,630 lb)
Normal T-O weight	6,100 kg (13,448 lb)
Max T-O weight	6,400 kg (14,110 lb)
Max disc loading	33.06 kg/m² (6.77 lb/sq ft)
PERFORMANCE (at normal T-O weight at 500 m; 1,640 ft, ISA, except where indicated):	
Never-exceed speed (VNE)	
	145 knots (270 km/h; 167 mph)
Max level speed	138 knots (255 km/h; 158 mph)
Max cruising speed	127 knots (235 km/h; 146 mph)
Econ cruising speed	119 knots (220 km/h; 137 mph)
Max rate of climb at S/L	510 m (1,673 ft)/min
Rate of climb at S/L, one engine out:	
at 30 min rating	30 m (100 ft)/min
at 8 min emergency rating	96 m (315 ft)/min
at 2½ min emergency rating	186 m (610 ft)/min
Service ceiling:	
at normal T-O weight	5,100 m (16,725 ft)
at T-O weight below normal	
	up to 6,000 m (19,680 ft)
Service ceiling, one engine out:	
at 30 min rating	500 m (1,640 ft)
at 8 min emergency rating	1,800 m (5,905 ft)
at 2½ min emergency rating	
	approx 2,300 m (7,545 ft)
Hovering ceiling: IGE	3,000 m (9,845 ft)
OGE	2,100 m (6,890 ft)
Range:	
standard fuel, 5% reserves	
	367 nm (680 km; 422 miles)
standard fuel, no reserves	
	386 nm (715 km; 444 miles)
with auxiliary fuel, 5% reserves	
	626 nm (1,160 km; 721 miles)
with auxiliary fuel, no reserves	
	661 nm (1,225 km; 761 miles)
Endurance:	
standard fuel, 5% reserves	3 h 50 min
standard fuel, no reserves	4 h 5 min
with auxiliary fuel, 5% reserves	6 h 41 min
with auxiliary fuel, no reserves	7 h 5 min

Mockup of the PZL Swidnik SW-4 four/five-seat light helicopter *(Lech Zielaskowski)*

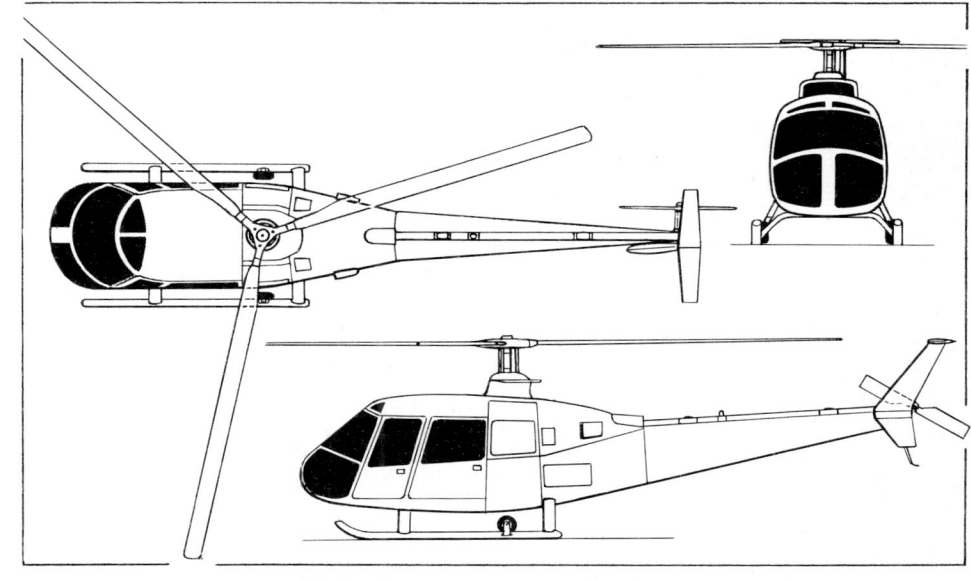

PZL Swidnik SW-4 (298 kW; 400 shp PZL Rzeszów GTD-350 turboshaft) *(Pilot Press)*

PZL SWIDNIK SW-4

Development of this 4/5-seat single-engined multi-purpose light helicopter began in 1985. Its general appearance is shown in the accompanying illustrations.

POWER PLANT: One 298 kW (400 shp) PZL Rzeszów GTD-350 turboshaft.

DIMENSIONS, EXTERNAL:

Main rotor diameter	9.00 m (29 ft 6⅓ in)
Main rotor blade chord	0.318 m (1 ft 0½ in)
Tail rotor diameter	1.40 m (4 ft 7 in)
Tail rotor blade chord	0.20 m (7.9 in)
Length:	
overall, both rotors turning	10.50 m (34 ft 5½ in)
fuselage	8.30 m (27 ft 2¾ in)
Height overall	2.75 m (9 ft 0¼ in)
Skid track	1.80 m (5 ft 11 in)
DIMENSIONS, INTERNAL:	
Cabin: Length	2.00 m (6 ft 6¾ in)
Max width	1.35 m (4 ft 5¼ in)
Max height	1.30 m (4 ft 3¼ in)
AREAS:	
Main rotor disc	63.62 m² (684.8 sq ft)
Tail rotor disc	1.54 m² (16.57 sq ft)
WEIGHTS AND LOADINGS:	
Weight empty	730 kg (1,609 lb)
Normal T-O weight	1,400 kg (3,086 lb)
Max T-O weight	1,500 kg (3,307 lb)
Max disc loading	23.58 kg/m² (4.83 lb/sq ft)

PERFORMANCE (estimated, at normal T-O weight):

Max level speed at 500 m (1,640 ft)	
	129 knots (240 km/h; 149 mph)
Max cruising speed	119 knots (220 km/h; 137 mph)
Service ceiling	5,000 m (16,400 ft)
Hovering ceiling: IGE	3,000 m (9,850 ft)
OGE	2,000 m (6,560 ft)
Range:	
with max payload and standard fuel, 5% reserves	
	216 nm (400 km; 248 miles)
with auxiliary fuel tank	485 nm (900 km; 559 miles)

PZL WARSZAWA-OKECIE

PANSTWOWE ZAKŁADY LOTNICZE WARSZAWA-OKECIE (State Aviation Works, Warsaw-Okecie)

Aleja Krakowska 110/114, 00-973 Warsaw
Telephone: 48 (22) 460031/9 and 465061/9
Fax: 48 (22) 465479
Telex: 817735
GENERAL MANAGER: Ryszard Leja, MSc
EXPORT MANAGER: Andrzej Jaworowski, Eng MSc

The Okecie factory, founded in 1928, is responsible for light aircraft development and production, and for the design and manufacture of associated agricultural equipment for its own aircraft and for those built at other factories in the Polish aviation industry. It has produced more than 3,500 aircraft since 1945.

PZL-104 WILGA (ORIOLE) 35 and 80

The PZL-104 Wilga is a light general purpose aircraft for a wide variety of general aviation and flying club duties. The prototype Wilga 1 flew for the first time on 24 April 1962. This aircraft, and other early models, were described in the 1968-69 *Jane's*.

Production of the improved Wilga 35 and Wilga 32 began in 1968, and both received a Polish type certificate on 31 March 1969; the Wilga 32 was described in the 1974-75 *Jane's*, and its Indonesian built modified version, the Lipnur Gelatik, in the 1975-76 edition.

The aircraft is currently manufactured in two basic versions: the **Wilga 35** (first flight 28 July 1967), which

meets the requirements of British BCAR regulations, and the **Wilga 80** (first flown on 30 May 1979), which conforms to US FAR Pt 23 requirements. The latter has the carburettor air intake located further aft. Aeroclub versions (Wilga 35A and 80A) are fitted with a glider towing hook; Wilgas with agricultural equipment are designated 35R and 80R, and aircraft with twin Airtech (Canada) LAP-3000 floats are known as Wilga 35H and 80H.

Wilgas have been sold to customers in Australia, Austria, Belgium, Bulgaria, Canada, Cuba, Czechoslovakia, Denmark, Egypt, Finland, Germany, Hungary, Indonesia, Italy, North Korea, Poland, Romania, Spain, Sweden, Switzerland, Turkey, the UK, the USA, the USSR (379 by 15 January 1989), Venezuela and Yugoslavia.

Total sales of the Wilga (all versions) had reached 890 by 1 January 1990.

Under study in 1990 was the STOL multi-purpose **Wilga 35M**, a variant of the Wilga 35A with extended operational range. With a max T-O and landing weight of 1,300 kg (2,866 lb), it would be powered by a 260.5 kW (360 hp) M-14P nine-cylinder radial engine, driving (on the prototype) a W530TA-D35 two-blade constant-speed propeller or (on any production version) a PZL-144 propeller.

The following description applies to the Wilga 35 and 80, except where a specific version is indicated:

TYPE: Single-engined general purpose aircraft.

WINGS: Cantilever high-wing monoplane. Wing section NACA 2415. Dihedral 1°. All-metal single-spar structure, with leading-edge torsion box and beaded metal skin.

Each wing attached to fuselage by three bolts, two at spar and one at forward fitting. All-metal aerodynamically and mass balanced slotted ailerons, with beaded metal skin. Ailerons can be drooped to supplement flaps during landing. Manually operated all-metal slotted flaps with beaded metal skin. Fixed metal slat on leading-edge along full span of wing and over fuselage. Tab on starboard aileron.

FUSELAGE: All-metal semi-monocoque structure in two portions, riveted together. Forward section incorporates main wing spar carry-through structure. Rear section is in the form of a tailcone. Beaded metal skin. Floor in cabin is of metal sandwich construction, with a paper honeycomb core, covered with foam rubber.

TAIL UNIT: Braced all-metal structure, with sweptback vertical surfaces. Stressed skin single-spar tailplane attached to fuselage by a single centre fitting and supported by a single aluminium alloy strut on each side. Stressed skin two-spar fin structure of semi-monocoque construction. Rudder and one-piece elevator are aerodynamically horn balanced and mass balanced. Trim tab at centre of elevator trailing-edge.

LANDING GEAR: Non-retractable tailwheel type. Semi-cantilever main legs, of rocker type, have oleo-pneumatic shock absorbers. Low-pressure tyres size 500 × 200 mm on mainwheels. Hydraulic brakes. Steerable tailwheel, tyre size 255 × 110 mm, carried on rocker frame with oleo-pneumatic shock absorber. Metal ski landing gear, and Airtech Canada LAP-3000 twin-float landing gear, optional.

PZL-104 Wilga 35 in the insignia of the Soviet flying training organisation DOSAAF

POWER PLANT: One 194 kW (260 hp) PZL AI-14RA nine-cylinder supercharged radial aircooled engine (AI-14RA-KAF in Wilga 80), driving a PZL US-122000 two-blade constant-speed wooden propeller. Two removable fuel tanks in each wing, with total capacity of 195 litres (51.5 US gallons; 43 Imp gallons). Refuelling point on each side of fuselage, at junction with wing. For longer-range operation, an additional 90 litre (23.8 US gallon; 19.8 Imp gallon) fuel tank can be installed in place of the rear pair of seats. Oil capacity 16 litres (4.2 US gallons; 3.5 Imp gallons).

ACCOMMODATION: Passenger version accommodates pilot and three passengers, in pairs, with adjustable front seats. Baggage compartment aft of seats, capacity 35 kg (77 lb). Rear seats can be replaced by additional fuel tank for longer-range operation. Upward opening door on each side of cabin, jettisonable in emergency. In the parachute training version the starboard door is removed and replaced by two tubular uprights with a central connecting strap, and the starboard front seat is rearward facing. Jumps are facilitated by a step on the starboard side and by a parachute hitch. A controllable towing hook can be attached to the tail landing gear permitting the Wilga, in this role, to tow a single glider of up to 650 kg (1,433 lb) weight or two or three gliders with a combined weight of 1,125 kg (2,480 lb).

SYSTEMS: Hydraulic system pressure 39 bars (570 lb/sq in). Engine starting is effected pneumatically by a built-in system of 7 litres (0.25 cu ft) capacity with a pressure of 49 bars (710 lb/sq in). Electrical system powered by DC generator and 24V 10Ah battery.

AVIONICS: VHF transceiver and blind-flying instrumentation standard; RS-6102 (of Polish design), R-860 II, R860 IIM, Bendix/King KY 195 or other radio; and ARL-1601 VHF, ARK-9, Bendix/King KR 85 or AV-200 ADF, GB-1 gyro compass, K2-715 airspeed and altitude recorder, optional.

EQUIPMENT: Sun visors, exhaust silencer and windscreen wiper optional.

DIMENSIONS, EXTERNAL:
Wing span: 35	11.12 m (36 ft 5¾ in)
80	11.13 m (36 ft 6¼ in)
Wing chord, constant	1.40 m (4 ft 7¼ in)
Wing aspect ratio	8.0
Length overall: 35	8.10 m (26 ft 6¾ in)
80	8.03 m (26 ft 4¼ in)
Height overall	2.96 m (9 ft 8½ in)
Tailplane span	3.70 m (12 ft 1¾ in)
Wheel track	2.75 m (9 ft 0¼ in)
Wheelbase	6.70 m (21 ft 11¾ in)
Propeller diameter	2.65 m (8 ft 8 in)
Passenger doors (each): Height	1.00 m (3 ft 3¼ in)
Width	1.50 m (4 ft 11 in)

DIMENSIONS, INTERNAL:
Cabin: Length	2.20 m (7 ft 2½ in)
Max width	1.20 m (3 ft 10 in)
Max height	1.50 m (4 ft 11 in)
Floor area	2.20 m² (23.8 sq ft)
Volume	2.40 m³ (85 cu ft)
Baggage compartment	0.50 m³ (17.5 cu ft)

AREAS:
Wings, gross	15.50 m² (166.8 sq ft)
Ailerons (total)	1.57 m² (16.90 sq ft)
Trailing-edge flaps (total)	1.97 m² (21.20 sq ft)
Fin	0.97 m² (10.44 sq ft)
Rudder	0.92 m² (9.90 sq ft)
Tailplane	3.16 m² (34.01 sq ft)
Elevator, incl tab	1.92 m² (20.67 sq ft)

WEIGHTS AND LOADINGS (Wilga 35A and 80):
Weight empty, equipped	870 kg (1,918 lb)
Max T-O and landing weight	1,300 kg (2,866 lb)
Max wing loading	83.9 kg/m² (17.18 lb/sq ft)
Max power loading	6.70 kg/kW (11.02 lb/hp)

PERFORMANCE (Wilga 35A, at max T-O weight):
Never-exceed speed(VNE)	150 knots (279 km/h; 173 mph)
Max level speed	105 knots (194 km/h; 120 mph)

Cruising speed (75% power)	85 knots (157 km/h; 97 mph)
Cruising speed for max range	74 knots (137 km/h; 85 mph)
Stalling speed: flaps up	35 knots (65 km/h; 41 mph)
flaps down	30 knots (56 km/h; 35 mph)
Max rate of climb at S/L	276 m (905 ft)/min
Time to 1,000 m (3,280 ft)	3 min
Service ceiling	4,040 m (13,250 ft)
T-O run (grass)	121 m (397 ft)
Landing run	106 m (348 ft)
Range with max fuel, 30 min reserves	275 nm (510 km; 317 miles)

PZL-105 FLAMING (FLAMINGO)

Although referred to at first as the Wilga 88, the PZL-105 is an entirely new design, developed as a successor to the Wilga 35/80 series to meet the needs of operators requiring STOL characteristics combined with greater speed, range and payload capacity. The design team was led by Roman Czerwiński, under the direction of Andrzej Frydrychewicz.

Intended to maintain the versatility of the Wilga, the PZL-105 will have a choice of power plants (**PZL-105M** with M-14P engine and **PZL-105L** with an IO-720) and landing gears, and will be suitable for such duties as light passenger or cargo transport, sport flying and aero club use, glider towing, parachute training, air ambulance, patrol or geophysical survey, and agricultural use. It can operate from unprepared airstrips, and is to be certificated to FAR Pt 23 (Amendments 1-28) in the Normal category.

A static test airframe (c/n 001) and three flying prototypes are being built, the first of the latter (SP-PRC, c/n 002) making its first flight on 19 December 1989 powered by an M-14P engine; c/n 003, with an IO-720, was expected to fly before the end of 1990. Certification of the PZL-105M was anticipated during 1991.

TYPE: Single-engined general purpose aircraft.

WINGS: All-metal high-wing monoplane, with wing section similar to NASA GA(W)-1. Single bracing strut on each side. Single-slotted Fowler trailing-edge flaps and flaperons, actuated electrically. Glassfibre wingtips. Construction generally similar to that of Wilga.

FUSELAGE: Conventional all-metal semi-monocoque structure.

TAIL UNIT: All-metal structure comprising sweptback fin and rudder, with low-set non-swept tailplane and elevators. Raked tips on fin and tailplane. Electrically actuated trim tab on port elevator; ground adjustable tab on rudder.

LANDING GEAR: Non-retractable type, with single mainwheels on cantilever self-sprung legs (glassfibre leaf springs) and a steerable tailwheel with oleo-pneumatic shock absorption. Low pressure tyres and hydraulic disc brakes on mainwheels. May also be fitted with floats, skis (with snow brakes) or wheel/skis.

POWER PLANT: Initial choice (PZL-105M) of one 268.5 kW (360 hp) Vedeneyev M-14P nine-cylinder aircooled radial engine, driving a W-530-TA-D35 two-blade constant-speed propeller. Provision for later use (PZL-105L) of 298 kW (400 hp) Textron Lycoming IO-720-A1B flat-eight engine and Hartzell propeller. Fuel in integral tanks in wings, total capacity 270 litres (71.3 US gallons; 59.4 Imp gallons).

ACCOMMODATION: Fully enclosed cabin, with seats for up to six persons (including pilot and optional second pilot) in three rows of two. Large door each side, with upward opening top half; downward opening lower halves incorporate steps. Dual controls optional. Cabin heated and ventilated.

DIMENSIONS, EXTERNAL:
Wing span	12.70 m (41 ft 8 in)
Wing aspect ratio	9.5
Length overall	8.60 m (28 ft 2½ in)
Height overall	2.80 m (9 ft 2¼ in)
Wheel track	3.10 m (10 ft 2 in)
Wheelbase	6.086 m (19 ft 11½ in)
Propeller diameter	2.40 m (7 ft 10½ in)
Cabin door: Height	1.10 m (3 ft 7¼ in)
Width	1.60 m (5 ft 3 in)

DIMENSIONS, INTERNAL:
Cabin: Length	2.80 m (9 ft 2¼ in)
Max width	1.10 m (3 ft 7¼ in)
Max height	1.20 m (3 ft 11¼ in)

AREAS:
Wings, gross	16.90 m² (181.9 sq ft)
Ailerons (total)	1.13 m² (12.16 sq ft)
Trailing-edge flaps (total)	1.95 m² (20.99 sq ft)

WEIGHTS AND LOADINGS:
Standard weight empty, equipped	1,100 kg (2,425 lb)
Max T-O weight	1,850 kg (4,078 lb)
Max wing loading	109.5 kg/m² (22.42 lb/sq ft)
Max power loading	6.89 kg/kW (11.32 lb/hp)

PERFORMANCE (estimated. A: at 1,250 kg; 2,756 lb AUW, B: at 1,650 kg; 3,637 lb, rest at max T-O weight):
Never-exceed speed (VNE)	165 knots (306 km/h; 190 mph)
Max level speed	140 knots (260 km/h; 161 mph)
Max cruising speed (134 kW; 180 hp)	116 knots (216 km/h; 134 mph)
Econ cruising speed (107.5 kW; 144 hp)	102 knots (190 km/h; 118 mph)
Stalling speed: A	45 knots (83 km/h; 52 mph)
B	52 knots (95 km/h; 59 mph)
Max rate of climb at S/L: A	523 m (1,716 ft)/min
B	396 m (1,299 ft)/min
T-O run: A	42 m (138 ft)
B	111 m (365 ft)
T-O to 15 m (50 ft): A	117 m (384 ft)
B	218 m (716 ft)
Landing from 15 m (50 ft): A	168 m (552 ft)
B	201 m (660 ft)
Landing run: A	66 m (217 ft)
B	94 m (309 ft)
Range with max fuel:	
at max cruising speed	533 nm (989 km; 614 miles)
at econ cruising speed	625 nm (1,159 km; 720 miles)
g limits	+3.8/−1.52

PZL-106B KRUK (RAVEN)

The PZL-106 was designed in early 1972 by a team led by Andrzej Frydrychewicz. The first prototype (SP-PAS) flew for the first time on 17 April 1973, powered by a 298 kW (400 hp) Textron Lycoming IO-720 engine. It was followed in October of that year by a second Textron Lycoming engined prototype (SP-PBG) and, from October 1974, by four prototypes fitted with the 441 kW (592 hp) PZL-3S radial engine that powers the PZL-106A and B. Production versions also have a low-mounted tailplane instead of the

Prototype PZL Warszawa-Okecie PZL-105M six-seat general utility aircraft (*Piotr Butowski*)

earlier T tail, and a greater chemical load in a larger hopper. Manufacture of some 600 aircraft for the member countries of the CMEA (Council for Mutual Economic Aid) is anticipated. A total of more than 246 (all versions) had been built by 1 January 1990, including 144 PZL-106As produced between 1976-81. Details of the PZL-106A, and of the AR and AT prototypes, can be found in the 1985-86 and earlier editions of *Jane's*.

The following versions of the Kruk are the most recent:

PZL-106AS: To increase the performance of PZL-106A Kruks operated by Pezetel in Egypt and the Sudan, PZL Warszawa-Okecie adapted the design to take a 746 kW (1,000 hp) PZL (Shvetsov) ASz-62IR nine-cylinder radial engine instead of the standard 441 kW (592 hp) PZL-3S. The prototype of this version (SP-PBD) flew for the first time on 19 August 1981. First ten re-engined in 1982; 44 converted by early 1987. Hopper load reduced to 750 kg (1,653 lb) initially, due to heavier engine. Re-certificated in July 1983 for operation at higher (Restricted) max T-O weight of 3,600 kg (7,936 lb). New-production aircraft with this engine are to PZL-106BS standard (which see).

PZL-106B: Prototypes for improved series, having redesigned wings with a new aerofoil section, increased span and area, trailing-edge flaps, and shortened V bracing struts. First prototype (SP-PKW) flew for the first time on 15 May 1981. Two further prototypes made their first flights in July and September 1981. Weights and performance data in 1985-86 and earlier *Jane's*.

PZL-106BR: Version with geared PZL-3SR engine; first flown on 8 July 1983. Tested also with wingtip vanes (three at each tip). Total of 64 built by 1 January 1990.

PZL-106BS: The prototype (SP-PBK) of this uprated version of the Kruk, with a PZL (Shvetsov) ASz-62IR radial engine, flew for the first time on 8 March 1982. Total of 15 built by 1 January 1990. For Restricted category operation, with higher max T-O weight and increased load of chemical.

PZL-106BT Turbo-Kruk: Turboprop version; described separately.

Armed version: Design study reportedly submitted to Polish Defence Ministry in late 1990; armour protection and six underwing weapon pylons.

The following description applies generally to the piston engined PZL-106B series, except where a specific version is indicated:

TYPE: Single-engined agricultural aircraft. Structure is corrosion resistant, and is additionally protected by an external finish of polyurethane enamel.

WINGS: Braced low-wing monoplane with upward cambered tips. NACA 2415 wing section throughout span. Dihedral 4° from roots. Incidence 6° 6′. Sweepback 1° at quarter-chord. All-metal two-spar duralumin structure, of constant chord. Metal and polyester fabric covering. Glassfibre wingtips, with upswept undersurfaces. Full span four-segment fixed leading-edge slats on each wing, of glassfibre sandwich construction with foam core. Slotted ailerons of duralumin, with polyester fabric covering. Trailing-edge flaps of similar construction. Ground adjustable tab on each aileron initially; aircraft from tenth production batch onward have electrically actuated trim tab in port aileron. Duralumin streamline section V bracing struts, with jury struts.

FUSELAGE: Welded steel tube structure, protected by several coats of polyurethane enamel and covered with quickly removable panels of light alloy and GFRP. Steel tube structure can be pressure tested for crack detection.

TAIL UNIT: Conventional duralumin structure, initially with single tailplane bracing strut each side; two struts each side from ninth production batch onward. Fixed surfaces metal covered; rudder and mass balanced elevators are polyester fabric covered. Trim tab in port elevator, automatic tab on rudder.

LANDING GEAR: Non-retractable tailwheel type, with oleo-pneumatic shock absorber in each unit. Mainwheels, with low-pressure tyres size 800 × 260 mm, each carried on side V and half-axle. Mainwheel tyre pressure 2.0 bars (29 lb/sq in). Pneumatically operated hydraulic disc brakes on mainwheels. Parking brake. Steerable tailwheel, with tubeless tyre size 350 × 135 mm, pressure 2.5 bars (36.25 lb/sq in).

POWER PLANT: *(PZL-106BR):* One 448 kW (600 hp) PZL-3SR seven-cylinder radial aircooled geared and supercharged engine, driving a PZL US-133000 four-blade constant-speed metal propeller. *(PZL-106BS):* One 746 kW (1,000 hp) PZL (Shvetsov) ASz-62IR nine-cylinder radial aircooled engine and AW-2-30 propeller. Fuel in two integral wing tanks, total capacity 560 litres (148 US gallons; 123 Imp gallons), can be increased to total of 950 litres (251 US gallons; 209 Imp gallons) by using hopper as auxiliary fuel tank. Gravity refuelling point on each wing; semi-pressurised refuelling point on starboard side of fuselage. Oil capacity 54 litres (14.3 US gallons; 11.9 Imp gallons) max in BR, 67 litres (17.7 US gallons; 14.7 Imp gallons) in BS. Carburettor air filter fitted.

ACCOMMODATION: Single vertically adjustable seat in enclosed, ventilated and heated cockpit with steel tube overturn structure. Provision for instructor's cockpit with basic dual controls, forward of main cockpit and offset to starboard, for training of pilots in agricultural duties. Optional rearward facing second seat (for

mechanic) to rear. Jettisonable window/door on each side of cabin. Pilot's seat and seat belt designed to resist 40g impact. Cockpit air-conditioning optional.

SYSTEMS: Pneumatic system, rated at 49 bars (710 lb/sq in), for brakes and agricultural equipment. Electrical power, from 3kW 27.5V DC generator and 24V 15Ah battery, for engine starting, pneumatic system control, aircraft lights, instruments, transceiver and semi-pressurised refuelling.

AVIONICS: VHF com transceiver standard; 720-channel UHF transceiver optional.

EQUIPMENT: Easily removable non-corroding (GFRP) hopper/tank, forward of cockpit, can carry more than 1,000 kg (2,205 lb) (see under Weights and Loadings paragraph) of dry or liquid chemical, and has a maximum capacity of 1,400 litres (370 US gallons; 308 Imp gallons). Turnround time, with full load of chemical, is in the order of 28 s. The hopper has a quick-dump system that can release 1,000 kg of chemical in 5 s or less. A pneumatically operated intake for the loading of dry chemicals is optional. Distribution system for liquid chemical (jets or atomisers) is powered by a fan driven centrifugal pump. A precise and reliable dispersal system, with positive on/off action for dry chemicals, gives effective swath widths of 30-35 m (100-115 ft). For ferry purposes, hopper can be used to carry additional fuel instead of chemical. When the Kruk is converted into a two-seat trainer (see Accommodation paragraph), standard hopper can be replaced easily by a special container with reduced capacity tank for liquid chemical. Steel cable cutter on windscreen and each mainwheel leg; steel deflector cable runs from top of windscreen cable cutter to tip of fin. Windscreen washer and wiper standard. Other equipment includes artificial horizon, gyro compass, engine hour meter, clock, rearview mirror, second (mechanic's) seat (optional), cockpit air-conditioning (optional), cockpit heating and ventilation, landing light, anti-collision light, and night working lights (optional).

DIMENSIONS, EXTERNAL:	
Wing span	14.90 m (48 ft 10½ in)
Wing chord, constant	2.16 m (7 ft 1 in)
Wing aspect ratio	6.9
Length overall: BR	9.25 m (30 ft 4½ in)
BS	9.34 m (30 ft 7¾ in)
Height overall	3.32 m (10 ft 10¾ in)
Tailplane span	5.77 m (18 ft 11¼ in)
Wheel track	3.10 m (10 ft 2¼ in)
Wheelbase	7.41 m (24 ft 3¾ in)
Propeller diameter: BR	3.10 m (10 ft 2 in)
BS	3.30 m (10 ft 10 in)
Propeller ground clearance (tail up)	0.39 m (1 ft 3¼ in)
Crew doors (each): Height	0.91 m (2 ft 11¾ in)
Width	1.06 m (3 ft 5¾ in)
Baggage door: Height	0.70 m (2 ft 3½ in)
Width	0.60 m (1 ft 11¾ in)

DIMENSIONS, INTERNAL:	
Cabin: Length	1.37 m (4 ft 6 in)
Max width	1.25 m (4 ft 1¼ in)
Max height	1.30 m (4 ft 3¼ in)
Floor area	1.12 m² (12.05 sq ft)
Rear cockpit/baggage compartment:	
Length	1.40 m (4 ft 7 in)
Width	1.00 m (3 ft 3¼ in)
Depth	0.60 m (1 ft 11¾ in)

AREAS:	
Wings, gross	31.69 m² (341.1 sq ft)
Ailerons (total)	4.34 m² (46.72 sq ft)
Trailing-edge flaps (total)	4.44 m² (47.79 sq ft)
Leading-edge slats (total)	4.25 m² (45.75 sq ft)
Fin	1.26 m² (13.56 sq ft)
Rudder, incl tab	1.62 m² (17.44 sq ft)
Tailplane	3.34 m² (35.95 sq ft)
Elevators, incl tab	4.22 m² (45.42 sq ft)

WEIGHTS AND LOADINGS:	
Weight empty, equipped: BR	1,790 kg (3,946 lb)
BS	2,080 kg (4,585 lb)
Max chemical payload: BR	1,300 kg (2,866 lb)
BS	1,150 kg (2,535 lb)
Max T-O and landing weight: BR, BS	3,000 kg (6,614 lb)
BR (Restricted category)	3,450 kg (7,606 lb)
BS (Restricted category)	3,500 kg (7,716 lb)
Max wing loading (Restricted category):	
BR	108.86 kg/m² (22.30 lb/sq ft)
BS	110.44 kg/m² (22.62 lb/sq ft)
Max power loading (Restricted category):	
BR	7.70 kg/kW (12.68 lb/hp)
BS	4.69 kg/kW (7.72 lb/hp)

PERFORMANCE (at max T-O weight):	
Never-exceed speed (VNE):	
BR, BS	145 knots (270 km/h; 167 mph)
Max level speed at S/L:	
BR, BS	116 knots (215 km/h; 134 mph)
Operating speed with max chemical load:	
BR	81-86 knots (150-160 km/h; 93-99 mph)
BS	86 knots (160 km/h; 99 mph)

PZL-106BR Kruk (PZL-3SR radial engine) *(R. J. Malachowski)*

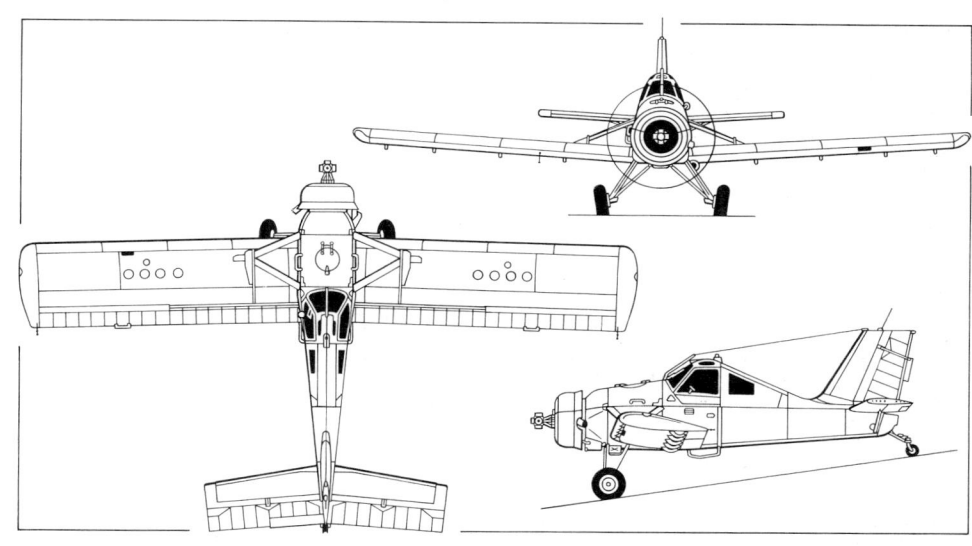

PZL-106BR Kruk single-seat agricultural aircraft *(Jane's/Mike Keep)*

PZL-106BT Turbo-Kruk, powered by a Czechoslovak turboprop engine (*R. J. Malachowski*)

Stalling speed at S/L:
BR, BS	54 knots (100 km/h; 62 mph)

Max rate of climb at S/L (with agricultural equipment):
BR	228 m (748 ft)/min
BS	372 m (1,220 ft)/min

T-O run (with agricultural equipment):
BR	250 m (820 ft)
BS	120 m (394 ft)

Landing run (with agricultural equipment):
BR, BS	200 m (656 ft)

Range with max standard fuel:
BR, BS	485 nm (900 km; 559 miles)

PZL-106BT TURBO-KRUK

This turboprop version of the Kruk was flown for the first time (prototype SP-PAA) on 18 September 1985. It has increased wing sweep, a taller fin, and carries a larger load of chemical. A total of 11 production aircraft had been built by 1 January 1990, at which time the Turbo-Kruk was operating in Egypt, Germany and Poland.

Differences from the piston engined Kruk are as follows:
WINGS: Sweepback 6° at quarter-chord. Dihedral 6°.
TAIL UNIT: Taller fin.
POWER PLANT: One 544 kW (730 shp) Walter M 601 D turboprop; Avia V 508 D three-blade propeller.
DIMENSIONS, EXTERNAL:
Wing span	15.00 m (49 ft 2½ in)
Wing chord, constant	2.16 m (7 ft 1 in)
Wing aspect ratio	7.1
Length overall	10.24 m (33 ft 7¼ in)
Height overall	3.82 m (12 ft 6½ in)
Propeller diameter	2.50 m (8 ft 2½ in)

AREAS:
Wings, gross	31.69 m² (341.1 sq ft)
Fin	1.82 m² (19.59 sq ft)

WEIGHTS AND LOADINGS:
Weight empty, equipped	1,680 kg (3,704 lb)
Max chemical payload	1,300 kg (2,866 lb)
Max T-O weight	3,500 kg (7,716 lb)
Max landing weight	3,000 kg (6,614 lb)
Max wing loading	110.44 kg/m² (22.62 lb/sq ft)
Max power loading	6.07 kg/kW (9.97 lb/shp)

PERFORMANCE (at max T-O weight):
Never-exceed speed (VNE)
	145 knots (270 km/h; 167 mph)

Max level speed at S/L:
without agricultural equipment	
	135 knots (250 km/h; 155 mph)
with agricultural equipment	
	116 knots (215 km/h; 134 mph)

Operating speed with max chemical load
	81-92 knots (150-170 km/h; 93-106 mph)
Stalling speed at S/L	49 knots (90 km/h; 56 mph)

Max rate of climb at S/L (with agricultural equipment)
	360 m (1,180 ft)/min
T-O run (with agricultural equipment)	230 m (755 ft)

Landing run (with agricultural equipment)
	130 m (427 ft)

Range with max standard fuel
	485 nm (900 km; 559 miles)

PZL-107

This designation is understood to apply to an agricultural aircraft (payload 1,200 kg; 2,645 lb) currently in the design stage. At press time, it was not clear whether this was a resurrection of the proposed PZL-106 replacement last mentioned in the 1983-84 edition.

PZL-110 KOLIBER (HUMMING-BIRD)

Under this designation, PZL Warszawa-Okecie is producing under licence a two/four-seat version of the Socata Rallye 100 ST, the lowest powered model in the Rallye light aircraft family. The first PZL-110, modified to receive an 86.5 kW (116 hp) PZL-F (Franklin) engine, made its initial flight on 18 April 1978, and the following versions have since been produced:

Koliber Series I: Initial version, first flown 8 May 1979 and certificated on 24 August that year; 10 built.

Koliber Series II: Special batch of 25 (built 1983-84) for Polish aeroclub use, approved for limited aerobatics.

Koliber Series III: Intended production batch of 45 aircraft; was awaiting availability of PZL-F 4A-235B31 engines in 1990.

Koliber 150: Current production version, differing in having Textron Lycoming O-320 engine and detail improvements. Prototype (SP-PHA) made first flight 27 September 1988; Polish type certificate awarded January 1989. Sales to date include customers in Belgium, Denmark, Germany, Norway, South Africa and Sweden.

The following description applies to the Koliber 150:
TYPE: Four-seat training and multi-purpose light aircraft.
WINGS: Cantilever low-wing monoplane. Wing section NACA 63A416 (modified). Dihedral 7° 7′ 30″. Incidence 4°. All-metal single-spar structure. Full span automatic leading-edge slats. All-metal ailerons (aerodynamically and mass balanced) and Fowler flaps with corrugated skins. Wing torsion box and trailing-edge segments electrically spot-welded. Ailerons actuated mechanically, flaps electrically. Ground adjustable aileron tabs. No anti-icing.
FUSELAGE: All-metal semi-monocoque structure, riveted and spot-welded.
TAIL UNIT: Cantilever all-metal structure, with corrugated skin on aerodynamically and mass balanced control surfaces. Fixed incidence tailplane. One controllable tab on elevator; ground adjustable tab on rudder.
LANDING GEAR: Non-retractable tricycle type, with leg fairings and oleo-pneumatic shock absorption. Castoring nosewheel, size 330 × 130 mm; mainwheels size 380 × 150 mm. Tyre pressures 1.4 and 1.8 bars (20.3 and 26.1 lb/sq in) respectively. Hydraulic disc brakes.
POWER PLANT: One 112 kW (150 hp) Textron Lycoming O-320-E2A flat-four engine, driving a Sensenich 74DM6-054, -056 or -058 two-blade constant-speed metal propeller. Fuel in two metal tanks in wings, with total capacity of 105 litres (27.7 US gallons; 23.1 Imp gallons). Refuelling points above wings. Oil capacity 6 litres (1.6 US gallons; 1.3 Imp gallons).
ACCOMMODATION: Two side by side seats, plus bench seat at rear, under large rearward sliding canopy. Dual controls. Heating and ventilation standard.
SYSTEMS: 12V electrical system, with 50A alternator and 30Ah battery.
AVIONICS: Bendix/King KX 155 or Narco Mk 12D UHF transceiver, ADF, VOR, electrically powered gyro attitude indicator, turn and bank indicator, and directional gyro.
EQUIPMENT: For training role, includes pupil's window blinds for instrument training, front seat backrests suitable for use with back type parachutes, safety belts, and accelerometers.
DIMENSIONS, EXTERNAL:
Wing span	9.75 m (31 ft 11¾ in)
Wing chord, constant	1.30 m (4 ft 3 in)

Wing aspect ratio	7.5
Length overall	7.37 m (24 ft 2¼ in)
Height overall	2.80 m (9 ft 2¼ in)
Tailplane span	3.67 m (12 ft 0½ in)
Wheel track	2.01 m (6 ft 7¼ in)
Wheelbase	1.71 m (5 ft 7¼ in)
Propeller diameter	1.78 m (5 ft 10 in)

AREAS:
Wings, gross	12.68 m² (136.5 sq ft)
Ailerons (total)	1.56 m² (16.79 sq ft)
Trailing-edge flaps (total)	2.40 m² (25.83 sq ft)
Vertical tail surfaces (total)	1.74 m² (18.73 sq ft)
Horizontal tail surfaces (total)	3.48 m² (37.50 sq ft)

WEIGHTS AND LOADINGS (U: Utility, N: Normal category):
Weight empty, equipped	548 kg (1,208 lb)
Max T-O weight: U	770 kg (1,697 lb)
N	850 kg (1,874 lb)
Max wing loading: U	60.72 kg/m² (12.44 lb/sq ft)
N	67.03 kg/m² (13.73 lb/sq ft)
Max power loading: U	8.90 kg/kW (14.63 lb/hp)
N	7.60 kg/kW (12.49 lb/hp)

PERFORMANCE (at max T-O weight):
Never-exceed speed (VNE):
U	145 knots (270 km/h; 167 mph)
N	134 knots (250 km/h; 155 mph)

Max level speed at S/L:
U, N	108 knots (200 km/h; 124 mph)

Max cruising speed at S/L:
U, N	92 knots (170 km/h; 106 mph)

Econ cruising speed:
U, N	75 knots (140 km/h; 87 mph)

Stalling speed:
U, N, flaps up	50 knots (92 km/h; 58 mph)
U, N, flaps down	45 knots (82 km/h; 51 mph)

Max rate of climb at S/L: U
U	264 m (866 ft)/min
N	216 m (708 ft)/min

Service ceiling: U, N	3,700 m (12,140 ft)
T-O run at S/L: U	140 m (459 ft)
N	167 m (548 ft)
T-O to 15 m (50 ft) at S/L: U	340 m (1,116 ft)
N	397 m (1,303 ft)
Landing from 15 m (50 ft) at S/L: U	290 m (952 ft)
N	320 m (1,050 ft)
Landing run at S/L: U	125 m (411 ft)
N	138 m (453 ft)

Range at 500 m (1,640 ft) with max fuel, no reserves
	324 nm (600 km; 373 miles)
g limits	+4.4/−1.76 (ultimate)

PZL-126 MRÓWKA (ANT)

Design of this very small agricultural aircraft, and of an innovatory new airborne spraying system, was initiated in the late 1970s by Dipl Eng Andrzej SJocinski of PZL Warszawa-Okecie; its propeller, rear fuselage and parts of the landing gear were built by students of the factory's training college. Preliminary design was completed in late 1982 and initial detail design work in the second quarter of 1983, but (as explained in the 1990-91 *Jane's*) the project was then delayed for some years until the first of three prototypes (SP-PMA) made its first flight on 20 April 1990.

The PZL-126 meets the requirements of FAR Pt 23 (USA) and BCAR Section K (UK). It can be dismantled quickly for long-distance transportation in the cabin of an An-2 biplane, or can be towed on its own landing gear by a light all-terrain vehicle. Landing gear is normally of tricycle type, with a 'taildragger' gear available optionally. Another option to be tested on the prototypes is a wing with full span flaps, airbrakes and spoilers, instead of the basic slotted flaps plus flaperons system. The dedicated agricultural spray system is in the form of vaned and pressurised wingtip pods of chemical, attached by quick-fastening locks to facilitate rapid replacement of empty pods by full ones. (These are replaced by extended wingtips on prototype, as illustrated, increasing span by 1.00 m; 3 ft 3¼ in.) A special retractable device for spreading biological agents is installed in the fuselage underside aft of the cockpit. Further details of individual dispersal systems are given in the Equipment paragraph.

PZL-110 Koliber 150, Polish built version of the Socata Rallye 100 ST (*R. J. Malachowski*)

The primary use intended for the Mrówka is as an economical small aircraft for use on farms and smallholdings, but it is considered suitable also for patrol and liaison missions (eg for detecting/controlling forest fires, identification of diseased vegetation, and monitoring areas of polluted land and water).

TYPE: Single-seat light agricultural and ecological support aircraft.

WINGS: Cantilever low-wing monoplane, of constant chord and NASA GA(W)-1 wing section. Single-spar metal structure, with trailing-edge single-slotted flaps inboard and flaperons outboard. Some components of glassfibre/epoxy construction. Alternative wings with full span flaps, airbrakes and spoilers also to be tested.

FUSELAGE: Conventional metal semi-monocoque structure, built in two portions. Some elements constructed of glassfibre/epoxy composite material.

TAIL UNIT: Cantilever all-metal structure, comprising rectangular fin and rudder and low-set tailplane with one-piece elevator. Trim tab on starboard half of elevator; ground adjustable tab on rudder.

LANDING GEAR: Non-retractable tricycle gear standard. Cantilever self-sprung mainwheel legs; shock absorber in nosewheel unit. Size 350 × 135 mm tyres on all three wheels, pressure 1.23 bars (17.8 lb/sq in) on main units and 0.78 bar (11.3 lb/sq in) on nose unit. Mainwheels fitted with differential hydraulic disc brakes. Tailwheel configuration optional.

POWER PLANT: One 44.7 kW (60 hp) PZL-F 2A-120-C1 flat-twin engine, driving a two-blade fixed-pitch wooden propeller. (Interchangeable propellers for agricultural flying or patrol mission.) Integral fuel tanks in wing torsion box. Fuel capacity 70 litres (18.5 US gallons; 15.4 Imp gallons).

ACCOMMODATION: Single adjustable seat under one-piece moulded canopy, opening sideways to starboard. Seat and canopy taken from SZD-51 Junior sailplane.

SYSTEMS: Hydraulic system for mainwheel brakes only; 12V DC electrical system.

AVIONICS: VFR instrumentation standard, plus 720-channel UHF com and 10-channel radio telephone.

EQUIPMENT: Dedicated system for spraying with low volume liquid chemicals (pyrethroids) consists of a 25 litre (6.6 US gallon; 5.5 Imp gallon) pod at each wingtip. Spraying is controlled electrically by a push-button on the throttle lever and effected by dispersing the liquid under pressure via an atomiser at the rear of each pod. An area of 25 ha (61.8 acres) can be covered with one pair of full pods. Biological agents, such as the eggs of the Trichogramma wasp, are carried in capsules in a paper tape wound on a reel which is housed in the lower fuselage behind the cockpit and extended through an openable hatch in the floor. One spreader holds a 3 kg (6.6 lb) package of eggs, on four reels, and at a drop rate of four capsules every 50 m (164 ft) can cover an area of 800 ha (1,977 acres) on a single loading. Like the spray system, the spreader's actuation is electrical, by means of a push-button on the throttle lever. Other equipment can include cameras and first aid appliances.

DIMENSIONS, EXTERNAL:

Wing span: excl pods	6.00 m (19 ft 8¼ in)
incl pods	6.30 m (20 ft 8 in)
Wing chord, constant	0.75 m (2 ft 5½ in)
Length overall	4.66 m (15 ft 3½ in)
Height overall	2.53 m (8 ft 3½ in)
Tailplane span	2.00 m (6 ft 6¾ in)
Wheel track	1.94 m (6 ft 4½ in)
Wheelbase	0.92 m (3 ft 0¼ in)
Propeller diameter	1.40 m (4 ft 7 in)
Propeller ground clearance	0.18 m (7 in)

AREAS:

Wings, gross: excl pods	4.50 m² (48.44 sq ft)
incl pods	5.12 m² (55.11 sq ft)
Flaps (total)	0.572 m² (6.16 sq ft)
Flaperons (total)	0.414 m² (4.46 sq ft)
Vertical tail surfaces (total)	0.68 m² (7.32 sq ft)
Horizontal tail surfaces (total)	1.02 m² (10.98 sq ft)

WEIGHTS AND LOADINGS:

Max T-O and landing weight	420 kg (926 lb)
Max wing loading:	
without pods (prototype)	93.33 kg/m² (19.12 lb/sq ft)
with pods	82.03 kg/m² (16.80 lb/sq ft)
Max power loading	9.39 kg/kW (15.43 lb/hp)

PERFORMANCE:

Operating speed	75 knots (140 km/h; 87 mph)

PZL-130 ORLIK (SPOTTED EAGLET)

Development of the piston-engined Orlik was discontinued in 1990 pending renewed availability of the Soviet-made Vedeneyev M-14Pm radial engine, which had been unsuccessfully transferred to Romania. The alternative Polish Kalisz K8-AA was not powerful enough. A full description of the piston-engined Orlik can be found in the 1989-90 Jane's.

PZL-130 TURBO ORLIK

This turboprop version of the Orlik (Spotted Eaglet), intended for home and export markets, was designed in 1985 by Mr Andrzej Frydrychewicz, the chief designer of PZL Warszawa-Okecie, initially in collaboration with the Canadian company Airtech Canada. In January 1986 work

First prototype PZL-126 Mrówka experimental agricultural aircraft *(R. J. Malachowski)*

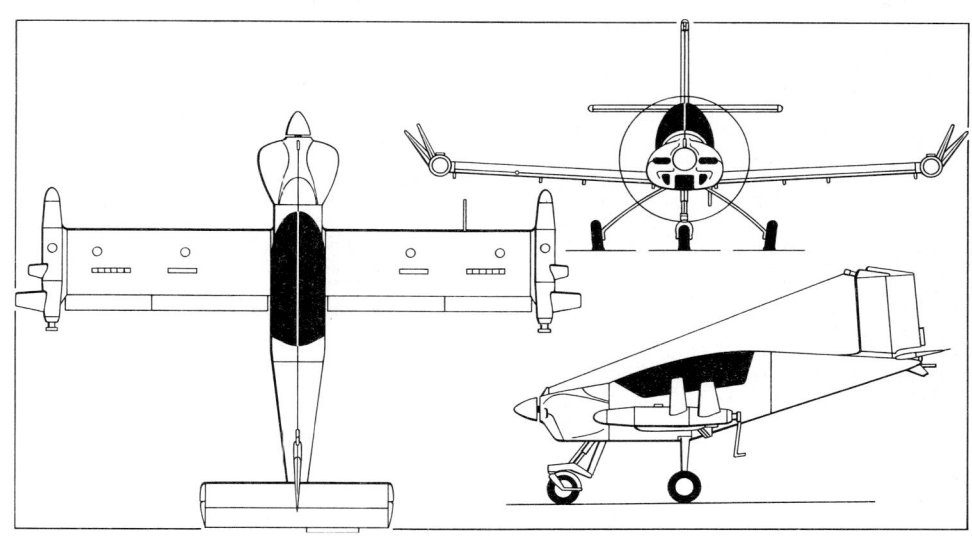

PZL-126 Mrówka experimental agricultural light aircraft *(Jane's/Mike Keep)*

began to convert the third PZL-130 (SP-PCC) to take a Pratt & Whitney Canada PT6A-25A engine. This aircraft made its first flight as the Turbo Orlik prototype on 13 July 1986, and received a provisional type certificate under FAR Pt 23 in January 1987, but later that month the aircraft and both occupants were lost. Airtech Canada is no longer involved in the programme.

Further development aircraft have flown, the first of them (c/n 007) being designated **PZL-130TM** (Motorlet) and powered by a 560 kW (751 shp) Motorlet Walter M 601 E engine and flying for the first time on 12 January 1989. A second PT6A-25A engined **PZL-130T** (SP-WCA) (c/n 008) was completed by December 1989. This was being intensively flight tested in early 1991. Then comes the **PZL-130TB Turbo Bis** (Motorlet M 601 E) for the Polish Air Force. The latter is a flying simulator and its cockpit resembles as closely as possible that of the Sukhoi Su-22. It is also intended for export to countries used to Soviet-made equipment; the fully aerobatic Walter M 601 T is an alternative engine. Following the May rollout, first flight of the TB was expected in mid-1991.

The PZL-130TB has a max T-O weight of 2,700 kg (5,952 lb), 1 m (3 ft 3¼ in) greater wing span, greater wing incidence to lower the nose in flight, double-slotted flaps, LFK-F1 ejection seats under a revised canopy, more powerful brakes and steerable nosewheel. Six underwing pylons can carry 800 kg (1,764 lb) of weapons for training or operational use.

There are three further versions. The most potent is the **PZL-130TC** powered by a P&WC PT6A-62 flat rated at 708 kW (950 shp) and fitted with extensive Bendix/King avionics. It is intended for export with foreign equipment. The **PZL-130TD**, also for export, is powered by the smaller 559 kW (750 shp) P&WC PT6A-25C and has the same equipment. Finally, the **PZL-130TE** is to be powered by the 410 kW (550 shp) PT6A-25 and, as a result, will have more limited equipment and no ejection seats. A 48-aircraft order for Turbo Orliks was reported in April 1991.

The following description applies to the PT6A-25A engined PZL-130T prototypes:

TYPE: Tandem two-seat primary, basic and multi-purpose trainer.

WINGS: Cantilever low-wing monoplane. Wing section NACA 64₂215 (modified). Dihedral 5° from roots. Incidence 0° at root, −3° at tip. One-piece all-metal (light alloy) multi-spar box structure. Torsion box, stiffened by riveted omega formers, forms integral fuel tanks.

Trailing-edge skin panels are stiffened by L formers, electrically spot welded. Tapered planform, with raked tips of glassfibre/epoxy. Leading-edges are detachable. All-metal constant chord three-position single-slotted trailing-edge flaps, actuated electrically. Frise differential ailerons are also all-metal and of constant chord, aerodynamically and mass balanced, and actuated mechanically via pushrods and torque tube in fuselage. Electrically actuated trim tab on port aileron. Provision for anti-icing system in leading-edges.

FUSELAGE: All-metal (light alloy) unpressurised semi-monocoque structure, with skin panels stiffened by electrically spot welded L formers.

TAIL UNIT: Cantilever light alloy structure, with sweptback vertical and non-swept horizontal surfaces. Fin integral with rear fuselage. Curved dorsal fin; shallow ventral strake under fuselage tailcone. One-piece two-spar fixed incidence tailplane. Elevators aerodynamically and mass balanced, controlled by rods and cables; electrically actuated trim tab on port elevator. Aerodynamically and mass balanced rudder, also with electrically actuated trim tab, is cable controlled.

LANDING GEAR: Hydraulically retractable tricycle type, all three units retracting into fuselage (mainwheels inward, nosewheel rearward). PZL Warszawa-Okecie oleo-pneumatic shock absorber in each unit (nosewheel on semi-fork with shimmy damper and centring device). Low pressure tubeless tyres (2.0 bars; 29 lb/sq in in all three), size 500 × 200 mm (main) and 400 × 140 mm (nose). Differential disc brakes, operated hydraulically. Parking brake. No anti-skid units.

POWER PLANT: One 410 kW (550 shp) Pratt & Whitney Canada PT6A-25A turboprop, driving a Hartzell HC-B3TN-3B/T10173K-11R three-blade constant-speed metal propeller with feathering and reverse pitch. Propeller blades de-iced electrically. Four integral fuel tanks (two of 110 litres; 29 US gallons; 24.2 Imp gallons and two of 100 litres; 26.5 US gallons; 22 Imp gallons capacity) in wing torsion box, plus a 9 litre (2.5 US gallon; 2.0 Imp gallon) collector tank in fuselage; total usable internal fuel capacity 420 litres (111 US gallons; 92.4 Imp gallons). Overwing refuelling point for each wing tank. Fuel and oil systems adapted for aerobatics, including up to 30 s of inverted flight. Electrically adjustable exhaust flaps for engine cooling air. Provision for two 150 litre (39.6 US gallon; 33 Imp gallon) auxiliary tanks on underwing stations.

ACCOMMODATION: Tandem seating for pupil and instructor under one-piece canopy, which opens sideways to starboard. Rear (instructor's) seat slightly elevated. Both seats are adjustable electrically, can accommodate back type and seat type parachutes, and are fitted with seat belts/harnesses. Full dual controls standard; rudder pedals are adjustable (three positions). Windscreen and canopy frames are of glassfibre/epoxy; windscreen is removable, canopy jettisonable. Cockpits heated (electric heater with blower) and ventilated. Baggage compartment aft of rear seat.

SYSTEMS: Hydraulic system for landing gear actuation. Electrical power (115V/400Hz) supplied by 6kW Lear Siegler starter/generator and two 24V 15Ah nickel-cadmium batteries, with three-phase 36V/400Hz AC converters. External DC power socket. Oxygen bottles and crew masks. Provision for anti-icing of wing leading-edges.

AVIONICS: Bendix/King VHF and UHF com, intercom and ADF.

ARMAMENT: Four underwing hardpoints, stressed for 200 kg (441 lb) each inboard, 160 kg (353 lb) each outboard.

DIMENSIONS, EXTERNAL:

Wing span	8.00 m (26 ft 3 in)
Wing chord: at root	2.00 m (6 ft 6¾ in)
mean aerodynamic	1.62 m (5 ft 3¾ in)
Wing aspect ratio	5.2
Length overall	8.68 m (28 ft 5¾ in)
Fuselage: Max width	0.90 m (2 ft 11½ in)
Height overall	3.53 m (11 ft 7 in)
Tailplane span	3.50 m (11 ft 5¾ in)
Wheel track	3.10 m (10 ft 2 in)
Wheelbase	2.22 m (7 ft 3½ in)
Propeller diameter	2.29 m (7 ft 6 in)

DIMENSIONS, INTERNAL:

Cockpits: Length	2.95 m (9 ft 8¼ in)
Baggage compartment volume	0.17 m³ (6.0 cu ft)

AREAS:

Wings, gross	12.28 m² (132.2 sq ft)
Ailerons (total, incl tab)	1.38 m² (14.85 sq ft)
Trailing-edge flaps (total)	1.37 m² (14.75 sq ft)
Fin, incl dorsal fin	1.20 m² (12.92 sq ft)
Rudder, incl tab	0.65 m² (6.97 sq ft)
Tailplane	1.81 m² (19.48 sq ft)
Elevators (total, incl tab)	0.94 m² (10.12 sq ft)

WEIGHTS AND LOADINGS (A: Aerobatic, U: Utility):

Weight empty, equipped, standard	1,150 kg (2,535 lb)
Max usable fuel (internal)	366 kg (807 lb)
Max T-O and landing weight: A	1,580 kg (3,483 lb)
U (no stores)	1,750 kg (3,858 lb)
U (with external stores)	2,155 kg (4,751 lb)
Max wing loading: A	128.66 kg/m² (26.35 lb/sq ft)
U (no stores)	142.51 kg/m² (29.19 lb/sq ft)
U (with external stores)	175.49 kg/m² (35.94 lb/sq ft)
Max power loading: A	3.85 kg/kW (6.33 lb/shp)
U (no stores)	4.27 kg/kW (7.01 lb/shp)
U (with external stores)	5.26 kg/kW (8.64 lb/shp)

PERFORMANCE (at max Aerobatic T-O weight except where indicated):

Max permissible diving speed (V_D)
302 knots (560 km/h; 347 mph)
Max level speed at 4,575 m (15,000 ft)
269 knots (499 km/h; 310 mph)
Max cruising speed at S/L
236 knots (438 km/h; 272 mph)
Stalling speed, power off:
flaps up, landing gear down
78 knots (144 km/h; 90 mph)
flaps and landing gear down:
A   63 knots (115 km/h; 72 mph)
U (no stores)   66 knots (122 km/h; 76 mph)
U (with external stores)
73 knots (135 km/h; 84 mph)
Max rate of climb at S/L   954 m (3,130 ft)/min
Service ceiling   10,060 m (33,000 ft)
T-O run   250 m (821 ft)
T-O to 15 m (50 ft)   410 m (1,345 ft)
Landing from 15 m (50 ft)   570 m (1,870 ft)
Landing run   370 m (1,214 ft)
Range with max internal fuel, AUW of 1,600 kg (3,527 lb):
U at 248 knots (460 km/h; 286 mph)
603 nm (1,117 km; 694 miles)
U at 140 knots (260 km/h; 161 mph)
694 nm (1,287 km; 800 miles)
Endurance with max internal fuel, AUW as above:
U at 248 knots (460 km/h; 286 mph)   2 h 26 min
U at 140 knots (260 km/h; 161 mph)   4 h 57 min
Range with max internal and external fuel, AUW of 1,977 kg (4,358 lb):
U at 245 knots (454 km/h; 282 mph)
1,166 nm (2,161 km; 1,343 miles)
U at 147 knots (272 km/h; 169 mph)
1,198 nm (2,220 km; 1,397 miles)
Endurance with max internal and external fuel, AUW as above:
U at 245 knots (454 km/h; 282 mph)   4 h 46 min
U at 147 knots (272 km/h; 169 mph)   8 h 10 min
g limits: +6/−3 at Aerobatic T-O weight
+4.4/−1.76 at max T-O weight

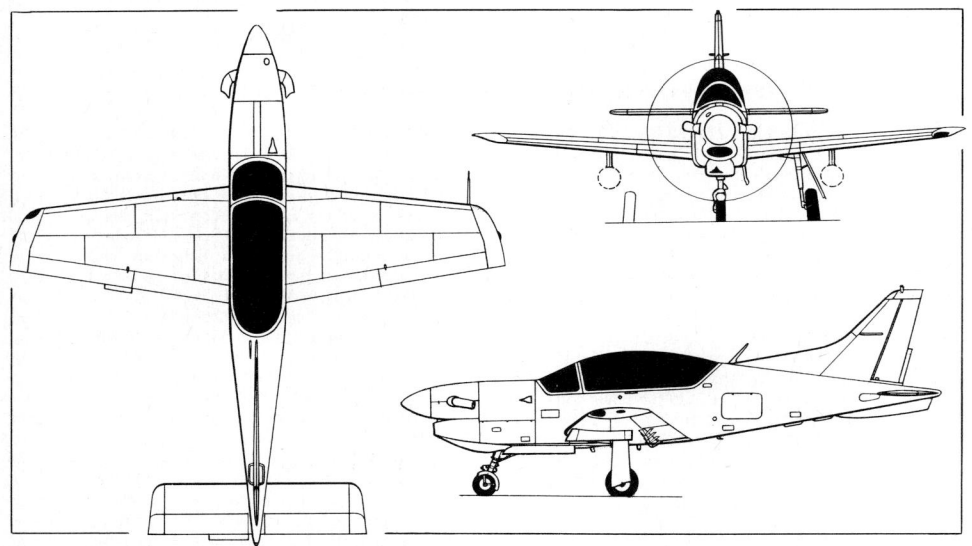

Pre-production PZL-130TM Turbo Orlik with Walter M 601 E turboprop *(R. J. Malachowski)*

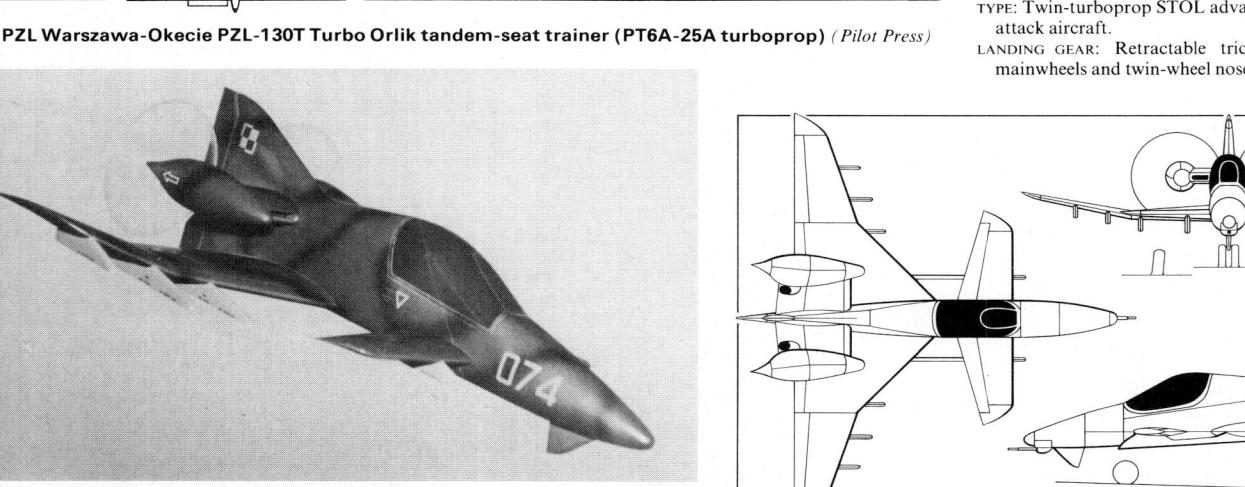

PZL Warszawa-Okecie PZL-130T Turbo Orlik tandem-seat trainer (PT6A-25A turboprop) *(Pilot Press)*

PZL-230 SKORPION

The Skorpion, designed under the leadership of Mr Andrzej Frydrychewicz, is in the preliminary concept stage according to first details released in early 1991. Several of its features, said to be based on Orlik technology, but also resembling the Scaled Composites ARES (see US section), can be seen in the accompanying picture and three-view drawing. The Skorpion would have a very high power/weight ratio and be able to fly a 180° turn with a radius of 150 m (490 ft) in 4.2 seconds. The inboard weapon pylon shown in one drawing runs from the main wing to the foreplane. A fin under the nose could provide side force control for weapon aiming. Structure would be mainly of composites. Israel and South Africa are seen as possible export customers. The following data are provisional:

TYPE: Twin-turboprop STOL advanced trainer and ground attack aircraft.

LANDING GEAR: Retractable tricycle type, with single mainwheels and twin-wheel nose unit.

This model of the PZL-230 Skorpion shows pylon-mounted pusher turboprops, single-seat cockpit, foreplane with separate stores pylon and a fin under the nose for side-force control

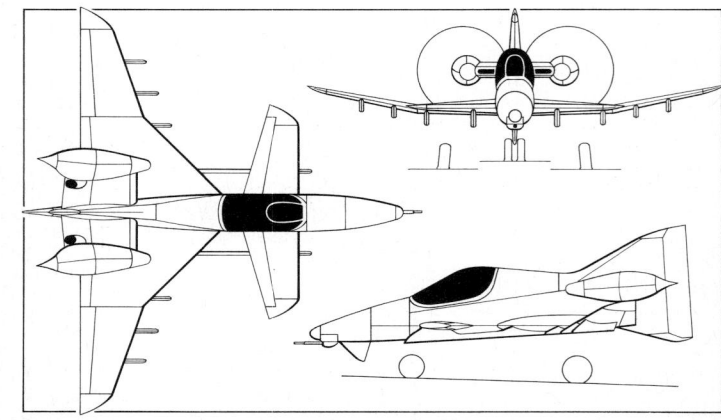

General configuration of the projected PZL-230 Skorpion *(Jane's/Mike Keep)*

POWER PLANT: Two Pratt & Whitney PT6A-67A turboprops, flat rated to 895 or 948 kW (1,200 or 1,272 shp), mounted on pylons on the rear fuselage, with intakes in pylon leading-edges, and driving pusher propellers. Max internal fuel capacity 900 litres (238 US gallons; 198 Imp gallons).

ACCOMMODATION: Crew of two in tandem, or single-seat.

ARMAMENT: Undernose gun; three external stores stations under each wing; possible fourth pylon inboard, running from wing to foreplane.

DIMENSIONS, EXTERNAL:

Wing span	10.00 m (32 ft 9¾ in)

Length overall	9.50 m (31 ft 2 in)
AREAS:	
Wings, gross	16.00 m² (172.20 sq ft)
Foreplanes (total)	4.00 m² (43.06 sq ft)
WEIGHTS AND LOADINGS:	
Weight empty	2,100 kg (4,630 lb)
Max external stores	2,000 kg (4,409 lb)
Max T-O weight	5,000 kg (11,023 lb)
Max wing/foreplane loading	250.0 kg/m² (51.20 lb/sq ft)
Max power loading	2.79 kg/kW (4.59 lb/shp)
PERFORMANCE (estimated):	
Max level speed at S/L	345 knots (640 km/h; 397 mph)

Stalling speed	59 knots (108 km/h; 68 mph)
Max rate of climb at S/L	3,000 m (9,850 ft)/min
Service ceiling	10,000 m (32,800 ft)
T-O run	250 m (821 ft)
Landing run	220 m (722 ft)
Combat radius, allowing 1 h for ground attack	
	162 nm (300 km; 186 miles)
g limits	+9/−4

PORTUGAL

OGMA
OFICINAS GERAIS DE MATERIAL AERONÁUTICO (General Aeronautical Material Workshops)

2615 Alverca
Telephone: 351 (1) 9581000
Fax: 351 (1) 9581288 and 9580401
Telex: 14479 OGMA P
DIRECTOR:
  Gen Eng Rui do Carmo da Conceição Espadinha
DEPUTY DIRECTOR AND COMMERCIAL MANAGER:
  Maj-Gen A. Leitão
PRODUCTION MANAGER: Col A. Nogueira
PUBLIC RELATIONS MANAGER: Jorge Pires

OGMA, founded in 1918, is the department of the Portuguese Air Force responsible for maintenance and repair, at depot level, of its aircraft, avionics, engines, ground communications and radar equipment, and can undertake similar work for civil or military national or foreign customers. OGMA has a total covered area of 116,000 m² (1,248,612 sq ft), and a workforce of approx 2,700 people.

Under a contract signed in 1959, OGMA undertakes IRAN, refurbishing and rehabilitation, periodic inspection and emergency maintenance and crash repair of US Air Force and US Navy aircraft. For Aerospatiale of France, OGMA has manufactured main and tail rotor structures for the SA 315B Lama and some components for other helicopters.

Ten Portuguese Air Force AS 330C Pumas were being upgraded and re-engined with Turbomeca Makila turboshafts early in 1991.

OGMA's engine repair and maintenance facility, with a covered area of 28,000 m² (301,390 sq ft), overhauls military and commercial turbojets and turbofans (up to 146.8 kN; 33,000 lb st), and turboprop and turboshaft engines of up to 5,667 kW (7,600 shp). In addition to two fully computerised test cells, this facility is equipped with plasma spray, two vacuum furnaces, complete cleaning and electroplating facilities, non-destructive testing, shot-peening and other specific equipment. Besides work for the Portuguese Air Force, OGMA also overhauls, under contract, Artouste III and Turmo IV turboshaft engines for Turbomeca of France; and, as a maintenance/overhaul centre for Allison, T56 engines and gearboxes for the USAF and other customers.

OGMA performs major maintenance on C-130/L-100 Hercules transport aircraft as a Lockheed Service Center, and on Alouette III, Puma and Ecureuil helicopters as an Aerospatiale Station-Service. It has recently been appointed as a line service centre for Dassault Falcon 20 and Falcon 50 aircraft and Garrett TFE731 engines.

The Avionics Division has premises covering an area of approx 6,400 m² (68,900 sq ft), fully equipped to the latest demands in the field of maintenance for new generation avionics, communications systems, test equipment and calibration laboratories. OGMA is licensed by Litton Systems of Canada to carry out level 2 and 2A maintenance on LTN-72 INS equipment.

ROMANIA

CNIAR
CENTRUL NATIONAL AL INDUSTRIEI AERONAUTICE ROMÂNE (National Centre of the Romanian Aeronautical Industry)

This body (see 1990-91 and earlier *Jane's*) was dissolved in December 1990 in order to give greater autonomy to individual aircraft factories, most of which have now been renamed.

Export sales of Romanian aerospace products are handled (though no longer exclusively) by:
Tehnoimportexport SA
2 Doamnei Street (PO Box 110), Bucharest
Telephone: 40 (0) 164570

Fax: 40 (0) 132526
Telex: 10254 TEHIE R
GENERAL DIRECTOR: Dipl Eng M. Bortes
DEPUTY DIRECTOR (AIRCRAFT DIVISION):
  Dipl Ec G. Popescu
CONTRACT MANAGER: Dipl Ec E. M. Preda

CONDOR
CONDOR SA (formerly IAv Bacau)

9 Condorilor Street, 5500 Bacau
Telephone: 40 (31) 30070
Fax: 40 (31) 40931
Telex: 21339
TECHNICAL DIRECTOR: Dipl Eng C. Craciun
COMMERCIAL DIRECTOR: Dipl Eng M. Gemine

This factory, originally a military aircraft, engine and avionics repair centre known as URA (later IRAv), has enlarged its product range and now manufactures the Soviet Yak-52 under USSR licence, plus a wide variety of landing gears for the Rombac 1-11, IAR-93, IAR-99, IAR-822, IAR-823, IAR-827 and AG-6 fixed-wing aircraft and Alouette, Puma, IAR-317 and Ka-126 helicopters. Other products include M-14P and M-14V26 piston engines, RU-19A-300 gas turbine APUs, Ka-26 and Ka-126 gears, avionics, hydraulic and pneumatic systems, fuel and air conditioning equipment, and various ground military items. Workforce is about 10,000.

A future contract for a new Yakovlev light aircraft was being negotiated in early 1991.

CONDOR (YAKOVLEV) Yak-52

Announced in late 1978, the Yak-52 is a tandem-cockpit variant of the Yak-50, with unchanged span and length, but with a semi-retractable tricycle landing gear to reduce damage in a wheels-up landing. It is a replacement for the Yak-18, and made its first flight less than a year after design was started. Production was entrusted to the Romanian aircraft industry under the Comecon (Council for Mutual Economic Assistance) programme.

Manufacture began at Bacau in 1979, and the aircraft is in series production; it does not have an IAR designation number. Bacau has now delivered more than 1,600 Yak-52s; production was continuing in 1991.

TYPE: Tandem two-seat piston engined primary trainer.

WINGS: Cantilever low-wing monoplane of single-spar stressed skin all-metal construction. Clark YN wing section, with thickness/chord ratio of 14.5 per cent at root, 9 per cent at tip. Dihedral 2° from roots. Incidence 2°. No sweepback; each wing comprises a single straight-tapered panel, attached directly to the side of the fuselage. Fabric covered slotted ailerons. Light alloy trailing-edge split flaps. Ground adjustable tab on each aileron.

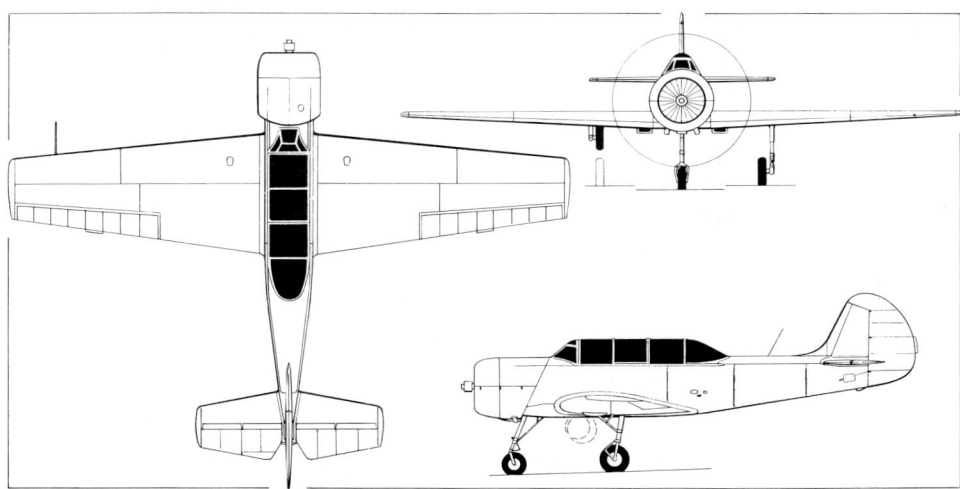

Yakovlev Yak-52 tandem two-seat primary trainer *(Pilot Press)*

FUSELAGE: Conventional light alloy semi-monocoque structure.

TAIL UNIT: Cantilever light alloy structure. Fin and fixed incidence tailplane metal covered; control surfaces fabric covered. Horn balanced rudder, with ground adjustable tab. Mass balanced elevators. Controllable tab in port elevator.

LANDING GEAR: Semi-retractable tricycle type, with single wheel on each unit. Pneumatic actuation, nosewheel retracting rearward, main units forward. All three wheels remain fully exposed to airflow, against the undersurface of the fuselage and wings respectively, to offer greater safety in the event of a wheels-up emergency landing. Oleo-pneumatic shock absorbers. Mainwheel tyre size 500 × 150; nosewheel tyre size 400 × 150. Tyre pressure (all units) 3.0 bars (43 lb/sq in). Pneumatic brakes. Skis can be fitted in place of wheels for Winter operations, permissible at temperatures down to −42°C.

POWER PLANT: One 268 kW (360 hp) Vedeneyev M-14P nine-cylinder aircooled radial, driving a two-blade variable-pitch propeller type V-530TA-D35, without spinner. Louvres in front of cowling to regulate cooling. Two-part cowling, split on horizontal centreline. Two fuel tanks, in wingroots forward of spar, each with capacity of 61 litres (16.1 US gallons; 13.5 Imp gallons). Collector tank in fuselage of 5.5 litres (1.45 US gallons; 1.25 Imp gallons) capacity supplies engine during inverted flight. Total internal fuel capacity 122 litres (32.2 US gallons; 27 Imp gallons). Oil capacity 22.5 litres (5.9 US gallons; 5 Imp gallons).

ACCOMMODATION: Tandem seats for pupil and instructor (at rear) under long 'glasshouse' canopy, with separate rearward sliding hood over each seat. Seats and dual flying controls are adjustable. Sides of cockpit have a soft synthetic lining. Heating and ventilation standard.

SYSTEMS: No hydraulic system. Independent main and emergency pneumatic systems, pressure 50 bars (725 lb/sq in), for flap actuation, landing gear actuation, engine starting, and wheel brake control. Pneumatic systems supplied by two compressed air bottles, mounted behind rear seat and recharged in flight by an AK-50T compressor. GSR-3000M 28.5V engine driven generator and (in port wing) 25V Varley battery for DC electric power; two static inverters in fuselage for 36V AC power at 400Hz. Oxygen system optional.

AVIONICS: Dual engine and flying instruments, including GMK-1A gyro compass, ARK-15M automatic radio compass, Baklan-5 VHF com and SPU-9 intercom.

DIMENSIONS, EXTERNAL:

Wing span	9.30 m (30 ft 6¼ in)
Wing chord: at root	1.997 m (6 ft 6¾ in)
at tip	1.082 m (3 ft 6½ in)
Wing aspect ratio	5.8
Length overall	7.745 m (25 ft 5 in)
Fuselage: Max width	0.90 m (2 ft 11½ in)
Height overall	2.70 m (8 ft 10¼ in)
Tailplane span	3.16 m (10 ft 4½ in)
Wheel track	2.715 m (8 ft 10¾ in)
Wheelbase	1.86 m (6 ft 1¼ in)
Propeller diameter	2.40 m (7 ft 10½ in)
Propeller ground clearance	0.36 m (1 ft 2¼ in)

DIMENSIONS, INTERNAL:

Cockpit: Max width	0.736 m (2 ft 5 in)
Max height	1.12 m (3 ft 8 in)

AREAS:

Wings, gross	15.00 m² (161.5 sq ft)
Ailerons (total)	1.98 m² (21.31 sq ft)
Trailing-edge flaps (total)	1.03 m² (11.09 sq ft)
Fin	0.609 m² (6.55 sq ft)
Rudder	0.871 m² (9.37 sq ft)
Tailplane	1.325 m² (14.26 sq ft)
Elevators (total, incl tab)	1.535 m² (16.52 sq ft)

WEIGHTS AND LOADINGS:

Weight empty	1,000 kg (2,205 lb)
Max fuel load	100 kg (220 lb)
Max T-O weight	1,290 kg (2,844 lb)
Max wing loading	86.0 kg/m² (17.61 lb/sq ft)
Max power loading	4.80 kg/kW (7.90 lb/hp)

PERFORMANCE:

Never-exceed speed (VNE)	194 knots (360 km/h; 223 mph)
Max level speed at 500 m (1,640 ft)	162 knots (300 km/h; 186 mph)
Max cruising speed at 1,000 m (3,280 ft)	145 knots (270 km/h; 167 mph)
Econ cruising speed at 1,000 m (3,280 ft)	102 knots (190 km/h; 118 mph)
Stalling speed: flaps up	60 knots (110 km/h; 69 mph)
flaps down:	
power on	54-57 knots (100-105 km/h; 62-66 mph)
engine idling	46-49 knots (85-90 km/h; 53-56 mph)
Max rate of climb at S/L	420 m (1,378 ft)/min
Service ceiling: without oxygen	4,000 m (13,125 ft)
with oxygen	6,000 m (19,685 ft)
Min ground turning radius	6.22 m (20 ft 5 in)
T-O run	170 m (558 ft)
Landing run	300 m (984 ft)
Range with max fuel	297 nm (550 km; 341 miles)
Endurance with max fuel	2 h 50 min
g limits	+7/–5

The 1,500th Yakovlev Yak-52 primary trainer built in Romania, rolled out on 23 June 1990

This new agricultural biplane, designated AG-6, was designed by the Institutul de Aviatie (Aviation Institute) in Bucharest. The prototype was built by Condor SA at Bacau *(Stefan Popa)*

IAR

IAR SA (formerly ICA)
PO Box 198, 2200 Brasov
Telephone: 40 (21) 92114037
Fax: 40 (21) 16938
Telex: 61 266
MANAGING DIRECTOR: Dipl Eng N. Banea

This factory, created in 1968, continues the work begun in 1926 by IAR-Brasov and undertaken in 1950-59 as URMV-3 Brasov. Today, it manufactures most types of Romanian designed light aircraft, plus Puma helicopters under licence from Aerospatiale of France (as the IAR-330); is undertaking the series manufacture of Ka-126 helicopters; and produces the IS-28/29 series of Romanian sailplanes and motor gliders. It also produces aircraft components and equipment. Workforce in 1990 was about 4,300.

IAR-503A
A new tandem-seat trainer with this designation is under design by the Institutul de Aviatie (Aviation Institute). Power plant is a Pratt & Whitney Canada PT6A-25C turboprop.

IAR IAR-825TP TRIUMF
Details of this turboprop military trainer can be found in the 1990-91 and earlier editions of *Jane's.* Development has ended.

IAR IAR-828
The IAR-828 began life, then known as the IAR-827TP, when the original prototype of the piston-engined IAR-827 (1987-88 *Jane's*) was refitted with a PT6A-15AG turboprop, making its first flight in this form on 7 September 1981. Flight testing towards certification was still continuing in 1985, but lack of subsequent news led to assumption that its further development had been suspended. Apparently, however, it is still an active programme, though some

Prototype IAR-828 agricultural aircraft with underwing spraybars

modifications have been made since it was last described in *Jane's.*

TYPE: Agricultural aircraft.

WINGS: Cantilever low-wing monoplane, of constant-chord NACA 23015 section. Incidence 6°. Dihedral 6° from roots. All-metal structure, with aluminium alloy skins, wet-riveted to fuselage. Electrically operated single-slotted Fowler flaps and mechanically actuated plain ailerons on trailing-edges. No tabs.

FUSELAGE: Forward structure of welded steel tube, including cockpit overturn structure, with aluminium alloy skins; rear fuselage is a light alloy monocoque. Entire structure corrosion treated.

TAIL UNIT: Angular, unbraced structure of aluminium alloy, with mechanically actuated control surfaces. Fixed incidence tailplane. Electrically actuated Flettner tab in each elevator; ground adjustable tab on rudder.

LANDING GEAR: Non-retractable 'taildragger' type, suitable for operation from unprepared strips and sandy terrain. Dunlop AH 52928 wheels, 615 × 225-10 tubeless tyres and oleo-pneumatic shock absorbers on main units; tailwheel has a 350 × 150 mm solid tyre. Independent hydraulic disc brakes and parking brake on mainwheels.

POWER PLANT: One 507 kW (680 shp), Pratt & Whitney Canada PT6A-15AG turboprop, driving a Hartzell HC-B3TN-3 three-blade constant-speed propeller. Integral fuel tank in each wing, combined capacity 450 litres (119 US gallons; 99 Imp gallons).

ACCOMMODATION: Single seat in heated and ventilated cockpit, with jettisonable window/door on each side. Two-seat cockpit optional.

SYSTEMS: Hydraulic system for brakes only; 24V electrical system, powered by 200A starter/generator and 40Ah lead-acid battery.

AVIONICS: VHF com transceiver standard, to customer's requirements. Directional and horizon gyros optional.

EQUIPMENT: GFRP hopper for 1,200 litres (317 US gallons; 264 Imp gallons) of liquid or 1,000 kg (2,205 lb) of dry chemical, with quick-release jettison system. Transland quick-disconnect pump mount. Wire cutters on cockpit and main landing gear legs, cable deflector from cockpit to fin. Anti-sand engine filter. Optional equipment includes second pilot seat and controls, windscreen wash/wipe, sprayboom pressure gauge, landing/taxying/ anti-collision lights, and clock.

DIMENSIONS, EXTERNAL:

Wing span	14.96 m (49 ft 1 in)
Wing chord, constant	2.10 m (6 ft 10¾ in)
Wing aspect ratio	7.14
Length overall	10.242 m (33 ft 7¼ in)
Fuselage: Max width	1.20 m (3 ft 11¼ in)
Height overall	3.79 m (12 ft 5¼ in)
Elevator span	5.12 m (16 ft 9 ½ in)
Wheel track	3.408 m (11 ft 2¼ in)
Wheelbase	6.186 m (20 ft 3½ in)

AREAS:

Wings, gross	31.332 m² (337.25 sq ft)

WEIGHTS AND LOADINGS:

Weight empty	1,470 kg (3,241 lb)
Max chemical payload	1,000 kg (2,205 lb)
Max T-O weight	2,800 kg (6,173 lb)
Normal landing weight	1,800 kg (3,968 lb)
Max wing loading	89.37 kg/m² (11.76 lb/sq ft)
Max power loading	5.52 kg/kW (9.08 lb/shp)

PERFORMANCE (at max T-O weight):

Normal working speed	86-97 knots (160-180 km/h; 99-112 mph)
Stalling speed	65 knots (120 km/h; 75 mph)
Max rate of climb at S/L	450 m (1,476 ft)/min
Service ceiling	9,000 m (29,525 ft)
T-O run	220 m (722 ft)
T-O to 15 m (50 ft)	360 m (1,182 ft)
Landing from 15 m (50 ft)	230 m (755 ft)
Landing run	120 m (394 ft)
Endurance with max payload	3 h

IAR IAR-831 PELICAN

The Pelican, the prototype of which (YR-IGA) made its first public appearance at the 1983 Paris Air Show, was essentially a modernisation of the IAR-825TP airframe with a 216 kW (290 hp) Textron Lycoming flat-six engine. This programme has also ended. All known details last appeared in the 1990-91 *Jane's*.

IAR IAR-317 AIRFOX

The Airfox is a tandem two-seat gunship conversion of the IAR-316B Alouette III, first flown in April 1984 but subsequently cancelled by the Ceausescu government. A detailed description and illustration last appeared in the 1988-89 *Jane's*. Reports in mid-1990 suggested that the programme may be receiving renewed consideration by the Romanian armed forces.

IAR (AEROSPATIALE) IAR-330L PUMA

An agreement for licence production of the Aerospatiale AS 330 Puma in Romania was concluded in 1977, an initial quantity of 100 being involved. A total of 160 had been completed by early 1991, most of them for the Romanian

Romanian Air Force armed IAR-330L Puma equipped with twin 20 mm cannon pods, four rocket pods, four AT-3 anti-tank missiles and roof mounted sight

Air Force but including exports to Pakistan and Sudan. Current production rate is about 10 a year. Romania is now the sole producer of this helicopter. Details of six early French-built versions of the Puma can be found in the 1976-77 *Jane's*. The final French production versions were the AS 330 civil (J) and military (L) introduced in 1976 with main rotor blades of composite materials. Increased max T-O weight, including certification at 7,500 kg (16,535 lb) for cargo-sling mission. Last described fully in 1982-83 *Jane's*. OGMA in Portugal (which see) is re-engining and upgrading 10 Portuguese Air Force AS 330Cs. A total of 697 AS 330 Pumas was built by Aerospatiale for delivery to 46 countries. Eleven were assembled by IPTN (Indonesia) from French CKD kits.

TYPE: Twin-turboshaft medium transport helicopter.

ROTOR SYSTEM: Four-blade main rotor, with fully articulated hub and integral rotor brake. Blade cuffs, equipped with horns, connected by link-rods to swashplate, which is actuated by three hydraulic twin-cylinder servo-control units. Each moulded blade has glassfibre roving spar, composite glassfibre/carbonfibre fabric skin and Moltoprene/honeycomb filler. Leading-edge covered with stainless steel protective section. Attachment of each blade to its sleeve by two quick-disconnect pins enables blades to be folded back quickly by manual methods. Five-blade tail rotor has flapping hinges only, and is located on starboard side of tailboom. Optional blade de-icing, with heating mat protected by titanium shielding on leading-edge of each main and tail rotor blade.

Mechanical shaft and gear drive. Main gearbox, mounted on top of cabin behind engines, has two separate inputs from engines and five reduction stages. First stage drives, from each engine, an intermediate shaft directly driving alternator and ventilation fan, and indirectly driving two hydraulic pumps. At second stage, action of the two units becomes synchronised on a single main driveshaft by means of freewheeling spur gears. If one or both engines are stopped, this enables drive gears to be rotated by remaining turbine or autorotating rotor, thus maintaining drive to ancillary systems when engines are stopped. Drive to tail rotor is via shafting and an intermediate angle gearbox, terminating at a right-angle tail rotor gearbox. Turbine output 23,000 rpm, main rotor shaft 265 rpm. Tail rotor shaft 1,278 rpm. Hydraulically controlled rotor brake, installed on main gearbox, permits stopping rotor 15 s after engine shutdown.

FUSELAGE: Conventional all-metal semi-monocoque structure. Local use of titanium alloy under engine installation, which is outside the main fuselage shell. Monocoque tailboom supports tail rotor on starboard side and horizontal stabiliser on the port side.

LANDING GEAR: Messier-Bugatti semi-retractable tricycle type, with twin wheels on each unit. Main units retract upward hydraulically into fairings on sides of fuselage; self-centring nose unit retracts rearward. When landing gear is down, nosewheel jack is extended and mainwheel jacks are telescoped. Dual-chamber oleo-pneumatic shock absorbers. All tyres same size (7.00-6), of tubeless type, pressure 6.0 bars (85 lb/sq in) on all units. Hydraulic differential disc brakes, controlled by foot pedals. Lever-operated parking brake. Emergency pop-out flotation units can be mounted on rear landing gear fairings and forward fuselage.

POWER PLANT: Two Turbomecanica Romanian-built Turbomeca Turmo IVC turboshafts, each with max rating of 1,175 kW (1,575 shp) and intake anti-icing. Engines mounted side by side above cabin forward of main rotor and separated by firewall. They are coupled to main rotor transmission box, with shaft drive to tail rotor, and form a completely independent system from fuel tanks up to main gearbox inputs. Fuel in four flexible tanks and one auxiliary tank beneath cargo compartment floor, total capacity 1,544 litres (408 US gallons; 339.5 Imp gallons). Provision for additional 1,900 litres (502 US gallons; 418 Imp gallons) in four auxiliary ferry tanks installed in cabin. External auxiliary tanks (two, each 350 litres; 92.5 US gallons; 77 Imp gallons capacity) are available. For long-range missions (mainly offshore) one or two special internal tanks (each 215 litres; 56.8 US gallons; 47.25 Imp gallons) can be fitted in cabin. Each engine supplied normally by two interconnected primary tanks, lower halves of which have self-sealing walls for protection against small-calibre projectiles. Refuelling point on starboard side of main cabin. Oil capacity 22 litres (5.8 US gallons; 4.8 Imp gallons) for engines, 25.5 litres (6.7 US gallons; 5.6 Imp gallons) for transmission.

ACCOMMODATION: Crew of one or two side by side on anti-crash seats on flight deck, with jump-seat for third crew member if required. Door on each side of flight deck. Internal doorway connects flight deck to cabin, with folding seat in doorway for extra crew member or cargo supervisor. Dual controls standard. Accommodation in main cabin for 16 individually equipped troops, six stretchers and six seated patients, or equivalent freight; number of troops can be increased to 20 in high-density version. Strengthened floor for cargo-carrying, with lashing points. Jettisonable sliding door on each side of main cabin. Removable panel on underside

IAR-317 Airfox prototype gunship helicopter *(Brian M. Service)*

of fuselage, at rear of main cabin, permits longer loads to be accommodated and also serves as emergency exit. Hatch in floor below centreline of main rotor for carrying loads of up to 3,200 kg (7,055 lb) on internally mounted cargo sling. A fixed or retractable rescue hoist (capacity 275 kg; 606 lb) can be mounted externally on starboard side of fuselage. Cabin and flight deck heated, ventilated and soundproofed. Demisting, de-icing, washers and wipers for pilots' windscreens.

SYSTEMS: Two independent hydraulic systems, each 172 bars (2,500 lb/sq in), supplied by self-regulating pumps driven by main gearbox. Each system supplies one set of servo unit chambers, left hand system supplying in addition the autopilot, landing gear, rotor brake and wheel brakes. Freewheels in main gearbox ensure that both systems remain in operation, for supplying servo-controls, if engines are stopped in flight. Other hydraulically actuated systems can be operated on ground from main gearbox, or through ground power receptacle. Independent auxiliary system, fed through handpump, can be used in emergency to lower landing gear and pressurise accumulator for parking brake on ground. Three-phase 200V AC electrical power supplied by two 15kVA 400Hz alternators, driven by port side intermediate shaft from main gearbox and available on ground under same conditions as hydraulic ancillary systems. 28.5V 10kW DC power provided from AC system by two transformer-rectifiers. Main aircraft battery used for self-starting and emergency power in flight. For latter purpose, an emergency 400VA inverter can supply essential navigation equipment from battery, permitting at least 20 min continued flight in event of main power failure. De-icing of engines and engine air intakes by warm air bled from compressor. Anti-snow shield for Winter operations.

AVIONICS: Optional VHF, UHF, tactical HF and HF/SSB com radio and intercom, radio compass, radio altimeter, VLF Omega, Decca navigator and flight log, Doppler, and VOR/ILS with glidepath. Autopilot, with provision for coupling to self-contained navigation and microwave landing systems. Full IFR instrumentation optional. Search and rescue version has nose-mounted Bendix/King RDR 1400 or Honeywell Primus 40 or 50 search radar, Doppler, and Decca self-contained navigation system, including navigation computer, polar indicator, roller-map display, hover indicator, route mileage indicator and ground speed and drift indicator. Roof mounted sight for AT-3 missiles in armed version.

ARMAMENT: Armed version equipped with two forward firing 20 mm cannon (540 rds/gun) in streamline pods attached to lower sides of fuselage at front; steel tube carriers attached to sides of main cabin can carry four eight-round (112 mm) or 16-round (57 mm) unguided air-to-ground rocket pods, plus four wire guided AT-3 (NATO 'Sagger') anti-tank missiles; 12.7 mm machine gun pintle mounted in each cabin doorway. Alternative loads on cabin outriggers include two or four 7.62 mm GMP-2 machine-gun pods (550 rds/pod) or four 100 kg bombs.

DIMENSIONS, EXTERNAL:

Main rotor diameter	15.00 m (49 ft 2½ in)
Tail rotor diameter	3.04 m (9 ft 11½ in)
Distance between rotor centres	9.20 m (30 ft 2¼ in)
Main rotor blade chord	0.60 m (1 ft 11½ in)
Tail rotor ground clearance	2.00 m (6 ft 6¾ in)
Length: overall	18.15 m (59 ft 6½ in)
fuselage	14.06 m (46 ft 1½ in)
blades folded	14.80 m (48 ft 6¾ in)
Height: overall	5.14 m (16 ft 10½ in)
to top of rotor head	4.38 m (14 ft 4½ in)
Width: blades folded	3.50 m (11 ft 5¾ in)
over wheel fairings	3.00 m (9 ft 10 in)
Wheel track	2.38 m (7 ft 10¾ in)
Wheelbase	4.045 m (13 ft 3 in)

Passenger cabin doors, each:

Height	1.35 m (4 ft 5 in)
Width	1.35 m (4 ft 5 in)
Height to sill	1.00 m (3 ft 3¼ in)

Floor hatch, rear of cabin:

Length	0.98 m (3 ft 2¾ in)
Width	0.70 m (2 ft 3½ in)

DIMENSIONS, INTERNAL:

Cabin: Length	6.05 m (19 ft 10 in)
Max width	1.80 m (5 ft 10¾ in)
Max height	1.55 m (5 ft 1 in)
Floor area	7.80 m² (84 sq ft)
Usable volume	11.40 m³ (403 cu ft)

AREAS:

Main rotor blades (each)	4.00 m² (43.06 sq ft)
Tail rotor blades (each)	0.28 m² (3.01 sq ft)
Main rotor disc	176.7 m² (1,902.1 sq ft)
Tail rotor disc	7.26 m² (78.13 sq ft)
Horizontal stabiliser	1.34 m² (14.42 sq ft)

WEIGHTS AND LOADINGS:

Weight empty, standard aircraft	3,615 kg (7,970 lb)
Max T-O and landing weight	7,400 kg (16,315 lb)
Max disc loading	41.88 kg/m² (8.58 lb/sq ft)

PERFORMANCE (A: at 6,000 kg; 13,230 lb AUW, B: at max T-O weight):

Never-exceed speed (VNE):

A	158 knots (294 km/h; 182 mph)
B	142 knots (263 km/h; 163 mph)

Max cruising speed: A		146 knots (271 km/h; 168 mph)
B		139 knots (258 km/h; 160 mph)
Max rate of climb at S/L: A		552 m (1,810 ft)/min
B		366 m (1,200 ft)/min

Service ceiling (30 m; 100 ft/min rate of climb):

A	6,000 m (19,680 ft)
B	4,800 m (15,750 ft)

Hovering ceiling IGE: A, ISA 4,400 m (14,435 ft)

A, ISA +20°C	3,700 m (12,135 ft)
B, ISA	2,300 m (7,545 ft)
B, ISA +20°C	1,600 m (5,250 ft)

Hovering ceiling OGE: A, ISA 4,250 m (13,940 ft)

A, ISA +20°C	3,600 m (11,810 ft)
B, ISA	1,700 m (5,575 ft)
B, ISA +20°C	1,050 m (3,445 ft)

Max range at normal cruising speed, no reserves:

A	309 nm (572 km; 355 miles)
B	297 nm (550 km; 341 miles)

IAR (KAMOV) Ka-126
NATO reporting name: Hoodlum-B

Work on a turboshaft version of the Kamov Ka-26 (see Soviet section of 1989-90 and earlier Jane's) began in 1981, and a photograph published in that year depicted an early mockup apparently identical to the piston engined version except for the substitution of a very small (and still unidentified), closely cowled turboshaft on each side of the cabin roof. A photograph of this version appeared in the 1986-87 Jane's.

Subsequently, it was decided to adopt a single turboshaft, installed above the passenger cabin. A ground test vehicle was completed in early 1986, and a prototype Ka-126 (SSSR-01963, illustrated in the 1988-89 Jane's) flew for the first time later that year. This was followed by four pre-production aircraft, the first of which made its initial flight in the USSR in October 1988; first flight by a Romanian built Ka-126 took place on 31 December 1988.

It had been announced in 1985 that conversion of Ka-26s to Ka-126 standard would be undertaken in Romania, but in fact the Ka-126 is a new-build aircraft. A total of 1,400 is to be built, of which ten had been completed by the Spring of 1991, the first of these being flown for the first time on 14 February 1989. Updated equipment includes new low-volume spraygear and pellet dispensing system and low-cost nav/com radio. A new pellet dispensing system, designed in Hungary, was undergoing certification in early 1991.

Compared with the Ka-26, the Ka-126 has a significant increase in payload, endurance and range capability and the ability for greater year-round utilisation. It can also hover with full load at 1,000 m (3,280 ft), whereas the Ka-26 can do so only at sea level.

The following description applies to the current production Ka-126:

TYPE: General purpose light helicopter.

ROTOR SYSTEM: Contra-rotating coaxial three-blade rotor system, with hydraulic dampers fitted to upper rotor head and rotor shafts inclined forward. Blades, made of glass-textolyte (plastics) materials, have advanced aerofoil section, are interchangeable, and are equipped with an anti-icing system. Energy storage system (two contra-rotating flywheels running at 28,400 rpm) are connected to shaft between engine and transmission. Depending on how pilot manages collective lever, this stored energy can keep helicopter flying for up to 40 s after engine failure.

FUSELAGE: Small extensively glazed crew cabin forward of rotor mast, and two tapered cylindrical plastics tailbooms.

TAIL UNIT: Tailplane mounted at extremity of tailbooms; twin endplate fins and rudders, toed inward at 15°.

LANDING GEAR: Non-retractable four-wheel landing gear. Main units, at rear, carried by stub wings. All four units embody oleo-pneumatic shock absorbers. Forward

IAR (Kamov) Ka-126 (537 kW; 720 shp Koptchenko TV-O-100 turboshaft) *(John Fricker)*

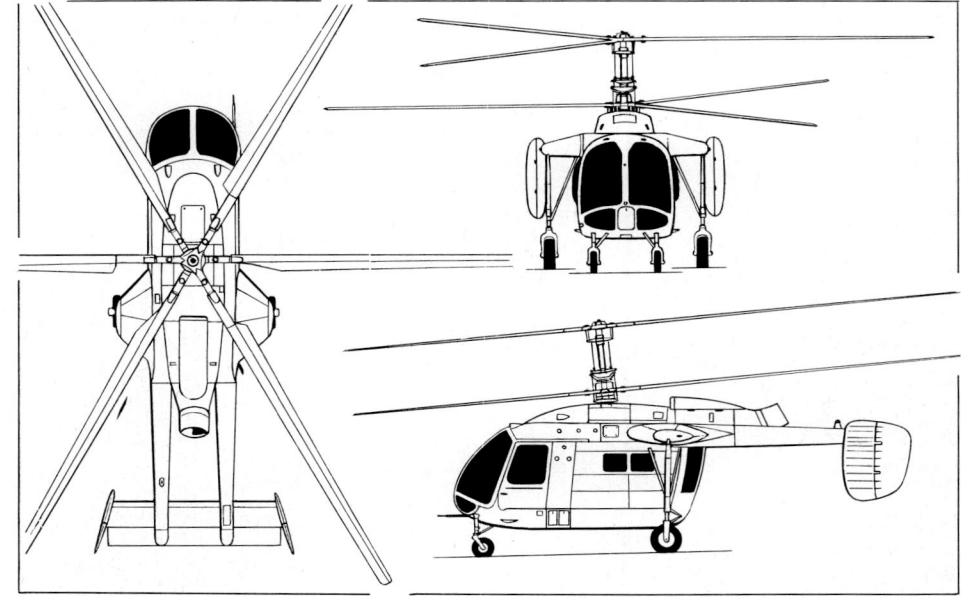

Kamov Ka-126 single-turboshaft helicopter, being produced in Romania by IAR *(Pilot Press)*

wheels of castoring type, not fitted with brakes. Rear wheels have pneumatically operated brakes. Provision for large inflatable pontoons, across front of aircraft forward of nosewheels and under each mainwheel unit.

POWER PLANT: One 537 kW (720 shp) Koptchenko TV-O-100 turboshaft, installed centrally in streamline fairing above cabin. Fuel capacity 800 litres (211.3 US gallons; 176 Imp gallons).

ACCOMMODATION: Fully enclosed cabin, with door on each side, fitted out normally for operation by single pilot; second seat and dual controls optional. Cabin warmed and demisted by air from combustion heater, which also heats passenger compartment when fitted. Air filter on nose of agricultural version. The space aft of the cabin, between the main landing gear units and under the rotor transmission, is able to accommodate a variety of interchangeable payloads. For agricultural work, a chemical hopper (capacity 1,000 litres; 264 US gallons; 220 Imp gallons) and dust spreader or spraybars are fitted in this position, on the aircraft's centre of gravity. This equipment is quickly removable and can be replaced by a cargo/passenger pod accommodating four or six persons,

with provision for a seventh passenger beside the pilot; or two stretcher patients, two seated casualties and a medical attendant in ambulance role. Alternatively, aircraft can be operated with either an open platform for hauling freight or a hook for slinging bulky loads at the end of a cable or in a cargo net.

SYSTEMS: Powered controls, actuated by single hydraulic system, with manual override in case of system failure. Anti-icing system for rotor blades and windscreen is activated automatically by radioisotope ice warning device and utilises an alcohol/glycerine mixture.

AVIONICS: The flying and navigation equipment is adequate for all-weather operation, by day and night. VHF and HF radio are fitted, together with a radio compass and radio altimeter.

DIMENSIONS, EXTERNAL:
Rotor diameter (each)	13.00 m (42 ft 7¾ in)
Length of fuselage	7.75 m (25 ft 5 in)
Height to top of rotor head	4.15 m (13 ft 7½ in)
Span over tail unit (rudder trailing-edges)	
	3.224 m (10 ft 7 in)

Wheel track: mainwheels	2.56 m (8 ft 4¾ in)
nosewheels	0.90 m (2 ft 11½ in)
Wheelbase	3.479 m (11 ft 5 in)

AREAS:
Rotor disc (each)	132.7 m² (1,428.7 sq ft)

DIMENSIONS, INTERNAL:
Passenger pod: Max length	2.04 m (6 ft 8¼ in)
Max width	1.28 m (4 ft 2½ in)
Max height	1.40 m (4 ft 7 in)

WEIGHTS AND LOADINGS:
Max payload	1,000 kg (2,205 lb)
Max T-O weight	3,250 kg (7,165 lb)
Max disc loading	24.49 kg/m² (5.02 lb/sq ft)

PERFORMANCE:
Max level speed	97 knots (180 km/h; 112 mph)
Cruising speed	81 knots (150 km/h; 93 mph)
Service ceiling	3,800 m (12,470 ft)
Hovering ceiling OGE	1,000 m (3,280 ft)
Max range	351 nm (650 km; 404 miles)
Endurance	4 h 30 min

IAv CRAIOVA
INTREPRINDEREA DE AVIOANE CRAIOVA (Craiova Aircraft Enterprise)

Str. Aeroportului 1, 1100 Craiova
Telephone: 40 (41) 24170
Fax: 40 (41) 24382
Telex: 41290 COCOR R
MANAGING DIRECTOR: Dipl Eng Grigore Leoveanu

This factory is responsible for Romanian manufacture of the IAR-93 close support/ground attack aircraft and operational trainer described under the SOKO/Craiova heading in the International section. Craiova's latest national product is the IAR-99 Şoim jet trainer.

IAR-99 ŞOIM (HAWK)

The existence of this Romanian designed advanced jet trainer/light ground attack aircraft first became known during the 1983 Paris Air Show. It was designed by the Institutul de Aviatie at Bucharest and built at Craiova.

Three prototypes were built, of which 002 was used for structural testing. First flight, by 001, was made on 21 December 1985. An initial batch of 20 IAR-99s was delivered to the Romanian Air Force, starting in 1987; a further 30 are reportedly on order. Jaffe Aircraft is supporting an Americanised Şoim in the USA.

TYPE: Advanced trainer and light ground attack aircraft.

WINGS: Cantilever low-wing monoplane, with 3° dihedral from roots. Wing section NACA 64₁A-214 (mod) at centreline, NACA 64₁A-212 (mod) at tip. Sweepback at quarter-chord 6° 35'. Incidence 1°. Each wing has two-spar all-metal structure, with machined skin panels forming integral fuel tanks; attached to fuselage by four bolts. All-metal single-slotted flaps, actuated by a single hydraulic jack. Flaps retract gradually when airspeed reaches 162 knots (300 km/h; 186 mph). Aluminium honeycomb ailerons, actuated by hydraulic servojacks (with manual reversion), are statically balanced along entire span. Electrically operated servo tab in port aileron. Flaps deflect 20° for take-off, 40° for landing; ailerons deflect 15° up or down.

FUSELAGE: Conventional all-metal semi-monocoque structure, of oval cross-section, consisting of frames, stringers, spars, skin panels and honeycomb panels for fuel tank compartments. Main (forward and centre) fuselage joined to rear fuselage by four bolts. Two hydraulically actuated airbrakes under rear fuselage.

TAIL UNIT: Cantilever metal structure. Tapered horizontal surfaces (one-piece tailplane and two horn balanced elevators). Sweptback vertical fin, with dorsal fairing and statically balanced rudder. Aluminium honeycomb rudder and elevators, actuated manually via push/pull rods. Electrically operated trim tabs in each elevator and rudder. Elevators deflect 20° up, 10° down; rudder 25° to right and left.

LANDING GEAR: Retractable tricycle type, with single wheel and oleo-pneumatic shock absorber on each unit. Mainwheels retract inward, non-steerable nosewheel forward, all wheels fully enclosed by doors when retracted. Landing light in port wingroot leading-edge. Mainwheels fitted with tubeless tyres, size 552 × 164-10, pressure 7.5 bars (108.8 lb/sq in), and hydraulic disc brakes with anti-skid system. Nosewheel has tubeless tyre size 445 × 150-6, pressure 4.0 bars (58.0 lb/sq in).

POWER PLANT: One Turbomecanica Romanian-built Rolls-Royce Viper Mk 632-41 M turbojet, rated at 17.79 kN (4,000 lb st). Fuel in two flexible bag tanks in centre-fuselage, capacity 900 litres (238 US gallons; 198 Imp gallons), and four integral tanks between wing spars, combined capacity 470 litres (124 US gallons; 103 Imp gallons). Total internal fuel capacity 1,370 litres (362 US gallons; 301 Imp gallons). Gravity refuelling point on top of fuselage. Provision for two drop tanks, each of 225 litres (59.5 US gallons; 49.5 Imp gallons) capacity, on inboard underwing stations. Max internal/external fuel capacity 1,820 litres (481 US gallons; 400 Imp gallons).

IAR-99 Şoim tandem-seat jet trainer *(Brian M. Service)*

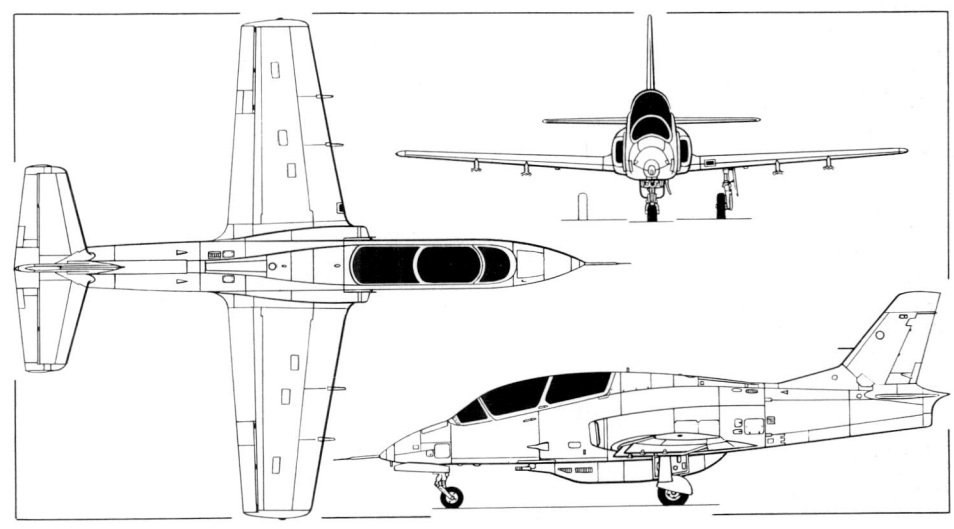

Romania's advanced jet trainer, the IAR-99 Şoim *(Pilot Press)*

ACCOMMODATION: Crew of two in tandem, on zero/zero ejection seats in pressurised and air-conditioned cockpit. Rear seat elevated 35 cm (13.8 in). Dual controls standard. One-piece canopy with internal screen (trainer), or (in ground attack version) individual canopies, all opening sideways to starboard.

SYSTEMS: Engine compressor bleed air for pressurisation, air-conditioning, anti-g suit and windscreen anti-icing system, and to pressurise fuel tanks. Hydraulic system, operating at pressure of 206 bars (2,990 lb/sq in), for actuation of landing gear and doors, flaps, airbrakes, ailerons and mainwheel brakes. Emergency hydraulic system for operation of landing gear, doors, flaps and wheel brakes. Main electrical system, supplied by 9kW 28V DC starter/generator, with 28.5V 36Ah nickel-cadmium battery, ensures operation of main systems, in case of emergency, and engine starting. Two static inverters, total output 1,500VA, supply two secondary AC networks: 115V/400Hz and 26V/400Hz. Oxygen system for two crew for 2 h 30 min.

AVIONICS: Standard avionics include VHF/UHF com radio, intercom, radio altimeter, marker beacon receiver, SRR-2 IFF, ADF, gyro platform and flight recorder.

ARMAMENT: Removable ventral gun pod containing 23 mm GSh-23 gun with 200 rds. Gun/rocket firing and weapon release controls, including electrically controlled AA-1F gyroscopic gunsight and AFCT-1 gun camera, in front

cockpit only. Four underwing hardpoints stressed for loads of 250 kg (551 lb) each. Typical underwing stores can include four 250 kg bombs; four triple carriers each for three 50 kg bombs (or two 100 kg and one 50 kg); four L 16-57 launchers each containing sixteen 57 mm air-to-surface rockets; four L 32-42 launchers each containing thirty-two 42 mm air-to-surface rockets; infra-red air-to-air missiles (inner pylons only); two twin-7.62 mm machine-gun pods with 800 rds/pod (inboard pylons only); and auxiliary fuel tanks (see under Power Plant) on the inboard pylons.

DIMENSIONS, EXTERNAL:
Wing span	9.85 m (32 ft 3¾ in)
Wing chord: at root	2.305 m (7 ft 6¾ in)
at tip	1.30 m (4 ft 3¼ in)
Wing aspect ratio	5.19
Length overall	11.009 m (36 ft 1½ in)
Height overall	3.898 m (12 ft 9½ in)
Tailplane span	4.12 m (13 ft 6¼ in)
Wheel track	2.69 m (8 ft 10 in)
Wheelbase	4.38 m (14 ft 4½ in)

AREAS:
Wings, gross	18.71 m² (201.4 sq ft)
Ailerons (total)	1.567 m² (16.87 sq ft)
Flaps (total)	2.54 m² (27.34 sq ft)
Fin, incl dorsal fin	1.919 m² (20.66 sq ft)
Rudder	0.629 m² (6.77 sq ft)

Tailplane 3.123 m² (33.62 sq ft)
Elevators (total) 1.248 m² (13.43 sq ft)

WEIGHTS AND LOADINGS:
Weight empty, equipped 3,200 kg (7,055 lb)
Max fuel weight: internal 1,100 kg (2,425 lb)
external 350 kg (772 lb)
Max T-O weight: trainer 4,400 kg (9,700 lb)
ground attack 5,560 kg (12,258 lb)
Max wing loading: trainer 235.2 kg/m² (48.17 lb/sq ft)
ground attack 297.2 kg/m² (60.86 lb/sq ft)
Max power loading: trainer 247.5 kg/kN (2.42 lb/lb st)
ground attack 312.7 kg/kN (3.06 lb/lb st)

PERFORMANCE:
Max Mach number 0.76
Max level speed at S/L 467 knots (865 km/h; 53 / mph)
Max rate of climb at S/L 2,100 m (6,890 ft)/min
Service ceiling 12,900 m (42,325 ft)
Min air turning radius 330 m (1,083 ft)
T-O run: trainer 450 m (1,477 ft)
ground attack 960 m (3,150 ft)
T-O to 15 m (50 ft): trainer 750 m (2,461 ft)
ground attack 1,350 m (4,430 ft)
Landing from 15 m (50 ft): trainer 740 m (2,428 ft)
ground attack 870 m (2,855 ft)
Landing run: trainer 550 m (1,805 ft)
ground attack 600 m (1,969 ft)
Typical combat radius (1 pilot, ventral gun, internal fuel only):
lo-lo-hi, four 16-round rocket pods, AUW 5,000 kg (11,023 lb)
189 nm (350 km; 217 miles)
hi-lo-hi, two 16-round rocket pods, two 50 kg and four 100 kg bombs, AUW 5,280 kg (11,640 lb)
186 nm (345 km; 214 miles)
hi-hi-hi, four 250 kg bombs, AUW 5,480 kg (12,081 lb)
208 nm (385 km; 239 miles)
Max range with internal fuel:
trainer 593 nm (1,100 km; 683 miles)
ground attack 522 nm (967 km; 601 miles)
Max endurance with internal fuel: trainer 2 h 40 min
ground attack 1 h 46 min

IAR-705A

The IAR-705A is a high-wing, 30-seat commuter transport with a twin-turboprop power plant (PW119 selected provisionally), with a second (50-seat) stretched variant. Design is by the Institutul de Aviatie in Bucharest; it will be built by IAv Craiova.

ROMAERO

ROMAERO SA (formerly IAv Bucuresti)

44 Bulevardul Ficusului, Sector 1 (PO Box 18), 71544 Bucharest
Telephone: 40 (0) 335082
MANAGING DIRECTOR: Dipl Eng Eugeniu Smirnov
TECHNICAL DIRECTOR: Dipl Eng Dan Gozia
COMMERCIAL DIRECTOR: Dipl Eng Anatolie Merling

Set up in 1951, this factory has operated successively under several names: ARMV-2 (1951-57), with headquarters at Pipera (Bucharest); CTIA (1958-61), first at Pipera and later at Baneasa; ICRMA-IRMA (1962-78); and IAv Bucuresti (1979-90: see 1990-91 *Jane's*). It became a commercial company under its present name on 20 November 1990. Romaero is currently responsible for manufacture of the Rombac 1-11 (components and complete aircraft) and the Pilatus Britten-Norman Islander. It specialises in the repair and overhaul of various large and small aircraft; is agent and repair centre for Textron Lycoming engines; and manufactures aircraft equipment.

ROMAERO ROMBAC 1-11 (BAC/BAe ONE-ELEVEN)

Romaero is the Romanian prime contractor for the licence manufacture of BAC/BAe One-Eleven twin-turbofan transports, under the Romanian designation Rombac 1-11. A corresponding programme provides for Romanian manufacture by Turbomecanica of the Rolls-Royce Spey engines. Details of British production of the One-Eleven can be found in the 1974-75 and 1981-82 *Jane's*.

Industrial transfer to the Romanian aircraft industry, preceded in 1981-82 by delivery of a BAe built Srs 487 freighter and two Srs 525/1s, was completed in 1986. The first flight by a Romanian assembled Srs 560 (YR-BRA) was made on 18 September 1982, and this aircraft entered service with Tarom in January 1983. Of the initial batch of 22 which were to be built in Romania, nine (all Series 560s) had been completed by 25 July 1990.

Romanian versions are designated as follows:

Series 495: Combines standard fuselage and accommodation of British built Series 400 with wings and power plant of Series 560 and a modified landing gear, using low-pressure tyres, to permit operation from secondary low-strength runways with poorer grade surfaces. The tenth Rombac 1-11 (c/n 410) will be the first convertible passenger/cargo **Model 497** (equivalent to BAC/BAe Series 475, but redesigned by Romaero and approved by BAe, using components from Series 487 and 560); delivery due in fourth quarter of 1991.

Series 560: Derived from British built Series 300/400; lengthened fuselage (2.54 m; 8 ft 4 in fwd of wing, 1.57 m; 5 ft 2 in aft) which accommodates up to 109 passengers. Wingtip extensions increases pan by 1.52 m (5 ft). Main landing gear strengthened and heavier wing planks used to cater for increased AUW. Nine built (c/n 401-409) by July 1990.

Series 2500: An agreement signed on 30 July 1990 with the British company Associated Aerospace, for the sale of 50 aircraft, was negated when AA went into receivership in the Spring of 1991. The Series 2500 is a Series 500 One-Eleven, seating 96-115 passengers and re-engined with Rolls-Royce Tay 650 turbofans to meet current noise and chemical pollution requirements. First example was originally due for delivery at the end of 1991; peak production rate of 10 aircraft per year anticipated in 1994.

The following description applies to the Series 495 and 560:

TYPE: Twin-turbofan short/medium-range transport.

WINGS: Cantilever low-wing monoplane. Modified NACA cambered wing section. Thickness/chord ratio 12½ per cent at root, 11 per cent at tip. Dihedral 2°. Incidence 2° 30′. Sweepback 20° at quarter-chord. All-metal structure of copper based aluminium alloy, built on fail-safe principles. Three-shear-web torsion box with integrally machined skin/stringer panels. Ailerons of Redux bonded light alloy honeycomb, manually operated through servo tabs. Port servo tab used for trimming. Hydraulically operated light alloy Fowler flaps. Light alloy spoiler/airbrakes on upper surface of wing, operated hydraulically. Hydraulically actuated lift dumpers, inboard of spoilers. Flaps on Series 495 have a glassfibre coating. Thermal de-icing of wing leading-edges with engine bleed air.

FUSELAGE: Conventional circular-section all-metal fail-safe structure with continuous frames and stringers. Skin made from copper based aluminium alloy.

TAIL UNIT: Cantilever all-metal fail-safe structure, with variable incidence T tailplane, controlled through duplicated hydraulic units. Fin integral with rear fuselage. Elevators and rudder actuated hydraulically through tandem jacks. Leading-edges of fin and tailplane de-iced by engine bleed air.

LANDING GEAR: Retractable tricycle type, with twin wheels on each unit. Hydraulic retraction, nose unit forward, main units inward. Oleo-pneumatic shock absorbers. Hydraulic nosewheel steering. Wheels have tubeless tyres, 5-plate heavy duty hydraulic disc brakes, and anti-skid units. Mainwheel tyres size 40 × 12 on Srs 560, pressure 11.03 bars (160 lb/sq in); size 44 × 16 on Srs 495, pressure 5.72 bars (83 lb/sq in). Nosewheel tyres size 24 × 7.25 on Srs 560, pressure 7.58 bars (110 lb/sq in); size 24 × 7.7 on Srs 495, pressure 7.24 bars (105 lb/sq in).

POWER PLANT: Two Rolls-Royce Spey Mk 512-14DW turbofans, each rated at 55.8 kN (12,550 lb st), pod-mounted on sides of rear fuselage. Fuel in integral wing tanks with usable capacity of 10,160 litres (2,684 US gallons; 2,235 Imp gallons) and centre-section tank of 3,968 litres (1,048 US gallons; 873 Imp gallons) usable capacity; total usable fuel 14,129 litres (3,732 US gallons; 3,108 Imp gallons). Executive versions can be fitted with auxiliary fuel tanks of up to 5,791 litres (1,530 US gallons; 1,274 Imp gallons) usable capacity. Pressure refuelling point in fuselage forward of wing on starboard side. Provision for gravity refuelling. Oil capacity (total engine oil) 13.66 litres (3.6 US gallons; 3 Imp gallons) per engine. Engine hush kits standard.

ACCOMMODATION (Srs 495): Crew of two on flight deck and up to 89 passengers in main cabin. Single class or mixed class layout, with movable divider bulkhead to permit any first/tourist ratio. Typical mixed class layout has 16 first class (four abreast) and 49 tourist (five abreast) seats. Galley units normally at front on starboard side. Coat space available on port side aft of flight deck. Ventral entrance with hydraulically operated airstair. Forward passenger door on port side incorporates optional power operated airstair. Galley service door forward on starboard side. Overwing emergency exit on each side. Two baggage and freight holds under floor, fore and aft of wings, with doors on starboard side. Upward opening forward freight door available at customer's option. Entire accommodation air-conditioned.

ACCOMMODATION (Srs 560): Crew of two on flight deck and up to 109 passengers in main cabin. Two overwing emergency exits on each side. One toilet on each side of cabin at rear. Otherwise generally similar to Srs 495.

SYSTEMS: Fully duplicated air-conditioning and pressurisation systems. Air bled from engine compressors through heat exchangers. Max pressure differential 0.52 bar (7.5 lb/sq in). Hydraulic system, pressure 207 bars (3,000 lb/sq in), operates flaps, spoilers, rudder, elevators, tailplane, landing gear, brakes, nosewheel steering, ventral and forward airstairs and windscreen wipers. No pneumatic system. Electrical system utilises two 30kVA AC generators, driven by constant speed drive and starter units, plus a similar generator mounted on the APU and shaft driven. Gas turbine APU in tailcone to provide ground electric power, air-conditioning and engine starting, also some system checkout capability. APU is run during take-off to eliminate performance penalty of bleeding engine air for cabin air-conditioning.

AVIONICS: Communications and navigation avionics generally to customers' requirements. Typical installation includes dual VHF com to ARINC 546, dual VHF nav to ARINC 547A, including glideslope receivers, marker beacon receiver, flight/service interphone system, ADF, ATC transponder to ARINC 532D, DME, weather radar. Compass system and flight director system (dual) are also installed. Autopilot system. Provision on the Srs 560 for additional equipment, including automatic throttle control, for low weather minima operation.

DIMENSIONS, EXTERNAL:
Wing span 28.50 m (93 ft 6 in)
Wing chord: at root 5.00 m (16 ft 5 in)
at tip 1.61 m (5 ft 5 in)
Wing aspect ratio 8.5
Length:
overall: Srs 495 28.50 m (93 ft 6 in)
Srs 560 32.61 m (107 ft 0 in)
fuselage: Srs 495 25.55 m (83 ft 10 in)
Srs 560 29.67 m (97 ft 4 in)
Height overall 7.47 m (24 ft 6 in)
Tailplane span 8.99 m (29 ft 6 in)
Wheel track 4.34 m (14 ft 3 in)
Wheelbase: Srs 495 10.08 m (33 ft 1 in)
Srs 560 12.62 m (41 ft 5 in)
Passenger door (fwd, port): Height 1.73 m (5 ft 8 in)
Width 0.84 m (2 ft 9 in)
Height to sill 2.08 m (6 ft 10 in)
Ventral entrance, bulkhead door:
Height 1.83 m (6 ft 0 in)
Width 0.66 m (2 ft 2 in)
Height to sill 2.08 m (6 ft 10 in)
Freight door (fwd, starboard):
Height (projected) 0.79 m (2 ft 7 in)
Width 0.91 m (3 ft 0 in)
Height to sill 1.04 m (3 ft 5 in)
Freight door (rear, starboard):
Height (projected) 0.71 m (2 ft 4 in)
Width 0.91 m (3 ft 0 in)
Height to sill 1.17 m (3 ft 10 in)
Freight door, main deck (optional, fwd, Srs 495):
Height 1.85 m (6 ft 1 in)
Width 3.05 m (10 ft 0 in)
Galley service door (fwd, starboard):
Height (projected) 1.22 m (4 ft 0 in)
Width 0.69 m (2 ft 3 in)
Height to sill 2.08 m (6 ft 10 in)

DIMENSIONS, INTERNAL (Srs 495):
Cabin, excl flight deck: Length 17.32 m (56 ft 10 in)
Max width 3.15 m (10 ft 4 in)
Max height 1.98 m (6 ft 6 in)
Floor area approx 47.4 m² (510 sq ft)
Freight hold: fwd 10.02 m³ (354 cu ft)
rear 4.42 m³ (156 cu ft)

DIMENSIONS, INTERNAL (Srs 560):
Cabin, excl flight deck: Length 21.44 m (70 ft 4 in)
Total floor area approx 59.5 m² (640 sq ft)
Freight holds (total volume) 19.45 m³ (687 cu ft)

AREAS (Srs 495, 560):
Wings, gross 95.78 m² (1,031.0 sq ft)
Ailerons (total) 2.86 m² (30.8 sq ft)
Flaps (total) 16.26 m² (175.0 sq ft)
Spoilers (total) 2.30 m² (24.8 sq ft)
Vertical tail surfaces (total) 10.91 m² (117.4 sq ft)
Rudder, incl tab 3.05 m² (32.8 sq ft)
Horizontal tail surfaces (total) 23.97 m² (258.0 sq ft)
Elevators, incl tab 6.54 m² (70.4 sq ft)

WEIGHTS AND LOADINGS:
Operating weight empty, typical:
Srs 495 (89 seats) 23,286 kg (51,339 lb)
Srs 560 (109 seats) 25,267 kg (55,704 lb)
Max payload, typical: Srs 495 10,733 kg (23,661 lb)
Srs 560 11,474 kg (25,296 lb)
Max T-O weight:
Srs 495: standard 41,730 kg (92,000 lb)
optional 44,680 kg (98,500 lb)
Srs 560: standard 45,200 kg (99,650 lb)
optional 47,400 kg (104,500 lb)
Max ramp weight:
Srs 495: standard 41,955 kg (92,500 lb)
optional 44,905 kg (99,000 lb)
Srs 560: standard 45,450 kg (100,200 lb)
optional 47,625 kg (105,000 lb)
Max landing weight:
Srs 495: standard 38,100 kg (84,000 lb)
optional 39,465 kg (87,000 lb)
Srs 560 39,465 kg (87,000 lb)
Max zero-fuel weight:
Srs 495: standard 33,110 kg (73,000 lb)

Romanian assembled Rombac 1-11-561RC of Tarom (two Rolls-Royce Spey Mk 512-14DW turbofans)

optional	34,020 kg (75,000 lb)	
Srs 560	36,740 kg (81,000 lb)	
Max wing loading: Srs 495	466.3 kg/m² (95.5 lb/sq ft)	
Srs 560	495.1 kg/m² (101.4 lb/sq ft)	
Max power loading: Srs 495	400.2 kg/kN (3.92 lb/lb st)	
Srs 560	424.5 kg/kN (4.16 lb/lb st)	

PERFORMANCE (at standard max T-O weights):
Design diving speed (S/L)
410 knots (760 km/h; 472 mph) EAS
Max level and max cruising speed at 6,400 m (21,000 ft)
470 knots (870 km/h; 541 mph)
Econ cruising speed at 10,670 m (35,000 ft)
410 knots (760 km/h; 472 mph)
Stalling speed (landing flap setting, at standard max landing weight):
Srs 495   98 knots (182 km/h; 113 mph) EAS
Srs 560   100 knots (186 km/h; 115 mph) EAS
Rate of climb at S/L at 300 knots (555 km/h; 345 mph)
EAS: Srs 495   786 m (2,580 ft)/min
Srs 560   722 m (2,370 ft)/min

Max cruising altitude   10,670 m (35,000 ft)
Min ground turning radius (to outer wingtip):
Srs 495   15.24 m (50 ft 0 in)
Srs 560   17.07 m (56 ft 0 in)
Runway LCN, rigid pavement (l 30): Srs 495   32
Srs 560   53
T-O run at S/L, ISA: Srs 495   1,676 m (5,500 ft)
Srs 560   1,981 m (6,500 ft)
Balanced T-O to 10.7 m (35 ft) at S/L, ISA:
Srs 495   1,798 m (5,900 ft)
Srs 560   2,225 m (7,300 ft)
Landing distance (BCAR) at S/L, ISA, at standard max landing weight: Srs 495   1,440 m (4,725 ft)
Srs 560   1,455 m (4,775 ft)
Max still air range, ISA, with reserves for 200 nm (370 km; 230 mile) diversion and 45 min hold:
Srs 495   1,933 nm (3,582 km; 2,226 miles)
Srs 560   1,897 nm (3,515 km; 2,184 miles)
Still air range with typical capacity payload, ISA, reserves as above:

Srs 495 at 44,680 kg (98,500 lb)
1,454 nm (2,694 km; 1,674 miles)
Srs 560 at 47,400 kg (104,500 lb)
1,327 nm (2,459 km; 1,528 miles)
Srs 495 executive aircraft with additional 5,602 litres (1,479 US gallons; 1,232 Imp gallons) fuel and 10 passengers   2,875 nm (5,325 km; 3,308 miles)

ROMAERO (PILATUS BRITTEN-NORMAN) ISLANDER

The Pilatus Britten-Norman Islander (see UK section) has been manufactured under licence in Romania, originally by IRMA, for many years. The first Romanian built example flew for the first time at Baneasa Airport, Bucharest, on 4 August 1969, and the initial commitment to build 215 Islanders was completed in 1976. A total of more than 450 had been delivered to Pilatus Britten-Norman by October 1990, and was expected to reach 480 by the end of that year.

SINGAPORE

SA
SINGAPORE AEROSPACE LTD

540 Airport Road, Paya Lebar, Singapore 1953
Telephone: 65 287 1111
Fax: 65 280 9713
Telex: RS 55851 SAERO
PRESIDENT: Quek Poh Huat
VICE-PRESIDENT MARKETING Michael Ng

Singapore Aerospace group (previously known as Singapore Aircraft Industries) consists of six subsidiaries, as follows:

Singapore Aerospace Engineering Pte Ltd,
Seletar West Camp, Singapore 2879
Telephone: 65 481 5955
Fax: 65 482 0245
Telex: RS 25507 SAMAIR
VICE-PRESIDENT/GENERAL MANAGER: Bob Tan

Maintenance, modification, repair and servicing of civil and military aircraft and helicopters. Authorised service centre for Beech Aircraft, Bell Helicopter Textron and Aerospatiale (Super Puma).

Singapore Aerospace Systems Pte Ltd,
505A Airport Road, Paya Lebar, Singapore 1953
Telephone: 65 287 2222
Fax: 65 284 4414
Telex: RS 55851 SAERO
VICE-PRESIDENT/GENERAL MANAGER: Foo Hee Liat

Service, maintenance, overhaul and repair of civil and military aircraft components and equipment. Authorised service centre for Hydraulic Research Textron, Allied Signal (Bendix/King), Rockwell Collins, J.E.T., Lucas Aerospace, GEC Ferranti, Sextant Avionique, Teledyne, ECE, Thomson-CSF, Astronautics, TRT, Superflexit, Kollsman, Revue Thommen and Aerospatiale.

Singapore Aerospace Engines Pte Ltd,
501 Airport Road, Paya Lebar, Singapore 1953
Telephone: 65 285 1111
Fax: 65 282 3010
Telex: RS 33268 SAENG
VICE-PRESIDENT/GENERAL MANAGER: Chong Kok Pan

Overhaul and repair of Pratt & Whitney JT8D and JT15D, Rolls-Royce Avon Mk 207, Wright J65, Allison T56/501, General Electric J85 and Textron Lycoming T53 aero engines.

Singapore Aerospace Manufacturing Pte Ltd,
503 Airport Road, Paya Lebar, Singapore 1953
Telephone: 65 284 6255
Fax: 65 288 0965 and 284 2704
Telex: RS 38216 SAMPL
VICE-PRESIDENT/GENERAL MANAGER: Goh Chin Khee

Manufacture of aircraft structure and aero engine components, external stores and composite structures.
Singapore Aerospace Supplies Pte Ltd,
540 Airport Road, Paya Lebar, Singapore 1953
Telephone: 65 287 2033
Fax: 65 284 1167 and 280 6179
Telex: RS 51158 SASUPP
VICE-PRESIDENT/GENERAL MANAGER: Donald Seow

Stocks and supplies a wide range of parts and components for civil and military aircraft, and is the material support specialist for Singapore Aerospace.

Singapore Aviation Services Company Pte Ltd,
540 Airport Road, Paya Lebar, Singapore 1953
Telephone: 65 2800817
Fax: 65 3821509
VICE-PRESIDENT/GENERAL MANAGER: Chiang Woon Seng

Specialises in commercial aircraft engineering and maintenance, especially Section 41 modification, heavy maintenance and structural modification, widebody interior conversions and refurbishment, ageing aircraft modification, avionics upgrade and modification, painting, finishing and corrosion control programme.

The Singapore Aerospace group was formed (as Singapore Aircraft Industries Pte Ltd) in early 1982 as a government owned industrial group under control of the Ministry of Defence's Singapore Technologies Holding Company Pte Ltd. It has a combined workforce of 2,936.

Major programmes have included rebuilding, refurbishing and A-4 to TA-4 conversion of Skyhawk aircraft for the RSAF and other air forces, and depot level maintenance, overhaul, repair and refurbishment of many types of aircraft including the C-130 Hercules, F-5E/F Tiger II, Hunter, Strikemaster and several models of Bell and Aerospatiale helicopters. The work started at Seletar, but a new 15,000 m² (161,450 sq ft) factory at Paya Lebar was opened in October 1983.

SA's subsidiaries have a substantial capability in the fields of aircraft and engine overhaul, maintenance and repair, component and equipment manufacture for civil and military aircraft and aero engines, external stores equipment and defence avionics.

In 1985, SA began assembly of 30 SIAI-Marchetti S.211 jet trainers (which see) for the RSAF. It also assembled 17 of the 22 Super Pumas ordered by the RSAF, and is a participant in the P120L helicopter programme described in the International section.

SA (MCDONNELL DOUGLAS) A-4S-1 SUPER SKYHAWK

In 1986, SA completed the re-engining of two McDonnell Douglas A-4S Skyhawks with General Electric F404-GE-100D non-afterburning turbofans. The engine increases dash speed by 15 per cent, but gives much greater improvement in acceleration, turn rate and take-off. Grumman and GE helped with the redesign work.

Phase I upgrade of 52 RSAF A-4S and TA-4S has been completed. Six of the single-seaters are flown by the RSAF's Black Knights display team. Phase II avionics upgrade with GEC Ferranti 4150 head-up display, new head-down display and Litton LN-93 laser inertial navigation system is now in progress. The RSAF has planned to increase the fleet of A-4/TA-4s powered by the F404 engine with the acquisition of additional engines and airframes from the US Navy. Conversion of these aircraft was expected to begin in 1991.

The following shortened description applies to the A-4S-1, except where stated; a more detailed one can be found in the 1989-90 edition.
TYPE: Single-seat attack aircraft.
POWER PLANT: One 48.04 kN (10,800 lb st) General Electric F404-GE-100D non-afterburning turbofan, with air intake each side of fuselage aft of cockpit. Internal fuel in integral wing tanks (combined capacity 2,142.5 litres; 566 US gallons; 471.3 Imp gallons) and self-sealing fuselage tank aft of cockpit (870.5 litres; 230 US gallons; 191.5 Imp gallons), giving total capacity of 3,013 litres (796 US gallons; 662.8 Imp gallons). One 1,136 or 1,514 litre (300 or 400 US gallon; 250 or 333 Imp gallon) drop tank can be carried on the underfuselage stores rack, and a 568 or 1,136 litre (150 or 300 US gallon; 125 or 250 Imp gallon) drop tank on each inboard underwing rack. Single-point refuelling receptacle in rear of engine compartment; all tanks have provisions for both pressure and gravity refuelling. When used as a tanker for other aircraft, fuel from the wing tanks and underwing drop tanks (but not that in the fuselage tank) can be transferred to the receiving aircraft via a refuelling store carried on the underfuselage centreline rack. This store contains a 1,136 litre (300 US gallon; 250 Imp gallon) fuel cell, a constant-speed ram air turbine driven hydraulic pump, a hydraulically operated hose reel and 18.3 m (60 ft) of hose with a drogue. It can transfer fuel to the receiver aircraft at approx 681 litres (180 US gallons; 150 Imp gallons)/min.
ACCOMMODATION: Pilot only, on McDonnell Douglas Escapac zero/zero lightweight ejection seat, under one-piece canopy hinged at rear and opening upward. (Two Escapac seats in tandem, under individual canopies,

Super Skyhawks of the Black Knights display team of the Republic of Singapore Air Force

Max zero-fuel weight	7,841 kg (17,287 lb)
Max wing loading	422.8 kg/m² (86.6 lb/sq ft)
Max power loading	212.6 kg/kN (2.08 lb/lb st)
Thrust/weight ratio	0.48

PERFORMANCE (at max T-O weight except where indicated):

Never-exceed speed (VNE) at S/L	
	628 knots (1,163 km/h; 723 mph)
Max level speed at S/L 609 knots (1,128 km/h; 701 mph)	
Max cruising speed at 9,150 m (30,000 ft)	
	445 knots (825 km/h; 512 mph)
Econ cruising speed at 10,670 m (35,000 ft)	
	424 knots (786 km/h; 488 mph)
Stalling speed at S/L	133 knots (247 km/h; 154 mph)
Max rate of climb at S/L	3,326 m (10,913 ft)/min
Combat ceiling	12,200 m (40,000 ft)
Min ground turning radius	3.76 m (12 ft 4 in)
T-O run	1,220 m (4,000 ft)
T-O to 15 m (50 ft)	1,768 m (5,800 ft)
Landing from 15 m (50 ft) at max landing weight	
	1,590 m (5,215 ft)
Landing run at max landing weight	1,372 m (4,500 ft)
Range, 113 kg (250 lb) fuel reserve:	
with max payload	625 nm (1,158 km; 720 miles)
with max internal/external fuel	
	2,046 nm (3,791 km; 2,356 miles)

for instructor and pupil in TA-4S-1). Bullet-resistant windscreen. Cockpit(s) pressurised and air-conditioned.

AVIONICS: The main Phase II upgrade is listed in the introductory copy.

ARMAMENT: Two 20 mm Mk 12 cannon in wingroots. Five external stores points (one on underfuselage centreline and two under each wing) for wide variety of bombs, rockets, gun pods, missiles and (except on outboard pair) drop tanks.

DIMENSIONS, EXTERNAL:

Wing span	8.38 m (27 ft 6 in)
Length overall	12.72 m (41 ft 8⅝ in)
Height overall	4.57 m (14 ft 11⅞ in)
Wheel track	2.37 m (7 ft 9½ in)
Wheelbase	3.64 m (11 ft 11⅛ in)

AREAS:

Wings, gross	24.14 m² (259.82 sq ft)

WEIGHTS AND LOADINGS:

Operating weight empty	4,649 kg (10,250 lb)
Max fuel weight: internal	2,364 kg (5,213 lb)
external (one 400 and two 300 US gallon tanks)	
	2,961 kg (6,529 lb)
Max T-O weight	10,206 kg (22,500 lb)
Max landing weight	7,257 kg (16,000 lb)

SA (NORTHROP) F-5E/RF-5E CONVERSION

Under a three-year programme started in 1990, eight of the RSAF's 28 F-5E Tiger II fighters are being converted to RF-5E TigerEye reconnaissance configuration. The modifications, which are undertaken by Singapore Aerospace with engineering and on-site technical support from Northrop, include changes to the forward part of the fuselage and installation of pallet-mounted cameras and other sensors, and updated com/nav equipment. The RF-5E was last described in the US section of the 1986-87 *Jane's*.

SOUTH AFRICA

ATLAS
ATLAS AIRCRAFT CORPORATION OF SOUTH AFRICA (PTY) LIMITED

PO Box 11, Atlas Road, 1620 Kempton Park, Transvaal
Telephone: 27 (11) 927 9111
Fax: 27 (11) 395 1103
Telex: 724403
GENERAL MANAGER: G. W. Ward

Atlas Aircraft Corporation, which was founded in 1963, has good manufacturing, design and development facilities for airframes, engines, missiles and avionics. It developed the Cheetah version of the Mirage III and the Rooivalk gunship helicopter as well as the V3B and V3C missiles and many weapons installations.

ATLAS MILITARY TRAINER

A new military turboprop trainer was flown on 29 April 1991. No details were released.

ATLAS CAVA

Some years ago Atlas began developing a new fighter/ground attack aircraft designated Cava for the South African Air Force, to enter service during the mid/late 1990s to replace early Mirage IIIs, the last Buccaneers retired in 1991, the eight Canberras also retired and, eventually, the South African Mirage F1s. It was to be based on the Mirage III/Cheetah design and powered by one or two licence built SNECMA Atar 9K-50 engines.

However, according to reports in early 1991 the Cava programme has been cancelled on cost grounds, the South African government expecting that international relations will have become more normalised by the time the new aircraft is needed. All known details of the Cava were given in the 1990-91 *Jane's*.

ATLAS CHEETAH

The Cheetah is a redesigned, upgraded version of the South African Air Force Mirage III, externally similar to the Israeli Kfir, but ostensibly modified independently by Atlas Aircraft. The Cheetah's existence was revealed in July 1985 and it became operational in Summer 1987.

About 15 Mirage III-EZ, four III-RZ and four III-R2Z single-seaters can be converted to Cheetah EZs, but they will probably equip only No. 5 Squadron at Louis Trichardt base. All existing South African Mirage IIIs are powered by 60.8 kN (13,670 lb st) SNECMA Atar 9Cs, except for the four Mirage III-R2Zs, which have 70.6 kN (15,873 lb st) Atar 9K-50s for which Atlas has had the manufacturing licence since the mid-1970s.

The mixture of Mirage III-CZs, two-seat III-BZ trainers and reconnaissance III-RZ/R2Zs in service with No. 2 (Cheetah) Squadron at Hoedspruit were not considered worth converting, having been in SAAF service since 1963. They were retired in October 1990.

The first Cheetahs were two-seat **DZs**, some of which are certainly intended for No. 85 Combat Flying School at Pietersburg, but a second crewman is probably also

Single-seat Cheetah EZ developed by Atlas from the Mirage III

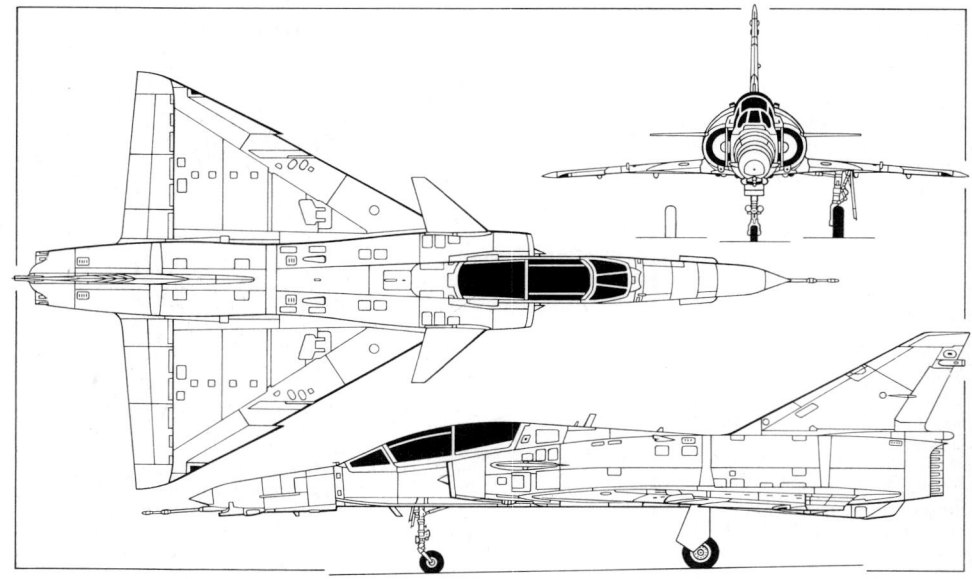

Atlas Cheetah DZ two-seat combat trainer, a redesigned and upgraded Mirage III *(Jane's/Mike Keep)*

envisaged for operational flying. The single-seat Cheetah has only a small nose-mounted ranging radar and no cooling-air intake or cable ducts connecting the nose with the centre fuselage equipment bay. The lateral strakes are mounted much closer to the nose. The two-seater is obviously more elaborately equipped and could be intended as a pathfinder for the single-seaters. The SAAF has 16 III-BZ, -DZ and D2Z two-seaters.

Conversion to Cheetah involves replacement of about 50 per cent of the airframe, fitting of the Atar 9K-50 engine and new avionics. Aerodynamic changes include two small strakes ahead of the cockpit, fixed canards aft of the intakes, short fences replacing the slot fences on the wing, dog-tooth outboard leading-edge extensions and possibly rephased control surfaces. The strakes probably smooth the airflow past the canopy and onto the fin at high angles of attack to ward off yaw departures. All these should greatly improve turning performance, though to nothing like the level of today's agile fighters.

The radome of the two-seater DZ is large enough to contain a basic lookdown search-and-track radar. The undernose fairing just aft of the pitot boom contains two radar warning antennae and a large cooling-air intake, suggesting powerful avionics with high heat output. The long lateral fairings further aft cover cable harnesses passing from the nose to the centre fuselage, skirting the pressure cabin, as on earlier Mirage III two-seaters.

The former rocket motor fairing under the tail of both versions is replaced by an enlarged fairing probably containing ECM equipment. There is an indication of a radar altimeter to assist in low flying. There is an Elbit head-up display, a helmet-mounted sight, possibly of South African design, and an Elbit nav/attack system probably including an inertial system.

Weapons include two 30 mm DEFA cannon in the wingroots and AIM-9 Sidewinder and Matra R.550 Magic that are now probably being replaced by Armscor V3B and then V3C Kukri air-to-air missiles. Matra R.530 medium-range missiles may still be in service. The South African AS.30 air-to-surface missiles might have been upgraded with laser guidance to form the basis, with a designator pod, of the unspecified South African smart weapon used to destroy the bridge at Cuito Cuanavale in 1988. The Cheetah has been seen loaded with eight 500 lb bombs, two underwing drop tanks and two V3B missiles.

ATLAS CSH-2 ROOIVALK (KESTREL)

Development begun in 1981 finally resulted in the public rollout on 15 January 1990 and first flight on 11 February of the XH-2 Rooivalk gunship escort helicopter based on the Aerospatiale AS 330 Puma, of which South Africa acquired 66 some years ago. Stages in development included the XH-1 Alpha based on the Alouette III, which appeared in 1984 and was flying in 1985, and the XTP-1 Puma-based experimental test platform, which appeared in 1986 and was used for weapons and system development. The development of the Rooivalk itself, as the XH-2, began in 1984; it has since been redesignated CSH-2 (for combat support helicopter), and had completed more than 30 hours of test flying by mid-1990. No orders from the South African armed forces are expected, but a possible joint development and production programme was being discussed with a number of potential overseas partners in 1990. An export order for five or more was reported in May 1991. A second prototype should fly during 1991.

The CSH-2 is based on the dynamics of the French AS 330 Puma, with the notable exception that the engines have had to be moved aft to leave a full field of view for the pilot in the rear seat. The rear drives from the Turmo engines are therefore probably taken up by a transverse combining gearbox to enter the main transmission through the former tail rotor drive coupling. The extensive mechanical modifications required for this new layout explain the South African claim to be capable of designing and manufacturing helicopter transmissions.

Atlas CSH-2 Rooivalk prototype, armed with V3B Kukri air-to-air missiles, pods of 68 mm unguided rockets, enclosed four-round 80 mm anti-tank missile pods and a chain-mounted 20 mm GA-1 gun. Fin above tail rotor is now tapered and more sweptback (*H. Heitman*)

The intakes are shielded from dust by adapted Puma particle separator assemblies. No self-protection system, such as cooled exhaust, IR jammer, flare/chaff dispensers or radar warning systems can be seen in early photographs. The tricycle landing gear of the Puma is replaced by a high-absorption main undercarriage forward and a tailwheel behind the ventral fin.

Although the Rooivalk is a combat support rather than a dedicated anti-tank helicopter, armament includes air-to-surface missiles, probably a South African weapon already used in Angola and possibly laser guided. The four-tube missile pods suggest that the front apertures may be intended to be covered by doors to shield the missile sensor heads before lock-on. Other weapons include pods of South African 68 mm unguided rockets, single V3-series air-to-air missiles on the tips of the pylons and the turreted GA-1 20 mm cannon first fitted to the experimental XH-1 Alpha. Both crewmen have a helmet mounted sight, probably a version of the sight developed for the V3 series and additionally adapted for the gun. The chin mounted optical turret seems unlikely to have direct-view optics, but is claimed to be stabilised and to contain FLIR with automatic tracking. There is a head-up display, almost certainly located in the rear cockpit to help the pilot aim the unguided rockets.

Only basic data have been released so far, as follows:

DIMENSIONS, EXTERNAL:

Main rotor diameter	15.08 m (49 ft 5¾ in)
Length overall	16.65 m (54 ft 7½ in)

AREAS:

Main rotor disc	178.6 m² (1,922.5 sq ft)

WEIGHTS AND LOADINGS:

Max T-O weight	over 8,000 kg (17,637 lb)
Max disc loading	over 44.8 kg/m² (9.17 lb/sq ft)

PERFORMANCE:

Max cruising speed over 145 knots (269 km/h; 167 mph)
Max range, with 30 min reserves
400 nm (741 km; 460 miles)

ATLAS (AEROSPATIALE) AS 330 PUMA CONVERSIONS

In addition to the XTP-1 testbed last described in the 1989-90 *Jane's*, at least two other conversions of SAAF Puma helicopters have been undertaken by Atlas:

Gemsbok: Combines the AS 330 airframe with the Makila power plant, uprated transmission, ventral fin and horizontal stabiliser of the AS 532 Cougar, and features also a nose radome. In service, reportedly as a replacement for the SAAF's SA 321 Super Frelons.

Gunship: Described as carrying "some of the equipment developed for the Rooivalk", including constant chord stub-wings each with two suspension pylons and a wingtip attachment for air-launched weapons. Laser designator for Atlas Swift anti-tank missiles in box fairing on nose; other weapons can include Darter or Viper infra-red air-to-air missiles. Three gunship conversions undergoing SAAF operational evaluation in mid-1990.

CELAIR

CELAIR (PTY) LTD
PO Box 77, Ermelo 2350
Telephone. 27 (1341) 4059
Fax: 27 (1341) 91925
MANAGING DIRECTOR: Peter Celliers
MANAGER: Francois Jordaan

Celair, whose GA-1 sailplane is described in the appropriate section of this edition, has also flown the prototype of a new lightplane known as the Eagle 300.

CELAIR EAGLE 300

Under development since August 1987, apart from a seven-month break in 1987 to concentrate on the GA-1 sailplane, the Eagle 300 is a light utility aircraft with good short-field and cruising performance. Construction uses the same LPET (low pressure/elevated temperature) technique as the GA-1, and the Eagle 300 is to be certificated to FAR Pt 23 by both the South African DCA and the US FAA. The prototype (ZS-WLD) made its first flight on 4 April 1990, and production is expected to start in early 1992.

TYPE: Single-engined STOL light utility aircraft.

WINGS: Cantilever high-wing monoplane. Wing sections NACA 64-313 at root, Wortmann FX-60-126 at tip. Dihedral 3°. Incidence 1° 30′. Fowler flaps (35° travel) and mechanically actuated. aerodynamically and mass balanced ailerons. No tabs. Single-spar (unidirectional glassfibre) structure; all other components manufactured from oven-cured pre-impregnated glassfibre cloth with Nomex honeycomb core.

FUSELAGE: Conventional box-section structure. Cabin has steel frame in wing attachment area; construction otherwise similar to that of wings.

TAIL UNIT: Conventional configuration, of similar construction to wings. Mechanically actuated one-piece elevator

Prototype Celair Eagle 300 six-seat light utility STOL aircraft

and rudder. Electrically actuated trim tab in starboard half of elevator.

LANDING GEAR: Non-retractable type, with self-sprung (composite) mainwheel legs and steel tube sprung, fully castoring tailwheel. Cleveland hydraulic mainwheel brakes. Float and ski gear to be developed.

POWER PLANT: One 224 kW (300 hp) Textron Lycoming IO-540-K flat-six engine, driving an MT-9V three-blade constant-speed propeller. Fuel in single tank in each wing, combined capacity 330 litres (87.2 US gallons; 72.6 Imp gallons); gravity fuelling point in top of each tank. Oil capacity 13.6 litres (3.6 US gallons; 3 Imp gallons).

ACCOMMODATION: Pilot and up to five passengers. Three forward hinged single doors (front, port and starboard, and rear starboard), plus upward hinged large cargo door on port side at rear. Passenger seats can be removed for carriage of cargo.

SYSTEMS: Hydraulic system for brakes only; 12V DC electrical system with battery and alternator.

AVIONICS: Narco IFR instrumentation standard.

DIMENSIONS, EXTERNAL:

Wing span	11.20 m (36 ft 9 in)
Wing chord: at root	1.60 m (5 ft 3 in)
at tip	1.00 m (3 ft 3¼ in)

Wing aspect ratio	7.74	Width	1.27 m (4 ft 2 in)	Max T-O and landing weight	1,750 kg (3,858 lb)	
Length overall	7.90 m (25 ft 11 in)	Height to sill	0.70 m (2 ft 3½ in)	Max wing loading	108.02 kg/m² (22.12 lb/sq ft)	
Fuselage: Max width	1.15 m (3 ft 9¼ in)	DIMENSIONS, INTERNAL:		Max power loading	7.83 kg/kW (12.86 lb/hp)	

DIMENSIONS, INTERNAL and the rest:

Wing aspect ratio 7.74
Length overall 7.90 m (25 ft 11 in)
Fuselage: Max width 1.15 m (3 ft 9¼ in)
Height over tail-fin (static) 2.50 m (8 ft 2½ in)
Tailplane span 3.50 m (11 ft 5¾ in)
Wheel track 2.50 m (8 ft 2½ in)
Wheelbase 6.00 m (19 ft 8¼ in)
Propeller diameter 2.08 m (6 ft 10 in)
Propeller ground clearance (tail down)
    0.67 m (2 ft 2¼ in)
Passenger doors (front, each):
  Height 1.07 m (3 ft 6 in)
  Width 0.75 m (2 ft 5½ in)
  Height to sill 0.90 m (2 ft 11½ in)
Passenger door (rear, stbd):
  Height 1.05 m (3 ft 5¼ in)
  Width 0.75 m (2 ft 5½ in)
  Height to sill 0.70 m (2 ft 3½ in)
Cargo door: Height 1.05 m (3 ft 5¼ in)

Width 1.27 m (4 ft 2 in)
Height to sill 0.70 m (2 ft 3½ in)
DIMENSIONS, INTERNAL:
Cabin: Length 1.80 m (5 ft 10¾ in)
  Max width 1.05 m (3 ft 5¼ in)
  Max height 1.33 m (4 ft 4½ in)
  Floor area 1.89 m² (20.34 sq ft)
  Volume 2.46 m³ (86.8 cu ft)
AREAS:
Wings, gross 16.20 m² (174.4 sq ft)
Ailerons (total) 0.93 m² (10.01 sq ft)
Flaps (total) 0.72 m² (7.75 sq ft)
Fin, incl dorsal fin 0.88 m² (9.47 sq ft)
Rudder 0.914 m² (9.84 sq ft)
Tailplane 1.581 m² (17.02 sq ft)
Elevator, incl tab 1.56 m² (16.79 sq ft)
WEIGHTS AND LOADINGS:
Weight empty, equipped 900 kg (1,984 lb)
Max fuel weight 256 kg (564 lb)

Max T-O and landing weight 1,750 kg (3,858 lb)
Max wing loading 108.02 kg/m² (22.12 lb/sq ft)
Max power loading 7.83 kg/kW (12.86 lb/hp)
PERFORMANCE (at max T-O weight):
Never-exceed speed (VNE) at S/L
  221 knots (409 km/h; 254 mph)
Max level speed at S/L 162 knots (300 km/h; 186 mph)
Max cruising speed at S/L
  140 knots (259 km/h; 161 mph)
Stalling speed at S/L, flaps down, engine idling
  57 knots (106 km/h; 66 mph)
Max rate of climb at S/L 405 m (1,330 ft)/min
Service ceiling not yet determined
T-O run 160 m (525 ft)
T-O to 15 m (50 ft) 256 m (840 ft)
Landing from 15 m (50 ft) 270 m (886 ft)
Landing run 120 m (394 ft)
Range with max fuel, 15% reserves
  588 nm (1,090 km; 677 miles)

SPAIN

AISA
AERONAUTICA INDUSTRIAL SA

Cuatros Vientos (Carretera del Aeroclub), Apartado 27094, Madrid 28044

Telephone: 34 (1) 6237000

Fax: 34 (1) 2083958

Telex: E 49872 MADRID

PRESIDENT: J. A. Pérez-Nievas

GENERAL MANAGER: Carlos Herraiz

DESIGN MANAGER: Rafael Moreno

PRESS RELATIONS: Enrique Gutierrez

This company was founded in 1923, assuming its present title in 1934. Its design office has, since the Second World War, been responsible for several liaison, training and sporting aircraft for the Spanish Air Force and aeroclub flying schools. The Cuatros Vientos factory has a covered area of 10,270 m² (110,545 sq ft) and employs about 200 people.

AISA repairs and overhauls US aircraft, in particular the Beechcraft B55 Barons and F33 Bonanzas operated by the Spanish Air Force and the National School of Aeronautics. It also repairs and overhauls Bell 47, 204, 205, 206 and 212, and Boeing CH-47, helicopters for the Spanish Army, Navy and Air Force and civilian operators. As a subcontractor to Messier-Bugatti, it is producing landing gear shock absorbers and hydraulic actuators for the Dassault Mirage F1, 2000 and Falcon series, Dassault/Dornier Alpha Jet, and other European aviation programmes. Under subcontract to CASA, it produces structural components for the C-212 Aviocar and Airbus transports; and, in offset programmes, helicopter structures and hydraulic components for Aerospatiale and Agusta. AISA modernises Spanish Air Force Mirage IIIs, and is also involved in the Eurofighter EFA programme. AISA is preparing to convert the Spanish Army's nine CH-47Cs to CH-47D standard, in co-operation with Boeing Helicopters.

CASA
CONSTRUCCIONES AERONAUTICAS SA

Rey Francisco 4, Apartado 193, 28008 Madrid

Telephone: 34 (1) 247 25 00

Fax: 34 (1) 248 88 85

Telex: 27418 CASA E

WORKS: Getafe, Ajalvir, Tablada, San Pablo, San Fernando, Puerto Real and Cádiz

PRESIDENT AND CHAIRMAN OF THE BOARD:
  Javier Alvarez Vara

PUBLIC RELATIONS AND PRESS MANAGER:
  José de Sanmillán

CASA was founded in 1923 and is now owned 96.41 per cent by the Spanish state holding company INI, 3.57 per cent by MBB and 0.02 per cent by other minority shareholders. The former 13 per cent holding by Northrop was acquired by INI, but it is reported that INI would be prepared to reduce its holding to 25 per cent to let another European company take a stake in CASA.

In 1989, CASA formed Industria de Turbopropulsores (ITP) to make parts for and assemble turbojet engines, including the EJ200 for the European Fighter Aircraft, the F404 for the F/A-18, possibly the R-R Pegasus for Spanish Matadors (Harriers) and the eventual engine for the CASA AX. A second company, Compania Espanola de Sistemas Aeronauticas (CESA) was formed with a 40 per cent holding by Lucas Aerospace. The CASA space division has been greatly expanded and a largely automated composites manufacturing plant has been set up at Iliescas, near Toledo.

The largest of CASA's present programmes is its 4.2 per cent share in Airbus (see International section). It makes horizontal tail surfaces, landing gear doors, wing ribs and skins, leading and trailing edges and passenger doors for the A300/310/320, many of them in composites. Similar work will be done for the A330/340.

Second-largest programme is CASA's share in the European Fighter Aircraft (EFA), also detailed in the International section. CASA is active in all four of EFA's joint teams for avionics, control systems, flight management system and structure. The last-named includes sharing the starboard wing with BAe and the rear fuselage with Alenia. CASA is responsible for integration and software creation of the EFA communication subsystem.

CASA's own aircraft programmes include the C-212 Aviocar and the C-101 Aviojet. The CN-235 is shared with IPTN under Airtech (see International section) and CASA is looking for a partner to produce the new AX operational trainer.

In October 1989, CASA won the competition to design, stress, test and manufacture the entire wing of the Saab 2000 turboprop commuter. CASA is using the same advanced metal bonding technique as used for the Saab 340, but more composites are included.

Early in 1990, CASA had preliminary talks with Ilyushin about developing and marketing a westernised version of the 60-passenger Il-114 turboprop commuter, possibly with western engines. In exchange, the CN-235 might be sold in the USSR.

CASA C-212-300M Aviocar used by the French Centre d'Essais en Vol *(Ivo Sturzenegger)*

CASA has designed and is manufacturing the tailplane of the McDonnell Douglas MD-11 and makes outer flaps for the Boeing 757. It is a member of the European Future Large Aircraft Group (see Euroflag entry in the International section), leads the team of Spanish companies that will update 18 single-seat Mirage IIIs for the Spanish Air Force, and is also to extend the service life of that service's 23 Northrop SF-5B trainers.

In past years, CASA has made centre-fuselages for Dassault Mirage F1s and components for McDonnell Douglas F/A-18s, both for the Spanish Air Force. It has assembled 57 MBB BO 105s for the Spanish Army and 19 more for Spanish government agencies, and two BK 117s for ICONA. It assembled 12 of the 18 AS 532B₁ Cougars for the Spanish Army and installed THORN EMI Searchwater AEW radars in three Spanish Navy Sikorsky SH-3Ds. CASA manufactures tail components for the Sikorsky S-70 and would assemble and test S-70s purchased for the Spanish armed forces. CASA has also assembled 40 ENAER T-35C Pillans for the Spanish Air Force under the designation E.26 Tamiz.

For many years, CASA has been maintaining and modernising US Air Force and Navy aircraft and helicopters. The main current types are the McDonnell Douglas F-15 and F-4.

CASA has seven factories covering 275,000 m² (2,960,075 sq ft) and employs about 10,700 people.

AIRTECH (CASA-IPTN) CN-235

Details of this twin-turboprop transport aircraft can be found in the International section.

CASA AX

Since early 1988 CASA has been working under successive contracts from the Spanish Ministry of Defence on pre-feasibility and feasibility studies for an AX advanced trainer and close support aircraft, intended to provide a replacement for the Spanish Air Force's F-5As and F-5Bs from about the year 2000.

CASA C-212 SERIES 300 AVIOCAR

The original C-212-5 Series 100 Aviocar (1981-82 and earlier *Jane's*), of which 135 examples (including ten development aircraft) were built by CASA and 29 under licence by Nurtanio (IPTN) in Indonesia, was followed in 1979 by the improved Series 200 with more powerful TPE331-10 engines and increased max T-O weight. Details of the latter version can be found in the 1987-88 *Jane's*. The standard model is now the Series 300, which was certificated in December 1987. Military variants are designated **C-212-300M**.

The C-212 is certificated under FAR Pt 25, can be operated under FAR Pt 121 and Pt 135 conditions, and is well within the noise requirements of FAR Pt 36. By January 1991 total sales of the Aviocar (all versions) had reached 436 (208 civil and 228 military), of which more than 400 had been delivered by CASA and IPTN, with production continuing. This total includes 13 Series 300 C-212-Ms for the air forces of Angola (four), Panama (three), France (five), Bolivia (one) and at least six civil Series 300s. Military customers (for all versions) include Abu Dhabi (Air Force four), Angola (Army 12), Argentina (Navy five), Bolivia (Air Force two), Chad (Air Force one), Chile (Army six, Navy four), France (CEV five), Ghana (Air Force one), Indonesia (Army four, Navy eight, Air Force 10), Jordan (Air Force four), Lesotho (Defence Force three), Mexico (Navy 10), Nicaragua (Sandinista Air Force four), Panama (Air Force seven), Portugal (Air Force 24), Spain (Army nine, Air Force 71), Sweden (Navy one, Coast Guard three), Uruguay (Air Force three), USA (DEA three), Venezuela (Navy eight), Zimbabwe (Air Force 14), and two undisclosed countries (one each).

Maritime patrol and elint/ECM versions of the Aviocar are described separately, as is the re-engined **C-212P**. The following description applies to the Series 300 transport and equivalent C-212-M:

TYPE: Twin-turboprop STOL utility transport.

WINGS: Cantilever high-wing monoplane. Wing section NACA 65_3-218. Incidence 2° 30′. No dihedral or sweepback on main wings, but wingtips have 45° dihedral. All-metal light alloy fail-safe structure. Light alloy ailerons and double-slotted trailing-edge flaps. Trim tab in port aileron. Pneumatic de-icing of leading-edges (rubber boots and engine bleed air).

FUSELAGE: Semi-monocoque non-pressurised fail-safe structure of light alloy construction. New nose section, compared with Srs 200, providing additional volume for baggage (civil) or avionics (special mission versions).

TAIL UNIT: Cantilever two-spar all-metal structure, with dorsal fin. Fixed incidence tailplane, mid-mounted on rear of fuselage. Trim tab in rudder and each elevator. Pneumatic de-icing of leading-edges (rubber boots and engine bleed air).

LANDING GEAR: Non-retractable tricycle type, with single mainwheels and single steerable nosewheel. CASA oleo-pneumatic shock absorbers. Goodyear wheels and tyres, main units size 11.00-12 Type III (10-ply rating), nose unit size 24-7.7 Type VII (8-ply rating). Tyre pressure 3.86 bars (56 lb/sq in) on main units, 3.72 bars (54 lb/sq in) on nose unit. Goodyear hydraulic disc brakes on mainwheels. No brake cooling. Anti-skid system optional.

POWER PLANT: Two Garrett TPE331-10R-513C turboprops, each flat rated at 671 kW (900 shp) and equipped with an automatic power reserve (APR) system providing 690 kW (925 shp) in the event of one engine failing during take-off. Dowty Aerospace R-334/4-82-F/13 four-blade constant-speed fully feathering reversible-pitch propellers. Fuel in four integral wing tanks, with total capacity of 2,040 litres (539 US gallons; 449 Imp gallons), of which 2,000 litres (528 US gallons; 440 Imp gallons) are usable. Gravity refuelling point above each tank. Single pressure refuelling point in starboard wing leading-edge. Additional fuel can be carried in one 1,000 litre or two 750 litre (264 or 198 US gallon; 220 or 165 Imp gallon) optional ferry tanks inside cabin, and/or two 500 litre (132 US gallon; 110 Imp gallon) auxiliary underwing tanks. Oil capacity 4.5 litres (1.2 US gallons; 1.0 Imp gallon) per engine.

ACCOMMODATION: Crew of two on flight deck; cabin attendant in civil version. For troop transport role, main cabin can be fitted with 25 inward facing seats along cabin walls, to accommodate 24 paratroops with an instructor/jumpmaster; or seats for 25 fully equipped troops. As an ambulance, cabin is normally equipped to carry 12 stretcher patients and four medical attendants. As a freighter, up to 2,700 kg (5,952 lb) of cargo can be carried in main cabin, including two LD1, LD727/DC-8 or three LD3 containers, or light vehicles. Cargo system, which is certificated to FAR Pt 25, includes roller loading/unloading system and 9*g* barrier net. Photographic version is equipped with two Wild RC-10A vertical cameras and a darkroom. Navigation training version has individual desks/consoles for instructor and five pupils, in two rows, with appropriate instrument installations. Civil passenger transport version has standard seating for up to 26 persons in mainly three-abreast layout at 72 cm (28.5 in) pitch, with provision for quick change to all-cargo or mixed passenger/cargo interior. Toilet, galley and 400 kg (882 lb) capacity baggage compartment standard, plus additional 150 kg (330 lb) in nose bay. VIP transport version can be furnished to customer's requirements. Forward and outward opening door on port side immediately aft of flight deck; forward/outward opening passenger door on port side aft of wing; inward opening emergency exit opposite each door on starboard side. Additional emergency exit in roof of forward main cabin. A two-section underfuselage loading ramp/door aft of main cabin is openable in flight for discharge of paratroops or cargo, and can be fitted with optional external wheels for door protection during ground manoeuvring. Interior of rear loading door can be used for additional baggage stowage in civil version. Entire accommodation heated and ventilated; air-conditioning optional.

SYSTEMS: Freon cycle or (on special mission versions) engine bleed air air-conditioning system optional. Hydraulic system, operating at a service pressure of 138 bars (2,000 lb/sq in), provides power via an electric pump to actuate mainwheel brakes, flaps, nosewheel steering and rear cargo ramp/door. Handpump for standby hydraulic power in case of electrical failure or other emergency. Electrical system is supplied by two 9kW starter/generators, three batteries and three static converters. Pneumatic boot de-icing of wing and tail unit leading-edges; electric de-icing of propellers and windscreens. Oxygen system for crew (incl cabin attendant); two portable oxygen cylinders for passenger supply. Engine and cabin fire protection systems.

AVIONICS: Standard avionics include Collins VHF com, VOR/ILS, ADF, DME, ATC transponder, radio altimeter, intercom (with Gables control) and PA system; Honeywell directional gyro and AFCS; Collins ADF; and Bendix/King weather radar. Blind-flying instrumentation standard. Optional avionics include second Collins ADF and transponder; Collins HF and UHF com; Global Omega nav; Honeywell weather radar; Dorne & Margolin marker beacon receiver; and Fairchild flight data and cockpit voice recorders.

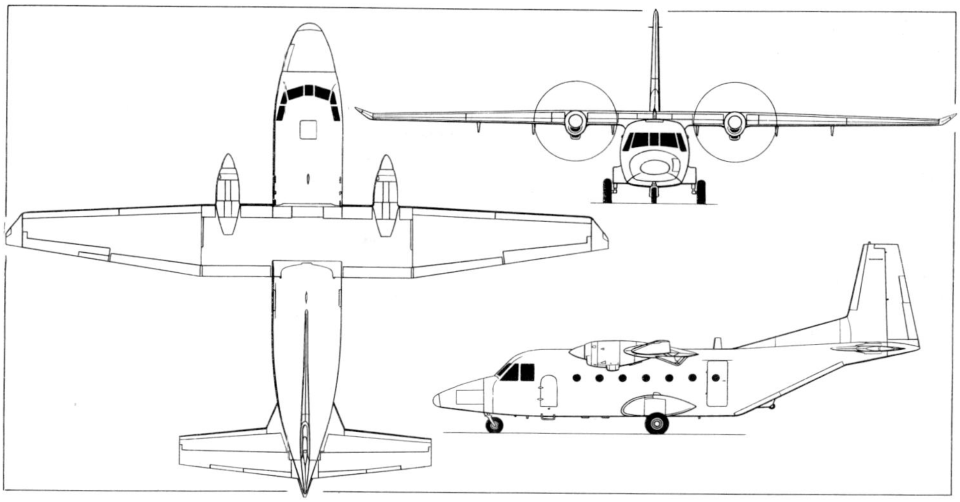

CASA C-212 Series 300 Aviocar, the current standard production version *(Pilot Press)*

ARMAMENT (military versions, optional): Two machine-gun pods or two rocket launchers, or one launcher and one gun pod, on hardpoints on fuselage sides (capacity 250 kg; 551 lb each).

DIMENSIONS, EXTERNAL:

Wing span	20.28 m (66 ft 6½ in)
Wing chord: at root	2.50 m (8 ft 2½ in)
at tip	1.25 m (4 ft 1¼ in)
Wing aspect ratio	10.0
Length overall	16.15 m (52 ft 11¾ in)
Fuselage: Max width	2.30 m (7 ft 6½ in)
Height overall	6.60 m (21 ft 7¾ in)
Tailplane span	8.40 m (27 ft 6¾ in)
Wheel track	3.10 m (10 ft 2 in)
Wheelbase	5.55 m (18 ft 2½ in)
Propeller diameter	2.74 m (9 ft 0 in)
Propeller ground clearance (min)	1.32 m (4 ft 4 in)
Distance between propeller centres	5.30 m (17 ft 4¾ in)
Passenger door (port, rear):	
Max height	1.58 m (5 ft 2¼ in)
Max width	0.70 m (2 ft 3½ in)
Crew and servicing door (port, fwd):	
Max height	1.10 m (3 ft 7¼ in)
Max width	0.58 m (1 ft 10¾ in)
Rear loading door: Max length	3.66 m (12 ft 0 in)
Max width	1.70 m (5 ft 7 in)
Max height	1.80 m (5 ft 11 in)
Emergency exit (stbd, fwd): Height	1.10 m (3 ft 7¼ in)
Width	0.58 m (1 ft 10¾ in)
Emergency exit (stbd, rear): Height	0.94 m (3 ft 1 in)
Width	0.55 m (1 ft 9¾ in)

DIMENSIONS, INTERNAL:

Cabin (excl flight deck and rear loading door):	
Length: passenger version	7.22 m (23 ft 8¼ in)
cargo/military	6.50 m (21 ft 4 in)
Max width	2.10 m (6 ft 10¾ in)
Max height	1.80 m (5 ft 11 in)
Floor area: passenger	13.51 m² (145.4 sq ft)
cargo/military	12.21 m² (131.4 sq ft)
Volume: passenger	23.7 m³ (837 cu ft)
cargo/military	21.3 m³ (752 cu ft)
Cabin: volume incl flight deck and rear loading door	27.0 m³ (953.5 cu ft)
Baggage compartment volume	3.6 m³ (127 cu ft)

AREAS:

Wings, gross	41.0 m² (441.33 sq ft)
Ailerons (total, incl tab)	3.75 m² (40.36 sq ft)
Trailing-edge flaps (total)	7.47 m² (80.41 sq ft)
Fin, incl dorsal fin	6.27 m² (67.49 sq ft)
Rudder, incl tab	2.05 m² (22.07 sq ft)
Tailplane	12.57 m² (135.31 sq ft)
Elevators (total, incl tabs)	3.56 m² (38.32 sq ft)

WEIGHTS AND LOADINGS:

Manufacturer's weight empty	3,780 kg (8,333 lb)
Weight empty, equipped (cargo)	4,400 kg (9,700 lb)
Max payload: cargo	2,700 kg (5,952 lb)
military	2,820 kg (6,217 lb)
Max fuel: standard	1,600 kg (3,527 lb)
with underwing auxiliary tanks	2,400 kg (5,291 lb)
Max T-O weight: standard	7,700 kg (16,975 lb)
military version	8,000 kg (17,637 lb)
Max ramp weight	7,750 kg (17,085 lb)
Max landing weight	7,450 kg (16,424 lb)
Max zero-fuel weight	7,100 kg (15,653 lb)
Max cabin floor loading	732 kg/m² (150 lb/sq ft)
Max wing loading: standard	187.8 kg/m² (38.46 lb/sq ft)
military version	195.1 kg/m² (39.96 lb/sq ft)
Max power loading: standard	5.74 kg/kW (9.43 lb/shp)
military version	5.96 kg/kW (9.80 lb/shp)

PERFORMANCE (at max T-O weight. A: passenger version, B: freighter, C: military version at 8,000 kg; 17,637 lb MTOGW):

Max operating speed (VMO):	
A, B, C	200 knots (370 km/h; 230 mph)
Max cruising speed at 3,050 m (10,000 ft):	
A, B, C	191 knots (354 km/h; 220 mph)
Econ cruising speed at 3,050 m (10,000 ft):	
A, B, C	162 knots (300 km/h; 186 mph)
Stalling speed in T-O configuration:	
A, B, C	78 knots (145 km/h; 90 mph)
Max rate of climb at S/L: A, B, C	497 m (1,630 ft)/min
Rate of climb at S/L, one engine out:	
A, B, C	95 m (312 ft)/min
Service ceiling: A, B, C	7,925 m (26,000 ft)
Service ceiling, one engine out:	
A, B, C	3,380 m (11,100 ft)
FAR T-O distance: A, B	817 m (2,680 ft)
FAR landing distance: A, B	866 m (2,840 ft)
MIL-7700C T-O distance to 15 m (50 ft):	
C	610 m (2,000 ft)
MIL-7700C landing distance from 15 m (50 ft):	
C	462 m (1,516 ft)
MIL-7700C landing run: C	285 m (935 ft)
Required runway length for STOL operation:	
C	384 m (1,260 ft)
Range (civil operation, IFR reserves):	
with 25 passengers, at max cruising speed	237 nm (440 km; 273 miles)
with 1,713 kg (3,776 lb) payload	773 nm (1,433 km; 890 miles)
Range (military operation):	
with max payload	450 nm (835 km; 519 miles)
with max standard fuel and 2,120 kg (4,674 lb) payload	907 nm (1,682 km; 1,045 miles)
with max standard and auxiliary fuel and 1,192 kg (2,628 lb) payload	1,446 nm (2,680 km; 1,665 miles)

CASA C-212 AVIOCAR (ASW and MARITIME PATROL VERSIONS)

Swedish Navy designation: Tp89

CASA has developed specialised versions of the C-212 equipped for anti-submarine and maritime patrol duties. They are generally similar to the standard C-212 except for addition of a nose radome and various external antennae.

Deliveries had been made by early 1991 to the Spanish Air Force (nine Series 100/200 for SAR duties), Spanish Ministry of Finance (five), Swedish Navy (one for ASW), Swedish Coast Guard (four, equipped with SLAR and IR/UV search gear), Venezuelan Navy (eight for maritime patrol), Mexican Navy (10 for maritime patrol), Argentine Prefectura Naval (five Series 300) and Uruguayan Air Force (one). These orders are included in the overall list of customers given in the previous entry. The orders by Sudan (two) and Portugal (three), listed in the 1990-91 *Jane's*, were subsequently cancelled.

TYPE: Twin-turboprop ASW and maritime patrol aircraft.

POWER PLANT: As for standard C-212. Auxiliary fuel tanks, total capacity 1,400 litres (370 US gallons; 308 Imp gallons).

ACCOMMODATION (ASW version): Pilot and co-pilot on flight deck, with OTPI and additional central console for radar repeater; controls for radio navigation, Doppler, DME, ADF, UHF/DF, Omega and VOR/ILS; weapons delivery controls; and intervalometer for rockets. Avionics rack on port side, aft of pilot, for com/nav equipment; second rack on starboard side, aft of co-pilot, contains avionics for mission equipment (radar, sonobuoys, MAD and ESM). Immediately aft of the latter rack, along the starboard side of the cabin, are three

Maritime patrol Series 300 Aviocar leased to the US Coast Guard in 1991

control consoles for the mission crew members. The first console has the radar control and display, ESM control and display, and intercom switch control. The second has the tactical display and control, MAD recorder and control, and intercom switch (ICS). The rearmost of the three incorporates intercom switch, sonobuoy receiver control unit, acoustic control panel, and acoustic control and display units.

ACCOMMODATION (maritime patrol version): Pilot and co-pilot on flight deck, with central console for radar repeater; control for radio navigation, Doppler, DME, ADF, UHF/DF, Omega, VOR/ILS and searchlight. Avionics rack on port side, aft of pilot, for com/nav and radar equipment. On starboard side of cabin is a console for the radar operator that incorporates radar PPI and ICS controls. Posts for two observers at rear of cabin.

AVIONICS: Communications equipment includes one HF and two VHF transceivers, single UHF, and interphone. Navigation equipment includes automatic flight control system, flight director, VOR/ILS (including VOR/LOC), glideslope and marker beacon receiver, DME, ADF, UHF/DF, radar altimeter, VLF/Omega, autopilot and compass. ASW version has underfuselage search radar with 360° scan, electronic support measures (ESM), sonobuoy processing system (SPS), OTPI, MAD, tactical processing system (TPS), IFF/SIF transponder; maritime patrol version has nose mounted AN/APS-128 100kW search radar with 270° scan and optional FLIR.

EQUIPMENT: Sonobuoy and smoke marker launcher, searchlight, smoke markers and camera in maritime patrol version.

ARMAMENT: Includes option to carry torpedoes such as Mk 46 and Sting Ray; air-to-surface missiles such as Sea Skua and AS15TT; and air-to-surface rockets.

CASA C-212 AVIOCAR (ELINT/ECM VERSION)

A version of the Aviocar for electronic intelligence and electronic countermeasures duties entered development in 1981. At least six (all Series 200s) have been ordered by undisclosed customers, and two C-212s previously delivered to the Portuguese Air Force were modified retrospectively for elint/ECM duties. This version is also available for the Series 300.

The elint/ECM version carries equipment for automatic signal interception, classification and identification in dense signal environments, data from which enable a map to be drawn plotting the position and characteristics of hostile radars. Emitters for the jamming part of the mission are also carried.

CASA C-212P AVIOCAR

Certificated in Spain in 1989, the C-212P is a Series 300 powered by 820 kW (1,100 shp) P&WC PT6A-65 engines to improve hot and high performance. CASA reported that initial orders were being negotiated in early 1991.

CASA C-101 AVIOJET

Spanish Air Force designation: E.25 Mirlo (Blackbird)

Chilean Air Force designations: T-36 and A-36 Halcón (Hawk)

The first of four prototypes of this basic and advanced military jet trainer made its initial flight on 27 June 1977. MBB (Germany) and Northrop (USA) collaborated in the design.

The first Spanish production aircraft flew in 1979. Export versions have been equipped for ground attack, either for training or combat.

In 1990, CASA began an 18-month modernisation of the C-101 weapon system for training or, as in Jordan and Chile, for front-line use. The system will include a GEC Ferranti head-up display.

The following versions have been built:

C-101EB: Initial production trainer version for Spanish Air Force, with 15.57 kN (3,500 lb st) TFE731-2-2J engine. Total of 88 delivered originally from 17 March 1980 (later increased to 92); now in service with one squadron of the Academia General del Aire at San Javier, two squadrons of the Grupo de Escuelas (41st Air Group) at Matacán, and

the Patrulla Aguila (Eagle Patrol) display team of the Spanish Air Force, which has seven aircraft. Described in 1983-84 *Jane's*.

C-101BB: Armed export version, with 16.46 kN (3,700 lb st) TFE731-3-1J engine, in service with air forces of Chile (14 **BB-02**) and Honduras (four **BB-03**, similar except for avionics). All BB-02s except first four were assembled under licence in Chile (see ENAER entry in Chilean section). Known as **T-36 Halcón** (Hawk) in Chilean service.

C-101CC: Light attack version, with more powerful TFE731-5-1J engine (normal rating 19.13 kN; 4,300 lb st, military power reserve (MPR) rating 20.91 kN; 4,700 lb st), and other modifications. First of two prototypes flown on 16 November 1983. Twenty-three **CC-02** ordered by Chile, of which 22 for assembly and partial manufacture by ENAER as **A-36 Halcón** (deliveries still in progress in 1991), and 16 **CC-04** delivered in 1987-88 to Royal Jordanian Air Force. These two operators hold options for a total of 14 more.

C-101DD: Enhanced training version, flown for the first time on 20 May 1985. Additional avionics include GEC Ferranti head-up display, weapon aiming computer and inertial platform. Power plant as for C-101CC. No orders announced up to Spring 1991.

The following description applies to the standard C-101CC except where indicated:

TYPE: Tandem two-seat basic and advanced trainer and light tactical aircraft.

WINGS: Cantilever low-wing monoplane. Norcasa 15 symmetrical wing section, thickness/chord ratio 15 per cent. Dihedral 5°. Incidence 1°. Sweepback at quarter-chord 1° 53′. All-metal (aluminium alloy) three-spar fail-safe stressed-skin structure, with six-bolt attachment to fuselage. Plain ailerons and slotted trailing-edge flaps, of glassfibre/honeycomb sandwich construction. Flap track guides of titanium. Ailerons actuated hydraulically, with electrically actuated artificial spring feel and manual backup. Ground adjustable tab on port aileron.

FUSELAGE: All-metal semi-monocoque fail-safe structure. Hydraulically operated aluminium honeycomb airbrake under centre of fuselage.

TAIL UNIT: Cantilever all-metal structure, with electrically actuated variable incidence tailplane. Aluminium honeycomb rudder and elevators, actuated manually via push/pull rods. Electrically actuated trim tab in rudder. Twin ventral strakes under jetpipe on armed versions.

LANDING GEAR: Hydraulically retractable tricycle type, with single wheel and oleo-pneumatic shock absorber on each unit. Forward retracting Dowty Aerospace nose unit, with non-steerable nosewheel and chined tubeless tyre size 457 × 146 (18 × 5.75-8). Inward retracting mainwheels with tubeless tyres size 622 × 216 (24.5 × 8.5-10) and hydraulically actuated multi-disc brakes.

POWER PLANT: One Garrett TFE731 non-afterburning turbofan (see variants for details), with lateral intake on each side of fuselage abreast of second cockpit. Fuel in one 1,155 litre (305 US gallon; 254 Imp gallon) fuselage bag tank, one 575 litre (152 US gallon; 126.5 Imp gallon) integral tank in wing centre-section, and two outer wing integral tanks, for ferry missions, each of 342 litres (90.4 US gallons; 75.25 Imp gallons). Total internal fuel capacity 1,730 litres (457 US gallons; 380.5 Imp gallons) normal, 2,414 litres (637.8 US gallons; 531 Imp gallons) maximum, of which 1,667 litres (440 US gallons; 367 Imp gallons) and 2,337 litres (617 US gallons; 514 Imp gallons), respectively, are usable. Fuel system permits up to 30 s of inverted flight. Pressure refuelling point beneath port air intake; gravity fuelling point for each tank. No provision for external fuel tanks. Oil capacity 8.5 litres (2.2 US gallons; 1.8 Imp gallons).

ACCOMMODATION: Crew of two in tandem, on Martin-Baker Mk 10L zero/zero ejection seats, under individual canopies which open sideways to starboard and are separated by internal screen. Rear (instructor's) seat elevated 32.5 cm (12¾ in). Cockpit pressurised and air-conditioned by engine bleed air. Dual controls standard.

SYSTEMS: Hamilton Standard three-wheel bootstrap type air-conditioning and pressurisation system, differential 0.28 bar (4.07 lb/sq in), using engine bleed air. Single hydraulic system, pressure 207 bars (3,000 lb/sq in), for landing gear, ailerons, flaps, airbrake, anti-skid units and wheel brakes. Backup system comprising compressed nitrogen bottle for landing gear extension and accumulator for aileron boosters and emergency braking. Pneumatic system for air-conditioning, pressurisation and canopy seal. Electrical system includes 28V 9kW DC starter/generator, two 700VA static inverters for 115/26V single phase AC power, and two 24V 23Ah nickel-cadmium batteries for emergency DC power and engine starting. High pressure gaseous oxygen system.

AVIONICS: C-101EB and BB as listed in earlier *Jane's*. Standard C-101CC equipped with Magnavox AN/ARC-164 UHF com, Collins 21B VHF com, Collins VIR-31A VOR/ILS, Collins DME-40, Collins ADF-60, Andrea AN/AIC-18 interphone, Teledyne/CASA AN/APX-101 IFF/SIF, Dorne and Margolin DMELT 8.1 ELT, Honeywell ZC-222 flight director, Honeywell AS-339 gyro platform, ADI-500C, RD-550A HSI, Avimo RGS2 gunsight (front and rear cockpit), and CASA SCAR-81 armament control system. Wide range of alternative avionics available for export versions, including Collins AN/ARN-118 Tacan, General Instrument AN/ALR-66 radar warning receiver and Vinten Vicon 78 chaff/flare dispenser. C-101DD specific equipment includes GEC Ferranti FD 4513 head-up display and weapon aiming computer, Litton LN-39 inertial platform, Alenia mission computer, all linked by MIL-1553 digital bus, FIAR P 0702 laser ranger, HOTAS controls, GEC Sensors AD 6601-12 Doppler velocity sensor, Collins AN/ARC-182(V) UHF/VHF-AM/FM com, Collins AN/ARC-186 VHF-AM/FM com, Collins VIR-130A VOR/ILS, Alenia radar altimeter, Fairchild video camera and Astronautics rear seat monitor.

ARMAMENT: Large bay below rear cockpit suitable for quick-change packages, including a 30 mm DEFA 553 cannon pod with 130 rds, a twin 12.7 mm Browning M3 machine-gun pod with 220 rds/gun, reconnaissance camera, ECM package or laser designator. Six underwing hardpoints, capacities 500 kg (1,102 lb) inboard, 375 kg (827 lb) centre and 250 kg (551 lb) outboard; total external stores load 2,250 kg (4,960 lb). Typical armament can include one 30 mm cannon with up to 130 rds, or two 12.7 mm guns, in the fuselage; and four LAU-10 pods of 5 in rockets, six 250 kg BR250 bombs, four LAU-3/A rocket launchers, four 125 kg BR125 bombs and two LAU-3/A launchers, two AGM-65

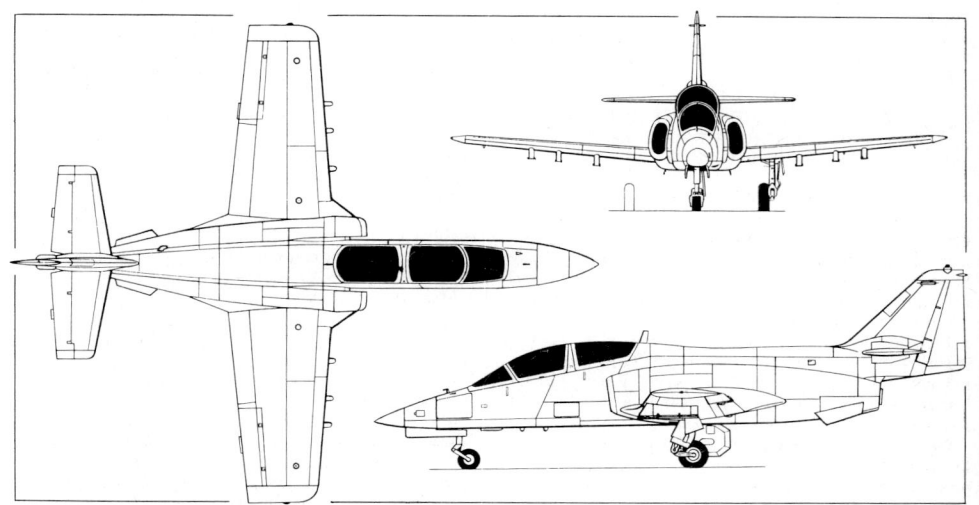

CASA C-101CC Aviojet light attack aircraft (*Pilot Press*)

Maverick missiles, or two AIM-9L Sidewinders or Matra Magic.

DIMENSIONS, EXTERNAL:

Wing span	10.60 m (34 ft 9⅜ in)
Wing chord: at c/1	2.36 m (7 ft 9 in)
at tip	1.41 m (4 ft 7½ in)
Wing aspect ratio	5.6
Length overall	12.50 m (41 ft 0 in)
Height overall	4.25 m (13 ft 11¼ in)
Tailplane span	4.32 m (14 ft 2 in)
Wheel track (c/1 of shock struts)	3.18 m (10 ft 5¼ in)
Wheelbase	4.77 m (15 ft 7¾ in)

AREAS:

Wings, gross	20.00 m² (215.3 sq ft)
Ailerons (total)	1.18 m² (12.70 sq ft)
Trailing-edge flaps (total)	2.50 m² (26.91 sq ft)
Fin	2.10 m² (22.60 sq ft)
Rudder	1.10 m² (11.84 sq ft)
Tailplane	3.44 m² (37.03 sq ft)
Elevators	1.00 m² (10.76 sq ft)

WEIGHTS AND LOADINGS:

Weight empty, equipped	3,500 kg (7,716 lb)
Max fuel weight: usable	1,822 kg (4,017 lb)
total	1,882 kg (4,149 lb)
Max external stores load	2,250 kg (4,960 lb)
T-O weight:	
trainer, clean: BB, CC	5,000 kg (11,023 lb)
DD	5,030 kg (11,089 lb)
ground attack: BB	5,600 kg (12,345 lb)
CC, DD	6,300 kg (13,890 lb)
Max landing weight:	
3.66 m (12 ft)/s sink rate	4,700 kg (10,361 lb)
3.05 m (10 ft)/s sink rate	5,800 kg (12,787 lb)
Wing loading:	
trainer, clean: BB, CC	250.0 kg/m² (51.20 lb/sq ft)
DD	251.5 kg/m² (51.51 lb/sq ft)
ground attack: BB	280.0 kg/m² (57.35 lb/sq ft)
CC, DD	315.0 kg/m² (64.52 lb/sq ft)
Power loading:	
trainer, clean: BB	303.7 kg/kN (2.98 lb/lb st)
CC (with MPR)	239.3 kg/kN (2.35 lb/lb st)
DD (with MPR)	240.7 kg/kN (2.36 lb/lb st)
ground attack: BB	340.8 kg/kN (3.34 lb/lb st)
CC, DD (with MPR)	301.0 kg/kN (2.95 lb/lb st)

PERFORMANCE (C-101BB at 4,400 kg; 9,700 lb AUW, C-101CC and DD at 4,350 kg; 9,590 lb, CC in training configuration with 50% normal fuel, except where indicated):

Max limiting Mach No. (all)	0.80
Never-exceed speed (V$_{NE}$) (all)	
	450 knots (834 km/h; 518 mph) IAS
Max level speed at S/L:	
BB	373 knots (691 km/h; 430 mph)
CC, DD	423 knots (784 km/h; 487 mph)

E.25 Mirlo (CASA C-101EB) of the Spanish Air Force

Max level speed at height:

BB at 7,620 m (25,000 ft)	
	430 knots (797 km/h; 495 mph)
CC and DD at 6,100 m (20,000 ft)	
	443 knots (821 km/h; 510 mph)
CC and DD at 4,575 m (15,000 ft) with MPR	
	450 knots (834 km/h; 518 mph)
Econ cruising speed at 9,145 m (30,000 ft) (all)	
	Mach 0.56 (330 knots; 612 km/h; 380 mph)
Unstick speed (all)	110 knots (204 km/h; 127 mph)
Touchdown speed (all)	92 knots (170 km/h; 106 mph)
Stalling speed (all):	
flaps up	99 knots (183 km/h; 114 mph) IAS
flaps down	88 knots (164 km/h; 102 mph) IAS
Max rate of climb at S/L: BB	1,152 m (3,780 ft)/min
CC and DD (normal)	1,517 m (4,975 ft)/min
CC and DD (with MPR)	1,939 m (6,360 ft)/min
Time to 7,620 m (25,000 ft): BB	8 min 30 s
CC, DD (at 4,500 kg; 9,921 lb)	6 min 30 s
Service ceiling: BB	12,200 m (40,000 ft)
CC, DD	13,410 m (44,000 ft)
T-O run: BB	630 m (2,065 ft)
CC, DD (at 4,500 kg; 9,921 lb)	560 m (1,835 ft)
T-O to 15 m (50 ft): BB	850 m (2,790 ft)
CC, DD (at 4,500 kg; 9,921 lb)	750 m (2,460 ft)
Landing from 15 m (50 ft) (all, at 4,000 kg; 8,818 lb)	
	800 m (2,625 ft)
Landing run (all, at 4,000 kg; 8,818 lb)	
	480 m (1,575 ft)

Typical interdiction radius (lo-lo-lo) with four 250 kg bombs and 30 mm gun:
CC and DD, 3 min over target, 30 min reserves
280 nm (519 km; 322 miles)

Typical close air support radius (lo-lo-lo):
CC and DD with four 19 × 2.75 in rocket launchers and 30 mm gun, 50 min loiter over battle area, 8 min over target, 30 min reserves
200 nm (370 km; 230 miles)
CC and DD, load as above plus two 125 kg bombs, 30 min loiter, 10 min attack (MPR thrust) and 7% reserves
170 nm (315 km; 196 miles)
CC and DD with two Maverick missiles and 30 mm gun, 8 min over target, 30 min reserves
325 nm (602 km; 374 miles)
Typical ECM mission radius:
BB and CC, 3 h 15 min loiter over target, 30 min reserves
330 nm (611 km; 380 miles)
Typical photo-reconnaissance radius (hi-lo-lo):
BB and CC, 30 min reserves
520 nm (964 km; 599 miles)
Armed patrol, no underwing stores, 100 nm (185 km; 115 mile) transit from base to patrol area:
BB, CC and DD with one 30 mm or two 12.7 mm guns, 45 min reserves
3 h 30 min at 200 knots (370 km/h; 230 mph) at S/L
Ferry range (all), 30 min reserves
2,000 nm (3,706 km; 2,303 miles)
Typical training mission endurance (all):
two 1 h 10 min general handling missions, incl aerobatics, with 20 min reserves after second mission

Max endurance (all)	7 h
g limits (all):	
at 4,900 kg (10,802 lb) AUW	+7.5/−3.9
at 6,300 kg (13,890 lb) AUW	+5.5/−2

SWEDEN

FFV

FFV AEROTECH
S-732 81 Arboga
Telephone: 46 (589) 800
Telex: 732 46 FFVA S

BA-14 STARLING

The BA-14 Starling two-seat light aircraft first flew on 25 August 1988 and was to be built and marketed jointly by MFI and FFV Aerotech, but this programe is not now going ahead. A detailed description and illustration of the BA-14 can be found in the 1990-91 *Jane's*; but see also pages 216-217 for details of the latest BA-14B version.

IG JAS

INDUSTRIGRUPPEN JAS AB

CHAIRMAN: Björn Svedberg (Ericsson)
PRESIDENT AND CHIEF EXECUTIVE OFFICER:
Hans Ahlinder (Saab-Scania)
PUBLIC RELATIONS DIRECTOR: Rolf Erichs (Saab-Scania)

Industrigruppen JAS (the JAS Industrial Group) was formed in 1981 to represent the activities of Saab-Scania, Ericsson, Volvo Flygmotor and FFV in the JAS 39 Gripen programme. IG JAS operates as the industry's contractual party to Försvarets Materielverk (the Defence Materiel Administration, FMV) and co-ordinates the activities of the group's companies in regard to development, manufacture, delivery and maintenance of the JAS 39 Gripen.

JAS 39 GRIPEN (GRIFFIN)

The Swedish government approved funding for project definition and initial development of this Viggen replacement in June 1980. Known as the JAS 39 (Jakt/Attack/Spaning: fighter/attack/reconnaissance), it is a multi-role combat aircraft to replace, successively, the AJ/SH/SF/JA 37 versions of the Viggen and all remaining Swedish Air Force J 35 Drakens. A similar financial commitment was made by Industri Gruppen JAS, a Swedish aerospace industry group formed in 1981 by Saab Aircraft Division, Volvo Flygmotor, Ericsson Radar Electronics and FFV Aerotech.

On 3 June 1981 the group submitted to the Swedish Defence Materiel Administration (FMV) its initial proposals for an aircraft to meet the JAS requirement. Power plant is a modified version of the General Electric F404 afterburning turbofan offering higher thrust and having a strengthened front fan to meet Swedish bird strike requirements. The engine was developed and is produced, as the RM12, by Volvo Flygmotor. Like the Viggen, the JAS 39 will be adapted to the specific Swedish defence profile, using 800 m (2,625 ft) V-90 airstrips and similar lengths of ordinary roads as air bases. It will require only simple maintenance, with turnround service handled mainly by conscripts.

The FMV evaluated the Swedish industry proposals against aircraft from other countries, and recommended adoption of the Saab design. The programme approved by the Swedish government on 6 May 1982 covers the development and procurement of 140 aircraft in two batches by the year 2000, and a contract for the first 30 was signed on 30 June 1982. Overall programme go-ahead was confirmed in the Spring of 1983, and prototype construction began in 1984. The ultimate requirement is for 21 to 23 squadrons totalling 340-350 aircraft. Gripen deliveries are scheduled to start in 1993. A design study of a two-seat JAS 39B tactical trainer was authorised in July 1989, and some of the first 140 Gripens may be two-seaters. The JAS 39B has a 0.5 m (1 ft 7¾ in) fuselage plug.

Contract tenders for the second production batch (110 aircraft), and for the JAS 39B, were made on 1 October 1990 and were valid until 30 June 1991. No commitment to batch 2 or the JAS 39B by the FMV is expected until mid-1992.

Five prototypes of the Gripen have been built, the first of which, 39-1, was rolled out on 26 April 1987 and made its first flight on 9 December 1988. It was lost on 2 February 1989, without major injury to its pilot, when it crashed while landing in gusty conditions after its sixth test flight, prompting considerable modification of the fly-by-wire system software. The first flight of 39-2 was made on 4 May 1990, followed by 39-4 (the third to fly) on 20 December 1990 and 39-3 on 25 March 1991. 39-5 was also due to fly in 1991, and the prototypes are being assisted by a Viggen for radar and display system testing plus, from 1992, the first production Gripen 39-101. Delays were caused in 1990 by a problem of slow acceleration of the RM12 engine, but all prototypes received modified RM12s early in 1991 and the time lost was being recovered. By 14 May 1991 the prototypes had made 83 flights, with 39-2 being fitted with an updated control system and 39-3 testing the radar and display system: 39-4 had a full avionic system except for radar and was being used to prove the installation.

The first three and a half sets of carbonfibre wings were manufactured for Saab by British Aerospace, but for all subsequent aircraft Saab is responsible for all CFRP components (30 per cent of the airframe) including the wings, canards, fin, and major (eg engine and landing gear) doors.

The following description applies to the single-seat prototypes:

TYPE: Single-seat all-weather, all-altitude fighter, attack and reconnaissance aircraft.

WINGS: Cropped delta main wings, mid-mounted on fuselage; leading-edge flaps with dog-tooth; inboard and outboard elevons on trailing-edges. Sweptback all-moving foreplanes, mounted on upper sides of engine air intake trunks. Leading-edge sweepback approx 43° on canards, 45° on main wings.

FUSELAGE: Area ruled structure. Airbrake on each side at rear.

TAIL UNIT: Fin and rudder only; no horizontal tail surfaces.

LANDING GEAR: AP Precision Hydraulics retractable tricycle gear, single mainwheels retracting hydraulically forward

Four of the five prototypes of the JAS 39 Gripen multi-role air defence, attack and reconnaissance aircraft

into fuselage; steerable twin-wheel nose unit retracts rearward. Goodyear wheels, tyres, carbon disc brakes and anti-skid units. Nosewheel braking. Entire gear designed for high rate of sink.

POWER PLANT: One General Electric/Volvo Flygmotor RM12 (F404-GE-400) turbofan, rated initially at approx 54 kN (12,140 lb st) dry and 80.5 kN (18,100 lb st) with afterburning. Near-rectangular intakes, each with splitter plate. Fuel in self-sealing main tank and collector tank in fuselage. Active control of CG location provided by Intertechnique fuel management system.

ACCOMMODATION: Pilot only, on Martin-Baker S10LS zero/zero ejection seat under teardrop canopy. Hinged canopy and one-piece windscreen by Lucas Aerospace.

SYSTEMS: BAe environmental control system for cockpit air-conditioning, pressurisation and avionics cooling. Hughes-Treitler heat exchanger. Two main Dowty hydraulic systems and one auxiliary system, with Abex pumps. Sundstrand main electrical power generating system (40kVA constant speed, constant frequency at 400Hz) comprises an integrated drive generator, generator control unit and current transformer assembly. Lear Astronics triplex digital fly-by-wire flight control system, with Moog electrically signalled servo-valves for primary flight control actuators, Lucas Aerospace rotary actuators ('geared hinges') for leading-edge flaps, and Saab Combitech aircraft motion sensors and throttle actuator subsystem. Single-channel analog backup system in the event of main FBW system failure. Lucas Aerospace auxiliary and emergency power system, comprising a gearbox mounted turbine, hydraulic pump and a 10kVA AC generator, to provide emergency electric and hydraulic power in the event of an engine or main generator failure. In emergency role, the turbine is driven by engine bleed or APU air; if this is not available the stored energy mode, using pressurised oxygen and methanol, is selected automatically. Microturbo TGA 15 APU and DA 15 air turbine starter for engine starting, cooling air and standby electric power.

AVIONICS: Bofors Aerotronics AMR 345 VHF/UHF-AM/FM com transceiver. Honeywell laser inertial navigation system. Ericsson EP-17 electronic display system in cockpit, using one Hughes Aircraft wide-angle head-up display with a GEC Ferranti FD 5040 video camera, for weapon aiming, and three interchangeable Ericsson head-down CRT displays, plus a minimum of conventional analog instruments for backup purposes only. The head-up display, using advanced diffraction optics, combines symbology and video images. Left hand (flight data) head-down display normally replaces all conventional flight instruments. Central display shows a computer generated map of the area surrounding the aircraft with tactical information superimposed. Right hand CRT is a multi-sensor display showing information on targets acquired by the video camera, radar and FLIR. An Ericsson SDS 80 computing system, incorporating more than 30 microcomputers, controls the aircraft's central air data computer, radar, electronic displays, fuel management, hydraulic, environmental

control and other systems, and allows for multi-mode use and flexibility for further development. A BAe three-axis strapdown gyro-magnetic unit provides standby attitude and heading information.

Ericsson/GEC Ferranti PS-05/A multi-mode pulse Doppler target search and acquisition (lookdown/shootdown) system, comprising a nose mounted I-band radar of 1kW output and (depending on mission) a pod mounted forward-looking infra-red sensor or a laser rangefinder pod. For fighter missions, this system provides fast target acquisition at long range; search and multi-target track-while-scan; quick scanning and lock-on at short ranges; and automatic fire control for missiles and cannon. In the attack and reconnaissance roles its operating functions are search against sea and ground targets; ground and sea target track-while-scan; mapping, with normal and high resolution; fire control for missiles and other attack weapons; and obstacle avoidance and navigation. The FLIR pod, carried externally under the starboard engine air intake trunk, forward of the wing leading-edge, is used for attack and reconnaissance missions at night, providing a heat picture of the target on the right hand head-down CRT. A radar warning receiver fairing is mounted near the tip of the fin. The JAS 39 will also carry advanced Ericsson ECM, both built-in and externally.

ARMAMENT: Internally mounted 27 mm Mauser BK27 automatic cannon in fuselage and infra-red dogfight missiles on the wingtips. Five other external hardpoints (two under each wing and one on the centreline). These stations can carry short and medium range air-to-air missiles such as RB71 (Sky Flash), RB74 (AIM-9L Sidewinder) or AMRAAM; air-to-surface missiles such as Maverick; anti-shipping missiles such as Saab RBS 15F; conventional or retarded bombs; or air-to-surface rockets. MBB is contracted to develop for the Gripen a submunitions dispenser based on its MDS that can glide towards its target before releasing its bomblets on command. The Swedish Defence Materiel Administration (FMV) has proposed developing a glide bomb known as TSA (Tungt Styrt Attackvapen; heavy guided attack weapon), with a warhead weighing several hundred kg, for attacking large targets such as bridges. There will be a series of mission pods.

DIMENSIONS, EXTERNAL (approx):

Wing span	8.00 m (26 ft 3 in)
Length overall	14.10 m (46 ft 3 in)
Height overall	4.70 m (15 ft 5 in)
Wheel track	2.60 m (8 ft 6½ in)
Wheelbase	5.30 m (17 ft 4¾ in)

WEIGHTS AND LOADINGS:

Design max T-O weight	approx 8,000 kg (17,635 lb)

PERFORMANCE:

Max level speed	supersonic at all altitudes
T-O and landing strip length	approx 800 m (2,625 ft)
g limit	+9

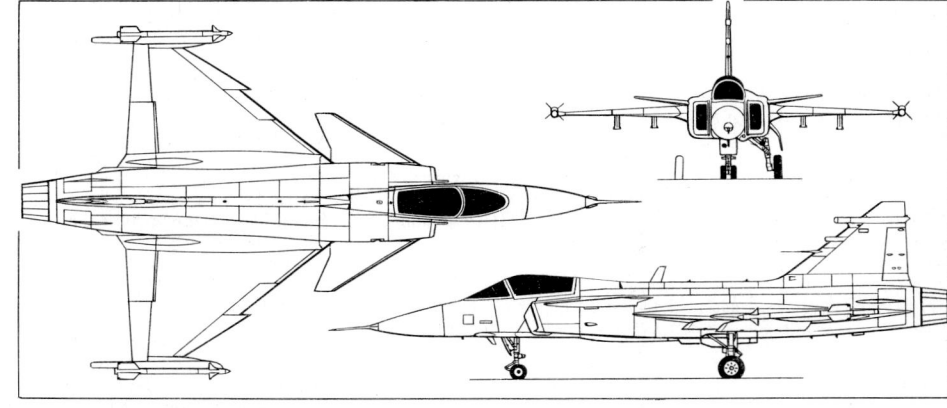

JAS 39 Gripen multi-role combat aircraft for the Swedish Air Force *(Pilot Press)*

MFI

MALMÖ FORSKNINGS & INNOVATIONS AB

Smedstorpsgatan 19, S-212 28 Malmö
Telephone: 46 (40) 18 07 05
Fax: 46 (40) 18 21 02
CHIEF DESIGNER: Hakan Langebro

MFI has put into production various light aircraft designed by Björn Andreasson, including the BA-12 Slandan (see Microlights), BA-14 and earlier MFI-9.

MFI BA-14B

Construction of the first prototype BA-14 Starling began in 1987 and the first flight was achieved on 25 August 1988. It had been designed by Björn Andreasson and became a joint venture project between MFI and FFV Aerotech. However, the much revised BA-14B appears to be solely an

MFI type. It has received certification under FAR Pt 23A standards and is being marketed. Other possible roles include ambulance, crop dusting and aerobatic training.

TYPE: Two/four-seat trainer and utility aircraft.

WINGS: Shoulder-wing monoplane, with single bracing strut each side. No dihedral. Sweepforward perhaps 3°. GFRP composite construction; spar caps reinforced with carbonfibre pultruded bars. Welded steel tube wing carry-through structure. Ailerons and flaps.

FUSELAGE: Semi-monocoque structure of GFRP/CFRP. Hatch for access to baggage/freight compartment in centre-fuselage.

TAIL UNIT: All-moving tailplane and fin/rudder (replaces V tail of original prototype).

LANDING GEAR: Non-retractable tricycle type. Mainwheels with brakes carried on an arched GFRP leaf spring. Optional floats.

POWER PLANTS: One 119 kW (160 hp) Textron Lycoming IO-320 flat-four engine, driving a Hoffmann HO-V72A

variable-pitch wooden/GFRP propeller. Fuel capacity 80 litres (21 US gallons; 17.6 Imp gallons).

ACCOMMODATION: Two persons side by side under large one-piece transparent canopy. Provision for two further seats. Baggage compartment aft of seats.

DIMENSIONS, EXTERNAL:

Wing span	9.00 m (29 ft 6½ in)
Length overall	7.20 m (23 ft 7½ in)
Height overall	2.90 m (9 ft 6¼ in)
Propeller diameter	1.85 m (6 ft 0¾ in)

AREAS:

Wings, gross	10.50 m² (113.02 sq ft)

WEIGHTS AND LOADINGS:

Weight empty	615 kg (1,356 lb)
Max T-O weight	900 kg (1,984 lb)
Max wing loading	85.71 kg/m² (17.55 lb/sq ft)
Max power loading	7.55 kg/kW (12.40 lb/hp)

PERFORMANCE:

Max level speed at S/L	124 knots (230 km/h; 143 mph)

Max cruising speed at S/L
         113 knots (210 km/h; 130 mph)
Econ cruising speed at S/L
         108 knots (200 km/h; 124 mph)
Stalling speed, power off
         46 knots (84 km/h; 53 mph)
Max rate of climb at S/L   335 m (1,100 ft)/min
T-O and landing run   250 m (821 ft)
g limits   +4.4/−2.2

MFI BA-14B training and utility aircraft
(Jane's/Mike Keep)

SAAB-SCANIA
SAAB-SCANIA AKTIEBOLAG
S-581 88 Linköping
Telephone: 46 (13) 18 00 00
Fax: 46 (13) 18 18 02
Telex: 50040 SAABLG S
PRESIDENT AND CHIEF EXECUTIVE OFFICER:
    Lars V. Kylberg
FIRST EXECUTIVE VICE-PRESIDENT: Bertil Krook
Saab Aircraft Division
Telephone: 46 (13) 18 00 00
GENERAL MANAGER: Christer Skogsborg
DIRECTOR OF COMMERCIAL AIRCRAFT SECTOR:
    Kurt Ahlborg
DIRECTOR OF MILITARY AIRCRAFT SECTOR:
    Tomy Ivarsson
PUBLIC RELATIONS DIRECTOR: Rolf Erichs
WORKS: Linköping, Malmö, Ödeshög, Norrköping and
    Kramfors
SAAB 340 MARKETING:
    Saab Aircraft International Ltd, Leworth House, 14-16
    Sheet Street, Windsor, Berkshire SL4 1BG, UK
    Telephone: 44 (753) 859991
    Fax: 44 (753) 858884
    Telex: 847 815 SFIWIN G
    PRESIDENT: Jeffrey Marsh
PUBLIC RELATIONS AND PROMOTIONAL SERVICES:
    Mike Savage
    Saab Aircraft of America Inc, Loudoun Tech Center,
    21300 Ridgetop Circle, Sterling, Virginia 22170, USA
PRESIDENT: Ove Dahlén
PUBLIC RELATIONS: Ron Sherman
Telephone: 1 (703) 406 7200
Fax: 1 (703) 406 7272

The original Svenska Aeroplan AB was founded at Trollhättan in 1937 for the production of military aircraft. In 1939 this company was amalgamated with the Aircraft Division (ASJA) of the Svenska Järnvägsverkstäderna rolling stock factory in Linköping, where the main aerospace factory is now located. The company's name was changed to Saab Aktiebolag in May 1965. During 1968 Saab merged with Scania-Vabis, to strengthen the two companies' position in automotive products. Malmö Flygindustri (MFI) was acquired in the same year.

Saab-Scania has more than 48,000 employees, organised in three operating divisions and one major subsidiary (Saab-Scania Combitech). Of these, nearly 6,800 are employed by the Saab Aircraft Division, including 5,800 at Linköping.

Production of the JA 37 Viggen ended in 1990. Saab-Scania's current aerospace activities include production of the Saab 340B, and development of the JAS 39 Gripen (see entry under IG JAS) and Saab 2000. Since 1949 the company has delivered more than 2,000 military jet aircraft and more than 1,500 piston engined aircraft. Since 1962, it has had a dealership for Schweizer (Hughes) helicopters in Scandinavia and Finland. Since 1978, it has manufactured inboard wing flaps and vanes for the McDonnell Douglas MD-80 series, and now also produces composite spoilers for the MD-82/83. A 25,000 m² (269,100 sq ft) factory at Linköping, for final assembly of the Saab 340, was completed in July 1982; an extension to this facility, to accommodate also the wing and tail unit production, was inaugurated on 26 June 1986. A further 15,000 m² (161,445 sq ft) expansion has taken place over the past year to accommodate increased production of the Saab 340B and assembly of the Saab 2000.

In the electronics field, current production items include computer systems, autopilots, fire control and bombing systems for piloted aircraft, and electronics for guided missiles. Spaceborne computers, electro-optical fire control systems and field artillery computer systems are also under development and in production.

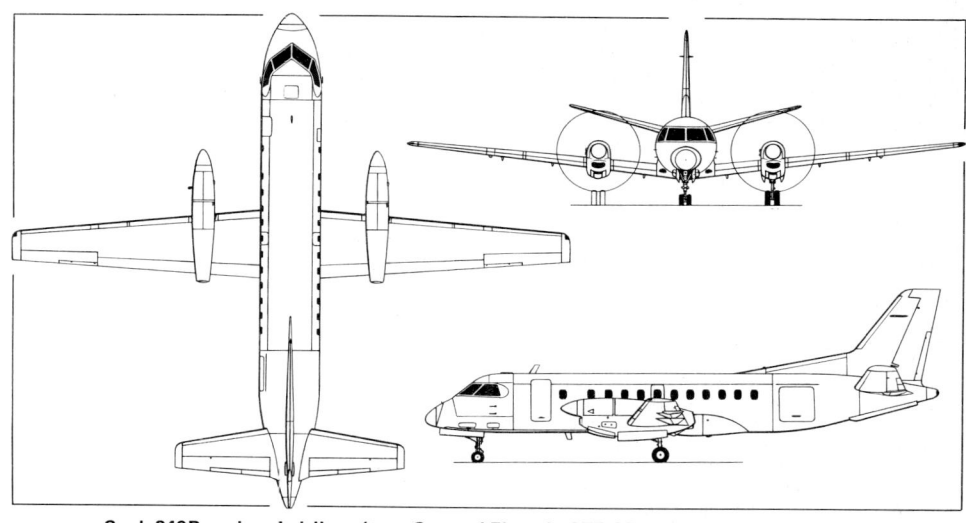

Saab 340B regional airliner (two General Electric CT7-9B turboprops) *(Pilot Press)*

SAAB 340B
Swedish Air Force designation: Tp100
First details of the 340, then called Saab-Fairchild 340, were announced in January 1980 and the go-ahead on joint design, development, manufacture and marketing was given in September 1980. Saab took complete control of the programme in November 1985 and Fairchild continued as a subcontractor until 1987, when the designation was changed to Saab 340.

The first prototype (SE-ISF) made the first flight on 25 January 1983. The fourth (first production) **340A** (SE-E04) flew on 5 March 1984. Ten European nations and the USA took part in the joint certification process to FAR/JAR 25, resulting in Swedish certification in May 1984 and virtually simultaneous certification by the other countries in June.

The 340A first went into service, with Crossair, in June 1984 and the first in the USA entered service in August that year. The first corporate 340A was delivered in November 1985. From mid-1985, engine power was increased from 1,215 kW (1,630 shp) to 1,294 kW (1,735 shp) and propeller diameter was increased. Earlier aircraft were retrofitted. An improved cabin with new lining and larger overhead bins, plus improved fittings, was introduced in mid-1988. It was designed and fitted by Metair Aircraft of the UK, meeting the FAA fire-resistance standards that became mandatory in August 1990. Full details of the Saab 340A were given in the 1989-90 *Jane's*.

The **340B** hot and high version was announced in late 1987 and replaced the 340A on the production line from c/n 160. It was certificated on 3 July 1989 and the first aircraft was delivered to Crossair in September 1989. The 340B is powered by General Electric CT7-9B turboprops with automatic power reserve (APR). Tailplane span is extended, operating weights increased and range with maximum payload improved.

By 1 February 1991, firm orders for the 340A and B totalled 354, of which more than half were for US customers and the rest for Europe, Australia, South East Asia and South America. The 200th 340 was handed over on 14 August 1990, and a total of 229 340As and 340Bs had been delivered by 31 March 1991.

TYPE: Twin-turboprop regional transport aircraft.
WINGS: Cantilever low-wing monoplane. Basic wing section NASA MS(1)-0313 with thickness/chord ratios of 16 and 12 per cent at root and tip respectively. Dihedral 7° from roots. Incidence 2° at root. Sweepback 3° 36′ at quarter-chord. Tapered two-spar wings embodying fail-safe principles. Stringers and skins of 2024/7075 aluminium alloy. Wingroot/fuselage fairings of Kevlar sandwich. Hydraulically actuated single-slotted trailing-edge flaps with aluminium alloy spars, honeycomb panels faced with aluminium sheet, and leading/trailing-edges of Kevlar. Ailerons have Kevlar skins and glassfibre leading-edges. Electrically operated geared/trim tab in each aileron. Pneumatic boot de-icing of leading-edges.
FUSELAGE: Conventional fail-safe/safe-life semi-monocoque pressurised metal structure, of circular cross-section. Built in three portions: nose (incl flight deck), passenger compartment, and tail section (incorporating baggage compartment). All doors of aluminium honeycomb. Nosecone of Kevlar; cabin floor of carbonfibre sandwich.
TAIL UNIT: Cantilever structure, with sweptback vertical and non-swept horizontal surfaces, the latter having marked dihedral. Fin integral with fuselage. Construction similar to that of wings, with tailplane and fin of aluminium honeycomb. Rudder and elevators have Kevlar skins and glassfibre leading-edges. Geared/trim tab in each elevator; spring/trim tab in rudder. Pneumatic boot de-icing of fin and tailplane leading-edges.
LANDING GEAR: Retractable tricycle type, of AP Precision Hydraulics design and manufacture, with twin Goodyear wheels and oleo-pneumatic shock absorber on each unit. Hydraulic actuation. All units retract forward, main units into engine nacelles. Mainwheel doors of Kevlar sandwich. Hydraulically steerable nose unit (60° to both left and right), with shimmy damper. Mainwheel tyres size 24 × 7.7-10, pressure 6.89 bars (100 lb/sq in); nosewheel tyres size 18 × 6.0-6, pressure 3.79 bars (55 lb/sq in). Independent Goodyear carbon hydraulic disc brakes on main units, with anti-skid control.
POWER PLANT: Two General Electric CT7-9B turboprops, each rated at 1,305 kW (1,750 shp) for normal T-O and 1,394 kW (1,870 shp) with automatic power reserve. Dowty (Hamilton Standard optional) four-blade slow-turning constant-speed propellers, with full auto-feathering and reverse pitch capability, each with glass-fibre/polyurethane foam/carbonfibre moulded blades. Fuel in integral tank in each outer wing; total capacity 3,220 litres (850.5 US gallons; 708 Imp gallons). Single-point pressure refuelling inlet in starboard outer wing panel. Overwing gravity refuelling point in each wing.

Saab 340B regional transport in the livery of KLM Cityhopper of the Netherlands

ACCOMMODATION: Two pilots and provision for observer on flight deck; attendant's seat (forward, port) in passenger cabin. Main cabin accommodates up to 37 passengers, in 12 rows of three, with aisle, and rearward facing seat(s) on starboard side at front. One or both rearward facing seats can be replaced by an optional galley module and/or baggage/wardrobe module. Seat pitch 76 cm (30 in). Standard provision for galley, wardrobe or storage module on port side at front of cabin, regardless of installations on starboard side. Toilet at front or rear of cabin. In former case, QC operation (conversion from passenger to freight interior or vice versa) is possible. Also available is a VIP-to-airliner convertible, as well as a fixed-installation combi with 19 passengers and 1,500 kg (3,307 lb) of cargo. Passenger door (plug type) at front of cabin on port side, with separate airstair. Type II emergency exit opposite this on starboard side, and Type III over wing on each side. Overhead crew escape hatch in flight deck roof. Baggage space under each passenger seat; overhead storage bins. Main baggage/cargo compartment aft of passenger cabin, with large plug type door on port side. Entire accommodation pressurised, including baggage compartment.

SYSTEMS: Hamilton Standard environmental control system (max pressure differential 0.48 bar; 7.0 lb/sq in) maintains a S/L cabin environment up to an altitude of 3,660 m (12,000 ft) and a 1,525 m (5,000 ft) environment up to the max cruising altitude of 7,620 m (25,000 ft). Single on-demand hydraulic system, operating between 138 and 207 bars (2,000-3,000 lb/sq in), for actuation of landing gear, nosewheel braking, nosewheel steering and wing flaps. System is powered by single 28V DC electric motor driven pump, rated delivery 9.5 litres (2.5 US gallons; 2.1 Imp gallons)/min. Self-pressurising main reservoir with 5.08 litres (0.18 cu ft) capacity, operating at pressure of 1.79-2.69 bars (26-39 lb/sq in). Hydraulic backup via four accumulators and pilot operated handpump, working via an emergency reservoir of 2.5 litres (0.09 cu ft) capacity. Electrical power supplied by two 28V 400A DC engine driven starter/generators, each connected to a separate busbar. Variable frequency 115/200V for heating circuits provided by two 26kVA AC generators; single-phase 115V and 26V AC at 400Hz for avionics provided by static inverters. Two 40Ah nickel-cadmium batteries for ground power and engine starting; standby 5Ah lead-acid battery for emergency use. External power receptacle. Pneumatic boot de-icing of wing and tail unit leading-edges, using engine bleed air. Flight deck windows have electric anti-icing and electrically driven windscreen wipers. Electric anti-icing is provided also for engine air intakes, propellers and pitot heads. Demisting by means of air-conditioning system. Plug-in connections for oxygen masks. Kidde engine fire detection system. Duncan/Garrett GTCP 36-150W APU kit certificated for installation as optional extra, to provide standby and emergency electrical power, main engine starting assistance, ground pre-heating and pre-cooling, and other power support functions.

AVIONICS: Standard avionics include all equipment required for FAR 121 operations. Aircraft is equipped with Bendix/King Gold Crown III or Collins Pro Line II com/nav radios, and a Collins integrated digital flight guidance and autopilot system (FGAS) consisting of attitude and heading reference units, electronic (CRT) flight display units, fail-passive autopilot/flight director system, colour weather radar, air data system with servo instruments, and radio altimeter. Lucas Aerospace electroluminescent flight deck instrument panel array. Dowty Aerospace microprocessor-based flight deck central warning system. Rosemount pitot static tubes, total temperature sensors and stall warning system. Provision for additional avionics to customer's requirements.

DIMENSIONS, EXTERNAL:

Wing span	21.44 m (70 ft 4 in)
Wing aspect ratio	11.0
Length overall	19.73 m (64 ft 8¾ in)
Fuselage: Max diameter	2.31 m (7 ft 7 in)
Height overall	6.91 m (22 ft 8 in)
Tailplane span	9.25 m (30 ft 4¼ in)
Wheel track	6.71 m (22 ft 0 in)
Wheelbase	7.14 m (23 ft 5 in)
Propeller diameter	3.35 m (11 ft 0 in)
Propeller ground clearance	0.51 m (1 ft 8 in)
Passenger door: Height	1.60 m (5 ft 3 in)
Width	0.69 m (2 ft 3¼ in)
Height to sill	1.63 m (5 ft 4 in)
Cargo door: Height	1.30 m (4 ft 3 in)
Width	1.35 m (4 ft 5 in)
Height to sill	1.68 m (5 ft 6 in)
Emergency exit (fwd, stbd): Height	1.32 m (4 ft 4 in)
Width	0.51 m (1 ft 8 in)
Emergency exits (overwing, each):	
Height	0.91 m (3 ft 0 in)
Width	0.51 m (1 ft 8 in)

DIMENSIONS, INTERNAL:
Cabin, excl flight deck, incl toilet and galley:

Length	10.39 m (34 ft 1 in)
Max width	2.16 m (7 ft 1 in)
Width at floor	1.70 m (5 ft 7 in)
Max height	1.83 m (6 ft 0 in)
Volume	33.4 m³ (1,179.5 cu ft)
Baggage/cargo compartment volume	
	6.8 m³ (240.0 cu ft)

AREAS:

Wings, gross	41.81 m² (450.0 sq ft)
Ailerons (total)	2.12 m² (22.84 sq ft)
Trailing-edge flaps (total)	8.07 m² (86.84 sq ft)
Fin (incl dorsal fin)	10.53 m² (113.38 sq ft)
Rudder (incl tab)	2.76 m² (29.71 sq ft)
Tailplane	14.57 m² (156.83 sq ft)
Elevators (total, incl tabs)	3.29 m² (35.40 sq ft)

WEIGHTS AND LOADINGS:

Typical operating weight empty	8,035 kg (17,715 lb)
Max payload (weight limited)	3,758 kg (8,285 lb)
Max fuel load	2,581 kg (5,690 lb)
Max ramp weight	13,063 kg (28,800 lb)
Max T-O weight	12,927 kg (28,500 lb)
Max landing weight	12,700 kg (28,000 lb)
Max zero-fuel weight	11,793 kg (26,000 lb)
Max wing loading	309.1 kg/m² (63.33 lb/sq ft)
Max power loading	4.64 kg/kW (7.62 lb/shp)

PERFORMANCE (at MTOW, ISA, except where indicated):

Max operating speed (V_{MO})	
	250 knots (463 km/h; 288 mph)
Max operating Mach No. (M_{MO})	0.5
Max cruising speed:	
at 4,575 m (15,000 ft)	282 knots (522 km/h; 325 mph)
at 6,100 m (20,000 ft)	280 knots (519 km/h; 322 mph)
Best range cruising speed at 7,620 m (25,000 ft)	
	252 knots (467 km/h; 290 mph)
Stalling speed: flaps up	106 knots (197 km/h; 123 mph)
T-O flap	95 knots (176 km/h; 110 mph)
approach flap	92 knots (171 km/h; 106 mph)
landing flap	88 knots (164 km/h; 102 mph)
Max rate of climb at S/L	625 m (2,050 ft)/min
Rate of climb at S/L, one engine out	160 m (525 ft)/min
Service ceiling: standard	7,620 m (25,000 ft)
optional	9,450 m (31,000 ft)
Service ceiling, one engine out (net)	3,445 m (11,300 ft)
FAR Pt 25 required T-O field length:	
at S/L	1,271 m (4,170 ft)
at S/L, ISA +15°C	1,364 m (4,475 ft)
at 1,525 m (5,000 ft)	1,585 m (5,200 ft)
at 1,525 m (5,000 ft), ISA +15°C	2,088 m (6,850 ft)

FAR Pt 25 required landing field length (at MLW):	
at S/L	1,049 m (3,440 ft)
at 1,525 m (5,000 ft)	1,183 m (3,880 ft)
Min ground turning radius	15.85 m (52 ft 0 in)
Runway LCN: flexible pavement	8
rigid pavement	10
Range with 35 passengers and baggage, reserves for 45 min hold at 1,525 m (5,000 ft) and 100 nm (185 km; 115 mile) diversion:	
at max cruising speed	820 nm (1,520 km; 945 miles)
at long-range cruising speed	
	975 nm (1,807 km; 1,123 miles)
Range with 30 passengers, reserves as above:	
at max cruising speed	
	1,095 nm (2,030 km; 1,261 miles)
at long-range cruising speed	
	1,310 nm (2,427 km; 1,509 miles)

OPERATIONAL NOISE LEVELS (FAR Pt 36, Appendix C):

T-O (with cutback)	77.8 EPNdB
Sideline	86.5 EPNdB
Approach	91.8 EPNdB

SAAB 2000

This programme was launched on 15 December 1988 with the simultaneous order for 25, plus options for 25, from Crossair. The first metal was cut in February 1990 and rollout was scheduled for November 1991; first flight is planned for Spring 1992, with deliveries following in the second half of 1993. By March 1991, the Crossair order had been followed by Salair (five plus five), Northwest Airlink (Express Airlines) (10), AMR Eagle (options for 50), Business Express (options for 10), Brit Air (options for four), Comair (options for 20), Skywest (options for 20), Hazelton Airlines (options for two), plus four orders and four options undisclosed. Orders (46) and options totalled 192 by 1 April 1991.

The 2000 retains the fuselage cross-section and many of the systems of the 340, but has a capacity for up to 58 passengers. For the 2000, the 340 wing is scaled up with 15 per cent more span and 33 per cent more area, but the same advanced aerofoil. The engine nacelles are located farther away from the fuselage. Saab is aiming at a cruising speed of 360 knots (667 km/h; 414 mph) and announced a memorandum of understanding with General Motors in July 1989 to adopt the Allison GMA 2100A turboprop based on the T406 turboshaft in the Bell/Boeing V-22 Osprey. Maximum output is 3,393 kW (4,550 shp) to FAR Pt 33 and JAR, but it will be flat rated to 2,722 kW (3,650 shp) for take-off.

It is intended that the 2000 should be able to climb to 6,100 m (20,000 ft) in 10 minutes and cruise at altitudes between 5,485 m and 9,450 m (18,000 ft and 31,000 ft), equalling jet speeds over short to medium-length stages, but retaining turboprop block fuel consumption. Economic range will be between 100 nm (185 km; 115 miles) and 1,000 nm (1,850 km; 1,150 miles) and cabin noise level will be 10 dB below that of the 340.

In late 1989, the Swedish government agreed to provide Saab with a loan of between $163 million and $187 million to cover development of the 2000 between 1989 and 1994, to be repaid by royalties from the 31st aircraft onwards until the year 2009. Saab has agreed to retain a high proportion of Saab 2000 work in Sweden. Flight testing will be from Skavsta airport, near Nyköping, in order to avoid conflict with the delayed development of the JAS 39 Gripen.

A number of major risk-sharing subcontractors have been recruited in addition to Allison. It was announced in November 1989 that Dowty is to supply to Allison a slow turning, high performance propeller with six swept blades. It includes a hydraulic control, hydraulic pump with mechanical overspeed protection, de-icing and an electric feathering pump. Propeller control is electric and integrated with the full authority digital engine control (FADEC) to allow single lever engine control. Dowty and Allison are already collaborating on a propeller for another T406 power plant.

In October 1989, CASA took on the design, stressing, testing and manufacture of the entire wing including movable surfaces and part of the engine nacelles. It will also equip, install and test the main undercarriage. The first wing was to be delivered to Linköping in late 1991. Wing geometry and basic structure were defined by Saab. The contract is worth $500,000, half of it funded by the Andalusian government in whose region much of the work will be concentrated.

Also in October 1989, Valmet signed to produce the fin, rudder, tailplane and elevators of the 2000 and take part in development. The production work will be done by its Flygplansfabriken division, with Advanced Composites Oy (ADCO) as a subcontractor for metal bonding. Flygplansfabriken will invest $8.4 million and ADCO $5.3 million. Total value of the agreement is $69.8 million. In January 1990, Westland received an order worth £40 million to produce the rear fuselage section of the 2000, delivering the first in March 1991. Hamilton Standard is to provide the environmental control system, incorporating the Recircair technique to economise on engine bleed. Sundstrand will provide the APU. Saab selected the Collins Pro Line 4 integrated avionics systems including autopilot, flight management and avionics maintenance system, all controlled from the integrated avionics processing system. Pro Line 4 also includes Collins com/nav/pulse and radio tuning units, digital air data and attitude heading reference, and solid-state weather radar. Options include TCAS, ACARS (the actual flight management system), and turbulence weather radar. Electronic flight instruments include the primary flight display and navigation display and engine indication and crew alerting system with checklist mode.

The following data were current in January 1991:

POWER PLANT: Two Allison GMA 2100A turboprops, each flat rated at 2,722 kW (3,650 shp). Dowty six-blade, slow turning, constant-speed propellers with full autofeathering and reverse pitch. Fuel in integral tank in each outer wing; total capacity 5,185 litres (1,370 US gallons; 1,140 Imp gallons). Single point pressure refuelling inlet in starboard outer wing panel. Overwing gravity refuelling point in each wing.

ACCOMMODATION: Flight crew of three or four, including cabin attendant(s). Standard accommodation for 50 (maximum 58) passengers in three-abreast seating with single aisle. Overhead baggage bins on starboard side. Range of galley options and locations, to customer's requirements. Toilet can be located at either end of cabin. Other passenger service options include wardrobe and stowage areas. Main cargo compartment aft of passenger cabin. Provision for additional, smaller cargo area at front of cabin on starboard side. Entire accommodation pressurised at 0.48 bar (7.0 lb/sq in). Main airstair door at front on port side, with smaller cargo door opposite. Main cargo door at rear on port side, with service door/emergency door on opposite side. Type III emergency exit over wing on each side.

DIMENSIONS, EXTERNAL:

Wing span	24.76 m (81 ft 2¾ in)
Wing aspect ratio	11.0
Length overall	27.03 m (88 ft 8¼ in)
Fuselage: Max diameter	2.31 m (7 ft 7 in)
Height overall	7.73 m (25 ft 4 in)
Wheel track	8.23 m (27 ft 0 in)
Wheelbase	10.97 m (36 ft 0 in)
Propeller diameter	3.81 m (12 ft 6 in)
Passenger door: Height	1.60 m (5 ft 3 in)
Width	0.69 m (2 ft 3 in)
Height to sill	1.63 m (5 ft 4 in)

Artist's impression of the Saab 2000 in the colours of launch customer Crossair

Cargo door (rear compartment, port):	
Height	1.30 m (4 ft 3 in)
Width	1.35 m (4 ft 5 in)
Height to sill	1.68 m (5 ft 6 in)
Stowage compartment door (fwd, stbd):	
Height	1.12 m (3 ft 8 in)
Width	0.51 m (1 ft 8 in)
Emergency exit/Service door (rear, stbd):	
Height	1.22 m (4 ft 0 in)
Width	0.61 m (2 ft 0 in)
Emergency exits (overwing, each):	
Height	0.91 m (3 ft 0 in)
Width	0.51 m (1 ft 8 in)

DIMENSIONS, INTERNAL:

Cabin, excl flight deck, incl toilet and galley:	
Length	16.70 m (54 ft 9½ in)
Max width	2.16 m (7 ft 1 in)
Width at floor	1.70 m (5 ft 7 in)
Max height	1.83 m (6 ft 0 in)
Volume	52.7 m³ (1,860.0 cu ft)
Baggage/cargo compartment:	
Volume	10.2 m³ (360.0 cu ft)

AREAS:

Wings, gross	55.74 m² (600.0 sq ft)

WEIGHTS AND LOADINGS:

Typical operating weight empty	12,700 kg (28,000 lb)
Max payload (weight limited)	5,896 kg (13,000 lb)
Max fuel load	4,155 kg (9,160 lb)
Max ramp weight	21,455 kg (47,300 lb)
Max T-O weight	21,320 kg (47,000 lb)
Max landing weight	20,410 kg (45,000 lb)
Max zero-fuel weight	18,600 kg (41,000 lb)
Max wing loading	382.3 kg/m² (78.33 lb/sq ft)
Max power loading	3.92 kg/kW (6.44 lb/shp)

PERFORMANCE (at max T-O weight ISA, except where indicated):

Max operating speed (V_{MO}):	
below 3,050 m (10,000 ft)	
	250 knots (463 km/h; 288 mph)
above 3,050 m (10,000 ft)	
	270 knots (500 km/h; 311 mph)
Max operating Mach No. (M_{MO})	0.62
Max cruising speed:	
at 7,620 m (25,000 ft)	366 knots (678 km/h; 421 mph)
at 9,450 m (31,000 ft)	353 knots (653 km/h; 406 mph)

Max operating speed (V_{MO}) and Max operating Mach No. (M_{MO})

Best range cruising speed at 9,450 m (31,000 ft)	
	300 knots (556 km/h; 345 mph)
Max rate of climb at S/L	707 m (2,320 ft)/min
Rate of climb at S/L, one engine out	183 m (600 ft)/min
Time to 6,100 m (20,000 ft)	10 min
Service ceiling	9,450 m (31,000 ft)
Service ceiling, one engine out (net)	6,220 m (20,400 ft)
FAR Pt 25 required T-O field length:	
at S/L	1,500 m (4,920 ft)
at S/L, ISA +15°C	1,640 m (5,380 ft)
at 1,525 m (5,000 ft)	1,854 m (6,080 ft)
at 1,525 m (5,000 ft), ISA +15°C	2,004 m (6,575 ft)
FAR Pt 25 required landing field length (at MLW):	
at S/L	1,195 m (3,920 ft)
at 1,525 m (5,000 ft)	1,345 m (4,410 ft)
Min ground turning radius	18.85 m (61 ft 10 in)
Runway LCN (paved runways)	max 15
Range with 50 passengers and baggage, reserves for 45 min hold at 1,525 m (5,000 ft) and 100 nm (185 km; 115 mile) diversion:	
at max cruising speed	
	1,345 nm (2,492 km; 1,550 miles)

SAAB JA 37 VIGGEN (THUNDERBOLT)

The Saab 37 Viggen multi-mission combat aircraft was produced to fulfil the primary roles of attack, interception, reconnaissance and training. In 1990, Viggens equipped eight fighter squadrons, five and a half fighter/attack and three reconnaissance squadrons of the Swedish Air Force. The Swedish Air Force plans to modify 115 Viggens into AJS 37s with a broader range of weapons and additional avionics.

The first of seven prototypes flew for the first time on 8 February 1967; the seventh was the prototype for the two-seat Sk37 operational trainer. First squadron delivery (of AJ 37s to F7) was made in June 1971.

Production deliveries of the AJ 37, SF 37, SH 37 and Sk37 versions totalled 180 (110, 26, 26 and 18). Details of these, and of the Saab 37X proposed export version, can be found in the 1980-81 and earlier editions of *Jane's*. The final version (149 built) was the JA 37 interceptor, the last of which was delivered on 29 June 1990, bringing overall Viggen production to 329.

A detailed description of JA 37 can be found in the 1990-91 *Jane's*. The following is a shortened version:

TYPE: Single-seat all-weather multi-purpose combat aircraft.

POWER PLANT: One Volvo Flygmotor RM8B turbofan, rated at 72.1 kN (16,203 lb st) dry and 125 kN (28,108 lb st) with afterburning. Thrust reverser doors actuated automatically by compression of oleo as nose gear strikes runway. Fuel in one tank in each wing, saddle tank over engine, one tank in each side of fuselage, and one aft of cockpit. Pressure refuelling point beneath starboard wing. Provision for jettisonable external tank on centreline pylon.

ACCOMMODATION: Pilot only, on Saab-Scania fully adjustable rocket assisted zero/zero ejection seat beneath rearward hinged clamshell canopy. Cockpit pressurisation, heating and air-conditioning by engine bleed air. Birdproof windscreen.

AVIONICS: Advanced target search and acquisition system, based on high performance long-range Ericsson PS-46/A pulse Doppler radar resistant to variations of weather, altitude, clutter and ECM. Automatic speed control system, Smiths electronic head-up display, Bofors Aerotronics aircraft attitude instruments, radio and fighter link equipment, Plessey Electronic SKC-2037 central digital computer, Garrett LD-5 digital air data computer, Plessey Electronic KT-70L inertial measuring equipment, Honeywell/Saab-Scania SA07 digital automatic flight control system, Honeywell radar altimeter, Decca Doppler Type 72 navigation equipment, SATT radar warning system, Ericsson radar display system and electronic countermeasures, and AIL Tactical Instrument Landing System (TILS). Most avionics connected to

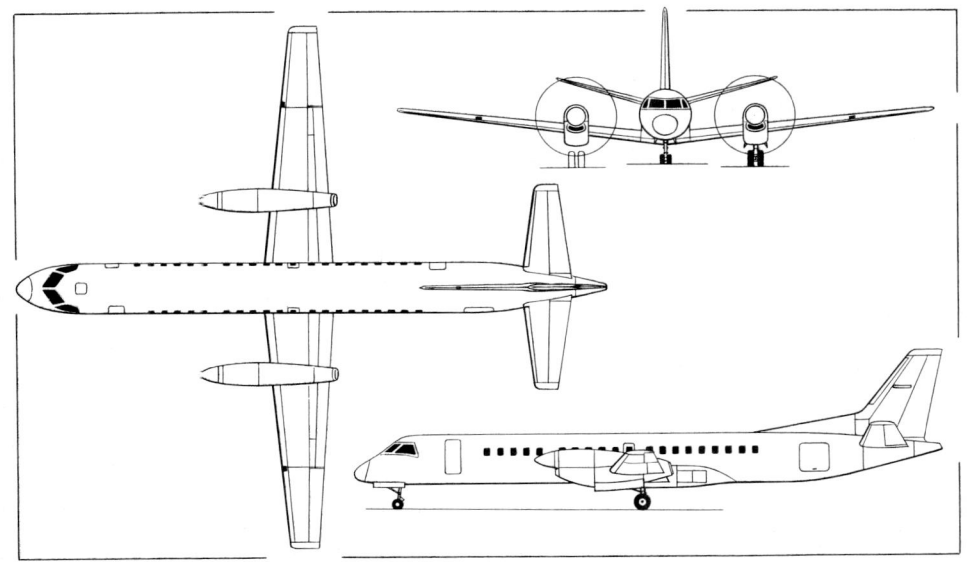

Saab 2000 short/medium-range 50/58-passenger transport *(Pilot Press)*

Saab JA 37 Viggen of the Swedish Air Force's F13 Wing

central digital computer, which is programmed to check out and monitor these systems both on ground and during flight. Ram air cooling for avionics compartment.
ARMAMENT: Permanent underbelly pack, offset to port side of centreline, containing one 30 mm Oerlikon KCA long-range cannon with 150 rounds. Three underfuselage and four underwing hardpoints. Armament can include two BAe Sky Flash (Swedish designation RB71) and six AIM-9L Sidewinder (RB74) air-to-air missiles. For air-to-surface attack, a total of twenty-four 135 mm rockets can be carried in four pods.

DIMENSIONS, EXTERNAL:
Main wing span	10.60 m (34 ft 9¼ in)
Main wing aspect ratio	2.4
Foreplane span	5.45 m (17 ft 10½ in)
Length: overall (incl probe)	16.40 m (53 ft 9¾ in)
fuselage	15.58 m (51 ft 1½ in)
Height: overall	5.90 m (19 ft 4¼ in)
main fin folded	4.00 m (13 ft 1½ in)
Wheel track	4.76 m (15 ft 7½ in)
Wheelbase (c/l of shock absorbers)	5.69 m (18 ft 8 in)

AREAS:
Main wings, gross	46.00 m² (495.1 sq ft)
Foreplanes, outside fuselage	6.20 m² (66.74 sq ft)

WEIGHTS AND LOADINGS (approx):
T-O weight: clean	15,000 kg (33,070 lb)
with normal armament	17,000 kg (37,478 lb)

PERFORMANCE:
Max level speed: at high altitude	above Mach 2
at 100 m (330 ft)	Mach 1.2
Approach speed	approx 119 knots (220 km/h; 137 mph)
Time to 10,000 m (32,800 ft) from brakes off, with afterburning	less than 1 min 40 s
T-O run	approx 400 m (1,310 ft)
Landing run	approx 500 m (1,640 ft)

Required landing field length:
conventional landing	1,000 m (3,280 ft)
no-flare landing	500 m (1,640 ft)

Tactical radius with external armament:
hi-lo-hi	over 540 nm (1,000 km; 620 miles)
lo-lo-lo	over 270 nm (500 km; 310 miles)

Swedish Air Force J 35J Draken of F10 Wing, showing the additional inboard underwing stores stations

SAAB 35 DRAKEN (DRAGON)

Under the revised designation **J 35J** (previously J 35F Mod or J 35F-Ny: new), 66 J 35F Draken fighters of F10 Wing of the Swedish Air Force, based near Ängelholm in southern Sweden, have been updated to extend their service life until the end of the 1990s, when they will be replaced by the JAS 39 Gripen. Saab Aircraft Division was responsible for modification and redelivery, with FFV Aerotech as subcontractor.

Two additional inboard underwing pylons are fitted, allowing four drop tanks and two air-to-air missiles, or four missiles (two RB24 Sidewinders and two RB27 Falcons) and two 550 litre (145.3 US gallon; 121 Imp gallon) tanks. Operation of the automatic gun and weapons electronics are changed, radar and IFF improved, infra-red missile target seeker upgraded, altitude warning system added, and instruments improved. F10 Wing will be the only unit operating this version of the Draken. Redeliveries were completed in 1991.

The J 35D and F were last described fully in the 1969-70 *Jane's*.

SAAB 105

Saab was completing a life extension programme on 142 Saab 105 trainer/light attack aircraft (Swedish Air Force Sk60) in early 1991. A development of the Saab 105 is also entered, as the **Saab 2060**, in the competition for the US Joint Primary Aircraft Training System (JPATS), for which a new engine, new escape system and new avionics would be fitted. No US partner had been announced at the time of going to press.

SWITZERLAND

DÄTWYLER

MDC MAX DÄTWYLER AG

Flugplatz, CH-3368 Bleienbach-Langenthal
Telephone: 41 (63) 28 31 11
Fax: 41 (63) 23 24 29
Telex: 982626 MDC CH
PRESIDENT: Max Dätwyler

Dätwyler has specialised for many years in the repair and modification of light aircraft. It has also manufactured components for the Pilatus Porter and Turbo-Porter and the B4-PC11 sailplane. Its latest design is the MD3 Swiss Trainer.

DÄTWYLER MD3 SWISS TRAINER

Dätwyler announced preliminary details of the Swiss Trainer in the late 1960s, and a description appeared in the 1974-75 *Jane's*. Since then considerable effort has been made to make the design genuinely modular, to facilitate manufacture by possible licensees in countries without a developed aircraft industry. In particular the pairs of ailerons, the flaps and the elevators and rudder are interchangeable with each other, as are the tailplane halves and fin, fin and tailplane tips, wing leading-edge sections (four per aircraft) and the central inner and outer portions of the wings.

The MD3-160 prototype (HB-HOH) made its first flight, with Mr Dätwyler at the controls, on 12 August 1983. The second prototype (HB-HOJ) was completed in 1990 and received Swiss FOCA certification to FAR Pt 23 on 8 April 1991.

Two versions of the Swiss Trainer are planned, as follows:
MD3-115: Two-seat primary training version, powered by an 82 kW (110 hp) Textron Lycoming O-235-N2A flat-four engine. Not yet flown.

Second prototype of the Dätwyler MD3-160 Swiss Trainer (*Roland Eichenberger*)

MD3-160: With more powerful Textron Lycoming O-320-D2A engine; particularly suitable for aerobatics and glider towing. Prototypes are of this version.

The following description applies to the MD3-160:
TYPE: Two-seat primary training aircraft.
WINGS: Cantilever mid-wing monoplane. Wing section NACA 64₂15414 (modified). Thickness/chord ratio 14 per cent. Dihedral 5° 30′. Incidence 2°. No sweepback. All-metal structure, with single main spar, each wing consisting of five modules of which the largest measures 3.45 × 0.67 × 0.21 m (136 × 26.4 × 8.3 in).

All-metal electrically operated two-segment flaps, and single-slotted mass balanced ailerons. Flap, aileron, rudder and elevator segments identical.
FUSELAGE: Mainly metal semi-monocoque structure, with glassfibre fairings and cowling. Tailboom detachable from fuselage aft of wing.
TAIL UNIT: Sweptback horizontal and vertical surfaces of all-metal two-spar construction, assembled from three equal modules. Dorsal fin. Mass balanced rudder and elevators, identical with aileron and flap modules. Trim tab in elevator.

LANDING GEAR: Non-retractable tricycle type with steerable nosewheel. Main-gear legs are cantilever steel struts, descending at 45° from fuselage main bulkhead. Nose gear fitted with oleo-pneumatic shock absorber. Cleveland 6.00-6 mainwheels and 5.00-5 nosewheel. Tyre pressure 2.41 bars (35 lb/sq in) on all units. Independent hydraulically operated Cleveland disc brake on each mainwheel. Speed fairings on all three wheels.

POWER PLANT: One 119 kW (160 hp) Textron Lycoming O-320-D2A flat-four engine, driving a Hoffmann HO-o23A-182-135 two-blade fixed-pitch wooden propeller. Exhaust system is extended full length under fuselage to extreme rear of tailcone exhaust gases being emitted through a narrow slot running along the pipe. (Aircraft meets noise requirements with short or long exhaust.) Integral fuel tank in each wing: total capacity 148 litres (39 US gallons; 32.6 Imp gallons). Refuelling point in top of each tank. Oil capacity 7.6 litres (2 US gallons; 1.7 Imp gallons).

ACCOMMODATION: Side by side adjustable seats for pilot and one passenger. Five-point fixed seat belts. Forward sliding canopy. Space behind seats for 50 kg (110 lb) of baggage. Dual controls, cabin ventilation and heating standard.

SYSTEMS: Hydraulic system for brakes only. 28V 60A engine driven alternator and 24V 30Ah battery provide electrical power for engine starting, lighting, instruments and com/nav equipment.

AVIONICS: Provision for VHF radio, VOR, ADF, transponder or other items at customer's option.

EQUIPMENT: Equipment for glider towing optional.

DIMENSIONS, EXTERNAL:
Wing span	10.00 m (32 ft 9¾ in)
Wing chord, constant	1.50 m (4 ft 11 in)
Wing aspect ratio	6.67
Length overall	7.10 m (23 ft 3½ in)
Height overall	2.92 m (9 ft 7 in)
Tailplane span	3.00 m (9 ft 10 in)
Wheel track	2.05 m (6 ft 8¾ in)
Wheelbase	1.56 m (5 ft 1½ in)
Propeller diameter	1.88 m (6 ft 2 in)

DIMENSIONS, INTERNAL:
Cabin, from firewall to rear bulkhead:
Length	1.30 m (4 ft 3¼ in)
Max width	1.12 m (3 ft 8 in)
Max height	1.08 m (3 ft 6½ in)

AREAS:
Wings, gross	15.00 m² (161.5 sq ft)
Ailerons (total)	1.13 m² (12.16 sq ft)
Trailing-edge flaps (total)	1.96 m² (21.10 sq ft)
Vertical tail surfaces (total)	1.40 m² (15.07 sq ft)
Rudder	0.51 m² (5.49 sq ft)
Horizontal tail surfaces (total)	2.75 m² (29.60 sq ft)
Elevators (total)	1.04 m² (11.19 sq ft)

WEIGHTS AND LOADINGS (A: Aerobatic, U: Utility):
Weight empty	633 kg (1,395 lb)
Max T-O and landing weight: A	840 kg (1,852 lb)
U	920 kg (2,028 lb)
Max wing loading: A	56.0 kg/m² (11.47 lb/sq ft)
U	61.3 kg/m² (12.56 lb/sq ft)

Max power loading: A		7.06 kg/kW (11.58 lb/hp)
U		7.73 kg/kW (12.68 lb/hp)

PERFORMANCE (A: Aerobatic at 840 kg; 1,852 lb AUW, B: Utility category at 920 kg; 2,028 lb):
Never-exceed speed (VNE):		
A		179 knots (331 km/h; 206 mph)
B		161 knots (298 km/h; 185 mph)
Max structural cruising speed:		
A		141 knots (261 km/h; 162 mph)
B		126 knots (233 km/h; 145 mph)
Max cruising speed (75% power) at 1,525 m (5,000 ft):		
A, B		130 knots (241 km/h; 149 mph)
Econ cruising speed (66% power) at 1,525 m (5,000 ft):		
A, B		124 knots (230 km/h; 143 mph)
Max normal manoeuvring speed:		
A		124 knots (230 km/h; 143 mph)
B		112 knots (207 km/h; 129 mph)
Max speed for flap extension:		
A		91 knots (168 km/h; 105 mph)
B		87 knots (161 km/h; 100 mph)
Stalling speed, engine idling:		
flaps up		56 knots (104 km/h; 65 mph)
flaps down		46 knots (85 km/h; 53 mph)
Max rate of climb at S/L		420 m (1,378 ft)/min
Max rate of climb (75% power) towing 365 kg (805 lb)		
sailplane		104 m (341 ft)/min
T-O run		108 m (354 ft)
Landing run		130 m (426 ft)
Range with max fuel, no reserves		
		588 nm (1,090 km; 677 miles)

FFA

FFA FLUGZEUGWERKE ALTENRHEIN AG

CH-9423 Altenrhein
Telephone: 41 (71) 43 51 11
Fax: 41 (71) 43 53 30
Telex: 88 29 06 FFA CH
PRESIDENT: Charles Brönimann
CHIEF ENGINEER: Hansjörg Candrian
DIRECTOR OF SALES AND MARKETING: Alex Quaite

This company had its origin in AG für Dornier Flugzeuge, the Swiss branch of the German Dornier company. In 1948 it became an entirely Swiss company named FFA (Flug-und Fahrzeugwerke AG). In January 1987 the complete aviation activity was sold to the Justus Dornier group in Zurich, and the present company name took effect on 1 June 1987.

Current activities, besides production of the AS 202 Bravo, consist of subcontracting for various aircraft manufacturers throughout the world, and licence production of components for Swiss built Northrop F-5E/F Tiger IIs. Overhaul, servicing and maintenance for the Swiss Air Force and for general aviation are also done at Altenrhein. FFA has 300 employees, approximately two-thirds of whom are engaged in aviation activities. Details of the FFA-2000 Eurotrainer are given under the FFT heading in the German section.

FFA AS 202/18A BRAVO

Following an agreement concluded with SIAI-Marchetti of Italy, FFA undertook production of the AS 202 Bravo light trainer and sporting aircraft.

The Swiss assembled AS 202/15 prototype (HB-HEA) flew for the first time on 7 March 1969. The Italian built second prototype flew on 7 May 1969. The third aircraft (HB-HEC) made its first flight on 16 June 1969, and the first production aircraft on 22 December 1971. The AS 202/15 (34 built: 1981-82 *Jane's*) and AS 202/26A (prototype only: 1985-86 and earlier editions) are no longer available.

The following version remained available in 1991:

AS 202/18A: Two/three-seat aerobatic version. First flew (HB-HEY) on 22 August 1974. Swiss certification granted on 12 December 1975; FAA certification awarded on 17 December 1976. Deliveries totalled 180 by early 1990, in Switzerland and to foreign customers as listed in the 1987-88 and earlier *Jane's*. A second pair of Bravos (A4s) was delivered to Oman during 1989. No further orders or deliveries have occurred since then.

Variants of the 18A include the A2 (higher max T-O/landing weight, extended canopy, electric trim), A3 (as A2 but with mechanical trim and 24V electrical system) and A4 (as A2 but with CAA approved special instrumentation). The 11 AS 202/18A4s for the BAe Flying College are known by the name **Wren**.

A Bravo was demonstrated to the US Air Force in July 1990 as part of that service's evaluation of candidates to meet its EFS (enhanced flight screener) requirement.

The following description applies to the AS 202/18A:

TYPE: Two/three-seat light aircraft.

WINGS: Cantilever low-wing monoplane. Wing section NACA 63_2618 (modified) at centreline, 63_2415 at tip. Thickness/chord ratio 17.63 per cent at root, 15 per cent at tip. Dihedral 5° 43' from roots. Incidence 3°. Sweepback at quarter-chord 0° 40'. Conventional aluminium single-spar fail-safe structure, with riveted

One of the final two FFA AS 202/18A4s delivered to Oman

honeycomb laminate skin. Aluminium single-slotted flaps and single-slotted ailerons. Ground adjustable tab on each aileron.

FUSELAGE: Conventional aluminium semi-monocoque fail-safe structure, with engine cowling and several fairings of glassfibre.

TAIL UNIT: Cantilever aluminium single-spar structure with sweptback vertical surfaces. Rudder mass balanced, with provision for anti-collision beacon. Fixed incidence tailplane. Two-piece elevator with full span electrically actuated trim tab on starboard side. Electrically actuated tab in rudder of current 202/18A4.

LANDING GEAR: Non-retractable tricycle type, with steerable nosewheel. Rubber cushioned shock absorber struts of SIAI-Marchetti design. Mainwheel tyres size 6.00-6; nosewheel tyre size 5.00-5. Tyre pressure (all units) 2.41 bars (35 lb/sq in). Independent hydraulically operated disc brake on each mainwheel.

POWER PLANT: One 134 kW (180 hp) Textron Lycoming AEIO-360-B1F flat-four engine, driving a Hartzell HC-C2YK-1BF/F7666A-2 two-blade constant-speed propeller. Hoffmann three-blade propeller optional. Two wing leading-edge rubber fuel tanks with total capacity of 170 litres (44.9 US gallons; 37.4 Imp gallons). Refuelling point above each wing. Starboard tank has additional flexible fuel intake for aerobatics. Christen 801 fully aerobatic oil system, capacity 7.6 litres (2 US gallons; 1.6 Imp gallons).

ACCOMMODATION: Seats for two persons side by side in Aerobatic versions, under rearward sliding jettisonable transparent canopy. Space at rear in Utility versions for a third seat or 100 kg (220 lb) of baggage. Dual controls, cabin ventilation and heating standard.

SYSTEMS: Hydraulic system for brake actuation. One 12V 60A engine driven alternator (24V in A3) and one 25Ah battery provide electrical power for engine starting, lighting, instruments, communications and navigation installations. 28V electrical system optional.

AVIONICS: Provision for VHF radio, VOR, ADF, Nav-O-Matic 200A autopilot, blind-flying instrumentation or other special equipment at customer's option.

EQUIPMENT: Clutch and release mechanism for glider towing optional.

DIMENSIONS, EXTERNAL:
Wing span	9.75 m (31 ft 11¾ in)
Wing chord: at root	1.88 m (6 ft 2 in)
at tip	1.16 m (3 ft 9½ in)
Wing aspect ratio	6.5
Length: overall	7.50 m (24 ft 7¼ in)
fuselage	7.15 m (23 ft 5½ in)
Height overall	2.81 m (9 ft 2¾ in)
Tailplane span	3.67 m (12 ft 0½ in)
Wheel track	2.25 m (7 ft 4½ in)
Wheelbase	1.78 m (5 ft 10 in)
Propeller diameter	1.88 m (6 ft 2 in)
Propeller ground clearance	0.31 m (1 ft 0¼ in)

DIMENSIONS, INTERNAL:
Cabin: Max length	2.15 m (7 ft 0½ in)
Max width	1.00 m (3 ft 4 in)
Max height	1.10 m (3 ft 7¼ in)
Floor area	2.15 m² (23.14 sq ft)

AREAS:
Wings, gross	13.86 m² (149.2 sq ft)
Ailerons (total)	1.09 m² (11.7 sq ft)
Trailing-edge flaps (total)	1.49 m² (16.04 sq ft)
Fin	0.45 m² (4.84 sq ft)
Rudder, incl tab	0.94 m² (10.12 sq ft)
Tailplane	1.88 m² (20.24 sq ft)
Elevators, incl tab	0.76 m² (8.18 sq ft)

WEIGHTS AND LOADINGS:
Weight empty, equipped	710 kg (1,565 lb)
Max useful load (incl fuel): Aerobatic	177 kg (390 lb)
Utility	248 kg (546 lb)
Max T-O and landing weight:	
Aerobatic: A/A1	950 kg (2,094 lb)
A2/A3	980 kg (2,160 lb)
A4	1,010 kg (2,226 lb)
Utility: current 18A models	1,080 kg (2,380 lb)
Max wing loading: Utility	75.8 kg/m² (15.52 lb/sq ft)
Max power loading: Utility	7.84 kg/kW (12.86 lb/hp)

PERFORMANCE (Utility category at max T-O weight):
Never-exceed speed (VNE):	
	173 knots (320 km/h; 199 mph)
Max level speed at S/L	
	130 knots (241 km/h; 150 mph)
Max cruising speed (75% power) at 2,440 m (8,000 ft)	
	122 knots (226 km/h; 141 mph)
Econ cruising speed (55% power) at 3,050 m (10,000 ft)	
	109 knots (203 km/h; 126 mph)

Stalling speed, engine idling:		T-O run at S/L	215 m (705 ft)	Range with max fuel, no reserves	
flaps up	62 knots (115 km/h; 71 mph)	T-O to 15 m (50 ft) at S/L	415 m (1,360 ft)		615 nm (1,140 km; 707 miles)
flaps down	49 knots (90 km/h; 56 mph)	Landing from 15 m (50 ft)	465 m (1,525 ft)	Max endurance	5 h 30 min
Max rate of climb at S/L	244 m (800 ft)/min	Landing run	210 m (690 ft)	g limits	+6/−3
Service ceiling	5,180 m (17,000 ft)				

GEPARD

GEPARD SENSOR TECHNOLOGIES SYSTEMS AG

Ludretikonerstrasse 44, CH-8800 Thalwil
Telephone: 41 (1) 721 1112
Fax: 41 (1) 720 3429
PRESIDENT: Andreas Reinhard
PROJECT MANAGER: Jürg Sommerauer

GEPARD S 10 gsm

Using the Stemme S 10 high performance motor glider (see German part of Sailplanes section) as the platform aircraft, this company has designed and developed the S 10 gsm (Gepard special mission) system enabling the aircraft to carry one or two interchangeable underwing pods which equip it for a wide variety of aerial sensor missions for both civil and military use. Virtual absence of platform vibration renders a complex stabilisation system unnecessary for most sensors. The S 10 has low thermal and radar signatures, and is given a state of the art (EFIS or FMS) instrument panel for the pilot, the right hand seat panel having a video monitor, observation equipment and associated avionics. An efficient data monitoring and recording system is installed for image, data and voice handling. The S 10 gsm is qualified for aerial reconnaissance, search and rescue, surveillance, and atmospheric or environmental research.

Types of underwing pod available include TV (high resolution CCD camera and Betacam SP); FLIR (high resolution IR scanner and Betacam SP); chemo (with air pollution monitoring equipment); radar (Doppler, low light camera and Betacam SP); photographic (various remotely controlled cameras); SAR (parachuting container); real-time (data transmission equipment); Nightsun (double-axis tracking searchlight and generator); meteorological (various atmospheric research sensors and DAT recorder); cargo; ferry (fuel tank); and an emergency engine pod with an 18.6 kW (25 hp) three-cylinder two-stroke autonomous power unit, three-blade folding propeller and other equipment.

The prototype S 10 gsm (D-KARD) was first displayed, with a FLIR pod and emergency engine pod attached, at the 1989 Paris Air Show. In January 1990 it made its first flight with two pods attached, at a T-O weight of 950 kg (2,094 lb).

S 10 motor glider with alternative Gepard pods for emergency engine (on wing pylon), photography (foreground) and cargo

It is currently certificated under JAR 22; special certification under JAR 22 and FAR AC 21.23-1 is under consideration for later.

DIMENSIONS, EXTERNAL: As for Stemme S 10, plus:

Pod: Length	2.26 m (7 ft 5 in)
Max diameter	0.345 m (1 ft 1½ in)

WEIGHTS AND LOADINGS:

Weight empty, no sensors	approx 640 kg (1,411 lb)
Cargo pod, empty	7 kg (15.4 lb)
Payload, each pod	60 kg (132 lb)
Max T-O weight: JAR 22	850 kg (1,874 lb)
JAR 22 & FAR AC 21.23-1:	
initially	908 kg (2,002 lb)
intended	980 kg (2,160 lb)

Wing loading at 850 kg (1,874 lb) AUW
45.36 kg/m² (9.29 lb/sq ft)
Power loading at 850 kg (1,874 lb) AUW
12.13 kg/kW (19.92 lb/hp)
PERFORMANCE (unpowered): As for Stemme S 10
PERFORMANCE (powered): As for Stemme S 10, except:
Range with 120 litres (31.7 US gallons; 26.4 Imp gallons) of internal fuel
933 nm (1,730 km; 1,075 miles)
Range with two ferry pods (280 litres; 74 US gallons; 61.6 Imp gallons fuel)
2,158 nm (4,000 km; 2,485 miles)

PILATUS

PILATUS FLUGZEUGWERKE AG

CH-6370 Stans
Telephone: 41 (41) 63 61 11
Fax: 41 (41) 613351
Telex: 866202 PIL CH
CHAIRMAN AND GENERAL MANAGER: W. Gubler
DIRECTOR OF PROGRAMMES: D. C. Klöckner
DIRECTOR OF PRODUCTION: W. Zbinden

Pilatus Flugzeugwerke AG was formed in December 1939; details of its early history can be found in previous editions of *Jane's*. It is part of the Oerlikon-Bührle Group. Current products are the PC-6 Turbo-Porter, the PC-7 Turbo-Trainer and PC-9. The PC-12 first flew on 31 May 1991.

On 24 January 1979 Pilatus purchased the assets of Britten-Norman (Bembridge) Ltd of the UK, which has operated since then under the name Pilatus Britten-Norman Ltd (which see) as a subsidiary of Pilatus Aircraft Ltd.

Pilatus PC-6 Turbo-Porter delivered to the Dubai Air Force

PILATUS PC-6 TURBO-PORTER
US Army designation: UV-20A Chiricahua

The PC-6 is a single-engined multi-purpose utility aircraft, with STOL characteristics permitting operation from unprepared strips under harsh environmental and terrain conditions. It can be converted rapidly from a freighter to a passenger transport, and adapted for a great number of missions, including supply dropping, search and rescue, ambulance, aerial survey and photography, parachuting, cropspraying, water bombing, rainmaking and glider or target towing. The PC-6 can operate from soft ground, snow, glacier or water.

The first piston engined prototype made its first flight on 4 May 1959, and details of piston engined production models can be found in contemporary editions of *Jane's*. The early PC-6/A, A1, A2, B, B1, B2 and C2-H2 Turbo-Porters, with various turboprop power plants, were last described in the 1974-75 edition, and the B2-H2 in editions up to and including 1986-87. The B1 and B2 can be fitted with an air inlet filter for operation in desert conditions and for agricultural applications.

Current version since 1985 is the **PC-6/B2-H4**, in which for CAR.3 operations (commercial operations with fare paying passengers) the maximum take-off weight is increased by 600 kg (1,323 lb), resulting in a payload increase of up to 570 kg (1,257 lb) compared with previous models. This was achieved by improving the aerodynamic efficiency of the wings with new tip fairings, enlarging the dorsal fin, installing uprated mainwheel shock absorbers and a new tailwheel assembly, and a slight strengthening of the airframe. While the H4 modification can be retrofitted to all existing PC-6/B2-H2 models equipped with electrically operated longitudinal trim, all new-production Porters since mid-1985 have been of the H4 version.

About 480 PC-6 aircraft, of all models, have been delivered (including US licence manufacture), and are operating in more than 50 countries. Military operators include the air forces of Angola, Argentina, Australia, Austria, Bolivia, Chad, Dubai, Ecuador, Iran, Myanmar, Oman, Peru, Sudan, Switzerland and Thailand, and the US Army.

Approx 40 Turbo-Porters (all H2 or earlier series) have been completed in agricultural configuration: these are in service in Indonesia, Sudan, Switzerland, Thailand and Zaïre. For liquid spraying, a stainless steel tank (capacity 1,330 litres; 351.5 US gallons; 292.5 Imp gallons) is installed behind the two front seats, and 46- or 62-nozzle spraybooms are fitted beneath the wings. In this configuration the aircraft can cover a swath width of 45 m (148 ft). An ultra-low-volume system, using four to six atomisers or two to six Micronairs, is also available, permitting increase in swath width up to 400 m (1,310 ft).

For dusting with granulated materials, the lower part of the standard tank can be replaced by a discharge and dispersal door permitting coverage of a swath width of up to 20 m (66 ft). A Transland spreader can be fitted for dust application (swath up to 30 m; 100 ft). Effective swath width of these versions is 13-40 m (43-131 ft), the optimum being approx 20 m (66 ft).

Both versions are fitted with small doors in the fuselage sides, giving access to the tank/hopper for servicing, removal or replenishment, and two single seats or a bench seat for three persons can be installed aft of the tank. Optional items include an engine air intake screen and a loading door for chemical in the top of the fuselage.

The structural description which follows is applicable to the standard B2-H4 version:

TYPE: Single-engined STOL utility transport.
WINGS: Braced high-wing monoplane, with single streamline-section bracing strut each side. Wing section NACA 64-514 (constant). Dihedral 1°; incidence 2°; single-spar all-metal structure, with span-increasing tip fairings.

Entire trailing-edge hinged, inner sections consisting of electrically operated all-metal double-slotted flaps and outer sections of all-metal single-slotted ailerons. No airbrakes or de-icing equipment.

FUSELAGE: All-metal semi-monocoque structure.

TAIL UNIT: Cantilever all-metal structure. Variable incidence tailplane. Flettner tabs on elevator. Enlarged dorsal fin.

LANDING GEAR: Non-retractable tailwheel type. Oleo shock absorbers of Pilatus design in all units. Steerable/lockable tailwheel. Goodyear Type II mainwheels and GA 284 tyres size 24 × 7 or 7.50 × 10 (pressure 2.21 bars; 32 lb/sq in); oversize Goodyear Type III wheels and tyres optional, size 11.0 × 12, pressure 0.88 bars (12.8 lb/sq in). Goodyear tailwheel with size 5.00-4 tyre. Goodyear disc brakes. Pilatus wheel/ski gear optional.

POWER PLANT: One 507 kW (680 shp) Pratt & Whitney Canada PT6A-27 turboprop (flat rated at 410 kW; 550 shp at S/L), driving a Hartzell HC-B3TN-3D/T-10178 C or CH, or T10173 C or CH constant-speed fully feathering reversible-pitch propeller with Beta mode control. Standard fuel in integral wing tanks, usable capacity 644 litres (170 US gallons; 142 Imp gallons). Two underwing auxiliary tanks, each of 245 litres (65 US gallons; 54 Imp gallons), available optionally. Oil capacity 12.5 litres (3.3 US gallons; 2.75 Imp gallons).

ACCOMMODATION: Cabin has pilot's seat forward on port side, with one passenger seat alongside, and is normally fitted with six quickly removable seats, in pairs, to the rear of these for additional passengers. Up to 11 persons, including the pilot, can be carried in 2-3-3-3 high density layout; or up to ten parachutists, who can be dropped from heights of up to 7,620 m (25,000 ft); or two stretchers plus three attendants in ambulance configuration. Floor is level, flush with door sill, and is provided with seat rails. Forward opening door beside each front seat. Large rearward sliding door on starboard side of main cabin. Port side sliding door optional. Double doors, without central pillar, on port side. Hatch in floor 0.58 × 0.90 m (1 ft 10¾ in × 2 ft 11½ in), openable from inside cabin, for aerial camera or for supply dropping. Hatch in cabin rear wall 0.50 × 0.80 m (1 ft 7 in × 2 ft 7 in) permits stowage of six passenger seats or accommodation of freight items up to 5.0 m (16 ft 5 in) in length. Walls lined with lightweight soundproofing and heat insulation material. Adjustable heating and ventilation systems provided. Dual controls optional.

SYSTEMS: Cabin heated by engine bleed air. Scott 8,500 oxygen system optional. 200A 30V starter/generator and 24V 34Ah (optionally 40Ah) nickel-cadmium battery.

EQUIPMENT: Generally to customer's requirements, but can include stretchers for ambulance role, aerial photography and survey gear, agricultural equipment (see earlier paragraphs) or an 800 litre (211 US gallon; 176 Imp gallon) water tank in cabin, with quick release system, for firefighting role. The 1,330 litre (351.5 US gallon; 292.5 Imp gallon) agricultural tank can also be used in the firebombing role.

DIMENSIONS, EXTERNAL:
Wing span	15.87 m (52 ft 0¾ in)
Wing chord, constant	1.90 m (6 ft 3 in)
Wing aspect ratio	8.4
Length overall	11.00 m (36 ft 1 in)
Height overall (tail down)	3.20 m (10 ft 6 in)
Elevator span	5.12 m (16 ft 9½ in)
Wheel track	3.00 m (9 ft 10 in)
Wheelbase	7.87 m (25 ft 10 in)
Propeller diameter	2.56 m (8 ft 5 in)
Cabin double door (port) and sliding door (starboard):	
Max height	1.04 m (3 ft 5 in)
Width	1.58 m (5 ft 2¼ in)

DIMENSIONS, INTERNAL:
Cabin, from back of pilot's seat to rear wall:	
Length	2.30 m (7 ft 6½ in)
Max width	1.16 m (3 ft 9½ in)
Max height (at front)	1.28 m (4 ft 2½ in)
Height at rear wall	1.18 m (3 ft 10½ in)
Floor area	2.67 m² (28.6 sq ft)
Volume	3.28 m³ (107 cu ft)

AREAS:
Wings, gross	30.15 m² (324.5 sq ft)
Ailerons (total)	3.83 m² (41.2 sq ft)
Flaps (total)	3.76 m² (40.5 sq ft)
Fin	1.70 m² (18.3 sq ft)
Rudder, incl tab	0.96 m² (10.3 sq ft)
Tailplane	4.03 m² (43.4 sq ft)
Elevator, incl tab	2.11 m² (22.7 sq ft)

WEIGHTS AND LOADINGS:
Weight empty, equipped	1,270 kg (2,800 lb)
Max fuel weight: internal	508 kg (1,120 lb)
underwing	392 kg (864 lb)
Max payload:	
with reduced internal fuel	1,130 kg (2,491 lb)
with max internal fuel	1,062 kg (2,341 lb)
with max internal and underwing fuel	
	571 kg (1,259 lb)
Max T-O weight, Normal (CAR 3):	
wheels (standard)	2,800 kg (6,173 lb)
skis	2,600 kg (5,732 lb)
Max landing weight: wheels	2,660 kg (5,864 lb)
skis	2,600 kg (5,732 lb)
Max cabin floor loading	488 kg/m² (100 lb/sq ft)

Max wing loading (Normal):
wheels	92.87 kg/m² (19.03 lb/sq ft)
skis	86.23 kg/m² (17.67 lb/sq ft)

Max power loading (Normal):
wheels	6.83 kg/kW (11.22 lb/shp)
skis	5.13 kg/kW (8.43 lb/shp)

PERFORMANCE (at max T-O weight, ISA, Normal category):
Never-exceed speed (VNE)	
	151 knots (280 km/h; 174 mph) IAS
Econ cruising speed at 3,050 m (10,000 ft)	
	115 knots (213 km/h; 132 mph)
Stalling speed, power off, flaps down	
	52 knots (96 km/h; 60 mph)
Max rate of climb at S/L	287 m (941 ft)/min
Max operating altitude	7,620 m (25,000 ft)
T-O run at S/L	197 m (646 ft)
Landing run at S/L	127 m (417 ft)
Max range at 115 knots (213 km/h; 132 mph) at 3,050 m (10,000 ft), no reserves:	
with max payload	394 nm (730 km; 453 miles)
with max internal fuel	500 nm (926 km; 576 miles)
with max internal and underwing fuel	
	870 nm (1,612 km; 1,002 miles)
g limits	+3.72/−1.5

PILATUS PC-7 TURBO-TRAINER
Swiss Air Force designation: PC-7/CH

The PC-7 Turbo-Trainer is a fully aerobatic two-seat training aircraft, powered by a 410 kW (550 shp) Pratt & Whitney Canada PT6A-25A turboprop. It can be used for basic, transition and aerobatic training and, with suitable equipment installed, for IFR and tactical training. It received FAA certification to FAR Pt 23 on 12 August 1983, and also meets the requirements of a selected group of US military specifications (Trainer category). As a single-seater, it is flown from the front seat. The PC-7 also holds type certificates in the Aerobatic and Utility categories from the Swiss Federal Office for Civil Aviation (5 December 1978/6 April 1979) and the French DGAC (16 May 1983).

The first production PC-7 was flown on 18 August 1978, and deliveries began in December of that year. Deliveries totalled over 400 by early 1991. Customers include 18 air forces: Abu Dhabi (24), Angola (18), Austria (16), Bolivia (36), Chad, Chile (10 for Navy), France (five for CEV), Guatemala (12), Iran (35), Iraq (52), Malaysia (44), Mexico (75), Myanmar (17), Netherlands (10), Switzerland (40) and three undisclosed countries. Other customers include CIPRA of France (two), Swissair (one), Contraves (one) and three US private owners (one each). From the 1987 air show season the French Patrouille Martini formation display team has flown three PC-7s, equipped with smoke generator pods.

The PC-7 is available with new, lightweight Mk CH 15A ejection seats developed in collaboration with Martin-Baker. These offer safe escape for both occupants at speeds between 60 knots on the runway and 300 knots in the air (111-556 km/h; 69-345 mph), and at altitudes up to 6,700 m (22,000 ft).

TYPE: Single-engined single/two-seat training aircraft.

WINGS: Cantilever low-wing monoplane. Wing section NACA 64₂A-415 at root, NACA 64₁A-612 at tip. Dihedral 7° on outer panels. Sweepback 1° at quarter-chord. One-piece all-metal single-spar structure, with auxiliary spar, ribs and stringer-reinforced skin. Constant chord centre-section and tapered outer panels. Alclad aluminium alloy (2022 or 2024) skin, reinforced by stringers. Some fairings of GFRP. Mass balanced ailerons; trailing-edge split flaps, extending under fuselage. Flaps actuated electrically, ailerons mechanically by pushrods. Trim tab in port aileron.

FUSELAGE: All-metal semi-monocoque structure, with stringers, bulkheads and aluminium alloy skin. Some fairings of GFRP.

TAIL UNIT: Cantilever all-metal structure, of similar construction to wings. Dorsal fin; small ventral fin under tailcone. Forward strakes ahead of leading-edges of tailplane. Trim tab in starboard half of elevator; anti-servo tab in rudder. All control surfaces mass balanced and cable operated.

LANDING GEAR: Electrically actuated retractable tricycle type, with emergency manual extension. Mainwheels retract inward, nosewheel rearward. Oleo-pneumatic shock absorber in each unit. Castoring nosewheel, with shimmy dampers. Goodrich mainwheels and tyres, size 6.50-8, pressure 4.5 bars (65 lb/sq in). Goodrich nosewheel and tyre, size 6.00-6, pressure 2.75 bars (40 lb/sq in). No mainwheel doors. Goodrich hydraulic disc brakes on mainwheels. Parking brake.

POWER PLANT: One 485 kW (650 shp) Pratt & Whitney Canada PT6A-25A turboprop, flat rated at 410 kW (550 shp at S/L), driving a Hartzell HC-B3TN-2/T10173C-8 three-blade constant-speed fully feathering propeller. Fuel in integral tanks in outer wing leading-edges, total usable capacity 474 litres (125 US gallons; 104 Imp gallons). Overwing refuelling point on each tank. Engine oil system permits up to 30 s of inverted flight. Provision for two 152 or 240 litre (40 or 63.5 US gallon; 33.5 or 52.75 Imp gallon) underwing drop tanks. Oil capacity 16 litres (4.2 US gallons; 3.5 Imp gallons).

ACCOMMODATION: Adjustable seats for two persons in tandem (instructor at rear), beneath rearward sliding jettisonable Plexiglas canopy. Martin-Baker Mk CH 15A lightweight ejection seats available optionally. Dual controls standard. Cockpits ventilated and heated by engine bleed air, which can also be used for windscreen de-icing. Space for 25 kg (55 lb) of baggage aft of seats, with external access.

SYSTEMS: Freon air-conditioning and oxygen systems standard. Hydraulic system for mainwheel brakes only. No pneumatic system. 28V DC operational electrical system, incorporating Lear Siegler 30V 200A starter/generator and Marathon 36Ah or 42Ah nickel-cadmium battery; two static inverters for AC power supply. Ground power receptacle in port side of rear fuselage. Goodrich propeller electric de-icing system optional.

AVIONICS: Basic flight and navigation instrumentation in both cockpits, except for magnetic compass (front cockpit only). Additional nav and com equipment to customer's requirements. Other optional equipment includes instrument flying hood to screen pupil from rear cockpit during IFR training.

EQUIPMENT: Landing/taxying light standard on each main-wheel leg.

DIMENSIONS, EXTERNAL:
Wing span	10.40 m (34 ft 1 in)
Wing chord: mean aerodynamic	1.64 m (5 ft 5 in)
mean geometric	1.60 m (5 ft 3 in)
Wing aspect ratio	6.5
Length overall	9.78 m (32 ft 1 in)
Height overall	3.21 m (10 ft 6 in)
Tailplane span	3.40 m (11 ft 2 in)
Wheel track	2.60 m (8 ft 6 in)
Wheelbase	2.32 m (7 ft 7 in)
Propeller diameter	2.36 m (7 ft 9 in)

AREAS:
Wings, gross	16.60 m² (179.0 sq ft)
Ailerons (total)	1.621 m² (17.45 sq ft)
Trailing-edge flaps (total)	2.035 m² (21.90 sq ft)
Fin, incl dorsal fin	1.062 m² (11.43 sq ft)
Rudder, incl tab	0.959 m² (10.32 sq ft)
Tailplane	1.783 m² (19.19 sq ft)
Elevators, incl tab	1.395 m² (15.02 sq ft)

WEIGHTS AND LOADINGS:
Basic weight empty	1,330 kg (2,932 lb)
Max T-O weight: Aerobatic	1,900 kg (4,188 lb)
Utility	2,700 kg (5,952 lb)
Max ramp weight: Utility	2,711 kg (5,976 lb)

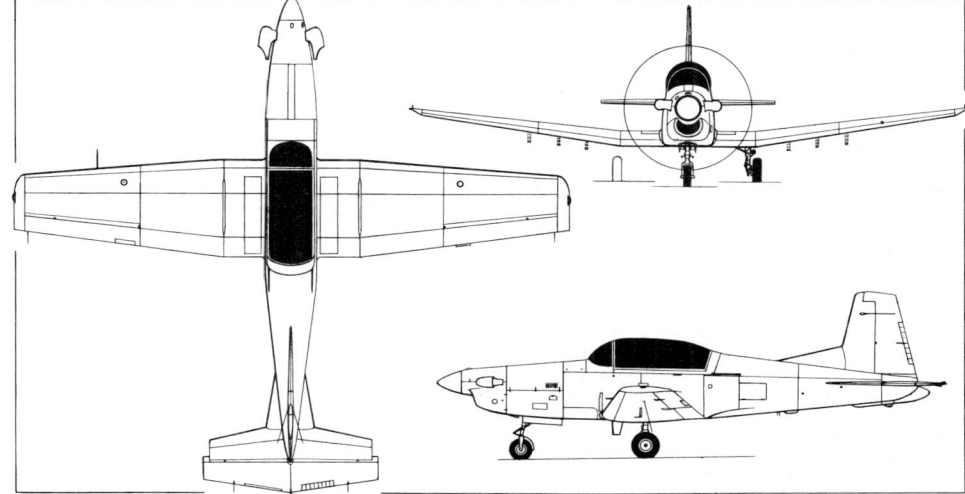

Pilatus PC-7 Turbo-Trainer (Pratt & Whitney Canada PT6A-25A turboprop) *(Pilot Press)*

Pilatus PC-7 Turbo-Trainer of the air force of Chad *(Ivo Sturzenegger)*

Max landing weight:

Aerobatic (military specification)	1,804 kg (3,977 lb)
Aerobatic (FAR Pt 23)	1,900 kg (4,188 lb)
Utility	2,565 kg (5,655 lb)
Max zero-fuel weight	1,664 kg (3,668 lb)

Max wing loading:

Aerobatic	114.5 kg/m² (23.44 lb/sq ft)
Utility	162.7 kg/m² (33.31 lb/sq ft)

Max power loading:

Aerobatic	4.63 kg/kW (7.61 lb/shp)
Utility	6.59 kg/kW (10.82 lb/shp)

PERFORMANCE (at max T-O weight, ISA, except where indicated. A: Aerobatic category, B: Utility category):

Never-exceed speed (VNE):		
A, B	270 knots (500 km/h; 310 mph) EAS	
Max operating speed:		
A, B	270 knots (500 km/h; 310 mph) EAS	
Max cruising speed at 6,100 m (20,000 ft):		
A	222 knots (412 km/h; 256 mph)	
B	196 knots (364 km/h; 226 mph)	
Econ cruising speed at 6,100 m (20,000 ft):		
A	171 knots (317 km/h; 197 mph)	
B	165 knots (305 km/h; 190 mph)	
Manoeuvring speed:		
A	175 knots (325 km/h; 202 mph) EAS	
B	181 knots (335 km/h; 208 mph) EAS	
Max speed with flaps and landing gear down:		
A, B	135 knots (250 km/h; 155 mph) EAS	
Stalling speed, flaps and landing gear up, power off:		
A	71 knots (131 km/h; 82 mph) EAS	
B	83 knots (154 km/h; 96 mph) EAS	
Stalling speed, flaps and landing gear down, power off:		
A	64 knots (119 km/h; 74 mph) EAS	
B	74 knots (138 km/h; 86 mph) EAS	
Max rate of climb at S/L: A	655 m (2,150 ft)/min	
B	364 m (1,195 ft)/min	
Time to 5,000 m (16,400 ft): A	9 min	
B	17 min	
Max operating altitude	7,620 m (25,000 ft)	
Service ceiling: A	10,060 m (33,000 ft)	
B	7,925 m (26,000 ft)	
T-O run at S/L: A	240 m (787 ft)	
B	780 m (2,560 ft)	
T-O to 15 m (50 ft) at S/L: A	400 m (1,312 ft)	
B	1,180 m (3,870 ft)	
Landing from 15 m (50 ft) at S/L at max landing weight:		
A	510 m (1,675 ft)	
B	800 m (2,625 ft)	
Landing run at S/L at max landing weight:		
A	295 m (968 ft)	
B	505 m (1,655 ft)	
Max range at cruise power at 5,000 m (16,400 ft), 5% fuel plus 20 min reserves:		
A	647 nm (1,200 km; 745 miles)	
B	1,420 nm (2,630 km; 1,634 miles)	
Endurance at 6,100 m (20,000 ft), with reserves:		
A, at max speed	3 h	
A, for max range	4 h 22 min	
B, at max speed	2 h 36 min	
B, for max range	3 h 45 min	
g limits: A	+6/−3	
B	+4.5/−2.25	

PILATUS PC-9

Design of the PC-9, as an advanced, high performance turboprop trainer suitable for all aspects from basic through to advanced flying, began in May 1982. Despite an external similarity to the PC-7, it has only about 10 per cent structural commonality with that aircraft, differences including a more powerful engine, stepped tandem cockpits with ejection seats, a ventral airbrake, modified wing profiles and tips, new ailerons, a longer dorsal fin, mainwheel doors, and larger wheels with high pressure tyres. The PC-9 complies with FAR Pt 23 (Amendments 1-28), plus special conditions as specified by the Swiss Federal Office for Civil Aviation, in both the Aerobatic and Utility categories, and also complies with selected parts of US military specifications.

Flight testing of major components, and aerodynamic optimisation of the new design, were completed during 1982-83 on a PC-7 technology demonstration aircraft, and were followed by two pre-production PC-9s (HB-HPA, first flight 7 May 1984, and HB-HPB, first flown on 20 July 1984) The second of these was more fully representative of the production version. Aerobatic certification was obtained on 19 September 1985. Sales now total about 140.

First customer for the PC-9 was the Union of Myanmar (then Burma) Air Force, which ordered four. It was followed by the Royal Saudi Air Force, which ordered 30 on 26 September 1985. The first of these was handed over to the RSAF on 15 December 1986, and all have now been delivered. On 16 December 1985 the Australian Defence Minister announced his government's decision to order PC-9s for the RAAF, and a contract for 67 aircraft, to be co-produced by Hawker de Havilland and ASTA, was signed on 10 July 1986. The Australian version is designated **PC-9/A**. For the Australian order, Pilatus supplied two complete aircraft in 1987; these were followed by six in kit form (first kit delivered 27 February 1987), and major components for a further 11; the remaining 48 are being built by HDH and ASTA. The two Swiss built aircraft, and the first two assembled in Australia, were handed over to the RAAF on 14 December 1987.

Ten **PC-9Bs** were delivered to Germany from September 1990, to replace OV-10B Broncos in the target towing role. Operated for the Luftwaffe by a private company, they differ from standard in having increased fuel capacity (giving 3 h 20 min mission endurance); two Southwest RM-24 winches on the inboard wing pylons, targets being stowed in a compartment aft of the winch; and a TAS 06 acoustic scoring system. Delivery of three PC-9s to the US Army began in Spring 1991.

Pilatus and Beech Aircraft Corporation of the USA are proposing a modified version of the PC-9 for the US Air Force/Navy Joint Primary Aircraft Training System (JPATS) requirement. Pilatus is to provide two PC-9s to Beech for development as Beech/Pilatus JPATS demonstrators; if selected, Pilatus would produce a major portion of the proposed aircraft, final assembly of which would take place at Beech's Kansas facilities.

The following description applies to the standard PC-9 unless otherwise indicated.

TYPE: Single/two-seat training aircraft.

WINGS: Cantilever low-wing monoplane. Wing section PIL15M825 at root, PIL12M850 at tip. Dihedral 7° from centre-section. Incidence 1° at root, washout −2° at tip. Sweepback 1° at quarter-chord. One-piece all-metal single-spar primary structure with auxiliary spar, ribs, and stringer-reinforced skin. Constant chord centre-section and tapered outer panels. Alclad aluminium alloy (2024) skin; some fairings of GFRP. Mass balanced plain ailerons; trailing-edge split flaps extending under fuselage with plate type airbrake at centre. Flaps and airbrake actuated hydraulically, ailerons mechanically by push-rods. Aileron trim is by an electrically actuated, movable centring spring on the control column.

FUSELAGE: All-metal semi-monocoque structure with stringers, bulkheads and aluminium alloy skin. Some fairings of GFRP.

Pilatus PC-9 single/two-seat trainer for delivery to the air force of Cyprus *(Ivo Sturzenegger)*

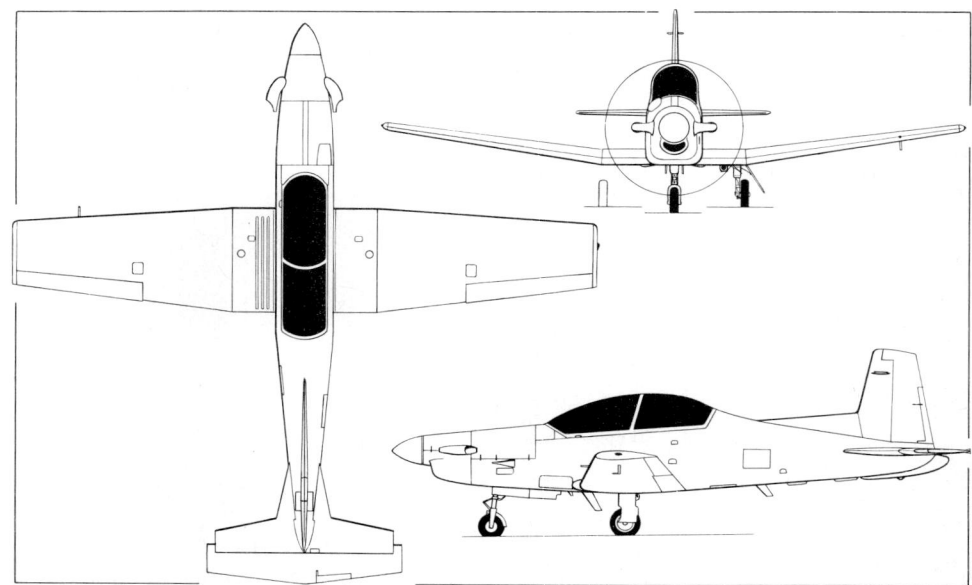

Pilatus PC-9 basic/advanced trainer (Pratt & Whitney Canada PT6A-62 turboprop) *(Pilot Press)*

TAIL UNIT: Cantilever all-metal structure with mass balanced cable operated rudder and elevator. Trim tab in starboard half of elevator, and trim/anti-balance tab in rudder, both mass balanced and electrically actuated.

LANDING GEAR: Retractable tricycle type, with hydraulic actuation in both normal and emergency modes. Mainwheels retract inward into wing centre-section, nosewheel rearward; all units enclosed by doors when retracted. Oleo-pneumatic shock absorber in each leg unit. Hydraulically actuated nosewheel steering. Goodrich wheels and tyres, with Goodrich multi-piston hydraulic disc brakes on mainwheels. RAAF version has low pressure tyres for grass field operation. Parking brake.

POWER PLANT: One 857 kW (1,150 shp) Pratt & Whitney Canada PT6A-62 turboprop, flat rated at 708 kW (950 shp), driving a Hartzell HC-D4N-ZA/09512A four-blade constant-speed fully feathering propeller. Single lever engine control. Fuel in two integral tanks in wing leading-edges, total usable capacity 535 litres (141.3 US gallons; 117.7 Imp gallons). Overwing refuelling point on each side. Fuel system includes a 12 litre (3.2 US gallon; 2.6 Imp gallon) aerobatics tank in fuselage, forward of front cockpit, which permits up to 60 s of inverted flight. Provision for two 154 or 248 litre (40.7 or 65.5 US gallon; 33.9 or 54.5 Imp gallon) drop tanks on the centre underwing attachment points. Total oil capacity 16 litres (4.2 US gallons; 3.5 Imp gallons).

ACCOMMODATION: Two Martin-Baker Mk CH 11A adjustable ejection seats, each with integrated personal survival pack and fighter-standard pilot equipment. Stepped tandem arrangement with rear seat elevated 15 cm (6.3 in). Seats operable, through canopy, at zero height and speeds down to 60 knots (112 km/h; 70 mph). Anti-g system optional. One-piece acrylic Perspex windscreen; one-piece framed canopy, incorporating rollover bar, opens sideways to starboard. Dual controls standard. Cockpit heating, ventilation and canopy demisting standard. Space for 25 kg (55 lb) of baggage aft of seats, with external access.

SYSTEMS: AiResearch environmental control system, using air cycle and engine bleed air, for cockpit heating/ventilation and canopy demisting. Fairey Systems hydraulic system, pressure 207 bars (3,000 lb/sq in), for actuation of landing gear, mainwheel doors, nosewheel steering, flaps and airbrake; system max flow rate 18.8 litres (4.97 US gallons; 4.14 Imp gallons)/min. Bootstrap oil/oil reservoir, pressurised at 3.45-207 bars (50-3,000 lb/sq in). Oil/nitrogen accumulator, also charged to 207 bars (3,000 lb/sq in), provides emergency hydraulic power for flaps and landing gear. Primary electrical system (28V DC operational, 24V nominal) powered by a Lear Siegler 30V 200A starter/generator and a 24V 40Ah battery; two static inverters supply 115/26V AC power at 400Hz. Ground power receptacle provided. Electric anti-icing of pitot tube, static ports and AOA transmitter standard; electric de-icing of propeller blades optional. Diluter demand oxygen system, selected and controlled individually from a panel in each cockpit.

AVIONICS: Both cockpits fully instrumented to standard customer specifications, with Kratos computer operated instrument system (COINS). RAAF aircraft have Bendix/King EFIS (see below) as standard. Single or dual system VHF, UHF and/or HF to customer's requirements. Audio integrating system controls audio services from com, nav and interphone systems. Customer-specified equipment provides flight environmental, attitude and direction data, and ground-transmitted position determining information. Optional equipment includes Bendix/King CRT displays (electronic ADI and HSI, standard on PC-9/A), J.E.T. head-up displays, encoding altimeter and emergency locator transmitter.

EQUIPMENT: Retractable 250W landing/taxying light in each main landing gear leg bay.

DIMENSIONS, EXTERNAL:

Wing span	10.124 m (33 ft 2½ in)
Wing chord: mean aerodynamic	1.65 m (5 ft 5 in)
mean geometric	1.61 m (5 ft 3½ in)
Wing aspect ratio	6.3
Length overall	10.175 m (33 ft 4¾ in)
Height overall	3.26 m (10 ft 8⅓ in)
Wheel track	2.54 m (8 ft 4 in)
Propeller diameter	2.44 m (8 ft 0 in)

AREAS:

Wings, gross	16.29 m² (175.3 sq ft)
Ailerons (total)	1.57 m² (16.90 sq ft)
Trailing-edge flaps (total)	1.77 m² (19.05 sq ft)
Airbrake	0.30 m² (3.23 sq ft)
Fin	0.86 m² (9.26 sq ft)
Rudder, incl tab	0.90 m² (9.69 sq ft)
Tailplane	1.80 m² (19.38 sq ft)
Elevator, incl tab	1.60 m² (17.22 sq ft)

WEIGHTS AND LOADINGS (A: Aerobatic, U: Utility):

Basic weight empty	1,685 kg (3,715 lb)
Max T-O weight: A	2,250 kg (4,960 lb)
U	3,200 kg (7,055 lb)
Max ramp weight: A	2,260 kg (4,982 lb)
U	3,210 kg (7,077 lb)
Max landing weight: A	2,250 kg (4,960 lb)
U	3,100 kg (6,834 lb)
Max zero-fuel weight: A	1,900 kg (4,188 lb)

First flight of the Pilatus PC-12 pressurised light transport

Max wing loading: A	138.1 kg/m² (28.3 lb/sq ft)
U	196.4 kg/m² (40.2 lb/sq ft)
Max power loading: A	3.18 kg/kW (5.22 lb/shp)
U	4.52 kg/kW (7.42 lb/shp)

PERFORMANCE (at appropriate max T-O weight, ISA, propeller speed 2,000 rpm):

Max permissible diving speed (V_D): A, U	
Mach 0.73 (360 knots; 667 km/h; 414 mph EAS)	
Max operating speed: A, U	
Mach 0.68 (320 knots; 593 km/h; 368 mph EAS)	
Max level speed:	
A at S/L	270 knots (500 km/h; 311 mph)
A at 6,100 m (20,000 ft)	
	300 knots (556 km/h; 345 mph)
Max manoeuvring speed:	
A	210 knots (389 km/h; 242 mph) EAS
U	200 knots (370 km/h; 230 mph) EAS
Max speed with flaps and/or landing gear down:	
A and U	150 knots (278 km/h; 172 mph) EAS
Stalling speed, engine idling:	
A, flaps and landing gear up	
	79 knots (147 km/h; 91 mph) EAS
U, flaps and landing gear up	
	93 knots (172 km/h; 107 mph) EAS
A, flaps and landing gear down	
	70 knots (130 km/h; 81 mph) EAS
U, flaps and landing gear down	
	86 knots (159 km/h; 99 mph) EAS
Max rate of climb at S/L: A	1,247 m (4,090 ft)/min
Time to 4,575 m (15,000 ft): A	4 min 30 s
Max operating altitude	7,620 m (25,000 ft)
Service ceiling	11,580 m (38,000 ft)
T-O run at S/L: A	227 m (745 ft)
T-O to 15 m (50 ft) at S/L: A	440 m (1,444 ft)
Landing from 15 m (50 ft) at S/L: A	530 m (1,739 ft)
Landing run at S/L:	
A (normal braking action)	417 m (1,368 ft)

Max range at cruise power at 7,620 m (25,000 ft), 5% fuel plus 20 min reserves	887 nm (1,642 km; 1,020 miles)
Endurance (typical mission power settings)	
2 sorties of 1 h duration plus 20 min reserves	
g limits: A	+7/-3.5
U	+4.5/-2.25

PILATUS PC-12

Pilatus announced its plan to develop a single-turboprop, pressurised, fast utility aircraft at the NBAA Show in October 1989, when it had already completed 60 per cent of full-scale engineering development. The first of two prototypes (HB-FOA) made its first flight on 31 May 1991; the second (production standard) aircraft was due to follow in late 1991 or early 1992. FAR Part 23 Amendment 36 certification is anticipated in 1992 and first deliveries in 1993. Australia's Royal Flying Doctor Service has signed options for two PC-12s, bringing total options to 27 by January 1991. Initial price is $1,627,000 (1989).

In terms of capacity, speed and economy, the PC-12 represents strong competition for the stretched Federal Express Cessna 208B Caravan I freighter and the Beech King Air 200 business aircraft, respectively in its PC-12F freighter and PC-12P passenger versions. Other possible missions include medevac, surveillance, border patrol, training and parachuting. About 60 per cent of sales are expected to come from North America.

The T tail keeps the tailplane clear of propeller slipstream and wing wake and easily compensates for the very wide CG range. It also avoids contact with loading vehicles. There is a large freight door aft, to port, and a separate airstair passenger door forward of the wing. The PC-12 will be cleared for single-pilot operation in IFR and have full de-icing for wings, tail, windscreen, propeller and engine intake. A three-axis autopilot and Bendix/King Gold Crown EFIS-based avionics will be standard.

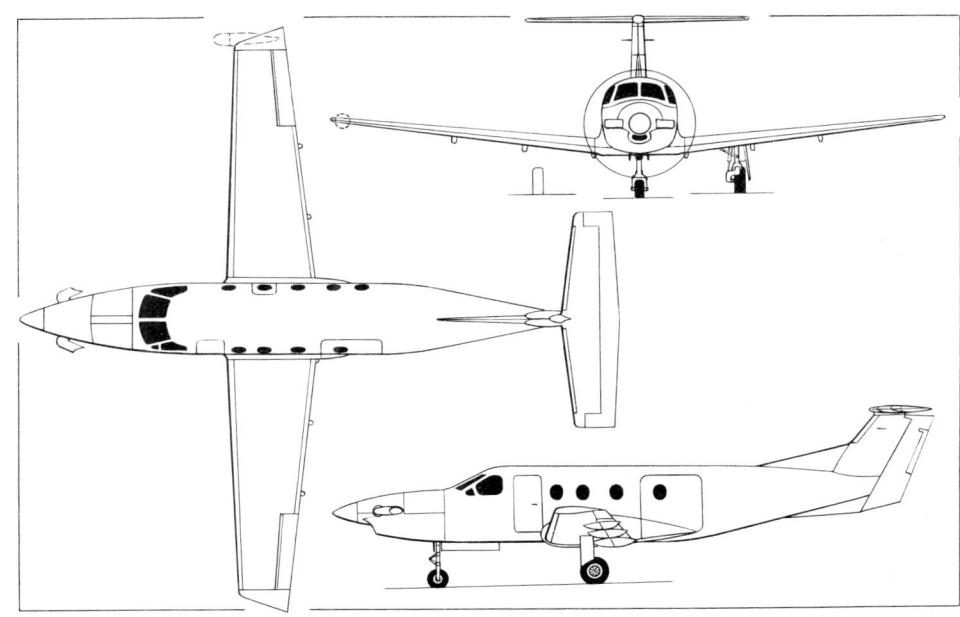

Pilatus PC-12 pressurised light utility and business transport *(Pilot Press)*

TYPE: Single-turboprop, pressurised utility/business transport.

WINGS: Conventional two-spar all-metal structure with internal fuel tankage. Aerofoil derived from NASA GAWA-1. Dihedral from roots. Fowler flaps over 67 per cent of trailing-edge. CG range 25 to 46 per cent MAC at 4,000 kg (8,818 lb). Pneumatic boot de-icing of leading-edges.

FUSELAGE: Oval section with flat floor from bulkhead behind flight deck to aft end of rear freight door.

TAIL UNIT: T tail with pivoting tailplane for trimming. Fin and rudder extend below rear fuselage. Rudder has trim tab. Pneumatic boot de-icing of leading-edges.

LANDING GEAR: Hydraulically retractable tricycle type, with single low pressure mainwheel tyres and single nosewheel. Propeller ground clearance maintained with nose leg compressed and nosewheel tyre flat. Main legs retract inward into wings and nose leg rearward under flight deck.

POWER PLANT: One 1,327 kW (1,780 shp) P&WC PT6A-67B turboprop, flat rated to 895 kW (1,200 shp) for T-O; 746 kW (1,000 shp) for climb and cruise. Hartzell four-blade composite propeller turning at 1,700 rpm. Usable fuel 1,514 litres (400 US gallons; 333 Imp gallons) in wings. Single-point pressure refuelling optional.

ACCOMMODATION: Two-seat flight deck: aircraft to be approved for single pilot, but dual controls and second flight instrument panel optional. Limit of nine passengers under FAR 23, or business layout for six with toilet. Forward airstair passenger door and upward opening rear freight door, both on port side.

SYSTEMS: Pressurised to 0.38 bar (5.5 lb/sq in) differential, giving 2,440 m (8,000 ft) cabin altitude at 7,620 m (25,000 ft). Vickers Systems (Germany) hydraulic system for landing gear actuation.

AVIONICS: Three-axis autopilot and Bendix/King EFIS-based IFR package as standard equipment.

DIMENSIONS, EXTERNAL:

Wing span	13.78 m (45 ft 2½ in)
Wing aspect ratio	8.4
Length overall	13.96 m (45 ft 9½ in)
Height overall	4.14 m (13 ft 7 in)
Tailplane span	5.15 m (16 ft 10¾ in)
Wheel track	4.53 m (14 ft 10½ in)
Wheelbase	3.48 m (11 ft 5 in)
Propeller diameter	2.67 m (8 ft 9 in)
Passenger door: Height	1.34 m (4 ft 4¾ in)
Width	0.62 m (2 ft 0½ in)
Cargo door: Height	1.36 m (4 ft 5½ in)
Width	1.32 m (4 ft 4 in)

DIMENSIONS, INTERNAL:

Cabin: Length, excl flight deck	5.16 m (16 ft 11 in)
Max width	1.51 m (4 ft 11½ in)
Floor width	1.26 m (4 ft 1½ in)
Height	1.45 m (4 ft 9 in)
Usable cargo volume (PC-12F)	9.24 m³ (326.3 cu ft)
Baggage compartment (PC-12P)	1.12 m³ (39.5 cu ft)

WEIGHTS AND LOADINGS:

Weight empty: PC-12F	2,183 kg (4,813 lb)
PC-12P standard	2,386 kg (5,260 lb)
Max payload: PC-12F	1,400 kg (3,086 lb)
PC-12P	1,150 kg (2,535 lb)
Max ramp weight	4,020 kg (8,862 lb)
Max T-O weight	4,000 kg (8,818 lb)
Max landing weight	3,800 kg (8,377 lb)
Max zero-fuel weight	3,700 kg (8,157 lb)
Max power loading	4.47 kg/kW (7.35 lb/shp)

PERFORMANCE (estimated):

Max cruising speed at 7,620 m (25,000 ft)	268 knots (497 km/h; 309 mph)
Stalling speed, landing configuration	61 knots (113 km/h; 71 mph)
Max operating altitude	7,620 m (25,000 ft)
Max rate of climb at S/L	625 m (2,050 ft)/min
T-O to 15 m (50 ft)	595 m (1,952 ft)
Landing from 15 m (50 ft)	490 m (1,608 ft)
Max IFR range, 45 min reserves	1,600 nm (2,965 km; 1,842 miles)

SWISS FEDERAL AIRCRAFT FACTORY (F+W)

EIDGENÖSSISCHES FLUGZEUGWERK—FABRIQUE FÉDÉRALE D'AVIONS—FABBRICA FEDERALE DI AEROPLANI

CH-6032 Emmen
Telephone: 41 (41) 59 41 11
Fax: 41 (41) 55 25 88
Telex: 868 505 FWE CH
MANAGING DIRECTOR: Hansjürg Kobelt

F + W is the Swiss government's official aircraft establishment for research, development, production, maintenance and modification of military aircraft and guided missile systems. It employs about 800 people in its works at Emmen, which cover 140,000 m² (1,506,946 sq ft). Research and development are divided among four departments: aerodynamics and flight mechanics, with appropriate test facilities which include four wind tunnels for speeds of up to Mach 4-5, test cells for piston engines and turbojets (with or without afterburners), all equipped with computerised data acquisition and processing; structural and systems engineering for aircraft, helicopters and space hardware, with a speciality in fatigue analysis and testing of entire aircraft structures; electronics and missile systems, covering all system aspects of aircraft and helicopter avionics and missiles; and prototype fabrication, flight test, instrumentation, and system and environmental testing.

The production department covers the whole field of production capabilities, from mechanical and sheet metal parts to composite parts and subassemblies (including leading-edge slats for the McDonnell Douglas MD-80 series and wingtips for the Airbus A320); electronics, electrical, electro-mechanical and electro-optical subassemblies; final assembly of missiles, missile systems, aircraft and helicopters. Recent major activities have included licence manufacture of aircraft, helicopters and missile systems, and co-fabrication with Contraves of all shrouds for the Ariane and Titan 3 space launchers. Nineteen of the 20 BAe Hawk Mk 66s ordered for the Swiss Air Force are being assembled by F + W; 12 Super Pumas are undergoing final integration.

F + W is general contractor for full licence production of the MDAC Dragon missile, completed a similar programme for the Rapier missile in 1987, began one for the TOW anti-tank missile in 1986 and one for the Stinger anti-aircraft missile in 1989. Missiles are assembled and tested at F + W and delivered to the Swiss government.

BAe Hawk Mk 66, assembled by F + W for the Swiss Air Force

F + W conducts wind tunnel tests for foreign aircraft manufacturers, ground transportation developers and users, and for the building industry. It develops and integrates internal stores and performs other modification work on military aircraft, including, currently, adding canard surfaces to Swiss Air Force Mirages. Subsonic wind tunnel tests have been made, and appropriate models built, of the Hermès spacecraft.

F + W proprietary products include a low-level dispenser bombing system and acoustic systems for failure and flight envelope warning; all-electronic linear angle of attack and *g* indicators; scoring indicators for air-to-air or ground-to-air shooting, with a microcomputer based ground station; multi-component strain gauge balances for testing purposes, covering forces from a few hundred grammes to several tons; water separators for aircraft conditioning; and POHWARO hot water rockets. (Details of these rockets can be found in the 1977-78 *Jane's*.) Co-operative development led to the Farner KZD 85 target drone described in the RPVs & Targets section of the 1987-88 *Jane's*. F + W has since developed, manufactured and delivered Ranger unmanned aerial vehicles (UAVs), together with a hydraulic launcher and appropriate ground support, and a first reconnaissance and surveillance Ranger system is now in operation. Services are offered for environmental testing, especially on F + W's own designed and proven test installation for high-shock long-duration tests.

F+W MIRAGE IMPROVEMENT PROGRAMME

The Swiss government approved funding in 1985 to retrofit Swiss Air Force Mirage IIIs. There are 30 III-S, 18 III-RS, two III-BS and two III-DS. Main items are a fixed canard and strake on each side of the nose. These improve manoeuvrability and increase stability in yaw near the upper limit of the flight envelope.

Other improvements include new audible warning and visual angle of attack monitoring systems, to alert the pilot when approaching limits of the flight envelope; Martin-Baker Mk 6 zero/zero ejection seats in place of the present Mk 4 seats; addition of infra-red and passive/active ECM; provision of more powerful VHF radios; wing refurbishing; ability to carry two underwing 500 litre (132 US gallon; 110 Imp gallon) drop tanks and a 730 litre (193 US gallon; 160.5 Imp gallon) centreline tank; mounting of improved blast deflectors for the two internal guns, to allow firing at high angles of attack; and a new camouflage paint scheme. The retrofit programme is continuing during the 1990s.

TAIWAN

AIDC

AERO INDUSTRY DEVELOPMENT CENTER
PO Box 90008-10, Taichung, Taiwan 40722
Telephone: 886 (4) 2523051 and 2523052
Fax: 886 (4) 2518302
Telex: 51140 AIDC
OTHER WORKS: Kang-Shan
DIRECTOR: Dr Hsichun M. Hua
DEPUTY DIRECTORS:
  Dr Shih-sen Wang (Research and Engineering)
  Y. L. Chang (Manufacturing)

The AIDC was established on 1 March 1969 as a successor to the Bureau of Aircraft Industry (BAI), which was formed in 1946 in Nanjing and moved to Taiwan in 1948. AIDC now employs more than 5,000 people, and is a subsidiary of the Chung Shan Institute of Science and Technology.

Between 1969 and 1976, the AIDC produced in Taiwan 118 Bell UH-1H (Bell Model 205) helicopters under licence for the Chinese Nationalist Army. From 1968 to 1974 it built a PL-1A prototype and 55 PL-1B Chienshou trainers (1975-76 *Jane's*), based on the US Pazmany PL-1, for the Nationalist Air Force. From 1974 to 1986 the AIDC was engaged in licence building 248 Northrop F-5E Tiger II tactical fighters (see 1986-87 *Jane's*) and 36 two-seat F-5Fs.

The AIDC designed and produced the T-CH-1 turboprop basic trainer (see 1981-82 *Jane's*). More recently, it has developed and produced the AT-3 twin-turbofan trainer, and has begun production of the Ching-Kuo, an indigenously designed jet fighter.

AIDC A-1 CHING-KUO

Taiwan's IDF (indigenous defensive fighter) programme is devoted to the development of an air superiority fighter intended primarily to replace about 100 F/TF-104G Starfighters of the Republic of China Air Force (RoCAF) in the middle to late 1990s. The need for an indigenous programme followed the US government's embargo on the sale to Taiwan of the Northrop F-20 Tigershark or any comparably advanced fighter. The same restrictions did not apply, however, to US technical assistance, and since May 1982, when the concept of an indigenous type was initiated, several US aerospace companies have collaborated with the AIDC in developing its own aircraft to meet the requirement.

Under the collective project name An Hsiang (Safe Flight), four subsidiary programmes were undertaken, including one named Tien Chien (Sky Sword) to develop the aircraft's primary missile armament. The airframe design was developed, with assistance from General Dynamics, under the title Ying Yang (Soaring Eagle), while the Yun Han (Cloud Man) programme involved the Chung Shan

Institute of Science and Technology, of which AIDC is a subsidiary, working with Garrett Turbine Engine Co to develop an afterburning version of the latter's TFE731 turbofan engine. The avionics for the aircraft are being acquired and integrated under the codename Tien Lei (Sky Thunder). In 1988, the aircraft itself was named after the late President of Taiwan, Chiang Ching-Kuo.

Four prototypes of the Ching-Kuo have been built, and the first of these (77-8001, designated A-1), was rolled out on 10 December 1988 and made its first flight on 28 May 1989. The nose landing gear and radome were seriously damaged due to a structural problem in the former during a take-off on 29 October 1989, but the aircraft resumed flying in December 1989 after repair. By January 1991 the A-1 had made more than 150 flights and had achieved its maximum speed at altitudes of up to 15,240 m (50,000 ft). The other three prototypes (two more single-seaters and a two-seater) made their first flights in late 1989 and early 1990; the total number of test flights had exceeded 400 by the end of 1990. The RoCAF is believed to require some 256 of these aircraft, including 40-50 two-seaters, by 1997. Series production is under way with a view to service entry in late 1992 or early 1993. Prototypes are of metal construction, but the possibility of later introduction of composites has been suggested.

TYPE: Single-seat air defence fighter.

WINGS: Shoulder-wing monoplane, of blended wing/body design. Moderately sweptback wings, extended forward at wingroot leading-edges. Wings have full span flaperons and leading-edge manoeuvring flaps.

TAIL UNIT: Sweptback fin and rudder; fuselage mounted all-moving tailplane.

LANDING GEAR: Retractable tricycle type of Menasco design, with single wheel and oleo-pneumatic shock absorber on each unit. Nose unit retracts forward, main units inward/upward into engine air intake trunks.

POWER PLANT: Two Garrett TFE1042-70 turbofans initially, side by side in rear fuselage, each developing 22.24 kN (5,000 lb st) dry and 37.14 kN (8,350 lb st) with afterburning. Later aircraft may have TFE1088 engine now under development. Elliptical air intakes, with splitter plates, mounted low on centre-fuselage beneath wingroots.

ACCOMMODATION: Pilot only, on Martin-Baker Mk 12 zero/zero ejection seat. One-piece bubble canopy, hinged at rear and opening upward. Two-seater canopy opens sideways to port. Cockpit(s) pressurised and air-conditioned.

SYSTEMS: AiResearch environmental control system. Lear Astronics fly-by-wire control system. Westinghouse variable-speed constant-frequency electrical power generating system.

AVIONICS: Golden Dragon 53 (GD-53) multi-mode pulse Doppler radar, a modified version of the GE Aerospace AN/APG-67 (V) incorporating also some elements of the Westinghouse AN/APG-66, has a range of approx 81 nm (150 km; 93 miles), capability for air and sea search, and lookdown/shootdown capability. Litton (LN-39?) inertial navigation system. Bendix/King cockpit displays (three multi-function and one head-up). Sidestick controller.

ARMAMENT: One 20 mm M61A Vulcan cannon in starboard side of fuselage, beneath extended wingroot leading-edge. Photo-Sonics gun camera. Six attachment points for external stores: two under fuselage, one under each wing and one at each wingtip. Prototype at rollout shown with four Sky Sword I short-range infra-red homing air-to-air missiles (two underwing and two at wingtips). Other combinations may include two medium-range Sky Sword II air-to-air missiles under fuselage in addition to four Sky Sword Is; or three Hsiung Feng II anti-shipping missiles (under wings and fuselage) plus two wingtip Sky Sword Is. In attack role, underwing and underfuselage hardpoints could be occupied by Maverick (or similar) missiles, single or cluster bombs, or rocket pods.

DIMENSIONS, EXTERNAL: Believed to be slightly smaller than General Dynamics F-16

PERFORMANCE (estimated):
Max level speed   approx Mach 1.2

AIDC AT-3
RoCAF name: Tsu-Chiang

In July 1975, AIDC was awarded a contract to design and develop prototypes of a new basic and advanced military jet training aircraft, designated XAT-3. Construction of two prototypes (0801 and 0802) began in January 1978, and these flew for the first time on 16 September 1980 and 30 October 1981 respectively. Following receipt of a contract for 60 production aircraft, AIDC began the manufacture of these in March 1982. The first production AT-3 (0803) made its initial flight on 6 February 1984. Deliveries began in the following month and were completed by early 1990.

The standard trainer version is now designated **AT-3A**. Following the conversion of two aircraft for 1989 prototype testing, 20 AT-3As have been modified as **AT-3B** close air support aircraft. Smiths Industries was prime contractor for this programme, which included the installation of a Westinghouse AN/APG-66 radar and fire control system. The AT-3B equips one squadron of the Republic of China Air Force. The proposed **A-3 Lui-Meng** single-seat

The two-seat version of the Taiwan AIDC Ching-Kuo fighter (two Garrett TFE1042-70 reheated turbofans) was first exhibited in late June 1990

The two-seat prototype of the AIDC Ching-Kuo indigenous defensive fighter

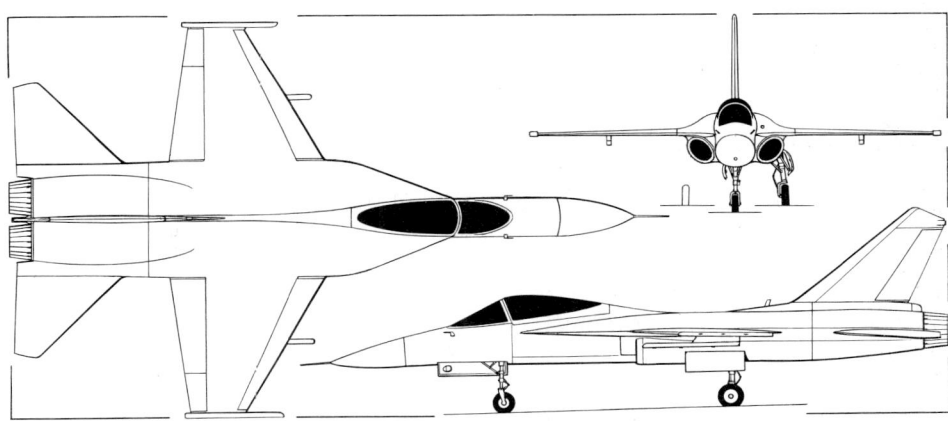

AIDC Ching-Kuo fighter (two Garrett TFE1042-70 turbofans) *(Pilot Press)*

ground attack/maritime strike variant, mentioned in the 1990-91 *Jane's*, is understood to have been abandoned.

The following description applies to the standard production AT-3A:

TYPE: Tandem two-seat twin-turbofan military trainer.

WINGS: Cantilever low-wing monoplane of supercritical section. Thickness/chord ratio 10 per cent. Dihedral 0° 46′. Incidence 1° 30′. Sweepback at quarter-chord 7° 20′. One-piece carry-through wing, with a machined torsion box, attached to fuselage by six bolts. Multi-spar light alloy structure, with heavy plate machined skin. Hydraulically powered light alloy honeycomb sealed-gap ailerons. Electrically operated light alloy single-slotted trailing-edge flaps. No anti-icing system.

FUSELAGE: Light alloy semi-monocoque basic structure, with steel, magnesium and graphite/epoxy used in certain areas. Built in three sections: forward fuselage, including cockpit; centre fuselage, including nacelles; and rear fuselage, including vertical and horizontal tail assembly. Two electrically controlled hydraulically actuated airbrakes, of laminated graphite/epoxy construction, mounted on fuselage undersurface forward of mainwheel wells. Fail-safe structure in pressurised cockpit section.

TAIL UNIT: Cantilever all-metal structure, integral with rear fuselage. One-piece all-moving tailplane; incidence varied by tandem hydraulic actuator. Dual hydraulic actuators

for rudder, with yaw stability augmentation. No trim tabs.

LANDING GEAR: Hydraulically retractable tricycle type, with single wheel on each unit. Main units retract inward into fuselage, nosewheel forward. Oleo-pneumatic shock absorber in each unit. Two-position extending nose leg increases static angle of attack by 3° 30′, to reduce T-O run, and is shortened automatically during retraction. Emergency extension by gravity. Mainwheels and tyres size 24 × 8.00-13, pressure 8.96 bars (130 lb/sq in). Hydraulically steerable nose unit, with wheel and tyre size 18 × 6.50-8, pressure 5.51 bars (80 lb/sq in). All-metal multi-disc brakes.

POWER PLANT: Two Garrett TFE731-2-2L non-afterburning turbofans (each 15.57 kN; 3,500 lb st), installed in nacelle on each side of fuselage. Inclined ram air intakes, each with splitter plate, abreast of rear cockpit. Engine starting by onboard battery or ground power. All fuel carried in fuselage, in two equal-size rubber impregnated nylon bladder tanks, with combined capacity of 1,630 litres (430.6 US gallons; 358.5 Imp gallons). Two independent fuel systems, one for each engine, with crossfeed to allow fuel from either or both systems to be fed to either or both engines. Pressure fuelling point forward of, and below, port air intake for internal and external tanks. A 568 litre (150 US gallon; 125 Imp gallon) auxiliary drop tank can

Camouflaged AT-3A of the Republic of China Air Force. Twenty similar aircraft have been converted as AT-3B close air support aircraft (*Denis Hughes*)

DIMENSIONS, EXTERNAL:	
Wing span	10.46 m (34 ft 3¾ in)
Wing chord: at root	2.80 m (9 ft 2¼ in)
at tip	1.40 m (4 ft 7 in)
Wing aspect ratio	5.0
Length overall, incl nose probe	12.90 m (42 ft 4 in)
Height overall	4.36 m (14 ft 3¾ in)
Tailplane span	4.83 m (15 ft 10¼ in)
Wheel track	3.96 m (13 ft 0 in)
Wheelbase	5.49 m (18 ft 0 in)

AREAS:	
Wings, gross	21.93 m² (236.05 sq ft)
Ailerons (total)	1.33 m² (14.32 sq ft)
Trailing-edge flaps (total)	2.53 m² (27.23 sq ft)
Fin	3.45 m² (37.14 sq ft)
Rudder	1.15 m² (12.38 sq ft)
Tailplane	5.02 m² (54.04 sq ft)

WEIGHTS AND LOADINGS:	
Weight empty, equipped	3,855 kg (8,500 lb)
Max fuel: internal	1,270 kg (2,800 lb)
external	884 kg (1,950 lb)
Max external stores load	2,721 kg (6,000 lb)
Normal T-O weight:	
trainer, clean	5,216 kg (11,500 lb)
Max T-O weight with external stores	
	7,938 kg (17,500 lb)
Max landing weight	7,360 kg (16,225 lb)
Max wing loading	362 kg/m² (74.14 lb/sq ft)
Max power loading	254.9 kg/kN (2.5 lb/lb st)

PERFORMANCE (at max T-O weight):	
Max limiting Mach No.	1.05
Max level speed:	
at S/L	485 knots (898 km/h; 558 mph)
at 11,000 m (36,000 ft)	
	Mach 0.85 (488 knots; 904 km/h; 562 mph)
Max cruising speed at 11,000 m (36,000 ft)	
	Mach 0.83 (476 knots; 882 km/h; 548 mph)
Stalling speed:	
flaps and landing gear up	
	100 knots (185 km/h; 115 mph)
flaps and landing gear down	
	90 knots (167 km/h; 104 mph)
Max rate of climb at S/L	3,078 m (10,100 ft)/min
Service ceiling	14,625 m (48,000 ft)
T-O run	458 m (1,500 ft)
T-O to 15 m (50 ft)	671 m (2,200 ft)
Landing from 15 m (50 ft)	945 m (3,100 ft)
Landing run	671 m (2,200 ft)
Range with max internal fuel	
	1,230 nm (2,279 km; 1,416 miles)
Endurance with max internal fuel	3 h 12 min

be carried on each inboard underwing pylon. Oil capacity 5.7 litres (1.5 US gallons; 1.25 Imp gallons) total, 1.9 litres (0.5 US gallon; 0.42 Imp gallon) usable. Fire warning and extinguishing systems for each engine bay.

ACCOMMODATION: Crew of two in tandem on zero/zero ejection (through canopy) seats, under individual manually operated canopies which open sideways to starboard. Crew separated by internal windscreen. Independent miniature detonation cord (MDC) system to break each canopy for ground and in-flight emergency egress. MDC can be operated from outside cockpit on ground. Rear seat elevated 30 cm (12 in). Dual controls standard.

SYSTEMS: AiResearch bootstrap air cycle environmental control system, for cockpit air-conditioning and pressurisation (max differential 0.34 bar; 5 lb/sq in), canopy seal, demisting, and pressurisation of g suits, hydraulic reservoirs and external fuel tanks. Two independent hydraulic systems, pressure 207 bars (3,000 lb/sq in), with engine driven pumps (flow rate 34.4 litres; 9.09 US gallons; 7.57 Imp gallons/min). Air type reservoir, pressurised at 2.41 bars (35 lb/sq in). Flight control hydraulic system provides power only for operation of primary flying control surfaces. Utility system serves primary flying control surfaces, landing gear, landing gear doors, airbrakes, wheel brakes, nosewheel steering, and stability augmentation system. Primary electrical power supplied by two 28V 12kW DC starter/generators, one on each engine. One 40Ah nickel-cadmium battery for engine starting. Two static inverters supply AC power at 400Hz. External DC power socket on starboard side of

centre fuselage. Hydraulic and electrical systems can be sustained by either engine. Liquid oxygen system, capacity 5 litres (1.3 US gallons; 1.1 Imp gallons), for crew.

AVIONICS: Most radio and nav equipment located in large avionics bays in forward fuselage. Standard avionics include UHF com, intercom, IFF/SIF, Tacan, panel mounted VOR/ILS/marker beacon indicator, attitude and heading reference system and angle of attack system, plus full blind-flying instrumentation. Wide range of optional avionics available.

EQUIPMENT: Can be equipped with A/A37U-15TTS aerial target system, carried on centreline and outboard pylons.

ARMAMENT (AT-3B): Manually adjustable gunsight and camera in forward cockpit. Large weapons bay beneath rear cockpit can house variety of stores, including quick-change semi-recessed machine-gun packs. Disposable weapons can be carried on a centreline pylon (stressed for 907 kg; 2,000 lb load), two inboard underwing pylons (each 635 kg; 1,400 lb and capable of accepting triple ejector racks), two outboard underwing pylons (each 272 kg; 600 lb), and wingtip launch rails (each of 91 kg; 200 lb capacity), subject to a max external stores load of 2,721 kg (6,000 lb). Weapons that can be carried include GP, SE, cluster and fire bombs; SUU-25A/A, -25C/A and -25E/A flare dispensers; LAU-3/A, -3A/A, -3B/A, -10/A, -10A/A, -60/A, -68A/A and -68B/A rocket launchers; wingtip infra-red air-to-air missiles; and rocket pods, practice bombs, and bomb or rocket training dispensers.

TAC
TAIWAN AEROSPACE CORPORATION

A committee was appointed in 1990 to create Taiwan Aerospace Corporation as the first step in an effort to establish a civil aerospace industry in Taiwan. The initial objective is to raise start-up capital from private investors (60 per cent) and the public sector (40 per cent).

THAILAND

IAC
INTERNATIONAL AIRCRAFT COMPANY LTD

RotorWay International has informed *Jane's* that the details given under this heading in previous editions were inaccurate. The name E-Tan (Wasp) applied only to the imported RotorWay Exec kits assembled by IAC, which were not modified in any way. Details of RotorWay's current range of small helicopters can be found in the US part of the Sport Aircraft section in this edition.

RTAF (SWDC)
ROYAL THAI AIR FORCE (Science and Weapon Systems Development Centre)
Office of Aeronautical Engineering, Don Muang Air Base, Praholyothin Road, Bangkok 10220
Telephone: 66 (2) 531 1824 or 241 2885
DIRECTOR OF SWDC: Air Marshal Prasert Ratanakan
CHIEF DESIGNER: Gp Capt Preecha Wannabhoom

The Office of Aeronautical Engineering was set up in 1975, and has been responsible for all subsequent design activity. Its most ambitious product to date, the RTAF-5 turboprop trainer and FAC aircraft, was designed and built entirely in Thailand and made its first flight on 5 October 1984. A full description appeared in the 1986-87 and earlier editions.

Eighteen RTAF CT4 Airtrainers, which remain in service from the 24 acquired in the early 1970s, are to receive wing modifications to extend their service life. The work will be undertaken by the RTAF with assistance from Pacific Aerospace of New Zealand (which see). Several of the CT4s have accumulated more than 8,000 flying hours.

RTAF (RFB) FANTRAINER 400 and 600
In 1984, the RTAF ordered 31 Fantrainer 400s and 16 Fantrainer 600s from RFB. One of each was delivered complete fitted with composite wings. The bare fuselages of another 15 Fantrainer 600s were delivered to Thailand and

RTAF metal winged Fantrainer 600 prototype

fitted there with composite wings bought from RFB. These 16 machines are established in service at the training base at Kampensaeng for RTAF pilot training, each aircraft flying an average of 50 hours per month. The RTAF was considering eliminating the intermediate training stage with Cessna T-37s before converting onto Northrop F-5s.

Production of the 400s began in 1986 with the design and manufacture of metal wings interchangeable with the German composite wings. The composite wing is 89 kg (196 lb) lighter. Incorporating centre fuselages sent from Germany, eight Fantrainer 400s had been completed by the end of 1989 and delivered to the RTAF for training flying instructors. Another 12 were to be assembled during 1990 and the final 11 during 1991, all with metal wings. The RTAF had not ordered composite replacement wings by April 1990. Neither was the additional batch of 15 armed Fantrainer 600s ordered. All Thai Fantrainers have the Yankee rocket-assisted escape system.

The description of the Fantrainer in the German section of the 1990-91 *Jane's* applies also to the RTAF aircraft, except as follows:

WINGS: All-metal stressed skin structure, with two-spar wing box forming integral fuel tank in each wing. Wings are bolted to each other at centre-section and attached to fuselage by two barrel pins on main spar and two shear bolts on rear spar. Corrugated skins at wingroots, over mainwheel bays.

WEIGHTS:

Weight empty: 400	1,275 kg (2,811 lb)	
600	1,325 kg (2,921 lb)	
Max internal fuel: 400, 600	365 kg (805 lb)	
Max T-O weight:		
400, Aerobatic	1,600 kg (3,527 lb)	
400, Utility	1,820 kg (4,012 lb)	
600, Aerobatic	1,650 kg (3,637 lb)	
600, Utility	1,870 kg (4,122 lb)	

PERFORMANCE (600 prototype at Utility max T-O weight):
Never-exceed speed (VNE)
220 knots (408 km/h; 253 mph)
Cruising speed (70% power) at 915 m (3,000 ft)
186 knots (345 km/h; 214 mph)
Stalling speed, 60° flap   82 knots (152 km/h; 95 mph)
Rate of climb at 610 m (2,000 ft)   579 m (1,900 ft)/min

TURKEY

KOC HOLDING

Istanbul

Through its Geneva-based Koc trading company Kofisa Trading SA, Koc Holdings formally agreed with Agusta to form a joint company in Turkey to promote the public and private aerospace sectors. Primary objective would be to start a Turkish helicopter industry, possibly providing the A 129 Mangusta or a licensed Bell 412 with uprated transmission designed to compete with the Sikorsky UH-60. In spite of the agreement, the 40 Agusta/SIAI-Marchetti SF.260Ds ordered for the Turkish Air Force in March 1990 are to be assembled by TAI.

TAI

TUSAŞ AEROSPACE INDUSTRIES INC (TUSAŞ Havacilik ve Uzay Sanayi A.Ş.)

PO Box 18, 06690 Kavaklidere, Ankara
Telephone: 90 (4) 523 1800
Fax: 90 (4) 523 1408/1425
Telex: 44640 TAIA TR
MANAGING DIRECTOR: J. R. Jones
F-16 PROGRAMME DIRECTOR: Kaya Ergenç

TAI is a majority owned Turkish company made up of Turkish (51 per cent) and American (49 per cent) partners and was formed on 15 May 1984. The major percentage shareholders are Turkish Aerospace Industries Inc (49) and General Dynamics (42); other shareholders are General Electric (7), the Turkish Armed Forces Foundation (1.9) and the Turkish Air League (0.1). The managing director post is the only one filled by a General Dynamics executive.

The objectives of TAI are to construct an aircraft facility capable of manufacturing modern weapon systems, helicopters and aerospace vehicles, modernise aircraft, perform research and development work in the field of aerospace, and to design, develop and manufacture total weapon systems for the Turkish armed forces.

TAI is under contract to General Dynamics to co-produce and deliver 152 of the 160 F-16C and D aircraft ordered by the Turkish Air Force (the Peace Onyx programme), and to fabricate and assemble rear and centre fuselages and wings of F-16 aircraft for the US Air Force. The first F-16C was delivered to the Turkish Air Force on 30 November 1987. By the end of 1990 a total of 59 aircraft had been delivered, a further 15 were on the assembly line or in flight status, and all work was continuing ahead of schedule. TAI will assemble and produce parts for 50 of the 52 CASA/IPTN CN-235s ordered by Turkey in 1991.

TAI facilities cover an area of 2.3 million m² (24,754,900 sq ft) with a factory floor area of over 100,000 m² (1,076,390 sq ft). The production facilities include fabrication and assembly, chemical processing, paint shops, fuel calibration and flight operations buildings, and are equipped with high-technology machinery and equipment capable of producing and assembling modern aircraft. The manufacturing and assembly building covers 62,500 m² (672,687 sq ft) under one roof. The fabrication area includes numerical control machining centres, complete forming capability

TAI-assembled General Dynamics F-16Cs over the TUSAŞ factory

including bladder press, detail fabrication shops, harness manufacture, hydraulic tubing and one of the largest chemical processing and chemical milling buildings of its kind. TAI also has one of the most up-to-date computer capabilities in the world.

The company had a workforce of 2,014 employees at the end of 1990. There is a modern training centre for electrical, hydraulic, airframe, avionics and other aircraft-related skills. General Dynamics had trained 347 Turkish employees at its Fort Worth Division, and another 859 have been trained in the TAI Training Centre in Mürted.

Research and development activities have already begun, and computer studies are being carried out under contract on projects such as turbulence models and jets in a cross-flow, in co-operation with General Dynamics, NASA, NATO-AGARD, METU and UDI. The company is involved in design and development of unmanned air vehicles and also participates in the development of the Future Large Aircraft (Euroflag: see International section) with six other European nations.

UNION OF SOVIET SOCIALIST REPUBLICS

ANTONOV
ANTONOV DESIGN BUREAU

Kiev 252062
Telephone: 7 (-) 442 6124
GENERAL DESIGNER: Pyotr Vasilyevich Balabuyev
DEPUTY CHIEF DESIGNER: Anatoli G. Bulanenko
ASSISTANT CHIEF DESIGNER: Ye. D. Goloborodjko
DIRECTOR GENERAL, KIEV WORKS: A. M. Malachine

Antonov OKB was founded in 1946 by Oleg
Konstantinovich Antonov, who died 4 April 1984, aged 78.
In current production are An-32 and An-124 at Kiev,
An-72/74 at Kharkov. An-124 wings are manufactured in
Tashkent, and airlifted to Kiev and Ulyanovsk for final
assembly. Any production of An-225 is likely to be at Kiev.
Small An-2 and An-28 are built by PZL Mielec, Poland.

ANTONOV An-2
NATO reporting name: Colt

TYPE: Single-engined general purpose biplane.
PROGRAMME: Prototype flew as SKh-1 on 31 August 1947.
More than 5,000 An-2s were built at Kiev, ending in
mid-1960s after limited manufacture of specialised
agricultural An-2M. Production transferred to PZL
Mielec, Poland, from where more than 11,730 delivered
since 1960. China acquired licence and has built
Yunshuji-5 (Y-5) versions 1957 to date. (See SAP, China,
and WSK-PZL Mielec, Poland.)

ANTONOV An-3

TYPE: Turboprop development of An-2 agricultural variant.
PROGRAMME: Reported Spring 1972 as expected competitor
to Polish turbofan WSK-PZL Mielec M-15 for standardised agricultural use in Soviet Union and eastern Europe;
confirmed 1979 that prototype produced by retrofitting
piston-engined An-2 with 706 kW (946 shp) Glushenkov
TVD-10 turboprop; state trials 1982-83, following
rejection of M-15, and announcement that production
An-3 would have 1,081 kW (1,450 shp) Glushenkov
TVD-20 turboprop; plans announced for large-scale
conversion of An-2s to An-3s, but no subsequent
confirmation of programme launch; announcement in
1988 that new 1,140 kW (1,528 shp) Glushenkov
TVD-1500 turboprop developed for An-3.
DESIGN FEATURES: Longer and slimmer nose than An-2,
housing turboprop, with small plugs fore and aft of wings
to lengthen fuselage; cockpit farther forward, sealed
and air-conditioned; multi-panelled starboard cockpit
windows replaced by single large blister window;
instrumentation, electrical and fuel systems new; access
to cockpit of agricultural version via small door on port
side; this door omitted on transport An-3, with access via
main cabin door and airtight door between cabin and
flight deck.
FLYING CONTROLS: As An-2.
STRUCTURE: As An-2.
LANDING GEAR: As An-2.
POWER PLANT: One 1,140 kW (1,528 shp) Glushenkov
TVD-1500 turboprop. Total of 1,200 litres (317 US
gallons; 264 Imp gallons) of fuel carried in six tanks in
upper wings.
ACCOMMODATION: As An-2.
EQUIPMENT: Chemical spraytank for agricultural duty has
capacity of 2,200 litres (581 US gallons; 484 Imp gallons),
more than 50 per cent increase over that of An-2. Dusting
equipment available.
DIMENSIONS, EXTERNAL: As for An-2, except:
Length overall   14.33 m (47 ft 0 in)
WEIGHTS AND LOADINGS:
Max T-O weight   5,800 kg (12,787 lb)
Max wing loading   81.10 kg/m² (16.61 lb/sq ft)
Max power loading   5.09 kg/kW (8.37 lb/shp)
PERFORMANCE:
Normal cruising speed   97 knots (180 km/h; 112 mph)
Rate of climb at S/L with max payload
                                  240 m (785 ft)/min

ANTONOV An-12
NATO reporting name: Cub

TYPE: Four-turboprop transport and electronic warfare
aircraft.
PROGRAMME: Prototype flew 1958, with Kuznetsov NK-4
turboprops, as rear-loading development of An-10
airliner; more than 900 built with AI-20K engines for
military and civil use, ending in USSR in 1973; standard
medium-range paratroop and cargo transport of Soviet
Military Transport Aviation (VTA) from 1959; replacement with Il-76 began 1974; Shaanxi Aircraft Company,
China, manufactures redesigned Yunshuji-8 (Y-8) transport version and derivatives (see SAC, China).
VARIANTS: **Cub (An-12BP):** Basic transport; fewer than
150 now with VTA, plus 200 with Soviet air armies and
air forces of military districts and groups of forces; 120
Aeroflot An-12s form military reserve; An-12BP has tail
gun turret.
  Cub-A: Elint version; as 'Cub' but blade aerials on
front fuselage, aft of flight deck, and other changes.
  Cub-B: Elint conversion of basic 'Cub' for Soviet
Naval Air Force; two additional radomes under forward

Antonov An-3 agricultural biplane (Glushenkov TVD-20 turboprop) *(Robert Senkowski)*

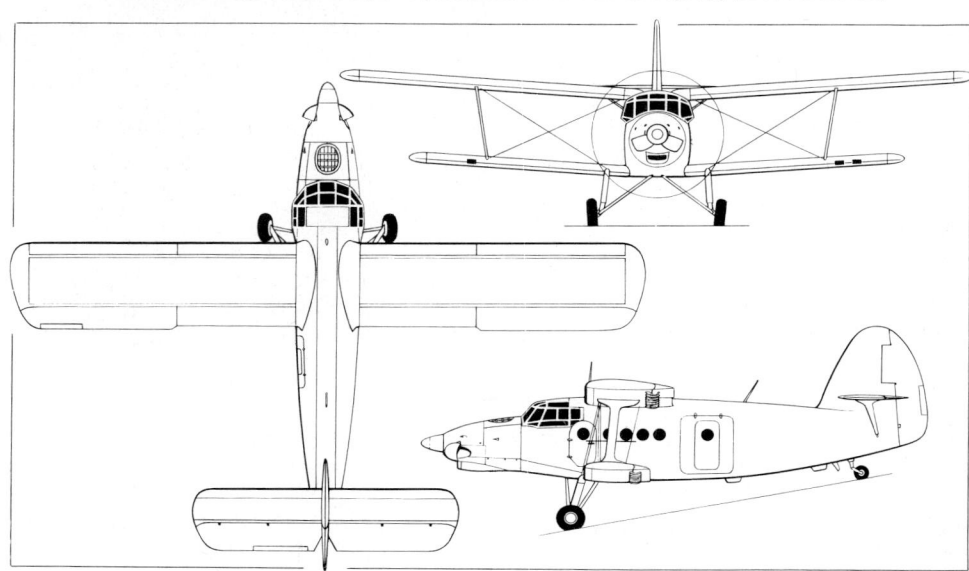

Antonov An-3 turboprop agricultural aircraft, with original flight deck side windows *(Pilot Press)*

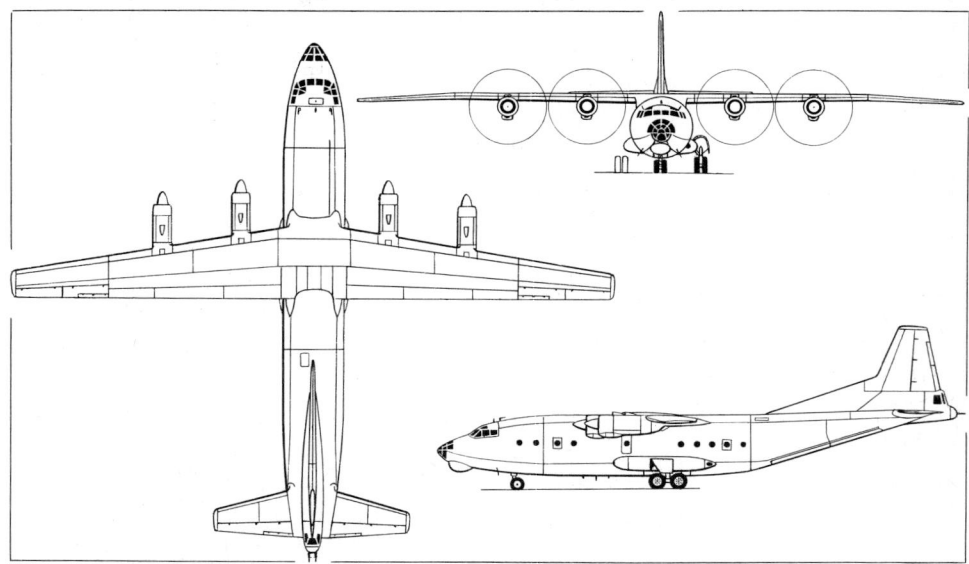

Antonov An-12BP ('Cub') four-turboprop general purpose military transport *(Pilot Press)*

and centre fuselage, plus other antennae; about 10
produced.
  Cub-C: ECM variant with several tons of electric
generation, distribution and control gear in cabin,
palletised jammers for at least five wavebands faired into
belly, and chaff/flare dispensers; glazed nose and

undernose radar of transport retained. Ogival 'solid'
fuselage tailcone, housing electronic equipment, replaces
usual gun position.
  Cub-D: ECM variant for active countermeasures,
with pods each side of front fuselage and tail fin. Soviet
Navy has about 20 'Cub-Cs and Ds'.

ECM variant of Antonov An-12 known to NATO as 'Cub-D' *(Soviet Wings/Alexander Dzhus)*

The following abbreviated details apply to the standard Soviet built military An-12BP transport. A full description last appeared in the 1979-80 *Jane's*.

POWER PLANT: Four 2,942 kW (3,945 ehp) Ivchenko AI-20K turboprops, driving AV-68 four-blade reversible-pitch propellers. All fuel in 22 bag tanks in wings, total normal capacity 13,900 litres (3,672 US gallons; 3,058 Imp gallons). Max capacity 18,100 litres (4,781 US gallons; 3,981 Imp gallons).

ACCOMMODATION: Pilot and co-pilot side by side on flight deck. Engineer's station on starboard side, behind co-pilot. Radio operator in well behind pilot, facing outward. Navigator in glazed nose compartment. Rear gunner in tail turret. Crew door on port side forward of wing. No integral rear loading ramp. Access to freight hold via large door under upswept rear fuselage, comprising two longitudinal halves which can be hinged upward inside cabin to provide access for direct loading of freight from trucks. Undersurface of fuselage aft of this door is formed by a further, rear-hinged, door which retracts upward into fuselage to facilitate loading and unloading. Equipped to carry 90 troops or 60 paratroops, all of whom can be despatched in under one minute, with rear door panels folded upward.

ARMAMENT: Two 23 mm NR-23 guns in tail turret.

DIMENSIONS, EXTERNAL:

Wing span	38.00 m (124 ft 8 in)
Wing chord (mean)	3.452 m (11 ft 4 in)
Wing aspect ratio	11.85
Length overall	33.10 m (108 ft 7¼ in)
Height overall	10.53 m (34 ft 6½ in)
Tailplane span	12.20 m (40 ft 0¼ in)
Wheel track	5.42 m (17 ft 9½ in)
Wheelbase	10.82 m (35 ft 6 in)
Propeller diameter	4.50 m (14 ft 9 in)
Rear loading hatch: Length	7.70 m (25 ft 3 in)
Width	2.95 m (9 ft 8 in)

DIMENSIONS, INTERNAL:

Cargo hold: Length	13.50 m (44 ft 3½ in)
Max width	3.50 m (11 ft 5¾ in)
Max height	2.60 m (8 ft 6¼ in)
Volume	97.2 m³ (3,432.6 cu ft)

AREAS:

Wings, gross	121.70 m² (1,310 sq ft)

WEIGHTS AND LOADINGS:

Weight empty	28,000 kg (61,730 lb)
Max payload	20,000 kg (44,090 lb)
Normal T-O weight	55,100 kg (121,475 lb)
Max T-O weight	61,000 kg (134,480 lb)
Max wing loading	501.2 kg/m² (102.6 lb/sq ft)
Max power loading	5.18 kg/kW (8.52 lb/shp)

PERFORMANCE:

Max level speed	419 knots (777 km/h; 482 mph)
Max cruising speed	361 knots (670 km/h; 416 mph)
Min flying speed	88 knots (163 km/h; 101 mph)
Landing speed	108 knots (200 km/h; 124 mph)
Max rate of climb at S/L	600 m (1,970 ft)/min
Service ceiling	10,200 m (33,500 ft)
T-O run	700 m (2,300 ft)
Landing run	500 m (1,640 ft)
Range:	
with max payload	1,942 nm (3,600 km; 2,236 miles)
with max fuel	3,075 nm (5,700 km; 3,540 miles)

ANTONOV An-22 ANTHEUS
NATO reporting name: Cock

TYPE: Long-range turboprop heavy transport.

PROGRAMME: Prototype first flew on 27 February 1965; production terminated early, in 1974; about 45 now used by VTA and Aeroflot.

VARIANTS: Early An-22s had small nose glazing, radar under starboard landing gear fairing; for production,

ECM version of the Antonov An-12 ('Cub-C'), operated temporarily in Egyptian Air Force insignia

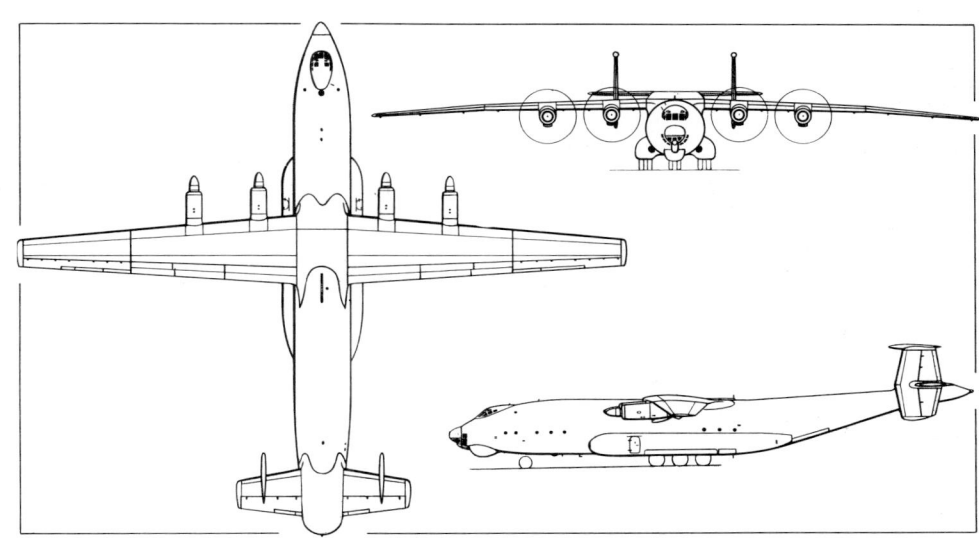

Antonov An-22 Antheus long-range heavy transport *(Pilot Press)*

weather/collision avoidance radar above new nose glazing, and undernose navigation/mapping radome. One An-22 (SSSR-64460), with original nose glazing and undernose radome, adapted to deliver An-124 wings non-stop 1,693 nm (3,136 km; 1,949 miles) from Valery Chkalov plant in Tashkent, where built, to Kiev assembly works; each 23 tonne wing carried over fuselage on mounts that prevent flexing of An-22 in flight being transmitted to An-124 wing; added central tail fin preserves An-22 handling qualities in flight.

The following abbreviated details apply to the standard production An-22. A full description last appeared in the 1982-83 *Jane's*.

POWER PLANT: Four 11,185 kW (15,000 shp) Kuznetsov NK-12MA turboprops, each driving a pair of four-blade contra-rotating propellers.

ACCOMMODATION: Crew of five or six on pressurised flight deck, with navigator's station in nose. Pressurised cabin for 28-29 passengers aft of flight deck, separated from main cabin by bulkhead containing two doors. Unpressurised main cabin, with reinforced titanium floor, tiedown fittings and rear loading ramp. When ramp lowers, a large door which forms the underside of the rear fuselage retracts upward inside fuselage to permit easy loading of tall vehicles. Rails in roof of cabin for four travelling gantries continue rearward on underside of this door. Two winches, used in conjunction with the gantries, each have a capacity of 2,500 kg (5,500 lb). Door in each landing gear fairing, forward of wheels, for crew and passengers.

DIMENSIONS, EXTERNAL:

Wing span	64.40 m (211 ft 4 in)

An-124 wing being delivered as external cargo above the fuselage of an An-22 transport *(Tass)*

Length overall	approx 57.92 m (190 ft 0 in)
Height overall	12.53 m (41 ft 1½ in)
Propeller diameter	6.20 m (20 ft 4 in)
DIMENSIONS, INTERNAL:	
Main cabin: Length	33.0 m (108 ft 3 in)
Max width	4.4 m (14 ft 5 in)
Max height	4.4 m (14 ft 5 in)
Volume	640 m³ (22,600 cu ft)
AREAS:	
Wings, gross	345 m² (3,713 sq ft)
WEIGHTS AND LOADINGS:	
Weight empty, equipped	114,000 kg (251,325 lb)
Max payload	80,000 kg (176,350 lb)
Max fuel	43,000 kg (94,800 lb)
Max T-O weight	250,000 kg (551,160 lb)
Max wing loading	724.6 kg/m² (148.4 lb/sq ft)
Max power loading	5.59 kg/kW (9.19 lb/shp)
PERFORMANCE:	
Max level speed	399 knots (740 km/h; 460 mph)
T-O run	1,300 m (4,260 ft)
Landing run	800 m (2,620 ft)
Range: with max fuel and 45,000 kg (99,200 lb) payload	5,905 nm (10,950 km; 6,800 miles)
with max payload	2,692 nm (5,000 km; 3,100 miles)
	2,692 nm (5,000 km; 3,100 miles)

ANTONOV An-24
NATO reporting name: Coke

Production of the An-24 twin-turboprop short-haul transport in the Soviet Union ended in 1978, after about 1,100 had been delivered. A version known as the **Y7-100** (which see) continues in production at Xian in China.

ANTONOV An-26
NATO reporting name: Curl

TYPE: Twin-turboprop pressurised short-haul transport.
PROGRAMME: First exhibited 1969 Paris Air Show; more than 1,000 built before superseded in production by An-32; derivative Y-7H-500 built by Xian Aircraft Company (see XAC, China).
VARIANTS: **An-26** ('Curl-A'): Original version; electrically/ manually operated conveyor flush with cabin floor for freight handling.

An-26B ('Curl-A'): Improved version, announced 1981, to carry three standard freight pallets, each 2.44 m (8 ft) long, 1.46 m (4 ft 9½ in) wide and 1.60 m (5 ft 3 in) high, with total weight of 5,500 kg (12,125 lb). Improved freight handling equipment.

'Curl-B': Signals intelligence (sigint) version; many short blade antennae mounted on fuselage (see accompanying illustration).
CUSTOMERS: Military An-26s assigned to air commands in Soviet regiments and squadrons; exported to at least 27 air forces; Angolan and Mozambique aircraft have bomb racks. Aeroflot has more than 200, available as military reserve. Civil customers include Aero Caribbean (Cuba), Aeronica (Nicaragua), Air Mongol, Alyemda (Yemen), Ariana Afghan Airlines, CAAC (China), Cubana, Syrianair and Tarom (Romania).
DESIGN FEATURES: Generally similar to earlier An-24RT specialised freighter, with auxiliary turbojet; more powerful turboprops and redesigned 'beaver-tail' rear fuselage. Oleg Antonov's special loading ramp forms underside of rear fuselage when retracted, slides forward under rear of cabin to facilitate direct loading and when airdropping cargo. Wing anhedral 2° on outer panels; incidence 3°; sweepback on outer panels 6° 50′ at quarter-chord, 9° 41′ on leading-edge; swept vertical and horizontal tail; tailplane dihedral 9°.
FLYING CONTROLS: Mechanical controls; mass balanced servo compensated ailerons with electrical glassfibre trim tabs; manual tab in each elevator; electrical trim/servo tab in rudder; hydraulically actuated tracked and slotted TsAGI flaps, single-slotted on centre-section, double-slotted outboard of nacelles.
STRUCTURE: Conventional light alloy; two-spar wing, built in centre, two inner and two detachable outer sections, with skin attached by electrical spot welding; bonded/ welded semi-monocoque fuselage in front, centre and rear portions, with 'bimetal' (duralumin-titanium)

bottom skin for protection during operation from unpaved airfields; blister on each side of fuselage forward of rear ramp carries track to enable ramp to slide forward; large dorsal fin; ventral strake on each side of ramp.
LANDING GEAR: Hydraulically retractable tricycle type, with twin wheels on each unit. Emergency extension by gravity. All units retract forward. Shock absorbers of oleo-nitrogen type on main units; nitrogen-pneumatic type on nose unit. Mainwheel tyres size 1,050 × 400 mm, pressure 5.9 bars (85 lb/sq in). Nosewheel tyres size 700 × 250 mm, pressure 3.9 bars (57 lb/sq in). Mainwheels fitted with hydraulic disc brakes and anti-skid units. Nosewheels can be steered hydraulically through 45° each side while taxying and are controllable through ±10° during take-off and landing.
POWER PLANT: Two 2,103 kW (2,820 ehp) Ivchenko AI-24VT turboprops, each driving a four-blade constant-speed fully feathering propeller. Electric de-icing system for propeller blades and hubs; hot air system for engine air intakes. One 7.85 kN (1,765 lb st) RU 19A-300 auxiliary turbojet in starboard nacelle for use, as required, at take-off, during climb and in level flight, and for self-contained starting of main engines. Two independent but interconnected fuel systems, with 5,500 kg (12,125 lb) of fuel, contained in integral tanks in inner wings and ten bag tanks in centre-section. Pressure refuelling socket in starboard engine nacelle. Gravity fuelling point above each tank area. Carbon dioxide inert gas system to create fireproof condition inside fuel tanks.
ACCOMMODATION: Basic crew of five (pilot, co-pilot, radio operator, flight engineer and navigator), with station at rear of cabin on starboard side for loading supervisor or load dispatcher. Optional domed observation window for navigator on port side of flight deck. Toilet on port

Antonov An-24RV fitted with equipment pannier for Polar service *(Paul R. Duffy)*

Antonov An-26 of the Hungarian Air Force *(Peter J. Cooper)*

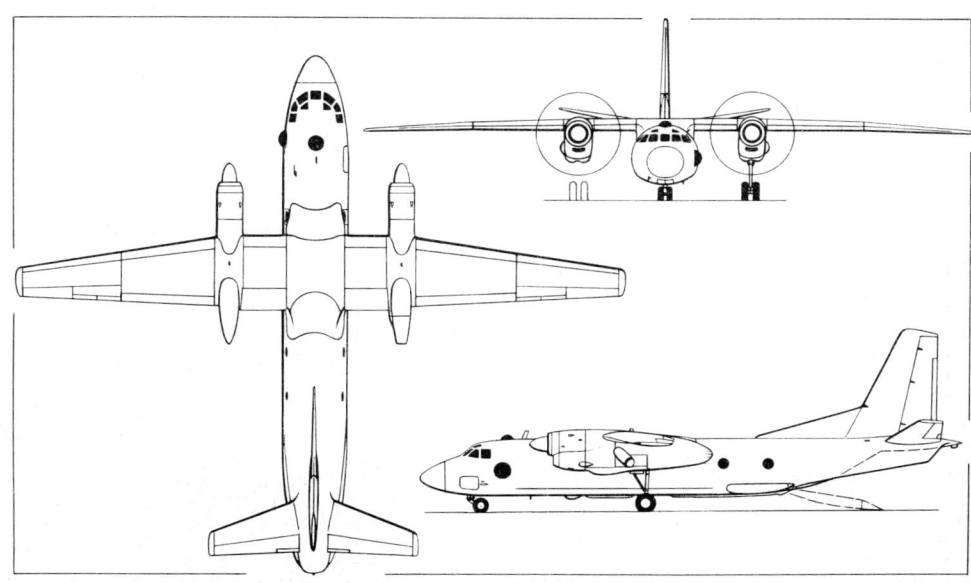

Antonov An-26 twin-turboprop short-haul transport *(Pilot Press)*

Sigint version of An-26 known to NATO as 'Curl-B' *(World Air Power Journal)*

side aft of flight deck; crew door, small galley and oxygen bottle stowage on starboard side. Emergency escape hatch in door immediately aft of flight deck. Large downward hinged rear ramp/door, hinged to an anchorage mounted on tracks running forward under the blister fairings. This enables ramp/door to slide forward under fuselage for direct loading on to cabin floor or for airdropping of freight. When doing so, its rear is supported by the pivoted swinging arm on each side which also raises and lowers door in the alternative fixed-hinge mode. Door can be locked in any intermediate position. Electrically powered mobile winch, capacity 2,000 kg (4,409 lb), hoists crates through rear entrance and runs on a rail in the cabin ceiling to position payload in cabin. Electrically and manually operated conveyor, capacity 4,500 kg (9,920 lb), built-in flush with cabin floor of original An-26, facilitates loading and airdropping of freight. An-26B has removable rollgangs, mechanism for moving pallets inside hold, and moorings, enabling two men to load and unload three pallets in 30 mins. Rollgangs can be stowed against sides of cabin. Both versions can accommodate a variety of motor vehicles, including GAZ-69 and UAZ-469 military vehicles, or cargo items up to 1.50 m (59 in) high by 2.10 m (82.6 in) wide. Height of rear edge of cargo door surround above the cabin floor is 1.50 m (4 ft 11 in). Cabin is pressurised and air-conditioned, and can be fitted with a row of tip-up seats along each wall to accommodate a total of 38 to 40 persons. Conversion to troop transport role, or to an ambulance for 24 stretcher patients and a medical attendant, takes 20 to 30 min in the field.

SYSTEMS: Air-conditioning system uses hot air tapped from the 10th compressor stage of each engine, with a heat exchanger and turbocooler in each nacelle. Cabin pressure differential 0.29 bar (4.27 lb/sq in). Main and emergency hydraulic systems, pressure 151.7 bars (2,200 lb/sq in), for landing gear retraction, nosewheel steering, flaps, brakes, windscreen wipers, propeller feathering and operation of cargo ramp and emergency escape doors. Handpump to operate doors only and build up pressure in main system. Electrical system includes two 27V DC starter/generators on engines, a standby generator on the auxiliary turbojet, and three storage batteries for emergency use. Two engine driven alternators provide 115V 400Hz single-phase AC supply, with standby inverter. Basic source of 36V 400Hz three-phase AC supply is two inverters, with standby transformer. Permanent oxygen system for pilot, installed equipment for other crew members and three portable bottles for personnel in cargo hold. Bleed air thermal de-icing system for wing and tail unit leading-edges. Electric windscreen de-icing.

AVIONICS: Standard com/nav avionics comprise two VHF transceivers, HF, intercom, two ADF, radio altimeter, glidepath receiver, glideslope receiver, marker beacon receiver, weather/navigation radar, directional gyro and flight recorder. Optional avionics include a flight director system, astrocompass and autopilot.

EQUIPMENT: Standard equipment includes parachute static line attachments and retraction devices, tiedowns, jack to support ramp sill, flight deck curtains, sun visors and windscreen wipers. Optional items include OPB-1R sight for pinpoint dropping of freight, medical equipment, and liquid heating system.

ARMAMENT: Provision for bomb rack on fuselage below each wingroot trailing-edge.

DIMENSIONS, EXTERNAL:
Wing span	29.20 m (95 ft 9½ in)
Wing aspect ratio	11.7
Length overall	23.80 m (78 ft 1 in)
Height overall	8.575 m (28 ft 1½ in)
Width of fuselage	2.90 m (9 ft 6 in)
Depth of fuselage	2.50 m (8 ft 2½ in)
Tailplane span	9.973 m (32 ft 8¾ in)
Wheel track (c/l shock struts)	7.90 m (25 ft 11 in)
Wheelbase	7.651 m (25 ft 1¼ in)
Propeller diameter	3.90 m (12 ft 9½ in)
Propeller ground clearance	1.227 m (4 ft 0¼ in)

Crew door (stbd, front): Height	1.40 m (4 ft 7 in)
Width	0.60 m (1 ft 11¾ in)
Height to sill	1.47 m (4 ft 9¾ in)
Loading hatch (rear): Length	3.40 m (11 ft 1¾ in)
Width at front	2.40 m (7 ft 10½ in)
Width at rear	2.00 m (6 ft 6¾ in)
Height to sill	1.47 m (4 ft 9¾ in)
Height to top edge of hatchway	3.014 m (9 ft 10¾ in)
Emergency exit (in floor at front):	
Length	1.02 m (3 ft 4¼ in)
Width	0.70 m (2 ft 3½ in)
Emergency exit (top): Diameter	0.65 m (2 ft 1½ in)
Emergency exits (one each side of hold):	
Height	0.60 m (1 ft 11¾ in)
Width	0.50 m (1 ft 7½ in)

DIMENSIONS, INTERNAL:
Cargo hold: Length of floor	11.50 m (37 ft 8¾ in)
Width of floor	2.40 m (7 ft 10½ in)
Max height	1.91 m (6 ft 3 in)

AREAS:
Wings, gross	74.98 m² (807.1 sq ft)
Vertical tail surfaces (total, incl dorsal fin)	
	15.85 m² (170.61 sq ft)
Horizontal tail surfaces (total)	19.83 m² (213.45 sq ft)

WEIGHTS AND LOADINGS:
Weight empty	15,020 kg (33,113 lb)
Normal payload	4,500 kg (9,920 lb)
Max payload	5,500 kg (12,125 lb)
Normal T-O and landing weight	23,000 kg (50,706 lb)
Max T-O and landing weight	24,000 kg (52,911 lb)
Max wing loading	320.1 kg/m² (65.6 lb/sq ft)
Max power loading	5.71 kg/kW (9.38 lb/ehp)

PERFORMANCE (at normal T-O weight):
Cruising speed at 6,000 m (19,685 ft)	
	237 knots (440 km/h; 273 mph)
T-O speed	108 knots (200 km/h; 124 mph) CAS
Landing speed	102 knots (190 km/h; 118 mph) CAS
Max rate of climb at S/L	480 m (1,575 ft)/min
Service ceiling	7,500 m (24,600 ft)
T-O run, on concrete	780 m (2,559 ft)
T-O to 15 m (50 ft)	1,240 m (4,068 ft)
Landing from 15 m (50 ft)	1,740 m (5,709 ft)
Landing run, on concrete	730 m (2,395 ft)
Min ground turning radius	22.3 m (73 ft 2 in)
Range, no reserves:	
with max payload	594 nm (1,100 km; 683 miles)
with max fuel	1,376 nm (2,550 km; 1,584 miles)

ANTONOV An-28
NATO reporting name: Cash

An-28 production takes place at the WSK-PZL Mielec works in Poland (see Polish section).

ANTONOV An-30
NATO reporting name: Clank

TYPE: Twin-turboprop aerial survey aircraft.
PROGRAMME: First flown 1974; built in small numbers.

VARIANTS: **An-30**: Basic photographic aircraft, as described in detail.

An-30M 'Sky Cleaner': Carries eight modular containers of granular carbon dioxide, instead of photographic equipment, in main cabin; this is seeded into clouds to induce precipitation over arable land, increase snow cover or fight forest fires; it can also protect specific areas, such as a large city, against excessive precipitation by causing it to be distributed in surrounding regions. External pod on each side of centre-fuselage houses six multiple dispensers (similar to military IRCM flare dispensers) for total of 384 meteorological cartridges that are fired into clouds. Capacity of each chemical modular container 130 kg (286 lb). Rate of discharge of carbon dioxide granules 0.8-6 kg (1.75-13.25 lb)/min. Chin radome standard.

CUSTOMERS: Bulgaria, Hungary, Romania, USSR and possibly Vietnam.

DESIGN FEATURES: Developed from An-24RT and An-26; nose extensively glazed for navigator; flight deck raised to improve access to navigator's compartment; fewer windows in main cabin; standard port side cabin door at rear, forward freight door on starboard side, and load hoisting/conveyor system retained.

FLYING CONTROLS: As An-26.

STRUCTURE: As An-26.

LANDING GEAR: As An-26.

POWER PLANT: Turboprops and auxiliary turbojet as An-26; water injection system for turboprops; AV-72T four-blade constant-speed fully feathering and reversible-pitch propellers; max fuel capacity 6,200 litres (1,638 US gallons; 1,364 Imp gallons).

ACCOMMODATION: Flight crew of five (pilot, co-pilot, flight engineer, radio operator and navigator); two photographer/surveyors; provision for conversion to transport by placing cover plates over camera apertures; toilet, buffet and crew rest area with armchairs and couches standard.

SYSTEMS: All accommodation pressurised and air-conditioned.

EQUIPMENT: Equipment for map-making and air survey described in previous editions of *Jane's*; provision for automatic or semi-automatic photography; cameras, control desk, darkroom and film storage in main cabin.

AVIONICS: Radar optional in chin fairing.

DIMENSIONS, EXTERNAL:
Wing span	29.20 m (95 ft 9½ in)
Wing aspect ratio	11.4
Length overall	24.26 m (79 ft 7 in)
Height overall	8.32 m (27 ft 3½ in)
Tailplane span	9.09 m (29 ft 10 in)
Fuselage, nominal diameter	2.90 m (9 ft 6¼ in)
Wheel track (c/l of oleos)	7.90 m (25 ft 11 in)
Wheelbase	7.65 m (25 ft 1¼ in)
Propeller diameter	3.90 m (12 ft 9½ in)
Propeller ground clearance	1.20 m (3 ft 11¼ in)

AREAS:
Wings, gross	74.98 m² (807.1 sq ft)
Vertical tail surfaces (total, incl dorsal fin)	
	15.85 m² (170.61 sq ft)
Horizontal tail surfaces (total)	17.23 m² (185.46 sq ft)

WEIGHTS AND LOADINGS:
Basic operating weight	15,590 kg (34,370 lb)
Weight of aerial photography equipment	
	650 kg (1,433 lb)
Max T-O and landing weight	23,000 kg (50,706 lb)
Max wing loading	306.75 kg/m² (62.8 lb/sq ft)
Max power loading	5.47 kg/kW (8.99 lb/ehp)

PERFORMANCE:
Max level speed	291 knots (540 km/h; 335 mph)
Cruising speed at 6,000 m (19,685 ft)	
	232 knots (430 km/h; 267 mph)
Landing speed	95 knots (175 km/h; 109 mph)
Service ceiling:	
with APU operating	8,300 m (27,230 ft)
without APU	7,300 m (23,950 ft)
T-O run on concrete	710 m (2,330 ft)
Landing run on concrete	670 m (2,198 ft)
Range with max fuel, no reserves	
	1,420 nm (2,630 km; 1,634 miles)

Antonov An-30 photographic aircraft of Hungarian Air Force *(Ivo Sturzenegger)*

Antonov An-32 in landing configuration *(Jacques Marmain/Aviation Magazine International, Paris)*

ANTONOV An-32

NATO reporting name: Cline
Indian Air Force name: Sutlej

TYPE: Twin-turboprop short/medium-range transport.

PROGRAMME: Prototype (SSSR-83966) first exhibited 1977 Paris Air Show; export deliveries to India began 1984; current production, 40 a year, largely for Soviet armed forces.

VARIANTS: Offered initially with choice of two AI-20 turboprops; all production An-32s have AI-20D Series 5 engines, as described in detail. Specialised versions available for firefighting, fisheries surveillance, agricultural, Polar (An-32P) and air ambulance use, last-named complete with operating theatre.

CUSTOMERS: Soviet air forces, Afghanistan, India (123, named Sutlej after a Punjabi river), and Peru (15); reported customers include Cape Verde, Nicaragua, Sao Tome and Principe, and Tanzania.

DESIGN FEATURES: Development of An-26, with triple-slotted trailing-edge flaps outboard of engines, automatic leading-edge slats, enlarged ventral fins and full-span slotted tailplane; improved landing gear retraction, de-icing and air-conditioning, electrical system and engine starting; large increase in power compared with An-26 improves take-off performance, service ceiling and payload under hot and high conditions; overwing location of engines reduces possibility of stone or debris ingestion, but requires nacelles of considerable depth to house underwing landing gear; operation possible from unpaved strips at airfields 4,000-4,500 m (13,125-14,750 ft) above sea level in ambient temperature of ISA +25°C; APU helps to ensure independence of ground servicing equipment, including onboard engine starting at these altitudes.

FLYING CONTROLS: As An-26 except for high-lift wings (see Design Features).

STRUCTURE: Generally as An-26.

LANDING GEAR: Hydraulically retractable tricycle type, basically as An-26. All shock absorbers of oleo-nitrogen type. Tyre sizes and pressures unchanged.

POWER PLANT: Two Ivchenko AI-20D Series 5 turboprops, each rated at 3,812 kW (5,112 ehp) and driving a four-blade constant-speed reversible-pitch propeller. One TG-16M APU in rear of starboard landing gear fairing.

ACCOMMODATION: Crew of three (pilot, co-pilot and navigator), with provision for flight engineer. Rear loading hatch and forward-sliding ramp/door, similar to those of An-26, plus winch and hoist with capacity of 3,000 kg (6,615 lb) for freight handling. Cargo or vehicles can be airdropped by parachute, including extraction of large loads by drag parachute, with the aid of removable roller conveyors and guide rails on the floor of the hold. Payloads include 12 freight pallets, 50 passengers or 42 parachutists and a jumpmaster on a row of tip-up seats along each cabin wall, or 24 stretcher patients and up to three medical personnel.

SYSTEMS: Accommodation fully pressurised and air-conditioned. Systems basically as An-26 but generally improved.

AVIONICS: Basically as An-26.

EQUIPMENT: Basically as An-26.

ARMAMENT: Provision for four bomb racks, two on each side of the fuselage below the wings (fitted to aircraft for Peru).

DIMENSIONS, EXTERNAL:	
As for An-26, except:	
Length overall	23.78 m (78 ft 0¼ in)
Height overall	8.75 m (28 ft 8½ in)
Tailplane span	10.23 m (33 ft 6¾ in)
Propeller diameter	4.70 m (15 ft 5 in)
Propeller ground clearance	1.55 m (5 ft 1 in)

DIMENSIONS, INTERNAL:	
Cargo hold: Length	15.68 m (51 ft 5¼ in)
Max width	2.78 m (9 ft 1¼ in)
Max height	1.84 m (6 ft 0½ in)
Volume	66.0 m³ (2,330 cu ft)
AREAS:	
Wings, gross	74.98 m² (807.1 sq ft)

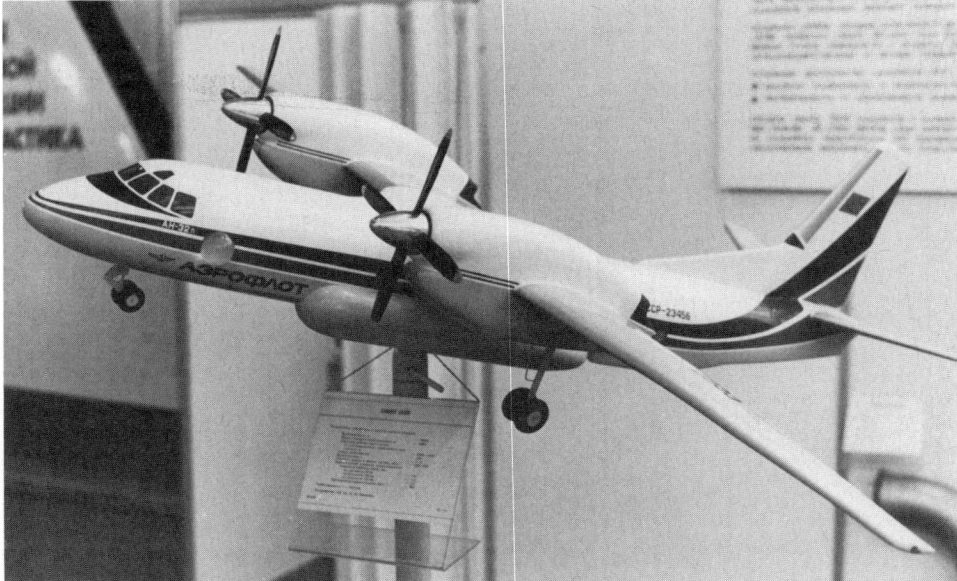

Model of Antonov An-32P with shorter pannier of same form as that fitted to Polar service An-24RV, page 232. This can carry skis, food, supplies and equipment *(Piotr Butowski)*

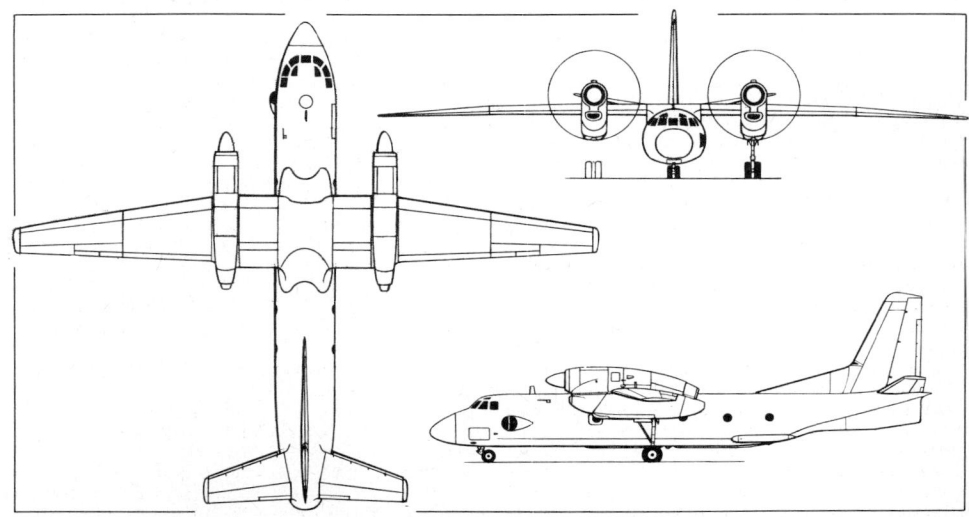

Antonov An-32 short/medium-range transport (two Ivchenko AI-20D turboprops) *(Pilot Press)*

Antonov An-74 ('Coaler-B') twin-turbofan STOL transport *(Jacques Marmain/Aviation Magazine International, Paris)*

Ailerons (total)	6.12 m² (65.88 sq ft)
Flaps (total)	15.00 m² (161.46 sq ft)
Vertical tail surfaces (total, incl dorsal fin)	
	17.22 m² (185.36 sq ft)
Horizontal tail surfaces (total)	20.30 m² (218.5 sq ft)

WEIGHTS AND LOADINGS:

Weight empty	16,800 kg (37,038 lb)
Weight empty, equipped	17,308 kg (38,158 lb)
Max payload	6,700 kg (14,770 lb)
Max fuel	5,445 kg (12,004 lb)
Max fuel with max payload	2,267 kg (4,998 lb)
Max ramp weight	27,250 kg (60,075 lb)
Max T-O weight	27,000 kg (59,525 lb)
Max landing weight	25,000 kg (55,115 lb)
Max wing loading	360.1 kg/m² (73.75 lb/sq ft)
Max power loading	3.54 kg/kW (5.82 lb/ehp)

PERFORMANCE:

Max cruising speed	286 knots (530 km/h; 329 mph)
Econ cruising speed	254 knots (470 km/h; 292 mph)
Landing speed	100 knots (185 km/h; 115 mph)
Optimum cruising height	8,000 m (26,250 ft)
Service ceiling	9,400 m (30,840 ft)
Service ceiling, one engine out	4,800 m (15,750 ft)
T-O run on concrete	760 m (2,495 ft)
T-O to 15 m (50 ft)	1,200 m (3,940 ft)
Landing run	470 m (1,542 ft)

Range, with 45 min reserves:

with max payload	464 nm (860 km; 534 miles)
with 5,500 kg (12,125 lb) payload	
	1,080 nm (2,000 km; 1,243 miles)

ANTONOV An-70

According to *Isvestia*, in its issue for 20 December 1988, an aircraft designated An-70 is under development to replace some of the remaining An-12s of the Soviet air forces. It was intended to enter production in 1988, but manufacture has been deferred until 1995.

ANTONOV An-72 and An-74
NATO reporting name: Coaler

TYPE: Twin-turbofan light STOL transport.

PROGRAMME: First of two prototype An-72s, built at Kiev, flew 22 December 1977; after eight pre-series aircraft, manufacture transferred to Kharkov; An-74 polar transport announced February 1984; production of An-72/74 variants currently 20 a year.

VARIANTS: **An-72A** ('Coaler-C'): Light STOL transport for military and civil use; extended wings, lengthened fuselage and other changes compared with An-72 ('Coaler-A') prototypes; crew of two or three.

An-72AT ('Coaler-C'): Cargo version of An-72A, able to carry international standard containers.

An-72S ('Coaler-C'): Three-compartment executive transport; toilets, wardrobe and galley for hot and cold meals at front; centre compartment has small table, three-place sofa, wardrobe and baggage space starboard, table, two pivoting armchairs and intercom port, with six armchairs optional in place of sofa and wardrobe; 12 pairs of armchairs in rear compartment. Provision for adapting to carry light vehicle, freight, 38 persons in seats

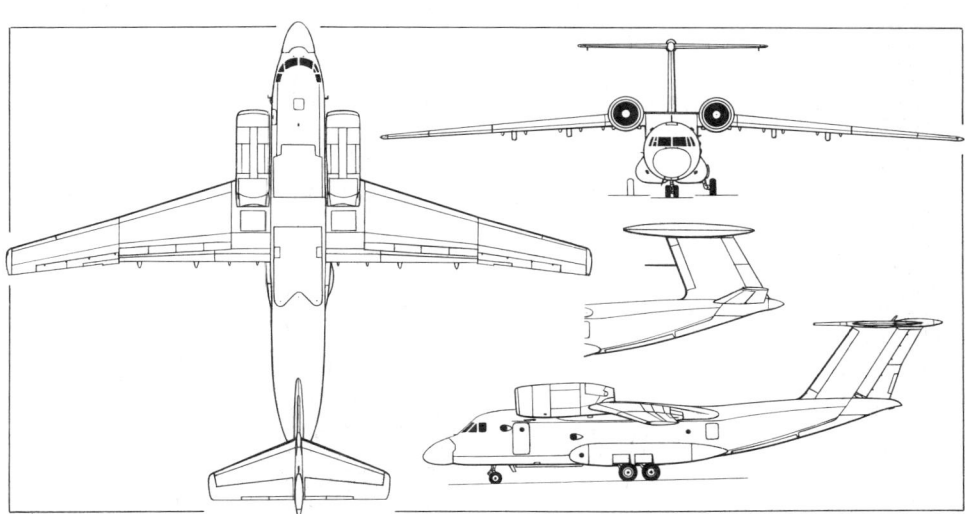

Antonov An-74 ('Coaler-B') STOL transport, with scrap view of 'Madcap' rotodome *(Pilot Press)*

along sidewalls and in centre row, or eight stretcher patients.

An-74 ('Coaler-B'): For all-weather operation in Arctic/Antarctic, to assist in setting up scientific stations on ice floes, airdrop supplies to motorised expeditions and observe changes in icefields; flight crew of five; wing, tail unit and engine air intake de-icing; advanced navigation aids, including inertial navigation system; provision for wheel/ski landing gear; much increased fuel capacity; airframe identical with An-72A except for two blister windows at rear of flight deck and front of cabin on port side, and larger nose radome.

An-74A ('Coaler-B'): As An-72A, but with avionics and larger radome of An-74.

An-74T ('Coaler-B'): Cargo version of An-74A.

An-74S ('Coaler-B'): Executive transport version of An-74A.

'Madcap': AEW&C version, described separately.

DESIGN FEATURES: Primary role as STOL replacement for turboprop An-26, with emphasis on freight carrying; ejection of exhaust efflux over upper wing surface and down over large multi-slotted flaps gives considerable increase in lift; special ramp/door as An-26; low-pressure tyres and multi-wheel landing gear for operation from unprepared strips, ice or snow; high-set engines avoid foreign object ingestion; wing leading-edge sweepback 17°; anhedral approx 10° on outer wings; normal T-O flap setting 25-30°, max deflection 60°; sweptback fin and rudder.

FLYING CONTROLS: Power actuated ailerons, with two tabs in port aileron, one starboard; double-hinged rudder, with tab in lower portion of two-section aft panel; during normal flight only lower rear rudder segment is used;

both rear segments used in low-speed flight; forward segment is actuated automatically to offset thrust asymmetry; horn balanced and mechanically actuated, aerodynamically balanced elevators, each with two tabs; hydraulically actuated full-span wing leading-edge flaps outboard of nacelles; trailing-edge flaps double-slotted in exhaust efflux, triple-slotted between nacelles and outer wings; four-section spoilers forward of triple-slotted flaps; two outer sections on each side raised before landing, remainder opened automatically on touchdown by sensors actuated by weight on main landing gear; inverted leading-edge slat on tailplane linked to wing flaps.

STRUCTURE: All-metal; multi-spar wings mounted above fuselage; wing skin, spoilers and flaps of titanium aft of engine nacelles; circular semi-monocoque fuselage, with rear ramp/door; tapered fairing forward of T-tail fin/tailplane junction, blending into ogival rear fairing.

LANDING GEAR: Hydraulically retractable tricycle type, made primarily of titanium. Twin wheels on rearward retracting steerable nose unit. Each main unit comprises two trailing-arm legs in tandem, each with a single wheel, retracting inward through 90° so that wheels lie horizontally in bottom of large fairings, outside fuselage pressure cell. Oleo-pneumatic shock absorber in each unit. Low pressure tyres, size 720 × 310 mm on nosewheels, 1,050 × 400 mm on mainwheels. Hydraulic disc brakes. Telescopic strut is hinged downward, from rear of each side fairing, to support fuselage during direct loading of hold with ramp/door under fuselage.

POWER PLANT: Initial versions have two Zaporozhye/Lotarev D-36 high bypass ratio turbofans, each rated at 63.74 kN (14,330 lb st). These have been superseded by two

An-74 after touchdown, with thrust reversers erected and flaps extended
(Paul Jackson)

AEW&C version of An-74 (background), known to NATO as 'Madcap'

Zaporozhye/Lotarev D-436 turbofans, each rated at 73.6 kN (16,550 lb st). Integral fuel tanks between spars of outer wings. Thrust reversers standard.

ACCOMMODATION: Pilot and co-pilot/navigator side by side on flight deck of An-72, plus a flight engineer, with provision for a fourth person; pilot, co-pilot, navigator, radio operator and flight engineer in An-74. Heated windows. Two windscreen wipers. Flight deck and cabin pressurised and air-conditioned. Main cabin designed primarily for freight, including four UAK-2.5 containers or four PAV-2.5 pallets each weighing 2,500 kg (5,511 lb); but An-72 has folding seats for 68 passengers along side walls and on removable central seats. It can carry 57 parachutists, and has provision for 24 stretcher patients, 12 seated casualties and an attendant in ambulance configuration. An-74 is able to carry eight mission staff in combi role, in two rows of seats, with tables, and with two bunks installed, one on each side of cabin aft of seats. Bulged observation windows on port side for navigator and hydrologist. Provision for wardrobe and galley. Movable bulkhead between passenger and freight compartments, with provision for up to 1,500 kg (3,307 lb) of freight in rear compartment. Large downward hinged and forward sliding rear ramp/door for loading trucks and tracked vehicles, and for direct loading of hold from trucks, as described under An-26 entry. It is openable in flight, enabling freight loads of up to 7,500 kg (16,535 lb), with a maximum of 2,500 kg (5,511 lb) per individual item, to be airdropped by parachute extraction system. Removable mobile winch, capacity 2,500 kg (5,511 lb), assists loading of containers up to 1.90 × 2.44 × 1.46 m (6 ft 3 in × 8 ft × 4 ft 9½ in) in size, pallets 1.90 × 2.42 × 1.46 m (6 ft 3 in × 7 ft 11 in × 4 ft 9½ in) in size, and other bulky items. Cargo straps and nets are stowed in lockers on each side of hold when not in use. Provision for building roller conveyors into floor. Main crew and passenger door at front of cabin on port side. Small emergency exit and servicing door at rear of cabin on starboard side.

SYSTEMS: Air-conditioning system provides comfortable environment to altitude of 10,000 m (32,800 ft), with independent temperature control in flight deck and main cabin areas. It can be used to refrigerate main cabin when perishable goods are carried. Hydraulic system for actuating landing gear, flaps and ramp. Electrical system powers auxiliary systems, flight deck equipment, lighting and mobile hoist. Thermal de-icing system for leading-edges of wings and tail unit (including tailplane slat), engine air intakes and cockpit windows. Provision for APU in starboard landing gear fairing. This can be used to heat the cabin; and, under cold ambient conditions, servicing personnel can gain access to major electric, hydraulic and air-conditioning components without stepping outside.

AVIONICS: HF com, VHF com/nav, ADF. Large radome over navigation/weather radar in nose. Doppler based automatic navigation system, linked to onboard computer, is pre-programmed before take-off on push-button panel to right of large map display. Failure warning panels above windscreen display red lights for critical failures, yellow lights for non-critical failures, to minimise time spent on monitoring instruments and equipment. 'Odd Rods' IFF standard. An-74 has enhanced avionics, including INS.

DIMENSIONS, EXTERNAL:
Wing span	31.89 m (104 ft 7½ in)
Length overall (An-72)	28.07 m (92 ft 1¼ in)

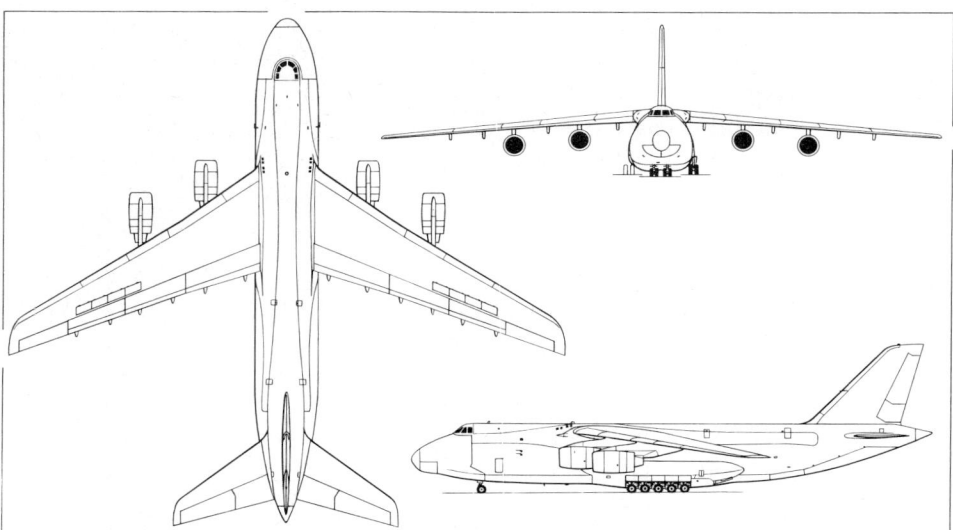

Antonov An-124 (four Zaporozhye/Lotarev D-18T turbofans) *(Pilot Press)*

Fuselage: Max diameter	3.10 m (10 ft 2 in)
Height overall	8.65 m (28 ft 4½ in)
Wheel track	4.15 m (13 ft 7½ in)
Wheelbase	8.12 m (26 ft 7¾ in)
Rear loading door: Length	7.10 m (23 ft 3½ in)
Width	2.40 m (7 ft 10½ in)

DIMENSIONS, INTERNAL:
Cabin: Length	10.50 m (34 ft 5¼ in)
Width at floor level	2.15 m (7 ft 0½ in)
Height	2.20 m (7 ft 2½ in)

AREAS:
Wings, gross	98.62 m² (1,062 sq ft)

WEIGHTS AND LOADINGS (D-36 engines):
Max payload: normal	10,000 kg (22,045 lb)
Max T-O weight:	
from 1,800 m (5,905 ft) runway	34,500 kg (76,060 lb)
from 1,500 m (4,920 ft) runway	33,000 kg (72,750 lb)
from 1,000 m (3,280 ft) runway	27,500 kg (60,625 lb)
Max wing loading	349.8 kg/m² (71.62 lb/sq ft)
Max power loading	270.6 kg/kN (2.65 lb/lb st)

PERFORMANCE (An-72A with D-36 engines. A: at T-O weight of 33,000 kg; 72,750 lb, B: at T-O weight of 27,500 kg; 60,625 lb on 1,000 m; 3,280 ft unprepared runway):
Max level speed at 10,000 m (32,800 ft):	
A	380 knots (705 km/h; 438 mph)
Cruising speed at 10,000 m (32,800 ft):	
A, B	297-324 knots (550-600 km/h; 342-373 mph)
Approach speed: A	97 knots (180 km/h; 112 mph)
Service ceiling: A	10,700 m (35,100 ft)
B	11,800 m (38,715 ft)
Service ceiling, one engine out: A	5,100 m (16,730 ft)
B	6,800 m (22,300 ft)
T-O run: A	930 m (3,052 ft)
B	620 m (2,035 ft)
T-O to 10.7 m (35 ft): A	1,170 m (3,840 ft)
B	830 m (2,725 ft)
Landing run: A	465 m (1,525 ft)
B	420 m (1,380 ft)
Range, with 45 min reserves:	
A with max payload	430 nm (800 km; 497 miles)
A with 7,500 kg (16,535 lb) payload	1,080 nm (2,000 km; 1,240 miles)
A with max fuel	2,590 nm (4,800 km; 2,980 miles)
B with 5,000 kg (11,020 lb) payload	430 nm (800 km; 497 miles)
B with max fuel	1,760 nm (3,250 km; 2,020 miles)

PERFORMANCE (An-74 with D-36 engines):
Generally as for An-72A, except:	
Range, with 2 h reserves:	
with max payload	620 nm (1,150 km; 715 miles)
with 1,500 kg (3,307 lb) payload	2,265 nm (4,200 km; 2,610 miles)

ANTONOV An-74 VARIANT
NATO reporting name: Madcap

TYPE: AEW&C development of An-72.

PROGRAMME: First seen in background of mid-1980s photograph taken during visit by Mr Gorbachev to Antonov OKB; only tail end shown, with rotodome at top of large sweptforward fin and rudder; development believed at early stage, with much work required to produce satisfactory avionics; Rear Admiral Thomas Brooks, US Director of Naval Intelligence, suggested 'Madcap' might be intended for operation from Soviet Navy aircraft carriers of 'Admiral Kuznetsov' class; production unlikely.

ANTONOV An-124
NATO reporting name: Condor

TYPE: Long-range heavy-lift four-turbofan freight transport.

PROGRAMME: Prototype (SSSR-680125) first flew 26 December 1982; second prototype (SSSR-82002 *Ruslan*, named after giant hero of Russian folklore immortalised by Pushkin) exhibited 1985 Paris Air Show; lifted payload of 171,219 kg (377,473 lb) to 10,750 m (35,269 ft) on 26 July 1985, exceeding by 53 per cent C-5A Galaxy's record for payload lifted to 2,000 m and setting 20 more records; entered service January 1986, transporting units of US/Canadian Euclid 154 tonne dumper truck for Yakut diamond miners; set closed circuit distance record 6-7 May 1987 by flying 10,880.625 nm (20,150.921 km; 12,521.201 miles) around the western USSR in 25 h 30 mins; deliveries to VTA to replace An-22, began 1987; production continues, at Ulyanovsk and Kiev.

CUSTOMERS: In early 1991 deliveries totalled 26, including prototypes: 23 to VTA, with three available to Air Foyle, UK, for charter operations.

DESIGN FEATURES: World's largest production aircraft; configuration similar to Lockheed C-5 Galaxy, except for low-mounted tailplane; upward hinged visor type nose and rear fuselage ramp/door for simultaneous front and rear loading/unloading; 100 per cent fly-by-wire control system; titanium floor throughout constant-section main hold, which is lightly pressurised, with a fully pressurised cabin for passengers above; landing gear for operation from unprepared fields, hard packed snow and ice covered swampland; steerable nose- and mainwheels permit turns on 45 m (148 ft) wide runway; supercritical wings, with anhedral; sweepback approx 35° on inboard leading-edge, 32° outboard; all tail surfaces sweptback.

FLYING CONTROLS: Fly-by-wire, with all surfaces hydraulically actuated; two-section aileron, three-section single-slotted Fowler flaps and six-section full-span leading-edge flaps on each wing; small slot in outer part of two inner flap sections each side to optimise

Antonov An-124 heavy freight transport, with landing gear extended *(Peter J. Cooper)*

aerodynamics; eight spoilers on each wing, forward of trailing-edge flaps; no wing fences, vortex generators or tabs; hydraulic flutter dampers on ailerons; rudder and each elevator in two sections, without tabs but with hydraulic flutter dampers; fixed incidence tailplane; control runs (and other services) channelled along fuselage roof.

STRUCTURE: Basically conventional light alloy, but 5,500 kg (12,125 lb) of composites make up more than 1,500 m² (16,150 sq ft) of surface area, giving weight saving of more than 2,000 kg (4,410 lb); each wing has one-piece root-to-tip upper surface extruded skin panel, strip of carbonfibre skin panels on undersurface forward of control surfaces, and glassfibre tip; front and rear of each flap guide fairing of glassfibre, centre portion of carbonfibre; central frames of semi-monocoque fuselage each comprise four large forgings; fairings over intersection of fuselage double-bubble lobes in line with wing, from rear of flight deck to plane of fin leading-edge, primarily of glassfibre, with central, and lower underwing, portions of carbonfibre; other glassfibre components include tailplane tips, nosecone, tailcone and most bottom skin panels forming blister underfairing between main landing gear legs; carbonfibre components include strips of skin panels forward of each tail control surface, nose and main landing gear doors, some service doors, and clamshell doors aft of rear loading ramp.

LANDING GEAR: Hydraulically retractable nosewheel type, with total of 24 wheels. Nose gear comprises two independent forward retracting and steerable twin-wheel units, side by side. Each main gear comprises five independent inward retracting twin-wheel units, of which the front two units on each side are steerable. Each mainwheel bogie is enclosed by separate upper and lower doors when retracted. Nosewheel doors and lower mainwheel doors close when gear is extended. All wheel doors are of carbonfibre. Main gear bogies can be retracted individually for repair or wheel change. Mainwheel tyres size 1,270 × 510 mm. Nosewheel tyres size 1,120 × 450 mm. Aircraft can 'kneel', by retracting nosewheels and settling on two extendable 'feet', giving floor of hold a 3.5° slope to assist loading and unloading. Rear of cargo hold can be lowered by compressing main gear oleos. Carbon brakes are normally toe operated, via rudder pedals. For severe braking, pedals are depressed by both toes and heels.

POWER PLANT: Four Zaporozhye/Lotarev D-18T turbofans, each rated at 229.5 kN (51,590 lb st). Thrust reversers standard. Engine cowlings of glassfibre; pylons have carbonfibre skin at rear end. All fuel in ten integral tanks in wings.

ACCOMMODATION: All crew and passenger accommodation on upper deck; freight and/or vehicles on lower deck. Flight crew of six, in pairs, on flight deck, with place for loadmaster in lobby area. Pilot and co-pilot on fully adjustable seats, which rotate for improved access. Two flight engineers, on wall-facing seats on starboard side, have complete control of master fuel cocks, detailed systems instruments, and digital integrated data system with CRT monitor. Behind pilot are the navigator and communications specialist, also on wall-facing seats. Between flight deck and wing carry-through structure, on port side, are toilets, washing facilities, galley, equipment compartment, and two cabins for total of up to six relief crew, with table and facing bench seats convertible into bunks. Aft of wing carry-through is a passenger cabin for up to 88 persons. Hatches in upper deck provide access to the wing and tail unit for maintenance in places where workstands may not be available. Flight deck and passenger cabin are each accessible from cargo hold by means of an hydraulic folding ladder, operated automatically with manual override. Rearward sliding and jettisonable window on each side of flight deck.

Primary access to flight deck via airstair door, with ladder extension, forward of wing on port side. Smaller door forward of this and slightly higher. Door from main hold aft of wing on starboard side. Upper deck doors at rear of flight deck on starboard side and at rear of passenger cabin on each side. Emergency exit from upper deck aft of wing on each side. Hydraulically operated visor type upward hinged nose takes 7 min to open fully, with simultaneous extension of folding nose loading ramp. When open, nose is steadied by reinforcing arms against wind gusts. No hydraulic, electrical or other system lines are broken when nose is open. Radar wiring passes through hollow tube in hinge. Hydraulically operated rear loading doors take 3 min to open, with simultaneous extension of three-part folding ramp. This can be locked in intermediate position for direct loading from truck or loading galley. Aft of ramp, centre panel of fuselage undersurface hinges upward; clamshell door to each side opens downward. Completely unobstructed lower deck freight hold has titanium floor, attached 'mobilely' to lower fuselage structure to accommodate changes of temperature, with rollgangs and retractable attachments for cargo tiedowns. A narrow catwalk along each sidewall facilitates access to, and mobility past, loaded freight. Payloads can include largest Soviet main battle tanks, complete missile systems, Siberian oil well equipment and earth movers. No personnel are carried normally on lower deck in flight, because of low pressurisation of hold. Two electric travelling cranes in roof of hold, each with two lifting points, offer total lifting capacity of 20,000 kg (44,100 lb). Two winches can each pull a 3,000 kg (6,614 lb) load.

SYSTEMS: Entire interior of aircraft is pressurised and air-conditioned. Max pressure differential 0.55 bars (7.8 lb/sq in) on upper deck, 0.25 bars (3.55 lb/sq in) on lower deck. Four independent hydraulic systems. Quadruple redundant fly-by-wire flight control system, with mechanical emergency fifth channel to hydraulic control servos. Special secondary bus electrical system. Landing lights under nose and at front of each main landing gear fairing. APU in rear of each landing gear fairing is used for engine starting, and can be operated in the air or on

the ground to open loading doors for airdrop from rear or normal ground loading/unloading, as well as for supplying electrical, hydraulic and air-conditioning systems. Bleed air anti-icing of wing leading-edges. Electro-impulse de-icing of fin and tailplane leading-edges.

AVIONICS: Comprehensive but conventional flight deck equipment, including automatic flight control system control panel at top of glareshield, weather radar screen and moving map display forward of throttle and thrust reverse levers on centre console. No electronic flight displays. Dual attitude indicator/flight director and HSIs, and vertical tape engine instruments. Two dielectric areas of nose visor enclose forward looking weather radar and downward looking ground mapping/navigation radar. Hemispherical dielectric fairing above centre fuselage for satellite navigation receiver. Quadruple INS, plus Loran and Omega.

EQUIPMENT: Small two-face mirror, of V form, enables pilots to adjust their seating position until their eyes are reflected in the appropriate mirror, which ensures an optimum field of view from the flight deck.

DIMENSIONS, EXTERNAL:

Wing span	73.30 m (240 ft 5¾ in)
Length overall	69.10 m (226 ft 8½ in)
Height overall	20.78 m (68 ft 2¼ in)

DIMENSIONS, INTERNAL:

Cargo hold: Length	36.0 m (118 ft 1¼ in)
Max width	6.4 m (21 ft 0 in)
Max height	4.4 m (14 ft 5¼ in)
Volume	1,000 m³ (35,315 cu ft)

AREAS:

Wings, gross	628.0 m² (6,760.0 sq ft)

WEIGHTS AND LOADINGS:

Operating weight empty	175,000 kg (385,800 lb)
Max payload	150,000 kg (330,693 lb)
Max fuel	230,000 kg (507,063 lb)
Max T-O weight	405,000 kg (892,872 lb)
Max zero-fuel weight	325,000 kg (716,500 lb)
Max wing loading	644.9 kg/m² (132.1 lb/sq ft)
Max power loading	441.2 kg/kN (4.32 lb/lb st)

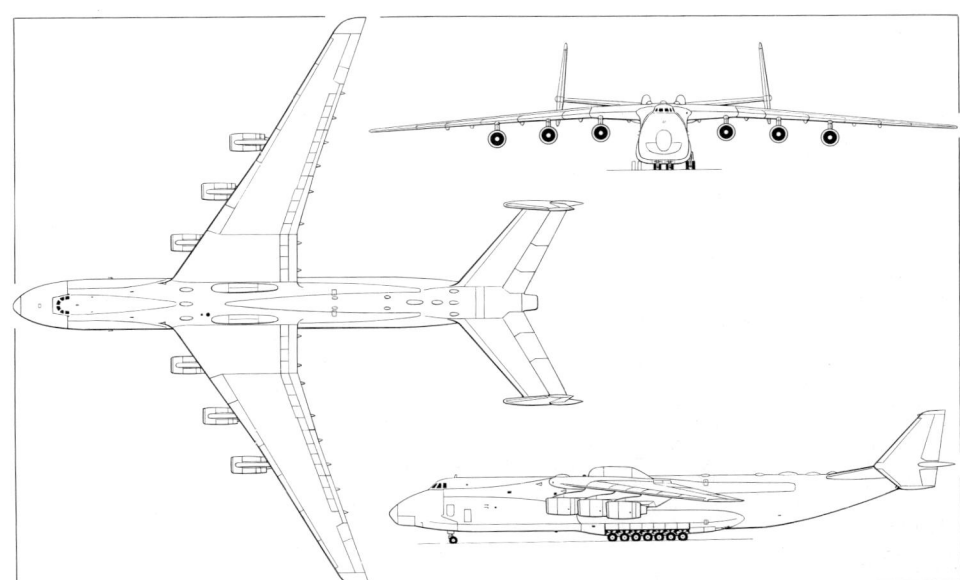

Antonov An-225 Mriya (NATO 'Cossack') six-turbofan heavy freight transport *(Pilot Press)*

Antonov An-225 at Farnborough 1990 air show *(Peter J. Cooper)*

World's largest aeroplane, the An-225, shows its agility *(Peter J. Cooper)*

Model showing projected carriage of British Hotol spacecraft on An-225 first-stage launch vehicle
(Piotr Butowski)

PERFORMANCE:
Max cruising speed   467 knots (865 km/h; 537 mph)
Normal cruising speed at 10,000-12,000 m (32,800-39,370 ft) 432-459 knots (800-850 km/h; 497-528 mph)
Approach speed
                    124-140 knots (230-260 km/h; 143-162 mph)
T-O balanced field length at max T-O weight
                                    3,000 m (9,850 ft)
Landing run at max landing weight   800 m (2,625 ft)
Range:
  with max payload   2,430 nm (4,500 km; 2,795 miles)
  with max fuel   8,900 nm (16,500 km; 10,250 miles)
OPERATIONAL NOISE LEVELS:
  Stated to meet ICAO requirements

ANTONOV An-218
See Addenda.

ANTONOV An-225 MRIYA (DREAM)
NATO reporting name: Cossack

TYPE: Six-turbofan heavy transport for internal/external payloads.

PROGRAMME: Design studies began mid-1985; prototype (SSSR-480182) made 75 min first flight "from 1,000 m (3,280 ft) runway" on 21 December 1988, three weeks after unveiling at Kiev; total of 106 records set on 22 March 1989 during 3½ h flight: taking off at 508,200 kg (1,120,370 lb), with 156,300 kg (344,576 lb) payload, flew 2,000 km closed circuit at 438.75 knots (813.09 km/h; 505.24 mph), with max altitude of 12,340 m (40,485 ft) *en route*; first flight carrying *Buran* orbiter on back made 13 May 1989 from Baikonur; one more An-225 funded to date; Antonov hopes to build 20 for commercial use.

DESIGN FEATURES: First aircraft built to fly at gross weight exceeding one million pounds; designed to replace Myasishchev VM-T Atlant as external load-carrier for space orbiters, components of Energiya rocket launch vehicles and other outsize loads; based on An-124, with extended wings and lengthened fuselage to permit 50 per cent increase in max T-O weight and payload; basic cabin cross-section and visor type nose door unchanged; rear loading ramp/door deleted and rear fuselage reconfigured with twin fins and rudders on dihedral tailplane to avoid airflow problems when carrying piggyback loads; main landing gear uprated from five to seven pairs of wheels on each side; six engines instead of four, of same type; basically standard An-124 wings attached to new centre-section; anhedral on outer wings only; sweepback 35° on inboard half-span, 32° outboard; all tail surfaces sweptback.

FLYING CONTROLS: Fly-by-wire, with all surfaces hydraulically actuated; each wing has two-section aileron, three-section single-slotted Fowler flaps on outer panels and single section on centre-section, and six-section leading-edge flaps on outer panels only; eight airbrakes (inboard) and eight spoilers (outboard) on each wing upper surface and centre-section forward of flaps; no wing fences, vortex generators or tabs; two-section rudder and three-section elevator on each side; control runs (and other services) channelled along fuselage roof.

STRUCTURE: Generally as for An-124.

LANDING GEAR: Hydraulically retractable nosewheel type. Nose gear comprises two independent forward retracting and steerable twin-wheel units, side by side. Each main gear comprises seven independent inward retracting twin-wheel units, with tyres size 1,270 × 510 mm. Rear four pairs of wheels on each side are steerable. Each mainwheel bogie is enclosed by separate upper and lower doors when retracted. Nosewheel doors and lower mainwheel doors close when gear is extended. Aircraft can 'kneel', by retracting nosewheels and settling on two extendable 'feet', giving floor a slope to assist loading and unloading.

POWER PLANT: Six Zaporozhye/Lotarev D-18T turbofans, each rated at 229.5 kN (51,590 lb st) and each fitted with thrust reverser. Engine cowlings of glassfibre. All fuel in integral tanks in wings, including additional tanks in new centre-section. Max capacity estimated at well over 300,000 kg (661,375 lb).

ACCOMMODATION: Flight crew of six, in pairs, on flight deck, with place for loadmaster in lobby area. Pilot and co-pilot on fully adjustable seats that rotate for improved access. Two flight engineers, on wall-facing seats on starboard side. Navigator and communications specialist behind pilot, also on wall-facing seats. Rest area for relief crew slightly larger than that of An-124. Cabin for 60–70 persons above hold aft of wing carry-through. Primary access to flight deck via airstair door, with ladder extension, forward of wing on port side. Door to main hold aft of wing on starboard side. Hydraulically operated visor type upward hinged nose takes 7 min to open fully, with simultaneous extension of folding nose loading ramp. Completely unobstructed lower deck freight hold, 43.0 m (141 ft) long, has titanium floor, attached 'mobilely' to lower fuselage structure to accommodate changes of temperature, with rollgangs and retractable attachments for cargo tiedowns. Interior

can be heated with warm air from a perforated tube above the floor on each side of hold. Internal loads can include vehicles, ground test and field maintenance equipment required by external loads. Two longitudinal mounting beams for external loads above wing centre-section. Small blister fairings forward of beams and forward of tailplane cover load attachments. Under consideration is a scheme to use the An-225 as a launcher for future space vehicles like the British Hotol or space combat aircraft.

AVIONICS: Generally similar to An-124, with comprehensive but conventional flight deck equipment including automatic flight control system and moving map display; no electronic flight displays. Two dielectric areas of nose visor enclose forward-looking weather radar and downward-looking ground mapping/navigation radar. Quadruple INS, plus Loran and Omega.

DIMENSIONS, EXTERNAL:
Wing span	88.40 m (290 ft 0 in)
Length overall	84.00 m (275 ft 7 in)

Height overall	18.10 m (59 ft 4¾ in)
Tailplane span	32.65 m (107 ft 1½ in)

DIMENSIONS, INTERNAL:
Cargo hold: Max width	6.4 m (21 ft 0 in)
Max height	4.4 m (14 ft 5¼ in)

WEIGHTS AND LOADINGS:
Max payload, internal or external	250,000 kg (551,150 lb)
Max T-O weight	600,000 kg (1,322,750 lb)
Max power loading	435.7 kg/kN (4.27 lb/lb st)

PERFORMANCE (estimated):
Cruising speed	378-458 knots (700-850 km/h; 435-528 mph)
Min turning radius about nosewheels	50 m (165 ft)
T-O run, carrying Buran	2,500–2,800 m (8,200–9,185 ft)
Range with 200,000 kg (440,900 lb) internal payload	2,425 nm (4,500 km; 2,795 miles)

BERIEV
BERIEV DESIGN BUREAU
Taganrog, Rostov

GENERAL DESIGNER: Alexander K. Konstantinov

This OKB was founded by Georgi Mikhailovich Beriev (1902–1979) in 1932; except during Second World War, 1942-45, it has been based at Taganrog, in northeast corner of Sea of Azov; since 1948 it has been the centre for all Soviet seaplane development. In addition to aircraft listed, Beriev OKB is investigating the feasibility of building aircraft with T-O weight between 200 and 600 tonnes for operation virtually anywhere in the Pacific, as well as supersonic flying-boats.

BERIEV Be-12 (M-12) TCHAIKA (SEAGULL)
NATO reporting name: Mail

TYPE: Twin-turboprop anti-submarine and maritime patrol amphibian.

PROGRAMME: First flew 1960; displayed publicly at 1961 Aviation Day Display, Tushino Airport, Moscow; production of estimated 100 began 1964 to replace Be-6s on anti-submarine and surveillance duties out to some 200 nm (370 km; 230 miles) from shore bases.

CUSTOMERS: Soviet Naval Aviation has an estimated 75 in 1991, with Northern and Black Sea Fleets; no exports, although Be-12 seen in temporary Egyptian insignia in early 1970s.

DESIGN FEATURES: General configuration inherited from piston-engined Be-6, with sharply cranked wing to raise propellers clear of water; single-step hull of high length to beam ratio, with spray dams on sides of nose.

FLYING CONTROLS: Mechanically actuated; hydraulically boosted ailerons, each with two electrically operated tabs; elevators and horn-balanced rudders hydraulically boosted; electrically operated trim tab in each elevator and rudder; hydraulically actuated trailing-edge flaps in two sections on each wing, passing under engine nacelle to wingroot.

STRUCTURE: Conventional all-metal; two-spar wings with considerable centre-section dihedral, slight anhedral on outer panels; semi-monocoque hull with conventional planing bottom; dihedral tailplane with endplate fins and rudders.

LANDING GEAR: Hydraulically retractable tailwheel type, comprising single-wheel main units which retract upward through 180° to lie flush within sides of hull, and a

rearward retracting steerable tailwheel. Oleo-pneumatic mainwheel shock absorbers. Except for top of each mainwheel, all units are fully enclosed by doors when retracted. Non-retractable wingtip floats.

POWER PLANT: Two Ivchenko AI-20M turboprops, each rated at 3,124 kW (4,190 ehp) and driving an AV-68I four-blade variable-pitch propeller. Metal cowlings open downward in halves, permitting their use as servicing platforms. Fuel tanks, between spars in wings and in fuselage, with total capacity of approx 11,000 litres (2,905 US gallons; 2,420 Imp gallons).

ACCOMMODATION: Not pressurised. Crew of five on flight deck. Glazed navigation and observation station in nose. Astrodome observation station in top of rear fuselage. Side hatches in rear fuselage permit loading while afloat.

SYSTEMS: Hydraulic system actuates flaps and landing gear. Two engine driven generators power 28V DC electrical system.

AVIONICS: No details available of com/nav systems or IFF. Radome above nose glazing. MAD (magnetic anomaly detection) sting extends rearward from tail.

EQUIPMENT: APU exhausts through aperture in port side of rear fuselage.

ARMAMENT: Internal weapons bay in bottom of hull aft of step. One large and one smaller external stores pylon under each outer wing panel, for torpedoes, depth charges, mines and other stores.

DIMENSIONS, EXTERNAL:
Wing span	29.71 m (97 ft 5¾ in)
Wing aspect ratio	8.4

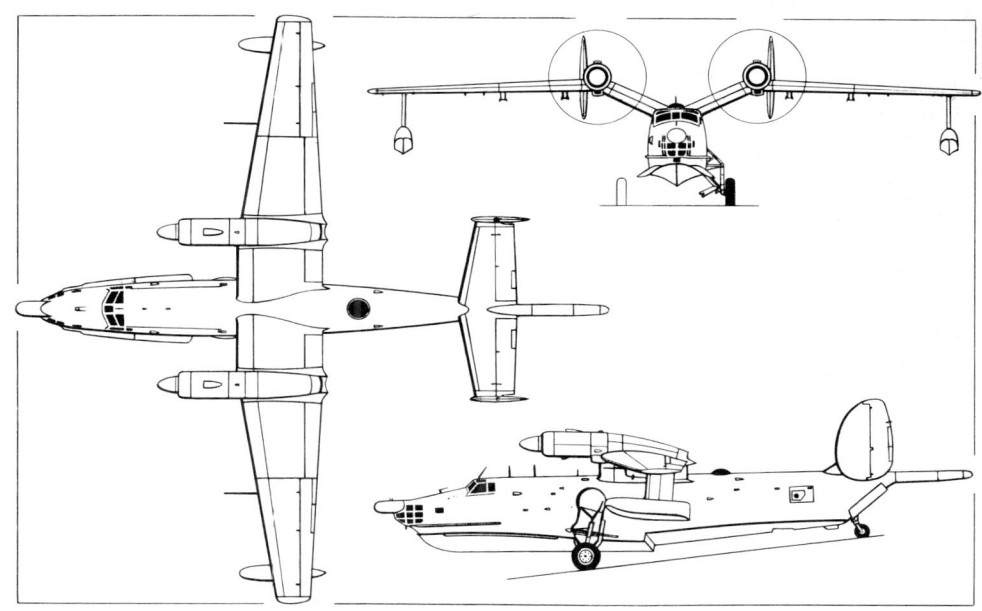

Beriev Be-12 Tchaika twin-turboprop maritime reconnaissance amphibian (Pilot Press)

Beriev Be-12 Tchaika anti-submarine and maritime patrol amphibian flying-boat of the Soviet Naval Air Force (Swedish Air Force, via FLYGvapenNYTT)

Beriev A-40 Albatross amphibian (two MKB [Perm]/Soloviev D-30KPV turbofans) *(AP/Viktor Yurchenko)*

Length overall	30.17 m (99 ft 0 in)
Height overall	7.00 m (22 ft 11½ in)
Propeller diameter	4.85 m (16 ft 0 in)
AREAS:	
Wings, gross	105 m² (1,130 sq ft)
WEIGHTS AND LOADINGS:	
Max operational load	10,000 kg (22,045 lb)
Max T-O weight	31,000 kg (68,345 lb)
Max wing loading	295.2 kg/m² (60.5 lb/sq ft)
Max power loading	4.96 kg/kW (8.16 lb/ehp)
PERFORMANCE:	
Max level speed	328 knots (608 km/h; 378 mph)
Normal operating speed	
	172 knots (320 km/h; 199 mph)
Rate of climb at S/L	912 m (2,990 ft)/min
Service ceiling	11,280 m (37,000 ft)
Range with max fuel	4,050 nm (7,500 km; 4,660 miles)

BERIEV Be-42 (A-40) ALBATROSS

TYPE: Twin-turbofan multi-role amphibian.

PROGRAMME: First mentioned Spring 1988 by Rear Adm William O. Studeman, then US director of naval intelligence, as seaplane with provisional Western designation 'Tag-D' (implying fourth unidentified type photographed by US reconnaissance satellite over Taganrog), for possible ASW/surveillance/minelaying role; identified as A-40 Albatross, designed by Alexander Konstantinov for search and rescue, when prototype flown over Tushino Airport during Aviation Day display, 20 August 1989; feature in *Krasnaya Zvezda*, 6 August 1989, stated that A-40 will be confined to SAR missions near coast, and next task confronting designers was to produce similar aircraft capable of operating anywhere in Pacific; Konstantinov said subsequently that seaplane development in USSR had halted because "if the West no longer builds them, we do not need them"; programme status therefore unknown, but prototype has set records (still to be confirmed), lifting payload of 5,000 kg to height of 13,300 m (43,635 ft) and 10,000 kg to 13,100 m (42,980 ft); 1989 completion of second prototype reported and 1990 edition of US Department of Defense's *Soviet Military Power* document states "The Soviets are still modernising their fixed-wing ASW force and are on the verge of deploying a jet amphibian" (the largest ever built). Designation Be-42 announced 1991.

DESIGN FEATURES: High-performance sweptwing amphibian; single-step hull of high length to beam ratio, with what the Soviet press describes as "the world's first development of a variable-rise bottom, providing a considerable improvement in stability and controllability in the water, as well as a reduction in g loads when landing and taking off at sea"; all-swept T-tail; high-mounted engines protected from spray by strakes on each side of nose and forward of step, and by wings; large underwing pod each side of hull, faired into wingroot; wing leading-edge sweep approx 27°; large dorsal fin.

FLYING CONTROLS: Entire span of each wing trailing-edge occupied by aileron and two-section area-increasing flaps; full-span leading-edge flaps; conventional rudder and elevators.

STRUCTURE: Details not yet known, but extensive use of bonded honeycomb structures and composites; double-chine planing bottom forward of step; water rudder at rear of hull.

LANDING GEAR: Retractable tricycle type. Main units retract into large underwing pods, aft of wing trailing-edge. Non-retractable stabilising float pylon-mounted under each wingtip.

POWER PLANT: Two MKB (Perm)/Soloviev D-30KPV turbofans (each 117.7 kN; 26,455 lb st), pylon-mounted above fuselage, aft of wings. Each exhaust efflux is toed outward. Flight refuelling probe above nose.

ACCOMMODATION: Conventional flight deck, with door to rear of this on port side. Three circular cabin windows between door and wingroot fairing, probably on each side. Rescue team of four or five specialists with power boats, LPS-6 liferafts and other specialised equipment can be carried, and there is room for up to 60 survivors, who enter the aircraft via hatches in the side of the hull with the aid of mechanised ramps. Medical team can include surgeon, therapeutist, anaesthetist and surgeon's assistant. Transport version could carry up to 95-100 passengers and/or freight.

AVIONICS: Large nose radome. Unidentified features include a slim container above each wingtip float pylon and a hemispherical fairing at rear of each wingroot pod.

EQUIPMENT: In SAR version, onboard equipment to combat hypothermia is available, together with resuscitation and surgical equipment and medicines; electro-optical sensors and searchlights to detect shipwreck survivors by day or night. Firefighting version could be equipped to drop firefighters and cargoes by parachute, and to drop up to 25,000 kg (55,115 lb) of water per sortie on a fire, at average concentration of 2.3 litres (0.60 US gallons; 0.50 Imp gallons)/m², while flying at 135 knots (250 km/h; 155 mph); water taken on board through scoops in planing bottom, from minimum 3,200 m (10,500 ft) stretch of water.

ARMAMENT: Stores bay, 6.10 m (20 ft) long, in bottom of hull, aft of step.

DIMENSIONS, EXTERNAL:

Wing span	41.8 m (137 ft 1½ in)
Length overall, excl noseprobe	43.0 m (141 ft 0 in)
Height overall, on wheels	11.0 m (36 ft 1 in)
Max depth of hull forward of wing	4.0 m (13 ft 2 in)
Tailplane span	12.0 m (39 ft 4 in)
PERFORMANCE:	
Max cruising speed	431 knots (800 km/h; 497 mph)
Patrol speed	
	173-215 knots (320-400 km/h; 200-250 mph)

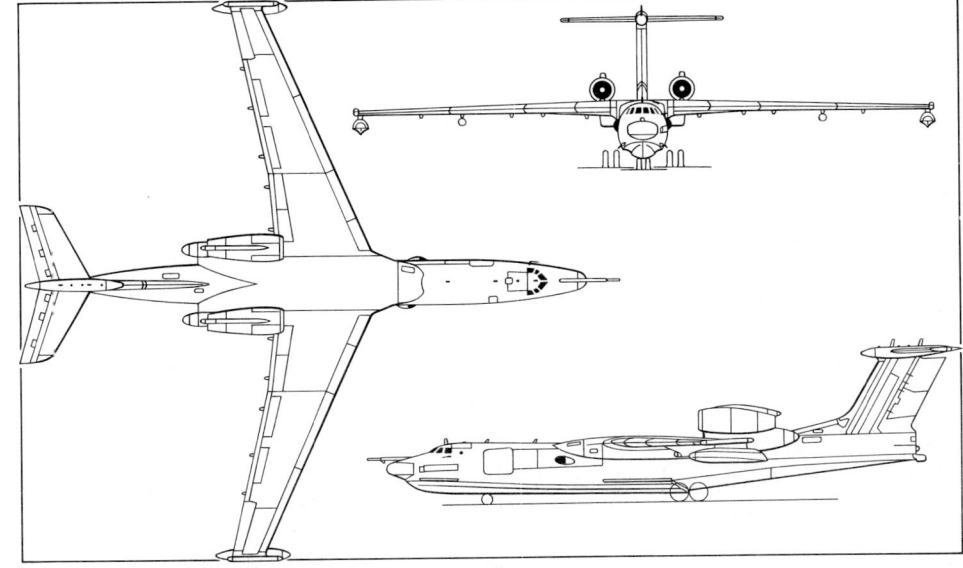

Beriev Be-42 Albatross twin-turbofan amphibian *(Jane's/Mike Keep)*

Balanced runway length   1,800 m (5,905 ft)
Max wave height for safe operation   2.0 m (6 ft 6½ in)
Range with 37 passengers and 6,500 kg (14,330 lb) cargo
                 2,700 nm (5,000 km; 3,100 miles)
Max patrol endurance   9 h

BERIEV Be-200

TYPE: Multi-role amphibian.

PROGRAMME: At design stage in early 1991.

DESIGN FEATURES: To operate from coastal waters, small inland lakes and reservoirs at T-O weight of 36,000 kg (79,365 lb): duties to include firefighting, passenger and cargo transport, ambulance; patrolling 200 nm (370 km; 230 mile) economic zones; servicing geological teams, expeditions, offshore oil rigs and fishery vessels; ice reconnaissance. (See Addenda.)

This photograph shows well the unique double-chine "variable rise bottom" of the Beriev A-40 Albatross *(Tass)*

ILYUSHIN

ILYUSHIN DESIGN BUREAU

Moscow 125319
Telephone: 155 30 60
Telex: 411956 Sokol
GENERAL DESIGNER: Genrikh V. Novozhilov
CHIEF DESIGNER: R. P. Papkovsky
HEAD OF SCIENTIFIC AND TECHNICAL INFORMATION DEPARTMENT: B. N. Tishunin
HEAD OF TECHNICAL PUBLICATIONS DEPARTMENT AND PUBLIC RELATIONS: A. A. Shakhnovich

Ilyushin OKB is named after Sergei Vladimirovich Ilyushin, who died 9 February 1977, aged 82. OKB was founded 1933.

ILYUSHIN Il-20

NATO reporting name: Coot-A

TYPE: Military elint/reconnaissance variant of Il-18 four-turboprop airliner.

PROGRAMME: First observed 1978; small number operational.

DESIGN FEATURES: Il-18 airframe basically unchanged; underfuselage container, approx 10.25 m (33 ft 7½ in) long and 1.15 m (3 ft 9 in) deep, assumed to house side-looking radar; container, approx 4.4 m (14 ft 5 in) long and 0.88 m (2 ft 10½ in) deep, on each side of forward fuselage contains door over camera or other sensor; antennae and blisters include eight on under-surface of centre and rear fuselage, with two large plates projecting above forward fuselage.

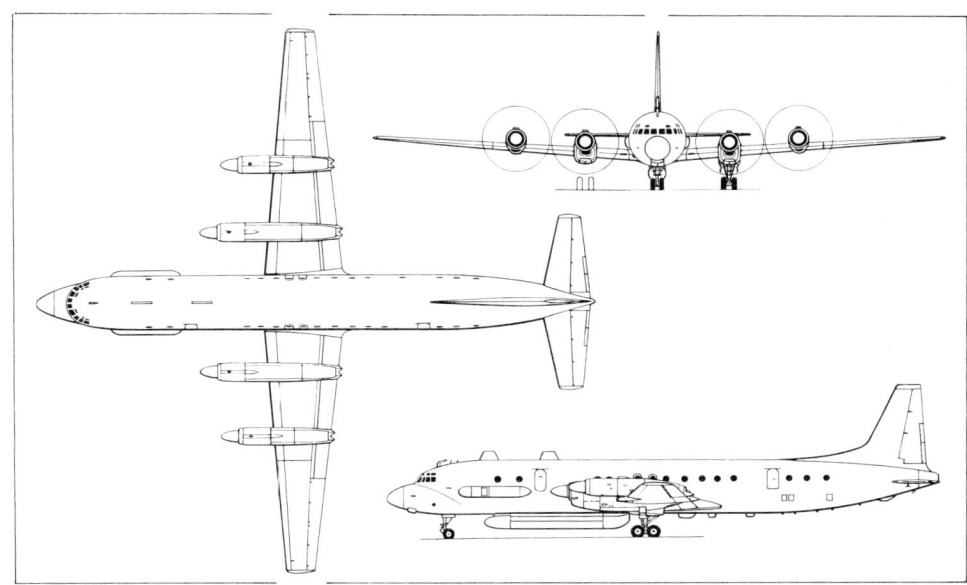

Ilyushin Il-20 (NATO 'Coot-A') elint/reconnaissance development of the Il-18 airliner *(Pilot Press)*

Ilyushin Il-20 (NATO 'Coot-A') electronic intelligence (elint) and reconnaissance aircraft *(Swedish Air Force, via FLYGvapenNYTT)*

Ilyushin Il-38 (four Ivchenko AI-20M turboprops) over the Mediterranean, escorted by an RAF Hawk in 63 Squadron markings *(Royal Air Force)*

Detailed description of Il-18 airliner in 1979-80 and earlier editions of *Jane's*; following abbreviated details of Il-18D indicate likely features retained by Il-20.

POWER PLANT: Four 3,169 kW (4,250 ehp) Ivchenko AI-20M turboprops, each driving an AV-68I four-blade reversible-pitch propeller. Ten flexible fuel tanks in inboard panel of each wing and integral tank in outboard panel, with a total capacity of 23,700 litres (6,261 US gallons; 5,213 Imp gallons). Some Il-18 airliners have additional bag tanks in centre-section, giving a total capacity of 30,000 litres (7,925 US gallons; 6,600 Imp gallons).

DIMENSIONS, EXTERNAL:

Wing span	37.42 m (122 ft 9¼ in)
Wing chord: at root	5.61 m (18 ft 5 in)
at tip	1.87 m (6 ft 2 in)
Wing aspect ratio	10
Length overall	35.9 m (117 ft 9 in)
Height overall	10.17 m (33 ft 4 in)
Tailplane span	11.80 m (38 ft 8½ in)
Wheel track	9.00 m (29 ft 6 in)
Wheelbase	12.78 m (41 ft 10 in)
Propeller diameter	4.50 m (14 ft 9 in)
Cabin doors (each): Height	1.40 m (4 ft 7 in)
Width	0.76 m (2 ft 6 in)
Height to sill	2.90 m (9 ft 6 in)

DIMENSIONS, INTERNAL:

Flight deck: Volume	9.36 m³ (330 cu ft)
Cabin, excl flight deck:	
Length	approx 24.0 m (79 ft 0 in)
Max width	3.23 m (10 ft 7 in)
Max height	2.00 m (6 ft 6¾ in)
Volume	238 m³ (8,405 cu ft)

AREAS:

Wings, gross	140 m² (1,507 sq ft)

WEIGHTS AND LOADINGS (Il-18D airliner):

Max payload	13,500 kg (29,750 lb)
Max T-O weight	64,000 kg (141,100 lb)
Max wing loading	457.1 kg/m² (93.6 lb/sq ft)
Max power loading	5.05 kg/kW (8.30 lb/ehp)

PERFORMANCE (Il-18D airliner, at max T-O weight):

Max cruising speed	364 knots (675 km/h; 419 mph)
Econ cruising speed	337 knots (625 km/h; 388 mph)
Operating height	8,000-10,000 m (26,250-32,800 ft)
T-O run	1,300 m (4,265 ft)
Landing run	850 m (2,790 ft)
Range, 1 h reserves:	
with max fuel	3,508 nm (6,500 km; 4,040 miles)
with max payload	1,997 nm (3,700 km; 2,300 miles)

ILYUSHIN Il-22
NATO reporting name: Coot-B

Many Il-22 airborne command post adaptations of the Il-18 transport are operational with Soviet air forces. No details are available, but it would be logical to expect a variety of external fairings and antennae.

ILYUSHIN Il-38
NATO reporting name: May

TYPE: Intermediate-range shore-based four-turboprop maritime patrol aircraft.

PROGRAMME: Development of Il-18 airliner, first reported 1970; about 59 serve currently with Soviet Naval Aviation; deployed periodically to Libya and Syria, and to Yemen for patrols over Red Sea, Gulf of Aden, Arabian Sea and Indian Ocean. India placed only export order 1975.

CUSTOMERS: Soviet Naval Aviation; Indian Navy (INAS 315 at Dabolim, Goa).

DESIGN FEATURES: Basic Il-18 airframe, with lengthened fuselage, and wings moved forward to cater for effect of

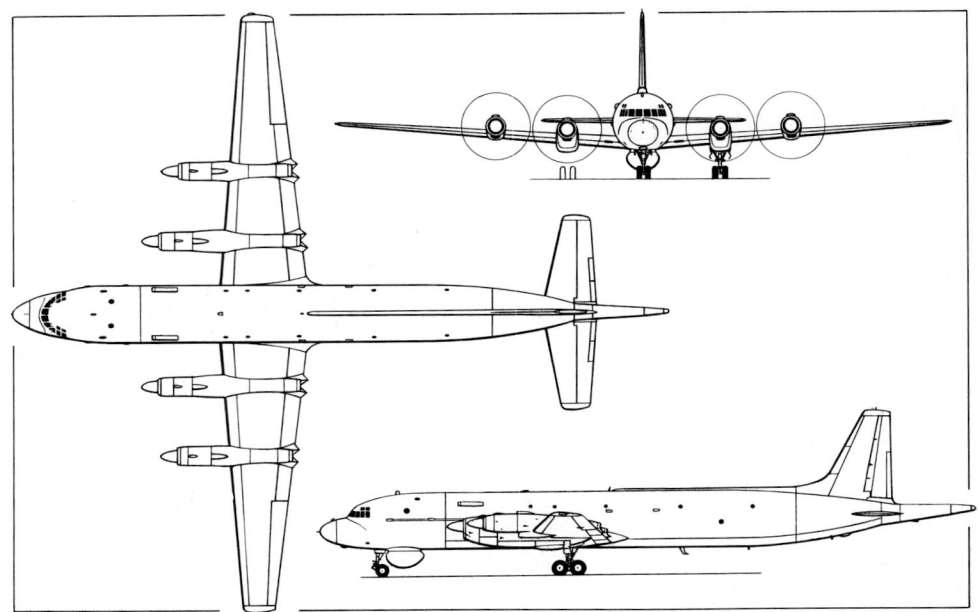

Ilyushin Il-38 anti-submarine/maritime patrol derivative of the Il-18 airliner *(Pilot Press)*

role equipment and stores on CG position; few cabin windows; large undernose radome; MAD tail sting; wing dihedral 3° from roots; mean thickness/chord ratio 14 per cent.

FLYING CONTROLS: Flying controls cable actuated; mass and aerodynamically balanced ailerons with electric trim tabs; hydraulically assisted elevators and rudder, each with electric trim tab; additional rudder spring tab; hydraulically actuated double-slotted wing trailing-edge flaps.

STRUCTURE: All-metal; three-spar wing centre-section, two spars in outer wings; circular-section fail-safe semi-monocoque fuselage, with rip-stop doublers around window cutouts, door frames and more heavily loaded skin panels.

LANDING GEAR: Retractable tricycle type, strengthened by comparison with that of Il-18. Hydraulic actuation. Four-wheel bogie main units, with 930 × 305 mm tyres and hydraulic brakes. Steerable (45° each way) twin nosewheel unit, with 700 × 250 mm tyres. Hydraulic brakes and nosewheel steering. Pneumatic emergency braking.

POWER PLANT: Four Ivchenko AI-20M turboprops, each rated at 3,169 kW (4,250 shp), driving AV-68I four-blade reversible-pitch metal propellers. Multiple bag type fuel tanks in centre-section and in inboard panel of each wing, and integral tank in outboard panel, with a total capacity of 30,000 litres (7,925 US gallons; 6,600 Imp gallons). Pressure fuelling through four international standard connections in inner nacelles. Provision for overwing fuelling. Oil capacity 58.5 litres (15.45 US gallons; 12.85 Imp gallons) per engine. Engines started electrically.

ACCOMMODATION: Pilot and co-pilot side by side on flight deck, with dual controls; flight engineer to rear. Number of operational crew believed to be nine, but unconfirmed. Flight deck is separated from main cabin by a pressure bulkhead to reduce hazards following sudden decompression of either. Main cabin has few windows and contains search equipment, electronic equipment and crew stations appropriate to role. Door is on

starboard side at rear of cabin (location of Il-18 service door).

SYSTEMS: Cabin pressurised to max differential of 0.49 bar (7.1 lb/sq in). Electrical system includes eight engine driven generators for 28V DC and 115V 400Hz AC supply. Hydraulic system, pressure 207 bars (3,000 lb/sq in), for landing gear retraction, nosewheel steering, brakes, elevator and rudder actuators, flaps, weapon bay doors and radar antennae. Electro-thermal de-icing system for wings and tail unit.

AVIONICS: Navigation/weather radar in nose. Search radar (NATO 'Wet Eye') in undernose radome. MAD tail 'sting'. Automatic navigation equipment, radio compasses and radio altimeter probably similar to those of Il-18.

ARMAMENT: Two weapons/stores bays forward and aft of wing carry-through structure on most aircraft, to accommodate a variety of attack weapons and sonobuoys.

DIMENSIONS, EXTERNAL:

As listed under Il-20 entry, except:

Length overall	39.60 m (129 ft 10 in)

WEIGHTS AND LOADINGS:

Weight empty	36,000 kg (79,367 lb)
Max T-O weight	63,500 kg (140,000 lb)
Max wing loading	453.6 kg/m² (92.9 lb/sq ft)
Max power loading	5.01 kg/kW (8.24 lb/ehp)

PERFORMANCE:

Max level speed at 6,400 m (21,000 ft)	
	390 knots (722 km/h; 448 mph)
Max cruising speed at 8,230 m (27,000 ft)	
	330 knots (611 km/h; 380 mph)
Patrol speed at 600 m (2,000 ft)	
	216 knots (400 km/h; 248 mph)
Min flying speed	103 knots (190 km/h; 118 mph)
T-O run	1,300 m (4,265 ft)
Landing run with propeller reversal	850 m (2,790 ft)
Range with max fuel	3,887 nm (7,200 km; 4,473 miles)
Patrol endurance with max fuel	12 h

Ilyushin Il-76T freight transport (four MKB [Perm]/Soloviev D-30KP-1 turbofans) in Aeroflot insignia *(Peter J. Cooper)*

ILYUSHIN Il-62
NATO reporting name: Classic

Brief details of the early history of this rear-engined four-turbofan long-range airliner can be found in the 1982-83 *Jane's*. Structural and specification details of the Il-62/62M/62MK series of production aircraft are contained in the 1989-90 and previous editions.

ILYUSHIN Il-76
NATO reporting name: Candid
Indian Air Force name: Gajaraj
TYPE: Four-turbofan medium/long-range transport.

PROGRAMME: Design began late 1960s, led by G. V. Novozhilov, to replace turboprop An-12; prototype (SSSR-86712) flew 25 March 1971; official 1974 film showed development squadron of Il-76s, with twin-gun rear turrets, as vehicles for Soviet airborne troops; series production began 1975, exceeded 680 by early 1991; delivery of more than 50 a year continues, from Tashkent plant.

VARIANTS: **Il-76** ('Candid-A'): Initial basic production version.

Il-76T ('Candid-A'): Developed version; additional fuel in wing centre-section, above fuselage; heavier payload; no armament.

Il-76M ('Candid-B'): As Il-76T but military; up to 140 troops or 125 paratroops carried as alternative to freight; rear gun turret (not always fitted on export aircraft) containing two 23 mm twin-barrel GSh-23L guns; small ECM fairings (optional on export aircraft) between centre windows at front of navigator's compartment, on each side of front fuselage, and each side of rear fuselage; packs of ninety-six 50 mm IRCM flares on landing gear fairings and/or on sides of rear fuselage of Soviet aircraft operating into combat areas.

Il-76TD ('Candid-A'): Unarmed; generally as Il-76T but with MKB (Perm)/Soloviev D-30KP-1 turbofans, maintaining full power to ISA +23°C against ISA +15°C for earlier models; max T-O weight and payload increased; 10,000 kg (22,046 lb) additional fuel increases max fuel range by 648 nm (1,200 km; 745 miles); first identified when SSSR-76467 passed through Shannon Airport, Ireland, November 1982; fully operational July 1983; one specially equipped with seats, soundproofing, buffet kitchen, toilet and working facilities, to carry members of Soviet Antarctic expeditions between Maputo, Mozambique, and Molodozhnaya Station, Antarctica (proving flight February 1986 with 94 passengers, 14,000 kg (30,865 lb) of scientific equipment, cargo and baggage containers).

Il-76MD ('Candid-B'): Military version; generally as Il-76M but with improvements of Il-76TD.

Il-76DMP: Firefighting conversion of Il-76 demonstrated first in 1990; up to 44 tonnes of water/fire retardant in two cylindrical tanks in hold; discharge, replenishment and draining systems; drop zone aiming devices; up to 384 meteorological cartridges in dispensers for weather modification; able to water-bomb an area of 500 × 100 m (1,650 × 330 ft) in 6 s, or to carry, and parachute when required, 40 firefighters; all airborne fire equipment (weight 5,000 kg; 11,025 lb) can be installed in standard Il-76, or removed, in four hours; tank replenishment time 10-15 min; discharge time 6-7 s, with option of successive discharge of tanks to cover 600 × 80 m (1,970 × 260 ft); airspeed during discharge 130-215 knots (240-400 km/h; 150-248 mph).

Il-76LL: Engine testbed conversion, carrying gas-turbine of up to 245 kN (55,100 lb st), including turboprops, in place of normal port inner D-30KP; provisions for five test engineers; four Il-76LLs are available, on commercial contract basis, from Gromov Flight Research Institute; engines tested by 1991 include

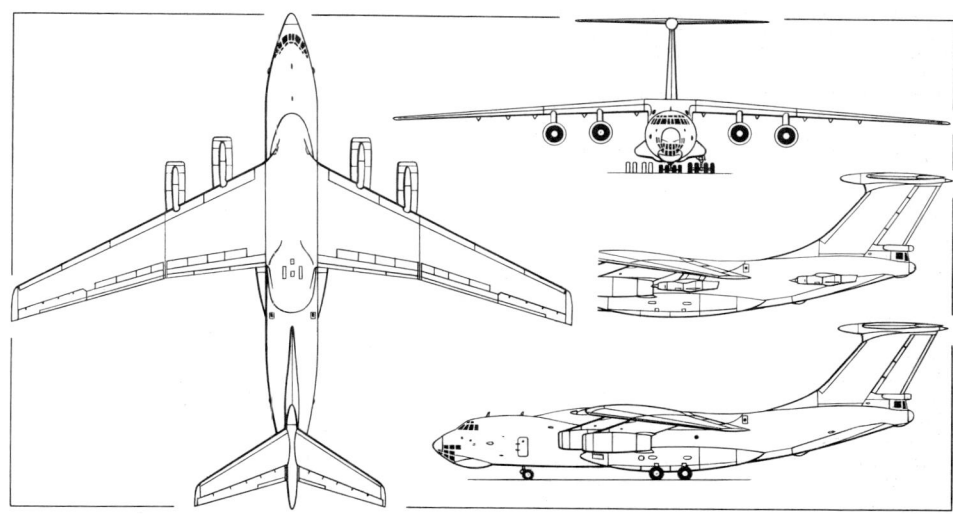

Ilyushin Il-76MD four-turbofan military transport, with added scrap view (centre right) of Il-78 tanker *(Pilot Press)*

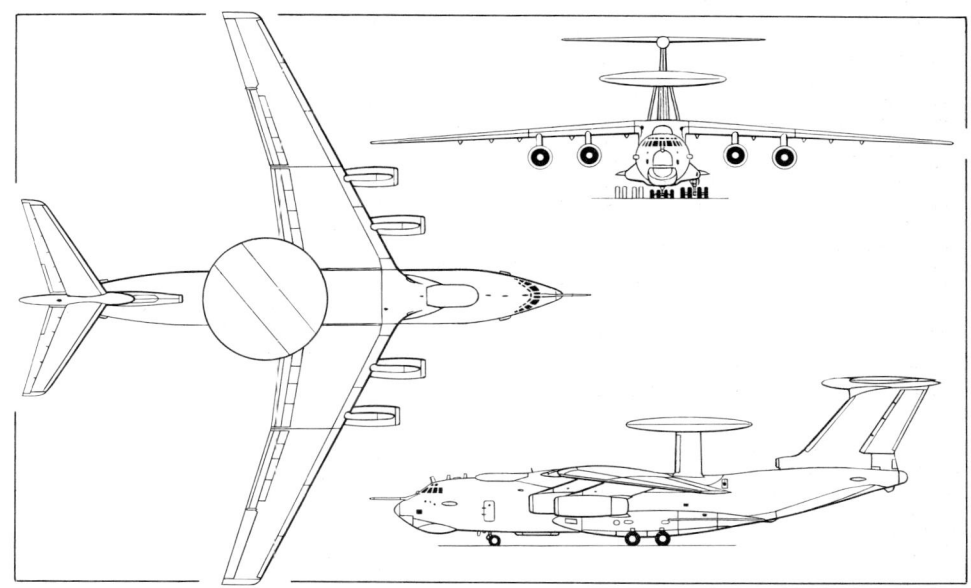

A-50 AEW&C version of Ilyushin Il-76, known to NATO as 'Mainstay' *(Pilot Press)*

NK-86, PS-90A and D-18T turbofans and D-236 propfan.

Specialised variants and developments of Il-76 include aircraft in which Soviet cosmonauts have experienced several tens of seconds of weightlessness during training; the AEW&C **A-50** known to NATO as 'Mainstay' (described separately); the **Il-78** (NATO 'Midas') flight refuelling tanker (described separately); the Iraqi-modified AEW&C **Adnan 1** and single-point flight refuelling tanker (described in Iraqi section). India is reportedly considering conversion of standard Il-76s for AEW duties.

CUSTOMERS: First-line units of Soviet Transport Aviation

force (VTA) (about 450 Il-76/76M/76MD); air forces of Algeria, India (24, given name Gajaraj), Iraq, Czechoslovakia, Poland; commercial operators include Aeroflot (more than 120, including Il-76Ts and Ms, forming military reserve), Iraqi Airways (about 30 Il-76Ts and Ms, operated for military), Jamahiriya Libyan Arab Airlines (21 Il-76Ts and Ms), Syrianair (2 Il-76Ts, 2 Ms); Il-76Ms of airlines have no guns in turret; first of at least two Il-76MDs delivered for Cubana had no tail turret.

DESIGN FEATURES: Late 1960s requirement was to carry 40 tonnes of freight 2,700 nm (5,000 km; 3,100 miles) in less than six hours, with ability to operate from short

A-50 'Mainstay', the AEW&C version of the Ilyushin Il-76 (*Swedish Air Force, via FLYGvapenNYTT*)

unprepared airstrips, in the most difficult weather conditions experienced in Siberia, the north of the Soviet Union and the Far East, while much simpler to service and able to fly much faster than An-12; wings mounted above fuselage to leave interior unobstructed; rear loading ramp/door; unique landing gear, with two large external fairings for each main gear; wing anhedral constant outboard of centre-section; sweepback 25° at quarter-chord; thickness/chord ratio 13 per cent at root, 10 per cent at tip; all tail surfaces sweptback.

FLYING CONTROLS: Hydraulically boosted; manual operation possible in emergency; mass balanced ailerons, with balance/trim tabs; two-section triple-slotted trailing-edge flaps over approx 75 per cent of each semi-span; eight upper-surface spoilers forward of flaps on each wing, four on each inner and outer panel; leading-edge slats over almost entire span, two on each inner panel, three on each outer panel; variable-incidence T tailplane; elevators and rudder aerodynamically balanced, each with tab.

STRUCTURE: All-metal; five-piece wing of multi-spar fail-safe construction, centre-section integral with fuselage; basically circular-section semi-monocoque fail-safe fuselage; underside of upswept rear fuselage made up of two outward hinged chamshell doors, upward hinged panel between doors, and downward hinged ramp; all tail surfaces sweptback.

The following description applies to the Il-76T:

LANDING GEAR: Hydraulically retractable tricycle type. Steerable nose unit made up of two pairs of wheels, side by side, with central oleo. Main gear on each side is made up of two units in tandem, each unit with four wheels on a single axle. Low-pressure tyres size 1,300 × 480 mm on mainwheels, 1,100 × 330 mm on nosewheels. Nosewheels retract forward. Main units retract inward into two large ventral fairings under fuselage, with an additional large fairing on each side of lower fuselage over actuating gear. During retraction mainwheel axles rotate around leg, so that wheels stow with axles parallel to fuselage axis (ie: wheels remain vertical but at 90° to direction of flight). All doors on wheel wells close when gear is down, to prevent fouling of legs by snow, ice, mud, etc. Oleo-pneumatic shock absorbers. Tyre pressure can be varied in flight from 2.5 to 5 bars (36-73 lb/sq in) to suit different landing strip conditions. Hydraulic brakes on mainwheels.

POWER PLANT: Four MKB (Perm)/Soloviev D-30KP turbofans, each rated at 117.7 kN (26,455 lb st), in individual underwing pods. Each pod is carried on a large forward-inclined pylon and is fitted with a clamshell thrust reverser. Integral fuel tanks between spars of inner and outer wing panels. Total fuel capacity reported to be 81,830 litres (21,617 US gallons; 18,000 Imp gallons).

ACCOMMODATION: Crew of seven, including two freight handlers. Conventional side by side seating for pilot and co-pilot on spacious flight deck. Station for navigator below flight deck in glazed nose. Crew door on port side of nose. Forward hinged main cabin door on each side of fuselage forward of wing. Two windows on each side of hold serve as emergency exits. Hold has reinforced floor of titanium alloys, with folding roller conveyors, and is loaded via rear ramp. Entire accommodation is pressurised, and advanced mechanical handling systems are provided for containerised and other freight, which can include standard ISO containers, each 12 m (39 ft 4½ in) long, building machinery, heavy crawlers and mobile

cranes. Typical loads include six containers measuring either 2.99 × 2.44 × 2.44 m (9 ft 9¾ in × 8 ft × 8 ft) or 2.99 × 2.44 × 1.90 m (9 ft 9¾ in × 8 ft × 6 ft 2¾ in) and with loaded weights of 5,670 kg (12,500 lb) or 5,000 kg (11,025 lb) respectively; or twelve containers measuring 1.46 × 2.44 × 1.90 m (4 ft 9¼ in × 8 ft × 6 ft 2¾ in) and each weighing 2,500 kg (5,511 lb) loaded; or six pallets measuring 2.99 × 2.44 m (9 ft 9¾ in × 8 ft) and each weighing 5,670 kg (12,500 lb); or twelve pallets measuring 1.46 × 2.44 m (4 ft 9¼ in × 8 ft) and each weighing 2,500 kg (5,511 lb). Folding seats along sidewalls in central portion of hold. Quick configuration changes can be made by the use of modules, each able to accommodate 36 passengers in four-abreast seating, litter patients and medical attendants, or cargo. Three such modules can be carried, each approx 6.10 m (20 ft) long, 2.44 m (8 ft) wide and 2.44 m (8 ft) high. They are loaded through the rear doors by means of two overhead travelling cranes, and are secured to the cabin floor with cargo restraints. Two winches at front of hold, each with capacity of 3,000 kg (6,615 lb). Cranes embody total of four hoists, each with capacity of 2,500 kg (5,511 lb). Ramp can be used as additional hoist, with capacity of up to 30,000 kg (66,140 lb) to facilitate loading of large vehicles and those with caterpillar tracks. Pilot's and co-pilot's windscreens can each be fitted with two wipers, top and bottom.

SYSTEMS: Flight deck only, or entire interior, can be pressurised; max differential 0.50 bar (7.25 lb/sq in). Hydraulic system includes servo motors and motors to drive the flaps, slats, landing gear and its doors, ramp, rear fuselage clamshell doors and load hoists. Flying control boosters are supplied by electric pumps and are independent of the central hydraulic system. Electrical system includes engine driven generators, auxiliary generators driven by an APU, DC converters and batteries. It powers the pumps for the flying control system boosters, radio and avionics, and lighting systems.

AVIONICS: Full equipment for all-weather operation by day and night, including a computer for automatic flight control and automatic landing approach. Weather radar in nose; navigation and ground mapping radar in undernose radome.

EQUIPMENT: APU in port side landing gear fairing for engine starting and to supply all aircraft systems on ground, making aircraft independent of ground facilities.

DIMENSIONS, EXTERNAL:

Wing span	50.50 m (165 ft 8 in)
Wing aspect ratio	8.5
Length overall	46.59 m (152 ft 10¼ in)
Fuselage: Max diameter	4.80 m (15 ft 9 in)
Height overall	14.76 m (48 ft 5 in)
Rear loading aperture: Width	3.40 m (11 ft 1¾ in)
Height	3.45 m (11 ft 4 in)

DIMENSIONS, INTERNAL:

Cabin: Length: excl ramp	20.00 m (65 ft 7½ in)
incl ramp	24.50 m (80 ft 4½ in)
Width	3.40 m (11 ft 1¾ in)
Height	3.46 m (11 ft 4¼ in)
Volume	235.3 m³ (8,310 cu ft)

AREAS:

Wings, gross	300.0 m² (3,229.2 sq ft)

WEIGHTS AND LOADINGS (A: Il-76T, B: Il-76TD):

Max payload: A	40,000 kg (88,185 lb)
B	50,000 kg (110,230 lb)

Max T-O weight: A	170,000 kg (374,785 lb)
B	190,000 kg (418,875 lb)
Max landing weight: B	151,500 kg (333,995 lb)
Permissible axle load (vehicles):	
A	7,500-11,000 kg (16,535-24,250 lb)
Permissible floor loading:	
A	1,450-3,100 kg/m² (297-635 lb/sq ft)
Max wing loading: A	566.7 kg/m² (116.05 lb/sq ft)
B	633.3 kg/m² (129.72 lb/sq ft)
Max power loading: A	361.1 kg/kN (3.54 lb/lb st)
B	403.6 kg/kN (3.95 lb/lb st)

PERFORMANCE (A: Il-76T, B: Il-76TD):

Max level speed: A, B	459 knots (850 km/h; 528 mph)
Cruising speed:	
A, B	405-432 knots (750-800 km/h; 466-497 mph)
T-O speed: A	114 knots (210 km/h; 131 mph)
Approach and landing speed:	
A	119-130 knots (220-240 km/h; 137-149 mph)
Normal cruising height:	
A, B	9,000-12,000 m (29,500-39,370 ft)
Absolute ceiling: A	approx 15,500 m (50,850 ft)
T-O run: A	850 m (2,790 ft)
B	1,700 m (5,580 ft)
Landing run: A	450 m (1,475 ft)
B	900-1,000 m (2,950-3,280 ft)
Range with max payload:	
B	1,970 nm (3,650 km; 2,265 miles)
Nominal range with 40,000 kg (88,185 lb) payload:	
A	2,700 nm (5,000 km; 3,100 miles)
Max range, with reserves:	
A	3,617 nm (6,700 km; 4,163 miles)
Range with 20,000 kg (44,090 lb) payload:	
B	3,940 nm (7,300 km; 4,535 miles)

ILYUSHIN A-50

NATO reporting name: Mainstay

TYPE: Four-turbofan airborne early warning and control aircraft.

PROGRAMME: Development began in 1970s to replace Tu-126s of APVO; production began early 1980s, now maintained at rate of five a year; first photographed by Royal Norwegian Air Force 1987.

CUSTOMERS: About 25 operational, primarily with MiG-29, MiG-31 and Su-27 counter-air fighters of Soviet APVO home defence force and tactical air forces, in 1991.

DESIGN FEATURES: Conversion of Il-76 transport, with conventionally located rotating 'saucer' radome, lengthened fuselage forward of wings, flight refuelling nose-probe, new IFF and comprehensive ECM; normal nose glazing around navigator's station replaced by non-transparent fairings; intake for avionics cooling at front of dorsal fin; no rear gun turret.

FLYING CONTROLS: As for Il-76.

STRUCTURE: As for Il-76, except as noted under Design Features.

LANDING GEAR: As for Il-76.

POWER PLANT: As for Il-76.

AVIONICS: Considered capable of detecting and tracking aircraft and cruise missiles flying at low altitude over land and water, and of helping to direct fighter operations over combat areas as well as enhancing air surveillance and defence of USSR.

ILYUSHIN Il-78
NATO reporting name: Midas
TYPE: Four-turbofan probe-and-drogue flight refuelling tanker.

PROGRAMME: Development began in mid-1970s, to replace modified Myasishchev M-3 (NATO 'Bison') used previously in this role; first operational Il-78 entered service 1987, supporting tactical and strategic combat aircraft.

CUSTOMERS: About 12 operational with Soviet air forces in early 1991.

DESIGN FEATURES: Development of basic Il-76MD; three-point tanker, with refuelling pods of same type under outer wings and on port side of rear fuselage; rear turret retained as flight refuelling observation station, without guns.

ILYUSHIN Il-86
NATO reporting name: Camber
TYPE: Four-turbofan medium-range wide-bodied passenger transport.

PROGRAMME: Construction of two prototypes started 1974; first flight 22 December 1976 from Ilyushin OKB headquarters at old Moscow Central Airport, Khodinka, from 1,820 m (5,970 ft) runway, to official flight test centre, by prototype SSSR-86000; first production Il-86 (SSSR-86002) flew at Voronezh assembly plant 24 October 1977; first delivery (SSSR-86004) to Aeroflot 24 September 1979; scheduled services began 26 December 1980; first international service, Moscow-East Berlin, 3 July 1981; 80 delivered; possible re-engining with MKB (Perm)/Soloviev PS-90A or CFM-56 turbofans being considered, to remedy disappointing range.

CUSTOMERS: Aeroflot only.

DESIGN FEATURES: Conventional low/mid swept wing; two-deck fuselage, intended to be entered via lower-deck doors, into stowage compartments for coats and hand baggage, and up stairways to passenger deck (deletion of lower-deck airstairs and internal stairways optional); additional centreline bogie between main landing gear units; dihedral from roots on wings and tailplane; wing sweepback 35° at quarter-chord; all tail surfaces swept.

FLYING CONTROLS: Hydraulic actuation, without manual reversion for primary surfaces; aileron and two-section double-slotted flaps occupy entire trailing-edge of each wing; multi-section upper-surface spoilers and airbrakes forward of each flap section; full-span leading-edge slats; variable-incidence tailplane; rudder and elevators each two-section.

STRUCTURE: All-metal; inner wings three-spar, outer panels two-spar; shallow fence above wing in line with each engine pylon; circular-section semi-monocoque fuselage; floors of both decks of honeycomb and carbonfibre reinforced plastics. Flaps, wing slats, engine pylons, tailplane and fin manufactured by PZL Mielec, Poland.

LANDING GEAR: Retractable four-unit type. Forward retracting steerable twin-wheel nose unit, and three four-wheel bogie main units. Two of the latter retract inward into the wingroot fairings; the third unit is mounted centrally under the fuselage, slightly forward of the others, and retracts forward. (Main landing gear made at Kuybyshev.) Mainwheel tyres size 1,300 × 480 mm; nosewheel tyres size 1,120 × 450 mm.

POWER PLANT: Four Kuznetsov NK-86 turbofans, each rated at 127.5 kN (28,660 lb st), mounted on pylons forward of wing leading-edges. Engines fitted with combined thrust reversers/noise attenuators. Integral fuel tanks in wings, capacity 70,000-80,000 litres (18,492-21,133 US gallons; 15,398-17,597 Imp gallons).

ACCOMMODATION: Standard flight crew comprises two pilots and a flight engineer, with provision for a navigator if required. Flight engineer's seat normally faces to starboard, aft of co-pilot, but can pivot to central forward-facing position to enable the engineer to operate the throttles. Upper deck, on which all seats are located, is divided into three separate cabins by wardrobes, a serving area connected by elevator to the lower deck galley, and cabin staff accommodation, with a total of eight toilets at front (2) and rear (6) of the aircraft. Cabins feature unusually large windows, indirect lighting in walls and in ceiling panels, and enclosed baggage lockers at top of side walls. Preponderance of metal and natural fibre materials rather than plastics throughout cabins to enhance safety in an emergency. Up to 350 passengers in basic nine-abreast seating throughout, with two aisles, each 55 cm (21.6 in) wide. Suggested mixed class alternative layout provides for 28 passengers six-abreast in the front cabin, and 206 passengers eight-abreast in the other two cabins. Passengers enter via three airstair doors (made in Kharkov), which hinge down from the port side of the lower deck. One of these doors is forward of the wing; the others are aft of the wing. Four further doors at upper deck level on each side, for emergency use (using dual inflatable escape slides) and for use at airports where the utilisation of high level boarding steps or bridges is preferred. Coats and hand baggage are stowed on the lower deck before passengers climb one of three fixed stairways to the main deck. (Optional deletion of lower deck airstair doors and stairways, reduces operating weight empty by 3,000 kg; 6,610 lb and permits installation of 25 more seats on upper deck.) Cargo holds on the lower deck are designed to accommodate heavy or registered baggage and freight in 8 standard LD3 containers, or 16 LD3 containers if some of the carry-on baggage racks are omitted. Access is via upward hinged doors forward of the starboard wingroot leading-edge and at the side of the rear hold. Containers can be loaded and unloaded by means of a self-propelled truck with built-in roller conveyor. Films can be shown in flight, and there is a choice of 12 tape recorded audio programmes. A bar-buffet can be provided on the lower deck in place of the baggage and freight accommodation in the forward vestibule.

SYSTEMS: Four completely self-contained hydraulic systems, each operated by one of the engines, for actuation of flying control surfaces, tailplane variable incidence,

Ilyushin Il-78 (NATO 'Midas') with only the fuselage-side refuelling pod fitted, photographed during a tanking mission with a 'Bear' bomber north of Finnmark, northern Norway (*Royal Norwegian Air Force*)

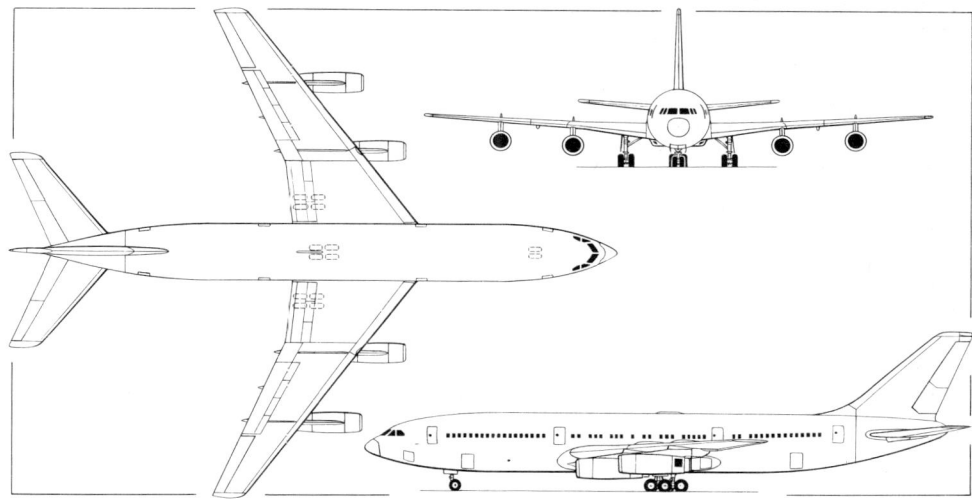
Ilyushin Il-86 four-turbofan wide-bodied passenger transport (*Pilot Press*)

Ilyushin Il-86 wide-bodied transport (four Kuznetsov NK-86 turbofans) in Aeroflot markings (*Paul R. Duffy*)

Prototype Ilyushin Il-96-300 at Sheremetyevo-1 Airport, Moscow, September 1990 *(Piotr Butowski)*

spoilers, airbrakes, slats, flaps, landing gear, nosewheel steering, wheel brakes, anti-skid system, and upper level doors when passenger gangways are used. All hot pipelines of air-conditioning system, and all fuel supply lines, outside pressure cell. Primary 200/155V 400Hz AC electrical system, powered by four 40kVA engine driven generators. Secondary 36V three-phase AC and 27V DC systems. Five accumulators and static transformer. Smoke detection system, with sensors in baggage, freight and equipment stowage areas. Pulse generating de-icing system consuming 500 times less energy than a conventional hot air or electrical system. APU in tailcone.

AVIONICS: All avionics equipment located within pressurised part of fuselage. Flight control and nav systems provide for automatic climb to the selected height, control of the rate of climb and automatic descent, and permit automatic landing in ICAO Cat IIIA conditions. Pre-programmable Doppler nav system with readout display screen on flight deck, on which microfilmed maps can be projected. Position of aircraft is indicated by cursor, driven by system computer. Nav system is updated automatically by inputs from VOR or VOR/ DME radio beacons.

DIMENSIONS, EXTERNAL:
Wing span	48.06 m (157 ft 8¼ in)
Length overall	59.54 m (195 ft 4 in)
Fuselage: Length	56.10 m (184 ft 0¾ in)
Max diameter	6.08 m (19 ft 11½ in)
Height overall	15.81 m (51 ft 10½ in)
Tailplane span	20.57 m (67 ft 6 in)
Wheel track (c/l of outer shock struts)	
	11.15 m (36 ft 7 in)
Wheelbase	21.34 m (70 ft 0 in)

DIMENSIONS, INTERNAL:
Main cabins: Height	2.61 m (8 ft 7 in)
Max width	approx 5.70 m (18 ft 8½ in)

AREAS:
Wings, gross	320 m² (3,444 sq ft)

WEIGHTS AND LOADINGS:
Max payload	42,000 kg (92,600 lb)
Max fuel	86,000 kg (189,600 lb)
Max T-O weight (dependent on size and type of runway)	190,000-208,000 kg (418,875-458,560 lb)

Max landing weight	175,000 kg (385,800 lb)
Max wing loading	650.0 kg/m² (133.1 lb/sq ft)
Max power loading	407.8 kg/kN (4.0 lb/lb st)

PERFORMANCE (designed):
Normal cruising speed at 9,000-11,000 m (30,000-36,000 ft) 486-512 knots (900-950 km/h; 559-590 mph)
Approach speed 130-141 knots (240-260 km/h; 149-162 mph)
Field length for T-O and landing 2,300-2,600 m (7,550-8,530 ft)
* Range: with 40,000 kg (88,185 lb) payload 1,944 nm (3,600 km; 2,235 miles)
* with max fuel 2,480 nm (4,600 km; 2,858 miles)
* *Reports suggest that these design ranges are not being achieved. The German airline Interflug quoted a max range of 1,350 nm (2,500 km; 1,550 miles) in its sales literature*

ILYUSHIN Il-90

TYPE: Twin-engined long-range passenger transport.
PROGRAMME: Design studies started at beginning of 1980s, in parallel with projects by Antonov and Tupolev; known originally by Ilyushin OKB as DMS (aircraft for long distances); first shown in model form at Moscow Aerospace '90 exhibition; then at preliminary design stage, with programme launch imminent.
DESIGN FEATURES: Conventional low-wing configuration; high aspect ratio swept wings of supercritical section, with winglets; podded underwing engines; basic requirement to carry 200 passengers 5,935 nm (11,000 km; 6,835 miles), with good field performance and clearance for Category IIIC operation.
POWER PLANT: Projected currently with two Kuznetsov NK-92 ducted propfans, each 177 kN (39,700 lb st).
ACCOMMODATION: Three arrangements proposed: (1) 20 first class passengers at 150 cm (59 in) seat pitch; 30 business class at 96 cm (38 in) pitch; 102 tourist class at 87 cm (34.25 in) pitch. (2) two tourist class cabins for 54 and 144. (3) two tourist class cabins for 61 and 159; twin aisles standard.
DIMENSIONS, EXTERNAL:
Wing span	47.70 m (156 ft 6 in)

WEIGHTS AND LOADINGS:
Weight empty, equipped	64,000 kg (141,100 lb)
Max payload	24,000 kg (52,900 lb)
Max T-O weight	125,000 kg (275,575 lb)

PERFORMANCE (estimated):
Cruising speed 458-470 knots (850-870 km/h; 528-540 mph)
Balanced T-O runway length 2,650 m (8,700 ft)
Balanced landing runway length 2,000 m (6,560 ft)
Range:
with 198 passengers 5,935 nm (11,000 km; 6,835 miles)
with 220 passengers 5,530 nm (10,250 km; 6,370 miles)

ILYUSHIN Il-96-300

TYPE: Four-turbofan wide-bodied passenger transport.
PROGRAMME: First of five prototypes (SSSR-96000) flew at Khodinka 28 September 1988, second on 28 November 1989; two used for static and fatigue testing; areas of commonality with Il-86 permitted planned test programme to be reduced to 750 flights totalling 1,200 hours; certification and first deliveries scheduled for 1992; Aeroflot to receive 70 during Soviet 1990-95 five-year plan.
CUSTOMERS: Aeroflot (more than 100); CSA of Czechoslovakia (intent to buy).
DESIGN FEATURES: Superficial resemblance to Il-86, but new design, with different engines to overcome performance deficiencies of Il-86; new structural materials and state of the art technology intended to provide life of 60,000 hours and 12,000 landings; no lower-deck passenger entry; winglets standard; wing and tailplane dihedral from roots; supercritical wings, with 30° sweep at quarter-chord; sweepback at quarter-chord 37° 30' on tailplane, 45° on fin.
FLYING CONTROLS: Triplex fly-by-wire, with manual reversion; each wing trailing-edge occupied by, from root, double-slotted inboard flap, small inboard aileron, two-section single-slotted flaps, and outboard aileron used only as gust damper and to smooth out buffeting;

Model of Ilyushin Il-90 twin-engined airliner
(Jacques Marmain/Aviation Magazine International, Paris)

Model of increased-capacity Ilyushin Il-96M *(Piotr Butowski)*

seven-section full-span leading-edge slats on each wing; three airbrakes forward of each inboard trailing-edge flap; six spoilers forward of outer flaps; inboard pair supplement ailerons, others operate as airbrakes and supplementary ailerons; variable-incidence tailplane; two-section rudder and elevators, without tabs.

STRUCTURE: Basically all-metal, including new high-purity aluminium alloy, with composites flaps, main-deck floors and underfloor holds of honeycomb and CFRP; inner wings three-spar, outer panels two-spar; each wing has seven machined skin panels, three top surface, four bottom, with integral stiffeners; circular-section semi-monocoque fuselage; leading- and trailing-edges of fin and tailplane of composites. Some components manufactured by PZL Mielec, Poland.

LANDING GEAR: Retractable four-unit type. Forward retracting steerable twin-wheel nose unit, and three four-wheel bogie main units. Two of the latter retract inward into the wingroot/fuselage fairings; the third unit is mounted centrally under the fuselage, to the rear of the others, and retracts forward after the bogie has itself pivoted upward 20°. Oleo-pneumatic shock absorbers. Nosewheel tubeless tyres size 1,260 × 460 mm; mainwheel tubeless tyres size 1,300 × 480 mm. Tyre pressure (all) 11.65 bars (169 lb/sq in).

POWER PLANT: Four Soloviev PS-90A turbofans, each rated at 156.9 kN (35,275 lb st). mounted on pylons forward of wing leading-edges. Thrust reversal standard. Integral fuel tanks in wings and fuselage centre-section, total capacity 152,620 litres (40,318 US gallons; 33,572 Imp gallons).

ACCOMMODATION: Crew of three on flight deck, comprising pilot, co-pilot and flight engineer, plus two seats for supplementary crew or an observer. Ten or 12 cabin staff. Basic all-tourist configuration has two cabins for 66 and 234 passengers respectively, nine-abreast at 87 cm (34.25 in) seat pitch, separated by a buffet counter, video stowage and two lifts from the galley on the lower deck. The two aisles are each 55 cm (21.65 in) wide. There are two toilets and a wardrobe at the front, six more toilets, a rack for cabin staff's belongings and seats for cabin staff at the rear. Seats recline, and are provided with individual tables, ventilation, earphones and attendant call button. Indirect lighting is standard. The 235-seat mixed class version has a front cabin for 22 first class passengers, six-abreast in pairs, at 102 cm (40 in) seat pitch and with aisles 75.5 cm (29.7 in) wide; a centre cabin with 40 business class seats, eight-abreast at 90 cm (35.4 in) seat pitch and with aisles 55.5 cm (22.25 in) wide; and a rear cabin for 173 tourist class passengers, basically nine-abreast at 87 cm (34.25 in) seat pitch, with an aisle width of 55 cm (21.65 in). Unlike the Il-86, the passenger cabin is entered through three doors on the port side of the upper deck, at the front and rear and forward of the wings. Opposite each door, on the starboard side, is an emergency exit door. The lower deck houses a front cargo compartment for six ABK-1.5 (LD3) containers or igloo pallets, a central compartment aft of the wing for ten ABK-1.5 containers or pallets, and a tapering compartment for general cargo at the rear. Three doors on the starboard side provide separate access to each compartment. The galley and lifts are located between the front cargo compartment and the wing, with a separate door aft of the door to the front cargo compartment.

SYSTEMS: Four independent hydraulic systems, using fire- and explosion-proof fluid, at pressure of 207 bars (3,000 lb/sq in). APU in tailcone.

AVIONICS: On the flight deck, conventional standby instruments are retained, but primary flight information is presented on dual twin-screen colour CRTs, fed by triplex INS, a satellite-based and Omega navigation system and other sensors. Triplex flight control and flight management systems, together with a head-up display, permit fully automatic en route control and operations in ICAO Cat IIIA minima. Duplex engine and systems monitoring and failure warning systems feed in-flight information to both the flight engineer's station and monitors on the ground. Autothrottle is based on IAS, without angle of attack protection. Another electronic system provides real-time automatic weight and CG situation data.

DIMENSIONS, EXTERNAL:

Wing span: excl winglets	57.66 m (189 ft 2 in)
over winglets	60.105 m (197 ft 2½ in)
Wing aspect ratio	9.5
Length overall	55.35 m (181 ft 7¼ in)
Fuselage: Length	51.15 m (167 ft 9¾ in)
Max diameter	6.08 m (19 ft 11½ in)
Height overall	17.57 m (57 ft 7¾ in)
Tailplane span	20.57 m (67 ft 6 in)
Wheel track	10.40 m (34 ft 1½ in)
Wheelbase	20.065 m (65 ft 10 in)
Passenger doors (three): Height	1.83 m (6 ft 0 in)
Width	1.07 m (3 ft 6 in)
Height to sill: Nos. 1 and 2	4.54 m (14 ft 10¾ in)
No. 3	4.80 m (15 ft 9 in)
Emergency exit doors (three):	
Height	1.825 m (5 ft 11¾ in)
Width	1.07 m (3 ft 6 in)
Cargo compartment doors (front and centre):	
Height	1.825 m (5 ft 11¾ in)

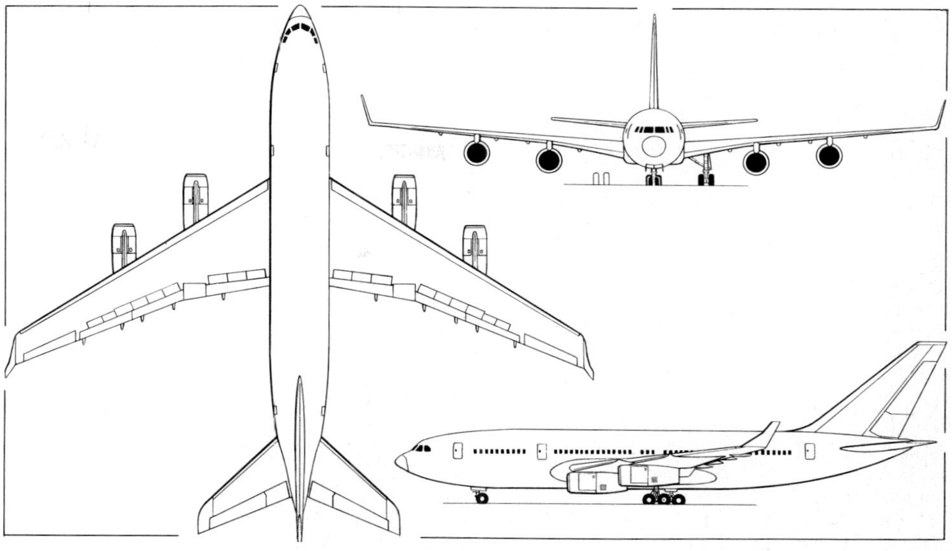

Ilyushin Il-96-300 four-turbofan long-range transport *(Pilot Press)*

Width	1.78 m (5 ft 10 in)
Height to sill: front	2.34 m (7 ft 8¼ in)
centre	2.48 m (8 ft 1¾ in)
Cargo compartment door (rear):	
Height	1.38 m (4 ft 6¼ in)
Width	0.972 m (3 ft 2¼ in)
Height to sill	2.74 m (9 ft 0 in)
Galley door: Height	1.20 m (3 ft 11¼ in)
Width	0.80 m (2 ft 7½ in)

DIMENSIONS, INTERNAL:

Cabins, excl flight deck:	
Height	2.60 m (8 ft 6¼ in)
Max width	approx 5.70 m (18 ft 8½ in)
Volume	350 m³ (12,360 cu ft)
Cargo hold volume: front	37.10 m³ (1,310 cu ft)
centre	63.80 m³ (2,253 cu ft)
rear	15.00 m³ (530 cu ft)

AREAS:

Wings, gross	391.6 m² (4,215 sq ft)
Vertical tail surfaces (total)	61.0 m² (656.6 sq ft)
Horizontal tail surfaces (total)	96.5 m² (1,038.75 sq ft)

WEIGHTS AND LOADINGS:

Basic operating weight	117,000 kg (257,940 lb)
Max payload	40,000 kg (88,185 lb)
Max T-O weight	216,000 kg (476,200 lb)
Max landing weight	175,000 kg (385,810 lb)
Max zero-fuel weight	157,000 kg (346,120 lb)
Max wing loading	551.6 kg/m² (113.0 lb/sq ft)
Max power loading	344.2 kg/kN (3.37 lb/lb st)

PERFORMANCE (estimated):

Normal cruising speed at 10,100-12,100 m (33,135-39,700 ft)
459-486 knots (850-900 km/h; 528-559 mph)
Approach speed 140 knots (260 km/h; 162 mph)
Balanced T-O runway length 2,600 m (8,530 ft)
Balanced landing runway length 1,980 m (6,500 ft)
Range, with UASA reserves:
with max payload 4,050 nm (7,500 km; 4,660 miles)
with 30,000 kg (66,140 lb) payload
4,860 nm (9,000 km; 5,590 miles)
with 15,000 kg (33,070 lb) payload
5,940 nm (11,000 km; 6,835 miles)

OPERATIONAL NOISE LEVELS:
Il-96-300 is designed to conform with ICAO Chapter 3 Annex 16 noise requirements

ILYUSHIN Il-96M

TYPE: Four-turbofan wide-bodied passenger transport.

PROGRAMME: Projected initially as Il-96-350; designation changed to Il-96M in 1990, when model exhibited at Moscow Aerospace '90; then at initial design stage and awaiting US clearance for planned Western power plant; scheduled 1993 first flight; planned certification to FAR 25 and ICAO Annex 16 noise levels.

DESIGN FEATURES: Basically as Il-96-300; lengthened fuselage of unchanged cross-section, permitting smaller tail fin; wings identical.

POWER PLANT: Four Pratt & Whitney PW2037 turbofans, each rated at 167.1 kN (37,565 lb st).

ACCOMMODATION: Three arrangements proposed: (1) 18 first class passengers at 152.4 cm (60 in) seat pitch; 44 business class at 91.5 cm (36 in) pitch; 250 tourist class at 86.4 cm (34 in) pitch. (2) 85 business class and 250 tourist class. (3) three tourist class cabins for 124, 162 and 89 passengers. Underfloor hold for 32 standard LD3 containers.

DIMENSIONS, EXTERNAL:

Wing span: excl winglets	57.66 m (189 ft 2 in)
over winglets	60.105 m (197 ft 2½ in)
Length overall	64.388 m (211 ft 3 in)
Fuselage: Length	60.50 m (198 ft 6 in)
Height overall	15.88 m (52 ft 1¼ in)

WEIGHTS AND LOADINGS:

Max payload	60,000 kg (132,275 lb)
Max T-O weight	265,000 kg (584,215 lb)
Max power loading	396.5 kg/kN (3.89 lb/lb st)

PERFORMANCE (estimated):

Normal cruising speed at 9,000-12,000 m (29,500-39,370 ft)
459-469 knots (850-870 km/h; 528-540 mph)
Balanced T-O runway length 3,200 m (10,500 ft)
Balanced landing runway length 2,150 m (7,055 ft)
Range 5,825-6,365 nm (10,800-11,800 km; 6,710-7,330 miles)

ILYUSHIN Il-103

TYPE: Two/four-seat light aircraft for primary training and general aviation.

PROGRAMME: Exhibited in model form at Moscow Aerospace '90; power plant not finalised then; first flight possibly 1992.

DESIGN FEATURES: Conventional low-wing monoplane, with non-retractable tricycle landing gear, to meet DOSAAF requirement for 500 military/civil pilot trainers; slight wing dihedral from roots; swept tail surfaces.

FLYING CONTROLS: Conventional ailerons, elevators, rudder and trailing-edge flaps.

STRUCTURE: Initially all-metal; use of composites and advanced materials possible in later versions.

POWER PLANT: Projected currently with 142 kW (190 hp) Teledyne Continental Voyager IOL-370 engine.

ACCOMMODATION: Two seats side by side, or four persons in pairs, in enclosed cabin; space for 220 kg (485 lb) freight with rear bench seat removed.

DIMENSIONS, EXTERNAL:

Wing span	10.60 m (34 ft 9 in)
Length overall	7.95 m (26 ft 1 in)
Height overall	3.00 m (9 ft 10 in)
Tailplane span	3.60 m (11 ft 9¾ in)
Wheel track	2.00 m (6 ft 6¾ in)

WEIGHTS AND LOADINGS:

Max T-O weight: two seats	720 kg (1,587 lb)
four seats	890 kg (1,962 lb)
Max power loading: four seats	5.97 kg/kW (9.81 lb/hp)

PERFORMANCE (estimated, A: two seats, B: four seats):

Max level speed: A, B	124 knots (230 km/h; 143 mph)
Max rate of climb at S/L: A	330 m (1,080 ft)/min
B	270 m (885 ft)/min
T-O run: A	150 m (492 ft)
B	230 m (755 ft)
Landing run: A	110 m (360 ft)
B	140 m (460 ft)
Endurance: A	1 h 30 min

ILYUSHIN Il-108

TYPE: Twin-turbofan business or third-level airline transport.

PROGRAMME: First shown in model form 1990; at initial design stage.

DESIGN FEATURES: Conventional low-wing/T-tail configuration, with rear-mounted engines; wings and tail unit swept; winglets added late 1990; retractable tricycle landing gear with twin wheels on each unit. Manual flying controls.

POWER PLANT: Two Zaporozhye/ZVL DV-2 turbofans, each 21.58 kN (4,852 lb st).

ACCOMMODATION: Proposed in two versions: (1) two crew and nine passengers, with facilities for work or relaxation on long flights. (2) 15 passengers, three-abreast with 40 cm (15.75 in) aisle; both versions with toilet, wardrobes, front and rear baggage compartments.

DIMENSIONS, EXTERNAL:

Wing span	15.00 m (49 ft 2½ in)
Length overall	15.85 m (52 ft 0 in)

Model of Ilyushin Il-108 business/regional transport
(Piotr Butowski)

Model of two/four-seat Ilyushin Il-103 lightplane
(Piotr Butowski)

forward of flaps; spoilers supplement ailerons differentially after engine failure during take-off; trim and servo tabs in rudder, trim tab in each elevator.

STRUCTURE: Approx 10 per cent of airframe by weight made of composites; two-spar aluminium-lithium wings; removable leading-edge on outer panels; circular-section aluminium alloy semi-monocoque fuselage built as five subassemblies; metal tail unit. Parts of wings manufactured in Romania, other airframe assemblies in Poland and Romania, tail unit in Bulgaria; power plant production involves Poland; final assembly at Tashkent.

LANDING GEAR: Retractable tricycle type, with twin wheels on each unit, manufactured by WSK-PZL Krosno. All units retract forward hydraulically, with emergency extension by gravity. Oleo-pneumatic shock absorber in each unit. Tyres size 620 × 80 mm on nosewheels, 880 × 305 mm on mainwheels. Nosewheels steerable ±55°. Disc brakes on mainwheels. All wheel doors remain closed except during retraction or extension of the landing gear.

Fuselage: Length	14.00 m (45 ft 11¼ in)
Max diameter	2.35 m (7 ft 8½ in)
Height overall	5.50 m (18 ft 0½ in)
Tailplane span	5.29 m (17 ft 4¼ in)
Wheel track	3.00 m (9 ft 10¼ in)

WEIGHTS AND LOADINGS:
Max payload	1,500 kg (3,306 lb)
Max T-O weight	14,300 kg (31,525 lb)
Max power loading	331.3 kg/kN (3.25 lb/lb st)

PERFORMANCE (estimated):
Econ cruising speed at 12,000 m (39,370 ft)
432 knots (800 km/h; 497 mph)
Balanced T-O runway length 1,800 m (5,905 ft)
Range at econ cruising speed:
with max payload 2,428 nm (4,500 km; 2,796 miles)
with 15 passengers and max fuel
2,615 nm (4,850 km; 3,010 miles)
with nine passengers 3,235 nm (6,000 km; 3,725 miles)

ILYUSHIN Il-114

TYPE: Twin-turboprop short-range passenger and freight transport.

PROGRAMME: Design finalised 1986, as replacement for aircraft in An-24 class; prototype (SSSR-54000) first flew at Zhukovsky flight test centre 29 March 1990; two more flying prototypes, two for static tests ordered; 100 test flights logged by October 1990; certification and first deliveries planned for 1993; scheduled production 100 a year, beginning 1996.

CUSTOMERS: Aeroflot (500).

DESIGN FEATURES: Conventional low-wing monoplane; only fin and rudder swept; slight dihedral on wing centre-section, much increased on outer panels; operation from unpaved runways practical.

FLYING CONTROLS: Manual actuation; each wing trailing-edge occupied entirely by aileron, with servo and trim tabs, and hydraulically actuated double-slotted trailing-edge flaps, inboard and outboard of engine nacelle; two airbrakes (inboard) and spoiler (outboard)

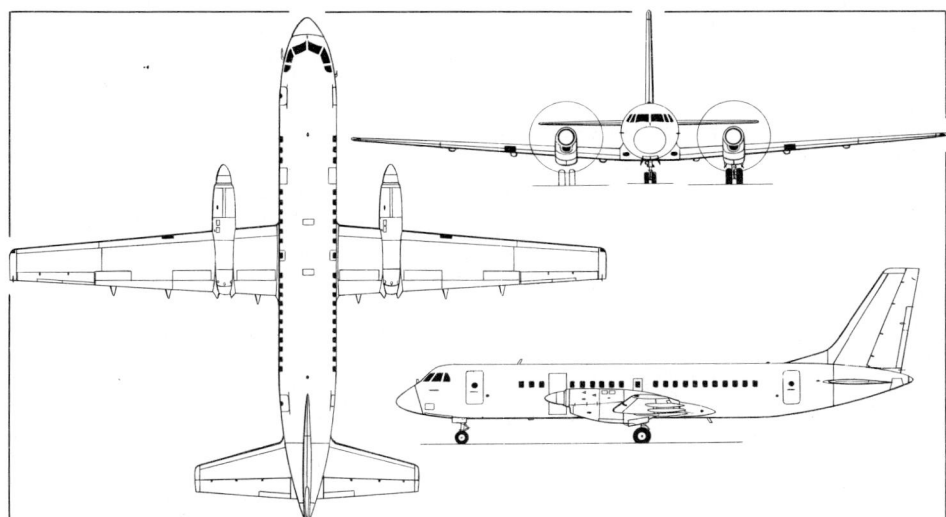

Production configuration of Ilyushin Il-114 commuter airliner *(Jane's/Mike Keep)*

Prototype Ilyushin Il-114 twin-turboprop airliner at Sheremetyevo-1 Airport, Moscow *(Piotr Butowski)*

POWER PLANT: Two 1,865 kW (2,500 shp) Leningrad/Klimov TV7-117 turboprops, each driving a low-noise six-blade CB-34 carbonfibre-reinforced composites propeller. Fuel in integral tanks in wings, total capacity 8,125 litres (2,146 US gallons; 1,787 Imp gallons). APU in tailcone.

ACCOMMODATION: Flight crew of two, plus stewardess. Emergency exit window on each side of flight deck. Four-abreast seats for 60 passengers in main cabin, at 75 cm (29.5 in) seat pitch, with central aisle 45 cm (17.72 in) wide. Provision for rearrangement of interior for increased seating, and lengthening of fuselage for 70-75 passengers. Airstair type passenger door at front of cabin on port side, further door at rear on port side, both opening outward. Galley, cloakroom and toilet at rear, with emergency escape slide by service door on starboard side. Type III emergency exit over each wing. Service doors at front and rear of cabin on starboard side. Baggage compartments forward of cabin on starboard side and to rear of cabin, plus overhead baggage racks. Optional large carry-on baggage shelves in lobby by main door at front of cabin.

SYSTEMS: Dual redundant pressurisation and air-conditioning system using engine bleed air from both engines. Two independent hydraulic systems, pressure 207 bars (3,000 lb/sq in), for landing gear actuation, wheel brakes, nosewheel steering and flaps. Three-phase 115/220V 400Hz AC electrical system powered by 40kW alternator on each engine. Secondary 24V DC system. Wing and tail unit leading-edges de-iced electrically. Electrothermal anti-icing system for propeller blades and windscreen. Engine air intakes de-iced by hot air.

AVIONICS: Digital avionics for automatic or manual control by day or night, including automatic approach and landing in limiting weather conditions (ICAO Cat I and II). Two colour CRTs for each pilot for flight and navigation information. Centrally mounted CRT for engine and systems data.

DIMENSIONS, EXTERNAL:
Wing span	30.00 m (98 ft 5¼ in)
Length overall	26.31 m (86 ft 4 in)
Diameter of fuselage	2.86 m (9 ft 4½ in)
Height overall	9.32 m (30 ft 7 in)
Tailplane span	11.10 m (36 ft 5 in)
Wheel track	8.40 m (27 ft 6½ in)
Wheelbase	9.13 m (29 ft 11½ in)
Propeller diameter	3.60 m (11 ft 9¾ in)
Propeller ground clearance	0.62 m (2 ft 0½ in)
Propeller fuselage clearance	0.97 m (3 ft 2¼ in)
Passenger doors (each): Height	1.70 m (5 ft 7 in)
Width	0.90 m (2 ft 11¼ in)
Service door (front): Height	1.30 m (4 ft 3¼ in)
Width	0.96 m (3 ft 1¾ in)
Service door (rear): Height	1.38 m (4 ft 6¼ in)
Width	0.61 m (2 ft 0 in)
Emergency exit (each): Height	0.91 m (2 ft 11¾ in)
Width	0.51 m (1 ft 8 in)

Model of Ilyushin Il-X business/regional transport *(Piotr Butowski)*

DIMENSIONS, INTERNAL:
Length between pressure bulkheads	22.24 m (72 ft 11½ in)
Cabin: Max height	1.92 m (6 ft 3½ in)

WEIGHTS AND LOADINGS:
Operating weight empty	13,700 kg (30,200 lb)
Max payload	6,000 kg (13,227 lb)
Max fuel	6,500 kg (14,330 lb)
Max T-O weight	21,000 kg (46,300 lb)
Max power loading	5.63 kg/kW (9.26 lb/shp)

PERFORMANCE (estimated):
Nominal cruising speed	270 knots (500 km/h; 310 mph)
Approach speed	100 knots (185 km/h; 115 mph)
Optimum cruising height	8,100 m (26,575 ft)
T-O run: paved	1,200 m (3,940 ft)
unpaved	1,400 m (4,600 ft)
Landing run: paved or unpaved	1,300 m (4,265 ft)

Range, with reserves:
with 5,760 kg (12,700 lb) payload (60 passengers)
540 nm (1,000 km; 621 miles)
with 3,600 kg (7,935 lb) payload
1,538 nm (2,850 km; 1,770 miles)
with 1,500 kg (3,300 lb) payload
2,590 nm (4,800 km; 2,980 miles)

ILYUSHIN Il-X

TYPE: Twin-turboprop business or commuter transport.
PROGRAMME: Development began May 1989; first exhibited in model form at 1990 Singapore air show; at preliminary design stage early 1991.
DESIGN FEATURES: Conventional low-wing/T-tail configuration, with rear-mounted pusher turboprops; wings and tail unit swept; retractable tricycle landing gear with twin wheels on each unit, for use from unprepared strips.
POWER PLANT: Two 1,156 kW (1,550 shp) Glushenkov

(Novikov/Rybinsk) TVD-1500 turboprops, each driving two four-blade pusher contraprops.
ACCOMMODATION: Proposed in two versions: (1) executive cabin layout, with five armchair seats, two of them facing with centre table, and three-place settee. (2) for 19 passengers, basically three-abreast at 78 cm (30.7 in) seat pitch. Each version has front and rear baggage compartments, aft toilet and buffet, main passenger door at front on port side, and folding seat at rear for attendant; cabin headroom 1.84 m (6 ft).

DIMENSIONS, EXTERNAL:
Wing span	18.00 m (59 ft 0½ in)
Length overall	17.77 m (58 ft 3½ in)
Fuselage: Length	16.30 m (53 ft 5¾ in)
Diameter	2.40 m (7 ft 10½ in)
Height overall	6.05 m (19 ft 10¼ in)
Tailplane span	6.00 m (19 ft 8¼ in)
Wheel track	3.60 m (11 ft 9¾ in)
Propeller diameter	2.60 m (8 ft 6½ in)

WEIGHTS AND LOADINGS (A: 19 passengers, B: 7 passengers):
Max payload: A, B	2,100 kg (4,630 lb)
Max T-O weight: A	8,700 kg (19,180 lb)
B	9,180 kg (20,238 lb)
Max landing weight: A	7,900 kg (17,415 lb)
B	7,200 kg (15,870 lb)
Max power loading: B	3.97 kg/kW (6.53 lb/shp)

PERFORMANCE (estimated):
Max cruising speed at 7,000 m (22,965 ft):
A, B	334 knots (620 km/h; 385 mph)

Econ cruising speed at 7,000 m (22,965 ft):
A, B	307 knots (570 km/h; 354 mph)
Balanced field length: A, B	800 m (2,625 ft)
Max range: A	810 nm (1,500 km; 932 miles)
B	2,158 nm (4,000 km; 2,485 miles)

KAMOV
KAMOV DESIGN BUREAU

GENERAL DESIGNER: Sergei V. Mikheyev
DEPUTY GENERAL DESIGNER: Veniamin Kasjanikov

Formed in 1947, this OKB continues the work of Prof Dr Ing Nikolai Ilyich Kamov, a leading designer of rotating wing aircraft from the late 1920s, who died on 24 November 1973, aged 71; all Kamov helicopters in current service have coaxial contra-rotating rotors; Ka-118 and Ka-62, under development, have single main rotor; design studies under continuous review include tilt-rotor types.

KAMOV Ka-25
NATO reporting name: Hormone

TYPE: Twin-turbine multi-purpose military helicopter.
PROGRAMME: Prototype flew 1961; shown in Soviet Aviation Day flypast, Tushino Airport, Moscow, July 1961, carrying two dummy air-to-surface missiles (ASMs not fitted to production aircraft); about 460 built 1966-75, of which 100 remain operational with Soviet Navy.
VARIANTS: Reportedly, more than 25 versions; three major variants in service:

Ka-25BSh ('Hormone-A'): Ship-based anti-submarine helicopter, operated from Soviet Navy missile frigates, cruisers, helicopter carriers *Moskva* and *Leningrad* and carrier/cruisers of 'Kiev' class; major shortcoming is lack of automatic hover capability, preventing night and adverse weather use of dipping sonar. Being replaced progressively by Ka-27PL ('Helix-A').

Ka-25 ('Hormone-B'): Special electronics variant, providing over-the-horizon target acquisition for ship-launched cruise missiles including SS-N-3B (NATO 'Shaddock') from 'Kresta I' cruisers, SS-N-12 ('Sandbox') from 'Kiev' class and 'Slava' class cruisers, SS-N-19 ('Shipwreck') from battle cruisers *Kirov* and *Frunze*, and SS-N-22 ('Sunburn') from 'Sovremenny' class destroyers. 'Kiev' and 'Kirov' class ships each carry three 'Hormone-Bs', other classes one; larger undernose radome (NATO 'Big Bulge') than Ka-25BSh, with spherical undersurface; cylindrical radome under rear

Kamov Ka-25BSh ('Hormone-A') anti-submarine helicopter of the Soviet Navy *(Piotr Butowski)*

cabin for data link; when radar operates, all landing gear wheels can retract upward to minimise interference to emissions; cylindrical fuel container each side of lower fuselage.

Ka-25PS ('Hormone-C'): As Ka-25BSh, but equipped for mid-course guidance of long-range ship-launched surface-to-surface missiles; Yagi aerial on nose;

with operational equipment removed, many used for utility and search and rescue duties.

CUSTOMERS: Soviet Naval Aviation, India (seven, ex-Soviet Navy), Syria, Vietnam and Yugoslavia.
DESIGN FEATURES: Use of folding three-blade coaxial rotors, requiring no tail rotor, and triple tail fins ensures compact stowed overall dimensions on board ship;

engines above cabin and external mounting of operational equipment and auxiliary fuel leaves interior uncluttered.

FLYING CONTROLS, STRUCTURE: See previous editions.

Following details apply to Ka-25BSh:

POWER PLANT: Two 671 kW (900 shp) Glushenkov GTD-3F turboshafts, mounted side by side above cabin, forward of rotor driveshaft, on early aircraft. Later aircraft have 738 kW (990 shp) GTD-3BM turboshafts. Independent fuel supply to each engine. Provision for carrying external fuel tank on each side of cabin.

ACCOMMODATION: Pilot and co-pilot side by side on flight deck, with rearward sliding door on each side. Entry to main cabin is via a rearward sliding door to rear of main landing gear on port side. Cabin large enough to contain 12 folding seats for passengers.

AVIONICS: Equipment available for all versions includes autopilot, navigational system, radio compass, radio communications, lighting system for all-weather operation by day or night, and hoist mounted above cabin door. IFF antennae (NATO 'Odd Rods') above nose and alongside central tail fin. Dipping sonar housed in compartment at rear of main cabin, immediately forward of tailboom, and search radar (NATO 'Short Horn') in flat-bottom undernose radome (diameter 1.25 m; 4 ft 1 in) on anti-submarine version, which can have a canister of sonobuoys mounted externally aft of the starboard main landing gear. Most aircraft have a cylindrical housing for ESM above the tailboom, with a shallow blister fairing to the rear of the cylindrical housing. Similar housing under rear of cabin for data link equipment.

EQUIPMENT: Cylindrical container on each side of lower fuselage for markers, smoke generators or beacons. The port side container has been seen housing reconnaissance cameras.

ARMAMENT: Doors under the fuselage of some aircraft enclose a weapons bay for two 450 mm (18 in) ASW torpedoes, nuclear or conventional depth charges and other stores.

DIMENSIONS, EXTERNAL:
Rotor diameter (each)	15.74 m (51 ft 7¾ in)
Length of fuselage	9.75 m (32 ft 0 in)
Height to top of rotor head	5.37 m (17 ft 7½ in)
Width over tail-fins	3.76 m (12 ft 4 in)
Wheel track: front	1.41 m (4 ft 7½ in)
rear	3.52 m (11 ft 6½ in)
Cabin door: Height	1.10 m (3 ft 7¼ in)
Width	1.20 m (3 ft 11¼ in)

DIMENSIONS, INTERNAL:
Cabin, excl flight deck:
Length	3.95 m (12 ft 11½ in)
Max width	1.50 m (4 ft 11 in)
Max height	1.25 m (4 ft 1¼ in)

AREAS:
Main rotor disc (each)	194.6 m² (2,095 sq ft)

WEIGHTS AND LOADINGS:
Weight empty	4,765 kg (10,505 lb)
Max T-O weight	7,500 kg (16,535 lb)
Max power loading	5.08 kg/kW (8.35 lb/shp)

PERFORMANCE:
Max level speed	113 knots (209 km/h; 130 mph)
Normal cruising speed	104 knots (193 km/h; 120 mph)
Service ceiling	3,350 m (11,000 ft)
Range, with reserves:	
with standard fuel	217 nm (400 km; 250 miles)
with external tanks	351 nm (650 km; 405 miles)

KAMOV Ka-26

NATO reporting name: Hoodlum-A

TYPE: Light twin-engined multi-purpose helicopter.

PROGRAMME: Prototype first flew 1965; production aircraft entered agricultural service in Soviet Union 1970; 850 built for many civil and military roles.

VARIANTS: Turbine-powered Ka-126 ('Hoodlum-B') described under IAR SA (Romanian section).

CUSTOMERS: Delivered for civilian use in 15 countries; military operators include air forces of Bulgaria and Hungary.

DESIGN FEATURES: Airframe comprises backbone structure carrying flight deck, coaxial contra-rotating rotors, landing gear, engine pods and twin tailbooms; space aft of flight deck, between main landing gear units and under rotor transmission, can accommodate interchangeable modules for passenger/freight transport, air ambulance, aerial survey, forest firefighting, mineral prospecting, pipeline and power transmission line construction, search and rescue, and (of primary importance) agricultural equipment.

Abbreviated details of Ka-26 follow; full description appeared last in 1987-88 edition.

POWER PLANT: Two 242.5 kW (325 hp) Vedeneyev M-14V-26 aircooled radial piston engines, mounted in pods on short stub wings at top of fuselage.

ACCOMMODATION: Fully enclosed cabin, with door on each side, fitted out normally for operation by single pilot; second seat and dual controls optional. Cabin warmed and demisted by air from combustion heater, which also heats passenger compartment when fitted. Air filter on nose of agricultural version. For agricultural work, a chemical hopper (capacity 900 kg; 1,985 lb) and dust

Passenger carrying version of Kamov Ka-26 in service with former East German Police *(Ivo Sturzenegger)*

spreader or spraybars are fitted in module space, on the aircraft's centre of gravity. This equipment is quickly removable and can be replaced by a cargo/passenger pod accommodating four or six persons, with provision for a seventh passenger beside the pilot; or two stretcher patients, two seated casualties and a medical attendant in ambulance role. Alternatively, the Ka-26 can be operated with either an open platform for hauling freight or a hook for slinging bulky loads at the end of a cable or in a cargo net.

DIMENSIONS, EXTERNAL:
Rotor diameter (each)	13.00 m (42 ft 7¾ in)
Vertical separation between rotors	1.17 m (3 ft 10 in)
Length of fuselage	7.75 m (25 ft 5 in)
Height overall	4.05 m (13 ft 3½ in)
Width: over engine pods	3.64 m (11 ft 11½ in)
over agricultural spraybars	11.20 m (36 ft 9 in)
Tailplane span	4.60 m (15 ft 1 in)
Wheel track: mainwheels	2.42 m (7 ft 11½ in)
nosewheels	0.90 m (2 ft 11½ in)
Wheelbase	3.48 m (11 ft 5 in)
Passenger pod door: Height	1.40 m (4 ft 7 in)
Width	1.25 m (4 ft 1¼ in)

DIMENSIONS, INTERNAL:
Passenger pod:
Length, floor level	1.83 m (6 ft 0 in)
Width, floor level	1.25 m (4 ft 1¼ in)
Headroom	1.40 m (4 ft 7 in)

AREAS:
Main rotor disc (each)	132.7 m² (1,430 sq ft)

WEIGHTS AND LOADINGS:
Operating weight, empty: stripped	1,950 kg (4,300 lb)
cargo/platform	2,085 kg (4,597 lb)
cargo/hook	2,050 kg (4,519 lb)
passenger	2,100 kg (4,630 lb)
agricultural	2,216 kg (4,885 lb)
Fuel weight: transport	360 kg (794 lb)
other versions	100 kg (220 lb)
Payload: transport	900 kg (1,985 lb)
agricultural duster	1,065 kg (2,348 lb)

agricultural sprayer	900 kg (1,985 lb)
with cargo platform	1,065 kg (2,348 lb)
flying crane	1,100 kg (2,425 lb)
Normal T-O weight: transport	3,076 kg (6,780 lb)
agricultural	2,980 kg (6,570 lb)
Max T-O weight: all versions	3,250 kg (7,165 lb)

PERFORMANCE (at max T-O weight):
Max level speed	91 knots (170 km/h; 105 mph)
Max cruising speed	81 knots (150 km/h; 93 mph)
Econ cruising speed	49-59 knots (90-110 km/h; 56-68 mph)
Agricultural operating speed range	16-62 knots (30-115 km/h; 19-71 mph)
Service ceiling	3,000 m (9,840 ft)
Service ceiling, one engine out	500 m (1,640 ft)
Hovering ceiling at AUW of 3,000 kg (6,615 lb):	
IGE	1,300 m (4,265 ft)
OGE	800 m (2,625 ft)
Range with 7 passengers, 30 min fuel reserves	215 nm (400 km; 248 miles)
Max range with auxiliary tanks	647 nm (1,200 km; 745 miles)
Endurance at econ cruising speed	3 h 42 min

KAMOV Ka-26 JET CONTROL TESTBED

TYPE: Testbed for anti-torque jet thruster control system to be used initially on Ka-118.

PROGRAMME: Converted from Ka-26; system operated on testbench and in wind tunnel from 1974, before installation and flight testing on testbed helicopter.

DESIGN FEATURES: Basically standard Ka-26, except interior of flight deck and passenger pod equipped for research programme; twin tailbooms and tail unit replaced by tubular boom housing fan and system of jet nozzles, tested in various forms.

FLYING CONTROLS: Pilot in left seat flew helicopter normally; before research phase, pilot trimmed aircraft by rudder input, then handed over to right-seat pilot, whose rudder pedals controlled jet thruster system similar to

Kamov Ka-26 jet control testbed helicopter *(Helicopter International)*

McDonnell Douglas Helicopters (USA) NOTAR (NO TAil Rotor); control capabilities proved comparable to those with tail rotor, with reduced danger for ground personnel, no hazard of tail rotor contact with natural or man-made objects on ground in restricted areas, and other advantages claimed for NOTAR.

KAMOV Ka-27 and Ka-28
NATO reporting names: Helix-A and D

TYPE: Twin-turbine multi-purpose military helicopter.
PROGRAMME: Design started 1969; first flight of prototype December 1974; first open reference in US Department of Defense's 1981 *Soviet Military Power* document, which stated that "Hormone variant" helicopters could be carried in a telescoping hangar on the new 'Sovremenny' class of Soviet guided missile destroyers, for ASW missions; photographs of two on stern platform of *Udaloy*, first of new class of Soviet ASW guided missile destroyers, taken by Western pilots during Baltic exercises, September 1981; at least 16 observed on 'Kiev' class carrier/cruiser *Novorossiysk* during ship's maiden deployment 1983, as stage in continuous replacement of Ka-25s with Ka-27s; will equip *Admiral of the Fleet Kuznetsov* and other large Soviet carriers.
VARIANTS: **Ka-27PL** ('Helix-A'): Basic ASW helicopter with three crew; operational since 1982; normally operated in pairs, one tracking hostile submarine, other dropping depth charges. Soviet Naval Aviation has more than 100.

Ka-27PS ('Helix-D'): Search and rescue and plane guard helicopter, first seen on *Novorossiysk*; as Ka-27PL, but some operational equipment deleted; external fuel tank each side of cabin, as civil Ka-32; winch beside port cabin door.

Ka-28 ('Helix-A'): Export version of Ka-27PL, said by Yugoslavia to have 1,618 kW (2,170 shp) TV3-117BK turboshafts and 3,680 kg (8,113 lb) of fuel in 12 tanks.

The Ka-29 ('Helix-B') and Ka-32 (civil 'Helix-C') are described separately.
CUSTOMERS: Soviet Naval Aviation; India (13 Ka-28, incl three for training) and Yugoslavia (Ka-28).
DESIGN FEATURES: Basic configuration very like Ka-25BSh, but longer and more capacious fuselage pod, no central tail fin and different undernose radome; similar overall dimensions with rotors folded enable Ka-27 to stow in shipboard hangars and use deck lifts built for Ka-25BSh.

The general description of the Ka-32 (which see) applies also to the Ka-27 and Ka-28.
ACCOMMODATION: Crew of three: pilot, tactical co-ordinator, ASW systems operator.
AVIONICS: Undernose 360° search radar; IFF (NATO 'Odd Rods'); directional ESM radomes above rear of engine bay fairing and at tailcone tip; Doppler box under tailboom; radar warning receivers on nose and above tailplane; dipping sonar behind clamshell doors at rear of fuselage pod; MAD; otherwise as Ka-32.
EQUIPMENT: Infra-red jammer (NATO 'Hot Brick') at rear of engine bay fairing; chaff/flare dispensers; colour coded identification flares; sonobuoys stowed internally; otherwise as Ka-32.
ARMAMENT: Ventral weapons bay for torpedoes, depth charges, other stores.
DIMENSIONS, EXTERNAL: As Ka-32
PERFORMANCE (Yugoslav Ka-28):
Max level speed at 10,700 kg (23,590 lb) AUW
135 knots (250 km/h; 155 mph)
Max cruising speed
124-129 knots (230-240 km/h; 143-149 mph)
Max rate of climb at S/L 750 m (2,460 ft)/min
Radius of action against submarine cruising at up to 40 knots (75 km/h; 47 mph) at depth of 500 m (1,640 ft)
108 nm (200 km; 124 miles)

KAMOV Ka-29
NATO reporting name Helix-B

TYPE: Twin-turbine assault transport and electronic warfare helicopter.
PROGRAMME: Entered service with Soviet Northern and Pacific Fleets 1985; photographed on board Soviet assault ship *Ivan Rogov* in Mediterranean 1987, thought to be Ka-27B and given NATO reporting name 'Helix-B'; identified as Ka-29TB (*Transportno Boyevoya* - combat transport) at Frunze (Khodinka) air show, Moscow, August 1989; EW version completed initial shipboard trials on aircraft carrier *Admiral of the Fleet Kuznetsov* (then *Tbilisi*) 1990; both versions expected to equip this ship and other carriers.
VARIANTS: **Ka-29TB** ('Helix-B'): Development of Ka-27 for transport and close support of seaborne assault troops.

EW version: Designation not yet known; basic airframe of Ka-29TB, but many equipment changes, suggesting EW jamming role in support of helicopter assault force; shallow pannier extends full length of underfuselage; two large panniers each side of cabin, fore and aft of main landing gear; starboard cabin door, aft of flight deck, reconfigured and carries box fairing in place of window; hatch window above starboard rear pannier deleted; APU repositioned above rear of engine bay fairing, with air intake at front of housing, displacing usual ESM and IR jamming pods; tailcone extended by conical, probably dielectric, fairing; no visible gun door

Kamov Ka-28 anti-submarine helicopter (NATO 'Helix-A') in Yugoslav service (*Ivo Sturzenegger*)

Ka-29TB (NATO 'Helix-B') combat transport helicopter (*Jane's Defence Weekly/Paul Beaver*)

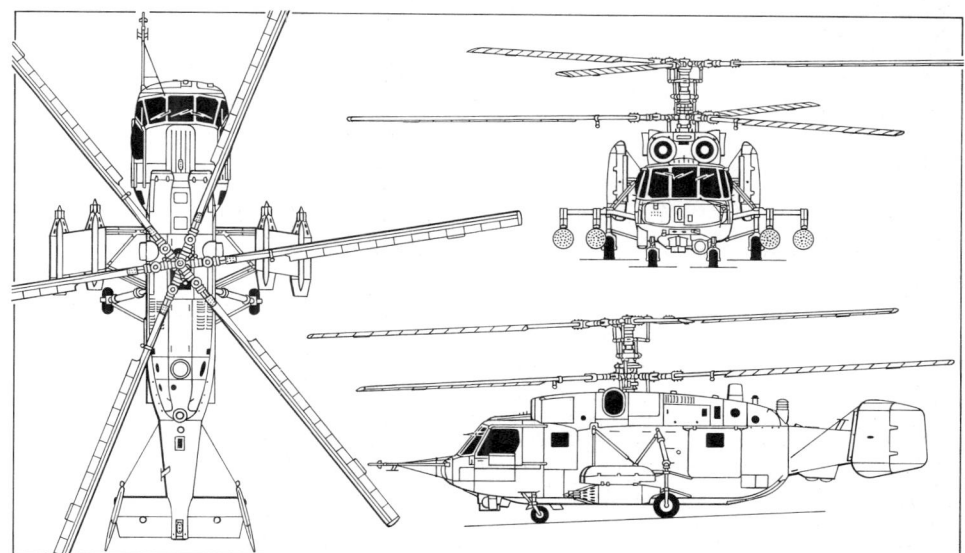

Kamov Ka-29TB combat transport helicopter (*Jane's/Mike Keep*)

on nose, or armour plating on flight deck and engine bay; no stores pylons or outriggers; unidentified structure at rear of fuselage.
CUSTOMERS: Soviet Naval Aviation (more than 30 Ka-29TBs).
General description of Ka-32 applies also to Ka-29TB, except as follows.
POWER PLANT: Two Klimov (Isotov) TV3-117VK turbo-shafts, each 1,660 kW (2,225 shp).
ACCOMMODATION: Wider flight deck than Ka-27 for two crew; windscreen comprises three flat-plate glazings

instead of two-piece curved transparency; main cabin port-side door, aft of landing gear, divided horizontally into upward and downward opening sections, to facilitate rapid exit of up to 16 assault troops; flight deck and engine bay heavily armoured.
AVIONICS: Undernose sensor pods appear similar to electro-optics and RF missile guidance pods of Mil Mi-24W; ESM 'flower pot' above rear of engine bay fairing, forward of infra-red jammer (NATO 'Hot Brick'); Doppler box under tailboom; radar warning receivers and IFF ('Slap Shot').

Unidentified version of Kamov Ka-29, assumed to have electronic warfare role *(Tass)*

short tailboom; twin turbines and APU above cabin, leaving interior uncluttered; lower fuselage sealed for flotation.

FLYING CONTROLS: Dual hydraulically powered flight control systems, without manual reversion; spring stick trim; yaw control by differential collective pitch applied through rudder pedals; mix in collective system maintains constant total rotor thrust during turns, to reduce pilot workload when landing on pitching deck, and to simplify transition to hover and landing; twin rudders intended mainly to improve control in autorotation, but also effective in co-ordinating turns; helicopter not designed for negative *g* loading; flight can be maintained on one engine at max T-O weight.

STRUCTURE: Titanium and composites used extensively, with particular emphasis on corrosion resistance; fully articulated three-blade coaxial contra-rotating rotors have all-composites blades with carbonfibre and glass-fibre main spars, pockets (13 per blade) of Kevlar type material, and filler similar to Nomex; blades have non-symmetrical aerofoil section; each has ground adjustable tab; each lower blade carries adjustable vibration damper, comprising two dependent weights, on root section, with further vibration dampers in fuselage; tip light on each upper blade; blades fold manually outboard of all control mechanisms, to folded width within track of main landing gear; rotor hub is 50 per cent titanium/50 per cent steel; rotor brake standard; all-metal semi-monocoque fuselage, with titanium primary components; composites tailcone; fixed-incidence tailplane, elevators, fins and rudders have aluminium alloy structure, composite skins; fins toe inward approx 25°; fixed leading-edge slat on each fin prevents airflow over fin stalling in crosswinds or at high yaw angles.

LANDING GEAR: Four-wheel type. Oleo-pneumatic shock absorbers. Nosewheels are smaller than mainwheels and of castoring type. Rear legs are pivoted on some versions, to retract upward about their wishbone supports so that the wheels can be moved to a position where they offer least interference to emissions from the undernose radar. Mainwheel tyres size 600 × 180 mm. Nosewheel tyres size 400 × 150 mm.

POWER PLANT: Two 1,660 kW (2,225 shp) Klimov (Isotov) TV3-117V turboshafts, with automatic synchronisation system, mounted side by side above cabin, forward of

ARMAMENT: Four-barrel Gatling type 7.62 mm machine gun flexibly mounted behind downward-articulated door on starboard side of nose; four pylons on outriggers, for four-round clusters of AT-6 ('Spiral') air-to-surface missiles and 57 mm UV-32-57 or 80 mm rocket packs.

DIMENSIONS, EXTERNAL:

Rotor diameter (each)	15.90 m (52 ft 2 in)
Blade length, aerofoil section (each)	
	5.45 m (17 ft 10½ in)
Blade chord	0.48 m (1 ft 7 in)
Vertical separation of rotors	1.40 m (4 ft 7 in)
Length overall, excl noseprobe and rotors	
	11.60 m (38 ft 0¾ in)
Height overall	5.40 m (17 ft 8½ in)
Width: between centrelines of outboard pylons	
	5.65 m (18 ft 6½ in)
over tail fins and centred rudders	
	3.65 m (12 ft 0 in)
flight deck	2.20 m (7 ft 2 in)
Mainwheel track	3.50 m (11 ft 6 in)
Nosewheel track	1.40 m (4 ft 7 in)
Wheelbase	3.00 m (9 ft 10 in)

AREAS:

Main rotor disc (each)	198.5 m² (2,138 sq ft)

WEIGHTS AND LOADINGS:

Weight empty	5,520 kg (12,170 lb)
Max T-O weight	12,600 kg (27,775 lb)

PERFORMANCE:

Max level speed at S/L	135 knots (250 km/h; 155 mph)
Service ceiling	5,000 m (16,400 ft)
Range	270-430 nm (500-800 km; 310-497 miles)

KAMOV Ka-32
NATO reporting name: Helix-C

TYPE: Twin-turbine civil utility helicopter.

PROGRAMME: Development of Ka-27/32 began 1969; first flight of common prototype December 1974; first Ka-32 (SSSR-04173) exhibited Minsk Airport late 1981, during fourth CMEA scientific/technical conference on use of aircraft in national economy, carrying slung truck in flying display; prototype of utility version (SSSR-31000, converted from Ka-27PL) shown at Paris Air Show, June 1985; in production.

VARIANTS: **Ka-32T** ('Helix-C'): Utility transport and flying crane; limited avionics; for carriage of internal or external freight, and passengers, along airways and over local routes.

Ka-32S ('Helix-C'): Maritime version; more comprehensive avionics, including undernose radar, for operation to IMC standards from icebreakers in adverse weather and over terrain devoid of landmarks; duties include ice patrol, guidance of ships through icefields, unloading and loading ships (up to 30 tonnes an hour, 360 tonnes a day), support of offshore drilling rigs, maritime search and rescue.

Ka-32K. Flying crane with retractable gondola for second pilot under cabin. Model shown 1990.

CUSTOMERS: Aeroflot (about 150 being delivered); Interflug (three ordered).

DESIGN FEATURES: Conceived as completely autonomous 'compact truck', to stow in much the same space as Ka-25

with rotors folded, despite greater power and capability, and to operate independently of ground support equipment; special attention paid to ease of handling with single pilot; overall dimensions minimised by use of coaxial rotors, requiring no tail rotor, and twin fins on

Kamov Ka-32S ('Helix-C') under automatic control, with no crew on flight deck

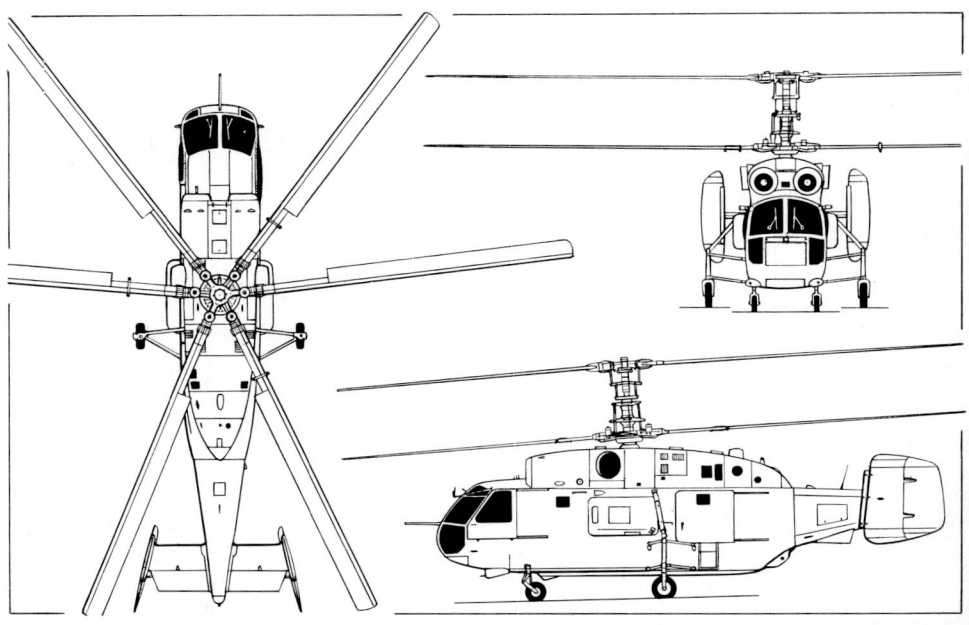

Kamov Ka-32T ('Helix-C') utility helicopter (two Klimov [Isotov] TV3-117V turboshafts) *(Pilot Press)*

Model of Kamov Ka-32K flying crane, with retractable rear pilot gondola *(Piotr Butowski)*

Full-scale mockup of Kamov Ka-62R utility helicopter *(Piotr Butowski)*

rotor driveshaft. Main gearbox brake standard. Oil cooler fan aft of gearbox. Electrothermal intake anti-icing. Cowlings hinge downward for use as maintenance platforms. All standard fuel in tanks under cabin floor and inside container on each side of centre fuselage. Provision for auxiliary tanks in cabin. Refuelling point behind small forward hinged door on port side, where bottom of tailboom meets rear of cabin.

ACCOMMODATION: Pilot and navigator side by side on large air-conditioned flight deck, in fully adjustable seats. Rearward sliding jettisonable door with blister window on each side. Seat behind navigator, on starboard side, for observer, loadmaster or rescue hoist operator. Electric windscreen anti-icing. Direct access to cabin from flight deck. Heated and ventilated main cabin can accommodate freight or 16 passengers, on three folding seats at rear, six along port sidewall and seven along starboard sidewall. Lifejackets under seats. Fittings to carry stretchers. No provisions for toilet or galley. Pyramid structure can be fitted on floor beneath rotor driveshaft to prevent swinging of external cargo sling loads. Rearward sliding door aft of main landing gear on port side, with steps below. Emergency exit door opposite. Door to avionics compartment on port side of tailboom.

SYSTEMS: Dual hydraulically powered flight control systems without manual reversion. Spring stick trim. Electro-thermal de-icing of the entire profiled portion of each blade, operating at all times when engines are running. Heat generated by rotor head prevents icing of droop stops. APU in rear of engine bay fairing on starboard side, for engine starting and to power all essential hydraulic and electrical services on the ground, eliminating need for GPU.

AVIONICS: Include electro-mechanical flight director controlled from autopilot panel, Doppler hover indicator, two HSI and air data computer. Autopilot is capable of providing automatic approach and hover at a height of 25 m (82 ft) over landing area, on predetermined course, using Doppler. Radar altimeter. Doppler box under tailboom.

EQUIPMENT: Doors at rear of fuel tank bay provide access to small compartment for auxiliary fuel, or liferafts which eject during descent in emergency, by command from flight deck. Container on each side of fuselage, under external fuel containers, for emergency flotation bags, deployed by water contact. Rescue hoist, capacity 300 kg (661 lb), can be installed between top of door opening and landing gear. Optional external load sling, with automatic release and integral load weighing and stabilisation systems.

DIMENSIONS, EXTERNAL:
Rotor diameter (each)	15.90 m (52 ft 2 in)
Length overall: excl rotors	11.30 m (37 ft 1 in)
rotors folded	12.25 m (40 ft 2¼ in)
Width, rotors folded	4.00 m (13 ft 1½ in)
Height to top of rotor head	5.40 m (17 ft 8½ in)
Wheel track: mainwheels	3.50 m (11 ft 6 in)
nosewheels	1.40 m (4 ft 7 in)
Wheelbase	3.02 m (9 ft 11 in)
Cabin door: Height	approx 1.20 m (3 ft 11¼ in)
Width	approx 1.20 m (3 ft 11¼ in)

DIMENSIONS, INTERNAL:
Cabin: Length	4.52 m (14 ft 10 in)
Max width	1.30 m (4 ft 3 in)
Max height	1.32 m (4 ft 4 in)

AREAS:
Main rotor disc (each)	198.5 m² (2,138 sq ft)

WEIGHTS AND LOADINGS:
Max payload: internal	4,000 kg (8,818 lb)
external	5,000 kg (11,023 lb)
Normal T-O weight	11,000 kg (24,250 lb)
Max flight weight with slung load	12,600 kg (27,775 lb)

PERFORMANCE (at AUW of 11,000 kg; 24,250 lb):
Max level speed	135 knots (250 km/h; 155 mph)

Max cruising speed	124 knots (230 km/h; 143 mph)
Service ceiling at normal T-O weight	
	6,000 m (19,685 ft)
Hovering ceiling OGE	3,500 m (11,480 ft)
Range with max fuel	432 nm (800 km; 497 miles)
Endurance with max fuel	4 h 30 min

KAMOV Ka-62

TYPE: Medium-sized twin-turbine multi-purpose helicopter.

PROGRAMME: Construction of prototype Ka-62 (then known as V-62) began early 1990; Ka-62R variant announced September 1990.

VARIANTS: **Ka-62:** Basic model for Soviet market, as described in detail; first flight planned for 1992, certification 1994.

Ka-62R: To be certificated to Western standards, for sale outside USSR; two 1,566 kW (2,100 shp) Rolls-Royce Turbomeca RTM322 turboshafts; first flight scheduled for late 1993, certification 1995.

DESIGN FEATURES: General configuration resembles closely such Western types as Aerospatiale Dauphin, with single main rotor and fan-in-fin similar to latter's fenestron; retractable tailwheel landing gear.

STRUCTURE: Between 50 and 55 per cent of structure made of composites, including four blades of main rotor. Main rotor head of GFRP and CFRP; cabin sides, floor and roof, tailboom, fin, vertical stabilisers, and fan blades of carbon reinforced Kevlar.

LANDING GEAR: Retractable tailwheel type; single main-wheels retract inward and upward into bottom of fuselage; twin tailwheels retract into tailboom; shock absorber in each unit.

POWER PLANT: Two Novikov/Rybinsk (Glushenkov) TVD-155 turboshafts, each 970 kW (1,300 shp); fuel tanks under floor and beneath rear seats, capacity 1,150 litres (304 US gallons; 253 Imp gallons).

ACCOMMODATION: Crew of one or two; optional bulkhead divider between flight deck and cabin; up to 14 passengers in four rows; forward hinged door on each side of flight deck; large sliding door each side of cabin; baggage hold to rear of cabin. VIP configuration to be available, typically with five seats, refreshment bar and toilet.

EQUIPMENT: As necessary for variety of roles, including transport of slung freight; air ambulance/operating theatre; search and rescue; patrol of highways, forests, electric power lines, gas and oil pipelines; survey of ice areas; surveillance of territorial waters, economic areas and fisheries; mineral prospecting; and servicing of offshore gas and oil rigs.

DIMENSIONS, EXTERNAL:
Main rotor diameter	13.00 m (42 ft 8 in)
Fuselage length	12.80 m (42 ft 0 in)
Height overall	3.70 m (12 ft 1¾ in)
Width: over endplate fins	3.00 m (9 ft 10¼ in)
over mainwheels	2.50 m (8 ft 2½ in)
Wheelbase	4.725 m (15 ft 6 in)

AREAS:
Main rotor disc	132.7 m² (1,429 sq ft)

WEIGHTS AND LOADINGS (A, Ka-62; B, Ka-62R):
Max payload: internal A, B	2,000 kg (4,409 lb)
external: A, B	2,500 kg (5,510 lb)
Normal T-O weight: B	6,000 kg (13,225 lb)
Max T-O weight: A	5,850 kg (12,900 lb)
B, internal load	6,250 kg (13,775 lb)
B, external load	6,500 kg (14,330 lb)
Max disc loading: A	44.08 kg/m² (9.03 lb/sq ft)

PERFORMANCE (estimated. A: Ka-62, B: Ka-62R at normal T-O weight):
Max level speed: A	156 knots (290 km/h; 180 mph)
B	162 knots (300 km/h; 186 mph)
Cruising speed: A	140 knots (260 km/h; 161 mph)
B	145 knots (270 km/h; 168 mph)
Max rate of climb at S/L:	
B, two engines	780 m (2,560 ft)/min
B, one engine out	300 m (985 ft)/min
Service ceiling: A, B	5,500 m (18,045 ft)
Hovering ceiling IGE: A	2,000 m (6,560 ft)
B	3,000 m (9,840 ft)
Range with 12 passengers at 1,220 m (4,000 ft), 35°C	
B	282 nm (523 km; 325 miles)
Range with standard fuel: A	323 nm (600 km; 372 miles)
B	315 nm (585 km; 363 miles)
Range with auxiliary tanks:	
B	540 nm (1,000 km; 621 miles)

KAMOV Ka-118

TYPE: Light multi-purpose turbine powered helicopter.

PROGRAMME: Decision to build Ka-118, utilising jet thruster control system developed on Ka-26 testbed (which see), announced at Helicopter Association International convention, Dallas, USA, 4 February 1990.

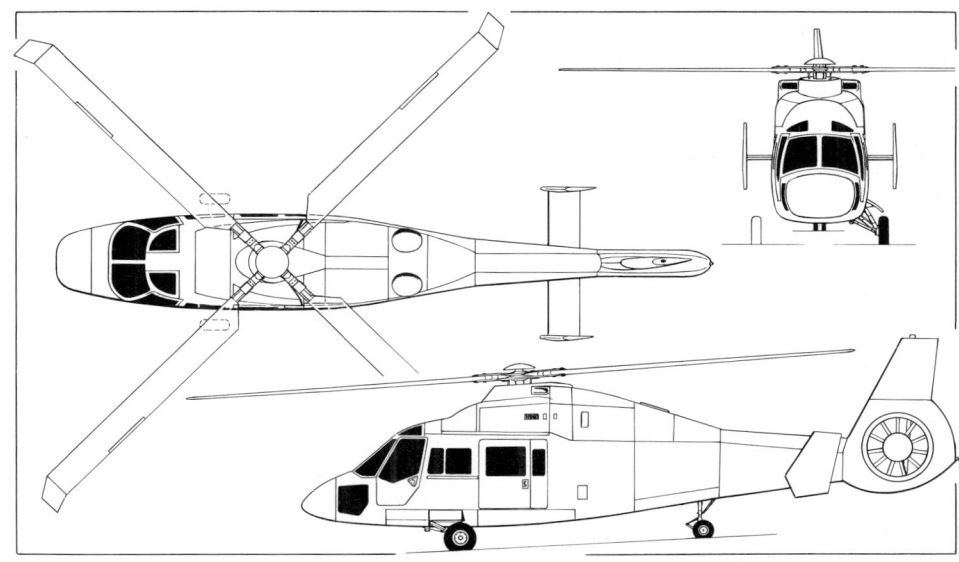

Kamov Ka-62 twin-turbine 12/14-passenger helicopter *(Pilot Press)*

DESIGN FEATURES: Single main rotor, with swept blade tips, breaks with Kamov traditional use of coaxial contra-rotating rotors; jet thruster control system (similar to US McDonnell Douglas NOTAR) eliminates need for tail rotor; highly streamlined, extensively glazed cabin; V tail with bridging tailplane; skid landing gear.

STRUCTURE: Four-blade rotor of composites construction.

POWER PLANT: Not decided early 1991; alternatives include one 530 kW (710 shp) Soyuz/Koptchyenko TV-O-100 turboshaft, or one or two engines of Allison, Pratt & Whitney Canada, Rolls-Royce or Turbomeca design; standard fuel capacity 700 litres (185 US gallons; 154 Imp gallons).

ACCOMMODATION: Pilot and four passengers in cabin.

EQUIPMENT: As necessary for day/night normal/adverse weather operation, on such duties as passenger transport, air ambulance, freight carrying, search and rescue, patrol of forests, highways, electric power lines, gas and oil pipelines.

Preliminary data for Ka-118 with TV-O-100 engine follow:

DIMENSIONS, EXTERNAL:
Rotor diameter	11.00 m (36 ft 1 in)
Fuselage length	10.00 m (32 ft 9¾ in)
Height overall	2.60 m (8 ft 6½ in)
Width over skids	2.60 m (8 ft 6½ in)

AREAS:
Rotor disc	95.03 m² (1,023 sq ft)

WEIGHTS AND LOADINGS:
Max payload: internal	800 kg (1,765 lb)
external	1,000 kg (2,205 lb)
Normal T-O weight	1,950 kg (4,300 lb)
Max T-O weight: internal load	2,150 kg (4,740 lb)
slung load	2,250 kg (4,960 lb)
Max disc loading	23.68 kg/m² (4.85 lb/sq ft)

PERFORMANCE (estimated):
Max level speed	162 knots (300 km/h; 186 mph)
Max cruising speed	145 knots (270 km/h; 168 mph)
Max rate of climb at S/L	660 m (2,165 ft)/min
Service ceiling	6,150 m (20,175 ft)
Hovering ceiling IGE	3,000 m (9,850 ft)
Range: max standard fuel	512 nm (950 km; 590 miles)
with auxiliary tanks	810 nm (1,500 km; 932 miles)

KAMOV Ka-126
NATO reporting name: Hoodlum-B

Responsibility for manufacture of the turbine powered Ka-126 has been allocated to IAR SA (see Romanian section and Addenda.)

KAMOV Ka-136 (Ka-34?)
NATO reporting name: Hokum

TYPE: Twin-turbine combat helicopter.

PROGRAMME: First reported Summer 1984, when flight testing had started; first photograph published in West 1989; production deliveries expected to begin 1991. OKB designation Ka-136 and service designation Ka-34 unconfirmed.

DESIGN FEATURES: Coaxial, contra-rotating and widely separated three-blade rotors, with swept blade tips; streamlined fuselage with tapered nose carrying pitot, transducer to provide data for fire control computer, and undernose sensor pack; retractable landing gear; stub-wings with endplates; underwing weapon pylons; horizontal stabiliser with endplate fins, supplementing swept tail fin; engines above wingroots.

POWER PLANT: Believed to comprise two Leningrad/Klimov TV3-117VK turboshafts, each 1,640 kW (2,200 shp).

ACCOMMODATION: At least one prototype reported to have side by side seating for two crew; US Department of Defense's *Soviet Military Power* document suggests definitive tandem two-seat gunship configuration, with raised rear cockpit under continuous glazed canopy.

EQUIPMENT: Infra-red suppressors, infra-red decoy dispensers, armour.

ARMAMENT: US Department of Defense states that 'Hokum' has not been observed carrying anti-tank guided weapons and that its primary armament of unguided rocket packs, air-to-air missiles and rapid-fire gun suggests suitability for employment as low-level helicopter intercept system by day and night and in adverse weather. Other combat roles could include "countering enemy attacks, preparing for and executing counter-offensives, and supporting combined-arms offensives into an opponent's territory". This suggests that 'Hokum' may be used as an escort for amphibious assault Ka-29TB 'Helix-Bs' based on Soviet Navy aircraft carriers, especially as Kamov military helicopters have always been produced for mainly maritime use.

DIMENSIONS, EXTERNAL:
Rotor diameter (each)	14.00 m (45 ft 10 in)
Length overall, excl noseprobes	13.50 m (44 ft 3½ in)
	13.50 m (44 ft 3½ in)
Height overall	5.40 m (17 ft 8 in)

WEIGHTS AND LOADINGS (estimated):
Max T-O weight	7,500 kg (16,500 lb)

PERFORMANCE (estimated):
Max level speed	189 knots (350 km/h; 217 mph)
Combat radius	135 nm (250 km; 155 miles)

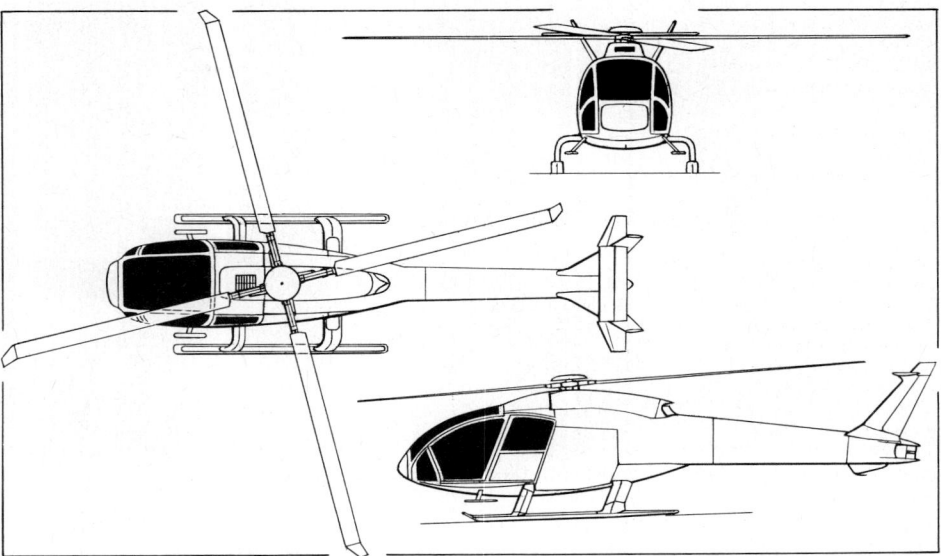

Provisional three-view drawing of Kamov Ka-118 five-seat helicopter (*Pilot Press*)

Kamov 'Hokum' combat helicopter (*US Department of Defense*)

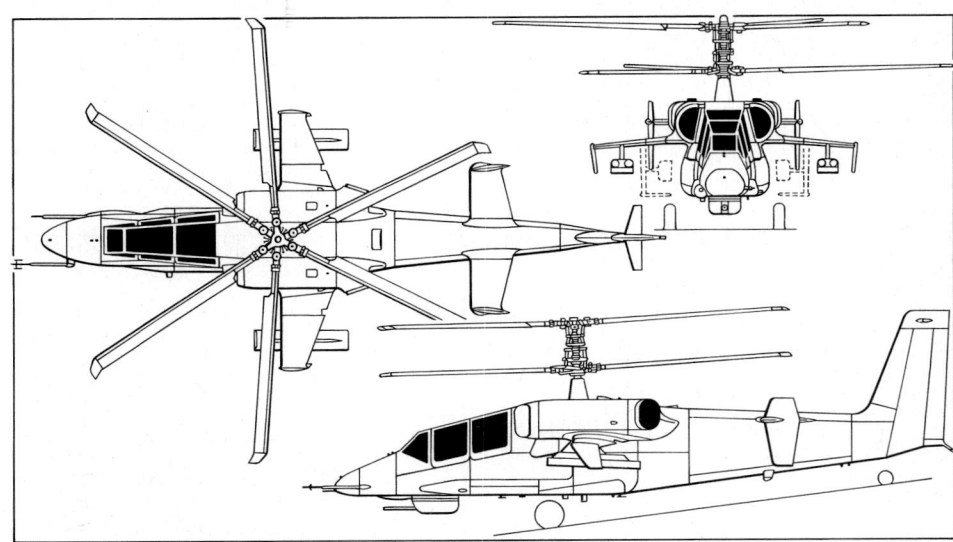

Updated three-view drawing of pre-production Kamov 'Hokum' (*Jane's/Mike Keep*)

KAMOV Ka-226

TYPE: Twin-turbine utility and agricultural helicopter.

PROGRAMME: Announced at 1990 Helicopter Association International convention, Dallas, USA; prototype expected to fly late 1990; delivery of production Allison engines scheduled to begin late 1991; FAA certification to be sought; production will be in USSR.

DESIGN FEATURES: Refined development of Ka-26/126; changes to shape of nose, twin tail fins and rudders, and passenger pod; passenger cabin has much larger windows and remains interchangeable with variety of payload modules including agricultural systems with hopper capacity of 1,000 litres (264 US gallons; 220 Imp gallons); new rotor system, interchangeable with standard coaxial system, will become available later.

LANDING GEAR: Non-retractable four-wheel type. Main units at rear, carried by stub-wings. All four units embody oleo-pneumatic shock absorbers. Forward units of castoring type, without brakes. Rear wheels have pneumatic brakes.

POWER PLANT: Two 313 kW (420 shp) Allison 250-C20B turboshafts, mounted side by side aft of the rotor mast, in the same position as the single turboshaft of the Ka-126, with individual driveshafts to the rotor gearbox. Standard fuel capacity 870 litres (230 US gallons; 191 Imp gallons).

ACCOMMODATION: Basic seating for pilot and seven passengers.

AVIONICS: Cockpit instrumentation and avionics to customer's choice.

EQUIPMENT: Specially equipped payload modules available for a variety of roles.

DIMENSIONS, EXTERNAL:
Rotor diameter (each)	13.00 m (42 ft 7¾ in)
Length overall, excl rotors	8.10 m (26 ft 7 in)
Width over stub-wings	3.22 m (10 ft 6¾ in)
Height to top of rotor head	4.15 m (13 ft 7½ in)
Wheel track: nosewheels	0.90 m (2 ft 11½ in)
mainwheels	2.56 m (8 ft 4¾ in)
Wheelbase	3.48 m (11 ft 5 in)
Passenger pod: Length	2.04 m (6 ft 8¼ in)
Width	1.28 m (4 ft 2¼ in)
Depth	1.40 m (4 ft 7¼ in)

AREAS:
Main rotor disc (each)	132.7 m² (1,430 sq ft)

WEIGHTS AND LOADINGS:
Max payload	1,000 kg (2,205 lb)
Normal T-O weight	3,100 kg (6,835 lb)
Max T-O weight	3,250 kg (7,165 lb)

PERFORMANCE (estimated):
Max level speed	110 knots (205 km/h; 127 mph)

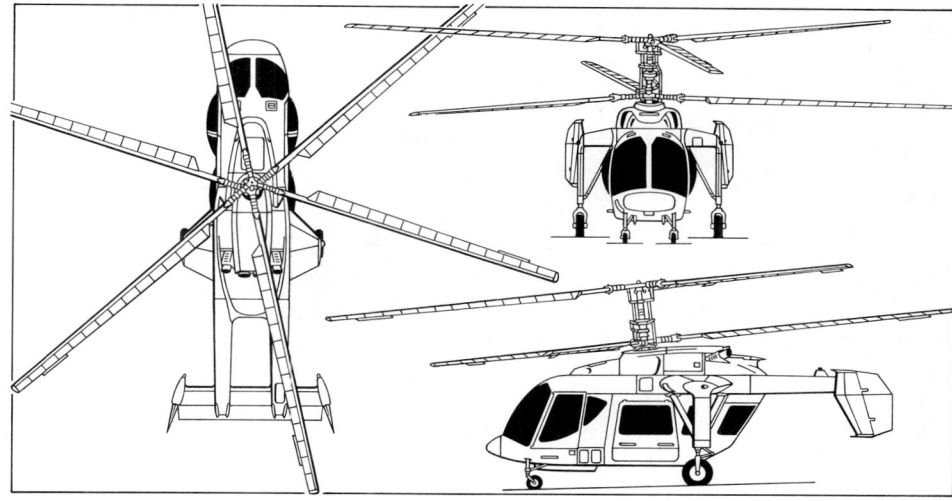

Kamov Ka-226, a refined development of the Ka-126 utility helicopter *(Jane's/Mike Keep)*

Max cruising speed	100 knots (185 km/h; 115 mph)	Range with max fuel	350 nm (650 km; 403 miles)
Service ceiling	5,250 m (17,225 ft)	Endurance with max fuel	4 h 30 min
Hovering ceiling IGE	1,950 m (6,400 ft)		

MiG
MIKOYAN DESIGN BUREAU
6 Leningradskoye Highway, PO Box 125171, Moscow
Telephone: 7 (95) 158 2452, 7 (95) 417 0504
GENERAL DESIGNER: Rostislav A. Belyakov
DEPUTY GENERAL DESIGNERS:
Mikhail Waldenburg
Anatoly A. Belosvet
PUBLIC RELATIONS: Boris B. Rybak

Colonel-General Artem Ivanovich Mikoyan, who died on 9 December 1970 aged 65, was head of the OKB responsible for the MiG series of fighter aircraft from 1939. With Mikhail Iosifovich Guryevich (1893-1976), a mathematician, he collaborated in design of the first really effective Soviet jet fighter, the MiG-15, which began to enter squadron service in numbers in 1949. Subsequent designs by the OKB have resulted in more MiGs entering worldwide service than any other fighter 'family' since the Second World War.

MIKOYAN MiG-21
NATO reporting names: Fishbed and Mongol
TYPE: Single-seat multi-role fighter and two-seat operational trainer.

PROGRAMME: Development began to meet Autumn 1953 official requirement for short-range interceptor; tailed delta configuration selected for production late 1956 after flight testing of prototypes with swept and delta wings; Ye-6 pre-production prototype flew late 1957; MiG-21 production authorised 1958; deliveries began late that year; production completed except in China, where developed versions manufactured by Chengdu Aircraft Corporation (CAC) and Guizhou Aviation Industry Corporation (GAIC) (see Chinese section).

VARIANTS: For details of early variants see 1985-86 and earlier editions of *Jane's*; major versions deployed currently with Soviet air forces of the military districts and groups of forces (MD/GOF), and their variants, are as follows.

MiG-21PFMA ('Fishbed-J'): Multi-role version, with four underwing pylons instead of former two; deepened dorsal spine fairing above fuselage; improved radar (NATO 'Jay Bird'); Tumansky R-11F2S-300 turbojet, rated at 38.25 kN (8,598 lb st) dry and 60.8 kN (13,668 lb st) with afterburning; zero/zero ejection seat; armament one GSh-23 twin-barrel 23 mm gun, two AA-2/2D ('Atoll') infra-red air-to-air missiles on inboard pylons, two radar-homing AA-2Cs ('Atolls') or drop fuel tanks on outboard pylons.

MiG-21R ('Fishbed-H'): Tactical reconnaissance version, basically as MiG-21PFMA; external pod for forward facing or oblique cameras, or elint sensors, on centreline pylon; suppressed ECM antenna at mid-point on dorsal spine; optional radar warning receivers in wingtip fairings.

MiG-21MF ('Fishbed-J'): As MiG-21PFMA, but with higher-rated, lighter weight, Tumansky R-13-300 turbojet; gun gas deflector beneath suction relief door forward of each wingroot; entered Soviet service 1969.

MiG-21M: Export variant of MiG-21MF; R-11F2S-300 engine; built as Indian Air Force Type 96 by Hindustan Aeronautics, with deliveries 1973-81.

MiG-21RF ('Fishbed-H'): Tactical reconnaissance version of MiG-21MF; equipment as MiG-21R.

MiG-21SMB ('Fishbed-K'): As MiG-21MF, but

MiG-21R ('Fishbed-H') of former East German Air Force *(Ivo Sturzenegger)*

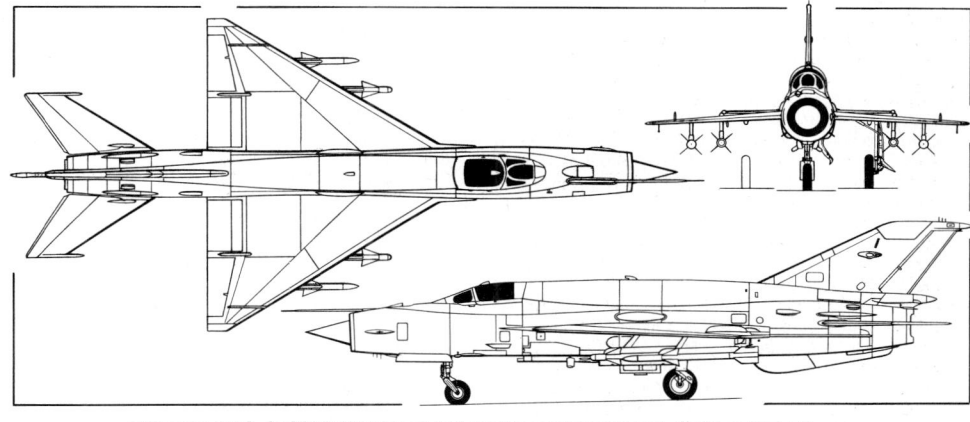

Mikoyan MiG-21SMB ('Fishbed-K') single-seat multi-role fighter *(Pilot Press)*

deep dorsal spine extends rearward as far as brake-chute housing, for maximum fuel tankage and optimum aerodynamic form; deliveries began 1971.

MiG-21bis-A ('Fishbed-L'): Third-generation multi-role air combat/ground attack version; Tumansky R-25-300 turbojet, rated at 73.6 kN (16,535 lb st) with afterburning; updated avionics; generally improved construction standards; wider and deeper dorsal fairing than MiG-21MF; capacity of seven internal self-sealing fuel tanks increased to 2,900 litres (766 US gallons; 638 Imp gallons); weight empty 5,353 kg (11,800 lb); max T-O weight 9,500 kg (20,940 lb).

MiG-21bis-B ('Fishbed-N'): Advanced version of 'Fishbed-L'; further improved avionics indicated by ILS antennae (NATO 'Swift Rod') under nose and on fin tip; two radar-homing AA-2C ('Atolls') outboard and two AA-8 ('Aphids') inboard, or four AA-8s; one version can carry nuclear weapons; rate of climb at AUW of 6,800 kg (15,000 lb), with 50 per cent fuel and two 'Atolls', is 17,700 m (58,000 ft/min; weight empty 6,000 kg (13,225 lb); max T-O weight clean 8,500 kg (18,740 lb); produced also by HAL, India, 1980-87.

MiG-21U ('Mongol'): Two-seat trainer; initial 'Mongol-A' generally similar to MiG-21F except for two cockpits in tandem with sideways hinged (to starboard)

double canopy, larger mainwheels and tyres of MiG-21PF, one-piece forward airbrake, above-intake pitot and no gun. 'Mongol-B' has broader-chord vertical tail surfaces and under-rudder brake-chute housing of later operational variants, deeper dorsal spine and no dorsal fin.

MiG-21US ('Mongol-B'): As later MiG-21U, but provision for SPS flap blowing; retractable periscope for instructor in rear seat; internal fuel capacity 2,400 litres (634 US gallons; 528 Imp gallons).

MiG-21UM ('Mongol-B'): Two-seat trainer counterpart of MiG-21MF; R-13 turbojet; four underwing stores pylons.

CUSTOMERS: At least 38 air forces (not all current); some have early MiG-21F/PF/PFM variants ('Fishbed-C/D/F').

Following details refer to MiG-21MF:

DESIGN FEATURES: Diminutive tailed delta with clipped tips to mid-mounted wings; circular-section fuselage with prominent dorsal spine; nose intake with large three-position centrebody; swept tail, with large vertical surfaces and ventral fin; 2° wing anhedral from roots; TsAGI section, thickness/chord ratio 5 per cent at root, 4.2 per cent at tip; leading-edge sweep 57°; no wing leading-edge camber.

MiG-21 bis ('Fishbed-N') armed with two AA-2C 'Atolls' outboard and two AA-8 'Aphids' inboard

MiG-23BN (NATO 'Flogger-H') of the Iraqi Air Force with added Dassault-type flight refuelling probe forward of windscreen. Such a system has not yet been observed on MiGs of the Soviet Air Force *(Jane's Defence Weekly/Tony Banks)*

FLYING CONTROLS: Manual operation, with autostabilisation in pitch and roll; hydraulically boosted inset ailerons; blown plain trailing-edge flaps, actuated hydraulically; forward hinged door type airbrake each side of underfuselage below wing leading-edge; third forward hinged airbrake under fuselage forward of ventral fin; airbrakes actuated hydraulically; hydraulically boosted rudder and all-moving horizontal surface with two gearing ratios for varying combinations of altitude and airspeed; tailplane trim switch on control column; no tabs.

STRUCTURE: All-metal; wings have two primary spars and auxiliary spar; semi-monocoque fuselage, with spine housing control pushrods, avionics, single-point refuelling cap and fuel tank; blister fairings on fuselage above and below each wing to accommodate retracted mainwheels.

LANDING GEAR: Hydraulically retractable tricycle type, with single wheel on each unit; all units housed in fuselage when retracted. Forward retracting non-steerable nosewheel unit, tyre size 500 × 180 mm; inward retracting mainwheels which turn to stow vertically inside fuselage. Size 800 × 200 mm tyres on mainwheels, inflated to approximately 7.93 bars (115 lb/sq in), ruling out normal operation from grass runways. Pneumatic disc brakes on all three wheels, supplied from compressed air bottles. Steering by differential mainwheel braking. Wheel doors remain open when legs are extended. Brake parachute housed inside acorn fairing at base of rudder.

POWER PLANT: One Tumansky R-13-300 turbojet, rated at 41.55 kN (9,340 lb st) dry and 64.73 kN (14,550 lb st) with afterburning. Fuel tanks in fuselage, and two integral tanks in each wing, with total capacity of 2,600 litres (687 US gallons; 572 Imp gallons), of which approx 1,800 litres (475 US gallons; 396 Imp gallons) are usable within CG limits at low speed. Provision for carrying one finned external fuel tank, capacity 490 litres (130 US gallons; 108 Imp gallons) or 800 litres (211 US gallons; 176 Imp gallons), on underfuselage pylon and two 490 litre drop tanks on outboard underwing pylons. Two jettisonable solid propellant JATO rockets can be fitted under rear fuselage, aft of wheel doors.

ACCOMMODATION: Pilot only, on zero/zero ejection seat with spring loaded arm at top which ensures that seat cannot be operated unless hood is closed. Canopy is sideways hinged, to starboard, and is surmounted by a small rearview mirror. Flat bulletproof windscreen. Cabin air-conditioned. Armour plating forward and aft of cockpit.

SYSTEMS: Duplicated hydraulic system, supplied by engine driven pump, with backup by battery powered electric pump, and emergency electric tailplane trim.

AVIONICS: Search and track radar (NATO 'Jay Bird') in intake centrebody, with search range of 10.8 nm (20 km; 12.5 miles). Other standard avionics include VOR, ARK automatic radio-compass, IFF and Sirena 3 radar warning system with an indicator marked in 45° sectors in front of and behind the aircraft. Gyro gunsight maintains precision up to 2.75 g. Automatic ranging can be fed into gunsight. Full blind-flying instrumentation, with attitude and heading indicators driven by remote central gyro platform.

ARMAMENT: One twin-barrel 23 mm GSh-23 gun, with 200 rounds, in belly pack. Four underwing pylons for weapons or drop tanks. Typical loads for interceptor role include two AA-2/2D (K-13A) 'Atoll' air-to-air missiles on inner pylons and two radar homing AA-2C 'Atolls' or two UV-16-57 rocket packs (each sixteen 57 mm rockets) on outer pylons; or two drop tanks and two AA-2/2D or AA-2C 'Atolls'. Typical loads for ground attack role are four UV-16-57 rocket packs; two 500 kg and two 250 kg bombs; or four 240 mm S-24 air-to-surface rockets.

DIMENSIONS, EXTERNAL (MiG-21MF):
Wing span 7.15 m (23 ft 5½ in)
Length, incl pitot boom 15.76 m (51 ft 8½ in)

Fuselage length, intake lip to jetpipe nozzle
12.30 m (40 ft 4¼ in)
Height overall 4.10 m (13 ft 5½ in)
Tailplane span 3.70 m (12 ft 8 in)
Wheel track 2.69 m (8 ft 10 in)
Wheelbase 4.81 m (15 ft 9½ in)
AREAS:
Wings, gross 23.0 m² (247.0 sq ft)
WEIGHTS AND LOADINGS (MiG-21MF):
Weight empty 5,843 kg (12,882 lb)
T-O weight:
 with four K-13A missiles 8,200 kg (18,078 lb)
 with two K-13A missiles and two 490 litre (130 US gallon; 108 Imp gallon) drop tanks
8,950 kg (19,730 lb)
 with two K-13As and three drop tanks
9,400 kg (20,725 lb)
Max T-O weight 9,800 kg (21,605 lb)
Max wing loading 426.0 kg/m² (87.5 lb/sq ft)
Max power loading 151.4 kg/kN (1.48 lb/lb st)
PERFORMANCE (MiG-21MF):
Max level speed above 11,000 m (36,000 ft)
Mach 2.05 (1,175 knots; 2,175 km/h; 1,353 mph)
Max level speed at low altitude
Mach 1.06 (701 knots; 1,300 km/h; 807 mph)
Landing speed 146 knots (270 km/h; 168 mph)
Design ceiling 18,000 m (59,050 ft)
Practical ceiling about 15,250 m (50,000 ft)
T-O run at normal AUW 800 m (2,625 ft)
Landing run 550 m (1,805 ft)
Combat radius (hi-lo-hi):
 with four 250 kg bombs, internal fuel
200 nm (370 km; 230 miles)
 with two 250 kg bombs and drop tanks
400 nm (740 km; 460 miles)
Range, internal fuel only 593 nm (1,100 km; 683 miles)
Ferry range, with three external tanks
971 nm (1,800 km; 1,118 miles)
PERFORMANCE (MiG-21US, clean):
Max level speed above 12,200 m (40,000 ft)
Mach 2.02 (1,159 knots; 2,150 km/h; 1,335 mph)
Max level speed at S/L
Mach 1.06 (701 knots; 1,300 km/h; 807 mph)
Max rate of climb at S/L 6,400 m (21,000 ft)/min
Rate of climb at 11,000 m (36,000 ft)
3,050 m (10,000 ft)/min
Time to 1,500 m (4,920 ft) 20 s
Turn rate at 4,575 m (15,000 ft):
 instantaneous (Mach 0.5) 11.1°/s
 instantaneous (Mach 0.9) 13.4°/s
 sustained (Mach 0.9) 7.5°/s
T-O run 700 m (2,297 ft)

MIKOYAN MiG-23/24
NATO reporting names: Flogger-A, B, C, E, F, G, H and K

TYPE: Single-seat variable-geometry air combat fighter and two-seat operational trainer.

PROGRAMME: Ye-231 (or Ye-23IG) prototype first displayed during Aviation Day flypast, Domodedovo Airport, Moscow, 9 July 1967, soon after first flight; pre-series aircraft delivered to Soviet air forces 1970; initial series production interceptors delivered 1973; with MiG-27, superseded MiG-21 as primary equipment Soviet tactical air forces and APVO home defence interceptor force; production in USSR ended mid-1980s, but continued in India; replacement of early variants with MiG-29s and Su-27s continues.

VARIANTS: Early versions last described in 1990-91 edition.

MiG-23MF ('Flogger-B'): Single-seat air combat fighter; first Soviet aircraft with demonstrated ability to track and engage targets flying below its own altitude; Tumansky R-29-300 turbojet, rated at 122 kN (27,500 lb st) with afterburning; J band radar (NATO 'High Lark');

Sirena-3 radar warning system; Doppler; small infra-red search/track pod under cockpit; standard in Soviet air forces from about 1975, and other Warsaw Pact air forces from 1978.

MiG-23UM ('Flogger-C'): Tandem two-seat operational training/combat version; Tumansky R-27F2M-300 turbojet, rated at 100 kN (22,485 lb st) with afterburning; individual canopy over each seat; rear seat raised, with retractable periscopic sight; deepened dorsal spine fairing aft of rear canopy.

MiG-23UB ('Flogger-C'): As MiG-23UM, but limited combat capability.

MiG-23MS ('Flogger-E'): Export version of 'Flogger-B'; R-27F2M-300 engine; equipped to lower standard; smaller radar ('Jay Bird', search range 15 nm; 29 km; 18 miles, tracking range 10 nm; 19 km; 12 miles) in shorter nose radome; no infra-red sensor or Doppler; armed with AA-2 ('Atoll') air-to-air missiles and GSh-23 gun.

MiG-23B ('Flogger-F'): Export single-seat fighter/bomber; nose shape, laser rangefinder, raised seat, cockpit external armour and larger, low-pressure tyres of Soviet air forces' MiG-27 ('Flogger-D'), but with R-29-300 turbojet, variable geometry intakes and GSh-23 gun of MiG-23MF interceptor; provision for AS-7 ('Kerry') air-to-surface missiles.

MiG-23ML ('Flogger-G'): Lightened version (L of designation for *logkiy*; light) first identified Summer 1978; basically as MiG-23MF, but Tumansky R-35F-300 turbojet; rear fuselage fuel tank deleted; much smaller dorsal fin; modified nosewheel leg; lighter weight radar; new undernose sensor pod on some aircraft.

MiG-23BN ('Flogger-H'): As 'Flogger-F' but small fairing for radar warning receiver each side of bottom fuselage, forward of nosewheel doors. Iraqi aircraft have Dassault-type fixed flight refuelling probe forward of windscreen. Max T-O weight 20,170 kg (44,465 lb); max level speed Mach 1.7; service ceiling 17,500 m (57,400 ft); combat radius 330 nm (610 km; 380 miles).

MiG-23MLD ('Flogger-K'): Development of 'Flogger-G' (D of designation for *dorabotannyy*; modified); identified by dogtooth notch at junction of each wing glove leading-edge and intake trunk, to generate vortices to improve stability in yaw at high angles of attack; this compensates for smaller ventral folding fin and small 'Flogger-G' type dorsal fin; new IFF antenna forward of windscreen; AA-11 ('Archer') close-range air-to-air missiles on fuselage pylons; pivoting pylons under outer wings.

MiG-24: Alternative designation for export MiG-23s, including those for former East Germany.

CUSTOMERS: Total of around 1,800 'Flogger-B/G/Ks' serving with Soviet strategic air defence force and tactical air force regiments in 1989 reduced considerably; most redundant aircraft placed in storage or assigned to training schools; late-generation versions serve with Vinnitsa and Legnica air armies and remain a major component of Frontal Aviation and APVO units; exported to Afghanistan, Algeria ('Flogger-E/F'), Angola ('C/E'), Bulgaria ('B/C/H'), Cuba ('C/E/F'), Czechoslovakia ('B/C/G/H'), Egypt ('C/F'), Ethiopia ('F'), East Germany ('B/C/G'), Hungary ('B/C'), India ('C/H'), Iraq ('E/H'), North Korea ('E'), Libya ('C/E/F'), Poland ('B/C/H'), Romania ('B/C'), Syria ('F/G'), Vietnam ('F'), Yemen ('F').

Details refer specifically to MiG-23ML of Soviet air forces.

DESIGN FEATURES: Shoulder-wing variable-geometry configuration; sweep variable manually in flight or on the ground to 16°, 45° or 72°; two hydraulic wing sweep motors driven separately by main and control booster systems; if one system fails, wing sweep system remains effective at 50 per cent normal angular velocity; rear fuselage detachable between wing and tailplane for engine servicing; lower portion of large ventral fin hinged to fold to starboard when landing gear extended, for ground clearance; leading-edge sweepback 72° on fixed wing panels, 57° on horizontal tail surfaces, 65° on fin.

FLYING CONTROLS: Hydraulically actuated; full-span single-slotted trailing-edge flaps, each in three sections; outboard sections operable independently when wings fully swept; no ailerons; two-section upper surface spoilers/lift dumpers, forward of mid and inner flap sections each side, operate differentially in conjunction with horizontal tail surfaces (except when disengaged at 72° sweep), and collectively for improved runway adherence and braking after touchdown; leading-edge flap on outboard two-thirds of each main (variable geometry) panel, coupled to trailing-edge flaps; all-moving horizontal tail surfaces operate differentially and symmetrically for aileron and elevator function respectively; ground adjustable tab on each horizontal surface; four door type airbrakes, two on each side of rear fuselage, above and below horizontal tail surface.

STRUCTURE: All-metal; two main spars and auxiliary centre spar in each wing; extended chord (dogtooth) on outer panels visible when wings swept; fixed triangular inboard wing panels; welded steel pivot box carry-through structure; basically circular section semi-monocoque fuselage, flattened each side of cockpit; lateral air intake trunks blend into circular rear fuselage; splitter plate, with boundary layer bleeds, forms inboard face of each intake; two rectangular suction relief doors in each trunk, under inboard wing leading-edge; pressure relief vents under rear fuselage; fin and forward portion of horizontal surfaces conventional light alloy structures; rudder and rear of horizontal surfaces have honeycomb core.

LANDING GEAR: Hydraulically retractable tricycle type, with single wheel on each main unit and steerable twin-wheel nose unit. Main units retract inward into rear of air intake trunks. Main fairings to enclose these units are attached to legs. Small inboard fairing for each wheel bay hinged to fuselage belly. Nose unit, fitted with small mudguard over each wheel, retracts rearward. Mainwheels fitted with brakes and anti-skid units. Brake parachute, area 21 m² (226 sq ft), in cylindrical fairing at base of rudder with split conic doors.

POWER PLANT: One Tumansky R-35F-300 turbojet, rated at up to 127.5 kN (28,660 lb st) with max afterburning in aircraft for Soviet Air Force. Water injection system, capacity 28 litres (7.4 US gallons; 6.15 Imp gallons). Four fuel tanks in fuselage, aft of cockpit, and two in wings. Max internal fuel capacity 5,750 litres (1,519 US gallons; 1,265 Imp gallons). Variable geometry air intakes and variable nozzle. Provision for carrying jettisonable external fuel tank, capacity 800 litres (211 US gallons; 176 Imp gallons), on underfuselage centreline pylon, and two more under fixed wing panels. Two additional external tanks of same capacity may be carried on non-swivelling pylons under outer wings for ferry flights, with wings in fully forward position. Attachment for assisted take-off rocket on each side of fuselage aft of landing gear.

ACCOMMODATION: Pilot only, on zero/zero ejection seat in air-conditioned and pressurised cockpit, under small hydraulically actuated rearward hinged canopy. Bullet-proof windscreen.

AVIONICS: J band multi-mode radar (NATO 'High Lark 2': search range 46 nm; 85 km; 53 miles, tracking range 29 nm; 54 km; 34 miles) behind dielectric nosecone. No radar scope; instead, picture is projected onto head-up display. RSBN-6S ILS, with antennae (NATO 'Swift Rod') under radome and at tip of fin trailing-edge; suppressed UHF antennae form tip of fin and forward fixed portion of ventral fin; yaw vane above fuselage aft of radome; angle of attack sensor on port side. SRO-2 (NATO 'Odd Rods') IFF antenna immediately forward of windscreen. Undernose infra-red sensor pod, Sirena-3 radar warning system, and Doppler equipment standard on Soviet Air Force version. Sirena-3 antennae in horns at inboard leading-edge of each outer wing and below ILS antenna on fin.

EQUIPMENT: Small electrically heated rearview mirror on top of canopy. Retractable landing/taxiing light under each engine air intake.

ARMAMENT: One 23 mm GSh-23L twin-barrel gun in fuselage belly pack, with large flash eliminator around muzzles; 200 rds. One pylon under centre-fuselage, one under each engine air intake duct, and one under each fixed inboard wing panel, for air-to-air missiles, bombs, rocket packs or other external stores. Use of twin launchers under air intake ducts permits carriage of four R-60 (AA-8 'Aphid') missiles, plus two R-23 (AA-7 'Apex') on underwing pylons.

DIMENSIONS, EXTERNAL:
Wing span: fully spread	13.965 m (45 ft 10 in)
fully swept	7.779 m (25 ft 6¼ in)
Length overall: excl nose probe	15.88 m (52 ft 1¼ in)
incl nose probe	16.71 m (54 ft 10 in)
Height overall	4.82 m (15 ft 9¾ in)

AREAS:
Wings, gross: spread	37.3 m² (401.5 sq ft)
swept	34.2 m² (368.1 sq ft)

WEIGHTS AND LOADINGS:
Weight empty	10,200 kg (22,485 lb)
Max external weapon load	3,000 kg (6,615 lb)
T-O weight	14,300-17,800 kg (32,625-39,250 lb)

MiG-23MF ('Flogger-B') of Polish Air Force, armed with AA-7 ('Apex') missiles (outboard) and paired AA-8s ('Aphids') inboard *(Ivo Sturzenegger)*

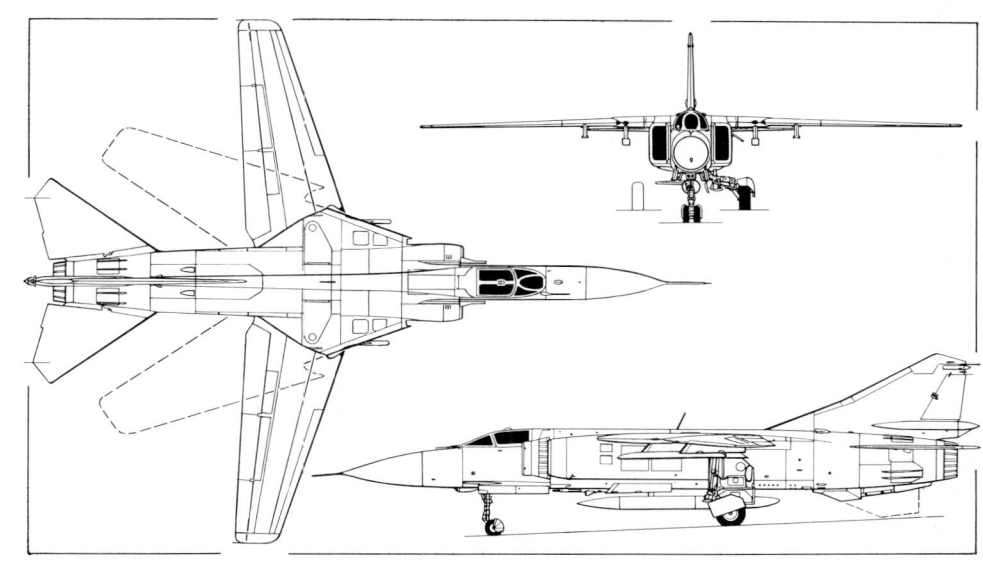

MiG-23MLD ('Flogger-K') single-seat variable-geometry interceptor *(Pilot Press)*

MiG-23UB two-seat trainer of Hungarian Air Force *(Ivo Sturzenegger)*

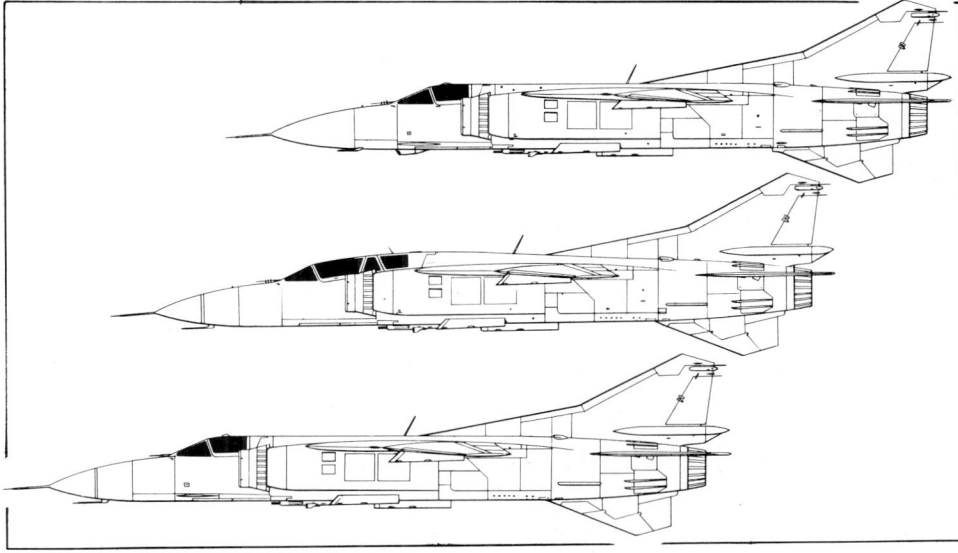

Top to bottom: Side views of the 'Flogger-B', 'Flogger-C' and 'Flogger-E' variants of the MiG-23 series *(Pilot Press)*

Nose of late production MiG-27M 'Flogger-J'
(Jane's Defence Weekly/Paul Beaver)

MiG-23BN ('Flogger-H') of Czechoslovak Air Force *(Ivo Sturzenegger)*

Max wing loading: spread	477.2 kg/m² (97.75 lb/sq ft)
swept	520.5 kg/m² (106.6 lb/sq ft)
Max power loading	139.6 kg/kN (1.37 lb/lb st)

PERFORMANCE:

Max level speed: at height, with weapons	Mach 2.35
at S/L	Mach 1.15
Max rate of climb at S/L	14,400 m (47,250 ft)/min
Service ceiling	18,000 m (59,055 ft)
T-O run	500 m (1,640 ft)
Landing run	750 m (2,460 ft)
Combat radius:	
with six air-to-air missiles	
	620 nm (1,150 km; 715 miles)
with 2,000 kg (4,410 lb) of bombs	
	378 nm (700 km; 435 miles)
Range:	
with max internal fuel	810 nm (1,500 km; 932 miles)
with external tanks	1,375 nm (2,550 km; 1,584 miles)
g limit	+8.5

MIKOYAN MiG-27
NATO reporting names: Flogger-D and J
Indian Air Force name: Bahadur (Valiant)

TYPE: Single-seat variable-geometry ground attack aircraft.
PROGRAMME: Based on MiG-23 airframe; entered service second half of 1970s; production in USSR completed mid-1980s, continues in India.
VARIANTS: **MiG-27** ('Flogger-D'): Initial version for Soviet tactical air forces; forward fuselage redesigned by comparison with MiG-23 interceptors; instead of ogival radome, nose sharply tapered in side elevation, with radar ranging antenna, and small sloping window over laser rangefinder; additional armour on flat cockpit sides; seat and canopy raised for improved view; wider low-pressure mainwheel tyres; ground attack armament.

MiG-27M ('Flogger-J'): First identified 1981; since delivered in successively upgraded variants; wider and deeper nose, with lip at top over less sloping window for laser rangefinder; blister fairing under nose of later aircraft, with rectangular window at front, providing added rearward laser designation capability for laser guided bomb delivery; IFF blade antenna under each side of nose aft of designator fairing; RSBN ILS antenna port side of nose; bullet shape antennae above wingroot glove pylons and external cockpit armour deleted; wingroot leading-edge extensions; export version built in India under licence by HAL, as Bahadur (see Indian section).

For somewhat similar 'Flogger-F and H' see MiG-23 entry.
CUSTOMERS: About 830 deployed with Soviet tactical air forces and Naval Aviation.

MiG-23 data (which see) apply also to MiG-27, except as noted above and below.
POWER PLANT: One Tumansky R-29B-300 turbojet, rated at 78.45 kN (17,635 lb st) dry and 112.8 kN (25,350 lb st) with max afterburning; fixed air intakes and two-position (on/off) afterburner nozzle consistent with primary requirement of transonic speed at low altitude.
AVIONICS: KN-23 inertial navigation system; Doppler navigation radar in nose; bullet shape antenna above each glove pylon of 'Flogger-D', associated with missile

guidance; radar warning receiver blister each side of front fuselage forward of nosewheel bay.
EQUIPMENT: Flare dispenser, in form of short fence, on fuselage each side of dorsal fin.
ARMAMENT: One GSh-6-30 six-barrel 30 mm underbelly gun; bomb/JATO rack each side of rear fuselage; five pylons for external stores, including tactical nuclear weapons and AS-7 (NATO 'Kerry'), AS-10 ('Karen'), AS-12 ('Kegler') and AS-14 ('Kedge') air-to-surface missiles; typical load six 500 kg bombs and two 800 litre

(211 US gallon; 176 Imp gallon) drop fuel tanks; or two 23 mm SPPU-22-01 gun pods, each with twin barrels that can be depressed to attack ground targets, and 260 rds.

DIMENSIONS, EXTERNAL: As MiG-23, plus:

Length overall	17.10 m (56 ft 1¼ in)
Tailplane span	5.75 m (18 ft 10¼ in)

AREAS:

Horizontal tail surfaces	6.88 m² (74.06 sq ft)

WEIGHTS AND LOADINGS:

Weight empty	10,700 kg (23,590 lb)
Max external load	4,500 kg (9,920 lb)
Max T-O weight	18,100-20,700 kg (39,900-45,635 lb)

Comparison of this photograph of a MiG-27M 'Flogger-J' with that of a 'Flogger-D' shows the restyled nose, absence of bullet shape antennae on the wing gloves, addition of wingroot leading-edge extensions, and depressed barrel of gun in port underwing pod

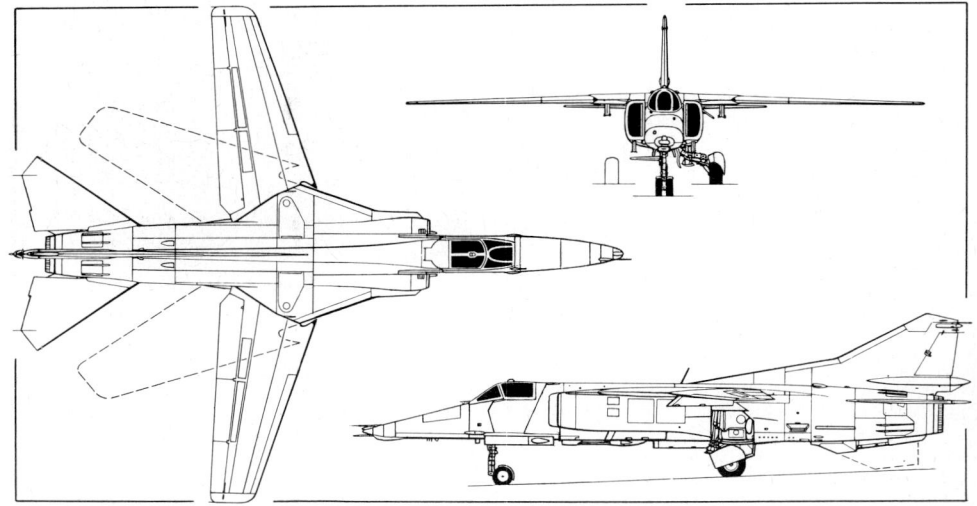

MiG-27M ('Flogger-J') single-seat ground attack aircraft *(Pilot Press)*

IRCM flare container on rear fuselage of MiG-27
(Jane's Defence Weekly/Paul Beaver)

MiG-27M ('Flogger-J') of Soviet Air Force *(Flieger Revue)*

MiG-25U ('Foxbat-C') after touchdown, with brake-chutes deployed *(Tass)*

Max wing loading: spread	555.0 kg/m² (113.7 lb/sq ft)
swept	605.3 kg/m² (124.0 lb/sq ft)
Max power loading	183.5 kg/kN (1.80 lb/lb st)

PERFORMANCE:

Max level speed: at height	Mach 1.77
at S/L	Mach 1.1
Max rate of climb at S/L	12,000 m (39,370 ft)/min
Service ceiling	14,000 m (45,900 ft)
T-O run	800 m (2,625 ft)
Landing run	950 m (3,120 ft)
Combat radius, with underbelly fuel tank, four 500 kg bombs and two 'Atoll' missiles, lo-lo-lo	
	210 nm (390 km; 240 miles)
Range with max internal fuel	
	944 nm (1,750 km; 1,087 miles)
Max ferry range with three external tanks	
	1,350 nm (2,500 km; 1,550 miles)
g limit	+7.0

MIKOYAN MiG-25
NATO reporting name: Foxbat

TYPE: Single-seat interceptor, reconnaissance aircraft and two-seat conversion trainer.

PROGRAMME: Designed as high-performance interceptor to counter B-70 Mach 3 strategic bomber under US development in early 1960s; early history in previous editions of *Jane's*; adapted for variety of roles; production completed mid-1980s.

VARIANTS: **MiG-25P** ('Foxbat-A'): Basic single-seat interceptor to engage high-flying targets; large radar (NATO 'Fox Fire') with estimated range of 45 nm (85 km; 52 miles) in nose; underwing missile armament; changed emphasis on intercepting low-altitude targets led to production cutback 1977-78; most Soviet air force and some Libyan 'Foxbat-As' replaced by 'Foxbat-Es'.

MiG-25R/RB ('Foxbat-B'): Basic reconnaissance version, able to accommodate any one of various photographic/radar modules in compartment aft of small dielectric nosecap for radar; standard 'Foxbat-B' module has five camera windows and flush dielectric panels for side looking airborne radar (SLAR); no armament; slightly reduced wing span; wing leading-edge sweep constant from root to tip; equipment believed to include Doppler navigation system.

MiG-25U ('Foxbat-C'): Two-seat conversion trainer; redesigned nose containing separate cockpit with individual canopy, forward of normal cockpit and at lower level; no search radar or reconnaissance sensors.

MiG-25R ('Foxbat-D'): Basically as 'Foxbat-B', but different reconnaissance module with larger SLAR dielectric panel, farther aft on nose, and no cameras.

MiG-25PDS ('Foxbat-E'): Single-seat interceptor; basically as 'Foxbat-A', but longer nose; changes to radar and equipment provide limited lookdown/shootdown capability comparable with MiG-23MF; undernose infra-red search/track pod; developed via experimental **Ye-266M**, which set three time-to-height records 1975 and holds aeroplane absolute height record of 37,650 m (123,524 ft).

MiG-25BM ('Foxbat-F'): Single-seat defence suppression aircraft, first illustrated USSR 1986; four AS-11 ('Kilter') anti-radiation missiles to attack surface-to-air missile sites over long stand-off ranges; generally as MiG-25 interceptors, but dielectric panel aft of radome each side of front fuselage; additional small blister at rear of radome each side; dielectric panel on front of each outboard weapon pylon; auxiliary tank for 5,500 kg (12,125 lb) fuel under rear fuselage; entered service 1988.

CUSTOMERS: Soviet APVO (400 'Foxbat-A/C/E'); Soviet tactical air forces (50 'Foxbat-A/E', 120 'Foxbat-B/D', some 'Foxbat-F'); Algeria ('Foxbat-A/B'); India ('Foxbat-B/C'); Iraq ('Foxbat-A'); Libya ('Foxbat-A/B/D/E'); Syria ('Foxbat-A/B').

Following details apply to MiG-25PDS ('Foxbat-E') except where indicated:

DESIGN FEATURES: Fastest combat aircraft yet identified in squadron service; agility less important for original role than high-speed high-altitude capability and weapon system for attack over considerable range; high swept wings with anti-flutter body (max diameter 30 cm; 11.8 in) at each tip; slim front fuselage, with ogival nosecone, blended into rectangular air intake trunks with wedge intakes; inner wall of intakes curved at top and not parallel with outer wall; hinged panel forms lower intake lip, enabling area to be varied electronically; fuselage undersurface dished between engines; all-swept tail surfaces; twin outward canted fins and twin outward canted ventral fins, all with large flush antennae; wing anhedral 4° from roots; leading-edge sweepback approx 40° inboard, 38° outboard of each outer missile pylon; sweepback at quarter-chord 32°; sweepback on tailplane 50°, fins 60°.

FLYING CONTROLS: Aileron at centre of each wing trailing-edge; plain flap on inboard 37 per cent; all-moving horizontal tail surfaces; inset rudders; no tabs; airbrake between ventral fins.

STRUCTURE: Airframe mainly of arc-welded nickel steel; titanium wing and tail unit leading-edges; rear tail

Camouflaged MiG-25R ('Foxbat-B') of the Soviet air forces *(P. R. Foster)*

MiG-25PDS ('Foxbat-E') interceptor of the Libyan Arab Air Force, armed with 'Acrid' and 'Aphid' air-to-air missiles *(US Navy)*

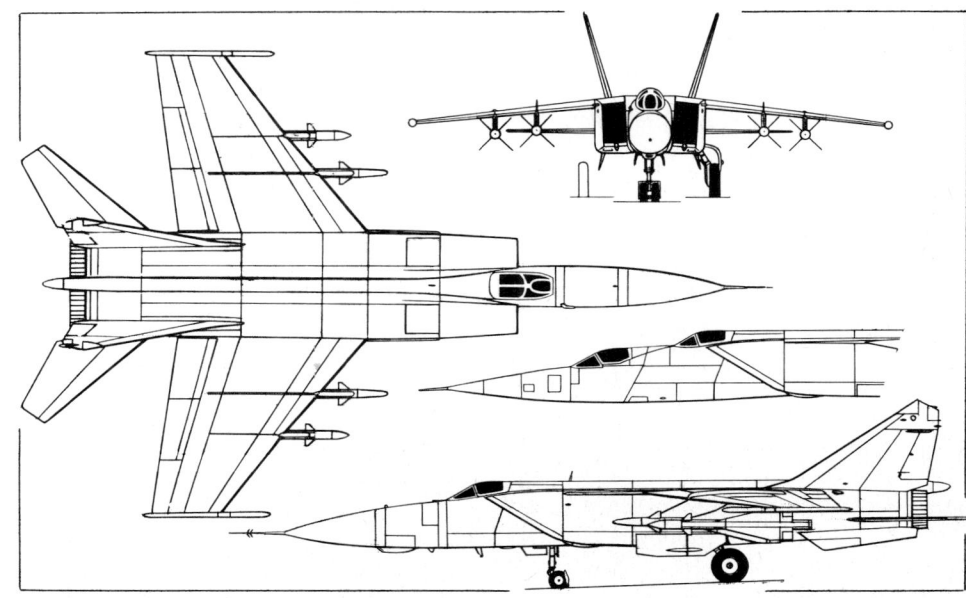

Mikoyan MiG-25PDS single-seat fighter (NATO 'Foxbat-E'), with scrap view of front fuselage of two-seat MiG-25U ('Foxbat-C') *(Pilot Press)*

Lengthened nose distinguishes the MiG-25PDS

'Foxbat-F' defence suppression version of the MiG-25 (*copied from Krasnaya Zvezda*)

sections light alloy; two shallow upper surface fences on each wing, in line with weapon pylons.

LANDING GEAR: Retractable tricycle type. Single wheel, with high pressure tyre of 1.20 m (47.25 in) diameter, on each forward retracting main unit. Wheel stows vertically between air intake duct and outer skin of each trunk. Twin-wheel forward retracting nose unit. Retractable sprung tailskid on each ventral fin. Twin brake-chutes in fairing above and between jet nozzles.

POWER PLANT: Two Tumansky R-15BD-300 single-shaft turbojets, each rated at 110 kN (24,700 lb st) with afterburning. Water-methanol injection standard. Fuel in two structural tanks in fuselage, between cockpit and engine bay, in saddle tanks around intake ducts, and in integral tank in each wing, filling almost the entire volume inboard of outer fence. Total fuel capacity approx 14,000 kg (30,865 lb) or 17,410 litres (4,600 US gallons; 3,830 Imp gallons).

ACCOMMODATION: Pilot only, on KM-1 zero-height/80 knot (150 km/h; 93 mph) ejection seat similar to that fitted to some versions of MiG-21. Canopy hinged to open sideways, to starboard.

AVIONICS: Main fire control radar in nose, forward of avionics compartment housing navigation radar. Infra-red search/track sensor pod under front fuselage. SRZO-2 (NATO 'Odd Rods') IFF and SOD-57M ATC/SIF, with antennae in starboard fin tip. Sirena-3 360° radar warning system with receivers in centre of each wingtip anti-flutter body and starboard fin tip. Unidentified ECCM, decoys and jammers. RSB-70/RPS HF, RSIU-5 VHF, R-831 UHF communications equipment, SP-50 (NATO 'Swift Rod') ILS, MRP-56P marker beacon receiver and ARK-15 radio compass.

EQUIPMENT: Retractable landing light under front of each intake trunk. Backup optical weapon sight.

ARMAMENT: Air-to-air missiles on four underwing attachments. These may comprise one infra-red and one radar homing example of the missile known to NATO as AA-6 'Acrid' under each wing. Alternatively, one AA-7 'Apex' and a pair of AA-11 'Archers' or AA-8 'Aphids' can be carried under each wing.

DIMENSIONS, EXTERNAL:
Wing span: 'Foxbat-A'	13.95 m (45 ft 9 in)
'Foxbat-B'	13.40 m (44 ft 0 in)
Wing aspect ratio: 'Foxbat-A'	3.4
Length overall	23.82 m (78 ft 1¾ in)
Length of fuselage	19.40 m (63 ft 7¾ in)
Height overall	6.10 m (20 ft 0¼ in)

AREAS:
Wings, gross: 'Foxbat-A'	56.83 m² (611.7 sq ft)

WEIGHTS AND LOADINGS (estimated):
Basic operating weight, empty:	
'Foxbat-A'	at least 20,000 kg (44,100 lb)
'Foxbat-B'	19,600 kg (43,200 lb)
Normal T-O weight	36,000 kg (79,365 lb)
Max T-O weight: 'Foxbat-A'	37,425 kg (82,500 lb)
'Foxbat-B'	41,000 kg (90,385 lb)
Max wing loading:	
'Foxbat-A'	658.5 kg/m² (134.9 lb/sq ft)

Max power loading:
'Foxbat-A'	170.1 kg/kN (1.67 lb/lb st)

PERFORMANCE:
Limiting Mach No.:	
all versions	Mach 2.82
Max level speed at low altitude: 'Foxbat-A', with four 'Acrid' missiles and 50% fuel	Mach 0.85
'Foxbat-B'	Mach 0.98
Landing speed:	
'Foxbat-A'	146 knots (270 km/h; 168 mph)
Max rate of climb at S/L:	
'Foxbat-A'	12,480 m (40,950 ft)/min
Time to 11,000 m (36,000 ft) with afterburning:	
'Foxbat-A'	2 min 30 s
Service ceiling: 'Foxbat-A'	24,400 m (80,000 ft)
'Foxbat-B, D'	23,000 m (75,450 ft)
T-O run: 'Foxbat-A'	1,380 m (4,525 ft)
'Foxbat-B'	1,250 m (4,100 ft)
Landing run: 'Foxbat-A'	2,180 m (7,150 ft)
'Foxbat-B'	800 m (2,625 ft)
Normal operational radius:	
'Foxbat-A'	610 nm (1,130 km; 700 miles)
Max combat radius, econ power:	
'Foxbat-A'	780 nm (1,450 km; 900 miles)
Range with max fuel:	
'Foxbat-B'	863 nm (1,600 km; 994 miles)
g limit	+5

MIKOYAN MiG-29
NATO reporting name: Fulcrum
Indian Air Force name: Baaz (Eagle)

TYPE: All-weather single-seat counter-air fighter, with attack capability, and two-seat combat trainer.

PROGRAMME: Technical assignment (operational requirement) issued 1972, to replace MiG-21, MiG-23, Su-15 and Su-17; initial order placed simultaneously; detail design began 1974; first of 11 prototypes flew 6 October 1977; photographed by US satellite, Ramenskoye flight

test centre, November 1977 and given interim Western designation 'Ram-L'; second prototype flew June 1978; second and fourth prototypes lost through engine failures; after major design changes (see previous editions of *Jane's*) production deliveries to Soviet Frontal Aviation began 1983; operational early 1985; first detailed Western study possible after visit of demonstration team to Finland July 1986; production in Moscow and Nizhny Novograd continues; former production plant at Znamja Truda converted to civil manufacture.

VARIANTS: **MiG-29** ('Fulcrum-A'): Land-based single-seat dual-role fighter, identified in three forms: (1) Initial production with two ventral tail fins like Su-27. (2) Ventral fins deleted; dorsal fins extended forward in form of overwing 'fences' containing IRCM flare dispensers. (3) As second variant, with extended-chord rudders. Described in detail.

MiG-29UB ('Fulcrum-B'): Combat trainer; second seat forward of normal cockpit, under continuous canopy, with periscope for rear occupant; nose radar replaced by radar rangefinder; underwing stores pylons retained.

MiG-29 ('Fulcrum-C'): As 'Fulcrum-A' variant 3, but deeply curved top to fuselage aft of cockpit, containing avionics, possibly transferred from lower fuselage to provide space for additional fuel; produced concurrently and operational in same units as 'Fulcrum-A'.

MiG-29K (K for *korabelnyy*; ship-based) ('Fulcrum-D'): Maritime version, used for ski-jump take-off and

MiG-29UB ('Fulcrum-B') two-seat combat trainer of Polish Air Force (*Ivo Sturzenegger*)

Rear view of MiG-25BM shows 5,500 kg underfuselage auxiliary fuel tank

AS-11 ('Kilter') missiles under wing of MiG-25BM ('Foxbat-F')

MiG-29K 'Fulcrum-D' on the deck of the carrier/cruiser *Admiral of the Fleet Kuznetsov*

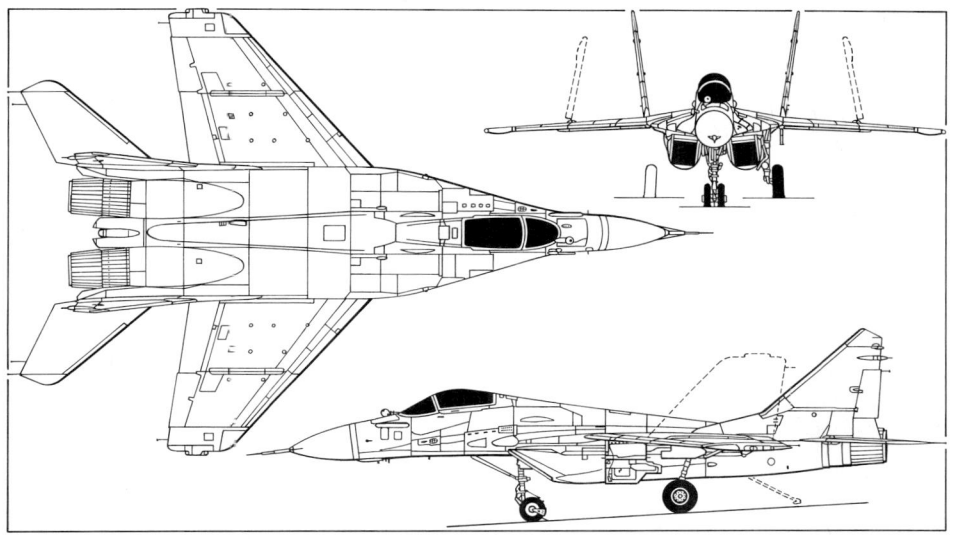

Naval MiG-29K with folding wings, arrester hook and bulged wingtips *(Jane's/Mike Keep)*

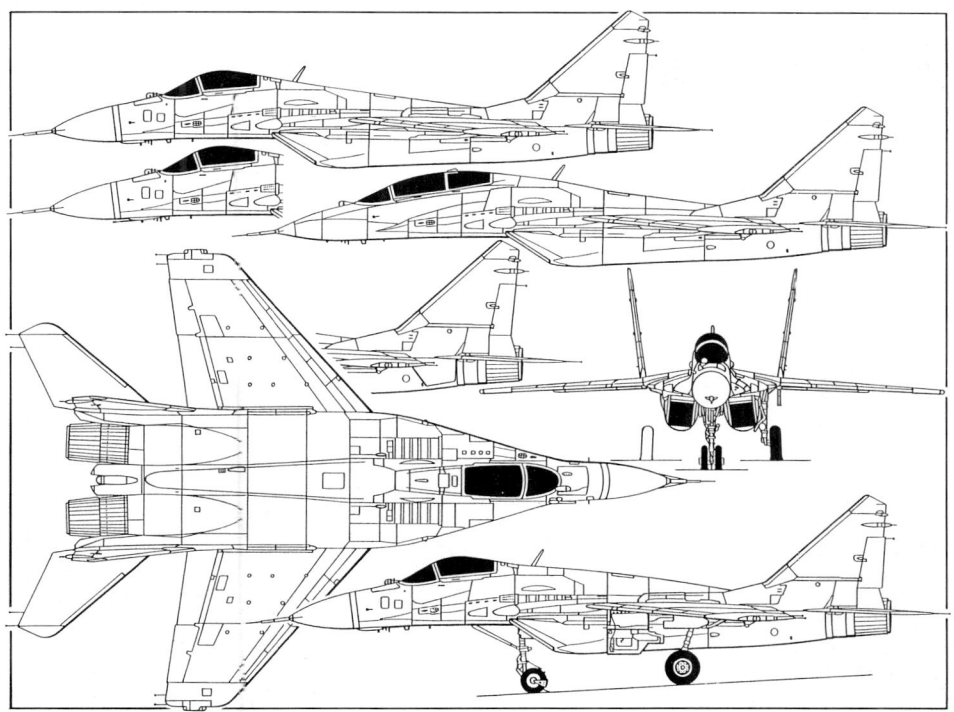

Three-view drawing of MiG-29 'Fulcrum-C' fighter, with scrap drawings of tail and nose of early production 'Fulcrum-A'. Additional side views at the top show main production 'Fulcrum-A' and two-seat 'Fulcrum-B' *(Jane's/Mike Keep)*

deck landing trials on board Soviet Navy carrier *Admiral of the Fleet Kuznetsov* (formerly *Tbilisi*), beginning 1 November 1989; two, converted from early 'Fulcrum-A'; upward folding outer wing panels with bulged tips, probably for ESM; eight underwing hardpoints; no intake doors required on deck, permitting deletion of overwing louvres and internal ducting in lightweight aluminium-lithium alloy centre-section, and providing increased fuel tankage (2,550 litres; 674 US gallons; 561 Imp gallons in centre-section); flight refuelling capability; strengthened landing gear; arrester hook; different IRST; expected to equip air wings of all large Soviet aircraft carriers.

MiG-29M: Advanced version with quadruplex digital fly-by-wire controls and 'glass' cockpit with CRTs; first flown late 1989; different horizontal tail surfaces; slightly changed wing position; modifications to extend aft centre of gravity limit for relaxed stability; claimed more comfortable to fly, with increased permissible angle of attack, better manoeuvrability, improved cruise efficiency; eight underwing hardpoints. Further details in Addenda.

CUSTOMERS: Soviet military districts and groups of forces (more than 500); Cuba; Czechoslovakia; Germany (18 single-seat, five two-seat delivered to former East Germany, now 5th Luftwaffe division); India (70, including two-seaters); Iran; Iraq (35 single-seat, six two-seat); North Korea; Poland; Romania; Syria; Yugoslavia.

DESIGN FEATURES: All-swept low-wing configuration, with wide ogival wing leading-edge root extensions, lift-generating fuselage, twin tail fins and widely spaced engines with wedge intakes; doors in intakes prevent ingestion of foreign objects during take-off and landing; fire control and mission computers link radar with laser rangefinder and infra-red search/track sensor, in conjunction with helmet mounted target designator; targets can be approached and engaged without emission of detectable radar or radio signals; sustained turn rate much improved over earlier Soviet fighters; thrust-to-weight ratio better than one; allowable angles of attack at least 70 per cent higher than previous fighters; difficult to get into stable flat spin, reluctant to enter normal spin, recovers as soon as controls released; wing leading-edge sweepback approx 42° on outer panels; anhedral approx 2°; tail fins canted outward approx 7°; leading-edge sweep approx 40° on fins, 50° on horizontal surfaces.

FLYING CONTROLS: Mechanical controls, hydraulically powered, with autopilot and rate dampers; computer controlled leading-edge manoeuvring flaps over full wing span except tips, and plain trailing-edge flaps; inset ailerons, each with manually adjustable trim tab; inset rudders and all-moving horizontal tail surfaces, without tabs; interconnect allows rudders to augment roll rate; mechanical yaw stability augmentation system; hydraulically actuated forward hinged airbrakes above and below rear fuselage between jetpipes.

STRUCTURE: Approx seven per cent of airframe, by weight, of composites; remainder metal, including aluminium-lithium alloys; trailing-edge wing flaps, ailerons and vertical tail surfaces of carbonfibre honey-comb; approx 65 per cent of horizontal tail surfaces aluminium alloy, remainder carbonfibre; semi-monocoque all-metal fuselage, sharply tapered and downswept aft of flat-sided cockpit area, with ogival dielectric nosecone; small vortex generator each side of nose helps to overcome early tendency to aileron reversal at angles of attack above 25°; tail surfaces carried on slim booms alongside engine nacelles.

LANDING GEAR: Retractable tricycle type, with single wheel on each main unit and twin nosewheels. Mainwheels retract forward into wingroots, turning through 90° to lie flat above leg. Nosewheels, on trailing-link oleo, retract rearward between engine air intakes. Hydraulic retraction and extension, with mechanical emergency release. Nosewheels steerable ±8° for taxying, T-O and landings, ±30° for slow speed manoeuvring in confined areas (selector in cockpit). Mainwheel tyres size 770 × 200 mm; nosewheel tyres size 530 × 100 mm. Pneumatic steel brakes. Mudguard to rear of nosewheels. Container for cruciform brake-chute in centre of boat-tail between engine nozzles.

POWER PLANT: Two Sarkisov (Leningrad/Klimov) RD-33 turbofans, each rated at 50 kN (11,240 lb st) dry and 81.4 kN (18,300 lb st) with afterburning. Engine ducts are canted at approx 9° and have wedge intakes, sweptback at approx 35°, under wingroot leading-edge extensions. Multi-segment ramp system, including top-hinged forward door inside each intake that closes the duct while the aircraft is taking off or landing, to prevent ingestion of foreign objects, ice or snow. Air is then fed to each engine through louvres in top of wingroot leading-edge extension and gap above top lip of intake. Integral fuel tanks in inboard portion of each wing and in fuselage between wings; total capacity 4,365 litres (1,153 US gallons; 960 Imp gallons). Attachment for a non-conformal external fuel tank under fuselage, between ducts, and another under each wing. Single-point pressure refuelling through receptacle in port wheel well. Overwing receptacles for manual fuelling. Airscoop for APU above rear fuselage on port side.

ACCOMMODATION: Pilot only, on 10° inclined K-36D zero/zero ejection seat, under rearward hinged transparent blister canopy in high-set cockpit. Sharply inclined one-piece curved windscreen. Three internal mirrors provide rearward view.

AVIONICS: NO-193 coherent pulse Doppler lookdown/ shootdown engagement radar (NATO 'Slot Back'; detection range 54 nm; 100 km; 62 miles); infra-red search/track sensor forward of windscreen (protected by removable fairing on non-operational flights) collimated with laser rangefinder; inertial navigation system; SRZO-2 (NATO 'Odd Rods') IFF; Sirena-3 360° radar warning system, with sensors on wingroot extensions, wingtips and port fin. Two SO-69 ECM antennae under conformal dielectric fairings in leading-edge of each wingroot extension; head-up display; and helmet-mounted target designation system for off-axis aiming of air-to-air missiles.

ARMAMENT: Six medium-range radar/infra-red homing R-27 (AA-10; NATO 'Alamo-A/B') and/or close-range R-73 (AA-11; 'Archer') air-to-air missiles, on three pylons under each wing. Provision for carrying AA-9 ('Amos') and R-60 (AA-8; 'Aphid') missiles. Able to carry bombs, submunitions dispensers and 57 mm, 80 mm and 240 mm rockets in attack role. One 30 mm GSh-30 gun in port wingroot leading-edge extension, with 150 rds.

DIMENSIONS, EXTERNAL:
Wing span	11.36 m (37 ft 3¼ in)
Wing chord: on centreline	5.60 m (18 ft 4½ in)
at tip	1.27 m (4 ft 2 in)
Length overall, incl nose probe	17.32 m (56 ft 10 in)
Height overall	4.73 m (15 ft 6¼ in)
Tailplane span	7.78 m (25 ft 6¼ in)
Wheel track	3.10 m (10 ft 2 in)
Wheelbase	3.67 m (12 ft 0½ in)

AREAS:
Wings, gross	35.20 m² (378.9 sq ft)

WEIGHTS AND LOADINGS:
Operating weight empty	10,900 kg (24,030 lb)
Normal T-O weight (interceptor)	15,600 kg (34,390 lb)
Max T-O weight	18,480 kg (40,740 lb)
Max wing loading	525.0 kg/m² (107.5 lb/sq ft)
Max power loading	113.5 kg/kN (1.11 lb/lb st)

PERFORMANCE:
Max level speed: at height	
Mach 2.35 (1,330 knots; 2,465 km/h; 1,530 mph)	
at S/L Mach 1.06 (700 knots; 1,300 km/h; 805 mph)	
Max rate of climb at S/L	19,800 m (65,000 ft)/min
Service ceiling	18,500 m (60,700 ft)
T-O run	240 m (790 ft)
Landing run	600 m (1,970 ft)
Range:	
with max internal fuel	810 nm (1,500 km; 932 miles)
with external tanks	1,345 nm (2,495 km; 1,550 miles)
g limits: above Mach 0.85	+7
below Mach 0.85	+9.5

MIKOYAN MiG-31
NATO reporting name: Foxhound
TYPE: Two-seat twin-engined strategic interceptor.

PROGRAMME: First flown, as Ye-155MP, 16 September 1975; development of improved interceptor based on MiG-25 first reported reliably by Lt Viktor Belyenko, Soviet defector to Japan in 'Foxbat-A', September 1976; NATO reporting name 'Foxhound' made public mid-1982; delivery to APVO began by early 1983; production continues at Nizhny Novograd.

VARIANTS: **MiG-31** ('Foxhound-A'): Two-seat interceptor.

MiG-31M ('Foxhound-B'): Improved interceptor; small side windows only for rear cockpit; wider dorsal spine; more rounded wingtips, with flush dielectric areas at front and rear; larger, curved fin root extensions; modified and extended wingroot leading-edge extensions; four new-type underwing pylons. See Addenda for three-view.

CUSTOMERS: Soviet air forces (more than 160).

Following details refer to MiG-31 ('Foxhound-A'):

DESIGN FEATURES: Basic MiG-25 configuration retained, with some strengthening to permit supersonic flight at low altitude; more powerful engines than MiG-25; upgraded avionics; radar said to embody technology found in US Hughes AN/APG-65 digital radar, providing true lookdown/shootdown and multiple target engagement capability for first time in Soviet interceptor; fuselage weapon mountings added; crew increased to two; wing anhedral 4° from roots; sweepback approx 40° on leading-edge, 32° at quarter-chord, with small sharply swept wingroot extensions; all-swept tail surfaces, with twin outward canted fins and dihedral horizontal surfaces.

FLYING CONTROLS: Large-span ailerons and flaps, wing leading-edge slats, all-moving horizontal tail surfaces, inset rudders.

STRUCTURE: Airframe 50 per cent arc-welded nickel steel, 16 per cent titanium, 33 per cent light alloy; three-spar wings; no wingtip fairings or mountings; small forward-hinged airbrake under front of each intake trunk; undersurface of centre-fuselage not dished between engine ducts like MiG-25; much enlarged air intakes; jet nozzles extended rearward; shallow fairing extends forward from base of each fin leading-edge; fence above each wing in line with stores pylon.

MiG-29 ('Fulcrum-A') of Soviet air forces, with full six-missile armament and underbelly fuel tank *(Swedish Air Force, via FLYGvapenNYTT)*

MiG-29 ('Fulcrum-A') of Polish Air Force, with rockets for ground attack role *(Ivo Sturzenegger)*

MiG-31 ('Foxhound-A') all-weather interceptor, with periscope raised above rear cockpit

LANDING GEAR: Retractable tricycle type. Staggered twin wheels on each main unit, retracting forward into air intake trunk. Rearward retracting twin nosewheel unit with mudguard.

POWER PLANT: Two Soloviev D-30F turbofans, each rated at 151.9 kN (34,170 lb st) with afterburning. Provision for two large external fuel tanks on outer underwing pylons. Semi-retractable flight refuelling probe on port side of front fuselage.

ACCOMMODATION: Pilot and weapon systems operator in tandem under individual rearward-hinged canopies. Rear canopy has only limited side glazing and blends into shallow dorsal spine fairing which extends to forward edge of jet nozzles.

AVIONICS: Main fire control radar (NATO 'Flash Dance') of pulse Doppler lookdown/shootdown type in nose, with reported search range of 165 nm (305 km; 190 miles) and tracking range of 145 nm (270 km; 167 miles). Radar reportedly capable of tracking ten targets and attacking four simultaneously. Retractable laser rangefinder under nose. Semi-retractable infra-red search/track sensor in top of fuselage forward of windscreen. Radar warning receivers.

EQUIPMENT: Active infra-red and electronic countermeasures.

ARMAMENT: Aircraft seen to date each had four AA-9 (NATO 'Amos') semi-active radar homing long-range air-to-air missiles in pairs under fuselage, and twin mounts for AA-8 ('Aphid') air-to-air missiles on one large pylon under each wing. These pylons plus outer underwing pylons (not yet observed) can probably increase the number of AA-9s carried by MiG-31 to reported total of eight. Front pair of AA-9s is semi-recessed in fuselage, rear pair on short pylons. GSh-6-23 six-barrel Gatling-type 23 mm gun is mounted inside a fairing on the starboard side of the lower fuselage, adjacent to the main landing gear, with 260 rds.

DIMENSIONS, EXTERNAL:

Wing span	13.464 m (44 ft 2 in)
Length overall	22.688 m (74 ft 5¼ in)
Height overall	6.15 m (20 ft 2¼ in)

AREAS:

Wings, gross	61.6 m² (663.0 sq ft)

WEIGHTS AND LOADINGS:

Weight empty	21,825 kg (48,115 lb)
Internal fuel	16,350 kg (36,045 lb)
Max T-O weight	46,200 kg (101,850 lb)
Max power loading	152.0 kg/kN (1.49 lb/lb st)

PERFORMANCE:

Max level speed: at 17,500 m (57,400 ft)	
	(1,620 knots (3,000 km/h; 1,865 mph)
at S/L	810 knots (1,500 km/h; 932 mph)
Max cruising speed	Mach 2.35
Service ceiling	20,600 m (67,600 ft)
T-O run at max T-O weight	1,200 m (3,940 ft)
Landing run	800 m (2,625 ft)
Max endurance: unrefuelled	3 h 36 min
refuelled inflight	6-7 h

MIKOYAN MiG 18-50

TYPE: Projected twin-turbofan long-range airliner/business transport.

PROGRAMME: Announced early 1990 as one of several designs by Mikoyan OKB under *konversiya* directives; at project design stage early 1991.

DESIGN FEATURES: Conventional all-swept low-wing transport with rear-mounted engines; digital navigation system for automatic and manual all-weather, all-season, round-the-clock flight and landing approach to ICAO Cat II; operation to be practicable from 1,800 m (5,906 ft) Soviet Class B airfields.

LANDING GEAR: Retractable tricycle type, with twin wheels on each unit.

POWER PLANT: Two Zaporozhye/Lotarev D-36 turbofans, each 63.74 kN (14,330 lb st).

ACCOMMODATION: Two variants projected: (1) Long-range regional airliner; 50 passengers four-abreast in pairs at 75 cm (29.5 in) seat pitch, with 40 cm (15.75 in) centre aisle. (2) Long-range 18-passenger business jet. Both versions with forward and rear baggage compartments and aft toilet. Increase to 75/100 passengers being studied for airliner, in lengthened fuselage.

DIMENSIONS, EXTERNAL:

Wing span	23.30 m (76 ft 5½ in)
Length overall	24.90 m (81 ft 8½ in)
Height overall	7.55 m (24 ft 9¼ in)
Fuselage diameter	2.80 m (9 ft 2¼ in)

DIMENSIONS, INTERNAL:

Passenger cabin: Length	10.66 m (34 ft 11½ in)
Width	2.60 m (8 ft 6¼ in)
Height	1.90 m (6 ft 3 in)

AREAS:

Wings, gross	64.00 m² (689.0 sq ft)

WEIGHTS AND LOADINGS (A: 50 seats, B: 18 seats):

Weight empty, equipped: A, B	20,200 kg (44,530 lb)

The more deeply curved back of 'Fulcrum-C' is seen clearly in this photograph
(Jon Lake/World Air Power Journal)

This MiG-31 has underbelly AA-9 ('Amos') and underwing AA-8 ('Aphid') missiles
(US Department of Defense)

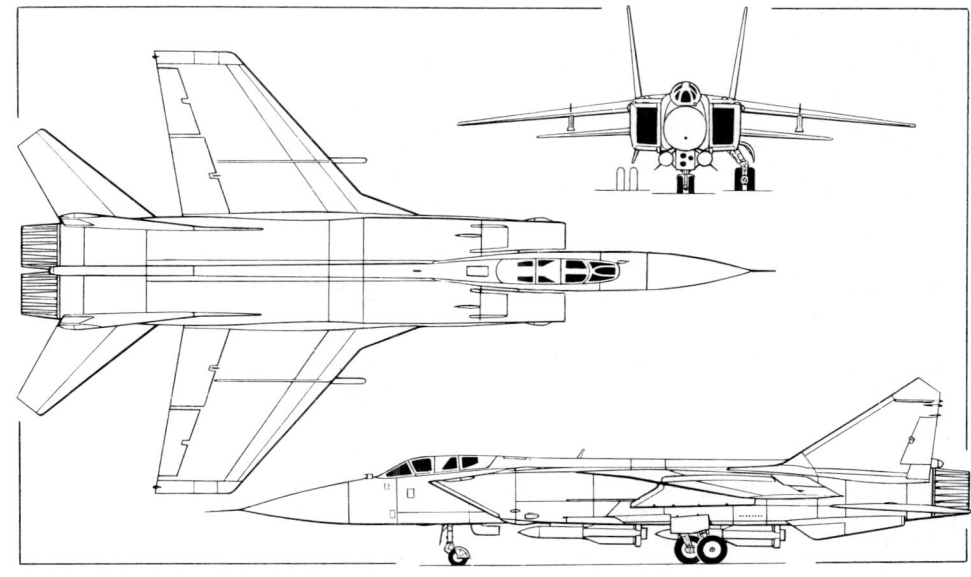

MiG-31 (NATO 'Foxhound-A') all-weather interceptor *(Pilot Press)*

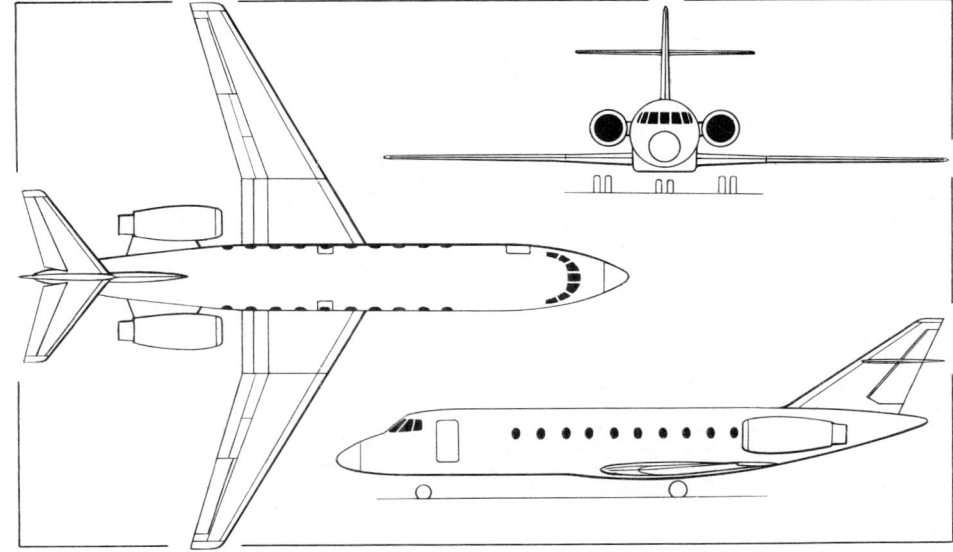

Mikoyan MiG 18-50 long-range airliner/business transport *(Pilot Press)*

Max payload: A	4,500 kg (9,920 lb)
B	1,620 kg (3,570 lb)
Max fuel: A, B	14,000 kg (30,865 lb)
Max T-O weight: A	39,000 kg (85,980 lb)
B	36,000 kg (79,365 lb)
Max wing loading: A	609.4 kg/m² (124.8 lb/sq ft)
Max power loading: A	305.9 kg/kN (3.0 lb/lb st)

PERFORMANCE (A: 50 seats, B: 18 seats; estimated):

Nominal cruising speed:	
A, B	458 knots (850 km/h; 528 mph)
Service ceiling: A	11,000 m (36,000 ft)
B	12,500 m (41,000 ft)
Balanced field length: A, B	1,800 m (5,906 ft)
Range, with 45 min reserves:	
A	4,530 nm (8,400 km; 5,220 miles)
B	5,395 nm (10,000 km; 6,215 miles)

MIKOYAN MiG SVB

TYPE: Pressurised twin-turboprop passenger/freight transport.

PROGRAMME: Announced early 1990 as Mikoyan konversiya project; at study stage early 1991.

DESIGN FEATURES: Requested by Soviet Asian Republics for operation into short fields at heights up to 4,000 m (13,125 ft) in hot mountainous regions; conventional high-wing configuration, with sweptback fin and rudder; large fairings on sides of fuselage for retracted landing gear. Digital avionics standard.

LANDING GEAR: Retractable tricycle type; main bogies each with two tandem pairs of wheels; twin-wheel nose unit.

POWER PLANT: Two 2,088 kW (2,800 shp) Leningrad/Klimov TV7-117 turboprops, each driving six-blade low noise level propeller.

ACCOMMODATION: Flight crew of two; two cargo handlers or cabin attendants, as appropriate; rear loading ramp, integral ceiling hoist and cargo floor for freight

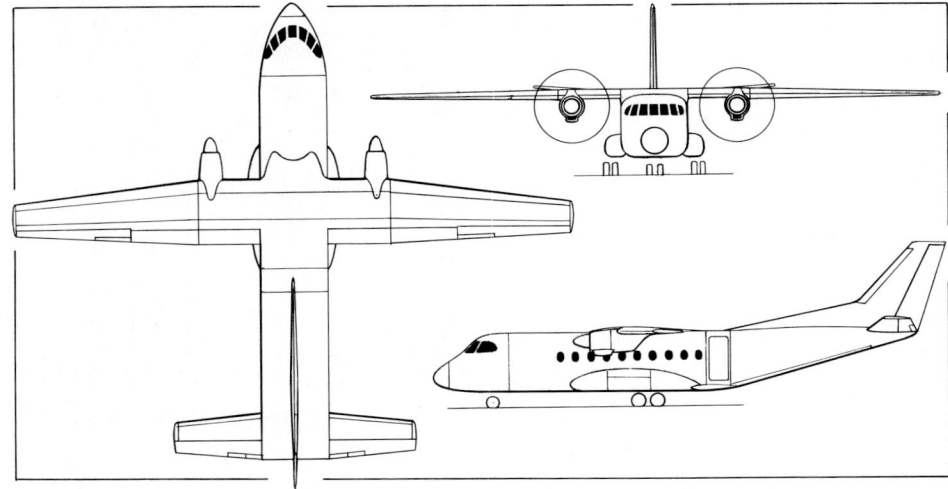

Mikoyan MiG SVB twin-turboprop pressurised passenger/freight transport (*Pilot Press*)

operations; optional seats for 50 passengers, five-abreast. All accommodation fully pressurised.

DIMENSIONS, EXTERNAL:

Wing span	25.90 m (84 ft 11¾ in)
Length overall	22.20 m (72 ft 10 in)
Height overall	8.07 m (26 ft 5¾ in)

WEIGHTS AND LOADINGS:

Max freight payload	5,000 kg (11,023 lb)
Max fuel	3,100 kg (6,835 lb)
Max T-O weight	19,400 kg (42,770 lb)

PERFORMANCE (estimated):

Nominal cruising speed at 7,000 m (22,965 ft)	
	297 knots (550 km/h; 342 mph)
T-O run at 3,000 m (9,850 ft) at ISA +15°C	
	840 m (2,756 ft)
Landing run at 3,000 m (9,850 ft) at ISA +15°C, with propeller reversal	700 m (2,300 ft)
Range with max fuel, 45 min reserves	
	1,187 nm (2,200 km; 1,367 miles)

MIL

MIL DESIGN BUREAU

2 Sokolnichyesky Val, Moscow 107113

Telephone: 7 (95) 264 3791

GENERAL DESIGNER: Marat N. Tishchenko

CHIEF DESIGNER: Alexei Ivanov

DEPUTY CHIEF DESIGNER: Mark V. Vineberg

This OKB was founded in 1947 by Mikhail Leontyevich Mil, who was involved with Soviet gyroplane and helicopter development from 1929 until his death on 31 January 1970, aged 60. His original Mi-1, first flown in September 1948 and introduced into service 1951, was the first Soviet series production helicopter.

MIL Mi-2 (V-2)

NATO reporting name: Hoplite

Built exclusively in Poland and described under Polish aircraft industry entry for WSK-PZL Swidnik. About 675 serve with Soviet military ground forces.

MIL Mi-6 and Mi-22

NATO reporting name: Hook

TYPE: Twin-turbine heavy transport helicopter.

PROGRAMME: Joint military/civil requirement issued 1954; prototype flew 5 June 1957 as, by far, world's largest helicopter of that time; five built for development testing; initial pre-series of 30; more than 800 built for civil/military use, ending 1981; developments included Mi-10 and Mi-10K flying cranes (which see); Mi-6 dynamic components used in duplicated form on V-12

(Mi-12) of 1967, which remains the largest helicopter yet flown.

VARIANTS: **Mi-6** ('Hook-A'): Basic transport, as described in detail.

Mi-6 ('Hook-B'): Command support version with dorsal 'clothesline' antenna.

Mi-22 ('Hook-C'): Developed command support version with single large dorsal blade antenna on forward part of tailboom.

CUSTOMERS: Soviet ground forces, primarily to haul guns, armour, vehicles, supplies, freight and troops in combat areas, but also in command support roles; air forces of Algeria, Iraq, Peru and Vietnam; Peruvian Army air force.

Abbreviated details follow. Full description last appeared in 1983-84 *Jane's*.

DESIGN FEATURES: Two small shoulder wings offload rotor by providing some 20 per cent of total lift in cruising flight. Removed when aircraft is operated as flying crane.

POWER PLANT: Two 4,101 kW (5,500 shp) Soloviev D-25V (TV-2BM) turboshafts, mounted side by side above cabin, forward of main rotor shaft. Eleven internal fuel tanks, with total capacity of 6,315 kg (13,922 lb), and two external tanks, on each side of cabin, with total capacity of 3,490 kg (7,695 lb). Provision for two additional ferry tanks inside cabin, with total capacity of 3,490 kg (7,695 lb).

ACCOMMODATION: Crew of five, consisting of two pilots, navigator, flight engineer and radio operator. Four jettisonable doors and overhead hatch on flight deck. Electro-thermal anti-icing system for glazing of flight deck and navigator's compartment. Equipped normally for cargo operation, with easily removable tip-up seats along side walls. When these seats are supplemented by

additional seats installed in centre of cabin, 65-90 passengers can be carried, with cargo or baggage in the aisles. Normal military seating is for 70 combat equipped troops. As an air ambulance, 41 stretcher cases and two medical attendants on tip-up seats can be carried. One of attendant's stations is provided with intercom to flight deck, and provision is made for portable oxygen installations for the patients. Cabin floor is stressed for loadings of 2,000 kg/m² (410 lb/sq ft), with provision for cargo tiedown rings. Rear clamshell doors and ramps are operated hydraulically. Standard equipment includes an electric winch of 800 kg (1,765 lb) capacity and pulley block system. Central hatch in cabin floor for cargo sling system for bulky loads. Three jettisonable doors, fore and aft of main landing gear on port side and aft of landing gear on starboard side.

AVIONICS: VHF and HF communications radio, intercom, radio altimeter, radio compass, three-channel autopilot, marker beacon receiver, directional gyro and full all-weather instrumentation.

ARMAMENT: Some military Mi-6s have a 12.7 mm machine gun in the nose.

DIMENSIONS, EXTERNAL:

Main rotor diameter	35.00 m (114 ft 10 in)
Tail rotor diameter	6.30 m (20 ft 8 in)
Length: overall, rotors turning	41.74 m (136 ft 11½ in)
fuselage, excl nose gun and tail rotor	33.18 m (108 ft 10½ in)
Height overall	9.86 m (32 ft 4 in)
Wing span	15.30 m (50 ft 2½ in)
Wheel track	7.50 m (24 ft 7¼ in)
Wheelbase	9.09 m (29 ft 9¾ in)
Rear loading doors: Height	2.70 m (8 ft 10¼ in)
Width	2.65 m (8 ft 8¼ in)

Mil Mi-6 heavy general purpose helicopter (two Soloviev D-25V turboshafts) of the Soviet air forces (*Lutz Freundt*)

Passenger doors:		AREAS:	
Height: front door	1.70 m (5 ft 7 in)	Main rotor disc	962.1 m² (10,356 sq ft)
rear doors	1.61 m (5 ft 3½ in)	WEIGHTS AND LOADINGS:	
Width	0.80 m (2 ft 7½ in)	Weight empty	27,240 kg (60,055 lb)
Sill height: front door	1.40 m (4 ft 7¼ in)	Max internal payload	12,000 kg (26,450 lb)
rear doors	1.30 m (4 ft 3¼ in)	Max slung cargo	8,000 kg (17,637 lb)
Central hatch in floor		Fuel load: internal	6,315 kg (13,922 lb)
	1.44 m (4 ft 9 in) × 1.93 m (6 ft 4 in)	with external tanks	9,805 kg (21,617 lb)
DIMENSIONS, INTERNAL:		Max T-O weight with slung cargo at altitudes under	
Cabin: Length	12.00 m (39 ft 4½ in)	1,000 m (3,280 ft)	38,400 kg (84,657 lb)
Max width	2.65 m (8 ft 8¼ in)	Normal T-O weight	40,500 kg (89,285 lb)
Max height: at front	2.01 m (6 ft 7 in)	Max T-O weight for VTO	42,500 kg (93,700 lb)
at rear	2.50 m (8 ft 2½ in)	Max disc loading	44.17 kg/m² (9.05 lb/sq ft)
Cabin volume	80 m³ (2,825 cu ft)		

PERFORMANCE (at max T-O weight for VTO):
Max level speed	162 knots (300 km/h; 186 mph)
Max cruising speed	135 knots (250 km/h; 155 mph)
Service ceiling	4,500 m (14,750 ft)

Range with 8,000 kg (17,637 lb) payload
334 nm (620 km; 385 miles)
Range with external tanks and 4,500 kg (9,920 lb) payload
540 nm (1,000 km; 621 miles)
Max ferry range (tanks in cabin)
781 nm (1,450 km; 900 miles)

MIL Mi-8 (V-8)
NATO reporting name: Hip
TYPE: Twin-turbine multi-purpose helicopter.
PROGRAMME: Development began May 1960, to replace piston-engined Mi-4; first prototype, with single AI-24V turboshaft and four-blade main rotor, flew June 1961, given NATO reporting name 'Hip-A'; second prototype ('Hip-B'), with two production standard TV2-117 engines and five-blade main rotor, flew August 1962; more than 10,000 Mi-8s and uprated Mi-17s (which see) delivered from Kazan and Ulan Ude plants in USSR for civil and military use; components produced also at Harbin, China; Mi-8 production completed; many converted to Mi-17 standard.
VARIANTS: **Mi-8** ('Hip-C'): Civil passenger helicopter; standard seating for 28-32 persons in main cabin with large square windows.

Mi-8T ('Hip-C'): Civil utility version; normal payload internal or external freight, but 24 tip-up passenger seats along cabin sidewalls optional; square cabin windows.

Mi-8 Salon ('Hip-C'): De luxe version of standard Mi-8; normally 11 passengers, on eight-place inward-facing couch on port side, two chairs and swivelling seat on starboard side, with table; square windows; air-to-ground radio telephone and removable ventilation fans; compartment for attendant, with buffet and crew wardrobe, forward of cabin; toilet (port) and passenger wardrobe (starboard) to each side of cabin rear entrance; alternative nine-passenger configuration; max T-O weight 10,400 kg (22,928 lb); range 205 nm (380 km; 236 miles) with 30 mins fuel reserve.

Military versions, with smaller circular cabin windows, are:

'**Hip-C**': Standard assault transport of Soviet army support forces; twin-rack for stores each side, to carry 128 × 57 mm rockets in four packs, or other weapons; more than 1,500 in Soviet army service; some uprated to Mi-17 standard as **Mi-8T** and **Mi-8TB**, with port-side tail rotor.

'**Hip-D**': Airborne communications role; as 'Hip-C' but rectangular section canisters on outer stores racks; added antennae above forward part of tailboom.

'**Hip-E**': Development of 'Hip-C'; flexibly mounted 12.7 mm machine gun in nose; triple stores rack each side, to carry total 192 rockets in six packs, plus four AT-2 (NATO 'Swatter') anti-tank missiles (semi-automatic command to line of sight) on rails above racks; about 250 in Soviet ground forces; some uprated to Mi-17 standard as **Mi-8TBK**, with port-side tail rotor.

'**Hip-F**': Export 'Hip-E'; missiles changed to six AT-3s ('Saggers'); manual command to line of sight).

'**Hip-G**': Airborne communications role; rearward inclined 'hockey stick' antennae projecting from rear of cabin, and from tailboom undersurface aft of Doppler box.

'**Hip-H**': See separate entry on Mi-17.

'**Hip-J**': ECM version; additional small boxes each side of fuselage, fore and aft of main landing gear legs.

'**Hip-K**': ECM communications jammer; rectangular container and array of six cruciform dipole antennae each side of cabin; no Doppler box under tailboom; some uprated to Mi-17 standard, with port-side tail rotor. See also Mi-17 'Hip-K derivative'.

Mil Mi-8 ('Hip-C') military helicopter of the Hungarian Air Force. This differs from the commercial versions in having circular cabin windows, and weapon carriers on outriggers *(Peter J. Bish)*

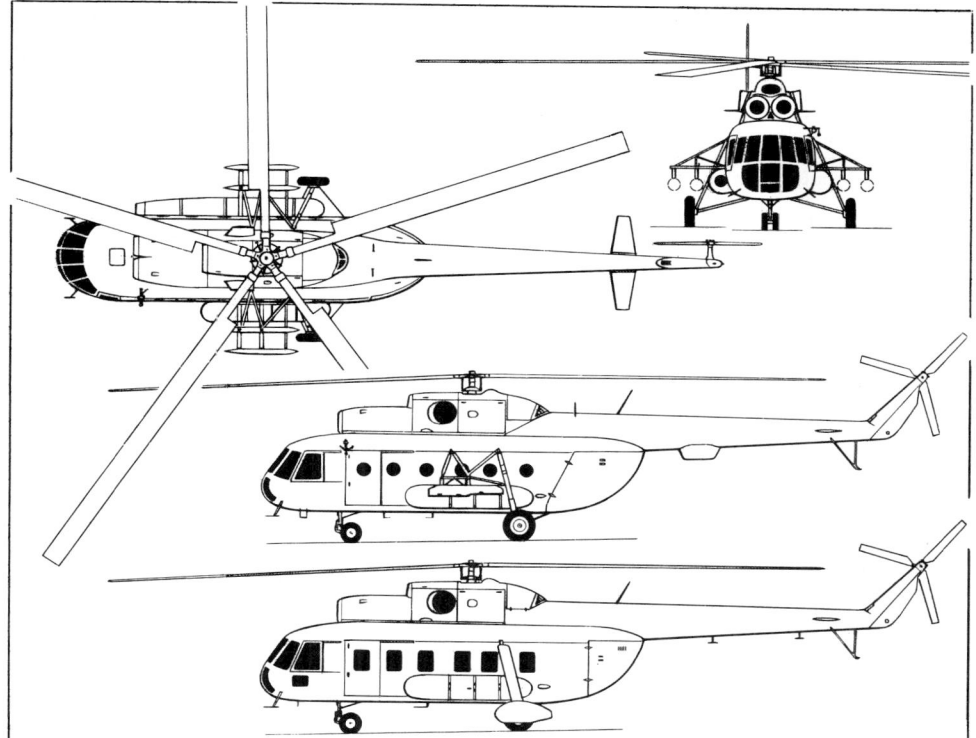

'Hip-C' military version of Mil Mi-8 twin-turbine helicopter, with additional side view (bottom) of commercial version *(Pilot Press)*

'Hip-J' ECM variant of the Mi-8

Infra-red suppressor and flare dispensers on Mi-8T *(Jane's Defence Weekly/Paul Beaver)*

'Hip-K' communications jamming variant of the Mi-8

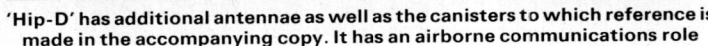

'Hip-D' has additional antennae as well as the canisters to which reference is made in the accompanying copy. It has an airborne communications role

CUSTOMERS: Soviet ground forces (estimated 2,400 Mi-8/17s); Soviet air forces; at least 39 other air forces; civil operators worldwide.

COSTS: Civil export price $2.5 million.

DESIGN FEATURES: Conventional pod and boom configuration; five-blade main rotor, inclined forward 4° 30′ from vertical; interchangeable blades of basic NACA 230 section, solidity 0.0777; spar failure warning system; drag and flapping hinges a few inches apart; blades carried on machined spider; three-blade starboard tail rotor; transmission comprises type VR-8 two-stage planetary main reduction gearbox giving main rotor shaft/engine rpm ratio of 0.016:1, intermediate and tail rotor gearboxes, main rotor brake, and drives off main gearbox for tail rotor, fan, AC generator, hydraulic pumps and tachometer generators; tail rotor pylon forms small vertical stabiliser; horizontal stabiliser near end of tailboom; clamshell rear-loading freight doors.

FLYING CONTROLS: Mechanical system, with irreversible hydraulic boosters; main rotor collective pitch control linked to throttles.

STRUCTURE: All-metal; main rotor blades each have extruded light alloy spar carrying root fitting, 21 honeycomb-filled trailing-edge pockets and blade tip; balance tab on each blade; each tail rotor blade made of spar and honeycomb filled trailing-edge; semi-monocoque fuselage.

LANDING GEAR: Non-retractable tricycle type, with steerable twin-wheel nose unit, which is locked in flight, and single wheel on each main unit. All units embody oleo-pneumatic (gas) shock absorbers. Mainwheel tyres size 865 × 280 mm; nosewheel tyres size 595 × 185 mm. Pneumatic brakes on mainwheels. Pneumatic system can also recharge tyres in the field, using air stored in main landing gear struts. Optional mainwheel fairings.

POWER PLANT: Two 1,267 kW (1,700 shp) Leningrad/Klimov (Isotov) TV2-117A turboshafts (1,454 kW; 1,950 shp TV3-117MTs in Mi-8T/TB/TBK). Main rotor speed governed automatically, with manual override. Single flexible internal fuel tank, capacity 445 litres (117.5 US gallons; 98 Imp gallons), and two external tanks, one each side of cabin, with capacity of 745 litres (197 US gallons; 164 Imp gallons) in the port tank and 680 litres (179.5 US gallons; 149.5 Imp gallons) in the starboard tank. Total standard fuel capacity 1,870 litres (494 US gallons; 411.5 Imp gallons). Provision for carrying one or two additional ferry tanks in cabin, raising max total capacity to 3,700 litres (977 US gallons; 814 Imp gallons). Fairing over starboard external tank houses optional cabin air-conditioning equipment at front. Engine cowling side panels form maintenance platforms when open, with access via hatch on flight deck. Engine air intake de-icing standard. Total oil capacity 60 kg (132 lb).

ACCOMMODATION: Two pilots side by side on flight deck, with provision for a flight engineer's station. Windscreen de-icing standard. Basic passenger version is furnished with 28 four-abreast track mounted tip-up seats at a pitch of 72-75 cm (28-29.5 in), with a centre aisle 32 cm (12.5 in) wide, a wardrobe and baggage compartment; or 32 seats without wardrobe. Seats and bulkheads of basic version are quickly removable for cargo carrying. Mi-8T and standard military versions have cargo tiedown rings in floor, a winch of 200 kg (440 lb) capacity and pulley block system to facilitate the loading of heavy freight, an external cargo sling system (capacity 3,000 kg; 6,614 lb), and 24 tip-up seats along the side walls of the cabin. All versions can be converted for air ambulance duties, with accommodation for 12 stretchers and a tip-up seat for a medical attendant. The large windows on each side of the flight deck slide rearward. The sliding, jettisonable main passenger door is at the front of the cabin on the port side. An electrically operated rescue hoist (capacity 150 kg; 330 lb) can be installed at this doorway. The rear of the cabin is made up of clamshell freight loading doors, which are

smaller on the commercial versions, with a downward hinged passenger airstair door inset centrally at the rear. Hook-on ramps are used for vehicle loading.

SYSTEMS: Standard heating system can be replaced by full air-conditioning system. Two independent hydraulic systems, each with own pump; operating pressure 44-64 bars (640-925 lb/sq in). DC electrical supply from two 27V 18kW starter/generators and six 28Ah storage batteries. AC supply for automatically controlled electro-thermal de-icing system and some radio equipment supplied by 208/115/36/7.5V 400Hz generator, with 36V three-phase standby system. Provision for oxygen system for crew and, in ambulance version, for patients. Freon fire extinguishing system in power plant bays and service fuel tank compartments, actuated automatically or manually. Two portable fire extinguishers in cabin.

AVIONICS: R-842 HF transceiver with frequency range of 2 to 8MHz and range of up to 540 nm (1,000 km; 620 miles), R-860 VHF transceiver operating on 118 to 135.9MHz over ranges of up to 54 nm (100 km; 62 miles), intercom, radio telephone, ARK-9 automatic radio compass, RV-3 radio altimeter with 'dangerous height' warning, and four-axis autopilot to give yaw, roll and pitch stabilisation under any flight conditions, stabilisation of altitude in level flight or hover, and stabilisation of pre-set flying speed, Doppler radar in box under tailboom.

EQUIPMENT: Instrumentation for all-weather flying by day and night, including two gyro horizons, two airspeed indicators, two main rotor speed indicators, turn indicator, two altimeters, two rate of climb indicators, magnetic compass, radio altimeter, radio compass and astrocompass for Polar flying. Military versions can be fitted with external flight deck armour, an infra-red suppressor above forward end of tailboom and flare dispensers above rear cabin window on each side.

ARMAMENT: See individual model descriptions of military versions.

DIMENSIONS, EXTERNAL:
Main rotor diameter	21.29 m (69 ft 10¼ in)
Tail rotor diameter	3.91 m (12 ft 9⅞ in)
Distance between rotor centres	12.65 m (41 ft 6 in)
Length: overall, rotors turning	25.24 m (82 ft 9¾ in)
fuselage, excl tail rotor	18.17 m (59 ft 7⅜ in)
Width of fuselage	2.50 m (8 ft 2½ in)
Height overall	5.65 m (18 ft 6½ in)
Wheel track	4.50 m (14 ft 9 in)
Wheelbase	4.26 m (13 ft 11¾ in)
Fwd passenger door: Height	1.41 m (4 ft 7¼ in)
Width	0.82 m (2 ft 8¼ in)
Rear passenger door: Height	1.70 m (5 ft 7 in)
Width	0.84 m (2 ft 9 in)
Rear cargo door: Height	1.82 m (5 ft 11½ in)
Width	2.34 m (7 ft 8¼ in)

DIMENSIONS, INTERNAL:
Passenger cabin: Length	6.36 m (20 ft 10¼ in)
Width	2.34 m (7 ft 8¼ in)
Height	1.80 m (5 ft 10¾ in)
Cargo hold (freighter):	
Length at floor	5.34 m (17 ft 6¼ in)
Width	2.34 m (7 ft 8¼ in)
Height	1.80 m (5 ft 10¾ in)
Volume	approx 23 m³ (812 cu ft)

AREAS:
Main rotor disc	356 m² (3,832 sq ft)
Tail rotor disc	12 m² (129.2 sq ft)

WEIGHTS AND LOADINGS:
Weight empty:	
civil passenger version	6,799 kg (14,990 lb)
civil cargo version	6,624 kg (14,603 lb)
military versions (typical)	7,260 kg (16,007 lb)
Max payload: internal	4,000 kg (8,820 lb)
external	3,000 kg (6,614 lb)
Fuel: standard tanks	1,450 kg (3,197 lb)
with 2 auxiliary tanks	2,870 kg (6,327 lb)
Normal T-O weight	11,100 kg (24,470 lb)

T-O weight: with 28 passengers, each with 15 kg (33 lb) of baggage 11,570 kg (25,508 lb)
with 2,500 kg (5,510 lb) of slung cargo 11,428 kg (25,195 lb)
Max T-O weight for VTO 12,000 kg (26,455 lb)
Max disc loading 33.7 kg/m² (6.90 lb/sq ft)

PERFORMANCE (civil Mi-8):
Max level speed at 1,000 m (3,280 ft):
  normal AUW 140 knots (260 km/h; 161 mph)
Max level speed at S/L:
  normal AUW 135 knots (250 km/h; 155 mph)
  max AUW 124 knots (230 km/h; 142 mph)
with 2,500 kg (5,510 lb) of slung cargo 97 knots (180 km/h; 112 mph)
Max cruising speed:
  normal AUW 122 knots (225 km/h; 140 mph)
  max AUW 97 knots (180 km/h; 112 mph)
Service ceiling 3,975 m (13,050 ft)
Hovering ceiling at normal AUW:
  IGE 1,900 m (6,235 ft)
  OGE 800 m (2,625 ft)
Ranges:
  cargo version at 1,000 m (3,280 ft), with standard fuel, 5% reserves:
    normal AUW 251 nm (465 km; 289 miles)
    max AUW 240 nm (445 km; 276 miles)
  with 28 passengers at 1,000 m (3,280 ft), with 20 min fuel reserves 270 nm (500 km; 311 miles)
  ferry range of cargo version, with auxiliary fuel, 5% reserves 647 nm (1,200 km; 745 miles)

PERFORMANCE (Mi-8MT):
Max cruising speed 129 knots (240 km/h; 149 mph)
Service ceiling 3,980 m (13,050 ft)
Range with max fuel, 5% reserves 267 nm (495 km; 307 miles)

MIL Mi-10 and Mi-10K
NATO reporting name: Harke

TYPE: Twin-turbine heavy-lift flying crane helicopter.

PROGRAMME: Development started February 1958; prototype of basic Mi-10 flew 1960; demonstrated as V-10 at 1961 Soviet Aviation Day display, Tushino; Mi-10K prototype flew 1966; displayed in Moscow 26 March 1966; total of approx 55 of both versions delivered by temporary end of production 1971; small-scale manufacture resumed briefly 1977.

VARIANTS: Mi-10 ('Harke-A'): Flying crane to transport bulk cargo too large for cabin of Mi-6; power plant and rotor systems identical to Mi-6; above line of cabin windows, fuselage very like Mi-6, but fuselage depth reduced considerably and tailboom deepened, so that flattened undersurface runs unbroken to tail; no fixed wings; tall long-stroke quadricycle landing gear, enabling Mi-10 to taxi over load it carries and accommodate loads as bulky as prefabricated building; wheel track exceeds 6.0 m (19 ft 8 in) with clearance under fuselage of 3.75 m (12 ft 3½ in) with full load; freight and vehicles normally carried on special platform locked hydraulically to landing gear legs.

Mi-10K ('Harke-B'): As Mi-10, but with short landing gear adequate for carrying only slung cargoes; more slender tail rotor support structure; operation by crew of only two pilots made possible by added cockpit gondola under front fuselage, with full flying controls and rearward facing seat; occupying this seat, one pilot can control the aircraft in hover and, at same time, have unrestricted view of cargo loading, unloading and hoisting, which are also under his control; max slung payload 11,000 kg (24,250 lb).

Abbreviated details of Mi-10K follow. More extensive description last appeared in 1983-84 *Jane's*.

POWER PLANT: Two 4,101 kW (5,500 shp) Soloviev D-25V turboshafts, mounted side by side above cabin, forward of main rotor driveshaft. Fuel capacity, in standard internal and two external tanks, on sides of cabin, 9,000

Mil Mi-10K (NATO 'Harke-B') preparing to lift a 10-tonne sheet steel drum to the top of a tower at the Sinarski pipe works in Kamensk-Uralskii *(Tass)*

litres (2,377 US gallons; 1,980 Imp gallons). Provision for ferry tanks in cabin.

ACCOMMODATION: Two pilots on flight deck, which has bulged side windows to provide an improved downward view. Flight deck is heated and ventilated and has provision for oxygen equipment. Additional cockpit gondola under front fuselage (see introductory notes). Crew door is immediately aft of flight deck on port side. Main cabin can be used for freight and/or passengers, 28 tip-up seats being installed along the side walls. Freight is loaded into this cabin through a door on the starboard side, aft of the rear landing gear struts, with the aid of a boom and 200 kg (440 lb) capacity electric winch. External sling gear standard, with hatch in the cabin floor, directly beneath main rotor shaft.

DIMENSIONS, EXTERNAL:

Main rotor diameter	35.00 m (114 ft 10 in)
Tail rotor diameter	6.30 m (20 ft 8 in)
Length: overall, rotors turning	41.89 m (137 ft 5½ in)
fuselage	32.86 m (107 ft 9¾ in)
Height overall	7.80 m (25 ft 7 in)
Wheel track (c/l of shock struts)	5.00 m (16 ft 4¾ in)
Wheelbase	8.74 m (28 ft 8 in)
Freight loading door: Height	1.56 m (5 ft 1½ in)
Width	1.26 m (4 ft 1½ in)
Height to sill	1.82 m (5 ft 11½ in)
Cabin floor hatch: Diameter	1.00 m (3 ft 3¼ in)

DIMENSIONS, INTERNAL:

Cabin: Length	14.04 m (46 ft 0¾ in)
Width	2.50 m (8 ft 2½ in)
Height	1.68 m (5 ft 6 in)
Volume	approx 60 m³ (2,120 cu ft)

AREAS:

Main rotor disc	962.1 m² (10,356 sq ft)

WEIGHTS AND LOADINGS:

Weight empty	24,680 kg (54,410 lb)
Max fuel load with ferry tanks in cabin	
	8,670 kg (19,114 lb)
Max T-O weight with slung cargo	38,000 kg (83,775 lb)
Max disc loading	39.5 kg/m² (8.09 lb/sq ft)

PERFORMANCE:

Cruising speed, empty	135 knots (250 km/h; 155 mph)
Max cruising speed with slung load	
	109 knots (202 km/h; 125 mph)
Service ceiling	3,000 m (9,850 ft)
Ferry range with auxiliary fuel	
	428 nm (795 km; 494 miles)

MIL Mi-14
NATO reporting name: Haze

TYPE: Twin-turbine shore-based amphibious helicopter.

PROGRAMME: Development of Mi-8; first flew September 1969, under designation **V-14** and with Mi-8 power plant; changed to Mi-17 engines for production, which continues.

VARIANTS: **Mi-14PL** ('Haze-A'): Basic ASW version; four crew; large undernose radome; OKA-2 retractable sonar in starboard rear of planing bottom, forward of two probable sonobuoy or signal flare chutes; APM-60 towed magnetic anomaly detection (MAD) bird stowed against rear of fuselage pod (moved to lower position on some aircraft); weapons include torpedoes, bombs and depth charges in enclosed bay in bottom of hull; WAS-5M-3 liferaft (in all versions).

Mi-14PW: Polish designation of Mi-14PL.

Mi-14BT ('Haze-B'): Mine countermeasures version; fuselage strake, for hydraulic tubing, and air-conditioning pod on starboard side of cabin; no MAD; container for searchlight to observe MCM gear during deployment and retrieval under tailboom, forward of Doppler box.

Mi-14PS ('Haze-C'): Search and rescue version, carrying ten 20-place liferafts; room for ten survivors in cabin; provision for towing many more survivors in liferafts; fuselage strake and air-conditioning pod as Mi-14BT; double-width sliding door at front of cabin on port side, with retractable rescue hoist able to lift up to three persons in basket; searchlight each side of nose and under tailboom.

CUSTOMERS: At least 230 delivered; most to Soviet armed forces; Bulgaria (10), Cuba (14), the former East Germany (8, incl Mi-14BT now converted for SAR), North Korea, Libya (12), Poland (12 Mi-14PW, 5 Mi-14PS), Romania (6), Syria (12), Yugoslavia.

DESIGN FEATURES: Developed from Mi-8; overall dimensions, power plant and dynamic components as Mi-17; new features include boat hull, sponson carrying inflatable flotation bag each side at rear and small float under tailboom; fully retractable landing gear with two forward retracting single-wheel nose units and two rearward retracting twin-wheel main units.

AVIONICS (Mi-14PL): Type 12-M undernose radar, R-842-M HF transceiver, R-860 VHF transceiver, SBU-7 intercom, RW3 radio altimeter, ARK-9 and ARK-U2 ADFs, DISS-15 Doppler, Chrom Nikiel IFF, AP34-B autopilot/autohover system and SAU-14 autocontrol system.

DIMENSIONS, EXTERNAL:

Main rotor diameter	21.29 m (69 ft 10¼ in)
Length overall, rotors turning	25.30 m (83 ft 0 in)
Height overall	6.93 m (22 ft 9 in)

AREAS:

Main rotor disc	356 m² (3,832 sq ft)

WEIGHTS AND LOADINGS:

Max T-O weight	14,000 kg (30,865 lb)
Max disc loading	39.3 kg/m² (8.05 lb/sq ft)

PERFORMANCE:

Max level speed	124 knots (230 km/h; 143 mph)
Max cruising speed	116 knots (215 km/h; 133 mph)
Normal cruising speed	110 knots (205 km/h; 127 mph)
Service ceiling	3,500 m (11,500 ft)
Range with max fuel	612 nm (1,135 km; 705 miles)
Endurance with max fuel	5 h 56 min

MIL Mi-17
NATO reporting names: Hip-H and K derivative

TYPE: Twin-turbine multi-purpose helicopter.

PROGRAMME: First displayed at 1981 Paris Air Show; successor to Mi-8; exports began (to Cuba) 1983; production continues.

Mil Mi-14PL ('Haze-A') with MAD bird mounted in new lower position *(Piotr Butowski)*

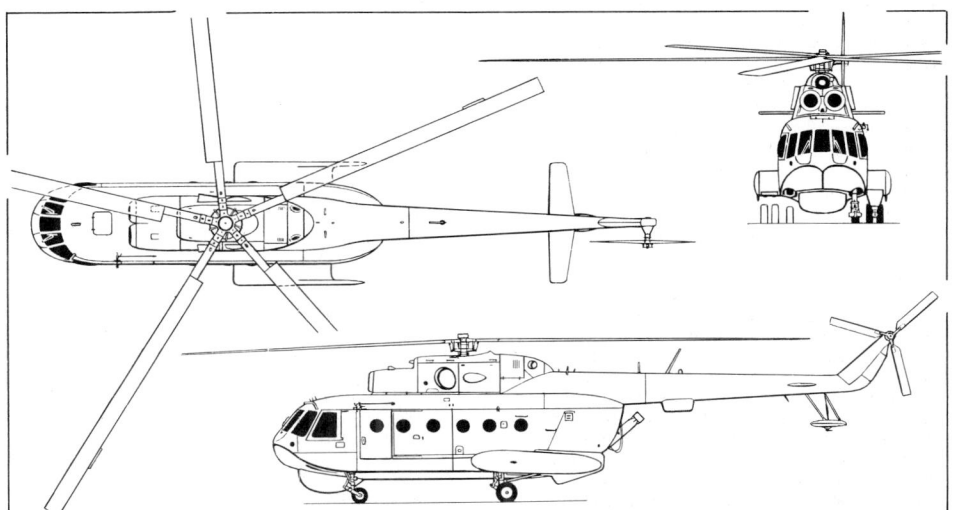

Mil Mi-14PL ASW helicopter (NATO 'Haze-A') *(Pilot Press)*

VARIANTS: **Mi-17** ('Hip-H'): Mid-life update of Mi-8 with more powerful turboshafts, giving overall performance improvement, particularly hover ceiling; many existing Mi-8s uprated to Mi-17 standard (see Mi-8 entry).

Mi-17P ('Hip-K derivative'): ECM communications jammer; two observed in Hungarian service in 1990; antenna array much more advanced than that of Mi-8 ('Hip-K'); large 32-element array, resembling vertically segmented panel, aft of main landing gear each side; four-element array to rear on tailboom each side; large radome each side of cabin, below jet nozzle; triangular container in place of rear cabin window each side; six heat exchangers under front fuselage.

Mi-17-1VA ('Hip-H'): First displayed 1989 Paris Air Show; more powerful TV3-117VM turboshafts, each 1,678 kW (2,250 shp); improved rates of climb and hover ceilings; other weights and performance generally unchanged; example displayed (SSSR-95043) had been produced for Soviet Ministry of Health as flying hospital equipped to highest practicable standards for relatively small helicopter; interior, with equipment developed in Hungary, had provision for three stretchers, operating table, extensive surgical and medical equipment, accommodation for doctor/surgeon and three nursing attendants. In production, initially for use in USSR.

CUSTOMERS: Many operational side by side with Mi-8s in Soviet armed forces; Angola, Cuba (16), Hungary, India, North Korea, Nicaragua, Papua New Guinea, Peru, Poland.

COSTS: Civil export price $5 million.

DESIGN FEATURES: Distinguished from Mi-8 by port-side tail rotor; shorter engine nacelles, with air intakes extending forward only to mid-point of door on port side at front of cabin; small orifice each side forward of jetpipe; correct rotor speed maintained automatically by system that also synchronises output of the two engines.

POWER PLANT (basic Mi-17): Two 1,454 kW (1,950 shp) Leningrad/Klimov (Isotov) TV3-117MT turboshafts; should one engine stop, output of the other increased automatically to contingency rating of 1,640 kW (2,200 shp), enabling flight to continue; APU for pneumatic engine starting; deflectors on engine air intakes prevent ingestion of sand, dust and foreign objects.

ACCOMMODATION: Configuration and payloads generally as Mi-8; but civilian Mi-17 described by Aviaexport as essentially a cargo carrying helicopter, with secondary passenger transport role.

EQUIPMENT: Options as for Mi-8, plus external cockpit armour, ASO-2 chaff/flare dispenser under tailboom and IR jammer (NATO 'Hot Brick') at forward end of tailboom.

ARMAMENT: Options as for Mi-8, plus 23 mm GSh-23 gun packs.

Following data apply to basic Mi-17:

DIMENSIONS, EXTERNAL: As for Mi-8, except:

Distance between rotor centres	12.661 m (41 ft 6½ in)
Length: overall, rotors turning	25.352 m (83 ft 2 in)
fuselage, excl tail rotor	18.424 m (60 ft 5⅜ in)
Height to top of main rotor head	4.755 m (15 ft 7¼ in)
Wheel track	4.510 m (14 ft 9½ in)
Wheelbase	4.281 m (14 ft 0½ in)

DIMENSIONS, INTERNAL: As for Mi-8
AREAS: As for Mi-8
WEIGHTS AND LOADINGS:

Weight empty, equipped	7,100 kg (15,653 lb)
Max payload: internal	4,000 kg (8,820 lb)
external, on sling	3,000 kg (6,614 lb)
Normal T-O weight	11,100 kg (24,470 lb)
Max T-O weight	13,000 kg (28,660 lb)
Max disc loading	36.5 kg/m² (7.48 lb/sq ft)

PERFORMANCE (A: at normal T-O weight, B: at max T-O weight):

Max level speed: B	135 knots (250 km/h; 155 mph)	
Max cruising speed: B	129 knots (240 km/h; 149 mph)	
Service ceiling: A	5,000 m (16,400 ft)	
B	3,600 m (11,800 ft)	
Hovering ceiling OGE: A	1,760 m (5,775 ft)	

Range with max standard fuel, 5% reserves:

A	267 nm (495 km; 307 miles)
B	251 nm (465 km; 289 miles)

Range with auxiliary fuel:

A	513 nm (950 km; 590 miles)

MIL Mi-22

See Mi-6 entry, page 264.

MIL Mi-24

NATO reporting name: Hind

TYPE: Twin-turbine gunship helicopter, with transport capability.

PROGRAMME: Development began second half of 1960s, as first Soviet fire support helicopter, with accommodation for eight armed troops; first reported in West 1972; photographs became available 1974, when two units of approx squadron strength based in East Germany; reconfiguration of front fuselage changed primary role to gunship; new version first observed 1977; used operationally in Chad, Nicaragua, Ceylon (Sri Lanka), Angola, Afghanistan and Iran/Iraq war, when at least one Iranian F-4 Phantom II destroyed by AT-6 (NATO 'Spiral') anti-tank missile from Mi-24; production

The Mi-14PS search and rescue helicopter ('Haze-C') in Polish service *(Helicopter International)*

Mil Mi-17 ('Hip-H') in Soviet army service *(Lutz Freundt)*

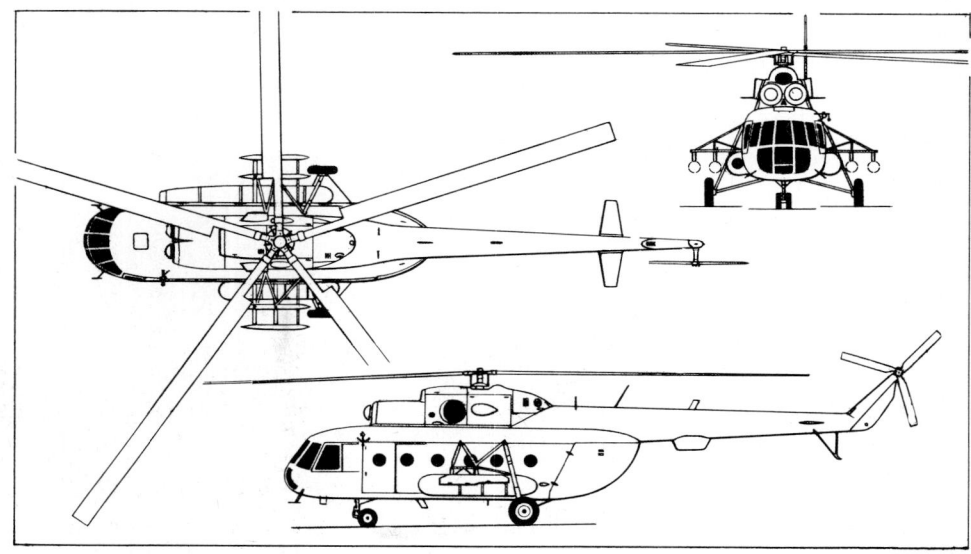
Mi-17 military general purpose helicopter, with external stores carriers *(Pilot Press)*

ECM jammer version of Mi-17P ('Hip-K derivative') of the Hungarian armed forces *(Flight/Sixma)*

Mi-24R ('Hind-G1'), with 'clutching hand' wingtip fittings for NBC warfare *(Lutz Freundt)*

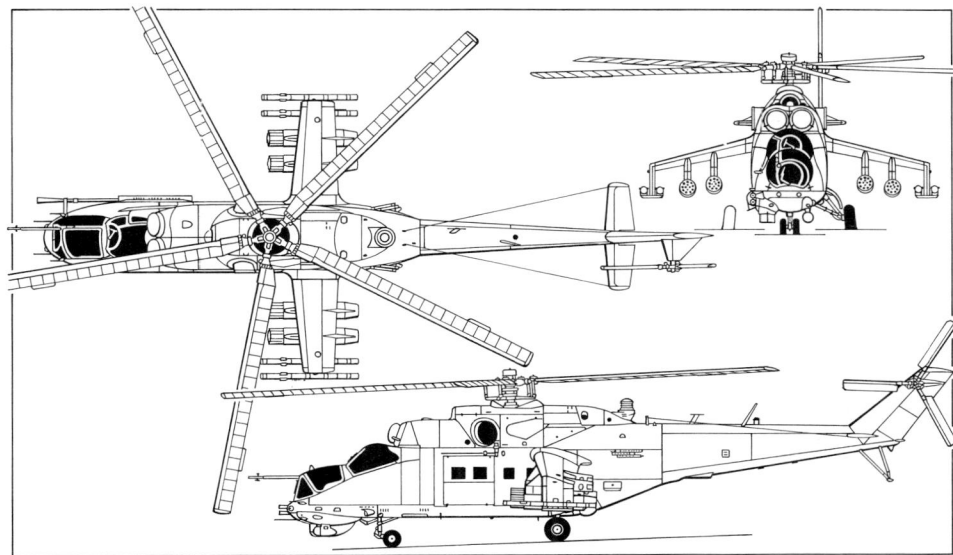

Mil Mi-24P gunship, known to NATO as 'Hind-F' *(Jane's/Mike Keep)*

Mil Mi-35P export version of 'Hind-F' helicopter gunship *(Peter J. Cooper)*

continues at rate much reduced from long-maintained 15 or more each month.

VARIANTS: **Mi-24** ('Hind-A, B and C'): Early versions with pilot and co-pilot/gunner side by side on large flight deck; last described in 1989-90 *Jane's*.

Mi-24D ('Hind-D'): First gunship version, observed 1977; basically as late model 'Hind-A' with TV3-117 engines and port-side tail rotor, but entire front fuselage redesigned above floor forward of engine air intakes; heavily armoured cockpits for weapon operator and pilot in tandem; flight mechanic in main cabin; transport capability retained; undernose Gatling-type 12.7 mm machine gun in turret, slaved to adjacent electro-optical sighting pod, for air-to-air and air-to-surface use; nosewheel leg extended to increase ground clearance of sensor pods; nosewheels semi-exposed when retracted. Training version has no gun turret. (See also Mi-25.)

Mi-24W ('Hind-E'): As 'Hind-D', but modified wingtip launchers and four underwing pylons for up to 12 AT-6 ('Spiral') radio guided tube-launched anti-tank missiles in pairs; enlarged undernose missile guidance pod on port side, with fixed searchlight to rear; AA-8 ('Aphid') air-to-air missiles optional on underwing pylons; pilot's HUD replaces former reflector gunsight. (See also Mi-35.)

Mi-24P ('Hind-F'): First shown in Soviet service in 1982 photographs; P of designation refers to *pushka* = cannon; as Mi-24W, but nose gun turret replaced by GSh-30-2 twin-barrel 30 mm gun (with 750 rds) in semi-cylindrical pack on starboard side of nose; bottom of nose smoothly faired above and forward of sensors.

Mi-24R ('Hind-G1'): Identified at Chernobyl after April 1986 accident at nuclear power station; no undernose electro-optical and RF missile guidance pods; instead of wingtip weapon mounts, has 'clutching hand' mechanisms on lengthened pylons, for NBC (nuclear/biological/chemical) warfare; lozenge shape housing with cylindrical insert under port side of cabin (purpose unknown); bubble window on starboard side; small rearward-firing marker flare pack on tailskid; deployed individually throughout Soviet ground forces.

Mi-24K ('Hind-G2'): As Mi-24R, but with large camera in cabin, lens on starboard side; believed for reconnaissance and artillery spotting.

Mi-25: Export Mi-24D, including those for Afghanistan, Cuba and India.

Mi-35: Export Mi-24W.

Mi-35P: Export Mi-24P.

CUSTOMERS: More than 2,300 produced at Arsenyev and Rostov; about 1,250 in Soviet army service, most with about 20 helicopter attack regiments of Mi-8/17s and Mi-24s; air forces of Afghanistan, Algeria, Angola, Bulgaria, Cuba, Czechoslovakia, the former East Germany, Hungary, India, Iraq, Libya, Mozambique, North Korea, Nicaragua, Peru, Poland, Vietnam, Yemen.

Following details refer to Mi-24D:

DESIGN FEATURES: Typical helicopter gunship configuration, with stepped tandem seating for two crew and heavy weapon load on stub-wings; fuselage unusually wide for role, due to requirement for carrying eight troops; dynamic components and power plant originally as Mi-8, but soon upgraded to Mi-17-type power plant and port-side tail rotor; main rotor blade section NACA 230; stub-wing anhedral 16°, incidence 20°; wings contribute approx 25 per cent of lift in cruising flight; fin offset 3°.

STRUCTURE: Five-blade constant-chord main rotor, on forged and machined steel head, with conventional flapping, drag and pitch change articulation; each blade has titanium spar, glassfibre skin and honeycomb core; spars nitrogen pressurised for crack detection; hydraulic lead/lag dampers; balance tab on each blade; aluminium alloy three-blade tail rotor; main rotor brake; all-metal semi-monocoque fuselage pod and boom; 8 mm hardened steel integral side armour on front fuselage; all-metal shoulder wings with no movable surfaces; swept fin/tail rotor mounting; variable incidence horizontal stabiliser.

LANDING GEAR: Tricycle type, with rearward retracting steerable twin-wheel nose unit, and single-wheel main units with oleo-pneumatic shock absorbers and low pressure tyres. Main units retract rearward and inward into the aft end of the fuselage pod, turning through 90° to stow almost vertically, discwise to the longitudinal axis of the fuselage, under prominent blister fairings. Tubular tripod skid assembly, with shock strut, protects tail rotor in a tail-down take-off or landing.

POWER PLANT: Two Leningrad/Klimov (Isotov) TV3-117 turboshafts, each with max rating of 1,640 kW (2,200 shp), mounted side by side above the cabin, with their output shafts driving rearward to the main rotor shaft through a combining gearbox. 8 mm hardened steel armour protection for engines. Main fuel tank in fuselage to rear of cabin, with bag tanks under cabin floor. Internal fuel capacity of 1,500 kg (3,307 lb) can be supplemented by 1,000 kg (2,205 lb) auxiliary tank in cabin. Provision for carrying (instead of auxiliary tank) up to four external fuel tanks, each with capacity of 500 litres (132 US gallons; 110 Imp gallons), on two inner pylons under each wing. Optional deflectors and separators for foreign objects and dust in air intakes; and infra-red suppression exhaust mixer boxes over exhaust ducts. APU mounted transversely inside fairing aft of rotor head.

ACCOMMODATION: Pilot (at rear) and weapon operator on armoured seats in tandem cockpits under individual canopies. Dual flying controls, with retractable pedals in front cockpit. Flight mechanic on jump-seat in narrow passage between flight deck and main cabin. Front canopy hinged to open sideways, to starboard; footstep under starboard side of fuselage for access to pilot's rearward hinged door. Rear seat raised to give pilot an unobstructed forward view. Anti-fragment shield between cockpits. Main cabin can accommodate eight persons on folding seats, or four stretchers. At front of passenger cabin on each side is a door, divided horizontally into two sections which are hinged to open upward and downward respectively, with integral step on lower portion. Optically flat bulletproof glass windscreen, with wiper, for each crew member. Cockpits heated and ventilated.

SYSTEMS: Dual electrical system, with three generators. Retractable landing/taxying light under nose. Navigation lights. Anti-collision light above tailboom. Stability augmentation system. Electro-thermal de-icing system for main and tail rotor blades. Cabin heating and ventilation systems.

AVIONICS: Include VHF and UHF radio, autopilot, radar altimeter, blind-flying instrumentation, and ADF navigation system with Doppler-fed mechanical map display. Air data sensor boom forward of top starboard corner of bulletproof windscreen at extreme nose. Undernose pods for electro-optics (starboard) and RF missile guidance (port). Many small antennae and blisters, including IFF (NATO 'Odd Rods') and radar warning antennae on each side of front fuselage and on trailing-edge of tail rotor pylon. Infra-red jammer in 'flower pot' container above forward end of tailboom.

EQUIPMENT: Gun camera on port wingtip. Colour-coded identification flare system. Decoy flare dispenser under tailboom forward of tailskid assembly initially; later triple racks (total of 192 flares) on sides of centre-fuselage.

ARMAMENT: One remotely controlled four-barrel Gatling type 12.7 mm machine gun in undernose turret, slaved to undernose sighting system. Rails for four AT-2 'Swatter' anti-tank missiles under endplate pylons at wingtips. Four underwing pylons for UV-32-57 rocket pods (each thirty-two S-5 type 57 mm rockets), pods each containing twenty 80 mm rockets, UPK-23 pods each containing a GSh-23 twin-barrel 23 mm gun, up to 1,500 kg (3,300 lb) of chemical or conventional bombs, PFM-1 mine dispensers, or other stores. Helicopter can be landed to install reload weapons carried in cabin. PKV reflector gunsight for pilot. Provisions for firing AK-47 guns from cabin windows.

DIMENSIONS, EXTERNAL (Mi-24P):

Main rotor diameter	17.30 m (56 ft 9 in)
Tail rotor diameter	3.908 m (12 ft 10 in)
Span over wingtip pylons	approx 6.65 m (21 ft 10 in)
Length overall:	
excl rotors and gun	17.506 m (57 ft 5¼ in)
rotors turning	21.50 m (70 ft 6½ in)
Height: to top of rotor head	3.97 m (13 ft 0½ in)
overall: rotors turning	6.50 m (21 ft 4 in)
Span of horizontal stabiliser	3.27 m (10 ft 9 in)
Wheel track	3.03 m (9 ft 11½ in)
Wheelbase	4.39 m (14 ft 5 in)

AREAS:

Main rotor disc	235 m² (2,530 sq ft)

WEIGHTS AND LOADINGS (Mi-24P):

Weight empty	8,200 kg (18,078 lb)
Max external stores	2,400 kg (5,290 lb)
Normal T-O weight	11,200 kg (24,690 lb)
Max T-O weight	12,000 kg (26,455 lb)
Max disc loading	51.1 kg/m² (10.5 lb/sq ft)

PERFORMANCE (Mi-24P):

Max level speed	180 knots (335 km/h; 208 mph)
Cruising speed	145 knots (270 km/h; 168 mph)
Econ cruising speed	117 knots (217 km/h; 135 mph)
Max rate of climb at S/L	750 m (2,460 ft)/min
Service ceiling	4,500 m (14,750 ft)
Hovering ceiling OGE	1,500 m (4,920 ft)
Combat radius:	
with max military load	86 nm (160 km; 99 miles)
with two external fuel tanks	
	121 nm (224 km; 139 miles)
with four external fuel tanks	
	155 nm (288 km; 179 miles)
Range:	
standard internal fuel	270 nm (500 km; 310 miles)
with auxiliary tanks	540 nm (1,000 km; 620 miles)
Max endurance	4 h

MIL Mi-25
NATO reporting name: Hind-D

Some export variants of the Mi-24D, including those for Angola, India and Peru, are designated Mi-25. Such a change presumably signifies different equipment standards.

MIL Mi-26
NATO reporting name: Halo

TYPE: Twin-turbine heavy transport helicopter.

PROGRAMME: Development started early 1970s; aim was payload capability 1.5-2 times greater than that of any

Mil Mi-26 heavy lift helicopter (two Zaporozhye/Lotarev D-136 turboshafts) in Soviet military service

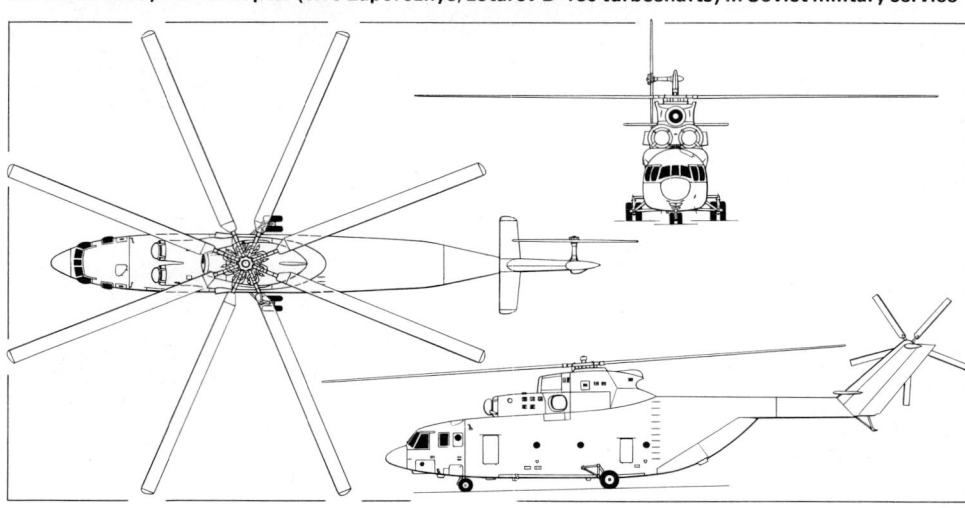

Mil Mi-26, first helicopter to operate successfully with an eight-blade main rotor *(Pilot Press)*

previous production helicopter; first prototype flew 14 December 1977; one of several prototype or pre-production Mi-26s (SSSR-06141) displayed at 1981 Paris Air Show; in-field evaluation, probably with military development squadron, began early 1983; fully operational 1985; export deliveries started (to India) June 1986; production continues.

VARIANTS: Only basic transport identified by early 1991; 1990 edition of US Department of Defense's *Soviet Military Power* states "New variants of 'Halo' are likely in the early 1990s to begin to replace 'Hooks' specialised for command support"; uprated transport version under development with more powerful engines, all-composites rotor blades, max payload 22,000 kg (48,500 lb).

CUSTOMERS: Soviet armed forces (more than 60), India (10).

DESIGN FEATURES: Largest production helicopter; empty weight comparable to that of Mi-6 and, as specified, approx 50 per cent max T-O weight; weight saved by in-house design of main gearbox providing multiple torque paths, glassfibre tail rotor blades, titanium main and tail rotor heads, main rotor blades of mixed metal and glassfibre, use of aluminium-lithium alloys in airframe; conventional pod and boom configuration, but first successful use of eight-blade main rotor, of smaller diameter than Mi-6 rotor; payload and cargo hold size similar to those of Lockheed C-130 Hercules; auxiliary wings not required; rear-loading ramp/doors; main rotor rpm 132.

FLYING CONTROLS: Hydraulically powered cyclic and collective pitch controls actuated by small parallel jacks, with redundant autopilot and stability augmentation system inputs.

STRUCTURE: Eight-blade constant-chord main rotor; flapping and drag hinges, droop stops and hydraulic drag dampers; no elastomeric bearings or hinges; each blade has one-piece tubular steel spar and 26 glassfibre aerofoil shape full-chord pockets, 'Nomex' filled, with ribs and stiffeners and non-removable titanium leading-edge abrasion strip; blades have moderate twist, taper in thickness toward tip, and are attached to small forged titanium head of unconventional design; each has ground adjustable trailing-edge tab; five-blade constant-chord tail rotor, starboard side, has glassfibre blades, forged titanium head; conventional transmission, with tail rotor shaft inside cabin roof; VR-26 fan-cooled main gearbox, rated at 14,914 kW (20,000 shp), with air intake above rear of engine cowlings; all-metal riveted semi-monocoque fuselage with clamshell rear doors; flattened tailboom undersurface; engine bay of titanium for fire protection; all-metal tail surfaces; swept vertical stabiliser/tail rotor support profiled to produce sideways lift; ground adjustable variable incidence horizontal stabiliser.

LANDING GEAR: Non-retractable tricycle type, with twin-wheels on each unit. Steerable nosewheels. Mainwheel tyres size 1,120 × 450 mm. Retractable tailskid at end of tailboom to permit unrestricted approach to rear cargo

doors. Length of main legs can be adjusted hydraulically to facilitate loading through rear doors and to permit landing on varying surfaces. A device on the main gear indicates take-off weight to flight engineer at lift-off, on panel on shelf to rear of his seat.

POWER PLANT: Two 8,380 kW (11,240 shp) Zaporozhye/Lotarev D-136 free-turbine turboshafts, mounted side by side above cabin, forward of main rotor driveshaft. Air intakes are fitted with particle separators to prevent foreign object ingestion, and have both electrical and bleed air anti-icing systems. Above and behind is a central oil cooler intake. There is a system for synchronising the output of the engines and maintaining constant rotor rpm. If one engine fails, output of the other is increased to maximum power automatically. Independent fuel system for each engine. Fuel in eight underfloor rubber tanks, feeding into two header tanks above engines, which permit gravity feed for a period in emergencies. Max fuel capacity 12,000 litres (3,170 US gallons; 2,640 Imp gallons). Two large panels on each side of main rotor mast fairing, aft of engine exhaust outlet, hinge downward as work platforms.

ACCOMMODATION: Crew of five on flight deck, consisting of pilot (on port side) and co-pilot side by side, with navigator's seat between pilots, and seats for flight engineer and loadmaster to rear. Four-seat passenger compartment aft of flight deck. Loads that can be accommodated in hold include two airborne infantry combat vehicles and a standard 20,000 kg (44,090 lb) ISO container. About 20 tip-up seats along each side wall of hold. Max military seating for about 85 combat equipped troops. Heated windscreen, with wipers. Four large blistered side windows on flight deck. Forward pair swing open slightly outward and rearward. Downward hinged doors, with integral airstairs, at front of hold on port side, and on each side aft of main landing gear units. Hold is loaded via a downward hinged lower door, with integral folding ramp, and two clamshell upper doors which form rear wall of hold when closed. Doors are opened and closed hydraulically, with backup handpump for emergency use. Two electric hoists on overhead rails, each with capacity of 2,500 kg (5,511 lb), enable loads to be transported along cabin. Winch for hauling loads, capacity 500 kg (1,100 lb). Roller conveyor in floor and load lashing points throughout hold. Flight deck and hold fully air-conditioned.

SYSTEMS: Two hydraulic systems, operating pressure 207 bars (3,000 lb/sq in). 28V DC electrical system. APU under flight deck, with intake louvres (forming fuselage skin when closed) and exhaust on starboard side, for engine starting and to supply hydraulic, electrical and air-conditioning systems on ground. Electrically heated leading-edge of main and tail rotor blades for anti-icing. Only flight deck pressurised. Four-axis autostabilisation.

AVIONICS: All items necessary for day and night operations in all weathers are standard, including weather radar in the hinged (to starboard) nosecone, Doppler, map display, HSI, and automatic hover system. Com/nav equipment generally similar to that of Yak-42.

EQUIPMENT: Hatch for load sling in bottom of fuselage, in line with main rotor shaft, enabling sling cable to be attached to internal winching gear. Closed circuit TV cameras to observe slung payloads. Operational equipment on military version includes infra-red jammers and suppressors, infra-red decoy dispensers and colour-coded identification flare system.

ARMAMENT: None.

DIMENSIONS, EXTERNAL:

Main rotor diameter	32.00 m (105 ft 0 in)
Tail rotor diameter	7.61 m (24 ft 11½ in)
Length: overall, rotors turning	40.025 m (131 ft 3¾ in)
fuselage, excl tail rotor	33.727 m (110 ft 8 in)
Height to top of rotor head	8.145 m (26 ft 8¾ in)
Width over mainwheels	8.15 m (26 ft 9 in)
Wheel track	7.17 m (23 ft 6¼ in)
Wheelbase	8.95 m (29 ft 4½ in)

DIMENSIONS, INTERNAL:
Freight hold:

Length: ramp trailed	15.00 m (49 ft 2½ in)
excl ramp	12.00 m (39 ft 4¼ in)
Width	3.25 m (10 ft 8 in)
Height	2.95-3.17 m (9 ft 8 in to 10 ft 4¾ in)
Volume	121 m³ (4,273 cu ft)

AREAS:

Main rotor disc	804.25 m² (8,657 sq ft)
Tail rotor disc	45.48 m² (489.6 sq ft)

WEIGHTS AND LOADINGS:

Weight empty	28,200 kg (62,170 lb)
Max payload, internal or external	20,000 kg (44,090 lb)
Normal T-O weight	49,500 kg (109,125 lb)
Max T-O weight	56,000 kg (123,450 lb)
Max disc loading	69.6 kg/m² (14.26 lb/sq ft)

PERFORMANCE:

Max level speed	159 knots (295 km/h; 183 mph)
Normal cruising speed	137 knots (255 km/h; 158 mph)
Service ceiling	4,600 m (15,100 ft)
Hovering ceiling OGE, ISA	1,800 m (5,900 ft)
Range with max internal fuel at max T-O weight, 5% reserves	432 nm (800 km; 497 miles)

MIL Mi-28
NATO reporting name: Havoc

TYPE: Twin-turbine all-weather combat helicopter.

PROGRAMME: Design started 1980; first prototype flew 10 November 1982; development 90 per cent complete by June 1989, when third prototype demonstrated at Paris Air Show; IOC planned for 1991-92.

VARIANTS: Members of Mil OKB stated that versions under development for naval amphibious assault support, night attack and air-to-air missions.

DESIGN FEATURES: Conventional gunship configuration, with two crew in stepped cockpits; original three-blade tail rotor superseded by 'scissors' type comprising two independent two-blade rotors set as narrow X (35°/145°) on same shaft, known in USA as Δ₃ (delta 3) type; resulting flapping freedom relieves flight loads; agility enhanced by doubling hinge offset of main rotor blades compared with Mi-24; survivability emphasised; crew compartments protected by titanium and composite armour and armoured glass transparencies; vital structural elements shielded by less vital; single hit will not knock out both engines; vital units and parts are redundant and widely separated; multiple fuel tanks in centre fuselage enclosed in composites second skin, outside metal fuselage skin; no explosion, fire or fuel leakage results if tanks hit by bullet or shell fragment; energy-absorbing seats and landing gear protect crew in crash landing at descent rate of 12 m (40 ft)/s; crew doors are rearward hinged, to open quickly and remain open in emergency; parachutes are mandatory for Soviet military helicopter aircrew; if Mi-28 crew had to parachute, emergency system would jettison doors, blast away stub wings, and inflate bladder beneath each door sill; as crew jumped, they would bounce off bladders and clear main landing gear; no provision for rotor separation; port-side door, aft of wing, provides access to avionics compartment large enough to permit combat rescue of two or three persons on ground, although it lacks windows, heating and ventilation; handcrank, inserted into end of each stub wing, enables stores of up to 500 kg (1,100 lb) to be winched on to pylons without hoists or ground equipment; current 30 mm gun is identical with that of Soviet Army ground vehicles and uses same ammunition; jamming averted by attaching twin ammunition boxes to sides of gun mounting, so that they turn, elevate and depress with gun; main rotor shaft has 5° forward tilt, providing tail rotor clearance; transmission capable of running without oil for 20-30 minutes; main rotor rpm 242; with main rotor blades and wings removed, helicopter is air transportable in An-22 or Il-76 freighter.

FLYING CONTROLS: Hydraulically powered mechanical type; horizontal stabiliser linked to collective; controls for pilot only.

STRUCTURE: Five-blade main rotor; blades have very cambered high-lift section and sweptback tip leading-edge; full-span upswept tab on trailing-edge of each blade; structure comprises numerically controlled, spirally wound glassfibre D-spar, blade pockets of

Third prototype of Mil Mi-28 ('Havoc') combat helicopter *(Peter J. Cooper)*

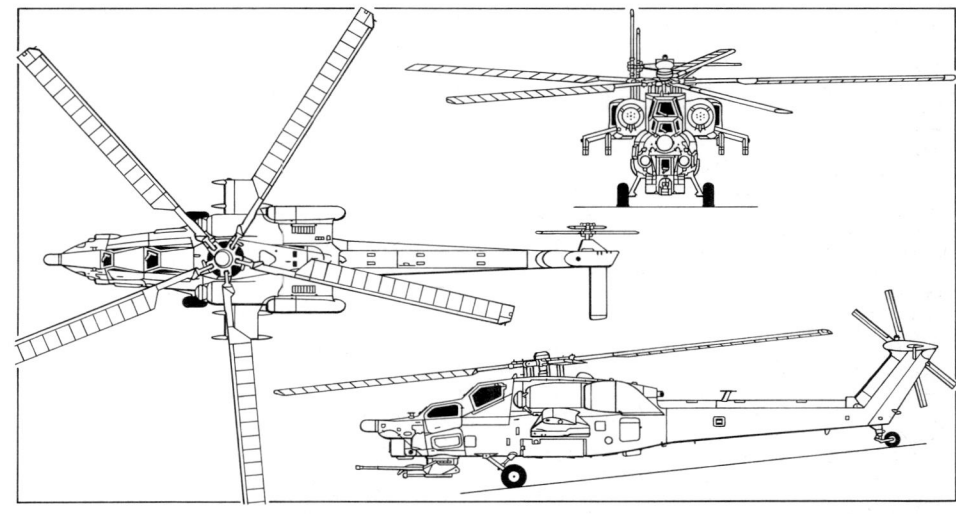

Mil Mi-28 combat helicopter (two Leningrad/Klimov [Isotov] TV3-117 turboshafts) *(Jane's/Mike Keep)*

Kevlar-like material with Nomex-like honeycomb core, and titanium erosion strip on leading-edge; each blade has single elastomeric root bearing, mechanical droop stop and hydraulic drag damper; four-blade glassfibre tail rotor with elastomeric bearings for flapping; rotor brake lever on starboard side of cockpit; strong and simple machined titanium main rotor head with automatic grease lubrication; power output shafts from engines drive main gearbox from each side; tail rotor gearbox, at base of tail pylon, driven by aluminium alloy shaft inside composite duct on top of tailboom; sweptback mid-mounted wings have light alloy primary box structure, leading- and trailing-edges of composites; no wing movable surfaces; tiedown in each wingtip; light alloy semi-monocoque fuselage, with titanium armour around cockpits and vulnerable areas; composites access door aft of wing on port side; swept fin has light alloy primary box structure, composites leading- and trailing-edges; two-position composites horizontal stabiliser.

LANDING GEAR: Non-retractable tailwheel type, with single wheel on each unit. Mainwheel tyres size 720 × 320 mm, pressure 5.4 bars (78 lb/sq in). Castoring tailwheel with tyre size 480 × 200 mm.

POWER PLANT: Two Leningrad/Klimov (Isotov) TV3-117 turboshafts, each rated at 1,640 kW (2,200 shp), in pod mounted above each wingroot. Three jetpipes inside downward deflected composites nozzle fairing on each side of third prototype shown in Paris. Upward deflecting type also tested. Ivchenko AI-9V APU in rear of main pylon structure supplies compressed air for engine starting and to drive a small turbine for pre-flight ground checks. Deflectors for dust and foreign objects forward of air intakes. Air intakes de-iced by engine bleed air. Internal fuel capacity approx 1,900 litres (502 US gallons; 418 Imp gallons). Provision for four external fuel tanks on underwing pylons.

ACCOMMODATION: Navigator/gunner in front cockpit; pilot behind, on elevated seat. Flat non-glint tinted transparencies of armoured glass.

SYSTEMS: Cockpits air-conditioned and pressurised by engine bleed air. Duplicated hydraulic systems, pressure 152 bars (2,200 lb/sq in). 200V AC electrical system supplied by two generators on accessory section of main gearbox, ensuring continued supply during autorotation. Low airspeed system standard, giving speed and drift via main rotor blade-tip pitot tubes at −7 to +42 km/h (−3.7 to +22 knots; −4.3 to +26 mph). Main and tail blades electrically de-iced.

AVIONICS: Conventional IFR instrumentation, with auto-stabilisation, autohover, and hover/heading hold lock in attack mode. Standard UHF/VHF nav/com. Pilot has head-up display and centrally mounted CRT for basic TV (and, later, FLIR/LLTV). Radio for missile guidance in nose radome. Radar warning receivers fitted. Small IFF fairing on each side of nose and tail. Daylight optical weapons sight and laser ranger/designator in double-glazed nose turret above gun, with which it rotates through ±110°. Wiper on outer glass which protects inner optically flat panel. Cylindrical container on each side of this turret for FLIR and low light level TV night vision systems (not fitted to aircraft in Paris). Aircraft designed for use with night vision goggles.

EQUIPMENT: Two slots, one above the other on port side of tailboom, for colour-coded identification flares. Three pairs of rectangular formation-keeping lights in top of tailboom and one further pair in top of main rotor pylon fairing. Infra-red suppressors and infra-red decoy dispensers.

ARMAMENT: One modified Type 2A42 30 mm turret mounted gun (with 300 rds) at nose, able to rotate ±110°, elevate 13° and depress 40°. Rates of fire 900 rds/min air-to-air, 300 rds/min air-to-ground. (A new specially designed gun is under development.) Two pylons under each stub wing, each with capacity of 480 kg (1058 lb), typically for a total of 16 improved AT-6 (NATO 'Spiral') radio guided tube-launched anti-tank missiles and two UV-20 pods of twenty 57 mm or 80 mm rockets. The gun is fired and guided weapons launched only from the front cockpit; unguided rockets can be fired from both cockpits.

DIMENSIONS, EXTERNAL:

Main rotor diameter	17.20 m (56 ft 5 in)
Tail rotor diameter	3.84 m (12 ft 7¼ in)
Length overall, excl rotors	16.85 m (55 ft 3½ in)
Width over stub wings	4.87 m (16 ft 0 in)
Height overall	4.81 m (15 ft 9½ in)

AREAS:

Main rotor disc	232.3 m² (2,501 sq ft)

WEIGHTS AND LOADINGS:

Weight empty	7,000 kg (15,430 lb)
Max T-O weight	10,400 kg (22,925 lb)
Max disc loading	44.77 kg/m² (9.17 lb/sq ft)

PERFORMANCE:

Max level speed	162 knots (300 km/h; 186 mph)
Max cruising speed	146 knots (270 km/h; 168 mph)
Service ceiling	5,800 m (19,025 ft)
Hovering ceiling OGE	3,600 m (11,800 ft)
Range with max fuel	253 nm (470 km; 292 miles)
Endurance with max fuel	2 h
g limits	+3/−0.5

MIL Mi-34
NATO reporting name: Hermit

TYPE: Lightweight two/four-seat multi-purpose helicopter.

PROGRAMME: First flight 1986; two prototypes and structure test airframe completed by mid-1987, when exhibited for first time at Paris Air Show; first Soviet helicopter to perform normal loop and roll; offered as replacement for DOSAAF's aging helicopter trainers, in competition with Polish turbine-powered PZL Swidnik SW-4; in 1989, quantity production said to be planned "for near future".

DESIGN FEATURES: Intended primarily for training and international competition flying; conventional pod and boom configuration; piston-engine of same basic type as that in DOSAAF's Yakovlev fixed-wing training aircraft and Kamov Ka-26 helicopters; suitable also for light utility, observation and liaison duties, and border patrol.

FLYING CONTROLS: Mechanical, with no hydraulic boost.

STRUCTURE: Semi-articulated four-blade main rotor with flapping and cyclic pitch hinges, but natural flexing in lead/lag plane; blades of glassfibre with carbonfibre reinforcement, attached by flexible steel straps to head like that of McDonnell Douglas MD 500; two-blade rotor of similar composites construction, on starboard side; riveted light alloy fuselage; sweptback tail fin with small unswept T tailplane.

LANDING GEAR: Conventional non-retractable skids on arched support tubes. Small tailskid to protect tail rotor.

POWER PLANT: One 242 kW (325 hp) Vedeneyev M-14V-26 nine-cylinder radial aircooled engine mounted sideways in the centre-fuselage. Fuel system for inverted flight.

ACCOMMODATION: Normally one or two pilots, side by side, in enclosed cabin, with optional dual controls. Rear of cabin contains low bench seat, available for two passengers and offering a flat floor for cargo carrying. Forward hinged door on each side of flight deck and on each side of rear cabin.

DIMENSIONS, EXTERNAL:
Main rotor diameter	10.00 m (32 ft 9¾ in)
Tail rotor diameter	1.48 m (4 ft 10¼ in)
Length of fuselage	8.71 m (28 ft 7 in)
Width of fuselage	1.42 m (4 ft 8 in)
Skid track	2.06 m (6 ft 9¼ in)

AREAS:
Main rotor disc	78.5 m² (845 sq ft)

WEIGHTS AND LOADINGS:
Fuel weight	120 kg (265 lb)
T-O weight, training and aerobatic missions:	
Normal	1,260 kg (2,777 lb)
Max	1,350 kg (2,976 lb)
Max disc loading	17.2 kg/m² (3.52 lb/sq ft)

PERFORMANCE (at T-O weight of 1,300 kg; 2,866 lb, except where indicated):
Max level speed	113 knots (210 km/h; 130 mph)
Max cruising speed	97 knots (180 km/h; 112 mph)
Normal cruising speed	86 knots (160 km/h; 99 mph)
Max speed rearward at AUW of 1,020 kg (2,249 lb)	70 knots (130 km/h; 80 mph)
Service ceiling	4,500 m (14,765 ft)
Hovering ceiling	1,500 m (4,920 ft)

Range at T-O weight of 1,250 kg (2,755 lb):
with 165 kg (363 lb) payload	97 nm (180 km; 112 miles)
with 90 kg (198 lb) payload	242 nm (450 km; 280 miles)

g limits at AUW of 1,020 kg (2,249 lb) and speeds of 27-81 knots (50-150 km/h; 31-93 mph)   +2.5/−0.5

MIL Mi-34V

The Mi-34V now in development is to be powered by two VAZ-430 twin-chamber rotary engines each giving 164 kW (220 hp) for take-off and 201 kW (270 hp) for contingency. They are produced by VAZ motorcar works in Togliattigrad and first flight is expected in 1993. The engines burn Mogas and have a power:weight ratio of 0.5 kg (1.1 lb)/hp. The Mi-34V should sell for under $400,000.

MIL Mi-35

The **Mi-35** is an export version of the Mi-24W. The **Mi-35P** is an export version of the Mi-24P.

MIL Mi-38

TYPE: Twin-turbine multi-role medium-range helicopter.

PROGRAMME: Model shown at 1989 Paris Air Show, when aircraft at mockup stage; first flight scheduled 1992-93; production planned to begin 1996.

COSTS: Civil export price about $30 million.

DESIGN FEATURES: Conventional pod and boom configuration; power plant above cabin; five-blade main rotor with considerable non-linear twist and swept tips; two independent two-blade tail rotors, set as narrow X on same shaft; large port-side passenger/freight door at front of cabin; clamshell rear loading doors and ramp; hatch in cabin floor, under main rotor driveshaft, for tactical/emergency cargo airdrop and for cargo sling attachment; optional windows for survey cameras in place of hatch; sweptback fin/tail rotor mounting, canted to starboard; small horizontal stabiliser; Mi-38 planned as Mi-8/17 series replacement; designed to FAR Pt 29 standards, for day/night operation over temperature range −60°C to +50°C: Western engines optional.

Prototype of the Mil Mi-34 (Vedeneyev M-14V-26 engine) *(Piotr Butowski)*

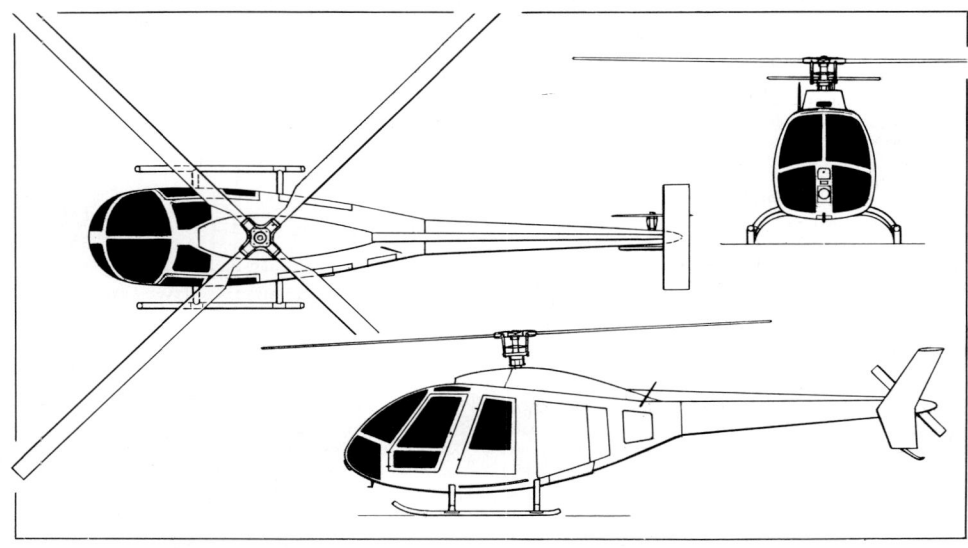

Mil Mi-34 two/four-seat training and competition helicopter *(Pilot Press)*

Model of projected twin-turbine Mil Mi-34V light helicopter *(Piotr Butowski)*

FLYING CONTROLS: Fly-by-wire, with manual backup.

STRUCTURE: Composites main and tail rotors, with elastomeric bearings; main rotor has hydraulic drag dampers; single lubrication point, at driveshaft; fuselage mainly composites.

LANDING GEAR: Retractable tricycle type, with twin wheels on each unit. Nose gear retracts forward under floor of flight deck. Main units retract into sponsons on sides of the cabin. Low-pressure tyres. Optional pontoons for emergency use in overwater missions.

POWER PLANT: Two Leningrad/Klimov TV7-117V turbo-shafts, each flat rated at 1,753 kW (2,350 shp) for T-O. Single-engine rating of 2,386 kW (3,200 shp) and transmission rated for same power. Power plant mounted above cabin, to rear of main reduction gear, with air intakes and filters in sides of cowling. Forward part of cowling houses VD-100 APU, hydraulic, air-conditioning, electrical and other system components. Bag fuel tanks beneath floor of main cabin. Provision for external auxiliary fuel tanks. Liquid petroleum gas fuel planned as alternative to aviation kerosene.

ACCOMMODATION: Crew of two on flight deck, separated from main cabin by compartment for majority of avionics. Single-pilot operation possible for cargo missions. Lightweight seats for up to 32 passengers as alternative to unobstructed hold for 5,000 kg (11,020 lb) of freight. Ambulance and air survey versions are planned. Provision for hoist over port-side passenger/

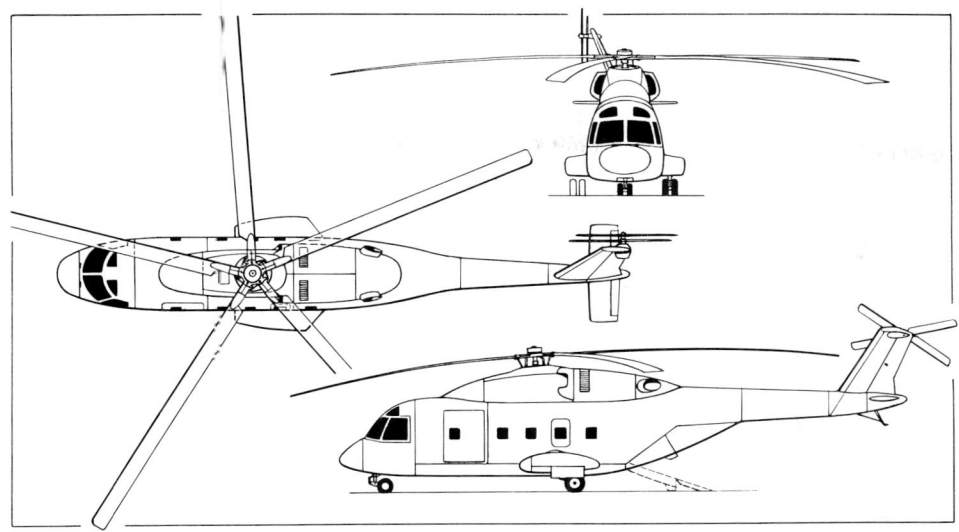

Mil Mi-38 medium-range helicopter to replace the Mi-8/17 *(Pilot Press)*

DIMENSIONS, EXTERNAL:	
Main rotor diameter	21.10 m (69 ft 2¾ in)
Tail rotor diameter	3.84 m (12 ft 7¼ in)
Length overall, excl rotors	19.70 m (64 ft 7½ in)
Stabiliser span	3.60 m (11 ft 9¾ in)
Wheel track, c/l of oleos	3.30 m (10 ft 10 in)
Wheelbase	6.61 m (21 ft 8¼ in)
Forward freight door: Width	1.50 m (4 ft 11 in)
Height	1.70 m (5 ft 7 in)
Floor hatch: Length	1.15 m (3 ft 9¼ in)
Width	0.75 m (2 ft 5½ in)
DIMENSIONS, INTERNAL:	
Main cabin: Length to ramp	6.70 m (22 ft 0 in)
Length, incl fwd part of tailboom	
	10.70 m (35 ft 1¼ in)
Max width	2.40 m (7 ft 10½ in)
Width at floor	2.20 m (7 ft 2½ in)
Height: centre	1.80 m (5 ft 11 in)
rear	1.85 m (6 ft 1 in)
AREAS:	
Main rotor disc	350 m² (3,764 sq ft)
WEIGHTS AND LOADINGS (provisional):	
Max payload	5,000 kg (11,020 lb)
Normal T-O weight	13,460 kg (29,672 lb)
Max T-O weight	14,500 kg (31,965 lb)
Max disc loading	41.4 kg/m² (8.49 lb/sq ft)
Max power loading	6.07 kg/kW (9.98 lb/shp)
PERFORMANCE (estimated at max T-O weight):	
Max level speed	148 knots (275 km/h; 171 mph)
Cruising speed	135 knots (250 km/h; 155 mph)
Service ceiling	6,500 m (21,325 ft)
Hovering ceiling OGE	2,500 m (8,200 ft)
Range, 30 min reserves:	
with 5,000 kg (11,020 lb) payload	
	175 nm (325 km; 202 miles)
with 4,500 kg (9,920 lb) payload (32 passengers and baggage)	286 nm (530 km; 329 miles)
with 3,500 kg (7,715 lb) payload and standard fuel	430 nm (800 km; 497 miles)
with 1,800 kg (3,965 lb) payload and auxiliary fuel	700 nm (1,300 km; 808 miles)

freight door, remotely controlled hydraulically actuated rear cargo ramp, powered hoist on overhead rails in cabin, and roller conveyor system in cabin floor and ramp.

SYSTEMS: Air-conditioning by compressor bleed air, or APU on the ground, maintains a temperature of not more than 25°C on flight deck in outside temperature of 40°C, and not less than 15°C on flight deck and in main cabin in outside temperature of –50°C. Three independent hydraulic systems, any one of which is able to maintain control of the helicopter in an emergency. Electrical system has three independent AC generators, two batteries, and transformer/rectifiers for DC supply. Electric rotor blade de-icing. Independent fuel system for each engine, with automatic cross-feed.

AVIONICS: Five colour CRTs on flight deck for use in flight and by servicing personnel on the ground. Pre-set flight control system allows full autopilot, autohover and automatic landing. Equipment monitoring, failure warning and damage control system. Avionics controlled by large central computer, linked also to automatic navigation system with Doppler, ILS, satellite navigation system, weather/navigation radar (range 54 nm; 100 km; 62 miles), autostabilisation system and automatic radio compass. Closed-circuit TV for monitoring cargo loading and slung loads. Other options include low-cost electro-mechanical instrumentation based on that of Mi-8, sensors for weighing and CG positioning of cargo in cabin, and for checking the weight of slung loads.

MYASISHCHEV
MYASISHCHEV DESIGN BUREAU

The Myasishchev OKB was founded in 1951, under the leadership of Professor Vladimir Mikhailovich Myasishchev, who died on 14 October 1978, aged 76. In the 1970s, responsibility for the OKB, and the Experimentalnyy Mashinostroitelnyy Zavod 'Serp i Molot' imeni V. Myasishcheva (V. Myasishchev Experimental Machine Factory 'Hammer and Sickle') that builds its designs, was taken over by the Molniya Scientific and Industrial Enterprise.

MYASISHCHEV M-4
NATO reporting name: Bison

TYPE: Single-point probe and drogue flight refuelling tanker.

PROGRAMME: Conversion of strategic bomber and maritime reconnaissance aircraft; being replaced by Il-78 (NATO 'Midas').

CUSTOMERS: Soviet air forces; about 40 remain, to service Tu-22/22M/95/142 attack force.

POWER PLANT: Four Mikulin AM-3D turbojets, each 85.3 kN (19,180 lb st).

Other details as for M-4 ('Bison') bomber, described in previous editions of *Jane's*.

DIMENSIONS, EXTERNAL (basic 'Bison-A' strategic bomber):
Wing span 50.48 m (165 ft 7½ in)
Length overall 47.20 m (154 ft 10 in)
Tailplane span 15.00 m (49 ft 2½ in)

WEIGHTS AND LOADINGS (basic 'Bison-A' strategic bomber):
Max T-O weight 158,750 kg (350,000 lb)

PERFORMANCE (basic 'Bison-A' strategic bomber, estimated):
Max level speed at 11,000 m (36,000 ft)
  538 knots (998 km/h: 620 mph)
Service ceiling 13,700 m (45,000 ft)
Max unrefuelled combat radius
  3,025 nm (5,600 km; 3,480 miles)
Range at 450 knots (835 km/h; 520 mph) with more than 5,450 kg (12,000 lb) of bombs
  4,320 nm (8,000 km; 4,970 miles)

MYASISHCHEV VM-T ATLANT

TYPE: Four-turbojet transport for outsize external payloads.

DESIGN FEATURES: Conversion of M-4 strategic bomber (SSSR-01502), to carry above its fuselage loads such as *Buran* space shuttle orbiter and large components of Energiya rocket launch vehicle; standard sweptback vertical tail surfaces replaced by twin endplate fins and rudders of rectangular shape; max payload 40 metric tons, requiring removal of *Buran*'s orbital manoeuvring system engines, tail fin and other components before it can be transported; later Antonov An-225, developed as replacement for VM-T Atlant, carries complete space shuttle orbiter.

Myasishchev VM-T Atlant, an M-4 bomber adapted to carry loads in canisters or sections of the Energiya launch vehicle *(Quadrant/Flight)*

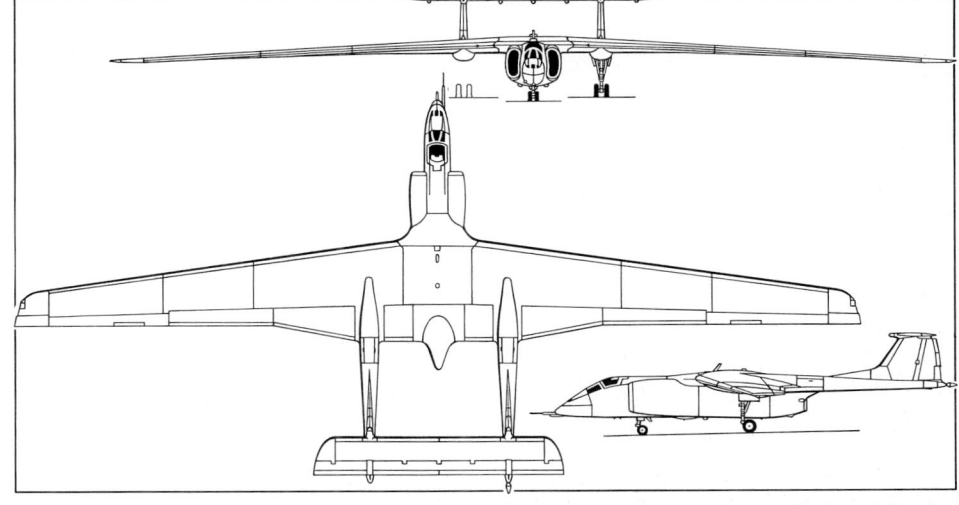

Myasishchev M-17 ('Mystic-A') reconnaissance and environmental research aircraft *(Jane's/Mike Keep)*

MYASISHCHEV M-17

NATO reporting name: Mystic

TYPE: Single-seat high-altitude research aircraft.

PROGRAMME: 'Mystic-A' prototype observed at Ramenskoye flight test centre 1982, given provisional US designation 'Ram-M'; two prototypes, plus two 'Mystic-B' prototypes, completed by 1990; publicised as civilian research aircraft; 25 international records set by 'Mystic-A' 28 March-14 May 1990, in classes Cli/j, for speed, climb and height, including 396 knots (734 km/h; 456 mph) around 500 km closed circuit and sustained height of 21,880 m (71,785 ft), subject to confirmation.

VARIANTS: **M-17 Stratosfera** ('Mystic-A'): First two aircraft, each with single RKBM RD-36-51V turbojet said to be developed from engine used in long-retired Tu-144 supersonic transport, rated at 68.6 kN (15,430 lb st) in non-afterburning form; aircraft SSSR-17401 used in 1989-90 for atmospheric research flights, including studies of ozone layer, and for record flying; aircraft SSSR-17103 in outdoor display of historic aircraft, Monino.

M-17 Geofizika ('Mystic-B'): Basically as Stratosfera, but with two Soloviev engines, each 49 kN (11,025 lb st), side by side at rear of fuselage pod; lengthened and more capacious nose; raised cockpit; small underfuselage radome forward of nosewheels; example in officially released photographs (SSSR-01552) has Aeroflot insignia and said to be for environmental research; smaller wing span than 'Mystic-A'. Designed probably for reconnaissance.

At design stage is M-17 variant with conventional fuselage, sweptback conventional tail unit, and twin engines on sides of fuselage beneath wingroots.

DESIGN FEATURES: High aspect ratio high-wing configuration, with central fuselage pod and twin tailbooms with bridging T-tailplane; side air ducts for engine(s), mounted at rear of fuselage pod; constant wing anhedral from roots; long and shallow ventral strake under port tailboom; assumed to have similar powered sailplane performance to US Lockheed U-2 series; large compartment in lower fuselage for cameras and other sensors.

FLYING CONTROLS: Aileron, with tab, and three-section flaps over most of each wing trailing-edge; elevators and twin rudders, with tabs.

LANDING GEAR: Retractable tricycle type; twin wheels on each unit; all units retract rearward, mainwheels into tailbooms.

POWER PLANT: See Variants.

ACCOMMODATION: Single seat under rearward hinged canopy.

DIMENSIONS, EXTERNAL (estimated. A: 'Mystic-A', B: 'Mystic-B'):

Wing span: A	40.7 m (133 ft 6½ in)
B	37.5 m (123 ft 0½ in)
Length overall: A	21.2 m (69 ft 6½ in)
B	22.7 m (74 ft 5¾ in)
Height overall: A	5.25 m (17 ft 3 in)
B	4.8 m (15 ft 9 in)
Wheel track: A	6.65 m (21 ft 10 in)
Wheelbase: A	5.6 m (18 ft 4½ in)

WEIGHTS AND LOADINGS (record flights):

Max T-O weight: A	19,950 kg (44,000 lb)
Power loading: A	290.8 kg/kN (2.85 lb/lb st)

PERFORMANCE:

Max level speed:	
B	377-405 knots (700-750 km/h; 435-466 mph)
Service ceiling	20,000 m (65,600 ft)
Max endurance at 17,000 m (55,775 ft)	6 h 30 min

MYASISHCHEV SL

TYPE: Projected two-seat light aircraft.

PROGRAMME: Shown in model form at Moscow Aerospace '90 exhibition; at design study stage.

DESIGN FEATURES: High-wing monoplane.

LANDING GEAR: Non-retractable; wheels or floats.

POWER PLANT: One 81 kW (108 hp) M-3 or 110 kW (148 hp) M-17 piston engine.

Myasishchev M-17 ('Mystic-A') single-engined high-altitude atmospheric research aircraft *(Tass)*

Twin-engined version of the Myasishchev M-17 ('Mystic-B') *(Tass)*

MYASISHCHEV SKIF

TYPE: Projected four/five-seat light aircraft.

PROGRAMME: Shown in model form at Moscow Aerospace '90 exhibition; at design study stage.

DESIGN FEATURES: Conventional cantilever high-wing monoplane; pod and boom fuselage; conventional tail unit with sweptback vertical surfaces.

LANDING GEAR: Non-retractable tricycle type, with single wheel on each unit; cantilever spring main legs.

POWER PLANT: One 221 kW (296 hp) M-16 piston engine, driving three-blade propeller.

ACCOMMODATION: Enclosed cabin for four or five persons.

MYASISHCHEV GJEL

TYPE: Projected four/five-seat turboprop light aircraft.

PROGRAMME: Shown in model form at Moscow Aerospace '90 exhibition; at design stage; first flight will be with 268 kW (360 hp) Vedeneyev M-14P radial piston engine, while awaiting definitive turboprop.

DESIGN FEATURES: Cantilever low-wing monoplane; slight wing forward sweep outboard of centre-section with sweptback leading-edge; enclosed cabin; V tail unit.

LANDING GEAR: Tricycle type; optional floats or skis.

POWER PLANT: Definitive engine will be 373 kW (500 shp) Lyulka AL-34 turboprop, currently under development.

ACCOMMODATION: Four or five persons.

MYASISHCHEV DELFINE

TYPE: Projected twin-turboprop four/nine-seat business aircraft.

PROGRAMME: Shown in model form at Moscow Aerospace '90 exhibition; at design study stage.

DESIGN FEATURES: High aspect ratio low-mounted wings, with slight sweepback; pressurised circular section fuselage; tailplane mid-mounted on sweptback fin; engines pylon-mounted above wing trailing-edge, with pusher propellers.

LANDING GEAR: Retractable tricycle type, with single wheel on each main unit.

POWER PLANT: Two 746 kW (1,000 shp) Lyulka AL-34 turboprops, each driving a five-blade pusher propeller.

ACCOMMODATION: Four to nine persons in enclosed cabin; door at front on port side; overwing emergency exit starboard side.

PERFORMANCE (estimated):

Max cruising speed	272 knots (505 km/h; 314 mph)
Range with max fuel	1,080 nm (2,000 km; 1,240 miles)

MYASISHCHEV/AVIASPETSTRANS YAMAL

TYPE: Twin-turboprop amphibious passenger/freight transport.

PROGRAMME: Development by Aviaspetstrans consortium, comprising Soviet Promstroyebank, Gazprom state enterprise, Okeangueologuiya engineering centre, Arctic and Antarctic research centre, Myasishchev OKB, civil aviation research centre; shown in model form at Moscow Aerospace '90 exhibition.

DESIGN FEATURES: Basically conventional small amphibian; unique power plant; two turboshafts mounted side by side at top of fuselage, driving a pusher propeller mounted behind the tail unit via separate angled driveshafts into a transmission gearbox with single output shaft; this protects engine air intakes from water and foreign object ingestion; flying boat hull and two fixed underwing stabilising floats; small water rudder at extreme rear of hull; servicing of power plant and some hydraulic and electric components possible from inside fuselage, in temperatures down to −35°C in Soviet Baltic, Siberia and Far Eastern regions; thimble nose radome.

LANDING GEAR: Retractable tailwheel type; all units retract upward, main units into fairings each side of hull; two wheels in tandem on each main unit.

POWER PLANT: Two 970 kW (1,300 shp) turboshafts, probably Glushenkov TVD-1500 series.

Myasishchev Skif projected four/five-seat light aircraft *(Tass)*

Model of Myasishchev Gjel turboprop powered light aircraft *(Tass)*

Model of projected Myasishchev Delfine twin-turboprop business aircraft
(Tass)

Myasishchev/Aviaspetstrans Yamal twin-turboshaft amphibian
(Jacques Marmain/Aviation Magazine International, Paris)

ACCOMMODATION: Nominal payloads are 2,000 kg (4,410 lb) of freight or 18 passengers.

DIMENSIONS, EXTERNAL:
Wing span	20.00 m (65 ft 7½ in)
Length overall	15.30 m (50 ft 2½ in)
Height overall	5.30 m (17 ft 4¾ in)

DIMENSIONS, INTERNAL:
Passenger cabin: Volume	23.4 m³ (826 cu ft)

AREAS:
Wings, gross	41.0 m² (442 sq ft)

WEIGHTS AND LOADINGS:
Weight empty, equipped	4,500 kg (9,920 lb)
Max T-O weight	7,200 kg (15,875 lb)
Max wing loading	175.6 kg/m² (35.9 lb/sq ft)
Max power loading	3.71 kg/kW (6.11 lb/shp)

PERFORMANCE (estimated at max T-O weight):
Max cruising speed	226 knots (420 km/h; 261 mph)
T-O run: unprepared field	225 m (740 ft)
water	230 m (755 ft)

Range:
with max payload	270 nm (500 km; 310 miles)
with 500 kg (1,100 lb) payload	
	1,618 nm (3,000 km; 1,864 miles)

SUKHOI
SUKHOI DESIGN BUREAU

23A Polikarpov Street, Moscow 125284
Telephone: 7 (95) 945 6525
Telex: 414716 SUHOI SU
GENERAL DESIGNER: Mikhail Petrovich Simonov
DEPUTY GENERAL DESIGNER: Alexander I. Blinov
CHIEF DESIGNERS:
Alexander I. Grigorenko
Konstantin Marbaschev
DEPUTY CHIEF DESIGNER: Nikolai Fedorovich Nikitin
PROJECT DESIGNER, Su-25: Vladimir P. Babak

This OKB is named for Pavel Osipovich Sukhoi, who headed it from 1939 until his death in September 1975. It remains one of the two primary Soviet centres for development of fighter and attack aircraft, and is widening its activities to include civilian aircraft, under the *konversiya* programme, in some cases with Western partners.

SUKHOI Su-15
NATO reporting name: Flagon
TYPE: Single-seat twin-jet all-weather interceptor and two-seat combat trainer.
PROGRAMME: Developed to 1962 requirement; T-5 prototype flew approx 1964; 10 development aircraft displayed on 1967 Soviet Aviation Day, Moscow; fully operational early 1970s; initial versions last described in 1983-84 *Jane's*; Su-15 now being replaced.
VARIANTS: **'Flagon-E':** Single-seat interceptor; longer span wings than earlier versions, with compound sweep; more powerful turbojets; additional fuel; uprated avionics (NATO 'Twin Scan' radar); major production version, operational second half 1973.

'Flagon-F': Final production version; ogival nose radome instead of earlier conical type; generally as 'Flagon-E' but different engines.

'Flagon-G': Tandem two-seat training version of 'Flagon-F'; probable combat capability; individual rearward hinged canopy over each seat; periscope above rear canopy to enhance forward view; overall length unchanged.
CUSTOMERS: Soviet APVO home defence units; less than 400 remain.
DESIGN FEATURES: Designed as Mach 2.5 interceptor to succeed Su-11; original mid-mounted wings of simple delta form replaced in current versions by wings with extended outer panels, giving compound sweep of 60° inboard, 47° outboard; no dihedral or anhedral; boundary layer fence above weapon pylon on each wing at approx 70 per cent span; basically circular cockpit section with large ogival dielectric nosecone; centre-fuselage faired into toed-in rectangular section air intake ducts; 60° leading-edge sweepback on all tail surfaces; anhedral tailplane with anti-flutter bodies near tips.
FLYING CONTROLS: Each wing trailing-edge comprises aileron and large-chord plain flap; all-moving tailplane; conventional rudder; no trim tabs; top and bottom door-type airbrakes each side of rear fuselage, forward of tailplane.
STRUCTURE: Conventional all-metal.

LANDING GEAR: Tricycle type, with single wheel on each main unit and twin nosewheels, all on levered-suspension legs. Mainwheels retract inward into wings and intake ducts; nosewheels retract forward, with blistered doors. Nosewheels steerable. Brake-chute at base of fin.
POWER PLANT: Two turbojets, with variable area nozzles, mounted side by side in rear fuselage. These are Tumansky R-13F2-300s, each rated at 64.73 kN (14,550 lb st) with afterburning. Ram air intakes, with variable ramps on splitter plates, embodying vertical slots for boundary layer control. Blow-in auxiliary inlets between main intake and wing leading-edge in side of each duct. Fuel tanks in centre-fuselage and wings.
ACCOMMODATION: Single zero/zero ejection seat in enclosed cockpit, with rearward sliding blister canopy. Rearview mirror above canopy of some aircraft.
AVIONICS: Large I-band radar (NATO 'Twin Scan') in nose, SOD-57M ATC/SIF nav system, SRO-2 (NATO 'Odd Rods') IFF, Sirena-3 radar warning system.
ARMAMENT: Two pylons for external stores under each wing. Normal armament comprises one radar homing and one infra-red homing AA-3 air-to-air missile (NATO 'Anab') on outboard pylons, and an infra-red homing AA-8 close-range missile ('Aphid') on each inboard pylon. Side by side pylons under centre-fuselage for weapons, including GSh-23L 23 mm gun pods, or external fuel tanks.

'Flagon-F' twin-jet interceptor, armed with 'Anab' missiles and gun pods *(Swedish Coast Guard/Air Patrol)*

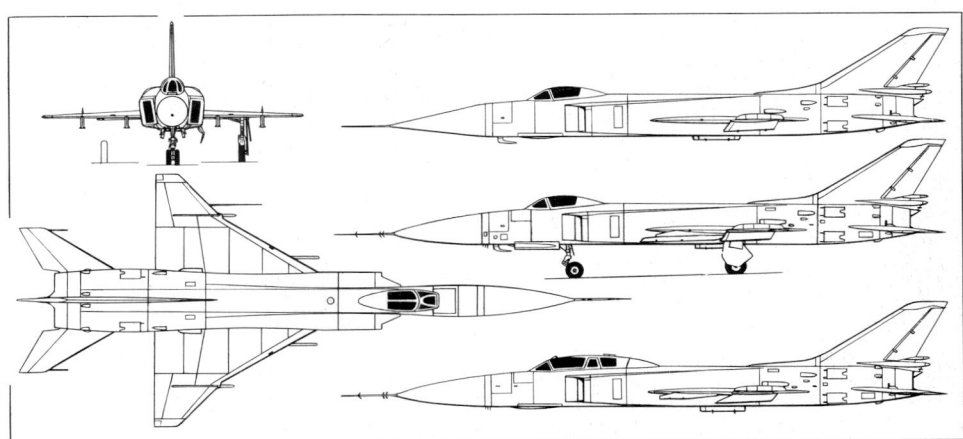

Sukhoi Su-15 ('Flagon-F') single-seat twin-jet all-weather interceptor, with additional side elevations of 'Flagon-E' (top) and 'Flagon-G' (bottom) *(Pilot Press)*

DIMENSIONS, EXTERNAL (estimated):
Wing span   9.15 m (30 ft 0 in)
Length overall   21.33 m (70 ft 0 in)
Height overall   5.10 m (16 ft 8½ in)
WEIGHTS AND LOADINGS (estimated):
Weight empty   11,000 kg (24,250 lb)
Max T-O weight   18,000 kg (39,680 lb)
Max power loading   139.0 kg/kN (1.36 lb/lb st)
PERFORMANCE (estimated):
Max level speed above 11,000 m (36,000 ft) with external
     stores   Mach 2.1
Time to 11,000 m (36,000 ft)   2 min 30 s
Service ceiling   20,000 m (65,600 ft)
Combat radius   538 nm (998 km; 620 miles)

Sukhoi Su-17 reconnaissance aircraft of the Polish Air Force (*Ivo Sturzenegger*)

SUKHOI Su-17, Su-20 and Su-22

NATO reporting names: Fitter-C, D, E, F, G, H, J and K

TYPE: Single-seat variable geometry ground attack fighter, reconnaissance aircraft and two-seat combat trainer.

PROGRAMME: Prototype S-22I or Su-7IG (*Izmenyaemaya Geometriya*; variable geometry) was minimal conversion of fixed-wing Su-7 (NATO 'Fitter-A'); only 4.2 m (13 ft 9 in) of each wing pivoted, outboard of large fence and deepened inboard glove panel; first flew 2 August 1966; shown at Aviation Day display July 1967; given NATO reporting name 'Fitter-B'; two squadrons 'improved Fitter-Bs' in Soviet air forces 1972; AL-21F-3 engine then replaced AL-7 in major Soviet air force production versions, beginning with 'Fitter-C'.

VARIANTS: **Su-17** (S-32, 'Fitter-C'): Single-seat attack aircraft; AL-21F-3 engine; eight stores pylons; additional wing fence on each glove panel; curved dorsal fin; operational with Soviet air forces and Naval Aviation since 1971 in relatively small numbers.

Su-17M (S-32M, 'Fitter-D'): Generally as Su-17, but forward fuselage lengthened by 0.38 m (15 in) and drooped 3° to improve pilot's view while keeping intake face vertical; added undernose Doppler navigation radar pod; laser rangefinder in intake centrebody.

Su-17U (U-32, 'Fitter-E'): Tandem two-seat trainer version of Su-17M, without Doppler pod; deepened dorsal spine fairing for additional fuel tankage; port wingroot gun deleted.

Su-17UM ('Fitter-G'): Two-seat trainer version of Su-17M-1 with combat capability; drooped forward fuselage and deepened spine like Su-17U; taller vertical tail surfaces; removable ventral fin; starboard wingroot gun only; laser rangefinder in intake centrebody.

Su-17M-1/M-2 ('Fitter-H'): Improved single-seater; same deepened spine and tail modifications as Su-17UM; Doppler navigation radar internally in deepened undersurface of nose; gun in each wingroot; total of approx 165 'Fitter-H/Ks' equipped for Soviet tactical reconnaissance carry, typically, centreline sensor pod, active ECM pod under port wing glove, two underwing fuel tanks.

Su-17M-3 ('Fitter-H'): As Su-17M-1, but improved avionics; launcher for AA-8 ('Aphid') air-to-air missile between each pair of underwing pylons.

Su-17M-4 ('Fitter-K'): Single-seat version, identified 1984; cooling air intake at front of dorsal fin; otherwise as Su-17M-3.

Su-20 ('Fitter-C'): Export version of basic Su-17.

All Su-17s and Su-20s have AL-21F-3 engine; other export aircraft have Tumansky R-29BS-300 (112.8 kN; 25,350 lb st with afterburning) in more bulged rear fuselage, with rearranged small external air intakes on rear fuselage and shorter plain metal shroud terminating fuselage, as follows:

Su-22U ('Fitter-E'): As Su-17U but Tumansky engine.

Su-22 ('Fitter-F'): Export Su-17M; modified undernose electronics pod, R-29 engine; gun in each wingroot; weapons include AA-2 ('Atoll') air-to-air missiles; aircraft supplied to Peru had Sirena-2 limited coverage radar warning system and virtually no navigation aids; some basic US-supplied avionics retrofitted.

Su-22 ('Fitter-G'): Export Su-17UM; R-29 engine.

Su-22M-2 ('Fitter-J'): As Su-17M-2 but R-29 engine; internal fuel tankage 6,270 litres (1,656 US gallons; 1,379 Imp gallons); more angular dorsal fin; AA-2 ('Atoll') air-to-air missiles.

Su-22M-4 ('Fitter-K'): As Su-17M-4 but R-29 engine.

CUSTOMERS: Soviet air forces (many of 1,060 Su-17s of all versions deployed in late 1980s since put into storage, assigned to training schools and passed to Soviet Naval Aviation to supplement 75 deployed originally for anti-shipping strike and amphibious support in Baltic Sea and Pacific areas); air forces of Afghanistan (Su-22), Algeria (Su-20), Angola (Su-22), Czechoslovakia (Su-20/22M-4), the former East Germany (Su-22/22M-4), Egypt (Su-20), Hungary (Su-22M-2), Iraq (Su-20), North Korea (Su-22), Libya (Su-22/22M-2), Peru (Su-22/22M-2), Poland (Su-20/22M-4), Syria (Su-22), Vietnam (Su-22), Yemen (Su-22).

Description applies to basic Su-17, except where indicated.

DESIGN FEATURES: Modest amount of variable geometry added to original fixed-wing Su-7 permitted doubled external load from strips little more than half as long,

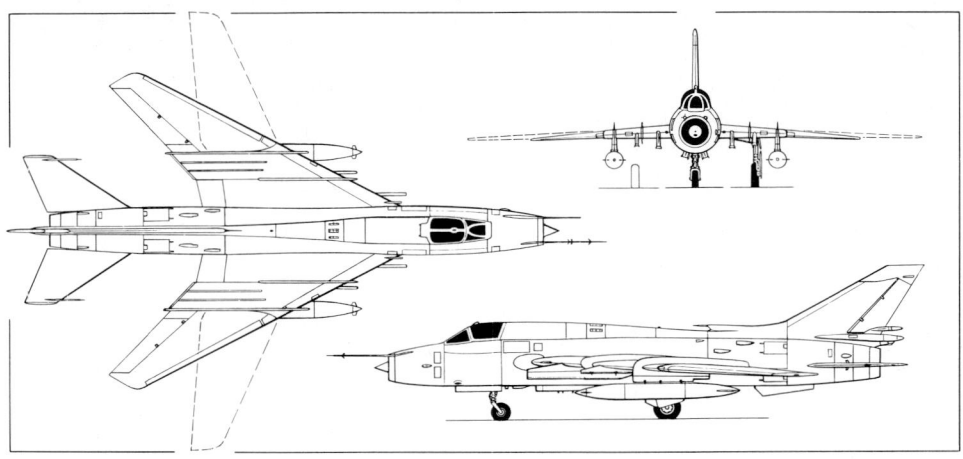

Su-17M-4 ('Fitter-K'), latest single-seat version of the variable geometry 'Fitter' series (*Pilot Press*)

Sukhoi Su-22M-4 ('Fitter-K') of the Polish Air Force (*Piotr Butowski*)

Sukhoi Su-22 ('Fitter-G') of former East German Air Force (*Ivo Sturzenegger*)

and 30 per cent greater combat radius; progressive refinements led to very effective final versions. Conventional mid-wing all-swept monoplane, except for variable geometry outer wings with manually selected positions of 28°, 45°, 63°; wide-span fixed centre-section glove panels; basically circular fuselage with dorsal spine; ram intake with variable shock-cone centrebody; pitot on port side of nose, transducer to provide pitch and yaw data for fire control computer starboard; anti-flutter bodies near tailplane tips.

FLYING CONTROLS: Slotted ailerons operable at all times; slotted trailing-edge flap on each variable geometry wing panel operable only when wings spread; area-increasing flap on each centre-section glove panel; full-span leading-edge slats on variable geometry wing panels; top and bottom door-type airbrakes each side of rear fuselage, forward of tailplane; all-moving horizontal tail surfaces; conventional rudder; no tabs.

STRUCTURE: All-metal; semi-monocoque fuselage; large main wing fence on each side, at junction of fixed and movable panels, square-cut at front, with attachment for external store; shorter fence above glove panel each side.

LANDING GEAR: Retractable tricycle type, with single wheel on each unit. Nosewheel retracts forward, requiring blistered door to enclose it. Main units retract inward into centre-section. Container for single cruciform brake-chute between base of rudder and tailpipe.

POWER PLANT: One Saturn/Lyulka AL-21F-3 turbojet, rated at 76.5 kN (17,200 lb st) dry and 110 kN (24,700 lb st) with afterburning. Fuel capacity increased to 4,550 litres (1,202 US gallons; 1,000 Imp gallons) by added tankage in dorsal spine fairing. Provision for carrying up to four 800 litre (211 US gallon; 176 Imp gallon) drop tanks on outboard wing pylons and under fuselage. When underfuselage tanks are carried, only the two inboard wing pylons may be used for ordnance, to a total weight of 1,000 kg (2,204 lb). Two solid propellant rocket units can be attached to rear fuselage to shorten T-O run.

ACCOMMODATION: Pilot only, on ejection seat, under rearward hinged transparent canopy. Rearview mirror above canopy.

AVIONICS: SRD-5M (NATO 'High Fix') I-band ranging radar in intake centrebody; ASP-5ND fire control system; HUD standard; Sirena-3 radar warning system providing 360° coverage, with antennae in slim cylindrical housing above brake-chute container and in each centre-section leading-edge, between fences; SRO-2M IFF; SOD-57M ATC/SIF, with transponder housing beneath brake-chute container; SP-50 ILS, RSB-70 HF and RSIU-5/R-831 UHF/VHF.

ARMAMENT: Two 30 mm NR-30 guns, each with 80 rds, in wingroot leading-edges. Total of nine weapon pylons (one on centreline, two tandem pairs under fuselage, one under each centre-section leading-edge, one under each main wing fence) for more than 3,175 kg (7,000 lb) of bombs, including nuclear weapons, rocket pods, 23 mm gun pods and guided missiles such as the air-to-surface AS-7 (NATO 'Kerry', AS-9 ('Kyle') and AS-10 ('Karen').

DIMENSIONS, EXTERNAL:

Wing span: fully spread	13.80 m (45 ft 3 in)
fully swept	10.00 m (32 ft 10 in)
Wing aspect ratio: fully spread	4.8
fully swept	2.7
Length overall, incl probes	18.75 m (61 ft 6¼ in)
Fuselage length	15.40 m (50 ft 6¼ in)
Height overall	5.00 m (16 ft 5 in)

AREAS (estimated):

Wings, gross: fully spread	40.0 m² (430.0 sq ft)
fully swept	37.0 m² (398.0 sq ft)

WEIGHTS AND LOADINGS (Su-17M-4):

Max external stores	4,250 kg (9,370 lb)
Normal T-O weight	16,400 kg (36,155 lb)
Max T-O weight	19,500 kg (42,990 lb)
Max wing loading: spread	487.5 kg/m² (100 lb/sq ft)
swept	527 kg/m² (108 lb/sq ft)
Max power loading	177.3 kg/kN (1.74 lb/lb st)

PERFORMANCE (Su-17M-4):

Max level speed: at height	Mach 2.09
at S/L	Mach 1.14
	(755 knots; 1,400 km/h; 870 mph)
Service ceiling	15,200 m (49,865 ft)
T-O run	900 m (2,955 ft)
Landing run	950 m (3,120 ft)
Range with max fuel:	
at high altitude	1,240 nm (2,300 km; 1,430 miles)
at low altitude	755 nm (1,400 km; 870 miles)

SUKHOI Su-24

NATO reporting name: Fencer

TYPE: Two-seat variable geometry 'frontal bomber', reconnaissance and EW aircraft.

PROGRAMME: Design started 1964 under Yevgeniy S. Felsner, Pavel Sukhoi's successor, to replace Il-28 and Yak-28 attack aircraft; T-6-1 prototype, now at Monino, had fixed delta wings with downswept tips, and four auxiliary booster motors mounted vertically in fuselage for improved take-off performance; T-6-21 variable geometry prototype, chosen for production, flew first 1969-70; initial production aircraft designated Su-19; changed to Su-24; by 1981 delivery rate 60-70 a year; by

Sukhoi Su-24 ('Fencer-D') with wings fully spread and landing gear extended *(US Department of Defense)*

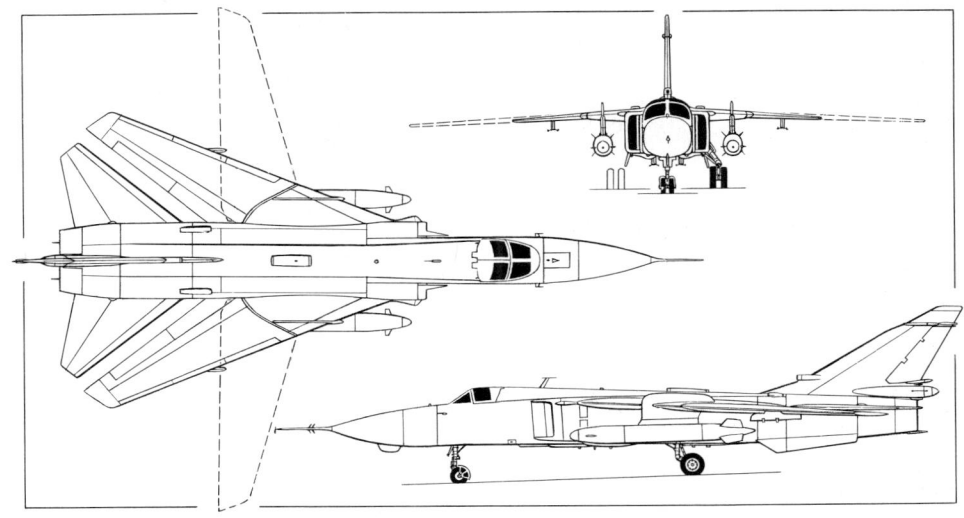

Sukhoi Su-24 ('Fencer-D') variable geometry attack aircraft *(Pilot Press)*

early 1991 many reassigned from Soviet first-line to rear echelon units, or passed to air forces of military districts and groups of forces.

VARIANTS: **'Fencer-A':** Has rectangular rear fuselage box enclosing jet nozzles. Few early aircraft only; deployed with trials unit 1974.

'Fencer-B': First operational version, 1976. Deeply dished bottom skin to rear fuselage box between jet nozzles; larger brake-chute housing.

'Fencer-C': Introduced 1981; important avionics changes; multiple nose fitting instead of former simple probe; triangular fairing for radar warning receiver on side of each engine air intake, forward of fixed wingroot, and each side of fin tip; kinked tail fin leading-edge.

'Fencer-D' (Su-24MK): First flew 1977; entered service 1983; believed to have terrain-following radar instead of earlier terrain avoidance system; added flight refuelling capability; nose approx 0.75 m (2 ft 6 in) longer to accommodate new avionics bay; large overwing fences with integral extended wingroot glove pylons when carrying AS-14 (NATO 'Kedge') missiles; undernose antennae deleted; laser ranger/designator housing aft of nosewheel bay; single long noseprobe.

'Fencer-E' (Su-24MR): Reconnaissance/EW version of 'Fencer-D'; antenna under nose radome; 'hockey stick' antenna at bottom of fuselage under each engine air intake nose section; air-to-surface missile capability retained; deliveries to Baltic fleet, replacing Tu-16s, began Summer 1985; tactical air force units include two squadrons on Chinese border.

'Fencer-F' (Su-24MP): Electronic jamming/sigint/reconnaissance version to replace 'Brewer-E' model of Yak-28.

CUSTOMERS: More than 800 delivered from Komsomolsk factory; 240 form primary strike element of Legnica and Vinnitsa air armies; 135 with Irkutsk air army in Pacific theatre; others for deep interdiction, maritime reconnaissance with Naval Aviation, etc; air forces of Iraq (15), Libya (15), Syria (12 ordered).

DESIGN FEATURES: Variable geometry shoulder wing; slight anhedral from roots; triangular fixed glove box; three-position (16°, 45°, 68°) pivoted outer panels; slab-sided rectangular section fuselage; integral engine air intake trunks, each with splitter plate and outer lip inclined slightly downward; chord of lower part of tail fin extended forward, giving kinked leading-edge; leading-edge sweepback 30° on inset rudder, 50° on horizontal tail surfaces; basic operational task, as Soviet-designated 'frontal bomber', to deliver wide range of air-to-surface missiles for defence suppression, with some hard target kill potential; specially developed

long-range navigation system and electro-optical weapons systems make possible penetration of hostile airspace at night or in adverse weather with great precision, to deliver ordnance within 55 m (180 ft) of target.

FLYING CONTROLS: Full-span leading-edge slats, aileron and two-section double-slotted trailing-edge flaps on each outer wing panel; differential spoilers forward of flaps for roll control at low speeds and use as lift dumpers on landing; airbrake under each side of centre-fuselage; inset rudder; all-moving horizontal tail surfaces operate collectively for pitch control, differentially for roll control, assisted by wing spoilers except when wings fully swept.

STRUCTURE: All-metal; semi-monocoque fuselage; two slightly splayed ventral fins.

LANDING GEAR: Retractable tricycle type, with twin wheels on each unit. Main units retract forward and inward into air intake duct fairings; nose unit retracts rearward. Trailing link type of shock absorbers in main units and low pressure tyres for operation from semi-prepared fields. Mudguard on nosewheels.

POWER PLANT: Two Saturn/Lyulka AL-21F-3A turbojets, each rated at 110 kN (24,700 lb st) with afterburning. Variable intake ramps. Internal fuel capacity, estimated at 13,000 litres (3,434 US gallons; 2,860 Imp gallons), can be supplemented by four 1,250 litre (330 US gallon; 275 Imp gallon) external tanks on underbelly and glove pylons. Probe-and-drogue flight refuelling capability, including operation as buddy tanker.

ACCOMMODATION: Crew of two (pilot and weapon systems officer) side by side on ejection seats. Cockpit width 1.65 m (5 ft 5 in). Jettisonable canopy, hinged to open upward and rearward in two panels, split on centreline.

AVIONICS: Large radar in nose. Laser ranger/designator under front fuselage. Radar warning receivers on sides of engine air intakes and tail fin. Active anti-radar suppression equipment.

ARMAMENT: Nine pylons under fuselage, each wingroot glove and outer wings for guided and unguided air-to-surface weapons, including TN-1000 and TN-1200 nuclear weapons, missiles such as AS-7 (NATO 'Kerry'), AS-10 ('Karen'), AS-11 ('Kilter'), AS-12 ('Kegler'), AS-13 ('Kingbolt') and AS-14 ('Kedge'), rockets of 57 mm to 370 mm calibre, bombs (typically 36 × 100 kg FAB-100), 23 mm gun pods or external fuel tanks. Two pivoting underwing pylons were the first of their kind observed on a Soviet aircraft. No internal weapons bay. One six-barrel 23 mm Gatling type gun inside fairing on starboard side of fuselage undersurface. Unidentified fairing on other side.

The first good photograph of a fully equipped Sukhoi Su-24 ('Fencer-E') maritime reconnaissance aircraft *(Swedish Air Force, via FLYGvapenNYTT)*

DIMENSIONS, EXTERNAL:
Wing span: spread	17.63 m (57 ft 10 in)
swept	10.36 m (34 ft 0 in)
Length overall, incl probe	24.53 m (80 ft 5¾ in)
Height overall	4.97 m (16 ft 3¾ in)
Wheel track	3.70 m (12 ft 1½ in)

AREAS:
Wings, gross	42.00 m² (452.1 sq ft)

WEIGHTS AND LOADINGS:
Weight empty, equipped	19,000 kg (41,885 lb)
Max external stores	8,000 kg (17,635 lb)
Normal T-O weight	36,000 kg (79,365 lb)
Max T-O weight	39,700 kg (87,520 lb)
Max wing loading	945.2 kg/m² (193.6 lb/sq ft)
Max power loading	180.5 kg/kN (1.77 lb/lb st)

PERFORMANCE:
Max level speed, clean: at height	Mach 2.18
at S/L	Mach 1.15
Service ceiling	17,500 m (57,400 ft)
T-O run	1,300 m (4,265 ft)
Landing run	950 m (3,120 ft)

Combat radius:
lo-lo-lo	over 174 nm (322 km; 200 miles)
lo-lo-hi with 2,500 kg (5,500 lb) of weapons	515 nm (950 km; 590 miles)
hi-lo-hi, with 3,000 kg (6,615 lb) of weapons and two external tanks	565 nm (1,050 km; 650 miles)

Sukhoi Su-25UB ('Frogfoot-B') operational conversion and weapons trainer *(Lutz Freundt)*

SUKHOI Su-25 and Su-28
NATO reporting name: Frogfoot

TYPE: Single-seat close support aircraft and two-seat trainer.

PROGRAMME: Development began 1968; prototype, known as T-8-1, flew 22 February 1975, with two 25.5 kN (5,732 lb st) non-afterburning versions of Tumansky RD-9 turbojet and integral twin-barrel gun with barrels that could be angled downward by pilot; second prototype, T-8-2, had more powerful non-afterburning versions of R-13, designated R-95Sh, and conventional fixed gun; observed by satellite at Ramenskoye flight test centre 1977, given provisional US designation 'Ram-J'; entered production 1978 with R-95 turbojets; trials unit, followed by squadron of 12, sent to Afghanistan for co-ordinated low-level close support of Soviet ground forces in mountain terrain, with Mi-24 helicopter gunships; fully operational 1984; current versions, built at Tbilisi, have upgraded R-195 turbojets, with pipe-like fitment at end of each engine tailcone; non-waisted undersurface to rear cowlings, which have additional small airscoops (as three-view).

VARIANTS: **Su-25** ('Frogfoot-A'): Single-seat close support aircraft; planned increase of max weapons load to 6,400 kg (14,100 lb). Export version **Su-25K** (*kommercheskiy*; commercial).

Su-25UB ('Frogfoot-B'): Tandem two-seat operational conversion and weapons trainer; first photographs Spring 1989; rear seat raised considerably, giving hump-back appearance; separate hinged portion of continuous framed canopy over each cockpit; taller tail fin, increasing overall height to 5.20 m (17 ft 0¾ in); new IFF blade antenna forward of windscreen instead of SRO-2 (NATO 'Odd Rods'); weapons pylons and gun retained. Export version **Su-25UBK**.

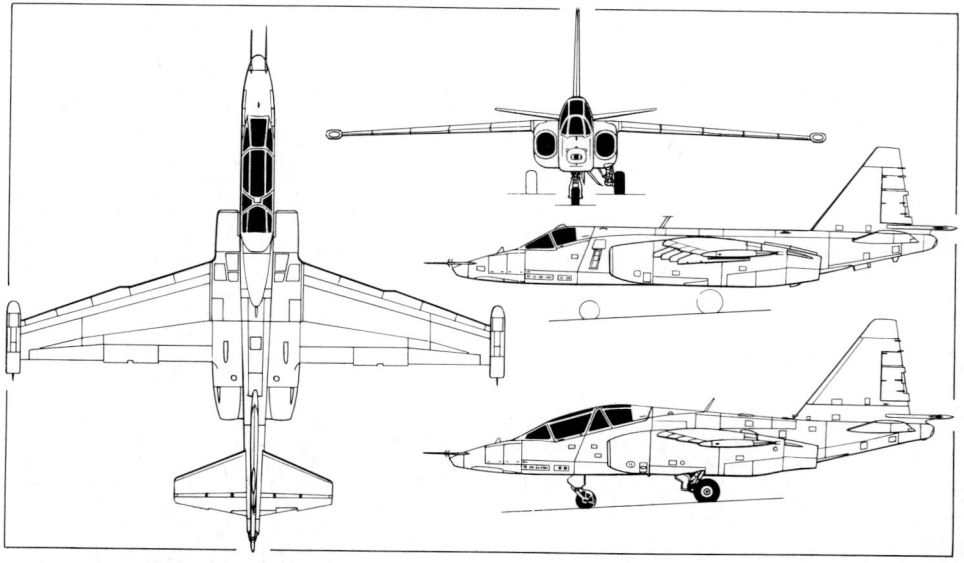

Sukhoi Su-28 (Su-25UT), with added side elevation (centre) of Su-25K *(Pilot Press)*

Sukhoi Su-25 ('Frogfoot-A') in lightly armed training configuration *(Lutz Freundt)*

Sukhoi Su-25K ('Frogfoot-A') combat aircraft of the Czechoslovak Air Force
(Letectvi + Kosmonautika/Václav Jukl)

Su-25UT ('Frogfoot-B'): As Su-25UB, but without weapons; prototype first flew 6 August 1985; demonstrated 1989 Paris Air Show as **Su-28**; overall length 15.36 m (50 ft 4¾ in); few only.

Su-25UTG (G for зak; hook) ('Frogfoot-B'): As Su-25UT, with added arrester hook under tail; used initially for deck landing training on dummy flight deck marked on runway at Saki naval airfield; on 1 November 1989 was third aircraft to land for trials on carrier *Admiral of the Fleet Kuznetsov* (formerly *Tbilisi*), after Su-27K and MiG-29K; one only.

Su-25T: Specialised anti-tank version; hump-back fuselage like Su-25UT: normal front cockpit only; fuselage faired aft of cockpit, to house fuel tankage, avionics and ammunition magazines for new gun; large cylindrical fairing above tailcone; photo of model only by early 1991; in production for 1993 export delivery.

Su-25T: Two-seat variant of above version shown in official Soviet photographs; underwing pylons for anti-tank guided missiles; underbelly gun (starboard) replaces internal gun; wider window for laser rangefinder/designator in more flattened nose; nosewheel offset further to port to clear gun.

Su-25BM (BM for buksir misheney; target towing aircraft): As Su-25 attack aircraft, with added underwing pylons for rocket propelled targets released for missile training by fighter pilots.

CUSTOMERS: More than 300 delivered; Soviet air forces lost 23 in Afghanistan, passed some to Soviet Naval Aviation 1990; exports to Afghanistan, Bulgaria, Czechoslovakia, Hungary and Iraq (45).

Following description applies basically to Su-25K:

DESIGN FEATURES: Shoulder-mounted wings; approx 20° sweepback; anhedral from roots; extended chord leading-edge dogtooth on outer 50 per cent each wing; wingtip pods each split at rear to form airbrakes that project above and below pod when extended; retractable landing light in base of each pod, outboard of small glareshield and aft of dielectric nosecap for ECM; semi-monocoque fuselage, with 24 mm (0.94 in) welded titanium armoured cockpit; pitot on port side of nose, transducer to provide data for fire control computer on starboard side; conventional tail unit; variable incidence tailplane, with slight dihedral.

Emphasis on survivability led to features accounting for 7.5 per cent of normal T-O weight, including welded

cockpit of titanium armour; pushrods instead of cables to actuate flying control surfaces (duplicated for elevators); damage-resistant main load-bearing members; widely separated engines in stainless steel bays; fuel tanks filled with reticulated foam for fire protection.

Maintenance system packaged into four pods for carriage on underwing pylons; covers onboard systems checks, environmental protection, ground electrical power supply for engine starting and other needs, and pressure refuelling from all likely sources of supply in front-line areas; engines can operate on any fuel likely to be found in combat area, including MT petrol and diesel oil.

FLYING CONTROLS: Hydraulically actuated ailerons, with manual backup; multiple tabs in each aileron; double-slotted two-section wing trailing-edge flaps; full-span leading-edge slats, two segments per wing; manually operated elevators and two-section inset rudder; upper rudder section operated through sensor vanes and transducers on nose probe and automatic electro-mechanical yaw damping system; tabs in lower rudder segment and each elevator.

STRUCTURE: All-metal; three-spar wings; semi-monocoque slab-sided fuselage.

LANDING GEAR: Hydraulically retractable tricycle type. Mainwheels retract to lie horizontally in bottom of engine air intake trunks. Single wheel with low-pressure tyre on each levered suspension unit. Oleo-pneumatic shock absorber in each unit. Mudguard on forward retracting steerable nosewheel, which is offset to port. Mainwheel tyres size 840 × 360 mm; nosewheel tyre size 660 × 200 mm. Brakes on mainwheels. Twin cruciform brake-chutes housed in tailcone.

POWER PLANT: Two non-afterburning Tumansky R-195 turbojets in long nacelles at wingroots, each rated at 44.18 kN (9,921 lb st). Fuel tanks in fuselage between cockpit and wing front spar, and between rear spar and fin leading-edge, and in wing centre-section. Provision for external fuel tank on each inboard underwing pylon.

ACCOMMODATION: Single K-36D zero/zero ejection seat under sideways hinged (to starboard) canopy, with small rearview mirror on top. Flat bulletproof windscreen. Folding ladder for access to cockpit built into port side of fuselage.

SYSTEMS: 28V DC electrical system, supplied by two engine driven generators.

AVIONICS: SRO-2 (NATO 'Odd Rods') IFF antennae forward of windscreen and under tail. Sirena-3 radar warning system antenna above fuselage tailcone.

EQUIPMENT: Chaff/flare dispensers (total of 256 flares) carried above root of tailplane and above rear of engine ducts. Strike camera in top of nosecone.

ARMAMENT: One twin-barrel 30 mm gun with rate of fire of 3,000 rds/min in bottom of front fuselage on port side, with 250 rds (sufficient for a one second burst during each of five attacks). Eight large pylons under wings for 4,400 kg (9,700 lb) of air-to-ground weapons, including 57 mm to 370 mm rockets, laser guided rocket-boosted 350 kg, 490 kg and 670 kg bombs, 500 kg incendiary, anti-personnel and chemical cluster bombs, and SPPU-22 pods each containing a 23 mm GSh-23 gun with twin barrels that can pivot downward for attacking ground targets, and 260 rds. Two small outboard pylons for AA-2D 'Atoll' or AA-8 'Aphid' air-to-air self-defence missiles. Laser rangefinder and target designator under flat sloping window in nose.

DIMENSIONS, EXTERNAL (Su-25K):
Wing span	14.36 m (47 ft 1½ in)
Length overall	15.53 m (50 ft 11½ in)
Height	4.80 m (15 ft 9 in)

AREAS:
Wings, gross	33.7 m² (362.75 sq ft)

WEIGHTS AND LOADINGS:
Weight empty	9,500 kg (20,950 lb)
Max T-O weight	14,600-17,600 kg (32,187-38,800 lb)
Max wing loading	522.2 kg/m² (107.0 lb/sq ft)
Max power loading	199.2 kg/kW (1.96 lb/lb st)

PERFORMANCE:
Max level speed at S/L	Mach 0.8
	(526 knots; 975 km/h; 606 mph)
Max attack speed, airbrakes open	
	372 knots (690 km/h; 428 mph)
Landing speed (typical)	108 knots (200 km/h; 124 mph)
Service ceiling	7,000 m (22,965 ft)
T-O run: typical	600 m (1,970 ft)
with max weapon load from unpaved surface	
	under 1,200 m (3,935 ft)
Landing run: normal	600 m (1,970 ft)
with brake-chutes	400 m (1,312 ft)
Range with 4,400 kg (9,700 lb) weapon load and two	
external tanks:	
at S/L	405 nm (750 km; 466 miles)
at height	675 nm (1,250 km; 776 miles)
g limits: with 1,500 kg (3,306 lb) of weapons	+6.5
with 4,400 kg (9,700 lb) of weapons	+5.2

SUKHOI Su-26M

TYPE: Single-seat aerobatic competition aircraft.

PROGRAMME: Su-26 prototype first flew June 1984; took part in World Aerobatic Championships, Hungary, August 1984 (details in 1985-86 *Jane's*); modified Su-26Ms, identified by sharp-cornered (rather than rounded) rudder and reduced fuselage side glazing, gained both men's and women's team prizes 1986 Championships, UK; further refined **Su-26M** shown 1989 Paris Air Show; Soviet pilots had won 61 gold medals in competitions when **Su-26MX** (X for export) appeared at Farnborough Air Show 1990; in production; planned for co-production by Mudry (see French section).

CUSTOMERS: Marketed worldwide, including USA and UK.

DESIGN FEATURES: Typical aerobatic competition aircraft; mid-wing of specially developed symmetrical section, variable along span, slightly concave in region of ailerons to increase their effectiveness; leading-edge somewhat sharper than usual to improve responsiveness to control surface movement; thickness/chord ratio 18 per cent at root, 12 per cent at tip; no dihedral, incidence or sweep at quarter-chord.

FLYING CONTROLS: Mechanical actuation, ailerons and elevators by pushrods, rudder by cables; each aileron has ground adjustable tab on trailing-edge and two suspended triangular balance tabs; no flaps; horn balanced rudder and elevators, each with ground adjustable tab.

STRUCTURE: Composites comprise more than 50 per cent of airframe weight; one-piece two-spar all-composites wing, without ribs, covered with honeycomb composite panels; foam filled front box spar with carbonfibre reinforced plastics (CFRP) booms and wound glassfibre webs; channel section rear spar of CFRP; plain ailerons have CFRP box spar, glassfibre reinforced plastics (GFRP) skin and foam filling; fuselage has basic welded truss structure of VNS-2 high strength stainless steel tubing; lower nose section of truss removable for wing detachment; quickly removable honeycomb composite skin panels; light alloy engine cowlings; fin and tailplane construction same as wings; rudder and elevator construction same as ailerons.

LANDING GEAR: Non-retractable tailwheel type. Arched cantilever mainwheel legs of titanium alloy. Mainwheels size 350 × 135 mm, with hydraulic disc brakes. Steerable tailwheel, on titanium spring, connected to rudder.

POWER PLANT: One 268 kW (360 hp) Vedeneyev M-14P nine-cylinder radial engine, driving a three-blade Gerd Mühlbauer variable-pitch metal propeller. Optional

V-530TA-D35 two-blade variable-pitch propeller. Steel tube engine mounting. Fuel tank in fuselage forward of front spar; capacity 60 litres (16 US gallons; 13 Imp gallons). Tank in each wing leading-edge, total capacity 200 litres (53 US gallons; 44 Imp gallons), for ferry flights. Oil capacity 22.6 litres (6 US gallons; 5 Imp gallons). Fuel and oil systems adapted for inverted flight. Pneumatic engine starting system.

ACCOMMODATION: One-piece pilot's seat of GFRP, inclined at 45° and designed for use with PLP-60 backpack parachute. Rearward hinged jettisonable canopy. Safety harness anchored to fuselage structure.

SYSTEMS: Electrical system of 24/28V, with 3kW generator, batteries and external supply socket.

AVIONICS: Briz VHF radio.

DIMENSIONS, EXTERNAL:
Wing span	7.80 m (25 ft 7 in)
Wing chord: at root	1.95 m (6 ft 4¾ in)
at tip	1.10 m (3 ft 7¼ in)
Wing aspect ratio	5.6
Length overall	6.845 m (22 ft 5½ in)
Height overall	2.78 m (9 ft 1½ in)
Tailplane span	2.95 m (9 ft 8¼ in)
Wheel track	2.20 m (7 ft 2½ in)
Wheelbase	5.05 m (16 ft 6¾ in)
Propeller diameter	2.40 m (7 ft 10½ in)

AREAS:
Wings, gross	11.80 m² (127.0 sq ft)
Ailerons (total)	1.18 m² (12.70 sq ft)
Fin	0.34 m² (3.66 sq ft)
Rudder	0.89 m² (9.58 sq ft)
Tailplane	1.10 m² (11.84 sq ft)
Elevators (total)	1.53 m² (16.47 sq ft)

WEIGHTS AND LOADINGS:
Weight empty	705 kg (1,554 lb)
Max T-O weight	1,000 kg (2,205 lb)
Max wing loading	84.75 kg/m² (17.36 lb/sq ft)
Max power loading	3.73 kg/kW (6.13 lb/hp)

PERFORMANCE:
Never-exceed speed (V$_{NE}$)	243 knots (450 km/h; 280 mph)
Max level speed at S/L	167 knots (310 km/h; 192 mph)
Normal cruising speed	140 knots (260 km/h; 161 mph)
T-O speed	65 knots (120 km/h; 75 mph)
Landing speed	62 knots (115 km/h; 72 mph)
Stalling speed	60 knots (110 km/h; 69 mph)
Max rate of climb at S/L	1,080 m (3,540 ft)/min
Service ceiling	4,000 m (13,125 ft)
Rate of roll	more than 360°/s
T-O run	160 m (525 ft)
Landing run	250 m (820 ft)
Ferry range at 1,000 m (3,280 ft)	432 nm (800 km; 497 miles)
g limits:	+12/−10 (operating)
	+23 (ultimate)

Sukhoi Su-26MX aerobatic competition aircraft *(Peter R. March)*

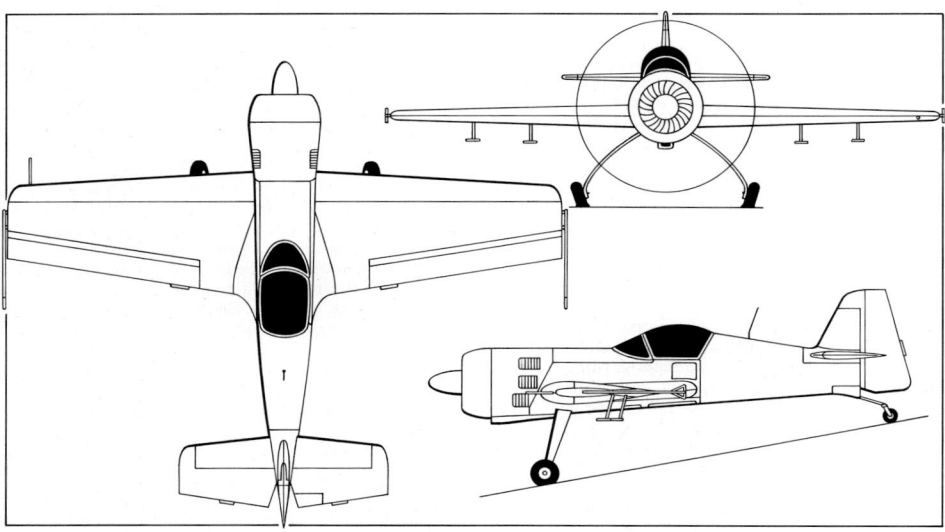

Sukhoi Su-26M single-seat competition aerobatic aircraft *(Jane's/Mike Keep)*

SUKHOI Su-27
NATO reporting name: Flanker

TYPE: Single-seat all-weather counter-air fighter and two-seat combat trainer.

PROGRAMME: Development began 1969 under leadership of Pavel Sukhoi; T-10-1 prototype, built under Mikhail Simonov's supervision, was flown 20 May 1977 by Vladimir Ilyushin; development was not easy; two pilots lost their lives before major airframe redesign resulted in production configuration; production centred in plant at Komsomolsk, Khabarovsk Territory; new versions being developed.

VARIANTS: **Su-27** ('Flanker-A'): Prototypes, with curved wingtips, rearward retracting nosewheel, tail fins mounted centrally above engine housings; first observed Ramenskoye by US satellite, given provisional designation 'Ram-J'.

Su-27 ('Flanker-B'): Single-seat land-based production version; square wingtips, carrying air-to-air missile launchers; tail fins outboard of engine housings; extended tailcone; forward retracting nosewheel; first flown 20 April 1981; standard Soviet air forces equipment.

Su-27UB ('Flanker-C'): Tandem two-seat trainer version of 'Flanker-B' with full combat capability; taller fin; overall height 6.357 m (20 ft 10¼ in).

Su-27K (K for *korabelnyy*; ship-based) ('Flanker-D'): Version for ramp-assisted operation from Soviet Navy carriers, first mentioned as 'Flanker-B variant 2' by Rear Adm William O. Studeman, USN, Spring 1988; basically similar to production Su-27 but with movable foreplanes, first tested on experimental Su-27 known as T-10-24; made first conventional (non-V/STOL) landing by Soviet aircraft on ship, the *Admiral of the Fleet Kuznetsov* (formerly *Tbilisi*) 1 November 1989; folding outer wing panels; strengthened landing gear with twin-wheel nose unit; added arrester hook; flight refuelling capability; long tailcone of land-based versions deleted to prevent tailscrapes during take-off and landing; can carry buddy flight refuelling pack on centreline pylon; carrier approach speed 130 knots (240 km/h; 150 mph).

Also used for trials on the *Admiral of the Fleet Kuznetsov* was a **side by side two-seat Su-27 variant** with foreplanes and twin nosewheels but without folding wings; wider nose; deep fairing behind the wide curved canopy; wing extensions taken forward as chines to tip of nose; louvres on air intake ducts reconfigured; nosewheel leg moved forward to retract rearward; four nosewheel doors replace usual single door; no ventral fins or deck arrester hook; no radar or IRST sensor; usual 30 mm gun and wingtip missile rails retained, but no other stores pylons during deck trials; described as deck landing trainer, but could form basis for reconnaissance or attack aircraft.

Two views of Su-27K ('Flanker-D') approaching to land on carrier

New versions, under development, will embody composites; current 1970s style cockpit instrumentation and conventional control column will be superseded by four CRTs and side-stick controller; vectoring nozzles have been evaluated on experimental Model 1024, independently of its foreplanes, and two-dimensional nozzles are likely on future Su-27 variants.

Trials have been conducted with retractable flight refuelling probe forward of cockpit on port side of single-seat and two-seat Su-27s; latter demonstrated endurance of up to 16 hours; one of the aircraft flew non-stop approx 7,550 nm (14,000 km; 8,700 miles) from Moscow to Soviet Pacific coast and back, proving compatibility with Il-78 tanker and Su-24 with buddy refuelling pack. The **P-42**, a specially prepared Su-27, holds 28 official world records, including climb to 12,000 m (39,370 ft) in 55.542 seconds; some records are in the FAI category for STOL aircraft.

CUSTOMERS: About 200 delivered to Soviet APVO home defence interceptor force and fighter components of Legnica and Vinnitsa air armies; China is expected to be first export customer.

Following data apply to basic land-based Su-27 ('Flanker-B'):

DESIGN FEATURES: Developed to replace Yak-28P, Su-15 and Tu-28P/128 interceptors in APVO, and to escort Su-24 deep-penetration strike missions; exceptional range on internal fuel made flight refuelling unnecessary until Su-24s received probes; external fuel tanks still not considered necessary; all-swept mid-wing configuration, with long curved wing leading-edge root extensions, lift-generating fuselage, twin tail fins and widely spaced engines with wedge intakes; doors in intakes prevent ingestion of foreign objects during take-off and landing; integrated fire control system with pilot's helmet mounted target designator; exceptional high-Alpha performance; basic wing leading-edge sweepback 42°; anhedral approx 2° 30′.

FLYING CONTROLS: Four-channel analog fly-by-wire, no mechanical backup; inherently unstable; no ailerons; full-span leading-edge flaps and plain half-span inboard flaperons controlled manually for take-off and landing, computer controlled in flight; differential/collective tailerons operate in conjunction with flaperons and rudders for pitch and roll control; flight control system limits g loading to +9 and normally limits angle of attack to 30-35°; angle of attack limiter can be overruled manually for certain flight manoeuvres; large door-type airbrake in top of centre-fuselage.

STRUCTURE: All-metal, with many titanium components but no composites; comparatively conventional two-spar wings; basically circular section semi-monocoque fuselage, sloping down sharply aft of canopy; cockpit high-set behind drooped nose; large ogival dielectric nosecone; long rectangular blast panel forward of gun on starboard side, above wingroot extension; uncanted vertical tail surfaces on narrow decks outboard of engine housings; fin extensions beneath decks form parallel, widely separated ventral fins.

LANDING GEAR: Retractable tricycle type, with single wheel on each unit. Mainwheels retract forward into wingroots. Nosewheel, with mudguard, also retracts forward. Mainwheel tyres size 1030 × 350 mm, pressure 12.25-15.7 bars (178-227 lb/sq in); nosewheel tyre size 680 × 260 mm, pressure 9.3 bars (135 lb/sq in). Brake-chute housed in fuselage tailcone.

POWER PLANT: Two Saturn/Lyulka AL-31F turbofans, each rated at 123.85 kN (27,557 lb st) with afterburning. Large auxiliary air intake louvres in bottom of each three-ramp engine duct near primary wedge intake. Two rows of small vertical louvres in each side wall of wedge, and others in top face. Fine-grille screen hinges up from bottom of each duct to shield engine from foreign object ingestion during take-off and landing.

ACCOMMODATION: Pilot only, on K-36MD zero/zero ejection seat, under large rearward opening transparent blister canopy, with low sill. Helmet-mounted target designation system.

AVIONICS: Track-while-scan coherent pulse Doppler lookdown/shootdown radar (antenna diameter approx 1.0 m; 3 ft 4 in) with reported search range of 130 nm (240 km; 150 miles) and tracking range of 100 nm (185 km; 115 miles). Infra-red search/track (IRST) sensor in transparent housing forward of windscreen. Sirena-3 (or later) 360° radar warning receivers, outboard of each bottom air intake lip and at tail. Integrated fire control system enables the radar, IRST and laser rangefinder to be slaved to the pilot's helmet mounted target designator and displayed on the wide-angle HUD.

EQUIPMENT: Three banks of chaff/flare dispensers in bottom of long tailcone extension.

ARMAMENT: One 30 mm GSh-30 gun in starboard wingroot extension, with 149 rds. Up to 10 air-to-air missiles, on tandem pylons under fuselage between engine ducts, beneath each duct, under each centre-wing and outer-wing, and at each wingtip. Typically, two short-burn semi-active radar homing AA-10A missiles (NATO 'Alamo-A') in tandem under fuselage; two short-burn infra-red homing AA-10B ('Alamo-B') missiles on the centre-wing pylons; and a long-burn semi-active radar homing AA-10C ('Alamo-C') or infra-red AA-10D ('Alamo-D') beneath each engine duct. The four outer pylons are able to carry either AA-11 ('Archer') or AA-8 ('Aphid') close-range infra-red missiles. AA-9 ('Amos') missiles optional in place of AA-10s.

Sukhoi Su-27UB ('Flanker-C') two-seat combat trainer *(Brian M. Service)*

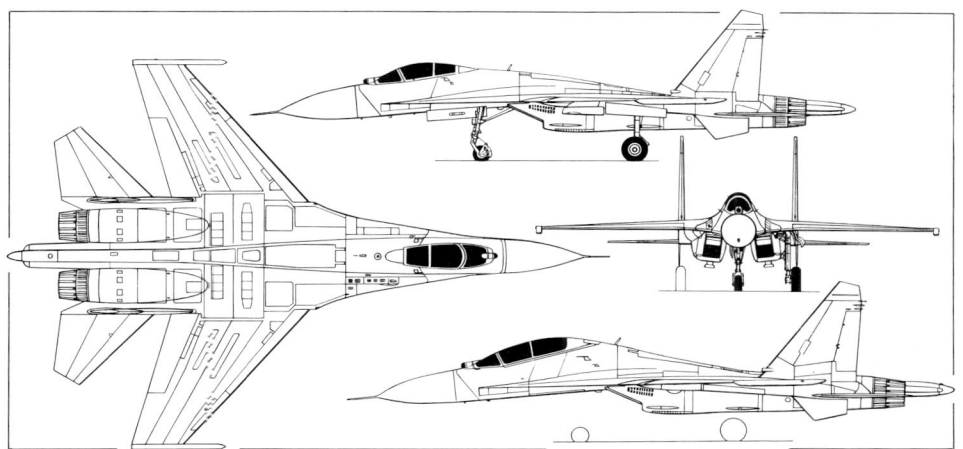

Sukhoi Su-27, with added side elevation (bottom) of two-seat Su-27UB *(Pilot Press)*

Sukhoi Su-27 ('Flanker-B') photographed from Swedish Air Force Viggen *(via FLYGvapenNYTT)*

Side by side two-seat version of Su-27 approaching to land on *Admiral of the Fleet Kuznetsov (Tass)*

DIMENSIONS, EXTERNAL ('Flanker-B'):

Wing span	14.70 m (48 ft 2¾ in)
Length overall, excl nose probe	21.935 m (71 ft 11½ in)
Height overall	5.932 m (19 ft 5½ in)
Fuselage: Max width	1.50 m (4 ft 11 in)
Tailplane span	9.90 m (32 ft 6 in)
Distance between fin tips	4.30 m (14 ft 1¼ in)
Wheel track	4.33 m (14 ft 2½ in)
Wheelbase	5.88 m (19 ft 3½ in)

WEIGHTS AND LOADINGS (B: 'Flanker-B', C: 'Flanker-C'):

Max T-O weight: B	22,000-30,000 kg (48,500-66,135 lb)
C	22,500 kg (49,600 lb)
Max power loading: B	121.1 kg/kN (1.20 lb/lb st)
C	90.8 kg/kN (0.90 lb/lb st)

PERFORMANCE:

Max level speed:	
at height: B, C	Mach 2.35
	(1,345 knots; 2,500 km/h; 1,550 mph)
at S/L: B, C	Mach 1.1
	(725 knots; 1,345 km/h; 835 mph)
Service ceiling: B, C	18,000 m (59,055 ft)

T-O run: B	500 m (1,640 ft)
C	550 m (1,805 ft)
Landing run: B	600 m (1,970 ft)
C	650 m (2,135 ft)
Combat radius: B	810 nm (1,500 km; 930 miles)
Range with max fuel:	
B	over 2,160 nm (4,000 km; 2,485 miles)
C	1,620 nm (3,000 km; 1,865 miles)
g limit (operational): B, C	+9

SUKHOI Su-29

TYPE: Tandem two-seat training/single-seat aerobatic aircraft.

PROGRAMME: Announced at Moscow Aerospace '90, when development was at advanced stage; mockup scheduled for display at 1991 Paris Air Show; prototype first flight later in 1991.

DESIGN FEATURES: Two-seat development of Su-26MX; wing span and overall length increased; continuous transparent canopy over both cockpits; wheel fairings optional; dual controls standard; tail unit unchanged.

POWER PLANT: One 268 kW (360 hp) Vedeneyev M-14P nine-cylinder radial engine.

DIMENSIONS, EXTERNAL:

Wing span	8.20 m (26 ft 10¾ in)
Length overall	7.32 m (24 ft 0¼ in)
Height overall	2.87 m (9 ft 5 in)

WEIGHTS AND LOADINGS (A: two persons, B: pilot only):

Max T-O weight: A	1,100 kg (2,425 lb)
B	850 kg (1,874 lb)
Max power loading: A	4.10 kg/kW (6.74 lb/hp)
B	3.17 kg/kW (5.21 lb/hp)

PERFORMANCE (estimated):

Never-exceed speed (VNE):	
A	215 knots (400 km/h; 248 mph)
B	226 knots (420 km/h; 261 mph)
Max level speed: A	161 knots (300 km/h; 186 mph)
B	172 knots (320 km/h; 199 mph)
Max rate of climb at S/L: A	960 m (3,150 ft)/min
B	1,080 m (3,543 ft)/min
Service ceiling: A, B	4,000 m (13,125 ft)
Unprepared runway length: A, B	600 m (1,970 ft)
Max ferry range: A, B	400 nm (740 km; 460 miles)

SUKHOI Su-31

TYPE: Single-seat advanced aerobatic aircraft.

PROGRAMME: Announced late 1990; under development.

DESIGN FEATURES: All-composites, more powerful, follow-on to Su-26M; unusual in having retractable tailwheel landing gear.

POWER PLANT: One 298 kW (400 hp) radial engine, driving four-blade propeller.

SUKHOI S-21 (SSBJ)

This designation was given to the supersonic business aircraft originally publicised under the joint feasibility study by Sukhoi and Gulfstream Aerospace of the USA. Further details of the SSBJ (supersonic business jet) as currently projected can be found under the Sukhoi/Gulfstream heading in the International section of this edition.

SUKHOI S-51

TYPE: Medium-size long-range supersonic transport.

PROGRAMME: At design study stage; initial letter of designation refers to Sukhoi General Designer Mikhail Simonov.

DESIGN FEATURES: General similarity to smaller SSBJ under joint development by Sukhoi and Gulfstream Aerospace, USA; rear-mounted sweptback low wings, with very long curved root extensions, carrying four engine ducts and tailplanes on wide rearward extension of inboard semi-span; small winglets; sweptback foreplanes; small diameter, long fuselage, with flush windscreen in conical nose; swept vertical tail surfaces.

LANDING GEAR: Retractable tricycle type; twin nosewheels; main bogies each two pairs of wheels in tandem.

POWER PLANT: Variable-cycle type.

ACCOMMODATION: Flexible, from 10 to 52 passengers.

DIMENSIONS, EXTERNAL:

Wing span	27.12 m (89 ft 0 in)
Length overall	42.70 m (140 ft 0 in)
Height overall	9.56 m (31 ft 4 in)

WEIGHTS AND LOADINGS:

Max T-O weight	88,500 kg (195,105 lb)

PERFORMANCE (estimated):

Max supersonic speed	Mach 2
	(1,150 knots; 2,125 km/h; 1,320 mph)
Max subsonic speed	Mach 0.9
	(540 knots; 1,000 km/h; 620 mph)
Service ceiling	17,000-18,000 m (55,775-59,055 ft)
Max range: subsonic or supersonic	
	4,855 nm (9,000 km; 5,600 miles)

SUKHOI S-80M

TYPE: Twin-turboprop multi-purpose STOL transport.

PROGRAMME: First new civilian aircraft of Sukhoi design scheduled for completion under Soviet industry's *konversiya* programme; shown in model form at 1989 Paris Air Show; power plant selected and overall size and weight increased 1990. Tentative agreement in March 1991 for licence manufacture by PADC in Philippines (which see).

DESIGN FEATURES: Tandem high-wing configuration; larger rear wing has anhedral on outer panels, and winglets; fuselage pod suspended from both wings; twin sweptback fins and rudders carried on two tailbooms that extend rearward from engine nacelles and connect both wings; horizontal tail surfaces bridge tips of toed-in tail fins; fuselage and many other components of composites.

LANDING GEAR: Retractable tricycle type, with single wheel on each unit. Mainwheels retract into sponsons, on each side of the cabin at the rear. Nosewheel retracts forward.

POWER PLANT: Two 1,156 kW (1,550 shp) Glushenkov TVD-1500 turboprops.

ACCOMMODATION: Two seats on flight deck. According to role, main cabin can have seats for 21 passengers or be equipped for air ambulance, freight transport or special

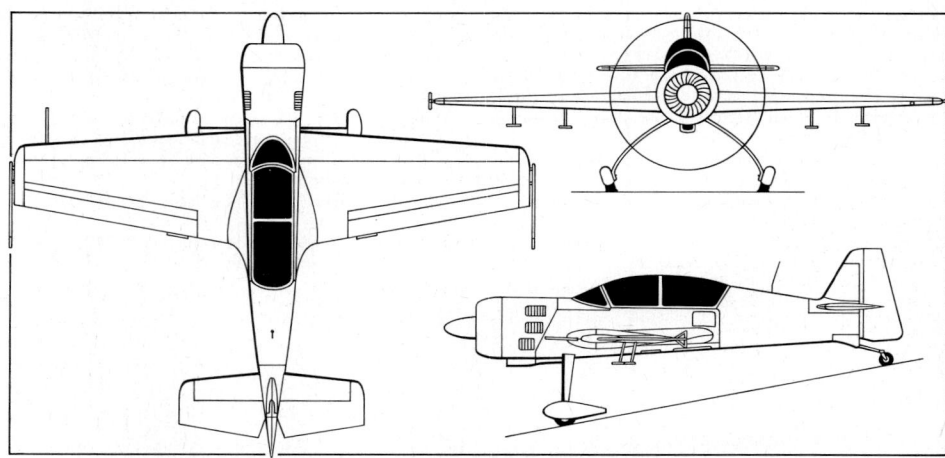

Sukhoi Su-29 training and aerobatic aircraft *(Jane's/Mike Keep)*

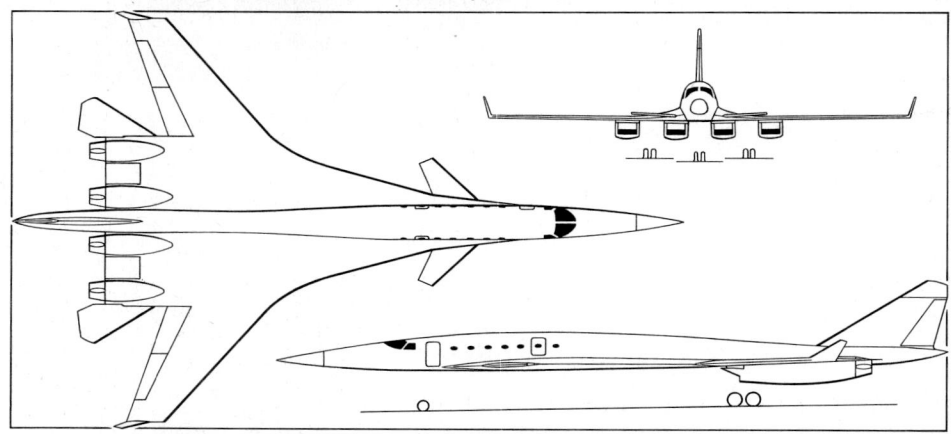

Sukhoi S-51 four-engined supersonic passenger airliner *(Jane's/Mike Keep)*

Model of Sukhoi Su-29 aerobatic aircraft *(Piotr Butowski)*

The projected Sukhoi S-51 supersonic transport *(Piotr Butowski)*

New Sukhoi S-84 concept shown at Moscow Aerospace '90. No details available *(Piotr Butowski)*

Model of Sukhoi S-86 light business transport *(Piotr Butowski)*

civilian and military tasks including air photography. Door at centre of cabin, on port side. Rear loading doors and ramp.

AVIONICS: Intended for IFR operation; autoland standard.

DIMENSIONS, EXTERNAL:
Span of rear wing	23.10 m (75 ft 9½ in)
Length overall	16.00 m (52 ft 6 in)
Height overall	4.90 m (16 ft 1 in)

WEIGHTS AND LOADINGS:
Max payload	2,100 kg (4,630 lb)
Max T-O weight	8,200 kg (18,075 lb)

SUKHOI S-84 (Original concept)

TYPE: Four-seat turboprop powered light aircraft.

PROGRAMME: Original S-84 concept (described below) revealed 1989; new design with same designation (no details available) shown in model form at Moscow Aerospace '90.

DESIGN FEATURES: High aspect ratio low-wing configuration, with forward sweep; dihedral from roots; streamlined bodies, probably for fuel, at wingtips, each carrying small winglet; slightly sweptback foreplanes immediately forward of wings, with dihedral; wide fuselage; enclosed cabin forms escape module that separates and descends by parachute in emergency; swept vertical tail surfaces, carrying high-mounted unswept tailplane and elevators; coupled twin-turboprop power plant.

LANDING GEAR: Retractable tricycle type; single wheel on each unit.

POWER PLANT: One 335 kW (450 shp) TVD-450 coupled twin turboprop, driving four-blade propeller.

ACCOMMODATION: Four persons, in pairs, in enclosed cabin; optional dual controls.

DIMENSIONS, EXTERNAL:
Wing span	14.00 m (45 ft 11¼ in)
Length overall	9.00 m (29 ft 6½ in)
Height	3.50 m (11 ft 6 in)

WEIGHTS AND LOADINGS:
Max payload	400 kg (882 lb)
Max T-O weight	1,500 kg (3,306 lb)
Max power loading	4.48 kg/kW (7.35 lb/shp)

PERFORMANCE (estimated):
Max level speed	270 knots (500 km/h; 310 mph)
T-O run	370 m (1,214 ft)
Landing run	430 m (1,410 ft)
Range with max fuel	647 nm (1,200 km; 745 miles)

SUKHOI S-86

TYPE: Six/eight-seat turboprop powered business aircraft.

PROGRAMME: First brief reference 1989; shown in model form at Moscow Aerospace '90; at mockup stage.

DESIGN FEATURES: High aspect ratio low-wing configuration, with forward sweep; optional streamlined bodies, probably for fuel, at wingtips, each carrying small winglet; wing centre-section carries fuselage pod with pusher turboprop at rear, foreplanes aft of flight deck, and twin tailbooms; twin sweptback tail fins bridged by tip mounted tailplane and elevator.

LANDING GEAR: Retractable tricycle type; single wheel on each unit.

POWER PLANT: One 522 kW (700 shp) Lyulka AL-34 turboprop, driving three-blade pusher contraprops; engine air intake on each side of rear fuselage.

ACCOMMODATION: Six or eight persons, in pairs, or alternative business interior; horizontally split upward/downward opening door at centre of cabin on port side; emergency exit at rear on starboard side.

DIMENSIONS, EXTERNAL:
Wing span	16.19 m (53 ft 1½ in)
Length overall	11.60 m (38 ft 0¾ in)
Height overall	3.56 m (11 ft 8¼ in)

Model of Sukhoi S-80M in ambulance form *(Piotr Butowski)*

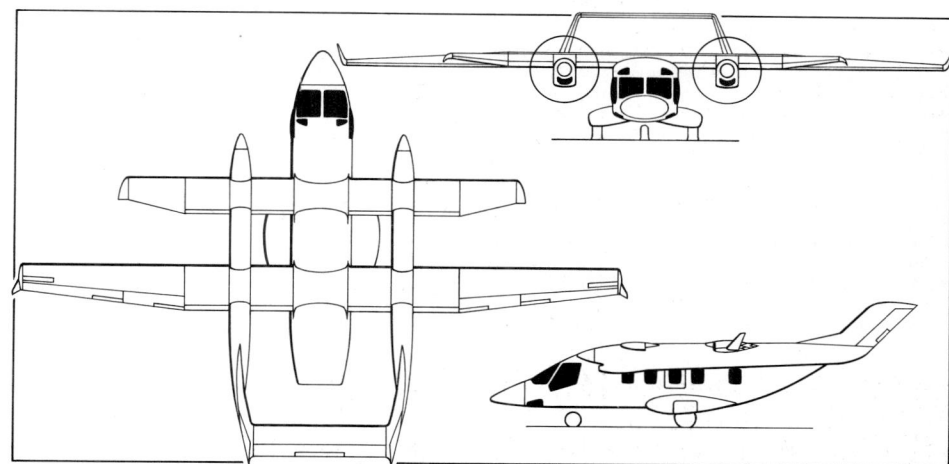

Sukhoi S-80M twin-turboprop STOL utility transport *(Jane's/Mike Keep)*

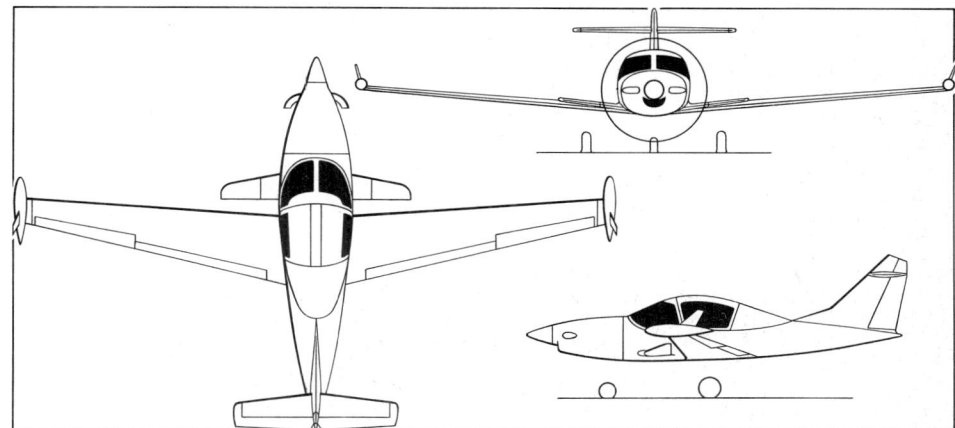

Original design for turboprop-powered Sukhoi S-84, as described *(Jane's/Mike Keep)*

WEIGHTS AND LOADINGS:

Max payload	700 kg (1,543 lb)
Max T-O weight	4,400 kg (9,700 lb)
Max power loading	8.43 kg/kW (13.86 lb/shp)

PERFORMANCE (estimated):

Max level speed	323 knots (600 km/h; 372 mph)
T-O and landing run	500 m (1,640 ft)
Range with max fuel	1,888 nm (3,500 km; 2,175 miles)

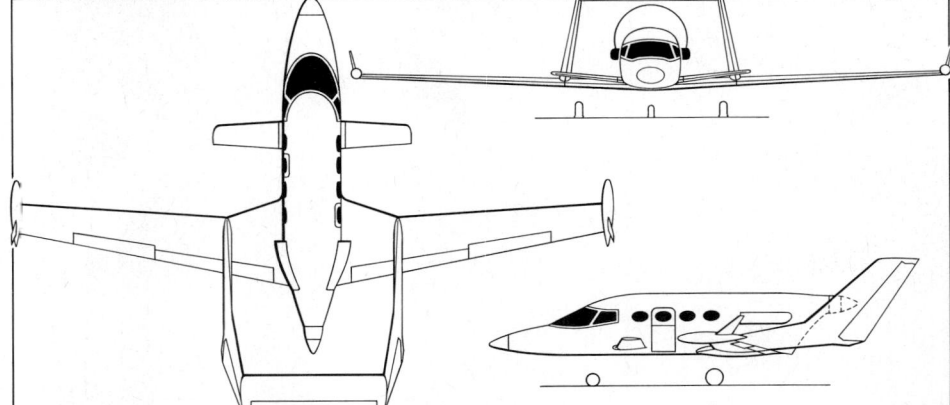

Sukhoi S-86 business aircraft. Cabin windows are rectangular in latest studies *(Jane's/Mike Keep)*

TUPOLEV
TUPOLEV DESIGN BUREAU
GENERAL DESIGNER: Dr Alexei Andreyevich Tupolev
DEPUTY CHIEF OF OKB: Andrei Kandolov
CHIEF DESIGNERS:
Lev Aronovich Lanovski (Commercial Aircraft)
Dmitry S. Markov
L. L. Selyakov

Andrei Nikolayevich Tupolev was a leading figure in the Central Aero-Hydrodynamic Institute (TsAGI) in Moscow from when it was founded, in 1929, until his death on 23 December 1972, aged 84. The Bureau that bears his name concentrates primarily on large military and civil aircraft.

TUPOLEV Tu-16
NATO reporting name: Badger
TYPE: Twin-jet medium bomber, maritime reconnaissance/attack and electronic warfare aircraft.
PROGRAMME: Prototype flown by N. S. Rybka, under OKB designation Tu-88, on 27 April 1952; achieved disappointing max speed of 510 knots (945 km/h; 587 mph) and was overweight; Andrei Tupolev delayed production until second prototype flew in 1953 with uprated AM-3A turbojets and 5,500 kg (12,125 lb) weight reduction; max speed increased to 535 knots (992 km/h; 616 mph) at cost of max IAS of only 378 knots (700 km/h; 435 mph) at low altitude instead of originally required Mach 0.9; deliveries began 1954; nine Tu-16s took part in May Day 1954 flypast over Moscow, 54 in Aviation Day flypast 1955; approx 2,000 produced in many versions; manufacture ended late 1950s; late versions all converted bombers; all but earliest have uprated AM-3M (RD-3M) engines.
VARIANTS: **Tu-16A** ('Badger-A'): Basic strategic jet bomber, with conventional or nuclear free-fall weapons; glazed nose, with small undernose radome; defensive armament of seven 23 mm AM-23 guns; licence production, as **H-6**, by Xian Aircraft Manufacturing Company (which see) continues in China.
Tu-16T: Torpedo bomber; externally identical to Tu-16A.
Tu-16N: As Tu-16A but equipped as flight refuelling tanker, using unique wingtip-to-wingtip transfer technique to refuel other Tu-16s, or probe-and-drogue system to refuel Tu-22s; added tankage in bomb bay.
Tu-16 Korvet: Tu-16A adapted for search and rescue duties; large radio-controlled rescue boat under fuselage; continues in use.
Tu-16KS-1 ('Badger-B'): First Naval Aviation missile carrying version; turbojet powered KS-1 (NATO AS-1 'Kennel') under each wing; free-fall bombing capability retained; first observed 1961; superseded 1968 by 'Badger-G'.
Tu-16K-10 ('Badger-C'): Anti-shipping version; first seen 1961 Soviet Aviation Day display, with Tu-16KS-1; longer-range Mikoyan K-10 (AS-2 'Kipper') turbojet powered missile in underbelly recess; wide nose radome (NATO 'Puff Ball') instead of glazing and nose gun of Tu-16A; no provision for free-fall bombs; about 100 supplied to Soviet Northern, Baltic, Black Sea and Pacific Fleet shore bases; some modified ('Badger-C Mod') to carry Mach 3 AS-6 ('Kingfish') missiles underwing, in addition to AS-2 capability.
Tu-16R ('Badger-D'): Maritime/electronic reconnaissance version, introduced early 1960s; nose as Tu-16K-10 but larger undernose radome; three elint radomes in tandem under weapons bay; large number of cameras in weapons bay. Tu-16Rs carry crew of eight to ten.
Tu-16 ('Badger-E'): Photographic/electronic reconnaissance version; as Tu-16A but cameras in weapons bay; two additional radomes under fuselage, larger one aft.
Tu-16R ('Badger-F'): Similar to 'Badger-E' but elint pod on pylon under each wing; late versions have various small radomes under centre-fuselage.

'Badger-J' ECM jamming version of Tu-16PP *(Swedish Air Force)*

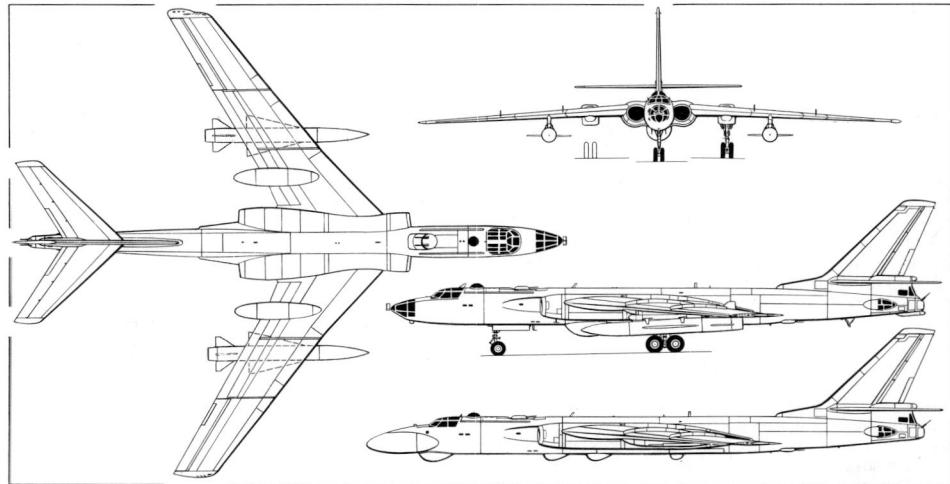

Tupolev Tu-16K 'Badger-G (Mod)' with additional side view (bottom) of Tu-16R 'Badger-D' *(Pilot Press)*

Tu-16 ('Badger-G'): Converted from Tu-16KS-1; two underwing rocket-powered AS-5 ('Kelt') missiles, which have larger radar and can be carried over range greater than 1,735 nm (3,220 km; 2,000 miles). Free-fall bombing capability retained; delivered mainly to Naval anti-shipping squadrons.
Tu-16K ('Badger-G Mod'): Modified to carry Mach 3 AS-6 ('Kingfish') missile, with nuclear or conventional warhead, under each wing; large radome, presumably associated with missile operation, under centre-fuselage, replacing chin radome; external device on glazed nose may help to ensure correct attitude of Tu-16 during missile launch; delivered to Northern, Black Sea and Pacific Fleets.

Tu-16PP (*Postanovchik Pomiekh*: jammer) ('Badger-H'): stand-off or escort ECM aircraft; primary function chaff dispensing to protect missile carrying strike force; two teardrop radomes, fore and aft of weapons bay, house passive receivers to identify enemy radar signals and establish length of chaff strips to be dispensed; dispensers with total capacity of up to 9,075 kg (20,000 lb) of chaff located in weapons bay, with three chutes in doors; hatch aft of weapons bay; two blade antennae aft of bay; glazed nose and chin radome.
Tu-16PP ('Badger-J'): ECM version specialised for active jamming in all frequencies; modified from standard bomber; some equipment in canoe shape radome protruding from weapons bay, surrounded by

Tupolev Tu-16R ('Badger-D') maritime/electronic reconnaissance aircraft *(Royal Navy)*

heat exchangers and exhaust ports; anti-radar noise jammers operate in A to I bands inclusive; glazed nose as Tu-16A; some aircraft (as illustrated) have large flat-plate antennae at wingtips.

Tu-16R ('Badger-K'): Electronic reconnaissance variant; nose as Tu-16A; two teardrop radomes, inside and forward of weapons bay (closer together than on 'Badger-H'); four small pods on centreline in front of rear radome; chaff dispenser aft of weapons bay.

Tu-16 ('Badger-L'): Soviet Navy electronic warfare variant, like 'Badger-G' but with equipment of the kind fitted to the Tu-95 'Bear-G', including an ECM nose thimble, pods on centre or rear fuselage, and 'solid' extended tailcone containing special equipment instead of tail gun position; sometimes has pod on pylon under each wing.

CUSTOMERS: In 1991, estimated 70 Tu-16s remain operational in strike role, mostly with Smolensk and Irkutsk air armies, plus 20 Tu-16N tankers, 90 ECM and 15 Tu-16R versions; Soviet Naval Aviation has estimated 100 attack models (mostly 'Badger-G'), 70 Tu-16Ns and up to 80 reconnaissance/ECM variants; further 175 former air army and Naval Tu-16s in storage; air forces of Egypt, Indonesia (retired), Iraq.

DESIGN FEATURES: All-swept high mid-wing configuration; heavy engine nacelles form root fairings; wing section PR-1-10S-9, with 15.7 per cent thickness/chord ratio, on inboard panels; SR-11-12 section, of 12 per cent thickness/chord, outboard; anhedral 3° from roots; incidence 1°; sweepback 41° inboard, 37° outboard at leading-edges, 35° at quarter-chord; 42° sweepback at quarter-chord on tail fin and tailplane; tailplane incidence −1° 30′.

FLYING CONTROLS: Conventional, with control wheel and rudder pedals; hydraulically boosted, with large trim tabs in each aileron, elevators and rudder; except in region of landing gear nacelles, entire wing trailing-edges comprise aerodynamically balanced Frise/TsAGI ailerons and electrically operated outboard and inboard sections of TsAGI (modified Fowler) flaps.

STRUCTURE: All-metal; two-spar wings made in centre-section (integral with fuselage), inner and outer sections; nacelle for landing gear at junction of inner and outer wing panels each side; circular semi-monocoque fuselage in five sections; nose houses navigator's pressure cabin with double-glazed nose panels in magnesium alloy frame, pilot's pressure cabin, forward gunner's cabin and radar equipment; second and fourth sections house fuel tanks, with weapon compartment between them; tail section contains pressure cabin for radio operator/gunner and rear gunner.

LANDING GEAR: Hydraulically retractable tricycle type. Twin-wheel nose unit retracts rearward. Main four-wheel bogies retract into housings projecting beyond the wing trailing-edge. Mainwheel tyres size 1,100 × 330 mm; nosewheel tyres size 900 × 275 mm. Anti-skid brakes on mainwheels.

POWER PLANT: Early Tu-16s have two Mikulin AM-3A turbojets, each rated at 85.21 kN (19,155 lb st) at sea level. Later aircraft fitted with RD-3M-500 (AM-3M) turbojets, each rated at 93.05 kN (20,920 lb st). Engines semi-recessed into sides of fuselage, giving unplanned area ruling. Divided air intake ducts: main duct passes through wing torque box between spars; secondary duct passes under wing to feed into primary airflow in front of engine. Engines separated from wings and fuselage by firewalls. Jetpipes inclined outward 3° to shield fuselage from effects of exhaust gases. Fuel in 27 wing and fuselage tanks, with total capacity of 43,800 litres (11,570 US gallons; 9,635 Imp gallons). Provision for underwing auxiliary fuel tanks and for flight refuelling. Tu-16 tankers trail hose from starboard wingtip; receiving equipment is in port wingtip extension.

ACCOMMODATION: Normal crew of six on ejection seats, with two pilots side by side on flight deck. Navigator/bombardier, on seat with armoured sides and base, in glazed nose of all versions except 'Badger-C and D'. Manned tail position plus lateral observation blisters in rear fuselage under tailplane. Entry via two hatches in bottom of fuselage, in front and rear structural sections.

AVIONICS: PBR-4 Rubin 1 mapping radar; SP-50M for IFR to ICAO Cat I standard; RSDN Chaika Loran; NavSat receiver; AP-6E autopilot, NAS-1 nav including DISS Trassa Doppler; R-807 and R-808 HF; RSIU-3M UHF; IFF, two ARK-15 ADFs, SPU-10 intercom; RV-5 and RV-18 radar altimeters; Sirena-2 radar warning receivers.

EQUIPMENT: Differs according to role; all Tu-16s can carry cameras in small section of fuselage, ahead of weapons bay, for reconnaissance.

ARMAMENT: PV-23 integrated armament firing control system. Forward dorsal and rear ventral barbettes each containing two 23 mm AM-23 guns. Two similar guns in tail position controlled by an automatic gun ranging radar set. Seventh, fixed, gun on starboard side of nose of versions with nose glazing. Bomb load of up to 9,000 kg (19,800 lb) delivered from weapons bay 6.5 m (21 ft) long in standard bomber, under control of navigator. Normal bomb load 3,000 kg (6,600 lb). Naval versions can carry air-to-surface winged standoff missiles.

DIMENSIONS, EXTERNAL ('Badger-G'):

Wing span	32.99 m (108 ft 3 in)
Mean aerodynamic chord	5.021 m (16 ft 5¾ in)
Length overall	34.80 m (114 ft 2 in)
Height overall	10.36 m (34 ft 0 in)
Basic diameter of fuselage	2.50 m (8 ft 2½ in)
Tailplane span	11.75 m (38 ft 6½ in)
Wheel track	9.775 m (32 ft 0¾ in)
Wheelbase	10.91 m (35 ft 9½ in)

AREAS:

Wings, gross	164.65 m² (1,772.3 sq ft)
Ailerons (total)	14.77 m² (159.0 sq ft)
Flaps (total)	25.17 m² (270.9 sq ft)
Vertical tail surfaces	23.30 m² (250.8 sq ft)
Horizontal tail surfaces	34.45 m² (370.8 sq ft)

WEIGHTS AND LOADINGS ('Badger-G'):

Weight empty, equipped	37,200 kg (82,000 lb)
Weight of max fuel	34,360 kg (75,750 lb)
Normal T-O weight	75,000 kg (165,350 lb)
Max landing weight	50,000 kg (110,230 lb)
Max wing loading	455.5 kg/m² (93.3 lb/sq ft)
Max power loading	403.0 kg/kN (3.95 lb/lb st)

PERFORMANCE ('Badger-G', at max T-O weight):
Max level speed at 6,000 m (19,700 ft)
566 knots (1,050 km/h; 652 mph)

Service ceiling	15,000 m (49,200 ft)

Range with 3,000 kg (6,600 lb) bomb load
3,885 nm (7,200 km; 4,475 miles)

TUPOLEV Tu-95 and Tu-142
NATO reporting name: Bear

TYPE: Four-turboprop long-range bomber and maritime reconnaissance aircraft.

PROGRAMME: Design studies began 1950; design frozen and mockup approved 1952; prototype, known as OKB Type 95, flew second half 1954; seven Tu-95s took part in 1955 Aviation Day flypast; operational with Soviet strategic attack force 1956; almost continuous, latterly small scale, production for more than 35 years.

VARIANTS: Major current versions identified by NATO reporting names are as follows:

Tu-95 ('Bear-D'): Maritime reconnaissance aircraft, first identified 1967; glazed nose; undernose radar (NATO 'Short Horn'); large underbelly radome for I band surface search radar ('Big Bulge'); elint blister fairing each side of rear fuselage; nose refuelling probe; variety of blisters and antennae, including streamlined fairing on each tailplane tip. Defensive armament comprises three pairs of 23 mm NR-23 guns in remotely controlled rear dorsal and ventral barbettes and manned tail turret; two glazed blisters on rear fuselage, under tailplane, used for sighting by gunner controlling all these guns; dorsal and ventral barbettes can also be controlled from station aft of flight deck. Housing for I band tail warning radar ('Box Tail') above tail turret is larger than on previous variants; no offensive weapons; tasks include pinpointing of maritime targets for missile launch crews on ships and aircraft that are themselves too distant for precise missile aiming and guidance; about 15 operational, probably converted from 'Bear-A' strategic bombers.

A 'Bear-D' was the first Tu-95 seen, 1978, with faired tailcone housing special equipment instead of normal tail turret and radome (similar tail on 'Bear-G').

Tu-95 ('Bear-E'): Reconnaissance conversion of 'Bear-A'; armament, refuelling probe and rear fuselage elint fairings as 'Bear-D'; six camera windows in weapons bay, in pairs in line with wing flaps; seventh window to rear on starboard side. Few only.

Tu-142 ('Bear-F'): Anti-submarine version; first of extensively redesigned Tu-142 series; highly cambered wings; double-slotted flaps; longer fuselage forward of wings; rudder of increased chord; space in longer pressure cabin for improved galley and relief crew on long missions. Deployed initially by Soviet Naval Aviation 1970; re-entered production mid-1980s. Initial 'Bear-Fs'

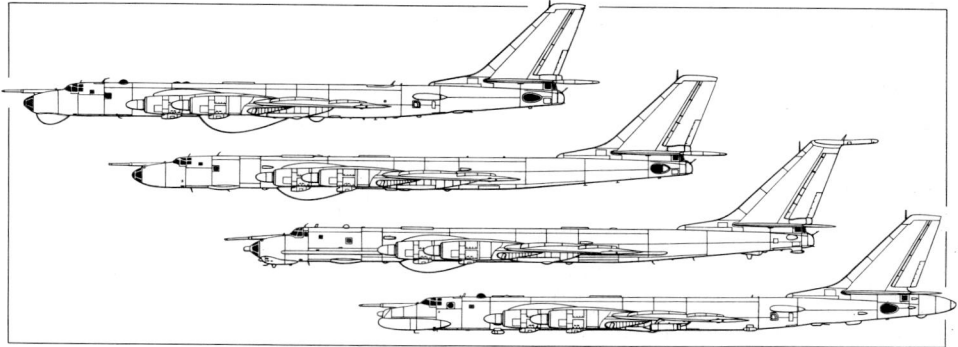

Top to bottom: Tu-95 'Bear-D', Tu-142 'Bear-F' Mod 1, Tu-142M 'Bear-F' Mod 4, Tu-95 'Bear-G'
(Pilot Press)

A 'Bear-F' Mod 3 seen over the Pacific in late 1988 shows the MAD sting on the fin and linear antenna above the fuselage adjacent to the wingroot. Soviet Naval Aviation has an air regiment of 'Bear-Fs' in the Pacific augmented by Il-38 'Mays'

The Tu-95 'Bear-G' is a reconfigured 'Bear-B or C' equipped to carry 'Kitchen' missiles *(UK Ministry of Defence)*

had 12-wheel main landing gear bogies, retracting into enlarged and lengthened fairings aft of inboard engine nacelles, and undernose radar; main underfuselage J band radar housing considerably farther forward than on 'Bear-D' and smaller; no large blister fairings under and on sides of rear fuselage; nosewheel doors bulged, suggesting larger or low-pressure tyres; two stores bays for sonobuoys, torpedoes, nuclear or conventional depth charges in rear fuselage, one replacing usual rear ventral gun turret and leaving tail turret as sole defensive gun position. Later 'Bear-Fs' identified as follows:

Mod 1: Reverted to standard size nacelles and standard four-wheel main landing gear bogies; chin mounted J band radar deleted; fewer protrusions.

Mod 2 (**Tu-142M**): Nose lengthened by 23 cm (9 in); roof of flight deck raised; angle of flight refuelling probe lowered by 4°.

Mod 3: MAD boom added to fin tip; fairings at tailplane tips deleted; rear stores bay lengthened and narrowed.

Mod 4: Chin radar reinstated; self-protection ECM thimble radome on nose; other fairings added; observation blister each side of rear fuselage deleted; entered service 1985.

Tu-95 ('Bear-G'): Bomber and elint conversion of 'Bear-B/C'; two AS-4 ('Kitchen') air-to-surface missiles, on pylon under each wingroot; new large undernose radome ('Down Beat'); ECM thimble under flight refuelling probe; streamlined ECM pod each side at bottom of both centre and rear fuselage; 'solid' tailcone containing special equipment, as on some 'Bear-Ds'; ventral gun turret sole defensive armament. More than 45 with Irkutsk air army.

Tu-142K ('Bear-H'): Late production version; Tu-142 airframe but fuselage same length as Tu-95; carries up to 10 AS-15 ('Kent') long-range cruise missiles, expected to be superseded by AS-19s early 1990s; six ALCMs on internal rotary launcher, pylons for two more under each wingroot; Built at Kuybyshev; achieved IOC 1984; larger and deeper radome built into nose; small fin tip fairing; no elint blister fairings on sides of rear fuselage; ventral gun turret deleted; some aircraft have single twin-barrel

gun instead of usual pair in tail turret. More than 70 operational.

Tu-142 ('Bear-J'): Identified 1986; Soviet counterpart of US Navy E-6A and EC-130Q Tacamo, with VLF communications avionics to maintain on-station/all-ocean link between national command authorities and nuclear missile armed submarines under most operating conditions; large ventral pod for VLF trailing wire antenna, several kilometres long, under centre-fuselage in weapons bay area; undernose fairing as 'Bear-F Mod 4'; fin-tip pod with trailing-edge of kind on some 'Bear-Hs';

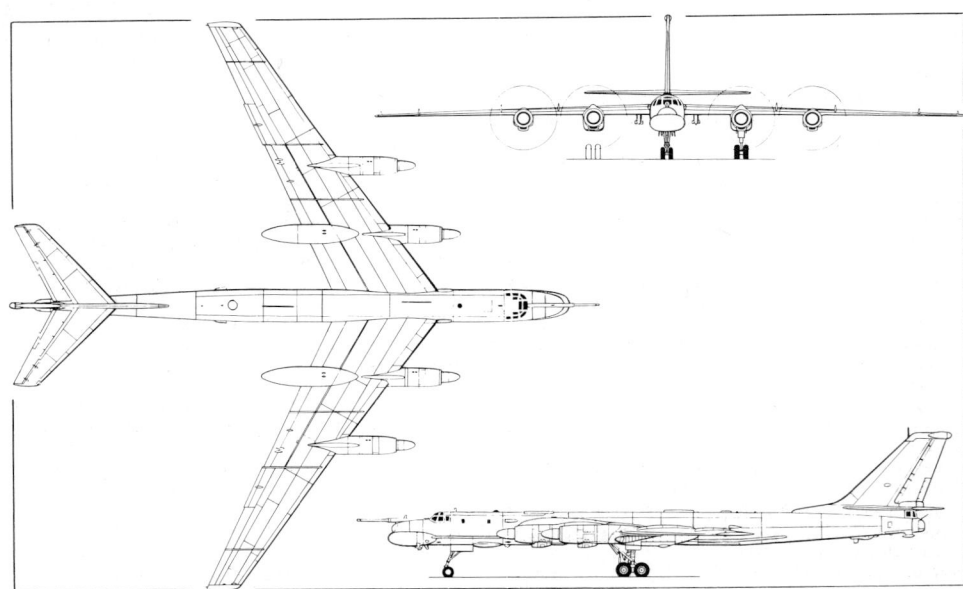

Tupolev Tu-142K strategic bomber, known to NATO as 'Bear-H' *(Pilot Press)*

satcom dome aft of flight deck canopy; modified 'Bear-F' airframe. With Northern and Pacific Fleets.

CUSTOMERS: Soviet air armies (159, mostly 'Bear-G/H'); Soviet Naval Aviation (15 'Bear-D', 55 'Bear-F' mostly Mod 3/4, few 'Bear-J'); Indian Navy (eight 'Bear-F' Mod 3).

DESIGN FEATURES: Unique large, high-performance, four-turboprop combat aircraft, able to carry largest air-launched missiles and outsize radars; all-swept mid-wing configuration; fuselage same diameter as US Boeing B-29/Soviet Tu-4, with similar crawlway linking crew

'Bear-J' version of Tupolev Tu-142, which maintains communications between Soviet national command authorities and the Soviet Navy's nuclear submarines, over long ranges. The ventral pod for the VLF trailing-wire antenna is under the centre-fuselage in the weapon bay area
(G. Jacobs/Jane's Intelligence Review)

'Bear-G' has two large pylons under the wingroots on which to carry 'Kitchen' missiles *(UK Ministry of Defence)*

Deep flight deck glazing and new undernose antennae are features of the 'Bear-H' cruise missile carrier *(UK Ministry of Defence)*

compartments fore and aft of weapons bay; main landing gear retracts into wing trailing-edge nacelles; contraprops with high tip speeds; wing section SR-5S, thickness/chord ratio 12.5 per cent at root; slight anhedral; sweepback at quarter-chord 37° on inner wings, 35° outer panels.

FLYING CONTROLS: All flying control surfaces hydraulically boosted; three-segment aileron and two-segment area-increasing flap each wing; trim tab in each inboard aileron segment; upper-surface spoiler forward of each inboard aileron; adjustable tailplane incidence; trim tab in rudder and each elevator.

STRUCTURE: All-metal; four spars in each inner wing, three outboard; three boundary layer fences above each wing; circular section semi-monocoque fuselage containing three pressurised compartments; tail gunner's compartment not accessible from others.

LANDING GEAR: Hydraulically retractable tricycle type. Main units consist of four-wheel bogies, with tyres approx 1.50 m (5 ft) diameter and hydraulic internal expanding brakes. Twin-wheels on steerable nose unit. All units retract rearward, main units into nacelles built on to wing trailing-edge. Retractable tail bumper consisting of two small wheels. Braking parachute may be used to reduce landing run.

POWER PLANT: Four Kuznetsov NK-12MV turboprops, each with max rating of 11,033 kW (14,795 ehp) and driving eight-blade contra-rotating reversible-pitch Type AV-60N propellers. Fuel in wing tanks, with normal capacity of 95,000 litres (25,100 US gallons; 20,900 Imp gallons). Flight refuelling probe above nose of most current operational aircraft.

ACCOMMODATION: See notes applicable to individual versions and under Design Features.

SYSTEMS: Thermal anti-icing of wing and tailplane leading-edges.

AVIONICS ('Bear-D'): Large I band radar (NATO 'Big Bulge') in blister fairing under centre-fuselage, for reconnaissance and to provide data on potential targets for anti-shipping aircraft or surface vessels. In latter mode, PPI presentation is data linked to missile launch station. Four-PRF range J band circular and sector scan navigation radar (NATO 'Short Horn'). I band tail warning radar (originally NATO 'Bee Hind'; later 'Box Tail') in housing at base of rudder. SRO-2 IFF (NATO 'Odd Rods'), A-321 ADF, A-322Z Doppler radar, A-325Z/321B Tacan/DME and ILS.

ARMAMENT: See notes applicable to individual versions.

EQUIPMENT ('Bear-D'): Two remotely controlled chaff/flare dispensers.

DIMENSIONS, EXTERNAL ('Bear-F'):
Wing span	51.10 m (167 ft 8 in)
Length overall	49.50 m (162 ft 5 in)
Height overall	12.12 m (39 ft 9 in)

WEIGHTS AND LOADINGS ('Bear-F', Mod 3):
Max fuel	87,000 kg (191,800 lb)
Max T-O weight	185,000 kg (407,850 lb)
Max power loading	4.19 kg/kW (6.89 lb/shp)

PERFORMANCE:
Max level speed at 7,620 m (25,000 ft)
    Mach 0.82 (500 knots; 925 km/h; 575 mph)
Over-target speed at 12,500 m (41,000 ft)
    Mach 0.78 (450 knots; 833 km/h; 518 mph)
Nominal cruising speed 384 knots (711 km/h; 442 mph)
Max unrefuelled combat radius
    4,475 nm (8,285 km; 5,150 miles)

TUPOLEV Tu-22
NATO reporting name: Blinder

TYPE: Twin-jet supersonic bomber and maritime reconnaissance aircraft.

PROGRAMME: First shown publicly 1961, when 10 took part in Aviation Day flypast, Moscow; one had AS-4 ('Kitchen') missile semi-recessed in weapons bay; 22 shown in 1967 display at Domodedovo, all with refuelling probes, most with AS-4s; total of about 250 manufactured.

VARIANTS: **Tu-22** ('Blinder-A'): Basic reconnaissance bomber with supersonic dash capability; fuselage weapons bay for free-fall nuclear and conventional bombs; entered limited service.

Tu-22 ('Blinder-B'): As 'Blinder-A' but weapons bay doors redesigned to carry AS-4 ('Kitchen') air-to-surface missile semi-recessed; larger radar and partially retractable flight refuelling probe on nose.

Tu-22 ('Blinder-C'): Maritime reconnaissance version; six camera windows in weapons bay doors; flight refuelling probe.

Tu-22U ('Blinder-D'): Training version; raised cockpit for instructor aft of standard flight deck, with stepped-up canopy.

Tu-22 ('Blinder-E'): Electronic warfare/reconnaissance version, with modifications to nosecone, additional dielectric panels, etc.

CUSTOMERS: Soviet air forces have approx 75 alongside

Tu-16s in Smolensk and Irkutsk air armies, most for ECM jamming and reconnaissance; Soviet Naval Aviation has approx 30 bombers and 20 maritime reconnaissance/ECM variants, mainly in southern Ukraine and Estonia to protect sea approaches; air forces of Libya and Iraq each have a few.

DESIGN FEATURES: All-swept mid-wing configuration; engine nacelles mounted above rear fuselage, each side of fin, with translating intake lips; main landing gear units retract into pods on wing trailing-edge; small wingtip pods; wing section modified TsAGI SR-5S; constant slight anhedral from roots; leading-edge sweepback approx 50° inboard of fence on each wing, 45° outboard, with small acutely swept segment at root; fuselage basically circular section, with area ruling at wingroots.

FLYING CONTROLS: Hydraulically powered control surfaces; two-section ailerons, with tab in each inboard section; tracked plain flaps inboard and outboard of each landing gear pod; all-moving horizontal tail surfaces at bottom of fuselage; aerodynamically balanced rudder, with inset tab.

STRUCTURE: All-metal; semi-monocoque fuselage.

LANDING GEAR: Retractable tricycle type. Wide track four-wheel bogie main units retract rearward into pods built on to wing trailing-edges. Oleo-pneumatic shock absorbers. Main legs designed to swing rearward for additional cushioning during taxying and landing on rough runways. Twin-wheel nose unit retracts rearward. Small retractable skid to protect rear fuselage in tail-down landing or take-off. Twin brake-chutes standard.

POWER PLANT: Two Koliesov VD-7 turbojets, each rated at 137.5 kN (30,900 lb st) with afterburning, mounted in nacelles above rear fuselage, on each side of tail fin. Lip of each intake is in the form of a ring which can be translated forward by jacks for take-off. Air entering ram intake is then supplemented by air ingested through annular slot between ring and main body of nacelle. Jetpipes have convergent-divergent nozzle inside outer fairing. Semi-retractable flight refuelling probe on nose of 'Blinder-B/C', with triangular guard underneath to prevent drogue damaging nosecone.

ACCOMMODATION: Crew of three in tandem. Row of windows in bottom of fuselage, aft of nose radome, at navigator/systems operator's station. Pilot has upward ejection seat; other crew members have downward ejection seats.

Tupolev Tu-22 photographed from an investigating interceptor of the Swedish Air Force *(via FLYGvapenNYTT)*

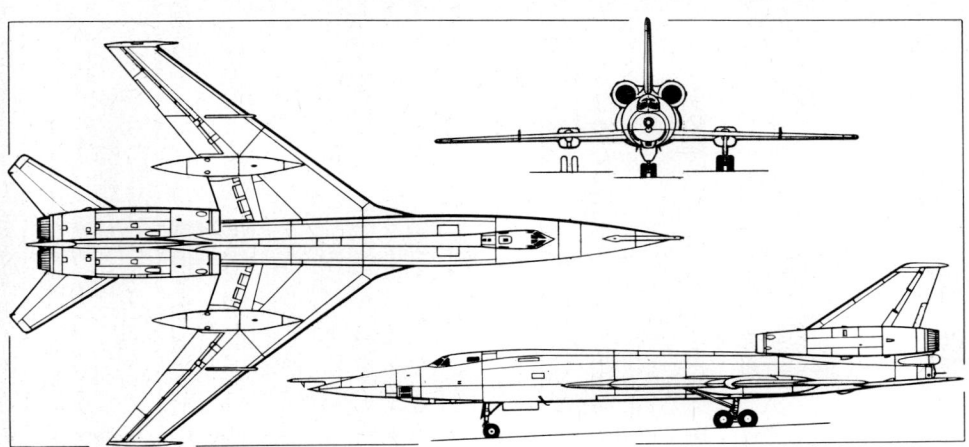

Tupolev Tu-22 twin-jet supersonic bomber ('Blinder-A') *(Pilot Press)*

AVIONICS: Nav/attack radar in nose; tail warning and gun fire control radar ('Bee Hind') at base of rudder.

EQUIPMENT: Chaff/flare countermeasures dispensers and bombing assessment cameras carried in rear of wheel pods of some aircraft.

ARMAMENT: Weapons bay in centre-fuselage, with double-fold doors on 'Blinder-A'. Special doors with panels shaped to accommodate recessed AS-4 ('Kitchen') missile on 'Blinder-B'. Single 23 mm NR-23 gun in radar directed tail turret.

DIMENSIONS, EXTERNAL (estimated):
Wing span	23.75 m (78 ft 0 in)
Length overall	40.53 m (132 ft 11½ in)
Height overall	10.67 m (35 ft 0 in)

WEIGHTS AND LOADINGS (estimated):
Max T-O weight	83,900 kg (185,000 lb)
Max power loading	305 kg/kN (3.0 lb/lb st)

PERFORMANCE (estimated):
Max level speed at 12,200 m (40,000 ft)	
	Mach 1.4 (800 knots; 1,480 km/h; 920 mph)
Service ceiling	18,300 m (60,000 ft)
Max unrefuelled combat radius	
	1,295 nm (2,400 km; 1,490 miles)

TUPOLEV Tu-22M
NATO reporting name: Backfire

TYPE: Twin-engined variable geometry medium bomber and maritime reconnaissance/attack aircraft.

PROGRAMME: NATO revealed the existence of a Soviet variable geometry bomber programme Autumn 1969; prototype observed July 1970 on the ground near Kazan manufacturing plant, western Russia; confirmed subsequently as twin-engined design by Tupolev OKB; at least two prototypes built, with first flight estimated 1971; up to 12 pre-production models by early 1973, for development testing, weapons trials and evaluation; production continues at long-established rate of 30 a year.

VARIANTS: **Tu-22M-1** ('Backfire-A'): Initial version, thought to have equipped one squadron; large pods on wing trailing-edges; these did not, as originally believed, house retracted main landing gear, which always

retracted into fuselage; slightly inclined lateral air intakes, with large splitter plates.

Tu-22M-2 ('Backfire-B'): First series production version; increased wing span; wing trailing-edge pods eliminated except for shallow underwing fairings, no longer protruding beyond trailing-edge; seen usually with optional flight refuelling nose probe removed and its housing replaced by long fairing. Initial armament was normally one AS-4 ('Kitchen') missile semi-recessed under fuselage; current aircraft have rack for a 'Kitchen' under each fixed wing centre-section panel, although fuselage mount retained; external stores racks seen frequently under engine air intake trunks; two GSh-23 twin-barrel 23 mm guns in tail mounting, initially beneath ogival radome, now with drum-shape radome of larger diameter.

Tu-22M-3 ('Backfire-C'): Advanced production version; entered service 1985, with Black Sea Fleet air force; operational in large numbers in long-range bomber and maritime roles; wedge type engine air intakes; upturned nosecone; no visible flight refuelling probe; single GSh-23 twin-barrel 23 mm gun, with barrels superimposed, in aerodynamically improved tail mounting, beneath large drum-shape radome.

CUSTOMERS: Smolensk and Irkutsk air armies have 170 to attack deep theatre targets; Soviet Naval Aviation's four Fleet air forces have total of 160.

Following details refer specifically to Tu-22M-2:

DESIGN FEATURES: Capable of performing nuclear strike, conventional attack and anti-ship missions; low-level penetration features ensure better survivability than for earlier Soviet bombers; not expected to become ALCM carriers, although used for development launches; deployment of AS-16 (NATO 'Kickback') short-range attack missiles in Tu-22Ms has recently increased significantly their weapon carrying capability. Low/mid-wing configuration; large-span fixed centre-section and two outer wing panels variable from 20° to 65° sweepback; no anhedral or dihedral, but wing section so thin that outer panels flex considerably in flight; leading-edge fence towards tip of centre-section each side; basically circular fuselage forward of wings, with ogival dielectric nosecone; centre-fuselage faired into rectangular section air intake trunks, each with large splitter plate and assumed to embody complex variable geometry ramps; no external area ruling of trunks; all-swept tail surfaces, with large dorsal fin.

FLYING CONTROLS: Full-span leading-edge slat, aileron and three-section slotted trailing-edge flaps aft of spoilers/lift dumpers on each outer wing panel; all-moving horizontal tail surfaces; inset rudder.

LANDING GEAR: Retractable tricycle type. Each mainwheel bogie comprises three pairs of wheels in tandem, with the two forward pairs of wheels on each bogie farther apart than the rear pairs. The bogies pivot inward from the

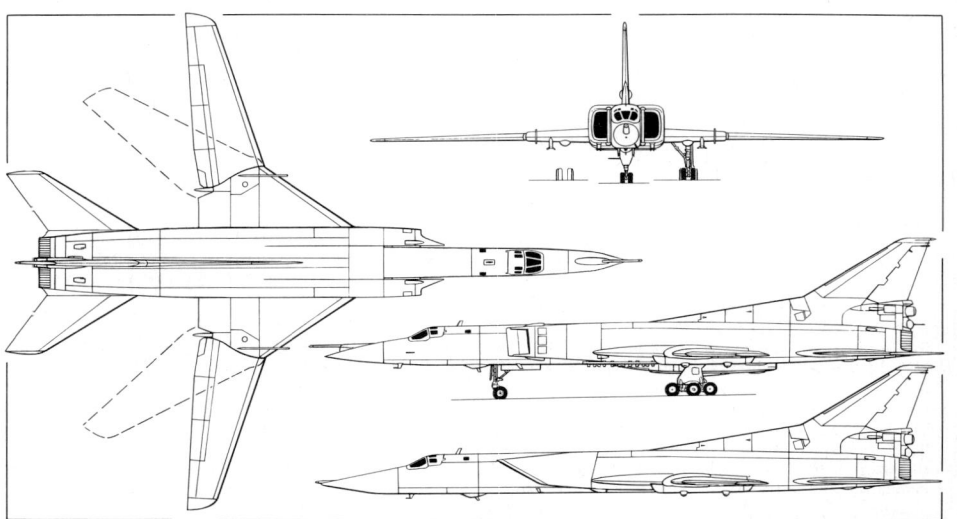

Tupolev Tu-22M-2 (NATO 'Backfire-B') bomber and maritime reconnaissance/attack aircraft, with additional side view (bottom) of Tu-22M-3 ('Backfire-C') *(Pilot Press)*

Tupolev Tu-22M-2 ('Backfire-B') with wings spread, photographed from an interceptor of the Swedish Air Force *(via FLYGvapenNYTT)*

Tupolev Tu-22M-3 ('Backfire-C') carrying an AS-4 'Kitchen' missile under its port wing *(Swedish Air Force, via FLYGvapenNYTT)*

vestigial fairing under the centre-section on each side into the bottom of the fuselage.

POWER PLANT: Two unidentified turbofans, mounted side by side in the rear fuselage, each with maximum rating of more than 200 kN (45,000 lb st) with afterburning. Fuel tankage is believed to include integral tanks in the entire fixed portion of the wings and much of the centre-fuselage above the weapon bay. Removable flight refuelling nose probe; after one observed refuelling, a 'Backfire' prototype remained airborne for a further 10 h.

ACCOMMODATION: Pilot and co-pilot side by side on flight deck, under upward opening gull-wing doors hinged on centreline. Two crew members further aft, as indicated by position of windows between flight deck and air intakes.

AVIONICS: Large bombing and navigation radar (NATO 'Down Beat') inside dielectric nosecone. Radar ('Fan Tail') for tail turret, above guns. Fairing with flat glazed front panel under front fuselage is believed to be for a video camera to provide visual assistance for weapon aiming. Very advanced ECM and ECCM.

ARMAMENT: Primary armament of two AS-4 (NATO 'Kitchen') air-to-surface missiles, carried under the fixed centre-section panel of each wing, or a single 'Kitchen' semi-recessed in the underside of the centre-fuselage, and/or AS-16 (NATO 'Kickback') short-range attack missiles. Multiple racks for twelve to eighteen 500 kg bombs sometimes fitted under air intake trunks. Alternative weapon loads include up to 12,000 kg (26,450 lb) of conventional bombs, carried internally. Two GSh-23 twin-barrel 23 mm guns, with barrels side by side horizontally, in radar directed tail mounting.

DIMENSIONS, EXTERNAL (estimated):

Wing span: fully spread	34.30 m (112 ft 6½ in)
fully swept	23.40 m (76 ft 9¼ in)
Length overall	39.60 m (129 ft 11 in)
Height overall	10.80 m (35 ft 5¼ in)

WEIGHTS AND LOADINGS:

Nominal weapon load	12,000 kg (26,450 lb)
Max T-O weight	130,000 kg (286,600 lb)
Max power loading	325 kg/kN (3.18 lb/lb st)

PERFORMANCE (estimated):

Max level speed: at high altitude	Mach 2.0
at low altitude	Mach 0.9
Max unrefuelled combat radius	
	2,160 nm (4,000 km; 2,485 miles)

TUPOLEV Tu-160
NATO reporting name: Blackjack

TYPE: Four-engined variable geometry long-range strategic bomber.

PROGRAMME: Designed under leadership of V. I. Bliznuk; prototype observed by satellite at Ramenskoye flight test centre 25 November 1981 (photograph in 1982-83 *Jane's*); US Defense Secretary Frank Carlucci invited to inspect twelfth aircraft built, at Kubinka air base, near Moscow, 2 August 1988; first operational squadron formed, Dolon air base, central USSR, 1988; West expected at least 100 to be delivered to Soviet air armies; production at huge Kazan airframe plant slowed during past year.

CUSTOMERS: Soviet air forces had received about 24 by early 1991, with two squadrons equipped.

DESIGN FEATURES: Intended for high altitude standoff role carrying ALCMs and for defence suppression, using

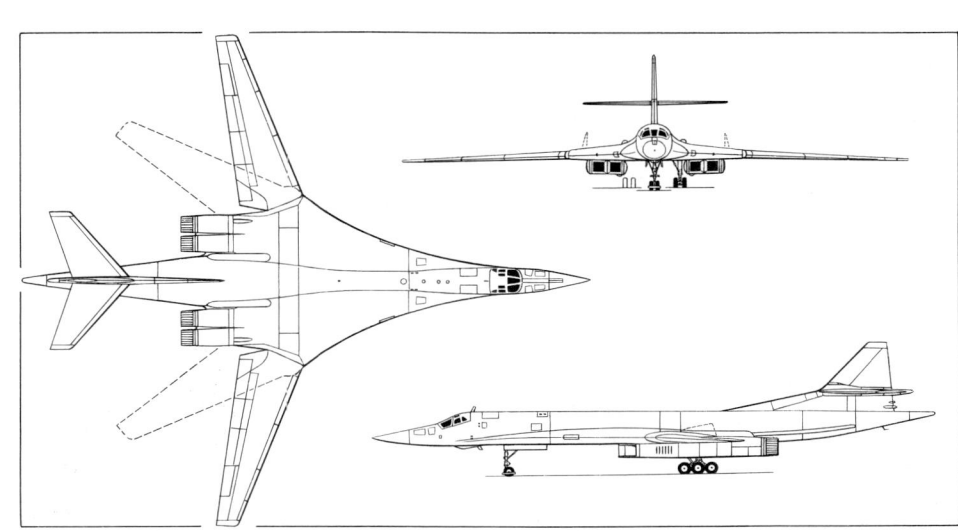

Provisional three-view drawing of Tupolev Tu-160 strategic bomber (NATO 'Blackjack') *(Pilot Press)*

Tupolev Tu-160 strategic bomber, known to NATO as 'Blackjack' *(Piotr Butowski)*

Tupolev Tu-160 ('Blackjack') bomber with wings in fully spread position *(Soviet Wings/Alexander Dzhus)*

short-range attack missiles similar to US Air Force SRAMs, along path of bomber making low altitude penetration to attack primary targets with free-fall nuclear bombs or missiles; this implies capability of subsonic cruise/supersonic dash at almost Mach 2 at 18,300 m (60,000 ft) and transonic flight at low altitude. About 20 per cent longer than USAF B-1B, with greater unrefuelled combat radius and much higher max speed; low-mounted variable geometry wings, with very long and sharply swept fixed root panel; small diameter circular fuselage; horizontal tail surfaces mounted high on fin, upper portion of which is pivoted one-piece all-moving surface; large dorsal fin; engines mounted as widely separated pairs in underwing ducts, each with central horizontal V wedge intakes and jetpipes extending well beyond wing centre-section trailing-edge; manually selected outer wing sweepback 20° to 65°; when wings fully swept, inboard portion of each trailing-edge flap hinges upward and extends above wing as large fence; unswept tail fin; sweptback horizontal surfaces, with conical fairing aft of intersection.

FLYING CONTROLS: Full-span leading-edge flaps, long-span double-slotted trailing-edge flap and inset drooping aileron on each wing; all-moving vertical and horizontal one-piece tail surfaces.

STRUCTURE: Slim and shallow fuselage blended with wingroots and shaped for maximum hostile radar signal deflection.

LANDING GEAR: Twin nosewheels retract rearward. Main gear comprises two bogies, each with three pairs of wheels. Retraction is very like that on Tu-154 airliner. As each leg pivots rearward, the bogie rotates through 90° around the axis of the centre pair of wheels, to lie parallel

with the retracted leg. Gear retracts into the thickest part of the wing, between the fuselage and inboard engine on each side; so track is relatively small.

POWER PLANT: Four Soloviev Type 'R' turbofans, each rated at 245 kN (55,115 lb st) with afterburning. Provision for in-flight refuelling assumed.

ACCOMMODATION: Four crew members in pairs, on individual ejection seats. One window on each side of flight deck can be moved inward and rearward for ventilation on ground. Flying controls use fighter type sticks rather than yokes or wheels. Crew enter via nosewheel bay.

AVIONICS: Radar in slightly upturned dielectric nosecone is claimed to provide terrain following capability. Fairing with flat glazed front panel, under forward fuselage, for video camera to provide visual assistance for weapon aiming. No head-up display. Single CRT for caution and warning data. Vertical tape engine instrumentation on centre console.

ARMAMENT: No guns. Internal stowage for up to 16,330 kg (36,000 lb) of free-fall bombs, short-range attack missiles or ALCMs. A rotary launcher can be installed in each of the two 10 m (33 ft) long weapon bays, carrying 12 AS-16 (NATO 'Kickback') SRAMs or six ALCMs, currently AS-15s (NATO 'Kent'), to be superseded by supersonic AS-19s.

DIMENSIONS, EXTERNAL (estimated):
Wing span: fully spread	55.70 m (182 ft 9 in)
fully swept	33.75 m (110 ft)
Length overall	54.00 m (177 ft)
Height overall	12.80 m (42 ft)

WEIGHTS AND LOADINGS:
Max weapon load	16,330 kg (36,000 lb)
Max T-O weight	275,000 kg (606,260 lb)
Max power loading	280 kg/kN (2.75 lb/lb st)

PERFORMANCE:
Max level speed at high altitude	approx Mach 1.88
Service ceiling	18,300 m (60,000 ft)
Max unrefuelled combat radius	
	3,940 nm (7,300 km; 4,535 miles)

TUPOLEV Tu-154M and Tu-154S
NATO reporting name: Careless

TYPE: Three-turbofan medium-range transport.

PROGRAMME: Basic Tu-154 announced Spring 1966 to replace Tu-104, Il-18 and An-10 on Aeroflot medium/long stages up to 3,240 nm (6,000 km; 3,725 miles); first of six prototype/pre-production models flew 4 October 1968; regular services began 9 February 1972; more than 600 Tu-154s and Tu-154As, Bs and B-2s with uprated turbofans and other refinements delivered, over 500 to Aeroflot (last described 1985-86 *Jane's*); prototype Tu-154M (SSSR-85317), converted from standard Tu-154B-2 (see 1990-91 *Jane's*), first flew 1982; first two production aircraft delivered to Aeroflot from Kuybyshev plant 27 December 1984; production continues.

VARIANTS: **Tu-154M:** Basic airliner with alternative standard configurations for up to 180 passengers; executive version available; with all passenger seats removed can carry light freight.

Tu-154S: Specialised freight version, announced Autumn 1982; offered primarily as Tu-154B conversion; unobstructed main cabin cargo volume 72 m³ (2,542 cu ft); freight door 2.80 m (9 ft 2¼ in) wide and 1.87 m (6 ft 1½ in) high in port side of cabin, forward of wing, with ball mat inside and roller tracks full length of cabin floor; typical load nine standard international pallets 2.24 ×

Tupolev Tu-154M medium-range airliner (three MKB [Perm]/Soloviev D-30KU-154-II turbofans) in service with CSA Czechoslovak Airlines
(Letectvi + Kosmonautika/Václav Jukl)

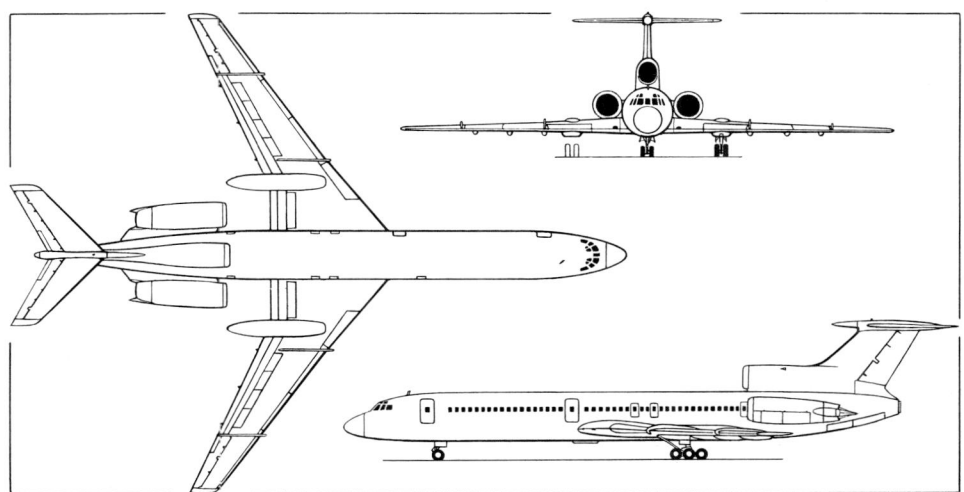

Tupolev Tu-154M medium-range three-turbofan transport *(Pilot Press)*

2.74 m (88 × 108 in) plus additional freight in standard underfloor baggage holds, volume 38 m³ (1,341 cu ft); nominal range 1,565 nm (2,900 km; 1,800 miles) with 20,000 kg (44,100 lb) cargo.

Following details apply to Tu-154M:

CUSTOMERS: Aeroflot; Aeronica, Nicaragua; Ariana Afghan Airlines (two); Balkan Bulgarian Airlines (seven); CAAC, China (more than 13); Chosonminhan Korean Airlines (two); Cubana (three); CSA, Czechoslovakia (seven); Jamahiriya Libyan Arab Airlines (three); LOT, Poland (13); Syrian Arab Airlines (three).

DESIGN FEATURES: Conventional all-swept low-wing configuration; two podded turbofans on sides of rear fuselage, third in extreme rear fuselage with intake at base of fin; nacelle to house retracted main landing gear on trailing-edge of each wing; wing sweep 35° at quarter-chord; anhedral on outer panels; geometric twist along span; circular section fuselage; sweepback at quarter-chord 40° on T tailplane; leading-edge sweep 45° on fin.

FLYING CONTROLS: Hydraulically actuated ailerons, triple-slotted flaps, four-section spoilers forward of flaps on each wing; electrically actuated slats on outer 80 per cent each wing leading-edge; tab in each aileron; electrically actuated variable incidence tailplane; rudder and elevators hydraulically actuated by irreversible servo controls; tab in each elevator.

STRUCTURE: All-metal; riveted three-spar wings, centre spar extending to just outboard of inner edge of aileron; semi-monocoque fail-safe fuselage; rudder and elevators of honeycomb sandwich construction.

LANDING GEAR: Retractable tricycle type. Hydraulic actuation. Main units retract rearward into fairings on wing trailing-edge. Each consists of a bogie made up of three pairs of wheels in tandem. Rearward retracting anti-shimmy twin-wheel nose unit, steerable through ±63°. Disc brakes and anti-skid units on mainwheels.

POWER PLANT: Three MKB (Perm)/Soloviev D-30KU-154-II turbofans, each rated at 104 kN (23,380 lb st), one in pod on each side of rear fuselage and one inside extreme rear of fuselage. Two lateral engines fitted with clamshell thrust reversers. Integral fuel tanks in wings: four tanks in centre-section and two in outer wings. For reasons of trim, all fuel is fed to a collector tank in the centre-section and thence to engines. Single-point refuelling.

ACCOMMODATION: Crew of three on flight deck, comprising two pilots and flight engineer, with provisions for navigator and five cabin staff. Two passenger cabins, separated by service compartments. Alternative configurations for 180 economy class passengers, 164 tourist class with hot meal service, or 154 tourist/economy plus a separate first class cabin seating eight to 24 persons. Mainly six-abreast seating with centre aisle. Washable non-flammable materials used for all interior furnishing. Fully enclosed baggage containers. Toilet, galley and wardrobe installations to customer's requirements. Executive and light cargo configurations available. Passenger doors are forward of the front cabin and between cabins on port side, with emergency and service doors opposite. All four doors open outward. Six emergency exits: two overwing and one immediately forward of engine nacelle on each side. Two pressurised baggage holds under floor of cabin, with two inward opening doors. Smaller unpressurised hold under rear of cabin.

SYSTEMS: Air-conditioning system pressure differential 0.58 bar (8.4 lb/sq in). Three independent hydraulic systems, working pressure 207 bars (3,000 lb/sq in), powered by engine driven pumps. Nos. 2 and 3 systems each have additional electric backup pump. Systems actuate landing gear retraction and extension, nosewheel steering, and operation of ailerons, rudder, elevators, flaps and spoilers. Three-phase 200/115V 400Hz AC electrical system supplied by three 40kVA alternators. Additional 36V 400Hz AC and 27V DC systems and four storage batteries. TA-92 APU in rear fuselage. Hot air anti-icing of wing, fin and tailplane leading-edges, and engine air intakes. Wing slats heated electrically. Engine fire extinguishing system in each nacelle. Smoke detectors in baggage holds.

AVIONICS: Avionics meet ICAO standards for Cat II weather minima and include updated navigation system with triplex INS. Automatic flight control system operates throughout flight except during take-off to 400 m (1,312 ft) and landing from 30 m (100 ft). Automatic go-round and automatic speed control provided by autothrottle down to 10 m (33 ft) on landing. Weather radar, transponder, Doppler, dual HF and VHF com and emergency VHF, cockpit voice recorder and GPWS standard.

DIMENSIONS, EXTERNAL:

Wing span	37.55 m (123 ft 2½ in)
Length overall	47.90 m (157 ft 1¾ in)
Height overall	11.40 m (37 ft 4¾ in)
Diameter of fuselage	3.80 m (12 ft 5½ in)
Tailplane span	13.40 m (43 ft 11½ in)
Wheel track	11.50 m (37 ft 9 in)
Wheelbase	18.92 m (62 ft 1 in)
Passenger doors (each): Height	1.73 m (5 ft 7 in)
Width	0.80 m (2 ft 7½ in)
Height to sill	3.10 m (10 ft 2 in)
Servicing door: Height	1.28 m (4 ft 2½ in)
Width	0.61 m (2 ft 0 in)
Emergency door: Height	1.28 m (4 ft 2½ in)
Width	0.64 m (2 ft 1¼ in)
Emergency exits (each): Height	0.90 m (2 ft 11½ in)
Width	0.48 m (1 ft 7 in)
Main baggage hold doors (each):	
Height	1.20 m (3 ft 11¼ in)
Width	1.35 m (4 ft 5 in)
Height to sill	1.80 m (5 ft 11 in)
Rear (unpressurised) hold:	
Height	0.90 m (2 ft 11½ in)
Width	1.10 m (3 ft 7¼ in)
Height to sill	2.20 m (7 ft 2½ in)

DIMENSIONS, INTERNAL:

Cabin: Width	3.58 m (11 ft 9 in)
Height	2.02 m (6 ft 7½ in)
Volume	163.2 m³ (5,763 cu ft)
Main baggage holds: front	21.5 m³ (759 cu ft)
rear	16.5 m³ (582 cu ft)
Rear underfloor hold	5.0 m³ (176 cu ft)

AREAS:

Wings, gross	201.45 m² (2,169 sq ft)
Horizontal tail surfaces (total)	42.20 m² (454.24 sq ft)

WEIGHTS AND LOADINGS:

Basic operating weight empty	55,300 kg (121,915 lb)
Max payload	18,000 kg (39,680 lb)
Max fuel	39,750 kg (87,633 lb)
Max T-O weight	100,000 kg (220,460 lb)
Max landing weight	80,000 kg (176,366 lb)
Max zero-fuel weight	74,000 kg (163,140 lb)
Max wing loading	496.4 kg/m² (101.6 lb/sq ft)
Max power loading	320.5 kg/kN (3.14 lb/lb st)

PERFORMANCE:

Max cruising speed	513 knots (950 km/h; 590 mph)
Max cruising height	11,900 m (39,000 ft)
Balanced field length for T-O and landing	
	2,500 m (8,200 ft)

Range:
with max payload 2,100 nm (3,900 km; 2,425 miles)
with max fuel and 5,450 kg (12,015 lb) payload
3,563 nm (6,600 km; 4,100 miles)

TUPOLEV Tu-155

Details of this experimental adaptation of a Tu-154, fuelled with liquid hydrogen, can be found in the 1990-91 *Jane's*.

TUPOLEV Tu-204

TYPE: Twin-turbofan medium-range passenger transport.

PROGRAMME: Development to replace Tu-154 announced 1983; preliminary details available Spring 1985; programme finalised 1986; first prototype (SSSR-64001) flown 2 January 1989 by Tupolev chief test pilot A. Talavkine; three more prototypes scheduled to fly before end 1990; two more for structural and fatigue testing; production at Ulyanovsk plant scheduled at 80 to 90 a year, to meet initial Aeroflot requirement for up to 500.

Prototype Tupolev Tu-204 twin-turbofan transport at Sheremetyevo-1 Airport, Moscow *(Piotr Butowski)*

VARIANTS: **Tu-204:** Basic version to carry 190-214 passengers, as described in detail.

Tu-204-100: Dimensions and internal arrangements unchanged; max T-O weight increased to 99,500 kg (219,355 lb) and max payload to 24,000 kg (52,910 lb), offering range of 2,860 nm (5,300 km; 3,293 miles) with full tanks and all seats occupied.

Tu-204-200: Dimensions and internal arrangements unchanged; max T-O weight increased further to 107,900 kg (237,875 lb), max landing weight to 87,500 kg (192,900 lb), max payload to 25,200 kg (55,555 lb) and max fuel load to 32,400 kg (71,428 lb); max range 4,047 nm (7,500 km; 4,660 miles) with 11,000 kg (24,250 lb) payload, or 2,805 nm (5,200 km; 3,230 miles) with max payload, in each case at Mach 0.78 at 11,100 m (36,400 ft) with reserves for 200 nm (370 km; 230 mile) diversion and 30 min hold; additional fuel carried in wing centre-section and adjacent baggage hold.

DESIGN FEATURES: Conventional low/mid-wing configuration, with all surfaces sweptback, and winglets; wing dihedral from roots; sweepback 28°; supercritical section; thickness/chord ratio 14 per cent at root, 9-10 per cent at tip; negative twist; semi-monocoque oval section pressurised fuselage; torsion box of fin forms integral fuel tank, used for automatic trimming of CG in flight; design life 45,000 flight hours and 20,000 landings, or 20 years.

FLYING CONTROLS: Triplex digital fly-by-wire, with triplex analog backup; conventional control yokes selected after evaluation of alternative sidestick on Tu-154 testbed; inset aileron outboard of two-section double-slotted flap on each wing trailing-edge; two-section upper surface airbrake forward of each centre-section flap; five-section spoiler forward of each outer flap; four-section leading-edge slat over full span of each wing; conventional rudder and elevators; no tabs.

STRUCTURE: Approx 18 per cent of airframe by weight of composites; three-piece two-spar wing, with metal structure, part composite skin; carbonfibre skin on spoilers, airbrakes and flaps; glassfibre wingroot fairings; all-metal fuselage, utilising aluminium-lithium and titanium; nose radome and some access panels of composites; extensive use of composites in tail unit, particularly for leading-edges of fixed surfaces and for rudder and elevators.

LANDING GEAR: Hydraulically retractable tricycle type. Electro-hydraulically steerable twin-wheel nose unit (±10° via rudder pedals; ±70° by electric steering control). Nosewheels retract forward; four-wheel bogie main units retract inward into wing/fuselage fairings. Carbon disc brakes, electrically controlled. Tyre size 1,070 × 390 mm on mainwheels, 840 × 290 mm on nosewheels.

POWER PLANT: Two Soloviev PS-90AT turbofans, each rated at 156.9 kN (35,275 lb st), mounted underwing in composite cowlings. Fuel in six integral tanks in wings and one in tail fin, total capacity 30,000 litres (7,925 US gallons; 6,600 Imp gallons). The torsion box of the fin forms an integral fuel tank which is used for automatic trimming of the CG in flight.

ACCOMMODATION: Can be operated by pilot and co-pilot, but Aeroflot has specified requirement for a flight engineer. Provision for fourth seat for instructor or observer. Three basic single-aisle passenger arrangements: (1) 190 seats, with 12 seats four-abreast in first class cabin at front at pitch of 99 cm (39 in), 35 business class seats six-abreast at pitch of 96 cm (38 in) in centre cabin, and 143 tourist class seats six-abreast at pitch of 81 cm (32 in) at rear; (2) 196 seats, with 12 seats four-abreast at pitch of 99 cm (39 in) in first class cabin at front and 184 six-abreast tourist class seats at pitch of 81 cm (32 in) at rear; (3) 214 seats, all

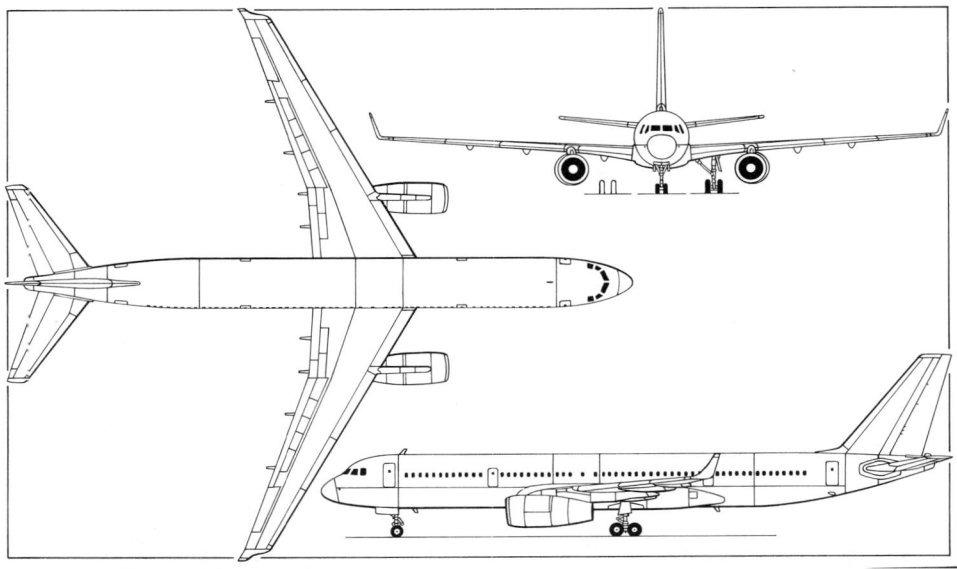

Tupolev Tu-204 medium-range transport (two Soloviev PS-90AT turbofans) *(Jane's/Mike Keep)*

six-abreast at tourist class pitch of 81 cm (32 in). All configurations have a buffet/galley and a toilet immediately aft of the flight deck, and two more toilets, a large buffet/galley and a service compartment at the rear of the passenger accommodation. Overhead stowage for hand baggage. Passenger doors at front and rear of cabin on port side, with service doors opposite. Type I emergency exit doors fore and aft of wing on each side. Inflatable slide for emergency use at each of the eight doors. Two underfloor baggage/freight holds: forward hold able to accommodate five type 2AK-0.7 or 2AK-0.4 containers; rear hold accommodates seven containers.

SYSTEMS: Triplex fly-by-wire digital control system, with triplex analog backup. Three independent hydraulic systems, pressure 207 bars (3,000 lb/sq in). Ailerons, elevators, rudder, spoilers and airbrakes are operated by all three systems; flaps, leading-edge slats, brakes and nosewheel steering are operated by two systems; landing gear retraction and extension are effected by all three systems. Electrical power supplied by two 200/115V 400Hz AC generators and a 27V DC system. Type TA-12-60 APU in tailcone.

AVIONICS: To ICAO Cat III approach standards. EFIS equipment comprises two colour CRTs for flight and navigation information for each pilot, plus two central CRTs for engine and systems data. Other equipment includes a triplex automatic flight control, automatic approach and landing system, permitting operation in ICAO Cat IIIA minima. VHF and HF radio, intercom, VOR, DME, inertial navigation system and satellite navigation system.

DIMENSIONS, EXTERNAL:

Wing span	42.00 m (137 ft 9½ in)
Length overall	46.22 m (151 ft 7¾ in)
Fuselage cross-section	
	3.80 m × 4.10 m (12 ft 5½ in × 13 ft 5½ in)
Height overall	13.88 m (45 ft 6½ in)
Tailplane span	15.00 m (49 ft 2½ in)
Wheel track	7.82 m (25 ft 8 in)
Wheelbase	17.00 m (55 ft 9¼ in)

Passenger doors (each): Height		1.85 m (6 ft 0¾ in)
Width		0.84 m (2 ft 9 in)
Service doors (each): Height		1.60 m (5 ft 3 in)
Width		0.65 m (2 ft 1½ in)
Emergency exit doors (each): Height		1.442 m (4 ft 8¾ in)
Width		0.61 m (2 ft 0 in)
Baggage holds: Height to sill		2.71 m (8 ft 10¾ in)

DIMENSIONS, INTERNAL:

Cabin, excl flight deck: Length	30.18 m (99 ft 0 in)
Max width	3.57 m (11 ft 8½ in)
Max height	2.15 m (7 ft 0½ in)
Fwd cargo hold: Height	1.162 m (3 ft 9¾ in)
Volume	11.00 m³ (388 cu ft)
Rear cargo hold: Height	1.162 m (3 ft 9¾ in)
Volume	15.4 m³ (544 cu ft)

AREAS:

Wings, gross	168.6 m² (1,814.8 sq ft)

WEIGHTS AND LOADINGS (basic Tu-204):

Operational weight empty	56,500 kg (124,560 lb)
Max payload	21,000 kg (46,300 lb)
Max baggage/freight: fwd hold	3,625 kg (7,990 lb)
rear hold	5,075 kg (11,190 lb)
Max fuel	24,000 kg (52,910 lb)
Max ramp weight	93,850 kg (206,900 lb)
Max T-O weight	93,500 kg (206,125 lb)
Max landing weight	86,000 kg (189,595 lb)
Max zero-fuel weight	77,500 kg (170,855 lb)
Max wing loading	507.7 kg/m² (104.0 lb/sq ft)
Max power loading	298.0 kg/kN (2.92 lb/lb st)

PERFORMANCE (estimated, basic Tu-204, at max T-O weight):

Cruising speed at 10,650-12,200 m (34,950-40,000 ft)	
	437-458 knots (810-850 km/h; 503-528 mph)
T-O speed	145 knots (269 km/h; 167 mph)
Approach speed	132 knots (245 km/h; 152 mph)
Time to cruising height after T-O	22-25 min
T-O run	1,230 m (4,035 ft)
T-O run, one engine out	2,030 m (6,660 ft)
Balanced T-O field length (30°C)	2,500 m (8,200 ft)
Balanced landing field length	2,130 m (6,990 ft)

Landing run   850 m (2,800 ft)
Range at Mach 0.78 at 11,000 m (36,100 ft) with max fuel
     and payload of 19,000 kg (41,887 lb), representing 196
     passengers   2,077 nm (3,850 km; 2,392 miles)

TUPOLEV Tu-334

TYPE: Twin-turbofan or twin-propfan medium-range passenger transport.

PROGRAMME: Under development as replacement for Tu-134s on some Aeroflot routes; first flight of turbofan version scheduled 1992; propfan version at early design stage.

VARIANTS: **Turbofan version:** For 86-102 passengers.

Propfan version: Basically similar; lengthened fuselage for 104-137 passengers; slightly reduced wing span and overall height; two rear-mounted pusher propfans, probably Zaporozhye (formerly Lotarev) D-227s, each 78.5-88.25 kN (17,635-19,840 lb st).

DESIGN FEATURES: To meet Aeroflot's urgent requirements, Tu-334's wings have much in common with those of the Tu-204 and its fuselage is a shortened version of that of

the Tu-204, with an identical flight deck; configuration is all-swept low/mid-wing, with rear-mounted engines and T tail; wings have supercritical section, with winglets; circular section semi-monocoque fuselage; wings have dihedral from roots, tailplane anhedral.

FLYING CONTROLS: Almost certainly fly-by-wire; aileron, two-section trailing-edge flap, two airbrakes forward of inner flap and four spoilers forward of outer flap on each wing; four-section leading-edge slat over full span each wing; inner flaps probably double-slotted, outer flaps single-slotted; conventional rudder and elevators; no tabs.

LANDING GEAR: Retractable tricycle type; twin-wheels on each unit; main units retract inward into wing/fuselage fairings; trailing-link mainwheel legs.

POWER PLANT: Two Zaporozhye/Lotarev D-436T turbofans, each rated at 73.5 kN (16,535 lb st), in initial version. Two propfans in later version.

ACCOMMODATION (turbofan): Crew of two or three on flight deck; provision for fourth seat for instructor or observer. Three basic single-aisle passenger arrangements: (1) 86

seats, with eight seats four-abreast in first class cabin at front, at pitch of 102 cm (40 in), 12 business class seats six-abreast at 96 cm (38 in) pitch in centre cabin, and 66 tourist class seats six-abreast at 81 cm (32 in) pitch at rear; (2) 92 seats, with eight first class and 84 tourist class at same pitches as 86-seater; (3) 102 seats, all tourist, at 81 cm (32 in) pitch. All configurations have a buffet/galley and toilet immediately behind the flight deck, a further buffet/galley, toilet and service compartment at the rear. Overhead stowage for hand baggage. Passenger doors at front and rear of cabin on port side, with service doors opposite. Underfloor baggage/freight holds, with doors on starboard side.

ACCOMMODATION (propfan): Flight deck unchanged. Four basic single-aisle passenger arrangements: (1) 104 seats, with eight first class, 12 business and 84 tourist at same seat pitches as in turbofan version; (2) 116 seats; with eight first class and 108 tourist; (3) 126 all-tourist; (4) 137 economy class at 75 cm (29.5 in) seat pitch. Facilities as turboprop version, plus emergency exit over wing on each side.

DIMENSIONS, EXTERNAL (T: turbofan, P: propfan):

Wing span: T	29.8 m (97 ft 9 in)
P	29.1 m (95 ft 5¾ in)
Length overall: T	33.0 m (108 ft 3 in)
P	36.9 m (121 ft 0¾ in)
Height overall: T	8.8 m (28 ft 10½ in)
P	8.4 m (27 ft 6½ in)

AREAS:

Wings, gross: T	83.2 m² (895.6 sq ft)

WEIGHTS AND LOADINGS:

Max payload: T	11,000 kg (24,250 lb)
P	13,500 kg (29,760 lb)
Max T-O weight: T	41,500 kg (91,490 lb)
P	47,400 kg (104,500 lb)
Max wing loading: T	498.8 kg/m² (102.2 lb/sq ft)
Max power loading: T	282.3 kg/kN (2.77 lb/lb st)

PERFORMANCE (estimated):
Nominal cruising speed:

T	431-442 knots (800-820 km/h; 497-510 mph)
P	431 knots (800 km/h; 497 mph)

Balanced runway length at 30°C:

T, P	2,200 m (7,220 ft)

Range:

T, with 9,251 kg (20,395 lb) payload (102 passengers)	1,079 nm (2,000 km; 1,242 miles)
P, with 11,430 kg (25,198 lb) payload (126 passengers)	1,860 nm (3,450 km; 2,143 miles)

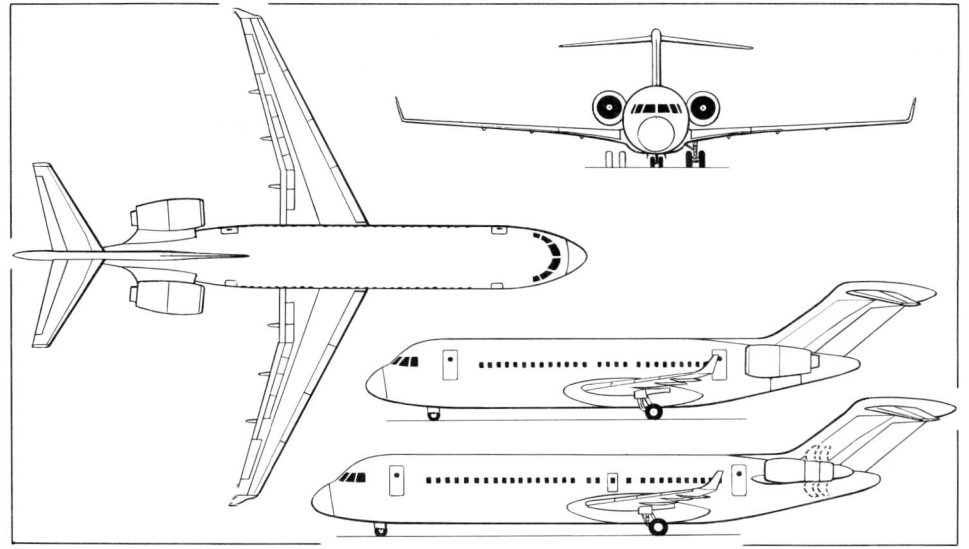

Provisional three-view drawing of the turbofan-powered Tupolev Tu-334, with additional side elevation (bottom) of version with propfan engines *(Pilot Press)*

YAKOVLEV
YAKOVLEV DESIGN BUREAU
Moscow
GENERAL DESIGNER: Sergei Alexandrovich Yakovlev
CHIEF DESIGNER, Yak-42: Alexei Vinogradov

The founder of this OKB, Alexander Sergeyevich Yakovlev, died on 22 August 1988, aged 84. He was one of the most versatile Soviet designers. Products of his OKB ranged from transonic long-range fighters to the Yak-24 tandem-rotor helicopter, an operational V/STOL carrier-based fighter and a variety of training, competition aerobatic and transport aircraft.

YAKOVLEV Yak-36MP/Yak-38
NATO reporting name: Forger
TYPE: Single-seat ship-based V/STOL combat aircraft and two-seat trainer.

PROGRAMME: Prototype **Yak-36MP** (*Morskoy Palubnyi*: maritime carrier-borne) flew 1971; production began 1975, as world's second operational V/STOL jet combat aircraft, after UK Harrier; deployed with Soviet Navy development squadron on *Kiev*, first of class of four 40,000 ton carrier/cruisers to put to sea 1976; subsequently on sister ships, *Minsk, Novorossiysk* and *Admiral of the Fleet Gorshkov* (then *Baku*), and 65,000 ton aircraft carrier *Admiral of the Fleet Kuznetsov*; experimental operation from specially configured Ro/Ro ships reported. Current designation Yak-38.

VARIANTS: **Yak-38** ('Forger-A'): Basic single-seat combat aircraft; primary roles reconnaissance, strikes against small ships and fleet defence against shadowing maritime reconnaissance aircraft; 12 on each 'Kiev' class ship.

Yak-38 ('Forger-B'): Two-seat trainer; second cockpit forward of normal cockpit, with ejection seat at lower level, under continuous transparent canopy; to compensate for longer nose, plug inserted in fuselage aft of wing, lengthening constant-section portion without modification of tapering rear fuselage; no ranging radar or weapon pylons; two on each 'Kiev' class ship.

CUSTOMERS: Soviet Naval Aviation (about 75 by October 1986; small number subsequently).

DESIGN FEATURES: Very small mid-mounted folding wings; thickness/chord ratio estimated maximum six per cent; constant anhedral from roots; leading-edge sweepback approx 45°; jet reaction control valve with upper and lower slots in each wingtip; basically oval section fuselage; integral engine air intake ducts, with boundary

The two-seat training version of the Yak-38 ('Forger-B')

layer splitter plates and downward inclined lips; row of small blow-in auxiliary intake doors short distance aft of each intake; rearward hinged door over liftjets, immediately aft of canopy, with 16 spring loaded louvres; location of corresponding side-hinged underfuselage doors conforms with forward tilt of lift engines; positions of these doors controlled automatically during take-off and landing as part of control system; fence on each side of door above liftjets, presumably to prevent ingestion of reflected exhaust efflux; yaw reaction control nozzle to each side of small tailcone; no reaction control system in nose; all-swept tail unit, with tailplane anhedral; air intake at front of long duct extending forward from base of fin, to cool avionics bay in rear fuselage.

FLYING CONTROLS: Aircraft appears to be extremely stable during take-off and landing; initially, take-off was always vertical, with rear vectored thrust nozzles up to 10° forward of vertical; this was followed by smooth conversion approx 5-6 m (15-20 ft) above deck, achieved by lowering aircraft's nose about 5° below horizon and maintaining this attitude until aircraft accelerated to 30-40 knots (55-75 km/h; 35-46 mph); at this speed, 5° nose-up attitude was assumed, and accelerating transition continued by vectoring aft the nozzles of the propulsion engine.

This VTO technique superseded by STOL take-off,

with short forward run, made possible by automatic control system which ensures that lift engines are brought into use, and thrust vectoring rear nozzles rotated, at optimum point in take-off run; STOL take-off can be assumed to offer improved payload/range.

Landing procedure begins with gradual descent from far astern, with final 400 m (1,300 ft) flown essentially level, about 30 m (100 ft) above water; aircraft crosses ship's stern with about 5 knot (10 km/h; 6 mph) closure rate, 10-14 m (35-45 ft) above flight deck, then flares gently to hover and descends vertically; precise landings are ensured by automatic control system, perhaps in association with laser devices lining each side of rear deck. Fully automatic control system ensures synchronisation of engine functioning, aerodynamic control operation, jet reaction nozzle operation, stabilisation and guidance.

Conventional aileron on each outer wing panel, with setback hinges and inset trim tab; large single-slotted Fowler flap on each inboard panel; no leading-edge flaps or slats; rudder and each elevator have setback hinges and trim tab.

STRUCTURE: All-metal; each wing comprises two light alloy panels of approx equal span; outer panel folds vertically upward for shipboard stowage; semi-monocoque fuselage and tail unit of light alloy.

Yakovlev Yak-42D short/medium-range transport (*Paul R. Duffy*)

LANDING GEAR: Retractable tricycle type. Single wheel on each unit, with legs of trailing link type with oleo-pneumatic shock absorption. Nose unit retracts rearward, main units forward into fuselage. Small bumper under upward curving rear fuselage.

POWER PLANT: Primary power plant is a Tumansky R-27V-300 turbojet (68 kN; 15,300 lb st), mounted in the centre-fuselage and exhausting through a single pair of hydraulically actuated vectoring side nozzles aft of the wings. No afterburner is fitted. Two RKBM RD-36-35FVR liftjets (each approx 30 kN; 6,725 lb st) in tandem immediately aft of cockpit, inclined forward at 13° from vertical, exhausting downward, and used also to adjust pitch and trim. Fuel tanks in fuselage, forward and aft of main engine. Drop tanks, each estimated to have capacity of 600 litres (158 US gallons; 132 Imp gallons), can be carried on underwing pylons.

ACCOMMODATION: Pilot only, on zero/zero ejection seat, under sideways hinged (to starboard) transparent canopy. Electronic system ejects pilot automatically if aircraft height and descent rate are sensed to indicate an emergency. Armoured glass windscreen.

AVIONICS: Ranging radar in nose. IFF (NATO 'Odd Rods') antennae forward of windscreen. Other avionics in rear fuselage.

ARMAMENT: No installed armament. Two pylons under fixed panel of each wing for 2,600-3,600 kg (5,730-7,935 lb) of external stores, including gun pods each containing a 23 mm twin-barrel GSh-23 cannon, rocket packs, bombs weighing up to 500 kg each, AS-7 short-range air-to-surface missiles (NATO 'Kerry'), armour-piercing anti-ship missiles, AA-8 air-to-air missiles ('Aphid') and auxiliary fuel tanks.

DIMENSIONS, EXTERNAL (estimated):

Wing span	7.32 m (24 ft 0 in)
Width, wings folded	4.88 m (16 ft 0 in)
Length overall: 'Forger-A'	15.50 m (50 ft 10¼ in)
'Forger-B'	17.68 m (58 ft 0 in)
Height overall	4.37 m (14 ft 4 in)
Tailplane span	3.81 m (12 ft 6 in)
Wheel track	2.90 m (9 ft 6 in)
Wheelbase	5.50 m (18 ft 0 in)

AREAS (estimated):

Wings, gross	18.5 m² (199 sq ft)

WEIGHTS AND LOADINGS (estimated):

Basic operating weight, incl pilot(s):	
'Forger-A'	7,485 kg (16,500 lb)
'Forger-B'	8,390 kg (18,500 lb)
Max T-O weight	11,700 kg (25,795 lb)
Max wing loading: 'Forger-A'	632.4 kg/m² (129.6 lb/sq ft)
Max power loading: 'Forger-A'	91.4 kg/kN (0.90 lb/lb st)

PERFORMANCE ('Forger-A', estimated, at max T-O weight):

Max level speed at height
Mach 0.95 (545 knots; 1,009 km/h; 627 mph)
Max level speed at S/L
Mach 0.8 (528 knots; 978 km/h; 608 mph)
Max rate of climb at S/L   4,500 m (14,750 ft)/min
Service ceiling   12,000 m (39,375 ft)
Combat radius:
with air-to-air missiles and external tanks, 75 min on station   100 nm (185 km; 115 miles)
with max weapons, lo-lo-lo
130 nm (240 km; 150 miles)
with max weapons, hi-lo-hi
200 nm (370 km; 230 miles)

YAKOVLEV Yak-41
NATO reporting name: Freestyle

TYPE: Single-seat carrier-based V/STOL fighter/attack aircraft.

PROGRAMME: Existence of this second-generation Yakovlev V/STOL combat aircraft revealed by Rear Adm William O. Studeman, USN, Spring 1988; general configuration shown in artist's impression of Yak-41 on deck of carrier *Admiral of the Fleet Kuznetsov*, in US Department of Defense's *Soviet Military Power* document; ship trials not, in fact, conducted by early 1991. New designation Yak-141 revealed June 1991 (see Addenda).

DESIGN FEATURES: Single artist's impression currently available, based on overhead satellite photography, gives no suggestion of key features such as power plant; press reports suggest use of vectored-thrust turbofan, designed under leadership of Eng Khachaturov, on lines of Harrier's Rolls-Royce Pegasus; a liftjet/vectored-thrust multi-engine power plant, similar to that of Yak-38, seems equally likely; evolutionary changes by comparison with Yak-38 include a refined airframe configuration, with twin tail fins, nose radar with lookdown/shootdown capability, and supersonic performance; purpose may be to supersede Yak-38s on four ships of 'Kiev' class, rather than operation from new 65,000 ton carriers capable of operating MiG-29 and Su-27.

YAKOVLEV Yak-42
NATO reporting name: Clobber

TYPE: Three-turbofan short/medium-range passenger transport.

PROGRAMME: Three prototypes ordered initially; first prototype (SSSR-1974) flew 7 March 1975, with 11° wing sweepback and furnished in 100-seat local service form, with carry-on baggage and coat stowage fore and aft of cabin; second prototype (SSSR-1975) had 23° sweepback and more cabin windows, representative of 120-seat version with three more rows of seats and no carry-on baggage areas; third prototype (SSSR-1976, later SSSR-42303) introduced small refinements (described in previous editions of *Jane's*); flight testing proved 23° wing superior; first series of production aircraft, built at Smolensk to replace some Aeroflot Tu-134s, generally similar to SSSR-42303 as exhibited 1977 Paris Air Show; changes for production included substitution of four-wheel main landing gear bogies for twin-wheel units on prototypes; scheduled service on Aeroflot's Moscow-Krasnodar route began late 1980.

VARIANTS: **Yak-42**: Basic standard, described in detail; Aeroflot had 72 in Autumn 1990.

Yak-42D: Increased fuel and rearranged interior; range increased to 1,185 nm (2,200 km; 1,365 miles) with 120 passengers; about 20 delivered by early 1991; production 15 a year, to continue five more years.

Yak-42E-LL: Test bed for D-236 propfan.

Yak-42M: See separate entry.

CUSTOMERS: 100 built by Autumn 1990, mostly for Aeroflot; two each for Cubana and China.

DESIGN FEATURES: Basic design objectives simple construction, reliability in operation, economy, and ability to operate in remote areas with widely differing climatic conditions; design is in accordance with Soviet civil airworthiness standards and US FAR 25; engines conform with international smoke and noise limitations, and aircraft is intended to operate in ambient temperatures from −50°C to +50°C; APU for engine starting and services removes need for ground equipment.

Conventional all-swept low-wing configuration; two podded turbofans on sides of rear fuselage, third in extreme rear fuselage with intake at base of fin; no wing dihedral or anhedral; sweepback 23° at quarter-chord; basically circular fuselage, blending into oval rear section; T tail.

FLYING CONTROLS: Hydraulically actuated; two-section ailerons, each with servo tab on inner section, trim tab on

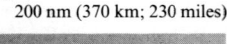

Yakovlev Yak-38 (NATO 'Forger-A') single-seat naval V/STOL combat aircraft (*Tass*)

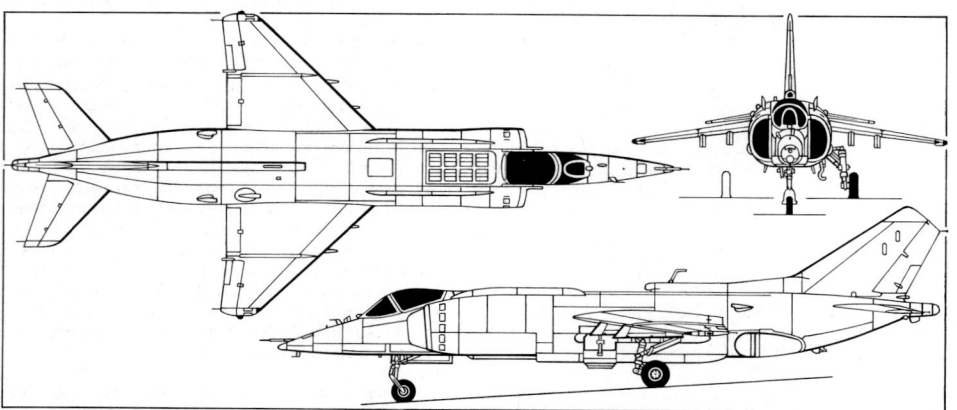

Yakovlev Yak-38 single-seat V/STOL carrier based combat aircraft (NATO 'Forger-A') (*Jane's/Mike Keep*)

outer section; two-section single-slotted trailing-edge flap, three-section spoiler forward of outer flap, full-span leading-edge flap on each wing; one-piece variable-incidence tailplane, variable from 4° up to 8° down; trim tab in each elevator, trim tab and spring servo tab in rudder.

STRUCTURE: All-metal; two-spar torsion box wing structure; riveted, bonded and welded semi-monocoque fuselage.

LANDING GEAR: Hydraulically retractable tricycle heavy-duty type. Four-wheel bogie main units retract inward into flattened fuselage undersurface. Twin nosewheels retract forward. Hydraulic backup system for extension only. Emergency extension by gravity. Oleo-nitrogen shock absorbers. Steerable nose unit of levered suspension type. Low pressure tyres; size 930 × 305 mm on nosewheels. Hydraulic disc brakes on mainwheels. Nosewheel brakes to stop wheel rotation after take-off.

POWER PLANT: Three Zaporozhye/Lotarev D-36 three-shaft turbofans, each rated at 63.74 kN (14,330 lb st). Centre engine, mounted inside rear fuselage, has S-duct air intake. Outboard engines are mounted in pod on each side of rear fuselage. No thrust reversers. Integral fuel tanks between spars in wings, capacity approx 23,175 litres (6,120 US gallons; 5,100 Imp gallons).

ACCOMMODATION: Crew of two side by side on flight deck, with provision for flight engineer if required, and two or three cabin attendants. Single passenger cabin, with total of 120 seats in six-abreast rows, at pitch of 75 cm (29.5 in), with centre aisle, 45 cm (17.7 in) wide, in high-density configuration. Alternative 104-passenger (96 tourist, eight first class) local service configuration, with carry-on baggage and coat stowage compartments fore and aft of

cabin. Main airstair door hinges down from undersurface of rear fuselage. Second door forward of cabin on port side, with integral airstairs. Service door opposite. Galley and crew coat stowage between flight deck and front vestibule. Passenger coat stowage and toilet between vestibule and cabin. Second coat stowage and toilet at rear of cabin. Two underfloor holds for cargo, mail and baggage in nets or standard containers, loaded through a door on the starboard side, forward of wing. Chain-drive handling system for containers built into cabin floor. Forward hold accommodates six containers, each with capacity of 2.2 m³ (77.7 cu ft); rear hold takes three similar containers. Provision for convertible passenger/cargo interior, with enlarged loading door on port side of front fuselage. Two emergency exits overwing on each side. All passenger and crew accommodation pressurised and air-conditioned, and furnished with non-flammable materials.

SYSTEMS: APU standard, for engine starting, and for power and air-conditioning supply on ground and, if necessary, in flight.

AVIONICS: Flight and navigation equipment for operation by day and night under adverse weather conditions, with landings on concrete or unpaved runways in ICAO Category II weather minima down to 40 m (131 ft) visibility at 300 m (985 ft). Type SAU-42 automatic flight control system and area navigation system standard.

DIMENSIONS, EXTERNAL:

Wing span	34.88 m (114 ft 5¼ in)
Wing aspect ratio	8.11
Length overall	36.38 m (119 ft 4¼ in)
Fuselage diameter	3.80 m (12 ft 5½ in)

Height overall	9.83 m (32 ft 3 in)
Tailplane span	10.80 m (35 ft 5 in)
Wheel track	5.63 m (18 ft 5¾ in)
Wheelbase	14.78 m (48 ft 6 in)
Passenger door (fwd):	
Height	1.81 m (5 ft 11¼ in)
Width	0.83 m (2 ft 8½ in)
Passenger entrance (rear): Height	1.78 m (5 ft 10 in)
Width	0.81 m (2 ft 7¾ in)
Cargo door (convertible version):	
Height	2.025 m (6 ft 7¾ in)
Width	3.23 m (10 ft 7 in)
Baggage/cargo hold door: Height	1.35 m (4 ft 5 in)
Width	1.145 m (3 ft 9 in)
Height to sill	1.45 m (4 ft 9 in)

DIMENSIONS, INTERNAL:

Cabin: Length	19.89 m (65 ft 3 in)
Max width	3.60 m (11 ft 9¾ in)
Max height	2.08 m (6 ft 9¾ in)
Baggage compartment volume (100-seater):	
fwd	19.8 m³ (700 cu ft)
rear	9.5 m³ (335 cu ft)

AREAS:

Wings, gross	150 m² (1,615 sq ft)
Vertical tail surfaces (total)	23.29 m² (250.7 sq ft)
Horizontal tail surfaces (total)	27.60 m² (297.1 sq ft)

WEIGHTS AND LOADINGS:

Weight empty, equipped:	
104 seats	34,555 kg (76,180 lb)
120 seats	34,580 kg (76,236 lb)
Max payload	13,000 kg (28,660 lb)
Max fuel	18,500 kg (40,785 lb)
Max T-O weight	56,500 kg (124,560 lb)
Max landing weight	50,500 kg (111,333 lb)
Max wing loading	376.7 kg/m² (77.1 lb/sq ft)
Max power loading	295.5 kg/kN (2.90 lb/lb st)

PERFORMANCE:

Max cruising speed at 7,620 m (25,000 ft)	
	437 knots (810 km/h; 503 mph)
Econ cruising speed	400 knots (740 km/h; 460 mph)
T-O speed	119 knots (220 km/h; 137 mph) IAS
Approach speed	114 knots (210 km/h; 131 mph) IAS
Max cruising height	9,600 m (31,500 ft)
T-O balanced field length	2,200 m (7,220 ft)
Landing from 15 m (50 ft)	1,100 m (3,610 ft)

Range at econ cruising speed, with 3,000 kg (6,615 lb) fuel reserves:

with max payload	702 nm (1,300 km; 807 miles)
with 120 passengers (10,800 kg; 23,810 lb payload)	
	1,025 nm (1,900 km; 1,180 miles)
with 104 passengers (9,360 kg; 20,635 lb payload)	
	1,240 nm (2,300 km; 1,430 miles)
with max fuel	2,105 nm (3,900 km; 2,423 miles)

Artist's impression of Yak-41 on deck of carrier *Admiral of the Fleet Kuznetsov* (*US Department of Defense*)

YAKOVLEV Yak-42M

TYPE: Three-turbofan short/medium-range passenger transport.

PROGRAMME: Development began 1987; prototype construction started 1991; first flight scheduled 1992; production to begin 1995, at Saratov.

VARIANTS: Three single-class configurations planned, for 150, 156 and 168 passengers; two mixed-class for 110 and 122 passengers.

CUSTOMERS: Aeroflot is considering purchase of 200.

DESIGN FEATURES: Much more than a stretched Yak-42, only general configuration and fuselage cross-section are not new; wings have supercritical section devised in collaboration with TsAGI, with sweepback of 25°, increased span and higher aspect ratio; double-slotted trailing-edge flaps, and winglets; together with new turbofans, this gives increased performance; fly-by-wire flight controls and five-CRT EFIS are standard; avionics are upgraded to permit operation to ICAO Cat IIIA minima.

FLYING CONTROLS: Fly-by-wire.

LANDING GEAR: Hydraulically retractable tricycle type; four-wheel bogie main units; twin nosewheels.

POWER PLANT: Three Zaporozhye/Lotarev D-436M turbofans, each rated at 73.5 kN (16,535 lb st) and fitted with thrust reverser.

ACCOMMODATION: Crew of two side by side on flight deck, with provision for flight engineer if required; basic accommodation for 156 tourist class passengers, six-abreast at 78 cm (30.7 in) seat pitch, with centre aisle; toilet and buffet/galley immediately aft of flight deck; two toilets at rear of cabin; alternative single class arrangements for 150 passengers at 81 cm (32 in) seat pitch, and 168 passengers; two mixed class configurations, for eight business and 114 tourist, or eight first class, 30 business and 72 tourist; main airstair door hinges down from undersurface of rear fuselage; second door forward of cabin on port side, with airstairs; service door opposite; emergency exit door forward of wing each side; two overwing emergency exit windows each side.

AVIONICS: TsPNK-42M digital flight control and navigation system and five-CRT EFIS standard.

DIMENSIONS, EXTERNAL:

Wing span	35.50 m (116 ft 5¾ in)
Wing aspect ratio	10.5
Length overall	40.47 m (132 ft 9½ in)

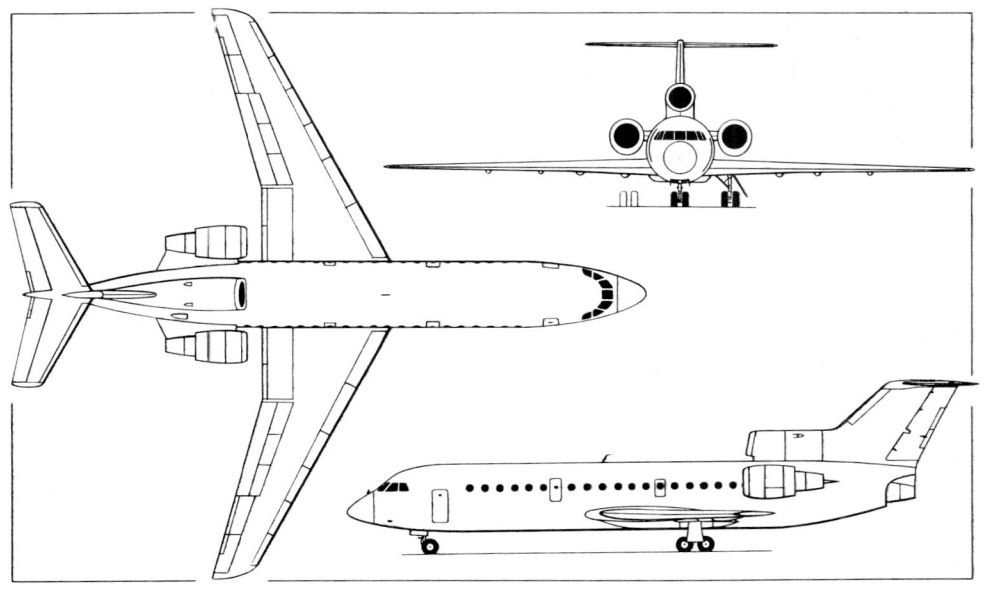

Yakovlev Yak-42 three-turbofan short/medium-range passenger transport (*Pilot Press*)

Model of stretched Yakovlev Yak-42M
(Jacques Marmain/Aviation Magazine International, Paris)

Projected Yakovlev Yak-46 twin-propfan airliner
(Jacques Marmain/Aviation Magazine International, Paris)

Yakovlev Yak-48, a projected 6/10-passenger business aircraft
(Jacques Marmain/Aviation Magazine International, Paris)

Yakovlev Yak-56 two-seat aerobatic aircraft
(Jacques Marmain/Aviation Magazine International, Paris)

AREAS:
Wings, gross	120.0 m² (1,292 sq ft)

WEIGHTS AND LOADINGS:
Weight empty, equipped	37,000 kg (81,570 lb)
Payload: with max fuel (156 passengers)	
	9,600 kg (21,165 lb)
normal	14,820 kg (32,672 lb)
max	16,500 kg (36,375 lb)
Max T-O weight	63,000 kg (138,890 lb)
Max wing loading	525 kg/m² (107.5 lb/sq ft)
Max power loading	285.7 kg/kN (2.8 lb/lb st)

PERFORMANCE (estimated):
Max cruising speed	448 knots (830 km/h; 515 mph)
Econ cruising speed	431 knots (800 km/h; 497 mph)
Normal cruising height	11,100 m (36,400 ft)
Balanced runway length at 30°C	2,200 m (7,220 ft)
Range, with reserves:	
with max payload	998 nm (1,850 km; 1,150 miles)
with normal payload	1,350 nm (2,500 km; 1,550 miles)
with max fuel	2,428 nm (4,500 km; 2,795 miles)

YAKOVLEV Yak-46 (Propfan)

TYPE: Twin-propfan short/medium-range passenger transport.

PROGRAMME: Design study and model shown at Moscow Aerospace '90 air show; prototype could fly 1995, given go-ahead.

VARIANTS: Four versions projected: single class with 168 tourist seats; mixed class for 12 first class and 114 tourist passengers; convertible passenger/freighter; casualty evacuation version.

DESIGN FEATURES: Airframe identical with Yak-42M, except for new rear fuselage and tail unit, with two side-mounted pusher propfans on pylons.

POWER PLANT: Two Zaporozhye D-27 propfans, each rated at 109.8 kN (24,690 lb st), driving contraprops, one with eight blades, other with six blades.

ACCOMMODATION: Generally similar to comparable versions of Yak-42M, except for deletion of rear underfuselage airstairs and addition of an emergency exit door at rear of cabin on each side.

DIMENSIONS, EXTERNAL: As Yak-42M, except:
Length overall	41.00 m (134 ft 6 in)
Propeller diameter (each)	3.80 m (12 ft 5¾ in)

WEIGHTS AND LOADINGS:
Weight empty, equipped	37,300 kg (82,230 lb)
Max payload	17,500 kg (38,580 lb)
Max T-O weight	61,300 kg (135,140 lb)
Max wing loading	510.8 kg/m² (104.6 lb/sq ft)
Max power loading	279.1 kg/kN (2.74 lb/lb st)

PERFORMANCE (estimated):
Nominal cruising speed	448 knots (830 km/h; 515 mph)
Nominal cruising height	11,100 m (36,400 ft)

Balanced runway length, ISA	2,100 m (6,890 ft)
Range: with max payload	
	971 nm (1,800 km; 1,118 miles)
with normal payload	1,888 nm (3,500 km; 2,175 miles)

YAKOVLEV Yak-46 (Turbofan)

TYPE: Twin-turbofan short/medium-range passenger transport.

PROGRAMME: Design study announced early 1991.

VARIANTS: As for Yak-46 (Propfan).

DESIGN FEATURES: Despite having same designation, this aircraft is entirely different from the Yak-46 (Propfan) except for having the same basic fuselage and accommodation; use of underwing advanced turbofans has necessitated moving the wings forward; in turn, this has permitted use of a conventional swept tail unit, with tailplane mounted on the tailcone; fly-by-wire flight controls and advanced avionics are as Yak-46 (Propfan).

POWER PLANT: Two unspecified high bypass turbofans, each rated at 107.9 kN (24,250 lb st).

DIMENSIONS, EXTERNAL:
Wing span	36.25 m (118 ft 11¼ in)
Length overall	38.80 m (127 ft 3½ in)

AREAS:
Wings, gross	120.0 m² (1,292 sq ft)

WEIGHTS AND LOADINGS:
Weight empty, equipped	34,840 kg (76,808 lb)
Max payload	17,500 kg (38,580 lb)
Max T-O weight	60,200 kg (132,715 lb)
Max wing loading	501.7 kg/m² (102.7 lb/sq ft)
Max power loading	278.7 kg/kN (2.74 lb/lb st)

PERFORMANCE (estimated):
Nominal cruising speed	
	448-458 knots (830-850 km/h; 515-528 mph)
Nominal cruising height	11,100 m (36,400 ft)
Balanced runway length, ISA	2,100 m (6,890 ft)
Range:	
with max payload	1,187 nm (2,200 km; 1,367 miles)
with normal payload	1,860 nm (3,450 km; 2,143 miles)

YAKOVLEV Yak-48

TYPE: Projected 6/10-passenger twin-turbofan business aircraft.

PROGRAMME: Design study and model at Moscow Aerospace '90.

DESIGN FEATURES: Conventional all-swept low-wing configuration, with rear podded turbofan engines and winglets; tailplane centrally mounted on tail fin; tricycle landing gear, with twin nosewheels and single mainwheels.

POWER PLANT: Two unspecified turbofans, each 18.15 kN (4,078 lb st).

ACCOMMODATION: Normal accommodation for six to ten persons in business configuration; convertible for freight

carrying or as ambulance for six patients; passenger door at front of cabin, port side; provision for large freight door opposite.

AVIONICS: Integrated digital flight control and navigation systems for flight to ICAO Cat II minima.

DIMENSIONS, EXTERNAL:
Wing span	16.25 m (53 ft 3¾ in)
Length overall	16.20 m (53 ft 1¾ in)
Height overall	5.15 m (16 ft 10¾ in)

WEIGHTS AND LOADINGS:
Max payload (cargo)	2,200 kg (4,850 lb)
Max fuel	3,500 kg (7,715 lb)
Max T-O weight	10,700 kg (23,590 lb)
Max power loading	295 kg/kN (2.9 lb/lb st)

PERFORMANCE (estimated):
Max cruising speed	448 knots (830 km/h; 515 mph)
Nominal cruising height	11,000 m (36,090 ft)
Balanced runway length	1,700 m (5,575 ft)
Range, 1 h fuel reserve	2,428 nm (4,500 km; 2,795 miles)

YAKOVLEV Yak-52

Production of this tandem two-seat piston engined primary trainer was entrusted to the Romanian aircraft industry. It is manufactured by Condor SA (which see).

YAKOVLEV Yak-55M

TYPE: Single-seat competition aerobatic aircraft.

PROGRAMME: Original Yak-55 made unanticipated appearance at 11th World Aerobatic Championships, Spitzerberg, Austria, August 1982; considerable subsequent refinement, including early change to stronger, tapered wings of thinner section for 1984 Championships; current Yak-55M, with further refinements, accompanied Soviet team to 1989 European Aerobatic Championships in Hungary.

DESIGN FEATURES: Mid-wing configuration; symmetrical section, no dihedral, anhedral or incidence; almost full-span ailerons, elevators and rudder all horn balanced, with ground adjustable tab; each aileron also has large suspended balance tab; bowed cantilever main landing gear with small wheels.

STRUCTURE: All-metal; two-spar wings; semi-monocoque fuselage; conventional tail unit; titanium spring main landing gear legs; rearward sliding canopy.

POWER PLANT: One 268 kW (360 hp) Vedeneyev M-14P nine-cylinder aircooled radial engine, driving two-blade controllable-pitch propeller; wing fuel tanks, capacity 120 litres (31.5 US gallons; 26 Imp gallons).

DIMENSIONS, EXTERNAL:
Wing span	8.10 m (26 ft 6¾ in)
Length overall	7.50 m (24 ft 7¼ in)
Tailplane span	3.15 m (10 ft 4 in)

Model of Yakovlev Yak-58 six-seat business aircraft
(Jacques Marmain/Aviation Magazine International, Paris)

Yakovlev Yak-112 four-seat multi-purpose lightplane
(Jacques Marmain/Aviation Magazine International, Paris)

AREAS:
Wings, gross	12.8 m² (137.8 sq ft)

WEIGHTS AND LOADINGS:
Max T-O weight	840 kg (1,852 lb)
Max wing loading	65.6 kg/m² (13.44 lb/sq ft)
Max power loading	3.13 kg/kW (5.14 lb/hp)

PERFORMANCE:
Max level speed	243 knots (450 km/h; 280 mph)
Stalling speed	57-60 knots (105-110 km/h; 66-69 mph)
Max rate of climb at S/L	900 m (2,959 ft)/min
Rate of roll	345°/s
g limits	+9/-6

YAKOVLEV Yak-56

TYPE: Tandem two-seat aerobatic light aircraft.

PROGRAMME: Announced 1990; model shown at Moscow Aerospace '90; prototype expected to fly 1992.

DESIGN FEATURES: Conventional low-wing configuration (see accompanying illustration); wings have no dihedral or anhedral; full-span trailing-edge control surfaces; unusual are retractable mainwheels; two seats in tandem under continuous transparent canopy; rectangular engine cowling.

POWER PLANT: One M-16 eight-cylinder two-row X piston engine, 224 kW (300 hp) driving AV-86 three-blade variable-pitch propeller.

EQUIPMENT: MIKBO-3 miniaturised and integrated instruments to display flight/navigation data and control power plant operation.

DIMENSIONS, EXTERNAL:
Wing span	8.30 m (27 ft 3 in)
Length overall	6.32 m (20 ft 9 in)
Height overall	1.92 m (6 ft 3½ in)

AREAS:
Wings, gross	11.53 m² (124.1 sq ft)

WEIGHTS AND LOADINGS:
Max T-O weight	830 kg (1,830 lb)
Max wing loading	72 kg/m² (14.75 lb/sq ft)
Max power loading	3.7 kg/kW (6.1 lb/hp)

PERFORMANCE (estimated):
Max level speed	248 knots (460 km/h; 285 mph)
Stalling speed	54 knots (100 km/h; 62 mph)
Rate of roll	345°/s
g limits	+9/-7

YAKOVLEV Yak-58

TYPE: Six-seat light multi-purpose aircraft.

PROGRAMME: Shown in model form at Moscow Aerospace '90; OKB claims receipt of 100 letters of intent to purchase. Could fly in 1992, given go-ahead.

DESIGN FEATURES: Constant-chord unswept wing with dihedral from roots and cambered tips; fuselage pod mounted above wing, with annular duct at rear to house aircooled pusher engine; short twin booms carry sweptback and slightly toed-in tail fins and bridging horizontal tail surface.

FLYING CONTROLS: Mechanical control system for ailerons, twin rudders and elevator; pneumatically operated trailing-edge flaps.

LANDING GEAR: Pneumatically actuated retractable tricycle type; single wheel and low-pressure tyre on each unit, for operation from unprepared strips. Mainwheels retract inward, nosewheel forward.

POWER PLANT: One 268 kW (360 hp) Vedeneyev M-14PR nine-cylinder radial engine enclosed in annular duct and driving three-blade variable-pitch pusher propeller. Location reduces noise in cabin.

ACCOMMODATION: Six persons in pairs in enclosed cabin, with large sliding door on starboard side, facilitating loading of freight when passenger seats removed, or despatch of parachutists. Planned uses include business, taxi and ambulance transport; surveillance of forests, high tension cables, oilfields and fisheries; and freight operation.

SYSTEMS: Two independent pneumatic systems for flaps and landing gear actuation and engine starting.

DIMENSIONS, EXTERNAL:
Wing span	12.70 m (41 ft 8 in)
Length overall	8.55 m (28 ft 0½ in)
Height overall	3.16 m (10 ft 4½ in)

AREAS:
Wings, gross	20.0 m² (215.3 sq ft)

WEIGHTS AND LOADINGS:
Weight empty	1,270 kg (2,800 lb)
Max payload	450 kg (992 lb)
Max T-O weight	2,080 kg (4,585 lb)
Max wing loading	104.0 kg/m² (21.3 lb/sq ft)
Max power loading	7.76 kg/kW (12.7 lb/hp)

PERFORMANCE (estimated):
Max level speed	162 knots (300 km/h; 186 mph)
Max cruising speed	153 knots (285 km/h; 177 mph)
Landing speed	68 knots (125 km/h; 78 mph)
Service ceiling	4,000 m (13,125 ft)
T-O run	610 m (2,000 ft)
Landing run	600 m (1,970 ft)
Range with max payload, 45 min reserves	more than 540 nm (1,000 km; 620 miles)

YAKOVLEV Yak-112

TYPE: Four-seat multi-purpose light aircraft.

PROGRAMME: Winner of 1988 official design competition for two-seat glider tug for Soviet sailplane clubs; developed subsequently to current four-seat configuration; model shown at Moscow Aerospace '90; prototype scheduled for completion 1992, in advance of M-17 engine availability.

VARIANTS: Basic glider tug, also intended for touring, training, ambulance, pipeline and cable patrol, fisheries surveillance and agricultural use.

DESIGN FEATURES: Conventional high-wing configuration; constant-chord unswept wing, without dihedral; cambered wingtips; single bracing strut each side; pod and boom fuselage, with heavily glazed cabin offering exceptional all-round view; swept tail fin.

LANDING GEAR: Non-retractable tricycle type; single wheel, with low-pressure tyre, on each unit; cantilever spring mainwheel legs; floats optional.

POWER PLANT: One 112 kW (150 hp) M-17 four-cylinder X piston engine, driving two-blade two-position propeller.

ACCOMMODATION: Four persons in pairs in enclosed cabin.

EQUIPMENT: MIKBO-3 miniaturised and integrated instruments to display flight/navigation data for VFR operation. Radio standard.

DIMENSIONS, EXTERNAL:
Wing span	10.46 m (34 ft 3¾ in)
Length overall	6.96 m (22 ft 10 in)
Height overall	2.90 m (9 ft 6 in)

AREAS:
Wings, gross	16.0 m² (172.2 sq ft)

WEIGHTS AND LOADINGS:
Weight empty	645 kg (1,422 lb)
Max payload	255 kg (562 lb)
Max T-O weight	1,050 kg (2,315 lb)
Max wing loading	65.6 kg/m² (13.4 lb/sq ft)
Max power loading	9.38 kg/kW (15.4 lb/hp)

PERFORMANCE (estimated):
Max level speed	113 knots (210 km/h; 130 mph)
Nominal cruising speed	81 knots (150 km/h; 93 mph)
Landing speed	65 knots (120 km/h; 75 mph)
Service ceiling	4,000 m (13,125 ft)
T-O run	490 m (1,608 ft)
Landing run	450 m (1,475 ft)
Range, 45 min reserves:	
with max payload	270 nm (500 km; 310 miles)
with max fuel	540 nm (1,000 km; 620 miles)

SOVIET AEROSPACECRAFT

SOVIET SPACE SHUTTLE

The Soviet space shuttle completed its first orbital mission successfully on 15 November 1988, in unmanned form. The orbiter, known as *Buran* (Snowstorm), was launched by an Energiya heavy-lift rocket vehicle from Baikonur Cosmodrome at 8 am local time. After two orbits, it was recovered 3 h 25 min later in a fully automatic landing on a runway 4,575 m (15,000 ft) long and 85 m (277 ft) wide, some 12 km (7.5 miles) from the launch pad.

Although the Soviet shuttle resembles its US counterpart superficially, there are significant differences. In particular, the four liquid oxygen/liquid hydrogen main engines are installed in the core component of Energiya instead of in the orbiter; and the four strap-on boosters run on oxygen/kerosene liquid propellants. Total thrust of the core component's four engines is about 5,783 kN (1,300,000 lb st). Each strap-on booster develops 7,117 kN (1,600,000 lb st). This configuration enables Energiya to be used as the launch vehicle for a variety of other payloads, as well as for shuttle missions. Thus, the Soviet Union has two vehicles rather than one, with the option of using Energiya by itself for payloads too large to be accommodated in the orbiter's payload bay.

The *Buran* orbiter flown on the first mission has a wing area and payload bay identical in size to those of the US orbiters. The wing is farther forward, to compensate for the

Space shuttle *Buran* **on Antonov An-225 transporter** *(Letectvi + Kosmonautika/Václav Jukl)*

absence of main engines in the rear fuselage, and the nosewheels are farther aft. The two-deck crew accommodation is slightly larger, with a volume of 70 m³ (2,472 cu ft), enabling up to ten cosmonauts to be carried on future manned flights, expected to begin in 1992. Four orbiters are being built under the current programme, for use in space station assembly missions, and for launching, retrieving and repairing satellites in orbit. Maximum payload is expected to be 30,400 kg (67,000 lb).

Buran weighed about 101,600 kg (224,000 lb) at lift-off in November 1988, but orbiters weighing up to 106,600 kg (235,000 lb) could be launched by the current configuration of Energiya. Total weight of the entire shuttle vehicle at lift-off was about 2,435,800 kg (5,370,000 lb). Its total thrust in vacuo built up to about 39,590 kN (8,900,000 lb) by the time the strap-on boosters separated. The four core engines continued running until a velocity of more than 7,620 m (25,000 ft)/s had been attained, eight minutes into the mission, at a height of 100 km (62 miles). Core separation was effected by firing *Buran's* reaction control system thrusters. Orbital velocity was then achieved by firing *Buran's* two rear-mounted orbital manoeuvring system engines as it climbed to a height of about 160 km (100 miles). A second firing of these engines, 45 min into the mission, established *Buran* in a 250 km (155 mile) circular orbit, at an inclination of 51.6°.

Off the coast of Chile, over the Pacific, 2 h 20 min after lift-off, the orbiter was turned tail-first, so that its orbital manoeuvring system engines could be retrofired to initiate re-entry. Temperatures on some areas of the 40° nose-up airframe reached 1,535°C (2,800°F) during re-entry into the atmosphere at Mach 25, when the orbiter was protected by 38,000 ceramic tiles. After a smooth touchdown on the runway at 183 knots (340 km/h; 211 mph), three cruciform braking parachutes were deployed to slow the orbiter.

DIMENSIONS, EXTERNAL (*Buran*):
Wing span	24.00 m (78 ft 9 in)
Length overall	36.40 m (119 ft 5 in)

DIMENSIONS, INTERNAL (*Buran*):
Payload bay: Length	18.30 m (60 ft 0 in)
Max width	4.60 m (15 ft 1 in)

AREAS (*Buran*):
Wings, gross	250.0 m² (2,691 sq ft)

Buran **space shuttle orbiter on its Energiya launch rocket at Baikonur Cosmodrome** *(Tass)*

SPIRAL PROJECT

During the period 1966-1988, the Soviet Union conducted considerable research on a project known as **Spiral** or **50-50**. Similar in some respects to the German Sänger project (which see), this involved the use of a hypersonic aircraft as the first stage of a launch vehicle that would place an aerospacecraft into Earth orbit. The first-stage aircraft had a designed wing span of 16.5 m (54 ft 1½ in), length of 38.0 m (124 ft 8 in), weight of 52,000 kg (114,640 lb) and speed of Mach 6. It was intended to carry on its back the second-stage Korolev rocket, weighing 53 tons, for launch at a height of 20,000-30,000 m (65,600-98,500 ft). This second stage was then to place into orbit the aerospacecraft that, in turn, it carried as payload. Designated **EPOS**, the aerospacecraft was to have a span of 7.4 m (24 ft 3 in), length of 8.0 m (26 ft 3 in), and weight of 10,000 kg (22,050 lb).

Prime contractor for the project, appointed on 29 June 1966, was Lozino-Lozinsky, an associate of the Mikoyan OKB. To develop the aerospacecraft, Mikoyan established a spaceflight subsidiary at Dubna, near Moscow.

EXPERIMENTAL AIRCRAFT 105

As a first stage in the development of its lifting-body aerospacecraft, Mikoyan built three half-scale and one-third-scale unpiloted models that could be launched from rocket vehicles at a height of 100 km (62 miles), to test the aerodynamic design and proposed thermal protection system during re-entry into the atmosphere. Known as **BOR-1, 2 and 3**, these models were tested at speeds between Mach 3 and Mach 14, and during re-entry at an angle of attack of 45°, when nose temperatures of up to 1,500-1,800°C were experienced. Together with wind tunnel, simulator and other testing, this qualified the stability and manoeuvrability of the EPOS design.

Next stage was to build three piloted aerodynamic test vehicles, or 'analogues', known as the subsonic **Aircraft 105-11**, supersonic **Aircraft 105-12** and hypersonic **Aircraft 105-13**. The first of these was manufactured in 1974, began its ground taxying tests in May 1976, and flew for the first time on 27 October 1977, piloted by Aviard Fastovetz. It was carried to height and launched by a

Mikoyan 105 experimental aircraft for Project Spiral *(Nigel Eastaway)*

modified Tu-95K aircraft. Further flights, by a team of four pilots, took place in 1977-78. Ground testing of Aircraft 105-13 indicated that EPOS could re-enter the atmosphere satisfactorily at an angle of attack of 53°, withstanding temperatures up to 1,500°C.

The airframe of Aircraft 105-13 was constructed of aluminium and titanium alloys. Heat protection was to be provided on the definitive EPOS vehicle by niobium alloy shielding; until this could be made available, steel plates like the scales of a fish were attached to a ceramic cushion that compensated for deformation caused by extreme heating. The 55° swept delta wings were designed to be folded upward through 45° during re-entry, giving the effect of two additional tail fins. Power plant of Aircraft 105 was a Koliesov RD-36-35K turbojet, basically as used in the Yak-38, and it had a take-off weight of 4,400 kg (9,700 lb). The hinged engine air intake door was above the rear fuselage. Wheels and skid landing gear were installed at different times. The pilot had an ejection seat.

Despite early progress, Project Spiral was terminated, and the Mikoyan team at Dubna was transferred to the Molniya enterprise at Tushino in 1981, where work on the *Buran* space shuttle orbiter was centred. Aircraft 105-11 is exhibited at the Soviet Air Force Museum, Monino.

BOR-4 and BOR-5

After the ending of tests with Aircraft 105, the Gromov Flight Research Institute was contracted to undertake a research programme with one-eighth scale models of two forms of aerospacecraft, as follows:

BOR-4: Identical in configuration to EPOS. Launched into orbit four times by rocket vehicles in 1982/84, as Cosmos satellites 1374, 1445, 1517 and 1614. Nominal orbital height 120/30 km (75/18.6 miles), with a speed of 7,500/1,200 m/s, corresponding to Mach 25/4.

BOR-5: Similar to BOR-4, but based on configuration of NASA Shuttle spacecraft. Used for five sub-orbital flights in 1986/88, the last on 22 June 1988. Designed for nominal orbital height of 120/10 km (75/6.2 miles), with a speed of 5,000/200 m/s, corresponding to Mach 16.6/0.8. These flights tested the heat shielding potential of carbon carbon and quartz fibre tiles.

Molniya is currently producing further BOR test vehicles, which are offered for export. One of the original series, which was launched by rocket into orbit and splashed down subsequently in the Indian Ocean, was illustrated in the 1989-90 and earlier editions of *Jane's*. It had a wing span of 2.35 m (7 ft 8½ in), length of 3.00 m (9 ft 10 in) and T-O weight of 1,000 kg (2,205 lb).

UNITED KINGDOM

BAe
BRITISH AEROSPACE PLC

HEADQUARTERS: 11 Strand, London WC2N 5JT
Telephone: 44 (71) 930 1020
Fax: 44 (71) 389 4774
Telex: 919221
CHAIRMAN: Professor Roland Smith, BA, MSc, PhD (Econ)
CHIEF EXECUTIVE: Richard Evans, CBE
DIRECTOR OF PUBLIC AFFAIRS: Jeremy Wooding
MANAGER, MEDIA RELATIONS: Irene Dodgson

British Aircraft Corporation (Holdings) Ltd, Hawker Siddeley Aviation Ltd, Hawker Siddeley Dynamics Ltd and Scottish Aviation Ltd nationalised and merged as British

Aerospace 1977; became private sector public limited company January 1981; residual HM Government shareholding sold May 1985; responsibility for business operations devolved 1989 to divisions and subsidiaries, currently employing 125,000. Subsidiaries comprise Military Aircraft, Commercial Aircraft, Space Systems and Dynamics Divisions, Royal Ordnance plc, Rover Group (Holdings) plc, BAe Enterprises Ltd (operating British Aerospace Flying College, Prestwick), Arlington Securities plc, British Aerospace Simulation Ltd; overseas subsidiaries are British Aerospace Australia Ltd, Steinheil Optronik GmbH, Arkansas Aerospace Inc, British Aerospace Inc, British Scandinavian Aviation AB, and Ballast Nedam BV.

Associated companies (details in International section) SEPECAT, Panavia Aircraft GmbH, Eurofighter Jagdflugzeug GmbH; others include British Aerospace (Holdings) Inc (formed to group aerospace, defence and automotive interests in North America), Arab-British Dynamics Co (formed 1977 for Egyptian manufacture of Swingfire missile); 20 per cent partner in Airbus Industrie, partner in Euromissile Dynamics Group (EMDG).

BRITISH AEROSPACE (COMMERCIAL AIRCRAFT) LTD

HATFIELD: Comet Way, Hatfield, Hertfordshire AL10 9TL
Fax: 44 (707) 275864
Telephone: 44 (707) 262345
Telex: 22411
CIVIL MARKETING OPERATIONS CENTRE: PO Box 81, Hatfield, Hertfordshire AL10 9PL
Telephone: 44 (707) 268123
Fax: 44 (707) 261696
Telex: 826 876
BRISTOL: Filton House, Bristol BS99 7AR
Telephone: 44 (272) 693831
Telex: 44163
CHADDERTON: Chadderton Works, Greengate, Middleton, Manchester M24 1SA
Telephone: 44 (61) 681 2020
Telex: 667015

CHESTER: Broughton, near Chester, Clwyd CH4 0DR
Telephone: 44 (244) 520444
Telex: 61201
PRESTWICK: Prestwick Airport, Ayrshire KA9 2RW
Telephone: 44 (292) 79888
Telex: 77432
WOODFORD: Woodford Aerodrome, Chester Road, Woodford, Cheshire SK7 1QR
Telephone: 44 (61) 439 5050
Telex: 668939/667545
CHAIRMAN: S. Gillibrand, MSc, CEng, FRAeS
MANAGING DIRECTOR: R. M. McKinlay
TECHNICAL DIRECTOR: J. B. Scott-Wilson, MA, FRAeS
EXECUTIVE VICE-PRESIDENT, MARKETING AND SALES: T. D. Rowlands
HEAD OF PUBLIC AFFAIRS: I. Woodward
DIRECTOR, PUBLIC RELATIONS AND PUBLICITY, AIRLINES DIVISION: David A. Dorman

PUBLIC RELATIONS MANAGER, AIRBUS DIVISION: H. Berry
PUBLIC RELATIONS MANAGER, CORPORATE AIRCRAFT DIVISION: A. Piper

Subdivided into three profit-accountable sections: Airbus Division at Filton and Chester; Airlines Division at Hatfield, Prestwick, Woodford and Chadderton; and Corporate Aircraft Division at Chester. Responsible for design, development, production, marketing and support of BAe 146, BAe 125, Jetstream Super 31, Jetstream 41 and Advanced Turboprop (ATP) transports; Rombac 1-11 licence manufacturing programme with Romania; design, development and production of wings for Airbus series; VC10 flight refuelling role conversion for RAF; and F-111 maintenance under USAF contract. Also supplies civil aircraft design, development, research, support, modification and refurbishing services.

BRITISH AEROSPACE (MILITARY AIRCRAFT) LTD

BROUGH: Brough, North Humberside HU15 1EQ
Telephone: 44 (482) 667121
Fax: 44 (482) 667121 extn 5758
Telex: 52634 BAEBRO G
DUNSFOLD: Dunsfold Aerodrome, Godalming, Surrey, GU8 4BS
Telephone: 44 (483) 272121
Telex: 859475 BAEDUN G
KINGSTON: Richmond Road, Kingston upon Thames, Surrey KT2 5QS
Telephone: 44 (81) 546 7741
Fax: 44 (81) 546 7741 extn 2942
Telex: 23726 BAEKIN G
PRESTON: Strand Road, Preston, Lancashire PR1 8UD
Telephone: 44 (772) 54722
Telex: 67616 BAEP G
SAMLESBURY: Samlesbury, Balderstone, Lancashire BB2 7LF

Telephone: 44 (25 481) 2371
Telex: 63435 BAES G
WARTON: Warton Aerodrome, Preston, Lancashire PR4 1AX
Telephone: 44 (772) 633333
Telex: 67627 BAEWAA G
CHAIRMAN: S. Gillibrand, MSc, CEng, FRAes
MANAGING DIRECTOR: J. P. Weston, MA(Eng)
TECHNICAL DIRECTOR: D. Gardner, BTech, DLC, CEng, FRAeS
VICE-PRESIDENT PUBLIC AFFAIRS: (BAe Defence Companies, Kingston): R. Gardner
HEAD OF PUBLIC AFFAIRS: David Mason
PUBLIC RELATIONS MANAGER, BROUGH: E. Barker
PUBLIC RELATIONS MANAGER, KINGSTON: J. Godden
PUBLIC RELATIONS MANAGER, WARTON: D. M. Kamiya

Military Aircraft headquarters transferred to and expanded at Warton 1989; departments established at other Military Aircraft sites.
Main activities include development of European Fighter

Aircraft (EFA) with Germany, Italy and Spain; design and development of Experimental Aircraft Programme (EAP) technology demonstrator; design, development, production and support of Panavia Tornado, with Deutsche Aerospace (MBB) and Alenia SpA (Aeritalia); design, development, production and support of V/STOL Harrier, Sea Harrier and, with McDonnell Douglas, AV-8B/GR. Mk 5/7 Harrier II; design, development, production and support of Hawk and, with McDonnell Douglas, T-45A Goshawk. Also updates RAF Phantoms and Buccaneers; undertakes Canberra conversion programmes; provides product support for earlier aircraft still in use and contributes to BAe 146 and Airbus programmes; offers defence support services and overseas and specialist training facilities, including technical and management courses.

BRITISH AEROSPACE (DYNAMICS) LTD

CHAIRMAN: R. H. Evans, CBE
MANAGING DIRECTOR: M. D. Parry, BSc(Eng), CEng, ACGI, FRAeS

Formed on 1 January 1989, incorporates former Air Weapons Division (Hatfield and Lostock), Army Weapons Division (Stevenage), and Naval and Electronic Systems Division (Bristol, Bracknell, Plymouth and Weymouth).

Details of missiles and weapon systems can be found in appropriate *Jane's* Yearbooks.

BRITISH AEROSPACE (SPACE SYSTEMS) LTD

STEVENAGE: Argyle Way, Stevenage, Hertfordshire SG1 2AS
Telephone: 44 (438) 313456
Telex: 82130/82197

BRISTOL: PO Box No. 5, Filton, Bristol BS12 7QW
Telephone: 44 (272) 693831
Telex: 449452
CHAIRMAN: Admiral Sir Raymond Lygo, KCB, RN (Retd)
MANAGING DIRECTOR: J. A. Holt, MSc, BSc, CEng, MRAeS
PUBLIC RELATIONS MANAGER: J. Humby

Responsible for Skynet 4 UK military communications satellite, civil communications satellites, and pallets for US Space Shuttle (see *Jane's Spaceflight Directory*). Also undertakes development of Hotol space transport.

BAe JETSTREAM SUPER 31

TYPE: Commuter/executive light transport.
PROGRAMME: Jetstream 31 development began 5 December 1978; first flight of development aircraft (G-JSSD), converted from Jetstream 1, 28 March 1980; production go-ahead announced January 1982; first flight of production aircraft (G-TALL) 18 March 1982; certificated to BCAR Section D in UK 29 June 1982, SFAR 41C in USA 30 November 1982, by LBA in Germany July 1983, DoA in Australia February 1984, BCA in Sweden December 1984. RLD in Netherlands January 1985 and DoT in Canada May 1987; customer deliveries began December 1982; 200th (first Super 31) handed over 3 October 1988; 300th to Pan Am Express at Farnborough 6 September 1990.

Jetstream Super 31 announced at 1987 Paris Air Show; certificated in FAA's 19-seat Commuter category (formulated under FAR Pts 23-24) 7 October 1988; also certificated by CAA 6 September 1988 under International Public Transport Category of BCAR Section D; Jetstream 31 and Super 31 fleet completed 1.74 million flying hours in 2.19 million flights by 31 October 1990.

VARIANTS: **Airliner:** 18/19 passengers. Up to 680 nm (1,260 km; 783 miles) stage length, without refuelling, with 18 passengers, baggage and full IFR reserves.

Quick-change (QC) facility allows conversion from 18-seat to 12/10-seat layouts in under 2 h; optional underfuselage baggage pod, 4.62 m (15 ft 2 in) external and 3.21 m (10 ft 6½ in) internal length, provides stowage for extra six cases and additional soft luggage; penalties of pod are 3-4 knot (6-7.5 km/h; 3.5-4.5 mph) reduction in TAS at cruise and 1.5 per cent reduction in specific air range; water methanol injection system developed for hot and high conditions; Super 31 cleared for use from unsealed runways.

Corporate: Executive version for 8/10 passengers; up to 1,050 nm (1,945 km; 1,208 miles) range with nine passengers, baggage and full IFR reserves; typical interior has six reclining/swivelling chairs, three-place divan, hot/cold meal galley, cocktail cabinet, wardrobe and washroom/toilet.

Executive Shuttle: Company and business charter version, with typically 1,050 nm (1,945 km; 1,208 mile) range with 12 passengers and full IFR reserves.

Special Role: Specialist application version, suited

to military communications, casualty evacuation, multiengine training, cargo carrying, airfield calibration, resources survey and protection. Jetstream **31 EZ** exclusive economic zone patrol version has 360° scan underbelly radar, increased fuel, observation windows and searchlight. Two Jetstream 31s, specially equipped with Tornado IDS avionics, delivered to Royal Saudi Air Force in 1987 for navigator training.

CUSTOMERS: Total of 347 Jetstream 31s (220) and Super 31s (127) ordered by 28 February 1991, of which 286 delivered; first Super 31 order announced 13 October 1987 by Wings West of USA (15); 59 Super 31s delivered in 1990. See Variants for RSAF navigation trainers.

DESIGN FEATURES: Current Super 31 has improvements in performance and passenger comfort, and wider flexibility for regional and interline operations; benefits derive from introduction of more powerful TPE331-12 turboprops, flat rated at 760 kW (1,020 shp) at temperatures up to 25°C, giving 8 per cent improvement at up to 20°C and up to 18 per cent power improvement at high altitude; max T-O weight increased by 400 kg (882 lb); zero-fuel weight increased by 200 kg (441 lb); internal changes include sidewash lighting, re-contoured furnishing panels giving

BAe Jetstream Super 31 light transport of American Eagle with underfuselage baggage pod

76 mm (3 in) increased width at head height, increased floor width and sunken aisle width, and reduced noise/vibration window panels.

Wing section NACA 63A418 at root, NACA 63A412 at tip; dihedral 7° from roots; incidence 2° at root, 0° at tip; sweepback 0° 34′ at quarter-chord; Goodrich rubber boot de-icing for wing and tail leading-edges; nose and tail sections unpressurised.

FLYING CONTROLS: Manually operated Frise ailerons, elevators and rudder, each with trim tab; hydraulically operated double-slotted flaps; no slats or leading-edge flaps; fixed incidence tailplane. AFCS optional (see Avionics).

STRUCTURE: Aluminium alloy construction; fail-safe wing structure of front, main and rear spars, with chordwise ribs; wing skins chemically etched and reinforced with bonded spanwise stringers; semi-monocoque fail-safe fuselage, with chemically milled skin panels.

LANDING GEAR: Retractable tricycle type, with nosewheel steering (±45°). Hydraulic retraction, mainwheels inward into wings, twin nosewheels forward. British Aerospace oleo-pneumatic shock absorbers in all units. Dunlop wheels and tyres: mainwheel tyres size 28 × 9.00-12, pressure 5.72 bars (83 lb/sq in); nosewheel tyres size 6.00-6, pressure 2.90 bars (42 lb/sq in). Anti-skid units.

POWER PLANT: Two 760 kW (1,020 shp) Garrett TPE331-12UAR turboprops, each driving a Dowty Aerospace four-blade variable- and reversible-pitch fully feathering metal propeller. Fuel in integral tank in each wing, total capacity 1,850 litres (489 US gallons; 407 Imp gallons). Refuelling point on top of each outer wing. Automatic power reserve (APR) and water methanol injection optional.

ACCOMMODATION: Two seats side by side on flight deck, with provision for dual controls, though aircraft can be approved (subject to local regulations) for single-pilot operation. Main cabin can be furnished in commuter layout for up to 19 passengers at 76/79 cm (30/31 in) pitch, or with executive interior for 8/10 passengers, but optional layouts are available, including a QC (quick change) option enabling an operator to change from an 18-seat layout to 12-seat executive configuration in around 1¼ hours. Downward opening passenger door, with integral airstairs, at rear of cabin on port side. Emergency exit over wing on each side. Baggage compartment in rear of cabin, aft of main door. Entire accommodation pressurised, heated, ventilated and air-conditioned. Toilet standard; galley and bar optional. Jetstream completion is by Field Aircraft at East Midlands Airport, Castle Donington, UK.

SYSTEMS: Air-conditioning system with cabin pressurisation at max differential of 0.38 bar (5.5 lb/sq in), providing a 2,440 m (8,000 ft) cabin altitude at 7,620 m (25,000 ft). Single hydraulic system, pressure 138 bars (2,000 lb/sq in), with two engine driven pumps, each capable of supplying 20.7 litres (5.46 US gallons; 4.55 Imp gallons)/min. One pump is capable of supplying all hydraulic systems. Combined air/oil reservoir, pressurised to 1.24 bars (18 lb/sq in), for main and emergency supply, for actuation of flaps, landing gear, brakes and nosewheel steering. APU optional.

AVIONICS: Standard Airliner avionics by Collins include dual VHF-22A com transceivers with CTL-22 controls; dual VIR-32 nav receivers with VOR/ILS/marker receivers and CTL-32 controls; dual RMI-36 radio magnetic indicators; ADF-60A with CTL-62 controller; DME-42 with IND-42C indicator; TDR-90 transponder with CTL-92 controller; WXR-270 colour weather radar with IND-270 display unit; dual Honeywell RD-450 horizontal situation indicators; dual Honeywell C-14 compass systems; dual Racal B692 communications

control and public address system and six cabin loudspeakers. Optional Enhanced Specification avionics package adds Honeywell SPZ-500 automatic flight control system; dual Honeywell RD-550 horizontal situation indicators (replacing RD-450s); Collins DCP-270 information display control panel; Honeywell AL-245 altitude alert controller; dual Honeywell VG-14A vertical gyro subsystems, and toilet loudspeaker, to above. Standard flight deck equipment includes dual Honeywell GH-14 gyro horizons; dual Kollsman MAAS 39948 airspeed indicators, A.32069 vertical speed indicators and B.45152 encoding altimeters; dual Davtron M811B digital clocks/stopwatches; Aerospace Optics 84-207-1 flight director mode indicator, dual Aerospace Optics 99-230 marker beacon lights; SFENA H.301 standby artificial horizons, and Sangamo Weston S149-1-169 OAT gauge. Enhanced Specification adds or substitutes Honeywell AD-550C attitude director indicator, BA-141 encoding altimeter, VS-200 vertical speed indicator and PC-500 autopilot controller to above.

DIMENSIONS, EXTERNAL:

Wing span	15.85 m (52 ft 0 in)
Wing chord: at root	2.19 m (7 ft 2½ in)
at tip	0.80 m (2 ft 7¼ in)
Wing aspect ratio	9.95
Length: overall	14.37 m (47 ft 1½ in)
fuselage	13.40 m (43 ft 11½ in)
Height overall	5.38 m (17 ft 8 in)
Fuselage: Max diameter	1.98 m (6 ft 6 in)
Tailplane span	6.60 m (21 ft 8 in)
Wheel track	5.94 m (19 ft 6 in)
Wheelbase	4.60 m (15 ft 1 in)
Propeller diameter	2.69 m (8 ft 10 in)
Passenger door: Height	1.42 m (4 ft 8 in)
Width	0.86 m (2 ft 10 in)
Emergency exits: Height	0.91 m (3 ft 0 in)
Width	0.56 m (1 ft 10 in)

DIMENSIONS, INTERNAL:

Cabin, excl flight deck: Length	7.39 m (24 ft 3 in)
Max width	1.85 m (6 ft 1 in)
Max height	1.80 m (5 ft 11 in)

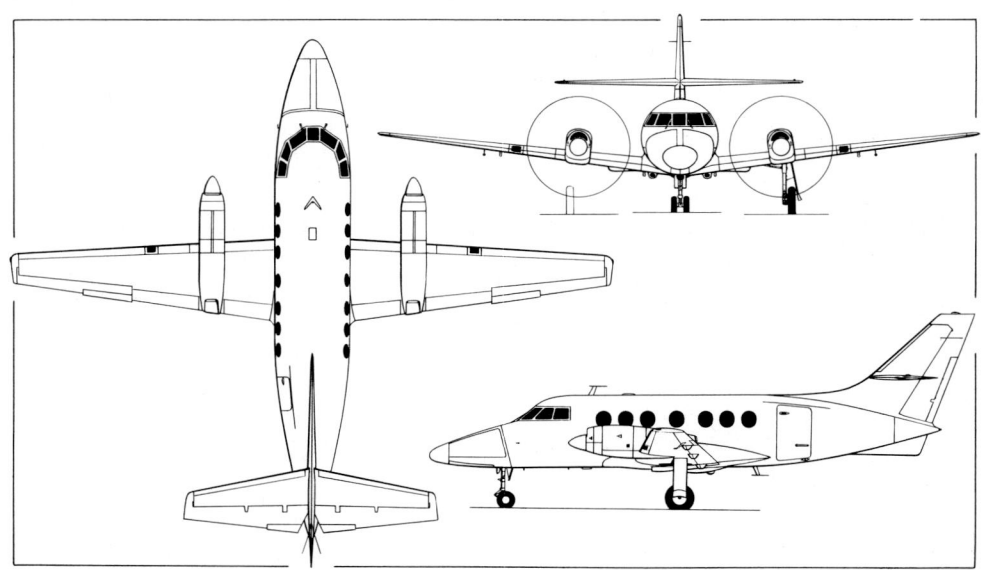

BAe Jetstream 31 twin-turboprop commuter/executive light transport (*Pilot Press*)

Floor area	8.35 m² (90 sq ft)
Volume (trimmed aircraft)	16.99 m³ (600 cu ft)
Baggage compartment volume:	
Airliner	2.13-2.74 m³ (75.2-96.7 cu ft)
Corporate	1.34-1.48 m³ (47.2-52.2 cu ft)
Baggage pod (optional)	1.39 m³ (49 cu ft)

AREAS:

Wings, gross	25.20 m² (271.3 sq ft)
Ailerons, aft of hinge line (total)	1.52 m² (16.4 sq ft)
Trailing-edge flaps (total)	3.25 m² (35.0 sq ft)
Vertical tail surfaces (total)	7.72 m² (83.1 sq ft)
Horizontal tail surfaces (total)	7.80 m² (84.0 sq ft)

WEIGHTS AND LOADINGS:

Operating weight empty	4,578 kg (10,092 lb)
Baggage pod weight empty	59 kg (130 lb)
Max fuel	1,372 kg (3,024 lb)
Max payload	1,805 kg (3,980 lb)
Max capacity of baggage pod	197 kg (435 lb)
Max T-O weight	7,350 kg (16,204 lb)
Max ramp weight	7,400 kg (16,314 lb)
Max landing weight	7,080 kg (15,609 lb)
Max zero-fuel weight	6,500 kg (14,330 lb)
Max wing loading	291.6 kg/m² (59.72 lb/sq ft)
Max power loading	4.84 kg/kW (7.94 lb/shp)

PERFORMANCE (at max T-O weight, except where stated):

Max cruising speed at 4,575 m (15,000 ft)	
	264 knots (489 km/h; 304 mph)
Econ cruising speed at 7,620 m (25,000 ft)	
	244 knots (452 km/h; 281 mph)
Stalling speed, flaps down	86 knots (159 km/h; 99 mph)
Max rate of climb at S/L	683 m (2,240 ft)/min
Rate of climb at S/L, one engine out	137 m (450 ft)/min
Certificated ceiling	7,620 m (25,000 ft)
Service ceiling, one engine out	3,660 m (12,000 ft)
Min ground turning radius about nosewheel	
	6.50 m (21 ft 4 in)
T-O field length: BCAR Section D	1,440 m (4,724 ft)
T-O to 15 m (50 ft): SFAR 41C	975 m (3,200 ft)
Landing field length, at max landing weight:	
BCAR Section D	1,235 m (4,052 ft)
SFAR 41C/FAR 135	1,165 m (3,820 ft)

Accelerate/stop distance:
SFAR 41C   1,362 m (4,470 ft)
Range with IFR reserves:
  19 passengers   700 nm (1,296 km; 805 miles)
  18 passengers, flight attendant and galley
         600 nm (1,111 km; 690 miles)

BAe JETSTREAM 41

TYPE: Commuter airliner.
PROGRAMME: Development announced 24 May 1989; full-scale cabin mockup displayed at 1989 Paris Air Show. Risk-sharing partners Field Aircraft Ltd of UK (electrical and avionics looms, interior furnishings) and Pilatus Flugzeugwerke AG of Switzerland (manufacture of tail assemblies and ailerons); Gulfstream Aerospace Technologies of Oklahoma, USA, to build 200 wing sets for 1990-2000 delivery; ML Slingsby Group to produce large composite components. Fuselage/wing mating 13 November 1990; rollout 27 March 1991; first flight (G-GCJL) anticipated June 1991; customer deliveries to begin Autumn 1992, following certification to FAR/JAR 25; production rate 35 aircraft per year by mid/late 1990s.
VARIANTS: **QC/Combi:** Proposed; Combi may be offered with 18 airliner or 10 executive shuttle seats, three containers loaded through rear baggage door. Incorporation of large freight door in parallel section of rear fuselage being evaluated, sized to accommodate standard containers; QC seat-rail mounted guide rollers and ballmats for 9g restrained rigid containers.
    Jetstream 51: Possible further-stretched version, under consideration. No details yet released.
CUSTOMERS: By March 1991, firm orders from Pan Am Express (10) and Manx Airlines (two), plus 92 options, incl 50 for American Eagle.
DESIGN FEATURES: Fuselage cross-section as Jetstream Super 31 but stretched 4.88 m (16 ft 0 in); forward plug 2.51 m (8 ft 3 in) with airstair door, rear plug 2.36 m (7 ft 9 in) with Type III emergency exit; large inward opening rear baggage door to 4.81 m³ (170 cu ft) hold; wing mounted below fuselage to permit clear cabin aisle; rearward extended fairing encloses 1.35 m³ (47.5 cu ft) baggage hold. Wing span increased, Super 31 wing extended inboard from nacelles; wing incidence 2.5°; revised ailerons, improved flaps, increased in span and chord; increased fuel capacity in wing, with pressure refuelling; lift spoilers inboard of nacelles. New nacelles for TPE331-14GR/HR turboprops with increased propeller/fuselage clearance; forward retracting main landing gear with twin wheels; increased chord rudder, increased tailplane area. V windscreen; duplicated control runs; floor mounted control columns replace yokes; Honeywell 4-tube EFIS, optional fifth tube.
FLYING CONTROLS: As for Super 31.
STRUCTURE: As for Super 31.
LANDING GEAR: Dunlop wheels and tyres: twin wheels on each main leg, size 22 × 6.75, tyre pressure 8.27 bars (120 lb/sq in); twin nosewheels, size 17 × 6.00, tyre pressure 2.9 bars (42 lb/sq in). Dunlop three-rotor steel brakes; anti-skid standard. Steerable nosewheels, maximum steering angle 45°.
POWER PLANT: Two 1,118 kW (1,500 shp) Garrett TPE331-14GR/HR flat rated turboprops, handed, each driving a five-blade constant-speed feathering McCauley metal propeller. Usable fuel capacity 3,273 litres (865 US gallons; 720 Imp gallons).
ACCOMMODATION: Flight crew of two; one attendant seated centrally at rear of cabin; and up to 29 passengers seated in ten double seats on right of cabin and nine singles on left at min seat pitch of 76.2 cm (30 in). Externally serviced toilet at rear on port side. Optional galley in 27-seat layout. Passenger door with integral airstair at front of cabin on port side. Emergency exit over wing on each side and at rear of cabin on starboard side. Stowage for carry-on baggage in forward cabin on right side, coat stowage at front and rear of cabin. Main baggage hold at rear of cabin, with external door; additional stowage in ventral wingroot fairing.
SYSTEMS: Normalair-Garrett air-conditioning system with cabin pressurisation at max differential of 0.39 bar (5.7 lb/sq in), providing 2,440 m (8,000 ft) cabin altitude at 7,925 m (26,000 ft) or 2,225 m (7,300 ft) at American max operating altitude of 7,620 m (25,000 ft). Hydraulic system, pressure 138 bars (2,000 lb/sq in), with variable delivery pump on each engine, one pump capable of supplying all services; system operates landing gear, nosewheel steering, flaps, spoilers and wheelbrakes. Emergency system operated by handpump on flight deck floor for flaps and landing gear. Electrical power by dual channel 28V DC system, provided by starter/generator on each engine, rated at 550A continuous, and two 27Ah batteries; 26V 400 Hz AC system powered by two 1.25VA static inverters for left and right hand instrument and navigation systems, either inverter capable of supplying 115V AC to flight data recorder. Electrical de-icing for propellers, pneumatic boot de-icing for wing, tailplane and fin leading edges. Electrical anti-icing for windscreen, pitot/static heads, airflow sensors and elevator horns. Engine intakes have bleed air anti-icing. Two-bottle fire extinguishing system in nacelles.
AVIONICS: Honeywell Primus II four-tube EFIS standard. Dual nav/com with VOR/ILS/markers; ADF; DME;

BAe Jetstream 41 twin-turboprop commuter airliner rolled out on 27 March 1991

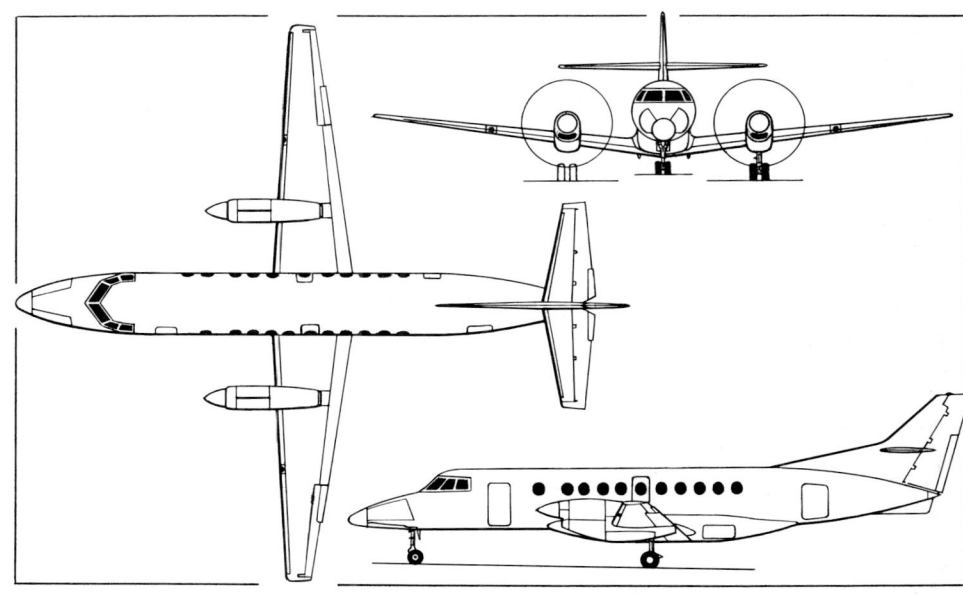

The 27/29-passenger BAe Jetstream 41 commuter airliner *(Pilot Press)*

dual transponders; flight director; and weather radar standard. Five-tube EFIS and autopilot optional.

DIMENSIONS, EXTERNAL:
Wing span	18.29 m (60 ft 0 in)
Wing chord: at root	2.70 m (8 ft 10½ in)
at tip	0.71 m (2 ft 4 in)
Wing aspect ratio	10.3
Length overall	19.25 m (63 ft 2 in)
Height overall	5.74 m (18 ft 10 in)
Tailplane span	6.68 m (21 ft 11 in)
Wheel track	6.10 m (20 ft 0 in)
Wheelbase	7.32 m (24 ft 0 in)
Propeller diameter	2.90 m (9 ft 6 in)
Propeller ground clearance	0.43 m (1 ft 5 in)
Passenger door: Height	1.42 m (4 ft 8 in)
Width	0.74 m (2 ft 5 in)
Height to sill	1.24 m (4 ft 1 in)
Baggage door: Height	1.22 m (4 ft 0 in)
Width	1.35 m (4 ft 5 in)
Height to sill	1.68 m (5 ft 6 in)
Emergency exits, overwing: Height	0.99 m (3 ft 3 in)
Width	0.51 m (1 ft 8 in)
Emergency exit, rear: Height	1.22 m (4 ft 0 in)
Width	0.51 m (1 ft 8 in)

DIMENSIONS, INTERNAL:
Cabin: Length	9.55 m (31 ft 4 in)
Max width	1.85 m (6 ft 1 in)
Max height	1.78 m (5 ft 10 in)
Volume	29.45 m³ (1,040 cu ft)
Baggage compartment volume:	
rear	4.81 m³ (170 cu ft)
ventral wingroot fairing	1.35 m³ (47.5 cu ft)

AREAS:
Wings, gross	32.59 m² (350.8 sq ft)
Ailerons (total)	1.94 m² (20.90 sq ft)
Trailing-edge flaps (total)	5.28 m² (56.80 sq ft)
Spoilers (total)	0.91 m² (9.78 sq ft)
Rudder, incl tab	2.03 m² (21.87 sq ft)
Tailplane	8.58 m² (92.35 sq ft)
Elevators, incl tabs	2.43 m² (26.18 sq ft)

WEIGHTS AND LOADINGS:
Weight empty	6,143 kg (13,544 lb)
Max fuel weight	2,612 kg (5,760 lb)
Max T-O weight	10,150 kg (22,377 lb)
Max ramp weight	10,200 kg (22,487 lb)
Max zero-fuel weight	9,000 kg (19,842 lb)
Max landing weight	9,850 kg (21,715 lb)
Max wing loading	311.5 kg/m² (63.8 lb/sq ft)
Max power loading	4.54 kg/kW (7.46 lb/shp)

PERFORMANCE (estimated, at max T-O weight, ISA, except where indicated):
Never-exceed speed (V$_{NE}$):	
to 5,300 m (17,400 ft)	
315 knots (583 km/h; 362 mph) CAS	
above 5,300 m (17,400 ft)	Mach 0.65
Max level speed at 6,100 m (20,000 ft)	
295 knots (547 km/h; 340 mph)	
Max cruising speed at 6,100 m (20,000 ft)	
292 knots (541 km/h; 336 mph)	
Econ cruising speed at 6,100 m (20,000 ft)	
260 knots (482 km/h; 299 mph)	
Max rate of climb at S/L	670 m (2,200 ft)/min
Service ceiling	7,925 m (26,000 ft)
Service ceiling, one engine out	4,575 m (15,000 ft)
Min ground turning radius, based on nosewheel	
10.67 m (35 ft 0 in)	
T-O run	1,525 m (5,000 ft)
Landing run	1,280 m (4,200 ft)
Range with 29 passengers, IFR reserves	
590 nm (1,093 km; 679 miles)	

BAe 125 SERIES 700-II

TYPE: Twin-turbofan business transport.
PROGRAMME: Announced 3 October 1990; first conversion N702BA.
COSTS: Standard aircraft approximately US$6 million.
DESIGN FEATURES: Update of Series 700 airframes (see 1983-84 *Jane's*) by Arkansas Aerospace Inc, Little Rock; refurbished flight deck and new cabin interior with five Aircraft Modular Products chairs and three-place sofa;

updated avionics package features dual Honeywell EDZ-605 EFIS, Honeywell Primus 870 weather radar, Global Wulfsberg GNS500-V with GPS (with provision for second system); Universal Navigation CVR and wiring provision for Fairchild F-800 FDR and NDB2 navigation data bank.

POWER PLANT: Two 16.46 kN (3,700 lb st) Garrett TFE731-3-1RH turbofans. Total fuel capacity (integral wing tanks, rear underfuselage tank and dorsal fin tank) 5,369 litres (1,418 US gallons; 1,171 Imp gallons).

DIMENSIONS, EXTERNAL:

Wing span	14.33 m (47 ft 0 in)
Wing chord (mean)	2.29 m (7 ft 6¼ in)
Wing aspect ratio	6.25
Length overall	15.46 m (50 ft 8½ in)
Height overall	5.36 m (17 ft 7 in)
Fuselage: Max diameter	1.93 m (6 ft 4 in)
Tailplane span	6.10 m (20 ft 0 in)
Wheel track	2.79 m (9 ft 2 in)
Wheelbase	6.34 m (20 ft 9½ in)
Passenger door: Height	1.30 m (4 ft 3 in)
Width	0.69 m (2 ft 3 in)
Emergency exits: Height	0.91 m (3 ft 0 in)
Width	0.51 m (1 ft 8 in)

DIMENSIONS, INTERNAL:

Cabin, excl flight deck: Length	6.50 m (21 ft 4 in)
Max width	1.80 m (5 ft 11 in)
Max height	1.75 m (5 ft 9 in)
Floor area	5.11 m² (55.0 sq ft)
Volume (trimmed aircraft)	17.10 m³ (604.0 cu ft)
Baggage compartment volume:	
Corporate	0.85 m³ (30.0 cu ft)

AREAS:

Wings, gross	32.79 m² (353.0 sq ft)

WEIGHTS AND LOADINGS:

Operating weight empty	6.532 kg (14,400 lb)
Max fuel	4.263 kg (9,400 lb)
Max payload	862 kg (1,900 lb)
Max ramp and max T-O weight	11,567 kg (25,500 lb)
Max landing weight	9.979 kg (22,000 lb)
Max zero-fuel weight	7,393 kg (16,300 lb)
Max wing loading	352.7 kg/m² (72.24 lb/sq ft)
Max power loading	351.6 kg/kN (3.45 lb/lb st)

PERFORMANCE (at max T-O weight, except where stated):

Max cruising speed at 8,380 m (27,500 ft)	436 knots (808 km/h; 502 mph)
Econ cruising speed at 12,500 m (41,000 ft)	390 knots (723 km/h; 449 mph)
Stalling speed, flaps down	84 knots (155 km/h; 96 mph) EAS
Certificated ceiling	12,500 m (41,000 ft)
Min ground turning radius about nosewheel	9.14 m (30 ft 0 in)
T-O field length: BCAR Section D	1,417 m (4,650 ft)
Landing field length at max landing weight:	
BCAR Section D	1,143 m (3,750 ft)
FAR 121	1,097 m (3,600 ft)
Range with NBAA reserves:	
6 passengers	2,150 nm (3,983 km; 2,475 miles)

BAe 125 SERIES 800
US Air Force designation: C-29A

TYPE: Twin-turbofan business transport.

PROGRAMME: First flight of prototype (G-BKTF) 26 May 1983 (max operating altitude achieved during the 3 h 8 min flight); type certificate gained 4 May 1984 and Certificate of Airworthiness, Public Transport Category, on 30 May 1984; FAA certification 7 June 1984.

VARIANTS: **Series 800A:** For North American market.

Series 800B: General version outside North America.

CUSTOMERS: By December 1990, 198 sold (784 BAe 125s of all versions ordered from 40 countries; 28 Series 800s delivered in 1990). First of six C-29As for USAF delivered on 24 April 1990, equipped with LTV Sierra Research Division inspection equipment for the combat flight inspection and navigation (C-FIN) mission, replacing CT-39A and C-140A calibration fleet with 1866th FCS at Scott AFB. Three JASDF aircraft also to be Sierra equipped, ordered in August 1989 for flight inspection (FC-X), for delivery from December 1992.

DESIGN FEATURES: Advanced version of BAe 125; other civil/military roles include communications, air ambulance, airways inspection and crew training; improvements compared with Series 700 include curved windscreen, sequenced nosewheel doors, extended fin leading-edge, larger ventral fuel tank, and increased wing span which reduces induced drag, improves aerodynamic efficiency and carries extra fuel; outboard 3.05 m (10 ft) of each wing redesigned. TFE731-5R-1H turbofans improve airfield/climb performance and increase maximum speed and range; redesigned interior, with increased headroom by relocating oxygen dropout units to sidewall panels, and 12.2 cm (4.8 in) extra width at shoulder level by sculpturing sidewall panels around fuselage frames; flight deck incorporates five-tube Collins EFIS-85, with centrally mounted multi-function display showing flight plans and checklists.

BAe wing sections; thickness/chord ratio 14 per cent at root, 8.35 per cent at tip; dihedral 2°; incidence 2° 5′ 42″ at root, −3° 5′ 49″ at tip; sweepback 20° at quarter-chord;

BAe 125 Series 700-II converted by Arkansas Modification Center

TKS liquid system de-icing/anti-icing on leading-edges of wings and tailplane; small fairings on tailplane undersurface eliminate turbulence around elevator hinge cutouts.

FLYING CONTROLS: Manually operated mass balanced ailerons, elevators and rudder, each with geared tab (servo assisted for ailerons); port aileron tab trimmed manually via screwjack. Hydraulically actuated four-position double-slotted flaps; mechanically operated hydraulic cutout prevents asymmetric flap operation; upper and lower airbrakes, with interconnected controls to prevent asymmetric operation, form part of flap shrouds and provide lift dumping for landing. Fixed incidence tailplane.

STRUCTURE: All-metal. One-piece wings, dished to pass under fuselage and attached by four vertical links, side link and drag spigot; two-spar fail-safe wings, with partial centre spar of approx two-thirds span, to form integral fuel tankage; singe-piece skins on each upper and lower wing semi-spans; detachable leading-edges; fail-safe fuselage structure of mainly circular cross-section, incorporating Redux bonding.

LANDING GEAR: Retractable tricycle type, with twin wheels on each unit. Hydraulic retraction: nosewheels forward, mainwheels inward into wings. Oleo-pneumatic shock absorbers. Fully castoring nose unit, steerable ±45°.

Dunlop mainwheels and 12-ply tubeless tyres, size 23 × 7-12. Dunlop nosewheels and 6-ply tubeless tyres, size 18 × 4.25-10. Dunlop triple-disc hydraulic brakes with Maxaret anti-skid units on all mainwheels.

POWER PLANT: Two 19.13 kN (4,300 lb st) Garrett TFE731-5R-1H turbofans, mounted on sides of rear fuselage in pods designed and manufactured by Grumman Aerospace. Optional thrust reversers developed by Dee Howard Company. Engine intake anti-icing by engine bleed air. Integral fuel tanks in wings, with combined capacity of 4,820 litres (1,273 US gallons; 1,060 Imp gallons). Rear underfuselage tank of 854 litres (226 US gallons; 188 Imp gallons) capacity, giving total capacity of 5,674 litres (1,499 US gallons; 1,248 Imp gallons). Single pressure refuelling point at rear of ventral tank. Overwing refuelling point near each wingtip.

ACCOMMODATION: Crew of two on flight deck, which is fully soundproofed, insulated and air-conditioned. Dual controls standard. Seat for third crew member. Standard executive layout has forward and rear baggage compartments, forward galley, wardrobe and toilet at rear. Individual recessed lights, air louvres and oxygen masks above each passenger position. Cabin styling offers the operator a choice of interchangeable furnishing units to suit individual requirements, with up to 14 seats. The wide seats swivel through 180°, are adjustable fore, aft

BAe 125 Series 800 business transport

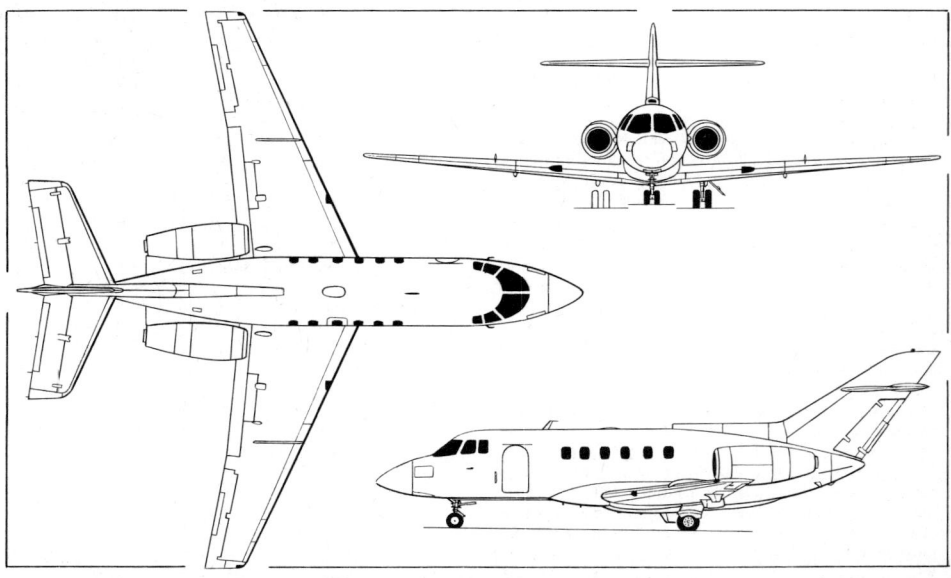

BAe 125 Series 800 (two Garrett TFE731-5R-1H turbofans) *(Pilot Press)*

and sideways, and can be reclined and used as a bed. Primary configuration since mid-1987 is an open plan layout, with the traditional club four seating moved to the rear of the cabin, the partial bulkhead at the front removed and the galley relocated behind the enlarged forward baggage area. Accommodation in the forward cabin comprises two individual swivelling chairs and a three-place settee. Outward opening door at front on port side, with integral airstairs. Emergency exit over wing on starboard side. Electric windscreen anti-icing. Optional heated baggage pannier in place of the rear underfuselage fuel tank.

SYSTEMS: AiResearch air-conditioning and pressurisation system. Max cabin differential 0.59 bar (8.55 lb/sq in). Oxygen system standard, with dropout masks for passengers. Hydraulic system, pressure 186-207 bars (2,700-3,000 lb/sq in), for operation of landing gear, mainwheel doors, flaps, spoilers, nosewheel steering, mainwheel brakes and anti-skid units. Two accumulators, pressurised by engine bleed air, one for main system pressure, the other providing emergency hydraulic power for wheel brakes in case of main system failure. Independent auxiliary system for lowering landing gear and flaps in the event of a main system failure. DC electrical system utilises two 30V 12kW engine driven starter/generators and two 24V 23Ah nickel-cadmium batteries. A 24V 4Ah battery provides separate power for standby instruments. AC electrical system includes two 1.25kVA static inverters, providing 115V 400Hz single-phase supplies, one 250VA standby static inverter for avionics, and two engine driven 208V 7.4kVA frequency-wild alternators for windscreen anti-icing. Ground power receptacle on starboard side at rear of fuselage for 28V external DC supply. Turbomach T-62T-40C8D-1 auxiliary power unit. Engine ice protection system supplied by engine bleed air. Graviner triple FD Firewire fire warning system and two BCF engine fire extinguishers. Stall warning system indicates approach to the stall, and an identification system operates a stick pusher to initiate a nose down pitching movement if the approach to the stall exceeds a predetermined rate.

AVIONICS: Digital avionics received FAA Cat II certification in 1987. Standard Collins avionics include dual VHF-22A com transceivers, 628T-3 HF com transceiver, dual VIR-32 VHF nav receivers with marker beacon indicator, dual ADF-60B, dual AHS-85 attitude and heading reference systems, dual DME-42 DME, dual TDR-90 ATC transponders, WXR-300 weather radar, dual ADS-82 air data systems, APS-85 autopilot, dual EFIS-85B-2 electronic flight instrument systems and ALT-55B radio altimeter, plus Baker M1045 audio system, Global GNS-1000 flight management system, Pioneer KE-8300 stereo tape and FM/AM radio. In 1988 Royal Air Force BAe 125s of earlier series were fitted with an infra-red jammer in an extended tailcone to deflect heat seeking missiles.

DIMENSIONS, EXTERNAL:
Wing span	15.66 m (51 ft 4½ in)
Wing chord (mean)	2.29 m (7 ft 6¼ in)
Wing aspect ratio	7.06
Length overall	15.60 m (51 ft 2 in)
Height overall	5.36 m (17 ft 7 in)
Fuselage: Max diameter	1.93 m (6 ft 4 in)
Tailplane span	6.10 m (20 ft 0 in)
Wheel track (c/l of shock absorbers)	2.79 m (9 ft 2 in)
Wheelbase	6.41 m (21 ft 0½ in)
Passenger door (fwd, port):	
Height	1.30 m (4 ft 3 in)
Width	0.69 m (2 ft 3 in)
Height to sill	1.07 m (3 ft 6 in)
Emergency exit (overwing, stbd):	
Height	0.91 m (3 ft 0 in)
Width	0.51 m (1 ft 8 in)

DIMENSIONS, INTERNAL:
Cabin (excl flight deck): Length	6.50 m (21 ft 4 in)
Max width	1.83 m (6 ft 0 in)
Max height	1.75 m (5 ft 9 in)
Floor area	5.11 m² (55.0 sq ft)
Volume	17.10 m³ (604.0 cu ft)
Baggage compartments:	
forward	0.74 m³ (26.0 cu ft)
rear	0.74 m³ (26.0 cu ft)
pannier (optional)	0.79 m³ (28.0 cu ft)

AREAS:
Wings, gross	34.75 m² (374.0 sq ft)
Ailerons (total)	2.05 m² (22.1 sq ft)
Airbrakes: upper (total)	0.74 m² (8.0 sq ft)
lower (total)	0.46 m² (5.0 sq ft)
Trailing-edge flaps (total)	4.83 m² (52.0 sq ft)
Fin (excl dorsal fin)	6.43 m² (69.2 sq ft)
Rudder	1.32 m² (14.2 sq ft)
Horizontal tail surfaces (total)	9.29 m² (100.0 sq ft)

WEIGHTS AND LOADINGS:
Basic weight empty	6,676 kg (14,720 lb)
Typical operating weight empty	6,858 kg (15,120 lb)
Max payload	1,306 kg (2,880 lb)
Max ramp weight	12,480 kg (27,520 lb)
Max T-O weight	12,430 kg (27,400 lb)
Max zero-fuel weight	8,164 kg (18,000 lb)
Max landing weight	10,590 kg (23,350 lb)
Max wing loading	357.69 kg/m² (73.26 lb/sq ft)
Max power loading	325.1 kg/kN (3.19 lb/lb st)

PERFORMANCE:
Max limiting Mach number	0.87
Max level speed and max cruising speed at 8,840 m (29,000 ft)	456 knots (845 km/h; 525 mph)
Econ cruising speed at 11,900-13,100 m (39,000-43,000 ft)	400 knots (741 km/h; 461 mph)
Stalling speed in landing configuration at typical landing weight	92 knots (170 km/h; 106 mph)
Max rate of climb at S/L	945 m (3,100 ft)/min
Time to 10,670 m (35,000 ft)	19 min
Service ceiling	13,100 m (43,000 ft)
Min ground turning radius about nosewheel	9.14 m (30 ft 0 in)
T-O balanced field length at max T-O weight	1,713 m (5,620 ft)
Landing from 15 m (50 ft) at typical landing weight (6 passengers and baggage)	1,372 m (4,500 ft)
Range:	
with max payload	2,870 nm (5,318 km; 3,305 miles)
with max fuel, NBAA VFR reserves	3,000 nm (5,560 km; 3,454 miles)

BAe 1000

TYPE: Twin-turbofan business transport.

PROGRAMME: Development initiated 1988 as BAe 125 Series 900, with larger cabin and increased range; substantial structural and systems changes, and modifications to meet latest FAR and JAR certification requirements; launched as BAe 1000 October 1989; first flight (G-EXLR) 16 June 1990 and of second aircraft 26 November 1990; 800 hour flight development programme in progress, to use three aircraft to achieve certification in second half 1991, with customer deliveries shortly after.

CUSTOMERS: Launch customers are J. C. Bamford Excavators Ltd (two) and The Yeates Group (one) in UK, United Technologies in USA (three, plus one for Pratt & Whitney Canada subsidiary); Aravco Ltd in UK ordered two for business jet charter; orders totalled 21 by December 1990.

DESIGN FEATURES: Intercontinental development of BAe 125 Series 800 (which remains in production) to offer 27 per cent increase in range and 15 per cent improvement in field performance; 0.84 m (2 ft 9 in) fuselage stretch via plugs forward and aft of wings; additional cabin window each side; PW305 turbofans with thrust reversers standard; fuel tank in extended forward wing fairing, capacity 614 litres (162 US gallons; 135 Imp gallons);

ventral fuel tank capacity increased by 136 litres (36 US gallons; 30 Imp gallons); new lightweight systems; re-styled cabin interior with increased headroom; improved modular galley facilities; external baggage hatch; Honeywell SPZ8000 digital avionics; underwing vortilon; TKS liquid de-icing/anti-icing.

BAe wing sections. Wing thickness/chord ratio 14 per cent at root, 8.35 per cent at tip; dihedral 2°; incidence 2° 5′ 42″ at root, –3° 5′ 49″ at tip; sweepback 20° at quarter-chord.

FLYING CONTROLS: Similar to BAe 125 Series 800. Split elevator circuit with normally locked break-out strut which splits automatically in event of control jam.

STRUCTURE: Similar to BAe 125 Series 800 but with upper fence on each wing replaced by underwing vortilon; intermediate fuselage frames fitted to meet latest FAR/JAR requirement; secondary rear pressure bulkhead forms forward bulkhead of rear baggage area (with baggage access door) allowing altitude certification to 13,100 m (43,000 ft) in USA; push-in/slide-up plug-type exterior baggage access door (63.5 × 35.5 cm; 25 × 14 in) on port side, interlocked to prevent engine start-up if open.

LANDING GEAR: Retractable tricycle type, with twin wheels on each unit. Hydraulic retraction, nosewheels forward, mainwheels inward into wings. Oleo-pneumatic shock absorbers. Fully castoring nose unit, steerable ±45°. Dunlop mainwheels and 12-ply tubeless tyres, size 23 × 7.12. Dunlop nosewheels and 6-ply tubeless tyres, size 18 × 4.25-10. Dunlop triple-disc hydraulic brakes with Maxaret anti-skid units on all mainwheels.

POWER PLANT: Two 23.13 kN (5,200 lb st) Pratt & Whitney Canada PW305 turbofans on sides of rear fuselage, in pods designed and manufactured by Rohr Aerospace. Rohr target-type thrust reversers fitted as standard. Engine intake anti-icing by engine bleed air. Integral fuel tanks in wings, with combined capacity of 4,800 litres (1,268 US gallons; 1,056 Imp gallons). Rear underfuselage ventral tank of 1,014 litres (268 US gallons; 223 Imp gallons) capacity and forward underfuselage ventral tank forming wingroot fairing, capacity 586 litres (155 US gallons; 129 Imp gallons), giving total capacity of 6,400 litres (1,691 US gallons; 1,408 Imp gallons). Single pressure refuelling point at rear of aft ventral tank. Overwing refuelling point near each wingtip.

British Aerospace 1000 twin-turbofan business aircraft

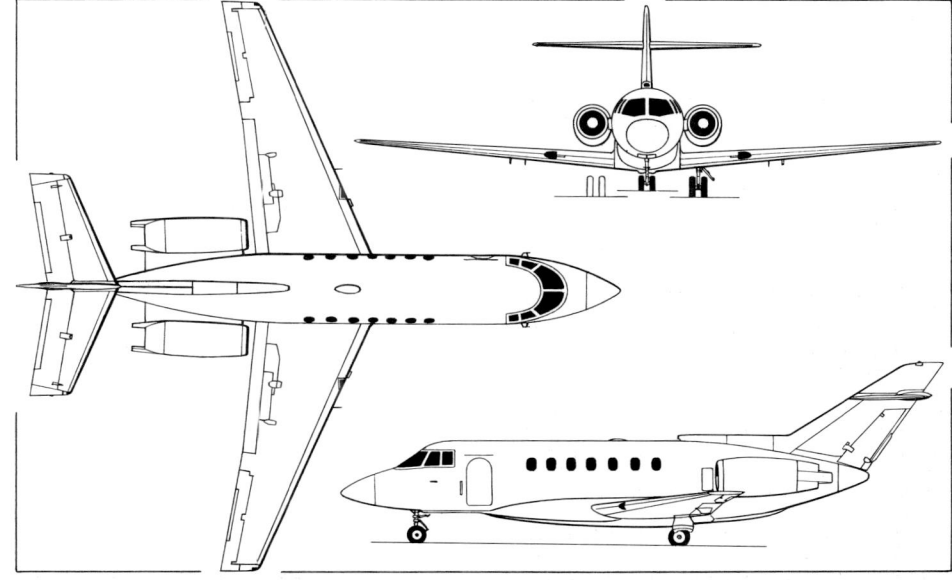

BAe 1000 stretched development of BAe 125 family (two P&WC PW305 turbofans) (*Pilot Press*)

ACCOMMODATION: Crew of two on flight deck, which is soundproofed, insulated and air-conditioned. Dual controls standard. Seat for third crew member. Standard executive layout has rear baggage compartment with forward wardrobe, forward galley comprising sink unit on port side, cooking and food stowage including fridge on starboard side, airliner style toilet at rear. Individual recessed lights, air louvres above each passenger position. Oxygen dropout masks in headliner. Cabin styling offers the operator a choice of interchangeable furnishing units to suit individual requirements, with up to 15 seats. The extra wide seats swivel through 360°, are adjustable fore, aft and sideways, and can be reclined and used as a bed. Standard seating for eight, with club four seating at the front of the cabin, a three-place settee on the port side, and single seat on the starboard side with an entertainment/bar unit behind, including video and compact disc player. Outward opening door at front on port side, with integral airstairs. Emergency exit over wing on starboard side.

SYSTEMS: AiResearch three-wheel turbine air-conditioning and pressurisation system. Maximum cabin differential 0.59 bar (8.55 lb/sq in). Oxygen system standard, with dropout masks for passengers. Hydraulic system, pressure 186-207 bars (2,700-3,000 lb/sq in), for operation of landing gear, mainwheel doors, flaps, spoilers, nosewheel steering, mainwheel brakes, anti-skid units and thrust reversers. Three accumulators, pressurised by engine bleed air, are for emergency hydraulic power for wheel brakes in case of main system failure. Independent auxiliary system for lowering landing gear and flaps in the event of a main system failure. DC electrical system utilises two 30V 12kW (restricted to 9kW) engine driven starter/generators and two 26V 43Ah nickel-cadmium batteries. A 24V 5Ah battery provides separate power for standby instruments. The AC system is deleted on the BAe 1000, those instruments requiring AC having their own dedicated inverter. Two engine driven 208V 7.4kVA frequency-wild alternators for windscreen anti-icing can also provide DC power through a standby transformer rectifier unit in emergency. Ground power receptacle on starboard side at rear of fuselage for 28V external DC supply. Turbomach T-62T-40C8D-1 APU standard. Engine ice protection system supplied by engine bleed air. Electric windscreen anti-icing. Graviner triple FD Firewire fire warning system and two BCF engine fire extinguishers standard. Stall warning system indicates approach to the stall, and an identification system operates a stick pusher to initiate a nose down pitching movement if the approach to the stall exceeds a predetermined rate.

AVIONICS: Standard Honeywell SPZ8000 avionics fit, includes dual EDZ-818 electronic flight instrument system; dual DFZ-800 automatic flight control system; dual SRZ-850 integrated radio/audio system; dual ADZ-810 air data system; dual Laseref III inertial reference system; DG-1086 global positioning system; dual FMZ-900 flight management system with colour display units; Primus 870 weather radar; AA-300 radio altimeter; dual HF com; Motorola N1335B Selcal, and LSZ-850 lightning detection system.

DIMENSIONS, EXTERNAL: As for BAe 125 Series 80 except:

Length overall	16.42 m (53 ft 10½ in)
Height overall	5.21 m (17 ft 1 in)
Wheelbase	6.91 m (22 ft 8 in)
Baggage door: Height	0.64 m (2 ft 1 in)
Width	0.36 m (1 ft 2 in)

DIMENSIONS, INTERNAL:

Cabin (excl flight deck): Length	7.44 m (24 ft 5 in)
Max width	1.83 m (6 ft 0 in)
Max height	1.75 m (5 ft 9 in)
Floor area	5.85 m² (62.95 sq ft)
Volume	approx 19.26 m³ (680.0 cu ft)

Baggage compartments, volume:

rear (main)	1.47 m³ (52.0 cu ft)
forward (wardrobe)	0.28 m³ (10.0 cu ft)
optional (wardrobe extension)	0.28 m³ (10.0 cu ft)

AREAS: As for BAe 125 Series 800

WEIGHTS AND LOADINGS:

Weight empty	7,629 kg (16,820 lb)
Typical operating weight empty	7,824 kg (17,250 lb)
Max payload	1,156 kg (2,550 lb)
Max T-O weight	14,060 kg (31,000 lb)
Max ramp weight	14,105 kg (31,100 lb)
Max zero-fuel weight	8,980 kg (19,800 lb)
Max landing weight	11,340 kg (25,000 lb)
Max wing loading	404.7 kg/m² (82.89 lb/sq ft)
Max power loading	304.1 kg/kN (2.98 lb/lb st)

PERFORMANCE (estimated, at max T-O weight, ISA, except where indicated):

Max limiting Mach number	0.87
Max level and max cruising speed at 8,840 m (29,000 ft)	468 knots (867 km/h; 539 mph)
Econ cruising speed at 11,890-13,100 m (39,000-43,000 ft)	402 knots (745 km/h; 463 mph)
Stalling speed in landing configuration at typical landing weight	89 knots (165 km/h; 103 mph)
Time to 10,670 m (35,000 ft)	22 min
Service ceiling	13,100 m (43,000 ft)
T-O balanced field length	1,830 m (6,000 ft)

British Aerospace ATP of SATA Air Acores

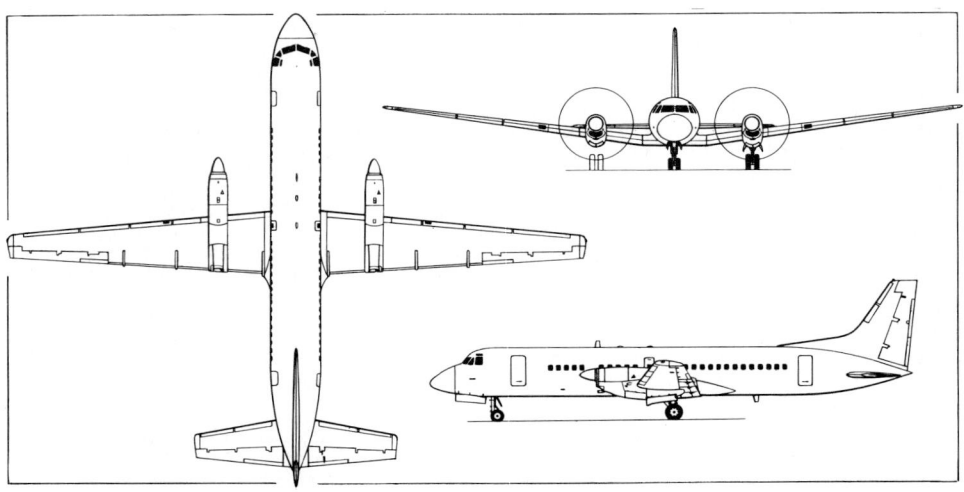

Three-view drawing of the twin-turboprop BAe ATP transport *(Pilot Press)*

Landing from 15 m (50 ft) at typical landing weight (6 passengers and baggage)   1,280 m (4,200 ft)

Range:

with max payload	3,440 nm (6,375 km; 3,961 miles)
with max fuel, NBAA VFR reserves	3,635 nm (6,736 km; 4,185 miles)

BAe ATP

TYPE: Twin-turboprop regional transport.

PROGRAMME: Announced 1 March 1984 to succeed Super 748; first flight of prototype (G-MATP) 6 August 1986; first production aircraft (G-BMYM) flew 20 February 1987; JAR 25 certification March 1988; first revenue service by British Midland Airways 9 May 1988.

VARIANTS: **BAe P132:** Proposed maritime warfare version; described separately.

CUSTOMERS: Launch customer Airlines of Britain (British Midland, Loganair and Manx Airlines) for eight. Other customers comprise Air Wisconsin (14); Bangladesh Biman (three); British Airways (eight); LAR of Portugal (three); SATA of Portugal (three). Total of 39 firm orders by 28 February 1991, of which 31 delivered.

DESIGN FEATURES: Retains Super 748 cross-section but fuselage lengthened by 5.03 m (16 ft 6 in); sill height of forward passenger door allows use of jetways at regional airports. Take-off and landing sound measurements have shown ATP to be 2-7 EPNdB quieter than any other airliner in class. Pneumatic boot de-icing of wings (outboard of engine nacelles), fin and tailplane leading-edges. Digital avionics system.

FLYING CONTROLS: Ailerons (horn balanced), elevators and rudder actuated mechanically (rudder power assisted); geared tab in each aileron, trim tab in each elevator, trim tab and spring tab in rudder. Fowler trailing-edge flaps (manufactured by HAI, Greece). Dual AFCS.

STRUCTURE: All-metal. Two spar fail-safe wings, generally similar to BAe 748; spars do not intrude into passenger cabin. Circular section semi-monocoque fail-safe fuselage, generally similar to BAe 748 but lengthened. Slightly swept vertical and non-swept horizontal tail surfaces.

LANDING GEAR: Retractable tricycle type, of Dowty design, with twin-wheel main units and twin-wheel steerable (±47°) nose unit. All units retract forward, main units into bottom of engine nacelles. Oleo-pneumatic shock absorbers. Mainwheels fitted with 34 × 11.75-14 tubeless tyres. Nosewheels fitted with 22 × 6.75-10 tubeless tyres. Mainwheels have fusible plugs operating at 199°C. All wheels have 'roll on rim' capability. Dunlop carbon brakes and Maxaret anti-skid units on mainwheels. Inner and outer brakes on each leg supplied from two hydraulically independent systems via engine driven pump or standby DC pump.

POWER PLANT: Two 1,978 kW (2,653 shp) Pratt & Whitney Canada PW126A turboprops. Max continuous rating 1,781 kW (2,388 shp). BAe/Hamilton Standard slow-turning propellers, each having six blades of advanced aerodynamic profile and lightweight composite construction. Max thrust in reverse pitch 2,948 kg (6,500 lb). Fuel in two integral wing tanks, with combined usable capacity of 6,364 litres (1,681 US gallons; 1,400 Imp gallons). Single pressure refuelling point under starboard outer wing. Max fuel transfer rate 636 litres (168 US gallons; 140 Imp gallons)/min.

ACCOMMODATION: Crew of two on flight deck; two cabin attendants. Main cabin has standard pressurised accommodation for 64 passengers, at seat pitch of 79 cm (31 in), in four abreast layout with central aisle. Alternative layouts provide 60 to 72 seats. Galley at rear of cabin on starboard side, toilet forward on port side. Separate passenger doors at front (with airstairs) and rear of cabin on port side. Compartment for carry-on baggage on port side of cabin, forward of front row of seats. Two baggage/freight compartments, one forward on starboard side and one aft of main cabin, both with external access. Overhead lockers above passenger seats. Forward cabin bulkhead can be moved on seat rails to permit flexibility for multi-sector or mixed passenger/cargo operations.

SYSTEMS: Hamilton Standard environmental control system with twin ECS packs offering sub-zero delivery temperature capability. Automatic pressurisation system, giving altitude equivalent to 2,440 m (8,000 ft) at 7,620 m (25,000 ft). Pressure differential 0.38 bar (5.5 lb/sq in). Each engine drives an Abex variable delivery hydraulic pump providing hydraulic power at a regulated pressure of 169 bars (2,450 lb/sq in) for landing gear actuation, nosewheel steering, brakes and airstairs. Auxiliary hydraulic power is supplied from a separate DC pump and reservoir for emergency operation of the landing gear and brakes. The system also provides hydraulic pressure for servicing when the engines are not running. Main system has a flow rate of 41 litres (11 US gallons; 9 Imp gallons)/min controlled to 169 bars (2,450 lb/sq in); emergency system has a flow rate of 2.25 litres (0.6 US gallon; 0.5 Imp gallon)/min controlled to 145 bars (2,100 lb/sq in). Air/oil reservoirs pressurised to 1.25 bars (18 lb/sq in). Electrical power provided by Lucas 200V 30/45kVA variable frequency alternators, mounted on each engine. 28V DC subsystem from either two TRUs or two 35Ah nickel-cadmium batteries. Second subsystem provides 1.5kVA 200/115V constant frequency power from two static inverters. Garrett Model GTCP36-150 APU for air-conditioning on the ground, and electrical power for battery charging, engine starting assist and other tasks.

AVIONICS: Digital avionics system using ARINC 429 data transmission, Smiths SDS-201 four-tube EFIS, Bendix/King avionics. Twin VHF com, twin VHF nav, scanning DME with additional frequency under R/Nav control, ADF, ATC transponder, CVR, FDR and digital GPWS. Bendix/King RDS-86 colour weather radar, with checklist facility, can display weather on EFIS nav display. Built-in test and recording facility. Dual AFCS, each with Litton LTR 81-01 AHRS and Smiths digital DADS, for Cat II ILS capability. Options include second DME, second ADF, second transponder, R/Nav, MLS and single HF.

DIMENSIONS, EXTERNAL:

Wing span	30.63 m (100 ft 6 in)
Length overall	26.00 m (85 ft 4 in)
Height overall	7.59 m (24 ft 11 in)
Wheel track	8.46 m (27 ft 9 in)
Wheelbase	9.70 m (31 ft 9¾ in)
Propeller diameter	4.19 m (13 ft 9 in)
Propeller fuselage clearance	0.80 m (2 ft 7½ in)
Passenger doors (each): Height	1.73 m (5 ft 8 in)
Width	0.71 m (2 ft 4 in)
Height to sill: fwd door	1.96 m (6 ft 5 in)
rear door	1.71 m (5 ft 7½ in)

DIMENSIONS, INTERNAL:

Cabin: Length	19.20 m (63 ft 0 in)
Max width	2.50 m (8 ft 2⅝ in)
Max height	1.93 m (6 ft 4 in)
Volume	75.1 m³ (2,652 cu ft)

Baggage/freight compartment volume (64 seats):

forward hold	3.62 m³ (128 cu ft)
rear hold	5.10 m³ (180 cu ft)
carry-on stowage	2.83 m³ (100 cu ft)
overhead lockers (max)	3.11 m³ (110 cu ft)

WEIGHTS AND LOADINGS:

Operating weight empty	14,193 kg (31,290 lb)
Max fuel	5,080 kg (11,200 lb)
Max payload	7,035 kg (15,510 lb)
Max ramp weight	22,997 kg (50,700 lb)
Max T-O weight	22,930 kg (50,550 lb)
Max landing weight	22,250 kg (49,050 lb)
Max zero-fuel weight	21,228 kg (46,800 lb)
Max power loading	5.80 kg/kW (9.52 lb/shp)

PERFORMANCE:

Cruising speed for 150 nm (278 km; 173 mile) sector, ISA:
high speed at 3,960 m (13,000 ft)
266 knots (493 km/h; 306 mph)
econ cruise at 5,485 m (18,000 ft)
236 knots (437 km/h; 272 mph)
Min ground turning radius about nosewheel
9.75 m (32 ft 0 in)
T-O field length:
at max T-O weight
1,463 m (4,800 ft)
for 250 nm (463 km; 288 mile) sector, 64 passengers, reserves for 100 nm (185 km; 115 mile) diversion, plus 45 min hold at 3,050 m (10,000 ft)
1,067 m (3,500 ft)
Landing field length at max landing weight
1,128 m (3,700 ft)
Range, with reserves for 100 nm (185 km; 115 mile) diversion and 45 min hold at 3,050 m (10,000 ft):
with max payload 340 nm (630 km; 391 miles)
with 68 passengers (6,169 kg; 13,600 lb)
800 nm (1,482 km; 921 miles)
Ferry range 2,320 nm (4,299 km; 2,671 miles)

The proposed BAe P132 ASW/ASV maritime variant of the ATP *(Pilot Press)*

OPERATIONAL NOISE LEVELS (BCAR Section N):

T-O	79.5 EPNdB
Approach	95.8 EPNdB
Sideline	82.7 EPNdB

BAe P132

Proposed anti-submarine warfare/anti-surface vessel warfare (ASW/ASVW) variant of ATP, to be configured to customer requirements. Equipment could include 360° scan maritime reconnaissance radar mounted under forward fuselage; undernose FLIR; internal/external magnetic anomaly detector (MAD); six stores hardpoints (four under wings, two under fuselage) for torpedoes, air-to-surface missiles, depth charges, bombs and mines; and total of 59 sonobuoys launched singly through pressurised launcher or in patterns of up to six through rotary launcher. Typical internal configuration provides accommodation for three systems operators, crew rest area with three bunks, wardroom, toilet, stowage of sonic equipment and sono-buoy racks, 14-man dinghy, and 43 cm (1 ft 5 in) diameter rear launch chute. Patrol endurance would be in excess of 8 hours.

BAe 146
RAF designation: BAe 146 CC. Mk 2
TYPE: Four-turbofan short-range transport.
PROGRAMME: Development with government support announced by former Hawker Siddeley Aviation August 1973, as HS 146; programme halted after few months because of UK economic problems, but research and design continued on limited basis; continued limited

funding by BAe allowed manufacture of assembly jigs, system test rigs, and continuing design and wind tunnel testing; BAe Board's decision to give programme full go-ahead as private venture approved by government 10 July 1978.

BAe 146 Series 100 prototype (G-SSSH) first flew 3 September 1981; type certificate gained 4 February 1983 and Transport category CAA certificate 20 May 1983. First Series 200 (G-WISC) flew 1 August 1982; type certificate gained 4 February 1983. Aerodynamic prototype of Series 300 (G-LUXE) flew 1 May 1987 (conversion of Series 100 G-SSSH); first production Series 300 flew June 1988 and certificated 6 September. 146-QC Convertible announced August 1988 and prototype displayed at 1989 Paris Air Show.

Production undertaken at Brough (fin and flaps), Filton (centre fuselage), Manchester (rear fuselage), Hamble (flap track fairings), Prestwick (engine pylons) and Hatfield (front fuselage and flight deck, and initially responsible for all final assembly and flight testing). Under risk sharing arrangements, Textron Aerostructures (USA) manufactures wings and Saab-Scania (Sweden) tailplanes and all movable control surfaces.

By 1990, construction of 40 aircraft a year was target, aided by second final assembly line at BAe Woodford, near Manchester; first Woodford assembled BAe 146 (c/n 2106) flew 16 May 1988; 16 were manufactured in 1990 to bring total to 29. In December 1989, Field Aircraft Ltd of East Midlands Airport appointed as approved maintenance, overhaul and completion centre. August

BAe 146 Series 100 in the insignia of Air Botswana

1990, 'New Generation' standard announced; introduction of more powerful LF5071H turbofans; structural strengthening of wings, fuselage and landing gear to permit increased design weights; optional Type III mid-cabin exits beneath wing, in conjunction with standard freight door, allow first combi versions to be offered; revised EFIS; Honeywell Cat IIIa digital flight guidance system; integrated windshear detection system; optional TCAS. First flight with LF507s (146-300) 2 March 1991; certification expected August, deliveries from first quarter 1992, initially to Crossair.

VARIANTS: **Series 100:** Designed to operate from short or semi-prepared airstrips with minimal ground facilities; normal seating for 82-94. Rollout 20 May 1981. Thicker skin on centre-fuselage of later production aircraft permits increased T-O weight if required. 'New Generation' optional max T-O weight 40,820 kg (90,000 lb), max landing weight 37,875 kg (83,500 lb), max zero-fuel weight 33,790 kg (74,500 lb), max payload range with optional fillet tanks 1,400 nm (2,594 km; 1,612 miles).

Series 200: Seating for 82-112; fuselage lengthened 2.39 m (7 ft 10 in) by five frame pitches; increased maximum T-O weight and zero-fuel weight; underfloor cargo volume increased by 35 per cent. 'New Generation' optional max T-O weight 44,000 kg (97,000 lb), max landing weight 38,555 kg (85,000 lb), max zero-fuel weight 35,830 kg (79,000 lb), max payload range with optional fillet tanks 1,300 nm (2,409 km; 1,497 miles).

Series 300: Development of Series 100; increased length by inserting 2.46 m (8 ft 1 in) forward fuselage plug and 2.34 m (7 ft 8 in) rear plug, accommodating 103 passengers five-abreast at 79 cm (31 in) pitch, with wardrobe and galley space; high-density seating for 128 passengers six-abreast at 74 cm (29 in) pitch, subject to incorporation of Type III emergency exits in centre-fuselage. Thicker centre-fuselage skin permits 44,225 kg (97,500 lb) T-O weight; first few have 43,090 kg (95,000 lb) max T-O weight, 37,648 kg (83,000 lb) max landing weight and 35,153 kg (77,500 lb) max zero-fuel weight. 'New Generation' optional max T-O weight 46,040 kg (101,500 lb), max landing weight 40,140 kg (88,500 lb), max zero-fuel weight 37,420 kg (82,500 lb), max payload range with optional fillet tanks 1,200 nm (2,224 km; 1,381 miles).

146-QT Quiet Trader: Freighter versions of all Series; cabin volume allows 146-200 freighter to carry six standard 2.74 × 2.24 m (108 × 88 in) pallets, with space for extra half pallet, or up to nine standard LD3 containers; minor modifications to standard floor allow maximum payload of 11,827 kg (26,075 lb), and floor stressing permits maximum individual pallet load of 2,721 kg (6,000 lb); additional capacity of 300-QT enables payloads of up to 12,490 kg (27,535 lb). First freighter conversion (a Series 200) undertaken by Hayes International Corporation (now Pemco Aeroplex) in USA, and entered service 5 May 1987 with TNT International Aviation Services (see Customers).

146-QC Convertible: Quick-change convertible passenger/freight version of Series 200-QT and 300-QT; 200-QC Convertible has 10,039 kg (22,132 lb) gross payload in freighter configuration and range with standard tankage of 1,045 nm (1,936 km; 1,203 miles); in passenger layout, 85 (five-abreast) can be carried up to 1,289 nm (2,388 km; 1,484 miles). Comparable data for 300-QC are 10,877 kg (24,002 lb) up to 1,087 nm (2,014 km; 1,251 miles); and 96 passengers up to 1,233 nm (2,285 km; 1,420 miles).

Statesman: Executive versions of all Series; cabin area allows flexibility of interior design; staterooms, staff quarters, additional galley and wardrobe space can be provided.

RJ70/RJ80: Regional jet versions based on Series 100 airframe; both achieve operating economies with LF 507 engine derated to 27.3 kN (6,130 lb st) and by reduced weight operation; to be offered in batches additional to production of existing variants to obtain maximum benefit of production economies and resulting lower first cost. **RJ70** is version for North American market; five-abreast seating for 70; max T-O weight 36,287 kg (80,000 lb), max landing weight 37,875 kg (83,500 lb), max zero-fuel weight 30,617 kg (67,500 lb), max range 800 nm (1,482 km; 921 miles). **RJ80** for European market; six-abreast seating for 80; max T-O weight 38,100 kg (84,000 lb), max landing weight 37,875 kg (83,500 lb), max zero-fuel weight 33,792 kg (74,500 lb), max range 1,100 nm (2,038 km; 1,266 miles).

BAe 146 NRA: Projected twin-engined New Regional Airliner version based on Series 300 fuselage with 4.27 m (14 ft) stretch; 125 passengers in single class, five-abreast layout, other mixed class and six-abreast 139-passenger layouts; new, larger wing, with winglets, permitting cruise speeds to Mach 0.82 and range of more than 2,171 nm (4,023 km; 2,500 miles); choice of GE/SNECMA CFM 56 or IAE V2500 high bypass ratio turbofans. BAe in discussion with potential international collaborative partners with intention of achieving entry into service 1996/7.

CUSTOMERS: First delivery to Dan-Air (Series 100) 21 May 1983; scheduled operations began 27 May. First production Series 200 delivered to Air Wisconsin June 1983, beginning scheduled services 27 June, following FAA certification of Series 100 and 200. First production

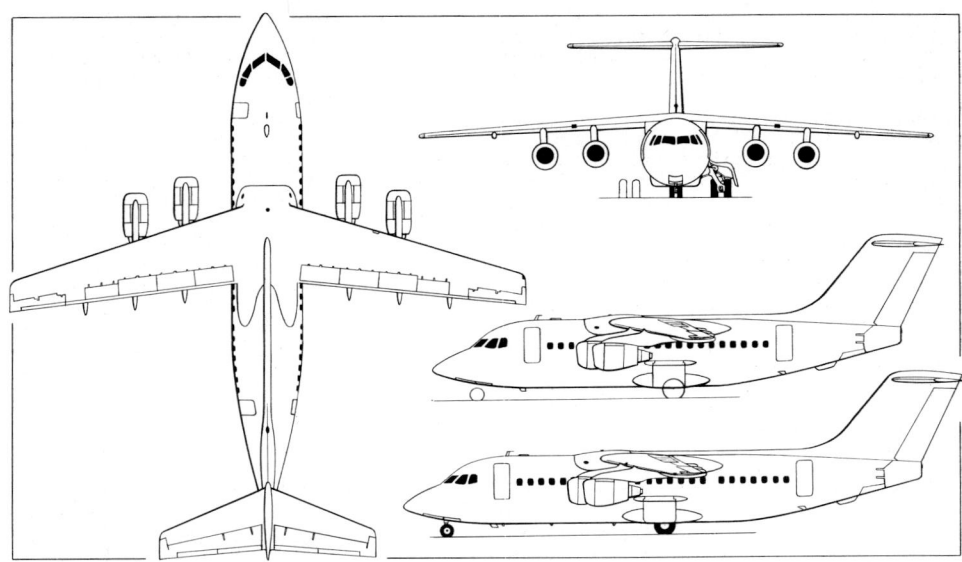

BAe 146 Series 200, with additional side view (centre) of Series 100 *(Pilot Press)*

BAe 146 Series 300 four-turbofan transport in the colours of Eastwest Airlines

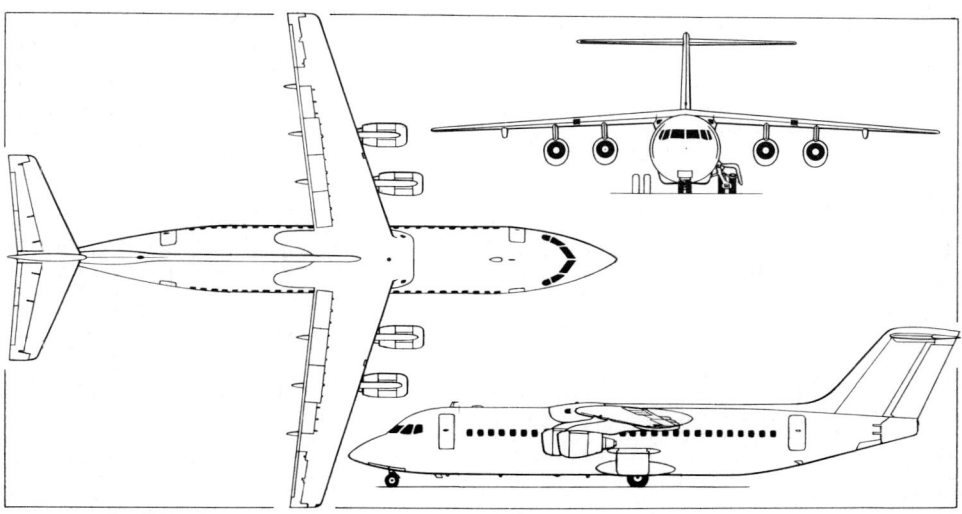

BAe 146 Series 300, the second stretched version of this regional transport *(Pilot Press)*

Artist's impression of BAe 146 NRA project

Series 300 delivered to Air Wisconsin 28 December 1988. In June 1987 TNT and BAe (see 146-QT under Variants) reached agreements for long-term commitment to purchase 72 146-QTs over five years; number for TNT freight network and remainder available for sale or lease through Ansett Worldwide Aviation Services. Firm orders by TNT increased to 23 by March 1990, when 11 Series 200-QTs delivered to TNT in Europe and two in Australia for Ansett Air Freight. First of 10 TNT Series 300-QTs delivered to Malmo Aviation of Sweden at end of 1989; seven were delivered to TNT in 1990. Prototype 146-QC Convertible sold to Ansett New Zealand in December 1989 after two months of service trials. First Statesman delivered in April 1986 as first of two BAe CC. Mk 2s for The Queen's Flight of RAF; third aircraft ordered 4 October 1989 and delivered in December 1990.

By 28 February 1991 orders totalled 30 Series 100s, 97 Series 200s, 39 Series 300s, 13 Series 200-QTs, 4 Series 200-QCs, 10 Series 300-QTs and 4 unannounced; total 197, of which 162 delivered (including 30 in 1990); fleet had then amassed over 1,000,000 flying hours in 1.2 million flights with 44 operators in 22 countries.

In March 1990, LAN-Chile BAe 146-200 became first commercial jet airliner to operate into Antarctica, a route-proving service from Punte Arenas to Chilean Air Force base at Teniente Marsh on King George Island. LAN-Chile's two Series 200s equipped with gravel runway all-terrain protection kit and serve nine Chilean cities from the capital of Santiago.

The following description applies to commercial Series 100, 200 and 300, except where indicated otherwise:

DESIGN FEATURES: Low operating noise levels; ability to operate from short or semi-prepared airstrips with minimal ground facilities. BAe high lift aerofoil section: thickness/chord ratio 15.3 per cent adjacent to fuselage, 12.2 per cent at tip; anhedral 3° at trailing-edge; incidence 3° 6′ at fuselage side, 0° at tip; sweepback 15° at quarter-chord; hot air de-icing of wing and tailplane leading-edges.

FLYING CONTROLS: Mechanically actuated balanced ailerons, with trim and servo tabs; manually operated balanced elevators, with trim and servo tabs; powered rudder. Single-section hydraulically actuated tabbed Fowler flaps, spanning 78 per cent of trailing-edges, with Dowty actuators; hydraulically operated roll spoiler outboard of three lift dumpers on each wing; no leading-edge lift devices; petal airbrakes form tailcone when closed. Smiths automatic flight control/flight guidance system.

STRUCTURE: All-metal; fail-safe wings with machined skins, integrally machined spars and ribs; fail-safe semi-monocoque fuselage with chemically etched skins; strengthened centre-section developed initially for Series 300 will be standard on all future Series 100s; flight deck and tailcone areas free of stringers; remainder of fuselage has top hat stringers bonded to skins above keel area; Z section stringers wet assembled with bonding agent and riveted to skin in keel area; T tail with chemically etched skins bonded to top hat section stringers; fixed incidence tailplane.

LANDING GEAR: Hydraulically retractable tricycle type, of Dowty design, with twin Dunlop wheels on each unit. Main units retract inward into fairings on fuselage sides; steerable (±70°) nose unit retracts forward. Oleo-pneumatic shock absorbers with wheels mounted on trailing axle. Simple telescopic nosewheel strut. Mainwheel tyres size 12.50-16 Type III, pressure (Series 100) 8.42 bars (122 lb/sq in). Nosewheel tyres size 7.50-10 Type III, pressure (Series 100) 7.80 bars (113 lb/sq in). Low pressure tyres optional. Dunlop multi-disc carbon brakes operated by duplicated hydraulic systems. Anti-skid units in both primary and secondary brake systems.

POWER PLANT: Four Textron Lycoming ALF 502R-5 turbofans, each rated at 31.0 kN (6970 lb st), installed in pylon mounted underwing pods. No reverse thrust. Fuel in two integral wing tanks and integral centre-section tank (the latter with a vented and drained sealing diaphragm above passenger cabin), having a combined usable capacity of 11,728 litres (3,098 US gallons; 2,580 Imp gallons). Optional auxiliary tanks in wingroot fairings, with combined capacity of 1,173 litres (310 US gallons; 258 Imp gallons), giving total capacity of 12,901 litres (3,408 US gallons; 2,838 Imp gallons). Single-point pressure refuelling, with coupling situated in starboard wing outboard of outer engine.

ACCOMMODATION: Crew of two pilots on flight deck, and two or three cabin staff. Optional observer's seat. Series 100 has accommodation in main cabin for 82 passengers with six-abreast seating at 84 cm (33 in) pitch, and up to 94 seats six-abreast at 74 cm (29 in) pitch. Series 200 has max capacity for 112 passengers with six-abreast seating at 74 cm (29 in) pitch. Series 300 has standard accommodation for 103 passengers, with five-abreast seating at 79 cm (31 in) pitch, and max seating for 128 passengers. All seating layouts have two toilets and a forward galley as standard. One outward opening passenger door forward and one aft on port side of cabin. Built-in airstairs optional. Servicing doors, one forward and one aft, on starboard side of cabin. Freight and baggage holds under cabin floor. All accommodation air-conditioned. Windscreen electrical anti-icing and demisting standard; rain repellent system optional.

SYSTEMS: BAe/Normalair-Garrett cabin air-conditioning and pressurisation system, using engine bleed air. Electro-pneumatic pressurisation control with discharge valves at fore and aft of cabin. Max differential 0.47 bar (6.75 lb/sq in), giving 2,440 m (8,000 ft) equivalent altitude at 9,450 m (31,000 ft). Hydraulic system, duplicated for essential services, for landing gear, flaps, rudder, roll and lift spoilers, airbrakes, nosewheel steering, brakes and auxiliary fuel pumps; pressure 207 bars (3,000 lb/sq in). Electrical system powered by two 40kVA integrated-drive alternators to feed 115/200V 3-phase 400Hz primary systems. 28V DC power supplied by transformer-rectifier in each channel. Hydraulically powered emergency electrical power unit. Garrett GTCP 36-150 APU (36-100 in early aircraft) for ground air-conditioning and electrical power generation. High pressure gaseous oxygen system, pressure 124 bars (1,800 lb/sq in). Stall warning and identification system, comprising stick shaker (warning) and stick force (identification) elements, providing soft and hard corrective stick forces at the approach of stall conditions. Series 100: stick force soft with flaps up; Series 200: force soft above 185 knots (343 km/h; 213 mph) regardless of configuration.

AVIONICS: Smiths SEP 10 automatic flight control and flight guidance system incorporates a simplex Cat I autopilot with a flight director display and separate attitude reference for each pilot. Addition of extra equipment and wiring permits coupled approaches to Cat II minima. Standard ARINC interface with radio nav system allows choice of radio equipment. Basic avionics include dual VHF com, audio system, passenger address system, cockpit voice recorder, dual compass systems, dual ADIs with separate attitude reference driven by single computer, marker beacon receiver, weather radar, dual radio altimeters, ground proximity warning system, dual DME, dual ATC transponders, dual VHF nav and dual ADF. Dowty-UEL flight deck warning system. Optional avionics include third VHF com, area navigation system, Selcal, tape reproducer, and single or dual HF com. Honeywell EFIS with Smiths LED engine instrument display incorporated as standard from Summer 1990, although electro-mechanical instruments continue to be available as customer option. Development under way of a digital flight deck incorporating Honeywell SPZ 1000 system to provide Cat III instrument landing capability.

DIMENSIONS, EXTERNAL:

Wing span: all versions except NRA, excl static dischargers 26.21 m (86 ft 0 in)
Note: Static discharger extends 6.3 cm (2½ in) from each wingtip
NRA 29.60 m (97 ft 1¼ in)
Wing aspect ratio: all versions except NRA 8.97
NRA 9.72
Wing chord: at root 2.75 m (9 ft 0 in)
at tip 0.91 m (3 ft 0 in)
Length overall: Series 100 26.20 m (85 ft 11½ in)
Series 200 28.60 m (93 ft 10 in)
Series 300 30.99 m (101 ft 8¼ in)
NRA 36.36 m (119 ft 3½ in)
Note: Static dischargers on elevator extend length of all series by 18.4 cm (7¼ in)
Height overall: Series 100 8.61 m (28 ft 3 in)
Series 200 8.59 m (28 ft 2 in)
Fuselage max diameter 3.56 m (11 ft 8 in)
Tailplane span 11.09 m (36 ft 5 in)
Wheel track 4.72 m (15 ft 6 in)
Wheelbase: Series 100 10.09 m (33 ft 1½ in)
Series 200 11.20 m (36 ft 9 in)
Series 300 12.52 m (41 ft 1 in)
Passenger doors (port, fwd and rear):
Height 1.83 m (6 ft 0 in)
Width 0.85 m (2 ft 9½ in)
Height to sill: fwd 1.88 m (6 ft 2 in)
rear 1.98 m (6 ft 6 in)
Servicing doors (stbd, fwd and rear):
Height 1.47 m (4 ft 10 in)
Width 0.85 m (2 ft 9½ in)
Height to sill: fwd 1.88 m (6 ft 2 in)
rear 1.98 m (6 ft 6 in)
Underfloor freight hold door (stbd, fwd):
Height 1.09 m (3 ft 7 in)
Width 1.35 m (4 ft 5 in)
Height to sill 0.78 m (2 ft 7 in)
Underfloor freight hold door (stbd, rear):
Height 1.04 m (3 ft 5 in)
Width 0.91 m (3 ft 0 in)
Height to sill 0.90 m (2 ft 11½ in)
Freight door (Freighter versions):
Height 1.93 m (6 ft 4 in)
Width: Series 100 2.92 m (9 ft 7 in)
Series 200 3.33 m (10 ft 11 in)
Height to sill 1.93 m (6 ft 4 in)

DIMENSIONS, INTERNAL:

Cabin (excl flight deck, incl galley and toilets):
Length: Series 100 15.42 m (50 ft 7 in)
Series 200 17.81 m (58 ft 5 in)
Series 300 20.20 m (66 ft 3¼ in)
Max width 3.42 m (11 ft 2½ in)
Max height 2.02 m (6 ft 7½ in)
Freight cabin, Series 200-QT:
Cargo floor: Length 16.08 m (52 ft 9 in)
Width 3.23 m (10 ft 7 in)
Volume: pallets/igloos 60.3 m^3 (2,145 cu ft)
LD3 containers 42.66 m^3 (1,422 cu ft)
Baggage/freight holds, underfloor:
Series 100 13.7 m^3 (479 cu ft)
Series 200 18.3 m^3 (645 cu ft)
Series 300 22.99 m^3 (812 cu ft)

AREAS:

Wings, gross:
all versions except NRA 77.30 m^2 (832.0 sq ft)
NRA 90.12 m^2 (970.0 sq ft)
Ailerons (total) 3.62 m^2 (39.0 sq ft)
Trailing-edge flaps (total) 19.51 m^2 (210.0 sq ft)
Spoilers (total) 10.03 m^2 (108.0 sq ft)
Fin 15.51 m^2 (167.0 sq ft)
Rudder 5.30 m^2 (57.0 sq ft)
Tailplane 15.61 m^2 (168.0 sq ft)
Elevators, incl tabs 10.03 m^2 (108.0 sq ft)

WEIGHTS AND LOADINGS (see also under Variants):

Operating weight empty:
Series 100 23,288 kg (51,342 lb)
Series 200 23,882 kg (52,651 lb)
Series 200-QT 22,310 kg (49,185 lb)
Series 300 24,878 kg (54,848 lb)
Series 300-QT 23,126 kg (50,985 lb)
Max payload: Series 100 7,783 kg (17,158 lb)
Series 200 10,138 kg (22,350 lb)
Series 200-QT 11,709 kg (25,815 lb)
Series 300 10,728 kg (23,652 lb)
Series 300-QT 12,707 kg (28,015 lb)
Max fuel weight:
All series: standard 9,362 kg (20,640 lb)
optional 10,298 kg (22,704 lb)
Max T-O weight: Series 100 38,102 kg (84,000 lb)
Series 200 42,184 kg (93,000 lb)
Series 300 44,225 kg (97,500 lb)
NRA 53,614 kg (118,200 lb)
Max ramp weight: Series 100 38,329 kg (84,500 lb)
Series 200 42,410 kg (93,500 lb)
Series 300 44,452 kg (98,000 lb)
Max zero-fuel weight: Series 100 31,071 kg (68,500 lb)
Series 200 34,019 kg (75,000 lb)
Series 300 35,607 kg (78,500 lb)
NRA 46,266 kg (102,000 lb)
Max landing weight: Series 100 35,153 kg (77,500 lb)
Series 200 36,741 kg (81,000 lb)
Series 300 38,328 kg (84,500 lb)
Max wing loading:
Series 100 493.0 kg/m^2 (101.0 lb/sq ft)
Series 200 545.7 kg/m^2 (111.8 lb/sq ft)
Series 300 572.2 kg/m^2 (117.2 lb/sq ft)
NRA 594.9 kg/m^2 (121.8 lb/sq ft)
Max power loading:
Series 100, standard 307.3 kg/kN (3.01 lb/lb st)
Series 200 340.2 kg/kN (3.34 lb/lb st)
Series 300 358.5 kg/kN (3.52 lb/lb st)

PERFORMANCE (at max standard T-O weight, except where indicated; NRA estimated):

Max operating Mach No.: all versions except NRA 0.73
NRA 0.82
Max operating speed:
Series 100 300 knots (555 km/h; 345 mph) CAS
Series 200, 300 295 knots (546 km/h; 339 mph) CAS
NRA 313 knots (580 km/h; 360 mph) CAS
Cruising speed at 8,840 m (29,000 ft) for 300 nm (556 km; 345 mile) sector:
Series 100/200:
high-speed 414 knots (767 km/h; 477 mph)
long-range 361 knots (669 km/h; 416 mph)
Series 300:
high-speed 426 knots (789 km/h; 491 mph)
long-range 377 knots (699 km/h; 434 mph)
Stalling speed, 30° flap:
Series 100 97 knots (180 km/h; 112 mph) EAS
Series 200, 300 102 knots (189 km/h; 118 mph) EAS
Stalling speed, 33° flap, at max landing weight:
Series 100 89 knots (165 km/h; 103 mph) EAS
Series 200, 300 92 knots (170 km/h; 106 mph) EAS
Min ground turning radius about nosewheels:
Series 100 11.53 m (37 ft 10 in)
Series 200 12.55 m (41 ft 2 in)
Series 300 13.97 m (45 ft 10 in)
T-O to 10.7 m (35 ft), S/L, ISA:
Series 100 1,219 m (4,000 ft)
Series 200, 300 1,509 m (4,950 ft)
FAR landing distance from 15 m (50 ft), S/L, ISA, at max landing weight: Series 100 1,067 m (3,500 ft)
Series 200 1,103 m (3,620 ft)
Series 300 1,228 m (4,030 ft)
Range with standard fuel:
Series 100 1,620 nm (3,002 km; 1,865 miles)
Series 200 1,570 nm (2,909 km; 1,808 miles)
Series 300 1,520 nm (2,817 km; 1,750 miles)
Range with max payload:
Series 100 880 nm (1,631 km; 1,013 miles)
Series 200 1,130 nm (2,094 km; 1,301 miles)
Series 200-QT 1,150 nm (2,131 km; 1,324 miles)
Series 300 1,040 nm (1,927 km; 1,197 miles)
Design range: NRA with 125 passengers
1,800 nm (3,335 km; 2,072 miles)
NRA with 139 passengers
1,490 nm (2,761 km; 1,715 miles)

OPERATIONAL NOISE LEVELS (FAR Pt 36-12, certificated):

T-O: Series 100	81.8 EPNdB
Series 200	85.2 EPNdB
Series 300	86.8 EPNdB
Approach: Series 100	95.6 EPNdB
Series 200	95.8 EPNdB
Series 300	96.1 EPNdB
Sideline: Series 100	87.7 EPNdB
Series 200	87.3 EPNdB
Series 300	86.9 EPNdB

BAe 146 MILITARY VARIANTS

TYPE: Multi-purpose transport.

PROGRAMME: Military developments of BAe 146 announced at 1987 Paris Air Show. Prototype 146STA (G-BSTA) converted by Pemco Aeroplex in USA from second 146 built (Series 100, c/n 1002); first flown 8 August 1988; displayed at Farnborough, then undertook sales tour of Far East and Australasia.

VARIANTS: **BAe 146M (Military Rear Loader):** Projected rear loading version (see Design Features).

BAe 146STA (Sideloading Tactical Airlifter): Derivative of 146-QT. Similar conversions of Series 200/300 offered. Missions envisaged include **paratrooping and supply dropping,** with 60 fully equipped paratroops deposited at 810 nm (1,501 km; 932 mile) radius on hi-lo-hi mission (lo phase 50 nm; 92 km; 58 miles each side of DZ) or standard 1.37 × 1.22 m (54 × 48 in) airdrop pallets carried in re-supply role; **troop transport** for up to 80 personnel, or 60 over 1,660 nm (3,076 km; 1,911 mile) range; **casualty evacuation,** with supplies outbound and 18 stretchers plus 26 seated wounded and four attendants returning over 780 nm (1,445 km; 898 mile) radius; **freight transport,** with floor loading of 976 kg/m² (200 lb/sq ft) throughout cargo hold, self-contained loading ramp, removable roller conveyor and ball-mat system, five pallet positions stressed to 1,814 kg (4,000 lb) and one to 3,175 kg (7,000 lb) with net palletised payload of 9,412 kg (20,750 lb); **aerial tanker** (optional role) with two wingtip hose-drum pods, disposable load of 11,340 kg (25,000 lb) of fuel at 200 nm (370 km; 230 mile) radius; **search and rescue** (optional role), with weather radar switched to surveillance mode and typically twelve 32-person dinghies airdropped through parachuting, door, offering 4.4 hours loiter on station at 200 nm (370 km; 230 miles) from base.

CUSTOMERS: Two ordered for Austrian Air Force for medical relief flights, paratroop dropping and ferrying Saab Draken power plants to Sweden for overhaul; first delivered early 1991.

DESIGN FEATURES: Large hydraulically operated rear loading ramp/doors on 146M allied to lowered main deck floor, accepting larger and heavier payloads; main landing gear redesigned to tandem configuration housed in fuselage sponsons. 146STA has large front-side freight door of 146-200QT; air-openable (outwards and forwards) parachuting door immediately behind freight door (one each side in production version). Either version can have over-cockpit in-flight refuelling probe.

Data for the 146-100STA are as for the civilian variant, except:

POWER PLANT: Four Textron Lycoming ALF 502R-MR turbofans. Fuel capacity 12,810 litres (3,384 US gallons; 2,818 Imp gallons).

DIMENSIONS, EXTERNAL:

Freight door: Height	1.93 m (6 ft 4 in)
Width	3.33 m (10 ft 11 in)

DIMENSIONS, INTERNAL:

Cabin: Unobstructed length	13.39 m (43 ft 11 in)
Width	3.33 m (10 ft 11 in)
Freight hold, underfloor:	
Volume	13.54 m³ (478.0 cu ft)

WEIGHTS AND LOADINGS:

Max payload	10,319 kg (22,750 lb)

BAe 146STA Sideloading Tactical Airlifter in low-visibility camouflage

Max T-O weight	42,184 kg (93,000 lb)
Max zero-fuel weight	33,565 kg (74,000 lb)
Max landing weight	37,684 kg (83,000 lb)

PERFORMANCE (at max T-O weight):

Service ceiling, one engine out	8,840 m (29,000 ft)
T-O to 15 m (50 ft)	1,174 m (3,850 ft)

BAe HAWK (TWO-SEAT VERSIONS)

RAF designations: Hawk T. Mks 1 and 1A
US Navy designation: T-45A Goshawk

TYPE: Two-seat basic and advanced jet trainer, with air defence and ground attack roles.

PROGRAMME: Early history of HS P1182 Hawk in 1989-90 *Jane's;* first generation Hawk in production, but marketing emphasis now on advanced 100 Series and single-seat 200 Series (detailed separately); Hawk design leadership transferred from Kingston to Brough 1988, and final assembly and flight test from Warton 1989; Hawk 50 Series exports made December 1980 to October 1985; Hawk 100 enhanced ground attack export model announced mid-1982; first flight of 100 Series aerodynamic prototype (G-HAWK/ZA101 converted as Mk 100 demonstrator) 21 October 1987; trials of wingtip Sidewinder rails started at Warton 1990.

VARIANTS: **Hawk T. Mk 1:** Basic two-seater for RAF flying and weapon training; 23.13 kN (5,200 lb st) Adour 151-01 (-02 in Red Arrows aircraft) non-afterburning turbofan; two dry underwing hardpoints; underbelly 30 mm gun pack; three-position flaps; simple weapon sight in aircraft of Nos. 1 and 2 Tactical Weapons Units; unarmed versions at No. 4 FTS and Central Flying School. Following basic Jet Provost or Tucano stage, future RAF fast-jet pilots fly 75 hours at No. 4 FTS and 54 hours' weapons and tactical training with one of TWUs; Hawks will be introduced to navigator training syllabus at No. 6 FTS, Finningley.

Hawk T. Mk 1A: Contract January 1983 to wire 89 Hawks of Nos. 1/2 TWUs and Red Arrows for AIM-9L Sidewinder on each inboard wing pylon and optional activation of previously unused outer wing hardpoints; last conversion redelivered 30 May 1986; 72 NATO-declared, for point defence and participation in RAF's Mixed Fighter Force, to accompany radar equipped Phantoms and Tornado ADVs on medium-range air defence sorties.

Hawk 50 Series: Initial export version with 23.75 kN (5,340 lb st) Adour 851 turbofan; max operating weight increased by 30 per cent, disposable load by 70 per cent, range by 30 per cent; revised tailcone shape to improve directional stability at high speed; larger nose equipment bay; four wing pylons, all configured for single or twin store carriage; each pylon cleared for 515 kg (1,135 lb) load; wet inboard pylons for 455 litre (122 US gallon; 100 Imp gallon) fuel tanks; improved nav/com; improved cockpit, with angle of attack indication, fully aerobatic twin gyro AHRS, slim seat head-boxes and weapon control panel; optional brake-chute; suitable for day VMC ground attack and armed reconnaissance with camera/sensor pod.

Hawk 60 Series: Development of 50 Series with 25.35 kN (5,700 lb st) Adour 861 turbofan; leading-edge devices and four-position flaps to improve lift capability; low-friction nose leg, strengthened wheels and tyres, and adaptive anti-skid system; 592 or 864 litre (156 or 228 US gallon; 130 or 190 Imp gallon) drop tanks; provision for Sidewinder or Magic AAMs; max operating weight increased by further 17 per cent over Mk 50 Series, disposable load by 33 per cent and range by 30 per cent; improved field performance, acceleration, rate of climb and turn rate. Deliveries complete, apart from seven for Finland, 20 hybrid Mk 60/100s (Mk 67s) ordered by South Korea and five improved Mk 60As being delivered in 1991 to Zimbabwe. Abu Dhabi plans upgrade of 15 existing Mk 63s to Mk 63A with Adour Mk 871, new wings, wingtip Sidewinders and possibly new avionics.

T-45A Goshawk: US Navy version (see McDonnell Douglas/BAe in International section).

Hawk 100 Series: Enhanced ground attack development of 60 Series, to exploit Hawk's five-pylon stores capability; two-seater, with perhaps pilot only on combat missions; 26.0 kN (5,845 lb st) Adour Mk 871 turbofan; combat wing incorporating fixed leading-edge droop for increased lift and manoeuvrability from Mach 0.3 to 0.7; full-width flap vanes; manually selected combat flap and fuselage-mounted smurfs (side-mounted unit horizontal root tail fin) ahead of tailplane leading-edge. MIL-STD-1553B databus integrating Plessey Electronic Systems SKN 2416 inertial navigation unit, as in F-16; advanced Smiths Industries HUD/WAC and new air data sensor package with optional laser ranging and FLIR; improved weapons management system allowing pre-selection in flight and display of weapon status; manual or automatic weapon release; passive radar warning; HOTAS controls; full colour multi-purpose CRT display in each cockpit; provision for ECM pod.

Max external load 3,084 kg (6,800 lb); T-O run reduced by typically 15 per cent; lo-lo-lo combat radius 129 nm (239 km; 148 miles) with four 1,000 lb bombs and gun pod or 111 nm (205 km; 128 miles) with eight 500 lb bombs and gun pod; in combat air patrol mission, can loiter on station at low level for 2¾ hours, 100 nm (185 km; 115 miles) from base, with two Sidewinder type AAMs, 30 mm gun pod and two 864 litre (228 US gallon; 190 Imp gallon) external tanks.

Hawk 200 Series: Single-seat multi-role version (described separately).

CUSTOMERS: See table.

Description below applies to current UK production Hawks for export:

DESIGN FEATURES: Fully aerobatic trainer, adaptable for point defence; design capable of other optional roles, with wing improvements on developed series to enhance combat efficiency; single non-afterburning engine; elevated rear cockpit to enhance forward view; underwing hardpoints; wingtip AAM rails, and/or extended wings with forward-facing optical flats for FLIR and laser rangefinder, optional for 100 Series.

Wing thickness/chord ratio 10.9 per cent at root, 9 per

The first (UK assembled) BAe Hawk Mk 66 for Switzerland escorted by one of the DH Vampire Trainers it has replaced

cent at tip; dihedral 2°; sweepback 26° on leading-edge, 21° 30′ at quarter-chord. Anhedral tailplane.

FLYING CONTROLS: Ailerons and one-piece all-moving tailplane actuated hydraulically by tandem actuators; rudder mechanically operated, with electrically actuated trim tab. Hydraulically actuated double-slotted flaps, outboard 300 mm (12 in) of flap vanes normally deleted; small fence on each wing leading-edge; 100 and 200 Series use special combat wing with full width flap vanes (refer Hawk 200 entry); large airbrake under rear fuselage, aft of wings; two small ventral fins known as smurfs (refer Hawk 200 entry) on 100 Series.

STRUCTURE: Aluminium alloy; one-piece wing, with machined torsion box of two main spars, auxiliary spar, ribs and skins with integral stringers; most of box forms integral fuel tank; honeycomb-filled ailerons; composites wing fences; frames and stringers fuselage; swept tail surfaces. Two-part programme of wing replacement for most RAF Hawks began 1989; initial 85 aircraft modified by BAe, 59 more out to tender for completion by mid-1990s.

LANDING GEAR: Wide track hydraulically retractable tricycle type, with single wheel on each unit. AP Precision Hydraulics oleos and jacks. Main units retract inward into wing, ahead of front spar; castoring nosewheel retracts forward. Dunlop mainwheels, brakes and tyres size 6.50-10, pressure 9.86 bars (143 lb/sq in). Nosewheel and tyre size 4.4-16, pressure 8.27 bars (120 lb/sq in). Tail bumper fairing under rear fuselage. Anti-skid wheel brakes. Tail braking parachute, diameter 2.64 m (8 ft 8 in), on Mks 52/53 and all 60 series aircraft.

POWER PLANT: One Rolls-Royce Turbomeca Adour non-afterburning turbofan, as described under Variants. Air intake on each side of fuselage, forward of wing leading-edge. Engine starting by Microturbo integral gas turbine starter. Fuel in one fuselage bag tank of 868 litres (229 US gallons; 191 Imp gallons) capacity and integral wing tank of 836 litres (221 US gallons; 184 Imp gallons) capacity; total fuel capacity 1,704 litres (450 US gallons; 375 Imp gallons). Pressure refuelling point near front of port engine air intake trunk; gravity point on top of fuselage. Provision for carrying one 455, 592 or 864 litre (120, 156 or 228 US gallon; 100, 130 or 190 Imp gallon) drop tank on each inboard underwing pylon, according to series.

ACCOMMODATION: Crew of two in tandem under one-piece fully transparent acrylic canopy, opening sideways to starboard. Fixed front windscreen and separate internal windscreen in front of rear cockpit. Improved front windscreen fitted retrospectively to RAF Hawks, able to withstand a 1 kg (2.2 lb) bird at 528 knots (978 km/h; 607 mph). Rear seat elevated. Martin-Baker Mk 10B zero/zero rocket assisted ejection seats, with MDC (miniature detonating cord) system to break canopy before seats eject. The MDC can also be operated from outside the cockpit for ground rescue. Dual controls standard. Entire accommodation pressurised, heated and air-conditioned.

SYSTEMS: BAe cockpit air-conditioning and pressurisation systems, using engine bleed air. Two hydraulic systems; flow rate: System 1, 36.4 litres (9.6 US gallons; 8 Imp gallons)/min; System 2, 22.7 litres (6 US gallons; 5 Imp gallons)/min. Systems pressure 207 bars (3,000 lb/sq in), for actuation of control jacks, flaps, airbrake, landing gear and anti-skid wheel brakes. Compressed nitrogen accumulators provide emergency power for flaps and landing gear at a pressure of 2.75 to 5.5 bars (40 to 80 lb/sq in). Hydraulic accumulator for emergency operation of wheel brakes. Pop-up Dowty ram air turbine in upper rear fuselage provides emergency hydraulic power for flying controls in the event of an engine or No. 2 pump failure. No pneumatic system. DC electrical power from single brushless generator, with two static inverters to provide AC power and two batteries for standby power. Gaseous oxygen system for crew.

AVIONICS: The RAF standard of flight instruments includes GEC Ferranti gyros and inverter, two Honeywell RAI-4 4 in remote attitude indicators and a magnetic detector unit, and Louis Newmark compass system. Radio and navigation equipment includes Sylvania UHF and VHF, Cossor CAT.7,000 Tacan, Cossor ILS with CILS.75/76 localiser/glideslope receiver and marker receiver, and IFF/SSR (Cossor 2720 Mk 10A IFF in aircraft for Finland). BAe LINS 300 INS in Omani 100 Series. GEC Ferranti F.195 weapon sight and camera recorder in each cockpit of about 90 RAF and all 50 and 60 series aircraft. (Saab RGS2 sighting system in aircraft for Finland.)

ARMAMENT: Underfuselage centreline mounted 30 mm Aden Mk 4 cannon with 120 rounds (VKT 12.7 mm machine gun beneath Finnish aircraft), and two or four hardpoints underwing, according to series. Provision for pylon in place of the ventral gun pack. In RAF training roles the normal max external load is about 680 kg (1,500 lb), but the uprated Hawk has demonstrated its ability to carry a total external load of 3,084 kg (6,800 lb). Typical weapon loadings on 60 series include a 30 mm or 12.7 mm centreline gun pod and four packs each containing eighteen 68 mm rockets; a centreline reconnaissance pod and four packs each containing twelve 81 mm rockets; seven 1,000 lb free fall or retarded bombs; four launchers each containing four 100 mm rockets; nine 250 lb or 250

BAe's original two-seat Hawk demonstrator, modified to the aerodynamic shape of the Hawk 100 series and fitted with wingtip Sidewinder rails

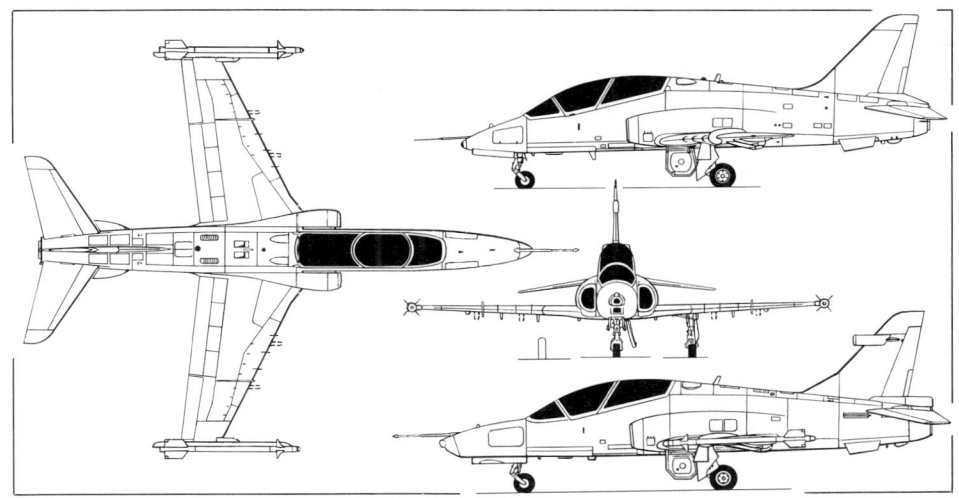

British Aerospace Hawk 100 with wingtip Sidewinders and additional side view (top) of Hawk 60 series
(*Pilot Press*)

BAe HAWK CUSTOMERS

Customer	Mark	Total	Deliveries	Squadrons
Abu Dhabi	63	18[8]	10.84-5.85	FTS
	102[6]	18*		On order
Dubai	61	8	3.83-9.83	Ftr Sqdn
	61	1	6.88	Ftr Sqdn
Finland	51	50[2]	12.80-10.85	11, 21, 31, Koul LLv
	51A	7*	1993	On order
Indonesia	53	20	9.80-3.84	103
Kenya	52	12	4.80-2.82	
S. Korea	67[6]	20*	1992-93	On order
Kuwait	64	12	11.85-87	
Malaysia	108	10*	1.94-	On order
	208[6]	18*	7.94-3.95	On order
Oman	103	8*		On order
	203	8*		On order
Saudi Arabia	65	30	8.87-10.88	21, 37
Switzerland	66	20[3]	11.89-	55, 255
UK	T. Mk 1	176[7]	11.76-2.82	4 FTS, Red Arrows 63, 79, 151, 234
USA	T-45A	302[4]		Requirement
Zimbabwe	60	3	7.82-10.82	2
	60A	10*	1991	On order
Demonstrator	60/102D	2[5]		
	200/200/200RDA	3[5]		
TOTAL		**756**		
Under negotiation:				
Brunei		8		100 Srs
		8		200 Srs
Saudi Arabia	205	60		

NOTES
* *Built at Brough, Hamble and Samlesbury; assembled at Warton; unless stated otherwise, remainder built at Kingston, assembled at Dunsfold (290) and Bitteswell (1)*

[1] *Conversions*
[2] *46 assembled by Valmet in Finland*
[3] *19 assembled by F + W in Switzerland*
[4] *Production by McDonnell Douglas in USA*
[5] *One assembled at Warton*
[6] *Wingtip Sidewinders*
[7] *89 converted to T. Mk 1A*
[8] *16 converted to 63A*

kg bombs; thirty-six 80 lb runway denial or tactical strike bombs; five 600 lb cluster bombs; four Sidewinder/Magic air-to-air missiles; four CBLS 100/200 carriers each containing four practice bombs and four rockets; or two 592 litre (156 US gallon; 130 Imp gallon) drop tanks and two Maverick air-to-surface missiles. Vinten reconnaissance pod available for centre pylon. A configuration demonstrated at the 1983 Paris Air Show included a Sea Eagle anti-ship missile on the centreline pylon, plus two Sidewinder missiles and two 864 litre (228 US gallon; 190 Imp gallon) drop tanks underwing.

DIMENSIONS, EXTERNAL:
Wing span: normal   9.39 m (30 ft 9¾ in)
incl tip Sidewinders   9.94 m (32 ft 7⅜ in)

Wing chord: at root	2.65 m (8 ft 8¼ in)
at tip	0.90 m (2 ft 11½ in)
Wing aspect ratio	5.3
Length overall: excl probe:	
Mk 1, 50 and 60 series	11.17 m (36 ft 7¾ in)
100 series	11.68 m (38 ft 4 in)
incl probe	11.86 m (38 ft 11 in)
Height overall:	
Mk 1, 50 and 60 series	3.99 m (13 ft 1¼ in)
100 series	4.16 m (13 ft 8 in)
Tailplane span	4.39 m (14 ft 4¾ in)
Wheel track	3.47 m (11 ft 5 in)
AREAS:	
Wings, gross	16.69 m² (179.6 sq ft)
Ailerons (total)	1.05 m² (11.30 sq ft)
Trailing-edge flaps (total)	2.50 m² (26.91 sq ft)
Airbrake	0.53 m² (5.70 sq ft)
Fin: Mk 1, 50 and 60 series	2.51 m² (27.02 sq ft)
100 series	2.61 m² (28.10 sq ft)
Rudder, incl tab	0.58 m² (6.24 sq ft)
Tailplane	4.33 m² (46.61 sq ft)
WEIGHTS AND LOADINGS:	
Weight empty: 60 series	3,750 kg (8,267 lb)
100 series	3,970 kg (8,752 lb)
T-O weight:	
60 series trainer, clean	5,150 kg (11,350 lb)
Max T-O weight: T. Mk 1	5,700 kg (12,566 lb)
50 series	7,350 kg (16,200 lb)
60, 100 series	8,500 kg (18,739 lb)
Max landing weight: T. Mk 1	4,649 kg (10,250 lb)
60 series	7,650 kg (16,865 lb)
Max wing loading:	
T. Mk 1	341.5 kg/m² (69.97 lb/sq ft)
50 series	440.4 kg/m² (90.2 lb/sq ft)
60,100 series	509.3 kg/m² (104.3 lb/sq ft)
Max power loading:	
T. Mk 1	246.5 kg/kN (2.42 lb/lb st)
50 series	309.47 kg/kN (3.03 lb/lb st)
60 series	335.3 kg/kN (3.29 lb/lb st)
100 series	326.9 kg/kN (3.21 lb/lb st)

PERFORMANCE:
Design max diving speed, clean:
  at S/L
    Mach 0.87 (575 knots; 1,065 km/h; 661 mph EAS)
  at and above 5,180 m (17,000 ft)
    Mach 1.2 (575 knots; 1,065 km/h; 661 mph EAS)

Max level speed:	
50 series	535 knots (990 km/h; 615 mph)
60, 100 series	560 knots (1,037 km/h; 644 mph)
Max level speed Mach number	0.88
Max rate of climb at S/L	3,600 m (11,800 ft)/min
Time to 9,145 m (30,000 ft), clean	6 min 6 s
Service ceiling	15,250 m (50,000 ft)
T-O run	550 m (1,800 ft)
Landing run: 60 Series	518 m (1,700 ft)
100 Series	524 m (1,720 ft)

Combat radius:
  with 2,268 kg (5,000 lb) weapon load
    538 nm (998 km; 620 miles)
  with 908 kg (2,000 lb) weapon load
    781 nm (1,448 km; 900 miles)
Ferry range: clean   1,313 nm (2,433 km; 1,510 miles)
  60 series, with two 864 litre (228 US gallon; 190 Imp
  gallon) drop tanks   2,200 nm (4,075 km; 2,530 miles)
Endurance, 100 nm (185 km; 115 miles) from base
    approx 4 h
g limits   +8/-4

BAe HAWK 200 SERIES (SINGLE-SEAT VERSIONS)

TYPE: Single-seat multi-role combat aircraft.
PROGRAMME: Intention to build demonstrator (ZG200) announced 20 June 1984; first flight 19 May 1986 but lost 2 July in g-induced loss of consciousness (GLOC) accident; replaced by first pre-production Hawk 200 (ZH200), first flown 24 April 1987; third demonstrator (200RDA) with full avionics and systems, including Westinghouse AN/APG-66H radar, flown 1991.
VARIANTS: Missions can include:
  Airspace denial: Two Sidewinders (more can be carried) and two 864 litre (228 US gallon; 190 Imp gallon) drop tanks, enabling 3 hour loiter on station at low level and 100 nm (185 km; 115 miles) from base, or one hour on station 550 nm (1,018 km; 633 miles) from base, or max intercept radius 720 nm (1,333 km; 828 miles).
  Close air support: Typically five 1,000 lb and four 500 lb bombs, precision delivered up to 104 nm (192 km; 120 miles) from base in lo-lo mission.
  Battlefield interdiction: Typically 1,360 kg (3,000 lb) load on hi-lo-hi mission over 510 nm (945 km; 587 mile) radius.
  Long-range photo reconnaissance: 1,723 nm (3,190 km; 1,982 mile) range, with two external tanks and pod containing cameras and infra-red linescan (rapid role change permits follow-on attack by same aircraft), or lo-lo day/night radius 510 nm (945 km; 586 miles).
  Long-range deployment: 1,950 nm (3,610 km; 2,244 mile) ferry range, using two 864 litre (228 US gallon; 190 Imp gallon) and one 592 litre (156 US gallon; 130 Imp gallon) external tanks, unrefuelled and with 864 litre tanks retained (reserves allow 10 min over destination at 150 m; 500 ft).

BAe pre-production Hawk 200 single-seat multi-role combat aircraft

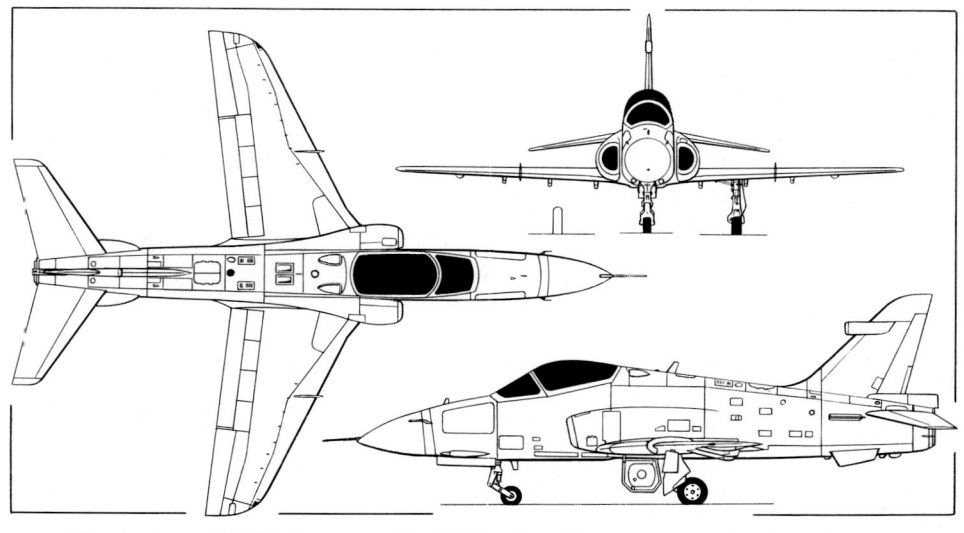

The single-seat British Aerospace Hawk 200 series with nose-mounted radar (*Pilot Press*)

Anti-shipping strike: Sea Eagle missile and two 864 litre (228 US gallon; 190 Imp gallon) tanks, enabling ship attack 666 nm (1,234 km; 767 miles) from base and return with 10 per cent fuel reserves (puts ships in wide area of North Atlantic within range of shore bases; weapon release could be beyond target's radar envelope).
Three standards of equipment envisaged, depending on customer's mission requirements:
  Day operation: Fit comprises gyro stabilised attack sight and attitude heading reference system, with radio aid navigation. Capabilities may be extended by adding INS, HUD/WAC; other options are HOTAS controls, laser rangefinder, IFF and RWR.
  Night operation: FLIR and laser rangefinder mounted in modified nosecone for precision ground attacks and tactical reconnaissance by day/night.
  All-weather operation: Westinghouse AN/APG-66H advanced multi-mode radar for all-weather target acquisition and navigational fixing capabilities (Sea Eagle, Sky Flash and other weapons employable).
CUSTOMERS: Oman (eight Mk 203 ordered July 1990), Malaysia (18 **Mk 208** ordered December 1990, for delivery from July 1994). Saudi Arabia signed MoU covering second batch of some 60 Hawks, substantial proportion **Mk 205** with APG-66H radar; Brunei negotiating for eight. All customers also ordered two-seat Hawks.
DESIGN FEATURES: Except for taller fin, fixed wing leading-edge droop to enhance lift and manoeuvrability at Mach 0.3 to 0.7, manually selected combat flaps (less than ¼-flap setting) available below 350 knots (649 km/h; 403 mph) IAS to allow sustained 5g+ at 300 knots (556 km/h; 345 mph) at sea level, full-width flap vanes reinstated and detail modifications to wing dressing, Hawk 200 virtually identical to current production Hawk two-seater aft of cockpit, giving 80 per cent airframe commonality. Intended to take advantage of new miniaturised, low-cost avionics and intelligent weapons; Hawk 100 type avionics fit allows radar, or FLIR and laser rangefinder. Built-in twin cannon frees centreline pylon for other stores, including 592 litre (156 US gallon; 130 Imp gallon) drop fuel tank; all four underwing pylons capable of 907 kg (2,000 lb) load, within max 3,493 kg (7,700 lb) external load; optional wingtip rails make possible six Sidewinders or similar AAMs.
FLYING CONTROLS: See Hawk two-seater; smurfs (strake ahead of each half of tailplane to restore control authority at high angles of attack).

LANDING GEAR: Mainwheel tyres size 559 × 165-279, pressure 16.2 bars (235 lb/sq in). Nosewheel tyre size 457 × 140-203, pressure 7.24 bars (105 lb/sq in). Optional single Tornado-type nosewheel for increased T-O weight.
POWER PLANT: One Rolls-Royce Turbomeca Adour Mk 871 non-afterburning turbofan, with uninstalled rating of 26.0 kN (5,845 lb st).
ACCOMMODATION: Pilot only, on Martin-Baker Type 10L zero/zero ejection seat, under side-hinged (to starboard) canopy.
SYSTEMS: 25kVA generator with DC transformer/rectifier. Fairey Hydraulics yaw control system added, comprising rudder actuator and servo control system, incorporating an autostabiliser computer. Lucas Aerospace artificial feel system.
AVIONICS: GEC Ferranti multi-function display in cockpit. HOTAS controls optional. BAe LINS 300 laser INS in Omani aircraft.
ARMAMENT: One or two internally mounted 25 mm Aden guns (with 100 rds each) beneath cockpit floor. GEC Ferranti ISIS sight or Smiths head-up display optional. Chaff/flare dispenser (Vinten Vicon 78 Srs 300 or equivalent) at base of fin. All weapon pylons cleared for 8g manoeuvres with 500 kg (1,102 lb) loads.

DIMENSIONS, EXTERNAL:
  As Hawk two-seater, except:

Length overall	11.38 m (37 ft 4 in)
Height overall	4.16 m (13 ft 8 in)
Wheelbase	3.298 m (10 ft 10 in)

AREAS:
  As Hawk two-seater, except:

Fin	2.61 m² (28.10 sq ft)

WEIGHTS AND LOADINGS:

Weight empty	4,510 kg (9,943 lb)
Max fuel: internal	1,360 kg (3,000 lb)
internal plus three drop tanks	3,210 kg (7,080 lb)
Max weapon load	3,493 kg (7,700 lb)
Max T-O weight	9,101 kg (20,065 lb)
Max wing loading	545.3 kg/m² (111.7 lb/sq ft)
Max power loading	350.04 kg/kN (3.43 lb/lb st)

PERFORMANCE (estimated; no external stores or role equipment unless stated):
Design max diving speed, clean:
  at S/L
    Mach 0.87 (575 knots; 1,065 km/h; 661 mph EAS)
  at and above 5,180 m (17,000 ft)
    Mach 1.2 (575 knots; 1,065 km/h; 661 mph EAS)

Max level speed at S/L
  551 knots (1,021 km/h; 634 mph)
Econ cruising speed at 12,500 m (41,000 ft)
  430 knots (796 km/h; 495 mph)
Stalling speed, flaps down
  106 knots (197 km/h; 122 mph) IAS
Max rate of climb at S/L   3,508 m (11,510 ft)/min
Service ceiling   15,250 m (50,000 ft)
Runway LCN: flexible pavement   15
  rigid pavement   10
T-O run with max weapon load   1,585 m (5,200 ft)
T-O to 15 m (50 ft) with max weapon load
  2,134 m (7,000 ft)
Landing from 15 m (50 ft) at landing weight of 4,550 kg
  (10,030 lb): with brake-chute   854 m (2,800 ft)
  without brake-chute   1,250 m (4,100 ft)
Radius of action, hi-hi with one Sea Eagle anti-ship
  missile and two 864 litre (228 US gallon; 190 Imp
  gallon) drop tanks   311 nm (576 km; 358 miles)
Range:
  with internal fuel only   482 nm (892 km; 554 miles)
  with internal fuel plus three drop tanks
  1,950 nm (3,610 km; 2,244 miles)
g limits   +8/−4

BAe HARRIER

RAF designations: Harrier GR. Mk 3 and T. Mks 4/4A
RN designations: T. Mks 4N/8N
Indian Navy designation: T. Mk 60
Spanish Navy designation: VA.1 Matador (AV-8S and TAV-8S)
TYPE: V/STOL close support and reconnaissance aircraft.
PROGRAMME: World's first operational fixed-wing V/STOL attack fighter; supplanted in production by AV-8B Harrier II/Harrier GR. Mks 5/7 (see International section: McDonnell Douglas/BAe), except limited manufacture as two-seat compatible trainer for Sea Harrier, as detailed below; following February 1990 order for two-seat Harrier IIs, plans abandoned to convert some RAF T. Mk 4s to T. Mk 6 standard with night vision equipment for training pilots of GR. Mk 7s fitted with FLIR.
  Two dual-control Harriers employed in test programmes, comprising XW175 at RAE Bedford as Vectored-thrust Advanced Aircraft Control (VAAC) Harrier (see 1987-88 Jane's Cranfield entry); and XW267 with 'Nightbird' night vision equipment (see 1990-91 edition).
VARIANTS: **Mk 54** and **Mk 55** Spanish Navy AV-8S and TAV-8S, in service; surplus RAF Harrier GR. Mk 3s withdrawn from 1988, last four operational aircraft based in Belize by January 1991; US Marine Corps **AV-8As** and **TAV-8As** retired 1985-87. Fuller details appeared in 1989-90 and earlier editions of Jane's. Principal variants are currently:
  Harrier T. Mk 4 and 4A and Harrier T. Mk 4N and 8N: Two-seat trainer version; RAF flies Mk 4A and laser-nosed Mk 4; three Royal Navy two-seaters designated Harrier T. Mk 4N. Two-seat Harrier production for UK totalled 31, including prototypes; some RAF trainers transferred to RN; approval awaited for some naval Harrier trainers to receive cockpits representative of Sea Harrier FRS. Mk 2 (but without radar), being re-designated T. Mk 8N.
  Harrier T. Mk 60: Two-seat operational trainer for Indian Navy; T. Mk 4A configuration, but complete Sea Harrier avionics except Blue Fox radar; four ordered, deliveries starting March 1984 (third delivered April 1990).
  Sea Harrier FRS. Mks 1, 2 and 51: Described separately.
CUSTOMERS: See Variants.
DESIGN FEATURES: See Programme and previous editions of Jane's.
  Technical details as for Sea Harrier, except:
LANDING GEAR: T. Mk 4 tyre pressures 6.90 bars (100 lb/sq in) on nose unit, 6.55 bars (95 lb/sq in) on main and outrigger units.
POWER PLANT: One Rolls-Royce Pegasus Mk 103 (or navalised Mk 104) vectored thrust turbofan (95.6 kN; 21,500 lb st).
ACCOMMODATION: Crew of two (Mk 4) on Martin-Baker Mk 9D zero/zero rocket ejection seats.
AVIONICS: GEC-Plessey U/VHF, Ultra standby UHF, GEC Avionics AD 2770 Tacan and Cossor IFF, GEC Ferranti FE 541 inertial navigation and attack system (INAS), with Honeywell C2G compass, Smiths electronic head-up display of flight information, and air data computer. Marconi ARI.18223 radar warning receiver. GEC Ferranti Type 106 laser ranger and marked target seeker (LRMTS) in most RAF Harriers.
DIMENSIONS, EXTERNAL: As for Sea Harrier except:
  Wing span   7.70 m (25 ft 3 in)
  Length overall:
    two-seat (laser nose)   17.50 m (57 ft 5 in)
  Height overall: two-seat   4.17 m (13 ft 8 in)
WEIGHTS AND LOADINGS:
  Weight empty (pilot/s plus four pylons; no guns):
    T. Mk 4   6,693 kg (14,755 lb)
    T. Mk 4A   6,568 kg (14,480 lb)
  Internal fuel   2,295 kg (5,060 lb)

Max T-O weight: two-seat   11,880 kg (26,200 lb)
Max wing loading   636.0 kg/m² (130.3 lb/sq ft)
Max power loading   124.27 kg/kN (1.22 lb/lb st)
PERFORMANCE (single-seat):
Max level speed at S/L 635 knots (1,176 km/h; 730 mph)
Max Mach number in a dive at height   1.3
Time to 12,200 m (40,000 ft) from vertical T-O
  2 min 23 s
Service ceiling   15,600 m (51,200 ft)
T-O run: with 2,270 kg (5,000 lb) payload at max T-O
  weight   approx 305 m (1,000 ft)
Range: hi-lo-hi with 1,995 kg (4,400 lb) payload
  360 nm (666 km; 414 miles)
  lo-lo with 1,995 kg (4,400 lb) payload
  200 nm (370 km; 230 miles)
Ferry range   1,850 nm (3,425 km; 2,129 miles)
Range with one in-flight refuelling
  more than 3,000 nm (5,560 km; 3,455 miles)
Endurance:
  combat air patrol 100 nm (185 km; 115 miles) from
  base   1 h 30 min
  with one in-flight refuelling   more than 7 h
g limits   +7.8/−4.2

BAe SEA HARRIER

RN designations: FRS. Mks 1 and 2
Indian Navy designation: FRS. Mk 51
TYPE: V/STOL fighter, reconnaissance and strike aircraft.
PROGRAMME: Development of P1184 Sea Harrier announced by British Government 15 May 1975; first flight (XZ450) 20 August 1978; first delivery to Royal Navy (XZ451) 18 June 1979; first ship trials (HMS Hermes) November 1979.
  Ski jump launching ramp (proposed by Lt Cdr D. R. Taylor, RN) take-off trials ashore 1977, and at sea from 30 October 1980; HMS Invincible and Illustrious first fitted with 7° ramps, HMS Ark Royal 12°; latter allows 1,135 kg (2,500 lb) increased load for same take-off run or 50-60 per cent shorter run at same weight; HMS Invincible recommissioned with 13° ramp 18 May 1989; HMS Illustrious to be similarly converted by 1993.
  UK MoD gave BAe project definition contract January 1985 for mid-life update of RN Sea Harrier FRS. Mk 1s; upgraded aircraft redesignated FRS. Mk 2s; aerodyamic development FRS. Mk 2 converted at Dunsfold from Mk 1 ZA195; first flight 19 September 1988; first flight of second development aircraft (XZ439) 8 March 1989; contract for conversion of further 33 Mk 1s to Mk 2s signed by UK MoD 7 December 1988; modifications begun at Kingston October 1990; redelivery 1991-94, augmenting newly built Mk 2s.

New FRS. Mk 2 AAM launch rail first tested by live AIM-9L (from Mk 1) 2 November 1988; AMRAAM trials began in USA (using XZ439) 1991; airborne testing of Blue Fox radar began in RAE One-Eleven (ZF433), completing 114 hour/121 sortie programme November 1987; development work transferred to RAE BAe 125 (XW930), first flown with A-version radar 26 August 1988; second 125-600B (ZF130) given full FRS. Mk 2 weapon system, including representative cockpit in co-pilot's position and Sidewinder acquisition round on underwing pylon (first flight at Woodford 20 May 1988; began development flying at Dunsfold December 1988; not fitted with B-version Blue Vixen radar until September 1989; first flight of B-version radar in Sea Harrier XZ439 24 May 1990. First Mk 2 deck landing, by ZA195 on HMS Ark Royal, 7 November 1990.
VARIANTS: **FRS. Mk 1:** Initial Royal Navy version; Pegasus 104 engine; first used operationally during Falkland Islands campaign 1982, from HMS Hermes and Invincible (29 flew 2,376 sorties, destroying 22 enemy aircraft in air-to-air combat without loss; four lost in accidents and two to ground fire). Total 38 remained, May 1991, including Mk 2 prototypes.
  FRS. Mk 51: Similar to Mk 1, for Indian Navy.
  FRS. Mk 2: Differs externally from Mk 1 by less pointed nose radome; longer rear fuselage, resulting from 35 cm (1 ft 1¾ in) plug aft of wing trailing-edge; revisions of antennae and external stores. Internal changes include Ferranti Blue Vixen pulse Doppler radar, offering all-weather lookdown/shootdown capability, with inherent track-while-scan, multiple target engagement, greatly increased missile launch range, enhanced surface target acquisition, and improved ECCM performance. Current weapons plus AIM-120 AMRAAM on Dowty/Frazer-Nash launch rails compatible with AIM-9L Sidewinder.
  Improved systems built around MIL-1553B databus, with dual redundant data highway, allowing computerised time sharing of information processed in databus control and interface unit.
  Redesign of cockpit includes new HUD and dual multi-purpose head-down displays; proposed JTIDS terminal will not be fitted (except as possible retrofit) following cancellation by US Navy of originally proposed equipment; all time-critical weapon systems controls positioned on up-front control panel, or on throttle and stick (HOTAS).
  Wingtip extensions of 20 cm (8 in) and 30 cm (1 ft 0 in) test-flown to enhance stability carrying AMRAAM, but proved unnecessary by 1990 trials.
CUSTOMERS: Royal Navy ordered three development aircraft

BAe Sea Harrier FRS. Mk 2 aerodynamic prototype carrying four AMRAAM missiles

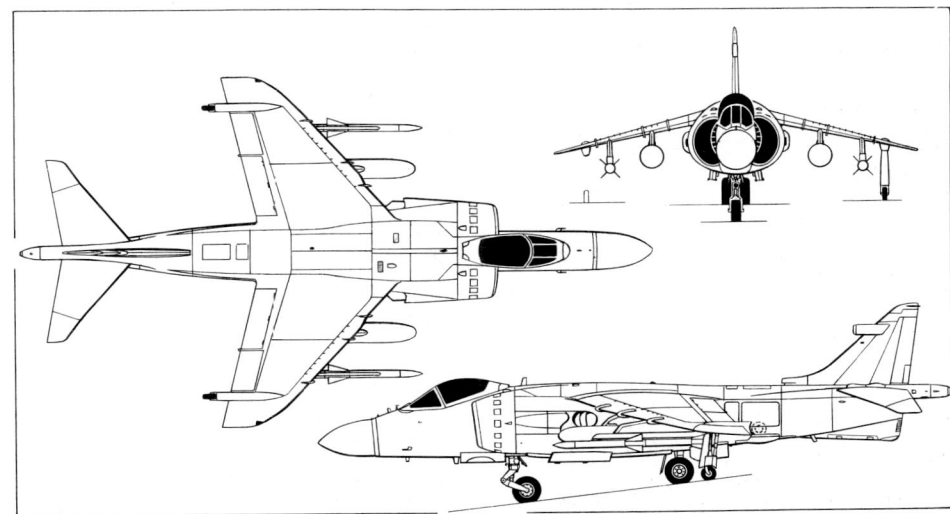

BAe Sea Harrier FRS. Mk 2 V/STOL fighter, reconnaissance and strike aircraft *(Pilot Press)*

plus batches of 21, 10, 14 and nine by September 1984; all built as Mk 1s, last completed June 1988; contract for 10 Mk 2s placed March 1990; Naval Intensive Flying Trials Unit (No. 700A Squadron) commissioned at RNAS Yeovilton 18 September 1979 and became normally shore based No. 899 HQ Squadron, April 1980; front line units Nos. 800 and 801 Squadrons, with eight aircraft each (previously five); non-radar T. Mk 4N two-seat trainers (three) received (see Harrier entry).

Six similar FRS. Mk 51s handed over to Indian Navy from January 1983; delivered (after pilot training in UK) from December 1983; used by No. 300 (White Tiger) Squadron from INS *Vikrant*; two T. Mk 60 two-seat trainers received (see Harrier entry); ten more FRS. Mk 51s and one T. Mk 60 ordered by Indian Government November 1985; letter of intent for seven more FRS. Mk 51s and one T. Mk 60 issued September 1986, to equip INS *Viraat* (former HMS *Hermes*); second batch deliveries began December 1989.

Following description applies to Sea Harrier FRS. Mk 1, except where indicated otherwise:

DESIGN FEATURES: Single-engined V/STOL system with four rotatable exhaust nozzles that can be set through 98.5° from fully aft position; short take-off made with nozzles initially fully aft, then turned partially downward for lift-off and continued forward acceleration; nozzles can be vectored at high speed to tighten turn radius or decelerate suddenly; control at less than wing-borne airspeed automatically transferred to puffer jets at wingtips, nose and tail, also enhancing combat manoeuvres.

Main differences from land-based Harriers include elimination of magnesium components, introduction of raised cockpit, revised operational avionics, and installation of multi-mode GEC Ferranti radar with air-to-air intercept and air-to-surface modes in redesigned nose that folds to port; Pegasus 104 turbofan of Mk 1 incorporates additional anti-corrosion features and generates more electrical power than land-based Pegasus 103. See Variants for FRS. Mk 2 features.

Wing section BAe (HS) design; thickness/chord ratio 10 per cent at root, 5 per cent at tip; anhedral 12°; incidence 1° 45′; and sweepback at quarter-chord 34°.

FLYING CONTROLS: Plain ailerons irreversibly operated by tandem hydraulic jacks; one-piece variable incidence tailplane, with 15° anhedral, irreversibly operated by tandem hydraulic jacks; manually operated rudder with trim tab; flaps; jet reaction control valve built into front of each outrigger wheel fairing and in nose and tailcone; large airbrake under fuselage; ventral fin under rear fuselage.

STRUCTURE: One-piece aluminium alloy three-spar safe-life wing with integrally machined skins (Brough built); entire wing unit removable to provide access to engine; revised inboard one-third of FRS. Mk 2 wing incorporates additional fence, kinked leading-edge, re-positioning of dog-tooth fillet closer to fuselage, and reduction of overwing vortex generators from 12 to 11; 67.3 cm (2 ft 2½ in) wing extensions available for ferrying; ailerons, flaps, rudder and tailplane trailing-edge of bonded aluminium alloy honeycomb construction; safe-life fuselage of frames and stringers, mainly aluminium alloy but with titanium skins at rear and some titanium adjacent to engine and other special areas; access to power plant through top of fuselage, ahead of wings; FRS. Mk 2 has deepened and stiffened nose structure, plus new rear fuselage, lengthened by 35 cm (1 ft 1¾ in); fin tip carries suppressed VHF aerial.

LANDING GEAR: Retractable bicycle type of Dowty Aerospace manufacture, permitting operation from rough unprepared surfaces of CBR as low as 3 to 5 per cent. Hydraulic actuation, with nitrogen bottle for emergency extension of landing gear. Single steerable nosewheel retracts forward, twin coupled mainwheels rearward, into fuselage. Small outrigger units retract rearward into fairings slightly inboard of wingtips. Nosewheel leg of levered suspension liquid spring type. Dowty telescopic oleo-pneumatic main and outrigger gear. Dunlop wheels and tyres, size 26.00 × 8.75-11 (nose unit), 27.00 × 7.74-13 (main units) and 13.50 × 6.4 (outriggers). Dunlop multi-disc brakes and Dunlop-Hytrol adaptive anti-skid system.

POWER PLANT: One Rolls-Royce Pegasus Mk 104 or (FRS. Mk 2) Mk 106 vectored thrust turbofan (95.6 kN; 21,500 lb st), with four exhaust nozzles of the two-vane cascade type, rotatable through 98.5° from fully aft position. Engine bleed air from HP compressor used for jet reaction control system and to power duplicated air motor for nozzle actuation. Low drag intake cowls each have eight automatic suction relief doors aft of leading-edge to improve intake efficiency by providing extra engine air at low forward or zero speeds. A 227 litre (60 US gallon; 50 Imp gallon) tank supplies demineralised water for thrust restoration in high ambient temperatures for STO, VTO and vertical landings. Fuel in five integral tanks in fuselage and two in wings, with total capacity of approx 2,865 litres (757 US gallons; 630 Imp gallons). This can be supplemented by two 455 litre (120 US gallon; 100 Imp gallon) jettisonable combat tanks, or two 864 litre (228 US gallon; 190 Imp gallon) tanks, or two 1,500 litre (396 US gallon; 330 Imp gallon) ferry tanks on the inboard wing pylons. Ground refuelling point in port rear nozzle fairing. Provision for in-flight refuelling probe above the port intake cowl.

ACCOMMODATION: Pilot only, on Martin-Baker Mk 10H zero/zero rocket ejection seat which operates through the miniature detonating cord equipped canopy of the pressurised, heated and air-conditioned cockpit. Sea Harrier seat raised 28 cm (11 in) compared with Harrier. Manually operated rearward sliding canopy. Birdproof windscreen, with hydraulically actuated wiper. Windscreen washing system.

SYSTEMS: Three-axis limited authority autostabiliser for V/STOL flight. Pressurisation system of BAe design, with Normalair-Garrett and Delaney Gallay major components; max pressure differential 0.24 bar (3.5 lb/sq in). Two hydraulic systems; flow rate: System 1, 36 litres (9.6 US gallons; 8 Imp gallons)/min; System 2, 23 litres (6 US gallons; 5 Imp gallons)/min. Systems, pressure 207 bars (3,000 lb/sq in), actuate Fairey flying control and general services and a retractable ram air turbine inside top of rear fuselage, driving a small hydraulic pump for emergency power. Turbine deleted from FRS. Mk 2. Hydraulic reservoirs nitrogen pressurised at 2.75 to 5.5 bars (40 to 80 lb/sq in). AC electrical system with transformer-rectifiers to provide required DC supply. Two 15kVA generators. Two 28V 25Ah batteries, one of which energises a 24V motor to start Lucas Mk 2 gas turbine starter/APU. This unit drives a 6kVA auxiliary alternator for ground readiness servicing and standby. Normalair-Garrett liquid oxygen system of 4.5 litres (1.2 US gallons; 1 Imp gallon) capacity. Bootstrap cooling unit for equipment bay, with intake at base of dorsal fin. Autopilot function on Fairey Hydraulics, giving throughput to aileron and tailplane power controls as well as to three-axis autostabs. British Oxygen liquid oxygen system of 4.5 litres (1.2 US gallons; 1 Imp gallon) capacity in Royal Navy aircraft; Indian Navy has gaseous oxygen system.

AVIONICS: Nose mounted GEC Ferranti Blue Fox multi-mode radar, with TV raster daylight viewing tube which conveys flight information, as well as radar data, to pilot. New and larger Smiths electronic head-up display and 20,000 word digital weapon aiming computer. Autopilot, radar altimeter and Decca Doppler 72 radar. GEC Ferranti self aligning attitude and heading reference platform and digital navigation computer. Radio navaids include UHF homing, GEC Avionics AD 2770 Tacan with offset facility and I band transponder. Radio com by multi-channel GEC-Plessey PTR 377 U/VHF, with VHF standby via D 403M transceiver. Passive electronic surveillance and warning of external radar illumination by receiver with forward and rear hemisphere antennae in fin and tailcone respectively.

EQUIPMENT: Optically flat panel in nose, on port side, for F.95 oblique camera, which is carried as standard. A cockpit voice recorder with in-flight playback facility supplements the reconnaissance cameras, and facilitates rapid debriefing and mission evaluation.

ARMAMENT: No built-in armament. Combat load carried on four underwing and one underfuselage pylons, all with ML ejector release units. Inboard wing points and fuselage point stressed for loads up to 907 kg (2,000 lb) each, and outboard underwing pair for loads up to 295 kg (650 lb) each; two strake fairings under the fuselage can each be replaced by a 30 mm Aden gun pod and ammunition or, on FRS. Mk 2, by two AIM-120 AMRAAMs. Aircraft cleared for operations with maximum external load exceeding 2,270 kg (5,000 lb), and has flown with weapon load of 3,630 kg (8,000 lb). FRS. Mk 2 outboard pylons re-stressed to 454 kg (1,000 lb). Able to carry 30 mm guns, bombs, rockets and flares of UK and US designs. Alternative stores loads of RN Sea Harriers include a WE177 nuclear bomb; free-fall (467 kg; 1,030 lb) and parachute-retarded (508 kg; 1,120 lb) bombs; Lepus flares; and ML CBLS 100 carriers for Portsmouth Aviation 3 kg and 14 kg practice bombs. Four AIM-9 Sidewinder missiles carried on the outboard underwing pylons (Matra Magic instead of Sidewinder on Indian Navy aircraft); provision for two air-to-surface missiles of Sea Eagle or Harpoon type. FRS. Mk 2 accommodates up to four AIM-120 AMRAAMs, or two AIM-120s and four AIM-9L Sidewinders. BAe ALARM anti-radiation missile may replace AIM-120.

DIMENSIONS, EXTERNAL:

Wing span: normal	7.70 m (25 ft 3 in)
ferry	9.04 m (29 ft 8 in)
Length overall: FRS. Mk 1	14.50 m (47 ft 7 in)
FRS. Mk 2	14.17 m (46 ft 6 in)
Length overall, nose folded:	
FRS. Mk 1	12.73 m (41 ft 9 in)
FRS. Mk 2	13.16 m (43 ft 2 in)
Height overall	3.71 m (12 ft 2 in)
Tailplane span	4.24 m (13 ft 11 in)
Outrigger wheel track	6.76 m (22 ft 2 in)
Wheelbase, nosewheel to mainwheels	approx 3.45 m (11 ft 4 in)

AREAS:

Wings, gross	18.68 m² (201.1 sq ft)
Fin (excl ventral fin): two-seat	3.57 m² (38.4 sq ft)
Rudder, incl tab	0.49 m² (5.3 sq ft)
Tailplane	4.41 m² (47.5 sq ft)

WEIGHTS AND LOADINGS (FRS. Mk 1):

Operating weight empty	6,374 kg (14,052 lb)
Max fuel: internal	2,295 kg (5,060 lb)
external	2,404 kg (5,300 lb)
Max weapon load: STO	3,630 kg (8,000 lb)
VTO	2,270 kg (5,000 lb)
Max T-O weight	11,880 kg (26,200 lb)
Max wing loading	636.0 kg/m² (130.3 lb/sq ft)
Max power loading	124.27 kg/kN (1.22 lb/lb st)

PERFORMANCE (FRS. Mk 1):

Max Mach No. at high altitude: 1.25

Max level speed at low altitude: above 640 knots (1,185 km/h; 736 mph) EAS

Typical cruising speed:
- high altitude, for well over 1 h on internal fuel: above Mach 0.8
- low altitude: 350-450 knots (650-833 km/h; 404-518 mph), with rapid acceleration to 600 knots (1,110 km/h; 690 mph)

STO run at max T-O weight, without ski-jump: approx 305 m (1,000 ft)

Time from alarm to 30 nm (55 km; 35 miles) combat area: under 6 min

High altitude intercept radius, with 3 min combat and reserves for VL: 400 nm (750 km; 460 miles)

Strike radius: 250 nm (463 km; 288 miles)

g limits: +7.8/–4.2

COMBAT PROFILES (FRS. Mk 2, from carrier fitted with a 12° ski-jump ramp, at ISA + 15°C and with a 20 knot; 37 km/h; 23 mph wind over the deck):

Combat air patrol: Up to 1½ hours on station at a radius of 100 nm (185 km; 115 miles), carrying four AMRAAMs, or two AMRAAMs and two 30 mm guns, plus two 864 litre (228 US gallon; 190 Imp gallon) combat drop tanks. Deck T-O run: 137 m (450 ft).

Reconnaissance: Low level cover of 130,000 nm² (446,465 km²; 172,380 sq miles) at a radius of 525 nm (970 km; 600 miles) from the carrier, with outward and return flights at medium/high level, carrying two 30 mm guns and two 864 litre (228 US gallon; 190 Imp gallon) combat drop tanks. Overall flight time 1 h 45 min.

Surface attack (hi-lo-hi): Radius of action to missile launch 200 nm (370 km; 230 miles), carrying two Sea Eagle missiles and two 30 mm guns.

Take-off deck run for the above missions is 137 m, 107 m and 92 m (450 ft, 350 ft and 300 ft) respectively, with vertical landing.

Interception: A typical deck-launched interception could be performed against a Mach 0.9 target at a radius of 116 nm (215 km; 133 miles), or a Mach 1.3 target at 95 nm (175 km; 109 miles), after initial radar detection of the approaching target at a range of 230 nm (425 km; 265 miles), with the Sea Harrier at 2 min alert status, carrying two AMRAAM missiles.

BAe EAP

Flight trials continue of the EAP advanced technology demonstrator in connection with development of the Eurofighter EFA (see International section). By January 1991, the aircraft had completed 221 flights (164 hours). Details, a photograph and drawing appeared in the 1990-91 and earlier editions of *Jane's*.

EUROFIGHTER (EFA)

Details of this military aircraft programme, in which British Aerospace is participating with companies from Germany, Italy and Spain, can be found in the International section.

F-111

In 1978, BAe's Filton plant began undertaking depot level maintenance on General Dynamics F-111 strike aircraft based in the UK with the USAF's 20th TFW (F-111E) and 48th TFW (F-111F). A second five-year contract, covering approximately 150 F-111s, was agreed with the USAF on 1 October 1988, this also including structural fatigue testing and avionics modifications as applied to US-based F-111s.

V-22 OSPREY

BAe and Bell/Boeing concluded an MoU in 1987 covering examination by the British company of the latter's V-22 tilt-rotor aircraft in both military and civilian applications within the European NATO area. In 1989, Aeritalia (now Alenia) and Dornier reached agreement with BAe to pursue the prospects of the V-22 tilt-rotor aircraft in collaborative tri-national projects.

Potential applications for a tilt-rotor aircraft in UK military service are foreseen by BAe as shore-based anti-submarine warfare (four Sting Ray torpedoes), ship-based AEW, commando assault (24 troops), air mobility and special forces (12 troops and extra fuel). Civilian uses include resource development (carrying 30+ oil/gas rig workers) and commuter transport.

E-3D SENTRY AEW. Mk 1

BAe selected by Boeing 1988 to perform installation and checkout (I&CO) duties on all except first of RAF's seven E-3Ds (assisted by Boeing team on first aircraft); responsible for reception of aircraft, installation and checking of some equipment, and maintenance in pre-delivery phase between arrival in UK and handover; most work undertaken at RAF Waddington; second RAF Sentry (ZH102) delivered to BAe 4 July 1990, followed by third on 9 January 1991. (First E-3D arrived fully equipped, 3 November 1990.) First handover to RAF following I&CO at Waddington was ZH102 on 26 March 1991. No. 8 Squadron converting from Shackleton AEW. Mk 2 (NATO's last piston-engined front-line aircraft) to Sentry on 1 July 1991.

BAe (BAC/VICKERS) VC10 C. Mk 1(K), K. Mk 2, 3 and 4 TANKERS

In addition to original VC10 C. Mk 1 transports (delivered 1966-68 and used by No. 10 Squadron), RAF's No. 101 Squadron operates tanker conversions of former airliners as five **VC10 K. Mk 2s** (delivered from July 1983) and four **Super VC10 K. Mk 3s** (delivered from February 1985).

Modification at BAe Filton involved installation of internal Flight Refuelling Mk 17B hose-and-drum unit (HDU), plus wing-mounted FR Mk 32/2800 HDUs; specific tanker modifications described in 1987-88 *Jane's*.

BAe (Civil Aircraft) Ltd at Manchester awarded two-part contract 1990 to modify 13 aircraft to tankers; first part (Air Staff Requirement 415) covers five unconverted Super VC10s stored at Abingdon to become **K. Mk 4s** with Mk 17B HDU in fuselage and two underwing Mk 32s; also included are general refurbishment, and installation of military avionics (including air-to-air Tacan) and closed-circuit TV; JTIDS terminals will be installed at later stage for relay of information between ground stations and AEW and interceptor aircraft. Work performed at Filton after aircraft returned to airworthy condition at Abingdon; ZD242 to Filton 27 July 1990, to launch conversion programme; service entry due 1992. Second part of programme (ASR 416), eight No. 10 Squadron transports to be converted into **C. Mk 1(K)s** by FR Aviation at Bournemouth, each having secondary tanker capability with two Mk 32 HDUs underwing (plus Tacan and TV); redelivery from Spring 1992; option held on similar rework of five remaining Mk 1s; neither Mk 1(K) nor Mk 4 conversions involve additional fuel tanks.

Details of previous modifications include:

WEIGHTS AND LOADINGS:

Max T-O weight: K. Mk 2		142,000 kg (313,056 lb)
K. Mk 3		151,900 kg (334,882 lb)
Theoretical max fuel weight*:		
K. Mk 2		78,170 kg (172,335 lb)
K. Mk 3		83,420 kg (183,909 lb)
Practical max fuel weight:		
K. Mk 2		74,000 kg (163,142 lb)
K. Mk 3		80,000 kg (176,370 lb)

* *Max T-O weight exceeded when all tanks full*

BAe HOTOL

TYPE: Space transport.

PROGRAMME: HOTOL (horizontal take-off and landing) is study by BAe's Warton, Brough, Stevenage and Filton divisions, in conjunction with Rolls-Royce, for producing reusable (initially unmanned) launch vehicle to carry satellites into orbit at one-fifth current costs; later to carry personnel to service low orbit space stations or other objects. Initial UK Department of Trade funds covered first six-month study 1987 (similar amount from industry); study maintained by additional BAe funds from October 1987 but UK Government announced funding halt July 1988.

FR Mk 32 underwing refuelling pods on an RAF VC10 K. Mk 2 *(Paul Jackson)*

Wind tunnel model of latest configuration of HOTOL aerospacecraft

Initial rig tests of critical engine components 1986; UK MoD declared RB545's technology secret December 1988. Alternative proposal under consideration, 1990, for 'Interim HOTOL' powered by Soviet rocket engine; air-launched at 9,145 m (30,000 ft) from upper fuselage mountings of Antonov An-225 (refer Soviet section); payload reduced to 7,000 kg (15,432 lb) for 300 km (162 mile) equatorial Earth orbit. Original design remains 'Mk 2' objective.

COSTS: British National Space Centre (Dept of Trade) announced £375,000 allocation February 1986, to begin two-year proof of concept study costing £3 million overall; also industry funding. 'Interim HOTOL' $2,300 million development; subsequently $8 million per mission.

DESIGN FEATURES ('Mk 2'): Take off and land as conventional aeroplane; relatively small cropped delta type wings under rear fuselage; jettisonable laser guided take-off trolley; on-board lightweight landing gear; Rolls-Royce RB545 Swallow hybrid power plant, acting as air-breathing turbofan in atmosphere and oxygen/hydrogen rocket in space (speed at transition from air-breathing to rocket power Mach 5 at 26,000 m; 85,000 ft); air inlet for power plant under rear fuselage; vertical surface above nose. 'Interim HOTOL' uses Soviet rocket technology and airborne launch.

STRUCTURE: Metal skin re-entry heat protection; titanium on upper surfaces.

DIMENSIONS, EXTERNAL (provisional):

Wing span	28.34 m (93 ft 0 in)
Length overall	62.97 m (206 ft 7¼ in)
Height overall	12.83 m (42 ft 1⅛ in)

WEIGHTS AND LOADINGS ('Mk 2', provisional):

T-O weight	250,000 kg (551,155 lb)
Landing weight	47,500 kg (104,719 lb)

PERFORMANCE ('Mk 2', provisional):

Payload into 300 km (162 mile) equatorial Earth orbit	
	8,000 kg (17,635 lb)
T-O speed	278 knots (515 km/h; 320 mph)
Landing speed	150 knots (278 km/h; 173 mph)
Landing run: dry runway	1,145 m (3,750 ft)
wet runway	1,500 m (4,925 ft)

BAF
BRITISH AIR FERRIES

Viscount House, Southend Airport, Essex SS2 6YL
Telephone: 44 (702) 354435
Fax: 44 (702) 331914
Telex: 995687 and 995576
MANAGING DIRECTOR, AIRLINE: R. Sturman
MANAGING DIRECTOR, ENGINEERING: B. Stone
SALES DIRECTOR: M. T. Sessions
FLIGHT OPERATIONS DIRECTOR: Capt W. Worthington

BAF's (lease and charter airline) engineering division is licensed by CAA and BAe to perform Viscount life-extension modifications; 11 Viscounts operated under contract by BAF on passenger and night freight services.

BAC VISCOUNT LIFE EXTENSION

By the end of 1990, fifteen 74-seat Viscount Series 800s comprehensively overhauled, including rib and fuselage reconditioning, to requirements formulated by BAF/BAe; now CAA certificated for further 15 years' service or 75,000 flights. Eleven are in service with BAF; approximately 50 other airworthy Viscounts eligible for rework worldwide.

BAC/Vickers Viscount Series 806 re-lifed by BAF for service into the 21st century *(John C. Cook)*

BROOKLANDS — *see Lovaux Ltd*

CMC

CHICHESTER-MILES CONSULTANTS LTD

West House, The Old Rectory, Ayot St Lawrence, Welwyn,
Hertfordshire AL6 9BT
Telephone: 44 (438) 820341
CHAIRMAN: Ian Chichester-Miles

Ian Chichester-Miles, formerly Chief Research Engineer
of BAe Hatfield, established Chichester-Miles Consultants
to develop Leopard high performance light business jet.

CMC LEOPARD

TYPE: Four-seat light business aircraft.

PROGRAMME: Design began January 1981; mockup completed early 1982; detail design and construction of prototype by Designability Ltd of Dilton Marsh, Wiltshire, began July 1982 under CMC contract; first flight of prototype (G-BKRL) 12 December 1988 at RAE Bedford; by September 1990 had made 40 flights investigating basic handling qualities at speeds up to 200 knots (371 km/h; 230 mph) IAS; new tailplane incorporating TKS liquid anti-icing system subsequently installed on prototype prior to resumption of flight testing aimed at expanding airspeed, altitude and CG envelopes.

Design of second prototype began April 1989; Slingsby Aviation to manufacture fuselage and wings in collaboration with Designability, both under CMC contract; expected to be completed September 1991, featuring reprofiled nose for EFIS avionics, substitution of oleo-pneumatic main landing gear legs for current rubber-in-compression units, and powered by demonstration versions of Noel Penny NPT 754 turbofans.

DESIGN FEATURES: Streamline composites airframe; sweptback supercritical technology wings; sweptback tail unit; twin low-cost turbofans; pressurised and air-conditioned cabin; TKS liquid de-icing and decontamination system on wing and tailplane leading-edges of production aircraft (see Programme); warm air de-icing of engine intake leading-edges. First prototype has lower-powered engines; lacks full pressurisation/air-conditioning system, advanced avionics and instrumentation of planned production model.

ARA designed wing section and 3D profiles combining laminar flow and supercritical technology; thickness/chord ratio 14 per cent at root, 11 per cent at tip; wing sweepback at quarter-chord 25°.

FLYING CONTROLS: All-moving fin; two independent tailplane sections operated collectively for pitch control and differentially for roll control; geared anti-servo tabs in fin and tailplane sections, adjustable for trim; no ailerons. Full-span electrically actuated trailing-edge plain flaps, with ± 45° deflections for high drag landing and airbraking/lift dumping; no spoilers.

STRUCTURE: Two-spar wings, primarily of GFRP, with some carbonfibre reinforcement; carbonfibre flaps; fuselage built in three sections as unpressurised nose housing avionics and nosewheel gear, pressurised cabin (production aircraft), and pressurised rear housing baggage bay, with fuel tanks below and equipment bays to rear; fuselage primarily GFRP with some carbonfibre reinforcement (fore and aft carbon bulkheads, engine and tailplane axle frames moulded in); pressure cabin section divided approximately along aircraft horizontal datum, with upper section formed by electrically actuated upward opening canopy hinged at windscreen leading-edge; bonded-in acrylic side windows carry pressurisation tension; nose opens for access to avionics; composites engine nacelles, with stainless steel firewalls; composites fin and tailplane; fin sternpost projects to bottom of rear fuselage; low-set tailplane in two independent sections, each mounted on steel axle projecting from side of rear fuselage; carbonfibre tabs.

LANDING GEAR: Electrically retractable tricycle type, main units retracting inward into wingroot wells, nosewheels forward. Well closure doors linked mechanically to landing gear units. Gravity extension assisted by bias springs and aerodynamic drag. Long-stroke shock absorber in each unit, using synthetic elastomers in compression. Main units, each with single Cleveland wheel, size 5.00-5, have tyres size 11 × 4, pressure 4.82 bars (70 lb/sq in) on prototype, 11.56 bars (170 lb/sq in) on production aircraft. Unpowered steerable twin-wheel nose unit has wheels size 4.00-3 and tyres size 8.5 × 2.75 in, pressure 2.75 bars (40 lb/sq in) on prototype, 3.8 bars (55 lb/sq in) on production aircraft. Hydraulic disc brakes. Parking brake. New, oleo-pneumatic main landing gear is being designed for production aircraft.

POWER PLANT: Prototype 001 has two Noel Penny Turbines NPT 301-3A turbojets each of nominal 1.33 kN (300 lb st) rating. Production aircraft will have two low-bypass Noel Penny Turbines NPT 754 turbofans, each of 3.78 kN (850 lb st). Each engine in nacelle, mounted on crossbeam located in rear fuselage. Fuel tanks in fuselage, below baggage bay. Prototype has total fuel capacity of 455 litres (120 US gallons; 100 Imp gallons). Production aircraft will have maximum capacity of 591 litres (156 US gallons; 130 Imp gallons). Refuelling point on upper surface of fuselage.

ACCOMMODATION: Cabin seats four, in two pairs, on semi-reclining (35°) seats beneath upward opening

Prototype of CMC Leopard business jet *(B. J. Cunnington/CMC)*

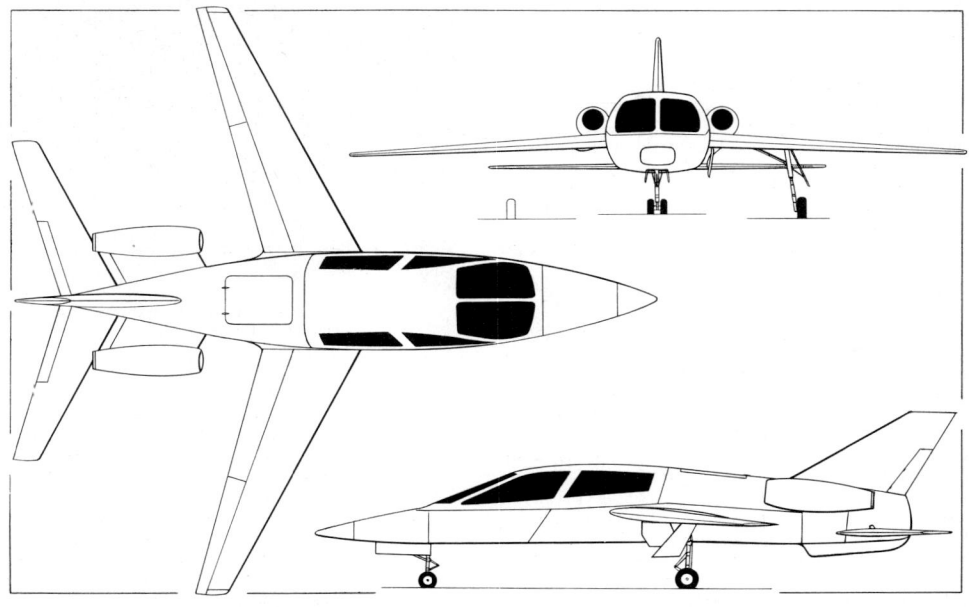

CMC Leopard (two Noel Penny Turbines NPT 301-3A turbojets) *(Pilot Press)*

jettisonable canopy. Options include dual controls, and accommodation for pilot, stretcher and attendant in medevac role. Unpressurised baggage bay aft of cabin, capacity 54 kg (120 lb), with external door in upper surface of fuselage.

SYSTEMS (production aircraft): Air-conditioning and pressurisation (max differential 0.66 bar: 9.6 lb/sq in) by engine bleed air, with simple Normalair-Garrett air cycle cold air/dehumidifier unit. Electrical system powered by dual engine driven 3kVA starter/generators. Hydraulic system for brakes only.

AVIONICS (production aircraft): Full nav/com and storm-avoidance systems. Bendix/King avionics, mounted in nose bay, supply EADI and EHSI information to two CRTs in pilot's instrument panel, together with weather radar. CRT displays can be transferred in the failure mode. Reduced scale electro-mechanical standby flight instruments. All avionics systems fully integrated with digital autopilot.

DIMENSIONS, EXTERNAL:

Wing span	7.16 m (23 ft 6 in)
Wing chord: at root	1.14 m (3 ft 9 in)
at tip	0.36 m (1 ft 2 in)
Wing aspect ratio	8.78
Length overall	7.52 m (24 ft 8 in)
Height: overall	2.06 m (6 ft 9 in)
to canopy sill	0.76 m (2 ft 6 in)
Tailplane span	3.91 m (12 ft 10 in)
Wheel track	3.45 m (11 ft 4 in)
Wheelbase	3.20 m (10 ft 6 in)

DIMENSIONS, INTERNAL:

Cabin: Length	2.74 m (9 ft 0 in)
Max width	1.14 m (3 ft 9 in)
Max height	0.94 m (3 ft 1 in)
Baggage bay volume	0.40 m³ (14 cu ft)

AREAS:

Wings, gross	5.85 m² (62.9 sq ft)
Trailing-edge flaps (total)	1.24 m² (13.3 sq ft)
Fin	0.86 m² (9.3 sq ft)
Tailplane (incl tabs)	2.14 m² (23.0 sq ft)

WEIGHTS AND LOADINGS (A: prototype, B: production aircraft, estimated):

Weight empty, equipped: A	862 kg (1,900 lb)
B	952 kg (2,100 lb)
Max fuel weight: A	367 kg (810 lb)
B	476 kg (1,050 lb)
Max T-O weight: A	1,156 kg (2,550 lb)
B	1,814 kg (4,000 lb)
Max zero-fuel weight: A	1,043 kg (2,300 lb)
B	1,315 kg (2,900 lb)
Max landing weight: A	1,156 kg (2,550 lb)
B	1,701 kg (3,750 lb)
Max wing loading: A	197.7 kg/m² (40.5 lb/sq ft)
B	310.3 kg/m² (63.6 lb/sq ft)
Max power loading: A	433.7 kg/kN (4.25 lb/lb st)
B	240.1 kg/kN (2.35 lb/lb st)

PERFORMANCE (production aircraft, estimated, ISA):

Never-exceed speed (VNE)	Mach 0.81
	(300 knots; 556 km/h; 345 mph) EAS
Max level speed at 9,450 m (31,000 ft)	
	469 knots (869 km/h; 540 mph)
Max and econ cruising speed at 15,545 m (51,000 ft)	
	434 knots (804 km/h; 500 mph)
Stalling speed, full flap, at AUW of 1,497 kg (3,300 lb)	
	84 knots (156 km/h; 97 mph)
Max rate of climb at S/L	1,660 m (5,450 ft)/min
Rate of climb at S/L, one engine out	
	685 m (2,250 ft)/min
Service ceiling	16,765 m (55,000 ft)
Service ceiling, one engine out	9,145 m (30,000 ft)
T-O to 15 m (50 ft)	727 m (2,385 ft)
T-O balanced field length	838 m (2,750 ft)
Landing from 15 m (50 ft) at AUW of 1,497 kg (3,300 lb)	
	778 m (2,550 ft)
Landing factored field length	854 m (2,800 ft)
Range with max fuel and max payload, with reserves	
	1,500 nm (2,775 km; 1,725 miles)

CRANFIELD
CRANFIELD INSTITUTE OF TECHNOLOGY, COLLEGE OF AERONAUTICS

Cranfield, Bedfordshire MK43 0AL
Telephone: 44 (234) 750111
Fax: 44 (234) 751181
Telex: 825072 C ITECH G

HEAD OF COLLEGE AND PROFESSOR OF AEROSPACE:
  Prof M. J. Rycroft
PROFESSOR OF AIRCRAFT DESIGN, CHIEF DESIGNER:
  Prof D. Howe
HEAD OF FLIGHT SYSTEMS AND MEASUREMENT
  LABORATORIES: D. A. Williams
  College of Aeronautics is CAA and MoD(PE) approved

design and manufacturing organisation based on Cranfield Institute of Technology airfield. Undertakes aeronautical and high technology tasks in support of aircraft and systems manufacturers, governments and research bodies, from feasibility studies to design, manufacture, installation and certification of aircraft modifications. Details of recent work appeared in 1989-90 *Jane's*.

CRANFIELD AERONAUTICAL SERVICES LIMITED

Cranfield Institute of Technology, Cranfield, Bedfordshire MK43 0AL

Telephone: 44 (234) 752746
Fax: 44 (234) 751181
CHAIRMAN: Prof D. Howe
  Cranfield Aeronautical Services is commercial arm

of Institute of Technology, College of Aeronautics, undertaking production work (see 1987-88, 1988-89 and 1989-90 editions of *Jane's*).

CROPLEASE
CROPLEASE PLC

Vicarage House, 58-60 Kensington Church Street, London W8 4DB
Telephone: 44 (71) 376 0448
Fax: 44 (71) 376 0340
CHAIRMAN: Richard Cox-Johnson
MANAGING DIRECTOR: Andrew Mackinnon
CHIEF DESIGNER: Desmond Norman, CBE

Following Norman Aeroplane Company receivership October 1988, design, manufacture and marketing rights to Fieldmaster acquired by Andrew Mackinnon of Irish-based Croplease Ltd; Croplease plc formed April 1989 and acquired Fieldmaster rights and Croplease Ltd business.

Croplease Firemaster 65 (Pratt & Whitney Canada PT6A-65AG) for French Alpes Maritimes region

CROPLEASE NAC 6 FIELDMASTER

TYPE: Two-seat agricultural, pollution control, or fire-fighting (Firemaster) aircraft.

PROGRAMME: Designed by Desmond Norman; financially supported by UK National Research Development Corpn; prototype (G-NRDC), built by Norman Aeroplane Co, first flown at Sandown (Isle of Wight) 17 December 1981; total 300 flight hours by March 1986 during tests, demonstrations and in-service spraying trials by an operator; first production Fieldmaster (G-NACL) flew 29 March 1987; certification received 27 April 1987; G-NACL flew 28 November 1989 with 917 kW (1,230 shp) PT6A-65AG turboprop driving five-blade Hartzell propeller, in **Firemaster** configuration; production of five Fieldmasters re-started using UTVA (Yugoslavia) manufactured components; to France Aviation at Cannes on permit for evaluation July-October 1990; returned for certification testing; CAA aerial work certification received late May 1991; two aircraft (G-NACM, G-NACN) to France Aviation 1 July 1991.

VARIANTS: **Fieldmaster:** Agricultural version. Optional PT6A-65AG engine as **Fieldmaster 65**.

Firemaster: Dedicated firefighting/water bombing variant (see Programme); firefighting modifications include additional 53 litre (14 US gallon; 11.6 Imp gallon) tank for fire retardant (mixed with water before release).

CUSTOMERS: Two production aircraft began season of fire patrol flights and water bombing sorties in Maritime Alps under France Aviation contract July 1987; turnaround time between sorties averaged 3 min; these two included in five Fieldmasters bought by Croplease Ltd of Shannon, Ireland.

DESIGN FEATURES: Structural titanium chemical hopper forming integral part of fuselage, outer surface contoured as part of fuselage skin; hopper capacity 2,032 kg (4,480 lb) of dry or 2,366 litres (625 US gallons; 520 Imp gallons) of liquid chemicals; power plant mounted on front of hopper; rear fuselage attached aft of hopper; wings attached directly to hopper sides; flaps embody liquid spray dispersal system (24 nozzles each wing; Micronair 12-nozzle system optional) discharging into flap down-

wash to ensure spray droplets achieve best crop penetration; strong rollover cockpit structure.

NACA 23012 aerofoil section, modified on inner panels, where forward extension of leading-edge reduces thickness/chord ratio of 8.6 per cent at wingroot; dihedral 4° 15′; incidence 4° 30′.

FLYING CONTROLS: Auxiliary aerofoil ailerons; servo tab in starboard aileron, linked mechanically to rudder pedals, ensuring some bank with rudder movement; fixed incidence tailplane; trim tab in port elevator; servo tab in rudder controlled by stick movement, moved automatically with bank; electrically actuated wide span auxiliary aerofoil trailing-edge flaps, incorporating spray nozzle plumbing. Removable dual controls available.

STRUCTURE: Overwing streamline section wing bracing struts; all-metal wings with corrosion proofing; forward fuselage section comprises structural titanium hopper incorporating large door, vent system, inspection windows and light; light alloy semi-monocoque rear fuselage section (corrosion proofed: see Design Features); braced light alloy tail unit.

LANDING GEAR: Non-retractable tricycle type, with single wheel on each unit. Nosewheel has alternative steerable or castoring facility. Main units of levered suspension type. Nosewheel tyre size 7.00-8, pressure 3.45 bars (50 lb/sq in); mainwheels have tubed tyres, diameter 736 mm (29 in), pressure 3.79 bars (55 lb/sq in). Cleveland hydraulic disc brakes. Landing gear incorporates wire cutters.

POWER PLANT: One 559 kW (750 shp) Pratt & Whitney Canada PT6A-34AG turboprop, driving a Hartzell type HC-B3TN-3/T10282+4 three-blade fully feathering reversible-pitch metal propeller. Optional 917 kW (1,230 shp) P&WC PT6A-65AG driving five-blade propeller.

Four integral fuel tanks, two per wing. Main tanks, each of 378.5 litres (100 US gallons; 83.3 Imp gallons), inboard; ferry tanks, each of 367 litres (97 US gallons; 80.7 Imp gallons), outboard. Total fuel capacity 1,491 litres (394 US gallons; 328 Imp gallons). Oil capacity 13 litres (3.5 US gallons; 2.9 Imp gallons). Engine air intake has a Centrisep filtration system.

ACCOMMODATION: Standard accommodation for pilot only, on fully adjustable seat in an enclosed cockpit, with rollover protective structure. Rear trainee/observer seat optional. Dual controls optional, those for pupil easily removable. Crew safety helmets with headsets optional. Baggage space in fuselage. Sideways hinged door on each side. Birdproof armoured glass windscreen, two-speed windscreen wiper and windscreen wash system optional. Accommodation ventilated; air-conditioning and heating system optional. Wirecutters forward of windscreen, and cable deflecting wire from top of windscreen to tip of fin.

SYSTEMS: Electrical system includes 24V 200A starter/generator. Hydraulic system for brakes only. Central warning system standard.

AVIONICS: Intercom standard. Avionics, and IFR instrument package, to customer requirements.

EQUIPMENT: Standard equipment includes an external power socket. Optional equipment includes airframe and engine hour meter; instrument lighting, navigation lights, fin and wingtip strobe lights; two forward looking retractable work lights, each 765,000 candlepower; automatic flagman installation; firefighting dump door and water scoop (see introductory copy); Transland gatebox, high volume spreader, quick disconnect flange kit, and side loading system; and Micronair installation, with flowmeter and rpm indicator.

DIMENSIONS, EXTERNAL (with PT6A-34AG):

Wing span	16.23 m (53 ft 3 in)
Wing chord (excl flaps): at root	2.01 m (6 ft 7¼ in)
at tip	1.45 m (4 ft 9 in)
Wing aspect ratio	7.96
Length overall	11.02 m (36 ft 2 in)
Height overall	4.12 m (13 ft 6 in)
Wheel track	5.28 m (17 ft 4 in)
Wheelbase	3.35 m (11 ft 0 in)
Propeller diameter	2.69 m (8 ft 10 in)

DIMENSIONS, INTERNAL:

Hopper volume	2.36 m³ (83 cu ft)

AREAS:

Wings, gross	33.25 m² (358.0 sq ft)

WEIGHTS AND LOADINGS:

Standard weight empty	2,266 kg (4,995 lb)
Max T-O and landing weight:	
BCAR Aerial Work Category	3,855 kg (8,500 lb)
UK CAA AN 90	4,535 kg (10,000 lb)
Max zero-fuel weight	3,855 kg (8,500 lb)
Max wing loading (AN 90)	136.37 kg/m² (27.93 lb/sq ft)
Max power loading (AN 90)	8.11 kg/kW (13.33 lb/shp)

PERFORMANCE (clean, with main landing gear fairings installed, at max Aerial Work Category T-O weight, S/L, ISA, except where indicated):

Never-exceed speed (V$_{NE}$)	
	172 knots (318 km/h; 198 mph)

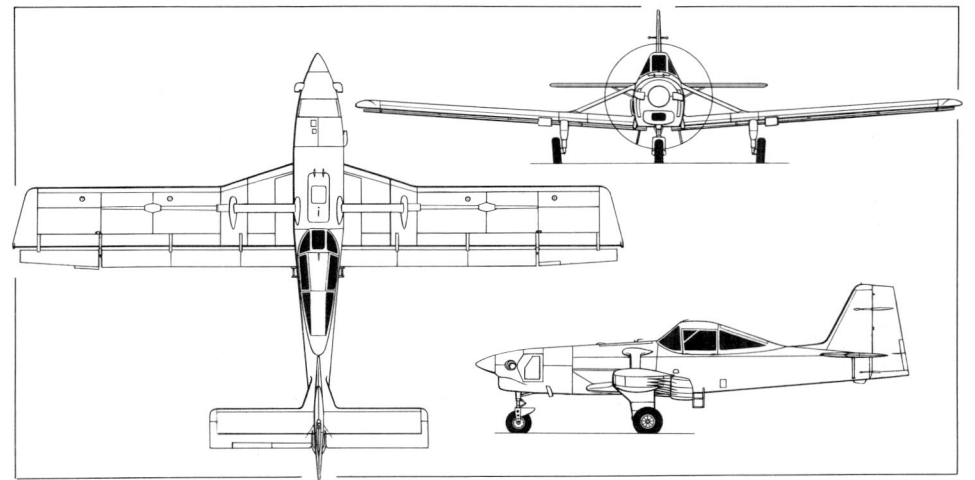

Croplease NAC 6 Fieldmaster agricultural aircraft (Pratt & Whitney Canada PT6A-34AG turboprop)
(Pilot Press)

Max level speed: at S/L	143 knots (265 km/h; 165 mph)	Service ceiling	5,550 m (18,200 ft)
at 1,830 m (6,000 ft)	147 knots (272 km/h; 169 mph)	T-O run	419 m (1,375 ft)
Design manoeuvring speed		T-O to 15 m (50 ft)	625 m (2,050 ft)
	126 knots (233 km/h; 145 mph)	Landing from 15 m (50 ft)	472 m (1,550 ft)
Stalling speed: flaps up	70 knots (129 km/h; 81 mph)	Landing run at typical landing weight of 2,720 kg	
30° flap	60 knots (111 km/h; 69 mph)	(6,000 lb), with propeller reversal	152 m (500 ft)
Max rate of climb at S/L	293 m (960 ft)/min		

Range at 3,050 m (10,000 ft) with two crew, 454 kg (1,000 lb) of equipment and max fuel, no reserves
1,000 nm (1,853 km; 1,150 miles)
g limits   +3.4/−1.7

ISLAND

ISLAND AIRCRAFT LTD
(Subsidiary of Taurus Aviation Ltd)

Company believed to have ceased trading. Full details of ARV-1 Super2 in 1990-91 *Jane's.*

LOVAUX

LOVAUX LIMITED (Subsidiary of FLS Aerospace)

Bournemouth International Airport, Christchurch, Dorset BH23 6NW
Telephone: 44 (202) 570380
Fax: 44 (202) 580380
Telex: 41500, 41530
CHAIRMAN AND MANAGING DIRECTOR: Peter Purdy
MARKETING DIRECTOR: Edward Searle
TECHNICAL DIRECTOR: Alan Doe

Wholly owned subsidiary of FLS Aerospace, division of F. L. Shmidt Group; specialises in deep maintenance and overhaul of military and civil aircraft, particularly of BAC One-Eleven, Shorts 360 and Boeing 737. Acquired assets of Brooklands Aerospace Group 27 July 1990, including Optica observation aircraft originally developed by Edgley Aircraft Ltd. Responsibility transferred from Brooklands' Old Sarum factory to Lovaux at Bournemouth for further engineering and operational improvements prior to certification. Early history, see Brooklands entry 1990-91 *Jane's.*

Optica Scout slow flying observation aircraft in representative Scoutmaster configuration
(John C. Cook)

LOVAUX OPTICA SCOUT Mk II and SCOUTMASTER

TYPE: Three-seat slow-flying observation and surveillance aircraft.
PROGRAMME: First flight 14 December 1979; production started 1983 (see Customers).
VARIANTS: **Optica:** Three-seat observation aircraft, suited particularly for pipeline and powerline inspection, forestry and coastal patrol, police duties, frontier patrol, aerial photography, film/TV and press reporting, and touring. Turbine powered version may be developed jointly with ASTA of Australia.

Scoutmaster: Electronic surveillance version, revealed as mockup 1988; developed with ASTA. Two models offered: **Scoutmaster I** basic model, with Bendix/King Silver Crown avionics for IFR operation and FLIR 2000G thermal imaging system; **Scoutmaster II** with comprehensive Gold Crown IFR nav/com, including radar altimeter and autopilot, Omega/VLF nav and Bendix/King RDR-1400C search radar plus FLIR 2000G.

CUSTOMERS: Excluding prototype, demonstrator and nine aircraft destroyed before delivery: six Opticas delivered by late 1989.
DESIGN FEATURES: 'Insect eye' cabin with outward visibility approximately 270° in vertical plane and 340° in horizontal plane, combining all-round vision of a helicopter with lower operating costs of fixed-wing aircraft; ducted propulsor power plant unit, offering very low vibration levels and exceptional quietness, both within cabin and from ground; claimed fuel consumption 16-24 per cent of comparable light turbine helicopter, and 31 per cent of operating costs (fixed and direct for 500 hours per year); low wing loading, pre-set inboard flaps and low stalling speed facilitate continuous low-speed *en route* flight; generous flap area provides good field performance from both hard and soft strips; stability increases at low speeds; stressed to BCAR Section K (non-aerobatic category) and FAR Pt 23 (Normal category).

Wing section NASA GA(W)-1; thickness/chord ratio of 17 per cent; dihedral 3° on outer panels; incidence 0°.
FLYING CONTROLS: Bottom hinged, mass balanced slotted ailerons outboard of outer flaps, operated by pushrods; balanced rudders; elevators with inset trailing-edge trim tab. Fowler trailing-edge flaps (29 per cent of total wing chord) inboard and outboard of tailbooms; electrically actuated outboard flaps can be set at angles up to 50° for landing, inboard flaps set permanently at 10°, giving effect of slotted wing, for continuous low speed flying; no spoilers or airbrakes; twin inward canted fins; fixed incidence tailplane.
STRUCTURE: Constant chord single-spar non-swept wings of L72 duralumin stressed skin construction; GFRP wingtips; aluminium alloy cabin with ICI Perspex windows (optionally tinted), attached to fan shroud and rest of airframe by six stators of steel tube and aluminium alloy shear web construction; steel tube and aluminium alloy nose beam supports cabin floor; horizontal window

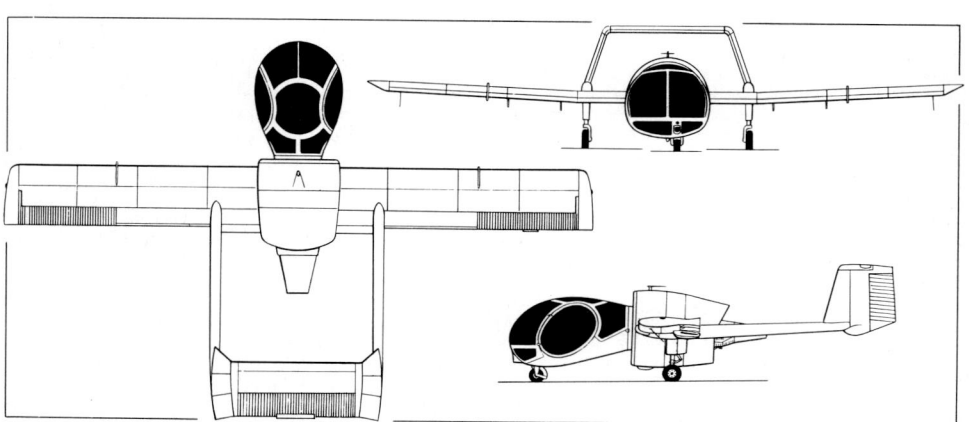

Lovaux Optica Scout (Textron Lycoming IO-540 engine) *(Pilot Press)*

frame member just above floor level, together with nosewheel box, designed to withstand 9g impact; two movable 7.5 kg (16.5 lb) ballast weights may be positioned on nose beam; landing lamp and taxi/standby landing lamp mounted in nose beam; aluminium alloy stressed skin tubular twin-tailboom; limited GFRP in non-load-bearing areas of tail unit, including fin/tailplane fillets; two movable 9 kg (20 lb) ballast weights may be positioned in fins.
LANDING GEAR: Non-retractable tricycle type, with steerable nosewheel offset to port. Mainwheel legs embody rubber in compression shock absorption. Nosewheel shock absorption by bungee rubber in tension. Single wheel on each unit, tyre sizes 6.00-6 (main) and 5.00-5 (nose). Hydraulic disc brakes on mainwheels. Parking brake. Nosewheel mudguard of GFRP.
POWER PLANT: Ducted propulsor unit, with engine and fan forming a power pod separate from the main shroud. Pod is attached to fan shroud with four Lord rubber mountings, and supported by four stators of steel channel and aluminium alloy shear web construction, with steel tube engine bearers. Some fairings of GFRP. Five-blade Hydulignum fixed-pitch fan, driven by a 194 kW (260 hp) Textron Lycoming IO-540-V4A5D flat-six engine, mounted in a duct downstream of the fan. Fuel tank of 128 litres (33.8 US gallons; 28 Imp gallons) capacity in each wing leading-edge, immediately outboard of tailbooms and forward of wing spar. Tanks are of full wing section, but are designed not to be stressed by wing bending and torsion. Total usable fuel capacity 250 litres (66 US gallons; 55 Imp gallons). Refuelling point in upper surface of each wing. Oil capacity 7.6 litres (2.0 US gallons; 1.7 Imp gallons).
ACCOMMODATION: Cabin designed to accommodate up to three persons side by side on fore and aft adjustable seats, with either single- or two-pilot operation (left hand and centre seats). Dual controls standard. Baggage space aft of seats. Single elliptical door on each side, hinged at front and opening forward. Can be flown with doors

removed. Cabin heated, by hot air from engine, and ventilated. A Janitrol combustion heater is offered as an extra.
SYSTEMS: Hydraulics for mainwheel brakes only. Electrical system (24V) includes engine driven alternator and storage battery for engine starting and actuation of flaps.
AVIONICS: Standard nav/com avionics by Bendix/King (Silver Crown). Alternative avionics could be provided.
EQUIPMENT: Special equipment which has been tested successfully includes FLIR, Barr & Stroud IR18 Mk II thermal imager and an air-to-ground video relay. Other equipment such as GEC Sensors TICM II, searchlights and loudspeakers is being assessed.

DIMENSIONS, EXTERNAL:

Wing span	12.00 m (39 ft 4 in)
Wing chord: basic, constant	1.32 m (4 ft 4 in)
over 10° fixed flaps	1.45 m (4 ft 9 in)
Wing aspect ratio	9.1
Length overall	8.15 m (26 ft 9 in)
Height over fan shroud (excl aerial)	1.98 m (6 ft 6 in)
Diameter of fan shroud	1.68 m (5 ft 6 in)
Diameter of fan	1.22 m (4 ft 0 in)
Shroud ground clearance	0.25 m (10 in)
Height over tailplane	2.31 m (7 ft 7 in)
Tailplane span:	
c/l of tailbooms	3.40 m (11 ft 2 in)
intersection fin chord	2.60 m (8 ft 6½ in)
Wheel track	3.40 m (11 ft 2 in)
Wheelbase	2.73 m (9 ft 0 in)
Doors (each): Long axis	1.35 m (4 ft 5 in)
Short axis	0.96 m (3 ft 1¾ in)
Height to sill	0.51 m (1 ft 8 in)

DIMENSIONS, INTERNAL:

Cabin: Length	2.44 m (8 ft 0 in)
Max width (to door Perspex)	1.68 m (5 ft 6 in)
Max height	1.35 m (4 ft 5 in)
Floor area	0.72 m² (7.75 sq ft)

AREAS:

Wings, gross	15.84 m² (170.5 sq ft)

Ailerons (total)	1.55 m² (16.68 sq ft)	
Trailing-edge flaps:		
inboard (total)	0.61 m² (6.57 sq ft)	
outboard (total)	1.59 m² (17.12 sq ft)	
Fins (total)	1.98 m² (21.31 sq ft)	
Rudders (total)	1.10 m² (11.84 sq ft)	
Tailplane	1.62 m² (17.44 sq ft)	
Elevator, incl tab	1.26 m² (13.56 sq ft)	

WEIGHTS AND LOADINGS: (A: Scout, B: Scoutmaster I, C: Scoutmaster II):

Weight empty, equipped: A	948 kg (2,090 lb)
B	1,050 kg (2,315 lb)
C	1,180 kg (2,600 lb)
Max cabin load: A	231 kg (510 lb)
Crew (pilot/observer): B, C	154 kg (340 lb)
Fuel: B	111 kg (245 lb)
C	206 kg (454 lb)
Max T-O weight: A, B	1,315 kg (2,900 lb)
C	1,540 kg (3,395 lb)
Max wing loading: A, B	83.0 kg/m² (17.0 lb/sq ft)
C	97.2 kg/m² (19.9 lb/sq ft)

Max power loading: A, B	6.78 kg/kW (11.2 lb/hp)
C	7.94 kg/kW (13.1 lb/hp)

PERFORMANCE (Scout, at max T-O weight, forward limit CG):

Never-exceed speed (VNE)	140 knots (259 km/h; 161 mph)
Max level speed	115 knots (213 km/h; 132 mph)
Cruising speed:	
50% power	86 knots (159 km/h; 99 mph)
70% power	103 knots (191 km/h; 119 mph)
Loiter speed (40% power)	70 knots (130 km/h; 81 mph)
Stalling speed, outboard flaps up	
	58 knots (108 km/h; 67 mph)
Max rate of climb at S/L	247 m (810 ft)/min
Service ceiling	4,275 m (14,000 ft)
T-O run	330 m (1,082 ft)
T-O to 15 m (50 ft)	472 m (1,548 ft)
Landing from 15 m (50 ft)	555 m (1,820 ft)
Landing run	278 m (912 ft)
Range with max fuel (45 min reserves):	
at 110 knots (204 km/h; 127 mph)	
	370 nm (685 km; 426 miles)

at 70 knots (130 km/h; 81 mph)	
	570 nm (1,056 km; 656 miles)
Endurance (45 min reserves):	
at 110 knots (204 km/h; 127 mph)	2 h 45 min
at 70 knots (130 km/h; 81 mph)	8 h
g limits	+3.8/−1.5

PERFORMANCE (B: Scoutmaster I, C: Scoutmaster II, at max T-O weight):

Operating speed range:	
B	70-113 knots (130-210 km/h; 80-130 mph)
C	75-118 knots (139-218 km/h; 86-136 mph)
Max rate of climb at S/L:	
B	244 m (800 ft)/min
C	216 m (710 ft)/min
Range (with IFR fuel reserves):	
B	200 nm (370 km; 230 miles)
C	400 nm (740 km; 460 miles)

MARSHALL

MARSHALL OF CAMBRIDGE (ENGINEERING) LTD (Aircraft Division)

Airport Works, Cambridge CB5 8RX
Telephone: 44 (223) 61133
Fax: 44 (223) 321032
Telex: 81208
CHAIRMAN: M. J. Marshall, DL
ENGINEERING DIRECTOR/CHIEF DESIGNER: R. E. Ward
SALES MANAGER: G. McA. Bacon
PUBLIC RELATIONS MANAGER: C. J. Buisseret

Aircraft Division (known as Marshalls Flying School Ltd until 1962) specialises in modification, overhaul and repair of aircraft, including design and installation of interior furnishing for business aircraft and avionics fits including complete calibration and ECM installations; appointed designated centre for RAF Hercules 1966; conversions have included one for long-range meteorological role (see 1979-80 *Jane's*), 29 C. Mk 1s stretched to C. Mk 3s (see 1987-88 *Jane's*), six others to C. Mk 1(K) flight refuelling tankers (see 1990-91 edition), and fitment of refuelling probe to entire RAF Hercules fleet; ex-airline TriStars converted to flight refuelling tanker/freighters for RAF. Major overhauls and embodiment of modifications continue in RAF and other C-130 Hercules. Fitting-out activities include BAe 146. Avionics modification completed on RAF Bulldog fleet.

MARSHALL (LOCKHEED) TRISTAR TANKER CONVERSIONS

TYPE: In-flight refuelling tanker/transport.
PROGRAMME: Six Lockheed L-1011-500 TriStar airliners purchased from British Airways 1982; converted to in-flight refuelling tankers or tanker/transports for RAF with slightly altered name; company also bidding for conversion of three more purchased from Pan Am 1984; work started 1983 (see Variants).
VARIANTS: **Tristar K. Mk 1:** Two interim (ZD950 and 953) and two full (ZD951 and 949) conversions to tanker/passenger standard; each has two Flight Refuelling Mk 17T hose-drum units (HDUs) and seven fuel tanks in fore and aft baggage compartments, totalling additional 45,386 kg (100,060 lb) of fuel; overall total fuel capacity 142,111 kg (313,300 lb); HDUs deliver fuel at 1,814 kg (4,000 lb)/min at 3.45 bars (50 lb/sq in); flight refuelling receiver probe above forward fuselage; closed

Marshall-modified Tristar K. Mk 1 in desert pink colour scheme used for combat support missions in Gulf War, early 1991 *(Paul Jackson)*

circuit TV for monitoring refuelling; first K. Mk 1 (ZD950) flight 9 July 1985; max T-O weight 244,940 kg (540,000 lb); received CA Release to Service 1 December 1988; ZD953 redelivered to RAF 25 March 1986, followed by ZD951 and 949 by mid-July 1986; interim models since converted to KC. Mk 1s.
Tristar KC. Mk 1: Tristars ZD948 and 952 converted to tanker/freighter role; ZD950 and 953 (see K. Mk 1) now this standard; additional modifications include 2.64 × 3.56 m (104 × 140 in) cargo door on port side, forward of wing leading-edge, and cargo handling system; passenger floor strengthened for high density loads; all items on cabin floor pallet mounted; seat pallets for 35 passengers (12 in forward area and 23 at rear); ZD948 redelivered to RAF 9 December 1988; ZD952 and 953 redelivered 1989 and ZD950 in December 1990.
Tristar C. Mk 2(K): Three ex-Pan Am airliners (ZE704-706), possibly to be converted to tanker/passenger role in early 1990s; ZE704 and 705 operated initially for trooping with airline accommodation; ZE706 stored at Cambridge; no extra fuel tanks or fuselage-mounted HDUs; normal tankage 96,724 kg

(213,240 lb) and underwing refuelling pods only. Marshall completed design study to fit FRL Mk 32B pods to K. Mk 1s, KC. Mk 1s and C. Mk 2(K)s; Mk 32 pods can deliver fuel simultaneously at 1,134 kg (2,500 lb)/min at 3.45 bars (50 lb/sq in).
General Instrument AN/ALR-66 radar warning receivers to be fitted to RAF Tristars; all assigned to No. 216 Squadron, RAF Brize Norton.

MARSHALL (LOCKHEED) TRISTAR and MD-11 MODIFICATION

Marshall offers freight door modification and additional fuel capacity; special fittings, including cockpit and cargo compartment modifications, under way for five American Airlines' McDonnell Douglas MD-11s; first arrival (N511MD) 17 July 1990. Delta Air Lines contract received August 1990 to install auxiliary 5,897 kg (13,000 lb) fuel tank in TriStars; tank and equipment weight approximately 907 kg (2,000 lb), of which 680 kg (1,500 lb) removable.
Satcom installations undertaken in wide-bodied airliners from 1990.

NASH

NASH AIRCRAFT LTD (A subsidiary of Kinetrol Ltd)

Trading Estate, Farnham, Surrey GU9 9NU
Telephone: 44 (252) 733838
Fax: 44 (252) 713042
Telex: 858567
DIRECTORS:
A. R. B. Nash (Managing)
Roy G. Procter
R. C. Nash

NASH PETREL

TYPE: Two-seat light aircraft.
PROGRAMME: First flight of prototype (G-AXSF) 8 November 1980 with O-320-D2A engine (replaced 1982 by 134 kW; 180 hp Textron Lycoming O-360-A3A); new high tailplane fitted 1983, upswept wingtips 1984 (further details in 1990-91 and earlier *Jane's*). Pre-production batch of five Petrels started in about 1986; by April 1991 one of these nearly complete and one other approx 75 per cent complete; structural test airframe also completed. Work towards certification proceeding, albeit slowly.
DESIGN FEATURES: Optimised for club/touring use, especially ease of handling and for glider towing.

Prototype of the Nash Petrel two-seat light aircraft

FLYING CONTROLS: Manual operation of primary surfaces and NACA slotted flaps.

STRUCTURE: See 1990-91 *Jane's* for prototype; pre-production aircraft; identical aerodynamically, but differ structurally.

OPERATION ABILITY

OPERATION ABILITY LTD

The Meadows, Firgrove Road, Whitehill, Bordon,
Hampshire GU35 9DY
Telephone: 44 (4203) 5062
CHAIRMAN AND MANAGING DIRECTOR: Philip Scott

Philip Scott, 85 per cent paralysed from an accident, formed Operation Ability to gain Private Pilot's Licence; without use of his legs, body, hands and much of arms, he became first tetraplegic to pass CAA medical examination as 'fit to learn'.

Venture began 1984; initially special Cranfield A3 aircraft designed; high costs led to alternative modification of French Aérodis G802 Orion, including jet power; other companies approached to produce Spur in Britain 1990.

Operation Ability since acquired ex-Luftwaffe Focke-Wulf-Piaggio P.149D trainer (G-BRKD); special hoist constructed to enable pilot to enter/exit cockpit. Aircraft modifications began early 1990 to enable him to fly it, including provision of servo actuator for rudder operation using either direct control or inputs from yaw damper; conversion of flap system from manual to hydraulic operation; new brake system; emergency backup system for lowering landing gear; and modifications to enable

Focke-Wulf-Piaggio P.149D for Operation Ability *(John C. Cook)*

operation of cockpit equipment/avionics (Racal Danac navigation computer will be installed in P.149D). More than 50 firms and numerous individuals sponsor Spur project.

ORCA

ORCA AIRCRAFT LTD

Placed under administration during Summer 1989, since when no further news received. Full details of Orca SAH-1 in 1990-91 *Jane's*.

PILATUS BRITTEN-NORMAN

PILATUS BRITTEN-NORMAN LTD (Subsidiary of Oerlikon-Bührle Holding Ltd)

The Airport, Bembridge, Isle of Wight PO35 5PR
Telephone: 44 (983) 872511
Fax: 44 (983) 873246
Telex: 86277 PBNBEM G
MANAGING DIRECTOR: Dr E. Haefliger
TECHNICAL DIRECTOR: R. Wilson
MARKETING DIRECTOR: A. Stansfeld
MARKETING SERVICES MANAGER: Richard M. Blake

Pilatus Aircraft Ltd of Switzerland acquired Britten-Norman (Bembridge) Ltd 1979, including Isle of Wight facilities and former Fairey SA Islander/Trislander production hardware at Gosselies, Belgium.

Previous company history appeared in 1978-79 and earlier *Jane's*. Final Trislander delivered to the Botswana Defence Force September 1984 but Fixed and Rotary Wing Engineering of Camden, New South Wales, to assemble 10 from components produced by Fairey at Gosselies (see Addenda).

PILATUS BRITTEN-NORMAN BN-2B ISLANDER

TYPE: Twin-engined feederline transport.
PROGRAMME: Detail design began April 1964; construction of prototype (G-ATCT) started September 1964; first flight 13 June 1965 with two 157 kW (210 hp) Rolls-Royce Continental IO-360-B engines and 13.72 m (45 ft) span wings; prototype subsequently re-engined with Textron Lycoming O-540s and flown 17 December 1965; wing span also increased by 1.22 m (4 ft) to initial production standard; production prototype BN-2 Islander (G-ATWU) flown 20 August 1966; domestic C of A received 10 August 1967; FAA type certificate 19 December 1967; Romanian manufacture (see Romaero entry) began 1969.
VARIANTS: **BN-2 Islander:** Initial piston engined production model (see earlier *Jane's*).

BN-2A Islander: Piston version built from 1 June 1969 (see 1977-78 *Jane's*). Still available to order.

BN-2B Islander: Current standard piston engined version; higher max landing weight; improved interior design; available with two engine choices and optional wingtip fuel tanks as **BN-2B-26** with O-540s and

BN-2B-20 with IO-540s (BN-2B-27 and -21 no longer available). Features include range of passenger seats and covers, more robust door locks, improved door seals and stainless steel sills, redesigned fresh air system to improve ventilation in hot and humid climates, smaller diameter propellers to decrease cabin noise, and redesigned flight deck and instrument panel.

Series of modification kits available as standard or option for new production aircraft and can be fitted retrospectively to existing aircraft; extended nose, incorporating 0.62 m³ (22 cu ft) additional baggage space, introduced as option 1972; Jonas Aircraft developed Rajay turbocharging installation, optional for 194 kW (260 hp) engines as bolt-on unit.

BN-2B Defender: Described separately.
BN-2B Maritime Defender: Described separately.
BN-2T Turbine Islander and Defender: Described separately.
BN-2T ASTOR Defender: Described separately.

CUSTOMERS: Deliveries began August 1967; various models, including military Defenders, supplied to operators in approx 120 countries; by January 1991 deliveries (all versions) totalled 1,132; 1990 customers for BN-2B included CAAC (one), Luftverkehr Friesland (one), Falklands Islands Government Air Service (two), Air Moorea (three), Monarch Aviation, Australia (one), Botswana Defence Force (one).
DESIGN FEATURES: Intended as replacement for aircraft in class of de Havilland Dragon Rapide, incorporating STOL characteristics; pneumatic de-icing boots optional on wings, tailplane and fin. NACA 23012 wing section; no dihedral; incidence 2°; no sweepback.
FLYING CONTROLS: Slotted ailerons with starboard ground adjustable tab, operated by pushrods and cables; mass balanced elevator; rudder and elevator actuated by pushrods and cables; trim tabs in rudder and elevator; single-slotted flaps operated electrically; fixed incidence tailplane.
STRUCTURE: L72 aluminium-clad aluminium alloys; two-spar wing torsion box in one piece; flared-up wingtips; integral fuel tanks in wingtips optional; four-longeron semi-monocoque fuselage of pressed frames and stringers; two-spar tail unit with pressed ribs.
LANDING GEAR: Non-retractable tricycle type, with twin wheels on each main unit and single steerable nosewheel. Cantilever main legs mounted aft of rear spar. All three

legs fitted with oleo-pneumatic shock absorbers. All five wheels and tyres size 16 × 7-7, supplied by Goodyear. Tyre pressure: main 2.41 bars (35 lb/sq in); nose 2.00 bars (29 lb/sq in). Foot operated aircooled Cleveland hydraulic brakes on main units. Parking brake. Wheel/ski gear available optionally.
POWER PLANT: Two Textron Lycoming flat-six engines, each driving a Hartzell HC-C2YK-2B or -2C two-blade constant-speed feathering metal propeller. Propeller synchronisers optional. Standard power plant is the 194 kW (260 hp) O-540-E4C5, but the 224 kW (300 hp) IO-540-K1B5 can be fitted at customer's option. Optional Rajay turbocharging installation on 194 kW (260 hp) engines, to improve high altitude performance. Integral fuel tank between spars in each wing, outboard of engine. Total fuel capacity (standard) 518 litres (137 US gallons; 114 Imp gallons). Usable fuel 492 litres (130 US gallons; 108 Imp gallons). With optional fuel tanks in wingtips, total capacity is increased to 855 litres (226 US gallons; 188 Imp gallons). Additional pylon mounted underwing auxiliary tanks, each of 227 litres (60 US gallons; 50 Imp gallons) capacity, available optionally. Refuelling point in upper surface of wing above each internal tank. Total oil capacity 22.75 litres (6 US gallons; 5 Imp gallons).
ACCOMMODATION: Up to 10 persons, including pilot, on side by side front seats and four bench seats. No aisle. Seat backs fold forward. Access to all seats via three forward opening doors, forward of wing and at rear of cabin on port side and forward of wing on starboard side. Baggage compartment at rear of cabin, with port side loading door in standard versions. Exit in emergency by removing door windows. Special executive layouts available. Can be operated as freighter, carrying more than a ton of cargo; in this configuration the passenger seats can be stored in the rear baggage bay. In ambulance role, up to three stretchers and two attendants can be accommodated. Other layouts possible, including photographic and geophysical survey, parachutist transport or trainer (with accommodation for up to eight parachutists and a dispatcher), firefighting, public health spraying and cropspraying.
SYSTEMS: Southwind cabin heater standard. 45,000 BTU Stewart Warner combustion unit, with circulating fan, provides hot air for distribution at floor level outlets and at windscreen demisting slots. Fresh air, boosted by propeller slipstream, is ducted to each seating position for on-ground ventilation. Electrical DC power, for instruments, lighting and radio, from two engine driven 24V 50A self-rectifying alternators and a controller to main busbar and circuit breaker assembly. Emergency busbar is supplied by a 24V 17Ah heavy duty lead-acid battery in the event of a twin alternator failure. Ground power receptacle provided. Optional electric de-icing of propellers and windscreen, and pneumatic de-icing of wing and tail unit leading-edges. Intercom system, including second headset, and passenger address system are standard. Oxygen system available optionally for all versions.
AVIONICS: Standard items include blind-flying instrumentation, autopilot, and a wide range of VHF and HF communications and navigation equipment.
EQUIPMENT: Dual flying controls and brake system standard.
DIMENSIONS, EXTERNAL:
Wing span   14.94 m (49 ft 0 in)

Pilatus Britten-Norman BN-2B Islanders for Air Moorea

Wing chord, constant	2.03 m (6 ft 8 in)
Wing aspect ratio	7.4
Length overall	10.86 m (35 ft 7¾ in)
Fuselage: Max width	1.21 m (3 ft 11½ in)
Max depth	1.46 m (4 ft 9¾ in)
Height overall	4.18 m (13 ft 8¾ in)
Tailplane span	4.67 m (15 ft 4 in)
Wheel track (c/l of shock absorbers)	3.61 m (11 ft 10 in)
Wheelbase	3.99 m (13 ft 1¼ in)
Propeller diameter	1.98 m (6 ft 6 in)
Cabin door (front, port):	
Height	1.10 m (3 ft 7½ in)
Width: top	0.64 m (2 ft 1¼ in)
Height to sill	0.59 m (1 ft 11¼ in)
Cabin door (front, starboard):	
Height	1.10 m (3 ft 7½ in)
Max width	0.86 m (2 ft 10 in)
Height to sill	0.57 m (1 ft 10½ in)
Cabin door (rear, port): Height	1.09 m (3 ft 7 in)
Width: top	0.635 m (2 ft 1 in)
bottom	1.19 m (3 ft 11 in)
Height to sill	0.52 m (1 ft 8½ in)
Baggage door (rear, port) Height	0.69 m (2 ft 3 in)

DIMENSIONS, INTERNAL:

Passenger cabin, aft of pilot's seat:	
Length	3.05 m (10 ft 0 in)
Max width	1.09 m (3 ft 7 in)
Max height	1.27 m (4 ft 2 in)
Floor area	2.97 m² (32 sq ft)
Volume	3.68 m³ (130 cu ft)
Baggage space aft of passenger cabin	
	1.39 m³ (49 cu ft)
Freight capacity:	
aft of pilot's seat, incl rear cabin baggage space	
	4.70 m³ (166 cu ft)
with four bench seats folded into rear cabin baggage	
space	3.68 m³ (130 cu ft)

AREAS:

Wings, gross	30.19 m² (325.0 sq ft)
Ailerons (total)	2.38 m² (25.6 sq ft)
Flaps (total)	3.62 m² (39.0 sq ft)
Fin	3.41 m² (36.64 sq ft)
Rudder, incl tab	1.60 m² (17.2 sq ft)
Tailplane	6.78 m² (73.0 sq ft)
Elevator, incl tabs	3.08 m² (33.16 sq ft)

WEIGHTS AND LOADINGS (A: 194 kW; 260 hp engines, B: 224 kW; 300 hp engines):

Weight empty, equipped (without avionics):	
A	1,866 kg (4,114 lb)
B	1,925 kg (4,244 lb)
Max payload: A	929 kg (2,048 lb)
B	870 kg (1,918 lb)
Payload with max fuel: A	692 kg (1,526 lb)
B	633 kg (1,396 lb)
Max fuel weight: standard: A, B	354 kg (780 lb)
with optional tanks in wingtips: A, B	585 kg (1,290 lb)
Max T-O and landing weight: A, B	2,993 kg (6,600 lb)
Max zero-fuel weight (BCAR):	
A, B	2,855 kg (6,300 lb)
Max wing loading: A, B	99.1 kg/m² (20.3 lb/sq ft)
Max floor loading, without cargo panels:	
A, B	586 kg/m² (120 lb/sq ft)
Max power loading: A	7.71 kg/kW (12.7 lb/hp)
B	6.68 kg/kW (11.0 lb/hp)

PERFORMANCE (at max T-O weight. A and B as above):

Never-exceed speed (VNE):	
A, B	183 knots (339 km/h; 211 mph) IAS
Max level speed at S/L:	
A	148 knots (274 km/h; 170 mph)
B	151 knots (280 km/h; 173 mph)
Max cruising speed (75% power) at 2,135 m (7,000 ft):	
A	139 knots (257 km/h; 160 mph)
B	142 knots (264 km/h; 164 mph)
Cruising speed (67% power) at 2,750 m (9,000 ft):	
A	134 knots (248 km/h; 154 mph)
B	137 knots (254 km/h; 158 mph)
Cruising speed (59% power) at 3,660 m (12,000 ft):	
A	130 knots (241 km/h; 150 mph)
B	132 knots (245 km/h; 152 mph)
Stalling speed:	
flaps up: A, B	50 knots (92 km/h; 57 mph) IAS
flaps down: A, B	40 knots (74 km/h; 46 mph) IAS
Max rate of climb at S/L: A	262 m (860 ft)/min
B	344 m (1,130 ft)/min
Rate of climb at S/L, one engine out:	
A	44 m (145 ft)/min
B	60 m (198 ft)/min
Absolute ceiling: A	4,145 m (13,600 ft)
B	6,005 m (19,700 ft)
Service ceiling: A	3,445 m (11,300 ft)
B	5,240 m (17,200 ft)
Service ceiling, one engine out: A	1,525 m (5,000 ft)
B	1,980 m (6,500 ft)
Min ground turning radius	9.45 m (31 ft 0 in)
T-O run at S/L, zero wind, hard runway:	
A	278 m (913 ft)
B	264 m (866 ft)
T-O run at 1,525 m (5,000 ft): A	396 m (1,299 ft)
B	372 m (1,221 ft)
T-O to 15 m (50 ft) at S/L, zero wind, hard runway:	
A	371 m (1,218 ft)
B	352 m (1,155 ft)

T-O to 15 m (50 ft) at 1,525 m (5,000 ft):	
A	528 m (1,732 ft)
B	496 m (1,628 ft)
Landing from 15 m (50 ft) at S/L, zero wind, hard	
runway: A, B	299 m (980 ft)
Landing from 15 m (50 ft) at 1,525 m (5,000 ft):	
A, B	357 m (1,170 ft)
Landing run at 1,525 m (5,000 ft): A, B	171 m (560 ft)
Landing run at S/L, zero wind, hard runway:	
A, B	140 m (460 ft)
Range at 75% power at 2,135 m (7,000 ft):	
A, standard fuel	622 nm (1,153 km; 717 miles)
A, with optional tanks	
	1,023 nm (1,896 km; 1,178 miles)
B, standard fuel	555 nm (1,028 km; 639 miles)
B, with optional tanks	920 nm (1,704 km; 1,059 miles)
Range at 67% power at 2,750 m (9,000 ft):	
A, standard fuel	713 nm (1,322 km; 822 miles)
A, with optional tanks	
	1,159 nm (2,147 km; 1,334 miles)
B, standard fuel	577 nm (1,070 km; 665 miles)
B, with optional tanks	975 nm (1,807 km; 1,123 miles)
Range at 59% power at 3,660 m (12,000 ft):	
A, standard fuel	755 nm (1,400 km; 870 miles)
A, with optional tanks	
	1,216 nm (2,253 km; 1,400 miles)
B, standard fuel	613 nm (1,136 km; 706 miles)
B, with optional tanks	
	1,061 nm (1,965 km; 1,221 miles)

PILATUS BRITTEN-NORMAN DEFENDER

TYPE: Government and military variant of civil Islander.

PROGRAMME: Developed to be adaptable for variety of roles such as search and rescue, internal security, long-range patrol, forward air control, troop transport, logistic support and casualty evacuation.

CUSTOMERS: Defenders/Islanders delivered to Abu Dhabi Defence Force, Belgian Army, Belize Defence Force, Botswana Defence Force, British Army Parachute Association, Ciskei Defence Force, Ghana Air Force, Guyana Defence Force, Haitian Air Corps, Indonesian Army, Iraqi Islamic Air Force, Israeli Air Force, Jamaica Defence Force, Malagasy Air Force, Presidential Flight of the Mexican Air Force, Royal Hong Kong Auxiliary Air Force, Panamanian Air Force, Qatar Emiri Air Force, Somali Aeronautical Corps, Royal Air Force of Oman, Suriname Air Force, Mauritania Islamic Defence Force, the Seychelles Ministry of Agriculture and Fisheries, the Malawi Army Air Wing, Venezuelan Army Air Regiment, Zaïre Air Force, Zimbabwe Air Force and the Rwanda Air Force. Those operated by Ciskei, Haiti, Indonesia, Iraq, Somalia, Venezuela, Zaïre, Zimbabwe, Israel and Qatar are military Islanders, and not equipped to carry offensive weapons.

DESIGN FEATURES: Same wing configuration choices as current civil Islander; wide range of sophisticated avionics, including nose mounted weather radar, providing maritime search capability. for electronic warfare role, equipment can range from simple radar warning receiver to comprehensive passive electronic intelligence gathering system, ESM, and ECM coupled to the ESM to provide radar jamming or defensive chaff/IR flare dispensing; other optional equipment includes four NATO standard underwing pylons for variety of external stores.

Passenger, stretcher or cargo capacity as for civil Islander.

The description given for the BN-2B Islander applies also to the Defender, except as follows:

POWER PLANT: Two 224 kW (300 hp) Textron Lycoming IO-540-K1B5 flat-six engines standard.

AVIONICS: Typical installation comprises 720 channel VHF nav/com transceivers with VOR/LOC and VOR/ILS, ADF, marker beacon receiver, transponder, HF com transceiver, weather radar and full autopilot. Optional equipment includes RWR, ESM and ECM.

ARMAMENT: Inboard pylons can each carry up to 340 kg (750 lb) and outboard pair up to 159 kg (350 lb). Typical underwing loads include twin 7.62 mm machine guns in pod packs, 250 lb or 500 lb GP bombs, Matra rocket packs, SURA rocket clusters, wire guided missiles, 5 in reconnaissance flares, anti-personnel grenades, smoke bombs, marker bombs and 227 litre (60 US gallon; 50 Imp gallon) drop tanks.

PILATUS BRITTEN-NORMAN MARITIME DEFENDER

TYPE: All-weather, day or night, coastal patrol, fishery and oil rig protection, and search and rescue aircraft.

CUSTOMERS: Cyprus National Guard, Indian Navy and Philippine Navy.

DESIGN FEATURES: Similar to Defender, except overall length increased to 11.07 m (36 ft 3¾ in). Modified nose with larger (Bendix/King RDR-1400) search radar, capable of detecting 100 m² (1,076 sq ft) target in sea state 4-5 at 36 nm (67 km; 41.5 miles) range; radar provides 60 nm (111 km; 69 miles) search width at optimum altitude while scanning 60° each side of flight path; interior layout provides for pilot and co-pilot, radar operator and two observers.

AVIONICS: Can include compass/HSI, horizon gyro (radar stabilisation), autopilot, ground mapping and weather

radar, VLF/Omega, radio altimeter, dual VHF com, dual VHF nav/ILS, VHF marine band com, ADF, transponder, DME, encoding altimeter and SSB HF com.

EQUIPMENT: Includes searchlight installation and hand-held camera. Loudspeaker pod, flares, parachute dinghy packs and variety of weapons on four underwing pylons.

PILATUS BRITTEN-NORMAN BN-2T TURBINE ISLANDER and DEFENDER

TYPE: Twin-turboprop development of piston engined Islander/Defender.

PROGRAMME: First flight of prototype (G-BPBN) 2 August 1980 with two Allison 250-B17C turboprops; British CAA certification received end of May 1981; first production aircraft delivered December 1981; FAR Pt 23 US type approval 15 July 1982; full icing clearance to FAR Pt 25 gained 23 July 1984.

CUSTOMERS: Total 37 delivered by December 1990, including three to Moroccan Ministry of Agriculture, one to Cyprus Police and two to British Army during 1990 (see also Special Role entry). Four delivered to Ghana Air Force 1990-91.

DESIGN FEATURES: Turboprops enable use of available low cost jet fuel instead of scarce and costly Avgas, and offer particularly low operating noise level; available for same range of applications as Islander, including military versions (described separately).

Description of the BN-2B Islander applies also to BN-2T, except as follows:

POWER PLANT: Two 298 kW (400 shp) Allison 250-B17C turboprops, flat rated at 238.5 kW (320 shp), and each driving a Hartzell three-blade constant-speed fully feathering metal propeller. Usable fuel 814 litres (215 US gallons; 179 Imp gallons). Pylon mounted underwing tanks, each of 227 litres (60 US gallons; 50 Imp gallons) capacity, are available optionally for special purposes. Total oil capacity 5.7 litres (1.5 US gallons; 1.25 Imp gallons).

ACCOMMODATION: Generally as for BN-2B. In ambulance role can accommodate, in addition to the pilot, a single stretcher, one medical attendant and five seated occupants; or two stretchers, one attendant and three passengers; or three stretchers, two attendants and one passenger. Other possible layouts include photographic and geophysical survey; parachutist transport or trainer (with accommodation for up to eight parachutists and a dispatcher); and pest control or other agricultural spraying. Maritime Turbine Islander/Defender versions available for fishery protection, coastguard patrol, pollution survey, search and rescue, and similar applications. Offered as an option is an in-flight sliding parachute door.

AVIONICS: Radar, VLF/Omega nav system, radar altimeter, marine band and VHF transceivers.

EQUIPMENT: Standard equipment generally similar to BN-2B. Other equipment, according to mission, includes fixed tail sting or towed bird magnetometer, spectrometer, or electro-magnetic detection/analysis equipment (geophysical survey); one or two cameras, navigation sights and appropriate avionics (photographic survey); 188.7 litre (50 US gallon; 41.5 Imp gallon) Micronair underwing spraypods complete with pump and rotary atomiser (pest control/agricultural spraying versions); dinghies, survival equipment and special crew accommodation (maritime versions).

DIMENSIONS, EXTERNAL:

As for BN-2B, except

Length overall: standard nose	10.86 m (35 ft 7¾ in)
weather radar nose	11.07 m (36 ft 3¾ in)
Propeller diameter	2.03 m (6 ft 8 in)

WEIGHTS AND LOADINGS:

Weight empty, equipped	1,832 kg (4,040 lb)
Payload with max fuel	608 kg (1,340 lb)
Max T-O weight	3,175 kg (7,000 lb)
Max landing weight	3,084 kg (6,800 lb)
Max zero-fuel weight	2,994 kg (6,600 lb)
Max wing loading	105.17 kg/m² (21.54 lb/sq ft)
Max power loading	5.33 kg/kW (8.75 lb/shp)

PERFORMANCE (standard aircraft and Turbine Defender, at max T-O weight, ISA, except where indicated):

Max cruising speed:	
at 3,050 m (10,000 ft)	170 knots (315 km/h; 196 mph)
at S/L	154 knots (285 km/h; 177 mph)
Cruising speed, 72% power:	
at 3,050 m (10,000 ft)	150 knots (278 km/h; 173 mph)
at 1,525 m (5,000 ft)	143 knots (265 km/h; 165 mph)
Stalling speed, power off:	
flaps up	52 knots (97 km/h; 60 mph) IAS
flaps down	45 knots (84 km/h; 52 mph) IAS
Max rate of climb at S/L	320 m (1,050 ft)/min
Rate of climb at S/L, one engine out	66 m (215 ft)/min
Service ceiling	over 7,620 m (25,000 ft)
Absolute ceiling, one engine out	
	over 3,050 m (10,000 ft)
T-O run	255 m (837 ft)
T-O to 15 m (50 ft)	381 m (1,250 ft)
Landing from 15 m (50 ft)	339 m (1,110 ft)
Landing run	231 m (757 ft)
Range (IFR) with max fuel, reserves for 45 min hold plus 10%	590 nm (1,093 km; 679 miles)
Range (VFR) with max fuel, no reserves	
	728 nm (1,349 km; 838 miles)

PILATUS BRITTEN-NORMAN ASTOR DEFENDER

TYPE: Twin-turboprop experimental battlefield surveillance aircraft.

PROGRAMME: ASTOR (Airborne STand-Off Radar) is current acronym for British MoD programme to develop airborne surveillance radar to provide overall picture of battle area; intended to operate in conjunction with Phoenix battlefield reconnaissance UAV (to obtain closer look at target/area shown by ASTOR to require detailed examination) and/or Joint STARS surveillance aircraft.

Two platforms being evaluated for ASTOR (BAC/English Electric Canberra the high-level option); more versatile BN-2T Defender could be selected for production systems if proven to acquire sufficient data from medium heights; radar trials included GEC equipment in Canberra and GEC Ferranti equipment in Defender (modified Thorn EMI Searchwater in Canberra testbed since 1982); up to 12 ASTOR platforms required.

Work on ASTOR (then CASTOR) Turbine Defender testbed (G-DLRA, c/n 2140; now ZG989) began 5 March 1984; converted aircraft first flight 12 May, with flat-bottomed undernose radome containing ballast only; new nose gives adequate performance and virtually unaltered handling characteristics; G-DLRA fitted with modified version of Thorn EMI Skymaster radar in AEW Defender type nose radome 1988; tests as low-level ASTOR platform continued 1989-90, flown at altitudes up to 3,050 m (10,000 ft).

DESIGN FEATURES: Nose radome considered best location for optimum lookdown capability for scanner; nosewheel leg lengthened by 30.5 cm (12 in) and Trislander main landing gear fitted to give necessary ground clearance. Tests involved new electrically driven antenna and additional signal processing techniques intended to provide required detection and azimuth resolution of slow moving targets against ground clutter background; data link trials 1990 evaluated system's interoperability with J-STARS (see Avionics).

STRUCTURE: See Programme for changes to nose.

Description of standard BN-2T Turbine Islander applies also to ASTOR Defender, except as follows:

LANDING GEAR: Modified BN-2A Mk III Trislander main landing gear. Longer nosewheel leg to provide adequate ground clearance for radome. Main landing gear tyre size 6.50 × 8, pressure 2.4 bars (35 lb/sq in).

AVIONICS: Thorn EMI Skymaster multi-mode radar in nose, modified to meet UK General and Air Staff Requirement 3956, to provide primary intelligence information in immediate battle zone and beyond, while operating well within friendly territory. Has 360° scan, and offers wide area of coverage against moving and fixed targets. Associated transmitter, receiver and processing equipment housed in fuselage of Defender, which is flown and operated by two-man crew. Data acquired are processed and transmitted automatically, via airborne link, to one or more ground stations.

DIMENSIONS, EXTERNAL:
Wing span	14.94 m (49 ft 0 in)
Wing aspect ratio	7.4
Length overall	12.37 m (40 ft 7¼ in)
Propeller diameter	2.03 m (6 ft 8 in)

WEIGHTS AND LOADINGS:
Design max T-O weight	3,630 kg (8,000 lb)

PILATUS BRITTEN-NORMAN SPECIAL ROLE BN-2T TURBINE ISLANDERS and DEFENDERS

British Army Air Corps designation: Islander AL. Mk 1

TYPE: Military special role adaptations of BN-2T Turbine Defender.

VARIANTS: **ASW/ASV Maritime Defender:** Equipped to customer's specifications, including 360° radar and FLIR; four underwing hardpoints for four Sea Skua missiles, ESM pods, survival packs, rockets, gun pods or other stores; three crew normal, with room for trainee.

ELINT Defender: Economically viable electronic warfare platform; programme jointly funded with Racal Radar Defence Systems Ltd; BN-2T (G-DEMO) fitted with Racal Kestrel lightweight EW avionics suite as demonstrator 1989.

Kestrel system provides ability to compile comprehensive library of electronic intelligence, constantly updated; offers total radar band coverage with instant onboard analysis and/or data recording for ground replay and analysis, and allows peacetime strategic intelligence role or tactical elint in active environment; flight crew plus equipment operator.

Underwing pods carry two outward-facing antenna units for Kestrel system; further two antennae opposite sides of tail fin; precision navigation system, such as Omega or an INS, standard; could remain on task at 87 nm (161 km; 100 miles) from base for four hours.

Internal Security Defender: Internal or underwing optical, thermal imaging and other types of camera equipment; armament options include guns, rockets and bombs underwing.

Dutch aircraft (see Customers) equipped with comprehensive Collins avionics fit, Bendix/King RDR 1400C

Pilatus Britten-Norman BN-2T for locust control duties with Moroccan Ministry of Agriculture

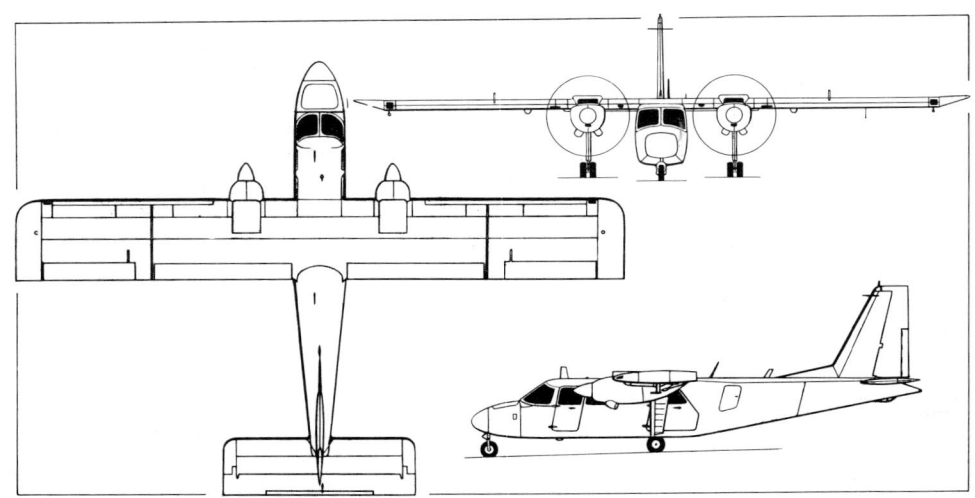

Pilatus Britten-Norman BN-2T Turbine Islander *(Pilot Press)*

Pilatus Britten-Norman Islander AL. Mk 1 of the British Army Air Corps

Pilatus Britten-Norman BN-2T Internal Security Defender of the Cyprus Police

radar, blister windows, in-flight-openable rear cabin door for camera and IR sensor platform, Racal R-NAV2 navigation management system, and external points for long-range auxiliary fuel tanks; UK AAC aircraft have R-NAV2, Doppler 91 velocity sensor, Mk 32 Airborne Decca Navigator receiver, and possibly Gepard Sensor Technologies Systems FLIR pod underwing (see Swiss section) for night surveillance.

AEW Defender: Lightweight high performance AEW system; Thorn EMI Electronics collaborated to install Skymaster radar into Defender airframe (G-TEMI); deeper nose radome, more bulbous and less angular than original ASTOR radome; long-range radar, using pulse Doppler processing, can acquire and track automatically many targets flying at all altitudes against land or sea background; for maritime reconnaissance (MR), operator selects non-coherent, frequency agile mode, optimising radar for detection of small surface targets in high sea states out to radar horizon. Production AEW Defenders would differ from standard aircraft in having increased wing span and all-up weight, plus additional fuel; higher-powered engines maintain performance.

Defender's STOL performance enables operation from forward unprepared strips; low radar cross-section aids survivability. **AEW/MR Defender** fitted with second console to increase operational flexibility and target handling capacity; air-to-air and air-to-ground data link, ESM, IFF, and navigation equipment can be fully integrated with radar display and control system.

ASTOR Defender: Described separately.

Defender 4000: General purpose military variant, with airframe and engine improvements developed for AEW Defender; new wing can lift 4,536 kg (10,000 lb), but 3,855 kg (8,500 lb) currently standard; 50 per cent greater internal fuel than standard aircraft at 3,855 kg; twice carrying capability of earlier BN-2s.

MSSA: Multi-sensor surveillance aircraft being developed with Westinghouse Electric Corporation as low-cost, off-the-shelf system for surveillance, border and fisheries patrol, drug interdiction and special operations/low-intensity conflict applications. Based on Defender 4000. Integrated multi-sensor system includes AN/APG-66 radar with 360° rotating antenna; WF-360 FLIR; dual UHF and VHF radios; ring laser gyro INS; high-resolution multi-function displays. Available for demonstration Autumn 1991.

CUSTOMERS: UK MoD purchased former Turbine Defender demonstrator (G-OPBN) in 1986, now ZF573, used by Royal Navy's Directorate-General of Underwater Weapons torpedo trials unit; Rijkpolitie (Netherlands National Police) received two Internal Security Defenders 1988; five **Islander AL. Mk 1s** to UK Army Air Corps February-March 1989, replacing DHC-2 Beavers, for Northern Ireland security (see Variants, Internal Security Defender); operational from May 1989 with 1 Flight at Aldergrove; two more delivered March 1990. Royal Air Force to acquire one **Islander CC Mk 2**, to be operational with No. 32 Squadron at RAF Northolt 1 August 1991 for large scale photographic mapping of small areas, with additional communications capability; to be fully airways-equipped and with Bendix/King weather radar.

DESIGN FEATURES: See Variants.

Following description refers to AEW Defender and Defender 4000 with increased span:

STRUCTURE: Similar to ASTOR Defender.

LANDING GEAR: Similar to ASTOR Defender.

POWER PLANT: Two Allison 250-B17F turboprops, each flat rated at 279.6 kW (375 shp). Usable internal fuel 912 kg (2,010 lb).

SYSTEMS: As for Islander/Turbine Islander.

AVIONICS: As for Islander/Turbine Islander, except Thorn EMI Skymaster I-band, frequency-agile AEW radar antenna in extended nose, providing pulse Doppler AEW lookdown, pulse AEW lookup, pulse maritime surveillance and pulse navigation weather warning modes. INS or similar precision navigation equipment. Operator's console (35 cm; 14 in display screen, plus two touch-sensitive control surfaces) in centre fuselage; second console optional. Radar transmitter, accumulators, equipment conditioning and transmitter conditioning systems all in rear fuselage.

DIMENSIONS, EXTERNAL:

Wing span	16.15 m (53 ft 0 in)
Length overall	12.37 m (40 ft 7¼ in)

WEIGHTS AND LOADINGS:

Max T-O weight	3,855 kg (8,500 lb)

PERFORMANCE:

Cruising speed	170 knots (315 km/h; 196 mph)

Pilatus Britten-Norman BN-2T Turbine Defender used for Marconi Sting Ray torpedo trials

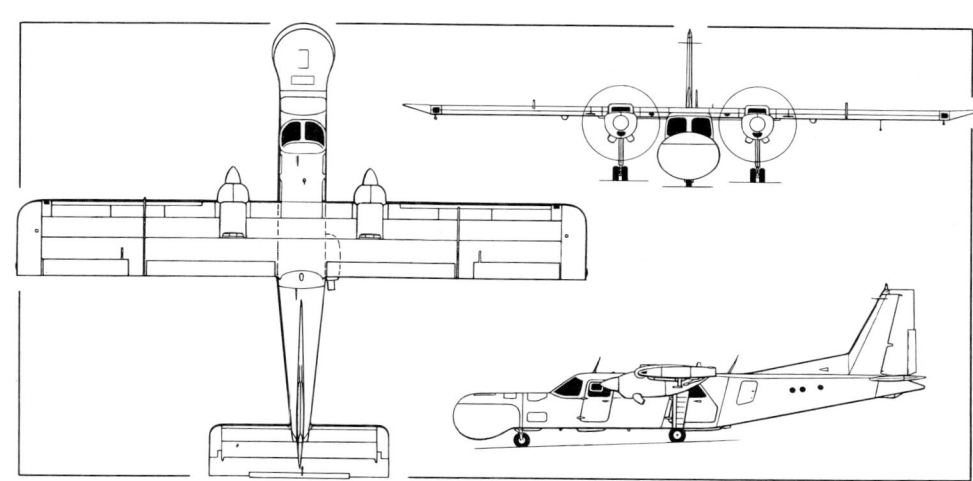

Pilatus Britten-Norman AEW Defender, a Turbine Islander development with Skymaster surveillance radar *(Pilot Press)*

Pilatus Britten-Norman ELINT Defender demonstrator with Racal Kestrel EW system

SHORTS
SHORT BROTHERS PLC

PO Box 241, Airport Road, Belfast BT3 9DZ, Northern Ireland
Telephone: 44 (232) 458444
Fax: 44 (232) 723974
Telex: 74688
OTHER WORKS: Newtownards, Castlereagh, Belfast (3), Dunmurry, Newtownabbey
LONDON OFFICE: Glen House, Stag Place, Victoria, London SW1E 5AG
Telephone: 44 (71) 828 9838
CHAIRMAN: Laurent Beaudoin

MANAGING DIRECTOR: R. W. R. McNulty
DEPUTY MANAGING DIRECTOR: A. F. C. Roberts, OBE
HEAD OF PUBLIC AFFAIRS: R. J. Gordon

Company's early history detailed in 1989-90 *Jane's*; UK government directly or indirectly owned 100 per cent of issued shareholding up to early 1989; announcement that Bombardier of Canada had purchased Shorts 7 June 1989; acquisition formally concluded 4 October 1989; Shorts remains single entity, and retains guided missile and UAV interests; employs over 8,500 people.

Company's current range no longer includes Skyvan (see 1987-88 *Jane's*); following Bombardier take-over, Shorts responsible for design, tooling and manufacture of

Canadair Regional Jet (which see) centre fuselage and plugs, plus other components including flaps, ailerons, spoilerons and inboard spoilers; first fuselage section delivered to Canadair on schedule in July 1990.

Important collaborative agreements between Shorts and Embraer of Brazil announced May 1984; first, Shorts marketing and manufacturing under licence modified version of EMB-312 Tucano turboprop basic trainer, selected for RAF; manufacture undertaken in Shorlac (Short Light Aircraft Company) facility at former Royal Naval Air Station Sydenham, Belfast.

Last refurbished Canberra PR. Mk 9 delivered to UK MoD December 1989; Shorts remains modification agency.

Two manufacturing centres, Newtownabbey and Dunmurry, cater for advanced composites programme; over 27.871 m² (300,000 sq ft) production floor area allocated to manufacture of components for Shorts aerostructure contracts with Boeing, Rolls-Royce, International Aero Engines and Fokker.

Internationally, Shorts collaborating as risk sharing partner with Fokker in Fokker 100 development and production, responsible for wings (39 sets produced 1990); it produces Boeing 747 main landing gear doors and Boeing 757 inboard trailing-edge flaps (respectively 851 and 368 by January 1991) and received £75 million follow-on order March 1990 for further components at higher delivery rate; also quality approved subcontractor to many major US and UK aerospace companies; conversely, Shorts 330/360 wing production undertaken jointly by CATIC (China) and Fokker.

Shorts began pod design/manufacture for Rolls-Royce jet engines 1967; currently podding RB211s for Boeing 747s, 757s and 767s (1,340 by January 1991, including over 600 524 nacelles and over 330 535E4 nacelles; pods for 757s since mid-1983 have utilised carbonfibre for outer skin barrel of nose cowl, offering 25 per cent weight saving compared with aluminium alloy; produces Textron Lycoming ALF 502 pods for BAe 146s, and designed/manufactured first flight test pod for PW2037 turbofan chosen for some 757s; also responsible for design, manufacture and production of nacelle components for RB211-524L Trent proposed for MD-11 and some versions of Boeing 767.

Shorts and Rohr Industries (USA) joined forces September 1984 to offer nacelle system for advanced International Aero Engines V2500 turbofan for 150-seat jetliners; team selected to produce V2500 pods for Airbus Industrie A320 January 1985 (assembly began 1987).

Company also develops and produces missiles and supersonic target drones, and manufactures Skeet target drone to UK MoD contract. Agreement with McDonnell Douglas Helicopters (USA) covers adaptation of Shorts Starstreak for airborne launch from Apaches; launch trials to start late 1991. Shorts also teamed with Boeing Aerospace & Electronics to market Starstreak to US armed forces; integration of Starstreak on Apache provides complementary missile to Stinger system; first successful two-stage firing of Starstreak from Apache announced September 1990.

Flying Services Division operates maintenance units and airfields for various civil and military organisations, and flies and maintains aircraft and target drones for UK MoD; subsidiary Short Brothers Air Services Ltd operates targets for MoD and overseas countries.

SHORTS 330

TYPE: Twin-turboprop transport.
PROGRAMME: Originally known as SD3-30; first flight of first prototype (G-BSBH) 22 August 1974; CAA certification to full Transport Category 18 February 1976; US FAR Pt 25 and Pt 36 approval 18 June 1976; subsequent approvals from Canadian Dept of Transport, German LBA and Australian Dept of Transport. First order (three), by Command Airways of Poughkeepsie, New York, 14 August 1974; deliveries began June 1976; first entered service, with Time Air, 24 August 1976.
VARIANTS: **330-200:** Standard passenger version, as detailed.
330-UTT: Military utility tactical transport version. Described separately.
Sherpa: Freighter version of 330, with ramp type full width rear loading door. Described separately.
CUSTOMERS: Orders and options for 330, 330-UTT and Sherpa totalled 179 by start of 1991; Sherpa used by US Air Force as **C-23A** and US Army National Guard as **C-23B** (described separately); US Army also leases six ex-airline 330s for operation in Kwajalein area of Pacific, four of which modified to military standards by Field Aircraft Services of Calgary, Alberta.
DESIGN FEATURES: Derived from smaller STOL Skyvan, retaining latter's proven characteristics, including large square-section unpressurised cabin with low floor level, braced high-mounted wings, twin tail unit, and safe-life concept and design philosophy for structural components; conforms with CAB Pt 298 (US); meets FAR Pt 36 noise requirements by substantial margin.

First 26 Shorts 330s powered by 875 kW (1,173 shp) PT6A-45As; next 40 given PT6A-45Bs; subsequent aircraft fitted with more powerful PT6A-45Rs and higher equipment standard; early aircraft had Goodrich pneumatic boot de-icing on wing and tail leading-edges.

NACA 63A series (modified) wing sections; thickness/chord ratio 18 per cent at root, 14 per cent on outer panels; dihedral 3° on outer panels.

Following description applies to standard 330-200 passenger version:
FLYING CONTROLS: Single-slotted ailerons with geared trim tabs; twin unshielded horn aerodynamic balance rudders; full span elevator, aerodynamically balanced by set-back hinges; geared trim tabs in elevator and starboard rudder (port rudder, trim only); single-slotted three-section flaps; fixed incidence tailplane.
STRUCTURE: All-metal safe-life construction; wing centre-section (integral with top of centre-fuselage) tapered on

leading- and trailing-edges, and is two-spar single-cell box with conventional skin and stringers; strut braced wing outer panels are reinforced Skyvan constant chord units, each with two-cell box and having smooth outer skin bonded to corrugated inner skin; fuselage in two main portions: nose portion (including flight deck, nosewheel bay and forward baggage compartment), centre (including main wing spar attachment frames and lower transverse beams carrying main landing gear and associated fairings), and rear portion (including aft baggage compartment and tail unit attachment frames); nose and rear fuselage of skin/stringer design, remainder smooth outer skin bonded to corrugated inner skin and stabilised by frames; two-spar twin-fin tail unit, with reinforced tailplane leading-edge.
LANDING GEAR: Menasco retractable tricycle type, with single wheel on each unit. Main units carried on short sponsons, into which the wheels retract hydraulically. Oleo-pneumatic shock absorbers. Nosewheel is steerable ±50°. Mainwheel tyre size 34 × 10.75-16; nosewheel tyre size 9-6. Normal tyre pressures: main units 5.45 bars (79 lb/sq in), nose unit 3.79 bars (55 lb/sq in).
POWER PLANT: Two 893 kW (1,198 shp) Pratt & Whitney Canada PT6A-45R turboprops, each driving a Hartzell five-blade constant-speed fully feathering metal low-speed propeller. Fuel tanks in wing centre-section/fuselage fairing; total usable capacity increased from original 2,182 litres (576 US gallons; 480 Imp gallons) to 2,546 litres (672.5 US gallons; 560 Imp gallons) in January 1985. Normal cross-feed provisions to allow for pump failure. Single pressure refuelling point in starboard landing gear fairing, backed by three gravity refuelling points in fuselage spine.
ACCOMMODATION: Crew of two on flight deck, plus cabin attendant. Dual controls standard. Standard seating for 30 passengers, in ten rows of three at 76 cm (30 in) pitch, with wide aisle. Seat rails fitted to facilitate changes in configuration. Galley, toilet and cabin attendant's seat at rear. Large overhead baggage lockers. Entire accommodation soundproofed and air-conditioned. Baggage compartments in nose and to rear of cabin, each with external access and capable of holding a combined total of 500 kg (1,100 lb) of baggage. Passenger door is at rear of cabin on port side. Passenger version has two emergency exits on the starboard side, two on the port side (including passenger door) and one in the flight deck roof. Mixed traffic version has full access to these emergency exits. For mixed passenger/freight operation a partition divides the cabin into a rear passenger area (typically for 18 persons) and a forward cargo compartment, the latter being loaded through a large port side door capable of admitting ATA 'D' type containers. In all-cargo configuration the cabin can

accommodate up to seven 'D' type containers, with ample space around them for additional freight. Cabin floor is flat throughout its length, and is designed to support loadings of 181 kg (400 lb) per foot run at 610.3 kg/m² (125 lb/sq ft). Locally reinforced areas of higher strength are also provided. Seat rails can be used as cargo lashing points. Freight loading is facilitated by the low level cabin floor.
SYSTEMS: Hamilton Standard air-conditioning system, using engine bleed air. Hydraulic system of 207 bars (3,000 lb/sq in), supplied by engine driven pumps, operates landing gear, nosewheel steering, flaps and brakes (at half pressure) and includes emergency accumulators. Air/oil reservoir pressurised to 1.72 bars (25 lb/sq in) at 20°C. Main electrical system, for general services, is 28V DC and is of the split busbar type with cross-coupling for essential services. Lucas 28V 250A DC starter/generator for engine starting and aircraft services, with separate 1.5kW 200V AC output for windscreen anti-icing and demisting. Special AC sources of 115V and 26V available at 400Hz for certain instruments, avionics and fuel booster pumps. Anti-icing standard for engine intake ducts, inlet lips and propellers. Optional de-icing of wing and tailplane leading-edges.
AVIONICS: Wide range of radio and navigation equipment available to customer's requirements. Typical standard avionics comprise duplicated VHF communications and navigation systems, two glideslope/marker beacon receivers, two ILS repeaters, two radio magnetic indicators, one ADF, one transponder, one DME, PA system and weather radar. Flight data recorder and voice recorder available as standard options.
EQUIPMENT: Passenger safety equipment standard.
DIMENSIONS, EXTERNAL:

Wing span	22.76 m (74 ft 8 in)
Wing chord (standard mean)	1.85 m (6 ft 0.7 in)
Length overall	17.69 m (58 ft 0½ in)
Width of fuselage	2.24 m (7 ft 4 in)
Height overall	4.95 m (16 ft 3 in)
Tailplane span	5.68 m (18 ft 7¾ in)
Wheel track	4.24 m (13 ft 10⅞ in)
Wheelbase	6.15 m (20 ft 2 in)
Propeller diameter	2.82 m (9 ft 3 in)
Propeller ground clearance	1.83 m (6 ft 0 in)
Cabin floor: Height above ground	0.94 m (3 ft 1 in)
Passenger door (port, rear):	
Height	1.57 m (5 ft 2 in)
Width	0.71 m (2 ft 4 in)
Height to sill	0.94 m (3 ft 1 in)
Cargo door (port, forward):	
Height	1.68 m (5 ft 6 in)
Width	1.42 m (4 ft 8 in)
Height to sill	0.94 m (3 ft 1 in)

Shorts C-23B Sherpa for the US Army National Guard

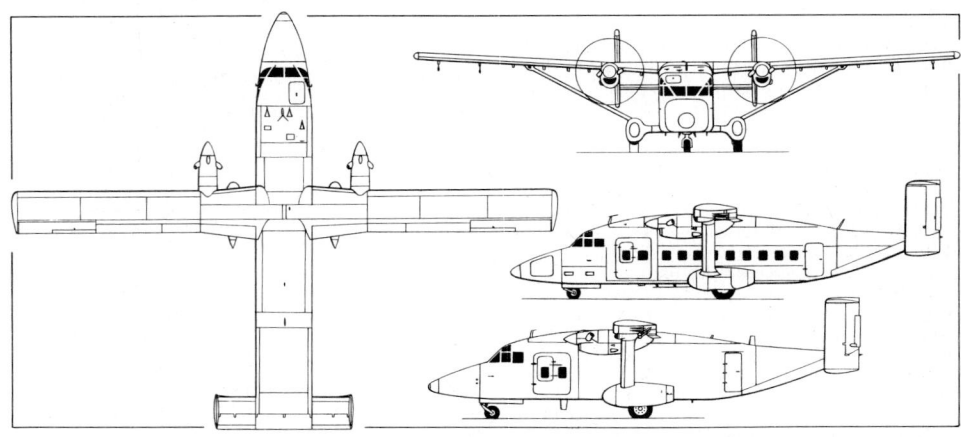

Shorts 330 twin-turboprop commuter and utility transport, with added side view (bottom) of C-23A Sherpa *(Pilot Press)*

DIMENSIONS, INTERNAL:

Cabin: Max length, incl toilet	9.47 m (31 ft 1 in)
Max width	1.93 m (6 ft 4 in)
Max height	1.93 m (6 ft 4 in)
Floor area	18.77 m² (202 sq ft)
Volume (all-cargo)	34.83 m³ (1,230 cu ft)
Baggage compartment volume:	
nose	1.27 m³ (45 cu ft)
rear of cabin	2.83 m³ (100 cu ft)
Cabin overhead lockers (total)	1.13 m³ (40 cu ft)

AREAS:

Wings, gross	42.1 m² (453.0 sq ft)
Ailerons (total, aft of hinges)	2.55 m² (27.5 sq ft)
Trailing-edge flaps (total)	7.74 m² (83.3 sq ft)
Fins (total)	8.65 m² (93.1 sq ft)
Rudders (total, aft of hinges)	2.24 m² (24.1 sq ft)
Tailplane (total)	7.77 m² (83.6 sq ft)
Elevator (total, aft of hinges)	2.55 m² (27.4 sq ft)

WEIGHTS AND LOADINGS:

Weight empty, equipped (incl crew of three):	
330-200 for 30 passengers	6,680 kg (14,727 lb)
Fuel	2,032 kg (4,480 lb)
Max payload for normal max T-O weight:	
30 passengers and baggage	2,653 kg (5,850 lb)
cargo	3,400 kg (7,500 lb)
Max T-O weight	10,387 kg (22,900 lb)
Max landing weight	10,251 kg (22,600 lb)
Max wing loading	246.8 kg /m² (50.55 lb/sq ft)
Max power loading	5.81 kg/kW (9.56 lb/shp)

PERFORMANCE (at max T-O weight, ISA at S/L, except where indicated):

Max cruising speed at 3,050 m (10,000 ft), AUW of 9,525 kg (21,000 lb)	190 knots (352 km/h; 218 mph)
Econ cruising speed at 3,050 m (10,000 ft), AUW of 9,525 kg (21,000 lb)	160 knots (296 km/h; 184 mph)
Stalling speed, flaps and landing gear up	90 knots (167 km/h; 104 mph) EAS
Stalling speed at max landing weight, flaps and landing gear down	73 knots (136 km/h; 85 mph) EAS
Max rate of climb at S/L	360 m (1,180 ft)/min
Service ceiling, one engine out, AUW of 9,072 kg (20,000 lb)	3,500 m (11,500 ft)
Min ground turning radius about nosewheel	7.77 m (25 ft 6 in)
T-O distance (FAR Pt 25 and BCAR Gp A):	
ISA	1,042 m (3,420 ft)
ISA + 15°C	1,295 m (4,250 ft)
Landing distance, AUW of 9,072 kg (20,000 lb):	
BCAR	1,143 m (3,750 ft)
FAR	1,030 m (3,380 ft)
Runway LCN at max T-O weight	10.7
Range with max passenger payload, cruising at 3,050 m (10,000 ft), no reserves	473 nm (876 km; 544 miles)
Range with max fuel, cruising at 3,050 m (10,000 ft), no reserves:	
passenger version, 1,966 kg (4,335 lb) payload	915 nm (1,695 km; 1,053 miles)
cargo version, 2,306 kg (5,085 lb) payload	758 nm (1,403 km; 872 miles)

OPERATIONAL NOISE LEVELS (FAR Pt 36):

T-O	88.9 EPNdB
Sideline	84.7 EPNdB
Approach	92.9 EPNdB

SHORTS 330-UTT

TYPE: Military utility tactical transport.

PROGRAMME: Military version of 330; production began 7 September 1982.

CUSTOMERS: Royal Thai Army received two and Royal Thai Border Police two 1984-85; latter now also operates one Army aircraft.

DESIGN FEATURES: Basic airframe and power plant of 330 unchanged; max payload increased to 3,630 kg (8,000 lb); max operational necessity T-O weight 11,158 kg (24,600 lb); strengthened cabin floor; reconfigured avionics panel.

ACCOMMODATION: Up to 33 troops, 30 paratroops plus jumpmaster (exit via inward opening rear door each side), or 15 stretchers plus four seated personnel.

PERFORMANCE:

Cruising speed at 3,050 m (10,000 ft), AUW of 9,979 kg (22,000 lb):	
high-speed cruise, max continuous power	201 knots (372 km/h; 231 mph)
long-range cruise	160 knots (296 km/h; 184 mph)
Max rate of climb at S/L at normal max T-O weight of 10,387 kg (22,900 lb):	
two engines	381 m (1,250 ft)/min
one engine	89 m (290 ft)/min
STOL T-O run at S/L, 15° flap	415 m (1,360 ft)
STOL T-O to 15 m (50 ft), 15° flap	644 m (2,110 ft)
STOL landing from 15 m (50 ft) at AUW of 9,525 kg (21,000 lb), flaps down, propeller reversal	488 m (1,600 ft)
STOL landing run, conditions as above	235 m (770 ft)
Range with 30 fully armed assault troops	600 nm (1,112 km; 691 miles)

SHORTS SHERPA

US Air Force designation: C-23A
US Army National Guard designation: C-23B

TYPE: Twin-turboprop freight/utility version of 330-200.

PROGRAMME: First flight of prototype 23 December 1982; first EDSA C-23A flown 6 August 1984; all 18 delivered by 6 December 1985; C-23A fleet based at Zweibrücken, Germany, for transporting high priority spares between over 20 peacetime USAF bases in Europe; initial contract included 10 years' logistic support and servicing; deliveries to ArNG began September 1990, first three to Missouri, Puerto Rico and Connecticut National Guard.

CUSTOMERS: Eighteen ordered by US Air Force March 1984, for 10th Military Airlift Squadron (MAC) in EDSA (European Distribution System Aircraft) role; US Department of Army ordered 10 C-23Bs October 1988 to replace DHC-4 Caribous with Army National Guard (mainly to carry Army aviation spares and components between ArNG bases and Aviation Classification Repair Activity Depots, but also suited to passenger, para-trooping and freight paradropping roles).

Civil-registered Sherpa delivered to Venezuelan government to support hydro-electric power development schemes (joined by 360-300 in 1988).

DESIGN FEATURES: Retains features of all-passenger 330-200, allowing utility passenger role; forward freight door and wide-body hold of 330-200 unchanged; power assisted full width rear cargo ramp/door for through loading (operated inside/outside aircraft, and lowered to variety of positions to simplify loading from range of ground equipment); forward baggage compartment of 330-200 retained; standard airline containers can be accommodated in main cabin, up to LD3 size, making aircraft particularly suited to short-haul cargo feeder services; loads can include two half-ton vehicles or bulky cargo; cabin also suitable for specialist role equipment; roller conveyor systems, including optional pallet locks picking up on aircraft's standard seat rails. No passenger cabin windows in C-23A.

ArNG aircraft embody strengthened wings, more powerful 1,061 kW (1,424 shp) PT6A-65AR turboprops and five-blade propellers of Shorts 360, plus uprated landing gear, more advanced flight deck instrumentation and air-openable rear freight doors for supply dropping; ramp upper section retracts inward and upward, while bottom section lowers to provide drop platform; max payload increased to 3,302 kg (7,280 lb).

Following details (except Avionics) apply to C-23B:

ACCOMMODATION: Crew of two on flight deck, plus optional jump seat facility. Dual controls standard. Aircraft air-conditioned throughout. Baggage compartment in nose with external access. Passenger door at rear of cabin on port side. Cargo door at front of cabin on port side. Power assisted full width rear loading ramp/door. In an all-cargo configuration the cabin can accommodate up to seven CO8 or four LD3 containers. Cabin floor is flat throughout its length and is designed to support 181 kg (400 lb) per foot run at 610.3 kg/m² (125 lb/sq ft). The locally reinforced centre cabin area is able to carry 272 kg (600 lb) per foot run at 732.4 kg/m² (150 lb/sq ft). A further 272 kg (600 lb) total load can be stowed on the ramp/door. Seat rails can be used as cargo lashing points. Freight loading is facilitated by the low level cabin floor. Alternative loads: seating capacity for 30 personnel in airline standard seats; 27 paratroops plus jumpmaster on side facing seats; 15 stretchers plus three attendants; two Land Rover/Jeep class vehicles; various aircraft engines and associated transport dollies.

AVIONICS: Avionics in the C-23As for the US Air Force include single UHF and HF radios, dual VHF-AM/FM, two flight directors, dual VOR/ILS, a Litton LTN-96 ring laser gyro inertial navigation system, Tacan and ADF, flight data recorder, cockpit voice recorder, IFF transponder, GPWS, radar altimeter, and a Collins RNS-300 colour weather radar with terrain mapping.

DIMENSIONS, EXTERNAL: As for 330-200 except:

Wing span	2.81 m (74 ft 10 in)
Height overall	5.00 m (16 ft 5 in)
Wheel track	4.26 m (14 ft 0 in)
Propeller ground clearance	1.82 m (5 ft 11½ in)
Main cabin door (port, rear):	
Height	1.59 m (5 ft 2½ in)
Width	0.69 m (2 ft 3 in)
Cargo door (port, forward):	
Height	1.66 m (5 ft 5½ in)
Width	1.41 m (4 ft 7½ in)
Rear ramp/door:	
opening inward, clear opening	1.56 m × 1.79 m (5 ft 1½in × 5 ft 10½ in)
opening outward, clear opening	1.92 m × 1.79 m (6 ft 3½ in × 5 ft 10½ in)

DIMENSIONS, INTERNAL:

Cabin: Max length	9.09 m (29 ft 10 in)
Width at side seat rails	1.89 m (6 ft 2½ in)
Height	1.97 m (6 ft 5½ in)
Floor area	17.18 m² (185.0 sq ft)
Volume	35.28 m³ (1,246 cu ft)
Baggage compartment volume (nose)	1.27 m³ (45 cu ft)

AREAS:

Ailerons (gross)	3.27 m² (35.2 sq ft)
Rudders (total)	2.86 m² (30.8 sq ft)
Elevator (total)	3.60 m² (38.8 sq ft)

WEIGHTS AND LOADINGS:

Operational weight empty (freight role)	7,276 kg (16,040 lb)
Max payload	3,302 kg (7,280 lb)
Max T-O weight	11,612 kg (25,600 lb)
Max landing weight	11,385 kg (25,100 lb)
Max wing loading	275.91 kg/m² (56.51 lb/sq ft)
Max power loading	6.50 kg/kW (10.68 lb/shp)

PERFORMANCE (at max T-O weight, ISA at S/L except where indicated):

Max cruising speed at 3,050 m (10,000 ft) and AUW of 9,980 kg (22,000 lb)	194 knots (359 km/h; 223 mph)
Normal cruising speed	180 knots (333 km/h; 207 mph)
Stalling speed, flaps and landing gear up	97 knots (179 km/h; 111 mph)
Stalling speed at max landing weight, flaps and landing gear down	78 knots (145 km/h; 90 mph)
Max rate of climb at S/L	445 m (1,460 ft)/min
Service ceiling, one engine out and AUW of 9,979 kg (20,000 lb)	3,660 m (12,000 ft)
T-O run at max T-O weight	564 m (1,850 ft)
T-O run to 15 m (50 ft)	802 m (2,630 ft)
Landing from 15 m (50 ft) at max landing weight	586 m (1,920 ft)
Landing run	345 m (1,130 ft)
Range: with max payload and no reserves	446 nm (827 km; 514 miles)
with 2,318 kg (5,110 lb) payload	1,031 nm (1,912 km; 1,188 miles)

SHORTS 360-300 and 360-300F

TYPE: Twin-turboprop commuter transport (300) and freighter (300F).

PROGRAMME: Details released 10 July 1980; first flight of prototype (G-ROOM) 1 June 1981 (PT6A-45 engines); PT6A-65Rs subsequently fitted; CAA certification 3 September 1982; FAA certification to FAR Pt 25 and Pt 36 early November 1982; first flight of production aircraft 19 August 1982; launch customer of 360-300F Rheinland Air Service of Dusseldorf, Germany (two delivered from March 1989).

VARIANTS: **360:** Initial production version with PT6A-65Rs.

360 Advanced: Production version from November 1985; 1,062 kW (1,424 shp) PT6A-65ARs.

360-300: Current production version; six-blade synchrophasing propellers; cambered wing lift struts; low-drag engine nacelle exhaust stubs; lightweight seats; PT6A-67R engines giving increased max cruising speed and improved weight/altitude/temperature limits, offering better hot and high performance, improved en route climb and allowing higher max T-O weight. Optional Category II autopilot; wet sink toilet facility; supplementary ground air-conditioning system; protective liners for freighting.

360-300F: Freighter adaptation of 360-300; up to 4,536 kg (10,000 lb) load; optional enlarged port forward cargo door enabling loading of five LD3-size containers; optional roller conveyor with pallet locks, directional

Shorts C-23A Sherpa in US Air Force service

transfer mat, side guidance rails, and forward cargo restraint barrier.

CUSTOMERS: 360 entered commercial service with Suburban Airlines of Pennsylvania 1 December 1982; first 360-300 to Philippine Airlines 18 March 1987; first 360-300 certificated for 39 passengers operated by Capital Airlines in UK from October 1987; by January 1991 over 160 Shorts 360s were in service worldwide.

DESIGN FEATURES: Stretched (0.91 m; 3 ft fuselage plug ahead of wings) development of 330, specifically for short haul airline operations over about 120 nm (222 km; 138 mile) average stage lengths; six extra passengers; strengthened outer wing panels and bracing struts; tapered rear fuselage with increased baggage capacity; drag-reducing single fin/rudder tail unit; more powerful, fuel efficient engines. 360-300F particularly suited to overnight parcel services.

FLYING CONTROLS: Single fin/rudder; constant chord tailplane; elevators and rudder with trim tabs.

STRUCTURE: Similar to 330-200 but lengthened fuselage, tapering for new all-metal two-spar tail unit; strengthened outer wing panels/struts; heavy duty floor panels for freighting.

LANDING GEAR: Similar to Shorts 330-200, but of Dowty design with Dunlop tyres. Mainwheel tyres size 37 × 11.75-16, pressure 5.38 bars (78 lb/sq in). Maxaret anti-skid units standard. Nosewheel steerable ± 55°.

POWER PLANT: Two 1,062 kW (1,424 shp) Pratt & Whitney Canada PT6A-67R turboprops, each driving a Hartzell advanced technology six-blade constant-speed fully feathering propeller. New engine nacelles with low-drag exhaust stubs on Series 300. Fuel capacity 2,182 litres (576 US gallons; 480 Imp gallons).

ACCOMMODATION: Crew of two on flight deck, plus cabin attendant. Dual controls standard. Main cabin accommodation similar to Shorts 330-200, but seating 36 passengers in 12 rows of three (optionally, 39 passengers). Standard ground and in-flight air-conditioning. Large overhead baggage lockers. Baggage compartments in nose and to rear of cabin, each with external access, giving equivalent of almost 0.17 m³ (6 cu ft) of baggage space per passenger (0.20 m³; 7.2 cu ft per passenger if locker space is included). Self-contained passenger stairs.

SYSTEMS: Generally as for Shorts 330-200 except for electrical system, which has Lear Siegler 28V 300A DC starter/generators and three 400VA single-phase static inverters for AC power. Full de-icing and anti-icing systems standard.

AVIONICS: From Collins Pro Line II range, including dual FDS-65 flight director systems, dual VHF-21A com, dual VIR-32 VHF nav, dual DME-42, dual TDR-90 transponders, dual RMI-36, ADF-60A, dual MCS-65 magnetic compasses, and WXR-220 colour weather radar, plus Sundstrand Mk II GPWS, Honeywell YG7500 radar altimeter, Fairchild A100A voice recorder and GEC-Plessey PV1584G data recorder. Options include Collins HF-230 HF com, APS-65 Cat II autopilot and second ADF.

DIMENSIONS, EXTERNAL: As for Shorts 330-200 except:

Wing span	22.80 m (74 ft 9½ in)
Length overall	21.58 m (70 ft 9⅝ in)
Height overall	7.27 m (23 ft 10¼ in)
Tailplane span	7.19 m (23 ft 7 in)
Wheelbase	7.06 m (23 ft 2 in)
Propeller diameter	2.74 m (9 ft 0 in)
Propeller ground clearance	1.78 m (5 ft 10 in)
Rear door sill height	0.98 m (3 ft 2¼ in)

DIMENSIONS, INTERNAL:

Cabin: Length	11.02 m (36 ft 2 in)
Max width	1.93 m (6 ft 4 in)
Max height	1.93 m (6 ft 4 in)
Passenger compartment volume	41.06 m³ (1,450 cu ft)

Baggage compartment volume:

forward	1.27 m³ (45 cu ft)
rear	4.81 m³ (170 cu ft)
lockers	1.47 m³ (52 cu ft)

AREAS: As for Shorts 330-200 except:

Wings, gross	42.18 m² (454.0 sq ft)
Vertical tail surfaces (total)	8.49 m² (91.4 sq ft)
Horizontal tail surfaces (total)	9.85 m² (106.0 sq ft)

WEIGHTS AND LOADINGS:

Typical operating weight empty	7,870 kg (17,350 lb)
Max payload:	
36 passengers and baggage	3,184 kg (7,020 lb)
cargo	3,765 kg (8,300 lb)
Max fuel load	1,741 kg (3,840 lb)
Max T-O weight	12,292 kg (27,100 lb)
Max ramp weight	12,337 kg (27,200 lb)
Max landing weight	12,020 kg (26,500 lb)
Max wing loading	291.4 kg/m² (59.7 lb/sq ft)
Max power loading	5.79 kg/kW (9.52 lb/shp)

PERFORMANCE (to FAR Pt 25: at max T-O weight except where indicated):

Cruising speed at 3,050 m (10,000 ft) and 11,340 kg (25,000 lb) aircraft weight	
	216 knots (400 km/h; 249 mph)
Max rate of climb at S/L: ISA	290 m (952 ft)/min
ISA +15°C	282 m (925 ft)/min
Service ceiling, one engine out	2,665 m (8,750 ft)
Min ground turning radius about nosewheel	
	8.21 m (26 ft 11 in)

Shorts 360-300 commuter transport

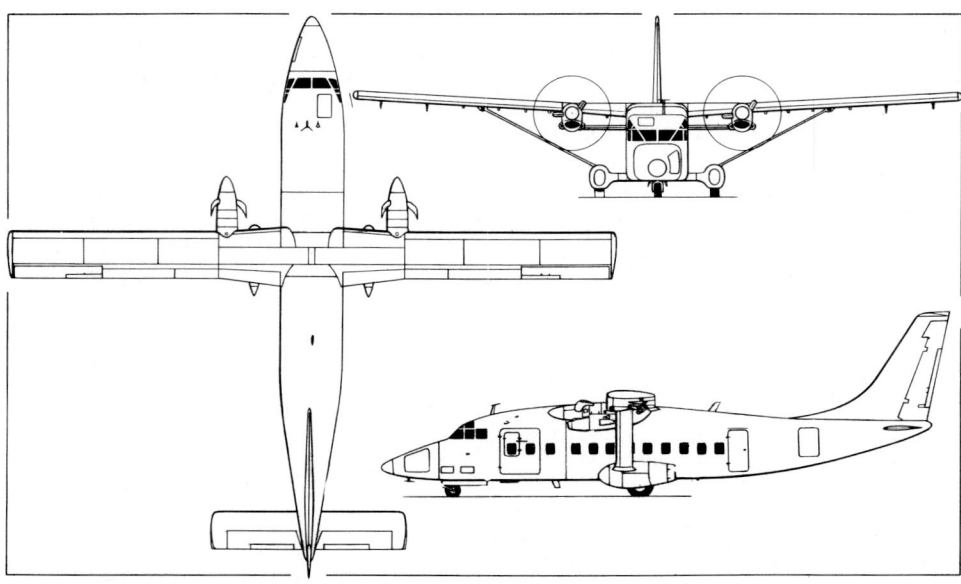

Shorts 360-300 commuter transport (two P&WC PT6A-67R turboprop engines) *(Pilot Press)*

Balanced T-O field length: ISA	1,305 m (4,280 ft)
ISA +15°C	1,402 m (4,600 ft)
Landing distance at max landing weight:	
ISA	1,220 m (4,000 ft)
Runway LCN	14.1

Range at 3,050 m (10,000 ft), cruising at 216 knots (400 km/h; 249 mph), 50 nm (93 km; 57 mile) diversion, 45 min hold, 54 kg (119 lb) fuel allowance, 36 passengers with baggage at 86 kg (190 lb) each

402 nm (745 km; 463 miles)

Range as above at 182 knots (337 km/h; 210 mph) with 31 passengers and baggage

636 nm (1,178 km; 732 miles)

SHORTS S312 TUCANO
RAF designation: Tucano T. Mk 1
TYPE: Basic trainer.

PROGRAMME: Co-operation agreement between Shorts and Embraer of Brazil to develop new version of EMB-312

Tucano (see Brazil), to meet or exceed all UK MoD Air Staff Target 412 requirements as Jet Provost replacement for RAF, announced May 1984; selected by UK Government 21 March 1985, partly because least expensive of competitors; first flight of EMB-312 with required Garrett engine (PP-ZTC) in Brazil 14 February 1986; airfreighted to UK after 14.35 flight test hours, reassembled as G-14-007 (later G-BTUC); first flight of G-14-007 in UK 11 April 1986; first flight of production T. Mk 1 (ZF135) 30 December 1986; formal rollout 20 January 1987; ZF135 delivered to Aeroplane & Armament Experimental Establishment, Boscombe Down, 26 June 1987 for provisional type certificate trials; ZF136 to Boscombe Down 1 October 1987; deliveries to Central Flying School, Scampton, began (with ZF138) 16 June 1988; flying by Tucano Course Design Team (CFS) started early August 1988; formal handover of first aircraft 1 September 1988; Shorts contracted January 1990 to modify first 50 completed aircraft with strengthened flying controls, revised communications/navigation

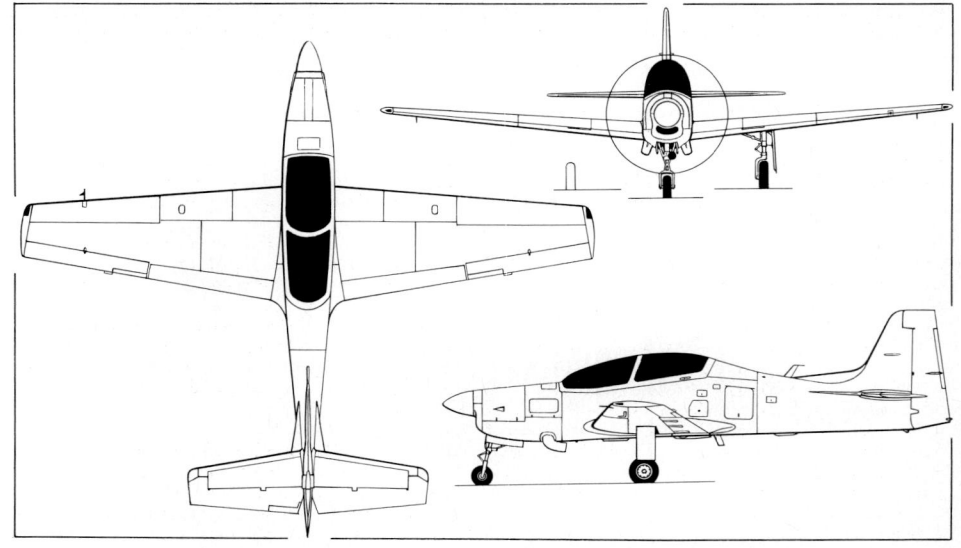

Shorts S312 Tucano basic trainer (Garrett TPE331-12B turboprop) *(Pilot Press)*

equipment and structural changes to extend fatigue life, as introduced on production line. Shorts also responsible for logistic supplies; Airwork has maintenance contract at Church Fenton and Field Aircraft at Cranwell; five GEC Ferranti simulators delivered to bases from 1990.

CUSTOMERS: Initially, 130 for RAF; student flying began at No. 7 FTS, Church Fenton, December 1989; first solo 11 January 1990; course completed 7 September 1990. Course Design Team disbanded November 1989 and CFS Tucano Squadron began working up to 15 aircraft; 30 aircraft to No. 3 FTS at RAF College, Cranwell, from December 1990 onwards; 39 to No. 1 FTS at Linton-on-Ouse 1991; final recipients, Refresher Flying Flight (Church Fenton) and navigator school, No. 6 FTS (Finningley); 50th RAF Tucano delivered 30 August 1990. RAF's baseline Tucano course 146 h 30 min for students with 30-60 hours previous piston-engine training; helicopter pilots receive 63½ Tucano hours; multi-engined aircraft pilots 140 hours. Exports to Kenya (12 armed **T. Mk 51s** for weapons training), ordered 1988 and first flown ('811', temporarily ZH203) 11 October 1989; delivered from 14 June 1990. Kuwait (16 **T. Mk 52s**) and support equipment, including simulator); first aircraft (temporarily ZH506) flown 21 September 1990.

Main description of Tucano under Embraer heading in Brazilian section. Shorts Tucano T. Mk 1 for RAF differs in following respects:

DESIGN FEATURES: Based on EMB-312, but only 25 per cent commonality. Modifications include TPE331-12B engine offering higher speed (particularly at low level) and increased rate of climb; ventral airbrake to control descent speed; structural strengthening for increased manoeuvre loads and fatigue life (12,000 hours); new cockpit layout; use of UK equipment; wing incidence 1° 13'; four wing strong-points for armament training/light attack (for exports).

FLYING CONTROLS: Strengthened; hydraulically actuated ventral airbrake.

STRUCTURE: 7075-T73511 and 7075-T76, and 2024-T3 sheet, aluminium alloy two-spar wing torsion box; strengthened wing leading-edges against bird strikes.

LANDING GEAR: Nosewheel unit supplied by Fairey Hydraulics. Dunlop wheels and tyres, size 22 × 6.75-10 on mainwheels, 5.00-5 on nosewheel. Dunlop hydraulic single-disc brakes on mainwheels.

POWER PLANT: One 820 kW (1,100 shp) Garrett TPE331-12B turboprop, driving a Hartzell four-blade constant-speed fully feathering reversible-pitch propeller. Additional 38 kW (51 ehp) derived from exhaust. Two integral fuel tanks in each wing, total capacity 694 litres (183.3 US gallons; 152.7 Imp gallons). Gravity refuelling point in each wing upper surface. Provision for two external tanks with total capacity of 640 litres (169 US gallons; 142 Imp

Shorts Tucano T. Mk 1 of the RAF's No. 7 Flying Training School *(Paul Jackson)*

gallons). Oil capacity 4.25 litres (1.13 US gallons; 0.94 Imp gallon).

ACCOMMODATION: Instructor and pupil in tandem, on Martin-Baker Mk 8LCP lightweight ejection seats under Lucas canopy. No pressurisation.

SYSTEMS: Cockpit air-conditioning by engine bleed air plus recirculated cockpit air through a regenerative turbofan system. Single hydraulic system, pressure 207 bars (3,000 lb/sq in), for landing gear extension and retraction, and airbrake. Accumulator to lower landing gear in emergency. DC electrical power provided by a 28V 200A starter/generator and two 24Ah alkaline batteries. Static inverter for 115V and 26V AC power at 400Hz. Normalair-Garrett oxygen system supplied from a single bottle, capacity 2,250 litres (80 cu ft). Emergency oxygen bottle, capacity 70 litres (2.5 cu ft), mounted on each ejection seat. Engine air intake de-iced by engine bleed air; propeller, pitot head, static vents, and stall warning system de-iced electrically.

AVIONICS: Standard avionics include VHF/UHF/audio by GEC-Marconi, GEC-Plessey and Dowty; gyromagnetic compass, VOR/ILS/marker beacon receiver, GEC Sensors AD2780 Tacan, and Narco transponder.

ARMAMENT: Optional provision on export variants for up to 1,000 kg (2,205 lb) of weapons distributed on four underwing pylons fitted with ML Aviation ejector release units. Details as for Embraer Tucano. Equipment specified for Kenya includes FN Herstal rocket pods and Forges de Zeebrugge 12.7 mm gun pods; and an ML Aviation stores management system, including Avimo weapon sights, Base Ten weapon control electronics and other equipment from Dowty and Guardian Electronics.

DIMENSIONS, EXTERNAL:

Wing span   11.28 m (37 ft 0 in)

Propeller diameter	2.39 m (7 ft 10 in)
Propeller ground clearance	0.32 m (12.6 in)

AREAS:

Wings, gross	19.33 m² (208.08 sq ft)
Fin, excl dorsal fin	2.08 m² (22.40 sq ft)
Rudder, incl tab	1.46 m² (15.70 sq ft)
Tailplane, incl fillets	4.57 m² (49.20 sq ft)

WEIGHTS AND LOADINGS (A: aerobatic configuration, B: full weapons configuration):

Basic weight empty: A	2,138 kg (4,713 lb)
Max internal fuel: A, B	545 kg (1,202 lb)
Max ramp weight: A	2,790 kg (6,151 lb)
B	3,610 kg (7,959 lb)
Max T-O weight: A	2,770 kg (6,107 lb)
B	3,600 kg (7,937 lb)
Max landing weight: A	2,770 kg (6,107 lb)
B	3,600 kg (7,937 lb)
Max zero-fuel weight: A	2,318 kg (5,110 lb)
Max wing loading: A	139.7 kg/m² (28.61 lb/sq ft)
B	186.2 kg/m² (38.14 lb/sq ft)
Max power loading: A	3.29 kg/kW (5.41 lb/shp)
B	4.39 kg/kW (7.21 lb/shp)

PERFORMANCE (at T-O weight of 2,700 kg; 5,952 lb, except where indicated):

Max operating speed
280 knots (518 km/h; 322 mph) EAS
Max level and max cruising speed at 3,050-4,575 m (10,000-15,000 ft) at 2,600 kg (5,732 lb)
274 knots (507 km/h; 315 mph)
Normal cruising speed (RAF)
240 knots (448 km/h; 276 mph)
Econ cruising speed at 6,100 m (20,000 ft)
211 knots (391 km/h; 243 mph)
Stalling speed, power off:
flaps and landing gear up
77 knots (143 km/h; 89 mph) EAS
flaps and landing gear down
70 knots (130 km/h; 81 mph) EAS
Max rate of climb at S/L   1,070 m (3,510 ft)/min
Service ceiling: theoretical   10,365 m (34,000 ft)
practical   7,620 m (25,000 ft)
T-O run   308 m (1,010 ft)
T-O to 15 m (50 ft)   533 m (1,750 ft)
Landing from 15 m (50 ft) at 2,600 kg (5,732 lb)
585 m (1,920 ft)
Landing run   314 m (1,030 ft)
Radius of action with 454 kg (1,000 lb) of weapons at T-O weight of 3,320 kg (7,319 lb) with 5 min over target
390 nm (722 km; 449 miles)
Range at 7,620 m (25,000 ft) with max fuel, 30 min reserves:
internal fuel only   990 nm (1,835 km; 1,140 miles)
with external fuel   1,790 nm (3,317 km; 2,061 miles)
Endurance at econ cruising speed at 7,620 m (25,000 ft), 30 min reserves   5 h 12 min
g limits: +7/-3.6 aerobatic
+4.4/-2.2 full weapons

Shorts Tucano T. Mk 51 delivered to Kenya for light attack duties *(Chris Webber/Flying Eye)*

SLINGSBY
SLINGSBY AVIATION LIMITED

Ings Lane, Kirkbymoorside, North Yorkshire YO6 6EZ
Telephone: 44 (751) 32474
Fax: 44 (751) 31173
Telex: 57597 SLINAV G

MANAGING DIRECTOR:
James S. Tucker, BSc (Eng), CEng, MRAeS
CHIEF DESIGNER: B. Mellers
MARKETING DIRECTOR, AIRCRAFT: John C. Dignan
PRODUCT SUPPORT MANAGER: Roger C. Bull, BSc (Eng)

Subsidiary of Aerospace Division of ML Holdings plc, specialising in application of modern composite materials; formerly manufacturer of sailplanes but now concentrating on development and production of T67 Firefly series; also major participant in Chichester-Miles Leopard business jet project (which see); approx 11,148 m² (120,000 sq ft) works area and 240 workforce early 1991.

Other activities include design and manufacture of hovercraft, large wind turbines and various marine structures and components; maintenance of type certif-

icates, and product support, for former Airship Industries Skyship 500 and 600; design and manufacture of major components for Westinghouse Sentinel 5000 airship for US Navy (which see) as main subcontractor; design and development of carbonfibre components for Bell/Boeing V-22 Osprey and metal assemblies for Boeing 747; design, development and production of ventral fairing/baggage bay of BAe Jetstream 41.

UK MoD work includes technical support and repair and maintenance facilities for RAF Air Cadet gliders/motor gliders, including full-scale dynamic fatigue test of Grob Viking, and re-covering and painting RAF/RN/Army Air Corps Chipmunks.

SLINGSBY T67 FIREFLY

TYPE: Two-seat aerobatic, training and sporting aircraft.
PROGRAMME: Current composites constructed Firefly developed from wooden Slingsby T67A (licence built version of French Fournier RF6B - see 1982-83 *Jane's*); T67B gained CAA certification 18 September 1984; T67C was CAA certificated 15 December 1987.

VARIANTS: **T67B**: Basic version; 86.5 kW (116 hp) Textron Lycoming O-235-N2A engine and two-blade fixed-pitch propeller.

T67C: Similar to T67B, but 119 kW (160 hp) AEIO-320-D1B engine, metal fixed-pitch propeller, 24V 70A engine driven alternator and 24V 15Ah battery. Subvariants **T67C1** with normal fuselage fuel tank and one-piece canopy; **T67C2** with fuselage tank and two-piece canopy; **T67C3** with wing fuel tanks and two-piece canopy.

T67M: Military variants; described separately.

CUSTOMERS: Over 90 civil/military T67s delivered to customers in 10 countries by January 1991. Nine T67C3 purchased by Netherlands Government Civil Aviation Flying School for KLM and Royal Netherlands Navy pilot training.

Following details apply to T67C:

DESIGN FEATURES: Wing section NACA 23015 at root, 23013 at tip; dihedral 3° 30'; incidence 3°.

FLYING CONTROLS: Manually operated mass balanced Frise-type ailerons, without tabs; mass balanced elevators with manually operated port trim tab; rudder; trailing-edge fixed hinge flaps; spin strakes forward of tailplane roots.

STRUCTURE: GFRP; single-spar wings with double skin (corrugated inner skin bonded to plain outer skin) and conventional ribs in heavy load positions; conventional frame and top-hat stringer fuselage; stainless steel firewall between cockpit and engine; fixed incidence tailplane of similar construction to wings (built-in VOR antenna); fin incorporates VHF antenna.

LANDING GEAR: Non-retractable tricycle type. Oleo-pneumatic shock absorber in each unit. Steerable nosewheel. Mainwheel tyres size 6.00-6, pressure 1.4 bars (20 lb/sq in). Nosewheel tyre size 5.00-5, pressure 2.5 bars (37 lb/sq in). Hydraulic disc brakes. Parking brake. GFRP mainwheel fairings optional.

POWER PLANT: One flat-four engine as described under Variants. Fuselage fuel tank, immediately aft of firewall, in T67C1 and T67C2, capacity 114 litres (30 US gallons; 25 Imp gallons). Refuelling point on fuselage upper surface, forward of windscreen. T67C3: wing fuel tanks as T67M. Oil capacity 4 litres (1.06 US gallons; 0.88 Imp gallon). Oil system permits short periods of inverted flight.

ACCOMMODATION: Two seats side by side, originally (T67C1) under one-piece transparent canopy, which swings upward and rearward for access to cockpit. T67C2/C3 have fixed windscreen, and rearward hinged upward opening rear section. Dual controls standard. Adjustable rudder pedals. Cockpit heated and ventilated. Baggage space aft of seats.

SYSTEMS: Hydraulic system for brakes only. Vacuum system for blind-flying instrumentation. Electrical power supplied by 24V engine driven alternator and 24V 15Ah battery (12V system in T67B).

AVIONICS: Standard avionics include artificial horizon and directional gyro, with vacuum system and vacuum gauge, electric turn co-ordinator, rate of climb indicator, recording tachometer, stall warning system, clock, outside air temperature gauge, accelerometer. Optional avionics, available to customer requirements, include equipment by Becker, Bendix/King and Narco, up to full IFR standard.

EQUIPMENT: Includes tiedown rings and towbar; cabin fire extinguisher, crash axe, heated pitot; instrument, landing, navigation and strobe lights. Optional equipment includes T67M-type blue tinted canopy, external power socket (not on T67B), and wingtip mounted smoke system (not T67B).

DIMENSIONS, EXTERNAL:

Wing span	10.59 m (34 ft 9 in)
Wing chord: at root	1.53 m (5 ft 0¼ in)
at tip	0.83 m (2 ft 8¾ in)
Wing aspect ratio	8.9
Length overall	7.32 m (24 ft 0¼ in)
Height overall	2.36 m (7 ft 9 in)
Tailplane span	3.40 m (11 ft 1¾ in)
Wheel track	2.44 m (8 ft 0 in)
Wheelbase	1.50 m (4 ft 11 in)
Propeller diameter	1.88 m (6 ft 2 in)

DIMENSIONS, INTERNAL:

Cockpit: Length	2.05 m (6 ft 8¾ in)
Max width	1.08 m (3 ft 6½ in)
Max height	1.08 m (3 ft 6½ in)

AREAS:

Wings, gross	12.63 m² (136.0 sq ft)
Ailerons (total)	1.24 m² (13.35 sq ft)
Trailing-edge flaps (total)	1.74 m² (18.73 sq ft)
Fin	0.80 m² (8.61 sq ft)
Rudder	0.82 m² (8.8 sq ft)
Tailplane	1.65 m² (17.76 sq ft)
Elevators (incl tab)	0.99 m² (10.66 sq ft)

WEIGHTS AND LOADINGS:

Weight empty (basic): T67B	610 kg (1,345 lb)
T67C2	649 kg (1,430 lb)
T67C3	658 kg (1,450 lb)
Max fuel: T67B, T67C1/C2	82 kg (181 lb)
T67C3	114 kg (252 lb)
Max baggage: T67B	18 kg (40 lb)
T67C	30 kg (66 lb)
Max T-O, landing and aerobatic weights:	
T67B	862 kg (1,900 lb)
T67C2	907 kg (2,000 lb)
T67C3	952 kg (2,100 lb)
Max wing loading: T67B	68.21 kg/m² (13.97 lb/sq ft)
T67C2	71.82 kg/m² (14.71 lb/sq ft)
T67C3	75.38 kg/m² (15.44 lb/sq ft)
Max power loading: T67B	9.97 kg/kW (16.38 lb/hp)
T67C2	7.62 kg/kW (12.50 lb/hp)
T67C3	8.00 kg/kW (13.13 lb/hp)

PERFORMANCE (at max T-O weight):

Never-exceed speed (VNE):	
T67B	165 knots (305 km/h; 190 mph)
T67C	180 knots (333 km/h; 207 mph)
Max level speed at S/L:	
T67B	115 knots (213 km/h; 132 mph)
T67C	133 knots (246 km/h; 153 mph)
Max cruising speed (75% power) at 2,440 m (8,000 ft):	
T67B	110 knots (204 km/h; 126 mph)
T67C	125 knots (231 km/h; 144 mph)
Stalling speed, power off, flaps up:	
T67B	55 knots (102 km/h; 64 mph)
T67C2	52 knots (97 km/h; 60 mph)
T67C3	53 knots (99 km/h; 61 mph)
Stalling speed, power off, flaps down:	
T67B	46 knots (85 km/h; 53 mph)
T67C	49 knots (91 km/h; 57 mph)
Max rate of climb at S/L: T67B	201 m (660 ft)/min
T67C2	287 m (940 ft)/min
Service ceiling: T67B	3,660 m (12,000 ft)
T-O run: T67B	223 m (733 ft)
T67C2	201 m (660 ft)
T-O to 15 m (50 ft): T67B	537 m (1,760 ft)
T67C2	442 m (1,450 ft)
Landing from 15 m (50 ft): T67B	521 m (1,710 ft)
T67C2	533 m (1,750 ft)
Landing run: T67B	213 m (700 ft)
T67C2	232 m (760 ft)
Range with max fuel (65% power at 2,440 m; 8,000 ft), allowances for T-O and climb, 45 min reserves at 45% power: T67B	451 nm (835 km; 519 miles)
T67C2	360 nm (666 km; 414 miles)
T67C3	565 nm (1,046 km; 650 miles)
Endurance at 65% power: T67B	4 h 20 min
T67C2	3 h 30 min
T67C3	4 h 50 min
g limits	+6/−3

SLINGSBY T67M Mk II FIREFLY

TYPE: Two-seat military basic trainer.

PROGRAMME: To speed T67M programme, T67A G-BJNG modified to Firefly 160 standard (119 kW; 160 hp engine and constant speed propeller) for tests including spinning trials at extreme CG limits; first flight of T67M Firefly 160 (G-BKAM) 5 December 1982; CAA certification 20 September 1983; designation changed to T67M Mk II as two-piece canopy introduced.

CUSTOMERS: Recent deliveries include five to Trent Air Services, Cranfield, and two to Japanese airline training academy.

DESIGN FEATURES: T67M based on T67B, except as detailed.

STRUCTURE: Generally as T67B.

LANDING GEAR: Generally as T67B.

POWER PLANT: One 119 kW (160 hp) Textron Lycoming AEIO-320-D1B flat-four engine, driving a Hoffmann HO-V72 two-blade constant-speed composite propeller. Fuel and oil systems suitable for inverted flight. Fuel tanks in leading-edge of wings, capacity 159 litres (42 US gallons; 35 Imp gallons). Refuelling point in upper wing surface. Oil capacity 7.7 litres (2.0 US gallons; 1.7 Imp gallons).

ACCOMMODATION: As for T67B, except that current aircraft have blue tinted canopy with fixed windscreen and upward hinged, rearward opening rear section. Inertia

Slingsby T67C3 Fireflies of Netherlands Government Civil Aviation Flying School *(John Dignan)*

reel lockable shoulder harness standard, air-conditioning optional.

AVIONICS: Avionics to customer requirements. Blind-flying instrumentation standard.

DIMENSIONS, EXTERNAL: As for T67B

AREAS: As for T67B

WEIGHTS AND LOADINGS:

Weight empty, equipped	658 kg (1,450 lb)
Max fuel weight	114 kg (252 lb)
Max T-O, aerobatic and landing weight	952 kg (2,100 lb)
Max wing loading	75.38 kg/m² (15.44 lb/sq ft)
Max power loading	8.00 kg/kW (13.12 lb/hp)

PERFORMANCE (at max T-O weight):

Never-exceed speed (VNE)	180 knots (333 km/h; 207 mph)
Max level speed at S/L	136 knots (252 km/h; 157 mph)
Max cruising speed, 75% power at 2,440 m (8,000 ft)	127 knots (235 km/h; 146 mph)
Stalling speed, power off, flaps down	49 knots (91 km/h; 57 mph)
Max rate of climb at S/L	335 m (1,100 ft)/min
Service ceiling	4,575 m (15,000 ft)
T-O run	190 m (623 ft)
T-O to 15 m (50 ft)	402 m (1,319 ft)
Landing from 15 m (50 ft)	533 m (1,750 ft)
Landing run	232 m (760 ft)
Range with max fuel at 75% power, at 2,440 m (8,000 ft), allowances for T-O, climb and 45 min reserves at 45% power	529 nm (980 km; 608 miles)
Range with max fuel at 65% power, at 2,440 m (8,000 ft), allowances as above	565 nm (1,047 km; 650 miles)
Endurance at 75% power	4 h 20 min
at 65% power	5 h 5 min
g limits at 884 kg (1,950 lb) AUW	+6/−3

SLINGSBY T67M200 FIREFLY

TYPE: Two-seat military basic trainer.

PROGRAMME: First flight 16 May 1985; CAA certification 13 October 1985; representative airframe underwent long term fatigue test to simulate 75,000 flying hours.

CUSTOMERS: 29 used in five countries by January 1991; first customer Turkish Aviation Institute, Ankara (16 delivered from 1985); Dutch operator King Air (three T67M200s, plus one T67M Mk II) as screening trainers for prospective RNethAF pilots; Royal Hong Kong Auxiliary Air Force (four); Norwegian Government's Flying Academy (six).

DESIGN FEATURES: Development of T67M; 149 kW (200 hp) Textron Lycoming AEIO-360-A1E engine; Hoffman HO-V123 three-blade variable-pitch composite propeller; fuel/oil systems for inverted flight.

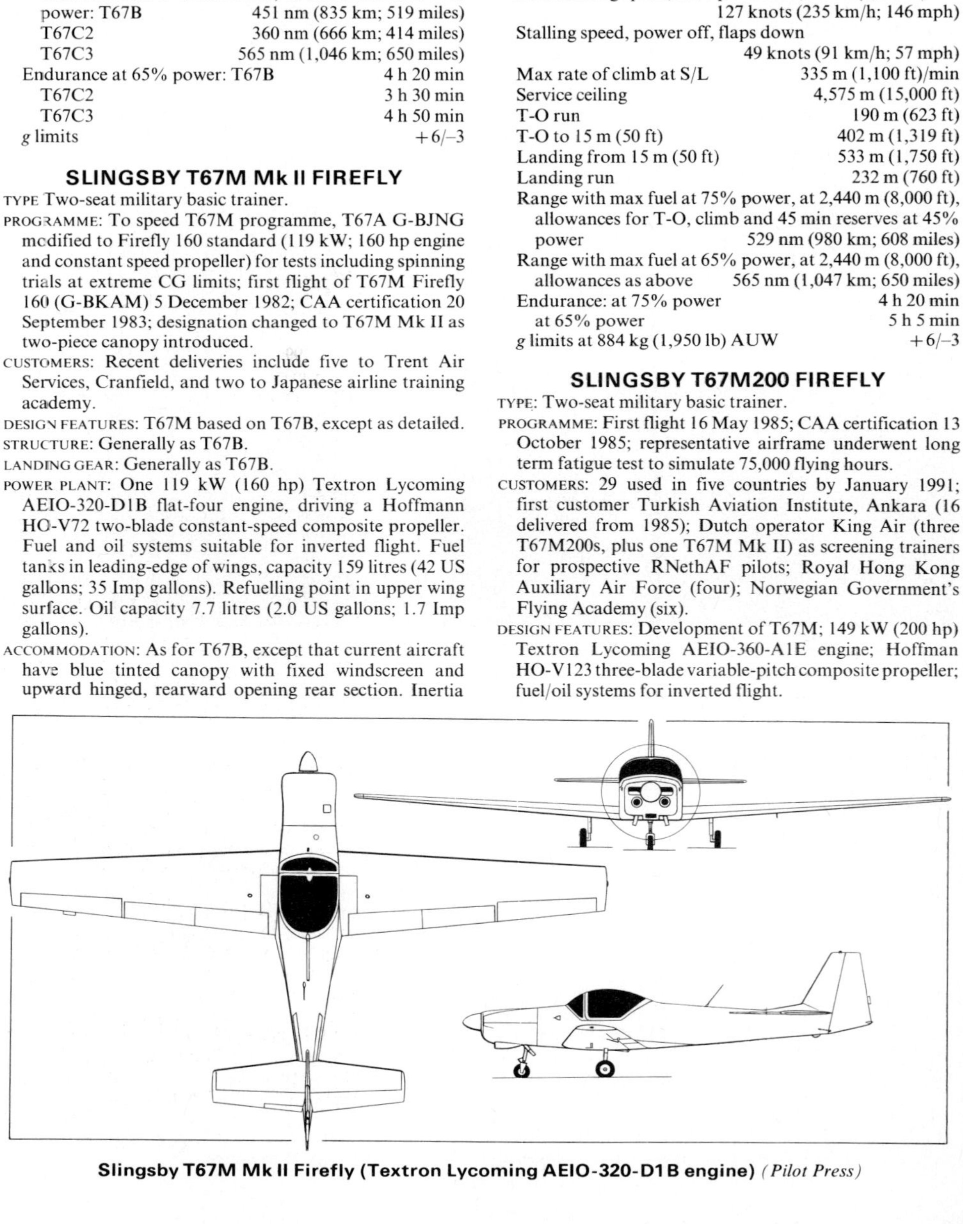

Slingsby T67M Mk II Firefly (Textron Lycoming AEIO-320-D1B engine) *(Pilot Press)*

DIMENSIONS, EXTERNAL: As for T67B/M except:
Propeller diameter   1.80 m (5 ft 11 in)
WEIGHTS AND LOADINGS:
Weight empty   698 kg (1,540 lb)
Max fuel   114 kg (252 lb)
Max baggage   30 kg (66 lb)
Max T-O weight: Utility   1,020 kg (2,250 lb)
                Aerobatic   975 kg (2,150 lb)
Max landing weight   975 kg (2,150 lb)
Max wing loading   80.75 kg/m² (16.54 lb/sq ft)
Max power loading   6.85 kg/kW (11.25 lb/hp)

PERFORMANCE:
Never-exceed speed (V_{NE})
                          180 knots (333 km/h; 207 mph)
Max level speed at S/L   140 knots (259 km/h; 161 mph)
Max cruising speed (75% power, at 2,440 m; 8,000 ft)
                          130 knots (241 km/h; 150 mph)
Stalling speed, power off, flaps down
                          51 knots (95 km/h; 59 mph)
Max rate of climb at S/L   350 m (1,150 ft)/min
T-O run   221 m (725 ft)
T-O to 15 m (50 ft)   409 m (1,340 ft)

Landing from 15 m (50 ft)   564 m (1,850 ft)
Landing run   265 m (870 ft)
Range with max fuel (75% power at 2,440 m; 8,000 ft),
  allowances for T-O and climb, 45 min reserves at 45%
  power   480 nm (889 km; 552 miles)
Range with max fuel (65% power at 2,440 m; 8,000 ft),
  allowances as above   500 nm (926 km; 575 miles)
Endurance: at 75% power   3 h 45 min
  at 65% power   4 h 10 min
g limits   +6/-3

WALLIS
WALLIS AUTOGYROS LTD
Reymerston Hall, Norfolk NR9 4QY
Telephone: 44 (362) 850418
MANAGING DIRECTOR: Wg Cdr K. H. Wallis, CEng, FRAeS,
FRSA, RAF (Retd)

First Wallis single-seat ultralight autogyro introduced
patented features, including rotor head with offset gimbal
system providing hands and feet off stability and eliminating
pitch-up and tuck-under hazards; a high speed flexible rotor
spin-up shaft with positive disengagement during flight; an
automatic rotor drive control on take-off allowing applied
power until last moment; centrifugal stops to control rotor
blade teetering; novel safe starting arrangement.

Many other Wallis autogyros since completed for
company operation; two WA-116s and WA-117 evaluated
by RARDE, Christchurch, in airfield battle damage
reconnaissance role.

Wallis WA-116/F/S
which holds Class E3
and E3a speed
records, showing
fixed foreplane
surfaces

WALLIS WA-116 and WA-116-T
TYPE: Single- and two-seat (WA-116-T) autogyros.
PROGRAMME: WA-116 original Wallis design; first flight of
prototype (G-ARRT) 2 August 1961; four built by Beagle
and five by Wg Cdr Wallis (see 1973-74 *Jane's*).
VARIANTS: **WA-116/Mc:** G-ARRT re-engined with 67 kW
(90 hp) McCulloch, plus G-ARZB; used for displays and
filming.
WA-116/F: Appeared 1971 (re-engined G-ASDY);
currently 44.5 kW (60 hp) Franklin 2A-120-B, driving
specially designed two-blade propeller; has performed
specialised aerial photographic work (see earlier *Jane's*
editions); G-ATHM holds nine world rotorcraft records
(see 1989-90 *Jane's*).
WA-116/F/S: G-BLIK 'Special' version of WA-116/
F; refinements, including small fixed foreplanes, holds
several world records (see 1989-90 *Jane's*), including first
ever for autogyros over 1,000 km closed circuit.
WA-116-T/Mc: Last WA-116 rebuilt as tandem
two-seater (G-AXAS); first flight 3 April 1969; recently
used for work utilising slow flight and STOL, and for
electrostatically charged spraying tests.
WEIGHTS AND LOADINGS (WA-116/F):
Weight empty   143 kg (316 lb)
Max T-O weight   317.5 kg (700 lb)
WA-116/F/S with long-range tank   331 kg (730 lb)
PERFORMANCE (WA-116/F):
Max level speed   not fully explored
Cruising speed without long-range tank
                          87 knots (161 km/h; 100 mph)
Max rate of climb at S/L   305 m (1,000 ft)/min
Max range with long-range tank (WA-116/F/S,
  estimated)   701 nm (1,300 km; 808 miles)

WALLIS WA-116/X
TYPE: Single-seat autogyro.
PROGRAMME: Development began for reconnaissance role
1985; emphasis on day and night all-weather capability,
and very low vibration levels; programme includes
current, modified and new technology engine tests;
WA-116 G-AVDG modified for flight tests, plus new
WA-116/X (G-BMJX, suffix X indicating unknown
quantity pending engine selection - Norton being
considered); expected to lead to next generation of Wallis
autogyros, with emphasis on easy adaptation to new
technology engines as available.
DESIGN FEATURES: Testing current, modified and new
technology engines (see Power Plant); future aircraft
equipped for night flying and sensor carrying, making
them adaptable for military, police and similar roles.
POWER PLANT: Current engines tested include special version
of 59.6 kW (80 hp) Limbach L 2000, 37 kW (50 hp) Fuji
440 cc two-cylinder aircooled two-stroke, and 47.7 kW
(64 hp) Rotax 520 Bombardier two-cylinder liquid-cooled
two-stroke; modified engines include Rootes Imp and
two-cylinder engine made from Rolls-Royce Continental
O-240 components; new technology engines include
special version of Norton Motors P62 twin-rotor Wankel
type and supercharged or turbocharged 1,360 cc
automobile engine. Radiator for Rotax and Norton
engines in cockpit nacelle nose, providing some cockpit
heating.

WALLIS WA-117/R-R
TYPE: Single-seat autogyro.
PROGRAMME: Details of WA-117 (Rolls-Royce Continental
O-200-B engine) appeared in 1986-87 *Jane's*; used to
demonstrate all-weather day and night military airfield
damage reconnaissance role 1987 under UK MoD
contracts.
DESIGN FEATURES: Equipped with BAe miniature infra-red
linescan and real-time ground link, and 70 mm camera.

WALLIS WA-120/R-R
WA-120 (G-AYVO); see 1987-88 *Jane's*.

WALLIS WA-121
TYPE: Single-seat experimental autogyro.
PROGRAMME: First flight of WA-121/Mc (G-BAHH) 28
December 1972; set Class E3 and E3a height records of
5,643.7 m (18,516 ft) at Boscombe Down 20 July 1982;
undertaking experimental flying using rotor blades
designed for high speeds, and to improve height record.
On 6 December 1990 set class time-to-height record of
8 min 8 s to 3,000 m (9,845 ft).
VARIANTS: **WA-121/Mc:** G-BAHH; about 74 kW (100 hp)
Wallis-McCulloch engine.
WA-121/F: Projected version; not yet built; 44.5 kW
(60 hp) Franklin 2A-120-B.
WA-121/M Meteorite 2: Supercharged 89 kW
(120 hp) Meteor Alfa 1 radial two-stroke engine;
transistorised ignition; not yet built.
DESIGN FEATURES: Smallest and lightest Wallis autogyro;

special rotor blades for high speed; WA-117 type rotor
head suspension features; high-mounted tailplane; open
cockpit; improved control system, giving greater stability
at speed, better head resistance and improved pilot
comfort; oxygen system and wide track main landing gear
now as for other Wallis autogyros.

WALLIS WA-122/R-R
TYPE: Two-seat training/single-seat long-range surveillance
autogyro.
PROGRAMME: First flight (G-BGGW) 16 July 1980; modified
into single-seater with camera for experimental long-
range surveillance 1988. Further details 1987-88 *Jane's*.
DESIGN FEATURES: Development of similar WA-116-T;
Rolls-Royce Continental engine; rear seat replaced by
F52 camera with 900 mm (35.4 in) lens, mounted in
shallow oblique position.

WALLIS WA-201
TYPE: Single-seat, twin-engined research autogyro.
PROGRAMME: Built as research vehicle (G-BNDG) for
twin-engined light autogyro; testing continued 1990.
DESIGN FEATURES: Two 47.7 kW (64 hp) Rotax 532
Bombardier geared two-cylinder liquid-cooled two-
stroke engines, mounted separately in tandem; counter-
rotating pusher and tractor propellers (front and rear
engines respectively) with no offset thrust; single-engine
power sufficient for take-off and flight; engines give
exceptional lift-to-empty-weight ratio and rate of climb.

Wallis WA-201 twin-engined research autogyro

WESTLAND
WESTLAND GROUP PLC

Yeovil, Somerset BA20 2YB
Telephone: 44 (935) 75222
Fax: 44 (935) 702131
Telex: 46277 WHL YEO G
LONDON OFFICE: 4 Carlton Gardens, Pall Mall, SW1
Telephone: 44 (71) 839 4061
CHAIRMAN: Sir Leslie Fletcher, DSC, FCA
DEPUTY CHAIRMAN: Alec Daly
CHIEF EXECUTIVE: Alan Jones, FEng, FIProdE, MA
PUBLIC RELATIONS DIRECTOR: Chris Loney

Westland Aircraft Ltd (now Westland Group plc) formed July 1935, taking over aircraft branch of Petters Ltd (known previously as Westland Aircraft Works) that had designed/built aircraft since 1915; entered helicopter industry having acquired licence to build US Sikorsky

S-51 as Dragonfly 1947; developed own Widgeon from Dragonfly; technical association with Sikorsky Division of United Technologies continued after decision to concentrate on helicopter design, development and construction.

Acquisition of Saunders-Roe Ltd 1959, Helicopter Division of Bristol Aircraft Ltd and Fairey Aviation Ltd 1960, and British Hovercraft Corporation's Aerospace Division 1983, plus subsequent restructuring into Divisions, detailed in 1989-90 *Jane's*; Divisions later consolidated into current limited liability companies, as Westland Helicopters Ltd, Westland Aerospace Ltd and Westland Technologies Ltd.

Financial reconstruction package approved February 1986, with United Technologies (USA) and Fiat (Italy) acquiring minority shareholdings; Fiat withdrew 1988; GKN acquired 22 per cent holding in Westland.

Current programmes include construction of Shorts 330/360 centre wing sections; composite engine cowlings for Boeing Canada DHC-8 Dash 8 and Dornier 328; missile and satellite structures; Boeing CH-47 Chinook fuel pods and transmission components; gears and gearboxes for other companies; composite structures for Airbus, Boeing and McDonnell Douglas aircraft.

EH Industries Ltd (see EHI in International section) is joint Westland/Agusta (Italy) management company supporting EH 101 helicopter; collaboration with Agusta extended to include design, manufacture and marketing across joint product range; EHI Inc (USA) and EHI Canada are subsidiaries of EHI Ltd; Westland Group activities in USA and Central America represented by wholly owned subsidiary, Westland Inc.

WESTLAND HELICOPTERS LIMITED

Yeovil, Somerset BA20 2YB
Telephone: 44 (935) 75222
Fax: 44 (935) 704201
Telex: 46277 WHL YEO G
MANAGING DIRECTOR: J. Varde
ENGINEERING DIRECTOR: R. I. Case
MARKETING DIRECTOR: A. Lewis
HEAD OF HM GOVERNMENT BUSINESS: G. N. Cole
HEAD OF EXPORT BUSINESS: D. L. Gardner
PUBLIC RELATIONS MANAGER: Mrs S. Eagles

Sea King and Lynx in production; Westland and Agusta of Italy collaborate on EH 101 development and manufacture (see EHI in International section); agreement with United Technologies permits Sikorsky Black Hawk production as WS 70. Other activities include construction of carbonfibre/glassfibre main rotor blades to replace metal blades on S-61s, SH-3s and Westland Sea Kings; advanced design composite main rotor blades successfully tested on Lynx, TT300 and EH 101.

Under June 1989 agreement, Westland obtained co-production rights for McDonnell Douglas AH-64 Apache; if selected for British Army Air Corps, production of up to 150 envisaged (Longbow Apache version preferred).

EH 101

Westland and Agusta of Italy are partners in programme; see EHI in International section.

WESTLAND SEA KING

TYPE: Anti-submarine, search and rescue and airborne early warning helicopter.
PROGRAMME: Licence to develop/manufacture Sikorsky S-61 obtained 1959; developed initially for Royal Navy as advanced ASW helicopter with prolonged endurance; SAR, tactical troop transport, casualty evacuation, cargo carrying, long-range self-ferry secondary roles; ordered for RN 1967; first flight of production HAS. Mk 1 (XV642) 7 May 1969.
VARIANTS: Current versions:
Sea King AEW. Mk 2A: Developed mid-1982 to give Royal Navy airborne early warning capability; 10 (plus trials vehicle) converted from HAS. Mk 2As; Thorn EMI Searchwater radar in air pressurised container on swivel mounting. See 1986-87 *Jane's*.
Sea King HAR. Mk 3: Uprated version for SAR with RAF; first flight 6 September 1977; 16 HAR. Mk 3s delivered by 1979, plus three in 1985 (follow-on order under discussion); operated by No. 202 Squadron at Finningly (HQ) and detachments at Boulmer, Brawdy, Manston, Lossiemouth and Leconfield, plus No. 78 Squadron on Falkland Islands; two flight crew, air electronics/winch operator and loadmaster/winchman; up to six stretchers, or two stretchers and 11 seated survivors, or 19 persons; nav system includes Decca TANS F computer, accepting Mk 19 Decca nav receiver and Type 71 Doppler inputs; MEL radar; No. 78 Squadron helicopters fitted with RWR and chaff/flare dispensers.
Sea King HC. Mk 4: Utility version of Commando Mk 2 (which see) for Royal Navy.
Sea King HAR. Mk 5: Four HAS. Mk 5s with ASW avionics stripped 1987-88 for SAR; operational from 1 April 1988 with No. 771 Squadron at Culdrose.
Sea King HAS. Mk 5: Updated ASW/SAR version for Royal Navy; 30 new aircraft handed over 2 October 1980 to July 1986; one HAS. Mk 1, 20 HAS. Mk 2s and 35 HAS. Mk 2As brought to same standard by 1987 at Fleet Air Arm workshops; four became HAR. Mk 5s and others HAS. Mk 6s (which see); nav/attack system utilises TANS G coupled to Decca 71 Doppler and MEL Sea Searcher radar (in larger radome); Racal MIR-2 Orange Crop ESM, passive sonobuoy dropping equipment, and associated GEC Avionics LAPADS acoustics processing and display equipment; four crew, with sonar operator also monitoring LAPADS as additional crew station; cabin enlarged by moving rear bulkhead 1.72 m (5 ft 7¾ in) aft; max T-O weight 9,525 kg (21,000 lb).

New equipment allows pinpoint of enemy submarine at greater range and attack with torpedoes; can monitor signals from own sonobuoys and those dropped by RAF

Westland Sea King HAS. Mk 6 conversion from Mk 5 (note blade aerial below forward fuselage)
(Royal Navy)

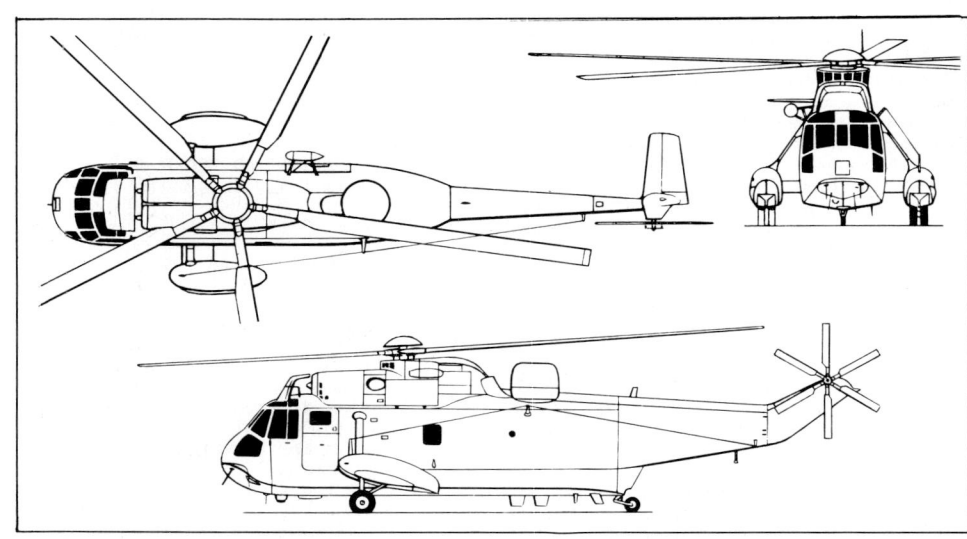

Westland Sea King HAS. Mk 5 anti-submarine helicopter *(Pilot Press)*

Nimrod in joint search; can remain on station for long periods up to 87 nm (160 km; 100 miles) from ship.
Sea King HAS. Mk 6: Uprated RN ASW version; large blade aerial under starboard side of nose; five new aircraft ordered from October 1987 and delivered January-August 1990; 25 HAS. Mk 5s being retrofitted to standard at RN Fleetlands workshop using Westland-supplied kits (44 more kits required by competitive tender); first flight of conversion (Mk 5 XZ581) 15 December 1987; first flight of new Mk 6 (ZG816) 7 December 1989; entered service (ZA136) with Intensive Flight Trials Unit within No. 824 Squadron (detached from Culdrose to Prestwick) 15 April 1988, squadron later disbanding; issued to 819 Sqn, Prestwick, April 1989; and Culdrose squadrons 810 (November 1989), 820 (January 1990), 826 (February 1990) and 814 (October 1990); 706 Sqn also to convert.
AQS-902G-DS enhanced sonar system (31 ordered from Maritime Aircraft Systems Division of GEC Avionics under 1987 contract, plus upgrade to standard of 112 previous AQS-902C sonobuoy processing systems), replacing Mk 5's analog computing element of Plessey 195 dipping sonar with digital processor (changing designation to GEC Ferranti 2069 : 44 ordered initially), and presenting integrated information from sonobuoys and dipping sonar on single CRT display; sonar dunking depth increased from 75 m (245 ft) to about 213 m (700 ft); GEC-Plessey PTR 446 improved IFF; upgraded ESM to Orange Reaper standard; two GEC Sensors AD3400 VHF/UHF secure speech radios;

CAE Electronics internal MAD retrofit anticipated (clearance trials completed 1989); 227-363 kg (500-800 lb) weight saving offers improved performance (equivalent to 30 min extra fuel).
Advanced Sea King: 1,092 kW (1,465 shp) Rolls-Royce Gnome H.1400-IT engines; uprated main gearbox with emergency lubrication and strengthened main lift frames; composite main and tail rotor blades; improved search radar; max AUW 9,752 kg (21,500 lb) for improved payload/range; through-life costs reduced.
Sea King Mk 42B: Advanced Sea King ASW version for Indian Navy; 20 ordered; GEC Avionics AQS-902 sonobuoy processor and tactical processing system; MEL Super Searcher radar; integrated Alcatel HS-12 dipping sonar; Chelton 700 series homing; Marconi Hermes ESM; BAe Sea Eagle missile capability; first flight (IN513) 17 May 1985; two handed over (IN515/516) 16 January 1989; last delivered 12 December 1989.
Sea King Mk 43B: Norwegian Air Force SAR helicopter; one ordered for June 1992 delivery, supplementing 11 Mk 43s received 1972-78 (nine survivors to be upgraded to Mk 43B standard with additional Bendix/King nose radar, Racal Doppler 91, R-NAV2 and Mk 32 Decca, plus 2000F FLIR; redelivery from August 1992).
CUSTOMERS: Royal Navy had fleet of 43 HAS. Mk 5s, 27 Mk 6 conversions, five new Mk 6s, 10 AEWs and four HAR. Mk 5s, plus single Sikorsky SH-3, January 1991. Total 320 Westland-built Sea Kings and Commandos ordered by 1 January 1991; 317 (including 89 Commandos: see

separate entry) delivered, two lost before delivery, one delivery outstanding. Four Sikorsky-built S-61Ds (one complete; three CKD) also received for development, 1966-67.

Details of other versions and customers where orders completed, see 1989-90 and 1983-84 *Jane's*. Recent developments to these include three German **Mk 41s** converted for anti-ship role (see MBB in German section); upgrade of Norwegian **Mk 43s** (see above); five Belgian Air Force **Mk 48s** (delivered 1976) given composite main rotor blades and new Doppler and TANS to upgrade nav systems (by Westland under 1989 contract; work completed early 1991); several other operators retrofitted composite blades.

Following details apply to current production Advanced Sea King:

DESIGN FEATURES: Based on SH-3 airframe and rotor system; Rolls-Royce Gnome turboshaft engines; transmission rating 2,200 kW (2,950 shp); specialised equipment to British requirements; composite rotor blades; new five-blade tail rotor for increased capability in side wind; unbraced tail stabiliser; increased fuel capacity. Automatic main rotor blade folding and spreading is standard; for shipboard operation the tail pylon can also be folded.

FLYING CONTROLS: Mk 31 AFCS provides radio altitude displays for both pilots; artificial horizon displays; three-axis stabilisation in pilot controlled manoeuvres; attitude hold, heading hold and height hold in cruising flight; controlled transition manoeuvres to and from the hover; automatic height control and plan position control in the hover; and an auxiliary trim facility.

POWER PLANT: Two 1,238 kW (1,660 shp) (max contingency rating) Rolls-Royce Gnome H.1400-1T turboshafts, mounted side by side above cabin. Fuel in six underfloor bag tanks, total capacity 3,714 litres (981 US gallons; 817 Imp gallons). Internal auxiliary tank, capacity 863 litres (228 US gallons; 190 Imp gallons), may be fitted for long range ferry purposes. Pressure refuelling point on starboard side, two gravity points on port side. Flat plate debris guard for engine air intakes. Optional Centrisep air cleaner unit.

ACCOMMODATION: Crew of four in ASW role; accommodation for up to 22 survivors — or 18 if radar fitted — in SAR role; and up to 28 troops in utility role. Alternative layouts for nine stretchers and two attendants; or 15 VIPs. Two-section airstair door at front on port side, cargo door at rear on starboard side. Entire accommodation heated and ventilated. Cockpit doors and windows, and two windows each side of cabin, can be jettisoned in an emergency.

SYSTEMS: Three main hydraulic systems. Primary and auxiliary systems operate main rotor control. System pressure 103.5 bars (1,500 lb/sq in); flow rate 22.7 litres/min at 87.9 bars (6 US gallons; 5 Imp gallons/min at 1,275 lb/sq in). Unpressurised reservoir. Utility system for main landing gear, sonar and rescue winches, blade folding and rotor brake. System pressure 207 bars (3,000 lb/sq in); flow rate 41 litres/min at 186.2 bars (10.8 US gallons; 9 Imp gallons/min at 2,700 lb/sq in). Unpressurised reservoir. Electrical system includes two 20kVA 200V three-phase 400Hz engine driven generators, a 26V single-phase AC supply fed from the aircraft's 40Ah nickel-cadmium battery through an inverter, and DC power provided as a secondary system from two 200A transformer-rectifier units.

AVIONICS (ASW models): As equipped for this role, the Sea King is a fully integrated all-weather hunter/killer weapon system, capable of operating independently of surface vessels, and the following equipment and weapons are used to achieve this task: GEC Ferranti 2069, GEC-Plessey Type 195, Bendix/King AN/AQS-13B or Alcatel HS-312 dipping sonar, GEC Avionics Doppler navigation system, MEL Super Searcher radar in dorsal radome, transponder beneath rear fuselage, Honeywell AN/APN-171 radar altimeter, BAe GM9B Gyrosyn compass system, Louis Newmark Mk 31 automatic flight control system. Observer/navigator has tactical display on which sonar contacts are integrated with search radar and navigational information. Radio equipment comprises Collins AN/ARC-182 UHF/VHF and homer, Ultra D 403M standby UHF, Collins 718U-5 HF radio, Racal B693 intercom, Telebrief system and IFF provisions. CAE Electronics AN/ASQ-504(V) internal MAD ordered for RN Sea Kings in 1987 and fitted from 1988 onwards. Whittaker Electronic Systems AN/ALQ-167 Yellow Veil modular jamming equipment installed internally in Mk 5 from about 1986.

AVIONICS (non-ASW models): A wide range of radio and navigation equipment may be installed, including VHF/UHF communications, VHF/UHF homing, radio compass, Doppler navigation system, radio altimeter, VOR/ILS, radar and transponder of Collins, GEC-Plessey, Honeywell and GEC Avionics manufacture. A Honeywell compass system and a Louis Newmark automatic flight control system are also installed.

EQUIPMENT: Two No. 4 marine markers, four No. 2 Mk 2 smoke floats, Ultra Electronics mini-sonobuoys, in ASW versions. Sea Kings equipped for search and rescue have a Breeze BL 10300 variable speed hydraulic rescue hoist of

Indian Sea King Mk 42B as operated from INS *Vikrant*

272 kg (600 lb) capacity mounted above the starboard side cargo door. Second electric hoist optional.

ARMAMENT: Up to four Mk 46, Whitehead A244S or Sting Ray homing torpedoes, or four Mk 11 depth charges or one Clevite simulator. For secondary role a mounting is provided on the rear frame of the starboard door for a general purpose machine gun.

DIMENSIONS, EXTERNAL:

Main rotor diameter	18.90 m (62 ft 0 in)
Tail rotor diameter	3.16 m (10 ft 4 in)
Length:	
overall, rotors turning	22.15 m (72 ft 8 in)
main rotor folded	17.42 m (57 ft 2 in)
rotors and tail folded	14.40 m (47 ft 3 in)
Height: overall, rotors turning	5.13 m (16 ft 10 in)
rotors spread and stationary	4.85 m (15 ft 11 in)
to top of rotor head	4.72 m (15 ft 6 in)
Fuselage: Length	17.02 m (55 ft 10 in)
Max width	2.16 m (7 ft 1 in)
Width: overall, rotors folded	
with flotation bags	4.98 m (16 ft 4 in)
without flotation bags	4.77 m (15 ft 8 in)
Wheel track (c/l of shock absorbers)	3.96 m (13 ft 0 in)
Wheelbase	7.14 m (23 ft 5 in)
Cabin door (port): Height	1.68 m (5 ft 6 in)
Width	0.91 m (3 ft 0 in)
Cargo door (stbd): Height	1.52 m (5 ft 0 in)
Width	1.73 m (5 ft 8 in)
Height to sill	1.14 m (3 ft 9 in)

DIMENSIONS, INTERNAL:

Cabin: Length	7.59 m (24 ft 11 in)
Max width	1.98 m (6 ft 6 in)
Max height	1.92 m (6 ft 3½ in)
Floor area (incl area occupied by radar, sonar etc)	13.94 m² (150 sq ft)
Volume	28.03 m³ (990 cu ft)

AREAS:

Main rotor disc	280.6 m² (3,020.3 sq ft)
Tail rotor disc	7.8 m² (83.9 sq ft)

WEIGHTS AND LOADINGS (A: anti-submarine, B: anti-surface vessel, C: airborne early warning, D: SAR, E: troop transport, F: external cargo, G: VIP):

Basic weight: with sponsons	5,393 kg (11,891 lb)
without sponsons	5,373 kg (11,845 lb)
Weight empty, equipped (typical): A	7,428 kg (16,377 lb)
B	7,570 kg (16,689 lb)
C	7,776 kg (17,143 lb)
D	6,241 kg (13,760 lb)
E	5,712 kg (12,594 lb)
F	5,686 kg (12,536 lb)
G	7,220 kg (15,917 lb)
Max T-O weight	9,752 kg (21,500 lb)
Max underslung or internal load	3,628 kg (8,000 lb)
Max disc loading	34.75 kg/m² (7.12 lb/sq ft)
Max power loading	4.44 kg/kW (7.29 lb/shp)

PERFORMANCE (at max T-O weight, ISA):

Never-exceed speed (V_NE, British practice) at S/L
122 knots (226 km/h; 140 mph)
Cruising speed at S/L   110 knots (204 km/h; 126 mph)
Max rate of climb at S/L   619 m (2,030 ft)/min
Max vertical rate of climb at S/L   246 m (808 ft)/min
Service ceiling, one engine out   1,220 m (4,000 ft)
Max contingency ceiling (1 hour rating)
1,067 m (3,500 ft)
Hovering ceiling: IGE   1,982 m (6,500 ft)
OGE   1,433 m (4,700 ft)
Radius of action:
A (2 h on station, incl three torpedoes)
125 nm (231 km; 144 miles)
B (2 h on station, incl two Sea Eagles)
110 nm (204 km; 126 miles)
C (2 h 24 min on station) 100 nm (185 km; 115 miles)
D (picking up 20 survivors)
220 nm (407 km; 253 miles)
E (28 troops)   range 300 nm (556 km; 345 miles)
F (1,814 kg; 4,000 lb external load)
225 nm (417 km; 259 miles)
G   580 nm (1,075 km; 668 miles)
Range with max standard fuel, at 1,830 m (6,000 ft)
800 nm (1,482 km; 921 miles)
Ferry range with max standard and auxiliary fuel, at 1,830 m (6,000 ft)   940 nm (1,742 km; 1,082 miles)

PERFORMANCE (at typical mid-mission weight):
Never-exceed speed (V_NE, British practice) at S/L
146 knots (272 km/h; 169 mph)
Cruising speed at S/L   132 knots (245 km/h; 152 mph)

WESTLAND COMMANDO

TYPE: Twin-turboshaft tactical military helicopter.

PROGRAMME: First flight 12 September 1973; first flight HC. Mk 4 (ZA290) 26 September 1979; HC. Mk 4s delivered November 1979 to October 1990; HC. Mk 4 ZF115 (28th delivery) first Commando type completed with composites main rotor blades (first flight 14 November 1985); composite blades retrofitted to HC. Mk 4s.

VARIANTS: See 1989-90 *Jane's* for Mk 1, Mk 2 and Mk 3 details.

Sea King HC. Mk 4: Royal Navy utility Commando Mk 2; folding main rotor blades; folding tail pylon; non-retractable landing gear; 28 equipped troops or 2,720 kg (6,000 lb) cargo internally; 3,628 kg (8,000 lb) max slung load; parachuting/abseiling equipment; Decca TANS with chart display and Decca 71 Doppler nav system; 7.62 mm cabin machine gun; can operate in Arctic or tropics; serves with Nos. 707, 845 and 846 (Naval Air Commando) and 772 (SAR) Squadrons. Additionally, No. 848 Squadron formed 16 November 1990 for Gulf War service. Two **Mk 4Xs** with less operational equipment delivered to RAE (incl for Blue

Westland Sea King Mk 4 (Commando) of the Empire Test Pilots' School (*Paul Jackson*)

Kestrel radar trials) 1982-83; one **Mk 4** to Empire Test Pilots' School 3 May 1989.

CUSTOMERS: Exports to Egypt (five Mk 1s, 17 Mk 2s, two Mk 2Bs, four Mk 2Es) and Qatar (three Mk 2As, one Mk 2C, eight Mk 3s; conversion began 1990 of Qatari Mk 2s to Mk 3 standard with new nav/com equipment). Six Indian Sea King Mk 42Cs and 40 RN Sea King HC. Mk 4s essentially Commandos (three of latter lost, all in Falklands conflict); three UK MoD Mk 4s. Total production 89; last delivery (HC. Mk 4 ZG822) 15 October 1990.

Following data apply to current production aircraft:

DESIGN FEATURES: Based on Sea King; optimised payload/ range and endurance for tactical troop transport, logistic support and cargo transport, and casualty evacuation primary roles, or air-to-surface strike and SAR secondary roles; five-blade composite main rotor, attached to hub by multiple bolted joint; NACA 0012 blade section; rotor brake; optional automatic main rotor blade folding; five-blade composite tail rotor; twin input four-stage reduction main gearbox, with single bevel intermediate and tail gearboxes; main rotor/engine rpm ratio 93.43; tail rotor/engine rpm ratio 15.26; unpressurised; stub wings instead of Sea King sponsons; non-retractable landing gear.

STRUCTURE: Light alloy stressed skin; optional tail pylon folding.

LANDING GEAR: Non-retractable tailwheel type, with twin-wheel main units. Oleo-pneumatic shock absorbers. Mainwheel tyres size 6.50-10, tailwheel tyre size 6.00-6.

POWER PLANT: As for current versions of Advanced Sea King.

ACCOMMODATION: Crew of two on flight deck. Seats along cabin sides, and single jump seat, for up to 28 troops. Overload capacity 45 troops. Two-piece airstair door at front on port side, cargo door at rear on starboard side. Entire accommodation heated and ventilated. Cockpit doors and windows, and two windows each side of main cabin, are jettisonable in an emergency.

SYSTEMS: Primary and secondary hydraulic systems for flight controls. No pneumatic system. Electrical system includes two 20kVA alternators.

AVIONICS: Wide range of radio, radar and navigation equipment available to customer's requirements.

EQUIPMENT: Cargo sling and rescue hoist optional.

ARMAMENT: Wide range of guns, missiles, etc may be carried, to customer's requirements: typically, pintle-mounted gun (7.62 mm or 20 mm) in cabin doorway and machine-gun pod (0.50 in or 7.62 mm) on each side of forward fuselage with reflector sight for pilot. If fitted, sponsons may mount one rocket pod each (FZ M159C 2.75 in; Matra F4 68 mm; Thomson-Brandt 68-22 68 mm; Medusa 81 mm; or SNIA HL-12 80 mm).

DIMENSIONS, EXTERNAL:
Main rotor diameter	18.90 m (62 ft 0 in)
Tail rotor diameter	3.16 m (10 ft 4 in)
Distance between rotor centres	11.10 m (36 ft 5 in)
Main rotor blade chord	0.46 m (1 ft 6¼ in)
Length: overall, rotors turning	22.15 m (72 ft 8 in)
fuselage	17.02 m (55 ft 10 in)
Height: overall, rotors turning	5.13 m (16 ft 10 in)
to top of rotor head	4.72 m (15 ft 6 in)
Wheel track (c/l of shock absorbers)	3.96 m (13 ft 0 in)
Wheelbase	7.21 m (23 ft 8 in)
Passenger door (fwd, port):	
Height	1.68 m (5 ft 6 in)
Width	0.91 m (3 ft 0 in)
Cargo door (rear, stbd): Height	1.52 m (5 ft 0 in)
Width	1.73 m (5 ft 8 in)

DIMENSIONS, INTERNAL: As Advanced Sea King (SAR version)

AREAS: As for Advanced Sea King, plus:
Main rotor blades (each)	4.14 m² (44.54 sq ft)
Tail rotor blades (each)	0.23 m² (2.46 sq ft)
Tailplane	1.80 m² (19.40 sq ft)

WEIGHTS AND LOADINGS:
Operating weight empty (troop transport, 2 crew, typical)	5,620 kg (12,390 lb)
Max T-O weight	9,752 kg (21,500 lb)
Max underslung load	3,628 kg (8,000 lb)

PERFORMANCE (at max T-O weight): As given for Advanced Sea King, plus:
Range with max payload (28 troops), reserves for 30 min standoff	214 nm (396 km; 246 miles)

WESTLAND LYNX

TYPE: Twin-engined multi-purpose helicopter.

PROGRAMME: Developed within Anglo-French helicopter agreement confirmed 2 April 1968; Westland given design leadership; first flight of first of 13 prototypes (XW835) 21 March 1971; first flight of fourth prototype (XW838) 9 March 1972, featuring production type monobloc rotor head; first flight of British Army Lynx prototype (XX153) 12 April 1972; first flight of French Navy prototype (XX904) 6 July 1973; first flight of production Lynx (RN HAS. Mk 2 XZ229) 20 February 1976; other development details and records in 1975-76 and subsequent *Jane's*. RN Lynx operations centred on Portland, Nos. 815 and 829 Squadrons providing detachments to warships, and No. 702 Squadron for

Westland Lynx HAS. Mk 3 aerodynamic prototype of Mk 8 with Sea Owl thermal imager and chin radome

Westland Lynx HAS. Mk 3 of HMS *London*, equipped for 1991 Gulf War service with Challenger IR jammers above cockpit and AN/ALQ-167 jamming pod on port pylon *(Jeremy Flack/API)*

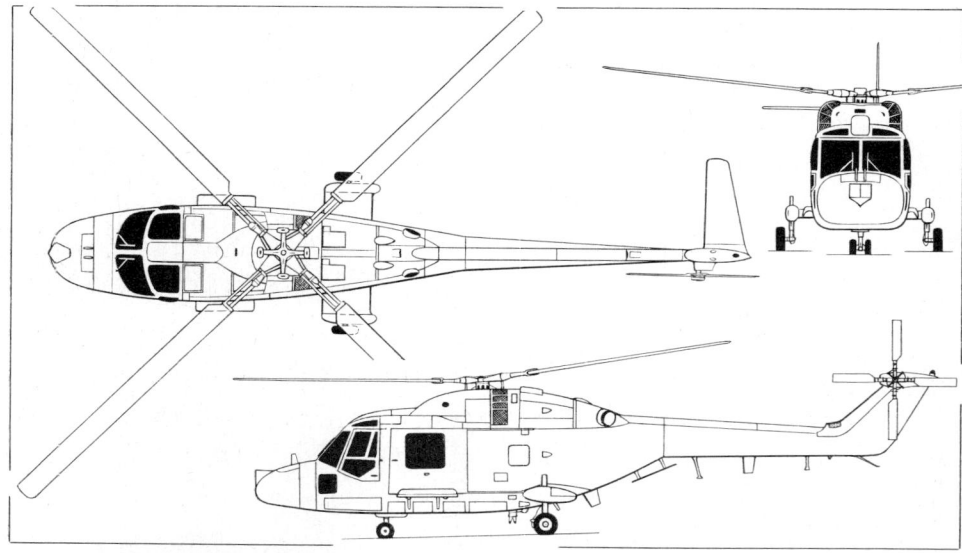
Westland Lynx HAS. Mk 3 anti-submarine helicopter for the Royal Navy *(Pilot Press)*

training; production shared 70 per cent Westland, 30 per cent Aerospatiale; for details of G-LYNX's 1986 world helicopter absolute speed record, and Lynx AH. Mk 7 XZ170's 1989 agility trials, see 1990-91 *Jane's*.

VARIANTS: **Lynx AH. Mk 1:** British Army general purpose and utility version; 113 built (107 remained January 1991

incl those converted to AH. Mk 7). Described in 1986-87 and earlier *Jane's*.

Lynx HAS. Mk 2: First Royal Navy version for advanced shipborne anti-submarine and other duties; Gem 2 engines; GEC Ferranti Seaspray search and tracking radar in modified nose; capable of anti-submarine classification and strike, air to surface vessel search and strike, SAR, reconnaissance, troop transport fire support, communications and fleet liaison, and vertrep; can carry Sea Skua; total 60 delivered, plus 26 to French Navy (**HAS. Mk 2(FN)**); first RN operational unit (No. 702 Squadron) formed on completion of intensive flight trials December 1977; all 53 RN aircraft then active modified to Mk 3 or later standards by 1989.

Lynx HAS. Mk 3: RN version; two 835 kW (1,120 shp) Gem 41-1 engines; 23 delivered March 1982 to April 1985; seven more in **HAS. Mk 3S** configuration (first flight, ZF557, 12 October 1987) delivered November 1987 to November 1988; additionally, ZD560 built in approx Mk 7 configuration, delivered to Empire Test Pilots' School April 1988; 18 used by Armilla Patrol in Arabian Gulf modified to **HAS. Mk 3GM** (Gulf Mod), with better cooling. Augmenting new-build Mk 3Ss, 23 modified by RN Aircraft Yard at Fleetlands from April 1989; Mk 3S is Phase 1 of Mk 8 conversion programme, involving secure speech radios (blade aerial beneath mid-point of tailboom) and upgraded ESM. Phase 2 is Lynx **HAS. Mk 3CTS**, adding RAMS 4000 central tactical system; prototype (XZ236 ex Mk 3) flew 25 January 1989; further six for RN trials (one ex Mk 3; five ex Mk 3S); deliveries to Operational Flight Trials Unit, Portland, from April 1989; unit became No. 700L Squadron 6 July 1990 with three Lynx; remaining three deployed to destroyers and frigates at sea from 3 December 1990 (HMS *Newcastle*); Mk 3CTS has flotation bag each side of nose. RN Lynx status January 1991: 32 Mk 3, 16 Mk 3GM, 25 Mk 3S, six Mk 3CTS and three Westland development helicopters.

Lynx Mk 4: Ordered May 1980 for French Navy; Gem 41-1s; uprated transmission allowing 4,763 kg (10,500 lb) AUW; 14 delivered 28 April 1982 to September 1983; equipment installed by Aerospatiale and subsidiaries.

Lynx AH. Mk 5: Similar to AH. Mk 1; two trials aircraft (ZD285/559, see 1989-90 *Jane's*); nine ordered for UK Army Air Corps; first flight (ZE375, used for engine trials) 23 February 1985; ZE376 flew as Mk 5 but became Mk 7; remainder transferred to AH. Mk 7 contract.

RAE Farnborough testbed ZD285 fitted 1989 with advanced fibre optic MIL-STD-1553B databus (hardware by STC); RAE Bedford testbed ZD559 received pressure sensors to support proposed Lynx active control technology (ACT) programme; ZD560 (see HAS. Mk 3) intended ACT recipient, to become world's first true FBW helicopter.

Lynx AH. Mk 7: Uprated British Army version, meeting GSR 3947; as Mk 5 but with improved systems, reversed-direction tail rotor with improved composite blades to reduce noise and enhance extended period hover at high weights; 4,876 kg (10,750 lb) AUW; 13 ordered, eight from Mk 5 contract (two cancelled); first flight (ZE376) 7 November 1985; 11th delivered July 1987.

RN workshops at Wroughton converting Mk 1s to Mk 7s; first conversion (XZ641) redelivered 30 March 1988; box-type exhaust diffusers added from early 1989; programme continues.

Lynx HAS. Mk 8: Proposed for RN; equivalent to export **Super Lynx**; passive identification system; 5,125 kg (11,300 lb) max T-O weight; improved (reversed-direction) tail rotor control; BERP composite main rotor blades; Racal RAMS 4000 central tactical system (CTS eases crew's workload by centrally processing sensor data and presents mission information on multi-function electronic display; 15 systems ordered 1987, 106 September 1989); original Seaspray Mk 1 radar re-positioned in new chin radome; GEC Sensors Sea Owl thermal imager (×5 or ×30 magnifying system on gimballed mount, with elevation +20° to −30° and azimuth +120° to −120°; ordered October 1989) in former radar position; MIR-2 ESM updated; three Mk 3s used in development programme as tactical system (XZ236), dummy Sea Owl/chin radome (ZD267) and avionics (ZD266) testbeds—see Lynx Mk 3 for Phases 1 and 2 of Lynx Mk 8 programme.

Definitive Mk 8 (Phase 3) conversions begin 1992 with addition of Sea Owl, CAE internal MAD, further radar and navigation upgrades, composites BERP main rotor blades and reversed-direction tail rotor.

Lynx AH. Mk 9: UK Army Air Corps equivalent of export **Battlefield Lynx**; tricycle wheel landing gear; max T-O weight 5,125 kg (11,300 lb); advanced technology composites main rotor blades; exhaust diffusers; no TOW capability; first flight of prototype (converted company demonstrator XZ170) 29 November 1989; 16 new aircraft (beginning ZG884, flown 20 July 1990) ordered for delivery from 1991, plus eight Mk 1 conversions; equipping Nos. 672 and 673 Squadrons of 9 Regiment, Dishforth, to support 24th Airmobile Brigade; some outfitted as advanced command posts, remainder for tactical transport role.

Other versions and operators where orders completed, see 1990-91 *Jane's*. Royal Netherlands Navy upgrading five UH-14As and eight SH-14Cs to **SH-14D** standard, with Alcatel dipping sonar, UHF radios, RWR, new navigation instruments, new radar altimeter and modified

Westland Lynx AH. Mk 7 conversion from Mk 1 with reversed-direction tail rotor and box-type exhaust diffusers (*Paul Jackson*)

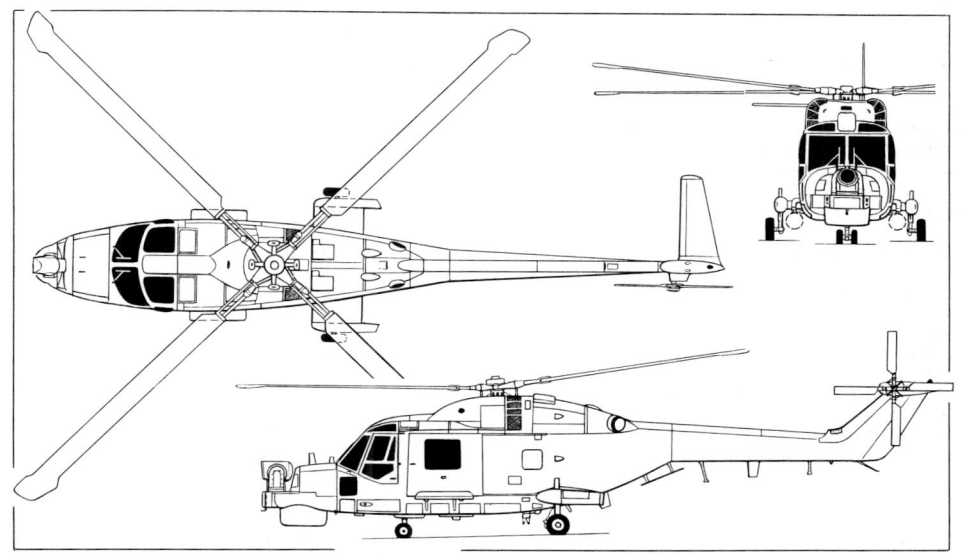
Westland Lynx HAS. Mk 8, based on the Super Lynx advanced export version (*Pilot Press*)

Prototype Lynx AH. Mk 9 conversion, fitted with wheel landing gear but lacking TOW sight and missiles

engines. Eight SH-14Bs, already with sonar, being raised to SH-14D standards.

CUSTOMERS: Production totalled 340 by 1 January 1991 (incl two demonstrators but not 13 prototypes); orders then 380. Versions and operators where orders completed, see 1989-90 *Jane's*.

Following description applies to military general purpose and naval versions with Gem 2 engines, except where indicated:

DESIGN FEATURES: Compact design suited to hunter-killer ASW and missile-armed anti-ship naval roles from frigates or larger ships (superseding ship-guided helicopters), armed/unarmed land roles with cabin large enough for squad, or other tasks; manually folding tail pylon on naval versions; single four-blade semi-rigid main rotor (foldable), each blade attached to main rotor hub by titanium root attachment plates and flexible arm; rotor drives taken from front of engines into main gearbox mounted above cabin ahead of engines; in flight, accessory gears (at front of main gearbox) driven by one of two through shafts from first stage reduction gears; four-blade tail rotor, drive taken from main ring gear; single large window in each main cabin sliding door; provision for internally mounted armament, and for exterior universal flange mounting each side for other weapons/stores.

FLYING CONTROLS: Rotor head controls actuated by three identical tandem servo jacks and powered by two independent hydraulic systems; control system incorporates simple stability augmentation system; each engine embodies independent control system providing full authority rotor speed governing, pilot control being limited to selection of desired rotor speed range; in event of one engine failure, system restores power up to single engine max contingency rating; main rotor can provide negative thrust to increase stability on deck after touchdown on naval versions; hydraulically operated rotor brake mounted on main gearbox; sweptback fin/tail rotor pylon, with starboard half-tailplane.

STRUCTURE: Conventional semi-monocoque pod and boom, mainly light alloy; glassfibre access panels, doors, fairings, pylon leading/trailing-edges, and bullet fairing over tail rotor gearbox; composites main rotor blades; main rotor hub and inboard flexible arm portions built as complete unit, as titanium monobloc forging; tail rotor blades have light alloy spar, stainless steel leading-edge sheath and rear section as for main blades.

LANDING GEAR (general purpose military version): Non-retractable tubular skid type. Provision for a pair of adjustable ground handling wheels on each skid. Flotation gear optional.

LANDING GEAR (naval versions): Non-retractable oleo-pneumatic tricycle type. Single-wheel main units, carried on sponsons, are fixed at 27° toe-out for deck landing, and can be manually turned into line and locked fore and aft for movement of aircraft into and out of ship's hangar. Twin-wheel nose unit can be steered hydraulically through 90° by the pilot to facilitate independent take-off into wind. Sprag brakes (wheel locks) fitted to each wheel prevent rotation on landing or inadvertent deck roll. These locks are disengaged hydraulically and will re-engage automatically in the event of hydraulic failure. Max vertical descent 2.29 m (7½ ft)/s; with lateral drift 0.91 m (3 ft)/s for deck landing. Flotation gear, and hydraulically actuated harpoon deck lock securing system, optional.

POWER PLANT: Two Rolls-Royce Gem 2 turboshafts, each with max contingency rating of 671 kW (900 shp) in Lynx AH. 1, HAS. 2 and early export variants. Later versions have Gem 41-1 or 41-2 engines, each with max contingency rating of 835 kW (1,120 shp), or Gem 42-1 engines, each with max contingency rating of 846 kW (1,135 shp). Engines of British and French Lynx in service being converted to Mk 42 standard during regular overhauls from 1987 onwards. Engine oil tank capacity 6.8 litres (1.8 US gallons; 1.5 Imp gallons). Main rotor gearbox oil capacity 28 litres (7.4 US gallons; 6.2 Imp gallons). Usable fuel capacity 973 litres (257 US gallons; 214 Imp gallons) in five internal tanks. Optional 214 litres (56.4 US gallons; 47 Imp gallons) beneath bench seat in rear of cabin. For ferrying, two tanks, each of 436 litres (115.3 US gallons; 96 Imp gallons) in cabin, replacing bench tank. Max usable fuel 1,845 litres (488 US gallons; 406 Imp gallons). Naval Lynx equipped with bench tank as standard, and ferry tanks for long-range surveillance, thus gross capacities: 1,200 litres (317 US gallons; 264 Imp gallons) standard; 1,862 litres (492 US gallons; 409.5 Imp gallons) maximum. Pressure or gravity refuelling.

ACCOMMODATION: Pilot and co-pilot or observer on side by side seats. Dual controls optional. Individual forward hinged cockpit door and large rearward sliding cabin door on each side; all four doors jettisonable. Cockpit accessible from cabin area. Maximum high density layout (general purpose version) for one pilot and 10 armed troops or paratroops, on lightweight bench seats in soundproofed cabin. Alternative VIP layouts for four to seven passengers, with additional cabin soundproofing. Seats can be removed quickly to permit the carriage of up to 907 kg (2,000 lb) of freight internally. Tiedown rings are provided. In the casualty evacuation role, with a crew of two, the Lynx can accommodate up to six Alphin stretchers and a medical attendant. Both basic versions have secondary capability for search and rescue (up to nine survivors) and other roles.

SYSTEMS: Two independent hydraulic systems, pressure 141 bars (2,050 lb/sq in). A third hydraulic system is provided in the naval version when sonar equipment, MAD or a hydraulic winch system is installed. No pneumatic system. 28V DC electrical power supplied by two 6kW engine driven starter/generators and an alternator. External power sockets. 24V 23Ah (optionally 40Ah) nickel-cadmium battery fitted for essential services and emergency engine starting. 200V three-phase AC power available at 400Hz from two 15kVA transmission driven alternators. Optional cabin heating and ventilation system. Optional supplementary cockpit heating system. Electric anti-icing and demisting of windscreen, and electrically operated windscreen wipers, standard; windscreen washing system optional.

AVIONICS: All versions equipped as standard with navigation, cabin and cockpit lights; adjustable landing light under nose; and anti-collision beacon. Avionics common to all roles (general purpose and naval versions) include GEC Avionics duplex three-axis automatic stabilisation equipment; BAe GM9 Gyrosyn compass system; Decca tactical air navigation system (TANS); Decca 71 Doppler, E2C standby compass; and Racal intercom system. Optional role equipment for both versions includes GEC Avionics Mk 34 automatic flight control system (AFCS); Collins VOR/ILS; DME; Collins AN/ARN-118 Tacan; I-band transponder (naval version only); GEC-Plessey PTR 446, Collins APX-72, Siemens STR 700/375 or Italtel APX-77 IFF; and vortex sand filter for engine air intakes. Additional units are fitted in naval version, when sonar is fitted, to provide automatic transition to hover and automatic Doppler hold in hover. British Army Lynx equipped with TOW missiles have roof mounted Hughes sight manufactured under licence by British Aerospace. The TOW roof sight is being upgraded to have a night vision capability in the far infra-red waveband to increase operational versatility in low-light night conditions or poor daylight visibility, and the first test firing of TOW with an added GEC Sensors thermal imager took place in October 1988. Sanders AN/ALQ-144 infra-red jammer installed beneath tail-boom of some British Army Lynx from 1987 pending availability of exhaust diffusers. Requirement for radar warning receiver satisfied by 1989 selection of GEC Ferranti AWARE-3 system. Optional equipment, according to role, can include lightweight sighting system with alternative target magnification, vertical and/or oblique cameras, flares for night operation, low light level TV, infra-red linescan, searchlight, and specialised communications equipment. Naval Lynx has specialised equipment for its primary duties. Detection of submarines is by means of dipping sonars or magnetic anomaly detector. The dipping sonars are operated by a hydraulically powered winch and cable hover mode facilities within the AFCS. CAE Electronics AN/ASQ-504(V) internal MAD ordered for RN Lynx in 1990. Tracor M-130 chaff/flare dispensers and Whittaker Microwave Systems AN/ALQ-167(V) D-J band anti-anti-ship missile jamming pods installed on RN Lynx patrolling Arabian Gulf, 1987. Two Loral Challenger IR jammers above cockpit of RN Lynx during 1991 Gulf War. GEC Ferranti ARI5979 Seaspray Mk 1 lightweight search and tracking radar, for detecting small surface targets in low visibility/high sea conditions.

ARMAMENT: For armed escort, anti-tank or air-to-surface strike missions, general purpose version can be equipped with two 20 mm cannon mounted externally so as to permit the carriage also of anti-tank missiles or a pintle-mounted 7.62 mm machine gun inside the cabin. External pylon can be fitted on each side of cabin for a variety of stores, including two Minigun or other self-contained gun pods; two rocket pods; or up to eight Aerospatiale/MBB HOT, Rockwell Hellfire, Hughes TOW, or similar air-to-surface missiles. An additional six or eight missiles can be carried in cabin, for rearming in forward areas, and a stabilised sight is fitted for target detection and missile direction. For search and rescue role, with three crew, both versions can have a waterproof floor and a 272 kg (600 lb) capacity clip-on hoist on starboard side of cabin. Cable length 30 m (98 ft). For ASW role, armament includes two Mk 44, Mk 46 or Sting Ray homing torpedoes, one each on an external pylon on each side of fuselage, and six marine markers; or two Mk 11 depth charges. Alternatively, up to four BAe Sea Skua semi-active homing missiles for attacking light surface craft; on French Navy Lynx, four AS.12 or similar wire guided missiles can be employed in conjunction with AF 530 or APX-334 lightweight stabilised optical sighting system. Self-protection FN HMP 0.50 in machine gun optional on RN Lynx.

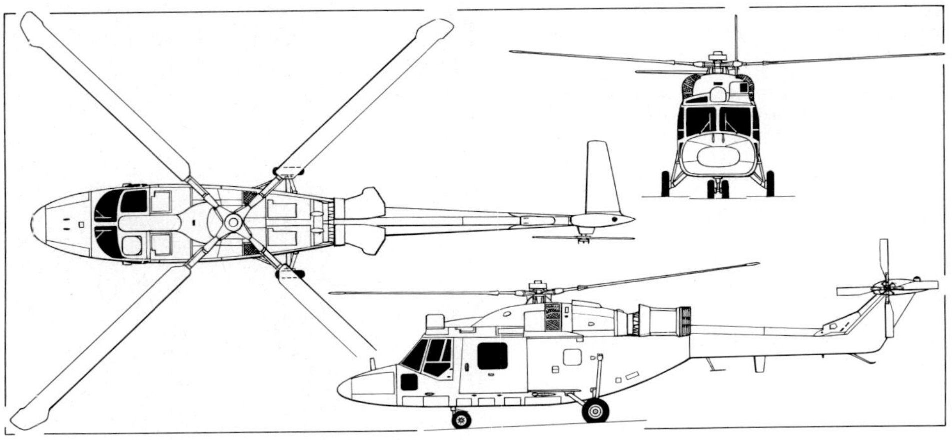

Westland Battlefield Lynx for export, equivalent to the British Army's Lynx AH. Mk 9 *(Pilot Press)*

DIMENSIONS, EXTERNAL (A: general purpose version, N: naval version):

Main rotor diameter (A, N) 12.80 m (42 ft 0 in)
Tail rotor diameter (A, N) 2.21 m (7 ft 3 in)
Length overall:
A, N, both rotors turning 15.163 m (49 ft 9 in)
N, main rotor blades and tail folded 10.618 m (34 ft 10 in)
Width overall, main rotor blades folded:
A 3.75 m (12 ft 3¾ in)
N 2.94 m (9 ft 7¾ in)
Height overall: both rotors stopped:
A 3.504 m (11 ft 6 in)
N 3.48 m (11 ft 5 in)
main rotor blades and tail folded:
N 3.20 m (10 ft 6 in)
Tailplane half-span 1.78 m (5 ft 10 in)
Skid track: A 2.032 m (6 ft 8 in)
Wheel track: N 2.778 m (9 ft 1.4 in)
Wheelbase: N 2.94 m (9 ft 7¾ in)

DIMENSIONS, INTERNAL:

Cabin, from back of pilots' seats:
Min length 2.057 m (6 ft 9 in)
Max width 1.778 m (5 ft 10 in)
Max height 1.422 m (4 ft 8 in)
Floor area 3.72 m² (40.04 sq ft)
Volume 5.21 m³ (184 cu ft)
Cabin doorway: Width 1.37 m (4 ft 6 in)
Height 1.19 m (3 ft 11 in)

AREAS:

Main rotor disc 128.7 m² (1,385.4 sq ft)
Tail rotor disc 3.84 m² (41.28 sq ft)

WEIGHTS AND LOADINGS (A: general purpose version, N: naval version):

Manufacturer's empty weight: A 2,578 kg (5,683 lb)
N 2,740 kg (6,040 lb)
Manufacturer's basic weight: A 2,658 kg (5,860 lb)
N 3,030 kg (6,680 lb)
Operating weight empty, equipped:
A, troop transport (pilot and 10 troops) 2,787 kg (6,144 lb)
A, anti-tank strike (incl weapon pylons, firing equipment and sight) 3,072 kg (6,772 lb)
A, search and rescue (crew of three) 2,963 kg (6,532 lb)
N, anti-submarine strike 3,343 kg (7,370 lb)
N, reconnaissance (crew of two) 3,277 kg (7,224 lb)
N, anti-submarine classification and strike 3,472 kg (7,654 lb)
N, air to surface vessel search and strike (crew of two and four Sea Skuas) 3,414 kg (7,526 lb)
N, search and rescue (crew of three) 3,416 kg (7,531 lb)
N, dunking sonar search and strike 3,650 kg (8,047 lb)
Max T-O weight: A 4,535 kg (10,000 lb)
N 4,763 kg (10,500 lb)
Max disc loading: A 35.24 kg/m² (7.22 lb/sq ft)
N 37.00 kg/m² (7.58 lb/sq ft)

PERFORMANCE (at normal max T-O weight at S/L, ISA, except where indicated. A: general purpose version, N: naval version):

Max continuous cruising speed:
A 140 knots (259 km/h; 161 mph)
N 125 knots (232 km/h; 144 mph)
A (ISA + 20°C) 130 knots (241 km/h; 150 mph)
N (ISA + 20°C) 114 knots (211 km/h; 131 mph)
Speed for max endurance:
A, N (ISA and ISA + 20°C) 70 knots (130 km/h; 81 mph)
Max forward rate of climb: A 756 m (2,480 ft)/min
N 661 m (2,170 ft)/min
A (ISA + 20°C) 536 m (1,760 ft)/min
N (ISA + 20°C) 469 m (1,540 ft)/min
Max vertical rate of climb:
A 472 m (1,550 ft)/min
N 351 m (1,150 ft)/min
A (ISA + 20°C) 390 m (1,280 ft)/min
N (ISA + 20°C) 244 m (800 ft)/min
Hovering ceiling OGE: A 3,230 m (10,600 ft)
N 2,575 m (8,450 ft)
Typical range, with reserves:
A, troop transport 292 nm (540 km; 336 miles)
Radius of action, out and back at max sustained speed, allowances for T-O and landing, 30 min loiter in search

area, 3 min hover for each survivor, and 10% fuel reserves at end of mission:

N, search and rescue (crew of 3 and 2 survivors)
115 nm (212 km; 132 miles)

N, search and rescue (crew of 3 and 7 survivors)
96 nm (178 km; 111 miles)

Time on station at 50 nm (93 km; 58 miles) radius, out and back at max sustained speed, with 2 torpedoes, smoke floats and marine markers, allowances for T-O and landing and 10% fuel reserves at end of mission:

N, anti-submarine classification and strike, loiter speed on station 2 h

N, anti-submarine strike, loiter on station 2 h 29 min

N, dunking sonar search and strike, 50% loiter speed and 50% hover on station 1 h 5 min

Time on station at 50 nm (93 km; 58 miles) radius, out and back at max sustained speed, with crew of 2 and 4 Sea Skuas, allowances and reserves as above:

N, air to surface vessel strike, en route radar search and loiter speed on station 1 h 36 min

Max range: A 340 nm (630 km; 392 miles)
N 320 nm (593 km; 368 miles)

Max endurance: A 2 h 57 min
N (ISA + 20°C) 2 h 50 min

Max ferry range with auxiliary cabin tanks:
A 724 nm (1,342 km; 834 miles)
N 565 nm (1,046 km; 650 miles)

WESTLAND SUPER LYNX and BATTLEFIELD LYNX

TYPE: Twin-engined multi-purpose export helicopters.

PROGRAMME: Battlefield Lynx mockup displayed at 1988 Farnborough air show (converted demonstrator G-LYNX), featuring wheeled landing gear, exhaust diffusers and provision for anti-helicopter missiles each side of fuselage; first flight of wheeled prototype (converted trials AH. Mk 7 XZ170) 29 November 1989; first flight of South Korean Super Lynx (90-0701, temporarily ZH219) 16 November 1989 (also first Lynx with Seaspray Mk 3).

VARIANTS: **Super Lynx:** Upgraded export naval Lynx, approx equivalent to Lynx HAS. Mk 8.

Battlefield Lynx: Upgraded export army Lynx; approx equivalent to Lynx AH. Mk 9; demonstrator G-LYNX fitted early 1991 with two 1,007 kW (1,350 shp) LHTEC T800 turboshafts as **Battlefield Lynx 800** private venture (LHTEC funding power plants and gearboxes, Westland providing airframe for full flight demonstration programme).

CUSTOMERS: Super Lynx ordered by South Korea 1988 (12 **Mk 99** with Racal Avionics Doppler 71/TANS N nav system, Seaspray Mk 3 360° radar and Sea Skua), handed over from 26 July 1991 for 'Sumner' and 'Gearing' class destroyers; Portugal ordered five Super Lynx **Mk 95** 1990 (plus three options) with Racal RNS252 and Doppler 91 navigation systems and some US equipment including AN/AQS-18 dipping sonar and Bendix/King 1500 radar; deliveries due in 1993 for 'Vasco da Gama' class (MEKO 200) frigates.

DESIGN FEATURES: Upgraded export Lynx; max T-O weight 5,125 kg (11,300 lb); all-weather day/night capability; extended payload/range; advanced technology swept-tip (BERP) composite main rotor blades offering improved speed and aerodynamic efficiency and reduced vibration; Mk 7's dynamic improvements (reversed direction tail rotor for improved control, etc); non-retractable wheeled landing gear.

STRUCTURE: Composite main and tail rotor blades.

LANDING GEAR: Battlefield Lynx equipped with non-retractable tricycle landing gear. Twin nosewheels; single mainwheels. Oleo-pneumatic struts capable of absorbing 1.83 m (6 ft)/s descent rate.

POWER PLANT: Two Rolls-Royce Gem 42-1 turboshafts, each rated at 835 kW (1,120 shp). Exhaust diffusers for infra-red suppression optional on Battlefield Lynx.

AVIONICS: Super Lynx has Seaspray Mk 3 or Bendix/King RDR 1500 360° scan radar in chin fairing. (UK Mk 8 has Seaspray Mk 1 re-packaged, plus GEC Sensors Sea Owl thermal imaging equipment above nose.) Vinten Vicon 78 chaff dispenser; Vinten Vipa 1 reconnaissance pod; or Agiflite reconnaissance camera system. Battlefield Lynx may be equipped with Goodyear AN/ALE-39 chaff/flare dispensers and (subject to development) Dalmo-Victor AN/APR-39 radar warning receiver. Secure speech radio. Decca Doppler 71 and TANS 9447 navigation; Honeywell/Smiths AN/APN-198 radar altimeter; Collins 206A ADF; Cossor 2720 IFF; Collins VIR 31A VOR/ILS. Sextant 250 sight for fixed armament. Vipa 1 and Agiflite cameras as Super Lynx.

ARMAMENT: Super Lynx as standard naval Lynx, including four Sea Skua or two Penguin anti-ship missiles; or four Stinger anti-helicopter missiles. Battlefield Lynx may carry two GIAT 20 mm cannon pods; two FN pods with two 7.62 mm machine guns each; or two M.159C pods containing nineteen 2.75 in rockets each. Eight TOW anti-tank missiles on modified mounting, with BAe sight for gunner. Optionally HOT or Hellfire missiles.

DIMENSIONS, EXTERNAL (A: Battlefield Lynx, N: Super Lynx):
Tail rotor diameter 2.36 m (7 ft 9 in)
Length overall:

Demonstrator for the Westland/Sikorsky WS 70L (two General Electric T700 turboshaft engines) in desert camouflage

Westland/Aerospatiale Puma in RAF's pink desert camouflage, fitted with chaff/flare dispensers, missile approach warning system, radar warning receiver (nose and beneath tailboom) and air intake sand filters (RAF)

A, N, both rotors turning 15.24 m (50 ft 0 in)
N, main rotor blades and tail folded
10.85 m (35 ft 7¼ in)
A, rotors folded 13.24 m (43 ft 5¼ in)
Width overall, main rotor blades folded:
A 3.29 m (10 ft 9½ in)
N 2.94 m (9 ft 7¾ in)
Height overall: tail rotor turning:
A 3.73 m (12 ft 3 in)
N 3.79 m (12 ft 5¼ in)
main rotor blades and tail folded:
N 3.25 m (10 ft 8 in)
Wheel track: A 2.80 m (9 ft 2¼ in)
Wheelbase: A, N 3.02 m (9 ft 11 in)
AREAS:
Tail rotor disc 4.37 m² (47.04 sq ft)
WEIGHTS AND LOADINGS:
Basic weight empty: A 3,178 kg (7,006 lb)
N 3,291 kg (7,255 lb)
Operating weight empty (including crew and appropriate armament):
A, anti-tank (eight TOW) 3,949 kg (8,707 lb)
A, reconnaissance 3,444 kg (7,592 lb)
A, transport (unladen) 3,496 kg (7,707 lb)
N, anti-submarine warfare 4,207 kg (9,276 lb)
N, ASV (four Sea Skua) 4,252 kg (9,373 lb)
N, ASV (two Penguin) 4,461 kg (9,834 lb)
N, surveillance and targeting 3,597 kg (7,929 lb)
N, search and rescue 3,658 kg (8,064 lb)
Max underslung load 1,361 kg (3,000 lb)
Max T-O weight 5,125 kg (11,300 lb)
PERFORMANCE:
Max continuous cruising speed:
A 138 knots (256 km/h; 159 mph)
Range:
A, tactical transport 370 nm (685 km; 426 miles)

Radius of action:
A, anti-tank, 2 h on station with four TOWs
25 nm (46 km; 29 miles)
N, anti-submarine, 2 h 20 min on station, dipping sonar and one torpedo 20 nm (37 km; 23 miles)
N, point attack with four Sea Skuas
148 nm (274 km; 170 miles)
N, surveillance, 4.1 h on station
75 nm (139 km; 86 miles)

WESTLAND WS 70

TYPE: Combat assault squad transport helicopter.

PROGRAMME: After full partnership agreement with United Technologies (USA), Westland received US State Department approval to produce Sikorsky Black Hawk as WS 70 (ZG468); demonstrator (ZG468) assembled from Sikorsky kit to US Army UH-60A battlefield transport standards; first flight 1 April 1987 (used for training and market support).

VARIANTS: **WS 70L:** Equivalent to US UH-60L.

CUSTOMERS: Saudi Arabia signed provisional agreement for 88 WS 70Ls July 1988 (part of larger equipment deal with UK Government); confirmation anticipated late 1991.

COSTS: Westland board assigned £3 million for demonstrator (ZG468).

POWER PLANT: Two 1,224 kW (1,641 shp) General Electric T700-GE-701C turboshafts.

Details for Sikorsky UH-60L apply to WS 70L, except as follows:

AVIONICS (recommended): Communications equipment includes UHF and V/UHF and VHF/FM homing. Navigation equipment includes AN/ASN-43 compass, Doppler, plus customer specified equipment.

WEIGHTS AND LOADINGS:

Weight empty	4,964 kg (10,943 lb)
Max T-O weight	9,979 kg (22,000 lb)

PERFORMANCE:

Range with 1,814 kg (4,000 lb) payload	
	300 nm (556 km; 345 miles)
Ferry range	1,145 nm (2,122 km; 1,318 miles)

WESTLAND/AEROSPATIALE PUMA

RAF Puma HC. Mk 1s, built by Westland under Anglo-French helicopter agreement of 1967, fitted in mid-1980s with GEC-Marconi ARI 18228 radar warning receivers from Vulcan bomber force. In late 1990, 20 prepared for participation in Gulf War with uprating of INS to Racal Super-TANS standard; night vision goggle compatible cockpit; two Tracor M-130 chaff/flare dispensers below junction of tailboom and cabin; and Honeywell AN/AAR-47 missile-approach warning sensors on nose (two) and each sponson.

Puma specification last appeared in 1983-84 *Jane's* (French section) and details of early versions in 1976-77 edition. See also IAR in Romanian section of this edition.

UNITED STATES OF AMERICA

AAC
AIRCRAFT ACQUISITION CORPORATION

Acquired manufacturing and sales rights for Taylorcraft and Helio aircraft ranges in 1989 (which see). Further information also under New Technik entry in this section and under Taylor Kits entry in Sport Aircraft section.

AASI (formerly ASI)
ADVANCED AERODYNAMICS AND STRUCTURES INC

10703 Vanowen Street, North Hollywood, California 91605
Telephone: 1 (818) 753 1888
Fax: 1 (818) 753 8554
CHAIRMAN: Song-gen Yeh
PRESIDENT: Dr Carl C. Chen
CHIEF EXECUTIVE OFFICER AND GENERAL MANAGER:
Darius Sharifzadeh
MARKETING MANAGER: Bill Hubbard

AASI has succeeded Aerodynamics & Structures Inc, formed by former airline pilot Darius Sharifzadeh to develop the Jet Cruzer.

AASI JET CRUZER 620
TYPE: Six-seat turboprop aircraft.
PROGRAMME: Prototype **Jet Cruzer 450** with 313 kW (420 shp) Allison 250-C20S first exhibited at NBAA Show October 1988; aerodynamic design undertaken in Britain 1984-85 by 'Sandy' Burns; layout prepared by Ladislao Pazmany; structural design by David Kent of Light Transport Design in Britain; wind tunnel tests by University of San Diego; first flight 11 January 1989 (N5369M) and had flown 150 hours by March 1991; production prototype made first flight April 1991; certification to FAR Pt 23 expected third quarter 1992.
VARIANTS: **Jet Cruzer 620:** Possible military and unmanned roles; external loads possible.
DESIGN FEATURES: Rear-mounted main wing using NACA 2412 aerofoil, with 20° sweepback at quarter-chord and 4° dihedral; tip-mounted fins; unswept foreplane using NASA LS 0417 (Mod) section. Compared to Jet Cruzer 450 prototype, Jet Cruzer 620 has 25 cm (10 in) fuselage stretch, addition of fuel-carrying strakes at wingroots, leading-edge slats on main wing, 43 cm (17 in) nose extension to allow forward retraction of nosewheel, and vertical tail surfaces canted 15° inboard to improve aileron control.
FLYING CONTROLS: Ailerons in main wing, elevators on foreplane, rudders in tip-mounted fins. No flaps.
STRUCTURE: Metal wings, foreplane and vertical tail surfaces; unpressurised monocoque fuselage of graphite epoxy/Nomex honeycomb sandwich.
LANDING GEAR: Retractable tricycle type. Main units have spring steel legs.
POWER PLANT: One 462 kW (620 shp) Pratt & Whitney Canada PT6A-27 turboprop, driving a Hartzell three-blade constant-speed pusher propeller at 2,200 rpm. Fuel capacity 624 litres (165 US gallons; 137 Imp gallons).

AASI Jet Cruzer six-seat business and utility aircraft with P&WC PT6A-27 turboprop

ACCOMMODATION: Standard seating for six, including pilot. Three cabin windows on each side. Door on each side.

DIMENSIONS, EXTERNAL:

Wing span	11.02 m (36 ft 2 in)
Wing aspect ratio	7.5
Foreplane span	4.83 m (15 ft 10 in)
Length overall	7.64 m (25 ft 1 in)
Fuselage length	4.45 m (14 ft 7 in)
Height overall	2.62 m (8 ft 7 in)
Propeller diameter	2.03 m (6 ft 8 in)
Propeller ground clearance	0.58 m (1 ft 11 in)
Cabin door (port): Height	1.09 m (3 ft 7 in)
Width	0.97 m (3 ft 2 in)
Cabin door (stbd): Height	1.09 m (3 ft 7 in)
Width	1.75 m (5 ft 9 in)

DIMENSIONS, INTERNAL:

Cabin: Length	3.61 m (11 ft 10 in)
Volume	4.15 m³ (146.5 cu ft)

AREAS:

Wings, gross	16.17 m² (174.0 sq ft)
Ailerons (total)	1.03 m² (11.1 sq ft)
Fins (total)	2.00 m² (21.5 sq ft)
Rudders (total)	0.85 m² (9.2 sq ft)
Foreplane, incl elevators	5.39 m² (58.0 sq ft)
Elevators (total, incl tabs)	1.79 m² (19.3 sq ft)

WEIGHTS AND LOADINGS:

Weight empty	1,111 kg (2,450 lb)
Max T-O weight	2,041 kg (4,500 lb)
Max wing loading	126.26 kg/m² (25.86 lb/sq ft)
Max power loading	4.42 kg/kW (7.26 lb/shp)

PERFORMANCE (estimated, at max T-O weight):

Max operating speed (V~MO~)	246 knots (457 km/h; 284 mph)
Stalling speed:	
slats extended	59 knots (109 km/h; 68 mph)
slats retracted	69 knots (128 km/h; 80 mph)
Service ceiling	8,230 m (27,000 ft)
T-O to 15 m (50 ft)	436 m (1,430 ft)
Landing from 15 m (50 ft)	594 m (1,950 ft)
Max range at 3,050 m (10,000 ft)	1,055 nm (1,957 km; 1,216 miles)

AAC
AEROSTAR AIRCRAFT CORPORATION
S 3608 Davison Bd, Spokane, Washington 99204
Telephone: 1 (509) 455 8872
PRESIDENT: Steve Speer

AAC AEROSTAR 3000
Company formed as offshoot of Machen Inc (which see) to re-engine pressurised Piper 601P, 602P and 700P with 8.45 kN (1,900 lb st) Williams FJ44 turbo-fans in underslung pods. Expected first flight July 1992; certification July 1993; price $975,000 (1991); cruising speed 400 knots (740 km/h; 460 mph); range 1,500 nm (2,780 km; 1,725 miles).

ACA
ACA INDUSTRIES INC
28603 Trailriders Drive, Rancho Palos Verdes, California 90274

Dr Julian Wolkovitch, President of ACA, died in January 1991, but ACA was not liquidated. In 1974, he flew proof-of-concept joined wing glider; configuration adopted for Summit Trident T-3 microlight (see Sport Aircraft section of 1987-88 *Jane's*). Defense Advanced Research Projects Agency (DARPA), NASA, US Army and US Navy have studied joined wing concept for aircraft and missiles: NASA awarded ACA contract to produce manned research aircraft (see below).

ACA JW-1, JW-2 and JW-3
TYPE: Joined wing research aircraft.
PROGRAMME: ACA began redesigning NASA AD-1 oblique wing research aircraft (see 1981-82 *Jane's*) as joined wing aircraft in March 1986; three variants planned; none flown.
JW-1 with wings joined at 60 per cent semi-span, **JW-2** joined at 80 per cent semi-span and **JW-3** joined at 100 per cent semi-span.
DESIGN FEATURES: Applications include transport and general aviation aircraft, fighters, VTOL aircraft, agricultural aircraft and UAVs. ACA was advising Rockwell International and other manufacturers. Claimed benefits include lighter weight, greater stiffness, less induced drag, lower wave drag, higher trimmed maximum lift coefficient, and inbuilt direct lift and side-force characteristics.

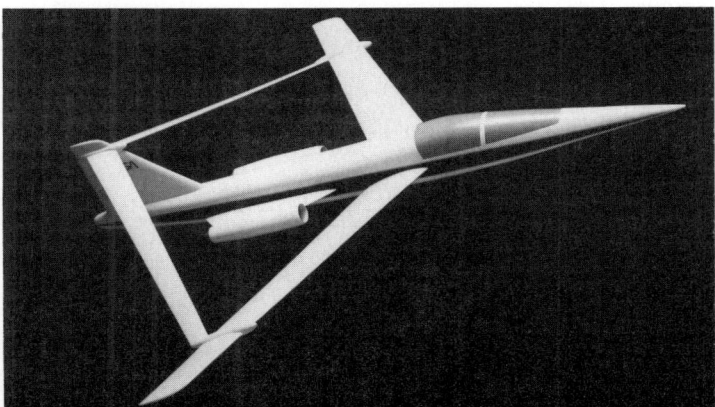

Models of the ACA JW-1 (left) and JW-2 long- and medium-span versions of NASA's joined wing research aircraft

FLYING CONTROLS: JW-1 has six trailing-edge control surfaces on front wing and four on rear wing, operating in a variety of combinations for pitch, roll and direct-lift control; single rudder on fin.

STRUCTURE: Fail-safe composites structure.

LANDING GEAR: Non-retractable tricycle type.

POWER PLANT: Two Ames Industrial Corporation TRS 18-046 turbojets, each rated at 0.978 kN (220 lb st), mounted in pods aft of front wing/fuselage junction.

ACCOMMODATION: Pilot only, in enclosed cockpit with canopy. Cockpit is not pressurised.

DIMENSIONS, EXTERNAL (A: JW-1, B: JW-2, C: JW-3):

Wing span, front: A		12.19 m (40 ft 0 in)
B		9.84 m (32 ft 3½ in)
C		7.31 m (24 ft 0 in)
rear, all		7.31 m (24 ft 0 in)

Wing chord: at root: all		1.19 m (3 ft 11 in)
at tip: A		0.48 m (1 ft 6¾ in)
B		0.61 m (2 ft 0 in)
C		0.76 m (2 ft 6 in)
Wing aspect ratio, front: A		11.18
B		8.07
C		5.21
AREAS:		
Wings, gross: A		13.29 m² (143.1 sq ft)
B		12.01 m² (129.3 sq ft)
C		10.27 m² (110.6 sq ft)
Front wing: A		10.17 m² (109.5 sq ft)
B		8.89 m² (95.7 sq ft)
C		7.15 m² (77.0 sq ft)
Rear wing: all		3.12 m² (33.6 sq ft)

WEIGHTS AND LOADINGS:		
Max T-O weight		973 kg (2,145 lb)
Max wing loading: A		73.21 kg/m² (14.99 lb/sq ft)
B		81.01 kg/m² (16.59 lb/sq ft)
C		94.74 kg/m² (19.39 lb/sq ft)
Max power loading		497.44 kg/kN (4.88 lb/lb st)
PERFORMANCE (estimated):		
Max level speed at 2,135 m (7,000 ft):		
A		276 knots (511 km/h; 318 mph)
B		283 knots (524 km/h; 326 mph)
C		291 knots (539 km/h; 335 mph)
Max rate of climb at S/L, ISA:		
A, B, C		518 m (1,700 ft)/min
Rate of climb at S/L, ISA, one engine out:		
A, B		152 m (500 ft)/min
C		91 m (300 ft)/min

ADVANCED AIRCRAFT
ADVANCED AIRCRAFT CORPORATION
2016 Palomar Airport Road, Carlsbad, California 92008
Telephone: 1 (619) 438 1964
Telex: 249075 ATSD UR
PRESIDENT: Neil F. Martin
GENERAL MANAGER: Leland L. Dimon III

Company formed 1 July 1983; acquired production facilities of Riley Aircraft Manufacturing Inc (see 1983-84 *Jane's*); two Cessna turbine conversions offered in 1987, since when no further details.

ADVANCED AIRCRAFT TURBINE P-210
TYPE: Cessna P-210 Pressurised Centurion powered by P&WC PT6A-135 turboprop.

PROGRAMME: Previously known as Spirit 750; conversion developed by Riley Aircraft Manufacturing; on offer 1987.

DESIGN FEATURES: Powered by 559 kW (750 shp) PT6A-135 turboprop flat rated to 335.5 kW (450 shp) driving Hartzell three-blade constant-speed fully feathering reversible-pitch Q-tip propeller. Conversion includes Flint wingtip fuel tanks with combined capacity of 62.5 litres (16.5 US gallons; 13.7 Imp gallons); modified control surfaces; ventral fin; glassfibre aerodynamic cowling with inertial separator and electric induction lip de-icing; electric propeller de-icing; FAA-approved 24V electrical system; Smiths 28V 200A starter/generator; 28V 50A standby generator; Gill 639T heavy duty battery; fuel computer; new engine instrument panel; 3M Stormscope weather radar.

DIMENSIONS, EXTERNAL: As for pressurised Centurion, except:

Length overall	9.17 m (30 ft 1 in)
Propeller diameter	1.98 m (6 ft 6 in)

WEIGHTS AND LOADINGS:

Weight empty	1,199 kg (2,621 lb)
Max ramp weight	1,822 kg (4,016 lb)
Max T-O weight	1,814 kg (4,000 lb)
Max landing weight	1,723 kg (3,800 lb)
Max wing loading	102.53 kg/m² (21.0 lb/sq ft)
Max power loading	5.41 kg/kW (8.88 lb/shp)

PERFORMANCE (at max T-O weight except where indicated):

Max cruising speed at 7,010 m (23,000 ft)	
	253 knots (470 km/h; 292 mph)
Econ cruising speed	213 knots (394 km/h; 245 mph)
Stalling speed:	
flaps up	67 knots (125 km/h; 78 mph) IAS
30% flap	63 knots (117 km/h; 73 mph) IAS
flaps down	58 knots (108 km/h; 67 mph) IAS
Max rate of climb at S/L	549 m (1,800 ft)/min
Service ceiling	above 7,010 m (23,000 ft)
T-O to 15 m (50 ft) at AUW of 1,542 kg (3,400 lb)	
	334 m (1,095 ft)
Landing from 15 m (50 ft) at AUW of 1,542 kg (3,400 lb)	
	394 m (1,291 ft)

Range with max fuel, ISA, max cruise power at 7,010 m (23,000 ft), allowances for start, taxi, take-off, climb and descent, 45 min reserves

1,008 nm (1,868 km; 1,160 miles)

ADVANCED AIRCRAFT REGENT 1500
TYPE: Cessna 421C Golden Eagle with P&WC PT6A turboprops.

PROGRAMME: Modification developed by Riley Aircraft Manufacturing Inc; first flight November 1979 at Palomar Airport; certificated 1980.

DESIGN FEATURES: Powered by two P&WC PT6A-135 turboprops, each flat rated at 559 kW (750 shp) and driving Hartzell three-blade, constant-speed autofeathering reversible-pitch propellers with Q-tips; fuel augmented by nacelle locker tanks with combined capacity of

Advanced Aircraft Turbine P-210 turboprop conversion of Cessna Pressurised Centurion, before addition of ventral fin

Advanced Aircraft Regent 1500, with Pratt & Whitney Canada PT6A-135 turboprops

568 litres (150 US gallons; 125 Imp gallons); optional all-glassfibre nacelle-end tanks increasing combined capacity to 605 litres (160 US gallons; 133 Imp gallons); advanced aerodynamic cowlings incorporating inertia separators; electric de-icing of intakes and propellers.

SYSTEMS: Generally as for Cessna 421C, except bleed air unit for pressurisation system; electrical system with 200A starter/generators and heavy duty battery; engine fire detection system; and pneumatic leading-edge de-icing boots for wings and tail unit.

WEIGHTS AND LOADINGS:

Weight empty	2,404 kg (5,300 lb)
Max T-O weight	3,447 kg (7,600 lb)
Max zero-fuel weight	2,993 kg (6,600 lb)
Max landing weight	3,266 kg (7,200 lb)
Max power loading	3.08 kg/kW (5.07 lb/shp)

PERFORMANCE (at max T-O weight except where indicated):

Max cruising speed, at max cruise power, AUW of 3,220 kg (7,100 lb):	
at 8,230 m (27,000 ft)	315 knots (584 km/h; 363 mph)
at 6,705 m (22,000 ft)	278 knots (515 km/h; 320 mph)
at 4,875 m (16,000 ft)	251 knots (465 km/h; 289 mph)
Max rate of climb at S/L:	
at max T-O weight	945 m (3,100 ft)/min

at 3,175 kg (7,000 lb) AUW	1,310 m (4,300 ft)/min
Service ceiling	9,145 m (30,000 ft)
Service ceiling, one engine out, at 3,175 kg (7,000 lb) AUW	7,620 m (25,000 ft)
T-O run	462 m (1,517 ft)
T-O to 15 m (50 ft)	694 m (2,277 ft)
Landing from 15 m (50 ft) with propeller reversal	606 m (1,988 ft)
Landing run with propeller reversal	324 m (1,064 ft)

Range with max fuel, ISA, allowances for start, taxi, take-off, climb and descent, 45 min reserves:

max cruise power:	
at 4,875 m (16,000 ft)	832 nm (1,542 km; 958 miles)
at 6,705 m (22,000 ft)	987 nm (1,829 km; 1,136 miles)
at 8,230 m (27,000 ft)	1,169 nm (2,166 km; 1,346 miles)
max range power:	
at 5,485 m (18,000 ft)	908 nm (1,682 km; 1,045 miles)
at 6,705 m (22,000 ft)	1,112 nm (2,060 km; 1,280 miles)
at 8,230 m (27,000 ft)	1,276 nm (2,364 km; 1,469 miles)

AERODIS
AERODIS AMERICA INC
D. W. Hooks Airport, 8319 Thora Spring, Texas 77379
Telephone: 1 (713) 370 0394
Fax: 1 (713) 251 3633
Telex: 792835
PRESIDENT: E. Glenn Walters

Company formed October 1982; commissioned David B. Thurston to design three all-composite aircraft based on common airframe; concluded agreement with PT Cipta Restu Sarana Svaha of Indonesia to manufacture components; marketing in Asia, Middle East and Pacific basin by Aerodis (HK) Company Ltd of Hong Kong.

AERODIS AA200 ORION
TYPE: Four-seat piston-engined light aircraft.

PROGRAMME: Design started April 1988; prototype construction began July 1989; first flight 7 April 1991. Not initially to be certificated, but design meets or exceeds FAR Pt 23 Amendment 34. Aerodis claims

AA200 Orion not related to French Grinvalds G-802 Orion homebuilt described in Sport Aircraft section of 1988-89 *Jane's*.

DESIGN FEATURES: Piston engine mounted aft of cabin, driving pusher propeller at tail through extension shaft; wing section NASA GA40U-A215 at root and GA37U-A212 at tip; dihedral 3°; incidence 1° 30′ at root.

FLYING CONTROLS: Frise-type ailerons, with differential deflection and actuated by pushrods; one-piece elevator carries electrically actuated trim tab at centre; rudder in ventral as well as in main fin; electrically actuated slotted flaps, maximum deflection 30°; dorsal and ventral fins; fixed tailplane.

STRUCTURE: Damage-tolerant two-spar wing with D-section leading-edge torque box and of graphite epoxy skins on Nomex core and graphite spars; ailerons and flaps of Rohacell foam/glassfibre; wings have quick-detach fittings in channels across the fuselage; damage-tolerant fuselage of graphite/glassfibre/Nomex honeycomb/Rohacell foam, made in two halves and bonded at centreline; stringers and seven bulkheads; roll-over protection over cabin; T tail of honeycomb core with glassfibre skins.

LANDING GEAR: Electro-hydraulically retractable tricycle type with steerable nosewheel. Mainwheels retract inward into wing, nosewheel forward. Oleo-strut shock absorbers in all units. Cleveland mainwheels, size 6.00-6, pressure 3.45 bars (50 lb/sq in). Cleveland nosewheel, size 5.00-5, pressure 2.76 bars (40 lb/sq in). Cleveland disc brakes.

POWER PLANT: One 134 kW (180 hp) Textron Lycoming O-360-A4A flat-four engine, mounted to rear of cabin and driving a three-blade constant-speed composite MT pusher propeller via a graphite/epoxy driveshaft and flexidyne coupler; 149 kW (200 hp) Textron Lycoming IO-360-A1B6 engine optional. Fuel contained in integral wing leading-edge tanks, maximum capacity 227 litres (60 US gallons; 50 Imp gallons). Fuel filler cap in upper surface of each wing. Oil capacity 7.6 litres (2 US gallons; 1.67 Imp gallons).

ACCOMMODATION: Enclosed cabin with four individual seats. Baggage compartment aft of seats. Single door on port side of fuselage, horizontally divided, upper half opening upwards while lower portion contains integral entrance step. Emergency exit in forward cabin window on starboard side. Cabin is stressed to withstand 20*g* impact. Inertia-reel shoulder harnesses and seatbelts, cabin soundproofing, heating and ventilation, standard.

SYSTEMS: Electrical system supplied by 28V 60A alternator.

AVIONICS: IFR avionics to customer choice.

EQUIPMENT: Dual controls (sticks) optional.

DIMENSIONS, EXTERNAL:
Wing span	9.13 m (29 ft 11½ in)
Wing chord: at root	1.60 m (5 ft 3 in)
at tip	1.12 m (3 ft 8 in)
Wing aspect ratio	6.55
Length overall	7.75 m (25 ft 5 in)
Height overall	2.62 m (8 ft 7 in)
Tailplane span	3.30 m (10 ft 10 in)
Wheel track	3.23 m (10 ft 7 in)

First prototype of Aerodis AA200 Orion (Textron Lycoming O-360-A4A)

Wheelbase	2.86 m (9 ft 4½ in)
Propeller diameter	1.88 m (6 ft 2 in)
Propeller ground clearance	0.53 m (1 ft 8¾ in)
Passenger door: Height	1.00 m (3 ft 3¼ in)
Width	1.00 m (3 ft 3¼ in)
Height to sill	0.65 m (2 ft 1½ in)

DIMENSIONS, INTERNAL:
Cabin: Length	2.48 m (8 ft 1½ in)
Max width	1.07 m (3 ft 6 in)
Height	1.14 m (3 ft 8¾ in)
Floor area	2.46 m² (26.43 sq ft)
Volume	2.62 m³ (92.5 cu ft)

AREAS:
Wings, gross	12,73 m² (137.0 sq ft)
Ailerons (total)	0.99 m² (10.67 sq ft)
Trailing-edge flaps (total)	1.68 m² (18.07 sq ft)
Vertical tail surfaces (total)	1.55 m² (16.7 sq ft)
Tailplane	3.14 m² (33.8 sq ft)
Elevator, incl tab	1.21 m² (13.0 sq ft)

WEIGHTS AND LOADINGS:
Weight empty	635 kg (1,400 lb)
Max fuel weight	163 kg (360 lb)
Max T-O weight	1,134 kg (2,500 lb)
Max wing loading	89.1 kg/m² (18.25 lb/sq ft)
Max power loading	8.46 kg/kW (13.89 lb/hp)

PERFORMANCE (estimated, at max T-O weight, ISA):
Never-exceed speed (V_NE)	190 knots (352 km/h; 218 mph)
Max level speed	180 knots (334 km/h; 207 mph)
Max cruising speed at 2,285 m (7,500 ft)	165 knots (306 km/h; 190 mph)
Stalling speed, landing gear and flaps down	54 knots (100 km/h; 62 mph)

Max rate of climb at S/L	311 m (1,020 ft)/min
Service ceiling	4,420 m (14,500 ft)
Range with max fuel	780 nm (1,445 km; 898 miles)

AERODIS AA300 RIGEL and AA330 THETA

TYPE: Two-seat military or civil jet trainer and single-seat tactical aircraft.

PROGRAMME: Two Rigel prototypes under construction (one with each engine option); entered for USAF/USN Joint Primary Aircraft Training System (JPATS) early 1991; first flight due early 1992. Theta design started September 1988; first flight not expected before mid-1993.

DESIGN FEATURES: Based on Orion airframe; detachable rear fuselage to facilitate engine change and servicing; both aircraft stressed for aerobatics; stores hardpoints on fuselage centreline and under each wing.

FLYING CONTROLS: Ventral fin and rudder replaced by small ventral strake; otherwise as AA200.

LANDING GEAR: Mainwheel size 18.5 × 5.5. Tyre pressures: mainwheels 5.86 bars (85 lb/sq in); nosewheel 2.07 bars (30 lb/sq in). Maximum nosewheel steering angle ±30°.

POWER PLANT: One 8.45 kN (1,900 lb st) Garrett TFE109-3 or Williams FJ44 turbofan, derated to 7.11 kN (1,600 lb st). Maximum internal fuel capacity 757 litres (200 US gallons; 166.5 Imp gallons). Refuelling point in each wingtip.

ACCOMMODATION: Two in tandem in pressurised and air-conditioned cockpit in Rigel, one in Theta, on Martin-Baker Mk 15 lightweight ejection seats. Upward opening bubble canopy, electro-hydraulically actuated. Headroom raised 10 cm (4 in). Windscreen arch tilted 6 cm (2.4 in) forward to improve rear-seat view. Sliding canopy optional on Theta.

SYSTEMS: 28V 300A electrical system. Pressurisation system, maximum differential 0.45 bar (6.5 lb/sq in). Oxygen system standard.

DIMENSIONS, EXTERNAL:
Wing span	8.85 m (29 ft 0½ in)
Wing aspect ratio	6.39
Length overall	7.90 m (25 ft 11 in)
Height overall	2.64 m (8 ft 8 in)
Tailplane span	3.30 m (10 ft 10 in)
Wheel track	2.95 m (9 ft 8 in)
Wheelbase	3.16 m (10 ft 4½ in)

DIMENSIONS, INTERNAL:
Cockpit (Rigel): Length	2.81 m (9 ft 2½ in)
Max width	0.78 m (2 ft 6½ in)
Height	1.12 m (3 ft 8 in)
Floor area	2.00 m² (21.5 sq ft)

AREAS:
Wings, gross	12.26 m² (132.0 sq ft)
Fin	1.05 m² (11.26 sq ft)
Rudder	0.365 m² (3.93 sq ft)

WEIGHTS AND LOADINGS:
Empty weight	1,030 kg (2,270 lb)
Max T-O weight	1,860 kg (4,100 lb)
Max wing loading	151.65 kg/m² (31.06 lb/sq ft)
Max power loading	220.12 kg/kN (2.16 lb/lb st)

PERFORMANCE (estimated, at max T-O weight, ISA):
Max level speed at 9,150 m (30,000 ft)	370 knots (686 km/h; 426 mph)
Max cruising speed at 9,150 m (30,000 ft)	335 knots (621 km/h; 386 mph)
Econ cruising speed at 9,150 m (30,000 ft)	220 knots (408 km/h; 253 mph)
Stalling speed, landing gear and flaps down	68 knots (126 km/h; 79 mph)
Max rate of climb at S/L	1,067 m (3,500 ft)/min
T-O to 15 m (50 ft)	314 m (1,030 ft)
Landing from 15 m (50 ft)	752 m (2,466 ft)
Range with max internal fuel, 45 min reserves	1,050 nm (1,945 km; 1,209 miles)
g limits	+9/−6

Artist's impression of Aerodis AA300 Rigel two-seat primary jet trainer

AERO UNION

AERO UNION CORPORATION

PO Box 247, Municipal Airport, 100 Lockheed Avenue, Chico, California 95926
Telephone: 1 (916) 896 3000
Fax: 1 (916) 893 8585
Telex: 171359 AEROUNION CICO
PRESIDENT: Dale P. Newton
SECRETARY-TREASURER/GENERAL MANAGER:
Victor E. Alvistur
DIRECTOR, SALES AND MARKETING: John Oswald
DIRECTOR, INTERNATIONAL MARKETING: John E. Gyarfas

Company established 1959 for aerial firefighting; manufactures tank systems for Douglas DC-3, DC-4, DC-6 and DC-7, Fairchild C-119, Grumman S-2, Lockheed C-130/L-100 Hercules, Lockheed P-3 Orion and Electra; also produces aircraft fuel tanks, airstairs, environmental control systems, cargo pallet roller systems, retardant delivery and aerial spraying systems, dorsal fins; sole manufacturer of Model 1080 Air Refuelling Store developed by Beechcraft and acquired by Aero Union in 1985.

AERO UNION MODULAR AERIAL FIREFIGHTING SYSTEM (MAFFS)

TYPE: Firefighting tank, control and dispensing modules to fit USAF 463L pallet system.
PROGRAMME: Some kits supplied to US Air Force.
CUSTOMERS: 16 sets of MAFFS delivered to US Air Force.
DESIGN FEATURES: Designed for aircraft such as Lockheed C-130 equipped for USAF 463L pallet system; MAFFS consists of five retardant tank modules, totalling 11,356 litres (3,000 US gallons; 2,498 Imp gallons), control module, dispensing module with two retractable nozzles making a swath 13-61 m (43-200 ft) wide and 180-610 m (590-2,000 ft) long according to height and speed. System empty weight is 2,177 kg (4,800 lb); powered by compressed air reservoir at each tank and battery power for control module; installed in C-130 in less than one hour; typical filling time 15 minutes; can be operated at 30-150 m (98-492 ft) at 130-140 knots (241-259 km/h; 150-161 mph).

AERO UNION C-130 AUXILIARY FUEL SYSTEM

TYPE: Transferable or usable extra fuel for C-130/L-100.
PROGRAMME: Development complete.
DESIGN FEATURES: Usable for in-flight refuelling, range extension or fuel transport; two cylindrical tanks mounted side by side on 6.1 m (20 ft) long platform loaded by 463L cargo handling system; total capacity 13,627 litres (3,600 US gallons; 2,998 Imp gallons); length 5.26 m (17 ft 3 in); width 3.0 m (9 ft 10¼ in); height, excluding plumbing, 1.68 m (5 ft 6 in); weight empty about 1,542 kg (3,400 lb); plumbing complies with MIL-F-17874; flow rate 1,136 litres (300 US gallons; 250 Imp gallons)/min. Unit interfaces with Lockheed air refuelling manifold; passage provided for crew access fore and aft of tanks.

AERO UNION C-130 FIRELINER

TYPE: Version of SP-2H Firestar conversion (which see) for C-130.
PROGRAMME: First flight early 1990; service entry Spring 1990, following FAA certification 29 March 1990.
DESIGN FEATURES: First conversion on C-130A, but adaptable to later marks. Retardant tank of 11,356 litres (3,000 US gallons; 2,498 Imp gallons), but otherwise system similar to that of SP-2H Firestar.

AERO UNION C-130 AERIAL SPRAY SYSTEM

TYPE: Modular spray kit for unmodified Lockheed C-130.
DESIGN FEATURES: Self-contained modular system with two Aero Union bulk fuel transfer tanks, each of 6,813 litres (1,800 US gallons; 1,498 Imp gallons), mounted on 463L pallet; tanks modified to supply liquid to a retractable spray module attached to cargo ramp; boom hydraulically extended into airstream; when boom retracted, ramp can be fully closed; interchangeable spray nozzles vary application rate; ultra-low-rate nozzles optional; pressure and flow rate to boom monitored and controlled by loadmaster using portable electronic control panel.

AERO UNION HELIBORNE AERIAL FIREFIGHTING SYSTEM (HAFFS)

TYPE: Designed for installation in large helicopters like Boeing CH-47/Model 234.
VARIANTS: Smaller system, capacity 2,650-3,785 litres (700-1,000 US gallons; 583-833 Imp gallons) being developed for CH-46/Kawasaki KV107. Also evaluating derivative designs for Aerospatiale AS 332, EHI EH 101, Mil Mi-8 and Sikorsky UH-60.
DESIGN FEATURES: Capacity of 7,571 litres (2,000 US gallons; 1,665 Imp gallons) delivered through remotely operated, variable pattern foam cannon capable of delivering 2,271 litres (600 US gallons; 500 Imp gallons)/min at stand-off distance of more than 61 m (200 ft). All or part of payload can also be dropped in 10 s. HAFFS will saturate half-acre area at density of 40.3 litres/m² (0.99 US gallons; 0.82 Imp gallons/sq ft). System empty weight 1,749 kg (3,857 lb).

Lockheed C-130 of the United States Air Force equipped with Aero Union MAFFS

Aero Union Firestar tanker conversion of the Lockheed SP-2H Neptune

Aero Union Aerostar conversion of Lockheed P-3A Orion

AERO UNION GRUMMAN HU-16B ALBATROSS TANKER CONVERSION

TYPE: Firefighting kit for HU-16B amphibian.
DESIGN FEATURES: Two tanks totalling 3,785 litres (1,000 US gallons; 833 Imp gallons) mounted side by side in fuselage and filled through two retractable probes extended while the aircraft is planing on the step; refilling takes 10 s at 70 knots (130 km/h; 81 mph); filling on land through single nozzle in fuselage side; tanks can be emptied individually or together.

WEIGHTS AND LOADINGS:
Weight empty	9,956 kg (21,950 lb)
Max T-O weight	15,036 kg (33,150 lb)

PERFORMANCE:
Max level speed	220 knots (408 km/h; 253 mph)
Cruising speed	162 knots (300 km/h; 186 mph)

AERO UNION SP-2H FIRESTAR

TYPE: Civilian air tanker version of Lockheed P2V-7/SP-2.
PROGRAMME: Prototype (N701AU) in service 1988.
DESIGN FEATURES: Westinghouse J34 booster turbojets and other military equipment removed; 7,571 litre (2,000 US gallon; 1,665 Imp gallon) capacity tank weighing 318 kg (700 lb) and two computer-controlled, electro-hydraulically actuated dispersal doors that can deliver precisely metered flow rates of 189-2,650 litres (50-700 US gallons; 41.6-583 Imp gallons) per second. One-eighth, one-quarter, one-half or whole tankful can be selected; computerised logic allows selection of coverage density and quantity; drops are precise and uniform without overlaps or gaps; flow is constant regardless of quantity remaining in tank; drop patterns 50 per cent longer than typical multi-door system claimed for same volume of retardant.

WEIGHTS AND LOADINGS:
Weight empty	16,692 kg (36,800 lb)
Max payload	8,164 kg (18,000 lb)
Max T-O and landing weight	30,617 kg (67,500 lb)

PERFORMANCE (at max T-O weight):
Never-exceed speed (V_{NE})

	270 knots (500 km/h; 311 mph)
Econ cruising speed	195 knots (361 km/h; 225 mph)
Max airdrop speed	145 knots (268 km/h; 167 mph)
Stalling speed, landing gear and flaps down	
	93 knots (172 km/h; 107 mph)
Max rate of climb at S/L	488 m (1,600 ft)/min
Rate of climb at S/L, one engine out	122 m (400 ft)/min
Certificated ceiling	5,485 m (18,000 ft)
Service ceiling, one engine out	5,365 m (17,600 ft)
Max ferry range, 30 min reserves	
	1,300 nm (2,409 km; 1,497 miles)

AERO UNION P-3A AEROSTAR

TYPE: Civil firefighting conversion of P-3A Orion.
PROGRAMME: First conversion early 1990 with temporary tank; installation of computer-controlled tank planned for Spring 1991.
DESIGN FEATURES: Initially 11,356 litre (3,000 US gallon; 2,498 Imp gallon) ventral tank with eight drop doors. Development planned of computer-controlled tank similar to those in SP-2H and C-130.

AERO UNION CESSNA 208/208B CARAVAN FIRE FIGHTER

TYPE: Cessna 208/208B Caravan I conversion.
DESIGN FEATURES: Ventrally mounted 1,893 litre (500 US gallon; 416 Imp gallon) aluminium tank attaches to standard cargo pod mountings; tank weighs 163 kg (360 lb) and has two drop doors over almost entire length of tank; preselected drop rates computer-modulated in eight increments to maintain flows of 3.8-30.3 litres (1-8 US gallons; 0.8-6.7 Imp gallons) per 9.3 m² (100 sq ft); integral injection system holds enough retardant for 10 drops; optional spray manifold kit for aerial insecticide spraying.

AIR TRACTOR

AIR TRACTOR INC

PO Box 485, Municipal Airport, Olney, Texas 76374
Telephone: 1 (817) 564 5616
Fax: 1 (817) 564 2348
Telex: 910 890 4792
PRESIDENT: Leland Snow

Air Tractor agricultural aircraft based on 30-year experience of Leland Snow, who produced Snow S-2 series, which later became Rockwell S-2R (see earlier *Jane's*); six models of Air Tractor available in 1991 powered by various P&WC PT6As.

AIR TRACTOR MODEL AT-401/401A AIR TRACTOR

TYPE: Single-seat agricultural aircraft.
PROGRAMME: AT-401 developed 1986 from AT-301, with increased wing span and larger hopper; combined production of AT-401/AT-502 (which see) running at nine a month in early 1991.
VARIANTS: **AT-401:** Original Pratt & Whitney R-1340 engined model; in production.

AT-401A: Powered by Polish 441.5 kW (592 hp) PZL-3S Series 2 radial engine driving four-blade constant-speed US-132000/A-4 Hydromatic propeller of 2.63 m (8 ft 7½ in) diameter; in development early 1990. PZL-3S engine specially fitted with enlarged cooling fins, to be offered as alternative to R-1340. Certification expected Spring 1991, to be followed by extensive Air Tractor dealer service testing before production.
CUSTOMERS: By 1991, 95 AT-401s delivered to Australia, Brazil, Colombia, Mexico, Spain and USA.
DESIGN FEATURES: Wing aerofoil NACA 4415; dihedral 3° 30'; incidence 2°.
FLYING CONTROLS: Ailerons, elevators and rudders have boost tabs; ailerons droop 10° when electrically operated Fowler flaps deflected to maximum 26°.
STRUCTURE: Two-spar wing structure of 2024-T3 light alloy, with alloy steel lower spar cap; bonded doubler inside wing leading-edge to resist impact damage; glassfibre wingroot fairings and skin overlaps sealed against chemical ingress; wing ribs and skins zinc chromated before assembly; flaps and ailerons of light alloy. Fuselage of 4130N steel tube, oven stress relieved and oiled internally, with skin panels of 2024-T3 light alloy attached by Camloc fasteners for quick removal; rear fuselage lightly pressurised to prevent chemical ingress; cantilever fin and strut braced tailplane of light alloy, metal-skinned and sealed against chemical ingress.
LANDING GEAR: Non-retractable tailwheel type. Cantilever heavy duty E-4340 spring steel main gear, thickness 28.6 mm (1.125 in); flat spring suspension for castoring and lockable tailwheel. Cleveland mainwheels with tyre size 8.50-10 (8-ply), pressure 2 83 bars (41 lb/sq in). Tailwheel tyre size 5.00-5. Cleveland four-piston brakes with heavy duty discs.
POWER PLANT: One remanufactured 447 kW (600 hp) Pratt & Whitney R-1340 aircooled radial engine with speed ring cowling in AT-401, driving a Pacific Propeller 22D40/AG200-2 Hydromatic two-blade constant-speed metal propeller. Hydromatic 23D40 three-blade propeller, diameter 2.59 m (8 ft 6 in), optional. AT-401A has 441.5 kW (592 hp) Pezetel PZL-3S Series 2, as detailed above. Fuel in two integral wing tanks with combined capacity of 477 litres (126 US gallons; 105 Imp gallons). Refuelling points on upper surface of wings at root. Oil capacity 30 litres (8 US gallons; 6.7 Imp gallons).
ACCOMMODATION: Single seat with nylon mesh cover in enclosed cabin which is sealed to prevent chemical ingress. Downward hinged window/door on each side. 'Line of sight' instrument layout, with swing-down lower instrument panel for ease of access for instrument maintenance. Baggage compartment in bottom of fuselage, aft of cabin, with door on port side. Cabin ventilation by 0.10 m (4 in) diameter airscoop.
SYSTEMS: Agricultural dispersal system comprises a 1,514 litre (400 US gallon; 333 Imp gallon) Derakane vinylester resin/glassfibre hopper mounted in forward fuselage with hopper window and instrument panel mounted hopper quantity gauge; 0.97 m (3 ft 2 in) wide Transland gatebox; Transland 5 cm (2 in) bottom loading valve; Agrinautics 6.4 cm (2½ in) spraypump with Transland on/off valve and two-blade wooden fan, and 41-nozzle stainless steel spray system with streamlined booms. 24V electrical system, supplied by 35A engine driven alternator.
AVIONICS: Optional avionics include Bendix/King KX 155 nav/com and Narco ELT-10 emergency locator transmitter.
EQUIPMENT: Standard equipment includes ground start receptacle and three-colour polyurethane paint finish. Optional equipment includes night flying package comprising strobe and navigation lights; night working lights; retractable 600W landing light in port wingtip, and ferry fuel system. Alternative agricultural equipment includes Transland 22358 extra high volume spreader, Transland 54401 NorCal Swathmaster, and 40 extra spray nozzles for high volume spraying.
DIMENSIONS, EXTERNAL:
Wing span	14.97 m (49 ft 1¼ in)
Wing chord, constant	1.83 m (6 ft 0 in)

Air Tractor Model AT-401A Air Tractor (PZL-3S Series 2 radial)

Wing aspect ratio	8.2
Length overall	8.23 m (27 ft 0 in)
Height overall	2.59 m (8 ft 6 in)
AREAS:	
Wings, gross	27.31 m² (294.0 sq ft)
Ailerons (total)	3.55 m² (38.2 sq ft)
Trailing-edge flaps (total)	3.75 m² (40.4 sq ft)
Fin	0.90 m² (9.7 sq ft)
Rudder	1.30 m² (14.0 sq ft)
Tailplane	2.42 m² (26.0 sq ft)
Elevators, incl tabs	2.36 m² (25.4 sq ft)
WEIGHTS AND LOADINGS:	
Weight empty, spray equipped	1,875 kg (4,135 lb)
Max T-O weight	3,565 kg (7,860 lb)
Max landing weight	2,721 kg (6,000 lb)
Max wing loading	130.51 kg/m² (26.73 lb/sq ft)
Max power loading	7.97 kg/kW (13.1 lb/hp)

PERFORMANCE (at max T-O weight, ISA, except where indicated):
Max cruising speed at S/L, hopper empty	135 knots (251 km/h; 156 mph)
Cruising speed at 1,220 m (4,000 ft)	124 knots (230 km/h; 143 mph)
Typical working speed	104-122 knots (193-225 km/h; 120-140 mph)
Stalling speed at 2,721 kg (6,000 lb):	
flaps up	64 knots (118 km/h; 73 mph)
flaps down	53 knots (98 km/h; 61 mph)
Stalling speed as usually landed	47 knots (87 km/h; 54 mph)
Max rate of climb at S/L:	
at max landing weight	335 m (1,100 ft)/min
at max T-O weight	158 m (520 ft)/min
T-O run	402 m (1,318 ft)
Range, econ cruising speed at 2,440 m (8,000 ft), no reserves	547 nm (1,014 km; 630 miles)

AIR TRACTOR MODEL AT-400 and 402 TURBO AIR TRACTOR

TYPE: Turboprop agricultural aircraft with choice of wing spans.
PROGRAMME: Following on from AT-400, AT-402 first flight August 1988; certificated November 1988; first delivery late 1988.
VARIANTS: **AT-400:** Basic version, with short-span wing.
AT-402: Combines fuselage, tail surfaces and landing gear of AT-400 with longer wing of AT-401.
CUSTOMERS: Total of 86 AT-400s and 27 AT-402s delivered by 1 January 1991.
DESIGN FEATURES: Both variants have 1,514 litre (400 US gallon; 333 Imp gallon) hopper with 0.97 m (3 ft 2 in) wide gatebox; both variants powered by 507 kW (680 shp) P&WC PT6A-15AG, -27 or -28, either new or customer-furnished, driving Hartzell three-blade constant-speed reversible-pitch propeller. All models have steel alloy lower wing spar caps for unlimited fatigue life and reinforced leading-edge to prevent bird strike damage, size 29-11 high-flotation tyres and wheels as

standard, 250A starter/generator and two 24V 21Ah batteries; standard fuel capacity 644 litres (170 US gallons; 142 Imp gallons); optional fuel tankage 818 litres (216 US gallons; 180 Imp gallons) or 886 litres (234 US gallons; 195 Imp gallons); optional equipment includes Transland extra high volume dispersal system.
DIMENSIONS, EXTERNAL:
Wing span: AT-400	13.75 m (45 ft 1¼ in)
AT-402	14.97 m (49 ft 1¼ in)
WEIGHTS AND LOADINGS:	
Weight empty, spray equipped	1,696 kg (3,739 lb)
Certificated gross weight (FAR 23)	2,721 kg (6,000 lb)
Typical operating weight (CAM 8)	3,538 kg (7,800 lb)
Max wing loading	141.1 kg/m² (28.9 lb/sq ft)
Max power loading	6.98 kg/kW (11.47 lb/shp)

PERFORMANCE (at max T-O weight except where indicated):
Max level speed at S/L, clean	174 knots (322 km/h; 200 mph)
Max level speed at S/L with dispersal equipment	160 knots (298 km/h; 185 mph)
Cruising speed at 283.3 kW (380 shp) at 2,440 m (8,000 ft)	142 knots (264 km/h; 164 mph)
Typical working speed	113-126 knots (209-233 km/h; 130-145 mph)
Stalling speed at 2,721 kg (6,000 lb) AUW:	
flaps up	64 knots (118 km/h; 73 mph)
flaps down	53 knots (99 km/h; 61 mph)
Stalling speed as usually landed	46 knots (86 km/h; 53 mph)
Max rate of climb at S/L, dispersal equipment installed, AUW of 2,721 kg (6,000 lb)	495 m (1,625 ft)/min
Max rate of climb at S/L, dispersal equipment installed, AUW of 3,565 kg (7,860 lb)	305 m (1,000 ft)/min
T-O run at AUW of 3,565 kg (7,860 lb)	247 m (810 ft)
Landing run as usually landed	122 m (400 ft)

AIR TRACTOR MODEL AT-501

TYPE: Single-seat agricultural aircraft.
PROGRAMME: Developed from AT-500 (see 1985-86 *Jane's*); certificated 23 June 1987.
VARIANTS: Can be converted to turboprop in the field.
CUSTOMERS: 11 delivered by early 1991.
DESIGN FEATURES: Powered by 447 kW (600 hp) P&W R-1340-S3H1G radial engine driving three-blade Hydromatic propeller; hopper capacity 1,900 litres (502 US gallons; 418 Imp gallons); fuel capacity 477 litres (126 US gallons; 105 Imp gallons).
DIMENSIONS, EXTERNAL:
Wing span	15.24 m (50 ft 0 in)
Wing chord, constant	1.83 m (6 ft 0 in)
Length overall	9.05 m (29 ft 8½ in)
Height overall	2.99 m (9 ft 9½ in)
Wheel track	3.11 m (10 ft 2½ in)
Propeller diameter	3.30 m (10 ft 10 in)
AREAS:	
Wings, gross	27.87 m² (300.0 sq ft)
WEIGHTS AND LOADINGS:	
Weight empty	2,086 kg (4,600 lb)

Air Tractor Model AT-501 with Pratt & Whitney radial engine

Design gross weight	3,629 kg (8,000 lb)
Normal operating weight	4,173 kg (9,200 lb)
Max wing loading	149.7 kg/m² (30.67 lb/sq ft)
Max power loading	9.33 kg/kW (15.33 lb/hp)

PERFORMANCE:

Max level speed, with spray equipment
    139 knots (257 km/h; 160 mph)

Cruising speed 121 knots (225 km/h; 140 mph)

Working speed
    104-121 knots (193-225 km/h; 120-140 mph)

Stalling speed at normal landing weight
    49 knots (91 km/h; 56 mph)

AIR TRACTOR MODEL AT-502

TYPE: Agricultural aircraft for low-density fertilisers.

PROGRAMME: First flight April 1987; certificated 23 June 1987; combined production of AT-401/AT-502 at nine a month in early 1991.

VARIANTS: Variety of P&WC PT6As can be installed.

CUSTOMERS: By 1 January 1991, 76 had been delivered.

DESIGN FEATURES: Larger chemical hopper than AT-400 to handle low-density nitrogen based fertilisers such as urea; safety glass centre windscreen with wiper. Differences from AT-400 include approx 1.52 m (5 ft 0 in) increase in wing span, alloy steel lower spar cap and bonded doubler on inside of wing leading-edge for increased resistance to impact damage, and glassfibre wingroot fairings; fuselage length increased by 0.56 m (1 ft 10 in), width increased by 0.25 m (10 in), and larger diameter tubular frame members used to cater for increased max T-O weight.

LANDING GEAR: Non-retractable tailwheel type. Heavy duty E-4340 spring steel main gear, thickness 37.2 mm (1.31 in); flat spring for castoring and lockable tailwheel. Cleveland mainwheels, tyre size 29.00-11, pressure 3.45 bars (50 lb/sq in); tailwheel tyre size 5.00-5; Cleveland six-piston brakes with heavy duty discs.

POWER PLANT: One 507 kW (680 shp) Pratt & Whitney Canada PT6A-15AG, PT6A-27 or PT6A-28, or 559 kW (750 shp) PT6A-34 or PT6A-34AG turboprop, driving a Hartzell HCB3TN-3D/T10282+4 three-blade metal propeller. Standard fuel capacity 644 litres (170 US gallons; 142 Imp gallons). Optional capacities 818 litres (216 US gallons; 180 Imp gallons) and 886 litres (234 US gallons; 195 Imp gallons).

ACCOMMODATION: As for AT-400, but with new quick-detachable instrument panel and removable fuselage skin panels for ease of maintenance.

SYSTEMS: Two 24V 42Ah batteries and 250A starter/generator.

AVIONICS: Optional avionics include Bendix/King KX 155 nav/com and KR 87 ADF, KY 196 com radio, KT 76A transponder and Narco ELT-10 emergency locator transmitter.

EQUIPMENT: Agricultural dispersal system comprises a 1,900 litre (502 US gallon; 418 Imp gallon) Derakane vinylester resin/glassfibre hopper mounted in forward fuselage with hopper window and instrument panel mounted hopper quantity gauge; 0.97 m (3 ft 2 in) wide Transland gatebox; Transland 6.4 cm (2½ in) bottom loading valve; Agrinautics 6.4 cm (2½ in) spraypump with Transland on/off valve and two-blade wooden fan, and 40-nozzle stainless steel spray system with streamlined booms. Optional dispersal equipment includes 7.6 cm (3 in) spray system with 119 spray nozzles, and automatic flagman. Standard equipment includes safety glass centre windscreen panel, ground start receptacle and three-colour polyurethane paint finish. Optional equipment includes night flying package comprising strobe and navigation lights; night working lights; retractable 600W landing light in port wingtip, windscreen washer and wiper, fuel flowmeter, fuel totaliser and ferry fuel system. Alternative agricultural equipment includes Transland 22356 extra high volume spreader, Transland 54401 NorCal Swathmaster, 41 extra spray nozzles for high volume spraying, and eight-unit Micronair Mini Atomiser unit.

DIMENSIONS, EXTERNAL:

Wing span	15.24 m (50 ft 0 in)
Wing chord, constant	1.83 m (6 ft 0 in)
Wing aspect ratio	8.3
Length overall	9.91 m (32 ft 6 in)
Height overall	2.99 m (9 ft 9½ in)
Wheel track	3.11 m (10 ft 2½ in)
Wheelbase	6.64 m (21 ft 9½ in)
Propeller diameter	2.69 m (8 ft 10 in)

AREAS:

Wings, gross	27.87 m² (300.0 sq ft)
Ailerons (total)	3.53 m² (38.0 sq ft)
Trailing-edge flaps (total)	3.75 m² (40.4 sq ft)
Fin	0.90 m² (9.7 sq ft)
Rudder	1.30 m² (14.0 sq ft)
Tailplane	2.41 m² (26.0 sq ft)
Elevators (total, incl tab)	2.44 m² (26.3 sq ft)

WEIGHTS AND LOADINGS:

Weight empty, spray equipped	1,870 kg (4,123 lb)
Max T-O weight (CAM 8)	4,173 kg (9,200 lb)
Max landing weight	3,629 kg (8,000 lb)
Max wing loading	138.36 kg/m² (28.33 lb/sq ft)
Max power loading	7.61 kg/kW (12.5 lb/shp)

PERFORMANCE (at max T-O weight, except where indicated, with spray equipment installed):

Air Tractor Model AT-502 agricultural aircraft

Air Tractor Model AT-503A dual-control agricultural and training aircraft

Never-exceed speed (VNE) and max speed at S/L, hopper empty
    156 knots (290 km/h; 180 mph)

Cruising speed at 2,440 m (8,000 ft), 283.3 kW (380 shp)
    136 knots (253 km/h; 157 mph)

Typical working speed
    104-126 knots (193-233 km/h; 120-145 mph)

Stalling speed at 3,629 kg (8,000 lb):

flaps up	72 knots (134 km/h; 83 mph)
flaps down	60 knots (111 km/h; 69 mph)

Stalling speed as usually landed
    46 knots (86 km/h; 53 mph)

Max rate of climb at S/L, AUW of 3,629 kg (8,000 lb):

with PT6A-15AG	311 m (1,020 ft)/min
with PT6A-34AG	360 m (1,180 ft)/min

Max rate of climb at S/L, AUW of 4,173 kg (9,200 lb):

with PT6A-15AG	232 m (760 ft)/min
with PT6A-34AG	282 m (925 ft)/min

T-O run at AUW of 3,629 kg (8,000 lb):

with PT6A-15AG	244 m (800 ft)
with PT6A-34AG	222 m (730 ft)

T-O run at AUW of 4,173 kg (9,200 lb):

with PT6A-15AG	356 m (1,170 ft)
with PT6A-34AG	302 m (990 ft)

Range with max fuel 435 nm (805 km; 500 miles)

AIR TRACTOR MODEL AT-503/AT-503A

TYPE: Two-seat agricultural and training aircraft.

PROGRAMME: Design begun September 1985 to meet US State Department requirement for anti-narcotics aerial application aircraft; first flight 25 April 1986; certificated 2 October 1986.

VARIANTS: **AT-503**: Single aircraft (see Customers).

    AT-503A: Production version, certificated 26 November 1990; AT-502 wings, tail unit, landing gear and engine installation. Prototype and first production aircraft with PT6A-34 turboprop engine rated at 559 kW (750 shp). Full dual controls; dry and liquid dispersal systems can be operated from either seat; empty weight 136 kg (300 lb) greater than otherwise comparable AT-502 due to extra weight of second cockpit and 68 kg (150 lb) ballast installed on engine mount ring. Specifications, external dimensions, areas, weights and performance identical to AT-502 except weight empty 2,032 kg (4,480 lb).

CUSTOMERS: Sole prototype AT-503 delivered to Spain, for fire suppression duties. Prototype AT-503A went to US customer in Spring 1991; first production aircraft to Brazil (Aviação Agricola), also in Spring 1991.

DESIGN FEATURES: AT-503 became two-seat Air Tractor; missions include anti-drug enforcement, fire bombing,

forest spraying in mountainous terrain, high-volume
seeding or fertiliser application.

FLYING CONTROLS: As for AT-401, but electrically operated
elevator trim tabs.

STRUCTURE: Wings as for AT-400 except increased wing
span and flaps and heavier gauge skins. Fuselage is 0.56
m (1 ft 10 in) longer, 0.25 m (10 in) wider and has larger
diameter structure tubes.

AIR TRACTOR MODEL AT-802

TYPE: Two-seat agricultural aircraft.

PROGRAMME: Design commenced July 1989; first flight
of prototype (N802LS) 14 November 1990; FAA
certification expected first quarter 1991; deliveries to start
late in second quarter.

DESIGN FEATURES: Largest model built by company to date;
full controls for training; also designed for firefighting;
programmable logic computer with cockpit control panel
and digital display enables pilot to select coverage level
and opens doors to prescribed width, closing them when
selected amount of retardant released. Wing aerofoil
section NACA 4415; dihedral 3° 30′; incidence 2°.

FLYING CONTROLS: Boost tabs in each elevator and rudder;
electrically operated Fowler trailing-edge flaps deflect to
maximum 30°.

STRUCTURE: Two-spar wing structure of 2024-T3 light alloy
with alloy steel upper and lower spar caps and bonded
doubler on inside of leading-edge for impact damage
resistance; ribs and skins zinc chromated before assembly;
glassfibre wingroot fairing and skin overlaps sealed
against chemical ingress; flaps and ailerons of light alloy.
Fuselage of 4130N steel tube, oven stress relieved and
oiled internally, with skin panels of 2024-T3 light alloy
attached by Camloc fasteners for quick removal; rear
fuselage lightly pressurised to prevent chemical ingress.
Cantilever fin and strut braced tailplane of light alloy,
metal skinned and sealed against chemical ingress.

LANDING GEAR: Non-retractable tailwheel type. Cantilever
heavy duty E-4340 spring steel main gear, thickness 39.6
mm (1.56 in); flat spring suspension for castoring and
lockable tailwheel. Cleveland mainwheels with tyre size
11.00-12 (8-ply), pressure 3.11 bars (45 lb/sq in).
Tailwheel tyre size 6.00-6. Cleveland four-piston brakes
with heavy duty discs.

POWER PLANT: One Pratt & Whitney Canada PT6A-67R
turboprop, rated at 1,062 kW (1,424 shp) at 99°F, driving
a Hartzell five-blade feathering and reversible-pitch
constant-speed metal propeller. Frakes Aviation Jet
Thrust exhaust outlets. Fuel in two integral wing tanks,
total usable capacity 931 litres (246 US gallons; 205 Imp

Air Tractor Model AT-802 two-seat agricultural aircraft

gallons). Engine air is filtered through two large pleated
paper industrial truck filters.

ACCOMMODATION: Two seats in tandem in enclosed cabin,
which is sealed to prevent chemical ingress and protected
with overturn structure. Four downward hinged doors,
two on each side. Windscreen is safety-plate auto glass,
with washer and wiper. Separate ram airscoops for
ventilation of each cockpit; air-conditioning system
optional.

SYSTEMS: Removable Derakane vinylester chemical hoppers
with total capacity 3,142 litres (830 US gallons; 691 Imp
gallons). Stainless steel foam tank mounted forward of
engine firewall, capacity 121 litres (32 US gallons; 26.6
Imp gallons). Foam tank with electric pump to inject up
to 4 per cent foam/water mixture.

DIMENSIONS, EXTERNAL:
Wing span	17.68 m (58 ft 0 in)
Wing chord, constant	2.03 m (6 ft 8 in)
Wing aspect ratio	8.75
Length overall	11.28 m (37 ft 0 in)
Height overall	3.35 m (11 ft 0 in)
Wheel track	3.11 m (10 ft 2½ in)
Wheelbase	7.25 m (23 ft 9½ in)
Propeller diameter	2.62 m (8 ft 7 in)

AREAS:
Wings, gross	35.72 m² (384.5 sq ft)

Ailerons (total)	4.61 m² (49.6 sq ft)
Trailing-edge flaps (total)	5.54 m² (59.6 sq ft)
Fin	1.24 m² (13.4 sq ft)
Rudder	1.57 m² (16.9 sq ft)
Tailplane	3.44 m² (37.0 sq ft)
Elevators (total, incl tab)	3.00 m² (32.3 sq ft)

WEIGHTS AND LOADINGS:
Weight empty, equipped	2,858 kg (6,300 lb)
Max T-O weight	6,804 kg (15,000 lb)
Max landing weight	5,670 kg (12,500 lb)
Max wing loading	190.48 kg/m² (39.01 lb/sq ft)
Max power loading	6.41 kg/kW (10.53 lb/shp)

PERFORMANCE (at max T-O weight except where indicated):
Max level speed at S/L	182 knots (338 km/h; 210 mph)
Max cruising speed at 1,675 m (5,500 ft)	
	174 knots (322 km/h; 200 mph)
Stalling speed, power off, flaps down, at max landing	
weight	69 knots (128 km/h; 79 mph)
Max rate of climb at S/L, no hopper load	
	915 m (3,000 ft)/min
Max rate of climb at S/L	366 m (1,200 ft)/min
Service ceiling	4,875 m (16,000 ft)
T-O run	488 m (1,600 ft)
Range with max fuel	434 nm (804 km; 500 miles)

ALLISON

ALLISON GAS TURBINE DIVISION GMC

Development of Turbine Mentor suspended. Last
mentioned in *Jane's* 1990-91.

AMECO-HAWK

AMECO-HAWK INTERNATIONAL

PO Box 6292, Olympia, Washington 98502
Telephone: 1 (206) 842 1093
PRINCIPALS:
    Ronald C. Karzmar
    Ronald W. Wright

Ameco, a holding company in aerospace engineering and
manufacturing, joined Hawk International in 1989 to
continue development of GafHawk 125 designed in 1977 by
Ernest Hawk.

AMECO-HAWK GAFHAWK 125-200

TYPE: Single-turboprop general aviation freighter.

PROGRAMME: Rebuilt Piper Tri-Pacer testbed flown as
MiniHawk prototype 1978; GafHawk 125 (N101GH)
first flight 19 August 1982, powered by 893 kW (1,198
shp) P&WC PT6A-45R turboprop; more than 75 flights
by early 1990; modifications then under way to revise
centre of gravity for better handling and to carry
containers; resulting GafHawk 125-200 to be certificated
to FAR Pt 23, limiting gross weight to 5,670 kg (12,500
lb) although T-O weight could be 6,577 kg (14,500 lb).

DESIGN FEATURES: Short-field operation with square fuselage
loaded under tail at truckbed height and capable of
accommodating vehicles or up to three LD3 containers.
NASA GAW-1 wing section; thickness/chord ratio 17
per cent; no dihedral. Single-pilot operation intended.

FLYING CONTROLS: Conventional controls with servo tabs
and electrically operated trim tabs on elevator and
rudder; spoiler ailerons (rollerons) over half wing span
ahead of full-span electrically actuated flaps; rollerons
move 60.5° up and 10.5° down; rolleron trimming by
bungee.

STRUCTURE: Wing braced by dual redundant struts and jury
struts faired with metal cuff; wing has leading-edge and
rear tubular spars with box spar between, 78 one-piece
ribs and light alloy skins. Rectangular-section fuselage of
welded square molybdenum tubes with non-structural
Alclad skins attached by clips. Fin and tailplane similar
to wing but without box spar.

Prototype Ameco-Hawk GafHawk 125 single-engined turboprop freighter

LANDING GEAR: Non-retractable tricycle type, with single
wheel on each unit. All units have shock absorption by
rubber elastomer in compression. Goodyear tyres and
wheels of the same size on all three units, tyre size
15.00-12. Dual mainwheels optional. Goodyear hydraulic
disc brakes. Parking brake.

POWER PLANT: One Pratt & Whitney Canada PT6A-65AR
turboprop, with a max continuous rating of 910 kW
(1,220 shp), driving a Hartzell five-blade reversible-pitch
constant-speed metal propeller. Fuel tank, made of light
alloy and with a capacity of 1,363 litres (360 US gallons;
300 Imp gallons), mounted above forward fuselage,
directly over the wing, and providing gravity feed to
engine. Refuelling point on upper surface of tank. Two
aluminium fuel tanks, with a combined capacity of 3,785
litres (1,000 US gallons; 833 Imp gallons), can be installed
in the main cargo hold for long ferry flights. Oil capacity
11.5 litres (3.5 US gallons; 2.9 Imp gallons). Engine air
intake incorporates an ice ramp and foreign particle

separator. Electrically heated de-icing boots for propeller
and engine air intake.

ACCOMMODATION: Pilot and co-pilot on flight deck. Dual
controls and full blind-flying instrumentation for both
pilots standard. Door to flight deck on each side of
fuselage; communicating door between flight deck and
cargo hold in forward bulkhead. Cabin door on each side,
aft of wing. Electrically actuated upward/inward-opening
main cargo door, in undersurface of upswept rear
fuselage, can be opened in flight. Heavy duty corrugated
light alloy floor in cargo hold, with cargo tiedowns along
walls at each fuselage gusset frame, and tailgate for
loading. Main cabin volume augmented by usable space
under flight deck, accommodating pipes and timber up to
9.14 m (30 ft) in length with rear loading door closed.
Accommodation heated and ventilated.

SYSTEMS: Electrical system powered by 28V 250A Smiths
starter/generator and 28V storage battery. Hydraulic

system for brakes only. Vacuum system standard. De-icing system optional.

AVIONICS: Standard avionics include Bendix/King dual nav/com, dual ILS, HSI on pilot's side, ADF, DME, radar altimeter, transponder, switching panel and VOR/localiser-coupled autopilot. Standard equipment includes dual blind-flying instrumentation including turn co-ordinator and rate of climb indicator, dual ASIs, dual altimeters (one encoding), OAT gauge.

EQUIPMENT: Compass, annunciator panel, eight-day clock, adjustable crew seats with armrests, instrument post lighting. landing, navigation, taxi and wingtip strobe lights, two rotating beacons, control locks, and heated pitot head.

DIMENSIONS, EXTERNAL:

Wing span	21.79 m (71 ft 6 in)
Wing chord, constant	2.08 m (6 ft 10 in)
Wing aspect ratio	10.4
Length overall	15.98 m (52 ft 5 in)
Height overall	5.49 m (18 ft 0 in)

Tailplane span	7.01 m (23 ft 0 in)
Wheel track (c/l outer tyres)	3.38 m (11 ft 1 in)
Wheelbase	4.39 m (14 ft 5 in)
Propeller diameter	2.74 m (9 ft 0 in)
Rear ramp/door: Height	1.93 m (6 ft 4 in)
Width	1.96 m (6 ft 5 in)

DIMENSIONS, INTERNAL:
Cabin: Length at floor level, excl flight deck

	6.40 m (21 ft 0 in)
Max width	1.96 m (6 ft 5 in)
Max height	2.36 m (7 ft 9 in)
Volume	26.9 m³ (950 cu ft)

Forward cargo hold under flight deck:

Height	0.66 m (2 ft 2 in)
Width	1.22 m (4 ft 0 in)

AREAS:

Wings, gross	45.8 m² (493.0 sq ft)

WEIGHTS AND LOADINGS:

Weight empty	3,085 kg (6,800 lb)
Max T-O weight	5,670 kg (12,500 lb)

Max wing loading	123.5 kg/m² (25.3 lb/sq ft)
Max power loading	6.23 kg/kW (10.24 lb/shp)

PERFORMANCE (prototype, at max design T-O weight):
Cruising speed (75% power) at 3,050 m (10,000 ft)
123 knots (229 km/h; 142 mph)
Econ cruising speed (55% power) at 3,050 m (10,000 ft)
113 knots (209 km/h; 130 mph)
Stalling speed, 30° flap, partial power
49 knots (91 km/h; 57 mph)

Max rate of climb at S/L	354 m (1,160 ft)/min
Service ceiling	5,485 m (18,000 ft)
T-O run	208 m (680 ft)
T-O to 15 m (50 ft)	506 m (1,660 ft)
Landing from 15 m (50 ft)	436 m (1,430 ft)
Landing run	201 m (660 ft)

AMERICAN GENERAL
AMERICAN GENERAL AIRCRAFT CORPORATION
PO Box 5757, Greenville, Mississippi 38704
Telephone: 1 (601) 332 2422
Fax: 1 (601) 334 9950
CHAIRMAN: Robert E. Crowley
PRESIDENT: James E. Cox
VICE-PRESIDENT, MARKETING: Robert R. Martin

Production and marketing rights for the Gulfstream American AA-1 Lynx, AA-5A Cheetah, AA-5B Tiger and GA-7 Cougar (see 1979-80 *Jane's* and earlier) were bought from Gulfstream Aerospace Corporation in June 1989. Producing trainer version of Tiger as AG-5B.

Agreement signed early 1991 for licence manufacture of GA-7 Cougar by Tbilisi Aircraft Manufacturing Association in the Soviet Dimitriov aircraft factory which

formerly produced Su-25s and MiG-21s. American General to supply materials and maintain quality control; aircraft will be assembled, furnished, painted and marketed in the USA; first aircraft scheduled for completion early 1992; cost $300,000.

AMERICAN GENERAL AG-5B TIGER
TYPE: Four-seat private aircraft.
PROGRAMME: Modified/updated version of AG-5B (1979-80 *Jane's*); certificated 1990; first AA-5B delivered September 1990; 35 delivered by April 1991; intended output 100 in 1991, using parts stored by Gulfstream and supplied by vendors.
CUSTOMERS: Include Florida Institute of Technology School of Aeronautics (up to 15).
DESIGN FEATURES: Changes from AA-5B include Sensenich propeller for 134 kW (180 hp) Textron Lycoming O-360-A4K flat-four engine; fuel capacity 199 litres (52.6

US gallons; 43.8 Imp gallons); CFRP engine cowling; four-point seat restraints; updated instrument panel, control yoke and throttle quadrant; 24V electrical system with circuit breakers; wingtip landing lights; recessed anti-collision light in fin.

DIMENSIONS, EXTERNAL:

Wing span	9.60 m (31 ft 6 in)
Length overall	6.71 m (22 ft 0 in)

WEIGHTS AND LOADINGS:

Weight empty	595 kg (1,311 lb)
Max T-O weight	1,088 kg (2,400 lb)
Max power loading	8.1 kg/kW (13.3 lb/hp)

PERFORMANCE:
Max cruising speed (75% power) at 2,590 m (8,500 ft)
143 knots (265 km/h; 165 mph)

Service ceiling	4,206 m (13,800 ft)

Range with max fuel (75% power)
550 nm (1,019 km; 633 miles)

AMI
AERO MODIFICATIONS INTERNATIONAL INC
2201 Scott Avenue Suite 102, Fort Worth, Texas 76103
Telephone: 1 (817) 535 1936
Fax: 1 (817) 536 2240

PRESIDENT: Dan H. Williams
CHIEF EXECUTIVE OFFICER: Theo W. Muller
DIRECTOR, PRODUCTION AND DESIGN: Earl Schafer

Marketing and engineering turboprop Douglas DC-3 conversions, based on original research and development by Schafer Aircraft Modifications of Waco, Texas (which

see). Obtained STC for such conversions 1987 and was to start converting two DC-3/C-47s in 1990 as **DC-3-65TPs** (P&WC PT6A-65AR engines). Other modifications to include 1.02 m (3 ft 4 in) fuselage stretch, all-new Bendix/King avionics and customer-specified interiors.

ARCTIC — *see Sport Aircraft section*

ASI — *see AASI*

AVIAT
AVIAT INC
Airport Box 1149, Afton, Wyoming 83110
Telephone: 1 (307) 886 3151
Fax: 1 (307) 886 9674
CHAIRMAN: Malcolm T. White
PRESIDENT: Verdean Heiner

Pitts Aerobatics company plus manufacturing and marketing rights of Pitts Special aircraft acquired by Christen Industries November 1983; Pitts Aerobatics factory at Afton, Wyoming, became headquarters of Christen Industries, which in turn acquired April 1991 by Aviat Inc of Delaware (wholly owned subsidiary of White International Ltd, Guernsey, Channel Islands). Aviat now owns production and type certificates for Christen range. See also Sport Aircraft.

AVIAT A-1 HUSKY
TYPE: Two-seat light utility aircraft.
PROGRAMME: Computer-aided design started November 1985; first flight (N6070H) 1986; FAA certification 1987, including Edo 2000 floats and skis, glider/banner towing hook approved.
CUSTOMERS: Total 170 delivered by January 1991, including 40 during 1990. US Border Patrol operates 15, replacing Piper Super Cubs.
DESIGN FEATURES: Missions include bush flying, border patrol, fish and wildlife protection and pipeline inspection. Wing has modified Clark Y US 35B section; drooped Plane Booster wingtips.
FLYING CONTROLS: Symmetrical section ailerons with spade-type mass balance; trim tabs in elevators; slotted flaps. Fixed tailplane; trim by adjustable bungee.
STRUCTURE: Wing has two aluminium spars, metal ribs and metal leading-edge, Dacron covering overall. Twin bracing struts each side of wing with wire and strut braced tail unit. Light alloy flaps and ailerons, with Dacron covering. Fuselage and tail have chrome molybdenum steel tube frames, covered in Dacron except for metal skin to rear fuselage.
LANDING GEAR: Non-retractable tailwheel type. Two faired side Vs and half-axles hinged to bottom of fuselage, with internal (under front seat) bungee cord shock absorption.

Cleveland mainwheels, tyres size 8.00-6 as standard; 6.00-6 or 8.50-6 tyres optional. Oversize 24 × 10-6 'tundra' tyres optional. Cleveland mainwheel brakes. Steerable leaf-spring tailwheel. Wheel-replacement or wheel-retract skis and floats optional.
POWER PLANT: One 134 kW (180 hp) Textron Lycoming O-360-C1G flat-four engine, driving a Hartzell two-blade constant-speed metal propeller. Fuel contained in two metal tanks, one in each wing, total capacity 208 litres (52 US gallons; 45.75 Imp gallons), of which 189 litres (50 US gallons; 41.6 Imp gallons) are usable. Fuel filler point in upper surface of each wing, near root.
ACCOMMODATION: Enclosed cabin seating two in tandem, with dual controls. Downward hinged door on starboard side, with upward hinged window above. Skylight window in roof.
SYSTEMS: Electrical system includes lights and 60A alternator.

DIMENSIONS, EXTERNAL:

Wing span	10.73 m (35 ft 2½ in)
Length overall	6.88 m (22 ft 7 in)
Height overall	2.01 m (6 ft 7 in)
Propeller diameter	1.93 m (6 ft 4 in)

AREAS:

Wings, gross	16.72 m² (180.0 sq ft)
Ailerons (total)	1.43 m² (15.4 sq ft)
Trailing-edge flaps (total)	2.09 m² (22.5 sq ft)
Fin	0.43 m² (4.66 sq ft)
Rudder	0.62 m² (6.76 sq ft)
Tailplane	1.48 m² (15.9 sq ft)
Elevators, incl tabs	1.31 m² (14.1 sq ft)

WEIGHTS AND LOADINGS:

Weight empty	540 kg (1,190 lb)
Max T-O weight	816 kg (1,800 lb)
Max baggage weight	22.7 kg (50 lb)
Max wing loading	48.8 kg/m² (10.0 lb/sq ft)
Max power loading	7.45 kg/kW (10.0 lb/hp)

PERFORMANCE:
Never-exceed speed (VNE)
132 knots (245 km/h; 152 mph)
Cruising speed:
75% power at 1,220 m (4,000 ft)
122 knots (226 km/h; 140 mph)
55% power   115 knots (212 km/h; 132 mph)
Stalling speed: flaps up   48 knots (80 km/h; 49 mph)

flaps down	37 knots (68 km/h; 42 mph)
Max rate of climb at S/L	457 m (1,500 ft)/min
Service ceiling	6,100 m (20,000 ft)
T-O run	46 m (150 ft)
T-O to 15 m (50 ft)	229 m (750 ft)
Landing from 15 m (50 ft)	427 m (1,400 ft)
Landing run, full flap	107 m (350 ft)

Range with max fuel, 75% power, 45 min reserves
550 nm (1,019 km; 633 miles)

PITTS S-1T SPECIAL
TYPE: Single-seat aerobatic biplane.
PROGRAMME: Original single-seat Pitts Special built and flown 1944; earlier factory-built S-1S described in 1987-88 *Jane's*. Production of current S-1T factory version started early 1981; FAA certification Autumn 1982.
CUSTOMERS: Total 58 delivered by January 1991, including four during 1990. Available to special order only.
DESIGN FEATURES: New features include more powerful engine and wings moved forward 11.5 cm (4½ in) to compensate; symmetrical wing and aileron sections. Wing section M6; thickness/chord ratio 12 per cent; dihedral upper wings 0°, lower wings 3°; incidence upper wing 1° 30′, lower wings 0°; sweepback 6° 40′ upper wing only.
FLYING CONTROLS: Symmetrical ailerons on upper and lower wings; lower with spade-type aerodynamic balance; trim tab on each elevator; fixed tailplane; no flaps.
STRUCTURE: Fabric covered wooden wing and ailerons; single interplane strut and duplicated flying and landing wires; fabric covered steel tube fuselage with wooden stringers and aluminium top decking and side panels, remainder fabric covered; tail surfaces fabric covered steel tube.
LANDING GEAR: Non-retractable tailwheel type. Rubber cord shock absorption. Cleveland mainwheels with 6-ply tyres, size 5.00-5, pressure 2.07 bars (30 lb/sq in). Cleveland hydraulic disc brakes. Steerable tailwheel. Glassfibre fairing on mainwheels.
POWER PLANT: One 149 kW (200 hp) Textron Lycoming AEIO-360-A1E flat-four engine, driving a Hartzell two-blade constant-speed propeller. Fuel tank aft of firewall, capacity 75 litres (20 US gallons; 16.6 Imp

gallons). Refuelling point on upper surface of fuselage, forward of windscreen. Oil capacity 7.5 litres (2 US gallons; 1.7 Imp gallons). Inverted fuel and oil systems standard.

ACCOMMODATION: Single seat. Sliding cockpit canopy standard.

DIMENSIONS, EXTERNAL:

Wing span, upper	5.28 m (17 ft 4 in)
Wing chord (constant, both)	0.91 m (3 ft 0 in)
Wing aspect ratio	5.8
Length overall	4.72 m (15 ft 6 in)
Height overall	1.91 m (6 ft 3 in)
Tailplane span	1.98 m (6 ft 6 in)
Propeller diameter	1.93 m (6 ft 4 in)

AREAS:

Wings, gross	9.15 m² (98.5 sq ft)

WEIGHTS AND LOADINGS:

Weight empty	376 kg (830 lb)
Max T-O weight	521 kg (1,150 lb)
Max wing loading	57.05 kg/m² (11.68 lb/sq ft)
Max power loading	3.50 kg/kW (5.75 lb/hp)

PERFORMANCE (at max T-O weight):

Never-exceed speed (V$_{NE}$)

	176 knots (326 km/h; 203 mph)
Max level speed at S/L	161 knots (298 km/h; 185 mph)
Max cruising speed at S/L	
	152 knots (282 km/h; 175 mph)
Stalling speed	56 knots (103 km/h; 64 mph)
Max rate of climb at S/L	853 m (2,800 ft)/min
Range with max fuel, 55% power, 30 min reserves	
	268 nm (497 km; 309 miles)
g limits	+6/−3.5

PITTS MODEL S-2B

TYPE: Two-seat aerobatic biplane; successor to S-2A. (1987-88 and earlier Jane's.)

PROGRAMME: Prototype completed September 1982; certificated in FAR Pt 23 aerobatic category Spring 1983; won first place Advanced Category of 1982 US Nationals with two occupants.

CUSTOMERS: Total 26 delivered during 1990, including 200th in December.

DESIGN FEATURES: 194 kW (260 hp) engine and wings moved 15 cm (6 in) forward to compensate: more front cockpit space. Wing sections NACA 6400 series on upper wing, 00 series on lower wings.

FLYING CONTROLS: Ailerons on upper and lower wings with aerodynamic spade-type balances on lower ailerons; trim tab on each elevator; fixed tailplane; no flaps.

STRUCTURE: Wings generally as S-1T; fuselage 4130 steel tube with wooden stringers, aluminium top decking and side panels; remainder Dacron covered. Steel tube, metal skinned fixed tail surfaces; Dacron covered control surfaces.

LANDING GEAR: Non-retractable tailwheel type. Rubber cord shock absorption. Steerable tailwheel. Streamline fairings on mainwheels.

POWER PLANT: One 194 kW (260 hp) Textron Lycoming AEIO-540-D4A5 flat-six engine, driving a Hartzell two-blade constant-speed metal propeller. Fuel tank in fuselage, immediately aft of firewall, capacity 110 litres (29 US gallons; 24 Imp gallons). Refuelling point on fuselage upper surface forward of windscreen. Oil capacity 11.35 litres (3 US gallons; 2.5 Imp gallons). Inverted fuel and oil systems standard.

ACCOMMODATION: Two seats in tandem cockpits, with dual controls. Sideways opening one-piece canopy covers both cockpits. Space for 9.1 kg (20 lb) baggage aft of rear seat when flown in non-aerobatic category.

SYSTEMS: Electrical system powered by 12V 40A alternator and non-spill 12V battery.

DIMENSIONS, EXTERNAL:

Wing span: upper	6.10 m (20 ft 0 in)
lower	5.79 m (19 ft 0 in)
Wing chord (constant, both)	1.02 m (3 ft 4 in)
Length overall	5.71 m (18 ft 9 in)
Height overall	2.02 m (6 ft 7½ in)

AREAS:

Wings, gross	11.6 m² (125.0 sq ft)

WEIGHTS AND LOADINGS:

Weight empty	521 kg (1,150 lb)
Max T-O weight	737 kg (1,625 lb)
Max wing loading	63.55 kg/m² (13.0 lb/sq ft)
Max power loading	3.80 kg/kW (6.25 lb/hp)

PERFORMANCE (at max T-O weight):

Never-exceed speed (V$_{NE}$)

	182 knots (338 km/h; 210 mph)
Max cruising speed	152 knots (282 km/h; 175 mph)
Stalling speed	52 knots (97 km/h; 60 mph)
Max rate of climb at S/L	823 m (2,700 ft)/min
Service ceiling	6,400 m (21,000 ft)
Range with max fuel, 55% power, 30 min reserves	
	277 nm (513 km; 319 miles)

PITTS MODEL S-2S

TYPE: Single-seat version of S-2A aerobatic biplane.

PROGRAMME: Production began late 1978; first flight of prototype 9 December 1977; full certification June 1981.

CUSTOMERS: Total 32 delivered by January 1991. Available to special order only.

DESIGN FEATURES: Forward fuselage shortened by 0.36 m (14 in) to accommodate 194 kW (260 hp) Textron Lycoming AEIO-540-D4A5 flat-six engine, driving Hartzell two-blade, constant-speed metal propeller; fuel capacity increased to 132.5 litres (35 US gallons; 29.1 Imp gallons); oil capacity increased to 11.4 litres (3 US gallons; 2.5 Imp gallons).

FLYING CONTROLS: Generally as for S-2A.

STRUCTURE: Generally as for S-2A.

DIMENSIONS, EXTERNAL: As for Model S-2B except:

Length overall	5.28 m (17 ft 4 in)

WEIGHTS AND LOADINGS:

Weight empty	499 kg (1,100 lb)
Max T-O weight	680 kg (1,500 lb)
Max wing loading	58.6 kg/m² (12.0 lb/sq ft)
Max power loading	3.51 kg/kW (5.77 lb/hp)

PERFORMANCE (at max T-O weight):

Never-exceed speed (V$_{NE}$)

	176 knots (326 km/h; 203 mph)
Max level speed at S/L	162 knots (301 km/h; 187 mph)
Max cruising speed at S/L	
	152 knots (282 km/h; 175 mph)
Stalling speed	51 knots (94 km/h; 58 mph)
Max rate of climb at S/L	853 m (2,800 ft)/min
g limits	+6/−3.5

AVSTAR

AVSTAR INC

Seattle, Washington

In co-operation with Chinese Shenyang Aircraft Corporation (which see), Pacific Marketing Consultants Inc of San Francisco and Plymouth Ltd of Hong Kong, Avstar planned to revive Temco TT-1 Super Pinto trainer, first built for US Navy in 1956 and temporarily revived by American Jet Industries in early 1970s. Philippine Aerospace Development Corporation was licensed by AJI to produce the aircraft as the T-160 Cali, but did not proceed. Avstar prototype, renamed Super Mustang T-100, was flight tested in USA 1988, but nothing heard since. All known details in 1990-91 Jane's.

AVTEK

AVTEK CORPORATION

4680 Calle Carga, Camarillo, California 93010
Telephone: 1 (805) 482 2700
Fax: 1 (805) 987 0068
Telex: 183218 AVTEK UD
PRESIDENT: Robert F. Adickes
SENIOR VICE-PRESIDENT. ENGINEERING: Niels Andersen
DIRECTOR OF MARKETING: Robert D. Honeycutt

Company founded 1982 to develop Avtek Model 400A; investors in Avtek Corporation now include E. I. DuPont de Nemours, Dow Chemical Company, Air Rotor GmbH of Germany, Nomura Securities of Japan and Valmet Corporation of Finland. In September 1988 Michigan state government went into partnership with Avtek and local development agencies to start assembly facility at W. K. Kellogg Regional Airport, Battle Creek, Michigan.

AVTEK MODEL 400A

TYPE: Six/ten-seat all-composite, turboprop multi-role twin.

PROGRAMME: Design started March 1981; proof-of-concept aircraft N400AV (see 1985-86 Jane's) flew 17 September 1984; N400AV then fitted with P&WC PT6A-135M engines (PT6A-35s with counter-rotating gearboxes from PT6A-66); extensive changes made Spring 1985, including fuselage stretch 20 cm (8 in) forward and 76 cm (2 ft 6 in) aft of front pressure bulkhead, widened cabin, new outer wing and enlarged fuel tanks in forward-swept root extensions, foreplane with greater span and reduced chord, ventral strakes (known as delta fins), relocated main landing gear legs, and specially developed P&WC PT6A-3s mounted closer to wings. Pre-production second prototype expected to fly 1991; FAA certification planned for 1992. DuPont has option to build first 100 production airframes using primarily proprietary polyaramid materials.

VARIANTS: **Model 400A:** Principal version, as detailed below.

Explorer: Valmet purchased option on 20 March 1985 to build Explorer derivative of Avtek 400A for maritime surveillance, liaison, coastal patrol, aerial survey, search and reconnaissance, and ESM, tailored to individual customer requirements. Fuel capacity increased by 208 litres (55 US gallons; 45.8 Imp gallons) and max T-O weight raised to 3,402 kg (7,500 lb).

Model 419 Express: Commuter aircraft to be certificated as a modification after FAR 23 gained by 400A; to be manufactured by Avtek Korean partner. Length increased to 14.87 m (48 ft 9½ in) and max T-O weight raised to 5,669 kg (12,499 lb).

CUSTOMERS: Avtek claims deposit payments received for more than 100 Avtek 400As.

DESIGN FEATURES: Initial design by Al W. Mooney, founder of Mooney Aircraft; refined by Niels Andersen, Ford Johnston and Irvin Culver; computer analysis of configuration and wind tunnel testing by NASA; materials research by Dow Chemical and Dr Leo Windecker; Dow Chemical basic patents on Windecker Eagle (first all-composites aircraft to receive civil certification) licensed to Avtek. Avtek 12 aerofoil section; anhedral 2° 30′ from roots; sweepback 50° inboard, 15° 30′ outboard; foreplane dihedral 1°; fuselage pressurised. De-icing of wing and foreplane pneumatic, electric or by engine bleed.

FLYING CONTROLS: Actuation by pushrods and cranks throughout; mass balanced elevators on foreplane; mass balanced rudder without trim tab; two-section ailerons, with inboard sections also electrically actuated as pitch-axis trim surfaces; no flaps.

STRUCTURE: All-composite structure, 72 per cent DuPont Kevlar and Nomex, 16 per cent graphite/carbonfibre, smaller quantities of R-glass, S-glass aluminium and nickel fibres; wire mesh incorporated to protect against lightning.

LANDING GEAR: Hydraulically retractable tricycle type, main units retracting inward and nosewheel forward. Emergency extension system. Oleo-pneumatic shock absorber in each unit. Single wheel on each unit, mainwheels size 6.00-6 with Goodyear tyres size 17.5-6.25 × 7.5, pressure 7.0 bars (102 lb/sq in). Steerable nosewheel unit with wheel size 5.00-5 and Goodyear tyre size 14.2-5.5 × 6.5, pressure 5.0 bars (73 lb/sq in). Cleveland hydraulic disc brakes.

POWER PLANT: Two Pratt & Whitney Canada PT6A-3L/R turboprops, derived from the PT6A-135 and flat rated at 507 kW (680 shp), one mounted within nacelle above each wing. Hartzell four-blade constant-speed fully feathering

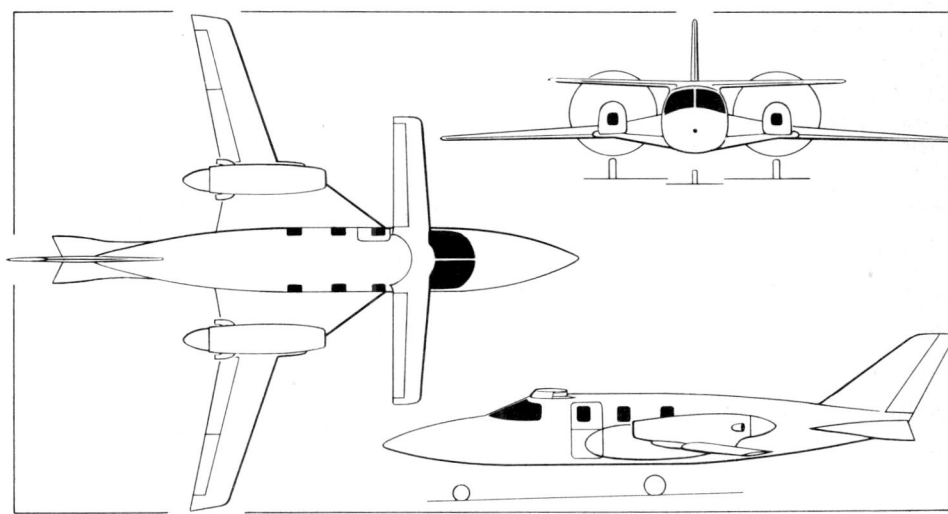

Avtek Model 400A six/ten-seat twin-turboprop aircraft *(Pilot Press)*

reversible-pitch pusher propellers (metal blades on prototype, Kevlar on production version). Propellers are opposite rotating, with automatic synchrophasing, full Beta control reversing and autofeathering. In-flight start capability. Integral fuel tank in each wingroot leading-edge. Total fuel capacity 1,003 litres (265 US gallons; 221 Imp gallons), of which 984 litres (260 US gallons; 216.5 Imp gallons) are usable. Refuelling point in upper surface of each wing. Dual anti-icing inlets for each engine.

ACCOMMODATION: Pilot and five to nine passengers according to interior layout. Optional configurations include eight-passenger Pullman or Salon; eight-passenger Lounge; six-passenger Conference; Ambulance with stretcher, medical equipment and seats for three ambulatory patients or medical attendants; and Cargo with seats for pilot and one passenger. Two-section door on port side of cabin, with step incorporated in lower half. Emergency exit on starboard side opposite cabin door. Baggage compartment at rear of cabin with internal access. Unpressurised baggage compartment in nose with external door on port side. Accommodation is pressurised, air-conditioned, heated and ventilated.

SYSTEMS: AiResearch bleed air pressurisation system with max differential of 0.52 bar (7.6 lb/sq in), and air cycle air-conditioning system. Electrically driven hydraulic pump provides pressure of 138 bars (2,000 lb/sq in) for landing gear actuation. Electrical system includes dual 28V 300A engine driven generators, dual 29Ah storage batteries and external power socket. Oxygen system of 1.39 m³ (49 cu ft) capacity, pressure 128 bars (1,850 lb/sq

:n), provides constant flow for passengers and demand flow for pilot. Anti-icing of windscreen by electrical system, of propellers by engine efflux; alcohol anti-icing of wing and fin leading-edges optional; electrically heated pitot. Engine fire extinguishing system optional.

AVIONICS: Wide range of optional avionics by Bendix/King, Collins and Honeywell, including EFIS and EICAS, and Honeywell colour weather radar. Full IFR instrumentation optional.

DIMENSIONS, EXTERNAL:

Wing span	10.67 m (35 ft 0 in)
Foreplane span	6.92 m (22 ft 8½ in)
Length: overall	11.99 m (39 ft 4 in)
fuselage	10.41 m (34 ft 2 in)
Height overall	3.47 m (11 ft 4¾ in)
Propeller diameter	1.93 m (6 ft 4 in)
Passenger door (port): Height	1.17 m (3 ft 10 in)
Width	0.76 m (2 ft 6 in)
Height to sill	0.76 m (2 ft 6 in)
Baggage door (port, nose): Height	0.51 m (1 ft 8 in)
Width	0.56 m (1 ft 10 in)
Height to sill	0.79 m (2 ft 7 in)
Emergency exit (stbd): Height	0.51 m (1 ft 8 in)
Width	0.67 m (2 ft 2½ in)

DIMENSIONS, INTERNAL:

Cabin: Length	3.14 m (10 ft 3½ in)
Max width	1.40 m (4 ft 7¼ in)
Max height	1.37 m (4 ft 6 in)
Baggage hold volume:	
nose	0.62 m³ (22.0 cu ft)
cabin	1.24 m³ (44.0 cu ft)

AREAS:

Wings, gross	13.40 m² (144.2 sq ft)
Foreplane, gross	4.52 m² (48.7 sq ft)
Elevators (total)	0.92 m² (9.9 sq ft)
Ailerons (total)	0.60 m² (6.5 sq ft)
Fin	1.16 m² (12.5 sq ft)
Rudder	0.90 m² (9.7 sq ft)

WEIGHTS AND LOADINGS:

Weight empty, equipped	1,714 kg (3,779 lb)
Max ramp weight	2,976 kg (6,560 lb)
Max T-O and landing weight	2,948 kg (6,500 lb)
Max wing loading	220.1 kg/m² (45.08 lb/sq ft)
Max power loading	2.91 kg/kW (4.78 lb/shp)

PERFORMANCE (estimated):

Max level speed at S/L	255 knots (473 km/h; 294 mph)
Max cruising speed:	
at 3,050 m (10,000 ft)	297 knots (550 km/h; 342 mph)
at 6,700 m (22,000 ft)	364 knots (675 km/h; 419 mph)
at 12,500 m (41,000 ft)	338 knots (626 km/h; 389 mph)
Stalling speed	83 knots (154 km/h; 96 mph)
Max rate of climb at S/L	1,411 m (4,630 ft)/min
Rate of climb at S/L, one engine out	
	578 m (1,897 ft)/min
Service ceiling	12,950 m (42,500 ft)
Service ceiling, one engine out	10,060 m (33,000 ft)
T-O to 15 m (50 ft)	463 m (1,520 ft)
Landing from 15 m (50 ft)	390 m (1,280 ft)
Range with max fuel:	
no reserves	2,276 nm (4,218 km; 2,621 miles)
NBAA IFR reserves	1,922 nm (3,562 km; 2,213 miles)

AYRES
AYRES CORPORATION

PO Box 3090, Albany, Georgia 31708-5201
Telephone: 1 (912) 883 1440
Fax: 1 (912) 439 9790
Telex: 547629 AYRESPORT ABN

SALES MANAGERS:
Marvin H. Wilson (Domestic)
Bill Brodbeck (International)

Ayres Corporation bought manufacturing and world marketing rights to Thrush Commander-600 and -800 from Rockwell International General Aviation Division in November 1977.

AYRES THRUSH S2R-R1340

TYPE: Single/two-seat agricultural aircraft.
PROGRAMME: In production.
VARIANTS: Following variants now offered:
Thrush S2R-R1340: Basic version, powered by Pratt & Whitney R-1340 Wasp aircooled radial engine and with one or two seats.
Thrush S2R-R1820: Powered by Pratt & Whitney R-1820 aircooled radial (described separately).
Turbo-Thrush S2R: Basic S2R powered by Pratt & Whitney Canada PT6A-11, -15, -34 or -65AG (described separately).
CUSTOMERS: Operating in 70 countries.
DESIGN FEATURES: Cantilever wing with 3° 30' dihedral; wingroots sealed against chemical entry; wing extensions adding 2.79 m² (30 sq ft) standard; deflector cable from cockpit to tip of fin.
FLYING CONTROLS: Plain ailerons; trim tab in each elevator; electrically actuated flaps.
STRUCTURE: Two-spar light alloy wing with 4130 chrome molybdenum steel spar caps; welded chrome molybdenum steel tube fuselage structure covered with quickly removable light alloy skin panels; underfuselage skin of stainless steel; all-metal tail surfaces with strut braced tailplane; metal ailerons and flaps.
LANDING GEAR: Non-retractable tailwheel type. Main units have rubber in compression shock absorption and 29 × 11.00-10 wheels with 10-ply tyres. Hydraulically operated disc brakes. Parking brakes. Wire cutters on main gear. Steerable, locking tailwheel, size 12.5 × 4.5 in.
POWER PLANT: One 447 kW (600 hp) Pratt & Whitney R-1340 Wasp nine-cylinder aircooled radial engine, driving a Hamilton Standard 12D40/EAC AG-100-2 two-blade constant-speed metal propeller. Fuel contained in wing tanks with combined capacity of 401 litres (106 US gallons; 88.3 Imp gallons).
ACCOMMODATION: Single adjustable mesh seat in 'safety pod' sealed cockpit enclosure, with steel tube overturn structure. Tandem seating optional, with forward or rear facing second seat. Dual controls optional with forward facing rear seat, for pilot training. Adjustable rudder pedals. Downward hinged door on each side. Tempered safety glass windscreen. Cockpit wire cutter. Dual inertia reel safety harness with optional second seat. Baggage compartment standard on single-seat aircraft. Windscreen wiper and washer.
SYSTEM: Electrical system powered by a 24V 50A alternator. Lightweight 24V 35Ah battery.
AVIONICS: To customer's requirements.
EQUIPMENT: Transland glassfibre hopper forward of cockpit with capacity of 1.50 m³ (53 cu ft) can hold 1,514 litres (400 US gallons; 333 Imp gallons) of liquid or 1,487 kg

Ayres Thrush S2R-R1820 (1,200 hp Wright R-1820 engine)

Ayres Thrush S2R-R1340 (600 hp Pratt & Whitney R-1340 Wasp engine)

(3,280 lb) of dry chemical. Hopper has a 0.33 m² (3.56 sq ft) lid, openable by two handles, and cockpit viewing window. Standard equipment includes Universal spray system with external 50 mm (2 in) stainless steel plumbing, 50 mm pump with wooden fan, Transland gate, 50 mm valve, quick-disconnect pump mount and strainer. Streamlined spraybooms with outlets for 68 nozzles. Micro-adjust valve control (spray) and calibrator (dry). A 63 mm (2.5 in) side loading system is installed on

the port side. Stainless steel rudder cables. Navigation lights, instrument lights and two strobe lights. Optional equipment includes a rear cockpit to accommodate aft facing crew member, or forward facing seat for passenger, or flying instructor if optional dual controls installed; space can be used alternatively for cargo. Other optional items are a Transland high-volume spreader, agitator installation; ten-unit AU5000 Micronair installation in lieu of standard booms and nozzles; Transland gatebox with stiffener casting; quick-disconnect flange and kit; night working lights including landing light and wingtip turn lights; cockpit fire extinguisher; and water bomber configuration.

DIMENSIONS, EXTERNAL:
Wing span	14.48 m (47 ft 6 in)
Length overall (tail up)	8.95 m (29 ft 4½ in)
Height overall	2.79 m (9 ft 2 in)
Tailplane span	5.18 m (17 ft 0 in)
Wheel track	2.72 m (8 ft 11 in)
Propeller diameter	2.74 m (9 ft 0 in)

AREAS:
Wings, gross	33.13 m² (356.6 sq ft)

WEIGHTS AND LOADINGS:
Weight empty, equipped	1,678 kg (3,700 lb)
Max T-O weight: CAR 3	2,721 kg (6,000 lb)
CAM 8	3,130 kg (6,900 lb)
Max wing loading	103.0 kg/m² (21.1 lb/sq ft)
Max power loading	7.0 kg/kW (11.5 lb/hp)

PERFORMANCE (with spray equipment installed and at CAR 3 max T-O weight, except where indicated):
Max level speed	122 knots (225 km/h; 140 mph)
Max cruising speed, 70% power	
	108 knots (200 km/h; 124 mph)
Working speed, 70% power	
	91-100 knots (169-185 km/h; 105-115 mph)
Stalling speed: flaps up	58 knots (108 km/h; 67 mph)
flaps down	55 knots (101 km/h; 63 mph)
Stalling speed at normal landing weight:	
flaps up	47 knots (87 km/h; 54 mph)
flaps down	45 knots (84 km/h; 52 mph)
Max rate of climb at S/L	317 m (1,040 ft)/min
Service ceiling	4,575 m (15,000 ft)
T-O run	215 m (705 ft)
Landing run	139 m (455 ft)
Ferry range with max fuel at 70% power	
	350 nm (648 km; 403 miles)

AYRES THRUSH S2R-R1820/510

TYPE: Single/two-seat agricultural aircraft (formerly Bull Thrush).

DESIGN FEATURES: As S2R-R1340 except for smaller wings, bigger hopper and more powerful engine.

Details as for S2R-R1340 except as follows:

POWER PLANT: One 895 kW (1,200 hp) Wright R-1820 Cyclone nine-cylinder aircooled radial engine, driving a Hamilton Standard three-blade constant-speed metal propeller. Fuel system as for S2R-R1340, but total usable fuel capacity 863 litres (228 US gallons; 190 Imp gallons).

EQUIPMENT: Generally as for S2R-R1340, except that the chemical hopper is of 1.93 m³ (68.2 cu ft) and 1,930 litres (510 US gallons; 425 Imp gallons) capacity.

DIMENSIONS, EXTERNAL: As for S2R-R1340, except:
Wing span	13.54 m (44 ft 5 in)
Length overall	9.60 m (31 ft 6 in)
Height overall	2.92 m (9 ft 7 in)
Wheel track	2.74 m (9 ft 0 in)

AREAS:
Wings, gross	30.34 m² (326.6 sq ft)

WEIGHTS AND LOADINGS:
Weight empty, equipped	2,263 kg (4,990 lb)
Typical operating weight (CAM 8)	4,536 kg (10,000 lb)
Max wing loading	149.5 kg/m² (30.62 lb/sq ft)
Max power loading	5.07 kg/kW (8.33 lb/hp)

PERFORMANCE (with spray equipment, at CAM 8 T-O weight, except where indicated):
Max level speed	138 knots (256 km/h; 159 mph)
Cruising speed, 50% power	
	135 knots (249 km/h; 155 mph)
Working speed, 30-50% power	
	87-130 knots (161-241 km/h; 100-150 mph)
Stalling speed: flaps up	61 knots (113 km/h; 70 mph)
flaps down	58 knots (107 km/h; 66 mph)
Stalling speed at normal landing weight:	
flaps up	52 knots (95 km/h; 59 mph)
flaps down	50 knots (92 km/h; 57 mph)
Max rate of climb at S/L	620 m (2,033 ft)/min
Service ceiling	8,535 m (28,000 ft)
T-O run	168 m (550 ft)
Landing run at normal landing weight	290 m (950 ft)
Ferry range at 40% power	
	582 nm (1,078 km; 670 miles)

AYRES TURBO-THRUSH S2R and TERR-MAR TURBO SEA THRUSH

TYPE: Single/two-seat turboprop agricultural and multi-role aircraft.

VARIANTS: **Turbo-Thrush S2R-T11:** Powered by 373 kW (500 shp) PT6A-11AG turboprop, with standard 1,514 litre (400 US gallon; 333 Imp gallon) chemical hopper.

Turbo-Thrush S2R-T15: Powered by 507 kW (680 shp) P&WC PT6A-15AG turboprop, with standard or optional 1,930 litre (510 US gallon; 425 Imp gallon) hopper.

Turbo-Thrush S2R-T34: Powered by 559 kW (750 shp) P&WC PT6A-34AG turboprop, with standard or optional hoppers.

Turbo-Thrush S2R-T65/400 NEDS: Narcotics Eradication Delivery System, powered by 1,026 kW (1,376 shp) P&WC PT6A-65AG turboprop and 2.82 m (9 ft 3 in) five-blade propeller; 19 delivered to US State

Ayres Turbo-Thrush S2R-T34 (Pratt & Whitney Canada PT6A-34AG turboprop)

Terr-Mar Aviation Corporation Turbo Sea Thrush conversion of the Ayres Turbo-Thrush agricultural aircraft

Department (see Customers). Has armoured two-seat cockpit, armour around engine, and 75.7 litre (20 US gallon; 16.7 Imp gallon) self-sealing fuel tank in bulletproof structure additional to normal wing tankage. NEDS aircraft dispense 'Roundup' herbicide from 1,514 litre (400 US gallon; 333 Imp gallon) hopper; delivery rate 265 litres (70 US gallons; 58.3 Imp gallons) per acre at 104-113 knots (193-209 km/h; 120-130 mph) working speed. NEDS equipment includes Bendix/King VLF/Omega 660, ADF, VOR, HF and VHF avionics.

V-1-A Vigilante: Multi-mission variant, described separately.

Terr-Mar Turbo Sea Thrush: FAA-approved water bomber fitted by Terr-Mar Aviation Corporation of Vancouver, Canada, with Wipline 6000 amphibious floats; optional large hopper can be filled with water in 10-15 s by scooping while planing.

CUSTOMERS: US State Department ordered 19 S2R-T65/400 NEDS during 1983-85 for use by International Narcotics Matters Bureau on 'Operation Roundup' eradication missions in Myanmar, Colombia, Thailand, Mexico, Belize and Guatemala. In Belize, the aircraft flew escorted by armed Pilatus Britten-Norman Islanders.

DESIGN FEATURES: All but NEDS and Vigilante variants have Hartzell three-blade, constant-speed, feathering and reversing propellers; usable fuel 863 litres (228 US gallons; 190 Imp gallons); claimed advantages include much improved take-off and climb, 454 kg (1,000 lb) higher payload because of lower engine weight, operation on aviation turbine fuel or diesel, 3,500 h TBO, quieter operation and ability to feather propeller without stopping engine while refuelling and reloading. Wing extensions (see S2R-R1340) optional on Turbo-Thrush.

DIMENSIONS, EXTERNAL: As for Bull Thrush S2R-R1820 except:
Length overall	10.06 m (33 ft 0 in)
Height overall	2.79 m (9 ft 2 in)

AREAS: As for Thrush S2R-R1820

WEIGHTS AND LOADINGS (A: standard hopper, B: optional 1,930 litre; 510 US gallon; 425 Imp gallon hopper):
Weight empty: A	1,633 kg (3,600 lb)
B	1,769 kg (3,900 lb)
Max T-O weight (CAR 3): A, B	2,721 kg (6,000 lb)
Typical operating weight (CAM 8):	
A	3,719 kg (8,200 lb)
B	3,856 kg (8,500 lb)
Max wing loading	127.1 kg/m² (26.0 lb/sq ft)

PERFORMANCE (A and B with PT6A-34AG power plant, at max T-O weight except where indicated):
Max level speed with spray equipment	
	138 knots (256 km/h; 159 mph)
Cruising speed, 50% power	
	130 knots (241 km/h; 150 mph)
Working speed, 30-50% power	
	82-130 knots (153-241 km/h; 95-150 mph)
Stalling speed: flaps up	61 knots (113 km/h; 70 mph)
flaps down	57 knots (106 km/h; 66 mph)
Stalling speed at normal landing weight:	
flaps up	51 knots (95 km/h; 59 mph)
flaps down	50 knots (92 km/h; 57 mph)
Max rate of climb at S/L	530 m (1,740 ft)/min
Service ceiling	7,620 m (25,000 ft)
T-O run	183 m (600 ft)
Landing run	152 m (500 ft)
Landing run with propeller reversal	91 m (300 ft)
Ferry range at 40% power	
	664 nm (1,231 km; 765 miles)

AYRES V-1-A VIGILANTE

TYPE: Multi-mission variant of Turbo-Thrush NEDS.

PROGRAMME: Developed in co-operation with US State Department and US Army Electro-Optical Survivability Programme; prototype (N3100A) flew May 1989; night surveillance trials flown for US Border Patrol in Arizona and Texas successfully detected several groups of illegal immigrants; Ayres sees market as low-cost surveillance and close-support aircraft in North Africa, Central and South America, but will not seek FAA certification without launch customer.

DESIGN FEATURES: Two-seat armoured cockpit and self-sealing auxiliary fuel tank; four standard NATO stores hardpoints under each wing and three tandem stores points under fuselage; three outer points have 159 kg (350 lb) capacity each, inner points 544 kg (1,200 lb) each. Stores include 0.50 in, 7.62 mm and 20 mm gun pods; 2.75 in rockets; 500 lb bombs; Stinger AAMs; land and sea mines; torpedoes; anti-tank missiles; and ECM. Surveillance systems installed in Vigilante include Honeywell, Westinghouse, Lockheed Gimbol/Texas Instruments and Lockheed Gimbol/Kollmorgen FLIR systems; multi-spectral LLTV and laser-gate LLTV cameras; Honeywell line scanner and BMS data link and receiver; on-board recorders for two sensors simultaneously and transmission to ground at up to 100 nm (185 km; 115 miles) in real time or as secure frozen imagery. Systems operator in rear cockpit. Wing section NACA 4412; dihedral 1.5°.

Otherwise as for Turbo-Thrush NEDS except as below:

LANDING GEAR: Cleveland mainwheels with 29 in tyres; rubber in compression suspension; dual caliper disc brakes, toe operated; castoring tailwheel locked central when stick held back. Tyre pressures: mainwheels 3.45 bars (50 lb/sq in); tailwheel 6.21 bars (90 lb/sq in).

POWER PLANT: One 1,026 kW (1,376 shp) emergency rating P&WC PT6A-65 turboprop; Hartzell five-blade quiet propeller turning at 1,000 to 1,700 rpm. Centrifugal air filtration system standard. Internal fuel capacity 1,135 litres (300 US gallons; 250 Imp gallons). External underwing fuel tanks, each capacity 1,514 litres (400 US gallons; 333 Imp gallons), optional.

SYSTEMS: 400A 28V DC electrical systems with AC inverter available. Parker Hannifin electric air-conditioning system and oxygen system standard. Wing and tail leading-edge, windscreen and propeller de-icing optional.

AVIONICS: Standard avionics include Bendix/King KY 196A nav/com, KNR 634 nav, dual KMA 24H audio panel, KDM 706A DME, dual KDI 573B DME indicators, KR 87 digital ADF, KT 76A transponder, KEA 130 encoding altimeter, KRA 10A radar altimeter, KI 250 altitude indicator, KA 35A marker beacon receiver, KCS 55A HSI, dual KI 229 RMI, KFS 564A, and KNS 660 VLF/Omega, HF, 3M Stormscope, Loran C, Rockwell Collins 182 UHF/VHF/FM multi-band transceiver with secure voice provisions, SATCOM, Have Quick and SINCGARS. Radar and IR warning receivers.

EQUIPMENT: IR paint, exhaust suppression system, hush kit and chaff/flare dispensers are optional. Armament and surveillance equipment as detailed above. BMS or other live video data link for images from various airborne sensors.

Ayres V-1-A Vigilante close air support and surveillance aircraft

DIMENSIONS, EXTERNAL:
Wing span	13.54 m (44 ft 5 in)
Wing chord, constant	2.29 m (7 ft 6 in)
Length overall	10.06 m (33 ft 0 in)
Height overall	2.90 m (9 ft 6 in)
Tailplane span	5.11 m (16 ft 9 in)
Wheel track	2.74 m (9 ft 0 in)
Wheelbase	5.31 m (17 ft 5 in)
Propeller diameter	2.69 m (8 ft 10 in)
Propeller ground clearance	0.91 m (3 ft 0 in)

AREAS:
Wings, gross	31.22 m² (336.0 sq ft)

WEIGHTS AND LOADINGS:
Weight empty	2,223 kg (4,900 lb)
Max fuel weight: internal	952 kg (2,100 lb)
external	1,270 kg (2,800 lb)
Max T-O and landing weight	4,762 kg (10,500 lb)

Max wing loading	151.36 kg/m² (31.01 lb/sq ft)
Max power loading	4.64 kg/kW (7.5 lb/shp)

PERFORMANCE (at max T-O weight, ISA, except where indicated):
Never-exceed speed (Vne)	
	191 knots (354 km/h; 220 mph) IAS
Max level speed	220 knots (408 km/h; 253 mph)
Max cruising speed	200 knots (371 km/h; 230 mph)
Max normal operating speed	
	163 knots (302 km/h; 187 mph)
Econ cruising speed	150 knots (278 km/h; 173 mph)
Stalling speed, flaps down	50 knots (93 km/h; 58 mph)
Max rate of climb at S/L:	
at AUW of 2,721 kg (6,000 lb)	1,067 m (3,500 ft)/min

at max T-O weight	610 m (2,000 ft)/min
Service ceiling	7,620 m (25,000 ft)
T-O run: at AUW of 2,948 kg (6,500 lb)	121 m (395 ft)
at max T-O weight	381 m (1,250 ft)
Landing run, with propeller reversal:	
at AUW of 2,948 kg (6,500 lb)	153 m (500 ft)
at AUW of 3,855 kg (8,500 lb)	229 m (750 ft)
Ferry range: with max internal fuel	
	900 nm (1,667 km; 1,036 miles)
with external fuel	1,750 nm (3,243 km; 2,015 miles)
Endurance, internal fuel, 60 knots (111 km/h; 69 mph)	
loiter speed	7 h

BASLER

BASLER TURBO CONVERSIONS INC

255 West 35th Avenue, PO Box 2305, Oshkosh, Wisconsin 54903-2305
Telephone: 1 (414) 236 7820
Fax: 1 (414) 236 0381
PRESIDENT: Warren L. Basler
VICE-PRESIDENT: Bob Clark

Company associated with Basler Flight Service Inc at same address. New 6,968 m² (75,000 sq ft) factory occupied 21 January 1990. Employees 142. Additional centres being set up in Taiwan and Poland.

BASLER TURBO-67 DC-3 CONVERSION

TYPE: Turboprop conversion and stretch of DC-3.

PROGRAMME: Multiple STC received 27 February 1990; full certification 11 December 1990. Seven Turbo-67s delivered in 1990; eight planned up to mid-1991. Capacity at Oshkosh for 14 conversions simultaneously.

CUSTOMERS: Air Colombia (three), El Salvador Air Force, via USAF (two), Bolivian Air Force (one), Colombian Air Force (one), US Forest Service (two), United Technologies (one).

DESIGN FEATURES: Pratt & Whitney Double Wasps replaced by Pratt & Whitney Canada PT6A-67R turboprops. Fuselage reinforced and stretched by 1.02 m (3 ft 4 in) plug forward of wing to retain centre of gravity; front cabin bulkhead also moved 1.52 m (5 ft 0 in) forward; wing reinforced to accept extra load; rear door can be enlarged by upward opening flap to take LD3 containers, of which five can be carried. New electrical system to FAR Pt 25 and upgraded hydraulics to give faster landing gear retraction; fuel system modified for jet fuel; optional additional tanks. Gross take-off and landing weight raised.

FLYING CONTROLS: All-metal control surfaces; lateral control improved; bob weight and down springs in elevator circuit; spring servo tab in rudder; drooped outboard leading-edge and new wingtips. Coupled autopilot to Cat II limits.

LANDING GEAR: As for DC-3.

POWER PLANT: Two 1,062 kW (1,424 shp) P&WC PT6A-67R turboprops rated at 955 kW (1,281 shp) at 32°C (91°F), driving 2.92 m (9 ft 7 in) diameter Hartzell metal five-blade feathering and reversing propellers. Standard usable fuel 2,918 litres (771 US gallons; 642 Imp gallons); optional 5,837 litres (1,542 US gallons; 1,284 Imp gallons).

Basler Turbo-67 DC-3 conversion (two P&WC PT6A-67R turboprops)

ACCOMMODATION: Two pilots in modernised cockpit. Normal 38 passengers or five LD3 containers with floor guides and rollers and upward opening door extension.

SYSTEMS: Variable delivery hydraulic pumps; two 300A starter/generators, four buses (main and emergency each side), two 12V 88Ah batteries; bleed air cabin heating; propeller and engine intake de-icing standard, pneumatic boots for wing and tail optional; fire detection and extinguisher system.

AVIONICS: Full Bendix/King com/nav and remote area system.

WEIGHTS AND LOADINGS:
Weight empty	6,804 kg (15,000 lb)
Basic operating weight (equipped)	7,121 kg (15,700 lb)
Max internal fuel	2,346 kg (5,172 lb)

Max T-O and landing weight	13,041 kg (28,750 lb)
Max zero-fuel weight	11,884 kg (26,200 lb)
Max power loading	6.83 kg/kW (11.22 lb/shp)

PERFORMANCE:
Max cruising speed at 7,620 m (25,000 ft), 80% torque
210 knots (389 km/h; 241 mph)
Service ceiling, one engine out 3,960 m (13,000 ft)
Max range, 45 min reserves:
with long-range tanks at 7,620 m (25,000 ft), 80% torque, or 4,575 m (15,000 ft), 90% torque
2,260 nm (4,188 km; 2,602 miles)
with standard tanks at 7,620 m (25,000 ft), 80% torque
1,000 nm (1,853 km; 1,150 miles)

BEECH

BEECH AIRCRAFT CORPORATION
(Subsidiary of Raytheon Company)

9709 East Central, Wichita, Kansas 67201-0085
Telephone: 1 (316) 676 7111
Fax: 1 (316) 676 8286
BRANCH DIVISION: Salina, Kansas
CHAIRMAN EMERITUS AND CHAIRMAN OF BEECH AIRCRAFT
  FOUNDATION: Mrs Olive Ann (Walter H.) Beech
PRESIDENT: Jack Braly
EXECUTIVE VICE-PRESIDENT: Charles W. Dieker (Marketing)
VICE-PRESIDENT, AEROSPACE: William R. Coughenour
VICE-PRESIDENT, ENGINEERING: Robert D. Dickerson
VICE-PRESIDENT, AIRCRAFT DESIGN: Joseph F. Furnish
VICE-PRESIDENT, MANUFACTURING: Cecil Miller
VICE-PRESIDENT, T-1A PROGRAMME: Dr William A. Edgington
DIRECTOR, CORPORATE AFFAIRS: James M. Gregory
MANAGER, PUBLIC RELATIONS: Michael S. Potts

Beech Aircraft Corporation founded 1932 by Mr and Mrs Beech; became wholly owned subsidiary of Raytheon 8 February 1980, but continues to operate separately building civil and military aircraft, missile targets and components for aircraft and missiles; Salina division supplies all wings, non-metallic interior components, ventral fins, nosecones and tailcones used in Wichita production and builds major subassemblies for the Beechjet. Additional Wichita products include subcontracted composites and metal winglets and composites landing gear doors for McDonnell Douglas C-17.

Wholly owned subsidiaries include Beech Aerospace Services Inc (BASI) of Madison, Mississippi (worldwide logistic support for Army/Air Force/Navy C-12s, Army U-21s and Beech MQM-107 targets, and of US Navy T-34C and T-44 trainers in the United States); Beech Acceptance Corporation Inc (business aircraft retail financing and leasing); Travel Air Insurance Company Ltd, Bermuda (aircraft liability insurance); Beech Holdings Inc (marketing support to parent company). Wholly owned sales outlets of Beech Holdings Inc include Beechcraft East Inc, Farmingdale, New York, and Bedford, Massachusetts; Hangar One Inc, Atlanta Hartsfield, De-Kalb Peachtree and Fulton County airports in Georgia; Birmingham in Alabama; and Opa Locka, Orlando and Tampa in Florida; United Beechcraft Inc, Wichita, Kansas; Beechcraft West, Ontario, Hayward, Van Nuys and Fresno, California; Hedrick Beechcraft in Houston, Dallas, Corpus Christi and San Antonio, Texas; Indiana Beechcraft Inc, Indianapolis, Indiana, the location of Beech Commuter Spare Parts Supply; Hartzog Aviation, Rockford in Illinois.

Beech aircraft has about 10,900 employees worldwide and occupies 350,700 m² (3,775,000 sq ft) of plant area at its two major facilities in Wichita and Salina, Kansas.

Total production by Beech reached 49,639 at start of 1991. Deliveries of Beech aircraft during 1990 included 207 Bonanzas, 33 Barons, 121 King Airs, four Model 1300s, 48 Model 1900s, eight Beechjets and 11 Starships.

BEECHCRAFT T-34C
US Navy designation: T-34C

Although production ended April 1990, numbers of T-34Cs remain in service. In addition to two prototypes, 353 were built for US Navy and 139 T-34C-1s for export to Argentine Navy, Republic of China (Taiwan) Air Force, Ecuador Air Force and Navy, Gabon Presidential Guard, Indonesian Air Force, Moroccan Air Force, Peruvian Navy, Uruguayan Navy; six civil Turbine Mentor 34Cs supplied to Algerian national pilot training school. Last described fully in *Jane's* 1989-90.

BEECHCRAFT BONANZA MODEL F33A/C

TYPE: Four/five-seat single-engined executive aircraft.
PROGRAMME: First flight 14 September 1959; known as Debonair until 1967; 1985 model introduced cargo door, three-blade propeller, super soundproofing, and full IFR avionics.
VARIANTS: **F33A:** Similar to Model V35B Bonanza (1984-85 *Jane's*), but with conventional vertical fin and tailplane. Certificated in Utility category.
  F33C: Aerobatic version without air-conditioning, big cargo door and fifth seat; produced to special order.
CUSTOMERS: F33C sales include three civilian F33Cs in 1986-87, Mexican Air Force (21), Imperial Iranian Air Force (16), Mexican Navy (five), Netherlands Government Flying School (16), and Spanish Air Force/Air Ministry (74). F33A special order trainers include Lufthansa (three) and Singapore International Airlines (four). Total 3,105 Model 33s built by 1 January 1991, including 126 in 1990.
DESIGN FEATURES: Beech modified NACA 23016.5 wing section at root, modified 23012 at tip; dihedral 6°; incidence 4° at root and 1° at tip.
FLYING CONTROLS: Mechanical flying controls; electrically actuated trim tab in each elevator; ground adjustable tabs in ailerons and rudder; single-slotted, three-position light alloy flaps.
STRUCTURE: Conventional light alloy, with two-spar wing torsion box and stressed-skin tail surfaces.
LANDING GEAR: Electrically retractable tricycle type, with steerable nosewheel. Mainwheels retract inward into wings, nosewheel rearward. Beech oleo-pneumatic shock

Beechcraft Model F33A Bonanza four/five-seat executive aircraft

absorbers in all units. Cleveland mainwheels, size 6.00-6, and tyres, size 7.00-6, pressure 2.28-2.76 bars (33-40 lb/sq in). Cleveland nosewheel and tyre, size 5.00-5, pressure 2.76 bars (40 lb/sq in). Cleveland ring-disc hydraulic brakes. Parking brake. Magic Hand landing gear system optional.
POWER PLANT: One 212.5 kW (285 hp) Continental IO-520-BB flat-six engine, driving a McCauley three-blade constant-speed metal propeller. Propeller de-icing optional. Manually adjustable engine cowl flaps. Two standard fuel tanks in wing leading-edges, with total usable capacity of 280 litres (74 US gallons; 61.6 Imp gallons). Refuelling points above tanks. Oil capacity 11.5 litres (3 US gallons; 2.5 Imp gallons).
ACCOMMODATION: Enclosed cabin with four individual seats in pairs as standard, plus optional forward facing fifth seat (F33A only). Baggage compartment and hatshelf aft of seats. Passenger door and baggage compartment door on starboard side. Heater standard. Large cargo door, on starboard side of fuselage, standard on F33A. F33C has removable seat cushions, to accommodate parachutes, and a quick-release passenger door.
SYSTEMS: Optional 12,000 BTU refrigeration type air-conditioning system (F33A only) comprises evaporator located beneath pilot's seat, condenser on lower fuselage, and engine mounted compressor. Air outlets on centre console, with two-speed blower. Electrical system supplied by 28V 60A alternator, 24V 15.5Ah battery; a 100A alternator is available as an option, as is a standby generator. Hydraulic system for brakes only. Pneumatic system for instrument gyros and refrigeration type air-conditioning system optional. Oxygen system and electric propeller de-icing optional.
AVIONICS: Standard avionics include Bendix/King KX 155 760-channel com transceiver, 200-channel nav/glideslope receiver/converter with KI 209 VOR/ILS indicator, Bendix/King KY 155 760-channel com transceiver, 200-channel nav receiver/converter with KI 208 VOR/

LOC indicator, KR 87 ADF with 227-00 indicator, KN 63 DME with KDI 572 indicator, DME hold and nav 1/nav 2 switching, KT 76A transponder, KEA-130A encoding altimeter, KMA 24-03 audio control/marker beacon receiver, microphone, headset, cabin speaker and static wicks. A wide range of optional avionics is available, including Bendix/King KFC 150 autopilot, and 3M/Ryan WX-1000 Stormscope.
EQUIPMENT: Standard equipment includes LCD digital chronometer, electric clock, exhaust gas temperature gauge, outside air temperature gauge, rate of climb indicator, turn co-ordinator, 3 in horizon and directional gyros, four fore and aft adjustable and reclining seats, armrests, headrests, single diagonal strap shoulder harness with inertia reel for all occupants, pilot's storm window, sun visors, ultraviolet-proof windscreen and windows, large cargo door (F33A only), emergency locator transmitter, stall warning device, alternate static source, heated pitot, rotating beacon, three-light strobe system, carpeted floor, super soundproofing, control wheel map lights, entrance door courtesy light, internally lit instruments, coat hooks, glove compartment, in-flight storage pockets, approach plate holder, utility shelf, cabin dome light, reading lights, instrument post lights, control wheel map light, electroluminescent sub-panel lighting, landing light, taxi light, full-flow oil filter, three-colour polyurethane exterior paint, external power socket and towbar. Optional equipment includes dual controls, co-pilot's wheel brakes, air-conditioning, fifth seat, fresh air vent blower and ground com switch. F33C has accelerometer, second boost pump with indicator light, non-baffled fuel cells, heavy-gauge rudder cables and reinforced fuselage, wings and tail surfaces as standard.
DIMENSIONS, EXTERNAL:

Wing span	10.21 m (33 ft 6 in)
Wing chord: at root	2.13 m (7 ft 0 in)
at tip	1.07 m (3 ft 6 in)

Beechcraft Model A36 Bonanza four/six-seat cabin monoplane

Wing aspect ratio	6.2
Length overall	8.13 m (26 ft 8 in)
Height overall	2.51 m (8 ft 3 in)
Tailplane span	3.71 m (12 ft 2 in)
Wheel track	2.92 m (9 ft 7 in)
Wheelbase	2.13 m (7 ft 0 in)
Propeller diameter	2.13 m (7 ft 0 in)
Passenger door: Height	0.91 m (3 ft 0 in)
Width	0.94 m (3 ft 1 in)
Baggage compartment door:	
Height	0.57 m (1 ft 10½ in)
Width	0.70 m (2 ft 3½ in)

DIMENSIONS, INTERNAL:

Cabin, aft of firewall: Length	3.07 m (10 ft 1 in)
Max width	1.07 m (3 ft 6 in)
Max height	1.27 m (4 ft 2 in)
Volume	3.31 m³ (117 cu ft)
Baggage space	0.99 m³ (35 cu ft)

AREAS:

Wings, gross	16.80 m² (181.0 sq ft)
Ailerons (total)	1.06 m² (11.4 sq ft)
Trailing-edge flaps (total)	1.98 m² (21.3 sq ft)
Fin	0.93 m² (10.0 sq ft)
Rudder, incl tab	0.52 m² (5.6 sq ft)
Tailplane	1.75 m² (18.82 sq ft)
Elevators, incl tabs	1.67 m² (18.0 sq ft)

WEIGHTS AND LOADINGS:

Weight empty	1,015 kg (2,237 lb)
Max T-O and landing weight	1,542 kg (3,400 lb)
Max T-O weight, F33C in Aerobatic category	1,270 kg (2,800 lb)
Max ramp weight	1,548 kg (3,412 lb)
Max wing loading	91.8 kg/m² (18.8 lb/sq ft)
Max power loading	7.26 kg/kW (11.93 lb/hp)

PERFORMANCE (at max T-O weight, except cruising speeds at mid-cruise weight):

Max level speed at S/L	182 knots (338 km/h; 209 mph)
Cruising speed:	
75% power at 1,830 m (6,000 ft)	
	172 knots (319 km/h; 198 mph)
66% power at 3,050 m (10,000 ft)	
	168 knots (311 km/h; 193 mph)
55% power at 3,660 m (12,000 ft)	
	157 knots (291 km/h; 181 mph)
45% power at 2,440 m (8,000 ft)	
	136 knots (253 km/h; 157 mph)
Stalling speed, power off:	
flaps up	64 knots (118 km/h; 74 mph) IAS
30° flap	51 knots (94 km/h; 59 mph) IAS
Max rate of climb at S/L	353 m (1,157 ft)/min
Service ceiling	5,443 m (17,858 ft)
T-O run	305 m (1,000 ft)
T-O to 15 m (50 ft)	530 m (1,740 ft)
Landing from 15 m (50 ft)	396 m (1,300 ft)
Landing run	232 m (760 ft)

Range with max usable fuel, allowances for engine start, taxi, T-O, climb and 45 min reserves at 45% power:

75% power at 1,830 m (6,000 ft)	
	715 nm (1,325 km; 823 miles)
66% power at 3,050 m (10,000 ft)	
	777 nm (1,440 km; 894 miles)
55% power at 3,660 m (12,000 ft)	
	838 nm (1,553 km; 964 miles)
45% power at 2,440 m (8,000 ft)	
	889 nm (1,648 km; 1,023 miles)

BEECHCRAFT BONANZA MODEL A36

TYPE: Four/six-seat, single-engined business and utility aircraft.

PROGRAMME: Developed from Bonanza Model V35B, but with vertical fin; current A36 introduced 3 October 1983, succeeding model powered by 212.5 kW (285 hp) Continental IO-520-BB; certificated in FAA Utility category.

CUSTOMERS: Saudi Arabian Airlines (four) in April 1985 for pilot training; Finnair Training Centre at Pori, Finland (three), in 1987; Japan Air Lines (five) in 1990. Orders in 1991 from Lufthansa (12, to replace existing F33As) and Japan Air Lines (23). Total 3,024 Model 36 Bonanzas delivered by 1 January 1991, including 70 in 1990.

DESIGN FEATURES: Structure as for F33A, but fuselage 0.25 m (10 in) longer; cabin volume increased by 0.54 m³ (18.9 cu ft); baggage volume increased by 0.28 m³ (10 cu ft); large double freight doors starboard side aft of wing; 1990 model has improved controls, lighting and systems; options same as for F33A, plus instrument post lights or internal instrument lighting; courtesy lights for entrance and step; co-pilot's vertically adjusting seat; refrigeration-type air-conditioning.

FLYING CONTROLS: As for F33A. Dual controls standard.

STRUCTURE: As for F33A, with addition of two vortex generators on wings.

LANDING GEAR: As for Model F33A; new landing gear warning system introduced in 1989.

POWER PLANT: One 224 kW (300 hp) Continental IO-550-B flat-six engine, driving a McCauley three-blade constant-speed propeller (Lufthansa aircraft derated to 212.5 kW; 285 hp and have smaller propeller). The engine is equipped with an altitude-compensating fuel pump which automatically leans and enriches the fuel/air

mixture during climb and descent respectively. Fuel capacity as for Model F33A.

ACCOMMODATION: Enclosed cabin seating four to six persons on individual seats. Pilot's seat is vertically adjustable. Dual controls standard. Two rear removable seats and two folding seats permit rapid conversion to utility configuration. Optional club seating with rear facing third and fourth seats, executive writing desk, refreshment cabinet, headrests for third and fourth seats, reading lights and fresh air outlets for fifth and sixth seats. Double doors of bonded aluminium honeycomb construction on starboard side facilitate loading of cargo. As an air ambulance, one stretcher can be accommodated with ample room for a medical attendant and/or other passengers. Extra windows provide improved view for passengers. Stowage for 181 kg (400 lb) of baggage.

SYSTEMS: Electrical system as for F33A. Hydraulic system for brakes only. Pneumatic system for instrument gyros, and refrigeration type air-conditioning system, optional.

AVIONICS: Standard avionics include Bendix/King KX 155 760-channel nav/com, with KI 208 VOR/LOC Omni converter/indicator, but a wide range of optional avionics is available, including Bendix/King KX 165 or KY 196A TSO/IFR transceiver, KAS 297. An optional ground communication switch permits use of one com radio without turning on the battery master switch.

EQUIPMENT: Optional equipment is as detailed for the F33A Bonanza, except as noted.

DIMENSIONS, EXTERNAL: As for F33A except:

Length overall	8.38 m (27 ft 6 in)
Height overall	2.62 m (8 ft 7 in)
Wheelbase	2.39 m (7 ft 10¼ in)
* Propeller diameter	2.03 m (6 ft 8 in)
Rear passenger/cargo door: Height	1.02 m (3 ft 4 in)
Width	1.14 m (3 ft 9 in)

* 1.93 m (6 ft 4 in) on Lufthansa aircraft

DIMENSIONS, INTERNAL:

Cabin, aft of firewall: Length, incl extended baggage compartment	3.84 m (12 ft 7 in)
Max width	1.07 m (3 ft 6 in)
Max height	1.27 m (4 ft 2 in)
Volume	3.85 m³ (135.9 cu ft)

AREAS: As for F33A

WEIGHTS AND LOADINGS:

Weight empty, standard	1,028 kg (2,266 lb)
Max T-O weight	1,655 kg (3,650 lb)
Max ramp weight	1,661 kg (3,663 lb)
Max wing loading	98.6 kg/m² (20.2 lb/sq ft)
Max power loading	7.40 kg/kW (12.2 lb/hp)

PERFORMANCE (max speed at minimum weight; cruising speeds at mid-cruise weight):

Max level speed	184 knots (340 km/h; 212 mph)
Max cruising speed:	
2,500 rpm at 1,830 m (6,000 ft)	
	176 knots (326 km/h; 202 mph)
2,300 rpm at 2,440 m (8,000 ft)	
	167 knots (309 km/h; 192 mph)
2,100 rpm at 1,830 m (6,000 ft)	
	160 knots (296 km/h; 184 mph)
2,100 rpm at 3,050 m (10,000 ft)	
	153 knots (283 km/h; 176 mph)
Stalling speed, power off:	
flaps up	68 knots (126 km/h; 78 mph) IAS
30° flap	59 knots (109 km/h; 68 mph) IAS
Max rate of climb at S/L	368 m (1,208 ft)/min
Service ceiling	3,640 m (18,500 ft)
T-O run: flaps up	360 m (1,182 ft)
12° flap	296 m (971 ft)
T-O to 15 m (50 ft): flaps up	640 m (2,100 ft)
12° flap	583 m (1,913 ft)
Landing from 15 m (50 ft)	442 m (1,450 ft)
Landing run	280 m (920 ft)

Range with max usable fuel, with allowances for engine start, taxi, T-O, climb and 45 min reserves at econ cruise power:

2,500 rpm at 3,660 m (12,000 ft)	
	875 nm (1,621 km; 1,008 miles)
2,300 rpm at 3,660 m (12,000 ft)	
	903 nm (1,672 km; 1,039 miles)
2,100 rpm at 1,830 m (6,000 ft)	
	914 nm (1,694 km; 1,052 miles)

BEECHCRAFT TURBO BONANZA MODEL B36TC

TYPE: Turbocharged version of A36 Bonanza.

PROGRAMME: Certificated as A36TC 7 December 1978; 271 A36TC delivered; improved B36TC introduced 1982.

CUSTOMERS: Total of 501 delivered by 1 January 1991.

DESIGN FEATURES: Compared with A36TC, B36TC has greater span; wing section NACA 23010.5 at tip; 0° incidence at tip; greater fuel capacity.

Data below summarise differences from A36TC:

POWER PLANT: One 223.7 kW (300 hp) Continental TSIO-520-UB turbocharged flat-six engine, driving a three-blade constant-speed metal propeller. Fixed engine cowl flaps. Two fuel tanks in each wing leading-edge, with total usable capacity of 386 litres (102 US gallons; 85 Imp gallons). Refuelling points above tanks. Oil capacity 11.5 litres (3 US gallons; 2.5 Imp gallons).

SYSTEMS: Air-conditioning optional.

AVIONICS: As for Model A36.

EQUIPMENT: As for Model A36, except that exhaust gas temperature gauge is not available. Turbine inlet temperature gauge is standard.

DIMENSIONS, EXTERNAL: As for Model A36, except:

Wing span	11.53 m (37 ft 10 in)
Wing chord at tip	0.91 m (3 ft 0 in)
Wing aspect ratio	7.6
Propeller diameter	1.98 m (6 ft 6 in)

DIMENSIONS, INTERNAL: As for Model A36

AREAS:

Wings, gross	17.47 m² (188.1 sq ft)

WEIGHTS AND LOADINGS:

Weight empty, standard	1,093 kg (2,410 lb)
Max T-O and landing weight	1,746 kg (3,850 lb)
Max ramp weight	1,753 kg (3,866 lb)
Max wing loading	100.1 kg/m² (20.5 lb/sq ft)
Max power loading	7.81 kg/kW (12.8 lb/hp)

PERFORMANCE (at max T-O weight, except speeds are at mid-cruise weight):

Max level speed at 6,700 m (22,000 ft)	
	213 knots (394 km/h; 245 mph)
Cruising speed at 7,620 m (25,000 ft):	
79% power	200 knots (370 km/h; 230 mph)
75% power	195 knots (361 km/h; 224 mph)
69% power	188 knots (348 km/h; 216 mph)
56% power	173 knots (320 km/h; 199 mph)
Stalling speed, power off:	
flaps up	65 knots (120 km/h; 75 mph) IAS
30° flap	57 knots (106 km/h; 66 mph) IAS
Max rate of climb at S/L	321 m (1,053 ft)/min
Service ceiling	over 7,620 m (25,000 ft)
T-O run, 15° flap	353 m (1,156 ft)
T-O to 15 m (50 ft), 15° flap	649 m (2,130 ft)
Landing run	298 m (976 ft)

Range with max fuel, allowances for engine start, taxi, T-O, cruise climb, descent, and 45 min reserves at 50% power:

79% power at 7,620 m (25,000 ft)	
	956 nm (1,770 km; 1,100 miles)
75% power at 7,620 m (25,000 ft)	
	984 nm (1,822 km; 1,132 miles)
69% power at 7,620 m (25,000 ft)	
	1,022 nm (1,892 km; 1,176 miles)
56% power at 6,100 m (20,000 ft)	
	1,092 nm (2,022 km; 1,256 miles)

BEECHCRAFT BARON MODEL 58

TYPE: Four/six-seat piston-twin business aircraft.

PROGRAMME: Developed from Baron D55; certificated in FAA Normal category 19 November 1969.

CUSTOMERS: Include Indonesian Civil Flying Academy, Java (four), Centre National de Formation Aviation Civile of M'Vengue, Gabon (three), US FAA staff pilot proficiency training programme (eight), Lufthansa pilot training (19); 1990 deliveries included Air France (three), Japan Air Lines (three), both for pilot training. Total 2,246 Baron 58s, including 58Ps and 58TCs, delivered by 1 January 1991, including 33 in 1990.

DESIGN FEATURES: Changes from Baron 55 include forward cabin extended by 0.254 m (10 in), wheelbase extended forward, double passenger/cargo doors starboard side, extended propeller hubs, redesigned nacelles for better cooling, and fourth window on each side. Wing section NACA 23015.5 at root, 23010.5 at tip; dihedral 6°; incidence 4° at root and 0° at tip. Optional pneumatic de-icing of wing and tailplane leading-edges.

FLYING CONTROLS: Manually operated trim tabs in elevators, rudder and port aileron; electrically operated single-slotted flaps.

STRUCTURE: Light alloy with two-spar wing box; elevators have smooth magnesium alloy skins.

LANDING GEAR: Electrically retractable tricycle type. Main units retract inward into wings, nosewheel aft. Beech oleo-pneumatic shock absorbers in all units. Steerable nosewheel with shimmy damper. Cleveland wheels, with mainwheel tyres size 6.50-8, pressure 3.59-3.96 bars (52-56 lb/sq in). Nosewheel tyre size 5.00-5, pressure 3.79-4.14 bars (55-60 lb/sq in). Cleveland ring-disc hydraulic brakes. Heavy duty brakes optional. Parking brake. New warning system introduced in 1989.

POWER PLANT: Two 224 kW (300 hp) Continental IO-550-C flat-six engines, each driving a McCauley three-blade constant-speed fully feathering metal propeller. The standard fuel system has a usable capacity of 514 litres (136 US gallons; 113 Imp gallons), with optional usable capacity of 628 litres (166 US gallons; 138 Imp gallons). Optional 'wet wingtip' installation also available, increasing usable capacity to 734 litres (194 US gallons; 161.5 Imp gallons).

ACCOMMODATION: Standard model has four individual seats in pairs in enclosed cabin, with door on starboard side. Single diagonal strap shoulder harness with inertia reel standard on all seats. Vertically adjusting pilot's seat is standard. Vertically adjusting co-pilot's seat, folding fifth and sixth seats, or club seating comprising folding fifth and sixth seats and aft facing third and fourth seats, are optional. Executive writing desk available as option with club seating. Baggage compartment in nose, capacity 136 kg (300 lb). Double passenger/cargo doors on starboard side of cabin provide access to space for 181 kg (400 lb) of baggage or cargo behind the third and fourth seats.

Beechcraft Baron Model 58 four/six-seat cabin monoplane

Pilot's storm window. Openable windows adjacent to the third and fourth seats are used for ground ventilation and as emergency exits. Cabin heated and ventilated. Windscreen defrosting standard.

SYSTEMS: Cabin heated by Janitrol 50,000 BTU heater, which serves also for windscreen defrosting. Oxygen system of 1.41 m³ (49.8 cu ft) or 1.87 m³ (66 cu ft) capacity optional. Electrical system includes two 28V 60A engine driven alternators with alternator failure lights and two 12V 25Ah batteries. Two 100A alternators optional. Hydraulic system for brakes only. Pneumatic pressure system for air driven instruments, and optional wing and tail unit de-icing system. Oxygen system, cabin air-conditioning and windscreen electric anti-icing optional.

AVIONICS: Standard avionics include Bendix/King KX 155-09 760-channel com transceiver with audio amplifier, 200-channel nav receiver with KI 208 VOR/LOC converter/indicator, KR 87 ADF with KI 227-00 indicator, Bendix/King combined loop/sense antenna, microphone, headset, cabin speaker, nav and com antennae. Bendix/King weather radar and/or Stormscope optional. Optional avionics by Bendix/King and Collins.

EQUIPMENT: Standard equipment includes dual controls, blind-flying instruments, control wheel clock, outside air temperature gauge, sensitive altimeter, turn co-ordinator, pilot's storm window, sun visors, ultraviolet-proof windscreen and cabin windows, armrests, adjustable rudder pedals (retractable on starboard side), emergency locator transmitter, heated pitot head, instrument panel floodlights, map light, lighted trim tab position indicator, step and entrance door courtesy lights, reading lights, navigation and position lights, steerable taxi light, dual landing lights, cabin carpeting and soundproofing, headrests, heated fuel vents, cabin dome light, door ajar warning light, nose baggage compartment light, heated fuel and stall warning vanes, external polyurethane paint finish, EGT and CHT gauges, synchroscope, engine winterisation kit, towbar and external power socket. Options include a true airspeed indicator, engine and flight hour recorders, instantaneous vertical speed indicator, alternate static source, internally illuminated instruments, digital beacon, strobe lights, electric windscreen anti-icing, wing ice detection light, static wicks, cabin club seating, executive writing desk, refreshment cabinet, cabin fire extinguisher, ventilation blower, super soundproofing, and approach plate holder.

DIMENSIONS, EXTERNAL:

Wing span	11.53 m (37 ft 10 in)
Wing chord: at root	2.13 m (7 ft 0 in)
at tip	0.90 m (2 ft 11.6 in)
Wing aspect ratio	7.2
Length overall	9.09 m (29 ft 10 in)
Height overall	2.97 m (9 ft 9 in)
Tailplane span	4.85 m (15 ft 11 in)
Wheel track	2.92 m (9 ft 7 in)
Wheelbase	2.72 m (8 ft 11 in)
Propeller diameter	1.98 m (6 ft 6 in)
Rear passenger/cargo doors:	
Max height	1.02 m (3 ft 4 in)
Width	1.14 m (3 ft 9 in)
Baggage door (fwd): Height	0.56 m (1 ft 10 in)
Width	0.64 m (2 ft 1 in)

DIMENSIONS, INTERNAL:

Cabin, incl rear baggage area:	
Length	3.84 m (12 ft 7 in)
Max width	1.07 m (3 ft 6 in)
Max height	1.27 m (4 ft 2 in)
Floor area	3.72 m² (40 sq ft)
Volume	3.85 m³ (135.9 cu ft)
Baggage compartment: fwd	0.49 m³ (17.2 cu ft)

AREAS:

Wings, gross	18.51 m² (199.2 sq ft)

Ailerons (total)	1.06 m² (11.40 sq ft)
Trailing-edge flaps (total)	1.98 m² (21.30 sq ft)
Fin	1.46 m² (15.67 sq ft)
Rudder, incl tab	0.81 m² (8.75 sq ft)
Tailplane	4.95 m² (53.30 sq ft)
Elevators, incl tabs	1.84 m² (19.80 sq ft)

WEIGHTS AND LOADINGS:

Weight empty	1,579 kg (3,481 lb)
Max T-O weight	2,495 kg (5,500 lb)
Max landing weight	2,449 kg (5,400 lb)
Max ramp weight	2,506 kg (5,524 lb)
Max wing loading	143.4 kg/m² (27.6 lb/sq ft)
Max power loading	5.60 kg/kW (9.2 lb/hp)

PERFORMANCE (at max T-O weight, except cruising speeds at average cruise weight):

Max level speed at S/L	208 knots (386 km/h; 239 mph)
Max cruising speed, 2,500 rpm at 1,525 m (5,000 ft)	
	203 knots (376 km/h; 234 mph)
Cruising speed, 2,500 rpm at 3,050 m (10,000 ft)	
	198 knots (367 km/h; 228 mph)
Econ cruising speed, 2,100 rpm at 3,660 m (12,000 ft)	
	163 knots (302 km/h; 188 mph)
Stalling speed, power off:	
flaps up	84 knots (156 km/h; 97 mph) IAS
flaps down	75 knots (139 km/h; 86 mph) IAS
Max rate of climb at S/L	529 m (1,735 ft)/min
Rate of climb at S/L, one engine out	119 m (390 ft)/min
Service ceiling	6,306 m (20,688 ft)
Service ceiling, one engine out	2,220 m (7,284 ft)
T-O run	427 m (1,400 ft)
T-O to 15 m (50 ft)	701 m (2,300 ft)
Landing from 15 m (50 ft)	747 m (2,450 ft)
Landing run	434 m (1,425 ft)

Range with 734 litres (194 US gallons; 161.5 Imp gallons) usable fuel, with allowances for engine start, taxi, T-O, climb and 45 min reserves at econ cruise power:

max cruising speed (power/altitude settings as above)	
	1,150 nm (2,130 km; 1,324 miles)
cruising speed (power/altitude settings as above)	
	1,411 nm (2,615 km; 1,625 miles)
econ cruising speed (power/altitude settings as above)	
	1,575 nm (2,919 km; 1,814 miles)

BEECHCRAFT KING AIR MODEL C90A

TYPE: Six/ten-seat turboprop pressurised business twin.

PROGRAMME: Superseded Models 90, A90, B90, C90, C90-1 King Air. Increased gross weight C90A announced April 1987, allowing two more passengers and extra baggage; deliveries began fourth quarter 1987.

CUSTOMERS: Include Japan Air Lines and Japan Civil Aviation College; 35 Model C90A delivered during 1990; total 1,261 commercial and 226 military King Air 90/A90/B90/C90/C90-1/C90A delivered by 1 January 1991.

DESIGN FEATURES: Wing section NACA 23014.1 (modified) at root, 23016.22 (modified) at outer end of centre section, 23012 at tip; dihedral 7°; incidence 4° 48′ at root, 0° at tip; tailplane 7° dihedral; automatic pneumatic de-icing of wing/fin/tailplane leading-edges standard.

FLYING CONTROLS: Trim tabs on port aileron, in both elevators and rudders; single-slotted aluminium flaps.

STRUCTURE: Generally light alloy; magnesium ailerons.

LANDING GEAR: Hydraulically retractable tricycle type. Nosewheel retracts rearward, mainwheels forward into engine nacelles. Mainwheels protrude slightly beneath nacelles when retracted, for safety in a wheels-up emergency landing. Fully castoring steerable nosewheel with shimmy damper. Beech oleo-pneumatic shock absorbers. Goodrich mainwheels with tyres size 8.50-10, pressure 3.79 bars (55 lb/sq in). Goodrich nosewheel with tyre size 6.50-10, pressure 3.59 bars (52 lb/sq in). Goodrich heat-sink and aircooled multi-disc hydraulic brakes. Parking brakes.

POWER PLANT: Two 410 kW (550 shp) Pratt & Whitney Canada PT6A-21 turboprops, each driving a Hartzell three-blade constant-speed fully feathering propeller. Propeller electrothermal anti-icing, auto ignition system, environmental fuel drain collection system, magnetic chip detector, automatic propeller feathering and propeller synchrophaser standard. Fuel in two tanks in engine nacelles, each with usable capacity of 231 litres (61 US gallons; 50.8 Imp gallons), and auxiliary bladder tanks in outer wings, each with capacity of 496 litres (131 US gallons; 109 Imp gallons). Total usable fuel capacity 1,454 litres (384 US gallons; 320 Imp gallons). Refuelling points in top of each engine nacelle and in wing leading-edge outboard of each nacelle. Oil capacity 13.2 litres (3.5 US gallons; 2.9 Imp gallons) per engine. Engine anti-icing system standard. Engine fire detection and extinguishing system optional.

ACCOMMODATION: Two seats side by side in cockpit with dual controls standard. Normally, four reclining seats in main cabin, in pairs facing each other fore and aft. Standard furnishings include cabin forward partition, with fore and aft partition curtain and coat rack, hinged nose baggage compartment door, seat belts and inertia reel shoulder harness for all seats. Optional arrangements seat up to eight persons, with lateral tracking chairs, and refreshment cabinets. Baggage racks at rear of cabin on starboard side, with optional toilet on port side. Door on port side aft of wing, with built-in airstairs. Emergency exit on starboard side of cabin. Entire accommodation pressurised, heated and air-conditioned. Electrically heated windscreen, windscreen defroster and windscreen wipers standard.

SYSTEMS: Pressurisation by dual engine bleed air system with pressure differential of 0.34 bar (5.0 lb/sq in). Cabin heated by 45,000 BTU dual engine bleed air system and auxiliary electrical heating system. Hydraulic system for landing gear actuation. Electrical system includes two 28V 250A starter/generators, 24V 45Ah aircooled nickel-cadmium battery with failure detector. Complete de-icing and anti-icing equipment. Oxygen system, 0.62 m³ (22 cu ft), 1.39 m³ (49 cu ft) or 1.81 m³ (64 cu ft) capacity, optional. Vacuum system for flight instruments.

AVIONICS: Standard Collins Pro Line II avionics package includes APS-65 autopilot/flight director with ADI-84 FDI and EFD-74 EHSI; dual VHF-22A transceivers with CTL-22 controls; dual VIR-32 VOR/LOC/GLS/MKR receivers with CTL-32 controls; ADF-60A with CTL-62 control; DME-42 with IND-42 indicator; RMI-30; dual MCS-65 compass systems; WXR-270

Beechcraft King Air Model C90A six/ten-seat business aircraft

colour weather radar; dual TDR-90 transponders; ALT-50A radio altimeter; dual DB systems Model 415 audio systems; pilot's United 5506-S encoding altimeter; dual Flite-Tronics PC-250 inverters; dual 2 in electric turn and bank indicators; co-pilot's 3 in horizon indicator; co-pilot's HSI; avionics master switch; edgelite radio panel; ELT; ground clearance switch to com 1; control wheel push-to-talk switches; dual hand microphones; dual Telex headsets; and sectional instrument panel. Optional avionics include Bendix/King Silver Crown and Gold Crown packages; Foster LNS-616B RNAV/Loran C; and 3M WX-1000+ Stormscope.

EQUIPMENT: Standard equipment includes dual blind-flying instrumentation with sensitive altimeters and dual instantaneous VSIs; standby magnetic compass; OAT gauge; LCD digital chronometer clock; vacuum gauge; de-icing pressure gauge; cabin rate of climb indicator; cabin altitude and differential pressure indicator; flight hour recorder; automatic solid state warning and annunciator panel; pilot and co-pilot's four-way adjustable seats with shoulder harness and lap belts; dual cockpit speakers; adjustable sun visors; map pocket; cigarette lighter; two ashtrays; fresh air outlets; coffee cup holders; oxygen outlets with overhead mounted diluter demand masks with microphones; pilot and co-pilot's approach plate/map cases; four fully adjustable cabin seats in club arrangement with removable headrests, shoulder harnesses, lap belts, adjustable reading lights, retractable inboard armrests, fresh air outlets, ashtrays and cupholders; cabin floor carpeting; adjustable polarised sunshades; cabin coat cable with hangers; magazine rack; removable low profile toilet with shoulder harness, lap belt; baggage webbing and relief tube; aisle-facing storage seat with air, light, ashtray, water tank, ice chest drawer, removable bottle/decanter rack and padded partition; two cabinets, forward left and right sides of cabin, with ice chest, heated liquid container and storage drawers; two cabin tables; cabin fire extinguisher; 'No smoking — Fasten seat belt' sign with audible chime; internal corrosion proofing; urethane exterior paint; towbar; propeller restraints; wing ice lights; dual landing lights; nosewheel taxi light; flush position lights; dual rotating beacons; dual map lights; indirect cabin lighting; two overhead cabin spotlights; entrance door light; aft compartment lights; primary and secondary instrument lighting systems; rheostat-controlled white cockpit lighting; entrance door step lights; wingtip recognition lights; wingtip and tail strobe lights; and vertical tail illumination lights. Optional equipment includes lateral tracking cabin seats; cabin door support cable; cabin partition sliding doors; central aisle carpet runner; electric flushing toilet; engine fire detection system; 1.81 m³ (64 cu ft) oxygen bottle; cockpit relief tube; co-pilot's control wheel digital chronometer; cabinet with three drawers and stereo tape deck storage; pilot-to-cabin paging with four stereo speakers; ADF audio to cabin paging; control wheel frequency transfer and memory advance switch; co-pilot's control wheel transponder ident switch; and passenger stereo headsets.

DIMENSIONS, EXTERNAL:

Wing span	15.32 m (50 ft 3 in)
Wing chord: at root	2.15 m (7 ft 0½ in)
at tip	1.07 m (3 ft 6 in)
Wing aspect ratio	8.6
Length overall	10.82 m (35 ft 6 in)
Height overall	4.34 m (14 ft 3 in)
Tailplane span	5.26 m (17 ft 3 in)
Wheel track	3.89 m (12 ft 9 in)
Wheelbase	3.73 m (12 ft 3 in)
Propeller diameter	2.36 m (7 ft 9 in)
Propeller ground clearance	0.305 m (1 ft 0 in)
Passenger door: Height	1.30 m (4 ft 3½ in)
Width	0.69 m (2 ft 3 in)
Height to sill	1.22 m (4 ft 0 in)

DIMENSIONS, INTERNAL:

Total pressurised length	5.43 m (17 ft 10 in)
Cabin: Length	3.86 m (12 ft 8 in)
Max width	1.37 m (4 ft 6 in)
Max height	1.45 m (4 ft 9 in)
Floor area	6.50 m² (70 sq ft)
Volume	8.88 m³ (313.6 cu ft)
Baggage compartment, rear	1.51 m³ (53.5 cu ft)

AREAS:

Wings, gross	27.31 m² (293.94 sq ft)
Ailerons (total)	1.29 m² (13.90 sq ft)
Trailing-edge flaps (total)	2.72 m² (29.30 sq ft)
Fin	2.20 m² (23.67 sq ft)
Rudder, incl tab	1.30 m² (14.00 sq ft)
Tailplane	4.39 m² (47.25 sq ft)
Elevators, incl tabs	1.66 m² (17.87 sq ft)

WEIGHTS AND LOADINGS:

Weight empty	2,985 kg (6,580 lb)
Max T-O weight	4,581 kg (10,100 lb)
Max ramp weight	4,608 kg (10,160 lb)
Max landing weight	4,354 kg (9,600 lb)
Max wing loading	167.7 kg/m² (34.4 lb/sq ft)
Max power loading	5.59 kg/kW (9.2 lb/shp)

PERFORMANCE (at max T-O weight except where indicated):

Max cruising speed at AUW of 3,855 kg (8,500 lb):

at 3,660 m (12,000 ft)	242 knots (448 km/h; 278 mph)

Beechcraft Super King Air B200 fourteen-passenger pressurised transport

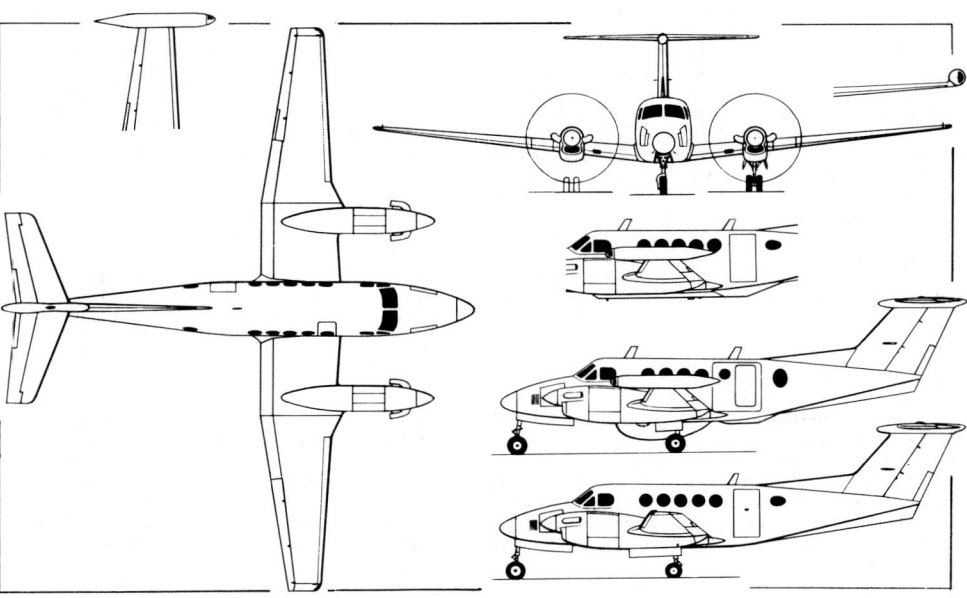

Beechcraft Super King Air B200 twin-turboprop transport, with additional side view of Maritime Patrol B200T (centre right); scrap views of wingtip tanks and centre-fuselage of photo survey aircraft for IGN *(Pilot Press)*

at 4,880 m (16,000 ft)	247 knots (457 km/h; 284 mph)
at 6,400 m (21,000 ft)	243 knots (450 km/h; 280 mph)

Stalling speed, power off:

wheels and flaps up	
	88 knots (163 km/h; 101 mph) IAS
wheels and flaps down	
	78 knots (144 km/h; 90 mph) IAS
Max rate of climb at S/L	610 m (2,003 ft)/min
Rate of climb at S/L, one engine out	169 m (554 ft)/min
Service ceiling	8,809 m (28,900 ft)
Service ceiling, one engine out	4,346 m (14,260 ft)
Min ground turning radius	10.82 m (35 ft 6 in)
T-O run	574 m (1,885 ft)
T-O to 15 m (50 ft)	785 m (2,577 ft)
Accelerate/stop distance	1,232 m (4,042 ft)

Landing from 15 m (50 ft) at max landing weight, with propeller reversal 633 m (2,078 ft)

Landing run at max landing weight, with propeller reversal 316 m (1,036 ft)

Range with max fuel at max cruising speed, incl allowance for starting, taxi, take-off, climb, descent and 45 min reserves at max range power, ISA, at:

6,400 m (21,000 ft)	1,075 nm (1,992 km; 1,238 miles)
4,875 m (16,000 ft)	933 nm (1,729 km; 1,074 miles)
3,660 m (12,000 ft)	866 nm (1,605 km; 997 miles)

Max range at econ cruising power, allowances as above, at:

6,400 m (21,000 ft)	1,277 nm (2,366 km; 1,470 miles)
4,875 m (16,000 ft)	1,155 nm (2,140 km; 1,330 miles)
3,660 m (12,000 ft)	1,054 nm (1,953 km; 1,214 miles)

BEECHCRAFT SUPER KING AIR B200
Swedish Air Force designation: Tp 101

TYPE: Twin-turboprop pressurised passenger, cargo or business light transport.

PROGRAMME: Design of Super King Air 200 began October 1970; first flight (c/n BB1) 27 October 1972; certificated FAR Pt 23 plus icing requirements of FAR Pt 25, 14 December 1973; design of B200 (prototype c/n BB343)

began March 1980; production started May 1980; FAA certification 13 February 1981; on sale March 1981.

VARIANTS: **Super King Air B200:** Basic version.

Super King Air B200C: As B200 but with 1.32 × 1.32 m (4 ft 4 in × 4 ft 4 in) cargo door.

Super King Air B200T: Standard provision for removable tip tanks, adding total 401 litres (106 US gallons; 88.25 Imp gallons), making total 2,460 litres (650 US gallons; 541 Imp gallons). Span without tip tanks 16.92 m (55 ft 6 in).

Super King Air B200CT: Combines tip tanks and cargo door as standard.

Maritime patrol: Described separately.

Super King Air 300 and 300LW: Described separately.

Super King Air 350: Described separately.

Raisbeck King Air: Performance modifications: see under Raisbeck Engineering.

CUSTOMERS: French Institut Géographique National acquired two B200T fitted with twin Wild RC-10 Superaviogon camera installations and Doppler navigation in February 1977; max endurance 10.3 h; high flotation landing gear; special French certification for max T-O weight 6,350 kg (14,000 lb) and max landing weight 6,123 kg (13,500 lb). Egyptian government acquired one Super King Air in 1978 for water, uranium and other natural resources exploration over Sinai and Egyptian deserts as follow-up to satellite surveys; fitted with remote sensing gear, specialised avionics and special cameras. Navaid checking versions of Super King Air used by Taiwan government (one) and Malaysian government (two). Special missions Super King Air delivered to Taiwan Ministry of Interior May 1979; Royal Hong Kong Auxiliary Air Force (two) 1986 and 1987; two Super King Air 200s operated by Swedish Air Force since 1989 as **Tp 101**. Total of 41 Super King Air B200s delivered in 1990, including two B200Cs. Total 1,480 commercial and private and 282 military (described separately) delivered to US armed forces and foreign customers by 1 January 1991.

DESIGN FEATURES: Pratt & Whitney Canada PT6A-41 turboprops of Super King Air 200 replaced by 634 kW (850 shp) P&WC PT6A-42s for better cruise and altitude performance; max zero-fuel weight raised by 272 kg (600 lb); cabin pressure differential increased from 0.41 bar (6.0 lb/sq in) to 0.44 bar (6.5 lb/sq in); pneumatic de-icing of wings and tailplane standard. Wing aerofoil NACA 23018 to 23016.5 over inner wing, 23012 at tip; dihedral 6°; incidence 3° 48′ at root, −1° 7′ at tip; swept vertical and horizontal tail.

FLYING CONTROLS: Trim tabs in port aileron and both elevators; anti-servo tab in rudder; single-slotted trailing-edge flaps; fixed tailplane.

STRUCTURE: Two-spar light alloy wing; safe-life semi-monocoque fuselage.

LANDING GEAR: Hydraulically retractable tricycle type, with twin wheels on each main unit. Single wheel on steerable nose unit, with shimmy damper. Main units retract forward, nosewheel rearward. Beech oleo-pneumatic shock absorbers. Goodrich mainwheels and tyres size 18 × 5.5, pressure 7.25 bars (105 lb/sq in). Oversize and/or 10-ply mainwheel tyres optional. Goodrich nosewheel size 6.50 × 10, with tyre size 22 × 6.75-10, pressure 3.93 bars (57 lb/sq in). Goodrich hydraulic multiple-disc brakes. Parking brake.

POWER PLANT: Two 634 kW (850 shp) Pratt & Whitney Canada PT6A-42 turboprops, each driving a Hartzell three-blade constant-speed fully feathering reversible-pitch metal propeller. Bladder fuel cells in each wing, with main system capacity of 1,461 litres (386 US gallons; 321.5 Imp gallons) and auxiliary system capacity of 598 litres (158 US gallons; 131.5 Imp gallons). Total usable fuel capacity 2,059 litres (544 US gallons; 453 Imp gallons). Two refuelling points in upper surface of each wing. Wingtip tanks optional, providing an additional 401 litres (106 US gallons; 88.25 Imp gallons) and raising maximum usable capacity to 2,460 litres (650 US gallons; 541 Imp gallons). Oil capacity 29.5 litres (7.8 US gallons; 6.5 Imp gallons). Anti-icing of engine air intakes by hot air from engine exhaust, electrothermal anti-icing for propellers and automatic feathering and synchrophaser standard.

ACCOMMODATION: Pilot only, or crew of two side by side, on flight deck, with full dual controls and instruments as standard. Six cabin seats standard, each equipped with seat belts and inertia reel shoulder harness; alternative layouts for a maximum of 13 passengers in cabin and 14th beside pilot. Partition with sliding door between cabin and flight deck, and partition at rear of cabin. Door at rear of cabin on port side, with integral airstair. Large cargo door optional. Inward opening emergency exit on starboard side over wing. Lavatory and stowage for up to 249 kg (550 lb) baggage in rear fuselage. Maintenance access door in rear fuselage; radio compartment access doors in nose. Cabin is air-conditioned and pressurised, with radiant heat panels to warm cabin before engine starting.

SYSTEMS: Cabin pressurisation by engine bleed air, with a maximum differential of 0.44 bar (6.5 lb/sq in). Cabin air-conditioner of 34,000 BTU capacity. Auxiliary cabin heating by radiant panels standard. Oxygen system for flight deck, and 0.62 m³ (22 cu ft) oxygen system for cabin, with automatic drop-down face masks; standard system of 1.39 m³ (49 cu ft); 1.81 m³ (64 cu ft) or 2.15 m³ (76 cu ft) optional. Dual vacuum system for instruments. Hydraulic system for landing gear retraction and extension, pressurised to 171-191 bars (2,475-2,775 lb/sq in). Separate hydraulic system for brakes. Pneumatic system for wing and tailplane de-icing. Electrical system has two 250A 28V starter/generators and a 24V 45Ah aircooled nickel-cadmium battery with failure detector. AC power provided by dual 250VA inverters. Engine fire detection system standard; engine fire extinguishing system optional.

AVIONICS: Standard Collins Pro Line II avionics and cockpit equipment generally as for King Air C90A except: dual DME-42, dual RMI-30; pilot's ALT-80A encoding altimeter; cockpit-to-cabin paging; dual maximum allowable airspeed indicators; flight director indicator; co-pilot's 24 hour clock; oxygen pressure indicator and blue-white cockpit lighting standard. Optional avionics include Collins Pro Line II with 5 in FCS; EFIS-85B(-14); Honeywell SPZ-4000 autopilot with 4 in or 5 in flight director systems or EDZ-605 three-tube EFIS; Bendix/King Gold Crown avionics packages; Bendix/King RDS-84VP colour weather radar; Fairchild 17M-700-274 flight data recorder; Fairchild A-100A cockpit voice recorder; Bendix/King KHF-950 or Collins HF-230 HF transceiver; Bendix/King CC-2024C or Collins DCP-270 radar checklist; Foster LNS-616B RNAV/Loran C; Bendix/King KNS-660 RNAV/VLF/Omega; 3M WX-1000+ Stormscope; and Wulfsberg Flitefone VI.

EQUIPMENT: Standard/optional equipment generally as for King Air C90A except fluorescent cabin lighting, one-place couch with storage drawers, flushing toilet (B200) or chemical toilet (B200C), cabin radiant heating, cockpit/cabin partition with sliding doors, and airstair door with hydraulic snubber and courtesy light, standard. FAR Pt 135 operational configuration includes cockpit fire extinguisher and 2.15 m³ (76 cu ft) oxygen bottle as standard. A range of optional cabin seating and cabinetry configuration is available, including quick-removable fold-up seats.

DIMENSIONS, EXTERNAL:
Wing span 16.61 m (54 ft 6 in)
Wing chord: at root 2.18 m (7 ft 1¾ in)
at tip 0.90 m (2 ft 11⅜ in)
Wing aspect ratio 9.8
Length overall 13.34 m (43 ft 9 in)
Height overall 4.57 m (15 ft 0 in)
Tailplane span 5.61 m (18 ft 5 in)
Wheel track 5.23 m (17 ft 2 in)
Wheelbase 4.56 m (14 ft 11½ in)
Propeller diameter 2.50 m (8 ft 2½ in)
Propeller ground clearance 0.37 m (1 ft 2½ in)
Distance between propeller centres 5.23 m (17 ft 2 in)
Passenger door: Height 1.31 m (4 ft 3½ in)
Width 0.68 m (2 ft 2¾ in)
Height to sill 1.17 m (3 ft 10 in)
Cargo door (optional): Height 1.32 m (4 ft 4 in)
Width 1.24 m (4 ft 1 in)
Nose avionics service doors (port and stbd):
Max height 0.57 m (1 ft 10½ in)
Width 0.63 m (2 ft 1 in)
Height to sill 1.37 m (4 ft 6 in)
Emergency exit (stbd): Height 0.66 m (2 ft 2 in)
Width 0.50 m (1 ft 7¾ in)

DIMENSIONS, INTERNAL:
Cabin (from forward to rear pressure bulkhead):
Length 6.71 m (22 ft 0 in)
Max width 1.37 m (4 ft 6 in)
Max height 1.45 m (4 ft 9 in)
Floor area 7.80 m² (84 sq ft)
Volume 11.10 m³ (392 cu ft)
Baggage hold, rear of cabin:
Volume 1.51 m³ (53.5 cu ft)

AREAS:
Wings, gross 28.15 m² (303.0 sq ft)
Ailerons (total) 1.67 m² (18.0 sq ft)
Trailing-edge flaps (total) 4.17 m² (44.9 sq ft)
Fin 3.46 m² (37.2 sq ft)
Rudder, incl tab 1.40 m² (15.1 sq ft)
Tailplane 4.52 m² (48.7 sq ft)
Elevators, incl tabs 1.79 m² (19.3 sq ft)

WEIGHTS AND LOADINGS:
Weight empty 3,656 kg (8,060 lb)
Max fuel 1,653 kg (3,645 lb)
Max T-O and landing weight 5,670 kg (12,500 lb)
Max ramp weight 5,710 kg (12,590 lb)
Max zero-fuel weight 4,990 kg (11,000 lb)
Max wing loading 201.6 kg/m² (41.3 lb/sq ft)
Max power loading 4.47 kg/kW (7.35 lb/shp)

PERFORMANCE (at max T-O weight ISA, except where indicated):
Never-exceed speed (V_{NE})
259 knots (480 km/h; 298 mph) IAS
Max operating Mach No. 0.52
Max level speed at 7,620 m (25,000 ft), average cruise weight 294 knots (545 km/h; 339 mph)
Max cruising speed at 7,620 m (25,000 ft), average cruise weight 289 knots (536 km/h; 333 mph)
Econ cruising speed at 7,620 m (25,000 ft), average cruise weight, normal cruise power
282 knots (523 km/h; 325 mph)
Stalling speed:
flaps up 99 knots (183 km/h; 114 mph) IAS
flaps down 75 knots (139 km/h; 86 mph) IAS
Max rate of climb at S/L 747 m (2,450 ft)/min
Rate of climb at S/L, one engine out 226 m (740 ft)/min
Service ceiling over 10,670 m (35,000 ft)
Service ceiling, one engine out 6,675 m (21,900 ft)
T-O run, 40% flap 566 m (1,856 ft)
T-O to 15 m (50 ft), 40% flap 786 m (2,579 ft)
Landing from 15 m (50 ft):
without propeller reversal 867 m (2,845 ft)
with propeller reversal 632 m (2,074 ft)
Landing run 536 m (1,760 ft)
Range with max fuel, allowances for start, taxi, climb, descent, and 45 min reserves at max range power, ISA:
max cruise power at:
5,485 m (18,000 ft)
1,190 nm (2,205 km; 1,370 miles)
8,230 m (27,000 ft)
1,550 nm (2,872 km; 1,785 miles)
9,450 m (31,000 ft)
1,750 nm (3,243 km; 2,015 miles)
10,670 m (35,000 ft)
1,965 nm (3,641 km; 2,263 miles)
econ cruise power at:
5,485 m (18,000 ft)
1,517 nm (2,811 km; 1,747 miles)
8,230 m (27,000 ft)
1,860 nm (3,447 km; 2,142 miles)
9,450 m (31,000 ft)
1,974 nm (3,658 km; 2,273 miles)

BEECHCRAFT MARITIME PATROL B200T

TYPE: Maritime patrol or multi-mission aircraft.

PROGRAMME: Maritime Patrol 200T announced 9 April 1979; current version B200T for surface and sub-surface monitoring of exclusive economic zones, pollution detection, inspecting offshore installations, search and rescue; special missions include aerial photography, environmental and ecological research, airways and ground-based navaid checking, target towing, ambulance flying.

CUSTOMERS: Japan Maritime Safety Agency (17), Algerian Ministry of Defence (two), Peruvian Navy (five), Puerto Rico (one), Uruguayan Navy (one).

DESIGN FEATURES: Modifications from standard Super King Air B200 include new outboard wings with provision for tip tanks, strengthened landing gear, two bubble observation windows at rear, hatch for dropping survival equipment, 360° radome under fuselage; standard avionics include VLF/Omega coupled to autopilot to allow programmed search patterns; integrated avionics, displays and controls; optional wingtip ESM antennae.

LANDING GEAR: Strengthened to cater for higher operating weights.

POWER PLANT: As for Super King Air B200, including removable wingtip tanks which increase maximum usable fuel capacity by 401 litres (106 US gallons; 88.25 Imp gallons) to a total of 2,460 litres (650 US gallons; 541 Imp gallons).

AVIONICS: Standard items as listed under Design Features. Optional avionics include ESM integrated with INS, VHF-FM com, HF and VHF com, Northrop Seehawk FLIR, LLLTV, sonobuoys and processor, OTPI, multi-spectral scanner, tactical navigation computer, and two alternative search radar systems, both with 360° scan and weather avoidance capability and integrated with INS.

DIMENSIONS, EXTERNAL: As for Super King Air B200, except:
Wing span over tip tanks 17.25 m (56 ft 7 in)
Wing aspect ratio 10.5

DIMENSIONS, INTERNAL: As for Super King Air B200, except:
Cabin: Length (excl flight deck) 5.08 m (16 ft 8 in)

WEIGHTS AND LOADINGS (A: Normal category, B: Restricted category):
Weight empty: A, B 3,744 kg (8,255 lb)
Max T-O weight: A 5,670 kg (12,500 lb)
B 6,350 kg (14,000 lb)
Max landing weight: A 5,670 kg (12,500 lb)
B 6,123 kg (13,500 lb)

PERFORMANCE (at max T-O weight except where indicated):
Max cruising speed, AUW of 4,990 kg (11,000 lb) at 4,265 m (14,000 ft) 265 knots (491 km/h; 305 mph)
Typical patrol speed 140 knots (259 km/h; 161 mph)
Range with max fuel, patrolling at 227 knots (420 km/h; 261 mph) at 825 m (2,700 ft), 45 min reserves
1,790 nm (3,317 km; 2,061 miles)
Typical endurance at 140 knots (259 km/h; 161 mph), at 610 m (2,000 ft), 45 min reserves 6 h 36 min
Max time on station, with wingtip fuel tanks 9 h

BEECHCRAFT SUPER KING AIR 200/B200 (US MILITARY VERSIONS)

US basic military designation: C-12

TYPE: Military versions of Super King Air 200/B200.

PROGRAMME: US Army acquired first three Super King Airs designated RU-21Js in 1974; US Army ordered 34 military passenger-carrying Super King Airs designated C-12A August 1974; worldwide deployment began July 1975.

CUSTOMERS: Total of 320 ordered by June 1991; 308 delivered by 1 January 1990.

VARIANTS: **C-12A:** Initial A200 version, powered by 559 kW (750 shp) P&WC PT6A-38 turboprops with Hartzell three-blade fully feathering reversible-pitch propellers; auxiliary tanks. Total 91 delivered (US Army 60; US Air Force 31, of which one transferred to Greek Air Force); entered service July 1975; details in 1980-81 *Jane's*. See C-12C and C-12E for C-12A re-engining.

UC-12B: US Navy/Marine Corps version (Model A200C) with 634 kW (850 shp) PT6A-41 turboprops, cargo door, high flotation landing gear. US Navy (49), US Marines (17), delivered by May 1982.

C-12C: As C-12A, but with PT6A-41 turboprops. Deliveries (US Army 14) complete; C-12A fleet re-engined as C-12Cs.

C-12D: Model A200CT. As US Army C-12C but cargo door, high flotation landing gear and provision for tip tanks. US Army (27), US Air Force (six); five others converted to RC-12D Guardrail for Israel and 13 for US Army. Wing span (over tip tanks) 16.92 m (55 ft 6 in).

RC-12D Improved Guardrail V: Model A200CT. US Army special mission version supplementing earlier unpressurised RU-21H Guardrail V and used in Europe; carries AN/USD-9 Improved Guardrail remote-controlled communications intercept and direction finding system with direct reporting to tactical commanders at corps level and below; aircraft survivability equipment (ASE) system, Carousel IV-E IN and Tacan system, radio data link, AN/ARW-83(V)5 airborne relay with antennae above and below wings, wingtip ECM pods; associated equipment includes AN/TSQ-105(V)4 integrated processing facility, AN/ARM-63(V)4 AGE flightline van and AN/TSC-87 tactical commander's terminal. System prime contractor ESL Inc; Beech was mission equipment integrator. US Army had 13 RC-12D Improved Guardrail Vs converted from C-12Ds, with deliveries starting in Summer 1983. Wing span (over ECM pods) 17.63 m (57 ft 10 in).

C-12E: Designation of 29 US Air Force C-12As retrofitted with PT6A-42 turboprops.

C-12F: Operational support aircraft (OSA), similar to Model B200C with PT6A-42 engines; payload choices include eight passengers, more than 1,043 kg (2,300 lb) freight, two litter patients plus attendants; cargo door standard. First delivery May 1984. US Air Force purchased 40 after initial five-year lease; US Army (17); Air National Guard (six).

UC-12F: US Navy equivalent of USAF C-12F with PT6A-42 turboprops. US Navy received first of 12 in 1986; two modified to **RC-12F** Range Surveillance Aircraft (RANSAC).

RC-12H Improved Guardrail V: US Army special mission aircraft, similar to RC-12D but max T-O weight increased to 6,804 kg (15,000 lb). Six delivered in 1988.

C-12J: Variant of Beechcraft 1900C (which see).

RC-12K Guardrail Common Sensor: PT6A-67 turboprops, large cargo door, oversized landing gear as standard; max T-O weight 7,257 kg (16,000 lb). US Army ordered nine in October 1985; further 12 ordered 1989 (nine) and 1991 (three), for delivery starting February 1992 and July 1993 respectively; current option for six more during FY 1992.

UC-12M: US Navy designation of C-12F. Twelve delivered from 1987; two conversions to **RC-12M** RANSAC ordered 1988.

CUSTOMERS: See under individual variants above.

BEECHCRAFT SUPER KING AIR 300

TYPE: Improved version of Super King Air Model B200.

PROGRAMME: Design started August 1980; first flight October 1981; production prototype first flight September 1983; certificated 24 January 1984. To be superseded by Model 350 in 1991.

VARIANTS: **Super King Air 300:** Basic version.

Super King Air 300AT: Airline training version; two ordered by Finnair.

Super King Air 300LW: Lightweight version, announced September 1988 at special European certification max T-O weight of 5,670 kg (12,500 lb) to limit airways user fees; max ramp weight 5,715 kg (12,600 lb); otherwise similar to Model 300; 15 delivered by 1 January 1991, including one in 1990.

CUSTOMERS: Include Finnair (two) for pilot training designated 300AT (Airline Training); US FAA (19) for airways calibration equipped with automatic flight inspection system (AFIS). Total of 215 delivered by 1 January 1991 including 10 in 1990.

DESIGN FEATURES: Two PT6A-60A turboprops; increased max T-O and landing weights to SFAR 41C; 'pitot cowl' engine intakes; aerodynamically faired exhausts; wing leading-edges extended 12.7 cm (5 in) forward; propellers moved forward 13.2 cm (5.2 in); hydraulically actuated landing gear; numerous interior equipment changes.

LANDING GEAR: Hydraulically retractable tricycle type. Goodrich mainwheels and tyres size 19 × 6.75-8, pressure 6.20 bars (90 lb/sq in) at max T-O weight. Goodrich nosewheel and tyre size 22 × 6.75-10, pressure 3.79-4.13 bars (55-60 lb/sq in). Beech brake de-icing optional.

POWER PLANT: Two 783 kW (1,050 shp) Pratt & Whitney Canada PT6A-60A turboprops, each driving a Hartzell four-blade constant-speed fully feathering reversible-pitch metal propeller. Bladder cells and integral tanks in each wing, with total capacity of 1,438 litres (380 US gallons; 316.5 Imp gallons); auxiliary tanks inboard of engine nacelles, capacity 601 litres (159 US gallons; 132.5 Imp gallons). Total fuel capacity 2,039 litres (539 US gallons; 449 Imp gallons). No provision for wingtip tanks. Oil capacity 30.2 litres (8 US gallons; 6.66 Imp gallons).

ACCOMMODATION: As for Model B200, except for additional emergency exit on port side of cabin, opposite starboard emergency exit and of the same dimensions. Pilot and co-pilot storm windows standard. Cabin features single-piece upper sidewall panels, indirect overhead lighting system with rheostat controls, stereo system with graphic equaliser and overhead speakers, larger executive tables incorporating magnetic game boards, seats with inflatable lumbar support adjustment, fore-and-aft, reclining and lateral tracking movement as standard. Crew seats have 2.5° or 5° tilt positions. Emergency exit lighting standard. Electric heating on ground standard. Optional radiant heat panels of B200 not available.

SYSTEMS: As for Model B200, except for automatic bleed air type heating and 22,000 BTU cooling system with high capacity ventilation system; 2.18 m³ (77 cu ft) oxygen system standard; hydraulic landing gear retraction and extension system; two 300A 28V starter/generators with triple bus electrical distribution system.

AVIONICS: Generally as for Model B200.

EQUIPMENT: Generally as for Model B200.

DIMENSIONS, EXTERNAL: As for Model B200 except:

Length overall	13.36 m (43 ft 10 in)
Height overall	4.37 m (14 ft 4 in)
Propeller diameter	2.67 m (8 ft 9 in)
Propeller ground clearance	0.25 m (10 in)

Emergency exit (each side of cabin, above wing):

Height	0.66 m (2 ft 2 in)
Width	0.95 m (1 ft 7¾ in)

US Army RC-12D in Improved Guardrail V configuration *(Ivo Sturzenegger)*

Beechcraft C-12F operational support aircraft of USAF Military Airlift Command *(Mike Jerram)*

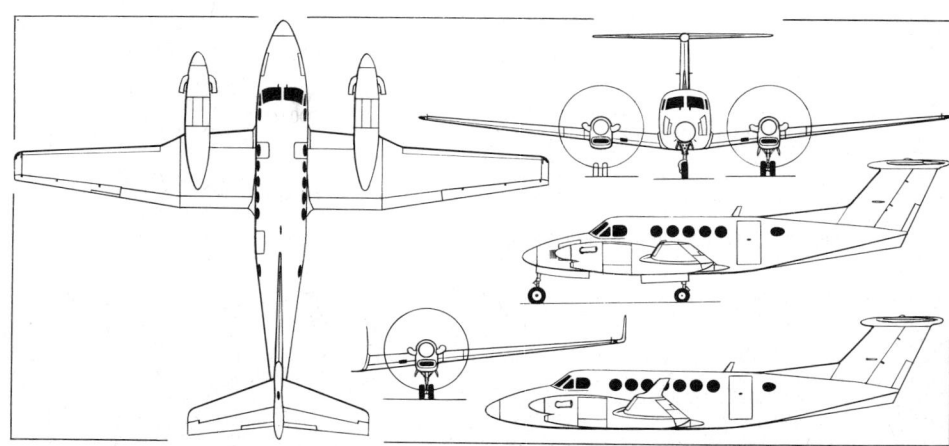

Beechcraft Super King Air 300, with side view (lower right) and scrap view of wing of Model 350
(Pilot Press)

WEIGHTS AND LOADINGS:

Weight empty	3,851 kg (8,490 lb)
Max baggage weight	249 kg (550 lb)
Max T-O and landing weight	6,350 kg (14,000 lb)
Max ramp weight	6,396 kg (14,100 lb)
Max zero-fuel weight	5,216 kg (11,500 lb)
Max wing loading	225.6 kg/m² (46.2 lb/sq ft)
Max power loading	4.05 kg/kW (6.7 lb/shp)

PERFORMANCE (A: Model 300, B: Model 300LW at max T-O weight, ISA):

Never-exceed speed (V_{NE})	
	259 knots (480 km/h; 298 mph) IAS
Max operating Mach No.	0.58
Max level speed	317 knots (587 km/h; 365 mph)
Max cruising speed	315 knots (583 km/h; 363 mph)
Econ cruising speed	307 knots (568 km/h; 353 mph)

Stalling speed:

flaps up	100 knots (185 km/h; 115 mph) IAS
flaps down	81 knots (150 km/h; 93 mph) IAS

Max rate of climb at S/L: A	867 m (2,844 ft)/min
B	999 m (3,277 ft)/min
Rate of climb at S/L, one engine out	264 m (867 ft)/min
Max certificated ceiling	10,670 m (35,000 ft)
Service ceiling, one engine out: A	6,970 m (22,875 ft)
B	7,882 m (25,855 ft)
T-O run, 40% flap, at T-O weight of 5,670 kg (12,500 lb)	411 m (1,350 ft)
T-O to 15 m (50 ft), 40% flap, at T-O weight of 5,670 kg (12,500 lb)	607 m (1,992 ft)
Accelerate/stop distance, 40% flap	1,122 m (3,682 ft)
Landing from 15 m (50 ft)	886 m (2,907 ft)
Landing run, without propeller reversal	514 m (1,686 ft)

Range with max fuel, allowances for start, taxi, T-O, climb, descent and 45 min reserves at max range power: max cruise power at:
5,485 m (18,000 ft)
1,055 nm (1,955 km; 1,215 miles)

7,315 m (24,000 ft)
    1,240 nm (2,298 km; 1,428 miles)
8,535 m (28,000 ft)
    1,400 nm (2,594 km; 1,612 miles)
10,670 m (35,000 ft)
    1,748 nm (3,235 km; 2,010 miles)
max range power at:
5,485 m (18,000 ft)
    1,429 nm (2,647 km; 1,645 miles)
8,535 m (28,000 ft)
    1,795 nm (3,326 km; 2,067 miles)
10,670 m (35,000 ft)
    1,959 nm (3,630 km; 2,256 miles)

Beechcraft Super King Air 350 eight/twelve-passenger turboprop business aircraft

BEECHCRAFT SUPER KING AIR 350

TYPE: Eight/twelve-passenger turboprop business aircraft.

PROGRAMME: Alternative to Super King Air 300; first flight (N120SK) September 1988; introduced at NBAA show 1989; certificated to FAR Pt 23 (commuter category); first delivery 6 March 1990.

VARIANTS: **King Air 350C:** Has 132 × 132 cm (52 × 52 in) freight door with built-in airstair passenger door.

CUSTOMERS: Total 42 Model 350s and one 350C delivered by 31 March 1991. First 350C delivery in 1990 to Rossing Uranium, Namibia.

DESIGN FEATURES: Compared with Super King Air 300, fuselage stretched 0.86 m (2 ft 10 in) by plugs 0.37 m (1 ft 2½ in) forward of main spar and 0.49 m (1 ft 7½ in) aft; wing span increased by 0.46 m (1 ft 6 in) with NASA winglets 0.61 m (2 ft 0 in) high; two additional cabin windows each side; double club seating for eight passengers; optionally two more seats in rear of cabin, one passenger on toilet seat and one in co-pilot seat if operating single-crew, making maximum 12 passengers. Can depart with full payload and full tanks.

FLYING CONTROLS: Automatic cable tensioner in aileron circuit and larger elevator bobweight; larger rudder anti-servo tab; ailerons and rudder cleaned up.

DIMENSIONS, EXTERNAL:
Wing span over winglets	17.65 m (57 ft 11 in)
Wing aspect ratio	10.79
Length overall	14.22 m (46 ft 8 in)
Height overall	4.37 m (14 ft 4 in)
Tailplane span	5.61 m (18 ft 5 in)
Passenger door: Height	1.31 m (4 ft 3½ in)
Width	0.68 m (2 ft 2¾ in)

DIMENSIONS, INTERNAL:
Cabin, excl cockpit: Length	5.94 m (19 ft 6 in)
Max width	1.37 m (4 ft 6 in)
Height	1.45 m (4 ft 9 in)

AREAS:
Wings, gross	28.80 m² (310.0 sq ft)

WEIGHTS AND LOADINGS:
Weight empty	4,105 kg (9,051 lb)
Max fuel weight	1,638 kg (3,611 lb)
Max T-O and landing weight	6,804 kg (15,000 lb)
Max ramp weight	6,849 kg (15,100 lb)
Max zero-fuel weight	5,670 kg (12,500 lb)
Max wing loading	236.3 kg/m² (48.4 lb/sq ft)
Max power loading	4.34 kg/kW (7.14 lb/shp)

PERFORMANCE:
Max level speed 315 knots (584 km/h; 363 mph)
Max cruising speed, AUW of 5,896 kg (13,000 lb) at:
7,315 m (24,000 ft) 313 knots (580 km/h; 360 mph)
10,670 m (35,000 ft) 295 knots (547 km/h; 340 mph)
Cruising speed, normal cruising power, AUW of 5,896 kg (13,000 lb) at:
7,315 m (24,000 ft) 311 knots (576 km/h; 358 mph)
10,670 m (35,000 ft) 290 knots (537 km/h; 334 mph)

Cruising speed, max range power, AUW of 5,896 kg (13,000 lb) at:
5,485 m (18,000 ft) 210 knots (389 km/h; 242 mph)
10,670 m (35,000 ft) 240 knots (445 km/h; 276 mph)
Stalling speed at max landing weight, flaps and wheels down 81 knots (150 km/h; 94 mph)
Max rate of climb at S/L, AUW of 6,804 kg (15,000 lb)
908 m (2,979 ft)/min
Rate of climb at S/L, one engine out, AUW of 6,350 kg (14,000 lb) 244 m (800 ft)/min
Service ceiling above 10,670 m (35,000 ft)
Service ceiling, one engine out, AUW of 6,804 kg (15,000 lb) 6,735 m (22,100 ft)
T-O balanced field length, AUW of 6,804 kg (15,000 lb)
1,139 m (3,737 ft)
Landing from 15 m (50 ft) at AUW of 6,804 kg (15,000 lb)
802 m (2,631 ft)
Landing run 408 m (1,338 ft)
Range with 2,040 litres (539 US gallons; 449 Imp gallons) usable fuel, allowances for start, T-O, climb and descent plus 45 min reserves: max cruising power at:
5,485 m (18,000 ft)
1,067 nm (1,977 km; 1,228 miles)
7,315 m (24,000 ft)
1,252 nm (2,320 km; 1,441 miles)
8,535 m (28,000 ft)
1,407 nm (2,607 km; 1,620 miles)
10,670 m (35,000 ft)
1,724 nm (3,195 km; 1,985 miles)
normal cruising power, allowances as above:
5,485 m (18,000 ft)
1,085 nm (2,010 km; 1,249 miles)
7,315 m (24,000 ft)
1,308 nm (2,424 km; 1,506 miles)
8,535 m (28,000 ft)
1,474 nm (2,731 km; 1,697 miles)
10,670 m (35,000 ft)
1,771 nm (3,282 km; 2,039 miles)
max range power, allowances as above:
5,485 m (18,000 ft)
1,421 nm (2,633 km; 1,636 miles)
8,535 m (28,000 ft)
1,756 nm (3,254 km; 2,022 miles)
10,670 m (35,000 ft)
1,894 nm (3,510 km; 2,181 miles)
NBAA VFR range, 4 passengers, 30 min reserves
2,031 nm (3,763 km; 2,338 miles)

BEECHCRAFT MODEL 1300 COMMUTER

No longer manufactured. See 1990-91 *Jane's* for details.

BEECHCRAFT MODEL 1900C AIRLINER and 1900 EXEC-LINER

US Air Force designation: C-12J

TYPE: Twin-turboprop commuter/cargo airliner and business aircraft.

PROGRAMME: Design of basic 1900 began 1979; first flight 3 September 1982; FAA certification to SFAR Pt 41C 22 November 1983, including single-pilot operation under FAR Pt 135 Appendix A; Model 1900C Airliner first delivered February 1984, and Model 1900 Exec-Liner first delivered Summer 1985. From aircraft c/n UC-1, all military and civil 1900s have wet wing, providing fuel capacity of 2,559 litres (676 US gallons; 563 Imp gallons); Model 1900C being replaced in 1991 by Model 1900D.

VARIANTS: **Model 1900C Airliner:** Basic airliner version with cargo door.

Model 1900 Exec-Liner: Corporate version.

Model 1900D: Announced March 1989; described separately.

CUSTOMERS: By 1 January 1991, 221 civil and military Airliners and Exec-Liners, including 45 in 1990, had been delivered to US regional airlines and operators overseas and to corporate operators in Africa, Australia, Europe and USA.

In March 1986, US Air Force ordered six C-12Js for delivery from September 1987 to replace Air National Guard Convair C-131s as mission support aircraft.

Eight Model 1900Cs delivered to Egyptian Air Force, six for electronic surveillance and two for maritime patrol; maritime equipment includes Litton search radar, Motorola sideways-looking airborne multi-mode radar (SLAMMR), Singer S-3075 ESM; 12 Model 1900Cs delivered to Republic of China Air Force (Taiwan) starting January 1988.

DESIGN FEATURES: Wing aerofoil NACA 23018 (modified) at root, 23012 (modified) at tip; dihedral 6°; incidence 3° 29′ at root, –1° 4′ at tip; no sweepback at quarter-chord; tailplane and fin swept; each tailplane carries small fin (tail-let) beneath, near tip; auxiliary horizontal fixed tail surface (stabilon) each side of rear fuselage; small horizontal vortex generator on fuselage ahead of wingroots. Pneumatic de-icing boots on wings, tailplane and stabilons.

Beechcraft Model 1900 Exec-Liner (two 821 kW; 1,100 shp P&WC PT6A-65B turboprops)

FLYING CONTROLS: Mechanical flying controls with automatic cable tensioner in aileron circuit; trim tabs on elevators, rudder and port aileron; single-slotted trailing-edge flaps in two sections on each wing.

STRUCTURE: Wing has continuous main spar with fail-safe structure riveted and bonded; fuselage pressurised and mainly bonded.

Description below applies to Models 1900C and Exec-Liner:

LANDING GEAR: Hydraulically retractable tricycle type. Main units retract forward and nose unit rearward. Beech oleo-pneumatic shock absorber in each unit. Twin Goodyear wheels on each main unit, size 6.50 × 10, with Goodyear tyres size 22 × 6.75-10, pressure 6.07 bars (88 lb/sq in); Goodrich steerable nosewheel size 6.75 × 8, with Goodrich tyre size 19.5 × 6.75-8, pressure 6.07 bars (88 lb/sq in). Multiple-disc hydraulic brakes. Beech/Hydro-Aire anti-skid units and power steering optional.

POWER PLANT: Two Pratt & Whitney Canada PT6A-65B turboprops, each flat rated at 820 kW (1,100 shp) and driving a Hartzell four-blade constant-speed fully feathering reversible-pitch composite propeller. Wet wing fuel storage, with a total capacity of 2,559 litres (676 US gallons; 563 Imp gallons), of which 2,525 litres (667 US gallons; 555 Imp gallons) are usable. Refuelling point in each wing leading-edge, inboard of engine nacelle. Oil capacity (total) 29.5 litres (7.8 US gallons; 6.5 Imp gallons).

ACCOMMODATION: Crew of one (FAR Pt 91) or two (FAR Pt 135) on flight deck, with standard accommodation in cabin of commuter version for 19 passengers, in single seats on each side of centre aisle. Forward and rear carry-on baggage lockers, underseat baggage stowage, rear baggage compartment and nose baggage compartment. Forward and rear doors, incorporating airstairs, on port side. Upward hinged cargo door instead of rear passenger door on Model 1900C. Two emergency exits over wing on starboard side, plus (1900C only) one on port side. Accommodation is air-conditioned, heated, ventilated and pressurised. Exec-Liner has 12/18-passenger cabin with forward and rear compartments, combination lavatory/passenger seat and two beverage bars at cabin compartment division. Club and double club seating optional. Customised interiors to customer choice.

SYSTEMS: Bleed air cabin heating and pressurisation, max differential 0.34 bar (5.0 lb/sq in). Air cycle and vapour cycle air-conditioning. Hydraulic system, pressure 207 bars (3,000 lb/sq in) for landing gear actuation. Electrical system includes two 300A engine driven starter/generators and one 22Ah nickel-cadmium battery. Constant flow oxygen system of 4.30 m³ (152 cu ft) capacity standard.

AVIONICS: Duplicated Bendix/King com/nav, glideslope receiver, transponder, audio, ADF, DME, marker beacon receiver and Bendix/King RDR-160 weather radar. Honeywell EFIS, and Collins autopilot and Pro Line II equipment, optional.

DIMENSIONS, EXTERNAL:

Wing span	16.60 m (54 ft 5¾ in)
Wing chord: at root	2.18 m (7 ft 1¾ in)
at tip	0.91 m (2 ft 11¾ in)
Wing aspect ratio	9.8
Length overall	17.63 m (57 ft 10 in)
Height overall	4.40 m (14 ft 5¼ in)
Tailplane span	5.64 m (18 ft 6 in)
Wheel track	5.23 m (17 ft 2 in)
Wheelbase	7.26 m (23 ft 10 in)
Propeller diameter	2.78 m (9 ft 1½ in)
Propeller ground clearance	0.36 m (1 ft 2 in)
Distance between propeller centres	5.23 m (17 ft 2 in)
Passenger doors (fwd and rear, port, each):	
Height	1.32 m (4 ft 4 in)
Width	0.68 m (2 ft 2¾ in)
Cargo door (rear, port): Height	1.32 m (4 ft 4 in)
Width	1.32 m (4 ft 4 in)
Emergency exits (two stbd; plus one port on 1900C only; all overwing): Height	0.53 m (1 ft 9 in)
Width	0.51 m (1 ft 8 in)

DIMENSIONS, INTERNAL:

Cabin, incl flight deck and rear baggage compartment:	
Length	10.38 m (34 ft 0¾ in)
Max width	1.37 m (4 ft 6 in)
Max height	1.45 m (4 ft 9 in)
Floor area	15.28 m² (164.5 sq ft)
Pressurised volume	21.10 m³ (745.14 cu ft)
Volume of passenger cabin	14.10 m³ (498 cu ft)
Baggage space:	
Cabin: 1900C: fwd	0.42 m³ (15.0 cu ft)
rear	4.36 m³ (154.0 cu ft)
Nose compartment	0.37 m³ (13.07 cu ft)

AREAS:

Wings, gross	28.15 m² (303.0 sq ft)
Ailerons (total)	1.67 m² (18.0 sq ft)
Trailing-edge flaps (total)	4.17 m² (44.9 sq ft)
Fin	3.42 m² (36.85 sq ft)
Rudder (incl tab)	1.106 m² (11.9 sq ft)
Tail-lets (total)	0.307 m² (3.30 sq ft)
Tailplane	4.52 m² (48.7 sq ft)

Beechcraft Model 1900C electronic surveillance aircraft of the Egyptian Air Force (*Ivo Sturzenegger*)

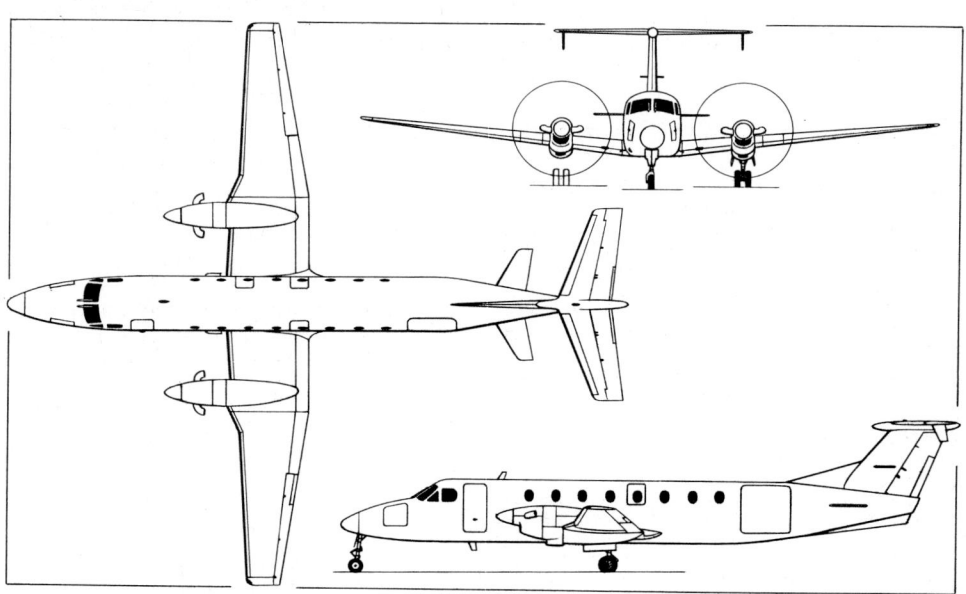

Beechcraft Model 1900C Airliner with rear cargo door (*Pilot Press*)

Elevator (incl tab)	1.79 m² (19.3 sq ft)
Stabilons (total, exposed)	1.44 m² (15.46 sq ft)

WEIGHTS AND LOADINGS:

Weight empty (typical)	4,468 kg (9,850 lb)
Max fuel (usable)	2,027 kg (4,469 lb)
Max baggage	866 kg (1,910 lb)
Max T-O weight	7,530 kg (16,600 lb)
Max ramp weight	7,580 kg (16,710 lb)
Max landing weight	7,302 kg (16,100 lb)
Max zero-fuel weight	6,350 kg (14,000 lb)
Max wing loading	267.5 kg/m² (54.8 lb/sq ft)
Max power loading	4.59 kg/kW (7.55 lb/shp)

PERFORMANCE (at max T-O weight except where indicated):

Max cruising speed at AUW of 6,350 kg (14,000 lb):	
at 2,440 m (8,000 ft)	267 knots (495 km/h; 307 mph)
at 4,875 m (16,000 ft)	267 knots (495 km/h; 307 mph)
at 7,620 m (25,000 ft)	254 knots (471 km/h; 292 mph)
T-O speed, 20° flap	105 knots (194 km/h; 121 mph) CAS
Approach speed at max landing weight	
	113 knots (209 km/h; 130 mph) CAS
Stalling speed at max T-O weight:	
wheels and flaps up	
	103 knots (191 km/h; 119 mph) IAS
wheels down and approach flaps	
	91 knots (169 km/h; 105 mph) IAS
Stalling speed at max landing weight, wheels and flaps down	88 knots (163 km/h; 102 mph) IAS
Max rate of climb at S/L	732 m (2,400 ft)/min
Rate of climb at S/L, one engine out	152 m (500 ft)/min
Service ceiling	
exceeds certificated ceiling of 7,620 m (25,000 ft)	
Service ceiling, one engine out	3,960 m (13,000 ft)
Turning radius based on nosewheel	8.13 m (26 ft 8 in)
T-O run, approach flap	671 m (2,200 ft)
T-O to 15 m (50 ft), approach flap	994 m (3,260 ft)
Landing from 15 m (50 ft) at max landing weight	
	780 m (2,560 ft)
Landing run at max landing weight	466 m (1,530 ft)
Accelerate/stop distance, 20° flap	1,158 m (3,800 ft)
Range with 10 passengers, at long range cruise power, with allowances for starting, taxi, T-O, climb and descent: with VFR reserves	
	1,569 nm (2,907 km; 1,806 miles)

BEECHCRAFT MODEL 1900D

TYPE: Development of Model 1900C.

PROGRAMME: Announced at US Regional Airlines Association meeting 1989; prototype (N5584B) first flight 1 March 1990; had flown more than 240 hours by late 1990; certification to FAR Pt 23 Amendment 34 received March 1991; planned production four per month; replacing earlier Model 1900C in current product line.

CUSTOMERS: Launch customer United Express partner Mesa Airlines (25 planned).

DESIGN FEATURES: Flat floor with stand-up headroom; cabin volume increased by 28.5 per cent; winglets for better hot and high performance; twin ventral strakes improve directional stability and turbulence penetration.

Data for Model 1900C Airliner apply to 1900D except as follows:

POWER PLANT: Two Pratt & Whitney Canada PT6A-67D turboprops, each flat rated at 954 kW (1,279 shp).

ACCOMMODATION: Airline-standard seats with underseat baggage stowage and forward wardrobe standard. Rear lavatory optional.

SYSTEMS: Engine inlet screen anti-ice protection, exhaust heated engine inlet lips, fuel vent heating, electric propeller and windscreen de-icing and pneumatic wing and tailplane leading-edge de-icing systems standard. Brake de-icing optional.

AVIONICS: EFIS, cockpit voice recorder and flight data recorder standard.

DIMENSIONS, EXTERNAL:

Wing span over winglets	17.65 m (57 ft 10¾ in)
Passenger door: Height	1.63 m (5 ft 4¼ in)
Width	0.69 m (2 ft 3¼ in)

DIMENSIONS, INTERNAL:

Passenger cabin: Max height	1.80 m (5 ft 11 in)
Volume	23.08 m³ (815.0 cu ft)
Pressurised volume, total, incl flight deck and rear baggage compartment	25.99 m³ (918.0 cu ft)
Baggage space:	
Cabin: underseat	0.91 m³ (32.3 cu ft)
forward	0.48 m³ (17.0 cu ft)
rear	4.96 m³ (175.0 cu ft)

WEIGHTS AND LOADINGS:
Typical operating weight empty 4,717 kg (10,400 lb)
Max baggage 857 kg (1,890 lb)
Max payload 2,087 kg (4,600 lb)
Max T-O weight 7,688 kg (16,950 lb)
Max ramp weight 7,738 kg (17,060 lb)
Max zero-fuel weight 6,804 kg (15,000 lb)
Max landing weight 7,303 kg (16,100 lb)
Max power loading 4.03 kg/kW (6.62 lb/shp)
PERFORMANCE (at 6,804 kg; 15,000 lb average cruise weight, ISA, except where indicated):
Max cruising speed:
at 3,050 m (10,000 ft) 271 knots (502 km/h; 312 mph)
at 3,960 m (13,000 ft) 290 knots (537 km/h; 334 mph)
at 7,620 m (25,000 ft) 287 knots (532 km/h; 330 mph)
Stalling speed, 35° flap, at max landing weight
87 knots (162 km/h; 100 mph)
Max rate of climb at S/L, at max T-O weight
800 m (2,625 ft)/min
Service ceiling, one engine out
above 5,335 m (17,500 ft)
Range with 19 passengers, high-speed cruise power at typical operating weight of 4,717 kg (10,400 lb), IFR reserves for diversion to 100 nm (185 km; 115 mile) alternate and 45 min hold:
at 2,440 m (8,000 ft) 500 nm (926 km; 575 miles)
at 3,660 m (12,000 ft) 540 nm (1,000 km; 621 miles)
at 4,880 m (16,000 ft) 570 nm (1,056 km; 656 miles)
at 7,620 m (25,000 ft) 690 nm (1,278 km; 794 miles)
Max range, VFR 1,380 nm (2,557 km; 1,589 miles)

BEECHCRAFT MODEL 2000 STARSHIP 1

TYPE: Eight/nine-passenger business turboprop.
PROGRAMME: Scaled Composites Inc (which see) flew first 85 per cent scale proof-of-concept demonstrator 29 August 1983; first flight of full-scale prototype (N2000S) at Wichita 15 February 1986, powered by Pratt & Whitney Canada PT6A-65A-4 engines while awaiting PT6A-67As; first flight second prototype (N3042S) 14 June 1986, fitted with Collins advanced integrated avionics intended for production aircraft; first flight of third prototype (N3234S; c/n NC-3) 5 January 1987, with furnished cabin and intended for function and reliability testing. N3234S appeared at Paris Air Show 1987; three other prototype airframes used for static, damage tolerance and pressure cycle testing.

Basic certification granted 14 June 1988; full certification for two-crew operation gained December 1989, followed by FAA crew determination study; single-pilot certification requiring functioning autopilot and flight management system granted May 1990; first flight of first full production aircraft (N2000S; c/n NC-4) 25 April 1989; used for demonstration flights; planned production of 10 Starship 1s in 1990; first overseas delivery, to Denmark, late 1990.
CUSTOMERS: Orders at January 1991 "not available at this time" from Beech; previously stated 40 from USA, Canada, UK and rest of Europe.
DESIGN FEATURES: Pusher turboprops with propellers aft of wing; integral fuel tanks are separate structures forming root extensions bolted to main wing; almost cylindrical cabin section mounted far forward of engines and propellers to reduce cabin noise; engines mounted close together reduce yaw moment under asymmetric thrust; wing has specially developed aerofoil; dihedral 1° 18′ 36″; incidence 2° at root; sweepback 24° 24′ at quarter-chord. B. F. Goodrich Silver Estane pneumatic de-icing boots on wing and foreplane.
FLYING CONTROLS: Pitch axis control by elevators on foreplane and elevons on main wing; directional control and yaw stabilisation through wingtip fins, called tipsails, and rudders; electrically actuated foreplane moved from 30° cruise sweep setting to 4° forward sweep as centre of lift moves when wing-mounted Fowler trailing-edge flaps are extended; vortex generators ahead of elevators energise flow over control surface when foreplane is swept. Trim tabs on elevators, rudders and elevons (for lateral trim); four vortillons under leading-edge of each outer wing and trailing-edge fences between flaps and elevons control airflow near stall; fixed ventral fin also acts as tail bumper.
STRUCTURE: Wing is continuous tip to tip structure of Nomex honeycomb and graphite epoxy monocoque, semi-monocoque and honeycomb sandwich with spars bonded to upper and lower skin assemblies; aluminium used in such points as integrally machined undercarriage attachments and tipsail mountings; fuselage structure similar to wings, manually laid-up and autoclaved; Bell Aerospace manufactures composites foreplanes.
LANDING GEAR: Retractable tricycle type, hydraulically operated with emergency extension. Main units retract inward, nose unit forward. Beech oleo-pneumatic shock absorbers. Twin Goodyear mainwheels with tyres size 19.5 × 6.75-10 8-ply rated, pressure 6.55 bars (95 lb/sq in). Single Goodrich nosewheel with tyre size 19.55 × 6.50-8 10-ply rated, pressure 4.48 bars (65 lb/sq in). Goodyear multi-disc anti-skid brakes with carbon heat sink.

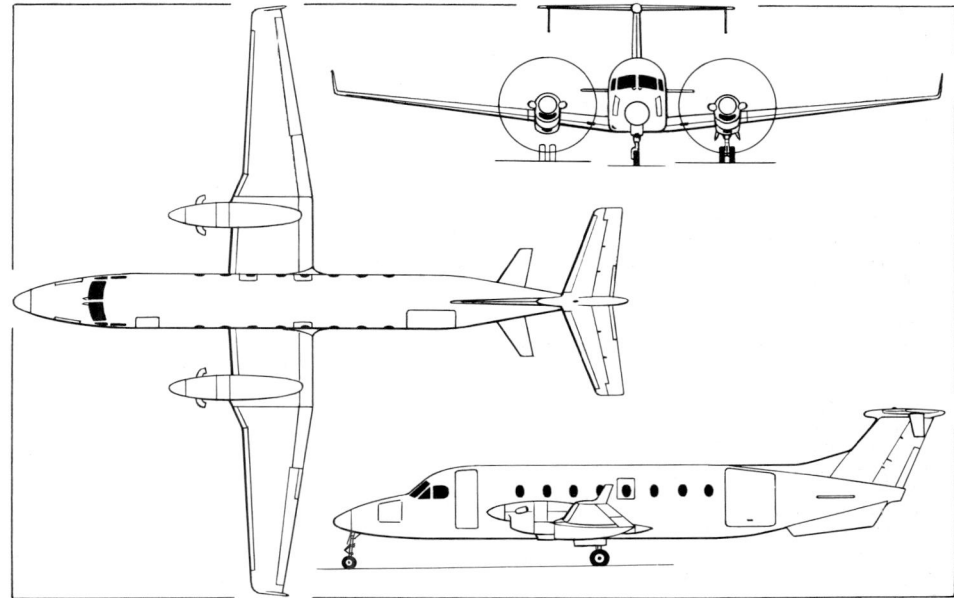

Retouched photograph and three-view drawing *(Pilot Press)* **of Beech Model 1900D commuter airliner**

First production Beechcraft Starship 1 all-composite twin-turboprop business aircraft

POWER PLANT: Two Pratt & Whitney Canada PT6A-67A turboprops, each flat rated at 895 kW (1,200 shp) and driving a McCauley five-blade fully feathering and reversible-pitch metal pusher propeller. Fuel, total usable capacity 2,021 litres (534 US gallons; 444.5 Imp gallons), contained in integral wing tanks with flush refuelling point in upper surface of each wing.
ACCOMMODATION: Certificated for single pilot operation, but provision for two crew with dual controls on four-way adjustable reclining seats on flight deck, separated from cabin by bulkhead with door. Standard seating for eight passengers, six in double club arrangement with centre aisle in reclining, lateral tracking, and

fore and aft adjustable seats with retractable inboard armrests, and two on forward facing couch at rear of cabin, each with shoulder harness, lap belt, adjustable headliner-mounted reading light and fresh air outlet, cup holder, ashtray. Four folding work tables with vinyl tops at forward and rear club seating positions. Fail-safe dual pane cabin windows with electrically powered Polaroid dimming. Upright refreshment cabinet with heated liquid container, cup dispenser, ice chest, four decanters, waste container and overboard drain on forward port side; low pyramid bar with ice and general stowage between each double club arrangement. Centre aisle stowage container. Low nap wool carpet, vinyl carpet protector, and No smoking and Fasten seat belt signs with audible chime, standard. Forward baggage compartment with flushing toilet, relief tube and cabin privacy door. Rear baggage compartment, accessible in flight via door in rear partition. Cabin is pressurised, bleed air heated, with vapour cycle cooling and high capacity ventilation systems. Single airstair door at forward end of cabin on port side, with courtesy light. Emergency exit at rear end of cabin on starboard side, over wing.

SYSTEMS: Pressurisation system with max differential of 0.58 bar (8.4 lb/sq in) to provide a cabin altitude of 2,440 m (8,000 ft) at 12,500 m (41,000 ft). Freon vapour cycle cooling system. Engine bleed air provides pressurisation, heating and ventilation. 28V DC three-bus electrical system supplied by single aircooled 34Ah battery and 300A 28V starter/generator mounted on each engine and connected in parallel. Oxygen cylinder capacity 2.18 m³ (77 cu ft) rated at 124 bars (1,800 lb/sq in), mounted in nose, provides passenger oxygen supply automatically via drop-down masks until cabin altitude reaches 4,115 m (13,500 ft). Quick-donning masks for crew. B.F. Goodrich fully automatic self-initiating ice detection and de-icing system with Silver Estane pneumatic boots on wing and foreplane leading-edges, and anti-icing systems for windscreen, engine air inlets, fuel vents, pitot static probes and stall warning sensor.

AVIONICS: Collins integrated avionics package comprising 12 colour and two monochrome CRT displays in 'all glass' cockpit. Pilot and co-pilot have duplicated instrument panels, each with two 15.2 × 17.8 cm (6 × 7 in) EFIS displays for primary flight and navigation functions and two 10.2 × 10.2 cm (4 × 4 in) airspeed indicator and altitude/vertical speed indicator CRTs. Monochrome sensor display units (SDUs) provide heading and VOR, FMS and ADF bearings, and serve as secondary nav display. Dual control/display units (CDUs) control EFIS, weather radar, navigation radios and flight management functions. Engine indication caution and advisory system (EICAS) provides nearly 100 specific pieces of information in analog or digital form on a 15.2 × 17.8 cm (6 × 7 in) colour CRT display, with a priority message system to override extraneous information. Dual multi-function displays (MFDs) provide weather radar images from Collins TWR-850 Doppler turbulence weather radar system, maps, checklists and diagnostic and maintenance data, and serve as backup to EICAS. Two radio tuning units provide gas discharge tube alphanumerics for displaying navigation and transponder frequencies and codes, and can be used for display of engine parameters if EICAS fails. Dual flight management system (FMS) keyboards control all navigation frequencies, selected from onboard microdisc storage which is updated every 28 days. Standard avionics also include dual Collins com and nav receivers, dual transponders, ADF, DME, radio altimeter, dual compass system with strapdown attitude/heading reference system, and dual audio system with pilot/co-pilot interphone, aural warnings to flight deck, cabin speaker system, and emergency locator transmitter. Dual altitude awareness panels, a course heading panel, reversionary switching panels and standby electromagnetic airspeed indicator, gyro horizon and altimeter are provided. Information from sensors and data acquisition units located throughout the aircraft is available to all instruments through an ARINC 429 digital databus system. Teledyne stall warning system. Stick pusher limits max attainable angle of attack.

EQUIPMENT: Standard cockpit equipment includes dual audio speakers, dual hand-held microphones and crew headsets, avionics master switch, primary and secondary instrument lighting systems, dual map lights, indirect cockpit lighting and overhead crew reading lights, electrically heated windscreen and cockpit side windows, hot air windscreen defroster, dual clocks, dual adjustable sun visors, cigarette lighter, two ashtrays, fresh air outlets, coffee cup holders, oxygen outlets and console mounted pressure/diluter demand crew oxygen masks with microphones, pilot and co-pilot map cases, and lighted control wheel approach plate holder. Other equipment includes nosewheel bay microphone/earphone jack plug and ground clearance switch linked to com 1, external power receptacle, external oxygen filler ports and pressure gauge, dual heated pitot and static heads, heated stall warning system, wing ice-detection lights, dual wing landing lights, nosewheel-mounted taxi and landing lights, position lights, selectable high- and low-intensity anti-collision strobe lights, entrance door light, aisle courtesy light, indirect cabin lighting, rear compartment lights, cabin fire extinguisher, towbar, pitot tube covers, static wicks, and control locks.

DIMENSIONS, EXTERNAL:
Wing span (reference)	16.60 m (54 ft 4¾ in)
Winglet height, each	2.45 m (8 ft 0½ in)
Foreplane span: sweptforward	7.82 m (25 ft 8 in)
sweptback	6.69 m (21 ft 11½ in)
Length overall	14.05 m (46 ft 1 in)
Fuselage: Length	13.67 m (44 ft 10 in)
Diameter (constant section)	1.78 m (5 ft 10 in)
Height overall	3.96 m (13 ft 0 in)
Wheel track	5.13 m (16 ft 10 in)
Wheelbase	6.86 m (22 ft 6 in)

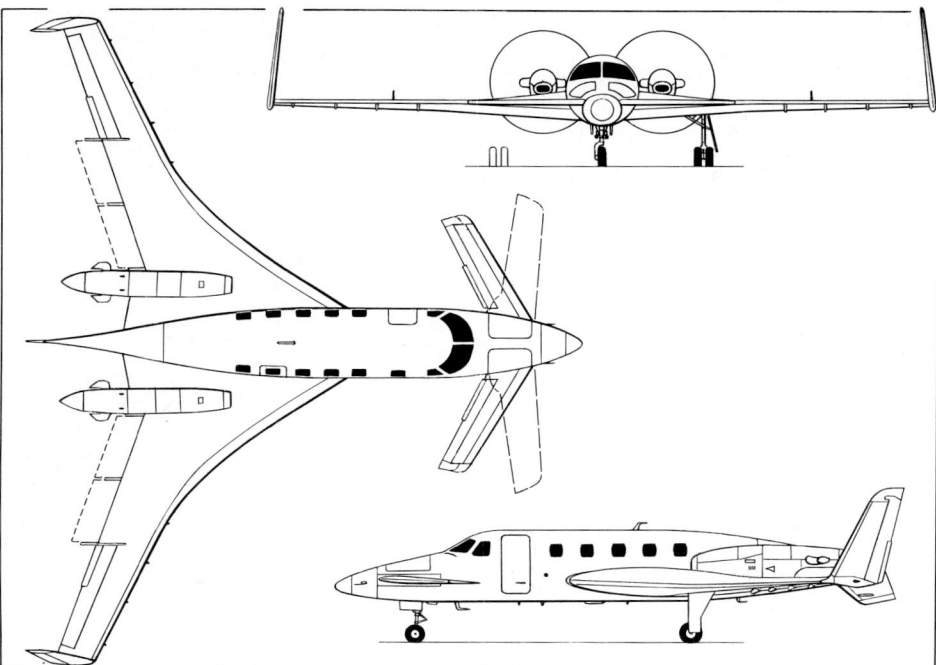

Beechcraft Starship 1 eight/nine-passenger business aircraft *(Pilot Press)*

Beechcraft Model 400A Beechjet twin-turbofan business aircraft

Propeller diameter	2.64 m (8 ft 8 in)
Propeller ground clearance	0.89 m (2 ft 11 in)
Distance between propeller centres	3.07 m (10 ft 1 in)
Passenger door: Height	1.28 m (4 ft 2½ in)
Width	0.71 m (2 ft 4 in)
Emergency exit: Height	0.56 m (1 ft 10 in)
Width	0.66 m (2 ft 2 in)

DIMENSIONS, INTERNAL:
Cabin, excl flight deck: Length	5.08 m (16 ft 8 in)
Max width	1.68 m (5 ft 6 in)
Max height	1.61 m (5 ft 3½ in)
Floor area	5.94 m² (64 sq ft)
Volume (between pressure bulkheads)	
	13.45 m³ (475 cu ft)
Baggage holds: forward	0.40 m³ (14.0 cu ft)
rear	0.99 m³ (35 cu ft)

AREAS:
Wings, gross	26.09 m² (280.9 sq ft)
Elevons (total)	1.59 m² (17.1 sq ft)
Trailing-edge flaps (total)	4.78 m² (51.5 sq ft)
Ventral fin	1.25 m² (13.5 sq ft)
Foreplane (forward position)	5.67 m² (61.0 sq ft)
Elevators (total)	1.01 m² (10.9 sq ft)
Winglets (total)	4.92 m² (53.0 sq ft)
Rudders (total, incl tabs)	1.04 m² (11.2 sq ft)

WEIGHTS AND LOADINGS:
Weight empty, equipped	4,574 kg (10,085 lb)
Max baggage weight	424 kg (935 lb)
Max payload	959 kg (2,115 lb)
Max fuel weight	1,623 kg (3,578 lb)
Max T-O weight	6,577 kg (14,500 lb)
Max ramp weight	6,627 kg (14,610 lb)
Max zero-fuel weight	5,534 kg (12,200 lb)
Max landing weight	6,205 kg (13,680 lb)
Max wing loading	251.93 kg/m² (51.6 lb/sq ft)
Max power loading	3.67 kg/kW (6.04 lb/shp)

PERFORMANCE (at max T-O weight, ISA, except where indicated):
Max limiting Mach number	0.60
Max cruising speed: at 7,620 m (25,000 ft)	
	335 knots (621 km/h; 386 mph)
at 10,670 m (35,000 ft)	
	304 knots (563 km/h; 350 mph)
Econ cruising speed at 10,670 m (35,000 ft)	
	295 knots (546 km/h; 340 mph)
Stalling speed: flaps up	99 knots (184 km/h; 114 mph)
flaps down	94 knots (175 km/h; 109 mph)
Max rate of climb at S/L	983 m (3,225 ft)/min
Rate of climb at S/L, one engine out	259 m (850 ft)/min
Max certificated altitude	12,500 m (41,000 ft)
Service ceiling	10,605 m (34,800 ft)
Service ceiling, one engine out	5,575 m (18,300 ft)
T-O to 11 m (35 ft)	1,248 m (4,093 ft)
Landing from 15 m (50 ft)	802 m (2,630 ft)

Range at 10,670 m (35,000 ft), max usable fuel, with reserves:
at max cruise power	1,373 nm (2,544 km; 1,581 miles)
at econ cruise power	1,394 nm (2,583 km; 1,605 miles)
at max range power	1,419 nm (2,629 km; 1,634 miles)

BEECHCRAFT MODEL 400A BEECHJET
US Air Force designation: T-1A Jayhawk

TYPE: Twin-turbofan business aircraft and military trainer.

PROGRAMME: Design of Diamond II acquired December 1985 from Mitsubishi Heavy Industries and Mitsubishi Aircraft International and renamed Beechjet; Beech has worldwide marketing rights outside Japan; transfer of all manufacturing operations to Beech factories at Salina and Wichita completed June 1989. Beech supporting all Mitsubishi-built Diamond I and IA delivered prior to acquisition. For information on Diamond series see 1985-86 *Jane's* and earlier editions. First Beech assembled Beechjet rolled out 19 May 1986; deliveries began June 1986.

VARIANTS: **Beechjet 400:** Initial production version (see earlier *Jane's*); superseded by 400A.

Beechjet 400A: Announced at 1989 NBAA show; production 400A first flight 22 September 1989; FAA certification received 20 June 1990; deliveries began November 1990.

Beechjet 400T/T-1A Jayhawk: US Air Force selected McDonnell Douglas, Beechcraft and Quintron to supply Tanker Transport Training System (TTTS) on 21 February 1990, including 211 Beechjet 400Ts designated T-1A Jayhawks. Deliveries to begin October 1991; with full options, deliveries will include 28 in 1992, 36 in 1993, 48 in 1994, 39 in 1995, 43 in 1996 and 16 in 1997. Beech Plant IV at Wichita being extended by 9,290 m² (100,000 sq ft) by mid-1991 for Jayhawk production.

IOC for USAF Jayhawks September 1992, for Air Training Command Specialised Undergraduate Pilot Training (SUPT) programme at Reese AFB. Jayhawks to be based at Williams AFB (Arizona), Columbus AFB (Mississippi), Vance AFB (Oklahoma), and Randolph, Reese and Laughlin AFBs (Texas) for 82nd, 14th, 71st, 12th, 64th and 47th FTWs respectively. T-1A will be used for training crews for KC-10, KC-135, C-5 and C-17.

CUSTOMERS: Total 64 Beechjet 400s and eight 400As delivered by 1 January 1991; total 105 Beechjet 400As ordered by December 1990 with delivery positions committed until mid-1993. US Air Force TTTS T-1A Jayhawk requirement covers 211 (see above).

COSTS: Jayhawk programme cost $1.3 billion; Beech contracts for first 43 aircraft, ordered by February 1991, $226.4 million. Civil 400A quoted at $4.3 million in October 1990.

DESIGN FEATURES: Wing has computer-designed Mitsubishi MAC510 aerofoil; thickness/chord ratio 13.2 per cent at root, 11.3 per cent at tip: dihedral 2° 30′; incidence 3° at root, −3° 30′ at tip; sweepback 20° at quarter-chord. New features of Beechjet 400A include increased payload and certificated ceiling, greater cabin volume achieved by moving rear-fuselage fuel tank forward under floor (balanced by moving toilet to rear of cabin), and improved soundproofing. Collins Pro Line 4 EFIS avionics standard.

T-1A Jayhawk features include student pilot in left seat, instructor on right and pupil/observer behind instructor; strengthened landing gear; more bird resistant windscreen and tail surfaces; fewer cabin windows; strengthened wing carry-through structure and engine attachment points to meet low-level flight stresses; rails for four passenger seats in cabin for personnel transport; avionics relocated from nose to rack in cabin to facilitate nose installation of air-conditioning; emergency door moved forward to position opposite main cabin door to allow straight-through egress; improved brakes; additional fuel tank; single point pressure refuelling; Rockwell Collins five-tube EFIS; digital autopilot; turbulence-detection radar; central diagnostic and maintenance system; Tacan with air-to-air capability.

FLYING CONTROLS: Variable incidence tailplane and elevators for pitch axis; lateral control by short-span ailerons and almost full semi-span, narrow chord spoilers; spoilers used also as airbrakes and lift dumpers; narrow chord Fowler type flaps, double-slotted inboard and single-slotted outboard, occupy most of trailing-edges and are hydraulically actuated; mid-span leading-edge fences on wing; small horizontal strakes on fuselage at base of fin; small ventral fin.

STRUCTURE: Wings include integrally machined metal upper and lower skins joined to two box spars forming integral fuel tank; tailplane and fin similar; fuselage fail-safe, fatigue resistant structure with multiple load paths and bonded doublers; flat cabin floor.

LANDING GEAR: Retractable tricycle type, with single wheel and oleo-pneumatic shock absorber on each unit. Hydraulic actuation, controlled electrically. Emergency free-fall extension. Nosewheel, which is steerable by rudder pedals, retracts forward; mainwheels retract inward into fuselage. Goodyear wheels, with Goodrich tyres, on all units. Goodyear brakes.

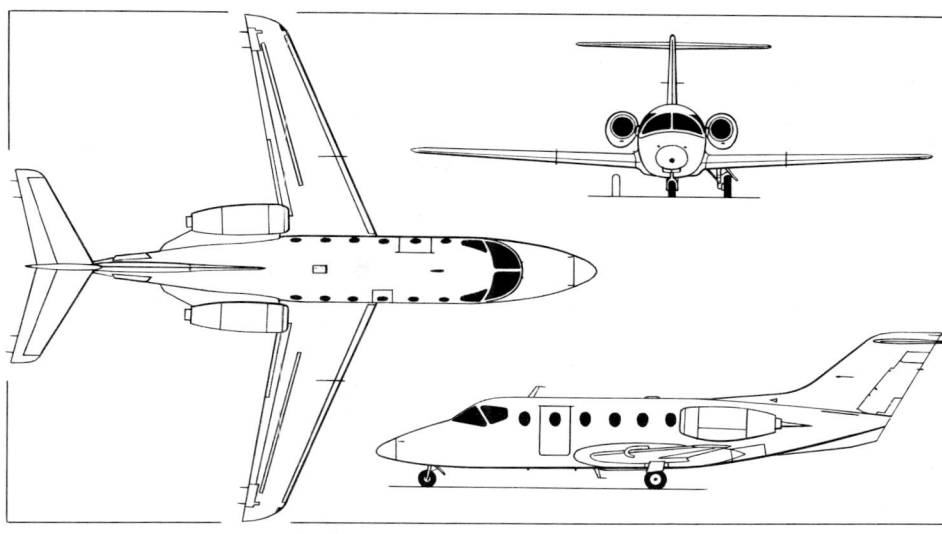

Beechcraft Model 400A (two P&WC JT15D-5 turbofans) *(Pilot Press)*

POWER PLANT: Two Pratt & Whitney Canada JT15D-5 turbofans, each rated at 12.9 kN (2,900 lb st) for take-off. Rohr thrust reversers optional. Total usable fuel capacity 2,790 litres (737 US gallons; 614 Imp gallons). One refuelling point in top of each wing, and one in rear fuselage for fuselage tank, capacity 806 litres (213 US gallons; 177 Imp gallons). Oil capacity 7.7 litres (2 US gallons; 1.7 Imp gallons).

ACCOMMODATION: Crew of two on flight deck. Standard double club layout seats eight passengers in pressurised cabin, with eight tracking, reclining seats in facing pairs, each with integral headrest and armrest and shoulder harness. Fold-out writing table between each pair of seats. Private flushing lavatory at rear with sliding doors and optional lighted vanity unit and hot water supply. With seat belts, this compartment can serve as an additional passenger seat. Interior options include substitution of carry-on baggage compartment, volume 0.34 m³ (12.0 cu ft), for one of the forward club seats, and hot and cold service refreshment centre with integral stereo entertainment system. Independent temperature control for flight deck and cabin heating systems standard. In-flight telephone optional. Rear baggage compartment with external access, capacity 204 kg (450 lb).

SYSTEMS: Pressurisation system, with normal differential of 0.63 bar (9.1 lb/sq in). Backup pressurisation system, using engine bleed air, for use in emergency. Hydraulic system, pressure 103.5 bars (1,500 lb/sq in), for actuation of flaps, landing gear and other services. Each variable volume output engine driven pump has a maximum flow rate of 14.76 litres (3.9 US gallons; 3.25 Imp gallons)/min, and one pump can actuate all hydraulic systems. Reservoirs, capacity 4.16 litres (1.1 US gallons; 0.9 Imp gallon), pressurised by filtered engine bleed air at 1.03 bars (15 lb/sq in). All systems are, wherever possible, of modular conception: for example, entire hydraulic installation can be removed as a single unit. Stick shaker as backup stall warning device.

AVIONICS: Standard avionics include pilot's integrated Collins Pro Line 4 EFIS featuring two-tube colour CRT primary flight display (PFD) and multi-function display (MFD) units mounted side by side, and control/display unit. PFD displays airspeed, altitude, vertical speed, flight director, attitude and horizontal situation information, while MFD displays navigation, radar, map, checklist and fault annunciation information. Smaller, single or dual CRTs mounted on central console function as independent navigation sensor displays or backup displays for main CRTs. Co-pilot's PFD/MFD optional. EFIS installation features EICAS engine instrumentation, strapdown attitude/heading referencing system, electronic map navigation display, airspeed trend information and V-speeds on Mach airspeed display, and solid state Doppler turbulence detection radar. Bendix/King three- or five-tube EFIS optional.

DIMENSIONS, EXTERNAL:
Wing span	13.25 m (43 ft 6 in)
Wing aspect ratio	7.5
Length overall	14.75 m (48 ft 5 in)
Fuselage: Length	13.15 m (43 ft 2 in)
Max width	1.68 m (5 ft 6 in)
Max depth	1.85 m (6 ft 1 in)
Height overall	4.19 m (13 ft 9 in)
Tailplane span	5.00 m (16 ft 5 in)
Wheel track	2.84 m (9 ft 4 in)
Wheelbase	5.86 m (19 ft 3 in)
Crew/passenger door: Height	1.27 m (4 ft 2 in)
Width	0.71 m (2 ft 4 in)

DIMENSIONS, INTERNAL:
Cabin:
Max length, incl flight deck	6.37 m (20 ft 11 in)
Length, excl flight deck	4.76 m (15 ft 7 in)
Max width	1.50 m (4 ft 11 in)
Max height	1.45 m (4 ft 9 in)
Volume: incl flight deck	11.69 m³ (413 cu ft)
excl flight deck	9.00 m³ (318 cu ft)
Baggage compartment volume	0.93 m³ (33 cu ft)

AREAS:
Wings, net	22.43 m² (241.4 sq ft)
Trailing-edge flaps (total)	5.22 m² (56.4 sq ft)
Spoilers (total)	0.57 m² (6.2 sq ft)
Fin, incl dorsal fin	5.91 m² (63.6 sq ft)
Rudder, incl yaw damper	1.12 m² (12.1 sq ft)
Tailplane	5.25 m² (56.5 sq ft)
Elevators, incl tab	1.56 m² (16.8 sq ft)

WEIGHTS AND LOADINGS:
Basic operating weight, incl crew, avionics and interior fittings	4,817 kg (10,620 lb)
Max fuel weight	2,240 kg (4,938 lb)
Max T-O weight	7,303 kg (16,100 lb)
Max ramp weight	7,393 kg (16,300 lb)
Max zero-fuel weight	5,896 kg (13,000 lb)
Max landing weight	6,450 kg (14,220 lb)
Max wing loading	325.6 kg/m² (66.69 lb/sq ft)
Max power loading	284.26 kg/kN (2.78 lb/lb st)

PERFORMANCE (at max T-O weight except where indicated):
Max limiting Mach number	0.785
Max level speed at 8,230 m (27,000 ft)	467 knots (865 km/h; 538 mph)
Typical cruising speed at 12,500 m (41,000 ft)	450 knots (834 km/h; 518 mph)
Long-range cruising speed at 12,500 m (41,000 ft)	395 knots (732 km/h; 455 mph)
Stalling speed, flaps down, idling power	87 knots (161 km/h; 100 mph) IAS
Max operating altitude	13,715 m (45,000 ft)
FAA (FAR 25) T-O to 10.7 m (35 ft) at S/L, ISA	1,245 m (4,082 ft)
FAA landing distance from 15 m (50 ft) at S/L, ISA, max landing weight	862 m (2,830 ft)
Range with four passengers, max fuel, ISA, zero wind, with allowance for climb and descent, long-range cruise power: NBAA VFR reserves	1,909 nm (3,537 km; 2,198 miles)

Beechcraft T-1A Jayhawk Tanker Transport Training System aircraft

BELL

BELL HELICOPTER TEXTRON INC
(Subsidiary of Textron Inc)

PO Box 482, Fort Worth, Texas 76101
Telephone: 1 (817) 280 2011
Fax: 1 (817) 280 8221
Telex: 758229 and 758313
PRESIDENT: Leonard M. Horner
SENIOR VICE-PRESIDENTS:
    COMMERCIAL BUSINESS, AND GENERAL MANAGER, CUSTOMER
        SUPPORT AND SERVICE DIVISION: Gainor J. Lindsey
    RESEARCH & ENGINEERING: Robert L. Lynn
    GOVERNMENT BUSINESS: Charles R. Rudning
VICE-PRESIDENTS:
    COMMERCIAL MARKETING: James A. Hamilton
    INTERNATIONAL MARKETING: Philip S. Prince
    ENGINEERING, V-22 JOINT PROGRAM OFFICE: Stanley Martin
    MILITARY BUSINESS DEVELOPMENT: Ray Swindell
DIRECTOR, PUBLIC AFFAIRS: Carl L. Harris

From 1970-81, Bell Helicopter Textron was an unincorporated division of Textron Inc; wholly owned subsidiary of Textron Inc from 3 January 1982. Bell Helicopter Canada (see Canada) formed at Montreal/Mirabel under contract with Canadian Government October 1983; transfer to Mirabel of Model 206B JetRanger and Model 206L LongRanger production completed January 1987 to make room for V-22 Osprey. Production of Models 212/412 transferred mid-1988 and early 1989 respectively; Model 230 programme also now transferred to Canada.

Bell employees in USA totalled 7,436 in early 1990; more than 30,000 Bell helicopters manufactured worldwide, including over 9,000 civilian.

Bell helicopters built in USA detailed here. Those built in Canada listed under Canada; several models built under licence by Agusta in Italy and Fuji in Japan (which see); Korea Bell Helicopter Company (KBHC) will co-produce helicopters with Bell Helicopter Textron in Republic of Korea; Bell Helicopter de Venezuela CA, joint venture with Maquinarias Mendoza CA and Aerotecnica SA, established early 1984 in Caracas for marketing and support; Bell Helicopter Asia (Pte) Ltd is wholly owned Singapore-based company for marketing and support in Southeast Asia.

BELL MODEL 205/UH-1 IROQUOIS and SUPER HUEY

Manufacture of the Bell 205 continues under licence in Japan by Fuji (which see).

Bell and Lycoming (both members of Textron group) offer Super Huey upgrade for some 12,000 Model 205s/UH-1s currently in service. Programme, costing some $1 million per aircraft, includes replacement of T53-L-13B power plant by -703 version for extra 298 kW (400 shp) of power and 3 per cent improved economy; fitment of 962 kW (1,290 shp) main gearbox; AH-1S HueyCobra tail rotor, driveshaft and gearboxes; Bell 212 main rotor system; and UH-1N style tailboom and tailplane. Japan Ground Self Defence Force upgrading HU-1H power plants to -703 standard during overhaul, adding 25 per cent to normal overhaul cost.

BELL MODEL 209 HUEYCOBRA (MODERNISED VERSIONS)
US Army designations: AH-1E, AH-1F, AH-1P, AH-1S and TH-1S

TYPE: Two-seat close support and attack helicopter.
PROGRAMME: AH-1S first ordered as TOW-capable version of AH-1G in 1975; programme included conversion of earlier AH-1Gs and three-stage production of new aircraft with various degrees of upgrading; all versions designated AH-1S until March 1987, when new-build AH-1s allotted dormant UH-1 Iroquois suffixes AH-1P, AH-1E and AH-1F; AH-1F production continues at three per month for export.
VARIANTS: **AH-1S:** Formerly AH-1S(MOD); 92 AH-1Qs (early TOW-capable AH-1G) upgraded by 1979; 87 AH-1Qs upgraded in 1986-88 with Textron Lycoming T53-L-703 engines, Kaman rotor blades (see AH-1P) and TOW system, but retaining original curved canopies; total includes 15 in **TH-1S** Night Stalker configuration for training AH-64 crews to operate night vision system and integrated helmet and display sighting system (IHADSS).

AH-1P: First batch of 100 new-production TOW Cobras (formerly called Production AH-1S), beginning with 76-22567, delivered 1977-78, two becoming AH-1F prototypes; improvements include flat-plate canopy, upturned exhaust, improved nap-of-the-earth (NOE) instrument panel, continental US (CONUS) navigation equipment, radar altimeter, improved communication radios, uprated engine and transmission, push/pull anti-torque control and, from 67th aircraft onwards, Kaman composite rotor blades with tapered tips.

AH-1E: Formerly Enhanced Cobra Armament System or Up-gun AH-1S; next 98 new-build aircraft, from 77-22673, with AH-1P improvements plus universal 20/30 mm gun turret (invariably fitted with long barrel 20 mm cannon); improved wing stores management system for 2.75 in rockets; automatic compensation for off-axis gun firing; 10kVA alternator for increased power. Delivered 1978-79.

Bell AH-1F HueyCobra of the US Army

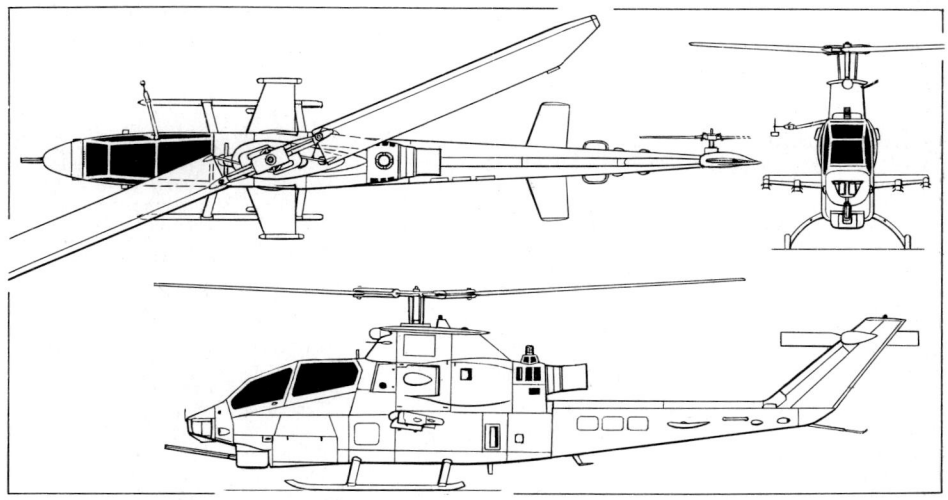

Bell AH-1F HueyCobra (Textron Lycoming T53-L-703 turboshaft) *(Pilot Press)*

AH-1F: Fully upgraded TOW version, previously designated Modernised AH-1S; 149 manufactured for US Army, beginning 78-23095, in 1979-86, including 50 transferred to Army National Guard; also 378 AH-1Gs converted to full AH-1F standard between November 1979 and June 1982, including 41 **TAH-1F** trainers; improvements of AH-1P and AH-1E added, plus new fire control system having laser rangefinder and tracker, ballistics computer, low airspeed sensor probe, Kaiser pilots' head-up display, Doppler navigation system, IFF transponder, infra-red jammer above engine, hot metal and plume infra-red suppressor, closed-circuit refuelling, new secure voice communications, Kaman composite rotor blades.

Retrofits: Later modifications have included C-Nite equipment fitted to 50 US Army AH-1Fs (reduced from planned 500), Air-to-Air Stinger (ATAS) and Cobra Fleet Life Extension (C-Flex), engine air filter, redesigned swashplate, M43 nuclear/biological/chemical mask, AN/AVR-2 laser warning and improved SCAS roll modifications. C-Nite FLIR for TOW sight delivered 1990 to US Army's 77 Aviation Battalion in South Korea. C-Flex items already completed include Nite Fix lighting, AH-1G-to-AH-1S upgrade and K-Flex driveshaft; remaining C-Flex work includes rotor improvements, improved TOW test set and radio upgrade.

Proposed retrofits: With sufficient orders, Bell is marketing upgrade package including kit to uprate engine to T53-L-703-70X offering 1,491 kW (2,000 shp); retrofit 14.02 m (46 ft 0 in) diameter Bell 412 four-blade main rotor with composite yoke instead of titanium hub; stretch tailboom by 51 cm (20 in); needle bearing tail rotor, as on Model 412 and Israeli AH-1F; three-axis digital stability augmentation; reliability and maintainability modifications. Such an AH-1F would carry 454 kg (1,000 lb) more weapons, manoeuvre down to 0.5g and achieve OGE hover ceiling of 1,067 m (3,500 ft) in ISA + 20°C at weight of 4,990 kg (11,000 lb).

CUSTOMERS: Japan received two AH-1Es and converted to AH-1F; AH-1F manufactured under licence by Fuji (which see) with 79 funded to end of FY 1991. Israel (six AH-1E, 30 AH-1F), Jordan (24 AH-1F), Pakistan (20 + 10 AH-1F on order), South Korea (42 AH-1F with C-Nite plus 20 ordered 1990), Thailand (four AH-1F).

COSTS: $9.85 million per unit (Korea, including spares and support), 1990.

DESIGN FEATURES: Transmission rated at 962 kW (1,290 shp) for take-off and 845 kW (1,134 shp) continuous; Kaman composite blades, fitted from 67th AH-1P onwards, tolerate hits by 23 mm shells, have tungsten carbide bearing sleeves and outer 15 per cent of blade is tapered in chord and thickness; tailboom strengthened against 23 mm hits; airframe has infra-red suppressant paint finish.

POWER PLANT: One 1,342 kW (1,800 shp) Textron Lycoming T53-L-703 turboshaft. Closed circuit refuelling on AH-1F. Fuel capacity 980 litres (259 US gallons; 216 Imp gallons). Upward facing exhaust on AH-1E; IR suppression nozzle on AH-1F.

ACCOMMODATION: Flat-plate canopy has seven planes of viewing surfaces, designed to minimise glint and reduce possibility of visual detection during nap-of-the-earth (NOE) flying; it also provides increased headroom for pilot. Improved instrument layout and lighting, compatible with use of night vision goggles. Improved, independently operating window/door ballistic jettison system to facilitate crew escape in emergency.

SYSTEMS: 10kVA 400Hz AC alternator with emergency bus added to electrical system. Hydraulic system pressure 103.5 bars (1,500 lb/sq in), maximum flow rate 22.7 litres (6 US gallons; 5 Imp gallons)/min. Open reservoir. Battery driven Abex standby pump, for use in event of main hydraulic system failure, can be used for collective pitch control and for boresighting turret and TOW missile system. Improved environmental control and fire detection systems.

AVIONICS: Standard lightweight avionics equipment (SLAE) includes AN/ARC-114 FM, AN/ARC-164 UHF/AM voice com, and E-Systems (Memcor Division) AN/ARC-115 VHF/AM voice com (compatible with KY-58 single-channel secure voice system). Other avionics include AN/ASN-128 Doppler nav system in AH-1F; HSI; VSI; radar altimeter; push/pull anti-torque controls for tail rotor; co-pilot's standby magnetic compass. C-Flex upgrade includes introduction of Magnavox AN/ARC-164(V) UHF/AM, Collins AN/ARC-186 VHF/AM-FM, ITT AN/ARC-201 (SINCGARS) VHF/FM, and LaBarge AN/ARN-89B D/F.

ARMAMENT: M65 system with eight Hughes TOW missiles, disposed as two two-round clusters on each outboard underwing station. Inboard wing stations remain available for other stores. Beginning with first AH-1E, M28 (7.62/40 mm) turret in earlier HueyCobras replaced by new electrically powered General Electric universal turret, designed to accommodate either 20 mm or 30 mm weapon and improve standoff capability, although only 20 mm M197 three-barrel cannon (with 750 rds) mounted in this turret. Rate of fire 675 rds/min. Turret position is controlled by pilot or co-pilot/gunner through helmet sights, or by co-pilot using M65 TOW missile system's telescopic sight unit. Field of fire up to 110° to each side of aircraft, 20.5° upward and 50° downward. Also from first AH-1E, helicopter equipped with Baldwin Electronics M138 wing stores management subsystem, providing means to select and fire, singly or in groups, any one of five types of external 2.75 in rocket store. These mounted in launchers each containing from seven to 19 tubes, additional to TOW missile capability.

In addition to these installations, first AH-1F introduced fire control subsystem which includes Kaiser head-up display for pilot, Teledyne Systems digital fire control computer for turreted weapon and underwing rockets, omnidirectional airspeed system to improve cannon and rocket accuracy, Hughes laser rangefinder (accurate over 10,000 m; 32,800 ft), and Rockwell AN/AAS-32 automatic airborne laser tracker. Other operational equipment includes Hughes LAAT stabilised sight (see 1987-88 *Jane's*). GEC Avionics M-143 air data subsystem, Bendix/King AN/APX-100 solid-state IFF transponder, Sanders AN/ALQ-144 infra-red jammer (above engine), suppressor for infra-red signature from engine hot metal and exhaust plume, and AN/APR-39 radar warning receiver.

DIMENSIONS, EXTERNAL:

Main rotor diameter	13.41 m (44 ft 0 in)
Main rotor blade chord (from 67th AH-1P onward)	
	0.76 m (2 ft 6 in)
Tail rotor diameter	2.59 m (8 ft 6 in)
Tail rotor blade chord	0.305 m (1 ft 0 in)
Wing span	3.28 m (10 ft 9 in)
Length overall, rotors turning	16.18 m (53 ft 1 in)
Width of fuselage	0.99 m (3 ft 3 in)
Height to top of rotor head	4.09 m (13 ft 5 in)
Width over TOW pods	3.56 m (11 ft 8 in)
Elevator span	2.11 m (6 ft 11 in)
Width over skids	2.13 m (7 ft 0 in)

AREAS:

Main rotor disc	141.26 m² (1,520.23 sq ft)
Tail rotor disc	5.27 m² (56.75 sq ft)

WEIGHTS AND LOADINGS (AH-1S):

Operating weight empty	2,993 kg (6,598 lb)
Mission weight	4,524 kg (9,975 lb)
Max T-O and landing weight	4,535 kg (10,000 lb)
Max disc loading	32.10 kg/m² (6.58 lb/sq ft)
Max power loading	4.72 kg/kW (7.75 lb/shp)

PERFORMANCE (AH-1S at max T-O weight, ISA):

Never-exceed speed (V_{NE}) (TOW configuration)
    170 knots (315 km/h; 195 mph)
Max level speed (TOW configuration)
    123 knots (227 km/h; 141 mph)
Max rate of climb at S/L, normal rated power
    494 m (1,620 ft)/min
Service ceiling, normal rated power 3,720 m (12,200 ft)
Hovering ceiling IGE 3,720 m (12,200 ft)
Range at S/L with max fuel, 8% reserves
    274 nm (507 km; 315 miles)
g limits +2.5/−0.5

BELL MODEL 209 IMPROVED SEACOBRA and SUPERCOBRA

US Navy/Marine Corps designations: AH-1J, AH-1T and AH-1W

TYPE: Two-seat, twin-engined close support and attack helicopter.

VARIANTS: **AH-1J SeaCobra:** Initial twin-engined version for US Marine Corps (67) and Imperial Iranian Army Aviation (202); production ended February 1975 (see 1987-88 *Jane's*).

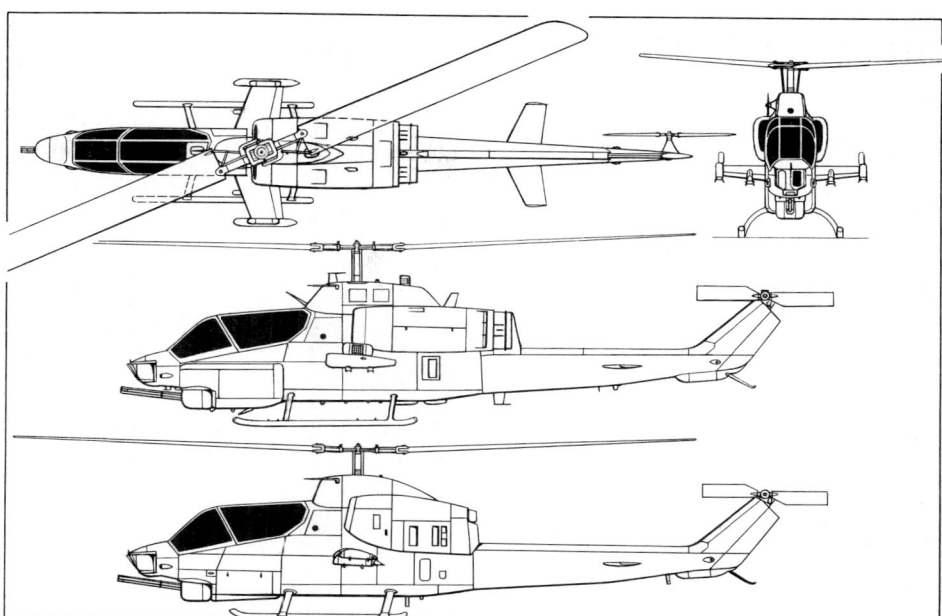

Bell AH-1W SuperCobra, with added side view (bottom) of AH-1T Improved SeaCobra *(Pilot Press)*

AH-1T Improved SeaCobra: Improved AH-1J for US Marine Corps (see 1987-88 and earlier *Jane's*); total 57 built, but upgrading of surviving 42 to AH-1W ordered March 1988. Final operator is HMT-303 at Camp Pendleton, California.

AH-1W SuperCobra: Bell flew AH-1T powered by two GE T700-GE-700; first flight of proposed improved AH-1T+, including GE T700-GE-401 engines, 16 November 1983. Congress approved 44 AH-1W Super-Cobras early 1984 for FYs 1985 and 1986; 44 AH-1Ws and one composite maintenance trainer delivered from 27 March 1986 to August 1988 to HML/A-169, 267, 367 and 369 at Camp Pendleton, California; 30 more AH-1W ordered August 1988 for delivery by end October 1991; 14 more funded FY 1990; 12 each planned for FYs 1992 and 1993; 42 AH-1Ts now being upgraded to AH-1W for HML/A-167 and 269 at New River, North Carolina; 23 delivered by December 1990.

AH-1(4B)W Viper: Described separately.

CUSTOMERS: US Marine Corps (see under Variants); Turkish Army received five AH-1Ws in 1990; four more planned for 1991; co-production agreement being negotiated.

COSTS: $10.7 million (1992) projected unit cost.

DESIGN FEATURES: Two-blade main rotor similar to that of Bell Model 214 with strengthened rotor head incorporating Lord Kinematics Lastoflex elastomeric and Teflon faced bearings. Blade aerofoil Wortmann FX69-H-098. Tail rotor also similar to that of Model 214 with greater diameter and blade chord. Rotor brake standard.

Missions of AH-1W include anti-armour, escort, multiple-weapon fire support, including air-to-air with Sidewinder, armed reconnaissance, search and target acquisition. Initial 25 US AH-1W being fitted with Kollsman laser Night Targeting System (NTS) based on Israeli Tamam CLNAS; testing of enhanced electronic warfare system began August 1989. Hughes AGM-65D Maverick ASM test-fired in August 1990; up to 12 Maverick-capable SuperCobras required.

STRUCTURE: Main rotor blades have aluminium spar and aluminium faced honeycomb aft of spar; tail rotor has aluminium honeycomb with stainless steel skin and leading-edge. Airframe conventional all-metal semi-monocoque.

Data below refer to AH-1W SuperCobra:

LANDING GEAR: Non-retractable tubular skid type. Ground handling wheels optional.

POWER PLANT: Two General Electric T700-GE-401 turbo-shafts, each rated at 1,212 kW (1,625 shp). Fuel contained in two interconnected self-sealing rubber fuel cells in fuselage, with protection from damage by 0.50 in ballistic ammunition, total capacity 1,153 litres (304.5 US gallons; 253.5 Imp gallons). Fire protection for wet area provided by passive powder filled panels and for ullage by onboard inert gas generating system (OBIGGS). Gravity refuelling point in forward fuselage, pressure refuelling point in rear fuselage. Provision for carriage on underwing stores stations of two or four external fuel tanks each of 295 litres (78 US gallons; 65 Imp gallons) capacity; or two 378 litre (100 US gallon; 83 Imp gallon) tanks; or two 100 and two 78 US gallon tanks. Oil capacity 19 litres (5 US gallons; 4.2 Imp gallons).

ACCOMMODATION: Crew of two in tandem, with co-pilot/gunner in front seat and pilot at rear. Cockpit is heated, ventilated and air-conditioned. Dual controls; lighting compatible with night vision goggles, and armour protection standard. Forward crew door on port side and rear crew door on starboard side, both upward opening.

SYSTEMS: Three independent hydraulic systems, pressure 207 bars (3,000 lb/sq in), for flight controls and other services. Electrical system comprises two 28V 400A DC generators, two 24V 34.5Ah batteries and three inverters: main 115V AC, 1kVA, single-phase at 400Hz, standby 115V AC, 750VA, three-phase at 400Hz and a dedicated 115V AC 365VA single-phase for AIM-9 missile system. AiResearch environmental control unit.

AVIONICS: Kaiser HUD compatible with PNVS-5 and ANVIS-6 night vision goggles. AN/ASN-75B compass set, AN/ARN-89B ADF, AN/APX-100(V) IFF transponder, AN/ARN-118 Tacan, AN/APN-154(V) radar beacon set, two AN/ARC-182(V) communication radios, AN/APN-194 radar altimeter, AN/APR-39(V) pulse radar signal detecting set, AN/APR-44(V) CW radar warning system, KY-58 TSEC secure voice set and AN/ALQ-144(V) IR countermeasures set. Improved countermeasures suite in USMC AH-1Ws replaces AN/APR-39 and AN/APR-44 by AN/APR-39(XE2) radar warning and adds AN/AVR-2 laser warner and AN/AAR-47 plume detecting set. Dual AN/ALE-39 chaff system with one MX-7721 dispenser mounted on each stub wing. From January 1991, new-build AH-1Ws have Teledyne AN/APN-217 Doppler-based navigation system with Collins CDU-800 control/display unit and dual Collins ICU-800 processors.

ARMAMENT: Electrically operated General Electric under-nose GTK4A/A turret housing an M197 three-barrel 20 mm gun. A 750-rd ammunition container is located in the fuselage directly aft of the turret; firing rate is 675 rds/min; a 16-round burst limiter is incorporated in the firing switch. Gun can be tracked 110° to each side, 18° upward, and 50° downward, but barrel length of 1.52 m (5 ft) makes it imperative that the M197 is centralised before wing stores are fired. Underwing attachments for up to four LAU-61A (19 tube), LAU-68A, LAU-68A/A, LAU-68B/A or LAU-69A (seven-tube) 2.75 in Hydra 70 rocket launcher pods; two CBU-55B fuel-air explosive weapons; four SUU-44/A flare dispensers; two M118 grenade dispensers; Mk 45 parachute flares; or two GPU-2A or SUU-11A/A Minigun pods. Provision for carrying totals of up to eight TOW missiles, eight AGM-114 Hellfire missiles, two AIM-9L Sidewinder or AGM-122A Sidearm missiles, on outboard underwing stores stations. Canadian Marconi TOW/Hellfire control system enables AH-1W to fire both TOW and Hellfire

Bell AH-1W SuperCobra test-firing a Maverick missile

missiles on same mission. Hughes AGM-65D Maverick capability demonstrated 1990; under consideration for USMC.

DIMENSIONS, EXTERNAL:

Main rotor diameter	14.63 m (48 ft 0 in)
Main rotor blade chord	0.84 m (2 ft 9 in)
Tail rotor diameter	2.97 m (9 ft 9 in)
Tail rotor blade chord	0.305 m (1 ft 0 in)
Distance between rotor centres	8.89 m (29 ft 2 in)
Wing span	3.23 m (10 ft 7 in)
Wing aspect ratio	3.74
Length: overall, rotors turning	17.68 m (58 ft 0 in)
fuselage	13.87 m (45 ft 6 in)
Width overall	3.28 m (10 ft 9 in)
Height: to top of rotor head	4.11 m (13 ft 6 in)
overall	4.32 m (14 ft 2 in)
Elevator span	2.11 m (6 ft 11 in)
Width over skids	2.13 m (7 ft 0 in)

AREAS:

Main rotor blades (each)	6.13 m² (66.0 sq ft)
Tail rotor blades (each)	0.45 m² (4.835 sq ft)
Main rotor disc	168.11 m² (1,809.56 sq ft)
Tail rotor disc	6.94 m² (74.70 sq ft)
Vertical fin	2.01 m² (21.70 sq ft)
Horizontal tail surfaces	1.41 m² (15.20 sq ft)

WEIGHTS AND LOADINGS:

Weight empty	4,627 kg (10,200 lb)
Mission fuel load	946 kg (2,086 lb)
Max useful load (fuel and disposable ordnance)	2,065 kg (4,552 lb)
Max T-O and landing weight	6,690 kg (14,750 lb)
Max disc loading	39.80 kg/m² (8.15 lb/sq ft)

PERFORMANCE (at max T-O weight, ISA):

Never-exceed speed (V_{NE})	190 knots (352 km/h; 219 mph)
Max level speed at S/L	152 knots (282 km/h; 175 mph)
Max cruising speed	150 knots (278 km/h; 173 mph)
Rate of climb at S/L, one engine out	244 m (800 ft)/min
Service ceiling	more than 4,270 m (14,000 ft)
Service ceiling, one engine out	more than 3,660 m (12,000 ft)
Hovering ceiling: IGE	4,495 m (14,750 ft)
OGE	915 m (3,000 ft)
Range at S/L with standard fuel, no reserves	317 nm (587 km; 365 miles)

BELL AH-1(4B)W VIPER

TYPE: Close support and attack helicopter with four-blade main rotor.

PROGRAMME: Prototype AH-1W (converted from AH-1T 161022) subsequently modified to AH-1(4B)W; first flight 24 January 1989; evaluated by US Marine Corps in 1990. Rotor retrofit planned for USMC AH-1Ws.

DESIGN FEATURES: Four-blade bearingless composite main rotor based on Bell 680 rotor (see 1989-90 *Jane's*), with blade roots of controlled flexibility to allow flapping, lead-lag and pitch-change movements without bearings; roots surrounded by rigid cuffs which transmit pitch-change commands from control rods to blade roots; two blades folded manually for compact storage; additional improvements include expanded *g* envelope; uprated transmission. Max weight increased by 930 kg (2,050 lb); speed increased by 20 knots (37 km/h; 23 mph); digital flight control system; night targeting sights; Doppler navigation.

Data generally as for AH-1W except as follows:

ARMAMENT: Cranked, six-station stub-wings, including overwing position for two AGM-122 Sidearm ARMs at each tip. Total ordnance capacity 1,444 kg (3,184 lb), including 750 rds for nose cannon and two chaff/flare dispensers.

DIMENSIONS, EXTERNAL:

Main rotor blade chord	0.63 m (2 ft 1 in)

WEIGHTS AND LOADINGS:

Max T-O and landing weight	7,620 kg (16,800 lb)

PERFORMANCE (at 6,120 kg; 13,494 lb mid-mission weight):

Never-exceed speed (V_{NE})	over 200 knots (371 km/h; 230 mph)
Max level speed	170 knots (315 km/h; 196 mph)
Max cruising speed	160 knots (297 km/h; 184 mph)
g limit	+3.39

BELL MODEL 206 JETRANGER and LONGRANGER

Model 206 is now produced in Canada by the Bell division (which see) in that country with dynamic components made by Bell in Texas.

BELL MODEL 406 (AHIP)

US Army designations: OH-58D Kiowa and Kiowa Warrior

TYPE: Two-seat scout and attack helicopter.

PROGRAMME: Bell won US Army Helicopter Improvement Program (AHIP) 21 September 1981; first flight of OH-58D 6 October 1983; deliveries started December 1985; first based in Europe June 1987. Production running at minimum economic rate of three a month, compared with capacity for 12.

VARIANTS: **Prime Chance:** Fifteen special armed OH-58Ds modified from September 1987 under Operation Prime Chance for use against Iranian high-speed boats in Gulf; delivery started after 98 days, in December 1987;

Bell AH-1(4B)W Viper demonstrating agility with Model 680 bearingless research rotor

Bell OH-58D Kiowa Warrior with weapons and mast-mounted sight

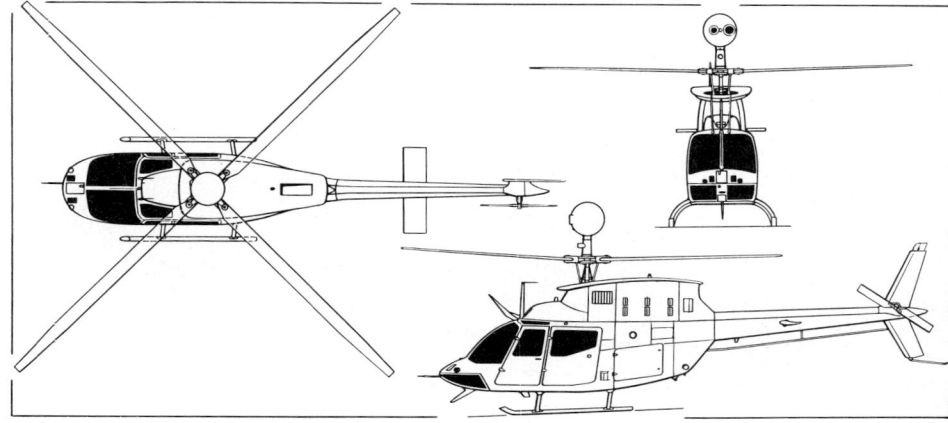

Bell OH-58D Kiowa scout and attack helicopter (*Pilot Press*)

firing clearance for Stinger, Hellfire, 0.50 in gun and seven-tube rocket pods completed in seven days; aircraft remained at sea in Gulf 1990.

Kiowa Warrior: Armed version, to which all 243 planned OH-58Ds are being modified; new engine diffuser raises power by 15 per cent; transmission uprated to 429 kW (575 shp); ultimate gross weight growth to 2,495 kg (5,500 lb); additional equipment as detailed below; armament same as Prime Chance; integrated avionics and lightened structure make Kiowa Warrior 113 kg (250 lb) lighter than Prime Chance.

Multi-Purpose Light Helicopter (MPLH): Features include squatting landing gear, quick-folding rotor blades and tilting fin to allow helicopter to be transported in cargo aircraft and flown to cover 10 minutes after unloading from C-130. Later additions include cargo hook for up to 907 kg (2,000 lb) slung load and fittings for external carriage of six outward-facing troop seats or four stretchers.

CUSTOMERS: US Army: initial plan to modify 592 OH-58A/B to OH-58D reduced to 477; again reduced to 207, but production Lot 7 funded in FY 1990 to bring total to 243 (Lots of 16, 44, 39, 36, 36, 36 and 36), of which 16 are new-build armed Kiowa Warriors. Main effort now is provision for armament and accompanying upgrades in new aircraft and retrofitting existing OH-58D to armed Kiowa Warrior configuration; 81 Kiowa Warriors to be raised to ultimate Multi-Purpose Light Helicopter (MPLH) standard for use by US Army quick reaction forces. Total of 163 delivered by February 1990, including 54 in Germany and six in South Korea. US Marine Corps to acquire 36 OH-58 airframes rebuilt as OH-58D Kiowa Warriors.

COSTS: $9.42 million (1990) programme unit cost.

DESIGN FEATURES: Four-blade Bell soft in plane rotor with carbon composites yoke, elastomeric bearings and composites blades. Transmission rating: Kiowa 339 kW (455 shp) continuous; Kiowa Warrior 429 kW (575 shp) continuous. McDonnell Douglas/Northrop mast-mounted sight containing TV and IR optics and laser designator/ranger; Honeywell integrated control of mission functions, navigation, communications, systems and maintenance functions based on large electronic primary displays for pilot and observer/gunner; hands-on cyclic and collective controls for all combat functions; automatic target hand-off system in some OH-58Ds operates air-to-air as well as air-to-ground using digital frequency hopping; system indicates location and armament state of other helicopters; some OH-58Ds have real-time video downlink capable of relaying to US Army Guardrail aircraft, to headquarters 22 nm (40 km; 25 miles) away or, via satellite, to remote locations.

Phase 1 improvements scheduled for OH-58D, beside basic armament fittings and wiring, include new software display menu pages and doubled computer memory capacity; this allows for Sanders AN/ALQ-144 IR jammer, Perkin Elmer AN/AVR-2 laser warning receiver, Tracor M130 chaff/flare dispenser and multi-target acquisition. Other additions include ITT SINCGARS VHF/FM secure radios; advanced ANVIS night vision goggles with display of horizon, airspeed, height and torque; video recorder; transmission upgrade to allow for added weight.

Stage 1 of Multi-Stage Improvement Program (MSIP) includes fitting Global Positioning System receiver, improved Doppler, digital data loader and MIL-STD-1750 processors.

FLYING CONTROLS: Full-powered controls, including tail rotor, with four-way trim and trim release; Stability and control augmentation system (SCAS) using AHRS gyro signals; automatic bob-up and return to hover mode; Doppler blind hover guidance mode; co-pilot/observer's cyclic stick can be disconnected from controls and locked centrally.

STRUCTURE: Basic OH-58 structure reinforced; armament cross-tube fixed above rear cabin floor; avionics occupy rear cabin area, baggage area and nose compartment.

LANDING GEAR: Light alloy tubular skids bolted to extruded cross-tubes.

POWER PLANT: One Allison 250-C30R turboshaft, with an intermediate power rating of 485 kW (650 shp) at S/L ISA. One self-sealing crash resistant fuel cell, capacity 399 litres (105.4 US gallons; 87.8 Imp gallons) located aft of the cabin area. Refuelling point on starboard side of fuselage. Oil capacity 5.7 litres (1.5 US gallons; 1.2 Imp gallons).

ACCOMMODATION: Pilot and co-pilot/observer seated side by side. Door on each side of fuselage. Accommodation is heated and ventilated.

SYSTEMS: Single hydraulic system, pressure 69 bars (1,000 lb/sq in), for main and tail rotor controls and SCAS system. Maximum flow rate 11.36 litres (3 US gallons; 2.5 Imp gallons)/min. Open-type reservoir. Primary electrical power provided by 10kVA 400Hz three-phase 120/208V AC alternator with 200A 28V DC transformer-rectifier unit for secondary DC power. Backup power provided by 500VA 400Hz single-phase 115V AC solid state inverter and 200A 28V DC starter/generator.

AVIONICS: Multi-function displays for vertical and horizontal situation indication, with mast mounted sight day/night viewing and communications control, with selection via

control column handgrip switches. Five com transceivers, data link and secure voice equipment. Plessey (PESC) AN/ASN-157 Doppler strapdown INS. Equipped for day/night VFR. Mast-mounted sight houses 12x magnification TV camera, auto-focusing IR thermal imaging sensor and laser rangefinder/designator, with automatic target tracking and in-flight automatic bore-sighting. Night vision goggles; AHRS; and airborne target handoff subsystem (ATHS). Germany-based OH-58Ds have real-time video downlink which can be relayed via Guardrail-capable aircraft. Phase 1 additions, introduced on production line in 1990, include doubled computer capacity to 88K, added weapons selection/aiming and multi-target acquisition/track displays, IR jammer, second RWR and laser warning, video recorder, data transfer system, SINCGARS and Have Quick II radios, ANVIS display and symbology system and EMV hardening.

EQUIPMENT: NBC mask in Phase 1 aircraft.

ARMAMENT: Four Stinger air-to-air or Hellfire air-to-surface missiles, or two seven-round 2.75 in rocket pods, or two Global Helicopter Technology CFD-5000 pods for 7.62 mm and 0.50 in machine guns, mounted on outriggers on cabin sides. IR jammer standard on armed version.

DIMENSIONS, EXTERNAL:

Main rotor diameter	10.67 m (35 ft 0 in)
Main rotor blade chord	0.24 m (9½ in)
Tail rotor diameter	1.65 m (5 ft 5 in)
Length: overall, rotors turning	12.85 m (42 ft 2 in)
fuselage, excl rotors	10.31 m (33 ft 10 in)
Width, rotors folded	1.97 m (6 ft 5½ in)
Height: to top of rotor head	2.59 m (8 ft 6 in)
overall	3.90 m (12 ft 9½ in)
Skid track	1.88 m (6 ft 2 in)
Cabin doors (port and stbd, each):	
Height	1.04 m (3 ft 5 in)
Width	0.91 m (3 ft 0 in)
Height to sill	0.66 m (2 ft 2 in)

AREAS:

Main rotor blades (each)	1.30 m² (13.95 sq ft)
Tail rotor blades (each)	0.13 m² (1.43 sq ft)
Main rotor disc	89.37 m² (962.0 sq ft)
Tail rotor disc	2.14 m² (23.04 sq ft)
Fin	0.85 m² (9.1 sq ft)

WEIGHTS AND LOADINGS:

Weight empty	1,281 kg (2,825 lb)
Max fuel weight	321 kg (707 lb)
Max T-O and landing weight: Kiowa	2,041 kg (4,500 lb)
Kiowa Warrior	2,495 kg (5,500 lb)
Max zero-fuel weight	1,711 kg (3,773 lb)
Max disc loading	22.95 kg/m² (4.7 lb/sq ft)
Max power loading: Kiowa	6.02 kg/kW (9.89 lb/shp)
Kiowa Warrior	5.82 kg/kW (9.56 lb/shp)

PERFORMANCE (at max T-O weight, clean):

Never-exceed speed (VNE)	
	130 knots (241 km/h; 149 mph)
Max level speed at 1,220 m (4,000 ft)	
	128 knots (237 km/h; 147 mph)
Max cruising speed at 610 m (2,000 ft)	
	120 knots (222 km/h; 138 mph)
Econ cruising speed at 1,220 m (4,000 ft)	
	110 knots (204 km/h; 127 mph)
Max rate of climb: at S/L, ISA	469 m (1,540 ft)/min
at 1,220 m (4,000 ft), 35°C (95°F)	
	over 366 m (1,200 ft)/min
Vertical rate of climb: at S/L, ISA	232 m (760 ft)/min
at 1,220 m (4,000 ft), 35°C (95°F)	
	over 152 m (500 ft)/min
Service ceiling	over 3,660 m (12,000 ft)
Hovering ceiling: IGE, ISA	over 3,660 m (12,000 ft)
OGE, ISA	3,415 m (11,200 ft)
OGE, 35°C (95°F)	1,735 m (5,700 ft)
Range with max fuel, no reserves	
	300 nm (556 km; 345 miles)
Endurance	2 h 30 min

BELL MODEL 406 CS COMBAT SCOUT

TYPE: Scout/attack helicopter for export.

PROGRAMME: Lighter, simplified OH-58D; first flight June 1984. Model 406 CS has OH-58D main rotor, high-thrust tail rotor and drive train; basic engine is 485 kW (650 shp) Allison 250-C30U; transmission with continuous rating 380 kW (510 shp) and transient rating 475 kW (637 shp); armament choices include two GIAT 20 mm M621 gun pods, four TOW 2 or Hellfire, or combinations of Stinger, 70 mm rockets and 7.62 mm or 0.50 in machine guns. Successful air-to-air combat trials flown at NAS Patuxent River 1987.

VARIANTS: **406 CS:** From June 1990, offered with fuel capacity increased to 455 litres (120 US gallons; 100 Imp gallons), transmission uprated to 410 kW (550 shp), max T-O weight of 2,268 kg (5,000 lb). Planned further upgrades include TOW armament, laser designator/ranger, 429 kW (575 shp) transmission, 2,495 kg (5,500 lb) gross weight.

MH-58D: See below.

CUSTOMERS: Saudi Arabia received 15 MH-58D Combat Scouts in 1990 with SFENA hybrid cockpit based on conventional instruments and electronic displays for TOW and communications control; roof-mounted Saab-Emerson HeliTOW sight has folding overhead direct-view optics tube; squatting undercarriage, folding rotor blades and tailplane. Deliveries began mid-1990.

COSTS: $5.73 million (1988) Saudi Arabia programme unit cost.

Bell Model 406 CS Combat Scout of the Royal Saudi Land Forces

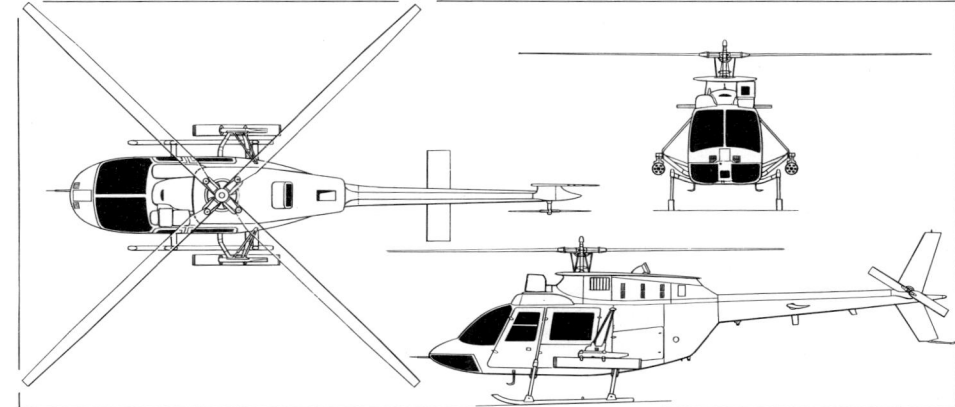

Bell Model 406 CS with roof-mounted HeliTOW sight, rocket pods and collapsible skid landing gear
(Pilot Press)

WEIGHTS AND LOADINGS:

Weight empty	1,030 kg (2,271 lb)
Max T-O weight	2,268 kg (5,000 lb)
Cargo hook capacity	680 kg (1,500 lb)
Max power loading	5.53 kg/kW (9.09 lb/shp)

PERFORMANCE (at max T-O weight):

Max level speed	125 knots (232 km/h; 144 mph)
Max cruising speed	120 knots (222 km/h; 138 mph)
Hovering ceiling: IGE	6,250 m (20,500 ft)
OGE	4,420 m (14,500 ft)
Range with max fuel	218 nm (404 km; 251 miles)
Endurance	2 h 48 min

BELL MODELS 212 and 412

Production lines transferred, respectively in mid-1988 and January 1989, to Bell Helicopter Textron division of Textron Canada in Montreal (which see).

BELL MODEL 214ST SUPERTRANSPORT

Production of the Model 214ST ceased in 1990, by which time 100 had been manufactured. Last described in 1990-91 *Jane's*.

BELL MODEL 222

Production of the Bell Model 222 ceased in 1989; 184 were manufactured, including 84 Model 222As, 26 Model 222Bs and 74 Model 222UTs. Last described in 1990-91 *Jane's*. Succeeded by Model 230, which see under Bell Helicopter of Canada.

Quick folding system for OH-58D Multi-purpose light helicopter and 406 CS Combat Scout

BELL MODEL 230

Production of this successor to the Model 222 has been assigned to Bell Helicopter Textron division of Textron Canada, at Montreal, which see.

BELL/BOEING V-22 OSPREY

Joint programme described under Bell/Boeing heading following this section.

BELL/BOEING
BELL HELICOPTER TEXTRON and BOEING HELICOPTERS
PROGRAMME MANAGER: Colonel James H. Schaeffer, USMC

BELL/BOEING V-22 OSPREY

TYPE: Twin-engined tilt-rotor multi-mission aircraft.

PROGRAMME: Based on Bell/NASA XV-15 tilt-rotor; initiated as US Department of Defense Joint Services Advanced Vertical Lift Aircraft (JVX), run by US Army, FY 1982; programme transferred to US Navy January 1983; 24-month US Navy preliminary design contract 26 April 1983; aircraft named V-22 Osprey January 1985; seven-year full-scale development (FSD) began 2 May 1986 with order for six prototypes (Nos. 1, 3 and 6 by Bell; Nos. 2, 4 and 5 by Boeing) plus static test airframes.

No. 1 (BuAer No. 163911) rolled out at Arlington, Texas, 23 May 1988; first flight 19 March 1989; achieved first transition from helicopter to aeroplane mode 14 September 1989. First flight No. 2 at Arlington 9 September and No. 4 at Wilmington, Delaware, 21 December 1989; first flight No. 3 on 9 May 1990 at Arlington. Test assignments include No. 1, flight envelope expansion and flight loads examination; No. 2, fly-by-wire development; No. 3, flight loads, vibration and acoustics and sea trials; No. 4, first with full avionics, initial shipboard compatibility and propulsion studies; No. 5, avionics, flight controls and associated equipment trials and initial US Air Force mission equipment tests; No. 6, flight-test fixes optimised for production configuration. Initial government trials, April 1990, involved 15 hours' flying by three military test pilots in No. 2.

Sea trials aboard USS *Wasp*, 4-7 December 1990, involved No. 3 in landing and take-off tests and No. 4 in fit and function tests. By end-1990, trials included transition landings and take-offs, wing stall tests, single-engine tests and flights up to 349 knots (647 km/h; 402 mph). V-22 awarded National Aeronautic Association's Collier Trophy in 1990 for "greatest achievement in aeronautics in past year"; claimed to meet or exceed 32 multi-service mission requirements. Trials programme is 4,000 hours, of which 430 hours flown by March 1991. Operational testing due to start in third quarter 1991; FSD due for completion June 1992, but may have slipped as much as two years.

Original schedule called for delivery to US Marines late 1991/early 1992, US Air Force 1993 and US Navy 1995. Production funding cut FY 1990, but development contract maintained; some long-lead items for production aircraft funded FY 1991, but might be transferred to development. HASC has proposed FY 1992-93 funding of six opeval 'production representative' aircraft.

Bell contributes wings, nacelles, proprotor and transmission systems and integrates engines. Boeing responsible for fuselage, tail unit, landing gear and fairings and integrates avionics.

VARIANTS: **MV-22A:** Basic US Marine Corps transport; original requirement for 552 to replace CH-46 Sea Knight and CH-53 Sea Stallion. Three-man crew and 24 combat-equipped troops or cargo carried at 250 knots (463 km/h; 288 mph) over radius of 200 nm (370 km; 230 miles), with ability to hover mid-way at 915 m (3,000 ft) OGE at 33°C (91.4°F).

HV-22A: US Navy combat search and rescue (CSAR), special warfare and fleet logistics model to replace HH-3s. Original requirement for 50.

CV-22A: US Air Force long-range special missions aircraft. Original requirement for 80 reduced to 55;

V-22 prototype No. 3 during deck trials in December 1990

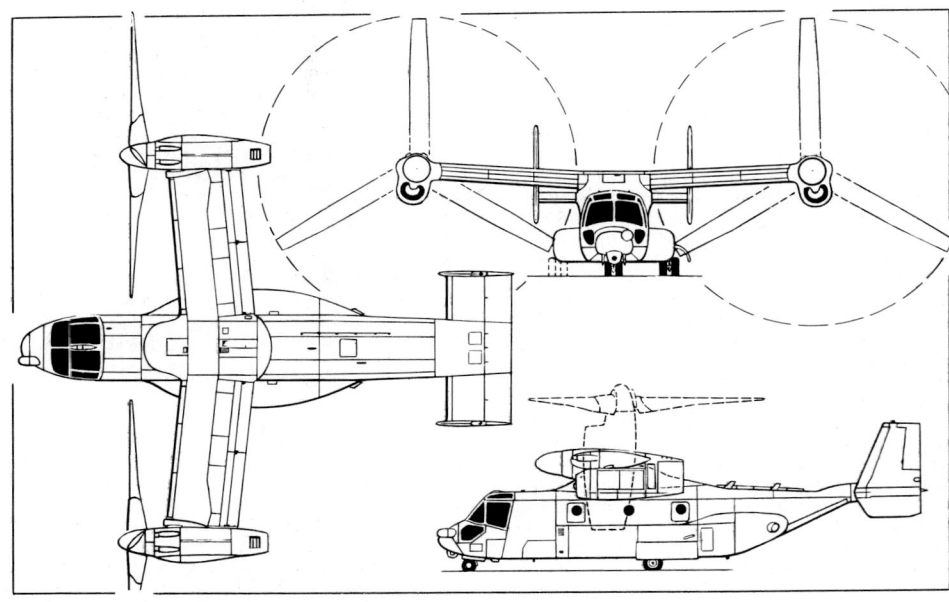

Bell/Boeing V-22 Osprey multi-mission tilt-rotor aircraft (*Pilot Press*)

should carry 12 troops or 1,306 kg (2,880 lb) internal cargo over 520 nm (964 km; 599 mile) radius at 250 knots (463 km/h; 288 mph), with ability to hover OGE at 1,220 m (4,000 ft) at 35°C (95°F).

SV-22A: Tentative US Navy ASW version to replace S-3 Viking. Original requirement for up to 300. Required to deposit and pick up recoverable large ASW sensors and operate them from high altitude.

US Army: Original requirement for 231 V-22s, based on USMC transport, withdrawn. Documented

requirement remains for V-22 in medevac, special operations and combat assault support roles.

CUSTOMERS: See above. Also European marketing co-operation with British Aerospace (which see), Dornier and Alenia. Japan Maritime Self Defence Force provisional commitment to fund two SAR Ospreys in 1994, plus two in 1995.

COSTS: FY 1991 budget assigned $238 million to continue R&D and $165 million former production money to start production tooling.

DESIGN FEATURES: Engines, transmission and proprotors tilt through 97° 30′ between forward flight and steepest approach gradient or tail-down hover; cross-shaft keeps both proprotors turning after engine loss; transmission rated at 3,408 kW (4,570 shp) normally and 4,415 kW (5,920 shp) with one engine inoperative; APU mounted in fuselage drives into cross-shaft for starting. Three-blade contra-rotating proprotors have special high-twist tapered format blades with elastomeric bearings and powered folding mechanisms; separate swashplates produce respectively yaw and fore-and-aft translation in hover and sideways flight in level attitude. Wing-fold sequence from helicopter mode involves power-folding of blades parallel to wing leading-edge, tilting engine nacelles down to horizontal and rotating entire wing/engine/proprotor group clockwise on stainless steel carousel to lie over fuselage.

FLYING CONTROLS: Three-lane fly-by-wire (Moog actuators) with automatic stabilisation, full autopilot and formation-flying modes. Automatic control of configuration change during transition and of transfer of control from aerodynamic surfaces to rotor-blade pitch changing; flaperons and ailerons droop during hover to reduce negative lift of wing.

Lateral attitude controlled in hover by differential rotor thrust, but lateral swashplate allows sideways flight in level attitude controlled by button on control column. Yaw control in hover by differential fore-and-aft cyclic. Integrated electronic cockpit with six electronic display screens; helicopter-style control columns rather than aileron wheels, but left-handed power levers move forward for full power in opposite sense to helicopter collective lever.

STRUCTURE: Approx 59 per cent of airframe is composites and just 454 kg (1,000 lb) of empty weight is metal; main composites are Hercules IM-6 graphite/epoxy in wings and AS4 in fuselage and tail. Fuselage mainly 'black aluminium' consisting of conventional stringers, frames and preformed skin, all in composites, assembled with metal fasteners. Wing box is high-strength, very stiff torsion box made up from one-piece upper and lower skins with moulded ribs and bonded stringers; two-segment graphite single-slotted flaperons with titanium fittings; three-segment detachable leading-edge of aluminium alloy with Nomex honeycomb core. Wing locking and unlocking with Lucas Aerospace actuators; fuselage sponsons contain landing gear, air-conditioning unit and fuel; tail unit of Hercules AS4 graphite/epoxy, built by Grumman.

LANDING GEAR: Dowty hydraulically actuated retractable tricycle type, with twin wheels and oleo-pneumatic shock absorbers on each unit, Menasco Canada steerable nose unit. Dowty Toronto two-stage shock absorption in main gear is designed for landing impacts of up to 3.66 m (12 ft)/s normal, 4.48 m (14.7 ft)/s maximum, and has been drop tested to 7.32 m (24 ft)/s. All units retract rearward, main gear into sponsons on lower sides of centre-fuselage. Manual and nitrogen pressurised standby systems for emergency extension. Parker Bertea wheels and multi-disc hydraulic carbon brakes.

POWER PLANT: Two Allison T406-AD-400 (501-M80C) turboshafts, each with T-O and intermediate rating of 4,586 kW (6,150 shp) and max continuous rating of 4,392 kW (5,890 shp), installed in Bell built tilting nacelles at wingtips. Each nacelle has GFRP cowling panels and pylon support structures, and a Garrett infra-red emission suppressor at the rear. Air particle separator and Lucas inlet/spinner ice protection system for each engine. Lucas Aerospace full authority digital engine control (FADEC) for each engine, with analog electronic backup control. Pratt & Whitney originally named as second production source for engines, starting with production lot 5. Internal fuel (JP-5) in up to 13 crash resistant, self-sealing (nitrogen pressurised) cells: one 1,431 kg (3,155 lb) forward cell in each sponson, a 925 kg (2,040 lb) cell in rear of starboard sponson, four 227 kg (500 lb) auxiliary cells in each wing leading-edge, and a 306 kg (675 lb) engine feed cell outboard of the auxiliary tanks in each wing. Total capacity 7,627 litres (2,015 US gallons; 1,678 Imp gallons). (Not all versions have all tanks.) Pressure refuelling point in starboard sponson leading-edge; gravity point in upper surface of each wing. Simmonds fuel management system. Provision for a further 7,427 kg (16,374 lb) of fuel to be carried in four additional joint services auxiliary fuel tanks, each 2,279 litres (602 US gallons; 501 Imp gallons), in main cabin for self-deployment mission. In-flight refuelling probe in lower starboard side of forward fuselage.

ACCOMMODATION: Normal crew complement of pilot (in starboard seat), co-pilot and crew chief in USMC variant. Flight crew accommodated on Simula Inc crashworthy armoured seats capable of withstanding strikes from 0.30 in armour piercing ammunition, 30*g* forward and 14.5*g* vertical decelerations. Seats are manufactured from a boron carbide/polyethylene laminate. Flight deck has overhead and knee-level side transparencies in addition to large windscreen and main side windows, plus an overhead rearview mirror. Main window frame is of titanium. Main cabin has composites floor panels, and can accommodate up to 24 combat-equipped troops, on inward facing crashworthy foldaway seats, plus two gunners; up to 12 litters plus medical attendants; or an equivalent cargo load with energy absorbing tiedowns. Cargo handling provisions include a 907 kg (2,000 lb) capacity cargo winch and pulley system and removable roller rails. Main cabin door at front on starboard side, top portion of which opens upward and inward, lower portion (with built-in steps) downward and outward. Full width rear loading ramp/door in underside of rear fuselage, operated by Parker Bertea hydraulic actuators. Emergency exit windows on port side; escape hatch in fuselage roof aft of wing.

SYSTEMS: Environmental control system, utilising engine bleed air; control unit in rear of port main landing gear sponson. Three hydraulic systems (two independent main systems and one standby), all at operating pressure of 345 bars (5,000 lb/sq in), with Parker Bertea reservoirs. Electrical power supplied by two 40kVA constant frequency AC generators, two 50/80kVA variable frequency DC generators (one driven by APU), rectifiers, and a 15Ah battery. GE Aerospace triple redundant digital fly-by-wire flight control system, incorporating triple primary FCS (PFCS) and triple automatic FCS (AFCS) processors, and triple flight control computers (FCC) each linked to a MIL-STD-1553B databus; two PFCSs and one AFCS are fail-operational. FBW system signals hydraulic actuation of flaperons, elevator and rudders, controls aircraft transition between helicopter and aeroplane modes, and can be programmed for automatic management of airspeed, nacelle tilting and angle of attack. FCCs provide interfaces for swashplate, conversion actuator, flaperon, elevator, rudder and pylon primary actuators, flight deck central drive, force feel, and nosewheel steering. Dual 1750A processors for PFCS and single 1750A for AFCS incorporated in each FCC. Non-redundant standby analog computer (in development aircraft only) provides control of aircraft, including FADEC and pylon actuation, in the event of FBW system failure. Sundstrand Turbomach 261 kW (350 shp) APU, in rear portion of wing centre-section, provides power for mid-wing gearbox which, in turn, drives two electrical generators and an air compressor. Anti-icing of windscreens and engine air intakes; de-icing of proprotors and spinners. Clifton Precision combined oxygen (OBOGS) and nitrogen (OBIGGS) generating systems for cabin and fuel tank pressurisation respectively. Systron Donner pneumatic fire protection systems for engines, APU and wing dry bays.

AVIONICS: VHF/AM-FM, HF/SSB and (USAF only) UHF secure voice com; Tacan, VOR/ILS, AHRS, radar altimeter and digital map displays; IFF; Honeywell AN/AAR-47 missile warning system; radar/infra-red warning system; J.E.T. ADI-350W standby attitude indicator; Aydin Vector data acquisition and storage system. Major tactical sensors are a Hughes Aircraft AN/AAQ-16 FLIR detector in undernose fairing and (USAF and USN only) a Texas Instruments AN/APQ-174 terrain following multifunction radar in offset (to port) nose thimble, with two Allied Signal IP-1555 full colour multifunction displays. Two Control Data AN/AYK-14 mission computers, with Boeing/IBM software. Pilots' night vision system and Honeywell integrated helmet display system.

EQUIPMENT: Chaff/flare dispensers. Provision for rescue hoist over forward (starboard) cabin door.

MV-22 development aircraft (prototype No. 4) in forward flight

DIMENSIONS, EXTERNAL:

Rotor diameter, each 11.58 m (38 ft 0 in)
Rotor blade chord: at root 0.90 m (2 ft 11½ in)
at tip 0.56 m (1 ft 10 in)
Wing span: excl nacelles 14.02 m (46 ft 0 in)
incl nacelles 15.52 m (50 ft 11 in)
Wing chord, constant 2.54 m (8 ft 4 in)
Distance between proprotor centres 14.25 m (46 ft 9 in)
Width: overall, rotors turning 25.78 m (84 ft 7 in)
folded 5.61 m (18 ft 5 in)
Length: fuselage, excl probe 17.47 m (57 ft 4 in)
overall, wings stowed/blades folded 19.09 m (62 ft 7½ in)
Height: over tail fins 5.28 m (17 ft 4 in)
wings stowed/blades folded 5.51 m (18 ft 1 in)
overall, nacelles vertical 6.90 m (22 ft 7½ in)
Nacelle ground clearance, nacelles vertical 1.31 m (4 ft 3¾ in)
Proprotor ground clearance, nacelles vertical 6.35 m (20 ft 10 in)
Tail span, over fins 5.61 m (18 ft 5 in)
Wheel track (c/l of outer mainwheels) 4.62 m (15 ft 2 in)
Wheelbase 6.59 m (21 ft 7½ in)
Dorsal escape hatch: Length 1.02 m (3 ft 4 in)
Width 0.74 m (2 ft 5 in)

DIMENSIONS, INTERNAL:

Cabin: Length 7.37 m (24 ft 2 in)
Max width 1.80 m (5 ft 11 in)
Max height 1.83 m (6 ft 0 in)
Usable volume 24.3 m^3 (858 cu ft)

AREAS:

Rotor discs, each 105.4 m^2 (1,134 sq ft)
Rotor blades (each) 12.15 m^2 (130.76 sq ft)
Wing, total incl flaperons and fuselage centre section 35.49 m^2 (382.0 sq ft)
Flaperons, total 8.25 m^2 (88.8 sq ft)
Tailplane 8.22 m^2 (88.5 sq ft)
Elevators, total 4.79 m^2 (51.54 sq ft)
Fins (each) 10.81 m^2 (116.4 sq ft)
Rudders (each) 1.64 m^2 (17.6 sq ft)

WEIGHTS AND LOADINGS:

Weight empty, equipped 14,463 kg (31,886 lb)
Max fuel weight: standard 6,215 kg (13,700 lb)
with self-ferry cabin tanks 13,641 kg (30,074 lb)
Max internal payload (cargo) 9,072 kg (20,000 lb)
Cargo hook capacity: single 4,536 kg (10,000 lb)
two hooks (combined weight) 6,804 kg (15,000 lb)
Rescue hoist capacity 272 kg (600 lb)
Normal mission T-O weight: VTO 21,545 kg (47,500 lb)
STO 24,947 kg (55,000 lb)
Max STO weight for self-ferry 27,442 kg (60,500 lb)
Max cabin floor loading (cargo) 1,464 kg/m^2 (300 lb/sq ft)
Max power loading 8.06 kg/kW (13.23 lb/shp)

PERFORMANCE (estimated):

Max cruising speed: at S/L, helicopter mode 100 knots (185 km/h; 115 mph)
at S/L, aeroplane mode 275 knots (509 km/h; 316 mph)
at optimum altitude, aeroplane mode 314 knots (582 km/h; 361 mph)
Max forward speed with max slung load 130 knots (241 km/h; 150 mph)
Service ceiling 7,925 m (26,000 ft)
T-O run at normal mission STO weight less than 152 m (500 ft)
Range:
VTO at 21,146 kg (46,619 lb) gross weight, incl 5,443 kg (12,000 lb) payload 1,200 nm (2,224 km; 1,382 miles)
STO at 24,947 kg (55,000 lb) gross weight, incl 9,072 kg (20,000 lb) payload 1,800 nm (3,336 km; 2,073 miles)
STO at 27,442 kg (60,500 lb) self-ferry gross weight, no payload 2,100 nm (3,892 km; 2,418 miles)

BOEING
THE BOEING COMPANY
PO Box 3707, Seattle, Washington 98124
Telephone: 1 (206) 655 2121
Fax: 1 (206) 655 1171
Telex: 329430
CHAIRMAN AND CHIEF EXECUTIVE OFFICER:
Frank A. Shrontz
Company founded July 1916. On 2 January 1990, Boeing Defense & Space Group (B. Dan Pinick, President) formed

to co-ordinate the Aerospace & Electronics, Helicopters, Military Airplanes and Advanced Systems divisions of The Boeing Company. Simultaneously, the former Military Airplanes divisions at Wichita reduced in size by the transfer of some activities to Boeing Commercial Airplane Group. Wichita now subsidiary of reorganised Military Airplanes division based in Seattle and absorbing Advanced Systems.

Operating components of The Boeing Company include:

BOEING DEFENSE & SPACE GROUP
Boeing Aerospace & Electronics
See next entry
Boeing Helicopters
Follows Boeing Aerospace & Electronics
Boeing Military Airplanes
Follows Boeing Helicopters
BOEING COMMERCIAL AIRPLANE GROUP
Follows Boeing Military Airplanes

BOEING AEROSPACE & ELECTRONICS
PO Box 3999, Seattle, Washington 98124
Telephone: 1 (206) 773 2121
Telex: 329430
PRESIDENT: B. Dan Pinick
EXECUTIVE VICE-PRESIDENT: John Sheridan
Boeing Aerospace & Electronics formed 1 May 1989 from Boeing Aerospace and Boeing Electronics divisions: headquarters at space centre at Kent, Washington. Four major divisions: Electronic Systems; Missile Systems; Space Systems; Huntsville. Subsidiaries: Boeing Aerospace & Electronics in Irving (Texas), Corinth (Texas) and Tennessee; UTL; Boeing Aerospace Electronics; Boeing Agri-Industrial Company; Boeing Technical Operations; Boeing Technical and Management Services; Boeing Petroleum Services. Major programme activities: airborne warning and control; E-6 Tacamo; participation in ATF programme (see entry for Lockheed F-22A); Inertial Upper Stage rocket motor for Space Shuttle; Minuteman ICBM; Peacekeeper ICBM ground support system; SRAM II air-launched attack missile; Avenger air defence system. Approx 20,000 employees.

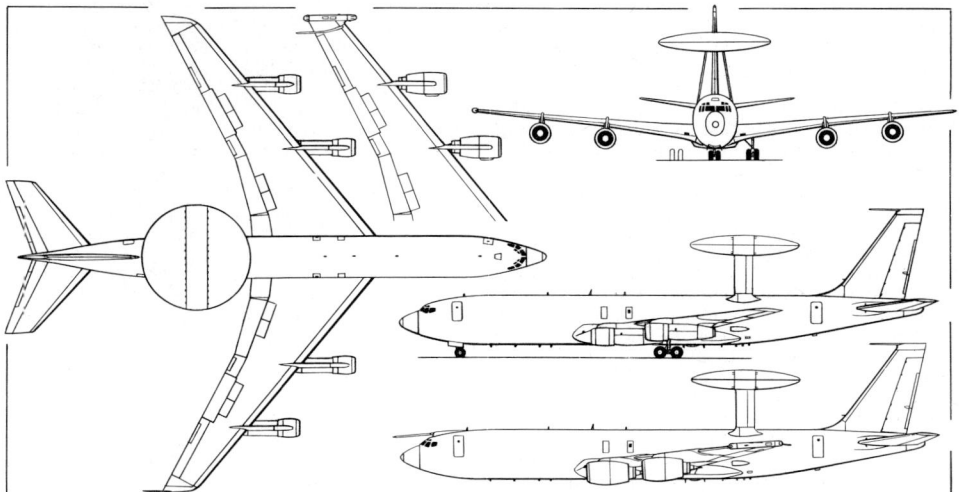

Boeing E-3A Sentry with lower side view and wing scrap view of Royal Air Force E-3D Sentry AEW. Mk 1 *(Pilot Press)*

BOEING E-3 SENTRY
TYPE: Mobile, flexible, survivable, jamming resistant, high capacity radar station and command, control and communications centre; Airborne Warning and Control System (AWACS).
PROGRAMME: Two prototype EC-137Ds used to test competing radars; Westinghouse selected; full-scale development completed 1976. USAF received 34 E-3s by June 1984, including two prototypes.
First production E-3A delivered to 552nd Airborne Warning and Control Wing, Tactical Air Command, at Tinker AFB, Oklahoma, on 24 March 1977; initial operational capability (IOC) April 1978. At various times, E-3s deployed to Iceland, Germany, Saudi Arabia (Detachment Elf One), Sudan, the Mediterranean area, South West Asia and the Pacific and in support of drug enforcement programme. E-3As began to work with NORAD continental air defence on 1 January 1979.
The 552nd Wing has three AWACS squadrons and supporting units. Overseas units include the 960th, 961st and 962nd AWAC squadrons based respectively at NAS Keflavik, Iceland, Kadena AB, Okinawa, Japan, and Elmendorf, Alaska, providing command and control capability to CINCLANT (through Commander, Iceland Defence Force) and CINCPAC.
VARIANTS: **Core E-3A:** Initial standard of 23 production USAF Sentries. Equipment detailed in 1987-88 *Jane's*.
E-3B: Block 20 modification updated two EC-137Ds and 22 USAF Core E-3As to E-3B standard by adding ECM-resistant voice communications, a third HF and five more UHF radios (making 12), faster IBM CC-2 computer with larger memory, five more SDCs (making 14), Westinghouse austere maritime surveillance capability to main radar, provision for Have Quick anti-jamming in UHF radios, self-defence, and radio teletype. First E-3B re-delivered to USAF 18 July 1984; remaining 23 modified with Boeing kits at Tinker AFB. Under Project Snappy, unspecified sensor installed in seven USAF E-3B/Cs by January 1991 for participation in Gulf War; eight further aircraft modified.

US/NATO Standard E-3A: Original standard for USAF aircraft Nos. 26 to 34 of which deliveries began December 1981, and of updated aircraft No. 3. Additions include full maritime surveillance capability, CC-2 computer, additional HF radios, ECM-resistant voice communications, radio teletype, provision for self defence, and ECM. Eighteen NATO E-3As are to this standard.
E-3C: USAF Block 25 modification of 10 USAF E-3As began 1984. Adds five more SDCs, five more UHF radios, and provision for Have Quick anti-jamming.
KE-3A, E-3D and E-3F: See Customers.
Other upgrades: USAF Electronic Systems Division proposed $425 million MSIP over five years for E-3s, adding improved radar detection, passive sensors and other features.
All USAF, NATO and RAF E-3s will in future have Joint Tactical Information Distribution System (JTIDS).
In May 1987, Boeing received $241.5 million USAF contract for full-scale development and integration into USAF and NATO E-3s of an ESM system to detect signals from hostile and friendly targets.
Block 30/35 programme additionally provides USAF E-3s with Radar System Improvement Programme (RSIP), upgrading of JTIDS to Tactical Digital Information Link-J (TADIL-J), CC-2 computer memory upgrade with VLSI circuitry and bubble memory and ability to use Global Positioning System (GPS). Planned initial operational capability for Block 30/35 is 1993.
All aircraft from No. 25 have a hardpoint for stores under each inner wing.
In 1989, Westinghouse awarded development contract for upgrading AN/APY-1/2 radars of USAF E-3s with new processors, displays and pulse compression to double performance against small targets like cruise

missiles. If successful, this will be applied to all 34 E-3B/Cs from 1994 onwards. In 1989, Boeing authorised to retrofit Have Quick A-NETS.

CUSTOMERS: Total of 68 ordered (USAF 34, NATO 18, Saudi Arabia five, UK seven, France four); 59 delivered by March 1991. First NATO production E-3A flew at Renton 18 December 1980 and delivered to system integrator Dornier at Oberpfaffenhofen 19 March 1981; all 18 delivered to NATO between 22 January 1982 and 25 April 1985. NATO E-3As assigned to Nos. 1, 2 and 3 Squadrons and Training Centre of E-3A component, NATO Airborne Early Warning Force, based at Geilenkirchen, Germany. Up to six NATO E-3As detached to forward operating locations (FOL) at Konya (Turkey), Previza (Greece), Trapani/Birgi (Italy) and Ørland (Norway). NAEWF has NATO Command status and is staffed by personnel from Belgium, Canada, Denmark, Greece, Italy, the Netherlands, Norway, Portugal, Turkey and USA, plus non-aircrew personnel from Luxembourg. ESM systems upgrade under way for 1995 completion. Seven-year E-3A modernisation plan agreed June 1990, subject to funding.
Sale of five E-3s to Royal Saudi Air Force approved October 1981 under **Peace Sentinel** programme: also included six **KE-3A** tanker/transports (increased to eight in 1984: see KC-135R entry, page 371). Selected CFM56-2A-2 with Hispano Suiza thrust reversers for E-3s in 1984. First E-3 handed over 30 June 1986; all 13 E-3s and KE-3s delivered by 24 September 1987.
British Government announced order for six E-3D, designated **E-3D Sentry AEW. Mk 1**, 18 December 1986 and exercised option for seventh in October 1987. CFM56-2A-3 power plants. First flight E-3D (ZH101) September 1989; first flight fully equipped 5 January

Boeing E-3D Sentry AEW. Mk 1 of the Royal Air Force escorted by a Tornado F. Mk 3

1990; flown to UK on 3 November 1990 after combined British-French airworthiness certification and in-flight refuelling trials. Second aircraft (ZH102) flown to Waddington 4 July 1990 for fitting out by a consortium led by British Aerospace (which see) and handed over to RAF as first receipt, 26 March 1991. Final UK E-3D (ZH107), the last airframe of the Boeing 707 family, to be rolled out May 1991 and delivered to RAF March 1992. Sentry Training Squadron formed at Waddington 1 June 1990. No. 8 Squadron, RAF, formed with E-3Ds at Waddington on 1 July 1991. RAF aircraft are E-3D component, NAEWF. Boeing giving UK 130 per cent industrial offset.

France ordered three **E-3Fs**, with CFM56-2A-3 power plants, February 1987; fourth aircraft ordered 1987, but options for two more dropped August 1988. First (No. 201) flown 27 June 1990; delivered UTA Industries at Le Bourget for fitting-out 10 October 1990; to Avord for integration trials and hand-over 19 December 1990; official delivery to CEAM for military acceptance, 22 May 1991. Delivery of remaining E-3Fs due July, September and November 1991. 36e Escadre de Détection Aéroportée formed at Avord 1 March 1990 as operating wing of two squadrons. Boeing giving France 130 per cent industrial offset.

COSTS: $129 million, flyaway, NATO 1982; $222 million programme unit cost, UK 1987; France $254 million, 1987. NATO ESM upgrade $230 million (1990); NATO E-3A modernisation $700 million (1990). E-3D programme cost $1.3 billion (1987); E-3F programme cost $550 million (1987).

DESIGN FEATURES: Construction details of the E-3 appeared in 1987-88 and earlier *Jane's*. Details below refer to USAF E-3s except where indicated:

FLYING CONTROLS: Essentially as for Boeing 707 family.

STRUCTURE: RAF aircraft have additional wing stringers outboard of outer engines because of wingtip pods and trailing-edge HF antennae.

POWER PLANT: Four Pratt & Whitney TF33-PW-100/100A turbofans, each rated at 93.4 kN (21,000 lb st), mounted in pods beneath the wings. Fuel contained in integral wing tanks. Usable fuel 90,528 litres (23,915 US gallons; 19,913 Imp gallons). Provision for in-flight refuelling, with receptacle for boom over flight deck. Four 106.8 kN (24,000 lb st) CFM56-2A-2/3 turbofans on French, Saudi and UK aircraft. SOGERMA in-flight refuelling probe on E-3D and E-3F (in addition to receptacle).

ACCOMMODATION: Basic operational crew of 17 includes a flight crew complement of four plus 13 AWACS specialists, though this latter number can vary for tactical and defence missions. Full crew complement is two pilots, navigator, flight engineer, tactical director, fighter allocator, two weapons controllers, surveillance controller, link manager, three surveillance operators, communications operator, radar technician, communications technician and computer display technician. Aft of flight deck, from front to rear of fuselage, are communications, data processing and other equipment bays; multi-purpose consoles; communications, navigation and identification equipment; and crew rest area, galley and parachute storage rack.

SYSTEMS: A liquid cooling system provides protection for the radar transmitter. An air cycle pack system, a draw-through system, and two closed loop ram-cooled environmental control systems ensure a suitable environment for crew and avionics equipment. Electrical power generation has a 600kVA capability. Distribution centre for mission equipment power and remote avionics in lower forward cargo compartment. Rear cargo compartment houses radar transmitter and an APU. External sockets allow intake of power when aircraft is on ground. Two separate and independent hydraulic systems

power essential flight and mission equipment, but either system can satisfy requirements of both equipment groups in an emergency.

AVIONICS: Elliptical cross-section rotodome of 9.14 m (30 ft) diameter and 1.83 m (6 ft) max depth, mounted 3.35 m (11 ft) above fuselage, comprises four essential elements: a turntable, strut mounted above rear fuselage, supporting rotary joint assembly to which are attached sliprings for electrical and waveguide continuity between rotodome and fuselage; structural centre-section of aluminium skin and stiffener supporting the Westinghouse AN/APY-1 surveillance radar (AN/APY-2 from No. 25 onwards, and in all export E-3s) and IFF/TADIL-C antennae, radomes, auxiliary equipment for radar operation and environmental control of the rotodome interior; liquid cooling of the radar antennae; and two radomes of multi-layer glassfibre sandwich material, one for surveillance radar and one for IFF/TADIL-C array. For surveillance operations rotodome is hydraulically driven at 6 rpm, but during non-operational flights it is rotated at only ¼ rpm, to keep bearings lubricated. Radar operates in E/F-band and can function as both a pulse and/or a pulse Doppler radar for detection of aircraft targets. A similar pulse radar mode with additional pulse compression and sea clutter adaptive processing is used to detect maritime/ship traffic. Radar is operable in six modes: PDNES (pulse Doppler non-elevation scan), when range is paramount to elevation data; PDES (pulse Doppler elevation scan), providing elevation data with some loss of range; BTH (beyond the horizon), giving long-range detection with no elevation data; Maritime, for detection of surface vessels in various sea states; Interleaved, combining available modes for all-altitude longer-range aircraft detection, or for both aircraft and ship detection; and Passive, which tracks enemy ECM sources without transmission-induced vulnerability. Radar antennae, spanning about 7.32 m (24 ft), and 1.52 m (5 ft) deep, scan mechanically in azimuth, and electronically from ground level up into the stratosphere. Heart of the data processing capability of the first 24 aircraft in their original core E-3A form is an IBM 4 Pi CC-1 high-speed computer (see 1987-88 *Jane's* for details). From 25th aircraft, the new and improved IBM CC-2 computer was installed from the start, with a main storage capacity of 665,360 words. Data display and control are provided by Hazeltine high resolution colour situation display consoles (SDC) and auxiliary display units (ADU). The E-3B carries 14 SDCs and two ADUs. Navigation/guidance relies upon two Delco AN/ASN-119 Carousel IV inertial navigation platforms, a Northrop AN/ARN-120 Omega set which continuously updates the inertial platforms, and a Teledyne Ryan AN/APN-213 Doppler velocity sensor to provide airspeed and drift information. Communications equipment provides HF, VHF and UHF channels through which information can be transmitted or received in clear or secure mode, in voice or digital form. A Bendix/King weather radar is carried in the nose. Identification is based on an Eaton (AIL) AN/APX-103 interrogator set which is the first airborne IFF interrogator to offer complete AIMS Mk X SIF air traffic control and Mk XII military identification friend or foe (IFF) in a single integrated system. Simultaneous Mk X and Mk XII multi-target and multi-mode operations allow the operator to obtain instantaneously the range, azimuth and elevation, code identification, and IFF status, of all targets within radar range. NATO E-3As carry, and USAF aircraft have provisions for, a radio teletype. All aircraft from No. 25 have an inboard underwing hardpoint on each side. There is no current requirement for either USAF or NATO AWACS to carry weapons; but on NATO E-3As these hardpoints can be

used to mount additional podded items of ECM equipment. E-3Ds carry Loral 1017 'Yellow Gate' ESM pods at the wingtips.

DIMENSIONS, EXTERNAL:

Wing span: normal	44.42 m (145 ft 9 in)
E-3D	44.98 m (147 ft 7 in)
Length overall	46.61 m (152 ft 11 in)
Height overall	12.73 m (41 ft 9 in)

WEIGHTS AND LOADINGS (E-3D):

Fuel weight (JP4)	70,510 kg (155,448 lb)
Normal T-O weight	147,417 kg (325,000 lb)
Max T-O weight	150,820 kg (332,500 lb)
Max ramp weight	151,953 kg (335,000 lb)

PERFORMANCE:

Max level speed	460 knots (853 km/h; 530 mph)
Service ceiling: TF33	over 8,850 m (29,000 ft)
CFM56	over 9,145 m (30,000 ft)
Endurance on station, 870 nm (1,610 km; 1,000 miles) from base	6 h
Max unrefuelled endurance: TF33	more than 11 h
CFM56	more than 10 h

BOEING E-6A TACAMO II

TYPE: Long endurance communications relay aircraft carrying US Navy airborne very low frequency (AVLF) system.

PROGRAMME: US Navy contract placed with Boeing Aerospace 29 April 1983 to replace EC-130Q Hercules TACAMO (take charge and move out); first full test flight of prototype (162782) 1 June 1987: two production E-6As ordered FY 1986; three, three and seven production E-6As ordered in FYs 1987-89, making 16; first two delivered to VQ-3 squadron, Barber's Point, Hawaii, 2 August 1989; VQ-3 withdrew last C-130 in August 1990, having eight E-6As for Pacific area; VQ-4 assigned seven at Patuxent River, Maryland, for Atlantic area; first of these delivered January 1991. By early 1991, continuous TACAMO airborne alert terminated; both squadrons to transfer to Tinker AFB, Oklahoma, in June 1992.

CUSTOMERS: US Navy 16, of which 10 delivered by May 1991.

DESIGN FEATURES: Substantially as for USAF E-3, but powered by four CFM International turbofans.

FLYING CONTROLS: Substantially as for E-3. Boeing contract 1991 to Bendix to develop digital AFCS.

STRUCTURE: 75 per cent common with E-3, including EMP nuclear hardening; radome support structure deleted. Additions include wingtip ESM/Satcom pods and HF antenna fairings, increased corrosion protection, forward freight door of 707-320C. Local strengthening to overcome stresses caused by banked orbit with antenna deployed: flap guide vanes modified; three minor changes to be made to cure tail fin flutter.

POWER PLANT: Four 106.76 kN (24,000 lb st) CFM International F108-CF-100 (CFM56-2A-2) turbofans in individual underwing pods, as on some export E-3s. Fuel contained in integral tanks in wings, with single-point refuelling. In-flight refuelling via boom receptacle above flight deck.

ACCOMMODATION: Basic militarised interior sidewalls, ceilings and lighting are similar to those of the E-3A. Interior divided into three main functional areas: forward of wings (flight deck and crew rest area), overwing (five-man mission crew), and aft of wings (equipment). Forward crew area, 50 per cent common with that of E-3A, accommodates a four-man crew on flight deck. Compartment immediately aft contains dining, toilet, and eight-bunk rest area for spare crew carried on extended or remote deployment missions. Crew enter by ladder and hatch in floor of this compartment. Overwing compartment with communications and other consoles,

Boeing E-6A TACAMO II prototype pictured during flight testing over Puget Sound, in Washington State

their operators, and an airborne communications officer (ACO). To the rear is compartment containing R/T racks, transmitters, trailing wire antennae and their reels. Bale-out door at rear on starboard side.

SYSTEMS: Some 75 per cent of the E-6A's systems are the same as the E-3. Among those retained are the liquid cooling system for the transmitters, 'draw-through' cooling system for other avionics, the 600kVA electrical power generation system, APU, liquid oxygen system, and MIL specification hydraulic oil.

AVIONICS: Three Collins AN/ARC-182 VHF/UHF com transceivers, all with secure voice capability; five Collins AN/ARC-190 HF com (one transceiver, one receive only); and Hughes Aircraft AN/AIC-32 crew intercom with secure voice capability. External aerials for Satcom UHF reception in each wingtip pod; fairings beneath each pod house antenna for standard HF reception. Navigation by triplex Litton LTN-90 ring laser gyro-based inertial reference system integrated with a Litton LTN-211 VLF/Omega system and duplex Smiths Industries SFM 102 digital/analog flight management computer system (FMCS). Bendix/King AN/APS-133 colour weather radar, in nosecone, with capability for short-range terrain mapping, tanker beacon homing, and waypoint display. Honeywell AN/APN-222 high/low-range (0-15,240 m; 0-50,000 ft) radio altimeter, and Collins low-range (0-762 m; 0-2,500 ft) radio altimeter, with ILS and GPWS. General Instrument AN/ALR-66(V)4 electronic support measures (ESM), in each wingtip pod, provide information on threat detection, identification, bearing and approximate range. In overwing compartment, overseen by ACO, is a new communications central console, which incorporates ERCS (emergency rocket communications system) receivers, cryptographic equipment, new teletypes, tape recorders, and other communications equipment, all hardened against electro-magnetic interference. In each operational area the E-6A links upward with airborne command posts and the Presidential E-4, to satellites, and to the ERCS; and downward to VLF ground stations and the SSBN fleet. Mean time between failures of complete mission avionics is less than 20 h, but the E-6 is able to carry spares, and a spare crew, to permit extended missions of up to 72 h with in-flight refuelling, and/or deployment to remote bases, where it is capable of autonomous operation.

EQUIPMENT: Main VLF antenna is a 7,925 m (26,000 ft) long trailing wire aerial (LTWA), with a 41 kg (90 lb) drogue at the end, which is reeled out from the middle part of the rear cabin compartment through an opening in the cabin floor. The LTWA, with its drogue, weighs about 495 kg (1,090 lb) and creates some 907 kg (2,000 lb) of drag when fully deployed. Acting as a dipole is a much shorter (1,220 m; 4,000 ft) trailing wire (STWA), winched out from beneath the tailcone. At patrol altitude, with the LTWA deployed, the aircraft enters a tight orbit and the wire stalls, causing it to be almost vertical (70 per cent verticality is required for effective sub-sea communications). Signals transmitted through the trailing wire antennae use 200kW of power, and can be received by submerged SSBNs via a towed buoyant wire antenna.

ARMAMENT: None.

DIMENSIONS, EXTERNAL:
Wing span	45.16 m (148 ft 2 in)
Length overall	46.61 m (152 ft 11 in)
Height overall	12.93 m (42 ft 5 in)
Wheel track	6.73 m (22 ft 1 in)
Wheelbase	17.98 m (59 ft 0 in)
Forward cargo door: Height	2.34 m (7 ft 8 in)
Width	3.40 m (11 ft 2 in)
Height to sill	3.20 m (10 ft 6 in)

AREAS:
Wings, gross	283.4 m² (3,050.0 sq ft)

WEIGHTS AND LOADINGS:
Operating weight empty	78,378 kg (172,795 lb)
Max fuel	70,305 kg (155,000 lb)

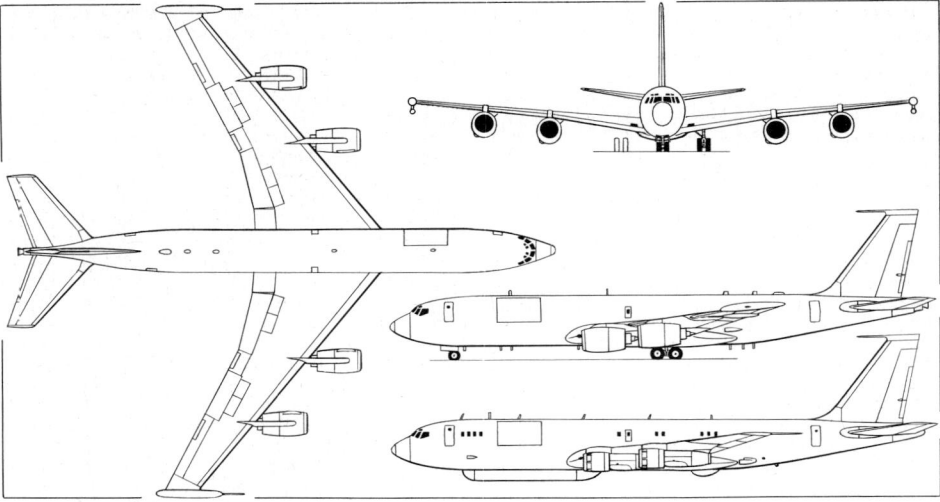

Boeing E-6A TACAMO II, with additional side view (lower) of E-8A J-STARS *(Pilot Press)*

Max T-O weight	155,128 kg (342,000 lb)
Max wing loading	547.4 kg/m² (112.13 lb/sq ft)
Max power loading	363.26 kg/kN (3.56 lb/lb st)

PERFORMANCE (S/L, ISA, estimated):
Dash speed	530 knots (981 km/h; 610 mph)
Cruising speed at 12,200 m (40,000 ft)	
	455 knots (842 km/h; 523 mph)
Patrol altitude	7,620-9,150 m (25,000-30,000 ft)
Service ceiling	12,800 m (42,000 ft)
Critical field length	2,042 m (6,700 ft)
Max effort T-O run	1,646 m (5,400 ft)
Max effort T-O run with fuel for 2,500 nm (4,630 km; 2,875 miles)	732 m (2,400 ft)
Landing run at max landing weight	793 m (2,600 ft)
Mission range, unrefuelled	
	6,350 nm (11,760 km; 7,307 miles)
Endurance: unrefuelled	15 h 24 min
on-station, 1,000 nm (1,850 km; 1,150 miles) from T-O	10 h 30 min
with one refuelling	28 h 54 min
with multiple refuelling	72 h

BOEING 767 AIRBORNE SURVEILLANCE TESTBED

Formerly US Army Airborne Optical Adjunct (AOA). Details appeared in 1990-91 *Jane's*. Testing of complete system began May 1990, following installation of the sensor earlier in the year. After test missions from Seattle, aircraft flew to US Army test site at Kwajalein Atoll, in the Pacific, for sensor tests, successfully conducted in late Summer, against inert ICBM warheads.

BOEING (LOCKHEED) P-3C UPDATE IV

TYPE: New ASW system for US Navy P-3 maritime aircraft.

PROGRAMME: Boeing won contract to develop Update IV system against Lockheed; contract placed 10 July 1987; P-3C Orion to Boeing for modification August 1987; to be re-delivered to US Naval Air Test Center, Patuxent River, mid-1992; plan to retrofit 109 P-3C Update I and II; Update IV was also destined for 125 P-7A LRAACA, since cancelled.

CUSTOMERS: US Navy.

BOEING/GRUMMAN E-8 (J-STARS)

TYPE: US Air Force/Army Joint Surveillance and Target Attack Radar System.

PROGRAMME: Grumman received full-scale development contract 27 September 1985; two former American Airlines Boeing 707-323Cs selected as EC-18C testbeds, later re-designated E-8A; first aircraft for modification reached Boeing Military Airplanes, Wichita, January 1986; delivered to Grumman Melbourne Systems Division 31 July 1987; second aircraft to Wichita June 1986 for delivery to Grumman Autumn 1988; first flight full J-STARS configuration (N770JS/86-0416) 22 December 1988; first flight second aircraft (N8411/86-0417) 31 August 1989; first instantaneous transmission to ground station August 1989; European trials February/March 1990 (N770JS) and September 1990 (86-0417); production decision on 22 aircraft and 100 ground stations expected early 1992; official initial operational capability (IOC) expected 1997, but interim capability achieved when two E-8As deployed to Saudi Arabia for Gulf War against Iraq, flying first mission with 4411th J-STARS Squadron, USAF (Provisional) 14 January 1991.

CUSTOMERS: US Air Force and US Army.

COSTS: $657 million (1985) full-scale development; $523 million award to Grumman, 1990, for conversion of third aircraft. $8,210 million (1990) complete programme (including ground stations).

DESIGN FEATURES: Two **E-8A** development aircraft are ex-American Airlines Boeing 707-323Cs. Third aircraft, also ex-civilian, designated **E-8B**. Because 707/C-18 production is to end, E-8 production aircraft (to have been based on E-6A TACAMO II airframe with F108 turbofans) will be designated **E-8C** and use re-engined second-hand 707 airframes.

Norden multi-mode side-looking radar with antenna in 9.1 m (30 ft) long canoe fairing under forward fuselage, offset to starboard. Synthetic aperture (SAR) mode used to detect stationary objects such as parked tanks up to 81-95 nm (150-175 km; 93-109 miles) behind front line, or can alternate between SAR and Doppler to locate slow-moving targets. Coverage, 1,000,000 km² (386,100 sq miles) in 8 h sortie, cruising at 9,145-12,200 m (30,000-40,000 ft). Radar can be instantaneously transmitted to ground stations, or attacks can be directed via Joint Tactical Information Distribution System (JTIDS). Two prototypes have 10 crew workstations; E-8B has 15; E-8C, 18.

BOEING HELICOPTERS

Boeing Centre, PO Box 16858, Philadelphia, Pennsylvania 19142

Telephone: 1 (215) 591 2121
Fax: 1 (215) 3873
Telex: 510 669 2217 BOEMORA MOR

PRESIDENT AND GENERAL MANAGER: Edward J. Renouard

VICE-PRESIDENT, RESEARCH AND ENGINEERING: John Diamond

DIRECTOR, COMMUNICATIONS: Robert Torgerson

Vertol Aircraft Corporation (formerly Piasecki Helicopter Corporation) purchased in 1960, becoming Vertol Division of Boeing; now Boeing Helicopters. Produced more than 2,500 tandem-rotor helicopters for US military services and export. Main production programme, modernisation of early CH-47s to CH-47D for US Army. Production of H-46 Sea Knight SR&M improvement kits for US Navy and Marine Corps completed January 1989.

Boeing Helicopters teamed with Bell Helicopter Textron in V-22 Osprey programme (see Bell/Boeing entry). Formed First Team with Sikorsky Aircraft 3 June 1985 to compete for US Army LH (RAH-66 Comanche) light helicopter,

with Boeing Military Airplanes integrating avionics; declared competition winner in April 1991 (see under separate Boeing/Sikorsky entry for details). All-composite rotor blade for Bell UH-1H developed for US Army; first blade delivered June 1989 to Army Engineering Flight Agency for interchangeability check with Bell-produced blade.

Boeing Helicopters produces fixed leading-edge components for Boeing 737/747/757/767 and metal leading-edge slats for 757.

Workforce 6,150 in early 1991. Manufacturing plant at Ridley Township, Pennsylvania has 325,150 m² (3,500,000 sq ft) of covered floor space; flight test centre at Greater Wilmington, Delaware, has 8,565 m² (92,200 sq ft). An 11,055 m² (119,000 sq ft) development facility and 17,466 m² (188,000 sq ft) office/computer centre added at Ridley Township early 1987.

BOEING MODEL 107
USN and USMC designations: CH-46/UH-46 Sea Knight

TYPE: Tandem-rotor, twin-turbine transport helicopter.

PROGRAMME: USN and USMC planning dynamic system upgrade of all H-46s in five-year programme. Total 261 CH/HH-46s remain with USMC plus 81 HH/UH-46s with US Navy.

DESIGN FEATURES: Details of previous H-46 upgrades given in 1989-90 and earlier *Jane's*. Rapid Emergency Flotation System (REFS) developed 1985 and fitted 1990-91; increased fuel capacity kits developed for 49 USMC H-46Es; AN/APN-217 Doppler navigation system for Marine Corps CH-46E contracted March 1990 (two dem/val kits); flight testing due to begin March 1991.

BOEING MODELS 114 and 414
US Army designation: CH-47 Chinook
Canadian Forces designation: CH-147
Royal Air Force designation: Chinook HC. Mk 1/2
Spanish Army designation: HT.17

TYPE: Tandem-rotor, twin-turbine transport helicopter.

PROGRAMME: Design of all-weather medium transport helicopter for US Army began 1956; first flight of first of five YCH-47As 21 September 1961; for details of

CH-47A (354 built for US Army) and CH-47B (108 built for US Army) see 1974-75 *Jane's*. Performance increased in CH-47C by uprated transmissions and 2,796 kW (3,750 shp) T55-L-11A; integral fuel capacity increased to 3,944 litres (1,042 US gallons; 867.6 Imp gallons); first flight 14 October 1967; 270 delivered to US Army from Spring 1968; 182 US Army CH-47Cs retrofitted with composite rotor blades; integral spar inspection system (ISIS) introduced 1973 together with crashworthy fuel system retrofit kit; full details in 1980-81 *Jane's*. Transmissions of some As and Bs upgraded to CH-47C standard.

VARIANTS: CH-47D: US Army contract to modify one each of CH-47A, B and C to prototype Ds placed 1976; first flight 11 May 1979; first production contract October 1980; first flight 26 February 1982; initial operational capability (IOC) achieved 28 February 1984 with 101st Airborne Div; second multi-year production contract for 144 CH-47Ds awarded 13 January 1989, bringing total CH-47D (and MH-47E) ordered to 472; deliveries reached 332 by November 1990; production rate four per month; programme completion due October 1993; US regular Army deliveries completed October 1990 with 17th operating unit (C Company, 228th Aviation Regiment, Fort Wainright, Alaska); remainder of CH-47Ds for Army Reserve and National Guard by late 1993; deliveries to National Guard (Texas) began 1988.

CH-47D update includes strip down to bare airframe, repair and refurbish, fit Textron Lycoming T55-L-712 turboshafts, uprated transmissions with integral lubrication and cooling, composite rotor blades, new flight deck compatible with night vision goggles (NVG), new redundant electrical system, modular hydraulic system, advanced automatic flight control system, improved avionics and survivability equipment, Solar T62-T-2B APU operating hydraulic and electrical systems through accessory gear drive, single-point pressure refuelling, and triple external cargo hooks. Composites account for 10 to 15 per cent of structure. About 300 suppliers involved.

At max gross weight of 22,680 kg (50,000 lb), CH-47D has more than double useful load of CH-47A. Sample loads include M198 towed 155 mm howitzer, 32 rounds of ammunition and 11-man crew, making internal/external load of 9,980 kg (22,000 lb); D5 caterpillar bulldozer weighing 11,225 kg (24,750 lb) on centre cargo hook; US Army Milvan supply containers carried at up to 130 knots (256 km/h; 159 mph); up to seven 1,893 litre (500 US gallon, 416 Imp gallon), 1,587 kg (3,500 lb) rubber fuel blivets carried on three hooks. Four CH-47Ds converted for in-flight refuelling from C-130 at up to 120 knots (222 km/h; 138 mph) by day and night and in moderate turbulence, approved July 1988; graphite fuel boom at lower starboard side contains telescoping aluminium tube and can accept flow rate of 568 litres (150 US gallons; 125 Imp gallons)/min to refuel completely in six minutes; first delivery to US Army July 1988.

CH-47D Special Operations Aircraft: Two battalions of 160th Special Operations Aviation Regiment (at Fort Campbell, Kentucky, and Hunter AAF, Georgia) equipped pending availability of MH-47E with CH-47D SOA fitted with refuelling probes, thermal imagers, Bendix/King RDR-1300 weather radar, improved communications and navigation equipment, and two pintle-mounted 7.62 mm machine guns. Navigator/commander's station fitted in some SOAs.

MH-47E: Special Forces variant. Prototype development contract 2 December 1987; 11 of intended 51 MH-47Es funded in FYs 1988-89 and taken from CH-47D re-manufacture; prototype (88-0267) flew 1 June 1990; first 11 (of 24 intended) to be delivered from November 1992 to 2 Battalion of 160th Special Operations Aviation Regt at Fort Campbell, Kentucky. Later helicopters earmarked for 3 Battalion/160 SOAR at Hunter AAF, Georgia, and 1/245th Aviation Battalion (SOA), Oklahoma National Guard, Lexington (eight and 16 MH-47Es respectively).

Mission profile 5½ hour covert deep penetration over 300 nm (560 km; 345 mile) radius in adverse weather, day or night, all terrain with 90 per cent success probability. Requirements include self deployment to Europe in stages of up to 1,200 nm (1,677 km; 1,042 miles), 44-troop capacity, powerful defensive weapons and ECM. Equipment includes IBM-Allied Bendix integrated avionics with four-screen NVG compatible EFIS; dual MIL-STD-1553 digital databuses; AN/ASN-145 AHRS; jamming-resistant radios; Rockwell-Collins CP1516-ASQ automatic target handoff system; inertial AN/ASN-137 Doppler, Rockwell-Collins AN/ASN-149(V)2 GPS/Navstar receiver and terrain referenced positioning navigation systems; Rockwell Collins ADF-149; laser (Perkin-Elmer AN/AVR-2), radar (E-systems AN/APR-39A) and missile (Honeywell AN/AAR-47) warning systems; ITT AN/ALQ-136(V) pulse jammer and Northrop AN/ALQ-162 CW jammer; Tracor M-130 chaff/flare dispensers; TI AN/APQ-174 radar with modes for terrain following down to 30 m (100 ft), terrain avoidance, air-to-ground ranging and ground mapping; Hughes AN/AAQ-16 FLIR in chin turret; digital moving map display; uprated T55-L-714 turboshafts with FADEC; increased fuel capacity; additional troop seating (44 max); OBOGS; rotor brake; 272 kg (600 lb) rescue hoist

CH-46E Sea Knight operating from Norfolk NAS, Virginia

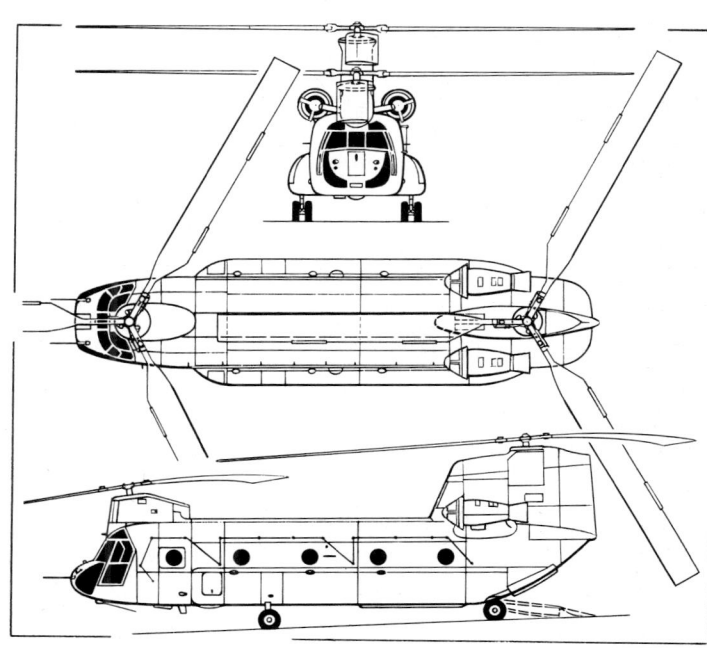

Boeing CH-47D military helicopter. Broken lines show rear loading ramp lowered
(*Pilot Press*)

MH-47E prototype showing extended nose and refuelling probe

with 61 m (200 ft) usable cable; two M-2 0.50 in window-mounted machine guns (port forward: starboard aft); provisions for Stinger AAMs using FLIR for sighting. This system largely common with equivalent Sikorsky MH-60K (which see).

MH-47E has nose of Commercial Chinook to allow for weather radar, if needed; forward landing gear moved 1.02 m (3 ft 4 in) forward to allow for all-composite

external fuel pods (also from Commercial Chinook) that double fuel capacity; Brooks & Perkins internal cargo handling system.

Chinook HC. Mk 1/2: RAF versions (35 of 41 remaining); designation CH47-352; all HC. Mk 1s upgraded to HC. Mk 1B (see 1989-90 and earlier *Jane's*); UK MoD authorised Boeing to update 33 Mk 1Bs to Mk 2, equivalent to CH-47D, October 1989; changes include new automatic flight control system, updated modular hydraulics, stronger transmission and improved T62-T-2B APU and airframe reinforcements. Conversion continues from 1991 (first aircraft to Boeing in March) to 1995. Chinook HC. Mk 1B ZA718 began flight testing Chandler Evans/Hawker Siddeley dual-channel, full-authority digital engine control system for Mk 2 in October 1989.

HT.17 Chinook: Spanish Army version. Ten CH-47Cs (one lost) and nine CH-47Ds delivered; agreed December 1989 to upgrade CH-47Cs to CH-47D after initial preparation in Spain by AISA; first re-delivery mid-1991, then four a year in 1992 and 1993.

Model 234: Commercial version, described opposite.

Model 414: Export military version, described in 1985-86 *Jane's*. Now superseded by CH-47D International Chinook (see below).

CH-47D International Chinook: Model 414-100 first sold to Japan; Japan Defence Agency ordered two for JGSDF and one for JASDF Spring 1984; first flight (N7425H) January 1986 and, with second machine, delivered to Kawasaki Heavy Industries April 1986 for fitting out; co-production arrangement (see under Japan: Kawasaki); final total of at least 54 expected. International Chinook available in four versions with combinations of standard or long range (MH-47E type) fuel tanks and T55-L-712 SSB or T55-L-714.

CUSTOMERS: Total 732 CH-47A/B/C built and 472 CH-47Ds authorised for US Army at January 1989. Exports include five CH-47Cs to Argentina; Australia 12 CH-47Cs with crashworthy fuel system; Canada nine CH-47Cs designated **CH-147**, delivered from September 1974 (details in 1985-86 *Jane's*); Chinese People's Liberation Army (PLA) ordered six CH-47D Internationals in January 1989, since embargoed; Japan (two, plus one CKD); Spanish Army 19, designated HT. 17, of which 10 CH-47Cs (one lost) and nine CH-47D International Chinooks delivered to 5th Helicopter Transport Battalion (Bheltra-V) at Colmenar Viejo, Madrid (last six have Bendix/King RDR-1400 weather radar); South Korea (18 delivered 1989-90); Taiwan (three, see Boeing 234MLR); Thailand (four ex-US Army plus three new-build); UK (41); 12 civilian, of which few left operating; two for trials, three to undisclosed operator; 45 in kits, comprising 40 for Italy and five for Japan; and 12 on order by undisclosed customers. Agusta sold licence-built CH-47Cs to Egypt (15), Greece (10), Iran (68), Italy (32), Libya (20), Morocco (nine) and Pennsylvania Army National Guard (11).

COSTS: $81.8 million (placed 1987) for development of MH-47E; $173.5 million (1991) contract for initial 11 MH-47Es; further 39 of this version planned.

DESIGN FEATURES: Two three-blade intermeshing contra-rotating tandem rotors; rotor transmissions driven by connecting shafts from combiner gearbox, which is driven by rear-mounted engines. Classic rotor heads with flapping and drag hinges; manually foldable blades, using Boeing Helicopters VR7 and VR8 aerofoils with cambered leading-edges; blades can survive hits from 23 mm HEI and API rounds; rotor brake optional; transmission capacity (CH-47D) 5,593 kW (7,500 shp) on two engines and 3,430 kW (4,600 shp) one engine inoperative; rotor rpm 225. Constant cross-section cabin with side doors at front and rear loading ramp that can be opened in flight; underfloor section sealed to give flotation after water landing; access to flight deck from cabin; main cargo hook mounting covered by removable floor panel so that load can be observed in flight.

FLYING CONTROLS: Dual hydraulic motor pitch-change actuators; secondary hydraulic actuators in control linkage behind flight deck for autopilot/autostabiliser input; autopilot provides stabilisation, attitude hold and outer-loop holds.

STRUCTURE: Blades based on D-shaped glassfibre spar, fairing assembly of Nomex honeycomb core and crossply glassfibre skin.

LANDING GEAR: Non-retractable quadricycle type, with twin wheels on each front unit and single wheels on each rear unit. Oleo-pneumatic shock absorbers in all units. Rear units fully castoring and steerable; power steering installed on starboard rear unit. All wheels are size 24 × 7.7-VII, with tyres size 8.50-10-III, pressure 4.62 bars (67 lb/sq in). Two single-disc hydraulic brakes. Provision for fitting detachable wheel-skis.

POWER PLANT: Two Textron Lycoming T55-L-712 turbo-shafts, pod-mounted on sides of the rear pylon, and each with a standard power rating of 2,796 kW (3,750 shp) and emergency rating of 3,356 kW (4,500 shp). Textron Lycoming T55-L-712 SSB engine has standard power rating of 3,264 kW (4,378 shp) and emergency rating of 3,451 kW (4,628 shp). Self-sealing pressure refuelled crashworthy fuel tanks in external fairings on sides of fuselage. Total fuel capacity 3,899 litres (1,030 US gallons; 858 Imp gallons). Oil capacity 14 litres (3.7 US gallons; 3.1 Imp gallons). Standard in MH-47E and optional in International Chinook are two Textron Lycoming T55-L-714 turboshafts, each with a standard power rating of 3,065 kW (4,110 shp) continuous and emergency rating of 3,749 kW (5,028 shp) and total fuel capacity 7,828 litres (2,068 US gallons; 1,722 Imp gallons). CH-47D SOA and MH-47E have 8.53 m (24 ft 0 in) refuelling probe on starboard side of forward fuselage. Provision for additional fuel cells in cabin.

RAF Chinook HC.Mk 1B, as used by Special Forces in 1991 Gulf War, retrofitted with fore and aft radar warning receiver antennae, chaff dispenser boxes each side of rear fuselage, flare dispensers each side of rear rotor mast and satellite communications antenna *(Paul Jackson)*

ACCOMMODATION: Two pilots on flight deck, with dual controls. Jump seat for crew chief or combat commander. Jettisonable door on each side of flight deck. Depending on seating arrangement, 33 to 55 troops can be accommodated in main cabin, or 24 litters plus two attendants, or vehicles and freight. Rear loading ramp can be left completely or partially open, or can be removed to permit transport of extra-long cargo and in-flight parachute or free-drop delivery of cargo and equipment. Main cabin door, at front on starboard side, comprises upper hinged section which can be opened in flight, and lower section with integral steps. Lower section is jettisonable. Triple external cargo hook system, as on Model 234, with centre hook rated to carry max load of 11,793 kg (26,000 lb) and the forward and rear hooks 7,711 kg (17,000 lb) each, or 10,433 kg (23,000 lb) in unison. Provisions are installed for a power-down ramp and water dam to permit ramp operation on water, for forward and rear cargo hooks, ferry fuel tanks, external rescue hoist, and windscreen washers.

SYSTEMS: Cabin heated by 200,000 BTU heater/blower. Hydraulic system provides pressure of 207 bars (3,000 lb/sq in) for flying controls. Max flow rate 53.0 litres (14 US gallons; 11.65 Imp gallons)/min. Spherical hydraulic reservoir, volume 5,326 cm³ (325 cu in), pressurised to 1.72 bars (25 lb/sq in). Utility hydraulic system, pressure 231 bars (3,350 lb/sq in), max flow rate 51.5 litres (13.6 US gallons; 11.3 Imp gallons)/min. Piston type reservoir, volume 7,014 cm³ (428 cu in), of which 5,326 cm³ (325 cu in) are usable, pressurised to 3.86 bars (56 lb/sq in). Electrical system includes two 40kVA air-cooled alternators driven by transmission drive system. Solar T62-T-2B APU runs accessory gear drive, thereby operating all hydraulic and electrical systems.

AVIONICS (International CH-47D: US Army CH-47D assumed to be generally similar. Avionics for RAF HC. Mk 1 listed in 1985-86 and earlier editions): Standard avionics include ARC-102 HF com radio, Collins ARC-186 UHF/AM-FM, Magnavox ARC-164 UHF/AM com; C-6533 intercom; Bendix/King AN/APX-100 IFF; APN-209 radar altimeter; AN/ARN-89B ADF; AN/ARN-118 Tacan; AN/ARN-123 VOR/glideslope/marker beacon receiver; and AN/ASN-43 gyromagnetic compass. Flight instruments are standard for IFR, and include an AN/AQU-6A horizontal situation indicator. AFCS maintains helicopter stability, eliminating the need for constant small correction inputs by the pilot to maintain desired attitude. The AFCS is a redundant system using two identical control units and two sets of stabilisation actuators. RAF Chinooks have GEC-Marconi ARI18228 RWR and (from 1990) Loral AN/ALQ-157 IR jammers, Racal RNS252 Super TANS INS and GPS. Tracor M-130 chaff/flare dispensers in RAF Chinooks.

EQUIPMENT: Hydraulically powered winch for rescue and cargo handling, rearview mirror, plus integral work stands and step for maintenance.

DIMENSIONS, EXTERNAL:

Rotor diameter (each)	18.29 m (60 ft 0 in)
Rotor blade chord (each)	0.81 m (2 ft 8 in)
Distance between rotor centres	11.86 m (38 ft 11 in)
Length: overall, rotors turning	30.14 m (98 ft 10¾ in)
fuselage	15.54 m (51 ft 0 in)
Width, rotors folded: CH-47D	3.78 m (12 ft 5 in)
MH-47E	4.78 m (15 ft 8 in)
Height to top of rear rotor head	5.68 m (18 ft 7¾ in)
Wheel track (c/l of shock absorbers):	
CH-47D	3.20 m (10 ft 6 in)
MH-47E	3.63 m (11 ft 11 in)
Wheelbase: CH-47D	6.86 m (22 ft 6 in)
MH-47E	7.87 m (25 ft 10 in)
Passenger door (fwd, stbd): Height	1.68 m (5 ft 6 in)
Width	0.91 m (3 ft 0 in)
Height to sill	1.09 m (3 ft 7 in)
Rear loading ramp entrance: Height	1.98 m (6 ft 6 in)
Width	2.31 m (7 ft 7 in)
Height to sill	0.79 m (2 ft 7 in)

DIMENSIONS, INTERNAL:

Cabin, excl flight deck:	
Length: CH-47D	9.19 m (30 ft 2 in)
MH-47E	9.30 m (30 ft 6 in)
Width: mean	2.29 m (7 ft 6 in)
at floor	2.51 m (8 ft 3 in)
Height	1.98 m (6 ft 6 in)
Floor area	21.0 m² (226.0 sq ft)
Usable volume	41.7 m³ (1,474 cu ft)
Length of fuselage: Army CH-47D	15.54 m (51 ft 0 in)
International CH-47D and MH-47E	
	15.87 m (52 ft 1 in)

AREAS:

Rotor blades (each)	7.43 m² (80.0 sq ft)
Rotor discs (total)	525.3 m² (5,655 sq ft)

WEIGHTS AND LOADINGS: See tables
PERFORMANCE: See tables

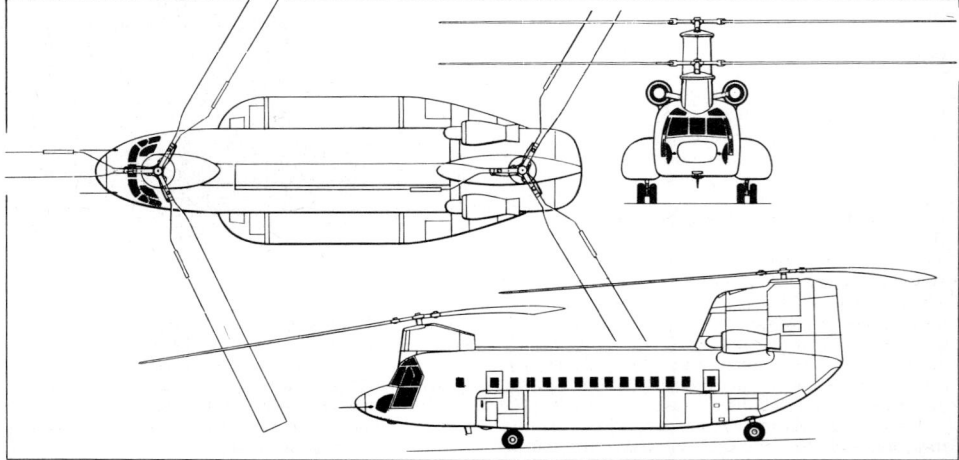

Boeing Model 234 LR long-range Commercial Chinook *(Pilot Press)*

US ARMY CH-47D CHINOOK WEIGHTS AND PERFORMANCE

	Condition 1	Condition 2	Condition 3	Condition 4
Take-off condition				
Altitude	1,220 m (4,000 ft)	Sea level	1,220 m (4,000 ft)	Sea level
Temperature	35°C (95°F)	15°C (59°F)	35°C (95°F)	15°C (59°F)
Empty weight	10,615 kg (23,402 lb)	10,615 kg (23,402 lb)	10,538 kg (23,232 lb)	10,151 kg (22,379 lb)
T-O weight	19,178 kg (42,280 lb)	22,679 kg (50,000 lb)	19,657 kg (43,336 lb)	22,679 kg (50,000 lb)
Payload: external	6,968 kg (15,362 lb)	10,341 kg (22,798 lb)	—	—
internal	—	—	6,308 kg (13,907 lb)	—
Max level speed, S/L, ISA, max continuous power, no external load	161 knots (298 km/h; 185 mph)	161 knots (298 km/h; 185 mph)	154 knots (285 km/h; 177 mph)	—
Average cruising speed	120 knots (222 km/h; 138 mph)	132 knots (245 km/h; 152 mph)	134 knots (248 km/h; 154 mph)	138 knots (256 km/h; 159 mph)
Max rate of climb, S/L, ISA, intermediate rated power	669 m (2,195 ft)/min	464 m (1,522 ft)/min	640 m (2,100 ft)/min	464 m (1,522 ft)/min
Hovering ceiling OGE, ISA, max power	3,215 m (10,550 ft)	1,524 m (5,000 ft)	2,972 m (9,750 ft)	1,524 m (5,000 ft)
Mission radius	30 nm (55.5 km; 34.5 miles)	30 nm (55.5 km; 34.5 miles)	100 nm (185 km; 115 miles)	—
Ferry range	—	—	—	1,093 nm (2,026 km; 1,259 miles)

Condition 1
T-O weight is gross weight for 61 m (200 ft)/min vertical rate of climb to hover OGE at 1,220 m/35°C (4,000 ft/95°F). External payload is carried outbound only. Fuel reserve is 30 min cruise fuel. Max speed shown is at T-O weight less external payload.

Condition 2
T-O gross weight is max structural T-O weight for which vertical climb capability at S/L, ISA is 271 m (890 ft)/min. Otherwise same as Condition 1.

Condition 3
T-O weight is gross weight for hover OGE at 1,220 m/35°C (4,000 ft/95°F). Radius is with inbound payload 50 per cent of outbound internal payload. Fuel reserve is 30 min cruise fuel. Max speed shown is at T-O weight.

Condition 4
T-O weight is max structural T-O weight. Max ferry range (internal and external auxiliary fuel). Optimum cruise climb to 2,440 m (8,000 ft) and complete cruise at 2,440 m (8,000 ft). Fuel reserve is 10 per cent of initial fuel.

INTERNATIONAL CHINOOK WEIGHTS AND PERFORMANCE

	International CH-47D/-712	International CH-47D/-714	International CH-47D(LR)/-712	International CH-47D(LR)/-714
Configuration designation Power plant	T55-L-712 SSB	T55-L-714	T55-L-712 SSB	T55-L-714
Fuel capacity	3,902 litres (1,030 US gallons; 858 Imp gallons)	3,902 litres (1,030 US gallons; 858 Imp gallons)	7,834 litres (2,068 US gallons; 1,723 Imp gallons)	7,834 litres (2,068 US gallons; 1,723 Imp gallons)
Take-off condition				
Altitude	1,220 m (4,000 ft)	1,220 m (4,000 ft)	1,220 m (4,000 ft)	1,220 m (4,000 ft)
Temperature	35°C (95°F)	35°C (95°F)	35°C (95°F)	35°C (95°F)
Mission T-O weight (hover OGE)	20,094 kg (44,300 lb)	22,426 kg (49,440 lb)	19,695 kg (43,420 lb)	21,918 kg (48,320 lb)
Empty weight	10,670 kg (23,523 lb)	10,693 kg (23,574 lb)	11,016 kg (24,286 lb)	11,039 kg (24,337 lb)
Payload[1]: internal (inbound payload = 50% outbound)	6,739 kg (14,857 lb)	8,895 kg (19,610 lb)	6,018 kg (13,268 lb)	8,081 kg (17,816 lb)
Mission radius[1]	100 nm (185 km; 115 miles)	100 nm (185 km; 115 miles)	100 nm (185 km; 115 miles)	100 nm (185 km; 115 miles)
Average cruise speed[1]	132 knots (245 km/h; 152 mph)	133 knots (246 km/h; 153 mph)	135 knots (250 km/h; 155 mph)	137 knots (254 km/h; 157 mph)
Max radius: full fuel (inbound payload = 50% outbound)	140 nm (259 km; 161 miles)	130 nm (241 km; 150 miles)	335 nm (621 km; 386 miles)	316 nm (585 km; 363 miles)
Max level speed, S/L, ISA[1] max continuous power, at T-O weight	156 knots (289 km/h; 180 mph)	161 knots (298 km/h; 185 mph)	153 knots (283 km/h; 176 mph)	157 knots (291 km/h; 181 mph)
Hover ceiling, OGE, max power: ISA, T-O weight[1]	3,080 m (10,100 ft)	2,415 m (7,930 ft)	3,050 m (10,000 ft)	2,395 m (7,850 ft)
35°C (95°F), 22,680 kg (50,000 lb) gross weight	244 m (800 ft)	1,128 m (3,700 ft)	91 m (300 ft)	844 m (2,900 ft)
Max T-O weight	24,494 kg (54,000 lb)	24,494 kg (54,000 lb)	24,494 kg (54,000 lb)	24,494 kg (54,000 lb)

[1]T-O weight is gross weight for hover OGE at 1,220 m/35°C (4,000 ft/95°F). Radius is with inbound payload 50 per cent of outbound payload. Fuel reserve is 30 min cruise fuel. Max speed shown is at T-O weight.

Boeing 234 Commercial Chinook of Trump Air, providing a shuttle service between New York and the casinos of Atlantic City, NJ

BOEING MODEL 234 COMMERCIAL CHINOOK

TYPE: Commercial tandem-rotor twin-turboshaft helicopter.
PROGRAMME: Launched by British Airways Helicopters order for three in 1978 (later increased to six) for North Sea off-shore operations: first flight 19 August 1980; FAA and CAA certification 19 and 26 June 1981 respectively; first service with BAH (now British International Helicopters) 1 July 1981; BAH deliveries completed 1 June 1982; FAA and CAA certificated 234 LR combi Summer 1982. Commercial Chinooks now withdrawn from service over the North Sea.

VARIANTS: **234 LR Long Range:** About twice CH-47 fuel load in composites tanks attached to fuselage flanks with anti-vibration mounts; flight deck floor on shock-mounts; 44-passenger interior (on shock mounts), with toilet and galley, based on Boeing airliners; walk-on baggage bins on rear ramp; alternative mixed passenger/cargo or all-cargo layouts.

234 ER Extended Range: Typical configurations are 17 passengers and two tanks for additional 875 nm (1,621 km; 1,008 miles) or 32 passengers and single cabin fuel tank; FAA certificated May 1983.

234 UT Utility: External fuel cells replaced by two cylindrical tanks in forward fuselage: FAA supplemental type certificate October 1981 at max gross weight 23,133

kg (51,000 lb) with external loads up to 12,700 kg (28,000 lb) on single hook; approved for 24 passengers and operation at up to 3,660 m (12,000 ft) at full gross weight. No known orders.

234 MLR Multi-purpose Long Range: Similar to 234 LR but with utility interior; can be reconfigured in eight hours; four men can handle cabin cylindrical fuel tanks and ramp baggage bins.

CUSTOMERS: Six 234 LR delivered to British BAH/BIH (one lost) and three to Helikopter Service SA of Norway 1981 to 1985; five former BIH aircraft now operated by Columbia Helicopters in Oregon for logging and firefighting; two second-hand 234s delivered to Trump Air 1989 for New York-Atlantic City service; two second-hand 234 ERs leased to Arco Alaska in 1983 and one to ERA Helicopters in 1985.

LANDING GEAR: As described for CH-47D, but with tyre pressures of 8.55 bars (124 lb/sq in) on forward gear, 7.20 bars (104.4 lb/sq in) on rear gear. Wheel/ski gear optional.

POWER PLANT: Two Textron Lycoming AL 5512 turboshafts, pod-mounted on sides of rear rotor pylon. Each engine has max T-O rating of 3,039 kW (4,075 shp), max continuous rating of 2,218.5 kW (2,975 shp), and 30 min contingency rating of 3,247 kW (4,355 shp). Long-range model has two fuel tanks, one in each fuselage side fairing, with total capacity of 7,949 litres (2,100 US gallons; 1,749 Imp gallons). Utility model has two drum-shape internal tanks, with total capacity of 3,702 litres (978 US gallons; 814 Imp gallons). Extended-range model has both fuselage side and internal drum tanks. Single-point pressure refuelling.

ACCOMMODATION: Two pilots side by side on flight deck, with dual controls. Passenger cabin of long-range model seats up to 44 persons four-abreast, with centre aisle. Each seat has overhead bin and underseat stowage for carry-on baggage; larger items are stowed over the rear ramp in the main baggage compartment. Galley, with cabin attendant's seat, and toilet, are standard, between flight deck and cabin. Basic FAA/CAA approved combi versions offer 8-32 passenger seats, with cargo at rear of cabin, loaded via rear ramp; or 22-32 passenger seats, with cargo stowed on only one side of cabin's centre aisle. All passenger facilities can be removed, and heavy duty floor installed, for freight-only service. Passenger door at front of cabin on starboard side. Crew door on each side of flight deck. Cabin floor supported by dynamically tuned fittings to reduce vibration. Hydraulically powered cargo ramp can be stopped at any intermediate position to match the level of the loading vehicle being used. Single central cargo hook is standard on utility model for carrying external loads of up to 12,700 kg (28,000 lb). Optional dual tandem hooks for precision operations and for load stability in high-speed flight; or three tandem hooks for delivering multiple loads.

SYSTEMS: Heating and ventilation systems maintain comfortable flight deck/cabin temperature in ambient temperatures down to −32°C. Duplicated flying control, hydraulic and electrical systems, as described for CH-47D/Model 414. Solar T62T-2B APU, rated at 71 kW (95 shp), drives auxiliary gearbox on rear transmission to start engines and provide power for two flying control system hydraulic pumps and two alternators. All critical systems heated to inhibit ice build-up.

AVIONICS: Duplicated full blind-flying instrumentation, weather radar, and dual four-axis automatic flight control system with built-in test equipment, provide all-weather capability.

EQUIPMENT: Optional equipment includes passenger interior furnishings for the utility model, combi interior, downward-shining cargo load light, rescue hoist of 272 kg (600 lb) capacity, glassfibre wheel-skis, an ice detector probe, and ditching equipment that includes two liferafts, each with an overload capacity of 36 persons. Standard items include integral work platforms, and a maintenance panel that allows 26 separate checks to be made from a single ground-level position.

DIMENSIONS, EXTERNAL: As CH-47D except:
Length of fuselage	15.87 m (52 ft 1 in)
Width over fuselage side fairings	4.78 m (15 ft 8 in)
Wheel track: fwd	3.20 m (10 ft 6 in)
rear	3.40 m (11 ft 2 in)
Wheelbase	7.87 m (25 ft 9.9 in)

DIMENSIONS, INTERNAL:
Passenger cabin	as for CH-47D
Baggage compartment volume	4.42 m³ (156.0 cu ft)
Utility model, cargo hold volume	41.03 m³ (1,449 cu ft)

WEIGHTS AND LOADINGS:
Manufacturer's weight empty:	
LR	11,748 kg (25,900 lb)
ER	12,020 kg (26,500 lb)
MLR	11,113 kg (24,500 lb)
UT	9,797 kg (21,600 lb)
Operating weight empty: LR	12,292 kg (27,100 lb)
ER	12,406 kg (27,350 lb)
MLR	11,400 kg (25,134 lb)
UT	10,002 kg (22,050 lb)
Fuel load: LR, MLR	6,391 kg (14,091 lb)
ER	9,368 kg (20,653 lb)
UT	2,976 kg (6,562 lb)
Max payload: LR, MLR, internal	9,072 kg (20,000 lb)

Boeing Model 360 advanced technology demonstrator

ER, UT, internal		8,731 kg (19,250 lb)
ER, MLR, UT, external		12,700 kg (28,000 lb)
Max T-O weight:		
ER, LR, MLR, internal load		22,000 kg (48,500 lb)
UT, internal load		19,051 kg (42,000 lb)
ER, LR, MLR, UT, external load		
		23,133 kg (51,000 lb)

PERFORMANCE:
Never-exceed speed (VNE):		
ER, LR, MLR	150 knots	(278 km/h; 173 mph)
UT	140 knots	(259 km/h; 161 mph)
Max cruising speed at 610 m (2,000 ft):		
ER, LR, MLR, internal load, at 20,411 kg (45,000 lb)		
AUW	145 knots	(269 km/h; 167 mph)
UT, internal load, at 19,051 kg (42,000 lb) AUW		
	140 knots	(259 km/h; 161 mph)
Cruising speed for optimum range, at 610 m (2,000 ft):		
ER, LR, MLR, UT, internal load, at all gross weights		
	135 knots	(250 km/h; 155 mph)
Max rate of climb at S/L at max T-O weight:		
ER, LR, MLR, internal load		360 m (1,180 ft)/min
UT, internal load		457 m (1,500 ft)/min
Operational ceiling:		
ER, LR, MLR, UT		4,575 m (15,000 ft)
Hovering ceiling IGE:		
ER, LR, MLR, internal load		2,590 m (8,500 ft)
UT, internal load		4,085 m (13,400 ft)
Hovering ceiling OGE:		
ER, LR, MLR, internal load		820 m (2,700 ft)
UT, internal load		3,505 m (11,500 ft)
Range with 45 min IFR reserves:		
LR, 44 passengers		530 nm (982 km; 610 miles)
ER, 17 passengers		830 nm (1,538 km; 956 miles)
LR, MLR, with max fuel		
		620 nm (1,149 km; 714 miles)
ER with max fuel	1,035 nm	(1,918 km; 1,192 miles)
UT with max internal load		
		229 nm (424 km; 264 miles)
UT with max external load		
		145 nm (269 km; 167 miles)
Max endurance: LR, MLR, internal load		5 h 18 min
ER, internal load		8 h 25 min
UT, external load		2 h 18 min

BOEING MODEL 360

TYPE: Experimental tandem rotor transport helicopter.

PROGRAMME: Built over several years as private venture technology demonstrator. First flight 10 June 1987; completed about 190 hours flying by early 1991; may attempt world speed record; testing will continue through 1990s.

DESIGN FEATURES: Designed to investigate aerodynamics, structures, vibration control, flight control and avionics of a helicopter designed to cruise at 200 knots (371 km/h; 230 mph). Maximum true airspeed of 214 knots (397 km/h; 246 mph) achieved 1990. World's largest all-composites helicopter. Tandem four-blade rotors driven by interconnecting shafts from combiner gearbox; composites hingeless rotor heads and composites rotor blades with Boeing VR12 and VR15 transonic rotor blade aerofoils; powered blade folding mechanisms integrated with drag dampers; engines mounted in base of rear pylon, originally drawing air through intake beneath rotor head, but now with individual pitot inlets.

FLYING CONTROLS: Fully powered main actuators at rotor heads with autostabilisation and autopilot inputs through secondary actuators aft of flight deck; dual Honeywell digital flight control computers based on MIL-1750A

processors (iterating at 40Hz) provide four-axis auto-stabilisation, holding of selected airspeed, heading and bank angle and in-flight tailoring of command responses; pitch-axis response rate automatically reduced with mainwheels on the ground; flight director/autopilot modes include heading select, VOR and Doppler navigation, ILS localiser, glideslope and back course hold, pressure and radar height hold, automatic downward transition and go-around, and automatic hover. Flight deck includes four-screen monochrome EFIS adapted for night vision goggles, and dual keyboards and displays for integrated control of avionics.

STRUCTURE: Main airframe structure Kevlar skin on Nomex honeycomb core with unidirectional carbonfibre composite frames and stringers; graphite composite reinforcement at panel edges and round cutouts; panels joined to structure by cold bonding supported by metal fasteners; cabin floor and underfloor fuel tank assembly attached to airframe by vibration isolators; flight deck similar. Airframe assembled using single jig. Carbon composites used for main rotor shafts, transmission casings, swashplates, rotor head structures, rotor blades and main undercarriage beams.

LANDING GEAR: Retractable tricycle type with twin wheels on each unit. Main landing gear retraction beams are of carbonfibre composites.

POWER PLANT: Two Textron Lycoming AL5512 turboshafts, mounted one in each side of the rear fuselage, each with a standard power rating of 3,132 kW (4,200 shp). Fuel in one 901 litre (238 US gallon; 198 Imp gallon) self-sealing tank at rear and two 1,109 litre (293 US gallon; 244 Imp gallon) tanks forward, giving total capacity of 3,119 litres (824 US gallons; 686 Imp gallons).

SYSTEMS: Hydraulic and electrical system components are modular in nature, and grouped to allow systems and structure to be integrated during construction.

AVIONICS: Full nav/com equipment. Doppler radar and optional remote map reader. Honeywell digital automatic flight control system forms part of Bendix/King integrated flight control and flight management system incorporating six CRT displays with multi-function keyboards, and computer controlled EADI and EHSI displays for pilot and co-pilot, linked to a heading and attitude reference system via a multiplex databus.

DIMENSIONS, EXTERNAL:
Length of fuselage	15.54 m (51 ft 0 in)
Height overall	5.91 m (19 ft 4¾ in)
Wheel track	3.96 m (13 ft 0 in)

DIMENSIONS, INTERNAL:
Cabin: Max width	1.93 m (6 ft 4 in)
Max height	1.80 m (5 ft 11 in)

WEIGHTS AND LOADINGS (estimated):
Design T-O weight	13,835 kg (30,500 lb)

PERFORMANCE (estimated):
Max design speed	235 knots (435 km/h; 270 mph)
Normal cruising speed	180 knots (334 km/h; 207 mph)

BELL/BOEING V-22 OSPREY

Boeing is teamed with Bell Helicopter Textron in development of the V-22 Osprey tilt-rotor transport. Full description in Bell/Boeing entry in this section.

BOEING/SIKORSKY RAH-66 COMANCHE (LH)

Boeing Helicopters formed First Team with Sikorsky in June 1985 to compete for US Army Light Helicopter (LH) programme. Full description in Boeing/Sikorsky entry after Boeing Commercial Airplane Group entries.

BOEING MILITARY AIRPLANES

PO Box 3707, Seattle, Washington 98124
PRESIDENT: C. G. King
WORKS: PO Box 7730, Wichita, Kansas 67277-7730
Telephone: 1 (316) 687 2020
Telex: 910 741 6900 BOEWICA WIC
VICE-PRESIDENT AND GENERAL MANGER: John Dempster
COMMUNICATIONS MANAGER: Richard L. Ziegler

On 2 January 1990 Boeing Military Airplanes, Wichita, was designated part of new Military Airplanes division based at Seattle and absorbing Boeing Advanced Systems. Civil airliner activities at Wichita subordinated to Boeing Commercial Airplane Group, Seattle (which see).

Boeing Military Airplanes programmes include B-52 Stratofortress, KC-135 tanker/transport, offensive avionics system of Rockwell B-1B, all-composites replacement wing for US Navy A-6 Intruder, and development of F-22A Advanced Tactical Fighter shared with Lockheed and General Dynamics (see under Lockheed in this section). Contracts for 179 new wing sets for A-6E placed by March 1988; options lapsed on two further batches of 72 each; 100 sets delivered by March 1991 and over 20 installed on new or rebuilt aircraft. Additional 120-150 wings required following cancellation of A-12 programme; Boeing to compete for contracts.

NASA ordered conversion of second 747-100 to carry Space Shuttle Orbiter vehicle early 1988; delivered 20 November 1990; Boeing Military Airplanes offers to upgrade McDonnell Douglas F-4 Phantoms with digital avionics and conformal fuel tanks or pylons; contracted to design and manufacture new navigation and weapon delivery system for 600 Air National Guard, Air Force Reserve and US Air Force F-4s.

LOCKHEED/BOEING/GENERAL DYNAMICS F-22A

F-22A design chosen 23 April 1991 to go forward into engineering and manufacturing development (EMD) to produce another 11 YF-22 development aircraft and up to 648 production aircraft. EMD phase to last 48 months; first production contract expected 1997; in production until 2014.

Boeing share includes wings, fuselage aft sections, engine installation, radar, infra-red search and track system (if adopted) and avionics ground prototype.

For details see F-22A entry under Lockheed.

BOEING B-52 STRATOFORTRESS

TYPE: Conventional nuclear bomber and missile launcher.
PROGRAMME: Serving with seven Bomb Wings of Eighth Air Force and three wings of Fifteenth Air Force. Full-scale development of system to carry AGM-86B air-launched cruise missile started early 1978; 98 B-52Gs and 95 B-52Hs modified to each carry 12 AGM-86B on inboard external pylons plus SRAM or other armament internally; first unit to reach IOC with AGM-86B was 416th Bomb Wing of SAC at Griffiss AFB December 1982; all aircraft fitted by late 1989; programme completed FY 1990.

Modification of B-52Hs to carry eight AGM-86B, SRAM, Advanced Cruise Missile or free-fall nuclear bombs on internal common strategic rotary launcher (CSRL) started 1982; first flight September 1985; 98 CSRLs to be produced; Boeing Military Airplanes manufactured 95 modification kits, plus support for US Air Force programme managed by Oklahoma City Air Logistics Center at Tinker AFB and conducted at Kelly AFB, Texas; first fully modified aircraft delivered to Carswell AFB April 1988; first full alert with internal and external stowage September 1989; operational status at all B-52H bases expected August 1993.

B-52H also being equipped for General Dynamics AGM-129A advanced cruise missile to augment AGM-86B; captive carry tests of 12 on underwing pylons began early 1989; IOC expected 1992. More B-52G/Hs may in future be assigned to the conventional role.

VARIANTS: **B-52G:** In 1991, 138 still in service with 2, 42, 93, 97 and 379 BWs; under Salt II agreement, B-52Gs capable of carrying cruise missiles have distinctive wingroot fairings known as strakelets; 40 B-52Gs not carrying cruise missiles modified for long-range conventional force projection including 30 also equipped to carry eight Harpoon anti-ship missiles in maritime role; two squadrons operational in 1990; all 40 being fitted with integrated conventional stores management system (ICSMS) by which weapon details can be entered in weapon computer by pre-recorded cassette. ALCM carriers to be withdrawn by 1993.

B-52H: In 1991, 95 still in service with 5, 92, 410 and 416 BWs; does not need strakelet fairings, as all carry cruise missiles.

STRUCTURE: See 1964-65 *Jane's*.

The following details apply to B-52G and B-52H:
POWER PLANT (B-52G): Eight 61.2 kN (13,750 lb st) J57-P-43WB turbojets. Fuel capacity 174,130 litres (46,000 US gallons; 38,303 Imp gallons) internally, plus two 2,650 litre (700 US gallon; 583 Imp gallon) underwing drop tanks.
POWER PLANT (B-52H): Eight 75.6 kN (17,000 lb st) Pratt & Whitney TF33-P-3 turbofans. Fuel capacity as for B-52G.

CSRL installed in weapons bay of a B-52H

ACCOMMODATION (B-52G/H): Crew of six (pilot and co-pilot, side by side on flight deck, navigator, radar navigator, ECM operator and gunner).
AVIONICS: Boeing OAS (offensive avionics system), introduced from 1980, is a digital solid state system, and includes Tercom (terrain comparison) guidance, a Teledyne Ryan Doppler radar, Honeywell AN/ASN-131 gimballed electrostatic airborne inertial navigation system (GEANS), IBM/Raytheon AN/ASQ-38 analog bombing/navigation system with IBM digital processing, Smiths attitude heading and reference system, Honeywell radar altimeter, Honeywell controls and displays, and Norden Systems modernised strategic radar. Under Phase II of the programme, completed by FY 1989, all 152 B-52Gs and 95 Hs were equipped with OAS. All currently operational B-52Gs and Hs have an AN/ASQ-151 electro-optical viewing system (EVS) to improve low level penetration capability. The EVS sensors are housed in two steerable, side by side chin turrets. The starboard turret houses a Hughes Aircraft AN/AAQ-6 forward-looking infra-red (FLIR) scanner, while the port turret contains a Westinghouse AN/AVQ-22 low light level TV camera. Phase VI avionics include Motorola AN/ALQ-122 SNOE (Smart Noise Operation Equipment) and Northrop AN/ALQ-155(V) advanced ECM; an AFSATCOM kit which permits worldwide communication via satellite; a Dalmo Victor AN/ALR-46 digital radar warning receiver; Westinghouse AN/ALQ-153 pulse Doppler tail warning radar; and ITT Avionics AN/ALQ-172(V) ECM.
ARMAMENT (B-52G): Four 0.50 in machine-guns in tail turret, remotely operated by AGS-15 fire control system, remote radar control, or closed circuit TV. Twelve AGM-86 cruise missiles, eight Boeing AGM-69 SRAM short-range attack missiles (on rotary launcher in internal weapons bay, plus nuclear free-fall bombs) on 98 aircraft. Other 40 aircraft equipped to carry conventional bombs and/or (on 30 aircraft) Harpoon air-to-surface missiles, as described under Variants. Aircraft of 42nd BW (Loring AFB) carry up to eight AGM-142A Have Nap conventional ASMs.
ARMAMENT (B-52H): Single 20 mm Vulcan multi-barrel cannon in tail turret instead of four machine-guns. All aircraft being equipped to carry 12 AGM-86 cruise missiles externally and eight internally on CSRL.
DIMENSIONS, EXTERNAL:
Wing span	56.39 m (185 ft 0 in)
Length overall	49.05 m (160 ft 10.9 in)
Height overall	12.40 m (40 ft 8 in)
Wheel track (c/l of shock struts)	2.51 m (8 ft 3 in)
Wheelbase	15.48 m (50 ft 3 in)
DIMENSIONS, INTERNAL:
Weapons bay volume	29.53 m³ (1,043 cu ft)
AREAS:
Wings, gross	371.6 m² (4,000 sq ft)
WEIGHTS AND LOADINGS:
Max T-O weight	more than 221,350 kg (488,000 lb)

Max wing loading   approx 595.7 kg/m² (122.0 lb/sq ft)
Max power loading (approx):
G	452.1 kg/kN (4.44 lb/lb st)
H	366.0 kg/kN (3.59 lb/lb st)
PERFORMANCE:
Max level speed at high altitude
    Mach 0.90 (516 knots; 957 km/h; 595 mph)
Cruising speed at high altitude
    Mach 0.77 (442 knots; 819 km/h; 509 mph)
Penetration speed at low altitude   Mach 0.53 to 0.55
    (352-365 knots; 652-676 km/h; 405-420 mph)
Service ceiling   16,765 m (55,000 ft)
T-O run: G   3,050 m (10,000 ft)
    H   2,900 m (9,500 ft)
Range with max fuel, without in-flight refuelling:
G	more than 6,513 nm (12,070 km; 7,500 miles)
H	more than 8,685 nm (16,093 km; 10,000 miles)

BOEING KC-135 STRATOTANKER

TYPE: Strategic flight refuelling tanker/transport with numerous C-135 special-mission variants (not all with tanker capability).
PROGRAMME: Between 1957 and 1965, the US Air Force received 729 KC-135A tankers, 18 C-135A and 30 C-135B transports, 14 EC-135C and three EC-135J command posts, four RC-135A and 10 RC-135C survey aircraft (B and C versions have turbofans). Current US Air Force fleet is 730 aircraft of all versions, including 411 KC-135A/R, two C-135As, one NC-135A, 10 NKC-135As (excluding two for the US Navy), four EC-135As, four C-135Bs, seven WC-135Bs, three C-135Cs, 13 EC-135Cs, four KC-135Ds, three EC-135Es, one NKC-135E, four EC-135Es, 163 KC-135Es, four EC-135Gs, four EC-135Hs, four EC-135Js, two EC-135Ks, five EC-135Ls, four EC-135Ps, 54 KC-135Qs, two RC-135Ss, one TC-135S, two RC-135Us, eight RC-135Vs, six RC-135Ws, one TC-135W, one RC-135X and two EC-135Ys.

From 1975 to 7 November 1988 Boeing extended life of every KC-135 by 27,000 hours (beyond year 2020) by replacing sections of underwing skins and other modifications; selection of 97.9 kN (22,000 lb st) CFM56-2B-1 turbofan for evaluation on a KC-135A announced 1980 (see KC-135R below); Air National Guard and AFRes KC-135As and 23 special missions aircraft re-engined with used airline JT3D-3B turbofans between 1981 and 1988 (see KC-135E below).
VARIANTS: **KC-135R:** CFM56-powered USAF tanker; first flight 4 August 1982; additional modifications include upgraded electrical and hydraulic systems, performance and fuel management system, upgraded flight control system, strengthened main landing gear, dual APUs for quick engine starting. First nine production conversions funded FY 1982; 306 modification kits (54,000 parts each) and 237 conversions funded by January 1990; 200th conversion re-delivered 25 April 1990; power plants on order for further 109 conversions. USAF Systems Command reported to have received funding to test Flight Refuelling Mk 32B hose-reel refuelling pod on one KC-135R. USAF considering Boeing offer of two-man EFIS cockpit modification costing under $1 million.

Compared with KC-135A, KC-135R can offload 65 per cent more fuel at 1,500 nm (2,775 km; 1,725 mile) radius and 150 per cent more fuel at 2,500 nm (4,630 km; 2,875 mile) radius at average gross weight; take-off run 762 m (2,500 ft) shorter; 90 EPNdB footprint 98 per cent smaller; max T-O weight increased from 136,800 kg (301,600 lb) to 146,285 kg (322,500 lb): max fuel load increased from 86,047 kg (189,702 lb) to 92,210 kg (203,288 lb).

KC-135E: Urgent re-engining of reserve refuelling squadrons based near built-up areas. USAF bought retired Boeing 707-100B/720B/320C airliners and spare JT3D-3B engines; between 1981 and January 1988, all 138 Air National Guard and Air Force Reserve KC-135As and 23 special missions aircraft re-engined (see 1987-88 and earlier *Jane's*); additional 14 conversions ordered September 1988 and completed by Boeing Louisiana Inc by September 1990 and shared between six squadrons; further nine completed by mid-1991; total 184; five-rotor Mark II/III wheel brakes also fitted.

Boeing KC-135R (62-3554) *Cherokee Rose*, **holder of 16 world time-to-height records** (*Paul Jackson*)

Four **KC-135Ds** received JT3Ds without change of designation.
Other variants: See under Programme and Customers.

CUSTOMERS: In addition to above, 12 **C-135F** delivered to France in 1964; one lost; structural modifications applied to remaining 11; converted to **C-135FR**s and re-delivered between 26 August 1985 and 13 April 1988 with CFM56 power plants; Dassault Electronique Adèle radar warning receivers installed from 1990; Flight Refuelling Ltd Mk 32B wing pods installed under each wing by Boeing from Spring 1991.

BOEING EC-18D

Designation for two US Air Force C-18As being modified as cruise missile control platforms by Chrysler Technologies Airborne Systems (CTAS) (which see).

BOEING 707 TANKER/TRANSPORT
Royal Saudi Air Force designation: KE-3A
Spanish Air Force designation: T.17

TYPE: Export tanker modification of 707-320 airliner.

PROGRAMME: Launched 1982; first flight of ex-TWA 707-320C converted demonstrator early 1983; earlier limited conversions completed before 1982; for details of 707-320C, see 1980-81 and earlier *Jane's*.

VARIANTS: See Design Features for choice of alternative quick-change roles.

CUSTOMERS: Only customers for new-build 707 tanker/transports were Saudi Arabia (eight illogically designated **KE-3A**s powered by CFM56-2A-2 engines, delivered September 1987) and Iran (four **707-3J9C**s with Beech 1800 wingtip pods installed by Boeing). Refurbished and converted 707 airliners supplied to Australia (four 707-338Cs with FRL Mk 32 wing pods fitted by ASTA using IAI conversion kits); Brazil (four **KC-137**s with Beech pods, converted by Boeing); Canada (two **CC-137**s with provision for Beech 1800 wingtip pods, converted by Boeing); Israel (six 707s converted by IAI with Sargent-Fletcher Co 34-000 pods); Italy (four 707-382Bs with SFC 34-000 pods and FR 480C fuselage HDU, being converted by Alenia Officine Aeronavali; first flight, by MM62148, 31 October 1990); Morocco (one 707-138B with Beech pods converted by AMIN); Peru (one 707-323C, IAI conversion with FRL pods); Spain (two **T.17**s with SFC 34-000 pods, converted by Boeing); Venezuela (one converted by IAI, 1990).

COSTS: $9.6 million per aircraft (Australia 1990) excluding value of airframe.

DESIGN FEATURES: When not refuelling, track-mounted interiors can be fitted for all-cargo, all-passenger or combi, aeromedical or VIP. Options include nose-mounted receiver probe; pods by Beech, Sargent-Fletcher Co or Flight Refuelling Ltd; rear fuselage hose and drogue unit; KC-135-type centreline boom. Systems can be mixed to give multiple capability.

Optional extra 19,040 litre (5,030 US gallon; 4,188 Imp gallon) underfloor fuel tank in rear cargo hold; with this and standard 90,301 litre (23,855 US gallon; 19,863 Imp gallon) wing tanks and triple refuelling points, 707 tanker/transport can transfer 55,878 kg (123,190 lb) of fuel at 1,000 nm (1,853 km; 1,150 mile) radius. Other basic modifications include refuelling control panel for flight engineer, improved hydraulic system and fuel pumps, strengthened outer wing, new wingtips, military avionics, TV monitor and boom operator's or pod observer's station. Quick-change cabin allows additional roles, such as coastal patrol, ECM, maritime missions, tactical command and control. Pylons or bays can be provided to dispense sonobuoys or other sensors, mines, bombs, air-to-air or stand-off missiles, and chaff or flares.

BOEING VC-25A 'AIR FORCE ONE'

TYPE: US Presidential transport.

PROGRAMME: Two Model 747-2G3Bs (-200Bs) converted by Boeing, Wichita, to replace Boeing VC-137Cs; delivery delayed by difficulties in laying 207 nm (384 km; 239 miles) of wiring (twice normal length for 747) and additional fire suppression; first flight of first converted VC-25A (contrived serial 82-8000) 26 January 1990; delivered to 89th Military Airlift Wing, Andrews AFB, 23 August 1990; second (92-9000) delivered 20 December 1990.

DESIGN FEATURES: Powered by four 252.4 kN (56,750 lb st) GE F103-GE-102 (CF6-80C2B1) turbofans; fuel capacity 202,940 litres (53,611 US gallons; 44,640 Imp gallons), giving range of 6,200 nm (11,490 km; 7,139 miles); fitted for flight refuelling; self-contained airstairs in lower fuselage lobe plus second Garrett GTCP331-200 APU in tail.

Avionics and equipment include Bendix/King Aerospace EFIS-10, secure voice terminals, cryptographic equipment, E-Systems and Rockwell-Collins mission communications kits installed by Boeing, and Litton ring laser INS. Each VC-25A accommodates 70 passengers and 23 crew, including ground crew. Floor area of 371.6

Spanish Air Force Boeing 707 (T.17) tanker with SFC 34-000 wingtip pods *(George W. Pennick)*

m² (4,000 sq ft) contains executive suite with presidential office, stateroom and lavatory, two galleys (each able to serve 50 people), emergency treatment medical facility, and work and rest areas for presidential staff, news reporters and USAF crew.

WEIGHTS AND LOADINGS:
Long-range mission T-O weight	364,552 kg (803,700 lb)
Max zero-fuel weight	238,816 kg (526,500 lb)
Design mission zero-fuel weight	202,302 kg (446,000 lb)
Max landing weight	285,763 kg (630,000 lb)

BOEING CARGO AIRCRAFT GROUND MOBILITY SYSTEM

TYPE: Strap-on ground cushion landing gear for C-130.

PROGRAMME: Boeing Military Airplanes and Textron Marine Systems developing ground cushion CAGMS to allow C-130 to operate from bomb-damaged airfields or rough surfaces. CAGMS illustrated 1989-90 *Jane's*.

DESIGN FEATURES: Strap-on unit enables a C-130 to clear obstacles 0.46 m (1 ft 6 in) high without damage. Normal landing gear lowered after touchdown to improve stability and manoeuvrability.

BOEING 720 AAT

TYPE: Advanced military avionics testbed.

PROGRAMME: Boeing 720B (N771BE) modified as Advanced Avionics Testbed (AAT) began Advanced Electronic Countermeasures (AECM) test programme 26 January 1989; Boeing believes AECM technology could be applied to special operations aircraft, tankers, transports and future upgrades of Rockwell B-1B. AECM contractor team led by Boeing includes US Air Force, ITT Avionics, Loral Electronic Systems, GEC Ferranti, FLIR Inc, Norden Systems, Raytheon Sedco Division, Tracor Aerospace and Electro-Radiation Inc. AECM first operated against ground-based tracking radar, SAM radars and airborne interceptors. Millimetre-wave radar, FLIR, terrain-referenced navigation system and two-crew operator station installed to demonstrate ability to navigate without constant radar emissions and to detect and identify typical strategic targets. Trials also involved ·

advanced system management with expert systems, real-time route planning, missile warning systems, and advanced integration and control concepts.

1990 programme included a positioned towed SRT sensor platform, sensor fusion for SRT applications, missile countermeasures and further integration concepts.

DESIGN FEATURES: Contributed systems, integrated by Boeing at Seattle, include ITT AN/ALQ-172 jamming equipment, Loral AN/ALR-56C ESM, Norden and Sedco monopulse jammers, and Tracor towed decoy.

Boeing provided core system with databus, flexible controls, displays and test instrumentation, making aircraft easily adaptable for various systems. Airframe modifications include provision for support systems, test equipment and new instrumentation in cabin, nose, wing and tail antennae, Tracor towed ECM equipment in tailcone.

F-4 PHANTOM NWDS

TYPE: Digital navigation and weapon delivery system for F-4E and RF-4C.

PROGRAMME: US Air Force order placed 1986; completed 1990. Details in 1990-91 *Jane's*.

BOEING 747 FREIGHTER CONVERSIONS

TYPE: Civil cargo conversion of passenger Boeing 747-100/200.

PROGRAMME: Boeing Military Airplanes proposed a production line at Wichita to produce up to five conversions per year, using parts and support from Boeing Commercial Airplane Group and Boeing Georgia Inc. Launch order for four required; second production line feasible.

VARIANTS: Similar to freighter conversions of 747-100s completed during 1970s. Upper decks converted to make passenger/cargo aircraft.

DESIGN FEATURES: Passenger interior and ceiling removed to accommodate 3.05 m (10 ft) high containers; floor and floor beams replaced; main deck floor strengthened; side cargo door and powered cargo handling system installed.

Retouched photograph showing final configuration of Boeing VC-25A (747-200B) 'Air Force One'

BOEING COMMERCIAL AIRPLANE GROUP

PO Box 3707, Seattle, Washington 98124
Telephone: 1 (206) 237 2121
Fax: 1 (206) 237 1706
Telex: 0650 329430 BOEING Co C
PRESIDENT: Dean D. Thornton
EXECUTIVE VICE-PRESIDENTS:
Philip M. Condit (General Manager, 777 Division)
R. R. Albrecht (Marketing and Sales)
R. L. Dryden (Manufacturing)
B. Gissing (Operations)
SENIOR VICE-PRESIDENT, ENGINEERING: Ben A. Cosgrove
SENIOR VICE-PRESIDENT, GOVERNMENT AND INTERNATIONAL
AFFAIRS: L. W. Clarkson
VICE-PRESIDENT, COMMUNICATIONS: Gerald A. Hendin

Boeing Commercial Airplane Group, headquartered at Renton, near Seattle, reorganised into three divisions in 1983: Renton Division produced 707 (until 1991) and produces 737 and 757; Everett Division produces 747 and 767; Fabrication Division provides manufacturing for other divisions. Materiel Division, created 1984, covers purchasing, quality control and vendor supplies.

Output in 1990, including military derivatives, was four 707s, 174 737s, 70 747s, 77 757s and 37 767s. Workforce in mid-1989 was 63,000. Delivered 6,000th Boeing jetliner 10 March 1990. Total 7,700 ordered at that date; total 8,173 ordered, 6,382 delivered at 31 March 1991.

BOEING 7J7/YXX

The agreement between Boeing and the Japan Aircraft Development Corporation concerning joint development of a new medium capacity airliner known by the Boeing designation 7J7 and Japanese designation YXX, which has been running since 1984, was renewed during February 1991 for a further period, though the project is not being very actively pursued at the engineering level. Further details under JADC in the Japanese section.

BOEING MODEL 707

USAF designations: VC-137, E-6A and E-8

First flight Model 367-80, original prototype of 707, 15 July 1954; developed version ordered in large numbers by US Air Force as KC-135 (Model 717); commercial developments of prototype were 707 and 720; details of many variants in 1980-81 and earlier *Jane's*; last commercial 707 was 707-320C for Moroccan Government delivered March 1982. Manufacture of military airframes continued (see other Boeing sections of this entry).

Total 1,010 commercial and military 707/720s ordered by 31 March 1991, with 991 delivered; production ended mid-1991. Boeing Military Airplane offers tanker/transport conversions of ex-airline 707s (which see); 707/720 conversions also offered by Israel Aircraft Industries (which see) and Comtran Ltd, USA (which see).

BOEING MODEL 727

First 727-100 rolled out 27 November 1962; first flight 9 February 1963; FAA certification 24 December 1963; into service with Eastern Air Lines 1 February 1964. 727-200 flew 27 July 1967; FAA certification 30 November 1967; into service with Northeast Airlines 14 December 1967. Last of 572 727-100s delivered October 1972 and of 1,260 727-200s September 1984. Current re-engining programmes by Valsan Partners and Dee Howard (which see). Model 727-100 last described in 1973-74 *Jane's* and 727-200 in 1983-84.

BOEING MODEL 737-100 and MODEL 737-200

Design of original 737 began 11 May 1964; first flight of 737-100, 9 April 1967; FAA certification 15 December 1967; 30 built. Superseded by 737-200; first flight 8 August 1967; added to 737-100 type certificate 21 December 1967; first delivery to United Air Lines 29 December 1967. Last of 1,114 737-200s delivered August 1988; total includes 19 **T-43A** navigation trainers for US Air Force and three **Surveillers** (now being upgraded) for Indonesian Air Force. Details of early versions and developments in 1974-75 *Jane's*; 737-200 last described in *Jane's* 1990-91.

BOEING MODEL 737-300

TYPE: Stretched and turbofan powered version of Advanced 737-200.
PROGRAMME: Production go-ahead March 1981; first flight 24 February 1984; certificated 14 November 1984; first delivery (to USAir) 28 November 1984. Model 737-300 for Ansett Worldwide (and subsequent lease to British Midland Airways) rolled out at Renton 19 February 1990 (as 1,833rd 737); 737 superseded 727 as world's most-produced commercial airliner. 120-minute EROPS approved November 1986; approval withdrawn July 1989 due to concerns related to operation in heavy rain and hail; approval restored September 1990.
VARIANTS: **737-300:** Basic airliner, as detailed below.
　Executive: Typically for about 20 passengers, with conference room, bedroom, bathroom and full dining facilities. Three sold by 31 December 1990, including one to Royal Thai Air Force.
CUSTOMERS: By 31 March 1991, 920 737-300s ordered and 659 delivered.
DESIGN FEATURES: Fuselage stretched 2.64 m (8 ft 8 in) compared with 737-200, by 1.12 m (3 ft 8 in) plug forward of wing box and 1.52 m (5 ft 0 in) aft; underfloor freight volume increased by 5.47 m³ (193 cu ft); wing aerofoil modified by new leading-edges outboard of engines, new flap sections and track fairings aft of engines; additional lateral control spoilers outboard; each wingtip extended by 28 cm (11 in); increased dorsal fin area and tailplane span; nosewheel mounting moved 13 cm (5 in) downwards to preserve engine ground clearance.
FLYING CONTROLS: All surfaces powered by two independent hydraulic systems with manual reversion for ailerons and elevator. Elevator servo tabs unlock on manual reversion. Rudder has standby hydraulic actuator and system. Three outboard powered overwing spoiler panels on each wing assist lateral control and also act as airbrakes. Variable incidence tailplane has two electric motors and manual standby.
　Leading-edge Krueger flaps inboard and three sections of slats outboard of engines. Two airbrake/lift dumper panels on each wing, inboard and outboard of engines. Triple-slotted trailing-edge flaps inboard and outboard of engines.
　FAA Category II landing minima system standard using SP-300 digital autopilot; Category IIIA capability optional.
STRUCTURE: Aluminium alloy dual-path fail-safe two-spar wing structure. Aluminium alloy two-spar tailplane. Graphite composite ailerons, elevators and rudders, latter built by Short Brothers (UK). Aluminium honeycomb spoiler/airbrake panels and trailing-edges of slats and flaps. Fuselage structure fail-safe aluminium. Some fins made by Xian Aircraft Co in China.
LANDING GEAR: Hydraulically retractable tricycle type, with Boeing oleo-pneumatic shock absorbers. Inward retracting main units have no doors, wheels forming

wheel well seal; nose unit retracts forward. Free-fall emergency extension. Compared with 737-200, nose unit is repositioned downwards by 13 cm (5 in) and modified to ensure adequate ground clearance for larger engine nacelles. Twin nosewheels have tyres size 27 × 7.75. Main units have heavy duty twin wheels, H40 × 14.5-19 heavy duty tyres, and Bendix or Goodrich heavy duty wheel brakes as standard. Mainwheel tyre pressure 13.45-14.00 bars (195-203 lb/sq in). Nosewheel tyre pressure 11-45-11.85 bars (166-172 lb/sq in).
POWER PLANT: Basic aircraft has two 88.97 kN (20,000 lb st) CFM International CFM56-3B-1 turbofans. Long-range option has two 97.86 kN (22,000 lb st) CFM56-3B-2. Engines pylon-mounted forward of wings, and higher than those of 737-200; each is fitted with an aerodynamic fence. Standard fuel capacity up to 20,104 litres (5,311 US gallons; 4,422 Imp gallons), with integral fuel cells in wing centre-section and integral wing tanks. Optional long-range fuel 23,830 litres (6,295 US gallons; 5,242 Imp gallons). Single-point pressure refuelling under leading-edge of starboard wing.
ACCOMMODATION: Crew of two side by side on flight deck (unchanged from 737-200). Alternative cabin layouts seat from 128 to 149 passengers. Typical arrangements offer 8 first class seats four-abreast at 96.5 cm (38 in) pitch and 120 tourist class seats six-abreast at 81 cm (32 in) in mixed class; and 141 or 149 all-tourist class at seat pitches of 81 cm (32 in) or 76 cm (30 in) respectively. One plug type door at each corner of cabin, with passenger doors on port side and service doors on starboard side. Airstair for forward cabin door optional. Overwing emergency exit on each side. One or two galleys and one lavatory forward, and one or two galleys and lavatories aft, depending on configuration. New lightweight interior, using advanced crushed core materials, providing total overhead baggage capacity of 6.80 m³ (240 cu ft), equivalent to 0.048 m³ (1.7 cu ft) per passenger. Underfloor freight holds forward and aft of wing, with access doors on starboard side.
SYSTEMS: Generally as for 737-200. AiResearch bleed air control system for air-conditioning and thermal anti-icing systems; Garrett GTCP 85-129(C) APU.
AVIONICS: Equipped to FAA Category II low weather minimum criteria as standard. Flight management computer system (FMCS), with performance and navigation functions, includes FAA Category II SP-300 digital autopilot with optional Category IIIA capability, inertial reference system (IRS) with laser gyros in lieu of gimbal type, 12.7 cm (5 in) electro-mechanical flight displays, 10 cm (4 in) electrical air data displays, dual digital air data computers, and full-range digital autothrottle. Other items include dual nav/com, VHF nav, colour digital radar, and digital autobrake. Optional equipment includes VLF/Omega nav system and dual INS. An EFIS installation received FAA certification on 24 July 1986. Also FAA approved is Boeing's windshear detection and guidance system.

DIMENSIONS, EXTERNAL:

Wing span	28.88 m (94 ft 9 in)
Wing chord at root	4.71 m (15 ft 5.6 in)
Length overall	33.40 m (109 ft 7 in)
Height overall	11.13 m (36 ft 6 in)
Tailplane span	12.70 m (41 ft 8 in)
Wheel track	5.23 m (17 ft 2 in)
Wheelbase	12.45 m (40 ft 10 in)
Main passenger door (port, fwd):	
Height	1.83 m (6 ft 0 in)
Width	0.86 m (2 ft 10 in)
Height to sill	2.62 m (8 ft 7 in)

Boeing 737-300 short-range transport of Aéromaritime of France

Passenger door (port, rear): Height	1.83 m (6 ft 0 in)	
Width	0.76 m (2 ft 6 in)	
Width with airstair	0.86 m (2 ft 10 in)	
Height to sill	2.74 m (9 ft 0 in)	
Emergency exits (overwing, port and stbd, each):		
Height	0.97 m (3 ft 2 in)	
Width	0.51 m (1 ft 8 in)	
Galley service door (stbd, fwd):		
Height	1.65 m (5 ft 5 in)	
Width	0.76 m (2 ft 6 in)	
Height to sill	2.62 m (8 ft 7 in)	
Service door (stbd, rear): Height	1.65 m (5 ft 5 in)	
Width	0.76 m (2 ft 6 in)	
Height to sill	2.74 m (9 ft 0 in)	
Freight hold door (stbd, fwd): Height	1.22 m (4 ft 0 in)	
Width	1.30 m (4 ft 3 in)	
Height to sill	1.30 m (4 ft 3 in)	
Freight hold door (stbd, rear): Height	1.22 m (4 ft 0 in)	
Width	1.22 m (4 ft 0 in)	
Height to sill	1.55 m (5 ft 1 in)	

DIMENSIONS, INTERNAL:

Cabin, incl galley and toilet:	
Length	23.52 m (77 ft 2 in)
Max width	3.45 m (11 ft 4 in)
Max height	2.13 m (7 ft 0 in)
Freight hold volume: fwd	12.03 m³ (425.0 cu ft)
rear	18.21 m³ (643.0 cu ft)

AREAS:

Wings, gross	105.4 m² (1,135.0 sq ft)
Ailerons (total)	2.49 m² (26.8 sq ft)
Trailing-edge flaps (total)	16.87 m² (181.6 sq ft)
Slats (total)	7.23 m² (77.8 sq ft)
Ground spoilers (total)	5.00 m² (53.8 sq ft)
Flight spoilers (total)	2.64 m² (28.4 sq ft)
Fin	23.13 m² (249.0 sq ft)
Rudder	5.22 m² (56.2 sq ft)
Tailplane	31.31 m² (337.0 sq ft)
Elevators, incl tabs (total)	6.55 m² (70.5 sq ft)

WEIGHTS AND LOADINGS (A: Basic aeroplane, B: Long-range option):

Operating weight empty: A	31,895 kg (70,320 lb)
B	32,459 kg (71,560 lb)
Max zero-fuel weight: A	47,627 kg (105,000 lb)
B	48,308 kg (106,500 lb)
Max landing weight: A	51,719 kg (114,000 lb)
B	52,526 kg (115,800 lb)
Max T-O weight: A	56,472 kg (124,500 lb)
B	62,823 kg (138,500 lb)
Max taxi weight: A	56,699 kg (125,000 lb)
B	63,050 kg (139,000 lb)

PERFORMANCE: (A: at brake release weight of 56,472 kg; 124,500 lb, B: at optional BRW of 62,822 kg; 138,500 lb):

T-O field length, S/L, at 29°C (84°F):	
A	2,027 m (6,650 ft)
B	2,749 m (9,020 ft)
Wet landing field length, 40° flap, at max landing weight:	
A, B	1,603 m (5,260 ft)
Still air range with 140 passengers, T-O at S/L:	
A	2,850 nm (5,280 km; 3,275 miles)
B	3,400 nm (6,300 km; 3,910 miles)

BOEING MODEL 737 SERIES ORDERS

Customers sometimes do not specify the individual model at time of ordering, or may adjust the models at a later date. This was the state of orders for the whole 737 series on 31 March 1991:

	Ordered	Delivered
737-100	30	30
737-200	1,114	1,114
737-300	920	659
737-400	307	149
737-500	240	62
Undecided	273	0

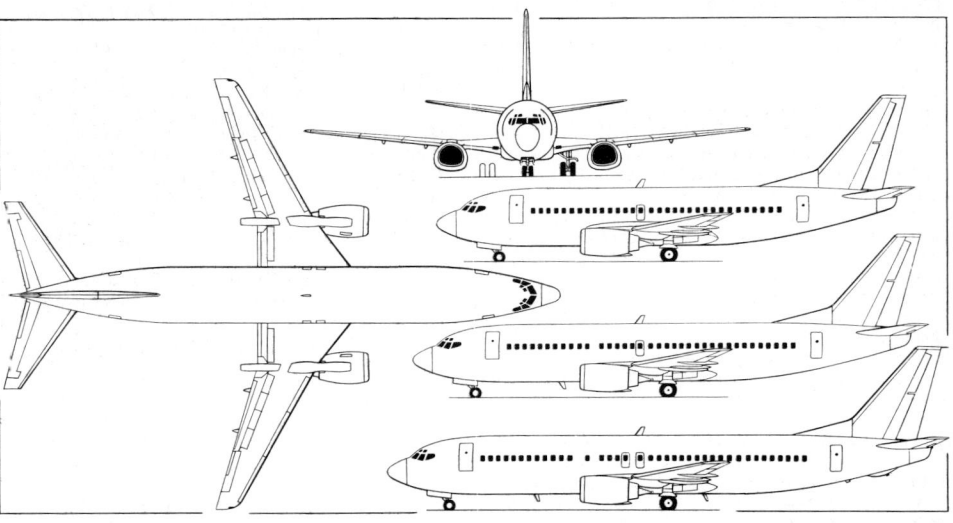

Three-view drawing of Boeing Model 737-400, with additional side elevations of 737-500 (top) and 737-300 (centre) *(Pilot Press)*

BOEING MODEL 737-400

TYPE: Stretched version of 737-300.

PROGRAMME: Announced June 1986; rolled out 26 January 1988; first flight 19 February 1988; certificated for up to 188 passengers 2 September 1988; first delivery (to Piedmont Airlines) 15 September 1988. 737-400 high gross weight structure variant rolled out 23 December 1988. EROPS approval granted September 1990.

VARIANTS: **High gross weight structure:** Strengthened wing and landing gear, revised avionics software, increased fuel capacity and CFM56-3C-1 engines; max ramp weight 68,265 kg (150,500 lb).

CUSTOMERS: By 31 March 1991, 307 firm orders and 149 delivered.

DESIGN FEATURES: Incorporates all the new technology of the 737-300. Fuselage has 1.83 m (6 ft 0 in) plug forward of wing and 1.22 m (4 ft 0 in) aft, totalling 3.05 m (10 ft); outer wings and landing gear strengthened for max landing weights from 54,885-56,245 kg (121,000-124,000 lb). Tail bumper standard on all 737-400s.

The general specification of the 737-300 applies also to the 737-400 except as follows:

POWER PLANT: Two 97.86 kN (22,000 lb st) CFM56-3B-2 or 104.5 kN (23,500 lb st) CFM56-3C-1 turbofans. Basic fuel capacity 20,105 litres (5,311 US gallons; 4,422 Imp gallons); long-range option fuel capacity, with Rogerson auxiliary tank, 23,830 litres (6,295 US gallons; 5,242 Imp gallons).

DIMENSIONS, EXTERNAL:

Length overall	36.45 m (119 ft 7 in)

DIMENSIONS, INTERNAL:

Cabin, incl galley and toilet:	
Length	27.18 m (89 ft 2 in)

WEIGHTS AND LOADINGS (A: Basic aeroplane, B: Long-range option):

Operating weight empty: A	33,434 kg (73,710 lb)
B	34,271 kg (75,555 lb)
Max zero-fuel weight: A	51,256 kg (113,000 lb)
B	53,070 kg (117,000 lb)
Max landing weight: A	54,885 kg (121,000 lb)
B	56,245 kg (124,000 lb)
Max T-O weight: A	62,822 kg (138,500 lb)
B	68,039 kg (150,000 lb)
Max taxi weight: A	63,049 kg (139,000 lb)
B	68,265 kg (150,500 lb)

PERFORMANCE (A: at T-O weight of 62,822 kg; 138,500 lb, B: at optional T-O weight of 68,039 kg; 150,000 lb):

T-O field length, S/L, at 30°C: A	2,315 m (7,600 ft)

B, with optional CFM56-3C engines	
	2,500 m (8,200 ft)
Wet landing field length, 40° flap:	
A at 54,885 kg (121,000 lb) landing weight	
	1,725 m (5,650 ft)
B at 56,245 kg (124,000 lb) landing weight	
	1,850 m (6,070 ft)
Range with 146 passengers, T-O at S/L:	
A	2,700 nm (5,000 km; 3,105 miles)
B	3,200 nm (5,930 km; 3,680 miles)

BOEING MODEL 737-500

TYPE: Short-body version of 737-300, replacing 737-200.

PROGRAMME: Initially known as 737-1000; announced as 737-500 on 20 May 1987; first flight 20 June 1989; certificated 12 February 1990 after 375 hour test programme; first delivery (to Southwest Airlines) 28 February 1990; EROPS approval September 1990.

VARIANTS: Max T-O weights ranging from 52,163 to 60,554 kg (115,000 to 133,500 lb).

CUSTOMERS: Firm orders totalled 240 by 31 March 1991. Launch customers were Braathens SAFE of Norway (25 firm) and Southwest Airlines (20 firm and 20 optioned); 62 delivered by 31 March 1991 (delivery to Lufthansa 25 February 1991 was 2,000th in 737 series).

DESIGN FEATURES: Incorporates advanced technology of 737-300 and -400, but fuselage shortened to overall length of 31.0 m (101 ft 9 in), similar to that of 737-200. With more powerful engines and auxiliary fuel, high gross weight 737-500 with mixed class 108-passenger load has max range of 2,996 nm (5,552 km; 3,450 miles).

POWER PLANT: Two CFM International CFM56-3B-1 turbofans, rated at 88.97 kN (20,000 lb st) or derated to 82.29 kN (18,500 lb st) according to gross weight. Basic fuel capacity 20,105 litres (5,311 US gallons; 4,422 Imp gallons); long-range option fuel capacity 23,830 litres (6,295 US gallons; 5,242 Imp gallons).

WEIGHTS AND LOADINGS (A: Basic aeroplane, B: Long-range option):

Operating weight empty: A	30,953 kg (68,240 lb)
B	31,515 kg (69,480 lb)
Max zero-fuel weight: A	46,493 kg (102,500 lb)
B	46,720 kg (103,000 lb)
Max landing weight: A, B	49,895 kg (110,000 lb)
Max T-O weight: A	52,163 kg (115,000 lb)
B	60,554 kg (133,500 lb)
Max taxi weight: A	52,617 kg (116,000 lb)
B	60,781 kg (134,000 lb)

Boeing 737-400 in the insignia of USAir

PERFORMANCE:

Range with 108 passengers:

A   1,700 nm (3,150 km; 1,955 miles)
B   2,420 nm (4,485 km; 2,785 miles)

BOEING MODEL 747 (DISCONTINUED MODELS)

TYPE: High capacity, wide-body, long-range airliner.

PROGRAMME: Programme announced 13 April 1966 (first-ever wide-body jet airliner), with Pan American order for 25; official programme launch 25 July 1966; first flight 9 February 1969; FAA certification 30 December 1969; first delivery (to Pan Am) 12 December 1969; first route service New York-London flown 22 January 1970. In May 1990 Boeing decided to market only the -400; at 31 March 1991, two 747-200F Freighters remained to be delivered.

VARIANTS: For all variants prior to 747-400, see 1990-91 and earlier editions. Produced as 747-100 (167), 747-100B (nine), 747SP (45), 747-100SR (29), 747-200B (226, incl two USAF VC-25A 'Air Force One'), 747-200C Convertible (13), 747-200F Freighter (73), 747-200M (77), 747-300 (56), 747-300M (21) and 747-300SR (four); total 720. Four other 747-200Bs modified by Boeing Aerospace as E-4 command post aircraft (see 1986-87 *Jane's*); 19 Pan American 747s modified as passenger/ cargo C-19As by Boeing Military Airplanes for Civil Reserve Air Fleet (see 1990-91 edition).

747 modification programmes: Major upgrade of 747-100 and -200B, including side cargo door, offered by Boeing to give main deck cargo capability. Alternatives include all-passenger or all-cargo Special Freighter; 6- or 12-pallet Combi; all-passenger or all-freight Convertible. Convertible can also be mixed passenger/cargo. Main elements of modification include cargo door measuring 3.05 m (10 ft 0 in) high by 3.4 m (11 ft 2 in) wide, strengthened floor, powered or manual cargo handling systems. Optional increase in gross weight.

747 can be produced or retrofitted with Boeing Delco performance management system (PMS), sensing onboard data to calculate best airspeed, engine power setting and altitude for best fuel burn or minimum cost. First complete system delivered June 1982.

Pending receipt of a detailed description of the 747-400, the following details of the -200B are retained for comparison:

FLYING CONTROLS: Low speed outboard ailerons, high speed inboard ailerons; eight overwing flight spoiler panels assist ailerons and act as airbrakes; variable incidence tailplane; no trim tabs; all surfaces fully powered hydraulic. High lift devices include triple-slotted trailing-edge flaps; 10 leading-edge flaps outboard; three sections Krueger flaps inboard; four overwing ground spoiler panels inboard.

STRUCTURE: Wing and tail surfaces are aluminium alloy dual-path fail-safe structures; aluminium honeycomb spoiler panels. Frame/stringer/stressed skin fuselage containing some bonding.

LANDING GEAR: Hydraulically retractable tricycle type. Twin-wheel nose unit retracts forward. Main gear comprises four four-wheel bogies: two, mounted side by side under fuselage at wing trailing-edge, retract forward; two, mounted under wings, retract inward. Disc brakes on all mainwheels, with individually controlled anti-skid units.

POWER PLANT: Four Pratt & Whitney, General Electric or Rolls-Royce turbofans, in pods pylon-mounted on wing leading-edges. Fuel in seven integral tanks: centre wing

Boeing 737-500 taking off from Boeing's Renton factory

tank, two inboard main tanks, two outboard main tanks and two inboard reserve tanks. Fuselage tank optional. Refuelling point on each wing between inboard and outboard engines.

ACCOMMODATION: Normal operating crew of three, on flight deck above level of main deck. Observer station and provision for second observer station are provided. Crew rest area available as option at rear of upper deck. Basic accommodation for 452 passengers, made up of 32 first class and 420 economy class, which includes a 32-passenger upper deck (extended on 747-400, which see). Alternative layouts accommodate 447 economy class passengers in nine-abreast seating or 516 ten-abreast, with 32 passengers on upper deck. All versions have two aisles. Five passenger doors on each side, of which two forward of wing on each side are normally used. Freight holds under floor, forward and aft of wing, with doors on starboard side. One door on forward hold, two on rear hold. Aircraft is designed for fully mechanical loading of baggage and freight. An optional side cargo door is available for passenger, convertible and freighter versions of the Model 747. Installed aft of door 4 on the port side of the fuselage, it allows the carriage of main deck cargo on passenger versions. Addition of this door to the freighter allows loads up to 3.05 m (10 ft) in height to be accommodated aft of the flight deck, and also makes possible simultaneous nose and side cargo handling.

SYSTEMS: Air cycle air-conditioning system. Pressure differential 0.61 bar (8.9 lb/sq in). Four independent hydraulic systems, pressure 207 bars (3,000 lb/sq in), maximum capacity 265 litres (70 US gallons; 58 Imp gallons)/min at 196.5 bars (2,850 lb/sq in), each with one engine driven and one pneumatically driven pump. The latter pumps supplement or substitute for engine driven pumps. Reservoir in each system, pressurised by engine bleed air via a pressure regulation module. Reservoir relief valve pressure is nominal 4.48 bars (65 lb/sq in). A small AC powered electric pump is installed to charge the brake accumulator during towing of the aircraft. Electrical supply from four aircooled 60kVA generators mounted one on each engine. Two 60kVA generators (supplemental cooling allows 90kVA each) mounted on APU for ground operation and to supply primary

electrical power when engine mounted generators are not operating. Three-phase 400Hz constant frequency AC generators, 115/200V output. 28V DC power obtained from transformer-rectifier units. 24V 36Ah nickel-cadmium battery for selected ground functions and as in-flight backup. Gas turbine APU for pneumatic and electrical supplies.

AVIONICS: Standard avionics include three ARINC 566 VHF communications systems, two ARINC 533A HF communications systems, one ARINC 531 Selcal, three ARINC 547 VOR/ILS navigation systems, two ARINC 570 ADF, marker beacon receiver, two ARINC 568 DME, two ARINC 572 ATC, three ARINC 552 low-range radio altimeters, two ARINC 564 weather radar units, three ARINC 561 inertial navigation systems, two heading reference systems, ARINC 573 flight recorder, ARINC 557 cockpit voice recorder, integrated electronic flight control system with auto-throttle and rollout guidance to provide automatic stabilisation, path control and pilot assist functions for Category II and III landing conditions, two ARINC 565 central air data systems, stall warning system, central instrument warning system, ground proximity warning system, attitude and navigation instrumentation, and standby attitude indication.

EQUIPMENT: ARINC 412 interphone, ARINC 560 passenger address system, multiple passenger service and entertainment system.

DIMENSIONS, EXTERNAL:

Wing span	59.64 m (195 ft 8 in)
Length: overall	70.66 m (231 ft 10 in)
fuselage	68.63 m (225 ft 2 in)
Height overall	19.33 m (63 ft 5 in)
Tailplane span	22.17 m (72 ft 9 in)
Wheel track	11.00 m (36 ft 1 in)
Wheelbase	25.60 m (84 ft 0 in)
Passenger doors (ten, each): Height	1.93 m (6 ft 4 in)
Width	1.07 m (3 ft 6 in)
Height to sill	approx 4.88 m (16 ft 0 in)
Baggage door (front hold): Height	1.68 m (5 ft 6 in)
Width	2.64 m (8 ft 8 in)
Height to sill	approx 2.64 m (8 ft 8 in)
Baggage door (forward door, rear hold):	
Height	1.68 m (5 ft 6 in)

The last Boeing 747-300 departing from Boeing's Everett Field

Width	2.64 m (8 ft 8 in)
Height to sill	approx 2.69 m (8 ft 10 in)

Bulk loading door (rear door on rear hold):

Height	1.19 m (3 ft 11 in)
Width	1.12 m (3 ft 8 in)
Height to sill	approx 2.90 m (9 ft 6 in)
Optional cargo door (port): Height	3.05 m (10 ft 0 in)
Width	3.40 m (11 ft 2 in)

DIMENSIONS, INTERNAL:

Cabin, incl toilets and galleys:

Length	57.00 m (187 ft 0 in)
Max width	6.13 m (20 ft 1½ in)
Max height	2.54 m (8 ft 4 in)
Floor area, passenger deck	327.9 m² (3,529 sq ft)
Volume, passenger deck	789 m³ (27,860 cu ft)
Baggage hold (fwd, containerised) volume	
	78.4 m³ (2,768 cu ft)
Baggage hold (rear, containerised) volume	
	68.6 m³ (2,422 cu ft)
Bulk volume	28.3 m³ (1,000 cu ft)

AREAS:

Wings, reference area	511 m² (5,500 sq ft)
Ailerons (total)	20.6 m² (222 sq ft)
Trailing-edge flaps (total)	78.7 m² (847 sq ft)
Leading-edge flaps (total)	48.1 m² (518 sq ft)
Spoilers (total)	30.8 m² (331 sq ft)
Fin	77.1 m² (830 sq ft)
Rudder	22.9 m² (247 sq ft)
Tailplane	136.6 m² (1,470 sq ft)
Elevators (total)	32.5 m² (350 sq ft)

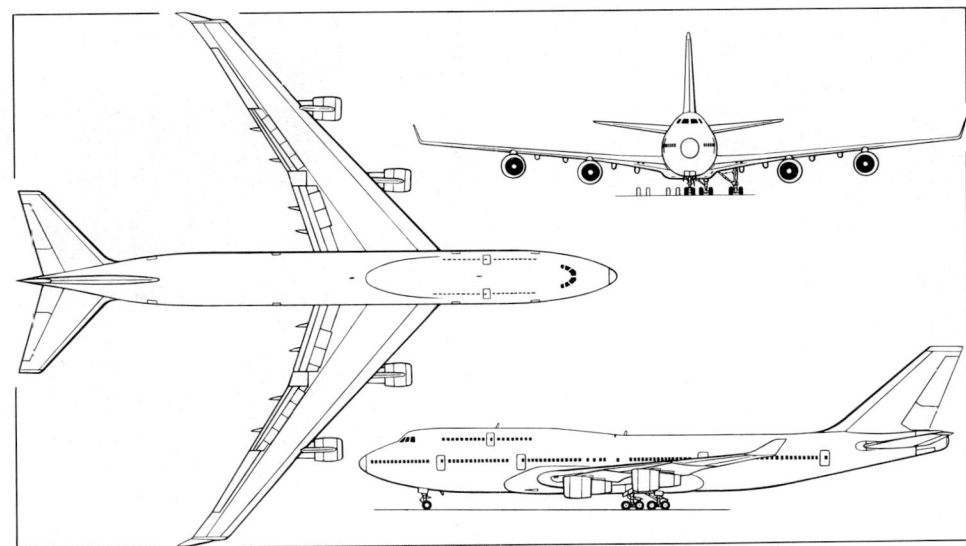

Boeing 747-400 advanced long-range version of the 747-300 (General Electric CF6-80C2 engines)
(Pilot Press)

BOEING MODEL 747-400

TYPE: 747 with extended capacity and range.

PROGRAMME: Announced May 1985; design go-ahead July 1985; rollout 26 January 1988; first flight 29 April 1988; certificated with P&W PW4056 9 January 1989; certificated with GE CF6-80C2 and R-R RB211-524G during 1989. Since May 1990, -400 is the only version marketed; orders now exceed those for -200 variants.

VARIANTS: **747-400:** Basic passenger version.

747-400M and 747-400F: Cargo/passenger and all-cargo versions respectively; launched 1989; carry 19,960 kg (44,000 lb) more than 747-200F at ranges up to 5,210 nm (9,656 km; 6,000 miles); no extended upper deck on -400F.

CUSTOMERS: Northwest Orient Airlines ordered 10 -400s with PW4000s and 420-passenger interior October 1985; first delivery 26 January 1989. Total orders, including 16 Freighters and 33 Combis, 412 by 31 March 1991; 116 delivered. Launch customer for 747-400F was Air France with five, powered by CF6-80C2s, for delivery from August 1993.

DESIGN FEATURES: Wing has special Boeing aerofoil and 3.66 m (12 ft 0 in) greater span than 747-200; sweepback at quarter-chord 37° 30′; thickness/chord ratio 13.44 per cent inboard, 7.8 per cent at mid-span, 8 per cent outboard; dihedral at rest 7°; incidence 2°. Winglets, canted 22° outward and swept 60°, increase range by three per cent. Engine choice includes 258.0 kN (58,000 lb st) class CF6-80C2, PW4056 or RB211-524G: fuel burn nine to 12 per cent lower than 747-300 according to engine: fuel burn per passenger 24 per cent lower than 747-200. Upper deck extended rearwards by 7.11 m (23 ft 4 in).

Advanced aluminium alloys save 2,721 kg (6,000 lb) wing weight; carbon brakes, wide wheels and low profile tyres save 816 kg (1,800 lb); new nacelles and pylons give

commonality with Model 767; two-crew, electronic display, digital flight deck. New tanks in tailplane torsion box, fuel capacity 12,492 litres (3,300 US gallons; 2,748 Imp gallons), which cannot be transferred to adjust longitudinal trim; greater fuel capacity, more economical engines and weight reduction result in 1,000 nm (1,853 km; 1,151 mile) increase in range.

STRUCTURE: Wing incorporates advanced aluminium alloys developed for Models 757 and 767; composites used for some components.

ACCOMMODATION: Two-crew flight deck. Upper deck economy seating for 69, six-abreast with single aisle, or 26 first class sleeper seats. Cabin improvements include increased overhead storage, alternative galley and toilet locations, audio and visual cabin entertainment transmitted without wires from floor, and quicker rearrangement of cabin interior. Optional overhead crew rest area above rear of main deck cabin (four bunks, four seats; eight bunks, two seats; two bunks, two seats, five sleeper seats).

DIMENSIONS, EXTERNAL: As for 747-200 except:

Wing span	64.31 m (211 ft 0 in)

WEIGHTS AND LOADINGS (letters are used to denote engine installations as follows: A: PW4056, B: CF6-80C2, C: RB211-524G):

Operating weight empty (approx) for max available gross weights:

A	180,849 kg (398,700 lb)
B	180,622 kg (398,200 lb)
C	181,983 kg (401,200 lb)
Max fuel weights: A, C	175,392 kg (386,674 lb)
B	174,553 kg (384,824 lb)

Max payload:

A	65,317 kg (144,000 lb)
B	65,453 kg (144,300 lb)
C	64,011 kg (141,120 lb)
Max T-O weight: A, B, C	362,875 kg (800,000 lb)
	or 385,555 kg (850,000 lb)
	or 394,625 kg (870,000 lb)
Max ramp weight: A, B, C	364,235 kg (803,000 lb)
	or 386,915 kg (853,000 lb)
	or 395,986 kg (873,000 lb)
Max zero-fuel weight: A, B, C	242,670 kg (535,000 lb)
Max landing weight: A, B, C	260,360 kg (574,000 lb)
	or 285,765 kg (630,000 lb)

PERFORMANCE (at T-O weight of 394,625 kg; 870,000 lb except where indicated. Engines as designated under Weights and Loadings):

Max level speed at 9,150 m (30,000 ft):

A	529 knots (979 km/h; 608 mph)
B	532 knots (985 km/h; 612 mph)
C	527 knots (976 km/h; 606 mph)

Approach speed, at highest optional landing weight:

A, B, C	152 knots (282 km/h; 175 mph)

Initial cruise altitude, at highest optional T-O weight:

A, B, C	9,845 m (32,300 ft)

FAR T-O field length at S/L, ISA, at highest optional T-O weight: A 3,475 m (11,400 ft)

B, C 3,490 m (11,450 ft)

FAR landing field length at max landing weight of 285,765 kg (630,000 lb): A, B, C 2,134 m (7,000 ft)

Design range, typical international rules, at highest optional T-O weight, 400 three-class passengers, full tanks:

A	7,340 nm (13,600 km; 8,450 miles)
B	7,230 nm (13,400 km; 8,325 miles)
C	7,200 nm (13,340 km; 8,290 miles)

BOEING MODEL 757

TYPE: Short/medium-range twin-turbofan airliner.

PROGRAMME: New-technology family designated 757/767/777 announced early 1978; medium/long-range 757 has 707/727/737 fuselage cross-section and two large turbofans; Eastern Air Lines and British Airways ordered 21 firm and 24 optioned and 19 + 18 respectively 13 August 1978; first flight (N757A) 19 February 1982

Boeing 747-400 of Canadian departing from Everett Field

Boeing 757-200 (Rolls-Royce 535E4 turbofans) in the insignia of Royal Brunei Airlines

powered by 166.4 kN (37,400 lb st) Rolls-Royce RB535Cs and designated 757-200; first Boeing airliner launched with foreign engine; FAA certification 21 December 1982; CAA certification 14 January 1983; revenue services began 1 January 1983 (EAL) and 9 February 1983 (BA). First flight of 757 powered by P&W PW2037s 14 March 1984; certificated October 1984 and delivered to Delta; first 757 with RB535E4s delivered to EAL 10 October 1984; first extended range model delivered to Royal Brunei Airlines May 1986; 757 with RB535E4 engines approved FAA EROPS December 1986 (extended to 180 min August 1990); 757 with PW2037/3040 EROPS approved April 1990; Boeing windshear guidance and detection system approved by FAA January 1987.

VARIANTS: **757-200:** First production passenger airliner; extended range available.

757-200PF Package Freighter: Large freight door forward, single crew door and no windows; up to 15 standard 2.24 × 3.18 m (88 × 125 in) cargo pallets on main deck.

757-200M Combi: Mixed cargo/passenger configuration with windows, upward opening cargo door to port (forward) 3.40 × 2.18 m (134 × 86 in); carries up to three 2.24 × 2.74 m (88 × 108 in) cargo containers and 150 passengers.

CUSTOMERS: By 31 March 1991, orders for 757-200/200M/200PF totalled 723, with 352 delivered. 59 Model 757-200PFs with PW2040s ordered by United Parcel Service; deliveries started 3 September 1987 and 24 delivered by March 1991; Ansett Worldwide ordered two; launch order for 757-200M Combi from Royal Nepal Airlines (one). First 757 kept by Boeing for flight test support in use early 1991 as avionics testbed for Lockheed YF-22.

DESIGN FEATURES: Special Boeing aerofoils; sweepback at quarter-chord 25°; dihedral 5°; incidence 3° 12′; wing thermally anti-iced.

FLYING CONTROLS: All-speed fully powered outboard ailerons assisted by five flight spoilers on each wing also acting variously as airbrakes and ground spoilers; one additional ground spoiler inboard on each wing; elevators and rudder; double-slotted trailing-edge flaps; full-span leading-edge slats, five sections each wing; variable incidence tailplane. EFIS instruments with EICAS; digital autopilot.

STRUCTURE: Aluminium alloy two-spar fail-safe wing box; centre-section continuous through fuselage; ailerons, flaps and spoilers extensively of honeycomb, graphite composites and laminates; tailplane has full-span light alloy torque boxes; fin has three-spar dual cell light alloy torque box; elevators and rudder have graphite/epoxy honeycomb skins supported by honeycomb and laminated spar and rib assemblies; graphite wing/fuselage and flap track fairings.

Subcontractors include Hawker de Havilland (wing inter-spar ribs), Shorts (inboard flaps), CASA (outboard flaps), Boeing Renton (leading-edge slats, main cabin sections), Boeing Helicopters (fixed leading-edges), Boeing Military Airplanes (flight deck), Grumman (overwing spoiler panels), Heath Tecna (wing/fuselage and flap track fairings), Schweizer (wingtips), LTV (fin and tailplane, extreme rear fuselage).

LANDING GEAR: Retractable tricycle type, with main and nose units manufactured by Menasco. Each main unit comprises a four-wheel bogie, fitted with Dunlop wheels, carbon brakes and tyres. Twin-wheel nose unit, also with Dunlop tyres. All landing gear doors of graphite/Kevlar.

POWER PLANT: Two 166.4 kN (37,400 lb st) Rolls-Royce 535C, 170 kN (38,200 lb st) Pratt & Whitney PW2037, 178.4 kN (40,100 lb st) Rolls-Royce 535E4, or 185.5 kN (41,700 lb st) Pratt & Whitney PW2040 turbofans,

mounted in underwing pods. Engine support struts supplied by Rohr Industries. Fuel capacity 42,597 litres (11,253 US gallons; 9,370 Imp gallons).

ACCOMMODATION: Crew of two on flight deck, with provision for an observer. Five to seven cabin attendants. Nine standard interior arrangements for 178 (16 first class/162 tourist), 186 (16 first class/170 tourist), 202 (12 first class/190 tourist), 208 (12 first class/196 tourist) mixed class passengers, or 214, 220, 223, 224 or 239 all-tourist passengers. First class seats are four-abreast, at 96.5 cm (38 in) pitch; tourist seat pitch is 81 or 86 cm (32 or 34 in), basically six-abreast, in mixed class arrangements. Large overhead bins of Kevlar provide approximately 0.054 m³ (1.9 cu ft) of stowage per passenger. Choice of two cabin door configurations, with either three passenger doors and two overwing emergency exits on each side (used with 186, 208, 220 and 224 seat interiors), or four doors on each side (used with 178, 202, 214, 223 and 239 seat interiors). All versions have a galley at the front on the starboard side and another at the rear (two on 178 and 186 passenger versions and three on the 239 version plus one amidships); a toilet at the front on the port side and three more at the rear (186, 202, 208, 220, 224 passengers) or two at the rear (239) or amidships (178, 214, 223 passengers). Coat closet at front of first class cabins and 214/220 passenger interiors. Baggage/cargo hold doors on starboard side.

SYSTEMS: AiResearch environmental control system; General Electric engine thrust management system; Honeywell-Vickers engine driven hydraulic pumps; four Abex electric hydraulic pumps. Hydraulic system maximum flow rate 140 litres (37 US gallons; 30.8 Imp gallons)/min at T-O power on engine driven pumps; 25.4-34.8 litres (6.7-9.2 US gallons; 5.6-7.7 Imp gallons)/min on electric motor pumps; 42.8 litres (11.3 US gallons; 9.4 Imp gallons)/min on ram air turbine. Independent reservoirs, pressurised by air from pneumatic system, maximum pressure 207 bars (3,000 lb/sq in) on primary pumps. Sundstrand electrical power generating system and ram air turbine; and Garrett GTCP331-200 APU.

AVIONICS: Collins FCS-700 autopilot flight director system (AFDS), EFIS-700 electronic flight instrument system, engine indication and crew alerting system (EICAS), RMI-743 radio distance magnetic indicator (RDMI) and optional radio magnetic indicator (RMI). Avionics also include a Honeywell inertial reference system (IRS). In this IRS, conventional mechanical gyroscopes are replaced by laser gyroscopes, and utilisation, in both the Models 757 and 767, represents their first commercial application. The IRS provides position, velocity and attitude information to flight deck displays, and the flight management computer system (FMCS) and digital air data computer (DADC) supplied by Honeywell. The

First Boeing 757-200PF Package Freighter for United Parcel Service

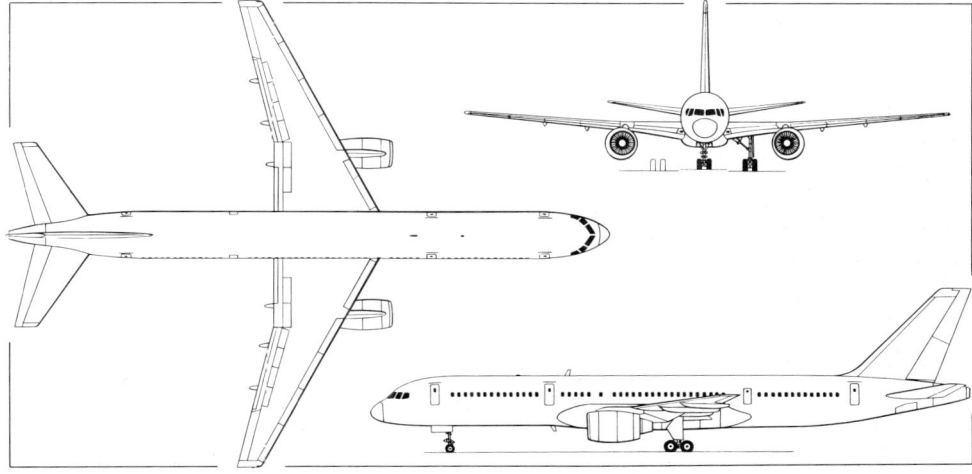

Boeing 757-200 twin-turbofan short/medium-range transport aircraft *(Pilot Press)*

Boeing 767-200ER of Air Mauritius photographed during a record-setting delivery flight in April 1988

FMCS provides automatic *en route* and terminal navigation capability, and also computes and commands both lateral and vertical flight profiles for optimum fuel efficiency, maximised by electronic linkage of the FMCS with automatic flight control and thrust management systems. Boeing windshear detection and guidance system is optional. Aircraft for British Airways and Monarch Airlines have Bendix/King ARINC 700 series avionics, including colour weather radar and seven digital com, nav and identification systems.

DIMENSIONS, EXTERNAL:

Wing span	38.05 m (124 ft 10 in)
Wing chord: at root	8.20 m (26 ft 11 in)
at tip	1.73 m (5 ft 8 in)
Wing aspect ratio	7.8
Length: overall	47.32 m (155 ft 3 in)
fuselage	46.96 m (154 ft 10 in)
Height overall	13.56 m (44 ft 6 in)
Tailplane span	15.21 m (49 ft 11 in)
Wheel track	7.32 m (24 ft 0 in)
Wheelbase	18.29 m (60 ft 0 in)
Passenger doors (two, fwd, port):	
Height	1.83 m (6 ft 0 in)
Width	0.84 m (2 ft 9 in)
Passenger door (rear, port): Height	1.83 m (6 ft 0 in)
Width	0.76 m (2 ft 6 in)
Service door (fwd, stbd): Height	1.65 m (5 ft 5 in)
Width	0.76 m (2 ft 6 in)
Service door (stbd, opposite second passenger door):	
Height	1.83 m (6 ft 0 in)
Width	0.84 m (2 ft 9 in)
Service door (rear, stbd): Height	1.83 m (6 ft 0 in)
Width	0.76 m (2 ft 6 in)
Emergency exits (four, overwing):	
Height	0.97 m (3 ft 2 in)
Width	0.51 m (1 ft 8 in)
Emergency exits, optional (two, aft of wings):	
Height	1.32 m (4 ft 4 in)
Width	0.61 m (2 ft 0 in)

DIMENSIONS, INTERNAL:

Cabin (aft of flight deck to rear pressure bulkhead):	
Length	36.09 m (118 ft 5 in)
Max width	3.53 m (11 ft 7 in)
Max height	2.13 m (7 ft 0 in)
Floor area	116.04 m² (1,249 sq ft)
Passenger section volume	230.50 m³ (8,140 cu ft)
Underfloor cargo volume (bulk loading):	
fwd	19.82 m³ (700 cu ft)
rear	30.87 m³ (1,090 cu ft)

AREAS:

Wings, gross	185.25 m² (1,994 sq ft)
Ailerons (total)	4.46 m² (48.0 sq ft)
Trailing-edge flaps (total)	30.38 m² (327 sq ft)
Leading-edge slats (total)	18.39 m² (198 sq ft)
Flight spoilers (total)	10.96 m² (118 sq ft)
Ground spoilers (total)	12.82 m² (138 sq ft)
Fin	34.37 m² (370 sq ft)
Rudder	11.61 m² (125 sq ft)
Tailplane	50.35 m² (542 sq ft)
Elevators (total)	12.54 m² (135 sq ft)

WEIGHTS AND LOADINGS (with 186 passengers. A: 535E4 engines, B: PW2037s, C: PW2040s):

Operating weight empty: A	57,180 kg (126,060 lb)
B, C	57,039 kg (125,750 lb)
Max basic T-O weight: A, B, C	99,790 kg (220,000 lb)
Max T-O weight (medium-range):	
A, B, C	104,325 kg (230,000 lb)
Max T-O weight (long-range):	
A, B, C	113,395 kg (250,000 lb)
Max landing weight: A, B, C	89,810 kg (198,000 lb)
757-200PF	95,255 kg (210,000 lb)

Max zero-fuel weight: A, B, C	83,460 kg (184,000 lb)
757-200PF	90,720 kg (200,000 lb)
Max wing loading:	
A, B, C at max basic T-O weight	
	538.5 kg/m² (110.3 lb/sq ft)
A, B, C at long-range max T-O weight	
	587.8 kg/m² (120.4 lb/sq ft)
Max power loading:	
at max basic T-O weight:	
A	279.68 kg/kN (2.74 lb/lb st)
B	293.5 kg/kN (2.88 lb/lb st)
C	268.97 kg/kN (2.64 lb/lb st)
at long-range max T-O weight:	
A	317.81 kg/kN (3.12 lb/lb st)
B	333.51 kg/kN (3.27 lb/lb st)
C	305.1 kg/kN (3.00 lb/lb st)

PERFORMANCE (nominal, with 186 passengers, US mixed class operations; at max basic T-O weight, except where indicated, and with engines as above):

Max operating speed: A, B, C	Mach 0.86
Cruising speed: A, B, C	Mach 0.80
Approach speed at S/L, flaps down, max landing weight:	
A, B, C	132 knots (245 km/h; 152 mph) EAS
Initial cruising height: A	11,880 m (38,970 ft)
B, C	11,675 m (38,300 ft)
Min ground turning radius: over wingtip	29.87 m (98 ft)
nose gear	21.64 m (71 ft)
Runway LCN at ramp weight of 100,244 kg (221,000 lb), optimum tyre pressure and subgrade C flexible pavement: H40 × 14.5-19.0 tyres	36
T-O field length (S/L, 29°C):	
at max basic T-O weight: A	1,646 m (5,400 ft)
B	1,791 m (5,875 ft)
C	1,637 m (5,370 ft)
at long-range max T-O weight: A	2,134 m (7,000 ft)
B	2,792 m (9,160 ft)
C	2,118 m (6,950 ft)
Landing field length at max landing weight:	
A	1,411 m (4,630 ft)
B, C	1,460 m (4,790 ft)
Range with 186 passengers:	
at max basic T-O weight:	
A	2,820 nm (5,226 km; 3,247 miles)

B, C	2,980 nm (5,522 km; 3,431 miles)
at long-range max T-O weight:	
A	3,820 nm (7,079 km; 4,399 miles)
B, C	4,000 nm (7,408 km; 4,603 miles)
757-200PF, max long-range T-O weight, 22,680 kg (50,000 lb) payload:	
A	3,700 nm (6,857 km; 4,261 miles)
B, C	3,885 nm (7,200 km; 4,474 miles)

OPERATIONAL NOISE LEVELS (FAR Pt 36 Stage 3):

T-O, at max basic T-O weight, cutback power:	
A	82.2 EPNdB
B	86.2 EPNdB
C (estimated)	84.7 EPNdB
Approach at max landing weight, 30° flap:	
A	95.0 EPNdB
B, C	97.7 EPNdB
Sideline: A	93.3 EPNdB
B	94.0 EPNdB
C (estimated)	94.6 EPNdB

BOEING MODEL 767

TYPE: Medium/long-range twin-turbofan airliner.

PROGRAMME: Launched on receipt of United Air Lines order for 30 on 14 July 1978; construction of basic 220-passenger 767-200 began 6 July 1979; first flight (N767BA) 26 September 1981 with P&W JT9D turbofans; first flight fifth aircraft with GE CF6-80A 19 February 1982; 767 with JT9D-7R4D certificated 30 July 1982; with CF6-80A 30 September 1982.

First delivery with JT9D (United Air Lines) 19 August 1982; first delivery with CF6 (Delta) 25 October 1982. 767-200 with JT9D-7R4 or CF6-80A or -80A2 approved for EROPS January 1987; EROPS approval for 767-200 and -300 with PW4000 obtained April 1990. Boeing windshear detection and guidance system FAA approved for 767-200 and -300 February 1987.

VARIANTS: **767-200:** Basic model. Medium-range variant has reduced fuel; higher gross weight variant certificated June 1983.

767-200ER: Extended range version; first flight 6 March 1984; basic -200ER with centre-section tankage and gross weight increased to 156,490 kg (345,000 lb) first delivered to Ethiopian Airlines 23 May 1984; optional

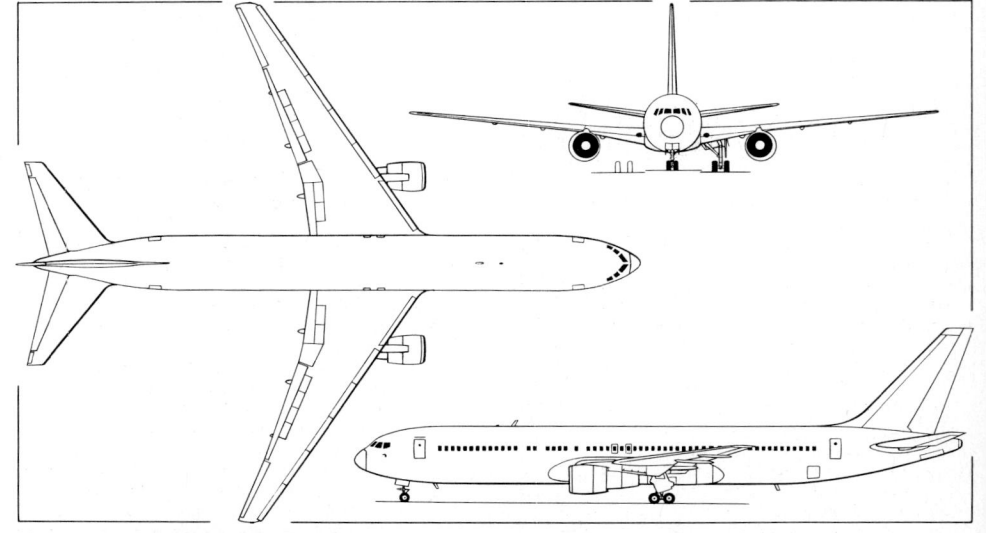

Boeing 767-300 wide-bodied medium-range commercial transport *(Pilot Press)*

Boeing 767-300 of the Dutch carrier Martinair

higher gross weights are 159,210 kg (351,000 lb), 172,365 kg (380,000 lb) and 175,540 kg (387,000 lb).

767-300: 269-passenger stretched version, with 3.07 m (10 ft 1 in) plug forward of wing and 3.35 m (11 ft) plug aft, and same gross weight as 767-200; strengthened landing gear and thicker metal in parts of fuselage and underwing skin; same flight deck and systems as other 767s; same engine options as 767-200ER; first ordered 29 September 1983. First flight with JT9D-7R4D engines 30 January 1986; certificated with JT9D-7R4D and CF6-80A2 22 September 1986; British Airways ordered 11 in August 1987, plus six more in October 1988, with Rolls-Royce RB211-524H, for delivery from November 1989.

767-300ER: Extended range, higher gross weight version; development began January 1985; optional gross weights 172,365 kg (380,000 lb), 175,540 kg (387,000 lb) and 181,439 kg (400,000 lb); increased centre-section tankage. Engine choice CF6-80C2, PW-4000, RB211-524H; structural reinforcement; certificated late 1987. Launch customer American Airlines (15), delivered from February 1988.

CUSTOMERS: Total orders for all versions 540 by 31 March 1991, with 352 delivered; original prototype became Boeing Aerospace & Electronics 767 Airborne Surveillance Testbed (formerly AOA) for US Army (see page 366). One reconfigured by E-Systems as medevac aircraft for Civil Reserve Air Fleet.

DESIGN FEATURES: Special Boeing aerofoils; quarter-chord sweepback 31° 30′; thickness/chord ratio 15.1 per cent at root, 10.3 per cent at tip; dihedral 6°; incidence 4° 15′. Anti-icing for outboard wing leading-edge; none on tail surfaces.

FLYING CONTROLS: Inboard all-speed and outboard low-speed ailerons supplemented by flight spoilers also acting as airbrakes and lift dumpers; single-slotted, linkage-supported outboard trailing-edge flaps, double-slotted inboard; track-mounted leading-edge slats; variable incidence tailplane, no trim tabs; all control surfaces hydraulically powered; roll and yaw trim through spring feel system; triple digital flight control computers and EFIS; Boeing windshear detection and guidance system optional.

STRUCTURE: Fail-safe structure; graphite composite wing spoilers; tailplane and fin contain aluminium honeycomb. Subcontractors include Grumman Aerospace (wing centre-section and adjacent lower fuselage section; fuselage bulkheads): LTV (horizontal tail): Canadair (rear fuselage): Alenia (wing control surfaces, flaps and leading-edge slats; wingtips): Fuji (wing fairings and main landing gear doors): Kawasaki (centre fuselage body panels; exit hatches; wing inter-spar ribs): Mitsubishi (rear-fuselage body panels; stringers; passenger and cargo doors; dorsal fin).

Following details apply to basic Model 767-200, except where indicated:

LANDING GEAR: Hydraulically retractable tricycle type. Menasco twin-wheel nose unit retracts forward. Cleveland Pneumatic main gear, comprising two four-wheel bogies which retract inward. Oleo-pneumatic shock absorbers. Bendix wheels and brakes. Mainwheel tyres size 45 × 17-20, pressure 12.6 bars (183 lb/sq in). Nosewheel tyres size 37 × 14-15, pressure 10.0 bars (145 lb/sq in). Steel disc brakes on all mainwheels. Electronically controlled anti-skid units.

POWER PLANT: Two high bypass turbofans in pods, pylon-mounted on the wing leading-edges. Alternative engines available for all models are the General Electric CF6-80A and Pratt & Whitney JT9D-7R4D, both rated

at 213.5 kN (48,000 lb st), and the CF6-80A2, JT9D-7R4E and JT9D-7R4E4, rated at 222.4 kN (50,000 lb st). Additionally, the 767-200, 767-200ER and 767-300 are available with the Pratt & Whitney PW4050 rated at 222.4 kN (50,000 lb st), PW4052 rated at 231.3 kN (52,000 lb st) and the General Electric CF6-80C2B2 rated at 233.5 kN (52,500 lb st). The General Electric CF6-80C2B4, rated at 257.5 kN (57,900 lb st), is available on the 767-200ER, 767-300 and 767-300ER. The Pratt & Whitney PW4056, rated at 252.4 kN (56,750 lb st), and the PW4060 and General Electric CF6-80C2B6 rated at 266.9 kN (60,000 lb st), are available only on extended range versions. Rolls-Royce RB211-524G, rated at 269.6 kN (60,600 lb st), available on 767s entering service from early 1990. Fuel in one integral tank in each wing, and in a centre tank, with total capacity of 63,216 litres (16,700 US gallons; 13,905 Imp gallons) in 200/300; 767-200ER has additional 14,195 litres (3,750 US gallons; 3,122 Imp gallons) in a second centre-section tank, raising total capacity to 77,412 litres (20,450 US gallons; 17,028 Imp gallons). The 767-300ER has a further expanded wing centre-section tank (optional on the -200ER), bringing total capacity to 91,039 litres (24,050 US gallons; 20,026 Imp gallons). Refuelling point in port outer wing. Anti-icing of engine air inlets.

ACCOMMODATION: Normal operating crew of two on flight deck, with third position optional. Basic accommodation in -200 models for 216 passengers, made up of 18 first class passengers in six-abreast seating at 96.5 cm (38 in) pitch, and 198 tourist class in mainly seven-abreast seating at 87 cm (34 in) pitch. Type A inward opening plug doors are provided at both the front and rear of the cabin on each side of the fuselage, with a Type III emergency exit over the wing on each side. A total of five toilets is installed, two centrally in the main cabin, two aft in the main cabin, and one forward in the first class section. Galleys are situated at forward and aft ends of the cabin. Alternative single class layouts provide for 230 tourist passengers, seated seven-abreast at 86 cm (34 in) pitch; 242 passengers seated seven-abreast at 81 cm (32 in) pitch; 255 passengers mainly seven-abreast (two-three-two) at 76 cm (30 in) pitch, or eight-abreast (two-four-two) at 81 cm (32 in) pitch. Max seating capacity in -200 models (requiring additional overwing emergency exit) is 290 passengers, mainly eight-abreast, at 76 cm (30 in) pitch; capacity in -300 is 290 passengers seven-abreast. Underfloor cargo holds of -200 versions can accommodate, typically, up to 22 LD2 or 11 LD1 containers. The 767-300 underfloor cargo holds can accommodate 30 LD2 or 15 LD1 containers. Forward and rear cargo doors of equal size are standard on the 767-200 and 767-300, but a larger (1.75 by 3.40 m; 5 ft 9 in by 11 ft 2 in) forward cargo door is standard on the 767-200ER and 767-300ER and optional on 767-200 and 767-300, to permit loading of Type 2 pallets, three such pallets being accommodated in the -200/200ER and four in the -300/300ER. Bulk cargo door at rear on port side. Overhead stowage for carry-on baggage. Cabin is air-conditioned, cargo holds heated.

SYSTEMS: AiResearch dual air cycle air-conditioning system. Pressure differential 0.59 bar (8.6 lb/sq in). Electrical supply from two engine driven 90kVA three-phase 400Hz constant frequency AC generators, 115/200V output. 90 kVA generator mounted on APU for ground operation or for emergency use. Three hydraulic systems at 207 bars (3,000 lb/sq in), for flight control and utility functions, supplied from engine driven pumps and a Garrett bleed air powered hydraulic pump or APU. Maximum generating capacity of port and starboard systems is 163 litres (43 US gallons; 35.8 Imp gallons)/min; centre

system 185.5 litres (49 US gallons; 40.8 Imp gallons)/min, at 196.5 bars (2,850 lb/sq in). Reservoirs pressurised by engine bleed air via a pressure regulation module. Reservoir relief valve pressure is nominally 4.48 bars (65 lb/sq in). An additional hydraulic motor driven generator, to provide essential functions for extended range operations, is standard on the 767-200ER and 767-300ER and optional on the 767-200 and 767-300. Nitrogen chlorate oxygen generators in passenger cabin, plus gaseous oxygen for flight crew. Anti-icing for air data sensors and windscreen. APU in tailcone to provide ground and in-flight electrical power and pressurisation.

AVIONICS: Standard avionics include ARINC 700 series equipment (Bendix/King VOR/marker beacon receiver, ILS receiver, radio altimeter, transponder, DME, ADF and RDR-4A colour weather radar in aircraft for All Nippon, Britannia and Transbrasil). Collins caution annunciator, dual digital flight management systems, and triple digital flight control computers, including FCS-700 flight control system, EFIS-700 electronic flight instrument system and RMI-743 radio distance magnetic indicator. Honeywell IRS, FMCS and DADC, as described in Boeing Model 757 entry. Options include Boeing's windshear detection and guidance system.

DIMENSIONS, EXTERNAL:

Wing span	47.57 m (156 ft 1 in)
Wing chord: at root	8.57 m (28 ft 1¼ in)
at tip	2.29 m (7 ft 6 in)
Wing aspect ratio	7.9
Length: overall: 200/200ER	48.51 m (159 ft 2 in)
300/300ER	54.94 m (180 ft 3 in)
fuselage: 200/200ER	47.24 m (155 ft 0 in)
300/300ER	53.67 m (176 ft 1 in)
Fuselage: Max width	5.03 m (16 ft 6 in)
Height overall	15.85 m (52 ft 0 in)
Tailplane span	18.62 m (61 ft 1 in)
Wheel track	9.30 m (30 ft 6 in)
Wheelbase: 200/200ER	19.69 m (64 ft 7 in)
300/300ER	22.76 m (74 ft 8 in)
Passenger doors (two, fwd and rear, port):	
Height	1.88 m (6 ft 2 in)
Width	1.07 m (3 ft 6 in)
Galley service door (two, fwd and rear, stbd):	
Height	1.83 m (6 ft 0 in)
Width	1.07 m (3 ft 6 in)
Emergency exits (two, each): Height	0.97 m (3 ft 2 in)
Width	0.51 m (1 ft 8 in)
Cargo doors (two, fwd and rear, stbd):	
Height	1.75 m (5 ft 9 in)
Width	1.78 m (5 ft 10 in)
Optional cargo door (fwd, port):	
Height	1.75 m (5 ft 9 in)
Width	3.40 m (11 ft 2 in)

DIMENSIONS, INTERNAL:

Cabin, excl flight deck:	
Length: 200/200ER	33.93 m (111 ft 4 in)
300/300ER	40.36 m (132 ft 5 in)
Max width	4.72 m (15 ft 6 in)
Max height	2.87 m (9 ft 5 in)
Floor area: 200/200ER	154.9 m² (1,667 sq ft)
300/300ER	184.0 m² (1,981 sq ft)
Volume: 200/200ER	428.2 m³ (15,121 cu ft)
300/300ER	483.9 m³ (17,088 cu ft)
Volume, flight deck	13.5 m³ (478 cu ft)
Baggage holds (containerised), volume:	
200/200ER	74.8 m³ (2,640 cu ft)
300/300ER	101.9 m³ (3,600 cu ft)
Bulk cargo hold volume:	
all models	12.2 m³ (430 cu ft)

Combined baggage hold/bulk cargo hold volume:
200/200ER   87.0 m³ (3,070 cu ft)
300/300ER   114.1 m³ (4,030 cu ft)
Total cargo hold volume:
200/200ER   111.3 m³ (3,930 cu ft)
300/300ER   147.0 m³ (5,190 cu ft)

AREAS:
Wings, gross   283.3 m² (3,050 sq ft)
Ailerons (total)   11.58 m² (124.6 sq ft)
Trailing-edge flaps (total)   36.88 m² (397.0 sq ft)
Leading-edge slats (total)   28.30 m² (304.6 sq ft)
Spoilers (total)   15.83 m² (170.4 sq ft)
Fin   30.19 m² (325.0 sq ft)
Rudder   15.95 m² (171.7 sq ft)
Tailplane   59.88 m² (644.5 sq ft)
Elevators (total)   17.81 m² (191.7 sq ft)

WEIGHTS AND LOADINGS (A: 767-200 basic/JT9D-7R4D engines, B: 767-200 basic/CF6-80A, C: medium-range version/JT9D-7R4D, D: medium-range version/CF6-80A, E: 767-200ER/PW4050, F: 767-200ER/CF6-80C2B2, G: 767-200ER/PW4056, H: 767-200ER/CF6-80C2B4, J: 767-300/PW4050, K: 767-300/CF6-80C2B2, L: 767-300 higher gross weight version/PW4050, M: 767-300 higher gross weight version/CF6-80C2B2, N: 767-300ER/PW4056, P: 767-300ER/CF6-80C2B4, Q: 767-300ER/PW4060):
Manufacturer's weight empty:
A, C   74,752 kg (164,800 lb)
B, D   74,344 kg (163,900 lb)
E   76,339 kg (168,300 lb)
F   76,249 kg (168,100 lb)
G   76,566 kg (168,800 lb)
H   76,476 kg (168,600 lb)
J, L   79,560 kg (175,400 lb)
K, M   79,379 kg (175,000 lb)
N   80,785 kg (178,100 lb)
P   80,603 kg (177,700 lb)
Q   81,374 kg (179,400 lb)
Operating weight empty: A, C   80,921 kg (178,400 lb)
B, D   80,512 kg (177,500 lb)
E   83,552 kg (184,200 lb)
F   83,461 kg (184,000 lb)
G   83,778 kg (184,700 lb)
H   83,688 kg (184,500 lb)
J, L   87,135 kg (192,100 lb)
K, M   86,953 kg (191,700 lb)
N   89,312 kg (196,900 lb)
P   89,131 kg (196,500 lb)
Q   89,902 kg (198,200 lb)
Max payload (767-200, 216 passengers; 767-200ER, 174 passengers; 767-300, 261 passengers; 767-300ER, 210 passengers): A, B, C, D   19,595 kg (43,200 lb)
E, F, G, H   16,574 kg (36,540 lb)
J, K, L, M   23,677 kg (52,200 lb)
N, P, Q   20,003 kg (44,100 lb)
Max fuel weight:
A, B, C, D, J, K, L, M   51,131 kg (112,725 lb)
E, F   62,613 kg (138,038 lb)
G, H, N, P, Q   73,635 kg (162,338 lb)
Max T-O weight: A, B   136,078 kg (300,000 lb)
C, D   142,881 kg (315,000 lb)
E, F, J, K   156,489 kg (345,000 lb)
G, H, N, P   175,540 kg (387,000 lb)
L, M   159,211 kg (351,000 lb)
Q   181,437 kg (400,000 lb)
Max ramp weight: A, B   136,985 kg (302,000 lb)
C, D   143,789 kg (317,000 lb)
E, F, J, K   157,396 kg (347,000 lb)
G, H, N, P   175,994 kg (388,000 lb)
L, M   159,664 kg (352,000 lb)
Q   181,890 kg (401,000 lb)
Max zero-fuel weight: A, B   112,491 kg (248,000 lb)
C, D   113,398 kg (250,000 lb)
E, F   114,757 kg (253,000 lb)
G, H   117,934 kg (260,000 lb)
J, K, L, M, N, P   126,098 kg (278,000 lb)
Q   130,634 kg (288,000 lb)
Max landing weight: A, B   122,470 kg (270,000 lb)
C, D   123,377 kg (272,000 lb)
E, F   126,098 kg (278,000 lb)
G, H   129,273 kg (285,000 lb)
J, K, L, M, N, P   136,078 kg (300,000 lb)
Q   145,149 kg (320,000 lb)
Max wing loading: A, B   480.24 kg/m² (98.36 lb/sq ft)
C, D   504.26 kg/m² (103.28 lb/sq ft)
E, F, J, K   552.25 kg/m² (113.11 lb/sq ft)
G, H, N, P   619.53 kg/m² (126.89 lb/sq ft)
L, M   561.87 kg/m² (115.08 lb/sq ft)
Q   640.33 kg/m² (131.15 lb/sq ft)

PERFORMANCE (at max T-O weight except where indicated):
Normal cruising speed, all versions   Mach 0.80
Approach speed at max landing weight:
A, B, C, D   136 knots (252 km/h; 157 mph)
E   138 knots (256 km/h; 159 mph)
F, G, H   140 knots (259 km/h; 161 mph)
J, K, L, M, N, P   141 knots (261 km/h; 162 mph)
Q   145 knots (269 km/h; 167 mph)
Initial cruise altitude: A   11,950 m (39,200 ft)
B   12,100 m (39,700 ft)
C   11,650 m (38,200 ft)
D   11,800 m (38,700 ft)

E   11,215 m (36,800 ft)
F   11,460 m (37,600 ft)
G   10,925 m (35,850 ft)
H   10,850 m (35,600 ft)
J, M   11,250 m (36,900 ft)
K   11,340 m (37,200 ft)
L   11,125 m (36,500 ft)
N, P   10,600 m (34,800 ft)
Q   10,400 m (34,100 ft)
Service ceiling, one engine out: A, C   6,525 m (21,400 ft)
B, D   6,430 m (21,100 ft)
E   6,850 m (22,500 ft)
F   7,200 m (23,600 ft)
G   7,250 m (23,800 ft)
H   7,375 m (24,200 ft)
J, L   6,035 m (19,800 ft)
K, M   6,150 m (20,200 ft)
N, P   6,615 m (21,700 ft)
Q   6,550 m (21,500 ft)
T-O field length: A, B   1,798 m (5,900 ft)
C   1,951 m (6,400 ft)
D   1,981 m (6,500 ft)
E   2,347 m (7,700 ft)
F   2,316 m (7,600 ft)
G, H   2,774 m (9,100 ft)
J   2,560 m (8,400 ft)
K   2,469 m (8,100 ft)
L, M   2,652 m (8,700 ft)
N   2,926 m (9,600 ft)
P   2,956 m (9,700 ft)
Q   2,774 m (9,100 ft)
Design range: A   3,160 nm (5,856 km; 3,639 miles)
B   3,220 nm (5,967 km; 3,708 miles)
C   3,795 nm (7,033 km; 4,370 miles)
D   3,850 nm (7,135 km; 4,433 miles)
E   5,365 nm (9,942 km; 6,178 miles)
F   5,410 nm (10,026 km; 6,230 miles)
G   6,770 nm (12,546 km; 7,796 miles)
H   6,805 nm (12,611 km; 7,836 miles)
J   4,000 nm (7,413 km; 4,606 miles)
K   4,020 nm (7,450 km; 4,629 miles)
L   4,230 nm (7,839 km; 4,871 miles)
M   4,260 nm (7,895 km; 4,905 miles)
N   5,740 nm (10,637 km; 6,610 miles)
P   5,760 nm (10,674 km; 6,633 miles)
Q   6,060 nm (11,230 km; 6,978 miles)

OPERATIONAL NOISE LEVELS (FAR Pt 36, Stage 3):
T-O at max basic T-O weight: B   87.1 EPNdB
H   90.4 EPNdB
Approach at max landing weight: B   101.6 EPNdB
H   101.7 EPNdB
Sideline: B   95.4 EPNdB
H   96.6 EPNdB

BOEING MODEL 777

TYPE: Long-range, high-capacity twin-turbofan airliner.
PROGRAMME: Formerly known as 767-X; brief details announced 8 December 1989; launch order by United Air Lines 15 October 1990 (see below); Boeing formal programme launch 29 October 1990; planned rollout Spring 1994; first flight July 1994; basic 777-200 certificated May 1995; first delivery June 1995; 777-200 Growth certificated December 1996.
VARIANTS: **777-200:** Basic aircraft with max gross weight of 229,520 kg (506,000 lb) and alternative max gross weight, 233,600 kg (515,000 lb); max payload 56,245 kg (124,000 lb); 375 to 400 two-class passengers or 305 to 325 three-class passengers; range with full passengers 4,050 nm (7,505 km; 4,660 miles).
777-200 Growth: Gross weight 263,085 kg (580,000

lb); alternative gross weight 267,620 kg (590,000 lb); max payload 55,338 kg (122,000 lb); same passenger capacity as basic aircraft; range with full passengers 6,350 nm (11,770 km; 7,310 miles).
777 Stretch: Intended as replacement for early 747s; about 370 passengers and nearly 5,000 nm (9,265 km; 5,755 miles) range.
CUSTOMERS: First firm order 34 plus options for 34 from United Air Lines 15 October 1990, to be powered by 325 kN (73,000 lb) Pratt & Whitney PW4073; United version has max T-O weight 234,000 kg (515,880 lb) carrying 363 passengers in two classes for up to 4,200 nm (7,785 km; 4,836 miles); other launch customer is All Nippon Airways with 15 firm plus options for 10 placed 19 December 1990 (engine not selected).
COST: Estimated development cost $4 billion (1990); aircraft cost $106 to 129 million (1991).
DESIGN FEATURES: New wing of 31.6° sweepback at quarter-chord incorporates new technology to allow Mach 0.83 cruise in combination with high thickness for economical structure and large internal volume, long span for improved take-off and payload/range and large area for high cruise altitude and low approach speed; no winglets. Boeing wants to achieve EROPS clearance at initial entry into service. Fuselage wider than 767 to allow twin aisle seating for from six to 10 abreast; toilets and overhead baggage bins designed to allow rapid change of layout. Outer 6.48 m (21 ft 3 in) of wings fold to vertical to reduce gate width requirement at airports.
FLYING CONTROLS: Hydraulic fully powered controls with electrical signalling from GEC Avionics fly-by-wire system; outboard low-speed aileron and inboard all-speed flaperon; five outboard and two inboard spoiler panels on each wing; seven leading-edge slats on each wing; double-slotted inboard flaps and single-slotted outboard flaps; variable-incidence tailplane; large rudder tab. Teijin Seiki primary flight control actuators; tailplane trim and optional wingtip folding controls by E-Systems.
Linked control columns and aileron wheels retained for crew familiarity; both back-driven by fly-by-wire system to let both pilots observe control demands; fly-by-wire system controls primary, secondary control and high-lift surfaces; full three-axis digital system with direct analog backup; conventional control characteristics with selected enhancement functions. Flight control integrated with aircraft information management system (AIMS) and ARINC 629 databus (see below).
STRUCTURE: Composites used for moving trailing-edge surfaces and spoiler panels, tail surfaces except leading-edges, wing fixed leading-edge, cabin floor beams, engine nacelles, wingroot fairings and main landing gear doors. Toughened materials for high damage resistance and to allow simple low temperature bolted repairs. Metal structure includes thick skins without need for tear straps; no bonding; single-piece fuselage frames.
Fully digital product definition with all parts created three-dimensionally on CAD/CAM and communicated to manufacturing and publications; structure and systems integration, tube and cable run design completed before design release.
Centre and rear fuselage barrel sections, tailcone, doors, wingroot fairing and landing gear doors made in Japan. Wing and tail leading-edges and moving wing parts, landing gear, floor beams, nose landing gear doors and nose radome made by Rockwell, Grumman, Alenia (Italy), HDH and ASTA (Australia), Korean Air and other subcontractors. Boeing manufactures flight deck and forward cabin, basic wing and tail structures and engine nacelles, and assembles and tests.
LANDING GEAR: Retractable tricycle type (Menasco/

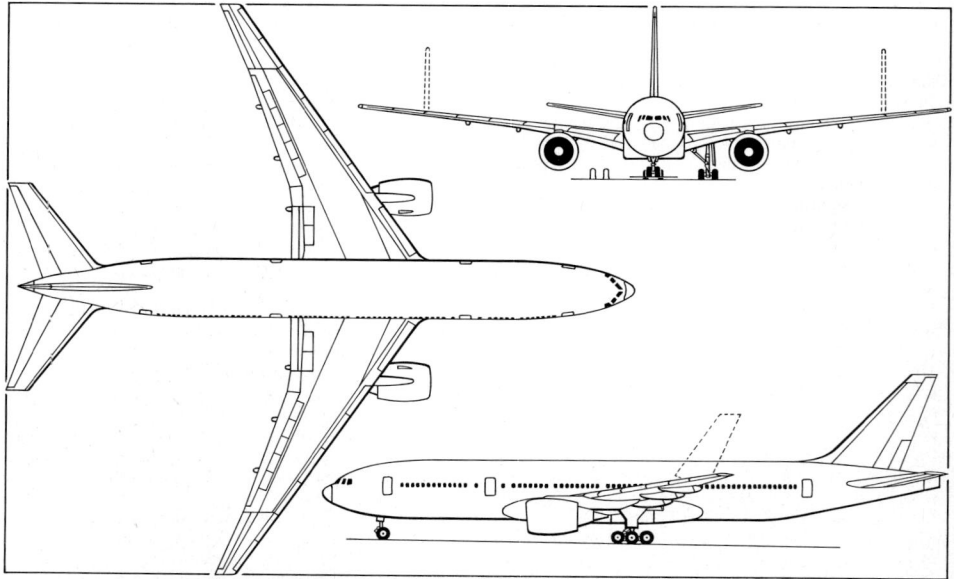

Boeing 777 (formerly 767-X) twin-turbofan high-capacity airliner (*Pilot Press*)

Messier-Bugatti joint design for main gear); two main legs carrying six-wheel bogies with steering rear axles; twin-wheel steerable nose gear; mainwheel tyres H49 × 19-22 with 28 bias ply rating; nosewheel tyres 44 × 18-18 (24 ply); carbon mainwheel brakes arranged so that initial toe-pedal pressure used during taxying applies brakes to alternate sets of three wheels to save brake wear; full toe-pedal pressure applies all six brakes together.

POWER PLANT: Boeing offers choice of Pratt & Whitney, Rolls-Royce and General Electric turbofans as follows: for 777-200, P&W 327 kN (73,500 lb st) PW4073A or PW4073; R-R 317 kN (71,200 lb st) Trent 870 or 871; GE 331 kN (74,500 lb st) GE90-B3 or -B2. For 777-200 Growth and 777 Stretch, P&W 366 kN (82,200 lb st) PW4082 or 376 kN (84,600 lb st) PW4084; R-R 366 kN (82,200 lb st) Trent 882 or 375 kN (84,400 lb st) Trent 884; GE 374 kN (84,100 lb st) GE90-B1 or 377 kN (84,700 lb st) GE90-B4. Fuel contained in integral tanks in wing torsion box and wing centre-section, with reserve tank, surge tank and fuel vent and jettison pipes all inboard of wing fold; combined capacity of main, centre and reserve tanks is 119,619 litres (31,600 US gallons; 26,312 Imp gallons) in 777-200 and 171,100 litres (45,200 US gallons; 37,637 Imp gallons) in 777-200 Growth.

ACCOMMODATION: Two-pilot crew. See under Variants for passenger capacities. Internal fuselage width 5.87 m (19 ft 3 in), designed to give wide choice of twin-aisle seat layouts from six to 10 abreast and easy adaptability of cabin for different combinations of classes and service locations; new pivoting and translating overhead baggage bins allow 0.08 m³ (3.0 cu ft) volume per passenger.

Underfloor compartments will accommodate containers from LD1 to LD6 and LD10 and LD11, as well as 96 in and 88 in wide pallets; capacity allows 18 LD3s in the forward compartment and 14 in the rear, or six 96 in wide pallets in front and 14 LD3s in the rear, or six pallets in front and four in rear (the latter requires the optional 2.64 m; 8 ft 8 in wide rear freight door). An optional

underfloor crew rest module with four bunks, two business class seats and stowage space, occupying same floor area as a 96 in wide pallet, requires only an electrical connection and access hatch in cabin floor.

SYSTEMS: GEC Avionics fly-by-wire AFCS; Sundstrand AC electrical power generating system, with two 120kVA integrated drive generators, one APU-driven generator and backup electrical power system.

AVIONICS: Honeywell aircraft information management system integrates flight management, flight and navigation display generators, onboard maintenance, communications management, engine data interface and data conversion gateway in two similar cabinets; AIMS results in 20 per cent weight reduction, 30 per cent power reduction and 100 per cent improvement in mean time between unscheduled removals (MTBUR) of avionic system line-replaceable units; ARINC 629 databus links all units to a single twisted wire pair, reducing wire bundles from 600 in the Model 767 to 400, connectors from 4,860 to 1,580, wire length from 114 km (71 miles) to 48 km (30 miles) and wire weight from 1,179 kg (2,600 lb) to 658 kg (1,450 lb). Honeywell air data inertial reference system (ADIRS), with ring-laser gyros.

DIMENSIONS, EXTERNAL:

Wing span	60.25 m (197 ft 8 in)
Wing span with tips folded	47.47 m (155 ft 9 in)
Length overall	63.72 m (209 ft 1 in)
Fuselage: Length	62.78 m (205 ft 11½ in)
Max width	6.20 m (20 ft 4 in)
Height	18.44 m (60 ft 6 in)
Tailplane span	21.35 m (70 ft 0½ in)
Wheelbase	25.87 m (84 ft 10½ in)
Passenger doors (four port, four stbd):	
Height	1.88 m (6 ft 2 in)
Width	1.07 m (3 ft 6 in)
Forward cargo door, stbd: Height	1.70 m (5 ft 7 in)
Width	2.72 m (8 ft 11 in)
Rear cargo door, stbd, standard	
Height	1.87 m (6 ft 2 in)
Width	1.77 m (5 ft 10 in)
Rear cargo door, stbd, optional width	
	2.63 m (8 ft 8 in)

DIMENSIONS, INTERNAL:

Cabin: Length	48.97 m (160 ft 8 in)
Max width	5.87 m (19 ft 3 in)
Floor area	279.1 m² (3,004 sq ft)
Underfloor cargo hold volume	162.5 m³ (5,740 cu ft)

AREAS:

Wings, projected	427.8 m² (4,605 sq ft)
Horizontal tail, projected	101.26 m² (1,090 sq ft)
Vertical tail, projected	53.23 m² (573 sq ft)

WEIGHTS AND LOADINGS:

Max payload: 777-200	56,245 kg (124,000 lb)
777-200 Growth	55,338 kg (122,000 lb)
Max T-O weight: 777-200, basic	229,520 kg (506,000 lb)
option	233,600 kg (515,000 lb)
Max T-O weight:	
777-200 Growth, basic	263,085 kg (580,000 lb)
option	267,620 kg (590,000 lb)
Max zero-fuel weight	190,510 kg (420,000 lb)
Max landing weight	201,850 kg (445,000 lb)

PERFORMANCE:

Cruising Mach number	0.83
Runway ACN (Flex, med subgrade, code B)	51.1

Range: 777-200, 375 two-class passengers, with allowances 4,050 nm (7,505 km; 4,660 miles)
777-200 Growth at optional weight, 305 three-class passengers, with allowances
6,700 nm (12,415 km; 7,705 miles)
777-200, max payload, with allowances
2,300 nm (4,260 km; 2,645 miles)
777-200 Growth at optional weight, max payload, with allowances 4,500 nm (8,340 km; 5,175 miles)

BOEING/SIKORSKY
BOEING HELICOPTERS and SIKORSKY AIRCRAFT

Boeing/Sikorsky LH Program Office, Scott Plaza II, Suite 635, Philadelphia, Pennsylvania 19142
Telephone: 1 (215) 591 8820
Fax: 1 (215) 591 8819
VICE-PRESIDENT, RAH-66 PROGRAMME: William W. Walls Jr

Boeing and Sikorsky began LHX collaboration June 1985; development centre initially Wichita, but transferred to Philadelphia in early 1990.

BOEING/SIKORSKY RAH-66 COMANCHE (LH)

TYPE: Two-seat reconnaissance/attack helicopter.

PROGRAMME: Light Helicopter Experimental (LHX) design concepts requested by US Army 1982; original plan for 5,000 to replace UH-1, AH-1, OH-58 and OH-6; reduced in 1987 to 2,096 scout/attack only, replacing 3,000 existing helicopters; to 1,292 in 1990 (with further 389 possible). LHX request for proposals issued 21 June 1988; 23-month demonstration/validation contracts issued to Boeing/Sikorsky First Team and Bell/McDonnell Douglas Super Team. Boeing/Sikorsky announced winner 8 April 1991; to build four demonstration/validation prototypes (first flight August 1994); if targets are met, this 52-month phase will be followed by 39-month FSD phase, involving two further prototypes, starting August 1995. LHTEC T800 engine specified October 1988. LHX designation changed to LH early 1990, then US Army designation RAH-66 Comanche in April 1991. Planned peak production 120 per year.

COSTS: $34,000 million programme, including $1,960 million dem/val and $900 million FSD; $8.9 million flyaway unit cost (1988 values).

DESIGN FEATURES: RAH-66 will be lighter, but only slightly smaller, than AH-64 Apache; mission equipment package has maximum commonality with F-22 ATF technology. Design has eight-blade Sikorsky fan-in-fin shrouded tail rotor and five-blade version of MBB all-composites bearingless main rotor system, and internal weapon stowage. Other members of Boeing/Sikorsky First Team include Boeing Aerospace and Electronics (flight control computer), General Electric Armament Systems Department, with GIAT of France (turreted gun and ammunition feed), Hamilton Standard (flight control computer, wide field-of-view helmet-mounted display system, air data system, environmental control and collective protection system, and air vehicle interface computer), Harris Corporation (3D digital map display, super high speed databus, sensor data distribution network, multi-function controls and displays), Kaiser Electronics (helmet-mounted display system), Link Flight Simulation (operator training systems), Martin Marietta (electro-optical night navigation and targeting systems), TRW Military Electronics Division with Westinghouse Defense and Electronics (signal and data processors and aircraft survivability equipment). Split torque transmission, obviating need for planetary gearing. T tail unit (upper

Mockup of the Boeing/Sikorsky RAH-66 Comanche with weapons bay closed

part folds down for air transportation). Detachable stub-wings for additional weapon carriage and/or auxiliary fuel tanks (EFAMS: external fuel and armament management system). Nose hinges to starboard for access to sensors and ammunition bay. Extremely low radar and infra-red signatures.

FLYING CONTROLS: Dual triplex fly-by-wire, with sidestick cyclic-pitch controllers and normal collective levers. Main rotor blades removable without disconnecting control system.

STRUCTURE: Largely composite airframe and rotor system. Fuselage built around composite internal box-beam; non-load-bearing skin panels, more than half of which can be hinged or removed for access to interior (eg, weapons bay doors can double as maintenance work platforms). Main rotor blades and tail section by Boeing, forward fuselage and final assembly by Sikorsky.

LANDING GEAR: Retractable tailwheel type, with single wheel on each unit. Main units can 'kneel' for air transportability.

POWER PLANT: Two 895 kW (1,200 shp) class LHTEC (Allison/Garrett) T800-LHT-800 turboshaft engines, with FADEC. Fuel capacity 1,018 litres (269 US gallons; 224 Imp gallons).

ACCOMMODATION: Pilot (in front) and WSO in identical stepped cockpits, pressurised for chemical/biological warfare protection.

AVIONICS: Martin Marietta Night Vision Pilotage System and Kaiser/Hamilton Standard helmet-mounted display; integrated cockpit, second-generation FLIR targeting, and digital map display. Dual anti-jam VHF-FM and UHF-AM Have Quick tactical communications,

VHF-AM, anti-jam HF-SSB, Airborne Target Handover System, Navstar-GPS, IFF and radar altimeter. Laser warning and radar warning receivers, RF and IR jammers. Miniaturised version of Longbow radar in one-third of LH fleet from 2000. Maximum avionics commonality required with USAF F-22 ATF programme. Two 15.2 × 20.3 cm (6 × 8 in) flat-screen LCDs in each cockpit (one monochrome for FLIR/TV, one colour for moving map, tactical situation and night operations), plus a 10.2 × 10.2 cm (4 × 4 in) monochrome LCD for fuel and armament information. Three redundant databases: one low-speed (MIL-STD-1553B), one high-speed and one very-high-speed (fibre-optic based) for signal data distribution.

ARMAMENT: General Electric/GIAT twin-barrel 20 mm cannon in undernose turret, with up to 500 rounds (320 rds normal for primary mission). Side-opening weapons bay door in each side of fuselage, on each of which can be mounted up to three Hellfire or six Stinger missiles or other weapons. Four more Hellfires or eight Stingers can be deployed from multiple carriers under tip of each optional stub-wing, or a 1,703 litre (450 US gallon; 375 Imp gallon) auxiliary fuel tank for self-deployment. All weapons can be fired, and targets designated, from push-buttons on collective and sidestick controllers.

DIMENSIONS, EXTERNAL:

Main rotor diameter	11.90 m (39 ft 0½ in)
Length: overall, rotor turning	14.48 m (47 ft 6⅛ in)
fuselage	13.22 m (43 ft 4½ in)
Height over tailplane	3.36 m (11 ft 0¼ in)
Width over mainwheels	2.31 m (7 ft 7 in)
Tailplane span	2.82 m (9 ft 3 in)

Internal arrangement of the Boeing/Sikorsky RAH-66 Comanche (LH)

WEIGHTS AND LOADINGS (estimated):
Weight empty, combat equipped	3,402 kg (7,500 lb)

T-O weight:
* primary mission	4,546 kg (10,022 lb)
max (hot/high)	5,080 kg (11,200 lb)
max (self-deployability)	7,620 kg (16,800 lb)

* with two crew, full internal fuel, 320 rds gun ammunition, four Hellfires and two Stingers

PERFORMANCE (estimated):
Max level (dash) speed	177 knots (328 km/h; 204 mph)
Vertical rate of climb at 1,220 m (4,000 ft) and 35°C (95°F)	360 m (1,182 ft)/min
Ferry range with external tanks	1,260 nm (2,335 km; 1,451 miles)
Endurance (standard fuel)	2 h 30 min

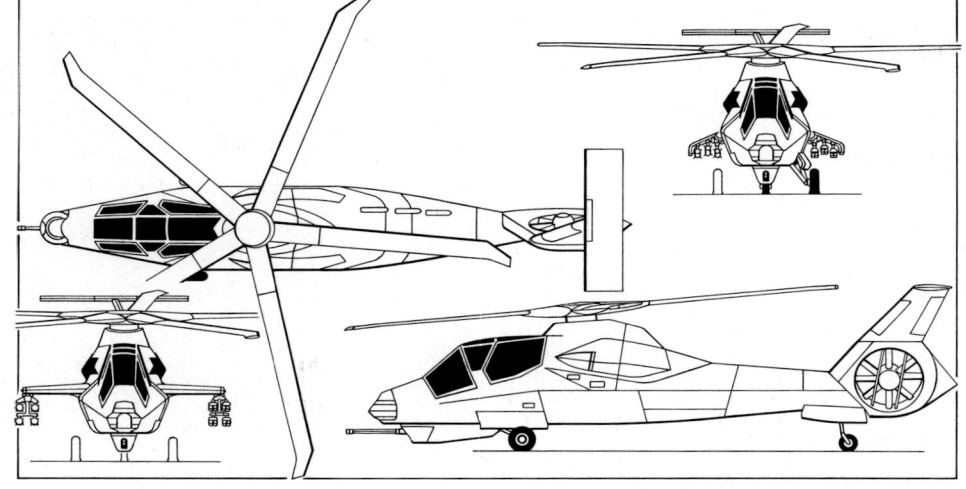

Boeing/Sikorsky RAH-66 Comanche. Upper head-on view shows internal weapons bay doors open; lower head-on view shows eight Stinger (port) and four Hellfire missiles (starboard) on detachable stub-wings *(Jane's/Mike Keep)*

BRANSON

BRANSON AIRCRAFT CORPORATION

3790 Wheeling Street, Denver, Colorado 80239
Telephone: 1 (303) 371 9112
Fax: 1 (303) 371 1813
Telex: 45-4577 BRANSON DVR
PRESIDENT: Carl F. Branson
EXECUTIVE VICE-PRESIDENT: Roger P. Kirwan

Founded in 1966 for special design and custom manufacturing of auxiliary fuel tanks, special interiors and equipment for civil aircraft.

CITATION EXTENDED RANGE FUEL SYSTEM

Branson holds FAA FAR Pt 25 supplemental type certificate for 454 litre (120 US gallon; 100 Imp gallon) fuel tank installation for Cessna Model 500 Citation, Citation I, II and S/II. Installation weighs 36 kg (80 lb) and allows 295 kg (650 lb) increase in gross weight; Citation I can carry three more passengers and 27 kg (60 lb) baggage and extend maximum range to 1,654 nm (3,065 km; 1,905 miles).

CITATION II WEIGHT INCREASE

FAA Part 25 supplemental type certificate held for 544 kg (1,200 lb) weight increase for Cessna Model 550 Citation II. New ramp and max T-O weights are 6,668 kg (14,700 lb) and 6,577 kg (14,500 lb) respectively; aircraft can carry full

fuel and up to seven passengers. Higher performance wheels, brakes and tyres available as part of STC kit for field installation. Quick-change cargo system (glassfibre liner and net/tiedowns restraints) also available, increasing cargo payload to 1,224 kg (2,700 lb).

CITATION EXTENDED WIDTH CARGO DOOR

Cabin door modification for Cessna Citation I, II and S/II provides 0.91 m (3 ft 0 in) wide opening for loading stretchers, palletised cargo, research equipment, large aerial cameras, etc; installation weighs 28.6 kg (63 lb), does not interfere with seating or furnishing, meets FAA FAR Pt 25, and takes six weeks.

CITATION AIR AMBULANCE EQUIPMENT

Medical equipment installation for Citation I, II and S/II includes wider cabin door, single or two stretchers, medical oxygen supply, compressed air, vacuum and electrical outlets; first installation in Citation II of Air Express of Oslo, Norway.

DIAMOND IA LONG-RANGE TANK

Auxiliary long-range tank for Mitsubishi Diamond IA holds 363 litres (96 US gallons; 80 Imp gallons) and is standard feature of Beech Model 400 Beechjet; tank

mounted against rear pressure bulkhead. Also for Diamond IA, a transfer system from wing tank to fuselage tank, avoiding need to fill fuselage tank separately. Branson 0.93 m³ (33 cu ft) tailcone baggage compartment holds maximum 204 kg (450 lb). FAA approval gained for Branson gross weight increase kit, raising max T-O weight to 7,031 kg (15,500 lb).

LEARJET 55 LONG-RANGE TANKS

Long-range tanks for Learjet Model 55 hold additional 378.5 litres (100 US gallons; 83.5 Imp gallons) or 757 litres (200 US gallons; 167 Imp gallons); installation takes about four weeks for smaller tanks and five weeks for larger tanks; latter extend range by 400 nm (741 km; 461 miles).

F27/FH-227 LARGE CARGO DOOR

FAA Part 25 supplemental type certificate for large cargo door in Fairchild FH-227 and Fokker F27 purchased by Branson from Fairchild Aircraft. Door measuring 1.83 m (6 ft 0 in) high by 2.30 m (7 ft 6½ in) wide located in port side just aft of flight deck; electrically operated and opens to 110° and 170°; crew door incorporated; conversion adds about 238 kg (525 lb) to aircraft empty weight; conversion possible in USA, Europe and Asia.

BRANTLY

BRANTLY HELICOPTER INDUSTRIES USA CO LTD

Wilbarger County Airport, 12399 Airport Drive, Vernon, Texas 76384
Telephone: 1 (817) 552 5451
Fax: 1 (817) 552 2703
PRESIDENT: James T. Kimura

Japanese-American businessman James T. Kimura planned to produce 100 B-2Bs and ten 305s during 1991. Production methods being continually improved. Turbine powered 305 planned.

Kimura acquired type certificates and manufacturing and marketing rights to Brantly B-2B and 305 from Hynes Aviation Industries March 1989; Brantly Helicopter Industries formed 8 May 1989; 2,787 m² (30,000 sq ft) facility established at Wilbarger County Airport.

Brantly Helicopter Industries B-2B two-seat light helicopter

BRANTLY B-2B

TYPE: Two-seat light helicopter.
PROGRAMME: 100 B-2Bs planned to be built in 1991; six in final assembly in December 1990 and first new production B-2B nearing first flight.
CUSTOMERS: Firm orders for 78 B-2Bs from overseas reported; first (of 30 ordered) handed over to Japanese customer 25 August 1990.
COSTS: Quoted at $136,500 (1990).
DESIGN FEATURES: Three-blade main rotor with flapping hinges close to hub and pitch-change/flap/lag hinges at 40 per cent blade length; symmetrical inboard blade section with 29 per cent thickness/chord ratio, outboard section NACA 0012; outer blade sections quickly removable for compact storage; rotor brake standard; two-blade anti-torque rotor. Transmission through automatic centrifugal clutch. Tail rotor drive through flexible couplings and intermediate gearbox. New lightweight starter and alternator replaces generator. Cabin will be streamlined.
FLYING CONTROLS: Conventional direct mechanical control; small fixed tailplane. .
STRUCTURE: Inboard blade section has stainless steel leading-edge spar; outboard portion has extruded aluminium spar, polyurethane core with bonded aluminium envelope riveted to spar. All-metal tail rotor. Fuselage steel tube centre-section with all-metal stressed skin tailcone.
LANDING GEAR: Alternative skid or float gear. Skid type has small retractable wheels for ground handling, fixed tailskid and four shock absorbers with rubber in compression. Inflatable pontoons, which attach to standard skids, are available to permit operation from water.
POWER PLANT: One 134 kW (180 hp) Textron Lycoming IVO-360-A1A flat-four engine, mounted vertically, with dual fan cooling system. Rubber bag type fuel tank under engine, capacity 117 litres (31 US gallons; 25.8 Imp gallons). Refuelling point on port side of fuselage. Oil capacity 5.7 litres (1.5 US gallons; 1.25 Imp gallons).
ACCOMMODATION: Totally enclosed circular section cabin for two persons seated side by side. Forward hinged door on each side. Dual controls, cabin heater and demisting fan standard. Compartment for 22.7 kg (50 lb) baggage in forward end of tail section.
AVIONICS: Provision for all standard nav/com radios.
EQUIPMENT: Blind-flying instrumentation available as an option, but the Model B-2B is not certificated for instrument flight. Twin landing lights in nose.

DIMENSIONS, EXTERNAL:
Main rotor diameter	7.24 m (23 ft 9 in)
Main rotor blade chord: inboard	0.225 m (8.85 in)
outboard	0.203 m (8.0 in)
Tail rotor diameter	1.30 m (4 ft 3 in)
Length: overall, rotors turning	8.53 m (28 ft 0 in)
fuselage	6.62 m (21 ft 9 in)
Height overall	2.06 m (6 ft 9 in)
Skid track	1.73 m (5 ft 8½ in)
Passenger doors (each): Height	0.79 m (2 ft 7 in)
Width	0.86 m (2 ft 9¾ in)
Baggage compartment door:	
Mean height	0.25 m (9¾ in)
Length	0.55 m (1 ft 9¾ in)

DIMENSIONS, INTERNAL:
Cabin: Length	1.83 m (6 ft 0 in)
Max width	1.19 m (3 ft 11 in)
Max height	0.99 m (3 ft 3 in)
Floor area	2.60 m² (28.0 sq ft)
Volume	2.78 m³ (98.0 cu ft)
Baggage compartment	0.17 m³ (6.0 cu ft)

AREAS:
Main rotor blades (each)	0.69 m² (7.42 sq ft)
Main rotor disc	41.16 m² (443.0 sq ft)
Tail rotor disc	1.32 m² (14.19 sq ft)

WEIGHTS AND LOADINGS:
Weight empty: with skids	463 kg (1,020 lb)
with floats	481 kg (1,060 lb)
Max T-O weight	757 kg (1,670 lb)
Max disc loading	18.40 kg/m² (3.77 lb/sq ft)

Brantly Helicopter Industries Model 305 five-seat light helicopter

PERFORMANCE (at max T-O weight):
Max level speed at S/L	87 knots (161 km/h; 100 mph)
Max cruising speed (75% power)	
	78 knots (145 km/h; 90 mph)
Max rate of climb at S/L	580 m (1,900 ft)/min
Service ceiling	3,290 m (10,800 ft)
Hovering ceiling IGE	2,040 m (6,700 ft)
Range with max fuel, with reserves	
	217 nm (400 km; 250 miles)

BRANTLY MODEL 305

TYPE: Five-seat light helicopter.
PROGRAMME: Production of 10 planned for 1991. Original first flight January 1964; FAA type approval 29 July 1965; about 44 built during mid-1960s. Improved prototype with redesigned rotor head and new blade aerofoil completed about 30 hours flying by mid-January 1990. New main rotor bearing fitted. Cabin to be streamlined.
VARIANTS: Turbine engines planned for a medevac version.
COSTS: Estimated $205,000 (1990).
DESIGN FEATURES: Rotor system and airframe as for B-2B, but enlarged.
FLYING CONTROLS: Conventional direct mechanical.
STRUCTURE: As for B-2B.
LANDING GEAR: Choice of skid, wheel or float gear. Skid type has four oleo struts, two on each side, and small retractable ground handling wheels. The wheel gear has single mainwheels and twin nosewheels, all with oleo-pneumatic shock absorbers. Goodyear mainwheels and tyres size 6.00-6, pressure 2.07 bars (30 lb/sq in); Goodyear nosewheels and tyres size 5.00-5, pressure 1.93 bars (28 lb/sq in). Goodyear single-disc hydraulic brakes on mainwheels.
POWER PLANT: One 227.4 kW (305 hp) Textron Lycoming IVO-540-B1A flat-six engine, mounted vertically, with dual cooling fans. One rubber fuel cell under engine, capacity 163 litres (43 US gallons; 35.8 Imp gallons). Refuelling point on port side of fuselage. Oil capacity 9.5 litres (2.5 US gallons; 2.1 Imp gallons).
ACCOMMODATION: Two individual seats side by side, with dual controls. Rear bench seat for three persons. Door on

each side. Rear compartment for 113 kg (250 lb) of baggage, with downward hinged door on starboard side.
AVIONICS: Bendix/King or Narco radio, to customer's specification.
EQUIPMENT: Blind-flying instrumentation is available, but helicopter is not certificated for instrument flight.

DIMENSIONS, EXTERNAL:
Main rotor diameter	8.74 m (28 ft 8 in)
Main rotor blade chord (constant)	0.254 m (10 in)
Tail rotor diameter	1.30 m (4 ft 3 in)
Length: overall, rotors turning	10.03 m (32 ft 11 in)
fuselage	7.44 m (24 ft 5 in)
Height overall	2.44 m (8 ft 1 in)
Wheel track	2.10 m (6 ft 10¾ in)
Wheelbase	2.15 m (7 ft 0½ in)
Passenger doors (each): Height	0.82 m (2 ft 8½ in)
Width	1.02 m (3 ft 3⅞ in)
Baggage compartment door:	
Mean height	0.30 m (1 ft 0¼ in)
Width	0.69 m (2 ft 3 in)

DIMENSIONS, INTERNAL:
Cabin: Length	2.30 m (7 ft 6½ in)
Max width	1.39 m (4 ft 6¾ in)
Max height	1.22 m (4 ft 0½ in)
Baggage compartment	0.47 m³ (16.7 cu ft)

AREAS:
Main rotor blades (each)	0.09 m² (11.79 sq ft)
Tail rotor blades (each)	0.05 m² (0.50 sq ft)
Main rotor disc	59.96 m² (645.4 sq ft)
Tail rotor disc	1.32 m² (14.19 sq ft)

WEIGHTS AND LOADINGS:
Weight empty	816 kg (1,800 lb)
Max T-O and landing weight	1,315 kg (2,900 lb)
Max disc loading	21.92 kg/m² (4.49 lb/sq ft)

PERFORMANCE (at max T-O weight):
Max level speed at S/L	104 knots (193 km/h; 120 mph)
Max cruising speed at S/L	
	96 knots (177 km/h; 110 mph)
Max rate of climb at S/L	297 m (975 ft)/min
Service ceiling	3,660 m (12,000 ft)
Hovering ceiling IGE	1,245 m (4,080 ft)
Range with max fuel and max payload, 15 min reserves	
	191 nm (354 km; 220 miles)

BUSH

BUSH CONVERSIONS INC

Box 431, Udall, Kansas 67146
Telephone: 1 (316) 782 3851
VICE-PRESIDENT: Barbara Williams
   Company offers 'Taildragger' conversions for Cessna
150/152, 172/Skyhawk, R172K and 175, designed by
former Ralph Bolen Inc.

BOLEN 'TAILDRAGGER' CONVERSIONS

TYPE: Tailwheel conversion of tricycle Cessnas (as listed).
DESIGN FEATURES: Average increase of 8.5-10.5 knots
   (16-19.5 km/h; 10-12 mph) in speed; better performance
   from short and rough fields; tighter turning radius on
   ground; simpler operation on floats and skis.
FLYING CONTROLS: Unchanged.
STRUCTURE: Two bulkheads and new landing gear attachment box added to forward fuselage; Cessna 172 and 175
   receive new cantilever landing gear legs; for Cessna 150
   series F, G, H, J and K, existing legs are retained, but
   fitted to new box; earlier Cessna 150s have to receive legs
   of newer models with 15 × 6.00-6 tyre and brake.
   Tailwheel unit includes Scott 3200 wheel; leg attached by
   stress plates and stringers, without removal of skin. CG
   not displaced; STC includes operation on Fluidyne snow
   skis; no weight penalty with Cessna 150/152; new main
   legs and extra structure of Model 172/175 modification
   increase weight by 13.6 kg (30 lb).

Bolen 'Taildragger' conversion of a Cessna Aerobat 135 *(John Cook)*

CALIFORNIA HELICOPTER

CALIFORNIA HELICOPTER INTERNATIONAL

2935 Golf Course Drive, Ventura, California 93003-7604
Telephone: 1 (805) 644 5800
Fax: 1 (805) 644 5132
Telex: 6831165 CHI UW
PRESIDENT: Bruce P. Mauldin
VICE-PRESIDENT AND GENERAL MANAGER:
   W. E. 'Jake' Dangle
   Rights to manufacture turbine conversion kits for
Sikorsky S-58 and spare parts, plus support of worldwide
S-58/S-58T fleet, bought from Sikorsky in 1981 after latter
had converted or produced conversion kits for about 146
S-58s. California Helicopter offers dynamic component
exchange service for S-58/S-58T.

CALIFORNIA HELICOPTER (SIKORSKY) S-58T

TYPE: Twin-turbine conversion of Sikorsky S-58.
CUSTOMERS: Civil customers include New York Airways
   (four) in 14-passenger layout for New York airports
   shuttle service. Government customers include Thai
   Ministry of Agriculture for VIP transport, Royal Thai
   Air Force (18), Indonesian Air Force (12), and South
   Korea (three).
DESIGN FEATURES: FAA and CAA approval for IFR
   operation. Details under Sikorsky in 1977-78 *Jane's*.
POWER PLANT: Pratt & Whitney Canada PT6T-6 Twin-Pac
   rated at 1,398 kW (1,875 shp) for T-O and 1,249 kW
   (1,675 shp) max continuous.
WEIGHTS AND LOADINGS:
   Weight empty   3,437 kg (7,577 lb)

California Helicopter conversion of Sikorsky S-58 to twin-turbine S-58T configuration

Max T-O and landing weight	5,896 kg (13,000 lb)	
Max disc loading	25.8 kg/m² (5.29 lb/sq ft)	

PERFORMANCE (at max T-O weight. A: PT6T-3, B: PT6T-6):
Max level speed at S/L:
A, B   120 knots (222 km/h; 138 mph)
Cruising speed:
A, B   110 knots (204 km/h; 127 mph)
Hovering ceiling OGE: A   1,433 m (4,700 ft)
   B   1,980 m (6,500 ft)

Single-engine absolute ceiling: A   640 m (2,100 ft)
   B   1,280 m (4,200 ft)
Range with 1,071 litres (283 US gallons; 236 Imp gallons)
   max usable fuel, including 20 min reserves at cruising
   speed:
A   260 nm (481 km; 299 miles)
B   242 nm (447 km; 278 miles)

CALIFORNIA MICROWAVE

CALIFORNIA MICROWAVE INC
(Government Electronics Division)

6036 Variel Avenue, PO Box 2800, Woodland Hills,
   California 91367
Telephone: 1 (818) 992 8000
Fax: 1 (818) 992 5079
Telex: 910 494 2794
PRESIDENT: J. Russell

BOEING CANADA DHC-7 ARL (AIRBORNE RECONNAISSANCE-LOW)

TYPE: US Army drug interdiction aircraft.
PROGRAMME: Prototype Grisly Hunter (now ARL) system,
   adapted from Developmental Sciences SkyEye UAV,
   installed in CASA C-212 (88-3210) by DSC; aircraft
   crashed 1 December 1989. Request for proposals issued
   February 1990 for 'production' prototype; options on
   further six; installation in any suitable twin-turboprop
   aircraft of off-the-shelf FLIR/TV turret, data link and IR

linescan, plus chaff/flare dispensers and self-protection
warning system(s); basing at Howard AFB, Panama, for
Caribbean patrols; range 1,200 nm (2,224 km; 1,382
miles) minimum. California Microwave chosen contractor August 1990; second-hand Boeing/de Havilland Dash
7 (out of production; last described fully in 1987-88
Jane's) as sensor platform; prototype due for completion
by February 1992.
COSTS: $19.8 million in FY 1990 for prototype; FY 1991
request for $10.4 million approved March 1991.

CAT

COMMUTER AIR TECHNOLOGY

14700 North Airport Drive, Suite 206, Scottsdale, Arizona
   85260
Telephone: 1 (602) 951 6288
Fax: 1 (602) 998 1239
PRESIDENT: Keith Nickels
VICE-PRESIDENT, AIRCRAFT MARKETING: Frank Rast

CAT TRANSREGIONAL 250 and ST 17

TYPE: Commuter developments of Beechcraft Super King
   Air 200.
PROGRAMME: Transregional 250 launched in mid/late 1980s
   (then as CAT 200) as 13-seat commuter modification of
   Super King Air; now marketed via Priority Aviation

Leasing; ST 17 due for first flight in late 1991, with
certification during 1992.
VARIANTS: **Transregional 250 CATPASS:** Basic
   13-passenger version, formerly CAT 200. Known by
   certification name CAT Performance and Safety System
   (CATPASS); incorporates most Raisbeck King Air
   modifications (which see); max zero-fuel weight increased to 4,990 kg (11,000 lb) also cargo version.
   ST 17: Fuselage stretched 1.22 m (4 ft 0 in) to hold 17
   passengers and 1.13 m³ (40 cu ft) nose baggage
   compartment; Beechcraft King Air 1.22 m (4 ft 0 in) wide
   cargo door optional; 2.12 m³ (75 cu ft) cargo pod
   optional.
CUSTOMERS: CAT 200 in service with Mesa Airlines, New
   Mexico; first PAL lease of Transregional 250 (to Elgaz of
   Poland; two, with third on option) announced March

1991; other leases then under negotiation with operators
in Africa (four), Brazil (four), Bulgaria (three) and
Mexico (six); PAL has ordered five conversions with
options for five from CAT. Unnamed French regional
airline has three options for ST 17.
COSTS: $2.2 million (1991) for ST 17.
PERFORMANCE (ST 17):
Max level speed   288 knots (534 km/h; 331 mph)
Typical cruising speed   270 knots (500 km/h; 311 mph)
Service ceiling   7,620 m (25,000 ft)
Service ceiling, one engine out   6,035 m (19,800 ft)
T-O field length, ISA +15°C   887 m (2,910 ft)
Landing field length, ISA +15°C   805 m (2,640 ft)
Max range, with reserves
                                  1,200 nm (2,224 km; 1,382 miles)

CAVENAUGH
CAVENAUGH AVIATION INC
15600 Drummet Boulevard, Suite 730, Houston, Texas 77302
Telephone: 1 (713) 442 3500
Fax: 1 (713) 442 3559
PRESIDENT: Dudley N. Cavenaugh
DIRECTOR OF MARKETING: William H. Reynolds

CAVENAUGH CARGOLINER
TYPE: Cargo conversion of Mitsubishi MU-2 series.
PROGRAMME: First conversion began mid-1984; FAA certificated; 20 conversions completed by November 1988.
DESIGN FEATURES: Cargoliner based on long-fuselage MU-2G, MU-2J, MU-2L, MU-2N and Marquise, last described under Mitsubishi International in US section of 1985-86 *Jane's*. Modifications include flight deck window replaced by forward hinged flight deck door and integral step on port or starboard side; bulkhead stressed to 9*g* between flight deck and cargo cabin; smooth plastic liner in cabin; cargo nets dividing cabin into three areas with access from front or rear; optional upward opening cargo door 1.22 m (4 ft 0 in) high × 1.42 m (4 ft 8 in) wide replacing standard rear cabin door. Pressurisation unchanged.

Cavenaugh Cargoliner conversion of the Mitsubishi MU-2, with optional rear cargo door

DIMENSIONS, EXTERNAL:

Crew door: Height	0.61 m (2 ft 0 in)		Max height: at forward bulkhead	1.29 m (4 ft 3 in)
Width: at top	0.41 m (1 ft 4 in)		at rear bulkhead	1.17 m (3 ft 10 in)
at bottom	0.84 m (2 ft 9 in)		Volume	7.64 m³ (270.0 cu ft)

DIMENSIONS, INTERNAL:

Cargo hold: Length	4.90 m (16 ft 1 in)

CESSNA
CESSNA AIRCRAFT COMPANY
(Subsidiary of General Dynamics Corporation)
PO Box 7704, Wichita, Kansas 67277
Telephone: 1 (316) 941 6000
Fax: 1 (316) 941 7812
Telex: 417 400
CHAIRMAN AND CHIEF EXECUTIVE: Russell W. Meyer Jr
SENIOR VICE-PRESIDENT, AIRCRAFT MARKETING:
Roy H. Norris
DIRECTOR OF PUBLIC RELATIONS: H. Dean Humphrey

Founded by late Clyde V. Cessna 1911; incorporated 7 September 1927; former Pawnee and Wallace aircraft divisions in Wichita consolidated in Aircraft Division mid-1984; acquired by General Dynamics as wholly owned subsidiary 1985.

Owned subsidiaries include McCauley Accessory Division, Dayton, Ohio; Cessna Finance Corporation in Wichita. Sold 49 per cent interest in Reims Aviation of France to Compagnie Française Chaufour Investissement (CFCI) February 1989; CFCI continues manufacturing Cessna F406 Caravan II and holds option to build Cessna single-engined aircraft when Cessna restarts production.

Total 177,553 aircraft produced by December 1990; 171 aircraft delivered in 1990, including 66 Caravan Is, four Caravan IIs, 30 Citation IIs, 15 Citation IIIs and 56 Citation Vs. Total employees 4,975 on 1 January 1991. Range includes Caravan I and II and seven variants of Citation.

CESSNA SUSPENDED PRODUCTION
Production of the types listed below was suspended during the mid-1980s; there are no restoration plans at present time.

Model 152: Total 7,500 Model 152 and Model 152 Aerobats produced by December 1986, including 640 by Reims Aviation in France. Both models described in 1984-85 *Jane's*.

Skyhawk: Total 35,773 civil Model 172/Skyhawks produced by 31 December 1987, including 2,144 F172s by Reims Aviation in France. Additional 864 T-41A, T-41B, T-41C and T-41D Mescaleros produced as military basic trainers from 1966 to 1983. Described in 1985-86 *Jane's*.

Cutlass RG: Airframe of Model 172 Skyhawk with retractable landing gear of Skylane RG. Total 1,159 Cutlass RGs sold by 31 December 1987. Described in 1985-86 *Jane's*.

Skylane: Total 19,812 Model 182/Skylanes of various models built by 31 December 1987, including 169 F182s produced by Reims Aviation. Described in 1985-86 *Jane's*.

Skylane RG and Turbo Skylane RG: Total 2,102 Skylane RGs produced by 31 December 1987, including 73 assembled in France as Reims 182 Skylane RGs. Described in 1985-86 *Jane's*.

Model 185 Skywagon: Total 4,356 Model 185 Skywagons produced by 31 December 1987, including 497 military U-17A/B/Cs. Described in 1985-86 *Jane's*.

AG Truck and AG Husky: Total 1,949 AG Trucks and 386 AG Huskys produced; production suspended 1985. Both models briefly described in 1985-86 *Jane's*; full description of AG Truck in 1984-85 *Jane's*.

Stationair 6 and Turbo Stationair 6 (US Air Force designation of Turbo Stationair: U-26A): Stationairs originated from U206 Skywagon and TU206 Turbo Skywagon; name changed to Stationair 6 and Turbo Stationair 6 in 1978, denoting six-seat capacity. Total 7,652 Model 206 Skywagons and Stationairs, including 643 de luxe Super Skylanes of similar design, produced by 31 December 1978. Descriptions in 1985-86 *Jane's*.

Centurion, Turbo Centurion and Pressurised Centurion: Total 8,453 Model 210/Centurions, plus 51 Pressurised Centurions, delivered by 31 December 1987. Described in 1985-86 *Jane's*.

Model T303 Crusader: Total 297 T303 Crusaders delivered by 31 December 1987. Described in 1985-86 *Jane's*.

Model 402C: Total 1,540 Model 402C Utililiners and 402C Businessliners delivered by 31 December 1987. Described in 1985-86 *Jane's*.

Model 414A Chancellor: Total 1,067 Model 414/Chancellors delivered by 31 December 1987. Model 414A described in 1985-86 *Jane's*.

Model 421 Golden Eagle: Total 1,909 early 421s, Model 421B Golden Eagle, 421B Executive Commuter and 421C Golden Eagle produced before production was suspended in 1985. Described in 1985-86 *Jane's*.

Model 425 Conquest I: Known as Corsair until late 1982; first deliveries 1980. Total 232 Corsairs and Conquest Is delivered by 31 December 1987, when production suspended. Described in 1986-87 *Jane's*.

Model 441 Conquest II: Total 360 delivered by 31 December 1987. Described, with brief details of P&WC PT6A-engined Model 435, in 1986-87 *Jane's*.

REIMS-CESSNA MODEL F406/ CARAVAN II
Turboprop version of Cessna Model 400 series developed in France by Reims Aviation, which see.

CESSNA MODEL 208 CARAVAN I/U-27A
TYPE: Single-turboprop civil and military multi-mission aircraft.
PROGRAMME: First flight of engineering prototype (N208LP) 9 December 1982; first production Caravan I rolled out August 1984; FAA certification October 1984; full production started 1985; amphibian float version certificated March 1986.
VARIANTS: **Model 208A:** Basic utility model for passengers or cargo. Commissioned by Federal Express Corporation as **Cargomaster** freighter with special features including T-O weight 3,629 kg (8,000 lb), Bendix/King avionics, no cabin windows or starboard rear door, more cargo tiedowns, additional cargo net, underfuselage cargo pannier of composite materials, 15.2 cm (6 in) vertical extension of fin/rudder, jetpipe deflected to carry exhaust clear of pannier.

Model 208B: Stretched version, developed at request of Federal Express. Commissioned by Federal Express as **Super Cargomaster**; first flight 3 March 1986; certificated October 1986; first delivery to Federal Express 31 October 1986; deliveries at three per month during 1990. Features include fuselage stretched by 1.22 m (4 ft), payload of 1,587 kg (3,500 lb) and 12.7 m³ (450 cu ft) of cargo volume.

Grand Caravan: Announced at NBAA 1990; stretched to accommodate up to 14 passengers in quick-change interior; powered by 503 kW (675 shp) P&WC PT6A-114A.

U-27A: Military utility/special mission derivative of 208A and 208B versions of Caravan I; announced Spring 1985; roles include cargo, logistic support, paratroop or supply dropping, medevac, electronic surveillance, forward air control, passenger/troop transport, C³I, maritime patrol, SAR, psychological warfare, radio relay/RPV control, military base support, range safety patrol, reconnaissance and fire patrol. Fittings can include six underwing and one centreline hard points, observation windows and bubble windows for downward view, centreline reconnaissance pod, 2.8 m³ (84 cu ft) cargo pannier from 208A and two-part electrically actuated upward and downward rolling shutter door with slipstream deflector.

Cessna offering U-27A as **Low Intensity Conflict Aircraft** (LICA); reconnaissance pod by General Dynamics contains variety of film and electronic sensors including Zeiss Avionics KS-153 80 mm Tri-Lens and 600 mm high resolution cameras, Texas Instruments RS730 IR linescanner, Honeywell four-channel encrypted data link, Fairchild RECCE interface unit, two RCA video recorders, Control Data video management system and Smiths 9000C or JET VG204 roll gyros, permitting real/near-real time reporting via voice or data link to control centres or battlefield commanders; pod could also house a SLAR unit for stand-off reconnaissance. Pod measures 4.39 m (14 ft 5 in) long, 0.72 m (2 ft 4½ in) deep and 0.63 m (2 ft 1 in) wide and weighs 454-567 kg (1,000-1,250 lb) depending on sensor configuration; is compatible with Advanced Tactical Air Reconnaissance

Turboprop powered Cessna Model 208 Caravan I

System (ATARS) and can be mounted on other aircraft, including F-16.

General Dynamics planned to install 360° FLIR turret in U-27A during 1989 and proposed Stinger armament for self-defence in combined reconnaissance/forward air control role. U-27A proposed for gunship requirement for USAF Special Operations Command equipped with door-mounted General Electric GECAL 50 12.7 mm three-barrel Gatling gun. U-27A LICA toured Europe after Farnborough Air Show 1988.

CUSTOMERS: Federal Express Corporation ordered first batch of 30 plus nine optioned Model 208As in December 1983; company ordered first 50 Model 208Bs in November 1989; 211 Caravans delivered by end December 1990; with all options, Federal Express total Caravan I fleet will be 349 when deliveries completed in October 1994, operating in Canada, France, Hawaii, Ireland, Sweden, the USA and US Virgin Islands.

Other customers include Royal Canadian Mounted Police (first amphibian float version); Brazilian Air Force (three plus four on order), Liberian Army (one), Royal Thai Army (10).

US State Department using two U-27As with VLF/Omega long-range navigation systems in anti-narcotics campaign. More than 10 per cent of Caravan Is are in military or paramilitary service, some with CIA.

Toyota Aviation (Toyota Motor Corporation subsidiary) appointed to market, distribute and support Caravan I and II in People's Republic of China.

Total of 438 Caravan Is delivered by December 1990.

DESIGN FEATURES: Claimed as first all-new single-engined turboprop general aviation aircraft; intended to replace de Havilland Canada Beavers and Otters, Cessna 180s, 185s and 206s in worldwide utility role.

Main qualities are high speed with heavy load, compatibility with unprepared strips, economy and reliability with minimum maintenance; can also carry weather radar, air-conditioning and oxygen systems; optional packs for firefighting, photography, spraying, ambulance/hearse, border patrol, parachuting and supply dropping, surveillance and government utility missions; optional wheel or float landing gear.

First single-engined aircraft to achieve FAA certification for ILS in Category II conditions (104 Federal Express aircraft to be equipped); approval for IFR cargo operations 1989 made France and Ireland first European countries to allow single-engined Public Transport day/night IFR operation.

Wing aerofoil NACA 23017.424 at root, 23012 at tip; dihedral 3° from root; incidence 2° 37′ at root, –0° 36′ at tip. Optional pneumatic de-icing of wings, tail and mainplane strut.

FLYING CONTROLS: Plain mechanical controls; lateral control by small ailerons and slot-lip spoilers ahead of outer section of flaps; aileron trim standard; all tail control surfaces horn balanced; fixed tailplane with vortex generators above, ahead of elevator; elevator trim tab; electrically actuated single-slotted flaps occupy more than 70 per cent of trailing-edge and deflect to maximum 30°.

STRUCTURE: Fail-safe two-spar wing; conventional fuselage.

LANDING GEAR: Non-retractable tricycle type, with single wheel on each unit. Tubular spring cantilever main units; oil-damped spring nosewheel unit. Mainwheel tyres size 6.50-10; nosewheel 6.50-8. Oversize tyres, mainwheels 8.50-10, nosewheel 22 × 8.00-8, and extended nosewheel fork, optional. Hydraulically actuated single-disc brake on each mainwheel. Certificated in floatplane and amphibian versions, with floats by Wipline.

POWER PLANT: One Pratt & Whitney Canada PT6A-114 turboprop, flat rated at 447 kW (600 shp) to 3,800 m (12,500 ft), and driving a Hartzell HC-B3MN3/M10083 three-blade constant-speed reversible-pitch and feathering composites propeller. Integral fuel tanks in wings, total capacity 1,268 litres (335 US gallons; 279 Imp gallons), of which 1,257 litres (332 US gallons; 276.5 Imp gallons) are usable.

ACCOMMODATION: Pilot and up to nine passengers or 1,360 kg (3,000 lb) of cargo. Maximum seating capacity with FAR Pt 23 waiver is 14. Cabin has a flat floor with Brownline cargo track attachments for a combination of two- and three-abreast seating, with an aisle between the seats. Forward hinged door for pilot, with direct vision window, on each side of forward fuselage. Airstair door for passengers at rear of cabin on starboard side. Cabin is heated and ventilated. Optional air-conditioning. Two-section horizontally split cargo door at rear of cabin on port side, flush with floor at bottom and with square corners. Upper portion hinges upward, lower portion forward 180°. Electrically operated, flight openable tambour roll-up door with airflow deflecting spoiler optional. In a cargo role cabin will accommodate typically two D-size cargo containers or up to ten 208 litre (55 US gallon; 45.8 Imp gallon) drums.

SYSTEMS: Electrical system is powered by 28V 200A starter/generator and 24V 45Ah lead-acid battery (24V 40Ah nickel-cadmium battery optional). Standby electrical system, with 95A alternator, optional. Hydraulic system for brakes only. Oxygen system, capacity 3.31 m³ (116.95 cu ft), optional. Vacuum system standard. Cabin air-conditioning system optional on c/n 208-00030 onwards. De-icing system, comprising electric propeller de-icing boots, pneumatic wing, wing strut and tail surface boots, electrically heated windscreen panel, heated pitot/static probe, ice detector light and standby electrical system, all optional.

AVIONICS: Standard avionics include Bendix/King Silver Crown package comprising a single nav/com, ADF, transponder and audio console. Optional avionics include Bendix/King RDS-82 colour weather radar in pod on starboard wing leading-edge.

EQUIPMENT: Standard equipment includes sensitive altimeter, electric clock, magnetic compass, attitude and directional gyros, true airspeed indicator, turn and bank indicator, vertical speed indicator, ammeter/voltmeter, fuel flow indicator, ITT indicator, oil pressure and temperature indicator, windscreen defrost, ground service plug receptacle, variable intensity instrument post lighting, map light, overhead courtesy lights (3) and overhead floodlights (pilot and co-pilot), approach plate holder, cargo tiedowns, internal corrosion proofing, vinyl floor covering, emergency locator beacon, partial plumbing for oxygen system, adjustable fore/aft/vertical/reclining pilot's seat with five-point restraint harness, tinted windows, control surface bonding straps, heated pitot and stall warning systems, retractable crew steps (port side), tiedowns and towbar. Optional equipment includes co-pilot's and passenger seats, stowable, folding utility seats, digital clock, fuel totaliser, turn co-ordinator, flight hour recorder, fire extinguisher, dual controls, co-pilot flight instruments, floatplane kit (on c/n 208-00030 onwards), hoisting rings (for floatplane), inboard fuel filling provisions (included in floatplane kit), ice detection light, courtesy lights on wing leading-edges, passenger reading lights, omniflash beacon, rudder gust lock, retractable crew step for starboard side, oversized tyres, electric trim system, oil quick drain valve and fan driven ventilation system.

Cessna Model 208B Caravan I operated by Union Flights of Sacramento, California, on behalf of Federal Express *(John Wegg)*

Cessna U-27A LICA aircraft with underfuselage reconnaissance pod, underwing hardpoints and roll-up cabin door

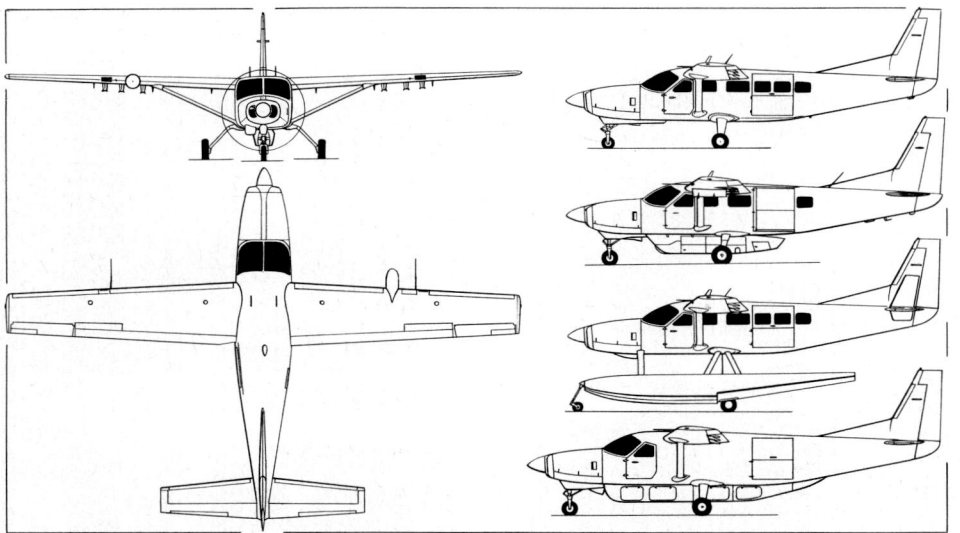

Three-view of Cessna U-27A Low Intensity Conflict Aircraft (LICA) with side views, top to bottom, of 208A Caravan I, U-27A, 208A amphibian and 208B Super Cargomaster for Federal Express *(Pilot Press)*

DIMENSIONS, EXTERNAL (Model 208):

Wing span	15.88 m (52 ft 1 in)
Wing chord: at root	1.98 m (6 ft 6 in)
at tip	1.22 m (4 ft 0 in)
Wing aspect ratio	9.6
Length overall: landplane	11.46 m (37 ft 7 in)
Height overall: landplane	4.32 m (14 ft 2 in)
amphibian (on land)	5.33 m (17 ft 6 in)
Tailplane span	6.25 m (20 ft 6 in)
Wheel track: landplane	3.56 m (11 ft 8 in)
amphibian	3.25 m (10 ft 8 in)
Wheelbase: landplane	3.54 m (11 ft 7½ in)
amphibian	4.44 m (14 ft 7 in)
Propeller diameter	2.54 m (8 ft 4 in)
Airstair door: Height	1.27 m (4 ft 2 in)
Width	0.61 m (2 ft 0 in)
Cargo door: Height	1.27 m (4 ft 2 in)
Width	1.24 m (4 ft 1 in)

DIMENSIONS, INTERNAL (Model 208):

Cabin: Length, excl baggage area	4.57 m (15 ft 0 in)
Max width	1.57 m (5 ft 2 in)
Max height	1.30 m (4 ft 3 in)
Volume	9.67 m³ (341.4 cu ft)

AREAS:

Wings, gross	25.96 m² (279.4 sq ft)
Vertical tail surfaces (total, incl dorsal fin)	
	3.57 m² (38.41 sq ft)
Horizontal tail surfaces (total)	
	6.51 m² (70.04 sq ft)

WEIGHTS AND LOADINGS (civil Model 208. L: landplane, F: floatplane, A: amphibian):

Weight empty: L	1,724 kg (3,800 lb)
F	2,020 kg (4,454 lb)
A	2,177 kg (4,799 lb)
Max baggage (all)	147 kg (325 lb)
Max fuel (all)	1,009 kg (2,224 lb)
Max ramp weight: L	3,327 kg (7,335 lb)
F, A	3,463 kg (7,635 lb)
Max T-O and landing weight, and max zero-fuel weight:	
L	3,311 kg (7,300 lb)
F, A	3,447 kg (7,600 lb)
Max wing loading: L	127.4 kg/m² (26.1 lb/sq ft)
F, A	132.8 kg/m² (27.2 lb/sq ft)
Max power loading: L	7.41 kg/kW (12.17 lb/shp)
F, A	7.71 kg/kW (12.7 lb/shp)

WEIGHTS AND LOADINGS (U-27A. L and A as above):

Weight empty, standard: L	1,752 kg (3,862 lb)
A	2,233 kg (4,922 lb)
Max ramp weight: L	3,645 kg (8,035 lb)
A	3,463 kg (7,635 lb)
Max T-O weight: L	3,629 kg (8,000 lb)
A	3,447 kg (7,600 lb)
Max landing weight: L	3,538 kg (7,800 lb)
A	3,311 kg (7,300 lb)
Max wing loading: L	139.8 kg/m² (28.6 lb/sq ft)
A	132.8 kg/m² (27.2 lb/sq ft)
Max power loading: L	8.11 kg/kW (13.33 lb/shp)
A	7.71 kg/kW (12.67 lb/shp)

PERFORMANCE (civil Model 208. L: landplane, F: floatplane, A: amphibian):

Max operating speed (all)	
	175 knots (325 km/h; 202 mph) IAS
Max cruising speed at 3,050 m (10,000 ft):	
L	184 knots (341 km/h; 212 mph)
F	159 knots (295 km/h; 183 mph)
A	153 knots (283 km/h; 176 mph)
Stalling speed, power off:	
L: flaps up	73 knots (135 km/h; 84 mph) CAS
flaps down	60 knots (111 km/h; 69 mph) CAS
F, A, landing configuration	
	58 knots (107 km/h; 67 mph) CAS
Max rate of climb at S/L: L	370 m (1,215 ft)/min
F	306 m (1,005 ft)/min
A	290 m (952 ft)/min
Service ceiling: L	8,410 m (27,600 ft)
F	7,285 m (23,900 ft)
A	7,010 m (23,000 ft)
Max operating altitude (all)	9,145 m (30,000 ft)
T-O run: L	296 m (970 ft)
T-O run, water: F	468 m (1,535 ft)
A	469 m (1,540 ft)
T-O to 15 m (50 ft): L	507 m (1,665 ft)
F, on water	843 m (2,765 ft)
A, on water	859 m (2,820 ft)
Landing from 15 m (50 ft): L	472 m (1,550 ft)
Landing run: L	197 m (645 ft)
Range with max fuel, at max cruise power, allowances for start, taxi and reserves stated:	
L at 3,050 m (10,000 ft), 45 min	
	970 nm (1,797 km; 1,117 miles)
L at 6,100 m (20,000 ft), 45 min	
	1,275 nm (2,362 km; 1,468 miles)
F at 3,050 m (10,000 ft), 30 min	
	898 nm (1,664 km; 1,034 miles)
A at 3,050 m (10,000 ft), 30 min	
	868 nm (1,608 km; 999 miles)
Range with max fuel at max range power, allowances as above:	
L at 3,050 m (10,000 ft)	
	1,115 nm (2,066 km; 1,284 miles)
L at 6,100 m (20,000 ft)	
	1,370 nm (2,539 km; 1,578 miles)
g limits	+3.8/-1.52

Cessna Citationjet six-seat light business jet during first flight

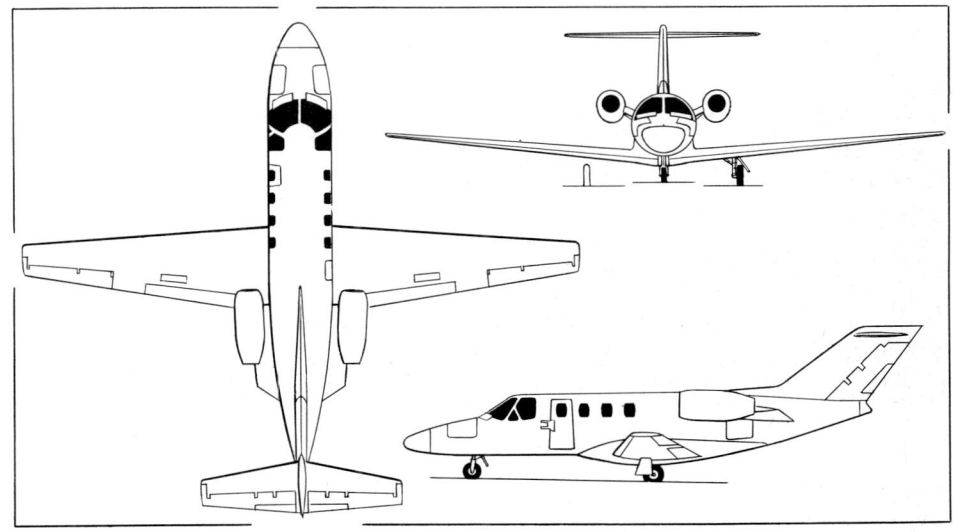

Cessna Citationjet (two Rolls-Royce/Williams International FJ44 turbofans (*Pilot Press*)

PERFORMANCE (U-27A. L and A as above):

Max cruising speed at 3,050 m (10,000 ft):	
L	184 knots (341 km/h; 212 mph)
A	163 knots (302 km/h; 188 mph)
Stalling speed in landing configuration:	
L	61 knots (113 km/h; 71 mph)
A	58 knots (107 km/h; 67 mph)
Max rate of climb at S/L: L	320 m (1,050 ft)/min
A	274 m (900 ft)/min
Service ceiling: L	7,770 m (25,500 ft)
A	6,100 m (20,000 ft)
T-O run at S/L: L	368 m (1,205 ft)
A, on water	500 m (1,640 ft)
T-O to 15 m (50 ft) at S/L: L	674 m (2,210 ft)
A, on water	872 m (2,860 ft)
Landing from 15 m (50 ft) at S/L, without propeller reversal: L	505 m (1,655 ft)
A	560 m (1,835 ft)
Landing run at S/L, without propeller reversal:	
L	227 m (745 ft)
A	297 m (975 ft)
Range at 3,050 m (10,000 ft) at max cruise power, allowances for T-O, climb, cruise, descent, and 45 min reserves: L	1,085 nm (2,011 km; 1,249 miles)
A	955 nm (1,770 km; 1,100 miles)

CESSNA MODEL 525 CITATIONJET

TYPE: Six-seat business jet.

PROGRAMME: Announced at NBAA convention 1989; to replace Citation 500 and I (production of which stopped 1985); first flight of FJ44 turbofans in Citation 500 April 1990; first flight of Citationjet 29 April 1991; first flight of second prototype Autumn 1991; FAA certification for single-pilot operation planned October 1992; first customer delivery December 1992. Anticipated market for 1,000 in 10 years.

CUSTOMERS: Orders for 50 placed at NBAA convention 1989; production sold for 18 months after first delivery.

DESIGN FEATURES: Compared with Citation I, Citationjet has fuselage shortened by 0.27 m (10¾ in) and wing span reduced by 0.57 m (1 ft 10½ in); cabin height increased by 13 cm (5 in) by lowering centre aisle. New supercritical laminar-flow wing aerofoil; high T-tail; two FJ44 turbofans; trailing link main landing gear.

POWER PLANT: Two 8.45 kN (1,900 lb st) Rolls-Royce/Williams International FJ44 turbofans.

Data below are provisional:

DIMENSIONS, EXTERNAL:

Wing span	13.78 m (45 ft 2½ in)
Wing aspect ratio	8.5
Length overall	12.98 m (42 ft 7¼ in)
Height overall	4.18 m (13 ft 8½ in)
Wheel track	3.84 m (12 ft 7¼ in)
Wheelbase	4.54 m (14 ft 10¾ in)
Tailplane span	4.99 m (16 ft 4¾ in)
Crew/passenger door:	
Height	1.29 m (4 ft 2¾ in)
Width	0.60 m (1 ft 11½ in)

DIMENSIONS, INTERNAL:

Cabin:	
Length between pressure bulkheads	
	4.85 m (15 ft 10¾ in)
Max width	1.49 m (4 ft 10¾ in)
Height	1.46 m (4 ft 9½ in)

AREAS:

Wings, gross	22.30 m² (240.0 sq ft)
Horizontal tail surfaces (total, incl tab)	
	5.03 m² (54.1 sq ft)
Vertical tail surfaces (total, incl tab)	
	4.74 m² (51.0 sq ft)

WEIGHTS AND LOADINGS:

Weight empty	2,599 kg (5,730 lb)
Max fuel weight	1,393 kg (3,070 lb)
Max T-O weight	4,536 kg (10,000 lb)
Max ramp weight	4,581 kg (10,100 lb)
Max zero-fuel weight	3,461 kg (7,630 lb)
Max landing weight	4,309 kg (9,500 lb)
Max wing loading	203.43 kg/m² (41.67 lb/sq ft)
Max power loading	268.4 kg/kN (2.63 lb/lb st)

PERFORMANCE (estimated):

Max operating speed:	
S/L to 9,300 m (30,500 ft)	
	260 knots (482 km/h; 299 mph) IAS
above 10,820 m (35,500 ft)	Mach 0.70
Max cruising speed at 10,670 m (35,000 ft)	
	380 knots (704 km/h; 438 mph)
Stalling speed, landing configuration	
	81 knots (150 km/h; 94 mph)
Rate of climb at S/L, one engine out	
	326 m (1,070 ft)/min
Service ceiling	12,500 m (41,000 ft)
T-O balanced field length (FAR Pt 25)	903 m (2,960 ft)
FAR Pt 25 landing field length at max landing weight	
	854 m (2,800 ft)
Range with one crew, four passengers, 45 min reserves	
	1,500 nm (2,780 km; 1,727 miles)

CESSNA MODEL 550 CITATION II

TYPE: Eight/twelve-seat twin-turbofan business jet.

PROGRAMME: Announced 14 September 1976; first flight (N550CC) 31 January 1977; FAR Pt 25 Transport Category certification for two-pilot crew March 1978; phased out in favour of Citation S/II 1984, after 503 Citation IIs delivered. Resumed production announced NBAA convention September 1985.

VARIANTS: **Model 550 Citation II**: First version for two-pilot operation.

Model 551 Citation II/SP: For single-pilot operation to FAR Part 23 with up to 10 passengers at max T-O weight 5,670 kg (12,500 lb).

CUSTOMERS: Total 607 Citation IIs delivered by 31 December 1990, including 30 in 1990. Production output into 1992 sold.

DESIGN FEATURES: Citation II 1.14 m (3 ft 9 in) longer than Citation I, greater wing span, increased fuel and baggage capacities. Wing aerofoil NACA 23014 (modified) at centreline, NACA 23012 at wing station 247.95; dihedral 4°; tailplane dihedral 9°. Wing leading-edges electrically de-iced ahead of engines; pneumatic de-icing boots on outer wings.

FLYING CONTROLS: Mechanically actuated ailerons; manual trim tab on port aileron; manual rudder trim; electric elevator trim tab with manual standby; electrically actuated single-slotted flaps; hydraulically actuated airbrake.

STRUCTURE: Two primary, one auxiliary metal wing spars; three fuselage attachment points; conventional ribs and stringers. All-metal pressurised fuselage with fail-safe design providing multiple load paths.

Data refer to current production Model 550 Citation II (c/n 0550 and later), unless otherwise indicated:

LANDING GEAR: Hydraulically retractable tricycle type with single wheel on each unit. Main units retract inward into the wing, nose gear forward into fuselage nose. Free-fall and pneumatic emergency extension systems. Goodyear mainwheels with tyres size 22.0 × 8-10, 10-ply rating, pressure 6.90 bars (100 lb/sq in). Steerable nosewheel (±20°) with Goodyear wheel and tyre size 18.0 × 4.4, 10-ply rating, pressure 8.27 bars (120 lb/sq in). Goodyear hydraulic brakes. Parking brake and pneumatic emergency brake system. Anti-skid system optional.

POWER PLANT: Two Pratt & Whitney Canada JT15D-4 turbofans, each rated at 11.12 kN (2,500 lb st) for take-off, pod-mounted on sides of rear fuselage. Integral fuel tanks in wings, with usable capacity of 2,808 litres (742 US gallons; 618 Imp gallons).

ACCOMMODATION: Crew of two on separate flight deck, on fully adjustable seats, with seat belts and inertia reel shoulder harness. Sun visors standard. Fully carpeted main cabin equipped with seats for six to ten passengers, with toilet in six/eight-seat versions. Main baggage area at rear of cabin. Second baggage area in nose. Total baggage capacity 522 kg (1,150 lb). Cabin is pressurised, heated and air-conditioned. Individual reading lights and air inlets for each passenger. Dropout constant-flow oxygen system for emergency use. Plug type door with integral airstair at front on port side and one emergency exit on starboard side. Doors on each side of nose baggage compartment. Tinted windows, each with curtains. Pilot's storm window, birdproof windscreen with de-fog system, anti-icing, standby alcohol anti-icing and bleed air rain removal system.

SYSTEMS: Pressurisation system supplied with engine bleed air, max pressure differential 0.61 bar (8.8 lb/sq in), maintaining a sea level cabin altitude to 6,720 m (22,040 ft), or a 2,440 m (8,000 ft) cabin altitude to 12,495 m (41,000 ft). Hydraulic system, pressure 103.5 bars (1,500 lb/sq in), with two pumps to operate landing gear and speed brakes. Separate hydraulic system for wheel brakes. Electrical system supplied by two 28V 400A DC starter/generators, with two 350VA inverters and 24V 40Ah nickel-cadmium battery. Oxygen system of 0.62 m³ (22 cu ft) capacity includes two crew demand masks and five dropout constant flow masks for passengers. High capacity oxygen system optional. Engine fire detection and extinguishing systems.

DIMENSIONS, EXTERNAL:
Wing span	15.76 m (51 ft 8½ in)
Wing aspect ratio	8.3
Length overall	14.39 m (47 ft 2½ in)
Height overall	4.57 m (15 ft 0 in)
Wheel track	5.36 m (17 ft 7 in)
Wheelbase	5.55 m (18 ft 2½ in)

DIMENSIONS, INTERNAL:
Cabin:
Length, front to rear bulkhead	6.37 m (20 ft 10¾ in)
Max height	1.46 m (4 ft 9½ in)
Baggage capacity	1.84 m³ (65.0 cu ft)

AREAS:
Wings, gross	30.00 m² (322.9 sq ft)
Horizontal tail surfaces (total, incl tab)	6.56 m² (70.6 sq ft)
Vertical tail surfaces (total)	4.73 m² (50.9 sq ft)

WEIGHTS AND LOADINGS:
Weight empty, equipped	3,351 kg (7,388 lb)
Max fuel weight	2,272 kg (5,009 lb)
Max T-O weight	6,033 kg (13,300 lb)
Max ramp weight	6,123 kg (13,500 lb)

Cessna Citation II business jet

Max zero-fuel weight: standard	4,309 kg (9,500 lb)
optional	4,990 kg (11,000 lb)
Max landing weight	5,760 kg (12,700 lb)
Max wing loading	201.1 kg/m² (41.19 lb/sq ft)
Max power loading	275.3 kg/kN (2.66 lb/lb st)

PERFORMANCE (at max T-O weight, ISA, except where indicated):
Max operating speed:
S/L to 4,265 m (14,000 ft)	
	262 knots (486 km/h; 302 mph) IAS
4,265 m (14,000 ft) to 8,530 m (28,000 ft)	
	277 knots (513 km/h; 319 mph) IAS
8,530 m (28,000 ft) and above	Mach 0.705

Cruising speed at average cruise weight of 4,990 kg (11,000 lb) at 7,620 m (25,000 ft)
385 knots (713 km/h; 443 mph)
Stalling speed, clean, at max T-O weight
94 knots (174 km/h; 108 mph) CAS
Stalling speed at max landing weight
82 knots (152 km/h; 95 mph) CAS
Max rate of climb at S/L	1,027 m (3,370 ft)/min

Rate of climb at S/L, one engine out
322 m (1,055 ft)/min
Max certificated altitude	13,105 m (43,000 ft)
Service ceiling, one engine out	7,680 m (25,200 ft)
T-O to 15 m (50 ft)	727 m (2,385 ft)
T-O balanced field length (FAR Pt 25)	912 m (2,990 ft)

FAR Pt 25 landing field length at max landing weight
692 m (2,270 ft)
Min ground turning radius about nosewheel
8.38 m (27 ft 6 in)
Range with max fuel, crew of two and six passengers, allowances for T-O, climb, cruise at 13,105 m (43,000 ft), descent, and 45 min reserves
1,662 nm (3,080 km; 1,914 miles)

OPERATIONAL NOISE LEVELS (FAR Pt 36):
T-O	80.1 EPNdB
Approach	90.5 EPNdB
Sideline	86.7 EPNdB

CESSNA MODEL S550 CITATION S/II
US Navy designation: T-47A

TYPE: Eight/ten-seat improved Citation II.

PROGRAMME: Announced 4 October 1983; first flight 14 February 1984; certificated with exemption for single-pilot operation July 1984; first delivery late Summer 1984; first delivery Citation S/II ambulance late 1985 to Province of Manitoba, Canada. High capacity brakes introduced as standard and offered as retrofit April 1987, reducing landing distance at max landing weight by 13 per cent.

VARIANTS: **Model S550**: Basic executive transport.

Ambulance: Carries single or double stretchers, up to four medical attendants and large quantities of medical oxygen.

T-47A (Cessna Model 552): Fifteen Citation S/IIs acquired by US Navy to replace T-39Ds in radar training role; part of five-year programme with three-year option, including provision of aircraft, simulators, maintenance and pilot services for training operators of air-to-air, intercept, air-to-ground and other radars. Differences from S/II include 12.89 kN (2,900 lb st) JT15D-5 turbofans, shorter wing to allow faster climb and Mach 0.733 at 12,200 m (40,000 ft), and Emerson nose-mounted AN/APQ-159 radar. Normal crew includes civilian pilot, Navy instructor, three students. First flight 15 February 1984; FAA certification 21 November 1984.

CUSTOMERS: US Navy (see above). Five specially equipped Citation S/IIs delivered to Flight Test Research Institute in Xian for Airborne Remote Sensing Centre of Chinese Academy of Sciences. 1,500th Citation, an S/II, delivered January 1988.

DESIGN FEATURES: Improvements, introduced on production line from c/n 506, include new wing aerofoil using Citation III supercritical technology, modified wing/fuselage fairing, extended inboard leading-edge, low drag engine pylon contours, sealed aileron/airbrake gaps, faired flap coves, hydraulically actuated flaps in two sections each side extending further inboard, TKS Glycol anti-icing system on wing, tail surface de-icing eliminated, P&WC JT15D-4B turbofans. New wing reduces cruise drag without sacrificing low speed and short-field capability.

Straight wing; incidence 2° 30′ at centreline, –0° 30′ at station 247.95; dihedral 4°; tailplane dihedral 9°.

Internal refinements include tailcone baggage volume

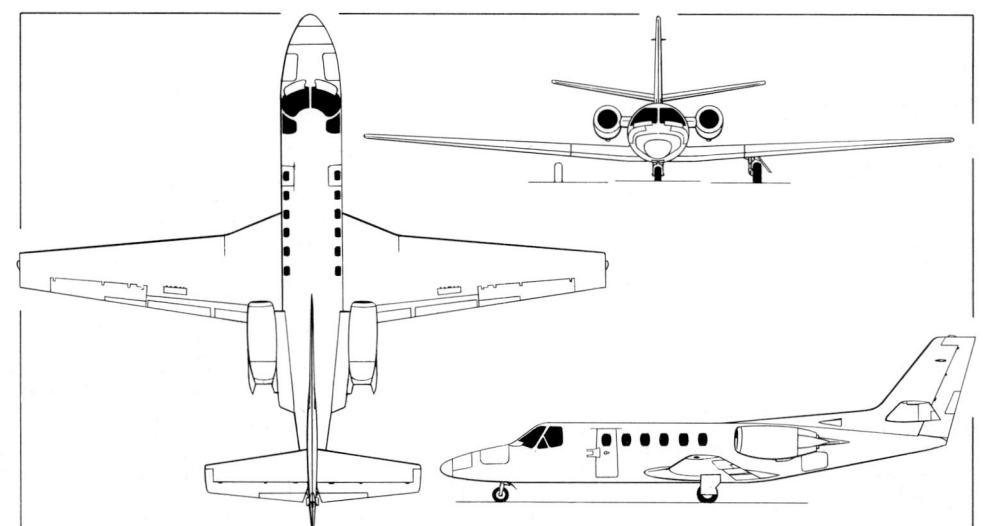

Cessna Citation S/II (Pratt & Whitney Canada JT15D-4B turbofans) *(Pilot Press)*

increased to 0.79 m³ (28 cu ft), 12.7 cm (5 in) extra headroom in totally private toilet, soft-touch sound deadening headliners, Citation III-style seats with shoulder harness, lateral seat tracking for better head and elbow room, built-in life jacket stowage, and redesigned sidewall air ducts giving greater insulation and heating and allowing more than 10 per cent extra aisle width.

Options include vanity unit for toilet, refreshment centres in composites, wide door for ambulance/cargo operations, Honeywell EFIS.

FLYING CONTROLS: Mechanically actuated ailerons assisted by geared trim tabs; elevator trim electrically actuated with mechanical standby; mechanical rudder trim; hydraulically actuated Fowler flaps; hydraulically operated airbrakes.

STRUCTURE: All-metal wing with two primary and one auxiliary spars, three fuselage attachments, conventional ribs and stringers. All-metal pressurised fuselage with multiple load path fail-safe design. Ailerons and flaps have graphite composite structure.

Data refer to current Citation S/II (c/n 0115 onwards) except where indicated:

LANDING GEAR: Hydraulically retractable tricycle type with single wheel on each unit. Main units retract inward into the wing, nose gear forward into fuselage nose. Free-fall and pneumatic emergency extension systems. Goodyear mainwheels with tyres size 22.0 × 8-10, 12-ply rating, pressure 8.27 bars (120 lb/sq in). Steerable nosewheel with Goodyear wheel and tyre size 18.0 × 4.4, 10-ply rating, pressure 8.27 bars (120 lb/sq in). High capacity brakes manufactured by Aircraft Wheel and Brake Division of Parker Hannifin Corporation. Parking brake and pneumatic emergency brake system. Anti-skid system optional.

POWER PLANT: Two Pratt & Whitney Canada JT15D-4B turbofans, each rated at 11.12 kN (2,500 lb st) for take-off, pod-mounted on sides of rear fuselage. Integral fuel tanks in wings, with combined usable capacity of 3,263 litres (862 US gallons; 718 Imp gallons).

ACCOMMODATION: Crew of two on separate flight deck, on fully adjustable seats, with seat belts and inertia reel shoulder harness, and sun visors. Seating for six to eight passengers in main cabin. Standard interior configuration provides for six passenger seats, two forward and four aft facing, each with headrest, seat belt and diagonal inertia reel harness; flushing toilet aft; tracked refreshment centre; forward cabin divider with privacy curtain, aft cabin divider with sliding doors. Passenger service units containing an oxygen mask, air vent and reading light for each passenger. Three separate baggage areas, one in nose section that is externally accessible, one in aft cabin area, and one in tailcone area, with a combined capacity of up to 658 kg (1,450 lb).

SYSTEMS: Pressurisation system supplied with engine bleed air, max pressure differential 0.61 bar (8.8 lb/sq in), maintaining a sea level cabin altitude to 6,962 m (22,842 ft), or a 2,440 m (8,000 ft) cabin altitude to 13,105 m (43,000 ft). Hydraulic system, pressure 103.5 bars (1,500 lb/sq in), with two pumps to operate landing gear and speed brakes. Pressurised reservoir. Separate hydraulic system for wheel brakes. Electrical system supplied by two 28V 300A engine driven DC starter/generators, with two 350VA inverters and 24V 40Ah nickel-cadmium battery. Otherwise as for Model 550 Citation II.

AVIONICS: Standard avionics package comprises Honeywell SPZ-500 integrated flight director/autopilot system, with single-cue command bars, Honeywell C-14D compass system, Honeywell RD-450 (starboard) HSI, dual Collins VHF-22A com transceivers, dual Collins VIR-32 nav receivers with VOR/LOC, glideslope and marker beacon receivers, dual Collins RMI-30, Collins DME-42 with 339F-12 indicator, TDR-90 transponder, Collins ADF-60, and Honeywell Primus 300SL colour weather radar. Optional advanced avionics and instrumentation are available according to customer choice, and include Bendix/King Series III integrated EFIS, nav/com and radar systems.

DIMENSIONS, EXTERNAL:
Wing span over lights: S/II	15.90 m (52 ft 2½ in)
T-47A	14.18 m (46 ft 6 in)
Wing chord (mean): S/II	2.06 m (6 ft 9 in)
Wing aspect ratio: S/II	7.8
Length overall: S/II	14.39 m (47 ft 2½ in)
T-47A	14.60 m (47 ft 10¾ in)
Height overall: S/II	4.57 m (15 ft 0 in)
T-47A	4.51 m (14 ft 9¾ in)
Wheel track	5.36 m (17 ft 7 in)
Wheelbase	5.55 m (18 ft 2½ in)
Tailplane span: S/II	5.79 m (19 ft 0 in)
Cabin door (S/II, optional): Height	1.14 m (3 ft 9 in)
Width	0.89 m (2 ft 11 in)

DIMENSIONS, INTERNAL (S/II):
Cabin:	
Length, front to rear bulkhead	6.37 m (20 ft 10¾ in)
Max height	1.45 m (4 ft 9½ in)
Max width	1.49 m (4 ft 10¾ in)
Baggage capacity (total)	2.27 m³ (80.0 cu ft)

AREAS (S/II):
Wings, gross	31.83 m² (342.6 sq ft)
Horizontal tail surfaces (total)	6.48 m² (69.8 sq ft)
Vertical tail surfaces (total)	4.73 m² (50.9 sq ft)

Cessna T-47A, a US Navy training version of the Citation S/II

WEIGHTS AND LOADINGS:
Weight empty, equipped: S/II	3,655 kg (8,059 lb)
T-47A	4,098 kg (9,035 lb)
Max baggage weight (S/II): internal	272 kg (600 lb)
external	385 kg (850 lb)
Max ramp weight: S/II	6,940 kg (15,300 lb)
Max fuel weight: S/II	2,640 kg (5,820 lb)
Max T-O weight: S/II	6,849 kg (15,100 lb)
T-47A	6,804 kg (15,000 lb)
Max landing weight: S/II	6,350 kg (14,400 lb)
Max zero-fuel weight: S/II	4,990 kg (11,200 lb)
Max wing loading: S/II	215.17 kg/m² (44.07 lb/sq ft)
Max power loading: S/II	1.42 kg/kN (3.02 lb/lb st)

PERFORMANCE (S/II at max T-O weight, except where indicated):
Max operating speed:
S/L to 2,440 m (8,000 ft)
  261 knots (483 km/h; 300 mph) IAS
2,440 m (8,000 ft) to 8,935 m (29,315 ft)
  276 knots (511 km/h; 318 mph)
above 8,935 m (29,315 ft) Mach 0.721
Cruising speed at mid-cruise weight of 5,443 kg (12,000 lb) at 10,670 m (35,000 ft)
  403 knots (746 km/h; 463 mph)
Stalling speed: clean, at max T-O weight
  94 knots (174 km/h; 108 mph) CAS
at max landing weight
  82 knots (152 km/h; 94 mph) CAS
Max rate of climb at S/L 926 m (3,040 ft)/min
Rate of climb at S/L, one engine out
  262 m (860 ft)/min
Max operating altitude 13,105 m (43,000 ft)
Service ceiling, one engine out 7,315 m (24,000 ft)
T-O balanced field length (FAR Pt 25)
  987 m (3,240 ft)
FAR 25 landing field length at max landing weight (high capacity brakes) 805 m (2,640 ft)
Range with four passengers, two crew and baggage, zero wind, IFR reserves 1,739 nm (3,223 km; 2,002 miles)
Range with max fuel 1,998 nm (3,701 km; 2,300 miles)

OPERATIONAL NOISE LEVELS (FAR Pt 36):
T-O	78.0 EPNdB
Approach	91.0 EPNdB
Sideline	90.4 EPNdB

CESSNA MODEL 560 CITATION V

TYPE: Stretched, eight-seat version of Citation S/II.
PROGRAMME: First flight of engineering prototype (N560CC) August 1987; announced at NBAA convention 1987; first flight of pre-production prototype early 1988; FAA certification 9 December 1988; first delivery April 1989.

CUSTOMERS: Order backlog at end 1990 covers production until mid-1992; total deliveries 89, including 56 in 1990.

DESIGN FEATURES: Fuselage stretched 0.61 m (2 ft) for eight-seat cabin and fully enclosed toilet/vanity area; seventh cabin window each side; two baggage compartments outside main cabin with total volume 1.16 m³ (41 cu ft) and capacity for 385 kg (850 lb) baggage. Other features include Global GNS-X navigation management system, advanced weather radar, dual transponders, encoding and radio altimeters, thrust reversers, engine synchronisers, 1.8 m³ (64 cu ft) oxygen system, recognition lights, and in-flight telephone. De-icing by engine bleed air for inboard wing leading-edges and 'silver' low profile pneumatic boots on outer wings and tailplane.

FLYING CONTROLS: Category II avionics standard, with integrated Honeywell autopilot and flight guidance system, and EFIS in captain's instrument panel.

POWER PLANT: Two Pratt & Whitney Canada JT15D-5A turbofans, each rated at 12.89 kN (2,900 lb st).

DIMENSIONS, EXTERNAL: As for Citation S/II except:
Length overall	14.90 m (48 ft 10¾ in)
Tailplane span	6.55 m (21 ft 6 in)
Wheelbase	6.06 m (19 ft 10¾ in)

DIMENSIONS, INTERNAL: As for Citation S/II except:
Length, front to rear bulkhead	6.89 m (22 ft 7¼ in)

AREAS: As for Citation S/II except:
Horizontal tail surfaces (total)	7.88 m² (84.8 sq ft)

WEIGHTS AND LOADINGS:
Weight empty, equipped	4,004 kg (8,828 lb)
Max fuel weight	2,640 kg (5,820 lb)
Max T-O weight	7,212 kg (15,900 lb)
Max ramp weight	7,303 kg (16,100 lb)
Max landing weight	6,895 kg (15,200 lb)
Max zero-fuel weight	5,080 kg (11,200 lb)
Max wing loading	226.6 kg/m² (46.41 lb/sq ft)
Max power loading	279.75 kg/kN (2.74 lb/lb st)

PERFORMANCE:
Max operating speed:
at 2,440 m (8,000 ft) to 8,810 m (28,900 ft)
  292 knots (541 km/h; 336 mph) IAS
above 8,810 m (28,900 ft) Mach 0.755
Cruising speed at 10,060 m (33,000 ft)
  427 knots (791 km/h; 492 mph)
Stalling speed, clean, at max T-O weight
  87 knots (161 km/h; 100 mph)
Max rate of climb at S/L 1,112 m (3,650 ft)/min
Rate of climb at S/L, one engine out
  360 m (1,180 ft)/min
Max operating altitude 13,700 m (45,000 ft)
Service ceiling, one engine out 9,480 m (31,100 ft)
T-O balanced field length (FAR 25) 963 m (3,160 ft)

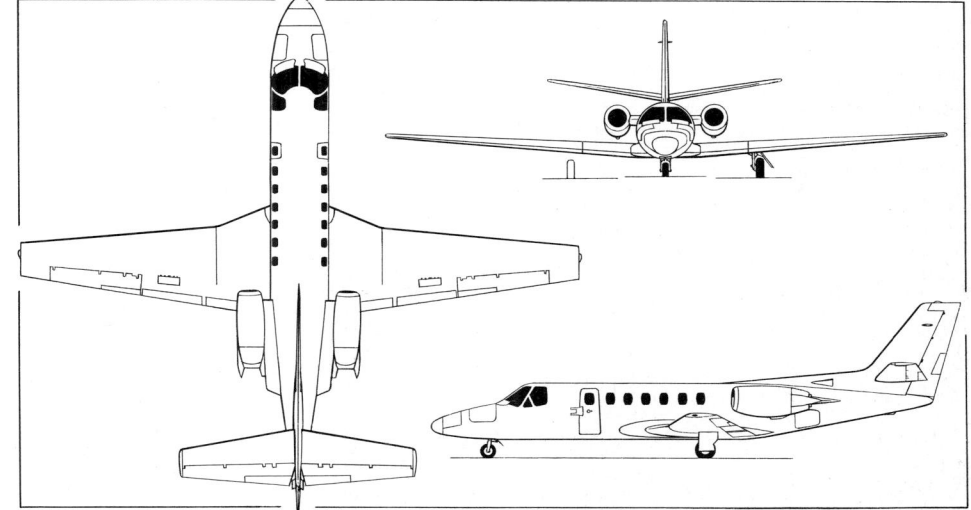

Cessna Model 560 Citation V (two Pratt & Whitney Canada JT15D-5A turbofans) *(Pilot Press)*

Cessna Model 560 Citation V eight-seat business jet

FAR 25 landing field length, S/L, ISA, at max landing weight   890 m (2,920 ft)
Range with six passengers, two crew, zero wind, at high-speed cruise speed with allowances for T-O, climb, cruise, descent and VFR reserves
                                    1,920 nm (3,558 km; 2,211 miles)

CESSNA MODEL 650 CITATION III

TYPE: Twin-turbofan eight/eleven-seat long-range business jet.
PROGRAMME: First flight of prototype (N650CC) 30 May 1979; first flight of second prototype 2 May 1980; FAR Pt 25 Transport Category certification 30 April 1982; first internal delivery December 1982; first customer delivery Spring 1983; CAA certification April 1988; European certifications include Austria, Denmark, France, Germany, Italy, Spain, Sweden, Switzerland. New Masterpiece interior introduced at NBAA convention 1988.
CUSTOMERS: Total 189 delivered by 31 December 1990, including 15 during 1990. Production of Citation III, VI and VII sold to end of 1991.
DESIGN FEATURES: Wing has NASA supercritical aerofoil; dihedral 3°; sweepback at quarter-chord 25°. Tailplane anhedral 3°. Wing leading-edges de-iced by engine bleed air; tailplane electrically de-iced; fin unprotected.
FLYING CONTROLS: Pitch axis, variable incidence tailplane and elevator; rudder boosted to counteract asymmetric thrust; hydraulically powered ailerons with manual reversion assisted after 3° movement by outboard spoiler panel; four hydraulically powered spoiler panels on each wing, of which outboard assists aileron, two centre panels act as airbrakes and all four panels used for emergency descent and lift dumping after touchdown. Electrically actuated trailing-edge flaps in three sections each side. Stall strips on inner and outer wings and small fence and turbulators ahead of outer flaps.

STRUCTURE: Conventional light alloy pressurised fuselage of circular section; fail-safe structure in pressurised area; light alloy tail surfaces; two-spar, fail-safe light alloy wing of bonded and riveted construction; wing built in three sections; flaps of Kevlar and graphite composites.
LANDING GEAR: Hydraulically retractable tricycle type. Main units retract inward into the undersurface of the wing centre-section, nosewheel forward and upward into the nose. Main units of trailing link type, each with twin wheels; steerable nose unit has a single wheel, max steering angle ±70-80°. Oleo-pneumatic shock absorber in each unit. Hydraulically powered nosewheel steering, with an accumulator to provide steering after a loss of normal hydraulic power. Emergency landing gear extension by manual release and free-fall to locked position; pneumatic blowdown system for backup. Mainwheel tyres size 22.0 × 5.75, 10-ply rating, pressure 10.20 bars (148 lb/sq in). Nosewheel tyre size 18.0 × 4.4, 10-ply rating, pressure 8.62 bars (125 lb/sq in). Fully modulated hydraulically powered anti-skid brake system. In the event of hydraulic system failure, an electrically driven standby pump provides pressure for the brakes. Emergency pneumatic brake system. Parking brake.
POWER PLANT: Two Garrett TFE731-3B-100S turbofans, each rated at 16.24 kN (3,650 lb st) for take-off, pod-mounted on sides of rear fuselage. Hydraulically operated Rohr target type thrust reversers standard. Two independent fuel systems, with integral tanks in each wing; usable capacity 4,183 litres (1,105 US gallons; 920 Imp gallons). Additional fuel cell behind rear fuselage bulkhead. Single-point pressure refuelling on starboard side of fuselage, to rear of wing trailing-edge. Gravity refuelling point on upper surface of each wing. A boost pump in the port wing fills the fuselage tank when pressure refuelling is not available. Engine intake anti-icing system.
ACCOMMODATION: Crew of two on separate flight deck, and up to nine passengers. Standard interior has six individual seats, with toilet at rear of cabin. The fuselage nose incorporates a radome, high resolution radar, avionics bay and a storage compartment for crew baggage. Electrically heated baggage compartment in rear fuselage with external door on port side. Airstair door forward of wing on port side. Overwing emergency

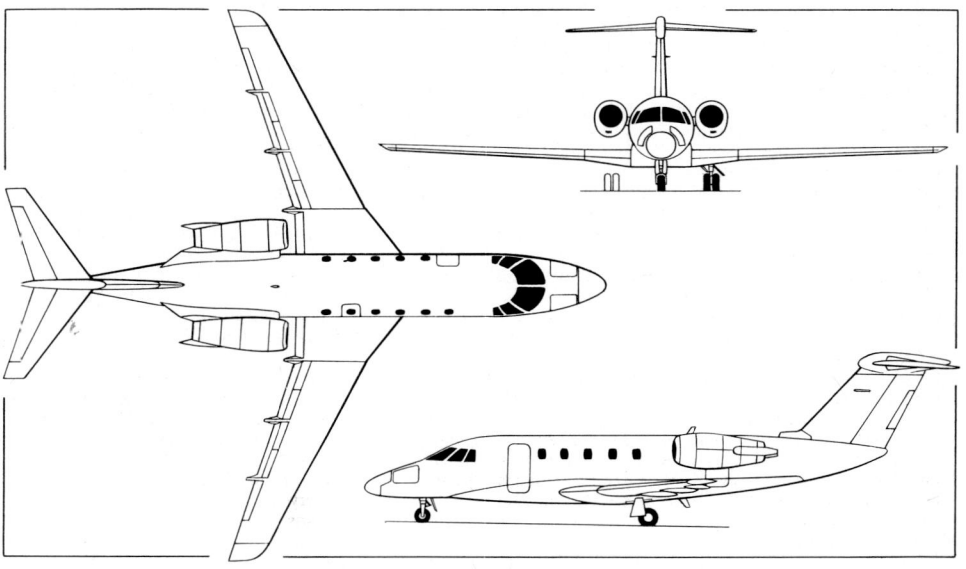

Cessna Citation III (two Garrett TFE731-3B-100S turbofans) *(Pilot Press)*

Cessna Citation III eight/eleven-seat business jet

escape hatch on starboard side. Cabin is pressurised, heated and air-conditioned. Windscreen anti-icing by engine bleed air, with alcohol spray backup for port side of the windscreen. Windscreen defogging by warm air, and rain removal by engine bleed air and a mechanically actuated airflow deflector.

SYSTEMS: Environmental control system, with separate control of flight deck and cabin conditions. Direct engine bleed pressurisation system, with nominal pressure differential of 0.67 bar (9.7 lb/sq in), provides 2,440 m (8,000 ft) cabin environment to max certificated altitude and can maintain a sea level cabin environment to approx 7,620 m (25,000 ft). Electrical system includes two 28V 400A DC starter/generators, two 200/115V 5kW three-phase engine driven alternators, two 115V 400Hz solid state static inverters, two 24V 22Ah nickel-cadmium batteries and an external power socket in the tailcone. Hydraulic system of 207 bars (3,000 lb/sq in) powered by two engine driven pressure compensated pumps for operation of spoilers, brakes, landing gear, nosewheel steering and thrust reversers. Hydraulic reservoir with integral reserve and an electrically driven hydraulic pump to provide emergency power. Oxygen system of 1.39 m³ (49 cu ft) capacity with automatic dropout constant-flow oxygen mask for each passenger and a quick-donning pressure demand mask for each crew member. Engine fire detection and extinguishing system.

AVIONICS: Standard avionics include a Honeywell SPZ-650 integrated flight director/autopilot system with AD650A ADI, RD650A HSI and C-14D compass system; Honeywell GH-14 ADI and RD450 HSI with C-14D compass system for co-pilot; AA-300 radio altimeter; dual Collins VHF-22A 720-channel com transceivers, dual VIR-32 nav receivers which include VOR, localiser, glideslope and marker beacon receivers, dual RMI-30, DME-42 DME, and TDR-90 transponder; Honeywell Primus 300SL colour weather radar; Collins ADF-60 ADF; J.E.T. standby attitude gyro; Teledyne angle of attack system; air data computer; dual Avtech audio amplifiers; and Telex microphones, headsets and speakers. A wide range of optional avionics is available including Bendix/King Series III integrated EFIS, nav/com and radar system.

EQUIPMENT: Standard equipment includes dual altimeters, Mach/airspeed indicators, angle of attack indicator, digital clock, instantaneous rate of climb indicators, outside air temperature gauge, crew seats with vertical, fore, aft and recline adjustments, seat belts, shoulder harnesses and inertia reels, six individual passenger seats, three forward and three aft facing with vertical, fore and aft adjustment, lateral tracking and recline adjustments, seat belts and shoulder harnesses, sun visors, flight deck divider with curtain, map case, openable storm windows, electroluminescent and edge-lit instrument panels, stall warning system, cockpit and cabin fire extinguishers, indirect cabin lighting, cabin aisle lights, door courtesy lights, 'Fasten seat belt'—No smoking' signs, refreshment centre, cup holders, ashtrays, executive table, aft cabin divider with curtain, emergency exit signs, internal corrosion proofing, emergency battery pack, emergency portable cabin oxygen, navigation and recognition lights, dual landing and taxi lights, dual anti-collision strobe lights, red flashing beacon, dual wing ice lights, lightning protection, static discharge wicks and tiedown provisions.

DIMENSIONS, EXTERNAL:
Wing span	16.31 m (53 ft 6 in)
Wing mean aerodynamic chord	2.08 m (6 ft 9¾ in)
Wing aspect ratio	8.9
Length overall	16.90 m (55 ft 5½ in)
Height overall	5.12 m (16 ft 9½ in)
Tailplane span	5.60 m (18 ft 4½ in)
Wheel track	2.84 m (9 ft 4 in)
Wheelbase	6.50 m (21 ft 4 in)
Cabin door: Width	0.61 m (2 ft 0 in)
Height	1.37 m (4 ft 6 in)

DIMENSIONS, INTERNAL:
Cabin:	
Length, front to rear bulkhead	7.01 m (23 ft 0 in)
Length, aft of cockpit divider	5.66 m (18 ft 7 in)
Max width	1.73 m (5 ft 8 in)
Max height	1.78 m (5 ft 10 in)
Baggage capacity (aft)	1.88 m³ (66.4 cu ft)
Crew baggage compartment (nose)	0.17 m³ (6.0 cu ft)

AREAS:
Wings, gross	29.00 m² (312.0 sq ft)
Horizontal tail surfaces (total)	6.26 m² (67.4 sq ft)
Vertical tail surfaces (total)	6.04 m² (65.0 sq ft)

WEIGHTS AND LOADINGS:
Weight empty, standard	5,357 kg (11,811 lb)
Max fuel weight	3,349 kg (7,384 lb)
Max payload	1,583 kg (3,489 lb)
Max T-O weight	9,979 kg (22,000 lb)
Max ramp weight	10,070 kg (22,200 lb)
Max landing weight	9,072 kg (20,000 lb)
Max zero-fuel weight	6,940 kg (15,300 lb)
Max wing loading	344.2 kg/m² (70.51 lb/sq ft)
Max power loading	307.24 kg/kN (3.01 lb/lb st)

PERFORMANCE (at max T-O weight, ISA, except where indicated):
Max operating speed:
S/L to 2,440 m (8,000 ft)	
	305 knots (565 km/h; 351 mph) IAS

at 11,130 m (36,525 ft)
	278 knots (515 km/h; 320 mph) IAS
above 11,130 m (36,525 ft)	Mach 0.851

Max cruising speed at 10,670 m (35,000 ft) and 7,257 kg (16,000 lb) cruise weight
	472 knots (874 km/h; 543 mph)

Stalling speed: clean, at max T-O weight
	125 knots (232 km/h; 144 mph) CAS

flaps and wheels down, at max landing weight
	97 knots (515 km/h; 112 mph) CAS
Max rate of climb at S/L	1,127 m (3,700 ft)/min
Rate of climb at S/L, one engine out	245 m (805 ft)/min
Time to 13,100 m (43,000 ft)	33 min
Certificated ceiling	15,545 m (51,000 ft)
Ceiling, one engine out	7,165 m (23,500 ft)
FAR 25 T-O field length at S/L	1,579 m (5,180 ft)

FAR 25 landing field length at max landing weight
	884 m (2,900 ft)
Turning circle based on nosewheel	6.63 m (21 ft 9 in)

Range, zero wind, with allowances for T-O, climb, descent and 45 min reserves (2 crew, 4 passengers)
	2,346 nm (4,348 km; 2,701 miles)
g limits	+3.2/−1

OPERATIONAL NOISE LEVELS (FAR Pt 36):
T-O	74.0 EPNdB
Approach	85.0 EPNdB
Sideline	81.0 EPNdB

CESSNA MODEL 670 CITATION IV

Announced 1989 as developed version of Citation III with longer range, better short-field performance, more fuselage space and all fuel in wings. Superseded by Citation VI and VII, which see.

CESSNA MODEL 650 CITATION VI

TYPE: Simplified, lower-cost version of Citation III.
PROGRAMME: Announced 1990; first aircraft rolled out 2 January 1991; first delivery scheduled March 1991; to share common production line with Citation III from c/n 0200 onwards.
DESIGN FEATURES: Citation III airframe; retains Garrett TFE731-3B-100 turbofans; empty weight (preliminary) 5,795 kg (12,775 lb). Avionics changes include replacement of Honeywell SPZ-8000 dual digital autopilot/FDS by dual SPZ-650; AHZ-600 AHRS replaced by VG14 and C14D gyros; single AZ-810 digital air data computer for pilot's single altitude encoding servoed altimeter in place of dual ADZ-810; Global/Wulfsberg GNS-X FMS with Loran C, full alpha/numeric monochrome CDU. Standard interiors only, choice of three layouts.
Specification otherwise as Citation III.

CESSNA MODEL 660 CITATION VII

TYPE: More powerful version of Citation III.
PROGRAMME: Announced 1990; engineering prototype first flew February 1991; test programme planned for 400 h in 225 flights; FAR 25 certification expected January 1992.
DESIGN FEATURES: Citation III airframe with 17.79 kN (4,000 lb st) Garrett TFE731-4R-2S turbofans for improved hot-and-high performance; MMO 0.85.
Specification otherwise as Citation III except:
WEIGHTS AND LOADINGS:
Weight empty, standard	5,301 kg (11,686 lb)
Max fuel weight	3,350 kg (7,385 lb)
Max T-O weight	10,183 kg (22,450 lb)
Max ramp weight	10,274 kg (22,650 lb)
Max landing weight	9,072 kg (20,000 lb)
Max zero-fuel weight	7,484 kg (16,500 lb)
Max wing loading	351.3 kg/m² (71.96 lb/sq ft)
Max power loading	286.20 kg/kN (2.81 lb/lb st)

PERFORMANCE (at max T-O weight, ISA, except where indicated):
Max operating speed:
S/L to 2,440 m (8,000 ft)	
	275 knots (509 km/h; 317 mph)
at 11,130 m (36,525 ft)	278 knots (515 km/h; 320 mph)

Max cruising speed at 10,670 m (35,000 ft) and 8,165 kg (18,000 lb) cruise weight
	478 knots (885 km/h; 550 mph)

Stalling speed, flaps and wheels down, at max landing weight
	97 knots (180 km/h; 112 mph)
Rate of climb at S/L, one engine out	253 m (830 ft)/min
FAR 25 T-O field length at S/L	1,509 m (4,950 ft)

FAR 25 landing field length at max landing weight
	914 m (3,000 ft)

Range, zero wind, with allowances for T-O, climb, cruise, descent and 45 min reserves
	2,200 nm (4,077 km; 2,533 miles)
g limits	+3.0/−1

OPERATIONAL NOISE LEVELS (FAR Pt 36):
T-O (7° flap)	69.3 EPNdB
Approach (full flap)	84.8 EPNdB

CESSNA MODEL 750 CITATION X

TYPE: High-speed long-range business jet.
PROGRAMME: Announced October 1990; first flight scheduled March 1993; service entry June 1995.
COSTS: $12.85 million equipped and furnished.
DESIGN FEATURES: High max operating Mach number; US transcontinental and transatlantic range. Forward fuselage/cockpit section derived from Citation VI. Wing sweepback 35-37°.
FLYING CONTROLS: Dual hydraulically powered non-reversible controls; one-piece all-moving horizontal tailplane; speed brakes and spoiler design optimised for drag control.
The following data are provisional:
LANDING GEAR: Trailing link main units, each with twin wheels; powered anti-skid brakes; steerable nose unit with twin wheels.
POWER PLANT: Two Allison GMA 3007A turbofans, each rated at 26.69 kN (6,000 lb st) for take-off, pod-mounted on sides of rear fuselage; full authority digital engine controls. Hydraulically operated target type thrust reversers standard. Single point refuelling.
ACCOMMODATION: Crew of two on separate flight deck, and up to 12 passengers; interior custom designed; cabin is pressurised, heated and air-conditioned; 1.79 m (5 ft 10½ in) stand-up headroom; heated and pressurised baggage compartment in rear fuselage with external door. Windscreen electrically heated and demisted.
DIMENSIONS, EXTERNAL:
Wing span	18.90 m (62 ft 0 in)
Length overall	19.66 m (64 ft 6 in)
Height overall	5.09 m (16 ft 8½ in)

DIMENSIONS, INTERNAL:
Cabin: Length, front to rear pressure bulkhead	
	8.38 m (27 ft 6 in)
Max width	1.74 m (5 ft 8½ in)
Max height	1.76 m (5 ft 9½ in)
Baggage compartment volume (aft)	2.04 m³ (72.0 cu ft)

WEIGHTS AND LOADINGS:
Weight empty, standard	8,437 kg (18,600 lb)
Max fuel weight	4,990 kg (11,000 lb)
Useful load	5,624 kg (12,400 lb)
Max T-O weight	14,061 kg (31,000 lb)
Max ramp weight	14,152 kg (31,200 lb)
Max landing weight	13,154 kg (29,000 lb)
Max power loading	263.41 kg/kN (2.58 lb/lb st)

PERFORMANCE (at max T-O weight, ISA, except where indicated):
Max operating Mach No.	0.90

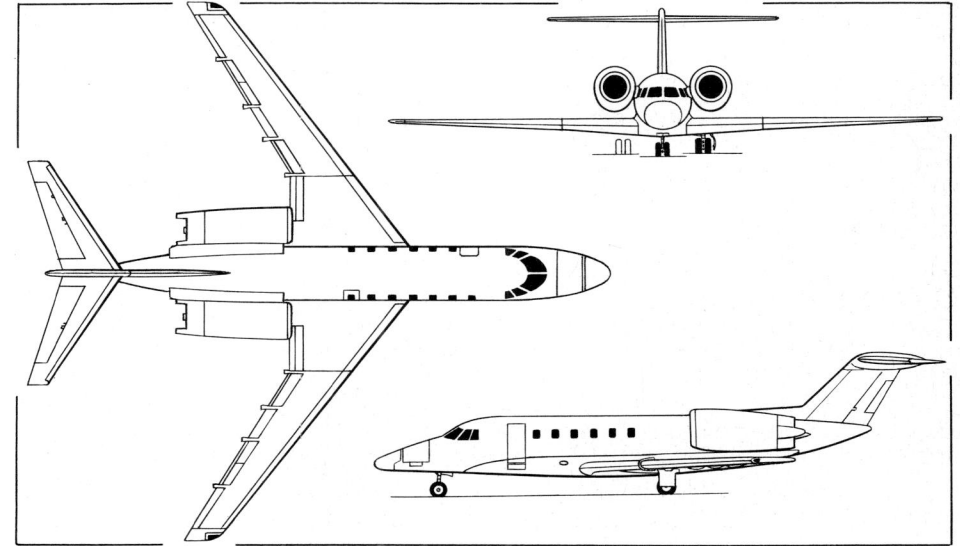

Cessna Model 750 Citation X high-speed long-range business jet *(Pilot Press)*

Max operating speed   350 knots (648 km/h; 403 mph)
Max cruising speed, mid-cruise weight at 11,275 m
    (37,000 ft)   Mach 0.88
Max rate of climb at S/L   1,340 m (4,400 ft)/min
Max operating altitude   15,545 m (51,000 ft)
T-O balanced field length (FAR Pt 25) 1,555 m (5,100 ft)
FAR Pt 25 landing field length   884 m (2,900 ft)
Range, with allowances for T-O, climb, cruise, descent
    and 45 min reserves 3,300 nm (6,115 km; 3,800 miles)

**Artist's impression of Cessna Model 750
Citation X business jet**

CHRISTEN INDUSTRIES — *see Aviat*

CHRYSLER

CHRYSLER TECHNOLOGIES AIRBORNE
SYSTEMS INC (CTAS)

PO Box 154580, Waco, Texas 76715-4580
Telephone: 1 (817) 867 4202
Fax: 1 (817) 867 4230
Telex: 163346
PRESIDENT: R. H. Pacey
VICE-PRESIDENT, BUSINESS DEVELOPMENT: J. L. Caldwell

CTAS formed April 1989 after Chrysler spun off
airborne systems business from Electrospace Systems Inc.
EC-24A conversion of DC-8 described in 1989-90 *Jane's*;
current programmes include C-27A and EC-18D (see
below). Services include major military airborne systems
integration, aircraft modification, special mission aircraft
(eg, Gulfstream SRA-4, which see) and airborne EW and
C³ systems, civil wide-body heavy maintenance and
modifications, and VIP completions.

CTAS (BOEING) EC-18D

TYPE: Cruise Missile Mission Control Aircraft (CMMCA).
PROGRAMME: Conversion of two C-18As (ex-airline Boeing
    707-320s) began July 1989; first flight November 1990;
    programme due to complete November 1991; operational
    with ASD's 4950th Test Wing in FY 1992.
COSTS: $42.6 million fixed-price contract awarded by USAF
    Aeronautical Systems Division October 1988.
DESIGN FEATURES: Intended to support Strategic Air
    Command and US Navy cruise missile test missions,
    including ability to fly missile as well as track and
    monitor. Forward fuselage structurally modified; avi-
    onics, including Hughes Aircraft AN/APG-63 radar,
    telemetry receiver and weather radar, installed and
    integrated.

CTAS (ALENIA) C-27A

TYPE: Mid-range pressurised transport.
PROGRAMME: US Air Force ordered five Alenia G222s
    (which see in Italian section) in 1990 to be fitted out by
    CTAS; first delivery scheduled for August 1991; order
    may be increased to 18.
COSTS: First five bought for about $80 million.
DESIGN FEATURES: Fitted for service in Panama and South
    America. See details under Alenia in Italian section.

US Air Force EC-18D Cruise Missile Mission Control Aircraft converted by CTAS

US Air Force C-27A transport version of the Alenia G222, fitted out by CTAS

CLASSIC

CLASSIC AIRCRAFT CORPORATION

Capital City Airport, Kansing, Michigan 48906
Telephone: 1 (517) 321 7500
Fax: 1 (517) 321 5845
PRESIDENT: Richard S. Kettles
ENGINEERING MANAGER: Donald P. Zurfluh
SALES MANAGER: Donald C. Kettles

CLASSIC WACO CLASSIC F-5

TYPE: Three-seat sport biplane.
PROGRAMME: Construction began March 1984 under type
    certificate of original Waco YMF-5; first flight of

prototype (N1935B) 20 November 1985; FAA certifi-
cation 11 March 1986.
VARIANTS: **F-5:** Standard version.
    F-5 Super: Enlarged front cockpit for commercial
    joyriding; enlarged forward door; front and rear cockpits
    10 cm (4 in) longer; front cockpit 6.3 cm (2½ in) wider.
CUSTOMERS: Total 35 delivered by 1 January 1991.
COSTS: Standard equipment aircraft $165,000.
DESIGN FEATURES: Wing section Clark Y; dihedral 2°,
    incidence 0° on upper and lower wings.
FLYING CONTROLS: Ailerons on upper and lower wings;
    no tabs. Tailplane incidence adjustable by screwjack
    actuator; ground adjustable trim tab on rudder; elevators.

STRUCTURE: Modern construction techniques, tolerances
    and materials applied to original design. N type
    interplane struts; streamlined stainless steel flying and
    landing wires; all-wood wing with Dacron covering;
    aluminium ailerons with external chordwise stiffening.
    Fuselage of 4130 welded steel tubes with internal oiling
    for corrosion protection; wooden bulkheads; Dacron
    covering. Braced welded steel tube tail surfaces with
    Dacron covering.
LANDING GEAR: Non-retractable tailwheel type. Shock
    absorption by oil and spring shock struts. Steerable
    tailwheel. Cleveland 30-67F hydraulic brakes on main-
    wheels only. Cleveland 40-101A mainwheels, tyre size

7.50-10; Cleveland 40-199A tailwheel, tyre size 3.50-4. Mainwheel fairings standard, tailwheel fairing optional. Float and amphibious landing gear optional.

POWER PLANT: One 205 kW (275 hp) Jacobs R-755-B2 aircooled radial engine (remanufactured), driving a two-blade fixed-pitch wooden propeller. Constant-speed propeller with spinner optional. Engine enclosed with streamline aluminium 'bump' (helmeted) cowling. Fuel contained in two aluminium tanks in upper wing centre-section, total capacity 182 litres (48 US gallons; 40 Imp gallons). Refuelling point for each tank in upper wing surface. Auxiliary tanks, capacity 45 litres (12 US gallons; 10 Imp gallons) each, optional in either or both inboard upper wing panels. Standard oil capacity 15 litres (4 US gallons; 3.33 Imp gallons); with auxiliary fuel tanks 19 litres (5 US gallons; 4.2 Imp gallons).

ACCOMMODATION: Three seats in tandem open cockpits, two side by side in front position, single seat at rear. Dual controls, seat belts with shoulder harness, and pilot's adjustable seat, standard. Front baggage compartment, capacity 11.3 kg (25 lb); rear baggage compartment, volume 0.2 m^3 (7.5 cu ft), capacity 34 kg (75 lb).

SYSTEMS: 24V electrical system with battery, alternator and starter for electrical supply to navigation, strobe and rear cockpit lights. Hydraulic system for brakes only.

AVIONICS: Emergency locator transmitter standard. VFR or IFR avionics packages to customer's choice including Bendix/King and Narco nav/com, ADF, DME, transponder and encoding altimeter; Apollo, Arnav, Foster, II Morrow and Northstar Loran C systems; 3M Stormscope WX-8 and 1000 series; Bendix/King KCS 55A slaved compass system with KN 72 VOR/LOC converter; NAT voice-activated intercom; Bendix/King KX 99 and TR 720 hand-held transceivers, and Astrotech LC-2 digital clock.

EQUIPMENT: Toe brakes standard in rear cockpit. Compass, airspeed indicator, turn and bank indicator, rate of climb indicator, sensitive altimeter, recording tachometer, cylinder head temperature gauge and oil pressure and oil temperature gauges standard in rear cockpit. Front cockpit instruments optional. Front and rear windscreens (front removable), front and rear cockpit covers, instrument post lighting, heated pitot, tiedown rings and three-colour paint scheme with choice of two designs, also standard. Optional equipment includes exhaust gas temperature gauge, carburettor temperature gauge, *g* meter, vacuum or electrically driven gyro system, Hobbs meter, outside air temperature gauge, manifold gauge, oil cooler for wooden propeller, ground service plug, landing and taxi lights, front and rear cockpit heaters, flight-approved metal front cockpit cover, map case, glider tow hook, deluxe interior with carpet, leather sidewalls and interior trim, and special exterior paint designs.

Classic Waco Classic F-5 re-creation of the Waco YMF-5 three-seat biplane *(Geoffrey P. Jones)*

DIMENSIONS, EXTERNAL (A: F-5, B: F-5 Super):
Wing span: upper: A, B 9.14 m (30 ft 0 in)
lower: A, B 8.18 m (26 ft 10 in)
Length overall: A 7.10 m (23 ft 3⅝ in)
B 7.26 m (23 ft 10 in)
Height overall: A 2.57 m (8 ft 5⅜ in)
B 2.59 m (8 ft 6 in)
Wheelbase: A, B 1.95 m (6 ft 5 in)
Propeller diameter: A, B 2.44 m (8 ft 0 in)

AREAS:
Wings, gross 21.69 m^2 (233.5 sq ft)

WEIGHTS AND LOADINGS (A: F-5, B: F-5 Super):
Basic weight empty: A 880 kg (1,940 lb)
B 900 kg (1,985 lb)
Max T-O and landing weight: A 1,256 kg (2,770 lb)
B 1,338 kg (2,950 lb)
Max wing loading: A 52.26 kg/m^2 (10.71 lb/sq ft)
B 61.67 kg/m^2 (12.63 lb/sq ft)
Max power loading: A 6.21 kg/kW (10.20 lb/hp)
B 6.53 kg/kW (10.73 lb/hp)

PERFORMANCE (at max T-O weight; A and B as above):
Never-exceed speed (VNE):
A, B 186 knots (344 km/h; 214 mph)
Max level speed at S/L:
A, B 117 knots (217 km/h; 135 mph)
Max cruising speed at S/L:
A, B 104 knots (193 km/h; 120 mph)
Econ cruising speed at 2,440 m (8,000 ft):
A, B 95 knots (177 km/h; 110 mph)
Stalling speed, power off: A 51 knots (94 km/h; 58 mph)
B 53 knots (97 km/h; 60 mph)
Max rate of climb at S/L: A, B 235 m (770 ft)/min
T-O run: A, B 152 m (500 ft)
Range, standard fuel, 30 min reserves:
A, B 286 nm (531 km; 330 miles)

COLEMILL

COLEMILL ENTERPRISES INC

PO Box 60627, Cornelia Fort Air Park, Nashville, Tennessee 37206
Telephone: 1 (615) 226 4256
Fax: 1 (615) 226 4702
Telex: 555 197
PRESIDENT: Ernest Colbert

Colemill specialises in performance improvements for single and twin-engined aircraft.

Colemill Panther Navajo with winglets

COLEMILL PANTHER NAVAJO

TYPE: Re-engined Piper Navajo and C/R Navajo.

VARIANTS: Optional Zip Tip winglets included in conversion or retrofitted under Supplemental Type Certificate awarded Summer 1982. Winglets improve stability at low airspeeds down to stall and add 4-9 knots (8-16 km/h; 5-10 mph) when cruising at between 45 per cent and 65 per cent power at 3,960-7,620 m (13,000-25,000 ft), resulting in fuel savings.

DESIGN FEATURES: Basic conversion with more powerful engines, new cowlings, continuous running fuel pumps, digital fuel totaliser, wingtip-mounted landing lights, heavy duty brakes and extended wingtips takes 10-14 days. Optional Zip Tip winglets increase wing span to 13.16 m (43 ft 2 in) and wing area by 0.56 m^2 (6 sq ft). Main data as for Piper Navajo in 1982-83 *Jane's*.

New data below refer to Panther Navajo:

LANDING GEAR: Cleveland four-spot heavy duty disc brakes.

POWER PLANT: Two 261 kW (350 hp) Textron Lycoming TIO-540-J2BD turbocharged engines, each driving a Hartzell four-blade constant-speed fully feathering metal propeller with Q-tips. Pressurised magnetos, Woodward propeller governors, synchrophasers and unfeathering accumulators standard. Fuel system as for basic Navajo, except for the addition of continuous running electrically operated fuel pumps.

EQUIPMENT: Generally as for standard Navajo, but existing fuel flow gauges are replaced by a Shadin Digiflow fuel management computer giving digital readout of fuel remaining/fuel consumed. Supplemental wingtip landing lights can be operated independently of the standard nosewheel mounted landing light, prior to lowering of landing gear.

DIMENSIONS, EXTERNAL:
Wing span (excl winglets) 13.00 m (42 ft 8 in)

WEIGHTS AND LOADINGS:
Max power loading 5.65 kg/kW (9.3 lb/hp)

PERFORMANCE (at max T-O weight):
Max level speed 269 knots (498 km/h; 309 mph)
Max cruising speed, 75% power at optimum altitude
248 knots (459 km/h; 285 mph)
Cruising speed, 65% power:
at 7,315 m (24,000 ft) 235 knots (435 km/h; 270 mph)
at 3,660 m (12,000 ft) 206 knots (381 km/h; 237 mph)
Max rate of climb at S/L 610 m (2,000 ft)/min
Rate of climb at S/L, one engine out 122 m (400 ft)/min
Short-field T-O run 229 m (750 ft)
T-O to 15 m (50 ft) 458 m (1,500 ft)
Landing from 15 m (50 ft) 427 m (1,400 ft)

COLEMILL PANTHER II

TYPE: Re-engined Piper Chieftain.

DESIGN FEATURES: Conversion includes new 261 kW (350 hp) Textron Lycoming TIO-540-J2BD and LTIO-540-J2BD (opposite rotation) turbocharged engines, driving four-blade constant-speed fully feathering metal propellers with Q-tips; digital fuel management computer; Woodward propeller governors and synchrophaser; and Cleveland four-spot heavy duty brakes. Zip Tip winglets optional.

COLEMILL EXECUTIVE 600

TYPE: Re-engined Cessna 310, Models F to Q.

DESIGN FEATURES: Conversion includes new 224 kW (300 hp) Teledyne Continental IO-520-E flat-six engines, driving McCauley three-blade propellers. Dimensions unchanged; empty weight increased by about 14 kg (30 lb).

WEIGHTS AND LOADINGS:
Max T-O weight 2,358 kg (5,200 lb)
Max power loading 5.26 kg/kW (8.67 lb/hp)

PERFORMANCE (at max T-O weight):
Max cruising speed, 75% power
205 knots (379 km/h; 236 mph)
Cruising speed, 65% power
195 knots (361 km/h; 224 mph)
Stalling speed, wheels and flaps down
64 knots (119 km/h; 74 mph)
Max rate of climb at S/L 762 m (2,500 ft)/min
Service ceiling 5,940 m (19,500 ft)
T-O to 15 m (50 ft) 518 m (1,700 ft)
Landing from 15 m (50 ft) unchanged
Range with max fuel, 45 min reserves
1,050 nm (1,944 km; 1,208 miles)

COLEMILL PRESIDENT 600

TYPE: Re-engined Beechcraft B55 Baron.

CUSTOMERS: About 250 President 600 conversions delivered.

DESIGN FEATURES: Conversion includes 224 kW (300 hp) Teledyne Continental IO-520-E flat-six engines, driving three-blade propellers. Dimensions unchanged; empty weight increased by about 14 kg (30 lb).

WEIGHTS AND LOADINGS:

Max T-O weight	2,313 kg (5,100 lb)
Max power loading	5.16 kg/kW (8.5 lb/hp)

PERFORMANCE (at max T-O weight):

Max cruising speed, 75% power	203 knots (376 km/h; 233 mph)
Cruising speed, 65% power	193 knots (357 km/h; 222 mph)
Stalling speed, wheels and flaps down	66 knots (123 km/h; 76 mph)
Max rate of climb at S/L	823 m (2,700 ft)/min
Service ceiling	5,940 m (19,500 ft)
T-O to 15 m (50 ft)	497 m (1,631 ft)
Landing from 15 m (50 ft)	unchanged
Range with max fuel, 45 min reserves	1,050 nm (1,944 km; 1,208 miles)

COLEMILL FOXSTAR BARON

TYPE: Re-engined Beechcraft Model 55 or 58 Baron.

DESIGN FEATURES: Conversion includes new 224 kW (300 hp) Teledyne Continental IO-550-C engines, driving Hartzell Sabre Blade four-blade Q-tip propellers; Woodward propeller governors and synchrophasers; Shadin Digiflow fuel computer; Zip Tip winglets; 60A alternators. Foxstar conversion FAA STC approved for all Model C55, D55, E55 and Model 58 Barons.

WEIGHTS AND LOADINGS:

Max T-O weight	2,449 kg (5,400 lb)
Max power loading	5.47 kg/kW (9.00 lb/hp)

PERFORMANCE (at max T-O weight):

Max cruising speed, 75% power	205 knots (380 km/h; 236 mph)
Cruising speed, 65% power	200 knots (371 km/h; 230 mph)
Stalling speed, landing gear and flaps down	74 knots (137 km/h; 85 mph)
Max rate of climb at S/L	561 m (1,840 ft)/min
Service ceiling	6,400 m (21,000 ft)
T-O to 15 m (50 ft)	610 m (2,000 ft)
Landing from 15 m (50 ft)	734 m (2,410 ft)
Range with max fuel, 45 min reserves	1,131 nm (2,096 km; 1,302 miles)

COLEMILL STARFIRE BONANZA

TYPE: Re-engined Beechcraft Bonanza.

DESIGN FEATURES: FAA STC approved for all Beechcraft Model C33A, E33A, F33A, S35, V35A, V35B and A36 Bonanzas. Conversion includes 224 kW (300 hp) Teledyne Continental IO-550-B engine, driving Hartzell Sabre Blade four-blade Q-tip propeller; Woodward propeller governor; Shadin Digiflow fuel computer/totaliser; Zip Tip winglets; 60A alternator.

PERFORMANCE:

Cruising speed	176 knots (326 km/h; 203 mph)
Max rate of climb at S/L	369 m (1,210 ft)/min
T-O run	296 m (971 ft)
T-O to 15 m (50 ft)	583 m (1,912 ft)

Colemill Panther II conversion with winglets

Colemill Foxstar Baron

Colemill Starfire Bonanza

COMMANDER

COMMANDER AIRCRAFT COMPANY

Wiley Post Airport, 7200 NW 63rd Street, Bethany, Oklahoma 73008

Telephone: 1 (405) 495 8080

Fax: 1 (405) 495 8383

PRESIDENT: Randall Greene

VICE-PRESIDENTS:

David R. Ellis (Engineering)

Lynn D. Jones (Manufacturing)

Roy D. Pickens (Operations)

Company acquired manufacturing, marketing and support rights for Rockwell Commander 112 and 114 from Gulfstream Aerospace Corporation Summer 1988; spares and support services for existing aircraft and manufacturing based in Oklahoma.

COMMANDER 114B

TYPE: New production version of four-seat, single-engined Commander 114A.

PROGRAMME: Certification expected March 1991; rollout of first production aircraft planned for April 1991; production rate of four per month planned for 1991.

VARIANTS: **Commander 114B**: Basic version, as detailed on next page.

Commander 114TCL: Powered by Teledyne Continental Voyager TSIOL-550-B liquid-cooled turbocharged engine, driving four-blade Hartzell propeller; engineering commenced April 1990; production scheduled for second quarter 1992. Increased gross weight; extended wing with sheared tips; larger dorsal fin; split rudder. Fuel capacity 322 litres (85 US gallons; 70.75 Imp gallons), of which 314 litres (83 US gallons; 69 Imp gallons) usable.

CUSTOMERS: Orders for 160 held in early 1990. Aircraft supplied in USA leased rather than sold.

COSTS: Standard IFR-equipped aircraft $147,500.

DESIGN FEATURES: Improvements in 114B include new cowling design, improved cooling and induction, specially developed McCauley three-blade metal propeller, NACA scoop in dorsal fin, new interior trim and seats, better soundproofing, inflatable door seals and strengthened tail surface and landing gear attachment fittings.

POWER PLANT: One 194 kW (260 hp) Textron Lycoming IO-540-T4B5 flat-six engine, driving a McCauley B3B 32C 419/82NHA-5 three-blade constant-speed metal propeller. Fuel in two integral wing tanks, max capacity 265 litres (70 US gallons; 58.3 Imp gallons), of which 257 litres (68 US gallons; 56.6 Imp gallons) are usable. Max oil capacity 7.6 litres (2 US gallons; 1.67 Imp gallons).

DIMENSIONS, EXTERNAL (A: Model 114B, B: Model 114TCL):

Wing span: A	9.98 m (32 ft 9 in)
B	11.20 m (36 ft 9 in)
Length overall: A	7.59 m (24 ft 11 in)
B	7.84 m (25 ft 8½ in)
Height overall: A	2.57 m (8 ft 5 in)
B	2.74 m (9 ft 0 in)
Tailplane span: A, B	4.10 m (13 ft 5½ in)
Wheel track: A, B	3.34 m (10 ft 11½ in)
Wheelbase: A, B	2.11 m (6 ft 11 in)
Propeller diameter: A	1.96 m (6 ft 5 in)
B	1.98 m (6 ft 6 in)
Propeller ground clearance: A, B	0.19 m (7½ in)

DIMENSIONS, INTERNAL (A and B):

Cabin: Length	1.91 m (6 ft 3 in)
Max width	1.19 m (3 ft 11 in)
Max height	1.24 m (4 ft 1 in)
Volume	2.83 m³ (100.0 cu ft)
Baggage compartment volume	0.62 m³ (22.0 cu ft)

AREAS:

Wings, gross: A	14.12 m² (152.0 sq ft)
B	14.77 m² (159.0 sq ft)

WEIGHTS AND LOADINGS:

Weight empty: A	927 kg (2,044 lb)
B	977 kg (2,155 lb)
Max T-O weight: A	1,474 kg (3,250 lb)
B	1,565 kg (3,450 lb)
Max ramp weight: A	1,479 kg (3,260 lb)
B	1,569 kg (3,460 lb)
Max wing loading: A	104.5 kg/m² (21.4 lb/sq ft)
B	105.9 kg/m² (21.7 lb/sq ft)

Commander Aircraft Commander 114B

Max power loading: A	7.62 kg/kW (12.54 lb/hp)
B	6.99 kg/kW (11.5 lb/hp)

PERFORMANCE (estimated, at max T-O weight, ISA, except where indicated):

Max level speed: A	174 knots (322 km/h; 200 mph)
B, at 7,315 m (24,000 ft)	
	228 knots (422 km/h; 262 mph)
Cruising speed:	
75% power: A	164 knots (304 km/h; 189 mph)
B, at 7,315 m (24,000 ft)	
	214 knots (396 km/h; 246 mph)
65% power: A	152 knots (282 km/h; 175 mph)
Stalling speed:	
flaps and wheels up: A	61 knots (113 km/h; 71 mph)
B	62 knots (115 km/h; 72 mph)

flaps and wheels down:	
A	56 knots (104 km/h; 65 mph)
B	57 knots (106 km/h; 66 mph)
Max rate of climb at S/L: A	335 m (1,100 ft)/min
B	518 m (1,700 ft)/min
Service ceiling: A, B	5,335 m (17,500 ft)
T-O run: A	317 m (1,040 ft)
B	293 m (960 ft)
T-O to 15 m (50 ft): A	610 m (2,000 ft)
B	561 m (1,840 ft)
Landing from 15 m (50 ft): A	366 m (1,200 ft)
Landing run: A	220 m (720 ft)
Range:	
at 75% power: A	672 nm (1,245 km; 773 miles)
B, at 7,315 m (24,000 ft)	
	940 nm (1,742 km; 1,082 miles)
at 65% power: A	705 nm (1,306 km; 811 miles)

COMTRAN

COMTRAN LTD

8507 Broadway, San Antonio, Texas 78217
Telephone: 1 (512) 821 6301
Fax: 1 (512) 822 7766
Telex: 767438 COMTRAN UD
PROGRAMME DIRECTOR: John T. Jennings

COMTRAN SUPER Q

TYPE: Boeing 707 upgrade.

DESIGN FEATURES: Includes engine noise reduction and cabin/flight deck updating. Comtran Q-707 nacelle hush kits include Rohr Industries DynaRohr liners with extended intake and fan exhaust ducts which meet FAR 36 Stage 2 and ICAO Annex 16 Chapter 2 requirements; 100 EPNdB footprint reduced from 5.6 nm (10.4 km; 6.4 miles) for standard Boeing 707 to 2.8 nm (5.2 km; 3.2 miles), without affecting anti-icing and thrust reversal.

Cabin has wide-body styling; lightweight seats; overhead bins; cabin entertainment system with video monitors and seat mounted controls; cabin soundproofing; cabin headliner with 'wash' lighting; emergency escape lighting; overhauled forward and aft galleys and toilets; new liferafts, lifejackets and emergency escape chutes; new floor and side panel liners in baggage compartment. Full range of interiors available with up to 186 passengers in four-class layout.

Cabin meets ICAO, FAA and European S-2000 fire, safety and toxicity standards by means of fireblocking materials in all seats, non-toxic polycarbonate composite materials for overhead panels and seat trim, plus supplementary emergency floor lighting.

Flight deck includes upgraded Collins avionics

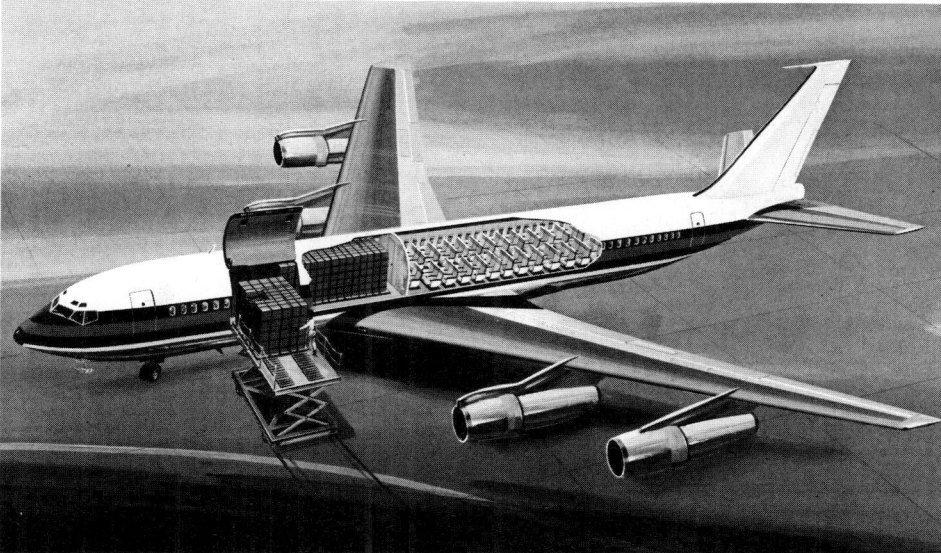

Cutaway drawing of Comtran Super Q conversion of the Boeing 707 in Combi configuration

including FD109Y flight directors, long-range navigation systems, colour weather radar, new cockpit audio, and new wiring and switching as required.

PERFORMANCE: For typical mission with full passengers, 65,075 kg (145,450 lb) fuel including 9,072 kg (20,000 lb) reserve, max brake release weight 150,955 kg (332,800 lb), cruising at Mach 0.8 at 10,670 m (35,000 ft), estimated range is 4,365 nm (8,089 km; 5,026 miles).

DAYTONA

DAYTONA AIRCRAFT CONSTRUCTION INC

1400 Flightline Boulevard, DeLand, Florida 32724
Telephone: 1 (904) 738 7222
Fax: 1 (904) 738 9472

Company established 1990 and acquired design rights to the Jamieson D-Series FAA-certificated light aircraft. A standard airframe is sold with a choice of eight Textron Lycoming engines, various propellers, choice of equipment and fixed or retractable landing gear.

DAYTONA D-SERIES

TYPE: Two/four-seat monoplane with choice of 89.5 to 223.9 kW (120 to 300 hp) engines.

PROGRAMME: Final development underway during 1991.

VARIANTS: Engine and equipment choices as listed below, with type designations D-120 to D-300 denoting horsepower.

DESIGN FEATURES: Conventional airframe with structure stressed for aerobatics at gross weight of 1,633 kg (3,600 lb).

FLYING CONTROLS: Mechanical, with push-pull rods with ball-race end bearings to ailerons and elevator; fixed tailplane; mass-balanced elevator with trim tab. Ground adjustable tabs on one aileron and rudder. Mechanically operated flaps.

STRUCTURE: All-metal, mainly 2024-T3 spars and skins. Composites wingtips.

LANDING GEAR: Option of retractable tricycle gear on all but 89.5 kW (120 hp) version; Air-oleo shock absorbers; nosewheel retracts rearwards and mainwheels inwards with full cover doors; gear operation electric with mechanical standby; Cleveland mainwheels and brakes;

all wheels have 600 × 6 tyres; dual pedal-operated brakes.

POWER PLANT: Choice of Textron Lycoming engines of 89.5 kW (120 hp), 119 kW (160 hp), 134 kW (180 hp), 149 kW (200 hp), 186 kW (250 hp), 194 kW (260 hp), 201 kW (270 hp) or 224 kW (300 hp) driving Hartzell or McCauley propellers. Two 117 litre (31 US gallon; 26 Imp gallon) fuel tanks in inner wing; two optional 57 litre (15 US gallon; 12 Imp gallon) tanks in outer wings in D-160 and above; overwing gravity refuelling.

ACCOMMODATION: Dual controls standard; all but 89.5 kW (120 hp) version will have rear two-seat bench; cabin access via steps aft of wing and two gull-wing doors; air-conditioning optional with D-180 and standard with larger engines.

SYSTEMS: 70A alternator; 33Ah 12V battery; vacuum pump and gauge.

AVIONICS: ELT standard; choice of radio.
EQUIPMENT: Standard equipment includes shoulder harness, full night lighting and beacon, stall warning light, door locks and two-colour urethane paint.

DIMENSIONS, EXTERNAL:

Wing span	10.97 m (36 ft 0 in)
Tailplane span	3.20 m (10 ft 2 in)
Wing chord: at root	1.90 m (6 ft 3 in)
at tip	0.78 m (2 ft 7 in)
Wing aspect ratio	7.96
Length overall	7.90 m (25 ft 11 in)
Height overall	2.33 m (7 ft 8 in)
Wheel track	3.36 m (11 ft 0¼ in)
Wheelbase	2.16 m (7 ft 1 in)

DIMENSIONS, INTERNAL:

Cabin: Length	2.43 m (8 ft 0 in)
Max width	1.07 m (3 ft 6 in)

AREAS:

Wing, gross	15.13 m² (162.8 sq ft)

WEIGHTS AND LOADINGS (A: D-200, B: D-300):

Weight empty: A	567 kg (1,250 lb)
B	773 kg (1,704 lb)
Max T-O weight: A	1,134 kg (2,500 lb)
B	1,636 kg (3,607 lb)
Max power loading: A	7.6 kg/kW (12.5 lb/hp)
B	7.3 kg/kW (12.0 lb/hp)

PERFORMANCE:

Max cruising speed: A	175 knots (324 km/h; 201 mph)
B	180 knots (333 km/h; 207 mph)
Cruising speed, 75% power:	
A	165 knots (305 km/h; 190 mph)
B	170 knots (315 km/h; 195 mph)
Stalling speed, flaps and gear down:	
A	51 knots (95 km/h; 59 mph)
B	58 knots (107 km/h; 67 mph)

Daytona Aircraft Construction DA-200 trainer/touring aircraft *(Geoffrey P. Jones)*

Max rate of climb: A	305 m (1,000 ft)/min	Range, standard fuel, no reserves:	
B	457 m (1,500 ft)/min	A	1,275 nm (2,360 km; 1,466 miles)
Service ceiling: A, B	5,486 m (18,000 ft)	B	702 nm (1,300 km; 807 miles)
T-O to 15 m (50 ft): A	402 m (1,319 ft)	Endurance with optional fuel: A	7 h 44 min
B	366 m (1,200 ft)	B	6 h 7 min
Landing from 15 m (50 ft): A	372 m (1,220 ft)	g limits: A and B	+6/−3
B	335 m (1,100 ft)		

DEE HOWARD
THE DEE HOWARD COMPANY

9610 John Saunders Road, International Airport, PO Box 17300, San Antonio, Texas 78217
Telephone: 1 (512) 828 1341
Telex: 767380
CHAIRMAN: Dee Howard
PRESIDENT AND CHIEF EXECUTIVE OFFICER:
   Philip Greco
VICE-PRESIDENT, ENGINEERING: David White
VICE-PRESIDENT, MARKETING AND SALES: Roger Munt
DIRECTOR OF MARKETING COMMUNICATIONS: Brian Loflin
   Alenia, formerly Aeritalia (see Italian section), took 60 per cent holding in Dee Howard in Spring 1989.

DEE HOWARD XR LEARJET

TYPE: Performance improvement for Learjet Models 24 and 25.
DESIGN FEATURES: Performance improvement package suitable for Learjet 24 and 25 powered by General Electric CJ610-6 or -8A. Improvements include new drag-reducing centre-section wing glove, which also accommodates additional 245 kg (540 lb) fuel; new engine pylon/nacelle shape that improves Mach characteristics and engine bay cooling; new engine exhaust nozzle that improves specific fuel consumption; fences, vortex generators and stall strips produce stall buffet and improve overall stall performance; modified ailerons, flaps and outer wing panels and tip tank fin cuffs improve cruise performance; new Teledyne angle of attack system, except for Century III wings, which retain Conrac system.
   Conversion gives 400 nm (741 km; 460 miles) more range at constant Mach 0.78 cruising speed, plus additional 680 kg (1,500 lb) take-off weight.

DEE HOWARD BAC 1-11 2400 and 2500

TYPE: Re-engined BAC One-Elevens.
PROGRAMME: Agreement signed with Rolls-Royce and British Aerospace February 1986; first converted 1-11 2400 rolled out March 1990; first flight 2 July 1990; FAA supplemental type certificate expected June 1991; UK CAA amended type certificate expected July 1991; avionics certification expected December 1991.

Dee Howard BAC 1-11 2400 with Rolls-Royce Tay 650 turbofans *(John Cook)*

VARIANTS: **1-11 2400:** Initial version, converted from One-Eleven Series 400 and 475.
   1-11 2500: Conversion of larger, heavier One-Eleven 500; separate certification required, anticipated 13 months from receipt of a launch order.
CUSTOMERS: Three corporate orders held for 2400; first due for delivery December 1991; market estimated at 75 to 100.
COSTS: Under $9 million at 1991 prices for Tay refit; plus $2.3 million for Honeywell EFIS cockpit refit.
DESIGN FEATURES: One-Eleven Series 400, 475 and 500 re-engined with 67.17 kN (15,100 lb st) Rolls-Royce Tay 650-14 and given new engine nacelles on new pylons; Dee Howard TR6500 thrust reversers fitted. Aircraft then meets FAR Pt 36 Stage 3 and ICAO Annex 16 Chapter 3 noise requirements; Tay installation adds 1,382 kg (3,407 lb) at rear of aircraft, requiring 740 kg (1,631 lb) additional weight (mainly heavier floor panels) in forward fuselage; max T-O weight increased to 41,540 kg (91,580 lb); corporate 400 Series One-Elevens should have NBAA IFR range of 3,100 nm (5,745 km; 3,570 miles) plus up to 30 per cent shorter field length in hot and high conditions. Conversion takes two to three months, depending on work required by customer.

AVIONICS: Refit includes Honeywell SPZ-8000 digital package, Primus 870 weather radar and LSZ-850 lightning sensor system. Options include TCAS 2, VLF/Omega with Lasertrak nav display, GPS, MLS and third IRS.

DEE HOWARD BOEING 727/DOUGLAS DC-8 UPDATE

PROGRAMME: Collins EFIS being installed in 40 Boeing 727-100s and 49 Douglas DC-8-70s as part of cockpit modernisation programme for United Parcel Service; 727s to have new air data system, DC-8s to have new inertial reference system; first 727 flew September 1990 and first DC-8 November 1990. Eight DC-8s to be converted 1991, then 10 each year until programme complete; 14 727s to be converted in 1991-92 and fleet to be completed in 1993. 727s also to be retrofitted with 67.17 kN (15,100 lb st) Rolls-Royce Tay 650 turbofans; re-engine design work may be completed in time for some aircraft to combine cockpit refit and new engine installation; first aircraft expected to fly April 1992, FAA approval to be obtained November 1992. 727-200 would have more powerful Tay 670, but not a current programme.

DMAV
DUAL MODE AIR VEHICLE INC

2205 West Division, Unit C-5, Arlington, Texas 76012
Telephone: 1 (817) 265 8843
Fax: 1 (817) 274 1379

CHIEF OF AERODYNAMICS: J. David Kocurek, PhD
   Responsible for design and wind tunnel testing of **TW-68** tilt-wing V/STOL aircraft being developed in conjunction with Ishida Aerospace Research in Texas and Ishida Corporation of Japan (which see).

ELECTROSPACE SYSTEMS — *See Chrysler Technologies Airborne Systems (CTAS)*

ENSTROM
THE ENSTROM HELICOPTER CORPORATION

PO Box 490, 2209 North 22nd Street, Twin County Airport, Menominee, Michigan 49858
Telephone: 1 (906) 863 9971
Fax: 1 (906) 863 6821
PRESIDENT AND CHIEF EXECUTIVE OFFICER: Robert M. Tuttle
VICE-PRESIDENT, MANUFACTURING: John E. Hansen
VICE-PRESIDENT, ENGINEERING: Robert L. Jenny
MANAGER, DOMESTIC MARKETING: James Zimmerman

Company history since foundation in 1959 detailed in earlier *Jane's*. Acquired by Bravo Investments BVC, Netherlands, January 1980; acquired by group of American investors headed by Mr Dean Kamen and Mr Robert Tuttle September 1984; in early 1990 acquired by investors based in Los Angeles. Total of more than 890 helicopters produced by 1 January 1991.

ENSTROM MODELS F28 and 280

TYPE: Three-seat light helicopter.
PROGRAMME: Basic Model F-28A and Model 280 described in 1978-79 *Jane's*; replaced by turbocharged Models F28C and 280C, certificated by FAA 8 December 1975 and last described in 1984-85 *Jane's*; production of these models ceased November 1981; succeeded by Models F28F and 280F Shark, described in 1985-86 *Jane's*, and Model 280FX; current models detailed below.
VARIANTS: **F28F Falcon:** Basic model certificated by FAA January 1981. Recent developments include redesigned main gearbox with heavy wall main rotor shaft (standard on all new F28s and retrofittable to all existing F models); optional lightweight exhaust silencer, reducing noise in hover by 40 per cent and by 30 per cent when flying at 152 m (500 ft) (can be retrofitted to existing F28F, 280F and 280FX); lightweight high efficiency starter motor recently introduced for all models.

Enstrom wet and dry agricultural kit comprises two side-mounted hoppers with quick-fill openings, total capacity 303 litres (80 US gallons; 67 Imp gallons); spraybar 9.04 m (29 ft 8 in) wide, extendable to 11.07 m (36 ft 4 in); manually operated clutch gives positive control of centrifugal pump with capacity for 227 litres (60 US gallons; 50 Imp gallons)/min; dry discharge rate variable from 0 to 272 kg (600 lb)/min; weight of entire quickly removable dispersal system 48 kg (105 lb).

F28F-P Sentinel: Dedicated police patrol version; first delivery October 1986; can be fitted with Locator B, Spectrolab SX-5 or Carter searchlight and specialised police radio; same specifications and performance as F28F.

Model 280FX: Certificated to FAA CAR Pt 6 on 14 January 1985. Features include new seats with lumbar support and energy-absorbing foam, new tailplane with endplate fins, tail rotor guard, covered tail rotor shaft, redesigned air inlet system, and completely faired landing gear; optional pneumatic door opener; optional internal tank extends range to 339 nm (627 km; 390 miles).
CUSTOMERS: Chilean Army operates 15 Model 280FXs for primary and instrument training; Peruvian Army to use 10 F28Fs for training duties.
DESIGN FEATURES: Three-blade fully articulated head with blades attached by retention pin and drag link; control rods pass inside tubular rotor shaft to swash plate inside fuselage; blade section NACA 0013.5; two-blade teetering tail rotor; blades do not fold. Poly V-belt drive system from horizontally mounted engine to transmission also acts as clutch.
STRUCTURE: Bonded light alloy blades. Fuselage has glassfibre and light alloy cabin section, steel tube centre section frame, and stressed skin aluminium tailboom.
LANDING GEAR: Skids carried on Enstrom oleo-pneumatic shock absorbers. Air Cruiser inflatable floats available optionally.
POWER PLANT: One 168 kW (225 hp) Textron Lycoming HIO-360-F1AD flat-rated engine with Rotomaster 3BT5EE10J2 turbocharger. Two fuel tanks, each of 79.5 litres (21 US gallons; 17.5 Imp gallons). Total standard fuel capacity 159 litres (42 US gallons; 35 Imp gallons), of which 151 litres (40 US gallons; 33.3 Imp gallons) are usable. Auxiliary tank, capacity 49 litres (13 US gallons; 10.8 Imp gallons), can be installed in the baggage compartment. Oil capacity 9.5 litres (2.5 US gallons; 2.1 Imp gallons).
ACCOMMODATION: Pilot and two passengers, side by side on bench seat; centre place removable. Fully transparent removable door on each side of cabin. Baggage space aft of engine compartment, capacity 49 kg (108 lb), with external access door. Cabin heated and ventilated.
SYSTEM: Electrical power provided by 12V 70A engine driven alternator; 24V 70A system optional on F28F, standard on 280FX.
AVIONICS: Variety of fits from AR Nav, Bendix/King II Morrow and Northstar.
EQUIPMENT: Standard equipment includes airspeed indicator, sensitive altimeter, compass, outside air temperature gauge, turn and bank indicator, rotor/engine tachometer, manifold pressure/fuel flow gauge, EGT gauge, oil pressure gauge, gearbox and oil temperature gauge, ammeter, cylinder head temperature gauge, and

Enstrom F28F-P Sentinel three-seat light helicopter

Enstrom Model 280FX three-seat light helicopter of the Chilean Army *(Kenneth Munson)*

fuel quantity gauge. Eight-light annunciator panel consisting of low rotor rpm, chip detectors (main and tail rotor transmissions), overboost, clutch not fully engaged, low fuel pressure, starter, and low voltage warning lights. Also standard are ground handling wheels with handle, kick-in service steps, floor carpeting, lap belts for all seats, shoulder harnesses for two seats, instrument lighting with dimmer control, position light on each horizontal stabiliser tip, anti-collision strobe light, landing lights, adjustable nose light, soundproofing, main and tail rotor covers and blade tiedowns. Additionally, the Model 280FX has as standard a graphic engine monitor and custom seating. Optional equipment includes dual controls, cabin heater, fire extinguisher, first aid kit, custom interior and custom paint scheme, floor switch, external power receptacle, third shoulder harness, auxiliary fuel tank, sliding vent windows, eight-day clock, baggage compartment, floats, cargo hook, hardpoints for agricultural equipment or night sign, and wet or wet/dry agricultural dispersal systems. Optional instrumentation includes R. C. Allen attitude gyro and turn co-ordinator, directional gyro, and instantaneous vertical speed indicator. Bose noise-attenuating headsets are optional on all models.

DIMENSIONS, EXTERNAL:

Main rotor diameter	9.75 m (32 ft 0 in)
Tail rotor diameter	1.42 m (4 ft 8 in)
Distance between rotor centres	5.56 m (18 ft 3 in)
Main rotor blade chord	0.24 m (9½ in)
Tail rotor blade chord	0.11 m (4½ in)
Length overall, rotors stationary	8.92 m (29 ft 3 in)
Height to top of rotor head	2.79 m (9 ft 2 in)
Skid track	2.21 m (7 ft 3 in)
Cabin doors (each): Height	1.04 m (3 ft 5 in)
Width	0.84 m (2 ft 9 in)
Height to sill	0.64 m (2 ft 1 in)
Baggage door: Height	0.55 m (1 ft 9½ in)
Width	0.39 m (1 ft 3½ in)
Height to sill	0.86 m (2 ft 10 in)

DIMENSIONS, INTERNAL (A: F28F, B: 280FX):

Cabin: Max width: A	1.55 m (5 ft 1 in)
B	1.50 m (4 ft 11 in)
Baggage compartment volume	0.18 m³ (6.3 cu ft)

AREAS:

Main rotor disc	74.69 m² (804.0 sq ft)
Tail rotor disc	1.66 m² (17.88 sq ft)

WEIGHTS AND LOADINGS (A: F28F Normal category, B: 280FX):

Weight empty, equipped: A	712 kg (1,570 lb)
B	719 kg (1,585 lb)
Max T-O weight: A, B	1,179 kg (2,600 lb)
Max disc loading: A, B	15.77 kg/m² (3.23 lb/sq ft)

PERFORMANCE (both versions at AUW of 1,066 kg; 2,350 lb, except where indicated):

Never-exceed speed (VNE):	
A	97 knots (180 km/h; 112 mph)
B	102 knots (189 km/h; 117 mph)
Max level speed, S/L to 915 m (3,000 ft):	
A	97 knots (180 km/h; 112 mph) IAS
B	102 knots (189 km/h; 117 mph) IAS
Max cruising speed: A	97 knots (180 km/h; 112 mph)
B	102 knots (189 km/h; 117 mph)
Econ cruising speed: A	89 knots (165 km/h; 102 mph)
B	93 knots (172 km/h; 107 mph)
Max rate of climb at S/L	442 m (1,450 ft)/min
Certificated operating ceiling	3,660 m (12,000 ft)
Hovering ceiling:	
IGE at AUW of 1,179 kg (2,600 lb)	2,345 m (7,700 ft)
OGE at AUW of 1,066 kg (2,350 lb)	2,650 m (8,700 ft)
Max range, standard fuel, no reserves:	
A	228 nm (423 km; 263 miles)
B	260 nm (483 km; 300 miles)
Max endurance	3 h 30 min

ENSTROM MODEL 480
Military designation: TH-28

TYPE: Four-seat turbine-powered helicopter.
PROGRAMME: Proof-of-concept 280FX, powered by Allison 250 turboshaft, flown December 1988; first flight of definitive wide-cabin four-seat prototype (N8631E) 7 October 1989; civil version shown at HAI's Heli Expo 1990; Model 480 entered as TH-28 in US Army new training helicopter (NTH) competition. Proof-of-concept 280FX and prototype had flown more than 500 hours by early 1991; entered certification test programme November 1990; civil certification expected second half 1991; initial production rate two per month.
VARIANTS: **Model 480:** Basic civil version, with four staggered seats or convertible to three-seat training/executive layout or single-seat for cargo carrying.
TH-28: Proposed US Army NTH pilot training version with three seats for instructor, student pilot and observing student; competing with Schweizer 330, modified Aerospatiale AS 350 AStar, and Imagineering/Global Helicopters Bell 206 with wheel landing gear. US Army requires 205 training helicopters.
CUSTOMERS: First batch of 40 sold; order book open for second batch.

COSTS: Civil Model 480 predicted price $385,000 (early 1990).

DESIGN FEATURES: Three-blade main rotor and dynamic system as for 280FX; 313 kW (420 shp) Allison 250-C20W turboshaft, derated to 212.5 kW (285 shp) for take-off and max continuous 186.4 kW (250 shp). New widened cabin able to seat three abreast behind pilot in single front seat. Civil cabin layout can be quickly rearranged (see Variants).

FLYING CONTROLS: As for 280FX.

DIMENSIONS, EXTERNAL: As for 280FX except:

Distance between rotor centres	5.64 m (18 ft 6 in)
Height to top of rotor head	2.90 m (9 ft 6 in)
Skid track	2.46 m (8 ft 1 in)

DIMENSIONS, INTERNAL:

Cabin: Max width	1.78 m (5 ft 10 in)

WEIGHTS AND LOADINGS:

Weight empty	712 kg (1,570 lb)
Max T-O weight	1,225 kg (2,700 lb)

PERFORMANCE (provisional, at max T-O weight, ISA, except where indicated):

Never-exceed speed (V_{NE})	
	123 knots (228 km/h; 142 mph)
Max cruising speed	108 knots (203 km/h; 126 mph)
Econ cruising speed	100 knots (185 km/h; 115 mph)
Max rate of climb at S/L:	
at AUW of 1,066 kg (2,350 lb)	494 m (1,620 ft)/min
at AUW of 1,225 kg (2,700 lb)	372 m (1,220 ft)/min
Service ceiling	4,570 m (15,000 ft)
Hovering ceiling:	
IGE:	
at AUW of 1,066 kg (2,350 lb)	4,635 m (15,200 ft)
at AUW of 1,225 kg (2,700 lb)	3,170 m (10,400 ft)
OGE:	
at AUW of 1,066 kg (2,350 lb)	3,870 m (12,700 ft)
at AUW of 1,225 kg (2,700 lb)	1,280 m (4,200 ft)
Max range	330 nm (611 km; 380 miles)
Endurance	4 h 12 min

Enstrom Model 480 four-seat turbine-powered light helicopter

EXCALIBUR

EXCALIBUR AVIATION COMPANY

8337 Mission Road, San Antonio, Texas 78214
Telephone: 1 (512) 927 6201
PRESIDENT: Michael M. Davis

Beechcraft Queen Air 65, A65 and 80 airframes are modified by Excalibur as Queenaire 800 and Queen Air A80s; B80 as Queenaire 8800. Conversion offers improved reliability, speed, range and reduced operating costs.

EXCALIBUR QUEENAIRE 800 and 8800

TYPE: Re-engined Beech Queen Air 65 and 80.

PROGRAMME: By early 1991, total of 170 Queenaire conversions, including four in 1990.

CUSTOMERS: Civil operators, notably in South America; more than 50 US Army U-8Fs modified for US National Guard Bureau.

DESIGN FEATURES: Installation of two 298 kW (400 hp) Textron Lycoming IO-720-A1B eight-cylinder engines; Hartzell three-blade constant-speed fully feathering metal propeller; new engine mountings; new exhaust system; new low drag engine nacelles; new (or zero time overhauled and certificated) accessories; Excalibur fully enclosed wheel well doors.

An Excalibur Queenaire 800 conversion of a Beech U-8F for the Missouri Army National Guard

WEIGHTS AND LOADINGS (A: Queenaire 800, B: Queenaire 8800):

Weight empty, equipped (average):	
A	2,449 kg (5,400 lb)
B	2,631 kg (5,800 lb)
Max T-O weight: A	3,628 kg (8,000 lb)
B	3,991 kg (8,800 lb)
Max landing weight: A	3,447 kg (7,600 lb)
B	3,792 kg (8,360 lb)
Max power loading: A	6.09 kg/kW (10.00 lb/hp)
B	6.70 kg/kW (11.00 lb/hp)

PERFORMANCE (at max T-O weight):

Cruising speed, 75% power:	
A, B at 2,530 m (8,300 ft)	
	201 knots (372 km/h; 231 mph)
Cruising speed, 65% power:	
A, B at 3,050 m (10,000 ft)	
	195 knots (362 km/h; 225 mph)
Cruising speed, 45% power:	
A, B at 3,050 m (10,000 ft)	
	172 knots (319 km/h; 198 mph)
Stalling speed:	
gear and flaps up:	
A	80 knots (148 km/h; 92 mph)
B	86 knots (160 km/h; 99 mph)
gear and flaps down:	
A	68 knots (126 km/h; 78 mph)
B	70 knots (129 km/h; 80 mph)
Max rate of climb at S/L: A	468 m (1,535 ft)/min
B	454 m (1,490 ft)/min

Rate of climb at S/L, one engine out:	
A	110 m (360 ft)/min
B	76 m (250 ft)/min
Service ceiling: A	6,005 m (19,700 ft)
B	5,700 m (18,700 ft)
Service ceiling, one engine out:	
A	3,595 m (11,800 ft)
B	3,110 m (10,200 ft)
T-O to 15 m (50 ft): A	520 m (1,706 ft)
B	625 m (2,050 ft)
Landing from 15 m (50 ft): A	663 m (2,176 ft)
B	747 m (2,450 ft)
Range with max fuel at 3,050 m (10,000 ft), with 113.5 litres (30 US gallons; 20.8 Imp gallons) reserves:	
A	1,322 nm (2,451 km; 1,523 miles)
B	1,547 nm (2,867 km; 1,782 miles)

FAIRCHILD

FAIRCHILD AIRCRAFT CORPORATION

PO Box 790490, San Antonio, Texas 78279-0490
Telephone: 1 (512) 824 9421
Fax: 1 (512) 820 8690
Telex: 76-7315
PRESIDENT: Carl Albert
VICE-PRESIDENT, AIRLINE SALES: Cal Humphrey

Fairchild Industries sold Metro Aviation, owning 97 per cent of Fairchild Aircraft Corporation, to GMF Investments Inc; Fairchild Aircraft sought Chapter 11 protection February 1990; at that time, 25 aircraft on order and 11 in final assembly, two of which delivered to Air Sardinia in February 1990. Purchase by Fairchild Acquisition Inc approved by US Bankruptcy Court; emerged Chapter 11 on 29 September 1990; new organisation effective 1 October 1990; order backlog quoted as $81.85 million.

FAIRCHILD MODEL SA227-DC METRO 23, SA227-AC METRO III and EXPEDITER I
Swedish Air Force designation: Tp88
US military designation: C-26A/B

TYPE: Twin-turboprop 19/20-passenger commuter airliner.

PROGRAMME: Metro III originally SFAR 41 approved; FAR 23 type approval June 1990 for version with TPE331-11 engines and September 1990 for Metro 23 with TPE331-12s; both types to remain in production under SFAR 41 until October 1991 when Metro III will be discontinued. British CAA certification August 1988; required modifications included dual-redundant stall warning system, dual continuous water/alcohol/water injection system, modified aileron aerofoil section, externally operable escape hatches.

VARIANTS: **SA227-DC Metro 23:** Current high gross weight aircraft.

Tp88: Swedish Air Force VIP transport; one delivered.
C-26A and C-26B: Six C-26As ordered March 1988 as US Air National Guard Operational Support Transport Aircraft (ANGOSTA), later increased to 13, delivered from March 1989; 10 delivered by 1 May 1990; one plus nine C-26Bs ordered FY 1990; these have quick-change passenger, medevac or cargo interiors and are due to be delivered by September 1995. Contract awarded January 1991 by USAF Aeronautical Systems Division for delivery/logistics support of up to 53 C-26s over five-year period from January 1992.

Expediter I: All-cargo version; air-conditioning ducts moved to increase cargo volume, reinforced cabin floor, cargo nets and guards; reduced empty weight allowing max payload of more than 2,268 kg (5,000 lb); first operator SAT-AIR on behalf of United Parcel Service; first of 10 Expediter Is delivered to DHL

Fairchild C-26 (two Garrett TPE331-12UAR-701G turboprops)

Worldwide Courier Express April 1985 with structurally reinforced landing gear and wing main spar for max T-O weight 7,257 kg (16,000 lb).

Merlin 23: Business aircraft version of Metro 23; launched November 1990 at RAA Fall Meeting, Phoenix, Arizona; meets new FAR 23 commuter certification requirements effective October 1991.

DESIGN FEATURES: Certificated to FAA SFAR 41 and 41B, which covers ICAO Annex 8, for operation at T-O weight over 5,670 kg (12,500 lb); Metro III cleared for T-O weight 6,577 kg (14,500 lb); optional high gross weight version 7,257 kg (16,000 lb). Metro 23, to which listed figures apply, has max T-O weight of 7,484 kg (16,500 lb).

Changes from Metro II include 3.05 m (10 ft 0 in) increase in wing span, improved handling, more powerful engines with slow-turning four-blade propellers, new main gear doors for better take-off and landing performance and easier maintenance, new streamlined nacelles with petal doors and quick-action latches, new fire prevention and containment with flammable fluid pipework isolated from electrical components and wiring. Certificated for flight into known icing; lightning strike protection claimed to be equal to that of latest commercial jet transports.

Wing section NACA 65_2A215 at root, 64_2A415 at tip; dihedral 5°; incidence 1° at root, −2° 30′ at tip; sweepback at quarter-chord 0° 54′. Goodrich automatic, bleed air operated pneumatic de-icing boots on wing, tailplane and fin.

FLYING CONTROLS: Mechanically operated, aerodynamically and mass balanced; manual trim tab in each aileron; electrically operated variable incidence tailplane; manual rudder trim tab; small ventral fin. Hydraulically operated double-slotted trailing-edge flaps.

STRUCTURE: Two-spar fail-safe wing made in one piece; main spar beams have laminated caps (titanium laminations in centre-section); pressurised cylindrical fuselage of 2024 aluminium alloy, flush riveted; glassfibre honeycomb nose cap can contain 0.46 m (18 in) diameter weather radar antenna.

LANDING GEAR: Retractable tricycle type with twin wheels on each unit. Hydraulic retraction, with dual actuators on each unit. All wheels retract forward, main gear into engine nacelles, nosewheels into fuselage. Ozone Aircraft Systems oleo-pneumatic shock absorber struts. Nosewheel steerable (±63° max). Free-fall emergency extension, with backup of hand operated hydraulic pump. Goodrich mainwheels with low-pressure tubeless tyres, size 19.5 × 6.75-8, type VII. Jay-Em nosewheels and Goodyear low-pressure tubeless tyres, size 18 × 4.40, type VII. Tyre pressures: nosewheel at standard T-O weight 3.79 bars (55 lb/sq in), at optional increased T-O weight 4.76 bars (69 lb/sq in); mainwheels at standard T-O weight 5.60 bars (87 lb/sq in), at optional T-O weight 7.10 bars (103 lb/sq in). Goodrich self-adjusting hydraulically operated disc brakes and anti-skid system.

POWER PLANT: Metro III has two 745.5 kW (1,000 shp) dry Garrett TPE331-11U-612G turboprops with propeller reversing. SA227-DC, C-26 and Metro 23 have TPE331-12UA-701Gs giving 745.5 kW (1,000 shp) dry and 820 kW (1,100 shp) with continuous alcohol/water injection system, driving a McCauley four-blade constant-speed fully feathering reversible-pitch metal propeller. Automatic propeller synchrophasing standard. In-flight windmill start capability. Integral fuel tank in each wing, each with a usable capacity of 1,226 litres (324 US gallons; 270 Imp gallons). Total usable fuel capacity 2,452 litres (648 US gallons; 540 Imp gallons). Refuelling point in each outer wing panel. Automatic fuel heating. Oil capacity

15.1 litres (4 US gallons; 3.3 Imp gallons). Alcohol/water tank in nose (except Metro III), capacity 60.5 litres (16 US gallons; 13.3 Imp gallons), with two pumps to pump fluid to engines. Engine inlet de-icing by bleed air. Electric oil cooler inlet anti-icing. Electric propeller de-icing. Flush mounted fuel vents. Single-point rapid defuelling provisions. Negative torque sensing, single red line/autostart, automatic engine temperature limiting, and engine fire extinguishing systems.

ACCOMMODATION: Crew of two on flight deck, each with four-way adjustable seat with folding armrests and shoulder harness, separated from passenger/cargo area by partial bulkhead on port side and armrest height curtain on starboard side. Dual controls standard. Bulkhead between cabin and flight deck optional.

Standard accommodation for 19-20 passengers seated two abreast, on each side of centre aisle. 'No smoking' and 'Fasten seat belt' signs. High-back, tracking, quickly removable passenger seats standard. Interior convertible to all-cargo or mixed passenger/cargo configuration with movable bulkhead between passenger and cargo sections. Snap-in carpeting. Self-stowing aisle filler. Tiedown fittings for cargo at 0.76 m (30 in) spacing. Integral-step passenger door on port side of fuselage, immediately aft of flight deck. Large cargo loading door on port side of fuselage at rear of cabin, hinged at top. Three window emergency exits, one on the port, two on the starboard side. Forward baggage/avionics compartment in nose, capacity 363 kg (800 lb). Pressurised rear cargo compartment, capacity 385 kg (850 lb). Cabin

Fairchild SA227-AC Metro III (two Garrett TPE331-IIU-612G turboprops)

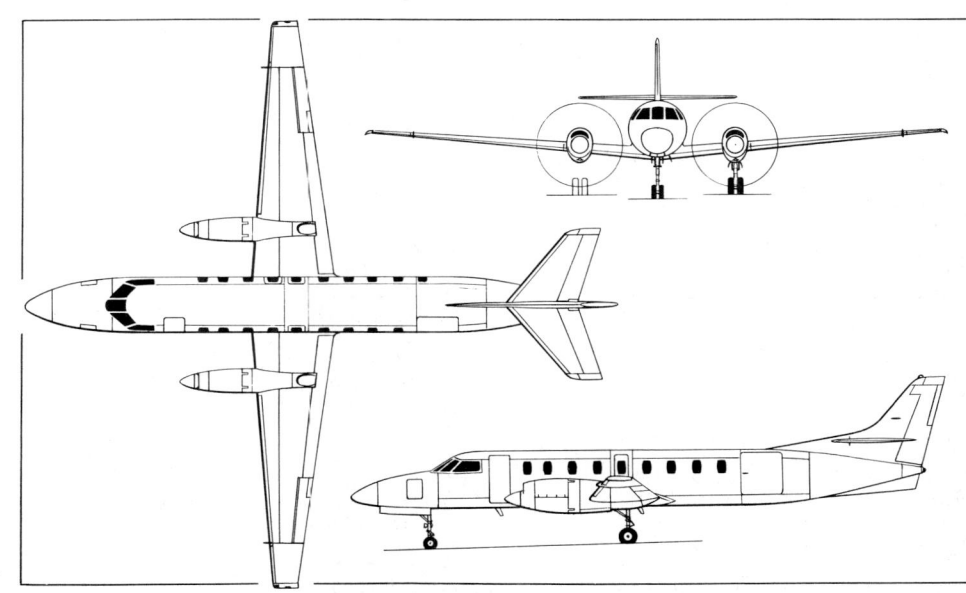

Fairchild Metro III commuter airliner (two Garrett TPE331 turboprops) *(Pilot Press)*

air-conditioned and pressurised. Electric windscreen de-icing. Two-speed windscreen wipers.

SYSTEMS: AiResearch automatic cabin pressure control system: max differential 0.48 bar (7.0 lb/sq in), providing a sea level cabin altitude to 5,120 m (16,800 ft). Engine bleed air heating, dual air cycle cooling system, with automatic temperature control. Air blower system for on-ground ventilation. Independent hydraulic system for brakes. Dual engine driven hydraulic pumps, using fire resistant MIL-H-83282 hydraulic fluid, provide 138 bars (2,000 lb/sq in) to operate flaps, landing gear actuators and nosewheel steering. Hydraulic system flow rates 30.3 litres (8 US gallons; 6.7 Imp gallons)/min at idle power, both engines; 46.7 litres (12.34 US gallons; 10.27 Imp gallons)/min at T-O and climb power. Air/oil reservoir, pressure 2.27 bars (33 lb/sq in). Electrical system supplied by two 300A 28V DC starter/generators. Fail-safe system with overload and overvoltage protection. Redundant circuits for essential systems. Two 350VA solid state inverters supply 115V and 26V AC. Two SAFT 24V 23Ah nickel-cadmium batteries for main services. Engine fire detection system and fire extinguishing system standard. Wing overheat detection system. Oxygen system of 1.39 m³ (49 cu ft) capacity with flush outlets at each seat; system with capacity of 5.04 m³ (178 cu ft) optional. Stall avoidance system comprising angle indicator, visual and aural warning.

AVIONICS: Two flight deck and four cabin speakers standard; provisions for installation of remotely mounted or panel mounted avionics, customer furnished weather radar and autopilot.

EQUIPMENT: Standard equipment includes pilot and co-pilot foot warmers; edge lit consoles, pedestal and switch panels; integrally lit instruments; annunciator panel with 48 indicators; internally operated control locks, individual reading lights and air vents for each passenger; heated pitot; heated static sources; baggage compartment, cargo compartment, entrance, map and instrument panel, ice inspection, retractable landing, navigation, rotating beacon and taxi lights; automatic engine start cycle; external power socket; and static wicks.

DIMENSIONS, EXTERNAL:

Wing span	17.37 m (57 ft 0 in)
Wing mean aerodynamic chord	1.84 m (6 ft 0⅓ in)
Wing aspect ratio	10.5
Length overall	18.09 m (59 ft 4¼ in)
Height overall	5.08 m (16 ft 8 in)
Tailplane span	4.86 m (15 ft 11½ in)
Wheel track	4.57 m (15 ft 0 in)
Wheelbase	5.83 m (19 ft 1½ in)
Propeller diameter	2.69 m (8 ft 10 in)
Passenger door (fwd): Height	1.35 m (4 ft 5 in)
Width	0.64 m (2 ft 1 in)
Cargo door (rear): Height	1.30 m (4 ft 3¼ in)
Width	1.35 m (4 ft 5 in)
Height to sill	1.30 m (4 ft 3¼ in)
Forward baggage doors (two, each):	
Height	0.64 m (2 ft 1 in)
Width	0.46 m (1 ft 6 in)
Emergency exits (three, each):	
Height	0.71 m (2 ft 4 in)
Width	0.51 m (1 ft 8 in)

DIMENSIONS, INTERNAL:

Cabin, excl flight deck and rear cargo compartment:

Length	7.75 m (25 ft 5 in)
Max width	1.57 m (5 ft 2 in)
Max height (aisle)	1.45 m (4 ft 9 in)
Floor area	13.01 m² (140.0 sq ft)
Volume	13.88 m³ (490.0 cu ft)

Rear cargo compartment (pressurised):

Length	2.34 m (7 ft 8 in)
Max width	1.57 m (5 ft 2 in)
Max height	1.32 m (4 ft 4 in)
Volume	4.06 m³ (143.5 cu ft)

Nose cargo compartment (unpressurised):

Length	1.75 m (5 ft 9 in)
Volume	0.85 m³ (30.0 cu ft)

AREAS:

Wings, gross	28.71 m² (309.0 sq ft)
Ailerons (total)	1.31 m² (14.12 sq ft)
Trailing-edge flaps (total)	3.78 m² (40.66 sq ft)
Fin, incl dorsal fin	3.40 m² (36.62 sq ft)
Rudder, incl tab	1.80 m² (19.38 sq ft)
Tailplane	5.08 m² (54.70 sq ft)
Elevators	1.98 m² (21.27 sq ft)

WEIGHTS AND LOADINGS (Metro 23):

Operating weight empty	3,935 kg (8,675 lb)
Max fuel weight	1,969 kg (4,342 lb)
Max T-O weight	7,484 kg (16,500 lb)
Max ramp weight	7,530 kg (16,600 lb)
Max zero-fuel weight	6,577 kg (14,500 lb)
Max landing weight	7,110 kg (15,675 lb)
Max wing loading	261 kg/m² (53.3 lb/sq ft)
Max power loading	4.56 kg/kW (7.5 lb/shp)

PERFORMANCE (Metro 23 at max T-O weight of 7,484 kg; 16,500 lb, ISA, except where indicated):

Design diving speed (V_D)
311 knots (576 km/h; 358 mph) CAS
Max operating speed (V_MO)
248 knots (459 km/h; 285 mph) CAS
Max operating Mach No. (M_MO)   0.52

Max cruising speed at 97% rpm, bleed low, max T-O weight at 3,353 m (11,000 ft)
288 knots (534 km/h; 331 mph)
Stalling speed:
flaps and wheels up
103 knots (191 km/h; 118 mph) IAS
flaps and wheels down
89 knots (165 km/h; 102 mph) IAS
Max rate of climb at S/L, bleed open
698 m (2,290 ft)/min
Rate of climb at S/L, one engine out, bleed closed
176 m (580 ft)/min
Service ceiling   7,666 m (25,150 ft)
Service ceiling, one engine out   3,505 m (11,500 ft)
T-O to 15 m (50 ft), wet power   1,414 m (4,640 ft)
Landing run   843 m (2,765 ft)
Range:
with 19 passengers and baggage, FAA IFR reserves   over 782 nm (1,450 km; 900 miles)
with 2,720 kg (6,000 lb), FAA IFR reserves
over 520 nm (967 km; 600 miles)
C-26 with 1,315 kg (2,900 lb) payload, 1,969 kg (4,342 lb) fuel, no reserves
1,740 nm (3,223 km; 2,000 miles)

FAIRCHILD SPECIAL MISSION AIRCRAFT

TYPE: Special mission versions of Metro III.

PROGRAMME: Development and production on demand.

VARIANTS: **Maritime patrol:** 360° scan Litton AN/APS-504(V), (V)5 or AIL AN/APS-128D radar in underbelly blister; Omega navigation linked to hand-held cameras; two bulged observation windows staggered one on each side of rear fuselage. Options include searchlight, IR linescanner, low light TV, FLIR, side-looking TV, Doppler radar, droppable liferafts, surival kits and two 288 litre (76 US gallon; 63 Imp gallon) underwing auxiliary tanks. At max T-O weight 7,257 kg (16,000 lb) with underwing tanks, surveillance variants can fly 10 hour mission over radius of 1,050 nm (1,946 km; 1,209 miles) from base at 7,620 m (25,000 ft) with 45 min fuel reserve.

Anti-submarine: Carries sonobuoys and sonobuoy signal processor, an OTP indicator, and MAD tailboom. Options as for maritime patrol variant.

Airborne early warning: Swedish Defence Materiel Administration (FMV) ordered Fairchild study of airborne early warning (AEW) version of Metro III in 1982, carrying dorsal active array radar antenna; initial wind tunnel testing by LTV in Dallas during 1983; FMV ordered Metro III to test Ericsson PS-890 (now FSR-890) Erieye early 1986; FSR-890 is fixed antenna, electronically scanned E/F band radar scanning to one side at a time over 120° arc; first flight with mockup antenna October 1986; delivered to Sweden after 116 hours aerodynamic and handling tests by Fairchild October 1987; exhibited at Farnborough Air Show 1988; first flight with operating radar due May 1991. Reported Swedish requirement for 10-15 aircraft, to enter service 1997-98; platform aircraft could be Saab 340 instead of Metro.

Antenna in composites housing approx 8 m (26 ft 3 in) long, mounted on pylons above fuselage with ram air cooling; antenna mounted at incidence –2° to allow for angle of attack at patrol speeds; auxiliary fins on tailplane; enlarged ventral fin; Turbomach T-62T APU, producing 60kVA electrical supply for radar, mounted in E-Systems pod on centreline pylon under wing; periscope sight in flight deck roof; larger emergency exit on port side of cabin. Data link to connect with Swedish STRIL60/90 not selected.

Loiter speeds include 135-146 knots (250-270 km/h; 155-168 mph) with flaps at 50 per cent, 164-175 knots (305-325 km/h; 189-202 mph) with flaps at 25 per cent; endurance 4-6 h in patrol area 100 nm (185 km; 115 miles) away from base.

Other variants include **flight inspection, photo reconnaissance, electronic intelligence** and **airborne critical care.**

CUSTOMERS: Total 35 delivered in various configurations.

FAIRCHILD MERLIN IV C (SA-227-AT)

TYPE: 11/14-passenger corporate version of Metro III airliner.

PROGRAMME: Certificated under SFAR Pt 41B and ICAO Annex 8 at max T-O weights of 6,577 kg (14,500 lb) or 7,257 kg (16,000 lb).

CUSTOMERS: Total 24 delivered by January 1990.

DESIGN FEATURES: Movable bulkheads and interchangeable furnishings allow cabin arrangement for variety of passenger numbers and cargo; interiors include reclining passenger seats, couches, more luxurious fittings, decor and lighting, large buffet cabinet with beverage and food storage and preparation facilities, television and stereo; toilet and baggage compartments at rear separated by bulkhead and hinged door.

Specifications of Merlin III apply to Merlin IV C, except that empty weight is 90-180 kg (200-400 lb) higher by reason of additional furnishings, and lower bleed air extraction results in higher cruising speeds.

AVIONICS: In late 1986 the Merlin IV C was certificated for a Bendix/King KFC 400 flight control system with KNS 660 flight management system integrated with the Bendix EFIS-10 five-tube electronic flight instrument system comprising two ADIs, two HSIs and a multi-function display.

WEIGHTS AND LOADINGS: As Metro III, except:
Weight empty, equipped   4,472 kg (9,860 lb)
PERFORMANCE (at max T-O weight, ISA, except where indicated):
Max cruising speed, at mid-cruise weight of 5,670 kg (12,500 lb):
at 3,050-4,575 m (10,000-15,000 ft)
283 knots (524 km/h; 326 mph)
at 6,100 m (20,000 ft)   281 knots (521 km/h; 323 mph)
at 7,620 m (25,000 ft)   273 knots (506 km/h; 314 mph)
Max rate of climb at S/L   803 m (2,635 ft)/min
Rate of climb at S/L, one engine out   198 m (650 ft)/min
Range with max standard fuel, max cruise power at 7,925 m (26,000 ft), 45 min reserves:
eight occupants   1,578 nm (2,924 km; 1,817 miles)
thirteen occupants   1,036 nm (1,920 km; 1,193 miles)
Ferry range, conditions and allowances as above, but with two flight crew only
2,071 nm (3,838 km; 2,384 miles)

Fairchild Metro Special Missions Aircraft with dorsal antenna housing for Ericsson PS-890 (FSR-890) radar (*Mike Jerram*)

Fairchild Merlin IV C twin-turboprop corporate transport

FARRINGTON

FARRINGTON AIRCRAFT CORPORATION

RT3, PO Box 319, Paducah, Kentucky 42001
Telephone: 1 (502) 898 2403
Telex: 204057
PRESIDENT: Don Farrington

AIR & SPACE 18A

TYPE: Two-seat autogyro.
PROGRAMME: Original aircraft (68 built) produced in mid-1960s (certificated 1965) until Air & Space Manufacturing Inc declared bankrupt in 1966. Farrington Aircraft announced in June 1990 that 30 of these had

been modernised under seven STCs and that it intended to restart production in this improved form, starting deliveries September 1990. Proposed applications include patrol/surveillance, environmental monitoring, law enforcement, pipeline inspection and broadcasting, as well as private flying.
COSTS: $75,000 flyaway (September 1990).
DESIGN FEATURES: Three-blade rotor, fully enclosed tandem-seat cabin, non-retractable tricycle landing gear, three-fin tail unit (all-moving central and two fixed outer). Original aircraft described in 1967-68 *Jane's*; Farrington improvements include trimmable two-position collective-pitch control, improved engine cowling, noise-reduced exhaust and strengthened nosewheel leg.

POWER PLANT: One 134 kW (180 hp) Textron Lycoming O-360 flat-four engine with Hartzell two-blade pusher propeller. Fuel capacity 113.5 litres (30 US gallons; 25 Imp gallons).
DIMENSIONS, EXTERNAL (original aircraft):
Rotor diameter	10.67 m (35 ft 0 in)
Length overall	6.05 m (19 ft 10 in)
Height overall	2.82 m (9 ft 3 in)

WEIGHTS AND LOADINGS (original aircraft):
Max T-O weight	816.5 kg (1,800 lb)

PERFORMANCE (original aircraft):
Max cruising speed	87 knots (161 km/h; 100 mph)
Service ceiling	3,660 m (12,000 ft)
Range	260 nm (483 km; 300 miles)

GARRETT

GARRETT GENERAL AVIATION SERVICES DIVISION
(Division of Allied Signal Aerospace Company)

Los Angeles International Airport, 6201 West Imperial Highway, Los Angeles, California 90045
Telephone: 1 (213) 568 3729
Fax: 1 (213) 568 3715
Telex: 181827 A/B AIRE AVI LSA
VICE-PRESIDENT, MARKETING & SALES: Richard A. Graser

GARRETT 731 FALCON 20 RETROFIT PROGRAMME

TYPE: Engine retrofit for in-service Falcon 20s.
PROGRAMME: Announced May 1987; new engine pylon developed by Dassault Aviation in France (which see); first flight development Falcon 20F (F-WTFE) from Bordeaux-Merignac 7 October 1988; first flight second aircraft (Falcon 20C F-WTFF) 26 January 1989; certificated USA and France March 1989.
CUSTOMERS: Total 42 Falcons of all models retrofitted by end January 1991, including first European conversion delivered by Europe Falcon Service on 6 July 1989.
DESIGN FEATURES: Original General Electric CF700s replaced initially with Garrett TFE731-5ARs with digital engine control, new pylons and nacelles identical with those of Falcon 900; suffix -5 added to identify retrofit, as

Garrett 731 Falcon 20C-5 (TFE731-5AR turbofans)

in Falcon 20F-5; new engine increases Falcon 20 range by 50 per cent and meets FAR Pt 36 Stage 3 noise levels. Range of Falcon 20C increased to 2,040 nm (3,780 km; 2,349 miles), Falcon 20D and E to 2,230 nm (4,132 km; 2,567 miles), and Falcon 20F to 2,260 nm (4,188 km; 2,602 miles); all calculated for eight passengers, cruising at Mach 0.72 with NBAA IFR reserves. From March 1991, 21.13 kN (4,750 lb st) TFE731-5BR fitted; available to operators of earlier 731 Falcon 20s; range of Falcon

20F increased to 2,500 nm (4,633 km; 2,878 miles). Optional Dee Howard TR-5020 thrust reversers are certificated.
Retrofit undertaken by Garrett General Aviation Services at Los Angeles, California, or Springfield, Illinois; Falcon Jet Service Center at Little Rock, Arkansas; Europe Falcon Service, Le Bourget Airport, Paris; and TransAirCo, Geneva, Switzerland.

GENERAL DYNAMICS

GENERAL DYNAMICS CORPORATION

Pierre Laclede Center, St Louis, Missouri 63105
Telephone: 1 (314) 889 8200
Fax: 1 (314) 889 8530
CHAIRMAN AND CHIEF EXECUTIVE OFFICER:
William A. Anders
PRESIDENT AND CHIEF OPERATING OFFICER: James R. Mellor
Fort Worth Division
PO Box 748, Fort Worth, Texas 76101
Telephone: 1 (817) 777 2000
Fax: 1 (817) 777 2115
GENERAL MANAGER: Herbert F. Rogers
VICE-PRESIDENT, F-16 PROGRAMME DIRECTOR: D. M. Hancock
VICE-PRESIDENT, RESEARCH AND ENGINEERING:
E. M. Petrushka
VICE-PRESIDENT, PROGRAMME DEVELOPMENT: A. D. Mayfield

General Dynamics US aerospace activities include Convair Division at San Diego, California; Fort Worth Division at Fort Worth, Texas; Pomona Division at Pomona, California; Electronics Division at San Diego, California; Valley Systems Division at Rancho Cucamonga, California; Space Systems Division at San Diego, California; and, since acquisition in March 1985, Cessna Aircraft Company at Wichita, Kansas (which see).
Convair Division designs, develops and produces offensive missile systems and aircraft structures. Fort Worth designs, develops and produces military aircraft and electronics. Pomona develops and produces tactical missile and gun systems. Electronics Division evolves new technology to support production of advanced electronic systems. Valley Systems Division produces Stinger and RAM missiles and is developing terminally guided submunitions.
Fort Worth activities include production of F-16 Fighting Falcon, shared development of F-22A ATF (with Lockheed [which see], and Boeing), provision of spares, support and modification/update for F-111 and various ground-based radar systems. Convair Division retains detailed tooling for high-usage spares for Convair-Liner 240/340/440 airliners and manufactures components for them.

GENERAL DYNAMICS F-111

Details of F-111 upgrade programmes can be found under Rockwell and US Air Force in USA, and BAe in the UK section. See also EF-111A upgrade under Grumman heading in this section.

GENERAL DYNAMICS/MCDONNELL DOUGLAS A-12

This aircraft was cancelled on 7 January 1991. Final details can be found under the separate General Dynamics/McDonnell Douglas heading following this entry.

GENERAL DYNAMICS F-16 FIGHTING FALCON

TYPE: Single-seat and two-seat multi-role fighter.
PROGRAMME: Emerged from YF-16 of US Air Force Lightweight Fighter prototype programme 1972 (details in 1977-78 and 1978-79 *Jane's*); first flight of prototype YF-16 (72-01567) 2 February 1974; first flight of second prototype (72-01568) 9 May 1974; selected for full-scale development 13 January 1975; day fighter requirement extended to add air-to-ground capability with radar and all-weather navigation; production of six single-seat F-16As and two-seat F-16Bs began July 1975; first flight of full-scale development aircraft 8 December 1976; first flight of F-16B 8 August 1977.
VARIANTS: **A-16:** Proposed Block 50/60 aircraft to be built for close air support (CAS)/battlefield air interdiction (BAI) in late 1990s; Falcon Eye head-steered FLIR, Pave Penny laser-ranger and 30 mm cannon pod. Project (and competing LTV A-7F) abandoned 1990. As replacement, 300-450 F-16Cs to receive CAS/BAI modifications from 1995, including DTS, Navstar GPS and automatic target handoff system (ATHS). First dedicated CAS/BAI aircraft are F-16As of ANG's 138th TFS at Syracuse, New York; operational 1989, equipment including fixed GPU-5/A 30 mm centreline cannon; first ATHS installed November 1990. Later version known as **F/A-16A.**
F-16A: First production version for air-to-air and air-to-ground missions; production for USAF completed March 1985, but still available for other customers; powered since late 1988 (Block 15OCU) by P&W F100-PW-220 turbofan; Westinghouse AN/APG-66 range and angle track radar; first flight of first aircraft (78-0001) 7 August 1978; entered service with 388th TFW at Hill AFB, Utah, 6 January 1979; combat ready October 1980, when named Fighting Falcon; most now serving ANG and AFRES. See also A-16, above. Also produced in Europe. Built in Blocks 01, 05, 10 and 15, of which Blocks 01 and 05 retrofitted to Block 10 standard 1982-84; Blocks 10 and 15 retrofitted to OCU standard from late 1987.
Operational Capabilities Upgrade (OCU): USAF/NATO co-operative programme to equip F-16A/B for next-generation BVR air-to-air and air-to-surface weapons; radar and software updated, fire control and

stores management computers improved, data transfer unit fitted, combined radar-barometric altimeter fitted, and provision for AN/ALQ-131 jamming pods. Ring laser INS and upgrade from P&W F100-PW-200 to F100-PW-220E planned for 1990s. FMS exports since 1988 to Block 15OCU standard with F-16C features including ring laser INS, AN/ALR-69 RWR, F100-PW-220 power plant and AIM-9P-4 Sidewinder AAM capability.
Mid-Life Update (MLU): Start of development planned for 1991; to be applied to 533 aircraft of USAF (130), Belgium (110), Denmark (63), Netherlands (172) and Norway (58) from 1996 in co-development/co-production programme. Includes cockpit similar to F-16C/D Block 50 with wide-angle HUD, night vision goggle compatibility, modular mission computer replacing three existing, digital terrain system, AN/APG-66(V2A) fire control radar, Navstar GPS, ATHS and provision for microwave landing system (MLS). Inlet hardpoints and wiring for FLIR pods will be added to Block 10 aircraft. Options include helmet-mounted display and advanced IFF interrogator/transponder.
F-16(ADF): Modification of 270 Block 15 F-16A/Bs as USAF air defence fighters to replace F-4s and F-106s with 11 Air National Guard squadrons; ordered October 1986. Modifications include upgrade of AN/APG-66 radar to improve small target detection, provision of AMRAAM data link, improved ECCM, Bendix/King AN/ARC-200 HF/SSB radio, Teledyne/E-Systems advanced IFF, provision for Navstar GPS Group A, low altitude warning, voice message unit, night identification light, and ability to carry and guide two AIM-7 Sparrow missiles. First successful guided launch of AIM-7 over Point Mugu range, California, February 1989; F-16(ADF) can carry up to six AIM-120 AMRAAM or AIM-9 Sidewinder or combinations of all three missiles; retains internal M61 20 mm Gatling gun. GD producing modification kits for installation by USAF Ogden Air Logistics Center, Utah, in conjunction with OCU programme. Development completed at Edwards AFB during 1990; operational test and evaluation with 57th Fighter Weapons Wing at Nellis AFB, Nevada; first F-16(ADF) delivered to 114th Tactical Fighter Training Squadron at Kingsley Field, Oregon, 1 March 1989; 194th Fighter Interceptor Wing, California ANG, Fresno, achieved IOC in 1989. Programme completed early 1991.
F-16B: Standard tandem two-seat version of F-16A; fully operational both cockpits; fuselage length unaltered; reduced fuel.
F-16C/D: Single-seat and two-seat USAF Multinational Staged Improvement Program (**MSIP**) aircraft

Visible LERX vortices and wing-tip smoke trails generated by a Netherlands F-16A in high *g* turn
(Paul Jackson)

Trial launch of an NFT Penguin anti-ship missile from an Edwards AFB F-16A

USAF Wild Weasel F-16C based in Europe with 52nd TFW *(Paul Jackson)*

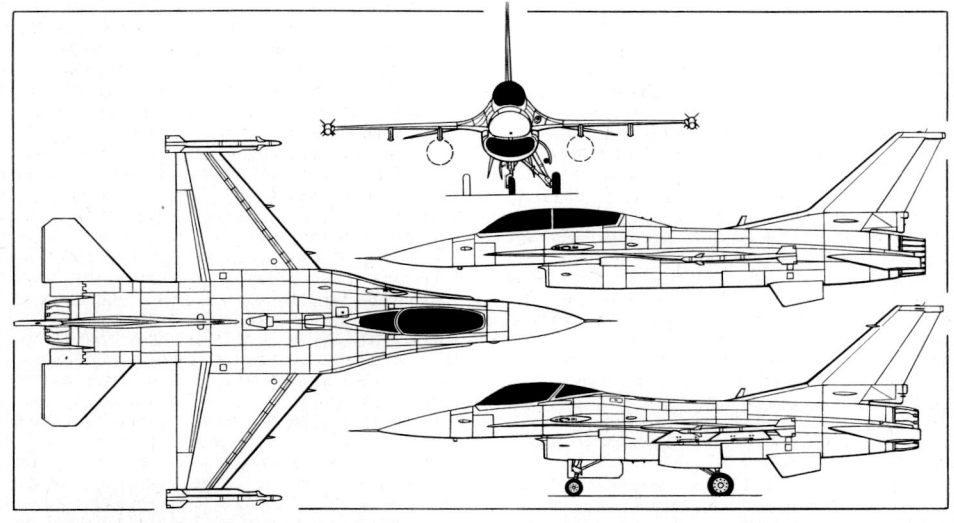

General Dynamics F-16C (GE F110 turbofan) with extra side view of two-seat F-16D (P&W F100 turbofan) *(Pilot Press)*

respectively, implemented February 1980. MSIP expands growth capability to allow for ground attack and beyond-visual-range missiles, and all-weather, night and day missions; **Stage I** applied to Block 15 F-16A/Bs delivered from November 1981 included wiring and structural changes to accommodate new systems; **Stage II** applied to Block 25 F-16C/Ds from July 1984 includes core avionics, cockpit and airframe changes. **Stage III** includes installation of systems as they become available. Changes include Westinghouse AN/APG-68 multi-mode radar with better range, resolution, more operating modes and better ECCM than AN/APG-66; advanced cockpit with better interfaces and up-front controls, GEC Avionics wide-angle HUD, two multi-function displays, Fairchild mission data transfer equipment and radar altimeter; expanded base of fin giving space for proposed later fitment of AN/ALQ-165 Airborne Self Protection Jamming system (since cancelled); increased electrical power and cooling capacity; structural provision for increased take-off weight and manoeuvring limits; and MIL-STD-1760 weapons interface for use of smart weapons such as AMRAAM and AGM-65D IR Maverick.

Common engine bay introduced at **Block 30/32** (deliveries from July 1986) to allow fitting of either P&W F100-PW-220 (Block 32) or GE F110-GE-100 (Block 30) Alternate Fighter Engine. Other changes include computer memory expansion and seal-bonded fuselage fuel tanks. First USAF wing to use F-16C/Ds with F110 engines was 86th TFW at Ramstein AB, Germany, from October 1986. Additions in 1987 included full Level IV multi-target compatibility with AMRAAM (as Block 30B), voice message unit, Shrike anti-radiation missiles (from August), crash survivable flight data recorder and modular common inlet duct allowing full thrust from F110 at low airspeeds.

Software upgraded for full Level IV multi-target compatibility with AMRAAM early 1988. Industry-sponsored development of radar missile capability for several European air forces resulted in firing of AIM-7F and AIM-7M missiles from F-16C in May 1988, to be introduced mid-1991; missiles guided using pulse Doppler illumination while tracking targets in a high PRF mode of the AN/APG-68 radar.

US Air Force F-16C/Ds of 52nd TFW at Spangdahlem AB, Germany, have interim HARM/Shrike capability and operate alongside F-4G Phantoms in Wild Weasel defence suppression role. Definitive version will have avionics housed in dorsal spine fairing between base of fin and canopy.

Fully combat capable F-16C/Ds bearing MiG-type camouflage started operating in 1989 with aggressor squadrons at Nellis AFB, Nevada, and RAF Bentwaters, UK. Budget cuts forced abandonment of planned aggressor squadrons at Kadena, Japan, and Tyndall AFB, Florida, and disbandment of 527th AS at Bentwaters, 26th AS at Clark AFB, Philippines, and 64th AS at Nellis.

Block 40/42 Night Falcon (deliveries December 1988) upgrades include AN/APG-68(V) radar allowing 100 h operation before maintenance, full compatibility with Martin Marietta low altitude navigation and targeting infra-red for night (LANTIRN) pods, four-channel digital flight control system, expanded capacity core computers, diffractive optics HUD, enhanced envelope gunsight, Navstar GPS, improved leading-edge flap drive system, improved cockpit ergonomics, high gross weight landing gear, structural strengthening, and provision for improved EW equipment. LANTIRN gives day/night standoff target identification, automatic target handoff for multiple launch of Mavericks, autonomous laser guided bomb delivery and precision air-to-ground laser ranging. Combat Edge pressure breathing system installed 1990 for higher pilot *g* tolerance.

Issue of first Block 40 F-16C/Ds to re-equip 50th TFW (Hahn, Germany) in late 1990 postponed; aircraft diverted to 363rd TFW (Shaw AFB, South Carolina).

Block 50/52 (deliveries begin F-16C 90-0801 in October 1991) upgrades include F110-GE-129 and F100-PW-229 increased performance engines (IPE), AN/APG-68(V5) radar with advanced programmable signal processor employing VHSIC technology, Have Quick IIA UHF radio, Have Sync VHF anti-jam radio and AN/ALR-56M advanced radar warning receiver. Changes planned for 1993 include full integration of HARM/Shrike anti-radiation missiles via Texas Instruments interface, upgraded programmable display generator with digital terrain system (DTS) provisions and scope for digital map capability, ring laser INS (Honeywell H-423 selected 1990) and AN/ALE-47 advanced chaff/flare dispenser. Upgrades being considered for 1994-95 include a digital terrain system with colour map, colour multi-function displays, modular core computer suite, head-steered FLIR with helmet-mounted display, self-protection jammer and onboard oxygen generating system (OBOGS).

NF-16D: Variable stability in-flight simulator test aircraft (VISTA) modified from Block 30 F-16D (86-0048) ordered December 1988 to replace NT-33A testbed. Features include vertical surface direct force generators above and below wings, variable stability flight control system, fully programmable cockpit controls and displays, additional computer suite, permanent flight test data recording system, variable feel centrestick and computer, and safety pilot in rear cockpit. Internal gun, RWR and chaff/flare equipment removed, providing space for Phase II and III growth including additional computer, reprogrammable display generator and customer hardware allowance. First flight due Spring 1991.

F-16N: US Navy supersonic adversary aircraft (SAA) modified from F-16C/D Block 30; selected January 1985; deliveries of 26 aircraft started 1987 and completed 1988; features include AN/APG-66 instead of AN/APG-68 radar, F110-GE-100 engine, deletion of M61 gun, AN/ALR-69 RWR, titanium in lower wing fittings instead of aluminium and cold working of lower wing skin holes to resist greater frequency of high *g*; wingtips fitted only for AIM-9 practice missiles and ACMI AIS pods, but normal tanks and stores on other stations. Four of 26 are two-seat **TF-16N**. F/TF-16Ns serve with Top Gun Fighter Weapons School (eight) and with VF-126 (six) at NAS Miramar, California, VF-45 (six) at NAS Key West, Florida, and VF-46 (six detached from VF-45) at NAS Oceana, Virginia.

F-16 Agile Falcon: Agile Falcon is proposed successor to F-16C/D with enlarged composites wings, lower weight, refined aerodynamics, updated avionics, and improved performance engine (IPE). Joint government/industry pre-FSD studies completed 1989 by US and four European user countries; no development funding allocated.

FS-X: F-16 derivative selected by Japan Defense Agency for its FS-X requirement 19 October 1987; details under Mitsubishi in Japan section.

F-16 Recce: Four existing European recce pods, including that for Tornado, demonstrated in flight on F-16 fighters with minimum changes; RNethAF reconnaissance F-16A(R) operational since 1983 with Orpheus pods. Specially designed General Dynamics ATARS pod extensively tested with near-real-time reconnaissance capability; ATARS semi-conformal centreline pod on an F-16B (75-0752) housed advanced electro-optical and IR sensors for day/night, all-speed, all-altitude operation and standoff capability; three multi-position sensors carried out work of seven fixed cameras; sensor positioning and real-time viewing in cockpit; in-flight imagery review/manipulation/frame selection followed by digital data linking of selected frames to ground stations. Operators on ground able to analyse, annotate and disseminate imagery and their reports electronically only minutes after images taken. US Air Force wants to replace RF-4C with 150 ATARS F-16s by mid-1990s; designation would be **RF-16**. Full-scale development planned for FY 1992, followed by retrofit of some Block 30 aircraft in 1995-97.

AFTI/F-16: Modified pre-series F-16A (75-0750) used for US Air Force Systems Command Advanced Fighter Technology Integration (AFTI); first flight 10 July 1982; digital flight control system and ventral foreplanes under intake allowed decoupled or six degrees of freedom manoeuvres and direct-force displacement (see 1986-87 *Jane's*); automated manoeuvre and attack system (AMAS) completed April 1987 (see 1987-88 *Jane's*). New programme began 1988 to improve communications between aircraft and troops during close air support; AFTI/F-16 CAS modifications include Rockwell Collins CP-1516 automatic target handoff system (ATHS) to forward air controllers, refinement of terrain management and display system and its Sandia software, head-steerable FLIR and pilot's helmet-mounted sight, AN/AAS-35 Pave Penny laser tracker, STARS digital terrain and display system, NVG-compatible lighting, Block 15 horizontal tail surfaces, Block 25 wing and Block 40 avionics. Trials programmes include automatic target designation and attack (1988), night navigation and map displays (1988-89), digital data link and two-aircraft operations (1989), autonomous attack (1989-91) and night attack (1989-92).

F-16XL: Two F-16XL prototypes, in flyable storage since 1985, leased from General Dynamics by NASA; first flight of single-seat No. 1, 9 March 1989; NASA modifying this aircraft at Dryden with wing glove having laser-perforated skin to smooth airflow over cranked arrow wing in supersonic flight, reducing drag and turbulence and saving fuel. Two-seat No. 2 with GE F110 engine expected at Edwards AFB in 1990. F-16XL described in 1985-86 *Jane's*.

F-16B-2: Second prototype F-16B (75-0752) converted to private-venture testbed of close air support and night navigation and attack systems; equipment includes F-16C/D HUD, helmet sight or GEC Avionics Cat's Eyes NVGs, Falcon Eye head-steered FLIR or LANTIRN nav/attack pod, digital terrain system (Terprom), and automatic target handoff system. Alternative nav/attack FLIR pods comprise GEC Avionics Atlantic and Martin Marietta Pathfinder (LANTIRN derivative). NVG compatible cockpit lighting. Equipment testing continues on AFTI testbed (which see).

Falcon Century: Programme to evaluate and monitor developments and maintain a master plan for F-16s into the next century.

The first Indonesian F-16A, TS-1605, handed over in December 1989

CUSTOMERS: See table. Total 3,530 production aircraft ordered by 1991, including planned USAF procurement of 2,204 and 71 assigned to Pakistan but embargoed; comprises 2,736 single-seat, 565 two-seat and 229 USAF Block 50/52 aircraft.

By August 1990 total of 2,146 delivered from Fort Worth and another 537 from assembly lines in Belgium, Netherlands and Turkey.

COSTS: $26.6 million, USAF unit cost, FY 1992 prices. $31.5 million for modification of one F-16D Block 30 as NF-16D, which see, placed December 1988.

DESIGN FEATURES (refers mainly to Block 40 F-16C/D): Cropped delta wings blended with fuselage, with highly swept vortex control strakes along fuselage forebody and joining wings to increase lift and improve directional stability at high angles of attack; wing section NACA 64A-204; leading-edge sweepback 40°; deep wingroots increase rigidity, save 113 kg (250 lb) structure weight and increase fuel volume; fixed-geometry engine intake; pilot's ejection seat inclined 30° rearwards; single-piece birdproof forward canopy section; two ventral fins below wing trailing-edge.

FLYING CONTROLS: Four-channel digital fly-by-wire (analog in earlier variants); pitch/lateral control by pivoting monobloc tailerons and wing-mounted flaperons (flaps/ailerons); maximum rate of flaperon movement 52°/s; automatic wing leading-edge manoeuvring flaps programmed for Mach number and angle of attack; flaperons and tailerons interchangeable left and right.

STRUCTURE: Wing, mainly of light alloy, has 11 spars, five ribs and single-piece upper and lower skins; attached to fuselage by machined aluminium fittings; leading-edge flaps are one-piece bonded aluminium honeycomb and driven by rotary actuators; fin is multi-spar, multi-rib with graphite epoxy skins; brake parachute or ECM housed in fairing aft of fin root; tailerons have graphite epoxy laminate skins, attached to corrugated aluminium pivot shaft and removable full-depth aluminium honeycomb leading-edge; ventral fins have aluminium honeycomb and skins; split speedbrakes in fuselage extensions inboard of tailerons open to 60°. Nose radome by Brunswick Corporation.

LANDING GEAR: Menasco hydraulically retractable type, nose unit retracting rearward and main units forward into fuselage. Nosewheel is located aft of intake to reduce the risk of foreign objects being thrown into the engine during ground operation, and rotates 90° during retraction to lie horizontally under engine air intake duct. Oleo-pneumatic struts in all units. Aircraft braking systems, mainwheels and brakes; Goodyear or Goodrich mainwheel tyres, size 27.75 × 8.75-14.5, pressure 14.48-15.17 bars (210-220 lb/sq in) at T-O weights less than 13,608 kg (30,000 lb). Steerable nosewheel with Goodyear, Goodrich or Dunlop tyre, size 18 × 5.7-8, pressure 20.68-21.37 bars (300-310 lb/sq in) at T-O weights less than 13,608 kg (30,000 lb). All but two main unit components interchangeable. Brake-by-wire system on main gear, with Aircraft Braking Systems anti-skid units. Runway arresting hook under rear fuselage. Landing/taxi lights on nose landing gear door.

POWER PLANT: One General Electric F110-GE-100, rated at 128.9 kN (28,984 lb st) with afterburning, or one Pratt & Whitney F100-PW-220 turbofan, rated at 105.7 kN (23,770 lb st) with afterburning, as alternative standard engines. Increased performance engines (IPE) for late 1991 incorporation are in 129.0 kN (29,000 lb st) class: F100-PW-229 in Block 52 aircraft; F110-GE-129 in Block 50. Over 70 per cent of FY 1984-91 production for USAF fitted with F110. Fixed geometry intake, with boundary layer splitter plate, beneath fuselage. F110-powered aircraft have enlarged intake. Israeli second-batch F-16D-30s have power plants locally modified by Bet-Shemesh Engines to F110-GE-110A with provision for up to 50 per cent emergency thrust at low level. Standard fuel contained in wing and five seal-bonded fuselage cells which function as two tanks; see under Weights and Loadings for quantities. Halon inerting system. In-flight refuelling receptacle in top of centre-fuselage, aft of cockpit. Auxiliary fuel can be carried in drop tanks: one 1,136 litres (300 US gallons; 250 Imp gallons) under fuselage; 1,402 litres (370 US gallons; 308 Imp gallons) under each wing. Optional 2,271 litre (600 US gallon; 500 Imp gallon) underwing tanks.

ACCOMMODATION: Pilot only in F-16C, in pressurised and air-conditioned cockpit. McDonnell Douglas ACES II zero/zero ejection seat. Bubble canopy made of polycarbonate advanced plastics material. Inside of USAF F-16C/D canopy (and most Belgian, Danish, Netherlands and Norwegian F-16A/Bs) coated with gold film to dissipate radar energy. In conjunction with radar-absorbing materials in air intake, this reduces frontal radar signature by 40 per cent. Windscreen and forward canopy are an integral unit without a forward bow frame, and are separated from the aft canopy by a simple support structure which serves also as the breakpoint where the forward section pivots upward and aft to give access to the cockpit. A redundant safety lock feature prevents canopy loss. Windscreen/canopy design provides 360° all-round view, 195° fore and aft, 40° down over the side, and 15° down over the nose. To enable the pilot to sustain high *g* forces, and for pilot comfort, the seat is inclined 30° aft and the heel line is raised. In normal operation the canopy is pivoted upward and aft by electrical power; the pilot is also able to unlatch the canopy manually and open it with a backup handcrank. Emergency jettison is provided by explosive unlatching devices and two rockets. A limited displacement, force sensing control stick is provided on the right hand console, with a suitable armrest, to provide precise control inputs during combat manoeuvres. The F-16D has two cockpits in tandem, equipped with all controls, displays, instruments, avionics and life support systems required to perform both training and combat missions. The layout of the F-16D second station is similar to the F-16C, and is fully systems-operational. A single-enclosure polycarbonate transparency, made in two pieces and spliced aft of the forward seat with a metal bow frame and lateral support member, provides outstanding view from both cockpits.

SYSTEMS: Regenerative 12kW environmental control system, with digital electronic control, uses engine bleed air for pressurisation and cooling of crew station and avionics compartments. Two separate and independent hydraulic systems supply power for operation of the primary flight control surfaces and the utility functions. System pressure (each) 207 bars (3,000 lb/sq in), rated at 161 litres (42.5 US gallons; 35.4 Imp gallons)/min. Bootstrap type reservoirs, rated at 5.79 bars (84 lb/sq in). Electrical system powered by engine driven Westinghouse 60kVA main generator and 10kVA standby generator (including ground annunciator panel for total electrical system fault reporting), with Sundstrand constant speed drive and powered by a Sundstrand accessory drive gearbox. 17Ah battery. Four dedicated, sealed cell batteries provide transient electrical power protection for the fly-by-wire flight control system. Application of the control configured vehicle (CCV) principle of relaxed static stability produces a significant reduction in trim drag, especially at high load factors and supersonic speeds. The aircraft centre of gravity is allowed to move aft, reducing both the tail drag and the change in drag on the wing due to changes in lift required to balance the download on the tail. Relaxed static stability imposes a requirement for a highly reliable, full-time-operating, stability augmentation system, including reliable electronic, electrical and hydraulic provisions. The signal paths in this quad-redundant system are used to control the aircraft, replacing the usual mechanical linkages. Pilot commands are processed by a four-channel Bendix/King digital flight control computer which generates the electrical signals for the servo actuators. An onboard Sundstrand/Solar jet fuel starter is provided for engine self-start capability. Simmonds fuel measuring system. Garrett emergency power unit automatically drives a 5kVA emergency generator and emergency pump to provide uninterrupted electrical and hydraulic power for control in the event of the engine or primary power systems becoming inoperative.

AVIONICS: Westinghouse AN/APG-68(V) pulse-Doppler range and angle track radar, with planar array in nose. Provides air-to-air modes for range-while-search, uplook search, velocity search, air combat, track-while-scan (ten targets), raid cluster resolution, single target track and (later) high PRF track to provide target illumination for AIM-7 missiles; and air-to-surface modes for ground mapping, Doppler beam sharpening, ground moving target, sea target, fixed target track, target freeze after pop-up, beacon, and air-to-ground ranging. Forward avionics bay, immediately forward of cockpit, contains radar, air data equipment, inertial navigation system, flight control computer, and combined altitude radar altimeter (CARA). Rear avionics bay contains ILS, Tacan and IFF, with space for future equipment. A Dalmo Victor AN/ALR-69 radar warning system (to be replaced in Block 50/52 by Loral AN/ALR-56M advanced RWR) is installed. Tracor AN/ALE-40(V)-4 chaff/flare dispensers (AN/ALE-47 in Block 50/52); provision for Westinghouse AN/ALQ-131 jamming pods and planned AN/ALQ-184. Communications equipment includes Magnavox AN/ARC-164 UHF Have Quick transceiver (AN/URC-126 Have Quick IIA in Block 50/52); provisions for a Magnavox KY-58 secure voice system; Collins AN/ARC-186 VHF AM/FM transceiver (AN/ARC-205 Have Cync Group A in Block 50/52); government furnished AN/AIC-18/25 intercom; and SCI advanced interference blanker. Honeywell central air

data computer. Litton LN-39 standard inertial navigation system (ring laser Litton LN-93 or Honeywell H-523 in Block 50/52 and current FMS F-16A/B); Gould AN/APN-232 radar altimeter; Collins AN/ARN-108 ILS; Collins AN/ARN-118 Tacan; Teledyne Electronics AN/APX-101 IFF transponder with a government furnished IFF control; government furnished National Security Agency KIT-1A/TSEC cryptographic equipment; Lear Astronics stick force sensors; GEC Avionics wide-angle holographic electronic head-up display with raster video capability (for LANTIRN) and integrated keyboard; Rockwell GPS/Navstar; General Dynamics enhanced stores management computer; Teledyne Systems general avionics computer; Honeywell multi-function displays; data entry/cockpit interface and dedicated fault display by Litton Canada and General Dynamics, Fort Worth; Fairchild data transfer set; and Astronautics cockpit/TV set. Cockpit and core avionics integrated on two MIL-STD-1553B multiplex buses. Optional equipment includes Collins VIR-130 VOR/ILS and ARC-190 HF radio. Essential structure and wiring provisions are built into the airframe to allow for easy incorporation of future avionics systems under development for the F-16 by the US Air Force. Israeli Air Force F-16s have been extensively modified with Israeli designed and manufactured equipment, as well as optional US equipment, to tailor them to the IAF defence role. This includes Elisra SPS 3000 self-protection jamming equipment in enlarged spines of F-16D-30s and Elta EL/L-8240 ECM in third batch F-16C/Ds, replacing Rapport. Fin-root fairing houses Loral Rapport ECM in Israeli F-16As; Irvin 7.01 m (23 ft 0 in) diameter braking parachute fitted in Greek, Indonesian, Netherlands (retrofit), Norwegian, Turkish and Venezuelan F-16s; Belgian F-16s have Dassault Electronique Carapace ECM; Pakistan F-16s carry Thomson-CSF Atlis laser designator pods. Turkish aircraft to share 60 LANTIRN pods. Historical details in 1986-87 and earlier *Jane's*.

ARMAMENT: General Electric M61A1 20 mm multi-barrel cannon in the port side wing/body fairing, equipped with a General Electric ammunition handling system and an enhanced envelope gunsight (part of the head-up display system) and 511 rounds of ammunition. There is a mounting for an air-to-air missile at each wingtip, one underfuselage centreline hardpoint, and six underwing hardpoints for additional stores. For manoeuvring flight at 5.5g the underfuselage station is stressed for a load of up to 1,000 kg (2,200 lb), the two inboard underwing stations for 2,041 kg (4,500 lb) each, the two centre underwing stations for 1,587 kg (3,500 lb) each, the two

outboard underwing stations for 318 kg (700 lb) each, and the two wingtip stations for 193 kg (425 lb) each. For manoeuvring flight at 9g the underfuselage station is stressed for a load of up to 544 kg (1,200 lb), the two inboard underwing stations for 1,134 kg (2,500 lb) each, the two centre underwing stations for 907 kg (2,000 lb) each, the two outboard underwing stations for 204 kg (450 lb) each, and the two wingtip stations for 193 kg (425 lb) each. There are mounting provisions on each side of the inlet shoulder for the specific carriage of sensor pods (electro-optical, FLIR, etc); each of these stations is stressed for 408 kg (900 lb) at 5.5g, and 250 kg (550 lb) at 9g. Typical stores loads can include two wingtip mounted AIM-9L/M/P Sidewinders, with up to four more on the outer underwing stations on Israeli F-16s from early 1991; centreline GPU-5/A 30 mm cannon; drop tanks on the inboard underwing and underfuselage stations; a Martin Marietta Pave Penny laser spot tracker pod along the starboard side of the nacelle; and bombs, air-to-surface missiles or flare pods on the four inner underwing stations. Stores can be launched from Aircraft Hydro-Forming MAU-12C/A bomb ejector racks, Hughes LAU-88 launchers, or Orgen triple or multiple ejector racks. Non-jettisonable centreline GPU-5/A 30 mm gun pods on dedicated USAF ground-attack F-16As. Weapons launched successfully from F-16s, in addition to Sidewinders and AMRAAM, include radar guided Sparrow and Sky Flash air-to-air missiles, French Magic 2 infra-red homing air-to-air missiles, AGM-65A/B/D/G Maverick air-to-surface missiles, HARM and Shrike anti-radiation missiles, Harpoon anti-ship missiles, and, in Royal Norwegian Air Force service, the Penguin Mk 3 anti-ship missile. F-16s can be equipped with a variety of reconnaissance pods (eg, Orpheus on RNethAF aircraft) and the Thomson-CSF Atlis laser designator pod, as carried by those of Pakistan Air Force.

DIMENSIONS, EXTERNAL (F-16C, D):

Wing span: over missile launchers	9.45 m (31 ft 0 in)
over missiles	10.00 m (32 ft 9¾ in)
Wing aspect ratio	3.0
Length overall	15.03 m (49 ft 4 in)
Height overall	5.09 m (16 ft 8½ in)
Tailplane span	5.58 m (18 ft 3¾ in)
Wheel track	2.36 m (7 ft 9 in)
Wheelbase	4.00 m (13 ft 1½ in)

AREAS (F-16C, D):

Wings, gross	27.87 m² (300.0 sq ft)
Flaperons (total)	2.91 m² (31.32 sq ft)

F-16 CUSTOMERS

Operator	Total	Single-seat	Quantity	Two-seat	Quantity	Power plant	First delivery	Squadrons (or base)
Bahrain	12	F-16C-40	8	F-16D-40	4	F110	March 1990	(Sheikh Isa)
Belgium	160[1]	F-16A-15	96	F-16B-15	20	F100	January 1979	23, 31, 349, 350
		F-16A-15OCU	40	F-16B-15OCU	4	F100	January 1988	1, 2
Denmark	70[1]	F-16A-15	46	F-16B-15	12	F100	January 1980	723, 727, 730
		F-16A-15OCU	8	F-16B-15OCU	4	F100	December 1987	726
Egypt[8]	128	F-16A-15	34	F-16B-15	7[2]	F100	March 1982	72, 74
		F-16C-32	36	F-16D-32	4	F100	August 1986	(Beni Sueif)
		F-16C-40	40	F-16D-40	7	F110	1991	
Greece	40	F-16C-42	34	F-16D-42	6	F110	November 1988	330, 346
Indonesia	12	F-16A-15OCU	8	F-16B-15OCU	4	F100	December 1989	3
Israel	210	F-16A-15	67	F-16B-15	8	F100	January 1980	101, plus two
		F-16C-30	51	F-16D-30	24	F110	December 1986	(Hatzor, Ramat David)
		F-16C-40	30	F-16D-40	30	F110	1991	
Korea, South[9]	40	F-16C-32	30	F-16D-32	10	F100	March 1986	161, 162
Netherlands	213[3]	F-16A-15	131	F-16B-15	31	F100	June 1979	306, 311, 312, 314, 316, 322, 323
		F-16A-15OCU	46	F-16B-15OCU	5	F100	February 1988	313, 315
Norway	74[3]	F-16A-15	60	F-16B-15	14	F100	January 1980	331, 332, 334, 338
Pakistan	111	F-16A-15	28	F-16B-15	12	F100	January 1983	9, 11, 14
		F-16A-15OCU	60	F-16B-15OCU	11	F100	1992	Embargoed
Portugal	20	F-16A-15OCU	17	F-16B-15OCU	3	F100	1993	201
Singapore	8	F-16A-15OCU	4	F-16B-15OCU	4	F100	February 1988	140
Thailand	18	F-16A-15OCU	12	F-16B-15OCU	6	F100	June 1988	103
Turkey	160[4]	F-16C-30	35	F-16D-30	9	F110	May 1987	141, 142
		F-16C-40	101	F-16D-40	15	F110	July 1990	161, 162 plus four
USAF	786	F-16A-15	665[5]	F-16B-15	121[6]	F100	August 1978	See note A
	1,189	F-16C[7]	1,009	F-16D[7]	180	both	July 1984	See note B
	229	F-16C-50/52		F-16D-50/52			October 1991	See note C
US Navy	26	F-16N-30	22	TF-16N-30	4	F110	June 1987	43, 45, 126, FWS
Venezuela	24	F-16A-15	18	F-16B-15	6	F100	September 1983	161, 162
TOTAL	3,530							

NOTES:

[1] Built by SABCA (Belgium)
[2] One built by Fokker (Netherlands)
[3] Built by Fokker
[4] 134 F-16Cs and 18 F-16Ds built by TAI (Turkey)
[5] Two built by Fokker
[6] Three built by SABCA
[7] 218 Block 25; 509 Blocks 30/32; 462 Block 40/42
[8] Fourth batch authorised February 1991: 46 Block 50 F-16C/Ds with F110-GE-129 power plants; delivery 1994-96 from original Turkish production
[9] Commitment in March 1991 to 140 further F-16C/Ds: 12 built in USA, 36 CKD kits and 72 produced locally by Samsung Aerospace (which see)

NOTE A: Currently operated by 31 and 58 TTWs; 89, 93, 465 and 466 squadrons of AFRES; 111, 114, 119, 134, 136, 159, 171, 178, 179 and 186 interceptor squadrons, ANG; 107, 121, 138, 148, 157, 160, 170, 182, 184 and 184 tactical fighter squadrons, ANG (141 and 169 forming 1991); Thunderbirds team.

NOTE B: Currently operated by 8, 50, 51, 52, 56, 86, 347, 363, 388 and 401 wings; 302 and 457 squadrons, AFRES; 127 and 161 squadrons, ANG.

NOTE C: FY 1991-93 multi-year procurement intended as 150 per annum (total 450). Plans announced January 1991 call for revised figures of 108, 48 and 24 (total 180) to

terminate USAF F-16 purchases. First 49 Block 50 aircraft funded in FY 1990.

REMARKS: Blocks 1 and 5 retrofitted to Block 10 standard 1982-84; Blocks 10 and 15 retrofitted to Block 15OCU from 1987. New build F-16As are Block 15OCU from November 1987.

Omitted are two YF-16s and eight pre-production aircraft (six F-16A; two F-16B).

Leading-edge flaps (total)	3.41 m² (36.72 sq ft)
Vertical tail surfaces (total)	5.09 m² (54.75 sq ft)
Rudder	1.08 m² (11.65 sq ft)
Horizontal tail surfaces (total)	5.92 m² (63.70 sq ft)

WEIGHTS AND LOADINGS:
Weight empty:

F-16C: F100-PW-220	8,273 kg (18,238 lb)
F110-GE-100	8,627 kg (19,020 lb)
F-16D: F100-PW-220	8,494 kg (18,726 lb)
F110-GE-100	8,853 kg (19,517 lb)
Max internal fuel: F-16C	3,104 kg (6,846 lb)
F-16D	2,567 kg (5,659 lb)
Max external fuel (both)	3,066 kg (6,760 lb)
Max external load (both)	5,443 kg (12,000 lb)
Typical combat weight:	
F-16C (F110)	10,780 kg (23,765 lb)

Max T-O weight:
air-to-air, no external tanks:

F-16C (F110)	12,331 kg (27,185 lb)
with external load:	
F-16C Block 30/32	17,010 kg (37,500 lb)
F-16C Block 40/42	19,187 kg (42,300 lb)

Wing loading:
at 12,927 kg (28,500 lb) AUW
464 kg/m² (95.0 lb/sq ft)
at 19,187 kg (42,300 lb) AUW
688 kg/m² (141.0 lb/sq ft)

Thrust/weight ratio (clean)	1.1 to 1

PERFORMANCE:
Max level speed at 12,200 m (40,000 ft)
above Mach 2.0
Service ceiling   more than 15,240 m (50,000 ft)
Radius of action:
F-16C Block 40, two 907 kg (2,000 lb) bombs, two

Sidewinders, 3,940 litres (1,040 US gallons; 867 Imp gallons) external fuel, tanks dropped when empty, hi-lo-lo-hi   740 nm (1,371 km; 852 miles)
F-16C Block 40, four 907 kg (2,000 lb) bombs, two Sidewinders, 1,136 litres (300 US gallons; 250 Imp gallons) external fuel, tanks retained, hi-lo-lo-hi
340 nm (630 km; 392 miles)
F-16C Block 40, two Sparrows and two Sidewinders, 3,940 litres (1,040 US gallons; 867 Imp gallons) external fuel, 2 h 10 min CAP
200 nm (371 km; 230 miles)
F-16C Block 40, as immediately above, point intercept
710 nm (1,315 km; 818 miles)
Ferry range, with drop tanks
more than 2,100 nm (3,890 km; 2,415 miles)
Max symmetrical design g limit with full internal fuel
+9

GENERAL DYNAMICS/ MCDONNELL DOUGLAS

PRINCIPAL PROGRAMME OFFICE: General Dynamics Corporation, Fort Worth Division, PO Box 748, Fort Worth, Texas 76101
Telephone: 1 (817) 777 2000
US Secretary of State for Defense announced cancellation of ATA programme 7 January 1991; final details of the programme are given below. Replacement for A-6 now covered by AX (Attack X) programme, described under US Navy heading in this section.

GENERAL DYNAMICS/MCDONNELL DOUGLAS ATA
US Navy designation: A-12A Avenger II

TYPE: Two-seat low-observable carrier-borne attack aircraft.
PROGRAMME: General Dynamics and McDonnell Douglas selected to develop A-12A Advanced Tactical Aircraft (ATA), as Grumman A-6E Intruder replacement, 23 December 1987 (contract awarded 13 January 1988); 11 month definition study for US Air Force version (leading possibly to F-111 replacement) ordered November 1988; first flight of prototype re-scheduled for December 1991 but since cancelled; US Navy required 450 ATAs by 2005; January 1989 plan called for 106 aircraft up to FY 1994; GD and McDonnell Douglas were expected to compete year by year after that date; total requirement of 858 cut to 620 before total cancellation.
VARIANTS: **A-12A Avenger II:** US Navy carrier-borne attack version. Now cancelled.
USAF A-12: Proposed as land-based version to supersede F-111. Now cancelled.
CUSTOMERS: US Navy; eight full-scale development aircraft (Bu 164526-533) funded FY 1989; six originally anticipated in first production lot FY 1990.
COSTS: $4.379 billion (ceiling $4.78 billion) allocated for development December 1987; $7.9 million contract for 11 month concept definition study of US Air Force version awarded November 1988; in January 1989, first 106 A-12As were to cost $10.2 billion. Programme 18 months late and $2.7 billion over estimates by January 1991. Projected programme cost over 620 aircraft: was $55 billion.

Artist's impression of General Dynamics/McDonnell Douglas A-12A Avenger II Advanced Tactical Aircraft

DESIGN FEATURES: A-12A had air-to-air and air-to-surface radar modes and weapons; two-man crew; two 60-65 kN (13,500-14,600 lb st) class General Electric F412-400 non-afterburning engines (F404 derivatives); subsonic pure delta planform with 48° sweep and no fins; integrated avionics and electronic warfare systems; engine intakes, weapons bay and numerous access panels in lower surface.
Subcontractors included, in alphabetical order, AiResearch and Ball Aerospace and Loral Randtron Systems (door mechanical drive group), Bendix (main landing gear, wheels and carbon brakes), Garrett (air data computer), Garrett Auxiliary Power Division (airframe-mounted accessory drive system), General Electric Aircraft Electronics Division (missile warning system), Harris (multi-function antenna system), Honeywell (digital flight control system), Honeywell/Litton (integrated inertial sensor system), Litton (inertial navigation and AN/ALD-11 electronic surveillance measures systems), Martin Marietta (navigational FLIR), Parker Bertea Aerospace (in-flight refuelling

probe), Pilkington PLC's Swedlow Inc subsidiary (cockpit transparencies), SCI Technology Inc (amplifier control intercommunications set), Sundstrand Turbomach Division (auxiliary power unit), Teledyne Ryan Electronics (radar altimeter), and Westinghouse (AN/APQ-183 multi-function radar and combined function FLIR).
FLYING CONTROLS: Trailing-edge flaperons doubled as drag-rudders in absence of vertical surfaces; pitch-trim 'beaver tail' as on B-2; slats or flaps on leading-edge of outboard (folding) wing panels.
STRUCTURE: Most structural loads carried on two spars; extensive use of composites materials.
DIMENSIONS, EXTERNAL (approx):

Wing span	20.19 m (66 ft 3 in)
Width, wings folded	9.83 m (32 ft 3 in)
Length overall	10.85 m (35 ft 7 in)

WEIGHTS AND LOADINGS:

Internal weapon load (24 Mk 82 bombs and four AIM-120 AMRAAM)	approx 6,123 kg (13,500 lb)
Design max T-O weight	27,000 kg (59,525 lb)

GLOBAL
GLOBAL HELICOPTER TECHNOLOGY INC
8900 Trinity Boulevard, Fort Worth, Texas 76053
Telephone: 1 (817) 284 1212
Fax: 1 (817) 284 8846
PRESIDENT: Clem Bailey
VICE-PRESIDENT, MARKETING: Mike Robbins
Company specialises in modifications to Bell helicopters, as recorded under Bell Helicopter Textron in Canadian section. Development of Cardoen CB 206L-III, in which Global was involved, stopped by FAA and US Customs.

GLOBAL HELICOPTER NIGHTRANGER
Armed version of 206L-3 LongRanger offered as conversion of new or remanufactured airframes; includes FLIR Systems FLIR 2000 infra-red system, Crouzet T100 sight, outrigger stores carriers from Bell Model 406 CS Combat Scout, armoured seats for pilot and co-pilot, cabin-mounted machine gun pintles with gunner's swivelling seats, sliding cabin doors, night vision goggle-compatible cockpit lighting; Saab-Emerson HeliTOW missile system, and SFENA mini-stab also offered. Armament includes two 7.62 mm machine guns with 2,000 rounds or two seven-tube or two 19-tube 2.75 in rocket pods. NightRanger equipped empty weight 1,134 kg (2,500 lb) and useful load 816 kg (1,800 lb). Weapons mounting system acceptable on any Bell 206/OH-58 airframe. Performance enhancement package developed to accommodate increased weight of armament: increased transmission T-O rating 236.4-261 kW (317-350 shp); mast torque measuring system; structural modifications.

Global NightRanger with Universal Pylon System, GIAT 20 mm gun, FN M240-E1 machine-gun, Global sliding door, and FLIR 2000 IR system

GLOBAL HELICOPTER UH-1HP
High Performance conversion of Bell UH-1H powered by 1,342 kW (1,800 shp) Textron Lycoming T53-L-703 with Bell Model 212 drive train, transmission upgraded to 962 kW (1,290 shp) and Frahm vibration absorber. Max T-O weight 5,080 kg (11,200 lb); useful load 2,540 kg (5,600 lb).

Conversion kit, developed with Southern Aero Corporation, also to upgrade T53-L-13 engines to L-703 standard.

TRIDAIR MODEL 206L-3ST GEMINI ST
Global Helicopter is participating with Tridair and Soloy Corporation (which see in this section) in development of this twin-engined version of the Bell Model 206L-3 LongRanger, which made its first flight on 16 January 1991 and was expected to be certificated in December 1991.

GRUMMAN
GRUMMAN CORPORATION
1111 Stewart Avenue, Bethpage, New York 11714-3580
Telephone: 1 (516) 575 0574
Telex: 961430
CHAIRMAN, PRESIDENT AND CHIEF EXECUTIVE OFFICER:
  Renso L. Caporali
SENIOR VICE-PRESIDENT: Martin Dandridge
VICE-PRESIDENT, MARKETING: David L. Walsh
VICE-PRESIDENT, PUBLIC AFFAIRS: Weyman B. Jones
  Grumman Aircraft Engineering Corporation incorporated 6 December 1929; Grumman Corporation formed as

small holding company 1969 for Grumman Aerospace Corporation, Grumman Allied Industries Inc and Grumman Data Systems Corporation. Ten operating divisions created February 1985 (see 1990-91 and earlier editions), followed by further re-organisations in 1987-88. Corporate structure further consolidated in early 1991 into four operating groups:
Aircraft Group, including former Aircraft Systems, Aerostructures and St Augustine divisions (see following entry).
Systems Group, including former Melbourne Systems, Electronics Systems, Space Systems, and Space Station

Program Support divisions (PRESIDENT: Albert Verderosa).
Data Systems and Services Group, including former Technical Services, Data Systems, and Systems Support divisions (PRESIDENT: Gerald Sandler).
Allied Group, including former Allied (Vehicles and Marine) division (PRESIDENT: Leonard Rothenberg).
  Systems Group is prime contractor and installs systems in E-8A Joint STARS modified Boeing 707 (see under Boeing Aerospace & Electronics in this section). A corporate services division covers legal, purchasing, contracts and other services common to all divisions.

GRUMMAN AIRCRAFT GROUP
PRESIDENT: Peter B. Oram
  Current products include versions of A-6 Intruder, EA-6B Prowler, E-2C Hawkeye and F-14 Tomcat for US Navy. Produced two X-29A forward-swept wing prototypes (1990-91 and earlier *Jane's*) for Defense Advanced Research Projects Agency (DARPA). Contracted in February 1984 to produce 270 shipsets of Tay turbofan nacelles and thrust reversers for Gulfstream IV and Fokker 100; design and manufacture of complete tail section of V-22 Osprey (see under Bell/Boeing) ordered August 1984; initial $28 million order for two sets of composites ailerons, elevators and rudders for McDonnell Douglas C-17A placed April 1987; responsible for engineering and logistic support for A-10 Thunderbolt II since October 1987. Has $155.8 million current contract to upgrade radar and communications jammers in EF-111A Raven Jamming aircraft.

GRUMMAN HAWKEYE
US Navy designations: E-2C and TE-2C
TYPE: Ship-borne and land-based airborne early warning and control aircraft.
PROGRAMME: First flight of first of three prototypes 21 October 1960; total 59 production E-2As, all updated to E-2B by end 1971 apart from two TE-2A trainers and two converted to E-2C prototypes (see earlier *Jane's*); first flight of E-2C prototype 20 January 1971; production started mid-1971; first flight production aircraft 23 September 1972; total 164 ordered, of which 130 delivered at start of 1990; planned production six per year until early 1990s; AN/APS-139 radar replaced AN/APS-125 and AN/APS-138 in new-built E-2Cs from 1989; all previously delivered USN aircraft being retrofitted.
  Evaluation of Grumman/General Electric AN/APS-145 began 1986; this radar tracks more targets at longer ranges, has improved jamming resistance and sharper overland detection; start of production expected 1991. Work continues on detection and processing capabilities, new IFF, and wing strengthening programme.
  E-2C entered service with VAW-123 at NAS Norfolk, Virginia, November 1973 and went to sea on board USS *Saratoga* late 1974; E-2C issued to 18 other squadrons, including two of Naval Reserve; two TE-2C in service, including 158639 assigned to JTIDS development. Squadrons are VAW-110 and 112 to 117 at Miramar, California, with VAW-88 of Reserves; VAW-120 to 127 and 132 with VAW-78 of Reserves at Norfolk, Virginia. VAW-110 and VAW-120 are training units. Also used by Coast Guard Air Wing One (CGAW-1) at St Augustine, Florida.
VARIANTS: **E-2B:** Withdrawn from USN service. See Taiwan under Customers.
  E-2C: Current service and production version (as detailed).
  TE-2C: Training model, based on E-2C.
  E-2T: E-2B conversion for Taiwan (see Customers).
CUSTOMERS: US Navy orders for E-2C totalled 147 by FY 1991, of which approx 120 delivered. US Navy transferred four to US Coast Guard and two (since returned) to US Customs Service for anti-narcotics operations. Exports to Israel (four delivered 1981), Japan (received four in 1982 and four in 1984, and ordered three in FY 1989 and two in FY 1990), Egypt (accepted five, beginning October 1987; ordered sixth in 1989), and Singapore (received four with AN/APS-138 in 1987). Singapore plans two more E-2Cs. Japan upgrading radars to AN/APS-145, 1991. Taiwan to buy six ex-USN E-2Bs for **E-2T** conversion with AN/APS-138 radar and ESM/IFF improvements; first conversion by Grumman, remainder by AIDC at Taichung.
COSTS: $60.5 million, flyaway, Japan 1990.
DESIGN FEATURES: Details here apply to E-2C. Hawkeye can cover naval task force in all weathers flying at 9,150 m (30,000 ft) and can detect and assess approaching aircraft at up to 260 nm (480 km; 300 miles); AN/APS-139 has total radiation aperture control antenna (TRAC-A) to

Grumman E-2C Hawkeye early warning and control aircraft of the US Navy *(Paul Jackson)*

reduce sidelobes to offset jamming; radar sweeps three million cubic mile envelope and simultaneously monitors surface ships; long range, automatic target track initiation and high-speed processing enable each E-2C to track more than 2,000 targets simultaneously and automatically, and control more than 40 intercepts; Randtron Systems AN/APA-171 antenna housed in 7.32 m (24 ft) diameter radome, rotating at 6 rpm above rear fuselage; Yagi radar arrays in rotodome provide radar sum and difference signals and IFF.
  AN/APS-139 and Allison T56-427 engines form Group 1 update; first operational aircraft (163538) delivered to VAW-112 on 8 August 1989; AN/APS-139 can detect cruise missiles at ranges over 145 nm (269 km; 167 miles); also monitors ships and land vehicles; radar coverage extended by AN/ALR-73 passive detection system (PDS), detecting electronic emitters at twice radar detection range; more detailed description in 1979-80 *Jane's*.
  Conventional airframe with nose-tow catapult attachment, arrester hook and tail bumper; parts of tail made of composites to reduce radar reflection; wings fold hydraulically on skewed hinges to lie parallel to fuselage; wing incidence 4° at root, 1° at tip; pneumatic boot de-icing on wings, tailplane and fins.
FLYING CONTROLS: Fully powered with artificial feel; tailplane has 11° dihedral; four fins and three double-hinged rudders; long-span ailerons droop automatically when hydraulically operated Fowler flaps are extended; autopilot provides autostabilisation or full flight control.

STRUCTURE: Wing centre-section has three beams, ribs and machined skins; hinged leading-edge provides access to flying and engine controls. Fuselage structure conventional light metal. Composites used in parts of tail.
LANDING GEAR: Hydraulically retractable tricycle type. Pneumatic emergency extension. Steerable nosewheel unit retracts rearward. Mainwheels retract forward, and rotate to lie flat in bottom of nacelles. Twin wheels on nose unit only. Oleo-pneumatic shock absorbers. Mainwheel tyres size 36 × 11 Type VII 24-ply, pressure 17.9 bars (260 lb/sq in) on ship, 14.5 bars (210 lb/sq in) ashore. Hydraulic brakes. Hydraulically operated retractable tailskid. A-frame arrester hook under tail.
POWER PLANT: Two 3,661 kW (4,910 ehp) Allison T56-A-427 turboprops, driving Hamilton Standard type 54460-1 four-blade fully feathering reversible-pitch constant-speed propellers. These have foam filled blades which have a steel spar and glassfibre shell. Spinners and blades incorporate electric anti-icing. Production E-2Cs delivered from 1989 onwards have T56-A-427 engines which provide a two per cent power increase and lower fuel consumption.
ACCOMMODATION: Normal crew of five on flight deck and in ATDS compartment in main cabin, consisting of pilot, co-pilot, combat information centre officer, air control officer and radar operator. Downward hinged door, with built-in steps, on port side of centre-fuselage.
AVIONICS: Randtron AN/APA-171 rotodome (radar and IFF antennae), General Electric AN/APS-139 advanced radar processing system (ARPS) with overland/overwater

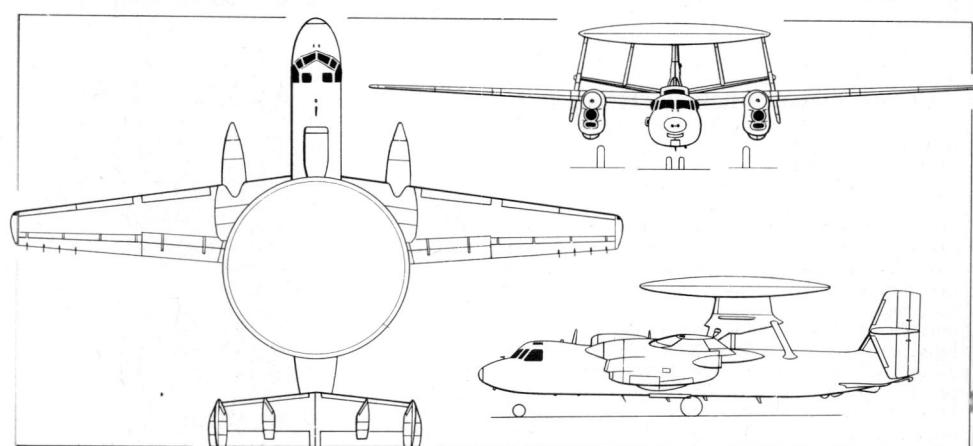

Grumman E-2C Hawkeye twin-turboprop airborne early warning and control aircraft *(Pilot Press)*

detection capability (with AN/APS-145 scheduled for introduction in 1991 and eventual retrofit in all E-2Cs), RT-988/A IFF interrogator with Hazeltine OL-76/AP IFF detector processor, Litton AN/ALR-73 passive detection system, Hazeltine AN/APA-172 control indicator group, Litton OL-77/ASQ computer programmer (L-304), AN/ARC-158 UHF data link, AN/ARQ-34 HF data link, ASM-440 in-flight performance monitor, Collins AN/ARC-51A UHF com, AN/AIC-14A intercom, Litton AN/ASN-92 (LN-15C) CAINS carrier aircraft inertial navigation system, GEC Avionics standard central air data computer, AN/APN-153 (V) Doppler, AN/ASN-50 heading and attitude reference system, AN/ARN-52 (V) Tacan, Collins AN/ARA-50 UHF ADF, AN/ASW-25B ACLS and Honeywell AN/APN-171 (V) radar altimeter.

DIMENSIONS, EXTERNAL:

Wing span	24.56 m (80 ft 7 in)
Wing chord: at root	3.96 m (13 ft 0 in)
at tip	1.32 m (4 ft 4 in)
Wing aspect ratio	9.3
Width, wings folded	8.94 m (29 ft 4 in)
Length overall	17.54 m (57 ft 6¾ in)
Height overall	5.58 m (18 ft 3¾ in)
Diameter of rotodome	7.32 m (24 ft 0 in)
Tailplane span	7.99 m (26 ft 2½ in)
Wheel track	5.93 m (19 ft 5¾ in)
Wheelbase	7.06 m (23 ft 2 in)
Propeller diameter	4.11 m (13 ft 6 in)

AREAS:

Wings, gross	65.03 m² (700.0 sq ft)
Ailerons (total)	5.76 m² (62.0 sq ft)
Trailing-edge flaps (total)	11.03 m² (118.75 sq ft)
Fins, incl rudders and tabs:	
outboard (total)	10.25 m² (110.36 sq ft)
inboard (total)	4.76 m² (51.26 sq ft)
Tailplane	11.62 m² (125.07 sq ft)
Elevators (total)	3.72 m² (40.06 sq ft)

WEIGHTS AND LOADINGS:

Weight empty	17,265 kg (38,063 lb)
Max fuel (internal, usable)	5624 kg (12,400 lb)
Max T-O weight	23,556 kg (51,933 lb)
Max wing loading	362.2 kg/m² (74.19 lb/sq ft)
Max power loading	3.22 kg/kW (5.29 lb/shp)

PERFORMANCE (at max T-O weight):

Max level speed	323 knots (598 km/h; 372 mph)
Max cruising speed	311 knots (576 km/h; 358 mph)
Cruising speed (ferry)	268 knots (496 km/h; 308 mph)
Approach speed	103 knots (191 km/h; 119 mph)
Stalling speed (landing configuration)	
	74 knots (138 km/h; 86 mph)
Service ceiling	9,390 m (30,800 ft)
Min T-O run	610 m (2,000 ft)
T-O to 15 m (50 ft)	793 m (2,600 ft)
Min landing run	439 m (1,440 ft)
Ferry range	1,394 nm (2,583 km; 1,605 miles)
Time on station, 175 nm (320 km; 200 miles) from base	
	3-4 h
Endurance with max fuel	6 h 6 min

GRUMMAN A-6E INTRUDER

US Navy designations: A-6E and KA-6D

TYPE: Carrier-based all-weather attack aircraft, with tanker variant.

PROGRAMME: More than 660 A-6s built; about 350 still in service with US Navy and Marine squadrons and three readiness training squadrons.

VARIANTS: **A-6A/B/C:** Only those converted to other variants still in service; described in 1978-79 Jane's.

EA-6B Prowler: Advanced electronics development of EA-6A; described separately.

KA-6D: Dedicated tanker; 78 converted from A-6A and seven from A-6E (see 1980-81 Jane's); latest configuration has no weapon capability and can carry five 1,514 litre (400 US gallon; 333 Imp gallon) drop tanks; fitted as probe and drogue receiver as well as tanker; drogue retracts into tunnel under rear fuselage.

A-6E Intruder: Began as advanced conversion of A-6A (240 converted) with multi-mode radar and IBM computer first fitted to EA-6B; first flight 10 November 1970; first deployed September 1972; approved for service November 1972. Total 202 new-build A-6Es funded by end FY 1988, of which final 21 have composites wings (see below).

A-6E/TRAM: Current production version equipped with Target Recognition Attack Multi-Sensor; first flight October 1974; delivery of fully equipped aircraft began 14 December 1978; first carrier deployment completed May 1980; all older A-6Es converted to TRAM by 1988; eight Grumman TC-4C (modified Gulfstream I) used for training.

US Navy A-6E squadrons are VA-52, 95, 115, 128 (training), 145, 165, 195, 196 at Whidbey Island, Washington, with two rotated to Atsugi, Japan; VA-34, 35, 36, 42 (training), 55, 65, 75, 85, and 176 at Oceana, Virginia; Reserves VA-205 at Atlanta, Georgia. Marine squadrons are VMA(AW)-224, 242, 332 and 533 at Cherry Point, North Carolina, including one rotated to Atsugi, Japan.

Grumman A-6E/TRAM Intruder of US Marine Corps Squadron VMA (AW)-224 (*Ivo Sturzenegger*)

A-6E Harpoon: 50 A-6Es each fitted to carry four McDonnell Douglas Harpoon anti-ship missiles; deployment began 1981; all subsequent new-build and converted aircraft also equipped.

Re-winged A-6E: Last metal-winged A-6E delivered September 1988; final 21 production aircraft being fitted with composites wings. Boeing Military Airplanes won competition to produce graphite/epoxy wing for A-6E (new build and retrofit) to overcome fatigue problems in service and give 8,800 hour service life; first flight 3 April 1989. Naval trials completed June 1990. Initial contract for 179 wing sets plus options for 327; up to 102 existing A-6Es were to be retrofitted but budget restrictions threatened cutback. Following A-12 cancellation in January 1991, re-winging and limited electrical modifications authorised for 30 A-6Es in both FYs 1992 and 1993 at total cost of $860 million.

A-6E SWIP: Systems Weapon Integration Program partially applied to last 21 production aircraft (see above). Features of Block 1 system, currently being applied also to earlier aircraft, include provision for AGM-88 HARM, AGM-84 Harpoon and AGM-65 Maverick, uprated P&W J52-P-408/409 turbojets, digital cockpit displays and controls, advanced multi-mode attack radar, GEC Avionics wide-angle HUD and night attack navigation system (NANS), provision for AMRAAM missile, additional chaff/flare and air-to-air weapons stations and various airframe improvements. SWIP Block 1A covers GPS, installation of GPS software in AN/ASN-139 INS, GEC Avionics standard central air data computer on MIL-STD-1553B digital databus, upgrade of Tacan from AN/ARN-84 to AN/ARN-118, HUD, wing fillet modifications containing antennae for Sanders AN/ALQ-126 ECM, and IDAP (Integrated Defence Avionics Program) combining chaff dispensers and radar warning receiver. Fillet trials A-6 flew Spring 1991; two avionics trials aircraft to fly September 1992 and May 1993; upgrade of 110 A-6s to follow.

A-6F and A-6G: Abandoned Intruder developments (see 1990-91 Jane's). Five pre-series A-6Fs employed for trials.

CUSTOMERS: US Navy and Marine Corps.

COSTS: $30.9 million (1987) system unit cost.

DESIGN FEATURES: Split fuel tanks to limit battle damage; better lightning and fire protection and easier repair and maintenance than earlier models. Wing sweepback 25° at quarter-chord; outer wing panels fold upward more than 90° for stowage; TRAM ball under nose, aft of radome.

FLYING CONTROLS: Hydraulic fully powered controls; slab tailplane; lateral control spoilers ahead of near-full span Fowler flaperons; split surface airbrakes in trailing-edge

outboard of flaperons; sharp-edged leading-edge stall strip next to fuselage with fixed droop section outboard, then long-span leading-edge slats. Fences near wingroot and near tip.

STRUCTURE: Conventional all-metal; graphite/epoxy wing being retrofitted; aluminium alloy control surfaces and titanium high strength fittings, such as wing-fold.

LANDING GEAR: Hydraulically retractable tricycle type. Twin-wheel nose unit retracts rearward. Single-wheel main units retract forward and inward into air intake fairings. A-frame arrester hook under rear fuselage; nose-tow catapult fitting.

POWER PLANT: Two 41.4 kN (9,300 lb st) Pratt & Whitney J52-P-408 turbojets. To be replaced by two 53.4 kN (12,000 lb st) J52-P-409s. Max internal fuel capacity 8,873 litres (2,344 US gallons; 1,952 Imp gallons). Provision for up to five external fuel tanks under wing and centreline stations, each of 1,135 litres (300 US gallons; 250 Imp gallons) or 1,514 litres (400 US gallons; 333 Imp gallons) capacity. Removable flight refuelling probe projects upward immediately forward of windscreen.

ACCOMMODATION: Crew of two on Martin-Baker GRU7 ejection seats, which can be reclined to reduce fatigue during low-level operations. Bombardier/navigator slightly behind and below pilot to starboard. Hydraulically operated rearward sliding canopy.

SYSTEMS: AiResearch environmental control system for cockpit and avionics bay. Dual hydraulic systems for operation of flight controls, leading-edge and trailing-edge flaps, wingtip speed-brakes, landing gear brakes and cockpit canopy, each rated at 119.4 litres (31.5 US gallons; 26.2 Imp gallons) per min, with air/oil separated reservoir, pressurised at 2.76 bars (40 lb/sq in). One electrically driven hydraulic pump provides restricted flight capability by supplying the tailplane and rudder actuators only, each rated at 11.4 litres (3 US gallons; 2.5 Imp gallons) per min, with internally pressurised reservoir, pressurised at 1.08 bars (15.7 lb/sq in). Electrical system powered by two Garrett constant speed drive units that combine engine starting and electric power generation, each delivering 30kVA. A Garrett ram air turbine, mounted so that it can be projected into the airstream above the port wingroot, provides in-flight emergency electric power for essential equipment.

AVIONICS: Single Norden AN/APQ-148 simultaneous multi-mode nav/attack radar. IBM and Fairchild nav/attack computer system and interfacing data converter. Conrac Corporation armament control unit. RCA video tape recorder for post-strike assessment of attacks. Litton AN/ALR-67 radar warning receiver. Radar provides

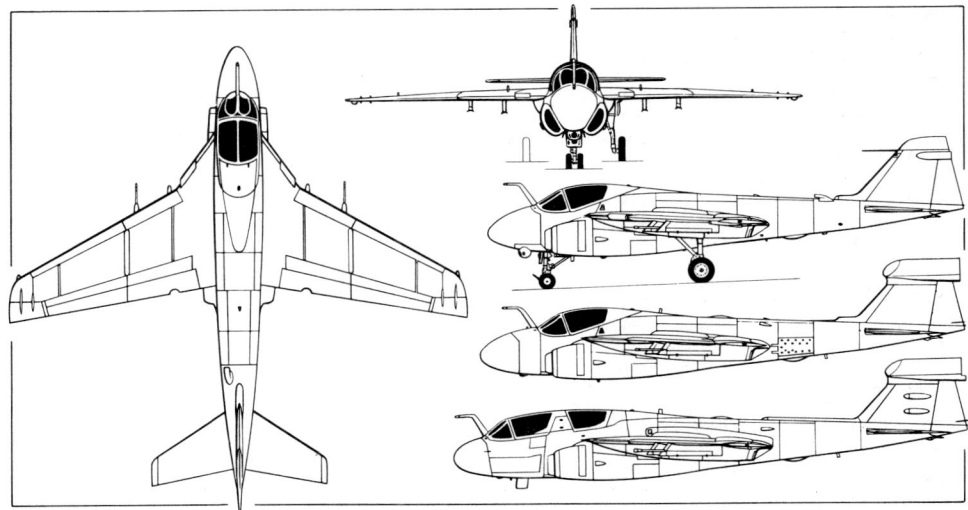

Grumman A-6E/TRAM, with additional side views of EA-6A (centre) and EA-6B (bottom) (*Pilot Press*)

simultaneous ground mapping; identification, tracking, and rangefinding of fixed or moving targets; and terrain clearance or terrain following manoeuvres. During 1981-83, it was updated by an improved AMTI (airborne moving target indication) to enhance its ability to detect moving targets. IBM AN/ASQ-133 solid state digital computer is coupled to A-6E's radar, inertial and Doppler navigational equipment, communications and AFCS. Fairchild signal data converter accepts analog input data from up to 60 sensors, converting data to a digital output that is fed into nav/attack system computer. Conrac armament control unit (ACU) provides all inputs and outputs necessary to select and release weapons. Kaiser AN/AVA-1 multi-mode display serves as a primary flight aid for navigation, approach, landing and weapons delivery. TRAM package includes undernose precision-stabilised turret, with a sensor package containing both infra-red and laser equipment; INS updated with Litton AN/ASN-92 CAINS; new communications-navigation-identification (CNI) equipment including AN/ARC-159 UHF, AN/ARN-84 Tacan and AN/APX-72 IFF transponder; and automatic carrier landing capability. Sensor package is integrated with multi-mode radar, providing capability to detect, identify and attack a wide range of targets (as well as view the terrain) under adverse weather conditions, and with improved accuracy, using either conventional or laser guided weapons. Bombardier/navigator operates TRAM system by first acquiring target on his radar screen. He then switches to FLIR (forward looking infra-red) system, using an optical zoom to enlarge target's image. After identifying and selecting his targets, bombardier uses a laser designator to mark target with a laser spot, on which his own laser guided weapons, or those from another aircraft, will home. Using TRAM's laser spot detector, A-6E can also acquire a target being illuminated from another aircraft, or designated by a forward air controller on the ground. Some A-6s modified for crew night vision goggles.

ARMAMENT: Five weapon attachment points, each with a 1,633 kg (3,600 lb) capacity (max external stores load 8,165 kg; 18,000 lb). Typical weapon loads are twenty-eight 500 lb bombs in clusters of six, or three 2,000 lb general purpose bombs plus two 1,135 litre (300 US gallon; 250 Imp gallon) drop tanks. AIM-9 Sidewinder missiles can be carried for air-to-air use. Harpoon missile capability added to weapons complement of A-6E/TRAM. The HARM missile has been test flown on the A-6E. Up to 20 Brunswick Defense TALD (Tactical Air-Launched Decoy) gliders, or two in addition to normal bomb load. Flight and firing tests have been carried out with the AGM-123A Skipper II, also on an A-6E.

DIMENSIONS, EXTERNAL:

Wing span	16.15 m (53 ft 0 in)
Wing mean aerodynamic chord	3.32 m (10 ft 10¾ in)
Width, wings folded	7.72 m (25 ft 4 in)
Length overall	16.69 m (54 ft 9 in)
Height overall	4.93 m (16 ft 2 in)
Tailplane span	6.21 m (20 ft 4½ in)
Wheel track	3.32 m (10 ft 10½ in)
Wheelbase	5.24 m (17 ft 2¼ in)

AREAS:

Wings, gross	49.1 m^2 (528.9 sq ft)
Flaperons (total)	3.81 m^2 (41.0 sq ft)
Trailing-edge flaps (total)	9.66 m^2 (104.0 sq ft)
Leading-edge slats (total)	4.63 m^2 (49.8 sq ft)
Fin	5.85 m^2 (62.93 sq ft)
Rudder	1.52 m^2 (16.32 sq ft)
Tailplane	10.87 m^2 (117.0 sq ft)

WEIGHTS AND LOADINGS:

Weight empty	12,132 kg (26,746 lb)
Fuel load: internal	7,230 kg (15,939 lb)
external (five tanks)	4,558 kg (10,050 lb)
Max external load	8,165 kg (18,000 lb)
Max T-O weight: catapult	26,580 kg (58,600 lb)
field	27,397 kg (60,400 lb)
Max zero-stores weight	20,166 kg (44,460 lb)
Max landing weight: carrier	16,329 kg (36,000 lb)
field	20,411 kg (45,000 lb)
Max wing loading	557. kg/m^2 (114.2 lb/sq ft)
Max power loading	330.88 kg/kN (3.25 lb/lb st)

PERFORMANCE (no stores, except where stated):

Never-exceed speed (VNE)	700 knots (1,297 km/h; 806 mph)
Max level speed at S/L	560 knots (1,037 km/h; 644 mph)
Cruising speed at optimum altitude	412 knots (763 km/h; 474 mph)
Approach speed	110 knots (204 km/h; 127 mph)
Stalling speed: flaps up	142 knots (264 km/h; 164 mph)
flaps down	98 knots (182 km/h; 113 mph)
Max rate of climb at S/L	2,323 m (7,620 ft)/min
Rate of climb at S/L, one engine out	646 m (2,120 ft)/min
Service ceiling	12,925 m (42,400 ft)
Service ceiling, one engine out	6,400 m (21,000 ft)
Min T-O run	1,185 m (3,890 ft)
T-O to 15 m (50 ft)	1,390 m (4,560 ft)
Landing from 15 m (50 ft)	774 m (2,540 ft)
Min landing run	521 m (1,710 ft)
Range with max military load	878 nm (1,627 km; 1,011 miles)
Ferry range with max external fuel: tanks retained	2,380 nm (4,410 km; 2,740 miles)
tanks jettisoned when empty	2,818 nm (5,222 km; 3,245 miles)

Grumman EA-6B Prowler tactical jamming aircraft *(Ivo Sturzenegger)*

GRUMMAN EA-6B PROWLER

TYPE: Four-seat carrier-borne ECM aircraft.

PROGRAMME: Development contract issued Autumn 1966; externally similar to basic A-6 except longer nose enclosing four-seat cockpit and large pod on fin; first flight 25 May 1968; delivery of first 12 production aircraft started January 1971; last of 164 delivered 1991; remanufacture continues.

Fourteen US Navy squadrons (VAQ-129 for training, 130, 131, 132, 133, 134, 135, 136, 137, 138, 139, 140, 141 and 142, all at Whidbey Island, Washington, including one rotated to Atsugi, Japan) were equipped with the Prowler by 1989. The first detachment of US Marine Corps Prowler squadron VMAQ-2 began training on the EA-6B in September 1977 and the detachment deployed in late 1978. Two additional detachments have since completed training, and at least one is deployed at all times from the main base at Cherry Point, North Carolina. Deployment with reserve units began in June 1989 with conversion of VAQ-309 at Whidbey, from EA-6As. VAQ-209 followed at Andrews AFB, 1991.

VARIANTS: **ICAP-1:** Improved capability variant; increased jamming capacity, now standard; 21 production EA-6B modified to ICAP-1 and all production aircraft to 1983 built to this standard; modifications include eight-band expanded onboard tactical jamming system, reduced response time and multi-format display, automatic all-weather carrier landing system (ALCS), new defensive ECM, new communications, navigation and identification (CNI) system.

ICAP-2: Introduced further improved jamming capacity; first flight 24 June 1980; newly built aircraft delivered since 1984 to this standard; IOC 1984; some earlier aircraft being modified to same standard; exciter in each of five external jamming pods can generate signals in one of seven different frequency bands instead of one and each pod can jam in two frequency bands simultaneously.

ADVCAP (advanced capability): Initiated 1983; Litton Industries Amecom Division with Texas Instruments and ITT contracted to produce new receiver/processor group for tactical jamming system; ADVCAP EA-6B can carry HARM (flight tested during 1989) or tanks on two inboard underwing pylons; additional outboard station under each wing for ECM pods (total six underwing stations); first flight of prototype (156482) rebuilt to ADVCAP 29 October 1989; retrofit of ADVCAP to 100 ICAP-2 Prowlers began 1991 with three aircraft to be delivered FY 1994; 12 conversions funded FY 1989, one in FY 1991 and three planned in FY 1993. Prime feature of ADVCAP is Lockheed-Sanders AN/ALQ-149 communications jammer with underfuselage antenna group; last of seven AN/ALQ-149 development models delivered for flight trials early 1989; AN/ALQ-149 contains eight assemblies in aircraft equipment bay including all antennae, receivers, signal recognisers, computers and controls needed to detect, identify, evaluate and jam hostile communications signals and long-range early warning radar systems; Sanders has options to supply 95 production AN/ALQ-149s. Other ADVCAP changes include AN/ALQ-99 jammer with 7-18 GHz transmitter complementing present 0.5-7 GHz, provision for Westinghouse AN/ALQ-165 self-defence jammer, two additional (making three) AN/ALE-39 chaff/flare dispensers, provision for JTIDS, Navstar GPS, disc-based recorder/onboard programme loader, improved cooling system, fitting of 53.4 kN (12,000 lb st) J52-P-409 turbojets to compensate for gross weight increase to nearly 29,500 kg (65,036 lb), fin height increased by 0.5 m (1 ft 7¾ in), recontoured slats and flaps, drooped wing leading-edges and new forward fuselage strakes.

VIP (vehicle improvement programme): Aimed at improving stall and manoeuvring limitations; one VIP testbed aircraft modified during 1988. Features include narrow triangular glove strakes forward of wingroot, fin extended by 0.46 m (1 ft 6 in), wingtip speed brakes modified to operate also as ailerons, droop of inboard and outboard slats increased, rear undersurface of wings including flaps recontoured; testbed also fitted with 53.4 kN (12,000 lb st) J52-P-409 turbojets.

CUSTOMERS: US Navy.

COSTS: $55.7 system unit cost, 1987.

DESIGN FEATURES: Generally as for A-6E; four crew and fin-tip antenna.

FLYING CONTROLS: As A-6E.

STRUCTURE: Wings as for A-6E, but reinforced to allow for greater gross weight, fatigue life and 5.5*g* load factor. Fuselage as for A-6E, but lengthened by 1.37 m (4 ft 6 in).

LANDING GEAR: As for A-6E, except for reinforcement of attachments, A-frame arrester hook, and upgrading of structure to cater for increased gross weight.

POWER PLANT: Two Pratt & Whitney J52-P-408 turbojets, each rated at 49.8 kN (11,200 lb st).

ACCOMMODATION: Crew of four under two separate upward opening canopies. Martin-Baker GRUEA 7 ejection seats for crew. The two additional crewmen are ECM Officers to operate the ALQ-99 equipment from the rear cockpit. Either ECMO can independently detect, assign, adjust and monitor the jammers. The ECMO in the starboard front seat is responsible for communications, navigation, defensive ECM and chaff dispensing.

SYSTEMS: Generally as for A-6E.

AVIONICS: AN/ALQ-99F tactical jamming system, in five integrally powered pods, with a total of 10 jamming transmitters. Each pod covers one of seven frequency bands. Sensitive surveillance receivers in the fin-tip pod for long-range detection of radars; emitter information is fed to a central digital computer (AN/AYK-14 in ICAP-2 aircraft) that processes the signals for display and recording. Detection, identification, direction-finding and jammer-set-on sequence can be performed automatically or with manual assistance from crew. PRB Associates AN/TSQ-142 tactical mission support system. Teledyne Systems AN/ASN-123 navigation system with digital display group.

ARMAMENT: Originally unarmed, but currently capable of carrying Texas Instruments AGM-88A HARM anti-radar missiles underwing. Four underwing hardpoints on ICAP-2 aircraft, six on ADVCAP EA-6B.

DIMENSIONS, EXTERNAL: As for A-6E, except:

Width, wings folded	7.87 m (25 ft 10 in)
Length overall	18.24 m (59 ft 10 in)
Height overall	4.95 m (16 ft 3 in)
Wheelbase	5.23 m (17 ft 2 in)

WEIGHTS AND LOADINGS:

Weight empty	14,588 kg (32,162 lb)
Internal fuel load	6,995 kg (15,422 lb)
Max external fuel load	4,547 kg (10,025 lb)
T-O weight from carrier in standoff jamming configuration (5 ECM pods)	24,703 kg (54,461 lb)
T-O weight from field in ferry range configuration (max internal and external fuel)	27,492 kg (60,610 lb)
Max T-O weight, catapult or field	29,483 kg (65,000 lb)
Max zero-fuel weight	17,708 kg (39,039 lb)
Max landing weight, carrier or field	20,638 kg (45,500 lb)
Max wing loading	600.5 kg/m^2 (123 lb/sq ft)
Max power loading	296.0 kg/kN (2.90 lb/lb st)

PERFORMANCE (A: no stores, B: 5 ECM pods):

Never-exceed speed (VNE)	710 knots (1,315 km/h; 817 mph)
Max level speed at S/L: A	566 knots (1,048 km/h; 651 mph)
B	530 knots (982 km/h; 610 mph)
Cruising speed at optimum altitude: A, B	418 knots (774 km/h; 481 mph)
Stalling speed: flaps up, max power: A	124 knots (230 km/h; 143 mph)
flaps down, max power: A	84 knots (156 km/h; 97 mph)
Max rate of climb at S/L: A	3,932 m (12,900 ft)/min
B	3,057 m (10,030 ft)/min

Rate of climb at S/L, one engine out:

A	1,189 m (3,900 ft)/min
Service ceiling: A	12,550 m (41,200 ft)
B	11,580 m (38,000 ft)
Service ceiling, one engine out: A	8,930 m (29,300 ft)
T-O run: B	814 m (2,670 ft)
T-O to 15 m (50 ft): A	869 m (2,850 ft)
B	1,065 m (3,495 ft)
Landing from 15 m (50 ft): A	823 m (2,700 ft)
Landing run: A	579 m (1,900 ft)
B	655 m (2,150 ft)

Range with max external load, 5% reserves plus 20 min at
S/L: B   955 nm (1,769 km; 1,099 miles)
Ferry range with max external fuel:
    tanks retained   1,756 nm (3,254 km; 2,022 miles)
    tanks jettisoned when empty
                            2,085 nm (3,861 km; 2,399 miles)

Grumman F-14A Tomcat of US Navy Squadron VF-33 from USS America *(Paul Jackson)*

GRUMMAN TOMCAT
US Navy designation: F-14

TYPE: Two-seat carrier-based long-range interceptor with attack capability.

PROGRAMME: Won US Navy VFX fighter competition 15 January 1969; first flight of first of 12 development aircraft 21 December 1970; original programme was for 497 Tomcats including 12 development aircraft; programme since extended into 1990s; 28 Tomcat squadrons scheduled by end 1987, including four reserve and two training squadrons, operating from 12 carriers and Naval Air Stations at Miramar (California), Oceana (Virginia), and Dallas (Texas).

Initial F-14A deployed with USN squadrons VF-1 and VF-2 October 1972; total 557, including 12 development aircraft, delivered to US Navy by April 1987, when production ended; final 102 aircraft delivered from FY 1983 powered by improved TF30-P-414A turbofans, having same rating as original 93 kN (20,900 lb st) TF30-P-412A.

F-14A squadrons are VF-1, 2, 21, 24, 51, 111, 114, 124 (training), 154, 211, 213, 301 (Reserve) and 302 (Reserve) at Miramar, California; VF-11, 14, 31, 32, 33, 41, 74, 84, 101 (training), 102, 103, 142, and 143 at Oceana, Virginia; VF-201 and 202 of the Reserve at Dallas, Texas.

VARIANTS: **F-14A:** Initial and main version, supplied to US Navy and Iran. Total of 557 built (last aircraft 162711), ending 13 March 1987; 32 being reworked to F-14A(Plus) and 18 to F-14D(R). Retrofit with Tape 115B started May 1991 (see under Avionics).

F-14A(Plus): Interim improved version re-engined with GE F110-GE-400 turbofans pending introduction of F-14D (see below). Development began July 1984; Grumman prime contractor with General Electric and Hughes Aircraft as subcontractors. F110 has 82 per cent parts commonality with F110-GE-100 in USAF F-15s and F-16s; 1.27 m (4 ft 2 in) plug inserted in afterburner section to match engine to F-14A inlet position and airframe contours; only secondary structure requires modification; new engine allows unrestricted throttle handling throughout flight envelope and fewer compressor stalls. NASA scoops for Vulcan cannon; glove vanes eliminated; cockpit modified. Full-scale development used two aircraft, including F-14B prototype (157986), which made first flight with definitive F110-GE-400 engines 29 September 1986; one F-14A(Plus) prototype was to be upgraded to full F-14D.

F-14A(Plus) followed F-14A into production; first flight production F-14A(Plus) 14 November 1987; 18, 15 and five funded in FY 1986-88; first delivery, to VF-101 at Oceana, Virginia, 11 April 1988; IOC with two US Navy squadrons achieved early 1989; F-14A(Plus) production deliveries (last aircraft 163411) completed May 1990. Additionally, 32 F-14As upgraded to F-14A(Plus); Plus variant issued to VF-24, 74, 101, 103, 142, 143 and 211. Tape 115B being retrofitted 1991.

F110 engine has 43 per cent more reheated thrust and 37 per cent more military thrust (without afterburning); results in 20 per cent more specific excess energy, 30 per cent lower specific fuel consumption in afterburner, 62 per cent greater deck launch intercept radius and 34 per cent more combat air patrol time; can be launched without afterburner; time to 10,670 m (35,000 ft) reduced by 61 per cent and acceleration time by 43 per cent.

F-14D Super Tomcat: Improved version with AN/APG-71 radar, NACES seats in NVG-compatible cockpits, twin IRST/TV pods, plus enhanced missile capability (AIM-120 AMRAAM, AIM-54C++ Phoenix). Total 37 out of 127 planned new F-14Ds funded (seven, 12 and 18 in FYs 1988-90) before programme cancelled as economy measure in 1989; plans continued for 400 F-14A and F-14A(Plus) to be remanufactured to F-14D; six **F-14D(R)** conversions funded FY 1990; Grumman working on four conversions; USN at Norfolk NADP, on two; FY 1991-95 funding plans for 12, 18, 20, 24 and 24 all cancelled February 1991, but FY 1991 dozen restored April 1991 (Grumman eight, NADP four); F-14D programme thus 37 new, 18 rebuilt. First flight of first of three development aircraft 24 November 1987; 36 months flight testing included a TA-3B Skywarrior. Prototype, 161867, delivered trials squadron VX-4 at Point Mugu, California, May 1990; first production F-14D (163412) rolled out 23 March 1990; last (163904) due May 1992. First F-14D(R) delivered June 1990. Training squadron, VF-124 (first user) October 1990; official acceptance 16 November 1990; first embarked squadrons, VF-51 and VF-111.

Quickstrike: Suggested first-stage development of F-14D for extended ground attack capability, including standoff weapons; potentially available (132-aircraft proposal) from 1994.

Super Tomcat-21: Company-funded study for US Navy multi-role fighter for next century as economic alternative to Navy version of USAF Advanced Tactical Fighter (ATF). Quickstrike improvements plus new slotted flaps, extended-chord leading-edge slats, enlarged wing glove fairings containing extra fuel, new frameless windscreen. Grumman claims Tomcat-21 can have 90 per cent of ATF capability for 60 per cent of cost. Conversion possible from F-14A.

Attack Super Tomcat-21 (AST-21): Suggested interim replacement for A-12 Avenger II with low-level penetration capability and nuclear as well as conventional armament. Terrain avoidance radar; two extra weapon stations.

ASF-14: Grumman proposal for alternative to Navalised ATF as F-14 evolutionary development including avionics, and possibly power plants, developed for ATF. Could be available by year 2000.

CUSTOMERS: US Navy (see Variants). Iran also acquired 79 F-14As in 1976-78; retained Phoenix missile system, but had slightly different ECM equipment.

COSTS: $984 million fixed-price contract in July 1984 for development of F-14(Plus) and F-14D Super Tomcats.

DESIGN FEATURES: Wing sweepback variable from 20° leading-edge to 68°; oversweep of 75° used for carrier stowage without wing fold; wing pivot point 2.72 m (8 ft 11 in) from aircraft centreline; fixed glove has dihedral to minimise cross-sectional area and reduce wave drag; small canards on F-14A known as glove vanes extend forward progressively to 15° from inboard leading-edge to balance supersonic trim change and unload tail surfaces.

FLYING CONTROLS: Lateral control by long-span spoilers ahead of flaps and tailerons; automatic leading-edge slats assist manoeuvring; automatic wing sweep has manual override; automatic scheduling of control with airspeed; autostabilisation and angle of attack protection; autopilot and automatic carrier landing system (ALCS). Airbrake panel above and below tail, between fins. All-flying tailplane and twin rudders.

STRUCTURE: Wing carry-through is one-piece electron beam-welded structure of Ti-6A1-4V titanium alloy with 7.60 m (22 ft) span. Fuselage has machined frames, titanium main longerons and light alloy stressed skin; centre fuselage is fuel-carrying box; radome hinges upwards for access to radar; fuel dump pipe at extreme tail; fins and rudders of light alloy honeycomb sandwich; tailplanes have multiple spars, honeycomb trailing-edges and boron/epoxy composites skins.

LANDING GEAR: Retractable tricycle type. Twin-wheel nose unit and single-wheel main units retract forward, main units inward into bottom of engine air intake trunks. Original beryllium brakes were replaced with Goodyear lightweight carbon brakes from Spring 1981. Arrester hook under rear fuselage, housed in small ventral fairing. Nose-tow catapult attachment on nose unit.

POWER PLANT (F-14A[Plus]/D): Two General Electric F110-GE-400 turbofans rated at 62.3 kN (14,000 lb st) dry and 102.75 kN (23,100 lb st) with afterburning. Garrett ATS200-50 air turbine starter. Integral fuel tanks in outer wings, each with capacity of 1,117 litres (295 US gallons; 246 Imp gallons); between engines in rear fuselage, with capacity of 2,453 litres (648 US gallons; 539 Imp gallons); and forward of wing carry-through structure, capacity 2,616 litres (691 US gallons; 575 Imp gallons); plus two feeder tanks with combined capacity of 1,726 litres (456 US gallons; 380 Imp gallons). Total internal fuel capacity 9,029 litres (2,385 US gallons; 1,986 Imp gallons). An external auxiliary fuel tank can be carried beneath each intake trunk, each containing 1,011 litres (267 US gallons; 222 Imp gallons). Retractable flight refuelling probe on starboard side of fuselage near front cockpit.

ACCOMMODATION: Pilot and naval flight officer seated in tandem on Martin-Baker NACES (or GRU7A in F-14A/A(Plus)) rocket assisted zero/zero ejection seats, under a one-piece bubble canopy, hinged at the rear and offering all-round view. NVG-compatible lighting in F-14D.

AVIONICS (F-14A): Hughes AN/AWG-9 weapons control system, with ability to detect airborne targets at ranges of more than 65-170 nm (120-315 km; 75-195 miles) according to their size, and ability to track 24 enemy targets and attack six of them simultaneously at varied altitudes and distances. Fairchild AN/AWG-15F fire control set; CP-1066/A central air data computer;

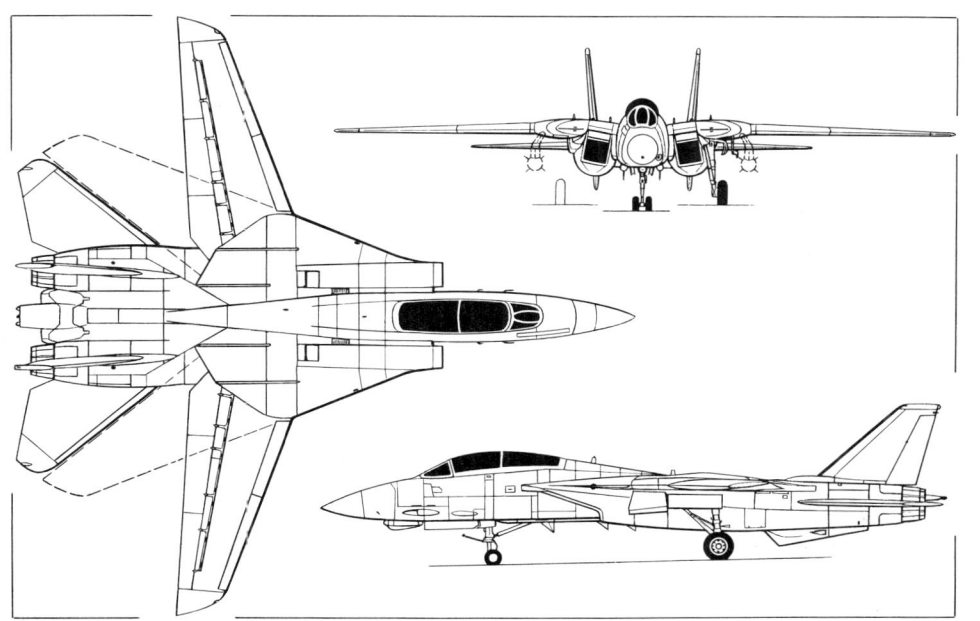

Grumman F-14A(Plus) Tomcat carrier-based multi-role fighter *(Pilot Press)*

CP-1050/A computer signal data converter; AN/ASW-27B digital data link; AN/APX-76(V) IFF interrogator;. AN/APX-72 IFF transponder; AN/ASA-79 multiple display indicator group; Kaiser Aerospace AN/AVG-12 vertical and head-up display system. AN/ARC-51 and AN/ARC-159 UHF com; AN/ARR-69 UHF auxiliary receiver; KY-28 cryptographic system; LS-460/B intercom; AN/ASN-92(V) INS; A/A24G39 AHRS; AN/APN-154 beacon augmentor; AN/APN-194(V) radar altimeter; AN/ARA-63A receiver-decoder; AN/ARN-84 micro Tacan; AN/ARA-50 UHF ADF; AN/APR-27/50 radar receiver; AN/APR-25/45 radar warning set. TV optical unit in undernose pod. Northrop Corporation television camera set (TCS) mounted beneath nose is closed-circuit TV system, offering both wide-angle (acquisition) and telescopic (identification) fields of view. TCS automatically searches for, acquires and locks on to distant targets, displaying them on monitors for the pilot and flight officer. Small undernose pod for Sanders AN/ALQ-100/126 deception jamming system, relocated under camera package of aircraft with Northrop TCS. During 1980-81, 49 F-14As were allocated to carry TARPS (tactical air reconnaissance pod system), containing a KS-87B frame camera, KA-99 low altitude panoramic camera, and AN/AAD-5 infra-red reconnaissance equipment, on underbelly attachment. In F-14D, some 60 per cent of analog avionics made digital, giving new weapons management, navigation, displays and control functions. MIL-STD-1553B digital bus interconnects Litton AN/ALR-67 threat warning and recognition system, Westinghouse/ITT AN/ALQ-165 airborne self-protection jammer (ASPJ), joint tactical information distribution system (JTIDS), General Electric Aerospace Electronic Systems infra-red search and track sensor (IRST) and television camera set (TCS); emphasis on commonality with FA-18 and latest A-6. New Hughes AN/APG-71 replaces AN/AWG-9 radar with improved ECCM, monopulse angle tracking, digital scan control, target identification and raid assessment. AN/APG-71 features non-co-operative target identification, and ECCM using low-sidelobe antenna and sidelobe blanking guard channel, frequency agility, new high-speed digital signal processor based on AN/APG-70 used in US Air Force multi-staged improvement programme for F-15. ECM equipment includes Goodyear AN/ALE-29 and AN/ALE-39 chaff and flare dispensers, with integral jammers.

All in-service Tomcats given Tape 115B computer software addition in May 1991 to allow full ground attack with iron bombs.

ARMAMENT: One General Electric M61A-1 Vulcan 20 mm gun mounted in the port side of forward fuselage, with 675 rounds of ammunition. Four AIM-7 Sparrow air-to-air missiles mounted partially submerged in the underfuselage, or four AIM-54 Phoenix missiles carried on special pallets which attach to the bottom of the fuselage. Two wing pylons, one under each fixed wing section, can carry four AIM-9 Sidewinder missiles or two additional Sparrow or Phoenix missiles with two Sidewinders. F-14D has bombing capability; AGM-88 HARM ARM integration in 1993; AIM-120 AMRAAM deferred.

DIMENSIONS, EXTERNAL:
Wing span: unswept	19.54 m (64 ft 1½ in)
swept	11.65 m (38 ft 2½ in)
overswept	10.15 m (33 ft 3½ in)

Retouched photograph showing engine configuration of Grumman S-2T Turbo Tracker with Garrett TPE331-15AW turboprops

Wing aspect ratio	7.28
Length overall	19.10 m (62 ft 8 in)
Height overall	4.88 m (16 ft 0 in)
Tailplane span	9.97 m (32 ft 8½ in)
Distance between fin tips	3.25 m (10 ft 8 in)
Wheel track	5.00 m (16 ft 5 in)
Wheelbase	7.02 m (23 ft 0½ in)
AREAS:	
Wings, gross	52.49 m² (565.0 sq ft)
Leading-edge slats (total)	4.29 m² (46.2 sq ft)
Trailing-edge flaps (total)	9.87 m² (106.3 sq ft)
Spoilers (total)	1.97 m² (21.2 sq ft)
Fins (total)	7.90 m² (85.0 sq ft)
Rudders (total)	3.06 m² (33.0 sq ft)
Horizontal tail surfaces (total)	13.01 m² (140.0 sq ft)
WEIGHTS AND LOADINGS (F-14A with TF30-P-414A):	
Weight empty	18,191 kg (40,104 lb)
Fuel (usable): internal	7,348 kg (16,200 lb)
external	1,724 kg (3,800 lb)
Max external weapon load	6,577 kg (14,500 lb)
T-O weight: clean	26,632 kg (58,715 lb)
with 4 Sparrow	27,086 kg (59,714 lb)
with 6 Phoenix	32,098 kg (70,764 lb)
max	33,724 kg (74,349 lb)
Design landing weight	23,510 kg (51,830 lb)
Max wing loading	642.5 kg/m² (131.59 lb/sq ft)
Max power loading	164.1 kg/kN (1.61 lb/lb st)
PERFORMANCE (-414A engines):	
Max level speed:	
at height	
Mach 2.34 (1,342 knots; 2,485 km/h; 1,544 mph)	
at low level	
Mach 1.2 (792 knots; 1,468 km/h; 912 mph)	
Max cruising speed	
400-550 knots (741-1,019 km/h; 460-633 mph)	
*Carrier approach speed	134 knots (248 km/h; 154 mph)
*Stalling speed	115 knots (213 km/h; 132 mph)
Max rate of climb at S/L	over 9,140 m (30,000 ft)/min
Service ceiling	above 15,240 m (50,000 ft)
Min T-O distance	427 m (1,400 ft)
Min landing distance	884 m (2,900 ft)

Max range with external fuel
approx 1,735 nm (3,220 km; 2,000 miles)
*carrier landing design gross weight

GRUMMAN (GENERAL DYNAMICS) RAVEN

US Air Force designation: EF-111A

TYPE: Electronic warfare aircraft.

PROGRAMME: Conversion of 42 F-111As (see 1986-87 and earlier *Jane's*). Avionics modernisation programme initiated with January 1987 contract (see 1989-90 edition); new $155.8 million contract March 1991 for FSD system improvement programme (SIP) to upgrade hardware and software to improve radar jamming capabilities; Grumman Aircraft Group (with team members Eaton/AIL, Astronautics Corp, IBM, Comptech and Smiths Industries) will design and install prototype upgrade kit at its Calverton facility; contract to be completed by January 1996.

GRUMMAN S-2T TURBO TRACKER

US Navy $260 million foreign military sales contract placed to fit S-2 Tracker with turboprops and fit new avionics, including GEC Avionics MAPADS 902F acoustic processor, AN/ASQ-504(V) magnetic anomaly detector, AN/APS-509 radar, AN/ARR-84 acoustic receivers, AN/ASN-150 tactical navigation system coupled with the 72R inertial navigation system, and Rockwell Collins radios. Tracor Aviation replaced 1,141 kW (1,530 hp) Curtiss-Wright R1820-82 piston engines with 1,227 kW (1,645 shp) Garrett TPE331-15AW turboprops driving Dowty advanced technology four-blade propellers; Turbo Tracker has 270 knot (500 km/h; 311 mph) maximum speed at 1,525 m (5,000 ft) and payload is increased by 500 kg (1,102 lb); cruising speed, field lengths and single-engined performance and engine TBO all improved.

Taiwan ordered 32 S-2Ts under US Navy FMS contract; Grumman converted two; remainder modified in Taiwan with kits. Refer to IMP Group (Canadian section) and Bedek Aviation (Israel) for details of other military turboprop Tracker conversions.

GULFSTREAM AEROSPACE

GULFSTREAM AEROSPACE CORPORATION

PO Box 2206, Savannah International Airport, Savannah, Georgia 31402-2206
Telephone: 1 (912) 964 3000
Fax: 1 (912) 964 3775 or 1 (912) 966 4171
Telex: 546470 GULF AERO
CHAIRMAN AND CHIEF EXECUTIVE OFFICER: Allen E. Paulson
PRESIDENT AND CHIEF OPERATING OFFICER: William C. Lowe
SENIOR VICE-PRESIDENT, ENGINEERING: Charles N. Coppi
SENIOR VICE-PRESIDENT, MARKETING: Robert H. Cooper
CORPORATE COMMUNICATIONS DIRECTOR: Alvin F. Balaban

Grumman Aerospace Corporation bought from Mr Allen Paulson by Chrysler Corporation August 1985; Mr Paulson and Forstmann Little and Company completed repurchase from Chrysler Corporation 19 March 1990.

AiResearch facility at Long Beach International Airport, California, bought by Gulfstream in 1986 and expanded from 9,290 m² (100,000 sq ft) to 20,438 m² (220,000 sq ft); can accommodate outfitting and completion of 17 Gulfstream IVs at a time.

GULFSTREAM AEROSPACE GULFSTREAM IV

TYPE: Twin-turbofan long-range business transport.

PROGRAMME: Design started March 1983; manufacture of four production prototypes (one for static testing) began 1985; first aircraft (N404GA) rolled out 11 September 1985; first flight 19 September 1985; first flight of second prototype 11 June 1986 and third prototype August 1986;

FAA certification 22 April 1987 after 1,412 hours flight testing. Westbound round-the-world flight from Le Bourget, Paris, on 12 June 1987, covering 19,887.9 nm (36,832.44 km; 22,886.6 miles), took 45 h 25 min at average 437.86 knots (811.44 km/h; 504.2 mph) and set 22 world records; eastbound round-the-world flight in N400GA from Houston, Texas, on 26/27 February 1988 covered 20,028.68 nm (37,093.1 km; 23,048.6 miles) in 36 h 8 min 34 s at average 554.15 knots (1,026.29 km/h; 637.71 mph), setting 11 records and bettering United Airlines 747SP circuit flown 30 days before; aircraft carried 3,629 kg (8,000 lb) optional internal long-range tank.

VARIANTS: **SRA-4:** Special missions aircraft, described separately.

CUSTOMERS: Total 162 Gulfstream IVs delivered by end 1990, including 26 in 1990; annual production rate 30 aircraft.

DESIGN FEATURES: Differences from Gulfstream III (1987-88 and earlier *Jane's*) include structurally redesigned wing with 30 per cent fewer parts, 395 kg (870 lb) lighter and carrying 453 kg (1,000 lb) more fuel; increased tailplane span; fuselage 1.37 m (4 ft 6 in) longer, with sixth window each side; rudder, ailerons and spoilers made of carbon composites; Rolls-Royce Tay Mk 611-8 turbofans; flight deck with electronic displays and digital avionics.

Advanced sonic rooftop aerofoil; sweepback at quarter-chord 27° 40′; thickness/chord ratio 10 per cent at wing station 50, 8.6 per cent at station 414; dihedral 3°; incidence 3° 30′ at root, −2° at tip; NASA (Whitcomb) winglets. Wing, tailplane and fin leading-edges anti-iced by engine bleed air.

FLYING CONTROLS: Hydraulically powered flying controls with manual reversion; trim tabs in port aileron, both elevators and rudder; three spoilers on each wing act differentially to assist aileron and collectively as airbrakes and lift dumpers; single-slotted Fowler flaps; four vortillons and a single 'tripper' strip under leading-edge of each wing ensure good stalling behaviour.

STRUCTURE: Wing manufactured by Textron Aerostructures. Light alloy airframe except for carbon composites ailerons, rudder and elevators, some tailplane parts, some cabin floor structure, and parts of flight deck; winglets of aluminium honeycomb.

LANDING GEAR: Retractable tricycle type with twin wheels on each unit. Main units retract inward, steerable nose unit forward. Mainwheel tyres size 34 × 9.25-16, pressure 12.07 bars (175 lb/sq in). Nosewheel tyres size 21 × 7.25-10, pressure 7.9 bars (115 lb/sq in). Loral aircooled carbon brakes, with Loral fully modulating anti-skid units. Loral digital electronic brake-by-wire system. Dowty electronic steer-by-wire system.

POWER PLANT: Two Rolls-Royce Tay Mk 611-8 turbofans, each flat rated at 61.6 kN (13,850 lb st) to ISA +15°C. Target type thrust reversers. Fuel in two integral wing tanks, with total capacity of 16,542 litres (4,370 US gallons; 3,639 Imp gallons). Single pressure fuelling point in leading-edge of starboard wing.

ACCOMMODATION: Crew of two or three. Standard seating for 14 to 19 passengers in pressurised and air-conditioned cabin. Galley, toilet and large baggage compartment, capacity 907 kg (2,000 lb), at rear of cabin. Integral airstair door at front of cabin on port side. Baggage compartment door on port side. Electrically heated

Gulfstream Aerospace Gulfstream IV twin-turbofan business transport

wraparound windscreen. Six cabin windows, including one overwing emergency exit, on each side.

SYSTEMS: Cabin pressurisation system max differential 0.65 bar (9.45 lb/sq in). Air-conditioning system. Two independent hydraulic systems, each 207 bars (3,000 lb/sq in). Maximum flow rate 83.3 litres (22 US gallons; 18.3 Imp gallons)/min. Two bootstrap type hydraulic reservoirs, pressurised to 4.14 bars (60 lb/sq in). Garrett GTCP36-100 APU in tail compartment, flight rated to 9,150 m (30,000 ft). Electrical system includes two 36kVA alternators with two solid state 30kVA converters to provide 23kVA 115/200V 400Hz AC power and 250A of regulated 28V DC power; two 24V 40Ah nickel-cadmium storage batteries and external power socket.

AVIONICS: Standard items include a Honeywell SPZ-8000 digital automatic flight control system, Honeywell FMZ-800 Phase II flight management system and six 20.3 cm × 20.3 cm (8 in × 8 in) colour CRT displays, two each for primary flight instruments, navigation and engine instrument and crew alerting systems (EICAS); dual fail-operational flight guidance systems including auto throttles; dual air data systems; dual flight management systems with vertical and lateral navigation and performance management, and digital colour radar. System integration is accomplished through a Honeywell avionics standard communications bus (ASCB). Other factory-installed avionics include dual VHF/HF com; dual VOR/LOC/GS and markers; dual DME; dual ADF; dual radio altimeters; dual transponders; dual cockpit audio; dual flight guidance and performance computers; dual laser INS; attitude/heading reference system; and cockpit voice recorder. The system is designed to provide growth potential for interface with MLS, GPS and VLF Omega in future developments. Optional avionics include Racal Satfone satellite communications equipment.

DIMENSIONS, EXTERNAL:

Wing span over winglets	23.72 m (77 ft 10 in)
Wing chord:	
at root (fuselage centreline)	5.94 m (19 ft 5⅞ in)
at tip	1.85 m (6 ft 0¾ in)
Wing aspect ratio	5.92
Length overall	26.92 m (88 ft 4 in)
Fuselage: Length	24.03 m (78 ft 10 in)
Max diameter	2.39 m (7 ft 10 in)
Height overall	7.57 m (24 ft 10 in)
Tailplane span	9.75 m (32 ft 0 in)
Wheel track	4.17 m (13 ft 8 in)
Wheelbase	11.61 m (38 ft 1¼ in)
Passenger door (fwd, port): Height	1.57 m (5 ft 2 in)
Width	0.91 m (3 ft 0 in)
Baggage door (rear): Height	0.72 m (2 ft 4½ in)
Width	0.91 m (2 ft 11¾ in)

DIMENSIONS, INTERNAL:

Cabin:	
Length, incl galley, toilet and baggage compartment	13.74 m (45 ft 1 in)
Max width	2.24 m (7 ft 4 in)
Max height	1.85 m (6 ft 1 in)
Floor area	22.9 m² (247 sq ft)
Volume	47.62 m³ (1682 cu ft)
Cabin volume	42.84 m³ (1,513 cu ft)
Passenger area volume	30.50 m³ (1,077 cu ft)
Flight deck volume	3.51 m³ (124.0 cu ft)
Rear baggage compartment volume	4.78 m³ (169.0 cu ft)

AREAS:

Wings, gross	88.29 m² (950.39 sq ft)
Ailerons (total, incl tab)	2.68 m² (28.86 sq ft)
Trailing-edge flaps (total)	11.97 m² (128.84 sq ft)
Spoilers (total)	7.46 m² (80.27 sq ft)
Winglets (total)	2.38 m² (25.60 sq ft)
Fin	10.92 m² (117.53 sq ft)
Rudder, incl tab	4.16 m² (44.75 sq ft)
Horizontal tail surfaces (total)	18.77 m² (202.0 sq ft)
Elevators (total, incl tabs)	5.22 m² (56.22 sq ft)

WEIGHTS AND LOADINGS:

Manufacturer's weight empty	16,102 kg (35,500 lb)
Typical operating weight empty	19,278 kg (42,500 lb)

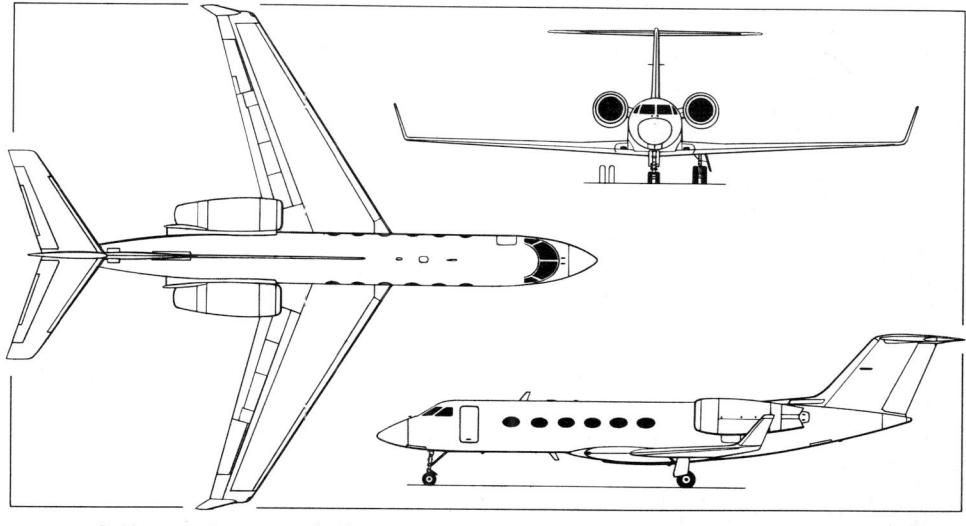

Gulfstream Aerospace Gulfstream IV twin-turbofan business transport *(Pilot Press)*

Max payload	1,814 kg (4,000 lb)
Max usable fuel	13,381 kg (29,500 lb)
Max T-O weight	33,203 kg (73,200 lb)
Max ramp weight	33,384 kg (73,600 lb)
Max zero-fuel weight	21,092 kg (46,500 lb)
Max landing weight	26,535 kg (58,500 lb)
Max wing loading	375.9 kg/m² (77.02 lb/sq ft)
Max power loading	269.6 kg/kN (2.64 lb/lb st)

PERFORMANCE (at max T-O weight, ISA, except where indicated):

Max operating speed	
	340 knots (629 km/h; 391 mph) CAS
	or Mach 0.88
Max cruising speed at 9,450 m (31,000 ft)	
	509 knots (943 km/h; 586 mph)
Normal cruising speed at 13,715 m (45,000 ft)	
	Mach 0.80 (459 knots; 850 km/h; 528 mph)
Stalling speed at max landing weight:	
wheels and flaps up	122 knots (227 km/h; 141 mph)
wheels and flaps down	
	108 knots (200 km/h; 124 mph)
Approach speed at max landing weight	
	140 knots (259 km/h; 161 mph)
Max rate of climb at S/L	1,220 m (4,000 ft)/min
Rate of climb at S/L, one engine out	
	337 m (1,105 ft)/min
Max operating altitude	13,715 m (45,000 ft)
Runway LCN	35
FAA balanced T-O field length at S/L	
	1,609 m (5,280 ft)
Landing from 15 m (50 ft)	1,032 m (3,386 ft)
Range:	
with max payload, normal cruising speed and NBAA IFR reserves	3,694 nm (6,845 km; 4,254 miles)
with max fuel, eight passengers, at Mach 0.80 and with NBAA IFR reserves	
	4,220 nm (7,820 km; 4,859 miles)

OPERATIONAL NOISE LEVELS (FAR Pt 36):

T-O	76.8 EPNdB
Approach	91.0 EPNdB
Sideline	87.3 EPNdB

GULFSTREAM AEROSPACE SRA-4

TYPE: Special missions version of G IV.

PROGRAMME: Development aircraft (N413GA) for electronic warfare support version, integrated by Electrospace Systems Inc (now CTAS: see under Chrysler heading), exhibited at Farnborough Air Show 1988.

VARIANTS: **Electronic warfare support:** Development aircraft had forward underfuselage pod for jamming antennae and small pod on top of fin for DF/omni antennae; cabin contains operators' consoles and microwave generator and amplifier rack, modulation generator rack, radio racks, and chaff supply and cutters to simulate EW from adversary aircraft and missiles; aircraft could be used to test and evaluate weapon systems and to develop electronic warfare tactics.

Electronic surveillance/reconnaissance: Possible sensors include side-looking synthetic aperture radar in belly-mounted pod under forward fuselage, long-range oblique photographic camera (LOROP), ESM, VHF/UHF/HF communications for C³, chaff dispensers, infra-red countermeasures in tailcone, SAR equipment and accommodation for operators for each system. Typical mission profile with 1,950 kg (4,300 lb) payload allows 10.5 hours on station at loiter altitudes between 10,670 m and 15,550 m (35,000 ft and 51,000 ft).

Maritime patrol: Equipment includes high definition surface search radar, forward looking infra-red detection system (IRDS), electronic support measures (ESM), flare/marker launch tubes, nav/com and ESM consoles, positions for up to eight observers/console operators, stowage and deployment for survival equipment, and crew rest area. SRA-4 with 1,950-4,173 kg (4,300-9,200 lb) mission payload including 272 kg (600 lb) expendable stores can operate at 600 nm (1,112 km; 690 mile) radius for four to six hours; outbound flight at 12,500 m (41,000 ft) and 454 knots (841 km/h; 523 mph); search at 3,050 m (10,000 ft), but spend one-third of time at 61 m (200 ft); return flight at 13,715 m (45,000 ft).

ASW: Equipment includes nose radar able to detect periscope and snorkels, FLIR, sonobuoy launchers, acoustic processor, magnetic anomaly detector (MAD) in tail, ESM, torpedo stowage in weapon bay under forward fuselage, and anti-shipping missile carried on each underwing hardpoint. Mission profile with six crew and 2,503 kg (5,518 lb) payload can stay 4.3 hours in hi-lo loitering and manoeuvring at 1,000 nm (1,853 km; 1,151 miles) radius. Mission profile for **anti-shipping** with two missiles allows 1,350 nm (2,502 km; 1,554 miles) outbound flight at high altitude; descent to 61 m (200 ft) for 100 nm (185 km; 115 mile) attack run at 350 knots (649 km/h; 403 mph); launch missile 50 nm (93 km; 57 miles) from target; return to base at 13,715 m (45,000 ft).

Medical evacuation: Accommodation for 15 stretchers and attendants.

Priority cargo transport: Cargo door (see below) plus floor-mounted cargo roller system.

DESIGN FEATURES: Missions include surveillance/reconnaissance, electronic warfare support, maritime patrol, anti-submarine warfare, medical evacuation, priority cargo and administrative transport. Cabin arranged for rapid role changes; upward-opening cargo door 1.6 m (5 ft 3 in) high by 2.1 m (6 ft 11 in) wide can be fitted to starboard ahead of wing to allow for bulky cargo, mission equipment or stretchers.

Development prototype of the Gulfstream SRA-4 electronic warfare support aircraft *(J.M.G. Gradidge)*

SUKHOI-GULFSTREAM AEROSPACE SSBJ

Discussions at Paris Air Show 1989 led to memorandum of understanding to investigate joint development of supersonic business jet. Lyulka and Rolls-Royce co-operating on suitable engine. Details in International section.

GULFSTREAM AEROSPACE TECHNOLOGIES
(Oklahoma Operations)

Wiley Post Airport, Box 22500, Oklahoma City, Oklahoma 73123
Telephone: 1 (405) 789 5000
Telex: 747193
PRESIDENT: Robert N. Buckley

Former Gulfstream Commander Jetprop factory 55,740 m² (600,000 sq ft) now used for subcontracted manufacture and engineering. Single-engined Commander 112 and 114 line sold to Commander Aircraft Company (which see) June 1988. Manufacturing and marketing rights for twin-engined Commanders sold December 1989 to Precision Airmotive of Everett, Washington (see Twin Commander Corporation in this section). Gulfstream

Aerospace authorised 2 May 1988 to produce spares for out-of-production Douglas airliners from DC-3 to DC-10. Contract announced 8 September 1989 to design, tool and manufacture 200 wing sets for British Aerospace Jetstream 41 for delivery between 1990 and 2000; first set delivered November 1990.

HAMILTON
HAMILTON AEROSPACE

San Antonio, Texas
PRESIDENT: George Hamilton

HAMILTON HX-1 and HXT-2

TYPE: Tandem two-seat tactical aircraft (HX-1) and primary trainer (HXT-2).
PROGRAMME: Hamilton designed an HX-321 two-seat homebuilt in 1987-88 (see Sport Aircraft section of

1988-89 *Jane's*), configured to resemble F-16-type fighter but powered by pusher piston engine. HX-1 appears to be scale-up of this, with cranked-arrow wings, canards, single rear-mounted LHTEC T800 turboprop and all-composites airframe; HXT-2 would be twin-turbofan (Garrett TFE109) derivative of HX-1. Prototype HX-1 said to be nearly ready for first flight by September 1990, but not confirmed.

DIMENSIONS, EXTERNAL (HX-1):
Wing span	8.79 m (28 ft 10 in)
Length overall	10.36 m (34 ft 0 in)

AREAS (HX-1):
Wings, gross	21.04 m² (226.47 sq ft)

WEIGHTS AND LOADINGS (HX-1):
Weight empty	907 kg (2,000 lb)
Fuel weight	816 kg (1,800 lb)
External weapon load	2,132 kg (4,700 lb)

PERFORMANCE (HX-1, estimated):
Max level speed	425 knots (787 km/h; 489 mph)
Max cruising speed	325 knots (602 km/h; 374 mph)

HELI-AIR
HELI-AIR (JAFFE HELICOPTER INCORPORATED)

119 Ida Road, Broussard, Louisiana 70518
Telephone: 1 (318) 837 2376
Fax: 1 (318) 837 2113
Telex: 5101010395
PRESIDENT: Gary J. Villiard
DIRECTOR OF OPERATIONS: David A. Brown
Member of Jaffe Group.

HELI-AIR BELL MODEL 222 CONVERSION

TYPE: Re-engined Bell Model 222.
PROGRAMME: First flight of Allison-engined Bell 222 test conversion (N5008Q) 10 November 1988; first flight of production conversion 12 January 1990; prototype had then flown 400 hours; FAA Supplemental Type Certificate for Bell 222A August 1990; Model 222B/UT certification expected March 1991.
CUSTOMERS: Heli-Air had delivered two aircraft by January 1991 and plans to deliver 12 in 1991 and 25 in 1992.
DESIGN FEATURES: Heli-Air-developed modification to replace standard 510 kW (684 shp) LTS 101-750C-1 turboshafts in Bell Model 222A, 222B and 222UT with

two 522 kW (700 shp) Allison 250-C30G. Performance unchanged except for improved engine-out performance and 36 kg (80 lb) greater useful load.

HELI-AIR MBB/KAWASAKI BK 117 CONVERSION

TYPE: Re-engined MBB/Kawasaki BK 117.
PROGRAMME: Certification expected June 1992.
CUSTOMERS: Rocky Mountain Helicopters ordered 33.
DESIGN FEATURES: Modification to replace standard 410 kW (550 shp) LTS 101-650B-1 turboshafts in MBB/Kawasaki BK 117 with two 522 kW (700 shp) Allison 250-C30Gs.

HELIO
HELIO AIRCRAFT CORPORATION

PO Drawer 3350, 165 Scott Avenue, Suite 102, Morgantown, West Virginia 26505
Telephone: 1 (304) 291 2376
Fax: 1 (304) 292 1902
PRESIDENT: Darus H. Zehrbach

Design, manufacturing and marketing rights of former Helio range of piston and turboprop-powered aircraft acquired by Aircraft Acquisition Corporation November 1989 (which see). Production restarted of Courier Models 600, 800 and 900 and turboprop-powered H-550A Stallion; new Courier 700 powered by liquid-cooled 224 kW (300 hp) Teledyne Continental Voyager piston engine and Super Courier powered by 300 kW (420 hp) Allison 250-B17C turboprop under development Spring 1990; certification of both types expected Autumn 1990. Early development of Courier and Stallion recorded in 1978-79 *Jane's*; full technical descriptions in 1976-77 *Jane's*.

Helio Courier 800 STOL utility aircraft on PK floats

HELIO COURIER 600, 700, 800 and 900

TYPE: Six-seat STOL utility aircraft.
DESIGN FEATURES: Unbraced parallel-chord wing; NACA 23012 aerofoil section; dihedral 1°. Power plants detailed below.
FLYING CONTROLS: Slab tailplane; wide-chord ailerons; two trim tabs on tailplane, one on rudder; automatic leading-edge slats in four sections; Fowler flaps.
STRUCTURE: All-metal fuselage and tail; cabin section has welded 4130 steel tube frame with metal skin; rear fuselage has light alloy bulkheads, stringers and skin.
LANDING GEAR: Non-retractable tailwheel or tricycle type with spring steel main legs and oleo-pneumatic shock absorber in nosewheel leg. Goodyear crosswind landing gear, Edo and PK floats, and amphibious floats, optional.
POWER PLANT: One 186.4 kW (250 hp) Textron Lycoming O-540 (Model 600), or liquid-cooled 224 kW (300 hp)

Teledyne Continental Voyager (Model 700), or 261 kW (350 hp) turbocharged Textron Lycoming TIO-540 (Model 800), or 298 kW (400 hp) Textron Lycoming IO-720-A1B (Model 900), each driving a Hartzell three-blade constant-speed metal propeller. Fuel in two wing tanks, total capacity 227 litres (60 US gallons; 50 Imp gallons). Auxiliary wing tanks optional, bringing total capacity to 454 litres (120 US gallons; 100 Imp gallons). Refuelling points in upper surface of each wing.
ACCOMMODATION: Standard seating for pilot and five passengers in three rows of two. Door at forward end of cabin on port side and at mid-cabin on starboard side. Four doors optional.
SYSTEMS: Electrical system power supplied by 50A 12V alternator.

AVIONICS: Standard avionics comprise VHF com transceiver, transponder and encoder. Full IFR avionics, II Morrow Loran C, GPS and INS optional.

DIMENSIONS, EXTERNAL:
Wing span	11.58 m (38 ft 0 in)
Wing chord, constant	1.83 m (6 ft 0 in)
Wing aspect ratio	6.6
Length overall	9.91 m (32 ft 6 in)
Height overall	4.32 m (14 ft 2 in)
Tailplane span	4.57 m (15 ft 0 in)
Wheel track	2.69 m (8 ft 10 in)
Wheelbase: tailwheel	7.26 m (23 ft 10 in)
nosewheel	3.10 m (10 ft 2 in)
Propeller diameter	2.44-2.57 m (8 ft 0 in-8 ft 5 in)
Propeller ground clearance	0.23 m (9 in)

AREAS:
Wings, gross	21.46 m² (231.0 sq ft)
Tailplane	3.48 m² (37.5 sq ft)

WEIGHTS AND LOADINGS (A: 600/700, B: 800/900):
Max T-O weight: A	1,542 kg (3,400 lb)
B	1,723 kg (3,800 lb)
Max zero-fuel weight: A	943 kg (2,080 lb)
B	1,146 kg (2,527 lb)
Max wing loading: A	71.87 kg/m² (14.72 lb/sq ft)
B	80.32 kg/m² (16.45 lb/sq ft)
Max power loading:	
Model 600	8.27 kg/kW (13.60 lb/hp)
Model 700	6.88 kg/kW (11.33 lb/hp)
Model 800	6.60 kg/kW (10.86 lb/hp)
Model 900	5.78 kg/kW (9.50 lb/hp)

PERFORMANCE (at max T-O weight, ISA, except where indicated. A: 600, B: 700, C: 800, D: 900):
Max level speed: A	139 knots (259 km/h; 160 mph)
B, C	145 knots (269 km/h; 167 mph)
D	147 knots (272 km/h; 169 mph)
Max cruising speed at 1,525 m (5,000 ft):	
A, C	132 knots (245 km/h; 152 mph)
B	143 knots (266 km/h; 165 mph)
D	133 knots (246 km/h; 153 mph)
Econ cruising speed at 1,525 m (5,000 ft):	
A	115 knots (214 km/h; 133 mph)
B	130 knots (241 km/h; 150 mph)
C	122 knots (225 km/h; 140 mph)
D	123 knots (229 km/h; 142 mph)
Stalling speed, flaps down, power on:	
A	26 knots (49 km/h; 30 mph)
B	27 knots (50 km/h; 31 mph)
Max rate of climb at S/L: A	364 m (1,195 ft)/min
B	381 m (1,250 ft)/min
C	360 m (1,180 ft)/min
D	341 m (1,120 ft)/min
Service ceiling: A	4,630 m (15,200 ft)
B	6,250 m (20,500 ft)
C	8,840 m (29,000 ft)
D	6,400 m (21,000 ft)
T-O run: A	92 m (300 ft)
B	75 m (245 ft)
C	89 m (290 ft)
D	87 m (285 ft)
T-O to 15 m (50 ft): A	229 m (750 ft)
B	186 m (610 ft)
C	211 m (690 ft)
D	189 m (618 ft)
Landing from 15 m (50 ft): A, B	151 m (493 ft)
C, D	223 m (730 ft)
Landing run: A, B	74 m (240 ft)
C, D	70 m (228 ft)
Range with max fuel:	
A	1,118 nm (2,072 km; 1,288 miles)
B	1,198 nm (2,220 km; 1,380 miles)
C	924 nm (1,712 km; 1,064 miles)
D	851 nm (1,577 km; 980 miles)

HELIO SUPER COURIER
Provisional details:

POWER PLANT: One 313 kW (420 shp) Allison 250-B17C turboprop.

WEIGHTS AND LOADINGS:
Weight empty	812 kg (1,790 lb)
Max fuel weight	381 kg (840 lb)
Max T-O weight	1,723 kg (3,800 lb)
Max power loading	5.50 kg/kW (9.04 lb/shp)

PERFORMANCE (estimated):
Max cruising speed at 5,180 m (17,000 ft), 70% power	152 knots (282 km/h; 175 mph)
Stalling speed	25 knots (45 km/h; 28 mph)
Max rate of climb at S/L	823 m (2,700 ft)/min
Service ceiling	7,620 m (25,000 ft)
T-O and landing run	46 m (150 ft)
Endurance	5 h 30 min

HELIO H-550A STALLION
US military designation: AU-24A
Details of Helio Courier apply also to Stallion except as follows:

TYPE: Eight/twelve-seat turboprop STOL utility aircraft.

DESIGN FEATURES: Military version has two hardpoints under each wing, capacity 680 kg (1,500 lb) each inboard and 612 kg (1,350 lb) each outboard; also centreline hardpoint for 227 kg (500 lb). Swept fin and rudder with dorsal fin.

FLYING CONTROLS: Lateral control spoilers above wing inboard of ailerons; elevators and rudder; electric aileron trim; manual rudder trim.

POWER PLANT: One 507 kW (680 shp) Pratt & Whitney Canada PT6A-27 turboprop, driving a three-blade constant-speed feathering and reversing Hartzell propeller. Fuel in four wing tanks, total capacity 454 litres (120 US gallons; 100 Imp gallons).

ACCOMMODATION: Standard seating for pilot and seven passengers in four rows of two. Three-abreast seating optional. Crew door on each side of cockpit, double cargo/passenger door on port side of cabin. Ventral airdrop hatch/emergency exit.

SYSTEMS: 150A 24V alternator.

AVIONICS: Bendix/King or Narco com transceiver, transponder, encoder and intercom standard. Full range of avionics by Bendix/King and Narco available to customer choice.

ARMAMENT: Military version has provision for the carriage of a range of weapons and stores including 20 mm and 7.62 mm miniguns, 500 lb Mk 82 bombs, FFARs, napalm and reconnaissance cameras.

DIMENSIONS, EXTERNAL:
Wing span	12.50 m (41 ft 0 in)
Wing aspect ratio	6.83
Length overall	12.07 m (39 ft 7 in)
Height overall	2.82 m (9 ft 3 in)
Tailplane span	5.49 m (18 ft 0 in)
Wheel track	2.95 m (9 ft 8 in)
Propeller diameter	2.82 m (9 ft 3 in)
Passenger/cargo door: Height	1.22 m (4 ft 0 in)
Width	1.63 m (5 ft 4 in)
Height to sill	0.76 m (2 ft 6 in)
Ventral hatch: Length	1.09 m (3 ft 7 in)
Width	0.58 m (1 ft 11 in)

DIMENSIONS, EXTERNAL:
Cabin: Length, incl cockpit	4.19 m (13 ft 9 in)
Max width	1.35 m (4 ft 5 in)
Height	1.47 m (4 ft 10 in)
Floor area	5.30 m² (57.0 sq ft)
Volume	6.46 m³ (228.0 cu ft)

AREAS:
Wings, gross	22.85 m² (246.0 sq ft)

WEIGHTS AND LOADINGS (A: civil, B: military):
Weight empty	1,297 kg (2,860 lb)
Max fuel weight	326.5 kg (720 lb)
Max T-O and landing weight: A	2,313 kg (5,100 lb)
B	2,857 kg (6,300 lb)
Max wing loading: A	101.21 kg/m² (20.73 lb/sq ft)
B	125.04 kg/m² (25.61 lb/sq ft)
Max power loading: A	4.56 kg/kW (7.50 lb/shp)
B	5.64 kg/kW (9.26 lb/shp)

PERFORMANCE (at max T-O weight, ISA, except where indicated. A: civil, B: military):
Max cruising speed at 3,050 m (10,000 ft):	
A	188 knots (348 km/h; 216 mph)
B	156 knots (289 km/h; 180 mph)
Econ cruising speed: A	139 knots (258 km/h; 160 mph)
Stalling speed: A	37 knots (69 km/h; 43 mph)
B	41 knots (76 km/h; 48 mph)
Max rate of climb at S/L: A	670 m (2,200 ft)/min
B	411 m (1,350 ft)/min
Service ceiling: A	8,840 m (29,000 ft)
B	5,790 m (19,000 ft)
T-O run: A	98 m (320 ft)
B	171 m (560 ft)
T-O to 15 m (50 ft): A	202 m (660 ft)
Landing from 15 m (50 ft): A	229 m (750 ft)
Landing run: A	77 m (250 ft)
B	98 m (320 ft)
Max range: A	640 nm (1,186 km; 737 miles)
B	450 nm (834 km; 518 miles)

HILLER — *see Rogerson*

HYNES — *see Brantly*

JAFFE
JAFFE AIRCRAFT INC
1770 Skyplace Boulevard, International Airport, San Antonio, Texas 78216
Telephone: 1 (512) 821 6301
Fax: 1 (512) 822 7766

Company has developed SA-32T Turbo Trainer; prototype built by Swearingen Engineering and Technology Inc; to be submitted for US Air Force JPATS programme. See also Jaffe Helicopter under Heli-Air.

JAFFE SA-32T TURBO TRAINER
TYPE: Two-seat training aircraft.

PROGRAMME: First flight of prototype 31 May 1989; displayed at 1989 Paris Air Show after 15 h North Atlantic ferry flight.

DESIGN FEATURES: Based on Ed Swearingen's SX300 light aircraft described and illustrated in 1987-88 *Jane's*; skin thickness increased by 50 per cent to cater for higher performance; new canopy with miniature detonating cord and either rocket extraction system or Martin-Baker lightweight ejection seats; larger wheels, tyres and brakes; NASA NLF 0416 laminar flow aerofoil section claimed to produce handling characteristics of jet aircraft.

FLYING CONTROLS: Ailerons have electric trim; electrically operated trim tab in elevator; hydraulically actuated trailing-edge flaps.

STRUCTURE: Mainly all-metal structure; single spar wings, composites used in wingtips and fuselage fairings; stressed skin fuselage, composites tailcone and engine cowling panels; composites in fin and tailplane tips.

LANDING GEAR: Hydraulically retractable tricycle type, with single wheel and oleo-pneumatic shock absorber on each

Prototype Jaffe SA-32T Turbo Trainer (*J. M. G. Gradidge*)

unit. Manual hydraulic pump for emergency extension, and gas-spring powered secondary emergency extension. Steerable nose unit, with shimmy damper. Mainwheel tyres size 6.00-6, nosewheel tyre size 5.00-5 (all three 6-ply). Hydraulic disc brakes and parking brake.

POWER PLANT: One 313 kW (420 shp) Allison 250-B17D turboprop, driving a three-blade constant-speed propeller. Inlet anti-iced by engine bleed air. Fuel in two integral wing tanks (each 128.5 litres; 34 US gallons; 28 Imp gallons usable) and a 72 litre (19 US gallon; 16 Imp gallon) fuselage header tank, giving total usable capacity of 329 litres (87 US gallons; 72 Imp gallons).

ACCOMMODATION: Side by side seats for instructor and pupil, with full-shoulder inertia reel safety harness for each occupant. Dual controls standard. Hydraulically actuated 'omnivision' canopy, with windscreen demisting.

Baggage space aft of seats. Accommodation heated (by engine bleed air) and ventilated.

SYSTEMS: Hydraulic system for actuation of flaps, landing gear and mainwheel brakes. Electrical system (28V DC), with lead-acid battery and 70A alternator, provides power for engine start, aileron and elevator trim, hydraulic pumps, navigation, strobe, landing and cockpit lights.

DIMENSIONS, EXTERNAL:
Wing span	7.43 m (24 ft 4½ in)
Wing aspect ratio	8.3
Length overall	6.86 m (22 ft 6 in)
Height overall	2.37 m (7 ft 9¼ in)

DIMENSIONS, INTERNAL:
Cockpit: Max width	1.04 m (3 ft 5 in)

AREAS:
Wings, gross reference	6.64 m² (71.5 sq ft)

WEIGHTS AND LOADINGS:
Average weight empty, equipped	707 kg (1,560 lb)
Fuel weight (usable)	264 kg (583 lb)
Baggage (max)	32 kg (70 lb)
Max T-O and landing weight	1,179 kg (2,600 lb)
Max power loading	3.77 kg/kW (6.19 lb/shp)

PERFORMANCE (estimated, at max T-O weight except where indicated):
Never-exceed speed (VNE)	348 knots (644 km/h; 400 mph)
Max level speed at S/L	288 knots (534 km/h; 332 mph)
Max manoeuvring speed	207 knots (383 km/h; 238 mph)
Normal cruising speed at 6,100 m (20,000 ft), 75% power	274 knots (508 km/h; 315 mph)
Max gear extension speed	170 knots (314 km/h; 195 mph)
Max full flap extension speed	135 knots (250 km/h; 155 mph)

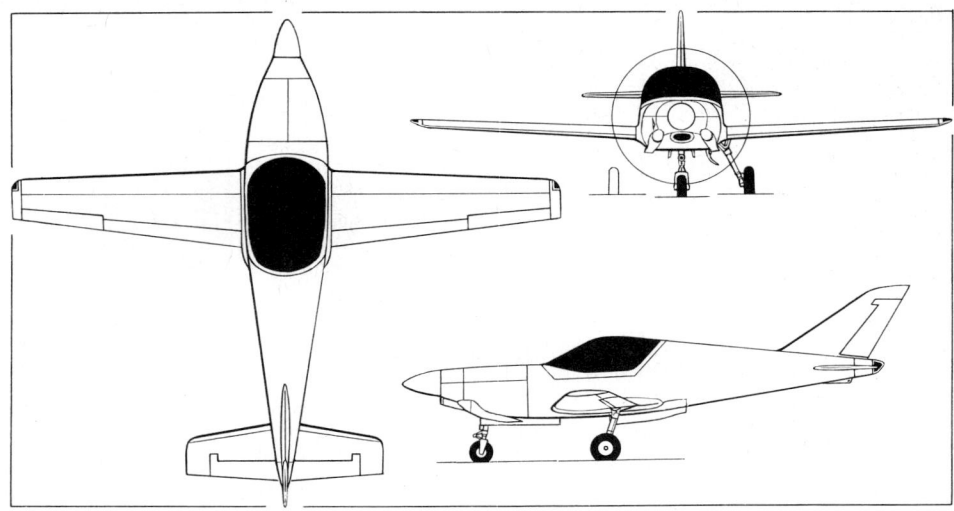

Jaffe SA-32T side by side two-seat turboprop trainer *(Pilot Press)*

Stalling speed at 1,134 kg (2,500 lb) AUW:	
gear and flaps up	86 knots (160 km/h; 100 mph)
gear and flaps down	66 knots (122 km/h; 76 mph)
Max rate of climb at S/L, at 1,134 kg (2,500 lb) AUW	1,128 m (3,700 ft)/min
Service ceiling	more than 7,620 m (25,000 ft)
T-O run	427 m (1,400 ft)

T-O to 15 m (50 ft)	518 m (1,700 ft)
Landing from 15 m (50 ft)	701 m (2,300 ft)
Landing run	335 m (1,100 ft)
Max range at normal cruising speed, no reserves	960 nm (1,779 km; 1,105 miles)
g limits	±6

KAMAN

KAMAN AEROSPACE CORPORATION
(Subsidiary of Kaman Corporation)
Old Windsor Road, PO Box No. 2, Bloomfield, Connecticut 06002
Telephone: 1 (203) 242 4461
Telex: 710 425 3411
PRESIDENT AND CHIEF EXECUTIVE OFFICER:
Walter R. Kozlow
VICE-PRESIDENT, ENGINEERING: David J. White
DIRECTOR, PUBLIC RELATIONS: Kenneth J. Nasshan

Founded in 1945 by Charles H. Kaman, now Chairman of the Board of Kaman Corporation. Developed servo-flap control of helicopter main rotor, still used in H-2 Seasprite naval helicopter. R&D programmes sponsored by US Army, Air Force, Navy and NASA include advanced design of helicopter rotor systems, blades and rotor control concepts, component fatigue life determination and structural dynamic analysis and testing. Kaman has undertaken helicopter drone programmes since 1953; is continuing advanced research in rotary wing unmanned aerial vehicles (UAVs).

Kaman is major subcontractor in many aircraft and space programmes, including design, tooling and fabrication of components in metal, metal honeycomb, bonded and composites construction, using techniques such as filament winding and braiding. Participates in programmes including Grumman A-6 and F-14, Bell/Boeing V-22, Boeing 737, 747, 757 and 767, Sikorsky UH-60 and SH-60, and NASA Space Shuttle Orbiter. Kaman also supplies acoustic engine ducts for P&W JT8D and thrust reversers for GE CF6-80C/E engines.

Kaman designed and, since 1977, has been producing all-composite rotor blades for Bell AH-1 Cobras for US and foreign armies; participated in AH-1 air-to-air Stinger (ATAS) programme. Personnel of Kaman Aerospace totalled 1,700 in January 1991.

KAMAN SEASPRITE and SUPER SEASPRITE
US Navy designation: SH-2
TYPE: Shipboard ASW helicopter with SAR, observation and utility capability.

PROGRAMME: First flight 2 July 1959; successive versions for US Navy described in earlier *Jane's*; SH-2F put back into production in 1981; from 1967 all single-engined SH-2A/B Seasprites progressively converted to twin-engined UH-2Cs with General Electric T58-GE-8Bs; later modified to Mk I Light Airborne Multi-Purpose System (LAMPS) standard to give small ships ASW, anti-ship surveillance and targeting (ASST), SAR and utility capability; all SH-2s subsequently upgraded to SH-2Fs, each with stronger landing gear, T58-GE-8F engines and improved rotor.

Operational deployment of LAMPS Mk I to HSL squadrons began 7 December 1971; by December 1990, more than 750,000 hours flown from ship classes FFG-7, DD-963, DDG-993, CG-47, FFG-1, FF-1052, FF-1040, CG-26, CGN-35, CGN-38 and BB-61; US Coast Guard WMEC and WHEC cutters being equipped to operate SH-2; eight active Navy LAMPS Mk I squadrons supplemented in 1984 by three Naval Air Reserve squadrons; 24 SH-2Fs transferred to HSL-74, 84 and 94

Production Kaman SH-2G Super Seasprite in new tactical light grey paint scheme

Reserve squadrons at South Weymouth (Massachusetts), North Island (California), and Willow Grove (Pennsylvania) as new aircraft delivered to HSLs; front-line squadrons are HSL-30, 32 and 34 at Norfolk, Virginia, and HSL-36 at Mayport, Florida, for Atlantic-based ships; and HSL-31, 33 and 35 at North Island, California, for the Pacific; active and Reserve LAMPS Mk I SH-2s will remain in service until 2010.

VARIANTS (in service 1991): **SH-2F:** LAMPS Mk I; 88 delivered between May 1973 and 1982, of which 75 operational February 1989; 16 SH-2Ds converted to SH-2F; first operational unit, HSL-33, deployed to Pacific 11 September 1973; 54 new SH-2Fs ordered FY 1982-86 (18, 18, six, six and six), delivered by December 1989; another six ordered in FY 1987, being completed as SH-2G (see below). SH-2F described in 1987-88 *Jane's*; SH-2F fleet to be upgraded to SH-2G.

For operation in Arabian Gulf since 1987, 16 SH-2Fs augmented standard AN/ALR-66A(V)1 RWR and AN/ALE-39 chaff/flare dispensers by Sanders AN/ALQ-144 IR jammers on starboard side of tail rotor driveshaft, Honeywell AN/AAR-47 missile warning equipment, Collins AN/ARC-182 secure VHF/UHF radios, AN/DLQ-3 missile warning and jamming equipment, and Hughes AN/AAQ-16 FLIR under nose.

SH-2G Super Seasprite: SH-2F upgrade initiated FY 1987; airframe changes included replacing T58 with T700-GE-401 engines and adopting all-composite main rotor blades with 10,000 hour life; fuel consumption improved by over 20 per cent. Avionics improvements include MIL-STD-1553B digital databus, onboard acoustic processor, multi-function raster display, AN/ASN-150 tactical navigation display, and 99-channel sonobuoys. SH-2G qualified for dipping sonar, air-to-

surface missiles, forward-looking infra-red sensors and various guns, rockets and countermeasures.

First flight of SH-2G 161653 as YSH-2G T700 engine testbed, April 1985; first flight with full avionics 28 December 1989; this helicopter to be delivered 1991, followed by six new-build SH-2Gs ordered FY 1987. June 1987 contract launched conversion programme from SH-2F to SH-2G; 20 conversion kits on order by January 1991, including six funded in 1990. First production SH-3G (163541) flown March 1990. Assigned to squadrons HSL-84, 33, 74 and 94, in order of conversion. Total 97 planned.

CUSTOMERS: SH-2G offered for export with various equipment from above; Greece and Thailand interested.

COSTS: USN planning expenditure on H-2 of $31.9, 8.9, 108.2 and 107.2 million in FYs 1990-93.

DESIGN FEATURES: Main rotor rpm 298; main and tail rotor blades folded manually; nose opens and folds back for shipboard stowage; lateral pylons for torpedoes or tanks; MAD bird in holder extending from starboard side.

FLYING CONTROLS: Main rotor blades fixed on hub; pitch changed by trailing-edge tabs.

STRUCTURE: All-metal airframe with flotation hull; titanium main rotor hub and all-composite main rotor blades.

LANDING GEAR: Tailwheel type, with forward retracting twin mainwheels and non-retractable tailwheel. Liquid spring shock absorbers in main gear legs; oleo-pneumatic shock absorber in tailwheel unit, which is fully castoring for taxying but locked fore and aft for T-O and landing. Mainwheels have 8-ply tubeless tyres size 17.5 × 6.25-11, pressure 17.25 bars (250 lb/sq in); tailwheel 10-ply tube-type tyre size 5.00-5, pressure 11.04 bars (160 lb/sq in).

POWER PLANT: Two 1,285 kW (1,723 shp) General Electric T700-GE-401/401C turboshafts, one on each side of rotor pylon structure. Basic fuel capacity of 1,802 litres (476 US gallons; 396 Imp gallons), including up to two external auxiliary tanks with a combined capacity of 757 litres (200 US gallons; 166.5 Imp gallons). Ship-to-air helicopter in-flight refuelling (HIFR).

ACCOMMODATION: Crew of three, consisting of pilot, co-pilot/tactical co-ordinator, and sensor operator. One passenger with LAMPS equipment installed; four passengers or two litters with sonobuoy launcher removed. Provision for transportation of internal or external cargo. Space for additional troop seats.

SYSTEMS: Include dual 30kVA electrical system and Solav T-62 gas turbine APU.

AVIONICS: LAMPS Mk I mission equipment includes Canadian Marconi LN-66HP surveillance radar; General Instruments AN/ALR-66A(V)1 radar warning/ESM; Teledyne Systems AN/ASN-150 tactical management system; dual Collins AN/ARC-159(V)1 UHF radios; Texas Instruments AN/ASQ-81(V)2 magnetic anomaly detector; Computing Devices AN/UYS-503 acoustic processor; Flightline Electronics AN/ARR-84 sonobuoy receiver and AN/ARN-146 on-top position indicator; Tele-Dynamics AN/AKT-22(V)6 sonobuoy data link; 15 DIFAR and DICASS sonobuoys; AN/ALE-39 chaff/flare dispensers; AN/ASQ-188 torpedo presetter. The US Navy plans to retrofit additional self-defence equipment in fleet SH-2Gs, consisting of Hughes AN/AAQ-16 FLIR, Sanders AN/ALQ-144 IR jammers, Loral AN/AAR-47 missile warning and Collins AN/ARC-182 VHF/UHF secure radio.

EQUIPMENT: Cargo hook for external loads, capacity 1,814 kg (4,000 lb); and folding rescue hoist, capacity 272 kg (600 lb).

ARMAMENT: One or two Mk 46 or Mk 50 torpedoes; eight Mk 25 marine smoke markers. Provision for pintle-mounted 7.62 mm machine gun in both cabin doorways.

DIMENSIONS, EXTERNAL:
Main rotor diameter	13.51 m (44 ft 4 in)
Main rotor blade chord	0.59 m (1 ft 11 in)
Tail rotor diameter	2.46 m (8 ft 1 in)

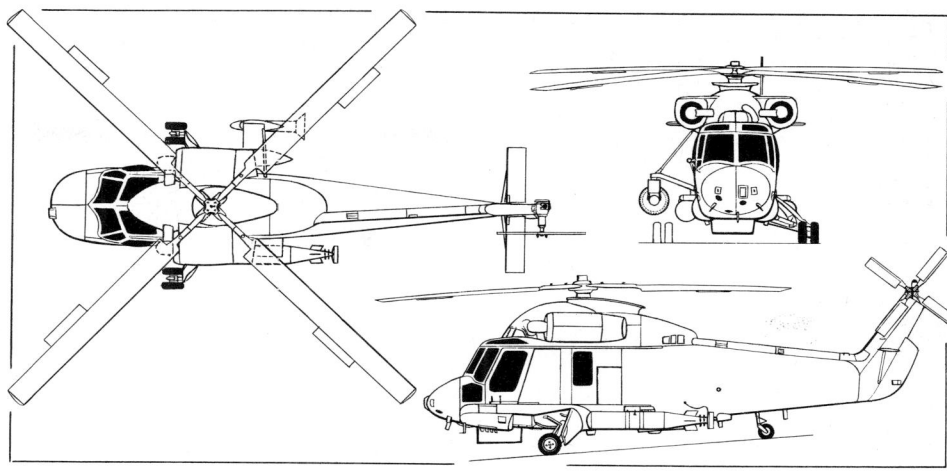

Kaman SH-2G Super Seasprite LAMPS Mk I helicopter *(Pilot Press)*

Tail rotor blade chord	0.236 m (9.3 in)
Length: fuselage, excl tail rotor	12.19 m (40 ft 0 in)
overall (rotors turning)	16.08 m (52 ft 9 in)
nose and blades folded	11.68 m (38 ft 4 in)
Height: overall (rotors turning)	4.58 m (15 ft 0½ in)
blades folded	4.14 m (13 ft 7 in)
Width overall, incl MAD	3.74 m (12 ft 3 in)
Stabiliser span	2.97 m (9 ft 9 in)
Wheel track (outer wheels)	3.30 m (10 ft 10 in)
Wheelbase	5.13 m (16 ft 10 in)
Tail rotor ground clearance	2.12 m (6 ft 11½ in)

AREAS:
Main rotor blades (each)	3.96 m² (42.63 sq ft)
Tail rotor blades (each)	0.295 m² (3.175 sq ft)
Main rotor disc	143.41 m² (1,543.66 sq ft)
Tail rotor disc	4.77 m² (51.32 sq ft)

WEIGHTS AND LOADINGS:
Weight empty	3,447 kg (7,600 lb)
Max T-O weight	6,124 kg (13,500 lb)
Max disc loading	42.72 kg/m² (8.75 lb/sq ft)

PERFORMANCE (ISA):
Max level speed at S/L	138 knots (256 km/h; 159 mph)
Normal cruising speed	120 knots (222 km/h; 138 mph)
Max rate of climb at S/L	762 m (2,500 ft)/min
Rate of climb at S/L, one engine out	530 m (1,740 ft)/min
Service ceiling	7,285 m (23,900 ft)
Service ceiling, one engine out	4,816 m (15,800 ft)
Hovering ceiling: IGE	6,340 m (20,800 ft)
OGE	5,486 m (18,000 ft)
Max range, 2 external tanks	478 nm (885 km; 500 miles)
Max endurance, 2 external tanks	5 h

KING'S

THE KING'S ENGINEERING FELLOWSHIP

Municipal Airport, Orange City, Iowa 51041
Telephone: 1 (712) 737 4444
PRESIDENT: Carl A. Mortenson

The Angel, developed by The King's Engineering Fellowship through donations and designed by Mr Carl Mortenson, follows the earlier Evangel (described in 1974-75 *Jane's*); of eight Evangels built, seven still served with missionaries in Alaska, Colombia, Micronesia and Peru in 1988.

KING'S MODEL 44 ANGEL

TYPE: Specialised light twin-engined utility aircraft.

PROGRAMME: Prototype (N44KE) built on production tooling; first flight January 1984; structural testing began 1990; production start planned for 1992.

DESIGN FEATURES: Intended for missionary aviation flying; design goals include low manufacturing costs, STOL capability, operation from soft and rough fields, easy repair in field, and easy loading of bulky cargo. Engines temporarily raised on pylons above wing, but returned to on-wing location and nacelles lengthened to increase cruising speed by 13 knots (24 km/h; 15 mph); other changes include outboard 'trimmerons' used to assist single-engined handling (normal lateral spoilers reduce lift when applied continually), and increased tailplane span. Wing section NACA 23018-23010 with modified leading-edge.

FLYING CONTROLS: Lateral control by multiple small-plate spoilers at maximum thickness point of wing; 'trimmerons' outboard of flaps to assist single-engined flight; elevators and rudder; almost full-span hydraulically actuated Fowler flaps deflecting to maximum 37°.

STRUCTURE: All-metal riveted structure; wing has built-up capstrip spars and 19 die-formed ribs each side; broad-chord fin and rudder with large dorsal fin.

LANDING GEAR: Retractable tricycle type. Electro-hydraulic retraction, mainwheels inward into wingroots, nosewheel rearward. Emergency extension by handpump or gravity. Tyre size: mainwheels 8.50-10, nosewheel 8.50-6. Cleveland brakes.

Prototype King's Angel light twin for missionary aviation duties *(Kenneth Munson)*

POWER PLANT: Two 224 kW (300 hp) Textron Lycoming IO-540-M flat-six engines, mounted on top of the inboard wings and each driving a Hartzell three-blade constant-speed feathering pusher propeller. Total usable fuel capacity 855 litres (226 US gallons; 188 Imp gallons). Oil capacity 22.7 litres (6 US gallons; 5 Imp gallons).

ACCOMMODATION: Enclosed cabin seating up to eight persons, including pilot. Five seats can be removed for carrying cargo, including four 208 litre (55 US gallon; 46 Imp gallon) drums. Rearmost bench seat is fixed. Four large windows and one smaller circular window on each side of cabin. Horizontally divided clamshell door on port side at front of cabin; emergency exit on starboard side. Heating and window air vents standard. Compartment for 90 kg (200 lb) of baggage at rear of fuselage, with door on port side.

SYSTEMS: Hydraulic system, with electric pump, for landing gear and flap actuation. Electrical system includes 12V battery in nose.

AVIONICS: Blind-flying instrumentation standard. Bendix/King avionics, including twin com/nav transceivers, glideslope, and dual ADF. Weather radar, Loran C and HF com optional.

DIMENSIONS, EXTERNAL:
Wing span	12.19 m (40 ft 0 in)
Wing chord at root	2.29 m (7 ft 6 in)
Length overall	10.13 m (33 ft 3 in)
Height overall	3.51 m (11 ft 6 in)
Wheel track	3.96 m (13 ft 0 in)
Wheelbase	4.57 m (15 ft 0 in)

WEIGHTS AND LOADINGS:
Weight empty	1,701 kg (3,750 lb)
Max T-O weight	2,631 kg (5,800 lb)
Max power loading	5.87 kg/kW (9.67 lb/hp)

PERFORMANCE:
Cruising speed, 65% power at 3,050 m (10,000 ft)	174 knots (322 km/h; 200 mph)
Landing speed	57 knots (105 km/h; 65 mph)
Service ceiling	5,790 m (19,000 ft)
Service ceiling, one engine out	2,135 m (7,000 ft)
T-O run	183 m (600 ft)
T-O to 15 m (50 ft)	366 m (1,200 ft)
Landing from 15 m (50 ft)	335 m (1,100 ft)
Landing run	183 m (600 ft)
Range with max fuel, with reserves	1,390 nm (2,575 km; 1,600 miles)
Endurance: with 8 occupants	4 h
with max fuel and 4 occupants	8 h

LAKE

LAKE AIRCRAFT INC

606 N. Dyer Boulevard, Kissimmee Airport, Kissimmee, Florida 34741
Telephone: 1 (407) 847 9000
Fax: 1 (407) 847 4516
PRESIDENT: Armand E. Rivard
EXECUTIVE VICE-PRESIDENT: Gordon Collins

SENIOR VICE-PRESIDENT, SEAWOLF DIVISION:
Maj Gen Frank J. Kelly Jr (Ret'd)
VICE-PRESIDENT, INTERNATIONAL: Haig Hagopian

LAKE LA4-200 AMPHIBIAN

TYPE: Single-engined four-seat amphibian.

PROGRAMME: First flight of original C-1 Skimmer prototype May 1948; led to improved C-2 Skimmer IV and Lake LA-4, LA-4A, LA-4P, LA-4S and LA-4T (described in previous *Jane's*); LA4-200 FAA certificated 1970; manufactured in two versions (see below).

VARIANTS: **LA4-200 EP:** Standard version (detailed below); new features include propeller shaft extended 13 cm (5 in) to increase efficiency and reduce cabin noise, dynamically balanced Textron Lycoming IO-360-A1B6, aerodynamically improved engine nacelle, wing trailing-edge fillets to improve low-speed stability and deflect water spray, hull hydro boosters for better water performance, reinforced floats and station 97 bulkhead, improved canopy, new instrument panel glareshield, new fresh air vents, additional corrosion proofing and new polyurethane paint.

LA4-200 EPR: As above, but with reversible-pitch, constant-speed propeller to simplify water operation.

CUSTOMERS: More than 1,300 delivered by 1990.

DESIGN FEATURES: Single-step all-metal double sealed boat hull; retractable water rudder in base of aerodynamic rudder. Tapered wings attached directly to sides of hull; wing section NACA 4415 at root, 4409 at tip; dihedral 5° 30′; incidence 3° 15′.

FLYING CONTROLS: Manually operated ailerons, elevators and rudder; ground adjustable aileron trim tabs; outer portion of port elevator separate from inboard and operated hydraulically as trimmer; hydraulically operated slotted flaps over 80 per cent of span.

STRUCTURE: Wing has duralumin leading- and trailing-edge torsion boxes separated by single main spar; wing floats light alloy monocoque; hull alodined and zinc chromated inside and out with polyurethane external paint; metal ailerons and tail surfaces.

LANDING GEAR: Hydraulically retractable tricycle type. Consolidated oleo-pneumatic shock absorbers in main gear, which retracts inward into wings. Nosewheel, with long-stroke oleo, retracts forward. Gerdes mainwheels with Goodyear tyres, size 6.00-6, pressure 2.41 bars (35 lb/sq in). Gerdes nosewheel with Goodyear tyre size 5.00-5, pressure 1.38 bars (20 lb/sq in). Gerdes disc brakes. Parking brake. Nosewheel is free to swivel 30° each side.

POWER PLANT: One 149 kW (200 hp) Textron Lycoming IO-360-A1B6 flat-four engine, mounted on pylon above hull and driving a Hartzell two-blade constant-speed metal pusher propeller. Rajay turbocharger, reversible-pitch and Q-tip propeller, optional. Standard usable fuel capacity 204 litres (54 US gallons; 45 Imp gallons); optional usable fuel capacity of 340 litres (90 US gallons; 75 Imp gallons). Oil capacity 7.5 litres (2 US gallons; 1.7 Imp gallons).

ACCOMMODATION: Enclosed cabin seating pilot and three passengers. Front and rear seats removable. Front seats have inertia reel shoulder harness as standard. Dual controls standard; dual brakes for co-pilot optional. Entry through two forward-hinged windscreen sections. Upward hinged gull wing cargo door standard. Baggage compartment, capacity 90.5 kg (200 lb), aft of cabin. Dual windscreen defroster system.

SYSTEMS: Vacuum system for flight instruments. Hydraulic system, pressure 86.2 bars (1,250 lb/sq in), for flaps, horizontal trim and landing gear actuation; handpump provided for emergency operation. Engine driven 12V 60A alternator and 12V 30Ah battery. Janitrol 30,000 BTU heater optional.

AVIONICS: Basic avionics installation includes com and nav antennae, cabin speaker, microphone and circuit breakers. An extensive range of avionics by Bendix/King, Collins and Narco, and autopilots by Brittain and Edo-Aire Mitchell, are available to customers' requirements.

EQUIPMENT: Standard equipment includes full blind-flying instrumentation, electric clock, manifold pressure gauge, outside air temperature gauge, recording tachometer, fuel pressure and quantity indicators, oil pressure and temperature indicators, cylinder head temperature gauge, ammeter, stall warning device, control locks, carpeted floor, four fresh air vents, tinted glass for all windows, dual windscreen defrosters, inertia reel shoulder harness on front seats, shoulder restraint on rear seats, map pocket on front seats, baggage tiedown straps, landing and taxi lights, navigation lights, strobe light, heated pitot, fuselage nose bumper, paddle, cleat, line, full flow oil filter, quick fuel drains, and inboard and outboard tiedown rings. Optional equipment includes hour meter, true airspeed indicator, shoulder harness for rear seats, alternate static source, manual/automatic bilge pump, cabin fire extinguisher, and external metallic paint finish.

DIMENSIONS, EXTERNAL:

Wing span	11.58 m (38 ft 0 in)
Wing chord, mean	1.35 m (4 ft 5.1 in)
Wing aspect ratio	8.7
Length overall	7.59 m (24 ft 11 in)
Height overall	2.84 m (9 ft 4 in)
Tailplane span	3.05 m (10 ft 0 in)
Wheel track	3.40 m (11 ft 2 in)
Wheelbase	2.69 m (8 ft 10 in)
Propeller diameter	1.88 m (6 ft 2 in)

DIMENSIONS, INTERNAL:

Cabin: Length	1.57 m (5 ft 2 in)
Max width	1.05 m (3 ft 5½ in)
Max height	1.32 m (3 ft 11½ in)
Floor area	approx 1.53 m² (16.5 sq ft)
Volume	approx 1.70 m³ (60.0 cu ft)
Baggage hold	0.24 m³ (8.5 cu ft)

AREAS:

Wings, gross	15.79 m² (170.0 sq ft)
Ailerons (total)	1.16 m² (12.5 sq ft)
Trailing-edge flaps (total)	2.28 m² (24.5 sq ft)
Fin	1.25 m² (13.5 sq ft)
Rudder	0.79 m² (8.5 sq ft)

Lake Renegade manoeuvring on water

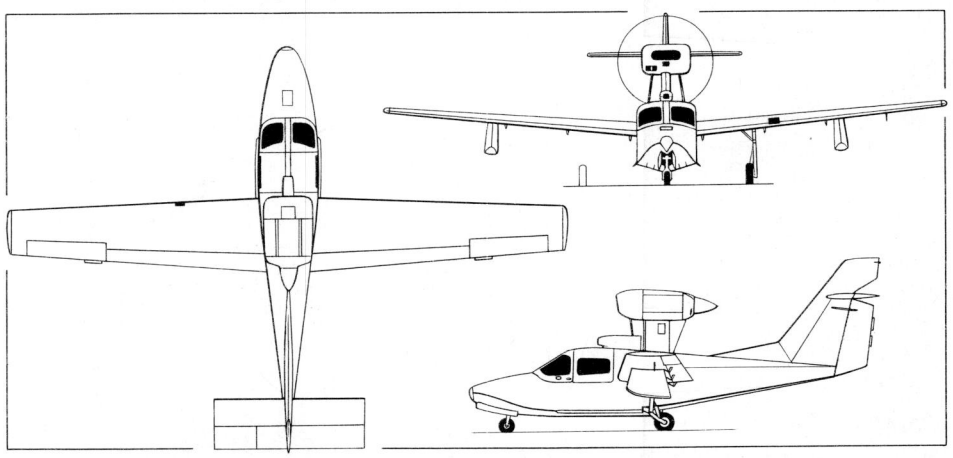

Lake LA-250 Renegade six-seat amphibian *(Pilot Press)*

Tailplane	1.45 m² (15.6 sq ft)
Elevators (total)	0.78 m² (8.4 sq ft)

WEIGHTS AND LOADINGS:

Weight empty, equipped	753 kg (1,660 lb)
Max T-O and landing weight	1,220 kg (2,690 lb)
Max wing loading	74.2 kg/m² (15.2 lb/sq ft)
Max power loading	8.19 kg/kW (13.45 lb/hp)

PERFORMANCE (at max T-O weight. A: EP/EPR, B: EP/EPR with turbocharger):

Max level speed at S/L:	
A	134 knots (248 km/h; 154 mph) IAS
Max cruising speed, 75% power:	
at 2,440 m (8,000 ft):	
A	130 knots (241 km/h; 150 mph)
at 6,100 m (20,000 ft):	
B	143 knots (265 km/h; 164 mph)
Stalling speed:	
A, B, flaps and landing gear up	
	53 knots (98 km/h; 61 mph)
A, B, flaps and landing gear down	
	39 knots (73 km/h; 45 mph)
Max rate of climb at S/L: A	299 m (980 ft)/min
Rate of climb at 2,440 m (8,000 ft):	
B	244 m (800 ft)/min
Service ceiling: A	3,810 m (12,500 ft)
Max operating altitude: B	6,100 m (20,000 ft)
T-O run: A, on land	183 m (600 ft)
A, on water	335 m (1,100 ft)
Landing run: A, on land	145 m (475 ft)
A, on water	183 m (600 ft)
Range with max fuel, at normal cruising speed, with reserves: A	564 nm (1,046 km; 650 miles)

Max range with max fuel, with reserves:	
A	716 nm (1,327 km; 825 miles)
Endurance (75% power):	
A at 2,440 m (8,000 ft)	5 h 36 min
B at 6,100 m (20,000 ft)	5 h 12 min

LAKE LA-250 RENEGADE and TURBO 270 RENEGADE

TYPE: Lengthened six-seat version of LA4-200.

PROGRAMME: LA-250 FAA certificated August 1983.

VARIANTS: **LA-250 Renegade:** Standard version, as described in detail.

Turbo 270 Renegade: Turbocharged version with 186 kW (250 hp) Textron Lycoming TIO-540-AA1AD. Set world altitude record of 7,465 m (24,500 ft) for small amphibians August 1983.

Special Edition Seafury: Renegade with salt water operating package including lifting rings, stainless steel brake discs, custom interior and survival package. Available from Summer 1990.

CUSTOMERS: Total of 23 Renegades delivered during 1989.

DESIGN FEATURES: Generally as for LA4-200, but fuselage lengthened 1.05 m (3 ft 5 in); deeper V hull bottom and additional strakes.

FLYING CONTROLS: As for LA4-200.

LANDING GEAR: As for LA4-200, except wheelbase increased by 0.43 m (1 ft 5 in), and oleo extension increased to provide greater ground clearance.

POWER PLANT: One 186 kW (250 hp) Textron Lycoming IO-540-C4B5 flat-six engine in Renegade and Seafury, driving a Hartzell three-blade constant-speed Q-tip

Lake Turbo 270 Renegade taxying up a slipway

metal pusher propeller. Turbocharged TIO-540-AA1AD engine in Turbo Renegade. Standard usable fuel capacity 204 litres (54 US gallons; 45 Imp gallons); optional usable capacity of 340 litres (90 US gallons; 75 Imp gallons).

ACCOMMODATION: As for LA4-200, but lengthened cabin provides seating for a pilot and five passengers, with increased baggage capacity. Gull wing cargo door standard.

DIMENSIONS, EXTERNAL:

Wing span	11.68 m (38 ft 4 in)
Length overall	8.64 m (28 ft 4 in)
Height overall	3.05 m (10 ft 0 in)
Wheel track	3.40 m (11 ft 2 in)
Wheelbase	3.13 m (10 ft 3 in)
Propeller diameter	1.93 m (6 ft 4 in)

DIMENSIONS, INTERNAL:

Cabin: Length	2.03 m (6 ft 8 in)

WEIGHTS AND LOADINGS:

Weight empty, equipped: Renegade	839 kg (1,850 lb)
Turbo Renegade	875 kg (1,930 lb)
Max usable fuel	240 kg (528 lb)
Max ramp, T-O and landing weight	1,383 kg (3,050 lb)
Max wing loading	87.6 kg/m² (17.94 lb/sq ft)
Max power loading	7.42 kg/kW (12.2 lb/hp)

PERFORMANCE (at max T-O weight, S/L, ISA):

Never-exceed speed (VNE):

Renegade	148 knots (274 km/h; 170 mph)

Max level speed at 1,980 m (6,500 ft):

Renegade	139 knots (258 km/h; 160 mph)

Max cruising speed:

Renegade, 75% power at 1,980 m (6,500 ft)
132 knots (245 km/h; 152 mph)

Turbo Renegade, 78% power at 6,100 m (20,000 ft)
148 knots (274 km/h; 170 mph)

Stalling speed, power off:

landing gear and flaps up
54 knots (100 km/h; 62 mph) IAS

landing gear and flaps down
48 knots (89 km/h; 56 mph) IAS

Max rate of climb at S/L	274 m (900 ft)/min
Service ceiling: Renegade	4,480 m (14,700 ft)
Turbo Renegade	6,100 m (20,000 ft)
T-O run: on land	268 m (880 ft)
on water	381 m (1,250 ft)

Range with max fuel, 30 min reserves:

Renegade	900 nm (1,668 km; 1,036 miles)

Endurance at 78% power: Turbo Renegade 5 h 18 min

LAKE SEAWOLF

TYPE: Single-engined military/maritime surveillance amphibian.

Lake Seawolf maritime patrol amphibian with underwing SAR pods

PROGRAMME: Introduced early 1985; prototype Seawolf (N1401G) first publicly shown at Paris Air Show 1985.

CUSTOMERS: None known.

DESIGN FEATURES: Generally similar to LA-250 Renegade; has Alkan underwing racks for bombs, rockets and machine-gun pods (see Armament); weapon boresighting preserved even after removal and replacement of racks; other underwing loads include droppable sea, land, desert or Arctic rescue pods; 28V electrical system. Possible mission profiles listed in 1990-91 *Jane's*.

FLYING CONTROLS: Similar to Renegade (which see).

STRUCTURE: As Renegade except optional interior LPS spray.

POWER PLANT: Standard fuel capacity 333 litres (88 US gallons; 73.3 Imp gallons); optional capacity, with external tanks, 568 litres (150 US gallons; 125 Imp gallons).

ACCOMMODATION: Enclosed cabin capable of seating up to six persons. All seats except pilot's removable, with a variety of optional internal configurations according to mission. Entry through two forward-hinged windscreen sections. Upward hinged gull wing cargo door standard.

AVIONICS: Various radars can be fitted in radome on front of engine, between cooling intakes; facilities include colour weather detection, range of 240 nm (445 km; 276 miles), and three search modes (Search 1 with sea clutter rejection circuitry for detecting small boats down to minimum range of 275 m; 900 ft, Search 2 for surface mapping with high target resolution, and Search 3 normal surface mapping for oil slick tracking, etc). Interfaces available for moving map display, waypoint designation, checklists, beacon navigation and multiple indicators. Loran and Omega available.

ARMAMENT: Standard Alkan 6091 stores mounts on underwing hardpoints, one inboard and one outboard of each wing balancer float, can accommodate a variety of stores, including external fuel tanks, parachute flares, SAR pods, ECM pods, gun pods, reconnaissance pods, rocket launchers, photo-reconnaissance pods, cartridge throwers, flare dispensers, hazardous material containers, practice and general purpose bombs. Inboard stores points can each carry up to 100 kg (220 lb), outboard points can each carry up to 35 kg (77 lb).

DIMENSIONS, EXTERNAL: As for Renegade

AREAS: As for Renegade

WEIGHTS AND LOADINGS:

Weight empty	998 kg (2,200 lb)
*Max ramp and T-O weight	1,565 kg (3.450 lb)
Max landing weight, on land	1,383 kg (3,050 lb)
Max wing loading	99.06 kg/m² (20.29 lb/sq ft)
Max power loading	8.41 kg/kW (13.80 lb/hp)

* *181 kg (400 lb) must be underwing stores*

PERFORMANCE: As for Renegade, except:

Cruising speed, 55% power
110 knots (204 km/h; 127 mph)

Landing distance, land and water	230 m (755 ft)

Range with standard fuel at 120 knots (222 km/h; 138 mph), with 38 litres (10 US gallons; 8.3 Imp gallons) fuel reserves 876 nm (1,622 km; 1,008 miles)

Range with external tanks at 120 knots (222 km/h; 138 mph), with 38 litres (10 US gallons; 8.3 Imp gallons) fuel reserves 1,500 nm (2,780 km; 1,727 miles)

Endurance: with standard fuel	8 h 30 min
with external tanks	14 h 30 min

LEARJET

LEARJET INC

Mid-Continent Airport, PO Box 7707, Wichita, Kansas 67277
Telephone: 1 (316) 946 2000
Fax: 1 (316) 946 2220
Telex: 417441
PRESIDENT AND CHIEF EXECUTIVE OFFICER: Brian Barents
VICE-PRESIDENT, INTERNATIONAL MARKETING: Robert C. Williams
VICE-PRESIDENT, DOMESTIC MARKETING: Ted Farid
VICE-PRESIDENT, OPERATIONS: Richard E. Hamlin
VICE-PRESIDENT, CORPORATE AFFAIRS: William G. Robinson
VICE-PRESIDENT, ENGINEERING: William W. Greer

Acquisition of Learjet by Canada's Bombardier announced April 1990 and concluded 22 June 1990 for $75 million; Bombardier assumed responsibility for Learjet's line of credit.

Company originally founded 1960 by Bill Lear Snr as Swiss American Aircraft Company (SAAC); transferred to Kansas 1962 and renamed Lear Jet Corporation; Gates Rubber Company bought about 60 per cent of company 1967; company renamed Gates Learjet Corporation; 64.8 per cent of company acquired by Integrated Acquisition Inc September 1987 and renamed Learjet Corporation; all manufacturing moved from Tucson, Arizona, to Wichita during 1988, leaving only customer service and modification centre. Wichita workforce 2,360 in 1990; total 2,760 at all locations.

Learjet is major subcontractor for Martin Marietta Manned Space Systems, Boeing, McDonnell Douglas, General Dynamics, Textron and LTV. Has subsidiary to maintain 83 Learjet 35As operating with US Air Force and Air National Guard (as C-21As). More than 1,600 Learjets produced to date.

Learjet bought manufacturing and marketing rights and tooling of Aeronca thrust reversers, for application to Learjet and other aircraft, March 1989.

Learjet achieved sales of $264 million and was to deliver 30 aircraft in 1990, compared with 25 in 1989.

LEARJET 35A and 36A

US Air Force designation: C-21A

TYPE: Light twin-turbofan business jet.

PROGRAMME: First flight of first turbofan Learjet (known as Model 26 and using Garrett TFE731-2s), 4 January 1973;

One of 80 Learjet C-21As sold to US Air Force for operational support missions *(Jay Miller/Aerofax)*

production 35 and 36, differing in fuel capacity and accommodation, announced May 1973; FAA certification July 1974; French and UK certification 1979.

VARIANTS: **Learjet 35A** and **36A**: Current production models of 35 and 36, with higher standard max T-O weight.

C-21A: USAF received 80 Model 35As on lease in 1984-85 and purchased them for $180 million in September 1986; used as Operational Support Aircraft for priority cargo, medevac and personnel transport, replacing T-39 Sabreliners; four more C-21As bought 1987 to replace T-39s at Andrews AFB, Maryland.

CUSTOMERS: Eight 35A/36A delivered 1990, bringing total to 720.

DESIGN FEATURES: Softflite package includes full-chord shallow fences bracketing ailerons, with arrowhead energisers on leading-edges and two rows of boundary layer energiser strips between fences. Wing section NACA 64A109 with modified leading-edge; dihedral 2° 30′; incidence 1°; sweepback at quarter-chord 13°. Wings de-iced by engine bleed air; tailplane electrically anti-iced.

Century III improvements, Softflite low-speed handling package and engine synchronisers now standard for both models; higher max T-O weight of 8,300 kg (18,300 lb), originally optional, now standard; improvements introduced in 1983 include T/R-4000 thrust reversers with standby hydraulic power reservoir, single-engined

reverse capability, quick removal hot section, prevention of reversal at high thrust, reverse available within two seconds of touchdown, throttle retard system and reverse thrust at reduced gas generator rpm. Special interior introduced 1985 offers better leg and headroom, Erda 10-way adjustable seats, stereo and in-flight telephone, lavatory enclosed by doors and electronically controlled washbasin cabinet.

FLYING CONTROLS: Manually actuated flying controls; balance tabs in both ailerons and electrically operated trim tab in port aileron; electrically actuated variable incidence tailplane; electric trim tab in rudder; small ventral fin; hydraulically actuated single-slotted flaps; hydraulically actuated spoilers ahead of flaps.

STRUCTURE: All-metal; eight spar wing with milled skins; fail-safe fuselage.

LANDING GEAR: Retractable tricycle type, with twin wheels on each main unit and single steerable nosewheel, maximum steering angle 45° either side of centreline. Hydraulic actuation, with backup pneumatic extension. Oleo-pneumatic shock absorbers. Goodyear multiple-disc hydraulic brakes. Pneumatic emergency braking system. Parking brakes. Fully modulated anti-skid system.

POWER PLANT: Two Garrett TFE731-2-2B turbofans, each rated at 15.6 kN (3,500 lb st), pod-mounted on sides of rear fuselage. Fuel in integral wing and wingtip tanks and a fuselage tank, with a combined usable capacity (Learjet

Special missions Learjet U-36A of the Japan Maritime Self-Defence Force

35A) of 3,500 litres (925 US gallons; 770 Imp gallons). Learjet 36A has a larger fuselage tank, giving a combined usable total of 4,179 litres (1,104 US gallons; 919 Imp gallons). Refuelling point on upper surface of each wingtip tank. Fuel jettison system. Engine nacelle leading-edges anti-iced by engine bleed air.

ACCOMMODATION: Crew of two on flight deck, with dual controls. Up to eight passengers in Learjet 35A; one on inward facing seat with toilet on starboard side at front, then two pairs of swivel seats which face fore and aft for take-off and landing, with centre aisle, and three on forward-facing couch at rear of cabin. Two forward storage cabinets, one on each side; refreshment cabinet with hot and cold cup storage, coffee warmer, water dispenser, ice chest and serving surfaces; and two folding tables, standard. Alternative arrangement, available optionally, places a refreshment area in the middle of the cabin, accessible from fore and aft club seating areas, each for four passengers. Learjet 36A can accommodate up to six passengers, one pair of swivel seats being removed. Toilet and stowage space under front inward facing seat which can be screened from remainder of cabin. Refreshment cabinet opposite this seat, aft of passenger door. Baggage compartment with capacity of 226 kg (500 lb) aft of cabin. Two-piece clamshell door at forward end of cabin on port side, with integral steps built into lower half. Emergency exit on starboard side of cabin. Birdproof windscreens.

SYSTEMS: Environmental control system comprises cabin pressurisation, ventilation, heating and cooling. Heating and pressurisation by engine bleed air, with a max pressure differential of 0.65 bar (9.4 lb/sq in), maintaining a cabin altitude of 1,980 m (6,500 ft) to an actual altitude of 13,715 m (45,000 ft). Freon R12 vapour cycle cooling system supplemented by a ram-air heat exchanger. Flight control system includes dual yaw dampers, dual stick pushers, dual stick shakers and Mach trim. Anti-icing system includes distribution of engine bleed air for wing, tailplane and engine nacelle leading-edges and windscreen; electrical heating of pitot heads, stall warning vanes and static ports; and alcohol spray on windscreen and nose radome. Hydraulic system supplied by two engine driven pumps, each pump capable of maintaining alone the full system pressure of 103.5 bars (1,500 lb/sq in), for operation of landing gear, brakes, flaps and spoilers. Hydraulic system maximum flow rate 15 litres (4 US gallons; 3.33 Imp gallons) per min. Cylindrical reservoir pressurised to 1.38 bars (20 lb/sq in). Electrically driven hydraulic pump for emergency operation of all hydraulic services. Pneumatic system of 124 to 207 bars (1,800 to 3,000 lb/sq in) pressure for emergency extension of landing gear and operation of brakes. Electrical system powered by two 30V 400A brushless generators, two 1kVA solid state inverters to provide AC power, and two 24V 37Ah lead-acid batteries. Oxygen system for emergency use, with crew demand masks and dropout masks for each passenger.

AVIONICS: Standard Collins avionics include dual FIS-84/EHSI-74 flight directors, integrated with J.E.T. FC-530 FCS and dual yaw dampers; dual VHF-22A com transceivers with CTL-22 controls; dual VIR-32 nav receivers with CTL-32 controls; ADF-60 with CTL-62 control; dual DME-42 with IND-42C indicators; dual TDR-90 transponders with CTL-92 controls; ALT-55B radio altimeter with DRI-55 indicator; dual Allen 3137 RMIs; UNS-1 long-range nav system; Honeywell Primus 450 colour weather radar; dual J.E.T. VG-206D vertical gyros; dual J.E.T. DN-104B directional gyros; pilot's IDC electric encoding altimeter with altitude preselect and IDC air data unit; co-pilot's IDC barometric altimeter; dual Teledyne SL2-9157-3 IVSIs; dual marker beacon lamps; dual D.B. audio systems; J.E.T. PS-835D emergency battery and AI-804 attitude gyro; dual Davtron 877 clocks; annunciator package; N_1 reminder; avionics master switch; chip detector; flap preselect; Wulfsberg Flitefone VI; Bendix/King KHF 950 HF; Frederickson Jetcal 5 Selcal; Rosemount air data system and SAS/TAT/TAS indicator.

EQUIPMENT: Standard equipment includes thrust reversers, dual angle of attack indicators, engine synchronisation meter, cabin differential pressure gauge, cabin rate of climb indicator, interstage and turbine temperature gauges, turbine and fan speed gauges, wing temperature indicator, alternate static source, depressurisation warning, engine fire warning lights, Mach warning system, dual stall warning system, fire axe, cabin fire extinguisher, cabin stereo cassette player, EEGO audio distribution system, flotation jackets for crew and passengers, sound-proofing; baggage compartment, courtesy, instrument panel, flood, map, cockpit dome, and reading lights; dual anti-collision, landing, navigation, recognition, strobe, taxi and maintenance lights, wing ice detection light; dual engine fire extinguishing systems with 'systems armed' and fire warning lights, maintenance interphone jack plugs, engine synchronisation system, control lock, external power socket, and lightning protection system.

DIMENSIONS, EXTERNAL:

Wing span over tip tanks	12.04 m (39 ft 6 in)
Wing chord: at root	2.74 m (9 ft 0 in)
at tip	1.55 m (5 ft 1 in)
Wing aspect ratio	5.7
Length overall	14.83 m (48 ft 8 in)
Height overall	3.73 m (12 ft 3 in)
Tailplane span	4.47 m (14 ft 8 in)
Wheel track	2.51 m (8 ft 3 in)
Wheelbase	6.15 m (20 ft 2 in)
Passenger door:	
Standard: Height	1.57 m (5 ft 2 in)
Width	0.61 m (2 ft 0 in)
Optional: Height	1.57 m (5 ft 2 in)
Width	0.91 m (3 ft 0 in)
Emergency exit: Height	0.71 m (2 ft 4 in)
Width	0.48 m (1 ft 7 in)

DIMENSIONS, INTERNAL (A: Learjet 35A, B: Learjet 36A):

Cabin: Length, incl flight deck: A	6.63 m (21 ft 9 in)
B	5.77 m (18 ft 11 in)
excl flight deck: A	5.21 m (17 ft 1 in)
B	4.06 m (13 ft 4 in)
Max width	1.50 m (4 ft 11 in)
Max height	1.32 m (4 ft 4 in)
Volume, incl flight deck: A	9.12 m³ (322.0 cu ft)
B	7.25 m³ (256.0 cu ft)
Baggage compartment: A	1.13 m³ (40.0 cu ft)
B	0.76 m³ (27.0 cu ft)

AREAS:

Wings, gross	23.53 m² (253.3 sq ft)

WEIGHTS AND LOADINGS (Learjet 35A and 36A):

Weight empty, equipped	4,462 kg (9,838 lb)
Max payload	1,361 kg (3,000 lb)
Max T-O weight	8,300 kg (18,300 lb)
Max ramp weight	8,391 kg (18,500 lb)
Max landing weight	6,940 kg (15,300 lb)
Max wing loading	347.1 kg/m² (71.1 lb/sq ft)
Max power loading	261.7 kg/kN (2.57 lb/lb st)

PERFORMANCE (Learjet 35A and 36A, at max T-O weight, except where indicated):

Max operating speed — Mach 0.81

Max level speed at 7,620 m (25,000 ft) — 471 knots (872 km/h; 542 mph)

Max cruising speed, mid-cruise weight, at 12,500 m (41,000 ft) — 460 knots (852 km/h; 529 mph)

Econ cruising speed, mid-cruise weight, at 13,700 m (45,000 ft) — 418 knots (774 km/h; 481 mph)

Stalling speed, wheels and flaps down, engines idling — 96 knots (178 km/h; 111 mph) IAS

Max rate of climb at S/L — 1,323 m (4,340 ft)/min

Rate of climb at S/L, one engine out — 390 m (1,280 ft)/min

Service ceiling — 13,715 m (45,000 ft)

Service ceiling, one engine out — 7,620 m (25,000 ft)

Min ground turning radius, about nosewheel — 6.43 m (21 ft 1 in)

T-O balanced field length, FAR Pt 25:
at 7,711 kg (17,000 lb) — 1,287 m (4,224 ft)
at 8,300 kg (18,300 lb) — 1,515 m (4,972 ft)

Landing distance, FAR Pt 25, at max landing weight — 937 m (3,075 ft)

Range with 4 passengers, max fuel and 45 min reserves:
Learjet 35A — 1,206 nm (2,236 km; 1,389 miles)
Learjet 36A — 1,437 nm (2,664 km; 1,655 miles)

OPERATIONAL NOISE LEVELS (FAR Pt 36):

T-O	83.9 EPNdB
Approach	91.4 EPNdB
Sideline	86.7 EPNdB

LEARJET 35A/36A SPECIAL MISSIONS VERSIONS

TYPE: Special mission adaptations for Learjet 35A/36A.

VARIANTS: **EC-35A:** Used for EW training simulation or as stand-off ECM/ESM platform.

PC-35A: Maritime patrol; equipment includes 360° sea surveillance digital radar, high resolution television, forward-looking infra-red (FLIR), infra-red linescanner (IRLS), electronic support measures (ESM), magnetic anomaly detector, integrated tactical displays, VLF Omega and other long-range navaids; hardpoint under each wing with Alkan 165B ejector for external stores up to 453 kg (1,000 lb); drop hatch for rescue gear, multi-track digital recorders, homing systems, ASW sonobuoy systems and data annotated hand-held cameras.

RC-35A and RC-36A: Reconnaissance versions; standard installations include long-range oblique photographic cameras (LOROP), side-looking synthetic aperture radars, and surveillance camera system in external pods. Geological versions delivered to China (see below).

UC-35A: Utility versions for transport, navaids calibration, medevac and target towing. Certificated tow systems include Hayes Universal Tow Target System (HUTTS) with or without MTR-101, Flight Refuelling LLHK, MRTT and EMT TGL targets, and Marquardt aerial target launch and recovery tow reel.

U-36A: Extensively modified for Japan Maritime Self-Defence Force (JMSDF). Four delivered for target towing, anti-ship missile simulation and ECM; tip pods extended, in association with Shin Meiwa, to house HWQ-1T missile seeker simulator, AN/ALQ-6 jammer and cameras. Additional equipment includes long-range ocean surveillance radar in underbelly fairing, AN/ALE-43 chaff dispenser, ARS-1-L high-speed tow sleeve with scoring, two-piece windscreen with electrical demisting for low-level missions, expanded underwing stores capability, greater max T-O and landing weights. Further deliveries to Japan expected during 1990s.

CUSTOMERS: 20 customer countries include Argentina, Australia, Bolivia, Brazil, Chile, People's Republic of China (two RC-36As delivered 1984, plus three RC-35As with geological equipment and Goodyear SLAR delivered 1985), Finland (three 35A target tugs also equipped for mapping, medevac, pollution control, oblique photography and SAR), Germany (four 35A/36A target tugs), Japan, Mexico, Peru, Saudi Arabia, Sweden, Switzerland, Thailand, UK, USA and Yugoslavia. Nearly 200 Learjet 30 Series aircraft now flying with or for military services, including 83 C-21As (which see).

DESIGN FEATURES: Civilian and paramilitary missions include aerial survey, aeronautical research, airways calibration, ASW, atmospheric research, border patrol, ESM/ECM, geophysical survey, maritime patrol, pilot training, radar surveillance, reconnaissance, search and rescue, and weather modification.

PERFORMANCE (PC-35A):

Operating speed:
at 11,275-12,500 m (37,000-41,000 ft) — 415 knots (769 km/h; 478 mph)
at 4,575-7,620 m (15,000-25,000 ft) — 319 knots (590 km/h; 367 mph)
S/L to 610 m (2,000 ft) — 250 knots (463 km/h; 288 mph)

Rate of climb at S/L — 1,380 m (4,525 ft)/min

Range:
at high altitude — 2,249 nm (4,168 km; 2,590 miles)
at medium altitude — 1,617 nm (2,996 km; 1,862 miles)
at low altitude — 1,060 nm (1,964 km; 1,220 miles)

LEARJET 31A

TYPE: Successor to Learjet 31.

PROGRAMME: Learjet 31 introduced September 1987; first flight of aerodynamic prototype 11 May 1987; first production aircraft (N311DF) used as systems testbed; FAA certification 12 August 1988. Learjet 31A and 31A/ER announced October 1990 to replace Learjet 31 from June 1991.

VARIANTS: **Learjet 31A/ER:** Optional extended range version with 2,597 litres (686 US gallons; 571 Imp gallons) fuel with higher max T-O weight.

CUSTOMERS: Total 15 Learjet 31s delivered during 1990.

COSTS: Standard Learjet 31A price $4,275,000 (April 1991); Learjet 31A/ER $4,392,600 (April 1991).

DESIGN FEATURES: Learjet 31 (1990-91 *Jane's*) combined fuselage/cabin/power plant of Learjet 35A/36A with wing of Learjet 55; Delta Fins added to eliminate Dutch roll, stabilise aircraft at high airspeeds, induce docile stall and reduce approach speeds and field lengths; stick pusher/puller and dual yaw dampers no longer required for departure; stick shaker and single yaw damper retained for comfort.

Additional features of Learjet 31A include cruise Mach number up to 12,500 m (41,000 ft) increased four per cent to 0.81 and VMO increased from 300 knots (556 km/h; 345 mph) to 325 knots (602 km/h; 374 mph). Increases mainly benefit descent from high altitudes. Learjet 31A also features integrated digital avionics package.

FLYING CONTROLS: All control surfaces mechanically actuated; ailerons have brush seals and geared tabs; electrically actuated trim tab on port aileron. Electrically actuated tailplane incidence control has separate motors for pilot and co-pilot and single-fault survival protection; aircraft can be manually controlled following tailplane runaway and landed with reduced flap. Rudder has electric trim tab; automatic electric rudder assist servo operates automatically if rudder pedal loads exceed 22.6 kg (50 lb). Full-chord fences bracket the ailerons; airflow between fences corrected by arrowhead energisers on leading-edge, row of round-head screws aft of leading-edge and two rows of energiser strips near ailerons. Single spoiler panel in each wing used as airbrake and lift dumper. Hydraulically actuated flaps extend to 40°. Optional drag parachute mounted on inside of baggage hatch under tail.

STRUCTURE: Multi-spar wing with machined skins.

LANDING GEAR: Retractable tricycle gear; main legs retract inward, nose leg forward; twin mainwheels with anti-skid disc brakes; nosewheel has full-time digital steer-by-wire replacing speed-limited steering of Learjet 31. Max airspeed with gear extended 260 knots (481 km/h; 299 mph); tyre limiting speed 183 knots (339 km/h; 210 mph).

POWER PLANT: Two 15.56 kN (3,500 lb st) Garrett TFE731-2 turbofans with digital electronic engine controller giving automatic retention of power settings above 4,570 m (15,000 ft) and special idling control for descent from 15,545 m (51,000 ft). Engine synchroniser fitted. Optional Dee Howard 4000 thrust reverser system weighs 109 kg (240 lb). One integral fuel tank in each wing holds 641 kg (1,413 lb); standard fuselage tank 608 kg (1,340 lb); ER fuselage tank 804 kg (1,773 lb); fuselage fuel transferred by pilots by gravity or pump; single-point pressure refuelling optional.

ACCOMMODATION: Cabin furnishings include a three-seat divan, four Erda 10-way adjustable individual seats, side facing seat with toilet, two folding tables, refreshment cabinet with ice chest, baggage compartment, coffee warmer, water dispenser, cup and miscellaneous storage, coat rod, forward privacy curtain, overhead panels with reading lights, indirect lighting, air vents and oxygen masks, and passenger lifejackets.

SYSTEMS: Hydraulic system operates flaps, landing gear, airbrake, wheelbrakes and thrust reversers; system pressure 68.95-120.6 bars (1,000-1,750 lb/sq in); pneumatic standby for gear extension and wheelbrakes. Normal cabin pressure differential 0.64 bar (9.4 lb/sq in) with automatic flood engine bleed if cabin altitude exceeds 2,820 m (9,250 ft); pop-out emergency oxygen for passengers and masks for crew. Electrical system based on two starter/generators, two nickel-cadmium batteries and two inverters; both buses can run from one engine; electrics operate tailplane incidence, rudder assister and nosewheel steering. De-icing by bleed air for wing, engine intakes and windscreen; tailplane electrically heated; fin not protected. Alcohol spray for radome to stop shed ice entering engines; controls prevent internal ice and condensation during long descents. Single engine at idle, burning 15.9 kg (35 lb) fuel every 10 minutes, acts as APU.

AVIONICS: Bendix/King integrated digital avionics package.

EQUIPMENT: Throttle-mounted landing gear warning mute and go-around switches, nacelle heat annunciator, engine synchroniser and synchroscope, recognition light, wing ice light, emergency press override switches, transponder ident switch in pilot's control wheel, engine synchroniser and synchroscope, flap preselect, crew lifejackets, cockpit dome lights, cockpit speakers, crew oxygen masks and fire extinguisher are standard.

DIMENSIONS, EXTERNAL:

Wing span	13.33 m (43 ft 9 in)
Length overall	14.83 m (48 ft 8 in)
Height overall	3.73 m (12 ft 3 in)

DIMENSIONS, INTERNAL (A: 31A, B: 31A/ER):

Cabin: Length		
incl flight deck: A		6.63 m (21 ft 9 in)
	B	6.27 m (20 ft 7 in)
excl flight deck: A		5.21 m (17 ft 1 in)
	B	4.85 m (15 ft 11 in)
Max width: A, B		1.50 m (4 ft 11 in)
Max height: A, B		1.32 m (4 ft 4 in)
Volume, incl flight deck: A		9.12 m³ (322.0 cu ft)
	B	8.83 m³ (312.0 cu ft)
Baggage compartment: A		1.13 m³ (40.0 cu ft)
	B	0.85 m³ (30.0 cu ft)

AREAS:

Wings, gross	24.57 m² (264.5 sq ft)

WEIGHTS AND LOADINGS (A: 31A, B: 31A/ER):

Weight empty: A		4,575 kg (10,087 lb)
	B	4,593 kg (10,126 lb)

The Learjet 31 eight-passenger twin-turbofan business aircraft (externally same as 31A)

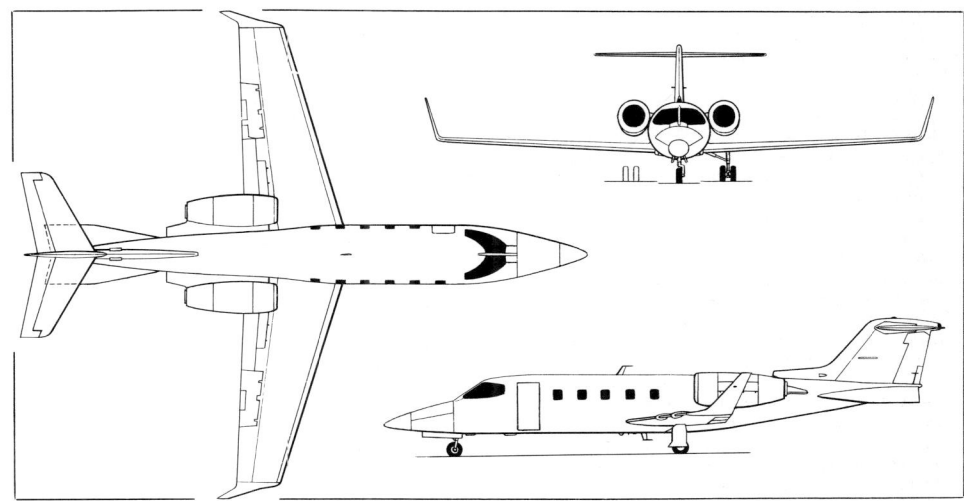

Learjet 31A business aircraft *(Pilot Press)*

Basic operating weight: A		4,758 kg (10,487 lb)
	B	4,775 kg (10,526 lb)
Max payload: A		1,037 kg (2,286 lb)
	B	1,019 kg (2,247 lb)
Payload with max fuel: A		595 kg (1,312 lb)
	B	791 kg (1,744 lb)
Max fuel weight: A		1,870 kg (4,124 lb)
	B	2,110 kg (4,653 lb)
Max T-O weight: A		7,030 kg (15,500 lb)
	B	7,484 kg (16,500 lb)
Max ramp weight: A		7,144 kg (15,750 lb)
	B	7,597 kg (16,750 lb)
Max zero-fuel weight		5,715 kg (12,600 lb)
Max landing weight		6,940 kg (15,300 lb)
Max wing loading: A		286.1 kg/m² (58.60 lb/sq ft)
	B	304.6 kg/m² (62.38 lb/sq ft)
Max power loading: A		225.32 kg/kN (2.21 lb/lb st)
	B	239.87 kg/kN (2.36 lb/lb st)

PERFORMANCE (at max standard T-O weight, S/L, ISA, except where indicated. A: 31A, B: 31A/ER):

Never-exceed speed (VNE)
300 knots (555 km/h; 345 mph) IAS

Max operating Mach number, up to 12,500 m (41,000 ft)
Mach 0.81

Cruising speed:
at 13,715 m (45,000 ft) 449 knots (832 km/h; 516 mph)
at 10,975-12,500 m (36,000-41,000 ft)
463 knots (855 km/h; 532 mph)

Stalling speed at typical landing weight
93 knots (173 km/h; 107 mph)

Max rate of climb at S/L: A		1,670 m (5,480 ft)/min
	B	1,555 m (5,100 ft)/min
Rate of climb at S/L, one engine out:		
A		576 m (1,890 ft)/min
B		466 m (1,530 ft)/min
Max certificated ceiling		15,545 m (51,000 ft)
Service ceiling, one engine out: A		9,510 m (31,200 ft)
	B	8,840 m (29,000 ft)
T-O balanced field length, FAR Pt 25:		
A		886 m (2,906 ft)
B		987 m (3,236 ft)

Ground turning radius, about nosewheel
11.91 m (39 ft 1 in)

FAR Pt 91 landing distance: A		844 m (2,767 ft)
	B	917 m (3,010 ft)

Range at econ cruising speed with four passengers, 45 min reserves: A   1,660 nm (3,076 km; 1,911 miles)
B   1,897 nm (3,515 km; 2,184 miles)

OPERATIONAL NOISE LEVELS (FAR Pt 36):

T-O	79.6 EPNdB
Approach	92.6 EPNdB
Sideline	87.2 EPNdB

LEARJET 55B and 55C

TYPE: Medium-range business jet.

PROGRAMME: First flight of first prototype Learjet 55 (N551GL) 19 April 1979; first flight of second prototype (N552GL) 15 November 1979; first flight of production aircraft 11 August 1980; FAR Pt 25 certification 18 March 1981; first delivery 30 April 1981. Phase I performance improvement package, certificated July 1983, included new triangular-wedge stall strips, automatic ground spoilers and automatic power reserve; Phase IA performance improvement package, introduced Spring 1984, includes high-energy, long-life brakes and modified landing gear; optional max T-O weight of 9,752 kg (21,500 lb) and max landing weight of 8,165 kg (18,000 lb) introduced from aircraft c/n 55-107; final Learjet 55C, No. 147, delivered December 1990 to UK; Learjet 55C being superseded by Learjet 60 in 1992.

VARIANTS: **Learjet 55B:** Announced September 1986; optional max T-O weight became standard, wing improved, new interior, all-digital flight deck; better take-off performance, increased range and better mission flexibility. Details in 1987-88 *Jane's*.

Learjet 55C: Announced September 1987; incorporated Delta Fins which improved stability at all speeds, eliminated Dutch roll, softened stall, reduced approach speeds and ended need for stick puller/pusher and dual yaw dampers at departure.

Learjet 55C/ER: Extended range version with additional 163 kg (359 lb) fuel tank in tailcone baggage compartment; can be retrofitted.

Learjet 55C/LR: As 55C/ER, but with additional 386 litre (102 US gallon; 85 Imp gallon) tank between standard fuselage tank and ER optional tank; can be retrofitted; typical seating for seven and two crew.

DESIGN FEATURES: Sweepback 13° at quarter-chord; advanced cambered leading-edge; Delta Fins, Softflite package and supercritical winglets. Anti-icing of wing leading-edge by engine bleed air and of tailplane leading-edge by electric heating.

FLYING CONTROLS: Manual flying controls with electric trim tabs on port aileron and rudder; electrically actuated variable incidence tailplane; hydraulically actuated slotted trailing-edge flaps; spoilers ahead of flaps.

Learjet 55C business transport

STRUCTURE: Multi-spar wing with cavity-milled skins; upper skin tapers in thickness towards tip; semi-monocoque fail-safe fuselage.

LANDING GEAR: Hydraulically retractable tricycle type, with twin wheels on each main unit and single steerable nosewheel (±55°). Mainwheel tyres size 17.5 × 5.75-8, 12 ply, pressure 12.4 bars (180 lb/sq in); nosewheel tyre size 18.0 × 4.4, 10 ply, pressure 7.24 bars (105 lb/sq in). High pressure pneumatic system for emergency extension. Oleo-pneumatic shock absorbers. Chined nosewheel tyre. Mainwheel doors are of composites construction. High energy hydraulic braking system, with pneumatic backup. Fully modulated anti-skid units.

POWER PLANT: Two Garrett TFE731-3A-2B turbofans, each rated at 16.46 kN (3700 lb st), plus 0.80 kN (180 lb st) automatic power reserve, pod-mounted on sides of fuselage aft of wing. Thrust reversers standard. Fuel in integral wing tanks and a fuselage bladder tank, with a combined usable capacity of 3,782 litres (999 US gallons; 832 Imp gallons) in standard Model 55C; 3,982 litres (1,052 US gallons; 876 Imp gallons) in Model 55C/ER; 4,353 litres (1,150 US gallons; 957 Imp gallons) in Model 55C/LR. Single-point refuelling. Engine nacelle leading-edges and fan hubs anti-iced by engine bleed air.

ACCOMMODATION: Crew of two on flight deck, with dual controls. IPECO fully adjustable crew seats. Seating for four to eight passengers in a choice of six interior layouts. Two folding tables. Carpeted floor. Galley refreshment cabinet. Toilet. Baggage space at rear of cabin, and in fuselage nose and tailcone of basic Model 55C. Tailcone baggage space reduced on long-range versions, but 55C/LR has baggage area at front of cabin. Two-piece clamshell door at forward end of cabin on port side, with integral steps built into the lower section. Emergency exit/baggage door on starboard side of cabin.

SYSTEMS: Environmental control system comprises cabin pressurisation, ventilation, heating and cooling. Heating and pressurisation are provided by engine bleed air, with a maximum pressure differential of 0.65 bar (9.4 lb/sq in), maintaining a cabin altitude of 2,440 m (8,000 ft) to 15,545 m (51,000 ft). Freon vapour-cycle cooling system, supplemented by a ram air system. Anti-icing system includes distribution of engine bleed air to wing leading-edges, engine nacelle leading-edges and fan hubs, and pilot and co-pilot windscreens; electric anti-icing of tailplane leading-edge, pitot heads, stall warning vanes and static ports; and alcohol anti-icing of windscreens. Hydraulic system supplied by two engine driven variable-volume constant-pressure pumps, one on each engine, each capable of maintaining alone the full system pressure of 103.5 bars (1,500 lb/sq in) for operation of landing gear, brakes, flaps and spoilers. Hydraulic system maximum flow rate 15 litres (4 US gallons; 3.33 Imp gallons) per min. Cylindrical reservoir pressurised to 1.38 bars (20 lb/sq in). Electrically driven hydraulic pump for emergency operation of all hydraulic services. Pneumatic system of 124 to 207 bars (1,800 to 3,000 lb/sq in) pressure for emergency extension of landing gear and operation of brakes. Electrical system powered by two 28V 400A engine driven brushless generators, either of which is capable of maintaining adequate DC power to operate all electrical services; two 1kVA solid state inverters to provide AC power; and two 24V 37Ah lead-acid batteries. Oxygen system of 1.08 m³ (38 cu ft) capacity, with crew demand masks; dropout mask for each passenger, which is presented automatically if cabin altitude exceeds 4,265 m (14,000 ft). Sundstrand Turbo-mach APU optional (not on 55C/ER or 55C/LR).

AVIONICS: From aircraft c/n 134 onwards standard avionics include a Collins five-tube EFIS-85L-12 electronic flight instrumentation system with dual AHS-85 AHRS; Collins APS-85 digital autopilot with glareshield controller and dual flight data computers; dual ADC-82 air data systems; dual VHF-22A nav/coms with CTL-22 controls; dual VIR-32 nav receivers with CTL-32 controls; dual DME-42 with IND-42C indicators; ADF-60 with CTL-62 control; dual RMI-30; dual TDR-90 transponders with CTL-92 controls; ALT-55B radio altimeter, Collins WXR-350 Sensor weather radar, Universal UNS-1A long-range nav system; Bendix/King KHF 950 HF; Frederickson Jetcal-5 secal; Collins flight profile advisory system; and Wulfsberg Flitefone VI. Other standard flight deck equipment includes dual Collins encoding altimeters; MSI-80 Mach/airspeed indicators; VSI-80 instantaneous vertical speed indicators; Collins altitude pre-selector/alerter; TAS/SAT/TAT temperature indicator; IDC two-inch standby Mach/IAS indicator and altimeter; J.E.T. PS-835D and AI-804 emergency battery and attitude gyro; dual marker beacon systems; dual Avtech audio systems; dual Davtron 877 clocks; yaw damper; dual stall warning indicators; engine synchroniser and synchroscope; annunciator panels; avionics master switch; N_1 reminder, chip detector and flap preselect.

EQUIPMENT: Standard equipment includes sun visors; map lights; life jackets; fire extinguisher; writing tables; dome lights; oxygen masks; manual storage compartments, and dividing panel between flight deck and cabin. Cabin equipment includes two folding tables; four individual seats with tracking, swivel, recline and sideways motions; three-seat forward facing divan with storage and tracking and recline motions, single side-facing seat, galley refreshment cabinet with decanters, bottle cooler, ice chest, oven, tray carrier, hot and cold liquid containers and storage area; forward coat closet; stereo and tape storage; magazine rack; convenience panel with reading lights, air vents, cabin speakers and oxygen masks; lighting control panel; opaque and tinted window shades; indirect lighting; aisle lighting; entrance step light; flushing toilet with vanity mirror and light; baggage compartment light; passenger life jackets; auxiliary cabin heater; fire extinguisher and axe; nose and tail baggage compartment lights; wing ice light and maintenance interphone jack plug sockets.

DIMENSIONS, EXTERNAL:

Wing span	13.34 m (43 ft 9 in)
Wing chord: at root	2.74 m (9 ft 0 in)
at tip	1.07 m (3 ft 6 in)
Wing aspect ratio	6.7
Length: overall	16.79 m (55 ft 1 in)
fuselage	15.93 m (52 ft 3 in)
Height overall	4.47 m (14 ft 8 in)
Tailplane span	4.47 m (14 ft 8 in)
Wheel track	2.51 m (8 ft 3 in)
Wheelbase	7.01 m (23 ft 0 in)
Cabin door: Height	1.70 m (5 ft 7 in)
Width	0.61 m (2 ft 0 in)

DIMENSIONS, INTERNAL:

Cabin: Length between pressure bulkheads:	
55C, 55C/ER	6.71 m (22 ft 0 in)
55C/LR	6.30 m (20 ft 8 in)
Length, cockpit/cabin divider to rear pressure bulkhead: 55C, 55C/ER	5.08 m (16 ft 8 in)
55C/LR	4.67 m (15 ft 4 in)
Max width	1.80 m (5 ft 11 in)
Max height	1.74 m (5 ft 8½ in)
Volume, incl flight deck:	
55C, 55C/ER	13.37 m³ (472 cu ft)
55C/LR	12.88 m³ (455 cu ft)
Baggage capacity: 55C, rear cabin	0.93 m³ (33.0 cu ft)
55C, nose	0.17 m³ (6.0 cu ft)
55C, tail	0.52 m³ (18.5 cu ft)
55C/ER, total	1.36 m³ (48.0 cu ft)
55C/LR, total	1.81 m³ (64.0 cu ft)

AREAS:

Wings, gross	24.57 m² (264.5 sq ft)
Ailerons (total)	1.09 m² (11.70 sq ft)
Trailing-edge flaps (total)	3.42 m² (36.85 sq ft)
Winglets (total)	1.11 m² (12.00 sq ft)
Spoilers (total)	0.65 m² (7.05 sq ft)
Fin	4.67 m² (50.29 sq ft)
Rudder	0.99 m² (10.65 sq ft)
Tailplane	5.02 m² (54.00 sq ft)
Elevators (total)	1.31 m² (14.13 sq ft)

WEIGHTS AND LOADINGS:

Weight empty: 55C	5,832 kg (12,858 lb)
55C/ER	5,861 kg (12,922 lb)
55C/LR	5,920 kg (13,052 lb)
Typical operating weight empty:	
55C	6,013 kg (13,258 lb)
55C/ER	6,042 kg (13,322 lb)
55C/LR	6,101 kg (13,452 lb)
Payload with max fuel: 55C	590 kg (1,302 lb)
55C/ER	625 kg (1,379 lb)
55C/LR	268 kg (591 lb)
Max payload: 55C	790 kg (1,742 lb)
55C/ER	761 kg (1,678 lb)
55C/LR	702 kg (1,548 lb)
Max fuel weight: 55C	3,035 kg (6,690 lb)
55C/ER	3,197 kg (7,049 lb)
55C/LR	3,496 kg (7,707 lb)
Max T-O weight: 55C	9,525 kg (21,000 lb)
55C/ER & LR	9,752 kg (21,500 lb)
Max ramp weight: 55C	9,639 kg (21,250 lb)
55C/ER & LR	9,865 kg (21,750 lb)
Max zero-fuel weight: all versions	6,804 kg (15,000 lb)
Max landing weight: all versions	8,165 kg (18,000 lb)
Max wing loading:	
55C	387.6 kg/m² (79.4 lb/sq ft)
55C/ER & LR	396.9 kg/m² (81.3 lb/sq ft)
Max power loading:	
55C	289.3 kg/kN (2.84 lb/lb st)
55C/ER & LR	296.2 kg/kN (2.90 lb/lb st)

PERFORMANCE (at max T-O weight except where indicated):

Never-exceed speed (VNE):	
below 2,440 m (8,000 ft)	300 knots (555 km/h; 345 mph) IAS
2,440 m (8,000 ft) to 11,275 m (37,000 ft)	350 knots (648 km/h; 403 mph) IAS
11,275 m (37,000 ft) to 13,715 m (45,000 ft)	Mach 0.81 to Mach 0.79
above 13,715 m (45,000 ft)	Mach 0.79
Max level speed at 9,150 m (30,000 ft)	477 knots (884 km/h; 549 mph)
Max cruising speed at 12,500 m (41,000 ft)	455 knots (843 km/h; 524 mph)
Econ cruising speed at 14,325 m (47,000 ft)	419 knots (776 km/h; 482 mph)
Stalling speed	106 knots (197 km/h; 122 mph)
Max rate of climb at S/L: 55C	1,273 m (4,176 ft)/min
55C/ER & LR	1,237 m (4,059 ft)/min
Rate of climb at S/L, one engine out:	
55C	378 m (1,240 ft)/min
55C/ER & LR	305 m (1,000 ft)/min
Max certificated ceiling	15,545 m (51,000 ft)
Min ground turning radius, about nosewheel	11.58 m (38 ft 0 in)
T-O balanced field length, FAR Pt 25:	
55C	1,536 m (5,039 ft)
55C/ER & LR	1,615 m (5,299 ft)
Landing distance, FAR Pt 91 at max landing weight	991 m (3,250 ft)
Range with crew of two, four passengers, allowances for taxi, T-O, climb, cruise at long-range power at 13,100 m (43,000 ft), descent and 45 min reserves:	
55C	2,189 nm (4,056 km; 2,520 miles)
55C/ER	2,305 nm (4,271 km; 2,654 miles)
55C/LR	2,397 nm (4,442 km; 2,760 miles)

OPERATIONAL NOISE LEVELS (FAR Pt 36):

T-O	86.3 EPNdB
Approach	90.7 EPNdB
Sideline	91.0 EPNdB

LEARJET 60

TYPE: Medium-range business jet.

PROGRAMME: Announced 3 October 1990 as Learjet 55C successor; first flight of proof-of-concept aircraft with one PW305 turbofan 18 October 1990; flight testing resumed 13 June 1991 with two PW305s and stretched fuselage; certification expected September 1992; first production delivery third quarter 1992.

COSTS: Standard aircraft price $7,900,000 (October 1990).

DESIGN FEATURES: Largest Learjet; P&WC PW305 engines; T-tail; winglets; Delta Fins.

FLYING CONTROLS: Spoilers can be partially extended to adjust descent rates.

POWER PLANT: Two P&WC PW305 turbofans, each flat-rated at 19.57 kN (4,400 lb st) at up to 27°C (80°F). Total fuel capacity 3,561 kg (7,850 lb).

ACCOMMODATION: Two crew and six to nine passengers; gross pressure cabin volume 15.49 m³ (547 cu ft); compared with 55C, main cabin is 0.71 m (2 ft 4 in) longer and rear baggage hold section 0.38 m (1 ft 3 in) longer; full-across aft toilet has flat floor, large mirror and external servicing; total 1.67 m³ (59 cu ft) baggage capacity divided between an externally accessible hold (larger than that of Learjet 55C) and internal pressurised, heated compartment that is accessible in flight; galley cabinet has storage for dinnerware, warming oven, cold liquid dispensers and ice storage; 10-way adjusting Erda seating is standard.

SYSTEMS: Windscreen demisted by electrically heated gold film which also diminishes sun heating in flight and on ground and produces warmth during prolonged flight at high altitude. Full-time digital steer-by-wire nosewheel control operates throughout taxying, take-off and landing.

AVIONICS: Standard fully integrated all-digital Collins Pro Line 4 avionics include EFIS, dual digital air data computers, dual navigation and communications radios, dual automatic heading and attitude reference systems (AHRS), advanced Collins autopilot and long-range navaid as standard; circuit breaker and controls panels redistributed, as in Learjet 31A.

DIMENSIONS, EXTERNAL:

Wing span	13.34 m (43 ft 9 in)
Wing chord: at root	2.74 m (9 ft 0 in)
at tip	1.12 m (3 ft 8 in)
Length: overall	17.88 m (58 ft 8 in)
fuselage	17.02 m (55 ft 10 in)
Height: overall	4.47 m (14 ft 8 in)
to cabin door sill	0.69 m (2 ft 3 in)
Tailplane span	4.47 m (14 ft 8 in)
Cabin door: Width	0.64 m (2 ft 1 in)

DIMENSIONS, INTERNAL:

Total baggage volume	1.67 m³ (59 cu ft)

WEIGHTS AND LOADINGS:

Max payload	816 kg (1,800 lb)
Max T-O weight	10,319 kg (22,750 lb)
Max power loading	263.64 kg/kN (2.58 lb/lb st)

PERFORMANCE:

Cruising speed	
	Mach 0.81 (463 knots; 858 km/h; 533 mph)
Max certificated ceiling	15,545 m (51,000 ft)

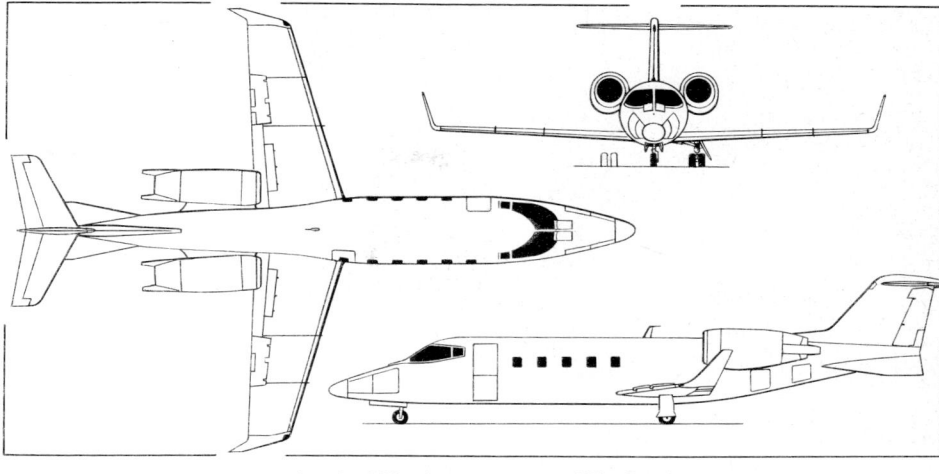

Learjet 60 business transport *(Pilot Press)*

Balanced field length	1,634 m (5,360 ft)
Range with VFR reserves	
	2,736 nm (5,071 km; 3,151 miles)

Range examples:
Can fly New York-Los Angeles against 85 per cent Boeing winds with NBAA reserves

Can reach either US coast after taking off from Aspen, Colorado, in ISA +20° with four passengers
Range with four passengers from runway shorter than 1,494 m (4,900 ft), is 2,497 nm (4,441 km; 2,760 miles)

LOCKHEED
LOCKHEED CORPORATION
4500 Park Granada Boulevard, Calabasas, California 91399-0610
Telephone: 1 (818) 712 2620
Fax: 1 (818) 712 2329
CHAIRMAN, PRESIDENT AND CHIEF EXECUTIVE OFFICER:
Daniel M. Tellep
VICE-CHAIRMEN:
Robert A. Fuhrman
Vincent N. Marafino

Former Lockheed Aircraft Corporation renamed Lockheed Corporation in September 1977. Activities include design and production of aircraft, electronics, satellites, space systems, missiles, ocean systems, information systems, and systems for strategic defence and for command, control, communications and intelligence.

Activities are administered by four subsidiary groups: Aeronautical Systems Group; Technology Services Group; Electronic Systems Group (comprising Lockheed Sanders Inc, CalComp and Lockheed Canada Inc); and Missiles and Space Systems Group (comprising Lockheed Missiles &

Space Company Inc, Lockheed Integrated Solutions Company and Lockheed Technical Operations Company).

Lockheed Corporation facilities cover more than 2,322,575 m² (25,000,000 sq ft); total employees 77,000 in 25 US states and worldwide.

LOCKHEED AERONAUTICAL SYSTEMS GROUP (LASG)
86 South Cobb Drive, Marietta, Georgia 30063
Telephone: 1 (404) 494 4411
Telex: 542642 LOCKHEED MARA
PRESIDENT: Kenneth W. Cannestra
EXECUTIVE VICE-PRESIDENTS:
H. Bard Allison (General Manager, Georgia Operations)
E. Lloyd Graham (General Manager, Programmes)
Sherman Mullin (President, Advanced Development Company)
EXECUTIVE VICE-PRESIDENT AND GENERAL MANAGER, TECHNOLOGY AND ENGINEERING: Bart Krawetz
VICE-PRESIDENT, CIEM AND MODERNISATION AND INFORMATION SERVICES: William R. Sorenson
PUBLIC INFORMATION: Joseph E. Dabney

LASG and its subsidiary Lockheed Aeronautical Systems Company is moving aircraft manufacturing from Burbank to Marietta and, to a lesser extent, to Palmdale. In May 1990, Lockheed Advanced Development Company (LADC or Skunk Works), employing 4,000 to 5,000 people, became autonomous as second component of LASG at Burbank and will move to Palmdale at a future date. LADC programmes have included F-117 (but see also under 'Strategic Reconnaissance Aircraft' in USAF entry).

Former Burbank Division produced P-3 Orion and made parts of TR-1 and Lockheed Georgia's C-5B. In April 1991, Lockheed won competition to produce F-22A Advanced Tactical Fighter with General Dynamics and Boeing Military Airplanes. Lockheed is studying advanced tactical surveillance aircraft (ATS) to replace E-2C, S-3B, ES-3A and EA-6B; advanced tactical transport (ATT) for 21st century tactical airlift; and advanced technology tactical transport (ATTT) small, low-cost STOL transport. Other experimental programmes include C-141 with electromechanical instead of hydraulic flying control actuators; four-year, four-phase investigation of integrated vehicle/propulsion concepts for supersonic cruise and of a supersonic STOVL fighter with hybrid fan vectored-thrust engine and gross weight of about 19,050 kg (42,000 lb) originated by NASA. P-7A LRAACA programme, based at Burbank, terminated by the US Navy July 1990.

Long-term activities at Marietta include production of C-130 Hercules. Re-winging of C-5A completed 1987 and new C-5Bs completed March 1989; new work will consist of P-3C line transferred from Burbank, subcontract for McDonnell Douglas C-17 and F-22. Several C-5As being fitted with hydraulic for rapid transport of large helicopters for US Air Force/Army special operations and US Navy minesweeping missions.

The Lockheed Have Blue stealth prototype, which first flew in December 1977, proved the feasibility of the faceted design

LOCKHEED TR-1 and U-2R
A full description of the TR-1 appeared in 1989-90 *Jane's* and a summary of production and world records in the 1990-91 edition. Replacement of Pratt & Whitney J75-P-13B turbojets in TR-1s and U-2Rs (including six of the latter from 1967-68 production) under consideration. General Electric F101-GE-F29 non-afterburning turbofan (derived from B-2's F118-GE-100) began flight trials in TR-1A July 1989; completed mid-1990 after 100 hours. Additional power from 84.5 kN (19,000 lb st) class replacement power plant increases range by 15 per cent and restores operational ceiling to above 24,380 m (80,000 ft); funding decision awaited.

LOCKHEED F-117A
TYPE: Precision attack fighter with stealth elements, optimised for radar energy dispersion and low IR emission.
PROGRAMME: Development began with USAF Flight Dynamics Laboratory contract to Lockheed Advanced Development Projects (Skunk Works), funded by DARPA under Have Blue programme; two **XST** (Experimental Stealth Technology) prototypes produced, each powered by two 11.12-12.46 kN (2,500-2,800 lb st) GE CJ610s; first flight at Groom Lake, Nevada, December 1977 by William C. Park; first prototype crashed 4 May 1978; second XST crashed at Tonopah Test Range 1980; similar to F-117 apart from inward-canted ruddervators. Span 6.71 m (22 ft 0 in); length

11.58 m (38 ft 0 in); max T-O weight 5,443 kg (12,000 lb); leading-edge sweep 72° 30'; four-transparency canopy.

Development and manufacture of operational F-117A started November 1978 under Senior Trend programme. First of five pre-series aircraft (Article numbers 780 to 784) flew 18 June 1981; one crashed 20 April 1982. Planned production of 100 reduced to 59 (Article numbers 785-843) of which 785 crashed on first flight 21 June 1982; first hand-over to USAF (Article 787) 23 August 1982; funding 13 in FY 1980 and 11, 10, 11 and 14 in FYs 1982-85; final assembly at Tonopah; deliveries seven, eight, eight, eight, eight, seven, five, four and three in calendar years 1982-90 (final delivery mid-July); first picture and designation released 10 November 1988; first operational deployment in Operation Just Cause over Panama, 21 December 1989, when two F-117As each dropped a 907 kg (2,000 lb) laser-guided bomb on barracks area at Rio Hato; all 56 in-service F-117As participated in 1991 Gulf War against Iraq, flying some 1,270 missions. Weapon system improvement began in 1989 and to continue to 2005; improvements installed by 1991 include 'four-dimensional' flight management system (time on waypoint ±1 second) and new cockpit instrumentation with full colour MFDs and digital moving map.

First F-117A unit, 4450th Tactical Group at Tonopah (122 nm; 225 km; 140 miles north-west of Las Vegas), Nevada, formed 1980 and equipped with 18 A-7D Corsair IIs until first F-117A arrived; initial operational capability achieved 26 October 1983; unit transferred

Lockheed F-117A of the 37th Tactical Fighter Wing *(Eric Schulzinger and Denny Lombard)*

Top view of F-117A showing facets which ensure stealth and vortex lift
(Eric Schulzinger and Denny Lombard)

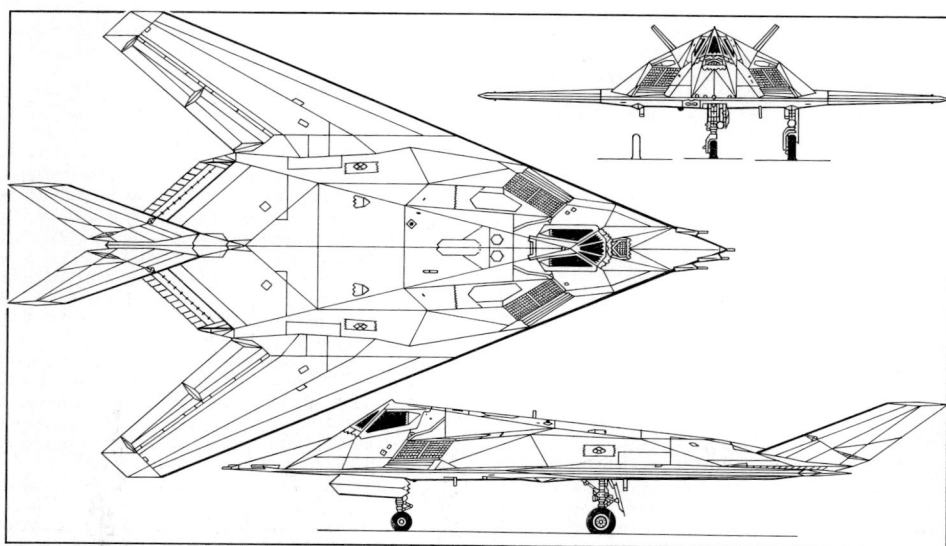

Lockheed F-117A stealth fighter *(Jane's/Mike Keep)*

from direct control of Tactical Air Command to Tactical Fighter Weapons Center at Nellis AFB 1985; first of several public air display appearances made April 1990; unit renamed 37th Tactical Fighter Wing of 12th Air Force October 1989; strength now 40 F-117As divided between 415th and 416th TFS; A-7Ds replaced in training and chase duty by eight T/AT-38 Talons of 417th TFTS, also with balance of 16 remaining F-117As; wing expected to move to Holloman AFB, New Mexico, 1992.

VARIANTS: None known, but Lockheed proposal submitted to USAF after 1991 Gulf War for potential upgrade (capable of retrofit) which could include bubble canopy, redesigned engine inlets, improved exhaust system, and a radar with 'smart skin' conformal antennae.

CUSTOMERS: USAF.

COSTS: $6,560 million programme (1990), including $2,000 million R&D, $4,270 million for procurement and $295.4 million for infrastructure. Average unit cost $42.6 million (then-year dollars).

DESIGN FEATURES: Multi-faceted airframe designed to reflect radar energy away from originating transmitter, particularly downward-looking AEW aircraft; vortexes from many sharp edges, including leading-edge of wing, designed to form co-ordinated lifting airflow pattern; wings have 67° 30′ sweepback, much greater than needed for subsonic performance, with aerofoil formed by two flat planes underneath and three on upper surface; forward underwing surface blends with forward fuselage; all doors and access panels have serrated edges to suppress radar reflection; internal weapon bay 4.7 m (15 ft 5 in) long and 1.75 m (5 ft 9 in) wide divided longitudinally by two lengthwise doors hinged on centreline; boom refuelling receptacle on port side of top plate, aft of cockpit. Frontal radar cross section estimated as 0.01 m² (0.1 sq ft).

FLYING CONTROLS: Four omnidirectional air probes at nose indicate GEC Astronics quadruplex fly-by-wire control system, similar to that of F-16, using two-section elevons and all-moving ruddervators together for control and stability; ruddervators swept about 65° and set at 85° to each other.

STRUCTURE: Material principally aluminium; two-spar wings; fuselage has flat facets mounted on skeletal subframe, jointed without contour blending; surfaces coated with various radar-absorbent materials. Ruddervators being replaced by new units of thermoplastic graphite composites construction, removing previous speed restriction due to flutter.

LANDING GEAR: Tricycle type by Menasco, with single wheels all retracting forward. Loral brakes and wheels; Goodyear tyres. All doors have serrated edges to suppress radar reflections. Emergency arrester hook with explosively jettisoned cover.

POWER PLANT: Two 48.0 kN (10,800 lb st) class General Electric F404-GE-F1D2 non-augmented turbofans. Rectangular overwing air intakes with 2.5 × 1.5 cm (1 × ⅝ in) heated grid for anti-icing and low observability. Auxiliary air intake doors in horizontal surface immediately to the rear. Part of cold air ingested bypasses engine and is mixed with exhaust gases for cooling. Narrow-slot 'platypus' exhausts in rear fuselage, 1.65 m (5 ft 5 in) long and 0.10 m (4 in) high, with extended lower lip, surrounded by heat tiles of type used on Space Shuttle and with 11 vertical, internal guide vanes. Sunstrand air turbine starter. In-flight refuelling receptacle in decking aft of cockpit, illuminated for night refuelling by lamp at apex of cockpit. Optional drop tank on internal weapon pylon.

ACCOMMODATION: Pilot only; McDonnell Douglas ACES II zero/zero ejection seat. Five individually framed flat-plate windows, including single-piece windscreen. Transparencies, gold-coated for radar dissipation, produced by Serracin/Sylmar Corporation. Canopy hinged to open upward and backward.

SYSTEMS: Allied Signal environmental control, auxiliary power and emergency power systems.

AVIONICS: Forward-looking infra-red (FLIR) sensor, with dual fields of view, in recessed emplacement, covered by fine mesh screen, below windscreen. Retractable downward-looking DLIR and laser designator beneath forward fuselage to starboard of nosewheel bay. HUD based on Kaiser AN/AVQ-28; large head-down display for FLIR imagery flanked by two multi-function CRTs. Retractable radio antennae beneath fuselage, ahead of port main landing gear, and on spine. Honeywell radar altimeter, INS, air data computer and multi-purpose display system; IBM mission computer; GEC Astronics flight control computer/navigation interface and auto-pilot computer (NIAC) system; SLI Avionic Systems Corp expanded data transfer system and AHRS. Digital moving map added as retrofit. Navstar GPS.

ARMAMENT: "Full range of USAF tactical fighter ordnance", principally two 907 kg (2,000 lb) bombs: BLU-109B low-level laser-guided or GBU-10/GBU-27 laser-guided glide weapons; alternatively, AGM-65 Maverick or AGM-88 HARM ASMs. Internal carriage on two extensible beams in weapon bay. (Only missiles with seeker heads extended below aircraft prior to launch; bombs released from within weapon bay.)

DIMENSIONS, EXTERNAL:

Wing span	13.20 m (43 ft 4 in)
Length overall	20.08 m (65 ft 11 in)
Height overall	3.78 m (12 ft 5 in)

AREAS (estimated):

Wing area	105.9 m² (1,140 sq ft)

WEIGHTS AND LOADINGS:

Weight empty (estimated)	13,608 kg (30,000 lb)
Max T-O weight	23,814 kg (52,500 lb)

PERFORMANCE (* = not confirmed by USAF):

Max level speed	Mach 1 + *
Normal max operating speed	Mach 0.9
T-O speed at normal combat weight	
	165 knots (306 km/h; 190 mph)*
Landing speed	150 knots (227 km/h; 172 mph)*
g limit	+ 6

LOCKHEED F-22 (ATF)

TYPE: US Air Force (originally also US Navy) advanced tactical fighter.

PROGRAMME: US Air Force requirement for McDonnell Douglas F-15 Eagle replacement incorporating low observables technology and supercruise (supersonic cruise without afterburner); parallel assessment of two new power plants; request for information issued 1981; concept definition studies awarded September 1983 to Boeing, General Dynamics, Grumman, McDonnell Douglas, Northrop and Rockwell; requests for proposals issued September 1985; submissions received by 28 July 1986; USAF selection announced 31 October 1986 of demonstration/validation phase contractors: Lockheed YF-22 and Northrop YF-23; each produced two prototypes and ground-based avionics testbed; first flights of all four prototypes 1990. Competing engine demonstration/validation programmes launched September 1983; ground testing began 1986-87; flight-capable Pratt & Whitney YF119s and General Electric YF120s ordered early 1988; all four aircraft/engine combinations flown.

Decision of 11 October 1989 extended evaluation phase by six months; draft request for engineering and manufacturing development (EMD) proposals issued April 1990; first artists' impressions released May 1990; final FSD requests issued for both weapon system and engine 1 November 1990; proposals submitted 2 January 1991; F-22 and F119 power plant announced by USAF as winning combination, 23 April 1991; EMD engineering, manufacture and development approval planned by late 1991 for 11 flying prototypes (including two tandem-seat) and two static test airframes; first flight 1995; first production batch of four aircraft to be awarded January 1996; to be followed by four, 12, 24, 36 and 48 in 1997-2001; service entry 2000; original requirement for 750 aircraft reduced to 648.

Lockheed teamed with General Dynamics (Fort Worth) and Boeing Military Airplanes to produce two YF-22 prototypes, civil registrations N22YF (with GE YF120) and N22YX (P&W YF119). N22YF rolled out at Palmdale 29 August 1990; first flight/ferry to Edwards AFB 29 September 1990; first air refuelling (11th sortie) 26 October 1990; thrust vectoring in flight 15 November 1990; anti-spin parachute for high angle of attack tests on 34th-43rd sorties; temporarily grounded 28 December 1990; 43 sorties/52.8 hours. N22YX first flight Palmdale-Edwards 30 October 1990; AIM-9M Sidewinder (28 November 1990) and AIM-120 AMRAAM (20 December 1990) launch demonstrations; achieved Mach 1.8 26 December 1990; temporarily grounded after 31 sorties/38.8 hours, 28 December 1990. Flight test demonstrations included 100 °/s roll rate at 120 knots (222 km/h; 138 mph) and 'supercruise' flight in excess of Mach 1.58 without afterburner.

Lockheed responsible for project control and systems integration; workload shared equally between three partners; Lockheed constructs forward fuselage and components, including cockpit, with avionics architecture and functional design, displays, controls, air data system and apertures. Boeing responsible for wings, fuselage aft sections, power plant installation, radar, infra-red search and track system (if fitted in production aircraft) and avionics ground prototype. Avionics flight tested in a modified Boeing 757 (N757A) (first flight 17 July 1989). General Dynamics concerned with mid-fuselage, tail assembly, landing gear and key systems including electrical, hydraulic, fuel, flight controls, environment and armament; also integrated electronic warfare system (INEWS), integrated communications/navigation/identification avionics (ICNIA) and INS subsystems. Programme involves 650 suppliers in 32 US states.

VARIANTS: US Navy variant (**NATF**) to replace Grumman F-14 Tomcat; original requirement for 546 had already been cut to 384. Concurrent development abandoned; option for programme re-start post-1997.

COSTS: $818 million contracts to both ATF teams, October 1986, for 54-month studies; each airframe team investing about $600 million; each engine contractor, about $50 million; total $3,800 million spent by USAF on both ATFs up to April 1991; programme cost (1992) for 648 aircraft is $13,000 million for development and $47,000 million for production; programme unit cost $61 million (1992).

DESIGN FEATURES: Low observables configuration and construction; stealth/agility trade-off decided by design team; target thrust/weight ratio 1.4 (achieved ratio possibly 1.1 at T-O weight); greatly improved reliability and maintainability for high sortie-generation rates, including 15 minute combat turn-round time; enhanced survivability through 'first-look first-kill' capability; short T-O and landing distances; supersonic cruise and manoeuvring (supercruise) in region of Mach 1.5 without afterburning; internal weapons storage and generous internal fuel; conformal sensors. Wing leading-edge sweep approximately 48°; trailing-edge some 17° forward; all-moving horizontal tail; canted outward approx 27°. Sidewinder AAMs stored internally in sides of intake ducts, with AMRAAMs in ventral weapons bay. Diamond-shaped cheek air intakes with straight-through air ducts; single-axis thrust vectoring available on PW119, but specified performance achievable without.

FLYING CONTROLS: Digital flight control system with fibre optic transmission handling 100 Mbytes/s. Ailerons and flaps occupy almost entire wing trailing-edge; leading-edge flaps; conventional rudders in vertical tail surfaces; slab taileron surfaces; upper fuselage airbrake. Digital flight control system by Lear Astronics.

Both Lockheed/GD/Boeing YF-22 prototypes in flight, the far one fitted with an anti-spin parachute

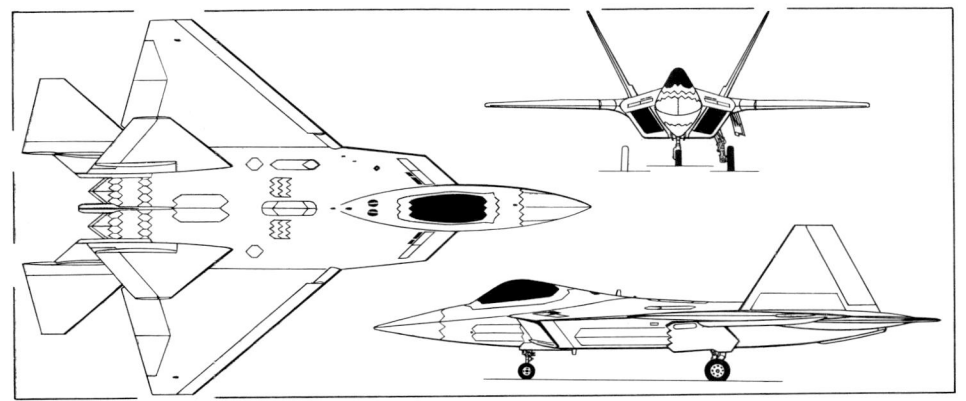

Lockheed/GD/Boeing YF-22 *(Pilot Press)*

Lockheed/GD/Boeing YF-22 with anti-spin parachute executes a roll to port with fly-by-wire system moving flaperons, ailerons, tailerons, rudders and wing leading-edges in response to a single pilot control input

STRUCTURE: Largely metal (aluminium/titanium/steel 33/24/5 per cent) in prototypes. Extensive use of thermoplastic composites (12 per cent) and thermoset structures (10 per cent); combined total increases to 35-40 per cent in production aircraft.

LANDING GEAR: Menasco retractable tricycle undercarriage, stressed for no-flare landings of up to 3.05 m (10 ft)/s.

POWER PLANT: Two 155 kN (35,000 lb st) class Pratt & Whitney F119-PW-100 advanced technology reheated engines reportedly developed from F100 turbofan. Two-dimensional convergent/divergent exhaust nozzles, for enhanced STOL performance and manoeuvrability, dropped from ATF specification, but installed in YF-22. Sundstrand Turbomach APU.

ACCOMMODATION: Pilot only in Weber zero/zero ejection seat and wearing Tactical Life Support System with upper and lower *g*-suits and pressure breathing; side-stick controller in prototype; central column in production version.

AVIONICS: Compared with F-15E, F-22 probably has three times as much computer memory and 16 times as many millions of computer operations per second; sensor outputs for display are managed by artificial intelligence or principles of Pilot's Associate system. GEC Avionics wide-angle HUD and sidestick; General Electric multi-purpose LCDs; Sanders/GE ESM suite; Texas Instruments mission and display processing computer; Hughes signal processors. Westinghouse and Texas Instruments in competition to provide electronically scanned, phased-array radar. Radar modes include precision landing. Integrated electronic warfare system (INEWS) and integrated communications/navigation/identification avionics (ICNIA).

ARMAMENT: Internal long-barrel M61A1 20 mm gun. Three internal bays (see Design Features) for eight AIM-9 Sidewinder and/or AIM-120 AMRAAM AAMs on 'revolutionary weapon racks'. Have Dash 2 AAM and Have Slick ASM under development.

DIMENSIONS, EXTERNAL:
Wing span	13.11 m (43 ft 0 in)
Wing aspect ratio	2.2
Length overall	19.56 m (64 ft 2 in)
Height overall	5.41 m (17 ft 8⅞ in)

AREAS (estimated):
Wings, gross	77.1 m² (830 sq ft)

WEIGHTS AND LOADINGS (YF-22, estimated):
Weight empty	over 13,608 kg (30,000 lb)
Max T-O weight	26,308 kg (58,000 lb)

PERFORMANCE (YF-22, demonstrated):
Max level speed: supercruise	Mach 1.58
with afterburning	Mach 1.7 at 9,150 m (30,000 ft)
Ceiling	15,240 m (50,000 ft)
g limit	+7.9

PERFORMANCE (F-22A, design target):
Max level speed at S/L 800 knots (1,482 km/h; 921 mph)	
g limit	+9

LOCKHEED MODEL 185/285 ORION

US Navy designation: P-3
CF designations: CP-140 Aurora/CP-140A Arcturus
TYPE: Land-based maritime patrol and ASW aircraft.
PROGRAMME: Lockheed won competition for off-the-shelf ASW aircraft 1958; first flight aerodynamic prototype 19 August 1958; first flight fully equipped YP-3A (YP3V-1) 25 November 1959; details of initial production P-3A and WP-3A in 1978-79 *Jane's*; details of P-3B and EP-3B in 1983-84 *Jane's*; South Korean order for eight P-3C Update III in December 1990 extends P-3 production beyond original 642 planned up to September 1991; assembly to be transferred from Burbank to Marietta, starting in 1992; first delivery to South Korea 1995; orders from European countries formerly expecting to order P-7, such as Germany, now probable.

Numbers built: one YP-3; 157 US Navy P-3As, of which 38 modified to UP-3A, seven to EP-3A, six to RP-3A, five to VP-3A (three via WP-3A), 12 to TP-3A, two to EP-3B and 10 to EP-3E; 124 USN P-3Bs, one converted to NP-3B and one under conversion in 1991 to RP-3B; 267 USN P-3Cs, 12 intended for EP-3E-II conversion; one USN RP-3D; two National Oceanographic and Atmospheric Administration WP-3Ds.

VARIANTS: **P-3C:** First flight 18 September 1968; in service 1969; introduced A-NEW system based on Univac computer integrating all ASW information for retrieval, display and transmission of tactical data without routine log-keeping; 267th and last US Navy P-3C (163295) delivered to VP-91 at Moffett Field NAS, California, one of two reserve squadrons (with VP-62 at Jacksonville, Florida) operating P-3C; 11 more Reserve squadrons operate **P-3B**, supporting 25 full-time patrol squadrons equipped with P-3C. (Final Reserve P-3A anti-submarine mission flown March 1990; final regular USN P-3B ASW mission, 11 September 1990.)

P-3C Update I: First 118 Baseline P-3Cs followed from January 1975 by 31 P-3C Update I; new avionics and software included magnetic drum to increase computer memory sevenfold, new versatile computer language, Omega navigation, improved directional acoustic frequency analysis and recording (DIFAR)

Current USV radar-absorbent tactical paint scheme on P-3B, devoid of unit markings and serial number *(Paul Jackson)*

processing sensitivity, AN/ASA-66 tactical displays for two sensor stations, and improved magnetic tape transport.

Update II: Applied to 44 aircraft built from August 1977; added infra-red detection system (IRDS) and sonobuoy reference system (SRS); Harpoon missile system incorporated from August 1977; 24 more USN P-3Cs received interim **Update II.5** of 1981 including more reliable navigation and communication systems; IACS submarine communications link; MAD compensation group adaptor; standardised wing pylons; and improved fuel tank vents.

Update III: Deliveries started May 1984; applied to last 50 USN P-3Cs; includes new IBM Proteus acoustic processor (doubling sonobuoy handling capacity), new sonobuoy receiver replacing DIFAR, improved APU, and higher capacity environmental control system. Baseline P-3C to III retrofit kit first installed in P-3C of VP-31 in 1987 (new designation **IIIR**); fitting of 18 more kits started June 1987; eventual total 113 planned.

Update IV: In full-scale development by Boeing Aerospace and Electronics for installation from early 1990s; originally intended for P-7A LRAACA; all P-3C Update II and II.5 to be retrofitted, equipping VP-8, 10, 11, 23, 26 and 44 at Brunswick, Maine, beginning FY 1994; one P-3C used for aerodynamic and functional testing of Eaton AIL Division AN/ALR-77 ESM system with 36 antennae mounted in four groups at wingtips; installation abandoned in favour of General Instrument AN/ALR-66(V)5 in same position; other features include improved processing, Texas Instruments AN/APS-137(V) radar and new family of acoustic sensors to detect quieter submarines.

EP-3C: Elint version of P-3C developed by Kawasaki for JMSDF; first aircraft funded 1987 for delivery March 1991; two more on order.

EP-3E Aries: Ten P-3A and two EP-3Bs converted to EP-3E; radars in large canoe-shaped fairings above and below fuselage and ventral radome forward of wing; avionics believed to include GTE-Sylvania AN/ALR-60 communications intercept and analysis system, Raytheon AN/ALQ-76 noise jamming pod, Loral AN/ALQ-78 automatic ESM system, Magnavox AN/ALQ-108 IFF jammer, Sanders AN/ALR-132 infra-red jammer, ARGO Systems AN/ALR-52 instantaneous frequency measuring equipment, Texas Instruments AN/APS-115

frequency agile search radar, Hughes AN/AAR-37 infra-red detector, Loral AN/ASA-66 tactical display, Cardion AN/ASA-69 scan converter and Honeywell AN/ASQ-114 computer.

EP-3E Aries II: Twelve low-houred P-3Cs replaced EP-3E Aries with USN special reconnaissance squadrons VQ-1 at Agana NAS, Guam, and VQ-2 at Rota, Spain; equipment transferred from original EP-3E; first conversion delivered November 1988; last aircraft due 1991; work by Lockheed Aircraft Service Company's Aeromod Center at Greenville, South Carolina.

P-3F: Six, similar to mid-1970s US Navy Baseline P-3C, delivered to Imperial Iranian Air Force.

CP-140 Aurora: Canadian Forces version (18 built); described in 1981-82 *Jane's*.

CP-140A Arcturus: Three P-3s for Canadian Forces completed by September 1991; no ASW equipment; for environmental and fishery patrol replacing CP-121 Trackers; equipment includes Texas Instruments AN/APS-134 radar, Honeywell AN/APN-194 RAWS, Bendix AN/ASW-502 AFCS, Canadian Marconi AN/APN-510 Doppler radar, Litton LN-33 INS and a Leigh AN/ASH-502 flight recorder.

P-3 AEW&C: Airborne Early Warning and Control; first flight of prototype (N91LC) converted from Australian P-3B and fitted with Randtron AN/APA-171 7.32 m (24 ft) diameter rotodome 14 June 1984; testing of installed General Electric AN/APS-138 radar began 1988; military version would have AN/APS-139 radar from Grumman E-2C Hawkeye. Other systems would include C³ system to receive, process and transmit tactical information on HF, UHF, VHF and Satcom channels; AN/ARC-187 satellite communication system; and Collins five-tube colour EFIS-86B flight instruments. General Electric AN/APS-145 radar available from late 1989.

First order from US Customs May 1987 for one plus option for three; first flight US Customs aircraft with AN/APS-125 radar 8 April 1988; aircraft called *Blue Eagle* delivered to NAS Corpus Christi, Texas, 17 June 1988 and used for anti-narcotics patrol over Caribbean and Gulf of Mexico; second P-3 AEW&C called *Blue Eagle II* fitted with improved AN/APS-138 radar delivered to US Customs June 1989; third on order; all are ex-Australian P-3Bs. Other systems include CDC AN/AYK-14 computer with Honeywell 1601M array

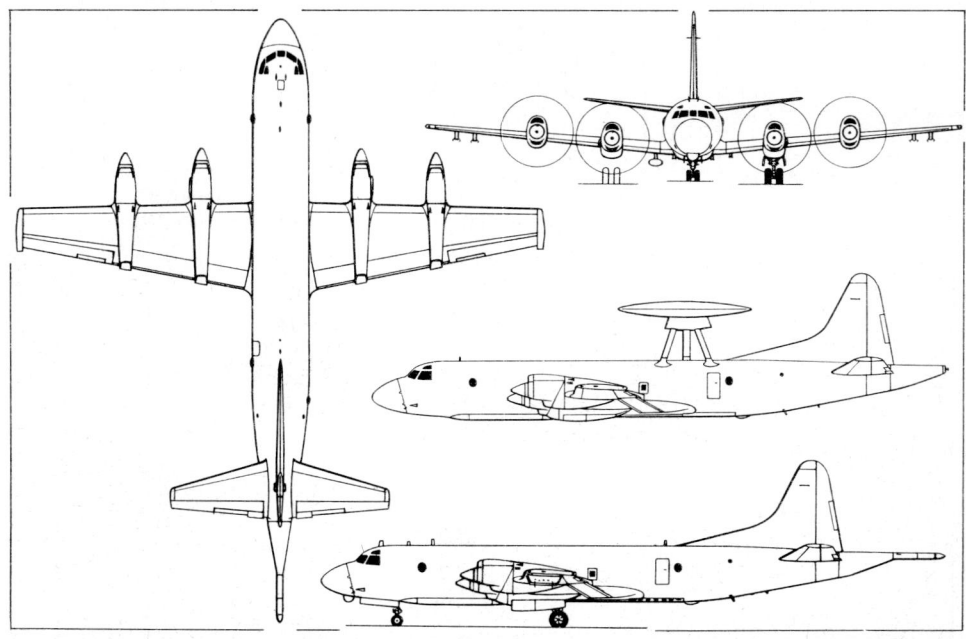

Lockheed P-3C Orion four-turboprop anti-submarine aircraft, with added side elevation (centre) of AEW & C version *(Pilot Press)*

processor, dual Sanders Miligraphics touch-sensitive colour display screens for digital target data, Hazeltine AN/TPX-54 IFF, dual AN/ARC-182 VHF/UHF com radios, dual AN/ARC-207 HF and dual Wulfsberg VHF/UHF-FM radios.

P-3H: Proposed P-3C upgrade to replace cancelled P-7A, submitted for FY 1992 budget approval. Update IV avionics plus new wings and engines and, possibly, HUDs and flat-panel cockpit displays. Decision awaited at press time.

P-3K: New Zealand P-3s. Planned ASW/avionics upgrade shelved 1990.

P-3N: Two P-3Bs retained by Norway, less some ASW equipment, for EEZ surveillance, SAR and training.

P-3P: Portuguese P-3Bs obtained from Australia; one converted by Lockheed and five converted by Portuguese OGMA (which see); MIL-STD-1553 digital bus and systems similar to Update II; operated by Esquadra 601 at Montijo.

P-3W: Australian P-3Cs; have AQS-901 processing system and Barra sonobuoys in place of Proteus and AN/AQA-7 equipment of USN P-3C.

NP-3: Various aircraft relegated to permanent test status. New-built NP-3E ordered from Kawasaki in FY 1991 Japanese defence budget.

UP-3: Various utility configurations. Japan requires two UP-3Cs from Kawasaki production.

CUSTOMERS: Total 90 P-3s exported from Burbank: to Australia (10 P-3Bs, one transferred from US Navy; 20 P-3C-IIs; five P-3Bs transferred to Portugal, one to New Zealand, three to US Customs for conversion to AEW&C), Canada (18 CP-140 Auroras, three CP-140A Arcturus), Iran (six P-3Es), Japan (three P-3C-IIs from Lockheed; Kawasaki produced 66 P-3C-IIs and has 32 P-3C-IIIs, three EP-3Es and one NP-3E on order; six further P-3Cs and two UP-3Cs will complete requirements; P-3C-II to be updated), Netherlands (13 P-3C-IIs), New Zealand (five P-3Ks), Norway (five P-3Bs, two transferred from US Navy, and four P-3C-IIIs; five P-3Bs transferred to Spain) and Pakistan (three P-3C-II.5s). Marietta production initially for South Korea (eight P-3C Update IIIs; deliveries from 1995). Four USN P-3As transferred to US Customs as UP-3As; others civilianised for various operators, including N406TP with Allison GMA 2100 turboprop and Dowty Aerospace R373 composite propeller in port outer nacelle, 1990. Thailand plans to buy three USN P-3Bs; Greece, six surplus P-3As.

COSTS: $600 million for eight P-3C for South Korea 1990; $840 million (1990) including engines, training and spares.

DESIGN FEATURES: Data below refer to P-3C. Pressurised cabin. Wing section NACA 0014 (modified) at root, NACA 0012 (modified) at tip; dihedral 6°; incidence 3° at root, 0° 30′ at tip. Anti-icing by bleed air on wing and electrical heating on tailplane and fin.

FLYING CONTROLS: Hydraulically boosted ailerons, elevators and rudder; fixed tailplane; Lockheed-Fowler trailing-edge flaps.

STRUCTURE: Conventional aluminium alloy with fail-safe box beam wing.

LANDING GEAR: Hydraulically retractable tricycle type, with twin wheels on each unit. All units retract forward, mainwheels into inner engine nacelles. Oleo-pneumatic shock absorbers. Mainwheels have size 40-14 type VII 26-ply tubeless tyres, pressures 7.58-12.41 bars (110-180 lb/sq in) at 36,287 kg (80,000 lb) T-O weight; 12.41 bars (180 lb/sq in) at 57,606 kg (127,000 lb) T-O weight; 13.10 bars (190 lb/sq in) at 61,235 kg (135,000 lb) max normal T-O weight. Nosewheels have size 28-7.7 type VII tubeless tyres, pressure 10.34 bars (150 lb/sq in). Hydraulic brakes. No anti-skid units.

POWER PLANT: Four 3,661 kW (4,910 ehp) Allison T56-A-14 turboprops, each driving a Hamilton Standard 54H60-77 four-blade constant-speed propeller. Fuel in one tank in fuselage and four wing integral tanks, with total usable

One of three Lockheed P-3C-II.5 Orions ordered by the Pakistan Navy

capacity of 34,826 litres (9,200 US gallons; 7,660 Imp gallons). Four overwing gravity fuelling points and central pressure refuelling point. Oil capacity (min usable) 111 litres (29.4 US gallons; 24.5 Imp gallons) in four tanks. Electrically de-iced propeller spinners.

ACCOMMODATION: Normal 10-man crew: pilot, co-pilot, flight engineer and nav/com operator on flight deck; tactical co-ordinator, two acoustic sensor operators, MAD operator, ordnance man and flight technician; up to 13 additional relief crew or passengers. Flight deck has wide-vision windows, and circular windows for observers are provided fore and aft in the main cabin, each bulged to give 180° view. Main cabin is fitted out as a five-man tactical compartment containing advanced electronic, magnetic and sonic detection equipment, an all-electric galley and large crew rest area.

SYSTEMS: Air-conditioning and pressurisation system supplied by two engine driven compressors. Pressure differential 0.37 bar (5.4 lb/sq in). Hydraulic system, pressure 207 bars (3,000 lb/sq in), for flaps, control surface boosters, landing gear actuation, brakes and bomb bay doors. Three hydraulic pumps, each rated at 30.3 litres (8.0 US gallons; 6.7 Imp gallons)/min at 0-152 bars (0-2,200 lb/sq in), 22.7 litres (6.0 US gallons; 5.0 Imp gallons)/min at 205 bars (2,975 lb/sq in). Class one non-separated air/oil reservoir, Type B pressurised. Electrical system utilises three 60kVA generators for 120/208V 400Hz AC supply. 24V DC supply. Integral APU with 60kVA generator for ground air-conditioning, electrical supply and engine starting.

AVIONICS: The AN/ASQ-114 general purpose digital computer is the heart of the P-3C system. Together with the AN/AYA-8 data processing equipment and computer controlled display systems, it permits rapid analysis and utilisation of electronic, magnetic and sonic data. Nav/com system comprises two LTN-72 inertial navigation systems; AN/APN-227 Doppler; AN/ARN-81 Loran A and C; AN/ARN-118 Tacan; two VIR-31A VOR/LOC/GS/MB receivers; AN/ARN-83 LF-ADF; AN/ARA-50 UHF direction finder; AN/AJN-15 flight director indicator for tactical directions; HSI for long-range flight directions; glideslope indicator; on-top position indicator; two AN/ARC-161 HF transceivers; two AN/ARC-143 UHF transceivers; AN/ARC-101 VHF receiver/transmitter; AN/AGC-6 teletype and high-speed printer; HF and UHF secure communication units; AN/ACQ-5 data link communication set and AN/AIC-22 interphone set; AN/APX-72 IFF transponder and AN/APX-76 SIF interrogator. Electronic computer controlled display equipment includes AN/ASA-70 tactical display; AN/ASA-66 pilot's display; AN/ASA-70 radar display and two auxiliary readout (computer stored data) displays. ASW equipment

includes two AN/ARR-72 sonar receivers, replaced in Update III by AN/ARR-78; two AN/AQA-7(V)8 DIFAR (directional acoustic frequency analysis and recording) sonobuoy indicator sets, replaced in Update III by AN/UYS-1 Proteus; hyperbolic fix unit; acoustic source signal generator; time code generator and AN/AQH-4(V) sonar tape recorder; AN/ASQ-81 magnetic anomaly detector; AN/ASA-64 submarine anomaly detector; AN/ASA-65 magnetic compensator; AN/ALQ-78 electronic countermeasures set; AN/APS-115 radar set (360° coverage); AN/ASA-69 radar scan converter; undernose AN/AAS-36 IRDS, KA-74 forward computer assisted camera; KB-18A automatic strike assessment camera with horizon-to-horizon coverage; RO-308 bathythermograph recorder. Additional items include AN/APN-194 radar altimeter; two AN/APQ-107 radar altimeter warning systems; A/A24G-9 true airspeed computer and AN/ASW-31 automatic flight control system. P-3Cs delivered from 1975 have the avionics/electronics package updated by addition of an extra 393K memory drum and fourth logic unit, Omega navigation, new magnetic tape transport, and an AN/ASA-66 tactical display for the sonar operators. To accommodate the new systems a new operational software computer programme was written in CMS-2 language. GEC Avionics AQS-901 acoustic signal processing and display system in RAAF P-3Ws. AN/ALR-66(V)5 passive radar detection system (ESM), to be housed in wingtip pods, is under development for Update IV P-3C by General Instrument, and will also provide targeting data for the aircraft's Harpoon missiles. AN/ALR-66(V)3 installed in Japanese and Nowegian P-3C and as retrofit in P-3P and CP-140. Wing span increased by some 0.81 m (2 ft 8 in) to accommodate ESM antennae and receivers. Similar Israeli Elta equipment for Australian retrofit. Loral AN/ALQ-157 IR jammers retrofitted each side of rear fuselage on USN P-3Cs. AN/ALR-66(V)5 replaces Loral AN/ALQ-78A pod on inboard wing pylon. Update IV FSED contract awarded to Boeing Aerospace and Electronics in Spring 1987, for completion in 1992. Subcontractors include Magnavox (acoustic system), Resdel (sonobuoy receiver), General Instrument (ESM), Honeywell (AN/AQH-4[V]2 data recorders) and M/A Com (satellite communications).

EQUIPMENT: Searchlight replaces one wing pylon, starboard. Search stores, such as sonobuoys and sound signals, are launched from inside cabin area in the P-3A/B. In the P-3C sonobuoys are loaded and launched externally and internally. Sonobuoys are ejected from P-3C aircraft with explosive cartridge actuating devices (CAD), eliminating the need for a pneumatic system. Australian P-3Ws use SSQ-801 Barra sonobuoys.

ARMAMENT: Bomb bay, 2.03 m wide, 0.88 m deep and 3.91 m long (80 × 34.5 × 154 in), forward of wing, and 10 underwing pylons. Maximum stores capabilities in weapons bay/underwing include Mk 46 torpedo 8/0; Mk 50 torpedo 6/0; Mk 54 depth bomb 8/10; B57 nuclear depth charge 3/0; Mk 82 560 lb bomb 8/10; Mk 83 980 lb bomb 3/8; Mk 36 destructor 8/10; Mk 40 destructor 3/8; LAU-68A pod (seven 2.75 in rockets), or LAU-69A (nineteen 2.75 in rockets), or LAU-10A/C (four 5 in rockets), or SUU-44A (eight flares) 0/4; Mk 52 mine 3/8; Mk 55 or Mk 56 mine 1/6; Mk 60 torpedo 0/6; AGM-86 Harpoon anti-ship missile 0/8. Two AIM-9L Sidewinder AAMs underwing for self-defence. Max total weapon load includes six 2,000 lb mines under wings and a 3,290 kg (7,252 lb) internal load made up of two Mk 101 depth bombs, four Mk 44 torpedoes, pyrotechnic pistol and 12 signals, 87 sonobuoys, 100 Mk 50 underwater sound signals (P-3A/B), 18 Mk 3A marine markers (P-3A/B), 42 Mk 7 marine markers, two B.T. buoys, and two Mk 5 parachute flares. Harpoon missiles are standard fit on a proportion of US Navy P-3Cs.

DIMENSIONS, EXTERNAL:

Wing span	30.37 m (99 ft 8 in)
Wing chord: at root	5.77 m (18 ft 11 in)
at tip	2.31 m (7 ft 7 in)

US Customs Service P-3 AEW & C Blue Eagle airborne early warning and control version of the Orion

Wing aspect ratio	7.5
Length overall	35.61 m (116 ft 10 in)
Height overall	10.27 m (33 ft 8½ in)
Fuselage diameter	3.45 m (11 ft 4 in)
Tailplane span	13.06 m (42 ft 10 in)
Wheel track (c/l shock absorbers)	9.50 m (31 ft 2 in)
Wheelbase	9.07 m (29 ft 9 in)
Propeller diameter	4.11 m (13 ft 6 in)
Cabin door: Height	1.83 m (6 ft 0 in)
Width	0.69 m (2 ft 3 in)

DIMENSIONS, INTERNAL:

Cabin, excl flight deck and electrical load centre:	
Length	21.06 m (69 ft 1 in)
Max width	3.30 m (10 ft 10 in)
Max height	2.29 m (7 ft 6 in)
Floor area	61.13 m² (658.0 sq ft)
Volume	120.6 m³ (4,260 cu ft)

AREAS:

Wings, gross	120.77 m² (1,300.0 sq ft)
Ailerons (total)	8.36 m² (90.0 sq ft)
Trailing-edge flaps (total)	19.32 m² (208.0 sq ft)
Fin, incl dorsal fin	10.78 m² (116.0 sq ft)
Rudder, incl tab	5.57 m² (60.0 sq ft)
Tailplane	22.39 m² (241.0 sq ft)
Elevators, incl tabs	7.53 m² (81.0 sq ft)

WEIGHTS AND LOADINGS (P-3B/C):

Weight empty	27,890 kg (61,491 lb)
Max fuel weight	28,350 kg (62,500 lb)
Max expendable load	9,071 kg (20,000 lb)
Max normal T-O weight	61,235 kg (135,000 lb)
Max permissible weight	64,410 kg (142,000 lb)
Design zero-fuel weight	35,017 kg (77,200 lb)
Max landing weight	47,119 kg (103,880 lb)
Max wing loading	507.0 kg/m² (103.8 lb/sq ft)
Max power loading	4.18 kg/kW (6.87 lb/ehp)

PERFORMANCE (P-3B/C, at max T-O weight, except where indicated otherwise):

Max level speed at 4,575 m (15,000 ft) at AUW of 47,625 kg (105,000 lb)	411 knots (761 km/h; 473 mph)
Econ cruising speed at 7,620 m (25,000 ft) at AUW of 49,895 kg (110,000 lb)	
	328 knots (608 km/h; 378 mph)
Patrol speed at 457 m (1,500 ft) at AUW of 49,895 kg (110,000 lb)	206 knots (381 km/h; 237 mph)
Stalling speed: flaps up	133 knots (248 km/h; 154 mph)
flaps down	112 knots (208 km/h; 129 mph)
Rate of climb at 457 m (1,500 ft)	594 m (1,950 ft)/min
Time to 7,620 m (25,000 ft)	30 min
Service ceiling	8,625 m (28,300 ft)
Service ceiling, one engine out	5,790 m (19,000 ft)
T-O run	1,290 m (4,240 ft)
T-O to 15 m (50 ft)	1,673 m (5,490 ft)
Landing from 15 m (50 ft) at design landing weight	
	845 m (2,770 ft)
Mission radius (3 h on station at 457 m; 1,500 ft)	
	1,346 nm (2,494 km; 1,550 miles)
Max mission radius (no time on station) at 61,235 kg (135,000 lb)	2,070 nm (3,835 km; 2,383 miles)
Ferry range	4,830 nm (8,950 km; 5,562 miles)
Max endurance at 4,575 m (15,000 ft):	
two engines	17 h 12 min
four engines	12 h 20 min

LOCKHEED LRAACA

US Navy designation: P-7A

TYPE: Intended successor to P-3; cancelled.

PROGRAMME: Lockheed selected to produce long-range air anti-submarine warfare capable aircraft (LRAACA), initially known as P-3G, in October 1988; requirement for 125 aircraft; development and two prototypes ordered January 1989 with P-7A designation; rollout scheduled for September 1991, with first flight December; second prototype was to be delivered March 1993 and first production aircraft 1994, with 18 aircraft a year from 1996 to 2001; commonality with P-3 declined from 20 per cent to near zero in 1989 and one to two year delay required for redesign; programme cancelled July 1990.

CUSTOMERS: German government signed MoU March 1989 to acquire 12 P-7As from 1997 to replace Dassault Atlantics; Dornier was to participate in programme. Outer wing panels subcontracted to Daewoo Heavy Industries of South Korea.

COSTS: Full-scale development contract of $52 million awarded January 1989; estimated unit cost $32-40 million.

DESIGN FEATURES: Four 3,729 kW (5,000 shp) class General Electric T407 turboprops, driving Hamilton Standard 15WF modular composite five-blade propellers; full authority digital controls; 37,703 litre (9,953 US gallon; 8,294 Imp gallon) fuel capacity.

DIMENSIONS EXTERNAL:

Wing span	32.49 m (106 ft 7¼ in)
Length overall	34.35 m (112 ft 8½ in)
Height overall	10.03 m (32 ft 8½ in)

WEIGHTS AND LOADINGS (estimated):

Weight empty	33,520 kg (73,900 lb)
Payload	17,411 kg (38,385 lb)
Max normal T-O weight (3.0 g)	74,843 kg (165,000 lb)
Max permissible weight	77,723 kg (171,350 lb)
Max power loading	5.02 kg/kW (8.25 lb/shp)

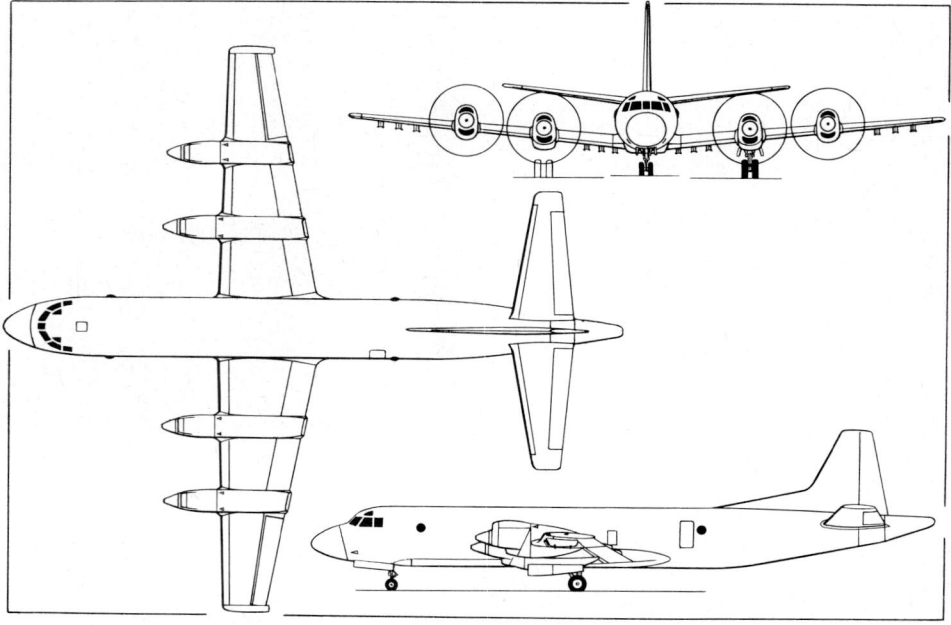

Lockheed P-7A long-range ASW capable aircraft (*Pilot Press*)

PERFORMANCE (estimated):

Cruise ceiling	10,668 m (35,000 ft)
Radius of action for 4 h on station	
	1,863 nm (3,453 km; 2,145 miles)
Time on station at 1,600 nm (2,965 km; 1,842 miles) from base	5 h 50 min

LOCKHEED VIKING

US Navy designation: S-3

TYPE: Carrier-borne ASW aircraft.

PROGRAMME: Production of 187 S-3As for US Navy ended mid-1978, tooling then stored at Burbank pending further orders; **US-3A** (COD) and **KS-3A** (dedicated tanker) demonstrators evaluated by US Navy early 1980; three earlier S-3As modified to US-3A 1982; KS-3A also converted to US-3A late 1983; S-3A fitted with Sargent-Fletcher buddy pack under port wing (to transfer fuel from internal tanks) and external tank under starboard wing: tested 1984 and adopted (ASW capability not affected).

VARIANTS: **S-3A:** Initial production ASW version (see 1978-79 *Jane's*).

S-3B: Lockheed defined Weapon System Improvement Program under US Navy contract 1980; full-scale development ordered 18 August 1981 and designated S-3B; first flight of first of two development S-3Bs 13 September 1984; flight testing completed August 1985 and six months' operational evaluation 1986; 22 kits plus spares and support ordered 28 April 1986 for installation at Cecil Field NAS, Florida; two prototype S-3B kits delivered 1987; 24 more kits ordered December 1988 for delivery by August 1992; first S-3B delivery to VS-27 17 December 1987; 42 S-3Bs completed for Atlantic Fleet by January 1990; VS-27, 30 and 32 re-equipped at Cecil Field, Florida, plus VS-28 and 31 in prospect; Lockheed has proposed kits for Pacific Fleet.

ES-3A: Contract for development of electronic reconnaissance E-3A awarded March 1988; S-3A for conversion (159401) delivered to Lockheed March 1988, scheduled to fly in Summer 1990 and be re-delivered May 1991; second YS-3A (157993) with 60 aerials and domes completed aerodynamic testing January 1990; original ES-3A development contract allowed for 15 production systems; nine modification kits ordered early 1989 for delivery by August 1991; airframe modification at Burbank and kit installation at LASG Aeromod Center at Greenville, South Carolina; two new squadrons, VQ-5 and VQ-6, formed at Agana NAS, Guam, 15 April 1991 and Cecil Field, Florida, August 1991; ES-3A will

supplement, but not replace, EA-3B Skywarrior in US Navy Battle Group Passive Horizon Extension System for long-range signals monitoring.

Weapons bay used for avionics as well as rear fuselage; starboard dual controls replaced by displays and controls for electronic warfare co-ordinating officer. Operational system, simplified from that of EP-3E Orion, includes AN/ALR-76 ESM, possibly AN/ALR-52 frequency measuring radar and AN/ALR-60 communications analysis system; other avionics include three AN/AYK-14 computers replacing one AN/AYK-10, MIL-STD-1553 databus, Navstar GPS and Omega navigation, Link 11 data link, AN/APX-76 IFF interrogator, AN/APS-137 radar, OR-236 FLIR and avionics cooling system; suppliers include Sanders Associates (cockpit display screens), Lockheed Missiles & Space (wiring and electronics racks).

COSTS: $66 million for prototype development of electronic reconnaissance installation awarded March 1988; $56.2 million for nine modification kits ordered early 1989.

AVIONICS (S-3B): AN/AYS-1 Proteus acoustic signal processor; modified Sanders AN/OL-320/AYS data processing memory group integrated with IBM AN/UYS-1; updated Honeywell AN/AYK-10A(V) air data computer, interfaced with Harpoon anti-ship missile and other new systems; improved electronic support measures (ESM); Hazeltine AN/ARR-78 sonobuoy receiver system; Precision Echo AN/AQH-7 analog tape recorder, Cubic AN/ARS-4 sonobuoy reference system; Texas Instruments AN/APS-137(V)1 radar, incorporating inverse synthetic aperture radar (ISAR) techniques; modified Goodyear AN/ALE-39 chaff/flare dispensing system; IBM AN/ALR-76 ESM; and provision for future advanced navigation and communications systems including GPS and JTIDS.

ARMAMENT: S-3A/B weapon options include four Mk 46/50 torpedoes, two B57 nuclear depth charges, four Mk 82 560 lb bombs or four Mk 36 destructors all stowed internally; plus underwing armament of six Mk 82/86s, two Mk 52/55/56 mines, two Mk 60 torpedoes, two AGM-84 Harpoon anti-ship missiles, or six LAU-10C/-68A/-69A rocket pods/SUU-44A flare pods.

LOCKHEED MODEL 382 HERCULES

US Air Force designations: C-130, AC-130, DC-130, EC-130, HC-130, JC-130, LC-130, MC-130, NC-130, RC-130 and WC-130

US Navy designations: C-130, DC-130, EC-130 and LC-130

Lockheed ES-3A aerodynamic prototype, showing some of 60 additional antennae

Lockheed C-130H of 64th Tactical Airlift Squadron of the US Air Force Reserve over its home town of Chicago

Lockheed EC-130H Compass Call jamming aircraft based at Sembach, Germany, with 43rd ECS, USAF
(Paul Jackson)

EC-130E *Volant Solo II* **in Rivet Rider psychological warfare configuration with 193rd SOS, USAF**
(Ivo Sturzenegger)

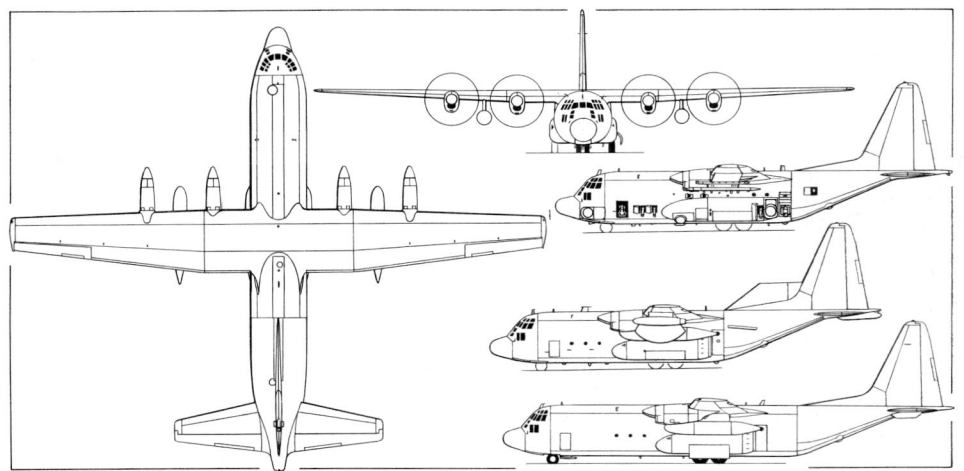

Lockheed C-130H-30 stretched Hercules (RAF C. Mk 3), with upper side view of AC-130U Spectre and centre side view of EC-130E *(Pilot Press)*

US Marine Corps designation: KC-130
US Coast Guard designation: HC-130
Canadian Forces designation: CC-130
RAF designations: Hercules C. Mk 1K, C. Mk 1P, W. Mk 2 and C. Mk 3P
Spanish designations: T.10, TK.10 and TL.10
Swedish designation: Tp 84
Export designations: C-130H, C-130H-30, KC-130H, C-130H-MP and VC-130H

TYPE: Tactical transport and multi-mission aircraft.

PROGRAMME: US Air Force specification issued 1951; first production contract for C-130A to Lockheed September 1952; two prototypes, 231 C-130As, 230 C-130Bs and 491 C-130Es manufactured (details in earlier *Jane's*). For later military versions, see below. Over 1,900 Hercules of all types produced by early 1991.

VARIANTS: **C-130H:** Deliveries started March 1965 to Royal New Zealand Air Force; in service with 50 countries. Features include updated avionics, improved wing, new corrosion protection, and Allison T56-A-15 engines flat rated at 3,362 kW (4,508 shp). Can deliver up to 22,680 kg (50,000 lb) by low altitude parachute extraction system (LAPES) or up to 11,340 kg (25,000 lb) by hook extraction and retardation on ground by Datron arrester cable system.

C-130H-MP: Maritime patrol version; one delivered to Indonesian Air Force and three to Royal Malaysian Air Force. Max T-O weight 70,310 kg (155,000 lb), max payload 18,630 kg (41,074 lb), and T56-A-15 engines; search time 2 h 30 min at 1,525 m (5,000 ft) at 1,800 nm (3,333 km; 2,070 miles) radius or 16 h 50 min at 200 nm (370 km; 230 miles) radius. Optional and standard search features include sea search radar, observer seats and windows, INS/Omega navigation, crew rest and galley slide-in module, flare launcher, loudspeaker, rescue kit airdrop platform, side-looking radar, passive microwave imager, low light TV, infra-red scanner, camera with data annotation and ramp equipment pallet with observer station.

C-130H-30: Stretched version similar to RAF Hercules C. Mk 3 (see C-130K). Convertible to 90-passenger transport with 15-seat pallets.

AC-130H Spectre: Gunship version with sideways-firing 105 mm recoilless gun, 40 mm cannon and two 20 mm Vulcan guns; infra-red and low light TV sensors, and side-looking head-up display for aiming at night while circling target; in-flight refuelling. Conversion by Lockheed Aircraft Service Co. New fire control computers and navigation and sensors under Special Operations/Forces Improvements (SOFI) being installed before transfer to 711th SOS, AFRes. Flight testing began September 1989; first upgrade completed mid-1990; last of current 10 due 1992. In service with 16th Special Operations Squadron at Hurlburt Field, Florida.

EC-130H Compass Call: Works with ground-based C³CM to jam enemy command, control and communications. Operated by 41st Electronic Combat Squadron at Davis Monthan AFB, Arizona, and 43rd Electronic Combat Squadron at Sembach, Germany. (Eight earlier EC-130Es of 7th ECCS being updated by UNISYS to ABCCC III standard in $34 million programme, 1990.)

HC-130H: Extended range USAF Aerospace Rescue and Recovery Service aircraft for aerial recovery of personnel or equipment and other duties; 43 delivered from October 1964; update announced Spring 1987 includes self-contained navigation, night vision goggles cockpit and new communications equipment; applied to 31 aircraft; 21 of these modified for in-flight refuelling; US Coast Guard ordered 35, final 10 as HC-130H-7 with T56A-7B power plants. Further three HC-130H(N)s funded FYs 1988-90 for 210th ARS, USAF, in Alaska, delivered from 28 November 1990.

JC-130H: Four US Air Force HC-130Hs equipped to recover re-entering space capsules.

DC-130H: Two US Air Force HC-130Hs modified for drone control.

KC-130H: Probe-drogue tanker similar to KC-130R; exported to Argentina (two), Brazil (two), Israel (two), Morocco (two), Saudi Arabia (eight), Spain (five) and Singapore (one).

LC-130H: Similar to LC-130R (which see); four acquired by 139th TAS, US Air Force Reserve.

MC-130H Combat Talon II: Conversion of new-build C-130H for day/night infiltration and exfiltration, resupply of Special Operations Forces, psychological warfare and aerial reconnaissance; terrain-following radar; five-man crew; 25 (including YMC-130H prototype) funded in FYs 1983-90; first flight by E-Systems (see below) at Greenville Spring 1988; 19-month flight testing began at Edwards AFB September 1988; MC-130Hs replaced MC-130Es with 8th SOS at Hurlburt Field from 1991.

Equipment includes Emerson Electric AN/APQ-170 precision ground mapping/weather/terrain following and avoidance radar in enlarged radome, inertial navigation, automatic computed air release point, high-speed low level release system, ground acquisition receiver/interrogator, Texas Instruments AN/AAQ-15 infra-red detection system, eight multi-function displays, secure voice UHF/VHF-FM radios, retractable FLIR pod, angle of attack probe, AN/ALQ-8 ECM pod under each

Lockheed KC-130T tanker of US Marine Corps Squadron VMGR-452 based at Stewart International Airport, Newburgh, New York *(Paul Jackson)*

wing, and in-flight refuelling. Defensive equipment includes Litton AN/ALR-69 radar warning receiver, ITT AN/ALQ-172 detector/jammer, Watkins Johnson WJ-1840 signal detector, Cincinnati Electronics AN/AAR-44 launch warning receiver, Northrop QRC-8402 IR jammer and chaff/flare dispensers. IBM Federal Systems Division is prime contractor for systems integration, with E-Systems as subcontractor for avionics installation and modification.

RC-130H: Unofficial designation for two Moroccan aircraft fitted with SLAR by Flight Systems Inc.

VC-130H: VIP transport.

C-130J: Advanced Hercules proposed in 1989 to replace US Air Force C-130Es from 1994; Series IV version of T56 allows deletion of external tanks without loss of range; two-crew flight deck with five liquid crystal displays, and two fold-down HUDs; carbon brakes with improved anti-skid. Flight-deck retrofit offered to USAF in competition with two-crew conversions tendered by other avionics manufacturers.

C-130K: RAF version of C-130H; much of avionics and instrumentation made in UK; 66 delivered as **Hercules C. Mk 1** beginning September 1966; one modified by Marshall of Cambridge for RAF Meteorological Research Flight as **Hercules W. Mk 2.** Thirty lengthened by 4.57 m (15 ft), equivalent to commercial L-100-30, and redesignated **Hercules C. Mk 3**; capacity increased from five to seven pallets; three Land Rovers and two trailers to four of each, from 92 to 128 troops, from 64 to 92 fully equipped paratroops and from 74 stretcher patients to 94; first aircraft modified at Marietta, remaining 29 by Marshall of Cambridge (see UK section).

HC-130N: US Air Force search and rescue version of C-130H for recovery of aircrew and space capsules; 15 delivered; advanced direction finding equipment.

HC-130P: C-130H modified for refuelling helicopters in flight and recovering parachute-borne payloads; 20 built for USAF; details in 1979-80 *Jane's.* HC-130N/Ps to be upgraded for refuelling operations in hostile airspace.

EC-130Q: Similar to earlier EC-130G, but with improved equipment and crew accommodation for TACAMO command communication with submarines; 18 built; HF and VLF SIMOP (simultaneous operation). Being replaced by Boeing E-6A.

TC-130Q: Surplus EC-130Q with trailing wire aerial removed to permit normal cargo loading via rear doors; wingtip pods retained; first (159348) noted 1990.

KC-130R: Probe-drogue tanker of C-130H; 14 delivered to US Marine Corps VMGR-252 and 352; changes from KC-130F (1975-76 *Jane's*) include 3,362 kW (4,508 shp) engines, higher T-O and landing weights, external fuel tanks for additional 10,296 litres (2,720 US gallons; 2,265 Imp gallons) fuel, and removable 13,627 litre (3,600 US gallon; 2,997 Imp gallon) fuel tank in cargo hold (all fuel can be used to increase tanker's range); single-point refuelling of normal and additional tanks from existing filler; operating weight empty 36,279 kg (79,981 lb); max T-O weight 79,378 kg (175,000 lb); can off-load up to 20,865 kg (46,000 lb) of fuel, equivalent to 26,790 litres (7,077 US gallons; 5,893 Imp gallons), at radius of 1,000 nm (1,850 km; 1,150 miles); maximum off-load capability 31,750 kg (70,000 lb), equivalent to 40,765 litres (10,769 US gallons; 8,967 Imp gallons).

LC-130R: C-130H with wheel-ski landing gear for US Navy Squadron VXE-6 in Antarctic; details in 1979-80 *Jane's.*

KC-130T: Tanker for US Marine Corps (Reserve), able to refuel helicopters and fighters; eight delivered to Marine Aerial Refueller Transport Squadron 234 (VMGR-234), starting November 1983; eight advanced KC-130Ts delivered to VMGR-452. Similar to KC-130R, but with updated avionics including INS, Omega and Tacan, new autopilot and flight director and solid-state search radar; KC-130Ts delivered in 1984 had Bendix AN/APS-133 colour radar, flush antennae and orthopaedically designed crew seats.

AC-130U Spectre: New gunship version of C-130H; details under Rockwell International entry.

CUSTOMERS (military C-130H variants only): Abu Dhabi (six), Algeria (10 and 10 H-30/L-100-30s), Argentina (five plus two KC- and one L-100-30), Australia (12), Belgium (12), Bolivia (two plus one L-100-30), Brazil (six plus two KC-), Cameroon (two plus one H-30), Canada (12), Chad (two), Chile (two), Colombia (two), Denmark (three), Dubai (one H-30, one L-100-30), Ecuador (three plus one L-100-30), Egypt (22 plus one VC- and three H-30s), France (three plus nine H-30s), Gabon (one plus one L-100-20 and two L-100-30s), Greece (12), Indonesia (three plus seven H-30s, one H-MP and one L-100-30), Iran (43), Israel (10 plus two KC-), Italy (14), Japan (15), Jordan (four), South Korea (three plus four H-30s), Kuwait (two L-100-20, two L-100-30), Libya (16, of which eight stored in US), Malaysia (six plus three H-MPs), Morocco (15 plus two KC- and two RC-), New Zealand (five), Niger (two), Nigeria (six H-30), Norway

(six), Oman (three), Peru (eight L-100-20s), Philippines (three plus four L-100s), Portugal (five plus one H-30 on order), Saudi Arabia (21 plus eight KC- and two VC- [10 plus seven KC- on order]), Singapore (six), Spain (seven plus five KC- and one H-30), Sudan (six), Sweden (six), Taiwan (12), Thailand (three plus three H-30 and two on order), Tunisia (two), United Kingdom (66 C-130K), Venezuela (eight), Yemen (two), Yugoslavia (two plus one H-30), Zaïre (seven).

Hercules in US service (including FY 1990 purchases and aircraft under conversion) at January 1991 were 12 C-130A, 10 AC-130A, five DC-130A, one NC-130A, 89 C-130B, 382 C-130E, 15 EC-130E, 13 MC-130E, seven WC-130E, 197 C-130H, 10 AC-130H, 12 AC-130U, 15 EC-130H, 12 HC-130H, three HC-130H(N), 15 HC-130N, 29 HC-130P, four LC-130H, one 24 MC-130H, one NC-130H, and six WC-130H with USAF; seven C-130F, 40 KC-130F, three LC-130F, three EC-130G, 15 EC-130Q, 14 KC-130R, six LC-130R and 16 KC-130T with USN/USMC; and 31 HC-130H with USCG.

COSTS: C-130H is $31.5 million (1988) flyaway; $48 million (1987) programme unit cost for AC-130H.

DESIGN FEATURES: Can deliver loads and parachutists over lowered rear ramp and parachutists through side doors; removable external fuel tanks outboard of engines are standard fittings; cargo hold pressurised. Wing section NACA 64A318 at root and NACA 64A412 at tip; dihedral 2° 30′; incidence 3° at root, 0° at tip. Leading-edges of wing, tailplane and fin anti-iced by engine bleed air.

FLYING CONTROLS: All control surfaces boosted by dual hydraulic units; trim tabs on ailerons, both elevators and rudder; elevator tabs have AC main supply and DC standby; Lockheed-Fowler trailing-edge flaps; strake under each tailplane root reduces cruise drag.

STRUCTURE: All-metal two-spar wing with integrally stiffened taper-machined skin panels up to 14.63 m (48 ft 0 in) long. Kevlar under-tailplane strakes.

LANDING GEAR: Hydraulically retractable tricycle type. Each main unit has two wheels in tandem, retracting into fairings built on to the sides of the fuselage. Nose unit has twin wheels and is steerable ± 60°. Oleo shock absorbers. Mainwheel tyres size 56 × 20-20, pressure 6.62 bars (96 lb/sq in). Nosewheel tyres size 39 × 13-16, pressure 4.14 bars (60 lb/sq in). Goodyear aircooled multiple disc hydraulic brakes with anti-skid units. Retractable combination wheel-skis available.

POWER PLANT: Four 3,362 kW (4,508 shp) Allison T56-A-15 turboprops, each driving a Hamilton Standard type 54H60 four-blade constant-speed fully feathering reversible-pitch propeller. Fuel in six integral tanks in wings, with total capacity of 26,344 litres (6,960 US gallons; 5,795 Imp gallons) and two optional underwing pylon tanks, each with capacity of 5,146 litres (1,360 US gallons; 1,132 Imp gallons). Total fuel capacity 36,636 litres (9,680 US gallons; 8,060 Imp gallons). Single pressure refuelling point in starboard wheel well. Overwing gravity refuelling. Oil capacity 182 litres (48 US gallons; 40 Imp gallons).

ACCOMMODATION: Crew of four on flight deck, comprising pilot, co-pilot, navigator and systems manager (fully performance qualified flight engineer on USAF aircraft). Provision for fifth man to supervise loading. Sleeping quarters for relief crew, and galley. Flight deck and main cabin pressurised and air-conditioned. Standard complements for C-130H are as follows: troops (max) 92, paratroops (max) 64, litters 74 and 2 attendants. Corresponding figures for C-130H-30 are 128 troops, 92 paratroops, and 97 litters. As a cargo carrier, loads can include heavy equipment such as a 12,080 kg (26,640 lb) type F.6 refuelling trailer or a 155 mm howitzer and its high-speed tractor, or up to five 463L pallets of freight (seven in C-130H-30). Hydraulically operated main loading door and ramp at rear of cabin. Paratroop door on each side aft of landing gear fairing. Two emergency exit doors standard; two additional doors optional on C-130H-30.

SYSTEMS: Air-conditioning and pressurisation system max pressure differential 0.52 bar (7.5 lb/sq in). Three independent hydraulic systems, utility and booster systems operating at a pressure of 207 bars (3,000 lb/sq in), rated at 65.1 litres (17.2 US gallons; 14.3 Imp gallons)/min for utility and booster systems, 30.3 litres (8.0 US gallons; 6.7 Imp gallons)/min for auxiliary system. Reservoirs are unpressurised. Auxiliary system has handpump for emergencies. Electrical system supplied by four 40kVA AC alternators, plus one 40kVA auxiliary alternator driven by APU in port main landing gear fairing. Four transformer-rectifiers for DC power. Current production aircraft incorporate systems and component design changes for increased reliability. There are differences between the installed components for US government and export versions. Babcock Power Ltd High Volume Mine Layer (HVML) system available as an option, using modular roll-on pallets.

AVIONICS: Dual 628T-2A HF com, dual 618M-3A VHF com, AN/ARC-164 UHF com, AN/AIC-13 PA system, AN/AIC-18 intercom, dual 621A-6A ATC transponders, DF-301E UHF nav, dual 51RV-4B VHF nav, CMA 771 Omega nav, LTN-72 INS, dual DF-206 ADF, 51Z-4

Potential C-130J cockpit for two-pilot operation includes five Litton Canada colour liquid crystal displays for flight, engine and systems information and four LCD tabular displays. This aircraft first flew on 28 February 1991

marker beacon receiver, dual 860E-5 DME, AL-101 radio altimeter, RDR-1F weather radar, dual C-12 compass systems, Mk II GPWS, AP-105V autopilot, and dual FD-109 flight directors.

DIMENSIONS, EXTERNAL:
Wing span	40.41 m (132 ft 7 in)
Wing chord: at root	4.88 m (16 ft 0 in)
mean	4.16 m (13 ft 8½ in)
Wing aspect ratio	10.1
Length overall:	
all except HC-130H and C-130H-30	
	29.79 m (97 ft 9 in)
C-130H-30	34.37 m (112 ft 9 in)
Height overall	11.66 m (38 ft 3 in)
Tailplane span	16.05 m (52 ft 8 in)
Wheel track	4.35 m (14 ft 3 in)
Wheelbase	9.77 m (32 ft 0¾ in)
Propeller diameter	4.11 m (13 ft 6 in)
Main cargo door (rear of cabin):	
Height	2.77 m (9 ft 1 in)
Width	3.05 m (10 ft 0 in)
Height to sill	1.03 m (3 ft 5 in)
Paratroop doors (each): Height	1.83 m (6 ft 0 in)
Width	0.91 m (3 ft 0 in)
Height to sill	1.03 m (3 ft 5 in)
Emergency exits (each): Height	1.22 m (4 ft 0 in)
Width	0.71 m (2 ft 4 in)

DIMENSIONS, INTERNAL:
Cabin, excl flight deck:	
Length without ramp:	
C-130H	12.22 m (40 ft 1¼ in)
C-130H-30	16.79 m (55 ft 1¼ in)
Length with ramp: C-130H	15.73 m (51 ft 8½ in)
C-130H-30	20.33 m (66 ft 8½ in)
Max width	3.12 m (10 ft 3 in)
Max height	2.81 m (9 ft 2¾ in)
Floor area, excl ramp: C-130H	39.5 m² (425.0 sq ft)
Volume, incl ramp: C-130H	127.4 m³ (4,500.0 cu ft)
C-130H-30	165.5 m³ (5,845.0 cu ft)

AREAS:
Wings, gross	162.12 m² (1,745.0 sq ft)
Ailerons (total)	10.22 m² (110.0 sq ft)
Trailing-edge flaps (total)	31.77 m² (342.0 sq ft)
Fin	20.90 m² (225.0 sq ft)
Rudder, incl tab	6.97 m² (75.0 sq ft)
Tailplane	35.40 m² (381.0 sq ft)
Elevators, incl tabs	14.40 m² (155.0 sq ft)

WEIGHTS AND LOADINGS:
Operating weight empty:	
C-130H	34,686 kg (76,469 lb)
C-130H-30	36,397 kg (80,242 lb)
Max fuel weight: internal	20,520 kg (45,240 lb)
external	8,020 kg (17,680 lb)
Max payload: C-130H	19,356 kg (42,673 lb)
C-130H-30	17,645 kg (38,900 lb)
Max normal T-O weight	70,310 kg (155,000 lb)
Max overload T-O weight	79,380 kg (175,000 lb)
Max normal landing weight	70,310 kg (155,000 lb)
Max overload landing weight	79,380 kg (175,000 lb)
Max zero-fuel weight, 2.5g	54,040 kg (119,142 lb)
Wing loading at max normal T-O weight	
	434.5 kg/m² (89 lb/sq ft)
Power loading at max normal T-O weight	
	5.23 kg/kW (8.6 lb/shp)

PERFORMANCE (C-130H at max normal T-O weight, unless indicated otherwise):
Max cruising speed	325 knots (602 km/h; 374 mph)
Econ cruising speed	300 knots (556 km/h; 345 mph)
Stalling speed	100 knots (185 km/h; 115 mph)
Max rate of climb at S/L	579 m (1,900 ft)/min
Service ceiling at 58,970 kg (130,000 lb) AUW	
	10,060 m (33,000 ft)
Service ceiling, one engine out, at 58,970 kg (130,000 lb) AUW	8,075 m (26,500 ft)
Min ground turning radius:	
C-130H:	
about nosewheel	11.28 m (37 ft 0 in)
about wingtip	25.91 m (85 ft 0 in)
C-130H-30:	
about nosewheel	14.33 m (47 ft 0 in)
about wingtip	27.43 m (90 ft 0 in)
Runway LCN: asphalt	37
concrete	42
T-O run	1,091 m (3,580 ft)

Lockheed L-100-30 Commercial Hercules of China Air Cargo

T-O to 15 m (50 ft)	1,573 m (5,160 ft)
Landing from 15 m (50 ft):	
at 45,360 kg (100,000 lb) AUW	731 m (2,400 ft)
at 58,967 kg (130,000 lb) AUW	838 m (2,750 ft)
Landing run at 58,967 kg (130,000 lb) AUW	
	518 m (1,700 ft)

Range with max payload, with 5% reserves and allowance for 30 min at S/L
2,046 nm (3,791 km; 2,356 miles)
Range with max fuel, incl external tanks, 7,081 kg (15,611 lb) payload, reserves of 5% initial fuel plus 30 min at S/L   4,250 nm (7,876 km; 4,894 miles)

LOCKHEED L-100 SERIES COMMERCIAL HERCULES

TYPE: Civilian version of C-130.

PROGRAMME: Initial variants described in earlier *Jane's*; current models below.

VARIANTS: **L-100-20 (Model 382E):** Fuselage stretched by 2.54 m (8 ft 4 in); certificated 4 October 1968; Allison 501-D22A engines; one L-100-20 is Lockheed HTTB testbed (which see); military/government operators listed under C-130 entry.

L-100-30 (Model 382G): Fuselage stretched 2.03 m (6 ft 8 in); military operators listed under C-130 entry; first operator Saturn Airways in December 1970.

L-100-30HS: Hospital version fitted by Lockheed Aircraft Service (which see), with operating theatre, intensive care, advanced anaesthesia and X-ray facilities; five delivered to Saudi Arabia; electrical generators and air-conditioners in underwing pods allow hospital to operate independently for 72 hours.

CUSTOMERS: See above. Total 111 commercial Hercules delivered (some in military use); operated at various times by 51 companies.

DESIGN FEATURES: Details of C-130H apply to L-100, except as detailed below. All C-130s and L-100s delivered since April 1984 have two 0.61 × 1.22 m (24 × 48 in) emergency exits which, together with rear personnel doors, allow carriage of 79 passengers; optional additional exit each side allows for 100 passengers; supplemental oxygen provided for passengers; various galley and toilet layouts available.

FLYING CONTROLS: As C-130H.

STRUCTURE: As C-130H.

LANDING GEAR: As for C-130H, except mainwheel tyre pressure 3.24-7.38 bars (47-107 lb/sq in) and nosewheel tyre pressure 4.14 bars (60 lb/sq in).

POWER PLANT: Four 3,362 kW (4,508 shp) Allison 501-D22A turboprops.

DIMENSIONS, EXTERNAL:
Length overall: L-100-20	32.33 m (106 ft 1 in)
L-100-30	34.37 m (112 ft 9 in)
Wheelbase: L-100-20	11.30 m (37 ft 1 in)
L-100-30	12.32 m (40 ft 5 in)
Crew door (integral steps): Height	1.14 m (3 ft 9 in)
Width	0.76 m (2 ft 6 in)
Height to sill	1.04 m (3 ft 5 in)

DIMENSIONS, INTERNAL:
Cabin, excl flight deck:

Length: L-100-20	15.04 m (49 ft 4 in)
L-100-30, excl ramp	17.07 m (56 ft 0 in)
incl ramp	19.93 m (65 ft 4¾ in)
Max height	2.74 m (9 ft 0 in)
Floor area, excl ramp: L-100-20	46.36 m² (499.0 sq ft)
L-100-30	52.30 m² (563.0 sq ft)
Floor area, ramp	9.57 m² (103.0 sq ft)
Volume, incl ramp: L-100-20	150.28 m³ (5,307 cu ft)
L-100-30	171.5 m³ (6,057 cu ft)

WEIGHTS AND LOADINGS:
Operating weight empty:	
L-100-20	34,781 kg (76,680 lb)
L-100-30	35,260 kg (77,736 lb)
Max payload: L-100-20	23,637 kg (52,110 lb)
L-100-30	23,158 kg (51,054 lb)
Max ramp weight	70,670 kg (155,800 lb)
Max T-O weight	70,308 kg (155,000 lb)
Max landing weight	61,235 kg (135,000 lb)
Max zero-fuel weight	58,420 kg (128,790 lb)
Max fuel weight	29,380 kg (64,772 lb)
Max wing loading	433.5 kg/m² (88.8 lb/sq ft)
Max power loading	5.23 kg/kW (8.6 lb/shp)

PERFORMANCE (at max T-O weight except where indicated):
Max cruising speed at 6,100 m (20,000 ft) at 54,430 kg (120,000 lb) AUW	308 knots (571 km/h; 355 mph)
Landing speed	124 knots (230 km/h; 143 mph)
Max rate of climb at S/L	518 m (1,700 ft)/min
Min ground turning radius: L-100-20	26.8 m (88 ft)
L-100-30	27.5 m (90 ft)
Runway LCN: asphalt	37
concrete	42
FAR T-O field length	1,905 m (6,250 ft)
FAR landing field length, at max landing weight	
	1,478 m (4,850 ft)
Range:	
with max payload, 45 min reserves	
	1,334 nm (2,472 km; 1,536 miles)
with zero payload	4,830 nm (8,951 km; 5,562 miles)

OPERATIONAL NOISE LEVELS (FAR Pt 36, Stage 2):
T-O sideline	96.7 EPNdB
T-O flyover: at T-O power	97.8 EPNdB
at cutback power	94.8 EPNdB
Approach flyover	98.1 EPNdB

LOCKHEED HTTB

TYPE: High technology testbed (HTTB) conversion of L-100-20.

PROGRAMME: First flight of prototype N130X 19 June 1984; early trials described in 1989-90 and earlier *Jane's*; 3,915 kW (5,250 shp) Allison T56 Series IV engines with 4.19 m (13 ft 9 in) Hamilton Standard propellers installed by LASC first quarter of 1989 to improve field performance and terrain following; trials demonstrating 460 m (1,509 ft) take-off and 365 m (1,198 ft) landing at 59,000 kg (130,073 lb) weight began November 1989.

DESIGN FEATURES: HTTB intended for STOL flight research in avionic systems, advanced flight controls, flight deck displays, navigation, guidance and *en route* survivability systems for future tactical transports; external features include long dorsal fin, 'horsals' (horizontal dorsals) ahead of tailplanes; composite material sensor booms at wingtips and greatly enlarged flaps; undercarriage reinforced for high-sink landings; non-Lockheed pilots and flight engineers have flown aircraft at each modification stage to accumulate opinions and assessments.

FLYING CONTROLS: Control system extensively adapted to simplify achievement of autonomous short field operation in all visibility conditions.

STRUCTURE: As C-130H, but extensively reinforced.

LOCKHEED ARTB

TYPE: Advanced radar testbed.

PROGRAMME: Modified Lockheed NC-141A StarLifter for USAF 4950th Test Wing at Wright-Patterson AFB,

Lockheed Advanced Radar Testbed conversion of C-141

Ohio, to evaluate response of modern airborne radars to jamming and other ECCM; first in-flight test 30 July 1990; for use until late 1990s.

DESIGN FEATURES: Modified by Lockheed at Greenville with Hughes and Westinghouse as subcontractors; interchangeable nose radomes; intended to improve anti-jamming capabilities of radars in B-1B, F-15, F-16 and F-22; modified cooling and electrical systems.

LOCKHEED AIRCRAFT SERVICE COMPANY (LAS)
(Division of Lockheed Technology Services Group)
PO Box 33, Ontario International Airport, Ontario, California 91761-0033
Telephone: 1 (714) 395 2411
PRESIDENT: Harold T. Bowling
EXECUTIVE VICE-PRESIDENT: John S. McLellan
VICE-PRESIDENT, ENGINEERING: George L. Morgan
VICE-PRESIDENT, NEW BUSINESS DEVELOPMENT:
John J. Bamberger
DIRECTOR, PUBLIC RELATIONS: John R. Dailey

Claims to be world's largest aircraft maintenance and modification unit; 3,000 employees; LAS has designed and installed major modifications and airborne mechanical and avionic systems, including cargo conversions in such aircraft as Boeing KC-135 and 707, Douglas DC-8, Lockheed C-130, C-141, L-188 Electra, L-1011 and P-3. LAS manufactures flight data recorders and portable airfield lighting and operates OMNILOG worldwide logistics support service tracking more than 20 million aircraft components. Lockheed Aeromod Center in Greenville, South Carolina, maintains and modifies military and civil aircraft; opened 21,740 m² (234,000 sq ft) facility for commercial aircraft modification at Tucson, Arizona, December 1990. Lockheed Commercial Aircraft Center Inc (LCAC) formed San Bernardino, California, June 1990 for maintenance and modification of Boeing 747s; Japan Air Lines has 14 per cent equity investment. Airod SDN BHD, a joint venture between LAS International and Aerospace Industries Malaysia, maintains, modifies, repairs and overhauls aircraft at Subang International Airport, Kuala Lumpur. Other components of Lockheed Technology Services Group are Lockheed Air Terminal Inc, Lockheed Information Management Services Co, Lockheed Engineering & Sciences Co and Lockheed Space Operations Co.

LOCKHEED C-130 CONVERSIONS
LASC specialises in design and application of special mission packages for electronic warfare, command, control and communication systems, and signals intelligence; 10 C-130s converted into rapid response mobile hospital systems for Saudi Arabia, including five L-100-30HS (which see); hospital fleet includes aircraft carrying

LOCKHEED GALAXY
Re-winging of remaining 77 of original 81 C-5As completed 1987; last of 50 C-5Bs delivered 17 April 1989 (details in 1989-90 and earlier *Jane's*). In November 1988 and October 1989, two C-5As redelivered to AFRes (433rd MAW, Kelly AFB, Texas) following Space Cargo Modification involving removal of upper troop deck aft of wing and redesign of rear ramp doors to provide same cargo volume as Space Shuttle. First 345-passenger conversion of

Lockheed AC-130H Spectre gunship re-delivered to 16th Special Operations Squadron after SOFI upgrade by LAS

four-wheel drive ambulance and evacuation aircraft for 52 patients; since 1985, LAS updating Special Forces AC-130H Spectre gunships with new navigation and fire control, including new software and improved reliability features; other special mission C-130s produced for USAF and gunships for export; first special operations forces improvement (SOFI Phase I) prototype MC-130E Combat Talon I delivered January 1988; first Phase II redelivered mid-1991, incorporating enhanced electronic warfare capabilities. First SOFI AC-130H (69-6568) redelivered July 1990; received new core avionics, HUD, secure communications, Navstar GPS, FLIR and improved gun mountings.

LOCKHEED P-3 CONVERSIONS
LASC modified US Customs anti-narcotics P-3A in 1984, including fittings of Hughes AN/APG-63 radar and infra-red detection; Lockheed Aeromod modified three more P-3As using LASC kits; all have inertial navigation and multi-standard com radios; LASC fitted rotodome radar antenna to P-3 AEW&C; two P-3s converted to US Navy VP special mission; order placed 1986 for conversion of EP-3E-II electronic surveillance Orion (which see).

LOCKHEED L-1011 (MODEL 385) TRISTAR CONVERSIONS
TYPE: Three-engined airliner.
PROGRAMME: Total 250 built; early history detailed in 1983-84 and earlier *Jane's*.
VARIANTS: **L-1011-150:** Four early TriStars being modified with Lockheed kits for First Chicago Leasing Corporation; conversion could be applicable to about 50 L-1011-1s; range increased from 2,800 nm (5,185 km; 3,220 miles) to 3,600 nm (6,665 km; 4,140 miles) and max T-O weight from 195,045 kg (430,000 lb) to 213,190 kg (470,000 lb).

L-1011-250: Extended range configuration available for 150 TriStars after CG range was extended at c/n 1052; six kits supplied by Lockheed for Delta Air Lines; wings, fuselage and landing gear strengthened to increase gross weight to 231,330 kg (510,000 lb); fuel capacity increased from 71,668 kg (158,000 lb) to 96,905 kg (213,640 lb) to extend range by 2,000 nm to 5,085 nm (9,415 km; 5,850 miles); original engines replaced by Rolls-Royce RB211-524B4 under separate arrangement.

L-1011 tanker-freighter for RAF: See under Marshall of Cambridge in UK section.

L-1011F: Freighter conversion by Pemco Aeroplex.

C-5A for bulk trooping (68-0225) flew initial service between McGuire AFB and Spangdahlem, Germany, 27 April 1990. $2.36 million contract to Lockheed, June 1990, for two special operations C-5 conversions in Pacer Snow programme; aircraft completed August and November 1990; equipped with Tracor AN/ALE-40 flare dispensers and Honeywell AN/AAR-47 missile warning system; trials at Eglin and Holloman AFBs.

LTV
LTV AEROSPACE AND DEFENSE COMPANY
(A unit of The LTV Corporation)
9314 West Jefferson, PO Box 655907, Dallas, Texas 75265-5907
Telephone: 1 (214) 266 2011
Fax: 1 (214) 266 4982
PRESIDENT AND CHIEF EXECUTIVE OFFICER, LTV AEROSPACE AND DEFENSE COMPANY: Richard J. Boyle
PRESIDENT, AIRCRAFT DIVISION: Gordon L. Williams
VICE-PRESIDENT, COMMERCIAL PROGRAMMES: L. Prine
VICE-PRESIDENT, B-2 PROGRAMME: Henry L. Spence
VICE-PRESIDENT, C-17 PROGRAMME: Thomas W. Jackson
VICE-PRESIDENT, PAMPA PROGRAMMES: Steve Yarborough
DIRECTOR, PUBLIC RELATIONS AND ADVERTISING, AIRCRAFT DIVISION: Lynn J. Farris
Chance Vought Aircraft Inc founded 1917; became Chance Vought Corporation 31 December 1960; merged with Ling-Temco Electronics 31 August 1961 to form Ling-Temco-Vought Inc (now The LTV Corporation); LTV aerospace/defence operations reorganised into two groups 29 September 1986; LTV Aircraft Products Group renamed LTV Aerospace and Defense Company in 1990; Aircraft Division works on airliner subcontracts, B-2, C-17 and A-7 programmes based in Dallas, Texas; LTV Missiles and Electronics Group renamed Missiles Division and includes AM General Division at South Bend, Indiana, Sierra Research Division at Buffalo, New York, and former Missiles Division at Grand Prairie, Texas. LTV Corporation filed further re-organisation plans with US Bankruptcy Court in late April 1991, including sale of aerospace and defence activities.

Current output includes about one-third of B-2 airframe by weight, the aft fuselage and tail surfaces of Boeing 747, tailplane of Boeing 767, tail surfaces of Boeing 757, engine nacelles and tail sections of Douglas C-17A and engine nacelles for Canadair Challenger and Regional Jet; work on YA-7F prototypes has now ceased; teaming agreement

existed with Aerospatiale Helicopter Corporation and LHTEC for possible production of Panther 800, a T800-powered version of AS 565 Panther for US government; LTV and FMA of Argentina teamed to promote IA 63 Pampa 2000 for USAF/USN JPATS programme.

LTV Sierra Research Division installed C-FIN flight inspection equipment in six BAe 125-800 (C-29s) for US Air Force, first of which delivered April 1990; Sierra inspection equipment sold to military organisations in 43 foreign countries; contract to study upgrade of 27 NASA Northrop T-38s awarded 1989; $1.7 million contract, May 1990, to produce prototype upgraded T-38, with work including improved safety and maintainability, weather radar, new radome, EFIS, area navigation system and navigation enhancements, extending useful life to 2010. Avionics upgrade offered to other F-5 operators as 'Tiger Paws', adding tactical capabilities of more modern fighters; first customer, Royal Norwegian Air Force, ordered upgrade of seven F-5As and eight F-5Bs of existing 20 aircraft fleet in January 1991; improvements include GEC Avionics HUD miniature standard central air data computer, laser INS with Litton or Honeywell laser gyro, colour video camera and recorder and MIL-STD-1553B digital databus; redelivery from May 1992 to February 1993. Sierra has also installed large, electronically steerable, dual polarised, phased-array airborne telemetry antenna in dorsal fin of an EP-3A Orion for Pacific Missile Test Range and converted two Boeing Canada Dash 8 to E-9A airborne telemetry configuration.

LTV A-7 CORSAIR II UPDATE PROGRAMMES
TYPE: Carrier-borne and land-based attack fighter.
PROGRAMME: Details of A-7A, A-7B (USN), A-7C, A-7D (USAF) and A-7E (USN) in 1979-80, 1983-84 and earlier *Jane's*; TA-7C, A-7H, TA-7H, A-7K, EA-7L and A-7P for Hellenic and Portuguese Air Forces described in 1989-90 *Jane's*. Total 1,545 new A-7s delivered before

production stopped in 1983; original A-7A ordered March 1964 and first flown 27 September 1965.
VARIANTS: **LANA:** Low-altitude night attack system applied to 83 Air National Guard A-7Ds and A-7Ks; first flight of first LANA aircraft, A-7K 81-0076 of 162nd TFTS, Arizona ANG, 2 October 1986; deliveries began Summer 1987.

FLIR: LTV retrofitted 75 A-7Ds and eight two-seat A-7Ks with forward-looking infra-red (FLIR) and manufactured 40 FLIR pods containing Texas Instruments AN/AAR-49 IR seekers; also fitted Singer tactical mission computer, automatic terrain following link between autopilot and Texas Instruments AN/APQ-126 nose radar, new GEC Avionics wide-angle HUD derived from unit in F-16C/D, to give round-the-clock and under-the-weather capability.

YA-7F/A-7 Plus CAS/BAI: Contract of 7 May 1987 for two LANA A-7Ds to be converted to YA-7Fs in programme to improve air-to-ground support capability, including Close Air Support/Battlefield Air Interdiction (CAS/BAI); prospect of 337 existing ANG Corsair IIs available for modificaton to A-7 Plus; first flights, 71-0334 on 29 November 1989 and 70-1039 on 3 April 1990; delivered to Edwards AFB 20 December 1989 and 6 April 1990 respectively. Modifications included common engine bay to take either P&W F100-PW-220 or GE F110-GE-100, but 105.7 kN (23,770 lb st) P&W engine fitted, giving YA-7F 50 per cent thrust increase; fuselage lengthened 75 cm (2 ft 5½ in) forward of wing and 46 cm (1 ft 6⅛ in) aft of wing; rear fuselage angled upwards 4° 20′; 25 cm (10 in) extension to fin and 5° 15′ anhedral on tailplane; re-skinned wings; airframe-mounted accessory drive unit; new technology flaps and lift dump/spoiler for shorter landing run on damaged airfields; wingroot strakes to boost directional stability at high angles of attack; avionics including GEC Avionics HUD and air data computer; improved environmental control; molecular sieve oxygen generating system (MSOGS).

Programme terminated November 1990 after 316.1 hours in 183 sorties; USAF CAS/BAI requirements instead to be met by GD F/A-16.

YA-7F capable of Mach 1.2 in level flight, sustained 6g turns at Mach 0.9 and has 45 per cent better take-off field length. Other features not incorporated in YA-7F include hands on throttle and stick (HOTAS), air-ground data link and automatic target handoff system (ATHS), improved radar warning, ground proximity warning, and improved landing gear warning.

WEIGHTS AND LOADINGS:
Operating weight empty: F100	10,463 kg (23,068 lb)
F110	10,825 kg (23,866 lb)
Max internal fuel	8,074 kg (17,800 lb)
Max stores weight	7,883 kg (17,380 lb)
Max T-O weight	20,865 kg (46,000 lb)
Max power loading	197.4 kg/kN (1.94 lb/lb st)

PERFORMANCE (typical mission, YA-7F with F100-PW-220 at T-O weight of 17,078 kg; 37,651 lb, with six Mk 82 bombs and 1,000 rds of 20 mm ammunition):
Max level speed at S/L	642 knots (1,190 km/h; 737 mph)
Time to 9,150 m (30,000 ft)	1 min 36 s
T-O run	640 m (2,100 ft)

Prototype YA-7F during trials at Edwards AFB

MACAVIA

MACAVIA INTERNATIONAL

2232 Airport Boulevard, Santa Rosa, California 95401
Telephone: 1 (707) 546 9435
Fax: 1 (707) 546 2037
Telex: 5106002077

MACAVIA TURBINE 207

TYPE: Turboprop conversion of Cessna 207.

PROGRAMME: At least one aircraft converted and flown.

CUSTOMERS: Single aircraft to Fliegerschule Eichenberger, Buttwil, Switzerland.

DESIGN FEATURES: Appears to be Soloy conversion with new Allison engine (replacing Teledyne Continental IO-520-F) inverted and reversed to position propeller drive high up; intake at rear and exhaust underneath cowling. Ergonomic pilot workstation includes new seats and soundproofing; standard avionics package of dual VOR, HSI and RMI; optional avionics include weather radar, 3M Stormscope, Loran C and HF. In cargo configuration, Turbine 207 offers 2.83 m² (100 cu ft) cargo space.

POWER PLANT: One 313 kW (420 shp) Allison 250C-20S turboprop, driving a Hartzell three-blade constant-speed propeller. Fuel capacity 333 litres (88 US gallons; 73.3 Imp gallons).

DIMENSIONS, EXTERNAL: As Cessna 207 except:
Length overall	10.36 m (34 ft 0 in)
Propeller ground clearance	0.30 m (1 ft 0 in)

MacAvia International Turbine 207 turboprop conversion of the Cessna 207 utility aircraft (*Mike Jerram*)

WEIGHTS AND LOADINGS:
Weight empty	1,088 kg (2,400 lb)
Max T-O weight	1,814 kg (4,000 lb)
Max landing weight	1,723 kg (3,800 lb)
Max power loading	5.80 kg/kW (9.52 lb/shp)

PERFORMANCE:
Max cruising speed:
at S/L	148 knots (274 km/h; 170 mph)
at 1,525 m (5,000 ft)	157 knots (291 km/h; 181 mph)
at 3,050 m (10,000 ft)	161 knots (298 km/h; 185 mph)
T-O run	225 m (736 ft)
Range with max fuel	910 nm (1,686 km; 1,047 miles)

MACHEN

MACHEN INC

South 3608 Davison Boulevard, Spokane, Washington 99204
Telephone: 1 (509) 838 5326
Fax: 1 (509) 838 0831
EXECUTIVE VICE-PRESIDENT: James S. Christy

Current output is conversion of Piper (Ted Smith) Aerostars to Superstar 650, 680 and 700; total of 175 Superstar conversions by 1 February 1991. See also AAC (Aerostar Aircraft Corporation).

MACHEN SUPERSTAR 650

TYPE: Performance enhancement for Piper (Ted Smith) Aerostar 600 series.

DESIGN FEATURES: Superstar 650 based on Piper Aerostar 600 (1982-83 *Jane's*), 601 and 601P (1981-82 *Jane's*) and 602P (1984-85 *Jane's*).

Conversion includes new turbochargers, controllers, fuel pumps, fuel injection servos, improved pressurisation components, and uprating of each Textron Lycoming TIO-540-S1A5 engine to 242 kW (325 hp); result is better twin- and single-engined rate of climb and single-engined service ceiling, reduced take-off distance and noise levels.

Machen markets and installs FAA-approved aerodynamic modification kit (SB 73-1) for Superstar 650 and Aerostar 600s to restore unrestricted use of flaps and the original CG limits after limits imposed by FAA in 1983; kit includes aileron and rudder hinge gap seals, strake on forward fuselage, leading-edge stall strips and vortex generators on underside of wings and on fin.

Compact turbo-intercooling system for turbocharged Aerostar 600s announced 1987; improves hot day take-off, cruise climb and single-engined climb.

PERFORMANCE: As for appropriate Aerostar model except:
Cruising speed, average cruise weight at 7,620 m (25,000 ft): 75% power
	240 knots (445 km/h; 276 mph)
65% power	226 knots (419 km/h; 260 mph)

Min single-engine control speed (VMC)
	79 knots (146 km/h; 91 mph)
Max rate of climb at S/L	596 m (1,955 ft)/min

Machen Superstar 650 conversion of the Piper Aerostar 601P

Rate of climb at S/L, one engine out	123 m (402 ft)/min
Service ceiling, one engine out	4,575 m (15,000 ft)
T-O to 15 m (50 ft)	604 m (1,980 ft)

MACHEN SUPERSTAR 680

TYPE: Further improvement of Piper (Ted Smith) Aerostar 601P.

PROGRAMME: Production began 1980.

DESIGN FEATURES: Induction intercoolers added; four-blade Hartzell propellers optional.

WEIGHTS AND LOADINGS:
Weight empty, equipped	1,863 kg (4,106 lb)
Max T-O and max ramp weight	2,812 kg (6,200 lb)
Max landing weight	2,721 kg (6,000 lb)
Max power loading	6.51 kg/kW (10.69 lb/hp)

PERFORMANCE (at max T-O weight except where indicated):
Max cruising speed at 7,620 m (25,000 ft)
	265 knots (491 km/h; 305 mph)

Cruising speed, average cruise weight at 7,620 m (25,000 ft):
75% power	250 knots (463 km/h; 288 mph)

65% power	242 knots (448 km/h; 279 mph)
55% power	232 knots (430 km/h; 267 mph)

Min single-engine control speed (VMC)
	79 knots (146 km/h; 91 mph)
Max rate of climb at S/L	596 m (1,955 ft)/min
Rate of climb at S/L, one engine out	122 m (402 ft)/min
Service ceiling	7,620 m (25,000 ft)
Service ceiling, one engine out	7,010 m (23,000 ft)
T-O to 15 m (50 ft)	603 m (1,980 ft)

Range: standard fuel, 45 min reserves
	1,137 nm (2,107 km; 1,309 miles)
auxiliary fuel	1,441 nm (2,670 km; 1,659 miles)

MACHEN SUPERSTAR 700

TYPE: Further conversion of Piper (Ted Smith) Aerostar 601P and 602P.

PROGRAMME: Production began 1988.

DESIGN FEATURES: Aerostar 601P and 602P described in 1981-82 *Jane's*; conversion includes fitting special Rotomaster automatic turbochargers, Machendeveloped nacelle-mounted intercoolers and low noise Hartzell three-blade propellers, raising engine output to 261 kW (350 hp); max T-O weight increased to 2,864 kg (6,315 lb), with 120 kg (265 lb) increase in useful load; other improvements include reduced cabin and external noise, increased cabin air volume, and more efficient pressurisation.

WEIGHTS AND LOADINGS:
Weight empty, equipped	1,862 kg (4,106 lb)
Max T-O and max ramp weight	2,864 kg (6,315 lb)
Max landing weight	2,721 kg (6,000 lb)
Max power loading	5.49 kg/kW (9.02 lb/hp)

PERFORMANCE (at max T-O weight except where indicated):
Max cruising speed at 7,620 m (25,000 ft)
270 knots (500 km/h; 311 mph)
Cruising speed, at average cruise weight at 7,620 m (25,000 ft):
75% power	261 knots (484 km/h; 300 mph)
65% power	245 knots (454 km/h; 282 mph)
55% power	230 knots (426 km/h; 265 mph)

Min single-engine control speed (VMC)
79 knots (146 km/h; 91 mph)
Max rate of climb at S/L
more than 610 m (2,000 ft)/min

Rate of climb at S/L, one engine out
	122 m (400 ft)/min
Service ceiling	7,620 m (25,000 ft)
Service ceiling, one engine out	4,575 m (15,000 ft)
T-O to 15 m (50 ft)	535 m (1,755 ft)

Range:
standard fuel, 45 min reserves
1,200 nm (2,224 km; 1,382 miles)
auxiliary fuel   1,560 nm (2,891 km; 1,796 miles)

MAGNUM
MAGNUM T/R
Salinas, California

Company plans to develop tilt-rotor transport based on wings, rotors, power train and flight controls of Bell Model 301 (XV-15, see 1990-91 and earlier *Jane's*), and on fuselage of Mitsubishi MU-2 turboprop twin; intended delivery date 1994; power plant to be two 1,305 kW (1,750 shp) P&WC turboshafts; predicted performance includes max cruising speed 300 knots (556 km/h; 345 mph) and range of 1,000 nm (1,853 km; 1,150 miles).

MARSH
MARSH AVIATION COMPANY
5060 East Falcon Drive, Mesa, Arizona 85205
Telephone: 1 (602) 832 3770
Fax: 1 (602) 985 2840
Telex: 165 028
PRESIDENT: Floyd D. Stilwell
EXECUTIVE VICE-PRESIDENT: Bill Walker Jr

MARSH S2R-T TURBO THRUSH
TYPE: Rockwell Thrush Commander agricultural aircraft with Garrett turboprop.
PROGRAMME: FAA STC issued September 1976 after 600 hours' flying by two prototypes; 75 delivered by February 1985 to Europe, Africa, Mexico, Middle East and USA; four more delivered in USA 1989.
DESIGN FEATURES: Fitted Garrett TPE331-1-101, flat rated to 447 kW (600 shp) and driving Hartzell constant-speed, feathering and reversing propeller; full 580 kW (778 shp) available in emergency; engine bleed air operates single-cycle air-conditioning and heating and spraypump; empty weight reduced by 227 kg (500 lb), giving greater payload and better performance; TPE331 can use ordinary automotive diesel fuel in remote areas. Rockwell Thrush Commander described in 1977-78 *Jane's*; weight and performance data for Turbo Thrush in 1987-88 *Jane's*.
Standard fuel capacity 401 litres (106 US gallons; 88.3 Imp gallons); standard hopper capacity 1.5 m³ (53 cu ft) or 1,514 litres (400 US gallons; 333 Imp gallons); optional hopper 1.89 m³ (66.8 cu ft) or 1,892.5 litres (500 US gallons; 416 Imp gallons).

Marsh Turbo Thrush conversion of the Rockwell International Thrush Commander

MARSH G-164 C-T TURBO CAT
Schweizer G-164 Super Ag-Cat C re-engined with Garrett TPE331-1-101, derated to 447 kW (600 shp). Certificated 1980; six completed by 1981; none since, but still available. Details of Schweizer Super Ag-Cat C in 1981-82 *Jane's* and of Turbo Cat in 1984-85 *Jane's*.

MARSH TURBO TRACKER S-2T
TYPE: Grumman S-2 re-engined with choice of Garrett turboprops.
PROGRAMME: First flight of Marsh S-2 conversion (N426DF) 24 November 1986; certificated 19 February 1990.
VARIANTS: **S-2AT Tracker:** With 932 kW (1,250 shp) TPE331-14 engines; firefighting retardant tank holds 3,028 litres (800 US gallons; 666 Imp gallons); with 1,227 kW (1,645 shp) TPE331-15s, tank holds 3,785 litres (1,000 US gallons; 83 Imp gallons).
S-2ET: ASW and maritime patrol version; first flight scheduled for 1 May 1991; flight testing to include carrier FCLP qualification in October, to be completed for first delivery late 1991.
CUSTOMERS: Evaluated by California Forestry Department; nine Turbo S-2s in conversion and seven military ASW versions on order by unnamed customers in 1990.
DESIGN FEATURES: Equipment for military maritime patrol and ASW includes search radar, FLIR, MAD, sonobuoy launchers, pictorial navigation avionics with automatic search and attack modes, six underwing stores points and torpedo bay. Basic conversion includes Hartzell five-blade reversing propellers of 2.92 m (9 ft 7 in) diameter, composite cowlings, max usable fuel 1,960 litres (518 US gallons; 431 Imp gallons), modern instrumentation, optional EFIS cockpit, multiple bus electrical with two batteries, Systron-Donner fire detection and halon extinguishers, optional environmental control system. Nacelles and fuselage streamlined to achieve 60 knot (111 km/h; 69 mph) increase in cruising

Prototype Marsh Turbo Tracker S-2T conversion of the S-2 Tracker

speed with 50 per cent lower fuel consumption; take-off and landing runs decreased by 25 per cent and single-engined rate of climb at gross weight increased by 230 m (750 ft)/min.

WEIGHTS AND LOADINGS:
Weight empty	6,278 kg (13,840 lb)
Max fuel weight	1,624 kg (3,580 lb)
Max T-O weight	11,340 kg (25,000 lb)
Max landing weight	11,113 kg (24,500 lb)
Max power loading (TPE331-14s)	
	6.08 kg/kW (10.00 lb/shp)

PERFORMANCE:
Cruising speed:
at 3,050 m (10,000 ft)	230 knots (426 km/h; 265 mph)
at 7,925 m (26,000 ft)	270 knots (500 km/h; 311 mph)
Retardant drop speed	130 knots (241 km/h; 150 mph)
Max rate of climb at S/L	518 m (1,700 ft)/min

Max range at cruising speed of 210 knots (389 km/h; 242 mph) at 7,620 m (25,000 ft), no reserves
1,468 nm (2,720 km; 1,690 miles)

MAULE

MAULE AIR INC

Lake Maule, Route 5, Box 319, Moultrie, Georgia 31768
Telephone: 1 (912) 985 2045
Fax: 1 (912) 890 2402
Telex: 804613 MAULE MOUL
PRESIDENT: Belford D. Maule
SALES MANAGER: Don Merrill

Original Maule Aircraft Corporation formed to manufacture M-4, a four-seat extrapolation of the Piper Cub; transferred to Moultrie, Georgia, 1968; production ceased 1975; Maule Air Inc formed 1984 to produce uprated M-5 Lunar Rocket and M-7 Super Rocket; Lunar Rocket discontinued, but variants listed below currently available.

MAULE STAR ROCKET and SUPER ROCKET

TYPE: Four/five-seat light aircraft.
VARIANTS: **M-6-235 Super Rocket:** Similar to M-5-235C (see 1983-84 *Jane's*), but with increased wing span and modified ailerons and flaps; certificated by FAA 25 June 1981; 175 kW (235 hp) Textron Lycoming six-cylinder O-540-J1A5D or fuel injected IO-540-W1A5D; choice of fixed landing gear or amphibious floats.

MX-7 Star Rocket: Fuselage of M-6 with shorter span wing of M-5 and glassfibre wingtips, greater fuel capacity, ailerons and seven-position flaps of M-7; certificated 9 November 1984.

MX-7-180: Alternative to above with 134 kW (180 hp) Textron Lycoming O-360-C1F.

MXT-7-180 Tri-Gear: As above with nosewheel landing gear. FAA certification November 1990; deliveries from following month.

MX-7-235: As MX-7-180 but with 175 kW (235 hp) Textron Lycoming O-540-J1A5D or IO-540-W1A5D.

M-7-235 Super Rocket: Five-seater developed in 1984 from M-6-235; wing span and weights increased; 175 kW (235 hp) Textron Lycoming O-540-J1A5D or IO-540-W1A5D; choice of wheels, Edo 797-2500 amphibious floats or Edo 2440B or Aqua 2400 standard floats, or FluiDyne 3000 Mk IIIA hydraulic wheel/skis.
CUSTOMERS: Total of more than 1,550 produced, including 40 sold in 1990.
DESIGN FEATURES: USA 35B (modified) wing section; dihedral 1°; incidence 0° 30′; cambered wingtips standard.
FLYING CONTROLS: Ailerons linked to rudder servo tab to allow normal flying with aileron wheel only; trim tab in port elevator; starboard rudder trim by spring to starboard rudder pedal; flap deflection 48° down for slow flight and 7° up for improved cruise performance; underfin on floatplane and amphibious versions.
STRUCTURE: All-metal two-spar wing with dual struts and glassfibre tips; fuselage frame of welded 4130 steel tube with Ceconite covering aft of cabin and metal doors and skin round cabin; glassfibre engine cowling.
LANDING GEAR: Non-retractable tailwheel type. Maule oleo-pneumatic shock absorbers in main units. Maule steerable tailwheel. Cleveland mainwheels with Goodyear or McCreary tyres size 17 × 6.00-6, pressure 1.79 bars (26 lb/sq in). Tailwheel tyre size 8 × 3.50-4, pressure 1.03-1.38 bars (15-20 lb/sq in). Cleveland hydraulic disc brakes. Parking brake. Oversize tyres, size 20 × 8.50-6 (pressure 1.24 bars; 18 lb/sq in), and fairings aft of mainwheels optional. Tricycle gear optional on MX-7-180. Provisions for fitting optional Edo Model 248B2440 floats or Edo Model 797-2500 amphibious floats, Aqua Model 2400 floats, or Federal Model C2200H or C3000 or Fli-Lite 3000 Mk IIIA skis.
POWER PLANT: One flat-four or flat-six engine, driving a Hartzell two-blade constant-speed propeller, as detailed under Variants. (Three-blade McCauley propeller optional.) Two fuel tanks in wings with total usable capacity of 151 litres (40 US gallons; 33 Imp gallons). Auxiliary fuel tanks in outer wings, to provide total capacity of 265 litres (70 US gallons; 58 Imp gallons), standard. Refuelling points on wing upper surface. Oil capacity 7.5 litres (2 US gallons; 1.7 Imp gallons) on all models except Super Rocket with O-540-J1A5D engine which has 9.5 litres (2.5 US gallons; 2.1 Imp gallons).
ACCOMMODATION: Pilot and three passengers in Star Rocket, four in Super Rockets, on two front bucket seats and rear bench seat, or optional quickly removed rear seat. One door on port side of fuselage, hinged at front edge and opening forward. Three doors on starboard side of fuselage, the forward and centre doors hinged at the front edge, the rear baggage door hinged at the rear edge. The centre and rear doors can be opened together to provide an opening 1.30 m (4 ft 3 in) wide to facilitate loading of bulky cargo. Plexiglas observation doors optional. Accommodation heated and ventilated. Tinted windscreen and windscreen defroster standard.
SYSTEMS: Hydraulic system for brakes only. Electrical system powered by 60A engine driven alternator. 28V electrical system optional.
AVIONICS: Standard avionics comprise Bendix/King KX 155 nav/com with glideslope and KI 208 indicator. Optional avionics include Bendix/King KX 155 digital nav/com; KN 62A DME; KR 21 marker beacon receiver; KR 87 ADF; KT 76A transponder; KN 75 glideslope receiver; KNS 80 integrated nav system; Narco ADF-841; AR-850 remote altitude encoder; AT-150 transponder; DME-890;

Maule M-7-235 Super Rocket five-seat STOL aircraft

IDME-891; Terra TX-720 com transceiver; AT-3000 altitude digitiser; TMA-230 audio panel; TRT-2350 transponder; David Clark Isocom or Sigtronics SPA-400 intercoms; Apollo II, ArNav 21 or North Star M1 Loran C, and Century 21 or IIB autopilots.
EQUIPMENT: Standard equipment includes airspeed indicator; altimeter; electric turn co-ordinator; full gyro panel; vertical speed indicator; tachometer; OAT, fuel pressure, oil pressure, oil temperature, manifold pressure, cylinder head temperature and electric fuel quantity gauges; compass; clock; ammeter; dual controls; cabin soundproofing; cloth velour upholstery; tinted windscreen with defroster; auxiliary cabin heater; ashtray; cigarette lighter; cabin steps; cargo tiedown straps; microphone and bracket; heated pitot; corrosion proofing; emergency locator transmitter; float reinforcements (235 models only); port wing landing light; instrument, dome, navigation and wingtip strobe lights; and tie-down rings. Optional equipment includes encoding altimeter; acoustic stall warner; engine hour meter; Alcor exhaust gas temperature gauge; cabin cool air kit; carburettor air temperature gauge; clear windscreen; observation window; swing-out window; Plexiglas door; skylight window; door pockets; dual caliper brakes; fire extinguisher; Schweizer tow-release kit; jump seat in baggage area; shoulder harnesses with lap belts; starboard wing landing light; control wheel push-to-talk switch; radio cooling kit; radio master switch; Telex headset; McCauley three-blade propeller (235 models only); wheel fairings, and ventral fin (floatplanes).

DIMENSIONS, EXTERNAL:

Wing span: M-6	10.03 m (32 ft 11 in)
M-7	10.26 m (33 ft 8 in)
MX-7	9.40 m (30 ft 10 in)
Wing chord, constant: all	1.60 m (5 ft 3 in)
Wing aspect ratio: M-6	6.5
M-7	6.4
MX-7	6.0
Length overall: MX-7-180, MX-7-235/O-540	7.16 m (23 ft 6 in)
all others	7.19 m (23 ft 7¼ in)
Height overall: all (landplane)	1.93 m (6 ft 4 in)
all (amphibian)	3.20 m (10 ft 6 in)
Tailplane span: all	3.28 m (10 ft 9 in)
Wheel track: all	1.83 m (6 ft 0 in)
Wheelbase: all	4.82 m (15 ft 10 in)
Propeller diameter:	
M-6, MX-7-235, M-7: two-blade	2.06 m (6 ft 9 in)
MX/MXT-7-180	1.93 m (6 ft 4 in)
Cabin doors: all (fwd, each):	
Height	0.84 m (2 ft 9 in)
Width	0.76 m (2 ft 6 in)
Height to sill	0.94 m (3 ft 1 in)
Cabin door: all (centre, stbd):	
Height	0.75 m (2 ft 5½ in)
Width	0.69 m (2 ft 3 in)
Height to sill	0.76 m (2 ft 6 in)
Baggage door: all (rear, stbd):	
Height	0.58 m (1 ft 11 in)
Width	0.56 m (1 ft 10 in)
Height to sill	0.61 m (2 ft 0 in)

DIMENSIONS, INTERNAL:

Cabin width: all	0.98 m (3 ft 2½ in)

AREAS:

Wings, gross: M-6	15.38 m² (165.6 sq ft)
M-7	16.44 m² (177.0 sq ft)
MX-7	14.67 m² (157.9 sq ft)
Ailerons (total): MX-7, M-7	1.17 m² (12.56 sq ft)
M-6	1.20 m² (12.92 sq ft)

Trailing-edge flaps (total): MX-7	2.12 m² (22.78 sq ft)
M-6	2.32 m² (25.0 sq ft)
M-7	2.44 m² (26.25 sq ft)
Fin: all	1.22 m² (13.14 sq ft)
Rudder, incl tab: all	0.54 m² (5.83 sq ft)
Tailplane: all	1.32 m² (14.2 sq ft)
Elevators, incl tab: all	1.58 m² (17.0 sq ft)

WEIGHTS AND LOADINGS (L: landplane, F: floatplane, A: amphibian):

Weight empty:	
M-6 (L), M-7 (L)	681 kg (1500 lb)
M-6 (F), M-7 (F), MX-7-235 (F)	794 kg (1,750 lb)
M-6 (A), M-7 (A), MX-7-235 (A)	907 kg (2,000 lb)
MX-7-180 (L)	613 kg (1,350 lb)
MX-7-235 (L)	669 kg (1,475 lb)
Max baggage (all)	45 kg (100 lb)
Max cargo (all)	317 kg (700 lb)
Max T-O and landing weight:	
all models (L)	1,134 kg (2,500 lb)
all models (F, A)	1,247 kg (2,750 lb)
Max wing loading:	
M-6 (L)	73.69 kg/m² (15.10 lb/sq ft)
M-6 (F, A)	81.06 kg/m² (16.61 lb/sq ft)
M-7 (L)	68.91 kg/m² (14.12 lb/sq ft)
M-7 (F, A)	75.83 kg/m² (15.54 lb/sq ft)
MX-7 (L)	77.25 kg/m² (15.83 lb/sq ft)
MX-7 (F, A)	85.01 kg/m² (17.42 lb/sq ft)
Max power loading:	
M-6 (L), M-7 (L), MX-7-235 (L)	6.48 kg/kW (10.64 lb/hp)
M-6 (F, A), M-7 (F, A), MX-7-235 (F, A)	7.12 kg/kW (11.70 lb/hp)
MX-7-180 (L)	8.45 kg/kW (13.89 lb/hp)

PERFORMANCE (at max T-O weight, ISA: L, F and A as for Weights and Loadings):

Max level speed at S/L:	
M-6/O-540 (L), M-7/O-540 (L), MX-7-235/O-540 (L)	144 knots (267 km/h; 166 mph)
M-6/IO-540 (L), M-7/IO-540 (L), MX-7-235/IO-540 (L)	147 knots (273 km/h; 170 mph)
M-6 (F, A)	126 knots (233 km/h; 145 mph)
M-7 (F, A), MX-7-235 (F, A)	130 knots (241 km/h; 150 mph)
MX-7-180 (L)	134 knots (248 km/h; 154 mph)
Max cruising speed (75% power) at optimum altitude:	
M-6 (L), M-7 (L), MX-7-235 (L)	139 knots (257 km/h; 160 mph)
M-6 (F, A)	121 knots (224 km/h; 139 mph)
M-7 (F, A), MX-7-235 (F, A)	125 knots (232 km/h; 144 mph)
MX-7-180 (L)	126 knots (233 km/h; 145 mph)
MXT-7-180	122 knots (225 km/h; 140 mph)
Stalling speed, flaps down, power off:	
M-6 (L), M-7 (L)	31 knots (57 km/h; 35 mph)
M-6 (F, A)	49 knots (91 km/h; 56 mph)
M-7 (F, A), MX-7-235 (F, A)	47 knots (87 km/h; 54 mph)
MX-7 (L), MXT-7-180	35 knots (65 km/h; 40 mph)
Max rate of climb at S/L:	
M-6 (L), MX-7-235, M-7 (L)	610 m (2,000 ft)/min
M-6 (F, A), MX-7-235 (F, A)	381 m (1,250 ft)/min
M-7 (F, A)	411 m (1,350 ft)/min
MX-7-180 (L), MXT-7-180	366 m (1,200 ft)/min
Service ceiling:	
M-6 (L), M-7 (L), MX-7-235 (L)	6,100 m (20,000 ft)
M-6 (F, A), M-7 (F, A), MX-7-235 (F, A)	5,180 m (17,000 ft)
MX-7-180 (L)	4,575 m (15,000 ft)

T-O run on land:
M-6 (L), M-7 (L), MX-7-235/IO-540 (L) 38 m (125 ft)
MX-7-235 (A), M-6 (A), M-7 (A) 69 m (225 ft)
MX-7-180 (L), MXT-7-180 61 m (200 ft)
MX-7-235/O-540 (L) 46 m (150 ft)

T-O run on water:
M-6 (F, A), M-7 (F, A) 305 m (1,000 ft)
MX-7-235 (F, A) 335 m (1,100 ft)

T-O to 15 m (50 ft) on land:
M-6 (L), M-7 (L), MX-7 (L), MXT-7-180 183 m (600 ft)
M-6 (A), M-7 (A), MX-7-235 (A) 152 m (500 ft)

T-O to 15 m (50 ft) on water:
M-6 (F, A), M-7 (F, A) 381 m (1,250 ft)
MX-7-235 (F, A) 412 m (1,350 ft)

Landing from 15 m (50 ft) on land:
M-6 (L), M-7 (L), MX-7 (L) 152 m (500 ft)
M-6 (A), M-7 (A), MX-7-235 (A) 305 m (1,000 ft)

Landing from 15 m (50 ft) on water:
M-6 (F, A), M-7 (F, A), MX-7-235 (F, A) 305 m (1,000 ft)

Landing run on land and water:
M-6 (A), M-7 (A), MX-7-235 (A) 244 m (800 ft)

Range with standard fuel:
M-6-235/O-540 (L), M-7-235/O-540 (L), MX-7-235/
O-540 (L) 425 nm (788 km; 490 miles)
M-6-235/IO-540 (L), M-7-235/IO-540 (L),
MX-7-235 (L) 460 nm (853 km; 530 miles)
MX-7-180 (L) 560 nm (1,038 km; 645 miles)
M-6-235/O-540 (F, A) 264 nm (490 km; 305 miles)
M-6-235/IO-540 (F, A) 299 nm (555 km; 345 miles)
M-7-235/O-540 (F, A) 286 nm (531 km; 330 miles)
M-7-235/IO-540 (F, A) 321 nm (595 km; 370 miles)

Range with auxiliary fuel:
M-6-235/O-540 (L), M-7-235/O-540 (L), MX-7-235/
O-540 (L) 746 nm (1,384 km; 860 miles)
M-6-235/IO-540 (L), M-7-235/IO-540 (L), MX-7-235
(L) 807 nm (1,496 km; 930 miles)
MX-7-180 (L) 977 nm (1,810 km; 1,125 miles)
M-6-235/O-540 (F, A) 586 nm (1,086 km; 675 miles)
M-6-235-IO-540 (F, A) 647 nm (1,199 km; 745 miles)
M-7-235/O-540 (F, A) 608 nm (1,126 km; 700 miles)
M-7-235/IO-540 (F, A) 668 nm (1,239 km; 770 miles)

MAULE M-7 and MX-7 STARCRAFT

TYPE: Turboprop powered variants.
PROGRAMME: Both versions certificated 1989.
VARIANTS: **MX-7-420:** Powered by Allison 250-B17C; similar to short wing span MX-7; choice of wheel, ski, float or Edo 797-2500 amphibious landing gear.

M-7-420: Powered by Allison 250-B17C; similar to long wing span M-7; choice of landing gears as above.
POWER PLANT: One 313 kW (420 shp) Allison 250-B17C turboprop, driving a Hartzell HC-B3TF-7A three-blade metal propeller with autofeathering, reverse pitch and Beta control. Intake anti-icing. Fuel capacity (usable) is 265 litres (70 US gallons; 58 Imp gallons) standard, increasable to 378 litres (100 US gallons; 83 Imp gallons) with optional outer-wing tanks.
SYSTEMS: 28V DC electrical system standard, with 150A starter/generator, solid state regulators and 24V 19Ah battery.
AVIONICS: Standard and optional avionics generally as for piston-engined models.

Turboprop powered Maule M-7-420 Starcraft with Edo 797-2500 amphibious landing gear

Maule MXT-7-180 with tricycle landing gear

EQUIPMENT: Additional equipment includes airspeed warning system; chip detector light; engine inlet heater; torque indicator; fuel filter light; propeller rpm indicator; 100A starter/generator, turbine temperature indicator; turbine percentage rpm indicator, and volt/amp meter, standard.
DIMENSIONS, EXTERNAL: As for piston engined M-7/MX-7 except:
Length overall: landplane 7.32 m (24 ft 0 in)
Propeller diameter: landplane 2.03 m (6 ft 8 in)
amphibian 2.29 m (7 ft 6 in)

WEIGHTS AND LOADINGS:
Weight empty:
M-7-420: landplane 626 kg (1,380 lb)
amphibian 907 kg (2,000 lb)
MX-7-420: landplane 626 kg (1,380 lb)
Max T-O weight:
M-7-420 (amphibian) 1,247 kg (2,750 lb)
M-7-420, MX-7-420 (landplane) 1,134 kg (2,500 lb)
Max wing loading:
M-7-420 75.83 kg/m² (15.54 lb/sq ft)
MX-7-420 77.25 kg/m² (15.83 lb/sq ft)
Max power loading:
M-7-420 (amphibian) 3.99 kg/kW (6.55 lb/shp)
MX-7-420 3.62 kg/kW (5.95 lb/shp)
PERFORMANCE (at max T-O weight. A: MX-7-420 landplane, B: M-7-420 amphibian):

Max level speed at S/L:
A 174 knots (322 km/h; 200 mph)
B 161 knots (298 km/h; 185 mph)
Cruising speed, 75% power at optimum altitude:
A 169 knots (314 km/h; 195 mph)
B 156 knots (290 km/h; 180 mph)
Cruising speed, 50% power at optimum altitude:
A 156 knots (290 km/h; 180 mph)
B 143 knots (266 km/h; 165 mph)
Stalling speed, flaps down, power off:
A 44 knots (81 km/h; 50 mph)
B 47 knots (87 km/h; 54 mph)
Max rate of climb at S/L: A 1,430 m (4,700 ft)/min
B 762 m (2,500 ft)/min
Service ceiling: A, B 6,100 m (20,000 ft)
T-O run: A 61 m (200 ft)
B (land) 77 m (250 ft)
B (water) 229 m (750 ft)
Landing run: A, B (land) 92 m (300 ft)
B (water) 107 m (350 ft)
Range, 75% power, no reserves:
A 456 nm (846 km; 526 miles)
B 422 nm (782 km; 486 miles)
Range, 50% power, no reserves:
A 644 nm (1,194 km; 742 miles)
B 590 nm (1,094 km; 680 miles)

MBB
MBB HELICOPTER CORPORATION
900 Airport Road, PO Box 2349, West Chester, Pennsylvania 19380
Telephone: 1 (215) 431 4150
Fax: 1 (215) 436 9618
Telex: 173102 MBB HELIC WCHR

PRESIDENT AND CHIEF EXECUTIVE OFFICER: David O. Smith
SENIOR VICE-PRESIDENT, MARKETING: Andreas Aastad
DIRECTOR OF COMMUNICATIONS: Lynda Kate
US subsidiary of MBB, member of Deutsche Aerospace (which see), formed 1979 for marketing and product support of BO 105 CBS, BO 105 LS and BK 117 helicopters (described respectively in German, Canadian and

International sections) in North and Central America and Peru; 3,716 m² (40,000 sq ft) completion centre, 3,252 m² (35,000 sq ft) maintenance and training centre, and 2,787 m² (30,000 sq ft) administration building located at Brandywine Airport, West Chester, Pennsylvania.

MCDONNELL DOUGLAS
MCDONNELL DOUGLAS CORPORATION
Box 516, St Louis, Missouri 63166
Telephone: 1 (314) 232 0232
Fax: 1 (314) 234 3826
Corporate Office
CHAIRMAN AND CHIEF EXECUTIVE OFFICER:
John F. McDonnell
PRESIDENT: Gerald A. Johnston
DIRECTOR, INTERNATIONAL PUBLIC RELATIONS:
Andrew Wilson

Formed 28 April 1967 by merger of Douglas Aircraft Co Inc and the McDonnell Company; encompasses their subsidiaries plus former Hughes Helicopter Company acquired in 1984 and renamed McDonnell Douglas Helicopter Company. Employees totalled about 120,000 worldwide in early 1991; total office, engineering, laboratory and manufacturing floor area was then 3.8 million m² (41 million sq ft).
Major operating units of McDonnell Douglas Corporation (MDC) Aerospace Group are:

McDonnell Aircraft Company (MCAIR)
Follows this entry
Douglas Aircraft Company (DAC)
Follows McDonnell Aircraft Co entry
McDonnell Douglas Helicopter Company (MDHC)
Follows Douglas Aircraft Co entry
McDonnell Douglas Missile Systems Company (MDMSC)
McDonnell Douglas Space Systems Company (MDSSC)

MCDONNELL AIRCRAFT COMPANY
(A Division of McDonnell Douglas Corporation)

Box 516, St Louis, Missouri 63166
Telephone: 1 (314) 232 0232
Fax: 1 (314) 234 3826
PRESIDENT: John P. Capellupo
EXECUTIVE VICE-PRESIDENT: James C. Restelli
VICE-PRESIDENT, MARKETING: Robert H. Trice
VICE-PRESIDENT, NEW AIRCRAFT PRODUCTS:
  James M. Sinnett
VICE-PRESIDENT, ENGINEERING: John W. Steurer
VICE-PRESIDENT, AIRCRAFT ENGINEERING:
  Donald D. Snyder
DIRECTOR OF COMMUNICATIONS: Jim Reed

Development and production continues to concentrate on F-15 Eagle, AV-8B Harrier and F/A-18 Hornet. McDonnell shared development of unsuccessful YF-23 Advanced Tactical Fighter prototypes with Northrop and played a part in development of McDonnell Douglas Helicopters/Bell Helicopter LH Light Helicopter. The US Navy A-12A Advanced Tactical Aircraft being developed by McDonnell Douglas and General Dynamics was cancelled in January 1991.

MCDONNELL DOUGLAS F-4 PHANTOM II

Total 5,057 Phantoms built by McDonnell to June 1979 and further 138 in Japan by May 1981, comprising 47 F-4As, 649 F-4Bs, 46 RF-4Bs, 635 F-4Cs, two YRF-4Cs, 503 RF-4Cs, 773 F-4Ds, 1,387 F-4Es, 132 RF-4Es, 14 RF-4EJs, 175 F-4Fs, 522 F-4Js, 52 F-4Ks, 118 F-4Ms and 140 F-4EJs. Some 1,750 remain operational (plus others in storage; or unserviceable in Iran) with the air arms of Egypt, Germany, Greece, Israel, Japan, South Korea, Spain, Turkey, UK and USA.

Foreign updating programmes detailed under DASA/MBB (Germany), IAI (Israel) and Mitsubishi (Japan). US programmes are given under Boeing Military Airplanes (1990-91 *Jane's*) and, in 1989-90 *Jane's*, under McDonnell Douglas.

MCDONNELL DOUGLAS/BAe AV-8B HARRIER II

Details of the Harrier II and current improvement programmes are given in the International section.

MCDONNELL DOUGLAS F-15C/D EAGLE

TYPE: Twin-turbofan air superiority fighter with secondary attack role.
PROGRAMME: First flight of YF-15 27 July 1972; first F-15C (78-468) 26 February 1979; first F-15D 19 June 1979; P&W F100-PW-220 standard since 1985; last of 894 F-15A/B/C/Ds delivered 3 November 1989; production restarted during 1991 to produce five for Israel and 12 for Saudi Arabia; production now concentrated on F-15E (which see).
VARIANTS: **F-15A:** Initial single-seat version (see 1981-82 *Jane's*).

  F-15B: Initial two-seat operational training version; first flight 7 July 1973.

  F-15C: Became standard single-seat production version from June 1979.

  F-15D: Standard two-seat production version from June 1979.

  F-15E: See separate entry.

  F-15J and DJ: Single- and two-seat versions for JASDF; former built by Mitsubishi in Japan (which see).

  MSIP: Multi-staged improvement programme, first funded 1983; testing began December 1984; first production MSIP F-15C unveiled 20 June 1985; all other F-15Cs retrofitted. MSIP included AN/APG-70 radar with memory increased to 1,000K and processing speed trebled; central computer capacity multiplied by four and processing speed three times as fast; original armament control system panel replaced by single Honeywell colour

McDonnell Douglas F-15C Eagle of the Royal Saudi Air Force *(Paul Jackson)*

video screen which, linked to computer, allows for advanced versions of AIM-7, AIM-9 and AIM-20 AMRAAM. Other improvements include Northrop enhanced AN/ALQ-135 internal countermeasures set, Loral AN/ALR-56C radar warning receiver, Tracor AN/ALE-45 chaff/flare dispenser, and Magnavox electronic warfare warning system. JTIDS Class 2 terminals to be installed from 1992.

  Conformal fuel tanks: All F-15Cs fitted to carry two 2,839 litre (750 US gallon; 624 Imp gallon) conformal fuel tanks (CFT) attached to fuselage sides aft of engine intakes; same load factors as main airframe and removable in 15 minutes; CFT can contain reconnaissance sensors, radar detection and jamming equipment, laser designator and low light TV as well as fuel; tangential carriage system includes rows of stub pylons carrying up to twelve 1,000 lb or four 2,000 lb class weapons or AIM-7F Sparrows.

  Reconnaissance pod: Centreline conformal reconnaissance pod developed as private venture by McDonnell Douglas and tested during Summer 1987; can transmit imagery via data link to ground stations in near real time.

  Follow-on Wild Weasel: Proposed replacement for USAF F-4G Wild Weasel.
CUSTOMERS: Including prototypes, 1,017 F-15A/Bs and C/Ds produced up to November 1989, when production temporarily halted; 366 F-15As, 58 F-15Bs, 409 F-15Cs and 61 F-15Ds for US Air Force; 19 F-15As (plus four ex-USAF), two F-15Bs, 24 F-15Cs and two F-16Ds for Israel Defence Force; 47 F-15Cs and 15 F-15Ds for Royal Saudi Air Force; and two F-15Js and 12 F-15DJs for Japan ASDF. Further 17 to be built in 1991-92, of which nine F-15Cs and three F-15Ds for Saudi Arabia, beginning June 1991 (in addition, USAF transferred 22 F-15Cs and two F-15Ds as emergency aid August 1990); Israel to receive five F-15Ds in 1992. Total production 1,034 (not including Japanese manufacture), plus F-15Es; including FY 1991 contracts, 191 JASDF F-15s ordered from Mitsubishi (which see) and McDonnell Douglas (noted above).
COSTS: $55.2 million, flyaway, Mitsubishi production in 1990.
DESIGN FEATURES: NACA 64A aerofoil section with conical camber on leading-edge; sweepback 38° 42′ at quarter-chord; thickness/chord ratio 6.6 per cent at root, 3 per cent at tip; anhedral 1°; incidence 0°. Twin fins positioned to receive vortex flow off wing and maintain directional stability at high angles of attack. Straight two-dimensional external compression engine air inlet each side of fuselage. Air inlet controllers by Hamilton Standard. Air inlet actuators by National Water Lift.
FLYING CONTROLS: Plain ailerons and all-moving tailplane with dog-tooth extensions, both powered by National Water Lift hydraulic actuators; rudders have Ronson

Hydraulic Units actuators; no spoilers or trim tabs; Moog boost and pitch compensator for control column; plain flaps; upward-opening airbrake panel mounted on fuselage between fins and cockpit.
STRUCTURE: Wing based on torque box with integrally machined skins and ribs of light alloy and titanium; aluminium honeycomb wingtips, flaps and ailerons; airbrake panel of titanium, aluminium honeycomb and graphite/epoxy composites skin.
LANDING GEAR: Hydraulically retractable tricycle type, with single wheel on each unit. All units retract forward. Cleveland nose and main units, each incorporating an oleo-pneumatic shock absorber. Nosewheel and tyre by Goodyear, size 22 × 6.6-10, pressure 17.93 bars (260 lb/sq in). Mainwheels by Bendix, with Goodyear tyres size 34.5 × 9.75-18, pressure 23.44 bars (340 lb/sq in). Bendix carbon heat-sink brakes. Hydro-Aire wheel braking skid control system.
POWER PLANT: Two Pratt & Whitney F100-PW-220 turbofans, each rated at 105.7 kN (23,770 lb st) with afterburning for take-off. Internal fuel in eight Goodyear fuselage tanks, total capacity 7,836 litres (2,070 US gallons; 1,724 Imp gallons). Simmonds fuel gauge system. Optional conformal fuel tanks attached to side of engine air intakes, beneath wing, each containing 2,839 litres (750 US gallons; 624 Imp gallons). Provision for up to three additional 2,309 litre (610 US gallon; 508 Imp gallon) external fuel tanks. Max total internal and external fuel capacity 20,441 litres (5,400 US gallons; 4,496 Imp gallons).
ACCOMMODATION: Pilot only, on McDonnell Douglas ACES II ejection seat. Stretched acrylic canopy and windscreen. Windscreen anti-icing valve by Dynasciences Corporation.
SYSTEMS: AiResearch air-conditioning system. Three independent hydraulic systems (each 207 bars; 3,000 lb/sq in) powered by Abex engine driven pumps; modular hydraulic packages by Hydraulic Research and Manufacturing Company. Smiths Industries generating system for electrical power, with Sundstrand 40/50kVA generator constant speed drive units and Electro Development Corpn transformer-rectifiers. The oxygen system includes a Simmonds liquid oxygen indicator. Garrett APU for engine starting, and for the provision of electrical or hydraulic power on the ground independently of the main engines.
AVIONICS: General Electric automatic analog flight control system standard. Hughes Aircraft AN/APG-63 X-band pulse Doppler radar (upgraded to AN/APG-70 under MSIP), equipped since 1980 with a Hughes Aircraft programmable signal processor, provides long-range detection and tracking of small high-speed targets operating at all altitudes down to treetop level, and feeds accurate tracking information to the IBM CP-1075 96K (24K on early F-15C/Ds) central computer to ensure effective launch of the aircraft's missiles or the firing of its internal gun. For close-in dogfights, the radar acquires the target automatically and the steering/weapon system information is displayed on a McDonnell Douglas Electronics AN/AVQ-20 head-up display. A Teledyne Electronics AN/APX-101 IFF transponder informs ground stations and other suitably equipped aircraft that the F-15 is friendly. It also supplies data on the F-15's range, azimuth, altitude and identification to air traffic controllers. A Hazeltine AN/APX-76 IFF interrogator informs the pilot if an aircraft seen visually or on radar is friendly. A Litton reply evaluator for the IFF system operates with the AN/APX-76. A Honeywell vertical situation display set, using a cathode ray tube to present radar, electro-optical identification and attitude director indicator formats to the pilot, permits inputs received from the aircraft's sensors and the central computer to be visible to the pilot under any light conditions. Honeywell also developed the AN/ASK-6 air data computer and AN/ASN-108 AHRS for the F-15, the latter also serving as a backup to the Litton AN/ASN-109 INS which provides the basic navigation data and is the aircraft's primary attitude reference. In addition to giving the

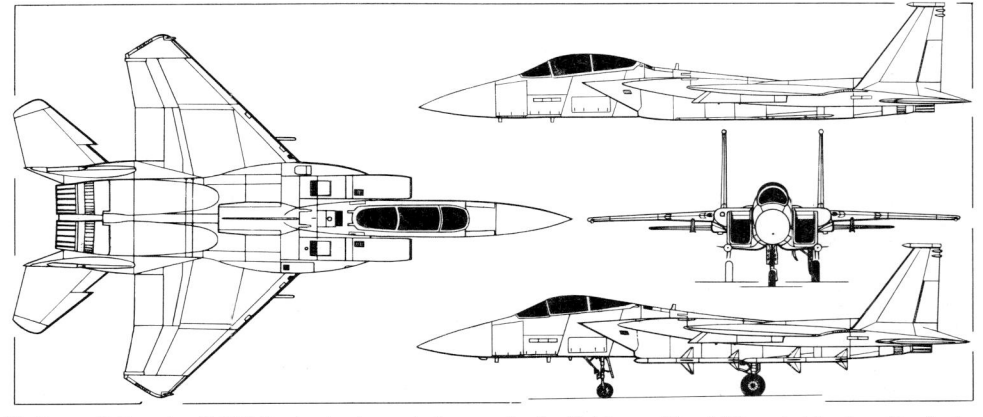

McDonnell Douglas F-15C Eagle single-seat air superiority fighter, with additional side view (top) of two-seat F-15B *(Pilot Press)*

aircraft's position at all times, the INS provides pitch, roll, heading, acceleration and speed information. Other specialised equipment for flight control, navigation and communications includes a Collins AN/ARN-118 Tacan; Collins HSI to present aircraft navigation information on a symbolic pictorial display; Collins ADF and AN/ARN-112 ILS receivers; Magnavox AN/ARC-164 UHF transceiver and UHF auxiliary transceiver. The communications sets have cryptographic capability. Dorne and Margolin glideslope localiser antenna, and Teledyne Avionics angle of attack sensors. Northrop (Defense Systems Division) Enhanced AN/ALQ-135(V) internal countermeasures set provides automatic jamming of enemy radar signals; Loral AN/ALR-56C radar warning receiver; Magnavox AN/ALQ-128 electronic warfare warning set; and Tracor AN/ALE-45 chaff dispenser. Bendix/King tachometer, fuel and oil indicators; Plessey feel trim actuators.

ARMAMENT: Provision for carriage and launch of a variety of air-to-air weapons over short and medium ranges, including our AIM-9L/M Sidewinders, four AIM-7F/M Sparrows or eight AIM-120 AMRAAM, and a 20 mm M61A1 six-barrel gun with 940 rounds of ammunition. General Electric lead-computing gyro. A Dynamic Controls Corporation armament control system keeps the pilot informed of weapons status and provides for their management. Three air-to-surface weapon stations (five if configured with conformal fuel tanks) allow for the carriage of up to 10,705 kg (23,600 lb) of bombs, rockets or additional ECM equipment. AN/AWG-20 armament control system.

DIMENSIONS, EXTERNAL:

Wing span	13.05 m (42 ft 9¾ in)
Wing aspect ratio	3.01
Length overall	19.43 m (63 ft 9 in)
Height overall	5.63 m (18 ft 5½ in)
Tailplane span	8.61 m (28 ft 3 in)
Wheel track	2.75 m (9 ft 0¼ in)
Wheelbase	5.42 m (17 ft 9½ in)

AREAS:

Wings, gross	56.5 m² (608.0 sq ft)
Ailerons (total)	2.46 m² (26.48 sq ft)
Flaps (total)	3.33 m² (35.84 sq ft)
Fins (total)	9.78 m² (105.28 sq ft)
Rudders (total)	1.85 m² (19.94 sq ft)
Tailplanes (total)	10.34 m² (111.36 sq ft)

WEIGHTS AND LOADINGS:

Weight empty, equipped (no fuel, ammunition, pylons or external stores)	12,973 kg (28,600 lb)
Max fuel load: internal	6,103 kg (13,455 lb)
CFTs (2, total)	4,422.5 kg (9,750 lb)
auxiliary tanks (3, total)	5,395.5 kg (11,895 lb)
max internal and external	15,921 kg (35,100 lb)
T-O weight (interceptor, full internal fuel and 4 Sparrows)	20,244 kg (44,630 lb)
T-O weight (incl three 2,309 litre; 610 US gallon; 508 Imp gallon drop tanks)	26,521 kg (58,470 lb)
Max T-O weight with CFTs	30,845 kg (68,000 lb)
Max wing loading	546.1 kg/m² (111.8 lb/sq ft)
Max power loading	147.87 kg/kN (1.45 lb/lb st)

PERFORMANCE:

Max level speed	more than Mach 2.5 (800 knots; 1,482 km/h; 921 mph CAS)
Approach speed	125 knots (232 km/h; 144 mph) CAS
Service ceiling	18,300 m (60,000 ft)
T-O run (interceptor)	274 m (900 ft)
Landing run (interceptor), without braking parachute	1,067 m (3,500 ft)
Ferry range: with external tanks, without CFTs	more than 2,500 nm (4,631 km; 2,878 miles)
with CFTs	3,100 nm (5,745 km; 3,570 miles)
Max endurance: with in-flight refuelling	15 h
unrefuelled, with CFTs	5 h 15 min
Design g limits	+9/−3

MCDONNELL DOUGLAS F-15E EAGLE

TYPE: Two-seat dual role attack/air superiority fighter.

PROGRAMME: Demonstration of industry-funded **Strike Eagle** prototype (71-291) modified from F-15B, including accurate blind weapons delivery, completed at Edwards AFB and Eglin AFB during 1982; product improvements tested in Strike Eagle, an F-15C and an F-15D between November 1982 and April 1983, including first take-off at 34,019 kg (75,000 lb), 3,175 kg (7,000 lb) more than F-15C with conformal tanks; new weight included conformal tanks, three other external tanks and eight 227 kg (500 lb) Mk 82 bombs; 16 different stores configurations tested, including 907 kg (2,000 lb) Mk 84 bombs, and BDU-38 and CBU-58 weapons delivered visually and by radar; full programme go-ahead announced 24 February 1984; first flight of first production F-15E (86-183) 11 December 1986; first delivery 29 December 1988 to 4th TFW at Seymour Johnson AFB, North Carolina; Wing declared operational October 1989, currently with 334, 335 and 336 Squadrons; 461st and 550th Tactical Fighter Training Squadrons of 405th TTW at Luke AFB, Arizona, equipped by end 1989 and others to part-squadron within 57th Fighter Weapons Wing at Nellis AFB, Nevada; two squadrons of 48th TFW at Lakenheath, UK, to equip

McDonnell Douglas F-15E Eagle dual role fighters from Luke Air Force Base

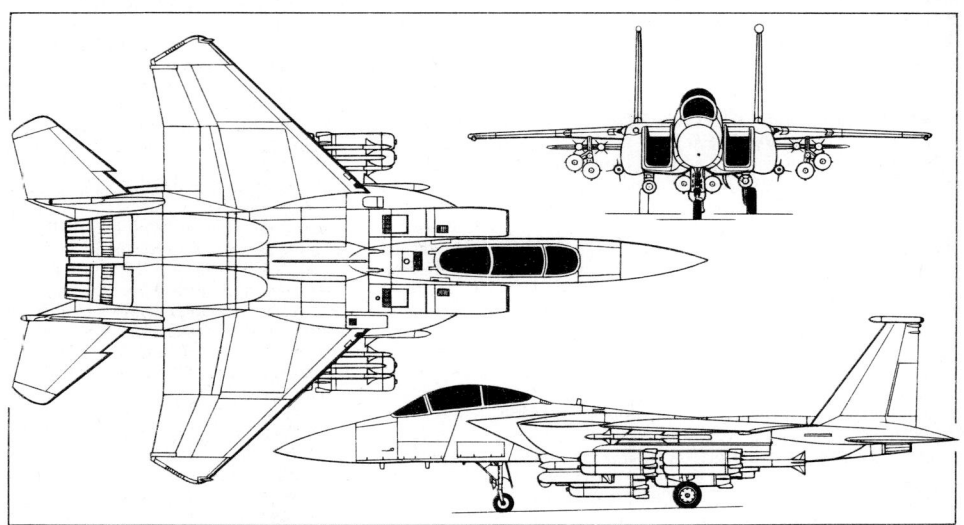

McDonnell Douglas F-15E Eagle equipped for high ordnance payload air-to-ground mission *(Pilot Press)*

with F-15Es from 1992 (gaining TASM armament in late 1990s). Small number of F-15Es used for trials with 3246th Test Wing at Eglin AFB, Florida, and 6510th TW at Edwards AFB, California; trials include 87-0180 with GE F110-GE-129 engines in place of F100s; P&W F100-PW-229 first flown in F-15E of 6510th TW 2 May 1990.

VARIANTS: **F-15E:** Basic version, as detailed.

F-15XX: Proposed alternative to USAF ATF; wing area increased to 62.2 m² (670 sq ft), fitted with camber-changing leading-edge slats; wing construction largely of composites; power plants and radar from ATF programme; additional fuel; supercruise capability. No USAF interest expressed in procurement.

F-15F: Single- or two-seat version, optimised for air combat; synthetic aperture high resolution ground mapping and attack modes deleted from AN/APG-70 radar to satisfy US export restrictions; no LANTIRN capability or conformal tanks; max T-O weight 36,741 kg (81,000 lb); re-designed cockpit with CRT displays and wide-angle HUD.

CUSTOMERS: Funding for 8, 42, 42, 36, 36 F-15Es in FYs 1986-90; originally planned 392 reduced to 200 with final order for 36 in FY 1991; deliveries to be completed May 1993, but request for additional funding in FY 1992 draft budget.

DESIGN FEATURES: Mission includes approach and attack at night and in all weather; main systems include new high resolution, synthetic aperture Hughes AN/APG-70 radar, wide field-of-view FLIR, Martin Marietta AN/AAQ-14 LANTIRN navigation and targeting pods; air-to-air capacity with AIM-7 Sparrow, AIM-9 Sidewinder and AIM-120 AMRAAM retained; rear cockpit has four multi-purpose CRT displays for radar, weapon selection, and monitoring enemy tracking systems;

front cockpit modifications include redesigned up-front controls, wide field-of-view HUD, colour CRT multifunction displays for navigation, weapon delivery, moving map, precision radar mapping and terrain following. Engines have digital electronic control, engine trimming and monitoring; fuel tanks are foam-filled; more powerful generators; better environmental control.

Internal fuel capacity slightly reduced to 7,643 litres (2,019 US gallons; 1,681 Imp gallons) to accommodate avionics; conformal tanks and tangential weapon carriage retained with up to three 2,309 litre (610 US gallon; 508 Imp gallon) external tanks.

FLYING CONTROLS: Digital triple-redundant Lear Astronics flight control system capable of automatic coupled terrain following.

STRUCTURE: 60 per cent of normal F-15 structure redesigned to allow 9g and 16,000 hours fatigue life; superplastic forming/diffusion bonding used for upper rear fuselage, rear fuselage keel, main landing gear doors, and some fuselage fairings, plus engine bay structure.

LANDING GEAR: Bendix wheels and Michelin AIR X radial tyres on all units. Nosewheel tyre size 22 × 7.75-9, mainwheel tyres size 36 × 11-18; tyre pressure 21.03 bars (305 lb/sq in) on all units. Bendix five-rotor carbon disc brakes.

POWER PLANT: Originally as F-15C/D, but option of General Electric F110-GE-129s. Aircraft built after August 1991 have 129.0 kN (29,000 lb st) Pratt & Whitney F100-PW-229s.

ACCOMMODATION: Two crew, pilot and weapon systems officer, in tandem on McDonnell Douglas ACES II ejection seats. Single-piece, upward-hinged canopy with increased bird resistance.

ARMAMENT: 20 mm M61A1 six-barrel gun in starboard wingroot, with 512 rds. General Electric lead computing gyro. Provision on underwing (one per wing) and centreline pylons for air-to-air and air-to-ground weapons and external fuel tanks. Wing pylons use standard rail and ejection launchers for AIM-9 Sidewinder and AIM-120 AMRAAM air-to-air missiles; AIM-7 Sparrow and AIM-120 AMRAAM can be carried on launchers on centreline station or on tangential stores carriers on conformal fuel tanks (maximum total load four each AIM-7 or AIM-9, up to eight AIM-120). Single or triple rail launchers for AGM-65 Maverick air-to-ground missiles can be fitted to wing stations only. Tangential carriage on CFTs provides for up to six bomb racks on each tank, with provision for triple ejector racks on wing and centreline stations. The F-15E can carry a wide variety and quantity of guided and unguided air-to-ground weapons, including Mk 20 Rockeye (26), Mk 82 (26), Mk 84 (seven), BSU-49 (26), BSU-50 (seven), GBU-10 (seven), GBU-12 (15), GBU-15 (two), GBU-24 (five), CBU-52 (25), CBU-58 (25), CBU-71 (25), CBU-87 (25), CBU-89 (25), CBU-90 (25), CBU-92 (25) or CBU-93 (25) bombs; LAU-3A rockets (nine); SUU-20 training weapons (five); A/A-37 U-33 tow target (one); and B57 and B61 series nuclear weapons (five). An AN/AXQ-14 data link pod is used in conjunction with the GBU-15; LANTIRN pod illumination is used to designate targets for the GBU-12 and -24 laser guided bombs. GBU-120 powered stand-off bomb to undertake qualification trials 1991-92. AN/AWG-27 armament control system.

WEIGHTS AND LOADINGS:
Basic operating weight empty	14,379 kg (31,700 lb)
Max weapon load	11,113 kg (24,500 lb)
Max fuel weight: internal	5,952 kg (13,123 lb)
external (two CFTs and three 610 US gallon drop	
tanks)	9,818 kg (21,645 lb)
Max T-O weight	36,741 kg (81,000 lb)
Max zero-fuel weight	28,440 kg (62,700 lb)
Max landing weight:	
unrestricted	20,094 kg (44,300 lb)
at reduced sink rates	36,741 kg (81,000 lb)
Max wing loading	650.5 kg/m² (133.2 lb/sq ft)
Max power loading	176.13 kg/kN (1.73 lb/lb st)

PERFORMANCE:
Max level speed at height	Mach 2.5
Max combat radius	685 nm (1,270 km; 790 miles)
Max range	2,400 nm (4,445 km; 2,765 miles)

MCDONNELL DOUGLAS F-15S/MTD

TYPE: One-off F-15 STOL/manoeuvring technology demonstrator for USAF.

PROGRAMME: Ordered October 1984; first prototype F-15B (71-0290) modified; first flight 7 September 1988; first flight with vectoring nozzles 10 May 1989; reverse thrust applied in flight 22 March 1990; demonstrated deceleration from Mach 1.6 to Mach 0.7. Since May 1991 participating in USAF/MDC integrated controls and avionics for air superiority (ICAAS) programme.

COSTS: $117.8 million cost-sharing contract placed October 1984.

DESIGN FEATURES: Designed to test Pratt & Whitney two-dimensional thrust vectoring and reversing nozzles, integrated flight/propulsion control, rough/soft field landing gear; advanced vehicle/pilot interfaces; controllable foreplanes based on F/A-18 Hornet tailplanes mounted on intake ducts increase g limit from 7.33 to 9; nozzles deflect thrust 20° up or down to improve take-off and for manoeuvring; aircraft has F-15E avionics and displays. Subcontractors include GE (flight control computers), National Water Lift (flight control actuators), Cleveland Pneumatic (landing gear modifications) and Hydro-Aire (anti-skid brake controls).

Performance improvements include take-off and landing on 457 m (1,500 ft) or 15 m (50 ft) wide, hard, wet, rough surface runway at night and adverse weather carrying fuel, gun, ammunition and a 2,721 kg (6,000 lb) external load; 6 to 7 per cent increase in manoeuvring performance over F-15 with 4,536 kg (10,000 lb) greater payload from 457 m (1,500 ft) runway; 39 per cent reduction in take-off run; 13 per cent longer range; 24 per cent faster roll rate; 100 per cent faster pitch rate. Autonomous landing guidance system for night/bad weather operations.

FLYING CONTROLS: Digital fly-by-wire system integrates foreplanes, flaperons, horizontal tail and vectoring nozzles for high precision control of flight path during approach; landing gear strengthened to accept 3.66 m (12 ft)/s landing impact; this aircraft serving as testbed for 552 bar (8,000 lb/sq in) hydraulic system development.

STRUCTURE: Engine nozzles made of carbonfibre; aluminium-lithium alloy skins are 5 per cent stronger, 9 per cent lighter.

MCDONNELL DOUGLAS F/A-18 HORNET
US Navy/Marine Corps designations: F/A-18A, B, C, D
Royal Australian Air Force designations: AF-18A and ATF-18A
Canadian Forces designations: CF-18A/B
Spanish Air Force designations: C.15 and CE.15
TYPE: Carrier-borne and land-based attack/fighter.

McDonnell Douglas F/A-18E proposed as a replacement for the cancelled US Navy A-12

PROGRAMME: US Navy study of VFAX low cost, lightweight multi-mission fighter accepted Spring 1974; VFAX study terminated August 1974 and replaced by derivative of either General Dynamics YF-16 or Northrop YF-17 lightweight fighter prototypes; McDonnell Douglas proposed F-17 derivative with Northrop as associate; resultant Navy Air Combat Fighter called Hornet accepted in two versions, F-18 fighter and A-18 attack aircraft; single F/A-18 selected to fill both roles; agreed 1985 McDonnell Douglas prime contractor and Northrop principal subcontractor for all versions; first Hornet flight (160775) 18 November 1978; 11 development aircraft flying by March 1980; delivery of US Navy F/A-18A/B (TF-18A designation dropped) to US Navy and Marines began May 1980 and completed 1987; millionth flying hour achieved 10 April 1990.

Total 1,000 Hornets delivered by 22 April 1991, of which over 700 to US forces; including FY 1991 procurement of 48, firm orders by March 1991 totalled 11 development and 848 production for USA and 325 export; USN proposed procurement of 48 each in FYs 1992-93 towards total of 1,157 production Hornets required.

Enhancements to Hughes AN/APG-65 radar funded ($65.7 million) May 1990; co-operative venture with USN, Canada and one other Hornet operator; new signal and data processors, upgraded receiver/exciter; available for FY 1994 installation, if production funded.

VARIANTS: **F/A-18A**: Single-seater. 369 F/A-18As and 41 two-seat F/A-18Bs (plus 11 prototypes, including two tandem-seat trainers) for USN and USMC as escort fighters to replace F-4s and as attack aircraft replacing A-7s under FYs 1979-85 contracts; first development squadron (VFA-125) formed at NAS Lemoore, California, November 1980; in service 7 January 1983 with Marine Fighter/Attack Squadron 314 at MCAS El Toro, California; first Atlantic Fleet squadrons formed NAS Cecil Field, Florida, 1 February 1985; same month VFA-113 'Stingers' and VFA-25 'Fist of the Fleet' embarked in USS Constellation.

US Navy squadrons with F/A-18A/Bs are VFAs 15, 87, 106 (also C/D), 132, 137 and Blue Angels display team at NAS Cecil Field, Florida; VFA-151, 192 and 195 at Atsugi, Japan; and USN Reserve squadrons VFA-203 at Cecil Field, VFA-204 at New Orleans, VFA-303 at Lemoore and VFA-305 at Point Mugu. Marine squadrons include VMFA-115, 122, 251, 312, 333, and 451 at Beaufort, South Carolina; and VMFA-314, 323, 531 and VMFAT-101 (also C/D) at El Toro, California. First combat experience by VFA-131, 132, 314 and 323 from USS Coral Sea attacking Libyan targets 1986.

F/A-18B: Combat capable two-seater; internal fuel capacity reduced by 6 per cent; production figures and US operating squadrons, see F/A-18A.

F/A-18C and F/A-18D: Single- and two-seat versions respectively. Purchased from FY 1986 onwards; 137 F/A-18Cs and 31 F/A-18Ds bought under 1986-87 procurements; overall total of 438 F/A-18C/Ds (including Night Attack - see below) funded between FY 1986 and FY 1991 (batches of 84, 84, 84, 72, 66 and 48), of which one-quarter two-seaters; first flight of production F/A-18C (163427) 3 September 1987. Squadrons with F/A-18C/Ds are VFA-37, 81, 82, 83, 86, 105, 131 and 136 at Cecil Field, Florida; VFA-22, 25, 27, 94, 97, 113, 125, 146 and 147 at Lemoore, California (VFA-46 and 72 converting in 1991); and Marine units VMFA-212, 232, and 235 at Kanehoe Bay, Hawaii. Modifications include provision for up to six AMRAAM missiles (two on fuselage and two on each outboard pylon); up to four imaging IR Maverick missiles (one on each wing pylon); provision for AN/ALQ-165 airborne self-protection jammer (ASPJ) interchangeable with AN/ALQ-126B; provision for reconnaissance equipment; upgraded stores management set with 128K memory, Intel 8086 processor, MIL-STD-1553B armament multiplex bus with MIL-STD-1760 weapons interface capability; flight incident recorder and monitoring set (FIRAMS), with integrated fuel/engine indicator, data storage set for recording maintenance and flight incidents data, signal data processor interfacing with fuel system to provide overall system control, enhanced built-in test capability and automatic CG adjustment as fuel is consumed; maintenance status panel isolating faults to card level;

Trial launch of a McDonnell Douglas SLAM from an F/A-18 Hornet of the Pacific Missile Test Center, Point Mugu

McDonnell Douglas F/A-18C Hornet of VFA-86 'Sidewinders' squadron, US Navy

and new faster XN-6 mission computer with twice memory of previous XN-5.

Small rectangular fence retrofitted to US Navy aircraft above LEX strake just ahead of wing leading-edge broadens LEX vortices, reduces fatigue and improves directional control at angles of attack higher than 45°.

F/A-18C/D Night Attack: First flight of prototype 6 May 1988; one Night Attack F/A-18C (163985) and one D (163986) delivered to Naval Air Test Center, Patuxent River, on 1 and 14 November 1989 respectively; all F/A-18Cs and Ds delivered subsequently (FY 1988 procurement) have all-weather night attack avionics. Marine Corps needs six squadrons of F/A-18Ds to replace Grumman A-6Es, McDonnell Douglas OA-4s and RF-4Bs in attack, reconnaissance and forward air controller roles; this requires 96 aircraft, of which only 48 authorised in 1990; deliveries began to VMFA(AW)-121 at El Toro, California, 11 May 1990, to be followed by VMFA(AW)-242, 225 (reconnaissance), 224, 232, and 553 in FYs 1991-95; Navy squadrons unchanged, with two-seaters used as trainers only.

Night Attack system includes pilot's night vision goggles, Hughes AN/AAR-50 thermal imaging navigation set (TINS) presenting forward view in Kaiser AN/AVQ-28 raster HUD, colour multi-function displays and Honeywell colour digital moving map; USMC version of F/A-18D has mission-capable rear cockpit with no control column, but two sidestick weapons controllers and two 12.7 cm (5 in) MFDs; may be converted to dual control, with stick and throttles, for pilot training.

F/A-18D(RC): Simple reconnaissance version launched 1982 and first flown 1984 included a twin-sensor package replacing guns in nose; now being developed is Advanced Tactical Airborne Reconnaissance System (ATARS) centreline pod containing Loral AN/UPD-8 SLAR high resolution synthetic aperture side-looking radar supplementing nose-mounted optical and IR sensors; images transmitted in real time by data link and also viewed in rear cockpit; pod has capacity for electro-optical camera; pod, data link and processing equipment flight tested in USMC RF-4B; F/A-18D(RC)

can be reconverted to fighter/attack overnight; IOC planned with USMC in FY 1994.

F/A-18E/F: Proposed single- and two-seat stretched versions offered as replacement for cancelled GD/MDC A-12; gross weight increased by 5,262 kg (11,600 lb); 86 cm (2 ft 10 in) fuselage plug; wing area increased by 9.29 m² (100 sq ft) and span by 1.3 m (4 ft 3½ in); larger tailplane; additional 1,361 kg (3,000 lb) of internal fuel and 1,406 kg (3,100 lb) of external fuel; 40 per cent extra range; non-afterburning power plants developed from GE F412 (intended for A-12); greater weapon load for primary strike/attack role; two more hardpoints and extra survivability features. USN requesting R&D funding of $435 million in FY 1992 and $1,000 million in FY 1993; first flight planned early 1996. See Addenda.

AF-18A and ATF-18A: Royal Australian Air Force version; decision to purchase 75 announced 20 October 1981; deliveries started 17 May 1985; first flight of ATF-18A assembled by Aerospace Technologies of Australia (ASTA, which see), 26 February 1985; first flight of Australian manufactured aircraft (ATF-18A, A21-104) 3 June 1985; last of 57 single-seat and 18 two-seat Hornets delivered 16 May 1990; Hornet replaced Dassault Mirage IIIO; units are No. 2 OCU, Williamtown, No. 3 Squadron (formed August 1986) and No. 77 Squadron at same base and No. 75 Squadron, Tindal. Weapons include AIM-9L, AGM-88 HARM, AGM-84 Harpoon and 2,000 lb LGBs; from 1990, remaining 74 aircraft being fitted with F-18C/D type avionics and provision for Ford Aerospace AN/AAS-38 IR tracking and laser designating pod.

CF-18A and B: Canada's purchase of 138 Hornets (finalised as 98 CF-18As and 40 two-seat CF-18Bs) announced 10 April 1980; first flight of CF-18 29 July 1982; deliveries between 25 October 1982 and September 1988; CAF units are No. 410 OCU and Nos. 416 and 441 Squadrons at CFB Cold Lake, Alberta, 425 and 433 at Bagotville, Quebec, and 439, 409 and 421 Squadrons of No. 4 Fighter Wing/No. 1 Air Division at Baden Sollingen, Germany. Unit strengths are six As and 20 Bs at the OCU, 10 As and three Bs in home-based squadrons and 43 As and six Bs shared by the German squadrons. Differences from US Navy F/A-18 include ILS, in-flight identification spotlight in port side of fuselage, and provision for LAU-5003 19-tube pods for CRV-7 70 mm (2.75 in) high velocity submunition rockets; other weapons are AIM-7M and AIM-9L air-to-air missiles, 227 kg (500 lb) Mk 82 bombs and Hunting BL755 CBUs. Pilot has comprehensive cold weather land survival kit.

EF-18A and B: Spanish version; purchase of 60 single-seat Hornets and 12 two-seaters, known respectively as **C.15** and **CE.15**, under Futuro Avion de Combate y Ataque programme announced 30 May 1983; financial restrictions reduced number from 84 and deliveries then stretched from 36, 24 and 12 from 1986 to 1988 to 11, 26, 15, 12 and eight from 1986 to 1990; maintenance performed in Spain by CASA, which also works on Canadian Hornets in Europe and USN Hornets with 6th Fleet in Mediterranean; first flight Spanish Hornet 4 December 1985; deliveries began 10 July 1986; all 12 trainers delivered by early 1987; armament includes AIM-7F and AIM-9L air-to-air missiles, AGM-84 Harpoon, AGM-88 HARM and free-fall bombs; AIM-120 AMRAAM ordered 1990. First 36 aircraft have Sanders AN/ALQ-126B deception jammers ordered in 1987; final 36 received Northrop AN/ALQ-162(V) systems. Units equipped are Ala de Caza 15 (15th Fighter Wing) formed at Zaragoza December 1985 and operational December 1987, with 30 A and six B shared between Escuadrones 151 and 152; Ala de Caza 12 at Torrejon (Escuadrones 121 and 122) completed re-equipping in July 1990.

CUSTOMERS: In addition to US Navy/Marine Corps, Australia, Canada and Spain (see Variants), Switzerland selected 26 F/A-18Cs and eight F/A-18Ds powered by GE F404-GE-402 engines in October 1988, as its Neue Jagdflugzeug to replace F-5Es; contract was expected late 1990 for entry into service 1994, but decision changed during 1990 to examine new offer of Mirage 2000-5 from Dassault. Kuwaiti contract signed September 1988 for 32 F/A-18Cs and eight F/A-18Ds together with AGM-65G Maverick, AGM-84 Harpoon, AIM-7F Sparrow and AIM-9L Sidewinder; deliveries January 1992-93; F404-GE-402 power plants. South Korea requirement for 120 F/A-18C/Ds, of which first 12 to fly in USA, announced December 1989; cancelled, March 1991, in favour of GD F-16.

COSTS: $12.2 million, flyaway unit cost, Kuwait contract in 1989. $55,632 million (1991) US programme, 1,168 aircraft.

DESIGN FEATURES: Sharp-edged, cambered leading-edge extensions (LEX), slots at fuselage junction and outward-canted twin fins are designed to produce high agility and docile performance at angles of attack over 50°; wings have 20° sweepback at quarter-chord; wings fold up 90° at inboard end of ailerons, even on land-based F/A-18s; landing gear designed for unflared landings on runways as well as on carriers.

FLYING CONTROLS: Full digital fly-by-wire controls using ailerons and tailerons for lateral control, plus flaps in flaperon form at low airspeeds; leading- and trailing-edge

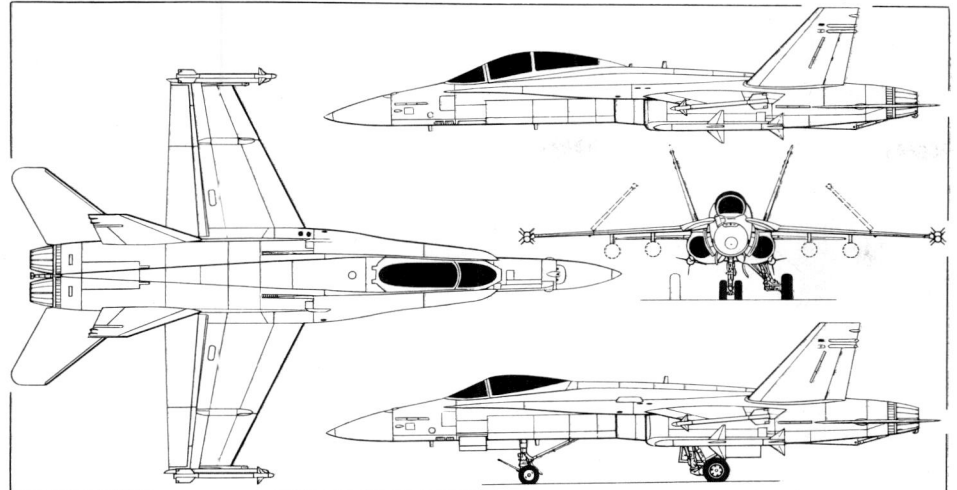

McDonnell Douglas F/A-18C Hornet with additional side view (top) of F/A-18D *(Pilot Press)*

flaps scheduled automatically for high manoeuvrability, fast cruise and slow approach speed; both rudders turned in at take-off and landing to provide extra nose-up trim effort; fly-by-wire returns towards 1*g* flight if pilot releases controls; lateral and then directional control progressively washed out as angle of attack reaches extreme values; height, heading and airspeed holds provided in fly-by-wire system; US Navy aircraft can land automatically using carrier-based guidance system; airbrake panel located on top of fuselage, between fins. Bertea hydraulic actuators for trailing-edge flaps; Hydraulic Research actuators for ailerons; National Water Lift actuators for tailerons.

STRUCTURE: Multi-spar wing mainly of light alloy, with graphite/epoxy inter-spar skin panels and trailing-edge flaps; tail surfaces mainly graphite/epoxy skins over aluminium honeycomb core; graphite/epoxy fuselage panels and doors; titanium engine firewall. Northrop produces rear and centre fuselages; assembly and test at McDonnell Douglas St Louis factory; CASA produces horizontal tail surfaces, flaps, leading-edge extensions, speedbrakes, rudders and rear side panels for all F/A-18s.

LANDING GEAR: Retractable tricycle type, with twin-wheel nose and single-wheel main units. Nose unit retracts forward, mainwheels rearward, turning 90° to stow horizontally inside the lower surface of the engine air ducts. Bendix wheels and brakes. Nosewheel tyres size 22 × 6.6-10, 20 ply, pressure 24.13 bars (350 lb/sq in) for carrier operations, 10.34 bars (150 lb/sq in) for land operations. Mainwheel tyres size 30 × 11.5-14.5, 24 ply, pressure 24.13 bars (350 lb/sq in) for carrier operations, 13.79 bars (200 lb/sq in) for land operations. Ozone nosewheel steering unit. Nose unit towbar for catapult launch. Arrester hook, for carrier landings, under rear fuselage.

POWER PLANT: Two General Electric F404-GE-400 low bypass turbofans, each producing approx 71.2 kN (16,000 lb st) with afterburning. F404-GE-402 EPE (Enhanced Performance Engine) installed from early 1992, with additional 20 per cent thrust. Self-sealing fuel tanks and fuel lines; foam in wing tanks and fuselage voids. Internal fuel capacity (JP5) approx 6,061 litres (1,600 US gallons; 1,333 Imp gallons). Provision for up to three 1,250 litre (330 US gallon; 275 Imp gallon) external tanks. Flight refuelling probe retracts into upper starboard side of nose. Simmonds fuel gauging system. Fixed ramp air intakes.

ACCOMMODATION: Pilot only, on Martin-Baker SJU-5/6 ejection seat, in pressurised, heated and air-conditioned cockpit. Upward opening canopy, with separate windscreen, on all versions. Two pilots in F/A-18B and USN F/A-18D; pilot and Naval Flight Officer in USMC F/A-18D.

SYSTEMS: Two completely separate hydraulic systems, each at 207 bars (3,000 lb/sq in). Max flow rate 212 litres (56 US gallons; 46.6 Imp gallons)/min. Bootstrap type reservoir, pressure 5.86 bars (85 lb/sq in). AiResearch air-conditioning system. General Electric electrical power system. Garrett GTC36-200 APU for engine starting and ground pneumatic, electric and hydraulic power. Oxygen system. Fire detection and extinguishing systems.

AVIONICS: Include an automatic carrier landing system (ACLS) for all-weather carrier operations; a Hughes Aircraft AN/APG-65 multi-mode digital air-to-air and air-to-ground tracking radar, with air-to-air modes which include velocity search (VS), range while search (RWS), track while scan (TWS), which can track ten targets and display eight to the pilot, and raid assessment mode (RAM). Loral AN/AAS-38 attack FLIR; Honeywell digital moving map display; Smiths Industries multi-purpose colour cockpit display; Collins AN/ARN-118 Tacan, AN/ARC-182 UHF/VHF com and DF-301E UHF/DF; Magnavox AN/ALR-50 and Litton AN/ALR-67 radar warning receivers; GEC Ferranti Type 117 laser designator; Goodyear AN/ALE-39 chaff dispenser; Sanders AN/ALQ-126B ECM; Harris AN/ASW-25 radio data link; Eaton AN/ARA-63 receiver/decoder; GEC Ferranti FID 2035 horizontal situation display; Bendix/King HSI; J.E.T. ID-1791/A flight director indicator; ITT/Westinghouse AN/ALQ-165 airborne self-protection jammer (ASPJ); General Electric quadruple-redundant fly-by-wire flight control system, with direct electrical backup to all surfaces and direct mechanical backup to tailerons; two Control Data AN/AYK-14 digital computers; Litton AN/ASN-130A inertial navigation system; two Kaiser multi-function CRTs, central GEC Ferranti-Bendix/King CRT and Kaiser AN/AVQ-28 head-up display; Conrac communications system control; Normalair-Garrett digital data recorder for Bendix/King maintenance recording system; flight incident recording and monitoring system (FIRAMS); Smiths standby altimeter; and Kearflex standby airspeed indicator, standby vertical speed indicator, and cockpit pressure altimeter. Night Attack F/A-18 has Hughes AN/ARR-50 thermal imaging navigation set, Honeywell colour digital moving map display (replacing film-strip map) and provision for GEC Cat's Eyes NVGs.

ARMAMENT: Nine external weapon stations, comprising two wingtip stations for AIM-9 Sidewinder air-to-air missiles; two outboard wing stations for an assortment of air-to-air or air-to-ground weapons, including AIM-7 Sparrows, AIM-9 Sidewinders, AIM-120 AMRAAMs, AGM-84 Harpoons and AGM-65F Maverick missiles; two inboard wing stations for external fuel tanks, air-to-ground weapons or Brunswick TALD tactical air-launched decoys; two nacelle fuselage stations for Sparrows or Martin Marietta AN/ASQ-173 laser spot tracker/strike camera (LST/SCAM) and Loral AN/AAS-38 FLIR pods; and a centreline fuselage station for external fuel or weapons. Air-to-ground weapons include GBU-10 and -12 laser guided bombs, Mk 82 and Mk 84 general purpose bombs, and CBU-59 cluster bombs. An M61 20 mm six-barrel gun, with 570 rounds, is mounted in the nose and has a McDonnell Douglas director gunsight, with a conventional sight as backup.

DIMENSIONS, EXTERNAL:

Wing span	11.43 m (37 ft 6 in)
Wing span over missiles	12.31 m (40 ft 4¾ in)
Wing chord: at root	4.04 m (13 ft 3 in)
at tip	1.68 m (5 ft 6 in)
Wing aspect ratio	3.5
Width, wings folded	8.38 m (27 ft 6 in)
Length overall	17.07 m (56 ft 0 in)
Height overall	4.66 m (15 ft 3½ in)
Tailplane span	6.58 m (21 ft 7¼ in)
Distance between fin tips	3.60 m (11 ft 9½ in)
Wheel track	3.11 m (10 ft 2½ in)
Wheelbase	5.42 m (17 ft 9½ in)

AREAS:

Wings, gross	37.16 m² (400.0 sq ft)
Ailerons (total)	2.27 m² (24.4 sq ft)
Leading-edge flaps (total)	4.50 m² (48.4 sq ft)
Trailing-edge flaps (total)	5.75 m² (61.9 sq ft)
Fins (total)	9.68 m² (104.2 sq ft)
Rudders (total)	1.45 m² (15.6 sq ft)
Tailplanes (total)	8.18 m² (88.1 sq ft)

WEIGHTS AND LOADINGS:

Weight empty	10,455 kg (23,050 lb)
Max fuel weight: internal (JP5)	4,926 kg (10,860 lb)
external F/A-18 (JP5)	3,053 kg (6,732 lb)
CF-18 (JP4)	4,246 kg (9,360 lb)
Max external stores load	7,710 kg (17,000 lb)
T-O weight: Fighter mission	16,651 kg (36,710 lb)
Attack mission	23,541 kg (51,900 lb)

Max wing loading (Attack mission)
600.83 kg/m² (123.06 lb/sq ft)
Max power loading (Attack mission)
156.80 kg/kN (1.54 lb/lb st)

PERFORMANCE:

Max level speed	more than Mach 1.8
Max speed, intermediate power	more than Mach 1.0
Approach speed	134 knots (248 km/h; 154 mph)

Acceleration from 460 knots (850 km/h; 530 mph) to 920 knots (1,705 km/h; 1,060 mph) at 10,670 m (35,000 ft)
under 2 min

Combat ceiling	approx 15,240 m (50,000 ft)
T-O run	less than 427 m (1,400 ft)

Combat radius, interdiction, hi-lo-lo-hi
290 nm (537 km; 340 miles)

Combat endurance	CAP 150 nm (278 km; 173 miles)
from aircraft carrier	1h 45 min

Ferry range, unrefuelled
more than 2,000 nm (3,706 km; 2,303 miles)

MCDONNELL DOUGLAS HORNET 2000
TYPE: Four configurations for internationally developed Hornet follow-on.

PROGRAMME: Company-funded studies, based on Hornet; various combinations of stretched fuselage, dorsal fuel tank and increased wing area (greater span and/or chord). Common features include 'Growth II' GE F404 power plants, active array radar and advanced electronic warfare systems. Further details in 1990-91 *Jane's*. Many features now included in proposed F/A-18E/F (which see).

MCDONNELL DOUGLAS/BAe T45TS
US Navy designation: T-45A Goshawk

Details under McDonnell Douglas/BAe entry in International section.

NORTHROP/MCDONNELL DOUGLAS YF-23 (ATF)
Unsuccessful candidate for US Air Force Advanced Tactical Fighter programme won by Lockheed/Boeing/General Dynamics on 23 April 1991. For details of YF-23, see under Northrop.

GENERAL DYNAMICS/MCDONNELL DOUGLAS A-12
See separate entry under General Dynamics/McDonnell Douglas heading in this section. Programme cancelled by US Navy January 1991.

DOUGLAS AIRCRAFT COMPANY
(Division of McDonnell Douglas Corporation)
HEADQUARTERS: 3855 Lakewood Boulevard, Long Beach, California 90846
Telephone: 1 (213) 593 5511
Fax: 1 (213) 496 8720
Telex: 674357
PRESIDENT: Robert H. Hood Jr

EXECUTIVE VICE-PRESIDENTS:
David Swain (C-17)
John D. Wolf (Commercial)

VICE-PRESIDENTS:
Joe Pirkle (General Manager, MD-11)

Russell L. Ray (General Manager, Commercial Marketing)
Walt Orlowski (General Manager, MD-90)
Bill Skibbe (General Manager, MD-80)
PUBLIC RELATIONS MANAGERS:
Don Hanson (Commercial Transports)
Richard Hill (Government Transports)

Douglas Aircraft Company operates plants at Long Beach and Torrance, California; Macon, Georgia; Columbus, Ohio; and Salt Lake City, Utah. DC designation superseded by MD designation in 1983; first designation change was DC-9 Super 80, becoming MD-80; existing DC-8, DC-9 and DC-10 remain unchanged.

Douglas delivered 976 DC-9s up to 1982 and its 1,500th twin-jet airliner, an MD-80, on 19 September 1988; total of 139 MD-80s delivered during 1990, and 31 in the first quarter of 1991. At end April 1991 undelivered firm orders for twin jets totalled 355 and for MD-11s 168.

MCDONNELL DOUGLAS MD-80 SERIES
TYPE: Twin-turbofan short/medium-range airliner.

PROGRAMME: Began as Super 80 higher capacity variant of DC-9; first flight 18 October 1979; first flight of second and third prototypes (N1002G and N1002W) 6 December 1979 and 29 February 1980 respectively; FAA certification 26 August 1980; first delivery to Swissair 12 September 1980.

VARIANTS: **MD-81**: Basic version with maximum seating for 172 passengers; P&W JT8D-209 engines with

First McDonnell Douglas MD-87 for Swiss carrier CTA *(Anton Wettstein)*

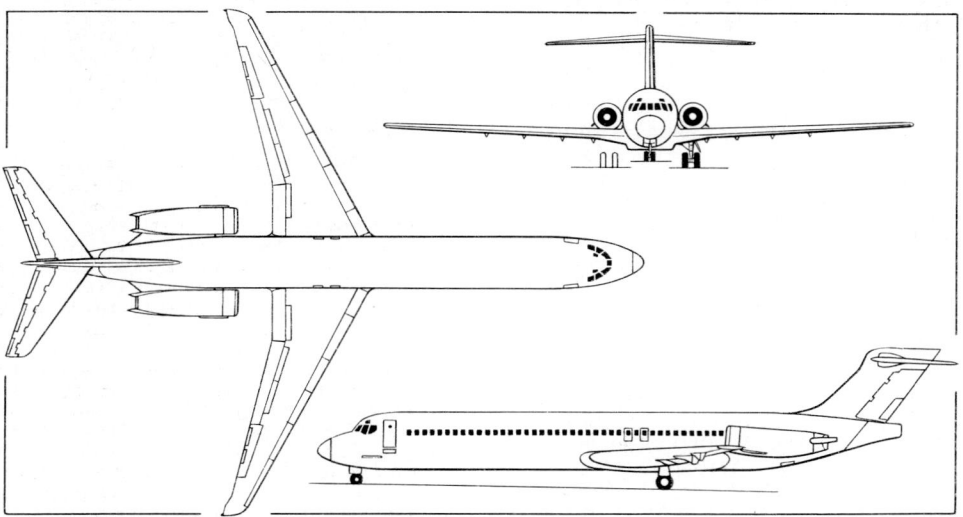

McDonnell Douglas MD-87, a short-fuselage variant of the MD-80 series of twin-turbofan transports
(Pilot Press)

automatic power reserve; two-man crew; maximum five-abreast passenger seating.

MD-82: Announced 16 April 1979; powered by P&W JT8D-217s for hot and high performance and increased payload/range; same size cabin; first flight 8 January 1981; certificated 31 July 1981 at max T-O weight 66,680 kg (147,000 lb); in service August 1981; same fuel capacity and landing weight as MD-81. Second version powered by JT8D-217As and with higher max T-O weight certificated mid-1982; available Autumn 1982.

Agreement signed 12 April 1985 for assembly by Shanghai Aircraft Manufacturing Factory of 25 out of 26 MD-82s ordered by China; another 10 aircraft approved April 1990; US-built first aircraft delivered 30 September 1985; first flight of SAMF assembled MD-82 2 July 1987; in service 4 August 1987; second aircraft delivered 18 December 1987; FAA certificate extended to Chinese-built aircraft 9 November 1987; 22 completed by SAMF by March 1991.

MD-83: Extended range version powered by JT8D-219s, announced 31 January 1983; two per cent better fuel consumption than -217As; two extra fuel tanks in cargo compartment. First flight 17 December 1984; FAA certification 1985; in service Alaska Airlines and Finnair early 1986; on 14 November 1985, Finnair MD-83 made longest MD-80 flight covering 3,404 nm (6,308 km; 3,920 miles) from Montreal to Helsinki in 7 h 26 min; first revenue transatlantic service flown by Transwede between Stockholm and Fort Lauderdale, Florida, with stops at Oslo and Gander.

MD-87: Short fuselage version for maximum 130 single-class passengers; fin height increased; powered by JT8D-217Cs with two per cent lower fuel consumption than 217As; other -200 series engines available; first flight 4 December 1986; certificated 21 October 1987; first deliveries to Finnair and Austrian Airlines; optional front and rear cargo compartment auxiliary fuel tanks each hold 2,139 litres (565 US gallons; 470.5 Imp gallons). MD-87 has MD-80 cruise performance improvement package including fillet fairing between engine pylons and fuselage, fairing on APU, improved sealing on horizontal tail, low drag flap hinge fairings, and extended low-drag tailcone; MD-87 also first of series with electronic flight instrument system, AHRS and head-up display as standard.

MD-88: Combines JT8D-219 power plant with EFIS cockpit displays, flight management system, onboard windshear detection system and increased use of composites in structure. Redesigned cabin interior for 142 passengers (14 first/128 coach class) five-abreast;

wider aisle; redesigned overhead bins. First flight 15 August 1987; FAA certification 9 December 1987; entered service 5 January 1988 with principal customer Delta Air Lines.

MD-80 Executive Jets: Corporate and executive versions of MD-83 and MD-87 offered; typically seating 20 passengers; MD-83 maximum range 4,100 nm (7,598 km; 4,721 miles); MD-87 maximum range 4,500 nm (8,339 km; 5,182 miles).

MD-80 Product improvement: Powered by quieter JT8D-290s with larger fan; alternative designations MD-80 Advanced or MD-90-20; expected delivery 1993; MD-90-style cabin; weights and ranges equivalent to MD-90-30; intended to extend MD-80 production beyond 1997.

CUSTOMERS: Total 1,500 MD-80 series ordered by 31 December 1990, of which 875 delivered by 1 June 1991.

DESIGN FEATURES: DC-9 wing span increased by centre-section plugs and 0.61 m (2 ft 0 in) wingtip extensions; fuselage extended by plugs fore and aft of wing; larger wing holds more fuel; systems improvements include digital integrated flight guidance and control system, 'dial a flap' control for more accurate flap settings, flow-through cooling of avionics compartment, larger capacity APU, recirculation of ventilating air, and advanced digital fuel gauging system. Performance management system similar to that of DC-10 standard from April 1983; optional flight management system giving horizontal and vertical guidance. Other features include increased use of composites, such as Kevlar wing/fuselage fillets introduced 1983. Flight deck changes include advanced attitude and heading reference system, optional Honeywell EFIS, flat LED displays, alternative flight management systems, and Honeywell windshear guidance system (certificated June 1989; now standard on all new MD-80s and retrofittable).

Wing sweepback at quarter-chord 24° 30′; mean thickness/chord ratio 11.0 per cent; dihedral 3°; incidence 1° 15′. Thermal anti-icing of leading-edges.

FLYING CONTROLS: Manual ailerons; elevators with assister tabs; electrically actuated variable incidence tailplane; hydraulically actuated rudder with manual standby; automatic landing available; full-span leading-edge slats; three spoilers per wing, of which outboard two for flight and ground braking and one for lift dumping; hydraulically actuated double-slotted flaps cover 67 per cent of span; one underwing vortillon fence on each wing.

STRUCTURE: All-metal two-spar wing with riveted spanwise stringers; glassfibre trailing-edges on wings, ailerons,

flaps, elevators and rudder; detachable wingtips; most of cabin floor made of balsa or Nomex core sandwich; engine pylons by Calcor and fuselage panels by Alenia (Aeritalia).

LANDING GEAR: Retractable tricycle type of Cleveland Pneumatic manufacture, with steerable nosewheels (±27° on MD-81/82/87/88; ±25° on MD-83). Hydraulic retraction, nose unit forward, main units inward. Twin Goodyear wheels and tyres on each unit. Mainwheel tyres size 44.5 × 16.5-20, pressure 11.38 bars (165 lb/sq in). Nosewheel tyres size 26 × 6.6-14, pressure 10.34 bars (150 lb/sq in). Goodyear disc brakes. Hydro-Aire Mk IIIA anti-skid units. Douglas ram air brake cooling.

POWER PLANT: Two Pratt & Whitney JT8D-209 turbofans in MD-81, pod mounted one each side of rear fuselage, and each rated at 82.3 kN (18,500 lb st), with emergency thrust reserve of 3.34 kN (750 lb st). MD-82 has JT8D-217s, each rated at 89 kN (20,000 lb st), with emergency thrust reserve of 3.78 kN (850 lb st), or -217As of similar rating. MD-83 has JT8D-219 engines of 93.4 kN (21,000 lb st). MD-87 has JT8D-217C engines of 89 kN (20,000 lb st), with an emergency thrust reserve of 3.78 kN (850 lb st). MD-88 has 93.4 kN (21,000 lb st) JT8D-219 turbofans. Standard fuel capacity in MD-81/82/87/88 is 21,876 litres (5,779 US gallons; 4,812 Imp gallons); increased in MD-83 (and, optionally, MD-87) to 26,260 litres (6,939 US gallons; 5,778 Imp gallons) by two 2,195 litre (580 US gallon; 483 Imp gallon) auxiliary tanks in cargo compartment. Pressure refuelling point in starboard wing leading-edge. Overwing gravity refuelling points.

ACCOMMODATION: Crew of two and observer on flight deck, plus cabin attendants. Seating arrangements are optional to meet specific airline requirements. Maximum optional seating capacity is for 172 passengers (130 in MD-87). Fully pressurised and air-conditioned. One toilet forward on port side, two at rear of cabin. Provisions for galley at both forward and rear ends of cabin. Passenger door at front of cabin on port side, with built-in electrically operated airstairs, and rear hydraulically operated ventral stairway, are standard. Servicing and emergency exit doors at starboard forward end and port rear end of cabin. Three cargo doors for underfloor holds on starboard side. Overwing emergency exits, two each side.

SYSTEMS: AiResearch dual air cycle air-conditioning and pressurisation system utilising engine bleed air, max differential 0.54 bar (7.77 lb/sq in). Two separate 207 bar (3,000 lb/sq in) hydraulic systems for operation of spoilers, flaps, slats, rudder, landing gear, nosewheel steering, brakes, thrust reversers and ventral stairway. Maximum flow rate 30.3 litres (8 US gallons; 6.7 Imp gallons)/min. Airless bootstrap type reservoirs, output pressure 2.07 bars (30 lb/sq in). Pneumatic system, for air-conditioning/pressurisation, engine starting and ice protection, utilises 8th or 13th stage engine bleed air and/or APU. Electrical system includes three 40kVA 120/208V three-phase 400Hz alternators, two engine driven, one driven by APU. Oxygen system of diluter demand type for crew on flight deck; continuous flow chemical canister type with automatic mask presentation for cabin passengers. Anti-icing of wing, engine inlets and tailplane by engine bleed air. Electric windscreen de-icing. APU provides pneumatic and electrical power on ground, and electrical power in flight.

AVIONICS: All-digital avionics, including dual Honeywell integrated flight systems; Honeywell Cat IIIA autoland; autopilot and stability augmentation; performance management system; speed command with digital full-time autothrottles; thrust rating indicator; dual Honeywell air data systems; automatic power reserve; colour weather radar. Sundstrand head-up display optional.

DIMENSIONS, EXTERNAL (all versions, except as indicated):

Wing span	32.87 m (107 ft 10 in)
Wing chord: at root	7.05 m (23 ft 1½ in)
at tip	1.10 m (3 ft 7½ in)
Wing aspect ratio	9.62
Length overall: except MD-87	45.06 m (147 ft 10 in)
MD-87	39.75 m (130 ft 5 in)

First McDonnell Douglas MD-88 taking off on its first flight, in the markings of Delta Air Lines

Length of fuselage:
except MD-87	41.30 m (135 ft 6 in)
MD-87	36.30 m (119 ft 1 in)

Height overall: except MD-87 9.04 m (29 ft 8 in)
MD-87 9.30 m (30 ft 6 in)
Tailplane span 12.24 m (40 ft 2 in)
Wheel track 5.08 m (16 ft 8 in)
Wheelbase: except MD-87 22.07 m (72 ft 5 in)
MD-87 19.18 m (62 ft 11 in)
Passenger door (port, fwd):
Height 1.83 m (6 ft 0 in)
Width 0.86 m (2 ft 10 in)
Height to sill 2.24 m (7 ft 4 in)
Servicing door (stbd, fwd): Height 1.22 m (4 ft 0 in)
Width 0.69 m (2 ft 3 in)
Height to sill 2.24 m (7 ft 4 in)
Servicing door (port, rear): Height 1.52 m (5 ft 0 in)
Width 0.69 m (2 ft 3 in)
Height to sill 2.67 m (8 ft 9 in)
Freight and baggage hold doors:
Height 1.27 m (4 ft 2 in)
Width 1.35 m (4 ft 5 in)
Height to sill: fwd 1.17 m (3 ft 10 in)
centre 1.30 m (4 ft 3 in)
rear 1.52 m (5 ft 0 in)
Rear cargo door (MD-87): Height 1.27 m (4 ft 2 in)
Width 0.91 m (3 ft 0 in)
Emergency exits (overwing, port and stbd):
Height 0.91 m (3 ft 0 in)
Width 0.51 m (1 ft 8 in)

DIMENSIONS, INTERNAL:
Cabin, excl flight deck, incl toilets:
Length 30.78 m (101 ft 0 in)
Max width 3.07 m (10 ft 1 in)
Max height 2.06 m (6 ft 9 in)
Floor area 89.65 m² (965.0 sq ft)
Volume 191.9 m³ (6,778 cu ft)
Freight holds (underfloor, MD-81/82):
fwd 13.14 m³ (464.0 cu ft)
centre 9.80 m³ (346.0 cu ft)
rear 12.54 m³ (443.0 cu ft)
Freight holds (underfloor, MD-83):
total 29.1 m³ (1,028 cu ft)

AREAS:
Wings, gross 118 m² (1,270 sq ft)
Ailerons (total) 3.53 m² (38.0 sq ft)
Fin, excl dorsal fin 9.51 m² (102.4 sq ft)
Rudder 6.07 m² (65.3 sq ft)
Tailplane 29.17 m² (314.0 sq ft)

WEIGHTS AND LOADINGS (A: MD-81, B: MD-82, C: MD-83, D: MD-87, E: MD-88):
Operating weight empty: A 35,580 kg (78,440 lb)
B 35,620 kg (78,528 lb)
C 36,395 kg (80,238 lb)
D standard fuel 33,628 kg (74,139 lb)
D optional fuel 34,357 kg (75,745 lb)
Fuel load:
A, B, D standard 17,748 kg (39,128 lb)
C, D optional 21,182 kg (46,699 lb)
Max payload (weight limited): A 17,944 kg (39,560 lb)
B 19,718 kg (43,472 lb)
C 18,943 kg (41,762 lb)
D standard 17,112 kg (37,727 lb)
D optional 16,445 kg (36,255 lb)
Max T-O weight: A (-217 engines), D standard
63,503 kg (140,000 lb)
A (-217A engines), B, D optional, E standard
67,812 kg (149,500 lb)
C, E optional 72,575 kg (160,000 lb)
Max zero-fuel weight: A 53,524 kg (118,000 lb)
B, C 55,338 kg (122,000 lb)
D 50,802 kg (112,000 lb)

Max landing weight:
A, D standard 58,060 kg (128,000 lb)
B, D optional 58,967 kg (130,000 lb)
C 63,276 kg (139,500 lb)
Max wing loading:
A, D standard 534.6 kg/m² (109.5 lb/sq ft)
B, D optional, E standard 574.7 kg/m² (117.7 lb/sq ft)
C, E optional 615.0 kg/m² (126.0 lb/sq ft)
Max power loading: A 385.8 kg/kN (3.78 lb/lb st)
B, D optional 381.0 kg/kN (3.74 lb/lb st)
C, E optional 388.5 kg/kN (3.81 lb/lb st)
D standard 356.8 kg/kN (3.50 lb/lb st)
E standard 363.3 kg/kN (3.56 lb/lb st)

PERFORMANCE (at max T-O weight except where indicated):
Max level speed (all) 500 knots (925 km/h; 575 mph)
Max cruising speed (all) Mach 0.80
Normal cruising speed (all) Mach 0.76
Min ground turning radius:
about nosewheels:
MD-81, 82, 83, 88 22.43 m (73 ft 7¼ in)
MD-87 19.54 m (64 ft 1¼ in)
about wingtip:
MD-81, 82, 83, 88 21.21 m (69 ft 7¼ in)
MD-87 20.64 m (67 ft 8½ in)
FAA T-O field length: A 1,954 m (6,410 ft)
B 2,315 m (7,595 ft)
C 2,462 m (8,075 ft)
D 1,913 m (6,275 ft)
FAA landing field length, at max landing weight:
A 1,451 m (4,760 ft)
B 1,463 m (4,800 ft)
C 1,540 m (5,050 ft)
D 1,451 m (4,760 ft)
Range with max fuel:
D standard 2,980 nm (5,522 km; 3,431 miles)
D optional 3,650 nm (6,764 km; 4,203 miles)
Range (A, B, C with 155 passengers, domestic reserves; D with 130 passengers, domestic reserves):
A 1,630 nm (3,020 km; 1,877 miles)
B 2,176 nm (4,032 km; 2,505 miles)
C 2,618 nm (4,851 km; 3,014 miles)
D standard 2,405 nm (4,457 km; 2,769 miles)
D optional 2,874 nm (5,326 km; 3,309 miles)

OPERATIONAL NOISE LEVELS (FAR Pt 36):
T-O: A, B, C 90.4 EPNdB
D estimated 88.7 EPNdB
Sideline: A, B, C 94.6 EPNdB
D estimated 92.8 EPNdB
Approach: A, B, C 93.3 EPNdB
D estimated 93.3 EPNdB

MCDONNELL DOUGLAS MD-90

TYPE: MD-80 follow-on powered by IAE V2500 turbofans.
PROGRAMME: Launched 14 November 1989; first flight early 1993; certification and first deliveries fourth quarter 1994; MD-90-10 certification expected first quarter 1995.
VARIANTS: **MD-90-10:** Basic version; same fuselage length as MD-87; 114 passengers in two classes; two 97.86 kN (22,000 lb st) International Aero Engines V2522-D5 turbofans; max fuel 22,107 litres (5,840 US gallons; 4,863 Imp gallons).
MD-90-30: Has MD-80 fuselage lengthened by 1.45 m (4 ft 9 in) ahead of wing; same tail as MD-87; 153 two-class passengers; two 111.21 kN (25,000 lb st) IAE V2525-D5 turbofans; max fuel 22,107 litres (5,840 US gallons; 4,863 Imp gallons).
MD-90-40: 180 mixed-class passengers; two 124.55 kN (28,000 lb st) IAE V2528-D5 turbofans; max fuel 22,107 litres (5,840 US gallons; 4,863 Imp gallons).
MD-90-40EC: Tentative European configuration, with increased fuel and payload.
CUSTOMERS: Launch customer Delta Air Lines (50 ordered plus 115 on option); other customers include Alaska Airlines (20 plus 20), International Lease Finance Corporation (15 plus 15) and Japan Air System (10). Candidate for Chinese 'trunkliner' requirement.
DESIGN FEATURES: MD-90 has same fuselage cross-section, advanced high-lift wing and EFIS flight instruments as MD-80; standardised modular fuselage components will allow MD-90 and -80 to be built on same production line.
DIMENSIONS, EXTERNAL (A: MD-90-10, B: MD-90-30, C: MD-90-40):
Wing span: A, B, C 32.87 m (107 ft 10 in)
Length overall: A 39.75 m (130 ft 5 in)
B 46.51 m (152 ft 7 in)
C 52.30 m (171 ft 7 in)
Height overall: A 9.30 m (30 ft 6 in)
B, C 9.42 m (30 ft 11 in)
Wheel track: A, B, C 5.09 m (16 ft 8½ in)
Wheelbase: A 19.17 m (62 ft 10¾ in)
B 23.52 m (77 ft 2 in)
C 26.91 m (88 ft 3½ in)
DIMENSIONS, INTERNAL:
Baggage volume (total): A 26.56 m³ (938.0 cu ft)
B 38.03 m³ (1,343 cu ft)
C 48.11 m³ (1,699 cu ft)
AREAS:
Wings, gross: A, B, C 112.32 m² (1,209 sq ft)
WEIGHTS AND LOADINGS:
Operating weight empty: A 36,690 kg (80,887 lb)

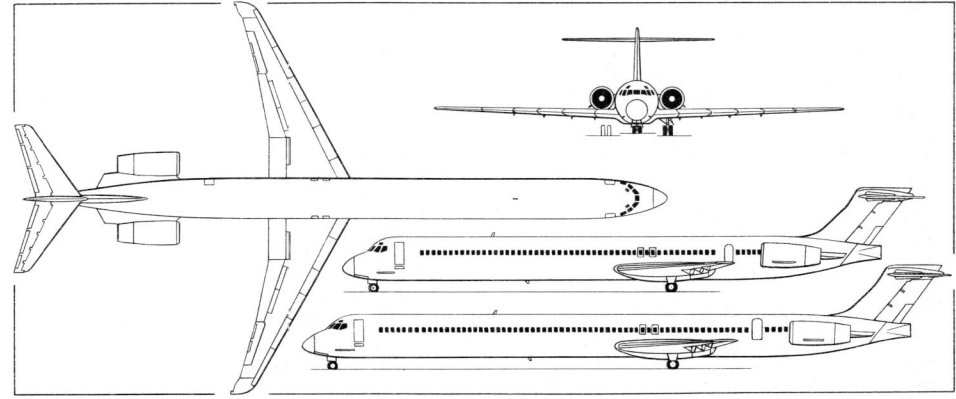

McDonnell Douglas MD-90-40EC with side view (upper) of MD-90-30 (two IAE V2525-D5 turbofans)
(Pilot Press)

Artist's impression of the McDonnell Douglas MD-90

B	39,275 kg (86,588 lb)
C	42,844 kg (94,455 lb)
Max T-O weight: A	63,050 kg (139,000 lb)
B	70,760 kg (156,000 lb)
C	74,160 kg (163,500 lb)
Max ramp weight: A	63,500 kg (140,000 lb)
B	71,215 kg (157,000 lb)
C	74,615 kg (164,500 lb)
Max zero-fuel weight: A	51,710 kg (114,000 lb)
B	58,965 kg (130,000 lb)
C	67,585 kg (149,000 lb)
Max landing weight: A	55,335 kg (122,000 lb)
B	64,410 kg (142,000 lb)
C	71,210 kg (157,000 lb)
Max wing loading: A	561.33 kg/m² (114.97 lb/sq ft)
B	629.98 kg/m² (129.03 lb/sq ft)
C	660.30 kg/m² (135.24 lb/sq ft)
Max power loading: A	322.14 kg/kN (3.16 lb/lb st)
B	318.14 kg/kN (3.12 lb/lb st)
C	297.71 kg/kN (2.92 lb/lb st)

PERFORMANCE (estimated, at max T-O weight, ISA, except where indicated):

Cruising speed at 10,670 m (35,000 ft): A, B, C

	Mach 0.76
FAA T-O field length: A	1,982 m (6,500 ft)
B	2,240 m (7,350 ft)
C	2,195 m (7,200 ft)

FAA landing field length, at max landing weight:

A	1,392 m (4,565 ft)
B	1,628 m (5,340 ft)
C	1,691 m (5,545 ft)

Range, with domestic reserves:

A	2,456 nm (4,551 km; 2,828 miles)
B	2,336 nm (4,329 km; 2,690 miles)
C	1,760 nm (3,261 km; 2,026 miles)

MCDONNELL DOUGLAS MD-XX

TYPE: MD-90 replacement.

PROGRAMME: Concept to be settled by end 1991; detailed design definition study to follow; discussed with Finnair, SAS and other airlines. Possible early 1996 launch, or earlier if customers reluctant to order MD-90 or interim MD-80 Advanced; first deliveries before year 2000.

DESIGN FEATURES: Technologically advanced short/medium-haul transport to improve passenger environment; designed to obviate excessively long cabin; provision of office facilities and modern communications techniques. Double-lobe fuselage section 4.4 m to 4.7 m (14 ft 5¼ in to 15 ft 5 in) wide with twin-aisle layout (2-3-2 seating); two-class cabin for 170-200 passengers; high aspect ratio (11.2) hybrid laminar flow wing; and two engines in 111.2-133.5 kN (25,000-30,000 lb st) thrust range, probably on underwing pylons. Possible technical features include composite primary and secondary structures in airframe; fly-by-light signalling; sidestick controls.

DIMENSIONS, EXTERNAL (provisional):

Wing span	39.3 m (128 ft 11¼ in)
Length of fuselage	46.0 m (150 ft 11 in)

PERFORMANCE (provisional):

Design max cruising speed	Mach 0.8
Max range	2,605 nm (4,828 km; 3,000 miles)

MCDONNELL DOUGLAS DC-10

TYPE: Three-turbofan medium-range airliner.

PROGRAMME: First flight of original DC-10 Series 10, 29 August 1970 (see also under Variants below); certificated 29 July 1971; last delivery Spring 1989. Described in 1990-91 and earlier *Jane's*.

VARIANTS: **DC-10 Series 10:** Initial version with max T-O weight 185,970 kg (410,000 lb) for US domestic services; three General Electric CF6-6D rated at 178 kN (40,000 lb st) each or -6D1 at 182.4 kN (41,000 lb st) each; later max T-O weight 206,385 kg (455,000 lb), with added centre wing fuel. Details in 1987-88 and earlier *Jane's*.

Series 15: Series 10 with 206,385 kg (455,000 lb) max T-O weight and 207 kN (46,500 lb st) GE CF6-50C2 engines; seven built. Details in 1987-88 *Jane's*.

Series 30: Intercontinental version; first flight 21 June 1972; certificated 21 November 1972; first deliveries to KLM and Swissair. Initial deliveries at max T-O weight 251,745 kg (555,000 lb); engines were CF6-50As rated at 218 kN (49,000 lb st) each or -50C at 227 kN (51,000 lb st) each. Later versions had max T-O weight up to 263,085 kg (580,000 lb) and powered by CF6-50C1s or -50C2s rated at 233.5 kN (52,500 lb st) each or CF6-50C2Bs at 236 kW (53,000 lb st) each; other features include more fuel, wing span increased by 3.05 m (10 ft 0 in), and additional two-wheel landing gear leg mounted on centreline.

Series 30ER: Further range extension with fuel tank in rear cargo compartment; powered by 240.2 kW (54,000 lb st) GE CF6-50C2B turbofans; first order (two) by Swissair July 1980 plus conversion of two existing Series 30s.

Series 30CF: Convertible freighter, also basis of USAF KC-10A Extender tanker/transport (which see). First flight 28 February 1973 powered by GE CF6-50A turbofans; first deliveries 1973 to Trans International Airlines and Overseas National Airways; total more than 30 Series 30CFs ordered. Similar to passenger Series 30 and 40 with capacity variable between 380 passengers plus baggage and 64,860 kg (143,000 lb) all-freight on intercontinental routes or up to 70,626 kg (155,700 lb) all-cargo on US transcontinental routes; two later Series 30CF powered by 233.5 kN (52,500 lb st) GE CF6-50C1s

delivered to Overseas National 1977. Features include overnight conversion; upward-opening side freight door 2.59 m high × 3.56 m wide (8 ft 6 in × 11 ft 8 in); maximum capacity 30 standard pallets on main deck and 132 m³ (4,670 cu ft) underfloor bulk cargo capacity.

Series 30F: Cargo-only version, generally similar to Series 30CF. Nine ordered by Federal Express delivered between 24 January 1986 and October 1988. Cargo capacity 80,282 kg (176,992 lb) with intercontinental range; powered by GE CF6-50C2 turbofans; main deck capacity 23 standard pallets; forward and centre underfloor bulk cargo compartments total 117.8 m³ (4,108 cu ft) volume.

Series 40: Extended range intercontinental version, powered by Pratt & Whitney JT9D turbofans; auxiliary fuel tank in rear of cargo compartment; first flight 28 February 1972; certificated 20 October 1972; Northwest Airlines received 22 early examples powered by 220 kN (49,400 lb st) JT9D-20s with water injection; first flight of later version for Japan Air Lines powered by 236 kN (53,000 lb st) JT9D-59As 25 July 1975. Delco Electronics performance management system (PMS) coupled to autothrottle and autopilot, saving 1 to 3 per cent fuel, certificated early 1983; first PMS-equipped DC-10 in service with JAL March 1983.

CUSTOMERS: Total 386 ordered.

DESIGN FEATURES: Three-man flight crew. Four integral wing fuel tanks with auxiliary fuel tank in wing centre section connected to bag tank in structural compartment; total fuel capacity about 138,165 litres (36,500 US gallons; 30,392 Imp gallons); optional tank in cargo area contains either 5,807 litres (1,534 US gallons; 1,277 Imp gallons) or 12,566 litres (3,317 US gallons; 2,762 Imp gallons).

MCDONNELL DOUGLAS EXTENDER

US Air Force designation: KC-10A

TYPE: Long-range military tanker/transport.

PROGRAMME: Selected as Advanced Tanker/Cargo Aircraft for USAF 19 December 1977; 60 ordered in annual lots and multi-year contract between November 1978 and 1987; first flight 12 July 1980; first delivery 17 March 1981; in service with 6th and 9th Air Refueling Squadron at March AFB, California, 2nd and 32nd ARS at Barksdale AFB and 344th and 911th ARS at Seymour Johnson AFB, North Carolina; some aircraft shared by AF Reserve 77th, 78th and 79th ARS (Associate); final aircraft delivered 4 April 1990 following trials with Flight Refuelling Mk 32B underwing hose-reel pods.

DESIGN FEATURES: Based on DC-10 Series 30CF (which see); can deliver 90,718 kg (200,000 lb) fuel to receivers at radius of 1,910 nm (3,540 km; 2,200 miles) from base; total onboard fuel, usable for own range or transferable, includes 108,062 kg (238,236 lb) of standard aircraft tankage plus seven fuel cells in underfloor cargo compartment totalling 53,446 kg (117,829 lb) fuel; max transfer rate 5,678 litres (1,500 US gallons; 1,249 Imp gallons) through boom and 1,590 litres (420 US gallons; 350 Imp gallons) through hose; Sargent-Fletcher FR600 hose/reel unit with max flow 2,271 litres (600 US gallons; 499.6 Imp gallons)/min in fuselage for US Navy/Marine receivers; KC-10A can be refuelled in flight through boom receptacle above flight deck; powered by three 233.53 kN (52,500 lb st) GE CF6-50C2 turbofans.

DIMENSIONS, EXTERNAL:

Wing span	50.40 m (165 ft 4½ in)
Wing chord: at root	10.71 m (35 ft 1¾ in)
at tip	2.73 m (8 ft 11½ in)
Wing aspect ratio	7.5
Length overall	55.35 m (182 ft 7 in)
Fuselage: Length	51.97 m (170 ft 6 in)
Max width	6.02 m (19 ft 9 in)
Height overall	17.70 m (58 ft 1 in)
Tailplane span	21.69 m (71 ft 2 in)

McDonnell Douglas DC-10 Series 30 in the insignia of Swissair, under charter to Air Afrique

The 60th production McDonnell Douglas KC-10A Extender, first to be equipped as a three-point tanker

Wheel track	10.57 m (34 ft 8 in)
Wheelbase	22.05 m (72 ft 4 in)

DIMENSIONS, INTERNAL:

Cabin: Length, from rear bulkhead of flight deck to rear	
cabin bulkhead	approx 41.45 m (136 ft 0 in)
Max width	5.72 m (18 ft 9 in)
Height (basic)	2.41 m (7 ft 11 in)

AREAS:

Wings, gross	367.7 m² (3,958 sq ft)
Ailerons: inboard (total)	7.68 m² (82.7 sq ft)
outboard (total)	9.76 m² (105.1 sq ft)
Trailing-edge flaps (total)	62.1 m² (668.2 sq ft)
Leading-edge slats (total)	43.84 m² (471.9 sq ft)
Spoilers (total)	12.73 m² (137.0 sq ft)
Fin	45.92 m² (494.29 sq ft)
Rudders (total)	10.29 m² (110.71 sq ft)
Tailplane	96.6 m² (1,040.2 sq ft)
Elevators (total)	27.7 m² (298.1 sq ft)

WEIGHTS AND LOADINGS:

Operating weight empty:	
tanker	109,328 kg (241,027 lb)
cargo	110,945 kg (244,591 lb)
Fuel at T-O: tanker	158,291 kg (348,973 lb)
Design fuel capacity	161,508 kg (356,065 lb)
Max cargo payload	76,843 kg (169,409 lb)
Design max T-O weight	267,620 kg (590,000 lb)
Max wing loading	727.8 kg/m² (149.06 lb/sq ft)
Max power loading	382.2 kg/kN (3.75 lb/lb st)

PERFORMANCE:

Critical field length	3,124 m (10,250 ft)
Max range with max cargo	
	3,797 nm (7,032 km; 4,370 miles)
Max ferry range, unrefuelled	
	9,993 nm (18,507 km; 11,500 miles)

MCDONNELL DOUGLAS MD-11

TYPE: Medium/long-range passenger and freight derivative of DC-10.

PROGRAMME: Revealed at Paris Air Show 1985; development began 1985; British Caledonian ordered nine 3 December 1986; official programme launch 30 December 1986; four-aircraft flight test programme (three with GE engines, one with P&W); first flight 10 January 1990 powered by CF6s; first flight of third prototype powered by P&W PW4460s 26 April 1990; certificated 8 November 1990; first delivery to Finnair 29 November 1990, entering service 20 December. Planned production 36 in 1991, 45 in 1992, 50 in 1993, 61 in 1994 and 62 in 1995. Certification with R-R Trent 650 planned for 1993.

VARIANTS: **MD-11:** Standard passenger version for 323 passengers in two-class layout; max range 7,008 nm (12,987 km; 8,070 miles).

MD-11 Combi: Mixed cargo/passenger version for four to 10 cargo pallets and 168 to 240 passengers; ranges from 5,210 nm (9,656 km; 6,000 miles) to 6,947 nm (12,875 km; 8,000 miles).

MD-11F: All-freight version.

CUSTOMERS: Firm orders for 184 aircraft, of which 15 delivered, and options for 208, by 6 June 1991.

COSTS: McDonnell Douglas backlog of firm MD-11 orders worth $17.8 billion in November 1990; development costs totalled $700 million; recurring costs were $2.8 billion.

DESIGN FEATURES: Winglets above and below each wingtip; tailplane has advanced cambered aerofoil, reduced sweepback and 7,571 litre (2,000 US gallon; 1,665 Imp gallon) fuel trim tank; extended tailcone of chisel profile; two-crew all-digital flight deck; restyled interior; choice of GE CF6-80C2D1F, P&W PW4460 or R-R Trent 650 engines; claimed 27 per cent greater range than DC-10-30 and 31 per cent lower seat-mile cost. Weight and drag of early aircraft above target. Wing has Douglas aerofoil section; sweepback at quarter-chord 35°; dihedral 6°; incidence at root 5° 51′.

Suppliers include Alenia (fin, rudder, fuselage panels, winglets), AP Precision Hydraulics (centreline and nose landing gear), Bendix Brake and Strut (mainwheels and carbon brakes), CASA (horizontal tail surfaces), General Dynamics Convair Division (fuselage sections), Embraer (outboard flap sections), Fischer GmbH (composite flap hinge fairings), Pneumo Abex Corporation (main landing gear), Rohr Industries (engine pylons), Honeywell (advanced flight deck and avionics), and Westland Aerospace (flap vane and inlet duct extension rings).

FLYING CONTROLS: Ailerons powered by National Water Lift actuators; electro-hydraulically actuated variable incidence tailplane with slotted elevators powered by Parker Hannifin and Teijin Seiki actuators; dual section rudder with rear section split into vertical segments; near full-span leading-edge slats, outer portions anti-iced by engine bleed air; double-slotted trailing-edge flaps with offset external hinges; five spoilers in groups of four and one on each wing; tailplane anti-iced by bleed from No. 2 engine; Category IIIb automatic landing (certificated April 1991) standard.

STRUCTURE: Composites used in virtually all control surfaces, engine inlets and cowlings and wing/fuselage fillets; wing has two-spar structural box with chordwise ribs and skins with spanwise stiffeners; upper winglet of ribs, spars and stiffened aluminium alloy skin with carbonfibre trailing-edge; lower winglet carbonfibre; inboard ailerons have metal structure with composites skin; outboard ailerons all-composites; inboard flaps composites-skinned metal; outboard flaps all-composites; spoilers aluminium honeycomb and skin; tailplane has carbonfibre trailing-edge; elevators carbonfibre.

LANDING GEAR: Hydraulically retractable tricycle type, with additional twin-wheel main unit mounted on the fuselage centreline. Nosewheel and centreline units retract forward, main units inward into fuselage. Twin-wheel steerable nose unit (±70°). Main gear comprises two four-wheel bogies. Oleo-pneumatic shock absorbers in all units. Loral nosewheels and Goodyear tyres size 40 × 15.5-16, pressure 13.44 bars (195 lb/sq in). Main and centreline units have Bendix wheels and Goodyear tyres size 54 × 21-24, pressure 13.79 bars (200 lb/sq in). Bendix carbon brakes with air convection cooling; Loral anti-skid system.

POWER PLANT: Three Pratt & Whitney PW4460 turbofans, each rated at 266.9 kN (60,000 lb st), or three General Electric CF6-80C2D1F turbofans, each rated at 273.57 kN (61,500 lb st), or three Rolls-Royce Trent 650 turbofans, each rated at 289-311 kN (65,000-70,000 lb st), two of which are mounted on underwing pylons, the third above the rear fuselage at the base of the fin. Rear engine inlet duct and fan cowl doors, and nose cowl outer barrels on wing-mounted engines, are of composites construction. Inner surfaces of engine nacelles are acoustically treated. Refuelling point in leading-edge of each wing.

ACCOMMODATION: Crew of two. Standard mixed class seating for 323 (MD-11) or 214 (Combi); max passenger capacity 410. Crew door and three passenger doors each side, all eight of which open sliding inward and upward. Two freight holds below cabin, forward and aft of wing, and one bulk cargo compartment in rear fuselage. Forward freight hold is heated and ventilated; rear freight hold heated only. MD-11 Combi has a cargo door in centre compartment on port side of fuselage for loading of pallets, a main deck cargo door on port rear side of cabin, and two additional emergency exit doors, one on each side of passenger cabin immediately forward of the main deck cargo door.

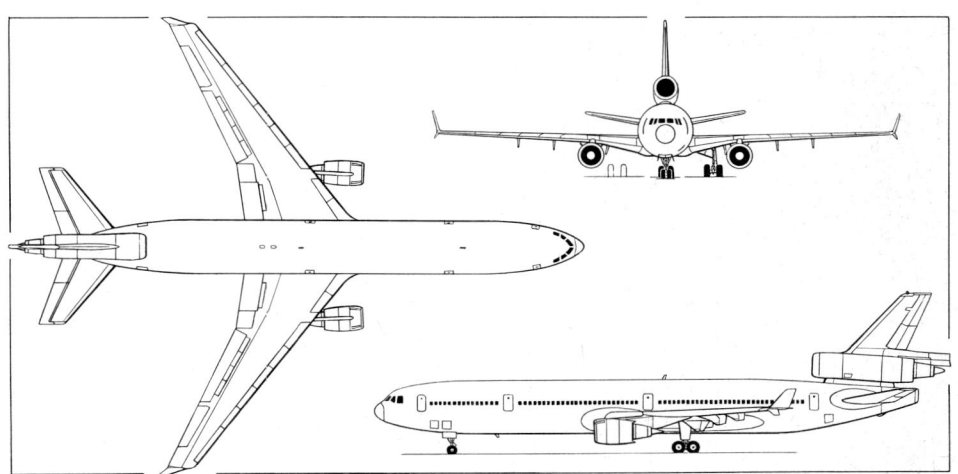

McDonnell Douglas MD-11 medium/long-range transport (*Pilot Press*)

The first McDonnell Douglas MD-11 prototype, powered by three General Electric CF6-80C2 turbofans

SYSTEMS: Air-conditioning system includes three AiResearch air bearing air cycle units with two automatic digital pressure controllers and electro-manual backup. Cabin max pressure differential 0.59 bar (8.6 lb/sq in). Three independent hydraulic systems for operation of flight controls and braking, with motor/pump interconnects to allow one system to power another. Electrical system comprises three 400Hz, 100/120kVA integrated drive generators, one per engine; one 90kVA generator in APU; 50Ah battery; four transformer-rectifiers to convert AC power to DC; and 25kVA drop-out air driven emergency generator. Pneumatic system, max controlled pressure 0.27-0.41 bar (4-6 lb/sq in) at 230°C, supplies air-conditioning, anti-icing for wing (outer slats) and tailplane leading-edges, galley vent jet pump, and cargo compartment floor heating. Plumbed gaseous oxygen system for crew, using EROS equipment; chemical oxygen generators with automatically deploying masks for passengers. Portable oxygen cylinders for attendants and first aid. Engine bleed air anti-icing for wing and tailplane leading-edges and engine cowlings. De-icing for windscreens, angle of attack sensors, TAT probe and static port plate. Garrett TSCP700-4E APU.

AVIONICS: Avionics integrator, Honeywell, responsible for flight guidance/flight deck system consisting of 44 line-replaceable units. These include aircraft system controllers (ASC) that perform flight engineering control and monitoring functions, providing automated hydraulic, electrical, environmental and fuel systems; a central fault display system (CFDS); an electronic instrument system (EIS) using six 20 × 20 cm (8 × 8 in) colour CRTs; a flight management system (FMS); an automatic flight system (AFS) featuring Cat IIIb autoland, windshear detection and guidance computer with escape capability and full-time longitudinal stability augmentation; a laser inertial reference system (IRS); and a digital air data computer (DADC).

DIMENSIONS, EXTERNAL:

Wing span	51.66 m (169 ft 6 in)
Wing chord: at root	10.71 m (35 ft 1¾ in)
at tip	2.73 m (8 ft 11½ in)
Wing aspect ratio	7.5
Length overall	61.21 m (200 ft 10 in)
Fuselage: Length	58.65 m (192 ft 5 in)
Max diameter	6.02 m (19 ft 9 in)
Height overall	17.60 m (57 ft 9 in)
Tailplane span	18.03 m (59 ft 2 in)
Wheel track	10.57 m (34 ft 8 in)
Wheelbase	24.61 m (80 ft 9 in)
Crew doors (two, each): Height	1.93 m (6 ft 4 in)
Width	0.81 m (2 ft 8 in)
Passenger doors (six, each): Height	1.93 m (6 ft 4 in)
Width	1.07 m (3 ft 6 in)
* Forward cargo door: Height	1.68 m (5 ft 6 in)
Width	2.64 m (8 ft 8 in)
Centre cargo door (standard): Height	1.68 m (5 ft 6 in)
Width	1.78 m (5 ft 10 in)
Bulk cargo door: Height	0.91 m (3 ft 0 in)
Width	0.76 m (2 ft 6 in)
Combi main deck cargo door (port, rear):	
Height	2.59 m (8 ft 6 in)
Width	4.06 m (13 ft 4 in)

* *Centre cargo door of Combi also this size*

DIMENSIONS, INTERNAL:

Cabin:	
Length, flight deck door to rear bulkhead	46.51 m (152 ft 7¼ in)
Max width	5.71 m (18 ft 9 in)
Max height	2.41 m (7 ft 11 in)
Floor area, incl galleys and toilets	244.7 m² (2,634.0 sq ft)
Volume, incl galleys and toilets	599.3 m³ (21,165 cu ft)
Baggage holds, volume:	
forward (containerised)	80.5 m³ (2,844 cu ft)
centre (containerised)	62.6 m³ (2,212 cu ft)
rear, bulk	14.4 m³ (510 cu ft)

AREAS:

Wings, gross	338.9 m² (3,648 sq ft)
Winglets (total)	7.42 m² (80.0 sq ft)
Vertical tail surfaces (total)	56.2 m² (605.0 sq ft)
Horizontal tail surfaces (total)	85.5 m² (920.0 sq ft)

WEIGHTS AND LOADINGS (A: MD-11, B: MD-11F, C: MD-11 Combi):

Operating weight empty: A	125,870 kg (277,500 lb)
B	111,580 kg (246,000 lb)
C	126,600 kg (279,100 lb)
Max payload: A	55,655 kg (122,700 lb)
B	92,215 kg (203,300 lb)
C	68,445 kg (150,900 lb)
Max fuel weight: A, B, C	117,525 kg (259,100 lb)
Max T-O weight: A, B, C	273,300 kg (602,500 lb)
Max zero-fuel weight: A	181,435 kg (400,000 lb)
B	204,700 kg (451,300 lb)
C	195,040 kg (430,000 lb)
Max landing weight: A	195,040 kg (430,000 lb)
B	213,870 kg (471,500 lb)
C	207,745 kg (458,000 lb)
Max wing loading: A, B, C	806.38 kg/m² (165.16 lb/sq ft)

PERFORMANCE (estimated: A: MD-11, B: MD-11F, C: MD-11 Combi):

Max Mach number (MMO): all	0.945
Max level speed at 8,230 m (27,000 ft): all	Mach 0.87 (519 knots; 962 km/h; 597 mph)
Max cruising speed at 9,150 m (30,000 ft): A, C	503 knots (932 km/h; 579 mph)
Econ cruising speed at 10,670 m (35,000 ft): all	473 knots (876 km/h; 544 mph)
Stalling speed, power on at max T-O weight:	
10° flap: A, B, C	148 knots (274 km/h; 171 mph)
25° flap: A, B, C	142 knots (263 km/h; 164 mph)
Max rate of climb at max T-O weight, at S/L: A, B, C	844 m (2,770 ft)/min
Rate of climb at S/L, one engine out: A, B, C	414 m (1,360 ft)/min
Service ceiling: A, B, C	9,935 m (32,600 ft)
Service ceiling, one engine out: A, B, C	6,310 m (20,700 ft)
Min ground turning radius:	
about nosewheel	26.67 m (87 ft 6 in)
about wingtip	35.90 m (117 ft 9½ in)
T-O run: A, B, C	2,207 m (7,240 ft)
T-O to 10.7 m (35 ft): A, B, C	2,926 m (9,600 ft)
Landing from 15 m (50 ft) at max landing weight:	
A	1,966 m (6,450 ft)
B	2,130 m (6,990 ft)
C	2,079 m (6,820 ft)
Runway LCN, rigid pavement, taxi weight of 276,010 kg (608,500 lb)	105
Runway ACN, conditions as above	65
Range with max payload, at max zero-fuel weight, with fuel to proceed to a 150 nm (278 km; 173 mile) alternate and make one missed approach, with FAR international reserves:	
A	5,002 nm (9,270 km; 5,760 miles)
B	3,542 nm (6,564 km; 4,079 miles)
C	4,024 nm (7,457 km; 4,634 miles)

MCDONNELL DOUGLAS MD-12X

TYPE: Longest range and highest capacity member of MD-11 family.

PROGRAMME: Programme launch probable in third quarter 1991 if about same commitments and customers exist as for MD-11; first flight possible in 1994, with certification in mid-1995; McDonnell Douglas looking for two partners each to take one-third risk share; Alenia (Italy) and CASA (Spain) possible.

VARIANTS: **Panoramic lower deck:** Total 440-passenger capacity, with 57 business class passengers in underfloor cabin forward of wing; cargo doors deleted and new keels and bulkheads to protect lower cabin; cargo capacity reduced; range reduced by 720 nm (1,334 km; 828 miles).

Advanced stretch: Range extended towards 8,000 nm (14,825 km; 9,200 miles) with same passenger capacity; optional panoramic underfloor cabin; basic passenger capacity 440 in three-class layout; six-wheel main landing gear trucks.

DESIGN FEATURES: Standard seating for 375 in three-class layout. Fuselage 10.66 m (35 ft) longer than MD-11; two Type A doors in 4.66 m (15.3 ft) plug aft of wing; max T-O weight 303,900 kg (670,000 lb); range with full passenger load about 8,000 nm (14,825 km; 9,212 miles); advanced wing design based on MD-11 but of much greater span and with chord extended aft of rear spar and re-designed flaps; three 275.8 kN (62,000 lb st) class turbofans; strengthened four-wheel centre landing gear; new APU; modified tail.

FLYING CONTROLS: Fly-by-wire control of wing control surfaces with automatic gust alleviation.

DIMENSIONS, EXTERNAL (approx):

Wing span	64.31 m (211 ft 0 in)
Length of fuselage	69.32 m (227 ft 5 in)

MCDONNELL DOUGLAS C-17A

TYPE: Long-range and intra-theatre heavy cargo transport.

PROGRAMME: US Air Force selected McDonnell Douglas to develop C-X cargo aircraft 29 August 1981; full-scale development called off January 1982 and replaced on 26 July 1982 by slow-paced preliminary development order; development and three prototypes (one flying) ordered 31 December 1985; fabrication of first C-17A (T-1/87-0025) began 2 November 1987; first production C-17A ordered 20 January 1988; assembly started at Long Beach 24 August 1988; assembly of first aircraft completed 21 December 1990; first flight scheduled for June 1991; second production C-17 (P-2) to fly 1992; production lot 3 (four aircraft, bringing total ordered to 10) ordered 1991; none funded in FY 1991; six and 12 planned for FY 1992-93; development to continue until 1993. First delivery in 1992 to 17th MAS at Charleston, South Carolina; IOC in 1994. By 1991, total requirement reduced from 210 to 120 aircraft; peak production target reduced from 24 to 18 per year; assembly in new 102,200 m² (1.1 million sq ft) facility at Long Beach, California. Feasibility study for hose-drogue tanker/transport combi under way Spring 1991.

COSTS: Originally expected unit cost $125 million. Programme unit cost now $294 million (1991), or $35,274 million for 120 aircraft.

DESIGN FEATURES: Externally blown flap system based on McDonnell Douglas YC-15 medium STOL transport prototypes (see 1979-80 *Jane's*), with extended flaps in exhaust flow from engines during take-off and landing; combines load-carrying capacity of C-5 with STOL performance of C-130; required to operate from 915 m (3,000 ft) long and 18.3 m (60 ft) wide runways, complete 180° three-point turn in 25 m (82 ft) and reverse up 1 in 50 gradient when fully loaded using thrust reversers. Structure designed to survive battle damage and protect crew; essential line-replaceable units (LRU) to be replaceable in flight; rear loading ramp. Supercritical wing with 25° sweepback; 2.90 m (9.5 ft) high NASA winglets.

FLYING CONTROLS: Outboard ailerons and four spoilers per wing; four elevator sections; two-surface rudder split into upper and lower segments; full-span leading-edge slats; single-slotted Fowler flaps over about two-thirds of trailing-edge; small strakes under tail. Quadruple-redundant digital fly-by-wire flight control system, with mechanical backup.

STRUCTURE: Major subassemblies produced in new factory at Macon, Georgia; subcontractors include Beechcraft (composites winglets), Delco Electronics Corporation (mission computer and electronic display system), Grumman Aerostructures (composites ailerons, rudder and elevators), GEC Avionics (advanced head-up displays), Lockheed (wing components up to sixth aircraft only), LTV (vertical and horizontal stabilisers, engine nacelles and thrust reversers), Reynolds Metals Company (wing skins), CC Industries (wing spars and stringers), Kaman Aerospace (wing ribs and bulkheads), Plessey (fuel pumps), Pyrotector Division of Graviner Inc (smoke detection systems), General Electric (electronic flight control system), Honeywell (air data computer), Martin Marietta (tailcone), Heath Tecna (wing-to-fuselage fillet), Aerostructures Hamble (composite flap hinge fairing and trailing-edge panels) and Northwest Composites (main landing gear pod panels).

LANDING GEAR: Hydraulically retractable tricycle type, with free-fall emergency extension. Twin-wheel Menasco nose unit and two six-wheel main units, designed for sink rate of 4.57 m (15 ft)/s and suitable for operation from paved runways or unpaved strips. Mainwheel units, each consisting of two legs in tandem with three wheels on each leg, rotate 90° to retract into fairings on lower fuselage sides; Menasco nose leg retracts forwards. Allied Signal wheels and carbon brakes.

POWER PLANT: Early aircraft will have four 185.5 kN (41,700 lb st) Pratt & Whitney F117-PW-100 turbofans with 181.0 kN (40,700 lb st) installed rating, pylon-mounted in individual underwing pods and each fitted with a directed-flow thrust reverser deployable both in flight and on the ground. Power plant contract open to competition for later C-17As. Provision for in-flight refuelling.

ACCOMMODATION: Normal flight crew of pilot and co-pilot, side by side on flight deck, plus a loadmaster in a station in the cargo hold. Provision for additional crew members if required for special missions. Access to flight deck via downward opening airstair door on port side of lower forward fuselage. Bunks for crew immediately aft of flight deck area; crew comfort station at forward end of cargo hold. Main cargo hold able to accommodate Army wheeled vehicles, including five-ton expandable vans in two rows, or three Jeeps side by side, or up to three AH-64A Apache attack helicopters, with straight-in loading via hydraulically actuated rear loading ramp which forms underside of rear fuselage when retracted. Alternatively, aircraft can be equipped as a troop transport, with rows of 27 stowable tip-up seats along each side wall and another 48 seats which can be erected along the centreline, or with litters for medical evacuation mission. Airdrop capability includes single platforms of up to 27,215 kg (60,000 lb), multiple platforms of up to 49,895 kg (110,000 lb), or up to 102 paratroops. Equipped for low altitude parachute extraction system (LAPES) drops. The C-17A will be the only aircraft able to airdrop outsize firepower the size of the US Army's new infantry fighting vehicle; it will also be able to carry the M1 main battle tank in combination with other vehicles. The cargo handling system includes rails for airdrops and rails/rollers for normal cargo handling. Each row of rails/rollers can be converted quickly by a single loadmaster from one configuration to the other. Cargo tiedown rings, each stressed for 11,340 kg (25,000 lb) all over cargo floor at 61 cm (24 in) intervals. Three quick-erecting litter stanchions, each supporting four litters, permanently carried. Main access to cargo hold is via rear loading ramp, which is itself stressed for 18,145 kg (40,000 lb) of cargo. Underfuselage door aft of ramp moves upward inside fuselage to facilitate loading and unloading. Paratroop door at rear on each side; two ditching exits overhead, aft of the paratroop doors, and two overhead forward of the wing box.

SYSTEMS: Include Allied Signal computer controlled integrated environmental control system and cabin pressure control system; quad-redundant flight control and four independent 276 bar (4,000 lb/sq in) hydraulic systems; independent fuel feed systems; electrical system; Allied Signal GTCP331 APU (at front of starboard landing gear pod), operable in flight, provides auxiliary power for environmental control system, engine starting, and on-ground electronics requirements; onboard inert gas generating system (OBIGGS) for the explosion protection system, pressurised by engine bleed air at 4.1 bars (60 lb/sq in) to produce NEA 4 gas and governed by a Gull Inc system controller; fire suppression system. All phases of cargo operation and configuration change capable of being handled by one loadmaster.

AVIONICS: General Electric digital fly-by-wire flight control system; Honeywell dual air data computers, with advanced digital avionics and four full-colour multifunction displays (MFDs), two GEC Avionics full flight regime head-up displays, plus integrated mission and communications keyboards (MCKs) and displays (MCDs). Primary flight data presented on HUD and a selectable mode for the MFD. Horizontal navigation situation, computer-generated flight plan and weather radar overlay selectable on MFD. Station keeping (SKE), engine and flight control configuration data available on MFDs. All frequency tuning for nav/com accomplished from glareshield control panel. MCDs have frequency and channel pre-storage facility and provide for flight plan entry manually or by preprogrammed cassette, permitting insertion of in-flight planning changes without disturbing ongoing navigation. All MCD information for flight and navigation monitoring is presented on the HUD and MFDs. Teledyne Controls warning and caution system. Master warning caution annunciator provides automatic monitoring of all main systems and provides visual alerts on glareshields, aural and voice alerts on intercom. Other equipment includes Allied Signal AN/APS-133[V] weather/mapping radar, Delco Electronics mission computer with MDC software; and electronic control system, Hamilton Standard aircraft and propulsion data management computer, General Dynamics automatic test equipment, and support equipment data acquisition and control system, LTV Sierra Research Division station keeping equipment, and Telephonic Corporation radio management system. Development of defensive electronic systems was authorised in 1988.

DIMENSIONS, EXTERNAL:
Wing span: wings only   50.29 m (165 ft 0 in)
          between winglet tips   52.20 m (171 ft 3 in)
Wing aspect ratio   7.16
Length overall   53.04 m (174 ft 0 in)
Height overall   16.79 m (55 ft 1 in)
DIMENSIONS, INTERNAL:
Cargo compartment:
Length, incl 6.05 m (19 ft 10 in) rear loading ramp
                                     26.82 m (88 ft 0 in)
Max width   5.49 m (18 ft 0 in)
Height under wing   3.76 m (12 ft 4 in)

First prototype McDonnell Douglas C-17A after completion at Long Beach

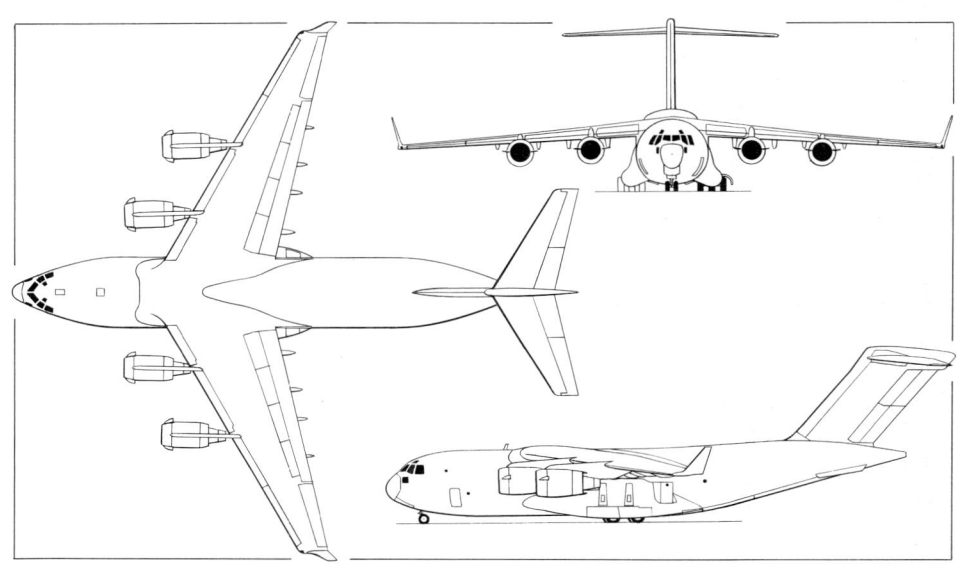

McDonnell Douglas C-17A long-range heavy lift transport *(Pilot Press)*

Max height   4.11 m (13 ft 6 in)
Volume   592 m³ (20,900 cu ft)
AREAS:
Wings, gross   353 m² (3,800 sq ft)
Ailerons (total)   11.83 m² (127.34 sq ft)
WEIGHTS AND LOADINGS (target):
Operating weight empty   122,016 kg (269,000 lb)
Typical payload:
  inter-theatre logistics mission (2.5g load factor)
                           56,245 kg (124,000 lb)
  heavy logistics mission (2.25g load factor)
                           69,535 kg (153,300 lb)
Max payload   78,108 kg (172,200 lb)
Max T-O weight   263,083 kg (580,000 lb)
Max wing loading   745.21 kg/m² (152.63 lb/sq ft)
Max power loading   363.37 kg/kN (3.56 lb/lb st)
PERFORMANCE (estimated, after USAF requirements reduced in early 1991):
Normal cruising speed at high altitude   Mach 0.77
Max cruising speed at low altitude
                    350 knots (648 km/h; 403 mph) CAS
Airdrop speed:
  at S/L
    115-250 knots (213-463 km/h; 132-288 mph) CAS
  at 7,620 m (25,000 ft)
    130-250 knots (241-463 km/h; 150-288 mph) CAS
Approach speed with max payload
                    115 knots (213 km/h; 132 mph) CAS
Min ground turning radius:
  three-point turn   25 m (82 ft)
  180° turn   34.74 m (114 ft)
  wingtip/tailplane clearance   72.24 m (237 ft)

Runway LCN (paved surface)   better than 49
T-O field length with 75,750 kg (167,000 lb) payload and fuel for 240 nm (445 km; 276 miles)
                                      2,286 m (7,500 ft)
Landing field length with 75,750 kg (167,000 lb) payload, using thrust reversal   915 m (3,000 ft)
Radius, T-O with 36,786 kg (81,100 lb) payload in 975 m (3,200 ft), land in 823 m (2,700 ft), T-O with similar payload in 853 m (2,800 ft) and land in 792 m (2,600 ft), all at load factor of 3g, no in-flight refuelling
                                      500 nm (925 km; 575 miles)
Radius, T-O with 56,245 kg (124,000 lb) payload in 2,012 m (6,600 ft) at load factor of 2.25g, land in 915 m (3,000 ft), T-O with zero payload (load factor of 3g) in 671 m (2,200 ft) and land in 701 m (2,300 ft), no in-flight refuelling   1,900 nm (3,520 km; 2,190 miles)
Range with payloads indicated, with no in-flight refuelling:
  75,750 kg (167,000 lb), T-O in 2,286 m (7,500 ft), land in 915 m (3,000 ft), load factor of 2.25g
                          2,400 nm (4,445 km; 2,765 miles)
  71,895 kg (158,500 lb), T-O in 2,320 m (7,600 ft), land in 885 m (2,900 ft), load factor of 2.25g
                          2,700 nm (5,000 km; 3,110 miles)
  56,245 kg (124,000 lb), T-O in 1,830 m (6,000 ft), land in 853 m (2,800 ft), load factor of 2.5g
                          2,800 nm (5,190 km; 3,225 miles)
  self-ferry (zero payload), T-O in 1,128 m (3,700 ft), land in 701 m (2,300 ft), load factor of 2.5g
                          4,700 nm (8,710 km; 5,412 miles)

MCDONNELL DOUGLAS HELICOPTER COMPANY
(Subsidiary of McDonnell Douglas Corporation)

5000 East McDowell Road, Mesa, Arizona 85205-9797
Telephone: 1 (602) 891 3000
Fax: 1 (602) 891 5599
Telex: 3719337 MD HC C MESA
OTHER WORKS: Culver City, California 90230
Telephone: 1 (213) 305 5000
Telex: 182436 HU HELI C CULV
PRESIDENT: Thomas M. Gunn
VICE-PRESIDENTS:
    Dean C. Borgman (MDX Programme)
    Jackie P. Brown (Production Division)
    Stuart D. Dodge (AH-64 Division)
    Ervin J. Hunter (Apache Programme)
    Andrew H. Logan (Advanced Product Development and Technology Division)
DIRECTOR, COMMUNICATIONS: Arnold Williams

Hughes Helicopters Inc became subsidiary of McDonnell Douglas Corporation 6 January 1984; name changed to McDonnell Douglas Helicopter Company 27 August 1985; 4,000 helicopters in service in 100 countries worldwide; series of new types under development; company teamed with Bell Helicopter Textron to develop one of two competing US Army Light Helicopter (LH) designs (declared unsuccessful April 1991: see under Bell/McDonnell Douglas in this section); Chain Gun systems manufactured at Culver City; research programmes include NOTAR (no tail rotor) system, composites rotor blades, hubs and tailbooms, metal insulation and IR suppression systems.

Main company base at Mesa, Arizona, with 52,955 m² (570,000 sq ft) AH-64 Apache assembly and testing factory and another 123,980 m² (1,334,500 sq ft) completed in 1986; workforce totalled 7,000 in 1990; MD 500/530 production line transferred to Mesa 1986-87.

Model 300 helicopter design rights sold to Schweizer Aircraft Corporation (which see) at Elmira, New York, 1986, following licence production by Schweizer since 1983; McDonnell Douglas helicopters produced under licence by RACA, Argentina (civil 500D and 500E), Kawasaki, Japan (civil and military 500D), Korean Air (civil and military 500D and 500E excluding TOW variants, and fuselages for all MD 500s sold worldwide), Agusta, Italy (500D, 500E and 530F civil variants).

McDonnell Douglas MD 530F used for search and rescue by the Chilean Army *(Kenneth Munson)*

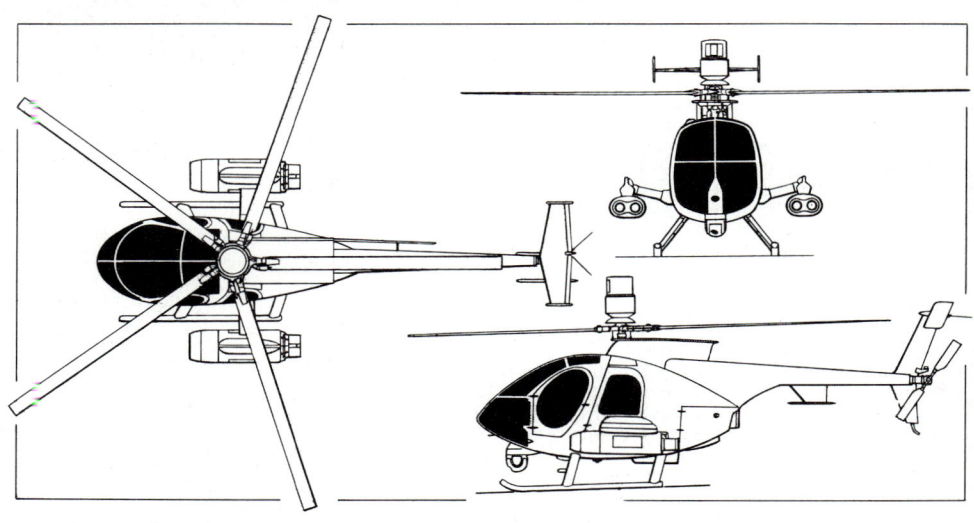

McDonnell Douglas 530MG Defender, with TOW missiles and mast-mounted sight *(Pilot Press)*

MCDONNELL DOUGLAS MD 500/530

TYPE: Single-engined utility helicopter.
PROGRAMME: Total 3,886 Model 500/530 series helicopters built by early 1991; MD 500 was initial basic civil production helicopter powered by Allison 250-C18A turboshaft; current 500E and 530F being produced at rate of 72 per year, increasing to 120 per year by 1992; military MD 500/530 and AH/MH-6 versions described separately; NOTAR 520N/530N also listed separately.

VARIANTS: **MD 500C:** US production ended 1978; powered by Allison 250-C20; produced under licence in Argentina (RACA) and Japan (Kawasaki).

MD 500D: Announced February 1975; first flight August 1974; first flight production aircraft 9 October 1975; powered by derated Allison 250-C20B; introduced five-blade main rotor and T tail; US production ended 1983; licence manufacture continues in Argentina (RACA), Italy (Agusta), Japan (Kawasaki) and Korea (Korean Air).

MD 500E: First flight (N5294A) 28 January 1982; replaced MD 500D in production 1982; deliveries started December 1982; 335.6 kW (450 shp) Allison 250-C20R became optional replacement for standard 250-C20B in late 1988; window area of forward canopy increased in 1991 model. Model MD 500E introduced more space for front and rear seat occupants, lower bulkhead between front and rear seats, new auxiliary fuel tank, T-layout flight instruments, better soundproofing around transmission, longer main rotor blade abrasion strips, new endplate fins, improved heating, optional air-conditioning and fore-and-aft litter kit. Four-blade Quiet Knight rotor optional to reduce external noise; dedicated law enforcement version can have 30 million candlepower SX-16 Nightsun searchlight, rescue net and steerable, stabilised infra-red sensor ball.

MD 530F Lifter: Powered by Allison 250-C30; transmission rating increased from 280 kW (375 shp) to 317 kW (425 shp) from 11 July 1985; diameter of main rotor increased by 0.3 m (1 ft 0 in) and of tail rotor by 5 cm (2 in); cargo hook for 907 kg (2,000 lb) external load available; first flight 22 October 1982; certificated 29 July 1983; first delivery 20 January 1984.

CUSTOMERS: Total 80 civil and military MD 500/530s delivered in 1990; outstanding orders totalled more than 90; Hungarian Police Aviation Force ordered six MD 500Es, delivered in 1990; Iraq received 26 MD 530Fs for civil training, transport and agricultural work.

DESIGN FEATURES: Fully articulated five-blade main rotor with blades retained by stack of laminated steel straps; blades can be folded after removing retention pins; two-blade tail rotor with optional X-pattern four-blade Quiet Knight tail rotor to reduce external noise; optional high skid landing gear to protect tail rotor in rough country; protective skid on base of lower fin; narrow-chord fin with high-set tailplane and endplate fins introduced with MD 500D. Main rotor rpm (500E/530F) 492/477 normal; main rotor tip speed 207-208 m (680-684 ft/s; tail rotor rpm, 2,933/2,848; MCP transmission rating 261 kW (350 shp).

FLYING CONTROLS: Flying controls plain mechanical without hydraulic boost. Pilot sits on left instead of normal right-hand seating.

STRUCTURE: Airframe based on two A frames from rotor head to landing gear legs enclosing rear-seat occupants; front-seat occupants protected within straight line joining rotor hub and forward tips of landing skids; engine mounted inclined in rear of fuselage pod with access through clamshell doors; main rotor blades have extruded aluminium spar hot-bonded to wraparound aluminium skin; tail rotor blades have swaged tubular spar and metal skin.

Data below refer to MD 500E and 530F, except where indicated:

LANDING GEAR: Tubular skids carried on McDonnell Douglas oleo-pneumatic shock absorbers. Utility floats, snow skis and emergency inflatable floats optional.

POWER PLANT: MD 500E is powered by a 313 kW (420 shp) Allison 250-C20B turboshaft, which is derated to 280 kW (375 shp) for T-O and has a max continuous rating of 261 kW (350 shp). Allison 250-C20R, rated at 280 kW (375 shp) for T-O and 261 kW (350 shp) max continuous, optional. MD 530F has a 485 kW (650 shp) Allison 250-C30 turboshaft, derated to 317 kW (425 shp) for take-off and 261 kW (350 shp) max continuous. Two interconnected bladder fuel tanks with combined usable capacity of 232 litres (61.3 US gallons; 51 Imp gallons). Self-sealing fuel tank optional. Refuelling point on starboard side of fuselage. Auxiliary fuel system, with 79.5 litre (21 US gallon; 17.5 Imp gallon) internal tank, available optionally. Oil capacity 5.7 litres (1.5 US gallons; 1.2 Imp gallons).

ACCOMMODATION: Forward bench seat for pilot and two passengers, with two or four passengers, or two litter patients and one medical attendant, in rear portion of cabin. Low-back front seats and individual front seats, with fabric or leather upholstery, optional. Baggage space, capacity 0.31 m³ (11 cu ft), under and behind rear seat in five-seat form. Clear space for 1.19 m³ (42 cu ft) of cargo or baggage with only three front seats in place. Two doors on each side. Interior soundproofing optional.

SYSTEMS: Aero Engineering Corporation air-conditioning system or Fargo pod mounted air-conditioner optional.

AVIONICS (MD 500E): Optional avionics include dual Bendix/King KY 195 com, KX 175 nav/com, KR 85 ADF, and KT 76 transponder; dual Collins VHF-251 com, VHF-251/351 nav/com, IND-350 nav indicator, ADF-650 ADF, and TDR-950 transponder; intercom system, headsets, microphones; and public address system.

EQUIPMENT: Standard equipment includes outside air temperature gauge, 8-day clock, engine hour meter, five sets inertia reel shoulder harness, cargo tiedown fittings, fire extinguisher, first aid kit, passenger steps, ground handling wheels, external power socket, landing light, skid-tip position light, anti-collision strobe lights, navigation lights, cockpit utility light, aft cabin light, and instrument lights. Optional equipment includes shatterproof glass, heating/demisting system, radios and intercom, attitude and directional gyros, rate of climb indicator, nylon mesh seats, dual controls, cargo hook, cargo racks, underfuselage cargo pod, heated pitot tube, extended landing gear, blade storage rack, litter kit, emergency inflatable floats and inflated utility floats. FAA supplemental certification has been received for installing a 30 million candlepower Spectrolab SX-16 Nightsun searchlight.

DIMENSIONS, EXTERNAL:

Main rotor diameter: 500E		8.05 m (26 ft 5 in)
530F		8.33 m (27 ft 4 in)
Main rotor blade chord		0.171 m (6¾ in)
Tail rotor diameter: 500E		1.37 m (4 ft 6 in)
530F		1.42 m (4 ft 8 in)
Distance between rotor centres:		
500E		4.67 m (15 ft 4 in)
530F		4.88 m (16 ft 0 in)
Length overall, rotors turning:		
500E		8.61 m (28 ft 3 in)
530F		8.97 m (29 ft 5 in)
Length of fuselage		7.49 m (24 ft 7 in)
Height to top of rotor head (standard skids: for extended skids add 0.27 m; 11¾ in): 500E		2.67 m (8 ft 9 in)
530F		2.67 m (8 ft 9 in)
Tailplane span		1.65 m (5 ft 5 in)
Skid track (standard)		1.91 m (6 ft 3 in)
Cabin doors (each): Height		1.13 m (3 ft 8½ in)
Max width		0.76 m (2 ft 6 in)
Height to sill: 500E		0.79 m (2 ft 7 in)
530F		0.76 m (2 ft 6 in)
Cargo compartment doors (each):		
Height		1.12 m (3 ft 8¼ in)
Width		0.88 m (2 ft 10½ in)
Height to sill: 500E		0.71 m (2 ft 4 in)
530F		0.66 m (2 ft 2 in)

DIMENSIONS, INTERNAL:

Cabin: Length	2.44 m (8 ft 0 in)
Max width	1.31 m (4 ft 3½ in)
Max height	1.52 m (5 ft 0 in)

AREAS:

Main rotor blades (each): 500E	0.62 m² (6.67 sq ft)
530F	0.65 m² (6.96 sq ft)
Tail rotor blades (each): 500E	0.063 m² (0.675 sq ft)
530F	0.066 m² (0.711 sq ft)
Main rotor disc: 500E	50.89 m² (547.81 sq ft)
530F	54.58 m² (587.50 sq ft)
Tail rotor disc: 500E	1.53 m² (16.47 sq ft)
530F	1.65 m² (17.72 sq ft)
Fin	0.56 m² (6.05 sq ft)
Tailplane	0.76 m² (8.18 sq ft)

WEIGHTS AND LOADINGS:

Weight empty: 500E	655 kg (1,445 lb)
530F	717 kg (1,580 lb)
Max normal T-O weight: 500E	1,361 kg (3,000 lb)
530F	1,406 kg (3,100 lb)
Max overload T-O weight:	
500E, 530F	1,610 kg (3,550 lb)
Max gross weight, external load:	
530F	1,701 kg (3,750 lb)
Max normal disc loading:	
500E	26.76 kg/m² (5.48 lb/sq ft)
530F	25.78 kg/m² (5.28 lb/sq ft)
Max normal power loading:	
500E	4.87 kg/kW (8.00 lb/shp)
530F	4.44 kg/kW (7.29 lb/shp)

PERFORMANCE (A: 500E, B: 530F, at max normal T-O weight):

Never-exceed speed (V_{NE}) at S/L:	
A, B	152 knots (282 km/h; 175 mph)
Max cruising speed at S/L:	
A	134 knots (248 km/h; 154 mph)
B	133 knots (246 km/h; 153 mph)
Max cruising speed at 1,525 m (5,000 ft):	
A	132 knots (245 km/h; 152 mph)
B	134 knots (248 km/h; 154 mph)
Econ cruising speed at S/L:	
A	129 knots (239 km/h; 149 mph)
B	131 knots (243 km/h; 151 mph)
Econ cruising speed at 1,525 m (5,000 ft):	
A, B	123 knots (228 km/h; 142 mph)
Max rate of climb at S/L: A	536 m (1,760 ft)/min
B	631 m (2,070 ft)/min
Vertical rate of climb at S/L: A	248 m (813 ft)/min
B	446 m (1,462 ft)/min
Service ceiling: A	4,575 m (15,000 ft)
B	4,875 m (16,000 ft)
Hovering ceiling IGE: ISA: A	2,590 m (8,500 ft)
B	4,360 m (14,300 ft)
ISA + 20°C: A	1,830 m (6,000 ft)
B	3,660 m (12,000 ft)
Hovering ceiling OGE: ISA: A	1,830 m (6,000 ft)
B	3,660 m (12,000 ft)
ISA + 20°C: A	975 m (3,200 ft)
B	2,970 m (9,750 ft)
Range, 2 min warm-up, standard fuel, no reserves:	
A at S/L	233 nm (431 km; 268 miles)
B at S/L	202 nm (374 km; 232 miles)
A at 1,525 m (5,000 ft)	258 nm (478 km; 297 miles)
B at 1,525 m (5,000 ft)	228 nm (422 km; 262 miles)

MCDONNELL DOUGLAS MODEL 500/530 DEFENDER

US Army designations: AH-6, MH-6

TYPE: Military derivatives of MD 500/530.

PROGRAMME: Earlier 500MD Scout Defender, TOW Defender, 500MD/ASW Defender and 500MD Defender II described in 1987-88 and earlier *Jane's*. Except for TOW Defender, military Defenders have same airframe as current civil 500/530; versions available detailed below.

VARIANTS: **500MG Defender:** As 530MG, but with 313 kW (420 shp) Allison 250-C20B and MD 500E rotor system.

TOW Defender: Retains round nose of original MD 500; M65 TOW sight in nose; carries four TOW missiles; available with Allison 250-C20, 250-C20B or 250-C30.

Paramilitary MG Defender: Introduced July 1985 as low-cost helicopter suitable for police, border patrol, rescue, narcotics control and internal security use; available in either 500E or 530F configurations.

530MG Defender: Based on MD 530F Lifter; first flight of prototype/demonstrator (N530MG) 4 May 1984; designed mainly for point attack and anti-armour, but also suitable for scout, day and night surveillance, utility, cargo lift and light attack; integrated crew station with multi-function display allows hands on lever and stick (HOLAS) control of weapon delivery, communications and flight control; HOLAS based on Racal RAMS 3000 designed for all-weather and NOE flight and connected to MIL-STD-1553B digital databus linking the processor interface unit (PIU), control and display unit (CDU) and data transfer unit (DTU); CDU used for flight planning, navigation, frequency selection and subsystem management and has its own monochrome display and keyboard; multi-function display is high definition monochrome tube with symbolic and

McDonnell Douglas 500MG Defender of the Philippine Air Force with seven-tube 2.75 in rocket launcher

alphanumeric capability; data input to DTU using ground loader unit inserted in cockpit receptacle.

Other equipment includes Astronics Corporation autopilot; Decca Doppler navigator with Racal Doppler velocity sensor; GEC Ferranti FIN 1110 AHRS; twin Collins VHF/UHF AM/FM radios; Bendix/King HF radio, ADF/VOR, radar altimeter and transponder; Telephonics intercom; SFENA attitude indicator. Options include mast-mounted Hughes TOW sight, FLIR, radar warning receiver, IFF, ground proximity warning system (GPWS) and laser ranger.

Weapons qualified or tested include TOW 2, FN pods containing 7.62 mm or 0.50 in machine gun and 2.75 in rockets in 7-tube or 12-tube launchers; stores attached by standard 14 in NATO racks. Future armament will include General Dynamics air-to-air Stinger and 7.62 mm McDonnell Douglas Chain Gun. Chaff and flare dispensers with automatic chaff discharge available. Both cyclic sticks have triggers for gun or rocket firing; co-pilot/gunner's visual image display has two handgrips for TOW/FLIR operation.

Nightfox: Introduced 1986 for low-cost night surveillance and military operations; equipment includes FLIR Systems Series 2000 thermal imager and night vision goggles, with same weapons as 530MG; available in both 500MG and 530MG forms.

AH-6 and MH-6: Total 12 AH-6s and 17 MH-6s believed in service with US Army 160th Special Operations Aviation Regiment (Night Stalkers) based at Fort Campbell, Kentucky; deployed in Gulf in September 1987 operating from USS *Jarrett*; identified variants include **MH-6B, AH-6C** and **EH-6B** conversions from OH-6A, of which most withdrawn from operational service; **AH-6F** and **MH-6E** based on MD 500MG; **AH-6G** and **MH-6F** based on MD 530MG; all can carry 7.62 mm Minigun, machine-gun and rocket pods with provision for air-to-air Stinger; MH-6E and MH-6F have multi-function displays and FLIR used in association with night vision goggles. US Army plans conversion of

up to 36 AH/MH-6s to NOTAR configuration (which see), plus single-axis (yaw only) stability augmentation system; first two returned to manufacturer April 1991.

CUSTOMERS: Include 22 500MG Defenders for delivery (August 1990 onwards) to Philippine Air Force, and four 500MG Nightfoxes reportedly delivered to Colombian Air Force.

DIMENSIONS, EXTERNAL (A: 500MD/TOW, B: 530MG):

As for 500E/530F except:

Length of fuselage: A	7.62 m (25 ft 0 in)
B	7.29 m (23 ft 11 in)
Height to top of rotor head: A	2.64 m (8 ft 8 in)
B	2.62 m (8 ft 7 in)
B with MMS	3.41 m (11 ft 2½ in)
Height over tail (endplate fins):	
A	2.71 m (8 ft 10½ in)
B	2.59 m (8 ft 6 in)
Width over skids: A	1.93 m (6 ft 4 in)
B	1.96 m (6 ft 5 in)
Width over TOW pods: A, B	3.23 m (10 ft 7¼ in)
Tailskid ground clearance: A	0.64 m (2 ft 1¼ in)
B	0.61 m (2 ft 0 in)

WEIGHTS AND LOADINGS:

Weight empty, equipped: A	849 kg (1,871 lb)
B	898 kg (1,979 lb)
Max T-O weight: A, normal	1,361 kg (3,000 lb)
A, max overload	1,610 kg (3,550 lb)
B, normal	1,406 kg (3,100 lb)
B, max overload	1,701 kg (3,750 lb)
Max disc loading: B	33.44 kg/m² (6.85 lb/sq ft)

PERFORMANCE (at max normal T-O weight, except where indicated):

Never-exceed speed (V_{NE}) at S/L:	
A, B	130 knots (241 km/h; 150 mph)
Max cruising speed at S/L:	
A, B	121 knots (224 km/h; 139 mph)
Max cruising speed at 1,525 m (5,000 ft):	
A	120 knots (222 km/h; 138 mph)
B	123 knots (228 km/h; 142 mph)

McDonnell Douglas AH-6F of the US Army's 160th Special Operations Aviation Regiment, fitted with Stinger missiles (*Ivo Sturzenegger*)

Max rate of climb at S/L, ISA: A	520 m (1,707 ft)/min
B	626 m (2,055 ft)/min
Vertical rate of climb at S/L: A	248 m (813 ft)/min
B	445 m (1,660 ft)/min
Service ceiling: A	4,635 m (15,210 ft)
B	over 4,875 m (16,000 ft)
Hovering ceiling IGE: ISA: A	2,590 m (8,500 ft)
B	4,360 m (14,300 ft)
ISA + 20°C: A	1,830 m (6,000 ft)
B	3,660 m (12,000 ft)
A, 35°C	1,341 m (4,400 ft)
B, 35°C	2,680 m (8,800 ft)
Hovering ceiling OGE: ISA: A	1,830 m (6,000 ft)
B	3,660 m (12,000 ft)
ISA + 20°C: A	975 m (3,200 ft)
B	2,970 m (9,750 ft)
A, 35°C	732 m (2,400 ft)
B, 35°C	2,120 m (6,950 ft)
Range, 2 min warm-up, standard fuel, no reserves:	
A at S/L	203 nm (376 km; 233 miles)
B at S/L	176 nm (326 km; 202 miles)
A at 1,525 m (5,000 ft)	227 nm (420 km; 261 miles)
B at 1,525 m (5,000 ft)	200 nm (370 km; 230 miles)
Endurance with standard fuel, 2 min warm-up, no reserves: A at S/L	2 h 23 min
B at S/L	1 h 56 min
A at 1,525 m (5,000 ft)	2 h 35 min
B at 1,525 m (5,000 ft)	2 h 7 min

McDonnell Douglas MD 530N with NOTAR tailboom

MCDONNELL DOUGLAS MD 520N and MD 530N NOTAR HELICOPTERS

TYPE: Light utility helicopter with no tail rotor.

PROGRAMME: First flight OH-6A NOTAR testbed 17 December 1981; programme details in 1982-83 *Jane's*; extensive modifications during 1985 with second blowing slot, new fan, 250-C20B engine and MD 500E nose; flight testing resumed 12 March 1986 and completed in June.

Commercial MD 520N and MD 530N NOTAR helicopters announced February 1988 and officially launched January 1989, to be powered by 335.6 kW (450 shp) 250-C20R-2 and 485 kW (650 shp) 250-C30 respectively; first flight of first MD 530N (N530NT) 29 December 1989; first flight 520N 1 May 1990; certification of 530N delayed from September 1990 to mid-1991 and of 520N from September 1990 to 'later in 1991'.

VARIANTS: **MD 520N:** NOTAR version of MD 500, offering more power, higher operating altitude and greater max T-O weight than MD 500E. Transmission take-off power 280 kW (375 shp); max continuous 261 kW (350 shp). Fuel capacity 235 litres (62 US gallons; 51.6 Imp gallons).

MD 530N: NOTAR companion to MD 520N, offering 40 per cent more power for high-altitude, hot day performance at max T-O weights. Transmission take-off power 317 kW (425 shp); max continuous 261 kW (350 shp). Fuel capacity as for MD 520N.

Military variants: Also being developed, including retrofit of some US Army AH/MH-6s.

CUSTOMERS: Orders for 160 MD 520N/530N received by January 1991, including seven MD 520Ns for Phoenix, Arizona, police. Planned production sold until 1994.

COSTS: Original $2.2 million 24-month contract from US Army Applied Technology Laboratory and Defense Advanced Research Projects Agency (DARPA) for modification of OH-6A (65-12917).

DESIGN FEATURES: NOTAR (no tail rotor) system provides anti-torque and steering control without an external tail rotor, thus eliminating the danger of tail strikes; air emerging through Coanda slots and steering louvres is cool and at low velocity. Main rotor rpm 477; main rotor tip speed 208 m (684 ft)/s; NOTAR system fan rpm 5,388.

FLYING CONTROLS: Flying controls unboosted mechanical, as in earlier models. Rotor downwash over tailboom deflected to port by two Coanda-type slots fed with low-pressure air from engine driven variable-pitch fan in root of tailboom; this counters normal rotor torque; some of fan air is also vented at tail through variable-aperture louvres controlled by pilot's foot pedals, giving steering control in hover and forward fight. Two moving fins on tailplane also connected to foot pedals, primarily to increase directional control during autorotation and allow touchdown at under 20 knots (37 km/h; 23 mph); additional fixed fin added under tailboom for spiral stability. Stability augmentation system installed 1991, to adjust starboard fin to offset unwanted yaw.

STRUCTURE: Same as for earlier models, but graphite composites tailboom; metal tailplane and fins; new high-efficiency fan with composites blades fitted in production aircraft.

DIMENSIONS, EXTERNAL (A: MD 520N, B: MD 530N):

Rotor diameter: A, B	8.33 m (27 ft 4 in)
Length: overall, rotor turning: A, B	8.69 m (28 ft 6 in)
fuselage: A, B	7.62 m (25 ft 0 in)
Height to top of rotor head:	
standard skids: A, B	2.74 m (9 ft 0 in)
extended skids: A, B	3.01 m (9 ft 10¾ in)
Height to top of fins: A, B	2.22 m (7 ft 4 in)
Tailplane span: A, B	2.07 m (6 ft 9½ in)
Skid track: A, B	1.98 m (6 ft 6 in)

AREAS:

Rotor disc	54.5 m² (586.8 sq ft)

WEIGHTS AND LOADINGS (A: MD 520N, B: MD 530N):

Weight empty: standard: A, B	742 kg (1,636 lb)
Max fuel weight: A, B	183 kg (404 lb)
Max hook capacity: A, B	1,004 kg (2,214 lb)
Max T-O weight: normal: A, B	1,519 kg (3,350 lb)
external load: A, B	1,746 kg (3,850 lb)
Max normal disc loading: A, B	27.87 kg/m² (5.71 lb/sq ft)
Max normal power loading:	
A	5.44 kg/kW (8.93 lb/shp)
B	4.80 kg/kW (7.88 lb/shp)

PERFORMANCE (A: MD 520N, B: MD 530N, at normal max T-O weight, ISA, except where indicated):

Never-exceed speed (VNE):	
A, B	152 knots (281 km/h; 175 mph)
Max cruising speed at S/L:	
A, B	135 knots (249 km/h; 155 mph)
Max rate of climb at S/L:	
A, B: ISA	564 m (1,850 ft)/min
A, B: ISA + 20°C	480 m (1,575 ft)/min
Service ceiling: A	4,320 m (14,175 ft)
B	4,875 m (16,000 ft)
Hovering ceiling IGE: ISA:	
A	2,753 m (9,034 ft)
B	3,596 m (11,800 ft)
Hovering ceiling OGE: ISA:	
A	1,537 m (5,043 ft)
B	2,896 m (9,500 ft)
ISA + 20°C:	1,292 m (4,241 ft)
Range at S/L: A	217 nm (402 km; 250 miles)
B	191 nm (354 km; 220 miles)
Endurance at S/L: A	2 h 24 min
B	1 h 54 min

MCDONNELL DOUGLAS MDX

TYPE: Eight/ten-seat light twin-engined helicopter.

PROGRAMME: Announced February 1988; launched January 1989; Hawker de Havilland Limited of Australia became partner in February 1989 to complete design and manufacture airframes for shipping to McDonnell Douglas Helicopter at Mesa, Arizona; transmissions to be manufactured by Kawasaki Heavy Industries, Japan; other partners being sought. First flight planned for July 1992, with certification by October 1993 and deliveries in December 1993.

CUSTOMERS: Certificates of interest held for 271 by end 1990, representing planned production until 1997; market estimated at 800 to 1,000 in first decade; planned production rate 108 a year by 1996.

COSTS: Target direct operating cost $243 (1991) per hour.

DESIGN FEATURES: NOTAR anti-torque system; HARP-type all-composite five-blade main rotor with bearingless flex-beam blade retention and pitch case for controlling blade pitch; tuned fixed rotor mast and mounting truss reduces vibration; frangible blade tips; NOTAR fan maintained on condition. Modified A frame structure from rotor mounting to landing skids protects passenger cabin. Engines widely spaced to prevent contagious failures.

FLYING CONTROLS: NOTAR has a tailboom slightly pressurised by a variable-pitch engine-driven fan; some air escapes through two Coanda effect slots to deflect rotor downwash to port and counteract torque; variable-area orifice at tail controlled by pilot's foot pedals produces side thrust for directional control. Auto-stabiliser and autopilot offered for IFR operation.

STRUCTURE: Cockpit, cabin and tail largely carbonfibre; top fairings Kevlar composites; no magnesium. Transmission overhaul life 5,000 hours; rotor blades and hub on condition.

LANDING GEAR: Fixed skids.

POWER PLANT: First 100 MDXs to be powered by two 450 kW (603 shp) P&WC PW206As; thereafter, Turbomeca TM319-2 Arrius at same power will be optional. Fuel contained in single tank under passenger cabin holding 553 litres (146 US gallons; 122 Imp gallons) or 666 litres (176 US gallons; 146 Imp gallons).

ACCOMMODATION: Two pilots or pilot/passenger in front; six passengers in club-type seating in main cabin; rear baggage compartment accessible through rear door. Impact absorbing seats. Cabin can accept long loads reaching from flight deck to rear door.

AVIONICS: Single- or two-pilot IFR avionics with appropriate instrument panels incorporating Integrated Instrumentation Display System electronic display of engine and system data; panel space for weather in IFR version or

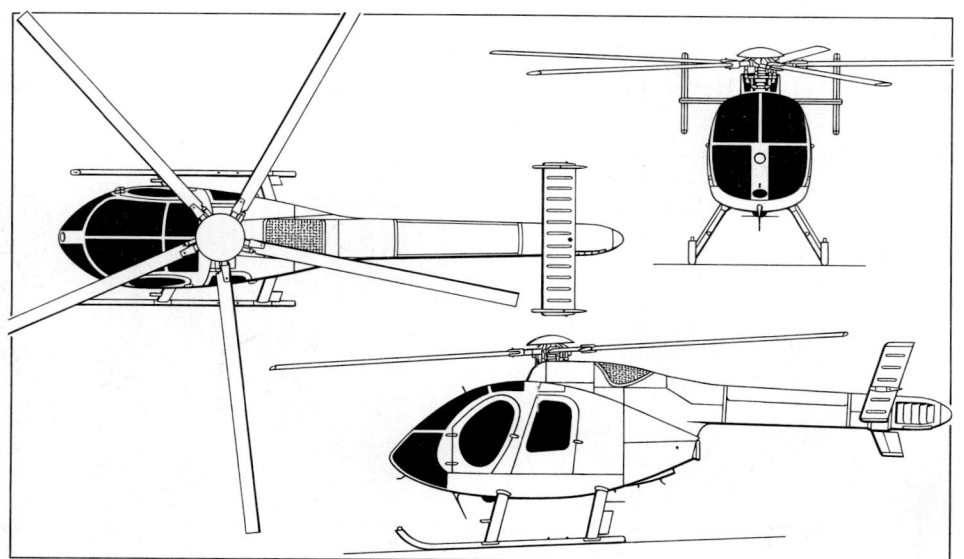

McDonnell Douglas MD 530N five-seat NOTAR helicopter *(Jane's/Mike Keep)*

FLIR display in law enforcement version; provision for radar altimeter.

EQUIPMENT: External cargo hook with 1,361 kg (3,000 lb) capacity.

DIMENSIONS, EXTERNAL:

Main rotor diameter	10.30 m (33 ft 9½ in)
Length: overall, rotor turning	11.64 m (38 ft 2½ in)
fuselage	9.66 m (31 ft 8½ in)
Fuselage width	1.70 m (5 ft 7½ in)
Height, incl rotor	3.74 m (12 ft 4 in)
Min ground clearance	0.42 m (1 ft 4¾ in)
Skid track	2.22 m (7 ft 3½ in)
Tailplane span	2.92 m (9 ft 7¼ in)

DIMENSIONS, INTERNAL:

Volumes: Cabin	3.43 m³ (121.2 cu ft)
Baggage compartment	1.10 m³ (38.8 cu ft)
Cabin door width	1.26 m (4 ft 2 in)

AREAS:

Main rotor disc	11.14 m² (120 sq ft)

WEIGHTS AND LOADINGS:

Weight empty	1,261 kg (2,780 lb)
Max T-O weight	2,540 kg (5,600 lb)
Max weight with slung load	2,812 kg (6,260 lb)
Internal payload, pilot and full fuel	771 kg (1,700 lb)
Useful load at T-O weight	1,279 kg (2,820 lb)
Max fuel load	485 kg (1,070 lb)
Max hook capacity	1,361 kg (3,000 lb)
Max disc loading	227.5 kg/m² (46.6 lb/sq ft)

PERFORMANCE:

Never-exceed speed, ISA, S/L	
	174 knots (322 km/h; 200 mph)
Max cruising speed, S/L 100°F	
	150 knots (278 km/h; 172 mph)
Hovering ceiling OGE: ISA + 20°C	3,048 m (10,000 ft)
ISA	3,962 m (13,000 ft)
ISA + 20°C	3,810 m (12,500 ft)
ISA	4,572 m (15,000 ft)
one engine, ISA	1,219 m (4,000 ft)
Range with full payload	315 nm (584 km; 507 miles)
Max range	343 nm (636 km; 395 miles)
Max endurance	4 h 6 min

MCDONNELL DOUGLAS APACHE
US Army designations: AH-64A and AH-64C
Israel Defence Force name: Petan (Cobra)

TYPE: Day/night twin-engined attack helicopter.

PROGRAMME: Original Hughes Model 77 entered for US Army advanced attack helicopter (AAH) competition; first flights of two development prototype YAH-64s 30 September and 22 November 1975; details of programme in 1984-85 and earlier *Jane's*; selected by US Army December 1976; named Apache late 1981.

Deliveries started 26 January 1984; 600th delivered 14 August 1990; 807th and final (plus five flying prototype and pre-production) due for delivery December 1993. Self deployment capability shown by 14th Apache with four 871 litre (230 US gallon; 191 Imp gallon) external tanks, which flew 1,020 nm (1,891 km; 1,175 miles) from Mesa to Santa Barbara with 30 minutes' fuel remaining on 4 April 1985; initial operating capability achieved by 3rd Squadron, 6th Cavalry Regiment, July 1986; 22 (half in US-based regular army) of 30 planned AH-64A battalions combat-ready by December 1990; first combat use (11 AH-64As) in operation Just Cause, Panama, December 1989; used extensively during January/February 1991 Gulf War against Iraq, including first air strike of conflict. First AH-64As issued to Army National Guard in 1987; fourth ArNG unit (1/211 AvRgt in Utah) established 1990; first overseas regiment 2/6 Cavalry Regiment, Illesheim, Germany, September 1987; eighth in Europe (3/4 AvRgt at Finthen) equipped 1990; battalion consists of 18 AH-64As and 13 Bell OH-58 Kiowas; more than 200 AH-64As to be based in Germany.

Eleven-month programme to integrate air-to-air Stinger began October 1987; four missiles mounted in pairs on wingtips; five firings early 1989; air-to-air development programme included firing two AIM-9 Sidewinders in hover and at 80 knots (148 km/h; 92 mph) at White Sands, New Mexico, November 1987; laser ranging and tracking tests on Bell UH-1 and LTV A-7 flown in 1989; M-230 Chain Gun being improved for air-to-air use; Matra Mistral captive carry tests completed and firings planned for late 1989; new missile control system by Base 10 Defense of Trenton, New Jersey, used for two more Stinger firings during 1990; Sidearm anti-radiation missile from AH-64A hit RF emitter on armoured vehicle at US Naval Weapons Test Center 25 April 1988; firings of Shorts Starstreak planned for 1991.

US Army ordered development of advanced composites main rotor hub for AH-64A, fibre reinforced thermoplastic secondary structure and artificial intelligence applications for system fault isolation and diagnosis; production AH-64A allocated for five-year vibration analysis funded by NASA Langley Research Center. General Electric and Lucas Aerospace teamed in June 1990 to produce fly-by-wire system for Apache.

VARIANTS:

Advanced Apache: Announced April 1987; would have been 75 per cent common with existing AH-64A; did not go ahead; new equipment included fly-by-wire flying

Artist's impression of the McDonnell Douglas MDX twin-turboshaft NOTAR helicopter

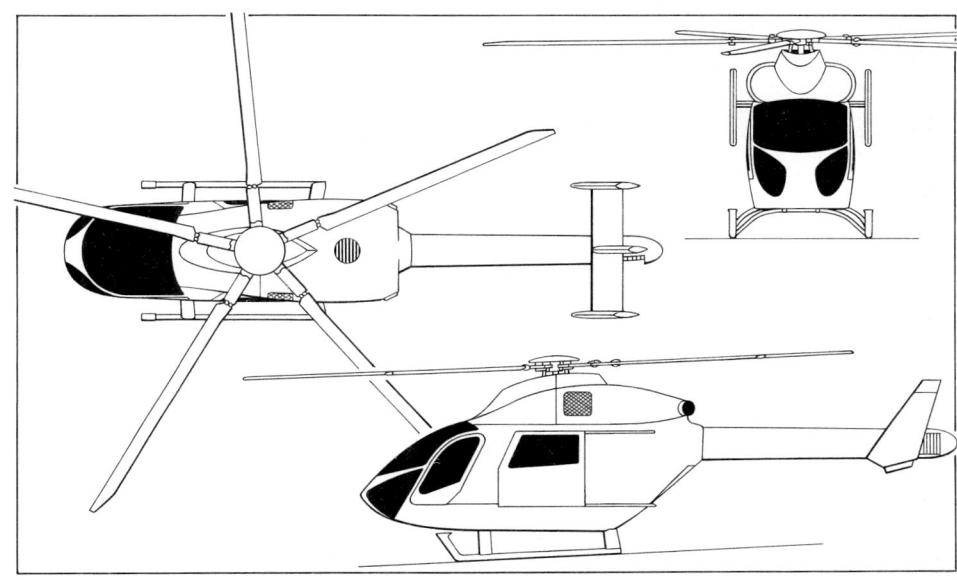

McDonnell Douglas MDX eight-seat commercial helicopter *(Jane's/Mike Keep)*

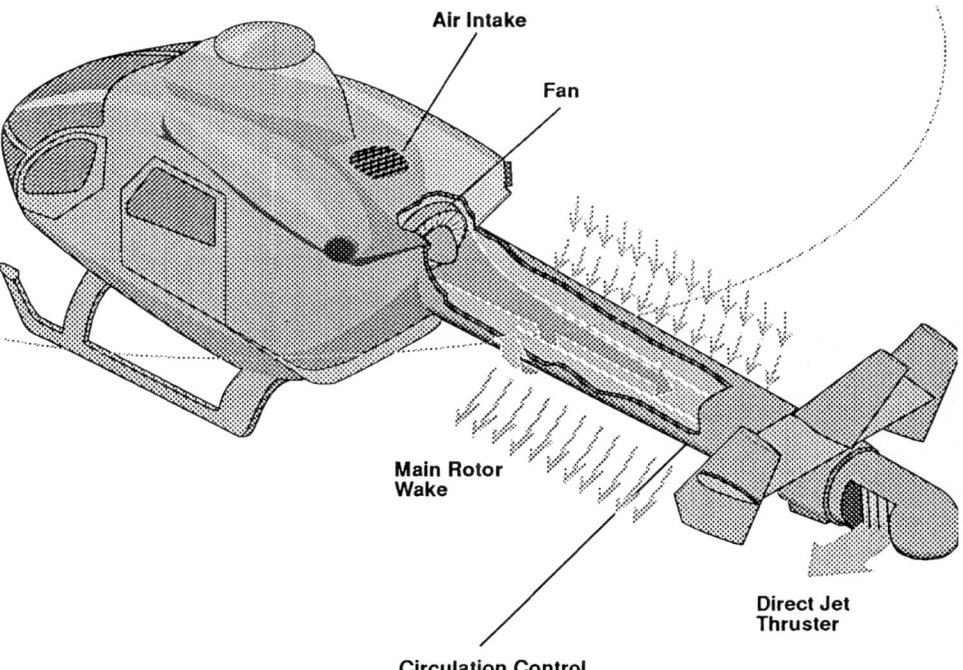

NOTAR operation in the MDX, shown here, is like that in the 520N and 530N

The six passengers in the MDX are within a protective cage, as in the 520N and 530N

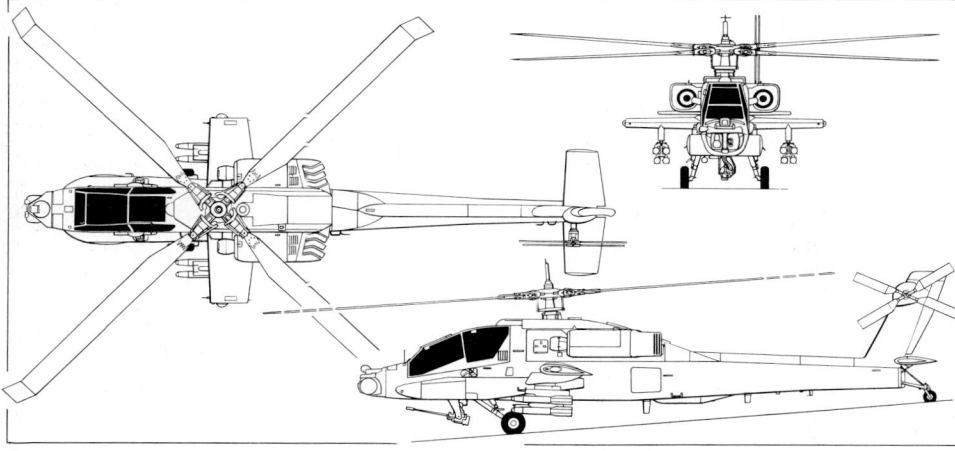

McDonnell Douglas AH-64A Apache armed with Hellfire ATMs and rocket pods

McDonnell Douglas AH-64A Apache tandem two-seat advanced attack helicopter *(Pilot Press)*

controls, Honeywell ring laser INS, cassette mission data loading system, ATHS (automatic target handover system), digitally controlled 1,491 kW (2,000 shp) engines, air-to-air gun, rearward-looking TV camera on fin and provision for air-to-air Stinger.

MSIP: Initially funded by FY 1988, but also failed to go ahead; equipment included upgraded weapon, sensor and fire control systems, digital databus and crew displays.

AH-64C Longbow Apache: Current improvement programme based on Westinghouse mast-mounted Longbow millimetre-wave radar and Martin Marietta Hellfire with RF seeker; required aircraft modifications include more powerful GE T700-GE-701 engines, a new Smiths electrical power distribution system, larger generator for doubled 70kVA load, Plessey AN/ASN-157 Doppler navigation, MIL-STD-1553 databus allied to dual 1750A processors, and a Parker Hannifin vapour cycle cooling system for avionics; early user tests completed April 1990 and seven RF Hellfires launched, of which six successful.

Fifty-month full-scale development programme authorised by Defense Acquisition Board December 1990, but airframe work postponed 19 months to coincide with missile development; supporting modifications being incorporated progressively; first flight of AH-64A with modified-shape mockup Longbow radome 11 March 1991; first AH-64C prototype due to fly early 1992, production deliveries to start 1996. Only 227 out of 330 available AH-64As will have Longbow because of budgetary restrictions. Longbow can track flying targets and see through rain, fog and smoke that defeat FLIR and TV; RF Hellfire can operate at shorter ranges; it can lock-on before launch or launch on co-ordinates and lock-on in flight; Longbow scans through 360° for aerial targets or scans over 270° in 90° sectors for ground targets; mast-mounted rotating antenna weighs 136 kg (300 lb).

Further possible modifications include 'man-print' cockpit with large displays, air-to-air Stinger, digital autostabiliser, integrated GPS/Doppler/INS/air data/laser/radar altimeter navigation system, digital communications, faster target hand-off system, and enhanced fault detection with data transfer and recording.

CUSTOMERS: Confirmed exports totalled 54 by 10 April 1991. Israel ordered 18 in March 1990; first two delivered 12 September 1990 to 'Wasp' Squadron, powered by T700-GE-701s. Deliveries expected to begin 1992 to Saudi Arabia (12) and 1994 to Egypt (24). Additional FMS requirements by April 1991 involved 32 firm orders

and 56 options: customers and quantities not identified officially, but thought to include Bahrain (eight) and United Arab Emirates (18).

COSTS: $10 million 11 month programme to integrate air-to-air Stinger started October 1987. Longbow radar costs $4 million (1990) without supporting modifications compared with $9 million flyaway cost of AH-64A. Longbow R&D contract (for four prototypes) $194.6 million. Programme cost (807 aircraft at 1991 values) $1,169 million.

DESIGN FEATURES: AH-64A is required to continue flying for 30 min after being hit by 12.7 mm bullets coming from anywhere in the lower hemisphere plus 20°; also survives 23 mm hits in many parts; Target Acquisition and Designation System (TADS) and Pilot Night Vision System (PNVS) sensors mounted in nose; low airspeed sensor above main rotor hub; avionics in lateral containers; chin-mounted chain gun fed from ammunition bay in centre fuselage; four weapon pylons on stub wings; engines mounted widely separated, with integral particle separators and built-in exhaust cooling fittings; four-blade main rotor with lifting aerofoil blade section and swept tips; blades can be folded or easily removed; tail rotor consists of two teetering two-blade units crossed at 55° to reduce noise; airframe meets full crash-survival specifications; two AH-64As will fit in C-141, six in C-5 and three in C-17A; Teledyne Ryan produces all fuselages, wings, tail, engine cowlings, canopies and avionics containers.

Telefunken Systemtechnik electric blade de-icing system; main transmission, by Litton Precision Gear Division, can operate for one hour without oil; tail rotor drive, by Aircraft Gear Corporation, has grease lubricated gearboxes with Bendix driveshafts and couplings; gearboxes and shafts can operate for one hour after ballistic damage; main rotor shaft runs within airframe-mounted sleeve, relieving transmission of flight loads and allowing removal of transmission without disturbing rotor; AH-64A has flown aerobatic manoeuvres and is capable of flying at 0.5g.

FLYING CONTROLS: Fully powered controls with stabilisation and automatic flight control system; automatic heading hold with feet off pedals; tailplane incidence automatically adjusted by Hamilton Standard control to streamline with downwash during hover and to hold best fuselage attitude during climb, cruise, descent and transition.

STRUCTURE: Main rotor blades (by Tool Research and Engineering Corporation, Composite Structures Divisions) have five U-sections forming spars and skins bonded with structural glassfibre tubes, laminated stainless steel skin and composites rear section; blades attached to hub by stack of laminated steel straps with elastomeric bearings.

LANDING GEAR: Menasco trailing arm type, with single mainwheels and fully castoring, self-centring and lockable tailwheel. Mainwheel tyres size 8.50-10, tailwheel tyre size 5.00-4. Hydraulic brakes on main units. Main gear is non-retractable, but legs fold rearward to reduce overall height for storage and transportation. Energy absorbing main and tail gears are designed for normal descent rates of up to 3.05 m (10 ft)/s and heavy landings at up to 12.8 m (42 ft)/s. Take-offs and landings can be made at structural design gross weight on terrain slopes of up to 12° (head-on) and 10° (side-on).

POWER PLANT: Two 1,265 kW (1,696 shp) General Electric T700-GE-701 turboshafts, derated for normal operations to provide reserve power for combat emergencies, and with automatic one engine inoperative rating of 1,285 kW (1,723 shp); 1,417 kW (1,900 shp) -701C engines from 600th AH-64A onward (1990). Engines mounted one on each side of fuselage, above wings, with key components armour-protected. Upper cowlings let down to serve as maintenance platforms. Two crash resistant fuel cells in fuselage, combined capacity 1,422 litres (376 US gallons; 313 Imp gallons). 'Black Hole' IR suppression system protects aircraft from heat-seeking missiles: this eliminates an engine bay cooling fan, by operating from engine exhaust gas through ejector nozzles to lower the gas plume and metal temperatures.

ACCOMMODATION: Crew of two in tandem: co-pilot/gunner in front, pilot behind on 48 cm (19 in) elevated seat. Crew seats, by Simula Inc, are of lightweight Kevlar. Teledyne Ryan canopy, with PPG transparencies and transparent acrylic blast barrier between cockpits, is designed to provide optimum field of view. Crew stations are protected by Ceradyne Inc lightweight boron armour shields in cockpit floor and sides, and between cockpits, offering protection against 23 mm high explosive and armour piercing rounds. Sierracin electric heating of windscreen. Seats and structure designed to give crew a 95 per cent chance of surviving ground impacts of up to 12.8 m (42 ft)/s.

SYSTEMS: AiResearch totally integrated pneumatic system includes a shaft driven compressor, air turbine starters, pneumatic valves, temperature control unit and environmental control unit. Parker Bertea dual hydraulic systems, operating at 207 bars (3,000 lb/sq in), with actuators ballistically tolerant to 12.7 mm direct hits. Redundant flight control system for both rotors. In the event of a flying control system failure, the system activates Honeywell secondary fly-by-wire control. Bendix electrical power system, with two 35kVA fully redundant engine driven AC generators, two 300A transformer-rectifiers, and URDC standby DC battery. Garrett GTP 36-55(H) 93 kW (125 shp) APU for engine starting and maintenance checking.

AVIONICS: Main avionics bays are adjacent to co-pilot/gunner's position, in large fairings on sides of fuselage. Communications equipment includes AN/ARC-164 UHF, AN/ARC-186 UHF/VHF, Tempest C-10414 intercom, KY-28/58/TSEC crypto secure voice, and C-8157 secure voice control. Plessey Electronic Systems AN/ASN-128 lightweight Doppler navigation system, with Litton LR-80 (AN/ASN-143) strapdown attitude and heading reference system (AHRS). Doppler system, with AHRS, permits nap-of-the-earth navigation and provides for storing target locations. Avionics fit includes an AN/ARN-89B ADF and an AN/APX-100 IFF transponder with KIT-1A secure encoding. Honeywell digital automatic stabilisation equipment (DASE). Aircraft survivability equipment (ASE) consists of an Aerospace Avionics AN/APR-39 passive radar warning receiver, an AN/AVR-2 laser warning receiver, a Sanders AN/ALQ-144 infra-red jammer, chaff dispensers, and an AN/ALQ-136 radar jammer. Other avionics include Astronautics Corpn HSI, an AN/APU-209 radar altimeter video display unit, and remote magnetic indicator, and Pacer Systems omnidirectional air data system. A Honeywell all-raster symbology generator processes TV data from IR and other sensors, superimposes symbology, and distributes the combination to CRT and helmet mounted displays in the aircraft. BITE fault detection/location system. Martin Marietta Orlando Aerospace target acquisition and designation sight and AN/AAQ-11 pilot's night vision sensor (TADS/PNVS) comprises two independently functioning systems mounted on the nose. The TADS consists of a rotating turret (±120° in azimuth, +30/−60° in elevation) that houses the sensor subsystems, an optical relay tube in the CPG's cockpit, three electronic units in the avionics bay, and cockpit-mounted controls and displays. It is used principally for target search, detection and laser designation, with the CPG as primary operator (though it can also provide backup night vision to the pilot in the event of a PNVS failure). Once acquired by the TADS, targets can be tracked manually or automatically for autonomous attack with gun, rockets or Hellfire missiles. The TADS daylight sensor consists of a TV camera with narrow (0.9°) and wide angle (4.0°) fields of view; direct view optics (4° narrow and 18° wide angle); a laser spot tracker; and an International Laser Systems laser rangefinder/designator. The night sensor, in the starboard half of the turret, incorporates a FLIR sight with narrow, medium and wide angle (3.1, 10.1 and 50.0°) fields of view. The PNVS consists of a FLIR sensor (30° × 40° field of view) in a rotating turret (±90° in azimuth, +20/−45° in elevation) mounted above the TADS; an electronics unit in the avionics bay; and the pilot's display and controls. It provides the pilot with thermal imaging that permits nap-of-the-earth flight to, from and within the battle area at night or in adverse daytime weather, at altitudes low enough to avoid detection by the enemy. PNVS imagery is displayed on a single monocle in front of one of the pilot's eyes; flight information such as airspeed, altitude and heading is superimposed on this imagery to simplify the piloting task. The monocle is a part of the Honeywell Avionics integrated helmet and display sighting system (IHADSS) worn by both crew members.

ARMAMENT: McDonnell Douglas M230 Chain Gun 30 mm automatic cannon, located between the mainwheel legs in an underfuselage mounting with Smiths Industries electronic controls. Normal rate of fire is 625 rds/min of Honeywell TP (target practice), HE or HEDP (high explosive dual purpose) ammunition, which is interoperable with NATO Aden/DEFA 30 mm ammunition. Max ammunition load is 1,200 rds. Gun mounting is designed to collapse into fuselage between pilots in the event of a crash landing. Four underwing hardpoints, with Aircraft Hydro-Forming pylons and ejector units, on which can be carried up to sixteen Rockwell Hellfire anti-tank missiles; or up to seventy-six 2.75 in FFAR (folding fin aerial rockets) in their launchers; or a combination of Hellfires and FFAR. Hellfire remote electronics by Rockwell; Bendix aerial rocket control system; multiplex (MUX) system units by Honeywell. Co-pilot/gunner (CPG) has primary responsibility for firing gun and missiles, but pilot can override his controls to fire gun or launch missiles.

DIMENSIONS, EXTERNAL:

Main rotor diameter	14.63 m (48 ft 0 in)
Main rotor blade chord	0.53 m (1 ft 9 in)
Tail rotor diameter	2.79 m (9 ft 2 in)

Hellfire-armed Apache testbed with mockup of radome for Longbow mast-mounted radar

Length overall: tail rotor turning	14.68 m (48 ft 2 in)	
both rotors turning	17.76 m (58 ft 3⅛ in)	
Wing span	5.23 m (17 ft 2 in)	
Height: over tail fin	3.52 m (11 ft 6½ in)	
over tail rotor	4.30 m (14 ft 1¼ in)	
to top of rotor head	3.84 m (12 ft 7 in)	
overall (top of air data sensor)	4.66 m (15 ft 3½ in)	
Distance between c/l of pylons:		
inboard pair	3.20 m (10 ft 6 in)	
outboard pair	4.72 m (15 ft 6 in)	
Tailplane span	3.40 m (11 ft 2 in)	
Wheel track	2.03 m (6 ft 8 in)	
Wheelbase	10.59 m (34 ft 9 in)	

AREAS:

Main rotor disc	168.11 m² (1,809.5 sq ft)
Tail rotor disc	6.13 m² (66.0 sq ft)

WEIGHTS AND LOADINGS:

Weight empty	4,881 kg (10,760 lb)
Max internal fuel weight	1,157 kg (2,550 lb)
Max external stores weight	771 kg (1,700 lb)
Structural design gross weight	6,650 kg (14,660 lb)
Primary mission gross weight	6,552 kg (14,445 lb)
Alternative mission gross weight	8,006 kg (17,650 lb)
Max T-O weight	9,525 kg (21,000 lb)
Max disc loading	56.69 kg/m² (11.61 lb/sq ft)

PERFORMANCE (at 6,552 kg; 14,445 lb AUW, ISA except where indicated):

Never-exceed speed (VNE)	197 knots (365 km/h; 227 mph)
Max level and max cruising speed	160 knots (296 km/h; 184 mph)
Max vertical rate of climb at S/L	762 m (2,500 ft)/min
Service ceiling	6,400 m (21,000 ft)
Service ceiling, one engine out	3,290 m (10,800 ft)
Hovering ceiling: IGE	4,570 m (15,000 ft)
OGE	3,505 m (11,500 ft)
Max range, internal fuel	260 nm (482 km; 300 miles)
Ferry range, max internal and external fuel, still air	918 nm (1,701 km; 1,057 miles)
Endurance at 1,220 m (4,000 ft) at 35°C	1 h 50 min
Max endurance, internal fuel	3 h 9 min
g limits at low altitude and airspeeds up to 164 knots (304 km/h; 189 mph)	+3.5/−0.5

WEIGHTS FOR TYPICAL MISSION PERFORMANCE (A: anti-armour at 1,220 m/4,000 ft and 35°C, 4 Hellfire and 320 rds of 30 mm ammunition; B: as A, but with 1200 rds; C: as A, but with 6 Hellfire and 540 rds; D: anti-armour at 610 m/2,000 ft and 21°C, 8 Hellfire and 1,200 rds; E: air cover at 1,220 m/4,000 ft and 35°C, 4 Hellfire and 1,200 rds; F: as E but at 610 m/2,000 ft and 21°C, 4 Hellfire, 19 rockets, 1,200 rds; G: escort at 1,220 m/4,000 ft and 35°C, 19 rockets and 1,200 rds; H: escort at 610 m/2,000 ft and 21°C, 38 rockets and 1,200 rds):

Mission fuel: A	727 kg (1,602 lb)
G	741 kg (1,633 lb)
E	745 kg (1,643 lb)
C	902 kg (1,989 lb)
B	1,029 kg (2,269 lb)
D	1,063 kg (2,344 lb)
H	1,077 kg (2,374 lb)
F	1,086 kg (2,394 lb)
Mission gross weight: A	6,552 kg (14,445 lb)
E	6,874 kg (15,154 lb)
G	6,932 kg (15,282 lb)
B, C	7,158 kg (15,780 lb)
D	7,728 kg (17,038 lb)
F	7,813 kg (17,225 lb)
H	7,867 kg (17,343 lb)

TYPICAL MISSION PERFORMANCE (A–H as above):
Cruising speed at intermediate rated power:

C	147 knots (272 km/h; 169 mph)
D	148 knots (274 km/h; 170 mph)
F	150 knots (278 km/h; 173 mph)
B	151 knots (280 km/h; 174 mph)
E, H	153 knots (283 km/h; 176 mph)
A	154 knots (285 km/h; 177 mph)
G	155 knots (287 km/h; 178 mph)

Max vertical rate of climb at intermediate rated power:

B, C	137 m (450 ft)/min
H	238 m (780 ft)/min
F, G	262 m (860 ft)/min
E	293 m (960 ft)/min
D	301 m (990 ft)/min
A	448 m (1,470 ft)/min
Mission endurance: A, E, G	1 h 50 min
C	1 h 17 min
D, F, H	2 h 30 min
B	2 h 40 min

MCDONNELL DOUGLAS/BELL LH

It was announced on 8 April 1991 that the Boeing Sikorsky First Team (which see) had been selected to continue development of the US Army RAH-66A LH. Details of the Bell and McDonnell Douglas Helicopters project are recorded under Bell/McDonnell Douglas.

MELEX

MELEX USA INC
1221 Front Street, Raleigh, North Carolina 27609
Telephone: 1 (919) 828 7645
Fax: 1 (919) 834 7290
Telex: 825868 MELEX UF

VICE-PRESIDENT: George Lundy
Subsidiary of Pezetel (PZL) of Poland (which see) responsible for sale and support of PZL Mielec M-18 and M-18A Dromader agricultural aircraft in western hemisphere.

TURBINES INC/MELEX T45 TURBINE DROMADER

TYPE: Turboprop version of Dromader.
PROGRAMME: First flight of prototype (N2856G) 17 August 1985; STC issued 25 April 1986.

VARIANTS: **Turbine Dromader:** Agricultural aircraft.
  Water bomber: Under development by Melex USA
during 1990; could replenish by scooping from water
troughs while taxying on land; hydroskis, for replenishing
on water without floats, under consideration.
DESIGN FEATURES: Converted by Turbines Inc of Terre
  Haute, Indiana, in co-operation with Melex USA Inc;
  895 kW (1,200 shp) P&WC PT6A-45AG derated to 735
  kW (986 shp), driving five-blade propeller; Dromader
  empty weight reduced by 363 kg (800 lb); normal
  operating speed increased by 20 knots (37 km/h; 23 mph)
  and take-off distance reduced by 0 per cent; standard
  fuel capacity increased to 719 litres (190 US gallons; 185
  Imp gallons); hydraulic and electrical systems improved;
  optional passenger in rearward-facing seat; two-seat pilot
  trainer available.
FLYING CONTROLS: As for M-18A Dromader, which see in
  Poland section.
STRUCTURE: As for M-18A Dromader.

**Prototype T45 Turbine Dromader conversion
with Pratt & Whitney Canada PT6A-45AG engine**

MID-CONTINENT
MID-CONTINENT AIRCRAFT
  CORPORATION
Drawer L, Highway 84 East, Hayti, Missouri 63851
Telephone: 1 (314) 359 0500
Fax: 1 (314) 359 0538
Telex: 447183
CHAIRMAN: Richard Reade
PRESIDENT: Ken Mauk
  Operator and distributor of Schweizer (Grumman)
Ag-Cats and Ayres Thrushes.

MID-CONTINENT KING CAT
TYPE: Re-engined Schweizer Ag-Cat.
PROGRAMME: Also certificated in Canada. Offered ready
  converted or as retrofit kit. Engineering work for STC by
  Serv-Aero Engineering Inc.
DESIGN FEATURES: Uses airframe of Super Ag-Cat C; hopper
  holds 1,893 litres (500 US gallons; 416 Imp gallons) liquid
  or 1,814 kg (4,000 lb) powder; powered by 895 kW
  (1,200 hp) Wright R-1820-202A radial engine driving
  three-blade metal propeller; improved hot and high
  performance. Options include upper wing installation
  height increased 20.3 cm (8 in), Serv-O ailerons, fuel
  capacity increased to 431.5 litres (114 US gallons; 95 Imp
  gallons), Collins cockpit air-conditioning, and a 1,893
  litre (500 US gallon; 416 Imp gallon) water bombing
  system.
FLYING CONTROLS: As for Schweizer Ag-Cat (which see).
STRUCTURE: As for Schweizer Ag-Cat.
WEIGHTS AND LOADINGS:

Mid-Continent King Cat, a Wright engined conversion of a Super Ag-Cat C

Weight empty: basic	2,184 kg (4,816 lb)	
spray equipped	2,257 kg (4,976 lb)	
dust equipped	2,225 kg (4,906 lb)	
Max T-O weight: FAR 23	2,857 kg (6,300 lb)	
CAM 8	3,855 kg (8,500 lb)	
Max wing loading:		
FAR 23	78.5 kg/m² (16.07 lb/sq ft)	
CAM 8	105.9 kg/m² (21.68 lb/sq ft)	
Max power loading:		
FAR 23	3.19 kg/kW (5.25 lb/hp)	
CAM 8	4.31 kg/kW (7.08 lb/hp)	
PERFORMANCE:		
Ferry speed	117 knots (217 km/h; 135 mph)	
Typical working speed		
	87-113 knots (161-209 km/h; 100-130 mph)	

Stalling speed, power off, at AUW of 2,857 kg
  (6,300 lb) 60 knots (111 km/h; 69 mph) CAS
T-O run with 907 kg (2,000 lb) hopper load
  293 m (960 ft)
T-O to 15 m (50 ft) with 907 kg (2,000 lb) hopper load
  427 m (1,400 ft)
Landing from 15 m (50 ft) at weight of 2,257 kg
  (4,976 lb) 363 m (1,190 ft)
Landing run at weight of 2,257 kg (4,976 lb)
  179 m (588 ft)

MOLLER
MOLLER INTERNATIONAL
1222 Research Park Drive, Davis, California 95616
Telephone: 1 (916) 756 5086
Fax: 1 (916) 756 5179
PRESIDENT: Dr Paul S. Moller
DIRECTOR OF MARKETING: Jack G. Allison
  Company formed in 1982 to develop Volantor VTOL
aircraft, including high power/weight ratio engines and
three-axis stabilisation; prototypes called **Discojet,
Model XM-4** and **Model 200X** were saucer-shaped with
multiple lift fans and centrally mounted cockpit; Model
200X made 150 flights from 1989 onwards; powered by
eight 37.3 kW (50 hp) Wankel engines. Four-seat Model 400
Volantor described below.

MOLLER 400 VOLANTOR
TYPE: Four-seat eight-engined VTOL private aircraft.
PROGRAMME: Work on prototype slowed down in 1988 while
  pilotless models were studied; limited number of Model
  400s expected to be available in 1992; certification in
  Powered-lift Aircraft category to follow.
VARIANTS:
  Moller 150: Tandem two-seat derivative with total
  installed 477.2 kW (640 hp) said to give cruising speed of
  287 knots (532 km/h; 330 mph).
CUSTOMERS: 75 delivery positions reserved at 31 January
  1991.
COSTS: Development costs (end 1990) $26 million.
DESIGN FEATURES: Pairs of ducted fans fore and aft each
  powered by two engines; small, slightly swept wing
  mounted on three fins on rear fuselage; lift at forward end
  provided by body contours; fan lift results in need for
  extremely high installed power, which appears to account

Partly completed prototype of the Moller 400 Volantor ducted fan VTOL aircraft

for very high cruising speed; rear passengers sit facing
rearwards.
FLYING CONTROLS: Triple redundant full-time roll, pitch and
  yaw fly-by-wire controls; ballistic parachute recovery
  system. Efflux from the four fixed ducted fans deflected
  downwards for hovering by flexible cascade vanes.

STRUCTURE: Largely composites.

POWER PLANT: Eight 111.8 kW (150 hp) aircooled rotary
  engines, two driving each ducted fan. Each engine said to
  weigh 38.5 kg (85 lb). Maximum fuel capacity 227 litres
  (60 US gallons; 50 Imp gallons).

DIMENSIONS, EXTERNAL:	
Wing span	3.96 m (13 ft 0 in)
Wing chord at tip	0.68 m (2 ft 3 in)
Wing aspect ratio	2.6
Length overall	5.48 m (18 ft 0 in)
Width overall	2.89 m (9 ft 6 in)
Height overall	1.68 m (5 ft 6 in)
Tailplane span	3.96 m (13 ft 0 in)
Wheel track	1.63 m (5 ft 4 in)
Wheelbase	3.25 m (10 ft 8 in)
DIMENSIONS, INTERNAL:	
Cabin: Length	2.90 m (9 ft 6 in)
Max width	1.17 m (3 ft 10 in)

Max height	1.17 m (3 ft 10 in)
Volume	2.43 m³ (85.8 cu ft)
Baggage compartment, forward fuselage	
	0.33 m³ (11.8 sq ft)
AREAS:	
Wings, gross	8.36 m² (90.0 sq ft)
Fins (total)	1.62 m² (17.5 sq ft)
Tailplane	2.69 m² (29.0 sq ft)
WEIGHTS AND LOADINGS:	
Operating weight, empty	624 kg (1,375 lb)
Max payload	498 kg (1,100 lb)
Max fuel weight	163.3 kg (360 lb)
Max T-O weight	1,123 kg (2,475 lb)

Max zero-fuel weight	959 kg (2,115 lb)
Max wing loading	134.3 kg/m² (27.5 lb/sq ft)
Max power loading	1.67 kg/kW (2.06 lb/hp)
PERFORMANCE:	
Max level speed	355 knots (658 km/h; 408 mph)
Cruising speed at 38% power	
	283 knots (524 km/h; 326 mph)
Rate of climb at 75% power	1,920 m (6,300 ft)/min
Hovering ceiling	2,896 m (9,500 ft)
Service ceiling	12,954 m (42,500 ft)
Max range, 20 min reserves	
	785 nm (1,455 km; 904 miles)

MOONEY

MOONEY AIRCRAFT CORPORATION

PO Box 72, Louis Schriner Field, Kerrville, Texas 78029-0072
Telephone: 1 (512) 896 6000
Fax: 1 (512) 257 4635
Telex: Easylink 62913770 OESL UD
CHAIRMAN AND PRESIDENT: Alexandre Couvelaire
EXECUTIVE VICE-PRESIDENT/GENERAL MANAGER:
Robert A. Kromer
SALES AND MARKETING:
8901 Wetmore Road, San Antonio International Airport, San Antonio, Texas 78216
Telephone: 1 (512) 824 2727
Fax: 1 (512) 824 4221
SALES MANAGER: Tim Mott

Original Mooney company formed in Wichita, Kansas, 1948; produced single-seat M-18 Mite until 1952; later history recorded in 1987-88 *Jane's*. Alexandre Couvelaire, President of Euralair/Avialair Paris, France, and Michel Seydoux, President of MSC, jointly acquired Mooney in 1985; Mooney and Aerospatiale (Socata) announced joint development of TBM 700 June 1987 (see under TBM in International section), but Mooney withdrew in spring 1991. Mooney delivered 135 aircraft during 1990.

Mooney 201SE four-seat light aircraft (Textron Lycoming IO-360-A3B6D engine)

MOONEY 201SE (M20J)

TYPE: Four-seat touring aircraft.
PROGRAMME: First flight of original Mooney 201 June 1976; certificated September 1976.
VARIANTS: **201AT**: Advanced trainer version of 201SE (Special Edition) produced 1989; main differences from standard aircraft include 14V DC electrics, 70A 12V alternator, dual brakes, hard-wearing interior, larger oil access door, instructor and pupil approach chart holders, white instrument panel, standby vacuum system, three strobe lights, high visibility paint scheme, Bendix/King IFR radio package, and David Clark four-position intercom system.
CUSTOMERS: Total of more than 1,800 model 201s delivered by early 1991, including 61 in 1990.
DESIGN FEATURES: High-efficiency touring aircraft originally designed by Mooney brothers; wing section NACA 63₂-215 at root, 64₁-412 at tip; dihedral 5° 30′; incidence 2° 30′ at root, 1° at tip; wing swept forward 2° 29′.
FLYING CONTROLS: Manually actuated; sealed gap, differentially operated ailerons; variable incidence tailplane; no trim tabs; electrically actuated single-slotted flaps.
STRUCTURE: Single-spar wing with auxiliary spar out to mid-position of flaps; wing and tail surfaces covered with stretch formed wraparound skins. Steel tube cabin section covered with light alloy skin; semi-monocoque rear fuselage with extruded stringers and sheet metal frames.
LANDING GEAR: Electrically retractable levered suspension tricycle type with airspeed safety switch bypass. Nosewheel retracts rearward, main units inward into wings. Rubber disc shock absorbers in main units. Cleveland mainwheels, size 6.00-6, and steerable nosewheel, size 5.00-5. Tyre pressure, mainwheels 2.07 bars (30 lb/sq in), nosewheel 3.38 bars (49 lb/sq in). Cleveland hydraulic single-disc brakes on mainwheels. Parking brake.
POWER PLANT: One 149 kW (200 hp) Textron Lycoming IO-360-A3B6D flat-four engine, driving a McCauley B2D34C214/90DHB-16 two-blade constant-speed metal propeller. Two integral fuel tanks in wings, with combined usable capacity of 242 litres (64 US gallons; 53.3 Imp gallons). Refuelling points in wing upper surface. Oil capacity 7.5 litres (2 US gallons; 1.7 Imp gallons).
ACCOMMODATION: Cabin accommodates four persons in pairs on individual vertically adjusting seats with reclining back, armrests and lumbar support. Dual controls standard. Overhead ventilation system. Cabin heating and cooling system, with adjustable outlets and illuminated control. One-piece wraparound windscreen. Tinted Plexiglas windows. Rear seats removable for freight stowage. Rear seats fold forward for carrying cargo. Single door on starboard side. Compartment for 54 kg (120 lb) baggage behind cabin, with access from cabin or through door on starboard side. Windscreen defrosting system standard.

SYSTEMS: Hydraulic system for brakes only. Electrical system includes 70A alternator, 28V 70Ah battery, voltage regulator and warning lights, together with protective circuit breakers.
AVIONICS: A complete range of digital IFR avionics, including autopilot and weather avoidance systems, is available as an option.
EQUIPMENT: Standard equipment includes 'Greystone' instrument panel, airspeed indicator, sensitive altimeter with blind encoder, vertical speed indicator, turn co-ordinator, magnetic compass, directional gyro, pictorial artificial horizon, emergency locator transmitter, ammeter, oil pressure gauge, oil temperature gauge, fuel pressure gauge, manifold pressure gauge, tachometer, FT101 digital fuel totaliser, fuel sight gauges in wings, two electric fuel quantity gauges, electric outside air temperature gauge, CHT and EGT gauges, alternate static source, instrument panel annunciator lights, internally lighted instruments, rheostat controlled glareshield post lights, navigation lights, landing/taxi light, cabin lighting, three high intensity strobe lights, grey tinted windscreen and cabin windows, seat belts and shoulder harnesses for all seats, assist straps and baggage straps, hatrack, multiple cabin fresh air vents, cargo tiedowns, wing jackpoints and external tiedowns, towbar, fuel tank quick drains and fuel sampler cup, auxiliary power plug, heated pitot tube, epoxy polyimide anti-corrosion treatment, and overall external polyurethane paint finish. Optional equipment includes export altimeter with millibar subscale, co-pilot's toe brakes, and deluxe control wheels.

DIMENSIONS, EXTERNAL:	
Wing span	11.00 m (36 ft 1 in)
Wing chord, mean	1.50 m (4 ft 11¼ in)
Wing aspect ratio	7.45
Length overall	7.52 m (24 ft 8 in)

Height overall	2.54 m (8 ft 4 in)
Tailplane span	3.58 m (11 ft 9 in)
Wheel track	2.79 m (9 ft 2 in)
Wheelbase	1.82 m (5 ft 11½ in)
Propeller diameter	1.88 m (6 ft 2 in)
Propeller ground clearance	0.24 m (9½ in)
DIMENSIONS, INTERNAL:	
Cabin: Length	2.90 m (9 ft 6 in)
Max width	1.10 m (3 ft 7½ in)
Max height	1.13 m (3 ft 8½ in)
Baggage door: Width	0.53 m (1 ft 9 in)
Height	0.43 m (1 ft 5 in)
Baggage compartment volume	0.38 m³ (13.5 cu ft)
AREAS:	
Wings, gross	16.24 m² (174.8 sq ft)
Ailerons (total)	1.06 m² (11.4 sq ft)
Trailing-edge flaps (total)	1.66 m² (17.9 sq ft)
Fin	0.73 m² (7.92 sq ft)
Rudder	0.58 m² (6.23 sq ft)
Tailplane	1.99 m² (21.45 sq ft)
Elevators (total)	1.11 m² (12.05 sq ft)
WEIGHTS AND LOADINGS:	
Weight empty	809 kg (1,784 lb)
Max T-O and landing weight	1,243 kg (2,740 lb)
Max wing loading	76.5 kg/m² (15.67 lb/sq ft)
Max power loading	8.34 kg/kW (13.7 lb/hp)
PERFORMANCE (at max T-O weight):	
Never-exceed speed (VNE)	
	196 knots (364 km/h; 226 mph)
Max level speed at S/L	175 knots (325 km/h; 202 mph)
Max cruising speed, 75% power at 2,470 m (8,100 ft)	
	168 knots (311 km/h; 193 mph)
Econ cruising speed, 55% power at 2,470 m (8,100 ft)	
	152 knots (282 km/h; 175 mph)

Mooney 201AT advanced trainer in high visibility colour scheme

Stalling speed:

flaps up	63 knots (117 km/h; 73 mph) IAS
wheels and flaps down	
	53 knots (98 km/h; 61 mph) CAS
Max rate of climb at S/L	314 m (1,030 ft)/min
Service ceiling	5,670 m (18,600 ft)
T-O to 15 m (50 ft)	463 m (1,517 ft)
Landing from 15 m (50 ft)	491 m (1,610 ft)
Landing run	235 m (770 ft)
Range: 55% power, no reserves	
	1,059 nm (1,962 km; 1,219 miles)
75% power, no reserves	
	951 nm (1,762 km; 1,095 miles)

MOONEY 252TSE (M20K)

TYPE: Four-seat Turbo Special Edition.

PROGRAMME: Introduced late 1985 to replace Turbo Mooney 231 (1985-86 *Jane's*).

CUSTOMERS: Total 245 Mooney 252TSEs delivered by early 1991, including 15 in 1990.

DESIGN FEATURES: Differences from Turbo 231 include Continental TSIO-360-MB-1 with intercooled Garrett TE04 supercharger and automatic waste gate; NACA induction intake; 28V electrics; fully enclosed landing gear; rounded cabin windows.

FLYING CONTROLS: As for 201SE, but with optional vacuum operated electrically controlled speed brakes in upper wing skin at quarter span/two-thirds chord.

STRUCTURE: As for 201SE.

LANDING GEAR: Electrically retractable tricycle type. Steerable nosewheel retracts rearward, main units inward into wings. All wheels faired by doors when retracted. Shock absorption of nosewheel and main wheel units by Lord rubber discs. Cleveland wheels. Mainwheel tyres size 6.00-6 (6-ply), pressure 2.90 bars (42 lb/sq in). Nosewheel tyre size 5.00-5 (6-ply), pressure 3.38 bars (49 lb/sq in). Cleveland hydraulic brakes. Parking brake.

POWER PLANT: One 156.5 kW (210 hp) Continental TSIO-360-MB-1 flat-six turbocharged and intercooled engine, driving a McCauley 2A34C216/90DHB-16E constant-speed metal propeller. Goodrich propeller de-icing optional. Two integral fuel tanks in inner wings, with combined capacity of 297.5 litres (78.6 US gallons; 65.4 Imp gallons), of which 286 litres (75.6 US gallons; 63 Imp gallons) are usable. Refuelling points in upper surface of the inboard section of each wing. Oil capacity 7.5 litres (2 US gallons; 1.7 Imp gallons).

ACCOMMODATION: Cabin accommodates four persons in pairs on individual seats. Front seats fully adjustable, with lumbar support. Rear seats fold flat for carriage of bulky items of cargo. Dual controls standard. Forward hinged door on starboard side. Baggage space aft of rear seat, accessible from cabin and via baggage door on starboard side. Accommodation heated and ventilated.

SYSTEMS: Hydraulic system for brakes only. 28V DC electrical system powered by a 70A engine driven alternator. Dual 70A alternators optional. 24V 22Ah battery. Electric standby vacuum system standard. Oxygen system, capacity 3.26 m³ (115.0 cu ft).

AVIONICS: Avionics options as for Mooney 201SE.

EQUIPMENT: Standard and optional equipment generally as for Mooney 201SE except that vacuum indicator, standby vacuum system with annunciator, push/pull vernier primary engine controls, turbine inlet temperature gauge, pressurised magnetos, air/oil separator, oil quick-drain, alternator loadmeter/voltmeter, fuel flow totaliser with memory, flight hour recorder, panel-mounted OAT gauge, electric clock, rheostat-controlled panel wash lighting, wingtip recognition lights, epoxy polyimide and zinc chromate anti-corrosion treatment and sun visor with power chart standard, and dual alternators, oxygen system, hot-prop de-icing system, speed brakes, and leather interior, optional.

DIMENSIONS, EXTERNAL: As Mooney 201SE, except:

Length overall	7.75 m (25 ft 5 in)
Cabin door (stbd, over wing):	
Height	1.13 m (3 ft 8½ in)
Width	0.74 m (2 ft 5 in)
Baggage door (stbd, aft): Height	0.52 m (1 ft 8½ in)
Width	0.43 m (1 ft 5 in)
Height to sill	1.17 m (3 ft 10 in)

DIMENSIONS, INTERNAL: As Mooney 201SE

AREAS: As Mooney 201SE except:

Fin	0.72 m² (7.80 sq ft)
Rudder	0.58 m² (6.25 sq ft)
Tailplane	1.99 m² (21.42 sq ft)
Elevators (total)	1.21 m² (13.0 sq ft)

WEIGHTS AND LOADINGS:

Weight empty	871 kg (1,920 lb)
Max baggage	54 kg (120 lb)
Max ramp, T-O and landing weight	1,315 kg (2,900 lb)
Max wing loading	80.97 kg/m² (16.6 lb/sq ft)
Max power loading	8.4 kg/kW (13.8 lb/hp)

PERFORMANCE (at max T-O weight):

Max level speed	219 knots (406 km/h; 252 mph)
Max cruising speed, 78.6% power at 8,535 m (28,000 ft)	
	202 knots (374 km/h; 233 mph)
Econ cruising speed, 55% power at 7,010 m (23,000 ft)	
	178 knots (330 km/h; 205 mph)

Mooney 252TSE (turbocharged Continental TSIO-360-MB-1 engine) *(John Cook)*

Stalling speed:

landing gear and flaps up	
	61 knots (113 km/h; 71 mph)
landing gear and flaps down	
	59 knots (110 km/h; 68 mph)
Max rate of climb at S/L	329 m (1,080 ft)/min
Certificated ceiling	8,535 m (28,000 ft)
T-O to 15 m (50 ft)	655 m (2,150 ft)
Endurance at max cruising speed	5 h 48 min

MOONEY PFM (M20L)

Design began April 1986; first flight May 1987; first flight production standard aircraft (N20PM) October 1987; certificated May 1988; powered by 162 kW (217 hp) Porsche 3200-N03 fan-cooled flat-six; stretched cabin; total 41 delivered, including eight in 1990; production stopped when engine went out of production. Last described in 1990-91 *Jane's*.

MOONEY 257TLS (M20M)

TYPE: Four-seat turbocharged light aircraft.

PROGRAMME: Announced 2 February 1989 as TLS (Turbocharged Lycoming Sabre); certificated 1989.

CUSTOMERS: Total of more than 90 delivered by early 1991, including 51 in 1990.

DESIGN FEATURES: Stretched PFM fuselage; turbocharged and intercooled engine. Other details of 252TSE apply to 257TLS except as below.

POWER PLANT: One 201.3 kW (270 hp) turbocharged and intercooled Textron Lycoming TIO-540-AF1A engine, driving a McCauley three-blade metal propeller. Two integral fuel tanks in inboard wing leading-edges, with a combined capacity of 363 litres (96 US gallons; 80 Imp gallons), of which 341 litres (90 US gallons; 75 Imp gallons) are usable. Two-piece nose cowling is of composite glassfibre/graphite construction.

ACCOMMODATION: All seats have centre and side armrests (removable in rear seats) and European-style headrests. Rear seats moved aft by 10 cm (4 in) to increase legroom. Pilot and co-pilot seats have inertia reel shoulder harnesses.

SYSTEMS: Oxygen system, capacity 3.26 m³ (115 cu ft), with masks and overhead outlets, standard.

AVIONICS: Full range of Bendix/King avionics packages available as options, including EFIS, EHI-40 coupled to KLN 88 Loran C with moving map display, flight director, altitude and vertical speed preselect, R/Nav, and weather avoidance systems.

EQUIPMENT: Standard equipment includes attitude indicator, IFR directional gyro, fuel flow indicator, annunciator panel with press-to-test, electric/manual elevator trim and electric rudder trim with console- or panel-mounted LED indicators, avionics master switch, forward centre console, console-mounted chart holder, pilot's and co-pilot's map lights, high speed electric starter, dual batteries, console-mounted weight-and-balance computer, chrome-plated collapsible towbar, cigarette lighter and ashtrays, cabin, baggage door and ignition locks, and speedbrakes.

DIMENSIONS, EXTERNAL: as for Model 252TSE except:

Length overall	8.15 m (26 ft 9 in)
Height overall	2.51 m (8 ft 3 in)
Propeller diameter	1.91 m (6 ft 3 in)

DIMENSIONS, INTERNAL:

Cabin: Length	3.20 m (10 ft 6 in)
Floor area	3.53 m² (38.0 sq ft)
Volume	3.88 m³ (137 cu ft)
Baggage compartment volume	0.64 m³ (22.6 cu ft)

WEIGHTS AND LOADINGS:

Weight empty	913 kg (2,012 lb)
Max T-O weight	1,451 kg (3,200 lb)
Max wing loading	89.35 kg/m² (18.3 lb/sq ft)
Max power loading	7.21 kg/kW (11.85 lb/hp)

PERFORMANCE (at max T-O weight, ISA, except where indicated):

Max cruising speed:	
at 3,960 m (13,000 ft)	200 knots (371 km/h; 230 mph)
at 7,620 m (25,000 ft)	223 knots (413 km/h; 257 mph)
Stalling speed:	
flaps and wheels up	65 knots (121 km/h; 75 mph)
flaps and wheels down	60 knots (111 km/h; 69 mph)
Max rate of climb at S/L	375 m (1,230 ft)/min
Certificated ceiling	7,620 m (25,000 ft)
Range with max fuel	1,070 nm (1,983 km; 1,232 miles)

MOONEY EFS (M20T)

TYPE: Two-seat aerobatic training aircraft.

PROGRAMME: Developed for US Air Force Enhanced Flight Screener requirement; prototype (N222FS) flew 6 February 1991; certification to aerobatic category FAR 23 Amendment 39 scheduled for December 1991; first deliveries May 1992.

VARIANTS: **EFS:** Military trainer.

M20T: Civil version, available from third quarter 1992.

CUSTOMERS: US Air Force requires up to 125 EFS to replace Cessna T-41As at Colorado Springs and Hondo (San Antonio) bases; request for proposals expected July 1991; selection and contract award expected December 1991.

COSTS: Under $200,000 anticipated for M20T.

DESIGN FEATURES: Modified M20 airframe (252TSE wing, 257TLS fuselage, cabin and tail unit); powered by 194 kW (260 hp) Textron Lycoming AEIO-540; engine moved 12 cm (4.7 in) aft; strengthened forward-fuselage tubular skeleton; composites wingtips replaced by metal components; fin and rudder extended by 15 cm (6 in); sliding one-piece canopy; side by side seating, instructor on left with second throttle; stressed to +6/−3g for aerobatics; target max T-O weight 1,315 kg (2,900 lb); design max cruising speed 180 knots (334 km/h; 207 mph); rate of climb 457 m (1,500 ft)/min; max range 850 nm (1,575 km; 979 miles) at 3,050 m (10,000 ft); max endurance 6 h.

Mooney 257TLS four-seat turbocharged light aircraft

MU-2

MU-2 MODIFICATIONS INC

Box 7331, Dallas, Texas 75209
Telephone: 1 (214) 358 3528
Fax: 1 (214) 350 9261
PRESIDENT: Steve Gage
MARKETING: Barron Thomas Aviation Inc, Love Field, Dallas, Texas 75209

MU-2 EXPRESS CONVERSIONS

TYPE: Conversions of long-fuselage Mitsubishi MU-2s.
PROGRAMME: First conversion began April 1985; crew and cargo door modifications STC-approved September/October 1985.
VARIANTS: **MU-2 Express:** Crew access door replaces left-hand flight deck side window; rear cargo door 1.22 m (4 ft 0 in) high by 1.35 m (4 ft 5 in) wide replaces standard cabin door on port side; cargo nets in cabin; cargo door can be single unit hinged at top or side-hinged double door with window in forward half; can be operated with or without pressurisation; total cargo volume 7.64 m³ (270.0 cu ft).

MU-2 Medi-Vac Express: Capacity for three stretcher patients, three medical attendants and life support equipment; incorporates crew door and pressurised rear cargo door.

Other variants: Ten-passenger commuter airliner,

MU-2 Modifications Inc MU-2 Express twin-turboprop cargo aircraft

combi passenger/cargo and Executive/Cargo quick-change.
DESIGN FEATURES: See Variants; optional weight reduction programme increases payload to 1,678 kg (3,700 lb).

FLYING CONTROLS: Full-span flaps and spoiler ailerons.
STRUCTURE: As for MU-2 (see Marquise/Solitaire under MAI heading in US section of 1985-86 *Jane's*).

MYERS

MYERS AVIATION

Ohio
PRESIDENT: Ralph Haven

MYERS MODEL 145

Modernised version of Myers two-seat tailwheel sporting aircraft described in 1947 and 1948 *Jane's*. Company reported to be planning to produce 50 in first year powered

by 156 kW (210 hp) Teledyne Continental IO-360; retractable tailwheel landing gear; version powered by 400 kW (550 hp) Teledyne Continental to be proposed as USAF Enhanced Flight Screener aircraft.

NASA

NATIONAL AERONAUTICS AND SPACE ADMINISTRATION (Office of Aeronautics and Space Technology)

600 Independence Avenue SW, Washington, DC 20546
Telephone: 1 (202) 453 1000
Fax: 1 (202) 426 4256
Telex: 89530 NASA WSH
ACTING ASSOCIATE ADMINISTRATOR:
  Dr William F. Ballhaus Jr
DIRECTOR OF AERONAUTICS: Cecil C. Rosen
DIRECTOR OF NASP OFFICE: Dr J. Robert Barthelmy

NASA's Convair NF-106B (see NASA Leading-Edge Vortex Flap Research; 1990-91 edition) was retired on 17 May 1991; General Dynamics F-16XL requested as replacement. Langley Research Center developing a design concept for a hypersonic (Mach 5+) next-generation reconnaissance aircraft.

NATIONAL AERO-SPACE PLANE (X-30)

Announced 4 February 1986 by President Reagan as aerospace plane that "could shrink travel times between Washington, DC, and Tokyo . . . to less than two hours"; NASA and US Department of Defense then initiated joint National Aero-Space Plane (NASP) research programme to develop economic, reusable NASP for 21st century; based on independent studies in 1984-85 by DoD, NASA and manufacturers working on Trans-Atmospheric Vehicle for Defense Advanced Research Projects Agency (DARPA).

US Air Force has overall responsibility for NASP, with NASA responsible for technology development and commercial applications; current contracts include airframe study by General Dynamics, McDonnell Douglas and Rockwell International (incorporating best features of six previous designs), and power plant work by Rocketdyne and Pratt & Whitney; The Marquardt Company received $18 million contract to assist P&W in developing scramjets July 1988; Rocketdyne successfully tested one-seventh scale model scramjet January 1989. Propulsion to be between three and five hydrogen-fuelled ramjet/scramjet engines with small rocket motors.

Contractor consortium formed January 1990, as second phase of programme, to develop advanced materials under Rockwell leadership; General Dynamics studying carbon structures, McDonnell Douglas silicon carbide reinforced titanium and Rockwell titanium aluminide honeycomb.

In third phase, the five manufacturers will build two flight research vehicles designated **X-30** of similar size to McDonnell Douglas MD-80 to demonstrate flight envelope to hypersonic cruise and acceleration to low Earth orbit; programme go-ahead expected 1993; first flight late 1990s.

Aero-space planes have both civil and military applications, as low-cost satellite and orbital payload launchers, long-range defence interceptors, and space platforms for Strategic Defence Initiative (SDI). NASP will be air-breathing hydrogen-fuelled aircraft using combination power plant with rockets for take-off and ramjets for cruise (scramjets); will take-off and land on normal runways to make single-stage entry into orbit; related vehicles might cruise in upper atmosphere at Mach 5 to 15 (5,250 to 15,750

Artist's impression of the X-30 National Aero-Space Plane in Earth orbit

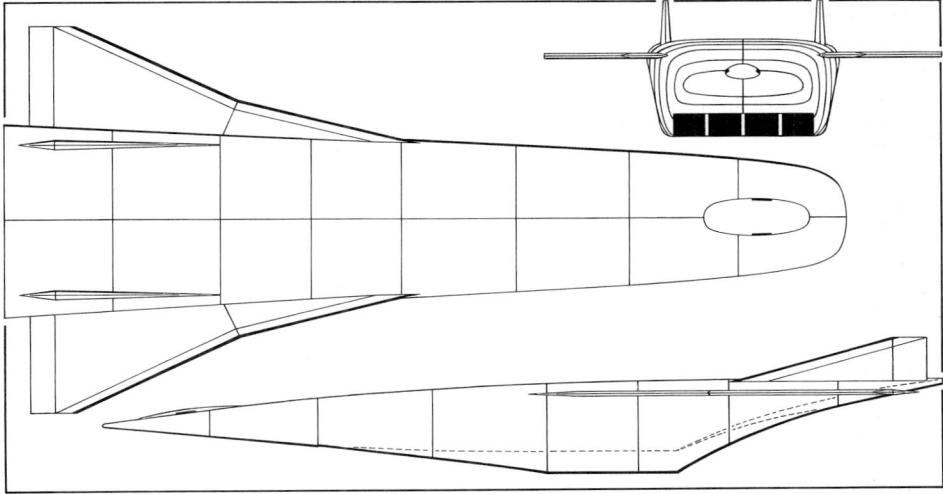

Provisional drawing of X-30 National Aero-Space Plane *(Jane's/Mike Keep)*

km/h; 3,000 to 10,000 mph) at altitudes around 32,000 m (105,000 ft).
DESIGN FEATURES: Twin-fin lifting body with small, compound-delta wings; propulsion by three to five scramjets in underfuselage pod, plus single booster rocket of 222-333 kN (50,000-75,000 lb) thrust for entry into

orbit and re-entry; side by side two-person crew compartment. Basic vehicle work-split gives McDonnell Douglas the centre-fuselage, overall aerodynamics, stability and control, and vehicle thermal control systems; GD responsible for rear fuselage and tail, crew compartment, airframe and airframe/engine integration;

Rockwell (North American Aircraft) for forward fuselage, wings, vehicle management system and subsystems; Rocketdyne leads on engine system integration, Pratt & Whitney for power plant controls. X-30 expected to be some 45.7-61 m (150-200 ft) long, with T-O gross weight in region of 113,400-136,080 kg (250,000-300,000 lb).

NASA HIGH-ALPHA RESEARCH VEHICLE (F/A-18A)

High-alpha (angle of attack) research programme began mid-1987 with standard F/A-18A Hornet (160780) loaned from USN; total 101 test flights up to 55° alpha. In second phase, McDonnell Douglas modified F/A-18A (161251/NASA840) with thrust vector system (TVS), comprising three Inconel (high-temperature nickel/steel alloy) paddles in each engine exhaust flow; existing nozzles removed; paddle movement −10° to +25° into exhaust gases; installation weight 652 kg (1,437 lb) plus 300 kg (661 lb) nose ballast. Test programme resumed December 1990; first flight with TVS installed (but not operating), 16 January 1991.

Afterburner exhaust flow from NASA high-alpha research F/A-18 deflected downwards by Inconel paddles during ground trials in February 1991

NEW TECHNIK
NEW TECHNIK INC
(Flight Vehicle Division)

PO Drawer 3350, 165 Scott Avenue, Suite 102, Morgantown, West Virginia 26505
Telephone: 1 (304) 291 2376
Fax: 1 (304) 292 1902
PRESIDENT: Darus H. Zehrbach

New Technik formed February 1990 by Aircraft Acquisition Corporation (which see), which had bought Taylorcraft Aircraft Corporation; objective to develop, market and support two-seat and four-seat light aircraft based on Taylorcraft Model L-2, 15 and 20, working in conjunction with West Virginia University Department of Mechanical and Aerospace Engineering and Concurrent Engineering Centre in Morgantown, West Virginia; new two-seat twin trainer being developed (see current types below).

NEW TECHNIK MODEL L-2M TECH 2

TYPE: Two-seat trainer/sport aircraft.
PROGRAMME: Under development 1990.
DESIGN FEATURES: Based on Taylorcraft L-2; tandem two-seater; rear seat can be rotated to face aft; two-spar wing with dual struts each side; wing section NACA 23013; dihedral 1°.
FLYING CONTROLS: Conventional, but Frise ailerons assisted by over-wing spoilers.
STRUCTURE: Strut braced wings have fabric covering, two aluminium I beam spars and stamped metal ribs; fabric covered steel tube fuselage and wire braced tail.
LANDING GEAR: Non-retractable tailwheel type. Bungee cord suspension. Mainwheel tyres size 6.00-6. Cleveland disc brakes. Wheel fairings or floats optional.
POWER PLANT: One 88 kW (118 hp) Textron Lycoming O-235-L2C flat-four engine, driving a Sensenich two-blade fixed-pitch metal propeller. One fuel tank in each wing, combined capacity 151 litres (40 US gallons; 33.3 Imp gallons). Oil capacity 5.7 litres (1.5 US gallons; 1.2 Imp gallons).
ACCOMMODATION: Two seats in tandem. Rear seat rotates 180° to face aft. Single door on starboard side.
SYSTEMS: Electrical system powered by 12V 35A engine driven alternator, with 12V 35Ah battery.
AVIONICS: Standard avionics comprise single com transceiver, transponder and encoder. IFR avionics optional.

DIMENSIONS, EXTERNAL:
Wing span	10.80 m (35 ft 5¼ in)
Wing chord, constant	1.60 m (5 ft 3 in)
Wing aspect ratio	5.1
Length overall	6.83 m (22 ft 5 in)
Height overall	1.98 m (6 ft 6 in)
Wheel track	1.93 m (6 ft 4 in)
Wheelbase	4.94 m (16 ft 2½ in)
Propeller diameter	1.83 m (6 ft 0 in)
Propeller ground clearance	0.23 m (9 in)

DIMENSIONS, INTERNAL:
Cabin: Max width	0.91 m (3 ft 0 in)

AREAS:
Wings, gross	17.07 m² (183.7 sq ft)
Spoilers (total)	0.19 m² (2.0 sq ft)

WEIGHTS AND LOADINGS:
Max T-O weight	794 kg (1,750 lb)
Max wing loading	46.38 kg/m² (9.5 lb/sq ft)
Max power loading	9.02 kg/kW (14.8 lb/hp)

PERFORMANCE (estimated, at max T-O weight, ISA:
Never-exceed speed (VNE)	
	134 knots (249 km/h; 155 mph)
Max level speed:	
at S/L	107 knots (198 km/h; 123 mph)
at 1,525 m (5,000 ft)	102 knots (188 km/h; 117 mph)
Econ cruising speed at 1,525 m (5,000 ft)	
	95 knots (175 km/h; 109 mph)
Stalling speed, power on	42 knots (78 km/h; 48 mph)
Max rate of climb at S/L	247 m (810 ft)/min
Service ceiling	5,485 m (18,000 ft)
T-O run	159 m (521 ft)
T-O to 15 m (50 ft)	214 m (700 ft)
Landing from 15 m (50 ft)	254 m (832 ft)
Landing run	170 m (556 ft)
Range with max fuel, 30 min reserves	
	590 nm (1,094 km; 680 miles)

NEW TECHNIK MODEL 20 TECH 4

TYPE: Four-seat light aircraft.
PROGRAMME: Under development in 1990.
DESIGN FEATURES: As for Tech 2, but with Fowler flaps.
FLYING CONTROLS: As for Tech 2.
STRUCTURE: As for Tech 2, but with glassfibre skin on fuselage, wings and tail; glassfibre flaps.
LANDING GEAR: Non-retractable tailwheel type. Tricycle landing gear optional. Bungee cord suspension on main gear for tailwheel type, spring steel main gear for tricycle configuration. Mainwheel tyres size 6.00-6; nosewheel tyre size 5.00-5. Cleveland disc brakes. Glassfibre wheel fairings standard.
POWER PLANT: One 171.5 kW (230 hp) Teledyne Continental O-470-U engine, driving a Hartzell or McCauley two-blade constant-speed metal propeller. One fuel tank in each wing, combined capacity 250 litres (66 US gallons; 55 Imp gallons). Auxiliary fuselage tank, capacity 83 litres (22 US gallons; 18.3 Imp gallons), optional. Oil capacity 7.6 litres (2 US gallons; 1.7 Imp gallons).
ACCOMMODATION: Two adjustable seats in front, with two-seat bench in rear. Single child's seat aft of bench optional. Baggage compartment behind rear seat. Four doors, one front and rear on each side of cabin. Small baggage door.
SYSTEMS: Electrical system powered by 12V 55A engine driven alternator, with 12V 35Ah battery.
AVIONICS: Standard avionics comprise single com transceiver, transponder and encoder. Full range of Bendix/King and Narco IFR avionics optional. II Morrow Loran C optional.

DIMENSIONS, EXTERNAL:
Wing span	10.57 m (34 ft 8 in)
Wing chord, constant	1.57 m (5 ft 2 in)
Wing aspect ratio	6.7
Length overall	7.42 m (24 ft 4 in)
Height overall	2.18 m (7 ft 2 in)
Propeller diameter	2.08 m (6 ft 10 in)
Propeller ground clearance	0.23 m (9 in)

AREAS:
Wings, gross	16.58 m² (178.5 sq ft)

WEIGHTS AND LOADINGS:
Max payload	510 kg (1,125 lb)
Max T-O weight	1,247 kg (2,750 lb)
Max wing loading	75.19 kg/m² (15.4 lb/sq ft)
Max power loading	7.27 kg/kW (11.96 lb/hp)

PERFORMANCE (estimated, at max T-O weight, ISA, except where indicated):
Never-exceed speed (VNE)	
	149 knots (277 km/h; 172 mph)
Max level speed at 1,525 m (5,000 ft)	
	139 knots (257 km/h; 160 mph)
Max cruising speed at 1,525 m (5,000 ft)	
	130 knots (241 km/h; 150 mph)
Econ cruising speed at 1,525 m (5,000 ft)	
	119 knots (220 km/h; 137 mph)
Stalling speed, power on	49 knots (90 km/h; 56 mph)
Max rate of climb at S/L	305 m (1,000 ft)/min
Service ceiling	4,575 m (15,000 ft)
T-O run	222 m (728 ft)
T-O to 15 m (50 ft)	278 m (912 ft)
Landing from 15 m (50 ft)	263 m (862 ft)
Landing run	196 m (643 ft)
Range, with max fuel, 30 min reserves	
	868 nm (1,609 km; 1,000 miles)

NEW TECHNIK TWIN TECH

TYPE: Two-seat twin-engined light trainer.
PROGRAMME: Design began January 1990; first flight expected August 1990.
DESIGN FEATURES: Basic Taylorcraft airframe has sufficient strength to take two engines, making very cheap and economical twin trainer; side by side seating; tricycle landing gear; aerodynamics as for Tech 2, except for ailerons drooping 11° 30' to assist flaps.
LANDING GEAR: Non-retractable tricycle type. Bungee cord suspension on main gear, oleo-pneumatic on nosewheel. Goodyear tyres, mainwheels size 6.00-6; nosewheel size 5.25-5. Cleveland disc brakes. Glassfibre wheel fairings standard.
POWER PLANT: Two 88 kW (118 hp) Textron Lycoming O-235-L2L flat-four engines, each driving a Sensenich two-blade fixed-pitch metal propeller. Two 119 kW (160 hp) Textron Lycoming O-320 or 134 kW (180 hp) O-360 engines optional, each driving a McCauley two-blade constant-speed metal propeller. One fuel tank in each wing, combined capacity 318 litres (84 US gallons; 70 Imp gallons). Oil capacity (O-235) 11.3 litres (3 US gallons; 2.5

Imp gallons), (O-320/O-360) 15 litres (4 US gallons; 3.3 Imp gallons).

ACCOMMODATION: Two individual bucket seats, side by side for pilot and pupil/passenger.

SYSTEMS: Electrical system powered by two 12V 35A engine driven alternators, with two 12V 25Ah batteries.

AVIONICS: Standard avionics comprise single com transceiver, transponder and encoder. Full range of Bendix/King and Narco IFR avionics optional. II Morrow Loran C optional.

DIMENSIONS, EXTERNAL:

Wing span	10.97 m (36 ft 0 in)
Wing chord, constant	1.60 m (5 ft 3 in)
Wing aspect ratio	7.1
Length overall	7.51 m (24 ft 7½ in)
Height overall	3.07 m (10 ft 1 in)
Tailplane span	3.05 m (10 ft 0 in)
Wheel track	1.98 m (6 ft 6 in)
Wheelbase	1.88 m (6 ft 2 in)
Propeller diameter: O-235	1.83 m (6 ft 0 in)
O-320/O-360	1.88 m (6 ft 2 in)
Propeller ground clearance	0.46 m (1 ft 6 in)

DIMENSIONS, INTERNAL:

Cabin: Length	2.74 m (9 ft 0 in)
Max width	1.02 m (3 ft 4¼ in)
Height	1.17 m (3 ft 10¼ in)
Floor area	2.42 m² (26.0 sq ft)
Volume	9.10 m³ (321.4 cu ft)
Baggage compartment volume	1.36 m³ (48.1 cu ft)

AREAS:

Wings, gross	17.19 m² (185.0 sq ft)
Ailerons (total)	1.86 m² (20.0 sq ft)
Trailing-edge flaps (total)	2.23 m² (24.0 sq ft)
Fin	1.23 m² (13.2 sq ft)
Tailplane	1.33 m² (14.3 sq ft)

WEIGHTS AND LOADINGS (O-320 engines):

Weight empty	640 kg (1,410 lb)
Max payload	373 kg (823 lb)
Max T-O weight	1,020 kg (2,250 lb)
Max ramp weight	1,027 kg (2,265 lb)
Max wing loading	59.57 kg/m² (12.2 lb/sq ft)
Max power loading	4.29 kg/kW (7.0 lb/hp)

PERFORMANCE (estimated, with O-320 engines and constant-speed propellers, at max T-O weight, ISA, except where indicated):

Never-exceed speed (VNE)	174.5 knots (323 km/h; 201 mph)
Max level speed at 1,525 m (5,000 ft)	174 knots (322 km/h; 200 mph)
Max cruising speed at 1,525 m (5,000 ft)	161 knots (298 km/h; 185 mph)
Econ cruising speed at 1,525 m (5,000 ft)	155 knots (286 km/h; 178 mph)
Stalling speed, power on	37 knots (68 km/h; 42 mph)
Max rate of climb at S/L	640 m (2,100 ft)/min
Rate of climb at S/L, one engine out	274 m (900 ft)/min
Service ceiling	7,010 m (23,000 ft)
Service ceiling, one engine out	3,355 m (11,000 ft)
T-O run	61 m (200 ft)
T-O to 15 m (50 ft)	98 m (320 ft)
Landing from 15 m (50 ft)	160 m (525 ft)
Landing run	77 m (250 ft)
Range with max fuel, 75% power, IFR reserves	771 nm (1,429 km; 888 miles)

NORDAM

NORDAM

PO Box 3365, 1200 East Pine Street, Tulsa, Oklahoma 7401-3365
Telephone: 1 (918) 587 4105
Fax: 1 (918) 438 9543
Telex: 158105

MARKETING DIRECTOR: Jack Arehart

Repairs, manufactures and modifies aircraft components and fits interiors.

Flight testing of hushkit with Boeing and Pratt & Whitney to make virtually all Boeing 737-200s meet FAA Stage 3 noise levels completed early 1991; reduces 75 dBA footprint at take-off by 69 per cent at 52,500 kg (115,750 lb)

and allows most 737-200s to use 40° flap during approach. Deliveries expected March 1992; 82 kits on order in April 1991; cost $3 million per aircraft.

NORTHROP

NORTHROP CORPORATION

1840 Century Park East, Los Angeles, California 90067-2199
Telephone: 1 (213) 553 6262
Fax: 1 (213) 201 3023, 553 2076 or 552 3104
Telex: 192893 NORTHROP 1
CHAIRMAN, PRESIDENT AND CHIEF EXECUTIVE OFFICER:
Kent Kresa
SENIOR VICE-PRESIDENT, PUBLIC AFFAIRS: Les Daly

Company formed 1939 by John K. Northrop to produce military aircraft; activities extended to missiles, target drones, electronics, space technology, communications,

support services and commercial products; name changed from Northrop Aircraft Inc to Northrop Corporation in 1959; company now organised in Aircraft, B-2 (formerly Advanced Systems) and Electronics Systems Divisions and subsidiary Northrop Worldwide Aircraft Services Inc. Workforce 39,000 in late 1990.

Aircraft Division (18,000 personnel) designs and manufactures fighters, produces fuselage sections for McDonnell Douglas F/A-18 (1,000th set delivered October 1990) and major subassemblies for commercial aircraft. Also operates Newbury Park (formerly Ventura Division) missile and unmanned target factory, which joined Aircraft Division in 1987 but is to close before end of 1991, transferring work to

Hawthorne and Pico Rivera, California; Northrop is prime contractor for Tacit Rainbow air-launched loitering anti-radar missile. B-2 Division manages a number of programmes and is prime contractor for B-2 advanced technology stealth bomber. Northrop Worldwide Aircraft Services Inc, Lawton, Oklahoma, provides technical and support services. Electronics Systems Division at Rolling Meadows, Illinois, produces strategic and tactical navigation and guidance equipment, passive sensor and tracking systems, electronic countermeasures (including internal countermeasures set for USAF F-15), rate and rate-integrating gyros and strapdown guidance systems.

AIRCRAFT DIVISION

One Northrop Avenue, Hawthorne, California 90250
Telephone: 1 (213) 332 1000
Telex: 181861 NORTHR HWTH A
VICE-PRESIDENT AND AIRCRAFT DIVISION GENERAL MANAGER:
Stephen R. Smith
VICE-PRESIDENT, ADVANCED DESIGN: Delbert H. Jacobs
VICE-PRESIDENT, ENGINEERING: Gene Hauser
VICE-PRESIDENT, INFORMATION RESOURCES: Robert W. Slusser
Newbury Park Site (closing late 1991)
1515 Rancho Conejo Boulevard, Newbury Park, California 91320
Telephone: 1 (805) 373 2000
Telex: 683 9403 NOCVNP

Principal subcontractor for F/A-18 (see McDonnell Douglas) and produces Boeing 747 main fuselage, upper deck, large cargo door and passenger doors; research projects involve advanced simulators and composite materials. Was prime contractor, with McDonnell Douglas as partner, for YF-23 unsuccessful contender in USAF's ATF competition.

Northrop/McDonnell Douglas YF-23 ATF *(Pilot Press)*

NORTHROP TIGER II

USAF designations: F-5E and F-5F

Production ended 1987, but five F-5E and three F-5F assembled from spares for Singapore Air Force and delivered by July 1989; total 3,805 of F-5/T-38 family produced; includes 617 F-5As, 89 RF-5As, 183 F-5Bs, 792 F-5Es, 12 RF-5Es, 149 F-5Fs and 1,187 T-38As. Canadair assembled 164 F-5As and 76 F-5B/Ds; CASA (Spain) 18 F-5As, 18 RF-5As and 34 F-5Bs; KA (South Korea) 48 F-5Es and 20 F-5Fs; F+W (Switzerland) 84 F-5Es and six F-5Fs; AIDC (Taiwan) 242 F-5Es and 66 F-5Fs. Separate are three prototypes each of T-38 and F-20 Tigershark; unmodified F-5 prototype (N.156F) and two F-5E fuselages used for Grumman X-29 forward sweep test aircraft. Details of aircraft in 1986-87 and earlier *Jane's.*

Total 560 F-5A/Bs and 1,080 F-5E/Fs remain in service with 31 air forces; several upgrade and life-extension programmes in hand or planned. Canadian Forces' CF-5s undergoing modernisation by Bristol Aerospace; Chilean F-5Es by Bedek (Israel); Jordanian and Thai F-5Es by Smiths Industries; Norwegian F-5As by LTV (Sierra Research); Venezuelan VF-5As by Singapore Aerospace Industries. Other avionics and rebuild contractors offer similar programmes.

NORTHROP YF-23 (ATF)

TYPE: Unsuccessful contender for US Air Force Advanced Tactical Fighter (ATF), for which Lockheed/Boeing/General Dynamics were selected on 23 April 1991. For programme details, see F-22 under Lockheed.

PROGRAMME: Northrop teamed with McDonnell Douglas to produce two YF-23 prototypes, serials 87-800 (with P&W YF119 power plant) and 87-801 (GE YF120). 87-800 rolled out at Edwards AFB 22 June 1990; first flight 27 August 1990; first air refuelling (fourth sortie) 14 September 1990; Mach 1.43 supercruise achieved 18 September 1990 (fifth sortie) with YF119s; 34th and final flight 30 November 1990, making total 43 hours. 87-801 first flight 26 October 1990; Mach 1.6 supercruise 29 November 1990; final flight 18 December 1990. Test programme (both aircraft) totalled 65 hours/50 sorties, demonstrating Mach 1.8 at 15,240 m (50,000 ft).

Northrop responsible for total systems integration and final assembly, construction of aft fuselage and empennage, defensive avionics and flight control system; McDonnell Douglas produced forward and centre fuselage, landing gear and wings, fuel and armament systems, offensive avionics, controls and displays. Crew station and pilot/vehicle interface were joint responsibility.

Avionics flight tested by modified BAe One-Eleven (N162W), beginning 17 July 1989.

DESIGN FEATURES: Low observables configuration and structure; stealth/agility trade-off decided by design team; target thrust/weight ratio 1.4 (achieved ratio possibly 1.1 at T-O weight); greatly improved reliability and maintainability for high sortie-generation rates, including 15 minute combat turn-round time; enhanced survivability through 'first-look first-kill' capability; short T-O and landing distances; supercruise performance in region of Mach 1.5 without afterburning; internal weapons storage and large internal fuel volume; conformal sensors. Cropped-diamond wing planform (leading- and trailing-edges at approximately 40° to fuselage) set low on hexagonal-section fuselage and blended into forebody chine; ruddervators opposed at included angle of approx 100°; no horizontal tail surfaces. Ventral weapon bays in tandem (Sidewinders forward, AMRAAMs aft). Fixed-geometry, inverted trapezoidal air intakes; S-shaped engine intake ducts lined with RAM; intakes below wing, exhausts above, latter reducing IR signature but restricting thrust-vectoring option. Auxiliary air inlet doors in upper wing surface.

VARIANTS: **US Navy NATF:** Discontinued early in 1991.

COSTS: $818 million contracts to both ATF teams, October 1986, for 54-month studies; each airframe team invested some $600 million; each engine contractor, some $50 million.

FLYING CONTROLS: Digital flight control system with fibre optic signal transmission. Ailerons and flaps cover 90 per cent of wing trailing-edge; leading-edge flaps; ruddervators combine pitch and yaw axis control.

STRUCTURE: Composites materials account for 25 per cent of prototype, compared with 40-50 per cent of planned production version.

LANDING GEAR: Strengthened for no-flare, short-field landings with up to 3.05 m (10 ft)/s sink rate. Nosewheel retracts forward; mainwheels rearward.

POWER PLANT: Two 155.7 kN (35,000 lb st) class Pratt & Whitney YF119-PW-100 or General Electric YF120-GE-100 advanced technology afterburning engines. F119 reportedly developed from F100 turbofan; F120 variable bypass power plant is turbofan at low speeds and turbojet at high speed.

ACCOMMODATION: Pilot only, on McDonnell Douglas NACES II zero/zero ejection seat.

AVIONICS: Wide-angle HUD and integrated cockpit displays; ITT/Westinghouse ESM suite; Unisys computer modules; Westinghouse and Texas Instruments competed to provide electronically scanned, phased-array radar. Radar modes included precision landing. Integrated electronic warfare system (INEWS) and integrated communications/navigation/identification avionics (ICNIA).

ARMAMENT: Internal long-barrel M61A1 20 mm gun. Internal bays for eight AIM-9 Sidewinder and/or AIM-120 AMRAAM AAMs on weapon racks of 'revolutionary' design. Have Dash 2 AAM and Have Slick ASM under development.

DIMENSIONS, EXTERNAL:

Wing span	13.29 m (43 ft 7¼ in)
Wing aspect ratio	2.01
Length overall	20.54 m (67 ft 4 ¾ in)
Height overall	4.24 m (13 ft 10¾ in)

AREAS (estimated):

Wings, gross	87.8 m² (945 sq ft)

The first Northrop/McDonnell Douglas YF-23 prototype (two P&W YF119 turbofans) during flight refuelling

WEIGHTS AND LOADINGS (estimated):

Operational weight empty	16,783 kg (37,000 lb)	Internal fuel weight	10,886 kg (24,000 lb)
		Combat T-O weight	29,030 kg (64,000 lb)

B-2 DIVISION

8900 East Washington Boulevard, Pico Rivera, California 90660-3737

Telephone: 1 (213) 942 3000

PRESIDENT AND GENERAL MANAGER: Oliver C. Boileau

NORTHROP B-2

TYPE: Low-observable strategic penetration bomber.

PROGRAMME: Development started 1978; contract for one prototype placed by USAF Aeronautical Systems Division October 1981; design modified for low altitude operation 1983; KC-135 testbed for B-2 avionics flying at Edwards AFB since January 1987; six B-2s assigned to trials; all but second will be refurbished for operational service; all but 12 of Strategic Air Command B-2s will have combined nuclear and conventional capability defined by MIL-STD-1760; six prototypes and two static airframes funded initially; first three production aircraft authorised at undisclosed date; three B-2s funded in FY 1989, two in FY 1990 and two in FY 1991; follow-on funding plan is four in FY 1992, seven each in FYs 1993-94, 11 each year in FYs 1995-97 and nine in FY 1998; delivery schedule, two in FY 1993, four each in FYs 1994-95, six in FY 1996, eight in FY 1997, 10 in FY 1998, 12 each in FYs 1999-2000 and five refurbished prototypes. First prototype B-2 (82-1066) rolled out USAF Plant 42 at Palmdale 22 November 1988; first flight (and delivery to Edwards AFB) 2 hours 20 min 17 July 1989; first flight refuelling (from KC-10A) 8 November 1989. Block 1 of test programme, up to 13 June 1990, comprised 67 hours in 16 flights, covering aerodynamic performance and airworthiness. Block 2 low observables testing began on 17th flight, 23 October 1990, after lay-up for preparation. Second B-2 (82-1067) first flew Palmdale to Edwards, 19 October 1990; loads test aircraft for performance and weapons carriage testing and envelope expansion. By mid-December 1990, first B-2 flown 91 hours in 23 sorties; second, 21 hours in six sorties; cleared half operational envelope; verified air data system and avionics and display systems; and completed initial validation of autopilot. Third and fourth B-2s to have full avionics and assigned to low-observability and weapons testing; fifth for climatic and weapons trials; sixth for operational test and evaluation, including low-observability.

CUSTOMERS: USAF originally wanted 133 B-2s including prototype, but budget cuts reduced this to 76. First B-2 unit to be 509th BW at Whiteman AFB, Missouri, where facilities are being built; one other base to be designated; Oklahoma Air Logistics Center is primary B-2 depot facility.

COSTS: $2 billion contract to start B-2 production 19 November 1987; programme cost $64,700 million ('then-year' prices) for 75 aircraft; $550 million, flyaway — but $776 million for each of first 15.

DESIGN FEATURES: Blended flying wing, with straight leading-edges, swept at 33°; centre and tip sections sharp, strongly under-cambered fixed leading-edges; four dielectric panels underwing outboard of flight deck

Northrop B-2 prototype viewed from a KC-10A tanker, showing air intakes and other details

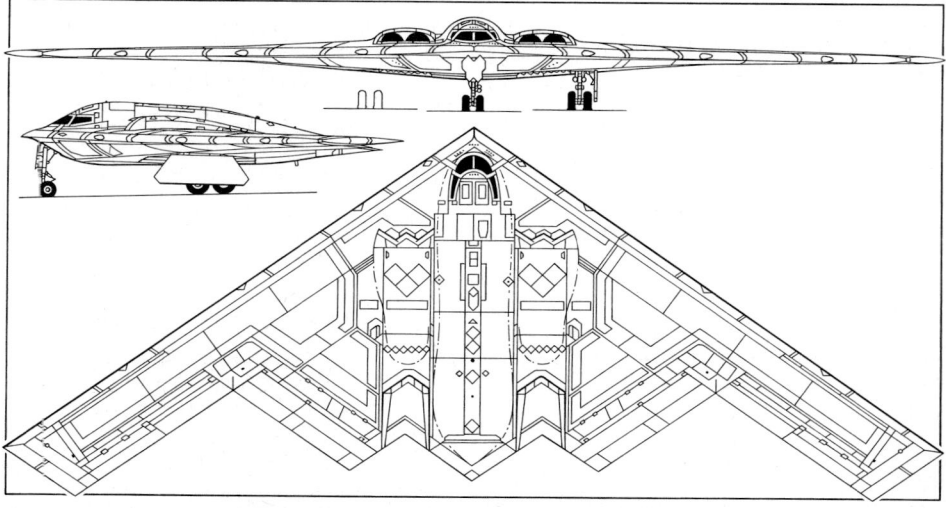

Northrop B-2 strategic penetration bomber *(Jane's/Mike Keep)*

probably cover Hughes radar antennae; 'double-W' trailing-edge incorporating elevons and drag rudders outboard of engines; two side by side weapons bays in lower centrebody; engines fed by S-shaped air ducts; irregular-shaped air intakes feed engines, with three-pointed splitter plates ahead of inlets which remove boundary layer and provide secondary airflow for cooling and IR emissions control; upper lip of intake has single point; two V-shaped overwing exhausts set well forward of trailing-edge; heat-resistant material on wing surface behind engine outlet; provision for mixing chloro-fluorosulfonic acid with exhaust gases to eliminate visible contrails; wingtips and leading-edges have dielectric covering of aerofoil section to mask radar-dissipating 'saw tooth' construction.

Northrop assisted by Boeing Advanced Systems, General Electric and LTV; planned 800,000 hours of testing aircraft's components include 24,000 hours wind tunnel tests, 44,000 hours avionics testing and 6,000 hours full-scale 'plastic bird' control system tests; flight testing to total 3,600 hours with six aircraft; all locations in airframe stored in CAD/CAM three-dimensional database used for machine tool, robot and tooling reference; prototype built on production tooling to accuracy of ±6.3 mm (¼ in) from tip to tip; nearing 900 new materials and processes developed; 131 Northrop subcontractors, plus 69 for Boeing, 52 for General Electric and 32 for LTV announced by late 1989.

Northrop builds forward centre section including cockpit, integrates and assembles aircraft; Boeing Military Airplanes produces aft centre section and outboard sections; LTV produces intermediate fuselage sections and aluminium and titanium structural components and composites parts; combined workforce is 26,000, including 10,000 at Boeing and 4,000 at LTV.

FLYING CONTROLS: Four control surfaces on each outer body/wing section, totalling approx 15 per cent of wing area combining aileron, elevator, rudder and flap functions; two inner pairs act in unison as elevons for slow-speed flight control; outboard elevon pair employed in normal flight; outermost surfaces, split horizontally, function as fast-moving drag rudders and speed-brakes, remaining partly deployed at most times (latter set at +45°/–45° on landing approach); for normal flight, lower halves of drag rudders deploy to 90°, followed by upper halves to extent required to execute manoeuvre; no high-lift devices; beaver tail behind centre fuselage acts as pitch-axis trimming surface and, with elevons, as gust alleviation system; elevons deflect at up to 100°/s; four groups of four pressure sensors around nose section indicate quadruplex full fly-by-wire flying control system.

STRUCTURE: Mostly of composites (extensively graphite/epoxy), radar absorbent honeycomb structure and skin; outer skin of materials and coatings designed to reduce radar reflection and heat radiation.

LANDING GEAR: Tricycle type, adapted from Boeing 757/767. Inward retracting four-wheel main bogies have large trapezoidal door of thick cross-section. Rearward-retracting two-wheel nose unit has small door with sawtooth edges and large rear door, also used for crew access. Two landing lights on nosewheel leg. Landing gear limiting speed 224 knots (415 km/h; 258 mph).

POWER PLANT: Four 84.5 kN (19,000 lb st) General Electric F118-GE-110 non-afterburning turbofans mounted in pairs within wing structure, each side of weapons bay, fed by S-shaped air ducts. Irregular-shaped air intakes feed each pair, with three-pointed splitter plates ahead of the inlets which draw in air, removing boundary layer and providing secondary airflow for cooling and infra-red emissions control. Upper lip of intake has single point. Two auxiliary air inlet doors mounted on top of intake trunks remain open on ground and in slow-speed flight. Two V-shaped overwing exhausts set well forward of trailing-edge. Heat-resistant material on wing surface behind engine outlet. In-flight refuelling receptacle in centrebody spine. Garrett APU outboard of port engine bay, covered by triangular door flush with wing surface.

ACCOMMODATION: Two crew, with upward firing ejection seats: pilot to port, mission commander/instructor pilot to starboard. Provision for third member. Both forward positions have conventional control columns. Flight, engine, sensor and systems information presented on nine-tube EFIS display. Either crew member capable of flying complete mission, although data entry panels biased towards weapon systems officer on starboard seat. Four flight deck windows.

Prototype Northrop B-2 banking with drag rudders in normal (slightly open) position and trailing static sensor cable extending from structure above the rear fuselage

SYSTEMS: Hydraulic system for flying controls operates at 276 bars (4,000 lb/sq in).

AVIONICS: Hughes AN/APQ-181 low-probability-of-intercept (LPI) J-band covert strike radar. AIL AN/ALQ-161A ECM. Rockwell Collins TCN-250 Tacan, VIR-130A ILS and ICS-150X intercom. To ease crew workload, three-position selector switch in cockpit activates/de-activates appropriate equipment for 'take-off' (transfer mission data tape, checklist and appropriate flight controls mode), 'go to war' (flight controls in 'stealthy' mode, weapons ready and radio emitters switched off) and 'land' (re-activate systems and perform checklist).

ARMAMENT: Boeing Advanced Applications Rotary Launcher in each of two side by side weapons bays in lower centrebody. Total capacity of 16 AGM-69 SRAM II or AGM-129 ACMs. Alternative weapons include B61 tactical/strategic and B83 strategic free-fall nuclear bombs, Mk 36 1,000 lb sea mines, Mk 82 500 lb bombs (maximum 80) and M117 750 lb fire bombs.

DIMENSIONS, EXTERNAL:
Wing span	52.43 m (172 ft 0 in)
Length overall	21.03 m (69 ft 0 in)
Height overall	5.18 m (17 ft 0 in)
Wheel track	12.20 m (40 ft 0 in)

AREAS (estimated):
Lower surface	over 464.5 m² (5,000 sq ft)

WEIGHTS AND LOADINGS:
Weight empty 45,360 kg-49,900 kg (100,000-110,000 lb)	
Max weapon load	22,680 kg (50,000 lb)
Max internal fuel capacity	
	81,650-90,720 kg (180,000-200,000 lb)
Normal T-O weight	168,433 kg (371,330 lb)
Max T-O weight	181,437 kg (400,000 lb)
Max wing loading	390.6 kg/m² (80.0 lb/sq ft)
Max power loading	536.80 kg/kN (5.26 lb/lb st)

PERFORMANCE:
Approach speed	140 knots (259 km/h; 161 mph)
Service ceiling	15,240 m (50,000 ft)

Range with eight SRAMs and eight B83 bombs, totalling 16,919 kg (37,300 lb), at max T-O weight:
hi-hi-hi	6,300 nm (11,675 km; 7,255 miles)
hi-lo-hi (1,000 nm; 1,853 km; 1,152 miles at low level)	
	4,400 nm (8,154 km; 5,067 miles)

Range with eight SRAMs and eight B61 bombs, totalling 10,886 kg (24,000 lb), at 162,386 kg (358,000 lb) T-O weight:
hi-hi-hi	6,600 nm (12,231 km; 7,600 miles)
hi-lo-hi (1,000 nm; 1,853 km; 1,152 miles at low level)	
	4,500 nm (8,339 km; 5,182 miles)

Range:
unrefuelled	6,300 nm (11,675 km; 7,255 miles)
with one aerial refuelling	
	over 10,000 nm (18,532 km; 11,515 miles)

ORLANDO
ORLANDO HELICOPTER AIRWAYS INC
2774 Carrier Avenue, Building 141, Sanford, Florida 32771
Telephone: 1 (305) 323 1756
Fax: 1 (407) 330 2647
Telex: 52 9450
PRESIDENT: Fred P. Clark

Founded at Sanford, Florida, 1964 to remanufacture, sell and operate Sikorsky helicopters; holds large parts stocks for Sikorsky S-52, S-55/H-19 and S-58/H-34, and holds FAA type certificates for all H-19 and H-34 models; affiliate company Rotorparts Inc holds world's largest stocks of S-55 parts and supplies components for S-55, S-58, S-61 and S-62; Orlando has remanufactured more than 100 Sikorsky helicopters; plans to convert military surplus S-61, S-62 and S-64, re-engine helicopters with turbines, and experiment with alternative gasoline/alcohol/propane fuels.

Agreement signed with Guangzhou Machinery Tool Company 27 October 1985 for manufacture of Orlando OHA-S-55 Bearcats in China; Guangzhou Orlando Helicopters (which see) formed to assemble parts supplied, but later to fabricate parts; 20 year joint venture includes establishment of passenger helicopter services in China and component overhaul for Far Eastern operators; plans to assemble larger helicopters in China. Orlando Helicopter Far East Ltd formed with Bates Associates of Hong Kong to sell Chinese-made helicopters.

ORLANDO/SIKORSKY S-55/H-19
TYPE: Remanufactured Sikorsky S-55/H-19.
VARIANTS: **Vistaplane:** Passenger/air ambulance seating eight passengers or 11 in high-density version; six stretchers and two attendants; optional cabin floor viewing window.

OHA-S-55 Heli-Camper: VIP model sleeping four; fully carpeted and soundproofed hot and cold water, refrigerator, two-burner stove, shower, wash basin, toilet, air-conditioning, AM/FM stereo radio and tape deck, roll-up awning, tinted windows, bar and storage cabinets, dual flight controls, full right lighting and dual landing lights, interphone system, com/nav radio and emergency locator beacon. Options include cargo sling, hydraulic hoist, floats, rotating spotlight and radio telephone. Heli-Camper sold with remanufactured airframe, new instruments, new or overhauled dynamics, overhauled 596 kW (800 hp) Wright Cyclone R-1300-3D engine. Fuel capacity 715 litres (189 US gallons; 157.5 Imp gallons); max T-O weight 3,266 kg (7,200 lb); cruising speed 78 knots (145 km/h; 90 mph); range 304 nm (563 km; 350 miles).

OHA-S-55 Nite-Writer: Aerial advertising model with 12.2 × 2.4 m (40 × 8 ft) Sky Sign Inc computerised electronic billboard, mounted 40° to helicopter side; displays running messages, logos and graphics; legible at up to 1.7 nm (3.2 km; 2 miles).

OHA-S-55 Bearcat: Carries Orlando-developed dry and spray dispensing systems, with quick conversion to fertilisers and seeds; 946 litre (250 US gallon; 208 Imp gallon) glassfibre chemical tank dry material can be carried internally; adaptable for firefighting. All Orlando-modified S-55s powered by P&W R-1340 engines FAA approved to use automotive fuel; 'superquiet' engine exhaust; optional Kysor cockpit air-conditioning. Certification of civil Bearcat II planned for July 1991.

OHA-S-55 Heavy Lift: External load model for logging, firefighting and construction; useful load 1,361 kg (3,000 lb).

OHA-AS-55/QS-55 Aggressor: Orlando has modified 15 S-55s to look like Mil Mi-24 'Hind-Es' for US Army Missile Command; used for training and as targets; dummy pilots in Mil cockpits when droned, or with pilot (when not droned) sitting high up and looking out through windows in Mi-24 type oil cooler fairings; retains S-55 four-wheel landing gear; new five-blade rotor being supplied by Rotaire; nose designed and supplied by 3D Industries; Honeywell drone flight control system; noise simulator will emulate sound of Mi-24; stub-wings each stressed to carry 227 kg (500 lb) of stores or ordnance; QS-55 fitted with defensive systems including flare/chaff dispensers. FAA Experimental certification May 1989.

OHA-AT-55 Defender: Low cost multi-role military helicopter, for use in troop transport, armoured assault or medevac duties; powered by 626 kW (840 shp) Garrett TPE331-3 turboshaft or Wright R-1300-3 radial. Incorporates much of technology developed for AS-55 Aggressor; five-blade main rotor; stub-wings with pylons; max T-O weight 3,583 kg (7,900 lb); max payload 952 kg (2,100 lb); max level speed 125 knots (231 km/h; 144 mph); max cruising speed 115 knots (213 km/h; 132 mph); max payload range 325 nm (602 km; 374 miles). Carries up to 10 fully equipped troops; entrances/exits on either side of cabin; medevac version carries up to six litters and two attendants; assault version with wing pylons each carrying up to 227 kg (500 lb) of missiles, armament or defensive systems. Design started August 1990; production aircraft to fly March 1991.

COSTS: Standard Bearcat $330,000; Aggressor under $1 million; Defender under $1 million.

ORLANDO/SIKORSKY S-58/H-34

TYPE: Remanufactured Sikorsky S-58/H-34.

VARIANTS: **Agricultural and Heavy Lift:** Powered by 1,137 kW (1,525 hp) Wright Cyclone R-1820-84; equipped as equivalent OHA-S-55 versions.

Heli-Camper: Equipped as OHA-S-55 Heli-Camper; additional features include 8.73 m² (94 sq ft) living area, sleeping for six, entertainment centre, separate bar, full-size four-burner stove, 0.11 m³ (3.9 cu ft) refrigerator, 3,500W generator, super soundproofing, tinted glass and wraparound windscreen; powered by 1,137 kW (1,525 hp) Wright Cyclone R-1820-84 radial engine; 992 litres (262 US gallons; 218 Imp gallons) fuel; max T-O weight 5,670 kg (12,500 lb); cruising speed 96 knots (177 km/h; 110 mph); range 304 nm (563 km; 350 miles).

Orlando Airliner: High-density 18-passenger version of Sikorsky twin-turbine S-58T (see California Helicopters entry in this section); standard equipment includes dual controls, toe brakes, hydraulic rotor brake, two independent powered control systems, full night lighting, rotating beacon, 24V battery, 1,071 litre (283 US gallon; 235.6 Imp gallon) fuel system, 2,268 kg (5,000 lb) cargo hook, extended passenger cabin, 18 additional cabin windows (tinted), Flightex soundproofing and ram-air cabin cooling; options include 272 kg (600 lb) rescue hoist, pop-out floats, 568 litre (150 US gallon; 125 Imp gallon) external auxiliary fuel tank, stereo system, toilet, air-conditioning, one-piece windscreen and choice of avionics; useful load is more than 2,268 kg (5,000 lb); maximum speed at S/L 120 knots (222 km/h; 138 mph); hover ceiling OGE 2,440 m (8,000 ft); range, with auxiliary fuel and 20 min reserve, 373 nm (692 km; 430 miles). 24 conversions completed.

COSTS: Standard Orlando Airliner $1.3 million.

Orlando Helicopter Airways Aggressor conversion of the Sikorsky H-19/S-55

Orlando Helicopter Airways OHA-S-55 Bearcat agricultural helicopter

Orlando Helicopter Airways OHA-AT-55 Defender

Orlando Helicopter Airways S-58T Orlando Airliner

PEMCO
PEMCO AEROPLEX
(Subsidiary of Precision Standard Inc)

PO Box 2287, Birmingham, Alabama 35201-2287
Telephone: 1 (205) 592 0011
Fax: 1 (205) 595 6631
Telex: (810) 733 3687

Former Hayes International Corporation acquired and renamed by Precision Standard Inc of Birmingham, Alabama, September 1988; still markets cargo aircraft conversions; besides those below, company has converted Convair 240, 340, 580, 640, Douglas DC-6, DC-8, Gulfstream I, Boeing 727-100/200.

PEMCO AEROPLEX BAe 146-200 CARGO CONVERSION

Appointed by BAe to make first conversion of 146-200 (see UK section) to all-cargo configuraton; installed port side upward opening 3.30 m × 1.98 m (10 ft 10 in × 6 ft 6 in) cargo door aft of wing; applied strengthening and fitted out cabin. Converted aircraft can operate as all-cargo or passenger carrier. Pemco Aeroplex obtained FAA supplemental type certificate and will make future conversions, but BAe markets; 146-200 and -300 also converted to QC quick change.

PEMCO AEROPLEX BOEING 737-300QC

Stronger floor-beam anchorages; additional fuselage doublers to accept new 3.55 m × 2.28 m (11 ft 7¾ in × 7 ft 5¾ in) cargo door. First aircraft scheduled for redelivery late April 1991, to joint venture company Aeropostale formed by Air France/Air Inter, La Poste, and TAT Group; four more on option. TNT Norge ordered three for delivery June 1991 to early 1992; to be flown by Falcon Aviation on Linjeflyg passenger services by day and Swedish postal/cargo operations at night.

PEMCO AEROPLEX BOEING 747-100 CARGO CONVERSION

Ex-TWA Boeing 747-100 converted to all-cargo configuration; 3.12 m × 3.48 m (10 ft 3 in × 11 ft 5 in) cargo door port side aft of wing; 9g bulkhead aft of flight deck; cargo compartment floor beams replaced; upper deck modified; windows blanked off; new interior cabin liner; provision for electric cargo handling system. Main deck can carry 29 cargo containers, with another 13 on lower deck; total payload 91,625 kg (202,000 lb). FAA supplemental type certificate gained April 1988; two modified in 1989; three more modified in 1990; sixth scheduled for completion April 1991.

PEMCO AEROPLEX LOCKHEED L-1011F TRISTAR

Ex-Eastern Air Lines L-1011-1 converted to all-cargo configuration for Aircraft Sales Company; 2.84 m × 4.32 m (9 ft 4 in × 14 ft 2 in) cargo door fitted port side forward of wing; 9g bulkhead aft of flight deck; windows blanked off; tracks and rollers on upper and lower decks; max payload 54,430 kg (120,000 lb); first flight 7 May 1987; FAA type approved; further conversions to order.

PEMCO AEROPLEX MCDONNELL DOUGLAS DC-9 CARGO CONVERSION

All-cargo conversion of DC-9; 2.06 m × 3.45 m (6 ft 9 in × 11 ft 4 in) cargo door port side aft of wing; 9g net barrier; cockpit emergency exit; smoke detection system; overhead storage rack/bin modification; altered interior panels and modifications to air-conditioning and oxygen systems; 15,876 kg (35,000 lb) cargo capacity in main cabin without operating restrictions.

PIASECKI
PIASECKI AIRCRAFT CORPORATION

West Terminus of 2nd Street, Essington, Pennsylvania 19029
Telephone: 1 (215) 521 5700
Fax: 1 (215) 521 9535
PRESIDENT: Frank N. Piasecki
VICE-PRESIDENT, ENGINEERING: Donald N. Myers
INDUSTRIAL ENGINEER: Kenneth R. Meenen

Formed in 1955 by Frank Piasecki, former Chairman of the Board and President of Piasecki Helicopter Corporation, now Boeing Helicopters; wholly owned subsidiary Piasecki Aircraft of Canada Ltd in Ottawa, Ontario; work on hybrid VTOL Heli-Stat ceased 1989.

PIASECKI 16H-4 PATHFINDER III

TYPE: Passenger-carrying compound helicopter.
PROGRAMME: Announced 29 March 1988; company is looking for domestic and foreign manufacturing and marketing partners; FY 1991 defence budget allocated $5.48 million for flight testing; possibility of modifying Westland 30-300 as prototype.
VARIANTS: **Attack helicopter:** Tentative gunship helicopter using vectored thrust ducted propeller and wing received US Army contract in April 1991.
DESIGN FEATURES: Pathfinder III to carry six passengers at 180 knots (333 km/h; 207 mph) competing with fixed-wing corporate and commuter aircraft; powered by 1,339 kW (1,796 shp) General Electric T700 turboshafts; has advanced version of Piasecki ring tail vectored thrust ducted propeller (VTDP) developed under US Army contract and demonstrated in Piasecki 16H-1A compound helicopter, which achieved maximum speed 195 knots (362 km/h; 225 mph) during 1966 trials.

DIMENSIONS, EXTERNAL:
Rotor diameter	13.48 m (44 ft 2¾ in)
Wing span	7.80 m (25 ft 7¼ in)
Wing chord: at root	1.77 m (5 ft 9½ in)
at tip	0.61 m (2 ft 0 in)
Wing aspect ratio	5.6
Length: overall, rotor turning	16.46 m (54 ft 0 in)
fuselage	15.73 m (51 ft 7¼ in)
Height overall	5.04 m (16 ft 6½ in)
Wheel track	2.32 m (7 ft 7¼ in)
Wheelbase	6.35 m (20 ft 9⅞ in)
Ducted propeller diameter	2.29 m (7 ft 6 in)
Passenger door: Height	1.40 m (4 ft 7 in)
Width	0.70 m (2 ft 3½ in)
Height to sill	0.58 m (1 ft 11 in)

Attack helicopter with vectored thrust ducted propeller and wing proposed by Piasecki Aircraft in 1991

DIMENSIONS, INTERNAL:
Cabin: Length	5.44 m (17 ft 10 in)
Max width	1.98 m (6 ft 6 in)
Max height	1.27 m (4 ft 2 in)

AREAS:
Wings, gross	10.87 m² (117.0 sq ft)

WEIGHTS AND LOADINGS:
Basic operating weight	5,512 kg (12,153 lb)
Max payload	1,064 kg (2,347 lb)
Max fuel weight	1,043 kg (2,300 lb)
Max ramp, T-O and landing weight	5,806 kg (12,800 lb)
Max zero-fuel weight	4,762 kg (10,500 lb)

PERFORMANCE (estimated at max T-O weight):
Never-exceed speed (VNE)	230 knots (426 km/h; 265 mph)
Max level speed at S/L	196 knots (363 km/h; 226 mph)
Max cruising speed at S/L	181 knots (335 km/h; 208 mph)
Econ cruising speed at S/L	140 knots (259 km/h; 161 mph)
Max rate of climb at S/L	594 m (1,950 ft)/min
Rate of climb at S/L, one engine out	46 m (150 ft)/min
Service ceiling	3,050 m (10,000 ft)
Range with max fuel, 15% sfc allowance, 10% reserves	290 nm (537 km; 334 miles)

PIPER
PIPER AIRCRAFT CORPORATION

2926 Piper Drive, PO Box 1328, Vero Beach, Florida 32960
Telephone: 1 (305) 567 4361
Fax: 1 (407) 562 0299
Telex: 441426
CHAIRMAN: M. Stuart Millar
PRESIDENT AND CHIEF EXECUTIVE OFFICER:
C. Raymond Johnson
VICE-PRESIDENT, MARKETING: Kevin T. Tracey
VICE-PRESIDENT, MANUFACTURING: William D. Polk

Piper purchased by Lear Siegler Inc effective 1 March 1984; Lock Haven and Piper facilities in Pennsylvania closed second half 1984; Lakeland, Florida, plant phased out October 1985. Activities concentrated at Vero Beach and new 12,077 m² (130,000 sq ft) plant completed October 1986 for Cheyenne IIIA and 400 production (transferred from Lakeland).

Company acquired by Mr M. Stuart Millar 12 May 1987 and became subsidiary of Romeo Charlie Inc; LoPresti Piper Advanced Engineering Group (which see) set up as subsidiary December 1987; Piper North Corporation (which see) subsidiary formed November 1989 at Lock Haven to re-establish aircraft manufacturing at former headquarters under loan guarantee agreement with Commonwealth of Pennsylvania. Increasing cash flow problems in second half of 1990 resulted in closure of both subsidiaries and reduced production. Sale of type certificates and manufacturing rights for number of out-of-production models being negotiated August 1990 and March 1991. Aerospatiale (Socata) negotiations to buy Piper finally broken off 22 March 1991, reportedly because of product liability uncertainties. January 1990 workforce of 1,600 had been reduced to fewer than 370 by April 1991.

Piper designs are manufactured in Argentina by Chincul SA (which see) and in Brazil by Embraer subsidiary Neiva (which see); PZL Mielec in Poland (which see) produces Seneca II as M-20 Mewa.

PIPER SUSPENDED PRODUCTION

By March 1991, Piper's cash flow and product liability difficulties were thought to have resulted in the effective suspension of production of all single-engined aircraft and twin piston-engined designs except the Malibu. The following were last fully described in 1990-91 *Jane's.*

Piper PA-18-150 Super Cub: Tandem two-seat light aircraft; original FAA Type Approval received 18 November 1949; rights acquired by WTA Inc 1982 but Piper resumed production 1988; 55 were delivered in 1989 and 1990, and 27 were on order on 1 January 1991.

Piper PA-28-161 Warrior II and Cadet: Development of four-seat PA-28 Cherokee Cruiser; longer span wings with tapered outer panels introduced, with 112 kW (150 hp) engine, on 1972 Warrior I; 119 kW (160 hp) engine introduced on 1976 Warrior II. Cadet two/four-seat version optimised for training, introduced 1988. Total 2,985 PA-28-161s sold by 1 January 1991.

Piper PA-28-181 Archer II: Introduced October 1972 as Cherokee Challenger, successor to PA-28 Cherokee 180;

became Cherokee Archer 1974; redesignated Cherokee Archer II in 1976; tapered wings of Warrior II introduced 1978. Total of 9,894 Cherokee 180s/Archer IIs delivered by 1 January 1991.

Piper PA-28R-201 Arrow and PA-28R-201T Turbo Arrow: Derived from Cherokee Arrow II, as retractable landing gear version of Archer II with more powerful engine; tapered wings of Archer II introduced 1977; turbo version flew December 1976; T tailed version introduced 1979 as Arrow IV but production of low-tail version later resumed. Total 33 Arrows and 10 Turbo Arrows delivered in 1989.

Piper PA-28-236 Dakota: Introduced 1978 as more powerful version of Warrior/Archer/Arrow range, with 175 kW (235 hp) Textron Lycoming O-540-J3A5D engine and increased fuel capacity. Total 742 sold by 1 January 1991.

Piper PA-32-301 Saratoga and PA-32R-301 Saratoga SP: Announced December 1979 as replacements for six-seat Cherokee Six 300 and T tail Lance; Saratoga SP has retractable landing gear. Total of 815 Saratogas delivered by 1 January 1991, including 55 in 1990.

Piper PA-34-220T Seneca III: PA-34 Seneca six-seat twin-engined light aircraft announced September 1971; redesignated Seneca II 1975 and PA-34-220T Seneca III, with more powerful engines, in 1981. Total of 4,464 Senecas delivered by 1 January 1991, including 50 in 1990.

Piper PA-44-180 Seminole: Four-seat twin-engined light aircraft first flown May 1976; production of basic Seminole and Turbo Seminole began 1978; production terminated 1982 after 361 Seminoles and 87 Turbo Seminoles built; basic Seminole restored to production 1988 and a further 29 delivered by 1 January 1991.

PIPER PA-42-720 CHEYENNE IIIA

TYPE: Seven/eleven-seat corporate and commuter airline transport and advanced trainer.

PROGRAMME: Announced as Cheyenne III; production prototype flew 18 May 1979; certification received early 1980; 89 built before replaced by Cheyenne IIIA; certificated March 1983; 56 Cheyenne IIIAs delivered by 1 January 1991.

VARIANTS: **Cheyenne IIIA Customs High Endurance Tracker (CHET):** Aircraft fitted with special sensors delivered to US Drug Enforcement Administration 15 February 1984; used for variety of day and night surveillance and identification missions; further eight ordered March 1985, delivered monthly intervals from September 1985. AN/APG-66 radar and Texas Instruments ventral FLIR turret.

CUSTOMERS: Advanced trainers delivered to Lufthansa (seven), with Collins five-tube EFIS on flight decks configured to resemble airline's Airbus A310s; also to Alitalia (three), Turkish Air League (two), All Nippon Airways (four), CAAC of China (four); Austrian Airlines ordered two for delivery early in 1991.

DESIGN FEATURES: Cheyenne III differences from Cheyenne I and II include increased wing span, lengthened fuselage, T tail and more powerful PT6A-41 engines; Cheyenne IIIA introduced PT6A-61 engines, increased max cruising speed, higher certificated ceiling, and improvements to interior layout, air-conditioning and electrical system. Wing section NACA 63$_2$A415 (modified) at root, NACA 63$_1$A212 at tip; dihedral 5°; incidence 1° 30′; no sweepback. Goodrich pneumatic de-icing boots standard for wing, tailplane and fin leading-edges.

FLYING CONTROLS: Manually actuated controls; servo tab in rudder; anti-servo tab on elevator.

LANDING GEAR: Hydraulically retractable tricycle type with single wheel on each unit. Main units retract inward, nosewheel forward. Pneumatic blow-down system for emergency extension, with manually operated hydraulic system as backup. Piper oleo-pneumatic shock absorbers. Cleveland mainwheels with tyres size 6.50-10 12-ply Type III, pressure 6.90 bars (100 lb/sq in). Cleveland steerable nosewheel with tyre size 17.5 × 6.25, 10-ply rating Type III, pressure 4.83 bars (70 lb/sq in). Goodrich hydraulically operated disc brakes. Parking brake.

POWER PLANT: Two Pratt & Whitney Canada PT6A-61 turboprops, each flat rated at 537 kW (720 shp) and driving a Hartzell three-blade constant-speed feathering and reversible-pitch metal propeller with Q-tips. Automatic propeller feathering system and synchrophaser optional. Each wing has four interconnected fuel cells and a tip tank, with a combined total capacity of 2,127 litres (562 US gallons; 468 Imp gallons), of which 2,120 litres (560 US gallons; 466 Imp gallons) are usable. NACA type anti-icing and non-siphoning fuel vents incorporating flame arresters. Refuelling points on upper surface of each tip tank and engine nacelle. Oil capacity 24.6 litres (6.5 US gallons; 5.4 Imp gallons). Electric intake anti-icing and propeller de-icing.

ACCOMMODATION: Pilot and co-pilot on four-way adjustable seats with armrests, headrests, shoulder safety belts with inertia reels, and stowage for oxygen mask beneath seats. Certificated for single pilot operation. Dual controls standard. Cabin seats up to nine passengers, but standard interior includes six reclining and adjustable passenger seats with armrests, headrests, and magazine storage on seat back, plus lavatory seat. Wide range of options for cabin furnishing available. Door with built-in airstair on

Piper Cheyenne IIIA used for advanced civil pilot training by China's CAAC

port side, with seven locking pins and inflatable pressurisation seal. Emergency exit window on starboard side. Baggage compartments in nose and rear of cabin, each with capacity of 136 kg (300 lb), and in each engine nacelle, with a capacity of 45 kg (100 lb), giving a maximum total baggage capacity of 363 kg (800 lb). Accommodation is pressurised, heated and air-conditioned. Pilot and co-pilot windscreen heated, wipers standard.

SYSTEMS: AiResearch pressurisation system with max differential of 0.43 bar (6.3 lb/sq in), maintaining a cabin altitude of 3,050 m (10,000 ft) to a height of 10,060 m (33,000 ft). Environmental control system, combining the functions of heater, air-conditioner and dehumidifier. Hydraulic system supplied by dual engine driven pumps. Pneumatic system and vacuum system supplied by engine bleed air. Electrical system includes two 28V 300A engine driven generators and 24V 40Ah storage battery. Oxygen system of 0.62 m³ (22 cu ft) capacity with ten outlets. Pneumatic wing and tailplane de-icing boots, electric anti-icing of engine air intakes, heated pitots, electric propeller de-icing, and windscreen heating.

AVIONICS: Standard Bendix/King avionics package includes 4 in EHSI, KFC-325 autopilot with flight director and altitude preselect, RDS-81 radar, dual slaved compass systems and audio panels. Alternative Collins package with same capabilities. Optional avionics include three-tube and five-tube EFIS, other Bendix/King and Collins weather radars, KNS-600 and UNS-1/1A flight management systems, plus a wide range of other options.

EQUIPMENT: Extensive standard installed equipment includes 'No smoking-Fasten seat belt' sign; carpeted floor; tinted cabin windows; pull-down window shades; wood divider between flight deck and cabin; two folding tables; oxygen system with individual masks in storage compartments; indirect fluorescent lighting, individual reading lights, and courtesy lights. Optional equipment includes cabin chimes; stereo system; cabin instrument cluster giving digital readouts of altitude, outside air temperature, time, and true airspeed; cabin fire extinguisher; emergency locator transmitter; and engine fire extinguishing systems.

DIMENSIONS, EXTERNAL:

Wing span over tip tanks	14.53 m (47 ft 8 in)
Wing chord: at root	3.12 m (10 ft 3 in)
at tip	0.97 m (3 ft 2 in)
Wing aspect ratio	7.8
Length overall	13.23 m (43 ft 4¾ in)
Height overall	4.50 m (14 ft 9 in)
Tailplane span	6.65 m (21 ft 10 in)
Wheel track	5.72 m (18 ft 9 in)
Wheelbase	3.23 m (10 ft 7¼ in)
Propeller diameter	2.41 m (7 ft 11 in)
Distance between propeller centres	5.38 m (17 ft 8 in)
Passenger door: Height	1.12 m (3 ft 8 in)
Width	0.73 m (2 ft 5 in)
Baggage doors:	
Nose: Height	0.51 m (1 ft 8 in)
Width	0.66 m (2 ft 2 in)
Utility door (aft): Height	0.76 m (2 ft 6 in)
Width	0.43 m (1 ft 5 in)
Nacelle locker doors: Height	0.86 m (2 ft 10 in)
Width	0.61 m (2 ft 0 in)

DIMENSIONS, INTERNAL:

Cabin (incl flight deck and rear baggage area):	
Length	6.99 m (22 ft 11 in)
Max width	1.30 m (4 ft 3 in)
Max height	1.32 m (4 ft 4 in)
Volume	approx 9.91 m³ (350.0 cu ft)
Baggage compartment volume:	
nose	0.46 m³ (16.25 cu ft)
rear	0.88 m³ (31.0 cu ft)
nacelle locker (two, each)	0.16 m³ (5.6 cu ft)

AREAS:

Wings, gross	27.22 m² (293.0 sq ft)
Ailerons (total)	1.25 m² (13.5 sq ft)
Trailing-edge flaps (total)	3.17 m² (34.1 sq ft)
Fin	4.26 m² (45.81 sq ft)
Rudder, incl tab	1.60 m² (17.25 sq ft)
Tailplane	4.39 m² (47.3 sq ft)
Elevators, incl tab	2.26 m² (24.3 sq ft)

WEIGHTS AND LOADINGS:

Basic weight empty	3,101 kg (6,837 lb)
Max T-O weight	5,080 kg (11,200 lb)
Max ramp weight	5,119 kg (11,285 lb)
Max zero-fuel weight	4,241 kg (9,350 lb)
Max landing weight	4,685 kg (10,330 lb)
Max wing loading	186.6 kg/m² (38.22 lb/sq ft)
Max power loading	4.73 kg/kW (7.78 lb/shp)

PERFORMANCE (at max T-O weight except where indicated):

Max level speed at average cruise weight of 4,127 kg (9,100 lb)   305 knots (565 km/h; 351 mph)

Cruising speed at max cruise power, at average cruise weight of 4,127 kg (9,100 lb):
at 6,700 m (22,000 ft)   305 knots (565 km/h; 351 mph)
at 7,620 m (25,000 ft)   302 knots (560 km/h; 348 mph)
at 9,460 m (31,000 ft)   293 knots (543 km/h; 337 mph)
at 10,670 m (35,000 ft)   282 knots (523 km/h; 325 mph)

Minimum single-engine control speed (VMC)   91 knots (169 km/h; 105 mph)

Stalling speed, engines idling, at 5,080 kg (11,200 lb):
flaps and gear up   100 knots (186 km/h; 115 mph) IAS
flaps and gear down   87 knots (162 km/h; 100 mph) IAS
Rotation speed   93 knots (172 km/h; 107 mph) IAS
Approach speed   109 knots (202 km/h; 126 mph) IAS
Max rate of climb at S/L   725 m (2,380 ft)/min
Rate of climb at S/L, one engine out   191 m (625 ft)/min
Service ceiling   10,925 m (35,840 ft)
Service ceiling, one engine out   6,460 m (21,200 ft)
T-O run   465 m (1,525 ft)
T-O to 15 m (50 ft)   726 m (2,380 ft)
Landing from 15 m (50 ft)   928 m (3,043 ft)
Landing from 15 m (50 ft) with propeller reversal   788 m (2,586 ft)
Landing run   583 m (1,914 ft)
Landing run with propeller reversal   444 m (1,457 ft)
Accelerate/stop distance   1,025 m (3,363 ft)

Range with max fuel, allowances for taxi, T-O, climb, descent, 45 min reserves at max range power, ISA:
max cruising power at:
6,700 m (22,000 ft)   1,372 nm (2,542 km; 1,580 miles)
7,620 m (25,000 ft)   1,510 nm (2,798 km; 1,739 miles)
9,460 m (31,000 ft)   1,850 nm (3,428 km; 2,130 miles)
10,670 m (35,000 ft)   2,060 nm (3,817 km; 2,372 miles)
max range power at:
6,700 m (22,000 ft)   1,803 nm (3,341 km; 2,076 miles)
7,620 m (25,000 ft)   1,945 nm (3,604 km; 2,240 miles)
9,460 m (31,000 ft)   2,200 nm (4,077 km; 2,533 miles)
10,670 m (35,000 ft)   2,270 nm (4,207 km; 2,614 miles)

PIPER PA-42-1000 CHEYENNE 400

TYPE: Seven/eleven-seat light business transport and advanced trainer.

PROGRAMME: Announced September 1982 as Cheyenne IV and later known as Cheyenne 400LS; first flight of

Cheyenne 400 prototype (N400PT) 23 February 1983; first flight of second prototype 23 June 1983; FAA certification received 13 July 1984; deliveries commenced July 1984.

CUSTOMERS: First delivery to Garrett Turbine Engine Company 26 July 1984; Korean Air received one advanced trainer in January 1990 and a second in early 1991; total of 43 Cheyenne 400s delivered by 1 January 1991; 1,000th aircraft of Cheyenne series was Cheyenne 400 delivered to customer in Connecticut.

DESIGN FEATURES: Similar to Cheyenne III but flush riveted throughout; wings adapted for TPE331 engines and strengthened inboard of wheel wells to accept new main landing gear; outer wing panels modified to incorporate integral fuel tanks and carry wingtip tanks; fuselage strengthened for increased pressurisation; new multi-ply stretched acrylic windows; minor modifications to tail unit to cater for higher speeds.

LANDING GEAR: Hydraulically retractable tricycle type, with single wheel on each unit. Main units retract inward into wings, nosewheel rearward. Redesigned by comparison with Cheyenne IIIA, for improved ground attitude and increased landing weight. Mainwheels and tyres size 6.50-10, 12-ply rating, pressure 7.58 bars (110 lb/sq in). Steerable nosewheel, size 6.00-6, with 17.5 × 6.25-6 tyre, 10-ply rating, pressure 5.52 bars (80 lb/sq in). Hydraulically actuated dual disc brakes, with multiple brake pads, on each mainwheel.

POWER PLANT: Two 1,226.5 kW (1,645 shp) Garrett TPE331-14A/14B counter-rotating turboprops, each flat rated at 746 kW (1,000 shp) and driving a Hartzell four-blade constant-speed reversible-pitch metal propeller. Blade design and construction incorporates protection from both erosion and lightning strike. Initial production (up to c/n 42) fitted with Dowty four-blade composite propellers; still available as an option. The installation of each engine includes new mountings, a new nacelle enclosing the exhaust system, new inlet incorporating bleed air anti-icing, and an exhaust system which discharges the efflux over the wing. Propeller synchrophaser standard. Fuel system as for Cheyenne IIIA, except usable fuel capacity is 2,158 litres (570 US gallons; 474.5 Imp gallons). The engines have automatic negative torque control, automatic start sequencing, and use a micro-computer system to record in-flight performance data for engine trend monitoring.

ACCOMMODATION: Although certificated for single pilot operation, provision for crew of two side by side on separate flight deck. Standard cabin has two rearward facing seats at front. Flat floor and table between these seats and two pairs of forward facing seats, with dropped aisle between each pair. Toilet, with solid divider and door, and walk-in baggage area (capacity 136 kg; 300 lb) at rear of cabin. Alternative cabin layouts available. Airstair door at rear of cabin on port side. Cargo door immediately aft of this, to provide unobstructed wide opening. Double glazed windows. Emergency exit over wing on starboard side. Nose baggage compartment, capacity 136 kg (300 lb), with two doors on port side.

SYSTEMS: Environmental control system utilises engine bleed air from both engines for heating, cooling and pressurisation. Max pressure differential 0.51 bar (7.5 lb/sq in), maintaining a cabin altitude of 3,040 m (9,980 ft) at a height of 12,500 m (41,000 ft). Independent emergency bleed air pressurisation system. Completely new electrical system includes two engine driven generators and two batteries. Automatic dropout oxygen masks.

AVIONICS: As for Cheyenne IIIA except standard autopilot is Bendix/King KFC-400 with air data system.

DIMENSIONS, EXTERNAL: As for Cheyenne IIIA, except:
Height overall	5.18 m (17 ft 0 in)
Propeller diameter	2.69 m (8 ft 10 in)
Nose baggage doors:	
Fwd: height	0.30 m (1 ft 0 in)
width	0.60 m (2 ft 0 in)
Rear: height	0.66 m (2 ft 2 in)
width	0.51 m (1 ft 8 in)

DIMENSIONS, INTERNAL: As for Cheyenne IIIA, except:
Cabin: Max height	1.42 m (4 ft 8 in)
Baggage compartment volume:	
nose	0.48 m³ (17.0 cu ft)
rear	0.88 m³ (31.0 cu ft)

WEIGHTS AND LOADINGS:
Weight empty, standard	3,412 kg (7,522 lb)
Max usable fuel	1,732 kg (3,819 lb)
Max T-O weight	5,466 kg (12,050 lb)
Max ramp weight	5,504 kg (12,135 lb)
Max landing weight	5,035 kg (11,100 lb)
Max zero-fuel weight	4,536 kg (10,000 lb)
Max wing loading	200.8 kg/m² (41.13 lb/sq ft)
Max power loading	2.23 kg/kW (3.66 lb/shp)

PERFORMANCE (at max T-O weight except where indicated):
Max operating speed
  Mach 0.62 (246 knots; 455 km/h; 283 mph EAS)
Cruising speed at max cruise power at AUW of 4,536 kg (10,000 lb):
  at 7,620 m (25,000 ft)   358 knots (663 km/h; 412 mph)
  at 12,500 m (41,000 ft)   335 knots (621 km/h; 386 mph)
Minimum single-engine control speed (VMC)
  99 knots (183 km/h; 114 mph) IAS

Piper Cheyenne 400 (Garrett TPE331-14A/14B turboprops)

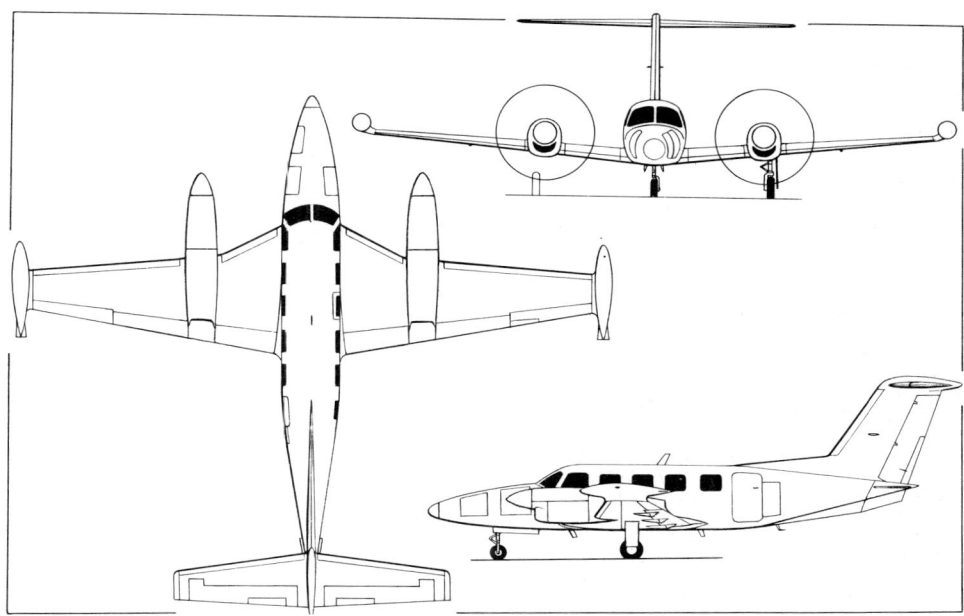

Piper Cheyenne 400 twin-turboprops seven/eleven-seat business transport
(Pilot Press)

Stalling speed, engines idling:
  flaps and landing gear up
  93 knots (172 km/h; 107 mph) IAS
  flaps and landing gear down
  84 knots (156 km/h; 97 mph) IAS
Max rate of climb at S/L   1,071 m (3,515 ft)/min
Rate of climb at S/L, one engine out
  314 m (1,030 ft)/min
Service ceiling   12,130 m (39,800 ft)
Service ceiling, one engine out   7,650 m (25,095 ft)
T-O run   606 m (1,987 ft)
T-O to 15 m (50 ft)   861 m (2,825 ft)
Landing from 15 m (50 ft) at max landing weight:
  without reverse thrust   860 m (2,820 ft)
  with reverse thrust (Dowty propellers only)
  622 m (2,038 ft)
Landing run:
  without reverse thrust   427 m (1,400 ft)
  with reverse thrust (Dowty propellers only)
  250 m (820 ft)
Accelerate/stop distance   1,113 m (3,650 ft)
Range at max cruise power at 10,670 m (35,000 ft), with allowances for start, taxi, T-O, climb, descent and 45 min reserves at max range power:
  with 8 passengers   1,167 nm (2,162 km; 1,343 miles)
  with 3 passengers   1,718 nm (3,183 km; 1,978 miles)
Max range, at max range power at 12,500 m (41,000 ft), allowances as above:
  with 8 passengers   1,547 nm (2,867 km; 1,781 miles)
  with 3 passengers   2,283 nm (4,230 km; 2,629 miles)

PIPER PA-46-350P MALIBU MIRAGE

TYPE: Six-seat light business transport.

PROGRAMME: Announced November 1982; FAA certification of original PA-46-310P Malibu received September 1988; production deliveries began November 1983; 402 built before replaced by PA-46-350P Malibu Mirage October 1988; Piper delivered 24 Malibu Mirages in 1990; total orders had reached 200 by May 1990 and combined deliveries 518 by Spring 1991, at which time FAA had imposed temporary ban on IMC flights.

DESIGN FEATURES: Teledyne Continental TIO-540-AE2A introduced on Malibu Mirage; other changes include dual 70A 28V alternators, split bus electrical system; redesigned flight deck; additional options include computerised fuel management system and pilot's electrically heated windscreen. Wing dihedral 4.5°. Optional pneumatic de-icing boots on wing and tailplane leading-edges.

FLYING CONTROLS: Conventional ailerons; horn balanced elevators and rudder; trim tab in elevator; electrically operated trailing-edge flaps.

STRUCTURE: Cantilever high aspect ratio all-metal wings; semi-monocoque light alloy fuselage, fail-safe construction in pressurised area; light alloy tail surfaces.

LANDING GEAR: Hydraulically retractable tricycle type with single wheel on each unit; main units retract inward into wingroots, nosewheel rearward, rotating 90° to lie flat under baggage compartment. Oleo-pneumatic shock absorber in each unit. Mainwheel tyres, size 6.00-6, 8-ply; nosewheel tyre, size 5.00-5, 6-ply. Hydraulic brakes on mainwheels. Parking brake.

POWER PLANT: One 261 kW (350 hp) Textron Lycoming TIO-540-AE2A turbocharged and intercooled flat-six engine, driving a Hartzell two-blade constant-speed propeller. Fuel system capacity 462 litres (122 US gallons; 101.6 Imp gallons), of which 454 litres (120 US gallons; 100 Imp gallons) are usable. Oil capacity 11.5 litres (3 US gallons; 2.5 Imp gallons).

ACCOMMODATION: Pilot and five passengers in pressurised, heated and ventilated cabin. Centre and rear contoured reclining seats in facing pairs. Foldaway writing table. Airstair door immediately to rear of wing trailing-edge on

Piper PA-46-350P Malibu Mirage cabin class, pressurised, single piston-engined aircraft

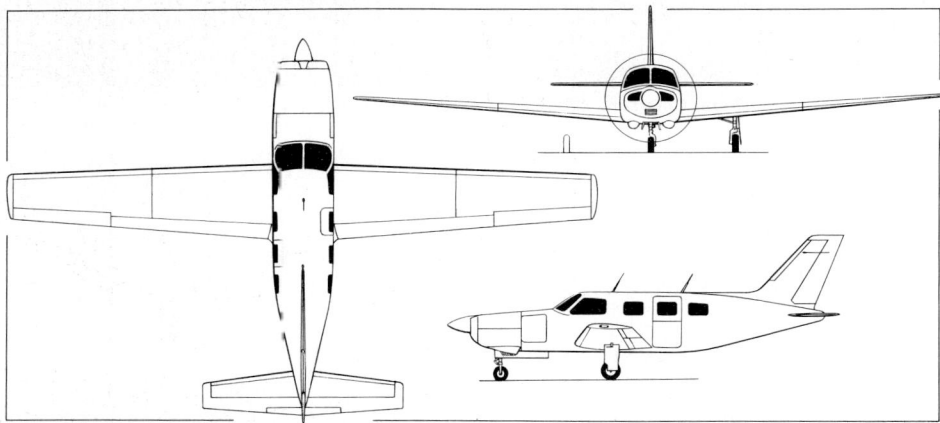

Piper PA-46-350P Malibu Mirage, powered by Textron Lycoming TIO-540-AE2A *(Pilot Press)*

port side. Overwing emergency exit on starboard side. Unpressurised baggage compartment in nose, and pressurised space at rear of cabin, each with capacity of 45 kg (100 lb). Heated pilot's windscreen optional.

SYSTEMS: Pressurisation system with max differential of 0.38 bar (5.5 lb/sq in), to provide a cabin altitude of 2,400 m (7,900 ft) to a height of 7,620 m (25,000 ft). Hydraulic system pressure 107 bars (1,550 lb/sq in). Dual engine driven vacuum pumps standard. Standard electrical system has two 70A alternators; 24V 10Ah battery. Full icing protection is optional, with pneumatic de-icing boots on wing and tail surfaces, electrically heated propeller, pilot's electrically heated anti-ice windscreen plate, wing ice inspection light, heated pitot head, heated lift detector, and dual alternators and vacuum pumps.

AVIONICS: Standard Bendix/King avionics package comprises KX 165-25 nav/com with VOR/LOC converter and glideslope receiver, KX 165-24 nav/com, KI 525A electric HSI with VOR/LOC/GS indicator for nav 1, KI 202-00 VOR/LOC indicator for nav 2, KG 258 horizon reference indicator, KCS 55A slaved compass system, KR 87 digital ADF with KI 227-00 indicator and K44B antenna, KT 76A transponder, KMA 24-03 audio selector panel with marker beacon receiver and lights, KN 62A DME, KAP 150 AFCS with electric pitch trim, VOR/LOC/GS coupling and KCS 55A HSI/compass system, United 5035P-P40 encoding altimeter, Piper avionics master switch, Telex 100T noise-cancelling microphone, Telex 600 OHM headset, and Truax static discharge wicks (16). Alternative Bendix/King package substitutes dual KY 196A-30 com, dual KN 53-01 nav 1, KN 53-01 nav 2, and nav 2 KI 203-00 VOR/LOC indicator, otherwise as above. Approved options to standard and alternative packages include KT 79 transponder, KNS 80 and KNS 81 integrated nav systems, second glideslope, nav 1/2 autopilot coupling switch, KI 227-01 slaved ADF indicator for use with KR 87, KN 63, DME, KMA 24H-70 audio control panel with intercom system, and KEA 346 encoding altimeter. Other avionics options include Bendix/King KFC 150 AFCS/flight director, KAS 297B altitude/vertical speed preselect/alerter, yaw damper, KA 185 autopilot mode

annunciator, EHI-40 EFIS, KDI 572 second DME indicator, KN 63 DME, KRA 10 radio altimeter, KI 229 and KNI 582 RMIs, Bendix/King KLN 88, II Morrow 612 and Northstar M1 Loran C systems, 3M Stormscope WX-1000/1000+, Bendix/King RDS-81 colour weather radar with Piper radome, Bendix/King KHF 950 HF, Wulfsberg Flitefone VI, Flite-Tronics PC-50 static inverter, ground clearance energy saver switch, pilot's boom microphone and control wheel button, pilot's and co-pilot's control wheel microphone and transponder ident buttons, and co-pilot's control wheel electric trim button.

EQUIPMENT: Standard equipment includes true airspeed indicator; magnetic compass; Piper pictorial turn rate indicator; eight-day clock; 3 in artificial horizon and pictorial navigation indicator; gyro air filter; vacuum gauge; luminous OAT gauge; heated pitot head; ammeter/voltmeter; annunciator panel with push-to-test; electric tachometer; two-in-one fuel quantity gauges; manifold pressure/fuel flow gauge; oil temperature/pressure gauge; cylinder head temperature gauge with individual cylinder monitoring; TIT gauge; Hobbs meter; cabin altitude and differential pressure indicator; cabin pressure rate of climb indicator; cabin altitude warning light; alternate static source; pilot's and co-pilot's toe brakes; stall warning computer and horn; landing light; two taxi lights; two navigation lights; two strobe lights; instrument panel, switch and circuit breaker panel lighting; solid state dimming; two cabin dome lights; seven overhead cabin lights; nose baggage compartment light; cabin entrance light; interior baggage compartment light; Piper Aire freon vapour cycle air-conditioning system; supplemental electric heater; windscreen defrosters; six cabin air controls with electric fan; six floor mounted cabin heating/ventilating vents; choice of four interior colours; fabric, leather and vinyl side panels; wool carpeting; sheepskin covered fore and aft and vertically adjustable and reclining pilot's and co-pilot's seats with inertia reel shoulder harnesses, seatbelts, map holders and ashtrays; pilot's storm window; emergency exit; pilot's and co-pilot's scuff pads and sun visors; compass card with holder; power setting table and

T-O/landing checklists on sun visor; four fabric and leather reclining passenger seats in club arrangement with inertia reel shoulder harnesses, seatbelts and ashtrays; executive writing table; super soundproofing and inner passenger windows; window shades for passenger windows; passenger briefing cards; luggage compartment security straps; rear cabin compartment luggage retaining net; cabin entrance door with integral steps and pneumatic extender on upper door; DuPont IMRON polyurethane enamel exterior paint finish with single- or two-tone base colour with choice of two schemes in two trim colours; epoxy primer and zinc chromate corrosion protection; stainless steel control cables; retractable tiedown rings; stowable towbar; two jack pads; external power receptacle; and emergency locator transmitter. Optional **Executive** group comprises forward refreshment centre, cassette player cabin entertainment system, lockable fuel caps, hand-held fire extinguisher, and vinyl floor runner. Other options available in addition to those listed for Executive group include panel mounted digital clock, Lewis digital TIT gauge, co-pilot's flight instruments, backup mechanical altimeter for co-pilot, six-cylinder CHT gauge, Shadin Mini Flow fuel management system, AIM 2 in standby attitude gyro, De-icing Group comprising wing and tail pneumatic de-icing boots, electric propeller de-icing, pilot's electrically heated windscreen and ice inspection light; polished propeller spinner, lightweight canister emergency oxygen system, all-leather crew and passenger seats, relief tube, CD player, third exterior trim colour, Infinity Designer Edition exterior styling, and shadowed registration numbers.

DIMENSIONS, EXTERNAL:
Wing span	13.11 m (43 ft 0 in)
Length overall	8.72 m (28 ft 7¼ in)
Height overall	3.51 m (11 ft 6 in)
Tailplane span	4.42 m (14 ft 6 in)
Wheel track	3.75 m (12 ft 3½ in)
Wheelbase	2.44 m (8 ft 0 in)
Propeller diameter	2.03 m (6 ft 8 in)
Passenger door (port, rear):	
Height	1.17 m (3 ft 10 in)
Width	0.61 m (2 ft 0 in)
Baggage door (port, nose):	
Height	0.58 m (1 ft 11 in)
Width	0.48 m (1 ft 7 in)

DIMENSIONS, INTERNAL:
Cabin: Length, instrument panel to rear pressure bulkhead	3.76 m (12 ft 4 in)
Max width	1.26 m (4 ft 1½ in)
Max height	1.19 m (3 ft 11 in)
Baggage compartment volume:	
nose	0.37 m³ (13.0 cu ft)
rear cabin	0.57 m³ (20.0 cu ft)

AREAS:
Wings, gross	16.26 m² (175.0 sq ft)

WEIGHTS AND LOADINGS:
Weight empty, standard (estimated)	1,265 kg (2,790 lb)
Max T-O weight	1,950 kg (4,300 lb)
Max ramp weight	1,958 kg (4,318 lb)
Max zero-fuel weight	1,860 kg (4,100 lb)
Max landing weight	1,860 kg (4,100 lb)
Max wing loading	119.9 kg/m² (24.6 lb/sq ft)
Max power loading	7.47 kg/kW (12.3 lb/hp)

PERFORMANCE:
Max level speed at mid-cruise weight	232 knots (430 km/h; 267 mph)
Cruising speed at optimum altitude, mid-cruise weight:	
high speed cruise power	225 knots (417 km/h; 259 mph)
normal cruise power	215 knots (398 km/h; 247 mph)
econ cruise power	199 knots (369 km/h; 229 mph)
long range cruise power	168 knots (311 km/h; 193 mph)
Stalling speed:	
flaps and wheels up	71 knots (132 km/h; 82 mph)
flaps and wheels down	60 knots (111 km/h; 69 mph)
Max rate of climb at S/L	371 m (1,218 ft)/min
Max certificated ceiling	7,620 m (25,000 ft)
T-O run	467 m (1,530 ft)
T-O to 15 m (50 ft)	724 m (2,375 ft)
Landing from 15 m (50 ft)	599 m (1,964 ft)
Landing run	311 m (1,018 ft)
Range with max fuel, allowances for start, T-O, climb and descent, plus 45 min reserves, at optimum altitude:	
high speed cruise power	990 nm (1,834 km; 1,140 miles)
normal cruise power	1,056 nm (1,957 km; 1,216 miles)
econ cruise power	1,184 nm (2,194 km; 1,363 miles)
long range cruise power	1,450 nm (2,687 km; 1,669 miles)

PIPER NORTH
PIPER NORTH CORPORATION
Lock Haven, Pennsylvania
PRESIDENT AND CHIEF EXECUTIVE OFFICER: John R. Piper
VICE-PRESIDENT: William H. Piper
VICE-PRESIDENT, OPERATIONS, AND GENERAL MANAGER:
Charles H. Bartholomew

Founded 17 November 1989 as wholly owned subsidiary of Piper's parent company, Romeo Charlie Inc; based at William T. Piper Memorial Airport, Lock Haven. Planned to produce Piper PA-31-350 Navajo Chieftain (see 1984-85 *Jane's*) and possibly LoPresti Piper SwiftFury (see next entry and 1990-91 *Jane's*); agreement to re-establish

production with loan guarantees from Commonwealth of Pennsylvania suspended July 1990.

LOPRESTI PIPER

LOPRESTI PIPER AIRCRAFT ENGINEERING COMPANY

3215 26th Avenue, Hangar 19, Vero Beach, Florida 32960
PRESIDENT: LeRoy P. LoPresti

This Piper subsidiary has been developing the **LP-1 SwiftFury**, a modernised and high-performance version of 1940s Globe/Temco Swift powered by 149 kW (200 hp)

Textron Lycoming IO-360; first flight (N217LP) 23 March 1989; reported 550 reservations by December 1990; certification originally expected late 1990 or early 1991 but delayed by suspension of operations December 1990. **SwiftThunder** tricycle landing gear version was under development for civil market and US Air Force EFS Enhanced Flight Screener training programme. **Swiftfire** is turbine version, powered by 313 kW (420 shp) Allison

250-B17C; first flight (N345LP) 19 July 1988; details in 1990-91 *Jane's*.

Investment capital, reportedly $15 million, being sought March 1991 to complete certification and commit to production; unit price then estimated as $125,000 direct from manufacturer.

RAISBECK

RAISBECK ENGINEERING INC

7675 Perimeter Road South, Boeing Field International, Seattle, Washington 98108
Telephone: 1 (206) 763 2000
Fax: 1 (206) 767 7726
CHIEF EXECUTIVE OFFICER: James D. Raisbeck
VICE-PRESIDENT, SERVICE AND SALES: Robert P. Steinbach
DIRECTOR, TECHNICAL SERVICES: Michael P. Tougher

Develops, certificates and sells general aviation advanced technology modifications to improve performance, safety and productivity of business aircraft.

HARTZELL/RAISBECK QUIET TURBOFAN PROPELLER SYSTEM FOR BEECHCRAFT KING AIRS

Four-blade propeller conversion known as Quiet Turbofan; first flight on Mark VI-equipped B200 June 1984; certificated on Super King Air 200 February 1985; also certificated for all King Air 90s. Flight deck and cabin noise reduced between 7 and 10 dBA; lower vibration; shorter take-off and landing; better climb. Uses advanced technology Hartzell lightweight Turbofan propellers of 2.39 m (7 ft 10 in) diameter, new timers, slip rings and Goodrich hot propeller de-icing system.

HARTZELL/RAISBECK QUIET TURBOFAN PROPELLER SYSTEM FOR DHC-6 TWIN OTTER

Similar to above applied to de Havilland Canada Twin Otter Series 300 of Scenic Airlines at Las Vegas, Nevada; cabin and flight deck noise reduced by 10-13 dBA; lower external noise, better engine inlet ram air recovery and lower engine temperatures; certificated May 1986; entire Scenic Airlines fleet converted; several European operators also converted to meet ICAO Annex 16 noise limits.

RAISBECK SHORT-FIELD ENHANCEMENT SYSTEM

New composites constructed inboard wing leading-edges, intercooler ducting, wing-to-fuselage fairings, and flush-mounted Goodrich de-icing boots. Announced June 1987 for Beech Super King Air 200/B200; when combined with Hartzell Quiet Turbofan propellers, gives 18 knot (33 km/h; 21 mph) reduction in flaps-up V_2 take-off speed, 35 per cent reduction in FAA T-O distance, 50 per cent reduction in FAA accelerate/go distance, better engine-out climb rate, reduced FAA reference and approach speeds, and 56 per cent reduction in stopping distance with maximum reverse thrust. Other benefits include better outer wing fatigue life, more efficient air-conditioning, higher cruising speeds, reduced stalling speed at all flap settings, and better low-speed handling and stall characteristics.
PERFORMANCE (at AUW of 5,670 kg; 12,500 lb, S/L, ISA. Super King Air 200/B200):

T-O speed (V_2)	103 knots (191 km/h; 119 mph)
Approach speed	97 knots (180 km/h; 112 mph)
T-O to 15 m (50 ft)	686 m (2,250 ft)
Accelerate/go distance	1,061 m (3,480 ft)
Accelerate/stop distance	988 m (3,240 ft)
Landing from 15 m (50 ft)	500 m (1,970 ft)

Raisbeck wing lockers and dual aft-body strake modifications on a Beechcraft Super King Air 200

RAISBECK DUAL AFT-BODY STRAKE SYSTEM

Dual ventral strakes to replace single strake on all Beechcraft King Air and Super King Air models; slightly increases cruising speeds and reduces rear cabin area vibration; with dual strakes, yaw damper no longer a mandatory dispatch item on King Air F90 and Super King Air 200.

RAISBECK WING LOCKERS

Engine nacelle wing lockers on Beechcraft King Air 90/100 and Super King Air 200/300; certificated to FAA FAR Part 135. Lockers can carry 272 kg (600 lb), increase baggage volume by 0.45 m³ (16 cu ft), improve climb and cruise performance, reduce stalling speed, and reduce pitch-axis trim changes in landing configuration.

RAISBECK FULLY ENCLOSED LANDING GEAR DOORS

Doors applied to Beechcraft King Air 90/100 and Super King Air 200s with high flotation landing gear; made of composites; increase high altitude cruising speed by 8-12 knots (15-22 km/h; 9-14 mph), increase climb rates, keep wheel wells clean and extend wheel, tyre and brake life.

RAISBECK SOOTLESS EXHAUST STACK FAIRINGS

Small fairings over fronts of exhaust stacks on all P&WC PT6A-powered Beechcraft King Air and Super King Air models; prevent power loss from hot air entering forward cowling and engine inlet, and reduce drag by streamlining propeller wake; fairing held in place by camlocks; two 'delta-wing' vortex generators on fairings divert high energy gases between exhaust and cowling, keeping exhaust soot from accumulating on nacelle and wing. Stainless steel or composites fairings available.

Raisbeck Short-Field Enhancement System modification for Beech Model 200 series Super King Airs

RAISBECK RAM AIR RECOVERY SYSTEM

RARS intended for Super King Air 200; developed in association with P&WC and certificated; more complete sealing of engine nacelle air inlet section, new fixed turning vane, addition of Coanda effect curved surface on rear portion of movable inertial separator vane, and new highly porous ice shedder screen; increases cruising speed, rates of climb, power plant flat rating and engine output with ice vanes deployed; reduces block fuel consumption and engine ITT at equal torque.

RAISBECK BEECHCRAFT KING AIR C90/C90A

FAA approval for operation at increased gross weight of early Beechcraft C90/C90As (serial nos. LJ-527 to LJ-1137) announced 1 October 1990; max T-O weight raised from 4,377 kg (9,650 lb) to 4,581 kg (10,100 lb) permits legal increase of three additional passengers with full tanks; max landing weight increased to 4,400 kg (9,700 lb). Approval requires Hartzell Quiet Turbofan propellers, Raisbeck Dual Aft Body Strakes and 10-ply tyres. Similar programme in progress to raise E90 gross weight to 4,762 kg (10,500 lb).

RAM

RAM AIRCRAFT CORPORATION

Waco Regional Airport, PO Box 5219, Waco, Texas 76708-0219
Telephone: 1 (817) 752 8381
Fax: 1 (817) 752 3307
Telex: 910 894 5248
PRESIDENT: Jack M. Riley Jr (Engineering)
INTERNATIONAL SALES:
  Dick Belanger
  Bob Neal
SALES MANAGER: David Seesing
PRESS RELATIONS: Chuck Morrow

RAM specialises in modification of selected single- and twin-engined general aviation aircraft for improved performance and efficiency. All modifications FAA approved by award of STC. Export STC modification kits available with new engines or RAM-remanufactured 100 per cent balanced versions of Teledyne Continental TSIO-520 engine (further details in 1990-91 *Jane's*). RAM Cessna 310, 320, 340 and 414A conversions designated Series I (310 hp) and Series III (325 hp) with Teledyne

Continental camshafts and Series II and Series IV respectively with RAM economy camshafts developed by Crane Cams Inc of Daytona Beach, Florida; these give easier starting, increased manifold pressure and smoother idling, together with claimed 3-5 per cent reduction in fuel consumption at cruise power. Refurbishing, repainting and maintenance also offered.

RAM/CESSNA 172

D to N Models fitted with 119 kW (160 hp) Textron Lycoming O-320-D2G or Textron Lycoming O-320-E2D engine with power increased from 112 kW (150 hp) to 119 kW (160 hp) when overhauled under RAM STC SE3692SW and installed under RAM STC SA2375SW.

RAM/PIPER PA-28-140/PA-28-151

Re-engined with 119 kW (160 hp) Textron Lycoming O-320-D3G under RAM STC SA2706SW for -140 and SA2969SW for -151.

RAM/CESSNA T206/210

Replacing TSIO-520-C/H in early models with 231 kW (310 hp) RAM-remanufactured TSIO-520-M/R; performance generally same as later models with 200 hours more overhaul life; optional Hartzell Q-tip or McCauley wide chord propellers.

RAM/CESSNA T310

Replaces 212 kW (285 hp) Teledyne Continental TSIO-520-Bs with either 224 kW (300 hp) TSIO-520-Es or RAM-remanufactured 242 kW (325 hp) TSIO-520-NBRs; with 242 kW (325 hp) engines, aircraft known as RAM 310 Series IV; T-O weight of 310P, Q and R models increased to 2,572 kg (5,670 lb), giving 122 kg (270 lb) greater useful load in 310P and 77 kg (170 lb) in 310Q and R; dual aerial mapping/reconnaissance ports available for cameras as large as Wild RC10 and Zeiss RMKA 15/23, but RAM will not install (will sell STC per aircraft).
PERFORMANCE (A: 224 kW; 300 hp, B: 242 kW; 325 hp engines, at max T-O weight of 2,572 kg; 5,670 lb):

Cruising speed, 75% power at 5,485 m (18,000 ft):
A	217 knots (402 km/h; 250 mph)
B	243 knots (450 km/h; 280 mph)

Max rate of climb at S/L: A   640 m (2,100 ft)/min
B	915 m (3,000 ft)/min

Rate of climb at S/L, one engine out:
A	152 m (500 ft)/min
B	183 m (600 ft)/min

RAM/CESSNA 340/340A

Replaces 212 kW (285 hp) TSIO-520-Ks with RAM-remanufactured 231 kW (310 hp) TSIO-520-Ns or 242 kW (325 hp) TSIO-520-NBRs. Series II modification has the 231 kW (310 hp) engines, 75 kg (165 lb) increase in useful load and max T-O weight increase of 68 kg (150 lb); Series IV has the 242 kW (325 hp) engines and 136 kg (300 lb) increases in useful load and max T-O weight; Series IV package also includes Hartzell Q-tip propellers.
PERFORMANCE (A: 231 kW; 310 hp engines with McCauley propellers, B: 242 kW; 325 hp engines, at max T-O weight of 2,853 kg; 6,290 lb):
Cruising speed, 75% power at 6,100 m (20,000 ft):
A	220 knots (408 km/h; 253 mph)
B	225 knots (417 km/h; 259 mph)

Max rate of climb at S/L: A   655 m (2,150 ft)/min
B	686 m (2,250 ft)/min

Rate of climb at S/L, one engine out:
A	105 m (345 ft)/min
B	114 m (375 ft)/min

Time to 5,485 m (18,000 ft): A   18 min
B	16 min

Acceleration to 87 knots (161 km/h; 100 mph): A   18 s
B	16 s

RAM/CESSNA 401/402A/402B/402C

Remanufactured 224 kW (300 hp) Teledyne Continental TSIO-520-E or 242 kW (325 hp) TSIO-520-VB engines installed in Cessna 401 and 402A-C; engine accessories replaced by new or overhauled parts; Slick 6220 pressurised magnetos; red silicone rubber baffle seal kit; Alcor 46158 exhaust gas temperature gauge and combustion analyser; options include electronic fuel flow management, Woodward propeller synchrophaser, RAM super soundproofing, Cleveland heavy duty brakes, polished and balanced propellers and three-colour polyurethane external paint finish.

RAM/CESSNA 414

Replaces 231 kW (310 hp) TSIO-520-J engines in 414s built between 1970-76 with 231 kW (310 hp) TSIO-520-Ns or 242 kW (325 hp) TSIO-520-NBRs; then known as RAM 414 Series II and IV; same options as Cessna 340A and 402C conversions; Hartzell Q-tip available only for 242 kW (325 hp) engines.
PERFORMANCE (A: 231 kW; 310 hp, B: 242 kW; 325 hp engines, at max T-O weight of 2,953 kg; 6,510 lb):
Cruising speed, 75% power at 6,100 m (20,000 ft):
A	210 knots (389 km/h; 241 mph)
B	215 knots (398 km/h; 247 mph)

Max rate of climb at S/L: A   503 m (1,650 ft)/min
B	610 m (2,000 ft)/min

Rate of climb at S/L, one engine out:
A	76 m (250 ft)/min
B	104 m (340 ft)/min

Time to 5,485 m (18,000 ft): A   20 min
B	18 min

Acceleration to 87 knots (161 km/h; 100 mph): A   22 s
B	19 s

RAM/CESSNA 414AW

Replaces 231 kW (310 hp) TSIO-250-Ns with remanufactured TSIO-520-N/NBs of same power (Series II) or (in 414AW Series IV) with 242 kW (325 hp) TSIO-520-NBRs, with Hartzell Q-tip propellers; certificated by FAA, with 0.89 m (2 ft 11 in) high winglets, 1 March 1983, and then by Australia; RAM/Cessna 414AW gross weight increased by 153 kg (337 lb) and useful load by 136 kg (300 lb).
PERFORMANCE (at max T-O weight. A with 231 kW; 310 hp engines, B with 242 kW; 325 hp engines):
Cruising speed at 6,100 m (20,000 ft):
75% power:
A	210 knots (389 km/h; 242 mph)
B	215 knots (398 km/h; 247 mph)

55% power:
A	188 knots (348 km/h; 216 mph)
B	195 knots (361 km/h; 224 mph)

Max rate of climb at S/L:
A	494 m (1,620 ft)/min
B	533 m (1,750 ft)/min

Rate of climb at S/L, one engine out:
A	91 m (300 ft)/min
B	98 m (320 ft)/min

Time to 5,485 m (18,000 ft):
A	22 min
B	18 min

Acceleration to 87 knots (161 km/h; 100 mph):
A	23 s
B	22 s

RAM/Cessna 414AW Series V conversion with Teledyne Continental Voyager liquid-cooled engines

RAM/CESSNA 414AW SERIES V

Replaces 231 kW (310 hp) Teledyne Continental TSIO-520-N/NB engines with new 261 kW (350 hp) liquid-cooled Teledyne Continental TSIO-550-A Voyager engines, driving new McCauley three-blade propellers. Modification includes installation of coolant radiator in extended rear of each nacelle baggage locker, each with flush non-icing NACA air intake scoop; new nacelle nose caps of graphite/glassfibre with flush-mounted recognition/landing lights; and winglets. Cockpit gauges provided for coolant temperature and pressure; coolant temperature thermostatically controlled. Same standard and optional items as Series IV; max T-O weight increased by 136 kg (300 lb) and useful load by 45.5 kg (100 lb). 414AW/V certificated 10 August 1989; deliveries at one per month; 14 delivered by early January 1991. RAM anticipated Voyager re-engining of Cessna 340A for delivery from November 1990.
PERFORMANCE:
Cruising speed at 75% power:
at 7,010 m (23,000 ft)   232 knots (430 km/h; 267 mph)
at 9,145 m (30,000 ft)   244 knots (452 km/h; 281 mph)
Rate of climb at S/L, one engine out   137 m (450 ft)/min
Time to 9,145 m (30,000 ft)   33 min

RAM/CESSNA 421C and 421CW

Cessna 421B and 421C Golden Eagle powered by RAM or Teledyne Continental GTSIO-520-L/N engines; 421C useful load increased by 50 kg (110 lb). Standard cooling baffles, exhaust risers, slip joints and magnetos replaced by RAM Reliability Package including new red silicone/glassfibre cooling baffle seal material, remanufactured exhaust system and slip joints, Bendix S6RN-1250 pressurised magnetos; also includes Hoskins computerised fuel management system and Alcor direct-reading exhaust gas temperature system.
Winglets for 421Cs up to factory serial number 0799 (becoming 421CW) approved by FAA November 1984, including flight into known icing; Australian certification 1987; winglets, incorporating wing extensions and winglet assembly and made of bidirectional carbon graphite cloth/epoxy with outer layer which includes interwoven aluminium cloth for electrical conductivity and lightning protection, increase wing span by 0.94 m (3 ft 1 in). First 421CW delivery October 1984; 35 conversions completed

by January 1991. 421CW useful load increased by 23 kg (50 lb); winglets increase rate of climb by 25 per cent. Planned installation of 317 kW (425 hp) Teledyne Continental Voyager series liquid cooled engines in Cessna 421C, March 1992.
DIMENSIONS, EXTERNAL: As for Cessna 421C except:
Basic wing span	13.47 m (44 ft 2½ ft)
Span, winglet tip to winglet tip	13.83 m (45 ft 4½ ft)
Wing aspect ratio (basic)	8.64
Effective wing aspect ratio, including winglets	9.74
Winglet cant angle	10°
Winglet toe-out angle	2°

AREAS:
Wings, gross (basic)	21.0 m² (226.0 sq ft)

WEIGHTS AND LOADINGS:
Max T-O weight	3,429 kg (7,560 lb)
Max zero-fuel weight	2,963 kg (6,533 lb)
Max wing loading	163.3 kg/m² (33.45 lb/sq ft)
Max power loading	6.12 kg/kW (10.06 lb/hp)

PERFORMANCE:
Cruising speed:
at 75% power at 6,100 m (20,000 ft)   228 knots (422 km/h; 262 mph)
at 65% power at 6,100 m (20,000 ft)   223 knots (413 km/h; 257 mph)
Rate of climb at 1,525 m (5,000 ft), ISA, one engine out   91 m (300 ft)/min
Time to 7,315 m (24,000 ft)   24 min

RAM/BEECH BARON 58

Baron 58P and 58TC re-engined with 231 kW (310 hp) Teledyne Continental TSIO-520-L/LB or 242 kW (325 hp) TSIO-520-WBs; standard equipment includes Alcor exhaust gas temperature gauge and combustion analyser, Airborne dry vacuum pumps, electronic fuel management and red silicone rubber baffle seals; options include Teflon fuel and oil hoses, balanced propellers and three-colour polyurethane exterior paint.
PERFORMANCE (Baron 58P. A: 231 kW; 310 hp, B: 242 kW; 325 hp):
Cruising speed, 75% power at 6,100 m (20,000 ft):
A	223 knots (413 km/h; 257 mph)
B	229 knots (424 km/h; 264 mph)

Max rate of climb at S/L: A   463 m (1,520 ft)/min
B	469 m (1,540 ft)/min

Rate of climb at S/L, one engine out:
A	67 m (220 ft)/min
B	97 m (320 ft)/min

RAM conversion of a Cessna 421C with winglets, known as RAM/Cessna 421CW

RILEY

RILEY INTERNATIONAL CORPORATION

2206 Palomar Airport Road, Suite B-2, Carlsbad,
California 92008
Telephone: 1 (619) 438 9089
Fax: 1 (619) 438 0578
PRESIDENT: Jack M. Riley

Company formed to continue marketing Riley conversions of production aircraft. Two types available in 1991 detailed below. Riley holds total of 120 STCs for conversions developed over 39 years. Future products will include unconventional power plants and turbine conversions of existing aircraft.

RILEY ROCKET CESSNA P-210

Riley conversion of Cessna P-210 Pressurised Centurion, announced 1983; FAA STC issued late 1984; 31 Rocket P-210s delivered by early 1991; current production two a month. Includes fitting remanufactured 231 kW (310 hp) turbocharged Teledyne Continental TSIO-520-AF with Riley intercooler system and flush NACA intake; induction air 45 per cent cooler and engine efficiency improved. Other equipment includes dynamically balanced, electrically de-iced three-blade McCauley propeller, heavy duty battery, dual vacuum pumps, alternative electrical system, Riley engine baffle system, new Cleveland wheels and brakes, new tyres, luxury interior, Bendix/King avionics including Loran, WX-1000 Stormscope, flush antennae, S-Tech autopilot system, Horton short take-off and landing modification and Riley custom soundproofing and interior. Options include radar, air-conditioning, speedbrakes, Flint wingtip fuel tanks increasing fuel capacity to 462 litres (122 US gallons; 102 Imp gallons), air-conditioning, full airframe de-icing and special law enforcement and govern-

Riley Rocket P-210 conversion of the Cessna Pressurised Centurion

ment communications systems. Intercooler also FAA approved for Cessna Turbo Stationair 6 and 7, Turbo Centurion and Pressurised Super Skymaster, and Piper Turbo Saratoga.

PERFORMANCE:
Cruising speed:
at 5,335 m (17,500 ft)   204 knots (378 km/h; 235 mph)
at 7,000 m (23,000 ft)   217 knots (402 km/h; 250 mph)
Stalling speed, power off, clean
42 knots (79 km/h; 49 mph)
Max rate of climb at S/L   305 m (1,000 ft)/min
Time to 7,000 m (23,000 ft)   23 min

Service ceiling   7,000 m (23,000 ft)
Range, with IFR reserves
1,129 nm (2,092 km; 1,300 miles)

RILEY SKY ROCKET CESSNA P-337

Riley was converting two Cessna pressurised P-337 twins a month in Spring 1991 and had then delivered 34. Basic conversion and optional features same as those listed for Rocket P-210 above. Max continuous cruising speed 220 knots (408 km/h; 253 mph); stalling speed, power off, clean, 50 knots (93 km/h; 58 mph).

ROBINSON

ROBINSON HELICOPTER COMPANY

24747 Crenshaw Boulevard, Torrance, California 90505
Telephone: 1 (213) 539 0508
Fax: 1 (213) 539 5198
Telex: 18-2554
PRESIDENT: Franklin D. Robinson
VICE-PRESIDENT, MARKETING: Barbara K. Robinson

ROBINSON MODEL R22 BETA, MARINER and POLICE

TYPE: Light two-seat helicopter.
PROGRAMME: Design began 1973; first flight 28 August 1975; first flight of second R22 early 1977; FAA certification 16 March 1979; UK certification June 1981; deliveries began October 1979; R22 Alpha certificated October 1983; R22 Beta announced 5 August 1985; 1,000th R22 delivered 30 March 1989.
VARIANTS: **R22 Beta:** Standard version from c/n 501 onwards; increased horsepower.
R22 Mariner: Has floats and ground wheels; first delivered for operation from tuna fishing boats off Mexico and Venezuela.
R22 Police: Special communications and other equipment (as listed under Equipment).
R22 IFR: Equipped with flight instruments and radio to allow training for helicopter IFR flying (see Equipment).
External load R22: Hook kit certificated for 181 kg (400 lb) produced by Classic Helicopter Corporation, Boeing Field, Seattle, Washington; weighs 2.3 kg (5 lb); used for slung load training; never-exceed speed with load in place limited to 75 knots (139 km/h; 86 mph).
CUSTOMERS: Production rate 10 per week in early 1991; total 380 delivered during 1990; total production 1,640 by 31 December 1990, when outstanding orders totalled 200 aircraft.
DESIGN FEATURES: Horizontally mounted multiple V belts and piston engine drives transmission through sprag-type overrunning clutch; main and tail gearboxes use spiral bevel gears; maintenance-free flexible couplings of proprietary manufacture used in both main and tail rotor drives. Two-blade semi-articulated main rotor, with tri-hinged underslung rotor head to reduce blade flexing, rotor vibration and control force feedback and an elastic teeter hinge stop to prevent blade-boom contact when starting or stopping rotor in high winds; blade section NACA 63-015 (modified); two-blade tail rotor on port side; rotor brake standard.
FLYING CONTROLS: Conventional mechanical except cyclic stick mounted between pilots with hand grips on swing arm for comfortable access.
STRUCTURE: All-metal bonded blades with stainless steel spar and leading-edge, light alloy skin and light alloy honeycomb filling; cabin section of steel tube with metal and plastics skinning; full monocoque tailboom.
LANDING GEAR: Welded steel tube and light alloy skid landing gear, with energy absorbing crosstubes. Twin float/skid gear on Mariner with additional tailplane surface on lower tip of fin.

Robinson R22 Beta two-seat helicopter (Textron Lycoming O-320-B2C)

POWER PLANT: One 119 kW (160 hp) Textron Lycoming O-320-B2C flat-four engine (derated to 97.5 kW; 131 hp for T-O), mounted in the lower rear section of the main fuselage with cooling fan. Light alloy main fuel tank in upper rear section of the fuselage on port side, usable capacity 72.5 litres (19.2 US gallons; 16 Imp gallons). Optional auxiliary fuel tank, capacity 39.75 litres (10.5 US gallons; 8.7 Imp gallons). Oil capacity 5.7 litres (1.5 US gallons; 1.25 Imp gallons).
ACCOMMODATION: Two seats side by side in enclosed cabin, with inertia reel shoulder harness. Curved two-panel windscreen. Removable door, with window, on each side. Police version has observation doors with bubble windows, which are also available as options on other models. Baggage space beneath each seat. Cabin heated and ventilated.
SYSTEMS: Electrical system, powered by 12V DC alternator, includes navigation, panel and map lights, dual landing lights, anti-collision light and battery. Second battery optional.
AVIONICS: A Bendix/King KY 197 com transceiver is standard; optional avionics include a KN 53 nav receiver, Apollo II, Bendix/King or Northstar Loran C, KT 76A transponder and KR 87 ADF.
EQUIPMENT: Standard equipment includes rate of climb indicator, sensitive altimeter, quartz clock, hour meter, low rotor rpm warning horn, temperature and chip warning lights for main gearbox and chip warning light for tail gearbox, high-capacity oil cooler, rotor brake, windscreen cover, rotor blade tiedowns, soundproofing, and ground handling wheels. Optional equipment includes Hamilton vertical compass, AIM 305-1AL artificial horizon, AIM-205-1AL directional gyro, remote altitude encoder, cabin heater/demister, engine primer, rotor rpm governor, removable port side controls, leather seats, ventral hardpoint and fire extinguisher.

Police version standard equipment as above, plus dual com control panel, Wulfsberg Flitefone 40 VHF or UHF radio, removable port side controls, 70A alternator and fire extinguisher. Police version optional equipment is searchlight with dual lamps, PA speaker and siren, second Wulfsberg Flitefone 40 VHF or UHF radio and Bendix/King KT 76A transponder.

IFR trainer standard equipment is same as for basic Beta. Avionics include AIM 305-1AL DVF artificial horizon, Bendix/King KEA 129 encoding altimeter, Astronautics DC turn co-ordinator, Bendix/King KCS 55A HSI, KR 87 ADF, KX 165 nav/com digital display radio, KT 76A transponder and KR 22 marker beacon receiver, and Astro Tech LC-2 digital clock. IFR trainer optional avionics include Bendix/King KN 63 DME. DME.

DIMENSIONS, EXTERNAL:
Main rotor diameter	7.67 m (25 ft 2 in)
Tail rotor diameter	1.07 m (3 ft 6 in)
Main rotor blade chord	0.18 m (7.2 in)
Distance between rotor centres	4.39 m (14 ft 5 in)
Length overall (rotors turning)	8.76 m (28 ft 9 in)
Length of fuselage	6.30 m (20 ft 8 in)
Fuselage: Max width	1.12 m (3 ft 8 in)
Height overall	2.67 m (8 ft 9 in)
Skid track	1.93 m (6 ft 4 in)

DIMENSIONS, INTERNAL:
Cabin: Max width	1.12 m (3 ft 8 in)

AREAS:
Main rotor blades (each)	0.70 m² (7.55 sq ft)
Tail rotor blades (each)	0.037 m² (0.40 sq ft)
Main rotor disc	46.21 m² (497.4 sq ft)
Tail rotor disc	0.89 m² (9.63 sq ft)
Fin	0.21 m² (2.28 sq ft)
Stabiliser	0.14 m² (1.53 sq ft)

WEIGHTS AND LOADINGS:

Weight empty (without auxiliary fuel tank)	
	379 kg (835 lb)
Fuel weight: standard	52 kg (115 lb)
auxiliary	28.6 kg (63 lb)
Max T-O and landing weight	621 kg (1,370 lb)
Max zero-fuel weight	569 kg (1,255 lb)
Max disc loading	13.43 kg/m² (2.75 lb/sq ft)
Max power loading	6.37 kg/kW (10.45 lb/hp)

PERFORMANCE (at max T-O weight):

Never-exceed speed (Vne) without sling load	
	102 knots (190 km/h; 118 mph)
Max level speed	97 knots (180 km/h; 112 mph)
Cruising speed, 75% power at 2,440 m (8,000 ft)	
	96 knots (177 km/h; 110 mph)
Econ cruising speed	82 knots (153 km/h; 95 mph)
Max rate of climb at S/L	366 m (1,200 ft)/min
Rate of climb at 1,525 m (5,000 ft)	
	323 m (1,060 ft)/min
Service ceiling	4,265 m (14,000 ft)
Hovering ceiling IGE	2,125 m (6,970 ft)
Range with auxiliary fuel and max payload, no reserves	
	319 nm (592 km; 368 miles)
Endurance at 65% power, auxiliary fuel, no reserves	
	3 h 20 min

Robinson R44 four-seat light helicopter

ROBINSON R44

TYPE: Four-seat version of R22.

PROGRAMME: Development began 1986; first flight 31 March 1990; by February 1991 prototype (N44RH) had flown 50 hours and second aircraft had joined test programme; certification expected early 1992; expected in production 1993-94 at new site in Los Angeles or Santa Maria, California; first 25 to be built at existing plant and supplied only to customers in south-western USA for easy recall if modification required.

DESIGN FEATURES: Direct extrapolation of R22 design.

LANDING GEAR: Fixed skids.

POWER PLANT: One 194 kW (260 hp) Textron Lycoming O-540 piston engine, derated to 165 kW (225 hp).

DIMENSIONS, EXTERNAL:

Main rotor diameter	10.06 m (33 ft 0 in)
Tail rotor diameter	1.47 m (4 ft 10 in)
Height overall	3.28 m (10 ft 9 in)
Skid track	2.18 m (7 ft 2 in)

DIMENSIONS, INTERNAL:

Cabin: Max width	1.28 m (4 ft 2½ in)

WEIGHTS AND LOADINGS:

Weight empty, standard	635 kg (1,400 lb)
Fuel weight: standard	85 kg (187 lb)
auxiliary	51.25 kg (113 lb)
Max T-O weight and landing weight	1,088 kg (2,400 lb)
Max power loading	6.59 kg/kW (10.66 lb/hp)

PERFORMANCE:

Cruising speed, 75% power	
	113 knots (209 km/h; 130 mph)
Max rate of climb at S/L	305 m (1,000 ft)/min
Service ceiling	4,270 m (14,000 ft)
Hovering ceiling: IGE	2,135 m (7,000 ft)
OGE	1,525 m (5,000 ft)
Max range, no reserves	347 nm (643 km; 400 miles)

ROCKWELL INTERNATIONAL

ROCKWELL INTERNATIONAL CORPORATION

2230 East Imperial Highway, El Segundo, California 90245
Telephone: 1 (213) 647 5000
Telex: 664465
CHAIRMAN AND CHIEF EXECUTIVE OFFICER:
    Donald R. Beall
EXECUTIVE VICE-PRESIDENTS AND CHIEF OPERATING OFFICERS:
    Kent M. Black
    Sam F. Iacobellis

North American Aviation founded 1928 and manufactured aircraft from 1934; merged with Rockwell-Standard Corporation of Pittsburgh, Pennsylvania (which manufactured Aero Commander aircraft) 22 September 1967; formed North American Rockwell Corporation; present name adopted 1973. Four major businesses comprise aerospace, automotive, electronics and graphics: aerospace includes production of military aircraft, manned and unmanned space systems, rocket engines, advanced space-based surveillance systems, and high energy laser and other directed energy programmes; electronics includes industrial automation equipment and systems, avionics products and communications-related systems for commercial and military aircraft, and communications, intelligence, and precision guidance and control systems.

NORTH AMERICAN AIRCRAFT

100 North Sepulveda Boulevard, El Segundo, California 90245
Telephone: 1 (213) 647 1000
PRESIDENT: John J. Pierro
Palmdale Facility:
2825 East Avenue P, Palmdale, California 93550
Telephone: 1 (805) 273 6000
VICE-PRESIDENT AND GENERAL MANAGER: C. W. Bright
Tulsa Facility:
2000 North Memorial Drive, Tulsa, Oklahoma 74158
Telephone: 1 (918) 835 3111
VICE-PRESIDENT AND GENERAL MANAGER:
    William P. Swiech
    In addition to detailed programmes, North American Aircraft is working on X-30 National Aero-Space Plane (NASP—see NASA entry); Rockwell teamed with Panavia to promote Tornado for USAF Follow-On Wild Weasel programme, and with MBB in X-31A programme and to offer Fan Ranger for JPATS training aircraft requirement (see International section).

ROCKWELL OV-10D-PLUS BRONCO

US Navy ordered modification (at Cherry Point MCAS, with Rockwell kits) of 23 US Marine Corps OV-10As and 14 OV-10Ds to OV-10D-Plus July 1988; modifications include fitting 775.5 kW (1,040 shp) Garrett T76-G-420/421 turboprops and composites propellers, new solid-state avionics with Rockwell-Collins cockpit management system, nose-mounted Texas Instruments AN/AAS-37 FLIR turret (already fitted to OV-10Ds), Sanders AN/ALQ-144 IR jammer, General Instrument AN/APR-39 RWR, complete re-wiring, quick-disconnect cargo door and structural strengthening for 4.28 m (14 ft)/s carrier landings; first carrier trial (by prototype OV-10D-Plus, 155468) on USS *Saratoga*, 7 June 1990; first production conversion (155499) completed June 1990 and redelivered to VMO-2 Squadron at Camp Pendleton; 15 converted OV-10s to be delivered 1991; details of OV-10 in 1986-87 *Jane's*.
    Eighteen ex-USAF OV-10A Broncos were bought by Venezuela in 1991.

GENERAL DYNAMICS F-111 UPGRADE

Pacer Strike update of 79 F-111Ds and 84 F-111Fs began September 1989, extending life to 2010; intended to bring F-111 fleet to essentially common avionics standard (F-111A, EF-111A and F-111E upgraded earlier by Grumman) but F-111D component cancelled 30 March 1990, and aircraft to retire. Modifications include integrated cockpit displays and complete re-wiring of avionics bay added to ring laser gyro INS and Navstar GPS; first flight of prototype expected April 1991; three months of manufacturer tests and one year of USAF trials; delivery of production conversion kits to start in August 1993; F-111Fs of 48th TFW at RAF Lakenheath, England, to be re-assigned to US-based wing by 1994; last F-111F overhaul by BAe at Bristol — coincidentally BAe's 300th F-111 re-work — completed 5 February 1991; BAe also converting F-111Es of 20th TFW at RAF Upper Heyford following testing of digital flight control system in FB-111A, to go to 27th TFW at Cannon AFB, New Mexico, replacing F-111Ds. Rockwell won Australian contract to update 22 Australian F-111s; announced 23 August 1990, with value of $160 million to Rockwell from total $320 million; AUP (avionics update programme) concerns 18 F-111Cs and four RF-111Cs; gaining digital avionics system and MIL-STD-1553B databus; prototype flown in USA, August 1990; Australian industry to manufacture 21 further kits to complete modification by late 1995. Details of other F-111 programmes under US Air Force heading.

ROCKWELL INTERNATIONAL B-1B LANCER

100th and final B-1B rolled out 20 January 1988; full details in 1989-90 *Jane's*; AIL proposed to improve AN/ALQ-161 defensive avionics suite, but USAF cancelled upgrade programme in March 1991; B-1B named Lancer May 1990; three lost in accidents.

ROCKWELL (LOCKHEED) AC-130U SPECTRE

Development of new gunship version of Lockheed C-130 Hercules launched 6 July 1987 with $155,233,489 contract to North American Aircraft Operations; prototype (87-0128) funded in FY 1986, six production aircraft in FY 1989 and five in FY 1990; prototype delivered to Rockwell as standard C-130 transport, 1988; first post-conversion flight on 20 December 1990 was also ferry to Edwards AFB, California, for trials; work on remaining AC-130Us began January 1991 for delivery from May 1992 onwards; assigned to 16th Special Operations Squadron at Hurlburt Field, Florida. Armament, firing to port, consists of (front to rear) General Electric GAU-12/U 25 mm six-barrel Gatling gun with 3,000 rounds, Bofors 40 mm gun and a 105 mm gun based on US Army howitzer; weapons can be slaved to Hughes AN/APG-80 (modified AN/APG-70)

Lockheed Hercules converted to AC-130U Spectre gunship by Rockwell

digital fire control radar, Texas Instruments AN/AAQ-117 FLIR or GEC Sensors All-Light Level Television (ALLTV), for night and adverse weather attack on ground targets; sideways-facing HUD for visual aiming. Attack method is to circle target at altitude firing into apex of turn on ground, but guns can now be trained, relieving pilot of absolute precision flying; flight path is also less predictable; can fire on two targets simultaneously; AC-130U can refuel in flight and fly escort, surveillance, search, rescue and armed reconnaissance/interdiction missions.

Prone observer's position on rear ramp; starboard side observer's window aft of flight deck and battle management centre in cabin with seven positions at monitoring consoles and four IBM AP-102 computers; crew totals 13, including flight crew and loaders. Defensive aids believed similar to those in MC-130H; modified fuel tank pylons contain IR countermeasures; total of 300 chaff bundles and 90 MJU7 or 180 M206 flares in three launchers under fuselage; ITT Avionics AN/ALQ-172 jammer in base of fin; other equipment includes combined INS and Navstar GPS, triple MIL-STD-1553B databuses and Spectra ceramic armour protection.

Full details of C-130H in LASC Georgia entry in this section.

AEROSPACE BUSINESSES

2230 East Imperial Highway, El Segundo, California 90245
Telephone: 1 (213) 647 5000
EXECUTIVE VICE-PRESIDENT AND CHIEF OPERATING OFFICER:
  Sam F. Iacobellis

Satellite & Space Electronics Division
2600 Westminster Boulevard, Seal Beach, California 90740-7644
Telephone: 1 (213) 797 3311
PRESIDENT: Richard E. Derr

Rocketdyne Division
6633 Canoga Avenue, Canoga Park, California 91303
Telephone: 1 (818) 710 6300
PRESIDENT: Robert D. Paster

Space Systems Division
12214 Lakewood Boulevard, Downey, California 90241
Telephone: 1 (213) 922 2111
PRESIDENT: Robert G. Minor
MANAGER, EXTERNAL COMMUNICATIONS AND MEDIA
  RELATIONS: Janet L. Dean

Group includes Downey and Palmdale facilities and contractual support groups in main national space centres; work includes development and fabrication of manned and unmanned space systems; Rockwell group produced four Shuttle Orbiter spacecraft for NASA and is building a fifth.

Space Operations Company

600 Gemini Avenue, Houston, Texas 77058
Telephone: 1 (713) 282 2000
PRESIDENT: Glynn S. Lunney

Formerly Shuttle Operations Company, SOC provides mission support for Johnson Space Center, consolidating work previously performed by 17 contractors; tasks include project management, maintenance and operations of Houston Mission Control Center, Shuttle Mission Simulator, Shuttle Avionics Integration Laboratory, Software Production Facility, Central Computing Facility, and Mockup and Integration Laboratory; also sustains engineering, flight preparation and direct mission operations, testing and support of Space Shuttle operations at Johnson Space Center. Rockwell team includes Bendix Field Engineering Corporation, Unisys, Omniplan Corporation, RMS Technologies Incorporated and System Management American Corporation. SOC holds Johnson Space Center's operations support contract; support related to operational concepts development and mission, flight crew and facility operations functions for *Freedom* space station and other programmes.

SPACE TRANSPORTATION SYSTEM

World's first reusable space transportation system; system includes Rockwell International spacecraft (see next entry), Martin Marietta external propellant tank and two Thiokol solid propellant rocket boosters. Shuttle launched vertically with all engines firing; booster stages separate at 43 km (27 miles) altitude and descend by parachute into sea for recovery; Shuttle continues under own power and jettisons external tank just before reaching orbit. In space, manoeuvres with two orbital manoeuvring engines; reaction control engines used for minor course corrections and attitude adjustments.

Main Shuttle tasks include placing satellites in orbit, retrieving satellites from orbit, repairing and servicing satellites in orbit, placing propulsive stages and satellites into precise low Earth orbit for subsequent transfer to geosynchronous orbit or escape path; can also be used for short-duration scientific and applications missions, as orbiting research laboratory or reconnaissance vehicle, tanker for space refuelling and to support orbiting space stations.

Pressurised seven-day Spacelab laboratory developed for European Space Agency by 10 European countries can be carried in payload bay for manned experiments; associated pallet used to expose experiments to space; pallet may be used alone with control from Shuttle or Earth.

At end of mission, Shuttle re-enters atmosphere using heat shielding designed to last for 100 missions; can glide for 950 nm (1,760 km; 1,100 miles) using aerodynamic controls inside atmosphere and land at one of several designated airfields, including Edwards AFB, California, and Kennedy Space Center, Florida.

Essential details of missions from 1981 to destruction of Space Shuttle *Challenger* in January 1986 given in previous editions of *Jane's*; launches resumed September 1988.

BOOSTERS (STS-8 and subsequent missions): Two Thiokol solid propellant rocket boosters (each 14,679 kN; 3,300,000 lb st for lift-off) are attached one on each side of the external propellant tank. The inert weight of each solid rocket booster is 87,090 kg (192,000 lb). The booster cases are designed for 20 re-uses.

EXTERNAL PROPELLANT TANK: Contains the main propellants for the Orbiter. It is of aluminium alloy semi-monocoque construction, with a 25 mm (1 in) thick foam external insulation. In the forward end of the tank is a 554 m³ (19,563 cu ft) tank holding 617,774 kg (1,361,936 lb) of liquid oxygen; in the rear end is a 1,514 m³ (53,518 cu ft) tank holding 103,257 kg (227,641 lb) of liquid hydrogen. Total propellant weight 721,031 kg (1,589,577 lb). Between propellant tanks is an unpressurised intertank which houses instrumentation and electrical components. Current missions use a lightweight tank weighing 750,980 kg (1,655,600 lb) when filled.

Basic dimensions and weights of the complete Space Transportation System are as follows:

DIMENSIONS, EXTERNAL:

Length: overall	56.14 m (184 ft 2⅜ in)
external tank	46.88 m (153 ft 9⅝ in)
boosters	45.46 m (149 ft 1⅝ in)
Height overall	23.35 m (76 ft 7¼ in)

WEIGHTS AND LOADINGS:

Shuttle system complete (STS-26)	2,051,334 kg (4,522,411 lb)
Shuttle spacecraft (STS-26, *Discovery* dry weight)	77,754 kg (171,419 lb)
External tank (full)	750,980 kg (1,655,600 lb)
Boosters (2), each	589,670 kg (1,300,000 lb)
Payload, for 177 km (110 mile) orbit	
due east (*Discovery* or *Atlantis*)	24,948 kg (55,000 lb)
eastwards 57° inclination	18,597 kg (41,000 lb)
98° polar orbit	13,426 kg (29,600 lb)

THRUST:

Total, at lift-off	34,613 kN (7,781,400 lb st)
Shuttle main engines (3), each at S/L at 104%	1,751 kN (393,800 lb st)
Boosters (2), each	14,679 kN (3,300,000 lb st)

ROCKWELL INTERNATIONAL SHUTTLE SPACECRAFT

TYPE: Reusable space transportation vehicle.
PROGRAMME: Missions resumed 29 September 1988 with STS-26, in which *Discovery* sent Tracking Data Relay Satellite TDRS-C into geosynchronous orbit using Inertial Upper Stage. Five Space Shuttles built so far are:

Columbia (OV-102): Made first successful test flight (36 orbits) April 1981 manned by John Young (commander) and Capt Robert Crippen (pilot); since completed nine more orbital missions; modified at Kennedy Space Center after mission STS-5 to carry Spacelab and six-person crew, returned to Rockwell at Palmdale after STS-9 for further modifications, including installation of operational systems, and returned to service early 1986.

Challenger (OV-099): Second vehicle, first flight 4 April 1983; first craft having all onboard systems qualified for 100 missions without major overhaul; destroyed in post launch explosion caused by booster burn-through at start of mission 51L on 28 January 1986.

Discovery (OV-103): First flight 30 August 1984.

Atlantis (OV-104): First flight 3 October 1985 on military mission 51J; *Discovery* and *Atlantis* are about

STS launching system at the Kennedy Space Center

3,116 kg (6,870 lb) lighter than *Columbia* through weight saving.

Endeavour (OV-105): Ordered by NASA on 31 July 1987 to replace *Challenger*; rollout scheduled for April 1991 and first flight May 1992.

DESIGN FEATURES: Lifts off vertically with boosters and re-enters atmosphere after mission for unpowered aerodynamic landing on airfield; wing of ogival planform with NACA 0010 section (modified), with blunt leading-edge and more than 1.52 m (5 ft) thick at thickest point; sweepback 81° on inner leading-edges, 45° on outer panels; dihedral 3° 30′ on trailing-edge; fin swept back 45°.

FLYING CONTROLS: Full fly-by-wire with manual or automatic modes for all phases; two orbit adjusting engines and reaction control engines for attitude adjustment in space; unpowered landing; two-segment powered elevons each side for pitch and roll control in atmosphere, with hinged panels on upper surface to seal wing/elevon gap; body flap used to protect engines during re-entry and as aerodynamic trimming surface; rudder divided into upper and lower halves and splits open to act as airbrake from Mach 10 to Mach 5 (with rudder locked) and for braking during landing.

STRUCTURE: Main wing, made by Grumman, mainly conventional aluminium alloy with corrugated spar webs, truss ribs, riveted skin/stringer and honeycomb skins; wing/elevon gap sealed by panels of titanium and Inconel sandwich, and are only airframe areas not

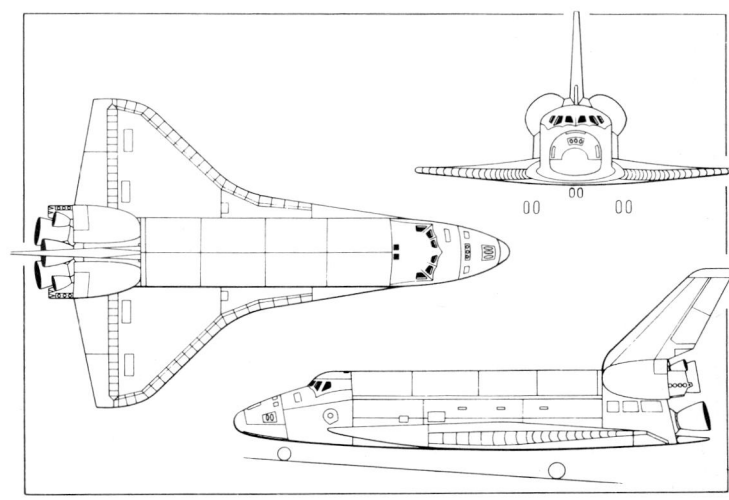

NASA/Rockwell International shuttle spacecraft
(*Michael A. Badrocke*)

covered by thermal protection tiles. Fuselage in three sections: forward section contains crew module with forward attitude controls, three avionics bays and nosewheel; centre section (primary load carrying structure; built by Convair Division of General Dynamics) includes wing carry-through structure, payload bay, and structural payload doors (in upper half) of graphite epoxy bonded honeycomb sandwich with Nomex core and incorporating deployable and fixed radiator panels; and rear section interfaces with removable orbital manoeuvring system (OMS)/reaction control system (RCS) pods, wing rear spar, vertical tail assembly (by Fairchild Republic), body flap, external tank rear supports, main propulsion system, launch umbilical panel, three rear avionics bays, and other discrete system equipment.

THERMAL PROTECTION SYSTEM: The thermal protection system (TPS) consists of materials applied externally to maintain the airframe outer skins within an acceptable temperature limit of 176°C (350°F) during re-entry. The TPS materials are designed to perform a minimum of 100 missions, in which temperatures will range from −156°C (−250°F) in space to re-entry temperatures of nearly 1,648°C (3,000°F). Reinforced carbon-carbon is used on the wing leading-edges, the nose cap (including chin panel area immediately aft on the lower surface), and the immediate area around the forward orbiter/external tank structural attachment. RCC protects areas where temperatures exceed 1,260°C (2,300°F) during entry. Coated Nomex felt reusable surface insulation (FRSI) is used where temperatures are less than 371°C (700°F), on the upper portion of the payload bay doors, mid and rear fuselage sides, upper wing, and part of the orbital manoeuvring system (OMS) pods. Low-temperature reusable surface insulation (LRSI) white tiles (about 700) are used where temperatures are below 649°C (1,200°F) and above 371°C (700°F) nominal. These tiles are used in selected areas on the forward, mid and aft sections of the fuselage, and the vertical tail, upper wing, and OMS/RCS pods. Advanced flexible reusable surface insulation (AFRSI) quilted fabric blankets are used in the majority of the areas below 649°C (1,200°F) and above 371°C (700°F) on the forward, mid and aft of fuselage, vertical tail, upper wing and OMS/RCS pods. High-temperature reusable surface insulation (HRSI) tiles are used where temperatures are below 1,260°C (2,300°F) and above 648°C (1,200°F). The areas are the forward fuselage, lower mid fuselage, lower wing, selected areas of the vertical tail, a portion of the OMS pods, and around the forward fuselage windows. The HRSI has two different densities: one weighs 4 kg/m³ (9 lb/cu ft) and is used in all areas except around the nose and main landing gear doors, nose cap interface, wing leading-edge, reinforced carbon-carbon/HRSI interface, external tank umbilical doors, vent doors, and fin leading-edge. These areas use HRSI tiles with a density of 9.9 kg/m³ (22 lb/cu ft) and have a black surface coating for entry emittance. When the higher density HRSI tiles have been expended, fibrous refractory insulation (FRCI) tiles will be used instead. The FRCI-12 tiles have a density of 5.4 kg/m³ (12 lb/cu ft), and improved strength, durability and resistance to cracking. A bulkhead heatshield at the rear of the vehicle protects the main engine system; a large body flap protects the main engine nozzles (see Flying Controls).

LANDING GEAR: Retractable tricycle type, with twin wheels and Menasco oleo-pneumatic shock absorbers on each unit. Hydraulic release, with a pyrotechnic backup for deployment in flight. Landing gear cannot be retracted in flight, after release. Nose unit is retracted forward into fuselage and main units forward into wings before launch. Nose unit is steerable; main units are fitted with Goodrich brakes and Hydro-Aire anti-skid units. All units have Goodrich wheels and tyres. Landing gear is designed to facilitate safe landing at speeds of up to 225 knots (415 km/h; 258 mph). The main gear tyres are rated at 20,410 kg (45,000 lb) and the brakes at 240 × 10⁶ ft-lb.

MAIN PROPULSION: Three Rocketdyne SSME (Space Shuttle Main Engines) high-pressure liquid oxygen/liquid hydrogen engines, each rated at 1,668 kN (375,000 lb st) at sea level and 2,091 kN (470,000 lb thrust) in vacuum at 100 per cent; 1,752 kN (393,800 lb) at sea level and 2,174 kN (488,800 lb) vacuum at 104 per cent; 1,856.2 kN (417,300 lb) at sea level and 2,283.0 kN (513,250 lb) vacuum at 109 per cent. The engines can be throttled over a range of 65 to 109 per cent of their rated power level. Each engine is designed for 7h 30 min of operation, with 55 starts.

ORBITAL MANOEUVRING ENGINES: Two Aerojet Liquid Rocket Company (ALRC) bipropellant liquid rocket engines, running on monomethylhydrazine (MMH) and nitrogen tetroxide (N_2O_4), are used for the Orbiter's orbital manoeuvring subsystem (OMS). These engines are housed in pods, one on each side of the Orbiter's rear fuselage. The OMS engines, for which a usable total of 10,830 kg (23,876 lb) of propellant is carried, are used to position the spacecraft in orbit; each develops 26.7 kN (6,000 lb thrust) in space.

REACTION CONTROL ENGINES: The reaction control subsystem (RCS) utilises 38 Marquardt R-40A bipropellant liquid rocket engines (each 3.88 kN; 872 lb vacuum thrust) and six Marquardt R-1E-3 bipropellant liquid rocket vernier thrusters (each 0.11 kN; 24 lb vacuum thrust). Fourteen of the R-40A engines are on the nose and 24 on the aft end, 12 in each OMS/RCS pod; there are two of the R-1E verniers on the nose and two in each aft pod. Propellants are the same as for the OMS engines; 1,096 kg (2,418 lb) is carried in the RCS tanks, and there is provision for crossfeed between the aft OMS and aft RCS tanks.

CREW COMPARTMENT: Self-contained crew module has a fuselage side hatch for access, a hatch into the airlock from the mid section, and a hatch from the airlock into the payload bay. It is divided into three levels, the upper (flight deck) level having side by side seating for two flight crewmen with dual controls. Behind them are seats for two mission specialists. On the middle deck provisions are made for three more seats, bunks and a galley, dependent upon particular flight requirements, hygiene section, airlock, three electronics bays, and payload bay access. For rescue missions, seats for three more persons can be fitted in place of the bunks. The lower deck contains environmental control equipment and crew equipment storage.

PAYLOAD BAY: In centre of fuselage, 18.29 m (60 ft) long and 4.57 m (15 ft) in diameter. Retractable manipulator arm on left hand side if required for a particular flight (with provision for a second one on the right), for deploying and retrieving payloads. Complete closed circuit TV system by RCA Astro-Electronics includes a colour camera in the crew compartment and several black and white and or colour cameras in the cargo bay and on the manipulator arm. These facilitate payload handling and provide TV coverage for engineers and the general public on Earth.

SYSTEMS: Environmental control and life support system, made up of four subsystems: atmosphere revitalisation subsystem (ARS), to control atmospheric environment for occupants and thermal environment for electronics; food, water and waste subsystem (FWW), to provide hygiene, and other life support functions; active thermal control subsystem (ATCS), to maintain subsystems and components within specified temperature limits and to provide, via payload door radiator panels, active heat rejection to protect payloads; and an airlock support subsystem. Three redundant hydraulic systems, each of 207 bars (3,000 lb/sq in), supply actuators for the elevons, body flap, rudder/speed brake, and power to actuate main engine thrust vector controls, landing gear, brakes and steering. Electrical power subsystem (EPS) consists, functionally, of a fuel cell power plant (FCP) subsystem, and a power reactant storage and distribution (PRSD) subsystem. There are three FCPs, each providing power at 27.5V to 32.5V DC over a power range of 2-12kW and each connected to one of the three main DC buses; these

supply the primary in-flight electrical power used by the Shuttle, generated through the chemical combination and conversion of cryogenic oxygen and hydrogen. In the PRSD subsystem, the cryogenic oxygen and hydrogen tanks are defined as a tank set. The tank sets installed are dependent upon specific flight requirements; up to five sets can be accommodated. Westinghouse remote power control system and master timing unit. Honeywell four channel fly by wire electrical flight control subsystem for operation of all control surfaces and main engine controls. APU subsystem consists of three Sundstrand independent APUs (each 100.7 kW; 135 shp), deriving their energy from the decomposition of hydrazine (N_2H_4).

AVIONICS: Fully fail-operational/fail-safe guidance, navigation and control system, including three Singer-Kearfott KT-70/SKN-2600 type inertial measuring units—due to be replaced by HAINS (High Accuracy Inertial Navigation System); triplex Ku-band microwave scan beam landing system, by the AIL Division of Eaton Corpn; head-up displays (HUD); three Northrop rate gyro assemblies; three Hoffman L-band Tacan—to be replaced by Collins Avionics TCN-252; three Bendix accelerometer assemblies; two Honeywell C-band radar altimeters; four AiResearch air data transducers; three Smiths attitude director indicators; two Collins horizontal situation indicators; two Honeywell alpha/Mach indicators; two Bendix/King altitude/vertical velocity indicators; two Bendix/King surface position indicators; two Honeywell barometric altimeters; and two Honeywell ATC transponders. Communications and tracking equipment includes one (optionally two) Ku-band rendezvous radar/satellite com on starboard side of cargo bay; two Ball star trackers; two 100W Watkins-Johnson S-band TWT amplifiers; two P-band UHF for EVA/ATC com; Conrac S-band FM for Orbiter/ground and Orbiter/payload com; and Ku-band radio for Orbiter/ground com and Ku band for rendezvous. Central data processing is by means of five IBM Advanced System/4 Pi Model AP-101 digital computers and two mass memory units. AP-101S retrofitted from March 1991 (STS-39/Discovery launch). Four of the computers are interconnected to process guidance, navigation and control inputs and to relay commands to FBW flight control systems; the fifth is provided for independent backup and systems management.

DIMENSIONS, EXTERNAL:

Wing span	23.79 m (78 ft 0.68 in)
Wing aspect ratio	2.265
Wing mean aerodynamic chord	12.06 m (39 ft 6.81 in)
Length overall	37.24 m (122 ft 2 in)
Height overall	17.27 m (56 ft 8 in)

DIMENSIONS, INTERNAL:

Payload bay: Length	18.29 m (60 ft 0 in)
Diameter	4.57 m (15 ft 0 in)
Crew module: Volume	74.33 m³ (2,625 cu ft)

AREAS:

Wings, gross	249.91 m² (2,690 sq ft)
Elevons (total)	38.38 m² (413.14 sq ft)
Rudder/speed brake	9.03 m² (97.15 sq ft)
Vertical tail surfaces (total)	38.39 m² (413.25 sq ft)
Body flap	12.61 m² (135.75 sq ft)

WEIGHTS AND LOADINGS:

Weight dry: Discovery (1988)	77,754 kg (171,419 lb)
Weight, incl cargo, at booster ignition (STS-26)	
	115,487 kg (254,606 lb)
Max landing weight	104,328 kg (230,000 lb)

PERFORMANCE:

Orbital speed
approx 15,285 knots (28,325 km/h; 17,600 mph)
Nominal touchdown speed (unpowered)
184-196 knots (341-363 km/h; 212-226 mph) EAS

ROCKY MOUNTAIN
ROCKY MOUNTAIN HELICOPTERS INC
PO Box 1337, Provo, Utah 84603
Telephone: 1 (801) 375 1124
Fax: 1 (801) 375 6712
PRESIDENT: James Burr
DIRECTOR OF MARKETING: David Dolstein
VICE-PRESIDENT, OPERATIONS: Don Andrews

ROCKY MOUNTAIN HELICOPTERS ALLSTAR AS350 CONVERSION
Programme to re-engine Aerospatiale AS 350 with 485 kW (650 shp) Allison 250-C30M turboshaft in place of standard Arriel or LTS101; supplemental type certificate purchased from Soloy 1990, since when weight has been reduced by 85 kg (187 lb) partly by use of composites in cowling; first conversion completed 1990 and certification

expected April 1991; conversion kit without engine costs $65,000; engine and installation by Rocky Mountain Helicopters $290,000; sold as conversion kit.

ROGERSON
ROGERSON HILLER CORPORATION
(Subsidiary of Rogerson Aircraft Corporation)
2140 West 18th Street, Port Angeles, Washington 98362
Telephone: 1 (206) 452 6891
Fax: 1 (206) 457 5426
PRESIDENT: Norman B. Hirsh
VICE-PRESIDENT, MARKETING: James Brown

Formed January 1973 as Hiller Aviation Inc to acquire from Fairchild Industries the design rights, production tooling and spares of Hiller 12E helicopters and support worldwide Hiller fleet; manufactured new 12Es and 12E4s and revived five-seat FH-1100 after 1980; Hiller Aviation became wholly owned subsidiary of Rogerson Aircraft April 1984; renamed Hiller Helicopters and began deliveries of redesignated UH-12E and RH-1100 July 1984; since

renamed Rogerson Helicopters; moved to new facility at Port Angeles November 1985; L.O.M. Corporation, which produces rotor blades, acquired September 1985 and renamed Aerobond; rotor blades manufactured at Port Angeles.

Production of UH-12E relaunched during 1991 and three-seat turbine-power UH-12ET being proposed for US Army New Training Helicopter (NTH) competition.

HILLER RH-1100

TYPE: Five-seat utility helicopter.

PROGRAMME: Original FH-1100 was refined development of OH-5A; 246 built before production ended 1974; production resumed, with initial deliveries July 1984.

VARIANTS: **RH-1100:** Civil version, derived from FH-1100.

RH-1100M Hornet: Military development shown at 1985 Paris Air Show; provision for autopilot, FLIR anti-missile warning systems; air-to-air missile system capability; chin or roof mounted sight; variety of approved armament includes two 2.75 in folding fin rocket pods, 7.62 mm machine guns, 0.50 calibre machine guns, and four TOW missiles.

DESIGN FEATURES: Improved RH-1100 has more powerful Allison 250-C20B; new main rotor blades with 76 mm (3 in) greater chord; larger diameter two-blade tail rotor; new drive coupling between engine and main rotor transmission for higher gross weight operation and increased max speed. Main rotor blade section NACA 63_2015; main rotor/engine rpm ratio 1:16.30; tail rotor/engine rpm ratio 1:2.47; rotor brake optional. Each main rotor blade attached to rotor head by single main retention bolt and drag link; droop stops standard.

FLYING CONTROLS: Conventional powered controls with electrically controlled trim system.

STRUCTURE: Aluminium alloy semi-monocoque fuselage; aluminium alloy and honeycomb vertical fin and fixed horizontal surface; main rotor blades each have rolled leading-edge bonded to aluminium trailing section with honeycomb core. Stainless steel and honeycomb tail rotor blades.

LANDING GEAR: Skid type with torsion tube suspension, with choice of standard or extended support struts. Extended struts necessary with optional inflatable float installation. Ground handling wheels standard.

POWER PLANT: One 313 kW (420 shp) Allison 250-C20B turboshaft, derated to 204 kW (274 shp). Single bladder fuel tank in bottom of centre-fuselage with usable capacity of 259 litres (68.5 US gallons; 57 Imp gallons). Refuelling point on starboard side of rear fuselage. Oil capacity 2.6 litres (0.7 US gallon; 0.6 Imp gallon).

ACCOMMODATION: Pilot and co-pilot side by side with three passengers to rear, or pilot and four passengers. Four forward hinged doors, two on each side of cabin, with removable centre door post for cargo loading. Dual internal stretcher kit optional. Baggage compartment to rear of cabin, capacity 0.30 m³ (10.5 cu ft). Accommodation ventilated. Cabin heater and windscreen defroster optional.

SYSTEMS: Hydraulic system for cyclic and collective pitch controls. Electrical system includes a 28V 60A DC starter/generator and nickel-cadmium battery.

AVIONICS: A range of nav/com systems is available to customer's requirements.

EQUIPMENT: Standard equipment includes clock, engine hour meter, outside air temperature gauge, fuel filter warning system, night lighting system including two rotating beacons, edge-lit instrument panel, seatbelts, shoulder harness on front seats, sliding rear windows, tinted windows, hardpoint for optional external cargo hook, external power socket, and choice of exterior paint schemes and interior trim. Optional equipment includes stability augmentation system, dual controls, rear seat shoulder harness, cabin fire extinguisher, first aid kit, strobe lights, engine auto relight, reverse scoop intake, heated pitot, loudspeaker/siren, quick-release cargo hook, cargo racks, ambulance kit, dual litter kit, searchlight and Simplex agricultural spraygear.

DIMENSIONS, EXTERNAL:

Main rotor diameter	10.80 m (35 ft 5 in)
Tail rotor diameter	1.83 m (6 ft 0 in)
Distance between rotor centres	6.29 m (20 ft 7½ in)
Main rotor blade chord	0.33 m (1 ft 1 in)
Length: overall, rotors turning	12.57 m (41 ft 3 in)
fuselage	9.08 m (29 ft 9½ in)
Width, rotors folded	1.32 m (4 ft 4 in)
Height overall	2.83 m (9 ft 3½ in)
Skid track	2.20 m (7 ft 2¾ in)

AREAS:

Main rotor disc	91.0 m² (979.0 sq ft)
Tail rotor disc	2.63 m² (28.3 sq ft)

WEIGHTS AND LOADINGS (A: RH-1100, B: RH-1100M):

Weight empty: A	687 kg (1,515 lb)
B (TOW)	1,048 kg (2,310 lb)
B (Scout)	726 kg (1,600 lb)
Max payload: A	462 kg (1,020 lb)
Max standard fuel weight: A, B	200.5 kg (442 lb)
Max T-O weight: A	1,292 kg (2,850 lb)
B	1,406 kg (3,100 lb)
Max disc loading: A	14.21 kg/m² (2.91 lb/sq ft)
B	15.48 kg/m² (3.17 lb/sq ft)
Max power loading: A	6.33 kg/kW (10.4 lb/hp)
B	6.89 kg/kW (11.31 lb/hp)

PERFORMANCE (at max T-O weight, A and B as above):

Max level speed at S/L:	
A, B	110 knots (204 km/h; 127 mph)
Max cruising speed at 1,525 m (5,000 ft):	
A	110 knots (204 km/h; 127 mph)
Econ cruising speed: A	106 knots (196 km/h; 122 mph)
Max rate of climb at S/L: A	488 m (1,600 ft)/min
Vertical rate of climb at S/L: A	244 m (800 ft)/min

Prototype RH-1100M Hornet with civilian RH-1100 in background

Service ceiling: A	5,275 m (17,300 ft)
Hovering ceiling: IGE: A	5,180 m (17,000 ft)
OGE: A	3,660 m (12,000 ft)
Range at 1,525 m (5,000 ft) with max fuel, no reserves:	
A	340 nm (629 km; 391 miles)
B (Scout)	534 nm (990 km; 615 miles)
Max endurance at 1,525 m (5,000 ft), no reserves:	
A	3 h 24 min
B	5 h

HILLER UH-12E HAULER

TYPE: Three/four-seat utility helicopter.

PROGRAMME: Resumed deliveries of original Hiller UH-12E; production rate one per month early 1991, to double October 1991. Proposed 1991 (as **UH-12ET**) for US Army New Training Helicopter (NTH) programme, with Soloy/Allison 250-C20B turboshaft.

CUSTOMERS: Deliveries of aircraft equipped for agricultural work to Government of India began May 1986; other orders from Hungary (three) and Taiwan (four).

DESIGN FEATURES: Blades interchangeable individually, bolted to forks which are retained at rotor head by tension-torsion bars; no blade folding. Main rotor blade thickness/chord ratio 12 per cent; main rotor/engine rpm ratio 1:8.66; tail rotor/engine rpm ratio 1:1.44. Mechanical drive through two-stage planetary main transmission; bevel gear drive to auxiliaries; tail rotor gearbox.

FLYING CONTROLS: Teetering two-blade main rotor controlled through stabiliser bar carrying aerodynamic paddles. Horizontal stabiliser incidence ground adjustable.

STRUCTURE: Aluminium alloy fully stressed semi-monocoque platform supporting non-stressed cabin structure, engine mounting and landing gear; beaded aluminium alloy sheet tailboom with no internal stiffeners; horizontal stabiliser with steel tube spar, aluminium alloy ribs and skin; horizontal stabiliser replaced on four-seat version by inverted-V surfaces of similar construction mounted forward of tail rotor.

LANDING GEAR: Wide track light alloy tube skids carried on spring steel cross members. Optional extended legs. Ground handling wheels standard. Optional 'zip-on' pontoons can be attached above the skids to permit water or land operations, but require extended landing gear.

POWER PLANT: One 253.5 kW (340 hp) Textron Lycoming VO-540-C2A flat-six engine, installed vertically and derated to 227.5 kW (305 hp). Engine muffler optional. Single bladder fuel cell, capacity 174 litres (46 US gallons; 38 Imp gallons), mounted in lower portion of rear

fuselage, beneath engine. Two optional auxiliary fuel tanks, mounted in fuselage on each side of engine; capacity 76 litres (20 US gallons; 16.6 Imp gallons) each. Oil capacity 12.5 litres (3.3 US gallons; 2.7 Imp gallons).

ACCOMMODATION: Three persons side by side on bench seat. Seat belts with provision for shoulder harness. Dual controls optional. Forward-hinged door on each side, with sliding window. Baggage compartment immediately aft of engine. Heater/defroster optional.

SYSTEMS: Electrical system includes a 72A alternator, nickel-cadmium battery, and battery temperature monitor.

AVIONICS: A range of optional avionics is available.

EQUIPMENT: Standard equipment includes engine hour meter, edge-lit instrument panel, outside air temperature gauge, eight-day clock, electrically controlled trim system, tinted glazing, cargo hook hardpoint, external power socket, and polyurethane paint finish. Optional equipment includes Mason cyclic control grip, fire extinguisher, first aid kit, night lighting equipment including two rotating beacons, strobe lights, 454 kg (1,000 lb) capacity quick-release cargo hook, twin heavy duty cargo racks, agricultural spray equipment, loudspeaker/siren, searchlight, and tropical doors. Agricultural equipment includes Simplex Model 3300 system with 9.75 m (32 ft) folding spraybooms and two glassfibre tanks, with total capacity of 416 litres (110 US gallons; 91 Imp gallons) or 530 litres (140 US gallons; 116 Imp gallons), designed for quick change to dry system; or Simplex Model 4500 system with single tank, capacity 530 litres (140 US gallons; 116 Imp gallons) and folding booms.

DIMENSIONS, EXTERNAL:

Main rotor diameter	10.80 m (35 ft 5 in)
Main rotor blade chord (constant)	0.33 m (1 ft 1 in)
Servo rotor diameter	3.05 m (10 ft 0 in)
Tail rotor diameter	1.68 m (5 ft 6 in)
Distance between rotor centres	6.17 m (20 ft 3 in)
Length: overall, rotors turning	12.41 m (40 ft 8½ in)
fuselage	8.69 m (28 ft 6 in)
Height to top of rotor head	3.08 m (10 ft 1¼ in)
Skid track	2.29 m (7 ft 6 in)
Cabin doors (standard, each):	
Height	1.13 m (3 ft 8½ in)
Max width	0.81 m (2 ft 8 in)
Height to sill	0.58 m (1 ft 11 in)

DIMENSIONS, INTERNAL:

Cabin: Length	1.52 m (5 ft 0 in)
Max width	1.50 m (4 ft 11 in)
Max height	1.35 m (4 ft 5 in)
Floor area	1.16 m² (12.5 sq ft)

New production Hiller UH-12E with Simplex cropspraying system

AREAS:

Tail rotor blades (each)	0.094 m² (1.01 sq ft)
Main rotor disc	91.97 m² (990.0 sq ft)
Tail rotor disc	2.57 m² (27.7 sq ft)

WEIGHTS AND LOADINGS:

Weight empty	798 kg (1,759 lb)
Max T-O weight	1,406 kg (3,100 lb)
Max disc loading	15.28 kg/m² (3.13 lb/sq ft)
Max power loading	6.18 kg/kW (10.16 lb/hp)

PERFORMANCE (at max T-O weight, except where indicated):

Never-exceed (VNE) and max level speed	
	83 knots (154 km/h; 96 mph)

Cruising speed		78 knots (145 km/h; 90 mph)
Max rate of climb at S/L		393 m (1,290 ft)/min
Vertical rate of climb at S/L		225 m (740 ft)/min
Service ceiling:		
at AUW of 1,270 kg (2,800 lb)		4,575 m (15,000 ft)
at max T-O weight		2,255 m (7,400 ft)
Hovering ceiling IGE:		
at AUW of 1,270 kg (2,800 lb)		3,170 m (10,400 ft)
at max T-O weight		2,315 m (7,600 ft)
Hovering ceiling OGE:		
at AUW of 1,270 kg (2,800 lb)		2,070 m (6,800 ft)
at max T-O weight		1,155 m (3,800 ft)

Range, 30 min reserves:		
standard fuel		150 nm (278 km; 173 miles)
auxiliary fuel		316 nm (585 km; 364 miles)
Endurance with auxiliary fuel, 30 min reserves		
		4 h 1 min

SABRELINER
SABRELINER CORPORATION
6161 Aviation Drive, St Louis, Missouri 63134
Telephone: 1 (314) 537 3660
Fax: 1 (314) 537 9053
Telex: 44-7227
OTHER WORKS: Perryvale Municipal Airport, Missouri
CHAIRMAN AND CHIEF EXECUTIVE OFFICER:
  F. Holmes Lamoreux
VICE-PRESIDENT, GOVERNMENT OPERATIONS: Reuben D. Best
VICE-PRESIDENT, COMMERCIAL MARKETING: Karl R. Childs
VICE-PRESIDENT, ENGINEERING: Bob D. Hanks

Sabreliner Corporation formed July 1983 after Wolsey & Co bought Sabreliner Division of Rockwell International; supports about 600 Sabreliners still in service; refurbishes and upgrades Lockheed T-33 and AT-33 for sale in Central and South America; two Sabreliner 40R and 24 AT-33s delivered to Ecuadorian Air Force; Sabreliner 40 and 60 re-engined with extended life P&W JT12s and fitted with Collins EFIS and new interior and exterior; contract for logistics support of US Navy Grumman TC-4Cs based at Whidbey Island (Washington), Oceana (Virginia), and Cherry Point (North Carolina) awarded early 1985; five-year contract for worldwide support of US Navy and Marine Corps CT-39 Sabreliner awarded September 1987; applying service life extension to two T-39As and eight T-39Bs, first of which was redelivered Spring 1988.

Excalibur programme for Sabreliner 40 and 60 with 10,000 flying hours introduced early 1989; refurbished aircraft became Sabreliner 40EX and 60EX and have 5,000 more airframe hours; alternative modifications give 30,000 hour/15,000 mission and 30,000 hour/30,000 mission life extension; service life extension contract for 644 Cessna T-37Bs for USAF Air Training Command awarded August 1989; modification includes replacement of wing carry-through structure, lower front wing spars, tail mounting structure and tailplane; after three Sabreliner-prepared prototypes, SLEP kits will be installed by US Air Force.

Sabreliner rebuilds Textron Lycoming T53 turboshafts for US Army Bell UH-1s and supports airborne and ground-based training systems for US Navy's Undergraduate Naval Flight Officer (UNFO) programme at NAS Pensacola, Florida. Plans to resume production of Model 65; preliminary design of Model 85 derivative completed Autumn 1990; investment partner being sought.

SADLER
SADLER AIRCRAFT COMPANY
8225 East Montebello, Scottsdale, Arizona 85253
Telephone: 1 (602) 994 4631
Fax: 1 (602) 481 0574
Telex: 285776 VAMP UR
PRESIDENT: William G. Sadler
MARKETING DIRECTOR: F. Brent Stewart

Formerly American Microflight Inc (see Skywise Ultraflight in Sport Aircraft section); developing series of low cost close support and patrol/reconnaissance derivatives.

SADLER A-22 LASA
TYPE: Light armed surveillance aircraft.
PROGRAMME: Design commenced June 1986; construction began January 1987; first flight of prototype (N22AB) 8 October 1989.
VARIANTS: **A-22-300F:** Fixed landing gear.
  A-22-300R: Retractable landing gear.
  T-22: Pod with two side by side seats and dual controls, fitted to same basic airframe.
COSTS: Programme cost $2.5 million (1989); average equipped cost of production aircraft $150,000.
DESIGN FEATURES: Wings unswept; constant chord with Hoerner droop tips; outer panels fold upward in two hinged sections for transportation or storage; NACA 63₃-A218 laminar flow aerofoil section; 18 per cent thickness/chord ratio; 3° dihedral; 4° incidence.
FLYING CONTROLS: Plain ailerons; twin rudders operating in unison; elevator with electrically operated trim tab; four-position electrically operated trailing-edge flaps.
STRUCTURE: Aluminium alloy wing with shear web main spar, tubular capstrips and spreaders, and aluminium alloy skin; Kevlar composite fuselage pod; twin aluminium alloy tailbooms; tail surfaces of aluminium alloy construction and skin.
LANDING GEAR: Tricycle type, with trailing link suspension. Retractable landing gear optional. Fully swivelling nosewheel with steering through differential braking of mainwheels.
POWER PLANT: One 224 kW (300 hp) watercooled Chevrolet V-6 all-aluminium fuel injected engine, modified for aircraft use, with custom forged crankshaft, stainless steel forged connecting rods, forged aluminium pistons, stainless steel inlet and exhaust valves, and a heavy duty reduction drive to a two- or four-blade composites pusher propeller. Standard fuel capacity 75.7 litres (20 US gallons; 16.6 Imp gallons). Turbocharged version available for high altitude operations.
ACCOMMODATION (A-22): Pilot only, in enclosed cockpit, with bullet resistant Lexan canopy.
EQUIPMENT: Demonstrated with stabilised video camera, low light level TV/infra-red sensor; video display in cockpit; real time video downlink. In light ground attack role, BEI Defense Systems M146 armament management system control panel for BEI Hydra-70 rocket systems with seven-tube launchers.
ARMAMENT: Four underwing hardpoints for up to 454 kg (1,000 lb) of stores; provision for 7.62 mm machine gun in each inboard wing section.

DIMENSIONS, EXTERNAL:

Wing span	6.70 m (22 ft 0 in)
Wing chord, constant	1.27 m (4 ft 2 in)
Wing aspect ratio	5.28
Length overall	4.78 m (15 ft 8 in)
Height overall	1.14 m (3 ft 9 in)

Prototype Sadler A-22 LASA single-seat light armed surveillance aircraft

Sadler A-22 LASA with wings folded

Height, wings folded	2.13 m (7 ft 0 in)
Width, wings folded	2.24 m (7 ft 4 in)
Propeller diameter	1.42 m (4 ft 8 in)

AREAS:

Wings, gross	8.51 m² (91.6 sq ft)

WEIGHTS AND LOADINGS:

Weight empty	386 kg (850 lb)
Max payload	454 kg (1,000 lb)
Max T-O weight	975 kg (2,150 lb)
Max wing loading	114.6 kg/m² (23.47 lb/sq ft)
Max power loading	4.35 kg/kW (7.17 lb/hp)

PERFORMANCE (estimated, at AUW of 975 kg; 2,150 lb, at S/L. A: A-22-300F, B: A-22-300R):

Max level speed at S/L:		
A		152 knots (282 km/h; 175 mph)
B		165 knots (306 km/h; 190 mph)
Stalling speed, flaps down:		
A, B		62 knots (115 km/h; 72 mph)
Max rate of climb at S/L: A		549 m (1,800 ft)/min
B		610 m (2,000 ft)/min
T-O run: A, B		153 m (500 ft)
Landing run: A, B		183 m (600 ft)
Range with standard fuel: A		239 nm (442 km; 275 miles)
B		260 nm (483 km; 300 miles)

SADLER OPV SERIES
TYPE: Optionally piloted patrol and observation aircraft.
PROGRAMME: Design of OPV series commenced January 1982; first model flew 27 August 1987. Since 1987 manned and unmanned tests conducted with autopilot, command uplink and autonomous guidance via GPS navigation.
VARIANTS: **OPV18-50 and OPV18-100:** Wing span 5.49 m (18 ft 0 in).
  OPV22-50 and OPV22-100: Wing span 6.71 m (22 ft 0 in); -50 models available with a 38 kW (51 hp) Bombardier-Rotax 532.2V two-stroke; -100 models have 71 kW (95 hp) Teledyne Continental GR-36 rotary engine.
COSTS: Programme cost $1.2 million (1988); manned version costs from $33,000 for basic OPV18-50 to $100,000 for fully equipped OPV22-100; high volume cost for drones from $10,000.
DESIGN FEATURES: Similar to A-22 except outer wings fold upward in single hinged sections; fixed landing gear when piloted; drone has none, for rail or zero-length launch and parachute recovery.
A-22 LASA description applies except as follows:

DIMENSIONS, EXTERNAL:

Wing span: OPV18	5.49 m (18 ft 0 in)
OPV22	6.71 m (22 ft 0 in)
Wing aspect ratio: OPV18	4.32

AREAS:

Wings, gross: OPV18		6.97 m² (75.0 sq ft)

WEIGHTS AND LOADINGS (A: OPV18-50, B: OPV22-50, C: OPV18-100, D: OPV22-100):

*Max payload: A	45 kg (100 lb)
B	91 kg (200 lb)
C	136 kg (300 lb)
D	181 kg (400 lb)
Max T-O weight: A	329 kg (725 lb)
B	397 kg (875 lb)
C	454 kg (1,000 lb)
D	521 kg (1,150 lb)
Max wing loading: A	47.21 kg/m² (9.67 lb/sq ft)
C	65.08 kg/m² (13.33 lb/sq ft)
Max power loading: A	8.66 kg/kW (14.22 lb/hp)
B	10.45 kg/kW (17.16 lb/hp)
C	6.39 kg/kW (10.53 lb/hp)
D	7.34 kg/kW (12.11 lb/hp)

PERFORMANCE (at max T-O weight):

Max level speed at S/L:	
A	100 knots (185 km/h; 115 mph)
B	102 knots (189 km/h; 117 mph)
C	130 knots (241 km/h; 150 mph)
D	128 knots (237 km/h; 147 mph)
Stalling speed, flaps down:	
A	47 knots (87 km/h; 54 mph)
B	40 knots (74 km/h; 46 mph)
C	56 knots (104 km/h; 65 mph)
D	46 knots (86 km/h; 53 mph)
Max rate of climb at S/L: A	183 m (600 ft)/min
B	213 m (700 ft)/min

Sadler OPV18-50 manned/unmanned patrol and surveillance aircraft

C	229 m (750 ft)/min		Range with standard fuel:	
D	244 m (800 ft)/min		A	282 nm (523 km; 325 miles)
T-O run: A	244 m (800 ft)		B	325 nm (603 km; 375 miles)
B	213 m (700 ft)		C	260 nm (482 km; 300 miles)
C	176 m (575 ft)		D	304 nm (563 km; 350 miles)
D	153 m (500 ft)		*Drone versions can carry additional 45-68 kg (100-150 lb) payload	
Landing run: A	213 m (700 ft)			
B	176 m (575 ft)			
C	244 m (800 ft)			
D	122 m (400 ft)			

SCALED

SCALED COMPOSITES INC

Hangar 78, Mojave Airport, Mojave, California 93501
Telephone: 1 (805) 824 4541
Fax: 1 (805) 824 4174
PRESIDENT: Elbert L. (Burt) Rutan
VICE-PRESIDENT AND GENERAL MANAGER:
Herbert A. Iversen

Scaled Composites Inc bought by Beech Aircraft Corporation June 1985; sold back to Burt Rutan November 1988 and integrated in joint venture with Wyman-Gordon Company of Worcester, Massachusetts; Scaled will produce composite aerospace structures for Wyman-Gordon and continue to provide R&D facilities to individuals and companies; several projects developed for Beechcraft retained by Scaled. Scaled associated with Wyman-Gordon Composites (formerly KDI of Buena Park, California) to offer series production capacity.

Past projects have included NASA AD-1 oblique wing research aircraft (see 1981-82 *Jane's*); Fairchild/Ames 62 per cent scale New Generation Trainer (see 1982-83 *Jane's*); M115-6.85 SCAT 1 85 per cent scale demonstrator for the Beech 2000 Starship (see Beech Aircraft in this section); prototype Aviation Composites Mercury canard microlight (see Sport Aircraft section 1987-88 *Jane's*); Model 120-9E proof-of-concept Predator 480 agricultural aircraft (see ATAC entry in 1985-86 *Jane's*); Rutan Model 81 Catbird (see Scaled entry in 1989-90 *Jane's*); full-scale demonstrator of California Microwave CM-44 manned UAV (see RPVs and Targets section of 1987-88 *Jane's*); short production run of Teledyne Ryan Aeronautical Scarab Mach 0.8 ground-launched reconnaissance UAV; composite wings and tail surfaces of Orbital Sciences/Hercules Pegasus air-launched space booster; sail for Americas Cup catamaran; and subscale radar cross-section models of aircraft such as Sukhoi Su-25.

Scaled 2,787 m² (30,000 sq ft) factory, next door to Rutan Aircraft Factory, has space and facilities for short-run production and flight testing.

SCALED COMPOSITES MODEL 133-4.62 POC ADVANCED TECHNOLOGY TACTICAL TRANSPORT (AT³)

TYPE: Scale proof-of-concept tactical transport.
PROGRAMME: First flight of prototype (N133SC) 29 December 1987, prior to commemorate first flight 20 January 1988; major modification late 1988; resumed flight testing early 1989; flight tests completed July 1989 after 150 hours; new flight tests started 1991.
CUSTOMERS: Defense Advanced Research Projects Agency (DARPA).
COSTS: $2.5 million development contract.
DESIGN FEATURES: Intended to provide tactical transport capacity between C-130 and helicopters; full-scale mission requirement to carry 14 troops and 2,268 kg (5,000 lb) cargo at 326 knots (604 km/h; 375 mph) over low-altitude unrefuelled range of 2,400 nm (4,448 km; 2,764 miles), while operating from unimproved strips 305 m (1,000 ft) long. Prototype is 62 per cent scale proof-of-concept demonstrator. Tandem high aspect ratio wings, originally connected fore and aft by pods carrying engines, main landing gear and fuel; front wing has dihedral, rear wing anhedral to avoid tip vortex interference; major modification substituted twin-boom tail with high tailplane for original fuselage-mounted tail

Scaled Composites AT³ in final configuration with rear loading ramp, twin fins and wingtip extensions

with mid-mounted tailplane; extra fins added to original tailplane after first flights, before modification.
FLYING CONTROLS: Defined as 'trimaran' system; eight fast-moving electrically actuated flaps extended rearwards, but are not deflected downwards, before take-off; these then deflected in 1.5 seconds at rotation to cause jump take-off.
STRUCTURE: Glassfibre/foam and carbonfibre structure.
LANDING GEAR: Tricycle retractable; mainwheels retract into outboard booms.
POWER PLANT: Two 559 kW (750 shp) P&WC PT6A-135A turboprops; all fuel contained in wings and booms.
ACCOMMODATION: Two-man flight deck; unobstructed cabin with rear loading doors.

DIMENSIONS, EXTERNAL (final configuration):

Wing span	16.21 m (53 ft 2 in)
Foreplane span	11.48 m (37 ft 8 in)
Length overall	13.67 m (44 ft 10 in)
Height overall	4.29 m (14 ft 1 in)

AREAS:

Main wing, gross	16.67 m² (179.48 sq ft)
Front wing, gross (total)	10.97 m² (118.08 sq ft)

WEIGHTS AND LOADINGS:

Max demonstrated T-O weight	5,216 kg (11,500 lb)
Max design T-O and landing weight	5,896 kg (13,000 lb)
Max wing loading, both wings	
	213.36 kg/m² (43.7 lb/sq ft)
Max power loading	5.27 kg/kW (8.67 lb/shp)

PERFORMANCE:

Max level speed	170 knots (315 km/h; 196 mph)
Min single-engine control speed (VMC)	
	63 knots (117 km/h; 73 mph)

RUTAN MODEL 143 TRIUMPH

TYPE: Proof-of-concept light business aircraft.
PROGRAMME: Design began 1985; first flight (N143SC) 14 July 1988; flight tests continued until potential to certificate under FAR Part 23 was demonstrated; used

until March 1990 by Scaled as flight test chase aircraft for ARES programme and then stored; flew about 110 hours; FJ44 engines returned to Williams; programme being offered to potential developers worldwide.
DESIGN FEATURES: Intended to explore range of piston, turboprop and turbofan powered six/eight-seat cabin class business aircraft for Beech Aircraft; only the turbofan powered prototype was completed; other prototypes stopped before Beech Aircraft sold Scaled Composites; 0.52 bar (7.5 lb/sq in) cabin pressurisation system incorporated later.
FLYING CONTROLS: Three-surface control system with pitch-axis control surfaces on foreplane and tailplane, and ailerons on wings.
STRUCTURE: Glassfibre/foam and carbonfibre.
LANDING GEAR: Retractable tricycle.
POWER PLANT: Prototype powered by two 8.00 kN (1,800 lb st) Williams International FJ44 turbofans mounted in pods above wing; 1,360 kg (3,000 lb) fuel in four cells in wing strakes and outboard wings.

DIMENSIONS, EXTERNAL:

Wing span	14.63 m (48 ft 0 in)
Wing aspect ratio	11.55
Foreplane span	3.11 m (10 ft 2½ in)
Length overall	11.89 m (39 ft 0 in)
Fuselage diameter	approx 1.52 m (5 ft 0 in)
Height overall	3.32 m (10 ft 10¾ in)
Tailplane span	3.11 m (10 ft 2½ in)

DIMENSIONS, INTERNAL:

Cabin: Length	5.92 m (19 ft 5 in)
Max width	1.42 m (4 ft 8 in)
Height	1.32 m (4 ft 4 in)

AREAS:

Wings, gross	18.49 m² (199.0 sq ft)

WEIGHTS AND LOADINGS:

Weight empty, equipped	approx 2,268 kg (5,000 lb)
Max usable fuel weight	1,356 kg (2,990 lb)
Max T-O weight	4,082 kg (9,000 lb)
Max wing loading	220.2 kg/m² (45.1 lb/sq ft)
Max power loading	255.13 kg/kN (2.50 lb/lb st)

Rutan Triumph light business jet prototype (two Williams FJ44 turbofans)

PERFORMANCE (at max T-O weight, ISA, except where indicated):
Max operating speed:
  below 7,620 m (25,000 ft)
        300 knots (556 km/h; 345 mph)
  above 7,620 m (25,000 ft)   Mach 0.75
Max level speed at 10,670 m (35,000 ft)
        400 knots (741 km/h; 460 mph)
Econ cruising speed at 10,670 m (35,000 ft)
        340 knots (630 km/h; 392 mph)
Stalling speed, power off   75 knots (139 km/h; 87 mph)
Max rate of climb at S/L   1,370 m (4,500 ft)/min
Rate of climb at S/L, one engine out
        305 m (1,000 ft)/min
Time to 10,670 m (35,000 ft)   13 min
Service ceiling   12,500 m (41,000 ft)
T-O run   381 m (1,250 ft)
T-O balanced field length   976 m (3,200 ft)
Landing run   671 m (2,200 ft)
Range with NBAA IFR reserves
        1,600 nm (2,965 km; 1,842 miles)

RUTAN MODEL 151 ARES

TYPE: Agile Response Effective Support (ARES) low cost military and paramilitary aircraft.
PROGRAMME: Rutan made design study of US Army Low Cost Battlefield Attack Aircraft (LCBAA) 1981; ARES design began 1985; first flight (N151SC) 19 February 1990; 120 hours flown by March 1991; speeds demonstrated to 305 knots (656 km/h; 351 mph) in level flight, 405 knots (750 km/h; 466 mph) at 7,620 m (25,000 ft); more than 1,000 nm (1,850 km; 1,150 miles) flown on internal fuel at 7,620 m (25,000 ft); live firing tests with GAU-12/U cannon scheduled for Summer 1991.
VARIANTS: ARES design can be produced in different sizes, with different armaments and in two-seat form.
CUSTOMERS: Potentially Pacific Rim nations; US Navy and Air Force interest.
COSTS: Initial development as private venture; no outside funding. Production aircraft would cost $1 million. Development prototypes could be supplied for $5 million each.
DESIGN FEATURES: Offset fuselage layout to prevent gun gases interfering with engine operation; General Electric five-barrel GAU-12/U 25 mm gun installed in 'focused depression' in starboard side of fuselage so that gun blast impinges on forward fuselage and counteracts recoil and cockpit canopy is shielded from blast; engine installed off-axis in rear fuselage, with curved duct from circular intake on port side; jetpipe curved to align efflux with fuselage axis; these curves hide compressor and turbine from radar; fuselage offset 76 mm (3.0 in) to port of wing centreline; fins and rudders mounted on short tailbooms, which shield jet efflux. Inner wing swept at 50°, outer wing at about 15°; foreplanes swept about 10° forward. Natural angle of attack limiting has been demonstrated.
   Rutan offering to produce prototypes for trials by potential customers in two years; potential roles include anti-helicopter, close air support, forward air control, operational trainer, armed border patrol and anti-narcotics.
FLYING CONTROLS: Elevators on foreplanes; ailerons on wings; airbrake/flaps on inner wings. Built-in aerodynamic angle of attack protection.
STRUCTURE: Extensive use of carbonfibre/epoxy over foam/PVC cores.
LANDING GEAR: Hydraulically retractable tricycle type, with single wheel on each unit. Main units retract rearward into tailbooms, nosewheel forward into fuselage.
POWER PLANT: One 13.12 kN (2,950 lb st) Pratt & Whitney JT15D-5 turbofan with electronic fuel control unit, offset 8° to port of centreline with thrust line corrected by curved jetpipe. Curved air intake on port side of centre fuselage only. Maximum internal fuel capacity 771 kg (1,700 lb). Provision for external fuel tank, capacity 227 kg (500 lb).

ACCOMMODATION: Pilot only, on Universal Propulsion Company SIIS-3ER ejection seat. Canopy hinged at rear. Two-seat version planned for training missions.
SYSTEMS: Oxygen system standard.
ARMAMENT: One internal 25 mm General Electric GAU-12/U five-barrel rapid-firing cannon on starboard side of fuselage, with 220 rounds. Provision for carriage of two AIM-9L Sidewinder or four AIM-92 Stinger air-to-air missiles on external stores hardpoints.
DIMENSIONS, EXTERNAL:
Wing span   10.67 m (35 ft 0 in)
Wing aspect ratio   6.5
Foreplane span   5.84 m (19 ft 2 in)
Foreplane aspect ratio   10.7
Length overall   8.97 m (25 ft 5¼ in)
Height overall   3.00 m (9 ft 10 in)
AREAS:
Wings, gross   17.49 m² (188.3 sq ft)
Foreplanes (total)   3.19 m² (34.3 sq ft)
WEIGHTS AND LOADINGS:
Weight empty, unarmed   1,308 kg (2,884 lb)
Max internal fuel weight   771 kg (1,700 lb)
Max T-O weight: unarmed   2,179 kg (4,804 lb)
  with GAU-12/U and 220 rds   2,767 kg (6,100 lb)
Max wing loading   158.17 kg/m² (32.40 lb/sq ft)
Max power loading   210.90 kg/kN (2.07 lb/lb st)
PERFORMANCE (estimated):
Max limiting Mach number   0.65
Max level speed at 10,670 m (35,000 ft)
        375 knots (695 km/h; 432 mph)

POND RACER PR-01

TYPE: Twin-piston-engined all-composites racer and record breaker.
PROGRAMME: Structurally complete in Summer 1989, awaiting special engines and gearboxes; first flight 22 March 1991; planned attempt on world propeller-driven speed record at Reno, Nevada, air races September 1991.
CUSTOMERS: Specially built for Mr Robert J. Pond and Bob Pond Racing by Voyager Aircraft Inc, Hangar 77, Mojave Airport, Mojave, California.
DESIGN FEATURES: Target maximum speed in excess of 460 knots (852 km/h; 530 mph); intended to break world piston-engined records. Twin-boom layout with cockpit module mounted on centre of forward-swept main wing and supporting central fin and tailwheel at rear; two fuselage booms carry engines, main landing gear, radiators and integral fuel tanks; low-set tailplane links rear of cockpit and booms. Exhaust, fuel and water lines do not pass near cockpit.
FLYING CONTROLS: Conventional ailerons, elevators and rudder; canted fins, called butterflies, above and below tips of tailplane, tailored to give pitch and yaw stability.
STRUCTURE: Carbonfibre/foam spars and skins.
LANDING GEAR: Retractable mainwheels; fixed steerable tailwheel.
POWER PLANT: Two 596/746 kW (800/1,000 hp) Electramotive VG-30 liquid-cooled, turbocharged and intercooled V-6 automobile racing piston engines with reduction gearing, driving highly modified Hartzell four-blade propellers rotating in opposite directions and designed to operate in Mach 0.98 airflow. Methanol fuel contained in six integral fuel tanks, three in each wing, combined capacity 318 litres (84 US gallons; 70 Imp gallons).

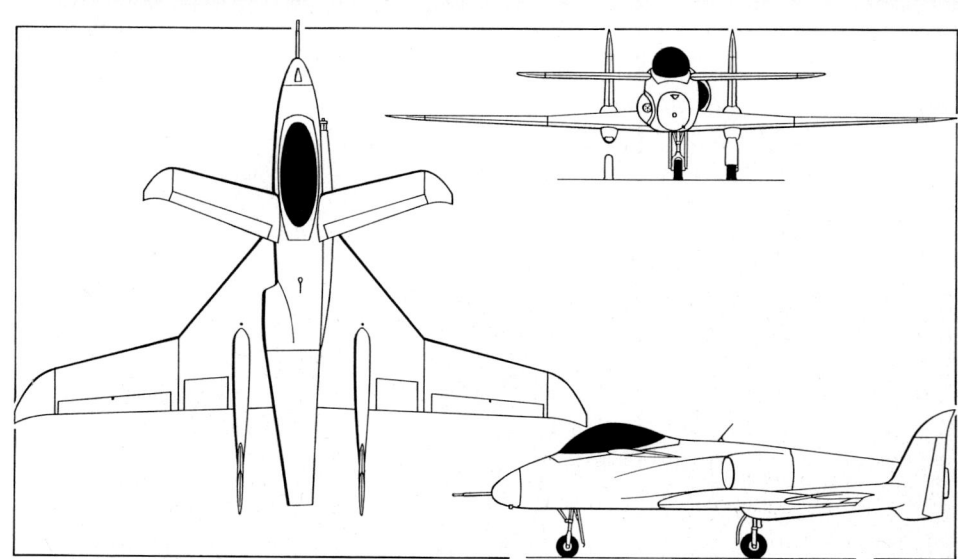

Photograph and three-view drawing *(Jane's/Mike Keep)* **of the Rutan Model 151 ARES turbofan powered agile combat aircraft**

ACCOMMODATION: Single-seat cockpit with 'space age' emergency egress system.

DIMENSIONS, EXTERNAL:

Wing span	7.74 m (25 ft 5 in)
Engine boom length	6.10 m (20 ft 0 in)
Cockpit length	1.68 m (5 ft 6 in)

WEIGHTS AND LOADINGS:

Empty weight	1,588 kg (3,500 lb)
Max T-O weight	1,882 kg (4,150 lb)
Max power loading (1,000 hp)	1.26 kg/kW (2.0 lb/hp)

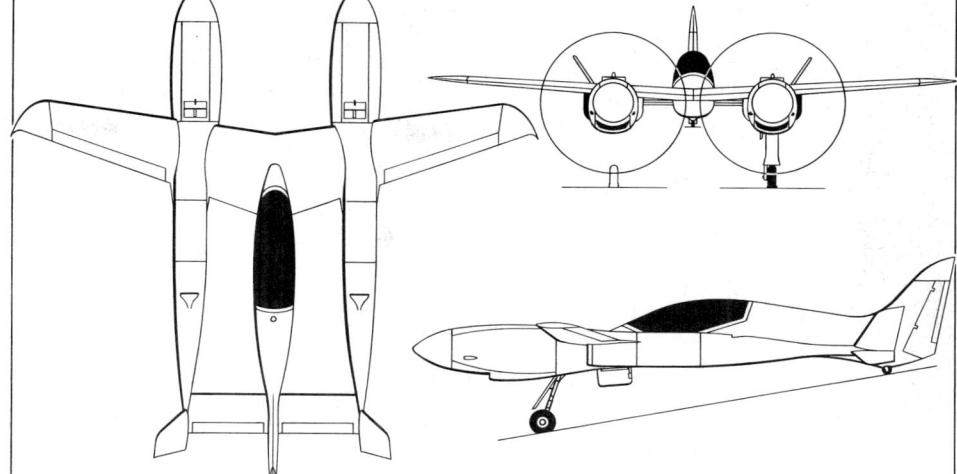

Pond Racer PR-01 designed by Mr Burt Rutan and made by Voyager Aircraft *(Jane's/Mike Keep)*

SCHAFER

SCHAFER AIRCRAFT MODIFICATIONS INC

Route 10, Box 301, Madison Cooper Airport, Waco, Texas 76708
Telephone: 1 (817) 753 1551
Fax: 1 (817) 753 8416
Telex: 795902 SCHAFER CFTO
PRESIDENT: Earl Schafer
EXECUTIVE VICE-PRESIDENT AND DIRECTOR OF MARKETING:
R. B. Stevens
Company formed 1977; originally manufactured auxiliary fuel tanks and modifications for Cessna 300 and 400 series aircraft; since 1979, has developed own modification programmes.

SCHAFER COMANCHERO

TYPE: Turbine powered Piper Pressurised Navajo.
PROGRAMME: Original piston engines replaced by turboprops; FAA STC received January 1981; Aerospatiale subsidiary SECA of France appointed sole modification and service centre for Europe, Middle East and Africa.
DESIGN FEATURES: Useful load increased by 345 kg (760 lb); optional dual camera port installation for high altitude photography.
FLYING CONTROLS: As for Navajo.
STRUCTURE: As for Navajo.
POWER PLANT: Two 559 kW (750 shp) P&WC PT6A-135 turboprops, flat rated at 462 kW (620 shp). Fuel capacity increased to 1,363 litres (360 US gallons; 300 Imp gallons).

WEIGHTS AND LOADINGS:

Weight empty	2,177 kg (4,800 lb)
Max baggage weight	218 kg (480 lb)
Max T-O weight	3,538 kg (7,800 lb)
Max wing loading	176.9 kg/km² (36.24 lb/sq ft)
Max power loading	4.07 kg/kW (6.7 lb/shp)

PERFORMANCE: As for Pressurised Navajo except:

Max cruising speed at 6,100 m (20,000 ft)	
	282 knots (522 km/h; 325 mph)
Max rate of climb at S/L	1,067 m (3,500 ft)/min
Rate of climb at S/L, one engine out	
	250 m (820 ft)/min
Service ceiling	more than 11,280 m (37,000 ft)
Service ceiling, one engine out	6,860 m (22,500 ft)
T-O to 15 m (50 ft)	533 m (1,750 ft)

Landing from 15 m (50 ft)	564 m (1,850 ft)
Max range at 8,840 m (29,000 ft), 45 min reserves	
	1,530 nm (2,835 km; 1,761 miles)

SCHAFER COMANCHERO 500

TYPE: Turboprop powered Piper Chieftain.
PROGRAMME: Original piston engines replaced by turboprops; programme launched mid-1980; flight testing started August 1981; licence to manufacture 50 Comanchero 500B sold to Neiva Industria Aeronautica of Brazil (see below) early 1984.
VARIANTS: **Comanchero 500A:** Powered by two 410 kW (550 shp) P&WC PT6A-20 turboprops; 132 litre (35 US gallon; 29 Imp gallon) extra fuel tank in each engine nacelle; max T-O weight increased; airframe inspected, bushings and hydraulic components replaced as necessary; options include special interiors, custom avionics, detachable underfuselage pod with capacity of 0.44 m³ (15.5 cu ft), and larger 341 litre (90 US gallon; 75 Imp gallon) nacelle tanks.
Comanchero 500B: Powered by two more expensive 533 ekW (715 ehp) P&WC PT6A-27 turboprops, flat rated at 431 ekW (578 ehp) for hot and high performance; other features and options as for Comanchero 500A.
Neiva Comanchero/NE-821 Carajá: Powered by 410 kW (550 shp) P&WC PT6A-34 turboprops; otherwise as Comanchero 500B; first two kits supplied by Schafer, remainder made by Neiva (see Brazilian section).
FLYING CONTROLS: As for Chieftain.
STRUCTURE: As for Chieftain.

WEIGHTS AND LOADINGS:

Max T-O weight	3,629 kg (8,000 lb)
Max power loading (500A)	4.43 kg/kW (7.27 lb/shp)

PERFORMANCE (A: Comanchero 500A, B: Comanchero 500B):

Max cruising speed: A, B at 3,660 m (12,000 ft)	
	240 knots (445 km/h; 276 mph)
Max rate of climb at S/L: A	853 m (2,800 ft)/min
B	732 m (2,400 ft)/min
Rate of climb at S/L, one engine out:	
A, B	259 m (850 ft)/min
Service ceiling: A	8,840 m (29,000 ft)
Service ceiling, one engine out: A, B	4,725 m (15,500 ft)
T-O to 15 m (50 ft): A	759 m (2,490 ft)
Landing from 15 m (50 ft): A	724 m (2,375 ft)
Range with pilot and ten passengers, 13.6 kg (30 lb) baggage allowance per passenger, and 45 min reserves,	

with standard fuel:

A, B	500 nm (926 km; 575 miles)
Range with pilot and 181 kg (400 lb) payload:	
B	1,300 nm (2,410 km; 1,500 miles)

SCHAFER COMANCHERO 750

TYPE: Re-engined Piper Cheyenne II.
PROGRAMME: FAA STC granted May 1981.
DESIGN FEATURES: Standard 462 kW (620 shp) P&WC PT6A-28 turboprops replaced by PT6A-135s flat rated at 559 kW (750 shp); optional dual camera port installation. Otherwise as for Cheyenne II.
PERFORMANCE:

Max cruising speed at 7,620 m (25,000 ft)	
	278 knots (515 km/h; 320 mph)
Max rate of climb at S/L	869 m (2,850 ft)/min
Rate of climb at S/L, one engine out	198 m (650 ft)/min
Max range, econ cruising power, at 8,840 m (29,000 ft)	
	1,630 nm (3,020 km; 1,877 miles)

SCHAFER/AMI DOUGLAS DC-3-65TP CARGOMASTER

TYPE: Turboprop Douglas DC-3.
PROGRAMME: Original piston engines replaced by turboprops; design began January 1985; first flight 1 August 1986; first production conversion started September 1986; by early 1989, Cargomasters operating in South America, South Africa and USA; demonstrated to US Air Force and Navy and Government agencies early 1989.
CUSTOMERS: Market estimated at 100 conversions in three years. Marketed by Aero Modifications International (which see).
DESIGN FEATURES: Conversion in association with Aero Modifications International of Fort Worth, Texas; re-engined with P&WC PT6A-65AR turboprops; fuselage stretched 1.02 m (3 ft 4 in) forward of wing, with or without extra window each side, to retain CG range; fuel capacity increased and hydraulics modified.
FLYING CONTROLS: Minor changes to horizontal tail to improve stability.
POWER PLANT: Two 1,062 kW (1,424 shp) Pratt & Whitney Canada PT6A-65AR turboprops, each flat rated at 917 kW (1,230 shp) and driving a Hartzell five-blade feathering and reversing propeller with de-icing. Engines have inertial separators and hot lip intake de-icing. One additional fuel tank, usable capacity 447 litres (118 US gallons; 98.25 Imp gallons), in each engine nacelle. One forward auxiliary fuel tank, usable capacity 765 litres (202 US gallons; 168 Imp gallons), and one rear auxiliary fuel tank, usable capacity 753 litres (199 US gallons; 166 Imp gallons), in each inboard wing, giving total usable fuel capacity of 3,930 litres (1,038 US gallons; 864 Imp gallons). Oil capacity 9.5 litres (2.5 US gallons; 2.1 Imp gallons).
SYSTEMS: Two engine driven 250A starter/generators. Redesigned electrical system with dual batteries providing simultaneous engine start capability.

DIMENSIONS, EXTERNAL: As for standard DC-3, except:

Length overall	20.34 m (66 ft 9 in)
Propeller diameter	2.79 m (9 ft 2 in)
Baggage door: Height	1.42 m (4 ft 8 in)
Width	2.13 m (7 ft 0 in)

DIMENSIONS, INTERNAL:

Cabin: Length	12.50 m (41 ft 0 in)
Max width	2.18 m (7 ft 2 in)
Max height	1.95 m (6 ft 5 in)
Floor area	26.72 m² (287.6 sq ft)
Volume	48.85 m³ (1,725 cu ft)

Schafer Comanchero 500 conversion of Piper Chieftain

WEIGHTS AND LOADINGS:

Basic operating weight	7,167 kg (15,800 lb)
Max fuel weight	3,154 kg (6,954 lb)
Max T-O and landing weight	12,202 kg (26,900 lb)
Max zero-fuel weight	11,793 kg (26,000 lb)
Max wing loading	132.8 kg/m² (27.2 lb/sq ft)
Max power loading	6.65 kg/kW (10.9 lb/shp)

PERFORMANCE:

Never-exceed speed (V~NE~)
187 knots (346 km/h; 215 mph) IAS

Max level speed at 3,050 m (10,000 ft)
217 knots (402 km/h; 250 mph)

Max cruising speed at 3,050 m (10,000 ft)
196 knots (363 km/h; 226 mph)

Econ cruising speed at 3,050 m (10,000 ft)
185 knots (343 km/h; 213 mph)

Stalling speed, flight idle power
52 knots (96 km/h; 60 mph) IAS

Max rate of climb at S/L	610 m (2,000 ft)/min
Rate of climb at S/L, one engine out	137 m (450 ft)/min
Service ceiling	7,620 m (25,000 ft)
Service ceiling, one engine out	3,685 m (12,100 ft)
T-O run	1,051 m (3,450 ft)
T-O to 15 m (50 ft)	1,122 m (3,680 ft)
Landing from 15 m (50 ft)	670 m (2,200 ft)

Range: with max fuel and 2,268 kg (5,000 lb) payload
1,300 nm (2,409 km; 1,497 miles)

with 4,536 kg (10,000 lb) payload
100 nm (185 km; 115 miles)

Schafer/AMI Douglas DC-3-65TP Cargomaster conversion with Pratt & Whitney Canada PT6A-65AR turboprops

SCHWEIZER

SCHWEIZER AIRCRAFT CORPORATION

PO Box 147, Elmira, New York 14902
Telephone: 1 (607) 739 3821
Fax: 1 (607) 796 2488
Telex: 932459 SCHWEIZER BIGF
PRESIDENT: Paul H. Schweizer
EXECUTIVE VICE-PRESIDENTS:
  Leslie E. Schweizer
  W. Stuart Schweizer
VICE-PRESIDENT: Michael D. Oakley
MARKETING DIRECTORS:
  Larry A. Brooks
  Truman C. Kosier
MANAGER, MARKETING AND COMMUNICATIONS:
  Barbara J. Tweedt

Established 1939 to produce sailplanes; present models described in appropriate section of this issue; from mid-1957 to 1979 Schweizer also made Grumman (later Gulfstream American) Ag-Cat under subcontract; all rights to Ag-Cat purchased January 1981; delivery of Ag-Cat Super-B, since supplemented by turboprop version, started October 1981; Ag-Cat marketing and support based at Elmira factory.

Schweizer acquired rights for sole US manufacture of Hughes 300 light helicopter 13 July 1983; Schweizer supporting earlier Hughes 300s and US Army TH-55 trainers; first Elmira-built 300C completed June 1984; Schweizer purchased US rights for whole 300C programme from McDonnell Douglas Helicopter Company (formerly Hughes Helicopters) 21 November 1986.

Schweizer subcontracts include work for Bell Helicopter, Boeing, Sikorsky and others; company is involved in design and prototyping, and in projects to develop heavy lift vehicles, aerial applications for pheromones, centrifuges and spatial disorientation trainers.

SCHWEIZER SA 2-37A
US military designation: RG-8A

TYPE: Two-seat quiet special missions aircraft.

PROGRAMME: First flight of SA 2-37A (N9237A) in 1986; three RG-8As (85-0047, 85-0048 and 86-0404) bought by US Army; one (85-0048) lost in accident; remaining two transferred to US Coast Guard for anti-narcotics operations; prototype fitted with Hughes AN/AAQ-16 and other manufacturers' thermal imaging systems.

CUSTOMERS: US Army and US Coast Guard.

DESIGN FEATURES: Modification of Schweizer SGM 2-37 motor glider (see Sailplanes section), but with slightly greater wing span, drooped leading-edge and leading-edge fences on outer wing panels to improve stall, much more powerful engine with large exhaust silencers on fuselage sides, three-blade quiet propeller, fuselage modified to accept bulged canopy and larger engine, streamlined fairings and hydraulic parking brake on mainwheels; more than treble standard fuel capacity, but optional extra tank also available; removable underfuselage skin and hatches give access to 1.84 m³ (65 cu ft) payload bay behind cockpit, in which pallets holding LLLTV, FLIR or camera payloads can be quickly removed and installed; other engines and larger payloads available for surveillance, basic and advanced training, operator training, glider and banner towing and priority cargo delivery. Certificated to FAR Pt 23 for day and night IFR; inaudible when overflying at 'quiet mode' speed at about 610 m (2,000 ft) using 38.8 kW (52 hp) from its 175 kW (235 hp) Textron Lycoming IO-540 engine.

Schweizer RG-8A two-seat drug interdiction aircraft of the US Coast Guard *(Ivo Sturzenegger)*

Wing section Wortmann FX-61-163 at root and FX-60-126 (modified) at tip; outer wing panels and horizontal tail can be removed for transport.

POWER PLANT: One 175 kW (235 hp) Textron Lycoming IO-540-W3A5D flat-six engine, driving a McCauley three-blade constant-speed propeller. Standard fuel capacity of 196.8 litres (52 US gallons; 43.3 Imp gallons), increasable optionally to 253.6 litres (67 US gallons; 55.8 Imp gallons). Shadin fuel flow system.

ACCOMMODATION: Seats for two persons side by side under two-piece upward opening canopy, hinged on centreline. Dual controls, seat belts and inertia reel harnesses standard. Compartment aft of seats enlarged to accommodate pallet containing up to 340 kg (750 lb) of sensors or other equipment.

SYSTEMS: 28V DC electrical system standard, with 100A alternator. A 300A generator and 110/120V 400Hz AC inverter are optional. Other options include air-conditioning and 1.81 m³ (64 cu ft) Scott oxygen system.

AVIONICS: Litton inertial navigation system. Standard Bendix/King avionics comprise dual KX 155 nav/com (one with VOR/ILS, one with VOR indicator) and single KG 258 artificial horizon, KEA 129 encoding altimeter, KR 87 ADF with indicator, KT 76 transponder, KR 21 marker beacon receiver, and KMA 24H audio control panel. Optional avionics include Bendix/King KNS 80 R/Nav, KCS 55A compass system, KFC 150 autopilot (requiring KCS 55A slave compass), and KRA 10A radar altimeter; Loran system; Stormscope WX-11.

EQUIPMENT: Flight and engine instrumentation includes compass, ASI, rate of climb indicator, altimeter, fuel pressure and quantity gauges, oil temperature and pressure gauges, tachometer and voltmeter. Other standard equipment includes directional gyro, turn and bank indicator, exhaust gas and cylinder head temperature gauges, vacuum system, two David Clark headsets, digital clock, dual engine mufflers with resonator quiet kit, navigation/strobe/landing lights, interior post lights, flood/map light, and static wicks. Optional equipment includes 56.8 litre (15 US gallon; 12.5 Imp gallon) auxiliary fuel tank; 25 cm (10 in) tailwheel; armour seat protection; tinted glass; and lighting compatible with night vision goggles.

DIMENSIONS, EXTERNAL:

Wing span	18.745 m (61 ft 6 in)
Wing aspect ratio	19.0
Fuselage length	8.46 m (27 ft 9 in)
Height overall (tail down)	2.36 m (7 ft 9 in)
Tailplane span	3.24 m (10 ft 7½ in)
Wheel track	2.79 m (9 ft 2 in)
Wheelbase	5.99 m (19 ft 8 in)
Propeller diameter	2.18 m (7 ft 2 in)
Propeller ground clearance (tail up)	0.55 m (1 ft 9.7 in)

AREAS:

Wings, gross	18.52 m² (199.4 sq ft)
Ailerons (total)	1.01 m² (10.90 sq ft)
Airbrakes (total)	0.82 m² (8.79 sq ft)
Vertical tail surfaces (total)	1.62 m² (17.43 sq ft)
Horizontal tail surfaces (total)	2.13 m² (22.95 sq ft)

WEIGHTS AND LOADINGS:

Weight empty	918 kg (2,025 lb)
Max mission payload	340 kg (750 lb)
Max T-O weight	1,587 kg (3,500 lb)
Max wing loading	85.65 kg/m² (17.55 lb/sq ft)
Max power loading	9.06 kg/kW (14.89 lb/hp)

PERFORMANCE (at max T-O weight):

Max permissible diving speed
176 knots (326 km/h; 202 mph) CAS

Cruising speed at 1,525 m (5,000 ft):

75% power	138 knots (256 km/h; 159 mph)
65% power	129 knots (239 km/h; 148 mph)
Approach speed	117 knots (217 km/h; 135 mph) CAS

Quiet mode speed
70-80 knots (130-148 km/h; 80-92 mph)

Optimum climbing speed
77 knots (142 km/h; 88 mph) CAS

Stalling speed:

airbrakes open	71 knots (132 km/h; 82 mph)
airbrakes closed	67 knots (124 km/h; 77 mph)
Max rate of climb at S/L	292 m (960 ft)/min
Service ceiling	5,490 m (18,000 ft)

T-O run (S/L, ISA): hard surface 387 m (1,270 ft)
grass 533 m (1,750 ft)

T-O to 15 m (50 ft) (S/L, ISA):

hard surface	612 m (2,010 ft)
grass	759 m (2,490 ft)

Landing from 15 m (50 ft) (S/L, ISA):

hard surface	680 m (2,230 ft)
grass	732 m (2,400 ft)
Best glide ratio	20
g limits	+6.6/-3.3

SCHWEIZER AG-CAT SERIES

TYPE: Agricultural aircraft.

PROGRAMME: First flight of original Grumman Ag-Cat 27 May 1957; first deliveries 1959; production resumed in October 1981 with improved G-164B designated Ag-Cat Super-B, later joined by Ag-Cat Super-B Turbine.

VARIANTS: **Ag-Cat Super-B/600 (G-164B):** Basic model powered by 447.5 kW (600 hp) P&W R-1340 radial engine, driving Pacific Propeller Type 12D40/AG100 two-blade constant-speed metal propeller; improvements in Super-B include 40 per cent more hopper capacity (1.51 m³; 53.5 cu ft) and 0.97 m (3 ft 2 in) wider stainless steel gatebox and bottom loader as standard equipment; upper wing raised 20 cm (8 in) to improve pilot's view and increase load carrying capability, operating speed and climb rate.

Ag-Cat 450B (G-164B): Generally similar alternative version, available to special order; powered by 335.5 kW (450 hp) P&W R-985 radial engine; usable fuel 242 litres (64 US gallons; 53.3 Imp gallons); hopper volume 1.23 m³ (43.5 cu ft) and capacity 1,230 litres (325 US gallons; 271 Imp gallons).

Ag-Cat Super-B Turbine (G-164B): Similar to basic Super-B, but powered by choice of 373 kW (500 shp) P&WC PT6A-11AG, 507 kW (680 shp) PT6A-15AG or 559 kW (750 shp) PT6A-34AG turboprop engines.

CUSTOMERS: Total 2,455 Ag-Cats built by Schweizer under contract, including 1,730 G-164As, 659 G-164Bs, 44 G-164Cs and 22 G-164Ds. Ag-Cat Super-B Turbine also being manufactured under licence by Ethiopian Airlines Technical Services Division in Addis Ababa (which see) since December 1986.

DESIGN FEATURES: Wing section NACA 4412; dihedral 3°; incidence 6°; uncowled piston engines.

FLYING CONTROLS: Mechanical, with trim tab on port elevator; ground adjustable tabs on one aileron, rudder and starboard elevator; no flaps.

STRUCTURE: Wing has two aluminium spars and sheet skin wrapped over whole upper surface and back to front spar on under surface; remainder of underside fabric covered; leading-edges in five panels to simplify repair; glassfibre wingtips; light alloy ailerons; wire-braced fabric covered tail surfaces on steel tube frame; welded steel tube fuselage with removable side panels.

LANDING GEAR: Non-retractable tailwheel type. Cantilever spring steel legs. Cleveland wheels with tyres size 8.50-10, 8-ply, pressure 2.42 bars (35 lb/sq in). Steerable tailwheel with tyre size 12.4-4.5, pressure 3.45 bars (50 lb/sq in). Cleveland heavy duty aircooled hydraulic disc brakes. Parking brake.

POWER PLANT: One Pratt & Whitney nine-cylinder aircooled radial engine with Pacific Propeller constant-speed propeller, or Pratt & Whitney Canada PT6A turboprop, as detailed under Variants. Fuel tanks in upper wing with combined usable capacity of 302 litres (80 US gallons; 66.6 Imp gallons). Single-point refuelling on upper surface of upper wing centre-section. Oil capacity 32.2 litres (8.5 US gallons; 7.1 Imp gallons).

ACCOMMODATION: Single seat in enclosed cockpit. Reinforced fairing aft of canopy for turnover protection. Canopy side panels open outward and down, canopy top upward and to starboard, to provide access. Baggage compartment. Cockpit pressurised against dust ingress and ventilated by ram air. Safety padded instrument panel. Air-conditioning by J.B. Systems optional.

SYSTEMS: Hydraulic system for brakes only. Optional electrical system with 24V alternator, navigation lights and/or strobe lights, external power socket, and electric engine starter.

EQUIPMENT: Radio optional. Standard equipment includes control column lock, instrument glareshield, seat belt and shoulder harness, tinted windscreen, stall warning light, refuelling steps and assist handles, tiedown rings, and urethane paint external yellow finish.

Forward of cockpit, over CG, is a 1.51 m³ (53.5 cu ft) glassfibre hopper, capacity 1,514 litres (400 US gallons; 333 Imp gallons), for agricultural chemicals (dry or liquid) with distributor beneath fuselage. Low-volume, ULV or high-volume spray system, with leading- or trailing-edge booms. Emergency dump system for hopper load; can be used also for water bomber operations.

DIMENSIONS, EXTERNAL (A: Super-B/600, B: Super-B Turbine, C: 450B):

Wing span: upper	12.92 m (42 ft 4½ in)
lower	12.36 m (40 ft 6¾ in)
Wing chord, constant	1.47 m (4 ft 10 in)
Wing aspect ratio: upper wing	8.7
biplane, effective mean	5.5
Length overall: A	7.44 m (24 ft 5 in)
B	8.41 m (27 ft 7¼ in)
C	7.54 m (24 ft 9 in)
Height overall: A, C	3.51 m (11 ft 6 in)
B	3.68 m (12 ft 1 in)
Tailplane span	3.96 m (13 ft 0 in)
Wheel track	2.44 m (8 ft 0 in)
Wheelbase	5.59 m (18 ft 4 in)
Propeller diameter (max)	2.74 m (9 ft 0 in)
Propeller ground clearance: A	0.27 m (10.8 in)
B	0.37 m (1 ft 2¾ in)

Schweizer Ag-Cat Super-B/600 agricultural aircraft

Cockpit door: Height	0.53 m (1 ft 9 in)
Width	0.64 m (2 ft 1 in)
Height to sill	0.71 m (2 ft 4 in)

DIMENSIONS, INTERNAL:

Cockpit: Length	1.27 m (4 ft 2 in)
Max width	0.76 m (2 ft 6 in)
Max height	1.14 m (3 ft 9 in)

AREAS:

Wings, gross	36.48 m² (392.7 sq ft)
Ailerons (total)	2.92 m² (31.4 sq ft)
Fin	1.67 m² (17.97 sq ft)
Rudder	1.12 m² (12.0 sq ft)
Tailplane	2.12 m² (22.8 sq ft)
Elevators	2.06 m² (22.2 sq ft)

WEIGHTS AND LOADINGS:

Weight empty equipped, spray and duster versions:

A	1,656 kg (3,650 lb)
B	1,429 kg (3,150 lb)
C	1,508 kg (3,325 lb)
Certificated gross weight	2,358 kg (5,200 lb)
Max T-O weight (CAM.8)	3,184 kg (7,020 lb)
Max wing loading	87.42 kg/m² (17.91 lb/sq ft)
Max power loading: A	7.12 kg/kW (11.71 lb/hp)
B	5.70-8.54 kg/kW (9.36-14.04 lb/shp)
C	9.49 kg/kW (15.6 lb/hp)

PERFORMANCE (A: Super-B/600, B: Super-B Turbine with PT6A-15AG engine, C: 450B):

Never-exceed speed (VNE)

	136 knots (252 km/h; 157 mph)
Working speed: A, C	100 knots (185 km/h; 115 mph)
B	113 knots (209 km/h; 130 mph)
Stalling speed, power off	56 knots (103 km/h; 64 mph)
T-O run	120 m (394 ft)
T-O to 15 m (50 ft) at 2,358 kg (5,200 lb) certificated gross weight: A	320 m (1,050 ft)
B	274 m (900 ft)
C	396 m (1,300 ft)
Landing from 15 m (50 ft)	407 m (1,333 ft)
Landing run	157 m (513 ft)
Range with max fuel	172 nm (318 km; 198 miles)
Design g limits, all versions	+4.2/−1

SCHWEIZER MODEL 300C

TYPE: Three-seat light utility helicopter.

PROGRAMME: First flight August 1969; first flight Hughes production model December 1969; FAA certification May 1970 (basic Model 300 described in 1976-77 *Jane's*). Production of 300C transferred from Hughes Helicopters to Schweizer July 1983; first flight Schweizer Model 300C June 1984; Schweizer bought entire programme November 1986.

VARIANTS: **300C Sky Knight:** Special police version; features include safety mesh seats with inertia reel shoulder harness, ballistic glassfibre armour under seats, high powered public address/siren system, high intensity steerable searchlight, integrated communications based on Bendix/King KY 195 VHF, heavy duty 28V 100A electrical system, cabin heater, night lights with strobe beacons, cabin utility light, external power socket, fire extinguisher, first aid kit and map case.

TH-300C: Military training version.

CUSTOMERS: $4.9 million US Army order for 30 Model 300Cs and spares placed in late 1985; two batches of 24 TH-300C training helicopters delivered to Royal Thai Army between March 1986 and mid-1989; 250th Schweizer 300C delivered late 1989; 80 produced in 1990; planned production of 110 in 1991. Hughes produced 2,800 of all versions, including TH-55A Osage for US Army before transfer to Schweizer. Recent Sky Knight customers include police departments of Baltimore, Maryland; Columbus, Ohio; Kansas City, Missouri; Hillsborough County Sheriff's Office, Florida; Clayton County Sheriff's Department, Georgia.

DESIGN FEATURES: Fully articulated three-blade main rotor; fully interchangeable blades; blade section NACA 0015; elastomeric dampers; two-blade teetering tail rotor; limited blade folding; no rotor brake; multiple V-belt and pulley reduction gear/drive system between horizontally mounted engine and transmission, with electrically controlled belt-tensioning system instead of clutch; braced tubular tailboom.

FLYING CONTROLS: Mechanical, with first pilot on left; electric cyclic trim; separate dihedral tailplane and fin.

STRUCTURE: Main rotor blades bonded with constant-section extruded aluminium spar, wrap around skin and trailing-edge; tail rotor blades have steel tube spar and glassfibre skin; steel tube cabin section with light alloy, stainless steel and Plexiglas skin.

LANDING GEAR: Skids carried on oleo-pneumatic shock absorbers. Replaceable skid shoes. Two ground handling wheels with 0.25 m (10 in) balloon tyres, pressure 4.14-5.17 bars (60-75 lb/sq in). Available optionally on

Schweizer Model 300C Sky Knight light utility helicopter of the Minnesota State Patrol

floats made of polyurethane coated nylon fabric, 4.70 m (15 ft 5 in) long and with a total installed weight of 27.2 kg (60 lb).

POWER PLANT: One 168 kW (225 hp) Textron Lycoming HIO-360-D1A flat-four engine, derated to 142 kW (190 hp), mounted horizontally aft of seats. Two aluminium fuel tanks, total capacity 185.5 litres (49 US gallons; 40.8 Imp gallons) mounted externally aft of cockpit. Crash resistant fuel tank optional. Oil capacity 9.5 litres (2.5 US gallons; 2.1 Imp gallons).

ACCOMMODATION: Three persons side by side on sculptured and cushioned bench seat, with shoulder harness, in Plexiglas enclosed cabin. Carpet and tinted canopy standard. Forward hinged, removable door on each side. Dual controls optional. Baggage capacity 45 kg (100 lb). Exhaust muff heating and ventilation kits available.

SYSTEMS: Standard electrical system includes 24V 70A alternator, 24V battery, starter and external power socket.

AVIONICS: Optional avionics include Collins VHF-253 or Bendix/King KY 196 com transceiver and headsets, ADF 650A or KR 86 ADFs, TDR 950 or KT 76A transponders.

EQUIPMENT: Standard equipment includes map case, first aid kit, fire extinguisher, engine hour meter, and main rotor blade tiedown kit. Optional equipment includes amphibious floats, litter kits, cargo racks with combined capacity of 91 kg (200 lb), external load sling of 408 kg (900 lb) capacity, Simplex Model 5200 agricultural spray or dry powder dispersal kits, Sky Knight law enforcement package, instrument training package, throttle governor, start-up overspeed control unit, night flying kit, dual controls, all-weather cover, heavy duty skid plates, single or dual exhaust mufflers, door lock and dual oil coolers.

DIMENSIONS, EXTERNAL:
Main rotor diameter	8.18 m (26 ft 10 in)
Main rotor blade chord	0.171 m (6¾ in)
Tail rotor diameter	1.30 m (4 ft 3 in)
Distance between rotor centres	4.66 m (15 ft 3½ in)
Length overall, rotors turning	9.40 m (30 ft 10 in)
Height: to top of rotor head	2.66 m (8 ft 8⅝ in)
to top of cabin	2.19 m (7 ft 2 in)
Width: rotor partially folded	2.44 m (8 ft 0 in)
cabin	1.30 m (4 ft 3 in)
Skid track	1.99 m (6 ft 6½ in)
Length of skids	2.51 m (8 ft 3 in)
Passenger doors (each): Height	1.09 m (3 ft 7 in)
Width	0.97 m (3 ft 2 in)
Height to sill	0.91 m (3 ft 0 in)

AREAS:
Main rotor blades (each)	0.70 m² (7.55 sq ft)
Tail rotor blades (each)	0.08 m² (0.86 sq ft)
Main rotor disc	52.5 m² (565.5 sq ft)
Tail rotor disc	1.32 m² (14.2 sq ft)
Fin	0.23 m² (2.5 sq ft)
Horizontal stabiliser	0.246 m² (2.65 sq ft)

WEIGHTS AND LOADINGS:
Weight empty	474 kg (1,046 lb)
Max T-O weight: Normal category	930 kg (2,050 lb)
external load	975 kg (2,150 lb)
Max disc loading: Normal category	17.67 kg/m² (3.62 lb/sq ft)
Max power loading: Normal category	6.55 kg/kW (10.8 lb/hp)

Prototype Schweizer Model 330 (Allison 250-C20 turboshaft)

PERFORMANCE (at max Normal T-O weight, ISA):
Never-exceed speed (VNE) at S/L	91 knots (169 km/h; 105 mph)
Max cruising speed	82 knots (153 km/h; 95 mph)
Speed for max range, at 1,220 m (4,000 ft)	67 knots (124 km/h; 77 mph)
Max rate of climb at S/L	229 m (750 ft)/min
Service ceiling	3,110 m (10,200 ft)
Hovering ceiling: IGE	1,800 m (5,900 ft)
OGE	840 m (2,750 ft)
Range at 1,220 m (4,000 ft), 2 min warm-up, max fuel, no reserves	194 nm (360 km; 224 miles)
Max endurance at S/L	3 h 24 min

SCHWEIZER MODEL 330

TYPE: Turbine powered three/four-seat light helicopter.

PROGRAMME: Announced 1987; first flight in public (N330T) 14 June 1988, entered in US Army New Training Helicopter (NTH) competition, but also intended for commercial sale; US Army requires FAA certification, which is expected by first quarter 1992, with commercial deliveries soon after.

CUSTOMERS: Launch customer Crescent Airways of West Hollywood, Florida, ordered five for tuna fish spotting; more than 20 ordered by early 1990.

COSTS: Approximately $400,000 anticipated for civil aircraft.

DESIGN FEATURES: Civil roles include law enforcement, scout/observation, aerial photography, light utility, agricultural spraying and personal transport; uses turbine fuel rather than scarcer Avgas; extremely low rating of Allison 250-C20 engine in Model 330 promises outstanding hot and high performance; third occupant seat moves forward to allow second student to observe instruction; three sets of flying controls can be fitted; streamlined external envelope and large tailplane with endplate fins added during development; rotor rpm 471.

FLYING CONTROLS: Similar to 300C.

STRUCTURE: Generally similar to 300C.

POWER PLANT: One Allison 250-C20 turboshaft capable of 313.2 kW (420 shp), flat rated at only 149 kW (200 shp). Max fuel capacity 227 litres (60 US gallons; 50 Imp gallons).

DIMENSIONS, EXTERNAL:
Main and tail rotor diameters:	As for Model 300C
Length overall, rotors turning	9.40 m (30 ft 10 in)
Height overall	2.89 m (9 ft 5¾ in)
Skid track	1.98 m (6 ft 6 in)

DIMENSIONS, INTERNAL:
Cabin: Width at seat	1.72 m (5 ft 7½ in)
Height at seat	1.35 m (4 ft 5¼ in)

WEIGHTS AND LOADINGS: As for Model 300C except:
Weight empty	476 kg (1,050 lb)

PERFORMANCE (at Normal T-O weight):
Max cruising speed	100 knots (185 km/h; 115 mph)
Normal cruising speed	91 knots (169 km/h; 105 mph)
Hovering ceiling: IGE	5,485 m (18,000 ft)
OGE	4,265 m (14,000 ft)
Max range at 1,220 m (4,000 ft), no reserves	221 nm (410 km; 255 miles)
Max endurance, no reserves	3 h 6 min

SEAPLANES INC — *see Turbotech*

SIERRA

SIERRA INDUSTRIES

Garner Municipal Airport, PO Box 5184, Uvalde, Texas 78802-5184
Telephone: 1 (512) 278 4381
Fax: 1 (512) 278 7649
Telex: 910 240 2612
PRESIDENT: Mark Huffstutler

Sierra Industries acquired assets of R/STOL Systems Inc 24 September 1986; assets included about 100 supplemental type certificates for STOL and performance modifications to 40 types of Beech, Cessna and Piper light and business aircraft (see tables in 1990-91 and earlier *Jane's*).

SIERRA IN-WING WEATHER RADAR

RCA Weather Scout I weather radar with truncated aerial and limited mapping capability installed in reinforced wing leading-edge bay behind dielectric leading-edge panel in Cessna 182, various 206 models and 210 series; total system weighs 10.5 kg (23.1 lb).

SIERRA INDUSTRIES CESSNA AUXILIARY FUEL SYSTEMS

Extra tankage for 204 litres (54 US gallons; 45 Imp gallons) of fuel fitted to Cessna 180, 182, 185, 206 and 207; three rubber fuel bladders installed outboard of each standard fuel tank; modification takes about 50 man hours and is certificated to FAR Pt 23.

Sierra/Cessna T210, showing clearly the high differential aileron droop Hi-Lift system

SIERRA INDUSTRIES CESSNA 210 LANDING GEAR DOOR MODIFICATION

FAA approved modification kit removes mainwheel doors and replaces them with metal fairings to cover gaps; advantages include 8.6 kg (19 lb) increase in useful load, faster gear retraction and extension, elimination of possible door-fouling problems, lower maintenance and improved appearance comparable to that of 1979 and later model Centurions; modification applicable to Cessna Model 210, T210 and P210 Centurions manufactured between 1970 and 1978 (c/n 21059200-21062954 inclusive).

SIERRA/BEECH, SIERRA/CESSNA and SIERRA/PIPER SAFETY and PERFORMANCE CONVERSIONS

Hi-Lift full span wing leading- and trailing-edge modification, which greatly improves landing and take-off distances; applicable to single- and smaller twin-engined Beech, Cessna and Piper aircraft; first applied to Cessna 182; ailerons linked to flaps to droop when flaps are lowered, virtually doubling lift at low airspeeds; ailerons continue to function for roll control; full span distributed camber leading-edge provides optimum spanwise lift distribution for maximum cruise efficiency; also reduces leading-edge pressure peak at high angle of attack, giving maximum resistance to stall and high manoeuvrability at low airspeeds; some Cessna singles built after 1972 have this leading-edge as standard.

Full span flap system, conical cambered wingtips, dorsal and ventral fins, belly mounted vortex generators and flap/elevator trim linkage can be applied to various models. Stall fences applied between flap and aileron to improve controllability at low airspeeds, and aileron gap sealed with aluminium or rubberised canvas strip; gives safe STOL take-offs and landings, even with novice pilots; cruising speed and range increased by 2-4 per cent.

Increased climb performance and slower take-off and landing speeds have allowed gross weight increases for small twin conversions such as Cessna Super Skymaster and Piper Twin Comanche.

Hi-Lift modification for Cessna 400 series involved complete redesign of wing aft of rear spar to accommodate 100 per cent Fowler flaps and flap-actuated aileron droop system; with flap/elevator trim linkage and double-hinged rudder, this modification led to FAA-certificated 40 per cent reduction in landing and take-off field lengths.

Sierra equipped Piper Seneca I was FAA certificated in 1974 with full span slotted flaps, upper surface spoilers for roll control, cambered wingtips and anti-servo rudder tab; roll response increased at all airspeeds, minimum control speed reduced by 16 per cent, best rate of climb speed lowered by 19 per cent and single-engined service ceiling increased by 213 m (700 ft). Similar modification for Seneca II certificated 1976.

Full span flaps and lateral control spoilers fitted to Piper Cherokee Six; high differential aileron droop Hi-Lift system developed for high performance singles, such as Cessna P210 Pressurised Centurion; new mechanism droops ailerons 15° when flaps lowered to 20° for take-off; with aileron wheel fully to starboard, starboard aileron moves up 47° (27° up from normal faired position); at same time, port aileron moves down another 12° to a total 27°; aileron droop with 30° flap remains 15°; benefits from Hi-Lift system include greatly reduced adverse yaw tendency in turns, high roll rate for more precise control when flaps are down and speed low, and control wheel forces reduced by aerodynamic effects on up-moving aileron and friction-reducing crossover control cable.

Four aluminium stall strips (rubber when fitted over de-icing boots) retain good stalling characteristics on all Hi-Lift systems; inboard strip produces warning and outboard strip initiates stall of inner and centre wing, leaving outboard section in good lift; aileron control continues into stall.

Sierra Hi-Lift systems can be applied to almost entire range of Cessna and Piper aircraft and to Beechcraft Bonanzas. Details of performance with Hi-Lift system of Beech Bonanzas and Cessna and Piper aircraft tabulated and listed in 1990-91 and many earlier *Jane's*.

SIERRA/CESSNA EAGLE SERIES
TYPE: R/STOL modifications to Cessna Citations.
PROGRAMME: See below.
VARIANTS: **Eagle:** Formerly Astec Eagle and R/STOL Eagle modifications applied to Cessna Citation 500 and Citation I; inner wing thickness increased and tips extended, as detailed below; fuel capacity increased by 392 kg (865 lb), accounting for about 75 per cent of range increase of 600 nm (1,112 km; 691 miles); remainder produced by improved aerodynamic efficiency.

Eagle SP: Modifications as above to Cessna Citation 501, which is certificated to FAR Pt 23 for single-pilot operation.

Longwing: Eagle wingtip extension without wingroot thickening; introduced 1983; increases fuel capacity by about 54 kg (120 lb) on aircraft c/n 001-213, giving 10 per cent range increase, better climb rate and lower approach speed.

Eagle 400B: Eagle modification plus 11.12 kN (2,500 lb st) JT15D-4Bs replacing JT15D-1 or -1As.

DESIGN FEATURES: Thickness/chord ratio of inboard wing increased from 14 to 19 per cent; supercritical technology applied to wing/fuselage flow; span increased by 0.51 m (1 ft 8 in) wingtip extensions.
FLYING CONTROLS: As for Citation.
STRUCTURE: As for Citation.
POWER PLANT: As for Citation 500, except increased fuel capacity provided in the thicker wing centre-section and wingtip extensions.
DIMENSIONS, EXTERNAL:
Wing span   14.35 m (47 ft 0½ in)

Sierra conversion of the Piper Seneca II features full span trailing-edge flaps, with wing upper surface spoilers for roll control

Beechcraft A36 Bonanza with Sierra Hi-Lift system, including full span flaps

Sierra/Cessna Century V Eagle, a Citation 500 conversion with advanced wing aerofoil section and JT15D-4 turbofans

Wing chord: at root	2.95 m (9 ft 8⅛ in)
at tip	0.93 m (3 ft 0½ in)
Wing aspect ratio	7.92
Length overall	13.26 m (43 ft 6 in)
Height overall	4.36 m (14 ft 3¾ in)
Wheel track	3.84 m (12 ft 7⅛ in)
Wheelbase	4.78 m (15 ft 8¼ in)

WEIGHTS AND LOADINGS (A: JT15D-1, B: JT15D-1A, C: JT15D-4B:

Weight empty: A, B	2,971 kg (6,550 lb)
C	3,180 kg (7,011 lb)
Max fuel weight: A, B, C	2,045 kg (4,510 lb)
Max T-O weight: A, B, C	5,670 kg (12,500 lb)
Max zero-fuel weight: A, B, C	4,309 kg (9,500 lb)
Max landing weight: A, B, C	5,148 kg (11,350 lb)
Max power loading: C	254.95 kg/kN (2.50 lb/lb st)

PERFORMANCE (at max T-O weight except where indicated):
Max cruising speed, AUW of 4,309 kg (9,500 lb), at 10,670 m (35,000 ft):

A	341 knots (631 km/h; 392 mph)
B	357 knots (661 km/h; 411 mph)

C (at 8,840 m; 29,000 ft)

	400 knots (741 km/h; 460 mph)
Cruising speed, AUW of 4,309 kg (9,500 lb), at 12,500 m (41,000 ft): A	317 knots (587 km/h; 365 mph)
B	336 knots (623 km/h; 387 mph)
C (at 13,100 m; 43,000 ft)	375 knots (695 km/h; 432 mph)

Stalling speed at max landing weight:

A, B, C	78 knots (145 km/h; 90 mph)
Max rate of climb at S/L: C	1,220 m (4,000 ft)/min

Rate of climb at S/L, one engine out:

C	442 m (1,450 ft)/min
Max certificated altitude: A	10,670 m (35,000 ft)
B	12,500 m (41,000 ft)
C	13,100 m (43,000 ft)
Balanced T-O field length: A, B	907 m (2,975 ft)
C	892 m (2,925 ft)
FAA landing field length at max landing weight: A, B, C	722 m (2,370 ft)

Max range, 45 min fuel reserves:

A	1,800 nm (3,336 km; 2,073 miles)
C	1,997 nm (3,700 km; 2,300 miles)

SIKORSKY
SIKORSKY AIRCRAFT, DIVISION OF UNITED TECHNOLOGIES CORPORATION
6900 North Main Street, Stratford, Connecticut 06601-1381
Telephone: 1 (203) 386 4000
Fax: 1 (203) 386 7300
Telex: 96 4372
OTHER WORKS: Troy, Alabama; South Avenue, Bridgeport, Connecticut; Shelton, Connecticut; West Haven,

Connecticut; Development Flight Test Center, West Palm Beach, Florida
PRESIDENT: Eugene Buckley
EXECUTIVE VICE-PRESIDENT, OPERATIONS AND ENGINEERING: Raymond P. Kurlack
SENIOR VICE-PRESIDENTS:
L. C. Kay (Administration)
Kenneth C. Mard (Programmes)

Ray D. Leoni (Research and Development Operations)
Robert R. Moore (Production Operations)
VICE-PRESIDENTS, INTERNATIONAL PROGRAMMES:
Robert M. Baxter (International Business)
David L. Powell (Japan)
Edward M. Francis (Korea)
Clement C. Peterson (Middle East)
James J. Satterwhite

VICE-PRESIDENT, RESEARCH AND ENGINEERING:
Dr Kenneth M. Rosen
VICE-PRESIDENT, COMMERCIAL PROGRAMMES:
Robert L. Kelly
VICE-PRESIDENT, GOVERNMENT BUSINESS DEVELOPMENT:
Gary F. Rast
VICE-PRESIDENT COMMUNICATIONS: James H. Lynch
MANAGER OF PUBLIC RELATIONS: William S. Tuttle

Founded as Sikorsky Aero Engineering Corporation by late Igor I. Sikorsky; has been division of United Technologies Corporation since 1929; began helicopter production in 1940s; has produced more than 6,000 rotating wing aircraft.

Headquarters and main plant at Stratford, Connecticut; employment at all Sikorsky facilities totalled 11,500 in 1990; main current programmes include UH-60 Black Hawk and derivatives, CH-53E Super Stallion and S-76 series. Sikorsky and Boeing Helicopters, associated in First Team, won US Army LH/RAH-66 Comanche light helicopter demonstration/validation order on 5 April 1991 (see under Boeing Sikorsky in this section).

Sikorsky licensees include Westland of the UK, Agusta of Italy, Aerospatiale of France, MBB of Germany, Mitsubishi of Japan and Pratt & Whitney Canada Ltd. Sikorsky and Embraer of Brazil signed agreement in Summer 1983 to transfer technology covering design and manufacture of composites components; Sikorsky and CASA of Spain signed memorandum of understanding in June 1984 covering long-term helicopter industrial co-operation programme. CASA builds tail rotor pylon, tailcone and stabiliser components for H-60 and S-70, with first CASA S-70 components delivered to Sikorsky January 1986.

Westland plc (see UK section) shareholders approved joint Fiat/Sikorsky plan involving financial and technical support and minor equity participation in Westland on 12 February 1986; Westland then licensed to manufacture S-70 series.

Plan to establish an S-76 production line in South Korea announced February 1988; Daewoo-Sikorsky Aerospace Ltd (DSA) formed with facility at Chang-Won to produce civil and military S-76/H-76. Licence to manufacture S-70 in Japan granted to Mitsubishi Heavy Industries in 1988.

BOEING/SIKORSKY RAH-66 COMANCHE

The Boeing/Sikorsky First Team submission for the US Army LH, now RAH-66 Comanche, was selected to proceed into demonstration/validation phase on 4 April 1991. Details under Boeing/Sikorsky in this section.

SIKORSKY S-61/SH-3 SEA KING

Sikorsky no longer manufactures S-61 series; military model remains in low-volume production by Westland in UK (which see). Production in Japan (185 aircraft: see Mitsubishi entry) completed 1990; Italian (Agusta) licence production of HH-3F version has been restarted.

SIKORSKY S-65/CH-53D

Production in USA and Germany completed; Israel Defence Force launched upgrade programme in 1989, designated **CH-53 2000**, to be applied by Mata Helicopters plant of IAI (which see). CH-53D last described in 1978-79 *Jane's*.

SIKORSKY S-65/MH-53J PAVE LOW III ENHANCED

US Air Force upgrade of Special Operations Forces combat rescue and recovery fleet; 31 HH-53Bs, HH-53Cs and CH-53Cs converted at NAS Pensacola, Florida, beginning 1986, to MH-53J Pave Low III Enhanced; similar to 11 HH-53H Pave Low III produced earlier, eight survivors of which also converted to MH-53Js; programme completed in 1990.

Modifications include Texas Instruments AN/AAQ-10 nose-mounted FLIR, inertial navigation, Doppler, computer-projected map display, Navstar GPS, Texas Instruments AN/APQ-158 terrain following/avoidance radar in offset nose radome, chaff/flare dispensers, Loral AN/ALQ-157 IR jammer on each outrigger pylon, 454 kg (1,000 lb) of extra titanium armour plating and Collins AN/AIC-3 intercom; armament includes three 7.62 mm or 0.50 in machine guns firing through windows on each side and from open rear ramp. Power plant is two 3,266 kW (4,380 shp) General Electric T64-GE-415 turboshafts; max T-O weight increased to 22,680 kg (50,000 lb).

Delivery of 15 MH-53J began mid-1987 to 20th SOS at Hurlburt Field, Florida; six delivered to 21st SOS at RAF Woodbridge, UK; four more issued to 1550th Combat Crew Training Wing at Kirtland AFB, New Mexico, in 1989 (unit also received four TH-53As—with two more in prospect—from US Marines; modified at Kirtland with T64-GE-416 power plant and some standard USAF avionics for commonality with MH-53J).

SIKORSKY S-80/H-53E
US Marine Corps and Navy designations: CH-53E Super Stallion and MH-53E Sea Dragon
TYPE: Three-engined heavy duty helicopter.

Sikorsky MH-53J Pave Low III Enhanced combat rescue and covert operations helicopter of the 21st Special Operations Squadron at RAF Woodbridge *(Paul Jackson)*

PROGRAMME: Phase I development funding for CH-53E Super Stallion allocated 1973; first flight of first of two prototypes 1 March 1974; first flight of first production prototype 8 December 1975; first flight of second production prototype March 1976; deliveries to US Marine Corps started 16 June 1981; 136 CH-53Es and 32 MH-53Es funded up to and including FY 1990; nil in FY 1991, but 20 H-53s planned in both FYs 1992 and 1993; total requirement is for 178 CH-53Es.

VARIANTS: **CH-53E Super Stallion:** Used by US Marine Corps for amphibious assault, carrying heavy equipment and armament, and recovering disabled aircraft; also used by US Navy for vertical onboard delivery and recovery of damaged aircraft from aircraft carriers; went into operation in Mediterranean area Summer 1983.

Planned improvements for CH-53E include composites tail rotor blades, uprated GE T64-416 engines, Omega navigation system, ground proximity warning system, flight crew night vision system, improved internal cargo handling system, missile alerting system, chaff/flare dispensers, nitrogen fuel inerting system, and facility for refilling hydraulic system inside cargo compartment; CH-53E will possibly be equipped with self-defence air-to-air missiles; initial trials of AIM-9 Sidewinder conducted at Naval Air Test Center, Patuxent River, Maryland. Total 117 delivered by June 1991.

Full-scale development of Helicopter Night Vision System (HNVS) for CH-53E began June 1986, in co-operation with Northrop Electro-Mechanical Division; HNVS includes Martin Marietta pilot night vision system and Honeywell integrated helmet and display sighting system (IHADSS) from Bell AH-1S surrogate trainer; HNVS will allow low level operations in night and adverse weather; HNVS ground testing began 1988; operational evaluation began August 1989.

MH-53E Sea Dragon: Airborne mine countermeasures helicopter able to tow through water hydrofoil sledge carrying mechanical, acoustic and magnetic sensors; early history in 1982-83 *Jane's*; nearly 3,785 litres (1,000 US gallons; 833 Imp gallons) extra fuel carried in enlarged sponsons made of composites; improved hydraulic and electrical systems; minefield, navigation and automatic flight control system with automatic towing and automatic down and up transition modes. First flight of first pre-production MH-53E 1 September 1983; first delivery to US Navy 26 June 1986; in operational service with HM-14 at Norfolk, Virginia, 1 April 1987; another MH-53E delivered to HM-12 (now AMCM training unit) in Spring 1987 was 100th H-53E; 29 delivered to USN by 29 June 1991, including some with HM-15 at Alameda, California, for Pacific Fleet; first carrier deployment by HM-15 on board USS *Tripoli*, 9 December 1989. Total requirement is 56.

CUSTOMERS: Japan has acquired helicopters similar to MH-53E (see S-80M entry). Over 570 of Sikorsky S-65/S-80/H-53 series built by 1990.

COSTS: $24.36 million (1992) projected average unit cost.

DESIGN FEATURES: Details below refer to CH-53E, but are applicable to MH-53E except as noted above. Fully articulated seven-blade main rotor; blade twist 14°; hydraulic powered blade folding for main rotor; tail pylon folds hydraulically to starboard; four-blade tail rotor on pylon canted 20° to port to derive some lift from tail rotor and extend CG range; cranked, strut-braced

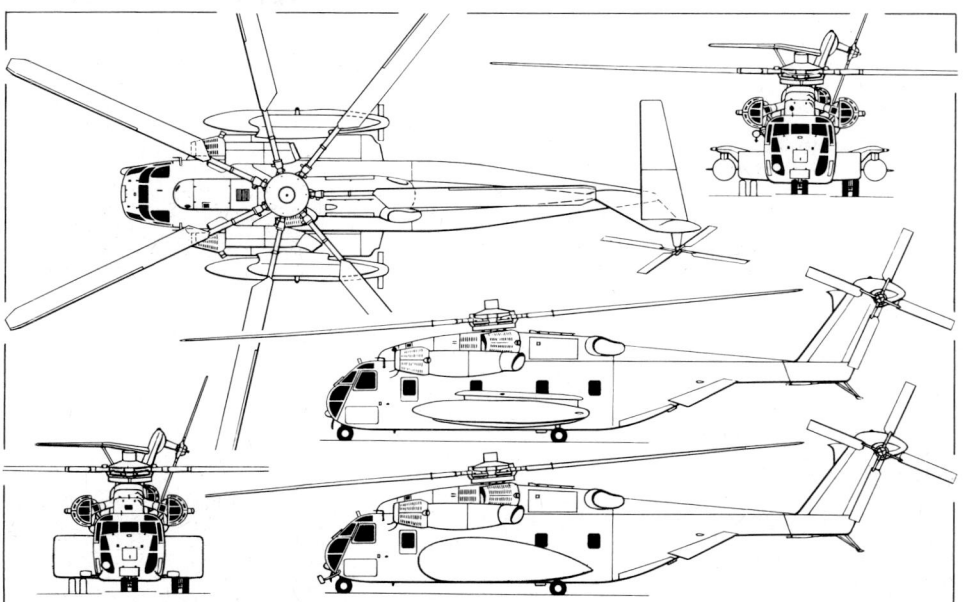

Sikorsky CH-53E Super Stallion, with additional lower side view and lower front view of MH-53E Sea Dragon *(Pilot Press)*

tailplane; transmission rated at 10,067 kW (13,500 shp) for take-off; rotor brake standard; fuselage stressed for 20g vertical and 10g lateral crash loads.

FLYING CONTROLS: Fully powered, with autostabilisation and autopilot.

STRUCTURE: Fuselage has watertight primary structure of light alloy, steel and titanium; glassfibre/epoxy cockpit section; extensive use of Kevlar in transmission fairing and engine cowlings; main rotor blades have titanium spar, Nomex honeycomb core and glassfibre/epoxy composites skin; titanium and steel rotor head; Sikorsky blade inspection method (BIM) sensors detect blade spar cracks occurring in service; tail rotor of aluminium; pylon and tailplane of Kevlar composites.

LANDING GEAR: Retractable tricycle type, with twin wheels on each unit. Main units retract into rear of sponsons on each side of fuselage. Fully castoring nosewheels.

POWER PLANT: Three General Electric T64-GE-416 turbo-shafts, each with a max rating of 3,266 kW (4,380 shp) for 10 min, intermediate rating of 3,091 kW (4,145 shp) for 30 min and max continuous power rating of 2,756 kW (3,696 shp). Self-sealing bladder fuel cell in forward part of each sponson, each with capacity of 1,192 litres (315 US gallons; 262 Imp gallons). Additional two-cell unit, with capacity of 1,465 litres (387 US gallons; 322 Imp gallons) brings total standard internal capacity to 3,849 litres (1,017 US gallons; 847 Imp gallons). (Total internal capacity of MH-53E is 12,113 litres; 3,200 US gallons; 2,664 Imp gallons.) Optional drop tank outboard of each sponson of CH-53E, total capacity 4,921 litres (1,300 US gallons; 1,082 Imp gallons). (MH-53E can carry seven internal range extension tanks, total capacity 7,949 litres; 2,100 US gallons; 1,748 Imp gallons.) Forward extendable probe for in-flight refuelling. Alternatively, aircraft can refuel by hoisting hose from surface vessel while hovering.

ACCOMMODATION: Crew of three. Main cabin of CH-53E will accommodate up to 55 troops on folding canvas seats along walls and in centre of cabin. Door on forward starboard side of main cabin. Hydraulically operated rear loading ramp. Typical freight loads include seven standard 1.02 × 1.22 m (3 ft 4 in × 4 ft) pallets. Single-point central hook for slung cargo, capacity 16,330 kg (36,000 lb).

SYSTEMS: Hydraulic system, with four pumps, for collective, cyclic pitch, roll, yaw and feel augmentation flight control servo mechanisms; engine starters; landing gear actuation; cargo winches; loading ramp; and blade and tail pylon folding. System pressure 207 bars (3,000 lb/sq in), except for engine starter system which is rated at 276 bars (4,000 lb/sq in). (Separate hydraulic system in MH-53E to power AMCM equipment.) Electrical system includes three 115V 400Hz 40-60kVA AC alternators, and two 28V 200A transformer-rectifiers for DC power. Solar APU.

AVIONICS: Hamilton Standard automatic flight control system, using two digital onboard computers and a four-axis autopilot.

EQUIPMENT: MH-53E equipment includes Westinghouse AN/AQS-14 towed sonar, AN/AQS-17 mine neutralis-ation device, AN/ALQ-141 electronic sweep, and Edo AN/ALQ-166 towed hydrofoil sled for detonating magnetic mines.

DIMENSIONS, EXTERNAL (CH-53E and MH-53E):

Main rotor diameter	24.08 m (79 ft 0 in)
Main rotor blade chord	0.76 m (2 ft 6 in)
Tail rotor diameter	6.10 m (20 ft 0 in)
Length overall: rotors turning	30.19 m (99 ft 0½ in)
rotor and tail pylon folded	18.44 m (60 ft 6 in)
Length of fuselage	22.35 m (73 ft 4 in)
Width of fuselage	2.69 m (8 ft 10 in)
Width overall, rotor and tail pylon folded:	
CH-53E	8.66 m (28 ft 5 in)
MH-53E	8.41 m (27 ft 7 in)
Height: to top of main rotor head	5.32 m (17 ft 5½ in)
tail rotor turning	8.97 m (29 ft 5 in)
rotor and tail pylon folded	5.66 m (18 ft 7 in)
Wheel track (c/l of shock struts)	3.96 m (13 ft 0 in)
Wheelbase	8.31 m (27 ft 3 in)

DIMENSIONS, INTERNAL (CH-53E and MH-53E):

Cabin:

Length (rear ramp/door hinge to fwd bulkhead)	9.14 m (30 ft 0 in)
Max width	2.29 m (7 ft 6 in)
Max height	1.98 m (6 ft 6 in)

AREAS (CH-53E and MH-53E):

Main rotor disc	455.38 m² (4,901.7 sq ft)
Tail rotor disc	29.19 m² (314.2 sq ft)

WEIGHTS AND LOADINGS:

Weight empty: CH-53E	15,072 kg (33,228 lb)
MH-53E	16,482 kg (36,336 lb)
Internal payload (100 nm; 185 km; 115 miles radius):	
CH-53E	13,607 kg (30,000 lb)
External payload (50 nm; 92.5 km; 57.5 miles radius):	
CH-53E	14,515 kg (32,000 lb)
Max external payload: CH-53E	16,330 kg (36,000 lb)
Useful load, influence sweep mission:	
MH-53E	11,793 kg (26,000 lb)
Max T-O weight (CH-53E and MH-53E):	
internal payload	31,640 kg (69,750 lb)
external payload	33,340 kg (73,500 lb)

Sikorsky CH-53E Super Stallion heavy lift helicopter of the US Marine Corps, in Saudi Arabia for Operation Desert Storm, 1991 *(Paul Jackson)*

Sikorsky MH-53E Sea Dragon towing an Edo minesweeping sled

Max disc loading:		
internal payload	69.47 kg/m² (14.23 lb/sq ft)	
external payload	73.21 kg/m² (14.99 lb/sq ft)	
Max power loading:		
internal payload	3.14 kg/kW (5.17 lb/shp)	
external payload	3.31 kg/kW (5.44 lb/shp)	

PERFORMANCE (CH-53E and MH-53E, ISA, at T-O weight of 25,400 kg; 56,000 lb):

Max level speed at S/L	170 knots (315 km/h; 196 mph)
Cruising speed at S/L	150 knots (278 km/h; 173 mph)
Max rate of climb at S/L, 11,340 kg (25,000 lb) payload	762 m (2,500 ft)/min
Service ceiling at max continuous power	5,640 m (18,500 ft)
Hovering ceiling at max power:	
IGE	3,520 m (11,550 ft)
OGE	2,895 m (9,500 ft)
Self-ferry range, unrefuelled, at optimum cruise condition for best range:	
CH-53E	1,120 nm (2,075 km; 1,290 miles)

SIKORSKY S-80E and S-80M

Export versions of CH/MH-53E available as **S-80E** basic heavy transport helicopter and **S-80M** mine countermeasures helicopter; S-80E has single-point cargo hook and VFR equipment; options include troop seats, cabin soundproofing, internal cargo winch, 272 kg (600 lb) external hoist, two-point external cargo attachment, automatic blade and tail folding, two 2,460.5 litre (650 US gallon; 541 Imp gallon) external tanks, ground-to-air or in-flight refuelling equipment, engine air particle separators, and wide selection of com/nav equipment.

Japan allocated funding for 11 S-80Ms (four in FY 1986, two in FY 1987, four in FY 1989 and one in FY 1991; further one required); first S-80M-1 (8623) completed 13 January 1989 and handed over to Japan Defence Agency 30 November 1989; six delivered by December 1990, initially to 51 Squadron at Atsugi for trials.

SIKORSKY S-2K

Feasibility studies for very large civil transport (VLCT) helicopter which could carry up to 100 passengers; the year 2000 is the target date for introduction; Sikorsky believes development work being undertaken for new Army Advanced Cargo Aircraft should produce refinements in helicopter rotor drive and other systems to satisfy civil requirements for reliability, comfort, operating economics and safety in large passenger carrying helicopters.

SIKORSKY TILT-ROTOR

Construction under way Spring 1991 of one-sixth scale wind tunnel test model of possible 30-passenger tilt-rotor design. Features include twin three-blade rotors able to retract from full 2.44 m (8 ft) diameter (max lift for T-O and hover) to 1.60 m (5 ft 3 in) diameter for reduced drag in forward flight. Tests of model scheduled for late 1991.

Sikorsky MH-60K special operations helicopter

SIKORSKY S-70A

US Army designations: UH-60A and UH-60L Black Hawk, EH-60C and MH-60K

US Air Force designations: UH-60A, MH-60G Pave Hawk

US Marine Corps designation: VH-60N

TYPE: Infantry squad transport helicopter; also adapted for other roles.

PROGRAMME: UH-60A declared winner of US Army Utility Tactical Transport Aircraft System (UTTAS) competition against Boeing Vertol YUH-61A 23 December 1976; first flight of first of three YUH-60A competitive prototypes 17 October 1974; early development history recorded in 1982-83 and earlier *Jane's*. For retrofitted improvements, see UH-60L below.

VARIANTS: **UH-60A Black Hawk:** Initial production version, designed to carry crew of three and 11 troops; also can be used without modification for medevac, reconnaissance, command and control, and troop supply; cargo hook capacity 3,630 kg (8,000 lb); one UH-60A can be carried in C-130, two in C-141 and six in C-5.

Medevac kits delivered from 1981; missile qualification completed June 1987, with day and night firing of Hellfire in various flight conditions; airborne target handover system (ATHS) qualified; cockpit lighting suitable for night vision goggles fitted to production UH-60s since November 1985 and retrofitted to those built earlier; US Army began testing Honeywell Volcano mine dispensing system July 1987; Volcano container is disposable and dispenses 960 Gator anti-tank and anti-personnel mines; usage monitor to measure certain rotor loads installed in 30 UH-60As; wire strike protection added to UH-60s and EH-60s during 1987; accident data recorders also fitted. Total 985 built before production change to UH-60L in 1989.

Enhanced Black Hawk: Incorporates active and passive self-defence systems, retrofitted by Corpus Christi Army Depot, Texas, to new build UH-60A/Ls; first 15 delivered to US Army in South Korea November 1989. Equipment includes Tracor AN/ARN-148 Omega navigation receiver, Motorola AN/LST-5B satellite UHF communications transceiver, Bendix/King AN/ARC-199 HF-SSB, and AEL AN/APR-44(V)3 specific threat RWR complementing existing AN/APR-39 general threat RWR; M134 Minigun can be fitted on each of two pintle mounts, replacing M60 machine gun.

JUH-60A: At least seven used temporarily for trials.

GUH-60A: At least nine grounded airframes for technical training.

HH-60D Night Hawk: One prototype completed for abandoned USAF combat rescue variant.

EH-60C: US Army ordered prototype YEH-60C in October 1980 to carry 816 kg (800 lb) Quick Fix IIB battlefield ECM detection and jamming system. TRW Electronic Systems Laboratories was prime contractor for AN/ALQ-151 ECM kit, with installation by Tracor Aerospace; four dipole antennae on fuselage and deployable whip antenna; Hover Infra-Red Suppressor Subsystem (HIRSS) standard. YEH-60C first flight 24 September 1981; order for Tracor Aerospace to modify 40 UH-60As to EH-60C standard under $51 million contract placed October 1984; first delivery July 1987 as part of US Army Special Electronics Mission Aircraft (SEMA) programme; 66 funded by FY 1987; programme completed 1989.

MH-60A: About 30 modified for Army 160th Special Operations Aviation Regt; believed to be fitted with FLIR, Omega/VLF navigation, multi-function displays, auxiliary fuel tanks and door-mounted Minigun; interim equipment, pending MH-60K.

VH-60N: Nine for US Marine Corps Executive Flight Detachment of squadron HMX-1 at Quantico, Virginia, to replace UH-1Ns; deliveries started November 1988; known as VH-60A until redesignated 3 November 1989; two standard UH-60As also supplied. Additional equipment includes more durable gearbox, weather radar, SH-60B-type flight control system and ASI, cabin soundproofing, VIP interior, cabin radio operator station, EMP hardening and extensive avionic upgrading.

MH-60G Pave Hawk: Replaced US Air Force HH-60D Night Hawk rescue helicopters, which were not funded (see 1987-88 *Jane's*); converted from UH-60A/L, including 10 originally delivered to 55th Aerospace Rescue and Recovery Squadron (now Special Operations Squadron) at Eglin AFB, Florida, in 1982-83, initially remaining as UH-60As; all progressively fitted by Sikorsky Support Services at Troy, Alabama, with aerial refuelling probe, 443 litre (117 US gallon; 97.5 Imp gallon) internal auxiliary fuel tank and fuel management panel; then to Pensacola NAD for mission avionics. All have Doppler/INS, electronic map display, Tacan, secure HF, Satcom, 0.50 in machine guns, and Pave Low III FLIR as fitted in MH-53H/J. Issued to the following Air National Guard squadrons: 210th ARS, Kulis, Alaska, in June 1990, followed by 102nd ARS at Suffolk County, New York, and 129th ARS at Moffett Field NAS, California; also in prospect for MH-60G are 301st ARS (AFRes) at Homestead AFB, Florida, 304th ARS (AFRes) at Portland, Oregon, 56th at Keflavik, Iceland, and new squadrons at Misawa, Japan, and Nellis AFB, Nevada. Nine conversions to MH-60G funded in FY 1989, followed by 24 and four in FYs 1990-91; further six and 10 planned for FYs 1992-93.

MH-60K: US Army special operations aircraft (SOA); prototype ordered in January 1988; first flight 10 August 1990. US Army initially expects to buy 23 MH-60Ks, with options for another 38; 11 conversions from UH-60As ordered from Sikorsky June 1989 for delivery to 160th Special Operations Aviation Group (part of 160 SOA Regiment) from November 1991; IOC in September 1992. Planned assignments to 1 Battalion/160 SOA Group at Fort Campbell, Kentucky; 3/160 Avn at Hunter AAF, Georgia; and 1/245 Avn,

Oklahoma ArNG. Features include two 870.5 litre (230 US gallon; 191.5 Imp gallon) external fuel tanks, provision for two extra internal 700 litre (185 US gallon; 154 Imp gallon) fuel tanks, flight refuelling capability, integrated avionics system with electronic displays, Hughes AN/AAQ-16 FLIR, Texas Instruments AN/APQ-174 terrain following/terrain avoidance radar, T700-GE-701C engines and uprated transmission, external hoist, wire-strike protection, rotor brake, tiedown points, folding tailplane, AFCS similar to that of SH-60B, strengthened pintle mounts for 0.50 in machine-guns, provision for Stinger missiles, AN/AAR-47 missile warning receiver, AN/ALQ-136 pulse radio frequency jammer, AN/ALQ-162 CW radio jammer, AN/APR-39A and -44 pulse/CW warning receivers, AN/AVR-2 laser detector, M130 chaff/flare dispensers, and AN/ALQ-144 IR jammer.

SH-60B Seahawk: US Navy ASW/ASST helicopter, described separately.

SH-60F Ocean Hawk: US Navy carrier-borne inner-zone ASW helicopter to replace SH-3D Sea King. See Seahawk entry.

HH-60H and HH-60J Jayhawk: Search and rescue/special warfare helicopters; see Seahawk entry.

UH-60L: Replaced UH-60A in production for US Army from October 1989; first flight 22 March 1988; first delivery 7 November 1989 to Texas ArNG. Powered by T700-GE-701C engines with uprated 2,535 kW, 3,400 shp) transmission. Current production aircraft fitted with Hover Infra-Red Suppression System (HIRSS) to cool exhaust in hover as well as forward flight; older UH-60s retrofitted.

UH-60M: Proposed enhanced version for US Army. Cancelled early 1989 in favour of UH-60L.

UH-60P: South Korean Army version of UH-60L with minor avionics modifications to meet local requirements; first of three UH-60Ls delivered by Sikorsky 10 December 1990; balance of 90 UH-60Ps to be assembled locally by Korean Air with increasing indigenous content, in $500 million, five-year programme.

S-70A: Export UH-60A; see under Customers below.

S-70C: Commercial version, described separately and under SH-60B Seahawk entry.

CUSTOMERS: Total 1,196 funded by US Army to end of FY 1991, including EH-60Cs and diversions to USAF, Colombia, Saudi Arabia and Philippines; 60 each planned in FYs 1992 and 1993; original target 2,262 cut by FY 1991 to less than 1,442; 1,000th accepted 17 October 1988; 1,150 built by January 1991; US Army Black Hawks in service in Hawaii, Korea, Panama, Germany and with Army National Guard and Army Reserve. Over 1,600 of S-70/H-60 family built by December 1990.

US Army loaned 12 UH-60As to the US Customs Service for anti-drug smuggling, augmenting four bought direct from Sikorsky.

Two export S-70A-5s delivered to Philippine Air Force. Royal Australian Air Force ordered 39 S-70A-9s to replace Bell UH-1s; deliveries ran from October 1987 to 1 February 1991; first S-70A-9 completed by Sikorsky, remainder assembled by Hawker de Havilland in Australia; aircraft transferred to Australian Army in February 1989, but RAAF continues to maintain them. Five UH-60As delivered to Colombian Air Force in July

Sikorsky MH-60G Pave Hawk air rescue helicopter

1988 for anti-narcotics operations; five more sold February 1989.

In May 1988, US Army ordered 13 S-70-A-1s under FMS deal for Royal Saudi Land Forces Army Aviation Command; 12 delivered January to April 1990 to squadron based at King Khaled Military City; modified to **Desert Hawk** and one (delivered December 1990) fitted with VIP interior; Desert Hawk has 15 troop seats, blade erosion protection using polyurethane tape and spray-on coating, Racal Jaguar 5 frequency-hopping radio, provision for searchlights, internal auxiliary fuel tanks, and external hoist. In September 1988, Turkish Jandarma (national police) ordered six S-70A-17s; deliveries completed December 1988; further six (including two VIP) delivered from late 1990. Two VIP Black Hawks delivered to Egypt during 1990; two UH-60Ls to Bahrain, early 1991; three S-70As to Jordan 1987.

COSTS: $5.87 million (1992) US Army unit cost.

DESIGN FEATURES: Represented new generation in technology for performance, survivability and ease of operation when introduced to replace UH-1 as US Army's main squad-carrying helicopter; adapted to wide variety of other roles, including several maritime applications. Four-blade main rotor; one-piece forged titanium rotor head with elastomeric blade retention bearings providing all movement and requiring no lubrication; hydraulic drag dampers; bifilar self-tuning vibration absorber above head; blades have 18° twist, and tips swept at 20°; thickness and camber vary over the length of blades, based on Sikorsky SC-1095 aerofoil; blades tolerant up to 23 mm hits and spar tubes pressurised with pressure gauges to indicate loss of pressure following structural degradation. Transmission rating 2,109 kW (2,828 shp) in UH-60A, uprated to 2,535 kW (3,400 shp) in models with T700-GE-701C engines.

Two pairs of tail rotor blades fastened in cross-beam arrangement mounted to starboard; tail rotor pylon tilted to port to produce lift as well as anti-torque thrust and to extend permissible CG range; fixed fin large enough to allow controlled run-on landing following loss of tail rotor.

FLYING CONTROLS: Rotor pitch control powered by two independent hydraulic systems; Hamilton Standard AFCS with digital three-axis autopilot provides speed and height control and coupled modes. Full-time autostabilisation includes feet-off heading hold cancelling torque-induced yaw at all airspeeds and during hover; positive fuselage attitude control provided by electrically driven variable incidence tailplane moving from +34° in hover to −6° during autorotation; angle is controlled by combined sensing of airspeed, collective-lever position, pitch attitude rate and lateral acceleration.

STRUCTURE: Main blade spar is formed and welded into oval titanium tube, with Nomex core, graphite trailing-edge, and covered by glassfibre/epoxy skin; titanium leading-edge abrasion strip and Kevlar tip. Cross-beam composites tail rotor, eliminating all rotor head bearings. Light alloy airframe designed to retain 85 per cent of its flight deck and passenger space intact after vertical impact at 11.5 m (38 ft)/s, lateral impact at 9.1 m (30 ft)/s, and longitudinal impact at 12.2 m (40 ft)/s; also withstands simultaneous 20g forward and 10g downward impact; glassfibre and Kevlar used for cockpit doors, canopy, fairings and engine cowlings; glassfibre Nomex floors; tailboom folds to starboard and main rotor mast can be lowered for transport/storage.

LANDING GEAR: Non-retractable tailwheel type with single wheel on each unit. Energy absorbing main gear with a tailwheel which gives protection for the tail rotor in taxying over rough terrain or during a high-flare landing. Axle assembly and main gear oleo shock absorbers by General Mechatronics. Mainwheel tyres size 26 × 10.00-11, pressure 8.96-9.65 bars (130-140 lb/sq in); tailwheel tyre size 15 × 6.00-6, pressure 6.21-6.55 bars (90-95 lb/sq in).

Sikorsky UH-60L in South Korean markings represents the UH-60P to be co-produced under licence by Korean Air

First of two Sikorsky VH-60 VIP transport helicopters delivered to the Egyptian Air Force in 1990

POWER PLANT: Two 1,151 kW (1,560 shp) General Electric T700-GE-700 turboshafts. From late 1989 (UH-60L), two T700-GE-701C engines, each developing 1,447 kW (1,940 shp). (T700-GE-701A engines with max T-O rating of 1,285 kW; 1,723 shp optional in export models.) Two crashworthy, bulletproof fuel cells, with combined usable capacity of 1,361 litres (360 US gallons; 299.5 Imp gallons), aft of cabin. Single-point pressure refuelling; or gravity refuelling via point on each tank. Auxiliary fuel can be carried internally in one of several optional arrangements, or externally by the ESSS system.

ACCOMMODATION: Two-man flight deck, with pilot and co-pilot on armour protected seats. A third crew member is stationed in the cabin at the gunner's position adjacent to the forward cabin windows. Forward hinged jettisonable door on each side for access to flight deck area. Main cabin open to cockpit to provide good communication with flight crew and forward view for squad commander. Accommodation for 11 fully equipped troops, or 14 in high density configuration.

Eight troop seats can be removed and replaced by four litters for medevac missions, or to make room for internal cargo. An optional layout is available to accommodate a maximum of six litter patients. Cabin heated and ventilated. External cargo hook, having a 3,630 kg (8,000 lb) lift capability, enables UH-60A to transport a 105 mm howitzer, its crew of five and 50 rounds of ammunition. Rescue hoist of 272 kg (600 lb) capacity optional. Large rearward sliding door on each side of fuselage for rapid entry and exit. Electric windscreen de-icing. (Executive interiors for 7-12 passengers available for the S-70A.)

SYSTEMS: Solar 67 kW (90 hp) T-62T-40-1 APU; Garrett engine start system. An optional winterisation kit provides a second hydraulic accumulator installed in parallel with the APU hydraulic start accumulator, maintaining engine start capability at low ambient temperatures; Bendix 30/40kVA and 20/30kVA electrical power generators; 17Ah nickel-cadmium battery. Engine fire extinguishing system. Rotor blade de-icing system standard on US Army aircraft, optional for export.

AVIONICS: Com equipment comprises E-Systems AN/ARC-186 VHF-FM, GTE Sylvania AN/ARC-115 VHF-AM, Magnavox AN/ARC-164 UHF-AM, Collins AN/ARC-186(V) VHF-AM/FM, Bendix/King AN/APX-100 IFF transponder, Magnavox TSEC/KT-28 voice security set, and intercom. Nav equipment comprises Emerson AN/ARN-89 ADF, Bendix/King AN/ARN-123(V)1 VOR/marker beacon/glideslope receiver, Honeywell AN/ASN-43 gyro compass, Plessey Electronic Systems AN/ASN-128 Doppler, and Honeywell AN/APN-209(V)2 radar altimeter. E-Systems Melpar/Memcor AN/APR-39(V)1 radar warning receiver and Sanders AN/ALQ-144 infra-red countermeasures set. Tracor M130 chaff/flare dispenser. Hamilton Standard AFCS with digital three-axis autopilot. Additional avionics and self-protection equipment installed in Enhanced Black Hawk, as described under Variants.

ARMAMENT: New production UH-60As and Ls from c/n 431 onward incorporate hardpoints for an external stores support system (ESSS). This consists of a combination of fixed provisions built into the airframe and four removable external pylons from which fuel tanks and a variety of weapons can be suspended. Able to carry more than 2,268 kg (5,000 lb) on each side of the helicopter, the ESSS can accommodate two 870 litre (230 US gallon; 191.5 Imp gallon) fuel tanks outboard, and two 1,703 litre (450 US gallon; 375 Imp gallon) tanks inboard. This

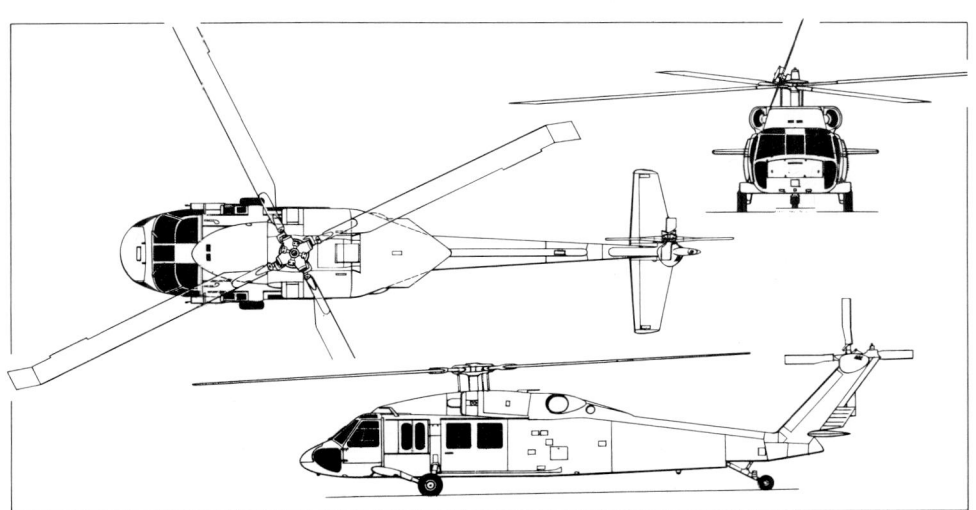

Sikorsky UH-60L Black Hawk combat assault helicopter *(Pilot Press)*

allows the UH-60A to self deploy 1,200 nm (2,220 km; 1,380 miles) without refuelling. The ESSS also enables the Black Hawk to carry Hellfire laser-guided anti-armour missiles, gun or M56 mine dispensing pods, ECM packs, rockets and motorcycles. Up to 16 Hellfires can be carried externally on the ESSS, with another 16 in the cabin to provide the capability to land and reload. (Laser designation provided by Bell OH-58 helicopter or ground troops.) Two pintle mounts in cabin, adjacent to forward cabin windows on each side, can each accommodate a 0.50 in calibre General Electric GECAL 50 or 7.62 mm six-barrel Minigun.

DIMENSIONS, EXTERNAL:

Main rotor diameter	16.36 m (53 ft 8 in)
Main rotor blade chord	0.53 m (1 ft 8¾ in)
Tail rotor diameter	3.35 m (11 ft 0 in)
Length overall: rotors turning	19.76 m (64 ft 10 in)
rotors and tail pylon folded	12.60 m (41 ft 4 in)
Length of fuselage:	
UH-60A/MH-60G, excl flight refuelling probe	
	15.26 m (50 ft 0¾ in)
MH-60G, incl retracted refuelling probe	
	17.38 m (57 ft 0¼ in)
Width: UH-60A fuselage	2.36 m (7 ft 9 in)
MH-60G with auxiliary tanks	5.46 m (17 ft 11 in)
Max depth of fuselage	1.75 m (5 ft 9 in)
Height: overall, tail rotor turning	5.13 m (16 ft 10 in)
to top of rotor head	3.76 m (12 ft 4 in)
in air transportable configuration	2.67 m (8 ft 9 in)
Tailplane span	4.38 m (14 ft 4½ in)
Wheel track	2.705 m (8 ft 10½ in)
Wheelbase	8.83 m (28 ft 11¾ in)
Tail rotor ground clearance	1.98 m (6 ft 6 in)
Cabin doors (each): Height	1.37 m (4 ft 6 in)
Width	1.75 m (5 ft 9 in)

DIMENSIONS, INTERNAL:

Cabin: Volume	11.61 m³ (410.0 cu ft)

AREAS:

Main rotor blades (each)	4.34 m² (46.70 sq ft)
Tail rotor blades (each)	0.41 m² (4.45 sq ft)
Main rotor disc	210.15 m² (2,262 sq ft)
Tail rotor disc	8.83 m² (95.03 sq ft)
Tailplane	4.18 m² (45.0 sq ft)
Vertical stabiliser	3.00 m² (32.3 sq ft)

WEIGHTS AND LOADINGS:

Weight empty: UH-60A	5,118 kg (11,284 lb)
Mission T-O weight: UH-60A	7,708 kg (16,994 lb)
Max alternative T-O weight:	
UH-60A, S-70A	9,979 kg (22,000 lb)
Max disc loading:	
UH-60A at mission T-O weight	
	36.68 kg/m² (7.51 lb/sq ft)
UH-60A/S-70A at max alternative T-O weight	
	47.49 kg/m² (9.73 lb/sq ft)
Max power loading:	
UH-60A at mission T-O weight	
	3.66 kg/kW (6.01 lb/shp)
UH-60A/S-70A at max alternative T-O weight	
	4.73 kg/kW (7.78 lb/shp)

PERFORMANCE (UH-60A at mission T-O weight, except where indicated):

Max level speed at S/L	160 knots (296 km/h; 184 mph)
Max level speed at max T-O weight	
	158 knots (293 km/h; 182 mph)
Max cruising speed at 1,220 m (4,000 ft) and 35°C (95°F)	
	145 knots (268 km/h; 167 mph)
Single-engine cruising speed at 1,220 m (4,000 ft), and 35°C (95°F)	105 knots (195 km/h; 121 mph)
Vertical rate of climb at S/L	over 137 m (450 ft)/min
Service ceiling	5,790 m (19,000 ft)
Hovering ceiling: IGE at 35°C	2,895 m (9,500 ft)
OGE, ISA	3,170 m (10,400 ft)
OGE at 35°C	1,705 m (5,600 ft)
Range with max internal fuel at max T-O weight, 30 min reserves	324 nm (600 km; 373 miles)
Range with external fuel tanks on ESSS pylons:	
with two 870 litre (230 US gallon; 191.5 Imp gallon) tanks	880 nm (1,630 km; 1,012 miles)
with two 870 litre (230 US gallon; 191.5 Imp gallon) and two 1,703 litre (450 US gallon; 375 Imp gallon) tanks	1,200 nm (2,220 km; 1,380 miles)
Endurance: UH-60A	2 h 18 min
MH-60G with max fuel	4 h 51 min

SIKORSKY S-70B
US Navy designations: SH-60B Seahawk, SH-60F Ocean Hawk and HH-60H
US Coast Guard designation: HH-60J Jayhawk
Spanish Navy designation: HS.23

TYPE: ASW and anti-ship surveillance and targeting helicopter.

PROGRAMME: Naval development of Sikorsky UTTAS (UH-60A Black Hawk) utility helicopter; won US Navy LAMPS Mk III competition for shipboard helicopter in 1977; first flight of first of five prototypes (BuAer No. 161169) 12 December 1979; development details in 1982-83 *Jane's*; first 18 SH-60Bs authorised FY 1982, plus 27 in 1984, rising to 159 by March 1991.

VARIANTS: **SH-60B:** Initial production version for ASW/ ASST, as detailed under main description. SH-60B

Sikorsky SH-60B Seahawk LAMPS Mk III helicopter with parent ship USS *Crommelin* (FFG-37)

interfaces with its mother ship via data link, but can also operate independently. Secondary missions include search and rescue (SAR), vertical replenishment (vertrep), medical evacuation (medevac), fleet support and communications relay.

XSH-60J: Japan Maritime Self-Defence Force (JMSDF) placed $27 million order for two XSH-60Bs for installation of Japanese avionics and mission equipment; first flights 31 August and early October 1987; two-year test programme by Japan Defence Agency Technical Research and Development Institute.

SH-60J: Mitsubishi (which see) is to manufacture SH-60J Seahawk for JMSDF in early 1990s to replace Sikorsky SH-3 Sea Kings by mid-1990s; total 80 required; 42 funded including FY 1991.

UH-60J: Japan Self-Defence Forces to obtain UH-60J version of Mitsubishi SH-60J for search and rescue. Sikorsky-built prototype (N7267D), plus two CKD kits, delivered late 1990. Air SDF requires 43, funded 11 up to FY 1991; Maritime SDF funded six up to FY 1991.

S-70B: Royal Australian Navy selected Seahawk, designated S-70B-2, for role adaptable weapon system (RAWS) full-spectrum ASW helicopter with autonomous operating capability; order for eight confirmed 9 October 1984; eight more ordered May 1986; operates from RAN 'Adelaide' class (FFG-7) guided missile frigates; first flight (N7265H) at West Palm Beach 4 December 1987; originally planned 14 would be assembled in Australia, but announced late 1988 Sikorsky would assemble first eight; ASTA in Australia (which see) designated to assemble remainder in early 1989; first S-70B-2 handed over in USA 12 September 1989; formal acceptance at Nowra, 4 October 1989; Seahawk Introduction and Transition Unit became HS-816 at Nowra, 1 June 1991; formed first ship's flight, September 1991. S-70B-2 has substantially different avionics to USN version: MEL Super Searcher radar (capable of tracking 32 surface targets) and Rockwell Collins advanced integrated avionics including cockpit controls and displays, navigation receivers, communications radios, airborne target hand-off data link and tactical data system (TDS).

Spanish Navy received six S-70Bs from December 1988 for operation from four FFG-7 frigates by Escuadrilla 010 at Rota; similar to USN SH-60B, but with Bendix/King AN/AQS-13F dipping sonar.

SH-60F Ocean Hawk: CV Inner Zone ASW helicopter, known as CV-Helo, designed for close-in

ASW protection of aircraft carrier groups; $50.9 million initial US Navy contract for full-scale development and production options placed 6 March 1985; replacing SH-3H Sea King; US Navy requires 175 SH-60Fs; Seahawk prototype modified as SH-60F test aircraft; total 61 on order, comprising seven pre-series plus 18 each in FYs 1988, 1989 and 1991; further 12 planned in both FYs 1992 and 1993; first flight SH-60F 19 March 1987 and two used for operational evaluation; five more delivered by September 1989; in service with HS-2, 6 and 10 squadrons NAS North Island, California, and HS-3 at Jacksonville, Florida; 36 delivered by June 1991; initial fleet deployment with USS *Nimitz* in 1991.

SH-60F has all LAMPS Mk III avionics, fairings and equipment removed, including cargo hook and RAST system main and tail probes, but installation provisions retained. Replaced by integrated ASW mission avionics including Allied Signal (Bendix Oceanics) AN/AQS-13F dipping sonar, MIL-STD-1553B databus, dual Teledyne Systems AN/ASN-150 tactical navigation computers and AN/ASM-614 avionics support equipment, automatic flight control system with quicker automatic transition and both cable and Doppler autohover, tactical data link with other aircraft, communications control system, multi-function keypads and displays for each of four crew members; internal/external fuel system and extra weapon station to port allowing carriage of three Mk 50 homing torpedoes; provision for surface search radar, FLIR, night vision equipment, passive ECM, MAD, air-to-surface missile capability, sonobuoy data link, chaff/ sonobuoy dispenser, attitude and heading reference system (AHRS), Navstar GPS, fatigue monitoring system and increase of max T-O weight to 10,659 kg (23,500 lb); secondary missions include SAR and plane guard.

HH-60H: US Navy ordered five (increased to 18) strike-rescue/special warfare support (HCS), designated HH-60H, in September 1986; first flight (163783) 17 August 1988; accepted by USN 30 March 1989; in service with HCS-4 at Norfolk, Virginia, January 1990; final delivery July 1991, completing HCS-5 at Point Mugu, California; both squadrons of Reserves; missions are to recover four-man crew at 250 nm (463 km; 288 miles) from launch point or fly 200 nm (371 km; 230 miles) and drop eight SEALs from 914 m (3,000 ft).

Close derivative of SH-60F with same T700-GE-401C engines and HIRSS as SH-60B/F; equipment includes

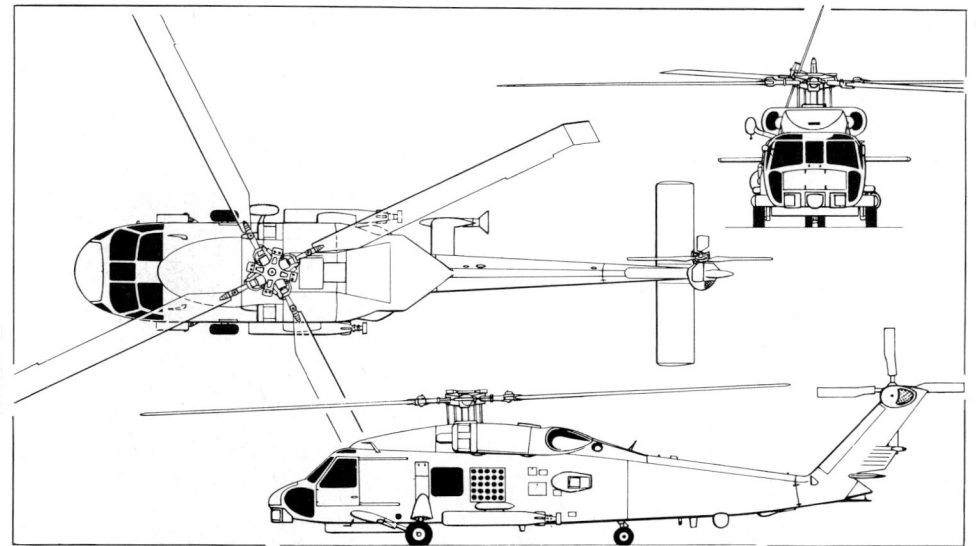

Sikorsky SH-60B Seahawk twin-turbine ASW/ASST helicopter *(Pilot Press)*

General Instrument AN/APR-39A(XE)2 radar warning receiver, Hughes AN/AVR-2 laser warning receiver, Honeywell AN/AAR-47 missile plume detector, Loral AN/ALE-47 chaff/flare dispenser, AN/ALQ-144 IR jammer, night vision goggle cockpit and two cabin-mounted M60D 7.62 mm machine guns; provision for weapon pylons; required to operate from decks of FFG-7, DD-963, CG-47 and larger vessels, as well as unprepared sites. Cubic AN/ARS-6 personnel locator system to be installed from FY 1991. Some equipped with Seahawk-type RAST (recovery assist, secure and traverse) equipment.

HH-60J Jayhawk: Ordered in parallel with HH-60H; adapted for US Coast Guard medium range recovery (MRR) role; 35 ordered for delivery by 1993; first flight (USCG 6001) 8 August 1989; first delivery to USCG (6002 at Elizabeth City CGAS) 16 June 1990. When carrying three 455 litre (120 US gallon; 100 Imp gallon) external tanks, HH-60J can fly out 300 nm (556 km; 345 miles), spend 45 min at scene and return with six survivors in addition to four-man crew or loiter for 1 h 30 min when investigating possible smugglers; other duties include law enforcement, drug interdiction, logistics, aids to navigation, environmental protection and military readiness; compatible with decks of 'Hamilton' and 'Bear' class USCG cutters. Equipment includes Bendix/King RDR-1300 search/weather radar, AN/ARN-147 VOR/ILS, KDF 806 direction finder, Tacan, VHF/UHF-DF, TACNAV, dual U/VHF-FM radios, HF radio, IFF, V/U/HF IFF crypto computers, NVG-compatible cockpit, rescue hoist and external cargo hook, and provision for Navstar GPS.

S-70C(M)-1: Delivery began July 1990 to Taiwanese Navy of 10 SH-60B Seahawks; given S-70C designations; shipboard deployment from 1993 aboard eight FFG-7 frigates.

CUSTOMERS: Total US Navy requirement 260 SH-60Bs, plus five prototypes; first flight production Seahawk 11 February 1983; deliveries at two a month; 159 SH-60Bs on order by March 1991, of which 147 delivered, and purchase of 34 under negotiation; first squadron was HSL-41 at NAS North Island, San Diego, California; operational deployment began 1984; 11 US Navy squadrons operating by March 1991 (HSLs 41, 43, 45, 47 and 49 at NAS North Island and 40, 42, 44, 46 and 48 at NAS Mayport, Florida; and 51 at Atsugi, Japan); SH-60Bs deployed in 'Oliver Hazard Perry' (FFG-7) class frigates, 'Spruance' class and Aegis equipped destroyers, 'Ticonderoga' class guided missile cruisers. Australia and Spain (see S-70B above) and Japan (see SH-60J). Greek Navy has requirement for five SH-60Fs equipped with Penguin anti-ship missiles.

COSTS: $20.25 million (1992) USN programme unit cost.

DESIGN FEATURES: SH-60B Seahawk designed to provide all-weather detection, classification, localisation and interdiction of surface ships and submarines, either controlled through data link from mother ship or operating independently; secondary missions include SAR, vertical replenishment, medevac, fleet support and communications relay.

New features include more powerful navalised GE T700-GE-401 engines, additional fuel, sensor operator's station, port-side internal launchers for 25 sonobuoys, pylon on starboard side of tailboom for MAD bird, lateral pylons for two torpedoes or external tanks, chin-mounted ESM pods, sliding cabin door, rescue hoist, electrically actuated blade folding, rotor brake, folding tail, short-wheelbase tailwheel landing gear with twin tailwheels stressed for lower crash impacts, DAF Indal RAST recovery assist, secure and traversing for haul-down landings on small decks and moving into hangar, hovering in-flight refuelling system, and emergency flotation system; pilots' seats not armoured. SH-60B gives 57 minutes more listening time on station and 45 minutes more ship surveillance and targeting time than LAMPS Mk I.

For operation in Gulf during Iran-Iraq war, 25 SH-60Bs fitted with upper and lower Sanders AN/ALQ-144 IR jammers, Tracor AN/ALE-39 chaff/flare dispensers, Honeywell AN/AAR-47 electro-optical missile warning and a single 7.62 mm machine-gun in door, for a weight penalty of 169 kg (369.5 lb); seven Seahawks fitted with Ford Aerospace AN/AAS-38 FLIR on port weapon pylon with instantaneous relay to parent ship.

First Block I SH-60B update, introduced in production Lot 9, includes provision for NFT AN/AGM-119 Penguin anti-ship missile, Mk 50 Advanced Lightweight Torpedo, Rospatch AN/ARR-84 99-channel sonobuoy receiver (replacing ARR-75), Chelton AN/ARC-182 V/UHF FM radio and Rockwell/Collins Class 3A Navstar GPS; 115 Penguin-capable Seahawks to come from retrofitting back to Lot 5; Block II development, including airborne low-frequency sonar and inverse synthetic aperture radar, was to begin in 1991 for retrofitting from 1999.

FLYING CONTROLS: As for UH-60.

STRUCTURE: Basically as for UH-60 with marine corrosion protection; single cabin door, starboard side, narrower than UH-60.

Sikorsky SH-60F Ocean Hawk CV-Helo, assigned to aircraft carrier USS *Nimitz*, lowering its sonar

Sikorsky HH-60H combat strike-rescue/special warfare support helicopter

POWER PLANT: Two 1,260 kW (1,690 shp) General Electric T700-GE-401 turboshafts in early aircraft; 1,417 kW (1,900 shp) T700-401C turboshafts introduced in 1988 and on HH-60H/J. Internal fuel capacity 2,233 litres (590 US gallons; 491 Imp gallons). Hovering in-flight refuelling capability. Two 455 litre (120 US gallon; 100 Imp gallon) auxiliary fuel tanks on fuselage pylons optional. (Three on HH-60J.) Hover infra-red suppressor subsystem (HIRSS) exhaust cowling fitted to HH-60H.

ACCOMMODATION: Pilot and airborne tactical officer/backup pilot in cockpit, sensor operator in specially equipped station in cabin. Dual controls standard. Sliding door with jettisonable window on starboard side. Accommodation heated, ventilated, air-conditioned.

SYSTEMS: Generally as for UH-60A.

AVIONICS: Com equipment comprises Collins AN/ARC-159(V)2 UHF and AN/ARC-174(V)2 HF, Hazeltine AN/APX-76A(V) and Bendix/King AN/APX-100(V)1 IFF transponders, TSEC/KY-75 voice security set, TSEC/KG-45(E-1) com security, Telephonics OK-374/ASC com system control group and Sierra Research AN/ARQ-44 data link and telemetry. Nav equipment comprises Collins AN/ARN-118(V) Tacan, Honeywell AN/APN-194(V) radar altimeter, Teledyne Ryan AN/APN-217 Doppler, and Collins AN/ARA-50 UHF DF. Mission equipment includes Sikorsky sonobuoy launcher, Edmac AN/ARR-75 and R-1651/ARA sonobuoy receiving sets, Texas Instruments AN/ASQ-81(V)2 MAD (CAE AN/ASQ-504(V) internal MAD in Australian Seahawks), Raymond MU-670/ASQ magnetic tape memory unit, Astronautics IO-2177/ASQ altitude indicator, Fairchild AN/ASQ-164 control indicator set and AN/ASQ-165 armament control indicator set, Texas Instruments AN/APS-124 search radar (under front fuselage), IBM AN/UYS-1(V)2 Proteus acoustic processor and CV-3252/A converter display, Control Data AN/AYK-14 (XN-1A) digital computer, and Raytheon AN/ALQ-142 ESM (in chin mounted pods). Pod mounted Texas Instruments AN/AAQ-17 FLIR deployed on one SH-60B during 1991 Gulf War; GEC Sensors Sea Owl IR turret being evaluated 1991.

EQUIPMENT: External cargo hook (2,722 kg; 6,000 lb) and rescue hoist (272 kg; 600 lb) standard.

ARMAMENT: Includes two Mk 46 torpedoes and (from 1989) NFT AGM-119B Penguin Mk 2 Mod 7 anti-shipping missiles. HH-60H has two pintle-mounted M60D machine guns.

DIMENSIONS, EXTERNAL: As UH-60A except:

Length overall, (rotors and tail pylon folded:	
SH-60B	12.47 m (40 ft 11 in)
HH-60H	12.51 m (41 ft 0⅝ in)
HH-60J	13.13 m (43 ft 0⅞ in)
Length of fuselage: HH-60J	15.87 m (52 ft 1 in)
Width (rotors folded)	3.26 m (10 ft 8½ in)
Height: to top of rotor head	3.79 m (12 ft 5⅜ in)
overall, tail rotor turning	5.18 m (17 ft 0 in)
overall, pylon folded	4.04 m (13 ft 3¼ in)
Wheelbase	4.83 m (15 ft 10 in)
Tail rotor ground clearance	1.83 m (6 ft 0 in)
Main/tail rotors clearance	6.6 cm (2⅝ in)

AREAS: as UH-60A

WEIGHTS AND LOADINGS:

Weight empty: SH-60B ASW	6,191 kg (13,648 lb)
HH-60H	6,114 kg (13,480 lb)
HH-60J	6,086 kg (13,417 lb)
Useful load: HH-60J	3,551 kg (7,829 lb)
Internal payload: HH-60H	1,860 kg (4,100 lb)
Mission gross weight:	
SH-60B ASW	9,182 kg (20,244 lb)
SH-60B ASST	8,334 kg (18,373 lb)
Max gross weight:	
SH-60B Utility and HH-60H	9,926 kg (21,884 lb)
HH-60J	9,637 kg (21,246 lb)
Max disc loading	47.26 kg/m² (9.68 lb/sq ft)

PERFORMANCE:

Cruising speed at S/L:	
HH-60H	147 knots (272 km/h; 169 mph)
HH-60J	146 knots (271 km/h; 168 mph)
Dash speed at 1,525 m (5,000 ft), tropical day:	
SH-60B	126 knots (234 km/h; 145 mph)
Vertical rate of climb at S/L, 32.2°C (90°F):	
SH-60B	213 m (700 ft)/min
Vertical rate of climb at S/L, 32.2°C (90°F), one engine out: SH-60B	137 m (450 ft)/min

SIKORSKY S-70C

TYPE: Commercial or military H-60 for non-FMS customers.

PROGRAMME: See Customers below.

CUSTOMERS: Delivery of 24, designated S-70C-2, with undernose radar to People's Republic of China completed December 1985; 14 supplied to Republic of China Air Force, Taiwan; other exports include Brunei (two) and one each for Westland plc (designated Westland WS-70L) and Rolls-Royce in UK; R-R aircraft used as testbed for R-R Turbomeca RTM 322 turboshafts; all based on Black Hawk. S-70C(M)-1 designation assigned to 10 Seahawks for Taiwan (see SH-60B entry).

DESIGN FEATURES: Certificated to FAR Pt 21.25; roles include utility transport, external lift, maritime and environmental survey, forestry and conservation, mineral

Sikorsky S-70C commercially available derivative of the UH-60 series

Sikorsky HH-60J Jayhawk rescue and law enforcement helicopter for the US Coast Guard

exploration and heavy construction support; powered by General Electric CT7-2C or -2D engines; options include de-icing kit for main and tail rotors, cargo hook for 3,630 kg (8,000 lb) loads, rescue hoist, aeromedical evacuation kit, and winterisation kit. Combined transmission rating (continuous) 2,334 kW (3,130 shp).

FLYING CONTROLS: As for UH-60.

STRUCTURE: As for UH-60.

POWER PLANT: Two 1,212 kW (1,625 shp) General Electric CT7-2C or 1,285 kW (1,723 shp) CT7-2D turboshafts, or equivalent military T700s. Rolls-Royce Turbomeca RTM 322 in demonstrator G-RRTM. Maximum fuel capacity 1,370 litres (362 US gallons; 301 Imp gallons).

ACCOMMODATION: Flight deck crew of two, with provision for 12 passengers in standard cabin configuration and up to 19 passengers in high density layout. Forward hinged door on each side of flight deck for access to cockpit area. Large rearward sliding door on each side of main cabin.

DIMENSIONS, INTERNAL:

Cabin: Length	3.84 m (12 ft 7 in)
Max width	2.34 m (7 ft 8 in)
Max height	1.37 m (4 ft 6 in)
Floor area	8.18 m² (88.0 sq ft)
Volume	10.96 m³ (387.0 cu ft)
Baggage compartment volume	0.52 m³ (18.5 cu ft)

WEIGHTS AND LOADINGS:

Weight empty	4,607 kg (10,158 lb)
Max external load	3,630 kg (8,000 lb)
Max T-O weight	9,185 kg (20,250 lb)
Max disc loading	43.73 kg/m² (8.96 lb/sq ft)
Max power loading	3.94 kg/kW (6.47 lb/shp)

PERFORMANCE (ISA, at max T-O weight):

Never-exceed speed (VNE)	195 knots (361 km/h; 224 mph)
Max level speed at S/L	157 knots (290 km/h; 180 mph)
Cruising speed at S/L	145 knots (268 km/h; 167 mph)
Max rate of climb at S/L	615 m (2,020 ft)/min
Service ceiling	4,360 m (14,300 ft)
Service ceiling, one engine out	1,095 m (3,600 ft)
Hovering ceiling OGE	1,204 m (3,950 ft)

Range at 135 knots (250 km/h; 155 mph) at 915 m (3,000 ft) with max standard fuel, 30 min reserves
255 nm (473 km; 294 miles)

Range, max fuel, no reserves
297 nm (550 km; 342 miles)

SIKORSKY S-76 MARK II

TYPE: Commercial twin-turbine helicopter.

PROGRAMME: Announced 19 January 1975; four prototypes begun May 1976; first flight (N762SA) 13 March 1977; certification to FAR Pt 29 in November 1978; deliveries started early 1979; delivery of Mk II began 1 March 1982; Mk II modification kits available for earlier S-76s.

VARIANTS: **S-76:** Original transport version delivered before 1 March 1982.

S-76 Mark II: Standard version since March 1982.

S-76A+: Unsold S-76s re-engined with Turbomeca Arriel 1S; described separately.

S-76B: Powered by P&W PT6B-36 engines; described separately.

S-76C: Powered by Turbomeca Arriel 1S1 engines; described separately.

S-76 Utility: More basic version of S-76 Mk II with sliding doors (one each side), dual controls and floors stressed for 976 kg/m² (200 lb/sq ft); options include fixed landing gear with low pressure tyres, crash-resistant fuel tanks, baggage compartment auxiliary tank for 416 litres (100 US gallons; 91.5 Imp gallons), armoured crew seats, cargo hook, rescue hoist, engine air particle separators, and provision for stretchers. Philippine Air Force received 17 military S-76 Utility, of which 12 AUH-76s fitted for COIN, troop/logistic support and medevac, two others for SAR, and three as 12 or eight passenger transports.

H-76 Eagle: Military development of S-76B; described separately.

H-76N: Naval development of H-76; described separately.

CUSTOMERS: Sikorsky delivered five S-76Bs and 13 S-76A+ during 1990 and expected to deliver 24 during 1991.

DESIGN FEATURES: Intended to increase share of civil market; conforms to FAR Pt 29 with Category A IFR; intended for offshore support, business transport, medical evacuation and general utility use; technology and aerodynamics of S-76 based on those of UH-60 Black Hawk; Mk II has more than 40 modifications including refinements in major dynamic components and blade retention fittings, more fuselage access panels and better cabin ventilation, all with no loss in performance.

Four-blade main rotor with high twist and varying section and camber based on Sikorsky SC-1095; tapered blade tip has 30° leading-edge sweep; fully articulated rotor head with single elastomeric bearings; hydraulic drag dampers; dual bifilar vibration absorber assemblies above rotor head; four-blade cross-beam tail rotor on port side; transmission rating 969 kW (1,300 shp); rotor brake optional.

Three quick-change medical kits offered February 1982 for single and dual patient intensive care transport with two attendants, and three-stretcher kit for civil defence or SAR ambulance use; Emergency Medical Service configuration with built-in redundant systems for gases, suction and electricity announced late 1986; many S-76s in civil ambulance use.

Unmodified production S-76 Mk II set 12 records in FAI Class E1d and E1e 4-9 February 1982; details in 1987-88 *Jane's*.

Experimental higher harmonic control (HHC) system, to damp vibration through control actuators at rotor head, tested Spring 1985; demonstrated 90 per cent vibration reduction. All-composite rotor head and blades developed during 1980s. Ice protection kit weighing 68 kg (150 lb), of which 45 kg (100 lb) could be removed in Summer, also under development.

FLYING CONTROLS: Dual powered hydraulic controls with autostabilisaton and autopilot; releasable spring-centring trim system for both cyclic and collective controls; full IFR instrument panel with optional EFIS and weather radar.

STRUCTURE: Main rotor blades have formed titanium oval-section tubular main spar with Nomex honeycomb aerofoil core, glassfibre composite outer skin and titanium/nickel leading-edge abrasion strips. Fuselage contains extensive Kevlar and honeycomb components.

LANDING GEAR: Hydraulically retractable tricycle type, with single wheel on each unit. Nosewheel retracts rearward, main units inward into rear fuselage; all three wheels are enclosed by doors when retracted. Mainwheel tyres size 14.5 × 5.5-6, pressure 11.38 bars (165 lb/sq in); nosewheel tyre size 13 × 5.00-4, pressure 9.31 bars (135 lb/sq in). Hydraulic brakes; hydraulic mainwheel parking brake. Non-retractable tricycle gear, with low pressure tyres, optional on Utility version.

POWER PLANT: Mk II has Allison 250-C30S (for Sikorsky) turboshafts, with 5 per cent higher take-off rating of 485 kW (650 shp) and 2½ minute contingency rating of 522 kW (700 shp); Allison 250-C34 also available to provide 10 per cent power increase; digital fuel control system developed by Hamilton Standard; with -C34 engines and uprated transmission, Mk II is certificated for max T-O weight of 4,989 kg (11,000 lb). Standard fuel system has a capacity of 1,064 litres (281 US gallons; 234 Imp gallons). Extended range fuel tanks, capacity 401 litres (106 US gallons; 88 Imp gallons), optional.

ACCOMMODATION: Pilot and co-pilot plus a maximum of 12 passengers. In this configuration passengers are seated on three four-abreast rows of seats, floor mounted at a pitch of 79 cm (31 in). A number of executive layouts are available, including a four-passenger 'office in the sky' configuration. Executive versions have luxurious interior trim, full carpeting, special soundproofing, radio telephone, and co-ordinated furniture. Dual controls optional. Two large doors on each side of fuselage, hinged at their forward edges; sliding doors are available optionally. Baggage hold aft of cabin, with external access door on each side of the fuselage. Cabin heated and ventilated. Windscreen demisting and dual windscreen wipers. Windscreen heating and external cargo hook optional.

SYSTEMS: Hydraulic system at pressure of 207 bars (3,000 lb/sq in) supplied by two pumps driven from main gearbox. Hydraulic system maximum flow rate 15.9 litres (4.2 US gallons; 3.5 Imp gallons) per minute. Bootstrap reservoir. Pump head pressure 3.45 bars (50 lb/sq in). In VFR configuration, electrical system comprises two 200A DC starter/generators and a 24V 17Ah nickel-cadmium battery. In IFR configuration, system comprises gearbox driven 7.5kVA generator, and a 115V 600VA 400Hz static inverter for AC power. 34Ah battery optional. Engine fire detection and extinguishing system.

AVIONICS: Wide range of optional avionics available, according to configuration, including Honeywell SPZS-7000 single-pilot digital AFCS with EFIS, Hamilton Standard AFCS, VHF nav receivers, transponder, compass system, weather radar, flight director system, radar altimeter, ADF, DME, VLF nav system, and ELT and sonic transmitters.

EQUIPMENT: Standard equipment includes provisions for dual controls; cabin fire extinguishers; cockpit, cabin, instrument, navigation and anti-collision lights; landing light; external power socket; first aid kit; and utility soundproofing. Collins VHF-20 com transceiver and intercom system standard. Optional equipment includes air-conditioning, cargo hook, rescue hoist, emergency flotation gear, engine air particle separators, full IFR instrumentation and litter installation.

DIMENSIONS, EXTERNAL (A: Mark II, B: Mark II Utility):
Main rotor diameter	13.41 m (44 ft 0 in)
Main rotor blade chord	0.39 m (1 ft 3½ in)
Tail rotor diameter	2.44 m (8 ft 0 in)
Tail rotor blade chord	0.16 m (6½ in)
Length overall, rotors turning	16.00 m (52 ft 6 in)

Sikorsky S-76 Mark II general purpose helicopter in service with the Royal Jordanian Air Force
(Ivo Sturzenegger)

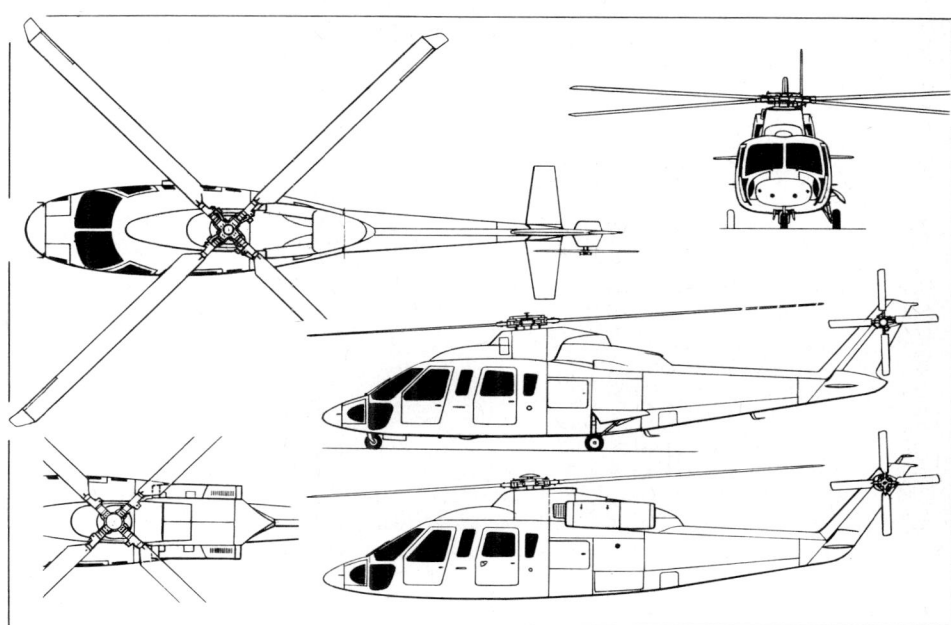

Sikorsky S-76 Mark II eight/twelve-passenger commercial transport helicopter, with lower side view and scrap detail of S-76B *(Pilot Press)*

Fuselage: Length	13.22 m (43 ft 4½ in)
Max width	2.13 m (7 ft 0 in)
Max depth	1.83 m (6 ft 0 in)
Height overall, tail rotor turning:	
A	4.41 m (14 ft 5¾ in)
B	4.52 m (14 ft 9¾ in)
Tailplane span: A	3.05 m (10 ft 0 in)
B	3.15 m (10 ft 4 in)
Wheel track: A	2.44 m (8 ft 0 in)
B	2.54 m (8 ft 4 in)
Wheelbase	5.00 m (16 ft 5 in)
Tail rotor ground clearance	1.97 m (6 ft 5¾ in)

DIMENSIONS, INTERNAL:
Cabin: Length	2.46 m (8 ft 1 in)
Max width	1.93 m (6 ft 4 in)
Max height	1.35 m (4 ft 5 in)
Floor area	4.18 m² (45.0 sq ft)
Volume	5.78 m³ (204.0 cu ft)
Baggage compartment volume	1.08 m³ (38.0 cu ft)

AREAS:
Main rotor disc	141.26 m² (1,520.53 sq ft)
Tail rotor disc	4.67 m² (50.27 sq ft)
Tailplane	2.00 m² (21.5 sq ft)

WEIGHTS AND LOADINGS:
Weight empty, standard equipment	2,540 kg (5,600 lb)
Max fuel weight: standard	861 kg (1,898 lb)
auxiliary	325 kg (716 lb)
Max payload	2,132 kg (4,700 lb)
Max external load	1,497 kg (3,300 lb)
Max T-O weight	4,672 kg (10,300 lb)
Max disc loading	33.07 kg/m² (6.77 lb/sq ft)
Max power loading	4.82 kg/kW (7.92 lb/shp)

PERFORMANCE (A: at gross weight of 4,536 kg; 10,000 lb, B: at gross weight of 3,810 kg; 8,400 lb):
Never-exceed speed (V$_{NE}$)
	155 knots (286 km/h; 178 mph)
Max cruising speed: A	145 knots (269 km/h; 167 mph)
B	155 knots (286 km/h; 178 mph)
Cruising speed for max range:	
A	125 knots (232 km/h; 144 mph)
Max rate of climb at S/L	411 m (1,350 ft)/min
Service ceiling: A	4,575 m (15,000 ft)
Service ceiling, one engine out: A	1,890 m (6,200 ft)
B	3,445 m (11,300 ft)

Hovering ceiling IGE: A	1,890 m (6,200 ft)
B	3,415 m (11,200 ft)
Range: with 12 passengers, standard fuel, 30 min reserves	404 nm (748 km; 465 miles)
with 8 passengers, auxiliary fuel and offshore equipment	600 nm (1,112 km; 691 miles)

SIKORSKY S-76A+

TYPE: Re-engined S-76A.

PROGRAMME: S-76A (F-WZSA) fitted with 522 kW (700 shp) Turbomeca Arriel 1S turboshafts 1987; FAA certificated April 1988; now available as new or retrofit with designation S-76A+; also certificated in Australia, France, Japan, UK and Germany.

CUSTOMERS: Hong Kong government ordered six S-76A+s and two S-76Cs for Royal Hong Kong Auxiliary Air Force in April 1989; all will have new sliding doors and rescue hoist; first three S-76A+s delivered April/May 1990 and two S-76Cs to be delivered 1991 and 1992 are standard; three S-76A+s, delivered November 1990, have FAA certification with Honeywell 7600 SAR flight control system with dual digital SPZ-7000 AFCS, EDZ-705 EFIS and integrated software for automatic search pattern flying, downward transition and Doppler hover in IFR conditions; other equipment includes GEC Sensors TICM II thermal imager in MRTS multi-role turret system, Honeywell Primus 701 mapping/weather radar, Racal 91 Doppler and NightSun searchlight.

Bond Helicopters, Scotland, ordered one S-76A+ and converted six S-76As; first machine used to test and gain FAA and CAA certification for S-76A+ at increased max T-O weight of 4,899 kg (10,800 lb); three further conversions to be completed for fleet of nine. Bristow Helicopters, England, had five conversions by February 1991, with five to follow 1991-92.

Other customers include Heli-Union of France, KK Marumasu Sangyo, Honda Airways and Seibu Shoji Company Ltd of Japan and Wiking Helicopters, Germany.

Sikorsky S-76A+ (Turbomeca Arriel 1S turboshafts)

Sikorsky S-76A+ SAR helicopter of Royal Hong Kong Auxiliary Air Force, with GEC MRTS FLIR turret under nose, searchlight under cabin, and cargo hook

DESIGN FEATURES: Modification originally applied to unsold S-76As; performance and reliability improved; for further development, see S-76C entry.

Details below represent differences from S-76 Mk II:

POWER PLANT: Two Turbomeca Arriel 1S turboshafts, with a max continuous rating of 508 kW (681 shp) and contingency rating of 544 kW (729 shp) for 2½ min.

WEIGHTS AND LOADINGS:

Weight empty, equipped	2,778 kg (6,126 lb)
Max T-O weight	4,898 kg (10,800 lb)

PERFORMANCE (at max T-O weight, S/L, ISA, except where indicated):

Max level speed	155 knots (287 km/h; 178 mph)
Max cruising speed	145 knots (269 km/h; 167 mph)
Max rate of climb at S/L	503 m (1,650 ft)/min
Service ceiling	4,318 m (14,167 ft)
Service ceiling, one engine out	1,370 m (4,500 ft)
Hovering ceiling OGE	564 m (1,850 ft)

Range at 135 knots (250 km/h; 155 mph) at 915 m (3,000 ft), with standard fuel:

no reserves	465 nm (861 km; 535 miles)
with 30 min reserves	397 nm (735 km; 457 miles)

SIKORSKY S-76B

TYPE: P & WC engined S-76 Mark II.

PROGRAMME: Initiated October 1983; first flight (N3123U) 22 June 1984; first flight of reworked ground test S-76B February 1985; certificated in FAA Category A early 1987; UK certification testing began July 1987; increase in max T-O weight to 5,307 kg (11,700 lb) approved by FAA in June 1988.

CUSTOMERS: S-76Bs operating in China, Germany, Japan, Netherlands, South Korea, UK and USA; five delivered in 1990.

DESIGN FEATURES: Additional power of P&WC PT6B-36 engines and transmission rating raised to 1,118 kW (1,500 shp) increases take-off power by 48 per cent; useful load increased 51 per cent in hot and high conditions; max T-O weight increased by 635 kg (1,400 lb); tail rotor pylon area reduced by 15 per cent and engine exhaust reconfigured.

Emergency medical service installation includes multiple-position pivoting primary patient litter, a second litter, and track-mounted seats for four attendants, forward and rear oxygen systems, and dual access to external power on ground; cabin volume 4,000 litres (141 cu ft).

STRUCTURE: Generally as for S-76 Mk II.

POWER PLANT: Two Pratt & Whitney Canada PT6B-36A turboshafts; five minute T-O rating 732 kW (981 shp); 30 minute single-engine rating 771 kW (1,033 shp); max continuous rating at 1,524 m (5,000 ft) and 30°C (77°F) 504 kW (676 shp). Standard fuel capacity 1,064 litres (281 US gallons; 234 Imp gallons); auxiliary tank capacity 208 litres (55 US gallons; 46 Imp gallons).

ACCOMMODATION: Two pilots and 12-13 passengers.

DIMENSIONS, EXTERNAL:

Main rotor diameter	13.41 m (44 ft 0 in)
Tail rotor diameter	2.44 m (8 ft 0 in)
Length: overall	16.00 m (52 ft 6 in)
fuselage	13.43 m (44 ft 0¾ in)
Width of fuselage	2.13 m (7 ft 0 in)
Wheel track	2.44 m (8 ft 0 in)
Wheelbase	5.00 m (16 ft 5 in)

DIMENSIONS, INTERNAL:

Passenger cabin: Length	2.46 m (8 ft 1 in)
Width	1.93 m (6 ft 4 in)
Height	1.35 m (4 ft 5 in)
Volume	5.78 m³ (204 cu ft)
Baggage compartment volume	1.08 m³ (38 cu ft)

WEIGHTS AND LOADINGS:

Weight empty, standard equipment	3,012 kg (6,641 lb)
Max T-O weight	5,307 kg (11,700 lb)
Max disc loading	37.6 kg/m² (7.69 lb/sq ft)
Max power loading	4.75 kg/kW (7.80 lb/shp)

PERFORMANCE (at 5,307 kg; 11,700 lb T-O weight, ISA, except where indicated):

Max level speed	155 knots (287 km/h; 178 mph)
Cruising speed	145 knots (269 km/h; 166 mph)
Max rate of climb at S/L	502 m (1,650 ft)/min
Max operating altitude	4,572 m (15,000 ft)
Service ceiling, one engine out	1,981 m (6,500 ft)
Hovering ceiling OGE	1,143 m (3,750 ft)

Range at 139 knots (257 km/h; 160 mph) at 915 m (3,000 ft) with standard fuel:

with no reserves	357 nm (661 km; 410 miles)
with 30 min reserves	288 nm (533 km; 331 miles)

SIKORSKY S-76C

TYPE: Arriel 1S1 engined S-76B.

PROGRAMME: Announced June 1989; first flight 18 May 1990; FAA certification and first deliveries April 1991.

CUSTOMERS: Two ordered for Royal Hong Kong Auxiliary Air Force and eight for Spanish Air Force (for IFR training at Ala 78 helicopter school, Granada/Armilla); Bond Helicopters, Scotland, ordered seven for delivery beginning second half 1991.

DESIGN FEATURES: Same airframe and power train as S-76B, but powered by two Turbomeca Arriel 1S1 turboshafts; initial certification intended for max T-O weight 5,171 kg (11,400 lb); useful load 342 kg (754 lb) greater than S-76A for same range; in typical UK CAA IFR off-shore configuration, S-76C can fly 12 passengers for 220 nm (407 km; 253 miles) or 10 passengers for 320 nm (593 km; 368 miles) with 45 min reserves.

POWER PLANT: Two Turbomeca Arriel 1S1 turboshafts, rated at 539 kW (723 shp) for take-off and 591 kW (792

Sikorsky S-76B (Pratt & Whitney Canada PT6B-36A turboshafts)

Artist's impression of Sikorsky S-76C twin-turboshaft helicopter

shp) max contingency for 2½ minutes on one engine and 498 kW (668 shp) for normal cruise. Standard fuel capacity 1,064 litres (281 US gallons; 234 Imp gallons).
ACCOMMODATION: Two pilots and 12-13 passengers.
DIMENSIONS, EXTERNAL: As for S-76B except:
Length of fuselage   13.22 m (43 ft 4½ in)
DIMENSIONS, INTERNAL: As S-76B
WEIGHTS AND LOADINGS: As S-76B except:
Weight empty, standard equipment   2,849 kg (6,282 lb)
PERFORMANCE (at max T-O weight, ISA, except where indicated):
Max level speed at S/L   155 knots (287 km/h; 178 mph)
Normal cruising speed at S/L
       145 knots (269 km/h; 166 mph)
Max rate of climb, T-O power, S/L   445 m (1,460 ft)/min
Service ceiling: two engines   3,505 m (11,800 ft)
   single engine at 30 min power   631 m (2,070 ft)
Fuel consumption at 138 knots (255 km/h; 159 mph) at 915 m (3,000 ft), 3,261 kg (10,700 lb) gross weight
       268 kg/h (593 lb/h)
Range at 138 knots (255 km/h; 159 mph) at 915 m (3,000 ft) with standard fuel:
   no reserves   430 nm (798 km; 494 miles)
   30 min reserves   366 nm (678 km; 421 miles)

SIKORSKY H-76 EAGLE

TYPE: Military armed utility derivative of S-76B.
PROGRAMME: First flight (N3124G) February 1985; weapon firing from four-station pitch-compensated armament pylon at Mojave, California, early 1987.
VARIANTS: H-76N: Naval version, described separately.
Demonstrator: Fitted with Boeing/Sikorsky First Team Fantail anti-torque system for RAH-66 Comanche (which see) and flown 6 June 1990; eight-blade tail rotor 1.20 m (3 ft 11¼ in) diameter, generating 737 kg (1,624 lb) max thrust at 610 m (2,000 ft) and 35°C (95°F).
CUSTOMERS: Selected for South Korean LUH (light utility helicopter) requirement; Daewoo-Sikorsky Aerospace Ltd formed 1988 with facility at Chang Won; production rate to meet Korean need for 150 to 175 helicopters would be 24 a year. First seven Phase 1 (Sikorsky built) aircraft delivered in 1990 (three), January (two) and March 1991 (two); Phase 2 was scheduled to begin June 1991 with delivery of one CKD kit, followed by two kits per month through remainder of year.
DESIGN FEATURES: Airframe modifications include armoured crew seats, sliding cabin doors, heavy duty floor, optical sight above instrument panel, self-sealing high-strength fuel tanks, and door-mounted weapons; main transmission, intermediate and tail rotor gearboxes uprated; main rotor hub and shaft strengthened; broader tail rotor blade chord; dual spars in tail pylon; fuselage side skin thickened to resist weapon blast; Strobex rotor blade tracker optional.
H-76 can be equipped for troop transport/logistic support, as gunship, or for airborne assault, air observation post, combat SAR, evacuation, ambulance and conventional SAR. Can carry either mast mounted or roof mounted sight, plus head-up display, laser ranger, and integrated armament management system; also provision for self-protection system including radar warning, infra-red jammer, and chaff/flare dispensers; high-clearance landing gear and Honeywell SPZ-7000 dual digital autopilot available.
Pitch-compensated armament pylon has faired leading-edge, giving 3-4 knots speed increase; weapons tested include GIAT 20 mm cannon pod, 7.62 mm and 12.7 mm machine-gun pods, VS-MD-H mine dispenser and 70 mm rockets; H-76 could carry 16 air-to-air missiles or eight AAMs and two cannon pods; integrated armament management system allows weapons to be selected from collective lever as well as from panel; system ready lights and sideslip trim ball on head-up display.
External/internal dimensions generally as for S-76B; details below show differences from civil S-76s:
POWER PLANT: As for S-76B, except fuel is contained in two high strength, optionally self-sealing, tanks located below the rear cabin, with a total capacity of 993 litres (262.4 US gallons; 218.4 Imp gallons). Gravity refuelling point on each side of fuselage. Engine ice protection by bleed air anti-icing system. Engine fire detection and extinguishing systems. Engine air particle separator optional.
ACCOMMODATION: Pilot and co-pilot, plus varying troop/passenger loads according to role. Armoured pilot seats optional. Ten fully armed troops can be transported, or seven troops when configured as an airborne assault vehicle with multi-purpose pylon system (MPPS) and one 7.62 mm door gun installed. For evacuation use the cabin can be equipped with 12 seats or, in emergency, all seats can be removed and 16 persons can be airlifted sitting on the cabin floor. For SAR use the cabin will accommodate three patients on litters, or six persons lying prone on the floor and on the rear cabin raised deck. The standard medevac layout provides for three litters and a bench seat for two medical attendants.
SYSTEMS: Generally as for S-76B, except electrical system has a 17 or optional 34Ah battery.
AVIONICS: Typical avionics include VHF-20A VHF transceiver, AN/ARC-186 VHF-AM/FM com, 719A UHF com, ADF-60A ADF, DF-301E UHF DF, VIR-30A

Sikorsky H-76 Eagle military utility helicopter (Pratt & Whitney Canada PT6B-36 turboshafts)

Artist's impression of Sikorsky H-76N naval helicopter with MEL Super Searcher radar and torpedoes

VOR with ILS, glideslope and marker beacon receivers, DME-40 DME, TDR-90 transponder and dual RMI-36 RMI, all by Collins, course deviation indicators, ELT, Andrea A301-61A intercom, cabin speaker system and loudhailer.
EQUIPMENT: Typical equipment includes dual controls and instrumentation, stability augmentation system, dual 5 in VGIs, Allen RCA-26 standby self-contained attitude indicator, Collins ALT-50A radio altimeter, soundproofing, 'Fasten seat belt—No smoking' sign, first aid kit, two cabin fire extinguishers, external power socket, provisions for optional emergency flotation system, and provisions for installation of cargo hook with certificated capacity of 1,497 kg (3,300 lb) and rescue hoist of 272 kg (600 lb) capacity. Standard lighting includes cockpit, cabin and instrument lights, navigation lights, anti-collision strobe light, and a battery operated cabin emergency light.
ARMAMENT: One 7.62 mm machine-gun can be pintle mounted in each doorway and fired with or without the MPPS system installed. Pintles incorporate field of fire limiters and will accept FN Herstal or Maramount M60D machine-guns. The MPPS can be installed on the cabin floor, providing the capability to carry and deploy pods containing single or twin 7.62 mm machine-guns, 0.50 in machine-guns, 2.75 in and 5 in rocket pods, Mk 66 2.75 in rockets, Oerlikon 68 mm rockets, mines, Hellfire, TOW, Sea Skua and Stinger missiles, and Mk 46 torpedoes (see also Design Features). Targeting equipment can include FLIR, Saab-Scania reticle sight, TOW roof sight or TOW mast mounted sight and laser rangefinder.
WEIGHTS AND LOADINGS:
Basic weight empty   2,545 kg (5,610 lb)
Weight empty, equipped (typical)   3,030 kg (6,680 lb)
Max fuel weight   792 kg (1,745 lb)
Max T-O weight   5,171 kg (11,400 lb)

PERFORMANCE: Similar to S-76B, but range highly variable according to loading and mission.

SIKORSKY H-76N

Announced 1984 as naval version of H-76, designed for anti-ship surveillance and targeting, ASW, surface attack, SAR and utility missions operating from frigate-sized ships; over-the-horizon targeting (OTHT) and anti-ship (ASV) versions offered with Ferranti Seaspray 3 or MEL Super Searcher radar in 360° pod; anti-ship armament is two Sea Skua missiles; ASW version would have dipping sonar, acoustic processor and two Gould Mk 46 or Marconi Sting Ray torpedoes. Choice of Allison 250-C34S or P&WC PT6B-36 engines.
Other features include dual digital AFCS with autohover, target information data link, tactical navigation, hover in-flight refuelling, roof or mast mounted FLIR, ECM pod, chaff/flare dispensers, strengthened high-clearance landing gear, folding main rotor blades and provision for deck securing.
Estimated empty weight (all versions) 2,812 kg (6,200 lb); max T-O weight for targeting version 4,473 kg (9,861 lb), for anti-ship version 4,968 kg (10,953 lb), and for H-76N equipped with 136 kg (300 lb) ECM pod for secondary jamming role 4,754 kg (10,481 lb). Total fuel capacity for all three versions 999 litres (264 US gallons; 210 Imp gallons).

SIKORSKY SHADOW

One-off modification (N765SA) of S-76; Sikorsky Helicopter Advanced Demonstrator and Operator Workload (Shadow) fitted with nose-mounted single-seat cockpit for US Army Rotorcraft Technology Integration (ARTI) programme; main cabin used for safety pilots and test operators; first flight 24 June 1985; trials of full cockpit

Sikorsky Helicopter Advanced Demonstrator of Operator Workload (SHADOW), based on an S-76

began Spring 1986; now has fly-by-wire side-arm control stick, voice interactive system, remote map reader, FLIR, head-up display with programmable symbol generator, visually coupled helmet-mounted display and dual CRT displays with touch-sensitive screens. Later modifications

include upgraded engines and dynamic components, NVG compatible cockpit and cabin, reconfigurable evaluation cockpit, and high visibility paint for night and NOE flying.

Partners in Shadow programme include Bendix/King, Kaiser, Litton, Northrop, Pacer Systems, Rockwell Collins,

Plessey Electronic Systems and United Technologies Hamilton Standard.

Used 1990 in Boeing/Sikorsky LH First Team programme to flight test NVPS (Night Vision Pilotage System) developed by Martin Marietta.

SNOW

SNOW AVIATION INTERNATIONAL INC

2228 South Third Street, Columbus Ohio 43207
Telephone: 1 (614) 443 2711
Fax: 1 (614) 443 2861
PRESIDENT: Harry T. Snow Jr
EXECUTIVE VICE-PRESIDENT: William G. Ferguson
VICE-PRESIDENT, ENGINEERING: Arthur E. Eckles
VICE-PRESIDENT, SALES: Emil E. Kluever

SNOW AVIATION SA-204C and SA-210AT

Transport aircraft with STOL and rough-field capability. Civil **204C** could carry 50 passengers (four-abreast at 76 cm; 30 in seat pitch) or equivalent cargo, or may be offered in optional combi and quick-change versions; military **SA-210AT** would accommodate 61 combat-equipped troops, or 38 paratroops, or 40 litters with attendants, or four 463L military pallets in all-cargo configuration.

FAA certification originally expected 1991; first flight now expected late 1991; planned production 321 aircraft in first five years at two/three a week.

Artist's impression of Snow Aviation SA-210AT STOL-C/AT Cargo/Assault Transport

Powered by two 2,050 kW (2,750 shp) P&WC PW127 turboprops, driving six-blade propellers; max fuel capacity 5,897 litres (1,558 US gallons; 1,297 Imp gallons). Max T-O weight would be 24,720 kg (54,500 lb).

Full details in 1990-91 *Jane's*.

SOLOY

SOLOY CORPORATION

450 Pat Kennedy Way SW, Olympia, Washington 98501-7298
Telephone: 1 (206) 754 7000
Fax: 1 (206) 943 7659
PRESIDENT: Joe E. Soloy
SALES MANAGER: J. T. Koester
ENGINEERING MANAGER: Nicholas R. Parkinson
MARKETING GROUP MANAGER: R. K. Furtick

Well known for re-engining of Hiller 12E and Bell 47G helicopters with the Allison 250-C20 turboshaft; Turbine Pac turboprop conversion for many fixed-wing aircraft developed in association with Allison. Also provides combiner gearbox for twin Allison installation in Tridair 260L-3ST Gemini ST conversion of Bell LongRanger (which see); this gearbox being adapted for re-engining single-engined business aircraft with coupled twin turbines driving single propeller for FAA certification as twins.

SOLOY TURBINE PAC and DUAL PAC CONVERSIONS

Turbine Pac based on 313 kW (420 shp) Allison 250-C20S, 373 kW (500 shp) 250-C28C or 485 kW (650 shp) 250-C30 turboprop, driving a 522 kW (700 shp) reduction gearbox with output; first flight 23 November 1981 in Cessna 185 (N5010Y) with Allison 250-C20 (see development details in 1987-88 and earlier *Jane's*); Cessna 206 and 207 and Beech A36 Bonanza are STC approved; Soloy Turbine Pac Cessna 185 available for government agencies able to operate without certification.

Royal Thai Army evaluated a Soloy Turbine Pac Cessna 185/U-17; Soloy Turbine Pac Cessnas used by US Drug Enforcement Administration and Government of Costa Rica; several Jet-Prop Beech A36 Bonanzas sold for private and business use (see under Tradewind); other installations include Allison Series IV being developed for single- and twin-engined aircraft and 485 kW (650 shp) Allison 250-C30M certificated in Aerospatiale AS 350D Astar in early 1986; Soloy installed Allison 250-B17 turboprop in Chilean Enaer Aucan prototype, first flight 12 February 1986 (see 1987-88 *Jane's*).

Soloy started development in early 1989 of **Dual Pac** twin-engine combining gearbox for both helicopter and fixed-wing applications, using either Allison 250-C20s or 250-C30s; each engine has separate freewheel so that Soloy expects FAA Pt 135 IFR certification of Dual Pac (granted 1991 for Cessna Caravan) as twin-engined power plant; both engines driving on aircraft centreline is important safety and performance factor. Tridair Helicopters (which see) uses Soloy Dual Pac for its twin-engined version of Bell 206L LongRanger. Dual Pac PT6B-35F for fixed-wing aircraft under joint development with Pratt & Whitney Canada.

Soloy has also installed two 380 kW (510 hp) Teledyne Continental TP-500E turboprops in Piper Chieftain; first flight in 1989; activity terminated prior to certification.

SOLOY CESSNA 206 TURBINE PAC

TYPE: Turbine powered Cessna 206.
PROGRAMME: FAA certificated 22 May 1984.
VARIANTS: **Civil:** Wheel or float landing gear; as detailed below.

Military: Additional fuel and 'super flotation' landing gear with oversize wheels for operation from unprepared terrain. Primarily for liaison and observation.

Soloy Turbine Pac installation in a Cessna 206 with PK amphibious floats

CUSTOMERS: Operating in Australia, Bolivia, Switzerland and USA; total of 62 Model 206/207 Turbine Pacs delivered by February 1991.
DESIGN FEATURES: Engine installed inverted and back to front to place output drive above, intake at rear top of nacelle and exhaust pipes under front of cowling. Approved for Wipline and PK floats and Edo 3500 amphibious floats.
FLYING CONTROLS: As for Cessna 206.
STRUCTURE: As for Cessna 206.
Main differences from standard Cessna 206 listed below:
POWER PLANT: One 313 kW (420 shp) Soloy Model 763 Turbine Pac/Allison 250-C20S turboprop, driving a Hartzell three-blade constant-speed fully feathering propeller. Fuel capacity 230-348 litres (61-92 US gallons; 51-77 Imp gallons), depending on airframe model. Extended range fuel tanks, total usable capacity 189 litres (50 US gallons; 42 Imp gallons), optional on military model. Oil capacity 7.1 litres (1.9 US gallons; 1.6 Imp gallons).

WEIGHTS AND LOADINGS:
Weight empty	866 kg (1,910 lb)
Max T-O weight	1,633 kg (3,600 lb)
Max power loading	5.22 kg/kW (8.57 lb/shp)

PERFORMANCE (at max T-O weight):
Never-exceed speed (V$_{NE}$)	148 knots (274 km/h; 170 mph) IAS
Max level speed and max cruising speed at 3,050 m (10,000 ft)	163 knots (302 km/h; 188 mph)
Econ cruising speed at 6,100 m (20,000 ft)	142 knots (263 km/h; 164 mph)
Stalling speed, power off:	
flaps up	58 knots (107 km/h; 67 mph) CAS
flaps down	52 knots (96 km/h; 60 mph) CAS
Max rate of climb at S/L	594 m (1,950 ft)/min
Service ceiling	6,100 m (20,000 ft)
T-O run	174 m (570 ft)
T-O to 15 m (50 ft)	324 m (1,063 ft)
Landing from 15 m (50 ft)	334 m (1,094 ft)
Landing run	168 m (553 ft)
Range with 333 litres (88 US gallons; 73 Imp gallons) usable fuel, max range power at 6,100 m (20,000 ft)	882 nm (1,635 km; 1,016 miles)

SOLOY CESSNA 207 TURBINE PAC

First flight of Cessna 207 (N21190) powered by 313 kW (420 shp) Allison 250-C20S 14 January 1984; second aircraft joined development Spring 1985; certificated early 1986; total of 62 Model 206/207 Turbine Pacs delivered by March 1991.

Main differences from standard Cessna 207 listed below:
WEIGHTS AND LOADINGS:
Weight empty	986 kg (2,175 lb)
Max T-O weight	1,814 kg (4,000 lb)
Max power loading	5.80 kg/kW (9.52 lb/shp)

PERFORMANCE:
Max level speed:		
at 1,525 m (5,000 ft)	157 knots (291 km/h; 181 mph)	
at 3,050 m (10,000 ft)	164 knots (304 km/h; 189 mph)	
Stalling speed:		
flaps up, power off		59 knots (109 km/h; 68 mph) CAS
flaps down, power off		53 knots (98 km/h; 61 mph) CAS
Max rate of climb at S/L	500 m (1,640 ft)/min	
Service ceiling	7,620 m (25,000 ft)	
T-O run	224 m (736 ft)	
Range with 303 litres (80 US gallons; 67 Imp gallons) usable fuel, max range power at 3,050 m (10,000 ft)		558 nm (1,034 km; 642 miles)

STODDARD-HAMILTON

T-9 Stalker turboprop version of Glasair III all-composite homebuilt intended for military training/ground support roles; prototype crashed 23 May 1989 and no further news received. Last described in 1990-91 *Jane's*. Further details of the company in Sport Aircraft section.

SUPER 580

SUPER 580 AIRCRAFT COMPANY
(Division of Flight Trails Inc)

2192 Palomar Airport Road, Carlsbad, California 92008
Telephone: 1 (619) 438 3600
Fax: 1 (619) 753 1531
Telex: 140414
PRESIDENT: Ted Vallas
SENIOR VICE-PRESIDENT: James Coleman
Licensed by Allison Gas Turbine Division of General Motors for turboprop conversion and remanufacturing of Convair 340/440/580 series transports into Super 580s.

SUPER 580 AIRCRAFT SUPER 580

TYPE: Re-engined Convair 340/440/580.
PROGRAMME: First Super 580 conversion by Hamilton Aviation, Tucson, Arizona; first flight 21 March 1984; FAA approval to CAR 4b by means of STC; delivered to The Way International June 1984. Super 580 ST stretch for 78 passengers or nine LD3 containers investigated 1984.
DESIGN FEATURES: Replaces piston engines of 340/440 or Allison 501-D13 of 580 with Allison 501-D22G turboprops, each flat rated at 2,983 kW (4,000 shp) and driving Hamilton Standard four-blade, constant-speed, feathering and reversing propeller; compared with 580, Super 580 has 2.5 per cent better sfc, improved engine-out performance, 13 per cent longer range, 40 per cent greater hot day payload, 40 per cent lower operating costs, and cruising speeds up to 325 knots (602 km/h; 374 mph). Further details in 1990-91 *Jane's*.

SWEARINGEN

SWEARINGEN ENGINEERING AND TECHNOLOGY INC

Suite A, 1234 99th Street, San Antonio, Texas 78214
Telephone: 1 (512) 921 1208
Fax: 1 (512) 921 0198
CHAIRMAN AND CHIEF EXECUTIVE OFFICER: E. J. Swearingen
PRESIDENT AND CHIEF OPERATING OFFICER: John R. Novak
VICE-PRESIDENTS:
 O. L Anderson (Marketing)
 T. Boardman (Engineering)
 K. Karwowski (Manufacturing)
 J. Lupia (Finance)
DIRECTOR, INTERNATIONAL MARKETING: John C. Maurer
'Ed' Swearingen is well known for designing Merlin and Metro commuter and business aircraft, and for engineering such aircraft as Piper Twin Comanche and Lockheed 731 JetStar II; also built prototype SA-32T for Jaffe (which see). Now developing Swearingen SJ30 small business jet.

SWEARINGEN SJ30

TYPE: Twin-turbofan small business jet.
PROGRAMME: Announced 30 October 1986 as SA-30 Fanjet; Gulfstream Aerospace, Williams International and Rolls-Royce announced they were joining programme in October 1988 and aircraft renamed Gulfstream SA-30 Gulfjet; Gulfstream withdrew from programme 1 September 1989; place taken by Jaffe Group of San Antonio, Texas, and aircraft renamed Swearingen/Jaffe SJ30; now solely a Swearingen project; first flight of prototype (N30SJ) 13 February 1991; certification expected before end 1992.
CUSTOMERS: Ishida Group and Toyota Tsusho of Japan appointed for marketing and service support for Asia-Oceania region.
DESIGN FEATURES: Six-seat pressurised business jet, powered by Williams International FJ44 turbofans; tapered, 30° sweptback wing of computer-designed section with integral fuel tanks in torsion box; wing and tailplane have TKS liquid de-icing systems.
FLYING CONTROLS: Mechanical flying controls with electric variable incidence tailplane and electrically actuated rudder and aileron trim tabs; two large outward-canted ventral fins under tail; slotted Fowler trailing-edge flaps actuated electrically; hydraulically actuated full span leading-edge slats; single electro-hydraulically actuated airbrake/lift dumper panel on each wing ahead of flap.
STRUCTURE: All-metal with chemically milled skins on fuselage.
LANDING GEAR: Retractable tricycle type, with twin wheels on each unit. Trailing-link oleo-pneumatic suspension on main units. Hydraulic actuation, main units retracting inward and rearward into fuselage, nose unit forward. Electrically steerable nose unit retracts forward.
POWER PLANT: Two 8.45 kN (1,900 lb st) Williams International FJ44 turbofans, pod-mounted on pylons on sides of rear fuselage. Inlets de-iced by engine bleed air. Fuel in three integral tanks, one in each wing and one in rear fuselage; combined capacity 1,893 litres (500 US gallons; 416 Imp ghallons). Single-point refuelling.
ACCOMMODATION: Pilot and one passenger (or co-pilot) on flight deck. Main cabin separated by a bulkhead; four chairs in facing pairs, each with adjustable reclining backs and retractable armrests, plus two foldaway tables; optional refreshment centre at front; toilet, washbasin and storage cabinets at rear. Other layouts optional. Airstair passenger door at front on port side. Baggage compartment aft of main cabin, with external access via port-side door aft of wing. Two-piece birdproof electrically heated wraparound windscreen.
SYSTEMS: Cabin pressurised to 0.69 bar (10.0 lb/sq in), and heated by engine bleed air; cooled by a Freon-cycle system. Hydraulic system (206.7 bars; 3,000 lb/sq in) for actuation of leading-edge slats, airbrake/lift dumpers, and landing gear extension/retraction. Two 300A engine driven starter/generators and static inverters. Redundant frequency-wild alternators provide power for windscreen heating.

Swearingen SJ30 business jet on its first flight on 13 February 1991

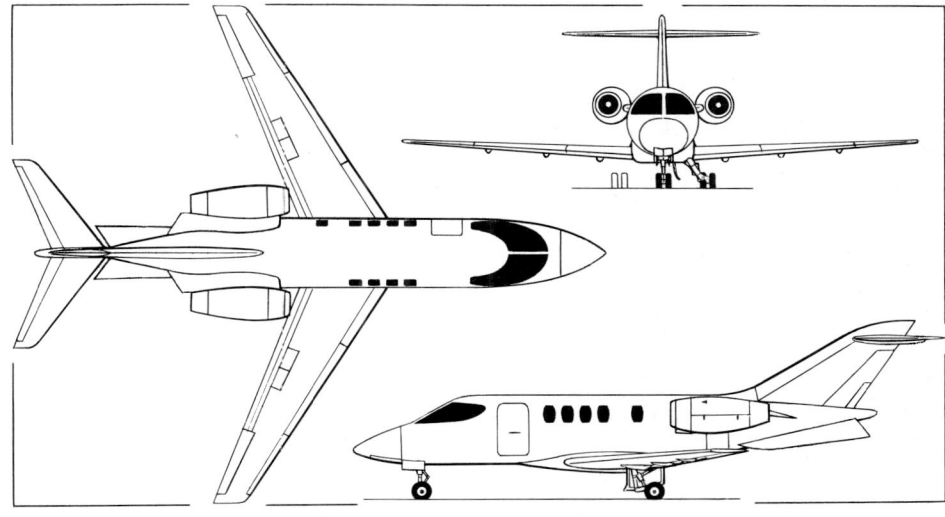

Swearingen SJ30 business jet *(Pilot Press)*

AVIONICS: Bendix/King Gold Crown III dual IFR avionics standard, with colour weather radar and autopilot/flight director.

DIMENSIONS, EXTERNAL:

Wing span	11.07 m (36 ft 4 in)
Wing aspect ratio	8.0
Length overall	12.90 m (42 ft 4 in)
Height overall	3.94 m (12 ft 11 in)

DIMENSIONS, INTERNAL:

Cabin: Length:	
between pressure bulkheads	4.97 m (16 ft 3½ in)
passenger section	3.41 m (11 ft 2½ in)
Max width	1.43 m (4 ft 8½ in)
Max height	1.31 m (4 ft 3½ in)
Volume	8.49 m³ (300.0 cu ft)

AREAS:

Wings, gross	15.33 m² (165.0 sq ft)

WEIGHTS AND LOADINGS:

Weight empty, equipped	2,585 kg (5,700 lb)
Fuel weight	1,519 kg (3,350 lb)
Max ramp weight	4,490 kg (9,900 lb)
Max zero-fuel weight	3,447 kg (7,600 lb)
Max T-O weight	4,468 kg (9,850 lb)
Max landing weight	4,309 kg (9,500 lb)
Max wing loading	291.5 kg/m² (59.7 lb/sq ft)
Max power loading	278.9 kg/kN (2.74 lb/lb st)

PERFORMANCE (estimated, at max T-O weight except where indicated):

Max operating speed	Mach 0.82 (470 knots; 871 km/h; 541 mph)
Max cruising speed	445 knots (824 km/h; 512 mph)
Long-range cruising speed	413 knots (765 km/h; 475 mph)
Stalling speed at max landing weight	80 knots (149 km/h; 93 mph)
Max rate of climb at S/L	1,195 m (3,920 ft)/min
Max operating altitude	12,500 m (41,000 ft)
FAA T-O balanced field length	1,015 m (3,330 ft)
FAA landing distance	762 m (2,500 ft)

Range at Mach 0.72 (413 knots; 765 km/h; 475 mph):
 NBAA VFR reserves
  2,076 nm (3,847 km; 2,390 miles)
 NBAA IFR reserves
  1,730 nm (3,206 km; 1,992 miles)

TAYLORCRAFT

TAYLORCRAFT AIRCRAFT CORPORATION

PO Drawer 3350, 165 Scott Avenue, Suite 102, Morgantown, West Virginia 26505
Telephone: 1 (304) 291 2376
Fax: 1 (304) 292 1902
WORKS:
820 East Bald Eagle Street, Lock Haven, Pennsylvania 17745
PRESIDENT: Darus H. Zehrbach
CHIEF ENGINEER: Darrel C. Romick
GENERAL MANAGER: Lee Anne Demus

Company re-formed 1 April 1968 mainly for product support, but also manufactured Model F-19 Sportsman 100 based on pre-Second World War Taylorcraft Model B; Model F-19 replaced by F-21 in 1980, F-21A in 1983 and F-21B in 1985 (see 1989-90 *Jane's*); company bought by group of former Piper employees 9 July 1985 and moved to Lock Haven, Pennsylvania; Taylorcraft bought manufacturing rights for Edo floats early 1986; production ceased August 1986 and company filed for Chapter 11 protection late 1986.

Taylorcraft acquired by Aircraft Acquisition Corporation (see also New Technik Corporation in this section and Taylor Kits in Sport Aircraft section) in November 1989; six new models, all based on same basic airframe, announced; Taylorcraft also plans to produce new long-wing design, plus single-strut and cantilever high-wing aircraft.

TAYLORCRAFT F-22A CLASSIC 118

TYPE: Two/three-seat trainer and sporting aircraft.
PROGRAMME: Construction began 29 December 1989; rolled out mid-January 1990; in production during 1990.
DESIGN FEATURES: Similar to Taylorcraft F-21B (see 1989-90 *Jane's*), but with flaps, larger door, new exhaust, choice of tricycle or tailwheel landing gear. Two-spar wing with dual struts either side and jury struts; NACA 23012 aerofoil section; dihedral 1°.
FLYING CONTROLS: Frise wide-span ailerons; trim tab in port elevator; split flaps.
STRUCTURE: Wings have aluminium I-beam spars with stamped metal ribs and Dacron covering; steel tube fuselage, with aluminium alloy skinned underside and Dacron elsewhere; wire braced steel tube tail surfaces, with Dacron covering.
LANDING GEAR: Non-retractable tailwheel type; tricycle optional. Two side Vs and half-axles. Mainwheels fitted with 6.00-6 4-ply tyres; swivelling tailwheel has 8 in pneumatic tyre as standard. Nosewheel has 5.00-5 4-ply tyre. Dual Cleveland hydraulic toe brakes standard. Wheel fairings optional. Edo or Aqua aluminium floats and Aero M1500 or M2000 skis optional.
POWER PLANT: One 88 kW (118 hp) Textron Lycoming O-235-L2C flat-four engine, driving a Sensenich 72CK-O-50 two-blade fixed-pitch metal propeller. One fuel tank in each wing, with combined capacity of 159 litres (42 US gallons; 35 Imp gallons), of which 151 litres (40 US gallons; 33.3 Imp gallons) are usable. Oil capacity 5.7 litres (1.5 US gallons; 1.2 Imp gallons).
ACCOMMODATION: Two adjustable seats, with shoulder harness, side by side in enclosed cabin. Folding rear seat optional, to accommodate one passenger. Dual controls standard. Metal door with sliding window each side. Standard equipment includes door locks and window latches, carpeted floor and cargo tiedown straps. Baggage compartment aft of seats, standard capacity 91 kg (200 lb), and side windows. Accommodation heated and ventilated.
SYSTEMS: Electrical system powered by 12V 35A engine driven alternator, with 12V storage battery. Wiring provisions for navigation lights. Engine driven vacuum pump when optional blind-flying instrumentation installed.
AVIONICS: Standard avionics include single com tranceiver, transponder with Mode C encoder and intercom. Full blind flying instrumentation, Bendix/King and Narco IFR avionics and II Morrow Loran C optional.
EQUIPMENT: Skylight and transparent doors optional.
DIMENSIONS, EXTERNAL:
Wing span   10.99 m (36 ft 1 in)

Taylorcraft Model F-22A Classic 118 two/three-seat light aircraft

Wing chord, constant	1.60 m (5 ft 3 in)
Length overall	6.90 m (22 ft 8½ in)
Height overall	1.98 m (6 ft 6 in)
Tailplane span	3.05 m (10 ft 0 in)
Wheel track	1.98 m (6 ft 6 in)
Propeller diameter	1.83 m (6 ft 0 in)
Passenger door: Height	0.95 m (3 ft 1½ in)
Width	0.76 m (2 ft 5¾ in)
Height to sill	0.60 m (1 ft 11½ in)

DIMENSIONS, INTERNAL:

Cabin: Length	2.68 m (8 ft 9½ in)
Max width	1.01 m (3 ft 3¾ in)
Max height	1.17 m (3 ft 10¼ in)
Floor area	2.14 m² (23.0 sq ft)
Volume	2.47 m³ (87.4 cu ft)
Baggage compartment:	
Volume	1.36 m³ (48.1 cu ft)

AREAS:

Wings, gross	17.07 m² (183.71 sq ft)
Ailerons (total)	1.86 m² (20.0 sq ft)
Trailing-edge flaps (total)	3.72 m² (40.0 sq ft)
Fin	0.49 m² (5.3 sq ft)
Rudder	0.59 m² (6.3 sq ft)
Tailplane	1.21 m² (13.0 sq ft)
Elevators (total, incl tab)	0.99 m² (10.66 sq ft)

WEIGHTS AND LOADINGS:

Weight empty	494 kg (1,090 lb)
Max T-O weight: Normal	794 kg (1,750 lb)
Utility	626 kg (1,380 lb)
Max wing loading	46.48 kg/m² (9.52 lb/sq ft)
Max power loading	9.02 kg/kW (14.83 lb/hp)

PERFORMANCE (at max T-O weight except where indicated):

Never-exceed speed (VNE)	128 knots (238 km/h; 148 mph)
Max level speed	108 knots (201 km/h; 125 mph)
Max cruising speed at 2,745 m (9,000 ft)	102 knots (188 km/h; 117 mph)
Econ cruising speed at 3,810 m (12,500 ft)	95 knots (175 km/h; 109 mph)
Stalling speed: flaps up	42 knots (78 km/h; 48 mph)
flaps down	36 knots (66 km/h; 41 mph)
Max rate of climb at S/L	229 m (750 ft)/min
Service ceiling	5,485 m (18,000 ft)
T-O run	220 m (720 ft)
T-O to 15 m (50 ft)	348 m (1,140 ft)
Landing from 15 m (50 ft)	221 m (725 ft)
Landing run	149 m (487 ft)
Range, 75% power with 30 min reserves	555 nm (1,028 km; 639 miles)

g limits:

Normal category, max T-O weight	+3.8/−1.52
Utility category at 626 kg (1,380 lb) AUW	+4.4/−1.76

TAYLORCRAFT MODEL AA-23 STOL 180 and AA-23A1 RANGER

TYPE: Two/three-seat light utility aircraft.
PROGRAMME: Construction started January 1990; first flight 23 February; certificated 1990; in production 1990.
VARIANTS: **AA-23 STOL 180**: Standard utility model.

AA-23A1 Ranger: Police/patrol version; one prototype built.
DESIGN FEATURES: Basically similar to F-22A Classic. Provision for three external stores racks under each wing. Details below show differences from F-22A Classic 118:
LANDING GEAR: Fixed tailwheel or tricycle type. Edo 1800 floats, and skis, optional.
POWER PLANT: One 134 kW (180 hp) Textron Lycoming O-360 flat-four, driving a Sensenich two-blade fixed-pitch metal propeller. Standard fuel capacity as for Classic 118; two auxiliary wing tanks optional, bringing total fuel capacity to 318 litres (84 US gallons; 70 Imp gallons). Oil capacity 7.6 litres (2 US gallons; 1.67 Imp gallons).
ACCOMMODATION: Pilot and observer in Ranger, with removable seats. Kevlar ballistic armour and bullet-resistant clear doors optional.
AVIONICS: VHF and police band transceivers optional.
EQUIPMENT: Kevlar armour, underwing dispensers for riot control agents, loudspeaker system, and searchlights, optional.
DIMENSIONS, EXTERNAL:

Propeller diameter	1.93 m (6 ft 4 in)
Propeller ground clearance	0.25 m (10 in)

PERFORMANCE:

Never-exceed speed (VNE)	128 knots (238 km/h; 148 mph)
Max level speed	124 knots (230 km/h; 143 mph)
Max cruising speed	119 knots (220 km/h; 137 mph)
Max rate of climb at S/L	more than 457 m (1,500 ft)/min
Service ceiling	5,485 m (18,000 ft)
T-O run	45 m (146 ft)
T-O to 15 m (50 ft)	65 m (213 ft)

TAYLORCRAFT MODEL AA-23B AEROBAT and AA-23B1 RS

TYPE: One/two-seat sport and competition aerobatic aircraft.
PROGRAMME: First of two prototypes begun December 1989; first flight March 1990.
VARIANTS: **AA-23B Aerobat:** Standard sport version. Tailwheel landing gear only.
AA-23B1 RS: RennSport limited edition aerobatic development, featuring napa leather interior, custom seats and Bendix/King IFR avionics. Optional tailwheel or nosewheel landing gear.
DESIGN FEATURES: As for STOL 180 except semi-symmetrical wing section (NACA 230 aerofoil) and reduced span, revised cowling design with ram air cooling intake, transparent cabin doors with quick-releases, and dual wire bracing on tail.
FLYING CONTROLS: As STOL 180 except two elevator trim tabs, one servo and one anti-servo.
STRUCTURE: As STOL 180.
LANDING GEAR: Tailwheel type only in Aerobat, tailwheel or nosewheel type in RS.
POWER PLANT: One 134 kW (180 hp) Textron Lycoming O-360-A1F6 flat-four engine, driving a Hartzell or McCauley three-blade constant-speed metal propeller. Auxiliary fuel tanks not available.
ACCOMMODATION: One/two-seat, interchangeable, in Aerobat; two/three seats in RS.
AVIONICS: Bendix/King IFR package comprising dual nav/com, ADF, DME, glideslope receiver, audio panel and II Morrow 604TCA or 618 Loran C standard in RS.
PERFORMANCE:

Never-exceed speed (VNE)	160 knots (297 km/h; 185 mph)
Max level speed	156 knots (290 km/h; 180 mph)
Max cruising speed	152 knots (282 km/h; 175 mph)
Econ cruising speed	139 knots (257 km/h; 160 mph)
Max rate of climb at S/L	701 m (2,300 ft)/min
Service ceiling	5,485 m (18,000 ft)
T-O run	77 m (252 ft)
T-O to 15 m (50 ft)	107 m (350 ft)

TAYLORCRAFT AGCRAFT

Agricultural variant of STOL 180 for ultra low volume aerial application; redesigned cockpit to protect pilot; hands on throttle and stick (HOTAS) controls. Certification had been expected late 1990.

Taylorcraft Model AA-23B Aerobat clipped wing aerobatic aircraft

TCM
TELEDYNE CONTINENTAL MOTORS
PO Box 90, Mobile, Alabama 36601
Telephone: 1 (205) 438 3411
Fax: 1 (205) 438 3411 ext 179
DIRECTOR OF OEM MARKETING: Tim Archer

Company is developing a Voyager liquid-cooled engine installation for later Beechcraft Bonanzas. An equivalent programme for the Piper Navajo Chieftain is in abeyance.

Bonanza: For late-production A36 and B36TC Bonanzas; replaces standard plain and turbocharged 212.5 kW (285 hp) and 224 kW (300 hp) engines with turbocharged liquid-cooled 224 kW (300 hp) Voyager T-550 engine driving a new three-blade McCauley propeller; new front cowling; radiator and oil cooler inside engine compartment; propeller arc moved forward about 7.6 cm (3 in); first flight of proof-of-concept prototype installation in A36 Bonanza (N9127Q) Summer 1989; if an STC is obtained, TCM would offer retrofits.

TELEDYNE RYAN
TELEDYNE RYAN AERONAUTICAL
PO Box 85311, San Diego, California 92186-5311
Telephone: 1 (619) 291 7311
Fax: 1 (619) 260 5400
Telex: 910 335 1180 TDYRYN SDG

PRESIDENT: Robert A. Mitchell
VICE-PRESIDENT, ENGINEERING: Darrel L. Hirsch
VICE-PRESIDENT, MARKETING: A. C. Richards

Flight testing of manned version of Model 410 UAV completed in 1988. Details in 1990-91 *Jane's*. Unmanned version described in *Jane's Battlefield Surveillance Systems*.

THORP
THORP AERO INC
Sturgis Airport Road, PO Box 237, Sturgis, Kentucky 42459
Telephone: 1 (502) 333 5440
Fax: 1 (502) 333 5860
PRESIDENT: Clifford Rock
MARKETING MANAGER: Marcos Monteiro

Formed to manufacture T-211 light aircraft, for markets outside North America only because of US product liability laws. Distributors appointed in Argentina, Australia, Brazil, Germany, Turkey and the United Kingdom.

THORP T-211
TYPE: Two-seat light trainer.
PROGRAMME: Original T-11 Sky Scooter, designed by John Thorp, flown 1946; powered by 48.5 kW (65 hp) engine; last described in 1950-51 *Jane's*. Limited production of Thorp T-211 with more powerful engine by Adams Industries 1964 after FAA certification 20 April 1964; rights purchased by Mr Tom Kurtz, Mr Harry Gehrke and Mr Earle McGuire in 1985 for production by Thorp 211 Aircraft Company; first flight of Thorp Aero aircraft 1990; production rate planned to reach 10 per month in July 1991, rising to 20-25 per month if sales justify.
COSTS: US$47,450.
DESIGN FEATURES: Improved version with aerodynamic glassfibre cowling, glassfibre wing and tailplane tips; new electrical system; larger wheels with Cleveland brakes.
FLYING CONTROLS: Plain ailerons; all-moving tailplane; wide-span manually operated three-position trailing-edge flaps.
STRUCTURE: Light alloy semi-monocoque fuselage; wing with main spar, false spar and ribbed skin; tailplane and rudder have ribbed skins.
LANDING GEAR: Non-retractable tricycle type; oleo-pneumatic shock absorber in each leg; all three wheels size 5.00-5, mainwheels with Cleveland brakes.

Thorp T-211 side by side two-seat light aircraft

POWER PLANT: One 74.5 kW (100 hp) Continental O-200A flat-four engine, driving a Sensenich two-blade fixed-pitch propeller. Fuel cell aft of cabin, capacity 79.5 litres (21 US gallons; 17.5 Im gallons).
ACCOMMODATION: Two seats side by side beneath rearward sliding transparent canopy. Baggage compartment behind seats, capacity 36 kg (80 lb).
SYSTEMS: Electrical system supplied by 12V 20A generator and 12V 2Ah storage battery.
AVIONICS: Single nav/com; ADF; transponder with Mode C.
DIMENSIONS, EXTERNAL:

Wing span	7.62 m (25 ft 0 in)
Length overall	5.49 m (18 ft 0 in)
Height overall	1.92 m (6 ft 3½ in)
Propeller diameter	1.70 m (5 ft 7 in)

AREAS:

Wings, gross	9.75 m² (105.0 sq ft)

WEIGHTS AND LOADINGS:

Weight empty	340 kg (750 lb)
Max T-O and landing weight	576 kg (1,270 lb)
Max wing loading	59.1 kg/m² (12.1 lb/sq ft)
Max power loading	7.73 kg/kW (12.7 lb/hp)

PERFORMANCE (at max T-O weight):

Max level speed at S/L	137 knots (254 km/h; 158 mph)
Cruising speed (75% power)	104 knots (193 km/h; 120 mph)
Stalling speed, flaps down	39 knots (73 km/h; 45 mph)
Max rate of climb at S/L	228 m (750 ft)/min
Service ceiling	5,790 m (19,000 ft)
T-O run	91 m (300 ft)
Landing run	61 m (200 ft)
Range at 55% power, with max fuel and reserves	347 nm (640 km; 400 miles)

TRADEWIND
TRADEWIND TURBINES CORPORATION
PO Box 31930, 4105 Tradewind Road, Amarillo, Texas 79120
Telephone: 1 (806) 376 5203
Fax: 1 (806) 376 9725
PRINCIPAL: Joe C. Boyd
CHIEF EXECUTIVE OFFICER: J. A. Whittenburg III

TRADEWIND PROP-JET BONANZA
TYPE: Turbine powered Beechcraft A36 Bonanza.
PROGRAMME: Allison Gas Turbine Division in conjunction with Soloy Corporation (which see) obtained STC for re-engining of Beechcraft A36 Bonanza in 1986; initially known as Allison Prop-Jet Bonanza; STC sold to Tradewind Turbines October 1989.
CUSTOMERS: Allison, DuPage Aviation and Tradewind had completed 24 conversions by April 1991. Production rate six a year.
COSTS: Fittings, engine and installation cost $352,932 (1991).
DESIGN FEATURES: Conversion available for post-1979 A36 and A36TC, but not for F33 Bonanzas; Teledyne Continental 212.5 kW (285 hp) piston engine replaced by Allison 250-B17D turboprop; two support spars added to lower fuselage and engine installed 0.53 m (1 ft 9 in) further forward to maintain centre of gravity; vacated space holds 54 kg (120 lb) of baggage. Other features include 24V electrical system with 150A starter/generator; dual actuators for elevator trim tabs; audible VMO overspeed warning; Goodrich propeller de-icing.
POWER PLANT: One 313 kW (420 shp) Allison 250-B17D turboprop driving a metal three-blade Hartzell feathering and reversing propeller running at 2,030 rpm. Total 424 litres (112 US gallons; 93 Imp gallons) fuel in two tanks in wings and two Osborne wingtip tanks.
DIMENSIONS, EXTERNAL:
Wing span, between tips of winglets 10.20 m (33 ft 5½ in)

Tradewind Prop-Jet Bonanza conversion of the Beechcraft Model A36 Bonanza with wingtip tanks and wing-mounted weather radar

Length overall	8.89 m (29 ft 2 in)
Height overall	2.62 m (8 ft 7 in)
Tailplane span	3.71 m (12 ft 2 in)
Wheel track	2.92 m (9 ft 7 in)
Propeller diameter	2.29 m (7 ft 6 in)
Propeller ground clearance	0.18 m (7¼ in)

WEIGHTS AND LOADINGS:

Weight empty	1,089 kg (2,400 lb)
Max ramp weight	1,746 kg (3,849 lb)
Max T-O weight	1,739 kg (3,833 lb)
Max landing weight	1,656 kg (3,650 lb)
Max power loading	5.56 kg/kW (9.13 lb/shp)

PERFORMANCE:

Max level speed	210 knots (389 km/h; 242 mph)
Cruising speed:	
at 4,575 m (15,000 ft)	200 knots (370 km/h; 230 mph)
at 6,100 m (20,000 ft)	195 knots (361 km/h; 224 mph)
Stalling speed, flight idle power:	
flaps up	65 knots (120 km/h; 75 mph)
flaps down	57 knots (106 km/h; 66 mph)
Max rate of climb at S/L, at max T-O weight	579 m (1,900 ft)/min
Service ceiling	above 7,620 m (25,000 ft)
T-O run, 15° flap	177 m (580 ft)

T-O to 15 m (50 ft), 15° flap	244 m (800 ft)	Range, with max fuel, allowances for start, taxi, T-O,		at 4,575 m (15,000 ft)	985 nm (1,825 km; 1,134 miles)
Landing from 15 m (50 ft), 30° flap	160 m (525 ft)	climb and 45 min reserves at max cruising power:		at 6,100 m (20,000 ft)	
Landing run, 30° flap with reverse pitch	99 m (325 ft)	at 3,050 m (10,000 ft)	820 nm (1,520 km; 944 miles)		1,065 nm (1,974 km; 1,226 miles)

TRIDAIR

TRIDAIR HELICOPTERS INC
3000 Airway Avenue, Costa Mesa, California 92626
Telephone: 1 (714) 540 3000
Fax: 1 (714) 540 1042
PRESIDENT: Douglas Daigle

TRIDAIR MODEL 206L-3ST GEMINI ST

TYPE: Twin-engined conversion of Bell 206L-3 LongRanger.
PROGRAMME: Announced at Helicopter Association International (HAI) show 1989; first flight of prototype N700TH 16 January 1991; two more prototype/demonstrators to be completed in 1991; final cowling profile decided April 1991; certification expected March 1992.
CUSTOMERS: Tridair ordered 25 new airframes from Bell Helicopter Canada for delivery at rate of two per month from November 1990; 18 delivery positions reserved by February 1991; 50 conversions expected by end of 1993; approved installation centres being established.
COSTS: Modification kit $575,000; new converted aircraft $1.4 million.
DESIGN FEATURES: Replaces single 485 kW (650 shp) Allison 250-C30P with two 335 kW (450 shp) 250-C20Rs with max continuous rating of 276 kW (370 shp) each; fuel capacity increased to 416 litres (110 US gallons; 91.6 Imp gallons); Soloy Dual Pac combining gearbox with individual freewheels concentrates engine outputs into original single input drive to transmission; transmission rating 325 kW (435 shp); will be certificated to fly single-engined in flight phases.

Tridair Helicopters Model 206L-3ST Gemini ST prototype without new top fairing

WEIGHTS AND LOADINGS:

Weight empty	1,175 kg (2,590 lb)	Service ceiling	6,100 m (20,000 ft)
Max fuel weight	340 kg (750 lb)	Hovering ceiling: IGE	4,815 m (15,800 ft)
Max external load	907 kg (2,000 lb)	OGE	1,675 m (5,500 ft)
Max T-O weight (internal load)	1,928 kg (4,250 lb)	Max range, with max payload and max internal fuel	
			347 nm (643 km; 400 miles)

PERFORMANCE (estimated):
Never-exceed speed (VNE)
130 knots (241 km/h; 150 mph)
Max cruising speed   117 knots (217 km/h; 135 mph)
Max rate of climb at S/L   472 m (1,550 ft)/min

TURBOTECH

TURBOTECH INC
2215 Parrott Way, Kelso, Washington 98666
Telephone: 1 (206) 423 7699
Fax: 1 (206) 423 7695
PRESIDENT: Nancy J. Soukup

Turbotech installs more powerful and more reliable engines in various aircraft; company holds more than 30 Supplemental Type Certificates for multiple conversions; also undertakes one-off engine changes and add-on turbo packages with FAA certification; recent examples include Grumman Widgeon fitted with 261 kW (350 hp) Textron Lycoming O-540 engines.

Supplemental Type Certificates obtained for two Cessna 185 modifications in 1982 to provide full performance to service ceilings; these covered alternatively installation of 261 kW (350 hp) Textron Lycoming TIO-540-J2BD or addition of a Garrett turbocharger to 224 kW (300 hp) Continental IO-520-D fitted in standard Cessna 185, which gave full performance to ceilings of 7,620 m (25,000 ft) and 7,315 m (24,000 ft) respectively; Cessna 206 also approved with TIO-540-J2BD turbocharged engine. Gross weight increased by 93 kg (250 lb) with installation of wingtip tanks, approved July 1983.

Other developments include modification to Grumman AA-5B Tiger with 134 kW (180 hp) Textron Lycoming O-360-A4K; 172 kW (230 hp) Teledyne Continental O-470 installed in Stinson 108. Current feasibility studies for Cessna 180, 182, 207 and 210 engine conversions; turbocharged Textron Lycoming C-540-L3C5D, with intercooler, automatic waste gate and magneto pressurisation, being installed in Cessna 182RG; latter also to be available for TR 182.

Turbotech Cessna 185 conversion

Turbotech Grumman Widgeon with 261 kW (350 hp) Textron Lycoming O-540 engines

TWIN COMMANDER

TWIN COMMANDER AIRCRAFT CORPORATION
19003 59th Drive NE, Arlington, Washington 98223
Telephone: 1 (206) 435 9797

Fax: 1 (206) 435 1112
PRESIDENT: Dan Montgomery

Purchased product support and manufacturing rights to former Commander series of piston and turboprop twins from Gulfstream Aerospace, December 1989 (production had been suspended since 1984); Twin Commander initially manufacturing and distributing spares, but negotiating with groups outside USA in 1990 to manufacture new aircraft.

USAF
UNITED STATES AIR FORCE SYSTEMS COMMAND

Aeronautical Systems Division, Wright-Patterson AFB, Dayton, Ohio 45433-6503
Telephone: 1 (513) 255 3334
PUBLIC AFFAIRS OFFICER: Capt Jamie S. Scearse
ATF PROGRAMME DIRECTOR: Col James A. Fain Jr

Merges with Logistics Command from 1 October 1991; becomes Materiel Command 1 July 1992.

ADVANCED TACTICAL FIGHTER (ATF)
US Air Force designation: F-22

Lockheed/Boeing/General Dynamics F-22 selected in place of the Northrop/McDonnell Douglas YF-23 as the US Air Force Advanced Tactical Fighter (ATF) on 23 April 1991. This launched a 48 month engineering and manufacturing development (EMD) phase to include production of 11 more YF-22s. Pratt & Whitney YF119 engine selected over GE YF120. First production contract expected 1997 with production of up to 648 F-22s to continue until 2014. Flyaway price (fully equipped aircraft excluding research and development, spares, training and support equipment) to be $61 million (1992).

For further details, see F-22 under Lockheed in this section.

ADVANCED TACTICAL AIRCRAFT (ATA)

USAF plans adoption of Navy's A-X (which see) as replacement for General Dynamics F-111, Lockheed F-117 and McDonnell Douglas F-15E. ATA joint concept definition and demonstration/validation phase to begin in 1994; full-scale development in 2000.

JOINT PRIMARY AIRCRAFT TRAINING SYSTEM (JPATS)

Replacement programme for USAF Cessna T-37s and USN Beech T-34Cs; selection in 1994; production to begin 1996; first of 495 aircraft due for delivery to USAF in 1998; 347 to USN from 2005 (carrier compatibility not required). Official contenders: Aermacchi/Lockheed MB-339, Agusta/Grumman S.211, FMA/LTV Pampa 2000, Pilatus/Beech PC-9 and DASA (MBB)/Rockwell Fan Ranger; interest also expressed for Enaer Turbo Pillán, Promavia ATTA 3000, Valmet Redigo, Shorts Tucano, Embraer Tucano, Soko Super Galeb, and Jaffe SA-32T Turbo Trainer.

ENHANCED FLIGHT SCREENER (EFS)

USAF programme for modern aerobatic aircraft, with side by side seats, to replace Cessna T-41A in student pilot screening and contract flight instruction roles; up to 125 required, at unit cost of around $200,000, as part of SUPT (specialised undergraduate pilot training) programme. Candidates include Mooney EFS (which see), Meyers Aviation 145, Grob 115T and several other aircraft including the now-suspended LoPresti Piper SwiftThunder (SwiftFury derivative).

C-27

STOL transport requirement; Chrysler CTAS (see this section) selected August 1990 to provide C-27 based on Alenia G222.

STRATEGIC RECONNAISSANCE AIRCRAFT

Follow-on to the Lockheed SR-71, reportedly being developed by same firm as project Aurora (*Jane's* 1990-91), is understood to have been cancelled by the US Congress in July 1990. However, NASA's Langley Research Center was reported in April 1991 to be developing a concept for a hypersonic (Mach 5+) reconnaissance aircraft "larger than the SR-71". Three SR-71s (including one two-seater) were allocated to NASA in 1990.

ADVANCED SURVEILLANCE AND TRACKING TECHNOLOGY/AIRBORNE RADAR DEMONSTRATOR (ASTT/ARD)

Part of AFSC's Electronics Systems Division programme to develop new AWACS aircraft for use in 21st century; wind tunnel test conducted late 1990; flight test demonstrator not expected before 1996. Current proposals envisage Boeing 747-200 platform aircraft, with GE Aerospace advanced L-band phased-array radar installed in huge E-Systems dorsal radome (40 × 14.5 × 3.8 m; 131.2 × 47.6 × 12.5 ft), called a 'synergistic plandome', supported by multiple-strut structure above fuselage.

GENERAL DYNAMICS F-111G

Strategic Air Command FB-111As being converted to dual nuclear/conventional role as F-111Gs, for transfer to Tactical Air Command following INF treaty of 1988; Short Range Attack Missile (SRAM) installation deleted; conventional weapon release system added, with controls on pilot's stick. Other features include Have Quick UHF radio, attachments for g-suits and structural changes for 6.5 g manoeuvres. First two conversions completed early 1989; programme to be completed by 1994 at 12 aircraft a year. FB-111As transferred to TAC between 1 June 1990 and early 1992 to serve primarily in training role with 27th TFW at Cannon AFB, New Mexico, replacing F-111Ds, following disbandment of SAC 509th (30 September 1990) and 380th Bomb Wings. USAF has 61 FB-111A/F-111Gs, including two for trials; 29 to TAC in 1990.

Other F-111 programmes detailed under Grumman and Rockwell headings.

F-111G (68-0286) following conversion from FB-111A, but still temporarily with SAC's 380th BW in 1989, pending transfer to TAC *(Paul Jackson)*

US ARMY
UNITED STATES ARMY AVIATION SYSTEMS COMMAND

400 Goodfellow Boulevard, St Louis, Missouri 63120-1798
Telephone: 1 (314) 263 1599

NEW TRAINING HELICOPTER

The US Army is leasing 180 three-seat (instructor and two pupils) turbine-powered helicopters with an option on 100 more. RFP was expected in August 1991. Candidate types were Schweizer 330, Enstrom 480, Bell/Imagineering/Global Helicopters 206 or similar, Aerospatiale AS 350B AStar, Rogerson Hiller UH-12ET and McDonnell Douglas MD 500.

USN
UNITED STATES NAVAL AIR SYSTEMS COMMAND

Jefferson Plaza 1, Washington, DC 20361-0001
Telephone: 1 (262) 693 2260
NAVAIR has over 46,000 military and civilian employees and an annual budget of $13,000 million.

A-X

Following January 1991 cancellation of General Dynamics/McDonnell Douglas A-12 naval attack aircraft, Tentative Operational Requirement issued for substitute aircraft to replace Grumman A-6 aboard USN carriers. Contenders may include variants of Lockheed F-22 and Northrop YF-23, derivative of A-12, and new designs. Demonstration/validation phase to begin 1994 followed by full-scale development in 1996. Between 400 and 500 A-Xs required.

NAVAL ADVANCED TACTICAL FIGHTER (NATF)

Plans for a naval adaptation of the winning contender for the USAF ATF competition were terminated in early 1991 by removal of funding until after 1997. IOC for a low-observables replacement for the Grumman F-14 Tomcat planned in 2005-2008, requiring concept definition for a new NATF to begin around 1999.

VALSAN
VALSAN PARTNERS

99 Washington Street, Norwalk, Connecticut 06854
Telephone: 1 (203) 866 6051
Fax: 1 (203) 855 0362
Telex: 6714726 DALAU UW
PRESIDENT: Robert E. Wagenfeld
VICE-PRESIDENT, MARKETING: Walter H. Johnson

VALSAN 727RE 'QUIET 727'

TYPE: Re-engined/quietened Boeing 727-100 and -200.
PROGRAMME: Prototype conversion of 727 (Sterling Airways 727-200 OY-SAS), to meet FAR Pt 36 Stage 3 and ICAO Annex 16 Chapter 3 noise limits, completed June 1988; first flight 12 July 1988; Supplemental Type Certificate awarded October 1988; certification of first customer 727-100 conversion July 1990; additional Winglet System conversions to be certificated in 1991.
CUSTOMERS: Firm orders for 52 and options for 138 reported by January 1991; 15 in service January 1991. Customers include Federal Express.
COSTS: Winglets $750,000 per set.

Valsan Partners 'Quiet 727' conversion of the Boeing 727-200 for Federal Express

DESIGN FEATURES: Modification work by Rockwell International, Palmdale and Sterling Airways; work includes acoustic treatment of centre engine and removal of thrust reverser, and replacement of outer engines by JT8D-217Cs; empty weight increased by 1,542 kg (3,400 lb), zero-fuel weight increased by 1,361 kg (3,000 lb), and max landing weight reduced by 907 kg (2,000 lb); performance improvements include 24 per cent higher

max S/L climb rate, 27 per cent shorter T-O distances and 300 nm (556 km; 345 miles) longer range; max range of executive configuration expected to be greater than 4,000 nm (7,412 km; 4,606 miles).

Flight testing of 727 with winglets completed November 1990; demonstrated specific fuel consumption reduction of at least five per cent and could be further improved when wing and flap testing completed.

Combined with re-engining, drag reduction modifications claimed to reduce fuel burn by 16-18 per cent. 727-100 winglets to be certificated January 1991 and -200 winglets March 1991.

OPERATIONAL NOISE LEVELS (727-200RE):

T-O	95.6 EPNdB
Approach	98.3 EPNdB
Sideline	97.4 EPNdB

VARDAX

VARDAX CORPORATION

3025 Eldridge Avenue, Bellingham, Washington 98225
Telephone: 1 (206) 671 7817
Fax: 1 (206) 671 7820
PRESIDENT: Dara Wilder

VARDAX VAZAR DASH 3

DHC-3 Otter re-engined with 559 kW (750 shp) P&WC PT6A-135 turboprop, giving improved performance and increasing useful load by 331 kg (730 lb); prototype (N9707B) completed 1986; orders for 10 conversions received by January 1990 and five completed; conversion takes six weeks; can operate on wheels skis or choice of Edo 7170 or 7490 amphibious floats. Details of standard DHC-3 in 1967-68 *Jane's* and of Vazar Dash 3 changes in 1990-91 *Jane's*.

DIMENSIONS, EXTERNAL: As for standard DHC-3, except:
Length overall	14.02 m (46 ft 0 in)

WEIGHTS AND LOADINGS:
Weight empty	3,770 kg (8,201 lb)
Max T-O weight	3,630 kg (8,000 lb)
Max power loading	6.49 kg/kW (10.67 lb/shp)

PERFORMANCE (at max T-O weight):
Max cruising speed at 3,050 m (10,000 ft)	
	144 knots (267 km/h; 166 mph)

Prototype Vardax Vazar Dash 3 turboprop conversion of a DHC-3 Otter STOL transport

Stalling speed: flaps up	63 knots (117 km/h; 73 mph)	T-O to 15 m (50 ft)	278 m (910 ft)
flaps down	50 knots (93 km/h; 58 mph)	Landing from 15 m (50 ft)	183 m (600 ft)
Max rate of climb at S/L	365 m (1,200 ft)/min	Landing run	95 m (310 ft)
Service ceiling, as tested by July 1988	4,875 m (16,000 ft)	Endurance	5 h 18 min
T-O run	171 m (560 ft)	Range	649 nm (1,203 km; 748 miles)

VOLPAR

VOLPAR AIRCRAFT CORPORATION

7701 Woodley Avenue, Van Nuys, California 91406
Telephone: 1 (818) 994 5023
Fax: 1 (818) 988 8324
Telex: 651482 VOLPAR B VAN
PRESIDENT: Andy Savva
VICE-PRESIDENTS:
Robert C. Dunigan (Maintenance and Engineering)
Joel Fogelson (Marketing)
Frank V. Nixon (Development)

Volpar Aircraft Corporation acquired by Gaylord Holdings of Switzerland in early 1990.

VOLPAR FALCON PW300-F20

Announced at Paris Air Show 1989; replaces GE CF700 engines on Falcon 20s with 23.24 kN (5,225 lb st) P&WC PW305 turbofans with variable inlet guide vanes for high altitude performance; Rohr Industries thrust reversers standard. Modified Falcons will meet FAR Pt 36 Stage 3 noise requirements and cruise 50 knots (93 km/h; 58 mph) faster at 12,500 m (41,000 ft); estimated max range with NBAA IFR reserves 2,600 nm (4,813 km; 2,994 miles). Baseline testing with CF700-2D2 engines completed Van Nuys August 1990; prototype then grounded for PW305 installation (first flight 12 February 1991). To be marketed by Advanced Falcon Aircraft Partnership of Greenwich, Connecticut. Cost $3.8 million, including thrust reversers and new paint.

VOLPAR T-33V

T-33V is upgraded and re-engined Lockheed T-33, being developed during 1990 in collaboration with William F. Chana Associates; Allison J33 would be replaced by P&WC PW300 turbofan, flat rated at 21.13 kN (4,750 lb st); aircraft weight reduced by 499 kg (1,000 lb) and fuel consumption reduced by up to two-thirds.

Artist's impression of the Volpar Falcon PW300-F20

Volpar estimates market for 250 modified T-33Vs and will also supply modification kits; about 1,000 T-33s thought to be in service worldwide.

WIPAIRE

WIPAIRE INC

South End Doane Trail, Inver Grove Heights, Minnesota 55075
Telephone: 1 (612) 451 1205
Fax: 1 (612) 451 1786
Telex: 297051
PRESIDENT: Robert Wiplinger

WIPAIRE BEAVER CONVERSIONS

Wipaire, well known for Wipline floats, offers conversion of customers' DHC-2 Beavers and produces Super Beaver rebuilds from surplus military DHC-2 or L-20 airframes.

Modifications to customers' aircraft, applied together or individually, include rearward extension of cabin by 0.71 m (2 ft 4 in), fitting a 0.85 m × 0.27 m (33½ in × 10½ in) baggage door, two extra Panaview windows each side, tinted forward skylight windows, articulating Cessna or Piper pilot's and co-pilot's seats with inertia reel shoulder harness, forward- or rearward-facing three-seat centre bench with underseat stowage, 3M cabin soundproofing, and hold-open door catches. Wipaire also offers electrically actuated flaps, customised IFR instrument panel, Digiflow fuel metering system, 3M Stormscope, S-Tech Series 50 autopilot with electric trim, altitude hold and flight director, Jasco alternator replacing generator, new battery location, Cessna electric fuel pump/primer, and Hartzell three-blade constant-speed propeller.

Super Beaver represents ex-military airframe completely dismantled, inspected and refurbished; new or overhauled 335.5 kW (450 hp) P&W R-985 engine and accessories; new oil, fuel tanks and instruments; also custom interiors and external paint; floats available. Modification also applicable to DHC Turbo Beavers. Wipline acquired ex-British Army Beavers.

WIPAIRE AMPHIBIOUS AZTEC

FAA certification obtained for Piper PA-23-250 Aztec with Wipline 6000A amphibious floats; airframe and wing spar strengthened for float attachment and additional door on port side. Amphibious Aztec has 680 kg (1,500 lb) useful load and cruising speed of 122-126 knots (225-233 km/h;

140-145 mph); future conversion may include more powerful 223.7 kW (300 hp) engines in place of standard 186.4 kW (250 hp) Textron Lycoming O-540-A1D5s.

Wipaire Super Beaver amphibian, converted from a former Army Air Corps aircraft *(Ian Burnett)*

WTA

WTA INC
Lubbock International Airport, Route 3, Box 48A, Lubbock, Texas 79401
Telephone: 1 (806) 765 7242
Telex: 744439

VICE-PRESIDENT: Larry T. Neal

WTA acquired marketing rights to Piper PA-18-150 Super Cub and PA-36 Brave; WTA delivered 250 Super Cubs before Piper itself put it back into production; WTA developed New Brave agricultural aircraft with 279 kW (375 hp) or 298 kW (400 hp) engines (see 1989-90 *Jane's*).

YUGOSLAVIA

EMIND

A company new to aircraft design, EMIND, based at Erevik, is to be responsible for producing prototypes of two agricultural aircraft. Neither appears to have met its target first flight date.

Development of agricultural spraying aircraft has been assigned the comparatively high priority of third in the government's 'Strategy of technological development of Yugoslavia to 2000', studies having indicated that local requirements can be met by two types of aircraft with payloads of 900 kg (1,984 lb) and 1,900 kg (4,189 lb). Early in 1990, construction was put in hand of prototypes of each aircraft. These designs were winners of an official competition, to which the UTVA-75AG11 was unsuccessfully tendered.

Funding of $6.3 million for two prototypes of each type frozen by the Yugoslav government; external finance being sought.

Both designed by Professor Dragoljub Stanojević, DSc, these are of modular concept, and share a common cockpit, instrumentation, equipment, power plant (with ducted propellers), landing gear and wing construction. Unusually for agricultural aircraft, both seat the pilot well forward, to provide a good view and eliminate chemical and exhaust fume penetration into the cockpit.

EMIND PPA-1

The smaller of the two designs is a twin-boom pusher aircraft, also available as a light transport with a cabin in place of the chemical hopper. The prototype was due to have flown before the end of July 1990, and a pre-production example before 30 September 1991.
POWER PLANT: One Turbomeca TP-319 turboprop, derated to 310 kW (416 shp), driving a ducted propeller.
DIMENSIONS, EXTERNAL:

Wing span	12.28 m (40 ft 3½ in)
Wing chord, constant	1.83 m (6 ft 0 in)
Wing aspect ratio	6.7

AREAS:

Wings, gross	22.50 m² (349.8 sq ft)

WEIGHTS AND LOADINGS:

Payload	900 kg (1,984 lb)
Max T-O weight	2,100 kg (4,630 lb)
Max wing loading	93.33 kg/m² (19.12 lb/sq ft)
Max power loading	6.77 kg/kW (11-13 lb/shp)

PERFORMANCE:

Never-exceed speed (V$_{NE}$)	151 knots (280 km/h; 174 mph)
Max cruising speed	130 knots (240 km/h; 149 mph)
Normal operating speed	65-97 knots (120-180 km/h; 75-112 mph)

Min flying speed, flaps down:

at 1,200 kg (2,646 lb)	37 knots (68 km/h; 42 mph)
at 1,875 kg (4,134 lb)	46 knots (85 km/h; 53 mph)

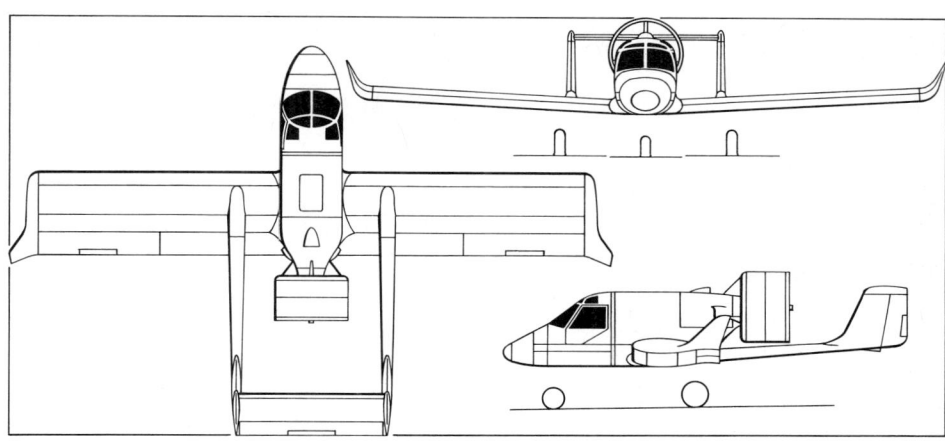

EMIND PPA-1 single-engined agricultural aircraft *(Jane's/Mike Keep)*

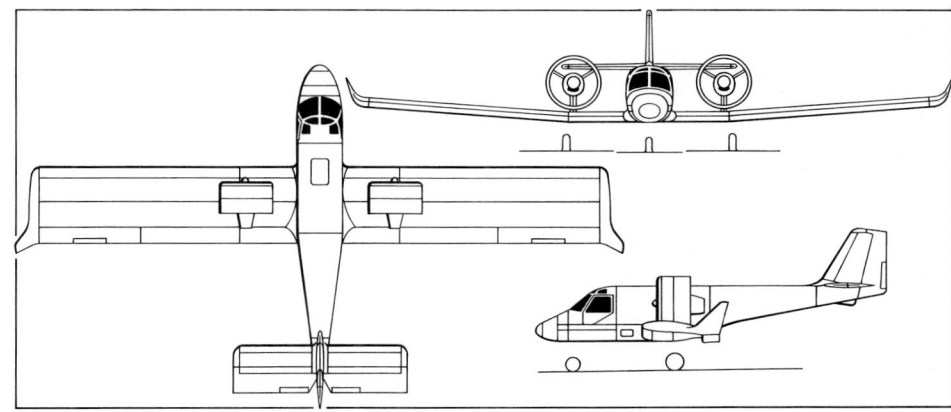

EMIND PPA-2 twin-engined agricultural aircraft *(Jane's/Mike Keep)*

EMIND PPA-2

The larger of Professor Stanojević's designs is a twin-engined, tricycle landing gear aircraft with a conventional fuselage and tail surfaces. A stretched version with a passenger cabin is projected. Completion of a PPA-2 prototype was due prior to 31 July 1990, and of the pre-production aircraft before 31 December 1991.
POWER PLANT: Two Turbomeca TP-319 turboprops, each derated to 310 kW (416 shp), driving ducted propellers.

DIMENSIONS, EXTERNAL:

Wing span	16.96 m (55 ft 7¾ in)
Wing chord, constant	1.83 m (6 ft 0 in)
Wing aspect ratio	9.3

AREAS:

Wings, gross	31.04 m² (334.1 sq ft)

WEIGHTS AND LOADINGS:

Payload	1,900 kg (4,189 lb)
Max T-O weight	4,000 kg (8,818 lb)

Scale models of the EMIND PPA-1 (left) and PPA-2 agricultural aircraft designed by Professor Dragoljub Stanojević *(Aerosvet)*

Max wing loading	128.86 kg/m² (26.39 lb/sq ft)	Max cruising speed	135 knots (250 km/h; 155 mph)	Min flying speed, flaps down:		
Max power loading	6.45 kg/kW (10.60 lb/shp)	Normal operating speed		at 2,100 kg (4,630 lb)	42 knots (78 km/h; 48 mph)	
PERFORMANCE:			76-103 knots (140-190 km/h; 86-118 mph)	at 3,525 kg (7,771 lb)	55 knots (102 km/h; 63 mph)	
Never-exceed speed (VNE)						
	167 knots (310 km/h; 193 mph)					

SOKO
VAZDUHOPLOVNA INDUSTRIJA SOKO
88 000 Mostar
Telephone: 38 (88) 22-121, 33-831, 35-244, 35-541, 37-943, 55-120
Telex: 46-180 YU SOKOMO
GENERAL MANAGER: Dipl OecN. Djurica
ASSISTANT GENERAL MANAGER: Dipl Ing B. Rogonja
DIRECTOR, COMMERCIAL: Dipl Oecc Neco Milović
DIRECTOR, ENGINEERING AND DEVELOPMENT:
Dipl Ing F. Dizdarević

Founded in 1951, this company manufactures aircraft of its own design and is participating, with Romania, in developing and producing the Orao/IAR-93 strike aircraft described under the SOKO/IAv Craiova heading in the International section. SOKO privatised March 1991; 3,000 of its 3,500 workers hold 20 per cent of the $110 million capital. Subcontract work for Aerospatiale, Boeing, McDonnell Douglas, DASA, IAI, Alenia, deHavilland Canada, Sogerma and Tupolev; US order backlog $203 million in May 1991.

Licence production continues of the Aerospatiale SA 342L and 342L₁ Gazelle. A Yugoslav source reports that SOKO is also planning a new small helicopter based on the Gazelle's dynamic system.

SOKO G-4 Super Galeb of the Myanmar Air Force

SOKO G-4 SUPER GALEB (SEAGULL)

This light attack and training aircraft was designed to replace the earlier G2-A Galeb and Lockheed T-33 in basic and advanced training units of the Yugoslav Air Force. The two Super Galeb prototypes (23004 and 23005) flew on 17 July 1978 and 18 December 1979, followed by the first of a small batch of pre-production aircraft (23601) on 17 December 1980. The production Super Galeb, for which the Yugoslav Air Force placed a substantial order, differs from the pre-production model in having an all-moving tailplane with considerable anhedral, instead of the original conventional horizontal tail surfaces with elevators and no anhedral. Super Galebs are operated by the Vojno-Vazduhoplovna Akademija (Air Force Academy) at Zemunite/Zadar for first 60 hours of pilot training syllabus up to streaming; an advanced training school at Pula providing further 120 hours for interceptor student stream; adanced training school at Titograd with 120 hour alternative ground attack course; and first public display 20 May 1990) the Academy's Letece Zvezde (Flying Stars) aerobatic team. Deliveries totalled at least 136 for local use by 1989, whilst a further six were supplied to Myanmar (Burma) from late 1990. Existing G-4s are to be upgraded with provision for AAMs (probably AA-8 and AA-11) and ASMs (probably AS-7 and AS-9), improved electronic equipment and better power plant de-icing.

Two prototypes were due to fly in early 1991 of the developed **G-4M**, featuring new avionics and nav/attack systems, but retaining (after consideration of a more modern turbofan) the Viper power plant. Addition is planned of a gyro platform, IFF, flight data recorder, an indigenous electronic sight, HUD, multi-function displays and wingtip missile rails. Weapon carrying capability will increase from 1,280 kg (2,822 lb) to 1,680 kg (3,704 lb) normal, or 1,800 kg (3,968 lb) overload. Production deliveries are due in 1992. The G-4M is intended to extend

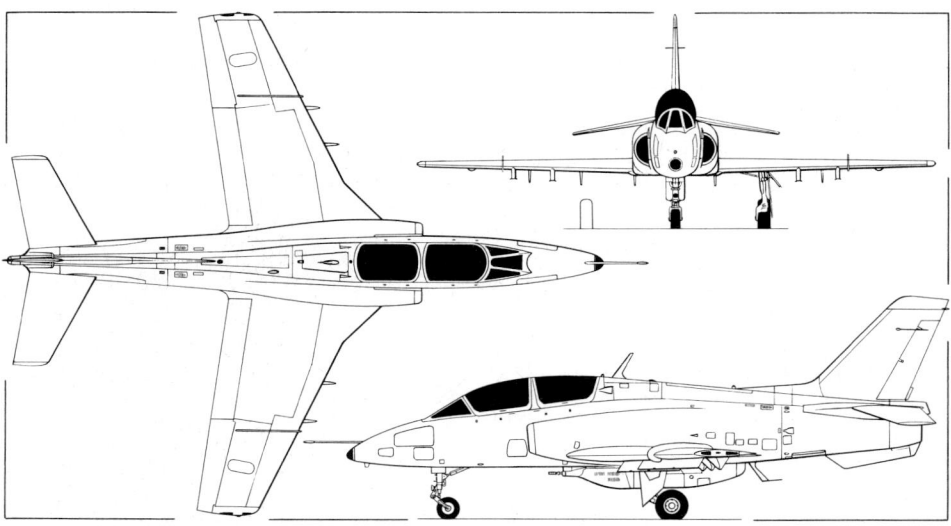

SOKO G-4 Super Galeb (Rolls-Royce Viper Mk 632 turbojet) *(Pilot Press)*

the training syllabus into areas currently covered by two-seat versions of front-line aircraft, and also to provide an improved anti-helicopter capability in wartime.
TYPE: Two-seat basic trainer and light attack aircraft.
WINGS: Cantilever low-wing monoplane. No dihedral. Sweepback at quarter-chord 22°; leading-edge sweep increased near wingroots. One-piece two-spar all-metal structure, with integrally machined skin panels inboard and chemically milled skin towards wingtips. Shallow boundary layer fence on upper surface of each wing, forward of inboard end of aileron. Wings attached to fuselage at six points. Entire trailing-edge made up of conventional all-metal sealed ailerons and flaps. Ailerons

actuated by hydraulic servo jacks, with artificial feel, flaps by electrically controlled hydraulic actuators. No slats or tabs.
FUSELAGE: All-metal semi-monocoque structure, with air intake trunk blended into each side. Rear portion, complete with tail surfaces, detachable for access to engine. Door type airbrake under rear fuselage. Landing light in nose, forward of large equipment bay. Some composite materials in secondary structure of G-4M.
TAIL UNIT: Conventional cantilever all-metal structure, with all surfaces sweptback. All-moving horizontal surfaces have 10° anhedral, and are actuated by hydraulic servo jacks, with artificial feel. Mechanically actuated rudder.

Dorsal fin. Ground adjustable tab on rudder. Two ventral strakes under jetpipe.

LANDING GEAR: Prva Petaletka hydraulically retractable tricycle type, with single wheel on each unit. Nosewheel retracts forward, main units inward into wings. Oleo-pneumatic shock absorber in each leg. Hydraulically steerable nose unit optional (not on current aircraft). Trailing link main units. Mainwheels fitted with Dunlop tyres size 615 × 225-10, pressure 4.4 bars (64 lb/sq in), and hydraulic brakes. Nosewheel has Dunlop tyre size 6.50-5.5 TC, pressure 3.0 bars (43.5 lb/sq in). Brake parachute container at base of rudder. Provision for attaching two assisted take-off rockets under centre-fuselage.

POWER PLANT: One Rolls-Royce Viper Mk 632 turbojet, rated at 17.8 kN (4,000 lb st). Fuel in three flexible bag tanks in centre-fuselage and an integral tank between the spars of each inner wing. Total internal fuel capacity 1,720 litres (454.4 US gallons; 378.5 Imp gallons). Provision for two underwing auxiliary tanks, on inboard pylons, total capacity 625 litres (165.1 US gallons; 137.5 Imp gallons). Max fuel capacity 2,345 litres (619.5 US gallons; 516 Imp gallons). Gravity refuelling system standard.

ACCOMMODATION: Crew of two in tandem on Martin-Baker zero/zero Mk J10 ejection seats (zero height/90 knot Mk J8 optional, but not on current aircraft), with ejection through the individual sideways hinged (to starboard) canopy over each seat. Rear seat raised by 25 cm (10 in) to give occupant forward view over front seat occupant. Cockpit pressurised and air-conditioned.

SYSTEMS: Engine compressor bleed air used for pressurisation, air-conditioning, anti-g suit and windscreen anti-icing systems, and to pressurise fuel tanks. Dual hydraulic systems, pressure 210 bars (3,045 lb/sq in), for flying control servos, flap and airbrake actuators, landing gear retraction and extension, and wheel brakes. Hydraulic system flow rate 45 litres (12 US gallons; 10 Imp gallons)/min for main system, 16 litres (4.2 US gallons; 3.5 Imp gallons)/min for flight control system. Electrical system supplied by 9kW 28V DC generator, with nickel-cadmium battery for ground/emergency power and self contained engine starting. Two static inverters, total output 600VA, provide 115V 400Hz AC power. Gaseous oxygen system adequate for two crew for 2 h 30 min.

AVIONICS: Dual controls and full blind-flying instrumentation in each cockpit. Standard nav/com equipment comprises EAS type ER4.671D or RC E163 Kondor VHF com radio, GEC Avionics AD 370B or Iskra VARK-01 ADF, Collins VIR-30 VOR/ILS, Iskra 75R4 VOR marker beacon receiver, Collins DME 40 and TRT AHV-6 radio altimeter. Optional UHF or V/UHF com, gyro platform and other equipment to customer's specification. INS optional in G-4M. GEC Ferranti D282 gyro gunsight standard. Other types of fire control system optional. Development of a photo reconnaissance/infra-red linescan pod and night illumination system, and selection of an alternative off-the-shelf reconnaissance pod, have been deferred pending identification of customer requirement.

ARMAMENT: Removable ventral gun pod containing 23 mm GSh-23L twin-barrel rapid fire cannon with 200 rds. Two attachments under each wing, with capacity of 500 kg (1,102 lb) inboard and 350 kg (772 lb) outboard. Total weapon load capability, with centreline gun pod, 1,280 kg (2,822 lb), or 1,800 kg (3,968 lb) for G-4M. In addition to standard high explosive bombs and napalm pods, typical Yugoslav stores include S-8-16 cluster bombs, each with eight 16 kg fragmentation munitions; KPT-150 expendable containers, each with up to 40 anti-personnel or 54 anti-tank bomblets; L-57-16MD pods, each with sixteen 57 mm rockets; L-128-04 pods, each with four 128 mm rockets; adaptors for twin 5 in HVAR rockets, single 57 mm VRZ-57 training rockets; SN-3-050 triple carriers for 50 kg bombs; SN-3-100 triple carriers for 100 kg bombs; KM-3 pods each containing a single 12.7 mm (0.50 in) gun; SAM Z-80 towed target system; and auxiliary fuel tanks on the inboard attachments. Provision to be added for air-to-air and air-to-surface missiles.

DIMENSIONS, EXTERNAL:

Wing span	9.88 m (32 ft 5 in)
Wing aspect ratio	4.73
Length overall	11.86 m (38 ft 11 in)
Height overall	4.28 m (14 ft 0½ in)
Tailplane span	3.97 m (13 ft 0¼ in)
Wheel track	3.49 m (11 ft 5½ in)
Wheelbase	4.15 m (13 ft 7½ in)

AREAS:

Wings, gross	19.5 m² (209.9 sq ft)
Ailerons (total)	1.358 m² (14.62 sq ft)
Trailing-edge flaps (total)	3.340 m² (35.95 sq ft)
Airbrake	0.438 m² (4.71 sq ft)
Fin	3.130 m² (33.69 sq ft)
Rudder	0.689 m² (7.42 sq ft)
Horizontal tail surfaces (total)	4.669 m² (50.26 sq ft)

WEIGHTS AND LOADINGS:

Weight empty, equipped	3,134 kg (6,909 lb)
Max fuel weight: internal	1,305 kg (2,877 lb)
external	500 kg (1,102 lb)

SOKO-manufactured SA 342L Gazelle, armed with AT-3 'Sagger' and SA-7 'Grail' missiles

SOKO G-4 Super Galeb jet training and light attack aircraft in blue/white/red colours of the Letece Zvezde aerobatic team

Model of the proposed Novi Avion combat aircraft

T-O weight: training mission   4,600 kg (10,141 lb)
  normal combat mission, with 1,350 kg (2,975 lb) of
  weapons   6,110 kg (13,470 lb)
Max T-O weight, combat overload   6,300 kg (13,889 lb)
Max wing loading   323.1 kg/m² (66.17 lb/sq ft)
Max power loading   353.93 kg/kN (3.47 lb/lb st)
PERFORMANCE (at AUW of 4,760 kg; 10,495 lb, except where
indicated):
  Max limiting Mach number   0.866
  Max level speed at 6,000 m (19,680 ft)
      491 knots (910 km/h; 565 mph)
  Landing speed   89 knots (165 km/h; 103 mph)
  Max rate of climb at S/L:
    AUW as above   1,800 m (5,905 ft)/min
    with 50% internal fuel (AUW of 3,890 kg; 8,575 lb)
      2,330 m (7,645 ft)/min
  Time to 8,000 m (26,240 ft)   6 min
  Absolute ceiling   15,000 m (49,200 ft)
  T-O run   532 m (1,745 ft)
  T-O to 15 m (50 ft)   850 m (2,790 ft)
  Landing from 15 m (50 ft) at landing weight of 3,800 kg
  (8,375 lb)   750 m (2,460 ft)

Landing run at above landing weight   550 m (1,805 ft)
Combat radius, with gun pack and full internal fuel, 10%
reserves:
  with four BL755 cluster bombs:
    lo-lo-lo   208 nm (386 km; 240 miles)
    hi-lo-hi   260 nm (483 km; 300 miles)
  with two BL755 and two aux fuel tanks:
    lo-lo-lo   321 nm (595 km; 370 miles)
    hi-lo-hi   438 nm (812 km; 504 miles)
Range at 11,000 m (36,000 ft), with two aux fuel tanks,
  10% reserves   1,420 nm (2,630 km; 1,635 miles)
Endurance at 11,000 m (36,000 ft), with two aux fuel
  tanks   4 h 20 min
g limits   +8/-4.2

NOVI AVION

Under the Novi Avion (New Aircraft) programme,
Yugoslavia has undertaken to produce an indigenous
successor to the MiG-21 multi-role fighter. By early 1990,
design definition had been completed at the Vazduhoplovno
Tehnicki Institut (Defence Technical Insitute) at Zarkovo,

near Belgrade, with assistance from several Western
aviation companies, notably Dassault. European and US
firms have held discussions concerning collaborative
airframe development and possible use of Rolls-Royce,
General Electric or Pratt & Whitney power plants.
Production is expected to be the responsibility of SOKO.

The Novi Avion is currently seen as a single-engined,
cranked-wing tailless delta with movable canards and
separate ventral air intakes resembling those of the Rafale.
Design requirements include a thrust:weight ratio in excess
of unity; speeds of Mach 1.1 + at sea level, Mach 1.4-1.6 at
4g at 6,100 m (20,000 ft), and Mach 1.8 at 11,000 m (36,100
ft); an instantaneous 24°/s or sustained 13-15°/s turn rate at
3,050 m (10,000 ft); and a sustained 4g capability at Mach
0.7 at 3,050 m (10,000 ft).

A decision on the future of the Novi Avion was due to
have been made at the end of 1989, but a year later the
design was reportedly still to be approaching finalisation.
The critical condition of the Yugoslav federation and its
economy is seen as a major obstacle to the programme,
which is expected to cost $150-200 million per year
throughout the 1990s.

UTVA
UTVA—SOUR METALNE INDUSTRIJE, RO FABRIKA AVIONA

Jabučki Put BB, 26 000 Pančevo
Telephone: 38 (13) 512584
Telex: 13250 UTVA YU
GENERAL MANAGER: Dipl Ing Milan Soso
MANAGER OF AIRCRAFT DEVELOPMENT:
  Dipl Ing Petar Stamatov
CHIEF DESIGNER: Dipl Ing Dragoslav Dimić

UTVA-75A

The **UTVA-75** (originally -75A21) side by side two-seat
training, glider towing and utility lightplane was projected,
designed and built in partnership by UTVA-Pančevo, Prva
Petoletka-Trstenik, Vazduhoplovno Tehnicki Institut and
Institut Masinskog Fakulteta of Belgrade. Design was
started in 1974, to the requirements of FAR Pt 23 (Utility
category). Construction of two prototypes was undertaken
in 1975; the first of these flew for the first time on 19 May
1976 and the second on 18 December 1976. Over 150
were built. Latest version (flown 1986) is the four-seat
UTVA-75A (previously -75A41), which has larger cabin
doors, eliminating the rear quarter-lights. This variant has
not yet entered production.
TYPE: Four-seat light aircraft.
WINGS: Cantilever low-wing monoplane, with short span
  centre-section and two constant chord outer panels.
  Wing section NACA 65₂415. Dihedral 0° on centre-
  section, 6° on outer panels. Conventional all-metal
  two-spar structure. Ailerons and flaps, with fluted skin,
  along entire trailing-edge of outer panels, except for tips.
  Flettner trim tab on each aileron.
FUSELAGE: Conventional all-metal semi-monocoque
  structure.
TAIL UNIT: Cantilever all-metal structure, with sweptback
  vertical surfaces. Fluted skin on fin, rudder and elevator.
  Rudder and elevator horn balanced. Controllable tab on
  elevator; ground adjustable tab on rudder.
LANDING GEAR: Non-retractable tricycle type, with single
  wheel on each unit, and small tail bumper. Prva
  Petoletka-Trstenik oleo-pneumatic shock absorbers.
  Dunlop tyres, size 6.00-6, pressure 2.2 bars (32 lb/sq in)
  on mainwheels; size 5.00-5, pressure 2.0 bars (29 lb/sq in)
  on nosewheel. Prva Petoletka-Trstenik hydraulic brakes.
POWER PLANT: One 134 kW (180 hp) Textron Lycoming
  IO-360-B1F flat-four engine, driving a Hartzell HC-
  C2YK-1BF/F7666A two-blade variable-pitch metal propeller. Two integral fuel tanks in wings, total capacity 150
  litres (39.6 US gallons; 33 Imp gallons). Provision for
  carrying two 100 litre (26.4 US gallon; 22 Imp gallon)
  drop tanks under wings, raising max total capacity to 350
  litres (92 US gallons; 77 Imp gallons). Oil capacity 10
  litres (2.6 US gallons; 2.2 Imp gallons).
ACCOMMODATION: Four seats in enclosed cabin, with large
  upward opening jettisonable canopy door over and to the
  rear of each seat, hinged on centre line. Dual stick type
  controls standard. Cabin heated and ventilated.
SYSTEMS: Dual hydraulic systems for brakes. 14V DC
  electrical system, with 35Ah battery, navigation lights,
  rotating beacon and landing lights as standard
  equipment.
AVIONICS: Bendix/King equipment standard, including dual
  KY 197 720-channel VHF com transceivers; KR 87
  digitally tuned ADF with integral electronic flight timer
  and pushbutton elapsed timer; panel mounted R/Nav
  system comprising a KNS 81 200-channel nav, 40-chan-
  nel glideslope indicator and 9-waypoint digital R/Nav
  computer, combined with a KI 525A pictorial nav
  indicator; KI 229 RMI; KN 53 200-channel VHF nav
  with integral 40-channel glideslope indicator and KI
  525A indicator; KN 62A 200-channel DME with digital
  distance, ground speed and time-to-station; KT 79 all
  solid state digital transponder featuring cross-check
  readout of encoded altitude and automatic VFR code

Prototype UTVA-75A four-seat touring aircraft *(R. J. Malachowski)*

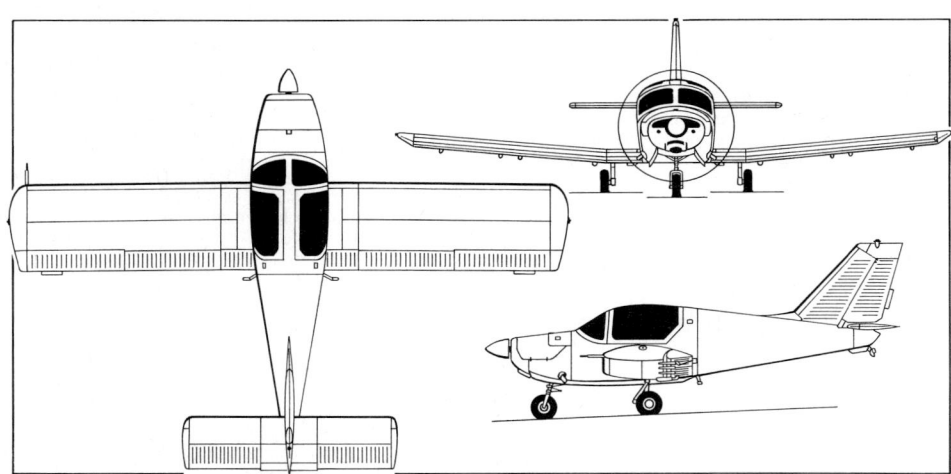

UTVA-75A four-seat tourer/trainer *(Jane's/Mike Keep)*

selection; and KMA 24 audio control console with
integral marker beacon receiver.
ARMAMENT: Two fittings for light weapon loads underwing
  on military UTVA-75s. Each can carry a bomb, 100 kg
  (220 lb) cargo container, two-round rocket launcher or
  machine gun pod.
DIMENSIONS, EXTERNAL:
Wing span	9.73 m (31 ft 11 in)
Wing chord, constant	1.55 m (5 ft 1 in)
Wing aspect ratio	6.5
Length overall	7.11 m (23 ft 4 in)
Height overall	3.15 m (10 ft 4 in)
Tailplane span	3.80 m (12 ft 5½ in)
Wheel track	2.58 m (8 ft 5½ in)
Wheelbase	1.99 m (6 ft 6¼ in)
Propeller diameter	1.93 m (6 ft 4 in)
Propeller ground clearance	0.295 m (11¾ in)

AREAS:
Wings, gross	14.63 m² (157.5 sq ft)
Ailerons (total)	1.38 m² (14.85 sq ft)
Flaps (total)	1.61 m² (17.33 sq ft)
Vertical tail surfaces (total)	1.78 m² (19.16 sq ft)
Horizontal tail surfaces (total)	3.34 m² (35.95 sq ft)

WEIGHTS AND LOADINGS:
Weight empty, equipped	720 kg (1,587 lb)
Luggage provision	20 kg (44 lb)
Max fuel: standard	108 kg (238 lb)
with drop tanks	251 kg (554 lb)
Max T-O weight	1,140 kg (2,513 lb)
Max wing loading	77.92 kg/m² (15.96 lb/sq ft)
Max power loading	8.50 kg/kW (13.96 lb/hp)

PERFORMANCE (at max T-O weight):
Max level speed	103 knots (190 km/h; 118 mph)
Max cruising speed	94 knots (175 km/h; 109 mph)
Stalling speed	54 knots (100 km/h; 62 mph)
Max rate of climb at S/L	240 m (787 ft)/min
Service ceiling	4,000 m (13,125 ft)
T-O run	200 m (656 ft)
T-O to 15 m (50 ft)	400 m (1,312 ft)
Landing from 15 m (50 ft)	340 m (1,115 ft)
Landing run	180 m (591 ft)
Range: with max standard fuel	
	324 nm (600 km; 373 miles)
with drop tanks, no reserves	
	755 nm (1,400 km; 870 miles)

UTVA-75AG11

The UTVA-75AG11 is an agricultural aircraft with an airframe almost identical to that of the UTVA-75 except for changes associated with the installation of a chemical hopper forward of a high-set single-seat cabin in the centre-fuselage. The landing gear is upgraded to cope with operations at a higher gross weight, from grass surfaces; and a more powerful engine is fitted. Although unsuccessful in a government design competition for agricultural aircraft, the UTVA-75AG11 continues to be offered as a private venture.

Design of the UTVA-75AG11 was started on 20 December 1986. Construction of the prototype (YU-XAF) began on 15 June 1987 and the first flight took place on 3 March 1989. No others built.

Differences by comparison with the UTVA-75 are as follows:

TYPE: Single-seat agricultural aircraft.

FUSELAGE: Basically as for UTVA-75, but greater use of composites, particularly for pilot's cabin. Chemical hopper, capacity 870 litres (230 US gallons; 191 Imp gallons), forward of cabin.

TAIL UNIT: Cantilever all-metal structure, with sweptback vertical surfaces. Fluted skin on fin and rudder. Elevator horn balanced. Tab on rudder and controllable tab on elevator, operated electrically by Teleflex actuator.

LANDING GEAR: Tyres size 7.00-8 on mainwheels, 6.00-6 on nosewheel.

POWER PLANT: One 224 kW (300 hp) Textron Lycoming IO-540-L1A5D flat-six engine, driving a Hartzell HC-C2YK-1BF/F8475D-4 propeller. Fuel and underwing tanks as UTVA-75A21.

ACCOMMODATION: Pilot only, in high-set cabin. Downward hinged canopy/door on each side. Cabin heated and ventilated.

SYSTEMS: Electrical system is 24V 60A DC, with a 19Ah nickel-cadmium battery. Vacuum system standard.

AVIONICS: Prototype has Rudičajavec VHF radio, blind-flying instrumentation, navigation and landing lights, and rotating beacon.

DIMENSIONS, EXTERNAL: As for UTVA-75A21 except:

Propeller diameter	2.03 m (6 ft 8 in)
Propeller ground clearance	0.47 m (1 ft 6 in)

WEIGHTS AND LOADINGS:

Weight empty, equipped	820 kg (1,808 lb)
Max chemical load	900 kg (1,984 lb)
Max fuel, internal	103 kg (227 lb)
Max T-O weight	1,800 kg (3,968 lb)
Max landing weight	1,400 kg (3,086 lb)
Max wing loading	123.03 kg/m² (25.20 lb/sq ft)
Max power loading	8.04 kg/kW (13.23 lb/hp)

PERFORMANCE (at max T-O weight, estimated):

Never-exceed speed (V$_{NE}$)	182 knots (338 km/h; 210 mph)
Max level speed	135 knots (250 km/h; 155 mph)
Max cruising speed	116 knots (215 km/h; 134 mph)
Econ cruising speed	89 knots (165 km/h; 102 mph)
Stalling speed, flaps down	54 knots (100 km/h; 62 mph)
Max rate of climb at S/L	240 m (787 ft)/min
Service ceiling	4,000 m (13,120 ft)
T-O run	340 m (1,115 ft)
T-O to 15 m (50 ft)	630 m (2,067 ft)
Landing from 15 m (50 ft)	540 m (1,772 ft)

Prototype of UTVA-75AG11 single-seat agricultural aircraft

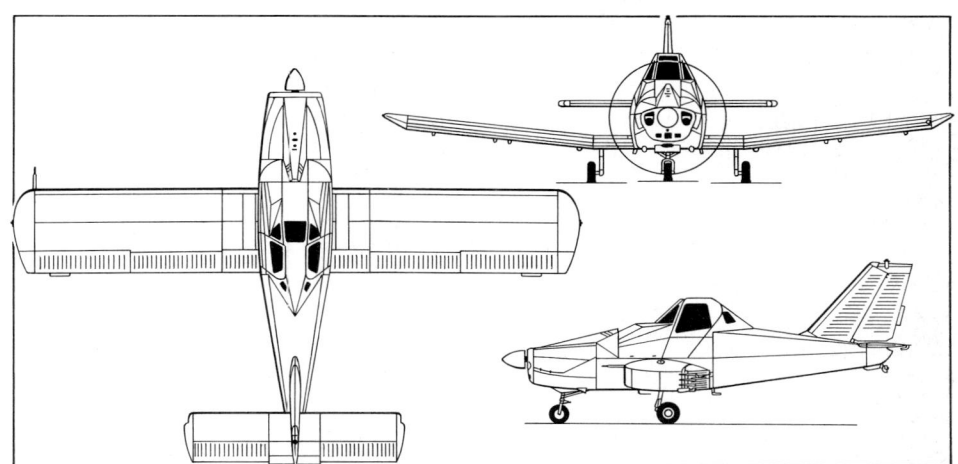

UTVA-75AG11 (Textron Lycoming IO-540-L1A5D engine) *(Jane's/Mike Keep)*

Landing run	250 m (820 ft)

Range:

with max internal fuel	162 nm (300 km; 186 miles)
with underwing tanks	442 nm (820 km; 510 miles)

UTVA LASTA (SWALLOW)

Two prototypes of this piston-engined military trainer were built in 1985-86, but despite reports to the contrary, none has been delivered to the Yugoslav Air Force. A considerably modified version, the Lasta 2, is described in the Addenda.

LOVAUX OPTICA, NAC 6 FIELDMASTER and ORCA SAH-1

Assembly lines have been established by UTVA for the Optica and Fieldmaster, of which further details will be found under Lovaux and Croplease in the United Kingdom section. Five Fieldmasters were said to be under construction in 1990. Agreement has also been reached to produce the Orca SAH-1 (see 1989-90 *Jane's*) in Yugoslavia.

SPORT AIRCRAFT
(incorporating Homebuilt and Microlight Aircraft)

ARGENTINA

BIGUÁ

Details regarding the constructor(s) and marketing of the Biguá have not been received. It is named after an Argentine water bird, and brings together the attributes of an amphibious sporting aircraft and a motor glider. Its construction uses both composite and more conventional materials, and is said to be easy to assemble.

BIGUÁ

TYPE: Tandem two-seat amphibious sporting aircraft/motor glider.
AIRFRAME: Mid-wing monoplane. Wing centre section attached to fuselage and constructed as GFRP/PVC foam/balsa sandwich, with torsion boxes having bulkheads to act as floats in emergency; Wortmann FX 61-184 aerofoil. Tapered outer wing panels of plywood. Fully enclosed fuselage/hull, with concave planing bottom and upswept tailboom supporting T tail with large rudder. Side floats retract behind wing spar and can be actuated as hydrodynamic or air brakes. Three-axis control, with fabric covered control surfaces. Retractable tricycle landing gear, with nosewheel possibly acting as nose-bumper.
POWER PLANT: One 78 kW (105 hp) Renault 12 converted motorcar engine with twin Weber carburettors, driving a two-blade wooden variable-pitch (ground adjustable) pusher propeller. Fuel capacity 95 litres (25 US gallons; 21 Imp gallons).

DIMENSIONS, EXTERNAL:
Wing span	16.00 m (52 ft 6 in)
Length overall	7.34 m (24 ft 1 in)
Height overall (on land)	2.98 m (9 ft 9¼ in)
Propeller diameter	1.83 m (6 ft 0 in)

AREA:
Wings, gross	19.80 m² (213.13 sq ft)

WEIGHTS:
Weight empty	450 kg (992 lb)
Max T-O weight	650 kg (1,433 lb)

PERFORMANCE (estimated, 35 litres fuel):
Range	156 nm (290 km; 180 miles)
Endurance, with 30 min reserves	2 h
g limits	+3/−1.2

CICARÉ
AUGUSTO CICARÉ

Augusto Cicaré designed a very lightweight single-seat helicopter, which became the prototype for the Mini 500 which is currently being marketed by Revolution Helicopter Corporation (which see) in the USA with the assistance of Dennis Fetters (of Air Command).

AUSTRALIA

CALAIR
CALAIR CORPORATION

Caloundra, Queensland
MANAGING DIRECTOR: Stuart Pryor

Calair, a public limited company listed on the Brisbane Stock Exchange in October 1989, is currently marketing a modified version of the US Denney Kitfox, known as the Skyfox. Future plans envisage production of a single-seat and a four-seat aircraft.

CALAIR SKYFOX

The Skyfox first flew on 15 September 1989. The aircraft has received CAA certification under CAO 101-55 regulations (under 450 kg empty weight). Fifty-five Skyfoxes were ordered over six months from April 1990 (no more recent figure received), and negotiations with a Taiwanese distributor had taken place, covering about 100 aircraft. Production then stood at about five/six units a month, but this was expected to rise to perhaps 10.

Compared to the Kitfox, the Skyfox is said to have 38 modifications. A 58.2 kW (78 hp) Aeropower engine driving a wooden propeller provides power, with dual ignition. The V bracing struts are attached further along the wings, and wing dihedral is increased. The fuselage steel tubing is of larger size, allowing an increase in payload. A taller tailfin is evident, the rudder is also taller and with greater chord, and the elevators also have increased chord. Fuel capacity is 50 litres (13.2 US gallons; 11 Imp gallons). Options include long-range fuel tanks and an underfuselage cargo pod.

WEIGHT:
Max payload	463 kg (1,020 lb)

PERFORMANCE (provisional):
Never-exceed speed (VNE)	112 knots (207 km/h; 129 mph)
Cruising speed	75 knots (139 km/h; 86 mph)

HUGHES
HOWARD HUGHES ENGINEERING PTY LTD

PO Box 89, 11 Smith Drive, Ballina, NSW 2478
Telephone: 61 (66) 86 3148
Fax: 61 (66) 86 8343

HUGHES LIGHTWING GR-582

The prototype LightWing first flew in June 1986, and many were sold conforming to ANO 95-25 requirements. Approval was sought to sell kits under homebuilt or CAO 101-28 regulations, in non-retractable tailwheel and twin-float configurations. About 10 kits have been completed. Construction of a prototype five-seater under CAO 101-31 is planned.

TYPE: Two-seat microlight, ARV and homebuilt.
AIRFRAME: Strut braced wings of 60E1-T6 aluminium alloy construction, and welded steel tube fuselage and tail unit, all Ceconite fabric covered. Modified Clark Y wing section. Glassfibre engine cowling. Three-axis control. Non-retractable tailwheel landing gear; optional amphibious floats with retractable mainwheels and non-retractable tailwheels (which double as water rudders), or skis.
POWER PLANT: One 47 kW (63 hp) Rotax 582, with 2.58 : 1 reduction gear. Fuel capacity 60 litres (15.9 US gallons; 13.2 Imp gallons).

DIMENSIONS, EXTERNAL:
Wing span	9.70 m (31 ft 10 in)
Length overall	5.80 m (19 ft 0½ in)
Height overall	1.90 m (6 ft 2¾ in)
Propeller diameter	1.68 m (5 ft 6 in)

AREA:
Wings, gross	14.55 m² (156.61 sq ft)

WEIGHTS:
Weight empty	240 kg (529 lb)
Max pilot weight	100 kg (220 lb)
Baggage capacity	11.3 kg (25 lb)
Max T-O weight	450 kg (992 lb)

PERFORMANCE:
Max level speed at 915 m (3,000 ft)	80 knots (148 km/h; 92 mph)
Econ cruising speed	70 knots (130 km/h; 81 mph)
Stalling speed	32 knots (60 km/h; 37 mph)
Max rate of climb at S/L	366 m (1,200 ft)/min
Service ceiling (CAO 101-55)	915 m (3,000 ft)
T-O run	31 m (100 ft)
Landing run	92 m (300 ft)
Range	150 nm (278 km; 172 miles)
g limits	+6/−3

HUGHES LIGHTWING GR-912

Similar to GR-582 but with a 59 kW (79 hp) water-cooled Rotax 912 engine with dual ignition. Empty weight is 275 kg (606 lb) and max level speed is 80 knots (148 km/h; 92 mph).

HUGHES LIGHTWING GA-55

The GA-55 is available in ready assembled and kit forms and produced under CAO 101-28 and 101-55 regulations; under Australian regulations, it can be owner built and registered as an ultralight or registered as a general aviation aircraft. The prototype first flew in March 1987 and a kit-built aircraft flew in the following year. By January 1991, 20 assembled GA-55s had been delivered (of 25 ordered), together with 15 kits (five built by that date). Airframe details are similar to those for the Rotax-engined LightWing GR-582.

TYPE: Two-seat homebuilt.
POWER PLANT: One 58.2 kW (78 hp) Aeropower or Limbach. Fuel capacity 60 litres (15.9 US gallons; 13.2 Imp gallons).

DIMENSIONS, EXTERNAL:
Wing span	9.11 m (29 ft 10½ in)
Length overall	5.70 m (18 ft 8½ in)
Height overall	1.90 m (6 ft 2¾ in)
Propeller diameter	1.50 m (4 ft 11 in)

WEIGHTS:
Weight empty	280 kg (617 lb)
Max pilot weight	90 kg (198 lb)
Max T-O weight	500 kg (1,102 lb)

PERFORMANCE:
Max level speed	80 knots (148 km/h; 92 mph)
Max and econ cruising speed	75 knots (139 km/h; 86 mph)
Stalling speed: flaps up	38 knots (71 km/h; 44 mph)
flaps down	34 knots (63 km/h; 39 mph)
negative flaps	40 knots (74 km/h; 46 mph)
Service ceiling	3,050 m (10,000 ft)
T-O run	153 m (500 ft)
Landing run	121 m (400 ft)
Range	217 nm (402 km; 250 miles)
Endurance	3 h 30 min
g limits	+6/−3

SKYTEK
SKYTEK AUSTRALIA PTY LTD

PO Box 238, Willetton, Western Australia 6155
Telephone: 61 (9) 310 3351
Fax: 61 (9) 332 3680
DESIGNER: Graham Swannell

SKYTEK MAVERICK

This aerobatic and cross-country homebuilt first flew as a prototype on 24 December 1987. Only the single prototype had been built by early 1991, and no marketing plans had been initiated by then. Details of the Maverick, and an illustration, can be found in the 1990-91 *Jane's*.

Hughes LightWing GR-582 in twin-float and landplane configurations

Epervier two-seat cabin monoplane in microlight form

SCWAL 101 two-seat light aircraft

SKYWISE

SKYWISE ULTRAFLIGHT PTY LTD
PO Box 226, Hornsby, NSW 2077

Details of the Skywise Ultraflight Sadler Vampire single-seat microlight can be found in the 1988-89 *Jane's*. A two-seat version has been developed, but it has been reported that the company is offering the design and manufacturing rights for sale, together with those for the single-seater if required.

THRUSTER

THRUSTER AIRCRAFT (AUSTRALIA) PTY LTD
458 The Boulevarde, Kirrawee, NSW 2232

Telephone: 61 (2) 542 1990
Fax: 61 (2) 542 3004
Telex: AA 73953
GENERAL MANAGER: Ken Asplin

In addition to its T300 and T500 microlights (see Microlight tables), Thruster began development of the T-88 two-seat lightplane. This is not being manufactured; details plus an illustration can be found in the 1989-90 *Jane's*.

BELGIUM

EPERVIER

EPERVIER AVIATION SA
Rue Delfosse, 1 bis, 1400 Nivelles
Telephone: 32 (67) 22 00 41
Fax: 32 (67) 22 10 38
INFORMATION: Yves Kimard

EPERVIER AVIATION EPERVIER

Construction of the first prototype Epervier began in September 1989, and this first flew in September of the following year. The aircraft is marketed in microlight and ARV forms, and is also said to be suitable for observation, medical and military roles, with equipment on request.

The following details refer to the ARV version:
TYPE: Side by side two-seat cabin ARV; conforms to JAR-VLA.
AIRFRAME: Strut braced wings with CFRP/epoxy spars, PVC foam/CFRP/epoxy ribs, and GFRP/epoxy skin. Wing section NACA 23012. Fuselage of GFRP/CFRP/epoxy construction. Three-axis control, with ailerons, flaps, elevators and rudder, of similar construction to wings. Baggage area behind seats. Non-retractable tricycle landing gear, with optional floats or skis.
POWER PLANT: One 56 kW (75 hp) Limbach L 2000, driving a Hoffmann two-blade, fixed-pitch, aluminium propeller. Total fuel capacity in two tanks 60 litres (15.9 US gallons; 13.2 Imp gallons).

DIMENSIONS, EXTERNAL:
Wing span	11.15 m (36 ft 7 in)
Length overall	6.82 m (22 ft 4½ in)
Height overall	2.55 m (8 ft 4½ in)

AREA:
Wings, gross	17.50 m² (188.37 sq ft)

WEIGHTS:
Weight empty	450 kg (992 lb)
Baggage capacity	70 kg (154 lb)
Max T-O weight	750 kg (1,653 lb)

EURONEF—*See Microlight tables*

SCWAL

SCWAL SA
77 Avenue Brugmann, 1060 Brussels
Telephone: 32 (2) 343 49 70
Fax: 32 (2) 344 67 94
Telex: 65892 GRYF B
MANAGING DIRECTOR: Charles Rifon

SCWAL, with offices in Brussels and a 2,000 m² (21,530 sq ft) manufacturing plant at Baileux, was established in 1985. In addition to producing its own SCWAL 101 light aircraft, it began manufacture and sale in September 1988 of improved versions of the American Aircraft Falcon, under licence from Sonaca (see Microlight tables).

SCWAL 101

The SCWAL 101 was designed to be a fully certificated aircraft fitting between microlights and conventional light

aeroplanes. Design goals were easy maintenance, road transportability, and the ability to use non-aviation fuel. Applications include civil and military training, surveillance, crop dusting and other work in addition to sport flying. A twin-engined version may follow. The first flight was achieved on 26 April 1984.
TYPE: Side by side two-seat monoplane; conforms to FAR Pt 23 normal category.
AIRFRAME: Bolted aluminium/steel tubular mainframe. All aluminium wing and tail surfaces. Wortmann wing section. Three-axis control, including flaps. Optional enclosed Perspex transparent cockpit pod with two doors. Non-retractable tricycle landing gear.
POWER PLANT: One 67 kW (90 hp) BMW converted motorcycle engine. Fuel capacity 60 litres (16 US gallons; 13.2 Imp gallons).

DIMENSIONS, EXTERNAL:
Wing span	11.00 m (36 ft 1 in)
Length overall	5.50 m (18 ft 0½ in)

AREA:
Wings, gross	13.75 m² (148.0 sq ft)

WEIGHTS:
Weight empty	280 kg (617 lb)
Max T-O weight	520 kg (1,146 lb)

PERFORMANCE:
Max level speed	75 knots (140 km/h; 87 mph)
Stalling speed: flaps up	38 knots (70 km/h; 44 mph)
flaps down	33 knots (60 km/h; 38 mph)
Max rate of climb at S/L	162 m (530 ft)/min
T-O run	125 m (410 ft)
Endurance	8 h
g limits	+5.7/−2.85 ultimate

BULGARIA

OPTIMUM
OPTIMUM AIRCRAFT GROUP
PO Box 74, 1404 Sofia
Telephone: 359 (2) 89 95 93
ENGINEERS: Georgi Dimanchev and Toshko Punchev

Bulgarian aeronautical engineers, Georgi Dimanchev and Toshko Punchev, conceived the **Optimum 88** as an inexpensive training aircraft for aero clubs and for sport flying. Designed to meet US FAR Pt 23 requirements, it became the first Bulgarian ultralight aircraft to fly, on 26 September 1989, and has successfully passed Bulgarian state acceptance tests. In April 1990 the editors of the Bulgarian aerospace magazine *Wings* awarded the designers the Icarus special prize and the *Wings* golden badge for its development. Max T-O weight is 420 kg (926 lb). Further details can be found in the Microlights section.

CANADA

CIRCA
CIRCA REPRODUCTIONS
8027 Argyll Road, Edmonton, Alberta T6C 4A9
Telephone: 1 (403) 469 2692 and 477 0024
DESIGNER/PROPRIETOR: Graham R. Lee
Circa Reproductions markets plans of ⅞th scale reproductions of First World War fighters.

CIRCA REPRODUCTIONS NIEUPORT 11
The prototype Nieuport 11 reproduction first flew on 25 July 1984. Plans, including drawings for a wooden replica Lewis gun, and kits are available; by December 1990 a total of 730 sets of plans had been sold. About 150 aircraft are reportedly under active construction and 25 have flown. A prefabricated engine cowling and fuel tank are available from the designer for the Experimental/microlight versions, plus an engine cowling and engine mount for the French ULM model (see below). Estimated building time is 600 working hours.

The Nieuport 11 is capable of meeting both Canadian and US ultralight regulations, and a version to conform to French ULM requirements became available in 1990 (prototype ULM model first flew in October 1989), though the company prefers that it be built as an Experimental category aircraft with a weight that makes it a homebuilt. If preferred the homebuilder can complete the aircraft as a Nieuport 16, 17, 24, 24*bis* or 27, the 17 onwards having a greater wing area of about 11.6 m² (125 sq ft), or as a German Siemens-Schuckert D.I.

TYPE: Single-seat replica fighter microlight or homebuilt; conforms as microlight to FAR Pt 103, Canadian regulations, and French ULM requirements.
AIRFRAME: Tubular 6061-T6 aluminium alloy structure, with 2024-T3 duralumin gussets and covered with Ceconite and aluminium sheet. Three-axis control. Non-retractable tailskid or tailwheel landing gear. Skis optional.
POWER PLANT: One 22.4 kW (30 hp) Cuyuna ULII-02. Optional engines include Rotax 503. French ULM version has one 31.3 kW (42 hp) Rotax 447 with 2.58 : 1 reduction gear as standard. Fuel capacity 48 litres (12.7 US gallons; 10.5 Imp gallons) or 19 litres (5 US gallons; 4.2 Imp gallons), according to US/Canadian regulation requirements; 30 litres (7.9 US gallons; 6.6 Imp gallons) for French ULM requirements.

DIMENSIONS, EXTERNAL:
Wing span	6.55 m (21 ft 6 in)
Length overall	4.98 m (16 ft 4 in)
Height overall	2.29 m (7 ft 6 in)
Propeller diameter	1.83 m (6 ft 0 in)

AREAS:
Wings, gross: standard	10.59 m² (114.0 sq ft)
French ULM	11.92 m² (128.3 sq ft)

WEIGHTS:
Weight empty: standard	113.5 kg (250 lb)
French ULM	119 kg (262 lb)
Max pilot weight	109 kg (240 lb)
Max T-O weight: standard	249 kg (550 lb)
French ULM	250 kg (551 lb)

PERFORMANCE (at 211 kg; 465 lb AUW):
Max level speed:	
Rotax engine	82 knots (153 km/h; 95 mph)
18.6 kW (25 hp) engine	67 knots (124 km/h; 77 mph)
French ULM	62 knots (115 km/h; 71 mph)
Econ cruising speed	43 knots (80 km/h; 50 mph)
Stalling speed:	
standard	23 knots (42 km/h; 26 mph) IAS
French ULM	22.5 knots (41 km/h; 25.5 mph)
Max rate of climb at S/L	137 m (450 ft)/min
T-O run: standard	76 m (250 ft)
French ULM	61 m (200 ft)
Landing run: standard and French ULM	61 m (200 ft)
Range with max fuel: standard	
	more than 173 nm (322 km; 200 miles)
Endurance: standard	4 h 45 min
g limits: standard	+ 5.5/–3.5
French ULM	+ 5/–3

CIRCA REPRODUCTIONS NIEUPORT 12
Plans of this ⅞th scale reproduction of the two-seat Nieuport 12C-2 are available, and 27 sets had been sold by December 1990; four aircraft were then under active construction. The prototype made its first flight in May 1989 on the power of a 38.8 kW (52 hp) Snowmobile engine.
TYPE: Two-seat replica homebuilt aircraft; conforms to US and Canadian Experimental regulations.
AIRFRAME: Braced sesquiplane, with UA-81 University of Alberta wing section. Sheet aluminium upper wing spars and oval tube lower spar. Remainder of airframe constructed of 6061-T6 aluminium alloy tubing, with aluminium gussets and fabric covering. Three-axis control. Non-retractable tailskid landing gear. Optional tailwheel.

POWER PLANT: One engine in 48.5-63.4 kW (65-85 hp) range preferred. Engines can include 38.8 kW (52 hp) Rotax 503 or a Teledyne Continental C65 or C85 of up to 63.4 kW (85 hp). Fuel capacity 50 litres (13.2 US gallons; 11 Imp gallons).
DIMENSIONS, EXTERNAL:
Wing span: upper	8.08 m (26 ft 6 in)
lower	6.93 m (22 ft 9 in)
Length overall	6.55 m (21 ft 6 in)
Height overall	2.59 m (8 ft 6 in)
Propeller diameter (prototype)	2.13 m (7 ft 0 in)

AREA:
Wings, gross	17.62 m² (189.7 sq ft)

WEIGHTS (prototype):
Weight empty	243 kg (536 lb)
Max T-O weight	454 kg (1,000 lb)

PERFORMANCE (Rotax 503, at 340 kg; 750 lb AUW):
Max level speed	56 knots (105 km/h; 65 mph)
Econ cruising speed	48 knots (89 km/h; 55 mph)
Stalling speed, flaps up, engine idling	
	29 knots (53 km/h; 33 mph)
Max rate of climb at S/L	137 m (450 ft)/min
T-O run	122 m (400 ft)
Landing run	153 m (500 ft)
Endurance	2 h-4 h 15 min
g limits	+ 5.7/–3

CIRCA REPRODUCTIONS SOPWITH TRIPLANE
A prototype of the ⅞th scale Sopwith Triplane has not yet been completed. Plans to allow amateur construction will become available in due course.
TYPE: Single-seat replica microlight; conforms to Canadian microlight regulations and Experimental aircraft category.
AIRFRAME: Structural materials, control and landing gear (with ski gear option) as for Nieuport 11 replica.
POWER PLANT: Prototype has one 30 kW (40 hp) Volkswagen modified motorcar engine. Max fuel capacity estimated at 45.5 litres (12 US gallons; 10 Imp gallons).
DIMENSIONS, EXTERNAL:
Wing span	7.06 m (23 ft 2 in)
Length overall	5.03 m (16 ft 6 in)
Height overall	2.82 m (9 ft 3 in)
Propeller diameter	1.83-2.01 m (6 ft 0 in-6 ft 7 in)

AREA:
Wings, gross	18.30 m² (197.0 sq ft)

WEIGHT:
Weight empty	147 kg (325 lb)

COWAN
PETER COWAN
132 Fenn Avenue, New York, Ontario M2P 1X6
Telephone: 1 (416) 224 5473

COWAN CEKADY
First flown as a prototype in 1983, the Cekady is a STOL utility monoplane using the wings, tail unit, boot cowl, landing gear legs and windscreen of a Cessna 170 or 172 married to a new steel tube fuselage. The prototype was fitted with a Textron Lycoming O-360 engine driving a constant-speed propeller, and has flown on wheels, floats and wheel/ski landing gears. It embodies a Horton STOL kit, and uses manual flaps (although electrically actuated can be chosen in conjunction with suitable wings).
Plans became available in 1989. Eventually, the design may be expanded to include Cessna 150 and 182 off-shoots with 74.5-186.4 kW (100-250 hp) engines.

ELMWOOD
ELMWOOD AVIATION
RR 4 Elmwood Drive, Belleville, Ontario K8N 4Z4
Telephone: 1 (613) 967 1853
DESIGNER/PROPRIETOR: Ronald B. Mason

ELMWOOD CA-05 CHRISTAVIA Mk I
The prototype Christavia Mk I (C-GENC) first flew on 3 October 1981. Elmwood Aviation is offering plans, and considers the aircraft suitable for the type of flying carried out by professional organisations like Mission Aviation Fellowship. More than 300 Christavia Mk Is are believed to be under construction; about 40 have flown. Those under construction include several for the mission field.
TYPE: Tandem two-seat homebuilt.
AIRFRAME: Braced two-spar wing structure of Sitka spruce, with truss ribs and Dacron covering. Aluminium can be used alternatively to fabricate spars and ribs. Computer designed wing section. Frise ailerons of wooden construction with Dacron covering. Fuselage of welded 4130 and 1025 steel tube, Dacron covered. Wire-braced tail unit of steel tube, with mild steel plate ribs, Dacron covered.

Non-retractable tailwheel landing gear. Optional floats or skis.
POWER PLANT: Prototype has a 48.5 kW (65 hp) Teledyne Continental A65. Engines of 37.25 to 112 kW (50 to 150 hp) can be fitted. Main fuel tank, capacity 57 litres (15 US gallons; 12.5 Imp gallons), in fuselage aft of firewall; auxiliary tank, capacity 23 litres (6 US gallons; 5 Imp gallons), in each wing.
DIMENSIONS, EXTERNAL:
Wing span	9.91 m (32 ft 6 in)
Length overall	6.30 m (20 ft 8 in)
Height overall	2.13 m (7 ft 0 in)
Propeller diameter	1.83 m (6 ft 0 in)

AREA:
Wings, gross	13.59 m² (146.25 sq ft)

WEIGHTS (48.5 kW; 65 hp engine, 15 US gallons fuel):
Weight empty	338 kg (745 lb)
Max T-O weight	590 kg (1,300 lb)

PERFORMANCE (at max T-O weight, engine and fuel as above):
Max level speed at S/L	104 knots (193 km/h; 120 mph)
Cruising speed at 610 m (2,000 ft), 45% power	
	74 knots (137 km/h; 85 mph)

Stalling speed: power off	37 knots (68 km/h; 42 mph)
power on	31 knots (57 km/h; 35 mph)
Rate of climb at S/L	259 m (850 ft)/min
Service ceiling	3,960 m (13,000 ft)
T-O run	107 m (350 ft)
Landing from 15 m (50 ft)	198 m (650 ft)
Range with standard fuel, 45% power	
	382 nm (708 km; 440 miles)
g limits	+ 4.5/–2.8

ELMWOOD CH-8 CHRISTAVIA Mk 4
This four-seat development of the Christavia Mk I first flew on 3 January 1986. Plans and an information kit are available, and about 50 are under construction.
TYPE: Four-seat homebuilt cabin monoplane.
AIRFRAME: Similar to Christavia Mk I.
POWER PLANT: One 112 kW (150 hp) Textron Lycoming O-320 or converted motorcar engine. Fuel capacity 136.4 litres (36 US gallons; 30 Imp gallons).
DIMENSIONS, EXTERNAL:
Wing span	10.67 m (35 ft 0 in)

Husky Norseman I single-seat utility aircraft *(Canadian Aviation)*

Circa Reproductions Nieuport 12 prototype replica (38.8 kW; 52 hp Snowmobile engine)

Prototype Cowan Cekady light aircraft using Cessna 170/172 components *(Geoffrey P. Jones)*

Kestrel Hawk two-seat biplane *(Geoffrey P. Jones)*

Elmwood Aviation CH-8 Christavia Mk 4 four-seat homebuilt

Length overall	7.01 m (23 ft 0 in)	PERFORMANCE:		Service ceiling	5,485 m (18,000 ft)
Height overall	1.98 m (6 ft 6 in)	Max level speed at 610 m (2,000 ft)		T-O run	91 m (300 ft)
Propeller diameter	1.78 m (5 ft 10 in)		111 knots (206 km/h; 128 mph)	Landing run	152 m (500 ft)
AREA:		Econ cruising speed, 65% power		Range with max fuel	548 nm (1,017 km; 632 miles)
Wings, gross	16.26 m² (175.0 sq ft)		102 knots (188 km/h; 117 mph)		
WEIGHTS (112 kW; 150 hp engine):		Stalling speed: flaps up	35 knots (65 km/h; 40 mph)		
Weight empty	522 kg (1,150 lb)	12° flap	31 knots (57 km/h; 35 mph)		
Max T-O weight	1,043 kg (2,300 lb)	Max rate of climb at S/L	244 m (800 ft)/min		

HUSKY
HUSKY MANUFACTURING LTD
Corman Air Park, Saskatchewan
PRESIDENT: Brian Heslin
VICE-PRESIDENT: Robert Ayres

HUSKY NORSEMAN
The Norseman, according to Husky's President, was designed for cropspraying and hard utility work from rough field strips. Mr Heslin was formerly the President of Sylvaire Manufacturing Ltd, producers of the Bushmaster ultralight described in the Sport Aircraft section of the 1987-88 *Jane's*, and the Norseman is based extensively on experience with that aircraft, the objective being to develop an aircraft with the low weight of an ultralight but the added strength needed for a robust working aeroplane.

The prototype Norseman flew for the first time in June 1987, and production began six months later in a 1,022 m² (11,000 sq ft) factory at Corman Air Park, Saskatchewan. The aircraft is available in both single-seat (Norseman I) and two-seat (Norseman II) forms, and is produced in both kit and ready to fly forms. The factory built Norseman conforms to FAR Pt 23 (Utility Category) requirements, and can be supplied for cropspraying with a 113.5 litre (30 US gallon; 25 Imp gallon) tank and accompanying spraygear.

Initial orders, including one from an unnamed US customer for 250 kits and another (for 50 aircraft) from the Aero Club of India, are said to be sufficient to ensure a production run of up to 600 aircraft. Deliveries to Canadian customers and to India began in 1988.

TYPE: Single-seat or two-seat lightweight utility aircraft.
AIRFRAME: Strut braced high-wing monoplane of constant chord, with two parallel streamline section struts each side and short jury struts. Slight dihedral. Wings constructed of Sitka spruce and glassfibre, with bonded Ceconite covering and polyurethane exterior finish. Full span differentially operating ailerons; no flaps or tabs. Riveted fuselage structure of aluminium alloy, with strong roll cage, covered with bonded Ceconite and polyurethane exterior finish. Conventional fin/rudder/tailplane/elevators, of similar construction to fuselage. Ground adjustable elevator trim. Non-retractable tailwheel landing gear; floats optional. Steerable tailwheel.
POWER PLANT: One 35 kW (47 hp) Rotax 503 two-cylinder two-stroke engine, with 2.58:1 geared reduction drive to a two-blade wooden fixed-pitch propeller. Three-blade propeller optional. Fuel capacity (petrol/oil mixture) 36.3 litres (9.6 US gallons; 8 Imp gallons).
ACCOMMODATION: Single upholstered glassfibre seat (adjustable fore and aft), or (Norseman II) two seats side by side with dual controls, in fully enclosed cabin. Large wrap-around windscreen. Reinforced transparent door on each side.

DIMENSIONS, EXTERNAL:	
Wing span	10.26 m (33 ft 8 in)
Length overall	6.07 m (19 ft 11 in)
Height overall	2.01 m (6 ft 7 in)
Propeller diameter (two-blade)	1.73 m (5 ft 8 in)
AREA:	
Wings, gross	14.07 m² (151.5 sq ft)

WEIGHTS (Norseman I, agricultural configuration):
Weight empty, equipped	144 kg (318 lb)
Fuel weight	26.1 kg (57.6 lb)
Max T-O weight	454 kg (1,000 lb)

PERFORMANCE (Norseman I at max T-O weight, agricultural configuration, hard runway, ISA at S/L):
Max level speed	89 knots (166 km/h; 103 mph)
Cruising speed, 75% power	78 knots (145 km/h; 90 mph)
Climbing speed:	
best climb angle	39 knots (72 km/h; 45 mph)
best climb speed	43 knots (80 km/h; 50 mph)
Stalling speed:	
power on	25 knots (45 km/h; 28 mph)
power off	29 knots (54 km/h; 33 mph)
T-O run	46 m (150 ft)
T-O to 15 m (50 ft)	76 m (250 ft)
Landing from 15 m (50 ft)	214 m (700 ft)
Endurance at 56 knots (105 km/h; 65 mph)	3 h
g limits	+6/−3

KESTREL
KESTREL SPORT AVIATION
PO Box 1808, Brockville, Ontario K6V 6K8
Telephone: 1 (613) 342 8366
Fax: 1 (613) 345 3567

KESTREL HAWK SERIES
Designed in several versions, the Hawk comes under ultralight and amateur-built regulations and is suited to sport flying and primary flight training, offering a fighter style cockpit and low operating costs. It is said to be capable of basic aerobatic manoeuvres such as loops and rolls.

Development began in about 1985 and an initial batch of 10 production aircraft was constructed that included four prototypes. The factory assembled ultralight is known simply as the Hawk, while the amateur-built version is the Kit Hawk. Both use a Rotax 503 engine. The amateur-built Sport Hawk and Float Hawk are versions with Rotax 532 engines for the US market, the latter featuring glassfibre amphibious floats. Delivery of Kit Hawks to customers in Canada was followed, from November 1988, by delivery of Sport Hawks and Float Hawks to US customers. Partial kits are also available. Construction from a kit takes between 300 and 400 working hours.

TYPE: Tandem two-seat ultralight and homebuilt biplane.

AIRFRAME: Equal-span biplane, with I interplane and diagonal struts. Pod and boom configuration, with conventional tail unit and controls. Homebuilt versions are all-metal construction; ultralight versions feature Tedlar polyurethane sheet wing skins. Semi-retractable landing gear with central monowheel, steerable tailwheel and balancer wheels beneath each lower wing.

POWER PLANT: Hawk and Kit Hawk use one 38.8 kW (52 hp) Rotax 503. Sport Hawk and Float Hawk use one 47.7 kW

(64 hp) Rotax 532LC. Two-blade pusher propeller. Design reportedly capable of accepting alternative engines of up to 93.2 kW (125 hp).

DIMENSIONS, EXTERNAL (all versions):

Wing span	7.47 m (24 ft 6 in)
Length overall	7.25 m (23 ft 9½ in)
Height overall	1.68 m (5 ft 6 in)
Propeller diameter	1.52 m (5 ft 0 in)

AREA (all versions):

Wings, gross	15.93 m² (171.5 sq ft)

WEIGHTS (A: Kit Hawk, B: Float Hawk):

Weight empty: A	179 kg (395 lb)
B	261 kg (575 lb)
Max T-O weight: A	376 kg (830 lb)
B	476 kg (1,050 lb)

PERFORMANCE (A and B as above):

Max level speed at S/L:	
A, B	87 knots (161 km/h; 100 mph)
Cruising speed, 75% power:	
A, B	71-74 knots (132-137 km/h; 82-85 mph)
Stalling speed: A	33 knots (61 km/h; 38 mph)
B	37 knots (68 km/h; 42 mph)
Max rate of climb at S/L: A, B	183 m (600 ft)/min
T-O run: A	69 m (225 ft)
B	92 m (300 ft)
B, from water	229 m (750 ft)
Landing run: A, B	107 m (350 ft)
B, on water	153 m (500 ft)
g limits: A	+6/−4
B	+4/−2

MACAIR
MACAIR INDUSTRIES INC

PO Box 1000, Baldwin, Ontario L0E 1A0
Telephone: 1 (416) 722 3411
Fax: 1 (416) 722 6457

MACAIR MERLIN

The Merlin is available in microlight and homebuilt versions, as a complete kit, in a series of partial kits, or ready assembled. The M50 version is available in Canada only and uses a Rotax 503 engine, while the Sport 65 uses the higher rated Rotax 582. Construction takes approximately 250 working hours.

TYPE: Side by side two-seat microlight and homebuilt.

AIRFRAME: Strut braced wings with aluminium D-cell and reinforced foam ribs, Ceconite 103 covered. Welded 4130 steel tube fuselage and tail unit, Falconar fabric

covered. Glassfibre engine cowling. Three-axis control. Non-retractable landing gear with tundra tyres; optional floats or skis. Brakes.

POWER PLANT: M50: one 37.3 kW (50 hp) Rotax 503. Sport 65: one 48.5 kW (65 hp) Rotax 582. Fuel capacity 19 litres (5 US gallons; 4.2 Imp gallons) and 38 litres (10 US gallons; 8.4 Imp gallons) respectively.

DIMENSIONS, EXTERNAL (A: M50, B: Sport 65):

Wing span: A, B	9.75 m (32 ft 0 in)
Length overall: A, B	6.10 m (20 ft 0 in)
Height overall: A, B	1.85 m (6 ft 1 in)
Propeller diameter: A	1.63 m (5 ft 4 in)
B	1.73 m (5 ft 8 in)

AREA:

Wings, gross: A, B	14.59 m² (157.0 sq ft)

WEIGHTS:

Weight empty: A	188 kg (415 lb)
B	193 kg (426 lb)
Max T-O weight: A	454 kg (1,000 lb)
B	499 kg (1,100 lb)

PERFORMANCE (two crew):

Max level speed:	
A	65-69 knots (121-129 km/h; 75-80 mph)
B	69-74 knots (129-137 km/h; 80-85 mph)
Cruising speed, 55% power:	
A	39-43 knots (72-80 km/h; 45-50 mph)
B	48-52 knots (89-97 km/h; 55-60 mph)
Stalling speed, power off:	
A, B	21 knots (39 km/h; 24 mph)
T-O run: A	46-61 m (150-200 ft)
B	23-46 m (75-150 ft)
Landing run: A, B	76 m (250 ft)
g limits	+6/−3

MOUNTAIN VALLEY
MOUNTAIN VALLEY AIR

Box 102, Lillooet, British Columbia V0K 1V0
Telephone: 1 (604) 256 4697

MOUNTAIN VALLEY AIR ARROW

This side by side two-seat Piper Cub look-alike is available as a Lazair conversion or as a complete kit offering new advanced wings with flaps. The fuselage has a 6061-T6 aluminium alloy structure of patented extrusion

fittings, and the aircraft is finished in Hipec except for the engine cowling, which is constructed of glassfibre. The crew sit on bush style safari seats in the semi-enclosed cabin and have a dual control stick and 'sun roof' opening. Power is provided by a 40.3 kW (54 hp) Rotax 503 engine with dual carburettors, reduction gear and electric starting. Fuel capacity is 22.7 litres (6 US gallons; 5 Imp gallons). The tailwheel of the non-retractable landing gear is of castoring type.

DIMENSIONS, EXTERNAL:

Wing span	11.89 m (39 ft 0 in)
Length of fuselage	5.94 m (19 ft 6 in)
Height overall	approx 2.03 m (6 ft 8 in)
Propeller diameter	1.73 m (5 ft 8 in)

WEIGHTS:

Weight empty	172 kg (380 lb)
Max T-O weight	385 kg (850 lb)

PERFORMANCE:

Cruising speed	56 knots (105 km/h; 65 mph)
Stalling speed:	
power off	22-24 knots (41-44 km/h; 25-27 mph)
power on	17-18 knots (31-32 km/h; 19-20 mph)
Max rate of climb at S/L	244 m (800 ft)/min
T-O run	76 m (250 ft)

MURPHY
MURPHY AVIATION LTD

8880-C Young Road South, Chilliwack, British Columbia V2P 4P5
Telephone: 1 (604) 792 5855
Fax: 1 (604) 792 8690
PRESIDENT: Darryl Murphy
SALES MANAGER: Dave Walker

In addition to the Renegade II and Renegade Spirit, Murphy has developed a new three-seat aircraft as the Rebel. This can be built as a homebuilt or ARV, or as a microlight in some countries.

MURPHY RENEGADE II

The prototype Renegade II first flew in May 1985. Ready assembled aircraft, plans and kits are available, the latter in four standards ranging from a partial parts kit to a 300-400 working hour quick build kit with all parts pre-manufactured plus partly assembled fuselage, wings and engine mounting. By 19 January 1991 a total of 10 assembled aircraft, 90 kits and 100 sets of plans had been delivered. Thirty aircraft had by then been completed.

TYPE: Two-seat dual-control ARV and homebuilt biplane; also conforms to microlight regulations in Canada and some European countries.

AIRFRAME: Strut and wire braced biplane of fabric covered all-metal construction. NACA 23012 wing section. Frise ailerons on lower only or all four wings. Optional extended wings with rounded tips. Non-retractable tailwheel landing gear. Optional floats, skis, agricultural spraygear and parachute.

POWER PLANT: One 35.8 kW (48 hp) Rotax 503 standard; 39.5 kW (53 hp) twin-carburettor Rotax 503.2V optional. Alternative engines include Rotax 532 and Teledyne Continental O65, O75 and O85. Fuel in two 29.5 litre (7.8 US gallon; 6.5 Imp gallon) tanks.

DIMENSIONS, EXTERNAL:

Wing span: upper	6.48 m (21 ft 3 in)
lower	6.05 m (19 ft 10 in)
Length overall	5.61 m (18 ft 5 in)
Height overall	2.08 m (6 ft 10 in)
Propeller diameter	1.73 m (5 ft 8 in)

AREA:

Wings, gross	14.29 or 15.61 m² (153.8 or 168.0 sq ft)

WEIGHTS:

Weight empty	163-181 kg (360-400 lb)
Max T-O weight	408 kg (900 lb)

PERFORMANCE (Rotax 503 engine and 2 crew, unless stated otherwise):

Max level speed at 305 m (1,000 ft)	
	69 knots (129 km/h; 80 mph)
Econ cruising speed	61 knots (113 km/h; 70 mph)
Stalling speed, power off	33 knots (61 km/h; 38 mph)
Max rate of climb at S/L	183 m (600 ft)/min
Service ceiling	3,660 m (12,000 ft)
T-O and landing run	61 m (200 ft)
Range with max payload	195 nm (362 km; 225 miles)
Endurance	4 h 30 min
g limits: pilot only	+10/−6
dual	+8.25/−4.5

MURPHY RENEGADE SPIRIT

The Renegade Spirit has the 47.7 kW (64 hp) Rotax 532 as its standard power plant, in a radial type cowling, and introduces a number of other internal and external refinements. The Rotax 912 flat-four and Norton rotary engines can be fitted. The prototype (C-IJLW) first flew on 6 May 1987. By 19 January 1991 a total of 26 assembled aircraft, 260 kits and 180 sets of plans had been delivered. About 100 aircraft had by then been completed.

DIMENSIONS, EXTERNAL AND WEIGHTS: As for Renegade II

PERFORMANCE (two crew):

Max level speed	78-82 knots (145-153 km/h; 90-95 mph)
Econ cruising speed	65 knots (120 km/h; 75 mph)
Stalling speed, power off	33 knots (62 km/h; 38 mph)
Max rate of climb at S/L	274 m (900 ft)/min
Service ceiling	3,660 m (12,000 ft)
T-O run	53 m (175 ft)
Landing run	61 m (200 ft)
Range with max payload	195 nm (362 km; 225 miles)
Endurance	4 h 30 min
g limits: pilot only	+10/−6 ultimate
dual	+8.25/−4.5

MURPHY REBEL

The Rebel is a three-seat high-wing cabin monoplane, suited to recreational, training, cross country, border patrol and other roles. It was designed to conform with FAR Pt 23 and JAR 22 Utility regulations at a gross weight of 385 kg (850 lb), the heavy payload and STOL performance being important features. Construction of the prototype started in October 1989, and this first flew in 1990. Building of production aircraft/kits began in October 1990, and by January 1991 49 had been ordered. Estimated assembly

time is 300-400 hours. The microlight version is being marketed only in some countries.

TYPE: Three-seat dual-control homebuilt, ARV and microlight.

AIRFRAME: Strut braced high-wing monoplane, with aluminium alloy structure; aluminium covered fuselage. Microlight version has fabric covered wings and control surfaces; Experimental version has aluminium covered wings. Modified NACA 4415 wing section. Conventional three-axis control, featuring full span flaperons. Non-retractable tailwheel landing gear, with brakes. Floats and skis optional.

POWER PLANT: One 59.7 kW (80 hp) Rotax 912, 48.5 kW (65 hp) Rotax 582, or 86.5 kW (116 hp) Textron Lycoming O-235 engine; 2.27 : 1 reduction gear with Rotax engines and direct drive with O-235. Ground adjustable wooden two-blade propeller. Standard fuel capacity 38 litres (10 US gallons; 8.3 Imp gallons); 152 litres (40 US gallons; 33.2 Imp gallons) in auxiliary tanks.

DIMENSIONS, EXTERNAL:

Wing span	9.14 m (30 ft 0 in)
Length overall	6.55 m (21 ft 6 in)
Height overall	1.98 m (6 ft 6 in)
Propeller diameter	1.78 m (5 ft 10 in)

AREA:

Wings, gross	13.94 m² (150.0 sq ft)

WEIGHTS:

Weight empty	295-329 kg (650-725 lb)
Baggage capacity	45.5-68 kg (100-150 lb)
Max T-O weight	658 kg (1,450 lb)

PERFORMANCE (A: Rotax 912, B: O-235):

Max level speed: A	100 knots (185 km/h; 115 mph)
B	113 knots (209 km/h; 130 mph)
Max cruising speed at S/L:	
A	82 knots (153 km/h; 95 mph)
B	96 knots (177 km/h; 110 mph)
Econ cruising speed: A	74 knots (137 km/h; 85 mph)
B	87 knots (161 km/h; 100 mph)
Stalling speed, flaps down:	
A, B with power off	28 knots (52 km/h; 32 mph)
A, B with 50% power	21 knots (39 km/h; 24 mph)
Max rate of climb at S/L: B	366 m (1,200 ft)/min
Service ceiling: B	3,960 m (13,000 ft)
T-O run: B	77 m (250 ft)
Landing run: B	92 m (300 ft)
Range: B	442 nm (820 km; 510 miles)
Endurance: B	6 h 45 min
g limits	+6.6/−4.4

Macair Merlin two-seat microlight/homebuilt *(Geoffrey P. Jones)*

Murphy Renegade Spirit two-seat biplane *(J. M. G. Gradidge)*

Mountain Valley Air Arrow two-seat light aircraft *(Peter M. Bowers)*

Murphy Rebel three-seat cabin monoplane *(J. M. G. Gradidge)*

Rotary Air Force GT 2000 *(Geoffrey P. Jones)*

NOVADYNE
NOVADYNE AIRCRAFT INC

The address for Novadyne Aircraft given in the 1990-91 *Jane's* is no longer current. Details of the company's Toucan Series II, and an illustration, can be found in that edition.

REPLICA PLANS
REPLICA PLANS
14752 90th Avenue, Surrey, British Columbia V3R 1A4

Details of the Replica Plans S.E.5A replica, and an illustration, can be found in the 1988-89 *Jane's*.

ROTARY AIR FORCE
ROTARY AIR FORCE INC
Hangar 3, Box 1205, Ponoka, Alberta T0C 2H0
Telephone: 1 (403) 783 8484
Fax: 1 (403) 783 6300
VICE-PRESIDENT: Pete Haseloh
Kits are available to construct the RAF 1000 and 2000 series autogyros.

ROTARY AIR FORCE GT 1000
TYPE: Single-seat homebuilt autogyro.
ROTOR SYSTEM: Two-blade rotor of composite/aluminium construction. Pre-rotator. Optional rotor brake to be developed.
AIRFRAME: Based on square section tubing. Vertical tail. Non-retractable tricycle landing gear.
POWER PLANT: One Subaru EA82 1,800 cc engine, rated at over 74.5 kW (100 hp), driving a Warp Drive composite pusher propeller via 2.10 : 1 belt reduction unit.

DIMENSIONS, EXTERNAL:
Rotor diameter	8.53 m (28 ft 0 in)
Length overall	3.71 m (12 ft 2 in)
Height overall	2.50 m (8 ft 2½ in)
Propeller diameter	1.68 m (5 ft 6 in)

WEIGHTS:
Weight empty	215 kg (475 lb)
Max payload	340 kg (750 lb)

PERFORMANCE:
Max level speed	109 knots (201 km/h; 125 mph)
Cruising speed, 75% power	78 knots (145 km/h; 90 mph)
Min flying speed	7-9 knots (13-16 km/h; 8-10 mph)
Will not stall	
Max rate of climb at S/L	366 m (1,200 ft)/min
T-O run	0-23 m (0-75 ft)
Landing run	0.3-3 m (1-10 ft)

ROTARY AIR FORCE SERIES 2000
TYPE: Side by side two-seat autogyro.
ROTOR SYSTEM: As for GT 1000.

AIRFRAME: As for GT 1000. Fully enclosed half-glazed cockpit pod.
POWER PLANT: As for GT 1000.
DIMENSIONS, EXTERNAL:
Rotor diameter	9.14 m (30 ft 0 in)
Length overall	4.14 m (13 ft 7 in)
Height overall	2.50 m (8 ft 2½ in)
Propeller diameter	1.68 or 1.73 m (5 ft 6 in or 5 ft 8 in)

WEIGHTS:
Weight empty	254 kg (560 lb)
Max payload	256 kg (565 lb)

PERFORMANCE (two persons):
Max level speed	78 knots (145 km/h; 90 mph)
Cruising speed	52 knots (97 km/h; 60 mph)
Min flying speed	9-13 knots (16-24 km/h; 10-15 mph)
Will not stall	
Max rate of climb at S/L (pilot only)	305 m (1,000 ft)/min
T-O run	23-107 m (75-350 ft)
Landing run	0-3 m (0-10 ft)
Endurance, with 30 min reserves	4 h 36 min

SEAWIND INTERNATIONAL — *See SNA Inc in USA*

ULTIMATE
ULTIMATE AIRCRAFT CORPORATION
Guelph Airpark, Guelph, Ontario N1H 6H8
Telephone: 1 (519) 836 8622
PRESIDENT: Gordon Price

ULTIMATE AIRCRAFT 10 DASH 100/300
Ultimate Aircraft is offering sets of plans, kits and ready assembled examples of three closely related single-seat biplanes of the 10 Dash series. The basic model is the **10 Dash 100**, designed to be an affordable sporting biplane with a 74.5 or 134 kW (100 or 180 hp) engine. Power plants between these ratings can be installed at the customer's option. A typical power plant is a 74.5 kW (100 hp) Teledyne Continental O-200. The prototype 10 Dash 100 flew for the first time on 6 October 1985.

The **10 Dash 200** was designed as a modern competition aerobatic aircraft, utilising a 134-149 kW (180-200 hp) engine with Ellison throttle body injector and a constant-speed Hoffmann or MT composites propeller. The final model in the range is the **10 Dash 300**, a state of the art competition aircraft, with longer-span wings, incorporating full-span symmetrical ailerons; a longer fuselage; and a 224 kW (300 hp) or 261 kW (350 hp) Textron Lycoming engine, driving a three-blade Hoffmann propeller.

TYPE: Single-seat homebuilt sporting and aerobatic biplane.

AIRFRAME: Braced biplane, with Ceconite covered wooden wings. Near symmetrical wing section. Upper and lower full-span ailerons of aluminium alloy. 'Macro flap' control (5° aileron droop with 30° 'up' elevator). Welded steel tube fuselage structure, aluminium alloy and Ceconite covered. Aluminium alloy turtledeck. Glassfibre nose cowlings. Braced steel tube tail unit, Ceconite covered. Non-retractable tailwheel landing gear.

POWER PLANT: See introduction. 10-100 has fuel capacity of 83 litres (22 US gallons; 18.3 Imp gallons). Optional 57 litre (15 US gallon; 12.5 Imp gallon) strap-on centre-section tank. Inverted fuel system.

DIMENSIONS, EXTERNAL:
Wing span: 10-100, 10-200	4.83 m (15 ft 10 in)
10-300	5.95 m (19 ft 6 in)
Length overall: 10-100	5.33 m (17 ft 6 in)
10-200	5.49 m (18 ft 0 in)
10-300	6.40 m (21 ft 0 in)
Height overall: 10-100, 10-200	1.68 m (5 ft 6 in)

AREAS:
Wings, gross: 10-100, 10-200	8.92 m² (96.0 sq ft)
10-300	11.15 m² (120.0 sq ft)

WEIGHTS:
Weight empty: 10-100	358 kg (790 lb)
10-200	420 kg (925 lb)
10-300	522 kg (1,150 lb)
Max T-O weight: 10-100, 10-200	612 kg (1,350 lb)
10-300	748 kg (1,650 lb)

PERFORMANCE:
Max level speed:	
10-100	165 knots (306 km/h; 190 mph)
10-200	191 knots (354 km/h; 220 mph)
10-300	217 knots (402 km/h; 250 mph)
Cruising speed, 75% power:	
10-100	122 knots (225 km/h; 140 mph)
10-200	148 knots (273 km/h; 170 mph)
10-300	165 knots (305 km/h; 190 mph)
Stalling speed:	
10-100: power off	46 knots (86 km/h; 53 mph)
power on	44 knots (81 km/h; 50 mph)
Max rate of climb at S/L: 10-100	350 m (1,150 ft)/min
10-300	915 m (3,000 ft)/min
T-O run: 10-100	180 m (590 ft)
Landing run: 10-100	155 m (510 ft)
Range: 10-100	564 nm (1,046 km; 650 miles)
10-200	434 nm (804 km; 500 miles)
10-300	520-781 nm (965-1,448 km; 600-900 miles)
Rate of roll: 10-200	360°/s
g limits: all	+7/−5 operating

ULTIMATE AIRCRAFT 20 DASH 300
The Ultimate Aircraft 20 Dash 300 is identical to the 10 Dash 300 except for having two seats in tandem under a one-piece bubble canopy. It offers the same choice of Textron Lycoming engines and other options, and is available in two forms: the **20 Dash 300T** is a two-seat aerobatic training aircraft; the **20 Dash 300E** is the exhibition model.

DIMENSIONS, EXTERNAL:
As for 10-300

WEIGHTS:
Weight empty	545 kg (1,200 lb)
Max T-O weight	907 kg (2,000 lb)

PERFORMANCE:
Max level speed	217 knots (402 km/h; 250 mph)
Cruising speed, 75% power	
	165 knots (305 km/h; 190 mph)
Range	434-608 nm (804-1,126 km; 500-700 miles)

ULTIMATE AIRCRAFT (PITTS) SPECIAL
The standard Pitts S-1 and S-2 Specials are mentioned under the Christen heading in the main US Aircraft section of this edition. Basic feature of the Ultimate versions of these aircraft is the use of new wings with larger control surfaces and significantly increased strength of construction. These make it possible to roll at 360°/s at normal flying speeds and 240°/s at low speeds, and to perform five vertical rolls on take-off. The wings are jig built to fit any Pitts Special without modification. Other features include low-profile glassfibre engine cowlings and Plexiglas cockpit canopy, and the option to build the fuselage up to 21 cm (8½ in) longer to increase comfort.

POWER PLANT: Conformal auxiliary fuel tanks, filled with Explosafe explosion-proof metal foil, strapped above centre-section of top wing. Capacity 34 or 57 litres (9 or 15 US gallons; 7.5 or 12.5 Imp gallons) for S-1; 68 litres (18 US gallons; 15 Imp gallons) for S-2.

DIMENSION, EXTERNAL (S-1):
Wing span (upper and lower)	4.77 m (15 ft 8 in)

WESTERN
WESTERN AIRCRAFT SUPPLIES
623 Markerville Road North-East, Calgary, Alberta T2E 5X1
Telephone: 1 (403) 276 3087
DIRECTOR: Jean J. Peters

WESTERN PGK-1 HIRONDELLE
The prototype Hirondelle first flew on 27 June 1976. Plans and wood kits are believed to be available, as well as some preformed components.

TYPE: Side by side two-seat, dual-control homebuilt aircraft.

AIRFRAME: Wing section NACA 23012. All wooden structure, with Dacron covering on wings and rear fuselage. Glassfibre cabin top. Non-retractable tailwheel landing gear.

POWER PLANT: One 86 kW (115 hp) Textron Lycoming O-235-C1B. Two fuel tanks, each 54.5 litres (14.4 US gallons; 12 Imp gallons) capacity.

DIMENSIONS, EXTERNAL:
Wing span	7.92 m (26 ft 0 in)
Length overall	6.27 m (20 ft 7 in)
Height overall	2.29 m (7 ft 6 in)
Propeller diameter	1.68 m (5 ft 6 in)

AREA:
Wings, gross	10.96 m² (118.0 sq ft)

WEIGHTS:
Weight empty, equipped	428 kg (944 lb)
Max T-O weight	669 kg (1,475 lb)

PERFORMANCE (at max T-O weight):
Max level speed	123 knots (228 km/h; 142 mph)
Max cruising speed	117 knots (217 km/h; 135 mph)
Stalling speed	53 knots (97 km/h; 60 mph)
Max rate of climb at S/L	over 305 m (1,000 ft)/min
Service ceiling	3,840 m (12,600 ft)
T-O run	approx 228 m (750 ft)
Endurance, with 45 min reserves	3 h 36 min

ZENAIR
ZENAIR AIRCRAFT LTD
Huronia Airport, Midland, Ontario L4R 4K8
Telephone: 1 (705) 526 2871
Fax: 1 (705) 526 8022
PRESIDENT AND DESIGNER: Christophe Heintz
MARKETING MANAGER: Sebastien C. Heintz

Founded in 1974, Zenair designs, develops and manufactures light aircraft. It began by marketing the Zénith two-seat homebuilt aircraft, and by early 1991 there were more than 1,000 Zenair aircraft flying in 47 different countries. It had licensed representatives in Africa, South America, France, Italy, Japan, Spain and the UK, and is currently developing a basic trainer for the primary recreational aircraft category. The company's 1991 production schedule concentrates mainly on the STOL CH 701 and Zodiac models.

ZENAIR MONO Z-CH 100
The single-seat Mono Z-CH 100 is of generally similar construction to the two-seat Zénith, but is smaller and less powerful. The prototype (C-GNYM) made its first flight on 8 May 1975.

Construction drawings and manual, materials, parts and complete kits are available by special order only. Building time is estimated at under 600 working hours.

TYPE: Single-seat homebuilt aircraft.

AIRFRAME: All-metal semi-monocoque construction. Wing section GAW-1 (modified). Non-retractable tricycle or, optionally, tailwheel landing gear.

POWER PLANT: One 41 kW (55 hp) 1,700 cc converted Volkswagen engine in prototype. Engines from 33.5 kW (45 hp) 1,600 cc Volkswagen to 74.5 kW (100 hp) Teledyne Continental O-200 optional. Fuel capacity 55 litres (14.4 US gallons; 12 Imp gallons).

DIMENSIONS, EXTERNAL:
Wing span	6.71 m (22 ft 0 in)
Length overall	5.94 m (19 ft 6 in)
Height overall	1.98 m (6 ft 6 in)
Propeller diameter	1.47 m (4 ft 10 in)

AREA:
Wings, gross	8.50 m² (91.5 sq ft)

WEIGHTS (48.5 kW; 65 hp engine):
Weight empty	286 kg (630 lb)
Baggage capacity	11.3 kg (25 lb)
Max T-O weight	435 kg (960 lb)

PERFORMANCE (engine as above):
Max level speed	109 knots (200 km/h; 125 mph)
Cruising speed (75% power)	
	95 knots (177 km/h; 110 mph)
Stalling speed	42 knots (77 km/h; 48 mph)
Max rate of climb at S/L	250 m (820 ft)/min
Service ceiling	over 3,660 m (12,000 ft)
T-O and landing run	168 m (550 ft)
Range with max fuel	350 nm (645 km; 400 miles)
g limits	±9 ultimate

ZENAIR ACRO-ZÉNITH CH 150
Developed from the Mono Z-CH 100, the CH 150 is intended for aerobatic training and competition flying. The prototype first flew on 19 May 1980. Kits, complete except for engine, are available to amateur constructors by special order only. All of the more critical parts, such as wing spars and ribs, are premanufactured.

TYPE: Single-seat homebuilt aircraft.

AIRFRAME: All-metal semi-monocoque construction. Wing section NACA 0015. Non-retractable tailwheel landing gear. Skis optional.

POWER PLANT: One 112 kW (150 hp) Textron Lycoming O-320 standard. Engines of 74.5-134 kW (100-180 hp) can be fitted. Fuel capacity 55 litres (14.4 US gallons; 12 Imp gallons). Can be increased to 136 litres (36 US gallons; 30 Imp gallons) by use of ferry tank. Fuel and oil systems equipped for inverted flight.

DIMENSIONS, EXTERNAL:
Wing span	6.15 m (20 ft 2 in)
Length overall	6.17 m (20 ft 3 in)
Height overall	1.52 m (5 ft 0 in)
Propeller diameter	1.78 m (5 ft 10 in)

AREA:
Wings, gross	7.83 m² (84.3 sq ft)

WEIGHTS (112 kW; 150 hp O-320 engine. Wooden propeller and ferry tank fitted. No electrics):
Weight empty	331 kg (730 lb)
Baggage capacity	20 kg (44 lb)
Typical aerobatic T-O weight	440 kg (970 lb)
Max T-O weight	522 kg (1,150 lb)

PERFORMANCE (conditions as above):
Max level speed at S/L	156 knots (290 km/h; 180 mph)
Econ cruising speed at 915 m (3,000 ft)	
	126 knots (233 km/h; 145 mph)
Stalling speed	48 knots (89 km/h; 55 mph)
Max rate of climb at S/L	670 m (2,200 ft)/min
Service ceiling	over 4,875 m (16,000 ft)
T-O run	213 m (700 ft)
Landing run	183 m (600 ft)

Ultimate Aircraft 10 Dash 100 *(J.M.G. Gradidge)*

Super Acro-Zénith CH 180 unlimited aerobatic aircraft *(Neil A. Macdougall)*

Prototype Western PGK-1 Hirondelle two-seat light aircraft

Zenair Zénith-CH 200 with float landing gear

Zenair Mono Z-CH 100 with optional tailwheel landing gear
(Neil A. Macdougall)

Range: with standard fuel 260 nm (483 km; 300 miles)
 with ferry fuel, 55% power
  660 nm (1,223 km; 760 miles)
Endurance with standard fuel 2 h
g limits ± 12 ultimate

ZENAIR SUPER ACRO-ZÉNITH CH 180

The first Super Acro-Zénith CH 180 (C-GZEN) was an unlimited aerobatic aircraft, powered by a 171.5 kW (230 hp) Textron Lycoming IO-360 engine. It differed from the Acro-Zénith CH 150 in several respects, apart from engine, the most obvious external changes being a revised tail unit and wings without dihedral. The front fuel tank capacity is 45.5 litres (12 US gallons; 10 Imp gallons) and the rear, with header, 77 litres (20.4 US gallons; 17 Imp gallons). It is available by special order only. Construction time is 800 working hours. Engines of up to 149 kW (200 hp) can be fitted.

DIMENSIONS, EXTERNAL:
 Wing span 6.15 m (20 ft 2 in)
 Length overall 6.17 m (20 ft 3 in)
 Height overall 1.65 m (5 ft 5 in)
AREA:
 Wings, gross 7.90 m² (85.0 sq ft)
WEIGHTS:
 Weight empty 363 kg (800 lb)
 Max T-O weight 521 kg (1,150 lb)
PERFORMANCE (149 kW; 200 hp engine):
 Cruising speed (75% power)
  165 knots (305 km/h; 190 mph)
 Stalling speed 42 knots (77 km/h; 48 mph)
 Max rate of climb at S/L 915 m (3,000 ft)/min
 Max rate of roll 270°/s
 Range with max fuel, 55% power
  565 nm (1,046 km; 650 miles)
 g limits: ± 8 normal
  ± 12 ultimate

ZENAIR ZÉNITH-CH 200

The prototype Zénith-CH 200 flew for the first time on 22 March 1970. Sets of plans and a constructional manual are

available to amateur builders, together with materials, parts and complete kits. Many hundreds of kits and plans have been sold to customers in 44 countries.

The following description applies to the standard Zénith-CH 200:

TYPE: Side by side two-seat, dual-control homebuilt aircraft.
AIRFRAME: All-metal semi-monocoque construction, except for glassfibre engine cowling and fairings. NACA 64A515 (modified) wing section. Plans show rudder only, with no fin. Conventional fin and rudder can be fitted if desired. Non-retractable tricycle or, optionally, tailwheel landing gear. Floats and skis optional.
POWER PLANT: Design suitable for engines from 63.5 kW (85 hp) to 119 kW (160 hp). Fuel capacity 90 litres (24 US gallons; 20 Imp gallons). Optional fuel tanks in wing leading-edges, total capacity 72.5 litres (19.2 US gallons; 16 Imp gallons).

DIMENSIONS, EXTERNAL:
 Wing span 7.00 m (22 ft 11¾ in)
 Length overall 6.25 m (20 ft 6 in)
 Height overall 2.11 m (6 ft 11 in)
 Propeller diameter 1.83 m (6 ft 0 in)
AREA:
 Wings, gross 9.80 m² (105.9 sq ft)
WEIGHTS (93 kW; 125 hp engine):
 Weight empty 422 kg (930 lb)
 Baggage capacity 35 kg (77 lb)
 Max T-O weight 680 kg (1,500 lb)
PERFORMANCE (at max T-O weight. 93 kW; 125 hp engine):
 Max level speed at S/L 131 knots (243 km/h; 151 mph)
 Cruising speed (75% power) at S/L
  122 knots (227 km/h; 141 mph)
 Stalling speed, flaps down 47 knots (87 km/h; 54 mph)
 Max rate of climb at S/L 335 m (1,100 ft)/min
 T-O and landing run 244 m (800 ft)
 Range with max fuel 391 nm (724 km; 450 miles)
 g limit +9 ultimate

ZENAIR ZÉNITH-CH 250

The Zénith-CH 250 is a de luxe version of the Zénith-CH 200 with two 65 litre (16.8 US gallon; 14 Imp gallon) fuel tanks in the wings and a 0.71 m³ (25 cu ft) baggage area. A

forward sliding canopy and rear windows similar to those of the Tri-Z CH 300 are fitted. Recommended engines are in the 86-119 kW (115-160 hp) range. A tailwheel or float landing gear can be fitted as alternatives to the standard tricycle type.

WEIGHTS (112 kW; 150 hp engine):
 Weight empty 449 kg (990 lb)
 Max T-O weight 730 kg (1,610 lb)
PERFORMANCE (engine as above):
 Max level speed 144 knots (267 km/h; 166 mph)
 Cruising speed (75% power)
  130 knots (241 km/h; 150 mph)
 Stalling speed 45 knots (84 km/h; 52 mph)
 Max rate of climb at S/L 518 m (1,700 ft)/min
 T-O and landing run 198 m (650 ft)
 Range with standard fuel 469 nm (869 km; 540 miles)

ZENAIR TRI-Z CH 300

The three-seat Tri-Z CH 300 is a stretched version of the two-seat CH 200, with an enlarged cabin to provide room for a rear bench seat able to carry a third adult, two children or 95 kg (210 lb) of baggage. Electrically actuated slotted flaps are fitted. Recommended power is in the 93-134 kW (125-180 hp) range. Fuel is carried in two 65 litre (16.8 US gallon; 14 Imp gallon) wing tanks. Extra fuel can be carried in further wing tanks. The prototype made its first flight on 9 July 1977.

Sets of plans and a constructional manual are available to amateur builders, as are materials, prefabricated component parts and complete kits. Construction from kits takes 1,000 working hours on average.

DIMENSIONS, EXTERNAL:
 Wing span 8.10 m (26 ft 6¾ in)
 Length overall 6.85 m (22 ft 5¾ in)
 Height overall 2.08 m (6 ft 10 in)
AREA:
 Wings, gross 12.00 m² (129.2 sq ft)
WEIGHTS (93 kW; 125 hp engine):
 Weight empty 476 kg (1,050 lb)
 Max T-O weight 816 kg (1,800 lb)
PERFORMANCE (engine as above):
 Max level speed 130 knots (241 km/h; 150 mph)

Econ cruising speed	109 knots (201 km/h; 125 mph)
Stalling speed, flaps down	45 knots (82 km/h; 51 mph)
Max rate of climb at S/L	244 m (800 ft)/min
Range (75% power)	521 nm (965 km; 600 miles)
g limits	±5.7 ultimate

ZENAIR ZODIAC CH 600

The first flight of the CH 60 was achieved in June 1984. Plans and a kit of component parts (45 per cent premanufactured) for the improved CH 600 are available to amateur builders. Construction from a kit takes about 400 working hours. It is suited to the first time builder. Depending on national regulations, it may be registered either as an Experimental homebuilt or as a microlight.

TYPE: Side by side two-seat, dual-control homebuilt or microlight aircraft.

AIRFRAME: All-metal construction. No fixed fin. Wing section NACA 65018. Non-retractable tricycle or tail-wheel landing gear. Skis and floats optional.

POWER PLANT: One 63.4 kW (85 hp) Rotax 912, with reduction gear, 47.7 kW (64 hp) Rotax 532, 48.5-74.5 kW (65-100 hp) Teledyne Continental, 37.3 kW (50 hp) Volkswagen without electric starting or 52 kW (70 hp) Volkswagen engine. Fuel capacity 60 litres (16 US gallons; 13.3 Imp gallons).

DIMENSIONS, EXTERNAL:	
Wing span	8.20 m (26 ft 10¾ in)
Length overall	5.65 m (18 ft 6½ in)
Height overall	1.90 m (6 ft 2¾ in)
Propeller diameter	1.52 m (5 ft 0 in)
AREA:	
Wings, gross	12.1 m² (130.2 sq ft)
WEIGHTS:	
Weight empty, equipped	268 kg (590 lb)
Max T-O weight	476 kg (1,050 lb)
PERFORMANCE (at max T-O weight):	
Max level speed at S/L	117 knots (217 km/h; 135 mph)
Econ cruising speed	104 knots (193 km/h; 120 mph)
Stalling speed	39 knots (71 km/h; 44 mph)
Max rate of climb at S/L	427 m (1,400 ft)/min
Service ceiling	more than 4,875 m (16,000 ft)
T-O run	122 m (400 ft)
Landing run	138 m (450 ft)
Range with max fuel, 75% power	
	416 nm (772 km; 480 miles)
Endurance	4 h
g limits	±6.9

ZENAIR ZODIAC CH 601

This new two-seater is very similar to the CH 600 but has been developed specifically to meet microlight/ARV regulations. New features include reduced empty weight, wider cabin (1.12 m; 3 ft 8 in), and standard wing lockers for baggage or extra fuel. A higher performance model was expected to follow in Autumn 1991, featuring a speed wing and larger engine.

Construction of the prototype began in September 1990 and it first flew in October that year. Kit production started in January 1991, by which time 20 aircraft had been ordered. All components are available to those selecting to build from plans. A military variant, suitable for surveillance, patrol and other roles, is designated **CH 601-M**.

TYPE: Side by side two-seat microlight, ARV and homebuilt; conforms to Canadian TP 10141 regulations.

AIRFRAME: Similar to CH 600.

POWER PLANT: One 59.7 kW (80 hp) Rotax 912. Fuel capacity 60 litres (16 US gallons; 13.3 Imp gallons). Two 28.4 litre (7.5 US gallon; 6.25 Imp gallon) auxiliary tanks optional.

DIMENSIONS, EXTERNAL:	
Wing span	8.23 m (27 ft 0 in)
Length overall	5.64 m (18 ft 6 in)

Height overall	1.52 m (5 ft 0 in)
Propeller diameter	1.73 m (5 ft 8 in)
AREA:	
Wings, gross	12.08 m² (130.0 sq ft)
WEIGHTS:	
Weight empty	249 kg (550 lb)
Baggage capacity	36 kg (80 lb)
Max T-O weight	476 kg (1,050 lb)
PERFORMANCE:	
Max level speed	100 knots (185 km/h; 115 mph)
Max and econ cruising speed at 915 m (3,000 ft)	
	91 knots (169 km/h; 105 mph)
Stalling speed	39 knots (71 km/h; 44 mph)
Max rate of climb at S/L	219 m (720 ft)/min
Service ceiling	more than 3,660 m (12,000 ft)
T-O run	168 m (550 ft)
Landing run	199 m (650 ft)
Range	278 nm (515 km; 320 miles)
Endurance	4 h
g limits	±6

ZENAIR STOL CH 701

The prototype of this Experimental category aircraft was flown for the first time in Summer 1986. The CH 701 is a strut braced high-wing cabin monoplane, capable of being completed with a tricycle or tailwheel landing gear, and with floats, amphibious and ski gears as options. Power is provided by a 37.3 kW (50 hp) Rotax 503 engine in the prototype, but a 59.7 kW (80 hp) Rotax 912, 48.5 kW (65 hp) Rotax 582, 44.7-52 kW (60-70 hp) VW, or 48.5-67 kW (65-90 hp) Teledyne Continental engine are optional; standard fuel capacity is 42 litres (11 US gallons; 9.2 Imp gallons). To achieve STOL performance, full span leading-edge flaps are fitted to the near constant chord wings (foldable). Plans, 49 or 85 per cent kits, or fully assembled aircraft are available. An agricultural version is available with a Micro AG spraying/dusting system. Aircraft are assembled by Zenair's Colombian subsidiary, Agricopteros Ltda (which see). In most countries, CH 701s can be registered either as microlights or as Experimental homebuilts.

DIMENSIONS, EXTERNAL:	
Wing span	8.23 m (27 ft 0 in)
Length overall	6.71 m (22 ft 0 in)
Propeller diameter	1.73 m (5 ft 8 in)
AREA:	
Wings, gross	11.33 m² (122.0 sq ft)
WEIGHTS:	
Weight empty	208 kg (460 lb)
Max T-O weight	435 kg (960 lb)
PERFORMANCE (48.5 kW; 65 hp engine, at max T-O weight):	
Max level speed at S/L	72 knots (134 km/h; 83 mph)
Max cruising speed	65 knots (121 km/h; 75 mph)
Stalling speed	25 knots (45 km/h; 28 mph)
Max rate of climb at S/L	250 m (820 ft)/min
Service ceiling	3,660 m (12,000 ft)
T-O run	35 m (115 ft)
Landing run	28 m (90 ft)
Range: standard fuel	217 nm (402 km; 250 miles)
with wing tanks	390 nm (724 km; 450 miles)
Endurance	1 h 40 min
g limits	+6/−3

ZENAIR SUPER STOL CH 801

Suitable for surveillance, patrol, training, crop spraying, light transport and other roles, the Super STOL CH 801 was designed as a light utility aircraft and carries the designation **CH 801-M** in military form. Construction of the first prototype began in January 1988 and the first flight was probably made in mid-1990. Production began that year.

TYPE: Four-seat utility monoplane.

AIRFRAME: All-metal strut braced high-wing monoplane, with steel tube fuselage structure and aluminium alloy wing structure, the whole skinned with aluminium alloy. Ailerons, flaps, fixed leading-edge slats, rudder and elevators. Non-retractable tricycle landing gear, with brakes. Optional floats, amphibious floats or skis.

POWER PLANT: One 112 kW (150 hp) Textron Lycoming O-320 standard. Optional engines in the 74.5-149 kW (100-200 hp) range. Two fuel tanks in wings, total capacity 75 litres (20 US gallons; 16.7 Imp gallons).

DIMENSIONS, EXTERNAL:	
Wing span	9.40 m (30 ft 10 in)
Length overall	7.06 m (23 ft 2 in)
Height overall	2.70 m (8 ft 10¼ in)
AREA:	
Wings, gross	15.00 m² (161.45 sq ft)
WEIGHTS:	
Weight empty	460 kg (1,014 lb)
Max T-O weight	890 kg (1,962 lb)
PERFORMANCE:	
Max level speed at 915 m (3,000 ft)	
	100 knots (185 km/h; 115 mph)
Econ cruising speed	89 knots (165 km/h; 103 mph)
Stalling speed, flaps down	34 knots (62 km/h; 39 mph)
Max rate of climb at S/L	320 m (1,050 ft)/min
Service ceiling	more than 6,100 m (20,000 ft)
T-O run	55 m (181 ft)
Landing run	47 m (155 ft)
Range	400 nm (741 km; 460 miles)
Endurance	5 h
g limits	+6/−3

ZENAIR ZÉNITH CH 2000

Fitting into the Zenair range as a side by side two-seat and smaller span derivative of the Tri-Z CH 300, the Zénith CH 2000 was designed to conform to Canadian Recreational category regulations, but is aimed at the primary training market.

AIRFRAME: All-metal construction. Wing section LS(1)0417 (mod). Non-retractable tricycle landing gear, with optional floats and skis.

POWER PLANT: One 74.5 kW (100 hp) Teledyne Continental O-200. Fuel capacity 100 litres (26.4 US gallons; 22 Imp gallons) standard, 200 litres (52.8 US gallons; 44 Imp gallons) optional.

DIMENSIONS, EXTERNAL:	
Wing span	7.60 m (24 ft 11¼ in)
Length overall	6.85 m (22 ft 5¾ in)
Height overall	2.30 m (7 ft 6½ in)
Propeller diameter	1.83 m (6 ft 0 in)
AREA:	
Wings, gross	11.00 m² (118.4 sq ft)

WEIGHTS (A: aerobatic category, B: standard):	
Max payload: A	180 kg (396 lb)
B, with baggage	230 kg (507 lb)
Max T-O weight: A	630 kg (1,389 lb)
B	680 kg (1,499 lb)
PERFORMANCE (estimated):	
Max level speed	124 knots (230 km/h; 143 mph)
Econ cruising speed	103 knots (190 km/h; 118 mph)
Stalling speed	42 knots (78 km/h; 49 mph)
Max rate of climb at S/L	259 m (850 ft)/min
Service ceiling	more than 3,660 m (12,000 ft)
T-O run	213 m (700 ft)
Landing run	183 m (600 ft)
Range with max standard and optional fuel:	
B	928 nm (1,720 km; 1,068 miles)
Range with max payload and standard fuel:	
B	464 nm (860 km; 534 miles)

CHINA, PEOPLE'S REPUBLIC

SAP
SHIJIAZHUANG AIRCRAFT PLANT

PO Box 164, Shijiazhuang, Hebei 050062
Telephone: 86 Shijiazhuang 744251
Telex: 26236 HBJXC CN

Details of the Qingting W-5 series (Dragonfly 5) of microlights can be found in the tables that follow this section.

SAP QINGTING W-6 (DRAGONFLY 6)

The Qingting W-6 is a three-axis control single-seat homebuilt of more refined design than the W-5 series of microlights. The structure is said to be all-metal. Power is provided by a Limbach L-2400 engine.

DIMENSIONS, EXTERNAL:	
Wing span	9.802 m (32 ft 2 in)
Length overall	6.676 m (21 ft 10¾ in)
Height overall	1.74 m (5 ft 8½ in)
AREA:	
Wings, gross	11.52 m² (124.0 sq ft)

WEIGHTS:	
Weight empty	253 kg (558 lb)
Max T-O weight	500 kg (1,102 lb)
PERFORMANCE:	
Max level speed	70 knots (130 km/h; 81 mph)
Normal cruising speed	51 knots (95 km/h; 59 mph)
Max rate of climb at S/L	180 m (590 ft)/min
Service ceiling	2,500 m (8,200 ft)
T-O run	118 m (388 ft)
Landing run	87 m (285 ft)
Range	162 nm (300 km; 186 miles)

Zenair Zodiac CH 600 with tricycle landing gear

Zenair STOL CH 701 in floatplane form

Zenair Zodiac CH 601 microlight/ARV/homebuilt

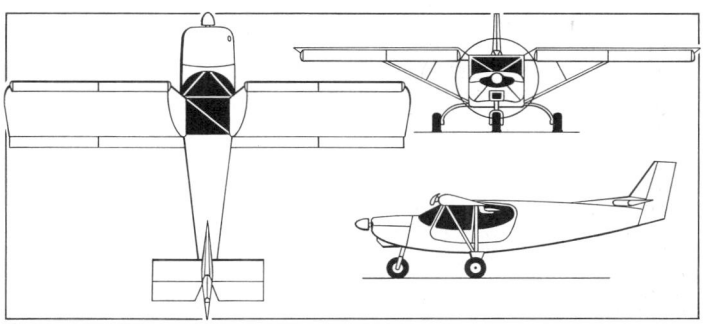

Zenair Super STOL CH 801 utility aircraft (Jane's/Mike Keep)

Martekno ATOL with optional wheeled landing gear

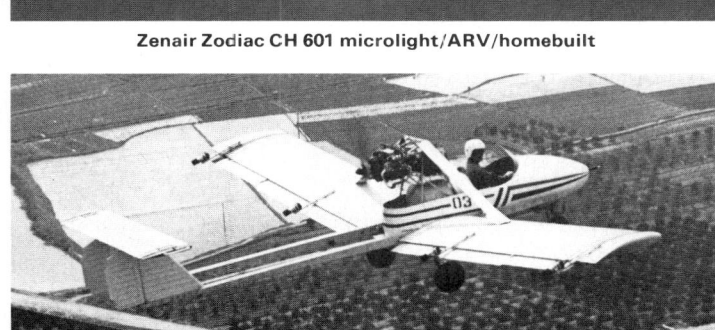

SAP Qingting W-6 homebuilt aircraft

FINLAND

MARTEKNO
MARTEKNO FINLAND OY

Nikkarinkuja 8, 96910 Rovaniemi
Telephone: 358 (60) 362 077
Fax: 358 (60) 362 388/362 394

MARTEKNO ATOL

The ATOL flying-boat amphibian is offered in two Experimental and three microlight versions, in assembled or kit forms. Microlight versions feature increased wing span. A retractable tailwheel landing gear with brakes and an electric engine starter (pull start standard) are available optionally. Kits include instruments (airspeed indicator, altimeter, variometer, ball-slip indicator, magnetic compass, tachometer and temperature gauge), and standard accessories are cabin heating, canopy defroster, dual controls and elevator trim. Estimated assembly time is 500-1,000 working hours, with mainly hand tools, a drill and grinder.

Reports in Spring 1991 suggested that Martekno was negotiating for licensed production with an airframe manufacturer, for distribution outside Europe.

TYPE: Side by side two-seat flying-boat/amphibian; conforms to Experimental and microlight requirements.

AIRFRAME: Mainly of plywood/PVC foam/plywood sandwich construction. Area between wing spars, the tailplane, elevator, fin and rudder are Dacron covered. Formed components and fuel tanks constructed of reinforced plastics (epoxy, glassfibre, carbonfibre and Kevlar). Three-axis control, with ailerons and flaps along entire span. Flying-boat hull plus outer-wing stabilising floats. Optional wheeled landing gear with brakes, the main units swinging rearward/upward to clear water when not required. Skis optional, but require wheeled landing gear for attachment.

POWER PLANT: **ATOL 450 S** (Experimental) and **ATOL 450 L** (microlight): one 47.7 kW (64 hp) Rotax 582; **ATOL 495 S** (Experimental) and **ATOL 475 L** (microlight): 59.7 kW (80 hp) Rotax 912; **ATOL 405 L** (microlight): 37.3 kW (50 hp) Rotax 503 engine, driving three-blade pusher propeller. Fuel capacity 75 litres (19.8 US gallons; 16.5 Imp gallons).

DIMENSIONS, EXTERNAL:

Wing span: 450 S and 495 S	9.60 m (31 ft 6 in)
405 L, 450 L and 475 L	10.80 m (35 ft 5¼ in)
Length overall	6.22 m (20 ft 5 in)

AREAS:

Wings, gross: 450 S and 495 S	14.40 m² (155.0 sq ft)
405 L, 450 L and 475 L	16.20 m² (174.4 sq ft)

WEIGHTS:

* Weight empty: 450 S	210 kg (463 lb)
495 S	230 kg (507 lb)
405 L	190 kg (419 lb)
450 L	214 kg (472 lb)
475 L	232 kg (511 lb)
Max T-O weight: 450 S and 450 L	450 kg (992 lb)
495 S	495 kg (1,091 lb)
405 L	405 kg (893 lb)
475 L	475 kg (1,047 lb)

PERFORMANCE:

Cruising speed: 450 S	76 knots (140 km/h; 87 mph)
405 L	59 knots (110 km/h; 68 mph)
Stalling speed:	
flaps up: 450 S	36 knots (66 km/h; 41 mph)
405 L	33 knots (61 km/h; 38 mph)
flaps down: 450 S	31 knots (57 km/h; 36 mph)
405 L	28 knots (52 km/h; 33 mph)
T-O to 15 m (50 ft):	
on water: 450 S	320 m (1,050 ft)
405 L	350 m (1,150 ft)
on land: 450 S	220 m (722 ft)
405 L	250 m (820 ft)
Landing from 15 m (50 ft):	
on water: 450 S	200 m (657 ft)
405 L	230 m (755 ft)
on land: 450 S	250 m (820 ft)
405 L	280 m (919 ft)
Range, no reserves:	
450 S	340 nm (630 km; 391 miles)
405 L	356 nm (660 km; 410 miles)
Endurance: 450 S	4 h 30 min
405 L	6 h

* *landing gear increases empty weight by 18 kg (40 lb), electric starter by 9 kg (20 lb) and radio/electrical system by 2 kg (4.4 lb)*

FRANCE

AÉRODIS

AÉRODIS SARL
Notaire, Allée de la Ronce, 10340 Les Riceys
Telephone: 33 25 29 30 34
Telex: 830 607F
EXECUTIVE: Alain Carsenti

GRINVALDS G-802 ORION

The original version of the Orion was the G-801, the prototype of which flew for the first time on 2 June 1981. A prototype of the developed G-802 first flew on 4 November 1983. Plans and kits of this version are believed still to be available.

The following description applies to the standard kit version of the G-802:

TYPE: Four-seat, dual-control homebuilt aircraft.
AIRFRAME: Wing and tail unit structures of glassfibre reinforced locally with Kevlar and carbonfibre. Wing section NACA 43015 at root, NACA 43012 at tip.

Composites fuselage of glassfibre/epoxy resin, Kevlar and graphite reinforced. Retractable tricycle landing gear.

POWER PLANT: One 134 kW (180 hp) Textron Lycoming IO-360 in first Orion, driving a 'tail-pusher' propeller. Suited to engines of 112-149 kW (150-200 hp). Two fuel tanks, total capacity 220 litres (58 US gallons; 48.4 Imp gallons). Long-range tanks available when flown with pilot and one passenger only, capacity 400 litres (106 US gallons; 88 Imp gallons), or 490 litres (129 US gallons; 108 Imp gallons) with pilot only.

DIMENSIONS, EXTERNAL:
Wing span	9.00 m (29 ft 6½ in)
Length overall	6.85 m (22 ft 5½ in)
Height overall	2.50 m (8 ft 2½ in)
Propeller diameter	1.50 m (4 ft 11 in)

AREA:
Wings, gross	11.22 m² (120.8 sq ft)

WEIGHTS (134 kW; 180 hp engine):
Weight empty, equipped	610 kg (1,345 lb)

Baggage capacity	30 kg (66 lb)
Max T-O weight	1,050 kg (2,315 lb)

PERFORMANCE (134 kW; 180 hp engine):
Max level speed at 2,440 m (8,000 ft)	178 knots (330 km/h; 205 mph)
Econ cruising speed at 2,440 m (8,000 ft)	135 knots (250 km/h; 155 mph)
Stalling speed: flaps up	54 knots (100 km/h; 63 mph)
20° flap	49 knots (90 km/h; 56 mph)
Max rate of climb at S/L	270 m (885 ft)/min
Service ceiling	4,500 m (14,775 ft)
T-O to 15 m (50 ft)	600 m (1,970 ft)
Landing run	200 m (655 ft)
Range at cruising speed, standard fuel	809 nm (1,500 km; 932 miles)
Max range with long range fuel tanks (65% power)	1,618 nm (3,000 km; 1,864 miles)

AVIASUD

AVIASUD ENGINEERING SA
Zone Industrielle la Palud, 83600 Fréjus
Telephone: 33 94 53 94 00
Telex: 461 172F AVIASUD
GENERAL MANAGER: Bernard d'Otreppe

AVIASUD SIROCCO

The first flight of the Sirocco was achieved in July 1982.
TYPE: Single-seat microlight aircraft; conforms to FAR Pt 103.
AIRFRAME: Mostly aluminium wing structure, with glassfibre front D spar, 6005A-T6 aluminium rear spar and ribs, and double surface Dacron covering. MacCready TK 7315 (modified) wing section. Fuselage boom of Kevlar reinforced glassfibre; fuselage pod of moulded glassfibre and polyester, with epoxy resin. Three-axis control. Integral tail fin stiffened with Klégécel PVC foam ribs. Non-retractable tricycle landing gear. Floats and skis optional.
POWER PLANT: One 26 kW (35 hp) Rotax 377, 17 kW (23 hp) König 430RD, 22.4 kW (30 hp) KFM 107ER or 19.4 kW (26 hp) JPX PUL 425. Fuel capacity 20 litres (5.3 US gallons; 4.4 Imp gallons) standard, 40 litres (10.6 US gallons; 8.8 Imp gallons) optional.

DIMENSIONS, EXTERNAL:
Wing span	10.12 m (33 ft 2½ in)
Length overall	5.85 m (19 ft 2¼ in)
Height overall	2.80 m (9 ft 2¼ in)
Propeller diameter (Rotax engine)	1.45 m (4 ft 9 in)

AREA:
Wings, gross	13.80 m² (148.5 sq ft)

WEIGHTS:
Weight empty	114-130 kg (251-286 lb)
Pilot weight range	55-120 kg (121-264 lb)
Baggage capacity	30 kg (66 lb)
Max T-O weight	250 kg (551 lb)

PERFORMANCE:
Max level speed	62 knots (115 km/h; 71 mph)
Econ cruising speed	43 knots (80 km/h; 50 mph)
Stalling speed, engine idling	21 knots (40 km/h; 25 mph)
Max rate of climb at S/L	300 m (985 ft)/min

Service ceiling	6,500 m (21,325 ft)
T-O run	35 m (115 ft)
Landing run	30-50 m (98-164 ft)
Range: with standard fuel	162 nm (300 km; 186 miles)
with max fuel	270 nm (500 km; 310 miles)
Endurance with max standard fuel	4 h
g limits	+6.7/−3.6

AVIASUD MISTRAL 532

The Mistral is designed for recreational flying but is also suited to professional activities normally performed by high-cost conventional aeroplanes and helicopters, such as pilot training, aerial photography, TV and surveillance, banner towing, and cropspraying. It is sold in ready to fly form. An agricultural example sold to a Spanish operator has a 125 litre (33 US gallon; 27.5 Imp gallon) underfuselage chemical tank.

TYPE: Side by side two-seat microlight and ARV aircraft; designed to FAR Pt 23.
AIRFRAME: Braced biplane, with NACA 23012 wing section. Duralumin wing spars and wooden ribs, double surface covered; tail unit similarly constructed. Glassfibre/carbonfibre/epoxy and polyester semi-monocoque fuselage. Three-axis control. Non-retractable tricycle landing gear, with optional floats and skis.
POWER PLANT: One 47 kW (63 hp) Rotax 532. Fuel capacity 68 litres (18 US gallons; 15 Imp gallons).

DIMENSIONS, EXTERNAL:
Wing span	9.40 m (30 ft 10 in)
Length overall	5.90 m (19 ft 4 in)
Height overall	2.20 m (7 ft 2½ in)
Propeller diameter	1.70 m (5 ft 7 in)

AREA:
Wings, gross	17.90 m² (192.7 sq ft)

WEIGHTS:
Weight empty	174 kg (383 lb)
Baggage capacity	20 kg (44 lb)
Max T-O weight	400 kg (882 lb)

PERFORMANCE (at max T-O weight):
Max level speed at S/L	81 knots (150 km/h; 93 mph)
Econ cruising speed	54 knots (100 km/h; 62 mph)
Stalling speed:	
power on	30 knots (55 km/h; 34.5 mph)
power off	33 knots (60 km/h; 38 mph)
Max rate of climb at S/L	240 m (785 ft)/min
Service ceiling	4,000 m (13,125 ft)
T-O and landing run	80 m (262 ft)
Range	270 nm (500 km; 310 miles)
Endurance	8 h
g limits	+4/−2 design
	+6/−3 ultimate

AVIASUD MISTRAL 462

Also in production is this later version of the Mistral, which offers improved economy. A superlight version, with an empty weight of 149.9 kg (330 lb), has been developed for the German market.

POWER PLANT: One 37.3 kW (50 hp) Rotax 462. Fuel capacity 33 litres (8.7 US gallons; 7.3 Imp gallons).

PERFORMANCE (two crew of 75 kg; 165 lb each, full fuel):
Max level speed	70 knots (130 km/h; 81 mph)
Max cruising speed	49 knots (90 km/h; 56 mph)
Stalling speed: power on	30 knots (55 km/h; 34 mph)
power off	32 knots (58 km/h; 36 mph)
Max rate of climb at S/L	180 m (590 ft)/min
Service ceiling	3,000 m (9,850 ft)
T-O run	100 m (330 ft)
Landing run	80 m (262 ft)
Range	162 nm (300 km; 186 miles)
Endurance	4 h
g limits	+4/−2 limit
	+6/−3 ultimate

AVIASUD MISTRAL (TWIN-ENGINED)

Developed specially for aerial advertising work, this is a standard Mistral fitted with either a Rotax 462 or 532 engine forward and carrying a Rotax 503 in pusher configuration above the upper wing. Fuel capacity is 68 litres (18 US gallons; 15 Imp gallons).

DIMENSION, EXTERNAL:
Wing span	9.60 m (31 ft 6 in)

WEIGHTS:
Weight empty	199-230 kg (439-507 lb)
Max T-O weight	450 kg (992 lb)

PERFORMANCE:
Max rate of climb at S/L	216 m (710 ft)/min

CENTRAIR

S. N. CENTRAIR
Aérodrome Le Blanc, BP 44, 36300 Le Blanc
Telephone: 33 54 37 07 96
Fax: 33 54 37 48 64
Telex: 750 272 F

S. N. CENTRAIR PARAFAN

Development of this parawing microlight was started in November 1984. Many Parafans have been delivered, some to the armed forces of France and foreign countries. This aircraft offers pendulum stability in flight, and can be landed safely power-off. The maximum acceptable wind

speed on the ground for take-off is a steady 12 knots (22 km/h; 14 mph), without major gusting.
TYPE: Single-seat parawing microlight.
AIRFRAME: Welded AG3 aluminium alloy trike unit, suspended under an eleven-cell NASA type ram air sports parachute wing (manufactured by PF and Aerazur) by two clusters of steering cables. Two-axis control. Non-retractable tricycle landing gear.
POWER PLANT: One 29.4 kW (39.4 hp) Rotax 447. Fuel capacity 20 litres (5.3 US gallons; 4.4 Imp gallons).

DIMENSIONS, EXTERNAL:
Parawing span	10.10 m (33 ft 1¾ in)
Trike: Length	2.40 m (7 ft 10½ in)
Width	1.70 m (5 ft 7 in)
Height	1.70 m (5 ft 7 in)

AREA:
Parawing, gross	31.40 m² (338.0 sq ft)

WEIGHTS:
Weight empty	105 kg (231 lb)
Max payload	100 kg (220 lb)

PERFORMANCE:
Cruising speed	22-24 knots (40-45 km/h; 25-28 mph)
Max rate of climb	90-120 m (295-395 ft)/min
Theoretical ceiling	3,500 m (11,480 ft)
T-O run (no wind):	
with ground assistance	20-40 m (66-131 ft)
without ground assistance	30-50 m (98-164 ft)
Landing run (no wind)	0-20 m (0-66 ft)

COLOMBAN

MICHEL COLOMBAN
37bis, rue Lakanal, 92500 Rueil-Malmaison
Telephone: 33 47 51 88 76

COLOMBAN MC 15 CRICRI

The MC 10 Cricri prototype was first flown on 19 July 1973. Early amateur-built Cricris were designated MC 12

and used Valmet SM 160J engines. The current model is the JPX powered MC 15. Plans are available in the French and English languages, with European standard metric dimensions; 506 sets had been sold by early 1991 to amateur builders in France and neighbouring countries, and 78 aircraft were then flying. Three are flown at air displays by the Brittany Ferries aerobatic team, whose leader, Yves Duval, set two new international records for aircraft weighing less than 300 kg in a Cricri on 7 June 1988; he

averaged 126.39 knots (234.226 km/h; 145.55 mph) over a 3 km course, and 121.98 knots (226.05 km/h; 140.46 mph) over 15/25 km.
TYPE: Single-seat light homebuilt aircraft.
AIRFRAME: Entire basic structure is of light alloy, except for Klégécel ribs in wings and tail unit, and Klégécel stringers in fuselage. Laminar-flow aerofoil derived from a Wortmann section. Full span auxiliary aerofoil wing flaps operate collectively as high-lift devices and

The first Grinvalds G-802 Orion all-plastics homebuilt aircraft

Colomban MC 15 Cricri built by Wolfgang Huber of Germany

Aviasud Mistral in twin-engined configuration for aerial advertising work

Croses EAC-3 Pouplume light aircraft (Moto engine)

Coupé-Aviation JC-01 two-seat lightplane

differentially as ailerons. Non-retractable tricycle landing gear.

POWER PLANT: Two JPX PUL 212 engines, each rated at 11 kW (15 hp). Fuel capacity 23 litres (6 US gallons; 5 Imp gallons).

DIMENSIONS, EXTERNAL:

Wing span	4.90 m (16 ft 0¾ in)
Length overall	3.91 m (12 ft 10 in)
Height overall	1.20 m (3 ft 11¼ in)
Propeller diameter	0.695 m (2 ft 3½ in)

AREA:

Wings, gross	3.10 m² (33.4 sq ft)

WEIGHTS:

Weight empty	80 kg (176 lb)
Max T-O and landing weight	170 kg (375 lb)

PERFORMANCE (MC 15 at max T-O weight):

Max speed measured in dive
159 knots (295 km/h; 183 mph)

Max cruising speed (75% power)
108 knots (200 km/h; 124 mph)

Stalling speed:

flaps up	50 knots (93 km/h; 58 mph)
flaps down	39 knots (72 km/h; 45 mph)
Max rate of climb at S/L	390 m (1,280 ft)/min
Service ceiling	5,000 m (16,400 ft)
T-O run	100 m (330 ft)
Landing run	150 m (495 ft)
Range with max fuel	215 nm (400 km; 248 miles)
g limits	+9/-4.5 ultimate

COUPÉ-AVIATION

JACQUES COUPÉ

La Trute, Azay-sur-Cher, 37270 Montlouis sur Loire
Telephone: 33 47 50 41 84

COUPÉ-AVIATION JC-01

The prototype JC-01 was flown for the first time on 16 March 1976. Plans were made available to amateur constructors, together with those for the more powerful JC-2.

TYPE: Two-seat, dual-control homebuilt sporting aircraft.

AIRFRAME: All-wood structure, with fabric covered wings, rear fuselage, and flying control surfaces. Non-retractable tailwheel landing gear.

POWER PLANT: One 48.5 kW (65 hp) Teledyne Continental A65-8F. Fuel capacity 60 litres (15.9 US gallons; 13 Imp gallons).

DIMENSIONS, EXTERNAL:

Wing span	8.35 m (27 ft 4¾ in)
Length overall	6.40 m (21 ft 0 in)

AREA:

Wings, gross	11.69 m² (125.83 sq ft)

WEIGHTS:

Weight empty	330 kg (728 lb)
Max T-O weight	580 kg (1,279 lb)

PERFORMANCE (as originally flown, at max T-O weight):

Max level speed	108 knots (200 km/h; 124 mph)
Econ cruising speed	76 knots (140 km/h; 87 mph)
T-O speed	27 knots (50 km/h; 31 mph)
Stalling speed	25 knots (45 km/h; 28 mph)
T-O run	90 m (295 ft)

COUPÉ-AVIATION JC-2

The JC-2 is generally similar to the JC-01 but has a more powerful engine and tricycle landing gear. The prototype first flew in May 1981. At least six JC-2s are under construction by amateurs or have flown, with 74.5 kW (100 hp) engines. It was intended to market the JC-2 also in kit form.

TYPE: Side by side two-seat homebuilt aircraft.

AIRFRAME: All-wood structure, with Dacron covered wings, ailerons, flaps, rear fuselage, elevators and rudder. Wing section NACA 23012. Non-retractable tricycle landing gear.

POWER PLANT: One 67 kW (90 hp) Teledyne Continental engine in prototype. Fuel capacity 90 litres (23.8 US gallons; 19.75 Imp gallons).

DIMENSIONS, EXTERNAL:

Wing span	8.35 m (27 ft 4¾ in)
Length overall	6.40 m (21 ft 0 in)

AREA:

Wings, gross	11.70 m² (126.0 sq ft)

WEIGHTS:

Weight empty	500 kg (1,103 lb)
Baggage capacity	20 kg (44 lb)
Max T-O weight	750 kg (1,653 lb)

PERFORMANCE (with 67 kW; 90 hp engine):

Max level speed	108 knots (200 km/h; 124 mph)
Econ cruising speed	86 knots (160 km/h; 99 mph)
Stalling speed: flaps up	27 knots (50 km/h; 31 mph)
flaps down	24 knots (45 km/h; 28 mph)

COUPÉ-AVIATION JC-3

The JC-3 differs from the JC-01 primarily in having a sweptback fin and a 51 kW (68 hp) Volkswagen 1,700 cc converted motorcar engine.

CROSES

EMILIEN CROSES

63 route de Davayé (Aérodrome), 71000 Charnay les Macon
Telephone: 33 85 38 07 31

CROSES EAC-3 POUPLUME

The Pouplume single-seat tandem-wing biplane has a fixed rear wing and a pivoted forward wing which dispenses with the need for ailerons and elevators. Construction is of wood, with fabric covered wings, and a non-retractable tailwheel landing gear is fitted. The prototype has a 7.8 kW (10.5 hp) Moto 232 cc motorcycle engine; fuel capacity is 10 litres (2.6 US gallons; 2.2 Imp gallons).

The EAC-3-01 Pouplume flew for the first time in June 1961. It was followed, in 1967, by a second prototype (EAC-3-02) with a 20 cm (8 in) longer fuselage. Plans were made available.

A version known as the **Pouplume Sport** differs in having a 1,500 cc Volkswagen engine and reduced span of 6.40 m (21 ft 0 in).

The following data apply to the standard Moto-powered Pouplume:

DIMENSIONS, EXTERNAL:

Wing span: forward wing	7.80 m (25 ft 7 in)
rear wing	7.00 m (23 ft 0 in)

Length overall	4.70 m (15 ft 3 in)
Height overall	1.80 m (5 ft 11 in)
AREA:	
Wings, gross	16.02 m² (172.2 sq ft)
WEIGHTS:	
Weight empty	110-140 kg (243-310 lb)
Max T-O weight	220-260 kg (485-573 lb)
PERFORMANCE (A: 7.8 kW; 10.5 hp engine, B: 13.4 kW; 18 hp engine):	
Max level speed: A	38 knots (70 km/h; 43 mph)
B	65 knots (120 km/h; 75 mph)
Econ cruising speed: A	27 knots (50 km/h; 31 mph)
B	38 knots (70 km/h; 43 mph)
T-O run: A	60 m (200 ft)
B	40 m (131 ft)
Landing run: A	24 m (80 ft)

CROSES EC-6 CRIQUET (LOCUST)

The Criquet is a side by side two-seater, using the same tandem-wing formula as the Pouplume. The EC-6-01 prototype flew for the first time on 6 July 1965. Plans were made available.

TYPE: Side by side two-seat tandem-wing homebuilt aircraft.

AIRFRAME: Wings have wooden structure, with plywood leading-edge, overall fabric covering and some components of glassfibre. NACA 23012 (modified) wing section. Wooden fuselage, covered with plywood. Glassfibre engine cowling. Plywood covered spruce fin and rudder. Non-retractable tailwheel landing gear.

POWER PLANT: One 67 kW (90 hp) Teledyne Continental engine. Fuel capacity originally 60 litres (15.9 US gallons; 13 Imp gallons); planned to be increased to 90 litres (23.8 US gallons; 19.75 Imp gallons).

DIMENSIONS, EXTERNAL:	
Wing span: forward wing	7.80 m (25 ft 7 in)
rear wing	7.00 m (22 ft 11½ in)
Length overall	4.65 m (15 ft 3 in)
AREA:	
Wings, gross	16.02 m² (172.2 sq ft)

WEIGHTS:	
Weight empty	290 kg (639 lb)
Max T-O weight	550 kg (1,213 lb)
PERFORMANCE (officially certificated, at max T-O weight):	
Max level speed at S/L	115 knots (213 km/h; 132 mph)
Econ cruising speed	86 knots (160 km/h; 99 mph)
Will not stall	
Time to 2,000 m (6,560 ft)	6 min 14 s

CROSES EC-8 TOURISME

This three-seat touring aircraft is generally similar to the standard wooden Criquet but can have an 'all-terrain' landing gear comprising two tandem pairs of mainwheels.

HYDROPLUM
HYDROPLUM SARL

Fior di Linu, Pietranera, 20200 Bastia, Corsica
Telephone: 33 95 31 67 67

M Claude Tisserand designed two amphibians: the single-seat Hydroplum monoplane and two-seat Hydroplum II sesquiplane. The Hydroplum II was purchased by S.M.A.N. in 1987 and is currently marketed in kit and ready assembled forms as the Petrel (which see).

TISSERAND HYDROPLUM

The Hydroplum first flew in September 1983. Plans are available.

TYPE: Single-seat amphibian; conforms to microlight and Experimental regulations.

AIRFRAME: Plywood construction. Wing section NACA 2415. Three-axis control with water rudder attached to heel of single-step hull. Retractable taildragger landing gear.

POWER PLANT: One 30 kW (40 hp) 440 cc Hirth. Fuel capacity 40 litres (10.6 US gallons; 8.8 Imp gallons).

DIMENSIONS, EXTERNAL:	
Wing span	9.25 m (30 ft 4¼ in)
Length overall	5.90 m (19 ft 4¼ in)
Height overall	1.40 m (4 ft 7 in)
Propeller diameter	1.40 m (4 ft 7 in)
AREA:	
Wings, gross	13.00 m² (139.93 sq ft)

WEIGHTS:	
Weight empty	145 kg (319 lb)
Pilot weight range	60-90 kg (133-198 lb)
Max T-O weight	260 kg (573 lb)
PERFORMANCE (at max T-O weight):	
Max level speed	59 knots (110 km/h; 68 mph)
Econ cruising speed	43 knots (80 km/h; 50 mph)
Stalling speed	30 knots (55 km/h; 34 mph)
Max rate of climb at S/L	300 m (985 ft)/min
T-O run: on land	80 m (262 ft)
on water	100 m (328 ft)
Landing run: on land	80 m (262 ft)
on water	50 m (164 ft)
Range with max standard fuel	145 nm (270 km; 167 miles)

JODEL
AVIONS JODEL SA

HEAD OFFICE: 37 Route de Seurre, 21200 Beaune
DESIGN OFFICE: 21-Darois
PRESIDENT-DIRECTOR GENERAL: Jean Delemontez

Jodel designs have been built both commercially and by amateurs, and more than 5,000 aircraft of Jodel type have flown throughout the world.

JODEL D.9 BÉBÉ SERIES

The prototype Bébé flew for the first time in January 1948. Construction can take as little as 500 working hours. An illustration can be found in the 1988-89 *Jane's*.

TYPE: Single-seat homebuilt aircraft.

AIRFRAME: All-wood construction, except for fabric covering on the wings, rudder and elevators. Non-retractable tailwheel or tailskid landing gear.

POWER PLANT: One modified Volkswagen engine is standard, but other engines of 18.6 to 48.5 kW (25 to 65 hp) may be fitted. Fuel capacity 25 litres (6.6 US gallons; 5.5 Imp gallons).

DIMENSIONS, EXTERNAL:	
Wing span	7.00 m (22 ft 11 in)
Length overall	5.45 m (17 ft 10½ in)
AREA:	
Wings, gross	9.0 m² (96.8 sq ft)
WEIGHTS:	
Weight empty	190 kg (420 lb)
Max T-O weight	320 kg (705 lb)
PERFORMANCE (30 kW; 40 hp engine, at max T-O weight):	
Max level speed at S/L	87 knots (160 km/h; 100 mph)
Cruising speed	74 knots (137 km/h; 85 mph)
Stalling speed	35 knots (65 km/h; 40 mph)
Max rate of climb at S/L	180 m (590 ft)/min
T-O run	110 m (360 ft)
Landing run	100 m (330 ft)
Range with max fuel	217 nm (400 km; 250 miles)

JODEL D.11 and D.119

The original D.11, with 33.6 kW (45 hp) Salmson engine, was the basic model in the series of Jodel two-seaters for amateur and commercial production. The version for amateur construction with 67 kW (90 hp) Teledyne Continental engine is designated D.119.

The wing is of wood, covered with Dacron, the fuselage and tail unit of wood covered with glassfibre. The following details refer to a D.11 which spans 8.23 m (27 ft 0 in), has an empty weight of 340 kg (750 lb) and loaded weight of 562 kg (1,240 lb), and is powered by a 48.5 kW (65 hp) Teledyne Continental A65-8 flat-four engine:

PERFORMANCE:	
Max level speed at S/L	93 knots (173 km/h; 108 mph)
Cruising speed	86 knots (161 km/h; 100 mph)
Max rate of climb at S/L	152 m (500 ft)/min
Service ceiling	4,875 m (16,000 ft)
T-O run	152 m (500 ft)
Landing run	244 m (800 ft)
Range with max fuel	260 nm (482 km; 300 miles)

JODEL D.112 CLUB and D.113

The D.112 is a two-seat dual-control version of the D.9. Except for increased overall dimensions, a wider fuselage and enclosed side by side cockpit, the D.112 conforms in layout and structure to the D.9, but is fitted normally with a 48.5 kW (65 hp) Teledyne Continental flat-four engine. Fuel capacity is 60 litres (15.9 US gallons; 13 Imp gallons).

The version built in Sweden as the D.113 differs from the D.112 in several minor respects.

DIMENSIONS, EXTERNAL:	
Wing span	8.20 m (26 ft 10 in)
Length overall	6.36 m (20 ft 10 in)
AREA:	
Wings, gross	12.72 m² (136.9 sq ft)
WEIGHTS:	
Weight empty	270 kg (600 lb)
Max T-O weight	520 kg (1,145 lb)
PERFORMANCE (at max T-O weight):	
Max level speed at S/L	102 knots (190 km/h; 118 mph)

Econ cruising speed	81 knots (150 km/h; 93 mph)
Stalling speed	38 knots (70 km/h; 44 mph)
Max rate of climb at S/L	193 m (632 ft)/min
T-O run	137 m (450 ft)
Landing run	120 m (395 ft)
Range with max fuel	323 nm (600 km; 373 miles)

JODEL D.18

The 1981-82 *Jane's* contained details of the Delemontez-Cauchy DC-1. No plans of this are available, but M Delemontez is marketing plans of a slightly modified version, known as the Jodel D.18, with a different wing section, revised ailerons, all-moving tailplane and other changes. It has a typical Jodel light wooden airframe, with coarse dihedral on the tapered outer wing panels. Installation of a 43 kW (58 hp) 1,600 cc Volkswagen engine, instead of the usual Teledyne Continental, has resulted in a more streamlined cowling and improved performance. Fuel capacity is 65 litres (17 US gallons; 14.3 Imp gallons).

The prototype D.18 was flown for the first time on 21 May 1984.

DIMENSIONS, EXTERNAL:	
Wing span	7.50 m (24 ft 7¼ in)
Length overall	5.70 m (18 ft 8½ in)
AREA:	
Wings, gross	9.83 m² (105.8 sq ft)
WEIGHTS:	
Weight empty	230-250 kg (507-551 lb)
Max T-O weight	460 kg (1,014 lb)
PERFORMANCE:	
Max level speed	135 knots (250 km/h; 155 mph)
Cruising speed	92 knots (170 km/h; 105 mph)
Stalling speed	39 knots (72 km/h; 45 mph)
Max rate of climb at S/L	180 m (590 ft)/min
T-O to 15 m (50 ft)	260 m (853 ft)
Landing from 15 m (50 ft)	450 m (1,477 ft)
Endurance	5 h

JODEL D.19

This is the designation of D.18s constructed with tricycle landing gear. An example built by M Vion is illustrated.

JUNQUA
ROGER JUNQUA

36 impasse d'Agen, 33800 Bordeaux
Telephone: (33) 56 91 81 17

In 1980, M Roger Junqua began the design of a tandem two-seat canard light aircraft known as the RJ-02 Volucelle. Construction of the prototype (F-WJCA) was started in the Spring of 1983 by M Jean-Yves Andreazza, assisted by M Junqua's son, Jean-Claude. This aircraft gained its French certificate of airworthiness on 9 December 1986, having first flown in July of that year.

The 'production' version of the RJ-02 became the RJ-03, of which the prototype was shown in public for the first time in July 1990, at the RSA rally in Moulins. It was then expected to fly in December of that year. No further news has been received.

JUNQUA IBIS RJ-03

The Ibis differs from the Volucelle in having a larger fuselage to accommodate two persons up to 1.90 m (6 ft 3 in) tall. It is equipped with an electrical system, heater, VHF and NDB. Plans may be made available in due course.

The following details are based on those that appeared in the 1987-88 *Jane's* and should now be considered provisional:

TYPE: Tandem two-seat homebuilt canard aircraft.

AIRFRAME: Cantilever shoulder-mounted wings, with large winglets and inset rudders, at rear of fuselage. All-wood, Styrodur foam filled constant chord structure, with ailerons and high-lift flaps. No dihedral. Foreplanes at nose, of similar construction, fitted with elevators. Conventional wooden truss fuselage, plywood covered. Non-retractable tricycle landing gear.

POWER PLANT: One 38 kW (51 hp) Volkswagen 1,600 cc modified motorcar engine.

DIMENSIONS, EXTERNAL:	
Wing span	6.00 m (19 ft 8¼ in)
Length overall	4.60 m (15 ft 1¼ in)
Height overall	1.60 m (5 ft 3 in)
WEIGHTS:	
Weight empty, equipped	225 kg (496 lb)
Max T-O weight	420 kg (926 lb)
PERFORMANCE (estimated):	
Max level speed	129 knots (240 km/h; 149 mph)
Max cruising speed	108 knots (200 km/h; 124 mph)
Econ cruising speed	97 knots (180 km/h; 112 mph)
Stalling speed	46 knots (85 km/h; 53 mph)
Range, with reserves	485 nm (900 km; 559 miles)

Croses EC-6 Criquet built by M Tissot of Beaune *(Geoffrey P. Jones)*

Jurca M.J.2N Tempête built by Mr Thomas Fahr of Gottmadingen, Germany (112 kW; 150 hp engine)

Hydroplum amphibian, designed by M Claude Tisserand

Jurca M.J.5L2 Sirocco with a retractable tailwheel, built by M Yves Guillou of Bretagne

First Jodel D.19 with tricycle landing gear, built by M Vion *(Geoffrey P. Jones)*

Junqua Ibis RJ-03 at the 1990 RSA rally *(Geoffrey P. Jones)*

JURCA

MARCEL JURCA

2 rue des Champs Philippe, 92250 La Garenne-Colombes
Telephone: 33 (1) 45 94 01 33

M Marcel Jurca is the designer of a series of high-performance light aircraft of which plans have been supplied to other constructors on a purely amateur non-profit making basis. More recently, he has produced plans for representations of Second World War fighters, which were fully detailed in earlier editions of *Jane's*.

For builders in North America, Australia and New Zealand, Jurca plans are available from Mr Ken Heit, 1733 Kansas, Flint, Michigan 48506, USA (telephone: 1 313 232 5395). Mr Simon Richards, a Briton living in France and builder of the M.J.100 prototype, supplies plans to UK builders (Ecorsaint, 21150 Les Laumes, France), while Claus Colling Ltd (Priel 5A, 8051 Gammelsdorf, Germany) manufactures all metal components, landing gears and flight controls for the Jurca representations of Second World War fighters.

JURCA M.J.2 and M.J.22 TEMPÊTE

The prototype **M.J.2** Tempête was flown for the first time on 27 June 1956. At least 45 Tempêtes are now flying.

The type of engine fitted to a particular aircraft is indicated by a suffix letter in its designation. Suffix letters are A for the 48.5 kW (65 hp) Teledyne Continental A65, B for the 56 kW (75 hp) Teledyne Continental A75, C for the 63.5 kW (85 hp) Teledyne Continental C85, D for the 67 kW (90 hp) Teledyne Continental C90-8/C90-14F, E for the 74.5 kW (100 hp) Teledyne Continental O-200-A, F for the 78.5 kW (105 hp) Potez 4 E-20, G for the 86 kW (115 hp) Potez 4 E-30, H for the 78.5-86 kW (105-115 hp) Textron Lycoming O-235, I for the 93 kW (125 hp) Textron Lycoming O-290-G, K for the 101-104 kW (135-140 hp) Textron Lycoming O-290-D2, N for the 112 kW (150 hp)

Textron Lycoming or Teledyne Continental, P for the 119 kW (160 hp) Textron Lycoming or Teledyne Continental, and R for the 134 kW (180 hp) Textron Lycoming or Teledyne Continental. The standard version is the M.J.2A. The M.J.2D cruises at 105 knots (195 km/h; 121 mph) and climbs to 1,000 m (3,280 ft) in 3 minutes. It can also perform aerobatics without loss of height.

A version known as the **M.J.22** has a 112 kW (150 hp) engine and strengthened airframe.

The Tempête is basically a single-seat aircraft, but the 112 and 134 kW (150 and 180 hp) versions have provision for carrying behind the pilot on cross-country flights a second person weighing not more than 55 kg (121 lb). This is not permitted by the DGAC in France. The suffix 'A' is added to the aircraft designation in two-seat configuration.

The following details apply generally to all basic single-seat M.J.2 models:

TYPE: Single-seat homebuilt aircraft.

AIRFRAME: All-wood construction, except for fabric covering on the wings, ailerons, elevators and rudder. NACA 23012 wing section. Non-retractable tailwheel (or tailskid) landing gear.

POWER PLANT: See introduction. Fuel capacity 60 litres (15.9 US gallons; 13.2 Imp gallons).

DIMENSIONS, EXTERNAL:

Wing span	6.00 m (19 ft 8 in)
Length overall	5.855 m (19 ft 2½ in)
Height overall	2.40 m (7 ft 10 in)

AREA:

Wings, gross	7.98 m² (85.9 sq ft)

WEIGHTS (48.5 kW; 65 hp engine):

Weight empty	90 kg (639 lb)
Max T-O weight	430 kg (950 lb)

PERFORMANCE (48.5 kW; 65 hp engine):

Max level speed	104 knots (193 km/h; 120 mph)
Cruising speed	89 knots (165 km/h; 102 mph)
Max rate of climb at S/L	170 m (555 ft)/min
Service ceiling	3,500 m (11,500 ft)
T-O run	250 m (820 ft)
Endurance	3 h 20 min

JURCA M.J.3 DART and M.J.4 SHADOW

These are versions of the basic M.J.2 Tempête design.

JURCA M.J.5 SIROCCO

The M.J.5 Sirocco is a tandem two-seat development of the M.J.2 Tempête. It is fully aerobatic when flown as a two-seater. The prototype M.J.5 flew for the first time on 3 August 1962, powered by a 78.5 kW (105 hp) Potez 4 E-20 engine. A factory built model was awarded subsequently a certificate of airworthiness in the Utility category.

The version of the Sirocco for amateur construction is generally similar to the factory built version, with non-retractable or retractable landing gear, including optional retractable tailwheel. The type of engine fitted to a particular aircraft is indicated by a suffix letter in its designation. Suffix letters are A for the 67 kW (90 hp) Teledyne Continental C90-8 or -14F, B for the 74.5 kW (100 hp) Teledyne Continental O-200-A, C for the 78.5 kW (105 hp) Potez 4 E-20, D for the 86 kW (115 hp) Potez 4 E-30, E for the 78.5 kW (105 hp) Hirth, F for the 93 kW (125 hp) Textron Lycoming, G for the 100.5 kW (135 hp) Regnier, H for the 119.5 kW (160 hp) Textron Lycoming, K for the 134 kW (180 hp) Textron Lycoming and L for the 149 kW (200 hp) Textron Lycoming. Addition of the numeral 1 indicates a non-retractable landing gear; the numeral 2 indicates a retractable main landing gear; 2A indicates that the tailwheel also retracts.

One aircraft has a 119 kW (160 hp) PRV modified motorcar engine and P-51 Mustang type underfuselage airscoop.

The details which follow refer to a Sirocco with an 86 kW (115 hp) Textron Lycoming O-235-C2B engine and 1.85 m (6 ft 0¾ in) diameter propeller, and a modified rudder of reduced height and greater chord:

DIMENSIONS, EXTERNAL:
Wing span	7.00 m (23 ft 0 in)
Length overall	6.15 m (20 ft 2 in)
Height overall, tail up:	
with modified rudder	2.60 m (8 ft 6¼ in)
standard rudder	2.80 m (9 ft 2¼ in)

AREA:
Wings, gross	10.00 m² (107.64 sq ft)

WEIGHTS:
Weight empty	430 kg (947 lb)
Max T-O weight	680 kg (1,499 lb)

PERFORMANCE (at max T-O weight):
Max level speed	127 knots (235 km/h; 146 mph)
Cruising speed	116 knots (215 km/h; 134 mph)
Stalling speed	44 knots (80 km/h; 50 mph)
Time to 1,000 m (3,280 ft)	4 min
Service ceiling	5,000 m (16,400 ft)
T-O run	250 m (820 ft)
Landing run	200 m (655 ft)
Endurance	4 h 20 min

JURCA M.J.5 SIROCCO (SPORT WING)

A special version of the Sirocco, with 86 kW (115 hp) engine and increased span, has been developed for the New Zealand and Australian market. The wing of this aircraft, known as a 'Sport' wing, embodies one additional rib and inter-rib bay each side. The modification is available in the English language set of Sirocco plans.

JURCA M.J.14 FOURTOUNA

The M.J.14 is an easy to build single-seat sport training aircraft of wooden construction. It uses an M.J.7 wing, has retractable landing gear, and is powered by a 119 kW (160 hp) Textron Lycoming engine. The prototype is under construction by M Yves Beliard of Coutances; a photograph of the Fourtouna under construction appeared in the 1989-90 Jane's.

JURCA M.J.51 SPEROCCO

The tandem two-seat Sperocco (the name being a contraction of 'Special Sirocco') is intended for high performance aerobatic and competition flying and incorporates features of the M.J.5 and M.J.7. The fuselage is of completely new design, with a basically triangular cross-section, but is of similar construction to that of the M.J.5. Landing gear is of the M.J.5 type and is fully retractable.

Any horizontally opposed engine of 112-179 kW (150-240 hp) may be installed. Fuel is contained in two wing tanks, each of 55 litres (14.5 US gallons; 12 Imp gallons) capacity, and one fuselage tank of 45 or 100 litres (11.9 or 26.4 US gallons; 10 or 22 Imp gallons) capacity.

The first M.J.51, powered by a 149 kW (200 hp) Textron Lycoming AIO-360 engine, is being constructed by M Serge Brillant at Melun.

DIMENSIONS, EXTERNAL:
Wing span	7.623 m (25 ft 0 in)
Length overall	7.24 m (23 ft 9 in)

AREA:
Wings, gross	11.00 m² (118.4 sq ft)

WEIGHT:
Max T-O weight	730 kg (1,653 lb)

PERFORMANCE (estimated, with 112 kW; 150 hp Textron Lycoming engine):
Max level speed	149 knots (275 km/h; 171 mph)
Max cruising speed, 75% power	
	135 knots (250 km/h; 155 mph)
Stalling speed	49 knots (90 km/h; 56 mph)
Time to 1,000 m (3,280 ft)	1 min 30 s

JURCA M.J.52 ZÉPHYR

The all-wooden M.J.52 Zéphyr is a very light two-seat monoplane, based on the M.J.5 Sirocco but using a converted Volkswagen motorcar engine or Teledyne Continental engine in the 30-48.5 kW (40-65 hp) range. It can have a non-retractable or retractable landing gear.

Plans of the M.J.52 have been available since Spring 1985, and a prototype is under construction. It has been designed to conform to FAR Pt 23 Utility category requirements, yet to be simple to construct in a garage or similar building and inexpensive in terms of materials and working hours.

DIMENSIONS, EXTERNAL:
Wing span	9.06 m (29 ft 8¾ in)
Length overall	6.28 m (20 ft 7¼ in)

AREA:
Wings, gross	13.50 m² (145.3 sq ft)

WEIGHTS:
Weight empty	333 kg (734 lb)
Max T-O weight	517 kg (1,140 lb)

PERFORMANCE (37.3 kW; 50 hp engine):
Max level speed	59 knots (110 km/h; 68 mph)
Stalling speed	22 knots (40 km/h; 25 mph)
Endurance	5 h
g limits	+8/-4 ultimate

JURCA M.J.53 AUTAN

The M.J.53 is a side by side two-seat version of the Sirocco. Two prototypes are under construction in Arles. It is suited to aerobatics in addition to touring.

POWER PLANT: One 134 kW (180 hp) Textron Lycoming flat-four. Fuel capacity 160 litres (42.3 US gallons; 35 Imp gallons) for touring and 80 litres (21.1 US gallons; 17.6 Imp gallons) for aerobatics.

DIMENSIONS, EXTERNAL:
Wing span	7.60 m (24 ft 11¼ in)
Length overall	6.50 m (21 ft 4 in)

AREA:
Wings, gross	11.20 m² (120.6 sq ft)

WEIGHTS:
Weight empty	600 kg (1,323 lb)
Max T-O weight, aerobatic	844 kg (1,860 lb)

PERFORMANCE:
Cruising speed, 75% power	
	130 knots (240 km/h; 149 mph)
Stalling speed	49-54 knots (90-100 km/h; 56-62 mph)
Max rate of climb at S/L	300 m (985 ft)/min
Endurance, at 75% power	4 h

JURCA M.J.7 and M.J.77 GNATSUM

The Gnatsum is a precise scale replica, for amateur construction, of the North American P-51D Mustang single-seat fighter of the Second World War. Its name 'Gnatsum' is 'Mustang' reversed. Drawings for two versions are available, the two-thirds scale M.J.7 and three-quarters scale M.J.77, the latter offering seating for two crew of up to 80 kg (176 lb) each. A reinforced model has a gross weight of 1,500 kg (3,307 lb). Engine options include a 313 kW (420 hp) supercharged Gipsy or 388-410 kW (520-550 hp) inverted Ranger. Specification details, and an illustration, can be found in the 1988-89 Jane's. Three are under construction in France, and one has flown in the USA with a 410 kW (550 hp) Double Ranger V12 engine (built by Ken Bard of Elmhurst, Wheeling, Illinois).

JURCA M.J.70

Full-size representation of the North American P-51 Mustang, currently at the design stage.

JURCA M.J.8 and M.J.80 1-NINE-OH

The M.J.8 is a single-seat sporting aircraft which was designed by M Jurca by scaling down to three-quarters of the original dimensions the airframe of the Focke-Wulf Fw 190A fighter. The M.J.80 is similar but is designed to full scale. One is under construction in Austria. Specification details, and an illustration, can be found in the 1988-89 Jane's.

JURCA M.J.9 ONE-OH-NINE

Three-quarter scale representation of the Messerschmitt Bf 109 fighter of the Second World War. The prototype is under construction.

JURCA M.J.90

This is a full-size representation of a Bf 109G, to which it is dimensionally the same. Its method of construction is similar to that of the M.J.9. Plans are available, and one is under construction in West Germany and two in France.

JURCA M.J.10 SPIT

The M.J.10 is a single-seat, three-quarter scale representation of the Supermarine Spitfire that can also be completed as a two-seater. Specification details, and an illustration, can be found in the 1988-89 Jane's.

JURCA M.J.100

Plans are available for a full-size representation of the Supermarine Spitfire, known as the M.J.100. Four are under construction in France, two in South Africa and one in the USA. The latter is of glassfibre construction, being built by Mr Allen Salberman with a 447 kW (600 hp) SNECMA 12T engine. Specification details can be found in the 1988-89 Jane's.

JURCA M.J.12 PEE-40

The M.J.12 is a three-quarter scale representation of the Curtiss P-40 single-seat fighter of the Second World War. Brief details can be found in the 1988-89 Jane's.

LEDERLIN

FRANÇOIS LEDERLIN

2 rue Charles Peguy, 38000 Grenoble

This aircraft was derived from the Mignet HM-380, but retains little of the original except for the wing section. First flight was made on 14 September 1965.

Plans of the 380-L, annotated in English and with both English and metric measurements, are available to amateur constructors.

LEDERLIN 380-L

TYPE: Side by side two-seat homebuilt aircraft.
AIRFRAME: Tandem-wing biplane. Wing section 3.40-13. Wooden wings, with plywood leading-edge and overall fabric covering. Variable incidence front wing. No ailerons or flaps. Welded steel tube fuselage, covered with light alloy to front of cabin and with fabric on rear fuselage, over wooden formers. Wooden tail unit with fabric covering. Non-retractable tailwheel landing gear.
POWER PLANT: One 67 kW (90 hp) Teledyne Continental C90-14F. Fuel capacity 85 litres (22.5 US gallons; 18.75 Imp gallons).

DIMENSIONS, EXTERNAL:
Wing span: forward	7.92 m (26 ft 0 in)
rear	6.00 m (19 ft 8¼ in)
Length overall	4.77 m (15 ft 7¾ in)
Height overall	2.08 m (6 ft 10 in)
Propeller diameter	1.83 m (6 ft 0 in)

AREAS:
Wings, gross: forward	9.92 m² (106.8 sq ft)
rear	7.43 m² (80.0 sq ft)

WEIGHTS:
Weight empty	360 kg (794 lb)
Max T-O weight	600 kg (1,323 lb)

PERFORMANCE (at max T-O weight):
Max level speed at 305 m (1,000 ft)	
	109 knots (201 km/h; 125 mph)
Econ cruising speed at 610 m (2,000 ft)	
	87 knots (161 km/h; 100 mph)
Stalling speed, power off	26 knots (49 km/h; 30 mph)
Max rate of climb at S/L	275 m (900 ft)/min
Service ceiling	over 3,660 m (12,000 ft)
T-O run	122 m (400 ft)
Landing run	153 m (500 ft)
Range at econ cruising speed	
	477 nm (885 km; 550 miles)

LENDEPERGT

PATRICK LENDEPERGT

112 rue de la Jarry, 94300 Vincennes
Telephone: 33 (1) 43 65 61 95

LENDEPERGT LP-01 SIBYLLE

The prototype of this amphibian was first flown in July 1984. It is available in kit form, and possibly ready assembled. In addition to sport flying, it can be adapted for surveillance (with nose mounted EAS ATAL TV system), stretcher carrying and other uses. The prototype is now equipped with GPS.

TYPE: Four-seat amphibious homebuilt aircraft.
AIRFRAME: All-composites, of pre-moulded carbonfibre, Kevlar and epoxy. Laminar flow wings. Single-step hull. Retractable tricycle landing gear, with water rudder.
POWER PLANT: Standard engine is now one 149 kW (200 hp) Textron Lycoming IO-360-1A1. Fuel capacity 290 litres (76.6 US gallons; 63.8 Imp gallons) standard; optional 80 litre (21 US gallon; 17.6 Imp gallon) auxiliary tank.

DIMENSIONS, EXTERNAL:
Wing span	9.40 m (30 ft 10 in)
Length overall	6.60 m (21 ft 8 in)
Height overall	2.50 m (8 ft 2½ in)
Propeller diameter	1.62 m (5 ft 3¾ in)

AREA:
Wings, gross	12.40 m² (133.5 sq ft)

WEIGHTS:
Weight empty	600 kg (1,323 lb)
Max T-O weight	1,300 kg (2,866 lb)

Lederlin 380-L two-seat light aircraft (Teledyne Continental C90-14F engine) *(Peter J. Bish)*

Four-seat Lucas L5 with retractable tricycle landing gear (O-320 engine)

Lendepergt LP-01 Sibylle amphibian (IO-360-1A1 engine driving an MTV 18B variable-pitch propeller)

Lucas L6 in final stages of construction

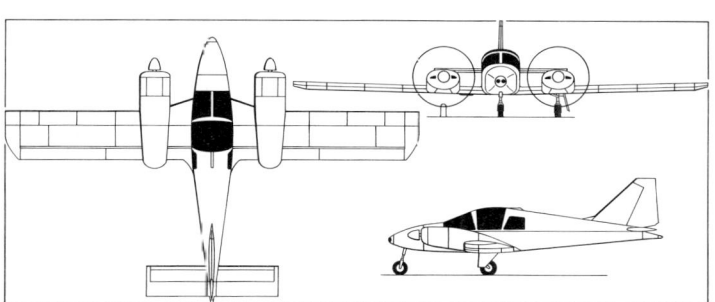

Lucas L10 four-seat lightplane

PERFORMANCE:

Max level speed	151 knots (280 km/h; 174 mph)	Max rate of climb at S/L	120 m (363 ft)/min	Landing run, on land	150 m (492 ft)
Econ cruising speed	130 knots (240 km/h; 149 mph)	Service ceiling	5,000 m (16,400 ft)	Range with max fuel	1,080 nm (2,000 km; 1,240 miles)
Stalling speed:		T-O run:		Endurance	8 h
flaps up	49 knots (90 km/h; 56 mph)	on land	600 m (1,970 ft)	g limits	+4/–3
flaps down	41 knots (75 km/h; 47 mph)	on water	750 m (2,460 ft)		

LUCAS

EMILE LUCAS

Corbonod, 01420 Seyssel
Telephone: 33 50 56 14 51

LUCAS L5

The prototype L5 was first flown on 13 August 1976. Plans are available to amateur builders, and more than 35 L5s are known to be flying or under construction, in four basic versions, as follows:

L5. Two/three-seat model, similar to prototype. Latest example has two seats, non-retractable tricycle landing gear and O-200 engine.

L5 200. Airframe generally similar to L5, but three seats standard. Suitable power plants include 70 kW (94 hp) Rolls-Royce Continental O-200-E and Textron Lycoming O-320. Fuel capacity 123 litres (32.5 US gallons; 27 Imp gallons). Accommodation for three persons and no baggage, or two persons and 65 kg (143 lb) baggage.

L5 320. As L5 360, but with Textron Lycoming O-320 engine and retractable tricycle landing gear (as illustrated).

L5 360. As basic L5, but with four seats in pairs. Prototype has 134 kW (180 hp) Textron Lycoming O-360. One fuel tank in fuselage, capacity 80 litres (21.1 US gallons; 17.6 Imp gallons) and two in wings, each 50 litres (13.2 US gallons; 11 Imp gallons). Space for 30 kg (66 lb) of baggage when carrying three persons.

The following details apply to the basic L5 but the airframe description is generally applicable to all versions:

TYPE: Two/three-seat homebuilt monoplane.

AIRFRAME: All-metal airframe of light alloy. Wing section NACA 23015 (mod). Non-retractable tricycle, or retractable tailwheel or (L5 320) retractable tricycle landing gear.

POWER PLANT: Prototype had one 85.75 kW (115 hp) Textron Lycoming O-235. Basic L5s built to plans can have an engine of between 93 and 134 kW (125-180 hp); see versions detailed. Fuel capacity 75 or 115 litres (19.8 or 30.4 US gallons; 16.5 or 25.3 Imp gallons) in L5; see model listings for other versions.

DIMENSIONS, EXTERNAL:

Wing span	9.20 m (30 ft 2¼ in)
Length overall	6.30 m (20 ft 8 in)
Height overall	2.10 m (6 ft 10¾ in)
Propeller diameter	1.70 m (5 ft 7 in)

AREA:

Wings, gross	11.90 m² (128.1 sq ft)

WEIGHTS (prototype):

Weight empty, equipped	505 kg (1,113 lb)
Max T-O weight	746 kg (1,644 lb)

PERFORMANCE (prototype):

Max level speed:
with retractable landing gear
146 knots (270 km/h; 168 mph)
with non-retractable gear
127 knots (235 km/h; 146 mph)
Econ cruising speed:
with retractable landing gear
116 knots (215 km/h; 134 mph)
with non-retractable gear
97 knots (180 km/h; 112 mph)

Max rate of climb at S/L	300 m (985 ft)/min
T-O to 15 m (50 ft)	280 m (920 ft)
Landing from 15 m (50 ft)	380 m (1,245 ft)
Range with max fuel	539 nm (1,000 km; 621 miles)

LUCAS L6

Design of this tandem two-seat light aircraft was started in 1981. Two prototypes have been built, one with a retractable tricycle and one with a retractable tailwheel landing gear. By adding wingtip extensions, it can be flown as a motor glider (see Sailplanes section). It will be marketed in the form of plans and kits.

TYPE: Two-seat homebuilt aircraft.

AIRFRAME: All-metal airframe of aluminium alloy. Wing section NACA 65₃618. Retractable tailwheel or tricycle landing gear.

POWER PLANT: One 62 kW (83 hp) Limbach. Optionally one 85.75 kW (115 hp) Textron Lycoming O-235, or 112 kW (150 hp) Textron Lycoming O-320 for aerobatic training. Fuel capacity 140 litres (37 US gallons; 30.8 Imp gallons).

DIMENSIONS, EXTERNAL (Sport aircraft):

Wing span	9.50 m (31 ft 2 in)
Length overall	7.00 m (22 ft 11½ in)
Height overall	1.85 m (6 ft 1 in)
Propeller diameter	1.61 m (5 ft 3½ in)

AREA (Sport aircraft):

Wings, gross	13.0 m² (140.0 sq ft)

WEIGHTS (Sport aircraft, Limbach engine):

Weight empty	350 kg (772 lb)
Max T-O weight	530 kg (1,168 lb)

PERFORMANCE (O-235 engine):

Max cruising speed	173 knots (320 km/h; 199 mph)
Econ cruising speed	146 knots (270 km/h; 168 mph)
T-O run	200 m (657 ft)
Landing run	160 m (525 ft)

LUCAS L7

The L7 is a cantilever high-wing cabin monoplane, offering side by side seating for two persons with dual controls. Construction is all-metal, with the conventional control surfaces including an all-moving tailplane. Power is provided by an engine in the 44.7-112 kW (60-150 hp) range. Fuel capacity in the two wing tanks is 80 litres (21 US gallons; 17.6 Imp gallons). A non-retractable tricycle landing gear is fitted.

DIMENSIONS, EXTERNAL:

Wing span	10.60 m (34 ft 9½ in)
Length overall	9.30 m (30 ft 6 in)

AREA:

Wings, gross	12.00 m² (129.17 sq ft)

WEIGHTS:

Weight empty	285 kg (628 lb)
Max T-O weight	495 kg (1,091 lb)

PERFORMANCE (44.7 kW; 60 hp engine):

Max cruising speed	100 knots (185 km/h; 115 mph)
Endurance	5 h

LUCAS L10

Construction of the prototype began in 1989 and the first flight is expected in 1992.

TYPE: Four-seat twin-engined monoplane.

AIRFRAME: Aluminium alloy construction. Wing section NACA 23015. Three-axis control. Retractable tricycle landing gear with brakes.

POWER PLANT: Two 85.75 kW (115 hp) Textron Lycoming O-235 engines, driving two-blade propellers. Fuel capacity 200 litres (52.8 US gallons; 44 Imp gallons).

DIMENSIONS, EXTERNAL:

Wing span	10.65 m (34 ft 11¼ in)
Length overall	8.32 m (27 ft 3½ in)
Height overall	2.50 m (8 ft 2½ in)
Propeller diameter (each)	1.80 m (5 ft 11 in)
AREA:	
Wings, gross	13.63 m² (146.71 sq ft)
WEIGHTS:	
Weight empty	700 kg (1,543 lb)
Baggage capacity	20 kg (44 lb)
Max T-O weight	1,150 kg (2,535 lb)
PERFORMANCE (estimated):	
Max level speed	189 knots (350 km/h; 217 mph)
Max cruising speed	146 knots (270 km/h; 168 mph)
Econ cruising speed	135 knots (250 km/h; 155 mph)
T-O run	450 m (1,475 ft)
Landing run	400 m (1,315 ft)
Range: with max standard fuel	539 nm (1,000 km; 621 miles)
with max payload	431 nm (800 km; 497 miles)
g limits	+6/–3

NICKEL & FOUCARD
RUDY NICKEL & JOSEPH FOUCARD
106 Avenue Château-Fleury, 26100 Romans

NICKEL & FOUCARD 001 ASTERIX

This unusually configured Experimental homebuilt aircraft has been designed to conform to FAR Pt 23 regulations. Construction of a prototype began in 1982 and the first flight was achieved in 1987. Plans are available.

TYPE: Tandem two-seat homebuilt monoplane.

AIRFRAME: Pod and boom type fuselage of wooden construction, providing enclosed accommodation. The strut braced pivoting parasol wing has a wooden structure, fabric and wood covered, and is foldable, with sweptback leading- and sweptforward trailing-edges, winglets of Araldite/Styrofoam construction, and small area triangular ailerons. The T tail has a steel tube structure, fabric covered, with an all-moving wire-braced tailplane. Non-retractable tailwheel landing gear.

POWER PLANT: One 27 kW (36 hp) Citroën Visa converted motorcar engine. Optional 650 cc BMW engine. Fuel capacity 28 litres (7.4 US gallons; 6.2 Imp gallons).

DIMENSIONS, EXTERNAL:

Wing span	7.50 m (24 ft 7¼ in)
Length overall	5.15 m (16 ft 10¾ in)
Height overall	2.10 m (6 ft 10¾ in)
Propeller diameter	1.24 m (4 ft 0¾ in)
AREA:	
Wings, gross	12.30 m² (132.4 sq ft)
WEIGHTS:	
Weight empty	200 kg (441 lb)
Pilot weight range	50-90 kg (110-198 lb)
Max T-O weight	374 kg (824 lb)
PERFORMANCE (two crew):	
Max level speed	78 knots (145 km/h; 90 mph)
Cruising speed	67-70 knots (125-130 km/h; 78-81 mph)
Econ cruising speed	59-62 knots (110-115 km/h; 68-71 mph)
Stalling speed	30-33 knots (55-60 km/h; 35-38 mph)
Max rate of climb at S/L	150 m (492 ft)/min
Service ceiling	3,000 m (9,840 ft)
T-O run	150 m (492 ft)
Landing run	70-150 m (230-493 ft)
Range	280 nm (520 km; 323 miles)
Endurance	4 h

NICOLLIER
AVIONS H. NICOLLIER
13 rue de Verdun, 25000 Besançon
Telephone: 33 81 53 57 01

NICOLLIER HN 433 MENESTREL

The prototype of this single-seat aircraft flew for the first time on 25 November 1962. Wing spars and kits of materials are available from the Siravia company, of Pons. Moulded canopies, cowlings and wheel fairings, together with plans, are available from Avions H. Nicollier.

TYPE: Single-seat homebuilt aircraft.

AIRFRAME: All-wood structure, with some plywood covering and Dacron overall. Non-retractable tailwheel landing gear.

POWER PLANT: One 22.4-37.3 kW (30-50 hp) converted Volkswagen motorcar engine; prototype adopted a 1,300 cc engine. Recommended are Rectimo-VW models.

DIMENSIONS, EXTERNAL:

Wing span	7.00 m (22 ft 11½ in)
Length overall	5.30 m (17 ft 4½ in)
Height overall	1.48 m (4 ft 10¼ in)
AREA:	
Wings, gross	8.20 m² (88.26 sq ft)
WEIGHTS:	
Weight empty	201 kg (443 lb)
Max T-O weight	330 kg (727 lb)
PERFORMANCE (with 29 kW; 39 hp Rectimo-VW engine, at max T-O weight):	
Max level speed at S/L	103 knots (190 km/h; 118 mph)
Max cruising speed	92 knots (170 km/h; 106 mph)
Stalling speed:	
engine idling	26 knots (48 km/h; 30 mph)
power on	22 knots (40 km/h; 25 mph)
Max rate of climb at S/L	180 m (590 ft)/min

NICOLLIER HN 434 SUPER-MENESTREL

A completely redesigned version of the Menestrel has been developed as the HN 434 Super-Menestrel, plans of which are available to amateur constructors. A 1,500 cc or 1,600 cc Volkswagen modified motorcar engine gives improved performance, although a 1,300 cc (22.4 kW; 30 hp) engine can be fitted, with which an 86 knots (160 km/h; 99 mph) cruising speed can be achieved. Fuel capacity is increased. Pilot comfort is improved. The Super-Menestrel is also simpler to construct.

NICOLLIER HN 700 MENESTREL II

This is basically a two-seat development of the HN 434, employing a 59.7 kW (80 hp) Limbach engine as standard but suitable for 1,600 cc to 2,000 cc Volkswagen converted motorcar engines.

DIMENSIONS, EXTERNAL:

Wing span	7.80 m (25 ft 7 in)
Length overall	5.30 m (17 ft 4¾ in)
Height overall	1.47 m (4 ft 10 in)
AREA:	
Wings, gross	9.80 m² (105.49 sq ft)
WEIGHTS:	
Weight empty	282 kg (622 lb)
Max T-O weight	500 kg (1,102 lb)
PERFORMANCE:	
Max cruising speed	101 knots (187 km/h; 116 mph)
Stalling speed	43 knots (80 km/h; 50 mph)
Service ceiling	3,800 m (12,475 ft)
T-O run	120 m (395 ft)
Max range	259-278 nm (480-515 km; 298-320 miles)
g limits	+4.4/–2.2
Max rate of climb at S/L:	
pilot only	420 m (1,380 ft)/min
dual	390 m (1,280 ft)/min
Range, with reserves for 45 nm (83 km; 52 miles)	
	539 nm (1,000 km; 621 miles)

NICOLLIER HN 600 WEEK-END

The HN 600 Week-end is a single-seat light aircraft, designed for economical construction and operation by amateurs. The structure is simple, of wood and fabric, with some components of Klégécel foam. Plans became available in 1981. A number of major components, such as the wing spar, ribs, cowlings and canopy, were to be made available in completed form from the Siravia company of Pons. Recommended power plant is a converted Volkswagen 1,500 cc motorcar engine.

DIMENSIONS, EXTERNAL:

Wing span	7.00 m (22 ft 11½ in)
Length overall	5.25 m (17 ft 2¾ in)
AREA:	
Wings, gross	8.20 m² (88.26 sq ft)
WEIGHTS:	
Weight empty	185 kg (408 lb)
Max T-O weight	310 kg (683 lb)
PERFORMANCE (estimated, at max T-O weight):	
Max level speed	108 knots (200 km/h; 124 mph)
Max cruising speed	92 knots (170 km/h; 106 mph)
Stalling speed	33 knots (60 km/h; 38 mph)
Max rate of climb at S/L	210 m (688 ft)/min
Range with max fuel at 86 knots (160 km/h; 99 mph)	
	345 nm (640 km; 397 miles)

PARENT
NORBERT PARENT
Le Mistral E5, 06150 La Bocca

PARENT NP2 BALADIN

Plans are on sale to construct this conventional side by side two-seat light homebuilt aircraft. It is a cantilever low-wing monoplane, with conventional control surfaces, and carries wingtip tanks. Cruising speed with a 67 kW (90 hp) engine is 124 knots (230 km/h; 143 mph).

PIEL
AVIONS CLAUDE PIEL
Le Mas de Darnetz, 19300 Egletons
Telephone: 33 55 93 09 79

PROPRIETOR: Mme Claude Piel

The authorised distributor for plans of Piel designs available to amateur constructors is:

M. E. Littner, 140 Philippe Goulet, Repentigny, Quebec J5Y 3M1, Canada.

PIEL EMERAUDE and SUPER EMERAUDE

More than 425 sets of plans of the Emeraude and Super Emeraude have been sold, and several versions have been factory-built. Current versions are as follows:

C.P.301. With 67 kW (90 hp) Teledyne Continental C90-12F engine.

C.P.304. With 63.4 kW (85 hp) Teledyne Continental C85-12F engine and wing flaps.

C.P.305. With 86 kW (115 hp) Textron Lycoming engine.

C.P.308. With 56 kW (75 hp) Teledyne Continental engine.

C.P.320. With Super Emeraude wings, a 74.5-85.75 kW (100-115 hp) Teledyne Continental engine and alternative tailwheel or tricycle landing gear.

C.P.320A. As C.P.320, but with sweptback fin.

C.P.321. As C.P.320, with 78.5 kW (105 hp) Potez engine.

C.P.323A. With 112 kW (150 hp) Textron Lycoming engine and sweptback fin. **C.P.323AB** has tricycle landing gear.

C.P.324 Emeraude Club. With 56 kW (75 hp) JPX 2100 engine.

C.P.328. As illustrated, with tailwheel landing gear.

TYPE: Side by side two-seat, dual-control homebuilt.

AIRFRAME: All-wood airframe, fabric covered except for wooden skins on tailplane. NACA 23012 wing section. Non-retractable tailwheel landing gear. Some aircraft have non-standard retractable landing gear.

POWER PLANT: Engine as in model listings. Fuel capacity 80 litres (21.1 US gallons; 17.6 Imp gallons). Provision for auxiliary tank, capacity 40 litres (10.6 US gallons; 8.8 Imp gallons).

DIMENSIONS, EXTERNAL:

Wing span	8.04 m (26 ft 4½ in)
Length overall: C.P.301	6.30 m (20 ft 8 in)
C.P.320	6.45 m (21 ft 2 in)
Height overall: C.P.301	1.85 m (6 ft 0¾ in)
C.P.320	1.90 m (6 ft 2¾ in)
Propeller diameter: C.P.301	1.80 m (5 ft 11 in)
C.P.320	1.78 m (5 ft 10 in)
AREA:	
Wings, gross	10.85 m² (116.7 sq ft)
WEIGHTS:	
Weight empty: C.P.301	380 kg (838 lb)
C.P.320	410 kg (903 lb)
Max T-O weight: C.P.301	650 kg (1,433 lb)
C.P.320	700 kg (1,543 lb)
PERFORMANCE (at max T-O weight):	
Max level speed:	
C.P.301	110 knots (205 km/h; 127 mph)
C.P.320	124 knots (230 km/h; 143 mph)

Nickel & Foucard 001 Asterix two-seat homebuilt monoplane

Piel C.P. 751 Beryl two-seat homebuilt *(Geoffrey P. Jones)*

Nicollier HN 700 Menestrel II

Piel C.P.328 Super Emeraude built by Nigel Reddish *(Geoffrey P. Jones)*

Econ cruising speed (65% power) at 1,200 m (3,940 ft):

C.P.301	101 knots (187 km/h; 116 mph)
C.P.320	110 knots (205 km/h; 127 mph)

Stalling speed:
flaps up:

C.P.301	51 knots (92 km/h; 58 mph)
C.P.320	53 knots (97 km/h; 61 mph)

flaps down:

C.P.301	46 knots (85 km/h; 53 mph)
C.P.320	49 knots (90 km/h; 56 mph)
Max rate of climb at S/L: C.P.301	168 m (551 ft)/min
C.P.320	240 m (787 ft)/min
Service ceiling: C.P.301	4,000 m (13,125 ft)
C.P.320	4,300 m (14,100 ft)
T-O run: C.P.301	250 m (820 ft)
C.P.320	230 m (755 ft)
Landing run: C.P.301	250 m (820 ft)
C.P.320	260 m (853 ft)

Range at econ cruising speed:

C.P.301, C.P.320	538 nm (1,000 km; 620 miles)

PIEL C.P.1320

Designed to combine the general characteristics of the Super Emeraude with the Super Diamant's three-seat cabin and fuel tanks in the wings, the C.P.1320 can be fitted with engines of 112 kW (150 hp) to 149 kW (200 hp).

TYPE: Three-seat homebuilt.

AIRFRAME: Wooden construction. NACA 23012 wing section. Retractable tailwheel landing gear.

POWER PLANT: Prototype has one 119 kW (160 hp) Textron Lycoming engine. Fuel capacity 140 litres (37 US gallons; 30.8 Imp gallons).

DIMENSIONS, EXTERNAL:

Wing span	7.90 m (25 ft 11 in)
Length overall	6.60 m (21 ft 8 in)
Height overall	1.80 m (5 ft 11 in)
Propeller diameter	1.80 m (5 ft 11 in)

AREA:

Wings, gross	11.10 m² (119.48 sq ft)

WEIGHTS:

Weight empty	470 kg (1,036 lb)
Max T-O weight	800 kg (1,764 lb)

PERFORMANCE:

Max level speed	162 knots (300 km/h; 186 mph)

Econ cruising speed (65% power)

132 knots (245 km/h; 152 mph)

Stalling speed: flaps up	54 knots (100 km/h; 62 mph)
flaps down	52 knots (95 km/h; 59 mph)
Max rate of climb at S/L	600 m (1,968 ft)/min
Service ceiling	5,000 m (16,400 ft)
T-O run	200 m (657 ft)
Landing run	300 m (984 ft)

Range with max fuel (65% power)

593 nm (1,100 km; 683 miles)

g limits: normal   +5/−2.5
aerobatic (two occupants, max T-O weight 720 kg; 1,585 lb)   +6/−3

PIEL SUPER DIAMANT

The Super Diamant is essentially a three/four-seat version of the Emeraude, of which more than 50 sets of plans have been sold. Current versions are as follows:

C.P.604. Prototype flown in Summer of 1964, with a 108 kW (145 hp) Teledyne Continental engine. Current version has swept vertical tail surfaces.

C.P.605. Much-modified four-seat ('2 + 2') version, with 112 kW (150 hp) Textron Lycoming O-320-E2A engine. Fully certificated for commercial production, as well as for amateur construction. Details in 1973-74 *Jane's*.

C.P.605B. Version of C.P.605 with retractable tricycle landing gear.

TYPE: Three/four-seat homebuilt.

AIRFRAME: All-wood airframe, fabric covered except for fixed tail surfaces which are plywood covered. Wing section NACA 23012. C.P.604 has non-retractable tailwheel landing gear. C.P.605B has retractable tricycle landing gear.

POWER PLANT: One flat-four engine (typically 119 kW; 160 hp Textron Lycoming IO-320-B1A or O-360-D1C). Fuel capacity 85 litres (22.5 US gallons; 18.7 Imp gallons). Provision for additional tankage to give total capacity of 160 litres (42.3 US gallons; 35 Imp gallons).

DIMENSIONS, EXTERNAL (C.P.605B):

Wing span	9.20 m (30 ft 2¼ in)
Length overall	7.00 m (22 ft 11¾ in)
Height overall	2.00 m (6 ft 6¾ in)
Propeller diameter	1.80 m (5 ft 11 in)

AREA:

Wings, gross	13.30 m² (143.2 sq ft)

WEIGHTS (C.P.605B):

Weight empty	520 kg (1,146 lb)
Max T-O weight	850 kg (1,873 lb)

PERFORMANCE (C.P.605B, at max T-O weight):

Max level speed	141 knots (260 km/h; 162 mph)

Econ cruising speed (65% power) at 1,200 m (3,940 ft)

124 knots (230 km/h; 143 mph)

Stalling speed: flaps up	49 knots (90 km/h; 56 mph)
flaps down	45 knots (82 km/h; 51 mph)
Max rate of climb at S/L	330 m (1,082 ft)/min
Service ceiling	5,000 m (16,400 ft)
T-O run	160 m (525 ft)
Landing run	270 m (886 ft)

Range at econ cruising speed

620 nm (1,150 km; 714 miles)

PIEL C.P.70, C.P.750 and C.P.751 BERYL

The **C.P.70 Beryl** combines the wing of the C.P.30 Emeraude, virtually unchanged, with a fuselage containing two seats in tandem, and non-retractable tricycle landing gear. It is powered by a 48.5 kW (65 hp) Teledyne Continental C65-8F engine. Plans of this version are not available from Canada.

Intended for aerobatic flying, the **C.P.750 Beryl** is also similar in general appearance to the Emeraude but has a longer, steel tube fuselage seating two persons in tandem, slightly reduced span, and other changes. The C.P.750 has been built principally by amateur constructors in Canada.

A further variant, the **C.P.751**, introduced several new design features and has a 134 kW (180 hp) Textron Lycoming O-360-A engine. Several are under construction or flying in Canada and the USA.

The following details refer to the C.P.750 Beryl:

TYPE: Two-seat homebuilt aerobatic monoplane.

AIRFRAME: All-wood wings, with fabric covering. Wing section NACA 23012. Fabric covered welded steel tube fuselage. Wooden tail unit; fixed surfaces plywood covered, control surfaces fabric covered. Non-retractable tailwheel landing gear.

POWER PLANT: One 112 kW (150 hp) Textron Lycoming O-320-E2A. Fuel capacity 70 litres (18.5 US gallons; 15.4 Imp gallons), with provision for two auxiliary tanks to give total capacity of 140 litres (37 US gallons; 30.75 Imp gallons).

DIMENSIONS, EXTERNAL (C.P.750):

Wing span	8.04 m (26 ft 4½ in)
Length overall	6.90 m (22 ft 7¾ in)
Height overall	2.10 m (6 ft 10¾ in)
Propeller diameter	1.80 m (5 ft 11 in)

AREA (C.P.750):

Wings, gross	11.00 m² (118.4 sq ft)

WEIGHTS:

Weight empty	480 kg (1,058 lb)
Max T-O weight	760 kg (1,675 lb)

PERFORMANCE (C.P.750, at max T-O weight):

Max level speed	151 knots (280 km/h; 174 mph)

Econ cruising speed (65% power) at 1,200 m (3,940 ft)

135 knots (250 km/h; 155 mph)

Stalling speed: flaps up	54 knots (100 km/h; 63 mph)
flaps down	52 knots (95 km/h; 59 mph)
Max rate of climb at S/L	390 m (1,280 ft)/min
Service ceiling	5,200 m (17,060 ft)
T-O run	190 m (623 ft)
Landing run	280 m (919 ft)

Range at econ cruising speed

593 nm (1,100 km; 683 miles)

PIEL C.P.80

The C.P.80 was designed as a single-seat racing aircraft for amateur construction. Details, and an illustration, can be found in the 1988-89 *Jane's*.

PIEL C.P.90 PINOCCHIO

The C.P.90 Pinocchio is essentially a smaller, single-seat development of the Emeraude, intended for aerobatic and general sporting flying.

AIRFRAME: All-wood, fabric covered. Wing section NACA 23012. Non-retractable tailwheel landing gear.

POWER PLANT: One 74.5 kW (100 hp) Teledyne Continental O-200. Fuel capacity 60 litres (15.9 US gallons; 13.2 Imp gallons).

DIMENSIONS, EXTERNAL:

Wing span	7.20 m (23 ft 7½ in)
Length overall	6.00 m (19 ft 8¼ in)
Height overall	1.80 m (5 ft 11 in)
Propeller diameter	1.80 m (5 ft 11 in)

AREA:

Wings, gross	9.65 m² (103.9 sq ft)

WEIGHTS:

Weight empty	335 kg (738 lb)
Max T-O weight	500 kg (1,102 lb)

PERFORMANCE (estimated, at max T-O weight):

Max level speed	141 knots (260 km/h; 162 mph)
Econ cruising speed (65% power) at 1,200 m (3,940 ft)	
	124 knots (230 km/h; 143 mph)

Stalling speed	41 knots (75 km/h; 47 mph)
Max rate of climb at S/L	480 m (1,575 ft)/min
Service ceiling	6,000 m (19,685 ft)
T-O run	180 m (590 ft)
Landing run	160 m (525 ft)
Range at econ cruising speed	
	296 nm (550 km; 341 miles)

PIEL C.P.150 ONYX

The Onyx was the last aircraft designed by the late M Claude Piel, and plans are currently available only from Mme Piel, in France. Construction of at least 110 Onyx is known to have been started, and several have flown.

TYPE: Single-seat tandem-wing microlight.

AIRFRAME: All-wood construction standard, except for Klégécel ribs in wings, fins and rudders, which are all Tergal fabric covered. Forward wing is pivoted for variable incidence. Rear wings have tip mounted fins and rudders and inset ailerons. Elevator in centre-section of forward wing. Non-retractable tricycle landing gear. Alternative glassfibre fuselage being utilised by some builders.

POWER PLANT: One 8.8 kW (12 hp) Solo.

DIMENSIONS, EXTERNAL:

Wing span	7.30 m (23 ft 11½ in)
Length overall	3.53 m (11 ft 7 in)

AREAS:

Wings, gross: rear wing	9.10 m² (97.95 sq ft)
front wing	3.70 m² (39.83 sq ft)

WEIGHTS:

Weight empty	70 kg (154 lb)
Max T-O weight	180 kg (397 lb)

POTTIER

JEAN POTTIER

4 rue de Poissy, 78130 les Mureaux
Telephone: 33 99 13 85

Details of the Pottier P.80S, P.100TS, P.110TS and P.105TS can be found in the 1987-88 *Jane's*, and of the P.50 Bouvreuil racing aircraft in the 1988-89 *Jane's*. Plans are available for the following types, plus the Bouvreuil:

POTTIER P.60 MINACRO

This biplane is available in normal sporting and aerobatic forms.

TYPE: Single-seat biplane.

AIRFRAME: Mainly wood with fabric covering. Wing bracing struts and wires. Three-axis control, with ailerons on lower wings only. Non-retractable tailwheel landing gear.

POWER PLANT: One engine of 48.5-93.2 kW (65-125 hp), driving a two-blade propeller. Aircraft illustrated has a Continental C90F. Fuel capacity 75 litres (20 US gallons; 16.5 Imp gallons).

DIMENSIONS, EXTERNAL:

Wing span	5.00 m (16 ft 5 in)
Length overall	4.60 m (15 ft 1 in)
Height overall, on ground	1.75 m (5 ft 9 in)

AREA:

Wings, gross	8.50 m² (91.5 sq ft)

WEIGHTS (67 kW; 90 hp engine):

Weight empty	280 kg (617 lb)
Max T-O weight	425 kg (937 lb)

PERFORMANCE (67 kW; 90 hp engine):

Max level speed	113 knots (210 km/h; 130 mph)
Max cruising speed	103 knots (190 km/h; 118 mph)
Stalling speed	46 knots (85 km/h; 53 mph)
Max rate of climb at S/L	
	more than 360 m (1,180 ft)/min
T-O run	100 m (328 ft)
Landing from 15 m (50 ft)	270 m (886 ft)
Range	308 nm (570 km; 354 miles)
Endurance	3 h

POTTIER P.70S

TYPE: Single-seat homebuilt sporting aircraft.

AIRFRAME: All-metal, of 2024 alloy. Wing section NACA 4415. Non-retractable tricycle landing gear.

POWER PLANT: One 30-44.7 kW (40-60 hp) Volkswagen converted motorcar engine. Fuel capacity 40 litres (10.6 US gallons; 8.75 Imp gallons).

DIMENSIONS, EXTERNAL:

Wing span	5.85 m (19 ft 2¼ in)
Length overall	5.15 m (16 ft 10¾ in)
Height overall	1.60 m (5 ft 3 in)
Propeller diameter	1.30 m (4 ft 3¼ in)

AREA:

Wings, gross	7.20 m² (77.5 sq ft)

WEIGHTS:

Weight empty, equipped	215 kg (474 lb)
Max T-O and landing weight	325 kg (716 lb)

PERFORMANCE (A: standard P.70S with 30 kW; 40 hp engine, B: 44.7 kW; 60 hp engine, at max T-O weight except where indicated):

Max level speed at S/L:		
A		97 knots (180 km/h; 112 mph)
B		116 knots (215 km/h; 133 mph)
Econ cruising speed at S/L:		
A		65 knots (120 km/h; 75 mph)
Stalling speed, flaps down:		
A, B		38 knots (70 km/h; 44 mph)
Max rate of climb at S/L: A		150 m (490 ft)/min
B		330 m (1,080 ft)/min
Service ceiling: A		4,500 m (14,775 ft)
T-O run: A		350 m (1,150 ft)
B		200 m (657 ft)
Range: A, B		215 nm (400 km; 248 miles)
g limit: A, B		+9 ultimate

POTTIER P.170S

The P.170S is a tandem two-seat version of the P.70S. It is of all-metal construction and has a retractable tricycle landing gear. Engine is a 37.3-52 kW (50-70 hp) Volkswagen.

TYPE: Two-seat sporting homebuilt.

DIMENSIONS, EXTERNAL:

Wing span	5.95 m (19 ft 6¼ in)
Length overall	5.70 m (18 ft 8½ in)
Height overall	1.65 m (5 ft 5 in)

AREA:

Wings, gross	7.40 m² (79.65 sq ft)

WEIGHTS:

Weight empty	230 kg (507 lb)
Max T-O weight	445 kg (981 lb)

PERFORMANCE (A: 37.3 kW; 50 hp engine, B: 52 kW; 70 hp engine):

Max level speed: A		95 knots (175 km/h; 109 mph)
B		108 knots (200 km/h; 124 mph)
Max cruising speed: A		84 knots (155 km/h; 96 mph)
B		102 knots (190 km/h; 118 mph)
Stalling speed: A, B		41 knots (75 km/h; 47 mph)
Max rate of climb at S/L: A		150 m (490 ft)/min
B		300 m (980 ft)/min
T-O run: A		380 m (1,250 ft)
B		220 m (722 ft)
Landing from 15 m (50 ft): A, B		350 m (1,150 ft)
Range with standard 50 litres (11 Imp gallons) of fuel, 45 min reserves: A, B		215 nm (400 km; 248 miles)
g limit: A, B		+6.6 ultimate

POTTIER P.180S

The P.180S is a side by side two-seat sporting aircraft, of all-metal construction and with a non-retractable tricycle landing gear. Power plant is a 41-67 kW (55-90 hp) Volkswagen.

TYPE: Two-seat sporting aircraft.

DIMENSIONS, EXTERNAL:

Wing span	6.50 m (21 ft 4 in)
Length overall	5.35 m (17 ft 6½ in)
Height overall	1.70 m (5 ft 7 in)

AREA:

Wings, gross	7.80 m² (83.96 sq ft)

WEIGHTS:

Weight empty	240 kg (529 lb)
Max T-O weight	470 kg (1,036 lb)

PERFORMANCE (estimated, 41 kW; 55 hp engine):

Max level speed	97 knots (180 km/h; 112 mph)
Max cruising speed	89 knots (165 km/h; 102 mph)
Stalling speed	41 knots (75 km/h; 47 mph)
Max rate of climb at S/L	168 m (550 ft)/min
T-O run	330 m (1,080 ft)
Landing from 15 m (50 ft)	350 m (1,150 ft)
Range	270 nm (500 km; 310 miles)
g limit	+5.7 ultimate

POTTIER P.200 SERIES

Five aircraft of basically similar layout make up this new series. offering accommodation for between one and four people (depending on version). Twenty-five kits were sold in 1990, when the first P.230S was flown. One or two P.220Ss and a P.250S were expected to fly in 1991.

The following versions are available:

P.210S Coati: Single-seater, with 37.3 kW (50 hp) Volkswagen modified motorcar engine.

P.220S Koala: Side by side two-seater, with 56 kW (75 hp) Volkswagen modified motorcar engine.

P.230S Panda: Three-seater, with 74.5 kW (100 hp) Teledyne Continental engine.

P.240S Saiga: Four-seater, with 112 or 134 kW (150 or 180 hp) Textron Lycoming engine.

P.250S Xerus: Tandem two-seater, with 48.5 kW (65 hp) Volkswagen modified motorcar engine.

TYPE: Single- to four-seat monoplanes.

AIRFRAME: All metal. Wing section NACA 4415. Non-retractable tricycle landing gear.

POWER PLANT: See model listings.

DIMENSIONS, EXTERNAL (A: P.210S, B: P.220S, C: P.230S, D: P.240S with 180 hp engine, and E: P.250S):

Wing span: A, E	6.40 m (21 ft 0 in)
B	6.50 m (21 ft 4 in)
C	8.10 m (26 ft 7 in)
D	9.50 m (31 ft 2 in)
Length overall: A	5.33 m (17 ft 5¾ in)
B	5.54 m (18 ft 2 in)
C	6.35 m (20 ft 10 in)
D	7.00 m (22 ft 11½ in)
E	5.82 m (19 ft 1¼ in)
Height overall: A	1.93 m (6 ft 4 in)
B, E	1.95 m (6 ft 4¾ in)
C	2.05 m (6 ft 8¾ in)
D	2.40 m (7 ft 10½ in)
Propeller diameter: A	1.45 m (4 ft 9 in)
B	1.44 m (4 ft 8¾ in)
C	1.72 m (5 ft 7¾ in)
D	1.82 m (5 ft 11¾ in)
E	1.50 m (4 ft 11 in)

AREAS (A to E as above):

Wings, gross: A	7.80 m² (83.96 sq ft)
B	8.00 m² (86.11 sq ft)
C	10.00 m² (107.64 sq ft)
D	12.40 m² (133.47 sq ft)
E	7.90 m² (85.03 sq ft)

WEIGHTS (A to E as above):

Weight empty: A	230 kg (507 lb)
B	275 kg (606 lb)
C	380 kg (838 lb)
D	550 kg (1,212 lb)
E	240 kg (529 lb)
Max T-O weight: A	350 kg (772 lb)
B	500 kg (1,102 lb)
C	700 kg (1,543 lb)
D	990 kg (2,182 lb)
E	470 kg (1,036 lb)

PERFORMANCE (A to E as above):

Max level speed: A		111 knots (205 km/h; 127 mph)
B		113 knots (210 km/h; 130 mph)
C		121 knots (225 km/h; 140 mph)
D		143 knots (265 km/h; 165 mph)
E		119 knots (220 km/h; 137 mph)
Cruising speed: A		100 knots (185 km/h; 115 mph)
B		103 knots (190 km/h; 118 mph)
C		113 knots (210 km/h; 130 mph)
D		121 knots (225 km/h; 140 mph)
E		108 knots (200 km/h; 124 mph)
Stalling speed:		
flaps up: A		41 knots (75 km/h; 47 mph)
B, C		49 knots (90 km/h; 56 mph)
E		48 knots (88 km/h; 55 mph)
flaps down: B, E		44 knots (80 km/h; 50 mph)
D		49 knots (90 km/h; 56 mph)
Max rate of climb at S/L: A, B		210 m (690 ft)/min
C		240 m (788 ft)/min
D		360 m (1,180 ft)/min
E		222 m (730 ft)/min
T-O run: A		150 m (493 ft)
B		200 m (657 ft)
C		210 m (690 ft)
D		360 m (1,180 ft)
E		180 m (591 ft)
Landing run: A		180 m (591 ft)
B		220 m (722 ft)
C		240 m (788 ft)
D		400 m (1,313 ft)
E		200 m (657 ft)
Range: A		242 nm (450 km; 279 miles)
B		377 nm (700 km; 435 miles)
C		404 nm (750 km; 466 miles)
D		539 nm (1,000 km; 621 miles)
E		350 nm (650 km; 404 miles)
g limits at max T-O weight: A		+6.6
B, C, D, E		+5.7

Piel C.P.150 Onyx with non-standard glassfibre fuselage *(Geoffrey P. Jones)*

Pottier P.230S built by C. Bire in France

Pottier P.60 built by M. Auboeck of Austria

Pottier P.180S two-seat sporting aircraft

Pottier P.70S with standard tricycle landing gear *(M.J. Hooks)*

S.M.A.N. Petrel with optional cockpit canopy

S.M.A.N.
SOCIÉTÉ MORBIHANNAISE D'AÉRO NAVIGATION

Anse de Mané Braz, Saint-Philibert, 56470 La Trinité-Sur-Mer
Telephone: 33 97 55 1063
Fax: 33 97 55 17 15
Telex: 740 043
GENERAL MANAGER: André Wydauw

Rights to M Claude Tisserand's two-seat Hydroplum II amphibian were purchased by S.M.A.N. in 1987, the prototype having first flown on 1 November 1986. S.M.A.N. markets kits to build the amphibian, known as the Petrel, requiring about 500 working hours to assemble. Ready to fly Petrels are also available.

S.M.A.N. PETREL
TYPE: Side by side two-seat microlight amphibian.
AIRFRAME: Wings have aluminium alloy tubular main spar, glassfibre/epoxy leading-edge and glassfibre/foam/epoxy ribs, with Dacron covering. Wing section NACA 2412. Three-axis control. Moulded monocoque single step hull of glassfibre/epoxy, with Kevlar reinforcement; carbonfibre/epoxy tailboom with water rudder at heel. Boom supports tail unit of wood with fabric covering on fin and control surfaces. Retractable tricycle landing gear. Optional fully enclosed cockpit.
POWER PLANT: One 47.7 kW (64 hp) Rotax 532. Four-stroke engine of same power can be installed for operation in homebuilt category. Fuel capacity 50 litres (13.2 US gallons; 11 Imp gallons).
DIMENSIONS, EXTERNAL:

Wing span: upper	8.90 m (29 ft 2½ in)
Length overall	5.90 m (19 ft 4¼ in)

Height overall	1.80 m (5 ft 11 in)
Propeller diameter	1.56 m (5 ft 1½ in)

AREA:

Wings, gross	17.30 m² (186.22 sq ft)

WEIGHTS:

Weight empty, equipped	195 kg (430 lb)
Min pilot weight	75 kg (166 lb)
Max T-O weight	400 kg (882 lb)

PERFORMANCE (at max T-O weight):

Max level speed	97 knots (180 km/h; 112 mph)
Cruising speed	81 knots (150 km/h; 93 mph)
Stalling speed	30 knots (55 km/h; 34 mph)
Max rate of climb at S/L	300 m (985 ft)/min
T-O run: on land	50 m (164 ft)
on water	100 m (328 ft)
Landing run: on land	70 m (230 ft)
on water	50 m (164 ft)
Endurance	4 h 10 min
g limits	+6/−3

SOYER/BARRITAULT
CLAUDE SOYER and JEAN BARRITAULT
Claude Soyer: BP 19, 49150 Longue-Jumelles
Jean Barritault: 10 rue G. Clémenceau, 49150 Baugé

SOYER/BARRITAULT SB1 ANTARÈS
The SB1 Antarès first flew on 24 May 1984. Plans available to amateur builders show an airframe of more simple design, a three-seat cabin with two side by side front seats and a rear bench, a non-retractable tricycle landing

gear, and 89.5 kW (120 hp) engine. The following description applies to the prototype:
TYPE: Tandem two-seat touring homebuilt.
AIRFRAME: Mostly all-wooden, with Dacron covering overall. Alternate wood and Klégécel wing nose ribs. Large polyester fairings over wing/fuselage junctions. Wing section NACA 4417. Retractable tricycle landing gear.
POWER PLANT: One 119 kW (160 hp) Textron Lycoming O-320-D2A. Fuel capacity 300 litres (79.25 US gallons; 66 Imp gallons).
DIMENSIONS, EXTERNAL:

Wing span	9.88 m (32 ft 5 in)

Length overall	7.20 m (23 ft 7½ in)
Height overall	1.90 m (6 ft 3 in)

AREA:

Wings, gross	12.20 m² (131.3 sq ft)

WEIGHTS:

Weight empty	642 kg (1,415 lb)
Max T-O weight	1,012 kg (2,231 lb)

PERFORMANCE:

Cruising speed	135 knots (250 km/h; 155 mph)
Range with max fuel, 45 min reserves	
	1,215 nm (2,250 km; 1,398 miles)

STERN

RENÉ STERN

10 rue du Château, 57730 Folschviller

STERN ST 80 BALADE

The ST 80 flew for the first time on 17 July 1983. Plans are available to amateur builders, together with kits containing major component parts.

TYPE: Single-seat homebuilt.

AIRFRAME: All-wood with fabric covering, except for fuselage which has wooden skins. Wing section NACA 43015 at root, NACA 43012 at tip. Non-retractable tricycle type.

POWER PLANT: One 45 kW (60 hp) Limbach 1,700 cc in prototype. Alternative Volkswagen modified motorcar engine in 1,600 cc to 2,000 cc range. Fuel capacity 32 litres (8.5 US gallons; 7 Imp gallons).

DIMENSIONS, EXTERNAL:
Wing span	6.40 m (21 ft 0 in)
Length overall	4.90 m (16 ft 0¾ in)
Propeller diameter	1.40 m (4 ft 7 in)

AREA:
Wings, gross	7.0 m² (75.35 sq ft)

WEIGHTS:
Weight empty	230 kg (507 lb)
Max T-O weight	340 kg (750 lb)

PERFORMANCE:
Max level speed	97-108 knots (180-200 km/h; 112-124 mph)
Max cruising speed	86 knots (160 km/h; 99 mph)
Stalling speed	44 knots (80 km/h; 50 mph)
Max rate of climb at S/L	240 m (785 ft)/min

GERMANY

AKAFLIEG MÜNCHEN

FLUGTECHNISCHE FORSCHUNGSGRUPPE an der TECHNISCHEN UNIVERSITÄT MÜNCHEN

Arcisstrasse 21, Postfach 202420, 8000 Munich 2

Although construction of the prototype **Mü 30 Schlacro** tandem two-seat aerobatic and towing aircraft began in 1985, it was not expected to fly until at least 1991. The wing span is now quoted as 8.82 m (28 ft 11¼ in), and max level speed is expected to be 216 knots (400 km/h; 248 mph). Details, and an illustration, appeared in the 1988-89 *Jane's*.

COSY

COSY EUROPE

Ahornstrasse 10, W-8901 Ried b. Augsburg
Telephone: 49 82 33/6 05 94
Fax: 49 82 33/2 01 50
OWNERS: Uli and Linda Wolter

Co Z Europe (now Cosy Europe) purchased the design rights to the Cozy side by side development of the Rutan Long-EZ in 1987, from the Co Z Development Corporation of the USA. Plans were made available but more recently Cosy Europe has undertaken some redesign of the aircraft, which is now named Classic. Plans, available since January 1990, are offered worldwide. The company also has an aircraft supply and import service, supporting homebuilders and general aviation.

COSY CLASSIC

The prototype of the original Cozy flew for the first time on 19 July 1982. Uli and Linda Wolter built and flew the first plans-built Cozy on 19 July 1985. The new Classic has a wider fuselage to provide more shoulder room, a larger canopy with more headroom, new turtleback with improved streamlining, R1145 rain canard as standard equipment, and the options of a fixed pitch or constant speed/variable pitch propeller.

The following modified details refer to the new Classic.

TYPE: Two/three-seat sporting homebuilt.

AIRFRAME: Wing and foreplane structures of unidirectional glassfibre with rigid styrofoam core. Modified Eppler wing section; foreplane has Roncz section. Composite fuselage comprising sheets of PVC foam, with wood strips as corner fillers, in a sandwich using internal and external covering of unidirectional glassfibre. Light alloy or steel extrusions used for engine mount. Tricycle landing gear, with retractable nosewheel.

POWER PLANT: One 112-119 kW (150-160 hp) Textron Lycoming O-320 or IO-320 engine. Fuel capacity 196 litres (51.8 US gallons; 43 Imp gallons).

DIMENSIONS, EXTERNAL:
Wing span	7.96 m (26 ft 1¼ in)
Length overall	5.12 m (16 ft 9½ in)
Height overall	2.30 m (7 ft 6½ in)
Propeller diameter	1.60 or 1.62 m (5 ft 3 in or 5 ft 3¾ in)

AREA:
Wings, gross	8.88 m² (95.6 sq ft)

WEIGHTS:
Weight empty, basic	410 kg (904 lb)
Max front seat load	160 kg (352 lb)
Max T-O weight	800 kg (1,763 lb)

PERFORMANCE:
Max level speed at S/L	165 knots (306 km/h; 190 mph)
Cruising speed (75% power) at 2,440 m (8,000 ft)	162 knots (300 km/h; 186 mph)
Econ cruising speed at 3,660 m (12,000 ft)	124 knots (230 km/h; 143 mph)
Stalling speed	53 knots (97 km/h; 60 mph)
Max rate of climb at S/L: solo	457 m (1,500 ft)/min
dual	305 m (1,000 ft)/min
Service ceiling: solo	7,620 m (25,000 ft)
dual	6,100 m (20,000 ft)
T-O run: solo	250 m (821 ft)
dual	450 m (1,477 ft)
Landing run: solo	300 m (985 ft)
dual	450 m (1,477 ft)
Range, 45 min reserves:	
at 45% power	1,025 nm (1,900 km; 1,180 miles)
at 75% power	863 nm (1,600 km; 994 miles)

HINZ

LUCIA AND BERNHARD HINZ

Bei der Kirche 17, D-7024 Filderstadt 1
Telephone: 49 (7158) 65441

HINZ BL1-KEA

First flown on 23 December 1989, the BL1-KEA is of GFRP/PVC foam sandwich construction. It has cantilever low wings (wing section FX-67-L150/30), a T tail with full span elevator, and a retractable landing gear comprising a monowheel, balancer wheels at about one-quarter span and a faired (non-retractable) tailwheel. Plans were expected to be made available in 1991.

TYPE: Side by side two-seat homebuilt.

POWER PLANT: One 70 kW (94 hp) Limbach L 2400 DA1B engine in nose, driving a Mühlbauer MTV-1-A/L160-03 two-blade variable-pitch propeller. Fuselage fuel tank, capacity 100 litres (26.4 US gallons; 22 Imp gallons).

DIMENSIONS, EXTERNAL:
Wing span	10.00 m (32 ft 9¾ in)
Length overall	6.75 m (22 ft 1¾ in)
Height overall	1.30 m (4 ft 3¼ in)
Propeller diameter	1.60 m (5 ft 3 in)

AREA
Wings, gross	12.00 m² (129.2 sq ft)

WEIGHTS:
Weight empty	480 kg (1,058 lb)
Max T-O weight	720 kg (1,587 lb)

PERFORMANCE:
Cruising speed, 75% power	135 knots (250 km/h; 155 mph)
Stalling speed	46 knots (85 km/h; 53 mph)
Max rate of climb at S/L	240 m (785 ft)/min
T-O and landing run	200 m (656 ft)
Range	863 nm (1,600 km; 994 miles)
g limits	+4.4/-2.2

IRAQ

CMI

UAV Department of CMI
Al Faris factory, Al Faris

CMI SAJA

As can be seen from the accompanying illustration, the Saja closely resembles the CFM Shadow tandem two-seat microlight (see UK part of Sport Aircraft section), and appears to be the modified Shadow II version formerly marketed by ASVEC (UK) Ltd as a manned aerial surveillance system. Stated roles are oil pipeline inspection and real-time video monitoring; a TV or thermal imaging package can be carried under the fuselage pod. Two examples had been completed by early 1989 but no more recent news has been received. Of pod and boom configuration, other features include a braced high-mounted wing, conventional tail unit comprising a tailplane and one-piece elevator, ventral fin and rudder, and a non-retractable nosewheel landing gear. Power is provided by a 47.7 kW (64 hp) Rotax 532 engine driving a three-blade pusher propeller; fuel load is 42 kg (92 lb).

DIMENSIONS, EXTERNAL:
Wing span	8.61 m (28 ft 3 in)
Length overall	6.40 m (21 ft 0 in)

WEIGHTS:
Weight empty	176 kg (388 lb)
Max T-O weight	408 kg (899 lb)

PERFORMANCE:
Max level speed	110 knots (204 km/h; 127 mph)
Service ceiling	7,010 m (23,000 ft)
Endurance	4 h 30 min
Range for videoing	108 nm (200 km; 124 miles)

ISRAEL

SCICRAFT

SCICRAFT LTD
(Subsidiary of Cyclone Aviation Products Ltd)

PO Box 114, Carmiel 20-100
Telephone: 972 (4) 960701
Fax: 972 (4) 962220
Telex: 471684 CYCLV
PRESIDENT: Gideon Goren
MARKETING: Baruch Lavanon

SCICRAFT GAMBIT

The Gambit, of which three models are available in kit form, is aimed mainly at private recreational pilots and training markets, though amphibious, agricultural and military applications are planned. Construction takes about 200 working hours. It was designed to FAR Pt 23 requirements, and was expected to gain full certification during the 1990s. Construction of a prototype began in 1986, and this flew in the following year. By January 1990 three prototypes and three ready assembled aircraft had been completed, but no more recent news has been received.

TYPE: Side by side two-seat homebuilt.

AIRFRAME: Wings have aluminium alloy leading-edges, composites cambered tips and winglets, and optional Tedlar or Ceconite skins. Composites ailerons on wings. Composites foreplane of glassfibre/graphite/foam core sandwich. Elevators on foreplane. Rudder on each winglet, deflecting outward only. Composites fuselage of

The SB1 Antarès designed and built in Baugé, France, by M Claude Soyer and M Jean Barritault

Stern ST 80 single-seat homebuilt aircraft with wings folded (*M.J. Hooks*)

Hinz BL1-KEA two-seat sporting homebuilt

First plans-built Cosy Europe Cozy, built by Uli and Linda Wolter

CMI Saja two-seat oil pipeline inspection microlight
(*Jane's Defence Weekly/Tony Banks*)

Prototype SciCraft Gambit two-seat homebuilt

glassfibre/Kevlar/graphite/foam core sandwich. Non-retractable tricycle landing gear, with brakes. Dual wheel controls.

POWER PLANT: Available as **Gambit 600** with 47.7 kW (64 hp) Rotax 582, **Gambit 700** with 56 kW (75 hp) Hewland, or **Gambit 900** with 59 kW (79 hp) Rotax 912 or 63.4 kW (85 hp) Norton rotary engine. Fuel capacity 60 litres (16 US gallons; 13.2 Imp gallons) standard; optional 30 litre (8 US gallon; 6.6 Imp gallon) auxiliary tank.

DIMENSIONS, EXTERNAL:
Wing span	10.01 m (32 ft 10 in)
Foreplane span	3.86 m (12 ft 8 in)
Length overall	5.13 m (16 ft 10 in)
Height overall	2.44 m (8 ft 0 in)
Propeller diameter	1.52 m (5 ft 0 in)

AREAS:
Wings, gross	13.65 m² (147.0 sq ft)
Foreplanes, gross	1.77 m² (19.1 sq ft)

WEIGHTS (A: Gambit 600, B: Gambit 900):
Weight empty: A	289 kg (637 lb)
B	299 kg (660 lb)
Max baggage: A	16 kg (35 lb)
B	25 kg (55 lb)
Max T-O weight: A	476 kg (1,050 lb)
B	506 kg (1,115 lb)

PERFORMANCE (A and B as above):
Max level speed: A	87 knots (161 km/h; 100 mph)
B	113 knots (209 km/h; 130 mph)
Max cruising speed: A	78 knots (145 km/h; 90 mph)
B	100 knots (185 km/h; 115 mph)
Stalling speed: A	41 knots (76 km/h; 47 mph)
B	42 knots (78 km/h; 48 mph)
Max rate of climb at S/L: A	183 m (600 ft)/min
B	259 m (850 ft)/min
T-O run: A	119 m (390 ft)

Range with standard fuel:
A	217 nm (402 km; 250 miles)
B	347 nm (643 km; 400 miles)
Endurance: A	3 h
g limits: A	+7/−2.64
B	+6.6/−2.64

ITALY

DEDALUS
DEDALUS Srl
Viale Campania 29, 20133 Milan
Telephone: 39 (2) 71 63 41
GENERAL MANAGER: Marco Baggi

DEDALUS POPPY
The prototype Poppy flew for the first time in May 1984. Kits are available, requiring about 300 working hours to assemble. Many completed aircraft are flying.
TYPE: Single-seat homebuilt.

AIRFRAME: Airframe is geodetic structure of Sitka spruce, with Dacron fabric covering, although aluminium alloy bracing struts are used and the engine cowling can be of glassfibre. Wing section Rhode St Genese 34. Non-retractable tailwheel landing gear.
POWER PLANT: One 18.6 kW (25 hp) KFM 107E. Fuel capacity 20 litres (5.3 US gallons; 4.4 Imp gallons).

DIMENSIONS, EXTERNAL:
Wing span	10.60 m (34 ft 9¼ in)
Length overall	5.90 m (19 ft 4¼ in)
Height overall	1.90 m (6 ft 2¾ in)
Propeller diameter	1.40 m (4 ft 7 in)

AREA:
Wings, gross	15.00 m² (161.5 sq ft)

WEIGHTS:
Weight empty	114 kg (252 lb)
Max T-O weight	210 kg (463 lb)

PERFORMANCE:
Max level speed	54 knots (100 km/h; 62 mph)
Econ cruising speed	43 knots (80 km/h; 50 mph)
Stalling speed	22 knots (40 km/h; 25 mph)
Max rate of climb at S/L	183 m (600 ft)/min
Service ceiling	3,050 m (10,000 ft)
T-O to 15 m (50 ft)	50 m (164 ft)
Landing from 15 m (50 ft)	100 m (328 ft)
Range with max fuel	108 nm (200 km; 124 miles)

IANNOTTA

DOTT ING ORLANDO IANNOTTA

Via Nicolardi 254, 80131 Naples
Telephone: 39 (81) 741 9324

In addition to the San Francesco, the 940 Zefiro microlight is available (see Microlight tables).

IANNOTTA I-66L SAN FRANCESCO

Plans to build the San Francesco are available; three are known to be flying.

TYPE: Two-seat, dual-control homebuilt motor glider.
AIRFRAME: All wood wings, with plywood leading-edges and fabric covering overall. Wing section NACA 23012. Fabric covered steel tube fuselage structure, with wooden formers. Wire braced tail unit of welded steel tube, fabric covered. Non-retractable tailwheel landing gear.
POWER PLANT: One 51 kW (68 hp) Limbach SL 1700E. Fuel capacity 70 litres (18.5 US gallons; 15.4 Imp gallons).
DIMENSIONS, EXTERNAL:

Wing span	9.34 m (30 ft 7¾ in)
Length overall	6.60 m (21 ft 8 in)
Propeller diameter	1.45 m (4 ft 9 in)

AREA:

Wings, gross	13.61 m² (146.5 sq ft)

WEIGHTS:

Weight empty	268 kg (591 lb)
Max T-O weight	462 kg (1,018 lb)

PERFORMANCE, POWERED:

Max level speed	81 knots (150 km/h; 93 mph)
Cruising speed at S/L	70 knots (130 km/h; 81 mph)
Landing speed	35 knots (65 km/h; 41 mph)
Max rate of climb at S/L	210 m (690 ft)/min
Service ceiling	3,800 m (12,470 ft)
Range with max fuel	378 nm (700 km; 435 miles)

PERFORMANCE, UNPOWERED:

Best glide ratio at 50 knots (93 km/h; 58 mph)	14
Min rate of sink at 48 knots (88 km/h; 55 mph)	
	84 m (275 ft)/min

NIKE

NIKE AERONAUTICA SRL

Via Ferrarese 10, 40013 Castelmaggiore, Bologna
Telephone: 39 (51) 765105
Fax: 39 (51) 765714
SALES MANAGER: Fabbri Giampiero

The Nike Italzair, a derivative of the Canadian Ultraflight Lazair microlight, was described and illustrated in the 1988-89 *Jane's*. Its latest design is the PUL 9.

NIKE AERONAUTICA PUL 9

Design of the PUL 9 started in October 1989. Construction began three months later, and the first flight was made in July 1990. No further examples had been built up to May 1991. Principal design parameters were high manoeuvrability and a wide operating speed range.

TYPE: Single-seat very light aircraft, suitable for recreational or military use and for piloted or unmanned operation.
AIRFRAME: Sweptback flying-wing configuration (30° on leading-edges), with thick, symmetrical aerofoil section (thickness/chord ratio 20 per cent); rounded tips, with washout. Pitch/roll control by pushrod-operated elevons. No vertical surfaces. Central cockpit/engine mount structure of steel tube; wings, including elevons, of glassfibre (spars) and carbonfibre/Kevlar construction. Non-retractable tricycle landing gear with rubber cord shock absorption; drum brakes on mainwheels.
POWER PLANT: One 31.3 kW (42 hp) Rotax 447UL engine, driving an Arplast 148GAM three-blade adjustable-pitch pusher propeller. Single 20 litre (5.3 US gallon; 4.4 Imp gallon) fuel tank in wing centre-section.
DIMENSIONS, EXTERNAL:

Wing span	9.00 m (29 ft 6⅓ in)
Length overall	3.90 m (12 ft 9½ in)
Height overall	1.60 m (5 ft 3 in)
Propeller diameter	1.48 m (4 ft 10¼ in)

AREA:

Wings, gross	approx 11.60 m² (124.86 sq ft)

WEIGHTS:

Weight empty	150 kg (331 lb)
Max T-O weight	300 kg (661 lb)

PERFORMANCE:

Max level speed at S/L	121 knots (225 km/h; 140 mph)
Max cruising speed at S/L	
	92 knots (170 km/h; 105 mph)
Econ cruising speed at S/L	76 knots (140 km/h; 87 mph)
Stalling speed, engine idling	30 knots (55 km/h; 35 mph)
Max rate of climb at S/L	305 m (1,000 ft)/min
T-O run	150 m (492 ft)

TERZI

TERZI AERODINE

Via Cesare Battisti 15, 20122 Milan
Telephone: 39 (2) 5518 0268
Fax: 39 (2) 5518 0268

This company has specialised in the construction and repair of glassfibre sailplanes.

TERZI T30 KATANA

This specialised aerobatic aircraft, designed by Pietro Terzi, made its first flight on 16 January 1991. It is available either in kit form or fully built and certificated to FAR 21 in the Experimental category. Terzi had delivered two kits by March 1991, one of them in the E version to which the data below refer.

TYPE: Single-seat competition aerobatic aircraft.
AIRFRAME: Aluminium alloy wings (detachable) and tail unit, and welded steel tube fuselage with removable composite shells of PVC core with Kevlar and carbon cloth facing. Three-axis control, with trim tab on starboard elevator. Non-retractable tailwheel landing gear.
POWER PLANT: The prototype flew with 224 kW (300 hp) Textron Lycoming O-540, but the definitive E version has 298 kW (400 hp) Textron Lycoming IO-720A, with Christen inverted operating kit, driving a Muhlbauer four-blade constant-speed propeller. An aerobatic fuel tank is mounted in the fuselage and two cruising tanks in the wing leading-edges: total capacity 195 litres (51.5 US gallons; 42.9 Imp gallons).
DIMENSIONS, EXTERNAL:

Wing span	7.77 m (25 ft 6 in)
Length overall	6.70 m (21 ft 11¾ in)
Height overall	2.57 m (8 ft 5¼ in)

AREA:

Wings, net	10.60 m² (114.1 sq ft)

WEIGHT (Aerobatic):

Max T-O weight	880 kg (1,940 lb)

PERFORMANCE:

Max level speed	205 knots (380 km/h; 236 mph)
Stalling speed	53 knots (98 km/h; 61 mph)
Max rate of climb at S/L	1,380 m (4,527 ft)/min
g limits	±12

LUXEMBOURG

WOLFF

ATELIERS PAUL WOLFF

1 Rue des Romains, L-8284 Kehlen
Telephone: 352 309 954

In addition to the Flash-3, this company has designed the four-seat Sky-Wolff, which is being built in the USA by Wolff Aircraft Engineering Ltd.

WOLFF FLASH-3

The Flash-3 was exhibited at the 1985 RSA meeting at Brienne in France, before it had made its first flight. It is offered in the form of a series of component kits, with an estimated construction time of 650 to 750 hours.
TYPE: Three-seat homebuilt aircraft.
AIRFRAME: Entire airframe constructed of vinylester and resin composites, partially strengthened with carbonfibre. Wing section NACA 43012⁵ at root, 43010 at tip. Retractable tricycle landing gear.
POWER PLANT: One 112 kW (150 hp) Textron Lycoming O-320. Other engines of up to 194 kW (260 hp) can be

fitted. Fuel capacity: standard tank 261 litres (69 US gallons; 57.4 Imp gallons); long range tank 541 litres (143 US gallons; 119 Imp gallons); long range tank with tip tanks 641 litres (169.3 US gallons; 141 Imp gallons).
DIMENSIONS, EXTERNAL:

Wing span, over tip tanks	8.53 m (27 ft 11¾ in)
Length overall	7.93 m (26 ft 0¼ in)
Height overall	2.11 m (6 ft 11 in)
Propeller diameter	1.93 m (6 ft 4 in)

AREA:

Wings, gross	10.00 m² (107.64 sq ft)

WEIGHTS:

Weight empty	508 kg (1,120 lb)
Baggage capacity	120 kg (264 lb)
Max T-O weight: without tip tanks	996 kg (2,196 lb)
with tip tanks	1,066 kg (2,350 lb)

PERFORMANCE (at max T-O weight):

Max level speed at S/L	197 knots (365 km/h; 227 mph)
Econ cruising speed at 3,050 m (10,000 ft)	
	180 knots (334 km/h; 207 mph)
Stalling speed, flaps down	44 knots (81 km/h; 50 mph)
Max rate of climb at S/L	366 m (1,200 ft)/min
Service ceiling	5,430 m (17,820 ft)
T-O run	230 m (755 ft)
Landing run	210 m (689 ft)
Range with standard fuel, two occupants and baggage	
	1,776 nm (3,291 km; 2,045 miles)

WOLFF SKY-WOLFF

The Sky-Wolff represents a redesign of the earlier Flash-3, offering seating for four adults in the larger fuselage. Assembly of this all-composites aircraft takes approximately 600 working hours. Cruising speed is 186 knots (346 km/h; 215 mph) IAS, and a range of up to 3,647 nm (6,759 km; 4,200 miles) can be achieved with 640 litres (169.3 US gallons; 141 Imp gallons) of fuel. A separate lock-up baggage compartment is provided, and the wings are removable for trailering.

NORWAY

LUNDS TEKNISKE

LUNDS TEKNISKE

Vikaveien 2, N-8600 Mo
Telephone: 47 (87) 52 100
Fax: 47 (87) 55 065
OWNER/MANAGER: Arne Lund

Rights to the Silhouette homebuilt aircraft were purchased from the US Silhouette Aircraft Inc, and Lunds Tekniske currently offers kits. The original prototype Silhouette first flew in the USA on 3 July 1984. By January 1990 (when the last update was received), 42 Silhouette kits had been sold, of which 15 had been assembled. Bolt-on wingtip extensions allow the Silhouette to be flown as a motor glider.

LUNDS TEKNISKE SILHOUETTE

TYPE: Single-seat sport/recreational homebuilt and motor glider; designed and tested to FAR Pt 23 standards.
AIRFRAME: Wings have glassfibre spars, pre-cut Styrofoam cores, glassfibre/epoxy skins and pre-moulded wingtips. Basic wings have half span ailerons of Styrofoam/glassfibre construction. Flaps will eventually be available. Provision for bolt-on wingtip extensions for use as motor glider. Centreline dive brake optional. Fuselage of glassfibre and Nomex honeycomb, pre-moulded in halves with integral tail fin, around plywood/Styrofoam/glassfibre bulkheads. Tail surfaces of foam and glassfibre. Non-retractable tricycle landing gear, with brakes.

POWER PLANT: One 30 kW (40 hp) Rotax 447 or 37.3 kW (50 hp) Rotax 503. Fuel capacity with standard wing 45 litres (12 US gallons; 10 Imp gallons).
DIMENSIONS, EXTERNAL:

Wing span: standard	9.75 m (32 ft 0 in)
with optional wing extensions	12.50 m (41 ft 0 in)
Length overall	5.87 m (19 ft 3 in)
Height overall	2.03 m (6 ft 8 in)
Propeller diameter	1.47 m (4 ft 10 in)

AREAS:

Wings, gross: standard	7.06 m² (76.0 sq ft)
with extensions	8.36 m² (90.0 sq ft)

Dedalus Poppy single-seat cabin monoplane *(Avio Data)*

Wolff Sky-Wolff homebuilt aircraft, designed in Luxembourg and manufactured in kit form in the USA *(Geoffrey P. Jones)*

Terzi T30 Katana single-seat aerobatic competition aircraft

Long-wing Lunds Tekniske Silhouette motor glider (foreground) and version with standard wings (rear) *(Howard Levy)*

Iannotta I-66L San Francesco

Alpha Marco J-5 in non-retractable landing gear form

Nike Aeronautica PUL 9 single-seat flying-wing

WEIGHTS:		Cruising speed	104 knots (193 km/h; 120 mph)	Landing run		183 m (601 ft)
Weight empty, standard wings	262 kg (578 lb)	Stalling speed	45 knots (84 km/h; 52 mph)	Range with max fuel, no reserves		
Max T-O weight	374 kg (824 lb)	Max rate of climb at S/L	244 m (800 ft)/min			390 nm (724 km; 450 miles)
PERFORMANCE (standard wings):		Service ceiling	4,265 m (14,000 ft)	g limits		+4.2/-2
Max level speed	122 knots (225 km/h; 140 mph)	T-O run	244 m (800 ft)			

POLAND

ALPHA
ALPHA
Balicka 176-190, 30-149 Kraków
Telephone: 48 (12) 37 44 17/37 40 00
Telex: 0322699
DESIGNER: Jaroslaw Janowski

The Marco J-5 first flew in Poland on 30 October 1983. An aircraft branch of the Marko-Elektronic Company was established in that country to construct export kits, now known as Alpha, and Alpha/USA Aviation Inc distributes aircraft (2016 Charter Point Drive, Arlington Heights, Illinois 60004, USA). Hewa Technics (detailed in the German section of the 1990-91 *Jane's*) had been appointed a distributor of company products in 1984.

The J-5 is the fifth aircraft designed by Mr Janowski (see Microlight section), and construction takes approximately 600 working hours.

ALPHA MARCO J-5
TYPE: Single-seat homebuilt.
AIRFRAME: Built almost entirely of glassfibre and epoxy; flaperons are glassfibre and duralumin. Wortmann FX 67-K170/17 wing section. Three-axis control. Landing gear comprises retractable mainwheel, non-retractable tailwheel and wingtip balancers or non-retractable tailwheel.
POWER PLANT: One 18.6 kW (25 hp) KFM 107ER. Fuel capacity 25 litres (6.6 US gallons; 5.5 Imp gallons).
DIMENSIONS, EXTERNAL:

Wing span	8.16 m (26 ft 9¼ in)
Length overall	4.66 m (15 ft 3½ in)
Height overall	1.40 m (4 ft 7¼ in)
Propeller diameter	1.15 m (3 ft 9¼ in)

AREA:

Wings, gross	6.3 m² (67.5 sq ft)

WEIGHTS:

Weight empty	165 kg (363 lb)
Pilot weight range	55-105 kg (122-231 lb)
Max T-O weight	290 kg (640 lb)

PERFORMANCE:

Cruising speed	91 knots (169 km/h; 105 mph)
Econ cruising speed	81 knots (150 km/h; 93 mph)
Stalling speed	42 knots (78 km/h; 48 mph)
Max rate of climb at S/L	182 m (600 ft)/min
Service ceiling	3,050 m (10,000 ft)
T-O run	200 m (656 ft)
Landing run	150 m (490 ft)
Range with max fuel	295 nm (547 km; 340 miles)
g limits	+6/-3

ORLIŃSKI
ROMAN ORLIŃSKI
ul Lesna 4, 82-200 Malbork

ORLIŃSKI RO-7 ORLIK (EAGLET)
The prototype Orlik was flown for the first time on 22 February 1987. Plans are available to amateur builders. Some glassfibre wing and fuselage components became available in 1989.

TYPE: Single-seat homebuilt.

AIRFRAME: Wing section NACA 23012. Wings of mostly wood construction, with plywood D-section leading-edge and fabric covering aft of spar. Welded steel tube forward fuselage; wooden semi-monocoque rear fuselage. Non-retractable tailwheel landing gear.

POWER PLANT: One 48.5 kW (65 hp) Walter Mikron III. Fuel capacity 30 litres (7.9 US gallons; 6.6 Imp gallons).

DIMENSIONS, EXTERNAL:

Wing span	7.60 m (24 ft 11¼ in)
Length overall	5.50 m (18 ft 0½ in)
Height overall	1.95 m (6 ft 4¾ in)
Propeller diameter	1.45 m (4 ft 9 in)

AREA:

Wings, gross	8.75 m² (94.18 sq ft)

WEIGHTS:

Weight empty	220 kg (485 lb)
Max T-O weight	320 kg (705 lb)

PERFORMANCE:

Max level speed at S/L	81 knots (150 km/h; 93 mph)
Econ cruising speed at S/L	49 knots (90 km/h; 56 mph)
Stalling speed	39 knots (71 km/h; 45 mph)
Max rate of climb at S/L	300 m (985 ft)/min
T-O run	100 m (328 ft)
Landing run	200 m (656 ft)
Range, 20 min reserves	215 nm (400 km; 248 miles)
Endurance, 20 min reserves	4 h 40 min

SWEDEN

ANDREASSON
BJÖRN ANDREASSON
Collins Väg 22B, 23600 Höllviksnäs

In addition to the aircraft described here, Mr Andreasson's BA-12 and BA-14B are detailed under MFI headings in the Microlight and main Aircraft sections respectively.

ANDREASSON BA-4B
Plans to build the BA-4B are available.

TYPE: Single-seat fully aerobatic homebuilt biplane.

AIRFRAME: Braced biplane. Alternative all-metal wings, or all-wood wing structure covered with heavy plywood skin. Ailerons, of simplified sheet metal construction, on lower wings only. Provision for detachable plastics wingtips. Sheet metal fuselage and tail unit. Turtledeck either sheet metal or reinforced plastics. Non-retractable tailwheel landing gear.

POWER PLANT: Prototype has 74.5 kW (100 hp) Rolls-Royce Continental O-200-A. Provision for other engines, including Volkswagen conversions. Standard fuel capacity 50 litres (13.2 US gallons; 11 Imp gallons). Provision for external 'bullet' tank of 50 litres (13.2 US gallons; 11 Imp gallons) capacity under fuselage.

DIMENSIONS, EXTERNAL:

Wing span: upper	5.34 m (17 ft 7 in)
lower	5.14 m (16 ft 11 in)
Length overall	4.60 m (15 ft 0 in)

AREA:

Wings, gross	8.30 m² (89.3 sq ft)

WEIGHT:

Max T-O weight	375 kg (827 lb)

PERFORMANCE (prototype, at max T-O weight):

Max level speed	122 knots (225 km/h; 140 mph)
Max cruising speed	104 knots (193 km/h; 120 mph)
Min flying speed	35 knots (64 km/h; 40 mph)
Max rate of climb at S/L	610 m (2,000 ft)/min
T-O and landing run	less than 100 m (330 ft)
Range with standard fuel	152 nm (280 km; 175 miles)

ANDREASSON MFI-9 HB
The prototype BA-7 made its first flight on 10 October 1958. It entered production, and was followed by the MFI-9 version which also went into production.

Plans for the MFI-9 HB, a redrawn version of the MFI-9 for amateur builders, are currently available and the description and data refer to this version. Kits of component parts were also made available from the Cana Aircraft Company in Singapore.

TYPE: Side by side two-seat, dual control homebuilt; conforms to FAR Pt 23 in Utility category.

AIRFRAME: All-metal construction, except for glassfibre reinforced plastics wingtips. Wing section NACA 23009, modified to have leading-edge droop. Non-retractable tricycle landing gear. Optional floats or skis.

POWER PLANT: One 74.5 kW (100 hp) Teledyne Continental O-200-A. Other engines of similar weight and power rating can be used. Fuel capacity 80 litres (21 US gallons; 17.6 Imp gallons).

DIMENSIONS, EXTERNAL:

Wing span	7.43 m (24 ft 4½ in)
Length overall	5.85 m (19 ft 2¼ in)
Height overall	2.00 m (6 ft 6¾ in)

AREA:

Wings, gross	8.70 m² (93.65 sq ft)

WEIGHTS:

Weight empty	340 kg (750 lb)
Baggage capacity	20 kg (44 lb)
Max T-O weight	575 kg (1,267 lb)

PERFORMANCE:

Max level speed	130 knots (240 km/h; 149 mph)
Econ cruising speed at S/L	113 knots (210 km/h; 130 mph)
Stalling speed, power off	44 knots (80 km/h; 50 mph)
Max rate of climb at S/L	270 m (885 ft)/min
Service ceiling	4,500 m (14,775 ft)
T-O run, on grass	150 m (492 ft)
Landing run	130 m (427 ft)
Range with max payload	431 nm (800 km; 497 miles)

SWITZERLAND

BRÄNDLI
MAX BRÄNDLI
Höheweg 2, CH-2553 Safnern
Telephone: 41 (32) 55 18 23

BRÄNDLI BX-2 CHERRY
The prototype Cherry made its first flight on 24 April 1982. Plans (written in German) are available, and 140 sets had been sold by early 1991. The canopy and main spar are available in prefabricated form.

TYPE: Two-seat homebuilt.

AIRFRAME: Wings and tail unit have wood spars and Styrofoam skins covered with glassfibre. Wing section NACA 747A15. Ailerons and flaps of foam and glassfibre construction. Optional folding wings and all-moving tailplane. Wood fuselage structure, plywood and glassfibre covered. Retractable tricycle landing gear, with brakes.

POWER PLANT: One 48.5 kW (65 hp) Teledyne Continental A65. Alternative engines include Limbach L 2400, Teledyne Continental A75 or C90-8F, or Rotax 912. Fuel capacity 84 litres (22.2 US gallons; 18.5 Imp gallons).

DIMENSIONS, EXTERNAL:

Wing span	7.00 m (22 ft 11½ in)
Length overall	5.25 m (17 ft 2½ in)
Height overall	2.05 m (6 ft 8½ in)
Propeller diameter	1.60 m (5 ft 3 in)

AREA:

Wings, gross	8.50 m² (91.5 sq ft)

WEIGHTS:

Weight empty, equipped	310 kg (683 lb)
Max payload	190 kg (419 lb)
Max baggage	40 kg (88 lb)
Max T-O and landing weight	550 kg (1,212 lb)

PERFORMANCE (with A65 engine, at max T-O weight, except where indicated):

Max level speed at 915 m (3,000 ft)	121 knots (225 km/h; 140 mph)
Max cruising speed at 915 m (3,000 ft)	113 knots (210 km/h; 130 mph)
Stalling speed, flaps down, engine idling, at AUW of 510 kg (1,125 lb)	45 knots (84 km/h; 52 mph)
Max rate of climb at S/L	180 m (590 ft)/min
Service ceiling	4,200 m (13,775 ft)
T-O run	300 m (985 ft)
Landing run	150 m (492 ft)
Range with max fuel	539 nm (1,000 km; 621 miles)
Endurance	6 h
g limits	+3.8/−1.9

BRÜGGER
MAX BRÜGGER
CH-1724 Zénauva
Telephone: 41 (37) 33 29 20

BRÜGGER MB-2 COLIBRI 2
The prototype Colibri 2 flew for the first time on 1 May 1970. Plans are available, and about 260 Colibri 2s are under construction or flying in Europe

TYPE: Single-seat homebuilt.

AIRFRAME: All-wood construction, except for fabric covering on wings and ailerons. No fixed fin. Wing section NACA 23012. Non-retractable tailwheel landing gear.

POWER PLANT: One 30 kW (40 hp) 1,600 cc Volkswagen engine (Brügger modification). Fuel capacity 33 litres (8.7 US gallons; 7.25 Imp gallons).

DIMENSIONS, EXTERNAL:

Wing span	6.00 m (19 ft 8¼ in)
Length overall	4.80 m (15 ft 9 in)
Height overall	1.60 m (5 ft 3 in)
Propeller diameter	1.38 m (4 ft 6⅓ in)

AREA:

Wings, gross	8.20 m² (88.25 sq ft)

WEIGHTS:

Weight empty	215 kg (474 lb)
Max T-O and landing weight	330 kg (727 lb)

PERFORMANCE (at max T-O weight):

Max speed at 1,000 m (3,280 ft)	97 knots (180 km/h; 111 mph)
Econ cruising speed (70% power) at 1,000 m (3,280 ft)	86 knots (160 km/h; 99 mph)
Stalling speed	33 knots (60 km/h; 38 mph)
Max rate of climb at S/L	180 m (590 ft)/min
Service ceiling	4,500 m (14,760 ft)
T-O and landing run	200 m (656 ft)
Range with max fuel	270 nm (500 km; 310 miles)

UNION OF SOVIET SOCIALIST REPUBLICS

AVIATECHNICA
CO-OPERATIVE DESIGN OFFICE AVIATECHNICA
K-45, A/R-32, Moscow 103045
Telephone: 7 (95) 207 25 19
CHAIRMAN: A. Koshelev

AVIATECHNICA SAMOLET
This twin-engined cabin biplane is delivered in two containers in partly knocked down form, and can be assembled by two persons in four to five hours. Production has been quoted at between 50 and 100 aircraft a year from 1991-93, to rise to between 100 and 500 a year from 1993-95.

TYPE: Possibly side by side two-seat biplane.

AIRFRAME: Constant chord wings with dihedral. I type interplane struts. Pod and boom fuselage. All moving tailplane and dorsal/ventral fin/rudder. Non-retractable tricycle landing gear.

Andreasson BA-4B single-seat fully aerobatic homebuilt biplane
(Geoffrey P. Jones)

Orliński RO-7 Orlik single-seat homebuilt aircraft *(Tomasz Szulc)*

MFI-9B (Andreasson) built in Sweden by MFI

Brügger MB-2 Colibri 2 built by Nadal Patrick *(Geoffrey P. Jones)*

Brändli BX-2 Cherry two-seat homebuilt aircraft

VK-8 Aushza agricultural homebuilt, built by Vladas Kensgaila

POWER PLANT: Two 24 kW (32 hp) PMS-640 engines, driving two-blade pusher propellers.	Height overall	2.30 m (7 ft 6½ in)	Stalling speed	38 knots (70 km/h; 44 mph)
	Propeller diameter (each)	1.60 m (5 ft 3 in)	Range	226 nm (420 km; 261 miles)
DIMENSIONS, EXTERNAL:	WEIGHTS: Unknown		Endurance	4 h
Wing span 8.20 m (26 ft 11 in)	PERFORMANCE (provisional):			
Length overall 5.00 m (16 ft 5 in)	Cruising speed	86 knots (160 km/h; 99 mph)		

FOTON

FOTON
Leningrader Prospekt 33A, Moscow 125284
Telephone: 7 (95) 945 56 54
Fax: 7 (95) 945 29 00
German distributor:
Flugzeugwerft Dresden GmbH, Königsbrücker
Landstrasse 38, Postfach 37, O-8080 Dresden
Telephone: 49 (51) 565 38 82
Fax: 49 (51) 565 31 01

FOTON MAI-89
This Soviet homebuilt is being marketed in Germany.

TYPE: Two-seat biplane.
AIRFRAME: Braced biplane of modern design. Slightly sweptback upper wing and dihedral lower wings, with interconnecting I struts. Pod and boom fuselage. Conventional tail unit with very large rudder. Non-retractable tricycle landing gear.
POWER PLANT: One 47.7 kW (64 hp) Rotax 532, driving a pusher propeller.
DIMENSIONS, EXTERNAL:
Wing span 8.11 m (26 ft 7¼ in)
Length overall 5.32 m (17 ft 5½ in)
Height overall 2.25 m (7 ft 4½ in)
AREA:
Wings, gross 14.29 m² (153.8 sq ft)

WEIGHTS:
Weight empty 235 kg (518 lb)
Max T-O weight 350 kg (771 lb)
PERFORMANCE:
Max level speed 75 knots (140 km/h; 87 mph)
Cruising speed 49-65 knots (90-120 km/h; 56-75 mph)
Stalling speed 34 knots (63 km/h; 39 mph)
T-O to 10 m (35 ft) 145 m (476 ft)
Landing from 15 m (50 ft) 300 m (985 ft)
Range 145 nm (270 km; 167 miles)
Endurance 3 h

KENSGAILA

VLADAS KENSGAILA
Roživ 87, Panevezhees 235306, Lithuania

KENSGAILA VK-8 AUSHZA
Design of this two-seat agricultural aircraft began in 1987 and construction of the prototype started in 1989. It won the 5th national homebuilt convention at Riga-89. At that time it was also the largest homebuilt in the USSR.

TYPE: Two-seat agricultural, transport and training aircraft; conforms to Experimental regulations.
AIRFRAME: Strut braced low-wing monoplane of composites construction. Three-axis control plus flaps and leading-edge slats. Spraybooms carried below wing trailing-edges, ahead of ailerons. Non-retractable tailwheel landing gear, with mainwheel brakes and large trouser fairings.
POWER PLANT: One 268 kW (360 hp) Vedeneyev M-14P radial piston engine, driving a two-blade variable-pitch wooden propeller via reduction gear. Fuel capacity 180 litres (47.6 US gallons; 39.6 Imp gallons).

DIMENSIONS, EXTERNAL:
Wing span 15.00 m (49 ft 3 in)
Length overall 9.57 m (31 ft 4¾ in)
Height overall 2.90 m (9 ft 6¼ in)
Propeller diameter 2.75 m (9 ft 0¼ in)
AREA:
Wings, gross 28.4 m² (305.7 sq ft)
WEIGHTS:
Weight empty 1,140 kg (2,513 lb)
Max payload 1,000 kg (2,204 lb)
Max T-O weight 2,300 kg (5,070 lb)

PERFORMANCE:

Max level speed	135 knots (250 km/h; 155 mph)
Max cruising speed	97 knots (180 km/h; 112 mph)
Econ cruising speed	86 knots (160 km/h; 99 mph)
Stalling speed, flaps down	38 knots (70 km/h; 44 mph)
Max rate of climb at S/L	300 m (985 ft)/min

Service ceiling	4,000 m (13,125 ft)
T-O run	35 m (115 ft)
Landing run	60 m (197 ft)
Range:	
with standard fuel	269 nm (500 km; 310 miles)
max payload	242 nm (450 km; 279 miles)

Endurance	3 h 40 min
g limits	+3.5/−2

WEWYNE
Lithuania

WEWYNE
First flown in 1989, this is a conventional two-seat strut braced high-wing homebuilt. It was said to be the most comfortable aircraft at the Riga-89 convention. No further details are known besides the few quoted figures below:

DIMENSIONS, EXTERNAL:

Wing span	11.35 m (37 ft 3 in)
Length overall	7.00 m (22 ft 11½ in)

AREA:

Wings, gross	17.00 m² (182.98 sq ft)

WEIGHT:

Max T-O weight	767 kg (1,691 lb)

PERFORMANCE:

Max level speed	97 knots (180 km/h; 112 mph)
Range	323 nm (600 km; 373 miles)

YAKOVLEV
Sazatov

YAKOVLEV KATTA
Little is known about this tiny strut braced cabin homebuilt, other than what can be gleaned from the accompanying illustration.

UNITED KINGDOM

AMF
AMF MICROFLIGHT LTD
Membury Airfield, Lambourn, Berkshire RG16 7TJ
Telephone: 44 (488) 72224
Fax: 44 (488) 72224
Telex: 848507 MIFLI
MANAGING DIRECTOR: Angus M. Fleming

AMF MICROFLIGHT CHEVVRON 2-32
The Chevvron was first flown in 1983. Production began in 1987 and deliveries have been in assembled form.
TYPE: Side by side two-seat microlight/trainer; conforms to BCAR Section S.
AIRFRAME: Airframe of glassfibre/carbonfibre/Kevlar and foam construction. Wortmann wing section. Three-axis control. Non-retractable tricycle landing gear, with brakes. Optional floats.
POWER PLANT: One 24 kW (32 hp) König SD 570; at least one seaplane powered by a 35.8 kW (48 hp) König engine. Standard fuel capacity 30 litres (7.9 US gallons; 6.6 Imp gallons). One auxiliary fuel tank optional, either of 30 litres or 20 litres (5.3 US gallons; 4.4 Imp gallons) capacity.

DIMENSIONS, EXTERNAL:

Wing span	13.41 m (44 ft 0 in)
Length overall	7.01 m (23 ft 0 in)
Height overall	1.52 m (5 ft 0 in)
Propeller diameter	1.52 m (5 ft 0 in)

AREA:

Wings, gross	17.56 m² (189.0 sq ft)

WEIGHTS:

Weight empty	175 kg (386 lb)
Pilot weight range	50-180 kg (110-396 lb)
Max T-O weight	382 kg (842 lb)

PERFORMANCE:

Max level and max cruising speed	65 knots (120 km/h; 75 mph)
Econ cruising speed	55 knots (102 km/h; 63 mph)
Stalling speed	30 knots (56 km/h; 35 mph)
Max rate of climb at S/L	128 m (420 ft)/min
Service ceiling	3,050 m (10,000 ft)
T-O run	91 m (300 ft)
Landing run	137 m (450 ft)
Range with standard fuel	200 nm (370 km; 230 miles)
Endurance	3 h
g limits	+4/−2

CFM
COOK FLYING MACHINES
(trading as CFM Metal-Fax Ltd)
Unit 2D, Eastlands Industrial Estate, Leiston, Suffolk IP16 4LL
Telephone: 44 (728) 832353/833076
Fax: 44 (728) 832 944
Telex: 9877703 CHACOM G
MANAGING DIRECTOR: David G. Cook

While continuing to produce the Shadow series of aircraft from its Suffolk works, CFM has licensed Larom Aviation Technologies of Portalis, New Mexico, to produce Shadow kits for the North and South American and Canadian market, and was negotiating in 1990-91 for licensed production at a plant at Bulembu Airport, near Bisho, Ciskei, for the African, Australasian and Far Eastern markets.

CFM SHADOW SERIES C and C-D
The Shadow first flew as a prototype in 1983. It has been in continuous production since 1984. Type approval to BCAR CAP 482 Section S was gained in May 1985. The current standard Shadow is designated Series C, with the C-D having dual controls.

ULV cropspraying trials demonstrated the suitability of the Shadow in this role, carrying a 64 litre (16.8 US gallon; 14 Imp gallon) chemical tank. A multi-function surveillance fit for photography (Hasselblad 'look down' camera platform), video recording, Linescan or thermal imagery, or closed-circuit TV microwave transmission to a command vehicle/station is also available.
TYPE: Tandem two-seat microlight; conforms to FAI and UK CAA requirements.
AIRFRAME: Wings constructed of aluminium alloy and wood, with foam/glassfibre ribs, plywood covering on forward section and polyester fabric aft. Wing design allows no 'defined stall' and will not permit spin. Fuselage pod of Fibrelam; aluminium tube tailboom. Three-axis control. Non-retractable tricycle landing gear, with brakes. Overseas options include floats, agricultural spraygear and other specialised equipment.
POWER PLANT: One 38 kW (51 hp) Rotax 503.2V. Standard fuel capacity 23 litres (6 US gallons; 5 Imp gallons). Options include a 73 litre (19.2 US gallon; 16 Imp gallon) auxiliary fuel tank.

DIMENSIONS, EXTERNAL:

Wing span	10.03 m (32 ft 11 in)
Length overall	6.40 m (21 ft 0 in)
Height overall	1.75 m (5 ft 9 in)
Propeller diameter	1.30 m (4 ft 3 in)

AREA:

Wings, gross	15.0 m² (162.0 sq ft)

WEIGHTS:

Weight empty	158 kg (349 lb)
Pilot weight range:	
front cockpit	54.5-100 kg (120-220 lb)
rear cockpit	0-100 kg (0-220 lb)
Max T-O weight	348 kg (767 lb)

PERFORMANCE (at max T-O weight):

Max level speed	89 knots (164 km/h; 102 mph)
Econ cruising speed	65 knots (121 km/h; 75 mph)
Min flying speed	22 knots (41 km/h; 25 mph)
Max rate of climb at S/L:	
pilot only	335-366 m (1,100-1,200 ft)/min
dual	213-244 m (700-800 ft)/min
Service ceiling	7,620 m (25,000 ft)
T-O run from metalled surface	90 m (295 ft)
Landing run, with brakes	75 m (246 ft)
Range, standard fuel	139 nm (257 km; 160 miles)
Endurance, standard fuel	2 h
g limits	+6/−3 static, ultimate

CFM STREAK SHADOW
This derivative version of the Shadow is designated a microlight in Europe and an Experimental homebuilt in the USA. It has a new wing design, light airframe weight and a more powerful engine. Fuel capacity is similar to the latest C version of the Shadow. The wing design continues to allow no 'defined stall' and is spin resistant.

Construction of a prototype started in 1987 and this first flew in June 1988. The first flight of a production aircraft followed that October, and by January 1991 40 kits had been delivered. Other roles can include surveillance and crop spraying.
TYPE: Tandem two-seat microlight/homebuilt; dual controls standard.
AIRFRAME: Similar to Shadow but with foam/glassfibre wings (CFM aerofoil section), and control surfaces with aluminium alloy ribs and polyester fabric covering (ailerons, flaps, rudder and elevators). Optional electric trim.
POWER PLANT: One 47.7 kW (64 hp) Rotax 582, or optional Norton 622. Standard fuel capacity 54.6 litres (14.4 US gallons; 12 Imp gallons). Optional 73 litre (19.2 US gallon; 16 Imp gallon) auxiliary fuel tank.

DIMENSIONS, EXTERNAL:

Wing span	8.53 m (28 ft 0 in)
Length overall	6.40 m (21 ft 0 in)
Height overall	1.75 m (5 ft 9 in)
Propeller diameter	1.32 m (4 ft 4 in)

AREA:

Wings, gross	13.01 m² (140.0 sq ft)

WEIGHTS:

Weight empty	176 kg (388 lb)
Max T-O weight	408 kg (900 lb)

PERFORMANCE:

Max level speed	105 knots (195 km/h; 121 mph)
Cruising speed:	
80% power	87 knots (161 km/h; 100 mph)
50% power	65 knots (121 km/h; 75 mph)
Min flying speed, engine idling	28 knots (52 km/h; 32 mph)
Max rate of climb at S/L:	
pilot only	549 m (1,800 ft)/min
dual	335-396 m (1,100-1,300 ft)/min
Service ceiling	9,150 m (30,000 ft)
Range	347 nm (643 km; 400 miles)
Endurance, standard fuel	4 h 30 min
g limits	+6/−3

CFM SHADOW II
This is a specialised single-seat version of the Shadow, which was marketed by ASVEC as a manned surveillance system aircraft for day and night use (two ordered by a NATO country in 1988, with six more on option). Uses one 44.7 kW (64 hp) Rotax 532 engine, and has a wing span of 8.53 m (28 ft 0 in). Further details can be found in *Jane's Battlefield Surveillance Systems.*

FULTON
FULTON AIRCRAFT LTD
Fulton House, Wood Wharf Business Park, Prestons Road, London Docklands, London E14 9SF
Telephone: 44 (71) 538 0751
Fax: 44 (71) 538 4743
Telex: 887951 FULCOL G
CHAIRMAN: A. Fulton

FULTON FA-1
Development of the FA-1 took place in Canada, where the prototype first flew in August 1985. A production prototype was built in the UK.
TYPE: Side by side two-seat, dual-control microlight trainer; conforms to FAI/CAA requirements, and to CAP 482 Section S.

Wewyne homebuilt monoplane *(Igor Krivoutsky)*

AMF Microflight Chevvron 2-32 two-seat microlight trainer

CFM Shadow Series C two-seat microlight

Fulton Aircraft FA-1 two-seat microlight trainer

Yakovlev Katta single-seat homebuilt monoplane *(Igor Krivoutsky)*

Wombat Gyrocopter, designed by Chris Julian

AIRFRAME: Constructed of rigid composite materials (glassfibre, epoxy and PVC foam plastics). Three-axis control. Non-retractable tricycle landing gear.
POWER PLANT: One 38.7 kW (52 hp) Rotax 503 2V. Fuel capacity 36.5 litres (9.6 US gallons; 8 Imp gallons).

DIMENSIONS, EXTERNAL:

Wing span	9.375 m (30 ft 9 in)
Length overall	6.08 m (19 ft 11 in)
Height overall	2.29 m (7 ft 6 in)
Propeller diameter	1.65 m (5 ft 5 in)

AREA:

Wings, gross	15.0 m² (161.5 sq ft)

WEIGHTS (open cockpit version):

Weight empty	148 kg (326 lb)
Crew weight range	50-180 kg (110-396 lb)
Max T-O weight	360 kg (794 lb)

PERFORMANCE (at max T-O weight):

Max level speed	70 knots (129 km/h; 80 mph)
Max cruising speed	65 knots (120 km/h; 75 mph)
Stalling speed	25 knots (46 km/h; 29 mph)
Max rate of climb at S/L	225 m (740 ft)/min
Endurance with max fuel, with reserves	2 h
g limits	+6/-3

ISAACS
JOHN O. ISAACS
23 Linden Grove, Chandler's Ford, Hampshire SO5 1LE
Telephone: 44 (703) 260885

Details of the Isaacs Fury II and Spitfire, and illustrations, can be found in the 1988-89 *Jane's*.

JULIAN
CHRIS JULIAN
The Chalet, Higher Fraddon, Indian Queens, St Columb, Cornwall
Telephone: 44 (726) 860662

JULIAN WOMBAT GYROCOPTER
Designed by Chris Julian, a pilot with some 20 years of autogyro experience, the single-seat Wombat Gyrocopter is powered by a Rotax 532 engine in prototype form but will be marketed with a Rotax 582. Rotor Hawk lightweight composite rotor blades have been adopted. The airframe structure is of metal tubing and carries a semi-enclosed cockpit fairing; a fully enclosed fairing/canopy is under development to provide extra comfort for cross-country flights. The large rudder gives good directional control at low speeds, and production aircraft will feature a conventional aircraft joystick. A range of more than 260 nm (482 km; 300 miles) can be achieved from the standard 77 litre (20.4 US gallon; 17 Imp gallon) fuel tank, and an endurance of four hours.

NIPPER
NIPPER KITS AND COMPONENTS LTD
Foxley, Blackness Lane, Keston, Kent BR2 6HL
Telephone: 44 (689) 58351
CHAIRMAN: D. P. L. Antill
DIRECTOR: A. F. Ayles

NIPPER Mk IIIb
This light aircraft was developed and manufactured originally by Avions Fairey in Belgium. Plans, kits of component parts and an advisory service are available. Approximately 60 Nippers are flying worldwide, with three under construction in early 1991. All non-wooden components are available prefabricated.
TYPE: Single-seat aerobatic homebuilt.

AIRFRAME: Wooden wing, aileron, tailplane and elevator structures, and welded steel tube fuselage and rudder structures, all fabric covered except for glassfibre underfuselage fairing and wood skins on tailplane and elevators. No fin. Modified NACA 43012A wing section. Non-retractable tricycle landing gear.
POWER PLANT: One 41 kW (55 hp) Rollason Ardem XI. Alternatively, Nipper recommends the 48.5 kW (65 hp)

Barry Smith aerobatic engine of 1,834 cc, with fuel and oil systems for inverted flight. Fuel capacity 34 litres (9 US gallons; 7.5 Imp gallons). Provision for two 16.5 litre (4.3 US gallon; 3.6 Imp gallon) wingtip fuel tanks.

DIMENSIONS, EXTERNAL:

Wing span: without tip tanks	6.00 m (19 ft 8 in)
with tip tanks	6.25 m (20 ft 6 in)
Length overall	4.56 m (15 ft 0 in)
Height overall	1.91 m (6 ft 3 in)

AREA:

Wings, gross	7.50 m² (80.70 sq ft)

WEIGHTS (Ardem engine):

Weight empty	210 kg (465 lb)
Max T-O weight: Aerobatic	310 kg (685 lb)
Normal	340 kg (750 lb)

PERFORMANCE (Ardem engine at max T-O weight, unless stated otherwise):

Max level speed at S/L:	
without tip tanks	93 knots (173 km/h; 107 mph)
Barry Smith engine	113 knots (209 km/h; 130 mph)
Econ cruising speed at S/L	
	78 knots (145 km/h; 90 mph)

Stalling speed, power off	33 knots (61 km/h; 38 mph)
Max rate of climb at S/L:	198 m (650 ft)/min
Barry Smith engine	305 m (1,000 ft)/min
Service ceiling	3,660 m (12,000 ft)
T-O run	85 m (280 ft)
Landing run	110 m (360 ft)
Range with tip tanks	390 nm (720 km; 450 miles)
g limits	+6/−3

NOBLE HARDMAN
NOBLE HARDMAN AVIATION LTD

Details of the Noble Hardman Aviation Snowbird, and an illustration, appeared in the 1989-90 edition of *Jane's*.

PFA
THE POPULAR FLYING ASSOCIATION
Terminal Building, Shoreham Airport, Shoreham-by-Sea, West Sussex BN4 5FF
Telephone: 44 (273) 461616

Fax: 44 (273) 463390
VICE-CHAIRMAN AND CHIEF EXECUTIVE: F. I. V. Walker
The PFA markets plans of the Currie Wot, Druine D31 Turbulent and Luton L.A.4a Minor, plus the Isaacs Fury, Evans VP-1 and VP-2, and Pazmany PL-4 detailed under

their designers' names in this section. Details of the Wot, Turbulent and Minor, plus illustrations, can be found in the 1988-89 *Jane's*.

TAYLOR
T. TAYLOR
79 Springwater Road, Eastwood, Essex SS9 5BW
Telephone: 44 (702) 521484

TAYLOR J.T.1 MONOPLANE
The prototype J.T.1 Monoplane first flew on 4 July 1959. Plans are available and by early 1991 about 800 sets had been sold. Approximately 110 plans-built Monoplanes have flown. Wood kits are available in Canada and the USA.
TYPE: Single-seat fully aerobatic homebuilt.
AIRFRAME: All-wood structure, with fabric covering part of wings, elevators and rudder, the remainder plywood covered. Wing section RAF 48. Non-retractable tailwheel landing gear standard.
POWER PLANT: One 30 kW (40 hp) Volkswagen 1,500 cc modified motorcar engine. Other engines fitted by constructors include a 30 kW (40 hp) Aeronca E 113, 48.5 kW (65 hp) Teledyne Continental A65, 48.5 kW (65 hp) Textron Lycoming, and a 53.7 kW (72 hp) McCulloch. Aircraft with the 48.5 kW (65 hp) engines have a 10 cm (4 in) longer nose and 25 cm (10 in) longer rear fuselage to maintain the correct CG position. Fuel capacity 32 litres (8.4 US gallons; 7 Imp gallons).

DIMENSIONS, EXTERNAL:

Wing span	6.40 m (21 ft 0 in)
Length overall	4.57 m (15 ft 0 in)
Height over tail	1.47 m (4 ft 10 in)
Propeller diameter	1.14 m (3 ft 9 in)

AREA:

Wings, gross	7.06 m² (76.0 sq ft)

WEIGHTS:

Weight empty	195 kg (430 lb)
Baggage capacity	4.5 kg (10 lb)
Max T-O weight	299 kg (660 lb)

PERFORMANCE:

Max level speed at S/L	100 knots (185 km/h; 115 mph)
Econ cruising speed	87 knots (161 km/h; 100 mph)
Stalling speed, power off:	
flaps up	35 knots (65 km/h; 40 mph)
flaps down	31 knots (57 km/h; 35 mph)
Max rate of climb at S/L	305 m (1,000 ft)/min
Service ceiling	4,115 m (13,500 ft)
T-O to 15 m (50 ft)	107 m (350 ft)
Landing from 15 m (50 ft)	229 m (750 ft)
Range	252 nm (466 km; 290 miles)
Endurance	3 h
g limits	±6

TAYLOR J.T.2 TITCH
The prototype Titch first flew on 4 January 1967. Plans are available and by early 1991 about 500 sets had been sold. Approximately 32 plans-built aircraft have flown. Wood kits are available in Canada and the USA.
TYPE: Single-seat homebuilt.
AIRFRAME: All-wood structure. Wings plywood and fabric covered. Fuselage and fixed tail surfaces plywood covered, except for aluminium cockpit side panels. Rudder and elevators fabric covered. Taylor modified NACA 23012 wing section. Non-retractable tailwheel landing gear.

POWER PLANT: One 63.5 kW (85 hp) Teledyne Continental C85. Plans-built Titches fitted with engines ranging from 33.6 kW (45 hp) Volkswagen 1,600 cc modified motorcar engine to 78.3 kW (105 hp) Textron Lycoming O-235. Fuel capacity 45.5 litres (12 US gallons; 10 Imp gallons). (1,834 cc VW engined version has 32 litre; 8.4 US gallon; 7 Imp gallon fuel tank.)

DIMENSIONS, EXTERNAL:

Wing span	5.72 m (18 ft 9 in)
Length overall	5.05 m (16 ft 7 in)
Height overall	1.42 m (4 ft 8 in)
Propeller diameter	1.52 m (5 ft 0 in)

AREA:

Wings, gross	6.60 m² (71.0 sq ft)

WEIGHTS (Teledyne Continental C85 engine):

Weight empty	229 kg (505 lb)
Baggage capacity	4.5 kg (10 lb)
Max T-O weight	345 kg (760 lb)

PERFORMANCE (engine as above):

Max level speed	174 knots (322 km/h; 200 mph)
Max and econ cruising speed	
	135 knots (250 km/h; 155 mph)
Stalling speed, power off:	
flaps up	51 knots (94 km/h; 58 mph)
flaps down	44 knots (81 km/h; 50 mph)
Service ceiling	5,485 m (18,000 ft)
Max rate of climb at S/L	488 m (1,600 ft)/min
T-O to 15 m (50 ft)	107 m (350 ft)
Landing from 15 m (50 ft)	274 m (900 ft)
Range	330 nm (611 km; 380 miles)
g limits	±6

UNITED STATES OF AMERICA

ACE
ACE AIRCRAFT COMPANY
05-134th Street, Chesapeake, West Virginia 25315
Telephone: 1 (304) 949 3098
OWNER: Denny Meadows
The Ace Aircraft Company offers plans, material kits and some pre-welded components for the Baby Ace Model D and Jr Ace Model E (see also Acro-Sport Corben Jr Ace).

BABY ACE MODEL D
The prototype of the redesigned Baby Ace Model D flew for the first time on 15 November 1956. About 350 have since been built by amateurs.
TYPE: Single-seat homebuilt.
AIRFRAME: Wing section Clark Y (modified). Wooden wings and ailerons, and welded steel tube fuselage and tail unit, all fabric covered. Non-retractable tailwheel landing gear. Optional floats.
POWER PLANT: One Teledyne Continental A65, A85, C65 or C85 engine of 48.5 or 63.5 kW (65 or 85 hp). Fuel capacity 63.6 litres (16.8 US gallons; 14 Imp gallons).

DIMENSIONS, EXTERNAL:

Wing span	8.05 m (26 ft 5 in)
Length overall	5.40 m (17 ft 8¾ in)
Height overall	2.02 m (6 ft 7¾ in)

AREA:

Wings, gross	10.43 m² (112.3 sq ft)

WEIGHTS (landplane, unless stated otherwise):

Weight empty, equipped	261 kg (575 lb)
Baggage capacity	4.5 kg (10 lb)
Max T-O weight: 48.5 kW (65 hp)	431 kg (950 lb)
63.5 kW (85 hp) landplane or seaplane	
	522 kg (1,150 lb)

PERFORMANCE (48.5 kW; 65 hp landplane, at max T-O weight):

Max level speed at S/L	96 knots (177 km/h; 110 mph)
Max cruising speed	
	87-91 knots (161-169 km/h; 100-105 mph)
Stalling speed	30 knots (55 km/h; 34 mph)
Max rate of climb at S/L	365 m (1,200 ft)/min
Service ceiling	4,875 m (16,000 ft)
T-O and landing run	76 m (250 ft)
Range with max fuel	304 nm (560 km; 350 miles)

JUNIOR ACE MODEL E
The Junior Ace Model E differs from the Baby Ace

Model D in being a side by side two-seater. It is powered usually by a 63.5 kW (85 hp) Teledyne Continental C85, and the details refer to a typical aircraft with this power plant that also has a cockpit 7.5 cm (3 in) wider and 10 cm (4 in) deeper than that of the standard Model E, a full electrical system and increased fuel capacity of 85 litres (22.5 US gallons; 18.75 Imp gallons).

DIMENSIONS, EXTERNAL:

Wing span	7.92 m (26 ft 0 in)
Length overall	5.50 m (18 ft 0 in)
Height overall	2.00 m (6 ft 7 in)

WEIGHTS:

Weight empty	367 kg (809 lb)
Max T-O weight	606 kg (1,335 lb)

PERFORMANCE:

Max level speed at S/L	113 knots (209 km/h; 130 mph)
Cruising speed	91 knots (169 km/h; 105 mph)
Landing speed	57 knots (105 km/h; 65 mph)
Service ceiling	3,050 m (10,000 ft)
T-O run	122 m (400 ft)
Landing run	183 m (600 ft)
Range with max fuel	304 nm (560 km; 350 miles)

ACRO SPORT
ACRO SPORT INC
PO Box 462, Hales Corners, Wisconsin 53130
Telephone: 1 (414) 529 2609
PRESIDENT: LaFonda Jean Kinnaman
The Acro Sport I, Super Acro Sport, Acro Sport II and Pober Pixie were all designed by Mr Paul H. Poberezny, President of the entirely separate Experimental Aircraft Association.

ACRO SPORT I
The Acro Sport I was designed specifically for construction by school students as a pupils' project. First flight of the prototype (N1AC) was made on 11 January 1972. Plans and construction manuals are available to homebuilders, and more than 1,300 sets had been sold by early 1991. More than sixty Acro Sport Is were then flying.
The following details apply to the prototype:
TYPE: Single-seat aerobatic homebuilt biplane.

AIRFRAME: Wooden wings and ailerons (on all four wings), fabric covered. Wing section Munk M-6. Glassfibre wingtips. Fuselage of welded steel tube, with wooden stringers, fabric covered. Glassfibre nose cowl and light alloy engine cowlings. Welded steel tube tail unit, with fabric covering. Non-retractable tailwheel landing gear, with main gear modified from Piper J-3 components.
POWER PLANT: Prototype has 134 kW (180 hp) Textron Lycoming engine. Basic power plant is a 74.5 kW (100 hp)

Nipper Mk IIIb single-seat light aircraft *(Tim Griffith)*

Baby Ace Model D with optional wheel spats and headrest fairing

Taylor J.T.1 Monoplane *(Geoffrey P. Jones)*

Acro Sport II owned by Bud Judy of Denton, Texas, with front cockpit covered and windscreen removed

Acro Sport Pober P-9 Pixie owned by Mr Mario Chabot of Drummondville, Quebec

Teledyne Continental O-200. Fuel capacity 104 litres (20 US gallons; 16.7 Imp gallons).

DIMENSIONS, EXTERNAL:

Wing span: upper	5.97 m (19 ft 7 in)
lower	5.82 m (19 ft 1 in)
Length overall	5.33 m (17 ft 6 in)
Height overall	1.83 m (6 ft 0 in)
Propeller diameter	1.93 m (6 ft 4 in)

AREA:

Wings, gross	10.73 m² (115.5 sq ft)

WEIGHTS:

Weight empty, equipped	335 kg (739 lb)
Baggage capacity	16 kg (35 lb)
Max T-O and landing weight	534 kg (1,178 lb)

PERFORMANCE (at max T-O weight):

Max level speed	132 knots (245 km/h; 152 mph)
Econ cruising speed	91 knots (169 km/h; 105 mph)
Stalling speed	44 knots (81 km/h; 50 mph)
Max rate of climb at S/L	518 m (1,700 ft)/min
T-O run	46 m (150 ft)
Landing run	244 m (800 ft)
Range with max fuel	304 nm (563 km; 350 miles)

SUPER ACRO SPORT

The Super Acro Sport prototype first flew on 21 March 1973. The aircraft is intended for unlimited International Class aerobatic competition at world championship level.

The differences by comparison with the standard Acro Sport I are covered in a supplement to the basic plans available from Acro Sport Inc. The description of the Acro Sport I applies also to the Super Acro Sport, except as follows:

TYPE: Single-seat homebuilt aerobatic biplane.
AIRFRAME: As for Acro Sport I, except wing section NACA 23012.
POWER PLANT: Prototype has 149 kW (200 hp) Textron Lycoming IO-360-A2A.
DIMENSIONS, EXTERNAL: As for Acro Sport I, except:

Length overall	5.30 m (17 ft 4½ in)

WEIGHTS:

Weight empty	401 kg (884 lb)
Max T-O weight	612 kg (1,350 lb)

PERFORMANCE (at max T-O weight):

Max level speed at S/L	135 knots (251 km/h; 156 mph)
Max cruising speed	117 knots (217 km/h; 135 mph)
Stalling speed	44 knots (81 km/h; 50 mph)
Max rate of climb at S/L	549 m (1,800 ft)/min
Service ceiling	4,575 m (15,000 ft)
T-O run	38 m (125 ft)
Landing run	244 m (800 ft)
Range with max fuel	260 nm (482 km; 300 miles)

ACRO SPORT II

The Acro Sport II is a two-seat aerobatic biplane derived from the Acro Sport I, for the pilot with only a low number of flying hours to his credit. The first flight was achieved on 9 July 1978. Plans are available to homebuilders and more than 2,300 sets had been sold by early 1991. More than 40 Acro Sport IIs are flying.

TYPE: Tandem two-seat homebuilt aerobatic biplane.
AIRFRAME: As for Acro Sport I.
POWER PLANT: Prototype has 134 kW (180 hp) Textron Lycoming O-360-A4B. Can be powered by engines of 74.5-149 kW (100-200 hp). Fuel capacity 98.4 litres (26 US gallons; 21.6 Imp gallons).

DIMENSIONS, EXTERNAL:

Wing span: upper	6.60 m (21 ft 8 in)
lower	6.32 m (20 ft 9 in)
Length overall	5.75 m (18 ft 10¼ in)
Height overall	2.03 m (6 ft 7¾ in)

AREA:

Wings, gross	14.12 m² (152.0 sq ft)

WEIGHTS:

Weight empty	397 kg (875 lb)
Baggage capacity	13.6 kg (30 lb)
Max T-O weight	689 kg (1,520 lb)

PERFORMANCE (prototype):

Max cruising speed	107 knots (198 km/h; 123 mph)
Stalling speed	46 knots (86 km/h; 53 mph)
Max rate of climb at S/L	457 m (1,500 ft)/min
T-O run	91 m (300 ft)
g limits	+6.5/−4.5

POBER P-9 PIXIE

The prototype Pixie made its first flight in July 1974, with a Volkswagen engine. Some Pixies currently flying use the 48.5 kW (65 hp) Teledyne Continental engine.

Plans are available to amateur constructors, and more than 1,100 sets had been sold by early 1991.

TYPE: Single-seat sporting homebuilt.
AIRFRAME: Wooden wing structure, plywood and fabric covered. Clark Y wing section. Welded fuselage of 4130 chrome molybdenum steel tubing with wood formers and fabric covering. Tail unit of welded 4130 chrome molybdenum steel tubing, fabric covered. Non-retractable tailwheel landing gear standard.
POWER PLANT: One 44.5 kW (60 hp) Limbach SL 1700 EA. Equally suited to other Volkswagen and 48.5 kW (65 hp) engines. Fuel capacity 46.6 litres (12.3 US gallons; 10.2 Imp gallons).

DIMENSIONS, EXTERNAL:

Wing span	9.09 m (29 ft 10 in)
Length overall	5.26 m (17 ft 3 in)
Height overall	1.88 m (6 ft 2 in)
Propeller diameter	1.35 m (4 ft 5 in)

AREA:

Wings, gross	12.47 m² (134.25 sq ft)

WEIGHTS:

Weight empty	246 kg (543 lb)
Baggage capacity	9 kg (20 lb)
Max T-O weight	408 kg (900 lb)

PERFORMANCE (at max T-O weight):

Max level speed at S/L	89 knots (166 km/h; 103 mph)
Max cruising speed	72 knots (134 km/h; 83 mph)
Stalling speed	26 knots (49 km/h; 30 mph)
Max rate of climb at S/L	213 m (700 ft)/min
Service ceiling	3,810 m (12,500 ft)
T-O and landing run	91 m (300 ft)
Range with max fuel	251 nm (466 km; 290 miles)

COUGAR MODEL 1

This aircraft was designed by Mr Robert E. Nesmith, to encourage aviation among teenage boys. More than 100 Cougars have been built from plans.

TYPE: Side by side two-seat homebuilt.

AIRFRAME: All-wood wings, using modified NACA 4900-series section. Ailerons of 4130 steel tubing with aluminium trailing-edges. Welded steel tube fuselage and tail unit, with fabric covering. Glassfibre nose cowling and light alloy engine cowlings. Non-retractable tailwheel landing gear.

POWER PLANT: Suitable engines range from 48.5 to 93.2 kW (65-125 hp), including the Teledyne Continental C65, C85 and O-200; and Textron Lycoming O-235 and O-290. Fuel capacity 11.4 kg (25 lb).

DIMENSIONS, EXTERNAL:

Wing span	6.25 m (20 ft 6 in)
Length overall	5.77 m (18 ft 11 in)
Height overall	1.68 m (5 ft 6 in)
Propeller diameter	1.63 m (5 ft 4 in)

AREA:

Wings, gross	7.62 m² (82.0 sq ft)

WEIGHTS:

Weight empty: standard	283 kg (624 lb)
with folding wings	312 kg (689 lb)
Max T-O weight	567 kg (1,250 lb)

PERFORMANCE (at max T-O weight):

Max level speed	152 knots (281 km/h; 175 mph)
Econ cruising speed	104 knots (193 km/h; 120 mph)
Stalling speed	46 knots (86 km/h; 53 mph)
Max rate of climb at S/L	396 m (1,300 ft)/min
T-O run	152 m (500 ft)
Landing run	183 m (600 ft)
Range with max fuel	521 nm (965 km; 600 miles)

POBER Jr ACE

The original Corben Jr Ace was designed by Mr O. G. Corben in the 1920s. The following details apply to the plans marketed by Acro Sport of an extensively modified and larger development (see also Ace Aircraft Company):

TYPE: Side by side two-seat homebuilt.

AIRFRAME: Wooden wings and ailerons, fabric covered. Wing section Clark Y. Fuselage structure of welded steel tube and wooden stringers, fabric covered. Light alloy engine cowling. Fabric covered steel tube tail unit. Non-retractable tailwheel landing gear.

POWER PLANT: One 33.6 kW (45 hp) Szekely, Aeromarine AR-350, Teledyne Continental C65 or similar engine. Fuel capacity 38 litres (10 US gallons; 8.3 Imp gallons).

DIMENSIONS, EXTERNAL:

Wing span	10.35 m (33 ft 11½ in)
Length overall	5.73 m (18 ft 9½ in)
Height overall	2.29 m (7 ft 6 in)
Propeller diameter	1.93 m (6 ft 4 in)

AREA:

Wings, gross	15.61 m² (168.0 sq ft)

WEIGHTS:

Weight empty	255 kg (563 lb)
Max T-O weight	442 kg (975 lb)

PERFORMANCE (at max T-O weight):

Max level speed at S/L	74 knots (137 km/h; 85 mph)
Econ cruising speed	61 knots (113 km/h; 70 mph)
Stalling speed	31 knots (57 km/h; 35 mph)
Max rate of climb at S/L	152 m (500 ft)/min
Service ceiling	over 3,960 m (13,000 ft)
T-O and landing run	46 m (150 ft)
Range with max fuel	173 nm (322 km; 200 miles)

POBER SUPER ACE

This single-seat homebuilt parasol-wing monoplane is a significantly modernised derivative of an aircraft designed by Mr O. G. Corben in the 1920s. It is powered by a 63.4 kW (85 hp) Teledyne Continental C85-8 engine (power plants of up to 112 kW; 150 hp can be installed) and carries 45.5 litres (12 US gallons; 10 Imp gallons) of fuel (doubled with wing tanks). Construction of the prototype began in 1987, and this first flew in October 1990.

AIRFRAME: Strut braced wooden (spruce) wing and ailerons. Stits Poly-Fiber fabric covered. Fuselage and tail unit of steel tubing with fabric covering, with an aluminium engine cowling and glassfibre nose bowl. Non-retractable tailwheel landing gear.

DIMENSIONS, EXTERNAL:

Wing span	8.32 m (27 ft 3½ in)
Length overall	5.61 m (18 ft 5 in)
Height overall	1.96 m (6 ft 5 in)
Propeller diameter	1.83 m (6 ft 0 in)

AREA:

Wings, gross	10.96 m² (118.0 sq ft)

WEIGHTS:

Weight empty	311 kg (685 lb)
Baggage capacity	5.4 kg (12 lb)
Max T-O weight	467 kg (1,030 lb)

PERFORMANCE:

Max level speed at S/L	87 knots (161 km/h; 100 mph)
Max cruising speed at S/L	74 knots (137 km/h; 85 mph)
Econ cruising speed at S/L	65 knots (121 km/h; 75 mph)
Stalling speed	34 knots (63 km/h; 39 mph)
Service ceiling	4,115 m (13,500 ft)
T-O run	107 m (350 ft)
Landing run	168 m (550 ft)
Range with standard fuel	208 nm (386 km; 240 miles)
Endurance	3 h

ADVANCED AVIATION

ADVANCED AVIATION INC

323 North Ivey Lane, PO Box 16716, Orlando, Florida 32811

Telephone: 1 (407) 298 2920

MARKETING MANAGER: Angel Matos

The Advanced Aviation range of aircraft includes the Cobra B (see Microlight tables) and the Sierra sailplane (see Sailplanes section).

ADVANCED AVIATION COBRA

The current standard model is the **B377 Cobra B**, which qualifies mainly under microlight regulations. The basically similar but more powerful **B447 Cobra VIP** is in the Experimental category, as is the **B532 AG Cobra** that is equipped for cropspraying. Many hundreds of Cobra kits have been sold. See Microlight tables.

ADVANCED AVIATION B532 KING COBRA B

This two-seat Experimental version of the Cobra is powered normally by a 47 kW (63 hp) Rotax 582, with optional engines of 32 kW (43 hp), 34.3 kW (46 hp) and 37.3 kW (50 hp). Fuel capacity is approximately 19 litres (5 US gallons; 4.2 Imp gallons). It flew for the first time in 1983 and is similar in construction to the single-seat Cobras. Construction from a kit takes about 50 working hours.

DIMENSION, EXTERNAL:

Wing span	10.54 m (34 ft 7 in)

AREA:

Wings, gross	13.56 m² (146.0 sq ft)

WEIGHTS:

Weight empty	147 kg (325 lb)
Crew weight range	50-190 kg (110-420 lb)
Max T-O weight	351 kg (775 lb)

PERFORMANCE (Cuyuna RR 430 cc engine):

Max level speed	55 knots (101 km/h; 63 mph)
Econ cruising speed	43 knots (80 km/h; 50 mph)
Stalling speed	27 knots (50 km/h; 31 mph)
Max rate of climb at S/L	198 m (650 ft)/min
Service ceiling	3,660 m (12,000 ft)
T-O run	76-107 m (250-350 ft)
Landing run	76 m (250 ft)
Range	65 nm (120 km; 75 miles)
Endurance	1 h 30 min

ADVANCED AVIATION CARRERA

This is a single-seat land-based-only derivative of the Buccaneer, with a non-retractable tricycle or tailwheel landing gear and elongated nose; with tricycle gear it is known as the **Carrera 150**. It is offered with four engine options, the models with a 20 kW (27 hp) Rotax 277, a 26 kW (35 hp) Rotax 377 and 30 kW (40 hp) Rotax 447 meeting FAR Pt 103-7 microlight requirements or coming under Experimental regulations, and the 34 kW (45.6 hp) Rotax 503 model being classified as an Experimental category type only. All have a fuel capacity of 19 litres (5 US gallons; 4.2 Imp gallons). Construction time is 50 hours.

DIMENSIONS, EXTERNAL:

Wing span	8.43 m (27 ft 8 in)
Length overall	6.22 m (20 ft 5 in)
Height overall	1.68 m (5 ft 6 in)
Propeller diameter	1.52 m (5 ft 0 in)

AREA:

Wings, gross	12.45 m² (134.0 sq ft)

WEIGHTS (Rotax 447 engine):

Weight empty	118 kg (260 lb)
Max pilot weight	113 kg (250 lb)
Max T-O weight	249 kg (550 lb)

PERFORMANCE (Rotax 447 and 77 kg; 170 lb pilot):

Max level speed	65 knots (121 km/h; 75 mph)
Cruising speed	52 knots (97 km/h; 60 mph)
Stalling speed	23 knots (42 km/h; 26 mph)
Max rate of climb at S/L	350 m (1,150 ft)/min
Service ceiling	4,265 m (14,000 ft)
T-O and landing run	46 m (150 ft)
g limits	+6/−3

ADVANCED AVIATION CARRERA 182

This two-seat version of the Carrera is available as a kit requiring 90 hours to assemble. The prototype Carrera 180 first flew in February 1989. Power is provided by a 34 kW (45.6 hp) Rotax 503.

DIMENSION, EXTERNAL:

Wing span	9.55 m (31 ft 4 in)

AREA:

Wings, gross	14.12 m² (152.0 sq ft)

WEIGHTS:

Weight empty	156 kg (345 lb)
Max T-O weight	431 kg (950 lb)

PERFORMANCE:

Cruising speed	52 knots (97 km/h; 60 mph)
Stalling speed	28 knots (52 km/h; 32 mph)
Max rate of climb at S/L	198 m (650 ft)/min

ADVANCED AVIATION BUCCANEER SX

This single-seat amphibian was based on the Carrera airframe but with a hull and wing floats. It superseded the earlier single-seat (Highcraft) Buccaneer (see Microlights section in 1990-91 *Jane's*). Construction from a kit takes about 75 working hours. Power is provided by a 34 kW (45.6 hp) Rotax 503.

DIMENSIONS, EXTERNAL:

Wing span	9.04 m (29 ft 8 in)
Length overall	6.22 m (20 ft 5 in)

AREA:

Wings, gross	13.29 m² (143.0 sq ft)

WEIGHTS:

Weight empty	144 kg (318 lb)
Max T-O weight	283 kg (625 lb)

PERFORMANCE:

Max level speed	69 knots (129 km/h; 80 mph)
Cruising speed	55 knots (101 km/h; 63 mph)
Stalling speed	25 knots (47 km/h; 29 mph)
Max rate of climb at S/L	274 m (900 ft)/min

ADVANCED AVIATION XA/650 BUCCANEER II

This side by side two-seat Experimental category derivative of the Buccaneer amphibian flew for the first time on 14 March 1986. The landing gear is retracted via a cockpit lever. Power plant is a 48.5 kW (65 hp) Rotax 582. Fuel capacity is 45 litres (12 US gallons; 10 Imp gallons). Kits are available and construction takes approximately 125 working hours.

DIMENSIONS, EXTERNAL:

Wing span	10.88 m (35 ft 8½ in)
Length overall	6.81 m (22 ft 4 in)
Height overall	2.06 m (6 ft 9 in)
Propeller diameter	1.73 m (5 ft 8 in)

AREA:

Wings, gross	15.89 m² (171.0 sq ft)

WEIGHTS:

Weight empty	249 kg (550 lb)
Max crew weight	190 kg (420 lb)
Max T-O weight	465 kg (1,025 lb)

PERFORMANCE:

Max level speed at S/L	65 knots (120 km/h; 75 mph)
Cruising speed	56 knots (105 km/h; 65 mph)
Econ cruising speed at S/L	50 knots (92 km/h; 57 mph)
Stalling speed, power off	27 knots (50 km/h; 31 mph)
Max rate of climb at S/L	244 m (800 ft)/min
T-O run: on land	77 m (250 ft)
on water	153 m (500 ft)

ADVANCED AVIATION EXPLORER

This two-seat landplane requires about 125 working hours to construct from a kit and is powered by a 34 kW (45.6 hp) Rotax 503.

DIMENSION, EXTERNAL:

Wing span	9.04 m (29 ft 8 in)

AREA:

Wings, gross	14.59 m² (157.0 sq ft)

WEIGHTS:

Weight empty	175 kg (385 lb)
Max T-O weight	408 kg (900 lb)

PERFORMANCE:

Max cruising speed	56 knots (105 km/h; 65 mph)
Stalling speed	25 knots (47 km/h; 29 mph)
Max rate of climb at S/L	198 m (650 ft)/min

AEROCAR

AEROCAR INC

PO Box 1171, Longview, Washington 98632

Telephone: 1 (206) 423 8260

PRESIDENT AND GENERAL MANAGER: Moulton B. Taylor

In February 1948 Aerocar Inc began developing a flying automobile designed by Mr M. B. Taylor. The prototype Aerocar, with a Textron Lycoming O-290 engine, was completed in October 1949. Design and theoretical work continue on the concept, now in its CRX fourth generation form. Aerocar anticipates developing a kit-built version in the near future if financing can be found. Having a span of 10.36 m (34 ft), the CRX is expected to cruise at 150 knots (278 km/h; 173 mph) on the power of its 313 kW (420 hp) Allison turbine engine.

Pober Super Ace prototype (Teledyne Continental C85 engine)

Cougar Model 1 owned by Mr Charles Warren Cronce of Florida

Buccaneer II two-seat homebuilt amphibian, marketed by Advanced Aviation *(Howard Levy)*

Advanced Aviation Carrera single-seat landplane *(Howard Levy)*

Advanced Aviation Explorer *(Howard Levy)*

Advanced Aviation Buccaneer SX amphibian *(Howard Levy)*

Two-seat Advanced Aviation King Cobra *(Brian M. Service)*

Aerocar Sooper-Coot Model A amphibian *(Peter M. Bowers)*

Fully active Aerocar programmes are detailed in this entry; separate entries for Brown and Holcomb cover other aircraft originated by Mr Taylor.

AEROCAR SOOPER-COOT MODEL A

The prototype Sooper-Coot flew for the first time in February 1971. Its 'float-wing' configuration permits rough-water operation and, since the close proximity of the wings to the water forms a 'pressure wedge', unusually low take-off and landing speeds are possible without recourse to flaps or other lift enhancing devices.

The structure is basically of wood, but the tailboom and tail unit can be of steel tube and fabric, wood monocoque or all-metal construction. Wing section is NACA 4415. The fabric covered ailerons are of metal construction. A

manually retractable tricycle landing gear is standard, but an alternative powered retraction system is shown on the plans.

Recommended power plant for the Sooper-Coot is a Franklin of either 134 or 164 kW (180 or 220 hp). However, other engines of 112-168 kW (150-225 hp) can be fitted. Many builders are using a 157 kW (210 hp) Teledyne Continental IO-360. To minimise expenditure, others are fitting Textron Lycoming O-320 and O-320-B engines of 119 kW (160 hp). Fuel capacity is 170 litres (45 US gallons; 37.5 Imp gallons).

Certain component parts (including the glassfibre engine cowls, glassfibre hull shell, foredeck, instrument panel, tail fairings, engine cooling fan blades and spring steel main landing gear legs), and plans, are available to amateur constructors. Many hundreds of Sooper-Coots are under construction, and more than 130 are known to be flying.

DIMENSIONS, EXTERNAL:
Wing span	10.97 m (36 ft 0 in)
Length overall	6.10 to 6.71 m (20 ft 0 in to 22 ft 0 in)
Height overall	2.44 m (8 ft 0 in)

AREA:
Wings, gross	16.72 m² (180.0 sq ft)

WEIGHTS:
Weight empty	658 kg (1,450 lb)
Max T-O weight	975 kg (2,150 lb)

PERFORMANCE (134 kW; 180 hp engine, at max T-O weight):
Max cruising speed	113 knots (209 km/h; 130 mph)
Econ cruising speed at 50% power	95 knots (177 km/h; 110 mph)
Max rate of climb at S/L	381 m (1,250 ft)/min
T-O run (land)	61 m (200 ft)

AEROCAR MINI-IMP

The Mini-Imp is a single-seat version of the Aerocar Imp (see Brown entry in 1989-90 *Jane's*). Features include an inverted V tail, tail pusher propeller, new NASA wing section with spoilers/flaps, and a retractable tricycle landing gear. The basic structure is all metal. Plans are available, together with parts kits. More than 250 amateur-built Mini-Imps are being constructed, and several are flying. Average time taken for construction is about 1,000 working hours.

TYPE: Single-seat sporting homebuilt.

POWER PLANT: Recommended engine is a 47 kW (63 hp) Rotax 532. Alternative engines in the 44.5-74.5 kW (60-100 hp) range may be installed. Fuel capacity 45.4 litres (12 US gallons; 10 Imp gallons), plus tip tanks, each of 34 litres (9 US gallons; 7.5 Imp gallons) capacity.

DIMENSIONS, EXTERNAL:
Wing span	7.62 m (25 ft 0 in)
Length overall	4.88 m (16 ft 0 in)
Height over fuselage	1.22 m (4 ft 0 in)
Propeller diameter	1.45 m (4 ft 9 in)

WEIGHTS:
Weight empty	227 kg (500 lb)
Baggage capacity	23 kg (50 lb)
Max T-O weight	385 kg (850 lb)

PERFORMANCE (51 kW; 68 hp Limbach 1,900 cc engine, except where indicated):
Max cruising speed at S/L	more than 130 knots (241 km/h; 150 mph)
Max cruising speed (Revmaster engine, estimated)	over 173 knots (322 km/h; 200 mph)
Stalling speed	44 knots (81 km/h; 50 mph)
Max rate of climb at S/L	305 m (1,000 ft)/min
T-O run	183 m (600 ft)
Range	over 434 nm (804 km; 500 miles)
g limits	±9

AEROCAR MICRO-IMP

The single-seat Micro-Imp is of similar configuration to the Mini-Imp, but is constructed primarily of glassfibre reinforced paper known as TPG (Taylor Paper Glass). The prototype made its first flight in the Summer of 1981. Drawings to allow amateur constructors to build the Micro-Imp are almost complete, but the programme has been delayed pending the availability of a suitable engine. A description appeared in the 1989-90 *Jane's*.

TAYLOR BULLET 2100

Following the success of the TPG method of construction for the Micro-Imp, Aerocar designed a two-seat counterpart also utilising TPG. It is known as the Taylor Bullet 2100, because of its similarity in configuration to the Gallaudet Bullet of 1912. The prototype was completed in February 1985.

Plans to allow amateur construction of the Bullet 2100 are not yet available, but are expected to be offered eventually, together with some difficult to fabricate component parts. A description appeared in the 1989-90 *Jane's*.

AERO COMPOSITE

AERO COMPOSITE TECHNOLOGY INC
Rt 3, Box 107B, Somerset, Pennsylvania 15501
Telephone: 1 (814) 445 8608
PRESIDENT: William D. Forrest

AERO COMPOSITE SEA HAWKER

Under the original owners, Aero Gare, design of the Sea Hawker began in 1981 and a prototype flew for the first time in July 1982. Aero Composite Technology Inc purchased the Sea Hawker from Aero Composites Inc in July 1987. Kits are marketed, comprising 22 pre-moulded components and all raw materials, with cadmium plating on all welded or machined parts. Average construction time from kits is 1,500 working hours. Plans are also available. By January 1991, 255 kits had been sold and 52 aircraft were flying.

The Sea Hawker's amphibious rough-field landing gear permits landings on water, asphalt, grass, snow, mud, and rough fields. The glassfibre covered rubbing strips on the hull allow a safe gear-up emergency landing on hard surfaces.

TYPE: Side by side two-seat homebuilt amphibious biplane.

AIRFRAME: NASA wing section. Composite wings of foam/GFRP/CFRP/Kevlar. Full-span slotted ailerons on lower wings deflect with slotted flaps on upper wings for take-off and landing. Single-step hull of similar composite materials to wings, with integral fin. Retractable tricycle landing gear. Water rudder under fin.

POWER PLANT: One 112 kW (150 hp) Textron Lycoming O-320 recommended, driving a two- or three-blade wooden pusher propeller. Two fuel tanks, each 132.5 litres (35 US gallons; 29 Imp gallons) capacity.

DIMENSIONS, EXTERNAL:
Wing span	7.32 m (24 ft 0 in)
Length overall	6.65 m (21 ft 10 in)
Height overall	2.29 m (7 ft 6 in)
Propeller diameter	1.63 m (5 ft 4 in)

AREA:
Wings, gross	10.59 m² (114.0 sq ft)

WEIGHTS (112 kW; 150 hp engine):
Weight empty	431 kg (950 lb)
Max T-O weight	726 kg (1,600 lb)

PERFORMANCE (112 kW; 150 hp engine):
Max level speed at S/L	122 knots (225 km/h; 140 mph)
Max cruising speed	117 knots (217 km/h; 135 mph)
Econ cruising speed	113 knots (209 km/h; 130 mph)
Stalling speed, power off	42 knots (78 km/h; 48 mph)
Max rate of climb at S/L	610 m (2,000 ft)/min
Service ceiling	3,660 m (12,000 ft)
T-O run: on land	153 m (500 ft)
on water	305 m (1,000 ft)
Landing run	122 m (400 ft)
Range	868 nm (1,609 km; 1,000 miles)
g limits	+6/-3

AERO DESIGNS

AERO DESIGNS INC
635 Blakeley, San Antonio, Texas 78209
Telephone: 1 (512) 650 3398
PRESIDENT: Mark Brown
MANAGER: Phil Durieux

AERO DESIGNS PULSAR

Aero Designs is marketing the Pulsar in kit form, including engine. It is basically a side by side two-seat version of the Star-Lite (see 1989-90 *Jane's*), designed also by Mark Brown. The prototype first flew on 3 April 1988. Construction takes about 1,000 working hours. By February 1991, 135 kits had been ordered, of which 110 had been delivered and 12 aircraft had flown.

AIRFRAME: Mostly wooden wing structure, but with polystyrene foam ribs and some use of unidirectional glassfibre. Ailerons and flaps. Wing section MS(1)-0313. Monocoque fuselage and tail unit of pre-moulded composite construction, using sandwich of pre-impregnated epoxy-glassfibre with PVC foam core. Non-retractable tricycle landing gear.

POWER PLANT: One 49.2 kW (66 hp) Rotax 582. Fuel capacity 60 litres (16 US gallons; 13.3 Imp gallons).

DIMENSIONS, EXTERNAL:
Wing span	7.62 m (25 ft 0 in)
Length overall	5.94 m (19 ft 6 in)
Height overall	1.91 m (6 ft 3 in)
Propeller diameter	1.42 m (4 ft 8 in)

AREA:
Wings, gross	7.43 m² (80.0 sq ft)

WEIGHTS:
Weight empty	343 kg (460 lb)
Baggage capacity	18 kg (40 lb)
Max T-O weight	408 kg (900 lb)

PERFORMANCE:
Max level speed	122 knots (225 km/h; 140 mph)
Cruising speed	113 knots (209 km/h; 130 mph)
Econ cruising speed at 1,525 m (5,000 ft)	87 knots (161 km/h; 100 mph)
Stalling speed, engine idling:	
flaps up	39 knots (73 km/h; 45 mph)
flaps down	37 knots (68 km/h; 42 mph)
Max rate of climb at S/L	305 m (1,000 ft)/min
Service ceiling	4,570 m (15,000 ft)
T-O and landing run	244 m (800 ft)
Range	347 nm (644 km; 400 miles)
g limits	+4/-2

AERO DYNAMICS

AERO DYNAMICS LTD

Details of the Sparrow Hawk Mk II and an illustration can be found in the 1990-91 *Jane's*.

AEROLITES

AEROLITES INC
Route 1, Box 187, Welsh, Louisiana 70591
Telephone: 1 (318) 734 3865
Telex: 6503079915 (via WUI)
PRESIDENT: Daniel J. Roché

In October 1986 the manufacturing rights to the Bearcat homebuilt aircraft were purchased from Litecraft by AeroLites Inc. A side by side two-seat version is currently under development.

AEROLITES BEARCAT

First flown in 1984, the Bearcat bears a close external resemblance to the Piper Cub. Kits are available. Estimated building time is 100-120 working hours.

TYPE: Single-seat homebuilt or microlight; conforms to Canadian and European microlight regulations.

AIRFRAME: Strut braced parasol-wing monoplane. Wing section Clark Y. Wings and fuselage constructed of aluminium alloy and 4130 chrome-molybdenum steel tubing respectively, and covered with Dacron (double surface on wings), polyester and glassfibre. Non-retractable tailwheel landing gear. Options include full cockpit enclosure, ballistic parachute, Spray Miser Ag system (with Rotax 582 engine only), hydraulic disc brakes, electric starter and high flotation tyres.

POWER PLANT: One 31.3 kW (42 hp) Rotax 447; 50 kW (67 hp) Rotax 582 available optionally. Fuel capacity 19 litres (5 US gallons; 4.2 Imp gallons).

DIMENSIONS, EXTERNAL:
Wing span	9.36 m (30 ft 8½ in)
Length overall	5.64 m (18 ft 6 in)
Height overall	1.96 m (6 ft 5 in)
Propeller diameter	1.73 m (5 ft 8 in)

AREA:
Wings, gross	14.86 m² (160.0 sq ft)

WEIGHTS:
Weight empty	136 kg (300 lb)
Pilot weight range	45.5-136 kg (100-300 lb)
Baggage capacity	13.6 kg (30 lb)
Max T-O weight	340 kg (750 lb)

PERFORMANCE (at max T-O weight):
Max level speed at 305 m (1,000 ft)	61 knots (113 km/h; 70 mph)
Econ cruising speed at 305 m (1,000 ft)	48 knots (89 km/h; 55 mph)
Stalling speed: power on	23 knots (42 km/h; 26 mph)
power off	24 knots (44 km/h; 27 mph)
Max rate of climb at S/L	213 m (700 ft)/min
Service ceiling	3,050 m (10,000 ft)
T-O run	31 m (100 ft)
Landing from 15 m (50 ft)	137 m (450 ft)
Landing run	46 m (150 ft)
Range with max standard fuel	104 nm (193 km; 120 miles)
Endurance	2 h 10 min
g limits	+6/-4

AEROLITES AG BEARCAT

The Ag Bearcat was created jointly by AeroLites and Louisiana AgriLites. Only slight modification was required to the airframe to accept the Spray Miser Ag system. The standard engine is a 50 kW (67 hp) Rotax 582; fuel capacity is 38 litres (10 US gallons; 8.3 Imp gallons). Alternative Sadler radial engines of 33.6-48.5 kW (45-65 hp). Full span trailing-edge ailerons help to improve pilot control. Standard equipment includes a 12V high volume electric pump capable of flow rates of over 30.3 litres (8 US gallons; 6.7 Imp gallons)/min at 1.38 bars (20 lb/sq in), a 91 litre (24 US gallon; 20 Imp gallon) glassfibre underbelly chemical tank with emergency dump, and welded aluminium 'wet' booms, offering a swath width of 9-30 m (30-100 ft). Options include a ballistic parachute, high flotation tyres and Mylar coated fabric.

Aerocar Mini-Imp single-seat sporting monoplane

AeroLites Ag Bearcat homebuilt agricultural aircraft

Aero Composite Sea Hawker amphibian

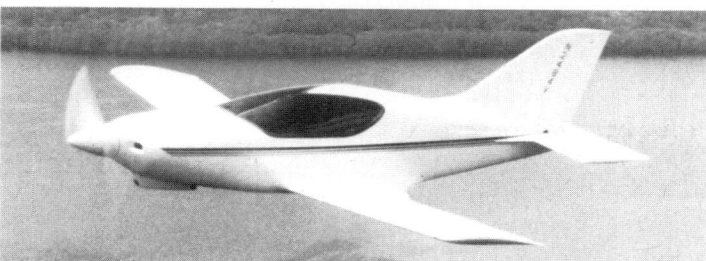

Aero Mirage TC-2 all-composites lightplane

Aero Designs Pulsar two-seat homebuilt *(J. M. G. Gradidge)*

Aerosport Scamp A biplane built by Mr Jack Stafford of Greenville, South Carolina

DIMENSIONS, EXTERNAL:		WEIGHTS:			
Wing span	9.25 m (30 ft 4 in)	Weight empty	172 kg (380 lb)	Stalling speed, power on	31 knots (57 km/h; 35 mph)
Length overall	5.64 m (18 ft 6 in)	Max T-O weight	408 kg (900 lb)	Max rate of climb at S/L	259 m (850 ft)/min
Height overall	1.96 m (6 ft 5 in)	PERFORMANCE (ISA, S/L with 88 kg; 195 lb pilot, except		Service ceiling	6,400 m (21,000 ft)
Propeller diameter	1.73 m (5 ft 8 in)	where indicated):		T-O run at max T-O weight	168 m (550 ft)
		Max level speed	78 knots (145 km/h; 90 mph)	Landing run	46 m (150 ft)
AREA:		Cruising and spraying speed		Range with max fuel	152 nm (282 km; 175 miles)
Wings, gross	14.77 m² (159.0 sq ft)		56 knots (105 km/h; 65 mph)	Endurance with max fuel	2 h 30 min
				g limits	+4.5/−2.5

AERO MIRAGE

AERO MIRAGE INC

3009 North-East 20th Way, Gainesville, Florida 32609
Telephone: 1 (904) 377 4145

AERO MIRAGE TC-2

The prototype of this high performance commuter homebuilt first flew on 16 May 1983 and the TC-2 is thought still to be available in kit form to amateur builders.

The following details refer to the prototype, unless stated otherwise:

TYPE: Side by side two-seat homebuilt.

AIRFRAME: Wing and tailplane spars of glassfibre reinforced plastics with foam core webs. Remainder of airframe constructed of Kevlar, Klégécel, S glass and vinylester resin. Wing section NACA 64415. Retractable tricycle landing gear.

POWER PLANT: One 74.5 kW (100 hp) Teledyne Continental O-200-A. Other engines recommended as suitable up to 74.5 kW (100 hp), though both a Textron Lycoming O-235 and O-290 are being fitted to Mirages. Standard fuel capacity 95 litres (25 US gallons; 20.8 Imp gallons); capacity with auxiliary tanks 144 litres (38 US gallons; 31.6 Imp gallons).

DIMENSIONS, EXTERNAL:

Wing span	6.40 m (21 ft 0 in)
Length overall	5.05 m (16 ft 7 in)
Height overall	1.78 m (5 ft 10 in)
Propeller diameter	1.57 m (5 ft 2 in)

AREA:

Wings, gross	5.95 m² (64.0 sq ft)

WEIGHTS (with 48.5 kW; 65 hp engine):

Weight empty	238 kg (525 lb)
Baggage capacity	18 kg (40 lb)
Max T-O weight	431 kg (950 lb)

PERFORMANCE (engine as above, unless stated otherwise):

Max level speed at S/L	157 knots (291 km/h; 181 mph)
Cruising speed, 75% power, at S/L	
	142 knots (264 km/h; 164 mph)
Stalling speed, prototype:	
flaps up	55 knots (102 km/h; 63 mph)
flaps down	50 knots (92 km/h; 57 mph)
Landing run	137 m (450 ft)

AEROSPORT

AEROSPORT LTD

Box 278, Holly Springs, North Carolina 27540
Telephone: 1 (919) 552 6375
PRESIDENT: E. B. Trent

AEROSPORT SCAMP A

The prototype Scamp flew for the first time on 21 August 1973. The Scamp A can be used for limited aerobatics; and emphasis has been placed on simple construction techniques to make it an easy project for the homebuilder.

Plans and parts were made available to amateur constructors, and a total of well over 900 sets of plans have been sold. More than 40 have flown, and some examples of an agricultural version, known as Scamp B, were assembled in South America (see under Colombia in main Aircraft section of the 1984-85 *Jane's*).

TYPE: Single-seat homebuilt biplane.

AIRFRAME: All-metal construction, with light alloy semi-monocoque fuselage. Wing section NACA 23012. Non-retractable tricycle landing gear.

POWER PLANT: Prototype has 44.5 kW (60 hp) 1,834 cc Volkswagen modified motorcar engine. Design suitable for Volkswagen engines of up to 2,100 cc, though Aerosport recommends 1,834 cc as optimum. Fuel capacity 30.5 litres (8 US gallons; 6.66 Imp gallons).

DIMENSIONS, EXTERNAL:

Wing span	5.33 m (17 ft 6 in)
Length overall	4.27 m (14 ft 0 in)
Height overall	1.69 m (5 ft 6½ in)
Propeller diameter	1.42 m (4 ft 8 in)

AREA:

Wings, gross	9.75 m² (105.0 sq ft)

WEIGHTS:

Weight empty	236-249 kg (520-550 lb)
Max T-O weight	348-362 kg (768-798 lb)

PERFORMANCE (1,834 cc engine):

Max level speed	91 knots (169 km/h; 105 mph)
Cruising speed	78 knots (145 km/h; 90 mph)
Stalling speed	39 knots (73 km/h; 45 mph)

Service ceiling (estimated)	3,660 m (12,000 ft)
T-O and landing run	122 m (400 ft)
Range at cruising speed	108 nm (201 km; 125 miles)
g limits	+6/−3

AEROVANT
AEROVANT AIRCRAFT CORPORATION
2342 Jonquil Place, Rockford, Illinois 61107
Telephone: 1 (815) 877 4508
PRESIDENT: Walt Peters

In April 1990 Aerovant Aircraft purchased the design rights to the SA-700 Acroduster 1 from Charles Sanford (formerly owned by the Stolp Starduster Corporation). Plans and component parts are offered for its construction but not kits.

AEROVANT SA-700 ACRODUSTER 1
Originally introduced by Stolp in 1973, the SA-700 is a single-seat fully-aerobatic biplane. Ailerons on both wings produce a roll rate in excess of 240°/s, and an interesting design feature is that the four ailerons are raised slightly when the control column is pulled back. This helps maintain aileron control when the aircraft is stalled in a normal attitude. Conversely, the ailerons are drooped slightly when the control column is pushed forward, which helps to maintain aileron control in an inverted stall.

TYPE: Single-seat aerobatic biplane.
AIRFRAME: Strut braced biplane. Wings have conventional structure, with two spruce spars, plywood ribs and fabric covering. Wing section Osborne A-1. Upper wing swept back 6°. Ailerons on both wings. All-metal semi-monocoque fuselage and metal cantilever tail unit. Non-retractable tailwheel landing gear.
POWER PLANT: Prototype had originally a 149 kW (200 hp) Textron Lycoming flat-four engine, driving a two-blade fixed-pitch propeller, but was re-engined subsequently with a 134 kW (180 hp) engine. Design is suitable for engines of 93-149 kW (125-200 hp). Fuel capacity 94.5 litres (25 US gallons; 20.8 Imp gallons).

DIMENSIONS, EXTERNAL:

Wing span	5.79 m (19 ft 0 in)
Length overall	4.80 m (15 ft 9 in)
Height overall	1.91 m (6 ft 3 in)

WEIGHTS (prototype with 149 kW; 200 hp engine):

Weight empty	335 kg (740 lb)
Baggage capacity	23 kg (50 lb)
T-O weight: aerobatic	476 kg (1,050 lb)
max	539 kg (1,190 lb)

PERFORMANCE (prototype with 149 kW; 200 hp engine, at AUW of 476 kg; 1,050 lb):

Max level speed	156 knots (290 km/h; 180 mph)
Cruising speed	143 knots (266 km/h; 165 mph)
Stalling speed	48 knots (88.5 km/h; 55 mph)
Max rate of climb at S/L	more than 915 m (3,000 ft)/min
Endurance at cruising speed, with reserves	2 h
g limits	±9 ultimate

AERO VISIONS
AERO VISIONS INTERNATIONAL
Route 2, Box 282, South Webster, Ohio 45682
Telephone: 1 (614) 778 3185
Fax: 1 (614) 778 3185
PRESIDENT: Michael E. Fisher

Aero Visions markets the Culex and Culite, which were formerly aircraft of Fisher Flying Products company, plus the Celebrity biplane and latest Horizon.

AERO VISIONS CULITE
The Culite is a development of the Culex, designed to use high power-to-weight ratio Rotax engines and a lighter airframe, with fabric covered wooden geodetic fuselage. Unlike the Culex, the Culite is available only with a non-retractable tricycle landing gear.
POWER PLANT: Two 35.8 kW (48 hp) Rotax 503s. Fuel capacity 60.5 litres (16 US gallons; 13.3 Imp gallons). Optional tankage of 121 litres (32 US gallons; 26.6 Imp gallons).
DIMENSIONS, EXTERNAL: As for Culex, except:

Wing span	8.53 m (28 ft 0 in)

AREA:

Wings, gross	13.00 m² (140.0 sq ft)

WEIGHTS:

Weight empty	249 kg (550 lb)
Max T-O weight	522 kg (1,150 lb)

PERFORMANCE (estimated):

Cruising speed (75% power)	104 knots (193 km/h; 120 mph)
Stalling speed: flaps up	37 knots (68 km/h; 42 mph)
flaps down	30 knots (55 km/h; 34 mph)
Max rate of climb at S/L	366 m (1,200 ft)/min
T-O run	76 m (250 ft)
Landing run	107 m (350 ft)

AERO VISIONS CULEX
The Culex is powered by two 59.6 kW (80 hp) Limbach L2000 engines, and has a fuel capacity of 174 litres (46 US gallons; 38.3 Imp gallons). Airframe is an all-wood semi-monocoque structure, plywood skinned. A choice of landing gears is offered: non-retractable tailwheel or tricycle, or retractable tailwheel type.

The Culex is offered in plans form, as partial or complete airframe kits, or in a number of separate prefabricated subassembly kits.
TYPE: Tandem two-seat homebuilt.
DIMENSIONS, EXTERNAL:

Wing span	9.40 m (30 ft 0 in)
Length overall	6.20 m (20 ft 4 in)
Height overall	1.93 m (6 ft 4 in)
Propeller diameter	1.60 m (5 ft 3 in)

AREA:

Wings, gross	13.94 m² (150.0 sq ft)

WEIGHTS:

Weight empty	454 kg (1,000 lb)
Payload with max fuel	215 kg (474 lb)
Max T-O weight: aerobatic	680 kg (1,500 lb)
utility	794 kg (1,750 lb)

PERFORMANCE (estimated, at utility T-O weight):

Max level speed	130 knots (241 km/h; 150 mph)
Cruising speed, 75% power	121 knots (225 km/h; 140 mph)
Stalling speed: clean	52 knots (97 km/h; 60 mph)
wheels and flaps down	42 knots (77 km/h; 48 mph)
Max rate of climb at S/L	457 m (1,500 ft)/min
Rate of climb at S/L, one engine out	107 m (350 ft)/min
T-O run	92-107 m (300-350 ft)
Landing run	76-92 m (250-300 ft)
Range with max fuel	651 nm (1,207 km; 750 miles)
g limits	+6.5/−3

AERO VISIONS CELEBRITY
This biplane is marketed in full, quick-build and partial kit forms, and optional prefabricated components are a J-3 type cowling, engine mount, mechanical or hydraulic brakes, and wheel fairings; plans are not sold separately.
TYPE: Tandem two-seat homebuilt and ARV biplane.
AIRFRAME: Strut and wire braced biplane of fabric-covered wooden construction; welded steel tube fuselage now available as option. NACA 23012 wing section. Conventional controls, with ailerons on upper and lower wings. Non-retractable tailwheel landing gear.
POWER PLANT: One 48.5-74.5 kW (65-100 hp) Teledyne Continental or 48.5-67 kW (65-90 hp) Volkswagen modified motorcar engine. Fuel capacity 49 litres (13 US gallons; 10.8 Imp gallons).
DIMENSIONS, EXTERNAL:

Wing span	6.71 m (22 ft 0 in)
Length overall	5.33 m (17 ft 6 in)
Height overall	1.83 m (6 ft 0 in)
Propeller diameter	1.83 to 1.88 m (6 ft 0 in to 6 ft 2 in)

AREA:

Wings, gross	16.35 m² (176.0 sq ft)

WEIGHTS:

Weight empty	238 kg (525 lb)
Baggage capacity	6.8 kg (15 lb)
Max T-O weight	453 kg (1,000 lb)

PERFORMANCE:

Max level speed	82 knots (153 km/h; 95 mph)
Econ cruising speed	69 knots (129 km/h; 80 mph)
Stalling speed, power off	35 knots (65 km/h; 40 mph)
Service ceiling	4,115 m (13,500 ft)
T-O run	107 m (350 ft)
Landing run	92 m (300 ft)
Range	208 nm (386 km; 240 miles)
Endurance	3 h
g limits	+6.5/−3.5

AERO VISIONS HORIZON
Construction of the prototype began in 1989, followed by prefabricated components for amateur constructors in 1990. The latter include ribs, spars, wingtip bows, fuselage sides, tail unit, engine cowling, landing gear and seats. The wings can be folded by one person in five minutes.
TYPE: Tandem two-seat cabin monoplane.
AIRFRAME: Strut braced high-wing monoplane of fabric-covered wooden construction. Three-axis control, with flaps. Non-retractable tailwheel landing gear. Optional floats, skis, wheel fairings and hydraulic or mechanical brakes.
POWER PLANT: One engine of 48.5-85.75 kW (65-115 hp), including Teledyne Continental, Textron Lycoming, Rotax 582 or 912, or Volkswagen modified motorcar types. Prototype has 59.7 kW (80 hp) Limbach. Fuel capacity 49 litres (13 US gallons; 10.8 Imp gallons).
DIMENSIONS, EXTERNAL:

Wing span	9.14 m (30 ft 0 in)
Length overall	5.69 m (18 ft 8 in)
Height overall	1.78 m (5 ft 10 in)
Propeller diameter	1.68 to 1.88 m (5 ft 6 in to 6 ft 2 in)

AREA:

Wings, gross	15.33 m² (165.0 sq ft)

WEIGHTS:

Weight empty	204-249 kg (450-550 lb)
Pilot weight range	61.5-113 kg (135-250 lb)
Max T-O weight	476 kg (1,050 lb)

PERFORMANCE:

Max level speed	91 knots (169 km/h; 105 mph)
Max cruising speed	82 knots (153 km/h; 95 mph)
Econ cruising speed	74-78 knots (137-145 km/h; 85-90 mph)
Stalling speed	33-35 knots (62-65 km/h; 38-40 mph)
Max rate of climb at S/L	366 m (1,200 ft)
T-O and landing run	92 m (300 ft)
Range	217 nm (402 km; 250 miles)
g limits	+4.5/−3 design

AIR COMMAND
AIR COMMAND MANUFACTURING INC
Liberty Landing Airport, Route 3, Box 197A, Liberty, Missouri 64068
Telephone: 1 (816) 781 9313
Fax: 1 (816) 781 9366
PRESIDENT: Dennis Fetters

Details of the 447 Commander and 447 Commander Sport can be found in the Microlight tables. Approximately 1,010 Air Command aircraft are flying worldwide, including some 15 used for observation by the military.

AIR COMMAND 503 COMMANDER and 503 COMMANDER SPORT
This gyroplane uses the same airframe as the 447 Commander, but has a 35 kW (47 hp) Rotax 503 engine as standard. It conforms to FAR Pt 103.

WEIGHTS:

Weight empty	122 kg (270 lb)
Max T-O weight	267 kg (590 lb)

PERFORMANCE (A: Commander, B: Commander Sport):

Max level speed: A	65 knots (121 km/h; 75 mph)
B	72 knots (134 km/h; 83 mph)
Econ cruising speed: A, B	43 knots (80 km/h; 50 mph)
Max rate of climb at S/L: A	274 m (900 ft)/min
B	290 m (950 ft)/min
Ceiling: A, B	3,050 m (10,000 ft)
T-O run: with pre-rotation: A, B	18 m (60 ft)
without pre-rotation: A, B	152 m (500 ft)
Range: A, B	87 nm (161 km; 100 miles)
Endurance: A, B	2 h
g limit	+9

AIR COMMAND 532 COMMANDER ELITE and 532 COMMANDER ELITE SPORT
The 532 Commander Elite became available in kit form in Spring 1985. It has the same airframe as the 447 Commander, but uses the 47.7 kW (64 hp) Rotax 532 engine as standard, with a three-blade propeller. It conforms to FAA Experimental homebuilt requirements, and as such the kit is less than 50 per cent completed. Options include a partial enclosure.

WEIGHTS:

Weight empty	125 kg (275 lb)
Max T-O weight	340 kg (750 lb)

PERFORMANCE:

Max level speed:	
Commander	82 knots (153 km/h; 95 mph)
Commander Sport	91 knots (169 km/h; 105 mph)
Econ cruising speed	61 knots (113 km/h; 70 mph)
Max rate of climb at S/L	366 m (1,200 ft)/min
Service ceiling	3,050 m (10,000 ft)
T-O run: with pre-rotation	18 m (60 ft)
without pre-rotation	152 m (500 ft)
Landing run	0-1.5 m (0-5 ft)
Endurance	1 h 30 min
g limit	+9

Aerovant SA-700 Acroduster 1 single-seat aerobatic biplane

Aero Visions Celebrity homebuilt biplane (J. M. G. Gradidge)

Aero Visions Culex twin-engined homebuilt

i Aero Visions Horizon two-seat homebuilt

New tandem two-seat Air Command gyroplane (Howard Levy)

Air Command 532 Commander Elite (Peter J. Cooper)

AIR COMMAND 532 COMMANDER ELITE TWO-SEATER

By means of a simple bolt-on conversion kit, a standard 532 Commander Elite can be modified into a side by side two-seater under homebuilt regulations. Fitting a second control stick makes it suitable for training purposes. A rotor of 7.62 m (25 ft) diameter is employed. A military version has also been developed.

WEIGHTS:
Weight empty	141 kg (310 lb)
Max T-O weight	340 kg (750 lb)

PERFORMANCE (two persons):
Max level speed	78 knots (145 km/h; 90 mph)
Cruising speed	48 knots (89 km/h; 55 mph)
Max rate of climb at S/L	152 m (500 ft)/min
T-O run: with pre-rotation	46 m (150 ft)
without pre-rotation	214 m (700 ft)
Landing run	0-1.5 m (0-5 ft)

AIR COMMAND TANDEM TWO-SEATER

First flown in Winter 1988, the tandem two-seater is reportedly available in kit form with a 47 kW (63 hp) Rotax 582 engine.

WEIGHTS:
Weight empty	143 kg (315 lb)
Max T-O weight	340 kg (750 lb)

PERFORMANCE:
Max level speed	82 knots (153 km/h; 95 mph)
Cruising speed, 50% power	56 knots (105 km/h; 65 mph)
Min flying speed	7 knots (13 km/h; 8 mph)
Max rate of climb at S/L	366 m (1,200 ft)/min
T-O run with pre-rotation	19 m (60 ft)
Landing run	0-1.5 m (0-5 ft)

AIRCRAFT DESIGNS
AIRCRAFT DESIGNS INC
25380 Boots Road, Monterey, California 93940
Telephone: 1 (408) 649 6212
Fax: 1 (408) 655 3912
PRESIDENT: Martin Hollmann

HOLLMANN HA-2M SPORTSTER
The Sportster prototype first flew in October 1974. Plans, materials and component parts are available.
TYPE: Side by side two-seat homebuilt gyroplane.
ROTOR SYSTEM: Two-blade rotor of NACA 8-H-12 section. Metal blades, each made up of a leading-edge extrusion, aluminium formed ribs and Alclad skin, riveted and bonded together. Pre-rotator and rotor brake standard.
AIRFRAME: All-aluminium alloy construction, except for glassfibre fairings and tail unit tips. Non-retractable tricycle landing gear.
POWER PLANT: One 97 kW (130 hp) Franklin Sport 4B on prototype. Most aircraft powered by a 112 kW (150 hp) Textron Lycoming O-320. Fuel capacity 45.4 litres (12 US gallons; 10 Imp gallons).
DIMENSIONS, EXTERNAL:

Rotor diameter	8.53 m (28 ft 0 in)
Length overall	3.66 m (12 ft 0 in)
Height to top of rotor head	2.34 m (7 ft 8 in)
Propeller diameter	1.68 m (5 ft 6 in)

WEIGHTS (112 kW: 150 hp engine, unless stated otherwise):

Weight empty, equipped (prototype)	281 kg (620 lb)
Max T-O weight	500 kg (1,100 lb)

PERFORMANCE (112 kW; 150 hp engine, unless stated otherwise):

Max cruising speed at S/L (prototype)	65 knots (121 km/h; 75 mph)
Econ cruising speed at S/L (prototype)	52 knots (97 km/h; 60 mph)
Stalling speed (prototype)	25 knots (45 km/h; 28 mph)
Max rate of climb at S/L	274 m (900 ft)/min
Service ceiling	2,440 m (8,000 ft)
T-O run	107 m (350 ft)
Landing run	0-6 m (0-20 ft)
Range: with max fuel	78 nm (145 km; 90 miles)
with max payload	61 nm (112 km; 70 miles)

HOLLMANN BUMBLE BEE
The Bumble Bee first flew in prototype form in January 1984 and is now available in bolt together kit form or can be built from plans, using prefabricated component parts.
TYPE: Single-seat microlight gyroplane; conforms to FAR Pt 103.
AIRFRAME: Fuselage structure of square aluminium alloy tubing, with glassfibre/foam sandwich cruciform tail surfaces. Two-blade rotor of NACA 8-H-12 section, with aluminium alloy leading-edges and glassfibre/foam/epoxy trailing-edges. Rotor pre-rotator standard. Non-retractable tricycle landing gear.

POWER PLANT: One 30 kW (40 hp) Rotax 447. Fuel capacity 19 litres (5 US gallons; 4.15 Imp gallons); optional 38 litres (10 US gallons; 8.3 Imp gallons).
DIMENSIONS, EXTERNAL:

Rotor diameter	7.01 m (23 ft 0 in)
Length overall	3.81 m (12 ft 6 in)
Height overall	2.29 m (7 ft 6 in)
Propeller diameter	1.52 m (5 ft 0 in)

AREA:

Rotor disc	38.55 m² (415.0 sq ft)

WEIGHTS:

Weight empty	104 kg (230 lb)
Pilot weight range	72.5-109 kg (160-240 lb)
Max T-O weight	227 kg (500 lb)

PERFORMANCE:

Max level speed	61 knots (113 km/h; 70 mph)
Econ cruising speed	34.5 knots (64 km/h; 40 mph)
Min flying speed	4.5 knots (8 km/h; 5 mph)
Max rate of climb at S/L	366 m (1,200 ft)/min
Service ceiling	3,660 m (12,000 ft)
T-O run, with 109 kg (240 lb) pilot	73 m (240 ft)
Range	34.5 nm (64 km; 40 miles)
Endurance	1 h
g limits	+3.5/-1

HOLLMANN NOVA
The Nova first flew as a prototype in June 1989. Ready to fly Novas and kits (produced by Pacific Composites of Salinas, California) will become available once test flying has been completed.
TYPE: Side by side two-seat Experimental monoplane.
AIRFRAME: Cantilever mid-wing monoplane of glassfibre/Nomex honeycomb/foam core sandwich construction. Wing section NLF 0215 Modified. Foreplane with elevators, wings with ailerons and flaps, and cruciform tail unit comprising straight tailplane with elevators, sweptback dorsal fin and sweptback ventral fin with rudder. Non-retractable tricycle landing gear, with brakes.
POWER PLANT: One 48.5 kW (65 hp) Rotax 532 with 2.5 : 1 reduction gear, driving a pusher propeller at the rear of the fuselage. Fuel capacity 68 litres (18 US gallons; 15 Imp gallons).
DIMENSIONS, EXTERNAL:

Wing span	6.10 m (20 ft 0 in)
Length overall	5.03 m (16 ft 6 in)
Height overall	2.22 m (7 ft 3½ in)
Propeller diameter	1.60 m (5 ft 3 in)

AREAS:

Wings, gross	5.57 m² (60.0 sq ft)
Foreplane	0.28 m² (3.0 sq ft)

WEIGHTS:

Weight empty	286 kg (630 lb)
Baggage capacity	4.5 kg (10 lb)
Max T-O weight	499 kg (1,100 lb)

PERFORMANCE:

Max level speed	126 knots (233 km/h; 145 mph)
Econ cruising speed	78 knots (145 km/h; 90 mph)

Stalling speed, flaps down	53 knots (98 km/h; 61 mph)

Max rate of climb at S/L:

pilot only	213 m (700 ft)/min
dual	137 m (450 ft)/min
T-O run	305 m (1,000 ft)
Landing run	275 m (900 ft)
Range: pilot only	521 nm (965 km; 600 miles)
dual	217 nm (402 km; 250 miles)
g limits	+4.4/-2.2

HOLLMANN STALLION
Construction of the prototype Stallion began in August 1990, with High Tech Composites Inc of Oxnard fabricating the fuselage plug and moulds and Snowline Engineering of Riverside producing the welded fuselage truss structure. Assembly by Aircraft Designs started in February 1991, allowing completion and the first flight before the end of that year. Assembled and kit aircraft will be delivered from the end of 1992.
The Stallion has been designed to FAR Pt 23 Utility category, and certification will either be under FAR Pt 23 or the Primary category. In addition to sport flying and touring, it can be used for cargo carrying, spotting, evacuation and similar roles.
TYPE: Four-seat utility high-wing monoplane.
AIRFRAME: Centre fuselage area of welded 4130 steel tubing; remainder of airframe constructed mainly of Kevlar/graphite/Nomex honeycomb core/epoxy. Wing section NACA 64212 at tip, Jacosky at root. Three-axis control. Retractable tricycle landing gear, with brakes. Optional floats or skis.
POWER PLANT: Prototype has 209 kW (280 hp) Teledyne Continental IO-550-G flat-six engine, driving a three-blade MT constant speed wood/glassfibre propeller. Fuel capacity 379 litres (100 US gallons; 83.25 Imp gallons).
DIMENSIONS, EXTERNAL:

Wing span	10.67 m (35 ft 0 in)
Length overall	7.47 m (24 ft 6 in)
Height overall	2.74 m (9 ft 0 in)
Propeller diameter	2.03 m (6 ft 8 in)

AREA:

Wings, gross	13.55 m² (145.83 sq ft)

WEIGHTS:

Weight empty	839 kg (1,850 lb)
Baggage capacity	22.7 kg (50 lb)
Max T-O weight	1,451 kg (3,200 lb)

PERFORMANCE:

Max level speed	234 knots (435 km/h; 270 mph)
Max cruising speed at S/L	226 knots (418 km/h; 260 mph)
Stalling speed, flaps down	57 knots (105 km/h; 65 mph)
Max rate of climb at S/L	457 m (1,500 ft)/min
T-O and landing run	244 m (800 ft)
Range, with 45 min reserves	1,129 nm (2,092 km; 1,300 miles)
Endurance	10 h
g limits	+4.4/-2.2

AIRCRAFT DYNAMICS
AIRCRAFT DYNAMICS CORPORATION
2978 East Euclid Place, Littleton, Colorado 80121
Telephone: 1 (303) 780 6021
PRESIDENT: Marilyn J. Bode

AIRCRAFT DYNAMICS NUWACO T-10
Aircraft Dynamics (formerly NuWaco Aircraft Company Inc) markets plans and kits of this modernised version of the pre-war Waco 10-T taperwing biplane; by January 1991, at least 30 ready assembled aircraft and 36 kits plus many sets of plans had been delivered. The prototype made its first flight on 5 May 1984. For those building from plans, the fuselage, tail assembly, landing gear, struts and fuel/oil tanks are available as individual components. Construction takes approximately 1,500 working hours.
TYPE: Three-seat homebuilt replica biplane.
AIRFRAME: Strut and wire braced structure of wood and welded steel tube construction, fabric covered. Wing

section Munk M-6. Non-retractable tailwheel landing gear. Options include floats and cockpit canopy.
POWER PLANT: Suited to engines of 164-336 kW (220-450 hp). Prototype fitted with (and recommended engine) 205 kW (275 hp) Jacobs R-755-B2 radial. Optional engines include Teledyne Continental W-670, Pratt & Whitney R-985, Wright R-975 or J5, and Jacobs R-755-A2. Fuel capacity 227 litres (60 US gallons; 50 Imp gallons). Two auxiliary fuel tanks in upper wing centre section optional, each with capacity of 66 litres (17.5 US gallons; 14.6 Imp gallons).
DIMENSIONS, EXTERNAL:

Wing span	9.22 m (30 ft 3 in)
Length overall	6.86 m (22 ft 6 in)
Height overall	2.74 m (9 ft 0 in)
Propeller diameter: standard	2.74 m (9 ft 0 in)
optional	2.72 m (8 ft 11 in)

AREA:

Wings, gross	21.09 m² (227.0 sq ft)

WEIGHTS:

Weight empty, average aircraft	855 kg (1,886 lb)
Baggage capacity	18 kg (40 lb)
Max T-O weight	1,179 kg (2,600 lb)

PERFORMANCE (at max T-O weight, Jacobs engine):

Max level speed at S/L	123 knots (229 km/h; 142 mph)
Max cruising speed at S/L, 65% power	113 knots (209 km/h; 130 mph)
Econ cruising speed at S/L	104 knots (193 km/h; 120 mph)
Stalling speed, power off	44 knots (81 km/h; 50 mph)
Max rate of climb at S/L	564 m (1,850 ft)/min
Service ceiling	more than 6,100 m (20,000 ft)
T-O run	122 m (400 ft)
Landing run	138 m (450 ft)
Range at 65% power	564 nm (1,046 km; 650 miles)
Endurance with max standard fuel	5 h
g limits	±10

AMERICAN AIR JET
AMERICAN AIR JET INC
710 Sunnywood Place, Woodland Park, Colorado 80863
Telephone: 1 (719) 633 5588
Fax: 1 (719) 632 8160
PRESIDENT: Stephen L. Willman
American Air Jet Inc was founded in 1987 with the purchased assets of the former Eagle Helicopter Corporation.

AMERICAN AIR JET AMERICAN
First flown in July 1988, this rotor-tip, cold air, pressure-jet helicopter was being offered initially in kit form, to be followed by ready assembled examples for export. FAA certification of production aircraft was expected to be sought if US demand proved sufficient. The

version of the American made available for purchase differs in some respects from the prototype, which is detailed here:
TYPE: Tandem or side by side two-seat homebuilt helicopter.
ROTOR SYSTEM: Single rotor with two hollow glassfibre blades, controlled by mechanical swashplate system. No tail rotor.
AIRFRAME: Aluminium alloy structure, with glassfibre nosecone and steel tube engine mounting. Non-moving tail surfaces. Twin skid landing gear, with optional ground handling wheels and floats.
POWER PLANT: Prototype has 209 kW (280 hp) Wankel rotary engine, driving a centrifugal compressor to provide compressed air to thrust-jets at trailing-edge of blade tips. 'Production' engine is a 268.5 kW (360 hp) rotary turbo, with alternative turbine engine of similar rating. Standard fuel capacity 182 litres (48 US gallons; 40 Imp gallons).

DIMENSIONS, EXTERNAL:

Rotor diameter	10.97 m (36 ft 0 in)
Length of fuselage	5.49 m (18 ft 0 in)
Height overall	2.44 m (8 ft 0 in)

WEIGHTS:

Weight empty	445 kg (980 lb)
Max T-O weight	726 kg (1,600 lb)

PERFORMANCE (estimated, with 209 kW; 280 hp engine):

Max level speed at S/L	78 knots (145 km/h; 90 mph)
Econ cruising speed at S/L	61 knots (113 km/h; 70 mph)
Service ceiling (tested)	3,050 m (10,000 ft)
Hovering ceiling: IGE	366 m (1,200 ft)
OGE	335 m (1,100 ft)
Range at optimum speed	260 nm (483 km; 300 miles)
Endurance at 61 knots (113 km/h; 70 mph)	4 h

Aircraft Designs (Hollmann) HA-2M Sportster two-seat gyroplane
(*J. M. G. Gradidge*)

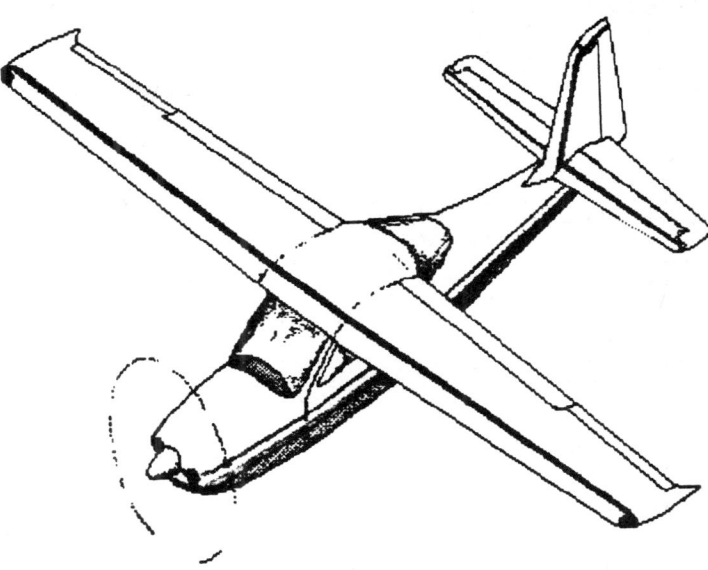

Drawing of the Aircraft Designs (Hollmann) Stallion four-seat utility aircraft

Aircraft Designs (Hollmann) Bumble Bee microlight gyroplane

Aircraft Dynamics NuWaco T-10 taperwing three-seat homebuilt biplane

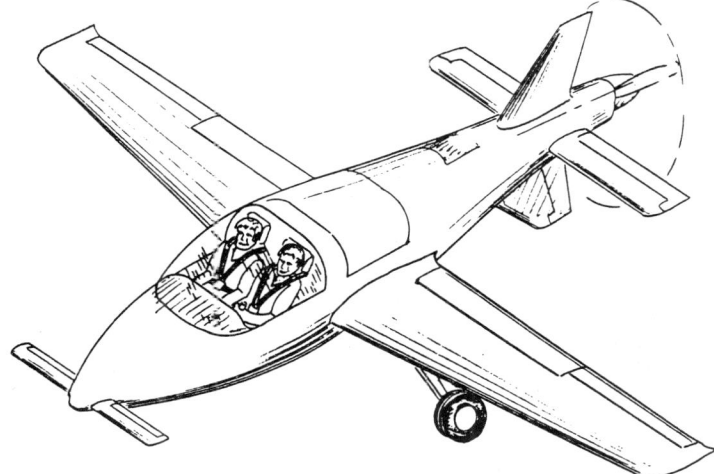

Drawing of the Aircraft Designs (Hollmann) Nova two-seat homebuilt

Prototype American Air Jet American pressure-jet helicopter

ANGLIN
ANGLIN ENGINEERING
Route 3, Box 189-A, Rutherfordton, North Carolina 28139
Telephone: 1 (704) 286 1415

Anglin Engineering is now also marketing a tandem two-seat version of the Spacewalker, known as the Spacewalker II.

ANGLIN SPACEWALKER I
The Spacewalker was designed to look like Ryan monoplanes of the late 1930s and early 1940s but is built of modern materials and uses a modern engine. Drawings, component parts and kits are available to amateur constructors and approximately 50 kits and 1,000 sets of drawings had been sold by 1990.

TYPE: Single-seat homebuilt.

AIRFRAME: Fabric covered wooden wings. Welded chrome-molybdenum steel tube fuselage and wire braced tail unit, also fabric covered. Non-retractable tailwheel landing gear.

POWER PLANT: One 48.5-63 kW (65-85 hp) Teledyne Continental. Fuel capacity 38 litres (10 US gallons; 8.3 Imp gallons).

DIMENSIONS, EXTERNAL:
Wing span	7.93 m (26 ft 0 in)
Length overall	5.49 m (18 ft 0 in)
Height overall	1.60 m (5 ft 3 in)

AREA:
Wings, gross	10.87 m² (117.0 sq ft)

WEIGHTS (48.5 kW; 65 hp Teledyne Continental):
Weight empty	245 kg (540 lb)
Max T-O weight	385 kg (850 lb)

PERFORMANCE (48.5 kW; 65 hp Teledyne Continental):
Max level speed at S/L	108 knots (201 km/h; 125 mph)
Cruising speed	97 knots (180 km/h; 112 mph)
Stalling speed: power off	37 knots (68 km/h; 42 mph)
power on	33 knots (61 km/h; 38 mph)
Max rate of climb at S/L	259 m (850 ft)/min
g limits	+6/–5

ANGLIN SPACEWALKER II
This is a new tandem two-seat version of the original Spacewalker, using similar methods of construction. Kits are available and several have been sold, this aircraft reportedly now being the customer preferred model of Spacewalker. The prototype is powered by a 48.5 kW (65 hp) Teledyne Continental engine; power plants ranging from a 63.4 kW (85 hp) Teledyne Continental to a 93 kW (125 hp) Textron Lycoming O-235 are recommended. Fuel capacity is 68 litres (18 US gallons; 15 Imp gallons).

DIMENSIONS, EXTERNAL:		WEIGHTS:		Stalling speed: power on	37 knots (68 km/h; 42 mph)
Wing span	8.53 m (28 ft 0 in)	Weight empty	318 kg (700 lb)	power off	44 knots (81 km/h; 50 mph)
Length overall	6.02 m (19 ft 9 in)	Max T-O weight	544 kg (1,200 lb)	Max rate of climb at S/L	259 m (850 ft)/min
Height overall	1.65 m (5 ft 5 in)	PERFORMANCE:		g limits	+5/–3.5
AREA:		Max level speed	109 knots (201 km/h; 125 mph)		
Wings, gross	11.71 m² (126.0 sq ft)	Cruising speed	97 knots (180 km/h; 112 mph)		

ARCTIC

ARCTIC AIRCRAFT COMPANY
PO Box 6-141, Anchorage International Airport, Alaska
99502
Telephone: 1 (907) 243 1580
PRESIDENT: William A. Diehl

The S1B2 Arctic Tern is an updated and much improved
version of the Interstate S1A, first flown in 1940. Built to
CAR.04a (aerobatic) standard, it was certificated for
operation on optional Edo floats on 20 January 1981. Both
the Arctic Tern and Privateer are being marketed only for
home construction.

ARCTIC AIRCRAFT INTERSTATE S1B2 ARCTIC TERN
TYPE: Tandem two-seat sporting and general utility aircraft.
AIRFRAME: Braced wings with Sitka spruce spars, light alloy
ribs and Dacron covering. Hoerner glassfibre wingtips.
Wing section NACA 23012. Welded steel tube fuselage
and tail unit structures, Dacron covered. Three-axis
control (ailerons, elevators, rudder, flaps). Non-
retractable tailwheel landing gear, with brakes. Optional
parking brake, floats or skis.
POWER PLANT: One 112 kW (150 hp) Textron Lycoming
O-320 flat-four engine. Fuel capacity 151 litres (40 US
gallons; 33.3 Imp gallons). Underbelly auxiliary fuel tank
optional.

DIMENSIONS, EXTERNAL:	
Wing span	11.18 m (36 ft 8 in)
Length overall: landplane	7.01 m (23 ft 0 in)
seaplane	7.32 m (24 ft 0 in)
Height overall	2.13 m (7 ft 0 in)
AREA:	
Wings, gross	17.30 m² (186.2 sq ft)

WEIGHTS (A: landplane, B: seaplane with Edo 2000 floats):

Weight empty: A	487 kg (1,073 lb)
B	521.5 kg (1,150 lb)
Baggage capacity	45 kg (100 lb)
Max T-O weight: A	862 kg (1,900 lb)
B	965 kg (2,127 lb)
PERFORMANCE:	
Max cruising speed at S/L, 75% power:	
A	102 knots (188 km/h; 117 mph)
B	91 knots (169 km/h; 105 mph)
Cruising speed, 65% power at optimum altitude:	
A	96 knots (178 km/h; 111 mph)
Stalling speed, flaps down:	
A, B	30 knots (55 km/h; 34 mph)
Max rate of climb at S/L, at max T-O weight:	
A	389 m (1,275 ft)/min
B	305 m (1,000 ft)/min
Service ceiling: A, B	5,790 m (19,000 ft)
T-O run at max T-O weight: A	99 m (325 ft)
Landing from 15 m (50 ft): A	137 m (450 ft)
Range with max fuel, 45 min reserves:	
A, 75% power	479 nm (888 km; 552 miles)
A, 65% power	566 nm (1,049 km; 652 miles)

Range with max fuel, no reserves:

B	499 nm (925 km; 575 miles)

ARCTIC AIRCRAFT INTERSTATE PRIVATEER
Four-seat development of the Arctic Tern. The following
details are provisional:
POWER PLANT: One 119 kW (160 hp) Textron Lycoming
O-320-B2B flat-four engine. Fuel capacity 151 litres (40
US gallons; 33.3 Imp gallons).

WEIGHTS:	
Weight empty	521 kg (1,148 lb)
Max T-O weight	1,021 kg (2,250 lb)
PERFORMANCE:	
Cruising speed:	
75% power at 1,065 m (3,500 ft)	
	107 knots (198 km/h; 123 mph)
65% power at 1,065 m (3,500 ft)	
	103 knots (191 km/h; 119 mph)
Stalling speed, flaps down	33 knots (61 km/h; 38 mph)
Max rate of climb at S/L	317 m (1,040 ft)/min
Service ceiling	5,790 m (19,000 ft)
T-O to and landing from 15 m (50 ft)	153 m (500 ft)
Range: at 75% power cruising speed at 915 m (3,000 ft),	
45 min reserves	600 nm (1,112 km; 691 miles)
at 65% power, reserves at above	
	650 nm (1,204 km; 748 miles)

ATI

ADVANCED TECHNOLOGIES
Newport News, Virginia

ATI, an R&D establishment, is working with Liteco
Helicopter Systems in the development of a two-seat
helicopter using a tip-jet power system. It is of pod and
boom design, with twin fins and a skid landing gear.

Construction of the blades is reportedly honeycomb
foam/composites, and the cabin (and presumably the
boom) is also of composites. Useful load may be about
181.4 kg (400 lb).

AUSTRALITE

AUSTRALITE INC
1301 Tower Square, Route 3, Ventura, California 93003
AUSTRALIAN DISTRIBUTOR:
Aeronautical Engineers Australia
Willeto, Western Australia
PRINCIPAL: Graeme Swannell

AUSTRALITE ULTRABAT
The Ultrabat, a mid-wing aerobatics competition aircraft
designed in Australia by Mr George Markey, is marketed
by this Australian-US company as an Experimental

category kit. High Tech Composites of Oxnard, California,
is manufacturing the components, which include an
all-composites tailboom and fully enclosed cockpit. In the
future higher powered engines are expected to be optional
(up to 89.5 kW; 120 hp), and a symmetrical wing has been
designed to allow upgrade to unlimited category. First flight
of the prototype took place in July 1988.
TYPE: Single-seat aerobatic competition aircraft.
AIRFRAME: Composites construction. Non-retractable tailwheel landing gear.
POWER PLANT: One 47.7 kW (64 hp) Rotax 532 or 52.2 kW
(70 hp) Rotax 583, driving a two-blade pusher propeller.
Fuel capacity 45.4 litres (12 US gallons; 10 Imp gallons).

DIMENSIONS, EXTERNAL:	
Wing span	6.40 m (21 ft 0 in)
Length of fuselage	4.88 m (16 ft 0 in)
Height over propeller	2.36 m (7 ft 9 in)
AREA:	
Wings, gross	4.88 m² (52.5 sq ft)
WEIGHTS:	
Weight empty	about 159 kg (350 lb)
Max T-O weight	295 kg (650 lb)
PERFORMANCE:	
g limits	±6

AVIAT

AVIAT INC
(Subsidiary of White International Ltd)
Airport Box 1149, Afton, Wyoming 83110
Telephone: 1 (307) 886 3151
Fax: 1 (307) 886 9674
PRESIDENT: Verdean G. Heiner
CHAIRMAN: Malcolm T. White

In 1991 the former Christen Industries Inc was taken over
by Aviat Inc (see also main Aircraft section).

AVIAT EAGLE II
The Eagle II flew for the first time in February 1977. By
1991, construction of more than 700 Eagle IIs had started
and about 350 were known to have been completed by
amateur builders. Each aircraft is built and maintained
from about 31 parts kits, requiring approximately 1,872
working hours to complete. In addition to airframe
construction and power plant, these include an electrical

system; instruments, nav/com, transponder and emergency
locator kits; seat belts; a flight kit with checklists, care
materials and flight test instructions; and a tiedown kit.
TYPE: Two-seat unlimited class homebuilt aerobatic biplane.
AIRFRAME: Wooden wing spars and ribs; moulded glassfibre
wingtip fairings; metal leading- and trailing-edges,
polyester fabric covered. Symmetrical wing section.
Ailerons on upper and lower wings, of similar construction to wings. Welded 4130N steel tube fuselage, covered
with removable light alloy panels from firewall to back of
rear seat and fabric over rear fuselage. Welded steel tube
tail unit, fabric covered. Non-retractable tailwheel
landing gear.
POWER PLANT: One 149 kW (200 hp) Textron Lycoming
AEIO-360-A1D. Fuel capacity 98.4 litres (26 US gallons;
21.6 Imp gallons). Fuel system allows unlimited inverted
flight.

DIMENSIONS, EXTERNAL:	
Wing span	6.07 m (19 ft 11 in)
Length overall	5.64 m (18 ft 6 in)
Height overall	1.98 m (6 ft 6 in)
Propeller diameter	1.93 m (6 ft 4 in)
AREA:	
Wings, gross	11.61 m² (125.0 sq ft)
WEIGHTS:	
Weight empty	465 kg (1,025 lb)
Baggage capacity	13.6 kg (30 lb)
Max T-O and landing weight	725 kg (1,600 lb)
PERFORMANCE:	
Max level speed at S/L	160 knots (296 km/h; 184 mph)
Econ cruising speed at 1,825 m (6,000 ft)	
	137 knots (254 km/h; 158 mph)
Stalling speed	51 knots (94 km/h; 58 mph)
Max rate of climb at S/L	645 m (2,120 ft)/min
Service ceiling	5,180 m (17,000 ft)
T-O run	244 m (800 ft)
Landing from 15 m (50 ft)	480 m (1,575 ft)
Range with max fuel and max payload	
	330 nm (611 km; 380 miles)
g limits	+9/–6

AVID

AVID AIRCRAFT INC
PO Box 728, 4823 Aviation Way, Caldwell, Idaho 83606
Telephone: 1 (208) 454 2600
Fax: 1 (208) 454 8608
PRESIDENT: Dean Wilson

AVID AIRCRAFT AVID FLYER
The Avid Flyer takes from 200 to 400 working hours to
assemble. It is available as a single kit, or as six separate kits
to spread the cost of purchase. It strongly influenced design
of the Indaer-Peru Chuspi light aircraft (see under Peru in
main Aircraft section).

The Avid Flyer features two forms of interchangeable
wings: the original high-lift STOL wings with unique near
full span auxiliary aerofoil flaperons and shorter span
Speed Wings using a new wing section. With the Speed
Wings fitted, cruising speed and stalling speed are raised.
The **Hauler** version has STOL wings and raised empty and
max T-O weights. The **Aerobatic** version is based on the
Speed Wings but with empty weight raised by 4.5 kg
(10 lb) and g limits of +6/–3. It is restricted to a max weight
of 386 kg (850 lb) during aerobatic manoeuvres (see also
Commuter).
TYPE: Side by side two-seat, dual-control homebuilt.
AIRFRAME: Aluminium wing spars and plywood ribs,

covered with heat shrunk Dacron. Welded fuselage,
rudder, tailplane and elevators of steel tubing, Dacron
covered except for fuselage nose which has pre-moulded
glassfibre cowlings. Fin integral with fuselage. Non-
retractable nosewheel or tailwheel landing gear. Optional
floats, skis and wheel-skis.
POWER PLANT: One 48.5 kW (65 hp) Rotax 582. Fuel
capacity 53 litres (14 US gallons; 11.7 Imp gallons) for
Flyer STOL and Hauler and 68 litres (18 US gallons; 15
Imp gallons) for Speed Wings, Commuter (see separate
entry) and Aerobatic. Similar capacity fuel tanks may be
added in port wing.

Anglin Engineering Spacewalker II built by Maxey Hester (*Howard Levy*)

Three-seat Avid Aircraft Avid Amphibian (*Anton Wettstein*)

Avid Aircraft Avid Commuter

Aviat Eagle II biplane built by Mr B. H. Grant McKay and Mr Bob Petryk of Calgary, Alberta, Canada (*Neil A. Macdougall*)

Australite Ultrabat single-seat aerobatics competition aircraft (*Geoffrey P. Jones*)

DIMENSIONS, EXTERNAL:
Wing span: STOL wings	9.11 m (29 ft 10½ in)
Speed wings	7.30 m (23 ft 11½ in)
Length overall	5.18 m (17 ft 0 in)
Height overall	1.70 m (5 ft 7 in)
Propeller diameter: STOL wings	1.80 m (5 ft 11 in)
Speed wings	1.63 m (5 ft 4 in)

AREAS:
Wings, gross: STOL wings	11.38 m² (122.46 sq ft)
Speed wings	9.04 m² (97.31 sq ft)

WEIGHTS (A: STOL, B: Speed Wings, C: Hauler, and D: Aerobatic):
Weight empty: A	193 kg (425 lb)
B	191 kg (420 lb)
C	200 kg (440 lb)
D	195 kg (430 lb)
Max T-O weight: A, B, D	413 kg (911 lb)
C	492 kg (1,085 lb)

PERFORMANCE (A: STOL, B Speed Wings, C: Hauler, and D: Aerobatic):
Max cruising speed: A, C	74 knots (137 km/h; 85 mph)
B, D	95 knots (177 km/h; 110 mph)
Stalling speed: A	28 knots (52 km/h; 32 mph)
B	29 knots (53 km/h; 33 mph)
C	31 knots (57 km/h; 35 mph)
D	35 knots (65 km/h; 40 mph)
Max rate of climb at S/L: A	427 m (1,400 ft)/min
B	366 m (1,200 ft)/min
C	270 m (886 ft)/min
D	259 m (850 ft)/min
Service ceiling: A	5,335 m (17,500 ft)
B	6,100 m (20,000 ft)

C	3,810 m (12,500 ft)
D	4,575 m (15,000 ft)
T-O run: A	34 m (110 ft)
B	39 m (125 ft)
C	191 m (625 ft)
D	92 m (300 ft)
Landing run: A	46 m (150 ft)
B, C	153 m (500 ft)
D	183 m (600 ft)
Range: A, C	295 nm (547 km; 340 miles)
B, D	491 nm (910 km; 566 miles)
g limits	+3.8 (+5.7 ultimate)

AVID AIRCRAFT AVID COMMUTER
Based on the Avid Flyer airframe and powered by a Rotax 582 CDI engine, the Commuter option includes Speed wings as standard, a 720-channel Terra nav/com, digital engine instrumentation, electric starter, compass, slip indicator and wheel fairings. Deliveries began in early 1990, with either tricycle or tailwheel landing gears.

AVID AIRCRAFT AVID AMPHIBIAN
The Avid Amphibian first flew on 12 July 1985. Kits are available. It can be built optionally for land operation only.
TYPE: Three-seat homebuilt amphibian or landplane.
AIRFRAME: Original high lift wing section. Wing structure comprises aluminium alloy tube spars, plywood ribs, and aluminium and steel drag tubes, covered with Ceconite.

Downward canted wingtips serve as stabilising floats on water. Full span trailing-edge flaperons of auxiliary aerofoil type, of similar construction to wings. Single-step flying-boat hull, with structure of steel tube, covered with glassfibre shells back to step and Ceconite over rear fuselage. Wire braced tail unit of steel tube covered with Ceconite. Retractable tailwheel landing gear.
POWER PLANT: One 48.5 kW (65 hp) Rotax 582. Fuel capacity 66 litres (17.5 US gallons; 14.6 Imp gallons). Optionally two 53 litre (14 US gallon; 11.7 Imp gallon) wing tanks.

DIMENSIONS, EXTERNAL:
Wing span	10.97 m (36 ft 0 in)
Length overall	5.92 m (19 ft 5 in)
Height overall	1.75 m (5 ft 9 in)
Propeller diameter	1.93 m (6 ft 4 in)

AREA:
Wings, gross	13.94 m² (150.0 sq ft)

WEIGHTS:
Weight empty	272 kg (600 lb)
Max T-O weight	544 kg (1,200 lb)

PERFORMANCE (at max T-O weight):
Max cruising speed	65 knots (120 km/h; 75 mph)
Stalling speed	29 knots (53 km/h; 33 mph)
Max rate of climb at S/L	286 m (940 ft)/min
Service ceiling	3,580 m (11,750 ft)
T-O run: on land	92 m (300 ft)
on water	230 m (756 ft)
Landing run: on land	183 m (600 ft)
on water	84 m (275 ft)
Range	278 nm (515 km; 320 miles)

BARNETT
BARNETT ROTORCRAFT
4307 Olivehurst Avenue, Olivehurst, California 95961
Telephone: 1 (916) 742 7416
Fax: 1 (916) 743 6866
PRESIDENT: K. Jerrie Barnett

Plans, materials, welded components and kits of parts are made available to construct the single-seat J 4B and two-seat J 4B-2 gyroplanes.

BARNETT J 4B and J 4B-2
The single-seat J 4B first flew in prototype form on 15

July 1968. For those wishing to construct a two-seat J 4B-2, a set of J 4B plans has to be purchased along with a set of modification plans which details the necessary changes to produce the two-seat configuration. The aluminium rotor blades, hand laid-up nacelle and engine cooling cowls are available ready fabricated.

TYPE: Single-seat (J 4B) and two-seat (J 4B-2) autogyros.
ROTOR SYSTEM: Two-blade autorotating rotor, of bonded aluminium alloy.
AIRFRAME: All-metal structure of welded 4130 chrome-molybdenum steel tubing, with fabric covered tail surfaces. Glassfibre fuselage nacelle. Non-retractable tricycle landing gear.

POWER PLANT: One 48.5-74.5 kW (65-100 hp) Teledyne Continental engine, of A65 through to O-200 type, for J 4B; 74.5 kW (100 hp) Teledyne Continental O-200 to a 134 kW (180 hp) Textron Lycoming O-360 for J 4B-2. Fuel capacity 51 litres (13.5 US gallons; 11.2 Imp gallons) in small tank or 64.4 litres (17 US gallons; 14.2 Imp gallons) in large tank.

DIMENSIONS, EXTERNAL (A: J 4B, B: J 4B-2):
Rotor diameter: A	7.01 m (23 ft 0 in)
B	7.72 m (25 ft 4 in)
Length overall, without rotor: A	3.76 m (12 ft 4 in)
B	4.17 m (13 ft 8 in)
Height overall: A	2.34 m (7 ft 8 in)
B	2.46 m (8 ft 1 in)

AREAS:		
Rotor disc: A		38.70 m² (416.59 sq ft)
B		46.95 m² (505.39 sq ft)
WEIGHTS (A and B as above):		
Baggage capacity: A		13.6 kg (30 lb)
B		9 kg (20 lb)
Normal T-O weight: A, no battery		333 kg (734.5 lb)
B		456 kg (1,005.5 lb)
Max T-O weight: A		363 kg (800 lb)
B		492 kg (1,085 lb)

PERFORMANCE (A and B as above):		
Max level speed: A		109 knots (201 km/h; 125 mph)
B		97 knots (180 km/h; 112 mph)
Cruising speed:		
A, A65 engine	69 knots (129 km/h; 80 mph) IAS	
B, O-200 engine		
	69-78 knots (129-145 km/h; 80-90 mph) IAS	
B, O-360 engine		
	87-104 knots (161-193 km/h; 100-120 mph) IAS	

Max rate of climb at S/L: A	457 m (1,500 ft)/min
B	152 m (500 ft)/min
Service ceiling: A	3,660 m (12,000 ft)
B	2,440 m (8,000 ft)
T-O run: A	107 m (350 ft)
B	183 m (600 ft)
Landing run: A	0-6 m (0-20 ft)
B	8 m (25 ft)

BARRACUDA
W. B. BUETHE ENTERPRISES INC
PO Box 486, Cathedral City, California 92234
Telephone: 1 (619) 324 9455
PRESIDENT: Dr William B. Buethe

BARRACUDA

The prototype Barracuda flew for the first time on 29 June 1975. Plans and kits are available, and about 30 Barracudas are flying from 530 sets of plans sold. The engine mount and cowling, and the landing gear are available as individual prefabricated components.
TYPE: Side by side two-seat, dual-control sporting homebuilt.
AIRFRAME: Plywood covered all-wood construction, except

for glassfibre used in ailerons and for tailplane tips. Wing section NACA 64₂415. Retractable tricycle landing gear.
POWER PLANT: One 186 kW (250 hp) Textron Lycoming IO-540-C4B5 or other engines including O-540s of 175-194 kW (235-260 hp), IO-360 or Teledyne Continental O-470. Fuel capacity 151 litres (40 US gallons; 33.3 Imp gallons). Provision for two 23 litre (6 US gallon; 5 Imp gallon) auxiliary tanks in outboard wing panels.

DIMENSIONS, EXTERNAL:	
Wing span	7.54 m (24 ft 9 in)
Length overall	6.55 m (21 ft 6 in)
Propeller diameter	2.13 m (7 ft 0 in)
AREA:	
Wings, gross	11.15 m² (120.0 sq ft)
WEIGHTS:	
Weight empty	698 kg (1,540 lb)
Baggage capacity	27 kg (60 lb)
Max T-O weight	1,043 kg (2,300 lb)

PERFORMANCE:	
Max level speed at 2,135 m (7,000 ft)	
	181 knots (335 km/h; 208 mph)
Max cruising speed	165 knots (306 km/h; 190 mph)
Econ cruising speed	143 knots (266 km/h; 165 mph)
Stalling speed: clean	56 knots (103 km/h; 64 mph)
wheels and flaps down	54 knots (100 km/h; 62 mph)
Max rate of climb at S/L	762 m (2,500 ft)/min
Service ceiling	4,875 m (16,000 ft)
T-O run	244 m (800 ft)
Landing run	458 m (1,500 ft)
Range with max payload	694 nm (1,287 km; 800 miles)
Endurance	4 h
g limits	+8/−6

BOAC
BARNEY OLDFIELD AIRCRAFT COMPANY
PO Box 228, Needham, Massachusetts 02192
Telephone: 1 (617) 444 5480
TECHNICAL DIRECTOR: R. M. Dick Lane

OLDFIELD 'BABY' LAKES

Plans and material kits are available for this scaled-down version of the Great Lakes Sport Trainer. More than 930 sets of plans have been sold and about 100 aircraft are flying.
TYPE: Single-seat homebuilt sporting biplane.
AIRFRAME: Wooden wings, fabric covered. Wing section modified M6, tapering to USA 27 46 cm (18 in) from tips. Ailerons on lower wings only. Welded steel tube fuselage and tail unit, fabric covered. Non-retractable tailwheel landing gear.
POWER PLANT: One 63.4 kW (85 hp) Teledyne Continental. Provision for alternative engines of between 37.25 and 74.5 kW (50 and 100 hp). Fuel capacity 45 litres (12 US gallons; 10 Imp gallons).

DIMENSIONS, EXTERNAL:	
Wing span, upper	5.08 m (16 ft 8 in)
Length overall	4.19 m (13 ft 9 in)
Height overall	1.37 m (4 ft 6 in)
AREA:	
Wings, gross	7.99 m² (86.0 sq ft)
WEIGHTS (59.5 kW; 80 hp A80 engine):	
Weight empty	215 kg (475 lb)
Max T-O weight	385 kg (850 lb)
PERFORMANCE (A80 engine, at max T-O weight):	
Max level speed at S/L	117 knots (217 km/h; 135 mph)
Cruising speed at S/L	102 knots (190 km/h; 118 mph)
Stalling speed	44 knots (81 km/h; 50 mph)

Max rate of climb at S/L	610 m (2,000 ft)/min
Service ceiling	5,200 m (17,000 ft)
T-O run	91 m (300 ft)
Landing run (no brakes)	122 m (400 ft)
Max range	217 nm (400 km; 250 miles)
g limits	±9

OLDFIELD 'SUPER BABY' LAKES

The prototype 'Super Baby' Lakes flew for the first time in 1976. It was developed as a more powerful and modified variant of the 'Baby' Lakes. Plans are available.
POWER PLANT: One Textron Lycoming engine in 80.5-93 kW (108-125 hp) range. Header tank fitted.

DIMENSIONS, EXTERNAL:	
As for 'Baby' Lakes, except:	
Length overall	4.34 m (14 ft 3 in)
WEIGHTS:	
Weight empty	218 kg (480 lb)
Max T-O weight	385 kg (850 lb)
PERFORMANCE:	
Max level speed	135 knots (249 km/h; 155 mph) IAS
Cruising speed, 75% power	
	117 knots (217 km/h; 135 mph) IAS
Stalling speed	48 knots (89 km/h; 55 mph) IAS
Max rate of climb at S/L	915 m (3,000 ft)/min
T-O run	69 m (225 ft)
Landing run	130 m (425 ft)
Max range, with wing tanks	260 nm (483 km; 300 miles)

OLDFIELD 'BUDDY BABY' LAKES

The two-seat 'Buddy Baby' utilises standard 'Baby' wings and tail unit. To prevent a significant increase in wing loading, a 41 cm (16 in) upper wing centre-section has been introduced, together with short stub-wings built integrally

with the fuselage to increase the lower span by a similar amount.

The fuselage has been widened and stretched to permit seating positions for two average-sized (77 kg; 170 lb) people in a configuration much like that of a 'buddy seat' on a motorcycle. Dual throttle, rudder pedals and brakes are provided, with a single dual-position joystick. The aircraft is flown solo from the rear seat and dual from the front position. The prototype first flew in July 1987. Plans, components, and material kits are available. A bubble canopy is optional.
POWER PLANT: One engine in 48.5-100.7 kW (65-135 hp) range.

DIMENSIONS, EXTERNAL:	
Wing span	5.49 m (18 ft 0 in)
Length overall	4.47 m (14 ft 8 in)
Height overall	1.91 m (6 ft 3 in)
Propeller diameter	1.70 m (5 ft 7 in)
AREA:	
Wings, gross	8.92 m² (96.0 sq ft)
WEIGHTS:	
Weight empty	243 kg (535 lb)
Max T-O weight	453 kg (1,000 lb)
PERFORMANCE (prototype with 85.75 kW; 115 hp Textron Lycoming engine and two crew):	
Max level speed at 1,065 m (3,500 ft)	
	135 knots (249 km/h; 155 mph)
Econ cruising speed at 1,065 m (3,500 ft)	
	113 knots (209 km/h; 130 mph)
Stalling speed, flaps up and engine idling	
	48 knots (89 km/h; 55 mph)
T-O run	92 m (300 ft)
Landing run	122 m (400 ft)
Range with wing tanks	260 nm (482 km; 300 miles)
Endurance	2 h 15 min
g limits	+7/−6

BOWERS
PETER M. BOWERS
10458 16th Avenue South, Seattle, Washington 98168
Telephone: 1 (206) 242 2582

BOWERS FLY BABY 1-A

The prototype Fly Baby monoplane was produced to compete in an Experimental Aircraft Association design contest, organised to encourage the development of a simple, low-cost, easy-to-fly aeroplane that could be built by inexperienced amateurs for recreational flying. It flew for the first time on 27 July 1960. Plans are available and about 4,300 sets had been sold by early 1991. Construction of well over 700 Fly Babys is known to have been undertaken, of which about 420 have flown.

Several individual amateur builders amended the plans during 1973 to allow for construction of two-seat versions of the Fly Baby. Although Mr Bowers does not recommend this conversion, he has made some additions to the plans to cater for it.

The following description applies to the original single-seat Fly Baby 1-A:
TYPE: Single-seat homebuilt.
AIRFRAME: All-wood construction, except for Dacron covering on wings and tail unit. Wing section NACA

4412. Non-retractable tailwheel landing gear. Examples have flown with floats and skis. Cockpit canopy optional.
POWER PLANT: One 63.5 kW (85 hp) Teledyne Continental C85. Suited to modified Volkswagen engines of over 1,800 cc. Fuel capacity 60.5 litres (16 US gallons; 13.3 Imp gallons).

DIMENSIONS, EXTERNAL:	
Wing span	8.53 m (28 ft 0 in)
Length overall	5.64 m (18 ft 6 in)
Height, wings folded	1.98 m (6 ft 6 in)
WEIGHTS:	
Weight empty	274 kg (605 lb)
Max T-O weight	419 kg (924 lb)
PERFORMANCE (at max T-O weight):	
Max level speed at S/L	
	over 104 knots (193 km/h; 120 mph)
Cruising speed	
	91-96 knots (169-177 km/h; 105-110 mph)
Landing speed	39 knots (73 km/h; 45 mph)
Max rate of climb at S/L	335 m (1,100 ft)/min
T-O and landing run	76 m (250 ft)
Range with max fuel	277 nm (515 km; 320 miles)

BOWERS FLY BABY 1-B

During 1968 Mr Bowers designed and built a set of interchangeable biplane wings for the original prototype

Fly Baby and with these fitted it flew for the first time on 27 March 1969. About 18 more biplanes, designated Fly Baby 1-B, have been completed and flown. The biplane wings have the same aerofoil section and incidence as those of the monoplane version, but incorporate aluminium alloy wingtip bows. Ailerons are fitted to the lower wings only. Changeover from monoplane to biplane configuration can be accomplished by two people in approximately one hour.

The biplane is intended to use the same engines as the monoplane, for which Mr Bowers does not recommend anything heavier than the Teledyne Continental O-200. Since some biplane builders have desired to use the 93 kW (125 hp) Textron Lycoming O-290, a modification has been authorised for the biplane, whereby the wing sweep is decreased by 5° for CG reasons.
TYPE: Single-seat homebuilt biplane.

DIMENSIONS, EXTERNAL:	
Wing span	6.71 m (22 ft 0 in)
Height overall	2.08 m (6 ft 10 in)
AREA:	
Wings, gross	13.94 m² (150.0 sq ft)
WEIGHTS:	
Weight empty	295 kg (651 lb)
Max T-O weight	440 kg (972 lb)
PERFORMANCE (at max T-O weight):	
Cruising speed	75 knots (140 km/h; 87 mph)
Max rate of climb at S/L	267 m (875 ft)/min

Barnett Rotorcraft J 4B-2 two-seater

Barracuda two-seat sporting monoplane, built by Dr W. B. Buethe
(Geoffrey P. Jones)

Oldfield (BOAC) 'Buddy Baby' Lakes *(Sally Lane)*

Bowers Fly Baby 1-A (Teledyne Continental A65 engine) built by Mr Eugene
Fisher of Seattle, Washington *(Peter M. Bowers)*

BX-200 cross-country homebuilt, designed by Mr Uriel Bristol

Ken Brock KB-2 Freedom Machine

BRISTOL
URIEL BRISTOL
1904 South West 85th Avenue, North Lauderdale, Florida
33068

BRISTOL BX-200
First flown as a prototype on 15 July 1986, the BX-200
has the general appearance of an enlarged Cassutt but is an
original design. Plans and kits are available; assembly time
for the kit is under 1,000 working hours.
TYPE: Side by side two-seat cross-country homebuilt.
AIRFRAME: Wooden wings, with NACA 2300 laminar flow
section, and Ceconite covered steel tube control surfaces.

Remainder of airframe has welded steel tube structure,
Ceconite covered except for glassfibre forward fuselage
skins, engine cowling and canopy frame. Non-retractable
tailwheel landing gear.
POWER PLANT: One 134 kW (180 hp) Textron Lycoming
O-360-A4A. Fuel capacity 102 litres (27 US gallons; 22.5
Imp gallons).
DIMENSIONS, EXTERNAL:

Wing span	6.10 m (20 ft 0 in)
Length overall	5.31 m (17 ft 5 in)
Height overall	1.50 m (4 ft 11 in)
Propeller diameter	1.83 m (6 ft 0 in)

AREA:

Wings. gross	8.36 m² (90.0 sq ft)

WEIGHTS:

Weight empty	363 kg (800 lb)
Baggage capacity	22.7 kg (50 lb)
Max T-O weight	612 kg (1,350 lb)

PERFORMANCE:

Max level speed at S/L	215 knots (398 km/h; 247 mph)
Econ cruising speed at 2,135 m (7,000 ft)	
	190 knots (352 km/h; 219 mph)
Max rate of climb at S/L	610 m (2,000 ft)/min
Service ceiling	6,100 m (20,000 ft)
T-O and landing run	457 m (1,500 ft)
Range	500 nm (926 km; 575 miles)
Endurance	2 h 30 min
g limits	+6/−3

BROCK
KEN BROCK MANUFACTURING INC
(Division of Santa Ana Metal Stamping)
11852 Western Avenue, Stanton, California 90680
Telephone: 1 (714) 898 4366
Fax: 1 (714) 894 0811
See also Microlight tables for KB-3 and Avion.

KEN BROCK KB-2 FREEDOM MACHINE
The KB-2 prototype flew in 1970. Manufacture of kits
began in 1979; several hundred have been sold.
The KB-2 is built from eight kits of parts. Assembly of the
basic airframe takes approximately 1½ hours, and the KB-2
can be assembled ready for testing in unpowered form in
one weekend.

TYPE: Single-seat homebuilt autogyro.
ROTOR SYSTEM: Single two-blade semi-rigid rotor, of
all-metal construction. Blade section modified Clark Y.
AIRFRAME: All-aluminium alloy construction, but with
alternative wooden tail unit. Non-retractable tricycle
landing gear.

POWER PLANT: One 53.7 kW (72 hp) McCulloch 4318A or Volkswagen modified motorcar engine (max power rating 74.5 kW; 100 hp). Patented seat/fuel tank, capacity 33.7 litres (8.9 US gallons; 7.4 Imp gallons).

DIMENSIONS, EXTERNAL:

Rotor diameter	6.70 m (22 ft 0 in)
Length of fuselage	3.43 m (11 ft 3 in)
Max height	2.03 m (6 ft 8 in)
Propeller diameter	1.22 m (4 ft 0 in)

AREA:

Rotor disc	35.32 m² (380.1 sq ft)

WEIGHTS:

Weight empty	109 kg (240 lb)
Max T-O weight	272 kg (600 lb)

PERFORMANCE (at max T-O weight):

Max level speed	78 knots (145 km/h; 90 mph)
Econ cruising speed	52 knots (97 km/h; 60 mph)
Min level speed	22 knots (40 km/h; 25 mph)
Max rate of climb at S/L	366 m (1,200 ft)/min
Service ceiling	3,050 m (10,000 ft)
T-O run	61 m (200 ft)
Landing run	3 m (10 ft)
Range with max fuel	130 nm (241 km; 150 miles)
Endurance	2 h

BROWN

MICHAEL BROWN

c/o Climber Aviation, 2909 Edgemoor Lane, Dayton, Ohio 45439
Telephone: 1 (513) 223 8730

Details of the Ascent I Tribute, and an illustration, can be found in the 1989-90 *Jane's*. Development is believed to continue.

BUSHBY

BUSHBY AIRCRAFT INC

674 Route 52, Minooka, Illinois 60447
Telephone: 1 (815) 467 2346
PRESIDENT: Robert Bushby

The Midget Mustang and M-II Mustang II are available in plans and kit forms.

BUSHBY M-1 and M-1A MIDGET MUSTANG

The prototype Midget Mustang was completed in 1948 by David Long. Robert Bushby developed new versions from the original design, of which the MM-1-85 (first flown in 1959) and MM-1-125 (first flown in 1963) were detailed in the 1990-91 and previous editions of *Jane's*. Current models are the M-1 and M-1A, for which prefabricated wing spars and ribs, and bulkheads, are available to those building from plans.

M-1. Basic version, with higher rated engine than previous MM-1 models.

M-1A. Development of the MM-1/M-1, with lowered turtledeck and bubble canopy. Suited to pilots up to 1.93 m (6 ft 4 in) tall, and offering better visibility. No performance changes. Alterations can be retrofitted to existing aircraft.

Approximately 360 Midget Mustangs had been completed by early 1991, with 1,100 more under construction throughout the world.

TYPE: Single-seat fully aerobatic sporting homebuilt.

AIRFRAME: All-aluminium alloy flush riveted construction. Wing section NACA 64A212 at root, NACA 64A210 at tip. Non-retractable tailwheel landing gear. Some examples built with retractable gear.

POWER PLANT: One 74.5 kW (100 hp) Teledyne Continental O-200 or Textron Lycoming O-290 or O-320 engine of up to 119 kW (160 hp). Fuel capacity 57 litres (15 US gallons; 12.5 Imp gallons). Optional integral wing fuel tanks, each with capacity of 47 litres (12.5 US gallons; 10.4 Imp gallons).

DIMENSIONS, EXTERNAL:

Wing span	5.64 m (18 ft 6 in)
Length overall	5.03 m (16 ft 6 in)
Height overall	1.37 m (4 ft 6 in)
Propeller diameter	1.52 m (5 ft 0 in)

AREA:

Wings, gross	6.32 m² (68.0 sq ft)

WEIGHTS:

Weight empty	249 kg (550 lb)
Baggage capacity	9 kg (20 lb)
Max T-O weight	408 kg (900 lb)

PERFORMANCE (O-200 engine):

Max level speed	182 knots (338 km/h; 210 mph)
Max cruising speed	174 knots (322 km/h; 200 mph)
Stalling speed, flaps down	50 knots (92 km/h; 57 mph)
Max rate of climb at S/L	488 m (1,600 ft)/min
Service ceiling	5,485 m (18,000 ft)
T-O and landing run	153 m (500 ft)
Range	390 nm (724 km; 450 miles)
Endurance	2 h 30 min
g limits	±9 ultimate

BUSHBY M-II MUSTANG II

This side by side two-seat derivative of the Midget Mustang flew for the first time on 9 July 1966. About 1,200 Mustang IIs were being built by amateurs in early 1991, at which time about 300 had been completed.

The description applies to the de luxe model, which is stressed for +6g. The empty weight quoted includes IFR instrumentation and nav/com equipment. The M-II can also be operated as an aerobatic aircraft in what Bushby Aircraft calls the 'Sport' configuration. This is identical to the de luxe model except that the electrical system, radio, additional IFR instrumentation, soundproofing and upholstery, wheel fairings, and some baggage capacity are deleted. The 'Sport' model has an empty weight of 340 kg (750 lb), T-O weight of 567 kg (1,250 lb) and is stressed for +9g.

TYPE: Two-seat, dual-control sporting homebuilt.

AIRFRAME: All-aluminium alloy flush riveted construction. Wing section NACA 64A212 at root, NACA 64A210 at tip. Standard version has non-retractable tailwheel landing gear. Alternative non-retractable tricycle gear.

POWER PLANT: Normally one 119 kW (160 hp) Textron Lycoming O-320. Provision for other engines including a 93 kW (125 hp) Textron Lycoming O-290. Fuel capacity 94.6 litres (25 US gallons; 21 Imp gallons). Optional integral wing fuel tanks, each with a capacity of 45 litres (12 US gallons; 10 Imp gallons). Provision for wingtip tanks.

DIMENSIONS, EXTERNAL:

Wing span	7.37 m (24 ft 2 in)
Length overall	5.94 m (19 ft 6 in)
Height overall	1.60 m (5 ft 3 in)
Propeller diameter: 93 kW (125 hp)	1.73 m (5 ft 8 in)
119 kW (160 hp)	1.83 m (6 ft 0 in)

AREA:

Wings, gross	9.02 m² (97.12 sq ft)

WEIGHTS:

Weight empty, equipped, 119 kW (160 hp) engine and tailwheel landing gear	420 kg (927 lb)
Baggage capacity	34 kg (75 lb)
*Max T-O weight	680 kg (1,500 lb)

*Except for countries that restrict max wing loading to 73.2 kg/m² (15 lb/sq ft), where T-O weight of 658 kg (1,450 lb) applies

PERFORMANCE (119 kW; 160 hp engine, tailwheel landing gear, at max T-O weight):

Max level speed at S/L	200 knots (370 km/h; 230 mph)
Max cruising speed at 2,285 m (7,500 ft)	181 knots (335 km/h; 208 mph)

Stalling speed:

flaps up	53 knots (96 km/h; 60 mph)
flaps down	51 knots (94 km/h; 58 mph)
Max rate of climb at S/L	670 m (2,200 ft)/min
Service ceiling	6,400 m (21,000 ft)
T-O run	137 m (450 ft)
Landing run	168 m (550 ft)

Range: with standard fuel, 75% power
373 nm (692 km; 430 miles)
with optional wingtip tanks
542 nm (1,005 km; 625 miles)

CABRINHA

CABRINHA ENGINEERING INC

7000 Merrill Avenue, Box 41, Chino Airport, Chino, California 91710
Telephone: 1 (714) 597 2888/722 3142
Fax: 1 (714) 722 6555
PRESIDENT: Richard Cabrinha

This company was formerly known as Free Spirit Aircraft Company Inc and later Cabrinha Aircraft Corporation.

CABRINHA FREE SPIRIT MARK II

The RC-412D Free Spirit Mark I prototype and test aircraft was powered by a 112 kW (150 hp) Textron Lycoming engine and flew for the first time in July 1986. Production of Mark II kits began in 1988. By late December 1990, 13 kits had been ordered and delivered, the first of which flew in January 1991. An order has been placed from Pakistan for aircraft to be used for training.

TYPE: Side by side two-seat, dual-control homebuilt.

AIRFRAME: Mostly of glassfibre and Nomex honeycomb composites construction, but with fiberfoam forming ailerons, flaps, elevators and rudder, and with glassfibre/balsa bulkhead and glassfibre/balsa/fiber fax/stainless steel firewall. Wing section NASA 0215. Retractable tricycle landing gear, with brakes.

POWER PLANT: One 156.6 kW (210 hp) Teledyne Continental IO-360ES. Fuel capacity 189 litres (50 US gallons; 41.6 Imp gallons).

DIMENSIONS, EXTERNAL:

Wing span	8.62 m (28 ft 3½ in)
Length overall	6.25 m (20 ft 6 in)
Height overall	2.13 m (7 ft 0 in)
Propeller diameter	1.83 m (6 ft 0 in)

AREA:

Wings, gross	7.62 m² (82.0 sq ft)

WEIGHTS:

Weight empty	420 kg (925 lb)
Baggage capacity	90 kg (200 lb)
Max T-O weight	839 kg (1,850 lb)

PERFORMANCE:

Max level speed at S/L	243 knots (450 km/h; 280 mph)
Max cruising speed at S/L	217 knots (402 km/h; 250 mph)
Econ cruising speed at 3,660 m (12,000 ft)	210 knots (389 km/h; 242 mph)
Stalling speed: clean, solo	55 knots (102 km/h; 63 mph)
max AUW, flaps down	52 knots (97 km/h; 60 mph)
Max rate of climb at S/L, solo	915 m (3,000 ft)/min
Service ceiling	7,010 m (23,000 ft)
T-O run: solo	119 m (390 ft)
max AUW	168 m (550 ft)
Landing run	153 m (500 ft)
Range	955 nm (1,770 km; 1,100 miles)
Endurance	4 h 30 min
g limits	+9/−6

CARLSON

CARLSON AIRCRAFT INC

50643 State Route 14, East Palestine, Ohio 44413
Telephone: 1 (216) 426 3934
Fax: 1 (216) 426 1144
PRESIDENT: Ernest W. Carlson

See also Microlight tables for the Sparrow.

CARLSON SPARROW SPORT SPECIAL

This Experimental category homebuilt is a single-seater, suited to engines of 28.3 to 38.8 kW (38 to 52 hp). It is the only version of the Sparrow to have a taildragger landing gear.

TYPE: Single-seat homebuilt.

POWER PLANT: See above. Fuel capacity 30 litres (8 US gallons; 6.66 Imp gallons).

DIMENSIONS, EXTERNAL:

Wing span	7.92 m (26 ft 0 in)
Length overall	5.11 m (16 ft 9 in)
Height overall	2.06 m (6 ft 9 in)

AREA:

Wings, gross	12.08 m² (130.0 sq ft)

WEIGHTS:

Weight empty	150 kg (330 lb)
Max T-O weight	311 kg (685 lb)

PERFORMANCE:

Max level speed	87 knots (161 km/h; 100 mph)
Cruising speed	74 knots (137 km/h; 85 mph)
Stalling speed	31 knots (57 km/h; 35 mph)
Max rate of climb at S/L	305 m (1,000 ft)/min
T-O run, min loading	23 m (75 ft)
Landing run	77 m (250 ft)
Range at cruising speed	260 nm (482 km; 300 miles)
g limits	+4/−3

CARLSON SPARROW II

This is basically an enlarged side by side two-seat derivative of the Sparrow Sport Special, offering dual controls, short field performance, 38 litre (10 US gallon; 8.3 Imp gallon) fuel capacity, and a baggage compartment with a 9 kg (20 lb) capacity. Options include different engines of 47.7 to 74.5 kW (64 to 100 hp), 91 litre (24 US gallon; 20 Imp

Bushby M-1 Midget Mustang built by Kit Sodergren of Sacramento
(Geoffrey P. Jones)

Carlson Sparrow II two-seat homebuilt *(Howard Levy)*

Bushby M-II Mustang II owned by A. G. Culvinor in Australia (O-320 engine)

Cirrus Design Corporation Cirrus VK30 four/five-seat homebuilt aircraft
(J. M. G. Gradidge)

Cabrinha Free Spirit Mark II two-seat homebuilt

---

gallon) total capacity wing tanks, and ski and float landing gears. Kits are available.

TYPE: Side by side two-seat homebuilt.

DIMENSIONS, EXTERNAL:

Wing span	9.50 m (31 ft 2¼ in)
Length overall	5.49 m (18 ft 0 in)
Height overall	2.36 m (7 ft 9 in)

AREA:

Wings, gross	13.00 m² (140.0 sq ft)

WEIGHTS:

Weight empty	231 kg (510 lb)
Max T-O weight	476 kg (1,050 lb)

PERFORMANCE (48.5 kW; 65 hp engine):

Cruising speed	78 knots (145 km/h; 90 mph)
Stalling speed	30 knots (55 km/h; 34 mph)
Max rate of climb at S/L	305 m (1,000 ft)/min
T-O run, min loading	39 m (125 ft)
Landing run	77 m (250 ft)
Range at cruising speed	260 nm (483 km; 300 miles)
g limits	+4/−3

CARLSON SPARROW-ETTE

Complying to the ARV category, the new Sparrow-ette is based on the Sparrow II but has been lightened, the wing chord extended and flaperons replace ailerons and flaps. Fuel capacity remains unchanged but engine power is between 35.8-47.7 kW (48-64 hp). The crew occupy a bench seat instead of bucket seats. Kits are available.

TYPE: Side by side two-seat ARV.

DIMENSIONS, EXTERNAL: As for Sparrow II

AREA:

Wings, gross	14.40 m² (155.0 sq ft)

PERFORMANCE:

Cruising speed	56 knots (105 km/h; 65 mph)
Stalling speed	27 knots (50 km/h; 31 mph)
Max rate of climb at S/L	305 m (1,000 ft)/min
T-O run, min loading	31 m (100 ft)
Landing run	77 m (250 ft)
g limits	+4/−3

CARLSON SKYCYCLE '87

Designed and built by Mr Neal K. Carlson, the original Skycycle first appeared in 1945. The fuselage was constructed from a Second World War drop tank. Only the prototype was built (with a 41 kW; 55 hp Textron Lycoming O-145A engine) and this was destroyed in a fire in about 1946.

The much refined Skycycle '87 became available in 1991 in ready assembled form. The basic structure is of welded steel tubing, with glassfibre skins and a Plexiglas bubble canopy. Anticipated empty weight was 134 kg (295 lb) with a 44.7 kW (60 hp) engine installed.

The following dimensions refer to the original Skycycle, but are likely to be close to those for the Skycycle '87.

DIMENSIONS, EXTERNAL (original Skycycle prototype):

Wing span	6.10 m (20 ft 0 in)
Length overall	4.83 m (15 ft 10 in)

CHRISTEN — *See Aviat*

CIRRUS

CIRRUS DESIGN CORPORATION

Baraboo-Dells Airport, S2440A Highway 12, Baraboo, Wisconsin 53913

Telephone: 1 (608) 356 3460
Fax: 1 (608) 356 2269
PRESIDENT: Alan Klapmeier

CIRRUS DESIGN CIRRUS VK30

First flown on 11 February 1988, the Cirrus is available in prefabricated kit form and 40 had been sold by early 1991, of which 20 had been delivered. Major design features include new laminar flow wing sections, large Fowler flaps, and a tail mounted pusher propeller. Three aircraft have flown, including an Allison 250-B17C turboprop powered version. However, the current model concentrates on the IO-550/TSIO-550 engine.

TYPE: Four/five-seat high-performance homebuilt.

AIRFRAME: Cantilever low-wing monoplane. Wing sections based on NASA NLF(1)-0414F. Wings constructed of glassfibre and PVC foam, with graphite spar. Fuselage has polyurethane foam core, graphite longerons and glassfibre skins. Ailerons/Fowler flaps/cruise flaps are of graphite/PVC/vinylester, and rudder/elevators of Kevlar/PVC/vinylester. Retractable tricycle landing gear.

POWER PLANT: One 224 kW (300 hp) Teledyne Continental IO-550-G or 261 kW (350 hp) TSIO-550-A engine, driving a Hoffman HO-V 123K or MT MTV-9 three-blade pusher propeller. Fuel capacity 397 litres (105 US gallons; 87.4 Imp gallons).

DIMENSIONS, EXTERNAL:

Wing span	12.04 m (39 ft 6 in)
Length overall	7.92 m (26 ft 0 in)
Height overall	3.25 m (10 ft 8 in)
Propeller diameter	1.88 m (6 ft 2 in)

AREA:

Wings, gross	11.71 m² (126.0 sq ft)

WEIGHTS:

Weight empty	1,089 kg (2,400 lb)
Max T-O weight	1,610 kg (3,550 lb)

PERFORMANCE (with TSIO-550-A engine):

Cruising speed, 75% power	more than 260 knots (483 km/h; 300 mph)
Stalling speed, flaps down, engine idling	56 knots (104 km/h; 65 mph)
Max rate of climb at S/L	503 m (1,650 ft)/min
T-O run	412 m (1,350 ft)
Landing run	328 m (1,075 ft)
Range with max fuel, 75% power, with reserves	1,346 nm (2,494 km; 1,550 miles)
g limits	+5/−3

CLASSIC

CLASSIC AIRCRAFT REPLICAS INC

c/o Building 411, Opa-Locka Airport, Opa-Locka, Florida 33054

PRESIDENT: Fred F. McCallum

CLASSIC AIRCRAFT REPLICAS LM-5X

This is a full-size representation of a Piper Super Cub type of braced high-wing monoplane, first flown on 7 April 1990. It uses a similar bonded aluminium alloy form of construction as the related Light Miniature Aircraft range, and this latter company is producing the kits under contract. Power is provided by a Rotax 532 engine, and control surfaces include flaps and flight trim. Empty weight is 227 kg (610 lb).

COBRA

COBRA HELICOPTERS

PO Box 396, Danville, Indiana 46122
Telephone: 1 (317) 252 3550

Cobra Helicopters is believed to market plans and kits to construct the single-seat Mustang and two-seat Cobra helicopters, of which brief details fo low.

COBRA HELICOPTERS COBRA

This streamline side by side two-seat helicopter can be assembled in a few weeks from a kit containing premoulded components forming the Kevlar structure. Power is provided by a 112 kW (150 hp) Textron Lycoming engine, which allows a cruising speed of 87 knots (161 km/h; 100 mph).

COBRA HELICOPTERS MUSTANG

The Mustang is a single-seat lightweight and low cost helicopter powered by a Rotax, Subaru or Volkswagen engine. If allowable weights for ultralights are raised in the USA, the Mustang will then comply with this category. An open structure is standard but an enclosed cabin is among options, as is agricultural spray gear.

COLLINS

COLLINS AERO

386 Fairville Road RD1, Chadds Ford, Pennsylvania 19317
Telephone: 1 (215) 388 2393
OWNER: Willard C. Collins

COLLINS AERO W-7 DIPPER

The Dipper prototype made its first flight on 24 August 1982. An information brochure and plans to allow construction of the Dipper are available to amateur constructors.

TYPE: Side by side two-seat homebuilt amphibious flying-boat.

AIRFRAME: Uses aluminium alloy wings from a Cessna 150, with floats added close to wingtips. Modified Cessna 150 basic fuselage, with instrument panel and windscreen moved forward by 0.91 m (3 ft 0 in) and glassfibre two-step boat hull and nose cowling added for water operations. Basic Cessna 150 tail unit, but with fin of increased height and tailplane raised by 0.46 m (1 ft 6 in). Dorsal fin added. Retractable tricycle landing gear.

POWER PLANT: One 134 kW (180 hp) Textron Lycoming O-360. Fuel capacity 148 litres (39 US gallons; 32.5 Imp gallons).

DIMENSIONS, EXTERNAL:

Wing span	10.16 m (33 ft 4 in)
Length overall	7.72 m (25 ft 4 in)
Height overall	2.84 m (9 ft 4 in)
Propeller diameter	1.88 m (6 ft 2 in)

AREA:

Wings, gross	14.86 m² (160.0 sq ft)

WEIGHTS:

Weight empty, equipped	481 kg (1,060 lb)
Max T-O weight	798 kg (1,760 lb)

PERFORMANCE:

Max level speed at 2,135 m (7,000 ft)	120 knots (222 km/h; 138 mph)
Econ cruising speed	100 knots (185 km/h; 115 mph)
Stalling speed	39 knots (73 km/h; 45 mph)
Max rate of climb at S/L	427 m (1,400 ft)/min
Service ceiling	6,700 m (22,000 ft)
T-O run	122 m (400 ft)
Landing run	152 m (500 ft)
Range with max fuel	500 nm (926 km; 575 miles)

Co Z

Co Z DEVELOPMENT CORPORATION

2046 North 63rd Place, Mesa, Arizona 85205
Telephone: 1 (602) 981 6401

Co Z COZY Mk IV

Details of Nathan D. Puffer's Cozy side by side two-seat development of the Rutan Long-EZ can be found in the 1987-88 *Jane's*. Design rights were sold to Co Z Europe in 1987 (see Cosy Europe under Germany in this section).

Reports have been received that Mr Puffer began selling plans and a construction manual for a Mk IV version of the Cozy at the start of 1991. The prototype, first displayed at Oshkosh '88, is powered by a 134 kW (180 hp) engine.

CVJETKOVIC

ANTON CVJETKOVIC

5324 West 121 Street, Hawthorne, California 90250
Telephone: 1 (213) 643 6931

CVJETKOVIC CA-61/-61R MINI ACE

The CA-61 can be built as a single-seat or side by side two-seat light aircraft, with any Teledyne Continental engine of between 48.5 and 63.5 kW (65 and 85 hp), and with non-retractable tailwheel landing gear or retractable gear (as the CA-61R). Alternatively, the single-seater can be fitted with a modified Volkswagen engine. Plans are available. Construction takes less than 1,000 h.

The following details refer specifically to the single-seat CA-61 prototype:

TYPE: Single-seat homebuilt.

AIRFRAME: All-wood construction, with fabric only over wings and ailerons. Wing section NACA 4415. Landing gear as detailed above.

POWER PLANT: Engine options as detailed above. Fuel capacity 64 litres (17 US gallons; 14.2 Imp gallons).

DIMENSIONS, EXTERNAL:

Wing span	8.38 m (27 ft 6 in)
Length overall	5.77 m (18 ft 11 in)
Height overall (in flying position)	2.08 m (6 ft 10 in)

AREA:

Wings, gross	11.75 m² (126.5 sq ft)

WEIGHTS:

Weight empty: single-seat	275 kg (606 lb)
two-seat	363 kg (800 lb)
Max T-O weight: single-seat	430 kg (950 lb)
two-seat	590 kg (1,300 lb)

PERFORMANCE:

Max level speed at S/L	104 knots (193 km/h; 120 mph)
Normal cruising speed	87 knots (161 km/h; 100 mph)
Min flying speed:	
single-seat	37 knots (68 km/h; 42 mph)
two-seat	44 knots (81 km/h; 50 mph)
Range with max fuel:	
single-seat	369 nm (685 km; 425 miles)
two-seat	321 nm (595 km; 370 miles)

CVJETKOVIC CA-65

The prototype CA-65 flew for the first time in July 1965. Plans are available.

TYPE: Two-seat, dual-control homebuilt.

AIRFRAME: All-wood construction, with fabric covering only on ailerons, elevators and rudder. Modified NACA 4415 wing section. Retractable tailwheel landing gear.

POWER PLANT: One 93 kW (125 hp) Textron Lycoming O-290-G. Other Textron Lycoming engines of 80.5-112 kW; (108-150 hp) can be fitted. Fuel capacity 106 litres (28 US gallons; 23.3 Imp gallons).

DIMENSIONS, EXTERNAL:

Wing span	7.62 m (25 ft 0 in)
Length overall	5.79 m (19 ft 0 in)
Height overall (in flying position)	2.24 m (7 ft 4 in)
Propeller diameter	1.73 m (5 ft 8 in)

AREA:

Wings, gross	10.03 m² (108.0 sq ft)

WEIGHTS:

Weight empty	408 kg (900 lb)
Max T-O weight	680 kg (1,500 lb)

CVJETKOVIC CA-65A

This is an all-metal version of the wooden CA-65.

POWER PLANT: Structure is designed to accommodate a Textron Lycoming engine of 80.5-112 kW (108-150 hp).

DIMENSIONS, EXTERNAL: As for Model CA-65 except:

Wing span	7.75 m (25 ft 5 in)
Length overall	5.99 m (19 ft 8 in)
Height overall	2.29 m (7 ft 6 in)

AREA:

Wings, gross	10.16 m² (109.4 sq ft)

PERFORMANCE (112 kW; 150 hp engine):

Max level speed	151 knots (280 km/h; 174 mph)
Normal cruising speed	130 knots (241 km/h; 150 mph)
Stalling speed	48 knots (89 km/h; 55 mph)
Max rate of climb at S/L	466 m (1,530 ft)/min
Service ceiling	4,570 m (15,000 ft)
T-O run	99 m (325 ft)
Landing run	183 m (600 ft)
Range with max fuel	460 nm (853 km; 530 miles)
g limits	+9/−6 ultimate

PERFORMANCE (at max T-O weight):

Max level speed	156 knots (290 km/h; 180 mph)
Normal cruising speed	135 knots (249 km/h; 155 mph)
Stalling speed	48 knots (89 km/h; 55 mph)
Max rate of climb at S/L	305 m (1,000 ft)/min
Service ceiling	4,575 m (15,000 ft)
T-O run	137 m (450 ft)
Landing run	183 m (600 ft)
Range with max fuel	434 nm (804 km; 500 miles)
g limits	+9/−6 ultimate

D 2

D 2 INC

PO Box 265, Bend, Oregon 97709
PROPRIETOR: Sidney L. Ellis

D 2 Inc acquired the designs of the Davis DA-2A and DA-5A and the Aerosport Quail, and is remarketing them.

D 2 (DAVIS) DA-2A

This two-seat homebuilt was flown for the first time on 21 May 1966. D 2 Inc offers both plans and kits of the DA-2A.

The DA-2A is of all-metal construction, with a V tail and non-retractable tricycle landing gear. Power plant in the prototype was a 48.5 kW (65 hp) Teledyne Continental A65-8, but the DA-2A is stressed for engines of up to 74.5 kW (100 hp). Fuel capacity 75 litres (20 US gallons; 16.7 Imp gallons).

There is baggage space aft of the side by side seats or, alternatively, a child's seat may be located in this position.

DIMENSIONS, EXTERNAL:

Wing span	5.86 m (19 ft 2¾ in)
Length overall	5.44 m (17 ft 10¼ in)
Height overall	1.65 m (5 ft 5 in)

AREA:

Wings, gross	7.66 m² (82.5 sq ft)

WEIGHTS (A65-8 engine):

Weight empty	277 kg (610 lb)
Max T-O weight	510 kg (1,125 lb)

PERFORMANCE (A65-8 engine):

Max level speed at S/L	104 knots (193 km/h; 120 mph)
Cruising speed	100 knots (185 km/h; 115 mph)
Range with max fuel	390 nm (725 km; 450 miles)

D 2 (DAVIS) DA-5A

The first flight of the DA-5A was made on 22 July 1974. Plans are available to amateur constructors.

TYPE: Single-seat homebuilt aircraft.

AIRFRAME: All-metal stressed-skin construction with a V tail. Wing section Clark Y. Non-retractable tricycle landing gear.

POWER PLANT: One 48.5 kW (65 hp) Teledyne Continental A65. Fuel capacity 64.3 litres (17 US gallons; 14.2 Imp gallons).

DIMENSIONS, EXTERNAL:

Wing span	4.76 m (15 ft 7¼ in)
Length overall	4.80 m (15 ft 9 in)
Height overall	1.35 m (4 ft 5¼ in)
Propeller diameter	1.52 m (5 ft 0 in)

AREA:

Wings, gross	5.31 m² (57.2 sq ft)

WEIGHTS:

Weight empty	208 kg (460 lb)
Max T-O weight	351 kg (775 lb)

PERFORMANCE (at max T-O weight):

Max level speed at S/L	139 knots (257 km/h; 160 mph)

Collins Aero W-7 Dipper amphibious flying-boat

D 2 (Aerosport) Quail single-seat homebuilt aircraft

D 2 (Davis) DA-2A built by Mr Wade Hammer of Augusta, Georgia
(*Geoffrey P. Jones*)

Cvjetkovic CA-65, with extended propeller shaft and landing gear doors

D 2 (Davis) DA-5A single-seat homebuilt sporting aircraft (*J. M. G. Gradidge*)

Davis DA-7, intended for FAA certification (*Howard Levy*)

Cobra Helicopters Cobra two-seat homebuilt helicopter

Econ cruising speed at S/L	
	104 knots (193 km/h; 120 mph)
Stalling speed	52 knots (97 km/h; 60 mph)
Max rate of climb at S/L	244 m (800 ft)/min
Service ceiling	4,420 m (14,500 ft)
T-O run	183 m (600 ft)
Landing run	183 m (600 ft)
Range with max fuel	390 nm (724 km; 450 miles)

D 2 (AEROSPORT) QUAIL

The Quail, designed by Aerosport Inc, flew for the first time in December 1971. Plans and kits are available from D 2 Inc.

TYPE: Single-seat homebuilt.

AIRFRAME: All-metal construction. Wing section NACA 23015. Non-retractable tricycle landing gear.

POWER PLANT: One 1,600 cc modified Volkswagen motorcar engine. Provision for other Volkswagen engines from 1,500 cc to 1,800 cc capacity. Fuel capacity 38 litres (10 US gallons; 8.3 Imp gallons).

DIMENSIONS, EXTERNAL:

Wing span	7.32 m (24 ft 0 in)
Length overall	4.85 m (15 ft 11 in)
Height overall	1.69 m (5 ft 6½ in)
Propeller diameter	1.37 m (4 ft 6 in)

AREA:

Wings, gross	7.8 m² (84.0 sq ft)

WEIGHTS:

Weight empty	242 kg (534 lb)

Baggage capacity	9 kg (20 lb)
Normal T-O weight	345 kg (762 lb)
Max T-O weight	359 kg (792 lb)

PERFORMANCE (at max T-O weight):

Max level speed at S/L	113 knots (209 km/h; 130 mph)
Econ cruising speed	96 knots (177 km/h; 110 mph)
Stalling speed, flaps down	42 knots (78 km/h; 48 mph)
Max rate of climb at S/L	259 m (850 ft)/min
Service ceiling (estimated)	3,660 m (12,000 ft)
T-O run	91 m (300 ft)
Landing run	122 m (400 ft)
Range with max fuel, no reserves	
	200 nm (370 km; 230 miles)

D'APUZZO
NICHOLAS E. D'APUZZO
102 Blue Rock Lane, Blue Bell, Pennsylvania 19422
Telephone: 1 (215) 646 4792

D'APUZZO D-201 SPORTWING

The D-201 is a development of the earlier PJ-260/D-260 Senior Aero Sport series. Plans and partial kits of the D-201 are available.

TYPE: Tandem two-seat homebuilt sporting biplane.

AIRFRAME: All-metal construction, except for fabric covering of the rear fuselage. Wing section NACA M-12 (modified). Non-retractable tailwheel landing gear.

POWER PLANT: One 119 kW (160 hp) Textron Lycoming IO-320-B1A. Design suitable for any Textron Lycoming engine from the 93 kW (125 hp) O-235 to the 149 kW (200 hp) O-360.

DIMENSIONS, EXTERNAL:

Wing span: upper	8.23 m (27 ft 0 in)
lower	7.86 m (25 ft 9½ in)
Length overall, tail up	6.59 m (21 ft 7½ in)
Height overall, tail down	2.34 m (7 ft 8 in)

AREA:

Wings, gross	17.14 m² (184.5 sq ft)

WEIGHTS:

Weight empty	591 kg (1,303 lb)
Design max T-O weight	862 kg (1,900 lb)

PERFORMANCE (at max T-O weight):

Max level speed at 2,135 m (7,000 ft)	
	115 knots (212 km/h; 132 mph)
Max cruising speed at 2,135 m (7,000 ft)	
	106 knots (196 km/h; 122 mph)
Stalling speed	41 knots (76 km/h; 47 mph)
Max rate of climb at S/L	320 m (1,050 ft)/min
T-O run	128 m (420 ft)
Landing run	168 m (550 ft)
Range with max fuel	313 nm (579 km; 360 miles)

DAVIS

LEEON D. DAVIS

PLANS AND PARTS: Joe Gauthier, GFG Enterprises, 9 Kowal Drive, Cromwell, Connecticut 06416
Telephone: 1 (203) 635 4058

DAVIS DA-7

The side by side two-seat DA-7 was designed for certification in the proposed Primary Aircraft category and subsequent commercial production in ready to fly form. It is of conventional light alloy construction, with a V tail. Wing section is USA 35B, and power is provided by an 86 kW (115 hp) Textron Lycoming O-235-L2C engine.

DIMENSIONS, EXTERNAL:

Wing span	6.25 m (20 ft 6 in)
Length overall	5.84 m (19 ft 2 in)

AREA:

Wings, gross	8.33 m² (89.7 sq ft)

WEIGHTS:

Weight empty	327 kg (720 lb)
Max T-O weight	576 kg (1,270 lb)

PERFORMANCE:

Max cruising speed, 75% power	
	126 knots (233 km/h; 145 mph)
Stalling speed	51 knots (94 km/h; 58 mph)

DAVIS WING

DAVIS WING LTD

PO Box 1103, Nampa, Idaho 83653-1103
PRESIDENT: Gilbert E. Davis

DAVIS WING STARCRUISER GEMINI

The single-seat prototype Davis Wing, known as *Alpha*, was flown for the first time on 10 June 1986. Kits are to be offered for a five-seat version, the Starcruiser Gemini.

TYPE: Five-seat homebuilt flying wing.

AIRFRAME: Majority of airframe built of pre-moulded composites, including glassfibre, Nomex honeycomb, aramid fibres, graphite fibres and various foams. Other materials include 4130 steel tubing, stainless steel and aluminium alloy. Elevons and split drag rudders. Retractable tricycle landing gear.

POWER PLANT: One 112 kW (150 hp) Textron Lycoming O-320. Fuel capacity 340 litres (90 US gallons; 75 Imp gallons) standard and 1,060 litres (280 US gallons; 233 Imp gallons) optional.

DIMENSIONS, EXTERNAL:

Wing span	12.19 m (40 ft 0 in)
Length overall	3.66 m (12 ft 0 in)
Height to top of canopy	1.52 m (5 ft 0 in)
Propeller diameter	1.73 m (5 ft 8 in)

AREA:

Wings, gross	20.09 m² (216.22 sq ft)

WEIGHTS:

Weight empty	445 kg (980 lb)
* Baggage capacity	285-517 kg (630-1,140 lb)
Max T-O weight	1,361 kg (3,000 lb)

PERFORMANCE (at max T-O weight):

Max level speed at S/L	161 knots (298 km/h; 185 mph)
Econ cruising speed at 3,660 m (12,000 ft)	
	133 knots (246 km/h; 153 mph)
Stalling speed	45 knots (84 km/h; 52 mph)
Max rate of climb at S/L	396 m (1,300 ft)/min
Max operating height	7,315 m (24,000 ft)
T-O run at normal T-O weight	137 m (450 ft)
Landing run	152 m (500 ft)
Range, max fuel, no reserves	
	1,736 nm (3,218 km; 2,000 miles)
Max endurance	15 h
g limits, normal T-O weight	+6/–3

* *Larger capacity with two people and 90 US gallons of fuel only.*

DENNEY

DENNEY AEROCRAFT COMPANY

Nampa Municipal Airport, 100 North Kings Road, Nampa, Idaho 83687
Telephone: 1 (208) 466 1711
Fax: 1 (208) 466 7194
PRESIDENT: Dan Denney

DENNEY AEROCRAFT KITFOX III

The Kitfox was designed to have exceptional short-field performance. The prototype first flew on 7 May 1984. In 1990 the latest Kitfox III version was introduced, featuring a stronger structure, enlarged tail unit, and a 45.4 kg (100 lb) increase in gross weight. Eighteen structural modifications were built into the Model III, allowing the option of a Rotax 912 engine and use of new all-composite Aerocet 1100 amphibious floats. Wings now fold for storage. Kits are available (Model III from July 1990 shipment), and by early 1991 more than 1,000 kits had been sold, of which more than 500 had been assembled. In addition, the aircraft is being manufactured under licence in Australia, Brazil, the Philippines (as the PAC Skyfox: see main Aircraft section), Portugal and South Africa. A specially equipped version has also been delivered for police duties.

TYPE: Side by side two-seat, dual control homebuilt.

AIRFRAME: Wings have extruded spars of aluminium alloy tubing, plywood ribs and drooped glassfibre tips, with Stits Poly-Fiber covering overall. Steel tube fuselage and tail unit, with Poly-Fiber covering. Non-retractable tailwheel landing gear, with brakes. Optional floats, amphibious floats, skis and underfuselage cargo pods.

POWER PLANT: One 48.5 kW (65 hp) Rotax 582 LC, with 3 : 1 reduction gear. Optional 59.7 kW (80 hp) Rotax 912. Fuel capacity 36 litres (9.5 US gallons; 8 Imp gallons) standard. Two 22.7 litre (6 US gallon; 5 Imp gallon) or one 51 litre (13.5 US gallon; 11.25 Imp gallon) optional fuel tanks in wings.

DIMENSIONS, EXTERNAL:

Wing span	9.75 m (32 ft 0 in)
Length overall	5.38 m (17 ft 8 in)
Height overall	1.73 m (5 ft 8 in)
Propeller diameter	1.68 m (5 ft 6 in)

AREA:

Wings, gross	12.16 m² (130.84 sq ft)

WEIGHTS:

Weight empty	200 kg (440 lb)
Pilot weight range	68-113 kg (150-250 lb)
Max recommended pilot and passenger weight	
	181 kg (400 lb)
Max T-O weight	476 kg (1,050 lb)

PERFORMANCE (two crew, unless stated otherwise):

Max level speed	87 knots (161 km/h; 100 mph)
Cruising speed	69-74 knots (129-137 km/h; 80-85 mph)
Stalling speed	26 knots (49 km/h; 30 mph)
Max rate of climb at S/L, at max T-O weight	
	396 m (1,300 ft)/min
Service ceiling, pilot only	6,100 m (20,000 ft)
T-O run, pilot only	23 m (75 ft)
Landing run	46 m (150 ft)
Range: standard fuel	195 nm (362 km; 225 miles)
max fuel	825 nm (1,528 km; 950 miles)
Endurance, standard fuel	3 h
g limits, pilot only	+6/–3

DURAND

DURAND ASSOCIATES INC

84th and McKinley Road, Omaha, Nebraska 68122
Telephone: 1 (402) 571 7058
PRESIDENT: W. H. Durand

DURAND Mk V

The prototype Durand Mk V flew for the first time on 28 June 1978. Plans are available to amateur builders, and at least 84 sets had been sold by early 1991.

TYPE: Two-seat, dual-control homebuilt biplane.

AIRFRAME: All-metal (light alloy) construction, with negative wing stagger. Full span flaps on upper wing. Anti-servo trim tabs on tailplane. Wing section NACA 23012. Non-retractable tricycle landing gear.

POWER PLANT: One 112-119 kW (150-160 hp) Textron Lycoming O-320. Fuel capacity 93 litres (24.5 US gallons; 20.4 Imp gallons). Two auxiliary wing tanks optional, each 15 litres (4 US gallons; 3.33 Imp gallons).

DIMENSIONS, EXTERNAL:

Wing span, both	7.47 m (24 ft 6 in)
Length overall	6.17 m (20 ft 3 in)
Height overall	2.03 m (6 ft 8 in)
Propeller diameter	1.83 m (6 ft 0 in)

AREA:

Wings, gross	13.38 m² (144.0 sq ft)

WEIGHTS:

Weight empty	549 kg (1,210 lb)
Baggage capacity	58 kg (128 lb)
Max T-O weight	834 kg (1,840 lb)

PERFORMANCE (at max T-O weight):

Max cruising speed at 2,285 m (7,500 ft)	
	117 knots (217 km/h; 135 mph)
Econ cruising speed at 2,285 m (7,500 ft)	
	109 knots (201 km/h; 125 mph)
Max rate of climb at S/L	366 m (1,200 ft)/min
Absolute ceiling, estimated	4,575 m (15,000 ft)
T-O run	168 m (550 ft)
Landing run	137 m (450 ft)
Range, no reserves:	
standard fuel	347 nm (644 km; 400 miles)
max optional fuel	451 nm (837 km; 520 miles)
g limits:	+3.8/–1.52
	+5.7/–2.28 ultimate design

DYKE

DYKE AIRCRAFT

2840 Old Yellow Springs Road, Fairborn, Ohio 45324
Telephone: 1 (513) 878 9832
DESIGNER: John W. Dyke

DYKE AIRCRAFT JD-2 DELTA

Plans of the JD-2 were made available to amateur constructors, and a total of about 360 aircraft are thought to be under construction. Hardware and tubing kits were made available.

TYPE: Delta-winged four-seat homebuilt.

AIRFRAME: Delta wing of modified NACA 63012 and 66015 section. Wings, fuselage and tail unit have welded steel tube structures. Wings use stainless steel capstrips to which laminated glassfibre skins are secured by pop rivets (optional aluminium skins). Fuselage similar except for steel tube capstrips and Poly-Fiber covering on undersurface. Elevons and tail unit Poly-Fiber covered. Optional all-moving T tail of all-metal construction for improved low-speed trim with heavier engine. Retractable tricycle landing gear.

POWER PLANT: Prototype has one 134 kW (180 hp) Textron Lycoming O-360. 149 kW (200 hp) engine installation optional. Fuel capacity 178 litres (47 US gallons; 39.1 Imp gallons), with pilot and two passengers. Fuel capacity reduced to 117 litres (31 US gallons; 26 Imp gallons) as a four-seat aircraft.

DIMENSIONS, EXTERNAL:

Wing span	6.87 m (22 ft 2½ in)
Length overall	5.79 m (19 ft 0 in)
Height overall	1.68 m (5 ft 6 in)
Propeller diameter	1.88 m (6 ft 2 in)

AREA:

Wings, gross	16.07 m² (173.0 sq ft)

WEIGHTS (with 134 kW; 180 hp or 149 kW; 200 hp engine):

Weight empty: basic equipped	481 kg (1,060 lb)
IFR equipped	490 kg (1,080 lb)
Baggage capacity	45.4 kg (100 lb)
Max T-O weight	884 kg (1,950 lb)

Prototype D'Apuzzo D-201 Sportwing, built by Mr Larry Stangil of Ferndale, Pennsylvania

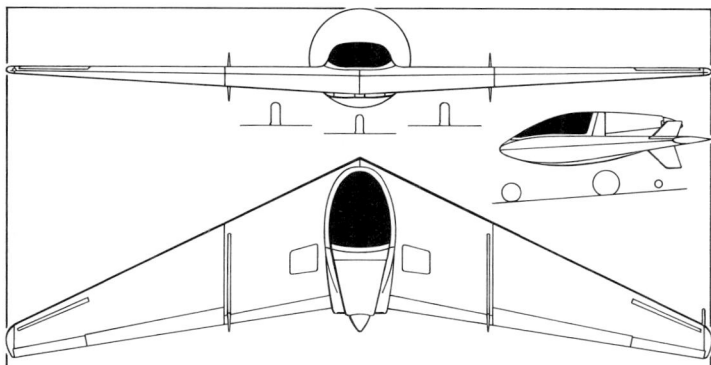

Davis Wing Starcruiser Gemini *(Jane's/Mike Keep)*

Eich JE-2 Gyroplane (C85 engine) with pre-rotation gear fitted

Earthstar Thunder Gull JX with two seats *(Julie Romo)*

Modified Dyke Delta built by Mr Bernie Schaknowski (Textron Lycoming O-360 engine) *(Peter M. Bowers)*

Durand Mk V all-metal two-seat biplane *(Howard Levy)*

Denney Kitfox III owned by Dan Denney

PERFORMANCE (at max T-O weight with 134 kW; 180 hp engine, except where indicated):
Max level speed at 2,285 m (7,500 ft), constant-speed propeller   174 knots (322 km/h; 200 mph)

Econ cruising speed at 2,285 m (7,500 ft)
135 knots (249 km/h; 155 mph)
Max rate of climb at S/L   610 m (2,000 ft)/min
Service ceiling   4,420 m (14,500 ft)
T-O run   213 m (700 ft)

Landing run   244-305 m (800-1,000 ft)
Range: with max fuel and pilot only, at 66% power
755 nm (1,400 km; 870 miles)
with max payload   576 nm (1,067 km; 663 miles)

EARTHSTAR
EARTHSTAR AIRCRAFT INC
Route 313, Santa Margarita, California 93453
Telephone: 1 (805) 438 5235
DESIGNER AND PRESIDENT: Mark H. Beierle
The Laughing Gull and Ultra Gull are no longer in production, having been superseded by the Thunder Gull J microlight and JX homebuilt.

EARTHSTAR THUNDER GULL JX
The Thunder Gull is of generally similar layout to the former Laughing Gull but has cantilever wings, an enlarged vertical tail and other changes. Two versions are offered, the J microlight (see tables) and the larger span, heavier and

more powerful Experimental JX, which can have one or two seats and an additional rear window. The prototype Thunder Gull first flew in 1988 and kits are available.
TYPE: Tandem two-seat homebuilt.
AIRFRAME: Aluminium alloy wings and welded 4130 fuselage structure with aluminium alloy skins. Glassfibre wingtips, nosecone, landing gear struts and seats. Wing section E-MBN713. Three-axis control (ailerons, all-moving tailplane and rudder), with optional flaps and trim. Non-retractable tricycle landing gear. Optional floats. Brakes standard.
POWER PLANT: One 39.5 kW (53 hp) Rotax 503.
DIMENSIONS, EXTERNAL:

Wing span	7.32 m (24 ft 0 in)
Length overall	5.03 m (16 ft 6 in)
Height overall	1.37 m (4 ft 6 in)

AREA:

Wings, gross	10.59 m² (114.0 sq ft)

WEIGHTS:

Weight empty	175 kg (385 lb)
Pilot weight range	45.5-113 kg (100-250 lb)
Max T-O weight	454 kg (1,000 lb)

PERFORMANCE:

Max level speed	109 knots (203 km/h; 126 mph)
Max cruising speed	89 knots (166 km/h; 103 mph)
Econ cruising speed at 1,830 m (6,000 ft)	
	81 knots (150 km/h; 93 mph)
Stalling speed, flaps down, engine idling	
	30 knots (55 km/h; 34 mph)
Max rate of climb at S/L	503 m (1,650 ft)/min

EICH
JAMES P. EICH
1820 West Grand Avenue, Alhambra, California 91801
Telephone: 1 (818) 289 1983

EICH JE-2 GYROPLANE
The prototype JE-2 first flew in 1977. Detailed drawings and instructions for building the aircraft are available from: Tech Man Company, 8525 E Duarte Road, San Gabriel, California 91775. At least 40 sets of plans have been sold.
The following details apply specifically to the prototype:
TYPE: Tandem two-seat, dual-control light autogyro.

ROTOR SYSTEM: Two-blade aluminium teetering rotor, with pre-rotation system.
AIRFRAME: Square section welded steel-tube girder fuselage, covered with Dacron. Dacron fin integral with fuselage covering. Stabiliser and rudder of sheet aluminium. Non-retractable tricycle landing gear.

POWER PLANT: One 63.5 kW (85 hp) Teledyne Continental C85. Optional engines from A65 to O-200. Fuel capacity 64.5 litres (17 US gallons; 14.2 Imp gallons).

DIMENSIONS, EXTERNAL:

Main rotor diameter	7.92 m (26 ft 0 in)
Length of fuselage	4.27 m (14 ft 0 in)
Height overall	2.59 m (8 ft 6 in)
Propeller diameter	1.78 m (5 ft 10 in)

WEIGHTS:

Weight empty	211 kg (465 lb)
Max T-O weight	417 kg (920 lb)

PERFORMANCE (with current rotor blades):

Max level speed at 915 m (3,000 ft)	
	70 knots (129 km/h; 80 mph)
Econ cruising speed at 915 m (3,000 ft)	
	48 knots (89 km/h; 55 mph)
Min flying speed (no stall)	39 knots (73 km/h; 45 mph)
Max rate of climb at 915 m (3,000 ft)	
	91 m (300 ft)/min
T-O run with pre-rotation	153 m (500 ft)
Landing run	15 m (50 ft)
Range with max fuel and max payload	
	156 nm (290 km; 180 miles)

EVANS
EVANS AIRCRAFT
PO Box 744, La Jolla, California 92038

Designed for easy building and safety to fly, the single-seat Evans VP-1 is available in plans form. Those for European customers are supplied through the Popular Flying Association (PFA) in the UK (which see). VP-2 plans are no longer available. Details of this aircraft, and an illustration, can be found in the 1988-89 *Jane's*.

EVANS VP-1
TYPE: Single-seat homebuilt.

AIRFRAME: Virtually all-wood structure, with fabric covered wings and tail unit, and plywood covered fuselage with glassfibre fairing aft of pilot's seat. Wing section NACA 4412. Non-retractable tailskid landing gear. Enclosed cockpit optional.

POWER PLANT: One 30 kW, 39.5 kW or 44.5 kW (40 hp, 53 hp or 60 hp) modified Volkswagen motorcar engine. Fuel capacity 30 litres (8 US gallons; 6.7 Imp gallons).

DIMENSIONS, EXTERNAL:

Wing span	7.32 m (24 ft 0 in)
Length overall	5.49 m (18 ft 0 in)
Height overall	1.56 m (5 ft 1½ in)
Propeller diameter	1.37 m (4 ft 6 in)

AREA:

Wings, gross	9.29 m² (100.0 sq ft)

WEIGHTS:

Weight empty	200 kg (440 lb)
Max T-O weight	295-340 kg (650-750 lb)

PERFORMANCE (30 kW; 40 hp engine, at T-O weight of 295 kg; 650 lb):

Max level speed	82 knots (153 km/h; 95 mph)
Cruising speed	65 knots (121 km/h; 75 mph)
Stalling speed	35 knots (65 km/h; 40 mph)
Max rate of climb at S/L	122 m (400 ft)/min
T-O run (average breeze)	137 m (450 ft)
Landing run (average breeze)	61 m (200 ft)

FIRST STRIKE
FIRST STRIKE AVIATION INC
4 Wade Avenue, Piggott, Arkansas 72454
Telephone: 1 (501) 598 5126
PRESIDENT: Bobby Baker

FIRST STRIKE BOBCAT and SUPER CAT
The first flight of the prototype Bobcat was achieved in May 1984. Kits and plans are available, together with those for the Experimental and stronger Super Cat. Estimated building time of a Bobcat and Super Cat is 150-200 and 300 working hours respectively. Individual component parts are available to builders using plans only.

TYPES: Single-seat microlight (Bobcat) and homebuilt (Super Cat) aircraft.

AIRFRAME: Fuselage uses spruce longerons and plywood bulkheads, the wings have spruce capped foam ribs with plywood D section leading-edges, all Ceconite 7600 fabric covered. Glassfibre engine cowling. Non-retractable tailwheel landing gear.

POWER PLANT: *Bobcat:* one 20 kW (27 hp) Rotax 277. *Super Cat:* one 26 kW (35 hp) Rotax 377; optional Rotax 447. Fuel capacity 19 litres (5 US gallons; 4.2 Imp gallons) in Bobcat, 30 litres (8 US gallons; 6.66 Imp gallons) in Super Cat.

DIMENSIONS, EXTERNAL:

Wing span	8.43 m (27 ft 8 in)
Length overall	4.65 m (15 ft 3 in)
Height overall	1.83 m (6 ft 0 in)
Propeller diameter: Bobcat	1.52 m (5 ft 0 in)
Super Cat	1.73 m (5 ft 8 in)

AREAS:

Wings, gross: Bobcat	10.41 m² (112.0 sq ft)
Super Cat	11.15 m² (120.0 sq ft)

WEIGHTS (A: Bobcat, B: Super Cat):

Weight empty: A	114 kg (251 lb)
B	150 kg (330 lb)
Max T-O weight: A	226 kg (500 lb)
B	283 kg (625 lb)

PERFORMANCE (A: Bobcat, B: Super Cat):

Max level speed: A	55 knots (101 km/h; 63 mph)
B	74 knots (137 km/h; 85 mph)
Max cruising speed:	
A	39-43 knots (72-80 km/h; 45-50 mph)
B	56 knots (105 km/h; 65 mph)
Stalling speed: A	24 knots (44 km/h; 27 mph)
B	32 knots (60 km/h; 37 mph)
Max rate of climb at S/L: A	213 m (700 ft)/min
B	259 m (850 ft)/min
T-O run: A	38 m (125 ft)
B	23 m (75 ft)
Landing run: A	61 m (200 ft)
g limits: A	±4
B	+5.5/−4.5

FISHER
FISHER FLYING PRODUCTS INC
PO Box 468, Edgeley, North Dakota 58433
Telephone: 1 (701) 493 2286

Details of the company's former Culex and Culite aircraft can be found under Aero Visions International. Kits continued to be available for the FP-202 Koala, FP-303, FP-404 Classic, FP-505 and FP-606 Sky Baby single-seat microlights and the two-seat Classic II and Super Koala (see also Microlight tables).

FISHER FLYING PRODUCTS SUPER KOALA
This larger and higher-powered two-seat variant of the Koala flew for the first time in the Spring of 1984. The standard kit takes about 400-500 working hours to complete; a quick-build kit requires only 150-250 working hours due to the large number of factory prefabricated components. Like the FP-202, the Super Koala can be fitted optionally with a pre-welded chrome-molybdenum steel tube fuselage.

TYPE: Side by side two-seat, dual-control STOL homebuilt/microlight; has training exemption to FAR Pt 103 and conforms to Canadian regulations.

AIRFRAME: High-lift wing. Geodetic wooden structure, fabric covered. Three-axis control, with flaps. Non-retractable tailwheel landing gear.

POWER PLANT: One 47 kW (63 hp) Rotax 582. Fuel capacity 30 litres (8 US gallons; 6.66 Imp gallons). Auxiliary tank can be carried, of up to 19 litres (5 US gallons; 4.2 Imp gallons) capacity.

DIMENSIONS, EXTERNAL:

Wing span	9.45 m (31 ft 0 in)
Length overall	5.51 m (18 ft 1 in)
Height overall	1.70 m (5 ft 7 in)
Propeller diameter	1.83 m (6 ft 0 in)

AREA:

Wings, gross	13.0 m² (140.0 sq ft)

WEIGHTS:

Weight empty	181 kg (400 lb)
Max T-O weight	376 kg (830 lb)

PERFORMANCE:

Cruising speed	65 knots (121 km/h; 75 mph)
Econ cruising speed	48 knots (88 km/h; 55 mph)
Stalling speed: power on	26 knots (49 km/h; 30 mph)
power off	28 knots (52 km/h; 32 mph)
Max rate of climb at S/L	244 m (800 ft)/min
T-O run	61 m (200 ft)
Landing run	76 m (250 ft)
Range with max standard fuel	
	126 nm (233 km; 145 miles)
Endurance	2 h
g limits	+4.6/−2.3

FISHER FLYING PRODUCTS FP-404 CLASSIC
This single-seat biplane has, like the Super Koala, a geodetic wooden fuselage and wings (semi-symmetrical section), all fabric covered, three-axis control, and a tailwheel landing gear. Either a 35.8 kW (48 hp) Rotax 503 or a 47 kW (63 hp) Rotax 582 engine can be fitted to the homebuilt version, or a 20 kW (27 hp) Rotax 277 to the microlight model. All use a 19 litre (5 US gallon; 4.2 Imp gallon) fuel tank. Construction takes 250-400 working hours.

DIMENSIONS, EXTERNAL:

Wing span	5.49 m (18 ft 0 in)
Length overall	4.42 m (14 ft 6 in)
Height overall	1.65 m (5 ft 5 in)

AREA:

Wings, gross	11.15 m² (120.0 sq ft)

WEIGHTS (A: microlight, B: homebuilt):

Weight empty: A	104-109 kg (230-240 lb)
B	122-127 kg (270-280 lb)
Max T-O weight: A	213 kg (470 lb)
B	245 kg (540 lb)

PERFORMANCE (A and B as above):

Max cruising speed: A	54 knots (100 km/h; 62 mph)
B	70 knots (128 km/h; 80 mph)
Econ cruising speed: A	48 knots (89 km/h; 55 mph)
B	52 knots (97 km/h; 60 mph)
Stalling speed: A	24 knots (44 km/h; 27 mph)
B	26 knots (49 km/h; 30 mph)
Max rate of climb at S/L: A	122 m (400 ft)/min
B	213-274 m (700-900 ft)/min
T-O run: A	54 m (175 ft)
B	38 m (125 ft)
g limits: A	+4/−2
B	+6/−3

FISHER FLYING PRODUCTS CLASSIC II
This is a tandem two-seat derivative of the FP-404 Classic, first flown on 25 March 1987. The standard engine is a 47 kW (63 hp) Rotax 582 but, alternatively, a 35.8 kW (48 hp) Rotax 503 can be fitted to kit-built aircraft. Construction takes about 350-500 working hours.

DIMENSIONS, EXTERNAL:

Wing span	6.71 m (22 ft 0 in)
Length overall	5.33 m (17 ft 6 in)
Height overall	1.88 m (6 ft 2 in)

AREA:

Wings, gross	14.31 m² (154.0 sq ft)

WEIGHTS:

Weight empty	181 kg (400 lb)
Max T-O weight	386 kg (850 lb)

PERFORMANCE:

Cruising speed	65 knots (121 km/h; 75 mph)
Stalling speed	31 knots (57 km/h; 35 mph)
Max rate of climb at S/L	305 m (1,000 ft)/min
T-O run	54 m (175 ft)
Landing run, without brakes	76 m (250 ft)
g limits	+6.5/−3.5

FLIGHTWORKS
FLIGHTWORKS CORPORATION
4211-C Todd Lane, Austin, Texas 78744
Telephone: 1 (512) 441 8844
Fax: 1 (512) 441 1997

FLIGHTWORKS CAPELLA
Kits are being marketed to construct the Capella. Two wing spans are believed to be available, offering high manoeuvrability or short-field operation.

TYPE: Single-seat homebuilt; conforms to FAR Pt 23.

AIRFRAME: All-aluminium alloy wing. Welded steel tube fuselage structure, the upper portion covered with aluminium alloy skins and the remainder with Dacron. Non-retractable tricycle or tailwheel landing gear. Floats optional.

POWER PLANT: One 34 kW (45.6 hp) Rotax 503. Fuel capacity 26.5 litres (7 US gallons; 5.8 Imp gallons).

DIMENSIONS, EXTERNAL:

Wing span:	
long span	9.52 m (31 ft 3 in)
short span	8.38 m (27 ft 6 in)
Length overall	5.28 m (17 ft 4 in)
Height overall	1.73 m (5 ft 8 in)

AREAS:

Wings, gross:	
long span	11.52 m² (124.0 sq ft)
short span	10.22 m² (110.0 sq ft)

Evans VP-1 Series 2 *(P. J. Cooper)*

Flightworks Capella XS two-seat homebuilt at Sun 'n Fun 91 *(Geoffrey P. Jones)*

First Strike Super Cat homebuilt cabin monoplane *(Geoffrey P. Jones)*

FLSZ Der Kricket DK-1 built by Reinhart Kuntz of Buford, Georgia
(Howard Levy)

Freedom Master Air Shark I four-seat homebuilt amphibian *(Joel Rieman)*

Fisher Flying Products Super Koala at Sun 'n Fun 91 *(Geoffrey P. Jones)*

WEIGHTS (short span wings):
Weight empty	154 kg (340 lb)
Max T-O weight	283 kg (625 lb)

PERFORMANCE (short span wings):
Max level speed	80 knots (148 km/h; 92 mph)
Cruising speed, 75% power	71 knots (132 km/h; 82 mph)
Stalling speed: flaps up	33 knots (61 km/h; 38 mph)
flaps down	29 knots (53 km/h; 33 mph)
Max rate of climb at S/L	253 m (830 ft)/min
T-O run	46 m (150 ft)
Landing run	31 m (100 ft)

FLIGHTWORKS CAPELLA XS

This is a new two-seat version of the Capella, model designated FW2C65 and FW2C80 when powered by either a Rotax 582 or 912 engine respectively. Construction from a kit is estimated to take about 350 working hours.

DIMENSIONS, EXTERNAL:
Wing span	8.69 m (28 ft 6 in)
Length overall	5.61 m (18 ft 5 in)
Height overall	1.73 m (5 ft 8 in)

AREA:
Wings, gross	10.59 m² (114.0 sq ft)

WEIGHTS (A: FW2C65, B: FW2C80):
Weight empty: A	193 kg (425 lb)
B	211 kg (465 lb)

Max T-O weight: A	420 kg (925 lb)
B	431 kg (950 lb)

PERFORMANCE (A and B as above; 2 crew):
Max level speed: A	93 knots (172 km/h; 107 mph)
B	100 knots (185 km/h; 115 mph)
Cruising speed, 75% power:	
A	82 knots (153 km/h; 95 mph)
B	91 knots (169 km/h; 105 mph)
Stalling speed, flaps down and power on:	
A	33 knots (60 km/h; 37 mph)
Max rate of climb at S/L: A	283 m (930 ft)/min
B	360 m (1,180 ft)/min
T-O run: A	77 m (250 ft)
Landing run, with brakes: A	54 m (175 ft)

FLSZ
FLIGHT LEVEL SIX-ZERO INC
4737 Shadowglen Drive. Colorado Springs, Colorado 80918
Telephone: 1 (303) 548 0822

FLSZ DER KRICKET DK-1
The prototype Der Kricket DK-1 first flew on 19 September 1978. Plans are available.
TYPE: Single-seat homebuilt sporting biplane.
AIRFRAME: Wing section NACA 4412. Wings and tail surfaces have light alloy structure, with pop riveted light alloy skins. Tips of Styrofoam covered with glassfibre. Ailerons on lower wings only. Basic fuselage structure of

bolted and riveted light alloy angle, covered by light alloy skins. Non-retractable tailwheel landing gear.
POWER PLANT: Modified Volkswagen motorcar engine of 37.3-48.5 kW (50-65 hp); 56 kW (75 hp) HAPI Magnum also reportedly fitted. Fuel capacity 30.3 litres (8 US gallons; 6.66 Imp gallons).

DIMENSIONS, EXTERNAL:
Wing span (both)	4.88 m (16 ft 0 in)
Length overall	4.88 m (16 ft 0 in)
Height overall	1.68 m (5 ft 6 in)
Propeller diameter	1.37 m (4 ft 6 in)

AREA:
Wings, gross	8.92 m² (96.0 sq ft)

WEIGHTS:
Weight empty	249 kg (550 lb)
Max T-O weight	354 kg (780 lb)

PERFORMANCE (VW engine at max T-O weight):
Max level speed	91 knots (169 km/h; 105 mph)
Econ cruising speed	74 knots (137 km/h; 85 mph)
Stalling speed, power off	46 knots (84 km/h; 52 mph)
Max rate of climb at S/L	229 m (750 ft)/min
Absolute ceiling	3,660 m (12,000 ft)
T-O run	213 m (700 ft)
Landing run	198 m (650 ft)
Range with max fuel	173 nm (322 km; 200 miles)

FLSZ VAGRANT II
Details of this aircraft last appeared in the 1990-91 *Jane's.*

FREEDOM MASTER
FREEDOM MASTER CORPORATION
450 Hamlin Avenue, Satellite Beach, Florida 32937
PRESIDENT: Ronald A. Lueck

FREEDOM MASTER FM-2 AIR SHARK I
The prototype Air Shark flew for the first time on 5 April 1985. Kits of pre-moulded parts were made available.
TYPE: Four-seat homebuilt sporting amphibian.

AIRFRAME: Wing section NASA NLF-0215-F. Wing spar caps of S-2 glassfibre or Kevlar rovings. All aerofoils are vacuum moulded. Wing upper shell and upper fuselage of glassfibre/epoxy and Clark foam plastics sandwich construction, with wing lower surfaces of Kevlar/epoxy. Hull and control surfaces of Kevlar/epoxy with Nomex honeycomb cores. Winglets of glassfibre/epoxy. Tail unit construction similar to wings. Retractable tricycle landing gear.

POWER PLANT: One 149 kW (200 hp) Textron Lycoming IO-360C1C. Alternative Porsche PFM 3200, Allison C250-B17 or Teledyne Continental IO-360 engine. Fuel capacity 227 litres (60 US gallons; 50 Imp gallons).

ARMAMENT: Hardpoints for weapons and other stores optional.

DIMENSIONS, EXTERNAL:

Wing span	9.96 m (32 ft 8 in)
Length overall	6.93 m (22 ft 9 in)
Height overall	2.49 m (8 ft 2 in)
Propeller diameter	1.83 m (6 ft 0 in)

AREA:

Wings, gross	12.31 m² (132.5 sq ft)

WEIGHTS:

Weight empty	680 kg (1,500 lb)
Baggage capacity	54 kg (120 lb)
Max T-O weight	1,270 kg (2,800 lb)

PERFORMANCE (at max T-O weight):

Max level speed at 2,285 m (7,500 ft)	178 knots (330 km/h; 205 mph)
Econ cruising speed at 2,285 m (7,500 ft)	148 knots (274 km/h; 170 mph)
Stalling speed, power off	55 knots (102 km/h; 63 mph)
Max rate of climb at S/L	380 m (1,250 ft)/min
Service ceiling	5,640 m (18,500 ft)
T-O run	488 m (1,600 ft)
Landing run	305 m (1,000 ft)
Range	1,736 nm (3,218 km; 2,000 miles)
Endurance	11 h 48 min
g limits	+10/−4

GREAT PLAINS
GREAT PLAINS AIRCRAFT SUPPLY CO INC
PO Box 1481, Palatine, Illinois 60067
Telephone: 1 (312) 359 6558

It has been reported that Great Plains Aircraft Supply has acquired the rights from HAPI Engines Inc to sell kits and components, and reproduce plans, for the Sonerai I and II.

GREAT PLAINS SONERAI I
The first flight by the prototype Sonerai was made in July 1971. Plans and certain components are available to amateur constructors, and the estimated building time is 800 working hours when a pre-welded fuselage and tail are not used.

TYPE: Single-seat homebuilt Formula V racing aircraft.

AIRFRAME: Wings of aluminium alloy construction, with NACA 64212 section. Full span aluminium alloy ailerons. Welded steel tube fuselage and tail unit, fabric covered except for glassfibre engine cowlings. Non-retractable tailwheel landing gear.

POWER PLANT: One 44.7, 56 or 61 kW (60, 75 or 82 hp) Volkswagen 1,600, 1,834 or 2,200 cc modified motorcar engine. Fuel capacity 38 litres (10 US gallons; 8.3 Imp gallons).

DIMENSIONS, EXTERNAL:

Wing span	5.08 m (16 ft 8 in)
Length overall	5.08 m (16 ft 8 in)
Height overall	1.52 m (5 ft 0 in)
Propeller diameter	1.27 m (4 ft 2 in)

AREA:

Wings, gross	6.97 m² (75.0 sq ft)

WEIGHTS:

Weight empty	199 kg (440 lb)
Max pilot weight	113 kg (250 lb)
Utility max T-O weight	340 kg (750 lb)
Max T-O weight	454 kg (1,000 lb)

PERFORMANCE (at max T-O weight):

Max level speed at S/L	148 knots (273 km/h; 170 mph)
Econ cruising speed	109 knots (201 km/h; 125 mph)
Stalling speed	35 knots (65 km/h; 40 mph)
Max rate of climb at S/L	305 m (1,000 ft)
T-O and landing run	183 m (600 ft)
Range, with reserves	217-260 nm (402-482 km; 250-300 miles)
g limits	±6g

GREAT PLAINS SONERAI II, IIL, II-LT and II-LTS
The prototype of the tandem two-seat Sonerai II made its first flight in July 1973 and at least 500 have since been built and flown. Many components, complete kits for fuselage, tail and wings, and materials, are available to amateur constructors. Estimated building time is 850 working hours.

One variant, first flown in June 1980, is the **Sonerai IIL**, with low-wing instead of mid-wing configuration and 3° of dihedral. Another variant, first flown in January 1983, is the **Sonerai II-LT**, which is similar to the Sonerai IIL but has a 2,200 cc VW engine as standard, a tricycle landing gear and larger front cockpit for a taller pilot. A retrofit kit was produced to allow existing Sonerais to be fitted with the tricycle gear. The **Sonerai II-LTS** is basically a stretched version of the Sonerai II-LT, first flown in June 1984.

The description of the Sonerai I applies also to Sonerai II, IIL, II-LT and II-LTS except as follows:

TYPE: Two-seat, dual-control sporting homebuilt.

POWER PLANT: One 44.7, 56 or 61 kW (60, 75 or 82 hp) HAPI converted Volkswagen 1,600, 1,834 or 2,200 cc motorcar engine. The 2,200 cc version is standard for the Sonerai II-LT and II-LTS. Fuel capacity 38 litres (10 US gallons; 8.3 Imp gallons) for all versions except Sonerai II-LTS, which has standard capacity of 68 litres (18 US gallons; 15 Imp gallons).

DIMENSIONS, EXTERNAL: As Sonerai I, except:

Wing span	5.69 m (18 ft 8 in)
Length overall:	
all, except Sonerai II-LTS	5.74 m (18 ft 10 in)
Sonerai II-LTS	6.20 m (20 ft 4 in)
Propeller diameter	1.32 to 1.37 m (4 ft 4 in to 4 ft 6 in)

AREA:

Wings, gross	7.80 m² (84.0 sq ft)

WEIGHTS (Sonerai II):

Weight empty	227 kg (500 lb)
Utility max T-O weight	431 kg (950 lb)
Max T-O weight	521 kg (1,150 lb)

PERFORMANCE (Sonerai II/IIL with 1,700 cc engine):

Max level speed at S/L	139 knots (257 km/h; 160 mph)
Econ cruising speed at S/L	113 knots (209 km/h; 130 mph)
Stalling speed	38 knots (71 km/h; 44 mph)
Max rate of climb at S/L	152 m (500 ft)/min
T-O run	274 m (900 ft)
Landing run	152 m (500 ft)
Range, with reserves	304 nm (563 km; 350 miles)
g limits: pilot only, aerobatic	±6
max T-O weight, utility	±4.4

GREGA
JOHN W. GREGA
355 Grand Boulevard, Bedford, Ohio 44146

In addition to the standard Aircamper design, of which plans are available from Mr Don Pietenpol (see 1988-89 *Jane's*), a modernised version has been developed by Mr John Grega. Plans of this are available to homebuilders, and by 1991 about 3,000 sets had been sold.

GREGA GN-1 AIRCAMPER
The prototype GN-1 Aircamper flew for the first time in November 1965. Builders can choose wood or steel tube fuselage construction.

TYPE: Tandem two-seat homebuilt.

POWER PLANT: One 48.5 kW (65 hp) Teledyne Continental A65-8. Other engines of up to 63.5 kW (85 hp) can be installed. Fuel capacity 68 litres (18 US gallons; 15 Imp gallons).

DIMENSIONS, EXTERNAL:

Wing span	8.84 m (29 ft 0 in)
Length overall	5.51 m (18 ft 1 in)
Height overall	2.06 m (6 ft 9 in)

AREA:

Wings, gross	13.94 m² (150.0 sq ft)

WEIGHT:

Max T-O weight	499 kg (1,100 lb)

PERFORMANCE (at max T-O weight):

Max level speed at S/L	100 knots (185 km/h; 115 mph)
Max cruising speed at S/L	78 knots (145 km/h; 90 mph)
Stalling speed	31 knots (56 km/h; 35 mph)
Max rate of climb at S/L	152 m (500 ft)/min
T-O run	122 m (400 ft)
Landing run	76 m (250 ft)
Range with max fuel	347 nm (640 km; 400 miles)

GROEN
GROEN BROTHERS AVIATION INC
1784 West 500 South, Salt Lake City, Utah 84104
Telephone: 1 (801) 973 0195
Fax: 1 (801) 973 4027
OWNERS: David and Jay Groen

Groen Brothers is developing a series of autogyros that will be FAA certificated but may be offered as kits at a later date. These comprise the single-seat **Hawk 1A** (134 kW; 180 hp Textron Lycoming O-360 engine), side by side two-seat **Hawk 2A** (possibly using a similar engine), and five-seat **Hawk 5A** (Textron Lycoming IO-540 engine).

Each will have enclosed accommodation, stub wings housing the main units of the retractable tricycle landing gear and supporting twin booms, inward canted twin fins and rudders forming a V, and a semi-rigid rotor. The Hawk 1A prototype was being test flown in early 1991.

GYRO
GYRO 2000 INC
Coronado Air Center, 10000 Pan American FWY North-East, Albuquerque, New Mexico 87113
Telephone: 1 (505) 293 7330
PROPRIETOR: David Gittens

The 1987-88 *Jane's* described and illustrated the Wind Dancer proof of concept gyroplane. The same company, now known as Gyro 2000, has developed the DAKI 530Z/Ikenga, Ikenga/Cygnus 21TX and Ikenga/Cygnus 21P.

GYRO 2000 DAKI 530Z/IKENGA
First flown in February 1988, this gyroplane is available on custom order only for light utility, surveillance, photography, commuter/courier and recreational uses. An illustration appeared in the 1990-91 *Jane's*.

TYPE: Single-seat autogyro.

ROTOR SYSTEM: Two-blade Skywheels composites rotor. Parsons offset gimbal rotor head and Kawasaki electric pre-rotator. Parsons jump capability rotor head to be optional.

AIRFRAME: Structure of aluminium alloy and steel tubing. Glassfibre cockpit fairing. Full cockpit enclosure, cargo pod, medical pod, surveillance pod, cropspraying equipment and provision for an additional passenger were under development.

POWER PLANT: One 71 kW (95 hp) Suzuki 530 engine, driving a ground adjustable Precision propeller. Fuel tank bucket seat, capacity 59 litres (15.5 US gallons; 13 Imp gallons).

DIMENSIONS, EXTERNAL:

Rotor diameter	7.01 m (23 ft 0 in)
Length overall	3.71 m (12 ft 2 in)
Height overall	2.26 m (7 ft 5 in)
Propeller diameter	1.42 m (4 ft 8 in)

WEIGHTS:

Useful load	252 kg (555 lb)
Max T-O weight	399 kg (880 lb)

PERFORMANCE (estimated):

Cruising speed	81 knots (150 km/h; 93 mph)
Min level speed	13 knots (24 km/h; 15 mph)
Max rate of climb at S/L	427 m (1,400 ft)/min
Service ceiling	4,265 m (14,000 ft)
T-O run	107 m (350 ft)
T-O run with pre-rotator	46 m (150 ft)
Range	315 nm (583 km; 362 miles)

GYRO 2000 IKENGA/CYGNUS 21P
This sports autogyro is kit-assembled (requires about 40 working hours), and was developed originally for distribution in Japan by Sumitomo Heavy Industries. The fairing and wheel covers can be retrofitted to Benson and Brock autogyros. It is registered in the microlight category in most countries and as an Experimental aircraft in the USA. Kits became available in the USA in Spring 1991.

TYPE: Single-seat autogyro.

ROTOR SYSTEM: Two-blade Rotordyne rotor of bonded aluminium. Parsons offset gimbal rotor head. Options include pre-rotator and rotor brake.

AIRFRAME: Structure of 6061-T6 aluminium alloy tubing, with aluminium tail unit and glassfibre fairings. Non-retractable tricycle landing gear, with hydraulic nosewheel brake. Options include a full cockpit enclosure.

POWER PLANT: One 71 kW (95 hp) Suzuki 530 engine, driving a three-blade ground adjustable Precision propeller. Brock 30 litre (8 US gallon; 6.7 Imp gallon) seat/fuel tank.

DIMENSIONS, EXTERNAL:

Rotor diameter	7.01 m (23 ft 0 in)
Length overall	3.35 m (11 ft 0 in)
Height overall	2.39 m (7 ft 10 in)
Propeller diameter	1.37 m (4 ft 6 in)

Grega GN-1 Aircamper (Teledyne Continental A80 engine) built by
Dr Samuel Meredith of West Memphis, Arkansas

Gyro 2000 Ikenga/Cygnus 21P autogyro

Great Plains Sonerai II built by Butch Mankovich of Clifton, New Jersey,
USA (Howard Levy)

Gyro 2000 Ikenga/Cygnus 21TX autogyro in latest configuration

Cygnet SF-2A, designed by Captain A. M. Sisler and marketed by HAPI
Engines (J. M. G. Gradidge)

WEIGHTS:

Useful load	254 kg (560 lb)
Max T-O weight	399 kg (880 lb)

PERFORMANCE:

Max level speed	100 knots (185 km/h; 115 mph)
Cruising speed	78 knots (145 km/h; 90 mph)
Min flying speed	13 knots (24 km/h; 15 mph)
Rate of climb at S/L	427 m (1,400 ft)/min
Service ceiling	4,420 m (14,500 ft)
T-O run: without pre-rotator	77 m (250 ft)
with pre-rotator	46 m (150 ft)
Range	143 nm (265 km; 165 miles)

GYRO 2000 IKENGA/CYGNUS 21TX

The Cygnus 21TX has replaced the 21T as the top of the range kit. It is suitable for utility and sports applications. Assembly takes about 40 working hours. Options include a full cockpit fairing, courier pod, Micro Ag cropspraying system, SWS intelligence gathering platform, and Life-Assist medical unit.

TYPE: Single-seat microlight autogyro.

ROTOR SYSTEM AND AIRFRAME: Similar rotor system and materials to Cygnus 21P. Triple tail surfaces.

POWER PLANT: One 71 kW (95 hp) Suzuki 530 engine, driving a five-blade Arrowprop or Precision tractor propeller. Hamilton 59 litre (15.5 US gallon; 13 Imp gallon) seat/fuel tank. Optional long-range tank.

DIMENSIONS, EXTERNAL:

Rotor diameter	7.01 m (23 ft 0 in)
Length overall	3.33 m (10 ft 11 in)
Height overall	2.13 m (7 ft 0 in)
Propeller diameter	1.37 to 1.52 m (4 ft 6 in to 5 ft 0 in)

WEIGHTS:

Weight empty	111 kg (244 lb)
Max T-O weight	399 kg (880 lb)

PERFORMANCE:

Cruising speed	78-82 knots (145-153 km/h; 90-95 mph)
T-O run: without pre-rotator	92 m (300 ft)
with pre-rotator	16-46 m (50-150 ft)
Landing run	0-3 m (0-10 ft)
Range	315 nm (583 km; 362 miles)

HAPI

HAPI ENGINES INC

Eloy Municipal Airport, RR 1 Box 1000, Eloy, Arizona 85231
Telephone: 1 (602) 466 9244

In October 1983 HAPI Engines acquired the rights to market Captain A. M. Sisler's Cygnet SF-2A. Plans and pre-welded airframe kits were made available. Also, in 1987, HAPI purchased the rights in the former INAV Sonerai, which have since been acquired by Great Plains Aircraft Supply (which see). HAPI also became a dealer for the Viking Dragonfly, quick-assembly 'Snap' Dragonfly, and Corby CJ-1 Starlet.

CYGNET SF-2A

TYPE: Two-seat homebuilt.

AIRFRAME: Wooden geodetic wing structure, with overall Dacron covering. Wing section NACA 3413. Welded chrome molybdenum steel tube fuselage and strut braced tail unit, Dacron covered. Non-retractable tailwheel landing gear. A float gear is under development.

POWER PLANT: One 44.7, 56 or 61 kW (60, 75 or 82 hp) HAPI converted Volkswagen 1,600, 1,834 or 2,200 cc motorcar engine. Fuel capacity 57 litres (15 US gallons; 12.5 Imp gallons).

DIMENSIONS, EXTERNAL:

Wing span	9.14 m (30 ft 0 in)
Length overall	5.79 m (19 ft 0 in)
Height overall	1.78 m (5 ft 10 in)
Propeller diameter	1.47 m (4 ft 10 in)

AREA:

Wings, gross	11.60 m² (124.8 sq ft)

WEIGHTS:

Weight empty	265 kg (585 lb)
Baggage capacity	23 kg (50 lb)
Max T-O weight	499 kg (1,100 lb)

PERFORMANCE (at max T-O weight):

Max level speed	94 knots (174 km/h; 108 mph)
Cruising speed at 2,440 m (8,000 ft)	87 knots (161 km/h; 100 mph)
Stalling speed: power off	42 knots (78 km/h; 48 mph)
power on	37 knots (68 km/h; 42 mph)
Max rate of climb at S/L	177 m (580 ft)/min
Service ceiling	3,660 m (12,000 ft)
T-O to and landing from 15 m (50 ft)	213 m (700 ft)
Range	304 nm (563 km; 350 miles)
g limit	+4

HATZ
HATZ AIRPLANE SHOP

Details of the Hatz CB-1 Biplane, and an illustration, appeared in the 1989-90 *Jane's*.

HELICRAFT
HELICRAFT INC
PO Box 50, Riderwood, MD 21139
Telephone: 1 (301) 557 8465
Fax: 1 (301) 692 5902
PRESIDENT: Joel Levin

HELICRAFT SKYLARK I
This is a new single-seat helicopter powered by a 47.7 kW (64 hp) Rotax 582 engine. The only known details at the time of going to press were:
WEIGHTS:

Weight empty	147 kg (325 lb)
Max T-O weight	318 kg (700 lb)

PERFORMANCE:

Max level speed	82 knots (153 km/h; 95 mph)
Cruising speed	61 knots (113 km/h; 70 mph)

HIPP'S
HIPP'S SUPERBIRDS INC
PO Box 266, I-26 Exit 28, Ozone Drive, Saluda, North Carolina 28773
Telephone: 1 (704) 749 9134 and 749 3986
Fax: 1 (704) 749 9803

In addition to the J-3 Kitten, Reliant and J-4 Sportster microlights, Hipp's Superbirds offers Experimental derivatives as follows.

HIPP'S SUPERBIRDS RELIANT II
This two-seat Experimental version of the Reliant strut braced cabin monoplane is powered by a 47.7 kW (64 hp) Rotax 532 or, optionally, a 48.5 kW (65 hp) Teledyne Continental. Kits were to be made available.
DIMENSIONS, EXTERNAL:

Length overall	6.10 m (20 ft 0 in)
Height overall	2.08 m (6 ft 10 in)

HIPP'S SUPERBIRDS RELIANT SX
The Reliant SX is an Experimental version of the Reliant, retaining the single-seat accommodation of the microlight. Kits are available.
TYPE: Single-seat cabin homebuilt.
AIRFRAME: Strut braced high wings, of fabric covered wooden construction (detachable). Fabric covered fuselage and tail unit have 4130 steel tube structures. Non-retractable tailwheel landing gear.
POWER PLANT: One 30 kW (40 hp) Rotax 447. Fuel capacity 19 litres (5 US gallons; 4.2 Imp gallons). Optional wing tanks.
DIMENSIONS, EXTERNAL:

Wing span	9.14 m (30 ft 0 in)
Length overall	4.98 m (16 ft 4 in)
Height overall	1.63 m (5 ft 4 in)
Propeller diameter	1.52 m (5 ft 0 in)

AREA:

Wings, gross	11.15 m² (120.0 sq ft)

WEIGHTS:

Weight empty	129 kg (285 lb)
Max T-O weight	272 kg (600 lb)

PERFORMANCE:

Max level speed	87 knots (161 km/h; 100 mph)
Econ cruising speed	63 knots (117 km/h; 73 mph)
Stalling speed, power off	26 knots (49 km/h; 30 mph) IAS
Max rate of climb at S/L	350 m (1,150 ft)/min
T-O run	31-46 m (100-150 ft)
Landing run	46-61 m (150-200 ft)
Range: standard	104 nm (193 km; 120 miles)
with wing tanks	225 nm (418 km; 260 miles)

HIPP'S SUPERBIRDS SUPER KITTEN
This is an Experimental derivative of the Kitten microlight. Kits are available.

AIRFRAME: As for Reliant SX. Wheel fairings.
POWER PLANT: As for Reliant SX. Fuel capacity 49 litres (13 US gallons; 10.8 Imp gallons).
DIMENSIONS, EXTERNAL: As for Reliant SX.
AREA:

Wings, gross	10.41 m² (112.0 sq ft)

WEIGHTS:

Weight empty	129-131 kg (285-290 lb)
Pilot weight range	55-131 kg (120-290 lb)
Max T-O weight	272 kg (600 lb)

PERFORMANCE:

Max level speed	87 knots (161 km/h; 100 mph)
Cruising speed	65 knots (121 km/h; 75 mph)
Stalling speed	27 knots (50 km/h; 31 mph)
Max rate of climb at S/L	274 m (900 ft)/min
T-O to 15 m (50 ft)	153 m (500 ft)
Range	104-225 nm (193-418 km; 120-260 miles)

HIPP'S SUPERBIRDS SUPER SPORTSTER
This is an Experimental derivative of the J-4 Sportster microlight. Kits are available.
AIRFRAME, POWER PLANT AND DIMENSIONS, EXTERNAL: As for Reliant SX.
WEIGHTS:

Weight empty	125-129 kg (275-285 lb)
Pilot weight range	55-131 kg (120-290 lb)

PERFORMANCE:

Max level speed	87 knots (161 km/h; 100 mph)
Range	104-225 nm (193-418 km; 120-260 miles)

HISTORIC
HISTORIC AIRCRAFT CORPORATION
PO Box 2218, Durango, Colorado 81302
Telephone: 1 (303) 259 1037

HISTORIC AIRCRAFT PZL P.11c
HAC offers kits to construct its 66 per cent scale replica of the Polish P.11c gull-wing fighter of circa 1939. It was developed jointly with Aircraft Spruce & Specialty and Geschwender Aeromotive, which supply raw materials and components for the kits that HAC fabricates and Pinto engine conversions respectively. Construction takes approximately 1,600 working hours.
TYPE: Scale fighter replica.
AIRFRAME: Spruce and ply wooden wings, and welded 4130 steel tube fuselage and tail unit (with wooden fuselage stringers), all heat shrink Ceconite 7600 fabric covered. Wing section NACA 2412. Three-axis control. Non-retractable tailwheel landing gear.
POWER PLANT: One 56 kW (75 hp) Ford Pinto converted motorcar engine. Fuel capacity 49 litres (13 US gallons; 10.8 Imp gallons).
DIMENSIONS, EXTERNAL:

Wing span	9.14 m (30 ft 0 in)
Length overall	5.33 m (17 ft 6 in)
Height overall	2.08 m (6 ft 10 in)

WEIGHT:

Max T-O weight	485 kg (1,070 lb)

PERFORMANCE:

Cruising speed	74 knots (137 km/h; 85 mph)
Stalling speed	42 knots (78 km/h; 48 mph)
Range	260 nm (482 km; 300 miles)

HOLCOMB
JERRY HOLCOMB
Perigee Associates, 1010 North-East 122nd Avenue, Vancouver, Washington 98684
Telephone: 1 (206) 892 7732

HOLCOMB PERIGEE
The Perigee (originally Ultra Imp) was conceived as a single-seat tail-pusher aircraft, utilising the TPG form of construction described under the Aerocar heading in this section. The prototype flew for the first time on 4 April 1987.

The Perigee is no longer offered in plans form, but component parts are still available. Currently the Perigee is undergoing modification to the wings, and a new engine will be installed. Details of the Perigee, and an illustration, appeared in the 1989-90 *Jane's*.

JAVELIN
JAVELIN AIRCRAFT COMPANY INC
Municipal Airport, Augusta, Kansas 67010
Telephone: 1 (316) 733 1011
PRESIDENT AND CHIEF ENGINEER: David D. Blanton

JAVELIN WICHAWK
The prototype Wichawk first flew on 24 May 1971. Plans and some components are available; by January 1991 at least 254 Wichawks were under construction and more than 30 were flying.
TYPE: Two/three-seat, dual-control homebuilt sporting biplane.
AIRFRAME: Wing section NACA 23015. Each wing has two wooden spars and light alloy ribs, fabric covered. Ailerons on lower wings only. Welded fuselage and tail unit of steel tube, with light alloy tubular fuselage stringers, fabric covered. Non-retractable tailwheel landing gear.
POWER PLANT: Prototype has 134 kW (180 hp) Textron Lycoming O-360. Provision for alternative horizontally opposed or radial engines from 112 kW (150 hp) to 224 kW (300 hp). Fuel capacity 151.5 litres (40 US gallons; 33.5 Imp gallons).
DIMENSIONS, EXTERNAL:

Wing span (upper)	7.32 m (24 ft 0 in)
Length overall	5.87 m (19 ft 3 in)
Height overall	2.18 m (7 ft 2 in)
Propeller diameter	1.93 m (6 ft 4 in)

AREA:

Wings, gross	17.2 m² (185.0 sq ft)

WEIGHTS (A: prototype with 134 kW; 180 hp engine; B: three-seat version with six-cylinder engine):

Weight empty: A	582.5 kg (1,284.5 lb)
B	635 kg (1,400 lb)
Baggage capacity	54.4 kg (120 lb)
*Max T-O weight: A	907 kg (2,000 lb)
B	978 kg (2,156 lb)

**Max T-O weight is increased to 998 kg (2,200 lb) with high-powered engines*

PERFORMANCE (prototype with 134 kW; 180 hp engine):

Max level speed at S/L	121 knots (225 km/h; 140 mph)
Max cruising speed	110 knots (204 km/h; 127 mph)
Stalling speed	50 knots (92 km/h; 57 mph) IAS
Max rate of climb at S/L	518 m (1,700 ft)/min
T-O run	46 m (150 ft)
g limits	+12/-6

KELLY
DUDLEY R. KELLY
Route 4, Versailles, Kentucky 40383
Telephone: 1 (606) 873 5253

KELLY-D
The prototype Kelly-D first flew on 20 December 1981. Plans are available.
TYPE: Tandem two-seat homebuilt aerobatic biplane.
AIRFRAME: Wing section NACA 4412. Wooden wings, with wooden ailerons on lower wings only. Welded steel tube fuselage and wire braced tail unit. All fabric covered. Non-retractable tailwheel landing gear.
POWER PLANT: One 86 kW (115 hp) Textron Lycoming O-235. Fuel capacity 91 litres (24 US gallons; 20 Imp gallons).
DIMENSIONS, EXTERNAL:

Wing span (both)	8.03 m (26 ft 4 in)
Length overall	5.87 m (19 ft 3 in)
Height overall	2.36 m (7 ft 9 in)
Propeller diameter	1.88 m (6 ft 2 in)

AREA:

Wings, gross	19.54 m² (210.38 sq ft)

WEIGHTS:

Basic operating weight empty	431 kg (950 lb)
Baggage capacity	18 kg (40 lb)
Max T-O and landing weight	726 kg (1,600 lb)

PERFORMANCE:

Cruising speed	78 knots (145 km/h; 90 mph)
Stalling speed	39 knots (73 km/h; 45 mph)
Max rate of climb at S/L, pilot only	274 m (900 ft)/min
Range with max fuel, 20 min reserves	243 nm (450 km; 280 miles)

Hipp's Superbirds Reliant SX homebuilt

Kelly-D two-seat aerobatic biplane

Historic Aircraft PZL P.11c scale replica *(J. M. G. Gradidge)*

Kennedy Skycycle autogyros in single- and two-seat forms *(Geoffrey P. Jones)*

Javelin Wichawk built by Mr Bill Taylor of Sydney, Australia

KENNEDY

KENNEDY AIRCRAFT COMPANY INC
2405 North Coolidge Street, Orlando, Florida 32804
PRESIDENT: Edward Kennedy

KENNEDY SKYCYCLE and FLYCYCLE

First flown as a prototype in 1960, the developed Skycycle autogyro is now marketed in plans and kit forms, in single and tandem two-seat versions. A lightweight variant is also available as the Flycycle. All are covered under Experimental regulations, while the Flycycle can also meet microlight requirements.

ROTOR SYSTEM: Rotor of aluminium alloy construction, with two McCutchin Sky Wheel blades for Skycycles. Lightweight Rotordyne rotor for Flycycle. Pre-rotator fitted.

AIRFRAME: Basic structure of bolted square light alloy tubing, with plywood fairing on single-seat Skycycle, aluminium on two-seater, and no fairing on Flycycle. Non-retractable tricycle landing gear.

POWER PLANT: Skycycle single-seater and Flycycle have 35 kW (47 hp) Rotax 503. Fuel capacity 19 litres (5 US gallons; 4.2 Imp gallons). Skycycle two-seater has 48.5 kW (65 hp) Rotax 532. Fuel capacity 23 litres (6 US gallons; 5 Imp gallons) standard; 49 litres (13 US gallons; 10.8 Imp gallons) optional.

DIMENSIONS, EXTERNAL:

Rotor diameter: single-seaters	7.01 m (23 ft 0 in)
two-seater	7.62 m (25 ft 0 in)
Length of fuselage:	
single-seat Skycycle	3.35 m (11 ft 0 in)
two-seater	3.66 m (12 ft 0 in)
Height overall	2.13 m (7 ft 0 in)

WEIGHTS:

Weight empty: single-seat Skycycle	121 kg (267 lb)
two-seater	141 kg (310 lb)
Max pilot weight: single-seaters	113 kg (250 lb)
Max T-O weight: two-seat Skycycle	317 kg (700 lb)

PERFORMANCE:

Max level speed:	
single-seat Skycycle	69 knots (129 km/h; 80 mph)
two-seater	100 knots (185 km/h; 115 mph)
Cruising speed: two-seater	
	61-65 knots (113-121 km/h; 70-75 mph)
Min forward speed: single-seaters	
	7-9 knots (13-16 km/h; 8-10 mph)
T-O run, with pre-rotator: single-seaters	
	30.5-61 m (100-200 ft)
Endurance with standard fuel: two-seater	2 h

KIMBREL

MICHAEL G. KIMBREL
1333 Garrard Creek Road, Oakville, Washington 98568
Telephone: 1 (206) 273 9203

Details of the Kimbrel Butterfly and Banty can be found in the Microlight tables. Details of the Bathtub Mk 1 and an illustration can be found in the 1988-89 *Jane's*.

KOLB

KOLB COMPANY INC

RD 3, Box 38, Phoenixville, Pennsylvania 19460
Telephone and Fax: 1 (215) 948 4136
PRESIDENT: Homer Kolb
   Details of the FireStar KX and KXP can be found in the Microlight tables.

KOLB TWINSTAR MARK III

The original TwinStar first flew as a prototype in August 1984. The current model is the Mark III, featuring 360° visibility and improved performance. The canopy can be removed for warm weather flying or special work such as photography, or the cockpit can be partially enclosed. The prototype Mark III first flew in February 1990 and kit production started in July that year. By early 1991, 45 kits had been ordered and 30 delivered.
TYPE: Side by side two-seat homebuilt.
AIRFRAME: Welded 4130 steel cage structure and aluminium boom. Quick-folding wings have aluminium tube spar with aluminium ribs, double surface Stits Dacron covered. Kolb aerofoil section. Three-axis control, plus flaps. Non-retractable tailwheel landing gear, with brakes. Options include ballistic recovery parachute, floats, skis, and full upholstery package.
POWER PLANT: One 38.8 kW (52 hp) Rotax 503, with 2.58 : 1 reduction gear. Optional Rotax 582 or 912, Volkswagen or other engines up to 67 kW (90 hp). Fuel in two 19 litre (5 US gallon; 4.2 Imp gallon) tanks. Optional wing tanks under development.

DIMENSIONS, EXTERNAL:

Wing span	9.15 m (30 ft 0 in)
Length overall	6.86 m (22 ft 6 in)
Height overall	1.88 m (6 ft 2 in)
Propeller diameter	1.68 m (5 ft 6 in)

AREA:

Wings, gross	14.86 m² (160.0 sq ft)

WEIGHTS:

Weight empty, without fairing	159 kg (350 lb)
Pilot weight range	59-104 kg (130-230 lb)
Max T-O weight: normal	363 kg (800 lb)
max	453 kg (1,000 lb)

PERFORMANCE (at max T-O weight):

Max level speed at S/L	78 knots (145 km/h; 90 mph)
Max cruising speed at S/L	69 knots (129 km/h; 80 mph)
Econ cruising speed at S/L	65 knots (121 km/h; 75 mph)
Stalling speed at S/L, power off	
	26 knots (49 km/h; 30 mph)
Max rate of climb at S/L (582 engine)	
	290 m (950 ft)/min
T-O and landing run, on grass	61 m (200 ft)
g limits	+4/−2

KOLB LASER

Intended to fit between very fast homebuilts and microlights, design goals for the Laser included low weight, low landing speed, good visibility and easy portability; set-up and take-down takes five minutes. Construction of the prototype began in February 1990 and it flew that year. Orders for kits have been taken from April 1991. Options include parachute, electric start, wheel fairings, strobe and blown canopy.

TYPE: Two-seat homebuilt monoplane.
AIRFRAME: Cantilever low-wing monoplane. Aluminium alloy wings and welded 4130 steel-tube fuselage structure, with Stits fabric covering. Wings fold. Wing section NACA 23012. Three-axis control, plus flaps. Non-retractable tailwheel landing gear.
POWER PLANT: One 48.5 kW (65 hp) Rotax 582 with 2.58 : 1 reduction gear. Alternative 59.7 kW (80 hp) Rotax 912; adaptable for a Volkswagen converted motorcar engine. Fuel capacity 38 litres (10 US gallons; 8.3 Imp gallons). Optional 19 litre (5 US gallon; 4.15 Imp gallon) auxiliary tank.

DIMENSIONS, EXTERNAL:

Wing span	6.71 m (22 ft 0 in)
Length overall	5.64 m (18 ft 6 in)
Height overall	1.50 m (4 ft 11 in)
Propeller diameter	1.60 m (5 ft 3 in)

AREA:

Wings, gross	9.29 m² (100.0 sq ft)

WEIGHTS:

Weight empty (582 engine)	159 kg (350 lb)
Baggage capacity	9 kg (20 lb)
Max T-O weight	385 kg (850 lb)

PERFORMANCE (estimated):

Max level speed at S/L	96 knots (177 km/h; 110 mph)
Max cruising speed at S/L	87 knots (161 km/h; 100 mph)
Econ cruising speed at S/L	78 knots (145 km/h; 90 mph)
Stalling speed, power off	39 knots (73 km/h; 45 mph)
Max rate of climb at S/L (582 engine)	
	290 m (950 ft)/min
T-O and landing run	122 m (400 ft)
g limits	+6/−3

LAVEN

JOE LAVEN

PO Box 415, Desert Hot Springs, California 92240
Telephone: 1 (619) 329 9354

LAVEN LACO-125, LACO-145 and SPECIAL

The original **LACO-125** prototype first flew on 29 May 1977. It was followed by the more powerful **LACO-145**. Plans for both models are available. The **Special** is a version of the LACO-145 being built to test minor structural changes for possible future inclusion on plans (including removable rear canopy). The main aim of these changes is to reduce the cost of construction.
TYPE: Two-seat homebuilt biplane.
AIRFRAME: Wing section NACA 2412. Wing structure has wooden spars and ribs, aluminium leading- and trailing-edges, and steel fittings. Modified Frise ailerons on lower wings only. Welded Warren truss fuselage of steel tubing, with wooden formers and stringers. Braced tail unit of welded steel tubing. Entire airframe fabric covered. Non-retractable tailwheel landing gear.
POWER PLANT: LACO-125: One 93 kW (125 hp) Teledyne Continental C-125-2. LACO-145: One 108 kW (145 hp) Teledyne Continental C-145. Fuel capacity 91 litres (24 US gallons; 20 Imp gallons).

DIMENSIONS, EXTERNAL:

Wing span: upper	6.93 m (22 ft 8¾ in)
lower	6.29 m (20 ft 7½ in)
Length overall	5.94 m (19 ft 6 in)
Height overall	2.18 m (7 ft 2 in)
Propeller diameter: LACO-125	1.83 m (6 ft 0 in)
LACO-145	1.93 m (6 ft 4 in)

AREA:

Wings, gross	13.94 m² (150.0 sq ft)

WEIGHTS:

Weight empty	390 kg (860 lb)
Max T-O weight	635 kg (1,400 lb)

PERFORMANCE (A: LACO-125, B: LACO-145):

Max level speed: A	108 knots (200 km/h; 124 mph)
B	115 knots (212 km/h; 132 mph)
Max cruising speed: A	98 knots (182 km/h; 113 mph)
B	104 knots (193 km/h; 120 mph)
Stalling speed:	
power off: A, B	49 knots (90 km/h; 56 mph)
power on: A	44 knots (81 km/h; 50 mph)
B	42 knots (78 km/h; 48 mph)
Max rate of climb at S/L: A	274 m (900 ft)/min
B	366 m (1,200 ft)/min
Range with max fuel	282 nm (523 km; 325 miles)

LIGHT MINIATURE

LIGHT MINIATURE AIRCRAFT INC

Building 411, Opa-Locka Airport, Opa-Locka, Florida 33054
Telephone: 1 (305) 681 4068
Fax: 1 (305) 687 9801
PRESIDENT: Fred F. McCallum

LIGHT MINIATURE AIRCRAFT LM-1

This is basically a single-seat three-quarter scale Piper J-3 Cub replica. The prototype first flew on 15 July 1983.
   Plans for the LM-1 are available. Estimated building time from plans is 600-750 working hours. Complete kits, partial kits and component parts for the LM-1 are available from Wicks Aircraft Supply, Highland, Illinois 62249.
TYPE: Single-seat homebuilt.
AIRFRAME: Wing section NACA 4412 modified. Dacron-covered all-wood airframe, except for aluminium alloy wing and aileron ribs. Non-retractable tailwheel landing gear.
POWER PLANT: One 29.4 kW (39.4 hp) Rotax 447 or 22.4 kW (30 hp) Cuyuna 430RR. Fuel capacity 21 litres (5.5 US gallons; 4.6 Imp gallons).

DIMENSIONS, EXTERNAL:

Wing span	8.23 m (27 ft 0 in)
Length overall	5.38 m (17 ft 8 in)
Height overall	1.70 m (5 ft 7 in)
Propeller diameter	1.27 m (4 ft 2 in)

AREA:

Wings, gross	11.29 m² (121.5 sq ft)

WEIGHTS:

Weight empty	152 kg (335 lb)
Max T-O and landing weight	272 kg (600 lb)

PERFORMANCE:

Max level speed and max cruising speed at 610 m (2,000 ft)	56 knots (105 km/h; 65 mph)
Econ cruising speed	43 knots (80 km/h; 50 mph)
Stalling speed, engine idling	
	21 knots (39 km/h; 24 mph)
Max rate of climb at S/L	152-183 m (500-600 ft)/min
T-O run	61 m (200 ft)
Landing run	91-107 m (300-350 ft)
Range, with 30 min reserves	139 nm (257 km; 160 miles)

LIGHT MINIATURE AIRCRAFT LM-1U and LM-1X

The prototype **LM-1U** microlight variant of the LM-1 flew for the first time on 7 April 1985. Kits are available, together with kits of an Experimental category homebuilt version, known as the **LM-1X**, which is identical except for having a 26 kW (35 hp) Rotax 377 engine and increased empty weight. Estimated construction time is 250-350 working hours.
   The following details refer to the LM-1U:
TYPE: Single-seat microlight: conforms to FAR Pt 103.
AIRFRAME: Wing section Göttingen 387 modified. Aluminium alloy airframe, except for wooden wing spars and overall Dacron covering. Three-axis control. Non-retractable tailwheel landing gear. Ballistic parachute and floats optional.
POWER PLANT: One 20 kW (27 hp) Rotax 277. Fuel capacity 20.4 litres (5.4 US gallons; 4.5 Imp gallons).

DIMENSIONS, EXTERNAL:

Wing span	9.14 m (30 ft 0 in)
Length overall	5.44 m (17 ft 10 in)
Height overall	1.70 m (5 ft 7 in)
Propeller diameter	1.52 m (5 ft 0 in)

AREA:

Wings, gross	10.87 m² (117.0 sq ft)

WEIGHTS (LM-1U):

Weight empty	114 kg (252 lb)
Pilot weight range	62-102 kg (135-225 lb)
Max baggage capacity	11.3 kg (25 lb)
Max T-O weight	238 kg (525 lb)

PERFORMANCE (LM-1U):

Max level speed at 305 m (1,000 ft)	
	61 knots (113 km/h; 70 mph)
Econ cruising speed at 305 m (1,000 ft)	
	47 knots (87 km/h; 54 mph)
Stalling speed, engine idling	
	23 knots (42 km/h; 26 mph)
Max rate of climb at S/L	168 m (550 ft)/min
T-O run	61 m (200 ft)
Landing run	91 m (300 ft)
Range, with 15 min reserves	
	156 nm (289 km; 180 miles)

LIGHT MINIATURE AIRCRAFT LM-2U, LM-2P and LM-2X

The single-seat LM-2U microlight appears to be very similar to the LM-1U, with reportedly identical dimensions, weights and engine. The LM-2P and LM-2X are two-seaters of similar type, reportedly powered by the Rotax 503. All are available in kit form, the two-seaters requiring an estimated 350-450 working hours to assemble.
   The following brief details refer to the two-seaters:
TYPE: Two-seat microlight or homebuilt monoplanes.

DIMENSION, EXTERNAL:

Wing span	9.94 m (32 ft 7¼ in)

WEIGHTS:

Weight empty	188 kg (415 lb)
Max T-O weight	397 kg (875 lb)

PERFORMANCE:

Max cruising speed	65 knots (121 km/h; 75 mph)
Stalling speed	28 knots (52 km/h; 32 mph)
Max rate of climb at S/L	229 m (750 ft)/min

LIGHT MINIATURE AIRCRAFT LM-3U and LM-3X

Identical except for engine and empty weight, the microlight **LM-3U** and Experimental category homebuilt **LM-3X** are three-quarter scale representations of the Aeronca 7AC Champ light aircraft. Kits to build the LM-3U and LM-3X include the appropriate Rotax engine and require an estimated 250-350 working hours to complete. The prototype LM-3 flew for the first time in July 1986.
TYPES: Single-seat microlight (LM-3U) and homebuilt (LM-3X); LM-3U conforms to FAR Pt 103 and LM-3X to Experimental category regulations.
AIRFRAME: Wing section Göttingen 387. Ceconite covered wings, with wooden spars, stamped aluminium ribs and glassfibre leading-edges. Aluminium alloy fuselage longerons, uprights and cross members, with wooden formers and stringers, Ceconite covered. Glassfibre engine cowling. Three-axis control. Non-retractable tailwheel landing gear. Optional floats and recovery parachute.

Kolb TwinStar Mark III

Light Miniature Aircraft LM-3X homebuilt aircraft

Kolb Laser two-seat homebuilt

Lightning Bug Aircraft Lightning Bug single-seat homebuilt
(J. M. G. Gradidge)

Laven LACO-145 two-seat light biplane

POWER PLANT: LM-3U: One 20 kW (27 hp) Rotax 277. LM-3X: One 26 kW (35 hp) Rotax 377. Fuel capacity 19 litres (5 US gallons; 4.2 Imp gallons). LM-3X has option of two 20.4 litre (5.4 US gallon; 4.5 Imp gallon) auxiliary fuel tanks fitted in wingroots.

AVIONICS: Hand-held radio.

DIMENSIONS, EXTERNAL:

Wing span	9.14 m (30 ft 0 in)
Length overall	5.33 m (17 ft 6 in)
Height overall	1.70 m (5 ft 7 in)
Propeller diameter: LM-3U	1.52 m (5 ft 0 in)
LM-3X	1.63 m (5 ft 4 in)

AREA:

Wings, gross: both	11.15 m² (120.0 sq ft)

WEIGHTS (A: LM-3U, B: LM-3X):

Weight empty: A	114 kg (252 lb)
B	147 kg (325 lb)
Pilot weight range: A, B	61.5-102 kg (135-225 lb)
Baggage capacity	11.3 kg (25 lb)
Max T-O weight: A	249 kg (550 lb)
B	272 kg (600 lb)

PERFORMANCE (A and B as above):

Max level speed: A, B	65 knots (121 km/h; 75 mph)
Econ cruising speed: A, B	48 knots (89 km/h; 55 mph)

Stalling speed:

A, B	19-24 knots (36-44 km/h; 22-27 mph)
Max rate of climb at S/L: A	168 m (550 ft)/min
B	183 m (600 ft)/min
T-O run: A, B	46-61 m (150-200 ft)
Landing from 15 m (50 ft): A, B	76-91 m (250-300 ft)

Range, standard fuel, with reserves:

A	130 nm (241 km; 150 miles)
B	95 nm (177 km; 110 miles)
Endurance: A	3 h
B	2 h
g limits: A, B	+5/-4.5

LIGHTNING BUG
LIGHTNING BUG AIRCRAFT CORPORATION
PO Drawer 40, Sheldon, South Carolina 29941
OWNER/DESIGNER: Nick Jones

LIGHTNING BUG AIRCRAFT LIGHTNING BUG

Kits are being made available to construct this single-seat sporting aircraft. The prototype was built by Johnny Murphy of Cape Canaveral, Florida, and now features a tailwheel landing gear (originally a monowheel and outriggers). However, kits feature the new tricycle landing gear.

The following details refer to kit-built aircraft:

TYPE: Single-seat sporting homebuilt.

AIRFRAME: Composites construction. Three-axis control, plus slotted flaps over 57 per cent of span. Non-retractable tricycle landing gear.

POWER PLANT: One 64-67 kW (86-90 hp) AMW three-cylinder two-stroke engine. Standard fuel capacity 83.3 litres (22 US gallons; 18.3 Imp gallons).

DIMENSIONS, EXTERNAL:

Wing span	5.38 m (17 ft 8 in)
Length overall	5.36 m (17 ft 7 in)

AREA:

Wings, gross	3.72 m² (40.0 sq ft)

WEIGHTS:

Weight empty	170 kg (375 lb)
Max T-O weight	340 kg (750 lb)

PERFORMANCE:

Max level speed	200 knots (370 km/h; 230 mph)
Stalling speed: clean	74 knots (137 km/h; 85 mph)
flaps down	54-65 knots (100-121 km/h; 62-75 mph)

LOEHLE
LOEHLE ENTERPRISES
'The Aviation Valley', Shipmans Creek Road, Wartrace, Tennessee 37183
Telephone: 1 (615) 857 3419
Fax: 1 (615) 857 3908
PRESIDENT: Michael Loehle
SALES: Mark Gonzales

Loehle Enterprises no longer produces microlight aircraft. Details of the Ritz Standard Model A, UFM of KY Aeroplane XP and The Fun Machine can be found in the 1989-90 and earlier editions of *Jane's*.

LOEHLE ENTERPRISES 5151 and 5151RG MUSTANG

The 5151 Mustang is an approximate ¾-scale representation of a Second World War North American P-51 Mustang fighter, offered in kit form under the Experimental category regulations. Construction time is approximately 400-500 working hours. A series of 11 partial kits are also available to help spread costs.

The prototype flew for the first time on 30 January 1986. The standard kit is for the non-retractable landing gear model but retractable gear is optional (as the 5151RG). Other optional items include auxiliary fuel tanks, brakes, remote/electric starter, custom upholstery, custom dorsal fin, moulded wing and tail tips, electric elevator trim, ballistic parachute, and a range of avionics and other equipment.

TYPE: Single-seat homebuilt aircraft.

AIRFRAME: Cantilever low-wing monoplane. Constructed primarily of wood, with both conventional and geodetic structures. The whole assembly is glued together, using a T-88 epoxy, and is fabric covered. NACA 44 series wing section. Three-axis control. Non-retractable or optional retractable tricycle landing gear. Optional brakes.

POWER PLANT: One 34 kW (46 hp) Rotax 503 on 5151 Mustang; Rotax 503 or 48.5 kW (65 hp) 582 on 5151RG Mustang. Standard fuel capacity 19 litres (5 US gallons;

4.2 Imp gallons). Optional 49 litres (13 US gallons; 10.8 Imp gallons) using two 15 litre (4 US gallon; 3.33 Imp gallon) auxiliary tanks in wings.

DIMENSIONS, EXTERNAL:

Wing span	8.36 m (27 ft 5 in)
Length overall	6.96 m (22 ft 10 in)
Height overall	1.83 m (6 ft 0 in)
Propeller diameter:	
Rotax 503 engine	1.73 m (5 ft 8 in)
Rotax 582 engine	1.83 m (6 ft 0 in)

AREA:

Wings, gross	12.08 m² (130.0 sq ft)

WEIGHTS (A: 5151, B: 5151RG):

Weight empty: A	233 kg (513 lb)
B	238 kg (525 lb)
B, with full options	266 kg (588 lb)
Max pilot weight: A, B	100 kg (220 lb)
Max T-O weight	401 kg (885 lb)

PERFORMANCE (A and B as above):

Max level speed at S/L:	
B	87 knots (161 km/h; 100 mph)
Cruising speed at S/L:	
A	65 knots (121 km/h; 75 mph)
B	74 knots (137 km/h; 85 mph)
Econ cruising speed at S/L:	
B	65 knots (121 km/h; 75 mph)
Stalling speed, engine idling	
	26 knots (49 km/h; 30 mph)
Max rate of climb at S/L:	
A	244-305 m (800-1,000 ft)/min
B	more than 366 m (1,200 ft)/min
Service ceiling: B	more than 3,050 m (10,000 ft)
T-O run	46 m (150 ft)
Landing run	77 m (250 ft)
Range: A, with 5 US gallons	100 nm (185 km; 115 miles)
A, with 13 US gallons	258 nm (478 km; 297 miles)
B, with 5 US gallons	108 nm (201 km; 125 miles)
B, with 13 US gallons	273 nm (507 km; 315 miles)
Endurance: B	3 h
g limits	+4.2/−2.7 standard
	+6/−3 ultimate

LUNDY
BRIAN LUNDY
c/o Steve Kotula, 1592 South 13th East, Salt Lake City, Utah 84105

LUNDY GRAFLITE
Mr Brian Lundy and Mr Steve Kotula, both mechanical engineers in composite construction, designed the Graflite with the first-time builder in mind. The prototype first flew on 11 July 1987 and kits became available in late 1988. An aerobatic version is optional.

The following details refer to the prototype. The kit-built version has as standard a Textron Lycoming O-360 engine and fuel capacity of 170 litres (45 US gallons; 37.5 Imp gallons).

TYPE: Side by side two-seat homebuilt.
AIRFRAME: Moulded and vacuum bagged components of graphite/epoxy/core sandwich construction. Wing section NACA 64212.5. Winglets standard. Retractable tricycle landing gear.
POWER PLANT: One 112 kW (150 hp) Textron Lycoming O-320-A2B. Fuel capacity 129 litres (34 US gallons; 28.3 Imp gallons).

DIMENSIONS, EXTERNAL:

Wing span over winglets	7.67 m (25 ft 2 in)
Length overall	6.32 m (20 ft 9 in)
Height overall	1.88 m (6 ft 2 in)
Propeller diameter	1.70 m (5 ft 7 in)

WEIGHTS:

Weight empty	449 kg (989 lb)
Max crew weight	154 kg (340 lb)
Baggage weight	41 kg (90 lb)
Max T-O weight	726 kg (1,600 lb)

PERFORMANCE:

Max level speed at S/L	180 knots (333 km/h; 207 mph)
Econ cruising speed at 2,440 m (8,000 ft)	
	156 knots (290 km/h; 180 mph)
Stalling speed, engine idling	
	56 knots (103 km/h; 64 mph)
Max rate of climb at S/L	457 m (1,500 ft)/min
Service ceiling	5,790 m (19,000 ft)
Range with max fuel	547 nm (1,014 km; 630 miles)
Endurance	3 h 30 min
g limits	+4.4/−3

MACFAM
MACFAM
Box 788, Great Falls, Montana 59403-0788
Telephone: 1 (403) 235 6331
Readopting an earlier name, MacFam (formerly McAsco) offers plans for its Cavalier range of homebuilts, plus the Jungsters designed by Mr Rim Kaminskas.

MACFAM SA 102.5 CAVALIER
The prototype SA 102.5 Cavalier was being reworked and refurbished in an effort to reduce empty weight from the original 477 kg (1,051 lb) to 408 kg (900 lb). Fitted with a Teledyne Continental O-200 engine and a new wooden propeller, it was anticipated that a true air speed of 139 knots (257 km/h; 160 mph) could be achieved at 2,450 rpm, at a maximum weight of about 658-680 kg (1,450-1,500 lb). This prototype was also to receive a front hinged 'swing up' windshield and canopy with a composites frame and new wing flaps. The flaps were expected to offer up to a 15 per cent increase in cruising speed. Both these innovations are shown on plans.
TYPE: Side by side two-seat homebuilt.
AIRFRAME: All-wood airframe except for Dacron covered outer wing panels, rear top decking and tail unit, plus glassfibre cockpit canopy frame and doors. Wing section NACA 23015 at root, NACA 23012 at tip. Non-retractable tricycle landing gear, with optional floats or skis.
POWER PLANT: Wide choice of four-cylinder engines, including 63.5, 67 or 74.5 kW (85, 90 or 100 hp) Teledyne Continental, 93-97 kW (125-130 hp) Franklin Sport 4A, 80.5 or 86 kW (108 or 115 hp) Textron Lycoming O-235, or 93 or 101 kW (125 or 135 hp) Textron Lycoming O-290. Wingtip fuel tanks, total capacity 151 litres (40 US gallons; 33.5 Imp gallons).

DIMENSIONS, EXTERNAL:

Wing span over tip tanks	8.33 m (27 ft 4 in)
Length overall	6.71 m (22 ft 0 in)
Height overall	2.23 m (7 ft 4 in)

AREA:

Wings, gross	10.87 m² (117.0 sq ft)

WEIGHTS:

Basic operating weight empty	408 kg (900 lb)
Baggage weight	56 kg (125 lb)
Max T-O weight	680 kg (1,500 lb)

PERFORMANCE (at max T-O weight, 93 kW; 125 hp Textron Lycoming engine):

Max level speed at 2,135 m (7,000 ft)	
	160 knots (297 km/h; 185 mph)
Econ cruising speed	134 knots (249 km/h; 155 mph)
Stalling speed:	
flaps up	44 knots (81 km/h; 50 mph) IAS
flaps down	35 knots (65 km/h; 40 mph) IAS
Max rate of climb at S/L	over 518 m (1,700 ft)/min
Service ceiling	4,875 m (16,000 ft)
T-O run	107 m (350 ft)
Landing run	183 m (600 ft)
Max range, no reserves	720 nm (1,335 km; 830 miles)

MACFAM JUNGSTER I
The primary design requirements of this aircraft were to duplicate as closely as possible the performance and flight characteristics of the Bücker Jungmeister. The prototype flew for the first time in October 1962. Sets of plans have been available to amateur constructors for many years, with several hundred sets sold.
TYPE: Single-seat sporting homebuilt.
AIRFRAME: Braced biplane with wood structure, plywood and fabric covered except for aluminium alloy engine cowling. Wing section NACA 4413. Non-retractable tailwheel landing gear.
POWER PLANT: Options include 63.4-74.5 kW (85-100 hp) Teledyne Continental C85, C90 or O-200; 93-97 kW (125-130 hp) Franklin Sport 4, 4A or 4B; 80.5-86 kW (108-115 hp) Textron Lycoming O-235-C or -C1; 93-100.6 kW (125-135 hp) Textron Lycoming O-290-D or -D2; 104.5-112 kW (140-150 hp) Textron Lycoming O-320; or European engines in the same weight/power class. Fuel capacity 62 litres (16.5 US gallons; 13.7 Imp gallons); optional 26 litre (7 US gallon; 5.8 Imp gallon) tank in upper wing centre-section, increasing total capacity to 88 litres (23.5 US gallons; 19.5 Imp gallons).

DIMENSIONS, EXTERNAL (prototype):

Wing span	5.08 m (16 ft 8 in)
Length overall	4.88 m (16 ft 0 in)
Propeller diameter	1.73 m (5 ft 8 in)

AREA:

Wings, gross	7.43 m² (80.0 sq ft)

WEIGHTS:

Weight empty	275 kg (606 lb)
T-O weight, aerobatic	385 kg (850 lb)
Max T-O weight	455 kg (1,000 lb)

PERFORMANCE (prototype, at max T-O weight, Textron Lycoming O-235 engine):

Max level speed at S/L	
	109 knots (201 km/h; 125 mph) IAS
Max cruising speed at S/L	
	103 knots (192 km/h; 119 mph)
Stalling speed	45 knots (84 km/h; 52 mph) IAS
Max rate of climb at S/L	455 m (1,500 ft)/min
Service ceiling	3,960 m (13,000 ft)
T-O run	91 m (300 ft)
Landing run	152 m (500 ft)
Range with max fuel (incl centre-section tank)	
	260 nm (482 km; 300 miles)
g limits	+9/−6

MACFAM JUNGSTER II
The prototype of this strut braced parasol monoplane flew for the first time in March 1966. Plans are available.
TYPE: Single-seat sporting homebuilt.
AIRFRAME: All-wood structure, plywood and fabric covered. Wing section NACA 2412. Non-retractable tailwheel landing gear.
POWER PLANT (prototype): One 134 kW (180 hp) Textron Lycoming O-360. Fuel capacity 75 litres (20 US gallons; 16.7 Imp gallons). Other engines available optionally include those listed under Jungster I description, plus 119 kW (160 hp) Textron Lycoming O-320 and 134 kW (180 hp) Textron Lycoming O-360.

DIMENSIONS, EXTERNAL:

Wing span	6.81 m (22 ft 4 in)
Length overall (tail up)	5.16 m (16 ft 11 in)
Height to top of wings (tail up)	2.06 m (6 ft 9 in)
Propeller diameter	1.68 m (5 ft 6 in)

MAGNUM
MAGNUM INDUSTRIES
9815 Lemona Avenue, Sepulveda, California 91343
Telephone: 1 (818) 893 9240
GENERAL MANAGER: Rodney E. Gage
In June 1987 Magnum Industries acquired from Delta Technology all assets related to the Nomad and Honcho series of microlights. An expanded manufacturing facility was established at Palmdale, California.

MAGNUM NOMAD II
Details of this microlight can be found in the Microlights section.

MAGNUM SUPER-HONCHO
The Honcho II is generally similar to the Nomad, except for a shorter fuselage and shorter span wings (detailed in the Microlights section). The Super-Honcho does not conform to FAA Part 103 but is an approved kit under Part 21. As nearly all Super-Honchos in the USA have received certification in the Experimental category, it is included in this section of the book.
TYPE: Single-seat microlight/homebuilt.
AIRFRAME: All-aluminium frame. Flying surfaces covered with Ceconite. Three-axis control. Non-retractable tricycle landing gear.
POWER PLANT: One 37.3 kW (50 hp) Rotax 503.

DIMENSIONS, EXTERNAL:

Wing span	9.80 m (32 ft 2 in)
Length overall	5.46 m (17 ft 11 in)
Height overall	3.02 m (9 ft 11 in)
Propeller diameter	1.37 m (4 ft 6 in)

AREA:

Wings, gross	12.20 m² (131.35 sq ft)

WEIGHTS:

Weight empty	110 kg (243 lb)
Max T-O weight	238 kg (525 lb)

PERFORMANCE (at max T-O weight):

Max level speed	55 knots (101 km/h; 63 mph) CAS
Max cruising speed	50 knots (93 km/h; 58 mph) CAS
Stalling speed	24 knots (44 km/h; 27 mph) CAS
Max rate of climb at S/L	481 m (1,580 ft)/min
Absolute power ceiling	5,335 m (17,500 ft)
T-O run, firm ground	18.5 m (60 ft)
Range with max fuel	121 nm (225 km; 140 miles)
Endurance with max fuel	2 h 24 min
g limits	+6.67/−3.5

Loehle Enterprises 5151RG Mustang homebuilt

Jungster II monoplane owned by Mr Ed Sullivan of Fresno, California
(*J. M. G. Gradidge*)

MacFam marketed Jungster I built by Mr Dave Clark of Renton, Washington

Marquart MA-5 Charger built by Mr Remo Galeazzi of Petaluma, California
(*John Wegg*)

Mirage Celerity (Textron Lycoming O-320)

Lundy Graflite all-composites homebuilt aircraft

MARQUART
ED MARQUART
PO Box 3032, Riverside, California 92519
Telephone: 1 (714) 683 9582

MARQUART MA-4 LANCER
Available in plans form only, the Lancer is a single-seat biplane powered by an engine in the 48.5-93.2 kW (65-125 hp) range. Construction is of wood, steel tube and fabric.

DIMENSIONS, EXTERNAL:
Wing span	6.10 m (20 ft 0 in)
Length overall	5.03 m (16 ft 6 in)
Height overall	1.98 m (6 ft 6 in)

AREA:
Wings, gross	10.78 m² (116.0 sq ft)

WEIGHTS:
Weight empty	295 kg (650 lb)
Max T-O weight	454 kg (1,000 lb)

PERFORMANCE (93.2 kW; 125 hp engine):
Max level speed	113 knots (209 km/h; 130 mph)
Cruising speed	104 knots (193 km/h; 120 mph)
Stalling speed	48 knots (89 km/h; 55 mph)
Max rate of climb at S/L	488 m (1,600 ft)/min
Service ceiling	3,050 m (10,000 ft)
T-O run	91 m (300 ft)
Landing run	244 m (800 ft)
Range	325 nm (603 km; 375 miles)

MARQUART MA-5 CHARGER
Plans and component parts of this popular homebuilt biplane are available.

TYPE: Two-seat homebuilt sporting biplane.

AIRFRAME: Wooden wings and steel tube fuselage, all fabric covered. Non-retractable tailwheel landing gear.

POWER PLANT: One engine of 74.6-134 kW (100-180 hp); typically, a 134 kW (180 hp) Textron Lycoming O-360-A1G6. Fuel capacity 98.4 litres (26 US gallons; 21.6 Imp gallons).

DIMENSIONS, EXTERNAL:
Wing span	7.32 m (24 ft 0 in)
Length overall	5.94 m (19 ft 6 in)
Height overall	2.29 m (7 ft 6 in)

AREA:
Wings, gross	15.8 m² (170.0 sq ft)

WEIGHTS:
Weight empty	454 kg (1,000 lb)
Baggage capacity	11.3 kg (25 lb)
Max T-O weight	703 kg (1,550 lb)

PERFORMANCE (134 kW; 180 hp engine):
Max level speed	126 knots (233 km/h; 145 mph)
Max cruising speed	117 knots (217 km/h; 135 mph)
Stalling speed	37 knots (68 km/h; 42 mph)
Max rate of climb at S/L	549 m (1,800 ft)/min
Service ceiling	4,260 m (14,000 ft)
T-O run	122 m (400 ft)
Landing run	244 m (800 ft)
Range with max fuel	390 nm (724 km; 450 miles)

MAXAIR
MAXAIR AIRCRAFT CORPORATION
1101 West Savannah Avenue, Valdosta, GA 31603
Telephone: 1 (800) 969 0771
Fax: 1 (912) 333 9608
DIRECTOR OF MARKETING AND SALES: Donald Jones

MAXAIR DRIFTER/ARV SERIES
In addition to five original versions of the Drifter, cable braced models of the XP503 and MU532 became available in August 1988. Each was provided with a single chrome molybdenum steel tube strut each side and stamped aluminium alloy ribs, plus full-span flaperons for STOL performance. Kits of all models were made available; by February 1990 a total of 1,796 Drifter kits had been delivered. It is believed that the latest current single- and two-seat models are known as ARVs, comprising ARV 277, ARV 503 and ARV 582.

DR277. Original single-seat model of the Drifter with Rotax 277 engine, introduced in early 1983 and the only version made available also in ready assembled form. Conforms to FAR Pt 103 requirements. **ARV 277** is believed to be the current designation. Assembly from a kit takes about 70 working hours.

DR377. More powerful Drifter single-seater, with Rotax 377 engine.

XP503. Tandem two-seat, dual control version of the basic Drifter. Higher weight made it an Experimental category homebuilt aircraft. **ARV 503** is believed to be the latest form. Assembly from a kit takes about 70 working hours.

MU532. Tandem two-seat, dual control utility counterpart of XP503, conceived for heavy duty applications such as floatplane operation and agricultural spraying.

Strengthened wings and landing gear permit a 245 kg (540 lb) useful load. Rotax 532 engine.

DR532 Rocket. High-performance single-seat version of Drifter with Rotax 532, shorter wing span and wide-chord full span ailerons for quick roll response. Classed as Experimental category homebuilt.

ARV 582. Believed to be the latest high-performance single-seater, with a Rotax 582 engine. Assembly from a kit takes about 70 working hours.

TYPE: DR277 and DR377 conform to FAR Pt 103, other models to FAA, ARV and Experimental requirements.

AIRFRAME: Braced mainframe of steel and aluminium alloy tube. Wings and tail surfaces have double surface Dacron/Stits Aerothane covering. Three-axis control. Non-retractable tailwheel landing gear. Options include skis, floats, amphibious gear and nose fairings.

POWER PLANT: DR277 and ARV 277: One 20 kW (27 hp) Rotax 277. DR377: One 26 kW (35 hp) Rotax 377. XP503 and ARV 503: One 34 kW (46 hp) Rotax 503. MU532 and DR532: One 47.7 kW (64 hp) Rotax 532. ARV 582: One 47 kW (63 hp) Rotax 582. Alternative engines may be 44.7 and 67 kW (60 and 90 hp) AMWs. Fuel capacity 19 litres (5 US gallons; 4.2 Imp gallons) standard; 38 litres (10 US gallons; 8.3 Imp gallons) optional.

DIMENSIONS, EXTERNAL (A: ARV 277, B: ARV 503, C: MU532, D: DR532, and E: ARV582):

Wing span: A, B, C		9.14 m (30 ft 0 in)
D, E		7.01 m (23 ft 0 in)
Length overall: A, B, C, D		5.79 m (19 ft 0 in)
Height overall: A		2.67 m (8 ft 9 in)
B, C		2.82 m (9 ft 3 in)
D		2.79 m (9 ft 2 in)
Propeller diameter: A, B, C, D		1.52 m (5 ft 0 in)

AREAS:

Wings, gross: A, B, C		14.12 m² (152.0 sq ft)
D, E		10.87 m² (117.0 sq ft)

WEIGHTS (A, B, C and D as above):

Weight empty: A		109 kg (240 lb)
B, D, E		156.5 kg (345 lb)
C		166 kg (365 lb)
Max pilot weight: A		104 kg (230 lb)
B, C		109 kg (240 lb)
D		104 kg (230 lb)
Max T-O weight: A		238 kg (525 lb)
B		340 kg (750 lb)
C		408 kg (900 lb)
D		272 kg (600 lb)
E		295 kg (650 lb)

PERFORMANCE (A and D with 79 kg; 175 lb pilot, B and C with two 79 kg; 175 lb crew):

Max level speed: A		55 knots (101 km/h; 63 mph)
B		65 knots (120 km/h; 75 mph)
C, D		82 knots (153 km/h; 95 mph)
Cruising speed: A		52 knots (97 km/h; 60 mph)
B		56 knots (105 km/h; 65 mph)
E		65 knots (120 km/h; 75 mph)
Econ cruising speed: A		35 knots (64 km/h; 40 mph)
Stalling speed: A		23 knots (42 km/h; 26 mph)
B		27 knots (50 km/h; 31 mph)
C		31 knots (57 km/h; 35 mph)
D, E		32 knots (60 km/h; 37 mph)
Max rate of climb at S/L: A, B		183 m (600 ft)/min
C		244 m (800 ft)/min
D, E		427 m (1,400 ft)/min
Service ceiling: A		3,050 m (10,000 ft)
T-O run: A		46-84 m (150-275 ft)
B		76-107 m (250-350 ft)
C		46-107 m (150-350 ft)
D		79 m (260 ft)
Landing run with brakes: A		69 m (225 ft)
B, D		76 m (250 ft)
C		91 m (300 ft)
Range, 65% power: A		104 nm (193 km; 120 miles)
B		87 nm (161 km; 100 miles)
C		74 nm (136 km; 85 miles)
D		69 nm (129 km; 80 miles)
Endurance with max fuel: A		2 h 30 min
g limits: A		+6/−3.3
B		+4.2 limit
B		+6/−3 ultimate

MILLER
MILLER AIR SPORTS INC
Bourne Stage Airfield, Route 3, Box 3450, Bourne, Texas 78006
Telephone: 1 (512) 755 8702

The 1988-89 *Jane's* gave brief details of the Texas Gem. This is no longer sold, but Jim Miller reportedly sells plans for the Gem 260.

MIRAGE
MIRAGE AIRCRAFT CORPORATION
3936 Austin Street, Klamath Falls, Oregon 97603
Telephone: 1 (503) 884 4011
PRESIDENT: Larry Burton

MIRAGE CELERITY
The prototype Celerity flew for the first time on 18 May 1985. It underwent considerable development, and was given a retractable landing gear, as shown on plans available from Mirage Aircraft. An inexperienced builder could take more than 3,000 working hours to build a Celerity from plans. Various kits and upholstery patterns to cut working time became available via Wicks Aircraft Supply (410 Pine Street, Highland, Illinois 62249). Prefabricated components listed by Mirage as being available are all metal parts, some glassfibre parts and some factory-built wooden components.
TYPE: Side by side two-seat homebuilt.

AIRFRAME: Wing section NACA 23015 at root, NACA 23010 at tip. Airframe structure of wood, with composite skins of foam, glassfibre and epoxy resin. Three-axis control, plus flaps. Retractable tailwheel landing gear, with brakes.
POWER PLANT: One 119 kW (160 hp) Textron Lycoming O-320-B1A. Fuel capacity 114 litres (30 US gallons; 25 Imp gallons). Two auxiliary tanks, each of 19 litres (5 US gallons; 4.15 Imp gallons) capacity. Engines of 112-134 kW (150-180 hp) optional, including the O-360.

DIMENSIONS, EXTERNAL:

Wing span over tip tanks	7.26 m (23 ft 10 in)
Length overall	6.55 m (21 ft 6 in)
Height overall	1.68 m (5 ft 6 in)
Propeller diameter	1.93 m (6 ft 4 in)

AREA:

Wings, gross	8.36 m² (90.0 sq ft)

WEIGHTS:

Weight empty	530 kg (1,169 lb)
Baggage capacity	27 kg (60 lb)
Max T-O weight	828 kg (1,825 lb)

PERFORMANCE (at max T-O weight):

Max level speed	191 knots (354 km/h; 220 mph)
Max cruising speed	178 knots (330 km/h; 205 mph)
Econ cruising speed	165 knots (306 km/h; 190 mph)
Stalling speed, flaps and landing gear down, engine idling	46 knots (86 km/h; 53 mph)
Max rate of climb at S/L	549 m (1,800 ft)/min
Service ceiling	6,100 m (20,000 ft)
T-O run	244 m (800 ft)
Landing run	305 m (1,000 ft)
Range with max standard fuel	781-868 nm (1,448-1,609 km; 900-1,000 miles)
Endurance	5 h 45 min
g limits	+6/−3

MITCHELL WING
MITCHELL AEROSPACE COMPANY
1900 South Newcomb, Porterville, California 93257
Telephone: 1 (209) 781 8100
DIRECTOR: James M. Meade
Details of the B-10, U-2 Superwing and A-10 Silver Eagle microlights can be found in the Microlight tables.

MITCHELL WING P-38 LIGHTNING
The P-38 was designed to be assembled by four people in about one day. It flew for the first time in late 1980 and is believed still to be available in plans and kit forms. Assembly time for the kit was quoted as 100 man-hours.

An **AG-38A Terrier** agricultural version, with a 12V battery, 53 litre (14 US gallon; 11.7 Imp gallon) ULV spraytank, two Beeco Mist sprayheads and an electric spraypump, is also available.

The following description applies to the standard P-38:
TYPE: Single-seat microlight; does not conform to FAR Pt 103.

AIRFRAME: Main structure of aluminium, with quick-fit ribs and Dacron covered wing and tail surfaces. Wing section NACA 23015. Three-axis control. Non-retractable tricycle landing gear. Optional cockpit 'podule', floats and skis.
POWER PLANT: One 22 kW (30 hp) 250 cc Cuyuna 430. Fuel capacity 5.7 litres (1.5 US gallons; 1.25 Imp gallons). Options include auxiliary fuel tank.

DIMENSIONS, EXTERNAL:

Wing span	8.53 m (28 ft 0 in)
Length overall	5.49 m (18 ft 0 in)
Height overall	1.52 m (5 ft 0 in)

AREA:

Wings, gross	11.52 m² (124.0 sq ft)

WEIGHTS:

Weight empty	136 kg (300 lb)
Max pilot weight	136 kg (300 lb)
Max T-O weight: standard	249 kg (550 lb)
Restricted category	340 kg (750 lb)

PERFORMANCE (at max standard T-O weight):

Max level speed	52 knots (97 km/h; 60 mph)
Max cruising speed	48 knots (88 km/h; 55 mph)
Stalling speed	28 knots (51 km/h; 32 mph)
Max rate of climb at S/L	76-91 m (250-300 ft)/min
T-O run	68 m (225 ft)
Landing run	61 m (200 ft)
Range: with max standard fuel	43 nm (80 km; 50 miles)
with auxiliary fuel	434 nm (805 km; 500 miles)
g limits	±6

MITCHELL WING AG-38-A WAR EAGLE
The AG-38-A War Eagle is an enlarged military version of the P-38/AG-38 series, with a more powerful engine, increased fuel and provision for a variety of operational equipment. An illustration appeared in the 1987-88 *Jane's*.

POWER PLANT: One 29.4 kW (39.4 hp) Rotax 447. Standard fuel capacity 24 litres (6.5 US gallons; 5.4 Imp gallons). Optional long-range fuel tank, capacity 151 litres (40 US gallons; 33.3 Imp gallons).
OPERATIONAL EQUIPMENT: Optional items include two M60 machine-gun mounts; four Strem 89 rocket mounts; wind-driven agricultural spraypump with full-span 25 nozzle spray system and 151 litre (40 US gallon; 33.3 Imp gallon) hopper capacity; ballistic parachute; radios; video camera, transmitter and antenna; Kevlar pilot protection and night vision goggles.

DIMENSIONS, EXTERNAL:

Wing span	10.36 m (34 ft 0 in)
Length overall	5.79 m (19 ft 0 in)
Height overall	2.11 m (6 ft 11 in)
Propeller diameter	1.47 m (4 ft 10 in)

AREA:

Wings, gross	14.86 m² (160.0 sq ft)

WEIGHTS:

Weight empty	168 kg (370 lb)
Max pilot weight	104 kg (230 lb)
Max T-O weight: Normal	363 kg (800 lb)
Restricted category	476 kg (1,050 lb)

PERFORMANCE (Normal category, 77 kg; 170 lb pilot):

Best cruising speed	60 knots (111 km/h; 69 mph)
Stalling speed, power off	30 knots (56 km/h; 35 mph)
Max rate of climb at S/L	152 m (500 ft)/min
T-O run	61 m (200 ft)
Endurance with max fuel	1 h 40 min

MONTANA
MONTANA COYOTE INC
3302 Airport Road, PO Box 9272, Helena, Montana 59604
Telephone: 1 (406) 449 3556
BUILT BY: Dick Sims and Jim Tomash

MONTANA COYOTE
TYPE: Two-seat homebuilt.
POWER PLANT: One 97 kW (130 hp) Honda Prelude modified motorcar engine. Fuel capacity 106 litres (28 US gallons; 23.3 Imp gallons).

DIMENSIONS, EXTERNAL:

Wing span	11.84 m (38 ft 10 in)
Length overall	6.71 m (22 ft 0 in)
Height overall	1.98 m (6 ft 6 in)

Maxair ARV 582, based on the Drifter DR 532

Demonstration of Mitchell Wing AG-38 cropsprayer in China

Mosler Super Pup (*J. M. G. Gradidge*)

First prototype Montana Coyote two-seat homebuilt at Sun 'n Fun 91
(*Geoffrey P. Jones*)

WEIGHTS:		PERFORMANCE:		T-O run	31 m (100 ft)
Weight empty	386 kg (850 lb)	Cruising speed	87 knots (161 km/h; 100 mph)	Landing run	61 m (200 ft)
Useful load	329 kg (725 lb)	Stalling speed	31 knots (57 km/h; 35 mph)	Range	521 nm (965 km; 600 miles)
Max T-O weight	726 kg (1,600 lb)	Max rate of climb at S/L	610 m (2,000 ft)/min		

MOSHIER

MOSHIER TECHNOLOGIES
334 State Street, Suite 106 (Dept KP1), Los Altos, California 94022

MOSHIER MANX
Moshier Technologies currently offers a two-seat, highly streamlined, coaxial twin-rotor homebuilt helicopter known as the Manx. It can achieve 130 knots (241 km/h; 150 mph) and a range of 521 nm (965 km; 600 miles).

MOSLER

MOSLER AIRFRAMES & POWER PLANTS
140 Ashwood Road, Hendersonville, North Carolina 28739
Telephone: 1 (704) 692 7713
Fax: 1 (704) 692 2008
PRESIDENT: John W. Martin

MOSLER N3 PUP, SUPER PUP and N3-2 PUP
Mosler's **N3 Pup** is a microlight representation of the Piper Cub, available in ready to fly and kit forms. It conforms to FAR Pt 103 regulations. Weight empty and max T-O weight are 115 kg (254 lb) and 242 kg (535 lb) respectively (see Microlight tables). Average construction time is 300 working hours. The **Super Pup** conforms to Experimental and ARV regulations and has clipped wings, wheel fairings, brakes and greater fuel capacity.

The **N3-2** is a tandem two-seat version of the N3, with 45 litres (12 US gallons; 10 Imp gallons) fuel capacity. The N3-2 kit comes under Experimental regulations. Max T-O weight of the N3-2 is 363 kg (800 lb), and cruising speed is 61 knots (113 km/h; 70 mph).

The designation **N3 EXP** applies to N3 Pups customised by Mosler to customers' requirements to incorporate some features of the Super Pup, possibly including clipped wings, D cell wing leading-edges, streamline (instead of round) wing struts, extra fuel tanks, door and window package, skylight, brakes, floats, ballistic parachute, extended landing gear and tundra tyres. Such changes would take the aircraft into the Experimental category.

The following details refer to the Super Pup:
TYPE: Single-seat homebuilt.
AIRFRAME: Strut braced, with stamped aluminium alloy wing ribs, aluminium alloy spars, welded 4130 steel tube fuselage and overall Stits Dacron covering. Glassfibre engine cowling. Three-axis control. Non-retractable tailwheel landing gear. Options include floats, skis and ballistic parachute.
POWER PLANT: One 26 kW (35 hp) Mosler MM-CB engine. Fuel capacity 45.5 litres (12 US gallons; 10 Imp gallons).
DIMENSIONS, EXTERNAL:

Wing span	7.92 m (26 ft 0 in)
Length overall	5.03 m (16 ft 6 in)
Height overall	1.52 m (5 ft 0 in)
Propeller diameter	1.37 m (4 ft 6 in)

AREA:

Wings, gross	11.43 m² (123.0 sq ft)

WEIGHTS:

Weight empty	150 kg (330 lb)
Max T-O weight	286 kg (630 lb)

PERFORMANCE:

Max level speed	82 knots (153 km/h; 95 mph)
Cruising speed, 75% power	more than 69 knots (129 km/h; 80 mph)
Stalling speed	31 knots (57 km/h; 35 mph)
Max rate of climb at S/L	213 m (700 ft)/min
Service ceiling	1,525 m (5,000 ft)
T-O and landing run	77 m (250 ft)
Range: cruising speed	364 nm (676 km; 420 miles)
max level speed	295 nm (547 km; 340 miles)
Endurance: cruising speed	5 h 30 min
max level speed	4 h
g limits	+10/−3

MOSLER N3-C and N3-2C CITABRIETTE
These are modified derivatives of the N3 Pup and N3-2 to represent scaled down Citabrias. Kits are available. Features include a modified more angular tail unit and a fully enclosed cowling for the Mosler engine.

NEICO
NEICO AVIATION INC
403 South Ojai Street, Santa Paula, California 93060
Telephone: 1 (805) 933 2747
Fax: 1 (805) 933 2093

NEICO AVIATION LANCAIR 200 and 235
The prototype Lancair 200 first flew in June 1984. The **Lancair 235** became the model offered in kit form with an 88 kW (118 hp) O-235 engine and 0.40 m³ (14.0 cu ft) baggage area. Glassfibre was replaced by Kevlar in subsequent form. Cruising speed compared to the Lancair 200 increased to 187 knots (346 km/h; 215 mph) at 75 per cent power, and empty weight became 399 kg (880 lb).

Several hundreds of Lancair kits of all versions have been delivered to customers in 18 countries.

The following details refer mainly to the Lancair 200:
TYPE: Side by side two-seat sporting and cross-country homebuilt.
AIRFRAME: Wing section NLF 0215F. Composite airframe of glassfibre, Nomex honeycomb, Polyimide Rohacell foam and epoxy resin. Retractable tricycle landing gear.
POWER PLANT: Originally one 74.6 kW (100 hp) Teledyne Continental O-200. Currently advertised with 88 kW (118 hp) O-235. Fuel capacity 106-114 litres (28-30 US gallons; 23.3-25 Imp gallons).
DIMENSIONS, EXTERNAL:
Wing span	7.16 m (23 ft 6 in)
Length overall	5.99 m (19 ft 8 in)
Width, wings folded	2.54 m (8 ft 4 in)
Height overall	1.85 m (6 ft 1 in)
Propeller diameter	1.47-1.52 m (4 ft 10 in-5 ft 0 in)

AREA:
Wings, gross	7.06 m² (76.0 sq ft)

WEIGHTS:
Weight empty	295 kg (650 lb)
Max T-O weight	578 kg (1,275 lb)

PERFORMANCE (100 hp engine):
Max level speed at S/L	185 knots (343 km/h; 213 mph)
Econ cruising speed	165 knots (306 km/h; 190 mph)
Stalling speed, engine idling	
	48 knots (89 km/h; 55 mph)
Max rate of climb at S/L	457 m (1,500 ft)/min
Service ceiling	5,485-6,100 m (18,000-20,000 ft)
T-O and landing run	183 m (600 ft)
Range with max fuel	868 nm (1,609 km; 1,000 miles)

NEICO LANCAIR 320
This version followed the Lancair 235 and has a 119 kW (160 hp) engine which allows a speed and max range of 217 knots (402 km/h; 250 mph) and 1,215 nm (2,253 km; 1,400 miles) respectively to be achieved. Layout remains similar although it is 'all new', providing a larger cockpit.

On 8 January 1990 Lancair received FAA approval under the 51 per cent rule for its new **Fast-Build** kit, which reduces construction time by between 600-700 working hours. Advanced Composite Technology (ACT) in the Philippines has produced Lancair 320 composite airframes since 1989 and now supplies Neico. ACT is also developing the **Apache I** military trainer version of the Lancair (of which Zaïre has reportedly ordered 30 as primary trainers — see also the Philippine Aerospace Development Corporation in the main Aircraft section).

NEICO LANCAIR IV
This is the latest version of the Lancair, of which initial kit deliveries were scheduled to begin in February 1991. It accommodates four persons and has particularly high performance.
TYPE: Four-seat homebuilt with dual controls.
AIRFRAME: Carbonfibre/Kevlar/epoxy airframe. Conventional control plus electrically actuated Fowler flaps. Retractable tricycle landing gear.
POWER PLANT: One 261 kW (350 hp) Teledyne Continental TSIO-550-A twin-turbocharged engine. Fuel capacity 299 litres (79 US gallons; 65.8 Imp gallons).
DIMENSIONS, EXTERNAL:
Wing span	9.60 m (31 ft 6 in)
Length overall	7.47 m (24 ft 6 in)
Height overall	2.44 m (8 ft 0 in)
Propeller diameter	1.93 m (6 ft 4 in)

AREA:
Wings, gross	9.10 m² (98.0 sq ft)

WEIGHTS:
Weight empty: prototype	794 kg (1,750 lb)
kit version	748 kg (1,650 lb)
Max T-O weight	1,259 kg (2,775 lb)

PERFORMANCE (estimated, unless stated otherwise):
Cruising speed: 75% power at 7,620 m (25,000 ft)
286 knots (529 km/h; 329 mph)
tested at 68% power, at 5,180 m (17,000 ft)
289 knots (536 km/h; 333 mph)
Stalling speed	62 knots (115 km/h; 71 mph)
Max range, 75% power at 7,620 m (25,000 ft), standard fuel, no reserves	1,259 nm (2,333 km; 1,450 miles)
g limits	+9/-4.4 ultimate

NUWACO — *See Aircraft Dynamics Corporation*

OSPREY
OSPREY AIRCRAFT
3741 El Ricon Way, Sacramento, California 95864
Telephone: 1 (916) 483 3004

PEREIRA GP3 OSPREY II
Developed from the Osprey I flying boat, the prototype Osprey II amphibian first flew from water in April 1973. Sets of plans, as well as material and component kits, are available to amateur constructors. By early 1991, more than 1,350 sets of plans had been sold to potential builders in 50 countries, and at least 250 Ospreys had flown.
TYPE: Side by side two-seat, dual-control homebuilt amphibian.
AIRFRAME: Wing section NACA 23012. All-wood wings, except for fabric covering aft of spar. Wingtip stabilising floats of polyurethane foam covered with glassfibre. All-wood hull covered with marine plywood. Hull undersurface contours formed from sculptured polyurethane foam, protected by several layers of glassfibre cloth bonded with resin. All-wood tail unit. Water rudder. Retractable tricycle landing gear.
POWER PLANT: One 112 kW (150 hp) Textron Lycoming O-320. Usable fuel capacity 98.4 litres (26 US gallons; 21.6 Imp gallons). Wing tanks available to replace standard fuselage tank, allowing increased baggage area.

DIMENSIONS, EXTERNAL:
Wing span	7.92 m (26 ft 0 in)
Length overall	6.25 m (20 ft 6 in)
Height overall (wheels down)	1.83 m (6 ft 0 in)
Propeller diameter	1.68 m (5 ft 6 in)

AREA:
Wings, gross	12.08 m² (130.0 sq ft)

WEIGHTS:
Weight empty	440 kg (970 lb)
Baggage capacity	41 kg (90 lb)
Max T-O weight	707 kg (1,560 lb)

PERFORMANCE (at max T-O weight except where indicated):
Max cruising speed at 75% power
113 knots (209 km/h; 130 mph)
Econ cruising speed at 55% power
94 knots (175 km/h; 109 mph)
Stalling speed	53 knots (97 km/h; 60 mph)

Max rate of climb at S/L, with pilot only
365 m (1,200 ft)/min
Rate of climb at S/L	305 m (1,000 ft)/min
T-O run: land	122 m (400 ft)
water	159 m (520 ft)
Range with wing tanks	313 nm (579 km; 360 miles)

PEREIRA GP4
This aircraft flew for the first time in 1984. Plans to construct the GP4 are available. In addition, pre-moulded glassfibre components and an airframe materials kit are available to reduce construction time.

TYPE: Two-seat cross-country homebuilt.
AIRFRAME: All-wood construction except for foam and glassfibre used in cowling and fairings. Wing section Laminar 63 series. Retractable tricycle landing gear.
POWER PLANT: One 149 kW (200 hp) Textron Lycoming IO-360. Fuel capacity 204 litres (54 US gallons; 45 Imp gallons).
DIMENSIONS, EXTERNAL:
Wing span	7.52 m (24 ft 8 in)
Length overall	6.55 m (21 ft 6 in)
Propeller diameter	1.83 m (6 ft 0 in)

AREA:
Wings, gross	9.66 m² (104.0 sq ft)

WEIGHTS:
Weight empty	566 kg (1,248 lb)
Baggage capacity	34 kg (75 lb)
Max T-O weight	900 kg (1,985 lb)

PERFORMANCE:
Cruising speed, 75% power
208 knots (386 km/h; 240 mph)
Stalling speed, clean	57 knots (105 km/h; 65 mph)

Max rate of climb at S/L:
2 crew, 50% fuel	670 m (2,200 ft)/min
max T-O weight	457 m (1,500 ft)/min
Range: 75% power	955 nm (1,770 km; 1,100 miles)
60% power (195 knots; 362 km/h; 225 mph)	1,085 nm (2,011 km; 1,250 miles)
g limits, at max T-O weight	+8/-6

PARAPLANE
PARAPLANE CORPORATION
5801 Magnolia Avenue, Pennsauken, New Jersey 08109
Telephone: 1 (609) 663 2234
PRESIDENT: Steve Snyder

PARAPLANE PM-2
The ParaPlane utilises a ram air parachute as its 'wing', attached to a 'powered trike' airframe. The aerofoil section parachute can be held open by two ground assistants before ground roll begins, though this is not necessary. It takes about five seconds to deploy as the lifting surface. Recreational flying is not recommended in winds in excess of 13 knots (24 km/h; 15 mph). Many hundreds have been sold.

TYPE: Single-seat microlight.
AIRFRAME: ParaPlane configuration has inherent pendulum stability with trike suspended beneath ram air parachute. Canopy made of F-111 ripstop nylon and having single-axis control through steering lines. Airframe consists of a T frame of aluminium alloy. Non-retractable tricycle landing gear.
POWER PLANT: Two 11.2 kW (15 hp) Solo 210 cc engines, driving counter-rotating pusher propellers on concentric shafts. Fuel capacity 17 litres (4.5 US gallons; 3.75 Imp gallons).
DIMENSIONS, EXTERNAL:
Parachute span	9.30 m (36 ft 6 in)
Airframe: Length	1.73 m (5 ft 8 in)
Height	1.70 m (5 ft 7 in)
Propeller diameter (each)	1.29 m (4 ft 3 in)

AREA:
Parachute	37.16 m² (400.0 sq ft)

WEIGHTS:
Weight empty	74.5 kg (164 lb)
Max pilot weight	84 kg (185 lb)
Max T-O weight	193 kg (425 lb)

PERFORMANCE:
Max level and max cruising speed
22 knots (41 km/h; 26 mph)
Glide speed, engine idling	18 knots (34 km/h; 21 mph)
Max rate of climb	150 m (495 ft)/min
Service ceiling	more than 1,525 m (5,000 ft)
T-O run	30-46 m (100-150 ft)
Range	43 nm (80 km; 50 miles)
Endurance	1 h 30 min

PARSONS
BILL PARSONS
PO Box 532, Lake Monroe, Florida 32747
Telephone: 1 (305) 323 9440

PARSONS TANDEM TRAINER
Kits are thought to be available for a tandem two-seat, dual-control autogyro known simply as the Tandem Trainer. It is of conventional configuration and metal tube construction, with a two-blade glassfibre rotor, a three-blade pusher propeller powered by a Rotax 532 or McCulloch engine, and a non-retractable tricycle landing gear.

Neico Aviation Lancair 235 *(John Wegg)*

UK registered Pereira Osprey II two-seat amphibian *(Peter J. Bish)*

Neico Aviation Lancair IV prototype *(J. M. G. Gradidge)*

ParaPlane in flight *(Howard Levy)*

Pereira GP4 prototype two-seat homebuilt cross-country aircraft
(Scott Kemper)

Pazmany PL-4A single-seat homebuilt *(Peter M. Bowers)*

Pazmany PL-2 built in Sweden by Hans Nielsen

PAZMANY

PAZMANY AIRCRAFT CORPORATION

PO Box 80051, San Diego, California 92138
Telephone: 1 (619) 224 73300
PROPRIETOR: Ladislao Pazmany

PAZMANY PL-2

The PL-2 was developed from the PL-1 (see 1979-80 *Jane's*), first flying on 4 April 1969. Plans are available and 400 sets had been sold by early 1991, with about 100 aircraft then flying. Individual prefabricated components available are the canopy, windshield and fairings. Aircraft built and flown include several examples for evaluation and use by foreign military training centres.

TYPE: Side by side two-seat, dual-control homebuilt.

AIRFRAME: All-aluminium alloy construction, except for glassfibre wingtips (including wingtip fuel tanks), wing fillets, tailcone, engine cowling, and the tips of the fin and tailplane. Wing section NACA 63_2615. Semi-monocoque fuselage has only flat or single-curvature skins. Conventional control, with ailerons, rudder, all-moving tailplane and flaps; trim tab on tailplane. Non-retractable tricycle landing gear, with brakes.

POWER PLANT: Recommended Textron Lycoming power plants include the 80.5 kW (108 hp) O-235-C1, 93 kW (125 hp) O-290-G (ground power unit), 101 kW (135 hp) O-290-D2B, 112 kW (150 hp) O-320-A and O-360 engines. Fuel capacity 95 litres (25 US gallons; 20.8 Imp gallons). Some PL-2s built with additional integral wing tanks, total capacity 94 litres (25 US gallons; 21 Imp gallons).

DIMENSIONS, EXTERNAL:

Wing span, over tip tanks	8.53 m (28 ft 0 in)
Length overall	5.90 m (19 ft 3½ in)
Height overall	2.44 m (8 ft 0 in)
Propeller diameter	1.52 m (5 ft 0 in)

AREA:

Wings, gross	10.78 m² (116.0 sq ft)

WEIGHTS (with 93 kW; 125 hp engine):

Weight empty	408 kg (900 lb)
Baggage capacity	9 kg (20 lb)
Max T-O weight	655 kg (1,445 lb)

PERFORMANCE (with 93 kW; 125 hp engine, at max T-O weight):

Max level speed at S/L	125 knots (232 km/h; 144 mph)
Econ cruising speed	111 knots (206 km/h; 128 mph)
Stalling speed, flaps down	47 knots (87 km/h; 54 mph)
Max rate of climb at S/L	457 m (1,500 ft)/min
Range (O-320-A engine)	330 nm (613 km; 381 miles)
Endurance (O-320-A engine)	2 h 48 min
g limits	+6/-4

PAZMANY PL-4A

The prototype of this economical single-seater flew for the first time on 12 July 1972. Sets of plans, kits of prefabricated components, glassfibre wingtips and fuel tank, and transparent cockpit canopy are available to amateur constructors.

TYPE: Single-seat sporting homebuilt.

AIRFRAME: All-aluminium alloy construction, except for glassfibre cambered wingtips, fairings, engine cowling, spinner, elevator trim kit and fuel tank. Wing section NACA 63_3418. Conventional three-axis control; rudder and elevator trim tabs. Non-retractable tailwheel landing gear.

POWER PLANT: One 1,600 cc modified Volkswagen motorcar engine, developing 40.3 kW (54 hp). Optional Volkswagen engine conversions from Revmaster, Limbach (50.7 kW; 68 hp SL-1700) and others, of up to 2,100 cc, or Continental A65 or C80. Fuel capacity 45 litres (12 US gallons; 10 Imp gallons).

DIMENSIONS, EXTERNAL:

Wing span	8.13 m (26 ft 8 in)
Length overall	4.93 m (16 ft 2 in)
Height overall	1.73 m (5 ft 8 in)
Propeller diameter	1.73 m (5 ft 8 in)

AREA:

Wings, gross	8.27 m² (89.0 sq ft)

WEIGHTS:
Weight empty	262 kg (578 lb)
Baggage capacity	9 kg (20 lb)
Max T-O and landing weight	385 kg (850 lb)

PERFORMANCE (37.5 kW; 50 hp engine, at max T-O weight):
Max level speed at S/L	96 knots (177 km/h; 110 mph)
Cruising speed	87 knots (161 km/h; 100 mph)
Econ cruising speed at S/L	78 knots (145 km/h; 90 mph)
Stalling speed: power on	40 knots (74 km/h; 46 mph)
power off	42 knots (78 km/h; 48 mph)
Max rate of climb at S/L	198 m (650 ft)/min
Service ceiling	3,960 m (13,000 ft)
T-O run	148 m (486 ft)
Landing run	133 m (436 ft)
Range with max fuel, no allowances	
	295 nm (545 km; 340 miles)
Endurance	3 h 48 min
g limits	±6

PAZMANY PL-9 STORK

The new PL-9 is a ¾-scale replica of the German Fieseler Fi-156 Storch of the Second World War. Design began in March 1990 and the prototype is flying. Plans and kits will be made available to amateur constructors.

TYPE: Tandem two-seat ¾-scale STOL replica.

AIRFRAME: Aluminium alloy structure, fabric covered. Braced wings and tail unit. Conventional three-axis control plus high lift devices. Non-retractable tailwheel landing gear.

POWER PLANT: One engine of 112 kW (150 hp), including Honda Prelude and Subaru Legacy converted motorcar types, and Textron Lycoming O-320. Fuel capacity 113.5 or 197 litres (30 or 52 US gallons; 25 or 43.3 Imp gallons).

DIMENSIONS, EXTERNAL:
Wing span	10.97 m (36 ft 0 in)
Length overall	7.40 m (24 ft 3½ in)

AREA:
Wings, gross	15.42 m² (166.0 sq ft)

WEIGHTS:
Weight empty	513 kg (1,132 lb)
Max T-O weight	817 kg (1,802 lb)

PERFORMANCE:
Max level speed	101 knots (187 km/h; 116 mph)
Cruising speed, 75% power	
	90 knots (167 km/h; 104 mph)
Stalling speed: flaps up	36 knots (66 km/h; 41 mph)
flaps down	30 knots (55 km/h; 34 mph)
Max rate of climb at S/L, at 85% power (30 US gallons of fuel) and 39 knots (72 km/h; 45 mph)	
	426 m (1,400 ft)/min
Service ceiling, 30 US gallons	4,600 m (15,100 ft)
T-O run, 52 US gallons	77 m (250 ft)
Landing run, 52 US gallons	28 m (90 ft)
Range, at 75% power:	
52 US gallons	357 nm (663 km; 412 miles)
30 US gallons	288 nm (534 km; 332 miles)

PIETENPOL
DONALD PIETENPOL
215, 21st Street SE, Rochester, Minnesota 55904

Details of the B4 Aircamper, and an illustration, can be found in the 1988-89 *Jane's*. Contact also **Pietenpol Aerial Biplane**, 5957 Seville Street, Lake Oswego, Oregon 97034.

POWERS BASHFORTH
POWERS BASHFORTH AIRCRAFT CORPORATION
4700 188th Street, North-East Ste, Arlington, Washington 98223
Telephone: 1 (206) 435 4356

Powers Bashforth markets in North America kits to construct its Mini Master; international marketing is undertaken by Sonoran Aviation Ltd, 7405 East, Camino Santo, Scottsdale, Arizona 85260 (1 [602] 998 5801).

POWERS BASHFORTH MINI MASTER 2+2

The Mini Master is configured as a small Cessna Skymaster representation, although having cantilever wings, a cockpit pod with wraparound glazing and a non-retractable tricycle landing gear. Kits and plans are available, requiring about 600 working hours to assemble.

TYPE: Side by side two-seat homebuilt.

AIRFRAME: All-metal construction. Three-axis control, with twin fins and rudders on booms and joining tailplane/elevator. Non-retractable tricycle type landing gear.

POWER PLANT: Two Rotax 582 engines, mounted in tractor and pusher configuration in fuselage pod. Fuel capacity 681 litres (180 US gallons; 150 Imp gallons).

DIMENSIONS, EXTERNAL:
Wing span	9.55 m (31 ft 4 in)
Length overall	7.09 m (23 ft 3 in)
Height overall	2.34 m (7 ft 8 in)

AREA:
Wings, gross	14.68 m² (158.0 sq ft)

WEIGHTS:
Weight empty	351 kg (775 lb)
Max T-O weight	657 kg (1,450 lb)

PERFORMANCE:
Max level speed	111 knots (206 km/h; 128 mph)
Cruising speed, 75% power	
	96 knots (177 km/h; 110 mph)
Stalling speed, flaps up	48 knots (88 km/h; 55 mph)
Max rate of climb at S/L	400 m (1,310 ft)/min
Service ceiling	6,100 m (20,000 ft)
Range, 75% power, with standard fuel	
	499 nm (925 km; 575 miles)

PROWLER
PROWLER AVIATION INC
3707 Meadow View Drive, Redding, California 96002
Telephone: 1 (916) 365 4524
PRESIDENT: George Morse Jr

PROWLER AVIATION (MORSE 364P) PROWLER

The prototype Prowler, reminiscent of a Supermarine Spitfire, made its first flight on 17 March 1985. Prowler Aviation offers kits to allow amateur construction of the aircraft; the original F-85 engine has now been discontinued, to be replaced by a new 261 kW (350 hp) engine.

TYPE: Tandem two-seat high-performance aerobatic homebuilt.

AIRFRAME: Aluminium alloy construction. Wing section NACA 64A-212 at roots, NACA 64A-210 at tips.

Three-axis control, plus electrically actuated flaps. Retractable tailwheel landing gear, with brakes.

POWER PLANT: One 261 kW (350 hp) modified motorcar engine based on a Chevrolet Rodeck block, with 1.67 : 1 reduction gear, under development for future kits. Originally fitted with 164 kW (220 hp) Auto Aviation modified Oldsmobile F-85 motorcar engine (discontinued for kits). Fuel capacity 227 litres (60 US gallons; 50 Imp gallons). Two external auxiliary fuel tanks possible.

DIMENSIONS, EXTERNAL:
Wing span	7.62 m (25 ft 0 in)
Length overall	6.40 m (21 ft 0 in)
Height overall	2.21 m (7 ft 3 in)
Propeller diameter	1.98 m (6 ft 6 in)

AREA:
Wings, gross	9.66 m² (104.0 sq ft)

WEIGHTS:
Weight empty	618 kg (1,362 lb)
Baggage capacity	22.7 kg (50 lb)
Max T-O weight	975 kg (2,150 lb)

PERFORMANCE (at max T-O weight, F-85 engine):
Max level speed at S/L	
	191 knots (354 km/h; 220 mph) IAS
Econ cruising speed at 2,135 m (7,000 ft)	
	148 knots (274 km/h; 170 mph)
Stalling speed, flaps up, power off	
	48 knots (89 km/h; 55 mph) IAS
Max rate of climb at S/L	549 m (1,800 ft)/min
Service ceiling	5,180 m (17,000 ft)
T-O and landing run	457 m (1,500 ft)
Landing from 15 m (50 ft)	610 m (2,000 ft)
Range: with max standard fuel	
	1,042 nm (1,931 km; 1,200 miles)
with auxiliary fuel	1,302 nm (2,414 km; 1,500 miles)
g limits	±6

PT
PROTECH AIRCRAFT INC
24215 F.M. 1093, Richmond, Texas 77469
Telephone: 1 (713) 341 9712

PROTECH PT-2 SASSY

The ProTech PT-2 is available in kit form, requiring about 300 working hours to assemble. By early 1991 approximately 80 kits had been delivered of over 100 ordered by customers in Australia, Canada, Italy, Mexico and the USA.

TYPE: Side by side two-seat, dual-control homebuilt STOL aircraft.

AIRFRAME: Strut braced monoplane. Wings have preformed aluminium alloy ribs, spars and skins. Wing section PS-1. Glassfibre wingtips, wingroot fillets, rear cabin fairing and engine cowlings. Steel tube and aluminium flaperons. Welded 4130 steel tube fuselage and tail surfaces, Ceconite covered. Non-retractable tailwheel landing gear.

POWER PLANT: One 56 kW (75 hp) Revmaster in prototype. Engines of 56-101 kW (75-135 hp) can be fitted. Standard fuel capacity 53 litres (14 US gallons; 11.7 Imp gallons). Optional auxiliary fuel tanks of similar capacity.

DIMENSIONS, EXTERNAL:
Wing span	9.68 m (31 ft 9 in)
Length overall	5.33 m (17 ft 6 in)
Propeller diameter	1.52 m (5 ft 0 in)

AREA:
Wings, gross	13.75 m² (148.0 sq ft)

WEIGHTS:
Weight empty	295 kg (650 lb)
Baggage weight	27 kg (60 lb)
Max T-O weight	569 kg (1,254 lb)

PERFORMANCE (Revmaster engine; pilot only):
Max level speed	100 knots (185 km/h; 115 mph)
Cruising speed	91 knots (169 km/h; 105 mph)
Stalling speed	26 knots (47 km/h; 29 mph)
T-O and landing run	61 m (200 ft)
Normal range at cruising speed, no reserves	
	364 nm (675 km; 420 miles)
g limits	+6/-4 computer evaluated

QUAD CITY
QUAD CITY ULTRALIGHT AIRCRAFT CORPORATION
3610 Coaltown Road, Moline, Illinois 61265
Telephone: 1 (309) 764 3515
Fax: 1 (309) 762 3920
Telex: 468556 CHALLENGER MOLINE
PRESIDENT: Dave Goulet

Details of the Challenger and Challenger II can be found in the Microlight tables.

QUAD CITY CHALLENGER SPECIAL and CHALLENGER II SPECIAL

These are higher performing versions of the Challenger and Challenger II microlights, with streamline wing struts, and landing gears, shortened wings covered with Stits Poly-Fiber or Ceconite, flaperons, Lexan door kits, and higher-powered Rotax engines as standard, to give a higher cruising speed and improved rate of roll. Kits are available. Construction time for the Specials is about 120 working hours.

TYPE: Single-seat (Challenger Special) and tandem two-seat (Challenger II Special) homebuilts.

POWER PLANT: Challenger Special: One 31.3 kW (42 hp) Rotax 447, with 19 litres (5 US gallons; 4.2 Imp gallons) fuel. Challenger II Special: One 38.8 kW (52 hp) Rotax 503, with 38 litres (10 US gallons; 8.3 Imp gallons) fuel.

DIMENSIONS, EXTERNAL: As for Challenger, except:
Wing span	7.92 m (26 ft 0 in)
Length overall:	
Challenger II Special	6.32 m (20 ft 9 in)
Propeller diameter:	
Challenger Special	1.35 m (4 ft 5 in)
Challenger II Special	1.37 m (4 ft 6 in)

Prowler Aviation Prowler all-metal two-seat homebuilt aircraft, with original engine

Questair Spirit two/three-seat sporting and cross-country monoplane

ProTech PT-2 Sassy two-seat homebuilt aircraft (Textron Lycoming O-290D engine) *(Howard Levy)*

Two-seat Quad City Challenger II Special

AREAS (A: Challenger Special, B: Challenger II Special):				
Wings, gross: A	11.15 m² (120.0 sq ft)	Cruising speed: A	69 knots (129 km/h; 80 mph)	
B	13.29 m² (143.0 sq ft)	B	74 knots (137 km/h; 85 mph)	
WEIGHTS (A and B as above):		Stalling speed:		
Weight empty: A	118 kg (260 lb)	A, flaperons up	29 knots (53 km/h; 33 mph)	
B	158 kg (350 lb)	B, flaperons up	32 knots (60 km/h; 37 mph)	
Pilot weight range: A	63.5-104 kg (140-230 lb)	A, flaperons down	25 knots (45 km/h; 28 mph)	
Max T-O weight: A	236 kg (520 lb)	B, flaperons down	28 knots (52 km/h; 32 mph)	
B	385 kg (850 lb)	Max rate of climb at S/L:		
PERFORMANCE (A and B as above):		A	305 m (1,000 ft)/min	
Max level speed: A	78 knots (145 km/h; 90 mph)	B	213 m (700 ft)/min	
B	82 knots (153 km/h; 95 mph)	Service ceiling: A, B	4,265 m (14,000 ft)	

T-O and landing run: A	31-46 m (100-150 ft)
B	61 m (200 ft)
Range with max fuel: A	130 nm (241 km; 150 miles)
B	191 nm (354 km; 220 miles)
Endurance: A	1 h 45 min
g limits: A	+8/–4 ultimate
B	+6/–4

QUESTAIR

QUESTAIR INC

7700 Airline Road, PO Box 18946, Greensboro, North Carolina 27419
Telephone: 1 (919) 668 7890 or (800) 852 3889
Fax: 1 (919) 668 7960
CHIEF EXECUTIVE OFFICER: Mark Chambers
DIRECTOR, SALES AND MARKETING: Charles S. Haupt

QUESTAIR M20 VENTURE

The prototype Venture flew for the first time on 1 July 1987. The aircraft is available for purchase in a series of four kits of component parts or as a single kit; the engine can be included with the kit.
TYPE: Side by side two-seat, dual-control sporting and cross-country homebuilt.
AIRFRAME: Wing sections 23017 at root and 23010 at tip. All-metal construction. Retractable tricycle landing gear.
POWER PLANT: One 209 kW (280 hp) Teledyne Continental IO-550-G. Fuel capacity 212 litres (56 US gallons; 46.6 Imp gallons).
DIMENSIONS, EXTERNAL:

Wing span	8.38 m (27 ft 6 in)
Length overall	4.95 m (16 ft 3 in)
Height overall	2.35 m (7 ft 8½ in)
Propeller diameter	1.73 m (5 ft 8 in)

AREA:

Wings, gross	6.76 m² (72.75 sq ft)

WEIGHTS:

Weight empty	544 kg (1,200 lb)
Max T-O weight	907 kg (2,000 lb)

PERFORMANCE:

Max cruising speed:	
at S/L	265 knots (491 km/h; 305 mph)
at 3,660 m (12,000 ft)	
	240 knots (445 km/h; 276 mph)
Stalling speed	61 knots (113 km/h; 71 mph)
Max rate of climb at S/L	762 m (2,500 ft)/min
T-O run	275 m (900 ft)
Landing run	305 m (1,000 ft)
Service ceiling	8,840 m (29,000 ft)
Range at 240 knots (444 km/h; 276 mph), at 3,660 m (12,000 ft), 45 min reserves	
	1,000 nm (1,853 km; 1,151 miles)
Endurance	4 h
g limits: solo	+6/–3
at max T-O weight	+5/–3

QUESTAIR SPIRIT

The Spirit is a new non-retractable landing gear derivative of the Venture, designed to be powered by a Teledyne Continental IO-360 engine but with a Textron Lycoming O-360 as the optional power plant. Construction of the prototype began in 1990 and this first flew in February 1991. Kits are available, with the engine included at the customer's request.

Details of the Venture apply also to the Spirit, except as follows:
TYPE: Side by side 2+1 seat sporting and cross-country homebuilt.
AIRFRAME: Non-retractable tricycle landing gear.
POWER PLANT: One 156.6 kW (210 hp) Teledyne Continental IO-360. Alternatively 134 kW (180 hp) Textron Lycoming O-360.
DIMENSION, EXTERNAL:

Height overall	2.34 m (7 ft 8 in)

WEIGHTS:

Weight empty	465 kg (1,025 lb)
Max T-O weight	771 kg (1,700 lb)

PERFORMANCE:

Max level speed at 2,135 m (7,000 ft)	
	195 knots (361 km/h; 225 mph)
Max cruising speed at 2,135 m (7,000 ft)	
	185 knots (343 km/h; 213 mph)
Stalling speed	56 knots (104 km/h; 65 mph)
Max rate of climb at S/L	518 m (1,700 ft)/min
Range	1,150 nm (2,131 km; 1,324 miles)
Endurance	6 h 10 min
g limits	+6/–3

RAND ROBINSON
RAND ROBINSON ENGINEERING INC
15641 Product Lane, Suite A-5, Huntington Beach, California 92649
Telephone: 1 (714) 898 3811

RAND ROBINSON KR-1
The KR-1 prototype flew for the first time in February 1972. Plans are available to amateur constructors; many thousands of sets have been sold and at least 200 KR-1s are known to be flying.
TYPE: Single-seat sporting homebuilt.
AIRFRAME: Wings have wooden spars and polyurethane foam ribs, polyurethane foam slab filling between ribs and Dynel reinforced epoxy covering. Pre-moulded wing skins are available. Wing section RAF 48. Ailerons of polyurethane foam, with Dynel reinforced epoxy covering; tail unit similar, with wooden spars. Lower half of fuselage of wooden construction, upper surface of carved Styrofoam covered with Dynel epoxy. Retractable (optionally non-retractable) tailwheel landing gear.
POWER PLANT: One Volkswagen modified motorcar engine. Prototype has a Rajay turbocharged 67 kW (90 hp) 2,074 cc VW. Fuel capacity with this engine is 190 litres (50 US gallons; 41.6 Imp gallons).

DIMENSIONS, EXTERNAL:
Wing span	5.18 m (17 ft 0 in)
Length overall	3.89 m (12 ft 9 in)
Height overall	1.07 m (3 ft 6 in)
Propeller diameter	1.35 m (4 ft 5 in)

AREA:
Wings, gross	5.76 m² (62.0 sq ft)

WEIGHTS (67 kW; 90 hp VW engine):
Weight empty, equipped	218 kg (480 lb)
Max T-O weight	408 kg (900 lb)

PERFORMANCE (67 kW; 90 hp VW engine, at max T-O weight):
Max level speed at S/L	191 knots (354 km/h; 220 mph)
Econ cruising speed at 5,485 m (18,000 ft)	217 knots (402 km/h; 250 mph)
Stalling speed	39 knots (73 km/h; 45 mph)
Max rate of climb at S/L	457 m (1,500 ft)/min
Service ceiling	9,145 m (30,000 ft)
T-O run	122 m (400 ft)
Landing run	152 m (500 ft)
Range with max fuel	2,600 nm (4,825 km; 3,000 miles)

RAND ROBINSON KR-2
The KR-2 is a slightly larger side by side two-seat version of the KR-1, to which it is generally similar in construction. The prototype flew for the first time in July 1974. More than 7,000 sets of plans and a great many kits have been sold; at least 350 KR-2s are known to be flying.
TYPE: Side by side two-seat sporting homebuilt.
POWER PLANT: Airframe designed to accept Volkswagen modified motorcar engines of 1,600 to 2,200 cc. Fuel capacity 144 litres (38 US gallons; 31.6 Imp gallons).

DIMENSIONS, EXTERNAL:
Wing span	6.30 m (20 ft 8 in)
Length overall	4.42 m (14 ft 6 in)
Height overall	1.07 m (3 ft 6 in)
Propeller diameter	1.32 m (4 ft 4 in)

AREA:
Wings, gross	7.43 m² (80.0 sq ft)

WEIGHTS (prototype, with turbocharger):
Weight empty, equipped with IFR and electrics	263 kg (580 lb)
Max T-O and landing weight	499 kg (1,100 lb)

PERFORMANCE (prototype, with turbocharger):
Max level speed at S/L	161 knots (298 km/h; 185 mph)
Max cruising speed at 5,485 m (18,000 ft)	191 knots (354 km/h; 220 mph)
Stalling speed, prototype without turbocharger	39 knots (73 km/h; 45 mph)
Max rate of climb at 5,485 m (18,000 ft)	244 m (800 ft)/min
Service ceiling	7,925 m (26,000 ft)
T-O run	122 m (400 ft)
Landing run	152 m (500 ft)
Range with max fuel	1,735 nm (3,215 km; 2,000 miles)

RAND ROBINSON KR-100
This was introduced as an entirely new single-seater of wood, foam and glassfibre construction, with a non-retractable tailwheel landing gear and powered in prototype form by a Teledyne Continental O-200 engine. Kits are to be made available, containing mostly moulded components of composites sandwich construction.

DIMENSIONS, EXTERNAL:
Wing span	5.79 m (19 ft 0 in)
Length overall	4.72 m (15 ft 6 in)

WEIGHT (estimated):
Weight empty	249 kg (550 lb)

PERFORMANCE (estimated):
Max level speed	208 knots (386 km/h; 240 mph)
Cruising speed	182 knots (338 km/h; 210 mph)
Stalling speed, flaps down	45 knots (84 km/h; 52 mph)

RANS
RANS INC
1104 East Highway 40 By-Pass, Hays, Kansas 67601
Telephone: 1 (913) 625 6346
Fax: 1 (913) 625 2795
PRESIDENT: Randy Schlitter

Details of the S-4 Coyote and S-6 Coyote II can be found in the Microlight tables, although both can also conform to Experimental homebuilt regulations.

RANS S-7 COURIER
RANS is offering standard kits (300-500 working hours to assemble) or a quick-build kit (150 working hours, approximately) for the Courier. Following the general configuration of the Coyote, the Courier is fitted with dual controls and is therefore suited to training, in addition to recreational flying and such utility tasks as agricultural spraying. The prototype first flew in October 1985. Estimated building time from the kit is 500 hours.
TYPE: Two-seat STOL homebuilt aircraft.
AIRFRAME: Fabric covered structure, with aluminium alloy wings, and welded 4130 steel fuselage and tail unit. Glassfibre engine cowling. Conventional control, with flaps. Non-retractable tailwheel landing gear. Optional floats and skis.
POWER PLANT: One 48.5 kW (65 hp) Rotax 582, with 2.58 : 1 reduction gear. Optional 67 kW (90 hp) AMW 636. Fuel capacity 49 litres (13 US gallons; 10.8 Imp gallons).

DIMENSIONS, EXTERNAL:
Wing span	8.92 m (29 ft 3 in)
Length overall	6.40 m (21 ft 0 in)
Height overall	1.91 m (6 ft 3 in)
Propeller diameter	1.73 m (5 ft 8 in)

AREA:
Wings, gross	14.03 m² (151.0 sq ft)

WEIGHTS:
Weight empty, equipped	204 kg (450 lb)
Max T-O weight	420 kg (925 lb)

PERFORMANCE (two persons):
Cruising speed	69 knots (129 km/h; 80 mph)
Stalling speed, power off:	
flaps up	31 knots (57 km/h; 35 mph)
flaps down	26 knots (49 km/h; 30 mph)
Max rate of climb at S/L	229 m (750 ft)/min
Service ceiling	4,115 m (13,500 ft)
T-O run	54 m (175 ft)
Landing run to safe turn speed	93 m (303 ft)
Range	208 nm (386 km; 240 miles)
Endurance	3 h
g limits	+6/–3

RANS S-9 CHAOS
The S-9 is currently offered only in Experimental category form. Construction from the kits is estimated to take 200-300 working hours.
TYPE: Single-seat aerobatic homebuilt aircraft.
AIRFRAME: Strut braced aluminium alloy wings with full-span ailerons, and pre-welded 4130 steel tube fuselage and tail unit (wire braced), Cooper Super-Flite fabric covered. Conventional control; optional flaperons. Pre-moulded engine cowling. Three-axis control. Non-retractable tailwheel landing gear. Optional brakes.

POWER PLANT: One 35 kW (47 hp) Rotax 503 standard; optional 48.5 kW (65 hp) Rotax 582 or 67 kW (90 hp) AMW 636. Fuel capacity 25 litres (6.5 US gallons; 5.4 Imp gallons). Optional 49 litre (13 US gallon; 10.8 Imp gallon) capacity.

DIMENSIONS, EXTERNAL:
Wing span	6.71 m (22 ft 0 in)
Length overall	4.78 m (15 ft 8 in)
Height overall	1.47 m (4 ft 10 in)
Propeller diameter	1.63 m (5 ft 4 in)

AREA:
Wings, gross	8.50 m² (91.5 sq ft)

WEIGHTS (with Rotax 503):
Weight empty	145 kg (320 lb)
Max T-O weight	304 kg (670 lb)

PERFORMANCE (with Rotax 503):
Max level speed	82 knots (153 km/h; 95 mph)
Cruising speed:	
80% power	74 knots (137 km/h; 85 mph)
50% power	65 knots (121 km/h; 75 mph)
Stalling speed: power on	18 knots (33 km/h; 20 mph)
power off	26 knots (47 km/h; 29 mph)
Max rate of climb at S/L	305 m (1,000 ft)/min
Service ceiling	4,725 m (15,500 ft)
T-O run	61 m (200 ft)
Landing run, no brakes	122 m (400 ft)
Endurance	2 h
g limits	+9/–6

RANS S-10 SAKOTA
The S-10 is basically a larger two-seat derivative of the S-9, with a welded 4130 steel fuselage and tail unit and aluminium alloy wings, fabric covered. Full span ailerons standard. Pre-moulded engine cowling. In addition to the kit, options available include flaperons and glassfibre wingtips.
TYPE: Side by side two-seat homebuilt.
POWER PLANT: One 48.5 kW (65 hp) Rotax 582, with 2.58 : 1 reduction gear standard. Optional 67 kW (90 hp) AMW 636. Fuel capacity 49 litres (13 US gallons; 10.8 Imp gallons).

DIMENSIONS, EXTERNAL:
Wing span	7.32 m (24 ft 0 in)
Length overall	5.44 m (17 ft 10 in)
Height overall	1.47 m (4 ft 10 in)
Propeller diameter	1.63 m (5 ft 4 in)

AREA:
Wings, gross	8.83 m² (95.0 sq ft)

WEIGHTS (Rotax 582 engine):
Weight empty	191 kg (420 lb)
Max T-O weight	397 kg (875 lb)

PERFORMANCE (Rotax 582 engine):
Max level speed	96 knots (177 km/h; 110 mph)
Cruising speed:	
80% power	87 knots (161 km/h; 100 mph)
50% power	56 knots (105 km/h; 65 mph)
Stalling speed, flaps down:	
power on	23 knots (42 km/h; 26 mph)
power off	33 knots (61 km/h; 38 mph)
Service ceiling	4,265 m (14,000 ft)
Max rate of climb at S/L	305 m (1,000 ft)/min
T-O run	92 m (300 ft)
Landing run, no brakes	152 m (500 ft)
g limits	+6/–3

RANS S-11 PURSUIT
This single-seater is entirely different from previous RANS aircraft, having cantilever low-mounted wings blended into the streamline fuselage, a bubble cockpit canopy, and a twin fin/rudder tail unit. Welded 4130 chromoly steel cockpit cage, aluminium alloy tail unit, composite ribs, and pre-moulded wing skins and engine cowling. Retractable tricycle landing gear, with brakes. Standard power plant is the 67 kW (90 hp) AMW 636. Fuel capacity is 76 litres (20 US gallons; 16.6 Imp gallons); inverted system is standard. Estimated building time 400 hours.

DIMENSIONS, EXTERNAL:
Wing span	6.10 m (20 ft 0 in)
Length overall	5.49 m (18 ft 0 in)
Height overall	1.63 m (5 ft 4 in)

WEIGHTS:
Weight empty	215 kg (475 lb)
Baggage capacity	13.6 kg (30 lb)
Max T-O weight	374 kg (825 lb)

PERFORMANCE:
Max level speed	143 knots (266 km/h; 165 mph)
Cruising speed:	
80% power	122 knots (225 km/h; 140 mph)
50% power	96 knots (177 km/h; 110 mph)
Stalling speed: power on	26 knots (49 km/h; 30 mph)
power off	35 knots (65 km/h; 40 mph)
Max rate of climb at S/L	610 m (2,000 ft)/min
Service ceiling	5,485 m (18,000 ft)
T-O run	61 m (200 ft)
Landing run, with brakes	153 m (500 ft)
g limits	±9

RANS S-12 AIRAILE
The S-12 is available in kit form with a choice of engines and an optional cockpit enclosure. Customers include those from Denmark, Finland, Germany, Israel, the UK and USA. Construction takes between 60 and 80 working hours.
TYPE: Side by side two-seat monoplane.
AIRFRAME: Strut braced aluminium alloy wings with ailerons and flaps, and aluminium alloy braced tail unit, both fabric covered. Welded 4130 steel tube cockpit cage, with optional transparent enclosure. Wing section NACA 2412 modified. Non-retractable tricycle landing gear.
POWER PLANT: One 35 kW (47 hp) Rotax 503, 48.5 kW (65 hp) Rotax 532 or Rotax 582. Fuel capacity 41.5 litres (11 US gallons; 9.2 Imp gallons).

DIMENSIONS, EXTERNAL:
Wing span	9.45 m (31 ft 0 in)
Length overall, without enclosure	6.02 m (19 ft 9 in)
Height overall	1.92 m (6 ft 3½ in)

AREA:
Wings, gross	12.26 m² (132.0 sq ft)

WEIGHTS (Rotax 532):
Weight empty	167 kg (368 lb)
Max T-O weight	408 kg (900 lb)

Rand Robinson KR-2 two-seat homebuilt (*J. M. G. Gradidge*)

Prototype RANS S-10

RANS S-7 Courier homebuilt aircraft

RANS S-11 Pursuit (*Geoffrey P. Jones*)

RANS S-9 Chaos homebuilt aircraft

RANS S-12 Airaile at Sun 'n Fun 91 (*Geoffrey P. Jones*)

RANS S-14 single-seater at Sun 'n Fun 91 (*Geoffrey P. Jones*)

PERFORMANCE (Rotax 532; no enclosure or fairings):
Cruising speed, 85% power
  52 knots (97 km/h; 60 mph)
Stalling speed, power off:
 flaps up 26 knots (49 km/h; 30 mph)
 flaps down 22 knots (41 km/h; 25 mph)

Max rate of climb at S/L 305 m (1,000 ft)/min
Service ceiling 4,575 m (15,000 ft)
T-O run 49 m (160 ft)
Landing run 40 m (130 ft)
Endurance 2 h 12 min
g limits +6/−3

RANS S-14

An accompanying illustration reportedly shows a RANS S-14 at the 1991 Sun 'n Fun meeting. It appears to be a single-seat version of the S-12 Airaile. No other details were available at the time of going to press.

R.D.

R.D. AIRCRAFT

PO Box 107, Mayville, New York 14757
Telephone: 1 (716) 753 2111
PRESIDENT: Robert G. Dart
ENGINEER: Emerson W. Stevens

Details of the Skycycle, Skycycle II and Skycycle Gypsy series can be found in the Microlight tables.

R.D. LITTLE DIPPER REPLICA

Construction of a prototype of this reproduction of the Lockheed Little Dipper (illustrated in 1947 *Jane's*) began in February 1988.

TYPE: Single-seat ARV and homebuilt; conforms to FAR Pt 23.
AIRFRAME: Aluminium alloy construction, with some use of glassfibre. Wing section NACA 4415. Three-axis control, plus flaps. Non-retractable tricycle landing gear. Options will include cockpit canopy.
POWER PLANT: One 30 kW (40 hp) Rotax 447FA. Fuel capacity 30 litres (8 US gallons; 6.7 Imp gallons). Rotax 503 optional.
DIMENSIONS, EXTERNAL:

Wing span	7.42 m (24 ft 4 in)
Length overall	5.49 m (18 ft 0 in)
Height overall	2.21 m (7 ft 7¼ in)
Propeller diameter	1.73 m (5 ft 8 in)

AREA:

Wings, gross	9.48 m² (102.0 sq ft)

WEIGHTS:

Weight empty	201 kg (443 lb)
Max T-O weight	300 kg (661 lb)

PERFORMANCE:

Max level speed at S/L	87 knots (161 km/h; 100 mph)
Stalling speed, power off	32 knots (58 km/h; 36 mph)
Max rate of climb at S/L	229 m (750 ft)/min
T-O run	76 m (250 ft)
Range	456 nm (845 km; 525 miles)
g limits	+4.6/−2.6

REVOLUTION

REVOLUTION HELICOPTER CORPORATION INC

20600 C East 210 Highway, Liberty, Missouri 64068
Telephone: 1 (816) 792 1011
Fax: 1 (816) 792 1011
PRESIDENT: Dennis Fetters

REVOLUTION HELICOPTER MINI 500

The Mini 500 is offered as a kit requiring only about 40 working hours to assemble by novice builders. It is based on the X101 prototype, a single-seat open structure helicopter designed by Argentine Augusto Cicaré and with whom Dennis Fetters (see Air Command) established Revolution Helicopters. The X101 is powered by a Rotax 582 engine and has two composite main rotor blades attached to a teetering semi-rigid articulated head and no flapping hinges. The Mini 500 in kit form has similar dynamics but incorporates a modified and lighter structure and features a moulded glassfibre cabin shell and unsupported tailboom with new tail surfaces. A military variant with outriggers for rocket launchers or perhaps other weapons is known as the **Aggressor**.

The following details refer to the Mini 500:
TYPE: Single-seat homebuilt helicopter, suited to recreational, inspection, utility and other roles.
ROTOR SYSTEM: Similar to X101, as described above. Main and tail composite rotor blades are manufactured by Revolution.
AIRFRAME: Welded steel tube and aluminium structure, with moulded glassfibre cabin enclosure. Twin skid landing gear.

POWER PLANT: One 50 kW (67 hp) Rotax 582. Fuel capacity 57 litres (15 US gallons; 12.5 Imp gallons).
DIMENSIONS, EXTERNAL:

Main rotor diameter	5.79 m (19 ft 0 in)
Length overall	6.71 m (22 ft 0 in)
Height overall	2.46 m (8 ft 1 in)

WEIGHTS:

Weight empty	143 kg (315 lb)
Max T-O weight	365 kg (805 lb)

PERFORMANCE:

Max level speed	82 knots (153 km/h; 95 mph)
Cruising speed	65 knots (121 km/h; 75 mph)
Max rate of climb at S/L	335 m (1,100 ft)/min
Range	195 nm (362 km; 225 miles)
Endurance	3 h

ROTEC

ROTEC ENGINEERING INC

PO Box 380220, Duncanville, Texas 75138
Telephone: 1 (214) 298 2505
Fax: 1 (214) 296 9614
Telex: 288777 ROTEC DCVL
PRESIDENT: William W. Adaska

Rotec's aircraft have been made available in kit and/or ready to fly forms. Details of its military Ground Troop Army Trainers can be found in the 1987-88 *Jane's*. Details of the Rally 2B, Rally 3, Rally Sport, Rally Champ and Panther can be found in the Microlight tables.

ROTEC PANTHER PLUS and SEA PANTHER

Rotec's follow-on aircraft to the Panther, the Panther Plus, is not a microlight but is covered by the FAA's Experimental homebuilt category. Construction from the optional kit takes about 40 hours.

The standard **Panther Plus** employs many features of the Panther, but has a fully enclosed cabin and a 31.3 kW (42 hp) Rotax 447. A twin-float variant of the Panther Plus is the **Sea Panther**, with foam core glassfibre floats of 3.45 m (11 ft 4 in) length. The Sea Panther has a maximum speed of 69 knots (129 km/h; 80 mph), a cruising speed of 65 knots (121 km/h; 75 mph), a range of 152 nm (281 km; 175 miles), and a useful load of 152 kg (335 lb). Military versions of the Panther have been proposed.

The description of the Panther in the Microlight tables applies also to the Panther Plus, except as detailed above and following.
AIRFRAME: As Panther but with fully enclosed cabin.

DIMENSIONS, EXTERNAL:

Wing span	10.36 m (34 ft 0 in)
Length overall	4.88 m (16 ft 10 in)
Height overall	2.06 m (6 ft 9 in)
Propeller diameter	1.52 m (5 ft 0 in)

AREA:

Wings, gross	13.75 m² (148.0 sq ft)

WEIGHTS:

Weight empty	134 kg (295 lb)
Pilot weight range	63.5-111 kg (140-245 lb)
Baggage capacity	18 kg (40 lb)
Max T-O weight	286 kg (630 lb)

PERFORMANCE:

Max level speed	65 knots (121 km/h; 75 mph)
Econ cruising speed	52 knots (97 km/h; 60 mph)
Stalling speed: full power	19 knots (34 km/h; 21 mph)
power off	23 knots (42 km/h; 26 mph)
Max rate of climb at S/L	244 m (800 ft)/min
Service ceiling	more than 3,050 m (10,000 ft)
T-O run	28 m (90 ft)
Landing run	23 m (75 ft)
Range with max fuel	152 nm (281 km; 175 miles)
Endurance	2 h 30 min
g limits	+3.5/−1.5

ROTEC PANTHER 2 PLUS

The Panther 2 Plus is basically a Panther Plus with a lengthened cabin to provide tandem seating for a pilot and passenger. The Rotax 447 engine remains the standard power plant; options are the 35.8 kW (48 hp) Rotax 503 and a 48.5 kW (65 hp) Rotax. An auxiliary 13.25 litre (3.5 US gallon; 2.9 Imp gallon) fuel tank is offered to supplement the standard 19 litre (5 US gallon; 4.2 Imp gallon) tank. Options include floats (**as Sea Panther 2 Plus**), skis, wheel fairings, dual controls and agricultural spraying equipment.
TYPE: Tandem two-seat cabin homebuilt; conforms to FAA Experimental category.
DIMENSIONS, EXTERNAL:

Wing span	10.36 m (34 ft 0 in)
Length overall	5.59 m (18 ft 4 in)
Height overall	2.13 m (7 ft 0 in)
Propeller diameter	1.65 m (5 ft 5 in)

AREA:

Wings, gross	17.09 m² (184.0 sq ft)

WEIGHTS:

Weight empty	179 kg (395 lb)
Pilot and passenger weight range (combined)	136-208 kg (300-460 lb)
Max T-O weight	422 kg (930 lb)

PERFORMANCE (standard aircraft, except where indicated):

Max level speed	69 knots (129 km/h; 80 mph)
Econ cruising speed	56 knots (105 km/h; 65 mph)
Stalling speed: power on	21 knots (39 km/h; 24 mph)
power off	25 knots (47 km/h; 29 mph)
Max rate of climb at S/L: 2 crew	167 m (550 ft)/min
pilot only	more than 274 m (900 ft)/min
Sea Panther	152 m (500 ft)/min
Service ceiling	more than 3,050 m (10,000 ft)
T-O run: Panther 2 Plus	54 m (175 ft)
Sea Panther	106 m (350 ft)
Landing run	38 m (125 ft)
Range with max fuel	173 nm (322 km; 200 miles)
Endurance	2 h 30 min
g limits	+3.5/−1.5

ROTORWAY

ROTORWAY INTERNATIONAL

300 South 25th Avenue, Phoenix, Arizona 85009
Telephone: 1 (602) 278 8899
Fax: 1 (602) 278 7657
PRESIDENT: John Netherwood

All assets of the former RotorWay Aircraft Inc have been purchased by Englishman John Netherwood, and a new company was established as Cobb International Inc on 1 June 1990, trading as RotorWay International.

The product line centres on the Exec 90, the former Exec with some 23 modifications. The Elete, detailed and illustrated in the 1990-91 *Jane's*, was never finished and is not in production.

ROTORWAY EXEC 90

RotorWay International currently manufactures Exec 90 helicopter kits for final assembly by amateur builders, powered by the company's own R.I. 2.66 litre (162 cu in) water-cooled engine. The kit comes complete and only requires paint, and there are no options offered (except for an agricultural spray system with an 8.53 m; 28 ft boom for this specific utility task) as all normal features are standard. Some foreign distributors also sell the helicopter fully assembled and test flown for delivery. It utilises asymmetrical aerofoil section, all-metal rotor blades, and an elastomeric bearing rotor hub system. RotorWay offers complete flight orientation and maintenance training, and a comprehensive customer service programme. It is currently marketed in the United States and in 33 foreign countries.
TYPE: Side by side two-seat homebuilt helicopter.
ROTOR SYSTEM: Asymmetrical aerofoil section two-blade main rotor. All-metal aluminium alloy blades are attached to aluminium alloy teetering rotor hub by retention straps. Teetering tail rotor, with two blades each comprising a steel spar and aluminium alloy skin. Elastomeric bearing rotor hub system with dual push/pull cable controlled swashplate for cyclic pitch control.
AIRFRAME: Basic 4130 steel tube structure, with wraparound glassfibre fuselage/cabin enclosure. Aluminium alloy monocoque tailboom. Basic twin skid landing gear.
POWER PLANT: One 113.3 kW (152 hp) RotorWay International R.I. engine with dual electronic ignition. Standard fuel capacity 64.4 litres (17 US gallons; 14.2 Imp gallons).

DIMENSIONS, EXTERNAL:

Main rotor diameter	7.62 m (25 ft 0 in)
Length of fuselage	6.71 m (22 ft 0 in)
Height to top of main rotor	2.44 m (8 ft 0 in)

WEIGHTS:

Weight empty	420 kg (925 lb)
Crew weight	181 kg (400 lb)
Max T-O weight	646 kg (1,425 lb)

PERFORMANCE (at max T-O weight):

Never-exceed (VNE) and max level speed	100 knots (185 km/h; 115 mph)
Normal cruising speed	82 knots (153 km/h; 95 mph)
Max rate of climb at S/L	305 m (1,000 ft)/min
Service ceiling	3,050 m (10,000 ft)
Hovering ceiling, with two persons:	
IGE	2,135 m (7,000 ft)
OGE	1,525 m (5,000 ft)
Range with max fuel at optimum cruising power	156 nm (290 km; 180 miles)
Endurance with max fuel at optimum cruising power	2 h

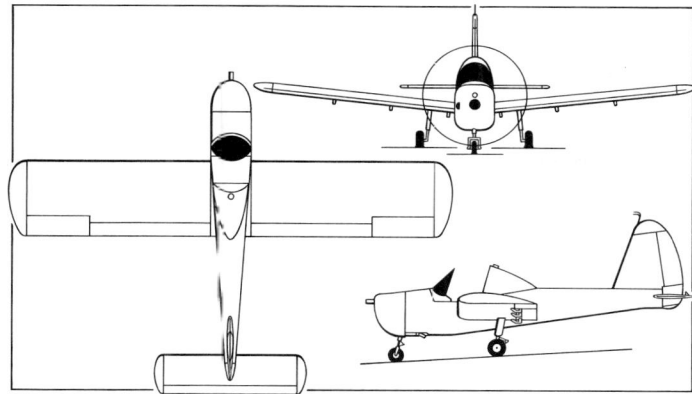

R.D. Little Dipper Replica *(Jane's/Mike Keep)*

Rotec Panther 2 Plus *(Geoffrey P. Jones)*

X101 prototype for Revolution Helicopter Corporation's Mini 500, designed by Augusto Cicaré

Mockup of Revolution Helicopter Corporation's Mini 500 single-seat helicopter at Sun 'n Fun 91 *(Geoffrey P. Jones)*

RotorWay International Exec 90 two-seat homebuilt helicopter

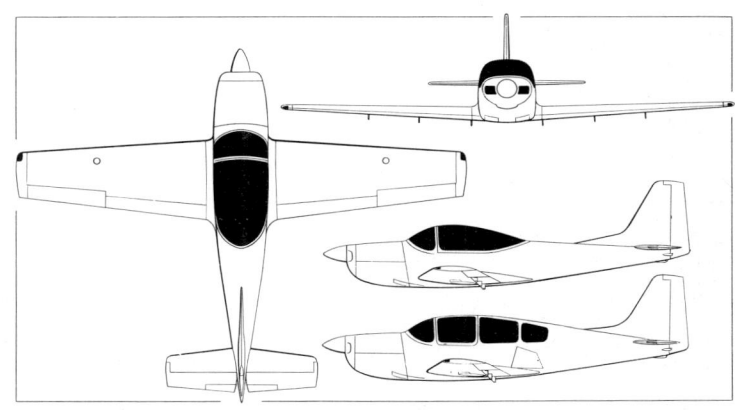

Model 300 Sequoia two-seat utility and aerobatic aircraft, with additional (lower) side view of Model 302 Kodiak *(Pilot Press)*

SEQUOIA

SEQUOIA AIRCRAFT CORPORATION

2000 Tomlynn Street, PO Box 6861, Richmond, Virginia 23230
Telephone: 1 (804) 353 1713
Fax: 1 (804) 359 2618
PRESIDENT: Alfred P. Scott

SEQUOIA MODEL 300 SEQUOIA

This aircraft is available in plan and kit forms.
TYPE: Side by side two-seat utility and aerobatic homebuilt.
AIRFRAME: Wing section NACA 64₂A215 at root, NACA 64A210 at tip. Wings, ailerons, slotted flaps and tail unit of flush riveted aluminium alloy construction. Wings have glassfibre tips. Welded steel tube fuselage, covered entirely with lightweight shell of glassfibre/PVC foam/glassfibre sandwich, attached to tubing with glassfibre and epoxy resin. Retractable tricycle landing gear.
POWER PLANT: One 224 kW (300 hp) Textron Lycoming TIO-540-S1AD. Other Textron Lycoming engines of 175-224 kW (235-300 hp) may be used. Fuel capacity 291.5 litres (77 US gallons; 64 Imp gallons). Provision for tip tanks of approximately 75 litres (20 US gallons; 16.7 Imp gallons) capacity each; and two underwing

attachment points for additional fuel tanks, radar or stores of up to 272 kg (600 lb) combined weight.

DIMENSIONS, EXTERNAL:
Wing span	9.14 m (30 ft 0 in)
Length overall	7.62 m (25 ft 0 in)
Height overall	2.90 m (9 ft 6 in)
Propeller diameter	2.03 m (6 ft 8 in)

AREA:
Wings, gross	12.08 m² (130.0 sq ft)

WEIGHTS:
Weight empty	816 kg (1,800 lb)
Baggage capacity	45 kg (100 lb)
Max T-O weight: utility	1,270 kg (2,800 lb)
aerobatic	1,088 kg (2,400 lb)

PERFORMANCE (estimated):
Max level speed at S/L	195 knots (362 km/h; 225 mph)
Max cruising speed at 2,440 m (8,000 ft)	185 knots (343 km/h; 213 mph)
Stalling speed: clean	75 knots (139 km/h; 86 mph)
flaps and wheels down	60 knots (111 km/h; 69 mph)
Max rate of climb at S/L	664 m (2,180 ft)/min
Service ceiling	7,620 m (25,000 ft)
T-O run	457 m (1,500 ft)
Landing run	548 m (1,800 ft)

Range at max cruising speed, with 45 min reserves
868 nm (1,609 km; 1,000 miles)

SEQUOIA MODEL 302 KODIAK

The Kodiak is a four-seat development of the Model 300 Sequoia with gull-wing doors to provide access to the enclosed cabin. It was designed to be fully aerobatic and is available in plan and kit forms (latter does not include prepared fuselage).

Power plant is in the 186-224 kW (250-300 hp) Textron Lycoming IO-540/TIO-540-S1AD range. Empty weight will be 839 kg (1,850 lb); max T-O weight 1,451 kg (3,200 lb); fuel capacity 341 litres (90 US gallons; 75 Imp gallons).

SEQUOIA FALCO F.8L

Sequoia Aircraft markets plans and kits to build an improved version of the Falco F.8L high-performance monoplane, designed in Italy by Ing Stelio Frati of General Avia and first flown on 15 June 1955. By February 1991, a total of 660 sets of plans had been sold and 30 Falcos had flown.
TYPE: Side by side two-seat, dual control homebuilt. Provision for child's seat in baggage space.
AIRFRAME: Entire airframe has plywood covered wood structure, with overall fabric covering and glassfibre wing fillets. Optional metal control surfaces. NACA 64₂212.5 wing section at root, NACA 64₂210 at tip. Retractable tricycle landing gear.

POWER PLANT: One 119 kW (160 hp) Textron Lycoming IO-320-B1A is standard for kit-built aircraft. Optional engines for which Sequoia offers installation kits are the 112 kW (150 hp) IO-320-A1A and 134 kW (180 hp) IO-360-B1E. Fuel capacity 151 litres (40 US gallons; 33.3 Imp gallons). Optional 7.6 litre (2 US gallon; 1.7 Imp gallon) header tank to permit inverted flight.

DIMENSIONS, EXTERNAL:

Wing span	8.00 m (26 ft 3 in)
Length overall	6.50 m (21 ft 4 in)
Height overall	2.29 m (7 ft 6 in)

AREA:

Wings, gross	10.00 m² (107.6 sq ft)

WEIGHTS (119 kW; 160 hp engine):

Weight empty	550 kg (1,212 lb)
Payload with max fuel	194 kg (428 lb)
Baggage capacity	40 kg (88 lb)
Max aerobatic weight	748 kg (1,650 lb)
Max T-O weight	853 kg (1,880 lb)

PERFORMANCE (119 kW; 160 hp engine):

Max level speed at S/L	184 knots (341 km/h; 212 mph)

Cruising speed at 1,830 m (6,000 ft), 75% power	
	165 knots (306 km/h; 190 mph)
Stalling speed, flaps and wheels down	
	54 knots (100 km/h; 62 mph)
Max rate of climb at S/L	347 m (1,140 ft)/min
Service ceiling	5,790 m (19,000 ft)
Range at econ cruising speed	
	868 nm (1,609 km; 1,000 miles)

SILHOUETTE — *See Lunds Tekniske of Norway*

SKYWAY
SKYWAY AIRCRAFT
Asheville, North Carolina
OWNERS: Carl McIntosh and Rosaly Sheppard

SKYWAY AIRCRAFT J-6 KARATOO
Formerly marketed by Grover and then Country Air, the Karatoo has been further developed by its present owners and the prototype currently uses a Subaru engine. Kits are available.

TYPE: Side by side two-seat homebuilt.
AIRFRAME: Wooden wing and welded 4130 steel tube fuselage and tail unit, all fabric covered. Wing section Clark Y. Non-retractable tailwheel landing gear.
POWER PLANT: One 48.5 kW (65 hp) Subaru EA 81 1,800 cc engine.

DIMENSIONS, EXTERNAL:

Wing span	9.96 m (32 ft 8 in)
Length overall	6.10 m (20 ft 0 in)
Height overall	1.70 m (5 ft 7 in)
Propeller diameter	1.83 m (6 ft 0 in)

AREA:

Wings, gross	13.84 m² (149.0 sq ft)

WEIGHTS:

Weight empty	332 kg (733 lb)
Max T-O weight	553 kg (1,220 lb)

PERFORMANCE:

Max level speed	95 knots (177 km/h; 110 mph)
Cruising speed	87 knots (161 km/h; 100 mph)
Max rate of climb at S/L	183 m (600 ft)/min
T-O and landing run	61 m (200 ft)
g limits	+5/−3.5

SMITH
S & H AIRCRAFT
1300 Rosney, Bloomington, Illinois 6 701
Telephone: 1 (309) 829 4656

SMITH TERMITE
Plans and an airframe kit are thought to be offered to construct this all-wooden parasol-wing monoplane. Advertising material has stated that more than 300 are flying worldwide.

SMYTH
JERRY SMYTH
ADDRESS FOR PLANS: Wicks Aircraft Supply, 410 Pine Street, Highland, Illinois 62249
Telephone: 1 (618) 654 7447
Fax: 1 (618) 654 6253

SMYTH MODEL 'S' SIDEWINDER
The prototype Sidewinder first flew on 21 February 1969. Plans and component parts were made available. The following description applies to the prototype:
TYPE: Side by side two-seat limited aerobatic homebuilt.
AIRFRAME: Aluminium alloy wings, ailerons and tail unit; wings filled with epoxy. Wing section NACA 64-612 at root, NACA 64-210 at tip. Welded steel tube fuselage, with aluminium formers and skin. Electrically operated speed brake may be fitted on lower fuselage. Non-

retractable tricycle landing gear. Aircraft have been completed with retractable landing gear (see 1975-76 *Jane's*) and tailwheel type landing gear (see 1980-81 *Jane's*).
POWER PLANT: Provision for installation of engines from 67 to 134 kW (90-180 hp). Prototype has a 93 kW (125 hp) Textron Lycoming O-290-G. Fuel capacity 66.2 litres (17.5 US gallons; 14.6 Imp gallons). Provision for wingtip tanks.

DIMENSIONS, EXTERNAL:

Wing span	7.57 m (24 ft 10 in)
Length overall	5.89 m (19 ft 4 in)
Height overall	1.66 m (5 ft 5½ in)
Propeller diameter	1.70 m (5 ft 7 in)

AREA:

Wings, gross	8.92 m² (96.0 sq ft)

WEIGHTS:

Weight empty	393 kg (867 lb)

Baggage capacity	41 kg (90 lb)
Max T-O and landing weight	657 kg (1,450 lb)

PERFORMANCE (at max T-O weight):

Max level speed at S/L	152 knots (282 km/h; 175 mph)
Max cruising speed, 75% power at 610 m (2,000 ft)	
	139 knots (257 km/h; 160 mph)
Stalling speed, flaps up	48 knots (89 km/h; 55 mph)
Max rate of climb at S/L: at 0°C	366 m (1,200 ft)/min
at 24°C	274 m (900 ft)/min
Service ceiling	4,575 m (15,000 ft)
T-O run	244 m (800 ft)
Landing run	457 m (1,500 ft)
Range with max fuel, no reserves	
	369 nm (684 km; 425 miles)
g limit	+9 design

SNA
SNA INC
Box 607, Kimberton, Pennsylvania 19442-0607
Telephone: 1 (215) 983 3377
Fax: 1 (215) 933 3335
PRESIDENT: Richard Silva

Rights to manufacture and market kits of the Seawind 2500 amphibian have been purchased from Seawind International by SNA Inc. A 224 kW (300 hp) Textron Lycoming IO-540K engine is now being offered as a further option.

SNA SEAWIND
The production prototype Seawind (C-GFNL) flew for the first time on 23 August 1982. An illustration can be found in the 1987-88 *Jane's*. The current Seawind is a much refined version of which kits are available, each containing pre-moulded components that are supplied as complete subassemblies where possible. Assembly takes about 1000 working hours.

TYPE: Four-seat dual-control homebuilt amphibian; exceeds FAR Pt 23 minimum performance requirements.
AIRFRAME: Wing section NLF(1)-0215F. Built-up GFRP wing spar and PVC foam ribs, covered with GFRP skins. Drooped ailerons linked with slotted flaps, wingtip floats and single-step flying-boat hull all of GFRP/PVC foam construction. GFRP tail unit. Electrically retractable tricycle landing gear.
POWER PLANT: One 186.5 kW (250 hp) Textron Lycoming IO-540 or 224 kW (300 hp) IO-540K engine. Two integral fuel cells in wings; total capacity 265 litres (70 US gallons; 58.3 Imp gallons) or optionally 393 litres (104 US gallons; 86.6 Imp gallons).

DIMENSIONS, EXTERNAL:

Wing span	10.67 m (35 ft 0 in)
Length overall	8.23 m (27 ft 0 in)
Height overall	2.90 m (9 ft 6 in)
Propeller diameter	1.98 m (6 ft 6 in)

AREA:

Wings, gross	14.86 m² (160.0 sq ft)

WEIGHTS:

Weight empty, 300 hp engine	953 kg (2,100 lb)
Max T-O weight	1,451 kg (3,200 lb)

PERFORMANCE (300 hp engine):

Max level speed at S/L	174 knots (322 km/h; 200 mph)
Cruising speed, 75% power	
	166 knots (307 km/h; 191 mph)
Stalling speed: flaps up	61 knots (113 km/h; 70 mph)
flaps and landing gear down	
	50 knots (92 km/h; 57 mph)
Max rate of climb at S/L	488 m (1,600 ft)/min
Service ceiling	6,100 m (20,000 ft)
T-O run: land	156 m (510 ft)
water	238 m (780 ft)
Range with max standard fuel, no reserves	
	807 nm (1,496 km; 930 miles)

SORRELL
SORRELL AIRCRAFT COMPANY LTD
16525 Tilley Road South, Tenino, Washington 98589
Telephone: 1 (206) 264 2866
Details of the SNS-8 Hiperlight and SNS-10 Intruder can be found in the Microlight tables.

SORRELL SNS-2 GUPPY
In 1967 the late Mr Hobie Sorrell flew his SNS-2 Guppy cabin biplane for the first time, powered by a 13.5 kW (18 hp) OMC Cushman Model 200 engine. Plans and kits for this 'back staggered' non-aerobatic single-seater are available from Sorrell Aircraft Company and/or from Mr Michael Kimbrel (see Microlights).
TYPE: Single-seat homebuilt cabin biplane.

AIRFRAME: Modified Grant X wing section. Wooden wings and fuselage, except for steel tube wingtips, aluminium fittings and wing drag member; Dacron covered. Full span ailerons on lower wings only, of aluminium tubing with riveted aluminium skins. Steel tube engine mounting, interplane struts and Dacron covered tail unit. Non-retractable tailwheel landing gear.
POWER PLANT: Engines of up to 27 kW (36 hp) can be fitted, including Volkswagen modified motorcar engines. Sorrell kit includes 24 kW (32 hp) Rotax 377. Fuel capacity 23 litres (6.5 US gallons; 5.4 Imp gallons).

DIMENSIONS, EXTERNAL:

Wing span	6.48 m (21 ft 3 in)
Length overall	4.70 m (15 ft 5 in)
Height overall	1.57 m (5 ft 2 in)

AREA:

Wings, gross	11.98 m² (129.0 sq ft)

WEIGHTS (prototype with Cushman engine):

Weight empty	159 kg (350 lb)
Max T-O weight	272 kg (600 lb)

PERFORMANCE (prototype with Cushman engine):

Max level speed	69 knots (129 km/h; 80 mph)
Cruising speed	61 knots (113 km/h; 70 mph)
Stalling speed, power off	26 knots (49 km/h; 30 mph)
Max rate of climb at S/L	91 m (300 ft)/min
Absolute ceiling	3,110 m (10,200 ft)
T-O run	91 m (300 ft)
Landing from 15 m (50 ft)	91 m (300 ft)
Range	182 nm (338 km; 210 miles)
g limit	+4 recommended

Sequoia Falco F.8L homebuilt aircraft

SNA Seawind four-seat homebuilt amphibian (*J.M.G. Gradidge*)

Skyway Aircraft J-6 Karatoo (*Howard Levy*)

Smyth Sidewinder with tailwheel landing gear (*J. M. G. Gradidge*)

Sorrell SNS-9 EXP II sport/trainer (*Peter M. Bowers*)

Spencer Amphibian four-seat amphibious homebuilt

Sorrell SNS-7 Hiperbipe two-seat aerobatic biplane (*Peter M. Bowers*)

SORRELL SNS-7 HIPERBIPE

The Hiperbipe made its initial flight as the SNS-6 prototype in March 1973. Plans and kits are available.

TYPE: Side by side two-seat, dual-control homebuilt aerobatic biplane.

AIRFRAME: Modified NACA 0012 wing sections. Welded steel interplane struts. Fabric-covered all-wood back-staggered wings, but with centre-section of upper wing skinned with transparent plastics to allow improved view for aerobatics. Cambered wingtips. Four full span flaperons of pop-riveted aluminium alloy. Fuselage and tail unit of welded steel tube, fabric covered. Glassfibre engine cowling. Non-retractable tailwheel landing gear.

POWER PLANT: One 134 kW (180 hp) Textron Lycoming IO-360-B1E. Fuel capacity 147.5 litres (39 US gallons; 32.5 Imp gallons).

DIMENSIONS, EXTERNAL:

Wing span	6.96 m (22 ft 10 in)
Length overall	6.35 m (20 ft 10 in)
Height overall	1.80 m (5 ft 10¾ in)
Propeller diameter	1.93 m (6 ft 4 in)

AREA:

Wings, gross (projected)	13.9 m² (150.0 sq ft)

WEIGHTS:

Weight empty	561 kg (1,236 lb)
Baggage capacity	36 kg (80 lb)
Max T-O weight: aerobatic	766 kg (1,690 lb)
normal	867 kg (1,911 lb)

PERFORMANCE (at max normal T-O weight):

Max level speed at S/L	149 knots (277 km/h; 172 mph)
Econ cruising speed	130 knots (241 km/h; 150 mph)
Stalling speed:	
flaperons down	43 knots (79 km/h; 49 mph)
flaperons up	51 knots (94 km/h; 58 mph)
Max rate of climb at S/L	457 m (1,500 ft)/min
Service ceiling, estimated	6,100 m (20,000 ft)
T-O run	122 m (400 ft)
Landing run	181 m (595 ft)
Range	436 nm (807 km; 502 miles)

SORRELL SNS-9 EXP II

First flown on 22 May 1985, the SNS-9 EXP II is a side by side two-seat sport/trainer, with dual controls and basic instrumentation as standard. Like other recent Sorrell designs, it is a small back-staggered biplane. The wings are made of pop riveted aluminium alloy, covered with Stits

Poly-Fiber. The welded steel tube fuselage is also Poly-Fiber covered. Power for the prototype is provided by a 31.3 kW (42 hp) Rotax 447. Standard fuel capacity is 34 litres (9 US gallons; 7.5 Imp gallons). Assembly from pre-welded component kits is said to require 300 hours of work.

TYPE: Two-seat homebuilt cabin biplane.

DIMENSIONS, EXTERNAL:

Wing span	7.11 m (23 ft 4 in)
Length overall	5.49 m (18 ft 0 in)
Height overall	1.63 m (5 ft 4 in)

AREA:

Wings, gross	13.75 m² (148.0 sq ft)

WEIGHTS:

Weight empty	162 kg (356 lb)
Max T-O weight	367 kg (810 lb)

PERFORMANCE (estimated at max T-O weight):

Max cruising speed	74 knots (136 km/h; 85 mph)
Stalling speed	34 knots (63 km/h; 39 mph)
Max rate of climb at S/L	183 m (600 ft)/min
T-O and landing run on grass	92 m (300 ft)
Range with max standard fuel	221 nm (410 km; 255 miles)
g limits	+3.8/−1.9

SPENCER

SPENCER AMPHIBIAN AIRCRAFT INC

PO Box 327, Kansas, Illinois 61933

Telephone: 1 (217) 948 5504/5505

Spencer Amphibian Air Car Inc was sold on 15 July 1988 to Robert F. Kerans.

SPENCER AMPHIBIAN AIRCRAFT MODEL S-12-E

This latest version of the S-12 series is available in plans form plus some glassfibre and all metal assemblies, while plans and certain components for the differently powered and earlier S-12-D may also be available. Plans and

components have been sold to amateur constructors in Brazil, Canada, Germany, Italy, the USA and elsewhere.

TYPE: Four-seat, dual control homebuilt amphibian.

AIRFRAME: Specially designed STOL (modified NACA 4415) wing section. Wing structure of wood, steel and glassfibre. Wooden ailerons and trailing-edge flaps.

Glassfibre stabilising float on strut beneath each wing. Single-stepped hull with wood frames, longerons and skin, sheathed in glassfibre and Kevlar (all glassfibre hull may become a future project). Welded steel tube structure to provide wing and engine mountings and attachment points for the retractable tricycle landing gear. Retractable water rudder.

POWER PLANT: One 212.5 kW (285 hp) Teledyne Continental Tiara 6-285. Also recommended is 224 kW (300 hp) Teledyne Continental IO-520. Development underway in 1988 to install a Ford 351-W converted motorcar engine. Fuel capacity 360 litres (95 US gallons; 79 Imp gallons).

DIMENSIONS, EXTERNAL:
Wing span	11.38 m (37 ft 4 in)
Length overall	8.05 m (26 ft 5 in)
Height overall	2.90 m (9 ft 6 in)
Propeller diameter	2.13 m (7 ft 0 in)

AREA:
Wings, gross	17.1 m² (184.0 sq ft)

WEIGHTS:
Weight empty	993 kg (2,190 lb)
Max T-O weight	1,451 kg (3,200 lb)

PERFORMANCE (at max T-O weight):
Cruising speed	122 knots (225 km/h; 140 mph)
Econ cruising speed at 3,050 m (10,000 ft)	109 knots (201 km/h; 125 mph)
Stalling speed, flaps down	38 knots (70 km/h; 43 mph)
Max rate of climb at S/L	320 m (1,050 ft)/min
Service ceiling	4,875 m (16,000 ft)
T-O run from calm water	213 m (700 ft)
Landing run	213 m (700 ft)
Range, 65% power at 2,315 m (7,600 ft), 20 min reserves	695 nm (1,285 km; 800 miles)
Endurance	7 h

SPORT
SPORT AIRCRAFT INC

44211 Yucca Avenue, Unit A, Lancaster, California 93534
Telephone: 1 (805) 949 2312
OWNER: Phil Tucker

SPORT AIRCRAFT (SUNDERLAND) S-18

Originating from the Thorp T-18 Tiger, the modified S-18 was offered in plans form by Sunderland Aircraft, while Sport Aircraft Inc made kits and prefabricated components available. Following the closure of Sunderland Aircraft, Sport Aircraft has taken over the sale of plans also and 130 sets for the S-18 have been sold.

TYPE: Side by side two-seat, dual-control homebuilt; provision for child's jump seat.
AIRFRAME: Aluminium alloy construction. Wing section LDS-4-212. Conventional controls, plus flaps. Optional electric aileron and pitch trim. Non-retractable tailwheel landing gear with brakes.
POWER PLANT: One Textron Lycoming engine in 100-134 kW (135-180 hp) category; typically 112 kW (150 hp) O-320. Optional Ford V6 motorcar engine modification by Blanton. Fuel capacity 110 litres (29 US gallons; 24.1 Imp gallons). Optional two integral tanks in wing leading-edges, each 47.3 litres (12.5 US gallons; 10.4 Imp gallons).

DIMENSIONS, EXTERNAL:
Wing span	6.35 m (20 ft 10 in)
Length overall	5.89 m (19 ft 4 in)
Height overall	1.55 m (5 ft 1 in)
Propeller diameter	1.73 m (5 ft 8 in)

AREA:
Wings, gross	8.0 m² (86.0 sq ft)

WEIGHTS (104.4 kW; 140 hp engine):
Weight empty	419 kg (923 lb)
Baggage capacity	36 kg (80 lb)
Max T-O weight	726 kg (1,600 lb)

PERFORMANCE (112 kW; 150 hp Textron Lycoming):
Max level speed at S/L	159 knots (295 km/h; 183 mph)
Max cruising speed (75% power) at 2,590 m (8,500 ft)	156 knots (290 km/h; 180 mph)
Econ cruising speed at 3,050 m (10,000 ft)	139 knots (257 km/h; 160 mph)
Stalling speed, flaps up and engine idling	55 knots (102 km/h; 63 mph)
Max rate of climb at S/L	366 m (1,200 ft)/min
Service ceiling	6,100 m (20,000 ft)
Range: with max fuel	460 nm (853 km; 530 miles)
with max payload	868 nm (1,609 km; 1,000 miles)
Endurance	3 h 12 min
g limits	+5/−2.5

STAR
STAR AVIATION INC

1901 North West Military Highway, Suite 200, San Antonio, Texas 78213

STAR AVIATION LONESTAR

Available in kit form, the LoneStar was designed by Tom Carlson and Ken Rehler and first flew as a prototype on 18 October 1989. Construction is said to take a few weeks using common tools.

TYPE: Single-seat homebuilt helicopter.
ROTOR SYSTEM: Two-blade main rotor, with composite blades manufactured by McCutchen Sky Wheels. Rotorhead uses bearings with Teflon and Kevlar liners. Conventional sticks and pedals linked with aircraft grade stainless steel push/pull cables for cyclic, collective and tail rotor control. Multi-belt transmission system.
AIRFRAME: Open structure of anodized aluminium alloy, with 10 cm (4 in) square vertical frame member providing mounting points for engine, main rotor shaft, idler shaft assembly, controls, pilot's seat, tailboom and non-retractable tricycle landing gear.
POWER PLANT: One 47.7 kW (64 hp) Rotax 582. Seat fuel tank capacity 33.7 litres (8.9 US gallons; 7.4 Imp gallons).

DIMENSIONS, EXTERNAL:
Main rotor diameter	6.20 m (20 ft 4 in)
Length of fuselage	4.04 m (13 ft 3 in)
Height overall	2.08 m (6 ft 10 in)

WEIGHTS:
Weight empty	168 kg (370 lb)
Max T-O weight	295 kg (650 lb)

PERFORMANCE:
Max level speed at S/L	78 knots (145 km/h; 90 mph)
Cruising speed	56 knots (105 km/h; 65 mph)
Max range	100 nm (185 km; 115 miles)

STARFIRE
STARFIRE AVIATION INC

3000 South Palo Verde Road, Buckeye, Arizona 85326
Telephone: 1 (602) 386 5019
PRESIDENT: H. G. McKenzie

STARFIRE FIREBOLT CONVERTIBLE

First flown on 15 May 1987, the Firebolt Convertible incorporates Skybolt features but is longer to give more cockpit room. Plans, kits, steel components and assemblies are available.

In addition to the standard Model A, as detailed below, the Model B has symmetrical ailerons (upper and lower) and elevator horns, and the Model C features a new fin and rudder shape, with dynamic balance to the rudder.

TYPE: Tandem two-seat aerobatic homebuilt biplane.
AIRFRAME: Wire braced wooden wings, steel tube Warren truss fuselage structure and steel tube tail unit, all Stits Poly-Fiber covered except for metal skin on fuselage forward of rear seat. Wing section NACA 63₂A015 on upper wing; NACA 0012 on lower wings. Non-retractable tailwheel landing gear, with brakes.
POWER PLANT: Prototype has one 134 kW (180 hp) Textron Lycoming IO-360-B1B. Fuel capacity 148 litres (39 US gallons; 32.5 Imp gallons). Optional 224 kW (300 hp) Textron Lycoming IO-540-K1A5 engine.

DIMENSIONS, EXTERNAL:
Wing span, both	7.32 m (24 ft 0 in)
Length overall	6.10 m (20 ft 0 in)
Height overall	2.18 m (7 ft 2 in)
Propeller diameter: 180-200 hp	1.88 m (6 ft 2 in)
300 hp	2.03 m (6 ft 8 in)

AREA:
Wings, gross	13.94 m² (150.0 sq ft)

WEIGHTS:
Weight empty	556 kg (1,225 lb)
Pilot weight range	68-113 kg (150-250 lb)

Baggage capacity	18 kg (40 lb)
Max T-O weight	907 kg (2,000 lb)

PERFORMANCE (134 kW; 180 hp engine, at 782 kg; 1,725 lb aerobatic weight):
Max level speed at S/L	143 knots (266 km/h; 165 mph) IAS
Max cruising speed at 1,980 m (6,500 ft)	148 knots (274 km/h; 170 mph) TAS
Econ cruising speed	109 knots (201 km/h; 125 mph)
Stalling speed, power off	51 knots (94 km/h; 58 mph)
Max rate of climb at S/L	548 m (1,800 ft)/min
Service ceiling	4,575 m (15,000 ft)
T-O run	138 m (450 ft)
Landing run	199 m (650 ft)
Range, no wind	590 nm (1,094 km; 680 miles)
Endurance	4 h 35 min
g limits	±6

STAR-LITE
STAR-LITE AIRCRAFT INC

The Star-Lite SL-1 is out of production. Details and an illustration can be found in the 1989-90 *Jane's*.

STEEN
STEEN AERO LAB INC

779 Ottawa Drive, Rock Hill, South Carolina 29732
Telephone: 1 (803) 366 9338
OWNER: Hale Wallace

Lamar Steen designed a two-seat fully aerobatic biplane named Skybolt, which was built as a class project in the Denver high school in which he was an aerospace teacher. Simplicity of construction was a primary aim of the design, begun in June 1968. Building began on 19 August 1969, and the first flight was made in October 1970. Plans were made available to amateur constructors (and components) and more than 3,500 sets were sold.

More recently, Stolp Starduster Corporation took over design and marketing rights for the Skybolt, developing a Mk II version. However, the aircraft is now owned by Hale Wallace and is being remarketed under the original Steen Aero Lab company name, with updated plans, materials, fuselage and wing kits, and technical assistance available.

STEEN SKYBOLT

The following description applies to the prototype with 134 kW (180 hp) Textron Lycoming engine.

TYPE: Tandem two-seat homebuilt aerobatic biplane.
AIRFRAME: Braced biplane. Symmetrical aerofoils: upper wing NACA 63₂A015, lower wing NACA 0012. Wooden two-spar wing structures with spruce spars, built-up ribs and fabric covering. Fabric covered Frise ailerons on upper and lower wings. Welded fuselage and wire braced tail unit of 4130 chrome molybdenum steel tube, with fabric covering. Adjustable trim tab in port elevator. Non-retractable tailwheel type, with brakes and glassfibre wheel fairings.
POWER PLANT: One 134 kW (180 hp) Textron Lycoming HO-360-B1B. Provision for alternative engines of 112-224 kW (150-300 hp). Fuselage fuel tank capacity 110 litres (29 US gallons; 24 Imp gallons). Optional tank of 37.8 litres (10 US gallons; 8.3 Imp gallons) capacity can be installed in centre-section of upper wing.

DIMENSIONS, EXTERNAL:
Wing span: upper	7.32 m (24 ft 0 in)
lower	7.01 m (23 ft 0 in)
Length overall	5.79 m (19 ft 0 in)
Height overall	2.13 m (7 ft 0 in)
Propeller diameter	1.88 m (6 ft 2 in)

AREA:
Wings, gross	14.2 m² (152.7 sq ft)

WEIGHTS:
Weight empty	490 kg (1,080 lb)
Baggage capacity	13.6 kg (30 lb)
Max T-O weight	748 kg (1,650 lb)

PERFORMANCE (at max T-O weight):
Max level speed	126 knots (233 km/h; 145 mph)
Cruising speed	113 knots (209 km/h; 130 mph)
Max rate of climb at S/L	762 m (2,500 ft)/min
Service ceiling	5,500 m (18,000 ft)
T-O run	122 m (400 ft)
Range with max fuel	390 nm (720 km; 450 miles)
g limits	+12/−10

Sport Aircraft S-18 two-seat homebuilt

Stoddard-Hamilton Glasair III (background) and Glasair II-S RG (foreground)

Starfire Firebolt Convertible two-seat aerobatic homebuilt

Steen Skybolt built in the UK by Mr Alexander and Mr Todd (*R. Kunert*)

STODDARD-HAMILTON
STODDARD-HAMILTON AIRCRAFT INC

18701 58th Avenue North-East, Arlington, Washington 98223
Telephone: 1 (206) 435 8533
Fax: 1 (206) 435 9525
PRESIDENT: Theodore E. Setzer
MARKETING AND SALES MANAGER: Bill Sprague

Approximately 1,150 kits for all models of the Glasair had been sold by the end of 1990, when about 300 were flying. The Glasair I and II have been superseded by the II-S and III. Details of the Glasair I can be found in the 1989-90 *Jane's*.

STODDARD-HAMILTON GLASAIR II-S

The Glasair II-S (stretched) is available in RG (retractable landing gear), FT (non-retractable tricycle gear) and TD (taildragger) forms to supersede the earlier Glasair series. One hundred kits had been sold by the end of 1990.
TYPE: Side by side two-seat dual control homebuilt.
AIRFRAME: Glassfibre and foam composite construction. Wing section NASA LS(1)-0413. Upswept Hoerner style trailing-edges. Three types of landing gear, as detailed above. Brakes.
POWER PLANT: One 119-134 kW (160-180 hp) Textron Lycoming O-360 series engine. Fuel capacity 182 litres (48 US gallons; 40 Imp gallons). Auxiliary tanks of 42 litres (11 US gallons; 9.2 Imp gallons) capacity in optional wingtip extensions.
DIMENSIONS, EXTERNAL:

Wing span, standard	7.10 m (23 ft 3½ in)
Length overall	6.16 m (20 ft 2½ in)
Height overall	2.07 m (6 ft 9½ in)

AREA:

Wings, gross	7.55 m² (81.3 sq ft)

WEIGHTS (A: RG, B: FT, C: TD):

Weight empty: A	601 kg (1,325 lb)
B	567 kg (1,250 lb)
C	544 kg (1,200 lb)
Baggage capacity	36 kg (80 lb)
Max T-O weight: A, B	953 kg (2,100 lb)
C	907 kg (2,000 lb)

PERFORMANCE (A: RG with 180 hp engine, B: FT with 160 hp, C: TD with 180 hp):
Max level speed at S/L:

A	217 knots (402 km/h; 250 mph)
B	207 knots (383 km/h; 238 mph)
C	208 knots (385 km/h; 239 mph)

Econ cruising speed at 2,440 m (8,000 ft):

A	189 knots (351 km/h; 218 mph)
B	178 knots (330 km/h; 205 mph)
C	179 knots (332 km/h; 206 mph)

Stalling speed, flaps down, power off:

A	43 knots (80 km/h; 50 mph)
B, C	42 knots (78 km/h; 49 mph)

Service ceiling: all versions	approx 5,790 m (19,000 ft)

Max rate of climb at S/L:

all versions	732 m (2,400 ft)/min

Range:

A, standard fuel	1,125 nm (2,085 km; 1,296 miles)
A, with auxiliary fuel	1,383 nm (2,563 km; 1,593 miles)
B, C, standard fuel	1,042 nm (1,931 km; 1,200 miles)
B, C, with auxiliary fuel	1,281 nm (2,373 km; 1,475 miles)

g limits at AUW of 708 kg (1,560 lb):

all versions	+6/−4 limit
	+9/−6 ultimate

STODDARD-HAMILTON GLASAIR III

The Glasair III is a recent addition to the company's range, retaining a similar configuration to the earlier models but designed to offer exceptional performance, constructional simplicity and economical kit price. The landing gear is retractable. Construction takes approximately 1,800 working hours.

The Glasair III has a longer and wider fuselage for increased baggage space, payload capacity and comfort, also improving the longitudinal and directional stability and thereby making it a better cross-country and IFR aircraft. It features a thicker windscreen to improve protection against bird strikes at its higher speeds, and has additional glassfibre laminates, integral longerons, and a lay-up schedule which provides a structurally stronger and torsionally stiffer fuselage. The Glasair III wing uses the LS(1)-0413 section, is strengthened, and carries more fuel than previous models. NACA style air vents provide cabin ventilation.

Under development is a turbocharging system to be offered as a retrofit kit option for IO-540-K engined Glasair IIIs. Projected max cruising speed with the system is 284 knots (526 km/h; 327 mph) at 5,485 m (18,000 ft).
POWER PLANT: One 224 kW (300 hp) Textron Lycoming IO-540-K1H5. Fuel capacity in wings 201 litres (53 US gallons; 44 Imp gallons). Fuselage header tank, capacity 30 litres (8 US gallons; 6.7 Imp gallons). Optional tanks in wingtip extensions, total capacity 41.6 litres (11 US gallons; 9.2 Imp gallons). Optional engine installation may be a 194 kW (260 hp) IO-540 eventually.
DIMENSIONS, EXTERNAL:

Wing span, standard	7.10 m (23 ft 3½ in)
Length overall	6.52 m (21 ft 4¾ in)
Height overall	2.29 m (7 ft 6 in)

AREA:

Wings, gross	7.55 m² (81.3 sq ft)

WEIGHTS:

Weight empty	703 kg (1,550 lb)
Baggage capacity	45 kg (100 lb)
Max T-O weight, without wingtip extensions	1,089 kg (2,400 lb)

PERFORMANCE (standard wings, except where indicated):

Max level speed at S/L	255 knots (473 km/h; 294 mph)
Cruising speed: 75% power at 2,440 m (8,000 ft)	247 knots (457 km/h; 284 mph)
50% power at 5,335 m (17,500 ft)	219 knots (406 km/h; 252 mph)
Stalling speed: pilot only, flaps and wheels up	65 knots (119 km/h; 74 mph)
flaps down, at max T-O weight	70 knots (129 km/h; 80 mph)
Max rate of climb at S/L	732 m (2,400 ft)/min
Service ceiling	approx 7,315 m (24,000 ft)

Range at 55% power:

standard fuel	1,112 nm (2,061 km; 1,281 miles)
with tip tanks	1,313 nm (2,433 km; 1,512 miles)

g limits at AUW of 962 kg (2,120 lb):

	+6/−4 limit
	+9/−6 ultimate

STODDARD-HAMILTON T-9 STALKER

Stoddard-Hamilton developed a low-cost military trainer version of the Glasair III, powered by an Allison turboprop engine. Details can be found in the main Aircraft section of the 1990-91 edition of *Jane's*.

STOLP
STOLP STARDUSTER CORPORATION

4301 Twining Flabob Airport, Riverside, California 92509
Telephone: 1 (714) 686 7943
Fax: 1 (714) 784 0072

PRESIDENT AND GENERAL MANAGER: William C. Clouse Jr

Stolp Starduster Corporation continues to market plans, kits and materials for the two-seat Starduster Too (well over 2,000 sets of plans sold), single-seat Starlet, aerobatic V-Star, Acroduster Too and Super Starduster.

STOLP SA-300 STARDUSTER TOO

Raw materials and certain prefabricated parts (such as glassfibre turtleback, nose cowling, wheel fairings, cockpit cowlings, aluminium fuel tank and Plexiglas windshield) are available.
TYPE: Tandem two-seat homebuilt sporting biplane.
AIRFRAME: Wing section M-6 modified. All-wood wing and aileron structures, fabric covered. Welded 4130 steel tube fuselage and tail unit, with fabric covering. Glassfibre turtleback. Non-retractable tailwheel landing gear.
POWER PLANT: One 134 kW (180 hp) Textron Lycoming O-360-A1A or 149 kW (200 hp) O-360 recommended. Horizontally opposed or radial engines of 93-194 kW (125-260 hp) may be fitted.
DIMENSIONS, EXTERNAL:

Wing span: upper	7.32 m (24 ft 0 in)
lower	6.22 m (20 ft 5 in)
Length overall	6.63 m (21 ft 9 in)
Height overall	2.21 m (7 ft 3 in)

AREA:

Wings, gross	15.05 m² (162.0 sq ft)

WEIGHTS (typical; with 149 kW; 200 hp engine):

Weight empty	517 kg (1,139 lb)
Max T-O weight	907 kg (2,000 lb)

PERFORMANCE (typical; with 149 kW; 200 hp engine):

Max level speed	174 knots (322 km/h; 200 mph)
Econ cruising speed	100 knots (185 km/h; 115 mph)
Stalling speed	51 knots (94 km/h; 58 mph)
Sustained rate of climb, with pilot only	548 m (1,800 ft)/min

STOLP SA-500 STARLET

The prototype Starlet flew for the first time on 1 June 1969. Available prefabricated components include glassfibre turtleback, nose cowling and wheel fairings; windshield; and aluminium fuel tank.

TYPE: Single-seat parasol wing homebuilt.

AIRFRAME: Dacron covered all-wood wings. Clark YH wing section. Welded 4130 steel tube fuselage and tail unit structures, Dacron covered; glassfibre turtleback. Non-retractable tailwheel landing gear.

POWER PLANT: Prototype has 1,500 cc Volkswagen converted motorcar engine. Other engines of 63.5-93 kW (85-125 hp) may be fitted, the 80.5 kW (108 hp) Textron Lycoming being recommended.

DIMENSIONS, EXTERNAL:

Wing span	7.62 m (25 ft 0 in)
Length overall	5.18 m (17 ft 0 in)
Height overall	2.03 m (6 ft 8 in)

AREA:

Wings, gross	7.71 m² (83.0 sq ft)

WEIGHT (prototype):

Max T-O weight	340 kg (750 lb)

PERFORMANCE (prototype, at max T-O weight):

Cruising speed	78 knots (145 km/h; 90 mph)
Landing speed	48-52 knots (89-97 km/h; 55-60 mph)

STOLP SA-750 ACRODUSTER TOO

The SA-750 is a two-seat aerobatic biplane generally similar to the Starduster Too. It has symmetrical wings. A fuel-injected 149 kW (200 hp) Textron Lycoming IO-360 engine is fitted to the prototype and is the optimum engine. The front cockpit is open and has a small windscreen, while the bubble canopy for the rear cockpit is faired to the turtledeck.

Raw materials, kits and prefabricated items are available.

DIMENSIONS, EXTERNAL:

Wing span: upper	6.53 m (21 ft 5 in)
Length overall	5.64 m (18 ft 6 in)
Height overall	2.08 m (6 ft 10 in)

AREA:

Wings, gross	12.1 m² (130.0 sq ft)

PERFORMANCE (prototype, at max T-O weight):

Cruising speed	139 knots (257 km/h; 160 mph)
Stalling speed	48 knots (89 km/h; 55 mph)
Max rate of climb at S/L	701 m (2,300 ft)/min
g limits	±9

STOLP SA-900 V-STAR

To meet the demand for low cost, low horsepower aircraft with aerobatic capability, Stolp introduced the SA-900 V-Star, which is essentially a biplane version of the SA-500 Starlet. The prototype has a 48.5 kW (65 hp) Teledyne Continental engine, but engines of 44.5-93 kW (60-125 hp) may be installed.

Raw material kits, cut tubing kits, and wing kits are available, together with prefabricated turtleback, nose cowling, wheel fairings, windshield and fuel tank.

AIRFRAME: Fabric covered wooden wings and welded steel tube fuselage. Clark YH wing section. Non-retractable tailwheel landing gear.

DIMENSIONS, EXTERNAL:

Wing span: upper	7.01 m (23 ft 0 in)
Length overall	5.23 m (17 ft 2 in)
Height overall	2.26 m (7 ft 5 in)

AREA:

Wings, gross	13.1 m² (141.0 sq ft)

PERFORMANCE (prototype, at max T-O weight):

Cruising speed	65 knots (121 km/h; 75 mph)
Stalling speed	31 knots (57 km/h; 35 mph)
Max rate of climb at S/L	183 m (600 ft)/min
g limits	±9

STOLP SUPER STARDUSTER

The Super Starduster is the first of a new series of special aerobatic aircraft for unlimited class aerobatic competition. The prototype, first flown on 1 April 1983, features a unique linkage between the ailerons and flaps, allowing the former to serve as flaps (down) with stick back, or flaps (up) with stick forward for outside loops.

TYPE: Single-seat homebuilt aerobatic biplane.

AIRFRAME: Osborne A-1 symmetrical wing section (modified). Dacron covered wooden wings and ailerons, the latter (on upper and lower wings) serving also as flaps during normal and inverted flight. Welded steel tube fuselage and tail unit, the former covered with fabric, aluminium alloy and glassfibre, and the latter with fabric. Non-retractable tailwheel landing gear.

POWER PLANT: One 149 kW (200 hp) Textron Lycoming IO-360-A1A. Fuel capacity 113.5 litres (30 US gallons; 25 Imp gallons).

DIMENSIONS, EXTERNAL:

Wing span	5.94 m (19 ft 6 in)
Length overall	4.88 m (16 ft 0 in)
Height overall	2.13 m (7 ft 0 in)
Propeller diameter	1.88 m (6 ft 2 in)

AREA:

Wings, gross	9.75 m² (105.0 sq ft)

WEIGHTS:

Basic operating weight empty	426 kg (940 lb)
Max T-O weight	680 kg (1,500 lb)

PERFORMANCE:

Max level speed at 2,440 m (8,000 ft)	156 knots (289 km/h; 180 mph) IAS
Econ cruising speed at 2,440 m (8,000 ft)	122 knots (225 km/h; 140 mph) IAS
Stalling speed, power off	48 knots (89 km/h; 55 mph) IAS
Max rate of climb at S/L	914 m (3,000 ft)/min
Service ceiling	3,810 m (12,500 ft)
T-O run	61 m (200 ft)
Landing run	335 m (1,100 ft)
Range with max fuel	440 nm (816 km; 507 miles)

STOLP SUPER SKYBOLT

Mr William Clouse Jr and Mr Eric Shilling developed a refined version of the Skybolt biplane. Brief details, and an illustration, can be found in the 1987-88 *Jane's*.

STOLP CABIN STARDUSTER

This is a new four-seat aircraft currently at the design stage, to be powered by a 335.6 kW (450 hp) engine.

STRIPLIN
STRIPLIN AIRCRAFT CORPORATION

PO Box 2001, Lancaster, California 93539-2001
Telephone: 1 (805) 256 2270
PRESIDENT: Kenneth Striplin

STRIPLIN LONE RANGER and SKY RANGER SERIES

The only microlight in this series is the single-seat **Lone Ranger Ultralight**; the remaining versions of the Lone Ranger and the **Sky Ranger** are Experimental homebuilt aircraft offered in **Silver Cloud STOL** form, with a tricycle landing gear; non-STOL **Silver Cloud X** form, with a tricycle landing gear and conventional inset ailerons, for higher-speed cross-country flying; and **Silver Cloud Husky STOL** form, with a tailwheel landing gear.

TYPES: Single-seat microlight and homebuilt (Lone Ranger) or two-seat homebuilt (Sky Ranger).

AIRFRAME: Wings constructed of wood, glassfibre and foam, with glassfibre skin on leading-edge and Dacron covering overall. NASA wing section. Full span flaperons on trailing-edges, of glassfibre/foam construction on all versions except the Silver Cloud X, which has in-wing ailerons. Pod and boom fuselage, the forward portion having base frame of unidirectional glassfibre, impregnated with epoxy resin, and moulded outer shell of glassfibre. At top of pod is U shaped channel, in which is buried a lightweight metal tube to which the wings are bolted and which also supports rear fuselage and tail unit. Tailboom is triangular section glassfibre and foam sandwich structure; tail surfaces of similar construction to wings. Removable fuselage side panels optional. Recovery parachute standard on all models. Non-retractable tricycle landing gear on all models except Husky which has tailwheel type. Tailwheel, float and ski landing gears optional on all models.

POWER PLANT: *Lone Ranger Ultralight*: One 20 kW (27 hp) Rotax 277. Fuel capacity 19 litres (5 US gallons; 4.2 Imp gallons). *Lone Ranger Silver Cloud STOL*: One 33.6 kW (45 hp) Rotax 503, 48.5 kW (65 hp) Rotax 532 or 48.5 kW (65 hp) Volkswagen 1,834 cc modified motorcar engine. *Lone Ranger Silver Cloud X* and *Husky STOL* have similar options to Silver Cloud STOL but with addition of 56 kW (75 hp) Volkswagen engine. *Sky Ranger* series all have same engine options as for Lone Ranger Silver Cloud STOL, plus 41 kW (55 hp) Volkswagen 1,600 cc engine. Fuel capacity for Lone Rangers (other than Ultralight) and Sky Rangers 38 litres (10 US gallons; 8.3 Imp gallons).

DIMENSIONS, EXTERNAL (A: Lone Ranger Ultralight, B: Lone Ranger STOL with Rotax 503, C: Lone Ranger Husky STOL with 75 hp VW, D: Sky Ranger Silver Cloud X with Rotax 532):

Wing span: A, B, C	10.36 m (34 ft 0 in)
D	10.67 m (35 ft 0 in)
Length overall: A, B, C	4.78 m (15 ft 8 in)
D	4.88 m (16 ft 0 in)
Height overall: D	2.13 m (7 ft 0 in)

AREAS (A, B, C, D as above):

Wings, gross: A, B, C	12.45 m² (134.0 sq ft)
D	10.22 m² (110.0 sq ft)

WEIGHTS (A, B, C, D as above):

Weight empty: A with parachute	125 kg (275 lb)
B	163 kg (360 lb)
C	200 kg (440 lb)
D	222 kg (490 lb)
Max T-O weight: A	272 kg (600 lb)
B	363 kg (800 lb)
C, D	454 kg (1,000 lb)

PERFORMANCE (A, B, C, D as above):

Max level speed: A	54 knots (100 km/h; 62 mph)
B	73 knots (135 km/h; 84 mph)
C	89 knots (164 km/h; 102 mph)
D	95 knots (177 km/h; 110 mph)
Cruising speed: A	48 knots (89 km/h; 55 mph)
B	65 knots (121 km/h; 75 mph)
C	78 knots (145 km/h; 90 mph)
D	87 knots (161 km/h; 100 mph)
Stalling speed:	
flaps up: A	26 knots (49 km/h; 30 mph)
B	30 knots (55 km/h; 34 mph)
C	32 knots (58 km/h; 36 mph)
D	42 knots (78 km/h; 48 mph)
flaps down: A	22 knots (41 km/h; 25 mph)
B	25 knots (45 km/h; 28 mph)
C	26 knots (47 km/h; 29 mph)
D	37 knots (68 km/h; 42 mph)
Max rate of climb at S/L: A	183 m (600 ft)/min
B	305 m (1,000 ft)/min
C	427 m (1,400 ft)/min
D	244 m (800 ft)/min
Service ceiling: A	2,895 m (9,500 ft)
B	3,505 m (11,500 ft)
C	4,265 m (14,000 ft)
D	3,810 m (12,500 ft)
T-O run: A	54 m (175 ft)
B	46 m (150 ft)
C	34 m (110 ft)
D	191 m (625 ft)
Range, no reserves:	
A, B, C	217 nm (402 km; 250 miles)
D	234 nm (434 km; 270 miles)

SUN AEROSPACE
SUN AEROSPACE GROUP INC

PO Box 317, Nappanee, Indiana 46550
Telephone: 1 (219) 773 3220

PRESIDENT: Russell A. McDonald

Details of the Sun Aerospace Sun Ray 100 series, and an illustration, can be found in the 1990-91 *Jane's*.

SUNRISE
SUNRISE ULTRALIGHT AIRCRAFT MANUFACTURING COMPANY

Rt 4, Box 336, New Caney, Texas 77357
Telephone: 1 (713) 354 1348

PRESIDENT: Kim A. Zorzi

Details of the Spitfire ultralight, Spitfire Super Sport, Sonic Spitfire, Spitfire II ultralight trainer vehicle, Clipper ultralight and Clipper Super Sport can be found in the Microlights tables in this edition. By early 1990, when the last update was received, a total of 430 kits of all versions, including the Experimental models detailed here, had been delivered.

Stolp SA-300 Starduster Too owned by Al Bird of Corona, California

Striplin Lone Ranger Husky STOL homebuilt

Stolp SA-500 Starlet single-seat homebuilt

Sunrise Ultralight Aircraft Manufacturing Spitfire II Elite

Stolp SA-750 Acroduster Too owned by Robert Hammond of Buffalo, New York

Taylor TA-2 Bird homebuilt

SUNRISE SPITFIRE II ELITE

This is basically a two-seat homebuilt version of the Spitfire I microlight and Spitfire II UTV. Construction from the kit takes 60 working hours.

TYPE: Side by side two-seat homebuilt; conforms to FAI/CAA Experimental aircraft category.

AIRFRAME: Strut or, optionally, wire braced high-wing monoplane, with optional kingpost. Aluminium alloy structure, with double skinned wing and tail surfaces using Dacron fabric. Glassfibre cockpit fairing and wheel fairings. Three-axis control, with flaps. Non-retractable tricycle landing gear, with brakes. Agricultural crop-spraying equipment and ballistic parachute optional.

POWER PLANT: One 48.5 kW (65 hp) Rotax 532. Fuel capacity 38 litres (10 US gallons; 8.3 Imp gallons).

Optional auxiliary fuel tank of 17.4 litres (4.6 US gallons; 3.8 Imp gallons) capacity.

DIMENSIONS, EXTERNAL:	
Wing span	9.14 m (30 ft 0 in)
Length overall	5.44 m (17 ft 10 in)
Height overall	2.29 m (7 ft 6 in)
Propeller diameter	1.68 m (5 ft 6 in)
AREA:	
Wing, gross	14.12 m² (152.0 sq ft)
WEIGHTS:	
Weight empty	175 kg (385 lb)
Pilot weight range	45.4-113 kg (100-250 lb)
Max T-O weight	378 kg (835 lb)
PERFORMANCE:	
Max level speed	74 knots (137 km/h; 85 mph)
Econ cruising speed	48 knots (89 km/h; 55 mph)
Stalling speed: flaps up	24 knots (44 km/h; 27 mph)
40% flap	19.5 knots (36 km/h; 22 mph)
Max rate of climb at S/L	244 m (800 ft)/min
Service ceiling	3,810 m (12,500 ft)
T-O run	31 m (100 ft)
Landing run	38 m (125 ft)
Range with max fuel	165 nm (305 km; 190 miles)
Endurance	3 h
g limits	+6/-4

SUNRISE CLIPPER II

This is an Experimental category derivative of the single-seat Clipper ultralight and Super Sport, with side by side seating for two persons with dual controls, Rotax 532 engine, hydraulic brakes and bush tyres.

TAYLOR

TAYLOR AERO INC

5855 State Route 40, Tipp City, Ohio 45371-9419
Telephone: 1 (513) 845 1226
PRESIDENT: Col Robert H. Taylor

TAYLOR TA-2/3 BIRD

Plans and additional data are available to homebuilders, who can complete the Taylor Bird in **TA-2** form, with non-retractable tailwheel landing gear, or **TA-3** form, with non-retractable tricycle gear. Optional floats and skis. Partial assembly kits are also available to amateur builders (fin, rudder, tailplane and elevators); difficult to fabricate components, such as castings, aluminium alloy formed parts (including the main load-bearing member and ribs) and pre-formed glassfibre fairings, can be purchased. Engine and propeller reduction drawings are available as a set of separate plans, plus a propeller reduction kit and plans for constructing a clamp-on towbar. By February 1991, 87 sets of plans and 11 'production' aircraft had been sold, of which two have been built from plans.

TYPE: Tandem two-seat homebuilt.

AIRFRAME: Wings have aluminium alloy structure, with pop riveted Alclad T3 skin and plastics composite root section. Wing section NACA 23015. Full span slotted metal ailerons. Main load-bearing member of fuselage comprises a 150 mm (6 in) diameter aluminium alloy tube, to which are bolted pylons for the cabin/landing gear/engine/wing group and the tail unit assembly. All fairings, including cabin enclosures, of glassfibre. Cantilever T tail has aluminium alloy spars and ribs, covered with Alclad T-3 skins. Non-retractable landing gear (see introduction), with brakes.

POWER PLANT: One 53.7 or 84.3 kW (72 or 113 hp) watercooled Subaru 1,600 cc or 1,800 cc converted motorcar engine. Optional Volkswagen modified motorcar or 48.5 kW (65 hp) Teledyne Continental engine. Fuel capacity 64.5 litres (17 US gallons; 14.2 Imp gallons).

DIMENSIONS, EXTERNAL:	
Wing span	7.92 m (26 ft 0 in)
Length overall	5.59 m (18 ft 4 in)
Height overall	1.68 m (5 ft 6 in)
Propeller diameter	1.52 m (5 ft 0 in)

AREA:					
Wings, gross	10.07 m² (108.42 sq ft)				

PERFORMANCE:

Max level speed	113 knots (209 km/h; 130 mph)
Econ cruising speed	82 knots (153 km/h; 95 mph)
Stalling speed	39 knots (73 km/h; 45 mph)
Service ceiling	4,265 m (14,000 ft)

T-O run	137 m (450 ft)
Landing run	122 m (400 ft)
Range, with max fuel, no reserves	
	295 nm (547 km; 340 miles)

WEIGHTS:

Weight empty	277 kg (610 lb)
Max T-O weight	526 kg (1,160 lb)

TAYLOR
TAYLOR KITS CORPORATION

PO Drawer 3350, 165 Scott Ave, Suite 102, Morgantown, West Virginia 26505
Telephone: 1 (304) 291 2376
Fax: 1 (304) 292 1902
PRESIDENT: Darus H. Zehrbach
CHIEF ENGINEER: Michael E. Renforth
GENERAL MANAGER: Lee Anne Demus

Aircraft Acquisition Corporation, owners of Helio Aircraft Corporation, Taylorcraft Aircraft Corporation and New Technik Corporation, formed the Taylor Kits Corporation in February 1990 to market aircraft, registered under the FAA 51 per cent owner built rule, based on the original C. G. Taylor designs.

Taylor Kits has drawn on the engineering, design and testing experience available through its parent corporation to produce kits which are equal to certificated production aircraft. The aircraft are manufactured to production specifications with a quality control system established.

All Taylor Kits use a 'Modular Mode' construction sequence, in which parts of the four major subassemblies are shipped in a staggered sequence based on the builder's available time and level of experience. This keeps construction and storage space to a minimum and helps ensure the proper order of assembly.

The first aircraft offered by Taylor Kits was based on the former Taylorcraft Model F21B. Although having the same basic structure as the Taylorcraft, the kit has replaced many of the original hard to fabricate parts with glassfibre and advanced composites components. The wooden spar has been augmented with an optional glassfibre/Kevlar unit, which has been shown to have better vibration damping and energy absorption characteristics and a slightly decreased weight. As the original aircraft was designed to operate with a 48.5 kW (65 hp) Franklin engine, the kit has been made available with engine options ranging from 67 to 93.2 kW (90 to 125 hp). A prototype has been flown with each engine.

An updated version of this same aircraft has been designed for those requiring higher levels of performance. This aircraft has slightly redesigned wing and tail surfaces as well as a more streamlined fuselage shape, offering speed increases of between 7 and 10 per cent over the original for a given engine installation.

Taylor Kits Corporation also began the design in January 1990 of a light twin-engined aircraft, construction of a prototype being scheduled to start in April of that year. Known as the Twin-T, kits could be available in 1991.

TAYLOR KITS T-CRAFT
TYPE: Side by side two-seat cabin homebuilt.
AIRFRAME: Strut braced high-wing monoplane. Fabric covered wings have wood and glassfibre/Kevlar spars, and aluminium ribs. Modified Frise type ailerons. NACA 23012 wing section. Warren truss fuselage structure of 4130 steel tubing, with aluminium alloy and fabric covering. Glassfibre nose cowling. Wire braced tail unit of steel tube and fabric construction. Trim tab on port elevator. Non-retractable tailwheel landing gear, with hydraulic disc brakes and optional mainwheel fairings and floats.
POWER PLANT: One engine of 67-119 kW (90-160 hp), with Rotax and Textron Lycoming engines recommended. Fuel capacity 91-152 litres (24-40 US gallons; 20-33.3 Imp gallons).

DIMENSIONS, EXTERNAL:

Wing span	10.97 m (36 ft 0 in)
Length overall	6.78 m (22 ft 3 in)
Height overall	2.08 m (6 ft 10 in)

WEIGHTS (88 kW; 118 hp engine):

Weight empty	476 kg (1,050 lb)
Max payload	312 kg (687.5 lb)
Max T-O weight	794 kg (1,750 lb)

PERFORMANCE (88 kW; 118 hp engine):

Max level speed at 1,145 m (3,750 ft)	
	108 knots (200 km/h; 124 mph)
Econ cruising speed at 1,525 m (5,000 ft)	
	89 knots (164 km/h; 102 mph)
Stalling speed, power off	39 knots (71 km/h; 44 mph)
Max rate of climb at S/L	230 m (756 ft)/min
Service ceiling	5,335 m (17,500 ft)
T-O run	116 m (380 ft)
Landing run	122 m (400 ft)
Range, no reserves	943 nm (1,747 km; 1,086 miles)

TAYLOR KITS TWIN-T
TYPE: Two/three-seat twin-engined homebuilt.
AIRFRAME: Strut braced high-wing monoplane. Fabric covered wings have glassfibre spars and aluminium ribs. Modified Frise type ailerons and slotted Fowler trailing-edge flaps, both of aluminium/glassfibre. NACA 23012 wing section. Warren truss 4130 steel tube fuselage structure with non-structural glassfibre skins. 4130 steel tube tail unit with glassfibre skins. Trim tabs on port elevator and rudder. Non-retractable tricycle landing gear, with hydraulic disc brakes and glassfibre wheel fairings.
POWER PLANT: Two engines of 67-119 kW (90-160 hp) each. Four fuel tanks, total capacity 182-303 litres (48-80 US gallons; 40-66.6 Imp gallons).

DIMENSIONS, EXTERNAL:

Wing span	10.97 m (36 ft 0 in)
Length overall	7.51 m (24 ft 7½ in)
Height overall	3.07 m (10 ft 1 in)

AREA:

Wings, gross	17.19 m² (185.0 sq ft)

WEIGHTS (two 119 kW; 160 hp engines):

Weight empty	639.5 kg (1,410 lb)
Max payload	373 kg (823 lb)
Max T-O weight	1,020 kg (2,250 lb)

PERFORMANCE (estimated, with two 88 kW; 118 hp engines):

Max level speed at 1,525 m (5,000 ft)	
	129 knots (240 km/h; 149 mph)
Econ cruising speed at 1,525 m (5,000 ft)	
	109 knots (201 km/h; 125 mph)
Stalling speed, flaps down, power off	
	37 knots (68 km/h; 42 mph)
Max rate of climb at S/L	511 m (1,675 ft)/min
Service ceiling	6,100 m (20,000 ft)
T-O run	70 m (227 ft)
Landing run	60 m (196 ft)
Range with max fuel, with IFR reserves	
	661 nm (1,224 km; 761 miles)

THURSTON
THURSTON AEROMARINE CORPORATION
24 Ledge Road, Cumberland Foreside, Maine 04110
Telephone: 1 (207) 829 6108
PRESIDENT: David B. Thurston

THURSTON TA16 TROJAN
The TA16 Trojan four-seat amphibian was conceived originally for the homebuilt market and plans became available from Thurston Aeromarine. A production version became the TA16 Seafire. The Trojan and Seafire are identical and the details of the Seafire given under the International Aeromarine Corporation entry in the main Aircraft section of the 1989-90 edition apply equally to the Trojan. By February 1991, a total of about 63 Trojans was under construction in Brazil, Canada, Norway and the USA, with at least five expected to fly by 1992. No new orders are being taken.

TURNER
TURNER AIRCRAFT INC
Route 4, Box 115AB3, Grandview, Texas 76050
Telephone: 1 (817) 783 5350
PRESIDENT: Eugene L. Turner

The original Turner T-40 first flew on 3 April 1961. Plans of the T-40, T-40A and Super T-40A are available to homebuilders; many hundreds of sets have been sold. An illustration of a T-40A accompanies this entry. Details can be found in the 1982-83 *Jane's*. In addition, development of the T-80 amphibian is to be completed once the first plans-built T-40 and the original T-40B have been restored (see 1982-83 *Jane's*). Also, Turner Aircraft has developed the T-100D Mariah (see Microlight tables) and the T-110.

TURNER T-110
This high-performance Experimental derivative of the T-100D is powered by a 32 kW (43 hp) engine. A prototype has been flight tested. Brief details and an illustration can be found in the 1987-88 *Jane's*.

V-8 SPECIAL
PLANS AND KITS FROM: Mizell Enterprises, 15749 Harvest Mile Road, Brighton, Colorado 80601
Telephone: 1 (303) 654 0049

The V-8 Special was first flown on 22 September 1978. Following the death of its designer, Mr Chris Beachner, rights in the aircraft were purchased by Mr Bill Mizell, who currently offers plans, kits, engine conversion plans and ready converted V-8 engines. Mr Mizell is also offering plans and kits of the **V-8 Special SXS**, a side by side seating model with optional non-retractable tricycle or tailwheel landing gear, or fully retractable gear.

The following details apply to the standard V-8 Special:

V-8 SPECIAL
TYPE: Tandem two-seat sporting homebuilt.
AIRFRAME: Wings, ailerons and tail unit of glassfibre/epoxy resin and polyurethane foam construction. Welded steel tube fuselage structure, covered with a shell of glassfibre/epoxy over a polyurethane foam core. Non-retractable or retractable tailwheel landing gear.
POWER PLANT: One 93.2 kW (125 hp) modified Buick watercooled motorcar engine. Alternatively, other engines in 93.2-186.4 kW (125-250 hp) range. Fuel capacity 132.5 litres (35 US gallons; 29 Imp gallons).

DIMENSIONS, EXTERNAL:

Wing span	7.32 m (24 ft 0 in)
Length overall	5.64 m (18 ft 6 in)
Propeller diameter	1.45 m (4 ft 9 in)

AREA:

Wings, gross	8.92 m² (96.0 sq ft)

WEIGHTS:

Weight empty	381 kg (840 lb)

Baggage capacity	18 kg (40 lb)
Max T-O weight	588 kg (1,296 lb)

PERFORMANCE:

Max cruising speed	
	more than 174 knots (322 km/h; 200 mph)
Cruising speed, 50% power	
	128 knots (238 km/h; 148 mph) IAS
Stalling speed:	
landing gear and flaps up	
	56 knots (103 km/h; 64 mph) IAS
flaps down	35 knots (65 km/h; 40 mph)
*Max rate of climb at S/L	over 762 m (2,500 ft)/min
*Depending on engine rating	

VANCRAFT
VANCRAFT COPTERS
7246 North Mohawk Avenue, Portland, Oregon 97203
Telephone: 1 (503) 286 5462

Details of the Lightning Sport Copter microlight autogyro can be found in the Microlight tables.

VANCRAFT COPTERS VANCRAFT
Kits to build this autogyro are available.
TYPE: Tandem two-seat autogyro.
ROTOR SYSTEM: Two-blade rotor, with steel spar, wooden core, and bonded and riveted aluminium alloy skins. Patented rotor head with no springs. Hydraulic pre-rotator.
AIRFRAME: Basic structure of 2 in square steel tubing, bolted and welded. Small horizontal stabiliser, fin, large-area rudder and mast supports constructed of circular-section tubing. Glassfibre cabin shell. Non-retractable tricycle landing gear.
POWER PLANT: One 74.6 kW (100 hp) SCAT modified Volkswagen 2,180 cc motorcar engine. Fuel capacity 34 litres (9 US gallons; 7.5 Imp gallons).

Prototype Taylor Kits Corporation T-Craft (88 kW; 118 hp Textron Lycoming engine)

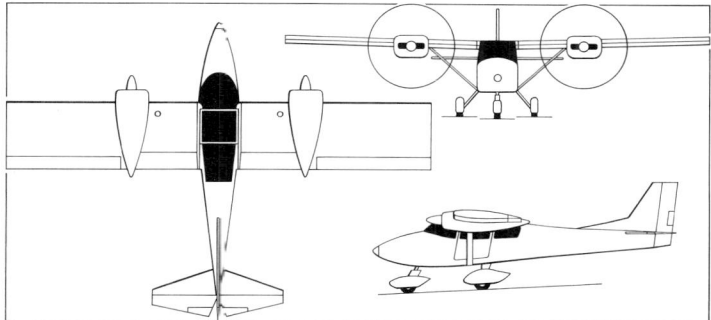

Taylor Kits Corporation Twin-T homebuilt (*Jane's/Mike Keep*)

Turner T-40A owned by Dean Beddow (*Geoffrey P. Jones*)

Tandem two-seat V-8 Special (*Howard Levy*)

Van's RV-4 tandem two-seat homebuilt aircraft built by Michael Betts of Victoria, Canada (*Neil Macdougall*)

Thurston TA16 Trojan owned by Mr Billy Johnson (*Billy Johnson*)

DIMENSIONS, EXTERNAL:		WEIGHTS:			
Rotor diameter	8.53 m (28 ft 0 in)	Weight empty	204 kg (450 lb)	Cruising speed	56-65 knots (105-121 km/h; 65-75 mph)
Length overall	3.96 m (13 ft 0 in)	Payload	159-181 kg (350-400 lb)	Max rate of climb at S/L	366 m (1,200 ft)/min
Height overall	2.29 m (7 ft 6 in)	PERFORMANCE:		T-O run	15-61 m (50-200 ft)
Propeller diameter	1.42 m (4 ft 8 in)	Max level speed	87 knots (161 km/h; 100 mph)	Range	261-304 nm (483-563 km; 300-350 miles)
				Endurance	3 h 30 min

VAN'S

VAN'S AIRCRAFT INC

PO Box 160, North Plains, Oregon 97133
Telephone: 1 (503) 647 5117
PRESIDENT: Richard VanGrunsven

VAN'S RV-3

More than 1,100 sets of plans of the RV-3 have been sold, with at least 200 aircraft under construction and over 150 RV-3s flying.
TYPE: Single-seat sporting homebuilt.
AIRFRAME: Built of light alloy, with glassfibre wing and tail unit tips and engine cowling. Wing section NACA 23012. Non-retractable tailwheel landing gear.
POWER PLANT: One 93 kW (125 hp) Textron Lycoming O-290-G (GPU). Fuel capacity 91 litres (24 US gallons; 20 Imp gallons).
DIMENSIONS, EXTERNAL:
Wing span	6.07 m (19 ft 11 in)
Length overall	5.79 m (19 ft 0 in)
Height overall	1.55 m (5 ft 1 in)
Propeller diameter	1.73 m (5 ft 8 in)
AREA:
Wings, gross	8.36 m² (90.0 sq ft)
WEIGHTS:
Weight empty	315 kg (695 lb)
Max T-O weight	476 kg (1,050 lb)
PERFORMANCE (at max T-O weight):
Max level speed at S/L	169 knots (314 km/h; 195 mph)

Econ cruising speed at 3,050 m (10,000 ft)
	139 knots (257 km/h; 160 mph)
Stalling speed: flaps up	46 knots (84 km/h; 52 mph)
flaps down	42 knots (78 km/h; 48 mph)
Max rate of climb at S/L	579 m (1,900 ft)/min
Service ceiling	6,400 m (21,000 ft)
T-O run	61 m (200 ft)
Landing run	91 m (300 ft)
Range, no reserves	520 nm (965 km; 600 miles)

VAN'S RV-4

The two-seat RV-4 is some 20 per cent larger than the RV-3 and there is no commonality of airframe components, although the configuration is unchanged. The first flight of the prototype was made on 21 August 1979. Plans and kits are available to homebuilders. By early 1991, over 2,500 sets of plans had been sold, with about 1,000 aircraft under construction and more than 260 RV-4s flying.
TYPE: Tandem two-seat sporting homebuilt.
AIRFRAME: As for RV-3, except wing section Van's Aircraft 135.
POWER PLANT: One 112 kW (150 hp) Textron Lycoming O-320-E1F. Fuel capacity 121 litres (32 US gallons; 26.6 Imp gallons).
DIMENSIONS, EXTERNAL:
Wing span	7.01 m (23 ft 0 in)
Length overall	6.21 m (20 ft 4½ in)
Height overall	1.60 m (5 ft 3 in)
Propeller diameter	1.73 m (5 ft 8 in)

AREA:
Wings, gross	10.22 m² (110.0 sq ft)
WEIGHTS:
Weight empty	404 kg (890 lb)
Baggage capacity	13.6 kg (30 lb)
Max T-O weight	680 kg (1,500 lb)
PERFORMANCE (at max T-O weight, and prior to prototype's aerodynamic clean-up):
Max level speed at S/L	175 knots (323 km/h; 201 mph)
Econ cruising speed, 55% power at 2,440 m; 8,000 ft	
	142 knots (264 km/h; 164 mph)
Stalling speed	47 knots (87 km/h; 54 mph)
Max rate of climb at S/L	503 m (1,650 ft)/min
Service ceiling	5,945 m (19,500 ft)
T-O run	137 m (450 ft)
Landing run	130 m (425 ft)
Range with max fuel, 55% power	
	695 nm (1,287 km; 800 miles)

VAN'S RV-6

This is basically a side by side two-seat derivative of the RV-4. The prototype first flew in June 1986. Plans and kits are available. By early 1991, more than 900 sets of plans had been sold, with more than 750 aircraft under construction and nine flying.
TYPE: Side by side two-seat sporting homebuilt.
AIRFRAME: Similar to RV-4.

POWER PLANT: One 119.3 kW (160 hp) Textron Lycoming O-320. Fuel capacity 140 litres (37 US gallons; 30.8 Imp gallons).

DIMENSIONS, EXTERNAL:

Wing span	7.01 m (23 ft 0 in)
Length overall	6.16 m (20 ft 2½ in)
Height overall	1.60 m (5 ft 3 in)
Propeller diameter	1.73 m (5 ft 8 in)

AREA:

Wings, gross	10.22 m² (110.0 sq ft)

WEIGHTS:

Weight empty	431 kg (950 lb)
Baggage capacity	27.2 kg (60 lb)
Max T-O weight	726 kg (1,600 lb)

PERFORMANCE (at max T-O weight):

Max level speed at S/L	175 knots (323 km/h; 201 mph)
Econ cruising speed, 55% power at 2,440 m (8,000 ft)	146 knots (270 km/h; 168 mph)
Stalling speed	47 knots (87 km/h; 54 mph)

Max rate of climb at S/L	503 m (1,650 ft)/min
Service ceiling	5,945 m (19,500 ft)
T-O run	160 m (525 ft)
Landing run	153 m (500 ft)
Range with max fuel (55% power)	803 nm (1,488 km; 925 miles)

VAN'S RV-6A

The RV-6A is a tricycle landing gear variation of the RV-6. Fuel capacity is 144 litres (38 US gallons; 31.6 Imp gallons). The prototype first flew in July 1988. Plans and kits are available. AIEP of Nigeria is constructing RV-6As as Air Beetle military trainers.

DIMENSIONS, EXTERNAL:

Wing span	7.01 m (23 ft 0 in)
Length overall	6.07 m (19 ft 11 in)
Height overall	2.13 m (7 ft 0 in)

AREA:

Wings, gross	10.22 m² (110.0 sq ft)

WEIGHTS:

Weight empty	451 kg (995 lb)
Baggage capacity	27.2 kg (60 lb)
Max T-O weight	726 kg (1,600 lb)

PERFORMANCE (two persons):

Max level speed	174 knots (322 km/h; 200 mph)
Econ cruising speed, 55% power at 2,440 m (8,000 ft)	144 knots (267 km/h; 166 mph)
Stalling speed	48 knots (89 km/h; 55 mph)
Max rate of climb at S/L	427 m (1,400 ft)/min
Service ceiling	4,970 m (16,300 ft)
T-O run	92 m (300 ft)
Landing run	153 m (500 ft)
Range, 55% power at 2.440 m (8,000 ft)	760 nm (1,408 km; 875 miles)

VAT
VERTICAL AVIATION TECHNOLOGIES INC
PO Box 2527, Sanford, Florida 32772-2527
Telephone: 1 (407) 322 9488
PRESIDENT: Bradley G. Clark
VICE-PRESIDENT: Ronald Mander
CONSULTANT ENGINEER: Ralph Alex

VAT HUMMINGBIRD
Vertical Aviation Technologies was formed to develop and market an improved and updated version of the Sikorsky S-52 four-seat helicopter in kit form. A prototype

(N9329R), fitted with a reconfigured glassfibre nosecone, new windscreen, restyled vertical tail and electric trim system, was first flown in February 1988 and was tested for compliance with FAA Supplemental Type Certificate requirements. Vertical Aviation replaced the S-52's standard 183 kW (245 shp) Franklin O-425-1 piston engine with a 231 kW (310 hp) watercooled Ford V-6 power plant on the prototype, but kits revert to the Franklin. Assembly time for the helicopter is estimated at 1,000 man hours, using some new components and also genuine Sikorsky parts zero time overhauled.

DIMENSIONS, EXTERNAL:

Main rotor diameter	10.06 m (33 ft 0 in)
Length overall, rotors turning	12.11 m (39 ft 9 in)

Length of fuselage	9.27 m (30 ft 5 in)
Height to top of rotor hub	2.62 m (8 ft 7 in)
Height overall	2.87 m (9 ft 5 in)

AREA:

Main rotor	79.46 m² (855.3 sq ft)

WEIGHTS:

Weight empty	771 kg (1,700 lb)
Max payload	408 kg (900 lb)
Max T-O weight	1,225 kg (2,700 lb)

PERFORMANCE S/L:

Cruising speed	85 knots (157 km/h; 98 mph)
Max rate of climb at S/L	335 m (1,100 ft)/min
Service ceiling	3,353 m (11,000 ft)
Range	approx 217 nm (402 km; 250 miles)

VELOCITY
VELOCITY AIRCRAFT
Sebastian, Florida 32958

VELOCITY AIRCRAFT VELOCITY
The prototype Velocity made its debut at the 1985 Sun 'n Fun meeting. Velocity Aircraft introduced the aircraft in kit form, with the glassfibre components pre-moulded.
TYPE: Two-plus-two homebuilt.
AIRFRAME: Built of foam cores, unidirectional/biaxial-triaxial glassfibre and epoxy resin. Rear mounted wings

use modified Eppler aerofoil section. Three Roncz 'vortilons' under leading-edge of each wing. Endplate fins and rudders. Speed brake under fuselage. Foreplanes on nose, of original section and with near full-span elevators. Non-retractable main landing gear. Retractable nosewheel.
POWER PLANT: Any Textron Lycoming engine of 112 to 149 kW (150 to 200 hp) or Teledyne Continental IO-360. Prototype has one 134 kW (180 hp) Textron Lycoming HIO-360. Fuel capacity of 277 litres (73 US gallons; 60.8 Imp gallons).

DIMENSIONS, EXTERNAL:

Wing span	8.72 m (28 ft 7½ in)

Length overall	5.49 m (18 ft 0 in)
Height overall	2.44 m (8 ft 0 in)
Propeller diameter	1.73 m (5 ft 8 in)

AREA:

Wings, gross	8.92 m² (96.0 sq ft)

WEIGHTS:

Weight empty	499 kg (1,100 lb)
Max T-O weight	1,020 kg (2,250 lb)

PERFORMANCE (prototype, at max T-O weight):

Max cruising speed at 610 m (2,000 ft)	191 knots (354 km/h; 220 mph)
Max rate of climb at S/L	305 m (1,000 ft)/min
Range with max fuel	1,736 nm (3,218 km; 2,000 miles)

VIKING
VIKING AIRCRAFT LTD
RR No. 1, PO Box 1000V, Eloy, Arizona 85231
Telephone: 1 (602) 466 7538
PRESIDENT: Rex Taylor

VIKING DRAGONFLY
The prototype Dragonfly first flew on 16 June 1980. Plans are available, together with a pre-formed engine cowling and canopy. Also, kits of prefabricated component parts, requiring no complex jigging or tooling, are available. In this form the aircraft is known as the 'Snap' Dragonfly. It is estimated that the kits save the builder more than 700 working hours.

In its original configuration, with the non-retractable mainwheels at the tips of the foreplane, the aircraft was designated **Dragonfly Mark I**. In parallel production, for operation from unprepared strips and narrow taxiways, was the **Dragonfly Mark II**. This has its main landing gear in the form of short non-retractable cantilever units under

the wings, with individual hydraulic toe brakes, and increased foreplane and elevator areas. In 1985 a **Dragonfly Mark III** version, with non-retractable tricycle landing gear, underwent flight trials.
TYPE: Side by side two-seat, dual control sporting homebuilt.
AIRFRAME: Composites wing, foreplane and tail unit structures of styrene foam, glassfibre, carbonfibre and epoxy. Wing section Eppler 1213. Foreplane of GU25 section. Semi-monocoque fuselage, formed (not carved) from 12.5 mm (½ in) thick urethane foam, with strips of 18 mm (¾ in) foam bonded along edges to allow large-radius external corners. Fuselage covered with glassfibre inside and out. (See introduction for landing gears.)
POWER PLANT: One 44.5 kW (60 hp) HAPI 1,835 cc modified Volkswagen motorcar engine; 1,600 cc engine, rated at 33.5 kW (45 hp), optional. Fuel capacity 56.8 litres (15 US gallons; 12.5 Imp gallons).

DIMENSIONS, EXTERNAL:

Wing span	6.71 m (22 ft 0 in)
Length overall	5.79 m (19 ft 0 in)

Height overall: Mk I	1.22 m (4 ft 0 in)
Propeller diameter	1.32 m (4 ft 4 in)

AREA:

Wings, gross	4.51 m² (48.5 sq ft)

WEIGHTS (Dragonfly Mk I with 1,835 cc engine):

Weight empty	274 kg (605 lb)
Max payload	184 kg (405 lb)
Max T-O weight	488 kg (1,075 lb)

PERFORMANCE (Dragonfly Mk I with 1,835 cc engine):

Max level speed at S/L	146 knots (270 km/h; 168 mph) IAS
Econ cruising speed at 2,285 m (7,500 ft)	121 knots (225 km/h; 140 mph)
Stalling speed, power on	39 knots (73 km/h; 45 mph) IAS
Max rate of climb at S/L	259 m (850 ft)/min
Service ceiling	5,640 m (18,500 ft)
T-O run	137 m (450 ft)
Landing run	213 m (700 ft)
Range with max fuel, 30 min reserves	434 nm (804 km; 500 miles)
g limits	+4.4/−2

VOLMER
VOLMER AIRCRAFT
Box 5222, Glendale, California 91201
Telephone: 1 (818) 247 8718
PRESIDENT: Volmer Jensen
Details of the VJ-23E Swingwing and VJ-24W Sunfun can be found in the Microlight tables.

VOLMER VJ-22 SPORTSMAN
The prototype Sportsman flew for the first time on 22 December 1958. Plans are available to amateur constructors. A total of 871 sets had been sold by January 1991 and more than 100 Sportsman amphibians are flying. Some have tractor propellers, but this modification is not recommended by Mr Jensen.

TYPE: Side by side two-seat, dual-control homebuilt amphibian.
AIRFRAME: Wings are standard Aeronca Chief or Champion assemblies with wooden spars, light alloy ribs and fabric covering, and carry stabilising floats under the tips. Plans of specially designed wing, with wooden ribs and spars, available. Flying-boat hull of wooden construction, coated with glassfibre. Steel tube tail unit, fabric covered. Retractable tailwheel landing gear. Water rudder.
POWER PLANT: One 63.5 kW (85 hp) Teledyne Continental C85, 67 kW (90 hp) or 74.5 kW (100 hp) Teledyne Continental O-200-B. Fuel capacity 76 litres (20 US gallons; 16.7 Imp gallons).

DIMENSIONS, EXTERNAL:

Wing span	11.12 m (36 ft 6 in)
Length overall	7.32 m (24 ft 0 in)
Height overall	2.44 m (8 ft 0 in)

AREA:

Wings, gross	16.3 m² (175.0 sq ft)

WEIGHTS (63.5 kW; 85 hp):

Weight empty	454 kg (1,000 lb)
Max T-O weight	680 kg (1,500 lb)

PERFORMANCE (63.5 kW; 85 hp, at max T-O weight):

Max level speed at S/L	83 knots (153 km/h; 95 mph)
Max cruising speed	74 knots (137 km/h; 85 mph)
Stalling speed	39 knots (72 km/h; 45 mph)
Max rate of climb at S/L	183 m (600 ft)/min
Service ceiling	3,960 m (13,000 ft)
Range with max fuel, no reserves	260 nm (480 km; 300 miles)

Prototype Vertical Aviation Technologies Hummingbird kit-built version of modified Sikorsky S-52 helicopter

Volmer VJ-22 Sportsman two-seat homebuilt amphibian

Viking Aircraft Dragonfly Mark I built in Germany as the Schneider TC-1 Dragonfly *(Geoffrey P. Jones)*

First Velocity all-composites four-seat aircraft built from a kit by Mr Neil Hunter *(Howard Levy)*

UK registered Wag-Aero Acro Trainer *(PFA)*

WAG-AERO
WAG-AERO INC

PO Box 181, 1216 North Road, Lyons, Wisconsin 53148
Telephone: 1 (414) 763 9586
PRESIDENT: Richard H. Wagner
MARKETING SUPERVISOR: Mary Pat Henningfield

WAG-AERO SPORT TRAINER

Wag-Aero plans and kits offer homebuilders the choice of four different modern versions of the Piper J-3.

Known as the **Sport Trainer**, the basic two-seat sporting aircraft follows the original design, but the wing has a wooden main spar and ribs, light alloy leading-edge and fabric covering. The fuselage and tail unit are of welded steel tube with fabric covering. The Sport Trainer can be powered by any flat-four Continental, Franklin or Textron Lycoming engine of between 48.5 and 93 kW (65 and 125 hp).

Also available are the **Acro Trainer**, which differs from the standard version by having a strengthened fuselage, shortened wings (8.23 m; 27 ft), modified lift struts, improved wing fittings and rib spacing, and a new leading-edge; the **Observer**, which is a replica L-4 military liaison aircraft; and the **Super Sport**, with structural modifications to accept engines of up to 112 kW (150 hp), making it suitable for glider towing, bush operations, or for operation as a floatplane.

The Sport Trainer first flew on 12 March 1975. The following details refer to this version:

DIMENSIONS, EXTERNAL:

Wing span	10.73 m (35 ft 2½ in)
Length overall	6.82 m (22 ft 4½ in)
Height overall	2.03 m (6 ft 8 in)

AREA:

Wings, gross	16.58 m² (178.5 sq ft)

WEIGHTS:

Weight empty	327 kg (720 lb)
Max T-O weight	635 kg (1,400 lb)

PERFORMANCE (at max T-O weight):

Max level speed at S/L	89 knots (164 km/h; 102 mph)
Cruising speed	82 knots (151 km/h; 94 mph)
Stalling speed	34 knots (63 km/h; 39 mph)
Max rate of climb at S/L	149 m (490 ft)/min
Service ceiling	over 3,660 m (12,000 ft)

T-O run	114 m (375 ft)

Range: at cruising speed with standard fuel (45.5 litres; 12 US gallons; 10 Imp gallons)
191 nm (354 km; 220 miles)
with auxiliary fuel (98.5 litres; 26 US gallons; 21.6 Imp gallons)
395 nm (732 km; 455 miles)

WAG-AERO WAG-A-BOND

The name Wag-A-Bond applies to a replica of the Piper PA-15 Vagabond, known as the **Classic**, and the **Traveler**. The latter is a modified and updated version of the Piper Vagabond with port and starboard doors, overhead skylight window, extended sleeping deck (conversion from aircraft to camper interior taking about two minutes and accommodating two persons), extended baggage area, engine of up to 85.7 kW (115 hp), and provision for a full electrical system.

The prototype Wag-A-Bond was completed by Wag-Aero in May 1978. The following details apply to both versions, unless stated otherwise:

TYPE: Side by side two-seat homebuilt.

AIRFRAME: All-wood wing and aluminium alloy aileron structures. Welded steel tube and flat plate fuselage structure, and steel tube tail unit. Complete airframe is fabric covered. Non-retractable tailwheel landing gear. Optional skis.

POWER PLANT: Traveler can be powered by a Textron Lycoming engine of 80.5-85.7 kW (108-115 hp). Classic can be powered by a Teledyne Continental engine of 48.5-74.5 kW (65-100 hp). Fuel capacity: Traveler 98.5 litres (26 US gallons; 21.6 Imp gallons), Classic 45.5 litres (12 US gallons; 10 Imp gallons).

DIMENSIONS, EXTERNAL:

Wing span	8.32 m (29 ft 3½ in)
Length overall	5.66 m (18 ft 7 in)
Height overall	1.83 m (6 ft 0 in)

AREA:

Wings, gross	13.70 m² (147.5 sq ft)

WEIGHTS (A: Traveler, B: Classic):

Weight empty: A	329 kg (725 lb)
B	290 kg (640 lb)

Baggage capacity:

A	27 kg (60 lb)
B	18 kg (40 lb)

Max T-O weight: A	658 kg (1,450 lb)
B	567 kg (1,250 lb)

PERFORMANCE (A: Traveler, B: Classic):

Max level speed: A	118 knots (219 km/h; 136 mph)
B	91 knots (169 km/h; 105 mph)
Cruising speed: A	108 knots (200 km/h; 124 mph)
B	83 knots (153 km/h; 95 mph)
Stalling speed: A, B	39 knots (73 km/h; 45 mph)
Max rate of climb at S/L: A	259 m (850 ft)/min
B	190 m (625 ft)/min

WAG-AERO 2+2 SPORTSMAN

The 2+2 Sportsman is based on the Piper PA-14 Family Cruiser. It is a true four-seater, with the option of a hinged rear fuselage decking to provide access to the baggage and rear seat areas. The rear seat itself can be removed so that cargo or a stretcher can be carried.

Plans and material kits are available for the 2+2 Sportsman. A pre-welded fuselage structure is also available.

TYPE: Four-seat homebuilt.

AIRFRAME: Similar construction to Wag-A-Bond, with glassfibre tips. Alternatively, drawings and materials provided to modify standard PA-12, PA-14 or PA-18 wings. Upper and lower spoilers.

POWER PLANT: Engine of 93-149 kW (125-200 hp). Usable fuel capacity 148 litres (39 US gallons; 32.5 Imp gallons).

DIMENSIONS, EXTERNAL:

Wing span	10.90 m (35 ft 9 in)
Length overall	7.12 m (23 ft 4½ in)
Height overall	2.02 m (6 ft 7½ in)

AREA:

Wings, gross	16.18 m² (174.12 sq ft)

WEIGHTS:

Weight empty	490 kg (1,080 lb)
Max T-O weight	998 kg (2,200 lb)

PERFORMANCE (typical; actual data depend on engine fitted):

Max level speed	112 knots (207 km/h; 129 mph)
Cruising speed	108 knots (200 km/h; 124 mph)
Stalling speed	33 knots (62 km/h; 38 mph)
Max rate of climb at S/L	244 m (800 ft)/min
Service ceiling	4,510 m (14,800 ft)
Range at cruising speed	582 nm (1,078 km; 670 miles)

WARNER
RICHARD WARNER AVIATION INC

Thunderhill Aerodrome, 82341 Highway 1129, Covington,
Louisiana 70433
Telephone: 1 (504) 892 3721
OWNER: Capt. Richard M. Warner

RICHARD WARNER (ANDERSON) W-1 SUPER KINGFISHER

The prototype EA-1 Kingfisher amphibian was designed
and built by Mr Earl Anderson. The first flight was made on
24 April 1969. Plans were made available to amateur
constructors via Anderson Aircraft Corporation; all rights
to the Kingfisher have since been transferred to Richard
Warner Aviation.

The latest version is the W-1 Super Kingfisher, the
prototype of which first flew on 25 December 1988. By early
1990 a total of about 250 sets of plans for the EA-1

Kingfisher and W-1 Super Kingfisher had been sold, and 75
plans-built aircraft were then flying. In comparison to the
Kingfisher, the Super Kingfisher has two doors, adjustable
seats, extended water rudder, skylight, greater fuel capacity,
larger spray rails, an O-320 engine, and larger baggage area.

The following details refer to the Super Kingfisher:
TYPE: Side by side two-seat homebuilt amphibian.
AIRFRAME: Standard J3, PA-11, PA-12, Super Cub or
homebuilt wing with aluminium alloy spars and ribs, and
Ceconite covering; plans include alternative wood wing.
Wing section USA 35B modified. Wing stabilising floats
and flying-boat hull of wooden construction, covered
with plywood and coated with glassfibre. Strut braced tail
unit of steel tubing, fabric covered. Retractable tailwheel
landing gear, with brakes.
POWER PLANT: One 112 kW (150 hp) Textron Lycoming
O-320-A2B in prototype. Fuel capacity 153 litres (40.5
US gallons; 33.7 Imp gallons).
DIMENSIONS, EXTERNAL:

Wing span	11.00 m (36 ft 1 in)
Length overall	7.16 m (23 ft 6 in)
Height overall	2.51 m (8 ft 3 in)
Propeller diameter	1.88 m (6 ft 2 in)

AREA:

Wings, gross	17.19 m² (185.0 sq ft)

WEIGHTS (O-320-A2B engine):

Weight empty	512 kg (1,129 lb)
Baggage capacity	22.7 kg (50 lb)
Max T-O weight	816 kg (1,800 lb)

PERFORMANCE (with O-320-A2B engine, at max T-O
weight):

Max level speed	109 knots (201 km/h; 125 mph)
Econ cruising speed at 305 m (1,000 ft)	74 knots (137 km/h; 85 mph)
Stalling speed, flaps down, power on	33 knots (61 km/h; 38 mph)
Max rate of climb at S/L	305 m (1,000 ft)/min
Service ceiling	3,660 m (12,000 ft)
T-O run	92 m (300 ft)
Landing run	153 m (500 ft)
Range	369 nm (684 km; 425 miles)
Endurance	5 h 15 min

WATSON
WATSON WINDWAGON COMPANY

Route 1, Box 51, Newcastle, Texas 75372
Telephone: 1 (817) 862 5615
OWNER: Gary Watson

Details of the GW-1 Windwagon, and an illustration, can
be found in the 1988-89 *Jane's*. Plans are believed to remain
available.

WHATLEY
VASCOE WHATLEY Jr

PO Box 474, Allendale, South Carolina 29810
Telephone: 1 (803) 584 2691

Details of the Whatley Special, and an illustration, can be
found in the 1988-89 *Jane's*. Plans are believed to remain
available.

WHEELER
WHEELER TECHNOLOGY INC

Dept 27, Tacoma-Narrows Airport, Gig Harbor,
Washington 98335
Telephone: 1 (206) 851 5793
Fax: 1 (206) 851 5916
PRESIDENT: Ken Wheeler

The factory closed down between August 1990 and
January 1991, but kits are again available.

WHEELER EXPRESS

The Express was CAD designed as a high speed
cross-country kitplane, with the unusual seating arrangement of one forward and one aft facing seat in the rear,
behind two front seats with dual controls. The prototype,
built from a kit of pre-moulded parts, flew for the first time
on 28 July 1987. The first, larger, production line Express
demonstrator flew for the first time in May 1990. It was
powered by a Teledyne Continental engine. Kits are
available.

TYPE: Four-seat, dual-control cross-country homebuilt;
conforms to FAR Pt 23.
AIRFRAME: Constructed of composites sandwich material,
comprising polyurethane foam core, glassfibre, unidirectional glassfibre tape and vinylester resin. Wing
section NASA NFL-1 0215-F (laminar flow). Non-
retractable tricycle landing gear. Retractable gear
optional.
POWER PLANT: Demonstrator fitted with 156.6 kW (210)
Teledyne Continental IO-360-ES1 engine; 119 or 134 kW
(160 or 180 hp) Textron Lycoming engine optional. Fuel
capacity 204 litres (54 US gallons; 45 Imp gallons);
optional 348 litres (92 US gallons; 76.6 Imp gallons).
DIMENSIONS, EXTERNAL:

Wing span	9.45 m (31 ft 0 in)
Length overall	7.62 m (25 ft 0 in)
Height overall	2.13 m (7 ft 0 in)

AREA:

Wings, gross	11.71 m² (126.0 sq ft)

WEIGHTS:

Weight empty	703 kg (1,550 lb)
Baggage capacity, with four 77 kg (170 lb) persons	29 kg (64 lb)
Max T-O weight	1,313 kg (2,895 lb)

PERFORMANCE (149 kW; 200 hp engine, retractable landing
gear):

Max level speed at S/L	204 knots (378 km/h; 235 mph)
Max cruising speed at S/L, 75% power and with 45 min reserves	183 knots (338 km/h; 210 mph)

Stalling speed at max T-O weight:

flaps up	55 knots (101 km/h; 63 mph)
flaps down	50 knots (92 km/h; 57 mph)
Max rate of climb at S/L	427 m (1,400 ft)/min
Service ceiling	6,100 m (20,000 ft)
Landing run	244 m (800 ft)

Range, 55% power, no reserves

	1,042 nm (1,931 km; 1,200 miles)
g limits	+4.4/−2.2
	+8.8/−4.4 ultimate

WHITE
E. MARSHALL WHITE

Meadowlark Airport, 5141 Warner Avenue, Huntington
Beach, California 92649
Telephone: 1 (714) 846 2409

Details of the WW-1 Der Jäger D.IX, and an illustration,
can be found in the 1988-89 *Jane's*. Plans, kits and some
components are believed to remain available.

WHITE LIGHTNING
WHITE LIGHTNING AIRCRAFT CORPORATION

Box 497, Walterboro, South Carolina 29488-0497
Telephone: 1 (803) 538 3999
PRESIDENT: Howell C. Jones Jr

WHITE LIGHTNING AIRCRAFT WHITE LIGHTNING

The first prototype White Lightning flew initially on 8
March 1986. In the same year it established several world
speed records in Classes C1b and C1c.

Kits are available, and 28 had been delivered by January
1991 of 35 ordered, by which time nine aircraft had flown.
Construction takes under 1,000 working hours for the
first-time builder and about 600 hours for the experienced
builder. Options include electrical various engine installation, light, strobe light, and interior kits, plus other items.

TYPE: Four-seat homebuilt.
AIRFRAME: Wing section NACA 66₂-215. Wings have
graphite tubular 'wet' main spar, and glassfibre/epoxy
front and rear spars and ribs, all pre-cast in the lower
glassfibre/epoxy skin. Fowler flaps. Glassfibre/epoxy
fuselage moulded in upper and lower halves. Tail unit has
spars and ribs of fin and tailplane pre-cast into one skin of
each. Retractable tricycle landing gear, with brakes.
Options include electrical kit and engine installation kit.
POWER PLANT: Prototype has 156.6 kW (210 hp) Teledyne
Continental IO-360 CB. Usable fuel capacity 257 litres
(68 US gallons; 56.6 Imp gallons).
DIMENSIONS, EXTERNAL:

Wing span	8.43 m (27 ft 8 in)
Length overall	7.11 m (23 ft 4 in)
Height overall	2.18 m (7 ft 2 in)
Propeller diameter	1.85 m (6 ft 1 in)

AREA:

Wings, gross	8.27 m² (89.0 sq ft)

WEIGHTS:

Weight empty	635 kg (1,400 lb)
Max baggage capacity	154 kg (340 lb)
Max T-O weight	1,088 kg (2,400 lb)

PERFORMANCE (at max T-O weight):

Max level speed at S/L	243 knots (450 km/h; 280 mph)
Max cruising speed at 2,440 m (8,000 ft)	230 knots (426 km/h; 265 mph)
Econ cruising speed at 3,350 m (11,000 ft)	221 knots (410 km/h; 255 mph)

Stalling speed: flaps up

flaps up	78 knots (145 km/h; 90 mph)
flaps down	58 knots (108 km/h; 67 mph)
Max rate of climb at S/L	579 m (1,900 ft)/min
Service ceiling	7,010 m (23,000 ft)
T-O run, full flap	381 m (1,250 ft)
Landing run	397 m (1,300 ft)
Range with max fuel	1,389 nm (2,575 km; 1,600 miles)
Endurance	6 h 10 min
g limits	+4.4/−2 utility

WINDRYDER
WINDRYDER ENGINEERING INC

555 Alter Street, Unit 15, Broomfield, Colorado 80020
Telephone: 1 (303) 466 6669
Fax: 1 (303) 469 2801

PRESIDENT: Jim McCutchen

WINDRYDER ENGINEERING HURRICANE

The first of two prototype Hurricane autogyros flew
initially in August 1985. Kits are available. Construction
takes about 100 working hours.

The Hurricane was demonstrated to the US Army, in
Florida, in April 1987. Possible non-sport uses include
surveillance, liaison and re-supply.

TYPE: Single-seat autogyro.
ROTOR SYSTEM: Skywheels two-blade rotor of 8H12 section,
constructed of unwoven bi-directional S-glass in a
vinylester matrix, with an extruded aluminium alloy spar
bonded inside the leading-edge. Unwoven bi-directional
S-glass pylon, manufactured in two halves, with tubular

Richard Warner Aviation (Anderson) W-1 Super Kingfisher amphibian

Prototype White Lightning Aircraft White Lightning four-seat composites homebuilts

First production-line demonstrator Wheeler Express four-seat homebuilt
(Geoffrey P. Jones)

Wittman Tailwind W-10 (inverted 93 kW; 125 hp 3,500 cc Oldsmobile F85 engine)

WindRyder Engineering Hurricane single-seat composites autogyro

---

D section forward half carrying most loads. 'Tilt spindle' rotor head. Pre-rotator.

AIRFRAME: Monocoque fuselage of pre-moulded inner and outer shells, factory bonded, using bi-directional unwoven S-glass and graphite in a polyester resin matrix, completed by installation of composite seat/fuel tank. Dihedral tailplane, three fins and large central rudder. Tail surfaces have NACA 0012 section. Non-retractable tricycle landing gear.

POWER PLANT: One 47.7 kW (64 hp) Rotax 532. Optional 74.5 kW (100 hp) Teledyne Continental O-200. Fuel capacity in seat tank 66 litres (17.5 US gallons; 14.6 Imp gallons). Optional 82 kW (110 hp) Hirth F30 engine.

DIMENSIONS, EXTERNAL:
Rotor diameter	8.84 m (29 ft 0 in)
Length overall (excl rotor)	3.38 m (11 ft 1 in)
Height overall	2.57 m (8 ft 5 in)
Propeller diameter	1.68 m (5 ft 6 in)

AREA:
Rotor disc	61.3 m² (660.0 sq ft)

WEIGHTS:
Weight empty	204 kg (450 lb)
Max payload	159 kg (350 lb)
Max T-O weight	363 kg (800 lb)

PERFORMANCE:
Max level speed at S/L	100 knots (185 km/h; 115 mph)
Econ cruising speed at S/L	69 knots (129 km/h; 80 mph)
Max rate of climb at S/L	305 m (1,000 ft)/min
Service ceiling	3,050 m (10,000 ft)
T-O run	46 m (150 ft)
Landing run	15 m (50 ft)
Range	173 nm (322 km; 200 miles)
Endurance	2 h
g limit	+3

WINDRYDER ENGINEERING HURRICANE 100

This is a high performance version of the Hurricane, with an 83.5 kW (112 hp) Arrow engine. The airframe is similar, except that carbonfibre replaces S-glass for the rotor and fuselage skins, and that the main landing gear units use compression struts and the nosewheel has a trailing arm for suspension. Standard fuel capacity is 64.4 litres (17 US gallons; 20.4 Imp gallons). Optional cargo pod.

DIMENSIONS, EXTERNAL:
Rotor diameter	8.84 m (29 ft 0 in)
Length overall (excl rotor)	3.56 m (11 ft 8 in)
Height overall	2.82 m (9 ft 3 in)
Propeller diameter	1.68 m (5 ft 6 in)

AREA:
Rotor disc	61.3 m² (660.0 sq ft)

WEIGHTS:
Weight empty	227 kg (500 lb)
Max T-O weight	499 kg (1,100 lb)

PERFORMANCE:
Max level speed	96 knots (177 km/h; 110 mph)
Econ cruising speed	69 knots (129 km/h; 80 mph)
Max rate of climb at S/L	305 m (1,000 ft)/min
Service ceiling	3,660 m (12,000 ft)
T-O run	31 m (100 ft)
Landing run	none
Range	173 nm (322 km; 200 miles)
Endurance	2 h
g limit	+3

WITTMAN
S. J. WITTMAN
7200 South-East 85th Lane, Ocala, Florida 32672

WITTMAN TAILWIND MODEL W-8

The prototype W-8 was built in 1952-53. Sets of plans and prefabricated components are believed still to be available, and more than 350 Tailwinds have flown. Some Tailwinds have been built with tricycle landing gear, retractable mainwheels and other design changes.

TYPE: Side by side two-seat cabin homebuilt.

AIRFRAME: Wing section is a combination of NACA 4309 (upper surface) and NACA 0006 (lower surface). Wooden wing structure with plywood and fabric covering. Ailerons, flaps and tail unit of steel and stainless steel construction. Steel tube fuselage, fabric covered. Non-retractable tailwheel landing gear standard.

POWER PLANT: Normally one 67 kW (90 hp) Teledyne Continental C90-12F. Alternative engines include the 63.5 kW (85 hp) Teledyne Continental C85, 74.5 kW (100 hp) Teledyne Continental O-200, 86 kW (115 hp) Textron Lycoming O-235 and 104.5 kW (140 hp) Textron Lycoming O-290. Fuel capacity 94.5-132.5 litres (25-35 US gallons; 20.8-29.1 Imp gallons).

DIMENSIONS, EXTERNAL:
Wing span	6.86 m (22 ft 6 in)
Length overall	5.87 m (19 ft 3 in)
Height overall	1.73 m (5 ft 8 in)
Propeller diameter	1.63 m (5 ft 4 in)

AREA:
Wings, gross	8.36 m² (90.0 sq ft)

WEIGHTS (74.5 kW; 100 hp Teledyne Continental O-200 engine):
Weight empty	318 kg (700 lb)

Baggage capacity 27 kg (60 lb)
Max T-O weight 590 kg (1,300 lb)
PERFORMANCE (74.5 kW; 100 hp Teledyne Continental O-200 engine at max T-O weight):
Max level speed at S/L 143 knots (265 km/h; 165 mph)
Econ cruising speed 113 knots (209 km/h; 130 mph)
Landing speed:
flaps up 57 knots (105 km/h; 65 mph)
flaps down 48 knots (89 km/h; 55 mph)
Max rate of climb at S/L 275 m (900 ft)/min
Service ceiling more than 4,875 m (16,000 ft)
T-O run 245 m (800 ft)
Landing run 183 m (600 ft)

Range with max payload at 3,050 m (10,000 ft), no reserves:
at 139 knots (257 km/h; 160 mph)
521 nm (965 km; 600 miles)
at 122 knots (225 km/h; 140 mph)
607 nm (1,125 km; 700 miles)

WITTMAN TAILWIND MODEL W-10

Revisions to the Tailwind plans (available as a separate package) produced a version known as the Model W-10. This is basically a W-8 with a 112 kW (150 hp) Textron Lycoming O-320, 108 kW (145 hp) Teledyne Continental, or aluminium block Oldsmobile F85 or Buick V-8 engine.

Fuel capacity is 114 litres (30 US gallons; 25 Imp gallons). Airframe improvements include a new and more efficient wingtip design and round spring steel landing gear legs with wood and fabric fairings. Empty and max T-O weights of this version, with Teledyne Continental O-300 engine, are 413 kg (910 lb) and 680 kg (1,500 lb) respectively.
PERFORMANCE (Teledyne Continental O-300 engine):
Max level speed at S/L 182 knots (338 km/h; 210 mph)
Econ cruising speed 156 knots (290 km/h; 180 mph)
Stalling speed: flaps up 38 knots (70 km/h; 43 mph)
flaps down 35 knots (65 km/h; 40 mph)
Service ceiling 4,875 m (16,000 ft)
T-O run 366 m (1,200 ft)

WOLF
DONALD S. WOLF
17 Chestnut Street, Huntington, New York 11743
Telephone: 1 (516) 427 9678

Details of the W-11 Boredom Fighter, and an illustration, can be found in the 1988-89 *Jane's*. Plans remain available.

WOLFF AIRCRAFT ENGINEERING LTD — *See Wolff in Luxembourg*

WOOD WING
WOOD WING SPECIALTY
PO Box 1258, Tehachapi, California 93561

PLUMB CJ-3D CRACKER JACK
The prototype Cracker Jack made its first flight on 6 October 1982. In addition to plans, Wood Wing Specialty made available four prefabricated components, comprising a glassfibre nose cowling, wingtips, windscreen and propeller.
TYPE: Single-seat homebuilt.
AIRFRAME: Fabric covered all-wood airframe structure, except for aluminium alloy tubing used for elevator and rudder curves. Wing section NACA 4413. Glassfibre nose cowling. Non-retractable tailwheel landing gear. Optional cockpit side windows.
POWER PLANT: One 28.3 kW (38 hp) Aero-DAF 95 950 cc converted motorcar engine. Main fuel tank capacity 17 litres (4.5 US gallons; 3.7 Imp gallons), plus header tank of 3.8 litres (1 US gallon; 0.83 Imp gallon) capacity. Optional half-Volkswagen converted motorcar engine (950-1,000 cc).
DIMENSIONS, EXTERNAL:
Wing span 8.53 m (28 ft 0 in)
Length overall 5.33 m (17 ft 6 in)
Propeller diameter 1.32 m (4 ft 4 in)

AREA:
Wings, gross 9.29 m² (100.0 sq ft)
WEIGHTS:
Weight empty 159 kg (350 lb)
Recommended max pilot weight 91 kg (200 lb)
Baggage capacity 9 kg (20 lb)
Max T-O weight 272 kg (600 lb)
PERFORMANCE:
Max level speed at S/L 74 knots (137 km/h; 85 mph)

Max and econ cruising speed at S/L
65 knots (121 km/h; 75 mph)
Stalling speed 34 knots (63 km/h; 39 mph)
Max rate of climb at S/L 244 m (800 ft)/min
Service ceiling 3,050 m (10,000 ft)
T-O and landing run 91 m (300 ft)
Range 173 nm (321 km; 200 miles)
Endurance 2 h 42 min
g limits +6/-4

Wood Wing Specialty CJ-3D Cracker Jack

MICROLIGHTS

Company & Address	Model	Wing span/ Rotor diameter m/ft in	Length overall m/ft in	Airframe F = flexwing R = rigid wing B = braced S = single surface fabric D = double surface fabric C = conventional fuselage O = open fuselage structure P = fuselage pod	Power plant	Weight empty kg/lb	Pilot weight range kg/lb	Max speed knots (km/h; mph)	Max range or endurance nm (km; miles)	Accom	Forms/Remarks K = kits P = plans A = assembled
ARGENTINA											
Pampa's Bull SA San Martin 969, piso 1°, 1004 Buenos Aires	AgStar, AviaStar and FlightStar	9.14/ 30-0 AgStar	5.02/ 16-5½ AgStar	R, B, D, P	FlightStar: one 30 kW (40 hp) Rotax 447. AgStar and AviaStar: 38.8 kW (52 hp) Rotax 503	n.k.	n.k.	78 (144; 89) AgStar	n.k.	Pilot in FlightStar and AgStar. Two seats in AviaStar	AgStar is agricultural model of FlightStar, with 106 litre (28 US gallon; 23.3 Imp gallon) chemical hopper and Micron X ultra low volume spray system.
AUSTRALIA											
Blue Max Ultralight PO Box 42, Nagambie, Victoria 3608	Blue Max	8.53/ 28-0	5.49/ 18-0	R, B, D, O, P	One 33.6 kW (45 hp) Rotax 447 or 21 kW (28 hp) König SD 570	115/254	95/210 max	59 (109; 68) with Rotax	2 h with Rotax	Pilot	A. Hirth engine fitted to one aircraft in early 1990.
Eastwood Aircraft Pty Ltd Stevens Road, PO Box 445 Goolwa, Currency Creek, South Australia 5214	Tyro Mk 2	8.90/ 29-2	5.33/ 17-6	R, B, D, O, P	One 20 kW (27 hp) Rotax 277 or 32 kW (43 hp) Rotax 447	113/250 with Rotax 277	54.4-91/ 120-200	69 (129; 80)	130 (241; 150)	Pilot	Materials K, P. Conforms to CAO 95-10.
Gareth J. Kimberley 211 Fowler Road, Illawong, New South Wales 2234	Sky-Rider	9.86/ 32-4	5.74/ 18-10 without elevator trim tab	R, B, S, O	One 13.4 kW (18 hp) 250 cc Fuji Robin or 8.9 kW (12 hp) McCulloch MC 101 or Rotax	95/210	91/200 max	43 (80; 50)	35 (64; 40)	Pilot	P. Conforms to CAO 95-10 and FAR Pt 103.
Robert Labahan 6 Victoria Street, Seville, Victoria 3139	Hitchiker	8.05/ 26-5	4.80/ 15-9	R, B, O and optional P	One 20 kW (27 hp) Rotax 277	100/220	n.k.	61 (113; 70)	156 (290; 180)	Pilot	A. Conforms to CAO 95-10.
Ligeti Aeronautical Pty Ltd 44 Wirraway Road, Essendon Airport, Victoria 3104	Stratos	5.36/ 17-7	2.49/ 8-2	R, D, P	Prototype: one 21 kW (28 hp) König SD 570. Optional engines up to 37.3 kW (50 hp)	78/172	55-83/ 121-183	108 (200; 124)	388 (720; 447)	Pilot	Conforms to CAO 95-10. All-composites construction. Joined tandem wing configuration. Business offered for sale or partnership about 1990.
Graham J. Percy PO Box 135, 50 Baxter- Tooradin Road, Pearcedale, Victoria 3912	Maya	8.48/ 27-10	5.33/ 17-6	R, B, D, C	One 21 kW (28 hp) König SD 570 or other two-stroke engine	112.5/248	91/200 max	55 (101; 63)	n.k.	Pilot	P. Conforms to CAO 95-10.
Skywise Ultraflight Pty Ltd PO Box 226, Hornsby, New South Wales 2077	Sadler Vampire SV-2	7.00/ 22-11½	5.14/ 16-10½	R, D, P	One 30.6 kW (41 hp) Rotax 447	166.5/367	91/200	88 (163; 101) IAS	n.k.	Pilot	Manufactured in Australia to US design. Fully enclosed pod and twin boom aircraft. New Skywise Vampire SV-200 two-seat aircraft was developed but design/manufacturing rights to this (and single-seater) offered for sale to overseas buyer.
SV Aircraft Pty Ltd PO Box 85, Nagambie, Victoria 3608	SV 11B Farmate	8.00/ 26-3	5.30/ 17-4¾	R, B, D, P	One 20 kW (27 hp) Rotax 277	150/331	75-95/ 165-209	80 (148; 92)	180 (333; 207)	Pilot	A. Glassfibre skins. No news received of SV 14 two-seat microlight.

Company & Address	Model	Wing span/ Rotor diameter m/ft in	Length overall m/ft in	Airframe F = flexwing R = rigid wing B = braced S = single surface fabric D = double surface fabric C = conventional fuselage O = open fuselage structure P = fuselage pod	Power plant	Weight empty kg/lb	Pilot weight range kg/lb	Max speed knots (km/h; mph)	Max range or endurance nm (km; miles)	Accom	Forms/Remarks K = kits P = plans A = assembled
AUSTRALIA *Contd.*											
Thruster Aircraft (Australia) Pty Ltd 458 The Boulevarde, Kirrawee, New South Wales 2232	T300	9.60/ 31-6	5.50/ 18-0	R, B, D, O, P	One 43.25 kW (58 hp) Rotax 503. Optional 47.7 kW (64 hp) Rotax 532	180/396	50-100/ 110-220	70 (130; 81)	195 (362; 226)	Two seats	K, A. T300 is current designation of TST microlight. Conforms to CAO 95-25, CASO 19 and BCAR Section S.
Thruster Aircraft (Australia) Pty Ltd	T500	As for T300	As for T300	R, B, D, C	As for T300	200/441	As for T300	As for T300	270 (500; 310)	Two seats	Version of T300 with enclosed rear fuselage, 55 litre (14.5 US gallon; 12 Imp gallon) fuel tank, electric starting and full instrument package.
Ron Wheeler Aircraft (Sales) Pty Ltd 152 Bellevue Parade, Carlton, New South Wales 2218	Scout Mk III	8.69/ 28-6 nominal	5.20/ 17-0¾	R, B, O	Mk III RN: one 13.4 kW (18 hp) Fuji Robin EC 25. Mk III RX: one 26 kW (35 hp) Rotax 337	Mk III RN: 68/150. Mk III RX: 82/181	79/175 max	57 (105; 65)	48 (90; 56)	Pilot	A. Several hundred Scouts sold in Mk I, II and III forms.
Scott Winton c/o J & P Heard, North Creek Road, Ballina, New South Wales 2478	Sapphire	8.84/ 29-0	4.93/ 16-2	R, D, P	Sapphire 10: one 26 kW (35 hp) Rotax 377. Sapphire LSA: one 30 kW (40 hp) Rotax 447	Sapphire 10: 104/230. Sapphire LSA: 141/310	n.k.	80 (148; 92)	n.k.	Pilot	Sapphire 10: K, A. Sapphire LSA: A.
BELGIUM											
Dynali SA 24 rue A. Delporte, 1050 Brussels	Chickinox	9.50/ 31-2	5.00/ 16-5	Semi-rigid, B, S, O, P	One 33.6 kW (45 hp) Rotax	155/342	n.k.	49 (90; 56) cruising	n.k.	Two seats	Side by side or tandem seating. Indian Air Force ordered 25 for training.
Epervier Aviation SA Rue Delfosse, 1 bis, 1400 Nivelles	Epervier	11.15/ 36-7	6.82/ 22-4½	R, B, D, C	One 37 kW (50 hp) Rotax 503-2V. Optional Rotax 582 and 912, or Limbach SL 1700 engines	175/386	n.k.	189/ (165; 103)	n.k.	Two seats	A. Side by side cabin monoplane of conventional layout. Construction of carbonfibre/ glassfibre/Nomex honeycomb/epoxy. Microlight model initially in production.
Euronef SA Chaussée de Grammont 79, B7860 Lessines	ATTL-1	12.11/ 59-8¾	6.45/ 21-2	R, B, D, C	One 38.8 kW (52 hp) Rotax	175/386	n.k.	65 (120; 75)	n.k.	Two seats	CAD designed. Constructed of carbonfibre/glassfibre/ Kevlar. Suited to agricultural and other roles. Can use electronic flight guidance display.
SCWAL SA 77 Avenue Brugmann, 1060 Brussels	Falcon B.1	10.97/ 36-0	5.30/ 17-4¾	R, B, D, P	One 20 kW (27 hp) Rotax 277 or 26 kW (35 hp) Rotax 377. Optionally other Rotax or Göbler-Hirth	113/249	40-100/ 88-222	63 (116; 72)	108 (200; 124) standard fuel	Pilot	A.
SCWAL SA	Falcon B.2	10.97/ 36-0	5.30/ 17-4¾	R, B, D, P	One 34.3 kW (46 hp) Rotax 503	174/384	100-200/ 220-441 crew	80 (148; 92)	270 (500; 310) standard fuel	Two seats	A. First production aircraft built in 1989.

Company & Address	Model	Wing span/ Rotor diameter m/ft in	Length overall m/ft in	Airframe F = flexwing R = rigid wing B = braced S = single surface fabric D = double surface fabric C = conventional fuselage O = open fuselage structure P = fuselage pod	Power plant	Weight empty kg/lb	Pilot weight range kg/lb	Max speed knots (km/h; mph)	Max range or endurance nm (km; miles)	Accom	Forms/Remarks K = kits P = plans A = assembled
BRAZIL Indústria Paranaense de Estruturas Ltda Rua Jerônimo Durski 357, Caixa Postal 7931, 80430 Curitiba, Paraná	IPE-06	10.00/ 32-9¾	6.35/ 20-10	R, B, D, C	One 48 kW (64 hp) Rotax 532 in two-seat microlight form	185/408 in two-seat micro-light form	n.k.	65 (120; 75) in two-seat micro-light form	n.k.	Two seats (see Remarks)	A. Available as a single-seat microlight (59.7 kW; 80 hp IMAER 2000 engine), two-seat microlight (Rotax), or two-seat Experimental type (IMAER 2000) with 250 kg (551 lb) weight empty. Twelve built in 1990.
BULGARIA Optimum Aircraft Group PO Box 74, 1404 Sofia	Optimum 88	11.30/ 37-1	5.70/ 18-8½	R, B, D, P	One 38.8 kW (52 hp) Rotax 503	220/485	160/352 crew	49 (90; 56) cruising	118 (220; 136)	Two seats	Suited to training, touring and recreational uses. Aluminium alloy structure, with cotton fabric covering over wings and tail unit; glassfibre pod.
CANADA Aces High Light Aircraft Ltd 3645 Bostwick Road, RR1, London, Westminster, Ontario N6A 4B5	Cuby I	9.75/ 32-0	n.k.	R, B, D, C	One 20 kW (27 hp) Rotax 277	113/250	136 (300) max	82 (153; 95)	86 (161; 100)	Pilot	K. Microlight or Experimental FAR Pt 103 acceptable. With Rotax 503 engine, can undertake cropspraying. Optional floats or skis. g limits +5/−3.
Aces High Light Aircraft	Cuby II	10.21/ 33-6	n.k.	R, B, D, C	One 30 kW (40 hp) Rotax 447, 35.8 kW (48 hp) Rotax 503, 47 kW (63 hp) Rotax 582 or other types	163/360	136 (300) max	87 (161; 100)	347 (643; 400)	Two seats	K. Microlight or Experimental FAR Pt 103 acceptable. g limits +4/−2 at 480 kg (1,058 lb) gross weight. Optional floats, amphibious floats, skis, cropspraying equipment and wing folding.
Airtech Canada PO Box 415, Peterborough Municipal Airport, Peterborough, Ontario K9J 6Z3	Skylark	10.97/ 36-0	5.49/ 18-0	R, B, D, O, P	One 21 kW (28 hp) König	129/284	n.k.	51 (95; 59)	n.k.	Pilot	K, A. Conforms to FAR Pt 23.
Beaver RX Enterprises Ltd 3-9531 192nd Street, Surrey, British Columbia V3T 4W2	RX-35 and RX-35 Floater	9.45/ 31-0	5.38/ 17-8	R, B, D, O, P	One 26 kW (35 hp) Rotax 377	RX-35: 121.5/ 268. Floater: 149/328	RX-35: 59-118/ 130-260. Floater: 59-102/ 130-225	RX-35: 56 (103; 64). Floater: 52 (97; 60)	RX-35: 78 (145; 90). Floater: 69 (128; 80)	Pilot	K. Assembly 50-75 h. Conform to BCAR Section S and JAR 22. Floater has amphibious landing gear. Optional full enclosure.
Beaver RX Enterprises Ltd	RX-550, RX-550 Floater and RX-550SP	10.67/ 35-0	6.30/ 20-8	R, B, D, O, P	RX-550: one 35.8 kW (48 hp) Rotax 503. Floater and RX-550SP: one 47 kW (63 hp) Rotax 582	179/395	54-104/ 120-130	69 (129; 80)	156 (290; 180) standard fuel	Two seats	K, A. Conform to BCAR Section S and JAR 22. Optional full enclosure. Assembly 100-160 h.
Beaver RX Enterprises Ltd	RX-650	10.06/ 33-0	6.63/ 21-9	R, B, D, P	One 35.8 kW (48 hp) Rotax 503 or 47.7 kW (64 hp) Rotax 532 standard; 67 kW (90 hp) Norton or Rotax 912 optional	172/380	50-113/ 110-250	59 (109; 68) cruising	217 (402; 250)	Two seats	K. Assembly 150-200 h. Conforms to BCAR Section S and JAR 22. Suitable for training, cropspraying and other roles. Optional amphibious floats. Tandem seats in enclosed cabin pod.

Company & Address	Model	Wing span/ Rotor diameter m/ft in	Length overall m/ft in	Airframe F = flexwing R = rigid wing B = braced S = single surface fabric D = double surface fabric C = conventional fuselage O = open fuselage structure P = fuselage pod	Power plant	Weight empty kg/lb	Pilot weight range kg/lb	Max speed knots (km/h; mph)	Max range or endurance nm (km; miles)	Accom	Forms/Remarks K = kits P = plans A = assembled
CANADA *Contd.* Canadian Ultralight Manufacturing Ltd PO Box 1385, St Paul, Alberta T0A 3A0	Chinook 1-S	10.67/ 35-0	5.34/ 17-6	R, B, P	One 20 kW (27 hp) Rotax 277 or 26.8 kW (36 hp) Rotax 377	113/250	50-113/ 110-250	52 (97; 60)	130-173 (241-321; 150-200)	Pilot	K.
Canadian Ultralight Manufacturing Ltd	Chinook Plus 2	9.75/ 32-0	5.46/ 17-11	R, B, D, P	One 30 kW (40 hp) Rotax 447 or 35 kW (47 hp) Rotax 503	172/380	n.k.	69 (129; 80) max cruising	n.k.	Two seats	K. Assembly 120 h.
Circa Reproductions (see main Sport section)	Nieuport 11			R, B, D, C						Pilot	K, P.
Falconar Aviation 19 Airport Road, Edmonton, Alberta T5G 0W7	HM-290E Flying Flea	6.10/ 20-0	n.k.	R, B, D, C	One 22.4 kW (30 hp) Hirth F263	109/240	n.k.	55 (101; 63)	n.k.	Pilot	K. Assembly 600 h.
Kestrel Sport Aviation (see main Sport section)	Hawk and Kit Hawk										
Macair Industries Inc (see main Sport section)	Merlin										
Magal Holdings Ltd 19 Pensville Road South East, Calgary, Alberta T2A 4K3 (see 1989-90 *Jane's*)	Cuby I and II										
Ronald M. B. Smith 5604 Waverly, Montreal, Quebec H2T 2Y1	Bumble Camel	6.30/ 20-8	4.27/ 14-0	R, B, D, C	One 18 kW (24 hp) König SC 430	91/200	84/185 max	39 (72; 45)	1 h 6 min	Pilot	Plans to become available. ¾-scale Sopwith F.1 Camel. Building time 1,000-1,500 h.
Snowbird Aviation 12624-124 Street, Edmonton, Alberta T5L 0N7	Bushmaster I Mk 2	10.21/ 33-6	n.k.	R, B, D, C	One 30 kW (40 hp) Rotax 447	115/253	n.k.	69 (129; 80)	n.k.	Pilot	K.
CHINA Beijing University of Aeronautics & Astronautics PO Box 85, 37 Xue Yuan Road, Haidian District, Beijing 100083	Mifeng-2 (Bee-2)	10.00/ 32-9¾	5.05/ 16-7	R, B, S, P	One 19.4 kW (26 hp)	100/220	65-80/ 143-176	40 (75; 47)	97 (180; 112)	Pilot	K, A.
Beijing University of Aeronautics & Astronautics	Mifeng-3 (Bee-3)	10.00/ 32-9¾	6.14/ 20-1¾	R, B, S, P	One 31.3 kW (42 hp) Rotax 447	140/310	65-80/ 143-176	51 (95; 59)	88 (163; 101)	Two seats or pilot and 70-100 kg (154-220 lb) payload	K, A. Sesquiplane development of Mifeng-2; first flight July 1983. Conforms to BCAR Section S-CAP 482. Used for agricultural, touring, training, forest protection and photography roles.

Company & Address	Model	Wing span/ Rotor diameter m/ft in	Length overall m/ft in	Airframe F = flexwing R = rigid wing B = braced S = single surface fabric D = double surface fabric C = conventional fuselage O = open fuselage structure P = fuselage pod	Power plant	Weight empty kg/lb	Pilot weight range kg/lb	Max speed knots (km/h; mph)	Max range or endurance nm (km; miles)	Accom	Forms/Remarks K = kits P = plans A = assembled
Beijing University of Aeronautics & Astronautics	Mifeng-3C (Bee-3C)	8.60/ 28-2½	6.10/ 20-0¼	R, B, D, P	One 31.3 kW (42 hp) Rotax 447	150/331	n.k.	65 (120; 75)	296 (550; 341)	Two seats	Derived from the Mifeng-3, but with increased speed, higher g limit, more flexibility and easier to assemble. Three flew in formation over a distance of 2,750 nm (5,100 km; 3,170 miles).
Beijing University of Aeronautics & Astronautics	Mifeng-4 and 4A (Bee-4 and 4A)	Mifeng-4: 10.44/ 34-3	6.15/ 20-2¼	R, B, D, P	One 31.3 kW (42 hp) Rotax 447	180/397	65-80/ 143-176	Mifeng-4: 54 (100; 62)	Mifeng-4: 86 (159; 99)	Two seats	K, A. Mifeng-4A has shorter wing span.
Beijing University of Aeronautics & Astronautics	Mifeng-5 (Bee-5)	n.k.	n.k.	R, B, D, P	n.k.	n.k.	n.k.	n.k.	n.k.	Three seats or pilot and 140 kg (309 lb) payload	First flown in September 1985, as light multi-purpose aircraft.
CCMI Central China Mechanical Institute Hubei	A-1 and A-1B	10.434/ 34-2¾	A-1: 5.917/ 19-5. A-1B: 6.087/ 19-11½	Semi-rigid, B, S, P	One 38.8 kW (52 hp) Rotax 503	160/353	n.k.	46 (85; 53)	70 (130; 81)	A-1: Pilot. A-1B: Two seats	Three-axis control. A-1B multi-purpose version for recreation, patrol, cropspraying, etc.
Shijiazhuang Aircraft Plant PO Box 164, Shijiazhuang, Hebei	W-5 and W-5A Qingting (Dragonfly)	10.55/ 34-7½	5.36/ 17-7	R, B, O. W-5A has P	One 22.4 kW (30 hp) engine	W-5: 123/271. W-5A: 135/298	n.k.	W-5: 47 (88; 54). W-5A: 42 (77; 48)	W-5: 56 (104; 64). W-5A: 46 (86; 53)	W-5: Pilot. W-5A: Two seats	W-5 has small nose fairing. W-5A has side by side seats.
Shijiazhuang Aircraft Plant	W-5B Qingting (Dragonfly)	10.62/ 34-10	5.75/ 18-10½	R, B, O, P	One 33.6 kW (45 hp) Rotax 447	150/331	n.k.	54 (100; 62)	65 (120; 74)	Two seats	Seating in tandem.
CZECHOSLOVAKIA Letov Ltd Beranovych 65, 19902 Prague 9, Letnany	LK-21 Sluka	9.20/ 30-2¼	5.12/ 16-9½	Semi-rigid, B, D, P	One 30 kW (40 hp) Rotax 447 standard	150/331	55-90/ 121.5-198	54 (100; 62)	129 (240; 149)	Pilot	First factory-built microlight from Czechoslovakia. Suited for sport and working roles. Ten production aircraft ordered by January 1991. Aluminium alloy/steel tubing, polyester covered. Pod and wheel fairings.
FRANCE Aermas (Automobiles Martini SA) ZI, 58470 Magny-Cours	Aermas 386	11.16/ 36-7½	7.20/ 23-7½	R, B, D, P	One 38 kW (51 hp) Rotax 462	174/384	n.k.	65 (120; 75) cruising	n.k.	Two seats	Conforms to FAR Pt 23, Normal category.
Aéronautic 2000 52 rue Galande, 75005 Paris	Baroudeur	10.90/ 35-9¼	5.60/ 18-4½	R, B, D, P	One 38 kW (51 hp) Rotax 462 or 37.3 kW (50 hp) Fuji Robin	175/385	n.k.	54 (100; 62)	54-151 (100-280; 62-174)	Two seats	20 or 40 litre fuel tank. Can be armed with 89 mm rocket launchers in military form.
Air Creation Aérodrome de Lanas, 07200 Aubenas	Fun GT 447	10.00/ 32-9¾	2.70/ 8-10¼	F, B, D (30%), O. Optional P	One 31.3 kW (42 hp) Rotax 447	137/302	40-120/ 88-264 with Quartz 18 flexwing	46 (85; 53)	n.k.	Two seats	A. Many hundreds of Fun GT 447/Quartz/ SX GT two-seaters sold (see entries below), combining two-seat Safari GT BI trikes with various Rotax engines and Fun 18, Quartz 18 and SX 16 flexwings. Optional 38 litre fuel tank.

Company & Address	Model	Wing span/ Rotor diameter m/ft in	Length overall m/ft in	Airframe F = flexwing R = rigid wing B = braced S = single surface fabric D = double surface fabric C = conventional fuselage O = open fuselage structure P = fuselage pod	Power plant	Weight empty kg/lb	Pilot weight range kg/lb	Max speed knots (km/h; mph)	Max range or endurance nm (km; miles)	Accom	Forms/Remarks K = kits P = plans A = assembled
FRANCE *Contd.*											
Air Creation	Quartz GT 503	10.00/ 32-9¾	2.70/ 8-10¼	F, B, D (80%), O. Optional P	One 38.8 kW (52 hp) Rotax 503	142/313	As above	57 (105; 65)	n.k.	Two seats	A. More than 600 sold.
Air Creation	Quartz GT 462	10.00/ 32-9¾	2.70/ 8-10¼	F, B, D (80%), O. Optional P	One 38.8 kW (52 hp) Rotax 462	142/313	As above	57 (105; 65)	n.k.	Two seats	A.
Air Creation	SX GT 462 and SX GT 503	10.00/ 32-9¾	2.70/ 8-10¼	F, B, D (90%), O. Optional P	SX GT 462: one 38.8 kW (52 hp) Rotax 462. SX GT 503: one Rotax 503	145/320	As above	65 (120; 75)	n.k.	Two seats	A. SX GT 462 is quiet version with low fuel consumption.
Air Creation	SX Racer and Fun Racer	10.00/ 32-9¾	2.50/ 8-2½	F, B, D, O. Optional P	One 31.3 kW (42 hp) Rotax 447	110/242 with SX 12 flexwing	50-120/ 110-265 with SX 12 flexwing	49 (90; 56) Fun Racer. 65 (120; 75) SX Racer	243 (450; 279) with SX 12 flexwing	Pilot	A. Combines Racer trikes with Fun 14 and SX 12 flexwings. Fun Racer 40% double surface. Optional 38 litre fuel tank.
Air International Service (A.I.R's SA) 26 rue des Roses, 75018 Paris	Allegro	9.00/ 29-6¼	5.50/ 18-0½	R, B, D, O, P	One 26 kW (35 hp) Rotax 377 or 38 kW (51 hp) Rotax	125/276	n.k.	75 (140; 87)	1 h 45 min	Pilot	A.
Air International Service (A.I.R's SA)	Maestro	10.50/ 34-5½	5.50/ 18-0½	R, B, D, O, P	One 34 kW (45.6 hp) Rotax 503. Optional 38 kW (51 hp) Rotax or 47 kW (63 hp) Rotax 532	167/368	n.k.	59 (110; 68)	1 h 30 min	Two seats	A. Agricultural version uses Rotax 532 engine.
ASL Club d'Avions Supers Légers du Cher 45 rue Guilbeau, 18000 Bourbes	ASL 18 La Guêpe	7.86/ 25-9½	6.24/ 20-5¾	R, B, D, C	One 37.3 kW (50 hp) 1,600 cc converted Volkswagen motorcar engine	175/386	50-90/ 110-198	76 (140; 87)	135 (250; 155)	Two seats	P. Biplane with pivoting lower wings for roll control. Can also be built as an Experimental homebuilt.
Aviasud Engineering SA (see main Sport section)	Sirocco and Mistral										
Bernard Broc Enterprise Route de Freycenet, Borne, 43350 St Paulien	Papillon	10.00/ 32-9¾	2.90/ 9-6¼	R, B, D, P	Two 17.9 kW (24 hp) König radials	170/375	n.k.	65 (120; 75) max cruising	323 (600; 372)	Pilot	Tandem wing aircraft with aluminium alloy wings (forward wings sweptback) and glassfibre fuselage pod.
SN Centrair Aérodrome Le Blanc, BP 44, 36300 Le Blanc (see main Sport section)	Parafan										
Yves Chasle 8 Lotissement-Concorde, Odos, 65310 Laloubére	YC-100/ 101/110/ 111 Hirondelle (Swallow)	8.30/ 27-2¾ for YC-100	5.43/ 17-9¾	R, B, D, C	One 16.4 kW (22 hp) JPX PUL 425/503 or 18 kW (24 hp) König SC 430 in YC-100	110/243 for YC-100	n.k.	70 (130; 80) for YC-100	n.k.	Pilot	P. YC-101 and YC-111 have 9.35 m (30 ft 8½ in) wing spans, and YC-110 has 8.25 m (27 ft 0¾ in) span. All higher powered models.
Ets D. Lascaud 41 rue de Crussol, 07500 Granges-les-Valence	Bifly	6.19/ 20-3¾	3.25/ 10-8	R, D, C	One 15 kW (20 hp) J-C-V 274 cc	65/143	n.k.	59 (110; 68)	89 (165; 102)	Pilot	K, A. Tandem wings, with rudder-only tail unit.

Company & Address	Model	Wing span/ Rotor diameter m/ft in	Length overall m/ft in	Airframe F = flexwing R = rigid wing B = braced S = single surface fabric D = double surface fabric C = conventional fuselage O = open fuselage structure P = fuselage pod	Power plant	Weight empty kg/lb	Pilot weight range kg/lb	Max speed knots (km/h; mph)	Max range or endurance nm (km; miles)	Accom	Forms/Remarks K = kits P = plans A = assembled
Société d'Exploitation des Aéronefs Henri Mignet Logis des Pierrières, Saint-Romain de Benêt, 17600 Saujon	HM-1000 Balerit	7.30/ 23-11½	5.00/ 16-5	R, B, D, O, P	One 34.3 kW (46 hp) Rotax 503, 44.7 kW (60 hp) Rotax 532, or 47.7 kW (64 hp) Rotax 582	175/386 with Rotax 503	110/242	78 (145; 90) with Rotax 582	215 (400; 248)	Two seats	Tandem wings. Pivoting forward wing and rudder control. Cannot spin or stall. Side by side seating. Suited to sport and working roles.
Ets Nion Aéronautiques RN 85, Châteauvieux, 05130 Tallard	Sirius	12.00/ 39-4½	5.90/ 19-4¼	R, B, D, P	One 13.4 kW (18 hp) JPX 425 or 17.9 kW (24 hp) König SC 430	135/298	100/220 max	62 (115; 71) with König engine	75.5 (140; 87)	Pilot	K, P, A. Microlight pod and boom motor glider.
GERMANY Composite Constructions GmbH Landsberger Strasse 414, 8000 Munich 60	Delta Dart II	6.24/ 20-5¾	5.53/ 18-1¾	R, D, C/P	One 48.5 kW (65 hp)	180/397	n.k.	119 (220; 137) max cruising	755 (1,400; 870)	Two seats	Prototype displayed. Rear delta wings with endplate fins/rudders (Styrofoam/glassfibre), foreplanes, glassfibre fuselage, retractable tricycle landing gear.
Dallach Flugzeuge GmbH Stauferstrasse 10, 7076 Wissgoldingen	Sunrise II	13.10/ 42-11¾	5.30/ 17-4¾	R, C	One 30 kW (40 hp) KKHD	150/330	n.k.	81 (150; 93)	143 (266; 165)	Pilot or two seats	K, A. Conventional low-wing monoplane.
Otto and Peter Funk Im Steigert 5, 6737 Böhl-Iggelheim	FK 9	10.00/ 32-10	5.85/ 19-2¼	R, B, D, C	One 26 kW (35 hp) Rotax 447 in German version. Other engines are Rotax 462 and 582	150/330	180/396 max	78 (145; 90) cruising	259 (480; 298)	Two seats	ATL version under development.
HFL-Flugzeug-bau GmbH Hohenhorststrasse 1B, 2120 Lüneburg	Stratos 300	12.60/ 41-4	6.30/ 20-8	R, D, P	One 17.9 kW (24 hp) König SC 430	150/330	n.k.	70 (130; 81)	216 (400; 248)	Pilot	Pod and twin boom motor glider.
Ikarus Deutschland Comco GmbH Tannenweg 20, 7042 Aidlingen/Württ	C22	10.40/ 34-1½	6.25/ 20-6	R, B, D, O, P	One 28.3 kW (38 hp) Rotax 462. Optional 38.8 kW (52 hp) Rotax or 30 kW (40 hp) Citroën Visa	170/374	65-200/ 143-441	59 (110; 68) max cruising	about 189 (350; 217)	Two seats	A. Side by side two-seat version of former Fox-D. High tailboom. 398 sold by January 1990 when last update received.
Ikarus Deutschland Comco GmbH	C22HF	10.40/ 34-1½	6.40/ 21-0	R, B, D, C	One 28.3 kW (38 hp) Rotax 447, 38.8 kW (52 hp) Rotax 462 or 30 kW (40 hp) Citroën Visa	185/408	65-185/ 143-408	62 (115; 71) max cruising	about 243 (450; 280)	Two seats	A. Side by side seating. Fully enclosed cabin. High Performance (HP).
Ikarusflug Bodensee Mennwanger Strasse 3, 7777 Salem-Altenbeuren	Mistral 53	9.40/ 30-10	5.88/ 19-3½	R, B, D, O, P	One 21 kW (28 hp) König SD 570	130/287	70-95/ 154-209	46 (85; 53)	172 (320; 198)	Pilot	A. Conforms to German national standards.

Company & Address	Model	Wing span/ Rotor diameter m/ft in	Length overall m/ft in	Airframe F = flexwing R = rigid wing B = braced S = single surface fabric D = double surface fabric C = conventional fuselage O = open fuselage structure P = fuselage pod	Power plant	Weight empty kg/lb	Pilot weight range kg/lb	Max speed knots (km/h; mph)	Max range or endurance nm (km; miles)	Accom	Forms/Remarks K = kits P = plans A = assembled
GERMANY *Contd.*											
Konsuprod GmbH & Co KG Gwinnerstrasse 13, 6000 Frankfurt am Main	ULM-1B Moskito	10.30/ 33-10	5.85/ 19-2¼	R, B, D, P	One 17 kW (23 hp) König SC 430	125/275	55-95/ 122-209	49 (90; 56) with two-blade propeller	182 (338; 210)	Pilot	A. Pod and boom design. Built mainly of composites; fabricated in Poland and assembled in Germany. Two-seat version under development.
Leichtflugzeug GmbH & Co KG Osemundstrasse 22, 5982 Neuenrade	Sky Walker II	10.15/ 33-3½	5.70/ 18-8½	R, B, D, O, P	One 38.8 kW (52 hp) Rotax 462, 48.5 kW (65 hp) Rotax 582 or Sauer UL 2100	178/392	65-200/ 144-441	65 (120; 75)	about 248 (460; 285)	Two seats	K, A. Can be used for photographic, banner towing and spraying work. Various float and amphibious landing gears available. Used by Netherlands police.
Saurier Flug Service Birk Meier, Leicht Flugzeug Bau Hunterburger Strasse 17, 4508 Bohmte 1	Vagabond II	7.55/ 24-9¼	6.70/ 21-11¾	R, B, D, C	One 22.4 kW (30 hp) Citroën Visa	170/375	75-180/ 166-396	65 (120; 75)	205 (380; 236)	Two seats	K, A. Wood and fabric biplane of conventional layout.
Tandem Aircraft KG Blumen Strasse 10, Postfach 1169, 7301 Deizisau	Sunny	7.00/ 22-11½	3.75/ 12-3½	R, B, D, O	One 28.3 kW (38 hp) Rotax 447 or 38.8 kW (52 hp) Rotax 462	150/331	n.k.	43-54 (80-100; 50-62) cruising	n.k.	Two seats	Biplane, with swept upper wing and interplane vertical surfaces at wingtips.
Ultraleicht- Fluggerätebau GmbH Twist 9, 4455 Wietmarschen	Wildente	10.50/ 34-5½	6.10/ 20-0	R, B, D, O	One 16.4 kW (22 hp) Göbler- Hirth F263	145/320	n.k.	54 (100; 62)	140 (260; 162)	Pilot	
Ultraleicht- Fluggerätebau GmbH	Wildente 2	11.00/ 36-1	7.10/ 23-3½	R, B, D, O	One 28 kW (38 hp) Göbler- Hirth F2702R	150/331	n.k.	n.k.	n.k.	Two seats	
Helmut Vogt Mörikestrasse 20, 7982 Baienfurt	LO-120	12.00/ 39-4½	7.00/ 22-11½	R, D, O	One 28.3 kW (38 hp) Rotax 337	150/331	60-130/ 132-286 crew	54 (100; 62)	215 (400; 248)	Two seats	K. Twin boom design, with inverted V tail.
Helmut Vogt	LO-150	15.00/ 49-2½	n.k.	R, D, P	One 28.3 kW (38 hp) or 38.8 kW (52 hp) Rotax	150/331	n.k.	81 (150; 93)	n.k.	Two seats	K. Twin boom design, with inverted V tail unit. Differs from LO-120 mainly in having fuselage pod and larger tapered wings.
Vulcan UL-Aviation Kiefernweg 13, 8011 Zorneding bei München	Albatros	9.60/ 31-6	6.00/ 19-8¼	R, B, D, O, P	One 28.3 kW (38 hp) Rotax 462 or 47 kW (63 hp) Rotax 532 for export floatplanes	150/331	n.k.	62 (115; 71)	162 (300; 186)	Two seats	
Heinrich Zettl Vor der Pfanne, 6293 Loehnberg	Götz 50	10.90/ 35-9½	6.15/ 20-2¼	R, B, D, C	One 17.2 kW (23 hp) Göbler- Hirth F263	145/320 estimated	n.k.	54 (100; 62)	n.k.	Pilot	
HUNGARY Air Service PO Box 1502, Köérberki út 36, H-1112 Budapest XI PF. 56	KSML-P1 Nemere	n.k.	n.k.	R, B, D, O	n.k.	n.k.	n.k.	n.k.	n.k.	Pilot	
Air Service	KSML-P2 Nyírség	10.20/ 33-5½	5.90/ 19-4¼	R, B, D, O	One 29.4 kW (39.4 hp) Rotax 447	150/331	n.k.	37 (68; 42) cruising	n.k.	Two seats	Suited to sport flying, training, agricultural spraying, etc.

Company & Address	Model	Wing span/ Rotor diameter m/ft in	Length overall m/ft in	Airframe F = flexwing R = rigid wing B = braced S = single surface fabric D = double surface fabric C = conventional fuselage O = open fuselage structure P = fuselage pod	Power plant	Weight empty kg/lb	Pilot weight range kg/lb	Max speed knots (km/h; mph)	Max range or endurance nm (km; miles)	Accom	Forms/Remarks K = kits P = plans A = assembled
J. Romain & Sons 111 Burnham Green Road, Burnham Green, Welwyn, Hertfordshire	Cobra Mk I	5.69/ 18-8	4.42/ 14-6	R, B, D, C	One 22.4 kW (30 hp) KFM	70/154	76/168 max	78 (145; 90)	87 (161; 100)	Pilot	Prototype only. Conventional biplane. Conforms to BCAR Section S-CAP 482.
Michael W. J. Whittaker Dawlish Cottage, Pincots Lane, Wickwar, Wotton-under-Edge, Gloucestershire GL12 8NY	MW5 Sorcerer	9.16/ 30-0½	4.80/ 15-9	R, B, D, O, P	One 37.3 kW (50 hp) Fuji Robin EC44 PM02, or Rotax 377 or 447, or other engine	140/308 with 44.7 kW (60 hp) engine	55-100/ 122-220	65 (120; 75) with 33.6 kW (45 hp) engine	150 (278; 172) with 33.6 kW (45 hp) engine	Pilot	P. Conforms to FAI/CAA requirements. Can be microlight or Experimental homebuilt.
Michael W. J. Whittaker	MW6 Merlin	9.75/ 32-0	5.33/ 17-6	R, B, D, O, P	One 37.3 kW (50 hp) Fuji Robin EC44PM, or Rotax 503 or 532	150/331	46-181/ 100-400 crew	55 (102; 63)	78 (144; 90)	Two seats	P. Microlight or homebuilt aircraft.
Michael W. J. Whittaker	MW7	6.71/ 22-0	4.57/ 15-0	R, B, D, O, P	One 47.7 kW (64 hp) Rotax 532	145/320	100/220 max	100 (185; 115)	220 (407; 253)	Pilot	P. Can also be Experimental homebuilt. First flown in August 1988.

UNITED STATES OF AMERICA

Company & Address	Model	Wing span/ Rotor diameter m/ft in	Length overall m/ft in	Airframe	Power plant	Weight empty kg/lb	Pilot weight range kg/lb	Max speed knots (km/h; mph)	Max range or endurance nm (km; miles)	Accom	Forms/Remarks
Advanced Aviation Inc 323 North Ivey Lane, Orlando, Florida 32811	Cobra B	10.57/ 34-8	5.46/ 17-10¾	R, B, D, O	One 30 kW (40 hp) Rotax 447. AG Cobra: one 48.5 kW (65 hp) Rotax 532LC (optional for Cobra VIP)	112-120/ 247-265	50-102/ 110-225	48-52 (88-97; 55-60)	78 (145; 90)	Pilot	K. Cobra B is a microlight, conforming to FAR Pt 103. Assembly 35h. Cobra VIP and AG Cobra conform to Experimental homebuilt category.
Advanced Aviation Inc (see main Sport section)	Cobra Carrera										K.
Advanced Aviation Inc (see main Sport section)	Buccaneer										
Aerolights Inc Route 1, Box 187, Welsh, Louisiana 70591	Air Master	8.74/ 28-8	n.k.	R, B, D, C	One 50 kW (67 hp) Rotax 582	159/350	n.k.	78 (145; 90)	n.k.	Pilot	K. Low-wing monoplane. Assembly 100 h.
Aerolights Inc (see main Sport section)	Bearcat										
Air Command Manufacturing Inc Liberty Landing Airport, Route 3, Box 197A, Liberty, Missouri 64068	447 Commander and 447 Commander Sport	7.01/ 23-0	Commander: 3.25/10-8 Commander Sport: 3.51/ 11-6	Gyroplane with P (optional)	One 30 kW (40 hp) Rotax 447	114/252	55-136/ 120-300	Commander: 55 (101; 63). Commander Sport: 63 (117; 73)	87 (161; 100)	Pilot	K (more than 900 sold). Conforms to FAR Pt 103.
Aircraft Designs Inc (see main Sport section)	Bumble Bee										
Aircraft Development Inc 1326 North Westlink Boulevard, Wichita, Kansas 67212	EZ-1	9.45/ 31-0	5.33/ 17-6	R, D	One 15 kW (20 hp) Zenoah G25B-1	106/234	45-102/ 100-225	43 (80; 50)	67 (124; 77)	Pilot	Conforms to FAR Pt 103. Composites and aluminium construction, using self-adhesive 'Scotch-A-Frame' bonding technique.

Company & Address	Model	Wing span/ Rotor diameter m/ft in	Length overall m/ft in	Airframe F = flexwing R = rigid wing B = braced S = single surface fabric D = double surface fabric C = conventional fuselage O = open fuselage structure P = fuselage pod	Power plant	Weight empty kg/lb	Pilot weight range kg/lb	Max speed knots (km/h; mph)	Max range or endurance nm (km; miles)	Accom	Forms/Remarks K = kits P = plans A = assembled
UNITED STATES OF AMERICA *Contd.*											
American Aircraft Inc 650 Sacramento Street, San Francisco, California 94111	Falcon	10.97/ 36-0	4.34/ 14-3	R, D, P	One 20 kW (27 hp) Rotax 277	113/250	50-95/ 110-210	55 (101; 63)	105 (194; 121)	Pilot	A. Conforms to FAR Pt 103. Much use of composites. Foreplane forward and high-mounted swept rear main wings. Planned military version is the Phalanx.
Avid Aircraft (see main Sport section)	Avid Flyer										
Brutsche Aircraft Corporation (BAC) 1800 West 1887 South, Woods Cross, Utah 84087	Freedom 28	8.48/ 27-0	5.31/ 17-5	R, B, D, C	One 20 kW (27 hp) Rotax 277	115/254	n.k.	55 (102; 63) cruising	2 h-3 h 30 min	Pilot	K. Homebuilt version with a Rotax 503 engine is the Freedom 48.
Ken Brock Manufacturing Inc 11852 Western Avenue, Stanton, California 90680	Avion	8.84/ 29-0	4.72/ 15-6	R, B, D, O	One 20 kW (27 hp) Rotax 277	109/240	59-95/ 130-210	45 (84; 52)	121 (225; 140)	Pilot	K. Conforms to FAR Pt 103 and AC 103-7.
Ken Brock Manufacturing Inc	KB-3	6.70/ 22-0	3.35/ 11-0	Autogyro, O	One 48.5 kW (65 hp) Rotax 532	113/250	n.k.	55 (101; 63)	65 (120; 75)	Pilot	K. Microlight version of the KB-2. Conforms to FAR Pt 103.
Carlson Aircraft Inc 50643 State Route 14, East Palestine, Ohio 44413	Sparrow	9.19/ 30-2	5.11/ 16-9	R, B, D, C	One 20 kW (27 hp) Rotax 277	115/254	n.k.	50 (93; 58) cruising	173 (321; 200)	Pilot	K. Conforms to FAR Pt 103. Useful load 113 kg (250 lb).
Carlson Aircraft Inc (see main Sport section)	Sparrow Sport Special, Sparrow II and Sparrow-ette										
CGS Aviation 8221 Brecksville Road, Brecksville, Ohio 44141	Hawk Classic and Arrow	8.79/ 28-10	6.30/ 20-8	R, B, D, P	One 26 kW (35 hp) Rotax 377 or 32 kW (43 hp) Rotax 447	Classic: 136/300. Arrow: 115/254	n.k.	74 (137; 85) for Arrow	n.k.	Pilot	K, A. Assembly 60-150 h. Fast kit assembly 25-35 h. Arrow features new moulded glassfibre cockpit pod.
CGS Aviation	Hawk II Classic and Arrow	8.84/ 29-0	6.53/ 21-5	R, B, D, P	One 35 kW (47 hp) Rotax 503	Classic: 152/335. Arrow: 188/415	n.k.	65 (121; 75) cruising for Classic	n.k.	Two seats	K, A. Two-seat versions of Hawk. Long wing span available (10.36 m; 34 ft), making weight empty for Classic 164 kg (362 lb). Assembly 60-100 h for Classic; 60-150 h for Arrow. Fast kit assembly 25-35 h.
CGS Aviation	SeaHawk										Floats added to Hawk or Hawk II.
CGS Aviation	Ag-Hawk	8.84/ 29-0	n.k.	R, B, D, P	One 35 kW (47 hp) Rotax 503	n.k.	n.k.	n.k.	n.k.	Pilot	With spraygear and 20 US gallon chemical tank.
Chuck's Aircraft Company 11845 Loop 107, Adkins, Texas 78101	Texan Chuck Bird	7.77/ 25-6	4.57/ 16-0	R, B, D, C	One 30 kW (40 hp) Chaparral	n.k.	n.k.	n.k.	n.k.	n.k.	K, A.
Coldfire Systems Inc 2235 First Street, Route 107, Simi Valley, California 93065	Ascender II+	10.06/ 33-0	5.08/ 16-8	R, B, D, O	One 26 kW (35 hp) Rotax 377	107/235	45.5-136/ 100-300	52 (97; 60)	87 (161; 100)	Pilot or two seats	Formerly marketed by Freedom Fliers Inc. Conforms to FAR Pt 103 with 5 US gallon fuel tank and pilot only.

Company & Address	Model	Wing span/ Rotor diameter m/ft in	Length overall m/ft in	Airframe F = flexwing R = rigid wing B = braced S = single surface fabric D = double surface fabric C = conventional fuselage O = open fuselage structure P = fuselage pod	Power plant	Weight empty kg/lb	Pilot weight range kg/lb	Max speed knots (km/h; mph)	Max range or endurance nm (km; miles)	Accom	Forms/Remarks K = kits P = plans A = assembled
Coldfire Systems Inc	Buckeye	10.21/ 33-6	n.k.	Parawing microlight with open trike	One 32 kW (43 hp) Rotax 447	86/189	38.5-84/ 85-185	22 (42; 26) cruising	Probably 43 (80; 50)	Pilot	K. Assembly 20 h. Formerly marketed by Freedom Fliers Inc. Standard and B models.
Diehl Aero-Nautical 1855 North Elm, Jenks, Oklahoma 74037	XTC Hydrolight	9.75/ 32-0	4.62/ 15-2	R, D, P	One 18.6 kW (25 hp) 294 cc KFM 107ER or 20 kW (27 hp) Rotax 277 or 32 kW (43 hp) Rotax 447	136/300	45-90/ 100-200	52 (97; 60) with KFM engine	130 (241; 150) with KFM engine	Pilot	K. Microlight or homebuilt landplane or amphibian. Conforms to FAR Pt 103 as microlight.
Earthstar Aircraft Inc Star Route 313, Santa Margarita, California 93453	Thunder Gull J	6.10/ 20-0	5.03/ 16-6	R, B, D, C	One 20 kW (27 hp) Rotax 277 or other Rotax up to 503	111/245	46-113/ 100-250	55 (101; 63)	156 (289; 180)	Pilot	K. Conforms to FAR Pt 103. g limits +6/−4. Optional aluminium alloy wing skins. Experimental category Thunder Gull JX similar (see main Sport section). Suitable for cropspraying.
Fisher Flying Products Inc PO Box 468, Edgeley, North Dakota 58433	FP-101	8.79/ 28-10	5.03/ 16-6	R, B, D, C	One 20 kW (27 hp) Rotax 277	109-113/ 240-250	45.5-100/ 100-220	52 (97; 60)	130 (241; 150)	Pilot	K. Conforms to FAR Pt 103 requirements. High-wing monoplane.
Fisher Flying Products Inc	FP-202 Koala	8.84/ 29-10	5.41/ 17-9	R, B, D, C	One 20 kW (27 hp) Rotax 277	109-113/ 240-250	n.k.	52 (97; 60) cruising	143 (265; 165)	Pilot	K, A. Assembly 250-500 h.
Fisher Flying Products Inc (see main Sport section)	Super Koala										
Fisher Flying Products Inc	FP-303	8.46/ 27-9	5.03/ 16-6	R, B, D, C	One 20 kW (27 hp) Rotax 277	104-109/ 230-240	45.5-95/ 100-210	52 (97; 60)	72 (133; 83)	Pilot	K. Low-wing monoplane. Conforms to FAR Pt 103 and FAI/CAA regulations. Assembly 300 h.
Fisher Flying Products Inc (see main Sport section)	FP-404 Classic and Classic II										
Fisher Flying Products Inc	FP-505 Skeeter	8.53/ 28-0	5.03/ 16-6	R, B, D, C	One 20 kW (27 hp) Rotax 277	109-113/ 240-250	n.k.	48-52 (89-97; 55-60)	n.k.	Pilot	K. Parasol wing. Assembly 200-400 h.
Fisher Flying Products Inc	FP-606 Sky Baby	8.79/ 28-10	n.k.	R, B, D, C	One 20 kW (27 hp) Rotax 277	115/254	n.k.	52 (97; 60) cruising	n.k.	Pilot	K, A. Assembly 250-500 h.
Flightworks (see main Sport section)	Capella										
Gemini International 20 Barnes Street, Daleville, Alabama 36322	Hummingbird 103	10.97/ 36-0	n.k.	R, B, D, O	Two 215 cc Solos	95/210	n.k.	48; (89; 55)	n.k.	Pilot	K.
Gemini International	Hummingbird Longwing	12.50/ 41-0	n.k.	R, B, D, O	Two 215 cc Solos	100/220	n.k.	43 (80; 50)	n.k.	Pilot	K.
Golden Circle Air 11691 North-West 46th Avenue, Grimes, Iowa 50111	T-Bird I	9.45/ 31-0	5.49/ 18-0	R, B, D, O	One 21 kW (28 hp) Rotax 277	115/252	55-113/ 120-250	54 (100; 62) cruising	104 (193; 120)	Pilot	K. Assembly 60 h. Ex-Teratorn Tierra

Company & Address	Model	Wing span/ Rotor diameter m/ft in	Length overall m/ft in	Airframe F = flexwing R = rigid wing B = braced S = single surface fabric D = double surface fabric C = conventional fuselage O = open fuselage structure P = fuselage pod	Power plant	Weight empty kg/lb	Pilot weight range kg/lb	Max speed knots (km/h; mph)	Max range or endurance nm (km; miles)	Accom	Forms/Remarks K = kits P = plans A = assembled
UNITED STATES OF AMERICA *Contd.*											
Golden Circle Air	T-Bird II	10.97/ 36-0	5.69/ 18-8	R, B, D, O	One 47 kW (63 hp) Rotax 582	159/350	n.k.	52 (97; 60) cruising	n.k.	Two seats	K. Assembly 60 h.
Hipp's Superbirds Inc PO Box 266, I-26 Exit 28, Ozone Drive, Saluda, North Carolina 28773	J-3 Kitten	9.14/ 30-0	4.98/ 16-4	R, B, D, C	One 21 kW (28 hp) Rotax 277	114/252	55-113/ 120-250	55 (101; 63)	104 (193; 120)	Pilot	K, P, A. Conforms to FAR Pt 103. Assembly 300 h.
Hipp's Superbirds Inc	Reliant II	9.14/ 30-0	4.98/ 16-4	R, B, D, C	One 21 kW (28 hp) Rotax 277	115/254	55-113/ 120-250	55 (101; 63)	104 (193; 120)	Pilot	K, A. Conforms to FAR Pt 103. Assembly 300 h.
Hipp's Superbirds Inc	J-4 Sportster	8.53/ 28-0	4.98/ 16-4	R, B, D, C	One 21 kW (28 hp) Rotax 277	109/240	55-113/ 120-250	55 (101; 63)	104 (193; 120)	Pilot	K, P, A. Parasol wing. Conforms to FAR Pt 103. Assembly 300 h.
Howland Aero Designs Box 233, Maryland, New York 12116	H-3 Pegasus	7.62/ 25-0	n.k.	R, D, C	One 21 kW (28 hp) Rotax 277	114/252	n.k.	52 (97; 60)	n.k.	Pilot	K. Conforms to FAR Pt 103. Assembly 250 h.
Robert W. Hovey Aircraft Specialties Co PO Box 1074, Canyon County, California 91351	Beta Bird	7.77/ 25-6	5.03/ 16-6	R, B, D, open P	One 33.5 kW (45 hp) Volkswagen motorcar engine	184/405	n.k.	74 (137; 85)	113 (209; 130)	Pilot	P. Pod and boom type.
Robert W. Hovey	Delta Bird	7.32/ 24-0	4.60/ 15-1	R, B, D, C	One 22.5 kW (30 hp) Cuyuna 430R	99/218	95/210 max	48 (88; 55)	61 (112; 70)	Pilot	K, P. Conforms to FAR Pt 103. Biplane.
Robert W. Hovey	Delta Hawk and Super Hawk	7.32/ 24-0	4.75/ 15-7	R, B, D, C	Delta Hawk: one 28.7 kW (38.5 hp) 440 cc Kawasaki 440. Super Hawk: Rotax	Delta Hawk: 112/248. Super Hawk: 113/250	54-100/ 120-220	55 (101; 63)	65 (120; 75)	Pilot	P, A. Conform to FAR Pt 103. Super Hawk has all-metal skin. Biplanes.
Robert W. Hovey	Whing Ding II (WD-II)	5.69/ 18-8	4.27/ 14-0	R, B, open P	One 10.5 kW (14 hp) McCulloch MC-101A	55/120	84/185 max	43 (80; 50)	17 (32; 20)	Pilot	P. Conforms to FAR Pt 103. Open pod and boom type biplane. Wing warping control.
Kennedy Aircraft Company Inc (see main Sport section)	Flycycle										
Michael G. Kimbrel 1333 Garrard Creek Road, Oakville, Washington 98568	Banty	9.75/ 32-0	5.74/ 18-10	R, B, D, C	One 20 kW (27 hp) Rotax 277	108/237	50-102/ 110-225	43 (80; 50) cruising	n.k.	Pilot	P.
Michael G. Kimbrel	Butterfly	11.13/ 36-6	6.55/ 21-6	R, B, D, P	One 20 kW (27 hp) Rotax 277	90/198	93/205 max	39 (72; 45) cruising	78 (145; 90)	Pilot	P. Conforms to FAR Pt 103.
Kolb Aircraft Inc RD3, Box 38, Phoenixville, Pennsylvania 19460	FireStar KX	8.43/ 27-8	6.17/ 20-3	R, B, D, P	One 26 kW (35 hp) Rotax 377. Alternative Rotax 447	115/254	55-119/ 120-264	61 (113; 70)	2 h	Pilot	K. Conforms to FAR Pt 103-7. More than 400 kits sold. Optional full cockpit enclosure. Alternative Rotax 503 engine in FireStar KXP version.

Company & Address	Model	Wing span/ Rotor diameter m/ft in	Length overall m/ft in	Airframe F = flexwing R = rigid wing B = braced S = single surface fabric D = double surface fabric C = conventional fuselage O = open fuselage structure P = fuselage pod	Power plant	Weight empty kg/lb	Pilot weight range kg/lb	Max speed knots (km/h; mph)	Max range or endurance nm (km; miles)	Accom	Forms/Remarks K = kits P = plans A = assembled
Kopy Kat 5453 East Airport Road, Mount Pleasant, Michigan 48858	Kopy Kat	n.k.	n.k.	R, B, D, C	One 20 kW (27 hp) Rotax 277	n.k.	n.k.	n.k.	n.k.	Pilot	K, P, A. Conforms to FAR Pt 103. Assembly 350 h. Microlight version of a conventional single-seat biplane.
Leader's International Inc 212 North Mecklenburg Avenue, South Hill, Virginia 23970	JB-1000	9.14/ 30-0	6.10/ 20-0	R, D, P	One 20 kW (27 hp) Rotax 277	113/250	63.5-100/ 140-220	52 (97; 60)	n.k.	Pilot	K, P, A. Conforms to FAR Pt 103. Carbonfibre/Kevlar construction.
Leading Edge Air Foils Inc 331 South 14th Street, Colorado Springs, Colorado 80904-4096	Nieuport 11	6.55/ 21-6	4.88/ 16-0	R, B, D, C	One 30 kW (40 hp) Rotax 447 or 34 kW (45.6 hp) Rotax 503	120/265	n.k.	72 (134; 83) with Rotax 503	143 (265; 165) with Rotax 503	Pilot	K, P, A. Useful load 129 kg (285 lb). Construction 400 h. Offered in microlight and Experimental forms.
Leading Edge Air Foils Inc	Nieuport 12	8.08/ 26-6	6.55/ 21-6	R, B, D, C	One 47.7 kW (64 hp) Rotax 532 or others incl VW, Teledyne Continental and Textron Lycoming	243/536	n.k.	74 (137; 85)	n.k.	Two seats	K, P, A. Construction 1,400 h. Microlight or Experimental forms.
Leading Edge Air Foils Inc	Jenny	8.38/ 27-6	5.59/ 18-4	R, B, D, C	One 34 kW (45.6 hp) Rotax 503 or similar up to 48.5 kW (65 hp)	190/419	n.k.	about 52 (97; 60)	156 (289; 180)	Two seats	K, P, A. Construction 400 h.
Light Miniature Aircraft Inc Building 411, Opa-Locka Airport, Opa-Locka, Florida 33054 (see main Sport section)	LM-1U and LM-3U										
Magnum Industries 9815 Lemona Avenue, Sepulveda, California 91343	Honcho II	9.80/ 32-2	5.35/ 17-6½	R, B, D, P	One 20 kW (27 hp) Rotax 277	108/239	n.k.	50 (93; 58) CAS.	139 (257 160)	Pilot	K. Conforms to FAR Pt 103. FAA approved kit for Pt 21. Super-Honcho in main Sport section.
Magnum Industries	Nomad II	11.00/ 36-1	5.75/ 18-10½	R, B, D, P	One 20 kW (27 hp) Rotax 277	97/214	n.k.	49 (90; 56) CAS	139 (257; 160)	Pilot	K. Conforms to FAR Pt 103. Meets Pt 21 but not pre-approved.
Maxair Aircraft Corporation (see main Sport section)	Drifter series										
Mc² Box 73415, Puyallup, Washington 98373	Chaser S	8.10/ 26-7	n.k.	F, B, O	One 26 kW (35 hp) Rotax 377	100/220	n.k.	80 (148; 92)	n.k.	Pilot	K.
Mitchell Aerospace Company (Mitchell Wing) 1900 South Newcomb, Porterville, California 93257	A-10 Silver Eagle	10.46/ 34-4	2.59/ 8-6	R, D, P	One 17.2 kW (23 hp) Zenoah	113/250	54.5-129/ 120-285	55 (101; 63)	131 (243; 151)	Pilot	A. Conforms to all FAA ultralight regulations, including FAR Pt 103.

Company & Address	Model	Wing span/ Rotor diameter m/ft in	Length overall m/ft in	Airframe F = flexwing R = rigid wing B = braced S = single surface fabric D = double surface fabric C = conventional fuselage O = open fuselage structure P = fuselage pod	Power plant	Weight empty kg/lb	Pilot weight range kg/lb	Max speed knots (km/h; mph)	Max range or endurance nm (km; miles)	Accom	Forms/Remarks K = kits P = plans A = assembled
UNITED STATES OF AMERICA *Contd.*											
Mitchell Aerospace Company (see main Sport section)	AG-38-A War Eagle, AG-38A Terrier and P-38 Lightning										
Mitchell Aerospace Company	B-10	10.36/ 34-0	n.k.	R, B, D, O and P (optional)	One 15 kW (20 hp) Honda	91/200	136/300	56 max (105; 65)	35-434 (64-805; 40-500) standard or auxiliary fuel	Pilot	K, P, A. Conforms to FAR Pt 103. B-10F is foot-launched version; B-10 has tricycle landing gear.
Mitchell Aerospace Company	TU-10 Double Eagle	n.k.	n.k.	n.k.	One 29.4 kW (39.4 hp) Rotax 447	n.k.	n.k.	n.k.	n.k.	Two seats	Two-seat version of the A-10 Silver Eagle.
Mitchell Aerospace Company	U-2 Superwing	10.36/ 34-0	2.84/ 9-4	R, D, P	One 15 kW (20 hp) Honda	136/300	136/300	74 max (137; 85)	39-434 (72-805; 45-500) standard or auxiliary fuel	Pilot	K, P. Does not conform to FAR Pt 103.
Mosler Airframes and Power Plants 140 Ashwood Road, Henderson, North Carolina 28739	N3 Pup	9.30/ 30-6	5.03/ 16-6	R, B, D, C	One 26 kW (35 hp) Mosler MM-CB	115/254	n.k.	55 (101; 63)	86-130 (161-241; 100-150)	Pilot	K. Assembly 300 h. With optional equipment, does not qualify under FAR Pt 103.
Mosler Airframes and Power Plants	Ultra Pup	9.30/ 30-6	n.k.	R, B, D, C	One 44.7 kW (60 hp) Mosler	175/385	n.k.	69 (129; 80) cruising	n.k.	Two seats	K. Assembly 350 h. High-wing cabin monoplane
Pago Jet North America PO Box 5147, Poughkeepsie, New York 12602	Pago Jet	9.22/ 30-3	n.k.	Parawing microlight	One 17 kW (23 hp) König	22/48	n.k.	22 (40; 25) cruising	n.k.	Pilot	K.
Paraplane Corporation (see main Sport section)	PM-2										
Phantom Sport Planes Inc 42295 Avenida Alvarado 1, Temecula, California 92390-3471	Phantom	8.69/ 28-6	5.11/ 16-9	R, B, D, O, P	One 31.3 kW (42 hp) Rotax 447	114/252	41-97/ 90-215	54 (100; 62)	126 (233; 145)	Pilot	K. Conforms to FAR Pt 103. Assembly 70 h.
Phantom Sport Planes Inc	Phantom F II	9.30/ 30-6	n.k.	R, B, D, O, P	One 35 kW (47 hp) Rotax 503DC	195/430	n.k.	51 (96; 60) cruising	n.k.	Two seats	K. Two-seat version of the Phantom. Assembly 120 h.
Pinaire Engineering Inc 1313 Newton Avenue, Evansville, Indiana 47715	Ultra- Aire I	7.92/ 26-0	4.32/ 14-2	R, B, O	One 26 kW (35 hp) Cuyuna ULII-02	109/240	n.k.	55 (101; 63)	n.k.	Pilot	K, A. Conforms to FAR Pt 103.
Powercraft Corporation 513 North 21st Avenue, Suite C, Yakima, Washington 98902	Parascender I	10.49/ 34-6	2.64/ 8-8	Parawing microlight with trike	One 31.3 kW (42 hp) Rotax 447 or optionally Rotax 503	104/230	86/190 with Rotax 447	23 (42; 26)	n.k.	n.k.	K.
Powercraft Corporation	Parascender II	11.13/ 36-6	2.69/ 8-10	Parawing microlight with trike	One 37.3 kW (50 hp) Rotax 503	113/250	158/350 max crew	28 max (51; 32)	n.k.	Two seats	K.

Company & Address	Model	Wing span/ Rotor diameter m/ft in	Length overall m/ft in	Airframe F = flexwing R = rigid wing B = braced S = single surface fabric D = double surface fabric C = conventional fuselage O = open fuselage structure P = fuselage pod	Power plant	Weight empty kg/lb	Pilot weight range kg/lb	Max speed knots (km/h; mph)	Max range or endurance nm (km; miles)	Accom	Forms/Remarks K = kits P = plans A = assembled
Quad City Ultralight Aircraft Corporation 3610 Coaltown Road, Moline, Illinois 61265	Challenger	9.60/ 31-6	5.64/ 18-6	R, B, D, C	One 20 kW (27 hp) Rotax 277 or optional Rotax 377, 447 or 503	107/235	n.k.	55 (101; 63) with Rotax 277	130 (241; 150)	Pilot	K. Conforms to FAR Pt 103 with Rotax 277 engine. With larger engine, becomes Experimental homebuilt. Assembly 60 h. Challenger Special version has clipped wings of 7.92 m (26 ft) span, Rotax 447 engine and 118 kg (260 lb) empty weight (see main Sport section).
Quad City Ultralight Aircraft Corporation	Challenger II	9.60/ 31-6	6.10/ 20-0	R, B, D, C	One 31.3 kW (42 hp) Rotax 447 or optionally Rotax 503	136/300	68-136/ 150-300 crew	74 (137; 85)	121 (225; 140) with two crew	Two seats	K. Microlight trainer to FAR Pt 103 or Experimental homebuilt. Assembly 60 h. Challenger II Special version has clipped wings of 7.92 m (26 ft) span, Rotax 503 engine and 159 kg (350 lb) empty weight.
Quicksilver Enterprises Inc PO Box 1572, 27495 Diaz Road, Temecula, California 92390	Quicksilver GT 400	9.14/ 30-0	6.20/ 20-4	R, B, D, O and P (optional)	One 31.3 kW (42 hp) Rotax 447	125/276	n.k.	50 (93; 58) cruising	n.k.	Pilot	K, A. Assembly 60 h.
Quicksilver Enterprises Inc	MX Sport and Sprint	8.53/ 28-0	n.k.	R, B, D, O	One 31.3 kW (42 hp) Rotax 447	Sport: 115/254. Sprint: 113/250	n.k.	Sport: 46 (85; 53) cruising	n.k.	Pilot	K. Assembly 40 h. Sprint has higher rate of climb and lower max and stalling speeds.
Quicksilver Enterprises Inc	Quicksilver MXL II Sport and Sprint	9.98/ 32-9	5.51/ 18-1	R, B, D, O and P (optional)	One 35 kW (47 hp) Rotax 503	Sport: 150/330. Sprint: 147/325	n.k.	Sport: 46 (85; 53) cruising	n.k.	Two seats	K. Assembly 50 h. Sport has higher performance.
Quicksilver Enterprises Inc	Quicksilver GT 500	9.14/ 30-0	6.21/ 20-4½	R, B, D, O and P (optional)	One 37.3 kW (50 hp) Rotax 503 or 48.5 kW (65 hp) Rotax 582	191/420	n.k.	65 (121; 75) cruising	n.k.	Two seats	K, A. First flown November 1989. Assembly 100 h.
RANS Inc 1104 East Highway 40 By-Pass, Hays, Kansas 67601	S-4 Coyote	8.99/ 29-6	5.18/ 17-0	R, B, D, C	One 31.3 kW (42 hp) Rotax 447	125/276	n.k.	55 (101; 63)	n.k.	Pilot	A and K. Conforms to FAR Pt 103-7 as a microlight. Optional Experimental category. Useful load 141 kg (311 lb). Assembly 75 h.
RANS Inc	S-6 Coyote II	9.45/ 31-0	6.10/ 20-0	R, B, D, C	One 35 kW (47 hp) Rotax 503 or 48.5 kW (65 hp) Rotax 532	172-191/ 380-420	n.k.	68-74 (126-137; 78-85) cruising	n.k.	Two seats	K. Microlight or Experimental categories. Useful load 217-235 kg (480-520 lb). Assembly 100-150 h.
R. D. Aircraft PO Box 211, Mayville, New York 14757	Skycycle	9.65/ 31-8	5.99/ 19-8	R, B, D, C	One 15 kW (20 hp) Snowmobile (or similar), Zenoah, 16.4 kW (22 hp) Yamaha 246 cc, or 18.6 kW (25 hp) KFM 107SR	112.5/248	50-118/ 110-260	48 (90; 56)	174 (322; 200)	Pilot	P, A and components. Conforms to FAR Pt 103.

Company & Address	Model	Wing span/ Rotor diameter m/ft in	Length overall m/ft in	Airframe F = flexwing R = rigid wing B = braced S = single surface fabric D = double surface fabric C = conventional fuselage O = open fuselage structure P = fuselage pod	Power plant	Weight empty kg/lb	Pilot weight range kg/lb	Max speed knots (km/h; mph)	Max range or endurance nm (km; miles)	Accom	Forms/Remarks K = kits P = plans A = assembled
UNITED STATES OF AMERICA *Contd.*											
R. D. Aircraft	Skycycle II	9.65/ 31-8	5.99/ 19-8	R, B, D, C	One 26 kW (35 hp) Cuyuna ULII-02 or 28.3 kW (38 hp) Kawasaki TA440 or 26 kW (35 hp) Rotax 377	n.k.	n.k.	n.k.	n.k.	Two seats	P, A and components. Microlight trainer.
R. D. Aircraft	Skycycle Gypsy, Skycycle Gypsy II, Skycycle Cabin Gypsy, and Wood Gypsy	9.65/ 31-8 Gypsy	6.20/ 20-4 Gypsy	R, B, D, C	One 15 kW (20 hp) Snowmobile (or other engine as for Skycycle). One 20 kW (27 hp) Rotax 277 also optional or (for Cabin Gypsy) standard	112/246 Gypsy	50-118/ 110-260 Gypsy	49 (90; 56) Gypsy	174 (322; 200) Gypsy	Pilot	P, A and components. Derived from Skycycle. Conform to FAR Pt 103. Gypsy II has tubular V bracing struts instead of kingpost, Cabin Gypsy has enclosed cabin and is smaller, and Wood Gypsy is constructed of wood.
R. D. Aircraft	Gypsy Trainer	9.35/ 30-8	6.17/ 20-3	R, B, D, C	One 30 kW (40 hp) Rotax 447	159/350	55-154/ 120-340	61 (113; 70)	174 (322; 200)	Two seats	First flown in 1989.
Roberts Ultralight Aircraft Jacksonville, Florida	RB-2	n.k.	n.k.	R, B, D, C	One Honda	n.k.	n.k.	n.k.	n.k.	Pilot	Conventional strut braced high-wing cabin monoplane.
Rotec Engineering Inc PO Box 380220, Duncanville, Texas 75138	Panther	10.36/ 34-0	5.13/ 16-10	R, B, D, P	One 20 kW (27 hp) Rotax 277, 377 or 477	113/250	45-91/ 100-200	50 (93; 58) cruising	149 (277; 172)	Pilot	K, A. Pod and boom type.
Rotec Engineering Inc	Rally 2B	9.45/ 31-0	5.13/ 16-10	R, B, S, O	One 28.3 kW (38 hp) Rotax 377	98/216	100/220 max	35 (64; 40) cruising	73 (135; 84)	Pilot	K, A. Conforms to FAR Pt 103.
Rotec Engineering Inc	Rally 3	11.58/ 38-0	5.28/ 17-4	R, B, S, O	One 35.8 kW (48 hp) Rotax 503	129/285	195/430 max crew	35 (64; 40) cruising	87 (161; 100)	Two seats	K, A. Two-seat version of Rally 2B.
Rotec Engineering Inc	Rally Champ	9.45/ 31-0	5.13/ 16-10	R, B, S, O and optional P	One 20 kW (27 hp) Rotax 277	92/202	55-91/ 120-200	35 (64; 40) cruising	74 (136; 85)	Pilot	K, A. Low cost version of Rally 2B.
Rotec Engineering Inc	Rally Sport	8.23/ 27-0	5.05/ 16-7	R, B, S, O and optional P	One 35.8 kW (48 hp) Rotax 503	112/248	45.5-100/ 100-220	52 (96; 60)	72 (133; 83)	Pilot	K, A. Version of Rally capable of aerobatic manoeuvres.
Saphir America PO Box 2343, New York, New York 10009	The Minimum	n.k.	n.k.	F, B, O	n.k.	n.k.	n.k.	n.k.	n.k.	Pilot	Flexwing hang glider and trike.
Sorrell Aircraft Company Ltd 16525 Tilley Road South, Tenino, Washington 98589	SNS-8 Hiperlight and Hiperlight EXP	6.71/ 22-0	4.72/ 15-6	R, B, D, C	Hiperlight: one 20 kW (27 hp) Rotax 277. Hiperlight EXP: one 26.8 kW (36 hp) Rotax 377	111.5/ 246 Hiperlight	104/230 Hiperlight	55 (101; 63) Hiperlight	174 (322; 200) Hiperlight	Pilot	K. Conforms to FAR Pt 103. Cabin biplane.
Sorrell Aircraft Company Ltd	SNS-10 Intruder	4.57/ 15-0	n.k.	R, B, D, C	n.k.	n.k.	n.k.	n.k.	n.k.	Pilot	Believed to be a strengthened version of Hiperlight for limited aerobatics.

Company & Address	Model	Wing span/ Rotor diameter m/ft in	Length overall m/ft in	Airframe F = flexwing R = rigid wing B = braced S = single surface fabric D = double surface fabric C = conventional fuselage O = open fuselage structure P = fuselage pod	Power plant	Weight empty kg/lb	Pilot weight range kg/lb	Max speed knots (km/h; mph)	Max range or endurance nm (km; miles)	Accom	Forms/Remarks K = kits P = plans A = assembled
Sport Flight Engineering Inc PO Box 2164, Grand Junction, Colorado 81502	Sky Pup	9.45/ 31-0	4.85/ 15-11	R, D, C	One 20 kW (27 hp) Rotax 277 or other engines in 13.5-20 kW (18-27 hp) range	91/200	86/190 max	53 (98; 61)	104 (193; 120)	Pilot	P. Conforms to FAR Pt 103.
Star Flight Aircraft Liberty Landing Airport, Route 3, Box 197, Liberty, Missouri 64066	XC series (data for XC 280 Stiletto)	8.69/ 28-6	5.18/ 17-0	R, B, D, O and P (optional)	One 24 kW (32 hp) Rotax 377 or 20 kW (27 hp) Rotax 277	107/235	59-113/ 130-250	42 (77; 48)	78 (145; 90)	Pilot or two seats	K, P and components? Conform to FAR Pt 103. Series includes XC 320 with larger wing, two-seat XC 2000 with larger wing and Rotax 447, and AgLite agricultural version of XC 2000.
Striplin Aircraft Corporation (see main Sport section)	Lone Ranger Ultralight										
Sunrise Ultralight Aircraft Manufacturing Company Route 4, Box 336, New Caney, Texas 77357	Clipper Ultralight and Clipper Super Sport	9.14/ 30-0	5.44/ 17-10	R, B, D, C	Clipper Ultralight: one 26 kW (35 hp) Rotax 377. Clipper Super Sport: one 38.8 kW (52 hp) Rotax 503	114/252 Clipper Ultralight. 122/270 Clipper Super Sport	46-113/ 100-250 Clipper Ultralight. Clipper Super Sport	52 (97; 60) Clipper Ultralight. 74 (136; 85) Clipper Super Sport	104 (193; 120) Clipper Ultralight. 165 (305; 190) Clipper Super Sport	Pilot	K. Conforms to FAR Pt 103. Conventional aeroplane layout. Assembly 45 h.
Sunrise Ultralight Aircraft Manufacturing Company	Spitfire Ultralight, Spitfire Super Sport, Spitfire Super Sport XE and Sonic Spitfire	9.14/ 30-0	5.44/ 17-10	R, B, D, O, P	Spitfire Ultralight: one 26 kW (35 hp) Rotax 377. Spitfire Super Sport XE and Sonic Spitfire: one 38.8 kW (52 hp) Rotax 503	112/248 Spitfire Ultralight. 122/270 Spitfire Super Sport	46-113/ 100-250 Spitfire Ultralight and Spitfire Super Sport	52 (97; 60) Spitfire Ultralight. 74 (136; 85) Spitfire Super Sport	104 (193; 120) Spitfire Ultralight. 165 (305; 190) Spitfire Super Sport	Pilot	K (see below). Conform to FAR Pt 103. Assembly 30 h. Sonic Spitfire and Spitfire Super Sport XE have twice the fuel capacity (10 US gallons). XE is factory built with full-span ailerons.
Sunrise Ultralight Aircraft Manufacturing Company	Spitfire II UTV	9.14/ 30-0	5.44/ 17-10	R, B, D, O, P	One 38.8 kW (52 hp) Rotax 503	159/350	46-113/ 100-250	52 (97; 60)	86 (161; 100)	Two seats	K. Assembly 50 h.
Tennessee Engineering and Manufacturing Inc (T.E.A.M.) State Route 53 and Ivy Bluff Road, Route 1, Box 338C, Bradyville, Tennessee 37026	Hi-MAX	7.62/ 25-0	4.72/ 15-6	R, B, D, C	One 20 kW (27 hp) Rotax 277	113/250	n.k.	52 (97; 60)	n.k.	Pilot	K, P. Conforms to FAR Pt 103. Assembly about 400 h. High wing and enclosed cabin version of miniMAX. Experimental version has Rotax 447.
Tennessee Engineering and Manufacturing Inc (T.E.A.M.)	miniMAX	7.62/ 25-0	4.72/ 15-6	R, B, D, C	One 20 kW (27 hp) Rotax 277	107/235	104/230	52 (97; 60)	95.5 (177; 110)	Pilot	K, P. Microlight to FAR Pt 103 or homebuilt to Experimental regulations (Rotax 447). Low-wing monoplane. Assembly about 300-400 h.
Tennessee Engineering and Manufacturing Inc (T.E.A.M.)	TA-3	n.k.	n.k.	R, B, D, C	One 35.8 kW (48 hp) Rotax 503 or 48.5 kW (65 hp) Rotax 532	181/400	n.k.	87 (161; 100)	n.k.	Two seats	K. Side by side two-seater with enclosed cockpit.

Company & Address	Model	Wing span/ Rotor diameter m/ft in	Length overall m/ft in	Airframe F = flexwing R = rigid wing B = braced S = single surface fabric D = double surface fabric C = conventional fuselage O = open fuselage structure P = fuselage pod	Power plant	Weight empty kg/lb	Pilot weight range kg/lb	Max speed knots (km/h; mph)	Max range or endurance nm (km; miles)	Accom	Forms/Remarks K = kits P = plans A = assembled
UNITED STATES OF AMERICA *Contd.*											
Turner Aircraft Inc Route 4, Box 115AB3, Grandview, Texas 76050	T-100D Mariah	9.75/ 32-0	5.18/ 17-0	R, D, P	Prototype: One 15 kW (20 hp) Cuyuna 215. Production model: KFM 105ER or Ultra	114/251	100/220 max	53 (98; 61)	3 h 35 min	Pilot	P, A. Conforms to FAR Pt 103. Pod and boom type.
Two Wings Aviation 821 3rd Street, Farmington, Minnesota 55024	Fury	8.64/ 28-4	3.96/ 13-0	R, B, D, C	See 'Forms'	115/254	46-113/ 100-250	over 52 (97; 60) cruising	n.k.	Pilot	K, A. Microlight with 30 kW (40 hp) Rotax 447; Experimental homebuilt with 37.3 kW (50 hp) Rotax. Biplane.
Two Wings Aviation	Mariner	9.55/ 31-4	5.92/ 19-5	R, B, D, C amphibious hull	One 30 kW (40 hp) Rotax 447 as microlight	138/304	up to 136/300	82 (153; 95)	n.k.	Pilot or two seats	K, A. Amphibious biplane. All-metal below waterline. Can be built as Experimental homebuilt using 37.3 kW (50 hp) or 47.7 kW (64 hp) Rotax engine, requiring 600-800 h to assemble from 51% kit.
Ultra Efficient Products Inc 1637 7th Street, Sarasota, Florida 34236	Demoiselle	8.23/ 27-0	6.40/ 21-0	R, D, O	One 15 kW (20 hp) Zenoah G25B	111/245	59-95/ 130-210	43 (80; 50)	86 (161; 100)	Pilot	P and some components.
Ultra Efficient Products Inc	Invader Mk III-B	9.45/ 31-0	5.49/ 18-0	R, D, P	One 20 kW (27 hp) Rotax 277	111/245	59-95/ 130-210	52 (97; 60)	217 (402; 250)	Pilot	P and components. Conforms to FAR Pt 103. Pod and boom type with shoulder wings and V tail.
Ultra Efficient Products Inc	Penetrater	7.32/ 24-0	4.88/ 16-0	R, D, P	One 15 kW (20 hp) Zenoah	79.5/175	59-81/ 130-180	52 (97; 60)	217 (402; 250)	Pilot	Pilot prone on boom type fuselage.
Ultralight Aircraft Inc 39416-264th Avenue, South East Enumclaw, Washington 98022	Sno-Bird	n.k.	n.k.	Autogyro	Rotax	n.k.	n.k.	n.k.	n.k.	Pilot	A?
US Aviation 265 Echo Lane, South St Paul, Minnesota 55075	Cloud Dancer	12.19/ 40-0	5.41/ 17-9	R, D, P	One 20 kW (27 hp) Rotax 277	115/253	50-111/ 110-245	55 (101; 63)	more than 173 (322; 200)	Pilot	A. Pod and boom low-wing soaring motor glider ultralight, with V tail. Weight empty 121 kg (267 lb) with ballistic parachute.
Vancraft Copters 7246 North Mohawk Avenue, Portland, Oregon 97203	Lightning Sport Copter	7.01 or 8.53/ 23-0 or 28-0	3.63/ 11-11	Autogyro	One 34.3 kW (46 hp) Rotax 503	114/252	68-100/ 150-220	55 (101; 63)	69-95 (128-177; 80-110)	Pilot	Conforms to FAR Pt 103. Semi-enclosed accommodation.
Volmer Aircraft Box 5222, Glendale, California 91201	VJ-23E Swingwing	9.93/ 32-7	5.31/ 17-5	R, B, D, O	One 7.5 kW (10 hp) McCulloch	54.5/120	45.5-91/ 100-200	n.k.	n.k.	Pilot	P. Foot launched powered sailplane.
Volmer Aircraft	VJ-24W Sunfun	11.13/ 36-6	5.64/ 18-6	R, B, D, O, P	One 11.2 kW (15 hp) Yamaha	75/165	81/180 max	24 (45; 28) cruising	n.k.	Pilot	P. All-metal with fabric covering. Three-axis control. g limit 3.
Weedhopper Inc PO Box 1377, 528 East College Street, Clinton, Mississippi 39056	Weedhopper C	8.53/ 28-0	5.64/ 18-6	Semi-rigid, B, S or D, O	One 20 kW (27 hp) Rotax 277	77/170	n.k.	35 (64; 40) cruising	n.k.	Pilot	K. Assembly 8 h. Weedhopper Inc acquired assets of Weedhopper of Utah Inc. Super Weedhopper version planned with a Rotax 447.
Weedhopper Inc	Weedhopper two-seater	8.53/ 28-0	5.64/ 18-6	Semi-rigid, B, S or D, O	One 34.3 kW (46 hp) Rotax 503	136/300	n.k.	43 (80; 50) cruising	n.k.	Two seats	K. Assembly 15 h. Experimental version planned.

SCWAL Falcon B.2 (Belgium)

Production IPE-06s (Brazil)

Optimum Aircraft Group Optimum 88 (Bulgaria)

Aces High Light Aircraft Cubys (Canada)

Beijing University Mifeng-3C (China)

CCMI A-1B multi-purpose microlight (China) *(Zhang Yi)*

Letov LK-21 Sluka (Czechoslovakia)

Henri Mignet HM-1000 Balerit with float landing gear (France)

Dallach Sunrise II (Germany) *(Mike Jerram)*

Funk FK 9 two-seater (Germany)

Korean Air Blue Sky-3 two-seater (South Korea)

Uhia Canelas Ranger (Spain)

Tamis Motor Industries Yuka (Turkey)

EPA Sky Ranger (Italy)

Janowski J-2 Polonez built by Mr Josef Leniec (Poland) *(Andrzej Glass)*

Antonov T-2 at Farnborough '90 (USSR) *(Peter J. Cooper)*

Hornet Microlights Hornet R (UK)

CGS Hawk Arrow with new glassfibre pod (USA) *(Howard Levy)*

Leading Edge Air Foils Jenny (USA)

T.E.A.M. miniMAX (USA) *(Geoffrey P. Jones)*

Howland Aero Designs H-3 Pegasus (USA) *(Geoffrey P. Jones)*

Quicksilver GT500 tandem two-seater (USA) *(Howard Levy)*

Vancraft Copters Lightning Sport Copter (USA)

SAILPLANES

Sailplanes are presented this year in the form of tables to make the information more readily accessible and pictures are grouped together throughout the section. Each entry runs across a double-page spread.

Company & Address	Model	Class	Wing span m/ft in	Wing aspect ratio	Wing area (gross) m²/sq ft	Length overall m/ft in	Height over tail m/ft in	Weight empty kg/lb	Max T-O weight kg/lb	Power plant
AUSTRIA										
HOAC Flugzeugproduktion und Entwicklung GmbH NA Ottostrasse 5, A 2700 Wiener Neustadt	H-36 Dimona (see 1990-91 *Jane's*)									
HOAC Flugzeugproduktion und Entwicklung GmbH	HK-36 Super Dimona (data for Limbach L 2400 EB engine)	—	16.20/ 53-1¾ or 17.60/ 57-9 with wingtip extensions	17.15 without wingtip extensions	15.30/ 164.69 without wingtip extensions	6.98/ 22-10¾	n.k.	574/ 1,265	770/ 1,697	One 59.7 kW (80 hp) Rotax 912A or 67 kW (90 hp) Limbach L 2400 EB
HOAC Flugzeugproduktion und Entwicklung GmbH	LF 2000 Turbo (see Aircraft section Addenda)									
BRAZIL										
Aeromot-Aeronaves e Motores SA Aeroporto Internacional Salgado F°, Portão 4-90201, Porto Alegre, RS	AMT-100 Ximango	—	17.47/ 57-3¾	16.3	18.70/ 201.3	7.89/ 25-10¾	1.93/ 6-4	600/ 1,323	800/ 1,764	One 59.7 kW (80 hp) Limbach L 2000 EO1
IPE-Industria, Projetos e Estruturas Aeronáuticas Ltda CP 7931, 80021, Curitiba, Paraná	IPE-02b Nhapecan II	—	16.60/ 54-5½	16.0	17.20/ 185-1	8.54/ 28-0¼	1.90/ 6-2¾	340/ 749	560/ 1,234	—
IPE-Industria, Projetos e Estruturas Aeronáuticas Ltda	IPE-04	—	n.k.	n.k.	n.k.	n.k.	n.k.	n.k.	n.k.	One 134 kW (180 hp) Textron Lycoming IO-320
IPE-Industria, Projetos e Estruturas Aeronáuticas Ltda	IPE-05 Quero-Quero III	15 m	15.00/ 49-2½	21.4	10.50/ 113.0	6.70/ 21-11¾	n.k.	120/ 265	240/ 529	—
IPE-Industria, Projetos e Estruturas Aeronáuticas Ltda	IPE-08	—	15.00/ 49-2½	n.k.	n.k.	6.60/ 21-7¾	n.k.	206/ 454	320/ 705	—
CHINA, PEOPLE'S REPUBLIC										
Chengdu Aircraft Corporation PO Box 800, Chengdu, Sichuan	X-7 Jian Fan (Sword Point)	—	13.07/ 42-10½	9.5	18.00/ 193.75	7.06/ 23-2	1.60/ 5-3	220/ 485	370/ 816	—
Shenyang Sailplane Factory No. 17 Shen-Liao East Road, Shenyang 110021	HU-1 Seagull	—	17.00/ 55-9¼	16.4	17.68/ 190.3	7.62/ 25-0	1.73/ 5-8	600/ 1,323	1,050/ 2,315 normal, 900/ 1,984 utility categories	One 86.5 kW (116 hp) Textron Lycoming O-235-N2A

n.k. = not known

Schempp-Hirth Nimbus 4 *(Peter F. Selinger)*

Performance (at max T-O weight except where indicated)

Best glide ratio	at (speed) knots (km/h; mph)	Min sink rate m (ft)/s	at (speed) knots (km/h; mph)	Stalling speed knots (km/h; mph)	Max speed (smooth air) knots (km/h; mph)	Max speed (rough air) knots (km/h; mph)	Max aero-tow speed knots (km/h; mph)	Max winch-launching speed knots (km/h; mph)	Remarks
27	56 (105; 65)	1.16/ 3.81	43 (80; 50)	39 (72; 45)	148 (275; 171) max permissible	—	—	—	Side by side two-seat motor glider. Alternative engines and fuel capacities.
30	54 (100; 62)	0.96/ 3.15	49 (90; 56)	39 (72; 45)	133 (245; 153) unpowered	97 (180; 112) unpowered	—	—	Two seats. Current production version of French Aérostructure (Fournier) RF-10 motor glider. Observation version is **AMT-100R** with dedicated VHF down/up link, underbelly pod for cameras or sensors, etc, and **AMT-100P** is military/police version.
better than 32	48 (88; 55)	0.75/ 2.46 with two crew	38 (70; 43)	37 (68; 43)	108 (200; 124)	n.k.	n.k.	n.k.	Tandem two seats. Prototype plus 79 production Model bs built; 80th being used for modifications leading to IPE-02c Nhapecan III.
n.k.	n.k.	n.k.	n.k.	n.k.	n.k.	n.k.	n.k.	n.k.	Side by side two-seat training and aerobatic motor glider. Prototype only by early 1991.
38 estimated	n.k.	0.69/ 2.26 estimated	42 (78; 48)	38 (70; 44) estimated	151 (280; 174) estimated	n.k.	n.k.	n.k.	Single seat. High performance sailplane project. Upper/lower surface spoilers.
32 estimated	46 (85; 53)	0.66/ 2.17 estimated	39 (72; 45)	33 (60; 38) estimated	n.k.	n.k.	n.k.	n.k.	Single-seat 'world class' sailplane, proposed as successor to KW1b2 Quero-Quero II (see 1989-90 *Jane's*). Prototype may be built in 1991.
12	34 (63; 39)	1.40/ 4.59	32 (60; 37)	25 (45; 28)	81 (150; 93)	54 (100; 62)	n.k.	43 (80; 50)	Tandem two-seat basic training glider. Status unknown. First flown 1966. May be built at Shenyang.
20	n.k.	1.50/ 4.92	43 (80; 50)	46 (85; 53) flaps up	121 (225; 140) max permissible	—	—	—	Side by side two-seat motor glider, primarily for aerial survey, aerial photography and forest patrol.

Company & Address	Model	Class	Wing span m/ft in	Wing aspect ratio	Wing area (gross) m²/sq ft	Length overall m/ft in	Height over tail m/ft in	Weight empty kg/lb	Max T-O weight kg/lb	Power plant
CHINA, PEOPLE'S REPUBLIC *Contd.*										
Shenyang Sailplane Factory	HU-2 Petrel 650B	—	14.92/ 48-11½	11.3	19.63/ 211.29	7.02/ 23-0½	2.14/ 7-0¼	485/ 1,069	750/ 1,653	One 59.7 kW (80 hp) Limbach L 2000 EO1
Shenyang Sailplane Factory	X-9 Jian Fan (Sword Point)	—	14.42/ 47-3¾	11	18.90/ 203.4	7.335/ 24-0¾	2.32/ 7-7¼	230/ 507	380/ 837	—
Shenyang Sailplane Factory	X-10 Qian Jin (Forward)	—	16.00/ 52-6	18.63	13.74/ 147.9	7.625/ 25-0¼	1.605/ 5-3¼	252/ 556	342/ 754	—
CZECHOSLOVAKIA										
Aerotechnik 68604 Uherské Hradiště-Kunovice	L-13SE Vivat	—	17.00/ 55-9¼	13.8	20.20/ 217.4	8.30/ 27-2¾	2.30/ 7-6½	470/ 1,036	690/ 1,521	One 48.5 kW (65 hp) Aerotechnik Mikron III AE
Aerotechnik	L-13SL Vivat	—	17.00/ 55-9¼	14.3	20.20/ 217.4	8.30/ 27-2¾	2.30/ 7-6½	487/ 1,074	720/ 1,587	One 52.2 kW (70 hp) Limbach L 2000 EO1
Aerotechnik	XL-113	—	17.00/ 55-9¼	14.3	20.20/ 217.4	8.30/ 27-2¾	n.k.	n.k.	890/ 1,962	One 58 kW (78 hp)
Let Koncernový Podnik (Let Concern Enterprise)	L-23 Super Blaník	—	16.20/ 53-1¾	13.7	19.15/ 206.1	8.50/ 27-10¾	1.90/ 6-2¾	310/ 683	510/ 1,124	—
VSO Vyvojová Skupina Orličan c/o Orličan Akciová Spoléčuost, 56537 Choceň	VSO 10 Gradient	Standard and Club	15.00/ 49-2½	18.75	12.00/ 129.2	7.00/ 22-11¾	1.38/ 4-6¼	250/ 551	380/ 837	—
FRANCE										
SN Centrair Aérodrome Le Blanc, BP 44, 36300 Le Blanc	101 Club	Club	15.00/ 49-2½	21.4	10.50/ 113.0	6.82/ 22-4½	1.42/ 4-8	245/ 540	455/ 1,003	—
SN Centrair	Pégase A and B	Standard	15.00/ 49-2½	21.4	10.50/ 113.0	6.82/ 22-4½	1.42/ 4-8	Pégase A: 251/ 553. Pégase B: 256/ 564	Pégase A: 455/ 1,003. Pégase B: 505/ 1,113	—
SN Centrair Centrair	Marianne	—	18.55/ 60-10¼	19.9	17.185/ 185.0	9.00/ 29-6½	1.55/ 5-1	430/ 948	650/ 1,433	—
Avions René Fournier Aérodrome d'Athée-Nitray, 37270 Montlouis-sur-Loire	RF-5	—	13.74/ 45-1	12.5	15.12/ 162.8	7.80/ 25-7¼	1.96/ 6-5	420/ 926	650/ 1,433	One 59.7 kW (80 hp) Limbach L 2000 EO1
Issoire-Aviation SA (Groupe Siren) Aérodrome d'Issoire-le-Broc (Puy-de-Dôme), BP No. 1, 63501 Issoire Cédex	PIK-20E2F	15 m	15.00/ 49-2½	22.5	10.00/ 107.6	6.53/ 21-5	1.47/ 4-10	310/ 683	470/ 1,036	One 32 kW (43 hp) Rotax 505 retracting into fuselage
Issoire-Aviation SA	PIK-30	17 m Open	17.00/ 55-9¼	27.2	10.63/ 114.42	n.k.	n.k.	310/ 683	460/ 1,014	One 32 kW (43 hp) Rotax 505 with automatic vertical positioning of propeller when engine stopped

n.k. = not known

Performance (at max T-O weight except where indicated)

Best glide ratio	at (speed) knots (km/h; mph)	Min sink rate m (ft)/s	at (speed) knots (km/h; mph)	Stalling speed knots (km/h; mph)	Max speed (smooth air) knots (km/h; mph)	Max speed (rough air) knots (km/h; mph)	Max aero-tow speed knots (km/h; mph)	Max winch-launching speed knots (km/h; mph)	Remarks
—	—	—	—	38 (70; 44)	73 (135; 84)	—	—	—	Three-seat strut braced cabin motor glider. Gained CAAC C of A. Substantial production.
17	36 (67; 42)	0.96/ 3.15	32 (60; 37)	25 (45; 28)	81 (150; 93)	54 (100; 62)	65 (120; 75)	54 (100; 62)	Tandem two-seat training sailplane, used extensively in China. About 150 built by 1980. Thought still to be in production.
26	38 (70; 43)	0.75/ 2.46	37 (68; 42)	32-33 (58-60; 36-38)	135 (250; 155)	97 (180; 112)	81 (150; 93)	59 (110; 68)	Single-seat high performance club sailplane. Licence built version of Polish SZD-8/14 Jaskolka, modernised with both wood and glassfibre structure.
24	51 (95; 59)	1.1/ 3.61	48 (90; 56)	34 (62; 39) unpowered. 33 (60; 38) powered	124 (230; 143) unpowered	86 (160; 99) unpowered	—	—	Side by side two-seat motor glider; 27 sold in Czechoslovakia, one to Canada and one to Finland.
24	51 (95; 59)	n.k.	n.k.	33 (60; 38)	116 (215; 134)	n.k.	—	—	Side by side two-seat motor glider. First flight 8 August 1990. Certification to JAR 22.
n.k.	n.k.	n.k.	n.k.	n.k.	108 (200; 124)	n.k.	—	—	Seen in European press as L-13SW Vivat with spraygear. Fin extension and more cockpit glazing. Prototype only.
28	46 (85; 53) IAS	0.82/ 2.69	43 (80; 50)	33 (60; 38) IAS	135 (250; 155) IAS	86 (160; 99)	81 (150; 93)	64 (120; 74)	Tandem two-seat training and performance soaring sailplane. Data as two-seater. Meets requirements of OSTIV 1986 and Utility category of JAR 22.
36	49 (90; 56)	0.64/ 2.10	39 (73; 45)	37 (68; 43)	135 (250; 155)	86 (160; 99)	n.k.	65 (120; 75)	Single-seater; 224 delivered to clubs by beginning of 1990 (incl 12 VSO 10C Club Class), when production ended.
38	50 (92; 57)	0.65/ 2.13	39 (72; 45)	n.k.	135 (250; 155)	97 (180; 112)	86 (160; 99)	86 (160; 99)	Single-seater. Basic version of 101/Pégase series, with non-retractable monowheel and no water ballast.
10	Pégase A: 53 (98; 61). Pégase B: 55 (102; 63)	Pégase A: 0.67/ 2.20. Pégase B: 0.65/ 2.13	Pégase A: 43 (80; 50). Pégase B: 45 (83; 51)	n.k.	135 (250; 155)	97 (180; 112)	86 (160; 99)	86 (160; 99)	Single-seater. Pégase A as 101 but with retractable monowheel. Over 400 built. Pégase B as for A, except standard 160 litre (42.3 US gallon; 35.2 Imp gallon) water ballast.
40	57 (105; 65)	0.65/ 2.13	46 (85; 53)	37 (67; 42)	135 (250; 155)	92 (170; 105)	92 (170; 105)	70 (130; 81)	Tandem two-seat sailplane; 250 expected to be acquired for French aero clubs.
n.k.	n.k.	n.k.	n.k.	43 (78; 49)	113 (210; 130) cruising	—	—	—	Tandem two-seat motor glider. Spanish company Aero-Jaen SA (Aerodromo El Curnicabral, 23280 Beas de Segura, Andalucia) is under licence to produce RF-5 in assembled and kit forms. No manufacture in France.
41	63 (117; 73)	0.70/ 2.30	47 (88; 55)	41 (75; 47)	154 (285; 177) unpowered	119 (220; 136) unpowered	105 (195; 121)	67 (125; 78)	Single-seat, self-launching sailplane. 80 kg (176 lb) max water ballast.
45	59 (110; 68)	0.54/ 1.77	41 (75; 47)	38 (70; 44)	n.k.	102 (190; 118)	102 (190; 118)	67 (125; 78)	Based on PIK-20E2F, with removable 1 m long glassfibre wingtips enabling it to qualify for 15 m or 17 m Classes. No longer in production.

Aeromot AMT-100 Ximango side by side two-seat motor glider

HOAC HK-36 Super Dimona

IPE-02b Nhapecan II sailplane

Chengdu X-7 Jian Fan two-seat glassfibre training glider *(Charles M. Gyenes)*

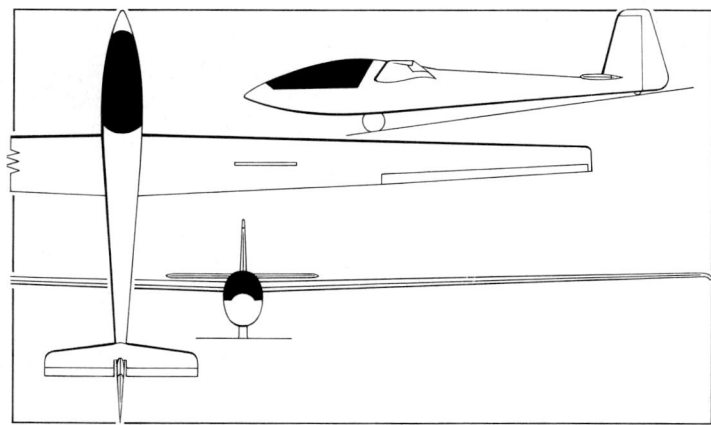

IPE-05 Quero-Quero III *(Jane's/Mike Keep)*

Shenyang HU-2 Petrel 650B cabin motor glider

Shenyang HU-1 Seagull two-seat motor glider carrying aerial survey equipment

Shenyang X-10 Qian Jin single-seat sailplane

Shenyang X-9 two-seat training glider, with enclosed cockpits
(Charles M. Gyenes)

Aerotechnik L-13SL Vivat (Limbach L 2000 EO1 engine and Mühlbauer MTV-1-A propeller *(Vladimir Janik)*

Aerotechnik XL-113 with spraygear

Let L-23 Super Blaník two-seat training sailplane

VSO 10C Club Gradient single-seat Club Class sailplanes

SN Centrair Pégase single-seat Standard Class sailplane

Prototype SN Centrair Marianne two-seat training and aerobatic sailplane

Fournier RF-5 tandem two-seat motor glider

Issoire built PIK-30 self-launching sailplane under power

Stralpes Aéro ST-11 prototype Club Class sailplane

Company & Address	Model	Class	Wing span m/ft in	Wing aspect ratio	Wing area (gross) m²/sq ft	Length overall m/ft in	Height over tail m/ft in	Weight empty kg/lb	Max T-O weight kg/lb	Power plant
FRANCE *Contd.* Sarl La Mouette 1 rue de la Petite Fin, 21121 Fontaine les Dijon	Atlas 21 m	—	10.60/ 34-9¼	5.2	21.5/ 231.4	n.k.	n.k.	42/ 93	350/ 771	n.k.
Sarl La Mouette	Chronos	—	10.00/ 32-9¾	7.1	14.00/ 150.7	n.k.	n.k.	130/ 287	300/ 661	One 47 kW (64 hp)
Stralpes Aéro Sarl BP 14, Aérodrome RN6, 73190 Challes-les-Eaux	ST-11	Club	11.60/ 38-0¾	20.6	6.54/ 70.4	5.55/ 18-2½	1.135/ 3-8¾	110/ 243	230/ 507	—
Stralpes Aéro Sarl	ST-15	15 m	15.00/ 49-2½	22.9	approx 9.80/ 105.5	n.k.	n.k.	240/ 529	440/ 970 with water ballast	—
GERMANY Akademische Fliegergruppe Berlin eV Technische Universität Berlin, Strasse des 17 Juni 135, 1000 Berlin 12	B 13	Open	23.20/ 76-1½	28.5	18.90/ 203.44	8.30/ 27-2¾	1.90/ 6-2¾	520/ 1,146	800/ 1,763	One 24 kW (32 hp) Rotax 377 in nose, with five-blade folding propeller
Akademische Fliegergruppe Braunschweig eV Flughafen Akafliegheim, 3300 Braunschweig	SB-13	Standard	15.00/ 49-2½	19.4	11.60/ 124.86	3.02/ 9-11 fuselage	1.96/ 6-5¼	285/ 628 incl rescue system	425/ 937	—
Akademische Fliegergruppe Darmstadt eV Technische Hochschule, Magdalenenstrasse 8, 6100 Darmstadt	D-41	n.k.	20.00/ 65-7½	28.6	14.00/ 150.7	8.30/ 27-2¾	0.85/ 2-9½	360/ 794	750/ 1,653	—
Akademische Fliegergruppe Hannover eV Welfengarten 1a, 3000 Hannover 1	AFH 24	Standard	15.00/ 49-2½	21.8	10.30/ 110.9	n.k.	n.k.	225/ 496	475/ 1,047	—
Akademische Fliegergruppe Karlsruhe eV Kaiserstrasse 12, 7500 Karlsruhe 1	AK-5	Standard	15.00/ 49-2½	21.1	10.656/ 114.7	6.80/ 22-3¾	1.45/ 4-9	245/ 540	485/ 1,069	—
Akademische Fliegergruppe Stuttgart eV Pfaffenwaldring 35, 7000 Stuttgart 80	Fs-32	15 m	15.00/ 49-2½	22.6	9.94/ 107.0	6.62/ 21-8½	n.k.	260/ 573 estimated	500/ 1,102 estimated	—
Doktor Fiberglas (Ursula Hänle) Postfach 1112, 5438 Westerburg	H 101 Salto	Standard and Club	Aerobatic: 13.30/ 43-7½. Utility optional: 15.50/ 50-10¼	Aerobatic: 20.6. Utility optional: 26.4	Aerobatic: 8.58/ 92.4. Utility optional: 9.10/ 98.0	5.70/ 18-8½	0.80/ 2-7½	Aerobatic: 182/ 401. Utility: 187/ 412	Aerobatic: 280/ 617. Utility: 310/ 683	—
Glaser-Dirks Flugzeugbau GmbH Im Schollengarten 19-20, Postfach 41 47, 7520 Bruchsal 4, Untergrombach	DG-400	—	15.00/ 49-2½ or 17.00/ 55-9¼ with add-on tips	22.5 or 27.3 with add-on tips	10.00/ 107.6 or 10.57/ 113.8 with add-on tips	7.00/ 22-11¾	1.40/ 4-7	305/ 672	480/ 1,058 or 460/ 1,014 with add-on tips	One 32 kW (43 hp) Rotax 505

n.k. = not known

Performance (at max T-O weight except where indicated)

Best glide ratio	at (speed) knots (km/h; mph)	Min sink rate m (ft)/s	at (speed) knots (km/h; mph)	Stalling speed knots (km/h; mph)	Max speed (smooth air) knots (km/h; mph)	Max speed (rough air) knots (km/h; mph)	Max aero-tow speed knots (km/h; mph)	Max winch-launching speed knots (km/h; mph)	Remarks
6	n.k.	1.80/ 5.91	n.k.	21 (38; 24) unpowered	65 (120; 74)	n.k.	—	—	Motor glider. At least 1,200 ordered.
8	33 (60; 38)	1.60/ 5.25	n.k.	25 (45; 28)	70 (130; 80) unpowered	n.k.	—	—	Motor glider. At least 1,000 built.
35	54 (100; 62)	0.65/ 2.13	43 (80; 50)	37 (68; 42)	124 (230; 143)	124 (230; 143)	89 (165; 102)	70 (130; 80)	Single-seat sailplane. Low cost for personal and club use. **ST-11M** powered version detailed in 1986-87 *Jane's*.
41.5	n.k.	n.k.	n.k.	n.k.	n.k.	n.k.	n.k.	n.k.	Single-seat sailplane. First flight 1986.
49	57 (105; 65)	0.55/ 1.80	40 (75; 47)	38 (70; 44)	151 (280; 174)	108 (200; 124)	75 (140; 87)	64 (120; 74)	Side by side two-seat motor glider. First flight was expected early 1991.
41.5	56 (103; 64)	0.58/ 1.90	42 (78; 48)	40 (74; 46) at 350 kg (770 lb) AUW	above 113 (210; 130)	above 113 (210; 130)	91 (170; 105)	81 (150; 93)	Single-seat sailplane. Tailless 'flying wing' design; first flight 1988.
n.k.	n.k.	n.k.	n.k.	n.k.	n.k.	n.k.	n.k.	n.k.	Side by side two-seat sailplane. 200 kg (441 lb) water ballast.
n.k.	n.k.	n.k.	n.k.	n.k.	146 (270; 168) estimated	n.k.	n.k.	n.k.	Single-seat sailplane. First flight expected 1991.
41	51 (95; 59)	0.60/ 1.97	45 (84; 52)	38 (70; 44)	146 (270; 168)	105 (195; 121)	105 (195; 121)	81 (150; 93)	Single-seat sailplane. Flight testing started early 1990; 160 kg (353 lb) max water ballast.
43 estimated	57 (105; 65)	0.60/ 1.97 estimated	46 (85; 53)	33 (60; 38) estimated	135 (250; 155) estimated	n.k.	n.k.	n.k.	Single-seat sailplane. Still under construction in 1991. Fowler type high lift slotted flaps (in two segments) and ailerons.
Aerobatic: 34.5 Utility: 37	51 (94; 58)	0.70/ 2.30 at max weight	39 (72; 45)	Aerobatic: 38 (70; 44). Utility: 34 (62; 39)	Aerobatic: 151 (280; 174). Utility: 135 (250; 155)	Aerobatic: 151 (280; 174). Utility: 135 (250; 155)	81 (150; 93)	70 (130; 81)	Single-seat sailplane. Based on Glasflügel Standard Libelle. Utility category uses either 13.3 m wings or extended to 15.5 m with detachable wingtips.
15 m span: 41. 17 m span: 44	59 (110; 68)	15 m span: 0.60/ 1.97. 17 m span: 0.50/ 1.64	43 (80; 50)	35 (65; 41) or 34 (63; 40) with add-on tips	146 (270; 168) unpowered	102 (190; 118) unpowered	102 (190; 118)	70 (130; 81)	Single-seat self-launching sailplane, developed from DG-202; 277 delivered by end of 1990.

Company & Address	Model	Class	Wing span m/ft in	Wing aspect ratio	Wing area (gross) m²/sq ft	Length overall m/ft in	Height over tail m/ft in	Weight empty kg/lb	Max T-O weight kg/lb	Power plant
GERMANY *Contd.* Glaser-Dirks Flugzeugbau GmbH	DG-500 Elan (data for DG-500/22 Elan, unless stated otherwise)	—	22.00/ 72-2	26.5	18.29/ 196.9	8.66/ 28-5	1.665/ 5-5½	445/ 981	750/ 1,653	DG-500M: One 44.7 kW (60 hp) Rotax 535C
Glaser-Dirks Flugzeugbau GmbH	DG-600 (data for DG-600, unless stated otherwise)	15 m	15.00/ 49-2½ or 17.00/ 55-9¼ with add-on tips	20.5 or 24.9 with add-on tips	10.95/ 117.9 or 11.59/ 124.75 with add-on tips	6.83/ 22-5	1.387/ 4-6½	255/ 562 or 260/ 573 with add-on tips	525/ 1,157	DG-600M: One 18.6 kW (25 hp) Rotax 275
Burkhart Grob Luft- und Raumfahrt GmbH & Co KG Postfach 1257, 8948 Mindelheim	G 103C Twin III (data for Twin III SL, unless stated otherwise)	—	18.00/ 59-0¾	18.5	17.50/ 188.4	8.18/ 26-10	1.55/ 5-1	460/ 1,014	710/ 1,565	One 36.5 kW (49 hp) Rotax 505
Burkhart Grob Luft- und Raumfahrt GmbH	G 109B	—	17.40/ 57-1	15.9	19.00/ 204.5	8.10/ 26-7	1.80/ 5-10¾	620/ 1,367	850/ 1,874	One 67 kW (90 hp) Grob 2500; **RAF Vigilant T.Mk1s** have 56 kW (75 hp) Limbach
Horst Havrda Sedanstrasse 21, 8998 Lindenburg/Allg	SH-2H	Aerobatic	10.40/ 34-1½	9.5	11.40/ 122.7	6.50/ 21-4	1.34/ 4-4¾	240/ 529	340/ 750	—
Jubi GmbH Sportflugzeugbau Robert-Kronfeldstrasse 2, 4811 Oerlinghausen	ASK 13	—	16.00/ 52-6	14.6	17.50/ 188.4	8.18/ 26-9½	1.60/ 5-3	290/ 640	480/ 1,060	—
Klotz	Moka 1	—	18.00/ 59-0¾ or 20.90/ 68-7	n.k.	n.k.	8.28/ 27-2	1.85/ 6-1	n.k.	765/ 1,686	Two Newbold engines; total output believed 74.5 kW (100 hp)
Rolladen-Schneider Flugzeugbau GmbH Postfach 1130, Mühlstrasse 10, 6073 Egelsbach/ Hessen	LS4	Standard	15.00/ 49-2½	21.4	10.50/ 113.0	6.83/ 22-5	1.26/ 4-1½	238/ 525	472/ 1,040	—
Rolladen-Schneider Flugzeugbau GmbH	LS6	15 m	15.00/ 49-2½ (see also Remarks)	21.4	10.50/ 113.0	6.65/ 21-9¾	1.30/ 4-3¼ with tailwheel	250/ 551	525/ 1,157	—
Rolladen-Schneider Flugzeugbau GmbH	LS7	15 m	15.00/ 49-2½	23	9.74/ 104.84	6.66/ 21-10¼	n.k.	235/ 518	486/ 1,071	—

n.k. = not known

Performance (at max T-O weight except where indicated)

Best glide ratio	at (speed) knots (km/h mph)	Min sink rate m (ft)/s	at (speed) knots (km/h; mph)	Stalling speed knots (km/h; mph)	Max speed (smooth air) knots (km/h; mph)	Max speed (rough air) knots (km/h; mph)	Max aero-tow speed knots (km/h; mph)	Max winch-launching speed knots (km/h; mph)	Remarks
47	59 (110; 68)	0.51/ 1.68	41 (75; 47)	31.5 (58; 36)	145 (270; 167)	106 (197; 122)	106 (197; 122)	75 (140; 87)	Two-seat sailplane in **DG-500/22 Elan** and **DG-500 Elan Trainer** forms, and motor glider as **DG-500M**. Elan Trainer has 18.00 m (59 ft 0¾ in) span and 615 kg (1,356 lb) max T-O weight. DG-500M has 22 m wings, 825 kg (1,819 lb) max T-O weight, and retractable engine. Six DG-500/22s, 5 DG-500 Elan Trainers and 12 DG-500Ms delivered by end of 1990.
15 m span: 44.5. 17 m span: 48.5 estimated	n.k.	15 m span: 0.56/ 1.84. 17m span: 0.50/ 1.64 estimated	n.k.	35 (64; 40) estimated	146 (270; 168)	108 (200; 124)	108 (200; 124)	81 (150; 93)	Single-seat sailplane. **DG-600M** is powered version with 440 kg (970 lb) max T-O weight for self-launching and same as DG-600 for tow launch. 50 DG-600s and 15 DG-600Ms delivered by end of 1990. Water ballast in wings (up to 180 kg; 397 lb) and fin (7 kg; 15.4 lb) for DG-600; 120 kg (265 lb) max wing water ballast for DG-600M.
38	57 (106; 66)	0.64/ 2.10	44 (82; 51)	37 (68; 43)	151 (280; 174) Acro	108 (200; 124) Acro and Twin III	100 (185; 115) Acro	75 (140; 87) Acro and Twin III	Twin III SL is tandem two-seat self-launching sailplane. Twin III and Acro are unpowered training/club sailplanes with 600 kg (1,323 lb) max T-O weight (see 1990-91 *Jane's* for further data). 70 Twin III SLs delivered by end of 1990; 30 more expected 1991.
28	62 (115; 71)	1.10/ 3.61	57 (105; 65)	40 (73; 46)	130 (240; 149)	130 (240; 149)	—	—	Side by side two-seat motor glider. RAF purchased **Vigilant T.Mk1s** for Air Cadets.
26	59 (110; 68)	1.05/ 3.44	46 (85; 53)	35 (65; 41)	194 (360; 223)	130 (240; 149)	108 (200; 124)	81 (150; 93)	Single-seat competition sailplane.
28	49 (90; 56)	0.80/ 2.62	38 (70; 43)	33 (61; 38)	108 (200; 124)	76 (140; 87)	76 (140; 87)	54 (100; 62)	Tandem two-seat sailplane. Schleicher ASK 13 built under licence.
n.k.	n.k.	n.k.	n.k.	n.k.	n.k.	n.k.	n.k.	n.k.	Side by side two-seat twin-engined motor glider, conforming to JAR 22. Displayed at Aero 91. Engines retract into fuselage for soaring.
40.5	54 (100; 62)	0.60/ 1.97	40 (75; 47)	37 (68; 43)	146 (270; 168)	97 (180; 112)	97 (180; 112)	70 (130; 81)	Single-seat sailplane. Provision for 140 litres (37 US gallons; 30.8 Imp gallons) water ballast in wings; **LS4-a** can have 160-170 litres (42.3-44.9 US gallons; 35.2-37.4 Imp gallons).
more than 40	n.k.	less than 0.60/ 1.97	n.k.	36 (65; 41)	146 (270; 168)	n.k.	n.k.	n.k.	Single-seat sailplane. 180 kg (397 lb) water ballast. **LS6-a** has 5.5 litre (1.45 US gallon; 1.2 Imp gallon) water tank in fin; **LS6-b** has carbonfibre (instead of foam/glassfibre) wings and optional fin tank; **LS6-17.5** has 17.5 m (57 ft 5 in) wing span.
43	n.k.	n.k.	n.k.	37 (68; 43)	146 (270; 168)	n.k.	n.k.	n.k.	Single-seat sailplane with enhanced handling qualities and good manoeuvrability.

Akaflieg Berlin B 13 side by side two-seat Open Class motor glider before completion

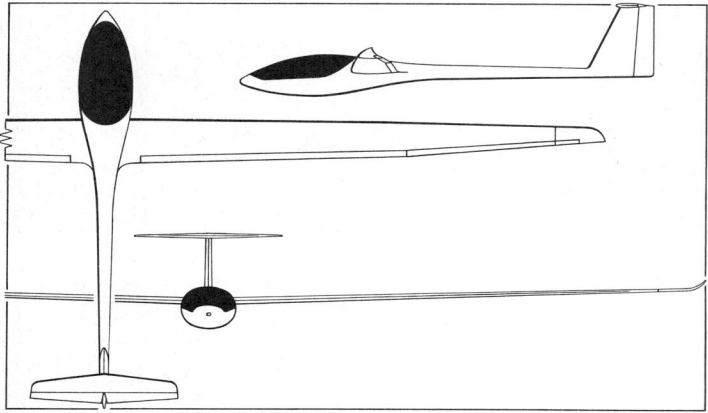

Akaflieg Darmstadt D-41 two-seat sailplane *(Jane's/Mike Keep)*

Akaflieg Karlsruhe AK-5 all-plastics Standard Class sailplane

Hänle (Doktor Fiberglas) H 101 Salto *(Peter F. Selinger)*

Akaflieg Braunschweig SB-13 prototype

Akaflieg Hannover's Standard Class AFH 24 sailplane

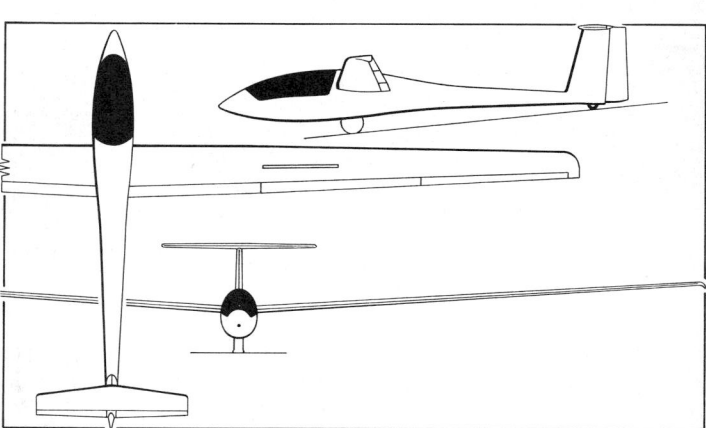

The 15 metre Class Akaflieg Stuttgart Fs-32 *(Jane's/Mike Keep)*

Glaser-Dirks DG-400

Glaser-Dirks DG-500M motor glider

Glaser-Dirks DG-600 with optional winglets to 15 m-span wings
(Peter F. Selinger)

Grob G 103C Twin III SL

RAF Grob G 109B Vigilant T. Mk 1 *(Paul Jackson)*

Havrda SH-2H competition sailplane *(W. Küchberg)*

Schleicher ASK 13, still in production by Jubi at Oerlinghausen
(Peter F. Selinger)

Rolladen-Schneider LS4 Standard Class sailplane *(Avio Data)*

15 m Class Rolladen-Schneider LS6 *(Martin Fricke)*

Rolladen-Schneider LS7 15 metre Class single-seat sailplane

Scheibe SF 25C-2000 two-seat motor glider with tricycle landing gear

Company & Address	Model	Class	Wing span m/ft in	Wing aspect ratio	Wing area (gross) m²/sq ft	Length overall m/ft in	Height over tail m/ft in	Weight empty kg/lb	Max T-O weight kg/lb	Power plant
GERMANY *Contd.* Scheibe Flugzeugbau GmbH August-Pfaltz-Strasse 23, Postfach 1829, 8060 Dachau, near Munich	SF 25C Falke 90	—	15.30/ 50-2½	13.8	18.20/ 195.9	7.60/ 24-11¼	1.85/ 6-0¾	approx 420/ 925	650/ 1,433	One 48.5 kW (65 hp) Limbach SL 1700 EA
Scheibe Flugzeugbau GmbH	SF 25E Super-Falke	—	18.00/ 59-0¾	17.8	18.20/ 195.9	7.50/ 24-7¼	1.85/ 6-0¾	440/ 970	650/ 1,433	One 48.5 kW (65 hp) Limbach SL 1700 EAI or 59.7 kW (80 hp) Limbach L 2000
Scheibe Flugzeugbau GmbH	SF 28A Tandem-Falke (see 1990-91 and 1985-86 *Jane's*)									
Scheibe Flugzeugbau GmbH	SF 34B	—	15.80/ 51-10	17	14.80/ 159.3	7.50/ 24-7¼	1.40/ 4-7	approx 330/ 727	540/ 1,190	—
Schempp-Hirth Flugzeugbau GmbH Krebenstrasse 25, Postfach 14 43, 7312 Kirchheim unter Teck	Discus (data for Discus a, unless stated otherwise)	Standard	15.00/ 49-2½	21.3	10.58/ 113.9	6.35/ 20-10	1.27/ 4-2	228/ 503	525/ 1,157	Discus bT only: One 15.3 kW (20.5 hp) Solo on retractable mount
Schempp-Hirth Flugzeugbau GmbH	Nimbus 3 (data for Nimbus 3 unless stated otherwise)	Open	22.90/ 75-1½	32.2	16.30/ 175.45	7.63/ 25-0½	1.55/ 5-1	392/ 864	750/ 1,653	Nimbus 3T: One Solo engine on retractable mount (removable) as retrieve system
Schempp-Hirth Flugzeugbau GmbH	Nimbus 3D (data for Nimbus 3D, unless stated otherwise)	Open	24.60/ 80-8½	35.9	16.85/ 181.4	8.70/ 28-6½	1.39/ 4-6¾	485/ 1,069	750/ 1,653	Nimbus 3DT: One 19.4 kW (26 hp) Solo 2350 on retractable mount. Nimbus 3DM: One 44.7 kW (60 hp) Rotax 535C on retractable mount
Schempp-Hirth Flugzeugbau GmbH	Nimbus 4 (data provisional)	Open	26.40/ 86-7½	38.8	17.86/ 192.24	7.83/ 25-8¼ fuselage	n.k.	approx 465/ 1,525	750/ 1,653	—
Schempp-Hirth Flugzeugbau GmbH	Janus (data for Janus B, unless stated otherwise)	—	18.20/ 59-8½ or 20.00/ 65-7½ for Janus C	20.0 or 23.0 for Janus C	16.60/ 178.7 or 17.40/ 187.3 for Janus C	8.62/ 28-3¼	1.45/ 4-9	365/ 805 or 355/ 783 for Janus C	620/ 1,366 or 700/ 1,543 for Janus C	Janus CM: One 44.7 kW (60 hp) Rotax 535C on retractable mount. Janus CT: One Solo engine on retractable mount

n.k. = not known

Performance (at max T-O weight except where indicated)

Best glide ratio	at (speed) knots (km/h; mph)	Min sink rate m (ft)/s	at (speed) knots (km/h; mph)	Stalling speed knots (km/h; mph)	Max speed (smooth air) knots (km/h; mph)	Max speed (rough air) knots (km/h; mph)	Max aero-tow speed knots (km/h; mph)	Max winch-launching speed knots (km/h; mph)	Remarks
23–24	n.k.	1.00/ 3.28	n.k.	36 (65; 41)	97 (180; 112)	—	—	—	Side by side two-seat motor glider. **SF 25C-2000** is version with 59.7 kW (80 hp) Limbach L 2000 EA engine.
28–29	46 (85; 53)	0.85/ 2.79	41 (75; 47)	37 (68; 43) unpowered	103 (190; 118) unpowered	103 (190; 118) unpowered	—	—	Side by side two-seat motor glider, developed from former SF 25C-S; 64 delivered by January 1991.
35	51 (95; 59)	0.70/ 2.30	41 (75; 47)	35 (65; 41)	135 (250; 155)	135 (250; 155)	86 (160; 99)	67 (125; 78)	Tandem two-seat training and sporting sailplane. 37 built by January 1991. Produced in Hungary.
43	54 (100; 62)	0.59/ 1.94	42 (78; 49)	36 (66; 41)	135 (250; 155)	108 (200; 124)	97 (180; 112)	81 (150; 93)	Single-seat sailplane; 360 built of all versions by early 1990. Provision for 180 litres (47.6 US gallons; 39.6 Imp gallons) of water ballast. **Discus b** has longer fuselage of Ventus b. **Discus bT** is powered 'Turbo' version (see Power Plant). **Discus CS** built under licence by VSO in Czechoslovakia (b version) since 1990.
55	51 (95; 59)	0.44/ 1.44	40 (75; 47)	33 (60; 38)	146 (270; 168)	108 (200; 124)	97 (180; 112)	81 (150; 93)	Single-seat sailplane; 135 built of all versions by early 1991. **Nimbus 3/24.5** has add-on wingtips (24.5 m; 80 ft 4½ in wing span). **Nimbus 3T** has 'Turbo' engine (see Power Plant). 280 litres (74 US gallons; 61.5 Imp gallons) of water ballast.
57	57 (105; 65)	0.45/ 1.48	43 (80; 50)	42 (77; 48)	148 (275; 171)	102 (190; 118)	97 (180; 112)	81 (150; 93)	Two-seat sailplane, combining modified Janus fuselage with Nimbus 3/24.5 wings and other changes. **3DT** is powered sailplane and **3DM** is self-launching sailplane; 40 Nimbus 3 series built by early 1991. Nimbus 3D water ballast 168 kg (370 lb).
60	59 (110; 68)	0.48/ 1.57	46 (85; 53)	approx 38 (70; 44)	148 (275; 171)	n.k.	n.k.	n.k.	Single-seat sailplane. Powered version has approx 800 kg (1,764 lb) max T-O weight. Water ballast. First flight 11 May 1990. Won German Open Class Nationals and Open Class World Championships for powered sailplanes in 1990.
39.5 or 43.5 for Janus C	59 (110; 68)	0.70/ 2.30 or 0.60/ 1.97 for Janus C	49 (90; 56)	38 (70; 43)	118 (220; 136)	118 (220; 136)	91 (170; 105)	65 (120; 75)	Tandem two-seat training sailplane. **Janus CM** is self-launching version and **Janus CT** has powered retrieve system; 270 Janus sailplanes built by early 1991.

Company & Address	Model	Class	Wing span m/ft in	Wing aspect ratio	Wing area (gross) m²/sq ft	Length overall m/ft in	Height over tail m/ft in	Weight empty kg/lb	Max T-O weight kg/lb	Power plant
GERMANY *Contd.* Schempp-Hirth Flugzeugbau GmbH	Ventus (data for Ventus a, unless stated otherwise)	15 m	15.00/ 49-2½	23.7	9.51/ 102.4	6.35/ 20-10	1.27/ 4-2	approx 240/ 529	525/ 1,157	Ventus bT: One 13.5 kW (18 hp) Solo on retractable mount (removable). Ventus cT: One 15.3 kW (20.5 hp) Solo 'Turbo' (removable). Ventus cM: One 22 kW (29.7 hp) Solo (removable)
Alexander Schleicher GmbH & Co Postfach 60, 6416 Poppenhausen/ Wasserkuppe	ASW 20B and 20 C (weights and performance data for 20B)	15 m	15.00/ 49-2½	21.4	10.50/ 113.0	6.82/ 22-4½	1.45/ 4-9	260/ 573	525/ 1,157	—
Alexander Schleicher GmbH & Co	ASW 20 BL and 20 CL (weights and performance data for BL)	Open	16.59/ 54-5¼	24.9	11.05/ 118.9	6.82/ 22-4½	1.45/ 4-9	265/ 584	430/ 948	—
Alexander Schleicher GmbH & Co	ASK 21	—	17.00/ 55-9¼	16.1	17.95/ 193.2	8.35/ 27-4¾	1.55/ 5-1	360/ 794	600/ 1,323	—
Alexander Schleicher GmbH & Co	ASW 22 B	Open	25.00/ 82-0¼	38.3	16.31/ 175.6	8.10/ 26-7	1.66/ 5-5½	450/ 992	750/ 1,653	—
Alexander Schleicher GmbH & Co	ASW 22 BE	—	25.00/ 82-0¼	38.3	16.31/ 175.6	8.10/ 26-7	1.66/ 5-5½	510/ 1,124	750/ 1,653	One 36 kW (48 hp) Rotax 505A
Alexander Schleicher GmbH & Co	ASK 23	—	15.00/ 49-2½	17.4	12.90/ 138.8	7.05/ 23-1½	1.37/ 4-6	approx 240/ 529	360/ 794	—
Alexander Schleicher GmbH & Co	ASW 24	Standard	15.00/ 49-2½	22.5	10.00/ 107.6	6.55/ 21-6	1.30/ 4-3¼	230/ 507	500/ 1,102	—
Alexander Schleicher GmbH & Co	ASW 24 E	Can be used in Standard Class competition	15.00/ 49-2½	22.5	10.00/ 107.6	6.55/ 21-6	1.37/ 4-6	275/ 606	500/ 1,102	One 18.6 kW (25 hp) Rotax 275
Alexander Schleicher GmbH & Co	ASW 24 TOP	—	15.00/ 49-2½	22.5	10.00/ 107.6	6.55/ 21-6	1.37/ 4-6	approx 270/ 595	500/ 1,102	One 18 kW (24 hp) König SC 430 on retractable mount

n.k. = not known

Performance (at max T-O weight except where indicated)

Best glide ratio	at (speed) knots (km/h; mph)	Min sink rate m (ft)/s	at (speed) knots (km/h; mph)	Stalling speed knots (km/h; mph)	Max speed (smooth air) knots (km/h; mph)	Max speed (rough air) knots (km/h; mph)	Max aero-tow speed knots (km/h; mph)	Max winch-launching speed knots (km/h; mph)	Remarks
43.5	56 (105; 65)	0.58/ 1.90	41 (75; 47)	36 (65; 41)	135 (250; 155)	108 (200; 124)	97 (180; 112)	81 (150; 93)	Single-seat sailplane. **Ventus b/16.6** has detachable wingtip extensions for Open Class. **Ventus c** can have 15 m (with optional winglets), 16.6 m or 17.6 m span wings, two fuselage sizes, extra water ballast in tail fin and more. **Ventus bT** is powered b/16.6 and **Ventus cT** is powered 17.6 m span Ventus c, for self retrieve. **Ventus cM** is self-launching 17.6 m span Ventus c. 500 Ventus built by early 1991.
43 with ballast	65 (120; 75)	0.59/ 1.93 without ballast	45 (84; 52)	35 (65; 41) without ballast	151 (280; 174)	103 (191; 118)	103 (191; 118)	70 (129; 80)	Single-seat sailplane. ASW 20 B has 160 kg (352 lb) of water ballast, 20 C has 120 kg (264 lb).
45 without ballast	48 (90; 56)	0.53/ 1.74	45 (84; 52);	35 (65; 41) without ballast	135 (250; 155)	97 (180; 112)	89 (165; 103)	70 (129; 80)	Single-seat sailplane. Version of ASW 20 with detachable outer wing panels. BL has 50 kg (110 lb) max water ballast.
35	46 (85; 53)	0.65/ 2.13	36 (67; 42)	34 (62; 39)	151 (280; 174)	135 (250; 155)	94 (175; 109)	70 (130; 81)	Tandem two-seat competition and training sailplane. Known as **Vanguard** to UK Air Cadets.
60 without ballast	51 (95; 59)	0.41/ 1.35 without ballast	43 (80; 50)	35 (65; 41) without ballast	151 (280; 174)	102 (190; 118)	102 (190; 118)	75 (140; 87)	Single-seat sailplane. Max water ballast 235 kg (518 lb). About 1,000 tubular apertures (tubulators) in wing underside over 17 m (55 ft 9¼ in) of span to provide a form of boundary layer control and improve performance at higher speeds.
60 without ballast	59 (110; 68)	0.44/ 1.44 without ballast	46 (85; 53)	41 (76; 48) unpowered	151 (280; 174) powered	n.k.	n.k.	n.k.	Self-launching version of ASW 22 B. Two (instead of four) water ballast wing tanks, giving max 120 kg (264 lb).
34	49 (90; 56)	0.66/ 2.17	40 (74; 46)	33 (60; 38)	116 (215; 134)	78 (145; 90)	78 (145; 90)	67 (125; 77)	Single-seat training and performance sailplane. ASK 20 B is suitable for cloud flying and aerobatic manoeuvres in accordance with JAR 22 Category U.
43	57 (105; 65) at 315 kg (694 lb) AUW	0.58/ 1.90	38 (70; 44)	38 (70; 44) at 315 kg (694 lb) AUW	145 (270; 168)	110 (205; 127)	110 (205; 127)	75 (140; 87)	Single-seat sailplane. Max water ballast 170 kg (375 lb).
43	59 (110; 68)	0.62/ 2.03	n.k.	41 (75; 47) powered	145 (270; 168) max permissible, powered	n.k.	—	—	Single-seat self-launching version of ASW 24. Conforms to JAR 22 Category U and preliminary LBA requirements for motor gliders of composite construction. Suited to experienced cross-country pilots or for training, competition, cloud flying and semi-aerobatics.
42	59 (110; 68)	0.62/ 2.03	n.k.	41 (75; 47) powered	145 (270; 168) max permissible, powered	n.k.	—	—	Single-seat self-launching sailplane. Conforms to JAR 22 Category U and preliminary LBA requirements for motor gliders of composite construction. Engine removable.

SF 34B completed at Scheibe's factory in Hungary

Schempp-Hirth Discus bT powered sailplane flown by the Chilean Air Force
(Kenneth Munson)

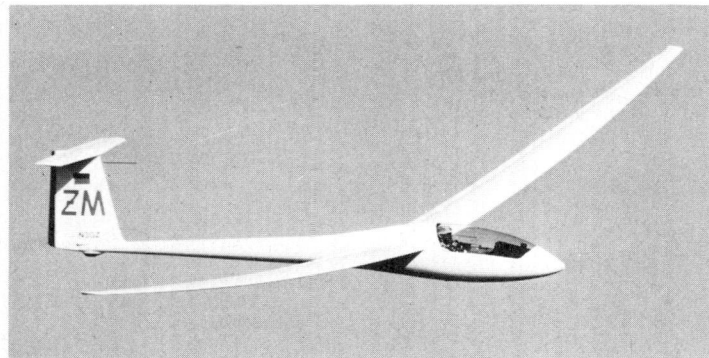

Schempp-Hirth Nimbus 3/24.5 *(Peter F. Selinger)*

Schempp-Hirth Nimbus 3DM *(Peter F. Selinger)*

Schempp-Hirth Janus B flown by the Chilean Air Force *(Kenneth Munson)*

Schempp-Hirth Ventus cM self-launching sailplane *(Peter F. Selinger)*

Schleicher ASW 20 C 15 metre Class sailplane *(Peter F. Selinger)*

Schleicher ASK 21 tandem two-seat sailplane *(Avio Data)*

Schleicher ASW 22 BE motor glider

Schleicher ASW 24 Standard Class sailplane

Stratos 500 non-flying airframe (*Mike Jerram*)

Technoflug Piccolo motor glider

TWI Kiwi with 'TOP' engine installation

Schleicher ASK 23 training and performance sailplane

ASH 25, designed by Schleicher's Martin Heide

Stemme S 10 with propeller deployed, carrying Gepard aerial pods under wings for trials (*Gepard*)

TWI Taifun 17 E II two-seat motor glider

Indian Civil Aviation Dept ATS-1 Ardhra two-seat training sailplane in Indian Air Force markings

Auto-Aero Góbé R-26SU two-seat training sailplane

Company & Address	Model	Class	Wing span m/ft in	Wing aspect ratio	Wing area (gross) m²/sq ft	Length overall m/ft in	Height over tail m/ft in	Weight empty kg/lb	Max T-O weight kg/lb	Power plant
GERMANY *Contd.*										
Alexander Schleicher GmbH & Co	ASH 25 (data for ASH 25 sailplane, unless stated otherwise)	Open	25.00/ 82-0¼	38.3	16.31/ 175.6	9.00/ 29-6¼	1.67/ 5-5¾	450/ 992	750/ 1,653	ASH 25 E: One 18.6 kW (25 hp) Rotax 277 on retractable mount
Alexander Schleicher GmbH & Co	ASH 26 E	—	18.00/ 59-0¾	27.69	11.70/ 125.94	7.55/ 24-9¼ fuselage	n.k.	325/ 716	585/ 1,289	n.k.
Alexander Schleicher GmbH & Co	ASW 27	15 m	15.00/ 49-2½	25.0	9.00/ 96.88	6.55/ 21-6	n.k.	225/ 496	500/ 1,102	—
Stemme GmbH & Co KG Gustav Meyer Allee 25, 1000 Berlin 65	S 10	—	23.00/ 75-5½	28.22	18.74/ 201.7	8.42/ 27-7½	1.79/ 5-10½	approx 635/ 1,400	850/ 1,874	One 70 kW (94 hp) Limbach L 2400
Stratos Unternehmensberatung GmbH Münchner Strasse 19, 8013 Haar b Munich	Stratos 500	—	16.50/ 54-1½	17.6	15.45/ 166.3	6.30/ 20-8	2.35/ 7-8½	445/ 981	680/ 1,499	One 59.7 kW (80 hp) Rotax 912
Technoflug Leichtflugzeugbau GmbH Dr-Kurt-Steim-Strasse 6, 7230 Schramberg 2	Piccolo	—	13.30/ 43-7½	16.6	10.60/ 114.1	6.28/ 20-7¼	1.02/ 3-4¼	180/ 397	297/ 655	One 17 kW (23 hp) Solo 2350 B
TWI Flugzeuggesellschaft mbH Postfach 85, Flugplatz, 7947 Mengen	Taifun 17 E II (Typhoon)	—	17.00/ 55-9¼	16.4	17.60/ 189.4	7.782/ 25-6½	2.30/ 7-6½	610/ 1,345	850/ 1,874	One 67 kW (90 hp) Limbach L 2400 EB1B
TWI Flugzeuggesellschaft mbH	Kiwi	—	15.00/ 49-2½	20.4	11.03/ 118.7	6.80/ 22-3¾	1.46/ 4-9½	205/ 452 without engine	380/ 838 with engine	One 17.9 kW (24 hp) König SC 430 in F + E Fischer 'TOP' retractable installation optional for self-launching
HUNGARY Autó-Aeró Közlekedéstechnikai Vállalat (Automobile and Aeronautical Technical Establishment) Szombathely H-9701 Zanati ut 4	Góbé R-26SU	—	14.00/ 45-11¼	10.9	18.00/ 193.75	9.00/ 29-6⅓	1.96/ 6-5¼	240/ 529	440/ 970	—
INDIA Technical Centre, Civil Aviation Department Opp. Safdarjung Airport, New Delhi 110003	ATS-1 Ardhra	—	16.50/ 54-1½	12.5	21.83/ 235.0	8.61/ 28-3	2.464/ 8-1	328/ 723	508/ 1,120	—
ITALY General Gliders Via Stadera a Poggioreale 62 80143, Naples	940A Zefiro (see Microlight tables)	—	—	—	—	—	—	—	230/ 507	—
NORWAY Lunds Tekniske Vikaveien 2, N-8600 Mo	Silhouette	—	12.50/ 41-0	18.92	8.36/ 90.0	5.87/ 19-3	2.03/ 6-8	271/ 597	374/ 824	One 30 kW (40 hp) Rotax 447 or 37 kW (50 hp) Rotax 503

n.k. = not known

Performance (at max T-O weight except where indicated)

Best glide ratio	at (speed) knots (km/h; mph)	Min sink rate m (ft)/s	at (speed) knots (km/h; mph)	Stalling speed knots (km/h; mph)	Max speed (smooth air) knots (km/h; mph)	Max speed (rough air) knots (km/h; mph)	Max aero-tow speed knots (km/h; mph)	Max winch-launching speed knots (km/h; mph)	Remarks
57	58 (108; 67)	0.45/ 1.48	43 (80; 50)	42-45 (77-84; 48-52)	151 (280; 174)	103 (190; 118)	103 (190; 118)	75 (140; 87)	Two-seat sailplane. Max water ballast 220 kg (485 lb). **ASH 25 E** is motor glider version with Rotax 277 engine but cannot self-launch.
50	about 62 (115; 71)	1.75/ 5.74	108 (200; 124)	39 (71; 45)	151 (280; 174)	n.k.	—	—	Self-launching sailplane. Will also be available without engine.
approx 48	54 (100; 62)	approx 0.52/ 1.71	n.k.	38 (70; 43)	151 (280; 174)	n.k.	n.k.	n.k.	Single-seat sailplane.
50	57 (105; 65)	0.55/ 1.80	n.k.	42 (78; 49) unpowered	145 (270; 167) unpowered	102 (190; 118) unpowered	—	—	Side by side two-seat motor glider. Engine in fuselage aft of seats, driving nose propeller via shaft. Propeller blades fold, being deployed after nosecone is extended forward. Ten sold by June 1991.
27	55 (101; 63)	1.0/ 3.28	46 (86; 53)	39 (72; 45)	135 (250; 155)	—	—	—	Side by side two-seat motor glider.
23	42 (78; 48)	0.90/ 2.95	35 (65; 40)	30 (54; 34) powered	74 (138; 86) powered	—	—	—	Single-seat microlight motor glider. Conforms to JAR 22. Pilot weight range 65-110 kg (144-242 lb). Modified and larger version of Neukom AN-20B.
30	62 (115; 71)	0.95/ 3.12	46 (85; 53)	39 (72; 45) unpowered	135 (250; 155) unpowered	100 (185; 115) unpowered	—	—	Side by side two-seat motor glider. Production by FFT.
37 or 35 with engine	n.k.	0.58/ 1.90 without engine	n.k.	34 (62; 39)	132 (245; 152)	—	n.k.	n.k.	Single-seat sailplane. Optional 'TOP' engine installation for self-launching and power for short periods of flying. Production by FFT.
23.2	43 (80; 50)	0.97/ 3.18	40 (75; 47)	34 (62; 39)	102 (190; 118)	77 (143; 89)	70 (130; 81)	59 (110; 68)	Tandem two-seat training sailplane; 190 built by early 1991.
26	47 (87; 54)	0.78/ 2.56	39 (72; 45)	33 (61; 38)	113 (210; 130)	69 (127; 79)	59 (110; 68)	59 (110; 68)	Tandem two-seat advanced training sailplane. HAL has completed production, but one being built at Technical Centre for Government Gliding Centre.
—	—	—	—	—	—	—	—	—	Single-seat kit built wood/fabric motor glider/sailplane.
almost 25	n.k.	n.k.	n.k.	44 (80; 50) IAS power off	87 (161; 100) IAS cruising	—	—	—	Single-seat Utility category motor glider, based on Silhouette sporting aircraft with wingtip extensions.

Company & Address	Model	Class	Wing span m/ft in	Wing aspect ratio	Wing area (gross) m²/sq ft	Length overall m/ft in	Height over tail m/ft in	Weight empty kg/lb	Max T-O weight kg/lb	Power plant
POLAND										
Politechnika Warszawska Institute of Aeronautics and Applied Mechanics, ul. Nowowiejska 22/24, 00-665 Warsaw	PW-2 Gapa	—	11.00/ 36-1	9.52	12.70/ 136.7	5.50/ 18-0¾	2.45/ 8-0½	110/ 243	220/ 485	—
Politechnika Warszawska	PW-3 Bakcyl	—	14.65/ 48-1¾	12.0	17.50/ 188.37	7.25/ 23-9½	2.50/ 8-2½	220/ 485	420/ 926	—
Politechnika Warszawska	PW-4	—	16.20/ 53-1¾	13.95	18.80/ 202.36	8.00/ 26-3	2.40/ 7-10½	500/ 1,102	720/ 1,587	One 59.7 kW (80 hp) Limbach L 2000 EC1
Swift Ltd c/o Vibrolot Ltd ul. 17 Stycznia 39, 00-906 Warsaw	S-1	—	13.00/ 42-7¾ for aerobatics or 15.00/ 49-2½ with wingtip extensions for cross country flying	n.k.	n.k.	n.k.	n.k.	584/ 1,287	838/ 1,847	—
SZD Przedsiebiorstwo Doświadczalno- Produkcyjne Szybownictwa PZL-Bielsko Ulica Cieszyńska 325, 43-303 Bielsko-Biala 1	SZD-48-3 Jantar Standard 3	Standard	15.00/ 49-2½	21.1	10.66/ 114.7	6.85/ 22-5¾	1.51/ 4-11½	274/ 604	540/ 1,190 with water ballast	—
SZD	SZD-50-3 Puchacz (Eagle Owl)	—	16.67/ 54-8¼	15.3	18.16/ 195.5	8.38/ 27-6	2.04/ 6-8¼	360/ 794	570/ 1,256	—
SZD	SZD-51-1 Junior	Club	15.00/ 49-2½	18	12.51/ 134.7	6.69/ 21-11½	1.57/ 5-1¾	215/ 474	380/ 838	—
SZD	SZD-55 (performance data at 50.5 kg/m²; 10.34 lb/sq ft wing loading)	Standard	15.00/ 49-2½	23.44	9.60/ 103.33	6.85/ 22-5¾	1.47/ 4-10	210/ 463	500/ 1,102	—
SZD	SZD-56	15 m	15.00/ 49-2½	27.6	8.16/ 87.83	6.88/ 22-7	1.35/ 4-5¼	165/ 364	410/ 904	—
WSK Wytwórnia Sprzetu Komunikacyjnego 'PZL-Krosno' 38-400 Krosno, ul. Zwirki i Wigury 6	KR-03A Puchatek	—	16.40/ 53-9¾	13.7	19.44/ 209.25	8.63/ 28-3¾	1.65/ 5-5	350/ 771	540/ 1,190	—
ROMANIA IAR SA Str Aeroportului 1, Căsuta Postală 198, 2200 Braşov	IS-28B2	—	17.00/ 55-9¼	15.8	18.24/ 196.3	8.45/ 27-8¾	1.87/ 6-1½	400/ 882	590/ 1,300	—
IAR SA	IS-28M2A	—	17.00/ 55-9¼	15.8	18.24/ 196.3	7.00/ 22-11½	2.15/ 7-0¾	560/ 1,234	760/ 1,675	One 59.7 kW (80 hp) Limbach L 2000 EO1

n.k. = not known

Performance (at max T-O weight except where indicated)

Best glide ratio	at (speed) knots (km/h; mph)	Min sink rate m (ft)/s	at (speed) knots (km/h; mph)	Stalling speed knots (km/h; mph)	Max speed (smooth air) knots (km/h; mph)	Max speed (rough air) knots (km/h; mph)	Max aero-tow speed knots (km/h; mph)	Max winch-launching speed knots (km/h; mph)	Remarks
6	37 (69; 43)	1.00/ 3.28	31 (58; 36)	27 (49; 31)	81 (150; 93)	64 (120; 74)	64 (120; 74)	54 (100; 62)	Single-seat ultralight sailplane. Produced by Doswiadczalne Warsztaty Lotnicze Konstrukcji Kompozytowych since 1990. First flight of production PW-2 January 1991.
20	49 (90; 56)	1.10/ 3.61	n.k.	30 (55; 34.5)	97 (180; 112)	n.k.	n.k.	n.k.	Two-seat sailplane developed from PW-2. Cannot be spun. Polish certification according to JAR 22 scheduled for 1991. Produced by same organisation as PW-2; two production PW-3s built by early 1991.
20	51 (95; 59)	1.20/ 3.94	46 (85; 53)	38 (70; 44)	n.k.	n.k.	—	—	Two-seat motor glider. First flight 23 December 1990.
30 with 13 m span or 35 with 15 m span	n.k.	n.k.	n.k.	n.k.	172 (320; 199)	n.k.	n.k.	n.k.	Single-seat aerobatic sailplane. Joint Polish/Swiss project. First flown 11 January 1991. Production expected in 1992.
40	66 (123; 76)	0.77/ 2.53	52 (97; 60)	45 (82; 51)	154 (285; 177)	108 (200; 124)	81 (150; 93)	67 (125; 77)	Single-seat sailplane. Provision for 150 litres (39.6 US gallons; 33 Imp gallons) of water ballast; 318 built by 1 January 1991.
30	46 (85; 53)	0.70/ 2.30	40 (75; 47)	33 (60; 38)	116 (215; 133)	86 (160; 99)	81 (150; 93)	59 (110; 68)	Tandem two-seat high performance training sailplane; 246 built by 1 January 1991.
35	43 (80; 50)	0.60/ 1.97	38 (70; 43)	33 (60; 38)	119 (220; 137)	81 (150; 93)	75 (140; 87)	69 (128; 79)	Single-seat sailplane; 170 built by 1 January 1991.
44.1	64 (119; 74)	0.686/ 2.25	54 (100; 62)	46 (84; 53)	137 (255; 158)	105 (195; 121)	n.k.	81 (150; 93)	Single-seat sailplane; 12 built by 1 January 1991.
48.7	60 (112; 70)	0.45/ 1.48 at 28.2 kg/m² (5.78 lb/sq ft) wing loading	39 (72; 45)	34 (63; 39.5)	154 (285; 177)	109 (203; 126)	75 (140; 87)	59 (110; 68)	Single-seat sailplane. First flight 23 November 1990. Prototype only by early 1991. Max water ballast 160 kg (353 lb).
27	n.k.	0.78/ 2.56	n.k.	32 (59; 37) IAS	108 (200; 124) IAS	n.k.	70 (130; 81) IAS	67 (125; 77) IAS	Tandem two-seat basic and advanced training sailplane. Up to 250 may be built for Polish aeroclubs.
34	54 (100; 62)	0.78/ 2.56	46 (85; 53)	39 (72; 45)	124 (230; 143)	91 (169; 105)	76 (140; 87)	59 (110; 68)	Tandem two-seat training and aerobatic sailplane. Over 385 built. Performance data as two-seater.
27	54 (100; 62)	1.20/ 3.94	43 (80; 50)	36 (66; 41) unpowered, flaps down	113 (210; 130) VNE	95 (177; 110) unpowered	—	—	Two-seat motor glider version of IS-28B2, with airframe changes. Undergoing French certification.

General Gliders (Iannotta) 940A Zefiro microlight motor glider/sailplane

Politechnika Warszawska PW-2 Gapa lightweight single-seat sailplane
(Robert Senkowski)

SZD-48-3 Jantar Standard 3 single-seat sailplane

SZD-55 single-seat Standard Class sailplane *(Wojciech Gorgolewski)*

Lunds Tekniske Silhouette in motor glider form

Politechnika Warszawska PW-3 Bakcyl two-seat sailplane *(W. Gorgolewski)*

SZD-50-3 Puchacz two-seat training sailplane

SZD-51-1 Junior Club Class sailplane

Production version of the PZL-Krosno KR-03A Puchatek sailplane

IAR IS-28M2A two-seat motor glider

Danish registered IAR IS-30 two-seat sailplane *(Peter F. Selinger)*

IAR IS-32 Open Class sailplane *(Air Photo Supply)*

Celair Celstar GA-1 aerobatic competition sailplane in inverted flight
(Peter F. Selinger)

IAR IS-28B2 tandem two-seat high performance training sailplane

IAR IS-29D2 single-seat sailplane

IAR IAR-35 Acro at Farnborough '90 *(Peter J. Cooper)*

Radab Windex 1200 powered sailplane

Company & Address	Model	Class	Wing span m/ft in	Wing aspect ratio	Wing area (gross) m²/sq ft	Length overall m/ft in	Height over tail m/ft in	Weight empty kg/lb	Max T-O weight kg/lb	Power plant
ROMANIA *Contd.*										
IAR	IS-29D2	Standard (IS-29D2 Club is Club Class version)	15.00/ 49-2½	21.6	10.40/ 111.9	7.30/ 23-11½	1.58/ 5-2¼	240/ 529	360/ 793	—
IAR	IS-30	—	17.00/ 55-9¼	15.8	18.24/ 196.3	8.45/ 27-8¾	2.27/ 7-5½	400/ 882	590/ 1,300	—
IAR	IS-32	Open	20.00/ 65-7½	27.25	14.68/ 158.0	8.36/ 27-5¼	2.27/ 7-5½	400/ 882	590/ 1,300	—
IAR	IAR-35 Acro	—	12.00/ 39-4½	13.3	10.80/ 116.2	6.47/ 21-2¾	1.72/ 5-7¾	270/ 595	380/ 838	—
SOUTH AFRICA Celair Manufacturing and Export (Pty) Ltd PO Box 77, Ermelo 2350, Transvaal	Celstar GA-1	—	11.20/ 36-9	10.9	11.54/ 124.22	6.50/ 21-4	1.65/ 5-5	265/ 584	385/ 849	—
SWEDEN AB Radab PO Box 92054, S-12006 Stockholm	Windex 1200C	—	12.10/ 39-8½	19.75	7.41/ 79.8	4.92/ 16-1¾	1.14/ 3-9	150/ 331	310/ 683 Utility. 250/ 551 Aerobatic	One 18.6 kW (25 hp) Radab
UNION OF SOVIET SOCIALIST REPUBLICS Oleg K. Antonov Design Bureau Kiev	Junior-1	—	10.56/ 34-7¾	7.3	15.60/ 167.92	5.60/ 18-4½	2.10/ 6-10¾	85/ 187	175/ 386	—
ESAG (Eksprimentine Sportines Avicijos Gamykla: Experimental Sport Aviation Plant) Pociūnai, Prienai, Lietuvos TSR (Lithuania)	LAK-12 Lietuva (Lithuania)	Open	20.42/ 67-0	28.5	14.63/ 157.5	7.23/ 23-8½	1.92/ 6-3½	360/ 794	650/ 1,433 with water ballast	—
ESAG	LAK-12 Lietuva 2R	Open	20.42/ 67-0	28.5	14.63/ 157.5	7.73/ 25-4¼	1.92/ 6-3½	400/ 882	690/ 1,521 with water ballast	—
ESAG	LAK-16	—	9.66/ 31-8¼	11.6	8.05/ 86.65	5.38/ 17-7¾	n.k.	88/ 194	175/ 386	—
SSAKTB (Specialus Sportines Avicijos Konstravimo-Technologinis Biuras: Special Sport Aviation Design and Technology Bureau) Pociūnai, Prienai, Lietuvos TSR (Lithuania)	SL-2P	Flying laboratory (see 1988-89 *Jane's*)	—	—	—	—	—	—	—	—
Oškinis	BRO-23KR Garnys (Stork)	—	8.20/ 26-10¾	6.5	10.40/ 111.9	6.40/ 21-0	2.20/ 7-2½	83.5/ 184	158.5/ 349	—
UNITED STATES OF AMERICA Advanced Aviation Inc 323 North Ivey Lane, Orlando, Florida 32811	Sierra	—	11.87/ 38-11½	11	12.17/ 131.0	6.57/ 21-6½	n.k.	70/ 155	181/ 400	—
Marske Aircraft Corporation 130 Crestwood Drive, Michigan City, Indiana 46360	Monarch	—	12.80/ 42-0	9.5	17.19/ 185.0	3.71/ 12-2	2.39/ 7-10	100/ 220	204/ 450	—

n.k. = not known

Performance (at max T-O weight except where indicated)

Best glide ratio	at (speed) knots (km/h; mph)	Min sink rate m (ft)/s	at (speed) knots (km/h; mph)	Stalling speed knots (km/h; mph)	Max speed (smooth air) knots (km/h; mph)	Max speed (rough air) knots (km/h; mph)	Max aero-tow speed knots (km/h; mph)	Max winch-launching speed knots (km/h; mph)	Remarks
37	50 (93; 58)	0.65/ 2.13	42 (78; 48)	36 (65; 41) flaps down	121 (225; 140)	93 (172; 107)	76 (140; 87)	70 (130; 81)	Single-seat sailplane; 215 IS-29D2s built by early 1990. **IS-29D2 Club** is Club Class version, without flaps and featuring non-retractable monowheel. Small number built.
33	54 (100; 62)	0.78/ 2.56	46 (85; 53)	41 (75; 47)	121 (225; 140)	86 (160; 99)	n.k.	67 (125; 78)	Tandem two-seat sailplane. Based on IS-28B2. No water ballast.
44.5	59 (110; 68)	0.62/ 2.03	49 (90; 56)	43 (78.5; 49)	105 (195; 121)	87 (161; 100)	76 (140; 87)	59 (110; 68)	Tandem two-seat sailplane. Developed from IS-28B2. No water ballast.
27	51 (95; 59)	0.85/ 2.79	46 (85; 53)	44 (80; 50)	205 (380; 236) VNE	109 (202; 125) estimated	n.k.	n.k.	Single-seat aerobatic and general-purpose sailplane. All-metal. Designed to JAR 22 requirements.
25	n.k.	0.90/ 2.95	n.k.	43 (78.5; 49)	161 (298; 185)	n.k.	n.k.	n.k.	Single-seat aerobatic competition sailplane; ± 10 g design. First flight 9 July 1989; 7 ordered by early 1991 (3 delivered).
38	54 (100; 62)	0.65/ 2.13	41 (75; 47)	35 (65; 41)	146 (270; 168) powered	109 (202; 125) unpowered	97 (180; 112)	—	Single-seat kit-built powered sailplane. Assembled aircraft may become available in 1992. Designed to JAR 22 Aerobatic requirements; +7/−5 g limits.
16.2	n.k.	0.95/ 3.12	n.k.	n.k.	48 (90; 56)	n.k.	n.k.	n.k.	Single-seat very basic strut braced sailplane.
48	61 (113; 70)	0.50/ 1.64	46 (85; 53)	36 (65; 41)	135 (250; 155)	n.k.	75 (140; 87)	n.k.	Single-seat sailplane. Lietuva in original form was first Soviet all-composites sailplane. Provision for 190 litres (50 US gallons; 41.8 Imp gallons) of water ballast.
48	62 (115; 71)	0.50/ 1.64	43 (80; 50)	38 (70; 44)	135 (250; 155)	94 (175; 108)	75 (140; 87)	n.k.	Two-seat version of Lietuva. Reinforced fuselage with modified control system, and other changes. Provision for 100 litres (26.4 US gallons; 22 Imp gallons) of water ballast.
12	29 (54; 34)	1.20/ 3.94	n.k.	26 (48; 30)	52 (96; 59)	n.k.	n.k.	n.k.	Single-seat primary training sailplane. Open fuselage frame. Production may have begun in 1987.
—	—	—	—	—	—	—	—	—	—
15	n.k.	1.00/ 3.28	n.k.	23 (42; 27)	54 (100; 62)	n.k.	n.k.	n.k.	Single-seat primary training sailplane.
approx 20	30 (56; 35)	0.86/ 2.83	n.k.	23 (42; 27)	n.k.	n.k.	n.k.	n.k.	Single-seat lightweight sailplane. Kit requiring 80 hours to assemble or ready assembled.
19	35 (64; 40)	0.82/ 2.70	26 (48; 30)	21 (39; 24)	61 (113; 70)	43 (80; 50)	43 (80; 50)	43 (80; 50)	Single-seat ultralight sailplane. Plans and kits available. Pilot weight range 45-104 kg (100-230 lb). Resistant to stalls and spins.

Company & Address	Model	Class	Wing span m/ft in	Wing aspect ratio	Wing area (gross) m²/sq ft	Length overall m/ft in	Height over tail m/ft in	Weight empty kg/lb	Max T-O weight kg/lb	Power plant
UNITED STATES OF AMERICA *Contd.*										
Marske Aircraft Corporation	Pioneer II	—	12.98/ 42-7	12.6	13.38/ 144.0	3.81/ 12-6	1.98/ 6-6	Pioneer II-C: 163/ 360	Pioneer II-C: 295/ 650	—
Jim Maupin Ltd Star Route 3, PO Box 4300-37, 24201 Rowel Court, Tehachapi, California 93561-9803	Carbon Dragon	—	13.41/ 44-0	12.9	13.94/ 150.0	approx 6.10/ 20-0	n.k.	66/ 145	136-152/ 300-335	—
Jim Maupin Ltd	Windrose (data for 12.65 m; 41 ft 6 in span version)	—	12.65/ 41-6	17.9	8.92/ 96.0	6.58/ 21-7	1.68/ 5-6	232/ 512	317-335/ 700-740	One 24.6 kW (33 hp) Cuyuna ULII-02
Jim Maupin Ltd	Woodstock One (data for 11.89 m; 39 ft span version)	—	11.89/ 39-0	14.5	9.73/ 104.7	5.87/ 19-3	1.30/ 4-3	111/ 245	206/ 455	—
Michna	Lite-N-Nite	n.k.	n.k.	n.k.	n.k.	n.k.	n.k.	n.k.	n.k.	n.k.
Schweizer Aircraft Corporation PO Box 147, Elmira, New York 14902	SGS 1-36 Sprite	—	14.07/ 46-2	15.1	13.07/ 140.72	6.27/ 20-7	1.45/ 4-9	215/ 475	322/ 710	—
Schweizer Aircraft Corporation	SGS 2-33A	—	15.54/ 51-0	11.8	20.39/ 219.48	7.85/ 25-9	2.83/ 9-3½	272/ 600	472/ 1,040	—
Schweizer Aircraft Corporation	SGM 2-37	—	18.14/ 59-6	18.1	18.18/ 195.71	8.38/ 27-6	2.37/ 7-9½	572/ 1,260	839/ 1,850	One 83 kW (112 hp) Textron Lycoming O-235-L2C or 112 kW (150 hp) O-320-E26 or 134 kW (180 hp) O-360-A
Prof Alex Strojnik 2337 East Manhatton Drive, Tempe, Arizona 85282	S-2A (data for S-2 prototype with Kohler K 340-2AX engine)	—	15.00/ 49-2½	19.1	11.80/ 127.0	6.88/ 22-7	1.65/ 5-5	280/ 617	444/ 980	One Kawasaki 440, or König SD 570, or Rotax 447
YUGOSLAVIA Elan Tovarna Športnegaorodja N.Sol.O Begunje 1, 64275 Begunje na Gorenjskem	DG-10 Elan (see 1989-90 *Jane's*)									

n.k. = not known

Performance (at max T-O weight except where indicated)

Best glide ratio	at (speed) knots (km/h; mph)	Min sink rate m (ft)/s	at (speed) knots (km/h; mph)	Stalling speed knots (km/h; mph)	Max speed (smooth air) knots (km/h; mph)	Max speed (rough air) knots (km/h; mph)	Max aero-tow speed knots (km/h; mph)	Max winch-launching speed knots (km/h; mph)	Remarks
35	52 (97; 60)	0.70/ 2.30	39 (72; 45)	31 (57; 35)	113 (209; 130)	113 (209; 130)	87 (161; 100)	61 (113; 70)	Single-seat sailplane. Plans available for amateur construction. Resistant to stalls and spins. **Pioneer II-D** is similar to II-C except has sweptback tail and modified wing leading-edge.
25	n.k.	0.51/ 1.67	n.k.	n.k.	n.k.	n.k.	—	—	Single-seat foot-launchable sailplane; 100 sets of plans sold to amateur constructors in Australia and USA by early 1991.
29	45 (84; 52)	0.70/ 2.30	40 (74; 46)	n.k.	114 (212; 132) at 317 kg (700 lb) AUW	87 (161; 100) at 317 kg (700 lb) AUW	—	—	Single-seat self-launching sailplane; 220 sets of plans sold to amateur constructors by early 1991; 14.88 m (48 ft 10 in) wings optional, coupled with use of 34.3 kW (46 hp) Rotax 503 engine (best glide ratio 38).
24	39 (72; 45)	0.79/ 2.60	35 (64; 40)	28 (52; 32)	87 (161; 100)	68 (125; 78)	56 (105; 65)	56 (105; 65)	Single-seat sailplane; 535 sets of plans sold to amateur constructors by early 1991. 13 m wing span available.
n.k.	n.k.	n.k.	n.k.	n.k.	n.k.	n.k.	n.k.	n.k.	Single-seat powered sailplane (see illustration).
31	46 (85; 53)	0.68/ 2.25	36 (68; 42)	31 (57; 35)	105 (195; 121)	105 (195; 121)	105 (195; 121)	68 (126; 78)	Single-seat multi-purpose sailplane, intended in part as Club Class type. **36903-1** and **36903-3** versions, latter recommended for school and club use where sturdiness and ease of ground handling are important considerations.
22.25	45 (84; 52) with two crew	0.95/ 3.10 with two crew	37 (68; 42)	31 (57; 35) with two crew	85 (158; 98)	85 (158; 98)	85 (158; 98)	60 (111; 69)	Tandem two-seat training sailplane. **2-33AK** is a kit version for amateur construction.
22	54 (100; 62)	1.16/ 3.80	52 (97; 60)	44 (81; 50)	115 (214; 133) unpowered	88 (162; 101) unpowered	—	—	Two-seat motor glider. At least 11 delivered to USAF Academy as **TG-7A**s. See also main Aircraft section for **SA 2-37A**.
34	48 (88; 55)	0.67/ 2.20	35 (64; 40)	33 (62; 38) flaps down	129 (240; 149) unpowered	87 (161; 100) unpowered	—	—	Single-seat motor glider. Plans and partial kits are available.

Company & Address	Model	Class	Wing span m/ft in	Wing aspect ratio	Wing area (gross) m²/sq ft	Length overall m/ft in	Height over tail m/ft in	Weight empty kg/lb	Max T-O weight kg/lb	Power plant
YUGOSLAVIA *Contd.*										
Elan Tovarna Športnegaorodja N.Sol.O	DG-300 Elan	Standard	15.00/ 49-2½	21.9	10.27/ 110.5	6.80/ 22-3¾	1.40/ 4-7	245/ 540	525/ 1,157	—
Jastreb Fabrika Aviona Jedrilica (Jastreb Aircraft and Sailplane Factory) ul. Podrvsanska 17, 26300 Vršac	Standard Cirrus 75-VTC	Standard and Club	15.00/ 49-2½	22.5	10.00/ 107.6	6.41/ 21-8½	1.32/ 4-4¾	220/ 485	390/ 860 with water ballast	—
Jastreb Fabrika Aviona Jedrilica	Standard Cirrus G/81	See Remarks	—	—	—	—	—	—	—	—
Jastreb Fabrika Aviona Jedrilica	VUK-T	—	15.00/ 49-2½	15	15.00/ 161.5	6.50/ 21-4	1.35/ 4-5¼	245/ 540	355/ 782	—

n.k. = not known

LAK-12 Lietuva 2R two-seat sailplane

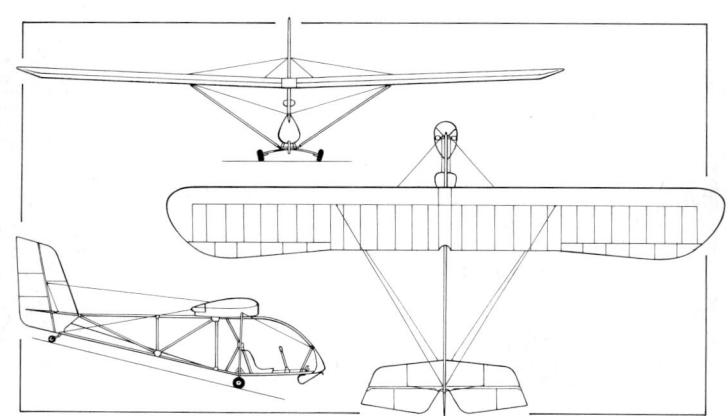

LAK-16 single-seat training glider *(Michael A. Badrocke)*

Advanced Aviation Sierra single-seat sailplane *(Geoffrey P. Jones)*

Oškinis BRO-23KR primary training glider (reproduced from *Krilya Rodini*)

Performance (at max T-O weight except where indicated)

Best glide ratio	at (speed) knots (km/h; mph)	Min sink rate m (ft)/s	at (speed) knots (km/h; mph)	Stalling speed knots (km/h; mph)	Max speed (smooth air) knots (km/h; mph)	Max speed (rough air) knots (km/h; mph)	Max aero-tow speed knots (km/h; mph)	Max winch-launching speed knots (km/h; mph)	Remarks
42	66 (122; 76) at 50 kg/m² (10.24 lb/sq ft) wing loading	0.59/ 1.94	39 (72; 45) at 32 kg/m² (6.55 lb/sq ft) wing loading	35 (65; 41) at 32 kg/m² (6.55 lb/sq ft) wing loading	147 (270; 168)	108 (200; 124)	108 (200; 124)	70 (130; 80)	Single-seat sailplane. Joint design by Elan and Glaser-Dirks; 476 ordered by end of 1990. Provision for 130 or 190 litres (34.3 or 50.2 US gallons; 28.6 or 41.8 Imp gallons) of water ballast in wings; optional 5.5 litre (1.5 US gallon; 1.2 Imp gallon) fin tank. Latest **DG-300 Club Elan** has non-retractable monowheel, no water ballast and no boundary layer distribution system.
38.5	49 (90; 56)	0.57/ 1.87	38 (70; 44)	34 (62; 39)	119 (220; 137)	119 (220; 137)	81 (150; 93)	65 (120; 75)	Single-seat sailplane designed by Schempp-Hirth. Licence manufacture in Yugoslavia since 1979. Provision for 60 kg (132 lb) of water ballast.
—	—	—	—	—	—	—	—	—	Developed by Jastreb from Standard Cirrus 75-VTC. Differences are no fixed monowheel option, new canopy, roomier cockpit, variable incidence T tailplane with separate elevator.
37.5	51 (95; 59)	0.65/ 2.13	42 (78; 49)	32 (59; 37)	129 (240; 149)	81 (150; 93)	70 (130; 80)	65 (120; 75)	Single-seat advanced training sailplane. Plastics stressed-skin construction and supercritical wing section. Cleared for cloud flying, aerobatics and spinning. No water ballast.

Marske Monarch E single-seat homebuilt glider

Marske Pioneer II-C homebuilt sailplane

Michna Lite-N-Nite powered sailplane *(J. M. G. Gradidge)*

Maupin Carbon Dragon foot launchable homebuilt glider

Rotax engined Maupin Windrose self-launching sailplane flying in Indonesia

Maupin Woodstock One homebuilt sailplane

Schweizer SGS 1-36 Sprite training and club sailplane (36903-3 version)

Schweizer SGS 2-33A two-seat general purpose sailplane
(Neil A. Macdougall)

Schweizer TG-7A (SGM 2-37) in service with the US Air Force Academy

First homebuilt Strojnik S-2A, constructed by Mr Thomas Sweeney of Salt Lake City, Utah, USA

Elan/Glaser-Dirks DG-300 Standard Class sailplane

Jastreb Standard Cirrus G/81, developed from the 75-VTC

Jastreb VUK-T all-plastics training sailplane

HANG GLIDERS

CONTRACTORS' ADDRESSES:

Country	Company	Address	Telephone/Fax/Telex
Australia	Moyes Delta Gliders Pty Ltd	173 Bronte Road, Waverley, Sydney, NSW 2024	Tel: 61 (2) 387 5114 Fax: 61 (2) 387 4472 Telex: 10101 INTSY AA
Austria	Steinbach-Delta Fun-Air GesmpH	6370 Kitzbühel/Tyrol, Achenweg 30	Tel: 43 (5356) 71233 Fax: 43 (5356) 72208
	VEGA-Drachenbau Pawel Wierzbowski	4563 Micheldorf, Hauptstrasse 43	Tel: 43 (7582) 4081 Fax: 43 (7582) 51259
Bulgaria	Optimum Aircraft Group	PO Box 74, 1404 Sofia	—
	Skraidykles	—	—
France	Aerotec SARL	68830 Oderen 21	Tel: 33 89 82 10 79
	SARL La Mouette	1 rue de la Petite Fin, 21 121 Fontaine les Dijon	Tel: 33 80 56 66 47 Fax: 33 80 55 42 01 Telex: 350 053 F
Germany	Drachen Studio Kecur GmbH	Zechenweg 9, 5603 Wülfrath	Tel: 49 (2058) 3000
	Finsterwalder GmbH	Pagodenburgstrasse 8, 8000 Munich 60	Tel: 49 (89) 811 65 28 Fax: 49 (89) 814 41 07
	Firebird Schweiger KG	Postfach 28, Hitzleriederstrasse 15, 8959 Seeg/Allgäu	Tel: 49 (8364) 1078/1079 Fax: 49 (8364) 1294 Telex: 541412
	Günter Rochelt	HBK, Lerchenfeld 2, 2000 Hamburg 76	Tel: 49 (40) 2984 3295 or 3233
	Thalhofer Team	Sudetenstrasse 10, 7449 Neckartenzlingen	Tel: 49 (7127) 187 95
	Wills Wing Deutschland (see USA for aircraft)	Am Burgblick 5, 7070 Schwäbisch Gmünd	Tel: 49 (7171) 40769 4945
Italy	Polaris Srl	Valdichiascio-Gubbio, (Perugia)	Tel: 39 (75) 92002930 Fax: 39 (75) 92003435 Telex: 564006 POLARE I
Poland	Akademicki Ośrodek Konstrukcyjny (AOK: Academic Design Centre)	Wydzial Doświadczalny Kompozytów Polimerowych ('Kompol'), Instytut Inżynierii Materiałowej Politechniki Warszawskiej, ul. Narbutta 85, 02-524 Warszawa	Tel: 48 (22) 250633
	Instytut Lotnictwa (Aviation Institute)	Al. Krakowska 110/114, 02-256 Warszawa-Okecie	Tel: 48 (22) 460011 and 460993 Telex: 813537
Switzerland	Swiss Aerolight	PO Box 22, Pt Lancy 1, CH-1213 Geneva	Tel: 41 (22) 793 3722
Union of Soviet Socialist Republics	O. K. Antonov Design Bureau	Kiev	
	Onpo Technologia	Obninsk	
United Kingdom	Airwave Gliders Ltd	Elm Lane, Shalfleet, Newport, Isle of Wight PO30 4JY	Tel: 44 (983) 78611 Fax: 44 (983) 78552 Telex: 869188 GLIDER G
	Pegasus Transport Systems Ltd/ Solar Wings Ltd	56 George Lane, Marlborough, Wiltshire SN8 4BY	Tel: 44 (672) 55066 Fax: 44 (672) 54492 Telex: 449 703
United States of America	Delta Wing Aviation	PO Box 483, Van Nuys, California 91408	Tel: 1 (818) 787 6000 Telex: 65-1425
	Pacific Airwave Inc	PO Box 4384, Salinas, California 93912	Tel: 1 (408) 422 2299 Fax: 1 (408) 758 3270 Telex: 4944863 PACWIN
	Seedwings	41 Aero Camino, Santa Barbara, California 93117	Tel: 1 (805) 968 7070 Fax: 1 (805) 968 0059
	UP Inc (Ultralite Products)	PO Box 659, Temecula, California 92390	Tel: 1 (714) 676 5652 Telex: 910 332 1306
	Volmer Aircraft	PO Box 5222, Glendale, California 91201	Tel: 1 (818) 247 8718
	Wills Wing Inc	1208 Unit H, East Walnut, Santa Ana, California 92701	Tel: 1 (714) 547 1344/6366 Fax: 1 (714) 547 0972

RIGID AND FLEXIBLE WING DATA

Manufacturer and Model	Rigid: R Flexwing: F	FAI or other class	Span: m/ft-in	Leading-edge (flexwing): m/ft-in	Length (rigid); Keel (flexwing): m/ft-in	Nose/Billow angle (flexwing): degrees
AUSTRALIA						
Moyes Delta						
Mars 150	F	1	8.84/29-0	5.10/16-9	2.54/8-4	125/0.5
Mars 170	F	1	9.45/31-0	5.51/18-1	2.62/8-7	125/0.5
Mars 190	F	1	10.06/33-0	5.87/19-3	2.74/9-0	125/0.5
GTR 148	F	1	9.75/32-0	4.80/15-9	1.98/6-6	130/0-1.5
GTR 162	F	1	10.36/34-0	5.14/16-10½	3.57/11-8½	130/0-1.5
GTR 175	F	1	10.97/36-0	5.49/18-0	2.13/7-0	130/0-1.5
GTR 210	F	1	10.97/36-0	5.49/18-0	2.90/9-6	130/0-1.5
Mission 170	F	1	9.55/31-4	5.51/18-1	2.62/8-7	125/0.5
AUSTRIA						
Steinbach-Delta Fun-Air						
Chiron 22	F	3 & 4 (DHV)	8.30/27-2¾	n.k.	n.k.	n.k.
Chiron 25	F	3 & 4 (DHV)	9.20/30-2¼	n.k.	n.k.	n.k.
Chiron 28	F	3 & 4 (DHV)	10.1/33-1½	n.k.	n.k.	n.k.
Condor 5+	F	n.k.	8.10/26-7	n.k.	3.10/10-2	n.k.
Divine 100	n.k.	n.k.	9.35/30-8	n.k.	n.k.	133/n.k.
Divine 200	n.k.	n.k.	9.35/30-8	n.k.	n.k.	135/n.k.
Euro III	F	n.k.	9.40/30-10	n.k.	n.k.	132/n.k.
Fun Air	F	n.k.	9.30/30-6¼	n.k.	n.k.	n.k.
Para Fun1	F	n.k.	9.10/29-10¼	n.k.	3.35/11-0	n.k.
Para Fun	F	n.k.	n.k.	n.k.	n.k.	n.k.
Para Safe	F	n.k.	n.k.	n.k.	n.k.	n.k.
SP	F	n.k.	10.40/34-1½	n.k.	n.k.	128/n.k.
SP Vario	F	n.k.	10.50/34-5½	n.k.	n.k.	126-130/n.k.
VEGA						
16/PR	F	1	10.50/34-5½	5.80/19-0¼	n.k.	132/n.k.
Alfa	F	1	9.75/32-0	5.70/18-8½	n.k.	120/n.k.
MX II	F	1	10.50/34-5½	5.80/19-0¼	n.k.	129-133/n.k.
BULGARIA						
Optimum						
Ephyr	F	n.k.	9.95/32-7¾	n.k.	n.k.	120/n.k.
Opit	F	n.k.	10.50/34-5½	n.k.	n.k.	128/n.k.
Skraidykles						
Favorit	F	n.k.	10.50/34-5½	n.k.	n.k.	123/n.k.
FRANCE						
Aerotec						
Rapace 15	F	n.k.	10.30/33-9½	n.k.	n.k.	130/n.k.
Rapace 16	F	n.k.	10.80/35-5¼	n.k.	n.k.	130/n.k.
La Mouette						
Atlas 14	F	1	9.30/30-6¼	5.36/17-7	3.50/11-5¾	120/0.5
Atlas 16	F	1	9.90/32-5¾	5.70/18-8½	3.50/11-5¾	120/0.5
Atlas 18	F	1	10.50/34-5½	6.10/20-0	3.50/11-5¾	120/0.5
Compact	F	n.k.	10.00/32-9¾	6.00/19-8¼	3.50/11-5¾	—
GERMANY						
Drachen						
Tropi 16	F	n.k.	10.60/34-9¼	n.k.	n.k.	130/n.k.
Tropi 17	F	n.k.	10.60/34-9¼	n.k.	n.k.	130/n.k.
Finsterwalder						
Bergfex	F	n.k.	n.k.	n.k.	n.k.	n.k.
Funfex	F	1 & 2 (DHV)	9.40/30-10	5.50/18-0½	2.40/7-10	120/0
Lightflex	F	n.k.	9.00/29-6⅓	5.20/17-0¾	2.30/7-6½	120/0
Minifex M2	F	2 (DHV)	9.14/29-11¾	n.k.	n.k.	130/0
Superfex	F	n.k.	9.80/32-1¾	n.k.	n.k.	n.k.
Topfex	F	2 & 3 (DHV)	10.40/34-1½	5.80/19-0¼	2.00/6-6¾	130/0
Firebird						
Classic	F	2 & 3 (DHV)	10.20/33-5½	5.80/19-0¼	n.k.	132/n.k.
New Wave 15	F	3 (DHV)	10.40/34-1½	5.80/19-0¼	n.k.	132/n.k.
New Wave 16	F	3 (DHV)	11.00/36-1	5.80/19-0¼	n.k.	132/n.k.
Quattro-S	F	2 & 3 (DHV)	9.92/32-6	5.75/18-10½	n.k.	125/n.k.
Quattro-S Piccolo	F	2 (DHV)	9.35/30-8	5.40/17-8½	n.k.	125/n.k.
Uno	F	1 & 2 (DHV)	9.95/32-7¾	5.75/18-10½	n.k.	125/n.k.
Uno Jumbo	F	2 (DHV)	10.80/35-5¼	5.80/19-0¼	n.k.	125/n.k.
Uno Piccolo	F	1 & 2 (DHV)	9.35/30-8	5.40/17-8½	n.k.	120/n.k.
Rochelt						
Flair	R	n.k.	12.00/39-4½	n.k.	n.k.	—
Schneid Air	F	n.k.	9.00/29-6⅓	n.k.	n.k.	n.k.
Thalhofer						
GT	F	n.k.	10.30/33-9½	n.k.	n.k.	124/n.k.
Joker	F	n.k.	9.65/31-8	n.k.	n.k.	122/n.k.
Swing	F	n.k.	10.40/34-1½	n.k.	n.k.	127/n.k.
ITALY						
Polaris						
FR 16	F	1	10.85/35-7¼	5.60/18-4½	3.60/11-9¾	132/0
*Ares	F	1	11.15/36-7	5.50/18-0½	3.30/10-10	130/0
*Gryps	F	1	10.60/34-9¼	5.50/18-0½	3.30/10-10	130/0
*Spit	Semi-R	1	10.60/34-9¼	5.50/18-0½	3.30/10-10	130/0
Touring 13	F	1	9.60/31-6	5.23/17-2	3.50/11-5¾	120/0
Touring 15	F	1	9.60/31-6	5.23/17-2	3.50/11-5¾	120/0

*Ares, Gryps and Spit are specifically for powered flying, using trikes or other attachable units (single- or two-seat).

n.k. = not known

Wing area: m²/sq ft	Wing aspect ratio	Weight: kg/lb	Glide ratio	Sink rate: m/ft per min	Pilot weight: kg (lb)	Stalling speed: knots (km/h; mph)	g limits
ITALY *Contd.*							
13.94/150.0	5.6	23.6/52	8.5	61/200	41-82 (90-180)	19 (34; 21)	+6/−4
15.98/172.0	5.6	28.1/62	8	61/200	57-109 (125-240)	23 (42; 26)	+6/−4
17.65/190.0	5.7	30/66.1	8	55/180	68-113 (150-250)	12 (21; 13)	+6/−4
13.75/148.0	6.9	30/66.1	10	61/200	54-100 (120-220)	14 (26; 16)	n.k.
15.05/162.0	7.2	30.8/68	10	55/180	59-104 (130-230)	15 (28; 18)	n.k.
16.26/175.0	7.4	35/77.2	10	55/180	68-113 (150-250)	13 (23; 14)	n.k.
19.51/210.0	6.2	40/88.2	10	55/180	73-118 (160-260)	11 (20; 12)	n.k.
16.16/174.0	5.8	29/63.9	9	58/190	59-95 (130-210)	11 (20; 12)	+6/−4
22.00/236.8	3.13	n.k.	7	66/216	50-75 (110-165)	12 (21; 13)	n.k.
25.00/269.1	3.38	n.k.	7	60/197	65-90 (144-198)	12 (21; 13)	n.k.
28.00/301.4	3.64	n.k.	7.1	54/177	80-115 (177-253)	11 (20; 12)	n.k.
26.00/279.9	n.k.	28/61.7	5	168/551	60-90 (132-198)	n.k.	n.k.
14.20/152.8	n.k.	28/61.7	n.k.	n.k.	60-90 (132-198)	n.k.	n.k.
14.20/152.8	n.k.	28/61.7	n.k.	n.k.	60-90 (132-198)	n.k.	n.k.
17.00/183.0	5.2	24/53	n.k.	n.k.	n.k.	n.k.	n.k.
29.00/312.2	n.k.	n.k.	5	114/374	50 (110) min	n.k.	n.k.
31.00/333.0	n.k.	32/70.5	n.k.	n.k.	60-100 (132-220)	n.k.	n.k.
29.00/312.2	n.k.	n.k.	n.k.	n.k.	n.k.	n.k.	n.k.
26.00/279.9	n.k.	n.k.	n.k.	n.k.	n.k.	n.k.	n.k.
15.80/170.1	6.85	29/63.9	n.k.	n.k.	n.k.	n.k.	n.k.
15.80/170.1	6.98	33/72.8	n.k.	n.k.	n.k.	n.k.	n.k.
16.00/172.2	6.9	31/68.3	n.k.	n.k.	56-99 (124-218)	13 (24; 15)	+6/−3
15.80/170.1	6	26/57.3	n.k.	n.k.	55-125 (122-275)	13 (24; 15)	+6/−3
13.80/148.5	8.0	31/68.3	n.k.	n.k.	55-85 (122-187)	13 (24; 15)	+6/−3
15.30/164.7	n.k.	27/60	8.5	60/197	55-90 (121-198)	12 (22; 14)	+4.5/−2.25
15.20/163.6	n.k.	30/66.1	10	59/194	65-95 (143-209)	14 (26; 16)	+6/−3
15.50/166.8	n.k.	30/66.1	7.11	n.k.	75-95 (166-209)	n.k.	n.k.
15.30/164.7	7	n.k.	n.k.	n.k.	60-90 (132-198)	12 (22; 14)	n.k.
15.80/170.1	7.2	n.k.	n.k.	n.k.	75-100 (165-220)	12 (22; 14)	n.k.
13.80/148.5	6.3	24.5/54	9	60/197	50-75 (110-165)	14 (25; 16)	+6/−4
15.80/170.0	6.2	25/55.1	9	60/197	65-95 (143-209)	14 (25; 16)	+6/−4
18.00/193.8	6.1	29/63.9	9	60/197	90-140 (198-308)	14 (25; 16)	+6/−4
14.00/150.7	7.1	n.k.	11	54/177	n.k.	14 (25; 16)	+6/−4
15.30/164.7	7.3	34/75	n.k.	n.k.	50-110 (110-242)	11 (20; 12)	n.k.
16.30/175.5	6.9	35/77.2	n.k.	n.k.	65-110 (143-242)	11 (20; 12)	n.k.
n.k.	n.k.	n.k.	n.k.	n.k.	n.k.	n.k.	n.k.
16.00/172.2	5.5	22/48.5	11	52/171	60-100 (132-220)	15 (28; 18)	n.k.
14.00/150.7	n.k.	20/44	10	60/197	45-75 (99-165)	14 (25; 16)	n.k.
14.00/150.7	5.7	22/48.5	10	54/177	45-65 (99-143)	15 (28; 18)	n.k.
16.80/180.8	n.k.	15.8/34.8	n.k.	72/236	65-95 (143-209)	16.5 (30; 19)	n.k.
16.10/173.3	6.7	29/63.9	12	54/177	65-110 (143-242)	18 (32; 20)	n.k.
15.50/166.8	6.7	32/70.5	n.k.	n.k.	60-100 (132-220)	18 (32; 20)	+6/−3
15.00/162.5	7.21	30.5/67.25	n.k.	n.k.	60-95 (132-209)	19 (35; 22)	+6/−3
16.00/172.2	7.56	33/72.8	n.k.	n.k.	70-100 (154-220)	19 (35; 22)	+6/−3
15.80/170.1	6.4	26/57.3	n.k.	n.k.	60-118 (132-260)	16.5 (30; 19)	+6/−3
14.00/150.7	6.24	25/55.1	n.k.	n.k.	45-70 (100-155)	16.5 (30; 19)	+6/−3
15.50/166.8	6.4	24.5/54	8.5	n.k.	50-100 (110-220)	12 (22; 14)	+6/−3
17.50/188.4	6.67	28/61.7	n.k.	n.k.	70-100 (154-220)	12 (22; 14)	+6/−3
14.00/150.7	6.25	20/44.1	n.k.	n.k.	75 (165) max	14 (25; 16)	+6/−3
11.00/118.4	n.k.	48/106	30	30/98	n.k.	17 (30; 19)	±6
n.k.	n.k.	19/42	n.k.	n.k.	n.k.	n.k.	n.k.
15.80/170.1	6.71	28/61.7	11	54/177	60-100 (132-220)	14 (25; 16)	n.k.
16.50/177.6	5.64	24.5/54	9.5	52/171	50-100 (110-220)	14 (25; 16)	n.k.
15.80/170.0	6.85	29/63.9	10	52/171	55-123 (121-271)	12 (22; 14)	n.k.
15.60/167.9	7.5	32/70.5	12	n.k.	80-95 (176-209)	14 (25; 16)	n.k.
20.50/220.7	6	42/92.6	8	n.k.	240 (529) max	15 (28; 18)	n.k.
18.50/199.1	6	42/92.6	9	n.k.	240 (529)	15 (28; 18)	n.k.
13.50/145.3	8.3	43/94.8	8	n.k.	240 (529)	15 (28; 18)	n.k.
13.50/145.3	6.8	23/50.7	10	54/177	55-72 (121-159)	14 (25; 16)	n.k.
15.00/161.5	6.14	24/52.9	10	54/177	68-86 (150-189)	14 (25; 16)	n.k.

RIGID AND FLEXIBLE WING DATA

Manufacturer and Model	Rigid: R Flexwing: F	FAI or other class	Span: m/ft-in	Leading-edge (flexwing): m/ft-in	Length (rigid); Keel (flexwing): m/ft-in	Nose/Billow angle (flexwing): degrees
POLAND						
AOK						
SB-1 WARS	F	1	9.50/31-2	6.00/19-8¼	4.20/13-9¼	105/0
Stratus E-2C I	F	1	10.60/34-9¼	6.10/20-0¼	3.60/11-9¾	126/variable
Stratus E-2C II	F	1	11.10/36-5	6.40/21-0	3.80/12-5½	126/variable
Stratus E-3C I	F	1	10.20/33-5½	5.90/19-4¼	3.60/11-9¾	126/variable
Stratus E-3C II	F	1	10.70/35-1¼	6.15/20-2¼	3.80/12-5½	126/variable
Stratus E-4 C	F	1	9.80/32-1¾	5.65/18-6½	3.60/11-9¾	126/0
Instytut Lotnictwa						
Zeta 87	Semi-R	1	11.60/38-0¾	6.00/19-8¼	3.60/11-9¾	134/-2
SWITZERLAND						
Swiss Aerolight						
Nimbus	R	n.k.	12.50/41-0¼	n.k.	n.k.	—
UNION OF SOVIET SOCIALIST REPUBLICS						
Antonov						
Slavutitch Sport	F	n.k.	10.50/34-5½	n.k.	3.90/12-9½	n.k.
Slavutitch-UT	F	n.k.	8.90/29-2½	5.72/18-9¼	4.235/13-10¾	104/1.0
Onpo Technologia						
Kompozit UT	F	n.k.	n.k.	n.k.	n.k.	n.k.
UNITED KINGDOM						
Airwave						
Calypso	F	1	9.30/30-6	5.30/17-4	3.66/12-0	120/0
Black Magic 22	F	3	8.53/28-0	n.k.	n.k.	n.k.
Black Magic 24	F	3	8.99/29-6	n.k.	n.k.	n.k.
Black Magic 27	F	3	9.91/32-6	n.k.	n.k.	n.k.
Magic 6	F	1	10.41/34-2	5.59/18-4	3.66/12-0	132/n.k.
K2	F	1	9.91/32-6	5.38/17-8	3.66/12-0	132/n.k.
K3	F	1	10.36/34-0	5.79/19-0	3.66/12-0	132/0
Pegasus/Solar Wings						
Ace/Ace RX (small)	F	1	9.60/31-6	n.k.	n.k.	122/variable
Ace/Ace RX (medium)	F	1	9.91/32-6	n.k.	n.k.	122/variable
Ace/Ace RX (large)	F	1	10.36/34-0	n.k.	n.k.	122/variable
Ace Fun	F	n.k.	n.k.	n.k.	n.k.	n.k.
Ace Sport	F	n.k.	n.k.	n.k.	n.k.	n.k.
Ace Supersport	F	n.k.	n.k.	n.k.	n.k.	n.k.
Rumour	F	n.k.	n.k.	n.k.	n.k.	n.k.
UNITED STATES OF AMERICA						
Delta Wing						
Dream 165	F	1	9.55/31-4	n.k.	n.k.	124/1.0
Dream 175	F	1	n.k.	n.k.	n.k.	n.k.
Dream 185	F	1	10.31/33-10	n.k.	n.k.	124/1.0
Mystic 155	F	n.k.	9.96/32-8	n.k.	n.k.	n.k.
Mystic 166	F	n.k.	10.39/34-1	n.k.	n.k.	n.k.
Mystic 177	F	n.k.	10.57/34-8	n.k.	n.k.	n.k.
Streak 130	F	1	8.84/29-0	n.k.	n.k.	133/0
Streak 160	F	1	10.62/34-10	5.56/18-3	3.35/11-0	133/0
Streak 180	F	1	11.38/37-4	n.k.	n.k.	133/0
Pacific Airwave						
Genesis	F	1	8.59/28-2	5.03/16-6	3.66/12-0	122/0
Magic Kiss 154	F	1	10.36/34-0	5.56/18-3	3.66/12-0	132/0
Vision Mk IV 17	F	1	9.19/30-2	5.33/17-6	3.66/12-0	122/0
Vision Mk IV 19	F	1	9.75/32-0	5.82/19-1	3.66/12-0	122/0
Seedwings						
Sensor 510E-160 VG	F	1	10.62/34-10	n.k.	2.11/6-11	135/0
UP						
Comet 2B 165	F	1	9.96/32-8	5.86/19-2¾	2.49/8-2	120/0
Comet 2B 185	F	1	10.57/34-8	6.22/20-4¾	2.62/8-7	120/0
Gemini M 134	F	1	8.78/28-9½	5.22/17-1½	2.18/7-2	120/1.0
Gemini M 164	F	1	9.91/32-6	5.86/19-2¾	2.49/8-2	120/1.0
Gemini M 184	F	1	10.49/34-5	6.22/20-4¾	2.62/8-7	120/1.0
Glidezilla 155	F	1	10.36/34-0	5.87/19-3	2.06/6-9	126/0
Volmer						
VJ-23 Swingwing	R	n.k.	9.93/32-7	9.93/32-7	5.31/17-5	—
VJ-24 Sunfun	R	n.k.	11.13/36-6	11.13/36-6	5.54/18-2	—
Wills Wing						
Skyhawk 168	F	1	9.19/30-2	5.49/18-0	3.66/12-0	115/0
Skyhawk 188	F	1	10.01/32-10	5.94/19-6	3.66/12-0	115/0
Spectrum 144	F	1	9.45/31-0	5.38/17-8	3.43/11-3	120/0
Spectrum 165	F	1	10.36/34-0	5.94/19-6	3.43/11-3	120/0
Sport AT 150	F	1	9.60/31-6	5.54/18-2	3.45/11-4	124/0
Sport AT 167	F	1	10.21/33-6	5.94/19-6	3.45/11-4	124/0
Sport AT 180	F	1	10.50/34-5½	6.10/20-0	3.45/11-4	128/0
Sport American 167	F	1	10.21/33-6	5.94/19-6	3.45/11-4	124/0
HP AT 145	F	1	10.13/33-3	5.54/18-2¼	3.43/11-3	130/0
HP AT 158	F	1	10.54/34-7	5.77/18-11¼	3.43/11-3	130/0

n.k. = not known

Wing area: m²/sq ft	Wing aspect ratio	Weight: kg/lb	Glide ratio	Sink rate: m/ft per min	Pilot weight: kg (lb)	Stalling speed: knots (km/h; mph)	g limits
UNITED STATES OF AMERICA *Contd.*							
18.90/203.4	4.8	25/55.1	8	75/246	50-110 (110-242)	16 (29; 19)	+6/−3
15.30/164.7	7.34	30/66	11	54/177	55-90 (121-198)	27 (50; 31)	n.k.
16.90/181.9	7.29	33/72.8	11	54/177	75-105 (165-231)	27 (50; 31)	n.k.
15.00/162.5	6.94	29/63.9	10	57/187	55-85 (121-187)	26 (48; 30)	n.k.
16.60/178.7	6.90	31/68.3	10	57/187	70-100 (154-220)	26 (48; 30)	n.k.
15.50/166.8	6.20	27/60	8.5	66/217	55-90 (121-198)	25 (47; 29)	n.k.
16.00/172.2	7.9	30-35/66-77	11-14	48-54/157-177	50-120 (110-264)	n.k.	+6/−3
16.20/174.4	n.k.	38/84	18	45/148	50-100 (110-220)	16 (28; 18)	+8/−6
16.30/175.5	n.k.	33.5/74	10+	60/197	n.k.	14 (25; 16)	+6/−3
17.50/188.4	n.k.	25/55	7	78/256	n.k.	14 (25; 16)	+4.5
17.00/183.0	6.2	19/42	9	60/197	65-95 (143-209)	10 (18; 11.5)	+5
15.05/162.0	6.6	26/57.3	n.k.	n.k.	45-60 (100-132)	15 (28; 18) estimated	+6/−3
21.93/236.0	3.34	n.k.	n.k.	n.k.	n.k.	n.k.	n.k.
23.97/258.0	3.38	n.k.	n.k.	n.k.	n.k.	n.k.	n.k.
26.94/290.0	3.63	n.k.	n.k.	n.k.	n.k.	n.k.	n.k.
14.30/154.0	7.55	29.4/64.9	n.k.	n.k.	60-95 (132-209)	n.k.	+6/−3
13.38/144.0	7.37	27/59.4	n.k.	n.k.	50-80 (110-176)	n.k.	+6/−3
14.86/160.0	7.22	31.4/69.3	n.k.	n.k.	74-120 (162-264)	n.k.	+6/−3
13.94/150.0	6.1	28.6/63	n.k.	n.k.	51-83 (113-183)	n.k.	n.k.
14.86/160.0	6.6	31.8/70	n.k.	n.k.	70-89 (154-196)	n.k.	n.k.
15.79/170.0	6.8	33.6/74	n.k.	n.k.	83-100 (183-220)	n.k.	n.k.
13.94/150.0 or 14.86/160.0	n.k.	n.k.	n.k.	n.k.	n.k.	n.k.	n.k.
13.94/150.0 or 14.86/160.0 or 15.79/170.0	n.k.	n.k.	n.k.	n.k.	n.k.	n.k.	n.k.
13.94/150.0 or 14.86/160.0	n.k.	n.k.	n.k.	n.k.	n.k.	n.k.	n.k.
13.47/145.0 or 14.40/155.0	n.k.	30/66 or 32.5/72	n.k.	n.k,	n.k.	n.k.	n.k.
15.33/165.0	6.4	28.1/62	n.k.	n.k.	59-91 (130-200)	n.k.	n.k.
16.26/175.0	n.k.	n.k.	n.k.	n.k.	n.k.	n.k.	n.k.
17.19/185.0	6.2	30.8/68	n.k.	n.k.	n.k.	n.k.	n.k.
14.49/156.0	6.7	29/64	n.k.	n.k.	45-77 (100-170)	n.k.	n.k.
15.42/166.0	6.8	29.9/66	n.k.	n.k.	64-95 (140-210)	n.k.	n.k.
16.26/175.0	6.8	32.2/71	n.k.	n.k.	77-109 (170-240)	n.k.	n.k.
12.08/130.0	6.6	24.9/55	n.k.	50/165	n.k.	n.k.	+8.5/−5
14.68/158.0	7.5	32.7/72	n.k.	50/165	59-100 (130-220)	n.k.	+8.5/−5
16.72/180.0	7.6	37.2/82	n.k.	50/165	n.k.	n.k.	+8.5/−5
12.82/138.0	6.4	21.3/47	11	55/180	43-75 (95-165)	17 (31; 19)	+6/−4
14.31/154.0	7.5	30.4/67	13	52/170	59-95.3 (130-210)	17 (31; 19)	+6/−4
15.05/162.0	5.4	26.8/59	11	55/180	52.5-88.5 (115-195)	17 (31; 19)	+6/−4
16.91/182.0	5.6	29/64	11	55/180	70.5-113 (155-250)	17 (31; 19)	+6/−4
14.77/159.0	7.64	30.8/68 Model SS	12-14	49/160	n.k.	n.k.	+6/−4.5
		31.8/70 Model ER	n.k.	n.k.	66-102 (145-225)	n.k.	n.k.
		32.7/72 Model FR	n.k.	n.k.	n.k.	n.k.	n.k.
15.33/165.0	6.5	29/64	10+	55/180	59-104 (130-230)	13.5 (25; 15) IAS	+6.5/−3.5
17.19/185.0	6.6	35.4/78	10+	55/180	68-113 (150-250)	13.5 (25; 15) IAS	+6.5/−3.5
12.45/134.0	6.2	24.9/55	8.5	64/210	43-75 (95-165)	12.5 (23; 14) IAS	n.k.
15.24/164.0	6.4	28.6/63	8.5	64/210	57-91 (125-200)	12.5 (23; 14) IAS	n.k.
17.09/184.0	6.4	34/75	8.5	64/210	68-104 (150-230)	12.5 (23; 14) IAS	n.k.
14.31/154.0	7.5	32.7/72	12.5	52/170	64-104 (140-230)	13 (24; 15)	+6.5/−3.5
16.63/179.0	5.9	45.5/100	9	n.k.	45.5-91 (100-200)	13 (24; 15)	+2 normal +3 ultimate
15.14/163.0	8.2	50/110	9	n.k.	91 (200) max	13 (24; 15)	+2.57 normal +3.87 ultimate
15.42/166.0	5.5	24.5/54	8.5	69/225	52-75 (115-165)	19 (36; 22)	+6/−3
17.47/188.0	5.7	29/64	8.5	69/225	66-88 (145-195)	19 (36; 22)	+6/−3
13.38/144.0	6.7	24.5/54	9	64/210	50-95 (110-210)	18 (32; 20)	+7.5/−3.5
15.33/165.0	7.0	27.2/60	9	64/210	64-108 (140-240)	18 (32; 20)	+7.5/−3.5
13.94/150.0	6.6	26/57	9	64/210	50-70 (110-154)	20 (37; 23)	+7.5/−3.5
15.51/167.0	6.8	28/62	9	64/210	60-90 (133-198)	20 (37; 23)	+7.5/−3.5
16.72/180.0	6.6	32/71	9	64/210	90-140 (198-308)	20 (37; 23)	+7.5/−3.5
15.51/167.0	6.7	29.9/66	9	64/210	64-109 (140-240)	20 (37; 23)	+7.5/−3.5
13.47/145.0	7.62	29.5/65	12.5	64/210	59-104 (130-230)	21 (39; 24)	+9/−4.5
14.68/158.0	7.57	31.3/69	12.5	64/210	68-113 (150-250)	21 (39; 24)	+9/−4.5

n.k. = not known

LIGHTER THAN AIR: AIRSHIPS

AUSTRALIA

ADA

AIRSHIP DEVELOPMENTS AUSTRALIA PTY LTD
96 Rankins Road, Kensington, Victoria 3031
Telephone: 61 (3) 879 5636
DESIGNER: Bruce N. Blake, c/o Advanced Airship Corporation Ltd, Jurby, Isle of Man, England
Telephone: 44 (624) 897962
Fax: 44 (624) 897006

Mr Bruce Blake, a consulting engineer, initiated a series of airship designs under the name of his Airship Developments Australia company, the latest of which is the LUA four/six-seat light utility airship. To demonstrate the airworthiness of this design, at minimal cost, while generating revenue, a one-third scale drone version of the LUA, named Albatross, was built during 1985.

ADA ALBATROSS

First flown on 6 November 1986, the Albatross RPMB (remotely piloted mini-blimp) introduced several innovative features, including a lifting outrigger with blown flap similar to one wind-tunnel tested in the USA for the GZ-16 non-rigid of the 1950s. Revenue is generated at outdoor displays, such as the Australian Bicentennial Air Show in October 1988, and other promotional opportunities.

The full scale version of the LUA, for which preliminary design work has been completed, is known as the **ADA-1200**. Efforts to attract venture capital for this airship were continuing in 1991.

A description of the Albatross one-third scale prototype can be found in the 1990-91 and earlier editions of *Jane's*.

One-thirtieth scale model (1m; 3.28 ft long) of the projected ADA-1200

CHINA, PEOPLE'S REPUBLIC

BUAA

BEIJING UNIVERSITY OF AERONAUTICS AND ASTRONAUTICS (Light Aircraft Design and Research Section)
37 Xue Yuan Road, Beijing 100083
Telephone: 86 (1) 2017251
Fax: 86 (1) 2010994
DIRECTOR AND SENIOR RESEARCH ENGINEER: Hu Jizhong

BUAA MIFENG-6 (BEE-6)

The BUAA's sixth Mifeng (Bee) design, started in September 1985, is a four-place hot-air airship. It has an envelope of lightweight high-strength nylon which can be

stored in a bag with a volume of only 1.5 m³ (53 cu ft). There are two vertical fins, each with a rudder for yaw control, and two horizontal stabilisers (without elevators). The gondola has a mainframe of chrome plated steel tube, covered with sheet aluminium. The envelope is inflated by the propulsion engine, two gas burners providing heat for buoyancy control. Propulsion is provided by a 31.3 kW (42 hp) Rotax 447 two-stroke engine driving a BUAA three-blade fixed-pitch pusher propeller. Fuel tank capacity is 50 litres (13.2 US gallons; 11.0 Imp gallons).

The prototype first flew on 20 December 1985. Three production Mifeng-6s had been completed by early 1988, but no further examples since then. Further details can be found in the 1990-91 and earlier *Jane's*.

BUAA Mifeng-6 four-place hot-air airship

HADG

HUAHANG AIRSHIP DEVELOPMENT GROUP
PO Box 307-10, Jingmen, Hubei 434535
DIRECTOR: Dong Xueping

HADG is a group organisation comprising several aircraft factories and design research institutes whose product range includes various lighter than air vehicles for domestic and overseas markets.

HADG FK-4

The FK-4 helium filled airship, which made its first flight on 10 August 1990, is the first passenger non-rigid ever built in China; MAS technical approval was awarded in late January 1991. Applications for production versions include advertising (two 108 m²; 1,163 sq ft panels available), TV relay, aerial photography/monitoring and powerline inspection. The gondola and twin vectoring ducted propulsion system appear similar to those of the UK Skyship series (which see).

DIMENSIONS, ENVELOPE:
Length overall	39.00 m (127 ft 11½ in)
Max diameter	10.00 m (32 ft 9¾ in)
Width over tail surfaces	12.00 m (39 ft 4½ in)
Height overall, incl gondola	14.00 m (45 ft 11¼ in)
Volume	2,000 m³ (70,629 cu ft)

WEIGHTS:
Max payload	300 kg (661 lb)
Max T-O weight	1,900 kg (4,189 lb)

Huahang (HADG) FK-4 non-rigid airship *(Zhang Yi)*

PERFORMANCE:
Max level speed	39 knots (73 km/h; 45 mph)
Max operating altitude	1,800 m (5,900 ft)
Max endurance	11 h

FRANCE

AERAZUR

AERAZUR (Member company of the Groupe Zodiac)
Division Equipements Aéronautiques
58 boulevard Galliéni, 92137 Issy-les-Moulineaux
Telephone: 33 (1) 45 54 92 80
Fax: 33 (1) 45 57 99 85
Telex: 270 887 F

CHIEF EXECUTIVE OFFICER: Jean Louis Gerondeau
INTERNATIONAL MARKETING MANAGER: Jean-Pierre Fetu

Aerazur began building lighter than air craft before the Second World War, and in the 1960s manufactured the world's largest non-rigid kite balloons (up to 15,000 m³; 529,720 cu ft), which were used for tests in the atmosphere of French nuclear weapons. It has made a series of small Vénus balloons for the French space agency CNES, as well as very large stratosphere research balloons of up to one

million m³ (35,314,720 cu ft) in volume. Other programmes have included development of a surveillance balloon carrying a Thomson-CSF radar, and barrage balloons for anti-aircraft defence. Aerazur designs and manufactures envelopes for the UK Skyship 500 and 600 series, and is associated in designing the envelope for the Sentinel 5000 airship for the US Navy.

GERMANY

GEFA-FLUG

GESELLSCHAFT ZUR ENTWICKLUNG UND FÖRDERUNG AEROSTATISCHER FLUGSYSTEME mbH
Weststrasse 14, 5100 Aachen
Telephone: 49 (241) 874026
Fax: 49 (241) 875206
MANAGING DIRECTOR: Karl Ludwig Busemeyer

Gefa-Flug has been operating advertising, filming and passenger-carrying balloons and airships since 1975. It has provided camera platforms for nationwide networks such as the BBC, WDR and ZDF. Various archaeological research projects have been undertaken in about a dozen countries including France, Germany, Italy, Oman, Pakistan, Syria and Turkey. The company currently operates seven hot-air balloons, one manned hot-air airship, and several remotely controlled LTA systems.

A leading part of Gefa-Flug's activities consists of aerial photogrammetry, in collaboration with the environmental research department of the German Mining Museum in Bochum, to obtain various kinds of data from low altitude. More than 70 of Gefa-Flug's remotely controlled balloons and airships have been sold worldwide; two of its airships used for such work were described and illustrated in the 1988-89 *Jane's*.

GEFA-FLUG AS 80 GD

Together with leading international environmental research organisations, Gefa-Flug completed in mid-1990 a two-seat hot-air airship designated AS 80 GD, to be used worldwide in various environmental research projects; two such projects were being prepared in early 1991 with the German Mining Technology concern. It is also expected to be a highly cost-effective advertising medium.

The AS 80 GD was extensively test-flown at the 1990 World Hot-Air Airship Championships, and currently operates under a provisional airworthiness certificate from the LBA.
POWER PLANT: One 38.8 kW (52 hp) Rotax 462 two-cylinder two-stroke engine.

Gefa-Flug AS 80 GD two-seat hot-air environmental research airship

DIMENSIONS:		WEIGHTS:	
Length overall	36.00 m (118 ft 1¼ in)	Max payload	100 kg (220 lb)
Height overall, incl gondola	13.50 m (44 ft 3½ in)	PERFORMANCE:	
Envelope volume	2,250 m³ (79,458 cu ft)	Max level speed	25 knots (46 km/h; 29 mph)
		Max endurance	3 h

WDL

WESTDEUTSCHE LUFTWERBUNG THEODOR WÜLLENKEMPER KG (WDL Flugdienst GmbH and WDL Luftschiff GmbH)
Flughafen Essen-Mülheim, 4330 Mülheim/Ruhr
Telephone: 49 (208) 378080
Fax: 49 (208) 3780833 (Management)
    49 (208) 3780841 (Operations)
Telex: 856810
OWNER: Theodor Wüllenkemper

Fifteen years after building its last (WDL 1) airship, WDL resumed airship construction in 1987 with the first batch of a new design known as the WDL 1B. In addition to its airship activities, WDL operates and maintains six Fokker F27 transport aircraft, based in Düsseldorf and used on passenger/cargo flights within Europe. It is reportedly planning an 86 m (282 ft) long, 10,000 m³ (353,147 cu ft), 16-passenger airship to follow the WDL 1B.

WDL 1B

The WDL 1B, of which four had been completed by early 1991 (including two for Mitsui in Japan), first flew (D-LDFP) on 30 August 1988. This airship, named *Asahi*, was delivered to Mitsui in mid-September of that year.

The largest fully certificated non-rigid airship in the world, the WDL 1B has two ballonets (40 per cent air-filled) and carries 300 litres (79.25 US gallons; 66 Imp gallons) of water ballast. The new-design gondola can accommodate up to seven passengers and features improved control instrumentation compared with the earlier WDL 1. Ballonet valves are actuated by a digital computer which indicates gas temperature and pressure; on *Asahi*, the coloured advertising graphics are also computer-controlled. This airship also carries a 9,000-bulb night sign.
POWER PLANT: Two 157 kW (210 hp) Teledyne Continental IO-360-CD flat-six engines, each driving a two-blade

WDL 1B seven-passenger non-rigids (two Teledyne Continental IO-360-CD flat-six engines)

propeller. Total fuel capacity (two tanks) 400 litres (105.7 US gallons; 88 Imp gallons).

DIMENSIONS, ENVELOPE:
Length overall	59.90 m (196 ft 6¼ in)
Max diameter	16.40 m (53 ft 9¾ in)
Volume	7,200 m³ (254,265 cu ft)

DIMENSIONS, GONDOLA:
Length overall	7.60 m (24 ft 11¼ in)

Width: top	2.10 m (6 ft 10¾ in)
bottom	1.30 m (4 ft 3¼ in)
Height: excl landing gear	2.53 m (8 ft 3½ in)
incl landing gear	3.68 m (12 ft 1 in)

WEIGHTS:
Hull weight	2,000 kg (4,409 lb)
Max payload	1,180 kg (2,601 lb)
Weight empty	5,100 kg (11,243 lb)

PERFORMANCE:
Never-exceed speed (V_{NE})	48 knots (90 km/h; 60 mph)
Max manoeuvring speed	35 knots (65 km/h; 40 mph)
Max endurance	22 h

ITALY

PAOLO BONANNO
BALLOONS SERVICE DI BONANNO LETTERIO
Via Volo 3/A, 12036 Revello (CN)
Telephone: 39 (175) 75666
Fax: 39 (175) 759313

BONANNO RBX-7
Mr Bonanno started work in 1988 on the prototype of this hot-air airship. First flight was scheduled to take place in July 1989, but no news of this venture has been received during the past two years. All known data can be found in the 1990-91 *Jane's*.

MEXICO

SPACIAL
SERVICIOS PUBLICITARIOS AÉREOS CONSTRUCCIÓN E INGENIERÍA DE AERONAVES LIGERAS SA de CV
Margaritas 312-8, Colonia Florida, Mexico DF 01030

Telephone: 52 (5) 524 7262

CHAIRMAN: Lic Ramón González Parra

CONSTRUCTION MANAGER: Arno Gjumlich Navarro

SPACIAL MLA-32-B TOLUCA
Research, development and design work on this unusual rigid airship began in 1973. The MLA-24-A prototype (see 1985-86 *Jane's*) was destroyed before its first flight, but by early 1986 construction of the larger MLA-32-A (XB-RGP: see 1988-89 *Jane's*) had begun. This made an inadvertent first flight on 12 February 1988, breaking free from its mooring mast while final adjustments for a crewed flight were being made. Although damage was confined to the gondola and one split gas cell, Spacial decided to build an

entirely new structure, designated MLA-32-B. This airship made its first flight on 24 June 1989. It was then re-engined, making a 2½ hour flight in June 1990 but being totally destroyed on landing. Following the death of Spacial's Director General, Ing Mario Sánchez Roldán, in a car accident in July 1990, the company is being reorganised and plans to design a more conventional airship. A description and illustrations of the MLA-32-B can be found in the 1990-91 *Jane's*.

UNION OF SOVIET SOCIALIST REPUBLICS

DEMENTYEV
Dolgoprudny, near Moscow
CHIEF DESIGNER: Pyotr Dementyev

DEMENTYEV DS-3
The DS-3 multi-purpose transport airship, currently under development in the USSR, is planned to make its first flight in 1992. It is a helium filled semi-rigid, with cruciform tail unit and an internally rigged envelope made of rubber coated Lavsan fabric. The gondola carries a crew of two, and can seat up to eight more people in its passenger version. As a cargo lifter, it can transport up to 3,000 kg (6,614 lb) in the cargo hold or up to 2,000 kg (4,409 lb) of externally slung bulky load. The twin engines, of unknown type, have ducted propellers, one each side of the rear of the gondola, that can be vectored 120° upward and 120° downward.

DIMENSIONS, ENVELOPE:
Length overall	62.00 m (203 ft 5 in)
Max diameter	15.00 m (49 ft 2½ in)
Volume	8,040 m³ (283,930 cu ft)

WEIGHTS:
Structural weight empty	4,500 kg (9,921 lb)

PERFORMANCE (estimated):
Max level speed	54 knots (100 km/h; 62 mph)

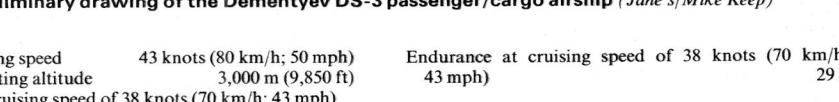

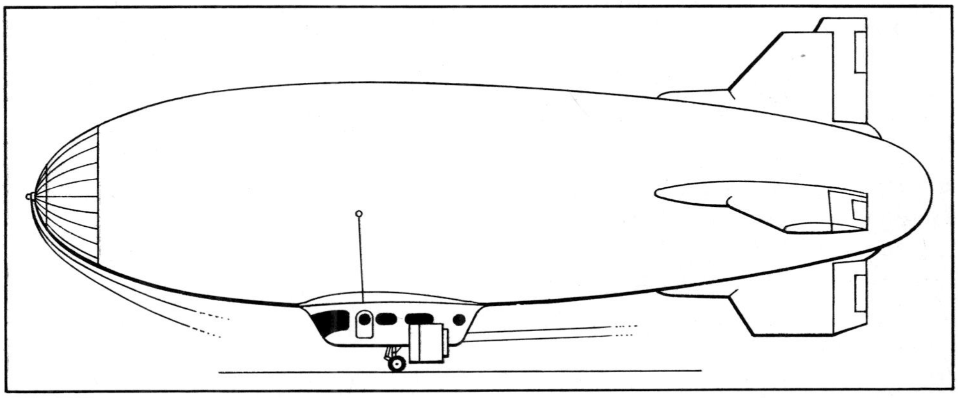

Preliminary drawing of the Dementyev DS-3 passenger/cargo airship *(Jane's/Mike Keep)*

Max cruising speed	43 knots (80 km/h; 50 mph)
Max operating altitude	3,000 m (9,850 ft)
Range at cruising speed of 38 knots (70 km/h; 43 mph)	
	1,080 nm (2,000 km; 1,243 miles)

Endurance at cruising speed of 38 knots (70 km/h; 43 mph)   29 h

MAI
MOSCOW AVIATION INSTITUTE
DIRECTOR: Yuri A. Ryzhov

THERMOPLANE
Currently in the design definition stage, with a proof-of-concept (POC) vehicle scheduled to fly in 1993, the Thermoplane is the subject of an extensively funded Soviet government programme to develop a heavy-lift airship to transport bulky cargo (eg for construction, logging or mining) in remote areas. It has a disc-shaped envelope with

elliptical cross-section, with a unique two-gas lift system. The centre portion of the envelope would be occupied by helium-filled spheres, while the remainder would be filled with natural gas. Hot air bled from the Thermoplane's twin turboshaft engines would be used to heat the natural gas, as required, to augment the basic lift provided by the helium spheres, while smaller engines fore and aft would generate additional lift and control in conjunction with horizontal and vertical control surfaces. Using this configuration, MAI has estimated that a full-size vehicle with a 200 m (656 ft) diameter should be able to lift a payload of some 550 t

(1.1 million lb), on a cargo platform slung beneath the gondola.

The POC Thermoplane is intended to utilise two 298 kW (400 shp) GTD-350 turboshafts from an Mi-2 helicopter as its primary power plant, with the flight deck/cabin portion of the Mi-2 serving as the gondola. This testbed will have an envelope diameter of about 36-40 m (118-131 ft), and a T-O weight of 8,500 kg (18,740 lb) including a 2,150 kg (4,740 lb) payload. Performance expectations include a max speed of 43 knots (80 km/h; 50 mph) and ceiling of 2,000 m (6,560 ft).

UNITED KINGDOM

AAC
ADVANCED AIRSHIP CORPORATION
Airship Facility, Jurby, Isle of Man
Telephone: 44 (624) 897962
Fax: 44 (624) 897006
Telex: 627835 AIRSHP G
EXECUTIVE DIRECTOR: John Hooper
MARKETING MANAGER: Brian Begley
The Advanced Airship Corporation is a CAA approved company for the design and manufacture of non-rigid airships and is currently building the Advanced Non-Rigid (ANR) airship at Jurby, Isle of Man, where development and flight testing are also undertaken.

The ANR is designed to fulfil many roles in the commercial, defence and paramilitary fields. Commercial roles are essentially tourism and civil flights, and the airship's high speed capability will allow the ANR to be a contender for regular scheduled flights. Defence and paramilitary uses are mainly as surveillance and sensor platforms. Possible applications range from airborne early warning and anti-submarine warfare to coastguard patrol and fishery law enforcement. Long time on station, excellent crew cabin accommodation and low noise enhance the usefulness of the ANR for the defence and paramilitary market.

ADVANCED AIRSHIP ANR
The ANR is a 14/28-passenger airship which can also operate in many defence and paramilitary roles. It has a potential on-station endurance of 77 hours at a patrol speed of 30 knots (56 km/h; 34 mph). The envelope is manufactured by Thunder & Colt. Final assembly was due to take place in the second half of 1991.
TYPE: Non-rigid helium filled airship.
ENVELOPE: Conventional non-rigid ellipsoidal design, manufactured from aramid fabric coated with titanium oxide pigmented polyurethane. Four catenary curtains and 24 catenary cables terminate at four vertical load

points on the gondola; 52 lateral load connections are also made to the gondola frames. Solid carapace replaces conventional batten arrangements at nose. One ballonet in nose and one in rear of hull, supplied by two single-stage axial flow fans each capable of delivering 170 m³ (6,000 cu ft)/min.

TAIL UNIT: Four equally spaced tail fins, in X configuration, all four with ruddervators for pitch and yaw control. The fins are made from metallic honeycomb ribs with tubular spars and are fabric covered. The ruddervators are built entirely from Kevlar faced honeycomb panels.

POWER PLANT: Two 313 kW (420 shp) Allison 250-B17C turboprops, mounted on stub-wings attached to gondola and each driving a Hartzell HC-B3TF-7A/T10173 three-blade propeller. Entire wing/propulsion unit can rotate from 0° to 75° upward to vector thrust. Standard fuel capacity 1,438 litres (380 US gallons; 316 Imp gallons), contained in three tanks in stub-wings and a collector tank at base of equipment bay. Provision for extra fuel in removable tanks in cargo hold.

ACCOMMODATION: Crew of two on gondola flight deck. Main cabin can accommodate a variety of passenger layouts, ranging from 14 in a 7-pair twin dining alcove arrangement to 28 in a four-abreast layout, all with a central aisle; provision for one or two cabin attendants. Toilet and galley installations to customer's requirements. Large baggage hold at rear of gondola. All-cargo interior available optionally. For military and paramilitary use, gondola can be equipped with crew quarters and fitted out with many sensors and recording devices. Radar antennae can be mounted inside the envelope, with the display located inside the gondola.

DIMENSIONS:

Length overall	60.96 m (200 ft 0 in)
Height overall, incl gondola	18.90 m (62 ft 0 in)
Envelope: Max diameter	15.24 m (50 ft 0 in)
Volume	7,270 m³ (256,724 cu ft)
Ballonet volume (two, total)	1,753 m³ (61,922 cu ft)
Fin area (total, net)	116.8 m² (1,257 sq ft)
Gondola: Length	13.66 m (44 ft 9½ in)
Max width	2.84 m (9 ft 4 in)
Max height	2.35 m (7 ft 8½ in)
Propeller diameter	2.29 m (7 ft 6 in)
Gondola passenger cabin:	
Length of seating area	6.71 m (22 ft 0 in)
Max width	2.67 m (8 ft 9 in)
Min height	2.35 m (7 ft 8½ in)

Model of the Advanced Airship ANR; first example was due to fly in 1991

WEIGHTS:

Weight empty	3,371 kg (7,432 lb)
Fuel: standard	1,134 kg (2,500 lb)
minimum	590 kg (1,300 lb)
Payload (typical):	
26 passengers, plus cabin attendants and baggage, or	
max cargo, with 50% fuel	3,074 kg (6,778 lb)
Max T-O weight	7,167 kg (15,800 lb)

PERFORMANCE (estimated, at 915 m; 3,000 ft, ISA):

Max level speed	80 knots (148 km/h; 92 mph)
Max cruising speed	78 knots (144 km/h; 90 mph)
Lower limit speed at max heaviness	
	24 knots (45 km/h; 28 mph)
Max rate of climb	610 m (2,000 ft)/min
Pressure ceiling: commercial	1,525 m (5,000 ft)
coastal patrol	1,830 m (6,000 ft)
Range with standard fuel load of 1,134 kg (2,500 lb):	
at 30 knots (56 km/h; 34 mph)	
	732 nm (1,356 km; 843 miles)
at 50 knots (93 km/h; 57 mph)	
	714 nm (1,323 km; 822 miles)

at 70 knots (130 km/h; 81 mph)
481 nm (891 km; 554 miles)
Range with increased fuel load of 3,402 kg (7,500 lb), provisions, and second crew:
at 30 knots (56 km/h; 34 mph)
2,316 nm (4,292 km; 2,667 miles)
at 50 knots (93 km/h; 57 mph)
2,166 nm (4,014 km; 2,494 miles)
at 70 knots (130 km/h; 81 mph)
1,443 nm (2,674 km; 1,662 miles)
Endurance, conditions as above:

with standard fuel:	
at 30 knots (56 km/h; 34 mph)	24 h 24 min
at 50 knots (93 km/h; 57 mph)	14 h 16 min
at 70 knots (130 km/h; 81 mph)	6 h 53 min
with additional fuel:	
at 30 knots (56 km/h; 34 mph)	77 h 12 min
at 50 knots (93 km/h; 57 mph)	43 h 19 min
at 70 knots (130 km/h; 81 mph)	20 h 37 min

AIRSHIP INDUSTRIES
AIRSHIP INDUSTRIES (UK) LTD

Airship Industries (see 1990-91 and earlier *Jane's*) went into receivership in early September 1990 and was liquidated on 28 September. In November 1990 it was announced that its assets had been purchased by three other companies. Slingsby Aviation (UK) acquired all work in progress, plus plant, tools, computers and type certificates for the civil versions of the Skyship 500HL and 600. Operating and sales rights in the USA for the civil 500/500HL/600 were purchased by Airship International of New York. Westinghouse Electric Corporation, USA, acquired AI's 50 per cent share of their joint venture company WAI (see US section), together with all military/defence applications of the Skyships 500/500HL/600 and the Sentinel 1000/5000. Five Skyship 500s and 10 Skyship 600s were built.

CAMERON
CAMERON BALLOONS LTD
St John's Street, Bedminster, Bristol BS3 4NH
Telephone: 44 (272) 637216
Fax: 44 (272) 661168
Telex: 444825 GASBAG G
MANAGING DIRECTOR:
D. A. Cameron, BSc (Aero Eng), MIE, MRAeS
SALES DIRECTOR: Philip Dunnington, BA

Cameron Balloons, which celebrated its 21st birthday in 1991, began manufacturing hot-air balloons in 1968 and holds CAA, FAA, French CNT and German Musterzulassungsschein type certificates for its balloons. It is now the world's largest manufacturer of hot-air balloons, and by 31 December 1990 had produced more than 2,500 balloons from a main factory in Bristol and a smaller unit at Harrogate. A sister company in Dexter, Michigan, USA, has produced a further 600 balloons under licence; a fledgling operation in Moscow, USSR, had completed 19 balloons by the end of 1990. In 1986-87 the O-120, N-133 and N-145 models were introduced to cater for increasing demand for passenger carrying balloons, and in August 1987 the N-850, with a double-deck basket, achieved a new world record of 45 passengers carried in a balloon. At the end of 1990 Cameron made the final modifications to the *Endeavour* envelope ordered by Mr Julian Nott for his planned global balloon flight. Cameron's current range of commercial balloons is listed in the tables at the end of this section.

Cameron Balloons Ltd also designs and produces hot-air airships, being the first company to develop a craft of this type. Production hot-air airships now include the pressurised DP series. Helium filled airships have included the DG-19 single-seater and DG-25 two-seater, both now superseded by the single-seat DG-14.

CAMERON DP SERIES
First flown in April 1986, the DP prototype (G-BMEZ) was the first of a new generation of pressurised hot-air airships, differing from earlier airships of this kind in utilising a single engine for both propulsion and pressure

A pair of Cameron DP 70 pressurised hot-air airships in formation

control. In the event of an engine failure the DP series can be flown unpressurised, and landed like a hot-air balloon. Twin silencers are fitted, to minimise the engine noise level. The DP series has a new, specially designed gondola, and is equipped with an ergonomically designed cockpit and a unique Cameron self-regulating pressure control system. The DP 60 and DP 70 can carry one or two persons, and Cameron has added the two-place DP 80 and DP 90 to the range for hot and high operation. Figures in the designations indicate approximate envelope volume in thousands of cubic feet.

By 1 January 1990 Cameron had completed, in addition to the DP 50 prototype, one DP 60 and 10 DP 70s; customer countries comprised Belgium, Chile, Luxembourg, Switzerland, the UK, the USA and Venezuela. DP 90s have been sold to customers in Australia, Brazil, Germany and Switzerland. The market for thermal airships was less buoyant in 1990, despite the fact that Cameron DP series craft were first, second and third in the World Hot-Air Airship Championships. However, at the start of 1991 three orders for DP airships were already in hand to add to the four sold in 1990.

GONDOLA: All-aluminium structure, seating one or two persons with full-harness seat belts. Full height polycarbonate windscreen.

POWER PLANT: One 21 kW (28 hp) König SD 570 four-cylinder two-stroke engine, driving a three-blade König shrouded pusher propeller. Fuel capacity 22.7 litres (6 US gallons; 5 Imp gallons) of 40:1 two-stroke mixture.

EQUIPMENT: Instrumentation comprises manometer, rev counter, fuel contents gauge, voltmeter, variometer, altimeter and thermistor. 12V 30Ah battery standard. Propane fuel in two Worthington, Cameron 599 or Cameron 426 tanks, according to model, with respective capacities of 77.3, 86.4 or 104.6 litres (20.4, 22.8 or 27.6 US gallons; 17, 19 or 23 Imp gallons) per tank. Manual piezo-electric or electronic ignition.

DIMENSIONS, ENVELOPE:

Length overall: DP 50	28.35 m (93 ft 0 in)
DP 60	30.48 m (100 ft 0 in)
DP 70	32.31 m (106 ft 0 in)
DP 80	33.83 m (111 ft 0 in)
DP 90	35.05 m (115 ft 0 in)
Height: DP 50	12.80 m (42 ft 0 in)
DP 60	13.72 m (45 ft 0 in)
DP 70	14.63 m (48 ft 0 in)
DP 80	15.24 m (50 ft 0 in)
DP 90	15.54 m (51 ft 0 in)
Max width: DP 50	10.67 m (35 ft 0 in)
DP 60	11.28 m (37 ft 0 in)
DP 70	11.89 m (39 ft 0 in)
DP 80	12.19 m (40 ft 0 in)
DP 90	12.80 m (42 ft 0 in)
Volume, gross: DP 50	1,415.8 m³ (50,000 cu ft)
DP 60	1,699.0 m³ (60,000 cu ft)
DP 70	1,982.2 m³ (70,000 cu ft)
DP 80	2,265.3 m³ (80,000 cu ft)
DP 90	2,548.5 m³ (90,000 cu ft)
Max display area per side: DP 50	77.02 m² (829 sq ft)
DP 60	86.96 m² (936 sq ft)
DP 70	95.97 m² (1,033 sq ft)
DP 80	91.97 m² (990 sq ft)
DP 90	99.03 m² (1,066 sq ft)

WEIGHTS:

Gondola (all models)	195 kg (430 lb)

Newest and smallest Cameron helium airship, the single-seat DG-14, about to land

Gondola of the Cameron DP series

Envelope: DP 60	146 kg (322 lb)
Useful passenger load (S/L, 15°C): DP 50	90 kg (198 lb)
DP 60	149 kg (328 lb)
DP 70	222 kg (489 lb)
DP 80	285 kg (628 lb)
DP 90	359 kg (791 lb)
Max T-O weight: DP 50	452 kg (997 lb)
DP 60: one person	469 kg (1,034 lb)
two persons	546 kg (1,204 lb)
DP 70: one person	485 kg (1,069 lb)
two persons	562 kg (1,239 lb)

PERFORMANCE:

Max level speed: DP 50	19 knots (35 km/h; 22 mph)
DP 60	15 knots (28 km/h; 17 mph)
Endurance: DP 50	1 h 30 min

CAMERON DG-14

Trials of the DG-14 one-man helium airship, which made its first flight (G-BRDU) in October 1989, were completed during 1990, and certification was received on 20 February 1991. At that time one example had been ordered by a customer in France.

Major use is expected to be for advertising, but the DG-14 could also find applications for surveillance or as a camera platform. It can be moored to a portable mast, but in adverse weather could be hangared without the loss of expensive helium that deflation would involve.

ENVELOPE: Helium-filled, with main and tail ballonets, 0.305 m (12 in) manual gas valves, main and overpressure patch-type rip panels and ball type mast connection.

POWER PLANT: One 21 kW (28 hp) König SD 570 four-cylinder two-stroke engine, driving a six-blade ducted fan with pitch adjustment, flow straighteners and 40° thrust vectoring. Electric starting. Fuel capacity 22.7 litres (6 US gallons; 5 Imp gallons).

GONDOLA: Single-seat, with welded steel frame and aluminium skin. Three-wheel landing gear.

DIMENSIONS, ENVELOPE:

Length overall	19.00 m (62 ft 4 in)
Max diameter	6.86 m (22 ft 6 in)
Height overall, incl gondola	8.23 m (27 ft 0 in)
Volume	396.4 m³ (14,000 cu ft)
Banner area (each side): Length	9.50 m (31 ft 2 in)
Height	2.59 m (8 ft 6 in)

SLINGSBY

SLINGSBY AVIATION LIMITED

Ings Lane, Kirkbymoorside, North Yorkshire YO6 6EZ
Telephone: 44 (751) 32474
Fax: 44 (751) 31173
Telex: 57597 SLINAV G
MANAGING DIRECTOR:
James S. Tucker, BSc(Eng), CEng, MRAeS
MARKETING DIRECTOR, AIRCRAFT: John C. Dignan

Slingsby Aviation was the principal subcontractor to Airship Industries (UK) Ltd, supplying gondolas, nosecones, fins and control surfaces made in composites materials for the Skyship range. Following the collapse of Airship Industries in September 1990, Slingsby acquired rights for the Skyship 500/500HL/600 range and is now responsible for maintaining the CAA and FAA type certificates, and for product support, of the civil versions of these airships.

The prime civil applications are for aerial advertising, promotional and pleasure flight operations. In all of these roles the extended endurance, low noise and vibration levels, large cabin space and low operating costs render the airship a cost-effective platform. By the beginning of 1990 Airship Industries had sold six airships, including two within the government agency market.

Due to the high volume of the gondola, which can house a thorough and sophisticated communications, navigation and sensor system, and the large dimensions of the envelope for mounting internal antennae, the airship also has considerable potential in such roles as maritime surveillance, electronic warfare and mine countermeasures.

Five Skyship 500s and ten 600s had been completed by the end of 1990.

SKYSHIP 500

The first production Skyship 500 (G-BIHN, c/n 02) made its first flight, at RAE Cardington, Bedfordshire, on 28 September 1981. Operation was under a British CAA aerial work C of A initially, with a full transport category certificate awarded on 21 November 1984, and on 23 April 1986 Skyship 500-02 inaugurated the first scheduled airship passenger service for 49 years when it took off from Leavesden Airport for the first of four daily sightseeing flights over central London. The service was repeated during 1987 and 1988 using the larger Skyship 600. The standard Skyship 500 civil configuration seats a pilot and up to seven passengers on five individual seats and a three-person seat at the rear.

Of the five Skyship 500s built, one was converted to the prototype 500HL (G-SKSB) by Airship Industries; one uncompleted HL conversion (500-04) has been acquired by Airship International, and one other (500-03) is to be converted to a 500HL by Slingsby. It is understood that Slingsby does not plan the manufacture of any further Skyship 500s.

ENVELOPE: The airship envelope is manufactured, by the Zodiac division of Aerazur in France, from a single ply polyester fabric, coated with a titanium dioxide loaded polyurethane to reduce ultraviolet degradation, and with a polyvinylidene chloride film bonded onto an inner coating of polyurethane on the inside of the envelope to minimise loss of helium gas. Two ballonets, which together comprise 26 per cent of the envelope volume, are installed fore and aft, so that differential inflation will provide static fore and aft trim. There is a ballonet air intake aft of each propulsor unit. Four parabolic arch load curtains carry multiple Kevlar 29 gondola suspension cables and peripheral bolt rope. The nose structure consists of a domed disc, moulded from GFRP and carrying the fitting by which the airship is moored to its mast. The tail unit is of conventional cruciform layout, each surface being attached to the envelope at its root and braced by wires on each side. All four surfaces are constructed from interlocking ribs and spars of Fibrelam and have GFRP skins: their hinged rudder and elevator control surfaces are cable operated, and each has a spring tab. A full-authority fly-by-light control system is also available (see Skyship 600 entry for details).

GONDOLA: One-piece moulding of Kevlar reinforced plastics, with flooring and bulkheads of Fibrelam panels; those which form the engine compartment at the rear are faced with titanium for fire protection. There is accommodation for a pilot and co-pilot, with dual controls, although the airship is designed to be flown by a single pilot. Ballast is contained in a box situated below the crew seats, and disposable water ballast is contained in tanks at the rear. On the ground, the airship rests on a single two-wheeled assembly with double tyres, mounted beneath the rear part of the gondola.

POWER PLANT: Two 152 kW (204 hp) Porsche 930/10 six-cylinder aircooled piston engines mounted in the rear of the gondola. Each drives a ducted propulsor consisting of a Hoffmann five-blade reversible-pitch propeller rotating within an annular duct constructed of GFRP, reinforced with carbonfibre. Each propulsor can be rotated about its pylon attachment to the gondola through an arc of 210°: 90° upward and 120° downward. The vectored thrust available gives the airship a V/STOL capability, as well as in-flight hovering ability. A fuel tank is mounted at the rear of the engine compartment. Engine modifications include provision of automatic mixture control, fuel injection and electronic ignition.

SYSTEMS: 28V electrical system, supplied by engine driven alternators.

AVIONICS: Include Bendix/King Silver Crown series dual nav/com, ADF, Omega, VOR/ILS and weather radar.

DIMENSIONS, ENVELOPE:

Length overall	52.00 m (170 ft 7¼ in)
Max diameter	14.00 m (45 ft 11¼ in)
Height overall	18.66 m (61 ft 2½ in)
Tail fin span	17.00 m (55 ft 9 in)
Volume: gross	5,153 m³ (181,977 cu ft)
ballonets (total)	1,334 m³ (47,102 cu ft)

DIMENSIONS, GONDOLA:

Length overall	9.24 m (30 ft 3½ in)
Max width	2.41 m (7 ft 10¾ in)
Cabin: Length	4.20 m (13 ft 9½ in)
Height	1.96 m (6 ft 5 in)

WEIGHTS:

Gross disposable load	1,260 kg (2,778 lb)

PERFORMANCE:

Max level speed	55 knots (101 km/h; 63 mph)
Cruising speed (50% power)	
	47 knots (87 km/h; 54 mph)
Pressure ceiling	3,050 m (10,000 ft)
Still air range at 40 knots (74 km/h; 46 mph)	
	470 nm (870 km; 541 miles)
Endurance	12 h

SKYSHIP 500HL

The 500HL, first flown on 30 July 1987, is a higher lift airship which can operate with a greater payload in hotter climates and at higher altitudes than the Skyship 500. It is powered by two 152 kW (204 hp) Porsche 930 engines; fuel tank capacity is 545 litres (144 US gallons; 120 Imp gallons).

One was converted by Airship Industries, and two others (see Skyship 500 entry) are to be completed.

DIMENSIONS, ENVELOPE: As for Skyship 600
DIMENSIONS, GONDOLA: As for Skyship 500
WEIGHTS:

Gross disposable load	2,190 kg (4,829 lb)

PERFORMANCE:

Max level speed	50 knots (93 km/h; 57 mph)
Cruising speed	up to 47 knots (87 km/h; 54 mph)
Pressure ceiling	3,050 m (10,000 ft)
Endurance at 35 knots (65 km/h; 40 mph)	17 h

Skyship 500HL (G-SKSB) heavy-lift airship at its Cardington base

SKYSHIP 600

The Skyship 600, first flown on 6 March 1984, accommodates up to 13 passengers in its civil configuration, and adding turbochargers to the Porsche engines increases the available power to 190 kW (255 hp) per engine. Fuel capacity is increased to 682 litres (180 US gallons; 150 Imp gallons), and auxiliary fuel tanks are available as optional equipment. A special category C of A was awarded by the UK CAA on 1 September 1984. Aerial work certification was received in the Spring of 1986, and on 8 January 1987 the Skyship 600 became the world's only airship with full passenger certification. This initiated the Skycruise aerial sightseeing service over London, San Francisco, Munich and Sydney in 1987, and over Paris in 1988. The first US FAA type certificate awarded to an airship for civil use was issued to the Skyship 600 in May 1989. A total of 10 Skyship 600s has so far been built.

The world's first full-authority fly-by-light system, developed in conjunction with GEC Avionics, was successfully flown on 23 October 1988 on Skyship 600-04 (G-SKSF) at Airship Industries' Weeksville base in the USA. The system incorporates a digital flight control computer, and is highly resistant to electromagnetic interference and lightning strikes, while greatly reducing pilot workload. The system will be fitted to the US Navy Sentinel 1000 and 5000 airships (see WAI in US part of this section), and can be incorporated into the specification for smaller airships as required. A sidestick control is fitted in place of the original conventional yoke control.

DIMENSIONS, ENVELOPE:

Length overall	59.00 m (193 ft 7 in)
Max diameter	15.20 m (49 ft 10½ in)
Height overall	20.30 m (66 ft 7¼ in)
Tail fin span	19.20 m (63 ft 0 in)
Volume: gross	6,666 m³ (235,400 cu ft)
ballonets (total)	1,733 m³ (61,200 cu ft)

DIMENSIONS, GONDOLA:

Length overall	11.67 m (38 ft 3½ in)
Max width	2.56 m (8 ft 4¾ in)
Cabin: Length	6.89 m (22 ft 7¼ in)
Height	1.92 m (6 ft 3½ in)
Floor area (usable)	12.00 m² (130.0 sq ft)

WEIGHTS (design):

Gross disposable load	2,343 kg (5,165 lb)

PERFORMANCE:

Max level speed	58 knots (107 km/h; 67 mph)
Cruising speed (70% power)	
	52 knots (96 km/h; 60 mph)
Pressure ceiling	3,050 m (10,000 ft)
Still air range at 40 knots (74 km/h; 46 mph), without	
auxiliary tanks	550 nm (1,019 km; 633 miles)

THUNDER & COLT

THUNDER & COLT LTD

Maesbury Road, Oswestry, Shropshire SY10 8HA
Telephone: 44 (691) 670644
Fax: 44 (691) 670617
Telex: 35503 COLT G
MANAGING DIRECTOR: Per Lindstrand
TECHNICAL DIRECTOR: Mark Broome
PRODUCTION DIRECTOR: Paul Dickinson
SALES AND MARKETING DIRECTOR: Chris Kirby
INFORMATION OFFICER: John Templeman

In addition to its current range of hot-air and helium airships described in this entry, Thunder & Colt is responsible for the envelope of the ANR airship described under the Advanced Airship Corporation heading in this section. Thunder & Colt manufactures an extensive range of hot-air balloons (see details in tables at the end of this section), of which the 300A is the world's largest passenger-carrying balloon for regular operation. Current output totals more than 250 hot-air balloons and airships per year, of which over 80 per cent are exported. The 1987 *Virgin Atlantic Flyer,* at 60,315 m³ (2.13 million cu ft) the largest hot-air balloon then manufactured and flown, was described in the 1987-88 *Jane's*; it has since been exceeded by the 73,624 m³ (2.6 million cu ft) *Pacific Flyer.* In a 16,990 m³ (600,000 cu ft) balloon named *Stratoquest* the company's managing director, Mr Per Lindstrand, reached approx 19,812 m (65,000 ft) after take-off from Laredo, Texas, on 1 June 1988, a new world altitude record for hot-air balloons. In the same year, with its sister company Airborne Industries, Thunder & Colt built a new gas balloon known as the GB-1. The envelope of this balloon is tested and certificated for hydrogen/helium, methane and coal gas. Appearing for the first time at the 1988 World Gas Balloon Championships, it gained first place, crewed by Jo Starkbaum and Gert Scholz. Two weeks later, with the same crew, it won the 32nd Gordon Bennett race by the greatest margin in recent times; and won the same race again in 1989.

COLT AS 80 Mk II and AS 105 Mk II

The Colt AS 80 Mk II is currently the most popular of the Colt hot-air airships in production. It was developed and certificated in 1988, and 10 had been built by 1990. The AS 105 Mk II uses the same gondola as the AS 80 Mk II, but has a larger envelope of 2,973.3 m³ (105,000 cu ft). An AS 80 Mk II won the Hot-Air Airship European Championships in France in 1989.

The envelope is manufactured in HTN90K high-tenacity and high temperature resistant fabric. It has a fineness ratio of 2.5, and four inflated fins in a cruciform configuration. Steering is by a single rudder on the bottom fin, operated by ropes connecting it to the gondola. The twin catenary load suspension system distributes the loads of gondola weight and power plant forces evenly into the envelope. The gondola is of aluminium panels over a stainless steel tubular spaceframe, with tricycle landing gear; pilot and passenger sit in tandem. In single-seat configuration, the passenger seat is exchanged for an extra fuel tank. The windscreen is made from polycarbonate sheet, forming a partially enclosed cockpit.

The power plant is a 38.8 kW (52 hp) Rotax 462 two-cylinder watercooled engine driving a two-blade pusher propeller. The engine also drives a generator supplying an electric fan used to pressurise the envelope. Additional air for pressurisation of the envelope is taken from a scoop situated in the propeller slipstream. The burners are situated inside the envelope and operated electrically with a manual override. Pilot lights are fitted with electric spark and piezo-electric ignition and are specially modified to operate directly underneath the inflating fan without blowing out. Standard instrumentation comprises an altimeter, variometer, envelope temperature and pressure gauges, propane volume gauge, petrol level gauge, voltmeter, engine water temperature and engine rpm gauge. A 720-channel VHF com transceiver option, with pilot-passenger intercom, is available.

DIMENSIONS, ENVELOPE (A: AS 80 Mk II, B: AS 105 Mk II):

Length overall: A	31.00 m (101 ft 8½ in)
B	34.00 m (111 ft 6½ in)
Max diameter: A	12.40 m (40 ft 8¼ in)
B	13.87 m (45 ft 6 in)
Volume: A	2,123.8 m³ (75,000 cu ft)
B	2,973.3 m³ (105,000 cu ft)

DIMENSIONS, GONDOLA (both):

Length overall	3.84 m (12 ft 7¼ in)
Max width	1.75 m (5 ft 9 in)
Height overall	1.80 m (5 ft 11 in)
Propeller diameter	1.57 m (5 ft 2 in)

WEIGHTS (A: AS 80 Mk II, B: AS 105 Mk II):

Envelope: A	190 kg (419 lb)
B	213 kg (469 lb)
Gondola, empty: A, B	210 kg (463 lb)
Propane fuel: A, B	60-110 kg (132-242 lb)
Gross lift: A	600 kg (1,323 lb)

PERFORMANCE (A and B as above):

Max level speed: A, B	20 knots (37 km/h; 23 mph)
Max endurance: A, B	2 h 30 min

COLT AS 56

Construction of this one-man hot-air airship largely follows the same lines as that of AS 80 Mk II, with a stainless steel tubular gondola and tricycle landing gear. The envelope is also of similar construction, with twin catenary curtains and cruciform tail surfaces. The power plant is a 21 kW (28 hp) König SC 570 four-cylinder two-stroke driving a two-blade pusher propeller.

The AS 56 envelope pressurisation system incorporates a similar system to that used in the AS 80 Mk II, with electric fan and automatic pressure relief system. An airship of this type won the first Hot-Air Airship World Championships in Luxembourg in 1988.

DIMENSIONS, ENVELOPE:

Length overall	28.00 m (91 ft 10½ in)
Max diameter	11.20 m (36 ft 9 in)
Volume	1,585.75 m³ (56,000 cu ft)

DIMENSIONS, GONDOLA:

Length overall	2.75 m (9 ft 0¼ in)
Max width	1.50 m (4 ft 11 in)

Height overall	1.40 m (4 ft 7 in)
Propeller diameter	1.32 m (4 ft 4 in)
WEIGHTS:	
Envelope	120 kg (265 lb)
Gondola	110 kg (242 lb)
Propane fuel	40 kg (88 lb)
Max T-O weight	365 kg (805 lb)
PERFORMANCE:	
Max level speed	15 knots (28 km/h; 17 mph)
Max endurance	1 h 30 min

COLT AS 261

The largest hot-air airship ever flown, the AS 261 is also the first with cargo carrying capability. It is a scaled-up version of the AS 80 Mk II, heated by triple Colt Mk 2 burners, and has the same power plant as the GA 42 airship. The prototype, flown extensively during 1989, has seats for a further three crew, and has been operated over the jungle in French Guyana. In this operation a huge netting platform, spread over an inflatable support frame, was lowered onto the rain forest canopy to support the four-man team of scientists and their equipment without disturbing or damaging the environment. The platform and scientific payload had a total weight of 740 kg (1,631 lb).

DIMENSIONS, ENVELOPE:	
Length overall	47.80 m (156 ft 10 in)
Max diameter	18.80 m (61 ft 8 in)
Height overall	20.40 m (66 ft 11 in)
Volume	7,391 m³ (261,000 cu ft)
DIMENSIONS, GONDOLA:	
Length overall	3.90 m (12 ft 9½ in)
Max width	1.70 m (5 ft 7 in)
Height overall	1.80 m (5 ft 11 in)
WEIGHTS (Tropics):	
Envelope	375 kg (827 lb)
Gondola	530 kg (1,168 lb)
Max T-O weight	2,100 kg (4,630 lb)

COLT GA 42

This helium filled dirigible is a project in which Thunder & Colt co-operates with its sister company Airborne Industries of Southend on Sea. Thunder & Colt undertook design and production of the gondola and design of the envelope; Airborne Industries was responsible for envelope manufacture.

The prototype (G-MATS) made its first flight on 2 September 1987. The type certificate was issued in May 1989 after an intensive testing and modification period. The design is certificated to BCAR CAP 471 Section Q in the aerial work category.

Six GA 42s had been built by September 1990, for customers in Finland, France, the UK and USA.

ENVELOPE: Helium-filled envelope of polyurethane coated polyamide, with ultra-violet blockage, hydrolysis proofed. Two air-filled ballonets (one forward, one aft), with max fill ratio of 25 per cent, inflated by an engine driven Porsche axial fan and controlled manually or (at pre-set levels) by an automatic pressure relief valve. Helium pressure relief valve operates automatically, but can be actuated manually in an emergency. Hull shape and stability maintained by two catenary curtains, which transfer weight loading to top of envelope. Four independent tail-fins, in cruciform configuration, are fabricated from GFRP composites and attached to hull by rigging wires. Movable control surface on all except upper vertical fin. Quick-release mooring by hard nose with 12 aluminium battens.

GONDOLA: All-aluminium riveted semi-monocoque structure, supported by seven catenary cables each side (three forward, four aft). Side by side bucket seats for crew of two, with full harnesses. on fully enclosed and heated flight deck; 180° single-curvature polycarbonate windscreen, plus observation window in roof for viewing airship interior. Fully castoring, rubber sprung single-wheel landing gear.

POWER PLANT: One 75 kW (100 hp) Teledyne Continental O-200-B flat-four engine, driving a Hoffmann four-blade fixed-pitch wood/composite pusher propeller. Fuel capacity 130 litres (34.3 US gallons; 28.6 Imp gallons).

SYSTEMS: Fly-by-wire flight control system, using three linear DC actuators; twin analog backup circuits. Electrical systems powered by a 25Ah wet cell battery, charged via engine mounted alternators capable of delivering 60A at 14V DC. Ample battery power available to supply control systems for landing in the event of alternator failure.

AVIONICS: VHF nav/com, ADF, transponder, VOR, and ADF indicators. Instrument panel is roof-mounted in order not to obstruct all-round field of view.

DIMENSIONS, ENVELOPE:	
Length overall	27.50 m (90 ft 2¾ in)
Max diameter	9.20 m (30 ft 2¼ in)
Height overall between fin-tips	11.20 m (36 ft 9 in)
Volume: gross	1,189.3 m³ (42,000 cu ft)
ballonets (total)	approx 311.5 m³ (11,000 cu ft)
Banner area (each side): Length	14.70 m (48 ft 2¾ in)
Height	7.50 m (24 ft 7¼ in)
DIMENSIONS, GONDOLA:	
Length overall	3.44 m (11 ft 3½ in)
Max width	1.54 m (5 ft 0½ in)
Height: excl wheel	1.55 m (5 ft 1 in)
incl wheel	2.14 m (7 ft 0¼ in)

Colt AS 80 Mk II single/two-person thermal airship, winner of the 1989 European Championships

World's largest hot-air airship, the AS 261, with netting and inflatable support platform for botanical investigation team

Colt GA 42 helium airships awaiting take-off on commercial advertising flights

WEIGHTS:			
Max static heaviness	100 kg (220 lb)	Max rate of climb	396 m (1,299 ft)/min
Design gross lift	1,100 kg (2,425 lb)	Max rate of descent	456 m (1,496 ft)/min
PERFORMANCE:		Pressure ceiling (ISA)	2,900 m (9,515 ft)
Cruising speed: max	40 knots (74 km/h; 46 mph)	Max endurance	7 h 30 min
normal	32 knots (60 km/h; 37 mph)	Pitch angle limits	+30°/−25°
econ	27 knots (50 km/h; 31 mph)		

UNITED STATES OF AMERICA

ABC

AMERICAN BLIMP CORPORATION

1900 North-East 25th Avenue (Suite 5), Hillsboro, Oregon 97124
Telephone: 1 (503) 693 1611
Fax: 1 (503) 681 0906
PRESIDENT: James Thiele

American Blimp Corporation A-60 Lightship

ABC A-60 and A-60 Plus LIGHTSHIP

The **A-60** Lightship, used primarily for advertising and promotion, is designed for cost-effective operation with a minimum ground support crew. It is illuminated internally for full-colour day and night advertising display.

The A-50 prototype (see 1990-91 *Jane's*) first flew on 9 April 1988, accumulating some 700 hours by the end of 1989. Development of the larger A-60 continued, with the first flight of the prototype in June 1989. This prototype and subsequent A-60 production airships have also flown over 700 hours. The A-60 was awarded FAA type certification on 18 May 1990, with full approval for day/night and VFR/IFR flight. ABC delivered the first production Lightship, to Virgin Lightships Ltd, in November 1990.

A chronology of events in December 1990 included successfully completed certification of an airborne, gyro-stabilised television camera mount complete with micro-wave downlink for live broadcast, and modification of the type certificate to include an APU capable of delivering 2,000W at 110V. The APU is used primarily to power the internal illumination lights, but can be used to power other airborne equipment. The camera and APU can be operated simultaneously. Delivery of the second production Lightship to Virgin took place in January 1991, and ABC was scheduled to deliver five additional Lightships in 1991.

The envelope has an outer structural skin with a separate inner gas-tight bladder and a single ballonet. All structural attachments to the sewn outer bag, such as nose mooring, fin base and guy wires, car catenary and handling lines, are made with webbing reinforcements sewn directly to the hull. The Lightship has four fins, in cruciform configuration, identical to each other and cable controlled from the gondola with a rotational clearance of 22.9 cm (9 in) during take-off. The Lightship is moored to a standard mooring mast.

The five-place A-60 Lightship gondola is suspended by 12 catenary cables each attached to external patches, eliminating the need for internal cables, gas-tight fittings and bellow sleeves. The Lightship can be inflated without a net, by attaching the ballasted car before adding helium, and the car can be removed from the inflated Lightship without a net by ballasting the catenary cables themselves. Primary flight controls are fitted for the front left-hand seat only.

Twin 60 kW (80 hp) Limbach L 2000 engines are pusher-mounted to enhance propulsive efficiency and reduce noise. Standard capacity of the rear-mounted fuel tank is 280 litres (74 US gallons; 61.6 Imp gallons), giving the Lightship a flight endurance of 8-15 hours. The Lightship can be refuelled in the field without mooring.

Final certification was expected in 1991 of the **A-60 Plus**, which incorporates the existing gondola, control surfaces and hardware with a higher volume envelope to enhance performance in hotter climates and at higher

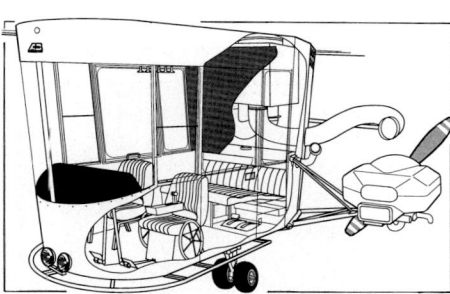

Gondola and power plant of the A-60 Lightship

altitudes. Future Lightship series will include even greater helium capacity with larger, nine-place gondolas.

ABC Lightship gondola (*Peter M. Bowers*)

DIMENSIONS, ENVELOPE (A: A-60, B: A-60 Plus):

Length overall: A, B	39.01 m (128 ft 0 in)
Max diameter: A	9.40 m (30 ft 10 in)
B	10.01 m (32 ft 10 in)
Fineness ratio: A	4.05
B	3.80
Fin area (total): A, B	42.74 m² (460.0 sq ft)
Volume: A	1,699 m³ (60,000 cu ft)
B	1,925.5 m³ (68,000 cu ft)

DIMENSIONS, GONDOLA (A-60 and A-60 Plus):

Length overall	3.96 m (13 ft 0 in)
Width	1.52 m (5 ft 0 in)
Height overall	2.90 m (9 ft 6 in)
Propeller diameter	1.52 m (5 ft 0 in)
Cabin: Length	2.74 m (9 ft 0 in)
Height	1.83 m (6 ft 0 in)

WEIGHTS (A and B as above):

Total weight empty: A	1,188 kg (2,620 lb)
B	1,216 kg (2,680 lb)
Max buoyancy: A, B	1,814 kg (4,000 lb)
Max dynamic lift: A, B	113 kg (250 lb)

Max useful lift, ISA at 656 m (2,000 ft):	
A	499 kg (1,100 lb)
B	680 kg (1,500 lb)
Max gross weight: A, B	1,993 kg (4,394 lb)

PERFORMANCE (A and B as above):

Max level speed: A	48 knots (89 km/h; 55 mph)
B	46 knots (85 km/h; 53 mph)
Max rate of climb: A	488 m (1,600 ft)/min
B	457 m (1,500 ft)/min
Service ceiling: A, B	2,225 m (7,300 ft)
Max rate of descent: A	427 m (1,400 ft)/min
B	396 m (1,300 ft)/min
Min T-O distance: A, B	112 m (366 ft)
Max range at 35 knots (65 km/h; 40 mph):	
A	564 nm (1,046 km; 650 miles)
B	521 nm (965 km; 600 miles)
Max endurance at 35 knots (65 km/h; 40 mph):	
A	16 h 18 min
B	15 h

AEROLIFT

AEROLIFT INC

AeroLift was founded in 1980. Originally funded by five major Canadian logging companies, AeroLift became publicly owned and held patents to develop a hybrid (aerostatic/aerodynamic) heavy lift vehicle known as the CycloCrane. Details of this unique vehicle have been well documented in the 1990-91 and earlier editions of *Jane's*. A number of trials were conducted by the proof-of-concept vehicle, under various US Defense Department contracts, but the cessation of these caused closure of the company in 1990.

BARNES

BARNES AIRSHIPS

Route 2, Box 86, Statesville, North Carolina 28677
Telephone: 1 (704) 876 2378

BARNES WHISPERSHIP

Due to become available in mid-1991, the Whispership is a single/two-place recreational non-rigid with an X-fin tail unit and pusher propeller. Features include water floats on the base of the gondola and lower fins.

POWER PLANT: One 3.73 kW (5 hp) four-stroke engine with electric starting.

DIMENSIONS, ENVELOPE:

Length overall	17.07 m (56 ft 0 in)
Max diameter	5.79 m (19 ft 0 in)
Height, incl gondola	7.01 m (23 ft 0 in)
Fineness ratio	2.94
Volume	269.0 m³ (9,500 cu ft)

WEIGHTS:

Weight empty	138 kg (304 lb)
Max payload	109 kg (240 lb)
Gross lift	273 kg (603 lb)

PERFORMANCE:

Max level speed	28 knots (51 km/h; 32 mph)
Cruising speed	21.5 knots (40 km/h; 25 mph)
Max rate of climb	305 m (1,000 ft)/min
Ceiling	915 m (3,000 ft)
Max rate of descent	244 m (800 ft)/min
Max endurance:	
with standard fuel, at 21.5 knots (40 km/h; 25 mph)	10 h
with auxiliary fuel tanks	36 h

GOODYEAR

GOODYEAR AEROSPACE CORPORATION
(Division of Loral Systems Group)

1210 Massillon Road, Akron, Ohio 44315
Telephone: 1 (216) 796 4635
Fax: 1 (216) 796 7886/4242
Telex: 986439, 810-431-2080 GDYRAERO AKRA
PRESIDENT: Robert W. Clark
EXECUTIVE VICE-PRESIDENT: Raymond E. Stankard
VICE-PRESIDENT, MARKETING: Willis S. Zeigler
DIRECTOR, PUBLIC RELATIONS: Lyle Schwilling

Goodyear has built over 310 airships, of which over 250 were constructed under contract for the US Army and Navy.

In March 1987 Goodyear's aircraft and aerospace subsidiary for more than 60 years, Goodyear Aerospace Corporation, was sold to Loral Corporation, and operates as a Division of Loral Systems Group. It provides airship manufacturing services and support to the Goodyear airship programme.

Goodyear Tire & Rubber Company operates three GZ-20A non-rigid airships in the USA for public relations and sales promotion activities: *America* (N3A), *Columbia* (N10A) and *Enterprise* (N1A).

GOODYEAR GZ-22

This latest airship flew for the first time on 9 October 1987, but numerous requests since that time have failed to yield either a photograph or any factual information from the company. All known details, culled from various press reports, were given in the 1990-91 *Jane's*.

MEMPHIS

MEMPHIS AIRSHIPS INC

Isle-A-Port Airport, 1720 Harbor Avenue, PO Box 13037,
Memphis, Tennessee 38113
Telephone: 1 (901) 775 0386
Fax: 1 (901) 775 0917
PRESIDENT: Steve Garner
EXECUTIVE VICE-PRESIDENT: Jim Groce

Memphis Airships was formed in 1981 as a producer of
small unmanned advertising airships and fan supported
inflatables, and continues to manufacture such items.

A prototype of the Ultrablimp small air recreation
vehicle was flown at the 1985 Sun 'n Fun and Oshkosh
meetings, and was described and illustrated in the 1987-88
Jane's. It was followed by a second prototype (Ultrablimp
II) in 1987. Details and a photograph of the one-off
Dreamfinder non-rigid single-place airship appeared in the
1986-87 *Jane's*. Memphis Airships' latest designs are the
two-place EXP-II and one-place Zephyr 200.

MEMPHIS EXP-II

Only one EXP-II was built. A description and photograph can be found in the 1990-91 *Jane's*.

MEMPHIS ZEPHYR 200

Light enough to meet FAR 103 (ultralight) criteria, the
Zephyr 200 began as a single-place sport/recreation airship,
powered by a single piston engine driving a shrouded
propeller aft of the gondola. The envelope is helium-filled,
with valves and ballasting for full control in ascent and
descent. It can be free ballooned for long periods in the
event of any control or engine failure. Four had been
ordered by early 1991, including one by Westinghouse
Electric Corporation for trials use in connection with a US
Army requirement for a remotely controlled observation
and communications platform.

In the following description, A refers to the Z-201
single-place sports version and B to the Z-203 optionally
piloted version:
POWER PLANT (A): One 7.5 kW (10 hp) Honda aircooled
four-stroke engine; fuel capacity 7.6 litres (2 US gallons;
1.66 Imp gallons).

Memphis Zephyr 200 in use by Westinghouse as a testbed for the US Army

POWER PLANT (B): One 17.9 kW (24 hp) König SC 430
two-cylinder two-stroke engine; fuel capacity 38 litres (10
US gallons; 8.3 Imp gallons).

DIMENSIONS, ENVELOPE:

Length overall: A	17.04 m (55 ft 10¾ in)
B	17.00 m (55 ft 9½ in)
Max diameter: A	5.24 m (17 ft 2½ in)
B	5.40 m (17 ft 8½ in)
Height overall, incl gondola: A, B	6.77 m (22 ft 2½ in)
Fineness ratio: A	3.25
B	3.15
Volume: envelope: A	236.2 m³ (8,340 cu ft)
B	249.6 m³ (8,813 cu ft)
ballonet(s): A	21.24 m³ (750 cu ft)
B	42.48 m³ (1,500 cu ft)

WEIGHTS:

Weight empty, incl gondola: A	114 kg (251 lb)
B	125 kg (275 lb)

Typical payload: A		95-122 kg (210-270 lb)
B		86-122 kg (190-270 lb)
Payload at max altitude: A		89 kg (197 lb)
B		84 kg (185 lb)
Max gross lift (ballonet/s 25% full): A		240 kg (530 lb)
B		249 kg (550 lb)

PERFORMANCE:

Max level speed: A		30 knots (56 km/h; 35 mph)
B		37 knots (69 km/h; 43 mph)
Cruising speed: A		23 knots (42 km/h; 26 mph)
B		28 knots (51 km/h; 32 mph)
Max rate of climb: A, B		244 m (800 ft)/min
Ceiling: A		975 m (3,200 ft)
B		1,705 m (5,600 ft)
Max rate of descent: A, B		213 m (700 ft)/min
Endurance at normal cruising speed:		
A		3 h
B		4 h

SKYRIDER

SKYRIDER AIRSHIPS INC

2840 Wilderness Place (Suite E), PO Box 1158, Boulder,
Colorado 80301
Telephone: 1 (303) 449 2190
Fax: 1 (303) 449 2074
PRESIDENT: Frank E. Rider

RIDER BA-3

Built in 14 months, the BA-3 prototype (N25FR) was
flown for the first time on 11 May 1988 and has been
described and illustrated in previous editions of *Jane's*. No
recent news has been received.

THOMPSON

JAMES THOMPSON, AIAA

1700 Citizens Plaza, Louisville, Kentucky 40202
Telephone: 1 (502) 589 0130
Telex: 204335

THOMPSON AIRSHIP

Construction of this small, two-person sport and
advertising airship was suspended during 1988-89. Completion was expected in 1990, but no confirmation of this
has been received.

The airship has a helium filled envelope, inside which are
two 56.6 m³ (2,000 cu ft) capacity air ballonets that will be
filled unequally to provide pitch trim. The tail unit is a fabric
covered aluminium tube inverted Y structure (all three
angles 120°), the elevators of which operate differentially to
control rolling moment. There are no catenary curtains:
cables attached to five finger patches on each side of the
envelope suspend the gondola slightly forward of the centre
of buoyancy, to compensate for pitch-up. The gondola itself
has a steel tube frame, with glassfibre and urethane foam
skin panels, and accommodates the crew, power plant and
two water ballast tanks. Propulsion is provided by a 1,200 cc
Honda liquid-cooled engine, with 2.2:1 toothed-belt
reduction drive to a two-blade shrouded wooden pusher
propeller. The gondola is stabilised by three cables attached
to the propeller shroud.

DIMENSIONS, ENVELOPE:

Length overall	24.91 m (81 ft 9 in)
Max diameter	7.91 m (25 ft 11¼ in)

Model of the Thompson two-person airship

Volume: helium	695.0 m³ (24,544 cu ft)
ballonets	97.9 m³ (3,456 cu ft)
design total	792.9 m³ (28,000 cu ft)
Fineness ratio	3.15

WEIGHTS:

Envelope	244 kg (538 lb)
Gondola	187 kg (412 lb)

Water ballast	81.5 kg (180 lb)
Max T-O weight	696 kg (1,534 lb)

PERFORMANCE (estimated):

Design speed	30 knots (55 km/h; 34 mph)

ULITA

ULITA INDUSTRIES INC (Manufacturing Division)

PO Box 412, Sheboygan, Wisconsin 53082-0412
Telephone: 1 (414) 458 2842

PRESIDENT AND TECHNICAL ADVISER: Thomas S. Berger

VICE-PRESIDENT, MARKETING: Mark R. Forss

Ulita has four current light utility airship programmes:
the UM20, UM25 and UM10, of which prototypes are
under construction, and the UM30, which is in the design
stage.

ULITA UM10-22 CLOUD CRUISER

Optimised for the ARV (air recreational vehicle)
category, the UM10-22 was conceived and designed by Mr
T. S. Berger, President and Technical Adviser of Ulita

Industries Inc. It is intended as a low-cost light utility
airship to appeal to a broad range of markets that larger
contemporary airships cannot satisfy.

Prototype construction was nearing completion in
January 1990. Certification was then being considered, but
in the meantime the UM10-22 is available only in kit form.
ENVELOPE: Non-rigid helium filled hull, with twin ballonets.
Attached directly to the hull are two stabiliser fin roots
which are located 45° below the horizontal plane of

symmetry, creating an inverted V. Attached to the ends of this inverted V are two vertical stabilisers each incorporating a movable control surface which operates as a rudder. The horizontal stabiliser is also attached to the ends of the inverted V and provided with movable control surfaces which operate as elevators. This fin arrangement provides for easy assembly and maintenance. One landing wheel at base of each fin.

GONDOLA: Side by side seating, with dual control wheels, for pilot and one student/passenger. Two landing wheels, mounted on outriggers. Accommodation ventilated, but not heated.

POWER PLANT: Two 18 kW (24 hp) König SC 340 three-cylinder two-stroke engines, each driving a three-blade fixed-pitch ducted propeller, mounted on an outrigger from gondola and capable of rotation to provide horizontal or vertical thrust. Main fuel tank is located in the control car, with provisions for auxiliary tanks on the outriggers. Maximum fuel capacity 60.6 litres (16 US gallons; 13.3 Imp gallons).

SYSTEMS: 12V DC battery and alternator.

DIMENSIONS, OVERALL:

Length	25.17 m (82 ft 6.8 in)
Width	8.05 m (26 ft 4.8 in)
Height	8.88 m (29 ft 1.8 in)

DIMENSIONS, ENVELOPE:

Length overall	24.69 m (81 ft 0 in)
Max diameter	6.86 m (22 ft 6 in)
Volume: ballonets (total)	140.2 m³ (4,950.75 cu ft)
gross	637.23 m³ (22,503.43 cu ft)

DIMENSIONS, GONDOLA:

Length: at top	3.12 m (10 ft 3 in)
overall	3.44 m (11 ft 3.6 in)
Width: at top	1.32 m (4 ft 4 in)
at floor	1.04 m (3 ft 4.9 in)
overall (incl propulsors)	4.33 m (14 ft 2.4 in)
Height: excl landing gear	1.71 m (5 ft 7.3 in)
incl landing gear	2.12 m (6 ft 11.4 in)
Propeller diameter (each)	1.07 m (3 ft 6 in)

WEIGHTS:

Weight empty	380 kg (838 lb)
Fuel (standard)	32.7 kg (72 lb)
Crew of 2	63.5 kg (140 lb)
Payload	52.5 kg (116 lb)
Total gross lift	620 kg (1,366 lb)

PERFORMANCE (estimated):

Max level speed	42 knots (78 km/h; 48 mph)
Econ cruising speed	26 knots (48 km/h; 30 mph)
Pressure ceiling	2,440 m (8,000 ft)

ULITA UM20-48

The UM20-48 (formerly LUA-1) has been designed primarily for advertising and training purposes. The prototype control car has been completed, and in early 1990 final work was being performed on the envelope and tail surfaces. The airship was due to be available, fully certificated, upon completion of flight tests by late 1991.

ENVELOPE: Non-rigid helium filled airship, with two ballonets. Tail unit, of inverted Y configuration, is a riveted aluminium truss structure with lightweight fabric covering. Trim tab on rudder and each ruddervator.

GONDOLA: Primary structure is a welded 4130 steel tube truss, with a skin of light gauge aluminium sheet riveted to aluminium angle and channel. It is fitted with a single non-retractable landing gear unit, carrying twin fully castoring and bungee sprung wheels of 244 mm (9.6 in) diameter, and has side by side seats for a pilot and one passenger. Storage space behind seats and under main cabin floor. Forward opening door on each side. Accommodation is heated and ventilated.

POWER PLANT: One 85.75 kW (115 hp) Textron Lycoming O-235-G1B flat-four engine, driving a two-blade reversible-pitch pusher propeller. Single 98 litre (26 US gallon; 21.6 Imp gallon) fuel tank standard; 38 litre (10 US gallon; 8.3 Imp gallon) auxiliary tank optional.

SYSTEMS: 12V DC battery and alternator.

DIMENSIONS, OVERALL:

Length	32.57 m (106 ft 10.4 in)
Width	9.33 m (30 ft 7.4 in)
Height	12.68 m (41 ft 7.1 in)

DIMENSIONS, ENVELOPE:

Length overall	31.95 m (104 ft 10 in)
Max diameter	8.88 m (29 ft 1.4 in)
Volume: ballonets (two)	271.8 m³ (9,600 cu ft)
gross	1,359.2 m³ (48,000 cu ft)

DIMENSIONS, GONDOLA:

Length overall	4.21 m (13 ft 9.6 in)
Width: at top	1.07 m (3 ft 6 in)
at floor	1.07 m (3 ft 6 in)

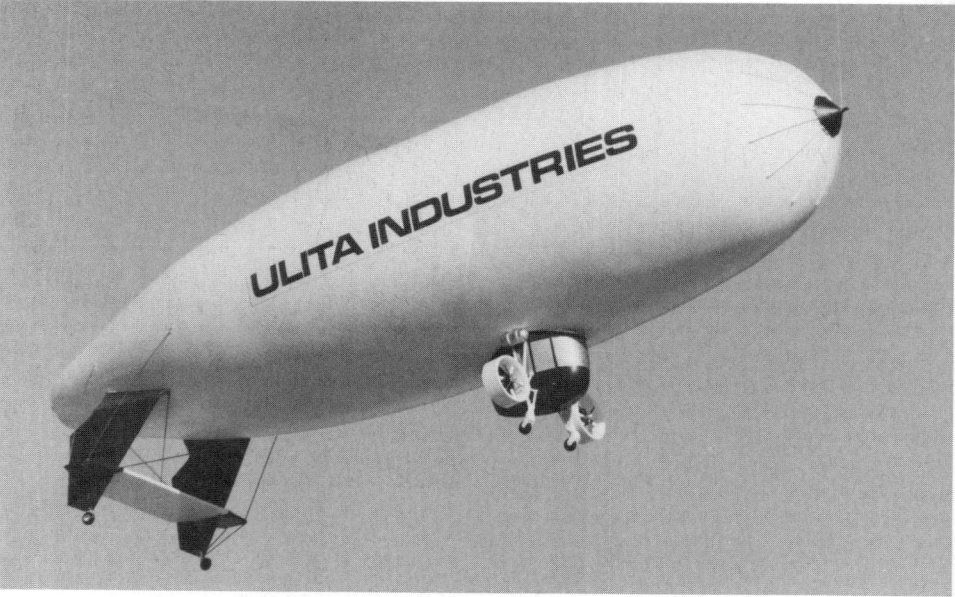

Model of the Ulita UM10-22 air recreation vehicle airship

Height: excl landing gear	2.01 m (6 ft 7.2 in)
incl landing gear	2.81 m (9 ft 2.6 in)

WEIGHTS (estimated):

Weight empty	974 kg (2,147 lb)
Fuel (standard)	72.5 kg (160 lb)
Payload (nominal)	83.5 kg (184 lb)
Total gross lift	1,284 kg (2,831 lb)

PERFORMANCE (estimated):

Max level speed	43 knots (80 km/h; 50 mph)
Econ cruising speed	26 knots (48 km/h; 30 mph)
Pressure ceiling	2,745 m (9,000 ft)

ULITA UM25-64

The four-seat UM25-64 is the latest addition to Ulita's line-up of specially designed airships. Designed specifically for today's multi-media advertising market, its simple design provides for low initial investment and low operating costs. Construction of the prototype envelope is currently well under way, with fabrication of the control car and fins being completed by mid-1990. Certification was planned to be completed by 1991, with availability to follow shortly afterward. Ulita Airship Operations intends eventually to operate five of these airships for training flight crews, advertising, and special purpose leasing operations.

ENVELOPE: Non-rigid, helium filled, with two ballonets. Tail unit, in a cruciform arrangement, is a riveted aluminium truss structure with lightweight fabric covering. Trim tab on rudder only.

GONDOLA: Primary structure is a welded 4130 steel tube truss, with a skin of light gauge aluminium sheet riveted to aluminium angle and channel. The car will incorporate a tricycle landing gear system. Shock absorption is provided by a shock cord system.

POWER PLANT: One Textron Lycoming O-320-D3G flat-four engine, rated at 119 kW (160 hp) at 2,700 rpm, mounted on back of car in pusher configuration. A twin-engined version, utilising two 59.7 kW (80 hp) Limbach engines, is also planned. Fuel is supplied from two 94.6 litre (25 US gallon; 20.8 Imp gallon) tanks and a 47.3 litre (12.5 US gallon; 10.4 Imp gallon) auxiliary tank.

SYSTEMS: 24V DC battery and alternator.

DIMENSIONS, OVERALL:

Length	35.73 m (117 ft 2.9 in)
Width	10.42 m (34 ft 2.4 in)
Height	14.41 m (47 ft 3.4 in)

DIMENSIONS, ENVELOPE:

Length overall	35.05 m (115 ft 0 in)
Max diameter	9.74 m (31 ft 11.3 in)
Volume: ballonets (two)	444.4 m³ (15,692.7 cu ft)
gross	1,851.5 m³ (65,386 cu ft)

DIMENSIONS, GONDOLA:

Length overall	5.18 m (17 ft 0 in)
Width: at top	1.83 m (6 ft 0 in)
at floor	1.37 m (4 ft 6 in)
Height: excl landing gear	2.47 m (8 ft 1.2 in)
incl landing gear	3.43 m (11 ft 3 in)

WEIGHTS (estimated):

Weight empty	1,224 kg (2,699 lb)
Fuel (standard)	136 kg (300 lb)
Payload (nominal)	67.5 kg (149 lb)
Total gross lift	1,737 kg (3,829 lb)

PERFORMANCE (estimated):

Max level speed	43 knots (80 km/h; 50 mph)
Econ cruising speed	36 knots (66 km/h; 41 mph)
Pressure ceiling	3,350 m (11,000 ft)

ULITA UM30-71

Still in the design stage, the UM30-71 (originally LUA-2) is a second-generation vehicle intended to offer greater payload capacity and in-flight endurance, opening up the market to such applications as harbour patrol, rescue/casevac and short-range maritime surveillance. Features will include vectored thrust propulsion, tricycle landing gear for improved ground handling, gondola accommodation for a pilot and three passengers, composite construction, and a fly-by-light control system with automated flight control capabilities.

POWER PLANT: One 149 kW (200 hp) Textron Lycoming IO-360 flat-four engine, driving two five-blade reversible-pitch ducted propellers with thrust vectoring. Fuel capacity (standard) 227 litres (60 US gallons; 50 Imp gallons).

DIMENSIONS, OVERALL:

Length	41.45 m (136 ft 0 in)
Width	9.94 m (32 ft 7.3 in)
Height	13.65 m (44 ft 9.4 in)

DIMENSIONS, ENVELOPE:

Length overall	41.15 m (135 ft 0 in)
Max diameter	9.87 m (32 ft 4.4 in)
Volume: ballonets (two)	404.4 m³ (14,283 cu ft)
gross	2,022.2 m³ (71,413 cu ft)

DIMENSIONS, GONDOLA:

Length overall	7.84 m (25 ft 8.6 in)
Width: at top	1.71 m (5 ft 7.2 in)
at bottom	1.22 m (4 ft 0 in)
Height: excl landing gear	2.50 m (8 ft 2.4 in)
incl landing gear	3.05 m (10 ft 0 in)

WEIGHTS (estimated):

Weight empty	1,386 kg (3,055 lb)
Fuel (standard)	163 kg (360 lb)
Payload	154 kg (340 lb)
Total gross lift	1,857 kg (4,095 lb)

PERFORMANCE (estimated):

Max level speed	54 knots (100 km/h; 62 mph)
Max cruising speed	48 knots (90 km/h; 56 mph)
Econ cruising speed	43 knots (80 km/h; 50 mph)
Pressure ceiling	2,135 m (7,000 ft)
Range at econ cruising speed, standard fuel	
	326 nm (605 km; 376 miles)
Endurance at econ cruising speed, standard fuel	
	7 h 30 min

US-LTA

US LIGHTER THAN AIR CORPORATION (A division of Aerotech)

6040 Hangar Road, Tillamook, Oregon 97141
Telephone: 1 (503) 842 3032
Fax: 1 (503) 842 7362
GENERAL MANAGER: Dix Evans
DIRECTOR OF AIRSHIP OPERATIONS: Lee Cermak
CHIEF PILOT: Hunter H. Harris

Originally known as Grace Aircraft Corporation, later (1985) as US Airship Corporation, and then (April 1986) as Aerotek Corporation, this company came under new ownership in July 1988 and is now known as US Lighter Than Air Corporation. Assets acquired by US-LTA included the prototype Aerotek USA 100 (originally Grace GAC-20) airship, which is now known as the US-LTA 138-S. Major components of this prototype were built at

Eugene; final assembly took place in the former US Navy airship hangars at Tillamook, Oregon.

US-LTA 138-S

The US-LTA 138-S is intended for commercial advertising, and as a testbed for further engineering and development of airship systems. It is designed and built in accordance with current FAA airworthiness standards for airships. First flight was made on 28 October 1987, and over 200 hours of flying had been completed by early 1990. FAA certification was received in 1990.

ENVELOPE: Non-rigid type of ellipsoidal configuration, made of polyurethane coated Dacron with a non-woven material laminated on the inside for bias stability. Seams are heat-sealed inside and out. Nose is stiffened by 16 battens to permit higher airspeeds and distribute mooring loads. Weight of gondola is supported by cables attached to two internal catenary curtains which hang from upper quarter of envelope over half of its length. Side loads and thrust from car are transmitted to envelope via the car catenary, a fabric doubler extending away from car perimeter in all directions to ensure uniform load distribution to envelope. Two air-filled ballonets within helium compartment, to compensate for variations in hull pressure and adjust in-flight trim, are made of heat sealed urethane coated nylon. Air is supplied to ballonets via ram air duct aft of propeller, with mechanically controlled valves to duct air to front or rear ballonet as required. A passive pressure relief valve is fitted to each ballonet and in the helium compartment to control and prevent accidental envelope overpressure. Manual cable control permits controlled venting of helium or air if required. Inverted Y tail unit, comprising three identical aluminium framework fins, covered with doped fabric; each fin is attached to envelope with 13 fan patches at its base and supported by three guy wires on each side.

GONDOLA: Control car is shaped as an ellipsoidal hyperbola with a circular end section, and has an exterior shell of glassfibre epoxy sandwich construction with a foam core, over a welded steel tube frame. Windows of Plexiglas. The cabin seats six persons, including the crew, in pairs, and is separated acoustically from the engine compartment at the rear. The single-wheel landing gear is of trailing link type, pivoting about a vertical axis.

POWER PLANT: One 224 kW (300 hp) Textron Lycoming IO-540-K1A5 flat-six engine, mounted aft of control car on a 4130 steel tube frame and driving a Hartzell HC-3YR-7LF three-blade constant-speed reversible-pitch pusher propeller within an annular duct. Fuel tanks at rear of car, combined capacity 386 litres (102 US gallons; 85 Imp gallons).

SYSTEMS: Electrical system is a standard light aircraft 28V 100A negative ground type, powered by an engine driven alternator. While moored, a blower system is powered by a ground based generator for automatic monitoring and control of envelope pressurisation. Flight control is cable driven and hydraulically boosted, using a conventional stick with pushrods in combination with an adjustable friction damper, hydraulic boost system and mechanical

Prototype of the US-LTA 138-S

mixer for the tail surfaces. System can be flown manually in the event of hydraulic failure.

AVIONICS: Dual nav/com radios with VOR/ILS, Loran, ADF, transponder, and marker beacon receivers. Standard instrumentation includes ASI, VSI, attitude indicator, barometric and radar altimeters, turn co-ordinator, directional gyro, magnetic compass, engine and fuel system instruments, inside and outside air temperature gauges, ballonet and helium envelope manometers, hydraulic system temperature and pressure gauges, and clock.

DIMENSIONS, OVERALL:
Length	48.77 m (160 ft 0 in)
Width	12.80 m (42 ft 0 in)
Height	17.37 m (57 ft 0 in)
Envelope volume	3,908 m³ (138,000 cu ft)

DIMENSIONS, GONDOLA:
External:
Length: incl power plant	6.55 m (21 ft 6 in)
excl power plant	approx 5.79 m (19 ft 0 in)
Max width	approx 1.83 m (6 ft 0 in)
Max height	approx 2.74 m (9 ft 0 in)

Internal (cabin):
Length	4.07 m (13 ft 4¼ in)
Max width: at floor	1.65 m (5 ft 4¾ in)
at ceiling	1.77 m (5 ft 9½ in)
Max height	1.93 m (6 ft 4 in)

WEIGHTS:
Weight empty	2,660 kg (5,865 lb)
Control car, empty	1,052 kg (2,320 lb)
Max fuel	278 kg (612 lb)
Payload with standard fuel	1,143 kg (2,520 lb)
Gross weight	3,804 kg (8,386 lb)

PERFORMANCE:
Max level speed	56 knots (104 km/h; 65 mph)
Demonstrated service ceiling	2,745 m (9,000 ft)
Range with max fuel, cruising at 30 knots (56 km/h; 35 mph)	434 nm (804 km; 500 miles)
Endurance with max fuel, speed as above	14 h 30 min

WAI
WESTINGHOUSE AIRSHIPS INC

PO Box 17193 (MS 8700), Baltimore, Maryland 21203
Telephone: 1 (301) 379 2144
Fax: 1 (301) 379 2124
ODM PROGRAMME MANAGER:
    Gordon T. Adams Sr
VICE-PRESIDENT, BUSINESS DEVELOPMENT:
    E. Judson Brandreth Jr

Following the collapse of Airship Industries (UK) Ltd in 1990, Westinghouse Electric Corporation acquired that company's 50 per cent share in their WAI joint venture company, together with all military/defence applications of the SK 500/500HL/600 Skyships and their Sentinel 1000/5000 derivatives.

WAI SENTINEL 1000

Driven by a market requirement for a vehicle with greater payload capability, endurance, speed and flexibility to better perform such military and naval roles as mine countermeasures, airborne early warning and anti-submarine warfare, Airship Industries in the UK began development of this addition to its product range. A derivative of the Skyship 600, the Sentinel 1000 (or **600S** as it is called in its civil variant) has a larger envelope, a higher performance engine, and the world's first fly-by-light optical fibre flight control system, developed by GEC Avionics.

As, in many respects, the Sentinel 1000 represents a half-linear-scale version of the YEZ-2A under development for the US Navy (see following entry), it will provide a useful tool for development and optimisation for the US Navy programme, and as such has been designated the official trials vehicle. Until the YEZ-2A is completed the Sentinel 1000 will be the largest non-rigid airship flying, combining substantial increase in payload, improved flight control through the autopilot/autostabilisation elements of the YEZ-2A flight control system, and upgrading of the general vehicle avionics. First flight of the Sentinel 1000 was made on 26 June 1991.

DIMENSIONS, ENVELOPE:
Length overall	67.50 m (221 ft 5½ in)
Max diameter	16.70 m (54 ft 9½ in)
Height overall	20.20 m (66 ft 3¼ in)
Volume: gross	10,000 m³ (353,150 cu ft)
ballonets (total)	2,405 m³ (84,932 cu ft)

DIMENSIONS, GONDOLA: As for Skyship 600 (see under Slingsby in UK section)
WEIGHTS (design):
Gross disposable load	4,200 kg (9,260 lb)

PERFORMANCE (estimated):
Max level speed	58 knots (107 km/h; 67 mph)
Cruising speed (70% power)	50 knots (92 km/h; 57 mph)
Still air range at 36 knots (67 km/h; 41 mph) with long-endurance tanks	2,400 nm (4,448 km; 2,764 miles)

WAI SENTINEL 5000
US Navy designation: YEZ-2A

A Naval Airship Program (NAP) was initiated by Naval Air Systems Command in 1985 to investigate the suitability of airships in the AEW role. A contract award was made to WAI in June 1987 selecting the Sentinel 5000 as the basis for an operational development model (ODM) airship. In October 1988 the NAP evolved from an exclusively US Navy programme to one by the Defense Advanced Research Projects Agency (DARPA). The lighter than air programme still focuses on the demonstration of a long-range, long-endurance surveillance system capable of seeing low-observable sea-skimming cruise missiles. However, OTH (over the horizon) third-party targeting now appears to be an evolving requirement for the US Navy battle group. In addition, drug surveillance and interdiction functions have a need for a surveillance platform that is fundamentally non-provocative, capable of sophisticated air and sea search in the detection of drug runners, and has the ability to act as a command and control centre for other

Ground test vehicle for the YEZ-2A Sentinel 5000 gondola and propulsion system, at Weeksville, North Carolina

government agencies. The Sentinel 5000 is a prime candidate for this role.

Six-month NAP study contracts were placed in mid-1985 with three US companies (Boeing Military Airplanes, Goodyear and Westinghouse), to investigate the suitability of airships for use by the US Navy in an independent airborne early warning role.

The original Navy requirement was for an independent airborne early warning system capable of operating with surface attack groups anywhere in the world. Primary functions were described by the Naval Air Development Center as "detection, classification, identification and tracking of surface and airborne targets, particularly those of low radar cross-section, flying at low altitude and high speed in a sea clutter environment, and communications connectivity between surface ships in a battle group". The surveillance system would warn surface ships of threats beyond the range of shipboard radars, including long-range sea-skimming cruise missiles.

All three study contractors responded initially to the USN request for proposals issued in August 1986, but Boeing (whose design was the only rigid airship submitted) subsequently withdrew, leaving Goodyear and the Westinghouse/Airship Industries partnership as the final contenders. Award of a $168.9 million contract to WAI for an operational development model (ODM) airship, based on the Airship Industries Sentinel 5000 design, was announced by NASC on 5 June 1987. Originally, the contract envisaged the installation of an E-2C Hawkeye avionics suite, but this is now unlikely to be used. The ODM vehicle will have an unrefuelled endurance of 2-3 days; by refuelling and replenishing from surface units within a task force, a mission capability of some 30 days is intended. Designated USN missions are surveillance and targeting, airborne early warning, and communications.

Two preliminary design reviews (PDRs) of the ODM programme were held in late January and June 1989, and the subsequent critical design review (CDR) was held in September 1989. These briefings, on the design status of the airship, were attended by representatives of the US Navy, DARPA and the Naval Air Development Center.

The NASC contract included options for up to five additional airships, and the potential production programme could involve up to 50 of these craft. Current activity is continuing as part of the US Department of Defense's Air Defense Initiative programme. First flight of the ODM prototype is now planned for 1994, with subsequent flight and operational test programmes to be decided when more is known about the proposed avionics suite. Final assembly and initial flight testing will take place in the USA.

General configuration of the YEZ-2A Sentinel 5000, with current X configuration tail unit

Based on earlier Airship Industries studies for very large airships, the Sentinel 5000 will be the largest non-rigid ever constructed, and will carry a crew of 10-15 in a multi-deck, wide-bodied and pressurised gondola. The upper deck will provide living accommodation for the crew, including double cabins, showers, separate wardroom galley, and a small gymnasium. Mission avionics, control information centre, galley, replenishment stores and refuelling equipment will occupy the lower deck. Below these two is a smaller flight deck containing the flight controls and instrumentation. The envelope will be made of a single-ply Dacron weave material, laminated with Tedlar and Mylar and bonded with Hytrel. The X configuration tail unit will have two control surfaces per fin, each control surface having two actuators and triple hinges. The control actuation will have full autostabilisation and autopilot provided by GEC Avionics computer controlled, optically signalled fly-by-light system. The system, using two MIL-STD-1750A standard computers and a MIL-STD-1553B databus, will provide redundant fail-safe actuation of the movable tail surfaces via fibre optic signalling, automatic stability and good handling characteristics throughout the flight regime, hands-off autopilot control for cruising, hovering and mooring, and automatic speed control.

An unpressurised engine room aft contains a CODAG (combined diesel and gas turbine) propulsion system, comprising an internally mounted pair of 1,394 kW (1,870 hp) ducted propulsion CRM diesel units, with thrust vectoring, plus a 1,394 kW (1,870 shp) General Electric CT7-9 turboprop, mounted on the gondola centreline at the rear, to provide additional power when a higher dash speed is required. A substantial winching bay is located between the engine room aft and pressurised accommodation section forward, from where refuelling, re-storing and personnel transfers will be conducted through a large opening in the base of the gondola.

DIMENSIONS, ENVELOPE:

Length overall	129.54 m (425 ft 0 in)
Max diameter	32.00 m (105 ft 0 in)
Height overall	46.33 m (152 ft 0 in)
Volume, gross	70,792 m³ (2,500,000 cu ft)

DIMENSIONS, GONDOLA:

Length overall	25.91 m (85 ft 0 in)
Max width	5.08 m (16 ft 8 in)
Max height	7.32 m (24 ft 0 in)

PERFORMANCE (estimated):

Max level speed (3 engines)	88 knots (163 km/h; 101 mph)
Operating height range	S/L to 3,050 m (10,000 ft)
Pressure ceiling	4,270 m (14,000 ft)
Max unrefuelled endurance at 40 knots (74 km/h; 46 mph) at 1,525 m (5,000 ft)	more than 60 h
Mission capability	30 days

LIGHTER THAN AIR: BALLOONS

CONTRACTORS' ADDRESSES:

Country	Company	Address	Telephone/Fax/Telex
Australia	Kavanagh Balloons Pty Ltd*	13/10 Pioneer Avenue, Thornleigh, NSW 2120	*Tel:* 61 (2) 484 3193 *Fax:* 61 (2) 484 4915
Canada	Fantasy Sky Promotions Inc	205 Bridge Street, New Dundee, Ontario N0B 2E0	*Tel:* 1 (519) 696 2414
Czechoslovakia	Aerotechnik*	Letiste Kunovice, 68604 Uherské Hradiště	*Tel:* 42 (623) 5122 *Telex:* 60380
France	Ballons Chaize	48 rue Balay, 42000 Saint-Étienne	*Tel:* 33/77 33 43 76 *Fax:* 33/77 38 19 01
Germany	Ballonfabrik See- und Luftausrüstung GmbH & Co KG*	Postfach 101327, Austrasse 35, 8900 Augsburg 1	*Tel:* 49 (821) 41 50 41 *Telex:* 17/821810
Hungary	Repülőgépes Szolgálat (RSZ)*	PO Box 56, Koérberki út 36, H 1112 Budapest XI	*Tel:* 36 (1) 185 1344 *Fax:* 36 (1) 166 8118 *Telex:* 22-5187
South Africa	Flamboyant Balloons (Pty) Ltd*	PO Box 149, Lanseria 1748, Transvaal	*Tel:* 27 (11) 659 2687 *Fax:* 27 (11) 659 1451
United Kingdom	Cameron Balloons Ltd	St John's Street, Bedminster, Bristol BS3 4NH	*Tel:* 44 (272) 637216 *Fax:* 44 (272) 661168 *Telex:* 444825 GASBAG G
	Thunder & Colt Ltd*	Maesbury Road, Oswestry, Shropshire SY10 8HA	*Tel:* 44 (691) 670644 *Fax:* 44 (691) 670617 *Telex:* 35503 COLT G
United States of America	Adams Balloon Loft Inc*	Building 27, Dekalb Peachtree Airport, Atlanta, Georgia 30341	*Tel:* 1 (404) 452 8066
	Aerostar International Inc (subsidiary of Raven Industries Inc)	Box 5057, Sioux Falls, South Dakota 57117-5057	*Tel:* 1 (605) 331 3500 *Fax:* 1 (605) 331 3520
	Avian Balloon Company	Building 101, Spokane Industrial Park, Spokane, Washington 99216	*Tel:* 1 (509) 928 6847
	The Balloon Works Inc	PO Box 827, 810 Salisbury Road, Statesville, North Carolina 28677	*Tel:* 1 (704) 878 9501 *Fax:* 1 (704) 878 9505
	Galaxy Balloons Inc	820 Salisbury Road, Statesville, North Carolina 28677	*Tel:* 1 (704) 878 9147 *Fax:* 1 (704) 878 9505

*1991 update not received

Representative hot-air balloon from Ballons Chaize

FireFly 77 (AX-7 class) from The Balloon Works

Thunder & Colt 17,000 cu ft Cloudhopper

HOT-AIR (AX), COMBINATION (AM)* AND GAS BALLOON (AA) DATA

Country	Company	Model	Volume m³/cu ft	Gores	Diameter m/ft	Height m/ft	Max gross weight kg/lb	Crew	Basket	Fuel cylinders/ Burners
FAI CLASS AA/AX-2 (250-400 m³; 8,829-14,126 cu ft)										
USA	Aerostar	MG-300	300/10,595	12	8.78/28.8	8.23/27	317/698	1	Mixed structure	NA
FAI CLASS AA/AM/AX-3 (400-600 m³; 14,126-21,189 cu ft)										
Germany	Ballonfabrik	K 630/1-Ri	630/22,248	?	10.64/34.91	18.0/59	?	3-4	Rattan	NA
UK	Cameron	Roziere R-15	424.8/15,000	24	10.3/33.8	12.01/39.4	442/975	2	Willow/Cane	2/2
UK	Cameron	Viva-20	566.3/20,000	8	9.14/30	9.75/32	181/400	1	Harness seat	1/1
UK	Thunder & Colt	Cloudhopper Midi	481.4/17,000	?	9.45/31	9.45/31	?	1	Harness seat	1/1
UK	Thunder & Colt	Cloudhopper Super	594.7/21,000	?	10.06/33	10.67/35	?	1	Harness seat	1/1
FAI CLASS AA/AX-4 (600-900 m³; 21,189-31,783 cu ft)										
Czechoslovakia	Aerotechnik	AB-3	890/31,430	?	12.0/39.37	14.0/45.93	?	1	Harness seat	1/1
Germany	Ballonfabrik	K 780/2-Ri	780/27,545	?	11.5/37.73	19.81/65	?	4	Rattan	NA
Germany	Ballonfabrik	B 800/2-Ri	800/28,252	?	11.5/37.73	20.12/66	?	4	Rattan	NA
Germany	Ballonfabrik	K 945/2-Ri	945/33,372	?	12.17/39.93	20.42/67	?	5-6	Rattan	NA
UK	Cameron	H-24 Skyhopper	680/24,000	15	11.19/36.7	13.69/44.9	218/480	1	Harness seat	1-2/1
UK	Cameron	N-31	878/31,000	24	12.5/41	14.63/48	285/629	1	Willow/Cane	2/1
UK	Cameron	O-31	878/31,000	12	12.5/41	14.63/48	285/629	1	Willow/Cane	2/1
UK	Cameron	Viva-31	878/31,000	8	12.5/41	14.63/48	285/629	1	Willow/Cane	2/1
UK	Thunder & Colt	31Z	890/31,430	?	12.19/40	14.63/48	?	1	Wicker/Cane	2/1
USA	Aerostar	S-40A	883/32,000	16	12.19/40	16.76/55	454/1,000	1	Aluminium chair	1/1
FAI CLASS AA/AM/AX-5 (900-1,200 m³; 31,783-42,378 cu ft)										
Germany	Ballonfabrik	K 1050/3-Ri	1,050/37,080	?	12.6/41.3	20.7/67.9	?	5-6	Rattan	NA
Germany	Ballonfabrik	K 1260/3-Ri	1,260/44,496	?	13.4/42	22.25/73	?	6	Rattan	NA
South Africa	Flamboyant	AX5-40M	1,132/40,000	?	12.9/42.32	14.0/45.93	?	1	Rattan	1/1
UK	Cameron	H-34 Skyhopper	963/34,000	15	12.56/41.2	15.21/49.9	308/680	1	Harness seat	1-2/1
UK	Cameron	N-42	1,189/42,000	24	14.26/46.8	12.07/39.6	?	2	Willow/Cane	2/1
UK	Cameron	O-42	1,189/42,000	12	14.26/46.8	12.07/39.6	381/840	2	Willow/Cane	2/1
UK	Cameron	Roziere R-42	1,189/42,000	24	14.97/49.1	17.47/57.3	1,238/2,730	5	Willow/Cane	2/2
UK	Cameron	Viva-42	1,189/42,000	8	14.26/46.8	12.07/39.6	?	1-2	Willow/Cane	2/1
UK	Thunder & Colt	42 Series 1	1,189/42,000	12	13.59/44.6	14.3/46.9	?	2	Wicker/Cane	2/1
UK	Thunder & Colt	42A	1,189/42,000	16	13.69/44.9	14.5/47.6	?	2	Wicker/Cane	2/1
USA	Adams	LD	964/34,029	?	12.95/42.5	15.54/51	?	1	Rattan	1-2/1
USA	Adams	LD-S	1,104/38,978	?	12.95/42.5	16.46/54	?	1-2	Rattan	1-2/1
USA	Aerostar	MG-1000	1,047/36,959	24	13.34/43.76	12.72/41.72	1,270/2,800	1-3	Rattan	NA
USA	Aerostar	S-45A	1,198/42,300	16	13.72/45	17.68/58	454/1,000	2	Wicker	2/1
USA	Avian	Sparrow	1,189/42,000	16	13.41/44	16.46/54	318/700	1	Wicker	2/1
USA	Balloon Works	FireFly 42	1,182/41,740	12	14.02/46	14.63/48	395/870	1-2	Wicker	3/2
FAI CLASS AA/AX-6 (1,200-1,600 m³; 42,378-56,503 cu ft)										
Australia	Kavanagh	C-56	1,586/56,000	?	15.2/49.87	17.25/56.6	?	2	Cane	1-4/1
Canada	Fantasy	Fantasy 6	1,597/56,400	16	15.24/50	?	?	1	Wicker/metal	?/1
France	Chaize	CS.1600	1,600/56,503	12	14.0/45.93	22.5/73.82	500/1,102	2	Rattan	2/1
Germany	Ballonfabrik	K1360/4-Ri	1,360/48,028	?	13.75/45.11	25.0/82.02	?	6	Rattan	NA
Germany	Ballonfabrik	K1680/4-Ri	1,680/59,329	?	14.78/48.5	24.4/80	?	6	Rattan	NA
South Africa	Flamboyant	AX6-56	1,586/56,000	?	15.0/49.2	18.0/59	?	2	Rattan	2/1
South Africa	Flamboyant	AX6-56M	1,586/56,000	?	15.0/49.2	18.0/59	?	2	Rattan	2/1
UK	Cameron	O-56	1,586/56,000	12	15.24/50	17.07/56	508/1,120	3	Willow/Cane	2/1
UK	Cameron	N-56	1,586/56,000	24	15.24/50	17.07/56	508/1,120	3	Willow/Cane	2/1
UK	Cameron	Viva-56	1,586/56,000	8	15.24/50	17.07/56	508/1,120	3	Willow/Cane	2/1
UK	Thunder & Colt	GB-1	1,050/37,080	?	13.0/42.65	21.0/68.9	?	5-6	Willow/Cane	NA
UK	Thunder & Colt	56 Series 1	1,586/56,000	12	15.39/50.5	16.31/53.5	?	3	Wicker/Cane	2-3/1
UK	Thunder & Colt	56A	1,586/56,000	20 or 28	15.61/51.2	16.4/53.8	?	3	Wicker/Cane	2-3/1
USA	Adams	A50	1,557/54,985	?	15.24/50	17.68/58	?	2	Rattan	1-4/1
USA	Aerostar	S-49A	1,529/54,000	16	14.94/49	17.68/58	499/1,100	1-2	Wicker	1/1
USA	Aerostar	S-50A	1,597/56,400	20	15.24/50	18.29/60	635/1,400	2-4	Wicker	3/1
USA	Aerostar	RX-6	1,597/56,400	12	15.24/50	17.68/58	648/1,430	2-3	Wicker	2/1
USA	Balloon Works	GadFly 56	1,576/55,660	12	15.3/50.1	16.1/52.8	476/1,050	3	Wicker	3/1
USA	Balloon Works	GadFly 560	1,576/55,660	12	15.24/50	16.46/54	476/1,050	1-3	Wicker	3/1
USA	Balloon Works	DragonFly 56	1,576/55,660	12	15.24/50	15.85/52	476/1,050	1-3	Wicker	3/1
USA	Balloon Works	DragonFly 560	1,576/55,660	12	15.24/50	15.85/52	476/1,050	1-3	Wicker	3/1
FAI CLASS AA/AM/AX-7 (1,600-2,200 m³; 56,503-77,692 cu ft)										
Australia	Kavanagh	C-65	1,840/65,000	?	15.9/52.16	17.95/58.9	?	2-3	Cane	1-4/1
Australia	Kavanagh	C-77	2,194/77,500	?	16.8/55.12	19.05/62.5	?	3-4	Cane	1-4/1-2
Australia	Kavanagh	D-77	2,194/77,500	?	16.8/55.12	19.05/62.5	?	3-4	Cane	1-4/1-2
Canada	Fantasy	Fantasy 7	2,194/77,500	20	16.76/55	?	?	3-4	Wicker/metal	2/1
Czechoslovakia	Aerotechnik	AB-2	2,190/77,339	12, 20 or 28	16.0/52.49	16.0/52.49	?	4	Rattan	2/2
France	Chaize	CS.1800	1,800/63,566	12	15.0/49.2	22.5/73.8	500/1,102	2-3	Rattan	3/1
France	Chaize	CS. 2000	2,000/70,629	12	16.5/54.1	22.5/73.8	750/1,653	3	Rattan	3/1
France	Chaize	CS. 2200	2,200/77,692	12 or 32	18.0/59	22.5/73.8	750/1,653	3-4	Rattan	4/2
Hungary	RSZ	RSZ-05	2,200/77,692	?	17.0/55.77	20.7/68	?	1-3	Rattan	2-4/2
South Africa	Flamboyant	AX7-65	1,840/65,000	?	16.0/52.49	20.0/65.6	?	3	Rattan	2/1
South Africa	Flamboyant	AX7-77M	2,180/77,000	?	16.0/52.49	20.0/65.6	?	3	Rattan	2/1
UK	Cameron	Roziere R-60	1,699/60,000	24	16.46/54	19.26/63.2	1,769/3,900	†	Basket or gondola	4+/3
UK	Cameron	O-65	1,840/65,000	12	16.15/53	18.0/59	590/1,300	3	Willow/Cane	3/1
UK	Cameron	N-65	1,840/65,000	24	16.15/53	18.0/59	590/1,300	3	Willow/Cane	3/1
UK	Cameron	Viva-65	1,840/65,000	8	16.15/53	18.0/59	590/1,300	3	Willow/Cane	2/1
UK	Cameron	O-77	2,180/77,000	12	17.07/56	18.9/62	703/1,550	4	Willow/Cane	4/1
UK	Cameron	N-77	2,180/77,000	24	17.07/56	18.9/62	703/1,550	4	Willow/Cane	4/1
UK	Cameron	Viva-77	2,180/77,000	8	17.07/56	18.9/62	703/1,550	4	Willow/Cane	2/1
UK	Thunder & Colt	65 Series 1	1,840/65,000	12	16.18/53.1	17.19/56.4	?	3	Wicker/Cane	2-3/1

NA: Not applicable (gas balloon).

* Roziere combination helium/hot-air balloon: small propane burner maintains helium efficiency at night when solar heating is absent, providing greatly extended flight duration without expending helium or sand ballast. A Cameron Roziere R-60 (see photo on page 660) made the first UK-USSR balloon flight in October 1990; Dutch team had previously crossed Atlantic (Canada-Holland) in an R-225.

HOT-AIR (AX), COMBINATION (AM)* AND GAS BALLOON (AA) DATA *(continued)*

Country	Company	Model	Volume m³/cu ft	Gores	Diameter m/ft	Height m/ft	Max gross weight kg/lb	Crew	Basket	Fuel cylinders/ Burners

FAI CLASS AA/AM/AX-7 (1,600-2,200 m³; 56,503-77,692 cu ft) *(continued)*

UK	Thunder & Colt	69A	1,954/69,000	24 or 30	16.31/53.5	17.31/56.8	?	3	Wicker/Cane	2-3/1
UK	Thunder & Colt	77 Series 1	2,180/77,000	12	16.79/55.1	18.11/59.4	?	4	Wicker/Cane	2-3/1-2
UK	Thunder & Colt	77A	2,180/77,000	24 or 32	17.01/55.8	18.29/60	?	4	Wicker/Cane	2-3/1-2
USA	Adams	A50S	1,755/61,977	?	15.24/50	18.59/61	?	3	Rattan	1-4/1
USA	Adams	A55	2,123/74,973	?	16.76/55	19.51/64	?	3	Rattan	1-4/1
USA	Aerostar	S-52A	1,840/65,000	20	15.85/52	18.29/60	635/1,400	2-3	Wicker	2-3/1-2
USA	Aerostar	S-55A	2,194/77,500	24	16.76/55	19.2/63	651/1,435	3-4	Wicker	2-3/1-2
USA	Aerostar	RX-7	2,194/77,500	12	16.76/55	19.2/63	671/1,480	3	Wicker	2-3/1-2
USA	Avian	Falcon II	1,699/60,000	20	15.54/51	18.59/61	454/1,000	1-3	Wicker	2/1
USA	Balloon Works	DragonFly 65	1,840/65,000	12	17.07/56	17.68/58	476/1,050	3-4	Wicker	3/1
USA	Balloon Works	DragonFly 650	1,840/65,000	12	17.07/56	17.68/58	476/1,050	3-4	Wicker	3/1
USA	Balloon Works	DragonFly 77	2,167/76,520	18	17.07/56	17.68/58	794/1,750	3-4	Wicker	3/1
USA	Balloon Works	DragonFly 770	2,167/76,520	18	17.07/56	17.68/58	794/1,750	3-4	Wicker	3/1
USA	Balloon Works	FireFly 65	1,840/65,000	12	17.07/56	17.68/58	476/1,050	3-4	Wicker	3/1
USA	Balloon Works	FireFly 650	1,840/65,000	12	17.07/56	17.68/58	476/1,050	3-4	Wicker	3/1
USA	Balloon Works	FireFly 77	2,167/76,520	18	17.07/56	17.68/58	794/1,750	3-4	Wicker	3/1
USA	Balloon Works	FireFly 770	2,167/76,520	18	17.07/56	17.68/58	794/1,750	3-4	Wicker	3/1
USA	Galaxy	Galaxy 7	2,170/76,633	16	17.07/56	17.68/58	762/1,680	3-4	Rattan/Wicker	4/1-2

FAI CLASS AX-8 (2,200-3,000 m³; 77,692-105,944 cu ft)

Australia	Kavanagh	D-84	2,378/84,000	?	17.4/57.1	19.55/64.1	?	4	Cane	1-4/1-2
Australia	Kavanagh	D-90	2,548/90,000	?	17.8/58.4	19.85/65.1	?	5	Cane	1-4/1-2
Australia	Kavanagh	D-105	2,973/105,000	?	18.7/61.4	20.95/68.7	?	6	Cane	2-4/2
Canada	Fantasy	Fantasy 8-90	2,548/90,000	20	17.37/57	?	?	3-5	Wicker/metal	?/1-2
Canada	Fantasy	Fantasy 8-105	2,973/105,000	20	18.29/60	?	?	3-5	Wicker/metal	?/1-2
Czechoslovakia	Aerotechnik	AB-8	2,950/104,178	?	18.5/60.7	18.0/59.06	?	6	Rattan	3/2
France	Chaize	CS.3000	3,000/105,944	16	19.44/63.8	25.0/82	1,000/2,204	5-6	Rattan	5/2
Hungary	RSZ	RSZ-03/1	3,000/105,944	?	18.7/61.35	22.9/75.13	?	5	Rattan	3-4/2
South Africa	Flamboyant	AX8-85	2,407/85,000	?	18.0/59	20.0/65.6	?	4	Rattan	2/1
South Africa	Flamboyant	AX8-105	2,973/105,000	?	19.0/62.3	21.0/68.9	?	6	Rattan	3/2
UK	Cameron	O-84	2,378/84,000	12	17.68/58	19.5/64	762/1,680	4	Willow/Cane	4/1
UK	Cameron	N-90	2,548/90,000	24	17.98/59	19.81/65	816/1,800	4-5	Wicker	6/2
UK	Cameron	O-90	2,548/90,000	12	17.98/59	19.81/65	?	5	Willow/Cane	6/2
UK	Cameron	Viva-90	2,548/90,000	8	17.98/59	19.81/65	?	5	Willow/Cane	6/2
UK	Cameron	A-105	2,973/105,000	20	18.9/62	20.73/68	953/2,100	6	Willow/Cane	6/2
UK	Cameron	N-105	2,973/105,000	24	18.9/62	20.73/68	953/2,100	6	Willow/Cane	6/2
UK	Cameron	O-105	2,973/105,000	12	18.9/62	20.73/68	953/2,100	6	Willow/Cane	6/2
UK	Thunder & Colt	84 Series 1	2,378/84,000	12	17.3/56.8	18.41/60.4	?	4	Wicker/Cane	2-3/1-2
UK	Thunder & Colt	90A	2,548/90,000	24	17.71/58.1	18.81/61.7	900/1,984	5	Wicker/Cane	2-4/2
UK	Thunder & Colt	90 Series 1	2,548/90,000	12	17.5/57.4	18.59/61	900/1,984	5	Wicker/Cane	2-4/2
UK	Thunder & Colt	90 Series 2	2,548/90,000	20	17.56/57.6	18.68/61.3	900/1,984	5	Wicker/Cane	2-4/2
UK	Thunder & Colt	105 Series 1	2,973/105,000	12	18.71/61.4	19.6/64.3	1,050/2,315	6	Wicker/Cane	2-6/2
UK	Thunder & Colt	105A	2,973/105,000	24	18.9/62	19.9/65.3	1,050/2,315	6	Wicker/Cane	2-6/2
UK	Thunder & Colt	105 Series 2	2,973/105,000	20	18.84/61.8	19.78/64.9	1,050/2,315	6	Wicker/Cane	2-6/2
USA	Adams	A55S	2,350/82,990	?	16.76/55	20.42/67	?	4	Rattan	1-4/1
USA	Adams	A60	2,973/105,000	?	18.59/61	22.25/73	?	5	Rattan	4/1-2
USA	Aerostar	RX-8	2,548/90,000	12	17.37/57	20.12/66	748/1,650	3-4	Wicker	2-4/1-2
USA	Aerostar	S-57A	2,548/90,000	24	17.37/57	20.12/66	660-748/ 1,455-1,650	3-4	Wicker	2-4/1-2
USA	Aerostar	S-60A	2,985/105,400	24	18.29/60	21.03/69	677-816/ 1,470-1,800	4-5	Wicker	2-4/1-2
USA	Avian	Skyhawk	2,265/80,000	20	16.76/55	20.12/66	635/1,400	1-4	Wicker	2/1
USA	Avian	Turbo 8	2,973/105,000	24	18.29/60	21.33/70	816/1,800	1-6	Wicker	4/2
USA	Balloon Works	DragonFly 90	2,600/91,818	18	17.98/59	18.75/61.5	753/1,660	3-4	Wicker	3/1
USA	Balloon Works	DragonFly 105	2,957/104,440	24	18.9/62	19.51/64	1,111/2,450	4-5	Wicker	6/2
USA	Balloon Works	DragonFly 900	2,600/91,818	18	17.98/59	18.75/61.5	753/1,660	3-4	Wicker	3/1
USA	Balloon Works	DragonFly 1050	2,957/104,440	24	18.9/62	19.51/64	1,111/2,450	4-5	Wicker	6/2
USA	Balloon Works	Firefly 8	2,965/104,708	24	19.4/63.65	20.5/67.26	1,111/2,450	5-6	Rattan/Wicker	6/2
USA	Balloon Works	FireFly 90	2,600/91,818	18	17.98/59	18.75/61.5	1,111/2,450	3-4	Wicker	3/1
USA	Balloon Works	FireFly 105	2,957/104,440	24	18.9/62	19.51/64	1,111/2,450	4-5	Wicker	6/2
USA	Balloon Works	FireFly 900	2,600/91,818	18	17.98/59	18.75/61.5	753/1,660	3-4	Wicker	3/1
USA	Balloon Works	FireFly 1050	2,957/104,440	24	18.9/62	19.51/64	1,111/2,450	4-5	Wicker	6/2
USA	Galaxy	Galaxy 8	2,965/104,708	24	19.4/63.65	20.5/67.26	1,088/2,400	5-6	Rattan/Plywood	6/2

FAI CLASS AX-9 (3,000-4,000 m³; 105,944-141,259 cu ft)

Australia	Kavanagh	E-120	3,398/120,000	?	19.3/63.3	21.75/71.4	?	7	Cane	2-4/2
Australia	Kavanagh	E-140	3,964/140,000	?	20.3/66.6	22.55/74	?	8	Cane/Stainless steel*	2-4/2
France	Chaize	CS.4000	4,000/141,259	16	22.0/72.2	27.5/90.2	1,100/2,425	8	Rattan	6/2
Hungary	RSZ	RSZ-04/1	4,000/141,259	?	20.6/67.6	24.7/81	?	8	Rattan	3-6/2
UK	Cameron	A-120	3,398/120,000	20	19.02/62.4	18.29/60	1,089/2,400	7	Stainless steel/Cane* (T)	6/2
UK	Cameron	N-120	3,398/120,000	24	?	?	?	7	Willow/Cane	6/2
UK	Cameron	O-120	3,398/120,000	12	20.24/66.4	17.07/56	1,089/2,400	7	Stainless steel/Cane* (T)	6/2
UK	Cameron	N-133	3,766/133,000	24	19.9/65.3	18.59/61	1,207/2,660	7	Stainless steel/Cane* (T)	6/2
UK	Cameron	A-140	3,964/140,000	20	20.73/68	21.95/72	1,270/2,800	8	Stainless steel/Cane* (T)	6/2
UK	Cameron	O-140	3,964/140,000	12	?	?	?	8	Stainless steel/Cane*	6/2
UK	Thunder & Colt	120A	3,398/120,000	24	19.51/64	21.03/69	?	7	Wicker/Cane	2-6/2
UK	Thunder & Colt	140 Series 2	3,964/140,000	20	20.48/67.2	21.3/69.9	1,200/2,645	8	Stainless steel/Cane*	2-6/2
USA	Adams	A60S	3,370/119,000	?	18.59/61	22.86/75	?	5-6	Rattan	4/2
USA	Adams	AB	3,540/125,000	?	19.51/64	23.16/76	?	6	Rattan	6/2
USA	Aerostar	S-66A	3,993/141,000	24	20.12/66	22.86/75	907-1,134/ 2,000-2,500	8	Wicker	6/2
USA	Avian	Magnum IX	3,964/140,000	24	20.12/66	23.16/76	1,134/2,500	1-8	Wicker	4/2
USA	Balloon Works	FireFly 140	3,964/140,000	36	20.12/66	22.86/75	1,490/3,285	5-6	Wicker	6-9/2
USA	Galaxy	AX9	3,964/140,000	36	20.12/66	22.86/75	1,361/3,000	6-8	Wicker	6-8/2

*Partitioned basket; (T) Partition in form of T or (TT) double T.

HOT-AIR (AX), COMBINATION (AM)* AND GAS BALLOON (AA) DATA *(continued)*

Country	Company	Model	Volume m³/cu ft	Gores	Diameter m/ft	Height m/ft	Max gross weight kg/lb	Crew	Basket	Fuel cylinders/ Burners
			FAI CLASS AX-10 (4,000-6,000 m³; 141,259-211,888 cu ft)							
Australia	Kavanagh	E-160	4,530/160,000	?	21.2/69.6	23.65/77.6	?	9	Cane/Stainless steel*	2-6/3
Australia	Kavanagh	E-200	5,663/200,000	?	22.8/74.8	25.15/82.5	?	10-11	Cane/Stainless steel*	2-6/3
Australia	Kavanagh	E-210	5,947/210,000	?	23.2/76.1	25.45/83.5	?	11	Cane/Stainless steel*	2-6/3
Czechoslovakia	Aerotechnik	AB-10	5,500/194,231	?	22.0/72.18	22.0/72.18	?	12	Rattan	4/3
South Africa	Flamboyant	AX10-150	4,248/150,000	?	21.0/68.9	22.0/72.18	?	8	Rattan	4/2
UK	Cameron	N-145	4,106/145,000	32	20.54/67.4	19.2/63	1,315/2,900	8	Stainless steel/Cane* (T)	6/2
UK	Cameron	A-160	4,530/160,000	20	?	?	?	9	Stainless steel/Cane* (T)	6/2
UK	Cameron	N-160	4,530/160,000	32	?	?	?	9	Stainless steel/Cane* (T)	6/2
UK	Cameron	O-160	4,530/160,000	12	21.0/69	22.25/73	1,451/3,200	8	Stainless steel/Cane* (T or TT)	6/2
UK	Cameron	A-180	5,097/180,000	20	?	?	?	10	Stainless steel/Cane* (T)	8/3
UK	Cameron	N-180	5,097/180,000	32	27.13/89	29.57/97	1,633/3,600	9	Stainless steel/Cane* (T or TT)	8/3
UK	Cameron	A-210	5,947/210,000	20	23.77/78	24.99/82	1,905/4,200	12	Stainless steel/Cane* (T or TT)	8/4
UK	Thunder & Colt	160 Series 1	4,530/160,000	12	21.61/70.9	22.71/74.5	1,300/2,866	9	Stainless steel/Cane*	2-8/3
UK	Thunder & Colt	160A	4,530/160,000	28	21.7/71.2	23.01/75.5	1,300/2,866	9	Stainless steel/Cane*	2-8/3
UK	Thunder & Colt	180 Series 1	5,097/180,000	12	22.48/73.75	23.62/77.5	1,300/2,866	9	Stainless steel/Cane*	2-8/3
UK	Thunder & Colt	180A	5,097/180,000	24	23.0/75.46	24.0/78.74	1,300/2,866	10	Stainless steel/Cane*	2-9/3
USA	Aerostar	S-71A	4,955/175,000	?	21.64/71	23.77/78	1,202/2,650	7	Wicker/Stainless steel	4/2
USA	Aerostar	S-77A	5,975/211,000	28	23.47/77	26.52/87	1,270/2,800	9	Wicker/Stainless steel	4/2
USA	Avian	Magnum Super Sport	5,097/180,000	28	21.95/72	24.99/82	1,361/3,000	9	Wicker	4/2-3
			FAI CLASS AM/AX-11 (6,000-9,000 m³; 211,888-317,832 cu ft)							
Australia	Kavanagh	E-240	6,796/240,000	?	23.8/78.1	26.45/86.8	?	12-13	Cane/Stainless steel*	2-6/3
Australia	Kavanagh	E-260	7,362/260,000	?	25.0/82.0	27.0/88.6	?	12-13	Cane/Stainless steel*	2-6/3
South Africa	Flamboyant	AX11-240	6,796/240,000	?	24.0/78.7	23.0/75.5	?	12	Willow/Cane	6/2
UK	Cameron	A-250	7,079/250,000	20	24.32/79.8	23.41/76.8	2,268/5,000	15	Stainless steel/Cane* (T)	8/3
UK	Cameron	A-300	8,495/300,000	20	25.85/84.8	24.81/81.4	2,722/6,000	18	Stainless steel/Cane* (TT)	8/3-4
UK	Cameron	A-375	10,619/375,000	20	27.86/91.4	26.73/87.7	3,402/7,500	22	?	8/4
UK	Cameron	Roziere R-225	6,371/225,000	40	26.21/86	30.48/100	6,634/14,625	†	Basket or gondola	8+/3
UK	Thunder & Colt	240A	6,796/240,000	28	24.51/80.4	25.79/84.6	1,600/3,527	12	Stainless steel/Cane*	2-10/3-4
UK	Thunder & Colt	300A	8,495/300,000	28	26.46/86.8	27.19/89.2	2,200/4,850	12	Stainless steel/Cane*	2-10/3-4
			FAI CLASS AX-12 (9,000-12,000 m³; 317,832-423,776 cu ft)							
UK	Thunder & Colt	400A	11,327/400,000	28	29.11/95.5	29.99/98.4	2,900/6,393	16	Stainless steel/Cane*	2-10/3
			FAI CLASS AX-13 (12,000-16,000 m³; 423,776-565,035 cu ft)							
UK	Cameron	A-530	15,008/530,000	20	31.21/102.4	29.99/98.4	4,808/10,600	30	Stainless steel/Cane* (2-deck)	10/4
			FAI CLASS AX-15 (22,000 m³; 776,924 cu ft and above)							
UK	Cameron	N-850	24,069/850.000	92	37.49/123	35.05/115	7,711/17,000	50	Stainless steel/Cane* (2-deck)	12/6
UK	Thunder & Colt	*Pacific Flyer*‡	73,624/ 2.6 million	?	?	?	?	2	Special gondola	6/?

*Partitioned basket; (T) Partition in form of T or (TT) double T.   †Generally used for special projects with minimal crew and additional equipment.

‡On 15-17 January 1991 made longest balloon flight in history (estimated 5,871 nm; 10,880 km; 6,760.5 miles), and first across the Pacific, crewed by Per Lindstrand and Richard Branson; took off from Miyakonojo, Japan, landed on frozen lake at Yellowknife, NW Territories, Canada.

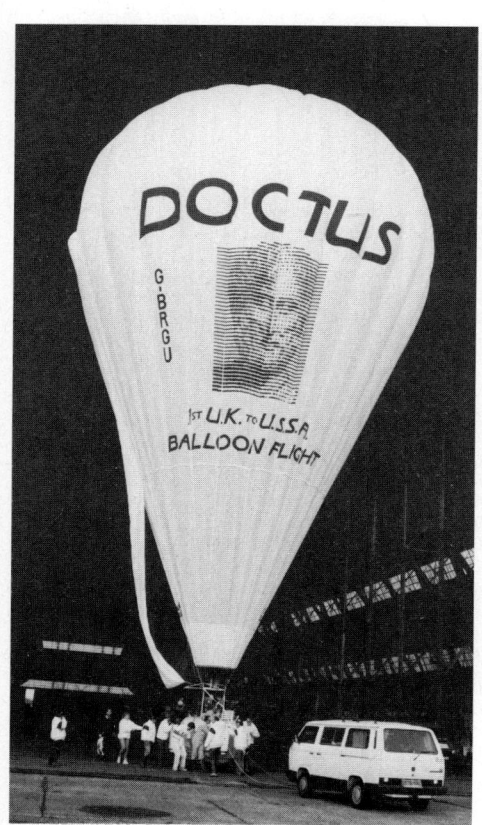

The Doctus Cameron R-60 (combined helium/hot-air) balloon used for October 1990 flight from UK to USSR

Thunder & Colt 300A of Transworld Safaris, Kenya

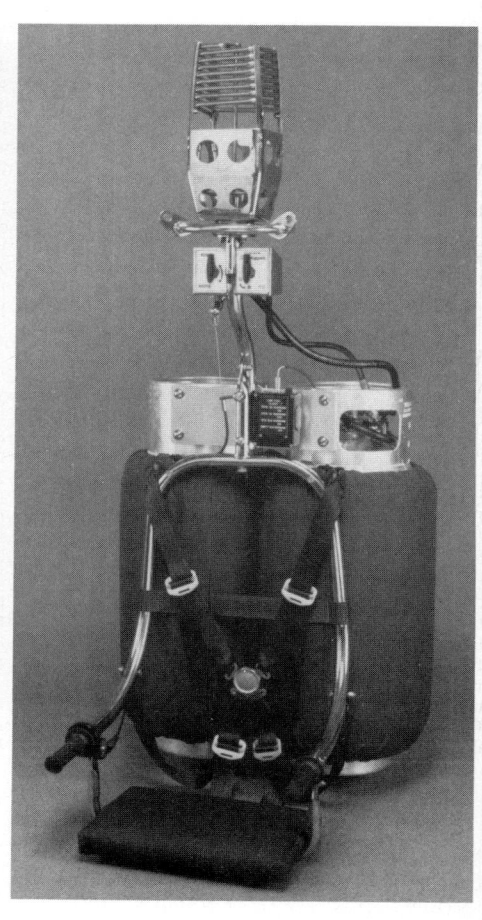

Twin tank/seat for Cameron Skyhoppers

AERO ENGINES

> This section includes all available details of engines of manned aircraft, including microlights, and aerospacecraft. Rocket engines and other propulsion systems used purely for UAVs, targets, missiles and unmanned spaceflight are no longer included. Readers are referred for these subjects to *Jane's Battlefield Surveillance Systems, World Unmanned Aircraft* by Kenneth Munson, and *Interavia Space Directory*.

AUSTRALIA

HDHV
HAWKER DE HAVILLAND VICTORIA LTD
Box 779H, GPO Melbourne, Victoria 3001
Telephone: 61 (3) 647 6111
Fax: 61 (3) 646 3431
Telex: AA 30721
OFFICERS: See HDH entry in Aircraft section

HDHV makes components for engines and airframes. It makes F404 blades and seals, and assembles and tests engines for the RAAF. It makes CF6-50 and -80 rings for GE, and CFM56 rings, and supports RAAF Atar 9C and Viper engines.

AUSTRIA

ROTAX
BOMBARDIER-ROTAX GmbH
Postfach 5, A-4623 Gunskirchen
Telephone: 43 (7246) 271-0
Fax: 43 (7246) 370
Telex: 25 546 BRG K A
PRODUCT MANAGER: Josef Fürlinger

This company is one of the world's largest producers of light piston engines. Those listed for light aircraft, microlights and gliders use 1:50 mix of oil with petrol (gasoline) of not below MON 83 or RON 90 grade. Customers have many options, including rewind manual or electric starter.

Rotax sustained an output of about 6,500 engines per year, all derived from snowmobile engines, until 1988 when it added the Model 912 that had been specially designed for aircraft.

Rotax 582 twin-cylinder piston engine

Rotax 912 four-cylinder piston engine

ROTAX LIGHT AIRCRAFT ENGINES

Engine Model	277	377	447	503	503.2V	462	508UL	532	582	912
Layout	1 cylinder (4,7)	2 cylinder (4,7)	2 cylinder (4,7)	2 cylinder (4,7)	2 cylinder (4,7)	2 cylinder (5,7)	2 cylinder (4,8)	2 cylinder (5,7)	2 cylinder (5,7)	4 cylinder (6,8)
	Piston port	Piston port	Piston port	Piston port	Piston port	Rotary valve	Overhead valve	Rotary valve	Rotary valve	Overhead valve
Bore/stroke mm (in)	72.0/66.0	62.0/61.0	67.5/61.0	72.0/61.0	72.0/61.0	69.5/61.0	71.0/64.0	72.0/64.0	76.0/64.0	79.5/61.0
	(2.83/2 60)	(2.44/2.40)	(2.66/2.40)	(2.83/2.40)	(2.83/2.40)	(2.74/2.40)	(2.79/2.52)	(2.83/2.52)	(2.99/2.52)	(3.13/2.40)
Capacity cc (cu in)	268.7	368.3	436.5	496.7	496.7	462.8	507.0	521.1	580.7	1211.2
	(16.397)	(22.475)	(26.637)	(30.310)	(30.310)	(28.242)	(30.8)	(31.799)	(35.44)	(73.912)
Weight, Dry (1) kg (lb)	19.0 (41.9)	27.5 (60.6)	27.5 (60.6)	30.2 (66.6)	30.2 (66.6)	27.0 (59.5)	38.0 (83.7)	28.0 (61.7)	28.4 (62.4)	60 (132) (9)
Weight, Dry (2) kg (lb)	24.0 (52.9)	32.5 (71.6)	32.5 (71.6)	36.2 (79.8)	36.2 (79.8)	32.0 (70.5)	48.5 (106.9)	33.0 (72.8)	33.8 (78.2)	59.9 (132.0)
Rating (3) kW (hp)	19 (25.5)	26 (34.9)	29.4 (39.4)	34 (45.6)	38 (51.0)	38 (51.0)	32 (43.0)	48 (64.0)	47 (63)	59 (79)
	6,500 rpm	6,500 rpm	6,500 rpm	6,500 rpm	6,500 rpm	6,500 rpm	7,800 rpm	6,500 rpm	6,500 rpm	5,500 rpm

Notes: 1, Bare, unequipped; 2, with carburettor (503.2V, twin carburettors), intake silencer and exhaust system; 3, standard bare engine; 4, aircooled; 5, liquid cooled; 6, liquid cooled heads, aircooled barrels; 7, two-stroke; 8, four-stroke; 9, with accessories and exhaust. The 503 and 503.2V are available with breakerless ignition.

WESTERMAYER
OSKAR WESTERMAYER
Hauptstrasse 11, A-2161 Poysbrunn
Telephone: 43 (2554) 405
Telex: 73379

This engineer has developed a piston engine with aircooled barrels but liquid-cooled heads. He claims that, compared with the Continental O-200 which was the basis for the engine, fuel consumption is reduced by 25 per cent. Compression ratio is raised to 8.6.

WESTERMAYER W 5/33

This flat-four engine has cylinder heads of cast aluminium alloy, cooled by pure ethylene glycol. The coolant pump feeds via a separate pipe to each head, and the return line passes through an air radiator. Certification to FAR 33 was completed in Austria in December 1986 and in Germany in October 1990. Current TBO is 1,500 h.

DIMENSIONS:
Length	730 mm (28.7 in)
Width	790 mm (31.1 in)
Height: carburettor	625 mm (24.6 in)
airbox	700 mm (27.6 in)

WEIGHT, DRY:
Bare	85 kg (187 lb)
With starter, alternator and silencer	102 kg (225 lb)

The 74.6 kW (100 hp) Westermayer W 5/33

Westermayer W 5/33 engine installation in Cessna 150

PERFORMANCE RATING:
T-O   74.6 kW (100 hp) at 2,750 rpm
FUEL CONSUMPTION:
T-O   25.5 litres (6.7 US gallons; 5.6 Imp gallons)/h

SPECIFIC FUEL CONSUMPTION:
T-O   71 µg/J (0.42 lb/h/hp)
OIL CONSUMPTION:
Overall   0.5 litre (0.1 Imp gallon) per 25 h

BELGIUM

FNMI
FN MOTEURS SA
(Subsidiary of Fabrique Nationale Nouvelle Herstal)
Route de Liers 121, B-4411 Herstal
Telephone: 32 (41) 784671
Fax: 32 (41) 785207 (general)
   32 (41) 786739 (sales & marketing)
Telex: B 41223 FABNA
DIRECTOR AND GENERAL MANAGER: P. Bourgeois
BUSINESS DEVELOPMENT: J. C. Morin

With long experience of piston engines, FN began jet engine production in 1949. Today's activity is equally distributed in three sectors: fighter engine production, medium/large transport and space propulsion production, and depot maintenance for air forces. FN Moteurs employs 1,650 people. Major programmes are:

FNMI is responsible for the production and assembly of the P&W F100 fan and engine core modules, and for assembly and test of complete engines.

FNMI is responsible for four major parts of the GE F110: fan discs 1 and 3, the HP turbine disc, and the fan stator case.

FNMI is a member of the consortium (RR, MTU, SNECMA, FNMI) producing Tyne 21 and 22 engines for the Atlantique and Transall, with a 9.5 per cent share.

After having produced parts for the JT8D and JT9D-7R4, FNMI signed a partnership agreement with Pratt & Whitney for a 3 per cent share in the PW4000 series. FNMI is responsible for the HP compressor case and various other components.

Since 1972, in association with SNECMA, FNMI has developed and produced the lubrication modules of all CFM56 versions. FNMI has increased its participation up to 10 per cent of the SNECMA share (5 per cent overall) in the -5A and -5C versions, to power respectively the Airbus A320 and A340. FNMI is responsible for the lubrication and shop modules and other stator or rotor parts. FNMI is also performing endurance testing of complete engines.

FNMI has signed a co-operation agreement with Turbomeca, and is developing several critical parts of the TM 333.

BRAZIL

CELMA
CELMA-CIA ELECTROMECANICA
Rue Alice Hervê 356, PO Box 90341, 25669 Petrópolis, RJ
Telephone: 55 (242) 43 4962
Fax: 55 (242) 42 3684
Telex: (021) 21271
PRESIDENT: Alexandre Gonçalves Silva
TECHNICAL DIRECTOR: Carlos A. R. Pereira

This company of 1,650 people has facilities totalling 45,000 m² (485,000 sq ft) in which it overhauls many kinds of jet engine and accessories. It shares in the production of components for the Rolls-Royce Spey 807 turbofan.

IMAER
INDÚSTRIA MECÂNICA E AERONÁUTICA LTDA
Aeroporto de Botucatú, PO Box 301, 18600 Botucatú, SP
Telephone: 55 (149) 22 1908 and 22 5938
Fax: 55 (011) 530 8924

IMAER manufactures four-stroke reciprocating engines for light aircraft, ultralights and powered gliders.

IMAER 2000
This engine is available in three models: the **2000 M1**, with single ignition, and the **ME1** and **ME2**, with dual ignition, all being JAR 22 certificated.
TYPE: Four-cylinder horizontally-opposed aircooled.
CYLINDERS: Bore 90.4 mm (3.56 in). Stroke 78.4 mm (3.09 in). Swept volume 2,017 cc (123.08 cu in). Compression ratio 8.7.
INDUCTION: Stromberg-Zenith 150 CD or Marvel-Schebler MA 3PA carburettor.

IMAER 2000 M1 four-cylinder piston engine

FUEL GRADE: Avgas 100/130.
IGNITION: Slick 4230 or Bendix S4RN21 magneto and/or Bosch electronic.

DIMENSIONS:	
Length	590 mm (23.23 in)
Width	764 mm (30.08 in)
Height	447 mm (17.60 in)
WEIGHT:	78-81 kg (172-178.6 lb)
PERFORMANCE RATING:	59.7 kW (80 hp) at 3,400 rpm

IMAER 1000
This engine is made in two models: the **1000 M1**, with magneto single ignition, not certificated, and the **1000 E1**, with electronic single ignition, not certificated.
TYPE: Two-cylinder horizontally-opposed aircooled.

DIMENSIONS:	
Length	370 mm (14.57 in)
Width	764 mm (30.08 in)
Height	410 mm (16.14 in)
WEIGHT:	39 kg (86 lb)
PERFORMANCE RATING:	30 kW (40 hp) at 3,600 rpm

CANADA

CAM
CANADIAN AIRMOTIVE INC
407-5940 No. 6 Road, Richmond, British Columbia V6V 1Z1
Telephone: 1 (604) 270 0188
Fax: 1 (604) 270 6048
Telex: 04 355779 SEI IND VCR

CAM TURBO 90
This is a three-cylinder in-line turbocharged four-stroke piston engine.
CYLINDERS: Overhead camshaft, aluminium head and block each in one piece. Bore 74 mm (2.91 in). Stroke 77 mm (3.03 in). Compression ratio 8.2. Capacity 993 cc (61 cu in).
INDUCTION: Turbocharger and carburettor with mixture control. Fuel 92 RON or 100LL.
IGNITION: Dual capacitive discharge electronic, self diagnostic.
COOLING: Water/glycol mix.
ACCESSORIES: Electric starter, 20A alternator, provision for controllable propeller.
PROPELLER DRIVE: Cam action silent chain in oil bath, normal ratio 2.23.

WEIGHT, DRY:	65 kg (144 lb)
PERFORMANCE RATING (T-O):	67 kW (90 hp) at 5,300 rpm
SPECIFIC FUEL CONSUMPTION (cruise):	
	64.2 µg/J (0.38 lb/h/hp)

ORENDA
HAWKER SIDDELEY CANADA INC
(Orenda Division)
3160 Derry Rd East, Mississauga, Ontario L4T 1A9
Telephone: 1 (416) 677 3250
Fax: 1 (416) 678 1538
Telex: 06-968727
VICE-PRESIDENT AND GENERAL MANAGER: R. J. Munro

Orenda has a 67,262 m² (724,000 sq ft) facility close to Toronto International Airport. It meets the maintenance needs of the Canadian Forces for General Electric J85 and F404 engines, and makes engine parts under subcontract.

In 1990 Orenda acquired two facilities for precision manufacture, Middleton Aerospace Corporation in Middleton, Massachusetts, and Windsor Aerospace Division in Emeryville, Ontario.

P&WC
PRATT & WHITNEY CANADA (Subsidiary of United Technologies Corporation)
1000 Marie Victorin, Longueuil, Quebec J4G 1A1
Telephone: 1 (514) 677 9411
Telex: 05 267509
PRESIDENT AND CHIEF EXECUTIVE OFFICER: L. D. Caplan
EXECUTIVE VICE-PRESIDENT: G. P. Ouimet
VICE-PRESIDENTS:
   C. Lloyd (Marketing and Customer Support)
   P. Henry (Communications)
   B. H. Sanders (Engineering)
PUBLIC RELATIONS MANAGER: Louise Boutin

Pratt & Whitney Canada is owned 97 per cent by United Technologies Corporation, Connecticut, USA, and is the P&W Group member responsible for engines for general aviation and regional transport. P&WC employs some 8,500 persons. By 1 January 1991 it had delivered 35,000 engines.

P&WC JT15D
Designed to power business aircraft, small transports and training aircraft, the JT15D first ran on 23 September 1967.

Initial application was the twin-engined Cessna Citation. Up to 1976 Cessna used the **JT15D-1**. Late that year it announced the Citation I powered by the **JT15D-1A** and the Citation II powered by the **JT15D-4**. During 1983 the D-1A was replaced by the **D-1B**.

Other twin-engined business jets powered by the JT15D-4 are the Aerospatiale Corvette and Mitsubishi Diamond I. TBO is 3,500 h for the JT15D-1/D-1A, and 3,000 h for the JT15D-4.

JT15D-4B. Altitude optimised variant for the Citation S/II.

JT15D-4C. Oil system for sustained inverted flight, and an electronic fuel control. Powers Agusta S.211.

JT15D-4D. Flat rated for improved hot/high performance for the Diamond IA.

JT15D-5. Growth version. A new fan with higher pressure ratio and flow, plus an improved boost stage and HP compressor, are combined to produce 25 per cent more altitude cruise thrust, with a 3 per cent improvement in sfc. HP turbine blades and electronic fuel control are also improved. Powers Cessna T-47A and Diamond II.

JT15D-5A. Hydromechanical fuel control. Selected for Citation V.

JT15D-5B. Dash-5A modified to suit Beech T-1A Jayhawk.

JT15D-5C. Oil system for sustained inverted flight. Powers Agusta S.211A.

By 1990 total deliveries of all JT15D engines had reached 3,687. Operating time totalled 11,179,919 h.

The following description relates to the JT15D-1B, except where indicated:
TYPE: Two-shaft turbofan.
FAN: Single-stage axial with 28 solid titanium blades with part-span shrouds. Mass flow, 34 kg (75 lb)/s; bypass ratio about 3.3; fan pressure ratio 1.5.
COMPRESSOR: Single stage titanium centrifugal. Overall pressure ratio about 10:1. (D-4 and D-5 have axial boost stage between fan and compressor.)

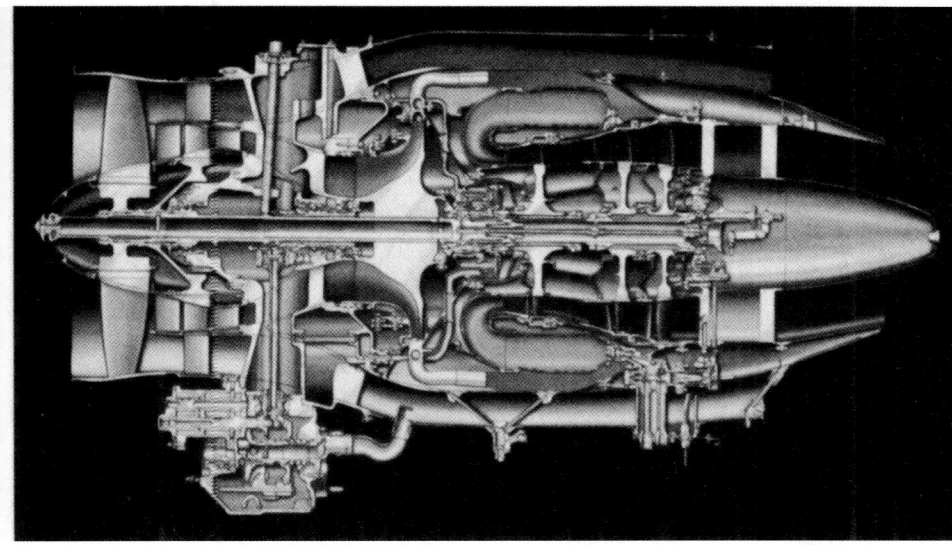

Longitudinal section of the P&WC JT15D-5 turbofan

COMBUSTION CHAMBER: Annular reverse flow type. Spark igniters at 5 and 7 o'clock (viewed from rear).

FUEL SYSTEM: Pump delivering at 44.8 bars (650 lb/sq in). D-1, 4, 4B, 5A have DP-L2 hydromechanical control; 4C, 4D and 5 have JFC 118 or 119 electronic system.

FUEL GRADES: JP-1, JP-4, JP-5 to CPW 204.

TURBINE: Single-stage HP with 71 solid blades; two-stage LP, first stage cast integrally with 61 blades and second carrying 55 blades in fir tree roots.

LUBRICATION SYSTEM: Integral oil system, with gear type pump delivering at up to 5.52 bars (80 lb/sq in). Capacity, 9.0 litres (2.4 US gallons; 2.0 Imp gallons).

OIL SPECIFICATION: PWA521 Type II, CPW 202.

STARTING: Air turbine starter or electric starter/generator.

DIMENSIONS:

Diameter: JT15D-1	691 mm (27.2 in)
JT15D-4	686 mm (27.0 in)
Length overall: JT15D-1	1,506 mm (59.3 in)
JT15D-4	1,600 mm (63.0 in)

WEIGHT, DRY:

JT15D-1, -1A	232.5 kg (514 lb)
JT15D-1B	235 kg (519 lb)
JT15D-4	253 kg (557 lb)
JT15D-4B	258 kg (568 lb)
JT15D-4C	261 kg (575 lb)
JT15D-4D	255 kg (560 lb)
JT15D-5, -5A	291.5 kg (632 lb)
JT15D-5B	288 kg (635 lb)
JT15D-5C	302 kg (665 lb)

PERFORMANCE RATINGS:

T-O: JT15D-1, -1A, -1B	9.79 kN (2,200 lb st)
JT15D-4, -4B, -4C, -4D	11.12 kN (2,500 lb st)
JT15D-5, -5A, -5B	12.9 kN (2,900 lb st)
JT15D-5C	14.19 kN (3,190 lb st)
Max continuous:	
JT15D-1, -1A, -1B	9.3 kN (2,090 lb st)
JT15D-4, -4B, -4D	10.56 kN (2,375 lb st)
JT15D-4C	9.45 kN (2,125 lb st)
JT15D-5, -5A, -5B	12.9 kN (2,900 lb st)
JT15D-5C	14.19 kN (3,190 lb st)

SPECIFIC FUEL CONSUMPTION (T-O):

JT15D-1, -1A, -1B	15.30 mg/Ns (0.540 lb/h/lb st)
JT15D-4, -4C	15.92 mg/Ns (0.562 lb/h/lb st)
JT15D-5, -5A, 5B	15.61 mg/Ns (0.551 lb/h/lb st)
JT15D-5C	16.23 mg/Ns (0.573 lb/h/lb st)

P&WC PW305

Planned for corporate aircraft of the 1990s, this engine is aimed at US coast-to-coast flights at Mach 0.75 at 14,325 m (47,000 ft). MTU of Germany will be responsible for the LP turbine section, as a partner sharing 25 per cent of the estimated development cost of $Can 500 million.

Certification was achieved in mid-1990. The PW305 powers the BAe 1000.

TYPE: Two-shaft turbofan.

FAN: Single-stage, overhung ahead of front bearing. Pointed rotating spinner. Bypass ratio (S/L, T-O) 4.5.

COMPRESSOR: Four axial stages followed by one centrifugal. Core pressure ratio 15.

COMBUSTION CHAMBER: Annular, fed around periphery by ring of separate curved pipes ducting air from diffuser case of centrifugal compressor.

CONTROL SYSTEM: Dowty and Smiths Industries full-authority digital, with dual channels.

HP TURBINE: Two axial stages, the first having aircooled blades.

LP TURBINE: Three axial stages joined via centre stage disc to fan shaft. Two main shaft bearings.

DIMENSIONS (estimated):

Diameter	869 mm (34.2 in)
Length	2,069 mm (81.4 in)

WEIGHT, DRY (installed): 441 kg (972 lb)

PERFORMANCE RATINGS (ISA, estimated):

T-O, S/L	23.29 kN (5,236 lb st) or flat rated at 21.13 kN (4,750 lb st) to 25°C
Cruise at Mach 0.8 at 12,200 m (40,000 ft)	4.95 kN (1,113 lb)

SPECIFIC FUEL CONSUMPTION (estimated):

T-O as above	11.50 mg/Ns (0.406 lb/h/lb st)
Cruise as above	19.12 mg/Ns (0.675 lb/h/lb)

P&WC PW100

The PW100 is a free turbine turboprop consisting of turbomachine and reduction gearbox modules connected by a torque-measuring driveshaft and integrated structural intake case.

Flight development of the PW100 began in February 1982. Principal versions are as follows:

PW115. T-O rated at 1,256 ekW; 1,193 kW (1,685 ehp; 1,600 shp) at 1,300 propeller rpm to 44°C. Selected for Embraer EMB-120 Brasilia. Certificated December 1983.

PW118. T-O rated at 1,411 ekW; 1,342 kW (1,892 ehp; 1,800 shp) at 1,300 propeller rpm to 33°C. Selected for EMB-120 Brasilia.

PW120. T-O rated at 1,566 ekW; 1,491 kW (2,100 ehp; 2,000 shp) at 1,200 propeller rpm to 27.7°C. Selected for Boeing Canada Dash 8-100, Aerospatiale/Alenia ATR 42 and Snow SA-210TA. Certificated December 1983.

PW120A. T-O rated at 1,566 ekW; 1,491 kW (2,100 ehp; 2,000 shp) at 1,200 propeller rpm to 29°C. Selected for Dash 8.

PW121. T-O rated at 1,679 ekW; 1,603 kW (2,252 ehp; 2,150 shp) at 1,200 propeller rpm to 26°C.

PW123. T-O rated at 1,866 ekW; 1,775 kW (2,502 ehp; 2,380 shp) at 1,200 propeller rpm to 35°C. Selected for Dash 8-300.

PW124. Growth version, with T-O rating of 1,880 ekW; 1,790 kW (2,522 ehp; 2,400 shp) to 34.4°C. **PW124A** is identical but has higher max continuous power rating.

PW124B. PW124 with PW123 turbomachinery to suit four-blade propeller. Selected for ATR 72.

PW125B. Growth PW124 with T-O rating of 2,095 ekW; 1,864 kW (2,810 ehp; 2,500 shp) at 1,200 propeller rpm to 30°C. Powers Fokker 50.

PW126. Growth engine, max contingency 2,078 ekW; 1,978 kW (2,786 ehp; 2,653 shp) at 1,200 propeller rpm to 32.4°C. Powers BAe ATP.

PW126A. Growth 124A with T-O rating of 2,073 ekW; 1,978 kW (2,780 ehp; 2,653 shp) at 1,200 propeller rpm to 29.2°C. Selected for BAe ATP.

PW127. Growth version under study for improved hot/high performance. Flat rated at 2,050 kW (2,750 shp) at 1,200 propeller rpm to 30.8°C.

By 1990 deliveries of engines of the PW100 family had reached 1,567. Operating time exceeded 4,379,414 h.

The following description applies to all PW100 series engines:

TYPE: Free turbine turboprop.

PROPELLER DRIVE: Twin-layshaft gearbox with propeller shaft offset above turbomachine. Max propeller speeds 1,300 rpm (PW115) and 1,200 rpm (PW120).

AIR INTAKE: S-bend duct. A secondary duct forms a flowing bypass to prevent foreign object ingestion.

COMPRESSOR: Two centrifugal impellers in series, each driven by its own turbine. Air guided through ring of curved pipes from LP diffuser to HP entry.

COMBUSTION CHAMBER: Annular reverse flow type, with 14 air blast fuel nozzles around periphery and two spark igniters.

FUEL SYSTEM: Hydromechanical control and electronic power management.

FUEL GRADES: JP-1, JP-4, JP-5 to PWA Spec 522.

TURBINES: Single-stage HP with 47 aircooled blades. Single-stage LP with 53 solid blades. Two-stage power turbine, first with 68 blades and second with 74, all with shrouded tips.

ACCESSORY DRIVES: Pads driven by HP compressor, for starter/generator, hydromechanical fuel control and hand turning. Pads on reduction gearbox for alternator, hydraulic pump, propeller control module, overspeed governor and electric auxiliary pump. Electric torque signal and auto power augmentation.

LUBRICATION SYSTEM: One pressure pump and two scavenge pumps, all driven off HP rotor. Integral tank, capacity 9.44 litres (2.5 US gallons, 2.08 Imp gallons).

OIL SPECIFICATION: CPW202 or PWA521 Type II.

STARTING: Electric starter/generator.

DIMENSIONS:

Length: PW115, 118	2,057 mm (81 in)
PW120, 123, 124, 124A	2,134 mm (84 in)
Width: PW115, 118, 120, 120A, 121	635 mm (25 in)
others	660 mm (26 in)
Height: all	787 mm (31 in)

WEIGHT, DRY:

PW115, 118	391 kg (861 lb)
PW120	417.8 kg (921 lb)
PW120A	423 kg (933 lb)
PW121	425 kg (936 lb)
PW123	450 kg (992 lb)
PW124, 125, 126 models	481 kg (1,060 lb)

PERFORMANCE RATINGS (S/L, static):

T-O: See under model listings	
Max continuous:	
PW115	1,256 ekW; 1,193 kW (1,685 ehp; 1,600 shp) at 1,300 rpm to 44°C
PW118	1,411 ekW; 1,342 kW (1,892 ehp; 1,800 shp) at 1,300 rpm to 33°C

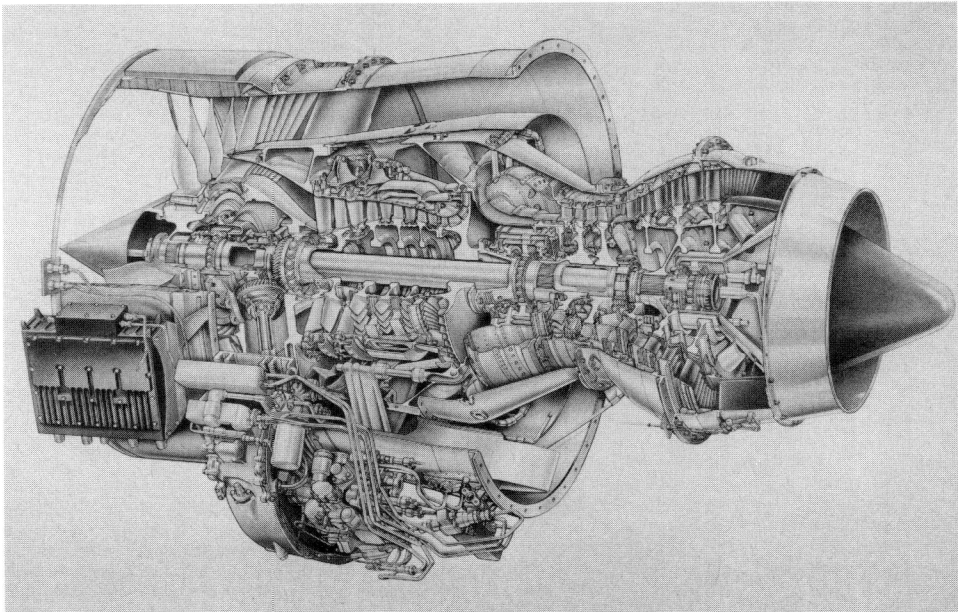

Cutaway P&WC PW305 turbofan

PW120	1,333 ekW; 1,268 kW
	(1,787 ehp; 1,700 shp) at 1,200 rpm to 32.7°C
PW120A	1,411 ekW; 1,342 kW
	(1,892 ehp; 1,800 shp) at 1,200 rpm to 33°C
PW121	1,524 ekW; 1,454 kW
	(2,044 ehp; 1,950 shp) at 1,200 rpm to 28°C
PW123, 124	1,686 ekW; 1,603 kW
	(2,261 ehp; 2,150 shp) at 1,200 rpm to 45°C
PW124A	1,749 ekW; 1,663 kW
	(2,345 ehp; 2,230 shp) at 1,200 rpm to 42°C
PW125B	2,095 ekW; 1,603 kW
	(2,810 ehp; 2,150 shp) at 1,200 rpm to 45°C
PW126	1,734 ekW; 1,648 kW
	(2,325 ehp; 2,210 shp) at 1,200 rpm to 27.9°C
PW127	as T-O

Max cruise:

PW115	1,178 ekW; 1,119 kW
	(1,580 ehp; 1,500 shp) at 1,300 rpm to 20°C
PW118	1,188 ekW; 1,128 kW
	(1,593 ehp; 1,512 shp) at 1,300 rpm to 20°C
PW120	1,271 ekW; 1,207 kW
	(1,704 ehp; 1,619 shp) at 1,200 rpm to 15°C
PW120A	1,296 ekW; 1,231 kW
	(1,738 ehp; 1,651 shp) at 1,200 rpm to 15°C
PW121	1,330 ekW; 1,268 kW
	(1,784 ehp; 1,700 shp) at 1,200 rpm to 15°C
PW123, 124, 124A	1,593 ekW; 1,514 kW
	(2,136 ehp; 2,030 shp) at 1,200 rpm to 22.2°C
PW125B	1,623 ekW; 1,513 kW
	(2,203 ehp; 2,030 shp) at 1,200 rpm to 22.2°C
PW126	1,635 ekW; 1,553 kW
	(2,192 ehp; 2,083 shp) at 1,200 rpm to 26.3°C
PW126A	1,632 ekW; 1,553 kW
	(2,188 ehp; 2,083 shp) at 1,200 rpm to 26.3°C
PW127	1,667 ekW; 1,591 kW
	(2,236 ehp; 2,134 shp) at 1,200 rpm to 22.7°C

SPECIFIC FUEL CONSUMPTION:

T-O rating:

PW115	87.2 µg/J (0.516 lb/h/ehp)
PW118	84.2 µg/J (0.498 lb/h/ehp)
PW120, 120A	82.0 µg/J (0.485 lb/h/ehp)
PW121	80.4 µg/J (0.476 lb/h/ehp)
PW123	79.4 µg/J (0.470 lb/h/ehp)
PW124, 124A	79.1 µg/J (0.468 lb/h/ehp)
PW125B, 126	78.2 µg/J (0.463 lb/h/ehp)
PW126A	76.6 µg/J (0.454 lb/h/ehp)
PW127	77.6 µg/J (0.459 lb/h/ehp)

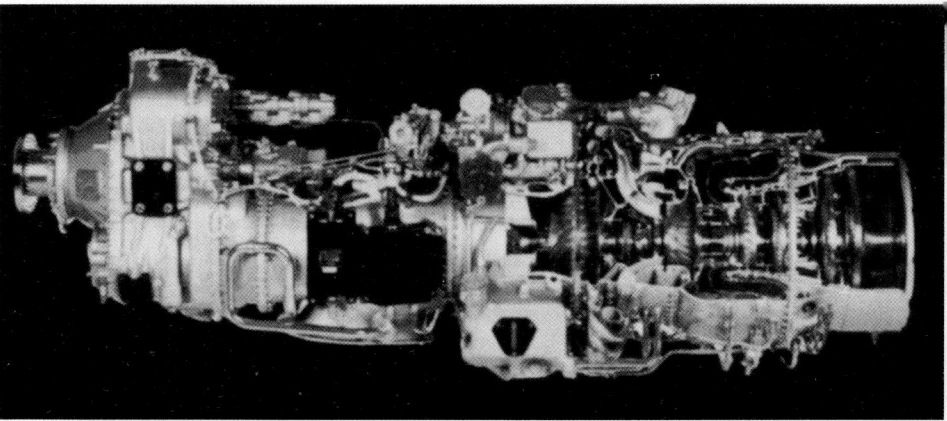

Cutaway P&WC PW100 turboprop

P&WC PT6A

US military designations: T74 (separate entry) and T101 (PT6A-45R)

The PT6A is a free turbine turboprop, built in many versions since November 1959. By 1990 a total of 22,068 had logged over 145 million hours in 10 113 aircraft of 4,419 customers.

Current versions of the PT6A are as follows:

PT6A-11. Flat rated at 394 ekW; 373 kW (528 ehp; 500 shp) at 2,200 propeller rpm to 42°C. Fitted to Piper Cheyenne I and IA, T-1040, original Claudius Dornier Seastar and Harbin Y-12 I.

PT6A-110. Flat rated at 374 ekW; 354 kW (502 ehp; 475 shp) at 1,900 propeller rpm to 38°C Fitted to Dornier 128-6.

PT6A-11AG. Flat rated at 394 ekW; 373 kW (528 ehp; 500 shp) at 2,200 propeller rpm to 42°C. Can use diesel fuel. Fitted to Ayres Turbo-Thrush, Schweizer Turbo Ag-Cat and Weatherly 620 TP.

PT6A-112. Flat rated at 394 ekW; 373 kW (528 ehp; 500 shp) at 1,900 propeller rpm to 56°C. Fitted to Cessna Conquest I, Reims-Cessna F 406 Caravan II, Claudius Dornier Seastar CD2 and AAC Turbine P-210 conversion.

PT6A-114. Flat rated at 471 ekW; 447 kW (632 ehp; 600 shp) at 1,900 propeller rpm to 54.4°C. Fitted to Cessna Caravan I, with single exhaust.

PT6A-15AG. Flat rated at 533 ekW; 507 kW (715 ehp; 680 shp) at 2,200 propeller rpm to 22°C. Can use diesel fuel. Fitted to Ayres Turbo-Thrush, Frakes Turbo-Cat, Schweizer Turbo Ag-Cat D, Air Tractor AT-400, and

prototypes of ICA Brasov IAR-827TP and IAR-825TP Triumf.

PT6A-21. Flat rated at 432.5 ekW; 410 kW (580 ehp; 550 shp) at 2,200 propeller rpm to 33°C. Mates A-20A power unit with A-20A gearbox. Fitted to Beechcraft King Air C90.

PT6A-25. Flat rated at 432.5 ekW; 410 kW (580 ehp; 550 shp) at 2,200 propeller rpm to 33°C. Oil system for sustained inverted flight. Fitted to Beechcraft T-34C and NAC Firecracker.

PT6A-25A. Some castings of magnesium alloy instead of aluminium alloy. Fitted to Pilatus PC-7.

PT6A-25C. Flat rated at 584 ekW; 559 kW (783 ehp; 750 shp) at 2,200 propeller rpm to 31°C. A-25 with A-34 hot end and A-27 first stage reduction gearing. Fitted to Embraer EMB-312.

PT6A-27. Flat rated at 553 ekW; 507 kW (715 ehp; 680 shp) at 2,200 propeller rpm to 22°C, attained by increase in mass flow, at lower turbine temperatures than in PT6A-20. Hamilton Westwind II/III (Beech 18) conversions, Beechcraft 99 and 99A, and U-21A and U-21D, DHC-6 Twin Otter 300, Pilatus/Fairchild Industries PC-6/B2-H2 Turbo-Porter, Frakes Aviation (Grumman) Mallard conversion, Let L-410A Turbolet, Saunders ST-27A conversion, Embraer EMB-110 Bandeirante (early), Harbin Y-12 II, SAC Spectrum-One, and Schafer Comanchero 500B/Neiva Carajá.

PT6A-28. Similar to PT6A-27, this has an additional cruise rating of 419 ekW (562 ehp) available to 21°C and max cruise up to 33°C. Beechcraft King Air E90 and A100, and 99A, Piper Cheyenne II, Avtek 400 and Embraer Xingu I.

PT6A-34. Flat rated at 584 ekW; 559 kW (783 ehp; 750 shp) at 2,200 propeller rpm to 31°C, this version has aircooled nozzle guide vanes. IAI 102/201 Arava, Saunders ST-28, Frakes Aviation (Grumman) Mallard conversion, Airmaster Avalon 680, Omni Turbo Titan, Spectrum-One, Embraer EMB-110P1/P2 and EMB-111, and Carajá.

PT6A-34B. Aluminium alloy replaces magnesium in major castings. Fitted to Beechcraft T-44A.

PT6A-34AG. Agricultural, certificated on diesel fuel. Frakes conversion of Ag-Cat and Ayres Turbo-Thrush. Selected for PZL-106AT/BT Turbo-Kruk, Schweizer Turbo Ag-Cat and Croplease Fieldmaster.

PT6A-135. Flat rated at 587 ekW; 559 kW (787 ehp; 750 shp) at 1,900 rpm. Changed drive ratio to reduce noise; higher cycle temperatures. JetCrafters Taurus, Embraer 121A1 Xingu II, Piper Cheyenne IIXL, Advanced Aircraft Turbine P-210 and Regent 1500, Airmaster Avalon 680, and Schafer Comanchero/Comanchero 750 conversions.

PT6A-135A. Higher thermodynamic ratings. Avtek 400, Beech F90-1, Dornier Seastar and OMAC Laser 300.

PT6A-36. Flat rated at 586 ekW; 559 kW (786 ehp; 750 shp) at 2,200 propeller rpm to 36°C. Similar to -34 but higher rating. Fitted to IAI 101B/202 Arava and Beechcraft C99.

PT6A-41. Higher mass flow, aircooled nozzle guide vanes and two-stage free turbine. T-O rating of 673 ekW;

634 kW (903 ehp; 850 shp) at 2,000 propeller rpm, to 41°C. Thermodynamic power 812 ekW (1,089 ehp). Beechcraft Super King Air 200 and C-12, and Piper Cheyenne III.

PT6A-41AG. For agricultural aviation. Frakes Turbo-Cat and Schweizer Turbo Ag-Cat.

PT6A-42. A-41 with increase in cruise performance. Beechcraft Super King Air B200.

PT6A-45A. A-41 with gearbox to transmit higher powers at reduced speeds. Rated at 916 ekW; 875 kW (1,229 ehp; 1,173 shp) at 1,700 rpm to 8°C, or to 21°C with water injection. Shorts 330 and Mohawk 298.

PT6A-45B. A-45A with increased water injection.

PT6A-45R. A-45B with reserve power rating and deleted water system.

T101-CP-100. A-45R for Shorts C-23A.

PT6A-50. A-41 with higher ratio reduction gear for quieter operation. T-O 875.5 ekW; 835 kW (1,174 ehp; 1,120 shp) with water up to 34°C at 1,210 propeller rpm. DHC-7.

PT6A-60. Flat rated to 522 kW (700 shp). TBM 700.

PT6A-60A. A-45B with jet flap intake and increased mass flow for high altitude cruise. Rated at 830 ekW; 783 kW (1,113 ehp; 1,050 shp) at 1,700 rpm to 25°C. Beech Super King Air 300 and OMAC Laser 300A.

PT6A-61. A-60 gas generator matched with A-41 power section with 2,000 rpm gearbox. T-O rating 673 ekW; 634 kW (903 ehp; 850 shp) to 46°C. Cheyenne IIIA.

PT6A-62. Flat rated to 708 kW (950 shp). Pilatus PC-9.

PT6A-64. A-67 gas generator with A-61 gearbox. Flat rated at 522 kW (700 shp) at 2,000 rpm to 63.5°C. TBM 700.

PT6A-65B. A-65R without reserve rating. Flat rated at 875.5 ekW; 820 kW (1,174 ehp; 1,100 shp) at 1,700 rpm to 51°C. Beechcraft 1900 and C-12J, and CASA Aviocar C-212P.

PT6A-65R. A-45R with four-stage compressor with jet flap intake, fuel control and fuel dump. Improved hot end and exhaust duct. Reserve power 1,087 ekW; 1,026 kW (1,459 ehp; 1,376 shp) at 1,700 rpm to 28°C. Alternative T-O at 975 ekW; 917 kW (1,308 ehp; 1,230 shp) at 1,700 rpm to 24°C. Shorts 360.

PT6A-65AR. Reserve power 1,125 ekW; 1,062 kW (1,509 ehp; 1,424 shp) at 1,700 rpm to 27.7°C. Shorts 360 and AMI DC-3.

PT6A-66. Flat rated at 674 ekW; 534 kW (905 ehp; 850 shp) at 2,000 rpm to 62.2°C. Piaggio Avanti with opposed rotation gearbox.

PT6A-67. Flat rated at 870 ekW; 820 kW (1,167 ehp; 1,100 shp) at 1,700 rpm to 60°C. Beechcraft Starship 2000 and RC-12K.

PT6A-67A. Flat rated at 948 ekW; 894 kW (1,272 ehp; 1,200 shp) at 1,700 rpm to 51°C. Powers Beech Starship 1 and 1900D.

PT6A-67AF. Flat rated at 1,125 ekW; 1,061 kW (1,509 ehp; 1,424 shp) at 1,700 rpm to 37.2°C. Powers Conair/IMP Turbo Firecat.

PT6A-67B. A-67 modified for medium altitudes. Flat rated at 895 kW (1,200 shp) at 1,700 rpm to 52°C. Pilatus PC-12.

PT6A-67CF. Growth version of A-67AF. Flat rated at 1,231 kW (1,650 shp) at 1,700 rpm to 37.8°C. Brazilian S-2 Turbine Tracker.

PT6A-67D. A-67B with A-67R gearbox. Flat rated at 909 kW (1,219 shp) at 1,700 rpm to 39°C. Beech 1900D.

PT6A-67R. A-67 with reserve power rating for commuter aircraft. Flat rated at 1,125 ekW; 1,061 kW (1,509 ehp; 1,424 shp) at 1,700 rpm to 37.2°C. Powers Shorts 360-300 and Basler Turbo 67.

The following data apply generally to the PT6A series.

TYPE: Free turbine axial-plus-centrifugal turboprop.

PROPELLER DRIVE (all models up to and including PT6A-41):
Two-stage planetary. Ratio 15. Higher ratio gears for A-45R, -50, -60, -65 and -67.

AIR INTAKE: Annular at rear with screen. Aircraft-supplied alcohol or inertial anti-icing.

COMPRESSOR: Three axial stages, plus single centrifugal (-65 series, four axial stages). PT6A-27: pressure ratio 6.7, mass flow 3.1 kg (6.8 lb/s). PT6A-65: pressure ratio 10, mass flow 4.3 kg (9.5 lb/s).

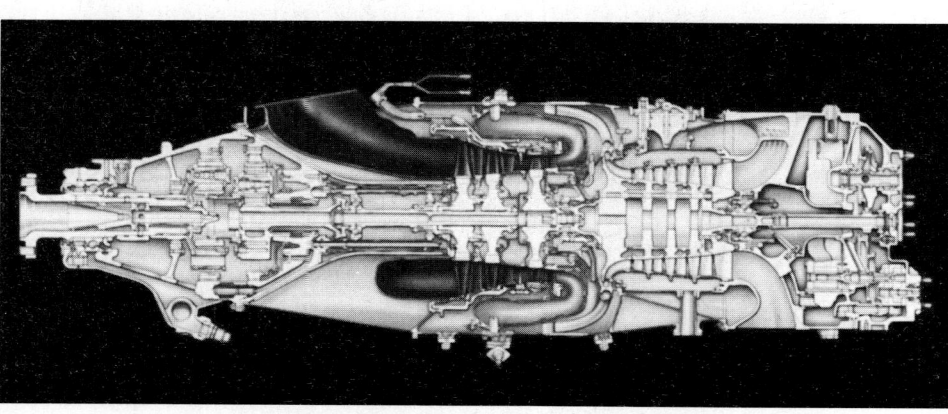

Longitudinal section of P&WC PT6A-67 turboprop

COMBUSTION CHAMBER: Annular reverse flow, with 14 simplex burners.

FUEL SYSTEM: Bendix DP-F2 pneumatic automatic fuel control. A-50 has DP-F3 with starting spill valve and motive flow systems; A-60 series (except -62) have Woodward 83212 hydromechanical system.

FUEL GRADE: JP-1, JP-4, JP-5, MIL-J-5624. Gasolines (MIL-G-5572) grades 80/87, 91/98, 100/130 and 115/145 for up to 150 h during any overhaul period. Agricultural use, diesel.

TURBINES: Up to A-34 two single-stage axial; HP (58 blades) drives compressor, and LP (41 shrouded blades) drives output shaft. A-41 onward have two-stage LP turbine. All blades have fir tree root.

ACCESSORIES: Pads on accessory case (rear of engine) for starter/generator, hydraulic pump, aircraft accessory drive, vacuum pump and tachometer generator. Pad on reduction gear for propeller governor, constant speed unit and tachometer.

LUBRICATION SYSTEM: One pressure and four scavenge elements driven by gas generator. Integral oil tank 8.75 litres (2.3 US gallons).

OIL SPECIFICATION: CPW202, PWA521 Type II (7.5 cs vis) (MIL-L-23699, MIL-L-7808 for military engines).

STARTING: Electric starter/generator on accessory case.

DIMENSIONS:

Max diameter	483 mm (19 in)
Length, excl accessories:	
PT6A-11 to -36	1,575 mm (62 in)
PT6A-41, 42, 61	1,701 mm (67 in)
PT6A-45, 60A	1,829 mm (72 in)
PT6A-50	2,133 mm (84 in)
PT6A-62, -66	1,778 mm (70 in)
PT6A-65B, -67	1,880 mm (74 in)
PT6A-65R, -65AR	1,905 mm (75 in)

WEIGHT, DRY:

PT6A-11	142.4 kg (314 lb)
PT6A-11AG	145.6 kg (321 lb)
PT6A-110	148.3 kg (327 lb)
PT6A-112	147.8 kg (326 lb)
PT6A-114	156.5 kg (345 lb)
PT6A-15AG	144.7 kg (319 lb)
PT6A-21	143.3 kg (316 lb)
PT6A-25	154.6 kg (341 lb)
PT6A-25A	150.1 kg (331 lb)
PT6A-25C	151.9 kg (335 lb)
PT6A-27, -28	142.4 kg (314 lb)
PT6A-34, -36	145.1 kg (320 lb)
PT6A-34B, -135, -135A	149.7 kg (330 lb)
PT6A-34AG	143.8 kg (317 lb)
PT6A-41, -42	177.3 kg (391 lb)
PT6A-41AG	181.4 kg (400 lb)
PT6A-45A	196.8 kg (434 lb)
PT6A-45R	197.7 kg (436 lb)
PT6A-50	275.3 kg (607 lb)
PT6A-60A	210.9 kg (465 lb)
PT6A-61	193.2 kg (426 lb)
PT6A-62	205.9 kg (454 lb)
PT6A-64	207.0 kg (456 lb)
PT6A-65B, -65R	218.2 kg (481 lb)
PT6A-65AR	220.4 kg (486 lb)
PT6A-66	216.4 kg (477 lb)
PT6A-67, -67A	229.5 kg (506 lb)
PT6A-67AF	241.0 kg (532 lb)
PT6A-67CF	253.0 kg (558 lb)
PT6A-67R, -67B, -67D	233.5 kg (515 lb)

PERFORMANCE RATINGS (S/L, static):

T-O: See under model listings

Max continuous:

PT6A-110	374 ekW; 354 kW (502 ehp; 475 shp) at 1,900 rpm (to 38°C)
PT6A-11, 11AG	394 ekW; 373 kW (528 ehp; 500 shp) at 2,200 rpm (to 42°C)
PT6A-112	394 ekW; 373 kW (528 ehp; 500 shp) at 1,900 rpm (to 56°C)
PT6A-114	471 ekW; 447 kW (632 ehp; 600 shp) at 1,900 rpm (to 54.4°C)
PT6A-15AG, -27, -28	533 ekW; 507 kW (715 ehp; 680 shp) at 2,200 rpm (to 22°C)
PT6A-21	432.5 ekW; 410 kW (580 ehp; 550 shp) at 2,200 rpm (to 33°C)
PT6A-25, -25A	432.5 ekW; 410 kW (580 ehp; 550 shp) at 2,200 rpm (to 33°C)
PT6A-25C	584 ekW; 559 kW (783 ehp; 750 shp) at 2,200 rpm (to 31°C)
PT6A-34	584 ekW; 559 kW (783 ehp; 750 shp) at 2,200 rpm (to 30°C)
PT6A-135	587 ekW; 559 kW (787 ehp; 750 shp) at 1,900 rpm (-135 to 29°C, -135A to 34°C)
PT6A-36	586 ekW. 559 kW (786 ehp; 750 shp) at 2,200 rpm (to 36°C)
PT6A-41	673 ekW; 634 kW (903 ehp; 850 shp) at 2,000 rpm (to 41°C)
PT6A-42	674 ekW; 634 kW (904 ehp; 850 shp) at 2,000 rpm (to 41°C)
PT6A-45A, -45B, -45R	798 ekW; 761 kW (1,070 ehp; 1,020 shp) at 1,700 rpm (to: -45A, 26.7°C; -45B, 29°C; -45R, 33°C)
PT6A-50	762 ekW; 725.5 kW (1,022 ehp; 973 shp) at 1,210 rpm (to 32°C)

PT6A-60A		830 ekW; 783 kW (1,113 ehp; 1,050 shp) at 1,700 rpm (to 25°C)
PT6A-61		673 ekW; 634 kW (902 ehp; 850 shp) at 2,000 rpm (to 46°C)
PT6A-62		751 ekW; 708 kW (1,008 ehp; 950 shp) at 2,000 rpm (to 37°C)
PT6A-64		557 ekW (747 ehp) at 2,000 rpm (to 63.5°C)
PT6A-65B		875 ekW; 820 kW (1,174 ehp; 1,100 shp) at 1,700 rpm (to 45°C)
PT6A-65R		931 ekW; 875 kW (1,249 ehp; 1,173 shp) at 1,700 rpm (to 38°C)
PT6A-66		675 ekW; 634 kW (905 ehp; 850 shp) at 2,000 rpm (to 62°C)
PT6A-67		870 ekW; 820 kW (1,167 ehp; 1,100 shp) at 1,700 rpm (to 45°C)
PT6A-67B		949 ekW (1,272 ehp) at 1,700 rpm (to 52°C)
PT6A-67CF		1,298 ekW (1,740 ehp) at 1,700 rpm (to 46°C)
PT6A-67D		1,009 ekW (1,353 ehp) at 1,700 rpm (to 39°C)
PT6A-67R		965 ekW; 910 kW (1,294 ehp; 1,220 shp) at 1,700 rpm (to 48°C)

Max cruise rating:

PT6A-110	374 ekW; 354 kW (502 ehp; 475 shp) at 1,900 rpm (to 19°C)
PT6A-11	394 ekW; 373 kW (528 ehp; 500 shp) at 2,200 rpm (to 37°C)
PT6A-11AG	394 ekW; 373 kW (528 ehp; 500 shp) at 2,200 rpm (to 36°C)
PT6A-112	394 ekW; 373 kW (528 ehp; 500 shp) at 1,900 rpm (to 48°C)
PT6A-114	471 ekW; 447 kW (632 ehp; 600 shp) at 1,900 rpm (to 31.1°C)
PT6A-15AG	as PT6A-27
PT6A-21, -25, -25A	432.5 ekW; 410 kW (580 ehp; 550 shp) at 2,200 rpm (to 47.2°C; 33°C; 33°C)
PT6A-25C	545 ekW; 522 kW (731 ehp; 700 shp) at 2,200 rpm (to 19°C)
PT6A-27	486 ekW; 462 kW (652 ehp; 620 shp) at 2,200 rpm (to 21°C)
PT6A-28	486 ekW; 462 kW (652 ehp; 620 shp) at 2,200 rpm (to 33°C)
PT6A-34	545 ekW; 522 kW (731 ehp; 700 shp) at 2,200 rpm (to 19°C)
PT6A-135	548 ekW; 522 kW (735 ehp; 700 shp) at 1,900 rpm (-135 to 37°C, -135A to 41°C)
PT6A-36	548 ekW; 522 kW (735 ehp; 700 shp) at 2,200 rpm (to 19°C)
PT6A-41	673 ekW; 634 kW (903 ehp; 850 shp) at 2,000 rpm (to 28°C)
PT6A-42	674 ekW; 634 kW (904 ehp; 850 shp) at 2,000 rpm (to 33°C)
PT6A-45	749 ekW; 713 kW (1,004 ehp; 956 shp) at 1,425 rpm (to 15°C)
PT6A-50	706 ekW; 671 kW (947 ehp; 900 shp) at 1,020-1,160 rpm (to 23°C)
PT6A-60A	791 ekW; 746 kW (1,061 ehp; 1,000 shp) at 1,700 rpm (to 28°C)
PT6A-61	as max continuous but to 43.8°C
PT6A-62	712 ekW; 671 kW (955 ehp; 900 shp) at 2,000 rpm (to 32°C)
PT6A-64	557 ekW (747 ehp) at 2,000 rpm (to 58°C)
PT6A-65B, -65R	762 ekW; 713 kW (1,022 ehp; 956 shp) at 1,425 rpm (to 27°C)
PT6A-65AR	762 ekW; 713 kW (1,022 ehp; 956 shp) at 1,425 rpm (to 29°C)
PT6A-66	675 ekW; 634 kW (905 ehp; 850 shp) at 2,000 rpm (to 56°C)
PT6A-67, -67A	792 ekW; 746 kW (1,062 ehp; 1,000 shp) at 1,700 rpm (to 50°C)

PT6A-67AF	808 ekW; 760 kW (1,083 ehp; 1,020 shp) at 1,700 rpm (to 37°C)
PT6A-67B	792 ekW (1,062 ehp) at 1,700 rpm (to 45°C)
PT6A-67CF	868 ekW (1,163 ehp) at 1,425 rpm (to 36°C)
PT6A-67D	837 ekW (1,122 ehp) at 1,700 rpm (to 34°C)
PT6A-67R	808 ekW; 761 kW (1,083 ehp; 1,020 shp) at 1,425 rpm (to 35°C)

SPECIFIC FUEL CONSUMPTION:

At T-O rating:

PT6A-110	111.0 µg/J (0.657 lb/h/ehp)
PT6A-11, -11AG	109.4 µg/J (0.647 lb/h/ehp)
PT6A-112	107.6 µg/J (0.637 lb/h/ehp)
PT6A-114	108.2 µg/J (0.640 lb/h/ehp)
PT6A-15AG, -27, -28	101.8 µg/J (0.602 lb/h/ehp)
PT6A-21, -25, -25A	106.5 µg/J (0.630 lb/h/ehp)
PT6A-25C, -34, -34B, -34AG	100.6 µg/J (0.595 lb/h/ehp)
PT6A-135, -135A	98.9 µg/J (0.585 lb/h/ehp)
PT6A-36	99.7 µg/J (0.590 lb/h/ehp)
PT6A-41, -61	99.9 µg/J (0.591 lb/h/ehp)
PT6A-42	101.5 µg/J (0.601 lb/h/ehp)
PT6A-45A, -45B	93.5 µg/J (0.554 lb/h/ehp)
PT6A-45R	93.4 µg/J (0.553 lb/h/ehp)
PT6A-50	94.6 µg/J (0.560 lb/h/ehp)
PT6A-60A	92.6 µg/J (0.548 lb/h/ehp)
PT6A-62	95.8 µg/J (0.567 lb/h/ehp)
PT6A-64	118.8 µg/J (0.703 lb/h/ehp)
PT6A-65B	90.6 µg/J (0.536 lb/h/ehp)
PT6A-65R	86.5 µg/J (0.512 lb/h/ehp)
PT6A-65AR	86.0 µg/J (0.509 lb/h/ehp)
PT6A-66	104.8 µg/J (0.620 lb/h/ehp)
PT6A-67	92.4 µg/J (0.547 lb/h/ehp)
PT6A-67A	92.8 µg/J (0.549 lb/h/ehp)
PT6A-67AF, -67R	87.9 µg/J (0.520 lb/h/ehp)
PT6A-67B	93.3 µg/J (0.552 lb/h/ehp)
PT6A-67CF	83.7 µg/J (0.495 lb/h/ehp)
PT6A-67D	89.6 µg/J (0.530 lb/h/ehp)

OIL CONSUMPTION:

Max	0.091 kg (0.20 lb)/h

P&WC T74

T74 is a US designation for military versions of the PT6A turboprop and PT6B turboshaft.

T74-CP-700. US Army PT6A-20. More than 300 delivered to Beech for 129 U-21A. Inertial separator system.

T74-CP-702. Rated at 580 ekW (778 ehp) and retrofitted in Beechcraft U-21.

P&WC PT6B/PT6C

The PT6B is the commercial turboshaft version of the PT6A and has a lower ratio reduction gear. Current versions are:

PT6B-36. Reverse drive 6,409 rpm gearbox. T-O rating 732 kW (981 shp) to 15°C, with 2½-min contingency 770 kW (1,033 shp) to 15°C. Sikorsky S-76B.

PT6B-36A. Identical to -36 but with different ratings.

PT6C. Direct drive from the power turbine.

DIMENSIONS:

Max diameter: PT6B-36, -36A	495 mm (19.5 in)
Length, excl accessories:	
PT6B-36, -36A,	1,504 mm (59.2 in)

WEIGHT, DRY:

PT6B-36	169 kg (372 lb)
PT6B-36A	171 kg (378 lb)

PERFORMANCE RATINGS:

T-O: See under model listings

Max cruise, continuous:

PT6B-36	640 kW (870 shp) to 15°C
PT6B-36A	652 kW (887 shp) to 15°C

The P&WC PT6B-36 turboshaft engine

SPECIFIC FUEL CONSUMPTION:
At T-O rating:

PT6B-36	100.5 µg/J (0.594 lb/h/shp)
PT6B-36A	98.2 µg/J (0.581 lb/h/shp)

OIL CONSUMPTION:

Max	0.091 kg (0.20 lb)/h

P&WC PT6T TWIN-PAC
US military designation: T400 (separate entry)
First run in July 1968, the Twin-Pac comprises two PT6 turboshaft engines side by side and driving a combining gearbox.

PT6T-3. T-O rating 1,342 kW (1,800 shp). For Bell and Agusta-Bell 212 and California/Sikorsky S-58T.

In these applications, shaft power is limited by the transmission. In the Model 212 the 1,342 kW (1,800 shp) PT6T-3 is restricted to a T-O rating of 962 kW (1,290 shp) and 843 kW (1,130 shp) for continuous power. In the S-58T the limits are 1,122 kW (1,505 shp) at T-O and 935 kW (1,254 shp) for continuous operation.

PT6T-3B. PT6T-3 with some T-6 hardware and improved single-engine performance. Bell 212 and 412.

PT6T-6. Improved compressor-turbine nozzle guide vanes and rotor blades. S-58T and AB 212. By 1989 18,448,884 equivalent PT6 hours had been flown by PT6T engines in 2,047 helicopters in 83 countries.

The following features differ from the PT6:

TYPE: Coupled free turbine turboshaft.

SHAFT DRIVE: Combining gearbox comprises three separate gear trains, two input and one output, each contained within an individual sealed compartment and all interconnected by driveshafts. Overall reduction ratio 5.

AIR INTAKES: Additional inertial particle separator to reduce ingestion. High frequency compressor noise suppressed.

FUEL SYSTEM: As PT6 with manual backup, and dual manifold for cool starts. Automatic power sharing and torque limiting.

FUEL GRADES: JP-1, JP-4 and JP-5.

ACCESSORIES: Starter/generator and tachogenerator on accessory case at front of each power section. Other drives on gearbox, including power turbine governors and tachogenerators, and provision for blowers and aircraft accessories.

OIL SPECIFICATION: PWA Spec 521. For military engines, MIL-L-7808 and -23699.

STARTING: Electrical, with cold weather starting down to −54°C.

DIMENSIONS:

Length	1,702 mm (67.0 in)
Width	1,118 mm (44.0 in)
Height	838 mm (33.0 in)

WEIGHT, DRY (standard equipment):

PT6T-3	292 kg (645 lb)
PT6T-3B, -6	298 kg (657 lb)

PERFORMANCE RATINGS:
T-O (5 min):
Total output, at 6,600 rpm:

PT6T-3, -3B	1,342 kW (1,800 shp)
PT6T-6	1,398 kW (1,875 shp) (to 21°C)

Single power section only, at 6,600 rpm:

PT6T-3, -3B	671 kW (900 shp)
PT6T-6, -3B (2½ min)	764 kW (1,025 shp)

30 min power (single power section), at 6,600 rpm:

PT6T-3B, -6	723 kW (970 shp)

Cruise A:
Total output, at 6,600 rpm:

PT6T-3, -3B	932 kW (1,250 shp)
PT6T-6	1,014 kW (1,360 shp)

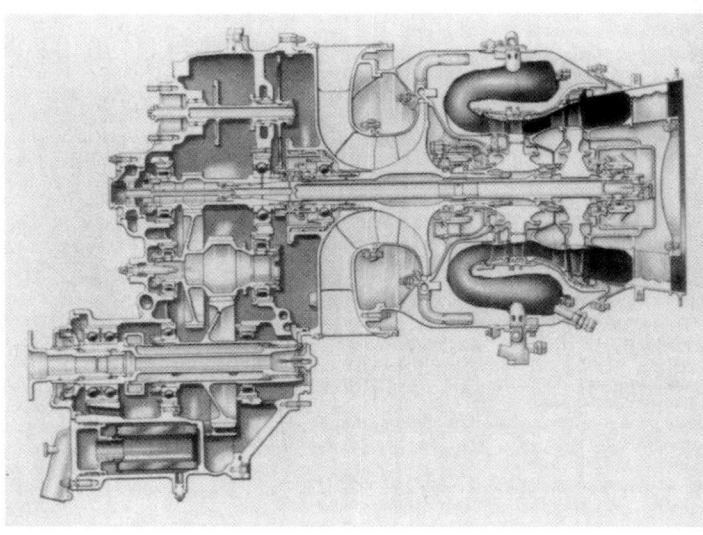

Cutaway drawing of the
P&WC PW206A
free turbine turboshaft

Single power section only, at 6,600 rpm:

PT6T-3, -3B	466 kW (625 shp)
PT6T-6	500 kW (670 shp)

Cruise B:
Total output, at 6,600 rpm:

PT6T-3, -3B	820 kW (1,100 shp)
PT6T-6	891 kW (1,195 shp)

Single power section only, at 6,600 rpm:

PT6T-3, -3B	410 kW (550 shp)
PT6T-6	440 kW (590 shp)
Ground idle, at 2,200 rpm	44.7 kW (60 shp) max

SPECIFIC FUEL CONSUMPTION:
At 2½-min rating (single power section):

PT6T-3B	100.7 µg/J (0.596 lb/h/shp)
PT6T-6	101.6 µg/J (0.602 lb/h/shp)

OIL CONSUMPTION:

Max (for both gas generators)	0.18 kg (0.4 lb)/h

P&WC T400
Military version of the PT6T Twin-Pac; castings of aluminium instead of magnesium and minimum infra-red signature. Produced from March 1970 for Bell UH-1N, AH-1J and CH-135. Deliveries totalled 799 engines.

The T400-WV-402 is the military PT6T-6 and is used in the AH-1T; 524 were delivered.

DIMENSIONS (CP-400 and WV-402):

Length	1,659 mm (65.3 in)
Width	1,115 mm (43.5 in)
Height	828 mm (32.6 in)

WEIGHT, DRY:

T400-CP-400	324 kg (714 lb)
T400-WV-402	338 kg (745 lb)

PERFORMANCE RATINGS:
Intermediate:

T400-CP-400	1,342 kW (1,800 shp) at 6,600 rpm
T400-WV-402	1,469 kW (1,970 shp) at 6,600 rpm

Max continuous:

T400-CP-400	1,141 kW (1,530 shp) at 6,600 rpm
T400-WV-402	1,248 kW (1,673 shp) at 6,600 rpm

SPECIFIC FUEL CONSUMPTION (Intermediate rating):

T400-CP-400	100.4 µg/J (0.594 lb/h/shp)
T400-WV-402	99.9 µg/J (0.591 lb/h/shp)

P&WC PW200
In 1983 P&WC announced the development of this new engine series. The basic design is flexible and is planned to permit increased power and reduced sfc without dimensional change. The first model in the series is the **PW206A**. Certification was due at the end of 1991.

TYPE: Free-turbine turboshaft.

AIR INTAKE: Inwards amidships through mesh screen.

COMPRESSOR: Single-stage centrifugal of machined titanium. Pressure ratio 8.

COMBUSTION CHAMBER: Reverse-flow annular with 12 air blast nozzles. Two capacitor discharge igniters.

FUEL SYSTEM: Hydromechanical with digital electronics powered by dedicated alternator.

FUEL GRADE: JP-1, JP-4, JP-5 or a range of gasolines.

TURBINES: Single-stage axial compressor and power turbines with blades held in dovetail slots. Cold junction temperature sensing.

GEARBOX: Front mounted combined reduction and accessory gearbox with 6,000 rpm output. Includes phase shift torquemeter and drives for starter/generator, hydraulic pump and alternator.

DIMENSIONS:

Length	912 mm (35.9 in)
Width	500 mm (19.7 in)
Height	566 mm (22.3 in)

PERFORMANCE RATINGS:

2½ min	476 kW (638 shp)
30 min and T-O	463 kW (621 shp)
Max continuous	410 kW (550 shp)

SPECIFIC FUEL CONSUMPTION:

2½ min	93.3 µg/J (0.552 lb/h/shp)
30 min and T-O	93.6 µg/J (0.554 lb/h/shp)
Max continuous	95.3 µg/J (0.564 lb/h/shp)

CHINA, PEOPLE'S REPUBLIC

MAS
MINISTRY OF AERO-SPACE INDUSTRY
PO Box 33, Beijing
Telephone: 86 (1) 440517
Telex: 211244 MAS CN
MINISTER: Lin Zongtang

CAREC
CHINA NATIONAL AERO-ENGINE CORPORATION
67 Jiao Nan Dajie, Beijing
Telephone: 86 (1) 4013322 ext 5401
Cables: 9696

INTERNATIONAL MARKETING:
CATIC (China National Aero-Technology Import and Export Corporation)
5 Liang Guo Chang Road, East City District (PO Box 1671), Beijing
Telephone: 86 (1) 445831, 442444
Fax: 86 (1) 4015381
Telex: 22318 AEROT CN
Cables: CAID BEIJING
PRESIDENT: Sun Zhaoqing
EXECUTIVE VICE-PRESIDENT: Tang Xiaoping

In the past 30 years China has enormously expanded its aero-engine industry. Today there are eight major engine manufacturing centres, five factory-managed design institutes and four engine research and design institutes. Over 48,000 engines of 25 types have been manufactured for the air force and navy, 756 engines of 10 types manufactured for CAAC, and smaller numbers for export. Not within the scope of this annual, nine types of large solid and liquid rocket engines have also been manufactured. Most factories are seeking foreign orders or partners.

The following survey is by alphabetical order in English of the design or manufacturing organisation.

BUAA
BEIJING UNIVERSITY OF AERONAUTICS AND ASTRONAUTICS

37 Xue Yuan Road, Beijing 100083
Telephone: 86 (1) 201 7251
Telex: 22036 BIAAT

This university's propulsion department is producing the **WP11** turbojet, for various manned and unmanned applications. It is derived from the Turbomeca Marboré II.

CEC
CHENGDU ENGINE COMPANY
PO Box 613, Chengdu, Sichuan
Telephone: 86 (28) 442470
Fax: 86 (28) 442470
Telex: 60142 CET CN
Cables: 4721
GENERAL MANAGER: Pei Hongbin

This company was formed in October 1958, and is also known as CEF (Chengdu Aero-Engine Factory). Most of the staff and resources came from the Shenyang Overhaul Factory, and the first task was to produce the **RD-500K** (RR Derwent derivative) turbojet for a cruise missile.

Today CEC has a site area exceeding 130 ha (321.2 acres) and a workforce of over 20,000. It produces the **WP6** turbojet (see LM), the **WP13** turbojet (see LMC) and components for the Pratt & Whitney **JT8D** turbofan,

including combustion liners. In 1988 the **WP13G** and **WP14** were announced, with annular combustion chambers, for later J-7 versions. In October 1988 SNECMA announced that it was assisting CATIC to develop the improved WP13G and WP14 for later F-7 versions. New annular combustion chambers will be produced. This work is thought to be the responsibility of the Chengdu Engine Company.

CLXMW
CHANGZHOU LAN XIANG MACHINERY WORKS
PO Box 37, Changzhou, Jiangxi
Telephone: 86 (596) 602095, 602097
Cables: 5046

DIRECTOR: Tian Taiwu

Also known as JHEF (Jiangxi Helicopter Engine Factory), this works has a payroll of over 5,000. Its main product is the **WZ6** turboshaft and the **WZ6G** industrial derivative. Rated at 1,145 kW (1,536 shp) and with a dry

weight of 300 kg (661 lb), the WZ6 is derived from the Turbomeca Turmo IIIC. Work began in 1975, testing occupied 1980-82 and WZ6 engines first flew in a Z-8 helicopter in 1986.

DEMC
DONGAN ENGINE MANUFACTURING COMPANY
PO Box 51, Harbin, Heilongjiang
Telephone: 86 (451) 61431
Telex: 87082 HEF CN
Cables: 0021
GENERAL MANAGER: Zhang Hongbiao

Also known as HEF (Harbin Engine Factory), this establishment was founded in 1948 and employs more than 10,000. Its first product was the 1,268 kW (1,700 hp) **HS7**, a 14-cylinder radial piston engine based on the Soviet Shvetsov ASh-82V. In parallel, in 1957-59, a few ASh-21 engines were made, but only the HS7 went into production, for the Z-5 helicopter. In the late 1950s there was a need for a better engine for the Il-12, Il-14, Tu-2 and Curtiss C-46,

with the main need on altitude performance. The result, produced from 1962 until 1980, was the **HS8**, which combined the main body and supercharger of the HS7 with the reduction gear of the ASh-82T. The HS8 is rated at 1,380 kW (1,850 hp).

A larger effort began in 1968 when development of the **WJ5** was transferred from ZEF. Rated at 1,901 ekW (2,550 ehp), this engine is derived from the Ivchenko AI-24A. Among problems solved were broaching of the turbine disc and welding of the annular combustion chambers. Following 5,678 test hours the WJ5 was certificated in January 1977. From 1969 an even larger project was development of the **WJ5A**, to meet the needs of the SH-5. The turbine section was almost completely redesigned, with aircooled rotor blades, and many other parts changed in design or material. The first 5A went on test in late 1970,

and certification was gained in January 1980. This modernised engine is rated at 2,350 ekW (3,150 ehp) up to 30°C. In 1979 work began on modifying the original WJ5 to enable the Y-7 series of aircraft to have better hot/high performance. The result, certificated in 1982, is the **WJ5A I**, basically a 5A flat rated at 2,162.5 ekW (2,900 ehp) to 38°C.

In 1988 an agreement was reached with General Electric of the USA for development of the **WJ5E** with reduced sfc. The prototype passed initial static tests in 1990, with sfc reduced from 98.7 µg/J (0.584 lb/h/shp) to 89.4 µg/J (0.529 lb/h/shp). The WJ5E is the engine of the Y7-200B.

In 1966 Harbin was assigned the task of modifying the WJ5 into the **WZ5** turboshaft engine for the Z-6 helicopter. After a prototype had been run this engine was transferred to ZARI (which see).

GADRI
GUIZHOU AERO-ENGINE DESIGN AND RESEARCH INSTITUTE

Supported by many companies, GADRI developed the **WP7B** fighter engine which, for convenience, is included in the main WP7 entry under LMC.

GEF — *See under LMC*

HEF — *See under DEMC*

JHEF — *See under CLXMW*

LM
LIMING ENGINE MANUFACTURING CORPORATION
PO Box 424 (6 Dongta St, Dadong District), Shenyang, Liaoning
Telephone: 86 (24) 443139
Fax: 86 (24) 732221
Cables: 4104
Telex: 80025 LMMCS CN
GENERAL MANAGER: Yan Guangwei

With site area exceeding 100 ha (247.1 acres), more than 200,000 m² (2,152,850 sq ft) covered area, and a workforce of over 20,000, Liming (Daybreak) is one of the largest and most experienced aero-engine centres in China. Alternatively known as SEF (Shenyang Aero-Engine Factory), or just as The New Factory, it was set up on the basis of the old overhaul factory in 1954-57. The first product was the **WP5** turbojet, a licensed version of the

Soviet Klimov VK-1F (Rolls-Royce Nene derivative). Production of the WP5 was achieved in June 1956. By 1957 the WP5A, based on the VK-1A, was in production, but in 1963, following increased demand to power the H-5, production was transferred to XEF (see XAE).

In 1956 SADO (Shenyang Aero-Engine Design Office) was established, later being restyled SARI. This undertook the design of the first Chinese turbojet, the **PF1A**, based on the WP5 but smaller and rated at 15.7 kN (3,527 lb st) to power the JJ-1 trainer. Design was complete in 1957 and the PF1A powered the prototype JJ-1 in July 1958, but later the requirement for the JJ-1 was dropped.

In early 1958 Soviet documents arrived for licence production of the Tumansky RD-9BF-811. This supersonic axial turbojet with afterburner, with 2,521 component parts, proved a major challenge, but the Shenyang **WP6** was first tested at the end of 1958. Tests were not successful, but following improvements in quality control trial

production restarted in 1961. Subsequently several thousand, with progressive upgrades, have been made for the J-6, JJ-6 and Q-5. Much further work led to the **WP6A** for the Q-5 I attack aircraft, with a variable inlet stator stage and increased turbine temperature. This engine was certificated in August 1973. A further variant was the **WP6B** for the J-12, not made in quantity.

The following is a description of the WP6A:

INLET: Cast assembly with four de-iced radial struts, one housing drive to accessory section above and projecting ahead of inlet. Central fixed bullet and front bearing.

COMPRESSOR: Welded ring construction with one row of variable inlet stators and nine rows of rotor blades. T-O airflow 46.2 kg (101.85 lb)/s. Pressure ratio 7.44.

COMBUSTION CHAMBER: Can-annular type with 12 flame tubes, each terminating in a section of turbine inlet periphery. Spill type burners. Two igniters fed from starting tank.

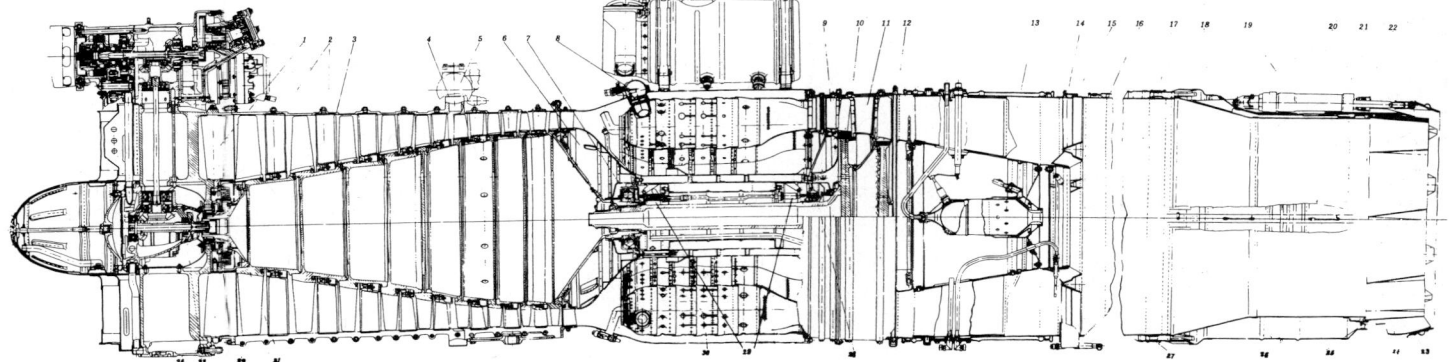

Longitudinal section through WP6A turbojet (afterburner shown shortened)
1 variable inlet stator, 2 stator vanes, 3 compressor case, 4 air bleed band, 5 bleed actuating cylinder, 6 rear load relief cavity, 7 centre bearing, 8 starting igniter, 9 stage 1 nozzle, 10 turbine rotor, 11 stage 2 nozzle, 12 quick-release ring, 13 diffuser, 14 quick-release ring, 15 front flange, 16 case, 17 shroud, 18 bracket, 19 actuating cylinder, 20 adjustable flap flange, 21 actuator and rod heat shield, 22 nozzle adjusting ring, 23 copper plate, 24 flap, 25 centring pin, 26 cylinder cowl, 27 clamp strip, 28 rear bearing, 29 oil jet, 30 flame tube, 31 compressor, 32 front load relief cavity, 33 front bearing, 34 front case

The WP6A afterburning turbojet

TURBINE: Two-stage type with blades inserted into large flat discs, driving compressor via tubular shaft.

AFTERBURNER: Constant diameter type with main starting burner in turbine rear cone and single ring of fuel nozzles and gutter flameholders around rear of cone. Ten adjustable nozzle flaps positioned by four rams.

DIMENSIONS:
Length	5,483 mm (215.9 in)
Max height	950 mm (37.4 in)
Diameter	668 mm (26.3 in)

WEIGHT, DRY: 725 kg (1,598 lb)

PERFORMANCE RATINGS (S/L, static):
Afterburner: WP6A	36.78 kN (8,267 lb st)
WP6B	39.72 kN (8,929 lb st)
Max dry: WP6A	29.42 kN (6,614 lb st)
Normal: WP6A	24.03 kN (5,401 lb st)
WP6B	24.51 kN (5,511 lb st)

SPECIFIC FUEL CONSUMPTION (WP6A):
Afterburner	0.163 kg/h/N (45.24 mg/Ns; 1.597 lb/h/lb st)
Max	0.1 kg/h/N (27.76 mg/Ns; 0.980 lb/h/lb st)
Normal	0.099 kg/h/N (27.48 mg/Ns; 0.970 lb/h/lb st)

To meet the needs of the J-7 fighter programme the Shenyang factory produced the Tumansky R-11F-300 afterburning turbojet under licence. Designated **WP7**, this Mach 2 engine was an even greater challenge as many key Soviet documents were not supplied, and 1,097 documents had errors or omissions. Eventually, using indigenous materials, the first WP7 went on test in October 1965. Dry and afterburning ratings were 38.2 kN (8,598 lb st) and 56.4 kN (12,676 lb st) respectively. By 1970 production of this engine was transferred to LMC. Shenyang continued to introduce design improvements, and a stall flutter problem was solved by using 24 larger blades in the first stage of the compressor instead of 31, while other changes were made to the HP turbine disc, bearing lubrication and afterburner nozzle flap design.

In 1964 a decision had to be made on how to power the J-8 fighter. No engine in the 120 kN (12 tonne) class could be produced in time, but Rong Ke, deputy director of Beijing Aeronautical Materials Institute, undertook to produce aircooled blades within a year to allow two uprated WP7 engines to be used. In May 1965 the resulting engine was authorised as the **WP7A**. After prolonged testing

WP7C afterburning turbojet (afterburner not fitted)

against forged blades with three large cooling holes the decision was taken to use nine-hole cast blades. Dry and afterburning ratings were established at 43.14 kN (9,698 lb st) and 59 kN (13,265 lb st), respectively. These engines powered the J-8 on its first flight in July 1969, and were certificated in June 1982. Subsequently LMC developed the **WP7B** and **WP7C**. The latter powers J-7 and J-7-II aircraft. Thrust ratings are: max 60.6 kN (13,623 lb st), max dry 42.65 kN (9,588 lb st) and normal 33.54 kN (7,540 lb st). TBO is 300 h.

Also in 1964 a meeting was held to select an engine for a new indigenous fighter. The choice fell on an augmented turbofan, the **WS6**. Drawings were produced in 1964-66,

and by 1969 two prototype engines had been made. Then the cultural revolution delayed the programme by about 10 years, but after 1978 further progress was possible. A two-spool engine with aircooled HP blades, it overcame many problems and reached design figures in 1980. Full details are not yet available, but dry and afterburning thrusts are respectively 71.3 kN (16,027 lb st) and 122.2 kN (27,470 lb st), and dry weight 2,100 kg (4,632 lb). In 1980-82 modifications were made, especially to the afterburner, to increase maximum thrust in the **WS6A** to 138.3 kN (31,085 lb st), giving a thrust/weight ratio close to 7. This engine is expected to power the H-7.

LMC
LIYANG MACHINERY CORPORATION
PO Box 207, Pingba, Guizhou
Telephone: 86 (34) Guiyang
Telex: 66044 LYNCG CN
Cables: 4099, 4101
GENERAL MANAGER: Hu Wenqin

With a covered area of 750,000 m² (8,073,200 sq ft), and a workforce exceeding 10,000, LMC is also known as GEF (Guizhou Aero-Engine Factory). The associated GADRI undertook the development of the **WP7B** afterburning turbojet, the programme being transferred to LMC because Shenyang was overloaded. The main change in the 7B concerned the structure and length of the afterburner. Severe problems were encountered with the cast aircooled turbine blades, which tended to crack, with the high reject rate of castings, and with burning of the rear fuselage caused by excessive afterburner wall temperatures. The 7B was eventually certificated in 1978 and succeeded the WP7 in production in 1980. Further changes enabled TBO to be increased from 100 h to 200 h. Guizhou then eliminated the separate petrol (gasoline) starter and its tank and supply system, which reduced weight and maintenance and improved air starting. The engine is known as the **WP7B (M batch)** and entered production in 1982. A further modification, in the **WP7B (BM)**, reduces weight by 17 kg

WP7B(BM) afterburning turbojet for the F-7M Airguard fighter

(37.5 lb), enabling the F-7M to add drop tanks. The following refers to the **WP7B (BM)**:

TYPE: Two-shaft turbojet with afterburner.

INLET: No inlet guide vanes, first LP compressor stage overhung ahead of front roller bearing.

COMPRESSOR: Three-stage LP compressor with pressure ratio of 2.74. Three-stage HP compressor giving overall pressure ratio of 8.1. All blades inserted into discs carried on short tubular shafts.

COMBUSTION CHAMBER: Can-annular, with ten flame tubes, Nos. 1 and 6 being of a different pattern and incorporating torch igniters. Air-film liners coated on both sides with ceramic material.

TURBINES: Single-stage HP with 96 inserted shrouded blades. Single-stage LP with shrouded blades. Outlet gas temperature 1,083°K (810°C).

AFTERBURNER: Multiple gutters and double-wall liner. Multi-flap nozzle driven by four hydraulic rams. Up to 40 h operation permitted in each 200 h overhaul period.

PERFORMANCE RATINGS (S/L, static):
Max afterburner	59.82 kN (13,448 lb st)
Max dry	43.15 kN (9,700 lb st)

SPECIFIC FUEL CONSUMPTION (as above):
Max afterburner	56.37 mg/Ns (1.99 lb/h/lb st)
Max dry	28.61 mg/Ns (1.01 lb/h/lb st)

The next major production of LMC was the **WP13**. Though this has some features in common with the Tumansky R-13 it is a Chinese development, based on experience with the WP7. A two-spool afterburning turbojet, it was developed to power the J-7 III and J-8 II. Compared with the WP7 the airflow is increased, work per stage improved, pressure ratio raised (the HP spool having five stages) and surge margin doubled. New titanium alloys were used for the compressor discs and blades, and in a major development two more new titanium alloys were used for the cast compressor casings. WP13 development began in 1978, and it was decided to make the engine a 50/50 joint project with CEC. Both factories tested engines, and certification was gained in 1985. Further development introduced aircooled HP turbine blades and modifications to the combustion chamber and afterburner, the afterburner of the **WP13A II** being longer.

DIMENSIONS:
Length overall:
WP13	4,600 mm (181.1 in)
WP13A II	5,150 mm (202.75 in)

LMC WP13A II turbojet (afterburner not fitted)

Diameter: both	907 mm (35.71 in)
Max height: WP13	1,085 mm (42.72 in)

WEIGHT, DRY:
WP13	1,211 kg (2,670 lb)
WP13A II	1,201 kg (2,648 lb)

PERFORMANCE RATINGS (S/L, static):
Max afterburner:
WP13	64.73 kN (14,550 lb st) at 11,156 LP rpm
WP13A II	65.9 kN (14,815 lb st)

Max dry:
WP13	40.21 kN (9,039 lb st) at 11,156 LP rpm
WP13A II	42.7 kN (9,590 lb st)

SPECIFIC FUEL CONSUMPTION (as above):
Max afterburner:
WP13	63.73 mg/Ns (2.25 lb/h/lb st)
WP13A II	62.32 mg/Ns (2.20 lb/h/lb st)

Max dry:
WP13	27.19 mg/Ns (0.96 lb/h/lb st)
WP13A II	28.04 mg/Ns (0.99 lb/h/lb st)

OVERHAUL LIFE:
WP13	500 h (total service life 1,500 h)
WP13A II	300 h (including up to 90 h in afterburner)

SAC
SHENYANG AERO-ENGINE COMPANY

This was formed in 1979 from the merger of SEF and SARI. Today it is part of LM.

SAMP
SHANGHAI AERO-ENGINE MANUFACTURING PLANT

PO Box 600, 600 Guangzhong Road, Shanghai
Telephone: 86 (21) 650644
Fax: 86 (21) 651482
Telex: 33136 SHAIR CN
Cables: 5834

DIRECTOR: Zhou Kecheng

This factory was built in 1971-74 and was originally the SAF (Shanghai Aero-Engine Factory). It has a covered area of 56,191 m² (604,855 sq ft) and workforce of 2,000. Apart from various non-aero engines and components, its main development effort was the **WS8** turbofan, to power the Y-10. Work proceeded quickly and the first engine went on test in June 1975. Eight engines were built, one running a

1,000 h test, one a 150 h certification test and one was flight tested, making eight flights totalling 22 h. A front-fan engine with a short bypass duct, the WS8 was rated at 80 kN (18,000 lb st). About 17 per cent was titanium, and new techniques included Ni-Cd anti-corrosion coating, graphite varnish of titanium parts and aluminised siliconising of turbine blades. The Y-10 was not put into production and the engine had no other application.

SARI
SHENYANG AVIATION ENGINE RESEARCH INSTITUTE

PO Box 428, Shenyang, Liaoning
Telephone: 86 (24) 443910
Fax: 86 (24) 445723
Telex: 80055 SARI CN
Cables: 4391 (national), SARI (international)

Originally (August 1956) SADO, the Shenyang Aero-Engine Design Office, SARI was merged into SAC in 1979. Responsible for R&D rather than manufacture, SARI was nevertheless charged with design and development of the **PF1A** (see LM) and in 1962 of the **WS5**. This was to be the first Chinese turbofan, developed by adding an aft fan to a **WP6** turbojet. Work began in January 1963. Compared with the WP6 the WS5 featured variable guide vanes ahead of the first three compressor stages instead of bleed valves, a

rear fan instead of an afterburner, and other related changes. The first engine was assembled in early 1965. Great difficulty was met in developing the double-deck turbine/fan blades, and in eliminating stall flutter. Seven engines were tested, and taxi tests carried out on an H-5. Take-off thrust reached 35 kN (7,940 lb st) with sfc reduced by 30 per cent. H-5 performance would have been greatly improved, but it was decided not to re-engine the aircraft and WS5 development ceased in 1973.

SEF — *Original abbreviation of SAC (see LM)*

SMPMC
SOUTH MOTIVE POWER AND MACHINERY COMPLEX

PO Box 211, Zhuzhou, Hunan 412002
Telephone: 86 (733) 21151
Fax: 86 (733) 24220
Telex: 995002 CHENF CN
Cables: 2820

SAEC (South Aero-Engine Company)
Address as above
GENERAL MANAGER: Wu Shenduo

With a covered area of nearly 300,000 m² (3,230,000 sq ft) and workforce of over 10,000, SMPMC is one of the larger MAS establishments. Until 1983 its aero-engine division, SAEC, was known as ZEF (Zhuzhou Aero-Engine Factory), and in 1951 was set up as the first aero-engine

factory in China. Its first product was the Soviet Shvetsov **M-11FR** radial piston engine rated at 119 kW (160 hp), the first three being completed in July 1954. Mass production followed. To meet the needs of the Y-5 (licensed An-2) ZEF began in September 1956 to work on the HS5 (licensed ASh-62IR). Over 2,600 of these 746 kW (1,000 hp) radial piston engines were produced by 1986, some being installed in CAAC Li-2s. Lacking the chosen Praga Doris B engine to power the CJ-6 trainer, the Soviet Ivchenko AI-14R radial piston engine was produced as the **HS6**. Rated at 191 kW (260 hp), the HS-6 entered production in June 1962, about 700 being produced. To improve performance, especially at altitude, ZEF increased rpm, compression ratio and supercharger gear ratio. The result, in 1963, was the **HS6A**, with T-O power increased to 212.5 kW (285 hp). About 3,000 were made by 1986. In 1975 the engine was again modified to power the Y-11; rpm were increased and the reduction gear strengthened. The resulting **HS6D**, with

power of 224 kW (300 hp), was certificated in August 1980. The **HS6E**, for the NAMC Haiyan, has a further increased compression ratio and modifed reduction gear, raising output to 261 kW (345 hp). In 1990 the simplified **HS6K** was certificated at 298 kW (400 hp) and is intended as the future engine of the N-5. Experimental models, in the 1963-70 period, were the turbocharged **HS6B** and the **HS6C** for helicopters, used in the 701 and Yan'an II helicopters.

Work on gas turbines began in January 1965 in support of the development by BIAA (Beijing Institute of Aeronautics and Astronautics) of the **WP11**. This simple turbojet, rated at 8.3 kN (1,874 lb st), powered the WZ-5 unmanned reconnaissance vehicle. The WP11 first ran in June 1971 and was certificated in 1980, manufacture then being transferred to ZEF. In September 1965 ZEF was selected to develop the **WJ5** turboprop, but this was transferred in 1968 to HEF (see DEMC). In 1969 ZEF was ordered to develop the **WJ6** turboprop, based on the Soviet Ivchenko AI-20M, to power the Y-8. Testing started in 1970, but various problems delayed certification until January 1977. Further changes (for example to compressor vane angle, igniter and lubrication clearances) resulted in TBO being raised in stages from 300 h to 3,000 h. T-O power was 3,169 ekW (4,250 ehp) and weight 1,200 kg (2,645 lb). In

1977 work began on the **WJ6A** to power the Y-8 with a pressure cabin and greater payload. By using aircooled blades and raising the rpm this engine was successfully run in 1983 at 3,393 ekW (4,550 ehp).

In 1980 ZEF began the assembly and test of the **WZ8** (Turbomeca Arriel 1C) for the Z-9 helicopter. ZEF gives the output as 522 kW (700 shp) for a weight of 118 kg (260 lb).

An all-Chinese WZ8 ran in 1985, and resulted in major technical upgrades at Zhuzhou (the high-voltage power unit was the only imported part). As part of the offset, 40 accessory gearboxes were supplied to France.

ZEF also produces solid rocket motors for air-to-air missiles.

XAE
XIAN AERO-ENGINE CORPORATION
PO Box 13, Xian, Shaanxi
Telephone: 86 (29) 61951, 63366
Fax: 86 (29) 72 2721
Telex: 70102 XIARO CN
Cables: 5411
GENERAL MANAGER: Yang Naishi

Construction of this factory began in August 1958, as XEF (Xian Aero-Engine Factory), and today its workforce exceeds 16,000. Its first task, undertaken in collaboration with HEF and SEF, was to develop and produce the **WP8** turbojet. Based on the Soviet Mikulin RD-3M, this large engine is rated at 93.17 kN (20,944 lb st) and weighs 3,133 kg

(6,906 lb). It posed the greatest challenge to the embryonic Chinese industry, especially as many questions were left unanswered by the licensor (for example, the composition and work processes for the nozzle guide vanes). In 1963 the whole WP8 programme was transferred to XEF, and the engine was certificated and put into production in January 1967.

In 1963 the increased demand for **WP5A** engines for the H-5 resulted in series production being transferred to XEF from SEF. In 1965, together with Chengdu Aircraft Corporation, XEF developed the modified **WP5D** for the JJ-5 trainer. In 1966 it developed the **WP5B** and produced it in quantity for Soviet-made MiG-15 bis fighters. In 1976 it developed and series-produced the **WP5C** to power Soviet-made MiG-17 all-weather fighters. XEF also

developed and produced WQJ-1 turbo-starters and WDZ-1 APUs.

In 1972 Premier Zhou Enlai called for a major upgrade in Chinese aeronautical quality and technology. As a result negotiations with Rolls-Royce began in May 1972, leading to a licence to produce the Spey 202 augmented turbofan signed on 13 December 1975. The work was assigned to XEF, the engine being designated **WS9**. After a great effort, of major benefit to the industry, four WS9 engines were successfully tested in China and Britain in 1979-80.

Since 1980 XEF has started business relations with Rolls-Royce, Pratt & Whitney (USA and Canada), GE, Textron Lycoming and Allison. Numerous types of engine parts are produced for these companies.

The WP8 single-shaft turbojet (Mikulin RD-3M)

The WS9 two-shaft augmented turbofan (Spey Mk 202)

YMF
YUHE MACHINE FACTORY
2 Jie Fang Lu, Nanjing
Telephone: 86 (25) 42133 and 41419
Cables: 1630 Nanjing
Yuhe Machine Factory produces small piston engines. The **YH40** is chiefly for models and UAVs, with two

aircooled two-stroke cylinders of 40 cc (2.44 cu in) capacity, giving an output of 2 hp at 7,000 rpm. The **YH280** powers light manned aircraft. It has four opposed two-stroke cylinders of 46 mm (1.81 in) bore and 42 mm (1.65 in) stroke, giving a capacity of 280 cc (17.09 cu in). It has two carburettors for the petrol/oil mix, and magneto flywheel ignition. Maximum rating is 11.2 kW (15 hp) at 6,000 rpm.

Yuhe YH280 two-stroke four-cylinder engine

ZAC
ZHUZHOU AERO-ENGINE COMPANY
This organisation, apparently an alternative or earlier title for SAEC (see SMPMC entry), was formed in 1983 by

merging ZEF and ZARI. Its main task so far has been to produce the **WJ9** turboprop to power a production version of the Y-12. This engine, rated at 507 kW (680 shp), is based on the WZ8 (Arriel 1C), but with a new reduction gear,

accessory drives and fuel and lubrication systems. The first engine ran in 1986 and met the design figures. A production WJ9 would probably also power agricultural and other special-purpose aircraft.

ZARI
ZHUZHOU AERO-ENGINE RESEARCH INSTITUTE
This organisation was established in 1968. From the start it has been tasked with R&D of shaft-drive gas-turbine

engines, starting with the **WZ5** (see DEMC). The poor payload and lack of twin-engine safety of the Z-5 and Z-6 led to a new helicopter, the Z-7, in 1970. This was powered by the twin-packaged **WZ5A**, developed at ZARI. Contingency power of each power section was 1,737 kW

(2,330 shp). Design was finished in 1971, but the cultural revolution caused a delay of eight years. The WZ5A then reached its design targets, but was cancelled upon the abandonment of the Z-7. ZARI was merged with ZEF in 1983 to form ZAC.

ZEF
ZHUZHOU AERO-ENGINE FACTORY
Established in 1951 as China's first aero-engine factory (see SMPMC entry), ZEF was amalgamated with ZARI in 1983 to form ZAC.

CZECHOSLOVAKIA

OMNIPOL
OMNIPOL FOREIGN TRADE CORPORATION
Nekázanka 11, 112 21 Prague 1
Telephone: 42 (2) 2140 111

Omnipol is responsible for exporting products of the Czechoslovak aviation industry and for supplying information on those products which are available for export.

AEROTECHNIK

68604 Uherské Hradiste, Kunovice
Telephone: 42 (632) 5122
Fax: 42 (632) 5128
Telex: 60380
TECHNICAL DEPT: Ing E. Parma

This company is now producing the long established inverted four-cylinder Walter Mikron piston engine, of 2,440 cc (149 cu in) capacity. The factory at Mor. Trebová calls it the **Mikron IIIS (A)**. It powers the Aerotechnik L-13SW Vivat motor glider. Since 1989 the **Mikron IIISE (AE)** has also been produced, with electric starter and alternator. This increases weight from 65.9 kg (145.3 lb) to 70.0 kg (154 lb).

PERFORMANCE RATINGS (both versions):
T-O	48.5 kW (65 hp) at 2,600 rpm
Cruise	35.5 kW (47.6 hp) at 2,350 rpm

Aerotechnik Mikron IIISE(AE) piston engine

AVIA

AVIA KŮNCERNOVÝ PODNIK

ul Beranovÿch 140, 199 03 Prague 9, Letňany
Telephone: 42 (2) 89 51 21
Fax: 42 (2) 85 85 740
Telex: Prague AVIA C 121 475

This company is at present engaged in series production of piston engines, propellers and spare parts.

AVIA M 137 A

Designed to power light aerobatic aircraft, the 134 kW (180 hp) M 137 A piston engine is a modification of the M 337 with fuel and oil systems for aerobatic operation and without a supercharger. It powers the Zlin 42 M and Z 526 F. The **M 137 AZ** is a modified version, with the air intake port at the rear so that a dust filter can be incorporated. Details are as M 337, with the following differences:

CRANKSHAFT: No oil holes for propeller control.

Avia M 137 A six-cylinder aircooled piston engine

FUEL SYSTEM: Type LUN 5150 pump; system designed for sustained aerobatics.
STARTER: LUN 2131 electric.
DIMENSIONS:
Length	1,344 mm (52.9 in)
Width	443 mm (17.44 in)
Height	630 mm (24.80 in)
WEIGHT (incl starter):	141.5 kg (312 lb)

PERFORMANCE RATINGS:
T-O	134 kW (180 hp) at 2,750 rpm
Max continuous	119 kW (160 hp) at 2,680 rpm
Max cruise	104.5 kW (140 hp) at 2,580 rpm

SPECIFIC FUEL CONSUMPTION:
At T-O rating	91.26 µg/J (0.540 lb/h/hp)
At max cruise rating	81.96 µg/J (0.485 lb/h/hp)

AVIA M 337 A

The M 337 A six-cylinder aircooled supercharged engine powers several types of light aircraft that were built in Czechoslovakia, including the L-200D Morava, Zlin 43 and Zlin 726K. It can be supplied with hubs for fixed-pitch or controllable-pitch propellers. The **M 337 AK** is fitted to the Zlin 142.

TYPE: Six-cylinder inverted in-line aircooled, ungeared, supercharged and with direct fuel injection.
CYLINDERS: Bore 105 mm (4.13 in). Stroke 115 mm (4.53 in). Swept volume 5.97 litres (364.31 cu in). Compression ratio 6.3 : 1. Steel cylinders with cooling fins machined from solid. Cylinder bores nitrided. Detachable cylinder heads are aluminium alloy castings.
PISTONS: Aluminium alloy with graphited surfaces.
CONNECTING RODS: Two split big ends bolted together.
CRANKSHAFT: Forged from chrome vanadium steel, machined all over. Nitrided crankpins.
CRANKCASE: Heat treated magnesium alloy (Elektron).
IGNITION: Shielded type. Two plugs per cylinder.
LUBRICATION: Dry sump pressure feed type. The M 337 AK has a system for sustained inverted operation.
SUPERCHARGER: Centrifugal, ratio 7.4 : 1.
FUEL SYSTEM: Low pressure injection system with nozzles in front of inlet valves. The M 337 A has a unified fuel injection pump.
FUEL GRADE: Minimum 72-78 octane.
STARTING: Electric, engaged by an electromagnet.
ACCESSORIES: One 600W 28V dynamo. Electric tachometer. Propeller control unit. Mechanical tachometer on oil pump. Hydraulic pump to special order.
PROPELLER DRIVE: Direct left hand tractor.
DIMENSIONS:
Length, excl propeller boss	1,410 mm (55.51 in)
Width	472 mm (18.58 in)
Height	628 mm (24.72 in)
WEIGHT, DRY:	148 kg (326.3 lb)

PERFORMANCE RATINGS:
T-O	157 kW (210 hp) at 2,750 rpm
Max cruise at 1,200 m (3,940 ft)	112 kW (150 hp) at 2,400 rpm

SPECIFIC FUEL CONSUMPTION:
At T-O rating	100.6 µg/J (0.595 lb/h/hp)
At max cruise rating at 1,200 m (3,940 ft)	72.7 µg/J (0.430 lb/h/hp)

MOTORLET

MOTORLET AERO-ENGINES LTD

Prague-Jinonice
Telephone: 42 (2) 521119 ·
Fax: 42 (2) 526060
GENERAL MANAGER: Ing Josef Krča

Motorlet operates the main aero engine establishment in Czechoslovakia, based on the former Walter factory. The Walter name continues as a trademark. The shareholding company listed above is a member of the Aero Group.

WALTER M 601

The M 601 was designed to power the L-410 transport. It drives an Avia V 508 propeller.

The first version, rated at 410 ekW (550 ehp), ran in October 1967. Development of the **M 601 B**, of increased diameter, started during 1968. The Let L-410M powered by M 601 B engines was in Aeroflot service by early 1979. The M 601B powers the L-410UVP. In 1982 a further variant, the **M 601 D**, entered production. This gives increased power and can be operated to longer TBO. It powers the PZL-106 BT-601.

By 1985 the **M 601 Z** had entered production to power the Z 137T agricultural aircraft. It drives an auxiliary piston compressor for the spraying/dusting installation. TBO is 1,500 h. The **M 601 E** powers the L-410UVP-E. It has a TBO of 2,000 h without hot-section inspection. It drives a VJ 8.508E five-blade propeller, and an alternator for anti-icing windshields and propeller blades. It is certificated to JAR and FAR Pt 33 in Czechoslovakia, and was expected to receive FAA certification in 1991.

The **M 601 T** is an aerobatic version for the PZL-130 Turbo Orlik. A new M 601 version to have a TBO of 3,000 to 4,000 h is under development.

Yakovlev Yak-40 testbed with M 601 E power plant on nose (*Letectvi + Kosmonautika/Vaclav Jukl*)

TYPE: Free turbine turboprop.
PROPELLER DRIVE: Reduction gear at front of engine with drive from free turbine. Reduction ratio 14.9.
AIR INTAKE: Annular, at rear (reverse flow engine).
COMPRESSOR: Two axial stages of stainless steel, plus single centrifugal stage of titanium. Pressure ratio (601 B) 6.4, (601 D) 6.55, (601 E) 6.65, at 36,660 rpm gas generator speed. Air mass flow (601 B) 3.25 kg (7.17 lb)/s, (601 D) 3.55 kg (7.83 lb)/s, (601 E) 3.6 kg (7.94 lb)/s.

COMBUSTION CHAMBER: Annular combustor with rotary fuel injection and low-voltage ignition.
COMPRESSOR TURBINE: Single stage with solid blades; inlet temperature 952°C.
POWER TURBINE: Single stage.
FUEL SYSTEM: Low pressure regulator, providing gas generator and power turbine speed controls.
FUEL GRADE: PL6, RT and Jet A-1 kerosene.

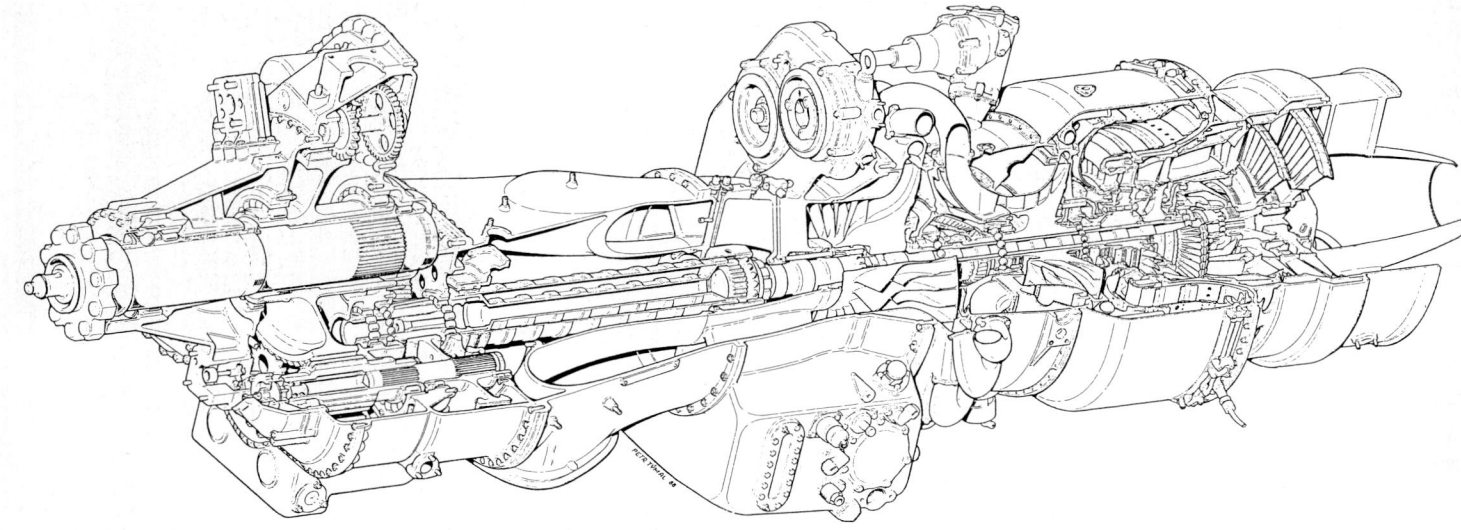

Cutaway drawing of the Walter M 602 turboprop

LUBRICATION SYSTEM: Pressure gear-pump circulation. Integral oil tank and cooler.
OIL SPECIFICATION: B3V synthetic oil or Aeroshell 550.
STARTING: LUN 2132-8 8kW electric starter/generator.
DIMENSIONS:

Length: 601 D	1,658 mm (65.27 in)
601 B, E, Z	1,675 mm (65.94 in)
Width	590 mm (23.23 in)
Height	650 mm (25.59 in)

WEIGHT, DRY:

601 B, D, E	193 kg (425.5 lb)
601 Z	197 kg (434.3 lb)

PERFORMANCE RATINGS (T-O):

601 B	515 kW (691 shp)
601 D	540 kW (724 shp)
601 E	560 kW (751 shp)
601 Z	360 kW (483 shp)

SPECIFIC FUEL CONSUMPTION (T-O):

601 B	109.55 µg/J (0.648 lb/h/ehp)
601 D	109.4 µg/J (0.647 lb/h/ehp)

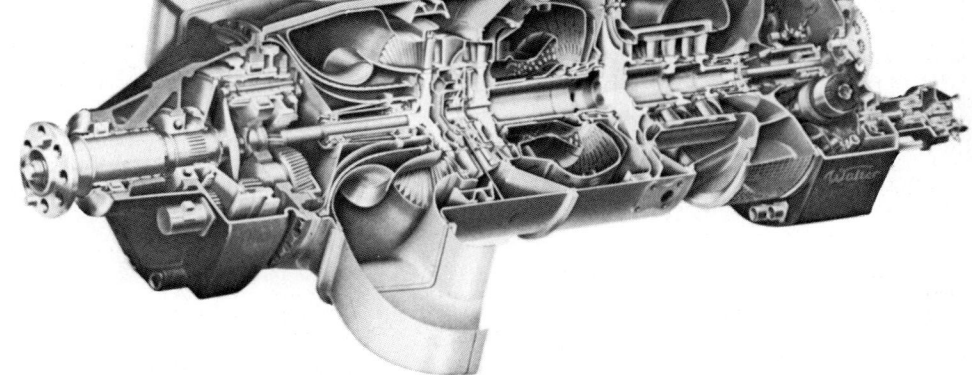

Cutaway drawing of the Walter M 601 E turboprop

WALTER M 602

This engine was developed to power the L 610, which first flew on 28 December 1988. Certification was expected in late 1991.
TYPE: Three-shaft turboprop.
PROPELLER DRIVE: Double spur reduction, ratio 12.58.
AIR INTAKE: At front, S duct from chin inlet passing up behind reduction gear.
COMPRESSORS: LP centrifugal, pressure ratio 4.15 at 25,000 rpm. HP centrifugal, pressure ratio 3.133 at 31,489 rpm. Overall pressure ratio 13. Mass flow 7.33 kg (16.16 lb)/s.
COMBUSTION CHAMBER: Short annular reverse flow with 14 simplex nozzles and low-voltage semiconductor ignition.
COMPRESSOR TURBINES: Single-stage HP, single-stage LP.

POWER TURBINE: Two-stage, 16,600 rpm.
FUEL SYSTEM: LP electrohydraulic regulator and electronic limiter.
FUEL GRADE: T-1, TS-1, RT, Jet A-1.
LUBRICATION SYSTEM: Pressure gear-pump circulation, integral oil tank and cooler.
OIL SPECIFICATION: B3V, AeroShell 500, 550.
STARTING: LUN 5362-8 pneumatic.
DIMENSIONS:

Length	2,669 mm (105.08 in)
Width	753 mm (29.65 in)
Height	872 mm (34.33 in)

WEIGHT, DRY (equipped):	570-580 kg (1,257-1,279 lb)

PERFORMANCE RATINGS (S/L):

T-O	1,360 kW (1,824 shp)
Max continuous	1,200 kW (1,608 shp)
Cruise	700 kW (938 shp)

SPECIFIC FUEL CONSUMPTION:

T-O	94.5 µg/J (0.559 lb/h/shp)

ZVL
ZÁVODY NA VÝROBU LOŽÍSK
01734 Považská Bystrica
Telephone: 42 (822) 23825
Telex: 075233, 075316
CHIEF DESIGNER: E. Jiři Bednář

ZVL is a major new design bureau which also includes the VUM research institute. It partnered the Progress/Lotarev (ZMKB) bureau in the Soviet Union (which see) in designing the DV-2.

EGYPT

AOI
AOI ENGINE FACTORY (135)
PO Box 12, Helwan
Telephone: 20 (2) 745090, 747984 and 781088
Telex: 92135 ENFAC UN

CHAIRMAN: Hassan El Gebali
Among other work, about 3,500 people are employed in assembly and test of the Larzac 04 and PT6A-25E, delivery of the first PT6 having been made in 1985. Following selection of a new fighter for the Egyptian Air Force, the factory is expected to assemble either the F100, F404 or M53-P2. Since 1980 AOI/EF has carried out complete overhaul, repair and test of Soviet APUs and the SNECMA Atar 9C and Larzac, GE T64 and Allison T56.

FRANCE

FAM
FRANCE AÉRO MOTEURS SARL
Roanne
CONTACT: Avions Pierre Robin (see Aircraft section)

This company, inaugurated on 29 April 1985, was formed on a 50/50 basis by Avions Pierre Robin and the Motorop division of Besson-Moteurs Sopart, to develop an aircraft version of the PRV (Peugeot-Renault-Volvo) V6 car engine.

It is still in the development phase. For the latest news see Robin 3000 (Aircraft section).

JPX
ATELIERS JPX

Z.I. Nord, BP 13, 72320 Vibraye
Telephone: 33 43 93 61 74
Fax: 33 43 93 62 71
Telex: 722151 F

PUL 212

The PUL 212 is a single-cylinder low-cost two-stroke, with bore of 66 mm (2.6 in), stroke of 62 mm (2.44 in) and capacity of 212 cc. Weighing 7.9 kg (17.42 lb) with pull cord inertia starter, it gives 11 kW (15 hp) at 6,000 rpm and is cleared to run at up to 6,500 rpm.

PUL 425

This is an opposed engine with two cylinders of the same size as in the PUL 212. Dry weight is 14.5 kg (32 lb), or 16.7 kg (36.8 lb) with silencer. Rated power is 16.4 kW (22 hp) at 4,600 rpm. With 0.5 reduction gear weight is 21 kg (46 lb).

JPX 4T60/A

Unlike previous JPX engines this is a four-stroke, with four opposed aircooled cylinders with bore 93.0 mm (3.66 in) and stroke 75.4 mm (2.97 in). Capacity 2,050 cc (125 cu in). Compression ratio 8.2. Overall length 650 mm (25.6 in). Width 805 mm (31.7 in). Weight, dry (without propeller hub) 73.0 kg (161 lb). Developed from the Volkswagen VW126A of smaller capacity, the 4T60/A has an electric starter and alternator, and is rated at 47.8 kW (65 hp) at 3,200 rpm, and 42.0 kW (57 hp) at 2,500 rpm. Using 4-star motor fuel or 100LL fuel, this engine was certificated by the DGAC on 9 January 1985, ready for production for the Robin ATL. The **4T60/AES** for ultralight aircraft weighs 61 kg (134 lb).

The lightweight JPX 4T60/AES

MICROTURBO
MICROTURBO SA

Chemin du Pont de Rupé, BP 2089, 31019 Toulouse Cédex
Telephone: 33 61 70 11 27
Fax: 33 61 70 75 40
Telex: 531442
MANAGEMENT:
  A. Halna du Fretay
  P. Calmels (General Manager)
  L. Pech (Deputy General Manager)

Microturbo operates as the gas turbine division of the Labinal group, in conjunction with Microturbo Ltd of Fareham, England, Microturbo North America of Bohemia, New York, USA, and Electromecanismes RFB in Paris. Total staff of the division is 800.

Details of Microturbo engines for missiles, UAVs and target drones can be found in the 1987-88 *Jane's*.

MICROTURBO TRB

Development of the **TRB 13** and **TRB 19** turbojets began in 1986. The former has a diameter of 230 mm (9.06 in), length of 480 mm (18.90 in), weight of 16 kg (35.3 lb) and thrust rating of 0.81 kN (182 lb st) with sfc of 32.5 mg/Ns (1.15 lb/h/lb st). The TRB 19 has a diameter of 280 mm (11.02 in), length of 580 mm (22.85 in), weight of 28 kg (61.7 lb) and thrust rating of 1.2 kN (270 lb st) with sfc of 33.0 mg/Ns (1.17 lb/h/lb st).

MICROTURBO TRS 18

This single-shaft turbojet is of modular construction. The forward module incorporates the intake, gearbox, electronic governing and start sequencing. The starter/generator is in the nose bullet. The oil tank, with submerged pump, is on the underside, and includes provision for inverted flight.

The turbine module comprises: the one-piece centrifugal compressor, with diffuser and straightener vanes; the axial turbine rotor and nozzle diaphragm; and the main frame. The aft module comprises: the turbine backplate, carrying the annular folded combustion chamber; 10 spill burners; two igniter plugs, and jetpipe.

The fuel pump is driven electrically. The lubrication system is a closed circuit, with pressure supply. The engine can be shut down and restarted in flight, and incorporates automatic fault and protection systems.

The following are current versions for piloted aircraft:
TRS 18 Model 046. Powered Bede BD-5J and various prototypes. 28V starter/generator up to 600W.
TRS 18 Model 046-1. Powered Microjet 90, A-21SJ Calif, NASA/Ames AD-1, Fairchild scaled NGT and other prototypes. 28V starter/generator up to 900W.
TRS 18-1 Models 081 and 083. Powers Microjet 200B and Caproni C-22J.
TRS 18-1 Model 202. For Caproni C-22J.
TRS 18-2. Uprated version of TRS 18-1, with unchanged dimensions.

DIMENSIONS:

Length: TRS 18	578 mm (22.75 in)
TRS 18-1	564 mm (22.20 in)
Width: TRS 18, 18-1	306 mm (12.05 in)
Height: TRS 18	349 mm (13.74 in)
TRS 18-1	339.5 mm (13.36 in)
WEIGHT, DRY:	
TRS 18	37.0 kg (81.5 lb)
TRS 18-1	38.5 kg (84.9 lb)
PERFORMANCE RATINGS (T-O, ISA, S/L):	
TRS 18	1.00 kN (225 lb st)
TRS 18-1	1.45 kN (326 lb st)
TRS 18-2	1.80 kN (405 lb st)
SPECIFIC FUEL CONSUMPTION (as above):	
TRS 18	34.5 mg/Ns (1.22 lb/h/lb st)
TRS 18-1	33.4 mg/Ns (1.18 lb/h/lb st)

MICROTURBO TFA

Two simple turbofans have been under study since 1986. The **TFA 66**, with a diameter of 350 mm (13.78 in) and length of 1,000 mm (39.37 in), will be rated at 3.60 kN (810 lb st) with sfc of 25.28 mg/Ns (0.892 lb/h/lb st). The **TFA 130**, with a diameter of 440 mm (17.32 in) and length 975 mm (38.39 in), will be rated at 3.57 kN (802 lb st) with sfc of 17.48 mg/Ns (0.617 lb/h/lb st). Projected weight for each of these engines is approx 60 kg (132 lb).

MUDRY
MOTEURS MUDRY-BUCHOUX (AVIONS MUDRY et CIE)

Aérodrome de Bernay, BP 47, 27300 Bernay
Telephone: 33 32 43 47 34
DIRECTOR: Auguste Mudry

MUDRY MB-4-80

This aircooled four-stroke flat-four incorporates some parts, such as piston rings, rocker arms, valves and springs, of standard auto industry type. Development is continuing.
CYLINDERS: Cast in pairs in light alloy with cast iron liners. Bore 93 mm (3.7 in). Stroke 92 mm (3.6 in). Capacity 2,498 cc (152.4 cu in).
VALVES: Flat cylinder heads with twin vertical overhead valves operated by pushrods.
PISTONS: Hypersilicate alloy, forming chamber in head. Three rings including U-Flex scraper.
CRANKCASE: AS7G-06 alloy divided on vertical centreline.

FUEL GRADE: 100LL or automobile gasoline.
ACCESSORIES: Generator, starter and alternator. Two 32 mm carburettors. Bendix dual ignition.
DIMENSIONS:

Length	730 mm (28.7 in)
Width	710 mm (28.0 in)
Height	420 mm (16.5 in)
WEIGHT, DRY (equipped):	83 kg (183 lb)
PERFORMANCE RATING (S/L):	
Max T-O	59.7 kW (80 hp) at 2,750 rpm

RECTIMO
RECTIMO AVIATION SA

Aérodrome de Chambéry, 73420 Savoie
Telephone: 33 79 54 40 06
Fax: 33 79 54 45 27
Telex: 980 202
DIRECTOR: André Rosselot

Rectimo has manufactured more than 500 **Type 4 AR 1200** single ignition derivatives of the Volkswagen four-cylinder aircooled car engine, which together with the larger 4 AR 1600 are used in the Sportavia RF4D motor glider and various lightweight aircraft. The 30 kW (40 hp) 4 AR 1200 engine has a 1,192 cc cubic capacity, 7:1 compression ratio and weighs 61.5 kg (136 lb). Fuel consumption under cruise conditions is 11 litres (2.9 US gallons; 2.4 Imp gal)/h. The **4 AR 1600** produces 45.5 kW (61 hp) at T-O and has a cubic capacity of 1,600 cc and an 8:1 compression ratio. Weight is 64 kg (141 lb). Both engines have a maximum speed of 3,600 rpm.

Rectimo 4 AR 1200 piston engine of 30 kW (40 hp)

SCOMA
SCOMA-ÉNERGIE

OFFICE: 11-13 rue Forest, 75018 Paris
Telephone: 33 (1) 43 87 55 79
WORKS: 58 rue de la Fosse aux Anglais, 77190 Dammarie-les-Lys (Melun)
Telephone: 33 (1) 64 37 46 17

This company, which specialises in diesel research and applications, has been flying a Cessna L-19 since June 1987 equipped with a **GMA 140 TK** geared diesel. This is a four-in-line liquid cooled engine of 2,068 cc (126 cu in) capacity, with turbocharger and geared drive. Installed weight is 180 kg (397 lb), and T-O power is 96 kW (136 hp) at 2,660 propeller rpm. At economic cruise of 2,300 propeller rpm the power is 65 kW (88 hp) and fuel consumption less than 22 litres (5.8 US gallons; 4.8 Imp gallons)/h. The engine has multi-fuel capability and is run mainly on Jet 1 or light diesel oil. Experience with this engine is being used to assist the design of a new range of engines called Comète (Comet), which are 170° V type engines with 1, 4, 6, 8, 12 or 16 cylinders each of 94 mm (3.7 in) bore and stroke. All are turbocharged and liquid cooled geared units, with ratings from 30 kW (40 hp) to 480 kW (653 hp).

Cessna L-19 powered by a
SCOMA GMA 140 TK diesel engine

SNECMA
SOCIÉTÉ NATIONALE D'ÉTUDE ET DE CONSTRUCTION DE MOTEURS D'AVIATION

2 boulevard du Général Martial Valin, 75724 Paris Cédex 15
Telephone: 33 (1) 40 60 80 80
Fax: 33 (1) 40 60 81 02
Telex: 600 700 SNECMA
CHAIRMAN AND CHIEF EXECUTIVE: Louis Gallois
SENIOR VICE-PRESIDENT:
  Pierre Alesi (Engineering and Production)
VICE-PRESIDENTS:
  Jean Bonnet (Military Programmes and Marketing)
  Dominique Hedon (Commercial Programme Management and Marketing)
COMMUNICATION MANAGER: Jean-Claude Nicolas

More than 5,200 Atar turbojets have been produced for Mirage fighters. SNECMA is now producing the M53 turbojet and developing the M88. It is also participating in international collaborative programmes, as described hereunder.

Today, SNECMA heads about 26,000 persons formed around its major subsidiaries: SEP (rocket motors, remote sensing and composites), Hispano-Suiza (aeronautical equipment, nuclear and robotic equipment), Messier-Bugatti (landing gears) and Sochata (engine repair).

SNECMA ATAR 9K50

The Atar is a single-shaft military turbojet first run in 1946 and subsequently developed and cleared for flight at Mach numbers greater than 2. The final version was the Atar 9K50, which powers all production Mirage F1 and Mirage 50 versions.

DIMENSIONS:
Diameter	1,020 mm (40.2 in)
Length overall	5,944 mm (234 in)

WEIGHT, DRY:
Complete with all accessories	1,582 kg (3,487 lb)

PERFORMANCE RATINGS:
With afterburner	70.6 kN (15,870 lb st) at 8,400 rpm
Without afterburner	49.2 kN (11,055 lb st)

SPECIFIC FUEL CONSUMPTION:
With afterburner	55.5 mg/Ns (1.96 lb/h/lb st)
Without afterburner	27.5 mg/Ns (0.97 lb/h/lb st)

OIL CONSUMPTION: 1.5 litres (3.2 US pints; 2.64 Imp pints)/h

SNECMA M53

The M53 is a single-shaft turbofan capable of propelling fighter aircraft to Mach 2.5, without any throttle limitations over the flight envelope. Its modular construction allows easier maintenance.

It includes a three-stage fan, five-stage compressor (pressure ratio 9.8 at 10,600 rpm), annular combustion chamber, two-stage turbine and an afterburner equipped with a multi-flap variable nozzle. The control system is monitored by an Elecma electronic computer. The following versions are in service:

M53-5. Produced in 1980-85 as the initial engine of the Mirage 2000.

M53-P2. Designed to power the Mirage 2000 from 1985; current production version.

DIMENSIONS:
Length, overall	5,070 mm (199.6 in)
Max diameter	1,055 mm (41.5 in)

WEIGHT, DRY:
M53-5	1,470 kg (3,240 lb)
M53-P2	1,500 kg (3,307 lb)

PERFORMANCE RATINGS:
Max with afterburner:	
M53-5	88.2 kN (19,830 lb st)
M53-P2	95.0 kN (21,355 lb st)
Max without afterburner:	
M53-5	54.4 kN (12,230 lb st)
M53-P2	64.3 kN (14,455 lb st)

SPECIFIC FUEL CONSUMPTION (without afterburner):
M53-5	24.64 mg/Ns (0.87 lb/h/lb st)
M53-P2	25.55 mg/Ns (0.90 lb/h/lb st)

SNECMA M88

The M88 is a family of advanced augmented turbofans, built around the same core, with thrust ranging from 75 kN (16,860 lb) to 105 kN (23,600 lb). In a six-year demonstration programme an uprated core with 1,850°K turbine entry temperature completed its first simulated altitude tests in February 1987.

M88-2. This is the basic engine of the family, under development since 1987 for the Rafale ACT/ACM aircraft for the French Air Force and Navy. The first engine went on test on 27 February 1989, afterburner operation began in April 1989 and one engine flew in the Rafale A in February 1990. Two engines were installed in the Rafale D to continue flight tests from the beginning of 1991.

The following relates to the basic M88-2:
TYPE: Two-shaft augmented turbofan.
COMPRESSOR: Variable inlet guide vanes, three-stage LP (fan), six-stage HP, with three variable stator stages.

SNECMA Atar 9K50 afterburning turbojet

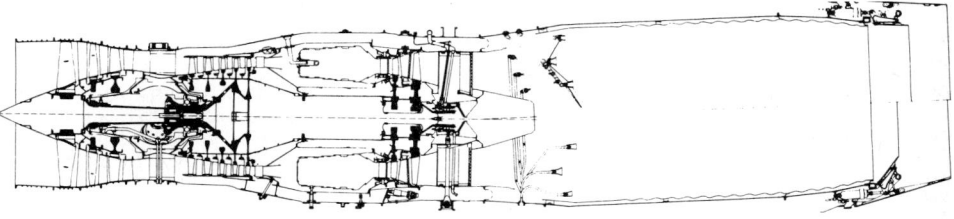

Longitudinal section through the SNECMA M53-P2 augmented bypass turbojet

SNECMA M53-P2 augmented bypass turbojet

SNECMA M88-2 augmented turbofan

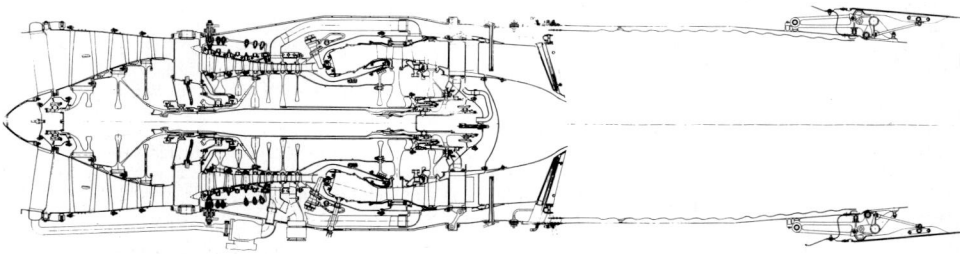

Longitudinal section through SNECMA M88 augmented turbofan

COMBUSTOR: Annular, with aerodynamic injection.
TURBINES: Single-stage HP, single-stage LP.
ACCESSORIES: Full-authority digital control system.
DIMENSION:

Length	3,540 mm (139.0 in)
WEIGHT, DRY:	897 kg (1,970 lb)

PERFORMANCE RATINGS (installed):

With afterburner	72.9 kN (16,400 lb st)
Without afterburner	48.7 kN (10,950 lb st)

SPECIFIC FUEL CONSUMPTION:

With afterburner	49.9 mg/Ns (1.76 lb/h/lb st)
Without afterburner	24.9 mg/Ns (0.88 lb/h/lb st)

GE/SNECMA GE90

SNECMA participates in the General Electric GE90 with a share of 25 per cent in all phases of the programme.

GE/SNECMA/MTU/VOLVO/FIAT CF6

As a continuation of the CF6-50 and CF6-80A programmes, SNECMA participates in the General Electric CF6-80C2, in the derived LM6000 industrial gas turbine with a share of 10 per cent, and in the CF6-80E1 with a share of 20 per cent.

CFM INTERNATIONAL CFM56

This programme is covered under CFM in the International part of this section.

GE/SNECMA GE36

SNECMA had a 35 per cent share in the GE36 UDF (unducted fan) programme, and was in charge of acoustic measurement during flight testing on a Boeing 727.

SNECMA participated in development of an improved engine for flight test on an MD-80. Jointly with GE, SNECMA was developing an advanced gas generator, and was in charge of the HP compressor, combustor, structural casings, fuel systems and nacelle.

SNECMA/TURBOMECA LARZAC

This appears under Turbomeca-SNECMA GRTS.

RR/SNECMA/MTU/FN TYNE

Under Rolls-Royce licence, the Tyne 22 turboprop for the Transall C-160 was put back into production in October 1977. The similar Tyne 21 is in production for the Dassault Atlantique 2. These 4,549 kW (6,100 ehp) engines were last described in the 1975-76 *Jane's*.

TURBOMECA

SOCIÉTÉ TURBOMECA

64511 Bordes
Telephone: 33 59 32 84 37
Fax: 33 59 53 15 12
Telex: 560928
PARIS OFFICE: 1 rue Beaujon, 75008 Paris
Telephone: 33 (1) 40 75 01 78
Fax: 33 (1) 40 75 01 79
Telex: 650347
CHIEF EXECUTIVE OFFICER: Jacques Marchand
PRESS RELATIONS MANAGER: Jacques Millepied

By 1 January 1990 more than 27,000 Turbomeca aircraft engines had been delivered to customers in 120 countries. Approximately 14,000 more engines have been built under licence by what are today Rolls-Royce plc in the UK, Teledyne CAE in the USA, ENMASA in Spain, Hindustan Aeronautics in India, Bet-Shemesh in Israel, SMPMC in China and factories in Romania and Yugoslavia.

A European Small Engines Co-operation Agreement signed in April 1985 joins Turbomeca, MTU of Germany and Rolls-Royce of the UK in promoting three complementary new engines: the Turbomeca TM 333, MTU-Turbomeca-RR MTR 390 and Rolls-Royce Turbomeca RTM 322. Other European small engine makers may join the collaboration, in which each partner may share in engines sold to its own government.

In March 1989 a UK marketing company was formed, Turbomeca Ltd. Address as for Rolls-Royce Turbomeca (see International part of this section); General Manager Michel Dubarry.

Total covered floor area for Turbomeca's three plants at Bordes, Mézières and Tarnos is 136,487 m² (1,134,469 sq ft). The company employs about 4,260 people.

ROLLS-ROYCE TURBOMECA ADOUR

This turbofan appears in the International part of this section.

TURBOMECA-SNECMA LARZAC

This turbofan appears under Turbomeca-SNECMA GRTS.

MTU-TURBOMECA-RR MTR 390

This appears in the International part of this section.

Turbomeca TM 319 Arrius free-turbine turboshaft

ROLLS-ROYCE TURBOMECA RTM 322

See International part of this section.

TURBOMECA TM 319 ARRIUS

This turboshaft is compact, there being no axial compressor. Initial rating is 340 kW (456 shp). The first TM 319 was run on the bench on 21 February 1983. Full authority digital electronic control is supplied by Elecma. Production deliveries for the AS 355 began in 1987, and were continuing in 1988 at the rate of 50 per year. Certification took place in 1988. The same gas generator is used in the TP 319 turboprop.

TM 319-1. Basic version to which data below apply. Twin TM 319s at a T-O rating of 358 kW (480 shp) are an alternative power plant for the MBB BO 108.

TM 319-2. Growth version, max T-O rating 473 kW (634 shp). Selected for McDonnell Douglas MDX.
DIMENSIONS:

Length	782 mm (30.78 in)
Width	360 mm (14.2 in)
Height	540 mm (21.26 in)
WEIGHT, DRY:	87 kg (192 lb)

PERFORMANCE RATINGS (TM 319-1, ISA, S/L):

Max contingency	408 kW (547 shp)
Max T-O	380 kW (509 shp)
Max continuous	295 kW (395 shp)

Turbomeca TP 319 Arrius free-turbine turboprop

TURBOMECA TP 319 ARRIUS

The turboprop version is fully aerobatic. The gas generator and power turbine modules are identical with those of the TM 319. The first TP 319 ran on 11 September 1985. Flight testing in an Epsilon began in November 1985, followed by a Valmet L-90 TP in December 1987. The TP 319 is flying in the Socata Oméga.
DIMENSIONS:

Length	826 mm (32.52 in)
Width	476 mm (18.74 in)
Height	590 mm (23.22 in)
WEIGHT, DRY (bare):	111 kg (245 lb)

PERFORMANCE RATINGS (ISA, S/L):

Twin T-O contingency	343 kW (460 shp)
T-O	313 kW (420 shp)
Cruise (6,100 m, 20,000 ft)	179 kW (240 shp)

TURBOMECA ARRIEL

This turboshaft powers the single-engined AS 350 and AS 550 Ecureuil, twin-engined AS 365 and AS 565 Dauphin, Agusta A 109K and Sikorsky S-76A + and S-76C.

The Arriel has modular construction. The first complete engine ran on 7 August 1974.

There are 13 qualified production versions, differing essentially only in power rating:

Arriel 1A, 1B. T-O rating 478 kW (641 shp); powers AS 350B and AS 365C.

Arriel 1C. T-O rating 492 kW (660 shp); powers AS 365N.

Arriel 1D. T-O rating 510 kW (684 shp); powers AS 350B and L₁.

Arriel 1C1, 1M, 1K, 1S. All have T-O rating of 522 kW (700 shp); power AS 365F and N₁, A 109K and S-76A +.

Arriel 1C2. T-O rating 550 kW (738 shp); powers AS 365N₂.

Arriel 1D1. T-O rating 558 kW (749 shp); powers AS 350B₂ and AS 550U₂.

Arriel 1M1. T-O rating 558 kW (749 shp); powers AS 565UA and AS 565MA.

Arriel 1S1. T-O rating 539 kW (723 shp); powers S-76C.

Arriel 2. Growth version with single-stage gas generator turbine. To provide at least 16 per cent more power than 1S. Candidate engine for P120L, Dauphin and S-76.

By 1 March 1990 a total of 2,406 Arriels had been delivered, with production continuing at the rate of 375 per year. These engines had then flown 2.9 million hours in 74 countries. These totals do not include engines produced under licence in China.

Turbomeca Arriel 1S free-turbine turboshaft

Turbomeca TM 333 free-turbine turboshaft

The following relates to the Arriel 1A, 1B:

TYPE: Single-shaft free turbine turboshaft.

COMPRESSOR: Single-stage axial and supersonic centrifugal. Pressure ratio 9.

COMBUSTION CHAMBER: Annular, with flow radially outwards and then inwards. Centrifugal fuel injection.

GAS GENERATOR TURBINE: Two integral cast axial stages with solid blades.

POWER TURBINE: Single axial stage with inserted blades.

REDUCTION GEAR: Light alloy gearbox, containing two stages of helical gears, giving drive at 6,000 rpm to front and rear. Hydraulic torquemeter.

ACCESSORY DRIVES: Main pad provides for optional 12,000 rpm alternator; other drives for oil pumps, tachometer generator, governor and starter.

LUBRICATION SYSTEM: Independent circuit through gear pump and metallic cartridge filter.

OIL SPECIFICATION: AIR 3512 or 3513A.

STARTING: Electric starter or starter/generator.

DIMENSIONS:

Length, excl accessories	1,090 mm (42.91 in)
Height overall	569 mm (22.40 in)
Width	430 mm (16.93 in)

WEIGHT, DRY:

With all engine accessories	120 kg (265 lb)

PERFORMANCE RATINGS: See variants list

SPECIFIC FUEL CONSUMPTION:

T-O	96.8 μg/J (0.573 lb/h/shp)

TURBOMECA ASTAZOU TURBOPROP

The Astazou turboprop is in production in its 761 kW (1,020 ehp) Astazou XVI (AZ16) version. The XVIG, equipped for sustained inverted flight, powers the Argentine IA 58 Pucará. By 1988 deliveries of all XVI versions totalled 367, against orders for 440.

The following data refer to the XVIG:

DIMENSIONS:

Diameter over intake cowl	546 mm (21.5 in)
Overall length, incl propeller	2,047 mm (80.6 in)

WEIGHT, DRY: 228 kg (502 lb)

PERFORMANCE RATINGS:

T-O	761 ekW; 720 kW
	(1,020 ehp; 965 shp) at 43,000 rpm
Max continuous	696 ekW; 654 kW
	(934 ehp; 877 shp) at 43,000 rpm

SPECIFIC FUEL CONSUMPTION:

At T-O rating	88.7 μg/J (0.525 lb/h/shp)

TURBOMECA ASTAZOU TURBOSHAFT

This turboshaft series is derived from the Astazou II turboprop. Variants are:

Astazou IIA. Rated at 390 kW (523 shp) for SA 318C. Total of 615 built.

Astazou IIIA. Derived from IIA but with revised turbine to match power needs of SA 341G. Produced jointly by Turbomeca and Rolls-Royce, with 1,008 delivered.

Astazou XIVB and XIVF. For SA 319B; XIVB is civil and XIVF military. Flat rated at 441 kW (591 shp) (1 h) up to 4,000 m (13,125 ft) or +55°C.

Astazou XIVH. For SA 342J/L, to remove altitude and temperature limitations; 1,146 delivered.

Astazou XVIIIA. Higher gas temperature. Powers AS 360C.

Astazou XX. Fourth axial compressor stage added. Designed for operation in hot and high countries.

The following description relates to the Astazou IIIN except where indicated:

TYPE: Single-shaft axial-plus-centrifugal turboshaft.

REDUCTION GEAR: Two-stage epicyclic having helical primary and straight secondary gears. Ratio 7.039 : 1 (XIVB/F, 7.345; XVIIIA, 7.375).

COMPRESSOR: Single-stage axial (IIA, IIN, IIIN), two-stage axial (XIV, XVIII) or three-stage axial (XX) followed by single-stage centrifugal. Mass flow 2.5 kg (5.5 lb)/s.

COMBUSTION CHAMBER: Reverse flow annular with centrifugal injector using rotary atomiser. Two ventilated torch igniters.

TURBINE: Three-stage axial with blades integral with discs.

ACCESSORIES: Five drive pads on casing forming rear of air intake.

FUEL SYSTEM: Automatic constant speed control.

LUBRICATION SYSTEM: Pressure type with gear type pumps. Oil tank of 8 litre (17 US pints; 14 Imp pint) capacity.

STARTING: Electrical, automatic.

DIMENSIONS:

Length overall: Astazou IIA	1,272 mm (50.0 in)
Astazou III, XIVB/F	1,433 mm (56.3 in)
Astazou XIVH	1,470 mm (57.9 in)
Astazou XVIIIA	1,327 mm (52.2 in)
Astazou XX	1,529 mm (60.22 in)
Height: Astazou IIA	458 mm (18.0 in)
Astazou III, XIVH	460 mm (18.1 in)
Astazou XVIIIA	698 mm (27.48 in)
Astazou XX	721 mm (28.4 in)
Width: Astazou IIA	480 mm (18.8 in)
Astazou III, XIVH	460 mm (18.1 in)

WEIGHTS:

Equipped: Astazou III	147 kg (324 lb)
Astazou III (suffix 2)	150 kg (330 lb)
Astazou XIVB/F	166 kg (366 lb)
Astazou XIVH	160 kg (353 lb)
Astazou XVIIIA	155 kg (341 lb)
Astazou XX	195 kg (430 lb)

PERFORMANCE RATINGS:

Max power: Astazou IIA	390 kW (523 shp)
Astazou III	441 kW (592 shp)
Astazou III (suffix 2)	481 kW (645 shp)
Astazou XX	749 kW (1,005 shp)
One hour: Astazou XIVB/F	441 kW (591 shp)
Astazou XVIIIA	651 kW (873 shp)
	maintained at sea level to 40°C
Max continuous: Astazou IIA	353 kW (473 shp)
Astazou III	390 kW (523 shp)
Astazou III (suffix 2)	441 kW (592 shp)
Astazou XIVB/F	405 kW (543 shp)
Astazou XIVH	flat rated in SA 341 at 440.7 kW
	(591 shp) to 55°C or 4,000 m (13,125 ft)
Astazou XVIIIA	600 kW (805 shp)
Astazou XX	675 kW (905 shp)

SPECIFIC FUEL CONSUMPTION:

At max power rating:

Astazou IIA	105.3 μg/J (0.623 lb/h/shp)
Astazou III	108.7 μg/J (0.643 lb/h/shp)
Astazou III (suffix 2)	109.9 μg/J (0.650 lb/h/shp)
Astazou XIVB/F	105.5 μg/J (0.624 lb/h/shp)
Astazou XVIIIA	91.3 μg/J (0.540 lb/h/shp)
Astazou XX	85.9 μg/J (0.508 lb/h/shp)

TURBOMECA ARTOUSTE III

The Artouste IIIB is a single-shaft turboshaft with two-stage axial-centrifugal compressor and three-stage turbine. Pressure ratio 5.2. Mass flow 4.3 kg/s (9.5 lb/s) at 33,300 rpm. Built under licence in India by Hindustan Aeronautics.

The IIIB powers the SA 315B and SA 316B/C. The uprated IIID has a reduction gear giving 5,864 rpm at the driveshaft (instead of 5,773) and in revised equipment. The IIID powers the SA 316C; data are for this version. A total of 2,525 Artouste III engines had been built by 1988.

DIMENSIONS:

Length	1,815 mm (71.46 in)
Height	627 mm (24.68 in)
Width	507 mm (19.96 in)

WEIGHT, DRY: 178 kg (392 lb)

PERFORMANCE RATING (T-O, maintained up to 55°C at S/L or up to 4,000 m; 13,125 ft): 440 kW (590 shp)

SPECIFIC FUEL CONSUMPTION: 126.2 μg/J (0.747 lb/h/shp)

TURBOMECA TM 333

This turboshaft was launched in July 1979 to power the AS 365 and other helicopters in the 4,000 kg (8,800 lb) class including the Indian ALH. French certification of the 1A version was obtained on 11 July 1986.

TM 333 1A. Basic version, composed of a gas generator module, free turbine module and reduction gear module.

TM 333 1M. For military AS 565.

TM 333 2B. Growth version with single crystal HP turbine, giving T-O rating of 747 kW (1,001 shp). First run 6 November 1984. Selected for HAL (India) ALH. First deliveries 1989.

The TM 333 is one of three new engines included in the European Small Engines Co-operation Agreement. Data are for the 2B:

TYPE: Free turbine turboshaft.

COMPRESSOR: Variable inlet guide vanes, two stage axial compressor, single stage centrifugal.

COMBUSTION CHAMBER: Annular, reverse flow.

GAS GENERATOR TURBINE: Single-stage with uncooled inserted blades.

POWER TURBINE: Single-stage axial with uncooled inserted blades.

GEARBOX: Two stages to give drive at 6,000 rpm to front output shaft.

LUBRICATION: Independent system. Oil passes through gear pump and metallic cartridge filter.

FUEL SYSTEM: Microprocessor numerical control.

DIMENSIONS:

Length, including accessories	1,045 mm (41.1 in)
Height overall	712 mm (28.0 in)
Width	454 mm (17.9 in)

WEIGHT, DRY: 156 kg (345 lb)

PERFORMANCE RATINGS:

Max contingency	788 kW (1,057 shp)
T-O	747 kW (1,002 shp)
Max continuous	663 kW (889 shp)

SPECIFIC FUEL CONSUMPTION:

Max contingency	88 μg/J (0.523 lb/h/shp)
T-O	89.4 μg/J (0.529 lb/h/shp)
Max continuous	91.7 μg/J (0.543 lb/h/shp)

TURBOMECA TURMO

The Turmo free turbine engine is in service in both turboshaft and turboprop versions.

Current variants are as follows:

Turmo IIIC₅, IIIC₆, IIIC₇. For SA 321F/G/H/Ja. Total production 549.

Turmo IIIE₆. Higher turbine temperature.

Turmo IVA. Civil engine derived from IIIC₄, with contingency rating of 1,057 kW (1,417 shp). The IVB is a military version.

TYPE: Free turbine turboshaft.

REDUCTION GEAR: IIIC₃, C₅ and E₃ fitted with rear mounted reduction gear; IIIC₄ direct drive.

COMPRESSOR: Single-stage axial followed by single-stage centrifugal. Pressure ratio 5.9 on IIIC₃. Mass flow 5.9 kg (13 lb)/s.

COMBUSTION CHAMBER: Reverse flow annular with centrifugal fuel injector using rotary atomiser. Two ventilated torch igniters.

GAS GENERATOR TURBINE: Two-stage axial.

POWER TURBINE: Two-stage axial unit in IIIC₃, C₅ and E₃, and single stage in IIIC₄.

ACCESSORIES: Pads for oil pump, fuel control, electric starter, tacho-generator and, on IIIC₄, oil cooler fan.

FUEL SYSTEM: Fuel control for gas generator on IIIC₃, C₅ and E₃, with speed limiter for power turbine on E₃. Constant-speed system on IIIC₄ power turbine.

FUEL GRADE: AIR 3405 for IIIC$_4$.
LUBRICATION SYSTEM: Pressure type with oil cooler and 13 litre (27.5 US pints; 23 Imp pint) tank.
OIL SPECIFICATION: AIR 3155A, or AIR 3513, for IIIC$_4$.
STARTING: Automatic system with electric starter motor.
DIMENSIONS:

Length:	
Turmo IIIC$_3$, C$_5$ and E$_3$	1,975.7 mm (78.0 in)
Turmo IIIC$_4$	2,184 mm (85.5 in)
Turmo IIID$_3$	1,868 mm (73.6 in)
Width:	
Turmo IIIC$_3$, C$_5$ and E$_3$	693 mm (27.3 in)
Turmo IIIC$_4$	637 mm (25.1 in)
Turmo IIID$_3$	934 mm (36.8 in)
Height:	
Turmo IIIC$_3$, C$_5$ and E$_3$	716.5 mm (28.2 in)
Turmo IIIC$_4$	719 mm (28.3 in)
Turmo IIID$_3$	926 mm (36.5 in)

WEIGHT, DRY:

Turmo IIIC$_3$ and E$_3$, fully equipped	297 kg (655 lb)
Turmo IIIC$_5$, IIIC$_6$ and IIIC$_7$	325 kg (716 lb)
Turmo IIIC$_4$, equipped engine	225 kg (496 lb)
Turmo IIID$_3$, basic engine	365 kg (805 lb)

PERFORMANCE RATINGS:

T-O: Turmo IIIC$_3$, D$_3$ and E$_3$	110 4 kW (1,480 shp)
Turmo IIIE$_6$	1,181 kW (1,584 shp)
Max contingency:	
Turmo IIIC$_4$ at 33,800 gas generator rpm	
	1,032 kW (1,384 shp)
Turmo IIIC$_6$ at 33,550 gas generator rpm	
	1,156 kW (1,550 shp)
Turmo IIIC$_7$ at 33,800 gas generator rpm	
	1,200 kW (1,610 shp)
Turmo IVA at 33,950 gas generator rpm	
	1,057 kW (1,417 shp)
Turmo IVC at 33,800 gas generator rpm	
	1,163 kW (1,560 shp)
T-O and intermediate contingency:	
Turmo IIIC$_5$	1,050 kW (1,408 shp)

SPECIFIC FUEL CONSUMPTION:

At T-O rating:	
Turmo IIIC$_3$ and E$_3$	101.9 µg/J (0.603 lb/h/shp)
Turmo IIID$_3$	104.1 µg/J (0.616 lb/h/shp)
At max contingency rating:	
Turmo IIIC$_4$, C$_5$, C$_6$, C$_7$ and IV	
	106.8 µg/J (0.632 lb/h/shp)
Turmo IVA	106.3 µg/J (0.629 lb/h/shp)

TURBOMECA MAKILA

This turboshaft powers the AS 332. Derived partly from the Turmo, it incorporates rapid-strip modular construction; three axial stages of compression plus one centrifugal; centrifugal atomiser; two-stage gas generator turbine with cooled blades; two-stage free power turbine; and lateral exhaust.

Makila 1A. Certificated 1980. OEI rating 1,310 kW (1,757 shp).

Turbomeca Makila 1A free-turbine turboshaft

Makila 1A1. Certificated 1984. OEI rating 1,400 kW (1,877 shp).

Makila 1A2. Under development. OEI rating (30 s) 1,569 kW (2,103 shp), (2 min) 1,433 kW (1,921 shp).

By the end of 1989 deliveries of Makila engines had reached 923, of which 100 were delivered in 1989.
DIMENSIONS:

Length, intake face to rear face	1,395 mm (54.94 in)
Max diameter	514 mm (20.25 in)

WEIGHT, DRY: Basic 210 kg (463 lb)
Equipped 243 kg (535 lb)
PERFORMANCE RATINGS (ISA, S/L):
Max contingency: see model listings
Cruise: 1A, 1A1, 1A2 700 kW (939 shp)
SPECIFIC FUEL CONSUMPTION:

Max contingency: 1A	83.9 µg/J (0.496 lb/h/shp)
1A1	81.4 µg/J (0.481 lb/h/shp)
Cruise: 1A	97.7 µg/J (0.578 lb/h/shp)
1A1	95.0 µg/J (0.562 lb/h/shp)

TURBOMECA-SNECMA
GROUPEMENT TURBOMECA-SNECMA (GRTS)

1 rue Beaujon, BP 37-08, 75362 Paris Cédex 08
Telephone: 33 (1) 49 24 18 61

Groupement Turbomeca-SNECMA is a company formed jointly by Société Turbomeca and SNECMA to manage the Larzac turbofan launched in 1968. GRTS has no capital and comprises primarily a joint management organisation.

TURBOMECA-SNECMA LARZAC

In February 1972 the **Larzac 04** turbofan was selected for a joint Franco-German programme to provide propulsion for the Alpha Jet (see under Dassault/Dornier in International part of Aircraft section). In addition to the two French engine partners, two German companies, MTU and KHD, shared in production and development. Complete engines were assembled in both countries.

Current versions are as follows:

Larzac 04-C6. Two-stage fan, four-stage HP compressor, annular combustion chamber, single-stage HP turbine with cooled blades and single-stage LP turbine. Maximum airflow 28 kg (62 lb)/s, pressure ratio 10.6 and BPR 1.13. First production delivery September 1977.

Larzac 04-C20. Growth version with increased mass flow compressor and higher temperature HP turbine. Pressure ratio 11.3 and BPR 1.04. First run March 1982; first flight December 1982; production deliveries from September 1984.

DIMENSIONS:

Overall length of basic engine	1,179 mm (46.4 in)
Overall diameter	602 mm (23.7 in)

WEIGHT, DRY: 302 kg (666 lb)

Turbomeca-SNECMA Larzac 04-C20 two-shaft turbofan

T-O THRUST (S/L, static):

Larzac 04-C6	13.19 kN (2,966 lb)
Larzac 04-C20	14.12 kN (3,175 lb)

SPECIFIC FUEL CONSUMPTION:

Larzac 04-C6	20.1 mg/Ns (0.71 lb/h/lb st)
Larzac 04-C20	20.95 mg/Ns (0.74 lb/h/lb st)

GERMANY

BMW RR
BMW ROLLS-ROYCE GmbH

Hohenmarkstrasse 60-70, Postfach 1246, D-6370 Oberursel
Telephone: 49 (61) 71 5000
Fax: 49 (61) 71 500485
Telex: 410727

This joint venture company was established in July 1990 by BMW AG of Munich (50.5 per cent) and Rolls-Royce plc of London (49.5 per cent) It is located at the facilities of the former KHD Luftfahrttechnik, with over 1,000 employees and capital of DM30 million. It is regarded as a German company.

It has taken over activities of the former KHD, including the Tornado secondary power system, T117 propulsion for the CL-289 UAV, T118 APU demonstrator and T128 low-cost turbojet. It has a 20 per cent share in the

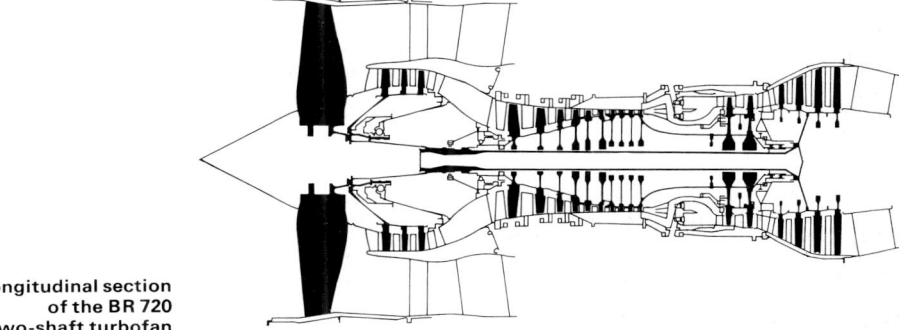

Longitudinal section of the BR 720 two-shaft turbofan

Rolls-Royce Tay programme, 5 per cent in the Rolls-Royce Trent, and 5 per cent in the SNECMA contribution to the CFM56-5.

Both partners are supporting the BR700 series, a new family of turbofans.

BMW ROLLS-ROYCE BR 700

Basic core, used in other engines of the family. A new design, to have been launched in March 1991 and to run in 1992. Ten-stage compressor with inlet guide vanes and next four stators variable. High-intensity smokeless annular combustor. Two-stage turbine. Together with the three currently projected derived engines, to be developed, manufactured, sold and supported by BMW Rolls-Royce.

BR 710. Turbofan for business jets and regional jet transports. Fan diameter 1,016 mm (40 in), driven by two-stage LP turbine. Ratings 35.6-62.3 kN (8,000-14,000 lb st).

BR 715. Turbofan for regional jet transports. Probably the first type to run, in 1994. Fan diameter 1,346 mm (53 in), plus two-stage LP booster, driven by three-stage LP turbine. Ratings 62.3-80.1 kN (14,000-18,000 lb st).

BR 720. Turbofan for larger jet aircraft. Fan diameter 1,397 mm (55 in), plus three-stage booster, driven by four-stage turbine. Ratings 80.1-97.9 kN (18,000-22,000 lb st).

F+E
FISCHER + ENTWICKLUNGEN GmbH
Sonnenring 38, D-8300 Landshut/Altdorf
Telephone: 49 (871) 32099
Fax: 49 (871) 32948

F+E TOP
TOP stands for Take-Off Power; three-cylinder two-stroke piston engine packaged as a bolt-on unit fitted in minutes on a mounting on top of sailplanes and raised above the fuselage or retracted by a control from the cockpit. Maximum power 18 kW (24 hp) at 4,200 rpm. Installed weight 44 kg (97 lb) including 30-start battery and fuel for one hour. Installations sold for Astir CS, CS77 and CSJEANS, all types of ASW 20, ASW 24, Cirrus, Cirrus 75 and Kiwi gliders.

HIRTH
GÖBLER-HIRTHMOTOREN GmbH
Postfach 20, Max Eyth Strasse 10, 7141 Benningen
Telephone: 49 (71) 44 6074
Fax: 49 (71) 44 5415
Telex: 7 264 530 GHIR D

This company produces small piston engines for microlights and other aircraft in the range 2.61-97 kW (3.5-130 hp). Except for the F 30, all are two-cylinder upright in-line two-strokes with carburettor, Bosch magneto ignition and direct drive. In mid-1990 it was planned to introduce a new engine series of 625 cc (38.1 cu in), weighing about 29 kg (64 lb), rated at 29.8-52.2 kW (40-70 hp) at 6,500 rpm.

HIRTH F 263 R 53
Cylinders 66 mm (2.598 in) bore and 56 mm (2.205 in) stroke, giving capacity of 383 cc (23.37 cu in). Compression ratio 9.5, using 25:1 fuel mix. Weight with electric starter 24.0 kg (52.8 lb), silencer adding 2.5 kg (5.5 lb). Max power 16.2 kW (22 hp) at 3,900 rpm.

HIRTH F 22
Cylinders as F 263. Weight with electric starter 20.0 kg (44 lb), silencer adding 3 kg (6.6 lb). Max power 17 kW (23 hp) at 5,000 rpm.

HIRTH F 23A
Cylinders 72 mm (2.835 in) bore and 64 mm (2.52 in) stroke, giving capacity of 521 cc (31.79 cu in). Compression ratio 10.5, using 50:1 fuel mix. Equipped weight 24.0 kg (52 lb), silencer adding 4.5 kg (10 lb). Max power 30 kW (40 hp) at 5,500 rpm.

HIRTH 2701 R 03
Cylinders 70 mm (2.756 in) bore and 64 mm (2.52 in) stroke, giving capacity of 493 cc (30.08 cu in). Compression ratio 11, using 50:1 fuel mix. Weight with fan and recoil starter 32.8 kg (72.5 lb). Max power 32 kW (43 hp) at 6,750 rpm.

HIRTH 2702 R 03
Cylinders as F 23A. Weight with fan and recoil starter 35.0 kg (77 lb). Max power 31 kW (41.6 hp) at 5,500 rpm.

HIRTH 2703
Similar to 2702 but twin carburettors. Max power 44 kW (59 hp) at 6,200 rpm.

HIRTH 2704
Again enlarged, to 625 cc (38.1 cu in). Max power 38 kW (51 hp) at 4,500 rpm.

Hirth F 30 flat-four piston engine

HIRTH F 30
Four-cylinder engine tested in two sizes, the smaller (1,042 cc) being a twinned 2702 but lighter. Both can have direct or geared drive, data being for the former.

1,042 cc (63.58 cu in) version. Weight dry 36.0 kg (79.4 lb). Max power 48.5 kW (65 hp) at 4,500 rpm, 82 kW (110 hp) at 6,500 rpm.

1,270 cc (77.50 cu in) version. Weight dry 35.0 kg (77 lb). Max power 59.5 kW (80 hp) at 4,500 rpm, 97 kW (130 hp) at 6,500 rpm.

KÖNIG
KÖNIG MOTORENBAU
Friedrich-Olbricht Damm 72, 1000 Berlin 13
Telephone: 49 (30) 344 3071
Fax: 49 (30) 344 1595

This company produces small two-stroke piston engines for microlights and other aircraft. All except the SF 930 have radial cylinders of 66 mm (2.598 in) bore and 42 mm (1.654 in) stroke, with natural air cooling. A 33:1 fuel mix is used, aspirated through a single bowl carburettor and with capacitor discharge ignition. The SC 430 and SD 570 have an electric starter and are available with direct drive or with 1.75 ratio Powergrip belt.

KÖNIG SC 430
This engine has three cylinders spaced at 120°, giving a capacity of 430 cc (26.24 cu in). Weight with full equipment is 16 kg (35.3 lb) and max power 18 kW (24 hp) at 4,000-4,200 rpm. It is used in the ASW 24 package by Fischer & Entwicklungen for sailplanes.

KÖNIG SD 570
This engine has four cylinders spaced at 90°, giving a capacity of 570 cc (34.78 cu in). Weight with full equipment is 18.5 kg (41 lb) and max power 21 kW (28 hp) at 4,000-4,200 rpm.

KÖNIG SF 930
Production of this larger four-cylinder radial began in April 1985. Bore and stroke are respectively 70 and 60 mm (2.756 and 2.362 in), giving a capacity of 930 cc (56.75 cu in); equipped weight is 36 kg (79.4 lb) and maximum power 35.8 kW (48 hp) at 4,000-4,200 rpm.

König SF 930 piston engine driving a four-blade propeller

LIMBACH
LIMBACH FLUGMOTOREN GmbH
Kotthausener Strasse 5, 5330 Königswinter 21, Sassenberg
Telephone: 49 (2244) 2322 and 3031
Fax: 49 (2244) 6976
Telex: 889574 plm d
PRESIDENT: Friedrich Welbhoff

In USA: **J. T. Consulting**
3114 N Sunset, Sand Springs, Oklahoma 74063
Telephone: 1 (918) 241 5468
Fax: 1 (918) 245 6910

This company manufactures four-stroke and two-stroke piston engines for light aeroplanes and powered gliders.

LIMBACH L 90E
Smallest of the company's range, this is an aircooled flat-twin two-stroke. Not yet available (1991).
CYLINDERS: Bore 42 mm (1.654 in). Stroke 31 mm (1.220 in). Capacity 86 cc (5.248 cu in). Compression ratio 9.5.
INDUCTION: Twin all-attitude diaphragm carburettors.
FUEL GRADE: 96 RON plus 25:1 oil.

Limbach L 275E two-stroke piston engine

IGNITION: Bosch solid state. single plugs.
WEIGHT, DRY: 4 kg (8.8 lb)
PERFORMANCE RATINGS:
T-O (5 min) 4.2 kW (5.6 hp) at 8,500 rpm
Continuous 2.9 kW (3.9 hp) at 7,000 rpm

LIMBACH L 275E

This engine is intended for low cost propulsion of UAVs, paraplanes and microlight aircraft.
TYPE: Two-cylinder horizontally opposed two-stroke air-cooled piston engine.
CYLINDERS: Cast aluminium alloy with Nicasil liner. Bore 66 mm (2.6 in). Stroke 40 mm (1.57 in). Capacity 274 cc (16.72 cu in).
INDUCTION: Two all-attitude diaphragm carburettors.
FUEL GRADE: 90 octane, mixed 25:1 with two-stroke oil.
IGNITION: 12V Bosch transistorised, one Bosch WK 175T6 plug per cylinder.
ACCESSORIES: Leistritz type turbo silencer (muffler).
DIMENSIONS:
Length overall 226 mm (8.89 in)
Width overall 390 mm (15.35 in)
Height overall 187 mm (7.36 in)
WEIGHT (with silencer): 7.5 kg (16.5 lb)
PERFORMANCE RATING: 18 kW (24 hp) at 7,300 rpm

LIMBACH L 550E

This is a four-cylinder version of the two-stroke L 275E. Capacity is thus 548 cc (33.5 cu in).
WEIGHT, DRY: 15.5 kg (34 lb)
PERFORMANCE RATING: 32 kW (43 hp) at 7,300 rpm

LIMBACH SL 1700

Several variants have been certificated by the LBA.
SL 1700D. Dual ignition. Not certificated. Fitted to Sportavia RF7.

Limbach SL 1700EA four-stroke piston engine

Sportavia-Limbach SL 1700E piston engine

SL 1700E. Fitted to Sportavia RF5 and RF5B.
SL 1700EA. Front-end starter and different induction system. Fitted to Scheibe SF-25C Falke.
SL 1700EAI. Hoffmann variable-pitch propeller. Fitted to Scheibe SF-28.
SL 1700EC. E with carburettor intake heating box. For pusher installation.
SL 1700 ECI. EC equipped to drive variable-pitch propeller.
SL 1700EI. E equipped to drive variable-pitch propeller. Optional for Sportavia RF5B.
Unless otherwise stated, the following description refers to the SL 1700E:
TYPE: Four-cylinder opposed aircooled four-stroke piston engine.
CYLINDERS: Bore 88 mm (3.46 in). Stroke 69 mm (2.71 in). Capacity 1,680 cc (102.51 cu in). Compression ratio 8.
INDUCTION: Stromberg-Zenith 150CD carburettor.
FUEL GRADE: 90 octane.
IGNITION: Single Slick 4230 magneto feeding one Bosch WB 240 ERT 1 plug in each cylinder.
STARTING: One Fiat 0.37 kW (0.5 hp) starter (EA, EAI, one Bosch 0.3 kW; 0.4 hp).
ACCESSORIES: Ducellier 250W alternator; APG 17.09.001 fuel pump (EA,EAI, 17.09.001A).
DIMENSIONS:
Length overall: SL 1700D 649 mm (25.6 in)
SL 1700EA, EAI 558 mm (22.0 in)
SL 1700E, EI, EC, ECI 618 mm (24.3 in)
Width overall: SL 1700D 800 mm (31.5 in)
SL 1700EA, EAI 770 mm (30.3 in)
other variants 764 mm (30.1 in)
Height overall: SL 1700D 451 mm (17.8 in)
SL 1700EA, EAI 392 mm (15.4 in)
other variants 368 mm (14.5 in)
WEIGHT, DRY:
SL 1700E, EI 73 kg (161 lb)
SL 1700EA, EAI 70 kg (154 lb)
SL 1700EC, ECI 74 kg (164 lb)
PERFORMANCE RATINGS:
T-O: SL 1700D 48.5 kW (65 hp) at 3,600 rpm
SL 1700E, EI, EC, ECI 51 kW (68 hp) at 3,600 rpm
SL 1700EA, EAI 44.7 kW (60 hp) at 3,550 rpm
Continuous:
SL 1700E, EI, EC, ECI 45.5 kW (61 hp) at 3,200 rpm
SL 1700EA, EAI 41.7 kW (56 hp) at 3,300 rpm

LIMBACH L 1800

Basically an L 2000 with reduced stroke. The **L 1800EA**, not certificated, is for experimental aircraft and ultralights.
CYLINDERS: Bore 90 mm (3.54 in). Stroke 69 mm (2.7 in). Capacity 1,756 cc (107 cu in). Compression ratio 7.5.
FUEL GRADE: 100LL or Mogas.
WEIGHT, DRY: about 70 kg (154 lb)

Limbach L 2000DA2 four-stroke piston engine

PERFORMANCE RATINGS (S/L):
T-O 49.2 kW (66 hp) at 3,600 rpm
Cruise 41 kW (55 hp) at 2,600 rpm

LIMBACH L 2000

This family is based on the SL 1700 with increased bore and stroke:
L 2000EO1. As 1700EI. Installed in Fournier RF-5, RF-9 and RF-10, IAR IS-28M2 and Aerotechnik L-13L Vivat motor gliders.
L 2000EA1. As 1700EAI. Installed in Scheibe SF-25C Falke 2000 and SF-36.
L 2000EB1. As 1700EBI. Installed in Grob G 109, Valentin Taifun and Hoffmann Dimona.
L 2000DA2. Compression ratio reduced to 8.5. JAR 22E certificated with TBO 1,000 h. Installed in Robin ATL II and Stiletto T-9.
Details as for SL 1700, except for following:
CYLINDERS: Bore 90 mm (3.54 in). Stroke 78.4 mm (3.09 in). Capacity 1,994 cc (120.26 cu in). Compression ratio 8.7 (EAI, 8.9).
FUEL GRADE: 100LL or Mogas.
WEIGHT, DRY (with all accessories):
L 2000EOI 70 kg (154 lb)
L 2000EAI 69 kg (152 lb)
L 2000EBI 71.5 kg (157.5 lb)
PERFORMANCE RATINGS:
T-O: all models 59 kW (80 hp) at 3,400 rpm
Continuous:
L 2000EOI, EAI 52 kW (70 hp) at 3,000 rpm
L 2000EBI 53 kW (72 hp) at 3,000 rpm

LIMBACH L 2400

Similar to L 2000 but larger. JAR 22 certificated. The EB1-D powers the Stemme S-10.
CYLINDERS: Bore 97 mm (3.82 in). Stroke 82 mm (3.23 in). Capacity 2,424 cc (147.91 cu in). Compression ratio 8.5.
INDUCTION: Twin Stromberg-Zenith 150 CD-3 carburettors.
FUEL GRADE: Minimum 96 RON.
IGNITION: Slick 4230 or Bendix S4RN21 magneto feeding single Bosch WB 240 ERT 1 plugs.
ACCESSORIES: 1.4 kW starter, 14-V 33 or 55 A generator, fuel pump and tachometer. Provision for Hoffmann or Mühlbauer variable-pitch propeller.
WEIGHT, DRY: 82 kg (181 lb)
PERFORMANCE RATINGS:
L 2400EB1-A, B and C:
T-O (5 min) 65 kW (87 hp) at 3,200 rpm
Continuous 63 kW (84.5 hp) at 3,000 rpm
L2400EB1-D:
T-O 70 kW (94 hp) at 3,400 rpm

MTU

MOTOREN- UND TURBINEN-UNION MÜNCHEN GmbH

Dachauer Str 655, Munich-Allach (Postal address, Postfach 500640, 8000 Munich 50)
Telephone: 49 (89) 1489 0
Fax: 49 (89) 1502621
Telex: 529 500-15 MT D
MTU München, a subsidiary of Deutsche Aerospace AG, is Germany's largest aero engine company. It produces engines for most classes of aircraft. In March 1990 it signed an agreement which gives Pratt & Whitney a firm foothold in Europe and makes MTU United Technologies' 'preferred partner worldwide'.

GENERAL ELECTRIC CF6

MTU has approximately a 12 per cent share in the manufacture of the CF6-50 for the A300, approximately an 8 per cent share of the CF6-80A/A1 for the A310 and 767 and a 9 per cent share of the CF6-80C2 for the A300-600, 747 and 767. MTU makes HP turbine parts.

PRATT & WHITNEY PW2000

MTU is a partner, with Fiat of Italy, in the PW2037 and 2040. It is responsible for the LP turbine, under an 11.2 per cent share.

IAE V 2500

MTU has a 12.1 per cent share in IAE (see International part of this section).

PRATT & WHITNEY JT8D-200

MTU has a 12.5 per cent share, being largely responsible for the LP turbine.

EUROJET EJ200

MTU has a 33 per cent share in this engine, described in the International part of this section.

TURBOMECA-SNECMA LARZAC

MTU has a 23 per cent share (see under France).

TURBO-UNION RB199

MTU has a 40 per cent share in this engine, described in the International part of this section.

ROLLS-ROYCE TYNE

MTU has a 28 per cent share in about 170 Tyne turboprops for the Transall. MTU supports all Tyne 21 engines (Atlantique) and Tyne 22 (Transall), as well as Tynes used by civil operators.

ALLISON 250-C20B

MTU licence built more than 700 engines, designated 250-MTU-C20B, for the PAH-1 and VBH military variants of the MBB BO 105 helicopter. MTU is converting C20Bs into C20Rs and is supporting engines used by civil operators.

MTU-TURBOMECA-RR MTR 390

Brief details of this three-nation helicopter engine are given in the International part of this section.

P&WC PW305

MTU has a 25 per cent share in this Canadian turbofan. One of its responsibilities is the LP turbine.

PARODI

PARODI MOTORSEGLERTECHNIK

Hauptstrasse 70, 7895 Klettgau-Erzingen
Telephone: 49 (7742) 7689

DIRECTOR: Roland Parodi

This company has developed a family of piston engines for ultralight aircraft and motor gliders. With various designations in the HP 45 and HP 60 series, these are derived from a Honda design, with a new crankcase and lubrication system.

Details were given in the 1984-85 *Jane's* of the HP 60

series engines of 44.7 kW (60 hp). These have been uprated to the 59.7 kW (80 hp) class, and are being used to support later engines for two-seat aircraft. Parodi hopes to produce two definitive engines: one with variable turbo pressure for 74.6 kW (100 hp), cruising at 55.9 kW (75 hp); and the other for 96.9 kW (130 hp), cruising at 74.6 kW (100 hp).

PIEPER

PIEPER MOTORENBAU GmbH

Postfach 1229, Viktoriastrasse 50, 4950 Minden
Telephone: 49 (571) 34088
Fax: 49 (571) 34454

STAMO MS 1500

Pieper manufactures the 33.5 kW (45 hp) Stamo MS 1500-1 modified Volkswagen four-cylinder aircooled piston

engine, applications for which have included the Scheibe SF-25B Falke two-seat motor glider. Capacity 1,500 cc, compression ratio 7.2 : 1, length 640 mm (25 in), width 745 mm (29.3 in), height 395 mm (15.5 in) and dry weight 52 kg (115 lb). The MS 1500-1 operates on 80/86 or 90 octane fuel, and is started by a pull-cord. The MS 1500-2, has electric starter and generator. This increases weight to 60 kg (132 lb).

Pieper built Stamo MS 1500-1 four-cylinder four-stroke engine, rated at 33.5 kW (45 hp)

PORSCHE

DR ING h c F. PORSCHE AG

Postfach 1140, 7251 Weissach

Porsche stopped producing its PFM range of four-stroke, geared, fan-cooled light aircraft engines during 1990. Details last appeared in 1990-91 *Jane's*.

SAUER

SAUER MOTORENBAU GmbH

Nieder-Olmer Str 16, 6501 Ober Olm
Telephone: 49 (61) 36/8 9377

This company is marketing three sizes of four-cylinder four-stroke piston engine.

SAUER SE 1800 E1S

Certificated by the LBA in December 1990, this is claimed to be the first motor glider engine to operate on Mogas 95 Unleaded.
CYLINDERS: Bore 90 mm (3.54 in). Stroke 69 mm (2.72 in). Capacity 1,754 cc (107.0 cu in). Compression ratio 8.8.
WEIGHT, DRY (with accessories): 63.1 kg (139 lb)
PERFORMANCE RATING: 40 kW (53.6 hp) at 3,000 rpm

SAUER SS 2100 H1S

This engine can have dual Slick 4230 magnetos and runs on 100LL Avgas or Mogas. It has twin Bing 64/32 carburettors, a 12V starter and 15A alternator.
CYLINDERS: Bore 90 mm (3.54 in). Stroke 84 mm (3.31 in). Capacity 2,135 cc (130.3 cu in). Compression ratio 9.5.
WEIGHT, DRY: 76 kg (168 lb)
PERFORMANCE RATING: 59.5 kW (80 hp) at 3,000 rpm

SAUER ST 2500 H1S

Similar to SS 2100 but increased bore. It has a 45A generator.
CYLINDERS: Bore 97 mm (3.82 in). Stroke 84 mm (3.31 in). Capacity 2,481 cc (151.3 cu in).
WEIGHT, DRY: 79 kg (174 lb)
PERFORMANCE RATING: 68 kW (91.2 hp) at 3,000 rpm

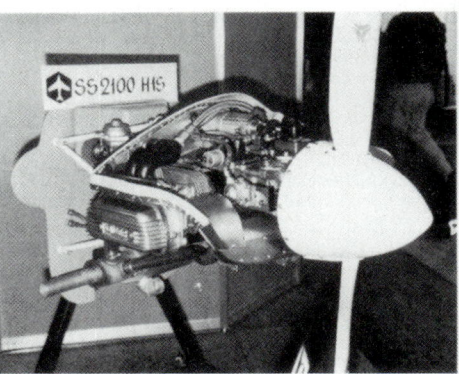

Sauer SS 2100 H1S four-cylinder piston engine
(Wolfgang Wagner)

ZOCHE

MICHAEL ZOCHE

Keferstrasse 13, 8000 Munich 40
Telephone: 49 (89) 34 45 91
Fax: 49 (89) 34 24 51
Telex: 523 402 ZOCHE D

This company's diesel aero engines incorporate the latest cylinder technology as well as such refinements as tungsten counterweights and full aerobatic pressure lubrication. Both engines have a propeller governor and four accessory drive pads. The weights given include starter, alternator, governor, vacuum pump and turbocharger.

ZOCHE ZO 01A

CYLINDERS: Four, arranged at 90°. Bore 95 mm (3.74 in). Stroke 94 mm (3.70 in). Capacity 2,665 cc (162.6 cu in). Compression ratio 17.
FUEL GRADES: Diesel No. 2, JP-4 or Jet A.

DIMENSIONS:
Length	720 mm (28 in)
Height or width	530 mm (20.9 in)
Diameter	640 mm (25.2 in)

WEIGHT, DRY: 89 kg (196 lb)
PERFORMANCE RATING: 110 kW (150 hp) at 2,500 rpm
SPECIFIC FUEL CONSUMPTION (above rating): 65.0 µg/J (0.385 lb/h/hp)

ZOCHE ZO 02A

This is a double-row eight-cylinder engine using 01A cylinders. It is 910 mm (35.8 in) long, weighs under 120 kg (265 lb) and has a T-O rating of 220 kW (300 hp).

Zoche ZO 01A four-cylinder diesel engine
(Howard Levy)

INDIA

GTRE

**GAS TURBINE RESEARCH
ESTABLISHMENT**

Suranjan Das Road, Post Bag 9302, C. V. Raman Nagar, Bangalore 560 093
Telephone: 91 (812) 570698
Telex: 0845 2438 GTRE IN
DIRECTOR: Arun Prasad

Established in 1959, the GTRE is one of 45 R&D establishments administered by the DRDO (Defence Research & Development Organisation). By far its biggest challenge is the design and development of a new engine for fighter aircraft.

GTRE GTX

This engine is planned as the power plant of the production LCA (Light Combat Aircraft). Although

influenced by existing engines, the GTX is a completely Indian project, and is being developed in the following versions:

GTX37-14U. This afterburning turbojet was the first designed in India. First run in 1977, it has a three-stage LP compressor and seven-stage HP compressor, both driven by single-stage turbines. It is flat rated to ISA +30°C at 44.5 kN (10,000 lb st) dry and 64.3 kN (14,450 lb st) with full reheat. A few engines will continue running to support later variants.

GTX37-14UB. Turbofan version with bypass ratio of 0.215. Max thrust 88.9 kN (19,990 lb st) with a larger frontal area.

GTX-35. Advanced turbojet with five-stage HP compressor, new annular combustor and increased turbine temperature. Offered required thrust for LCA, but higher fuel consumption due to higher thrust levels.

GTX-35VS. Improved turbofan planned as engine for LCA. Core was to run in early 1991, engine in mid-1992.
LP COMPRESSOR: Three stages, with transonic blading. Pressure ratio 3.22.
HP COMPRESSOR: Five stages with some variable stators. Pressure ratio 6.5. Overall pressure ratio 21.
COMBUSTION CHAMBER: Annular, with air-blast atomisers.
HP TURBINE: Heavily loaded single-stage with DS cooled blades. Entry gas temperature 1,377°C. Later to have thermal barrier coating.
LP TURBINE: Single-stage, cooled.
CONTROL SYSTEM: FADEC being developed by HAL Lucknow Division, in collaboration with DSIC Ltd.
PERFORMANCE RATINGS (flat rated to ISA +20°C, S/L):
Max: dry	50.6 kN (11,380 lb st)
with afterburning	80.07 kN (18,000 lb st)

HAL
HINDUSTAN AERONAUTICS LTD
PO Box 5150, 15/1 Cubbon Road, Bangalore 560 001
Telephone: 91 (812) 76901
OFFICERS: see Aircraft section

The Bangalore Engine and Koraput Divisions of HAL constitute the main aero engine manufacturing elements of the Indian aircraft industry.

BANGALORE COMPLEX (Engine Division)
Adour 811 engines are manufactured under Rolls-Royce Turbomeca licence. The Orpheus 701 and Dart 536-2T are manufactured under licence from Rolls-Royce. The Artouste IIIB is made under licence from Turbomeca.
KORAPUT DIVISION
This Division was established to manufacture under Soviet government licence the Tumansky R-11 afterburning turbojet. With help from the Soviet Union, the first engine

was run in early 1969. In 1977 production switched to the Soyuz/Tumansky R-25 for the MiG-21bis, followed in 1984 by the R-29B for the MiG-27M.

INTERNATIONAL PROGRAMMES

BMW ROLLS-ROYCE
See under Germany in this section.

CFM
CFM INTERNATIONAL SA
2 boulevard du Général Martial Valin, 75015 Paris, France
Telephone: 33 (1) 40 60 81 90
Fax: 33 (1) 40 60 81 47
CHAIRMAN AND CHIEF EXECUTIVE: J. Bilien
MARKETING DIRECTOR: Richard B. Shaffer

CFM International, a joint company, was formed by SNECMA (France) and General Electric (USA) in 1974 to provide management for the CFM56 programme and a single customer interface.

GE is responsible for design integration, the core engine and the main engine control. The core engine is derived from that of the F101 turbofan developed for the US military. SNECMA is responsible for the low-pressure system, gearbox, accessory integration and engine installation.

CFM INTERNATIONAL CFM56
US military designation: F108
In the late 1960s SNECMA and General Electric (now GE Aircraft Engines) concluded that a large market existed for a high bypass ratio engine in the ten ton class (97.9-106.8 kN; 22,000-24,000 lb st). The first CFM56 demonstrator ran at GE's Evendale plant on 20 June 1974.

The CFM56 designation covers a family of engines from 82.3 to 151.25 kN (18,500-34,000 lb st). By December 1990 a total of 4,300 engines had been delivered, against orders for more than 7,600. The following are current versions:

CFM56-2. Certificated 8 November 1979, under FAR Pt 33 and JAR-E, at 106.8 kN (24,000 lb st); but several applications use only a 97.9 kN (22,000 lb) T-O rating. CFM56-2 production was launched in 1979 to re-engine the DC-8-60 to Super 70 standard. Scheduled operations began on 24 April 1982 and 110 aircraft in service with 16 operators have logged more than 6,800,000 engine flight hours. Engine-caused shop visit rate is 0.14 and the dispatch reliability is 99.89 per cent. The CMF56-2 exists in several variants, differing by their ratings or configuration details.

CFM56-2A. Certificated 6 June 1985 at 106.8 kN (24,000 lb st), flat rated to 35°C (95°F), the CFM56-2A-2 powers the US Navy E-6 communications aircraft and the Royal Saudi Air Force KE-3 tanker, the E-3s for Saudi Arabia, the UK and France and the Boeing E-8A for the US Air Force and Army. These applications require long duration oiltank, reverser and gearbox for two high capacity integrated drive generators.

CFM56-2B. Certificated 25 June 1984 at 97.9 kN (22,000 lb st), flat rated to 32°C (90°F), the CFM56-2B1 was selected by the US Air Force for its KC-135A tanker re-engining programme on 22 January 1980. First flight of a KC-135R took place on 4 August 1982 and production **F108-CF-100** engines power KC-135R aircraft delivered from late 1983. CFM56-2B1 also powers the C-135FR tankers of the French Armée de l'Air.

CFM56-2C. Version of CFM56-2 for re-engining DC-8; T-O thrust of 97.9 kN (22,000 lb st), with flat rating to 30°C (86°F) in -2C1 to -2C6 subvariants.

CFM56-3B1. Derivative of CFM56-2, rated at 89.00 kN (20,000 lb st), flat rated to 30°C (86°F), with smaller fan. Powers Boeing 737-300. First ran in March 1982. US and French certification granted 12 January 1984. Entered airline service December 1984. Rerated at 82.3 kN (18,500 lb st), powers 737-500 which entered service February 1990.

CFM56-3B2. Certificated at 97.90 kN (22,000 lb st), flat rated to 30°C (86°F), on 20 June 1984. For 737-300 and 737-400 with improved payload/range from short, hot, high airfields. 737-400 entered service September 1988.

CFM56-3C1. Rated at 104.5 kN (23,500 lb st) for 737-300, -400 and -500. Certificated December 1986. Offered as common engine for all future 737 models.

By December 1990 more than 97 customers had ordered 4,034 CFM56-3 engines. Over 819 Boeing 737s in service had logged more than 13,200,000 engine flight hours. Engine-caused shop visit (12 month rolling averages) was 0.096, and dispatch reliability 99.96 per cent. All versions certificated for 120 min EROPS.

CFM56-5A1. Launched September 1984, for A320. Has fan diameter of –2, with improved aerodynamics in all LP and HP components, advanced clearance control features and FADEC. Nominal rating of 111.21 kN (25,000

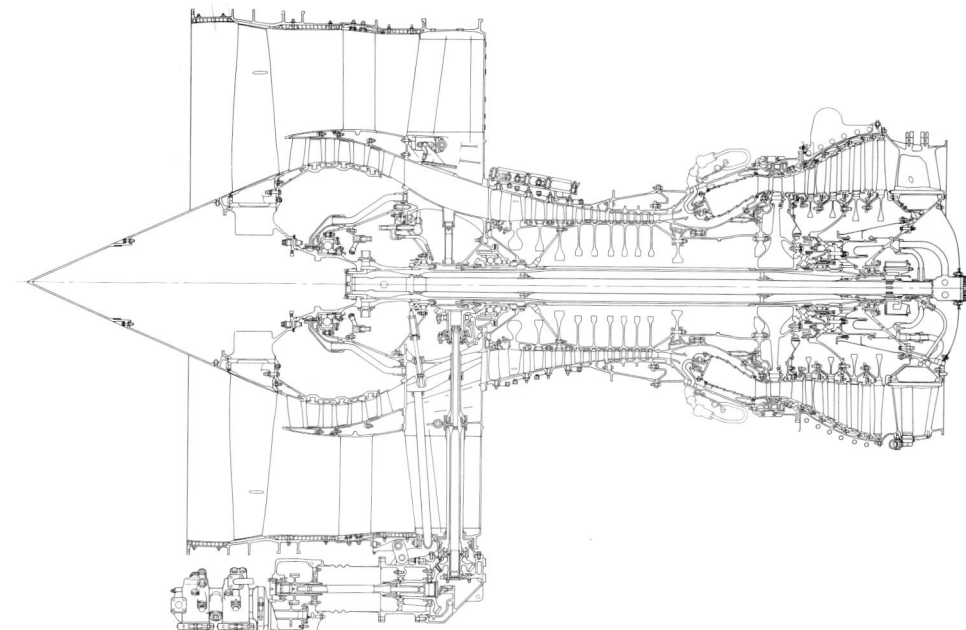

Longitudinal section of CFM56-5A1

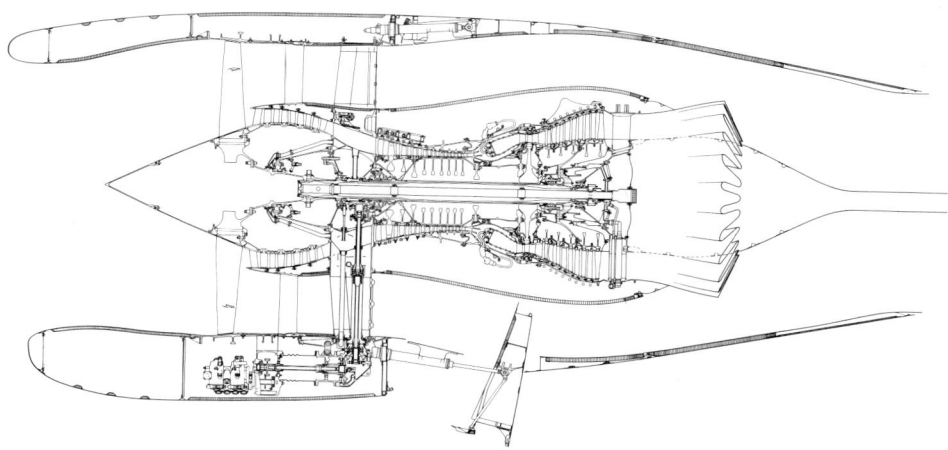

Longitudinal section of CFM56-5C complete nacelle, showing (lower half) reverser in operation

lb st), flat rated to 30°C (86°F). Certificated 27 August 1987 and entered service April 1989.

CFM56-5A3. Rated at 117.9 kN (26,500 lb st). To meet specific airline requirements for A320. Entered service December 1990.

CFM56-5B1. Four-stage LP compressor. Rated at 133.5 kN (30,000 lb st) to power A321.

CFM56-5B2. Rated at 137.9 kN (31,000 lb st) to power A321.

CFM56-5B4. Version of -5B derated to 117.9 kN (26,500 lb st); option for A320.

CFM56-5C2. Advanced fan, new four-stage LP compressor, active clearance control HP spool, new turbine section (5-stage LP, new frame, modulated clearance, new aerodynamics throughout), integrated mixer nozzle and FADEC. Rated at 138.8 kN (31,200 lb st). Powers A340, to enter service late 1992.

CFM56-5C3. Growth version rated at 144.6 kN (32,500 lb st). To enter service late 1993.

CFM56-5C4. Growth version to be rated at 151.25 kN (34,000 lb st) to provide increased range/payload capability for A340 from early 1995.

TYPE: Two-shaft subsonic turbofan.

FAN: Single-stage axial. Forged titanium disc holding (CFM56-2) 44 titanium blades, each with a tip shroud to form a continuous ring; (CFM56-3) 38 titanium blades, each with part-span shroud; (CFM56-5) 36 titanium blades, each with part-span shroud. Mass flow (-2A2) 370 kg (817 lb)/s, (-3B2) 312 kg (688 lb)/s, (-5A1) 386 kg (852 lb)/s, (-5B2) 434 kg (956 lb)/s, (-5C2) 466 kg (1,027 lb)/s. Bypass ratio (-2) 6, (-3) 5, (-5) 6, (-5C) 6.6.

LP COMPRESSOR: Three axial stages (4 on -5B and -5C), on titanium drum bolted to fan disc. A ring of bleed doors allows core airflow to escape into fan duct at low power settings.

HP COMPRESSOR: Nine-stage rotor with three stages of titanium blades and remainder of steel. Stator vanes are steel, with first four stators variable. Overall pressure ratio (-2) 25 class, (-3C) 30.6, (-5A) 31.3, (-5B) 35, (-5C2/-5C3, max climb) 37.4.

COMBUSTION CHAMBER: Machined ring, fully annular, with advanced film cooling.

HP TURBINE: Single-stage with aircooled stator and rotor airfoils, directionally solidified on -5. HP system carried in two bearings.

LP TURBINE: Four-stage (5 on -5C) with tip shrouds.

EXHAUST UNIT (FAN): Constant diameter duct of sound-absorbent construction. Outer cowl and engine cowl form convergent plug nozzle, with airframe mounted reverser.

EXHAUST UNIT (CORE): Fixed-area with convergent nozzle, mixer on -5C.

ACCESSORY DRIVE: (CFM56-2 and -5) Gearbox in front sump transmits drive from front of HP spool to transfer gearbox on underside of fan case. Air starter at transfer gearbox (-2) or accessory gearbox (-5). (CFM56-3) Side mounted accessory drive gearbox with transfer gearbox; air starter pad on accessory gearbox.

CONTROL SYSTEM: Hydromechanical with electronic trim (-2, -3); FADEC (-5).

LUBRICATION: Non-pressure-regulated system.

DIMENSIONS:

Length, excl spinner:

CFM56-2	2,430 mm (95.7 in)
CFM56-3	2,360 mm (93.0 in)
CFM56-5A1, -5A3	2,422 mm (95.4 in)
CFM56-5B1, -5B2	2,601 mm (102.4 in)
CFM56-5C	2,616 mm (103 in)

Fan diameter:

CFM56-2, -5A, -5B	1,735 mm (68.3 in)
CFM56-3	1,524 mm (60.0 in)
CFM56-5C	1,836 mm (72.3 in)

WEIGHT, DRY:

CFM56-2A2	2,187 kg (4,820 lb)
CFM56-2B1	2,120 kg (4,674 lb)
CFM56-2C series	2,102 kg (4,635 lb)
CFM56-3B1	1,940 kg (4,277 lb)
CFM56-3B2, -3C	1,951 kg (4,301 lb)
CFM56-5A1	2,259 kg (4,980 lb)
CFM56-5A3	2,266 kg (4,996 lb)
CFM56-5B1, -5B2	2,381 kg (5,250 lb)
CFM56-5C	2,492 kg (5,494 lb)

PERFORMANCE RATINGS:

Max T-O: see under model listings

Cruise, installed, 10,670 m (35,000 ft), Mach 0.8, ISA:

CFM56-2A2	25.62 kN (5,760 lb)
CFM56-2B1	22.10 kN (4,970 lb)
CFM56-2C series	22.15 kN (4,980 lb)
CFM56-3B1	20.67 kN (4,650 lb)

CFM International CFM56-5C two-shaft turbofan

CFM56-3B1 rerate	19.13 kN (4,300 lb)	CFM56-2B1	18.77 mg/Ns (0.662 lb/h/lb)
CFM56-3B2	22.42 kN (5,040 lb)	CFM56-2C series	18.44 mg/Ns (0.651 lb/h/lb)
CFM56-3C	23.88 kN (5,370 lb)	CFM56-3 (all)	18.72 mg/Ns (0.661 lb/h/lb)
CFM56-5A1, -5A3	22.23 kN (5,000 lb)	CFM56-5A1, -5A3, -5B1, -5B2	
CFM56-5B1, -5B2	25.96 kN (5,836 lb)		16.87 mg/Ns (0.596 lb/h/lb)
CFM56-5C (with mixer)	30.78 kN (6,920 lb)	CFM56-5C (with mixer)	16.06 mg/Ns (0.567 lb/h/lb)

SPECIFIC FUEL CONSUMPTION (cruise, as above):

CFM56-2A2	18.83 mg/Ns (0.665 lb/h/lb)

EUROJET

EUROJET TURBO GmbH

Arabellastrasse 13, D-8000 Munich 81, Germany
Telephone: 49 (89) 9210050
Fax: 49 (89) 92100539 and 92100562
Telex: 5212124 EJET D
MANAGING DIRECTOR: D. A. Marsh

Formed in August 1986 by a consortium of Fiat Aviazione of Italy, MTU-München GmbH of (then) West Germany, Rolls-Royce of the UK and Sener of Spain, this company became operational on 1 January 1987 as EUROJET Turbo GmbH. It was established to co-ordinate the design, development and manufacture of the EJ200 engine for the European Fighter Aircraft.

The workshare is proportional to the expected aircraft requirements of the four nations, and has been agreed as follows: Fiat (21 per cent), LP turbine and shaft, interstage support, reheat system, gearbox, oil system, and participation in the intermediate casing; MTU (33 per cent), LP compressor, HP compressor, participation in HP turbine, and FADEC (full authority digital electronic control) design responsibility; Rolls-Royce (33 per cent), combustion system, HP turbine, intermediate casing, and participation in LP and HP compressors, LP turbine, interstage support, reheat system and nozzle; Sener (13 per cent), nozzle, jetpipe, exhaust diffuser and bypass duct.

Engine build and test during development and production will be at each partner's facilities. Each partner will provide comprehensive support for engines of its own national air force. The initial requirement of the four nations is for nearly 800 aircraft, including about 2,000 engines. The contract for full scale development was signed in November 1988. In the same month the first Design Verification Engine began running at MTU.

EJ200 engine DV02 on test at Fiat, Turin

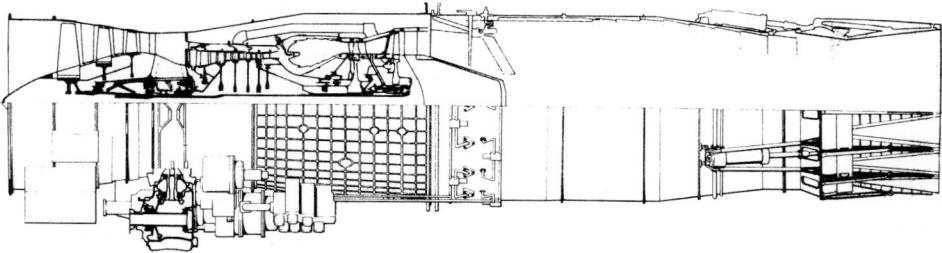

Longitudinal half-section through the EUROJET EJ200 two-shaft augmented turbofan

EUROJET EJ200

This engine will be an advanced turbofan designed for Mach numbers of about 2. It is fully modular, and allows for on-condition maintenance with built-in engine health monitoring and test equipment. Low maintenance and life-cycle cost along with high reliability have been prime design criteria. The total number of aerofoils is only approximately 60 per cent of those used in the RB199. The EJ200 programme has achieved all technical milestones on time and cost. This includes 150 h of accelerated mission endurance testing at full temperature rating. Entry into service is expected to be in 1996.

TYPE: Two-shaft augmented turbofan.

LP COMPRESSOR: Three stages, with 3-D transonic blades of robust large-chord section. No inlet guide vanes. Third stage blisks. Overhung ahead of high-capacity ball bearing and forward roller bearing. Bypass ratio about 0.4. Pressure ratio 4-plus.

HP COMPRESSOR: Five stages, with first-stage variable inlet guide vanes and blisk rotor stage. Shaft supported between front ball and rear roller bearings. Overall pressure ratio more than 25.

COMBUSTOR: Fully annular, with vaporising burners.

HP TURBINE: Single-stage, with powder metallurgy disc and low density aircooled single crystal blades.

LP TURBINE: Single-stage, with powder metallurgy disc and single crystal blades. Both turbine bearings in single interstage support frame.

EXHAUST SYSTEM: High efficiency augmentor of burn-then-mix type, with fully variable convergent-divergent nozzle.

ACCESSORIES: Central gearbox driven via tower shaft in interstage support. Full authority digital electronic control. Integrated health monitoring system. Rotating-tank oil system to give artificial positive gravity at all times.

DIMENSIONS: Smaller throughout than RB199.

WEIGHT: In 1,000 kg (2,000 lb) class.

PERFORMANCE RATING: In 90 kN (20,000 lb st) class.

IAE

INTERNATIONAL AERO ENGINES AG

OFFICES: Corporate Center II, 628 Hebron Avenue, Glastonbury, Connecticut 06033, USA
Telephone: 1 (203) 652 1800
Fax: 1 (203) 659 1410
Telex: 4436031 INTLAERO
PRESIDENT: Roland P. Dilda
EXECUTIVE VICE-PRESIDENT: J. M. S. Keen
VICE-PRESIDENT, BUSINESS: Phillip Aldred
VICE-PRESIDENT, MARKETING: C. R. Nelson
PUBLIC RELATIONS MANAGER: Robert Nuttall

IAE is a management company set up on 14 December 1983 to direct the entire programme for the V2500 turbofan worldwide. The following shareholders signed a 30-year agreement: Rolls-Royce, UTC (P&W), Japanese Aero Engines (IHI, KHI, MHI), MTU and Fiat Avio. Responsibility for each module is allocated according to shareholding. Overall engineering direction is delegated to Pratt & Whitney. Rolls-Royce manages the nacelle programme. Engines are assembled and tested by Pratt & Whitney and Rolls-Royce.

JAEC is responsible for the fan (derived from 535E4) and LP compressor, Rolls-Royce for the HP compressor, Pratt & Whitney for the combustor and HP turbine, MTU for the LP turbine and Fiat for the gearbox. Turbines, gearbox and FADEC use PW2000 technology.

IAE V2500

V2500-A1. In service on the A320. IAE supplies the complete package, including the nacelle (by Rohr/Shorts). Testing of the engine began in December 1985. A flight programme on a Boeing 720B in Canada was completed in 35 h in Spring 1988, and every ingestion and fan-blade-off test was passed first time (believed an industry record). The first pair of propulsion systems was delivered to Airbus Industrie in March 1988, and the V2500 was certificated in June 1988.

The first V2500-powered A320 made its first flight on 28 July 1988. The aircraft entered service with Adria Airways in May 1989.

Subsequent development to higher thrust is being achieved by increasing the core airflow and aerodynamic changes. Pressure ratio of the LP compressor is increased by adding a fourth stage. All engines in the A (Airbus) and D (Douglas) series have common fans and cores, and fit into a common nacelle which for the MD-90 is modified for fuselage side mounting.

V2522-D5. Rated at 99.79 kN (22,000 lb st). Four-stage LP compressor, as in all A5 and D5 versions. Bypass ratio 4.9. Pressure ratio 24.9. For MD90-10.

V2525-A5. Flat rated at 111.25 kN (25,000 lb st). Bypass ratio 4.8. Pressure ratio 27.7. For A320.

V2525-D5. Flat rated at 111.25 kN (25,000 lb st). Bypass ratio 4.8. Pressure ratio 27.7. For MD90-30.

V2528-D5. Rated at 124.55 kN (28,000 lb st). Bypass ratio 4.7. Pressure ratio 30.4. For MD90-40.

V2530-A5. Rated at 133.4 kN (30,000 lb st). Bypass ratio 4.6. Pressure ratio 32.5. For A321.

By 1 February 1991 a total of 22 customers had specified the V2500 for 649 aircraft, comprising 402 A320/321s and 247 MD-90s.

IAE V2500 two-shaft turbofan

The primary features of the V2500-A1 are as follows:

TYPE: Two-spool subsonic turbofan.

FAN: Single-stage with wide-chord shroudless blading. Diameter 1,600 mm (63.0 in). Pressure ratio 1.70. Bypass ratio 5.42. Mass flow 355 kg (783 lb)/s.

LP COMPRESSOR: Three stages, bolted to rear of fan to boost inlet to core. (Four stages in A5 and D5 versions.)

HP COMPRESSOR: Ten stages of blading supported by a drum rotor. Inlet guide and first three vane stages variable. Overall pressure ratio 29.4.

COMBUSTOR: Annular segmented construction eliminates hoop stresses and provides low emissions and uniform exit temperatures.

HP TURBINE: Two stages of aircooled single-crystal blading in powder metallurgy discs. Active tip clearance control.

LP TURBINE: Five stages of uncooled blading in welded and bolted rotor. Active clearance control.

GEARBOX: Modular unit, fan-case mounted.

CONTROL SYSTEM: Full authority digital electronic control (FADEC) to provide command outputs for engine fuel flow, stator vane angle, bleed modulation, turbine and exhaust case cooling, oil cooling, ignition and reverser functions. Supplied by Hamilton Standard.

NACELLE: Full length nacelle with reverser. Cowl load sharing to minimise case deflections. Acoustically treated.

DIMENSIONS:
Length (flange to flange)	3,200 mm (126 in)
Fan diameter	1,600 mm (63 in)

WEIGHT, DRY (with original single-stage LP compressor):
Bare engine	2,242 kg (4,942 lb)
Complete power plant, incl nacelle	3,311 kg (7,300 lb)

PERFORMANCE RATINGS (installed):
T-O, S/L, ISA 111.25 kN (25,000 lb st) to ISA + 15°C
Cruise Mach 0.8, 10,670 m (35,000 ft) 21.6 kN (4,850 lb)

SPECIFIC FUEL CONSUMPTION (Cruise Mach 0.8, 10,670 m; 35,000 ft, installed) 16.29 mg/Ns (0.575 lb/h/lb)

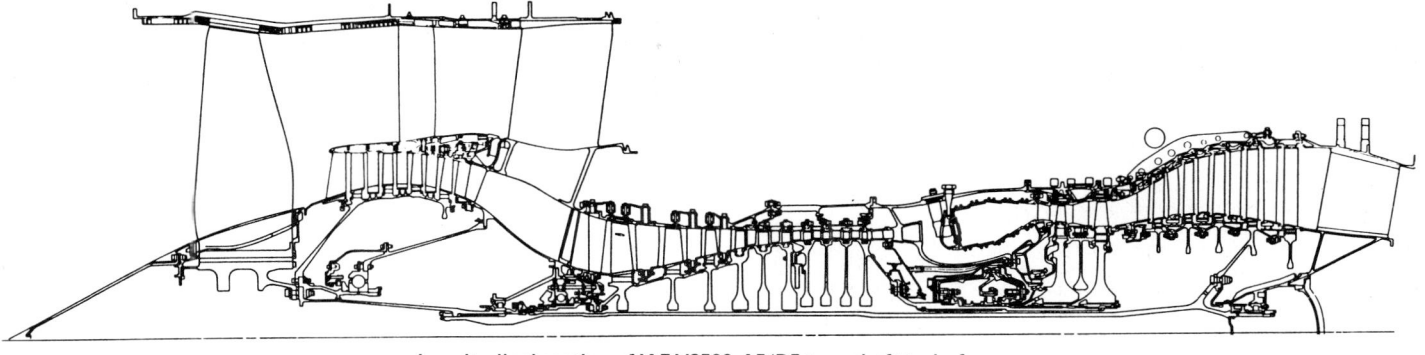

Longitudinal section of IAE V2500-A5/D5 two-shaft turbofan

MTR

MTU-TURBOMECA-ROLLS-ROYCE GmbH

Arabellastrasse 13, D-8000 Munich 81, Germany
Telephone: 49 (89) 910 2017
Fax: 49 (89) 910 1543

MTR 390

This turboshaft engine is being developed by a joint company owned equally by MTU, Turbomeca and Rolls-Royce. The engine was selected to power the Franco-German Tiger anti-tank and escort/support helicopters. The engine is suitable for military and civil applications in helicopters and fixed-wing aircraft in the form of single and twin installations.

The main characteristics of the modular engine are: ample emergency power reserve for OEI operation, high alternating output shaft power capability, low fuel consumption under part load, good acceleration, low life-cycle cost, easy handling and simple maintenance. It has a high performance FADEC and an engine monitoring system for flight and maintenance crew support.

Design studies have been extended to derivatives for other applications. A 6,000 rpm drive version (MTR 390L) and a direct-drive version (MTR 390T) have been defined.

First run took place at MTU in December 1989, and the first flight engines for the first Tiger prototypes were delivered in September 1990. First flights in a Dauphin testbed and the prototype Tiger helicopter were to follow in 1991.

TYPE: Free-turbine turboshaft.

COMPRESSOR: Two centrifugal stages for erosion and FOD resistance. Mass flow 3.2 kg (7.05 lb)/s. Pressure ratio 13.

COMBUSTION CHAMBER: Annular reverse-flow, with airblast fuel injectors for low emissions.

HP TURBINE: Single-stage gas generator turbine with high performance blade cooling, single-crystal blades and powder-metal disc.

LP TURBINE: Two-stage free power turbine with shrouded blades.

GEARBOX: Reduces the speed of the power turbine to the output shaft speed of 8,000 rpm. The accessory gearbox in the upper part provides the support and drive for the front and top mounted engine equipment.

CONTROL SYSTEM: A FADEC, with engine monitoring system.

LUBRICATION SYSTEM: Integral oil system, with engine-mounted tank and oil cooler with fan.

DIMENSIONS:
Length overall	1,078 mm (42.4 in)
Width overall	442 mm (17.4 in)
Height overall	682 mm (26.9 in)

WEIGHT, DRY: 169 kg (372.6 lb)

PERFORMANCE RATINGS (uninstalled, ISA, S/L):
Super contingency (OEI, 20 s)	1,160 kW (1,556 shp)
T-O	958 kW (1,285 shp)
Max continuous	873 kW (1,171 shp)

SPECIFIC FUEL CONSUMPTION:
T-O	75.88 µg/J (0.449 lb/h/shp)
Max continuous	76.73 µg/J (0.454 lb/h/shp)

Cutaway drawing of MTR 390 turboshaft

PROGRESS/LOTAREV/ZVL

PROGRESS/LOTAREV (ZMKB): see under USSR
ZVL: see under Czechoslovakia

The DV-2 turbofan is a joint programme by these two organisations. It is described under Progress.

ROLLS-ROYCE SATURN

ROLLS-ROYCE: see under UK
LYULKA: see under Saturn/Lyulka in USSR

It was announced on 16 May 1990 that a preliminary agreement has been signed between Rolls-Royce, the Lyulka (Saturn) engine design bureau and the Sukhoi aircraft design bureau which is intended to lead to the joint development of an engine for a supersonic business jet. By May 1991 the two engine teams were to have determined the engine configuration and main characteristics. Further progress will then depend on a business evaluation, finance, and the approval of the two governments to launch the programme.

ROLLS-ROYCE TURBOMECA

ROLLS-ROYCE TURBOMECA LIMITED
4/5 Grosvenor Place, London SW1X 7HH, England
Telephone: 44 (71) 235 3641
Fax: 44 (71) 245 6385
Telex: 918944

This joint company was formed in June 1966 to control design, development and production programmes for the Adour two-shaft turbofan.

In 1980 Rolls-Royce Turbomeca launched the RTM 321 turboshaft demonstrator, leading to the RTM 322.

ROLLS-ROYCE TURBOMECA ADOUR
US military designation: F405

The Adour was designed for the SEPECAT Jaguar. The whole engine is simple and robust and of modular design.

Bench testing began at Derby on 9 May 1967. Engines for Jaguars were assembled at Derby (RR) and Tarnos (Turbomeca) from parts made at single sources in Britain and France. Turbomeca makes the compressors, casings and external pipework (to preserve Anglo-French parity the afterburner is subcontracted to SNECMA); Rolls-Royce makes the remainder.

Following selection of the Adour for the Mitsubishi T-2 trainer and F-1 fighter/support aircraft, Ishikawajima-Harima Heavy Industries has been producing the Adour since 1970 under a licence agreement. In 1972 a non-afterburning Adour was selected to power the British Aerospace Hawk advanced trainer. More than 2,300 engines have been produced, including licence manufacture in Japan, India and Finland. Flight hours exceed 3.5 million.

Current versions of the engine are as follows:

Mk 102. Original production engine for Jaguars in service with RAF and Armée de l'Air. Qualified in 1972.

Mk 104. Uprated RT172-26 version similar to Mk 804; RAF Mk 102 engines were converted to this standard.

Mk 151. Non-afterburning version for Hawk. Internal components and certification temperatures identical to Mk 102 and Mk 801A. Qualified in 1975.

Mk 801A. Japanese designation TF40-IHI-801A. For Mitsubishi T-2 and F-1. Qualified in 1972. (See Ishikawajima-Harima in Japanese section.)

Mk 804. Uprated engine for Jaguar International. Rating with full afterburner at Mach 0.9 at S/L, ISA, increased by 27 per cent. Qualified in 1976.

Mk 811. Uprated version for Jaguar International. Revised compressor aerodynamics and hot-end improvements. Assembled by Hindustan Aeronautics, with increasing Indian manufactured content.

Mk 815C. Mk 804 uprated to Mk 811 performance level by conversion at overhaul.

Mk 851. Non-afterburning version of Mk 804 for export Hawk.

Cutaway drawing of Rolls-Royce Turbomeca Adour 871 turbofan

Mk 861. Non-afterburning version of Mk 811, first deliveries 1981.

Mk 861-49. US designation **F405-RR-400.** Derated version of Mk 861, for prototype McDD/BAe T-45A Goshawk for US Navy. Certificated 1988.

Mk 871. Uprated version for BAe Hawk Series 100 and 200. Certificated late 1990.

F405-RR-401. US version of Mk 871 with minor changes for production T-45A Goshawk.

The following refers to non-afterburning versions, except where indicated:

TYPE: Two-shaft turbofan for subsonic aircraft.

FAN: Two-stage. Full length bypass duct. Bypass ratio, 0.75-0.80.

COMPRESSOR: Five stages. Overall pressure ratio 11 : 1.

COMBUSTION CHAMBER: Annular, with 18 air spray fuel nozzles and two igniter plugs. Lucas engine fuel system.

HP TURBINE: Single-stage, aircooled.

LP TURBINE: Single-stage. Squeeze-film bearings.

DIMENSIONS:
Length overall:	
Mks 102, 801A, 804, 811	2,970 mm (117 in)
Mks 151, 851, 861, 861-49, 871	1,956 mm (77 in)
Inlet diameter (all)	559 mm (22 in)
Max width (all)	762 mm (30 in)
Max height (all)	1,041 mm (41 in)

WEIGHT, DRY:
Mk 102, 801A	704 kg (1,552 lb)
Mk 104, 804	713 kg (1,571 lb)
Mk 151	553 kg (1,220 lb)
Mk 851	568 kg (1,252 lb)
Mk 861	577 kg (1,273 lb)
Mk 811	738 kg (1,627 lb)
Mk 871	603 kg (1,330 lb)

PERFORMANCE RATINGS (S/L T-O):
Mk 102, 801A	32.5 kN (7,305 lb st)*
Mk 104	35.1 kN (7,900 lb st)*
Mk 151, 851	23.1 kN (5,200 lb st)
Mk 804	35.8 kN (8,040 lb st)*
Mk 861	25.4 kN (5,700 lb st)
Mk 861-49	24.2 kN (5,450 lb st)
Mk 811	37.4 kN (8,400 lb st)*
Mk 871	26.2 kN (5,900 lb st)

With afterburner

SPECIFIC FUEL CONSUMPTION (Mk 102):
S/L static, dry	21 mg/Ns (0.74 lb/h/lb st)
Mach 0.8, 11,890 m (39,000 ft)	27 mg/Ns (0.955 lb/h/lb st)

ROLLS-ROYCE TURBOMECA RTM 322

Rolls-Royce and Turbomeca combined their extensive experience in helicopter gas turbines to produce the RTM 322 family of engines. Since 1986, Piaggio of Italy has been a 10 per cent participant. The launch engine is the RTM 322-01 turboshaft, which is conservatively rated at 1,566 kW (2,100 shp) with easy growth potential to 2,237 kW (3,000 shp).

The family, which will include turboprop and turbofan derivatives, is configured to combine simple design, reliability, low fuel consumption, light weight and low cost of ownership. A turboprop using the RTM 322-01 core would produce 1,193-1,491 kW (1,600-2,000 shp), with potential for growth to 2,088 kW (2,800 shp). It is therefore suitable for aircraft in the 35-70 seat range.

The turboshaft itself has full-authority digital electronic control, availability of different output drive configurations, a choice of three starting systems, and options for an inlet particle separator and infra-red suppressor. Combined with engine mounts configured for compatibility with a number of existing airframes, these features give the unit a wide range of potential civil and military applications in the 7 to 15 tonne class. Examples are: EH 101, Sikorsky Black Hawk and Seahawk series, European NH 90, Westland WS-70 and AH-64 Apache. The engine has been studied by the US Army as a potential growth power plant for the Black Hawk and Apache, and during 1987 the US Navy carried out an operability study in an SH-60B. In 1985 UTC (Pratt & Whitney) signed a licence agreement for US and Canadian markets.

In 1988 a major competition was held between Rolls-Royce Turbomeca and General Electric for the production engine contract of all UK EH 101 helicopters. In September 1988 the Minister of Defence Procurement announced that Rolls-Royce Turbomeca had won this competition for approximately 500 engines, as it provided 'the best value for money'. The first flight on the EH 101 is planned for 1992.

The first complete RTM 322-01 ran on 4 February 1985. Over 1,790 kW (2,400 shp) has been demonstrated. A total of over 10,000 hours running have been completed, which includes 1,100 hours of flight development in the S-70C (from 14 June 1986) and then in the SH-60B. UK military certification was completed in October 1988, and was to be followed by civil certification in 1991.

The following particulars apply to the RTM 322-01 turboshaft:

COMPRESSOR: Three-stage axial and single-stage centrifugal.
COMBUSTOR: Annular reverse flow. Ignition by Lucas Aerospace exciter.

Rolls-Royce Turbomeca RTM 322-01 turboshaft

TURBINES: Two-stage gas generator turbine. Cooling is applied to the 1st and 2nd stage stators and 1st stage rotor. The 2nd stage rotor is made of single crystal material and is uncooled. Two-stage power turbine with drive to front or rear.
DIMENSIONS:

Length overall	1,171 mm (46 in)
Diameter	604 mm (23.8 in)

WEIGHT, DRY:	240 kg (538 lb)
PERFORMANCE RATINGS (S/L):	
Max contingency	1,724 kW (2,312 shp)
Max T-O	1,566 kW (2,100 shp)
Typical cruise	940 kW (1,260 shp)
SPECIFIC FUEL CONSUMPTION:	
Cruise (as above)	81 µg/J (0.48 lb/shp/h)

TURBO-UNION

TURBO-UNION LTD
PO Box 3, Filton, Bristol BS12 7QE, England
Telephone: 44 (272) 791234
Fax: 44 (272) 797575
Telex: 44185 RR BSLG
MUNICH OFFICE: Arabellastrasse 13, D-8000 Munich 81, Germany
Telephone: 49 (89) 9242 1
Fax: 49 (89) 915870
Telex: 524151 TUD
CHAIRMAN: Dr G. C. Boffetta
MANAGING DIRECTOR: Kurt Münzenmaier

Formed in 1969 as a European engine consortium comprising Rolls-Royce plc (40 per cent) of the United Kingdom, MTU Motoren-und Turbinen-Union München GmbH (40 per cent) of Germany and Fiat Avio SpA (20 per cent) of Italy. The consortium was established to design, develop, manufacture and support the RB199 turbofan for the Panavia Tornado aircraft.

TURBO-UNION RB199
The RB199 is a three-spool turbofan offering low fuel consumption for long-range dry cruise and approximately 100 per cent thrust augmentation with full afterburner for short take-off, combat manoeuvre and supersonic acceleration. An integral thrust reverser system is available. It was the first military engine with FADEC without hydromechanical backup.

In-service experience of over 1,400,000 flying hours, at low level in the most arduous conditions, has proven the resilience of the RB199 to birdstrike and foreign object damage (FOD). This is a direct result of the relatively short, rigid rotating assemblies held between the small bearing spans in a three-spool layout.

Over 2,400 engines have been produced, with the present engine family comprising:

Mk 103. Standard production engine, with integral thrust reverser, for Panavia Tornado IDS variants.

Mk 104. Identical to the Mk 103 other than the jetpipe, which is extended by 360 mm (14 in) to provide up to 10 per cent greater thrust and reduced specific fuel consumption. The Mk 104 is the standard production engine for Tornado ADV variants.

Mk 104D. The power plant for the BAe experimental aircraft programme (EAP) advanced technology demonstrator.

Mk 104E. Selected as the interim engine for the European Fighter Aircraft (EFA) programme, the RB199 will be used to conduct flight test work on early EFA prototypes.

Mk 105. Similar to the Mk 103, the Mk 105 incorporates an increased mass flow LP compressor producing higher pressure ratios, and single-crystal HP turbine blades. In addition to a 10 per cent thrust increase, these improvements also give significant reductions in life-cycle cost. In service as the power plant for the Tornado ECR.

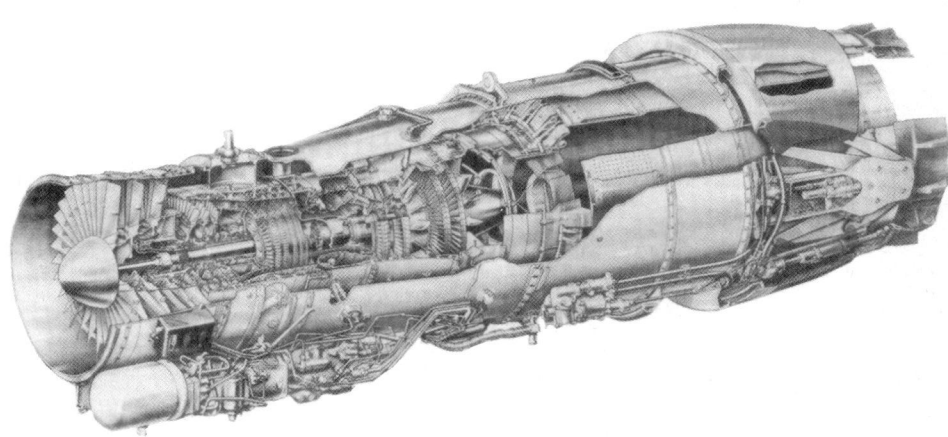

Cutaway drawing of Turbo-Union RB199 Mk 104 three-shaft augmented turbofan

The following description refers to the Mk 105:
TYPE: Three-shaft turbofan with afterburner and reverser.
LP COMPRESSOR: Three-stage axial of titanium alloy. Casing of three bolted sections. Rotor of three discs welded together. Rotor blades secured by dovetail roots, all with snubbers. Mass flow approx 74.6 kg (164 lb)/s. Bypass ratio about 1:1.
IP COMPRESSOR: Three stages of titanium alloy. Rotor has welded discs in which blades are secured by dovetails.
HP COMPRESSOR: Six-stage; material changes from titanium at front to heat resisting alloy at rear, except stator blades are heat resisting steel throughout. Rotor discs secured by ten through-bolts, carrying blades by dovetail roots. Bevel drive to gearbox. Overall pressure ratio greater than 23.
BYPASS DUCT: Fabricated in titanium.
COMBUSTION CHAMBER: Annular flame tube fabricated from nickel alloy, bolted at rear end between outer casing, forged and chemically milled in nickel-iron alloy, and inner casing of nickel alloy. Carries 13 double-headed fuel vaporisers which give combustion without visible smoke. Two igniter plugs. Hot-streak injector for afterburner ignition.
HP TURBINE: Shrouded single stage. Entry temperature over 1,327°C. Rotor blades and stator vanes aircooled.
IP TURBINE: Shrouded single stage. Aircooled stator vanes and rotor blades.
LP TURBINE: Two-stage with shrouded hollow uncooled rotor blades.
AFTERBURNER: Front end of titanium fabricated jetpipe carries afterburner in which bypass air and core gas burn concurrently, without a mixing section. For core flow, two gutter flameholders fed by upstream atomisers. For bypass flow, reverse colander with radial extensions, each containing vaporising primary burner, between which multiple jets inject remainder of afterburner fuel. Fully modulated augmentation.

NOZZLE: Variable area, short petal, convergent nozzle operated by shroud actuated by four screwjacks, driven by fourth stage HP air motor via flexible shafting. Each of 14 master and 14 secondary petals is precision cast in cobalt alloy which minimises friction.
REVERSER: External two bucket type driven via flexible shafts by motor using HP air. In stowed position outer skins form aircraft profile. Deployment takes 1 s at any thrust setting from idle to max dry.
ACCESSORY DRIVES: Accessory gearbox on underside of intermediate casing (quick attach/detach coupling) carries hydromechanical portions of main and afterburner fuel systems, oil tank and pump, and output shaft to aircraft gearbox carrying KHD gas turbine starter/APU.
FUEL SYSTEM: Electronic main engine control unit uses signals from pilot's lever and power plant sensors. Afterburner fuel from engine driven vapour core pump.
DIMENSIONS:

Length overall: Mk 103	3,251 mm (128 in)
Mk 104	3,607 mm (142 in)
Mk 105	3,302 mm (130 in)
Intake diameter: Mk 103	719 mm (28.3 in)
Mk 104	719 mm (28.3 in)
Mk 105	752 mm (29.6 in)
WEIGHT, DRY (excl reverser):	
Mk 103	965 kg (2,107 lb)
Mk 104	976 kg (2,151 lb)
Mk 105	980 kg (2,160 lb)
PERFORMANCE RATINGS (S/L, ISA):	
Max dry: Mk 103	40.48 kN (9,100 lb st)
Mk 104	40.48 kN (9,100 lb st)
Mk 105	42.95 kN (9,656 lb st)
Max afterburning: Mk 103	71.17 kN (16,000 lb st)
Mk 104	72.95 kN (16,400 lb st)
Mk 105	74.73 kN (16,800 lb st)

ISRAEL

BSEL
BET-SHEMESH ENGINES LTD
Mobile Post Haela, Bet-Shemesh 99000
Telephone: 972 (2) 911661-6
Fax: 972 (2) 911970 or 915117
Telex: 25590 BSENG IL

Bet-Shemesh Engines is partly owned by the Israeli Government. Its 400 employees produce Turbomeca Marboré VI and Bet-Shemesh Sorek 4 turbojets (not included as it powers missiles and UAVs) and parts for the F100, J52, J79 and JT8. Support is provided for the Allison 250, F100, J79, Marboré and PW1120. There is an important investment casting division. BSEL is one of the few companies with experience of the F100 upgrading programme to the 220-E version.

IAI
ISRAEL AIRCRAFT INDUSTRIES LTD
Ben-Gurion International Airport, 70100
Telephone: 972 (3) 97131111
Fax: 972 (3) 972290
Telex: ISRAV-IL 371133

The Engine Overhaul Plant is part of IAI's Bedek Aviation Division. It produces J79 engines and performs extensive overhaul and maintenance of civil and military engines.

J79-IAI-J1E
The J79-IAI-J1E powers the IAI Kfir and is produced by IAI under GE licence. It is a J79-GE-19 incorporating 102 per cent engine speed at high aircraft Mach number, smokeless combustors, and a T_5 reset for fast acceleration. Accessories and gearboxes are relocated, and a titanium heatshield covers the afterburner. A Combat Plus system increases T-O thrust from 78.9 kN (17,750 lb) to 83.4 kN (18,750 lb).

Details of the J79 can be found in the 1978-79 edition of *Jane's*.

Data for the J1E include:	
MASS FLOW:	77.1 kg (170 lb)/s
PRESSURE RATIO:	12.4
DIMENSIONS:	
Max diameter	995.7 mm (39.2 in)
Length	5,283 mm (208 in)
WEIGHT, DRY:	1,699 kg (3,746 lb)
MAX RATINGS (T-O, S/L):	
With augmentation	83.4 kN (18,750 lb st)
Dry	49.4 kN (11,110 lb st)

ITALY

ALFA ROMEO AVIO
ALFA ROMEO AVIO SpA
80038 Pomigliano D'Arco, Naples
Telephone: 39 (81) 8430111
Telex: 710083 ARAVIO
CHAIRMAN: Gen Fulvio Ristori
MANAGING DIRECTOR: Ing Filippo De Luca

Alfa Romeo Avio was prime contractor for the manufacture, under General Electric licence, of the J85, J79 and T58. It manufactures CF6 combustors and JT9D components, and assembles PT6T engines for the AB 212. Under GE licence it is responsible for the hot section of the T64-P4D, co-produced with Fiat, and participates in the RB199. The company is a partner in Italian production of the Rolls-Royce Spey 807. In November 1988 it became a 6.4 per cent partner in the Rolls-Royce Tay programme.

In February 1986 it began deliveries of GE T700-401 engines for EH 101 prototypes. It supplies components for T700 engines fitted to American helicopters and is developing new versions. It is also involved, with Fiat, in the development of the GE CT7-6, aimed at the EH 101, NH 90 and a new version of the A 129.

ALFA ROMEO AVIO AR.318
Alfa Romeo Avio is developing this simple turboprop to cover powers from 298 to 596 kW (400-800 shp). The programme draws upon Rolls-Royce under a contract for technical support. RAI (Italian civil) certification was achieved in April 1985, and production engines with FAA certification are now available.

TYPE: Single-shaft turboprop.
REDUCTION GEAR: Epicyclic, driven by muff coupling from compressor forward shaft. Accessory gear train driven from first reduction stage. Phase displacement torque-meter and torque/speed sensing unit.
COMPRESSOR: Single-stage centrifugal. Pressure ratio 5.4.
COMBUSTION CHAMBER: Annular reverse flow type, with eight T shape vaporiser tubes. Two igniters and three starter spray nozzles.
TURBINE: Two-stage axial. Each IGV row is a one-piece investment casting. Rotors and blades are integral solid castings, joined by a curvic coupling.

Alfa Romeo Avio AR.318 single-shaft turboprop

OIL SYSTEM: One pressure and two scavenge pumps. Provision for engine mounted tank, fuel heater and temperature/pressure transducers.
FUEL SYSTEM: Single assembly of filters, pumps, metering and overspeed protection. Optional beta control, top temperature and torque limiting, and autofeather.
FUEL GRADE: JP-1, JP-4.

DIMENSIONS:	
Length	1,061 mm (41.8 in)
Width	534 mm (21.0 in)
Height	658 mm (25.9 in)

WEIGHT, DRY:	140.6 kg (310 lb)
PERFORMANCE RATINGS (S/L, ISA):	
T-O (no time limit)	453 kW (608 shp)
Max continuous	420 kW (564 shp)
Cruise	394 kW (529 shp)
SPECIFIC FUEL CONSUMPTION:	
T-O	97.7 µg/J (0.578 lb/h/shp)
Max continuous	99.2 µg/J (0.587 lb/h/shp)
Cruise	102.4 µg/J (0.606 lb/h/shp)

ARROW
ARROW snc
Via Badiaschi 25, 29100 Piacenza
Telephone: 39 (523) 41932
Fax: 39 (523) 34367
Telex: 530112 CC PC1
CHAIRMAN: Tullio Osellini
ENGINEERING MANAGER: G. Polidoro

This company produces modular aircooled piston engines for microlights and homebuilts. In 1985 Arrow powered the winners of the French ULM championship and the Grande Course for two-seat microlights.

ARROW GT250
Single-cylinder geared two-stroke. Cast light alloy cylinder with ceramic coated interior. Bore 74.6 mm (2.94 in). Stroke 57.0 mm (2.24 in). Capacity 250 cc (15.25 cu in). Induction through 36 mm Dell'Orto carburettor of 100 grade fuel mixed with 2 per cent oil. Electric starter and 12V electronic ignition with one or two plugs. Planetary reduction gear of 0.335 ratio.

DIMENSIONS:	
Length	460 mm (18.12 in)
Width	370 mm (14.60 in)
Height	380 mm (15.0 in)

Arrow GT250 single-cylinder engine

WEIGHT, READY TO RUN:	26.0 kg (57.26 lb)
PERFORMANCE RATING:	25.33 kW (34 hp) at 6,800 rpm
FUEL CONSUMPTION:	4 to 6 litres (1.06-1.58 US gallons; 0.88-1.32 Imp gallons)/h

ARROW GT500
This is the opposed-twin version of the GT250. A 38 mm carburettor is used.

Arrow GT500 two-cylinder engine

DIMENSIONS:	
Length	500 mm (19.65 in)
Width	500 mm (19.65 in)
Height	451 mm (17.70 in)
WEIGHT, READY TO RUN:	36.0 kg (79.3 lb)
PERFORMANCE RATING:	48.5 kW (65 hp) at 6,800 rpm
FUEL CONSUMPTION:	6 to 10 litres (1.58-2.64 US gallons; 1.32-2.20 Imp gallons)/h

ARROW GT1000

This is the flat-four version, using the same cylinders as in the foregoing engines. Two 38 mm carburettors are fitted.

DIMENSIONS:
Length	521 mm (20.45 in)
Width	500 mm (19.65 in)
Height	451 mm (17.70 in)
WEIGHT, READY TO RUN:	54.0 kg (119 lb)
PERFORMANCE RATING:	82 kW (110 hp) at 6,200 rpm
FUEL CONSUMPTION:	8 to 14 litres (2.11-3.70 US gallons; 1.76-3.08 Imp gallons)/h

ARROW GT654

This is a 90° V twin four-stroke based on the Moto Guzzi V65 motorcycle engine. The light alloy cylinders have Nicasil liners. Bore 80.0 mm (3.15 in). Stroke 64.0 mm (2.52 in). Capacity 650 cc (39.66 cu in). Fuel is 100 mogas fed through twin 30 mm Dell'Orto carburettors. A 12V starter is fitted, and the planetary geared drive has a ratio of 0.335.

DIMENSIONS:
Length	702 mm (27.6 in)

Arrow GT1000 four-cylinder engine

Arrow GT654 V-twin engine

Width	431 mm (17.0 in)
Height	460 mm (18.12 in)
WEIGHT, READY TO RUN:	60.0 kg (132 lb)

PERFORMANCE RATING:	41.0 kW (55 hp) at 6,500 rpm
FUEL CONSUMPTION:	4 to 6 litres (1.06-1.58 US gallons; 0.88-1.32 Imp gallons)/h

CRM

CRM

Via Manzoni 12, 20121 Milan
Telephone: 39 (02) 708326

This company is famous for high-speed diesel engines for patrol boats and yachts, derived from the Isotta-Fraschini Asso 1000 W-18 aero engine of 1928. One version has been selected by the US Navy for the Sentinel 5000 airship.

CRM 18D/SS

This engine is a four-stroke turbocharged diesel. It has 18 cylinders in W formation, three banks of six, with precombustion chambers.

CYLINDERS: Water-cooled. Bore 150 mm (5.91 in). Stroke 180 mm (7.09 in). Capacity 57,260 cc (3,495 cu in). Compression ratio 16.25. Two turbochargers.

DIMENSIONS:
Length	3,370 mm (132.68 in)
Width	1,350 mm (53.15 in)
Height	1,304 mm (51.34 in)
WEIGHT, DRY:	about 1,700 kg (3,745 lb)
PERFORMANCE RATING:	1,380 kW (1,850 hp) at 2,100 rpm

CRM 18D/SS 18-cylinder diesel engine

FIAT

FIAT AVIAZIONE SpA

Via Nizza 312, 10127 Turin
Telephone: 39 (11) 69311
Telex: 221320 FIATAV
MANAGING DIRECTOR: P. Torricelli

Fiat Aviazione's main aircraft engine programmes now concern the IAE V2500, Turbo-Union RB199, Rolls-Royce Spey 807 and Viper 600, Pratt & Whitney PW2037/2040 and PW4000, and General Electric CF6 (including CF6-80C2), CT7 and T64. It is a partner in EUROJET Turbo. Fiat Aviazione makes the FA150-Argo APU for the AMX, transmissions for Aerospatiale helicopters and many other aviation products.

EUROJET TURBO EJ200

Fiat is responsible for 21 per cent of this programme. Its duties include design, development and manufacture of the LP turbine and shaft, rear bearing support, gearbox, oil tank and pump, afterburner and some accessories including the nozzle control unit and part of the DECU software.

TURBO-UNION RB199

Fiat holds 20 per cent of the shares of Turbo-Union Ltd. Its responsibility is the LP turbine and shaft, exhaust diffuser, jetpipe and nozzle.

IAE V2500

The V2500 is being developed by the IAE consortium. Fiat is responsible for the accessory gearbox, oil tank and pumps, exhaust case and No. 5 bearing compartment.

ROLLS-ROYCE SPEY 807

This turbofan is produced for the AMX, under a Rolls-Royce licence to the Italian government, by Fiat (prime contractor in Italy) and CELMA (prime contractor in Brazil). It underwent type testing in the first half of 1987. Fiat carries out bench testing in support of the prototype aircraft, and rig testing of the engine Group-A parts.

PRATT & WHITNEY PW2037/2040 and PW4000

Since 1974 Fiat has been responsible for design and development of the accessory drive gearbox for these Pratt & Whitney engines.

GENERAL ELECTRIC CF6

Fiat produces components for the CF6 for GE and SNECMA. For GE the company supplies accessory gearboxes, inlet gearboxes and shafts. SNECMA is supplied with gearbox components and shafts for CF6-50 engines. Fiat is collaborating with GE on CF6-80C/C2 engines.

GENERAL ELECTRIC T64-P4D

This turboprop powers the Alenia G222. Under a licence agreement between GE and the Italian government, the engine is manufactured in Italy, with Fiat as prime contractor.

GENERAL ELECTRIC T700/CT7

Parts of the T700 are made by Fiat, while for the EH 101 helicopter the CT7-6 is being developed by GE, Fiat Aviazione and Alfa Romeo Avio.

ROLLS-ROYCE VIPER 600

Development of this turbojet was undertaken in collaboration with Rolls-Royce. For most versions, components rearward of the compressor (except turbine discs and blades) are Fiat's responsibility. However, the Mk 632-43 is licensed to Piaggio.

IAME

ITAL-AMERICAN MOTOR ENGINEERING

Via Lisbona 15, 24040 Zingonia
Telephone: 39 (35) 883022
Fax: 39 (35) 885744
Telex: 301205

IAME light piston engines are known as KFM (Komet Flight Motors). They were launched in 1981, the chief market being US homebuilders and microlight aircraft manufacturers.

KFM 107 MAXI

Two-cylinder two-stroke engine for microlights, motor gliders, UAVs and similar uses. Available as: **107E**, direct drive, with electric starter and alternator; and **107ER**, with V belt reduction gear (2 : 1).

CYLINDERS: Bore 64 mm (2.52 in). Stroke 52 mm (2.05 in). Capacity 334 cc (20.38 cu in).

DIMENSIONS:
Length	435 mm (17.13 in)
Width (over plugs)	440 mm (17.32 in)
Height	253 mm (9.96 in)

WEIGHT, DRY:
Maxi 107E	19.0 kg (41.8 lb)
Maxi 107ER	22.5 kg (49.6 lb)

PERFORMANCE RATINGS:
Max T-O	22.4 kW (30 hp) at 6,300 rpm
Max continuous	20.1 kW (27 hp) at 6,080 rpm

FUEL CONSUMPTION:
Cruise	8.3 litres (2.19 US gallons; 1.83 Imp gallons)/h

KFM 107E Maxi two-stroke piston engine

KFM 112

This is the only KFM four-stroke engine currently in production.

CYLINDERS: Bore 90 mm (3.54 in). Stroke 64 mm (2.52 in). Capacity 1,628.6 cc (99.4 cu in).

DIMENSIONS:

Length	583 mm (22.95 in)
Width	603 mm (23.74 in)
Height	380 mm (14.96 in)

WEIGHT, DRY (with starter and dual ignition):
54 kg (119 lb)

PERFORMANCE RATINGS:

Max rated (3 min)	44.16 kW (60 hp) at 3,200 rpm
Max continuous	39.74 kW (54 hp)

FUEL CONSUMPTION:

Max continuous
16.3 litres (4.3 US gallons; 3.6 Imp gallons)/h
70 per cent cruise
11.2 litres (2.97 US gallons; 2.47 Imp gallons)/h

KFM 112 flat-four piston engine

OFFMAR

OFFMAR AVIO srl

Borgo Valentino 1, 10020 Arignano (TO)
Telephone: 39 (11) 946 2159
Fax: 39 (11) 946 2237

This company is producing a piston engine for the ultralight market.

OFFMAR LEM 2fm 17

The unusual feature of this engine is that it comprises two single-cylinder two-stroke aircooled engines side by side, the overall appearance being that of a flat twin.

CYLINDERS: Each side has one two-stroke aircooled cylinder, served by its own starter, fuel pump and carburettor. Combining gearbox provides single output. Bore 72.5 mm (2.85 in). Stroke 58.0 mm (2.28 in). Capacity 478.8 cc (29.22 cu in). Compression ratio 9.

DIMENSIONS:

Length	464 mm (18.27 in)
Width	690 mm (27.17 in)
Height	330 mm (12.99 in)

WEIGHT, DRY: 39 kg (86.0 lb)
PERFORMANCE RATING: 31.64 kW (42.4 hp) at 5,550 rpm
FUEL CONSUMPTION:
Cruise   5 litres (1.32 US gallons; 1.1 Imp gallons)/h

Offmar LEM 2fm 17 coupled two-stroke piston engine *(Howard Levy)*

PIAGGIO

INDUSTRIE AERONAUTICHE E MECCANICHE RINALDO PIAGGIO SpA

Via Cibrario 4, 16154, Genoa
Telephone: 39 (10) 600 41
Fax: 39 (10) 603378
Telex: 270695 AERPIA I

WORKS AND OFFICERS: see Aircraft section

The Aero Engine Division of Piaggio manufactures the following engines under licence agreements: Rolls-Royce Viper 11, 526, 540 and 632-43 turbojets; Textron Lycoming T53-L-13, T55-L-11 and -712 turboshafts; and Rolls-Royce 1004 turboshaft. Piaggio also participates in co-production under licence of the Rolls-Royce Spey 807 turbofan and has joined Rolls-Royce Turbomeca in development and production of the RTM 322-01 turboshaft. The Engine Division also produces IR suppression devices.

VM

VM MOTORI SpA

Via Ferrarese 29, 44042 Cento (Fe)
Telephone: 39 (51) 908511
Fax: 39 (51) 908517
Telex: 511642

VM Motori specialises in high speed lightweight diesel engines. Following automotive production, the company entered the aeronautical field with a range of horizontally opposed engines. All are aircooled four-stroke compression ignition engines, cooled by a propylenic glycol mixture and burning Jet A-1, JP-4, JP-5, JP-8 or similar fuel with direct injection by camshaft-driven plunger pumps. Each engine is turbocharged for operation to 8,850 m (29,000 ft). The engines are fully modular and are being offered with an initial TBO of 3,000 h. Cylinder size is 130 mm (5.1 in) by 110 mm (4.33 in) and compression ratio 18. Specific fuel consumption (econ cruise) is 106.4 µg/J (0.63 lb/h/hp).

VM TPJ 1304HF

Four cylinders, capacity 5.84 litres (356 cu in). Weight, dry with electrical system, 185 kg (408 lb). Maximum power 154 kW (206 hp) at 2,640 rpm.

VM TPJ 1306HF

Six cylinders, capacity 8.76 litres (535 cu in). Weight, dry with electrical system, 243 kg (536 lb). Maximum power 235 kW (315 hp) at 2,640 rpm.

VM TPJ 1306HF six-cylinder diesel engine

VM TPJ 1308HF

Eight cylinders, capacity 11.68 litres (713 cu in). Weight, dry with electrical system, 298 kg (657 lb). Maximum power 316 kW (424 hp) at 2,640 rpm.

JAPAN

IHI

ISHIKAWAJIMA-HARIMA JUKOGYO KABUSHIKI KAISHA

(Ishikawajima-Harima Heavy Industries Co Ltd)

Shin Ohtemachi Bldg 2-1, Ohtemachi 2-chome, Chiyoda-ku, Tokyo 100

Aero-Engine and Space Operations (ASO):

ADDRESS: As above
Telephone: 81 (3) 3224 5331
Fax: 81 (3) 3244 5668
Telex: 22232 IHIHQT J
PRESIDENT, ASO: Shozo Ojimi
GENERAL MANAGER, BUSINESS PLANNING: Satoshi Maeda

IHI's Aero-Engine & Space Operations specialises in the development and manufacture of aero-engines, space-related equipment, and land/marine gas turbines, as well as maintenance and repair. It has three plants and 3,600 employees. The number of jet engines so far produced totals about 3,100.

IHI began production of the J3 turbojet using Japan's own technology in 1959. This was followed by the licensed production of the J79, T64, T58 and TF40 (Adour) engines. In recent years, the F100, T56, F3 and T700 have been added to the product line.

The company has been involved in numerous engine development projects including the national project for the FJR710 and the Japan-Britain joint project for the RJ500. Currently, as the leader of a Japanese consortium, IHI is participating in the IAE V2500.

IHI is actively involved in many aspects of spaceflight.

IHI F3

Development of this turbofan began in 1976, with funding by the JDA's Technical Research & Development

F3-IHI-30 two-shaft turbofan

Institute. The Phase 1 **XF3-1** form has a single-stage fan with bypass ratio of 1.9, five-stage transonic compressor, and single-stage HP and LP turbines. Rating is 11.79 kN (2,650 lb st).

In 1977 JDA contracted with IHI for the **XF3-20**, with reduced bypass ratio and higher turbine temperature to give a rating of 16.28 kN (3,660 lb st). This was followed by the **XF3-30**, which in 1982 was selected by the JASDF as the engine for the T-4 trainer. XF3-30 qualification was completed in March 1986. The engine is now redesignated **F3-IHI-30**, and the first production engine was delivered to JDA on 17 December 1987.

TYPE: Two-shaft turbofan.
FAN: Two-stage axial. No inlet guide vanes. Mass flow 34 kg (75 lb)/s. Pressure ratio 2.6. Bypass ratio 0.9.
COMPRESSOR: Five stages. First two stators variable. Overall pressure ratio 11.

COMBUSTION CHAMBER: Annular, with 12 duplex fuel nozzles.
HP TURBINE: Single-stage, aircooled rotor blades.
LP TURBINE: Two-stage, tip shrouded.
FUEL SYSTEM: Hydromechanical, with electronic supervisor.
DIMENSIONS:
Length   1,340 mm (52.76 in)
Inlet diameter   560 mm (22.0 in)
WEIGHT, DRY: 340 kg (750 lb)
PERFORMANCE RATING (T-O, S/L):
   16.37 kN (3,680 lb st) class
SPECIFIC FUEL CONSUMPTION:
   19.83 mg/Ns (0.7 lb/h/lb st)

KAWASAKI

KAWASAKI JUKOGYO KABUSHIKI KAISHA

(Kawasaki Heavy Industries Ltd)

1-18 Nakamachi-dori 2-chome, Chuo-ku, Kobe 650-91
Telephone: 81 (78) 371 9530
Jet Engine Division: World Trade Centre, 4-1 Hamamatsu-cho 2-chome, Minato-ku, Tokyo
Telephone: 81 (3) 3435 2111
Fax: 81 (3) 3578 3519
OFFICERS: see Aircraft section

In 1967 KHI started manufacturing T53 turboshafts. Deliveries of the resulting KT5311A, KT5313B and T53-K-13B engines totalled 324 by 1989. KHI now licence-builds the T53-K-703 for AH-1S HueyCobras (58 by 1989) and T55-K-712 for CH-47J Chinooks (72 by 1989). Kawasaki shares in parts manufacturing for the Adour, F100 and JT8D and IHI-assembled T56. It is a member of the IAE consortium (see under International heading), and is a risk-sharing partner on the PW4000 and RR Trent.

KHI is developing a helicopter turboshaft engine in the 597-746 kW (800-1,000 shp) class, but no details were known by mid-1991.

KAWASAKI KJ12

This simple low cost turbojet has been developed as the core of various future engine programmes. In its present form it is suited to UAVs and sporting aircraft. Component testing began in 1979 and the first KJ12 ran in early 1981. It has a centrifugal compressor driven by a single-stage axial turbine; the combustion chamber is annular and the control system of the electronic type.

DIMENSIONS:
Length   653 mm (25.71 in)
Max diameter   314 mm (12.36 in)
WEIGHT, DRY: 40 kg (88.2 lb)
PERFORMANCE RATINGS:
T-O   1.47 kN (331 lb st)
Cruise (9,145 m; 30,000 ft at Mach 0.9)
   0.716 kN (161 lb)

Kawasaki KJ12 single-shaft turbojet

MITSUBISHI

MITSUBISHI JUKOGYO KABUSHIKI KAISHA (Mitsubishi Heavy Industries Ltd)

HEAD OFFICE: 5-1, Marunouchi 2-chome, Chiyoda-ku, Tokyo 100
NAGOYA WORKS: 10 Oye-cho, Minato-ku, Nagoya 455
Telephone: 81 (52) 611 2111
Fax: 81 (52) 611 2681

OFFICERS: see Aircraft section

Between January 1973 and June 1981, under licence agreement with Pratt & Whitney, MHI delivered 72 JT8D-M-9 turbofans. MHI entered into a risk- and revenue-sharing agreement on the JT8D-200 in 1984, and on the PW4000 in 1989.

In collaboration with IHI and Kawasaki, MHI participates in the V2500 (see IAE in the International part of this section). Like IHI and KHI, Mitsubishi is developing a turboshaft in the 597-746 kW (800-1,000 shp) class. One of these engines is expected to power the planned medium helicopter.

NAL

NATIONAL AEROSPACE LABORATORY

7-44-1 Jindaijihigashi-machi, Chofu City, Tokyo 182
Telephone: 81 (422) 47 5911
DIRECTOR: Dr Kazuyuki Takeuchi
HEAD OF AERO-ENGINE DIVISION: Hiroyuki Nouse

The NAL is a government establishment responsible for research and development. In 1971 the Ministry of International Trade and Industry (MITI) funded a high bypass ratio turbofan development programme.

MITI/NAL FJR710

NAL manages the design of the FJR710. Manufacture of development engines was contracted to IHI, Kawasaki and Mitsubishi. The first engine ran in May 1973.

Phase 2 of the programme began in 1976, and the first of three FJR710/600s had been completed by December 1978. This version was followed by the lower-rated **FJR710/600S**, rated at 47 kN (10,582 lb st), which powers the experimental Asuka QSTOL aircraft. By early 1990

FJR710/600S two-shaft turbofan

total FJR710 running time had reached 7,100 h. The
following description applies to the /600 engine:
TYPE: Two-shaft turbofan.
FAN: Single-stage, with inserted titanium blades with part
span shrouds. Bypass ratio 6.5.
COMPRESSOR: Twelve-stage axial with inserted blades of
titanium and high nickel alloy. Five rows of variable
stator blades.
COMBUSTION CHAMBER: Smokeless annular type.

TURBINE: Two-stage HP with cooled blades; gas temperature
1,250°C. Four-stage LP.
DIMENSIONS (approx):
Length (flange to flange)   2,350 mm (93 in)
Diameter (inlet)   1,240 mm (49 in)
WEIGHT, DRY: 980 kg (2,160 lb)
PERFORMANCE RATINGS (ISA):
T-O   50 kN (11,243 lb st)

Cruise at 7,600 m (25,000 ft) at Mach 0.75
                                     13.24 kN (2,976 lb)
SPECIFIC FUEL CONSUMPTION:
T-O   10.5 mg/Ns (0.370 lb/h/lb st)
Cruise, as above   19.3 mg/Ns (0.680 lb/h/lb st)

POLAND

PZL
POLSKIE ZAKŁADY LOTNICZE
ul. Miodowa 5, 00251 Warsaw
Telephone: 48 (22) 261441
Telex: 814281

Pezetel Foreign Trade Enterprise Co:
00-991 Warsaw 44, Al. Stanów Zjednoczonych 61,
PO Box 6
Telephone: 48 (22) 108001
Telex: 813314

The Polish aircraft and diesel engine industry is managed
by the association of aviation and engine producers 'PZL'.
Pezetel handles all exports of Polish aeronautical material
and diesel engines.

IL
INSTYTUT LOTNICTWA (Aviation Institute)
HEADQUARTERS: Al. Krakowska 110/114, 02-256 Warsaw-
Okecie
Telephone: 48 (22) 460993
Fax: 48 (22) 464232
MANAGING DIRECTOR: Roman Czerwiński
CHIEF CONSULTANT FOR SCIENTIFIC AND TECHNICAL CO-
OPERATION: Jerzy Grzegorzewski
The Aviation Institute is concerned with aeronautical
research and testing. It can construct prototypes to its own
design.

IL K-15
This turbojet was announced in Summer 1988.
TYPE: Single-shaft turbojet.
COMPRESSOR: Six stages. Rotor blades and shrouded stator
blades of stainless steel. Two blow-off valves. Pressure
ratio 5.3. Mass flow 23 kg (50.7 lb)/s.
COMBUSTION CHAMBER: Short annular type, with 18
vaporising burners and six starting atomisers. Electric
ignition.
FUEL SYSTEM: Hydromechanical, with electronic blow-off
valve control and overspeed and overtemperature
limiters.
FUEL GRADE: Kerosene PSM-2 or TS-1.
TURBINE: Single-stage. Disc attached by Hirth coupling.
LUBRICATION SYSTEM: Self-contained recirculatory system.
Fully aerobatic.
OIL SPECIFICATION: Type SDF synthetic.
ACCESSORY DRIVES: Gearbox at bottom of intake casing
driven by bevel gear from front of compressor.
STARTING: 27V starter/generator in nose bullet.
DIMENSIONS:
Length overall   1,560 mm (61.42 in)
Width   725 mm (28.54 in)
Height   892 mm (35.12 in)
WEIGHT, DRY: 350 kg (772 lb)
PERFORMANCE RATINGS:
T-O   14.7 kN (3,305 lb st) at 15,900 rpm
Max continuous 11.5 kN (2,585 lb st) at 15,025 rpm
SPECIFIC FUEL CONSUMPTION:
At T-O rating   28.49 mg/Ns (1,006 lb/h/lb st)

IL SO-1
The Aviation Institute designed the SO-1 turbojet to
power the TS-11 trainer. Guaranteed overhaul life is 200 h.
Production was handled by the WSK-Rzeszów, as noted in
that organisation's entry.
TYPE: Single-shaft axial-flow turbojet.
COMPRESSOR: Seven-stage axial, all-steel. Stator blades
bonded with resin into slots in carrier rings. Pressure ratio
4.8.
COMBUSTION CHAMBER: Annular with 24 vaporisers.
FUEL SYSTEM: Starting system has six injectors. Main system
has 12 twin injectors with outlets towards the vaporisers.
FUEL SPECIFICATION: Kerosene P-2 or TS-1.
TURBINE: Single-stage axial.
LUBRICATION SYSTEM: Open type for rear compressor and
turbine bearings. Closed type for all other points.
OIL SPECIFICATION: Type AP-26 (synthetic).
ACCESSORY DRIVES: Gearbox at bottom of air intake casing
and driven by bevel shaft.
STARTING: 27V starter/generator.
DIMENSIONS:
Length overall   2,151 mm (84.7 in)
Width   707 mm (27.8 in)
Height   764 mm (30.1 in)
WEIGHT, DRY: 303 kg (668 lb)
PERFORMANCE RATINGS:
T-O   9.8 kN (2,205 lb st) at 15,600 rpm
Max continuous 8.7 kN (1,958 lb st) at 15,100 rpm
SPECIFIC FUEL CONSUMPTION:
At T-O rating   29.6 mg/Ns (1.045 lb/h/lb st)
OIL CONSUMPTION: 0.8 litre (1.7 US pints; 1.4 Imp pints)/h

IL K-15 single-shaft turbojet

IL SO-3W22 single-shaft turbojet

IL SO-3
This improved SO-1 replaced the earlier type in
production. Intended for tropical use, it incorporates minor
changes in compressor, combustion chamber and turbine,
data remaining the same as for the SO-1. The **SO-3B** is now
the standard TS-11 engine, with TBO of 400h. It also
powers the PZL I-22, with the designation **SO-3W22**. A
revised vaporising burner and flame tube result in more
uniform gas temperature entering the turbine. Data are as
for the SO-1 except:

OIL SPECIFICATION: AW-30 synthetic.
WEIGHT, DRY: 321 kg (708 lb)
PERFORMANCE RATINGS:
T-O   10.8 kN (2,425 lb st) at 15,600 rpm
Max continuous   9.8 kN (2,205 lb st) at 15,100 rpm
OIL CONSUMPTION:
1.0-1.2 litres (2.1-2.5 US pints; 1.7-2.1 Imp pints)/h

REFRIGERATION EQUIPMENT
REFRIGERATION EQUIPMENT WORKS
ul. Metalowców 25, 39-200 Debica
Telephone: 48 (146) 2031
Telex: 066617 WUCH PL

PZL-F ENGINES
In 1975 Pezetel acquired rights to manufacture and market the entire range of aircooled piston engines formerly produced by the Franklin Engine Company (Aircooled Motors) of the USA. These engines, known as PZL-F, are being produced in Poland for light aircraft and motor gliders. Previously manufactured by WSK-PZL Rzeszów, they were transferred in 1985 to the Debica works.

Current applications include the SZD-45-2 Ogar F motor glider (2A-120C), PZL-126 Mrówka (2A-120C), PZL-110 Koliber (4A-235B3), and PZL Mielec M-20 Mewa (6A-350C). The 2A-120C, 4A-235B3 and 6A-350C each have a Polish CACA certificate.

All models are of the horizontally opposed type, with cylinders of 117.48 mm (4.625 in) bore and 88.9 mm (3.5 in) stroke. All have direct drive and operate on 100/130 grade fuel. Accessories normally include electric starter, alternator and fuel pump. Other details are tabulated.

PZL-F 4A-235B four-cylinder piston engine

PZL-F 2A-120C two-cylinder piston engine

PZL-F 6A-350 six-cylinder piston engine

PZL-F ENGINES

Engine model	Cylinder arrangement	Capacity cc (cu in)	Compression ratio	Max T-O rating at S/L kW (hp) at rpm	Overall dimensions mm (in) length	width	height	Weight, dry kg (lb)
2A-120C	2 horiz	1,916 (117)	8.5	45 (60) at 3,200	581 (22.9)	795 (31.3)	515 (20.3)	75.8 (167)
4A-235B	4 horiz	3,850 (235)	8.5	93 (125) at 2,800	774 (30.5)	795 (31.3)	637 (25.1)	117.6 (259)
6A-350C	6 horiz	5,735 (350)	10.5	164 (220) at 2,800	952 (37.5)	795 (31.3)	641 (25.25)	167 (367)

WSK-PZL KALISZ
WYTWÓRNIA SPRZETU KOMUNIKACYJNEGO-PZL KALISZ
ul. Czestochowska 140, 62-800 Kalisz
Telephone: 48 (62) 77351
Fax: 48 (62) 37084
Telex: 046 2231
GENERAL MANAGER: Dipl Ing Jan Kolodziej

In 1952 the Soviet Union transferred responsibility for manufacture and service support of Soviet aircooled radial piston engines to the WSK (transport equipment manufacturing centre) at Kalisz. Current production is centred on the following, plus the TWD-10B turboprop (described under WSK-PZL Rzeszów), which is supplied to the USSR. Kalisz also overhauls the TWD-10B.

PZL (IVCHENKO) AI-14R
The original 260 hp AI-14R version of this nine-cylinder aircooled radial engine was produced in very large quantities, in the Soviet Union, China and Poland. Subsequent versions are:

AI-14RA. Rated at 191 kW (256 hp). Piston compressor drive and pneumatic starter. For Yak-12, Yak-18, PZL-101A Gawron and PZL-104 Wilga 35.

AI-14RA-KAF. RA with carburettor further aft, for Wilga 80.

AI-14RD. Rated at 206 kW (276 hp). Electric starter. For PZL-104 Wilga.

AI-14RDP. With pneumatic starter. For PZL-104 Wilga.

K8-AA. Rated at 246 kW (330 hp). Direct drive and pneumatic starter. Aerobatic. For PZL-130 Orlik until piston engine abandoned in favour of turboprop.

The following description refers to the AI-14RA:
TYPE: Nine-cylinder aircooled radial.
CYLINDERS: Bore 105 mm (4.125 in). Stroke 130 mm (5.125 in). Capacity 10.16 litres (620 cu in). Compression ratio 5.9.
FUEL GRADE: 91 to 100 octane.
PROPELLER DRIVE: Planetary gears, ratio 0.787.
DIMENSIONS:
Length   956 mm (37.63 in)
Diameter   985 mm (38.78 in)
WEIGHT, DRY: 200 kg (441 lb)
PERFORMANCE RATINGS:
T-O   191 kW (256 hp) at 2,350 rpm
Rated   162 kW (217 hp) at 2,050 rpm

PZL K8-AA (M-14Pm) nine-cylinder piston engine

SPECIFIC FUEL CONSUMPTION:
T-O   95-104.3 µg/J (0.562-0.617 lb/h/hp)

PZL (SHVETSOV) ASz-62R
Power plant of the An-2 transport biplane, the ASz-62R was developed in the Soviet Union as the ASh-62. Current versions are:

ASz-62IR-16. Centrifugal oil filter. For An-2 and PZL-106 Kruk.

ASz-62IR-M18. Hydraulic airframe pump drive. For PZL M-18 Dromader.

ASz-62IR-M18/DHC-3. As M18 plus vacuum pump. For DHC-3 Otter.

K9-AA. Uprated engine designed at Kalisz, 860 kW (1,170 hp) at 2,300 rpm. Electric starter and hydraulic airframe pump. For PZL M-24 Super Dromader.

K9-BA. First of B-series, with improved cylinders and piston rings. Provision for feathering propeller, for C-47/DC-3 conversion.

K9-BB. Improved engine for M-24 Super Dromader.

K9-BC. Improved engine for An-2 and PZL-106 Kruk.

PZL ASz-62IR nine-cylinder piston engine

TYPE: Nine-cylinder aircooled radial.
CYLINDERS: Bore 155 mm (6.10 in). Stroke 174 mm (6.85 in). Capacity 29.87 litres (1,823 cu in). Compression ratio 6.4.
FUEL GRADE: 91 to 100 octane.
PROPELLER DRIVE: Planetary gears, ratio 0.687.
The following relates to the IR-16:
DIMENSIONS:
Length overall   1,130 mm (44.50 in)
Diameter   1,375 mm (54.13 in)
WEIGHT, DRY:
Without power take-off   579 kg (1,276 lb)
PERFORMANCE RATINGS:
T-O   735 kW (985 hp) at 2,200 rpm
Rated power   603 kW (809 hp) at 2,100 rpm
SPECIFIC FUEL CONSUMPTION:
T-O   112 µg/J (0.661 lb/h/hp)

WSK-PZL RZESZÓW
WYTWÓRNIA SPRZETU KOMUNIKACYJNEGO-PZL RZESZÓW
ul. Hetmańska 120, 35-078 Rzeszów, PO Box 340
Telephone: 48 (17) 46100
Fax: 48 (17) 42625
Telex: 0633353
GENERAL MANAGER: Eng Tadeusz Cebulak

Current production at WSK Rzeszów is centred on the TWD-10 turboprop supplied to PZL for the An-28. The engine is also produced by WSK-PZL Kalisz (which see), and GTD-350 turboshaft, together with WR-2 reduction gear for Mi-2 helicopters; the tropicalised SO-3 turbojet for the TS-11 Iskra trainer; and the PZL-3S piston engine for agricultural aircraft. The SO-3 is described under the IL heading.

TWD-10B
The Soviet designed OMKB/Glushenkov TVD-10B turboprop, rated at 716 kW (960 shp), is made under licence in Poland for the An-28 STOL light transport built at WSK-PZL Mielec. TBO is 1,000 h.
TYPE: Free turbine turboprop.
AIR INTAKE: Three radial struts, inlet guide vanes and starter de-iced by bleed air from combustion chamber.

COMPRESSOR: Six axial stages and one centrifugal. Stage 1 has front bearing journal, bolted to stages 2 to 6 which are pinched by compressor shaft used as tie bolt. Blades in dovetail roots. Pressure ratio 7.4. Mass flow 4.6 kg (10.14 lb)/s at 29,600 rpm.

COMPRESSOR CASING: Forward upper and lower halves in titanium; rear section welded from sheet steel and containing anti-surge bleed valve and radial diffuser.

COMBUSTION CHAMBER: Annular with centrifugal burner, and two starting units each with semiconductor igniter and auxiliary burner.

FUEL SYSTEM: Comprises supply pump, filter, pump governor, acceleration control, signalling block and thermocorrector.

FUEL GRADE: T-1, TS-1 or RT.

COMPRESSOR TURBINE: Two-stage axial. Blades held by fir tree roots. Inlet guide vanes of hollow sheet with air cooling. Casing has ceramic liner.

POWER TURBINE: Single-stage axial, blades with fir tree roots, held in front roller and rear ball bearing.

REDUCTION GEARS: Single-stage spur high speed gear to accessory box and propeller gear; under the high speed gear is the feathering pump oil tank. Accessory box drives 16kW alternator, propeller tachometer and reduction gear oil pump, with propeller brake. Upper driveshaft to single-stage planetary reduction gear.

ENGINE ACCESSORIES: Box contains oil centrifuge; and drives tachometer, oil pump, fuel pump and pump governor. The starter is on the front with a claw clutch.

OIL SYSTEM: Closed and pressurised. Gas generator and reduction gear pumps. Oil tank capacity 16 litres (3.5 Imp gallons).

OIL GRADE: Oil mixture: 25 per cent MK-22 or MS-20, 75 per cent MK-8 or MS-8p.

DIMENSIONS:
Length without airframe jetpipe	2,060 mm (81.1 in)
Width	555 mm (21.9 in)
Height	900 mm (35.4 in)

WEIGHT, DRY: Bare 230 kg (507 lb)
Complete engine 300 kg (661 lb)

PERFORMANCE RATINGS:
T-O	754 kW (1,011 shp)
Nominal	613 kW (823 shp)
Max cruise	543 kW (728 shp)

SPECIFIC FUEL CONSUMPTION (T-O):
96.4 µg/J (0.570 lb/h/shp)

OMKB TWD-10B licensed to PZL Rzeszów

PZL GTD-350 free-turbine turboshaft

PZL-10W

This is the helicopter version of the TWD-10B, two of which power the PZL Swidnik Sokól. It uses the same gas generator, with the following differences:

TYPE: Free-turbine turboshaft engine.

POWER TURBINE: Single-stage axial, with blades held in fir tree roots. Speed maintained at 22,490 rpm.

FUEL SYSTEM: Pump governor provides automatic operation at selected constant helicopter rotor speeds, as well as control of anti-surge bleed valve, maintaining constant fuel flow in starting cycle, limiting shaft speed and gas temperature and automatic switch-off of faulty engine and selection of emergency power on remaining unit.

FUEL GRADE: T1, T2, TS-1, RT, PSM-2a, Jet A-1.

OIL SYSTEM: Closed and pressurised, with one delivery and four-section scavenge pump. Oil tank airframe-mounted, normal capacity 14 litres (3.08 Imp gallons).

OIL GRADE: B-3W synthetic, Castrol 599 or oil mixture 25 per cent MK22 or MS20 and 75 per cent MK8 or MS-8P.

ACCESSORIES: Integral cast box drives 5kW starter, starter unit, electronic temperature limiter, vibration sensor, tachometer generator, oil pumps and centrifuge, phase torquemeter, de-icing valve, power-turbine speed limiter and operation time counter.

DIMENSIONS:
Length with jetpipe	1,875 mm (73.8 in)
Width	740 mm (29.0 in)

WEIGHT, DRY: 141 kg (310 lb)

PERFORMANCE, RATINGS (ISA):
OEI 1	858 kW (1,150 shp)

OEI 2	736 kW (987 shp)
T-O	671 kW (900 shp)
One hour	615 kW (825 shp)
Nominal	582 kW (780 shp)
Continuous	515 kW (691 shp)

SPECIFIC FUEL CONSUMPTION:
T-O 101.11 µg/J (0.60 lb/h/shp)

PZL GTD-350

The **GTD-350** is a helicopter turboshaft. In the Mi-2, the drive is taken from the rear. Though developed by the Isotov bureau in the Soviet Union, it is in production only in Poland. PZL Rzeszów has developed a new version rated at 331 kW (444 shp) and designated **GTD-350P**. Technical life of the GTD-350 is 4,000 h.

TYPE: Axial/centrifugal-flow free-turbine turboshaft.

AIR INTAKE: Stainless steel. Automatic de-icing of inlet guide vanes and bullet by air bleed.

COMPRESSOR: Seven axial stages and one centrifugal, all of steel. Pressure ratio 6.05. Mass flow 2.19 kg (4.83 lb)/s at 45,000 rpm.

COMBUSTION CHAMBER: Reverse-flow type with air supply through two tubes. Centrifugal duplex single-nozzle burner. Semiconductor igniter plug.

FUEL SYSTEM: NR-40TA pump governor; RO-40TA power turbine governor, DS-40 controlling bleed valves; and electromagnetic starting valve.

FUEL GRADE: TS-1, TS-2 or Jet A-1.

COMPRESSOR TURBINE: Single stage. Shrouded blades with fir tree roots. Temperature before turbine 940°C (GTD-350P, 985°C).

POWER TURBINE: Two-stage constant speed (24,000 rpm). Shrouded blades with fir tree roots. Discs bolted together. Turbine stators integrally cast.

REDUCTION GEARING: Two sets of gears, with ratio of 0.246 : 1, in magnesium alloy casing. Output speed 5,900 rpm.

LUBRICATION SYSTEM: Closed type. Gear type pump with one pressure and four scavenge units. Cooler and tank, capacity 12.5 litres (2.75 Imp gallons).

OIL GRADE: B3-W (synthetic), Castrol 98 or 5000, Elf Turbojet II or Shell Turbine Oil-500.

ACCESSORIES: STG3 3kW starter/generator, NR-40TA governor pump, D1 tachometer and oil pumps driven by gas generator. RO-40TA speed governor, D1 tachometer and centrifugal breather driven by power turbine.

STARTING: STG3 starter/generator suitable for operation at up to 4,000 m (13,125 ft) altitude.

DIMENSIONS:
Length overall	1,385 mm (54.53 in)
Max width	520 mm (20.47 in)
Width (with jetpipes)	626 mm (24.65 in)
Max height	630 mm (24.80 in)
Height (with jetpipes)	760 mm (29.9 in)

WEIGHT, DRY:
Less jetpipes and accessories 139.5 kg (307 lb)

PERFORMANCE RATINGS:
T-O rating (6 min) at 96% max gas generator rpm:
GTD-350	298 kW (400 shp)
GTD-350P	331 kW (444 shp)

Nominal rating (1 h) at 90% gas generator rpm:
GTD-350	238.5 kW (320 shp)
GTD-350P	261 kW (350 shp)

Cruise rating (I)
212.5 kW (285 shp) at 87.5% gas generator rpm

Cruise rating (II)
175 kW (235 shp) at 84.5% gas generator rpm

SPECIFIC FUEL CONSUMPTION:
T-O	136 µg/J (0.805 lb/h/shp)
Nominal	146 µg/J (0.861 lb/h/shp)
Cruise (I)	154 µg/J (0.913 lb/h/shp)
Cruise (II)	165 µg/J (0.978 lb/h/shp)

OIL CONSUMPTION:
Max 0.3 litre (0.63 US pint; 0.53 Imp pint)/h

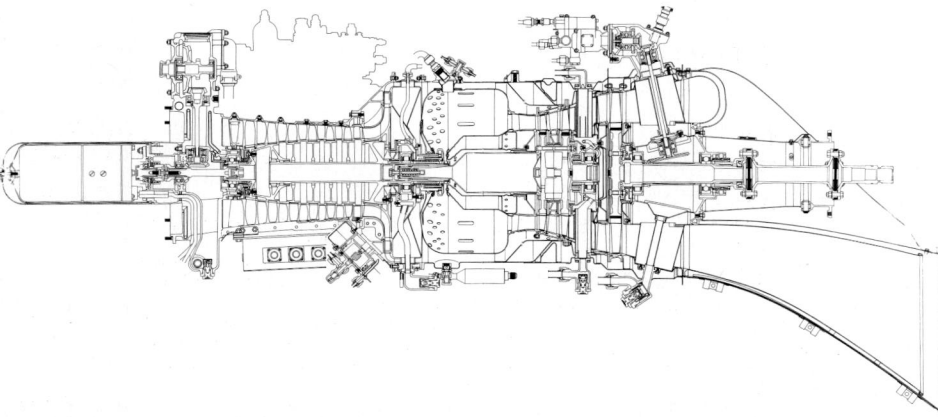

Longitudinal section through PZL-10W turboshaft

PZL-3S

Derived from Soviet AI-26W via LiT-3. Applications include PZL-106A Kruk, IAR-827A and conversions of Grumman/Schweizer Ag-Cat A, B and C, Thrush Commander, DHC-2 Beaver and DHC-3 Otter.

TYPE: Seven-cylinder aircooled radial.
CYLINDERS: Bore 155.5 mm (6.12 in). Stroke 155 mm (6.1 in). Capacity 20.6 litres (1,265 cu in). Comp ratio 6.4.
PISTONS: Forged aluminium.
INDUCTION SYSTEM: Float type carburettor. Mechanically driven supercharger.
FUEL GRADE: Aviation gasoline, minimum 91 octane.
LUBRICATION: Gear type oil pump. Oil grade Aero Shell 100 or other to MIL-L-6082.
PROPELLER DRIVE: Direct. Provision for constant-speed US-132000A propeller.
ACCESSORIES: ANG 6423 Prestolite alternator and two output shafts, one 20 kW (27 hp) (26 kW; 35 hp max) for spraying pump and the other 3.7 kW (5 hp).
STARTING: Electric.
DIMENSIONS:

Diameter	1,267 mm (49.88 in)
Length	1,177 mm (46.34 in)

WEIGHT, DRY: 411 kg (906 lb)

PERFORMANCE RATINGS:

Max T-O	447 kW (600 hp) at 2,200 rpm
Max continuous	410 kW (550 hp) at 2,050 rpm
Cruise (75 per cent)	310 kW (415 hp) at 2,000 rpm

SPECIFIC FUEL CONSUMPTION:

T-O, max continuous	105 µg/J (0.61 lb/h/hp)
Cruise	86 µg/J (0.51 lb/h/hp)

PZL-3SR

This is the geared version of the PZL-3S. Applications include the PZL-106AR and BR and M-21. The following are the main differences:
PROPELLER DRIVE: Planetary gear of 0.7 ratio. Provision for constant-speed propeller, Type US-133000.
DIMENSION:
Length   1,271 mm (50.06 in)
WEIGHT, DRY: 446 kg (983 lb)

Cutaway PZL-3S seven-cylinder piston engine

ROMANIA

AEROSTAR
AEROSTAR SA
ADDRESS: Formerly Condor. See Aircraft section and Addenda.

This reorganised factory is manufacturing under licence the Soviet VMKB (Vedeneyev) M-14P and M-14V26 piston engines, and the Soyuz/Tumansky RU-19A-300 gas turbine.

TURBOMECANICA
INTREPRINDEREA TURBOMECANICA BUCURESTI

c/o Centrul National Aeronautic, Bulevardul Dacia 13, Casuta Postala 22-149, R-70185 Bucharest
Telephone: 40 (0) 12 08 78
Telex: 10660 CNAER

This factory produces under licence the Rolls-Royce Spey 511-14W and Viper 632/633, and the Turbomeca Turmo IVC.

SINGAPORE

SA
SINGAPORE AEROSPACE LTD
ADDRESSES: See Aircraft section

SA manufactures engine parts for General Electric and Turbomeca. It has 2 per cent of the PW4000 programme and is sole source of eleven high-precision parts, mainly in the compressor section.

SOUTH AFRICA

ATLAS
ATLAS AIRCRAFT CORPORATION OF SOUTH AFRICA (PTY) LTD
PO Box 11, Atlas Road, Kempton Park 1620, Transvaal

Atlas is manufacturing the Rolls-Royce Viper 540 turbojet under sublicence from Piaggio of Italy, for use in Atlas Impala attack trainers.

SPAIN

ITP
INDUSTRIA DE TURBOPROPULSION SA
Zamudio Industrial Park, Bilbao
The Spanish Government approved the establishment of this company in April 1989. Three state-owned Spanish

companies—Sener, CASA (see Aircraft section) and Bazan—hold 51 per cent of the shares. Rolls-Royce plc holds 45 per cent, and the remaining 4 per cent is held by the Banco Bilbao. The Spanish Government is providing $34 million, described as 'subsidies'.

ITP will make parts for civil and military jet engines. Its main work is expected to include a share (probably 13 per cent) in the EJ200 programme, described under Eurojet in this section.

SENER
SENER-INGENIERIA Y SISTEMAS SA
Raimundo Fernández Villaverde 65, Madrid 28003
Telephone: 34 (1) 456 7062

Sener, engaged in NATO programmes and ESA space activities, was to have been the Spanish partner in the consortium that will build the EJ200 engine of the

Eurofighter EFA. This role has now been assumed by ITP, in which Sener is a shareholder, as briefly referred to above and in the International part of this section.

SWEDEN

FLYGMOTOR
VOLVO FLYGMOTOR AB
S-461 81 Trollhättan
Telephone: 46 (520) 94000
Fax: 46 (520) 34010
Telex: 420 40 VOLFA S
Volvo Flygmotor produces aircraft engines and space propulsion components. Since 1980 it has been a risk and revenue sharing partner with General Electric on the CF6-80A and -80C for wide-body transports. Volvo Flygmotor also participates in development and production of the Garrett TFE731-5 turbofan and TPE331-14/15 turboprop. The company also has agreements with Pratt & Whitney on the JT8D-200, PW2000 and V2500, and with Rolls-Royce on the Tay, making combustors for the Tay 610-650 and compressor intermediate casings for the Mk 670.

FLYGMOTOR RM8
The RM8 is a Swedish military version of the Pratt & Whitney JT8D turbofan which Flygmotor developed to power the Saab 37 Viggen. Following the RM8A for the AJ 37, SF 37, SH 37 and SK 37, the RM8B was developed for the JA 37. The major change to improve functional stability at high altitude involved replacing the first stage of the LP compressor by a third stage on the fan. To increase thrust the RM8B has a four-nozzle burner combustion system and a new HP turbine. Delivery of RM8B engines was completed on 19 September 1988.
The following description refers to the RM8A:
TYPE: Two-spool turbofan with modulated afterburner.
FAN: Two-stage front fan. Titanium blades.
LP COMPRESSOR: Four-stage integral with fan.

HP COMPRESSOR: Seven-stages. Overall pressure ratio 16.5. Bypass ratio approximately 1. Mass flow 145 kg (320 lb)/s.
COMBUSTION CHAMBER: Cannular with nine flame tubes. Two spark plugs, each with its own igniter.
HP TURBINE: Single-stage with cast aircooled blades.
LP TURBINE: Three-stage axial flow, with cast blades.
AFTERBURNER: One hot streak igniter. Hydraulically (fuel) actuated nozzle.
CONTROL SYSTEMS: Bendix hydromechanical controls for gas generator and for afterburner and nozzle.
ACCESSORY DRIVE: Via gearbox driven from HP shaft.
DIMENSIONS:

Length overall: RM8A	6,153 mm (242.2 in)
RM8B	6,223 mm (245 in)

Max diameter (both versions)	1,349 mm (53.1 in)
Inlet diameter (both)	1,030 mm (40.55 in)
WEIGHT, DRY:	
RM8A	2,100 kg (4,630 lb)
RM8B	2,220 kg (4,894 lb)
PERFORMANCE RATINGS (ISA, S/L):	
Max T-O, augmented:	
RM8A	115.6 kN (25,990 lb st)
RM8B	125 kN (28,110 lb st)
Max T-O, dry:	
RM8A	65.6 kN (14,750 lb st)
RM8B	72.1 kN (16,200 lb st)
SPECIFIC FUEL CONSUMPTION:	
Max augmented:	
RM8A	70.0 mg/Ns (2.47 lb/h/lb st)
RM8B	71.4 mg/Ns (2.52 lb/h/lb st)
Max dry:	
RM8A	17.6 mg/Ns (0.63 lb/h/lb st)
RM8B	18.1 mg/Ns (0.64 lb/h/lb st)
Max continuous (both)	17.3 mg/Ns (0.61 lb/h/lb st)

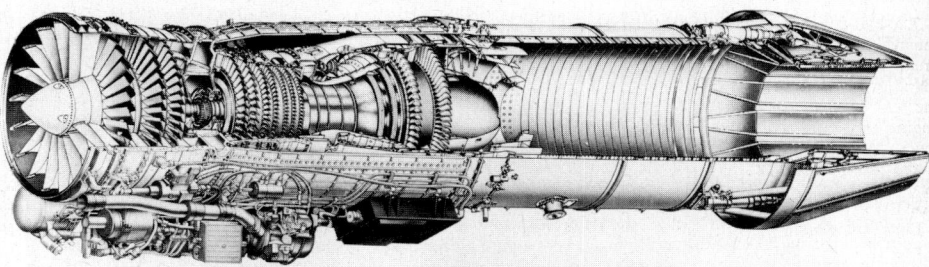

Cutaway drawing of Flygmotor RM12 two-shaft augmented turbofan

FLYGMOTOR RM12

The RM12 is a version of the F404 developed jointly by General Electric and Volvo Flygmotor to power the JAS 39 Gripen. General Electric retains rights to the design, and supplies approximately 60 per cent by value of parts.

Volvo Flygmotor is a partner in all F404 applications. Volvo Flygmotor will supply parts to General Electric similar to those parts that it manufactures for the RM12.

The RM12 thrust improvement has been achieved by increasing the turbine inlet temperature by up to 105°C and by increasing fan airflow. The fan meets more stringent bird strike requirements, and this has required changes to the control system, with built-in redundancy to ensure get-home power. Increased temperature and pressure have required changes to hot section materials. RM12 testing started at

GE in June 1984, and the Gripen first flew on 9 December 1988. Production deliveries are due in 1993.

The following are features of the RM12:
FAN: Variable first-stage stator. Airflow 68 kg (150 lb)/s. Bypass ratio 0.28.

WEIGHT, DRY:	1,050 kg (2,315 lb)
PERFORMANCE RATINGS:	
Max T-O: dry	54 kN (12,140 lb st)
augmented	80.5 kN (18,100 lb st)

TURKEY

TEI
TUSAS ENGINE INDUSTRIES
Muttalip Mevkii Mrk, PK 610 Eskisehir
Telephone: 90 (222) 22 030
Fax: 90 (222) 22 057
Telex: 35356 tmco tr
MANAGING DIRECTOR: G. R. Levesque

TEI is a joint venture between US General Electric and Turkish shareholders. The factory produces the F110 fighter engine, and had delivered 87 engines by the end of 1990. TEI also produces numerous other aircraft engine components.

UNION OF SOVIET SOCIALIST REPUBLICS

Since 1989 the entire industry of the Soviet Union has been undergoing great changes. These changes are generally intended to increase commercial viability, and they are superimposed on changes of name caused by the replacement of deceased or retired chief constructors by their successors. For nearly 70 years the procedure was for new engines to be designed at a KB (construction bureau)

always identified by the name of the bureau head, or chief constructor. Their work had the benefit of support from the laboratories of the Central Institute of Aviation Motors. Once cleared for production, an engine would be assigned to a factory for series production. The factory (or factories) remained anonymous, though its GAZ (state aviation factory) number might become known (eg, see introduction

to Klimov). Today the production plants are being named, many even have a chief designer, and they are taking display stands at exhibitions alongside the KBs. Meanwhile, confusion is increased further by the fact that some of the KBs have received names in honour of former chief designers or based on the city where they are located.

BAKANOV

This designer, at Voronezh, is working on four completely new piston engines for general aviation.

BAKANOV M-16
Largest of the new engines, this is intended to replace the M-14P radial. It has eight aircooled cylinders in double-X

form (tandem pairs of cylinders forming a 90° X seen from the front). Maximum rating is 224 kW (300 hp). Applications include the Yak-56, Yak-57 and Yak-58.

BAKANOV M-17
Fifty years ago one of the Soviet Union's most important engines, this designation now applies to an X-4 engine produced by taking half an M-16. To be rated in 1993 at 112 kW (150 hp), the M-17 could power the Yak-112.

BAKANOV M-18
This engine has two cylinders, smaller than those of the M-16 and M-17. To be rated at 30 kW (40 hp), it will power microlights.

BAKANOV M-19
This engine has four cylinders of the type used in the M-18. It will be rated at up to 59.7 kW (80 hp) for various light aircraft.

CHERNYSHOV
MOSCOW MACHINE-BUILDING PRODUCTION ASSOCIATION NAMED FOR V. V. CHERNYSHOV
121362 Moscow

Telephone: 491 57 22
Telex: ELIKA

The RD-33, engine of the MiG-29, is manufactured at this factory (see Klimov).

GLUSHENKOV — *see OMKB*

ISOTOV — *see Klimov*

IVCHENKO — *see Progress*

KKBM
KUIBYSHEV ENGINE DESIGN BUREAU
This is the bureau formerly named for N. D. Kuznetsov.

NK-12M
Designed at Kuibyshev in 1947-52 under N. D. Kuznetsov and former German engineers, the NK-12M is the most powerful turboprop in the world. The **NK-12M** developed 8,948 ekW (12,000 ehp). The **NK-12MV** is rated at 11,033 ekW (14,795 ehp) and powered the Tu-114, driving four-blade contra-rotating propellers of 5.6 m (18 ft 4 in) diameter. As the **NK-12MA**, rated at 11,185 kW

(15,000 shp), it powers the An-22, with propellers of 6.2 m (20 ft 4 in) diameter. A further application is in the Tupolev Tu-95/-142 bomber and its derivatives, and Tu-126, both believed to be powered by the NK-12MV.

The NK-12M has a 14-stage axial-flow compressor. Pressure ratio varies from 9 to 13 according to altitude, and variable inlet vanes and blow-off valves are necessary. A can-annular type combustion system is used: each flame tube is mounted centrally on a downstream injector, but all tubes merge at their maximum diameter to form an annular secondary region. The single turbine is a five-stage axial. Mass flow is 65 kg (143 lb)/s.

The casing is made in four portions, from sheet steel, precision welded. An electric control for variation of propeller pitch is incorporated, to maintain constant speed.

DIMENSIONS:	
Length	6,000 mm (236.2 in)
Diameter	1,150 mm (45.3 in)
WEIGHT, DRY:	2,350 kg (5,181 lb)
PERFORMANCE RATINGS (NK-12MV):	
T-O	11,033 ekW (14,795 ehp)
Nominal power	8,826 ekW (11,836 ehp) at 8,300 rpm
Idling speed	6,600 rpm

NK-8

The NK-8 was developed through a number of variants, the most powerful of which is the NK-144. Basic versions are the 99.1 kN (22,273 lb st) **NK-8-4**, later uprated to 103 kN (23,150 lb st), which originally powered the Il-62, and the 93.2 kN (20,950 lb) **NK-8-2** which was the original engine of the Tu-154. The NK-8-4 remains in service with several Il-62 (not Il-62M) operators, including LOT. It led to the NK-86 described later.

TYPE: Two-shaft turbofan.

FAN: Two-stage axial, with anti-flutter sweptback blades on first rotor stage. Pressure ratio 2.15 at 5,350 rpm. Bypass ratio 1.02 (NK-8-2, 1.00).

COMPRESSOR: Two IP stages on fan shaft. Six-stage HP compressor. Construction almost wholly of titanium. Core pressure ratio, 10.8 at 6,950 HP rpm (NK-8-2, 10 at 6,835 rpm).

COMBUSTION CHAMBER: Annular, with 139 burners.

FUEL GRADE: T-1 and TS-1 to GOST 10227-62 or T-7 to GOST 12308-66 (equivalent to Avtur 50).

TURBINE: Single-stage HP turbine, two-stage LP turbine, all with shrouded rotor blades, aircooled discs and hollow nozzle blades (stators). Gas temperature, not over 870°C (1,143°K) ahead of turbine, not over 670°C (NK-8-2, 650°C) downstream.

JETPIPE: Mixer leads bypass flow into common jetpipe which may be fitted with blocker/cascade type reverser giving up to 48 per cent (NK-8-2, 45 per cent) reverse thrust, and noise suppressor.

LUBRICATION: Continuous pressure feed and recirculation. Pressure not less than 2.28 bars (33 lb/sq in).

OIL GRADE: Mineral oil MK-8 or MK-8P to GOST 6457-66 (DERD.2490 or MIL-O-6081B).

ACCESSORIES: These include automatic flight deck warning of vibration, ice and fire. All grouped beneath fan duct casing. RTA-26-9-1 turbine temperature controller by Smiths Industries.

STARTING: HP spool driven by constant-speed drive type PPO-62M, or started pneumatically by air from TA-6 APU from ground hose or by air bleed (NK-8-2, pneumatic only).

DIMENSIONS:

NK-8-4: Length, no reverser	5,100 mm (201 in)
NK-8-2: Length, with reverser	5,288 mm (208.19 in)
Length, no reverser	4,762 mm (187.48 in)
Diameter	1,442 mm (56.8 in)

WEIGHT, DRY:

NK-8-4: no reverser	2,100 kg (4,629 lb)
with reverser	2,400 kg (5,291 lb)
NK-8-2: no reverser	2,100 kg (4,629 lb) max
with reverser	2,350 kg (5,180 lb) max

PERFORMANCE RATINGS:

NK-8-4: T-O rating	103.0 kN (23,150 lb st)
Cruise rating at 11,000 m (36,000 ft) and 458 knots (850 km/h; 530 mph)	27.0 kN (6,063 lb)
NK-8-2: T-O rating	93.2 kN (20,950 lb st)
NK-8-2U: T-O rating	103.0 kN (23,150 lb st)

SPECIFIC FUEL CONSUMPTION:
At cruise rating at 11,000 m (36,000 ft) and 458 knots (850 km/h; 530 mph):

NK-8-4	22.1 mg/Ns (0.78 lb/h/lb)
NK-8-2	21.53 mg/Ns (0.76 lb/h/lb)

NK-86

Though described by the Ilyushin aircraft bureau as a new engine, this turbofan of 127.5 kN (28,660 lb st) is closely related to the NK-8 series. Four power the Il-86 with combined reversers and noise attenuators.

NK-88

Almost certainly another derivative of the NK-8 series, the NK-88 is the engine fitted to the Tu-155 (Tu-154 development) fuelled by liquid hydrogen, which first flew on 15 April 1988. No major modification is needed for the cryogenic fuel (other than to the aircraft and engine fuel systems), nor to burn LNG (liquefied natural gas) which

KKBM NK-86 two-shaft turbofan *(Flight International)*

was expected to be used in 1988 in the same aircraft. Engine performance is unlikely to differ materially from the NK-8-2U.

NK-92

Under development in 1991, this ducted propfan (or turbofan of ultra-high BPR) has been selected to power the projected Il-90 twin-engined 150/220-seat airliner. Thrust rating is in the 177 kN (39,785 lb st) class.

NK-93

This is the most powerful propfan currently in advanced development in the world. It would power the double-deck four-engined Il-96-500. The Ilyushin bureau expect an engine for test and development in late 1992.

TYPE: Three-shaft propfan.

FANS: Contra-rotating. Front, eight thin titanium scimitar blades, rear 10 blades, all with variable pitch. Bypass ratio 16.6 (later 17).

COMPRESSORS: Low-pressure seven stages. High-pressure eight stages. Overall pressure ratio 37.

FAN DRIVE: By three-stage LP turbine via differential planetary gearbox.

ACCESSORIES: Full-authority electronic control, but with hydromechanical standby system. Closed-loop oil system.

DIMENSIONS:

Fan diameter	2,900 mm (114 in)
Length	5,972 mm (235 in)

WEIGHT, DRY: 3,650 kg (8,047 lb)

PERFORMANCE RATING (S/L):
T-O 176.5 kN (39,683 lb st)

SPECIFIC FUEL CONSUMPTION:
T-O as above 13.89 mg/Ns (0.49 lb/h/lb st)

NK-144

This augmented turbofan was derived from the NK-8 to power the Tu-144 SST. A version of the NK-144 is believed to be the engine of at least the first subtype of the Tupolev Tu-22M supersonic bomber known to NATO as 'Backfire'.

The NK-144 is reported to have a two-stage titanium fan, three-stage IP compressor, eleven-stage HP compressor, annular combustion chamber, single-stage HP turbine and two-stage LP turbine. Aircooled blades are used in the HP turbine, and titanium is used extensively in construction of

the engine. Bypass ratio is reported to be 1 : 1, maximum mass flow 250 kg (551 lb)/s, and pressure ratio 15 : 1. The jetpipe incorporates an afterburner, with hydraulically actuated variable area nozzle. Gas temperature at turbine entry is 1,050°C.

DIMENSIONS:

Length overall	5,200 mm (204.7 in)
Diameter	1,500 mm (59 in)

WEIGHT:
Without jetpipe, but with afterburner
2,850 kg (6,283 lb)

PERFORMANCE RATINGS:

Max: without afterburning	127.5 kN (28,660 lb st)
with afterburning	196.1 kN (44,090 lb st)

KKBM P-020

The first new Soviet piston engine to be revealed for many years, the P-020 is a small but highly rated two-cylinder two-stroke opposed aircooled engine for manned and unmanned applications. T-O power 14.9 kW (20 hp) at 7,300 rpm. Sfc 133.5 μg/J (0.79 lb/h/hp). Dry weight 9 kg (19.8 lb). In production at Kuibyshev MPO named for M. V. Frunze. It powers the Yak Shmel-1 UAV.

KKBM P-020 flat-twin two-stroke piston engine

KLIMOV

LENINGRAD NPO IM. KLIMOV

GENERAL DESIGNER: Alexander Alexandrovich Sarkisov

The great design bureau and factory at Leningrad, the former Factory No. 117, was a major centre for high-power piston engines developed under Vladimir Yakovlyevich Klimov. In 1946 it was selected to build the Rolls-Royce Nene turbojet, later developed as the Klimov VK-1. Klimov was succeeded by his deputy, Sergei Pietrovich Isotov, who developed gas turbines mainly for helicopters but which in 1968 moved into the field of fighters. Isotov died in 1983 and was succeeded by Vladimir Styepanov (who retired early) and Alexander Sarkisov, but today the bureau has been renamed for its founder, and is also often simply called the Leningrad bureau.

Engines designed by NPO Klimov are manufactured at Perm (Sverdlov) and Zaporozhye (Motorostroitel).

TV2-117

The power plant of the Mi-8 comprises two **TV2-117A** engines coupled through a VR-8A gearbox. The complete package incorporates a control system (separate from the control system of each gas generator) which maintains desired rotor speed, synchronises the power of both engines, and increases the power of the remaining engine if the other should fail.

TV2-117TG. Qualified to operate on all normal gas-turbine fuels, and on gasoline (petrol), benzine, diesel oil, liquefied natural gas, propane or butane gas. Flown on Mi-8TG, ratings unchanged, and selected as interim engine for Mi-38. A foreign production facility is sought.

TYPE: Free turbine helicopter turboshaft.

COMPRESSOR: Ten-stage axial. Inlet guide vanes and stators of stages 1, 2 and 3 are variable. Pressure ratio 6.6 at 21,200 rpm.

COMBUSTION CHAMBER: Annular, with eight burner cones.

FUEL GRADE: T-1 or TS-1 to GOST 10227-62 specification (Western equivalents, DERD.2494, MIL-F-5616).

TURBINE: Two-stage axial compressor turbine with solid blades. Two-stage free power turbine.

OUTPUT SHAFT: Conveys torque from the free turbine to the overrunning clutch of the main gearbox (VR-8A) and also to the speed governor. Max output speed 12,000 rpm; main rotor speed 192 rpm.

ACCESSORIES: Engine control system includes fuel, hydraulic, anti-icing, gas temperature restriction, engine electric supply and starting, and monitoring systems. Up to 1.8 per cent of the mass flow can be used to heat the intake and other parts liable to icing. Fire extinguishant can be released by the pilot.

LUBRICATION: Pressure circulation type. Oil is scavenged from the five main bearings by the lower pump, returned through the air/oil heat exchanger and thence to the tank.

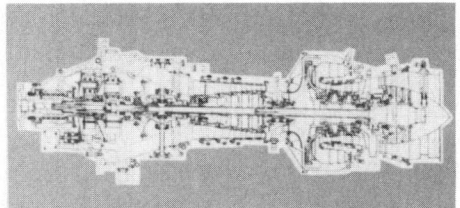

**Longitudinal section of Klimov TV7-117V
helicopter turboshaft**

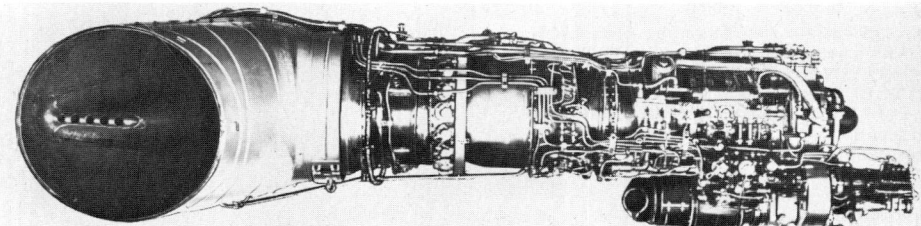

Klimov (Isotov) TV2-117A free-turbine turboshaft

OIL GRADE: Synthetic, Grade B-3V to MRTU 38-1-157-65 (nearest foreign substitute Castrol 98 to DERD.2487).

STARTING: The SP3-15 system comprises DC starter/ generator, six storage batteries, control panel, ground supply receptacle, and control switches and relays; airframe mounted except the GS-18TP starter/generator. The ignition unit comprises a control box, two plugs, solenoid valve, and switch. The starting fuel system comprises an automatic unit on the NR-40V pump, constant-pressure valve, and two igniters.

DIMENSIONS:

Length overall	2,835 mm (111.5 in)
Width (without jetpipe)	547 mm (21.5 in)
Height	745 mm (29.25 in)

WEIGHT, DRY:

Engine, without generator, etc	338 kg (745 lb)
VR-8A gearbox, less entrapped oil	745 kg (1,642 lb)

PERFORMANCE RATINGS:

Max	1,267 kW (1,700 shp)
T-O (S/L, static)	1,118 kW (1,500 shp)
Max continuous	895 kW (1,200 shp)
Cruise (122 knots; 225 km/h; 140 mph at 500 m; 1,640 ft)	746 kW (1,000 shp)

SPECIFIC FUEL CONSUMPTION:

T-O, as above	102.4 µg/J (0.606 lb/h/shp)
Cruise, as above	115.4 µg/J (0.683 lb/h/shp)

**Klimov TV3-117
free-turbine turboshaft**

TV3-117

This second-generation turboshaft has been produced in very large numbers. Bench testing began in 1974, the first flight was in 1976 and series production began in 1978.

TV3-117BK. Electronic control. Rated at 1,618 kW (2,170 shp). Powers some Ka-27s and Ka-28.

TV3-117MT. 1,417 kW (1,900 shp). Powers Mi-8T/TB/ TBK, -14, -17, -24.

TV3-117V. 1,660 kW (2,225 hp). Powers some Ka-27s, -29 and -32.

TV3-117VK. Electronic control. Rated at 1,640 kW (2,200 shp). Powers Kamov 'Hokum'.

TV3-117VM. Electronic control. Rated at 1,678 kW (2,250 shp) to 3,600 m (11,810 ft). Powers Mi-17-1VA, -25, -28 and -35.

Data below refer mainly to the MT:

TYPE: Free-turbine turboshaft.

COMPRESSOR: Ten-stage axial. Inlet guide vanes and first three stators variable. Pressure ratio 7.5.

COMBUSTION CHAMBER: Annular, improved version of TV2-117.

TURBINES: Two-stage gas generator turbine, improved from TV2-117. Two-stage power turbine.

OUTPUT: As TV2-117 but more compact jetpipe.

STARTING: BK, MT, pneumatic air turbine; V, VK, VM, electric.

DIMENSIONS:

Length	2,085 mm (82.1 in)
Width	640 mm (25.2 in)
Height	725 mm (28.5 in)

WEIGHT, DRY: 285 kg (628 lb)

PERFORMANCE RATINGS (S/L, max T-O): See variants

SPECIFIC FUEL CONSUMPTION:

Max T-O, TV3-117V 96.3 µg/J (0.57 lb/h/shp)

TV7-117

Described as a third-generation engine, the TV7-117 has a modular core incorporating advanced features and materials, and envisaged as the basis for various jet and shaft engines.

TV7-117C. Turboprop version, selected to power the Il-114, produced in collaboration with Polish industry. Also selected at 1,866 kW (2,250 shp) for MiG-101M and at 2,090 kW (2,800 shp) for MiG SVB freighter driving SV-346 six-blade propellers.

TV7-117V. Turboshaft version. Flat rated at 1,753 kW (2,350 shp) to 2,700 m (8,860 ft); OEI contingency 2,536 kW (3,400 shp) at S/L only. Powers Mi-38.

A growth core with two centrifugal stages is under development. Output will be in the 2,985 kW (4,000 shp) class.

TYPE: Free-turbine turboprop.

COMPRESSOR: Annular ram inlet around reduction gear tapers to entry to five-stage axial compressor, with variable inlet guide vanes and next two stators, followed by centrifugal stage on same shaft. Pressure ratio 16.

COMBUSTION CHAMBER: Annular folded reverse flow. Minimum pollution with wide range of fuels.

Klimov TV7-117 turboprop (test fairing on left in place of propeller)
(Jacques Marmain, Aviation Magazine International, Paris)

Klimov RD-33 augmented bypass turbojet

TURBINES: Two-stage gas generator turbine with cooled blades. Entry temperature 1,242°C. Two-stage power turbine.

REDUCTION GEAR: Planetary type, with new tooth profiles and anti-vibration mountings.

CONTROL SYSTEM: Full-authority electronic, with separate automatic control for ground and flight operation.

STARTING: Pneumatic air turbine, mass flow 0.2 kg (0.44 lb)/s.

DIMENSIONS:

Length	2,143 mm (84.37 in)
Width	886 mm (34.88 in)
Height	940 mm (37.0 in)

WEIGHT, DRY: 520 kg (1,146 lb)

PERFORMANCE RATINGS:
Max T-O
  1,865 kW (2,500 shp) to 35°C and 250 m (820 ft)
  Cruise (6,000 m; 19,685 ft at 270 knots; 500 km/h;
  311 mph)   1,342 kW (1,800 shp)
SPECIFIC FUEL CONSUMPTION:
  Cruise, as above   68.95 µg/J (0.408 lb/h/shp)

RD-33

This important fighter engine was designed before Isotov's death. Detail design began in 1968, meeting the requirements of the MiG-29, and the first bench run took place in 1972. Deliveries were initiated in 1976, and mass production followed in 198_. It powers all known MiG-29 versions and is offered as the engine of an upgraded MiG-21.

TYPE: Two-shaft afterburning bypass turbojet (low ratio turbofan).

LP COMPRESSOR: Four stages. Front bearing carried in four-strut nose, but no inlet guide vanes. Bypass ratio 0.4.

HP COMPRESSOR: Nine stages. Overall pressure ratio 20.

COMBUSTION CHAMBER: Annular with air-blast fuel nozzles giving generally smokeless combustion of a range of fuels.

TURBINES: Single-stage HP turbine with single-crystal cooled blades. Single-stage LP turbine.

AFTERBURNER: Combustion in both core and bypass flows. Nozzle with fully variable area and profile in primary and secondary flows. Outer nozzle has 24 flaps.

ACCESSORIES: Oil tank, hydromechanical fuel control and auxiliaries grouped above engine to reduce cross-section.

DIMENSIONS:
  Length   4,127 mm (162.5 in)
  Max diameter   1,000 mm (39.37 in)

WEIGHT, DRY:
  Bare engine   980 kg (2,160 lb)
  Complete power plant   1,217 kg (2,683 lb)

PERFORMANCE RATINGS (S/L):
  Max augmented   81.4 kN (18,300 lb st)
  Max dry   50.0 kN (11,240 lb st)

SPECIFIC FUEL CONSUMPTION:
  Max augmented   59.48 mg/Ns (2.10 lb/h/lb st)
  Max dry, S/L   21.8 mg/Ns (0.77 lb/h/lb st)

KOPTCHYENKO — see OMKB

KUZNETSOV

Kuibyshev

Kuznetsov was deputy to General V. Ya. Klimov during the Second World War. In the late 1940s his own bureau developed large turboprops and turbofans. The NK-4 was transferred to Ivchenko, and is described under Progress as the AI-20. Later engines, see KKBM.

LOTAREV — see Progress

LYULKA

During the late 1930s A. M. Lyulka, who died in June 1984, worked on an axial turbojet that became an early war casualty. Brief details of his subsequent work have appeared in previous editions of *Jane's*. His first major success was achieved with the AL-7. Based in Moscow, the bureau is today known as the Saturn, or Saturn/Lyulka, NPO (which see).

MIKULIN

A. A. Mikulin was a leading designer of engines from 1916. The bureau is today called Soyuz.

MKB

MOTOROSTROITELNOYE KONSTRUKTORSKOYE BURO

93 Komsomolsky Prospect (PO Box 624), Perm 614600
Telephone: 7 (83422) 452019
Fax: 7 (83422) 459777
Teletype: 134135 LAVA
Telex: 134802
Cables: Perm 10 LAVA
GENERAL DESIGNER: Yuri E. Reshetnikov

This large design bureau was founded 40 years ago by Shvetsov (which see), who was followed in 1953 by Soloviev. On the same site are MKB, PPO Aviadvigatel (aviation engine) and PPO Motorostroitel (motor manufacture) named for Ya. M. Sverdlov. Today many of its new projects are based on the core of the PS-90A turbofan. One group, beginning with the PS-90 GP-1 and GP-2, are for industrial and marine applications. Some are shaft engines for aircraft, with ratings up to 16,000 kW (21,400 shp). Another series are advanced propfans, particular attention being paid to aft-fan derivatives with contra-rotating shrouded fans with a bypass ratio in the region of 30.

D-15

This engine was first reported, in 1959, as that fitted to the Type 201-M which gained world records for speed and altitude. This aircraft was a special Myasishchev M-4, and the engine was standard in some versions of this aircraft. Details of the D-15 are still unknown in the West, but it is probably a two-shaft turbojet. It laid the foundation upon which Soloviev's bureau produced the civil D-20 and D-30.

PERFORMANCE RATING:
  T-O   128.6 kN (28,660 lb st)

D-20

The D-20 was the first turbofan in the world to enter scheduled airline service. A two-shaft engine, it was qualified in 1962 as the **D-20P** to power the Tu-124 at a rating of 52.96 kN (11,905 lb st). A full description last appeared in *Jane's* in 1987-88.

The engine used in the twin-engined version of the Myasishchev M-17 (NATO 'Mystic-B') is almost certainly a version of the D-20. Thrust is given as 49 kN (11,023 lb st).

D-25V

D-25V is the Soloviev designation for the turboshaft which powers the Mi-6 and Mi-10 helicopters. It is usually referred to by its official designation of **TV-2BM**.

The helicopter power plant comprises two D-25V engines, identical except for handed jetpipes, and an R-7 gearbox. The latter has four stages of large gearwheels

MKB (Soloviev) D-25V free-turbine turboshaft

providing an overall ratio of 69.2. The R-7 is 2,795 mm (110.04 in) high, 1,551 mm (61.06 in) wide and 1,852 mm (72.91 in) long. Its dry weight is 3,200 kg (7,054 lb).

The D-25V is flat rated to maintain rated power to 3,000 m (10,000 ft) or to temperatures up to 40°C at sea level.

The **D-25VF** is uprated to 4,847 kW (6,500 shp). These engines are believed to incorporate a zero stage on the compressor and to operate at higher turbine gas temperatures. They power the Mi-10K crane helicopter.

The following details apply to the basic D-25V:

TYPE: Single-shaft turboshaft with free power turbine.

COMPRESSOR: Nine-stage axial, with fixed inlet guide vanes and blow-off valves. Pressure ratio 5.6 at T-O power, 10,530 rpm.

COMBUSTION CHAMBER: Can-annular with 12 flame tubes.

FUEL GRADE: T-1, TS-1 to GOST 10227-62 (DERD.2494, MIL-F-5616).

TURBINE: Single-stage compressor turbine, overhung behind rear roller bearing. Two-stage power turbine, overhung on end of rear output shaft. Normal power turbine rpm, 7,800-8,300; maximum 9,000.

LUBRICATION: Pressure circulation at 3.45-4.41 bars (50-64 lb/sq in). Separate systems for gas generator and for power turbine, transmission and gearbox.

OIL GRADE: Gas generator, MK-8 to GOST 6457-66 or GOST 982-56. Power turbine and gearbox, mixture (75-25 Summer, 50-50 Winter) of MK-22 or MS-20 to GOST 1013-49 and MK-8 or 982-56.

ACCESSORIES: SP3-12TV electric supply and starting system; fuel supply to separate LP and HP systems; airframe accessories driven off upper and lower gearboxes.

STARTING: The SP3-12TV comprises an STG-12TM starter/generator on each engine, igniter unit, two spark plugs with cooling shrouds, two contactors, solenoid air valve, pressure warning, PSG-12V control panel and electro-hydraulic cutout switch of the TsP-23A centrifugal governor.

DIMENSIONS:
  Length overall, bare   2,737 mm (107.75 in)
  Length overall with transmission shaft
                  5,537 mm (218.0 in)
  Width   1,086 mm (42.76 in)
  Height   1,158 mm (45.59 in)

WEIGHT, DRY:
  With engine mounted accessories   1,325 kg (2,921 lb)

PERFORMANCE RATINGS:
  T-O   4,101 kW (5,500 shp)
  Rated power   3,504 kW (4,700 shp)
  Cruise (1,000 m; 3,280 ft, 135 knots; 250 km/h; 155 mph)   2,983 kW (4,000 shp)

SPECIFIC FUEL CONSUMPTION:
  T-O, as above   108 µg/J (0.639 lb/h/shp)
  Cruise, as above   118.1 µg/J (0.699 lb/h/shp)

D-30

Since about 1972 the standard engine of the Tu-134A has been the **D-30-II**, with reverser. One Tu-134 was flown with D-30 engines with a zero stage on the LP compressor; the existing ratings were obtained at reduced gas temperature and maintained to ISA + 25°C.

TYPE: Two-shaft turbofan (bypass turbojet).

FAN: Four-stage axial (LP compressor). First stage has shrouded titanium blades in disc by pinned joints. Pressure ratio (T-O rating, 7,700 rpm, S/L, static), 2.65. Mass flow 125 kg (265 lb)/s. Bypass ratio 1.

COMPRESSOR: Ten-stage axial (HP compressor). Drum and disc construction, largely of titanium. Pressure ratio (T-O rating, 11,600 rpm, S/L, static), 7.1. Overall pressure ratio, 17.4.

COMBUSTION CHAMBER: Can-annular, with 12 flame tubes fitted with duplex burners.

FUEL GRADE: T-1 and TS-1 to GOST 10227-62 (equivalent to DERD.2494 or MIL-F-5616).

TURBINE: Two-stage HP turbine. First stage has cooled blades in both stator and rotor. LP turbine also has two stages. All blades shrouded and bearings shock mounted.

JETPIPE: Main and bypass mixer with curvilinear ducts. D-30-II engine of Tu-134A fitted with twin-clamshell reverser.

LUBRICATION: Open type, with oil returned to tank.

OIL GRADE: Mineral oil MK-8 or MK-8P to GOST 6457-66 (equivalent to DERD.2490 or MIL-O-6081B).

ACCESSORIES: Automatic ice protection system, fire extinguishing for core and bypass flows, vibration detectors on casings, oil chip detectors and automatic limitation of exhaust gas temperature to 620°C at take-off or when starting and to 630°C in flight (5 min limit). Shaft driven accessories driven via radial bevel gear shafts in centre casing, mainly off HP spool. D-30-II carries constant speed drives for alternators.

STARTING: Electric DC starting system incorporating STG-12TVMO starter/generators

DIMENSIONS:
Overall length	3,983 mm (156.8 in)
Base diameter of inlet casing	1,050 mm (41.3 in)

WEIGHT, DRY: 1,550 kg (3,417 lb)

PERFORMANCE RATINGS:
T-O	66.68 kN (14,990 lb st)
Long-range cruise rating, 11,000 m (36,000 ft) and Mach 0.75	12.75 kN (2,866 lb)

SPECIFIC FUEL CONSUMPTION:
T-O	17.56 mg/Ns (0.62 lb/h/lb st)
Cruise, as above	21.81 mg/Ns (0.77 lb/h/lb)

D-30K

Despite its designation, this turbofan is much larger and more powerful than the D-30. The basic **D-30KU**, to which the specification details apply, replaced the NK-8-4 as power plant of the Il-62M. The **D-30KU-154-II** is configured to suit the Tu-154M and is derated to 104 kN (23,380 lb st). The **D-30KP**, rated at 117.7 kN (26,455 lb st), was the original engine of all versions of the Il-76. Clamshell reversers are fitted to all four engines of this aircraft, and to the outer engines of the Il-62M. These reversers are airframe assemblies incorporated in the nacelle. In 1980 the KP was replaced in production by the **KP-1** which maintains full power to ISA +23°C. The **D-30KPV**, rated at 147.1 kN (33,070 lb st) powers the Beriev A-40 Albatross, with reversers superficially resembling those of the Il-76.

TYPE: Two-shaft turbofan, with mixer and reverser.

FAN (LP COMPRESSOR): Three stages, mainly of titanium alloy. First-stage rotor blades with part-span snubbers. Mass flow, 269 kg (593 lb)/s at 4,730 rpm (87.9 per cent), with bypass ratio of 2.42.

HP COMPRESSOR: Eleven stages, first two having part-span snubbers. Guide vanes turn 30° over 7,900-9,600 rpm, while air is bled from fifth and sixth stages. Overall pressure ratio (S/L, static) 20 at HP speed of 10,460 rpm (96 per cent).

COMBUSTION CHAMBER: Can-annular type with 12 flame tubes. Each tube comprises hemispherical head and eight short sections welded with gaps for dilution air. Single swirl type main/pilot burner centred in each tube. Igniter plugs in two tubes.

FUEL GRADE: T-1, TS-1, GOST-10227-62, A-1 (D1655/63t), DERD.2494 or 2498, Air 3405/B or 3-GP-23e.

TURBINES: Two-stage HP turbine with cooled blades in both stages. Second-stage rotor blades tip shrouded. Max gas temperature 1,122°C. Four-stage LP turbine with shrouded blades.

LUBRICATION: Closed type. Fuel/oil heat exchanger and centrifugal air separator with particle warning.

OIL GRADE: MK-8 or MK-8P to GOST 6467-66 (mineral) or BNII NP-50-1-4F to GOST 13076-67 (synthetic).

ACCESSORIES: Front and rear drive boxes under engine carry all shaft driven accessories. Differential constant speed drive to alternator and air turbine starter.

STARTING: Pneumatic starter fed by ground supply, APU or cross-bleed.

DIMENSIONS:
Length with reverser	5,700 mm (224 in)
Inlet diameter	1,464 mm (57.6 in)
Maximum diameter of casing	1,560 mm (61.4 in)

WEIGHT, DRY:
With reverser	2,650 kg (5,842 lb)
Without reverser	2,300 kg (5,071 lb)

PERFORMANCE RATINGS (ISA):
T-O	107.9 kN (24,250 lb st) to 21°C
Cruise at 11,000 m (36,000 ft) and Mach 0.8	27 kN (6,063 lb)

SPECIFIC FUEL CONSUMPTION:
At T-O rating	13.88 mg/Ns (0.49 lb/h/lb st)
Cruise, as above	19.83 mg/Ns (0.70 lb/h/lb)

TYPE R

Powers the Tupolev Tu-160 'Blackjack'. Also designated **Type 15**. Rated at 245 kN (55,075 lb st) with afterburning.

PS-90A (D-90A)

This high bypass ratio turbofan is not derived from any existing engine. It is assembled from 11 modules, and is designed for long life, high reliability and low fuel burn.

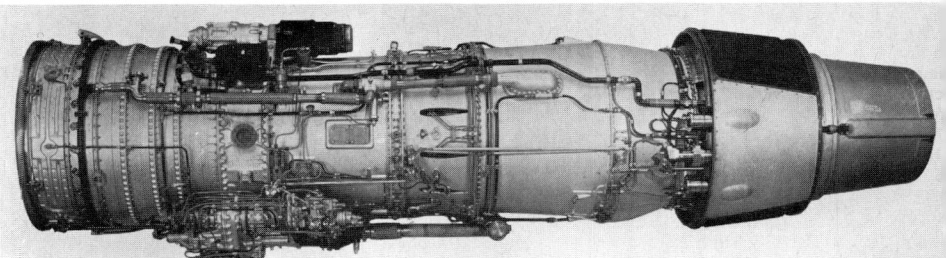

MKB (Soloviev) D-30 Series II two-shaft turbofan with reverser

MKB (Soloviev) D-30KU two-shaft turbofan with reverser

MKB (Soloviev) PS-90A two-shaft turbofan *(Brian M. Service)*

Bench testing began in 1985. Flight testing was in progress in 1987 with an engine replacing a D-30KP in an Il-76. Certification was due in 1989. The PS-90A powers the Il-96-300, first flown on 28 September 1988 with engines derated to 132.4 kN (29,762 lb st), and the Tu-204, first flown on 2 January 1989 with fully rated PS-90As. This engine is the first to have a designation reflecting the name of the General Designer (Soloviev).

In 1990 Mr Reshetnikov stated that the sfc so far achieved is 16.85 mg/Ns (0.595 lb/h/lb), and that remedial measures include adding a third stage to the LP booster and modifying blade profiles. The improved engine is to be certificated in 1993.

TYPE: Two-shaft turbofan with mixer and fan reverser.

FAN: Single-stage, with 28 wide-chord (at root 250 mm; 9.84 in) titanium blades, without snubbers or shrouds. Hub/tip ratio 0.34. Bypass ratio (T-O) 4.6, (cruise) 4.8.

LP COMPRESSOR: Three-stage booster bolted to rear of fan.

HP COMPRESSOR: 13-stage spool with variable inlet guide vanes and first two stators. Overall pressure ratio (T-O) 36.4, (cruise) 35.5. Speed (max) 11,820 rpm.

COMBUSTION CHAMBER: Fully annular with vaporising burners and two igniters.

HP TURBINE: Two stages, with advanced aircooled blades. Entry gas temperature 1,565°K (1,292°C).

LP TURBINE: Four stages.

JETPIPE: Mixer combines core and bypass flows to single nozzle.

CONTROL SYSTEM: Full-authority digital electronic.

REVERSER: Multiple blocker doors close off fan duct as translating mid-section of cowl moves to rear, to uncover all-round reverser cascades. No core reverser.

DIMENSIONS:
Fan diameter	1,900 mm (74.8 in)
Overall length	5,329 mm (209.8 in)

WEIGHT, DRY: 2,800 kg (6,173 lb)

PERFORMANCE RATINGS (ISA):
T-O, S/L	156.9 kN (35,275 lb st) to 30°C
Cruise at 11,000 m (36,000 ft) and Mach 0.8	34.36 kN (7,716 lb)

SPECIFIC FUEL CONSUMPTION:
Cruise, as above	16.43 mg/Ns (0.58 lb/h/lb)

D-100/110

The D-100 and D-110 are turbofans for the 1990s, based on the PS-90A core. The **D-100** would have a fan with a diameter of 2,333 mm (91.85 in), the bypass ratio being between 6 and 8. Overall pressure ratio would be 35 to 5, TET 1,287°-1,327°C, dry weight 3,350-3,550 kg (7,385-7,826 lb), T-O thrust 19-21 tonnes (186.3-205.9 kN, 41,890-46,300 lb st) and sfc (cruise, 11 km/36,000 ft, M 0.8) of 15.30 mg/Ns (0.54 lb/h/lb st).

The **D-110** is a more advanced engine with a geared fan of 2,670 mm (105 in) diameter, giving a bypass ratio of 9 to 12. Overall pressure ratio would be 31 to 44, TET 1,327°C, dry weight 3,500-4,000 kg (7,716-8,820 lb), T-O thrust 20-24 tonnes (196.1-235.3 kN, 44,090-52,900 lb st) and sfc (cruise, same conditions) 14.73 mg/Ns (0.52 lb/h/lb st).

An accompanying illustration shows the two engines together with the planned next generation propfan. This has some features resembling the Garrett ATF3, with the same double reverse-flow arrangement, accessories being at the rear and the core jet being turned 180° to escape into the fan duct.

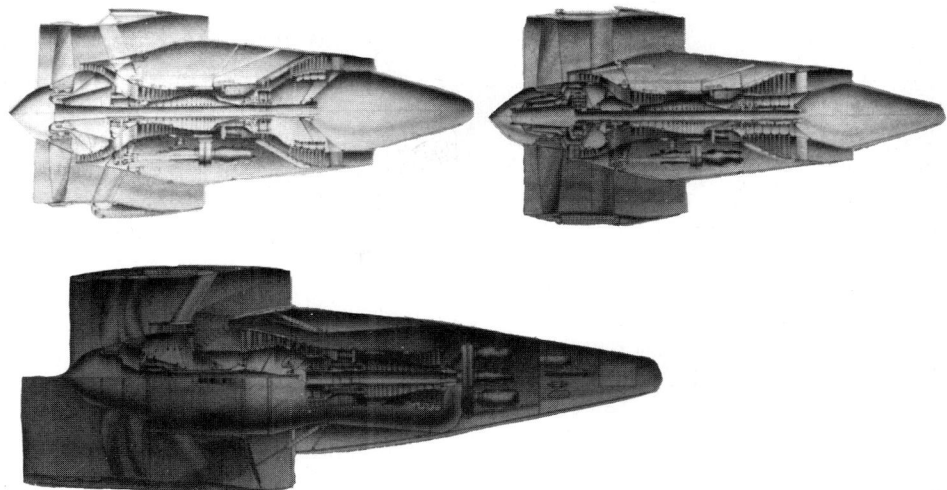

MKB projects based on the PS-90A: from the top, D-100, D-110 and an advanced propfan

---

NOVIKOV — *see RKBM*

OMKB
OMSK AIRCRAFT ENGINE DESIGN BUREAU
644021 Omsk
Telephone: 33 49 81, 33 00 84
Telegraph: Omsk-21 MARS
Teletype: Omsk-3274 MARS
Telex: 133112 + MARS SU

This bureau was formerly headed by Glushenkov. The current General Designer is Koptchyenko. Development, in partnership with TsIAM (Central Institute for Aviation Motors) began in 1957. The first product was the 224 kW (300 hp) GTD-1, followed by the GTD-5 and -5M, which continue in production. The first major engine for aircraft propulsion was the GTD-3, produced from 1964 as a twin package plus common reduction gear for helicopters. In 1970 came the TVD-10 turboprop. Apart from APUs the latest OMKB engines are the TVD-20 and TV-O-100.

TVD-10
Military designation: GTD-3
This free turbine engine was developed to power the Kamov Ka-25 helicopter. The civil turboshaft was licensed to Poland for production, and a description appears under WSK-PZL Rzeszów. Ka-25 engines were made in the Soviet Union, the **GTD-3F** being rated at 671 kW (900 shp) and the **GTD-3BM** at 738 kW (990 shp).

The **TVD-10B** is the turboprop version selected to power the An-28. This engine is produced in Poland as the **TWD-10B**, as described under WSK-PZL Rzeszów.

TV-O-100
This engine was developed to provide a modern core in the 537 kW (720 shp) class. Its initial application is in the single-turbine Ka-126 helicopter produced under licence in Romania. Development has been partly transferred to Romania, and in 1991 was in difficulties. Future development of the engine to 619 kW (830 shp), with pressure ratio about 10.2 and turbine entry temperature of 1,077°C, may be carried out in collaboration with that country. A derated version (530 kW; 710 shp) is a candidate engine for the Ka-118. TsIAM, the national aero-engine research organisation, is testing a heat exchanger with which specific fuel consumption may be reduced by 15-20 per cent.
TYPE: Free-turbine turboshaft. Modular construction.
COMPRESSOR: Inlet above engine leads via large dust/sand extractor to two-stage axial compressor, with inlet and

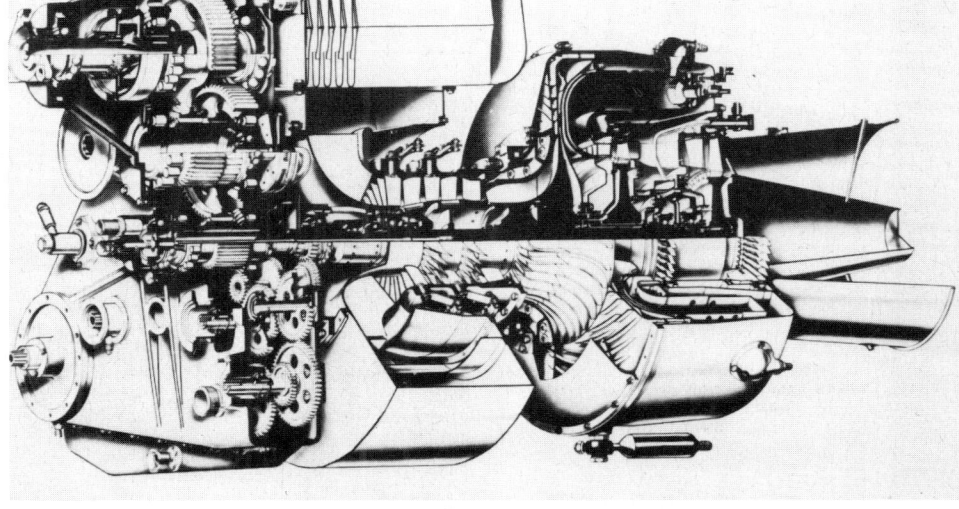

Cutaway drawing of OMKB TV-O-100 turboshaft
(Jacques Marmain, Aviation Magazine International, Paris)

intermediate stator stages variable, and single centrifugal stage. Pressure ratio 9.2.
COMBUSTION CHAMBER: Annular folded reverse flow.
TURBINES: Single-stage gas generator turbine with uncooled blades. Turbine entry temperature 1,027°C. Single-stage power turbine.
CONTROL SYSTEM: Dual-channel electronic.
OUTPUT SHAFT: Central quill shaft drives gear train at front, with triple spur gears to output shaft at top.
WEIGHT, DRY: 156 kg (344 lb)
PERFORMANCE RATINGS (S/L):
Maximum	537 kW (720 shp)
Cruise	343 kW (460 shp)

SPECIFIC FUEL CONSUMPTION:
Cruise	109.2 µg/J (0.646 lb/h/shp)

TVD-20
This turboprop is fitted to the An-3. It uses a derivative of the TVD-10B gas generator, with a zero stage (to a total of seven) on the compressor and a second stage on the power turbine.

COMPRESSOR: Seven axial stages plus one centrifugal. Inlet faces aft.
COMBUSTION CHAMBER: As TVD-10B.
TURBINES: Two-stage gas-generator turbine. Two-stage free power turbine.
PROPELLER DRIVE: Quill shaft leads forward from power turbine to drive two-stage gearbox with accessory drives above. Drive to AV-17 propeller incorporates brake.
ACCESSORIES: Two 27 V electric starters, provision for dusting or spraying pumps.
DIMENSIONS:
Length	1,770 mm (69.7 in)
Width	850 mm (33.5 in)
Height	845 mm (33.3 in)

WEIGHT, DRY: 285 kg (628 lb)
PERFORMANCE RATING (S/L):
T-O	1,067 kW (1,430 shp)

SPECIFIC FUEL CONSUMPTION:
T-O as above	85.4 µg/J (0.506 lb/h/shp)

PPO AVIADVIGATEL

Together with Motorostroitel and MKB (which see) at the same address, this organisation, the Scientific and Production Organization 'Aircraft Engines', manufactures the Reshetnikov D-30F6 fighter engine.

D-30F6
This large supersonic engine was designed from 1972 expressly for the MiG-31. Requirements included supersonic speed at sea level, Mach 3 at high altitude and, predominantly, the lowest possible fuel consumption.
TYPE: Two-shaft augmented turbofan (bypass turbojet).

LP COMPRESSOR: Five stages, no inlet guide vanes, variable stators or snubbers. Pressure ratio 3. Bypass ratio 3.
HP COMPRESSOR: 10 stages, first row variable stators and bypass doors behind stages 4 and 5. Pressure ratio 7.05.
COMBUSTION CHAMBER: Can-annular with 12 interlinked flame tubes.
TURBINES: Two-stage HP, with entry temperature 1,660°K (1,387°C). Two-stage LP.
AFTERBURNER: High-volume, unrestricted length, with four flameholder rings.
NOZZLE: Multi-flap con-di type with very large secondary and cooling flows. Area and profile varied over unprecedented range by 18 rams. Flow stabilised by auxiliary valve plates in divergent petals.

AUXILIARIES: Independent gas-turbine APU under compressor used for starting (two per aircraft). Independent lubrication system, IPM-10 synthetic oil.
WEIGHT, DRY: 2,416 kg (5,326 lb)
PERFORMANCE RATINGS (S/L static):
Dry	93.2 kN (20,944 lb st)
Augmented	151.96 kN (34,171 lb st)
Frontal (max)	186.1 kN (41,843 lb st)
Power/frontal area	18,900 kg/m² (3,871 lb/sq ft)

SPECIFIC FUEL CONSUMPTION:
Dry	20.4 mg/Ns (0.72 lb/h/lb st)
Augmented	53.8 mg/Ns (1.9 lb/h/lb st)

PROGRESS

330064 Zaporozhye 64
Telephone: 7 650327
Telex: 127464
GENERAL DESIGNER: Feodor Mikhailovich Muravtchyenko

For many years the name of the engine KB (experimental construction bureau) at Zaporozhye, formerly headed by Ivchenko and then by Lotarev, Progress is an alternative to ZMKB. See introduction to Klimov.

AI-20

This turboprop was developed as the NK-4 at the Kuznetsov bureau in 1947-52, with the assistance of German engineers. Eventually preferred to the VK-2, the Zaporozhye collective was charged with refinement and production. Redesignated AI-20 (for Ivchenko), it was produced from 1955, with series deliveries from late 1958.

AI-20K. Rated at 2,942 ekW (3,945 ehp). Used in Il-18V, An-10A and An-12. Produced at Shanghai as **WJ6**.

AI-20M. Initial T-O rating of 3,124 ekW (4,190 ehp), later increased to 3,169 ekW (4,250 ehp). Fitted to An-12 and Il-18/20/22/38.

AI-20D. Rated at 3,124 ekW (4,190 ehp); navalised engine fitted to Beriev M-12.

AI-20DM. Rated at 3,812 ekW (5,112 ehp). Fitted to An-32. In 1985 this engine was reported to the FAI as the **AM-20**. Another designation is **AI-20D Series 5**.

The AI-20 was designed to operate from −60°C to +55°C. The rotor speed is at 12,300 rpm by automatic variation of propeller pitch. TBO is 4,000 or 4,750 h for AI-20K versions but only 1,000 h for the D family. Excluding China, total deliveries exceed 19,000 engines, and these have flown well over 60 million hours.

The following description refers to the AI-20M:
TYPE: Single-shaft turboprop.
COMPRESSOR: Ten stages. Magnesium alloy stator casing in upper and lower halves. Pressure ratio 9.45. Mass flow 20.7 kg (45.6 lb)/s.
COMBUSTION CHAMBER: Annular with ten burner cones. Pilot burners and ignition plugs at top of casing.
FUEL GRADE: T-1 or TS-1 to GOST-10227-62 (DERD.2492, JP-1 to MIL-F-5616).
TURBINE: Three stages. Rotor blades shrouded at inner and outer ends and installed in pairs in slots in aircooled discs. Entry temperature, AI-20D series 930°C, AI-20K series 850°C.
REDUCTION GEAR: Planetary type, incorporating six-cylinder torquemeter and negative-thrust transmitter (type IKM), for autofeathering AV-68I propeller. Ratio 0.08732 (input speed 12,300 rpm except ground-idle 10,400 rpm).
LUBRICATION: Pressure-feed type with full recirculation.
OIL GRADE: 75 per cent GOST 982-56 or MK-8 to GOST 6457-66 (DERD.2490 or MIL-O-6081B) and 25 per cent MS-20 or MK-22 to GOST 1013-49 (DERD.2472 or MIL-O-6082B).
STARTING: Two electric starter/generators, Type STG-12 TMO-1000, supplied from ground or TG-16 APU.
DIMENSIONS:

Length	3,096 mm (121.89 in)
Width	842 mm (33.15 in)
Height	1,180 mm (46.46 in)

WEIGHT, DRY: 1,040 kg (2,292 lb)
PERFORMANCE RATINGS:

T-O	3,169 ekW (4,250 ehp)
Cruise (350 knots; 650 km/h; 404 mph at 8,000 m; 26,000 ft)	2,013 ekW (2,700 ehp)

SPECIFIC FUEL CONSUMPTION:

T-O	104.3 μg/J (0.617 lb/h/ehp)
Cruise, as above	73.3 μg/J (0.434 lb/h/ehp)

AI-24

This turboprop powers the An-24 and its derivatives. Production began in 1960 and the following data refer to engines of the second series, which were in production by the Spring of 1966.

The **AI-24** of 1,875 ekW (2,515 ehp) powered the An-24V Series I, and was followed by the **AI-24A** with provision for water injection; produced at DEMC (China) as the **WJ5A**.

The **AI-24T** of 2,103 ekW (2,820 ehp) with water injection is used in the An-26 and An-30. Vibration monitoring, automatic relief of overloads and gas temperature and autofeathering. From 1980, designated **AI-24VT** with improved fuel economy.

The AI-24 is maintained at 15,100 rpm by automatic variation of propeller pitch. The engine is flat rated to 3,500 m (11,500 ft). TBO is 3,000 h (original AI-24, 4,000 h). Deliveries, excluding Chinese production, total 14,800. Total flight time in 1988 was nearly 51 million hours.

Following the flight testing of propellers with eight blades on an An-24, a research programme has been under way on propfans, with emphasis on contra-rotating configurations. Two full scale examples have been run with an AI-24 engine. Typical configurations have 6+6, 7+7 and 8+8 blades.
TYPE: Single-shaft turboprop.
COMPRESSOR: Ten-stage axial. Pressure ratio, AI-24T 7.55, VT 7.65. Mass flow 14.4 kg (31.7 lb)/s.
COMBUSTION CHAMBER: Annular, with eight simplex burners and two starting units, each comprising a body, pilot burner and igniter plug.

Progress (Ivchenko) AI-20M single-shaft turboprop *(Aviation Magazine International, Paris)*

Progress (Ivchenko) AI-24 single-shaft turboprop *(Aviation Magazine International, Paris)*

FUEL GRADE: T-1, TS-1 to GOST 10227-62 (DERD.2494 or MIL-F-5616).
TURBINE: Three-stage axial with solid blades. Rotor/stator sealing effected by soft inserts mounted in grooves in nozzle assemblies. Entry temperature 797°C.
REDUCTION GEAR: Planetary type, incorporating hydraulic torquemeter and electromagnetic negative thrust transmitter for propeller autofeathering. Type AV-72 propeller (AI-24T drives AV-72T propeller). Ratio 0.08255.
LUBRICATION: Pressure circulation system.
OIL GRADE: 75 per cent GOST 982-56 or MK-8 (DERD.2490 or MIL-O-6081B) and 25 per cent MS-20 or MK-22 (DERD.2472 or MIL-O-6082B).
ACCESSORIES: Mounted on front casing are starter/generator, alternator, aerodynamic probe, ice detector, negative-thrust feathering valve, torque transmitter, oil filter, propeller speed governor and centrifugal breather. Below casing are oil unit, air separator, LP and HP fuel pumps and drives to hydraulic pump and tachometer generators.
STARTING: Electric STG-18TMO starter/generator supplied from ground power or from TG-16 APU.
DIMENSIONS:

Length overall	2,346 mm (92.36 in)
Width	677 mm (26.65 in)
Height	1,075 mm (42.32 in)

WEIGHT, DRY: 600 kg (1,323 lb)
PERFORMANCE RATINGS:

T-O: AI-24A	1,875 ekW (2,515 ehp)
AI-24VT	2,103 ekW (2,820 ehp)

Cruise rating at 243 knots (450 km/h; 280 mph) at 6,000 m (19,685 ft):

AI-24A	1,156 ekW (1,550 ehp)
AI-24T	1,178 ekW (1,580 ehp)

SPECIFIC FUEL CONSUMPTION:

At cruise rating: AI-24A	91.3 μg/J (0.540 lb/h/ehp)
AI-24T	90.1 μg/J (0.533 lb/h/ehp)
AI-24VT	76.4 μg/J (0.452 lb/h/ehp)
OIL CONSUMPTION:	0.85 kg (1.87 lb)/h

AI-25

This turbofan powers the Yak-40. Yak-40Bs of the Soviet Air Force have an AI-25 with an aircooled HP turbine and rating of 17.13 kN (3,850 lb st). The AI-25TL powers the Czech L-39 trainer but will be replaced in the L-59 by the DV-2. Deliveries since 1967 have reached 9,800, flight time exceeding 40 million hours.
TYPE: Two-shaft turbofan.
FAN: Three-stage axial. Drum/disc construction with pin-jointed blades. Casing and fan duct of magnesium alloy. Pressure ratio, 1.695 at 10,750 rpm. Bypass ratio 2.
COMPRESSOR: Eight-stage axial. Drum/disc construction of titanium, with aluminium and magnesium casing. Dovetailed blades. Peak pressure ratio, 4.68 at 16,640 rpm. Overall pressure ratio 8.
COMBUSTION CHAMBER: Annular. Inner and outer casings joined upstream to 12 burner heads with stabilisers.
FUEL GRADE: T-1, TS-1 to GOST 10227-62 (DERD.2494, MIL-F-5616).

Progress (Ivchenko) AI-25TL two-shaft turbofan

TURBINE: Single-stage HP turbine; two-stage LP turbine. Shrouded solid rotor blades held by fir tree roots in cooled discs.
LUBRICATION: Self-contained, pressure circulating.
OIL GRADE: MK-8 to GOST 6457-66 or MK-6 to GOST 10328-63 (Western equivalents, DERD.2490 or MIL-O-6081B). Consumption 0.3 litres (0.63 US pints; 0.53 Imp pints)/h.
ACCESSORIES: All mounted on gearbox driven off HP spool. Equipment includes automatic fire extinguishing (agent can be supplied into oil-contacted labyrinth cavities), ice protection, automatic starting and control system, oil system chip detector and casing vibration monitor.
STARTING: Pneumatic. Air starter type SV-25 is supplied from ground hose or AI-9 APU or an operating engine bleed.
DIMENSIONS:

Length overall	1,993 mm (78.46 in)
Width overall	820 mm (32.28 in)
Height overall	895 mm (35.24 in)

WEIGHT, DRY:

Without accessories	290 kg (639 lb)

PERFORMANCE RATINGS:

T-O	14.71 kN (3,307 lb st)
Long-range cruise rating, 6,000 m (20,000 ft) and 296 knots (550 km/h; 342 mph)	3.49 kN (785 lb st)

SPECIFIC FUEL CONSUMPTION:

T-O	15.86 mg/Ns (0.56 lb/h/lb st)
Cruise, as above	23.71 mg/Ns (0.837 lb/h/lb)

DV-2

This small turbofan was designed jointly with ZVL (which see, under Czechoslovakia) to replace the AI-25TL as the engine of the Aero L-59 (previously L-39 MS) trainer. The engine was designed to fit the existing engine bay, so that L-39s can be re-engined.

The same core is to be used in several engines:

DV-2. Basic turbofan. The description below applies to this engine. Will power L-59 and selected to power Il-108 business jet and China/Pakistan K-8 single-engined trainer/attack aircraft.

DV-2B. Larger fan, with bypass ratio 2. T-O rating 25 kN (5,610 lb st); sfc 15.26 mg/Ns (0.539 lb/h/lb st); dry weight about 500 kg (1,102 lb).

DV-2F. Afterburning engine for supersonic applications. Bypass ratio 1.4; maximum thrust 36 kN (8,085 lb st); sfc 61.1 mg/Ns (2.16 lb/h/lb st); dry weight about 600 kg (1,323 lb).

DV-12. Turboshaft for helicopters and tilt-rotor aircraft. Large curved jetpipe to side and rear gearbox and output shaft. Max contingency power 5,480 kW (7,346 shp); sfc 68.1 μg/J (0.403 lb/h/shp); dry weight about 580 kg (1,279 lb).

DV-22. Turbofan for transport aircraft. Mass flow 122 kg (269 lb)/s; bypass ratio 5; T-O thrust 35.1 kN (7,900 lb st); sfc 11.1 mg/Ns (0.391 lb/h/lb st); dry weight 675 kg (3,062 lb). Planned for later Il-108.

DV-32. Turboshaft for helicopters and tilt-rotor aircraft. As DV-12 but front drive. Same weight.

DV-X. Projected core for pusher turboprop or propfan. T-O rating 4,425 kW (5,932 shp) plus 2.4 kN (540 lb st) to 30°C; sfc 75.4 μg/J (0.446 lb/h/shp).
TYPE: Two-shaft turbofan.
FAN: Single stage, overhung, with 15 titanium blades of large chord, without snubbers, hub/tip ratio 0.37, bypass ratio 1.46. Diameter 645 mm (25.4 in). Mass flow 49.5 kg (109 lb)/s.
LP COMPRESSOR: Two stages, rotating with fan.
HP COMPRESSOR: Seven stages. Pressure ratio 13.5.
COMBUSTION CHAMBER: Annular, giving low emissions.
HP TURBINE: Single stage, max gas temperature 1,127°C.
LP TURBINE: Uncooled, two-stage.
STARTING: Air turbine.
DIMENSIONS:

Length	1,721 mm (67.75 in)
Width	994 mm (39.1 in)
Height	1,050 mm (41.3 in)

WEIGHT, DRY: 475 kg (1,047 lb)
PERFORMANCE RATING (S/L, T-O): 21.58 kN (4,852 lb st)
SPECIFIC FUEL CONSUMPTION: 16.7 mg/Ns (0.59 lb/h/lb st)

D-36

As successor to Ivchenko at Zaporozhye, Lotarev developed the turbofan that powers the An-72, An-74 and Yak-42. Bench testing began in 1971, flight testing in 1974 and series production in 1977. The D-36 has also been selected for the MiG-18-50 long range business jet. Several of its modules, with more than 1.2 million hours flying, have been used in the D-136, D-236, D-336 and D-436, all of which are described separately.
TYPE: Three-shaft turbofan. Made of 12 modules.
FAN: Single-stage; 29 inserted titanium blades with part-span shrouds (snubbers). Mass flow 260 kg (573 lb)/s. Bypass ratio 5.6. Speed (max) 5,300 rpm.
LP COMPRESSOR: Six stages with variable inlet vanes and four blow-off valves. Speed (max) 11,200 rpm.
HP COMPRESSOR: Six stages, titanium and steel. Speed (max) 14,300 rpm. Overall engine pressure ratio at T-O, S/L ISA static, 20.

Progress/ZVL DV-2 two-shaft turbofan *(Brian M. Service)*

Progress (Lotarev) D-18T three-shaft turbofan with reverser *(Brian M. Service)*

COMBUSTION CHAMBER: Annular, with 28 burners and with integral inlet guide vanes to HP turbine.
HP TURBINE: Single-stage; aircooled blades. Max inlet temperature 1,177°C (1,450°K).
LP TURBINE: Single-stage. (Called IP in Western engines.)
FAN TURBINE: Two-stage. (Called LP in Western engines.)
BYPASS DUCT: Short-length, comprising forward module (fan contravane) and rear module (intermediate case). Contravane contains 49 vanes to remove twist. Provision for reverser downstream of intermediate case.
ACCESSORIES: Shaft driven units mounted on gearbox mounted around underside of intermediate case.
DIMENSIONS:

Length	3,470 mm (136.6 in)
Diameter	1,390 mm (54.7 in)

WEIGHT, DRY: 1,106 kg (2,438 lb)
PERFORMANCE RATINGS (ISA):

T-O static	63.74 kN (14,330 lb st)
Max continuous	49.0 kN (11,025 lb st)
Max cruise at 8,000 m (26,250 ft) at Mach 0.75	15.7 kN (3,527 lb)

SPECIFIC FUEL CONSUMPTION:

T-O	10.195 mg/Ns (0.360 lb/h/lb st)
At max cont rating	9.83 mg/Ns (0.347 lb/h/lb st)
Max cruise as above	18.4 mg/Ns (0.65 lb/h/lb)

D-18T

For many years the main gap in the spectrum of available Soviet engines was a large HBPR (high bypass ratio) turbofan. In the 1970s the Lotarev bureau produced such engines in two sizes, the smaller (D-36) on an earlier timescale. The linear scale is about 2 : 1; so, in terms of airflow and thrust, the ratio is about 4 : 1.

The bigger engine is more advanced than the small one, its pressure ratio and turbine entry temperature being higher. The D-18T also has an integral fan duct reverser. It first ran in 1981 and four were fitted to the An-124 prototype which made its first flight on 26 December 1982. The D-18T has been produced in quantity for the An-124, and also powers the An-225. Selected for An-218.
TYPE: Three-shaft turbofan for large subsonic aircraft.
FAN: Single-stage with 33 inserted titanium blades with part-span shrouds. Mass flow 765 kg (1,687 lb)/s. Bypass ratio 5.7 at Mach 0.75 at 9,144 m (30,000 ft). Speed (max) 3,300 rpm.

IP COMPRESSOR: Seven-stage axial with variable inlet vanes. Speed (max) 5,750 rpm.
HP COMPRESSOR: Seven-stage axial. Speed (max) 9,000 rpm. Overall engine pressure ratio 27.5.
COMBUSTION CHAMBER: Annular, with forged and machined outer case and 28 vaporising burners.
FUEL GRADE: T-1, TS-1 or T-7 (Avtur equivalent).
HP TURBINE: Single-stage with aircooled directionally solidified blades with tip shrouds and raised root platforms. Max inlet temperature 1,327°C (1,600°K); temperature at cruise (as below) 1,080°C (1,353°K).
IP TURBINE: Single-stage with aircooled blades with tip shrouds.
LP TURBINE: Four stages with tip shrouded blades.
BYPASS DUCT: Comprises forward module, called contra-vane, with inserted blades (vanes) to remove twist from flow, followed by rear case with six large radial struts carrying pipes and shaft drives.
REVERSER: Attached to rear fan duct case, with multiple blocker doors pulled inwards by axial movement of translating cowl section, which simultaneously opens peripheral cascade rings directing expelled air forwards.
ACCESSORIES: Oil tank and all shaft driven accessories are grouped around lower half of rear fan case.
DIMENSIONS:

Length	5,400 mm (212.6 in)
Fan diameter	2,330 mm (91.73 in)

WEIGHT, DRY: 4,100 kg (9,039 lb)
PERFORMANCE RATINGS:

T-O (S/L, ISA + 13°C)	229.5 kN (51,590 lb st)
Max cruise (11,000 m; 36,100 ft, Mach 0.75, ISA)	50.47 kN (11,345 lb)

SPECIFIC FUEL CONSUMPTION:

T-O	10.195 mg/Ns (0.360 lb/h/lb st)
Cruise as above	16.142 mg/Ns (0.570 lb/h/lb)

D-27

In engineering design in 1991, the D-27 has been selected in its definitive pusher form to power the Yak-46 twin-engined passenger airliner. It is a 109.8 kN (24,683 lb st) propfan. Free internal turbines downstream of the core drive contra-rotating unducted propulsor blades, the front unit having eight blades and the rear unit six, the diameter being 3.8 m (12 ft 5½ in). S. A. Yakovlev claims the Yak-46 will burn 14 g of fuel per passenger/km, compared with the Yak-42M (D-436 engines) figure of 21 g. The tractor D-27, available earlier, has been selected to power the An-180. In this case the rating is expressed in shaft power at 10,180 kW (13,646 shp). It also powers the four-engined An-70 airlifter.

D-136

This turboshaft was developed for the Mi-26 helicopter. Aviaexport stresses its background of over 20,000 h running prior to certification to standards which included FAR and BCAR. Bench testing started in 1979 and series production began in 1982. It is composed of nine modules, some of which are identical with those of the D-36, though the LP compressor runs faster.

TYPE: Two-spool free turbine turboshaft.
LP COMPRESSOR: Six stages, with one row of variable inlet guide vanes. Faces for bleed ducts for anti-icing the Mi-26 air inlets. Mass flow 36 kg (79.4 lb)/s. Speed (max) 11,350 rpm.
HP COMPRESSOR: Six stages, in casing with large bleed pipes and carrying main gearbox and mounting points. Speed (max) 14,300 rpm. Overall pressure ratio 18.3.
COMBUSTION CHAMBER: Annular, with 28 burners and incorporating inlet guide vanes for HP turbine.
HP TURBINE: Single-stage with aircooled blades. Max inlet temperature 1,205°C (1,478°K).
LP TURBINE: Single-stage, separated from HP rotor by large intermediate case with 26 guide vanes (stators).
POWER TURBINE: Two stages forming separate module; casing with 12 long-chord radial struts. Speed (max) 8,300 rpm.
DRIVE SHAFT: Flexibly mounted shaft at rear.
ACCESSORIES: Mounted on gearbox above HP compressor.
DIMENSIONS:

Length	3,715 mm (146.26 in)
Width	1,382 mm (54.41 in)
Height	1,133 mm (44.61 in)

WEIGHT, DRY: 1,050 kg (2,315 lb)
PERFORMANCE RATINGS (ISA, S/L):

Max T-O at 8,300 rpm	8,380 kW (11,240 shp)
Max cont at 7,500 output rpm	8,230 kW (11,100 shp)

SPECIFIC FUEL CONSUMPTION:
Max T-O 73.8 µg/J (0.4365 lb/h/shp)

D-236

This engine uses a core similar to that of the D-136 turboshaft, but it incorporates a reduction gearbox to drive a contra-rotating propfan. As exhibited in 1987, the front propeller only, with eight composite blades, weighed 380 kg (838 lb). This propeller turned at 960 rpm and demonstrated propulsive efficiency of 87 per cent at Mach 0.7, the diameter being 4.2 m (13 ft 10 in). This engine first ran in 1984 and flew in 1987, replacing one of the engines of an Il-76.

By this time the propellers had been redesigned, the front unit retaining eight blades but the rear having only six. Blades are epoxy-bonded glassfibre, without metal reinforcement along the leading-edge. Speed has increased to 1,100 rpm. The production D-236 pusher version is expected to be an alternative power plant for the Tu-334.

Progress D-236 turboprop *(Jacques Marmain, Aviation Magazine International, Paris)*

Yakovlev has been working on propfan integration since 1987 and the Yak-42E-LL testbed with a D-236 replacing the starboard D-36 turbofan first flew on 15 March 1991. The engine was rated at 8,195 kW (11,000 shp) and was driving a 4.2 m (18 ft 9½ in) SV-36 tractor contra-rotating propeller with eight and six blades.
GAS GENERATOR: Generally as D-136.
REDUCTION GEAR: Planetary, giving contra-rotating output. Drive ratio 7.5.
CONTROL SYSTEM: Hydromechanical, with electronic computer.
WEIGHT, DRY: 1,600 kg (3,527 lb) with propellers
PERFORMANCE RATINGS:
T-O, S/L
7,459 kW (10,000 shp); 8-9 tonnes (17,635-19,840 lb st)
Cruise thrust 1.6 tonnes (3,527 lb)
SPECIFIC FUEL CONSUMPTION:
Cruise, at height 81.97 µg/J (0.485 lb/h/shp)

D-336

An example of this free turbine turboshaft engine was exhibited in Moscow in 1990. No details were given but it was clearly an uprated D-136, presumably intended to enhance the performance of the Mi-26 helicopter.

D-436

This advanced derivative of the D-36 was developed chiefly to match the requirements of the initial version of the Tu-334. The **D-436K** first ran, without reverser, in 1985. Series production was due to begin in 1989, initially for An-72 and An-74 aircraft. At this time service experience

with the D-36 and D-136 core exceeded 1 million hours. The **D-436M** has a thrust of 73.5 kN (16,535 lb st).

The definitive engine is the **D-436T**, with aerodynamic improvements. This engine is expected to fly in the first Tu-334-1 in 1991. It has also been selected for the 156-seat Yak-42M; the Aeroflot Yak-42 fleet will probably be re-engined.
TYPE: Three-shaft turbofan.
FAN: As D-36 but with improved performance. Mass flow 285 kg (628 lb)/s. Bypass ratio 5.49, rising to 6.2 at Mach 0.75 at 9,144 m (30,000 ft). Speed (max) 5,850 rpm.
COMPRESSORS: As D-36, except seven HP stages. Overall pressure ratio 20.97.
TURBINES: As D-36 but new HP turbine based on D-18T for entry temperature increased to 1,207°C, and fan turbine has three stages and speed increased to 5,850 rpm.
REVERSER: Based on that of D-18T.
DIMENSIONS:

Length	3,030 mm (119.3 in)
Diameter	1,390 mm (54.72 in)

WEIGHT, DRY:

D-436K	1,250 kg (2,756 lb st)
D-436T	1,490 kg (3,285 lb st)

PERFORMANCE RATINGS:
S/L, T-O 73.6 kN (16,550 lb st)
Cruise (8,000 m; 26,250 ft, Mach 0.75)
19.26 kN (4,330 lb)
SPECIFIC FUEL CONSUMPTION:
T-O 10.57 mg/Ns (0.373 lb/h/lb st)
Cruise, as above:

D-436K	18.3 mg/Ns (0.646 lb/h/lb)
D-436T	17.84 mg/Ns (0.63 lb/h/lb)

Progress (Lotarev) D-136 free-turbine turboshaft *(Brian M. Service)*   **Lotarev (Progress) D-436K three-shaft turbofan** *(Brian M. Service)*

RKBM

RKBM (RYBINSK ENGINE-BUILDING DESIGN OFFICE)

152903 Rybinsk, Jaroslavskaya obl.
Telephone: 4 31 44
Telex: Start

This large engine design office has produced over 50 types of engine under a succession of General Designers. The latter were: Dobrynin, Koliesov, Gulguzr and, now, Alexander S. Novikov.

KOLIESOV VD-7

This large single-shaft turbojet was fitted to at least the final Myasishchev M-50 supersonic bomber (NATO reporting name 'Bounder'), with afterburners on the inner

engines. Maximum thrust was estimated in the 137.5 kN (30,900 lb st; 14 tonne) class. It is commonly supposed that a derived version powers the Tu-22 (NATO 'Blinder') family.

RD-36-35FVR

This was the first of the Rybinsk lift engines to go into production. Designed under Koliesov, it provides lift for the Yak-38.
TYPE: Single-shaft turbojet for operation in almost vertical attitude.
COMPRESSOR: Five stages. Part composite construction.
COMBUSTION CHAMBER: Annular, with 12 burners.
TURBINE: Single-stage, air-impingement starting.
WEIGHT, DRY: 210 kg (463 lb)
PERFORMANCE RATING: 31.87 kN (7,165 lb st)

RKBM RD-36-51A

This large afterburning turbojet has no connection with the RD-36-35FVR, despite the similarity of designation. It powered the Tu-144D supersonic transport, and thus was designed to cruise at Mach 2.2. It has several features in common with the Olympus engine of Concorde.
TYPE: Two-shaft turbojet with afterburner.
LP COMPRESSOR: Six stages. Inlet guide vanes and all stator stages variable. Titanium and steel.
HP COMPRESSOR: Five stages. All stators variable. Mainly refractory steel.
COMBUSTION CHAMBER: Annular with 20 vaporising burners.
TURBINES: Single-stage HP with cooled blades, two-stage LP. TET 1,160°C.
AFTERBURNER: Close-coupled, with con/di nozzle driven by 12 hydraulic rams. Not used in cruising flight.

Cutaway RKBM RD-36-35FVR turbojet
(Flight International)

ACCESSORIES: Airframe mounted, driven off HP spool (see photograph).

DIMENSIONS:

Length	5,228 mm (205.8 in)
Diameter	1,486 mm (58.5 in)

WEIGHT, DRY: 4,125 kg (9,094 lb)

PERFORMANCE RATING:

T-O	196.12 kN (44,090 lb st)

SPECIFIC FUEL CONSUMPTION (Cruise, hi-alt, Mach 2.2):
24.93 mg/Ns (0.88 lb/h/lb st)

RKBM RD-36-51V

Another puzzle is provided by this engine, a non-afterburning turbojet or turbofan, which powers the single-engined version of the Myasishchev M-17 (NATO 'Mystic-A'). Its rating is given as 68.65 kN (15,430 lb st), so it cannot have much in common with the RD-36-51A.

RD-38

This turbojet is a derivative of the RD-36-35 modified for operation in the horizontal attitude, with a long-life lubrication system and other changes. It is the take-off booster fitted to the original Beriev A-40. It will not be fitted to later variants.

PERFORMANCE RATING: 27.46 kN (6,173 lb st)

RD-41

The next generation beyond the RD-36-35, this lift engine is fitted to the Yak-141 shipboard V/STOL aircraft. As in the Yak-38, two engines in tandem are installed pointing slightly aft.

PERFORMANCE RATING: 40.78 kN (9,171 lb st)

RKBM PROJECT

In 1990 RKBM revealed plans for a range of engines based on a core already developed. This single-shaft core has a nine-stage compressor driven by a single-stage turbine. Mass flow is 22.5 kg (49.6 lb)/s, pressure ratio 12.4 and TET 1,547°C. Three derived engines would be: a helicopter turboshaft rated at 4,480-5,970 kW (6,000-8,000 shp), a high bypass ratio turbofan in the 12 tonne (117.5 kN, 26,455 lb) class, and an advanced propfan, with three core booster stages, giving a thrust of 12-15 tonnes (117.5-147.1 kN, 26,455-33,070 lb st).

TVD-1500

This new gas turbine has been developed as a core suitable to power turboshaft, turboprop and turbofan engines. Features include minimal number of parts, advanced materials (new titanium alloys, new refractory materials and new composites), full-authority digital control and modular construction. Prototypes are running

RKBM RD-36-51A afterburning turbojet *(Flight International)*

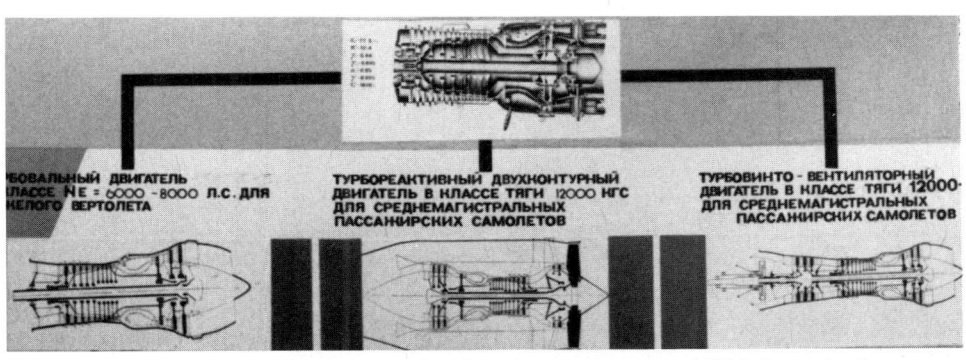

RKBM exhibit showing future engines based on a common core *(Flight International)*

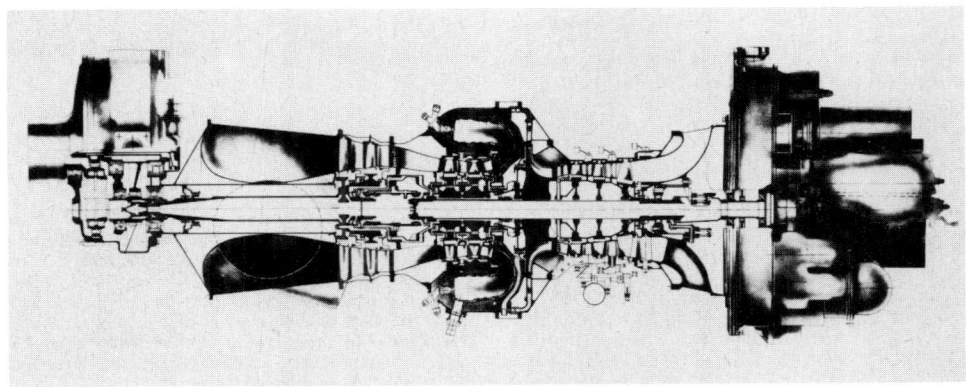

Longitudinal section of TVD-1500 turboshaft (air inlet at right)
(Jacques Marmain, Aviation Magazine International, Paris)

of the shaft and propeller versions. There is no immediate plan to build a turbofan, but this would be in the 7.85-9.81 kN (1,764-2,205 lb st) class.

The basic engine will power the Antonov An-38. Certification in this application is scheduled for 1995. The **TVD-1500S** turboprop would power the Sukhoi S-80. The **TVD-1500SKh** would power the Antonov SKhS agricultural aircraft. The **TVD-1500I** pusher propfan would power the Ilyushin Il-Kh. Two **TVD-1500A** turboshaft engines would be installed in the rear fuselage of the Myasishchev Yamal amphibian, driving via shafts to a pusher propeller behind the rudder. The **TVD-1500V** turboshaft will power the Kamov V-62 helicopter, a near-term programme, and the later Ka-52.

TYPE: Free-turbine turboshaft or turboprop.

COMPRESSOR: Three axial stages with inlet guide vanes and both stators variable, followed by one centrifugal. Pressure ratio 14.4. Electrochemically machined blades, electron-beam welded rotors and precision-cast casing.

COMBUSTION CHAMBER: Annular reverse-flow. Multi-fuel capability.

TURBINES: Two-stage compressor turbine with monocrystal or directionally solidified blades. Entry temperature 1,227°C. Two-stage power turbine with shaft passing through the engine to front drive.

REDUCTION GEAR: On turboprop, two-stage spur gear followed by single-stage planetary.

DIMENSIONS:

Width	620 mm (24.4 in)
Height	760 mm (29.9 in)
Length: Turboprop	1,965 mm (77.4 in)
Turboshaft	1,250 mm (49.2 in)

WEIGHT, DRY:

Turboprop	240 kg (529 lb)

PERFORMANCE RATINGS (S/L):

T-O	970 kW (1,300 shp)
Contingency (TVD-1500V)	1,156 kW (1,550 shp)
Cruise (7,500 m; 24,600 ft, Mach 0.65)	559 kW (750 shp)

SPECIFIC FUEL CONSUMPTION:

Cruise, as above	63.2 µg/J (0.374 lb/h/hp)

DN-200

Designated for Diesel Novikov, this unusual piston engine is hoped to be the most economical in the world. It is being designed to replace American engines in light aircraft, beginning with the Yak-112. Five single-cylinder test engines had been built by 1991 to assist in reaching the target fuel consumption. The first DN-200 was to run in 1991, and certification is due in 1994-95.

TYPE: Two-stroke liquid-cooled diesel piston engine.
CYLINDERS: Opposed pistons driving crankshafts along each side. Bore 72 mm (2,835 in). Stroke of each piston 72 mm (2.835 in). Capacity 1,759 cc (107.3 cu in).
WEIGHT, DRY: 165 kg (364 lb)

PERFORMANCE RATING (S/L):
T-O   149 kW (200 hp)
Cruise   119 kW (160 hp)
SPECIFIC FUEL CONSUMPTION:
T-O   45.5 μg/J (0.27 lb/h/hp)

Rybinsk Novikov DN-200 149 kW (200 hp) opposed piston Diesel engine

SALYUT

This name (Good health) is that of the MMPO (production factory) making the Lyulka AL-31F.

SATURN
NPO SATURN

13 Kasatkin St, 129301 Moscow
Telephone: 283 09 13
Fax: 286 7 566

This bureau is named for its famous founder, Arkhip M. Lyulka (which see). President and Chief Executive Officer is Viktor M. Chepkin. In addition to the engines listed below this bureau is collaborating with Rolls-Royce on the engine to power the Gulfstream/Sukhoi SSBJ (see International section).

AL-7
Service designation: TRD-31

The first AL-7 ran on the bench in late 1952 and the first production version was cleared for use in 1954 at a design rating of 63.74 kN (14,330 lb st). The main innovation in this engine was supersonic flow through the first two stages of the compressor. In the mid-1950s the afterburning **AL-7F** powered the initial production Su-7, and the Tu-98, Il-54 and La-250. Later versions were the **AL-7RV** and **AL-7PB** without afterburner, the latter powering the Be-10. By 1963 production had been transferred to an uprated afterburning version designated **AL-7F-1** to power the Su-7BM and later versions and the Su-9 series. The final production version was the **AL-7F-2**.
TYPE: Single-shaft turbojet, with or without afterburner.
COMPRESSOR: Ten-stage axial (eight stages in original AL-7 design). First two stages widely separated axially, with variable stators ahead of first two stages. Mass flow 114 kg (251 lb)/s. Pressure ratio 9.1.
COMBUSTION CHAMBER: Annular type with perforated inner flame tube. Multiple downstream fuel injectors inserted through cups in forward face of liner.
TURBINE: Two-stage axial-flow type. Both wheels overhung behind rear bearing; front disc bolted to flange on hollow tubular driveshaft. Entry temperature 927°C.
AFTERBURNER (AL-7F): Comprises upstream diffuser and downstream combustion section. Pilot combustor includes single nozzle ring and flame holder; main spray ring and gutter flame holder assembly downstream at

greater radius. Refractory liner in combustion section. Variable-area nozzle, with 24 hinged flaps.
ACCESSORIES: Fuel pump and control unit, oil pumps, hydraulic pump, electric generator, tachometer and other items grouped into quickly replaceable packages beneath compressor casing.
DIMENSIONS (AL-7F-1):
Length   6,810 mm (268 in)
Max diameter   1,250 mm (49.2 in)
WEIGHT, DRY:
AL-7F-1   2,010 kg (4,431 lb)
AL-7F-2   2,103 kg (4,636 lb)
PERFORMANCE RATINGS:
AL-7F   63.0 kN (14,250 lb st)
AL-7F, with afterburner   88.25 kN (19,840 lb st)
AL-7PB, RV   63.74 kN (14,330 lb st)
AL-7F-1   68.65 kN (15,432 lb st)
AL-7F-1, with afterburner   90.22 kN (22,282 lb st)
AL-7F-2, with afterburner   97.08 kN (21,825 lb st)
SPECIFIC FUEL CONSUMPTION:
Al-7F-1, max continuous rating
                                  25.49 mg/Ns (0.90 lb/h/lb st)

AL-21

This important engine, in its **AL-21F-3** version, has been produced in thousands for such aircraft as the MiG-23, Su-24, Su-17/20/22 and Su-15. Developed in the early 1970s, and cleared for production in 1970-74, it is noteworthy for its major advances in the design of the compressor, combustion chamber, turbine and afterburner.
COMPRESSOR: 14-stage axial. Inlet frame carries front bearing, with hot-air de-icing of fixed inlet vanes. Variable stators downstream pivoted to casing and central bullet. Variable stators ahead of stages 2, 3 and 4. Parallel HP section with independently scheduled variable stators ahead of stages 10, 11, 12, 13 and 14. Mass flow 104 kg (229 lb)/s. Pressure ratio 14.6.
COMBUSTION CHAMBER: Can-annular type, with 12 flame tubes each with duplex downstream burner.
TURBINE: Three stages with aircooled first stage blades. Entry temperature 1,112°C. Rotor assembly supported

by rear bearing held in eight-strut rear frame and drives via cone coupled to rear of compressor shaft.
AFTERBURNER: Rapid combustion downstream of three injector/flameholder rings. Corrugated insulated liner with ceramic coating. Fully variable nozzle with 24 flaps driven by six rams. Full-regime control giving smooth lightup and modulated power over whole range from flight idle to max afterburner.
WEIGHT, DRY: 1,720 kg (3,792 lb)
PERFORMANCE RATINGS (S/L):
Military power   76.5 kN (17,200 lb st) at 8,400 rpm
Max afterburner   110.5 kN (24,800 lb st)
SPECIFIC FUEL CONSUMPTION (S/L):
Military power   22.6 mg/Ns (0.80 lb/h/lb st)

AL-31

This was A. Lyulka's last and greatest engine. With afterburner, as the **AL-31F**, it powers all known versions of the Su-27, for which it entered series production in 1984. Slightly modified engines might power the prototype Sukhoi/Gulfstream SSBJ. Engines designated **R-32** (almost certainly the Service designation for all AL-31 engines) were fitted to the P-42, an Su-27 development aircraft, which set rate of climb records in 1986. A high proportion of the engine is titanium or stainless steel. Production by Salyut MMPO.
TYPE: Two-shaft augmented turbofan.
FAN: Inlet has 23 variable guide vanes. Four fan stages slotted into discs. Bypass ratio 0.4.
COMPRESSOR: Variable inlet guide vanes followed by nine-stage HP spool with first three stators variable. Easy field replacement of damaged blades. Overall pressure ratio 20.
COMBUSTION CHAMBER: Annular, with 24 downstream burners fed from inner manifold. Auto continuous ignition during missile launch.
TURBINES: Single-stage HP with cooled blades, using air/air heat exchanger in bypass duct. Two-stage LP with cooled blades. Both turbines have active tip clearance control.

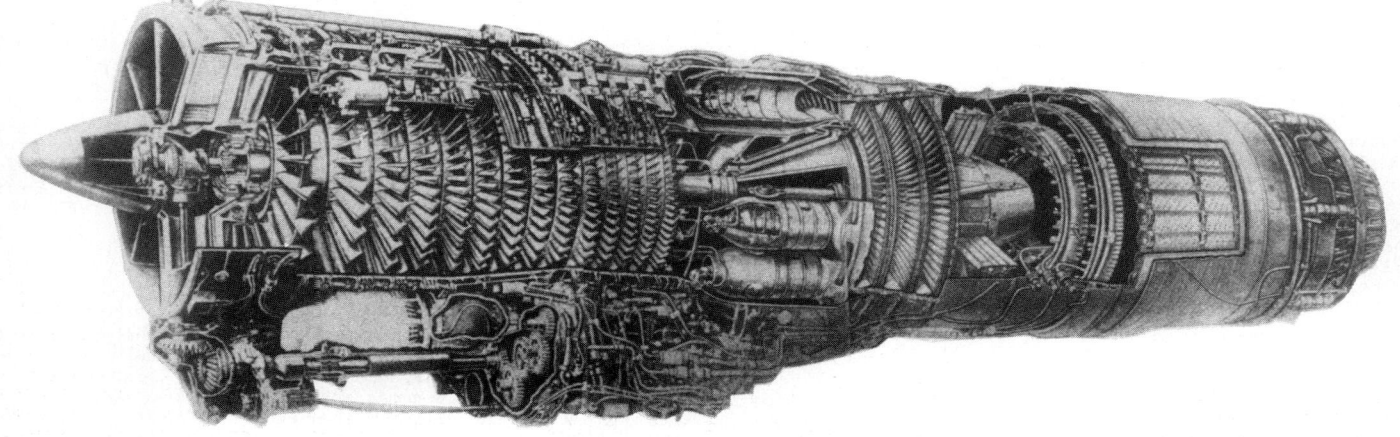

Lyulka AL-21F-3 single-shaft afterburning turbojet

JETPIPE: Short mixer section to combine core and bypass flows upstream of afterburner.

AFTERBURNER: Two flameholder rings downstream of multiple radial spray bars. Interlinked primary and secondary multi-flap nozzles are angled about 5° downwards.

CONTROL SYSTEM: Hydromechanical full-regime control giving smooth power from flight idle to max afterburner in all manoeuvre conditions. Auto elimination of surge "at Mach numbers 2-2.5 when normal, flat and inverted spins occur". Linked via software to Su-27 fly by wire flight control system. All accessories grouped above engine.

DIMENSIONS:

Length	4,950 mm (195 in)
Diameter	1,220 mm (48.0 in)

WEIGHT, DRY:

	1,530 kg (3,373 lb)

PERFORMANCE RATINGS:

Max augmented	123.85 kN (27,560 lb st)
Max dry	79.42 kN (17,857 lb st)

SPECIFIC FUEL CONSUMPTION:

Max dry	18.98 mg/Ns (0.67 lb/h/lb st)

AL-34

This turboprop in the 410 kW (550 shp) class was reported in 1990 to have been selected to power the Sukhoi S-86 executive aircraft (rated at 522 kW; 700 shp), Myasishchev Gjel (rated at 373 kW; 500 shp) and the Ross-Aeroprogress T-601 utility transport. In the S-86, the AL-34 would drive a pusher contraprop.

SATURN RTWD-14

The RTWD-14 is the primary source of shaft power on the Buran spacecraft. Three are installed, two active and one on standby. These engines run on the liquid oxygen/liquid hydrogen main propellants.

Saturn (Lyulka) AL-31F sectioned display engine *(Piotr Butowski)*

Saturn (Lyulka) AL-31F two-shaft augmented bypass turbojet

SHVETSOV

FOUNDER OF BUREAU: Arkadiya Dmitrievich Shvetsov

A. D. Shvetsov was responsible for the M-11 five-cylinder aircooled radial engines made in enormous numbers in 1928-59 at powers from 74 6 kW (100 hp) to 149 kW (200 hp). He later developed larger radials, the most important being the ASh-82, which at ratings up to 1,491 kW (2,000 hp) powered Lavochkin fighters, the Tu-2 and Tu-4 bombers, Il-12 and -14 transports and Mi-4 and Yak-24 helicopters. The ASh-62 was made in large numbers at ratings in the 750 kW (1,000 hp) class for the Li-2 and An-2. The ASh-62M agricultural version, developed by Vedeneyev, and all An-2 engines after 1952, were transferred to Poland (see WSK-PZL Kalisz and WSK-PZL Rzeszów). Another important engine was the 545 kW (730 hp) ASh-21, fitted to the Yak-11. All these have been described in earlier editions. The ASh-62 and ASh-82 have been produced under licence in China, as described in the Chinese entry in this section. Today the bureau is MKB (PPO) Perm.

SOLOVIEV — *see MKB*

SOYUZ

GENERAL DESIGNER: Koptchyenko
DEPUTY GENERAL DESIGNER: Alexander Girnov

This design bureau is today known as the **MNPK**, Moscow Scientific Production Corporation 'Soyuz' (Alliance). The longest established engine KB in the Soviet Union, it was founded by A. A. Mikulin, who was General Constructor during the design of the AM-3 (see below). He was succeeded, successively, by Tumansky, Favorski (briefly) and now by Koptchyenko.

AM-3
Service designation: TRD-3

The AM-3M single-spool turbojet was developed under the leadership of P. F. Zubets from the Mikulin M-209 (civil RD-3 or AM-3) which powers the Tu-16 and early M-4 bombers and was adapted for the USSR's first jet transport, the Tu-104. Current M-4s are believed to have the **AM-3D**, while the usual engine of Tu-16s is the **AM-3M-500**. This engine was produced at the Xian factory in China as the WP8 (see under XAE, China).

It has a simple configuration, with an eight-stage compressor, annular combustion system with 14 flame tubes, and a two-stage turbine. The compressor casing is made in front, centre and rear portions, the front casing housing a row of inlet guide vanes. The inlet bullet houses an S-300M gas turbine starter, developing 75 kW (100 hp) at 31,000-35,000 rpm. Pressure ratio is 6.4; temperature after turbine 720°C.

DIMENSIONS:

Length overall	5,340 mm (210.23 in)
Diameter	1,400 mm (55.12 in)

PERFORMANCE RATINGS (T-O):

AM-3	85.8 kN (19,285 lb st)
AM-3D	85.3 kN (19,180 lb st)
AM-3M-500	93.19 kN (20,950 lb st)

TUMANSKY RD-9

First axial turbojet of wholly Soviet design to be placed in production, this engine was designed under Tumansky in the Mikulin bureau in 1950-51 and received the TsIAM designation AM-5. The afterburning **AM-5F** was selected for the MiG-19 and the unaugmented engine for the Yak-25. After Mikulin's removal in 1956 the engine was redesignated **RD-9**, the afterburning type being called **RD-9B**. In 1957 the **RD-9BM** entered production, with a hydraulically actuated three-step nozzle. All variants have a nine-stage compressor, can-annular combustor and two-stage turbine; pressure ratio at take-off is 7.14. Production in the Soviet Union tapered off in 1958 in favour of the R-11. In China, production of the RD-9BM began in 1960 and has continued for the J-6 and Q-5. Diameter of all models is 813 mm (32.0 in). Maximum T-O rating of the BM is 32.36 kN (7,275 lb st).

A detailed description and drawing will be found under the designation **WP6** in the Chinese (**LM**) part of this section.

TUMANSKY R-11
Service designation: TRD-37

The first R-11 turbojets (known as the R-37 series by the armed forces) ran in 1953 and entered production in 1956. The R-11 is a two-spool engine, with accessories grouped on the underside of the compressor. It was one of the first engines to have an overhung first rotor stage without inlet guide vanes. Other features include a can-annular combustion chamber with ten flame tubes, which in some versions provides large air bleed couplings for flap blowing, and, in most installations, a large afterburner with multi-flap variable nozzle. All early versions (but not the Chinese derivative) are started on petrol (gasoline) fed from a separate tank, and gaseous oxygen can be fed to the burners to increase relight altitude from 8 to 11.9 km (26,250 to 39,000 ft). Considerably more than 20,000 of all versions have been delivered from Soviet plants, to power many types of aircraft including versions of the MiG-21 and Yak-28. Many more have been produced by Hindustan Aeronautics in India, and by the Chinese as the LEMC WP7. Known Soviet versions are:

R-11. Initial production series, rated at 38.25 kN (8,600 lb st) dry and 50.0 kN (11,240 lb st) with afterburner. Three-stage transonic LP compressor and three-stage HP, each driven by single-stage turbine.

R-11-300. Fitted with enlarged afterburner and new nozzle. Powered speed-record Ye-66 in 1959. Dry thrust unchanged but maximum increased to 58.4 kN (13,120 lb st). Believed to power Yak-28 versions.

R-11F. Original engine uprated, with small afterburner; dry thrust unchanged, maximum 56.4 kN (12,676 lb st).

d **R-11FS, F2S.** Suffix S signifies provision for flap blowing. Final version was the **R-11F2S-300**. According to a Polish magazine this powers not only various MiG-21s but also initial versions of the Sukhoi T-37, with dry and maximum ratings of 38.2 kN (8,588 lb st) and 60.8 kN (13,668 lb st). The F2S-300 was until at least 1986 still in production in India and China. Details will be found in the entry on the Chinese WP7.

TUMANSKY R-13

This two-spool turbojet supplanted the R-11 as the MiG-21 engine in the late 1960s, before giving way to the R-25. It has an advanced afterburner, and a new five-stage HP compressor handling a greater airflow. An unaugmented version powers the Su-25 (see R-195 below). The **PDM** fitted to the record breaking Ye-66B of 1974 may have been an R-13. The standard ratings for the **R-13-300** are 41.55 kN (9,340 lb st) dry and 64.73 kN (14,550 lb st) with afterburner. Fuller details will be found in the entry on the Chinese WP13.

TUMANSKY R-195

This tough and simple turbojet was developed from the R-13 to power the Su-25 and Su-28 family of attack and training aircraft. Originally designated **R-95**, it was further developed into the R-195 before entering production in about 1979. The entire engine was designed to offer considerable resistance to 23 mm gunfire, and to continue to operate after suffering damage in eight places.

TYPE: Two-shaft turbojet.
LP COMPRESSOR: Three stages. No inlet guide vanes or variable stators.
HP COMPRESSOR: Five stages. No variable stators, but auto bleed valves.
COMBUSTION CHAMBER: Can-annular with multiple duplex burners. Cleared for kerosene, diesel oil and MT petrol.
TURBINES: Single-stage HP, single-stage LP.
JETPIPE: No afterburner, simple fixed-area nozzle.
DIMENSIONS:
Length	3,300 mm (130 in)
Diameter	914 mm (36 in)
WEIGHT, DRY: | 990 kg (2,183 lb)
PERFORMANCE RATING:
T-O	44.18 kN (9,921 lb st)

TUMANSKY R-15

In early 1990 it was announced that the engine of the MiG-25R variants is an afterburning turbojet designated **R-15BD-300**, rated at 110 kN (24,700 lb st). Presumably it is related to the R-31.

Another MiG-25 engine is the **R-15B-300** illustrated.

Soyuz (Tumansky) R-11F2S-300 two-shaft turbojet, with afterburner removed

Tumansky R-195 two-shaft turbojet *(Flight International)*

Cutaway Tumansky R-15B-300 single-shaft afterburning turbojet *(Piotr Butowski)*

TUMANSKY RU-19

Service designation: TRD-29

This single-shaft turbojet has been used to power aircraft and as an APU and emergency booster (in the An-26). When used as an APU its thrust is reduced depending upon the shaft power extracted. The fully rated **RU-19-300** has a thrust of 8.83 kN (1,985 lb st). This is installed in the An-24RV and An-24RT. The **RU-19A-300** is rated at 7.85 kN (1,765 lb st) and is installed in the An-26 and An-30. When providing full electrical power the residual thrust is only 2.16 kN (485 lb st). An RU-19 was selected as the APU/booster for the MAI-Tashkent Semurg, the rating in this application being 3.1 kN (697 lb st). Another RU-19, equipped as a turbojet and fully rated, powers the La-17 target (see RPVs and Targets in 1977-78 *Jane's*). The RU-19 powered the Yak-30 and Yak-32 jet trainers.

TUMANSKY R-25

This two-spool turbojet was a new design, and its compressor of high pressure ratio confers a markedly lower sfc than the R-13. The R-25 has redesigned accessory systems but is installationally interchangeable with the R-13. The first LP compressor stage has 21 titanium blades of large chord. The afterburner has two stages (the R-11 and R-13 having one) and so can be used in combat at high altitudes. The **R-25-300** powers the MiG-21bis, with ratings of 52 kN (11,700 lb st) dry and 74.5 kN (16,755 lb st) with afterburner. No longer made, except under licence by HAL of India for MiG-21bis.

TUMANSKY R-266/R-31

The R-26 sub-type 6 is a single-shaft afterburning turbojet designed for the MiG-25. It stemmed from the P-166 fitted to the Ye-166 which set a world speed record in 1962. The P-166 had a thrust with afterburner of 98.06 kN (22,046 lb st). This was also the thrust of the original R-266, announced under its service designation of **R-31** as being fitted to prototypes of the MiG-25 (designated Ye-266).

Constructed mainly of steel, the R-266 has a five-stage compressor with T-O pressure ratio of about 7, driven by a single-stage turbine with uncooled blades. Special T-6 fuel is used, with freezing point of –62.2°C and flash point of 54.4°C. In the MiG-25, water/methanol is injected into the variable inlet duct at supersonic speeds. At Mach 3 most of the thrust is generated by the three-ring afterburner and multi-flap variable nozzle.

RD-F. This is an uprated R-266 fitted to the Ye-266M (MiG-25 variant) which set time-to-height records in 1975. According to a Polish magazine the R-26 powers the MiG-25M, with dry and maximum ratings of 90 kN (20,230 lb st) and 138 kN (31,025 lb st). This engine may have the military designation TRD-31F.

R-31-300. This is the production engine of the MiG-25 fighter versions. Ratings are 91.18 kN (20,500 lb st) dry and 120 kN (27,010 lb st) with afterburner.

TUMANSKY R-27

This engine was a natural growth development from the R-11, -13, -25 series. It entered production in about 1970 to power the initial series versions of the MiG-23.

R-27V-300. Afterburner replaced by bifurcated nozzles each rotating through about 100° (cycle time 8 s), driven by two hydraulic motors linked by cross-shaft. Provides lift/cruise propulsion of Yak-38. Displayed 1990 by Mikulin/Soyuz bureau.

TYPE: Two-shaft turbojet.

LP COMPRESSOR: Five stages. No inlet guide vanes or variable stators.

HP COMPRESSOR: Six stages. No variable stators.

COMBUSTION CHAMBER: Annular, burners fed from inner manifold. Water injection with max afterburner.

Tumansky R-25 two-shaft turbojet, with afterburner removed

TURBINES: Single-stage HP with aircooled blades, single-stage LP.

JETPIPE: Afterburner with profiled multi-flap primary and secondary nozzles. R-27V, plenum chamber and two vectoring nozzles.

DIMENSIONS:

Length: R-27	4,850 mm (191 in)
R-27V	3,700 mm (146 in)
Diameter	915 mm (36 in)

WEIGHT, DRY:

R-27	1,500 kg (3,300 lb)
R-27V	1,350 kg (2,976 lb)

PERFORMANCE RATINGS:

R-27 max with afterburner and water injection	100 kN (22,485 lb st)
R-27 max dry	68.65 kN (15,430 lb st)
R-27V-300 max T-O	68.0 kN (15,300 lb st)

TUMANSKY R-29

This augmented turbojet is simpler than the corresponding American F100, with fewer compressor stages and a lower pressure ratio; but it is more powerful and costs much less. Different subtypes are fitted to all current MiG-23 and MiG-27 versions for Warsaw Pact front-line use, and to the Su-22. In all these aircraft water injection is used on take-off, the MiG-23MF water tank having a capacity of 28 litres (7.4 US gallons; 6.2 Imp gallons).

The following versions have been identified:

R-29B. Original full-rated production engine for MiG-23MF and related versions.

R-29PN. This replaced the R-29B as the standard engine of non-export MiG-23 aircraft.

R-29B-300. Simplified engine with small afterburner and short two-position nozzle for subsonic low-level operation. Fitted to all MiG-27 versions, with fixed or variable inlet ducts.

R-29BS-300. This is the engine of the Su-22 (export Su-17 versions).

COMPRESSOR: Five-stage LP, six-stage HP. Overall pressure ratio (29B) 12.4, (29-300) 13. Mass flow (29B) 105 kg (235 lb)/s, (R-29-300) 110 kg (242.5 lb)/s.

COMBUSTION CHAMBER: Annular, vaporising burners.

TURBINES: HP has single stage with aircooled blades; max 8,800 rpm. Two-stage LP; max 8,500 rpm.

AFTERBURNER: Fuel rings with separate light-up give modulated fully variable augmentation. Fully variable nozzles differ in different installations (see variants).

DIMENSIONS (R-29-300):

Length	4,960 mm (195 in)
Max diameter	912 mm (35.9 in)

WEIGHT, DRY:

R-29B	1,760 kg (3,880 lb)
R-29-300	1,880 kg (4,145 lb)

PERFORMANCE RATINGS:

Max S/L unaugmented	78.45 kN (17,635 lb st)
Min with afterburner	97.1 kN (21,825 lb st)
Max T-O, wet (R-29B-300)	112.8 kN (25,350 lb st)
Max T-O, wet (MiG-23MF)	122.0 kN (27,500 lb st)

TUMANSKY R-35

In early 1990 it was announced that the MiG-23ML, MLA and MLD are powered by the the **R-35F-300**, rated at 127.5 kN (28,660 lb st). It is not yet known how closely this engine resembles the R-29.

SOYUZ GTE-400

This new turboshaft, rated at 298 kW (400 shp), has been selected for the twin-engined version of the Ka-118.

Two views of the Tumansky R-27V-300 vectored-thrust turbojet (box above left nozzle is added for demonstration purposes)
(Flight International)

SOYUZ TVD-450

This turboprop may use the same core as the GTE-400. A twinned version, driving through a coupling gearbox to a single propeller, powers the Sukhoi S-86, as an alternative to the Saturn AL-34. Each power section is rated at 336 kW (450 shp).

SOYUZ TV116-300

This turboprop is being designed for pusher installations, and has much in common with the Garrett TPF351. To be rated in the 895 kW (1,200 shp) class, it has two centrifugal compressors in series and a free power turbine driving the rear gearbox.

Tumansky R-29B built under licence by HAL (rear view with afterburner removed)

SVERDLOV

This is the name of the production factory at Perm, the principal source of helicopter engines of Klimov (Leningrad, previously Isotov) design.

TRUD

Meaning Truth, this is the name of the production factory on the Samara at Kuibyshev for Kuznetsov engines.

TUMANSKY

Academician Sergei Konstantinovich Tumansky, who died in 1973, was a noted designer of piston engines. His RD-9 axial turbojet went into production in 1953. On Mikulin's disgrace in 1956, Tumansky was appointed head of the bureau. Production of his subsequent engines easily exceeds that of any other family of aircraft gas turbines in the post-1955 era. His engines are produced by Soyuz and UMKPA (which see).

UMKPA

CHIEF DESIGNER: Alexei Ryzhov

The Ufa Engine-Manufacturing Production Association is a principal source of engines designed by the Tumansky KB. Their catalogue and exhibit material makes no mention of Tumansky, but lists engines as 'products'. **Product 25-11** (69.2 kN; 15,555 lb st combat rating) is the R-25-300; **Product 55B** (117 kN; 26,300 lb st combat rating) is the R-35F-300; **Product 95-I** (64.5 kN; 14,500 lb st 'first reheat rating') is the R-13-300; and **Product 95-III** (T-O 40.2 kN; 9,037 lb st) is the R-195.

VAZ

The Togliatti (Fiat) car plant has designed two RC (rotary combustion) Wankel type engines for surface applications, and has now produced a fresh design for aircraft.

VAZ-430

This twin-rotor engine has been developed to run on Mogas. Its first application is the Mi-34V helicopter, in which it is intended to replace the Vedeneyev M-14V radial with two rotary engines. Mil general designer Marat Tischenko said "We could not find a gas turbine small enough". The VAZ-430 was running in early 1991 and is expected to fly in 1993. TBO is to be set at 600 h, rising quickly to 1,000 h.

WEIGHT, DRY:	130 kg (287 lb)
PERFORMANCE RATINGS (S/L):	
T-O	164 kW (220 hp)
Contingency	202 kW (270 hp)

VEDENEYEV

FORMER GENERAL DESIGNER: Ivan M. Vedeneyev

This designer was responsible for improvement of the AI-14 piston engine designed by the Ivchenko bureau. He also developed the ASh-62M, produced in Poland as the ASz-62M, from Shvetsov's ASh-62IR. His engines are now produced by the VMKB.

VMKB

Engines of Vedeneyev design are now attributed to the MKB (motor construction bureau) at Voronezh.

VMKB M-14V-26

Derived from the AI-14 engines for fixed-wing aircraft, the M-14V-26 powers the Ka-26 helicopter. In this installation the stub wing carries an engine on each tip. Beneath the rotor an R-26 gearbox combines the power of the engines and distributes it equally between the two coaxial main rotors. The same engine in a revised installation powers the initial single-engined Mi-34 helicopter. Production of the M-14 has apparently been transferred to the Romanian aerospace industry.

The engine has forced cooling by an axial fan driven via a friction clutch and extension shaft ahead of the main output bevel box at 1.452 times crankshaft speed. The planetary gearbox has a ratio of 0.309 and incorporates friction and ratchet clutches. The central R-26 gearbox has a ratio of 0.34; it also drives the generator, hydraulic pump, oil pump and tachometer generator.

DIMENSIONS:

Length	1,145 mm (45.08 in)
Diameter	985 mm (38.78 in)
WEIGHT, DRY:	245 kg (540 lb)

PERFORMANCE RATINGS:

T-O	242 kW (325 hp) at 2,800 rpm
Max continuous I	205 kW (275 hp) at 2,450 rpm
Max continuous II	142 kW (190 hp) at 2,350 rpm
Cruise I	142 kW (190 hp) at 2,350 rpm
Cruise II	108 kW (145 hp) at 2,350 rpm

SPECIFIC FUEL CONSUMPTION:

At cruise ratings	77.7 μg/J (0.46 lb/h/hp)

VMKB M-14P

For fixed-wing applications, the M-14P was used with direct drive in the original version of the OSKB-1-3PM Kwant, at a T-O rating of 242 kW (325 hp). Currently, the Kwant has an M-14 II of 268 kW (360 hp). The same rating is quoted for the M-14P fitted to the Yak-18T, -50, -52, -53 and -55 and Su-26 and -26M, all of which have a controllable-pitch propeller.

VMKB M-18

This engine has been produced for homebuilts, microlights and hang gliders.

TYPE: Two-stroke piston engine with two horizontally opposed aircooled cylinders.

WEIGHT, DRY:

Geared	28 kg (61.7 lb)
Ungeared	13.7 kg (30.2 lb)

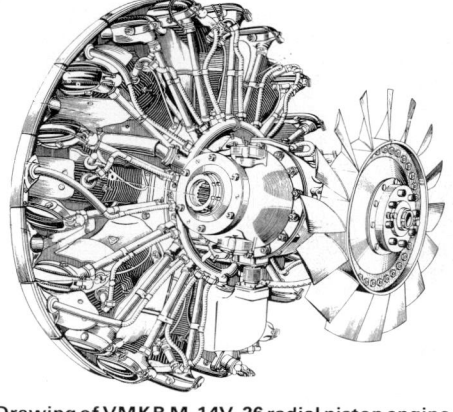

Drawing of VMKB M-14V-26 radial piston engine, with cooling fan

PERFORMANCE RATING (T-O):

Geared	40 kW (53.6 hp)
Ungeared	30 kW (40.2 hp)

ZMKB — see Progress

UNITED KINGDOM

EMDAIR
EMDAIR LTD

Harbour Road, Rye, E Sussex TN31 7TH
Telephone: 44 (797) 223460
Fax: 44 (797) 224615
Telex: 957116 FOR EMDAIR

Activities centre on lightweight four-stroke flat-twin engines. These aircooled engines run on Avgas and have four-valve heads, electronic management systems, central and side spark plugs, direct injection, alternator and electric starter. They are intended to combine high specific output at low rpm with low sfc, low costs and long life. Each engine is available in A (direct drive) and B (geared, torsional damping and extension shaft) versions.

EMDAIR CF 077A

Crankshaft rotation counterclockwise, seen from the front. An exhaust muffler (silencer) is optional. Conforms to JAR 22.

CYLINDERS: Bore 95.0 mm (3.74 in). Stroke 88.9 mm (3.50 in). Capacity 1,261 cc (76.91 cu in). Compression ratio 9.5.

DIMENSIONS:

Length	400 mm (15.75 in)
Width	698 mm (27.5 in)
Height	447 mm (17.75 in)
WEIGHT, DRY (with starter):	47.27 kg (104 lb)

PERFORMANCE RATINGS:

Max	44.8 kW (60 hp) at 3,600 rpm
Max cruise	33.6 kW (45 hp) at 3,090 rpm

FUEL CONSUMPTION:

Max cruise	13.25 litres (3.5 US gallons; 2.9 Imp gallons)/h

EMDAIR CF 077B

This version powers the Verilite Sunbird, designed to FAR Pt 23. Geared output with torsional vibration damping, reducing propeller speed to 2,600 rpm.

EMDAIR CF 092A

CYLINDERS: Bore 104.0 mm (4.094 in). Stroke 88.9 mm (3.50 in). Capacity 1,511 cc (92.17 cu in). Compression ratio 9.5. The **092B** is a geared version.

DIMENSIONS:

Length	401 mm (15.8 in)
Width	698 mm (27.5 in)
Height	447 mm (17.75 in)
WEIGHT, DRY (with starter):	51.0 kg (112 lb)

PERFORMANCE RATINGS:

Max	52.2 kW (70 hp) at 3,600 rpm
75 per cent cruise	39.1 kW (52.5 hp) at 3,075 rpm

FUEL CONSUMPTION:

Max cruise	14.4 litres (3.8 US gallons; 3.2 Imp gallons)/h

EMDAIR CF 112

The **112B** has an epicyclic gearbox giving a propeller speed of 2,500 rpm at a crankshaft speed of 3,600 rpm. The following relates to the **112A**:

CYLINDERS: Bore 110 mm (4.35 in). Stroke 96.0 mm (3.78 in). Capacity 1,834 cc (112 cu in). Compression ratio 9.5.

DIMENSIONS:

Length	412.75 mm (16.25 in)
Width	711.2 mm (28.0 in)
Height	425 mm (16.75 in)

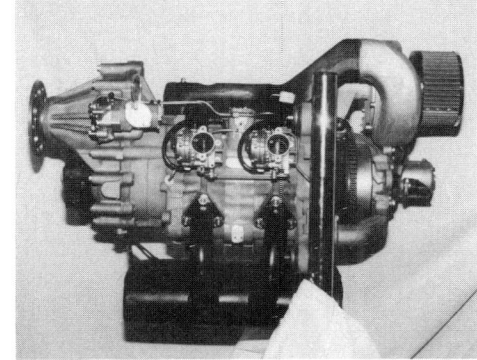

Emdair CF 092B two-cylinder piston engine

WEIGHT, DRY (with starter):	57.28 kg (128 lb)

PERFORMANCE RATINGS:

Max	63.4 kW (85.0 hp) at 3,600 rpm
75 per cent cruise	47.5 kW (63.75 hp) at 3,270 rpm

FUEL CONSUMPTION:

Max cruise	15.5 litres (4.1 US gallons; 3.4 Imp gallons)/h

NORTON
NORTON MOTORS LTD

Lynn Lane, Shenstone, Lichfield, Staffs WS14 0EA
Telephone: 44 (543) 480101
Fax: 44 (543) 480814
Telex: 335998 NORTON G
MANAGING DIRECTOR: Graham Williams
DIRECTOR OF ENGINEERING: David W. Garside
DIRECTOR OF MARKETING: David T. Morris

Norton designs and produces a range of rotary engines in the power band 15 to 89.5 kW (20 to 120 bhp). Increased power to weight, elimination of radial vibration and reduced maintenance requirements are just some features of rotary engines.

The feasibility of jet and diesel burning versions of the rotary engine has been proved on a US DoD Contract. Durability testing is continuing. It is feasible to turbocharge the range of engines to achieve power retention at altitude. A device is now available to correct fuel/air mixture at altitude automatically.

NORTON NR642

The NR642 is a fan-rotor-cooled highly silenced twin-rotor engine. The housing is water-cooled. The engine

Norton NR642 twin-rotor engine

incorporates a heavy duty reduction gearbox with various ratio options, and is designed to meet JAR-E and FAR Pt 23. The NR642 is in production and has been selected by a range of light aircraft and UAV manufacturers.

DIMENSIONS:

Length	702 mm (27.6 in)
Width	457 mm (18.0 in)
Height	444 mm (17.2 in)
WEIGHT (complete, wet with accessories):	64 kg (140 lb)

PERFORMANCE RATING: 67 kW (90 bhp)

SPECIFIC FUEL CONSUMPTION:

Full power	91 μg/J (0.54 lb/bhp/hp)
Cruise	84 μg/J (0.50 lb/bhp/hp)

NORTON NR622

Twin rotors cooled by induction air, water-cooled housings, incorporating 2:1 or 3:1 reduction gearbox. Suitable for ultralights, autogyros and light aircraft. Capacity 2 × 294 = 588 cc (35.9 cu in).

DIMENSIONS:

Length	550 mm (21.6 in)
Width	330 mm (13.0 in)
Height	350 mm (13.8 in)
WEIGHT, READY TO RUN:	52 kg (115 lb)

PERFORMANCE RATING: 61 kW (82 hp) at 7,500 rpm
SPECIFIC FUEL CONSUMPTION: As NR642

Norton NR622 twin-rotor engine

NR612 twin-rotor engine

Norton NR801 single-rotor engine

Norton NR731 single-rotor engine

NORTON NR612

Similar to NR622 but without gearbox. Applications include light aircraft with or without reduction drive. For UAV/RPV applications can be tuned to 89.5 kW (120 hp).

DIMENSIONS:
Length	432 mm (17 in)
Width	330 mm (13 in)
Height	305 mm (12 in)

WEIGHT, READY TO RUN:	48 kg (105 lb)
PERFORMANCE RATING:	62.6 kW (84 hp) at 7,500 rpm
SPECIFIC FUEL CONSUMPTION:	
Full power	88 μg/J (0.52 lb/h/hp)
Cruise	81.12 μg/J (0.48 lb/h/hp)

NORTON NR801

This single-rotor engine with fan or exhaust-ejector rotor cooling, liquid-cooled housings and without reduction gearbox was originally developed for UAVs. The standard engine has a 900W or 1,500W generator. It is anticipated that a version with revised accessories and with a reduction drive will be developed for the ultralight market.

DIMENSIONS:
Length	305 mm (12 in)
Width	325 mm (12.8 in)
Height	249 mm (9.8 in)
WEIGHT, READY TO RUN (with generator):	22.7 kg (50 lb)
PERFORMANCE RATING:	39 kW (52 bhp) at 7,500 rpm
SPECIFIC FUEL CONSUMPTION:	
Full power	91 μg/J (0.54 lb/h/hp)
Cruise	84 μg/J (0.50 lb/h/hp)

NORTON NR731

This single-rotor engine with ram-air cooled housings and rotor has the highest power-to-weight ratio ever achieved by a standard production rotary engine. It is available in tractor or pusher configurations. Generators can be added, and two or more engines can be coupled together.

DIMENSIONS:
Length	190 mm (7.4 in)
Width	237 mm (9.3 in)
Height	262 mm (10.3 in)
WEIGHT, READY TO RUN:	10 kg (22 lb)
PERFORMANCE RATING:	28.3 kW (38 bhp)
SPECIFIC FUEL CONSUMPTION:	
Max rating	96 μg/J (0.57 lb/bhp/hp)
At cruise	88 μg/J (0.52 lb/bhp/hp)

NPT

NOEL PENNY TURBINES LTD

Siskin Drive, Toll Bar End, Coventry CV3 4FE
Telephone: 44 (203) 301528
Fax: 44 (203) 302025
Telex: 312285 PENNY G
CHAIRMAN AND CHIEF EXECUTIVE: R. N. Penny

NPT specialises in small gas turbines for aerospace, industrial and marine applications. The aerospace range comprises turboprops of 18.64-387.76 kW (25-520 shp), turbofans of 3.781-7.562 kN (850-1,700 lb st) and turbojets of 0.222-4.448 kN (50-1,000 lb st).

NPT 301

The 301 family was developed for re-usable drones and target vehicles requiring thrusts in the range 1.3 to 2 kN (300 to 450 lb st) at up to 13,850 m (45,000 ft). One version, the NPT 301-3/4, has a manned aircraft application: the prototype CMC Leopard light business aircraft, first flown in January 1989.

TYPE: Single-shaft turbojet.
COMPRESSOR: Centrifugal, aluminium alloy. Air mass flow 2.27 kg (5.0 lb)/s. Pressure ratio 4.5.
COMBUSTION CHAMBER: Reverse flow annular, with vaporising burners.
FUEL SYSTEM: LP pressurised inlet electric pump. Analog or digital electronic control.
FUEL GRADES: Jet A-1, JP-5.
TURBINE: Single-stage axial with integral blades.
STARTING: External air source impingement on compressor.
ACCESSORY DRIVE: Alternator, currently 2.5 kW.

Cutaway NPT 301 turbojet

LUBRICATION: Total loss pulsed oil flow.
DIMENSIONS:
Length	1,000 mm (39.6 in)
Diameter	343 mm (13.5 in)
WEIGHT, DRY:	45.4 kg (100 lb)
PERFORMANCE RATING (S/L):	1.334 kN (300 lb st)
SPECIFIC FUEL CONSUMPTION:	30.6 mg/Ns (1.08 lb/h/lb st)

NPT 754

This engine is one of a family of advanced, lightweight two-shaft turbofans using common technology and component interchangeability. The design flight envelope of this particular engine is 0-16,764 m (0-55,000 ft) and Mach 0-0.85. It has been selected to power the production CMC Leopard.

TYPE: Two-shaft turbofan.
FAN: Single stage with wide-chord blades, overhung ahead of high-capacity ball bearing.
COMPRESSOR: Four axial stages with interstage labyrinth seals. Shaft supported at front by ball bearing.
COMBUSTION CHAMBER: Throughflow annular. Vaporising burners and high-energy igniter.
TURBINES: Single-stage HP and single-stage LP, both driving via tubular shafts with squeeze-film rear roller bearings. Each rotor is a single monolithic casting.
JETPIPE: Exhaust mixer and single nozzle.
STARTING: Via tower shaft inside one of the five main support struts, with bevel drive to front of HP spool.
ACCESSORIES: Remote gearbox driven via tower shaft. HP air bleed offtake.
CONTROL SYSTEM: Full-authority digital.
DIMENSIONS:
Length	762 mm (30.0 in)
Diameter	330 mm (13.0 in)
WEIGHT, DRY:	54.43 kg (120.0 lb)
PERFORMANCE RATING (ISA, S/L):	3.781 kN (850 lb st)

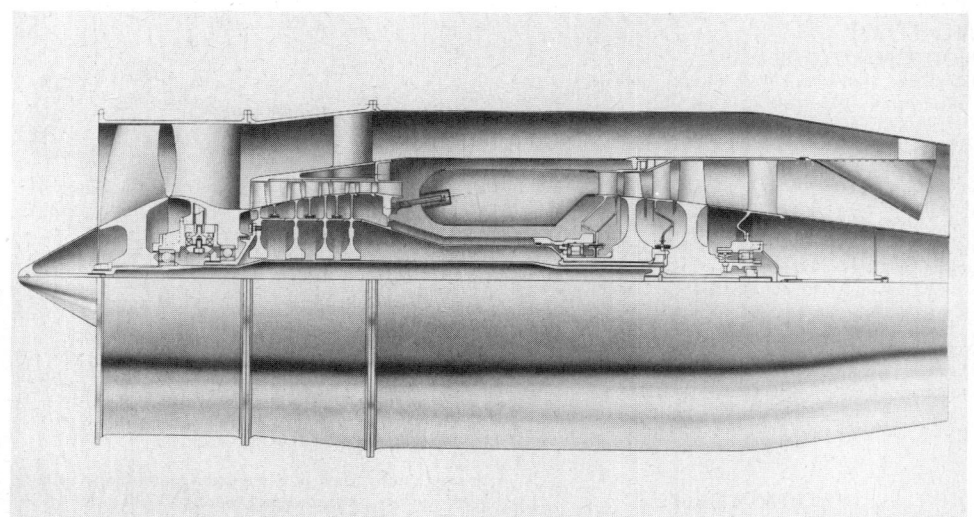

Longitudinal section of NPT 754 turbofan

ROLLS-ROYCE

ROLLS-ROYCE plc
65 Buckingham Gate, London SW1E 6AT
Telephone: 44 (71) 222 9020
Fax: 44 (71) 233 1733
Telex: 918091
MAIN LOCATIONS:
  PO Box 31, Moor Lane, Derby DE2 8BJ
  Telephone: 44 (332) 242424
  Fax: 44 (332) 249936/7
  PO Box 3, Filton, Bristol BS12 7QE
  Telephone: 44 (272) 791234
  Fax: 44 (272) 797575
  Leavesden, Watford WD2 7BZ
  Telephone: 44 (923) 674000
  Fax: 44 (923) 661939
CHAIRMAN: Lord Tombs of Brailes
CHIEF EXECUTIVE AND DEPUTY CHAIRMAN:
  Sir Ralph Robins
DIRECTOR OF PUBLIC AFFAIRS: Michael Farlam

More than 336 million hours have been accumulated with
Rolls-Royce civil and military gas turbines, which are used
by over 310 airlines, over 110 armed forces and more than
700 executive customers.

The main activities are at Derby, Glasgow, Bristol,
Coventry and Leavesden, where aircraft gas turbines are
produced, and at Ansty, where aircraft gas turbine
techniques are applied to industrial and marine uses.
Employees total 64,000.

In April 1985 Rolls-Royce joined with Turbomeca and
MTU in the European Small Engines Co-operation
Agreement. This involves the Rolls-Royce Turbomeca
RTM 322, MTU-Turbomeca-RR MTR 390, and Turbo-
meca TM 333. Further details are given under Turbomeca
(France) and in the International part of this section. The
company is a partner in IAE, EUROJET, Turbo-Union,
Rolls-Royce Turbomeca and Williams-Rolls Inc. Through
NEI the group designs and builds heavy capital plant and
equipment.

In 1990, BMW Rolls-Royce was formed, which see in
German part of this section.

ROLLS-ROYCE TURBOMECA ADOUR

See the International part of this section.

TURBO-UNION RB199

See the International part of this section.

EUROJET EJ 200

See the International part of this section.

IAE V2500

See the International part of this section.

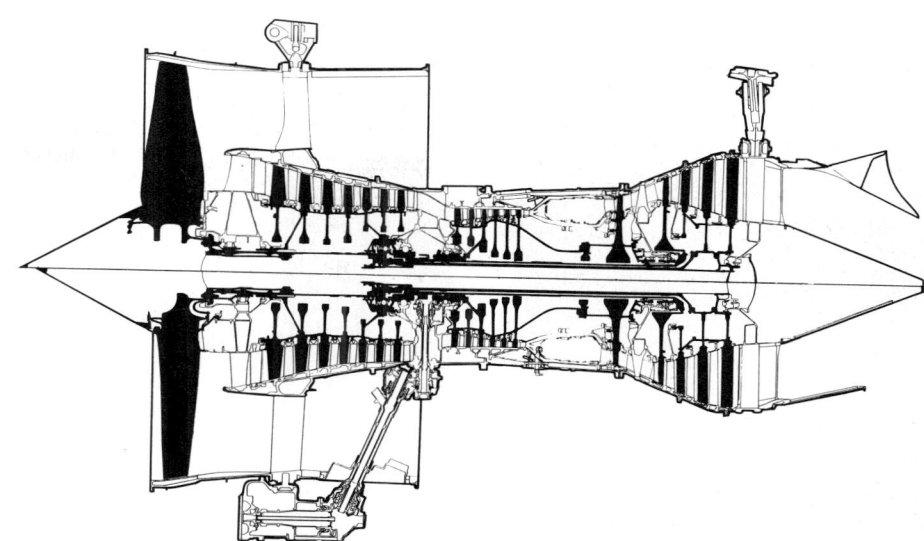

Longitudinal sections of the Rolls-Royce RB211-524G (upper half) and RB211-524D4 Upgrade (lower)

ROLLS-ROYCE RB211

The designation RB211 applies to a family of three-shaft
turbofans of high bypass ratio and high pressure ratio,
ranging in thrust from 166.4 kN (37,400 lb st) to 422.6 kN
(95,000 lb st). These ratings include the derived 535 and
Trent, which are described separately.

For all announced applications Rolls-Royce retains
responsibility for the complete propulsion system, comprising the engine, fan airflow reverser, pod cowlings and
related systems, and noise attenuation for the intake, fan
cowl and turbine exhaust duct. The engine is built up of
seven modules, each changed easily.

The **RB211-22B**, fitted to the L-1011-1 and -100
TriStar, is flat rated at 186.8 kN (42,000 lb st) to 29°C.
Certificated in February 1973 by the CAA and in April 1973
by the FAA. Production ceased in 1982 when over 670
engines had been delivered. By 1991 engine flight hours in
service exceeded 19 million.

The **RB211-524** series of engines was developed from
the RB211-22B and covers a range of thrusts from 222.4 kN
(50,000 lb) to 280.2 kN (63,000 lb). The -524 entered airline
service in 1977 with the L-1011 and 747. By the beginning of
1991 nearly 900 engines had been delivered, and service
experience of nearly 17 million hours achieved.

The **RB211-524B**, which powers the L-1011-200,
L-1011-500 and 747, is certificated at 222.4 kN (50,000 lb) to
28.9°C. Further developments at the same thrust but
offering better fuel consumption include the **RB211-
524B3**, giving a 3.5 per cent improvement over the
-524B, and which entered service in May 1980; and the

RB211-524B4, which offers up to 4.8 per cent better sfc
than the 524B and entered service in February 1981.
Further savings are obtained from the **524B4 Improved**
and the **524B4-B**, which incorporate additional sfc and
component life improvements. These engines can be
installed new or by modifying existing engines in the
L-1011-250.

The **RB211-524C** offers increased thrust ratings for the
747. It entered service in April 1980 with a rating of 229.1
kN (51,500 lb).

The **RB211-524D4** is an improved engine rated at
235.75 kN (53,000 lb) for the 747, and offering a 4.8 per cent
better fuel consumption relative to the -524B. Certification
was followed by entry into service in November 1981.

The **RB211-524D4 Upgrade** offers 2.6 per cent lower
sfc than the D4 and is rated at 235.75 kN (53,000 lb) for the
747. This engine entered service in 1984. Variants entering
service from 1987 increased the sfc improvements to around
5 per cent.

The **RB211-524G** incorporates advanced features
proven on the 535E4, such as the wide-chord fan, 3-D
aerodynamics, directionally solidified HP and IP turbine
blades and integrated mixer nozzle. Another new feature is
a full-authority digital control system. It is rated at 258 kN
(58,000 lb st), with sfc 5 per cent lower than the D4 Upgrade,
and was certificated in March 1988 for the 747-400, entering
service in June 1989.

The **RB211-524H**, rated at 269.6 kN (60,600 lb st)
entered service on the Boeing 747-400 and 767-300 in
February 1990, and is mechanically identical to the 524G.

A lighter and even more efficient G/H version will enter
service in 1992.

The following description relates to the 1991 standard of
G/H:

TYPE: Three-shaft axial turbofan. Overall pressure ratio 33.
FAN: Single-stage overhung, driven by LP turbine. Composite nosecone, 24 hollow wide-chord blades in titanium
  alloy, supercritical outlet guide vanes. Aluminium casing,
  with Armco containment ring. Mass flow 728 kg (1,604
  lb)/s. Bypass ratio 4.3.
IP COMPRESSOR: Seven-stage, driven by IP turbine. Two
  drums, one of titanium discs welded together and the
  other of welded steel discs, bolted to form one rotor,
  carrying titanium blades. Aluminium and steel casings
  carry steel stator blades. Single-stage titanium variable
  inlet guide vanes.
HP COMPRESSOR: Six-stage, driven by HP turbine. Welded
  titanium discs, single steel disc and welded nickel alloy
  discs bolted together carrying titanium, steel and nickel
  alloy blades. Steel casing carries steel and Nimonic stator
  blades.
COMBUSTION CHAMBER: Fully annular, with steel outer
  casings and nickel alloy combustor. Downstream fuel
  injection by 18 airspray burners with annular atomisers.
  High energy igniter plugs in Nos 8 and 12 burners.
HP TURBINE: Single-stage, with directionally solidified nickel
  alloy rotor blades, both convection and film cooled,
  mounted in nickel alloy disc by fir tree roots.
IP TURBINE: Single-stage, with directionally solidified nickel
  alloy rotor blades fir tree mounted in nickel alloy disc.
LP TURBINE: Three-stage, with nickel alloy rotor blades fir
  tree mounted in steel discs.
EXHAUST NOZZLE: Integrated nozzle with deep-chute forced
  mixer.
ACCESSORY DRIVES: Radial drive from HP shaft to gearbox
  on fan casing. Accessories include integrated drive
  generator and aircraft hydraulic pumps.
LUBRICATION SYSTEM: Continuous circulation dry sump
  system supplying oil to four bearing chambers with a
  combination of ball and roller bearings. 27 litre (57.6 US
  pint; 48 Imp pint) oil tank integral with gearbox.

Rolls-Royce RB211-524G three-shaft turbofan

DIMENSIONS:
Length overall:

RB211-22B, -524C2	3,033 mm (119.4 in)
RB211-524B4, -524D4	3,106 mm (122.3 in)
RB211-524G, -524H	3,175 mm (125.0 in)

Fan diameter:

RB211-22B, -524C2	2,154 mm (84.8 in)
RB211-524B4, -524D4	2,180 mm (85.8 in)
RB211-524G, -524H	2,192 mm (86.3 in)

WEIGHT, DRY:

RB211-22B	4,171 kg (9,195 lb)
RB211-524B4, B4 Improved	4,452 kg (9,814 lb)
RB211-524C2	4,472 kg (9,859 lb)
RB211-524D4, D4 Upgrade, -524G/H	
	4,479 kg (9,874 lb)
RB211-524G/H (1992)	4,309 kg (9,499 lb)

PERFORMANCE RATINGS:
T-O: see model listings
Cruise at 10,670 m (35,000 ft) and Mach 0.85 (uninstalled):

RB211-22B	42.2 kN (9,495 lb)
RB211-524B4, B4 Improved	48.9 kN (11,000 lb)
RB211-524C2	51.1 kN (11,490 lb)
RB211-524D4 (all models)	50.0 kN (11,230 lb)
RB211-524G, -524H	52.5 kN (11,813 lb)

SPECIFIC FUEL CONSUMPTION (cruise):

RB211-22B	17.79 mg/Ns (0.628 lb/h/lb)
RB211-524B4	17.56 mg/Ns (0.620 lb/h/lb)
RB211-524B4 Improved	17.16 mg/Ns (0.606 lb/h/lb)
RB211-524C2	18.21 mg/Ns (0.642 lb/h/lb)
RB211-524D4	17.48 mg/Ns (0.617 lb/h/lb)
RB211-524D4 Upgrade (1987)	
	17.02 mg/Ns (0.601 lb/h/lb)
RB211-524G, -524H	15.95 mg/Ns (0.563 lb/h/lb)
RB211-524G/H (1992)	15.66 mg/Ns (0.553 lb/h/lb)

Rolls-Royce Trent three-shaft turbofan

ROLLS-ROYCE TRENT

Originally known as the RB211-524L, this is the most powerful conventional aircraft engine currently under firm contract in the world. Its detailed engineering design began in 1988 to meet the propulsion requirements of wide-bodied aircraft planned for the 1990s, including the MD-11, A330 and Boeing 777. To meet the requirements for these aircraft a range of Trent engines is being developed.

Trent Designation	Take-off Thrust
665	285.4 kN (64,150 lb st)
668	302.3 kN (67,950 lb st)
768	300.3 kN (67,500 lb st)
772	316.3 kN (71,100 lb st)
871	317.2 kN (71,300 lb st)
882	366.1 kN (82,300 lb st)

The Trent is a low risk derivative of the RB211-524, employing advances in design techniques and material. It incorporates the first increase in diameter of the fan since the entry into service of the RB211-22B in April 1972, even though power at this size has increased by nearly 45 per cent due to design and material improvements.

Another change in the Trent design is that, whilst the successful modular design of the RB211 has been retained, the order of module removal has been altered for increased ease of maintenance. With the RB211 design the IP compressor and intermediate casing are removed from the front of the fan case assembly, with all other modules being removed rearwards. On the Trent all modules are removed rearwards, facilitating complete gas generator removal from the fan case and further improving maintenance flexibility.

The Trent 600 was launched in February 1989 by an order from Air Europe to power the MD-11. For this aircraft the engine will be certificated in June 1992 at the Trent 668 rating, although Air Europe intend to commence operation at the Trent 665 rating. A growth version of the MD-11, the MD-12X, is expected to require a thrust level offered by the Trent 700. In April 1989 Cathay Pacific selected the Trent 700 for their A330 aircraft. For this application the Trent 700 will be certificated in December 1993 and cleared to operate at both 768 and 772 ratings. June 1989 saw TWA order the Trent 772 to enable their A330s to fly long distances, for example from the US west coast to Europe, with maximum payloads. The Trent 800, designed to meet the thrust requirements of the Boeing 777, will be certificated at the thrust rating of the Trent 882 in August 1994.

The following outlines major differences between the Trent and the RB211-524G/H:

FAN: Single stage with 26 wide chord blades of hollow titanium. Blades made by superplastic forming the diffusion bonding to form integral canted spars running from root to tip.

IP COMPRESSOR: Eight stages, giving increased core airflow. Variable inlet guide vanes and first two stator stages.

HP COMPRESSOR: New six-stage design offering greater efficiency, with improved tip clearance control based on V2500 technology.

COMBUSTION CHAMBER: Based on latest technology optimised for reduced emissions.

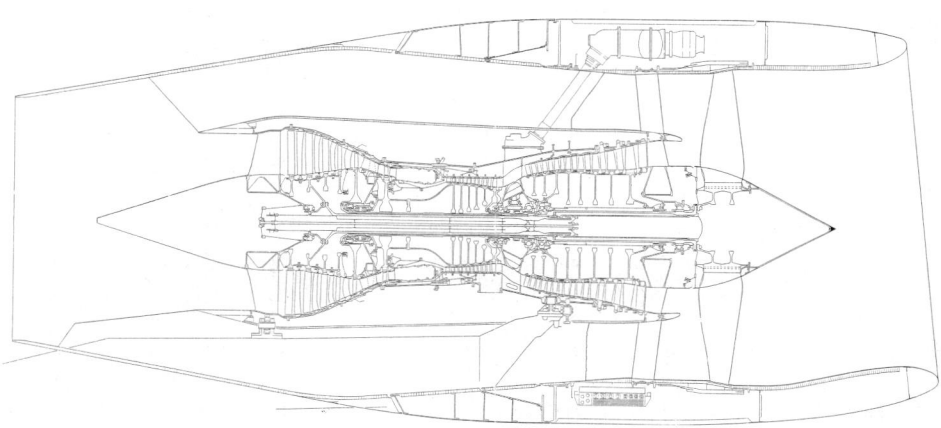

Longitudinal section of Rolls-Royce Trent and nacelle

HP TURBINE: Fitted with blading of the latest three-dimensional design, with directionally solidified blades. Complete HP module common with 1992 524G/H.

IP TURBINE: Increased annulus design with single-crystal uncooled blades.

LP TURBINE: Trent 600 and 700 have a new four-stage design with three-dimensional blading. Trent 800 features a five-stage turbine.

GEAR BOX: Single-piece casting with gear and bearings individually replaceable without disturbance of adjacent gears. Separate oil tank and filler.

REVERSER: Hurel Dubois four-door type with Lucas hydraulic actuation, governed by main engine FADEC.

MOUNTING: Trent 600 and 700 core mounted. Trent 800 front fan case mount, rear core mount with thrust struts to front of core. Designed for enhanced rigidity, reduced distortion of the fan case and reduced engine weight.

ENGINE CONTROL: Lucas Full Authority Digital Engine Control (FADEC). Gives improved fuel consumption, better engine control and reduces pilot work load by interacting with aircraft computers.

DIMENSIONS:
Length overall:

600, 700	3,912 mm (154 in)
800	4,369 mm (172 in)

Fan diameter:

600	2,403 mm (94.6 in)
700	2,474 mm (97.4 in)
800	2,794 mm (110 in)

WEIGHT, DRY:

600, 700	4,513 kg (9,950 lb)
800	5,447 kg (12,010 lb)

PERFORMANCE RATINGS:
T-O: See above
Cruise (10,670 m; 35,000 ft, Mach 0.82 (0.83 for Trent 800)):

665	57.9 kN (13,020 lb)
668	55.9 kN (12,570 lb)
768, 772	64.8 kN (14,570 lb)
871, 882	72.2 kN (16,233 lb)

SPECIFIC FUEL CONSUMPTION (cruise):

600	15.75 mg/Ns (0.556 lb/h/lb)
700	15.55 mg/Ns (0.549 lb/h/lb)
800	15.66 mg/Ns (0.553 lb/h/lb)

ROLLS-ROYCE 535

The **535C** was launch engine for the Boeing 757. It has an HP module based on the RB211-22B, six-stage IP compressor without variable stator vanes, and a scaled down -524 fan. Fan airflow is 18 per cent lower than that of the -22B, and core airflow 12 per cent lower. The engine runs at moderate temperatures, pressures and velocities, resulting in low noise and outstanding reliability for short-haul operation. The 535C entered service on 1 January 1983. The 100 engines of this model had accumulated 1.2 million hours by 1 January 1991.

Max cruise (10,670 m; 35,000 ft, Mach 0.80):
535C   37.6 kN (8,453 lb)
535E4   38.7 kN (8,700 lb)
SPECIFIC FUEL CONSUMPTION (cruise, as above):
535C   18.30 mg/Ns (0.646 lb/h/lb)
535E4   17.19 mg/Ns (0.607 lb/h/lb)

ROLLS-ROYCE RB163 CIVIL SPEY
US military designation: F113

Design of the Spey began in September 1959. The first engine ran at the end of December 1960. Civil Speys are the subject of a collaborative production programme between Rolls-Royce and the government of Romania. The **F113-RR-100** is the Mk 511-8 which powers the Gulfstream C-20A C-SAM aircraft. A total of 2,155 civil Speys were produced in Britain, logging 28.3 million hours by 1 January 1991.

The following details refer to the Spey Mk 512-14DW, as fitted to the BAe and Rombac One-Eleven Series 500, except where indicated:

TYPE: Two-spool turbofan.
COMPRESSOR: Two spools. Five-stage (four-stage on Mks 505 and 506) low pressure (LP) and 12-stage high pressure (HP). First-stage HP stator vanes variable incidence. Pressure ratio 21.2. Mass flow 94.4 kg (208 lb)/s. Bypass ratio 0.64.
COMBUSTION CHAMBER: Tubo-annular with 10 Nimonic sheet liners. Duplex downstream burners, one per chamber. High energy igniters in chambers 4 and 8.
FUEL SYSTEM: Plessey LP pump feeding through fuel cooled oil cooler and Marston Excelsior fuel heater to LP filter at inlet to Lucas GD pump.
FUEL GRADE: DERD.2482 or 2486.
WATER INJECTION SYSTEM (engines bearing 'W' suffix): Water supplied by Lucas air turbopump to injector passages in fuel spray nozzles.
TURBINES: Two two-stage. First HP aircooled. Nickel alloy blades attached by fir tree roots.
REVERSER AND SUPPRESSOR: Normally internal clamshell (Gulfstream II and III target type). Five- or six-chute silencing nozzles available.
ACCESSORY DRIVES: Port gearbox, driven from LP rotor, carries LP governor and LP tacho. Starboard gearbox, driven from HP rotor, carries LP and HP fuel pumps, fuel regulator, main oil pumps, airflow control rpm signal transmitter, starter and HP tacho. Provision in starboard gearbox for aircraft ancillaries.
LUBRICATION SYSTEM: Self-contained continuous circulation. Tank capacity 6.8 litres (14.4 US pints; 12 Imp pints). Normal pressure 2.41-3.45 bars (35-50 lb/sq in).
OIL SPECIFICATION: DERD.2487.
STARTING: Plessey 220 air turbine starter.
DIMENSIONS:
Length, less tailpipe   2,911 mm (114.6 in)
Diameter   942 mm (37.1 in)
WEIGHT, DRY: 1,168 kg (2,574 lb)
PERFORMANCE RATINGS:
Max T-O   55.8 kN (12,550 lb st)
Max continuous
                51.5 kN (11,580 lb st) at 12,450 rpm
Typical cruise rating at 450 knots (834 km/h; 518 mph) at 9,750 m (32,000 ft)   13.7 kN (3,070 lb)
SPECIFIC FUEL CONSUMPTION (cruise as above)
                22.7 mg/Ns (0.800 lb/h/lb)
OIL CONSUMPTION:
Max (all Marks)
                0.42 litre (0.89 US pint; 0.75 Imp pint)/h

ROLLS-ROYCE RB183

Developed for the Fokker F28, this derivative engine has a similar configuration to the Spey but has a four-stage LP compressor. Pressure ratio 15.4, mass flow 90.27 kg (199 lb)/s and bypass ratio 1. The 613 engines produced had by 1 January 1991 achieved almost 10 million hours. The following versions are in use:

Mk 555-15. Basic model, rated at 43.8 kN (9,850 lb st).
Mk 555-15H. Hot-day version, flat rated at 44.0 kN (9,900 lb st) to 29.7°C. Entered service 1973.
Mk 555-15N. Mk 555-15 with 10-lobe mixer.
Mk 555-15P. More fuel-efficient -15H with 10-lobe mixer. Entered service 1982.

The following data refer to the 555-15P:
DIMENSIONS:
Length   2,553 mm (100.5 in)
Diameter   940 mm (37.0 in)
WEIGHT, DRY: 1,024 kg (2,257 lb)
PERFORMANCE RATINGS:
T-O: see model listings
Cruise at 7,620 m (25,000 ft) at 440 knots (815 km/h; 507 mph)   16.59 kN (3,730 lb)
SPECIFIC FUEL CONSUMPTION:
T-O   15.9 mg/Ns (0.560 lb/lb st)
Cruise (as above)   22.7 mg/Ns (0.800 lb/h/lb)

ROLLS-ROYCE RB168 SPEY

The RB168 military versions of the Spey are as follows:
Mk 101. Basic engine, but with air offtake for BLC. Fitted to BAe Buccaneer.

Rolls-Royce 535E4 three-shaft turbofan

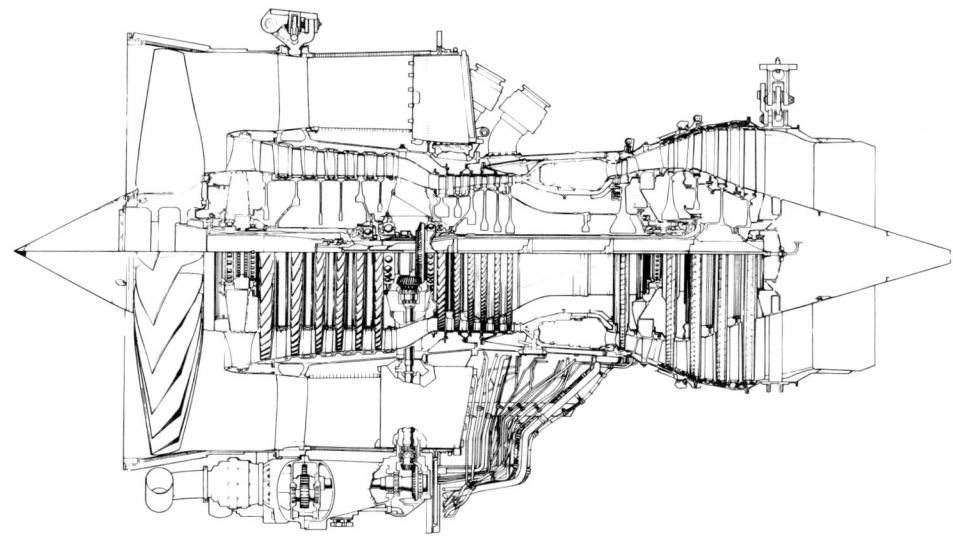

Longitudinal section and cutaway of Rolls-Royce 535E4

The **535E4** is an advanced version offering increased thrust, together with reduced fuel consumption relative to the 535C. It has a new wide chord fan blade without snubbers, together with advanced compressor and turbine blading and an integrated nozzle. Revenue service began in October 1984. The E4 reliability rates surpass those of its predecessor. In the sixth year of service the total engine-caused removal and shutdown rates were 0.06 and 0.02 per 1,000 h. The E4 allowed 757s powered by it to be cleared for 120 minute extended-range operations (EROPS) in December 1986, extended to 180 minutes in 1990.

An uprated 535E4 entered service in August 1989. Its T-O rating of 191.7 kN (43,100 lb) enables the 757 to carry heavier payloads from the most noise-sensitive airports. By 1 January 1991 a total of 330 E4 engines had accumulated 2.4 million hours in service.

The **535E5** is basically an E4 with a higher-efficiency HP compressor, resulting in reduced fuel burn. It was due to be certificated in mid-1991 and to enter service before the end of the year.

The following description relates to the 535E4:
TYPE: Three-shaft turbofan.
FAN: Single-stage, with only 22 wide chord blades, without snubbers, each of activated diffusion bonded titanium skins on titanium honeycomb core. Fan case of Rohrbond with Kevlar containment. Mass flow 522 kg (1,150 lb)/s. Bypass ratio 4.3 (535C, 4.4).
IP COMPRESSOR: Six stages of controlled diffusion design. No variable vanes.
HP COMPRESSOR: Six stages of end-bend blading, with stage -4, -5 and -6 discs in titanium super alloy. Low expansion casing for improved tip clearance control. Overall engine pressure ratio 25.8 (535C, 21.1).

COMBUSTION CHAMBER: Annular, 18 airspray nozzles, flexible liner mountings, heatshields and thermal barrier coatings.
HP TURBINE: Single-stage. Rotor blades, directionally solidified, cast with HP leading-edge cooling, HP and LP internal air cooling passages both with triple pass system. Nozzle guide vanes with curved stacking, highly cooled and with thermal barrier coating on platforms.
IP TURBINE: Single stage. Cooled NGVs with multi-lean stacking for improved airflow onto high aspect ratio blades.
LP TURBINE: Three stages. All turbine casings double wall and cooled.
JETPIPE: Core and bypass flows mixed in integrated nozzle.
REVERSER: Fan reverser only. Jacks move translating cowl to rear, blocker deals seal fan duct and uncover cascade vanes. Over expansion reduces core thrust.
GEARBOX: Mounted under fan case, driven from HP spool.
DIMENSIONS:
Length: 535C   3,010 mm (118.5 in)
        535E4   2,995 mm (117.9 in)
Inlet diameter: 535C   1,877 mm (73.9 in)
                535E4   1,892 mm (74.5 in)
WEIGHT, DRY:
        535C   3,309 kg (7,294 lb)
        535E4   3,295 kg (7,264 lb)
PERFORMANCE RATINGS (note: flexible T-O ratings involving considerable derating are used in operation):
T-O (S/L, ISA): 535C   166.4 kN (37,400 lb st)
        535E4   178.4-192 kN (40,100-43,100 lb st)
Max climb (10,670 m; 35,000 ft, Mach 0.80):
        535C   40.1 kN (9,023 lb)
        535E4   41.4 kN (9,300 lb)

Rolls-Royce Spey Mk 807 two-shaft turbofan

HP TURBINE: All Mks except 650 and 670, two stages as RB183 Mk 555. Tay 650 and 670, advanced two-stage design.

LP TURBINE: New design with three stages.

BYPASS DUCT: Carbonfibre composite.

MIXER: Forced deep chute type with 12 lobes.

DIMENSIONS:

Length	2,405 mm (94.7 in)
Inlet diameter: Tay 611/620	1,118 mm (44.0 in)
Tay 650	1,138 mm (44.8 in)
Tay 670	1,245 mm (49.0 in)

WEIGHT, DRY:

Tay 611	1,406 kg (3,099 lb)
Tay 650	1,514 kg (3,338 lb)

PERFORMANCE RATING (T-O):

Tay 611, 620-15	61.61 kN (13,850 lb st) to 30°C
Tay 650	67.17 kN (15,100 lb st) to 30°C
Tay 670	80.1 kN (18,000 lb st) to 30°C

SPECIFIC FUEL CONSUMPTION (cruise):

Tay 611 (13,100 m; 43,000 ft, Mach 0.8)
20.1 mg/Ns (0.709 lb/h/lb)

Tay 620 and 650 (9,145 m; 30,000 ft, Mach 0.73)
19.5 mg/Ns (0.69 lb/h/lb)

Tay 670 (10,669 m; 35,000 ft, Mach 0.76)
19.9 mg/Ns (0.704 lb/h/lb)

Mk 202. Augmented engine for supersonic aircraft, with shaft/disc LP compressor and fully modulated afterburner. Fitted to Phantom FGR.2 (F-4M) and licensed to China. Phantom FG.1 (F-4K) has **Mk 203.**

Mk 250. Fully navalised. Fitted to BAe Nimrod MR.1, R.1 and MR.2.

Mk 807. Mk 101 rotors within RB183 structure, with BLC deleted and fitted with manual emergency fuel control. Produced under licence in Italy with Brazilian participation for AMX aircraft.

DIMENSIONS:

Length: Mk 101	2,911 mm (114.6 in)
Mk 202	5,204 mm (204.9 in)
Mk 250, 251	2,972 mm (117.0 in)
Mk 807	2,456 mm (96.7 in)
Diameter	825 mm (32.5 in)

WEIGHT, DRY:

Mk 101	1,121 kg (2,471 lb)
Mk 202	1,857 kg (4,093 lb)
Mk 250, 251	1,243 kg (2,740 lb)
Mk 807	1,096 kg (2,417 lb)

PERFORMANCE RATINGS (max T-O):

Mk 101, 807	49.1 kN (11,030 lb st)
Mk 202: dry	54.5 kN (12,250 lb st)
augmented	91.2 kN (20,515 lb st)
Mk 250, 251	53.3 kN (11,995 lb st)

ROLLS-ROYCE TAY

The Tay turbofan is designed around the core and external gearbox of the RB183 Mk 555. The LP system has been tailored to complement this by maintaining core inlet and outlet conditions similar to those of the original engine. The wide-chord fan and three-stage IP compressor are driven by a three-stage LP turbine which uses the latest proven technology. The cold bypass air and hot exhaust are combined in a forced mixer. The bypass duct is carbonfibre composite.

The initial production versions are the **Tay 611** and **620.** The **Tay 650** gives a 9 per cent increase in maximum take-off thrust and a 15 per cent increase in maximum continuous, climb, and cruise thrusts, achieved by a small increase in fan diameter and an advanced HP turbine.

The initial versions received certification from the CAA in June 1986. Over 400 of these had accumulated 430,000 hours in service by 1 January 1991. Certification of the Tay 650 was achieved ahead of schedule in June 1988. The **Tay 670** is an uprated version, under review for re-engining 727, 737 and DC-9 aircraft.

The Tay easily meets all current emission standards, and enables the Fokker 100, Gulfstream IV and re-engined BAe One-Eleven to comply with FAR Pt 36 Stage 3 noise requirements. In May 1990, the Tay 650 was selected to re-engine the 727-100 fleet of United Parcel Service. All versions are subject to a collaborative agreement with Volvo Flygmotor of Sweden (which see).

Tay 610-8. Selected for Gulfstream IV. Certificated on 26 June 1986. All replaced by **Tay 611** (see data).

Tay 620-15. Selected for Fokker 100. Entered service April 1988.

Tay 650-14. Selected to re-engine BAe One-Eleven.

Tay 650-15. Specified for higher-performance versions of Fokker 100. Entered service October 1989.

Tay 651-54. Selected to re-engine 727-100.

Tay 670. Rated at 80 kN (18,000 lb st) for re-engining DC-9, 737-200 and 727.

TYPE: Two-shaft turbofan.

FAN: Single-stage with wide chord blades. Diameter (620) 1,118 mm (44 in), (650) 1,143 mm (45 in).

LP COMPRESSOR: New design with three stages on fan shaft.

HP COMPRESSOR: 12-stage axial (RB183 Mk 555).

COMBUSTION CHAMBER: Tubo-annular with 10 flame tubes, each with one burner.

FUEL SYSTEM: As RB183 Mk 555 but with improved fuel control unit.

ROLLS-ROYCE TYNE

The 4,549 ekW (6,100 ehp) Tyne two-shaft turboprop is being produced by a consortium comprising SNECMA and MTU (prime contractors carrying out assembly and test), Rolls-Royce and FN. The Mk 21 engine powers the Atlantique and the Mk 22 the Transall.

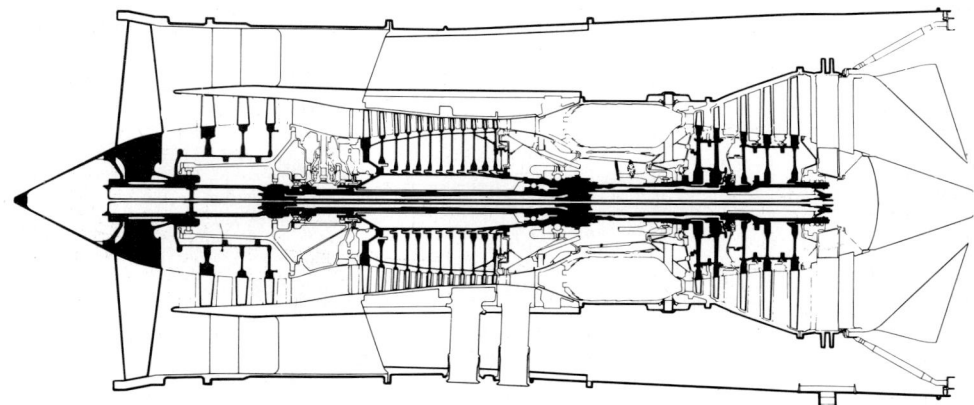

Longitudinal section of Rolls-Royce Tay two-shaft turbofan

Rolls-Royce Tay two-shaft turbofan

ROLLS-ROYCE VIPER

This turbojet remains in production. More than 5,000 are in civil and military operation.

Current versions are as follows:

Viper 11 (Mk 200 Series). Single-shaft seven-stage axial compressor driven by single-stage turbine. Mass flow 20 kg (44 lb)/s. Type tested at 11.12 kN (2,500 lb st) and powers Jindivik Mk 3 drone, Jet Provost T.4 and 5, SOKO Galeb and HJT-16 Kiran Mk I/IA.

A Viper 11 version, the 22-1, was built under licence in Italy by Piaggio for the Aermacchi MB-326 and by Atlas of South Africa and HDHV of Australia.

Viper 500 Series. Development with zero stage on compressor. Major applications include early HS 125 (Mks 521, 522) and PD-808 executive aircraft (Mk 526) and Strikemaster (Mk 535), MB-326 (Mk 540) and Jastreb (Mk 531) training and light combat aircraft. Mk 540 built under licence by Piaggio and Atlas.

Viper 600 Series. Eight-stage compressor driven by two-stage turbine; annular vaporising combustion chamber. Take-off rating 16.7 kN (3,750 lb st) civil and 17.8 kN (4,000 lb st) military. Agreement signed with Fiat (Italy) in July 1969 for technical collaboration (see Fiat).

The civil Viper 601 powers the BAe 125-600; the military 632 is fitted to the G-4 Super Galeb, MB-326K and MB-339. The 632-41 powers the Orao/IAR-93A and IAR-99. The 632 is built under licence in Italy, Romania and Yugoslavia. The 633 has an afterburner of the two-gutter type, with hot streak ignition; rating 22.3 kN (5,000 lb).

The **Viper 680** is the latest variant for the MB-339. It produces 20 per cent more thrust than the Viper 632.

The following details apply to the Viper 600 Series:

TYPE: Single-shaft axial turbojet.
COMPRESSOR: Eight-stage. Steel drum type rotor with disc assemblies. Magnesium alloy casing with blow-off valve. Pressure ratio 5.8 : 1. Mass flow 26.5 kg (58.4 lb)/s.
COMBUSTION CHAMBER: Short annular type with 24 vaporising burners and six starting atomisers. Electric ignition.
FUEL SYSTEM: Hydromechanical, with pump, barometric control and air/fuel control.
FUEL GRADE: JP-1 or JP-4.
TURBINE: Two-stage axial. Shrouded blades attached to discs by fir tree roots and locking strips.
ACCESSORY DRIVES: Gearbox driven from front of compressor by bevel gear.
LUBRICATION SYSTEM: Self contained recirculatory system. Military version fully aerobatic.
OIL SPECIFICATION: Mobil Jet 2, Shell ASTO 500 and Castrol 98.
STARTING: 24V starter/generator.
DIMENSIONS:

Length (flange to flange):	
Viper 11	1,626 mm (64.0 in)
Viper 531, 535, 540, 632	1,806 mm (71.1 in)
Max casing diameter:	
all versions	622 mm (24.5 in)

WEIGHT, DRY:

Viper 11	284 kg (625 lb)
Viper 531	345 kg (760 lb)
Viper 535	331 kg (730 lb)
Viper 540	342 kg (755 lb)
Viper 601, 632 and 680	358 kg (790 lb)

PERFORMANCE RATINGS (T-O):

Viper 11	11.12 kN (2,500 lb st)
Viper 531	13.9 kN (3,120 lb st)
Viper 535, 540	14.9 kN (3,360 lb st)
Viper 601	16.7 kN (3,750 lb st)
Viper 632	17.8 kN (4,000 lb st)
Viper 680	21.7 kN (4,870 lb st)

SPECIFIC FUEL CONSUMPTION (T-O):

Viper 11	30.3 mg/Ns (1.07 lb/h/lb st)
Viper 500 series	28.3 mg/Ns (1.00 lb/h/lb st)
Viper 601	26.6 mg/Ns (0.94 lb/h/lb st)
Viper 632	27.5 mg/Ns (0.97 lb/h/lb st)

OIL CONSUMPTION (max):

all versions	0.71 litre (1.5 US pints; 1.25 Imp pints)/h

ROLLS-ROYCE XG40

XG40 is a technology programme which encompasses rig testing, core engine running and two demonstrator engines. Launched in 1983, the programme objectives are to demonstrate life prediction methodology and assess new materials for the EJ200 (see Eurojet in International section).

ROLLS-ROYCE PEGASUS
USMC designations: F402

The Pegasus is a turbofan for STOVL applications. It has two main rotating systems which rotate in opposite directions, thus minimising gyroscopic effects. Thrust vectoring is achieved by four rotatable nozzles simultaneously operated and symmetrically positioned on each side of the engine. The total thrust is divided between the four nozzles, and the resultant thrust passes through a fixed point irrespective of nozzle angle, thus minimising aircraft control problems. HP bleed air is used for aircraft stabilisation.

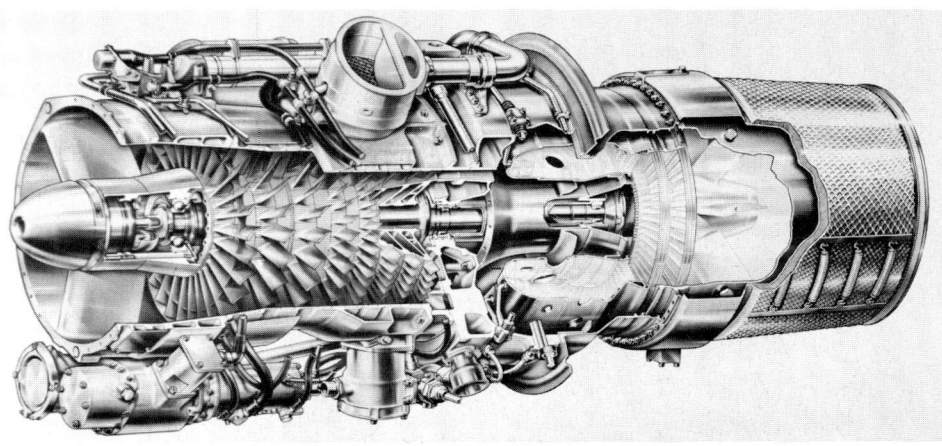

Cutaway drawing of Rolls-Royce Viper 632 single-shaft turbojet

The Pegasus ran in August 1959. The engine entered service in the BAe Harrier in 1969 as the **Pegasus 11 Mk 103**, (US designation **F402-RR-402**). A maritime version, designated **Mk 104**, for the Sea Harrier embodies material changes to the LP and intermediate casings, sacrificial protective coatings on ferrous components, and an increased capacity gearbox.

The **Pegasus 11-21** developed for the McDonnell Douglas/BAe Harrier II has the US designation **F402-RR-406** and UK designations **Mk 105** and **Mk 106**; it includes improved HP turbine cooling, a new shrouded LP turbine, revised swan-neck intermediate casing and changes to suit the revised airframe. Delivery of Mk 105 engines began in December 1984. Since 1986 production engines for the AV-8B and Harrier GR.5 and GR.7 have been fitted with a DECS (digital engine control system), replacing the previous hydromechanical system.

To enhance the Harrier II's hot-day vertical landing capability, and to cater for future growth, the **Pegasus 11-61 (F402-RR-408)** is now in production. It offers greater thrust, improved reliability and maintainability, and lower life-cycle costs. Its new fan has Dunlop blade root dampers of silicone rubber, Nomex textiles and titanium.

For future combat aircraft Rolls-Royce is studying vectored-thrust engines (with and without PCB) together with other advanced V/STOL systems such as a hybrid fan, remote augmented lift and ejector lift. The company is also studying lift fan engines for advanced transports and UAVs.

The following data apply specifically to the Pegasus 11-61 (F402-RR-408):

TYPE: Two-shaft vectored thrust turbofan.
FAN: Three-stage, overhung ahead of front bearing. Titanium blades with part-span snubbers. Mass flow 200 kg (441 lb)/s. Pressure ratio 2.7. Bypass ratio 1.2.

HP COMPRESSOR: Eight-stage with titanium rotor blades. Overall pressure ratio 14.85.
COMBUSTION SYSTEM: Annular, with LP vaporising burners.
FUEL SYSTEM: DSIC duplicated digital electronic control with emergency manual backup.
TURBINES: Two-stage HP with cooled blades and two-stage LP.
THRUST NOZZLES: Two steel zero-scarf cold nozzles and two Nimonic hot nozzles, actuated by duplicated air motors through shafts and chains under pilot command.
LUBRICATION SYSTEM: Self contained, with fuel cooled oil cooler.
STARTING: Gas turbine starter/APU on intermediate casing.
DIMENSIONS:

Width, with nozzles	2,510 mm (98.83 in)
Length, with nozzles	3,485 mm (137.2 in)
Diameter, fan casing	1,220 mm (48.05 in)

WEIGHT, DRY (without nozzles):

11 (Mk 105)	1,470 kg (3,240 lb)
11-21	1,796 kg (3,960 lb)
11-61	1,896 kg (4,180 lb)

PERFORMANCE RATINGS (ISA, S/L static):

Max lift thrust:	
Mks 104, 105, 106	95.64 kN (21,500 lb st)
11-21 (except Mk 106)	97.86 kN (22,000 lb st)
11-61	105.07 kN (23,620 lb st)

ROLLS-ROYCE TURBOMECA RTM 322

See the International part of this section.

MTU TURBOMECA RR-MTR 390

See the International part of this section.

Rolls-Royce Pegasus 11-61 (F402-RR-408) vectored-thrust turbofan

Cutaway drawing of Rolls-Royce Gem 60 free turbine turboshaft

ROLLS-ROYCE GEM

The Gem was developed at Leavesden, for the Westland Lynx helicopter. Subsequent applications are the Westland 30 and advanced Lynx versions, and Agusta A 129. The Gem 41 and 60 have been civil certificated.

Choice of a two-spool gas generator gives fast response to power demand without the need for a complex control system. There are seven major modules, each assembled, tested and released as an interchangeable unit.

Provision is made for in-flight and on-ground condition monitoring systems. Features include access ports for intrascope inspection of each LP compressor stage, HP compressor, combustor, LP turbine and power turbine, and mountings for vibration pickups.

The following versions have been announced:

Gem Mk 1001. Engine change unit for Lynx of British services and French Navy. Rated at 671 kW (900 shp).

Gem 2. Export military, rated at 671 kW (900 shp).

RR 1004. For Agusta A 129. Direct drive in place of reduction gearbox and electronic instead of hydromechanical control. Production under licence by Piaggio.

Gem 41 series. Modified compressor to increase mass flow by about 10 per cent plus small increase in TET.

Gem 42 series. Same ratings as Gem 41, but improved reliability and power retention.

Gem Mk 510. Civil Gem 41 for Westland 30.

Gem 60 series. Further increase in mass flow of approximately 26 per cent over Gem 41, derived from LP compressor incorporating new blades. TET also increased.

Gem Mk 531. Civil Gem 60 for Westland 30.

The following description relates to the Gem Mk 1001:

TYPE: Free turbine turboshaft.

SHAFT DRIVE: Single-stage double-helical reduction gear with rotating planet cage carried by ball bearing at front and roller bearing at rear. Alternative of direct drive output at 27,000 rpm or gearbox giving governed output speed of 6,000 rpm.

LP COMPRESSOR: Four-stage axial.

HP COMPRESSOR: Single-stage centrifugal. Overall pressure ratio 12.0.

COMBUSTION CHAMBER: Annular reverse flow with air atomiser fuel sprays. High energy ignition.

HP TURBINE: Single-stage close-coupled to HP impeller.

LP TURBINE: Single-stage with shrouded blades.

POWER TURBINE: Two-stage axial with shrouded blades.

ACCESSORY DRIVES: Bevel gear on front of HP shaft drives starter/generator, fuel pump, oil cooler fan and other accessories.

FUEL SYSTEM: Plessey fluidics automatic control, and power matching for multi-engine installation. Hamilton Standard electronic control fitted to RR 1004 and Gem 60.

LUBRICATION SYSTEM: Engine mounted oil tank and cooler. Magnetic chip detectors. Oil filter in accessory wheelcase.

DIMENSIONS:

Length overall	1,099 mm (43.2 in)
Width overall	575 mm (22.6 in)
Height overall	596 mm (23.5 in)

WEIGHT, DRY:

Gem 1001, 2	178 kg (393 lb)
Gem 41, 42	183 kg (404 lb)
RR 1004	163 kg (360 lb)
Gem 60	185 kg (407 lb)

PERFORMANCE RATINGS: see table

SPECIFIC FUEL CONSUMPTION:

50 per cent max T-O:

Except Gem 60	110 μg/J (0.65 lb/h/shp)
Gem 60	103 μg/J (0.61 lb/h/shp)

ROLLS-ROYCE GNOME

Gnome is the name given to the General Electric T58 turboshaft which Rolls-Royce manufactures. More than 2,300 have been delivered in the following versions:

H.1000. Initial version, rated at 783 kW (1,050 shp) for Whirlwind and Agusta-Bell 204B.

H.1200. Rated at 932 kW (1,250 shp). Used in Agusta-Bell 204B, Boeing 107 and some Kawasaki KV107-II-5s. Coupled version for Wessex comprises two H.1200s driving through a coupling gearbox.

H.1400. Rated at 1,044 kW (1,400 shp). Based on the H.1200, with modified compressor to increase airflow.

H.1400-1. Rated at 1,145 kW (1,535 shp). Increased gas generator speed and improved gas generator turbine blades. In production for Sea King and Commando.

H.1400-1T. Tropical model; turbine nozzle adjusted for better high ambient performance.

The following description refers to the H.1400-1:

TYPE: Free turbine turboshaft.

COMPRESSOR: Ten-stage axial. Variable inlet guide vanes and first three stator rows. Mass flow 6.26 kg (13.8 lb)/s.

COMBUSTION CHAMBER: Annular with 16 Simplex injectors, eight on each of two sets of manifolds. One Lodge high energy igniter.

FUEL SYSTEM: Lucas hydromechanical controlled by HSDE computer.

FUEL GRADE: DERD.2452, 2453, 2454, 2486, 2494 and 2498 (NATO F44, F34, F40, F35 and F43).

GAS-PRODUCER TURBINE: Two-stage.

POWER TURBINE: Single-stage free turbine.

REDUCTION GEAR: Optional double helical gear providing reduction from nominal 19,500 rpm power turbine speed to 6,600 rpm at left or right output shaft.

ACCESSORY DRIVES: Fuel and lubrication systems mounted beneath compressor casing. Power take-off shaft up to 100 shp.

LUBRICATION: Scavenged gear pumps. Serck oil cooler.

STARTING: Rotax electric starter in nose bullet.

DIMENSIONS:

Length:	H.1400-1	1,392 mm (54.8 in)
Max height:	H.1400-1	549 mm (21.6 in)
Max width:	H.1400-1	577 mm (22.7 in)

WEIGHT, DRY:

H.1400-1	148 kg (326 lb)

PERFORMANCE RATINGS (at power turbine shaft):

Max contingency (2½ min; multi-engine aircraft only):

H.1400-1	1,238 kW (1,660 shp)
H.1400-1T	1,092 kW (1,465 shp) to 45°C

Max one-hour (single engine):

H.1400-1	1,145 kW (1,535 shp)
H.1400-1T	1,030 kW (1,380 shp) to 45°C

Max continuous:

H.1400-1	932 kW (1,250 shp)
H.1400-1T	783 kW (1,050 shp) to 45°C

SPECIFIC FUEL CONSUMPTION:

At max contingency rating:

H.1400-1	102.75 μg/J (0.608 lb/h/shp)
H.1400-1T (30°C)	105.8 μg/J (0.626 lb/h/shp)

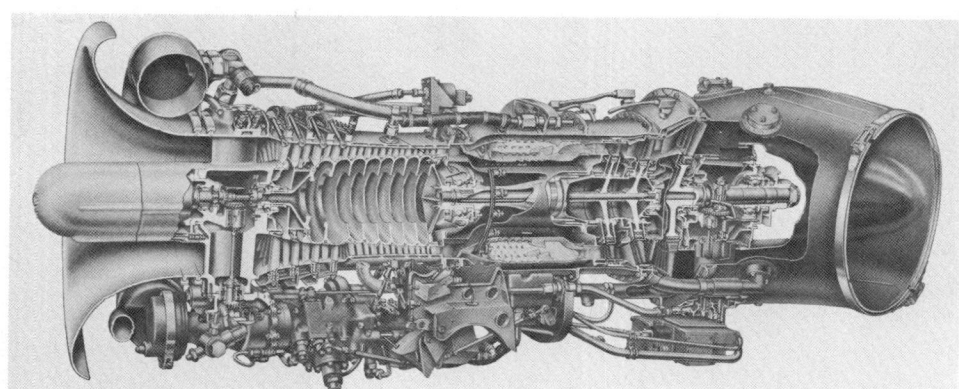

Cutaway drawing of Rolls-Royce Gnome H. 1400-1 free turbine turboshaft

GEM ENGINE RATINGS, kW (shp) ISA S/L STATIC

			One Engine Inoperative			Normal Twin Operation		
Designation	Date In Service	Emergency (20 s)	Max Contingency (2½ min)	Intermediate Contingency (60 min)	Max (T-O) (30 min)	Max (T-O) (5 min)	Max Continuous
Gem 2, Mk 1001	1976	N/A	671 (900)	619 (830)	N/A	619 (830)	559 (750)
RR 1004	1990	759 (1,018)	704 (944)	657 (881)	657 (881)	N/A	615 (825)
Gem 41-1, Mk 1014	1978	N/A	835 (1,120)	790.5 (1,060)	N/A	746 (1,000)	664 (890)
Gem 42, Mk 1017	1987	N/A	835 (1,120)	790.5 (1,060)	N/A	746 (1,000)	664 (890)
Gem 60-3/1 Mk 530	1983	N/A	897 (1,203)	844 (1,132)	N/A	844 (1,132)	821.75 (1,102)
Gem 60-3/3 Mk 531	1983	N/A	897 (1,203)	844 (1,132)	N/A	821.75 (1,102)	821.75 (1,102)

N/A: Not applicable

UNITED STATES OF AMERICA

AEROJET

AEROJET-GENERAL
(Subsidiary of GenCorp Inc)

10300 N Torrey Pines Road, La Jolla, California 92037
Telephone: 1 (619) 455 8500
PRESIDENT: R. I. Ramseier
VICE-PRESIDENT, PUBLIC AFFAIRS: Tom Sprague

Aerojet is a major aerospace and defence contractor with expertise in solid and liquid rocket propulsion, electronics and ordnance.

AEROJET TECHSYSTEMS CO

Sacramento, California: Development and manufacture of all liquid fuel engines for the US Air Force's Titan family of vehicles; second stage propulsion for the Japanese Space Agency (NASDA) N-II launch vehicles; and Orbiter Manoeuvring System (OMS) engines for the Space Shuttle.

AEROJET SPACE SHUTTLE OMS ENGINE

The Space Shuttle Orbiter has two Orbiter Manoeuvring System (OMS) engines, in pods each side of the vertical stabiliser (fin). They provide thrust for orbit insertion, circularisation and plane change, rendezvous and de-orbit manoeuvres. The propellants are monomethylhydrazine (MMH) and nitrogen tetroxide. At launch the basic system carries 4,087 kg (9,010 lb) of usable MMH and 6,743 kg (14,866 lb) of usable oxidiser. Fully qualified OMS engines have flown on all Shuttle missions to date. The following are chief characteristics:

THRUST (in vacuo):	26.7 kN (6,000 lb)
CHAMBER PRESSURE (in vacuo):	8.62 bars (125 lb/sq in)
SPECIFIC IMPULSE:	316 s
MIXTURE RATIO:	1.65 : 1
NOZZLE AREA RATIO (flight):	55 : 1
WEIGHT, DRY:	118 kg (260 lb)
THRUST VECTOR LIMITS:	±7°
STORAGE LIFE:	10 years
FIRING LIFE (100 missions):	15 h
NUMBER OF STARTS:	500
LONGEST SINGLE FIRING:	1,250 s

Aerojet Space Shuttle OMS rocket engine

ALLISON

ALLISON GAS TURBINE DIVISION, GENERAL MOTORS CORPORATION

Indianapolis, Indiana 46206-0420
Telephone: 1 (317) 230 2000
GENERAL MANAGER: Dr F. Blake Wallace

Allison Gas Turbine Division has 7,500 employees producing gas turbine engines and components for aircraft, vehicular and industrial/marine applications.

Collaboration on the T800 engine with Garrett is described under LHTEC on a later page. Collaboration with MTU is reported under the International heading.

ALLISON MODEL 250
US military designations: T63 and T703

The Model 250 is a small turboshaft/turboprop. Deliveries exceed 23,000, logging over 66 million hours.

A development contract for the T63 military version was received by Allison in June 1958. Details of early versions last appeared in the 1978-79 *Jane's*; the following are current models:

T63-A-720. Military turboshaft engine with hot-end improvements, increasing T-O rating to 313 kW (420 shp), for the Bell OH-58C.

T703-A-700. Military turboshaft engine corresponding to 250-C30R, for Bell OH-58D.

250-B17. Uprated version of B15 turboprop. The **B17B** operates at 17°C higher turbine gas temperature with hot-end improvements which maintain full power at high ambient temperatures. Produced from 1974 for Turbostar 402 conversions, Turbostar 414, ASTA Nomad N22 and 24, SIAI-Marchetti SM.1019E and various agricultural aircraft. **B17C** introduced improved gearbox allowing use of 313 kW (420 shp) on T-O. Produced for Nomad N22 and 24, SF.260TP and 600TP, Turbostar 402/414, Allison Bonanza, Bobby Aerostar, Par Turbine Aerostar, LoPresti

Piper/Globe/Temco Swift, ASI Jet Cruzer, Glasair III, Advanced Airship, BN-2T Turbine Islander, Composite Eagle, P.68TP Viator. **B17D** produced for SF.260TP, Aucán, Redigo, KM-2 Fuji T-5, HTT-34, Mentor 420 and SA.32T. **B17F**, with new compressor as in -C20R for increased T-O power, introduced in 1985 for BN-2T, SM600TP, HX-1, Redigo and Turbine P-210.

250-C20B. Introduced 1974, and rated at 313 kW (420 shp). For Bell and Agusta-Bell 206B JetRanger III and 206L LongRanger, MD 500D and E, Kitty Hawk, FH-1100 and UH-12E, Ka-226, RFB Fantrainer 400 and Bell 47G conversions.

250-C20F. For AS 355 Ecureuil 2/Twinstar.

250-C20J. For Bell and Agusta-Bell 206B JetRanger III.

250-C20R. Derivative of C20B with new axial-centrifugal compressor. **C20R/1** with redundant overspeed system for twin-engine applications certificated September 1986 for A 109A Mk II and BO 108. **C20R/2** for single-engine helicopters certificated early 1987 for MD 500ER, JetRanger III and LongRanger, and selected for MD 520N.

250-C20S. Turboprop for Soloy Turbine Pac conversions of Cessna 185, 206 and 207. Powers prototype ASI Jet Cruzer.

250-C28. Major redesign with single centrifugal compressor only, with increased airflow. Reduced noise and emissions, and minimal infra-red signature. New main gearbox. Certificated December 1977.

250-C28B. With particle separator; 2½-min rating of 410 kW (550 shp). Powers Bell LongRanger I.

250-C28C. Improved model with plain inlet; 2½-min rating of 410 kW (550 shp). Powers MBB BO 105 LS.

250-C30. Advanced single-stage compressor and dual ignition. Initial rating 485 kW (650 shp), with a 2½ min rating of 522 kW (700 shp). Certification completed March 1978. Produced for S-76 and MD 530G.

250-C30G. Produced for Heli-Air Bell 222.

250-C30L. With digital control, produced for Bell 406CS.

250-C30M. Produced for AS 350.

250-C30P. Produced for LongRanger III.

250-C30R. With digital control, produced for AHIP OH-58D.

250-C30S. Produced for S-76.

TYPE: Light turboshaft or turboprop.

COMPRESSOR: C20, C20B and B17B have six axial stages and one centrifugal. B17F and C20R have four axial stages and one centrifugal. Other models have single-stage centrifugal compressor only. Pressure ratio: C20B, B17, 7.2: C28B/C, C30, 8.4. Mass flow: C20B, B17C, 1.56 kg (3.45 lb)/s; C28B/C, 2.02 kg (4.45 lb)/s; C30, 2.54 kg (5.6 lb)/s.

COMBUSTION CHAMBER: Single can type at rear. Single duplex fuel nozzle in rear face. One igniter on C20B, B17C, C28B/C and C30L/M/P/R. Dual igniters on C30 and C30S; optional on C28B/C.

TURBINES: Two-stage gas producer turbine and two-stage free power turbine. Integrally cast rotor blades and wheels.

CONTROL SYSTEM: Pneumatic-mechanical system (B17C, hydromechanical; C20B, C28, C30/30M/P/S, pneumatic-mechanical; C30L, C30R, supervisory electronic).

FUEL: Primary fuels are ASTM-A or A-1 and MIL-T-5624, JP-4, JP-5 and die sel fuel.

LUBRICATION: Dry sump.

OIL SPECIFICATION: MIL-L-7808 and MIL-L-23699.

DIMENSIONS:

Length: B17C	1,143 mm	(45.0 in)
C20B, R	985 mm	(38.8 in)
C28C	1,201 mm	(47.3 in)
C30	1,041 mm	(41.0 in)
Width: B17C, C20B	483 mm	(19.0 in)
C28, C30	557 mm	(21.94 in)

Allison Model 250-B17C free-turbine turboprop

Allison Model 250-C20R free turbine turboshaft

Height: B17C	572 mm (22.5 in)
C20B	589 mm (23.2 in)
C28, C30	638 mm (25.13 in)
WEIGHT, DRY: B17C	88.4 kg (195 lb)
C20B	71.5 kg (158 lb)
C20R	76.0 kg (168 lb)
C28	99.3 kg (219 lb)
C28B, C	104 kg (230 lb)
C30	109.3 kg (240 lb)

PERFORMANCE RATINGS (S/L, ISA):

T-O: B17C, C20B, C20J, C20S (5 min)	313 kW (420 shp)
B17F, C20R (5 min, to 26.7°C)	335 kW (450 shp)
C20F	317 kW (425 shp)
C28, 28B, 28C (30 min)	373 kW (500 shp)
C30 (5 min)	485 kW (650 shp)
Max continuous: B17C (cruise)	275 kW (369 shp)
C20B	276 kW (370 shp)
C20R	283 kW (380 shp)
C28	368 kW (494 shp)
C30	415 kW (557 shp)
Cruise B (75 per cent): B17C	206 kW (277 shp)
C20B	207 kW (278 shp)
C20R	236 kW (317 shp)
C28	274 kW (367 shp)
C30	312 kW (418 shp)

SPECIFIC FUEL CONSUMPTION:

At T-O rating: B17C	111 µg/J (0.657 lb/h/shp)
C20B	110 µg/J (0.650 lb/h/shp)
C20R	103 µg/J (0.608 lb/h/shp)
C28	102.5 µg/J (0.606 lb/h/shp)
C30	100 µg/J (0.592 lb/h/shp)
At cruise B rating: B17C	120.8 µg/J (0.715 lb/h/shp)
C20B	120 µg/J (0.709 lb/h/shp)
C20R	112.5 µg/J (0.666 lb/h/shp)
C28	112 µg/J (0.664 lb/h/shp)
C30	111 µg/J (0.657 lb/h/shp)

ALLISON T56 and 501

US military designation: T56

Current versions of the T56 are as follows:

T56-A-14. Rated at 3,661 ekW (4,910 ehp). Generally similar to T56-A-15, but seven-point suspension and detail changes. Powers the P-3B and C Orion.

T56-A-15. Rated at 3,661 ekW (4,910 ehp). Introduced aircooled turbine blades. Powers current C-130.

T56-A-423 and **A-16.** Rated at 3,661 ekW (4,910 ehp). Powers US Navy versions of the C-130.

T56-A-425. Rated at 3,661 ekW (4,910 ehp). Powers C-2A Greyhound and early E-2C Hawkeye.

T56-A-427. Increased power and 13 per cent improvement in specific fuel consumption. Digital electronic supervisory control and modified propeller drive to maintain 1,106 rpm output with 14,239 power section rpm. Powers E-2C delivered since 1987.

501-D22A. Rated at 3,490 ekW (4,680 ehp). Commercial version of T56-A-15. Powers Lockheed L-100.

501-D39. Commercial derivative of T56-A-427 with modified propeller drive to provide 1,020 rpm output with 14,239 power section rpm.

Including the Model 501 commercial engines, production of these engines reached 14,864 by 1 January 1991.

The following details apply to the T56-A-15:

TYPE: Axial-flow turboprop.

PROPELLER DRIVE: Combination spur/planetary gear type. Overall gear ratio 13.54. Power section rpm 13,820. Weight of gearbox approximately 249 kg (550 lb) with pads on rear face for accessory mounting.

COMPRESSOR: Fourteen-stage axial flow. Pressure ratio 9.5. Mass flow 14.70 kg (32.4 lb)/s. Constant speed 13,820 rpm.

COMBUSTION CHAMBER: Six stainless steel can-annular type perforated combustion liners within one-piece stainless steel outer casing. Two ignitors in diametrically opposite combustors.

FUEL SYSTEM: High pressure type. Bendix control system. Water/alcohol augmentation system available.

FUEL GRADE: MIL-J-5624, JP-4 or JP-5.

TURBINE: Four-stage. Rotor assembly consists of four stainless steel discs, with first stage having hollow aircooled blades, secured by fir tree roots. Gas temperature before turbine 1,076°C.

ACCESSORY DRIVES: Accessory pads on rear face of reduction gear housing at front end of engine.

LUBRICATION SYSTEM: Low pressure. Dry sump. Pesco dual-element oil pump. Normal oil supply pressure 3.8 bars (55 lb/sq in).

OIL SPECIFICATION: MIL-L-7808.

MOUNTING: Three-point suspension.

STARTING: Air turbine, gearbox mounted.

DIMENSIONS:

Length (all current versions)	3,708 mm (146 in)
Width (all current versions)	686 mm (27 in)
Height: A-15, A-16, A-425, D-22A	991 mm (39 in)
A-14	1,118 mm (44 in)
WEIGHT, DRY: A-14	855 kg (1,885 lb)
A-15	828 kg (1,825 lb)
A-16	835 kg (1,841 lb)
A-425	860 kg (1,895 lb)
D22A	832 kg (1,834 lb)

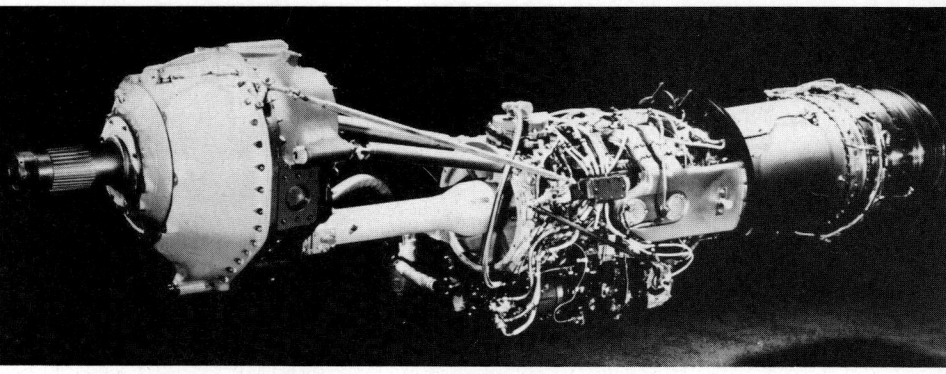

Allison T56-A-427 single-shaft turboprop

PERFORMANCE RATINGS (S/L, ISA, static):

T-O: A-14, A-15, A-16, A-423, A-425	3,661 ekW; 3,424 kW (4,910 ehp; 4,591 shp)
A427	3,915 kW (5,250 shp)
501-D22A	3,490 ekW (4,680 ehp)
Normal: A-14, A-15, A-16, A-425, D22A	3,255 ekW; 3,028 kW (4,365 ehp; 4,061 shp)

SPECIFIC FUEL CONSUMPTION:

At max rating:	
A-14, A-15, D22A	84.67 µg/J (0.501 lb/h/ehp)
At normal rating:	
A-14, A-15	87.4 µg/J (0.517 lb/h/ehp)

OIL CONSUMPTION:

A-14, A-15
    1.3 litres (0.35 US gallon; 0.29 Imp gallon)/h

ALLISON GMA 1100

US military designation: T406-AD-400

The T406 turboshaft, developed for the tilt-rotor V-22 Osprey, is the basis for the GMA 1100 turboshaft, GMA 2100 turboprop and GMA 3000 turbofan. The last two are described separately. All rest on 140 million T56 hours built into the core.

The T406-AD-400 is a free-turbine, front drive 4,588 kW (5,150 shp) turboshaft incorporating high efficiency components and reduced maintenance features required for operation in the V-22 Osprey. It features six rows of variable compressor stators, dual full-authority digital electronic fuel controls, self-contained oil system capable of engine operation in the vertical position and modular construction. The T406 has completed its flight rating tests and 21 engines have been delivered for the V-22 flight test programme. Full production is scheduled for 1993.

The T406 is applicable to other helicopter and tilt-rotor aircraft as the **GMA 1007.** This engine was in 1990 undergoing certification for use on a commercial derivative of the V-22.

TYPE: Axial flow turboshaft.

COMPRESSOR: Fourteen-stage axial flow, with variable inlet guide vanes and first five stator rows. Pressure ratio 14. Mass flow 16.1 kg (35.5 lb)/s.

COMBUSTOR: Annular convection film cooled, with 16 air-blast-type fuel nozzles providing smoke-free operation. Dual capacitor discharge ignition.

CONTROL SYSTEM: Full-authority digital, with analog backup.

FUEL GRADE: MIL-T-5624; grades JP-4, JP-5 and MIL-T-83188; JP-8.

TURBINE: Gas generator turbine has two axial stages with aircooled single-crystal blading; both stages overhung to the rear of the gas generator thrust bearing. Power turbine has two axial stages on a straddle-mounted shaft which runs the entire length of the engine. Film-damped bearings eliminate the need for a centre bearing.

OUTPUT: Power turbine forward shaft drives a torquemeter assembly which is directly coupled to the V-22 rotor gearbox. The torque tube housing serves as the main engine mount.

ACCESSORY DRIVES: An engine accessory gearcase is mounted beneath the air inlet housing. It provides for engine starter, generator, oil pump and fuel pump metering unit drives.

LUBRICATION SYSTEM: Self contained, featuring positive scavenging sumps, 3-micron filtration, quantitative debris monitor and a bottom-mounted, all-attitude oil reservoir with service scuppers on each side of the engine.

OIL GRADE: MIL-L-7808 or MIL-L-23699.

DIMENSIONS:

Length overall, without gearbox	1,958 mm (77.08 in)
Length from inlet flange	1,521 mm (59.88 in)
Width	671 mm (26.40 in)
Height	864 mm (34.00 in)
WEIGHT, DRY:	440.4 kg (971 lb)

PERFORMANCE RATINGS:

Max power (S/L)	4,586 kW (6,150 shp) to 43°C
Max cont power (static 1,219 m; 4,000 ft)	
	4,391 kW (5,888 shp) to 25°C

SPECIFIC FUEL CONSUMPTION:

Max cont power	71.0 µg/J (0.42 lb/h/shp)

ALLISON GMA 2100

The GMA 2100 turboprop is being developed for the new generation of high-speed regional aircraft as well as military transports and maritime patrol aircraft. The engine combines the T406 power section with a new propeller reduction gearbox based on the highly successful T56/501 design. The GMA 2100 is scheduled for certification in 1991 and has been selected by Saab (derated to 3,393 kW; 4,550 shp) to power their Saab 2000 and by IPTN to power their N-250 aircraft.

The first GMA 2100 went on test in June 1988. A prototype GMA 2100 engine successfully completed flight testing on a P-3A aircraft in late 1990. The prototype consisted of a T406 power section, the new reduction gearbox and a flange-mounted Dowty Aerospace six-bladed propeller.

TYPE: Free-turbine, axial flow turboprop.

COMPRESSOR: Fourteen-stage, axial flow, with variable inlet guide vanes and first five stator rows.

COMBUSTER: Annular design with 16 airblast fuel nozzles.

CONTROL SYSTEM: Full-authority digital (FADEC), co-ordinating engine and propeller functions.

HP TURBINE: Two-stage axial design with aircooled single-crystal blading.

POWER TURBINE: Two uncooled stages on straddle-mounted shaft.

Allison T406-AD-400 free-turbine turboshaft

PROPELLER DRIVE: Completely new design saving 68 kg (150 lb) weight, with life of 30,000 h. Accessories grouped on rear face.
DIMENSIONS:
Overall diameter   1,151 mm (45.3 in)
Overall length   2,743 mm (108 in)
WEIGHT, DRY: 702.2 kg (1,548 lb)
PERFORMANCE RATINGS:
S/L, T-O   4,474 kW (6,000 shp)
SPECIFIC FUEL CONSUMPTION:
S/L, T-O   69.31 µg/J (0.41 lb/h/shp)

ALLISON GMA 3007

This turbofan derivative of the T406 utilises the same high-pressure core as the GMA 2100 and is being developed to power regional airliners and large business-jet aircraft. The GMA 3007 was selected in 1990 by Embraer to power the EMB-145, and by Cessna for their Citation X. The 31.14 kN (7,000 lb) thrust class turbofan is scheduled to be qualified for production in 1992. Growth versions are planned with thrust ratings exceeding 48.93 kN (11,000 lb st).
TYPE: Two-shaft subsonic turbofan.
FAN: Single-stage, direct drive featuring wide chord, clapperless blades. Bypass ratio of 5.0.
HP COMPRESSOR: Fourteen-stage axial flow, with variable inlet guide vanes and first five stator rows. Overall pressure ratio 24.
COMBUSTOR: Annular design with 16 airblast fuel nozzles. Dual capacitor-discharge ignition.
CONTROL SYSTEM: Full-authority digital (FADEC).
HP TURBINE: Two-stage axial with aircooled single-crystal blading.
LP TURBINE: Three-stage axial uncooled design.
BYPASS DUCT: Single-piece full-length composite with provisions for thrust reverser.
DIMENSIONS:
Overall diameter   1,105 mm (43.5 in)
Length   2,705 mm (106.5 in)
WEIGHT, DRY (with bypass duct):   717.1 kg (1,581 lb)
PERFORMANCE RATINGS:
S/L, T-O   31.81 kN (7,150 lb st) to 30°C
SPECIFIC FUEL CONSUMPTION:
S/L, T-O   65.93 µg/J (0.39 lb/h/lb)

ALLISON MODEL 578

This is described later under the entry for PW-Allison Engines.

Allison GMA 2100 free-turbine turboprop

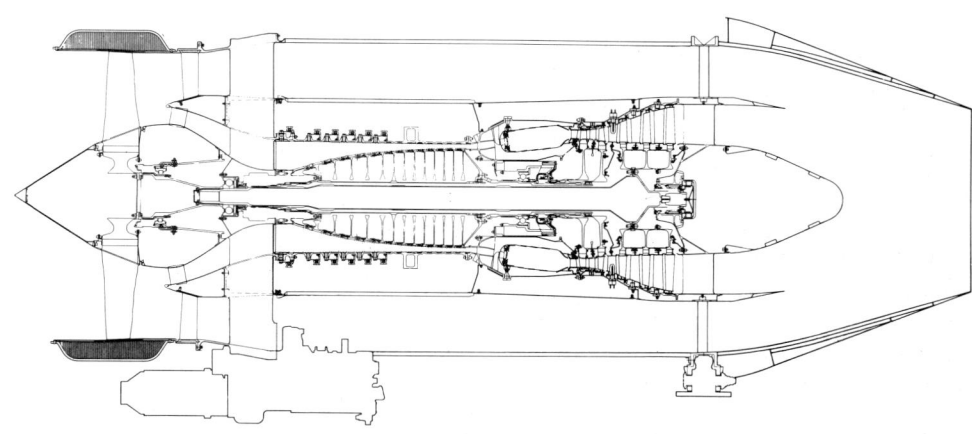

Longitudinal section of Allison GMA 3007 turboshaft

ALTURDYNE
ALTURDYNE

8050 Armour Street, San Diego, California 92111
Telephone: 1 (619) 565 2131
Fax: 1 (619) 279 4296
Telex: (910) 335-2000
PRESIDENT: Frank G. Verbeke

This company has developed small gas turbines for UAVs and very light aircraft. It was formed in 1970 and employs 100 people.

At present it purchases the basic gas generator and incorporates this into a complete engine for various purposes. The two main products are of 112 kW (150 hp) and 157 kW (210 hp). These are based upon the Sundstrand Turbomach T62 Titan single-shaft gas turbine (last described in the 1975-76 *Jane's*). A company funded lightweight rotary combustion aircraft engine is under development in two sizes up to 186.5 kW (250 hp). The first engines were tested in December 1984. Tests are being conducted with a reduction gearbox and using diesel fuel, the diesel ratings being 70 per cent of those using petrol (gasoline).

AMI
AEROMOTION INC

1224 S Park Ave, Oshkosh, Wisconsin 54901
Telephone: 1 (414) 233 0773

This company has produced a light two-cylinder opposed piston engine tailored to light aircraft. It uses some off the shelf automotive parts. The first AeroMotion Twin ran in April 1982 and has shown high reliability since then. Pre-production engines flew in a Heath Parasol in March 1984 and in a Ken Brock autogyro a month later.

AEROMOTION TWIN

TYPE: Two-cylinder opposed four-stroke aircooled piston engine.

CYLINDERS: Bore 104.8 mm (4.125 in). Stroke 95.25 mm (3.75 in). Capacity 1,650 cc (100 cu in).
IGNITION: Twin Slick magnetos, dual plugs.
DIMENSIONS:
Length   451 mm (17.75 in)
Width   787 mm (31.0 in)
Height   470 mm (18.5 in)
WEIGHT, DRY (equipped):   45 kg (100 lb)
PERFORMANCE RATING (S/L):
  37-39.5 kW (50-53 hp) at 3,100 rpm

AeroMotion Twin two-cylinder piston engine

CFE
CFE COMPANY

111 South 34th Street, PO Box 5274, Phoenix, Arizona 85010
Telephone: 1 (602) 231 3285
Fax: 1 (602) 231 7722

This company was formed jointly by Garrett Engine Division and General Electric Aircraft Engines in June 1987. It is managing all phases of the development, manufacture, marketing and support of the CFE738 turbofan.

CFE738

This turbofan is being developed to power regional airliners and large business jet aircraft. The CFE738 is being designed to the latest airline standard technology, with modular construction for 'on wing' maintenance. Its core is essentially that of the GE27, developed under the US Army's MTDE (Modern Technology Demonstrator Engine) programme and part of the T407/GLC38 programme. Designed to have an initial time between overhauls of 3,000 h for the hot section and 6,000 h for the remainder of the core. Cores will be shipped to Garrett complete with the engine control system. Garrett is responsible for the fan, LP turbine and accessory gearbox, and for engine assembly and test. Complete engine testing for certification programmes will be shared equally by the two partners. Deliveries of the first version, CFE738-1, are due in 1993 after 5,000 hours of testing.

In April 1990 the CFE738 was selected to power the Dassault Falcon 2000. The thrust was announced as 26.69 kN (6,000 lb).

The following data relate to the CFE738-1. Growth versions are planned with thrust ratings exceeding 31.1 kN (7,000 lb).
TYPE: Two-shaft subsonic turbofan.
FAN: Single stage with 28 inserted titanium blades with part-span dampers and rotating pointed spinner. Front end of LP shaft held in large-capacity ball bearing. Mass flow 109 kg (240 lb)/s. Pressure ratio 1.7. Bypass ratio 5.3.
HP COMPRESSOR: Five axial stages followed by one centrifugal. First three stator stages variable. Overall pressure ratio 35.
COMBUSTION CHAMBER: Centrifugal diffuser leads into annular chamber with 15 fuel injectors.
HP TURBINE: Two stages with cooled blades.
LP TURBINE: Three stages.
JETPIPE: Fixed mixer assembly with 20 chutes for combining the hot and cold flows from core and bypass duct. Provision for reverser.

DIMENSIONS:
Overall diameter   902 mm (35.5 in)
Length   1,735 mm (68.3 in)
WEIGHT, DRY: 550.7 kg (1,214 lb)
PERFORMANCE RATINGS (ideal installation):
S/L, T-O   24.87 kN (5,600 lb st) to 30°C (86°F)
Cruise, 12,200 m (40,000 ft), Mach 0.8
     5.83 kN (1,310 lb)
SPECIFIC FUEL CONSUMPTION:
S/L, T-O   10.54 mg/Ns (0.372 lb/h/lb st)
Cruise (as above)   18.27 mg/Ns (0.645 lb/h/lb)

Full-scale model of CFE738 two-shaft turbofan

CSD
CHEMICAL SYSTEMS DIVISION
(A division of United Technologies Corporation)

PO Box 49028, San Jose, California 95161-9028
Telephone: 1 (408) 281 1122
DIVISION EXECUTIVE VICE-PRESIDENT AND GENERAL MANAGER:
David E. Lee

In 1986 CSD joined the Booster Production Company (BPC) and a newly formed unit, Space Flight Systems (SFS), to create Space Transportation Systems, an operating unit of UTC's Defense & Space Group. CSD is formed into four units: Strategic and SDI Booster Systems; Space Launch Booster Systems; Space Maneuvering Systems; and Tactical Systems; as well as an Advanced Propulsion Technology group. Its only current product with a manned application is the Shuttle booster separation motor. Many of its activities are now covered by other *Jane's* publications.

CSD AIR-BREATHING PROPULSION

CSD spearheads the efforts of its parent, United Technologies Corporation, in the research and development of ramjet propulsion systems. In 1973 it was awarded a contract by the US Navy to develop an integral rocket/ramjet (IRR) which operates as a solid rocket booster until it reaches supersonic speeds. At that point, through a series of mechanical changes, it becomes a ramjet. These changes involve the opening of air inlets, an increase in the nozzle diameter and a switch to the burning of liquid fuel and air in the combustion chamber.

DYNA-CAM
DYNA-CAM INDUSTRIES

105 N Irena 1, Redondo Beach, CA 90277
Telephone: 1 (213) 543 2917
Fax: 1 (213) 543 2917

The Dyna-Cam engine has been under development for more than 60 years. It appeared as the Herrmann cam engine in *Jane's* for 1950-51. Today it is fully certificated, and installed in a Piper Arrow has increased rate of climb from 274 to 457 m (from 900 to 1,500 ft)/min. The engine's

production depends on the arrangement of funding.
TYPE: Axial-piston cam engine.
CYLINDERS: Six liquid-cooled cylinders at each end house double-ended pistons containing large rollers driving a sinusoidal cam on the central drive shaft. Bore 82.55 mm (3.25 in). Stroke 95.25 mm (3.75 in). Capacity 6,112 cc (373 cu in). Compression ratio 8.
DIMENSIONS:
Length   1,016 mm (40.0 in)
Diameter   330 mm (13.0 in)

WEIGHT, DRY: about 136 kg (300 lb)
PERFORMANCE RATINGS:
Max T-O (fuel injected) 186.5 kW (250 hp) at 2,000 rpm
Torque   112 kg/m (810 lb/ft) at 1,200 rpm
SPECIFIC FUEL CONSUMPTION:
Cruise 1,700 rpm   67.5 µg/J (0.40 lb/h/hp)

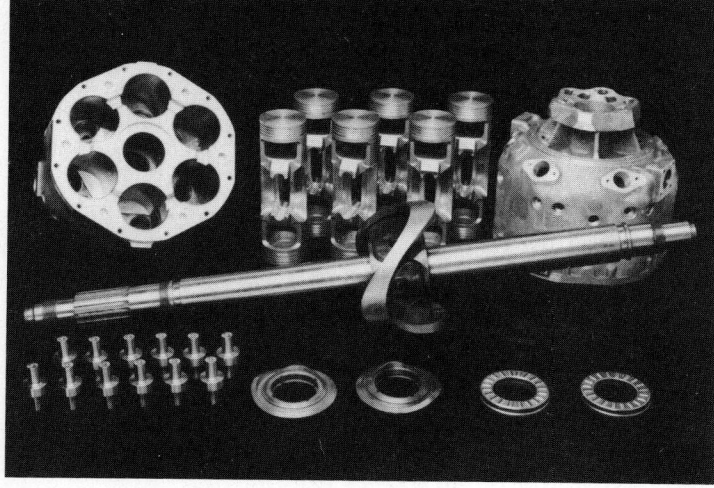

Piper Arrow used for Dyna-Cam development

Dyna-Cam engine dismantled

EMG
EMG ENGINEERING COMPANY

PO Box 1368, Hesperia, California 92345
Telephone: 1 (714) 247 8519

Eugene M. Gluhareff, a pioneer of ultra-lightweight rotorcraft, has been developing a simple air-breathing jet engine for rotor tip drive. The first model is the G8-2, which was designed in 1955 and developed for tip drive or sailplane auxiliary propulsion. Production has been hard pressed to keep up with demand, a fast growing market being radio controlled flight vehicles. Manned platforms, hang gliders and small helicopters are also proving to be a large market for EMG engines.

GLUHAREFF G8-2

The design is based on propane. Tank pressure delivers the fuel, via a needle valve throttle, to the burner. The fuel is vaporised in a heat exchanger. Vapour passes to the injector where its residual pressure is converted to kinetic energy. The high velocity gas jet induces air through three 'supercharger' intakes, each synchronised to the internal flow, which gives the correct fuel/air ratio for the combustion chamber. Here the mixture is initially ignited by a spark plug and thereafter burns continuously.

Since 1979 four more models have been available, the G8-2-20, -80, -130 and -700, rated respectively at 0.09, 0.36, 0.58 and 3.11 kN (20, 80 130 and 700 lb st). The best sfc has

been reduced dramatically from 170 mg/Ns (6 lb/h/lb st) to only 21.8 mg/Ns (0.77 lb/h/lb st). Some, such as the G8-2-130R, are used for rotor tip drive. The biggest unit (-700) weighs 36.3 kg (80 lb).

The units are manufactured by Gluhareff's subsidiary EMG Engineering Co. Customers have the option of buying plans, a construction package, an assembly kit or finished engine.

FISHER

FISHER RESEARCH CORPORATION

Two Cairn Street, Rochester, New York 14611-2476
Telephone: 1 (716) 235 5993
Fax: 1 (716) 328 1984

This organisation has developed an aircraft engine, the Fisher Tornado, based on the automotive Ford 3.8 litre V-6, using a Kevlar-reinforced toothed belt giving a choice of two reduction ratios. Changes include: fitting forged pistons, regrinding the camshaft, fitting a twin-throat downdraught carburettor, fitting harder aluminium main and camshaft bearings and adding a second electronic ignition module. The Tornado is being flight tested in a PA-28-140 Cherokee, with the 50/50 water/glycol coolant piped to a radiator in the rear fuselage fed through NACA inlets in the fuselage sides. Fuel can be premium automotive or 100LL. Engine dry weight is 177 kg (390 lb) and S/L performance includes: T-O, 205 kW (275 hp) at 5,000 rpm (propeller 3,125 or 2,500 rpm) with consumption of 57 litres (15 US gallons; 12.5 Imp gallons)/h, and 75 per cent cruise, 155 kW (206 shp) at 4,200 rpm with consumption of 29 litres (7.7 US gallons; 6.4 Imp gallons)/h. Converted engines will have TBO of over 1,500 h and a factory warranty.

GARRETT

GARRETT ENGINE DIVISION
(a division of Allied Signal Aerospace Company)

Sky Harbor Airport, 111 South 34th Street, PO Box 5217, Phoenix, Arizona 85010
Telephone: 1 (602) 231 1000
Fax: 1 (602) 231 7722
PRESIDENT: Malcolm E. Craig

Garrett Engine Division has been called the world's largest producer of small gas turbines.

At the end of 1984 Garrett announced its collaboration with Allison on the T800-LHT-800 turboshaft for the LH helicopter programme. This is mentioned under LHTEC.

The CFE738 turbofan, being developed jointly by Garrett and General Electric, is to be found under CFE.

GARRETT ATF3
US military designation: F104-GA-100

The ATF3 was the first engine to combine three-spool design with a reverse-flow combustion system and turbines, and mixed-flow exhaust.

The arrangement of components allows the fan design to be determined largely independently of the gas generator, and permits operation at optimum fan speed. Omission of inlet guide vanes, mixing of the exhaust with the fan airflow, and double reversal of the airflow, enable the ATF3 to offer reductions in noise and IR signature.

In May 1976 it was announced that the **ATF3-6A** had been selected by Dassault to power the Falcon 200 business jet. FAA certification was achieved on 24 December 1981, and Falcon 200 deliveries began in 1983. It also powers the HU-25A Guardian.

TYPE: Three-shaft axial-flow turbofan.
LOW PRESSURE (FAN) SYSTEM: Single-stage titanium fan, driven by three-stage IP turbine. Bypass ratio 2.8 at take-off. Mass flow 73.5 kg (162 lb)/s.
INTERMEDIATE PRESSURE SYSTEM: Five-stage titanium compressor, driven by two-stage LP turbine. Airflow is delivered to rearward facing HP compressor via eight tubes feeding into annular duct. Core airflow 18.15 kg (40 lb)/s.
HIGH PRESSURE SYSTEM: Single titanium centrifugal compressor, driven by single-stage HP turbine. IP airflow enters the impeller from the rear. Overall pressure ratio (T-O) 21, (high altitude cruise) 25.
COMBUSTION SYSTEM: Reverse-flow annular type.
TURBINES: Single-stage HP, three-stage IP and two-stage LP turbines drive, respectively, the HP, fan (LP) and IP compressors. IP and LP turbines have shrouded blades. Aircooled HP rotor blades. Exhaust gases turned 180° through eight sets of cascades to mix with fan bypass flow.
FUEL SYSTEM: Electromechanical, incorporating solid state computer. Manual emergency backup system.
ACCESSORY DRIVES: Three drive pads on rear-mounted gearbox driven by HP shaft, providing for hydraulic pump, starter/generator and one spare.
EXHAUST SYSTEM: Mixed fan and turbine exhaust discharged via annular nozzle surrounding combustion section.
LUBRICATION SYSTEM: Hot tank integral with gearbox.
STARTING: Electric or pneumatic.
DIMENSIONS:
Length	2,591 mm (102.0 in)
Max diameter	853 mm (33.6 in)

WEIGHT, DRY: 510 kg (1,125 lb)
PERFORMANCE RATINGS (uninstalled):
T-O (ISA, S/L, static)	24.20 kN (5,440 lb st)
Cruise (12,200 m; 40,000 ft at Mach 0.8)	4.69 kN (1,055 lb)

SPECIFIC FUEL CONSUMPTION:
At T-O rating (S/L, ISA static)	14.33 mg/Ns (0.506 lb/h/lb st)
At cruise (as above)	23.51 mg/Ns (0.83 lb/h/lb)

GARRETT TFE109
US military designation: F109-GA-100

Based on the core of the T76/TPE331 turboprops, with performance improvements, this turbofan was selected in July 1982 as the engine of the US Air Force's Fairchild T-46A. This was subsequently cancelled, but the engine was certified and production engines delivered.

TFE109-1. Basic engine, as described below. Powers Jet Squalus 1300.

TFE109-2. Rated at 6.7 kN (1,500 lb st). Selected for twin-engined Promavia ATTA 3000.

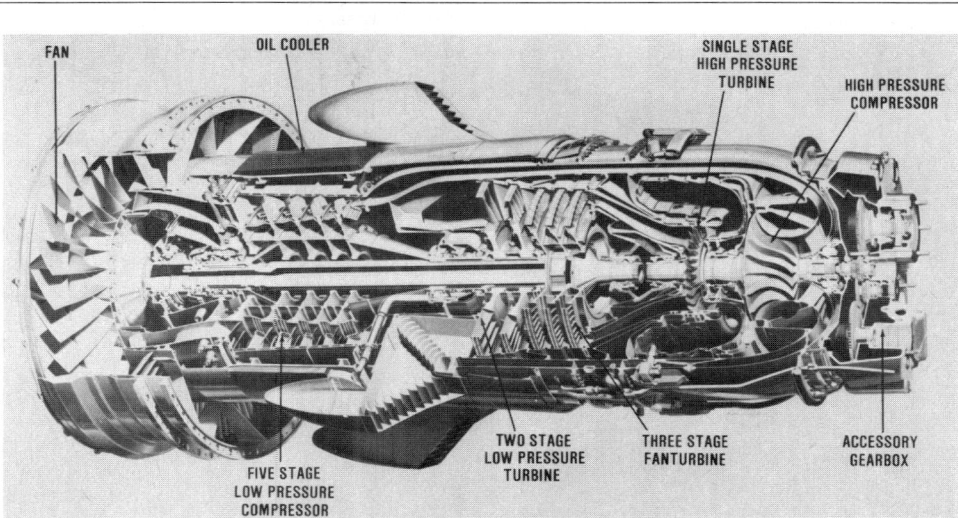

Cutaway drawing of Garrett ATF3-6A three-shaft turbofan

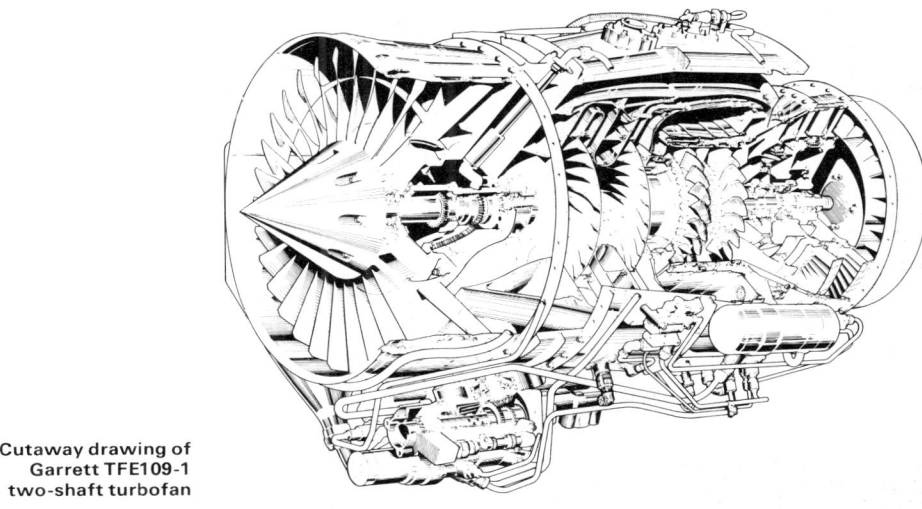

Cutaway drawing of
Garrett TFE109-1
two-shaft turbofan

TFE109-3. Uprated to 7.12 kN (1,600 lb st). Powers Jet Squalus 1600.

The core of the TFE109 is used in the T800 helicopter engine, described under LHTEC.

TYPE: Two-shaft turbofan.
FAN: Single-stage, with 28 blades with part-span shrouds (snubbers) inserted in self-de-icing rotating spinner.
COMPRESSOR: Tandem two-stage centrifugal with titanium impellers. LP and HP bleeds.
COMBUSTION CHAMBER: Annular reverse flow type, with piloted air blast nozzles for low emissions.
HP TURBINE: Two-stage axial, with single-pass cooling.
LP TURBINE: Two-stage axial, with tip shrouds.
CONTROL SYSTEM: Full-authority digital with hydro-mechanical backup.
ACCESSORIES: Mounted on one-piece gearbox, under intermediate case, with drive from HP shaft taken through one of five main aerofoil struts spaced at 72°.
DIMENSIONS:
Length	1,130 mm (44.495 in)
Diameter	597 mm (23.51 in)

WEIGHT, DRY: 199 kg (439 lb)
PERFORMANCE RATINGS (ISA):
T-O	5.92 kN (1,330 lb st)
Max continuous (9,145 m; 30,000 ft, Mach 0.5)	1.78 kN (400 lb)

SPECIFIC FUEL CONSUMPTION:
Max T-O as above	11.10 mg/Ns (0.392 lb/h/lb)

GARRETT TFE731

Announced in April 1969, the TFE731 is a two-spool geared turbofan designed for business jet aircraft. Use of a geared fan confers flexibility in operation and yields optimum performance at up to 15,545 m (51,000 ft).

TFE731-2. First production model. Deliveries for the Falcon 10 took place in August 1972.

TFE731-3. Increased turbine temperature. First delivered in 1974 for re-engined JetStar II. Also selected for the Learjet 54/56, Cessna Citation III, Dassault Falcon 50, BAe 125-700, IAI Westwind 1 and 2 and Astra, Rockwell International's Sabreliner 65A, CASA C-101 and Argentine IA 63.

TFE731-4. Selected to power Citation VII. Certification scheduled for late 1991.

TFE731-5. Higher bypass ratio fan driven by new LP turbine. Certificated in November 1983 for BAe 125-800 and CASA C-101.

TFE731-5A. Mixer nozzle reducing sfc and raising standard thrust to that of the APR rating. Certificated in December 1984 for Dassault Falcon 900, and offered as retrofit for Falcon 20. Volvo Flygmotor has a 5.6 per cent share of the 731-5 production programme.

TFE731-5B. Uprated version, certificated in 1990 for Falcon 900B and Falcon 20 retrofit.

TYPE: Turbofan with two shafts and geared front fan.
FAN: Single-stage axial titanium fan, with inserted blades. The fan shaft is connected directly to the planetary gearbox ring gear. Mass flow, sea level static, TFE731-2, 51.26 kg (113 lb)/s; -3, 53.7 kg (118.3 lb)/s; -5, 64.86 kg (143 lb)/s. Bypass ratio, -2, 2.66; -3, 2.80; -5, 3.48.
COMPRESSOR: Four-stage LP, followed by centrifugal HP on separate shaft running at higher speeds. Overall pressure ratio (S/L, static): -2, 14.0; -3, 14.6.
COMBUSTION CHAMBER: Annular reverse flow type, with 12 nozzles injecting tangentially. Meets EPA/FAA emission requirements.
FUEL SYSTEM: Hydro-electronic, with single lever control.
TURBINES: Single-stage HP and three-stage LP. Average HP inlet gas temperature, S/L, max T-O, -2, 860°C; -3, 907°C; -5, 952°C.
ACCESSORY DRIVES: Pads provided for hydraulic pump, starter/generator or starter motor and alternators. Pads on back side of drive fuel control and oil pump.

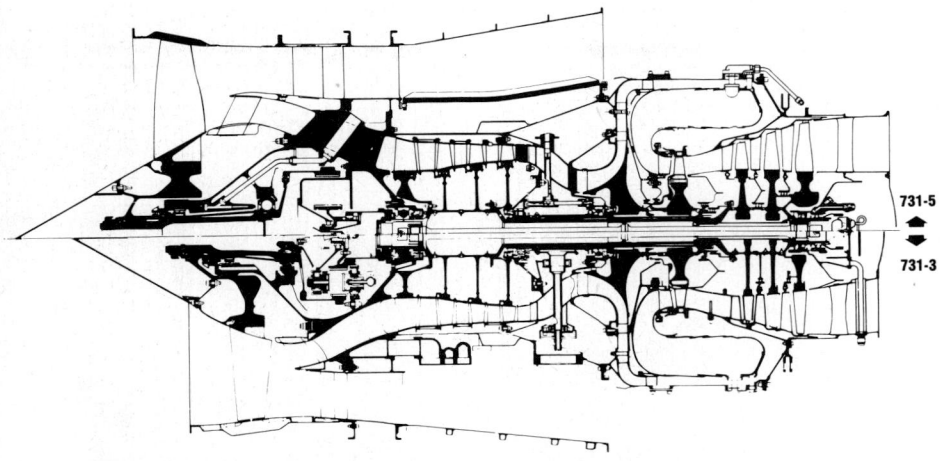

Longitudinal section of TFE731-5 (top half) and TFE731-3 (bottom half) geared turbofans

DIMENSIONS:
Length overall:
-2, -3	1,520 mm (59.83 in)
-3A, -3B	1,440 mm (59.70 in)
-4	1,477 mm (58.15 in)
-5	1,665 mm (65.54 in)
-5A, -5B	2,314 mm (91.10 in)
Intake diameter	716 mm (28.20 in)

Width:
-2, -3, -3A, -3B, -4	869 mm (34.20 in)
-5, -5A, -5B	858 mm (33.79 in)

Height overall:
-2, -3, -3A, -3B, -4	1,000 mm (39.36 in)
-5, -5A, -5B	1,029 mm (40.52 in)

WEIGHT, DRY:
-2	332 kg (730 lb)
-3	337 kg (742 lb)
-3A	345 kg (758 lb)
-3B	346 kg (760 lb)
-4	373 kg (822 lb)
-5	387 kg (852 lb)
-5A	402 kg (884 lb)
-5B	408 kg (899 lb)

PERFORMANCE RATINGS:
Max T-O (S/L, 24.4°C):
-2	15.57 kN (3,500 lb st)
-3, -3A	16.46 kN (3,700 lb st)
-3B	16.24 kN (3,650 lb st)
-4	18.15 kN (4,080 lb st)
-5	19.15 kN (4,304 lb st)
-5A	20.02 kN (4,500 lb st)
-5B	21.13 kN (4,750 lb st)

Max T-O (APR, auto performance reserve):
-3, -3A, -3B	17.13 kN (3,850 lb st)
-5, -5A	20.02 kN (4,500 lb st)
-4, -5B: as above	

Cruise (12,200 m; 40,000 ft at Mach 0.8):
-2	3.36 kN (755 lb)
-3	3.64 kN (817 lb)
-3A	3.73 kN (838 lb)
-3B	3.75 kN (844 lb)
-4	4.13 kN (929 lb)
-5	4.25 kN (955 lb)
-5A	4.39 kN (986 lb)
-5B	4.68 kN (1,052 lb)

SPECIFIC FUEL CONSUMPTION:
Cruise (as above):
-2	23.08 mg/Ns (0.815 lb/h/lb)
-3	23.65 mg/Ns (0.835 lb/h/lb)
-3A	23.30 mg/Ns (0.823 lb/h/lb)
-3B	23.11 mg/Ns (0.816 lb/h/lb)
-4	22.55 mg/Ns (0.796 lb/h/lb)
-5	22.72 mg/Ns (0.802 lb/h/lb)
-5A	21.84 mg/Ns (0.771 lb/h/lb)
-5B	21.41 mg/Ns (0.756 lb/h/lb)

GARRETT TFE1042/1088
US military designation: F124-GA-100

This derivative of the TFE731 was launched in 1978 as a co-operative programme with Volvo Flygmotor of Sweden. Details last appeared in the 1982-83 *Jane's*, when it was described as a family of related engines, with lower bypass ratio than the TFE731. The TFE1042-7, with afterburner, was stated to have dry and maximum augmented ratings of 21.44 kN (4,820 lb st) and 37.1 kN (8,340 lb st) respectively.

The engine was then withdrawn from our pages, even after it had been announced as the power plant of the AIDC Ching-kuo IDF (Indigenous Defensive Fighter). But at the 1989 Paris Air Show Garrett showed the engine and revealed that it had been working on it with Taiwan since 1982. Fully modular, it has matured as a family of engines to be marketed by Garrett as the TFE1088. The basic engine, the 1042-70/1088-11, had by late 1990 completed over 10,000 hours of testing. Initial flight release was achieved in February 1989, with full qualification in February 1991. Garrett claim the basic engine as "the most reliable and efficient in this power class".

The following are existing and planned versions:
TFE1042-70. Basic version, fitted to Ching-kuo IDF. Description below applies to this version.
TFE1088-11. USAF F125-GA-100. Similar to TFE1042-70. Being marketed by Garrett at 29.49 kN (6,630 lb st) intermediate thrust and 41.81 kN (9,400 lb st) maximum.
TFE1088-12. Growth version for 1994. Turbine inlet 1,454°C; maximum rating 54.49 kN (12,250 lb st).
TFE1088-13. Growth engine for 1997. Turbine inlet 1,566°C; maximum thrust 62.28 kN (14,000 lb st).

TFE1088-16. Fully rated dry version, with USAF designation F124-GA-100. Details as below except: length 1,511 mm (59.5 in); dry weight 454 kg (1,001 lb); corrected airflow 43 kg (94.8 lb)/s; maximum thrust 29.8 kN (6,700 lb st).
TFE1088-17. F124 growth engine for 1994. Turbine inlet 1,454°C; maximum thrust 36.12 kN (8,120 lb st).
TFE1088-18. F124 dry growth engine for 1998. Turbine inlet 1,566°C; maximum thrust 43.82 kN (9,850 lb st).
TYPE: Two shaft augmented turbofan.
FAN: Three stages with rotating spinner. Maximum airflow 43.29 kg (95.4 lb)/s. Bypass ratio 0.3.
COMPRESSOR: Four axial stages followed by one centrifugal.
COMBUSTION CHAMBER: Reverse flow annular.
TURBINES: Single-stage HP and LP turbine. HP entry gas temperature 1,343°C.
AUGMENTOR: Reheat in bypass and core flows. Three mechanical actuators drive 10-flap variable nozzle.
DIMENSIONS:
Inlet diameter	605 mm (23.8 in)
Length	2,880 mm (134.0 in)
Maximum nozzle diameter	782 mm (30.8 in)

WEIGHT, DRY: 603 kg (1,330 lb)
PERFORMANCE RATINGS:
Intermediate	22.24 kN (5,000 lb st)
Maximum augmented	37.14 kN (8,350 lb st)

SPECIFIC FUEL CONSUMPTION:
TFE1042-70 (intermediate) 23.79 mg/Ns (0.84 lb/h/lb st)

GARRETT TPE331
US military designation: T76

Based upon experience with APUs, this was the first Garrett engine for aircraft propulsion. By January 1988 deliveries of all versions had passed 11,000.

The following are major versions:
TPE331 series I, II. FAA certificated in February 1965. Rated at 451 ekW; 429 kW plus 0.33 kN (605 ehp; 575 shp plus 75 lb st). Redesignated **TPE331-25/61** and **-25/71** and produced until 1970. Powers MU-2 (A to E models), Porter, Jet Liner, Super Turbo 18, FU-24, Hawk Commander and 680, and Turbo Beaver.
TPE331-1 series. Certificated December 1967 at 526 ekW; 496 kW plus 0.44 kN (705 ehp; 665 shp plus 100 lb st). Powers MU-2 (F and G), Turbo-Porter and AU-23A Peacemaker, CJ600, Turboliner, Interceptor 400, Turbo Commander and (customer option) Thrush Commander, Merlin IIB and Fletcher 1284, Turbo Thrush and Turbo Ag-Cat.
TPE331-2 series. Certificated in December 1967 at 563 ekW; 533 kW plus 0.45 kN (755 ehp; 715 shp plus 102 lb st). Powers Skyvan, CASA 212 pre-series, Turbo Goose and Turbo Beaver.
TPE331-3 series. Certificated in March 1970 at 674 ekW; 626 kW plus 0.71 kN (904 ehp; 840 shp plus 159 lb st). Uprated gas generator with increased airflow and pressure ratio, but same turbine temperature as in original TPE331. Powers Merlin III, IV and Metro, and Jetstream III.
TPE331-5/6 series. The -5 was certificated in March 1970; this matches the gas generator of the -3 with the 715 shp gearbox, and is flat rated to 2,135 m (7,000 ft). Powers MU-2, King Air B100 (-6), CASA 212 (-5), Dornier 228 (-5), and Commander 840/900. The -5 designation indicates output speed of 1,591 rpm; the -6 has an output speed of 2,000 rpm.
TPE331-8. Matches compressor and gearbox of -3 with new turbine section. Thermodynamic power of 676 ekW; 645 kW (905 ehp; 865 shp) plus 0.47 kN (105 lb st), but flat rated at 533 kW (715 shp) to 36°C. Certification received in November 1976. Powers Conquest II.
TPE331-9. Thermodynamic rating 645 kW (865 shp).
TPE331-10. Rated at 746 kW (1,000 shp). Certificated January 1978. Powers Marquise and Solitaire, Commander 980/1000, Merlin IIIC, CASA 212-200 and Jetstream 31.
TPE331-11. Certificated 1979. Higher gearbox limit; wet rating 820 kW (1,100 shp). Powers Metro III.
TPE331-12. Same size as -10 but offers 834 kW (1,119 shp). Certificated December 1984. Powers Jetstream Super 31 and Metro 23. The **TPE331-12B**, powers the Shorts Tucano. Rolls-Royce makes 30 per cent by value of engines for Shorts, and supports RAF engines in service.
TPE331-14/15. Scaled-up models, with thermodynamic power in the 1,227 kW (1,645 shp) class. The -14 was certificated in April 1984 and is flat rated at 746 kW (1,000 shp) for the Cheyenne 400. TPE331-15AW powers re-engined S-2 Tracker.
TPE331-14GR/HR (clockwise/anti-clockwise) handed engine, flat rated at 1,119 kW (1,500 shp) to 35°C, selected for Jetstream 41.
T76. Military engine, with gas generator similar to TPE331-1 but with front end inverted, to give inlet above spinner. All models power OV-10 Bronco.

Except for the TPE331-14, all versions are of similar frame size, and the following data apply generally to all:
TYPE: Single-shaft turboprop.
PROPELLER DRIVE: Two-stage reduction gear, one helical spur and one planetary, with overall ratio of 20.865 or 26.3.
COMPRESSOR: Tandem two-stage centrifugal made from titanium. Mass flow, 2.61 kg (5.78 lb)/s for -25/61, -25/71, 2.81 kg (6.2 lb)/s for -1, 2.80 kg (6.17 lb)/s for -2 and T76,

Garrett TFE1042/1088 two-shaft augmented turbofan

3.52 kg (7.75 lb)/s for -5 and 3.54 kg (7.8 lb)/s for -3. Pressure ratio 8.0 for -25/61, -25/71, 8.34 for -1, 8.54 for -2 and T76, 10.37 for -5 and -3.

COMBUSTION CHAMBER: Annular, with capacitor discharge igniter plug on turbine plenum.

FUEL SYSTEM: Woodward or Bendix control with Beta propeller control. Max fuel pressure 41.4 bars (600 lb/sq in).

FUEL GRADE (TPE331): ASTM designation D1655-64T types Jet A, Jet B and Jet A-1; MIL-F-5616-1, Grade JP-1.

TURBINE: Three-stage axial. In early models, blades cast integrally with disc. In -10, -11, -12 first-stage disc with inserted blades. In -14/-15 inserted blades in all three stages. Inlet gas temperature, 987°C for -25/61, -25/71, 993°C for T76, 1,005°C for all other models.

ACCESSORIES: AND 20005 Type XV-B tachometer generator, AND 20002 Type XII-D starter/generator, AND 20010 Type XX-A propeller governor and AND 20001 Type XI-B hydraulic pump.

LUBRICATION SYSTEM: Medium pressure dry sump system. Normal oil supply pressure 6.90 bars (100 lb/sq in).

OIL SPECIFICATION: MIL-L-23699-(1) or MIL-L-7808.

STARTING: Pad for 399A starter/generator.

DIMENSIONS (approx):

Length overall:	
TPE331	1,092 to 1,333 mm (43-52.5 in)
T76	1,118 mm (44 in)
Width: TPE331	533 mm (21 in)
T76	483 mm (19 in)
Height: TPE331	660 mm (26 in)
T76	686 mm (27 in)

WEIGHT, DRY:

TPE331-25/61, 71	152 kg (335 lb)
TPE331-1, -2	152.5 kg (336 lb)
T76	155 kg (341 lb)
TPE331-3	161 kg (355 lb)
TPE331-5	163 kg (360 lb)
TPE331-8	168 kg (370 lb)
TPE331-10	172 kg (380 lb)
TPE331-11	182 kg (400 lb)
TPE331-12	176 kg (387 lb)
TPE331-14/15	256 kg (565 lb)

Cutaway drawing of Garrett TPE331-14 turboprop

PERFORMANCE RATINGS:

T-O	see under model listings

Military (30 min): T76-G-410/411
533 kW; 563 ekW (715 shp) (755 ehp)

Normal: T76-G-410/411
485 kW; 514.5 ekW (650 shp) (690 ehp)

Max cruise (ISA, 3,050 m; 10,000 ft and 250 knots; 463 km/h; 288 mph):

TPE331-25/61, 71	332 kW (445 shp)
TPE331-1	404 kW (542 shp)
TPE331-2, T76	430 kW (577 shp)
TPE331-3, -5	530 kW (710 shp)

SPECIFIC FUEL CONSUMPTION:

At T-O rating:

TPE331-25/61, 71	111.5 µg/J (0.66 lb/h/shp)
TPE331-1	102.2 µg/J (0.605 lb/h/shp)
TPE331-2	99.4 µg/J (0.588 lb/h/shp)
TPE331-3	99.7 µg/J (0.59 lb/h/shp)
TPE331-5	105.8 µg/J (0.626 lb/h/shp)
TPE331-8	96.7 µg/J (0.572 lb/h/shp)
TPE331-10	94.6 µg/J (0.560 lb/h/shp)
TPE331-11	94.3 µg/J (0.558 lb/h/shp)
TPE331-12	92.8 µg/J (0.549 lb/h/shp)
TPE331-14/-15	84.8 µg/J (0.502 lb/h/shp)
T76-G-410/411	101.4 µg/J (0.60 lb/h/shp)

OIL CONSUMPTION:

Max	0.009 kg (0.02 lb)/h

GARRETT TPF351

This is Garrett's first free-turbine turboprop. It is being developed initially as the **TPF351-20** for pusher installation in the Embraer/FAMA CBA-123. The engine is modular, and arranged for clockwise (CW) or counter-clockwise (CCW) propeller rotation (both forms of gearbox are shown in the drawing).

TYPE: Free-turbine pusher turboprop.

AIR INLET: Ram inlet at front of nacelle with duct passing above accessory gearbox.

COMPRESSOR: Tandem two-stage centrifugal. Mass flow 6.35 kg (14.0 lb)/s. Pressure ratio 13.3.

COMBUSTION CHAMBER: Annular reverse flow with dual-channel ignition system.

FUEL SYSTEM: FADEC with mechanical backup fuel control unit and integral electrical shutoff valve.

TURBINES: Two-stage gas generator turbine. Three-stage power turbine; inter-turbine temperature 805°C (1,481°F), EGT 571°C (1,061°F).

JET PIPE: Bifurcated with diagonal outlet on each side (depicted in drawing as above and below).

PROPELLER DRIVE: Epicyclic with drive to auxiliary gearbox.

DIMENSIONS:

Length overall	1,954 mm (76.94 in)
Width	606 mm (23.84 in)
Height	838 mm (33.0 in)

WEIGHT, DRY:

CW	340.2 kg (750.1 lb)
CCW	347.0 kg (765.1 lb)

PERFORMANCE RATING (ISA, S/L, T-O):

Thermodynamic 1,566 kW (2,100 shp), torque-limited to 1,081 kW (1,450 shp)

SPECIFIC FUEL CONSUMPTION (T-O):

83.66 µg/J (0.495 lb/h/shp)

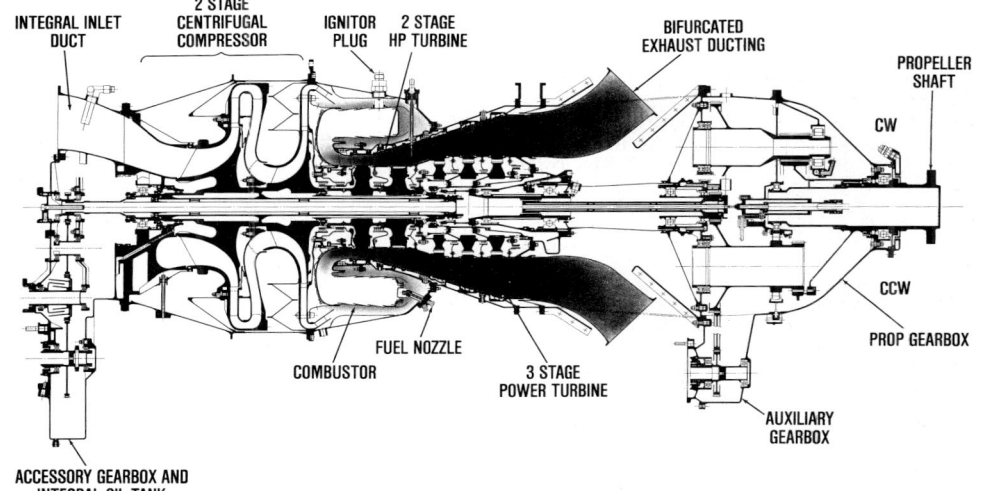

INTEGRAL INLET DUCT — 2 STAGE CENTRIFUGAL COMPRESSOR — IGNITOR PLUG — 2 STAGE HP TURBINE — BIFURCATED EXHAUST DUCTING — PROPELLER SHAFT — CW — CCW — PROP GEARBOX — AUXILIARY GEARBOX — 3 STAGE POWER TURBINE — FUEL NOZZLE — COMBUSTOR — ACCESSORY GEARBOX AND INTEGRAL OIL TANK

Longitudinal section of Garrett TPF351-20 free-turbine pusher turboprop

GENERAL ELECTRIC
GE AIRCRAFT ENGINES

Neumann Way, Evendale, Ohio 45215-6301
Telephone: 1 (513) 243 6136
Fax: 1 (513) 786 1568
Telex: 212078 GEAEG UR
1000 Western Avenue, Lynn, Massachusetts 01910
Telephone: 1 (617) 594 4809
Fax: 1 (617) 594 1596
Telex: 6817065
SENIOR VICE-PRESIDENT: B. H. Rowe

Current products of GE Aircraft Engines include the F103, F110, F118, F120, F404, F412, T64, T700 and TF34 for military use, and the GE90, CF6, CF34, CT7 and GLC38 for the commercial and general aviation market. A new turbofan is being developed in partnership with Garrett and appears under CFE. In partnership with SNECMA of France a company was formed to develop and market the CFM56 turbofan, as described in the International part of this section under CFM International.

Details of the CF700, CJ610, F101, J79, J85, T58 and TF39 engines, which are no longer in production, can be found in earlier editions of *Jane's*.

GENERAL ELECTRIC F404

In May 1975 the US Navy selected the McDonnell Douglas/Northrop team to develop its F/A-18 Hornet, powered by two F404-GE-400 engines.

First F404 engine test took place in December 1976. Preliminary flight rating test took place in May 1978, first F/A-18 flight in November 1978 and MQT (model qualification test) in July 1979. The first production delivery took place in December 1979.

The following are current versions of the F404:

F404-GE-400. Original production engine for all F/A-18 models. Also powers the Grumman X-29, Dassault Rafale and Rockwell/MBB X-31. Max rating 71.2 kN (16,000 lb st).

F404-GE-402. Enhanced Performance Engine (EPE) in the 79 kN (17,700 lb st) class; combines a 2,000-h hot section with a 10 to 20 per cent increase in thrust, achieving this performance through improved design and materials in the turbines and afterburner. Designed to replace the F404-GE-400, the EPE was to be delivered in 1991 for F/A-18 aircraft for Kuwait, and from 1992 to the US Navy.

F404-GE-100D. A 49 kN (11,000 lb st) non-afterburning derivative of the F404-GE-400 powering the Singapore Air Force A-4 Super Skyhawk.

F404-GE-F1D2. A non-afterburning turbojet derivative of the F404-GE-400 powering the US Air Force F-117A.

F404/RM12. An 80 kN (18,100 lb st) F404 derivative. Fan handles five per cent greater airflow and has increased resistance to foreign-object damage. Increased turbine inlet temperature provides operating margin for lower right hand corner of flight envelope. Modified control system for single-engined JAS 39 Gripen. Interim engine for Indian Light Combat Aircraft and proposed for re-engining Chinese F-7 and J-8. Candidate for Yugoslav Novi Avion and other programmes. See Volvo Flygmotor, Sweden.

F404-GE-400D. Unaugmented version of F404-GE-400 rated at 48.0 kN (10,800 lb st). Powered Grumman A-6F prototype.

The following description applies to the F404-GE-402:

TYPE: Two-shaft augmented low bypass ratio turbofan (turbojet with continuous bypass bleed).

FAN: Three-stage. Bypass ratio 0.27. Mass flow 66.2 kg (146 lb)/s.

HP COMPRESSOR: Seven-stage. Overall pressure ratio, 26 : 1 class.

COMBUSTION CHAMBER: Single-piece annular.

HP TURBINE: Single-stage with aircooled blades.

LP TURBINE: Single-stage.
EXHAUST SYSTEM: Close coupled afterburner. Convergent-divergent exhaust nozzle with hydraulic actuation.
CONTROL SYSTEM: Electrical-hydromechanical.
DIMENSIONS:

Length overall	4,030 mm (158.8 in)
Max diameter	880 mm (34.8 in)

WEIGHT, DRY:

	1,016 kg (2,240 lb)

PERFORMANCE RATING:

Max T-O	79 kN (17,700 lb st)

GENERAL ELECTRIC F412

GE was developing the F412-GE-400 engine for the US Navy's A-12 aircraft programme, which was terminated in January 1991.

GENERAL ELECTRIC TF34

This turbofan won a 1965 US Navy competition. In August 1972 the **TF34-GE-2**, the initial variant for the Lockheed S-3A Viking, completed its model qualification test (MQT) and entered fleet service in February 1974. In January 1975 GE began shipment of the **TF34-GE-400A/B**, which replaced the GE-2 as S-3A engine. In 1970 the TF34 was selected to power the A-10A attack aircraft as the **TF34-GE-100**, with a long fan duct and side mountings.

In 1974 a third version was selected to provide auxiliary (thrust) power for the Sikorsky S-72 research aircraft.
TYPE: Two-shaft high bypass ratio turbofan.
FAN: Single-stage fan has blades forged in titanium. Mass flow (TF34-400A/B) 153 kg (338 lb)/s at 7,365 rpm with pressure ratio 1.5. Bypass ratio 6.2.
COMPRESSOR: 14-stage axial on HP shaft. Inlet guide vanes and first five stators variable. First nine rotor stages titanium, remainder high nickel alloy. Performance at max S/L rating, core airflow 21.3 kg (47 lb)/s at 17,900 rpm with pressure ratio 14 : 1, overall pressure ratio 21.
COMBUSTION CHAMBER: Annular Hastelloy liner and front dome, with 18 carburetting burners.
TURBINE: Two-stage HP; four-stage LP with tip-shrouded blades. EGT 1,225°C maximum.
FUEL SYSTEM: Hydromechanical with electronic amplifier. Fuel grade JP-4 or JP-5.
DIMENSIONS:
Max diameter:

TF34-GE-400A/B	1,321 mm (52.0 in)
TF34-GE-100	1,245 mm (49.0 in)
Basic length (both)	2,540 mm (100.0 in)

WEIGHT, DRY:

TF34-GE-400A/B	670 kg (1,478 lb)
TF34-GE-100	653 kg (1,440 lb)

PERFORMANCE RATING (max T-O; S/L static):

TF34-GE-400A/B	41.3 kN (9,275 lb st)
TF34-GE-100	40.3 kN (9,065 lb st)

SPECIFIC FUEL CONSUMPTION (max T-O, S/L static):

TF34-GE-400A/B	10.3 mg/Ns (0.363 lb/h/lb st)
TF34-GE-100	10.5 mg/Ns (0.370 lb/h/lb st)

GENERAL ELECTRIC CF34

The CF34 is a commercial adaptation of the TF34. Total airflow at take-off with automatic power reserve (APR) is 151 kg (332 lb)/s. Bypass ratio is 6.3. Certificated in August 1982, the **CF34-1A** powers the Challenger 601-1A and the **CF34-3A1** the Challenger 601-3A and Canadair RJ.

General Electric F404-GE-100D unaugmented turbofan

DIMENSIONS:

Length (overall)	2,616 mm (103.0 in)
Max diameter (at mounts)	1,245 mm (49.0 in)

PERFORMANCE RATINGS (S/L, static):

T-O (APR)	41.0 kN (9,220 lb st)
T-O (Normal)	38.8 kN (8,729 lb st)

SPECIFIC FUEL CONSUMPTION (as above):

T-O (Normal)	10.11 mg/Ns (0.357 lb/h/lb st)

GENERAL ELECTRIC GE90

On 16 January 1990 General Electric announced it is developing a high-bypass turbofan with thrust in the range 333-422 kN (75,000-95,000 lb st) capable of powering all new and derivative widebody aircraft that may enter the market in the mid-1990s.

The GE90 is scheduled for certification at 355.5 kN (80,000 lb st) in May 1994, and entry into service at 311-333 kN (70,000-75,000 lb st) on the Boeing 777 in mid-1995.

General Electric GE90 nacelle mockup

This new design is based on a compressor scaled directly from GE's Energy Efficient Engine programme, a joint GE/NASA-funded project aimed at establishing a technology base for engines of the 1990s. It will feature the largest fan yet built, with composite wide-chord blades.

The large fan diameter increases the bypass ratio to 10, higher than that of any engine yet developed. The higher bypass ratio will help achieve a 10 per cent improvement in specific fuel consumption compared to today's large turbofan engines, while providing reduced noise levels.

Improvements to the combustor design will result in significantly improved emissions (oxides of nitrogen).

The engine will feature a composite, structural, load-sharing nacelle, integrating the design of the engine and the nacelle. As a result, a complete propulsion system will be provided, incorporating substantial weight savings, improved performance retention, and reduced airline maintenance costs.

The compressor permits a shorter, lighter, stiffer engine with a high overall cycle pressure ratio that also contributes to the significantly improved specific fuel consumption. The double-dome combustor was designed specifically for low NO_x emissions. Under low thrust, the outer combustor nozzles are used; as thrust is increased, the inner set of main nozzles begins operation. The high-pressure turbine will feature single-crystal blades, and the turbine discs are boltless, with smooth side plates for low windage losses.

GE's partners include SNECMA, Fiat Aviazione and IHI. Among the GE90's features are:
FAN: Low speed, low pressure ratio with bypass ratio of approximately 10; composite, unshrouded wide-chord rotor blades; structural outlet guide vanes. Blade/vane quantities and spacing optimised for low acoustics.
LP COMPRESSOR: Three stages; low speed; moderate pressure ratio; low noise features.
HP COMPRESSOR: Ten stages; pressure ratio 23; derived from GE/NASA Energy Efficient Engine (E^3) technology demonstrator. Overall pressure ratio over 40.
COMBUSTOR: Double annular design for low NO_x emissions; derived from E^3 technology demonstrator.
HP TURBINE: Two stages with monocrystal blades and powdered metal discs.
LP TURBINE: Seven stages with relatively low stage loading for improved efficiency, low noise features.
FUEL SYSTEM: FADEC control of fuel flow, variable geometry and active clearance control systems.
DIMENSIONS:

Fan diameter	3,048 mm (120 in)
Length, flange to flange	4,775 mm (188 in)

GENERAL ELECTRIC CF6
US military designation (CF6-50E): F103-GE-100

On 11 September 1967 General Electric announced the commitment of corporate funding for development of the CF6 turbofan for wide-body transports. The CF6-6D for the DC-10-10 was selected by United and American on 25 April 1968. Details of this and other early versions appeared in the 1987-88 *Jane's*. The following are current versions:
CF6-50C2/E2. Rated 233.5 kN (52,500 lb st) to 30°C. Certification 1978. Military -50C2 powers KC-10; -50E2 powers Boeing E-4.

CF6-80A/A3. Improved sfc and performance retention, with length and weight reduced by elimination of turbine mid frame and reduction in combustor and diffuser length. Engine rated at 213.5 kN (48,000 lb) as the -80A/A1, and 222.4 kN (50,000 lb) as the -80A2/A3. Fitted to 767 and A310. Programme launched November 1977, first engine ran October 1979 and certification October 1981. Production split between GE and SNECMA. The -80A and -80C2 on the 767 were first to receive FAA approval (January 1989) for 180 min EROPS operations.

General Electric CF34-3A two-shaft turbofan

CF6-80C2. Described separately.

The following data relate to the CF6-50C2/E2, with -80 differences noted:

TYPE: Two-shaft high bypass ratio turbofan.

FAN: Single-stage with three-stage LP compressor both driven by LP turbine. The 38 fan rotor blades have anti-vibration shrouds at two-thirds span. Blades, discs, spool of titanium; exit guide vanes of aluminium; fan frame and shaft of steel; spinner and fan case of aluminium alloy. Total airflow 591 kg (1,303 lb)/s, bypass ratio 5.7. CF6-80A/A1 has better efficiency and bird strike resistance, with Kevlar containment in fan case. Fan diameter 2,195 mm (86.4 in). Mass flow, CF6-80A/A1, 651 kg (1,433 lb)/s; -80A2/A3, 663 kg (1,460 lb)/s. Bypass ratio, -80A/A1, 4.7; -80A2/A3, 4.6.

LP COMPRESSOR: Three core booster stages; 12 bypass doors maintain flow matching between fan/LP and core by opening at low power settings, closed during take-off and cruise.

HP COMPRESSOR: Fourteen-stage with inlet guide vanes and first six stator rows having variable incidence. Core airflow 125 kg (276 lb)/s. CF6-80A series incorporate bore cooling for blade/casing clearance control, and one-piece steel casing with insulated aft stages and short diffuser section. Overall pressure ratio (T-O), 29.13 (-50C), 30.1 (-50E), 28.0 (-80A/A1), 29.0 (-80A2/A3).

COMBUSTOR: Fully annular. CF6-80A has rolled ring combustor, 152 mm (6.0 in) shorter, mounted at aft flange.

HP TURBINE: Two-stage aircooled, TET 1,330°C. CF6-80A has no turbine mid-frame and eliminates one main bearing, and HP case has active clearance control.

LP TURBINE: Four-stage constant tip diameter with nominal 871°C inlet temperature. Rotor blades tip-shrouded and not aircooled. CF6-80A, new turbine with active clearance control.

THRUST REVERSER (FAN): Rear portion of fan outer cowl translates aft on rotating ballscrews to uncover cascade vanes. Blocker doors (16) flush-mounted in cowl on link arms hinged in inner cowl, rotate inwards to expose cascade vanes and block fan duct. CF6-80A1/A3 (A310) similar; 767 reverser by Boeing.

ACCESSORY DRIVE: Inlet gearbox in forward sump transfers energy from the core. Transfer gearbox on bottom of fan frame with starter, fuel pump, main engine control, lubrication pump and tachometer. Pads for aircraft hydraulic pumps, constant speed drive and alternator. CF6-80A gearbox in environmental enclosure on core; -80A1 on fan case.

FUEL SYSTEM: Hydromechanical, schedules acceleration and deceleration fuel flow, variable stator vane position and LP compressor variable bypass doors. CF6-80, electronic trimming.

FUEL GRADES: Fuels conforming to ASTM-1655-65T, Jet A, Jet A1 and Jet B, and MIL-T-5624G2 grades JP-4 or JP-5 are authorised, but Jet A is primary specification.

LUBRICATION SYSTEM: Dry sump centre-vented nominal pressure is 2.07-6.21 bars (30-90 lb/sq in).

STARTING: Air turbine starter mounted on the front of the accessory gearbox at the through shaft.

NOISE SUPPRESSION: Acoustic panels integrated with fan casing, fan front frame and thrust reverser.

DIMENSIONS:

Max height (over gearbox)	2,675 mm (105.3 in)
Length overall (cold):	
CF6-50 series	4,394 mm (173.0 in)
CF6-80A	3,998 mm (157.4 in)

WEIGHT, DRY:

Basic engine:	
CF6-50C2	3,960 kg (8,731 lb)
CF6-50E, -E1	3,851 kg (8,490 lb)
CF6-50E2	3,977 kg (8,768 lb)
CF6-80A, -80A2	3,854 kg (8,496 lb)
CF6-80A3	3,819 kg (8,420 lb)
Reverser:	
CF6-50E	962 kg (2,121 lb)

PERFORMANCE RATINGS:

Max T-O, uninstalled ideal nozzle: See under model listings

Max cruise thrust at 10,670 m (35,000 ft), Mach 0.85, flat rated to ISA + 10°C, uninstalled, real nozzle:

CF6-50C2, -E2	50.3 kN (11,300 lb)
CF6-80A, -80A1	45.9 kN (10,320 lb)

SPECIFIC FUEL CONSUMPTION:

At T-O thrust, as above:

CF6-50E	10.65 mg/Ns (0.376 lb/h/lb st)
CF6-50C2, -E2	10.51 mg/Ns (0.371 lb/h/lb st)
CF6-80A	9.74 mg/Ns (0.344 lb/h/lb st)

OIL CONSUMPTION: 0.9 kg (2.0 lb)/h

GENERAL ELECTRIC CF6-80C2

This engine is a major redesign for higher thrust and improved sfc, based on the CF6-80A1/A3 but with a 2,362 mm (93 in) diameter fan. It has a four-stage LP compressor and LP turbine redesigned aerodynamically with 5½ stages. The first CF6-80C2 ran in May 1982, and exceeded 276 kN (62,000 lb) corrected thrust. Flight test on an A300 took place between August and December 1984, leading to certification on 28 June 1985. The engine entered revenue service on 5 October 1985.

General Electric CF6-80C2 two-shaft turbofan

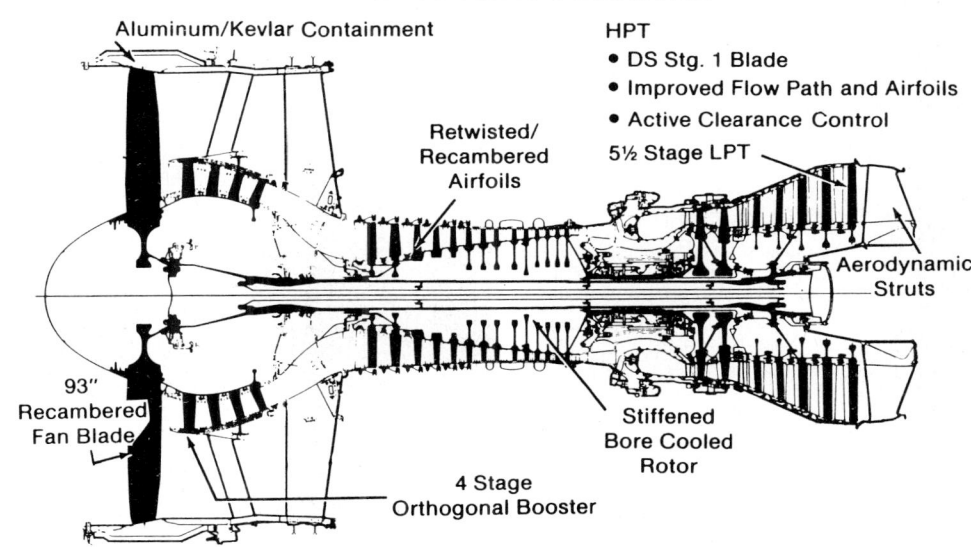

Features of General Electric CF6-80C2 two-shaft turbofan

CF6-80C2 and -80E1 MODELS

Model	Thrust		Application
	Ideal nozzle	Real nozzle	
CF6-80C2A2	238 kN (53,500 lb)	233.5 kN (52,460 lb) to 43.9°C	A310-200, -300
CF6-80C2A3	268 kN (60,200 lb)	262 kN (58,950 lb) to 30°C	A300-600
CF6-80C2A5	272.5 kN (61,300 lb)	267.5 kN (60,100 lb) to 30°C	A300-600R
CF6-80C2A8	262.4 kN (59,000 lb)	257.4 kN (57,860 lb) to 35°C	A310-300
CF6-80C2B1	252 kN (56,700 lb)	249 kN (55,980 lb) to 30°C	747-200, -300
CF6-80C2B1F	258 kN (58,000 lb)	254 kN (57,160 lb) to 32.2°C	747-400
CF6-80C2B2	233.5 kN (52,500 lb)	231 kN (51,950 lb) to 32.2°C	767-200ER, -300ER
CF6-80C2B2F	234.5 kN (52,700 lb)	231.5 kN (52,010 lb) to 32.2°C	767-300ER
CF6-80C2B4	257.5 kN (57,900 lb)	254.5 kN (57,180 lb) to 32.2°C	767-200ER, -300ER
CF6-80C2B4F	258 kN (58,100 lb)	255 kN (57,280 lb) to 32.2°C	767-300ER
CF6-80C2B6	270 kN (60,800 lb)	267 kN (60,070 lb) to 30°C	767-300ER
CF6-80C2B6F	270 kN (60,800 lb)	267 kN (60,070 lb) to 30°C	767-300ER
CF6-80C2D1F	273.5 kN (61,500 lb)	268 kN (60,240 lb) to 30°C	MD-11
CF6-80E1A1	287 kN (64,500 lb)	281.5 kN (63,290 lb) to 30°C	A330
CF6-80E1A2	292.5 kN (65,800 lb)	287 kN (64,530 lb) to 30°C	A330
CF6-80E1A3	309 kN (69,500 lb)	303.5 kN (68,240 lb) to 30°C	A330

Programme sharing agreements have been signed with SNECMA of France, MTU of Germany, Volvo Flygmotor of Sweden and Fiat Aviazione of Italy. Applications are shown in table on this page.

The CF6-80C2 differs from earlier CF6 engines in the following features:

FAN: Single-stage, with integrally mounted four-stage booster (LP compressor). Mainly titanium except for steel mid-fan shaft, aluminium spinner and blade-containment shroud of layers of Kevlar around aluminium case. Eighty composite exit guide vanes canted for better aerodynamic efficiency. Mass flow 802 kg (1,769 lb)/s; bypass ratio 5.05.

LP COMPRESSOR: Four stages with blades and vanes mounted orthogonally, with dovetail offset from centre of pressure to reduce bending.

HP COMPRESSOR: 14-stage, with inlet guide vanes and first five stator rows with variable incidence. Blades in stages 1-5 titanium, 6-14 steel; vanes all steel. One-piece steel casing with insulated aft stages. Core airflow 154 kg (340 lb)/s. Overall pressure ratio 30.4.

COMBUSTOR: Annular, rolled ring construction, aft-mounted with film cooling.

HP TURBINE: Two-stage. Stage one blades directionally solidified. Casing with active and passive clearance control. No midframe.

LP TURBINE: Five stages, with cambered struts in rear frame to reduce exit swirl, effectively producing another half-stage. Rear hub heated by exhaust gas to reduce thermal stress.

FUEL SYSTEM: FADEC or hydromechanical fan speed control with electronic supervision; one throttle position corresponds to each engine rating in all flight conditions.

DIMENSION:
Length	4,087 mm (160.9 in)

WEIGHT, DRY: 4,144 kg (9,135 lb)

PERFORMANCE RATINGS (uninstalled, ideal nozzle):
Max T-O	See table
Max cruise (10,670 m; 35,000 ft, Mach 0.85)	
	50.4 kN (11,330 lb)

SPECIFIC FUEL CONSUMPTION:
T-O, as above	9.32 mg/Ns (0.329 lb/h/lb st)

GENERAL ELECTRIC CF6-80E1

This engine is a major redesign for higher thrust and improved sfc, based on the CF6-80C2 but with a 2,438 mm (96 in) diameter fan. It has a four-stage LP compressor and LP turbine redesigned aerodynamically with 5½ stages. The first CF6-80E1 ran in December 1990 at 335.8 kN (75,500 lb st) corrected thrust. Flight test on an A300 is planned for late 1991 and early 1992, leading to certification in December 1992. The engine will enter revenue service in 1993 on the A330.

The CF6-80E1 development is being shared with SNECMA of France, MTU of Germany, Volvo Flygmotor of Sweden, and Fiat Aviazione of Italy.

The CF6-80E1 differs from the CF6-80C2 in the following features:

FAN: Diameter increased; number of blades reduced from 38 to 34.

LP COMPRESSOR: Flow capacity increased 9 per cent at a 12 per cent increased pressure ratio.

HP COMPRESSOR: High-temperature alloys in last stage. Overall pressure ratio: E1A1, 32; E1A2, 32.6; E1A3, 34.6.

COMBUSTOR: No change.

HP TURBINE: High-temperature alloys and improved cooling.

LP TURBINE: High-temperature alloys, improved cooling changes and aerodynamic changes.

FUEL SYSTEM: Surface-mounted FADEC; a higher-capacity system with an externally valved staging system (50 per cent of nozzles can be turned off) for low thrust operability.

DIMENSIONS:
Length: Engine	4,405 mm (173.5 in)
Propulsion system	7,356 mm (289.6 in)

WEIGHT, DRY:
Engine	4,818 kg (10,600 lb)
Propulsion system	6,532 kg (14,400 lb)

PERFORMANCE RATINGS: See table

SPECIFIC FUEL CONSUMPTION (Max T-O):
E1A1	9.18 mg/Ns (0.324 lb/h/lb st)
E1A2	9.26 mg/Ns (0.327 lb/h/lb st)
E1A3	9.63 mg/Ns (0.340 lb/h/lb st)

GENERAL ELECTRIC F110

The **F110** (previously F101 DFE) is a fighter engine derivative of the F101. The first ran in late 1979. In early 1984 the USAF selected the F110 to power future F-16 aircraft.

The following are current versions of the F110:

F110-GE-100. Initial USAF engine, also selected by Israel (100 engines) and Turkey (177 engines). Other orders have been received from Bahrain, Egypt and Greece. Delivery of production F-16C/D aircraft with F110 engines began in mid-1986. The US Navy selected the Dash-100 to power its F-16Ns for the adversary role in its Top Gun programme.

F110-GE-400. Powers F-14A (Plus) and F-14D Tomcat for the US Navy. First production aircraft with this engine delivered to Navy in November 1987. Tomcats powered with this engine show a significant improvement in fuel consumption and the ability to catapult launch without use of an afterburner, resulting in a 61 per cent time-to-climb reduction and a 62 per cent improvement in mission range. Ratings are: maximum 120.2 kN (27,000 lb st), dry 71.2 kN (16,000 lb st).

F110-GE-129. Rated at 129 kN (29,000 lb st), the GE IPE (Improved Performance Engine) is the successor to the F110-GE-100. Through the use of improved design and materials, higher operating temperatures, speeds and pressures, the GE IPE increases thrust levels by as much as 30 per cent in certain areas of the flight envelope, while retaining more than 80 per cent parts commonality. The IPE's digital electronic control has 50 per cent fewer parts than previous controls, and offers substantially improved reliability. The IPE first flew in an F-16C/D in August 1988, and a USAF field service evaluation programme began in the latter half of 1990. Service entry was scheduled for 1991. The engine has also been selected to power Japan's FSX fighter.

General Electric F110-GE-129 two-shaft augmented turbofan

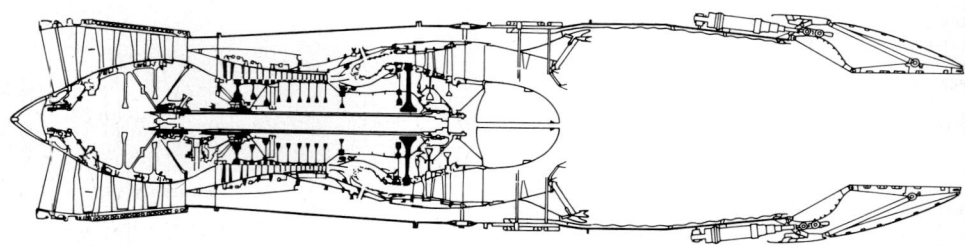

Longitudinal section of General Electric F110 two-shaft augmented turbofan

General Electric F120-GE-100 variable cycle fighter engine with vectoring nozzle

The following refers to the F110-GE-129:

FAN: Three stages. Bypass ratio 0.76. Airflow 122 kg (270 lb)/s.

HP COMPRESSOR: Nine stages. Overall pressure ratio, 31 : 1 class.

COMBUSTOR: Annular scroll.

HP TURBINE: Single stage with aircooled blades.

LP TURBINE: Two stages, drives fan.

AUGMENTOR: Close coupled mixed-flow linear thrust afterburner.

EXHAUST NOZZLE: Convergent/divergent exhaust nozzle with hydraulic actuation.

DIMENSIONS:
Length	4,626 mm (182.3 in)
Diameter	1,180 mm (46.5 in)

PERFORMANCE RATINGS (S/L):
T-O	129 kN (29,000 lb st)
Max dry	75.7 kN (17,000 lb)

GENERAL ELECTRIC F120

The F120-GE-100 is GE Aircraft Engines' propulsion candidate for the USAF's Advanced Tactical Fighter (ATF). The engine features advanced variable-cycle capability, counter-rotating turbine and a two-dimensional, vectoring exhaust nozzle. The variable-cycle technology enables the F120 to operate as a conventional turbojet at supersonic speeds, while maintaining the characteristics of a more fuel-efficient turbofan at subsonic speeds. The use of advanced materials and design technology enable the F120 to achieve a higher thrust-to-weight ratio than GEAE's current production aircraft fighter engines. In 1990 prototype engines completed flight testing on the Lockheed YF-22A and Northrop YF-23A ATF prototype aircraft. The demonstrator engines completed testing in 1988.

GENERAL ELECTRIC F118

This unaugmented turbofan has been developed under USAF contract to meet the demanding propulsion requirements of the Northrop B-2A bomber. An 84.52 kN (19,000 lb set) thrust class derivative of the F101 and F110 engines, the non-afterburning **F118-GE-100** employs new long-chord fan technology with the compressor and turbine used on the F110. The F118 has a higher airflow capacity and higher air pressure ratio than the F110, resulting in higher thrust. The engine was fully qualified in 1987, has successfully powered the B-2A in the USAF flight test programme since July 1989, and has accumulated more than 6,000 test hours to date. A feature is the use of common F101/F110 production tooling for low cost.

The accompanying photograph shows the actuation ring for the trailing flaps of the inlet guide vanes, a large inlet bleed-air de-icing pipe, and the ribbed bypass duct. The cooled jets issue across what appear to be carbon areas above the B-2A wing.

In Autumn 1989 a Lockheed TR-1 began a flight test programme powered by a derivative of the F118, designated **F101-GE-F29**. This engine is lighter and shorter but delivers more dry thrust than the J75-P-13B normally fitted.

GENERAL ELECTRIC UDF

Using thin scimitar-like blades, the unducted fan (UDF) engine has a bypass ratio of 36. The proof of concept demonstrator used an F404 core and was rated in the 111.2 kN (25,000 lb st) class. Flight testing on a Boeing 727 started on 20 August 1986, and was completed in February 1987. Flight testing on an MD-80 began on 18 May 1987 and was completed in September 1988.

After accomplishing all flight objectives, GE started development of the product engine, which it considered suitable for use on the projected MD-91, MD-92 and 7J7. On 30 May 1985 GE and SNECMA signed an agreement assigning to the French company a 35 per cent share of the UDF programme. SNECMA participated in the proof of concept demonstration, and was to be involved in the design and development of major portions of the product engine.

The key to the light weight and low fuel consumption of the UDF lies in elimination of a drive gearbox. Instead, the gas from the core passes through large multi-stage contra-rotating turbines downstream. This substitutes rotor blades for what would normally be the turbine stators, and the visible propulsor blades are mounted directly on the two rotors of the power turbine. Blade loading for the LP power turbines is normal, but speed is low and the resulting modest stress levels allow the unique construction at low risk.

The external propulsor blades are designed using techniques established with fan blades, the hub radius ratio of more than 0.45 being more than twice that common for propellers. The composite blades change pitch from flight settings through feather to reverse, and the pitch is set to control speed and power output.

In June 1989 GE announced completion of UDF development, pending a time when a market might appear. Should work be resumed at a future date, about four years and about $1.3 billion would be needed for certification.

GENERAL ELECTRIC GLC38

The GLC38 is a member of the T407/GLC38/CFE738 engine family, which includes turboprop, turboshaft, turbofan, and unducted fan (UDF) versions. The **T407-GE-400** turboprop was selected to power the Lockheed P-7A ASW aircraft, a programme terminated in 1990. The **GLC38** is the commercial turboprop engine. The following refers to the basic GLC38 power plant (including the propeller gearbox):

TYPE: Two-shaft modular turbine engine.
COMPRESSOR: Five axial stages followed by one centrifugal stage.
COMBUSTION CHAMBER: Short annular type with 15 injectors.
TURBINES: Two-stage aircooled compressor turbine. Three-stage power turbine.
DIMENSIONS:

Max envelope length	2,972 mm (117 in)
Max envelope diameter	838 mm (33 in)

PERFORMANCE RATING (S/L, T-O):
T407   4,475 kW (6,000 shp) class
SPECIFIC FUEL CONSUMPTION:
"15-30 per cent better than engines in its class"

GENERAL ELECTRIC T64

The T64 was developed initially for the US Navy. It is available as a turboshaft or turboprop. Current versions are:

T64-GE-100. -7A with improved turbine. Powers CH-53C and MH-53J. Also being upgraded by kit from -7A.

T64-GE-413. Powers CH-53D.

T64-GE-415. Improved combustion liner and turbine cooling. Powers RH-53D.

T64-GE-416. As -415. Powers CH/MH-53E.

T64-GE-416A. As -416, improved turbine.

T64-GE-419. As -416A, with integral fuel/oil heat exchanger, and OEI emergency power on a 32.2°C day. To power CH/MH-53E from 1993.

CT64-820-4. Turboprop, powers DHC-5D.

T64/P4D. Turboprop, powers G222 and C-27A. Production by Fiat, supported by Alfa Romeo Avio from 1975.

TYPE: Free turbine turboshaft/turboprop.
COMPRESSOR: Fourteen-stage axial-flow, single-spool steel rotor for -820/-1/2/3, titanium and steel compressor for -100, -413, -415, -416, -416A, -419, -P4D and CT64-820-4. Inlet guide vanes and first four stages of stator vanes variable, air mass flow per second: -100, -413, -415, -416, -416A, -419, 13.3 kg (29.4 lb); -820-4, 11.9 kg (26.2 lb); P4D, 12.2 kg (27.0 lb). Pressure ratio: -820-4, 12.5; -100, -413, -415/-416/-416A, -419, 14.0; P4D, 13.0.
COMBUSTION CHAMBER: Annular type. Double fuel manifold feeds twelve duplex type fuel nozzles.
GAS GENERATOR TURBINE: Two-stage, coupled directly to compressor rotor by spline connection. Engines rated 3,228 kW (4,330 shp) or over have aircooled first-stage blades.
POWER TURBINE: Two-stage, independent of gas generator.
REDUCTION GEAR: Remotely mounted for turboprop, offset and accessible for inspection and replacement. Ratio 13.44.
STARTING: Mechanical, airframe supplied.
DIMENSIONS:
Length: T64-GE-100, -413, -415, -416, -416A, -419
                          2,006 mm (79 in)
   T64/P4D, CT64-820-4   2,793 mm (110 in)
Width: T64-GE-100, -413, -415, -416, -416A, -419
                          660 mm (26.0 in)
   T64/P4D, CT64-820-4   683 mm (26.9 in)
Height: T64-GE-100, -413, -415, -416, -416A, -419
                          825 mm (32.5 in)
   T64/P4D, CT64-820-4   1,168 mm (46 in)
WEIGHT, DRY:
   T64-GE-100, -413, -415, -416, -416A   327 kg (720 lb)
   T64-GE-419   343 kg (755 lb)
   CT64-820-4   520 kg (1,145 lb)
   T64/P4D   538 kg (1,188 lb)
PERFORMANCE RATINGS (max rating (S/L)):
   T64-GE-100   3,229 kW (4,330 shp) to 29.4°C
   T64-GE-413   2,927 kW (3,925 shp)
   T64-GE-415, -416, -416A   3,266 kW (4,380 shp)
   T64-GE-419   3,542 kW (4,750 shp)
   CT64-820-4   2,336 kW (3,133 shp)
   T64/P4D   2,535 kW (3,400 shp)
SPECIFIC FUEL CONSUMPTION (max rating (S/L)):
   T64-GE-100, -413, -415, -416, -416A, -419
                      79.4 µg/J (0.47 lb/h/shp)
   CT64-820-4, T64/P4D   81 µg/J (0.48 lb/h/shp)

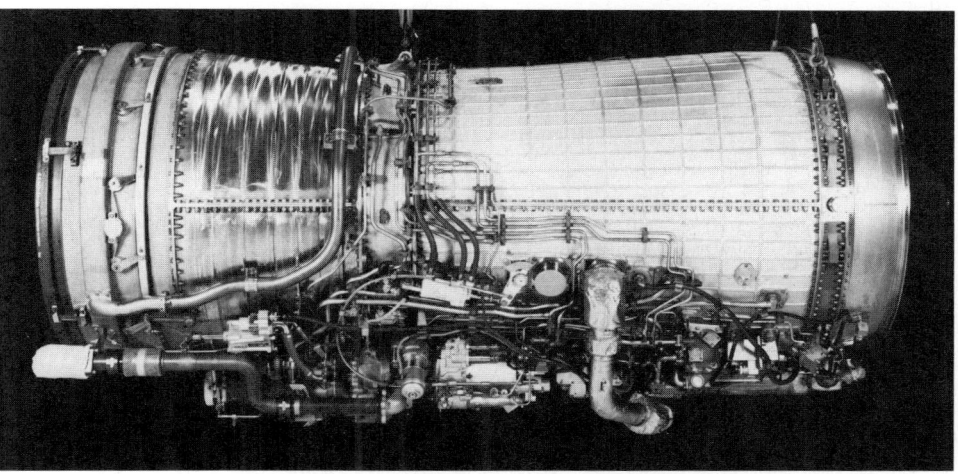

General Electric F118-GE-100 two-shaft unaugmented turbofan

General Electric UDF engine installed on MD-80

General Electric T64-GE-415/416 turboshaft

General Electric T407/GLC38 basic core

General Electric GLC38 turboprop mockup

General Electric T700-401 free-turbine turboshaft

GENERAL ELECTRIC T700

The T700 was selected in 1971 to power the US Army's utility tactical transport aircraft system (UTTAS). The first T700 went to test in 1973, and in 1976 it was the first turboshaft to pass current US military qualification standards. The engine went into production in 1978. Of the following models, only the Step 2 growth derivatives are in production.

T700-GE-700. First production model delivered from early 1978. Following description refers to this version, except where otherwise noted. Powers UH-60A Black Hawk.

T700-GE-701. First-step growth derivative. Upgrade of 10 per cent. Powers AH-64 Apache.

T700-GE-401. Navalised first-step derivative. Powers SH-60B Seahawk, SH-2G Super Seasprite and AH-1W SuperCobra.

T700-GE-701C. Second-step growth derivative. Provides 20 per cent more power than -700. Went into production in 1989 for Black Hawk and Apache. Offered for future S-70/WS-70 Black Hawk derivatives for international sales.

T700-GE-401C. Navalised second-step growth derivative. Chosen by US Navy for future Seahawks and derivatives. First production engines delivered in 1988 to power HH-60H; Royal Australian Navy also a launch customer.

GE alliances on T700 engines include: agreements with Ruston Gas Turbines of Great Britain that result in a UK-manufactured T700; a licence agreement with Alfa Romeo Avio (with additional participation of Fiat Avio) for manufacture and assembly of T700/CT7 engines in Italy; a licence agreement with Australia to assemble T700s; another with Japan to build and test T700s for Black Hawks and Seahawks and a licence agreement for manufacture of test of T700 engines for Black Hawks in South Korea.

TYPE: Ungeared free turbine turboshaft engine.

INTAKE: Annular, with anti-iced separator designed to remove 95 per cent of sand, dust and foreign object ingestion. Extracted matter discharged by blower driven from accessory gearbox.

COMPRESSOR: Combined axial/centrifugal. Five axial stages and single centrifugal stage mounted on same shaft. Each axial stage is one-piece 'blisk' (blades plus disc) in AM355

steel highly resistant to erosion. Inlet guide vanes and first two stator stages variable. Pressure ratio about 15. Mass flow about 4.5 kg (10 lb)/s at 44,720 rpm.

COMBUSTION CHAMBER: Fully annular. Central fuel injection to maximise acceptance of contaminated fuel and give minimal smoke generation. Ignition power from separate winding on engine mounted alternator serves dual plugs.

TURBINE: Two stage gas generator (HP) turbine. Rated speed (S/L, ISA, max T-O), 44,720 rpm. Two stage free power turbine, with tip shrouded blades and segmented nozzles. Output speed, 21,000 rpm.

CONTROLS: Hydromechanical control can be replaced in less than 12 minutes. Electrical control provides twin-engine speed and torque matching.

ACCESSORIES: Grouped at top of engine, together with engine control system. Integral oil tank, plus emergency mist lubrication. Torque sensor provides signal to electrical control.

DIMENSIONS:

Length overall	1,168 mm (46.0 in)
Width	635 mm (25 in)
Height overall	584 mm (23 in)

WEIGHT, DRY (with particle separator):

T700-700	198 kg (437 lb)
T700-401	197 kg (434 lb)
T700-701C	207 kg (456 lb)
T700-401C	208 kg (458 lb)

PERFORMANCE RATINGS (ISA, S/L, static):

T700-700:	
intermediate	1,210 kW (1,622 shp)
continuous	987 kW (1,324 shp)
T700-401:	
contingency	1,285 kW (1,723 shp)
intermediate	1,260 kW (1,690 shp)
continuous	1,072 kW (1,437 shp)
T700-701C:	
maximum	2,534 kW (1,890 shp)
intermediate	2,414 kW (1,800 shp)
continuous	2,229 kW (1,662 shp)
T700-401C:	
contingency	2,600 kW (1,940 shp)
intermediate	2,414 kW (1,800 shp)
continuous	2,229 kW (1,662 shp)

SPECIFIC FUEL CONSUMPTION (ISA, S/L, static):

T700-700:	
continuous	79.41 µg/J (0.470 lb/h/shp)
T700-401:	
intermediate	78.40 µg/J (0.464 lb/h/shp)
T700-701C:	
continuous	77.56 µg/J (0.459 lb/h/shp)
T700-401C:	
continuous	77.56 µg/J (0.459 lb/h/shp)

GENERAL ELECTRIC CT7

Commercial engine based on the T700. Certification in April 1977. The **CT7-2A** turboshaft powers the Bell 214ST. The **CT7-2D** and **-2D1** power S-70 Black Hawks. The CT7-2D is the commercial equivalent of the -701/-401. The CT7-2D1 is the commercial equivalent of the -701C/-401C and received FAA certification in June 1989.

The **CT7-6** is a Step 2 growth engine, co-developed by Alfa Romeo Avio, Fiat Avio and GE for the EH 101 and other helicopter applications, such as the NH 90. First delivery for the EH 101 took place in April 1988; first flight of a CT7-6 powered EH 101 took place in September 1988. The marinised **CT7-6A** powers the Italian Navy's EH 101 prototype. The CT7-6/-6A has received FAA certification, as well as RAI and BCAA validation.

The same core is used in the CT7 turboprop, which has a remote propeller gearbox. This engine received FAA certification in August 1983 and is in production as the **CT7-5A** for the Saab 340 and as the **CT7-7A** for the Airtech CN 235.

CT7 turboprop growth engines include the **CT7-9B** and **-9C** flat rated at 1,395 kW (1,870 shp). Increased power is obtained by improvements in aerodynamics, materials and turbine cooling. These engines power advanced versions of the CN 235 and Saab 340. The -9B has also been selected as the power plant for the Let L-610.

GE is also discussing a compact Dash-9 flat rated at 1,119 kW (1,500 shp). This **CT7-3** would have a Hamilton Standard gearbox located on the front of the engine, saving 660 mm (26 in) in length and 56.7 kg (125 lb) in weight.

Data below are for the current turboshaft versions:

DIMENSIONS:

Length	1,168 mm (46.0 in)
Diameter (max envelope)	635 mm (25.0 in)

WEIGHT, DRY:

CT7-2A	202 kg (444 lb)
CT7-2D/2B	201 kg (442 lb)
CT7-6	209 kg (460 lb)

PERFORMANCE RATINGS (S/L, static, 15°C):

Contingency (2½ min OEI):	
CT7-2A, 2B, -2D	1,287 kW (1,725 shp)
CT7-6	1,491 kW (2,000 shp)
T-O (5 min) and en route contingency (30 min):	
CT7-2A, 2B, -2D	1,211 kW (1,623 shp)
CT7-2B	1,212 kW (1,625 shp)
CT7-6	1,491 kW (2,000 shp)

SPECIFIC FUEL CONSUMPTION:
  Max continuous:
  CT7-2A, -2B   79.9 µg/J (0.473 lb/h/shp)
  CT7-6 (15°C)   77.4 µg/J (0.458 lb/h/shp)
  CT7-6 (35°C)   82.8 µg/J (0.490 lb/h/shp)
  Table below right shows data for the current turboprop
versions:

**Full scale model of General Electric CT7-6
turboshaft** *(Brian M. Service)*

General Electric CT7-9 free-turbine turboprop

CT7 turboprops				
	-5A	-7A	-9B	-9C
Length mm (in)	2,438 (96)	2,438 (96)	2,438 (96)	2,438 (96)
Max diameter mm (in)	737 (29)	737 (29)	737 (29)	737 (29)
Weight, dry kg (lb)	349.3 (770)	351.5 (775)	360.6 (795)	360.6 (795)
PERFORMANCE RATINGS:				
S/L T-O kW (shp)	1,294 (1,735)	1,268 (1,700)	1,305 (1,750)	1,305 (1,750)
APR auto power reserve kW (shp)	—	—	1,394 (1,870)	1,394 (1,870)
Max cruise at 4,575 m (15,000 ft)				
ekW (ehp)	978 (1,312)	978 (1,312)	1,052 (1,411)	1,118 (1,499)

IN-TECH
IN-TECH INTERNATIONAL INC
West 7510 Hall Avenue, Spokane, Washington 99204-5708
Telephone: 1 (509) 455 6116
Fax: 1 (509) 747 1701
  In September 1985 In-Tech International acquired the
Merlyn engine (see Machen in 1985-86 *Jane's*). Due to
product liability exposure, the Merlyn will be available for
aircraft only after experience shows that the risk can be
minimised.

IN-TECH MERLYN
  Research shows a need for a new piston engine in the
373-522 kW (500-700 hp) class, with liquid cooling. Design
goals included a power: weight ratio better than 0.34 kg/kW
(1 lb/hp); ability to use multifuels (Jet A, JP-4, JP-5, Nos. 1
and 2 diesel); an sfc 20 per cent lower than small turboprops;
low frontal area and drag; and at least six accessory pads.
TYPE: Three-cylinder inline two-stroke diesel.
CYLINDERS: Bore 130 mm (5.125 in). Stroke 86 mm (3.388
  in). Capacity 3.47 litres (210 cu in). Twin overhead
  camshaft and four exhaust valves per cylinder. Offset
  crankshaft.
DIMENSIONS:
  Length   1,283 mm (50.5 in)
  Width   457 mm (18.0 in)
  Height   648 mm (25.5 in)
WEIGHT, DRY: 263 kg (580 lb)

**In-Tech Merlyn
three-cylinder
two-stroke diesel**

PERFORMANCE RATINGS:
  T-O   485 kW (650 hp) at 4,800 rpm
  Max continuous   448 kW (600 hp)

JAVELIN

JAVELIN AIRCRAFT COMPANY INC

Municipal Airport, Augusta, Kansas 67010
Telephone: 1 (316) 733 1011

Javelin has a long-term programme to produce liquid cooled aircraft engines. Extensive work has been done on the Javelin Ford 140 (cu in capacity). A completely engineered power plant with turbocharger was flight tested in a Cessna 172. The 140T continues in demand for replica fighters, but most homebuilders need the smaller Ford Escort/Lynx 98 of 1,607 cc (98 cu in). Six Ford 98s are on test, one being a 'hi-drive' for amphibians with the engine and radiator inside the hull and propeller above. The conventional installation weighs about 129 kg (285 lb) with toothed belt drive. By early 1982 one 98-size engine was flying in a Cessna 150, held to 93 kW (125 hp) and cruising at 44.8 kW (60 hp) with sfc of 62 µg/J (0.37 lb/h/hp). In 1983 intensive flight development was in progress on the Ford 230 (Windsor) V-6, with a continuous rating of 149 kW (200 hp) for a weight, with reduction gear and all accessories, of 176 kg (387 lb).

Javelin Ford 230 six-cylinder piston engine

LHTEC

LIGHT HELICOPTER TURBINE ENGINE COMPANY

The Paragon Building, Suite 400, 12400 Olive Boulevard, St Louis, Missouri 63141
MEMBER COMPANIES: **Allison Gas Turbine Division**
PO Box 420, Indianapolis, Indiana 46206
Garrett Engine Division
PO Box 5217, Phoenix, Arizona 85010

These two companies have combined their resources to develop the T800-LHT-800 975 kW (1,300 shp) class turboshaft engine for the multi-service LH (AH-66) programme. The CTS800 is a version for commercial applications.

LHTEC T800-LHT-800

This fully metric, high power density helicopter engine stems from programmes that the two partners started prior to 1983. Garrett's core engine based on the F109 had extensive running time. Allison's engine was developed under the Army's Advanced Technology Demonstrator Engine (ATDE) programme. The blending of these two engines produced the T800 technology prototypes, which exceeded 940 kW (1,260 shp) in December 1984, with lower than specified fuel consumption. After fierce competition, LHTEC was selected by the US Army in October 1988 to continue the engine development and subsequent production. By December 1990 civil CTS800 and military T800 engines had run more than 1,000 hours of flight testing.

The CTS800/T800 is designed for unprecedented reliability, maintainability and supportability, and low specific fuel consumption. Its basic design philosophy includes module/LRU removal and replacement times of less than 15 minutes using six basic hand tools, and on-condition maintenance and TBOs.

Twin CTS800s have been flying in an Agusta A129 since 1988. In 1991 CTS800s were to fly in a Bell UH-1, Westland Lynx, Coast Guard HH-65 (Aerospatiale SA366) and LTV/AHC Panther 800. The CTS800/T800 is to receive FAA certification and military qualification in April 1992. Production engines will be available in mid-1992. Turboprop, ground power and armoured-vehicle derivatives are expected.

INLET: Annular, with solids extracted by particle separator of over 97 per cent efficiency.

Cutaway drawing of LHTEC T800 free-turbine turboshaft

COMPRESSOR: Two centrifugal stages in tandem. One-piece titanium impellers.
COMBUSTION CHAMBER: Annular reverse flow.
COMPRESSOR TURBINE: Two axial stages with single-pass cooling.
POWER TURBINE: Two axial stages with tip shrouds.
LUBRICATION SYSTEM: Self-contained, with tank of 4.1 litres (1.08 US gallons, 0.90 Imp gallons), air/oil heat exchanger.
OIL GRADES: MIL-L-7808, MIL-STD-23699.
FUEL GRADES: MIL-T-5624, MIL-T-83133, JP-4, JP-5, JP-8 (emergency DF-A, DF-1, DF-2).
CONTROL SYSTEM: FADEC.
ACCESSORIES: Mounted above engine with drive from core. Self-contained electrical system.
REDUCTION GEAR: Drive at 23,000 rpm to front or rear. Reduction gearbox gives output at 6,000-6,600 rpm.

DIMENSIONS:	
Length	800 mm (31.5 in)
Width	549 mm (21.6 in)
Height	658 mm (25.9 in)
WEIGHT, DRY T800:	143 kg (315 lb)
CTS800 with gearbox	163 kg (360 lb)
PERFORMANCE RATINGS:	
Contingency (2 min)	1,007 kW (1,350 shp)
T-O (5 min)	969 kW (1,300 shp)
T-O (30 min)	895 kW (1,200 shp)
Continuous	764 kW (1,025 shp)
FUEL FLOW:	
Contingency	285 kg (630 lb)/h
5 min	274 kg (603 lb)/h
30 min	256 kg (565 lb)/h
Continuous	219 kg (483 lb)/h

MARQUARDT

THE MARQUARDT COMPANY (subsidiary of International Signal and Control Group)

16555 Saticoy Street, Van Nuys, California 91409
Telephone: 1 (818) 989 6400
Telex: (910) 4951710
PRESIDENT: F. X. Marshall

Marquardt's main business continues to be advanced aerospace propulsion and the supply of ram air turbine power systems. Marquardt is developing composite rocket/air breathing propulsion systems for the US Air Force and Navy. Marquardt has developed bipropellant rockets for spacecraft since 1959, as described in the 1984-85 and earlier editions of *Jane's*.

MARQUARDT RAMJETS

Marquardt continues to be a principal developer of advanced ramjet systems. This activity has included the development of an integral rocket/ramjet for an advanced strategic air launched missile, the development of fixed and variable flow ducted rockets and small scale integral rocket/ramjets for air-launched missile applications.

MARQUARDT R-40A

This precision control rocket was developed and qualified for the Shuttle Orbiter and is being used as an orbit

Marquardt R-40A reaction control rocket

insertion engine for the US Navy's Shuttle Launch Dispenser.
TYPE: Liquid propellant reaction control rocket.
PROPELLANTS: Nitrogen tetroxide and monomethyl hydrazine.
THRUST CHAMBER ASSEMBLY: Single chamber. Area ratio 20. Made of silicide coated columbium, with welded-on orthogonal and scarfed nozzle extension in same material. Internal film cooling. Multiple doublet injector with hypergolic ignition.

Marquardt R-1E vernier long scarf thruster

PROPELLANT FEED SYSTEM: Pressurised tanks, with feed of 0.526 kg (1.16 lb)/s fuel and 0.838 kg (1.85 lb)/s oxidant at 16.4 bars (238 lb/sq in abs).

DIMENSIONS:	
Length overall	472 mm (18.6 in)
Nozzle exit diameter	267 mm (10.5 in)
WEIGHT, DRY:	9.5 kg (21.0 lb)
PERFORMANCE RATINGS:	
Max thrust (vacuum)	3.87 kN (870 lb)
Chamber pressure	10.5 bars (152 lb/sq in)
Specific impulse: area ratio 20	281
area ratio 120	306

MARQUARDT R-1E

This small high performance rocket was qualified as the vernier for the Shuttle Orbiter.

TYPE: Liquid bipropellant rocket for use in space.

PROPELLANTS: Nitrogen tetroxide and monomethyl hydrazine.

THRUST CHAMBER: Single chamber. Minimum area ratio 26 with orthogonal and scarfed nozzles. Made of silicide coated columbium. Insulated for buried installation. Single doublet injector with hypergolic ignition.

PROPELLANT FEED SYSTEM: Pressurised tank. Flow rate 0.016 kg (0.0354 lb)/s fuel and 0.0256 kg (0.565 lb)/s oxidant.

DIMENSIONS:

Length overall	279 mm (11.0 in)
Width	147 mm (5.8 in)
Height (depth)	145 mm (5.7 in)

WEIGHT, DRY: 3.7 kg (8.2 lb)

PERFORMANCE RATINGS:

Max thrust (vacuum)	0.11 kN (25.0 lb)
Chamber pressure	7.45 bars (108 lb/sq in)
Specific impulse (area ratio 100)	290

MOLLER
MOLLER INTERNATIONAL

1222 Research Park Drive, Davis, California 95616
Telephone: 1 (916) 756 5086
Fax: 1 (916) 756 5179
PRESIDENT: Dr Paul S. Moller
DIRECTOR OF MARKETING: Jack G. Allison

This company, builders of Volantors, has developed an RC (rotating combustion) engine of remarkable power/weight ratio. The twin-rotor 1,300 cc (79.3 cu in) unit, only 305 mm (12 in) long, has an output of 'over 150 hp' (112 kW) yet weighs 'under 85 lb' (38.5 kg).

MTI
MICROTURBO INC

2707 Forum Drive, Grand Prairie, Texas 75051-7027
Telephone: 1 (214) 660 5545
Fax: 1 (214) 660 7181
Telex: (510) 228 7320

PRESIDENT: Robert P. Schiller

This company was established in 1970 as the US subsidiary of Microturbo SA (see under France). It makes, overhauls and repairs Microturbo turbojets, APUs and other products.

NELSON
NELSON AIRCRAFT CORPORATION

PO Box 454, 8075 Pennsylvania Ave, Irwin, Pennsylvania 15642
Telephone: 1 (412) 863 5900
PRESIDENT: Charles R. Rhoades
DEVELOPMENT DEPARTMENT: 420 Harbor Drive, Naples, Florida 33940
Telephone: 1 (813) 263 1670
Fax: 1 (813) 434 5993

Nelson Aircraft Corporation, among its many industrial activities, produces to order the Nelson H-63 four-cylinder two-cycle aircooled engine, which is certificated by the FAA as a power unit for single-seat helicopters, and is also available as a power plant for propeller driven aircraft. These engines are capable of sustained inverted flight. Recommended overhaul period is 800 h.

The affiliated Sport Plane Power Inc in Naples, Florida, is the subject of a separate entry.

Nelson H-63C four-cylinder two-stroke engine

NELSON H-63
US military designation: YO-65

Developed originally as a power unit for single-seat helicopters, the H-63 is now available in two versions, as follows:

H-63C. Basic helicopter power unit for vertical installation. Battery/electronic ignition and direct drive. Certificated by FAA. Supplied as complete power package, including clutch, cooling fan and shroud.

H-63CP. Basically as H-63C, but without clutch, fan and shroud. Intended primarily for installation in horizontal position, with direct drive to propeller. FAA certificated.

Nelson has developed a 1.07 m (42 in) wooden propeller with glassfibre covering for use with the H-63. It is suitable for either tractor or pusher installation.

TYPE: Four-cylinder horizontally opposed aircooled, two-stroke.

CYLINDERS: Bore 68.3 mm (2^{11}/$_{16}$ in). Stroke 70 mm (2$\frac{3}{4}$ in). Total capacity 1.03 litres (63 cu in). Compression ratio 8 : 1.

PISTONS: Aluminium alloy casting. Two piston rings. Two needle roller bearings pressed in boss.

CONNECTING RODS: Alloy steel forging. Caged roller bearing at big-end.

CRANKSHAFT: Four-throw. Nitralloy shaft on ball and roller bearings.

CRANKCASE: Two-piece magnesium alloy cast case divided on horizontal centreline.

INDUCTION: Nelson diaphragm type all-angle fuel control carburettor. Fuel/oil mixture valves from crankcase through rotary valve driven by crankshaft. Intake to and exhaust from cylinders through ports.

FUEL: 80/87 octane gasoline and SAE 30 ash-free-base oil in 16 : 1 mixture.

IGNITION: Battery/electronic dual ignition with two Champion D-9 or 5 COM spark plugs per cylinder.

LUBRICATION: See under 'Fuel'.

POWER TAKE-OFF (H-63C): Hollow shaft extension from Salisbury centrifugal clutch output drive.

STARTING: 12V DC Autolite electric motor and Bendix drive.

COOLING: (H-63C): Centrifugal aluminium fan and two-piece glassfibre shrouding for FAA hot day of 37.8°C. (H-63CP): by propeller slipstream.

Nelson H-63CP four-cylinder engine for fixed-wing aircraft

DIMENSIONS (H-63C):

Length	508 mm (20.0 in)
Height	376 mm (14.8 in)
Width	605 mm (23.8 in)

WEIGHT, DRY (with accessories):

H-63C	34.5 kg (76 lb)
H-63CP	30.8 kg (68 lb)

POWER RATINGS:

T-O:

H-63C	32 kW (43 hp) at 4,000 rpm
H-63CP	35.8 kW (48 hp) at 4,400 rpm

Max continuous:

H-63C	32 kW (43 hp) at 4,000 rpm
H-63CP	33.6 kW (45 hp) at 4,000 rpm

PRATT & WHITNEY
UNITED TECHNOLOGIES PRATT & WHITNEY

HEADQUARTERS: East Hartford, Connecticut 06108
Telephone: 1 (203) 565 4321
Fax: 1 (203) 565 8896

Government Engines and Space Propulsion
PO Box 109600, W Palm Beach, Florida 33410-9600
Telephone: (PR) 1 (407) 796 6796
Fax: (PR) 1 (407) 796 7258
PRESIDENT: Arthur E. Wegner

Pratt & Whitney Aircraft was formed in 1925. Today Pratt & Whitney is the world's largest producer of gas turbine engines. Excluding P & W Canada (which see) it had by 1989 delivered over 70,000 aircraft gas turbines, including more than 25,000 airline jet engines.

PRATT & WHITNEY JT8
US military designation: J52

The J52 is a two-spool turbojet, with 12 compressor stages, a can-annular combustion system fed by 36 dual orifice injectors and single-stage HP and LP turbines. The P-408 has two-position inlet guide vanes and aircooled first-stage turbine vanes and blades. P-8 and P-408 can be upgraded to P-409 by field retrofit.

J52-P-6A, 6B, 8A, 8B. Rated at 37.8 kN (8,500 lb st) (6A, 6B) or 41.4 kN (9,300 lb st) (8A, 8B). Powers A-4, and A-6.

J52-P-408. Rated at 49.8 kN (11,200 lb st). Powers A-4F, A-4M, some export A-4 versions, EA-6B.

J52-P-409. Rated at 53.4 kN (12,000 lb st). Powers upgraded A-6E.

Data below are for the P-408:

DIMENSIONS:

Diameter	814.3 mm (32.06 in)
Length	3,020 mm (118.9 in)

WEIGHT, DRY: 1,052 kg (2,318 lb)

PRATT & WHITNEY JT8D

This turbofan was developed to power the Boeing 727. Military versions have been developed in Sweden by Volvo Flygmotor (see RM8 in that company's entry).

The JT8D entered commercial service on 1 February 1964. It has since become the most widely used commercial jet engine, almost 14,000 having logged more than 400 million flight hours by January 1991.

The following are current versions:

JT8D-9, -9A. Develops 64.5 kN (14,500 lb st) to 28.9°C at S/L. Specified for 727-100, -100C and -200, 737-200, -200C and T-43A, DC-9-20, -30, -40, C-9A, C-9B and VC-9C, Caravelle 12 and Kawasaki C-1. Produced under licence in Japan (see Mitsubishi).

JT8D-11. Develops 66.7 kN (15,000 lb st) to 28.9°C at S/L. Specified for DC-9-20, -30 and -40.

JT8D-15. Develops 69 kN (15,500 lb st) to 28.9°C. Powers Mercure, Advanced 727 and 737, and DC-9.

JT8D-15A. In 1982 new components in the Dash-15 resulted in a 5.5 per cent reduction in cruise fuel consumption. The same parts in the Dash-17 produce the **JT8D-17A**, and when fitted to the Dash-17R the **JT8D-17AR**.

JT8D-17. Develops 71.2 kN (16,000 lb st) to 28.9°C. Powers Advanced Boeing 727 and 737, and DC-9.

JT8D-17R. Normal T-O rating 72.95 kN (16,400 lb st) but has capability of providing 4.448 kN (1,000 lb) additional thrust in the event of significant thrust loss on any other engine.

JT8D-200 Series. Described separately.

Since February 1970 all new JT8D engines have incorporated smoke reduction hardware, and conversion kits are also available. Two noise reduction options are also available.

TYPE: Two-spool turbofan.

FAN: Two-stage front fan. Mass flow: -9, -9A, 145 kg (319 lb)/s; -11, -15, 146 kg (322 lb)/s; -17, 147 kg (324 lb)/s; -17R, 148 kg (326 lb)/s. Bypass ratio: -9, -9A, 1.04; -11, 1.05; -15, 1.03; -17, 1.02; -17R, 1.00.

LP COMPRESSOR: Six-stage, integral with fan.

HP COMPRESSOR: Seven-stage. Overall pressure ratio: -9, -9A, 15.9; -11, 16.2; -15, 16.5; -17, 16.9; -17R, 17.3.

COMBUSTION CHAMBER: Can-annular type with nine cylindrical flame tubes, each with a single Duplex burner.

HP TURBINE: Single-stage. Solid blades in -9, aircooled in -11 and later.

LP TURBINE: Three-stage.

DIMENSIONS:

Diameter	1,080 mm (42.5 in)
Length	3,137 mm (123.5 in)

WEIGHT, DRY:

JT8D-9, -9A	1,532 kg (3,377 lb)
JT8D-11	1,537 kg (3,389 lb)
JT8D-15	1,549 kg (3,414 lb)
-15A	1,576 kg (3,474 lb)
JT8D-17	1,556 kg (3,430 lb)
-17A	1,577 kg (3,475 lb)
JT8D-17R	1,585 kg (3,495 lb)
-17AR	1,588 kg (3,500 lb)

PERFORMANCE RATINGS:

T-O thrust (S/L, static)   see model descriptions

Max cruise thrust (10,670 m; 35,000 ft):

JT8D-9, -9A	18.2 kN (4,100 lb)
JT8D-11	17.6 kN (3,950 lb)
JT8D-15, -15A	18.2 kN (4,100 lb)
JT8D-17, -17R, -17A, -17AR	18.9 kN (4,240 lb)

SPECIFIC FUEL CONSUMPTION:

T-O rating:

JT8D-9, 9A	16.85 mg/Ns (0.595 lb/h/lb st)
JT8D-11	17.56 mg/Ns (0.620 lb/h/lb st)
JT8D-15	17.84 mg/Ns (0.630 lb/h/lb st)
-15A	16.63 mg/Ns (0.587 lb/h/lb st)
JT8D-17	18.27 mg/Ns (0.645 lb/h/lb st)
-17A	17.05 mg/Ns (0.602 lb/h/lb st)
JT8D-17R	18.55 mg/Ns (0.655 lb/h/lb st)
-17AR	17.31 mg/Ns (0.611 lb/h/lb st)

Max cruise rating, as above:

JT8D-9, -9A	22.86 mg/Ns (0.807 lb/h/lb)
JT8D-11	23.14 mg/Ns (0.817 lb/h/lb)
JT8D-15	22.97 mg/Ns (0.811 lb/h/lb)
JT8D-17, -17R	23.37 mg/Ns (0.825 lb/h/lb)

PRATT & WHITNEY JT8D-200 SERIES

This reduced noise derivative of the JT8D combines the HP compressor, HP turbine spool and combustion section of the JT8D-9 with advanced LP technology. It offers increased thrust with reduced noise and specific fuel consumption. The fan has increased diameter. The new six-stage LP compressor, integral with the fan, offers increased pressure ratio. The LP turbine has 20 per cent greater annular area and achieves a higher efficiency. Surrounding the engine is a new bypass duct. The exhaust system includes a 12 lobe mixer. FAA certification of the JT8D-209 was awarded in June 1979.

The following are current models:

Pratt & Whitney J52-P-408 two-shaft turbojet

JT8D-209. Rated at 82.2 kN (18,500 lb st) to 25°C, and 85.6 kN (19,250 lb st) following loss of thrust on any other engine. Entered service in October 1980, powering the MD-81.

JT8D-217. Rated at 88.96 kN (20,000 lb st), and 92.75 kN (20,850 lb st) following loss of thrust on any other engine. Powers MD-82.

JT8D-217A. T-O thrust available to 28.9°C or up to 1,525 m (5,000 ft). Powers MD-82.

JT8D-217C. Incorporates JT8D-219 performance improvements to reduce sfc. Powers MD-82 and -87.

JT8D-219. Rated at 93.4 kN (21,000 lb st), with a reserve power of 96.5 kN (21,700 lb st). Powers MD-83 and other MD-80 aircraft.

TYPE: Two-spool turbofan.

FAN: Single-stage front fan has 34 titanium blades, with part-span shrouds. Mass flow: -209, 213 kg (469 lb)/s; -217 (all), 219 kg (483 lb)/s; -219, 221 kg (488 lb)/s. Bypass ratio: -209, 1.78; -217 (all), 1.73; -219, 1.77.

LP COMPRESSOR: Six-stage axial, integral with fan.

HP COMPRESSOR: Seven-stage axial. Overall pressure ratio: -209, 17.1; -217 (all), 18.6; -219, 19.2.

COMBUSTION CHAMBER: Nine can-annular low-emissions burners with aerating fuel nozzles.

HP TURBINE: Single-stage. Aircooled blades in -217 and -219.

LP TURBINE: Three-stage.

DIMENSIONS:

Diameter	1,250 mm (49.2 in)
Length	3,911 mm (154 in)

WEIGHT, DRY:

JT8D-209	2,012 kg (4,435 lb)
JT8D-217, -217A	2,028 kg (4,470 lb)
JT8D-217C, -219	2,048 kg (4,515 lb)

PERFORMANCE RATINGS:

T-O (S/L static):   see model descriptions

Max cruise thrust (10,670 m; 35,000 ft at Mach 0.8):

JT8D-209	22.0 kN (4,945 lb)
JT8D-217, -217A, -217C	23.31 kN (5,240 lb)
JT8D-219	23.35 kN (5,250 lb)

SPECIFIC FUEL CONSUMPTION:

Max cruise rating, as above:

JT8D-209	20.50 mg/Ns (0.724 lb/h/lb)
JT8D-217, -217A	21.32 mg/Ns (0.753 lb/h/lb)
JT8D-217C	20.84 mg/Ns (0.736 lb/h/lb)
JT8D-219	20.87 mg/Ns (0.737 lb/h/lb)

PRATT & WHITNEY PW4000

The PW4000 is a third generation turbofan for wide-body transports. Ratings range from 213.5 kN (48,000 lb) to 373.7 kN (84,000 lb). The first engine achieved 275 kN (61,800 lb) thrust during initial testing in April 1984. First flight test on an A300B took place on 31 July 1985. Certificated July 1986 at 249 kN (56,000 lb st) and in 1988 at 266.9 kN (60,000 lb st). Entered service on Pan Am A310 on 20 June 1987. The last two numbers denote thrust (thus, the initially certificated 56,000 lb st engine is the PW4056). Programme sharing agreements have been signed with FN (Belgium), Fiat (Italy), Norsk Jet Motors (Norway), Kawasaki (Japan), Samsung (South Korea), Eldim (Netherlands), Mitsubishi (Japan) and Singapore Aircraft Industries.

Fuel consumption was initially reduced seven per cent compared with the JT9D-7R4. There are about half as many parts, promising reductions in maintenance cost exceeding 25 per cent. HP compressor pressure ratio is increased by 10 per cent and the HP rotor operates at 27 per cent higher speed.

The PW4000 incorporates single-crystal turbine blades, aerodynamically enhanced aerofoils, and a full-authority digital electronic engine control (FADEC). The PW4000 was the first FADEC engine approved for ETOPS operations beyond 120 min from alternates.

Thrust beyond 275.8 kN (62,000 lb) is achieved by changing materials and modifying the HP turbine cooling airflow (the improved turbine is retrofittable). For the A330 the **PW4168** will have a fan diameter increased to 2,535 mm (99.8 in) and an extra stage on the LP compressor and LP turbine. Initial A330 deliveries will be at 284.7 kN (64,000 lb st) in 1994. For the Boeing 777 the **PW4084** will have a fan of 2,845 mm (112 in) diameter, six-stage LP compressor and seven-stage LP turbine. Initial 777 deliveries in 1995 will be at 324.7 kN (73,000 lb st).

The following data apply to the basic PW4000 except where indicated:

TYPE: Two-shaft turbofan.

FAN: Single-stage. Titanium alloy hub retains 38 titanium alloy blades with aft part-span shrouds. Diameter 2,377 mm (93.6 in). Data for 249 kN (56,000 lb st) rating: mass flow 773 kg (1,705 lb)/s. Fan pressure ratio 1.7. Bypass ratio 4.85.

LP COMPRESSOR: Four stages with controlled diffusion aerofoils.

HP COMPRESSOR: Eleven stages with first four vane rows variable. Clearance control accomplished via rotor/case thermal matching.

Overall pressure ratio at 249 kN rating, 29.7.

COMBUSTOR: Annular, forged nickel alloy roll-ring with double-pass cooling. 24 air-blast anti-coking injectors. Segmented Floatwall burner liner to be introduced in 1993.

HP TURBINE: Two stages with aircooled blades cast as single crystal (PWA 1480) in first row and directional crystal (PWA 1422) in second row, retained in double-hub nickel alloy rotor with active clearance control. Vane aerofoils thermal barrier coated.

LP TURBINE: Four stages with active clearance control.

CONTROL SYSTEM: Full authority digital electronic with dual channel computer.

DIMENSIONS:

Length: PW4000	3,371 mm (132.7 in)
PW4168	4,143 mm (163.1 in)
PW4084	4,868 mm (191.7 in)
Fan case diameter: PW4000	2,463 mm (96.98 in)
PW4168	2,718 mm (107.0 in)

WEIGHT, DRY:

Basic PW4000	4,264 kg (9,400 lb)
PW4168 (complete system)	6,350 kg (14,000 lb)
Basic PW4084	6,214 kg (13,700 lb)

RATINGS: See table

SPECIFIC FUEL CONSUMPTION (ISA, ideal nozzle, Mach 0.8, 10,670 m/35,000 ft):

PW4000	15.21 mg/Ns (0.537 lb/h/lb)

Pratt & Whitney JT8D-219 two-shaft turbofan

Pratt & Whitney PW4000 two-shaft turbofan

PW4000 MODELS

Model	Thrust (ideal nozzle)	Application
PW4152	231.3 kN (52,000 lb) to 42.2°C	A310-300
PW4156	249.1 kN (56,000 lb) to 30°C	A300-600
PW4158	258.0 kN (58,000 lb) to 30°C	A300-600R
PW4168	302.5 kN (68,000 lb) to 30°C	A330
PW4052	232.2 kN (52,200 lb) to 33.3°C	767-200/-200ER
PW4056	252.4 kN (56,750 lb) to 33.3°C	767-300/-300ER/747-400
PW4060	266.9 kN (60,000 lb) to 30°C	767-300ER/747-400
PW4084	373.7 kN (84,000 lb)	777
PW4460	266.9 kN (60,000 lb) to 30°C	MD-11

Ratings are S/L static, no bleed or power extraction

PRATT & WHITNEY JT9D

This was the first of the new era of large, high bypass ratio turbofans on which the design of wide-body commercial transports rests. First run was in December 1966. The first flight of the Boeing 747 was on 9 February 1969.

Current versions include:

JT9D-3A. Water injection rating of 200.8 kN (45,150 lb) to 26.7°C. Powers 747-100 and -200B.

JT9D-7. Higher thrust version with aircooled DS HP turbine blades; powers 747-200B, C, F and SR.

JT9D-7A. Aerodynamic improvements; powers 747-200 and 747SP.

JT9D-7F, -7J. Improved DS blades, 7J with shower-head cooled first stage, giving -7F T-O rating without water injection.

JT9D-7Q, -7R. Described later.

JT9D-20, -20J. D-7A and D-7J with accessory gearbox under fan case.

JT9D-59A, -70A. Fan diameter approximately 25.4 mm (one inch) larger, with re-profiled blades; LP compressor has zero (fourth) stage and is redesigned; burners recontoured, HP turbine carbon seal added, HP blades directionally solidified, and HP annulus larger. Both configured for common nacelle for 747 (-70A) or DC-10 and A300B (-59A). The **-59D** and **-70D** are higher thrust versions.

JT9D-7Q Series. As -59A and -70A but configured like -7 for 747-200 nacelle. Thrust 236-249 kN (53,000-56,000 lb).

JT9D-7R4 Series. Seven models (7R4D to 7R4H), with larger fan with wide chord blades, zero stage on LP compressor, improved combustor, H has single crystal HP turbine blades, increased diameter LP turbine, supervisory electronic fuel control and many smaller changes. 7R4D, 7R4E and 7R4E4 for Boeing 767; 7R4D1 and 7R4E1 for A310; -7R4G2 for 747; -7R4H1 for the A300B-600.

Deliveries exceed 3,265 and flight time in early 1989 was in excess of 90 million h.

The following applies to early versions, with later models in parentheses.

TYPE: Two-shaft turbofan of high bypass ratio.

FAN: Single stage, with 46 titanium blades of 4.6 aspect ratio (-7R4, 40 blades of 4.0 a.r.) and two part-span shrouds (-7R4, one shroud) dovetailed in titanium LP rotor. Mass flow 684 kg (1,509 lb)/s at 3,650 rpm (-7, 698 kg; 1,540 lb/s at 3,750 rpm; -59A, -70A, -7Q, 744 kg; 1,640 lb/s at 3,430 rpm; -7R4G/H, 769 kg; 1,695 lb/s at 3,530 rpm). Pressure ratio typically 1.6 : 1. Bypass ratio: -3A, 5.17; -7, 5.15; -59A, -70A, 4.9; -7R4D, E, 5.0; -7R4G2, H1, 4.8.

LP COMPRESSOR: Three stages (JT9D-59A, -70A, -7Q, -7R4, four stages), rotating with fan. Rotor stages have 104, 132 and 130 (-7Q, -59A, -70, -7R4, 108, 120, 112, 100) dovetailed blades of titanium alloy. Core airflow typically 118 kg (260 lb)/s (all versions).

HP COMPRESSOR: Eleven stages. Rotor stages have 60, 84, 102, 100, 110, 108, 104, 94 and 100 dovetailed titanium blades and 102 and 90 nickel alloy blades. First three stator stages are variable, plus intermediate IGV stage. Max HP speed: -3A, 7,850 rpm; -7, 8,000 rpm; -7R4E4/G/H, 8,080 rpm. Overall pressure ratio: -3A, 21.5; -7, 22.2; -7Q, -59A, -70, 24.5; -7R4D, D1, 23.4; -7R4E/E1/E4, 24.2; -7R4G2, 26.3; -7R4H1, 26.7.

COMBUSTION CHAMBER: Annular, nickel alloy. Ignition by dual AC 4-joule capacitor system serving two plugs.

FUEL SYSTEM: Hydraulic control operating at up to 76 bars (1,100 lb/sq in). (-7R4 except G2 has digital electronic system to control hydromechanical control; engine is operational with or without electronic system functioning.) Water injection adds 18.1 kg (40 lb) to weight (not fitted to -7R4).

FUEL GRADE: P&W specification PWA 522.

HP TURBINE: Two stages. First has 116 aircooled blades and second has 138 solid blades (aircooled in -D7 and subsequent; -7R4, DS to G2, single crystal first and second blades and two vanes for H). Turbine inlet temperature (-3A, max T-O), typically 1,243°C (-59A, -70A, 1,350-1,370°C, -7R4 1,200-1,300°C).

LP TURBINE: Four stages. Solid nickel alloy blades held in fir tree roots in discs of nickel alloy (fifth disc, iron alloy). In 1982 an improved LP turbine was introduced to -7R4 production.

REVERSER: Fan reverser comprises a translating sleeve which moves aft, causing links to close blocker doors and simultaneously pulling aft the cascade vanes. Primary (core) reverser, uses fixed cascades uncovered by aft movement of translating sleeves. No primary reverser on -59A, -70A, -7Q or -7R4.

ACCESSORY DRIVES: Main accessory gearbox driven from front of HP spool and mounted under central diffuser case (-20, -59A, -70A, under fan discharge case). Accessories include CSD (IDG on -7R4 except G2) fuel pump and control, starter, hydraulic pump, alternator and N_2 tachometer; Boeing 747 includes primary reverser motor and DC-10-40 a second hydraulic pump and fuel boost pump.

LUBRICATION SYSTEM: Pressure feed through fuel/oil cooler to four main bearings and return to 18.8-37.6 litre (5-10 US gallon; 4.16-8.32 Imp gallon) tank.

OIL GRADE: PWA 521C.

STARTING: Pneumatic, by HamStan PS 700 or AiResearch ATS100-384 (DC-10, PS 700 only).

DIMENSIONS:
JT9D-3A, -7, -7A, -7F, -7J, -20:
Diameter	2,427 mm (95.56 in)
Length (flange to flange)	3,255 mm (128.15 in)

JT9D-59A, -70A, -7Q:
Diameter	2,464 mm (97.0 in)
Length	3,358 mm (132.2 in)

JT9D-7R4D to H:
Diameter	2,463 mm (96.98 in)
Length	3,371 mm (132.7 in)

WEIGHT, DRY:
Guaranteed, including standard equipment:
JT9D-3A	3,905 kg (8,608 lb)
JT9D-7, -7A, -7F, -7J	4,014 kg (8,850 lb)
JT9D-20	3,833 kg (8,450 lb)
JTRD-20J	3,883 kg (8,560 lb)
JT9D-59A	4,146 kg (9,140 lb)
JT9D-70A	4,153 kg (9,155 lb)
JT9D-7Q	4,216 kg (9,295 lb)
JT9D-7R4D, E, E4	4,039 kg (8,905 lb)
JT9D-7R4D1, E1	4,029 kg (8,885 lb)
JT9D-7R4G2	4,143 kg (9,135 lb)
JT9D-7R4H1	4,029 kg (8,885 lb)

PERFORMANCE RATINGS (ideal nozzle):
T-O, dry:
JT9D-3A	193.9 kN (43,600 lb st) to 26.7°C
JT9D-7	202.8 kN (45,600 lb st) to 26.7°C
JT9D-7A	205.7 kN (46,250 lb st) to 26.7°C
JT9D-7F	213.5 kN (48,000 lb st) to 26.7°C
JT9D-7J, -20J	222.4 kN (50,000 lb st) to 30°C

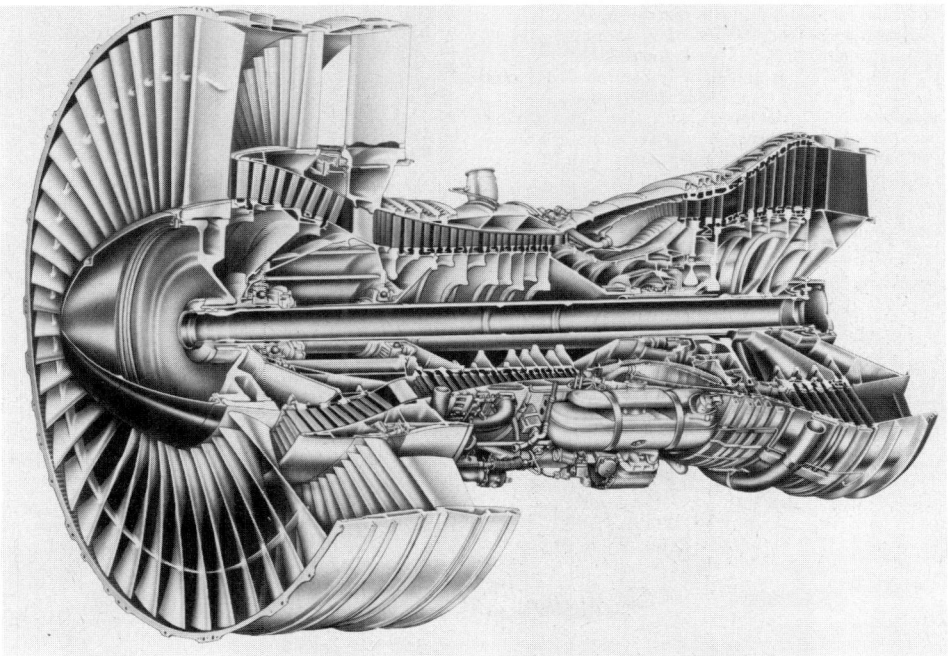

Cutaway drawing of Pratt & Whitney JT9D-7R4 two-shaft turbofan

JT9D-20	206.0 kN (46,300 lb st) to 28.9°C
JT9D-59A, -70A, -7Q	
	236.0 kN (53,000 lb st) to 30°C
JT9D-7R4D, D1	213.5 kN (48,000 lb st) to 33°C
JT9D-7R4E, E1	222.4 kN (50,000 lb st) to 33°C
JT9D-7R4E4	222.4 kN (50,000 lb st) to 45.6°C
JT9D-7R4G2	243.4 kN (54,750 lb st) to 30°C
JT9D-7R4H1	249.0 kN (56,000 lb st) to 30°C

T-O, wet:

JT9D-3A	200.8 kN (45,150 lb st) to 26.7°C
JT9D-7	210.0 kN (47,200 lb st) to 30°C
JT9D-7A	212.4 kN (47,750 lb st) to 30°C
JT9D-7F	222.4 kN (50,000 lb st) to 30°C
JT9D-20	220.0 kN (49,400 lb st) to 30°C

Max cruise, 10,670 m (35,000 ft) at Mach 0.85:

JT9D-3A, -7	45.4 kN (10,200 lb)
JT9D-7A	48.2 kN (10,830 lb)
JT9D-7F, -7J	49.2 kN (11,050 lb)
JT9D-20, -20J	47.5 kN (10,680 lb)
JT9D-59A, -70A, -7Q	53.2 kN (11,950 lb)
JT9D-7R4D, D1	50.0 kN (11,250 lb)
JT9D-7R4E, E1	52.0 kN (11,700 lb)
JT9D-7R4G2, H1	54.5 kN (12,250 lb)

SPECIFIC FUEL CONSUMPTION (ideal nozzle):
Max cruise, ISA + 10°C, Mach 0.85 at 10,670 m
(35,000 ft):

JT9D-3A	17.67 mg/Ns (0.624 lb/h/lb)
JT9D-7	17.55 mg/Ns (0.620 lb/h/lb)
JT9D-7A	17.69 mg/Ns (0.625 lb/h/lb)
JT9D-7F, -7Q, -59A, -70A	
	17.87 mg/Ns (0.631 lb/h/lb)
JT9D-20, -20J	17.67 mg/Ns (0.624 lb/h/lb)
JT9D-7R4D, D1	17.42 mg/Ns (0.615 lb/h/lb)
JT9D-7R4E, E1	17.55 mg/Ns (0.620 lb/h/lb)
JT9D-7R4G2	18.10 mg/Ns (0.639 lb/h/lb)
JT9D-7R4H1	17.79 mg/Ns (0.628 lb/h/lb)

PRATT & WHITNEY PW2000
US military designation: F117

The PW2000 is a third generation turbofan upon which major changes have been made since 1972. In mid-1980 it was scaled up to be compatible with the Boeing 757-200, at 170.1 kN (38,250 lb st). The first model was given the designation **PW2037**, the last two digits denoting thrust in thousands of pounds. The first engine test run took place in December 1981. FAA certification was achieved in December 1983, and the first flight was made on the prototype 757 on 14 March 1984.

Companies participating are MTU of Germany and Fiat of Italy. Pratt & Whitney bears 80.8 per cent of the programme, MTU 11.2 per cent and Fiat 4 per cent. A collaboration agreement between these companies was signed in July 1977. In 1987 Volvo of Sweden joined the programme as a 4 per cent manufacturing partner.

Current applications are in versions of the Boeing 757 and McDonnell Douglas C-17A. The PW2037-powered 757 was certificated on 25 October 1984 and entered revenue service on 1 December. An uprated engine, the **PW2040**, was certificated in January 1987 and entered service in September 1987 powering the 757PF. The C-17A will be powered by four **F117-PW-100** engines similar to the PW2040. The F117 was certificated in December 1988.

The PW2000 engine family is expected to consist ultimately of a series of models which will span a take-off thrust range of 151.2 to 195.7 kN (34,000 to 44,000 lb).

TYPE: Two-shaft turbofan of high bypass ratio.
FAN: Single-stage. Titanium forged hub, with 36 inserted titanium alloy blades with part-span shrouds. Tip diameter 1,994 mm (78.5 in). Mass flow 608 kg (1,340 lb)/s. Pressure ratio 1.7. Bypass ratio 6.0.
LP COMPRESSOR: Four stages, with controlled diffusion aerofoils with thick leading- and trailing-edges.
HP COMPRESSOR: Twelve stages, with controlled diffusion aerofoils. Variable vanes on first five stages and active clearance control on last eight stages. Overall cruise pressure ratio 31.8.

COMBUSTION CHAMBER: Annular, with flame tube fabricated in nickel alloy. Single-pipe fuel nozzles.
HP TURBINE: Two stages with aircooled blades cast as single crystals in PW 1480 alloy. Rotors with active clearance control. Both discs of PW1100 nickel based powder.
LP TURBINE: Five stages, with active clearance control.
CONTROL SYSTEM: Full authority digital electronic with two redundant computers.
DIMENSIONS:

Length	3,729 mm (146.8 in)
Fan case diameter	2,154 mm (84.8 in)

WEIGHT, DRY:

PW2000	3,311 kg (7,300 lb)
F117	3,220 kg (7,100 lb)

PERFORMANCE RATING (T-O, S/L):

PW2037	170.1 kN (38,250 lb st)
PW2040	185.5 kN (41,700 lb st)

SPECIFIC FUEL CONSUMPTION (ideal nozzle, cruise at Mach 0.8 at 10,670 m; 35,000 ft): 15.95 mg/Ns (0.563 lb/h/lb)

PRATT & WHITNEY JTF10A
US military designation: TF30

Development of this military engine began in 1958. It was chosen as the power plant for the F-111 and A-7A.

A third application is the F-14A Tomcat, powered by the **TF30-P-414**, since converted to **-414A** standard which significantly improves engine stability and extends overhaul interval to 2,400 h.

The following description refers to the P-414A:

TYPE: Two-shaft turbofan.
FAN: Three stages. Rotor and stator and casings all of titanium, except for steel containment case.
LP COMPRESSOR: Six stages integral with fan. Titanium, except steel stator blades.
HP COMPRESSOR: Seven stages, mainly nickel alloy.
COMBUSTION CHAMBER: Can-annular, with eight Hastelloy combustors, each with four dual-orifice burners.

FUEL SYSTEM: HP system (above 69 bars; 1,000 lb/sq in) with conventional hydromechanical control and electronic turbine temperature limiter.
FUEL GRADES: JP-4, JP-5, JP-8.
HP TURBINE: Single stage, with 40 aircooled nozzle guide vanes (stators) of single-crystal nickel based material and aircooled rotor blades of nickel-based alloy.
LP TURBINE: Three stages of nickel based alloys.
AFTERBURNER: Double wall outer duct and inner liner carrying five-zone combustion system. Ignition by auxiliary squirt, coupled with main squirt in No. 4 burner can which produces hot streak through turbine. Max gas temperature 1,677°C.
NOZZLE: Primary nozzle has six hinged segments actuated by fuel rams. Ejector nozzle has 18 iris segments.
ACCESSORY DRIVES: Main gearbox under compressor, driven by bevel shaft from HP spool.
LUBRICATION SYSTEM: Self contained dry sump system.
OIL GRADE: MIL-L-7808, MIL-L-23699.
STARTING: Air turbine starter on left forward drive pad.
DIMENSIONS:

Max diameter	1,293 mm (50.9 in)
Length overall	5,987 mm (235.7 in)

WEIGHT, DRY: 1,905 kg (4,201 lb)
PERFORMANCE RATING:
T-O, S/L 93 kN (20,900 lb st)
SPECIFIC FUEL CONSUMPTION (T-O):
78.75 mg/Ns (2.78 lb/h/lb st)

PRATT & WHITNEY F100

The F100 is a military turbofan with afterburner for supersonic applications. In February 1970 the decision was taken to use the JTF22 core as the basis for the engine to power the F-15 Eagle.

F100-PW-100. Initial production version for F-15A and B. More than 6 million hours flown by 1991.

F100-PW-200. Initial production engine for F-16A and B. Backup fuel control for single-engine application.

Pratt & Whitney PW2000 series two-shaft turbofan

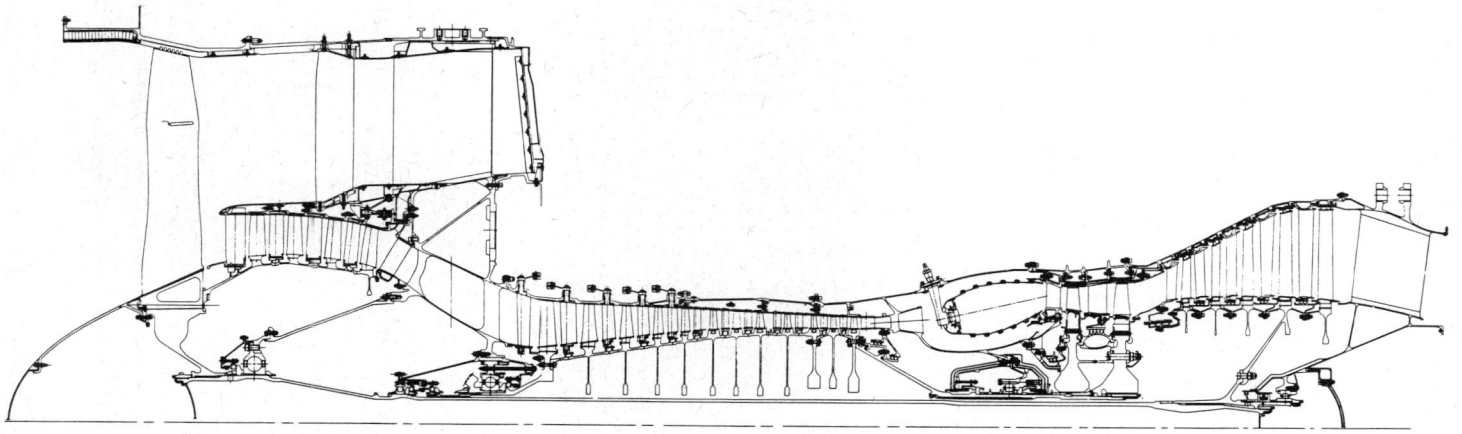

Longitudinal section of Pratt & Whitney PW2000 two-shaft turbofan

Cutaway drawing of Pratt & Whitney F100-PW-229 two-shaft augmented turbofan

Cutaway drawing of Pratt & Whitney F100-PW-220 two-shaft augmented turbofan

F100-PW-220. Qualified mid-1985 for F-15C and D and F-16C and D. Digital control, gear type main fuel pump and increased-life core. Intended to provide 4,000-cycle (about seven-year) inspection interval.

F100-PW-220E. Upgrade packages for PW-100 and -200 to provide capability and life equivalent to -220.

F100-PW-229. Previously known as the PW1129, this was designed as an IPE (Increased-Performance Engine) for the F-15 and F-16. It features components of the F100-PW-220 and of the PW1128 (see 1984-85 *Jane's*). Major improvements include a new compressor and a Float-wall combustor. Thrusts in excess of the figure given below have been demonstrated. The PW-229 entered production in 1989, Field Service Evaluations in both fighters took place in 1990, and the engine was to become operational in August 1991.

F100-PW-200P. This configuration is being developed to incorporate PW-229 technology into PW-220 and PW-220E engines, to improve safety, reliability and performance. The upgrade is modular and is claimed to increased capability at modest cost. The upgraded engines can power any F-15 or F-16. Non-augmented versions are being evaluated for other applications.

Except where otherwise indicated the following refers to the PW-100:

TYPE: Two-shaft turbofan with afterburner.

FAN: Three stages. Fan blades have part-span shrouds. Entry diameter 884 mm (34.8 in). Bypass ratio 0.6.

COMPRESSOR: Ten-stage axial, on HP shaft. First three stages have variable stators. Pressure ratio 8. Overall pressure ratio 25.

COMBUSTION CHAMBER: Annular. Cobalt based alloy with film cooling. Air blast fuel nozzles. Capacitor-discharge ignition.

HP TURBINE: Two stages. Discs forged IN-100. Blades and vanes directionally solidified Mar M200/Hf alloy with aluminide coating; first rotor transpiration convectively cooled, second with HP bleed only. Max gas temperature 1,399°C. Maximum speed 13,450 rpm.

LP TURBINE: Two stages. Discs forged IN-100. Blades, uncooled, cast in IN-100 with aluminide coating. Max speed 10,400 rpm.

AFTERBURNER: Five spray rings in flow from core and two downstream in bypass airflow. Flameholder downstream with high energy ignition to give modulated light-up.

NOZZLE: Multi-flap balanced beam articulated nozzle.

CONTROL SYSTEM: (Dash-100, -200) unified hydromechanical fuel and nozzle area control, with electronic supervisory control. Dash-220, digital electronic control.

DIMENSIONS:

Overall diameter	1,181 mm (46.5 in)
Length:	
F100-PW-100, excl bullet	4,855 mm (191.2 in)
F100-PW-220, -229, -200P	5,280 mm (208 in)

WEIGHT, DRY:

F100-PW-100	1,386 kg (3,055 lb)
F100-PW-200	1,410 kg (3,108 lb)
F100-PW-220	1,459 kg (3,218 lb)
F100-PW-229	1,681 kg (3,705 lb)
F100-PW-200P	1,526 kg (3,365 lb)

PERFORMANCE RATINGS (S/L, ISA):

Intermediate:

F100-PW-100	65.2 kN (14,670 lb st)
F100-PW-220	64.9 kN (14,590 lb st)
F100-PW-229	79.2 kN (17,800 lb st)
F100-PW-200P	74.3 kN (16,700 lb st)

Max T-O, augmented:

F100-PW-100	106.0 kN (23,830 lb st)
F100-PW-220	105.7 kN (23,770 lb st)
F100-PW-229	129.4 kN (29,100 lb st)
F100-PW-200P	120.1 kN (27,000 lb st)

SPECIFIC FUEL CONSUMPTION:

Intermediate:

F100-PW-229	20.96 mg/Ns (0.74 lb/h/lb st)

Max T-O:

F100-PW-229	58.07 mg/Ns (2.05 lb/h/lb st)
F100-PW-200P	58.35 mg/Ns (2.06 lb/h/lb st)

PRATT & WHITNEY PW1120

The PW1120 is a turbojet derivative of the F100. Its development was initiated in June 1980. It retains the F100 core module, gearbox, fuel pump and forward ducts, as well as the F100 digital electronic control, with only minor modifications.

Unique PW1120 components include a wide chord LP compressor, single-stage uncooled LP turbine, simplified single stream augmentor, and a lightweight convergent/divergent nozzle. Mass flow is 80.9 kg (178 lb)/s and pressure ratio 26.8.

Full scale testing was initiated in June 1982, and the engine completed flight clearance testing in August 1984. The PW1120 was selected to power the Israeli Lavi, later cancelled. Flight demonstration in an F-4 began on 30 July 1986. The engine is a candidate for F-4 re-engining as well as for other fighter projects.

A cutaway drawing appeared in the 1990-91 *Jane's*.

DIMENSIONS:

Max diameter	1,021 mm (40.2 in)
Length	4,110 mm (161.8 in)

WEIGHT, DRY:

	1,292 kg (2,848 lb)

Pratt & Whitney F119, with 2D (two-dimensional) nozzle and fairing for F-22A

PERFORMANCE RATINGS (S/L, ISA):

Max T-O	91.7 kN (20,620 lb st)
Intermediate	60.3 kN (13,550 lb st)

SPECIFIC FUEL CONSUMPTION:

Maximum	52.65 mg/Ns (1.86 lb/h/lb)
Intermediate	22.7 mg/Ns (0.8 lb/h/lb)

PRATT & WHITNEY PW5000
US military designation: F119

This advanced augmented turbofan was selected by the US Air Force over the rival General Electric F120 to power the Lockheed F-22A Advanced Tactical Fighter in April 1991. Basic requirements were the simplest and most robust design for maximum reliability and maintainability, supercruise (supersonic persistence) capability without afterburner and a 2D (two-dimensional) nozzle incorporating limited thrust vectoring. The rival companies began formal development of their competing designs in 1983. From the outset Pratt & Whitney chose to offer a mature low-risk engine, even if in some respects it might appear to be less advanced than the rival F120. This philosophy was followed when, as the result of weight growth in the competing ATF aircraft, the thrust requirements were upgraded in early 1988. By this time the PW5000 design had long been fixed and the first YF119 demonstrator was about to run. The decision was taken not to change the engine, but to meet the extra thrust requirement by a subsequent slight increase in fan diameter, leaving the rest of the engine unaltered.

Bench testing began in December 1988. In the Summer of 1990, F119 engines made 65 flights totalling 153 h, with no stalls or shutdowns. By April 1991, engines on ground test had run over 3,000 h, including 1,500 with the 2D nozzle. Production engines are due for delivery from 1997, the full programme total exceeding 1,500 engines priced at over $12 billion.

TYPE: Two-shaft low-bypass ratio augmented turbofan.

FAN: Three stages of snubberless wide-chord blades.

COMPRESSOR: Multi-stage spool with integrally bladed rotors turning in opposition to the fan.

COMBUSTION CHAMBER: High-intensity short annular with smokeless burning.

TURBINES: Single-stage contra-rotating HP and LP turbines.

CASING: Integrally stiffened bypass duct and inner compressor casing both split for easy maintenance access.

AUGMENTOR: Single spray ring for combustion downstream of both bypass duct and core.

NOZZLE: Two-dimensional (rectangular) with external flaps to meet aircraft aerodynamic and LO (low observables) requirements and internal flaps to match engine operating parameters. Hydraulic control to ±20°. No reversing capability.

ACCESSORIES: Grouped for immediate access from below. All LRUs mounted one-deep. FADEC control.

DIMENSIONS: Generally similar to PW1129

WEIGHT: Lighter than PW1120

PERFORMANCE RATING (S/L):   155.6 kN (35,000 lb st) class

PW-ALLISON

MEMBER COMPANIES:

Allison Gas Turbine Division, GMC
Indianapolis, Indiana 46206

Pratt & Whitney, UTC
East Hartford, Connecticut 06108

United Technologies' Pratt & Whitney and General Motors' Allison Gas Turbine Division formed a joint partnership in 1986 to develop propfan propulsion technology.

PW-ALLISON MODEL 578-DX

PW-Allison developed the Model 578-DX geared counter-rotation propfan propulsion system for testing and technology demonstrations. The initial flight test demonstrator is rated at 88.97 kN (20,000 lb st). This incorporates a three-stage LP compressor, modified Allison 571 core engine, and an advanced technology 9,698 kW (13,000 shp) differential planetary gear system. The latter drives two 3.53 m (11 ft 7 in) six-blade Hamilton Standard propfans. A modified PW-HamStan full-authority digital electronic engine control regulates fuel flow, variable compressor stators and propfan blade angles. The 578-DX made its first flight on an MD-80 on 13 April 1989, and successfully completed the programme in the same quarter of 1989.

PW-Allison propfan installed on MD-80 aircraft

ROCKETDYNE
ROCKETDYNE DIVISION OF ROCKWELL INTERNATIONAL

6633 Canoga Avenue, Canoga Park, California 91303
Telephone: 1 (818) 710 6300
Fax: 1 (818) 710 2866
Telex: 698478
PRESIDENT: R. D. Paster

Rocketdyne is devoted primarily to rocket engines for the US Air Force and the National Aeronautics and Space Administration. It was established as a separate division in November 1955. Rocketdyne liquid propellant engines have powered more than three-quarters of all large US space vehicle stages.

ROCKETDYNE SSME

On 13 July 1971 Rocketdyne was selected by NASA to develop the main engine for the Shuttle Orbiter. Three of these engines provide a total of 6,523 kN (1,466,400 lb) vacuum thrust, and power the vehicle to near orbit.

The SSME (Space Shuttle Main Engine) was designed for high reliability, reusability, multiple re-start capability and low cost. It is designed for 7½ h of burn time, or 55 flights.

The design combines the merits of high pressure operation, an optimum bell nozzle, and a regeneratively cooled thrust chamber, capable of 11° gimballing. The chamber wall is cooled to 567°C, although the combustion temperature is about 3,300°C. No propellants are wasted in the cooling process. The combustion chamber wall is made of slotted metal, rather than tubes, using Rocketdyne developed NARloy-Z, copper alloy.

The SSME is controlled by a unique system incorporating dual redundant digital computers. This system monitors engine parameters such as pressure and flow rate, and the engine is adjusted automatically to operate at the required thrust and mixture ratio. The system also develops a record of engine operating history for maintenance purposes.

Flight certification was achieved in December 1980. Another cycle in the FPL (full power level) certification programme was completed in April 1983. Certification required four test series of 5,000 s each, involving engine power levels normally at 104 per cent. This testing provided flight readiness certification for engine sets for the *Challenger*, *Columbia*, *Discovery* and *Atlantis* orbiters.

The Shuttle programme began its operational phase with the STS-5 launch of the *Columbia* on 11 November 1982. On 4 April 1983 a second vehicle, *Challenger*, powered by SSMEs rated at 104 per cent thrust, was launched on STS-6. The third Orbiter, *Discovery*, was launched on 30 August 1984. A total of 24 launches, all successful, had been accomplished prior to the loss of *Challenger* on 28 January 1986. Excellent flight-to-flight performance repeatability had been achieved.

Testing is being continued to extend the life of the HP turbomachinery, increase performance margin by reducing flow losses, and investigate other modifications that could allow uprating or life extension.

COMBUSTION CHAMBER: Channel wall construction with regenerative cooling by the hydrogen fuel. Concentric element injector.

TURBOPUMPS: Two low pressure pumps boost the inlet pressures for two high pressure pumps. Dual pre-burners provide turbine drive gases to power the high-pressure pumps. Hydrogen pump discharge pressure is 485.4 bars (6,445 lb/sq in) at 35,080 rpm; it develops 51,528 kW (69,100 hp).

CONTROLLER: Honeywell digital computer provides closed loop control, in addition to data processing and signal conditioning for control, checkout, monitoring engine status, and maintenance data acquisition.

CONTROLS: Hydraulic actuation. Dual redundant self-monitoring servo actuators respond to signals from the controller to position the ball valves. A pneumatic system provides backup for engine cut-off.

MAINTENANCE: Airline type maintenance procedure for on-the-vehicle servicing. Planned life between overhauls 55 flights.

DIMENSIONS:

Length	4,242 mm (167 in)
Diameter at nozzle exit	2,388 mm (94 in)

SSME undergoing FPL test

PERFORMANCE:

S/L thrust (one engine, 104%)	1,751.7 kN (393,800 lb)
Vacuum thrust	2,174.3 kN (488,800 lb)
Specific impulse	453 s
Chamber pressure	215.5 bars (3,126 lb/sq in)
Throttling ratio	1.67
Expansion ratio	77.5

ROTORWAY

ROTORWAY AIRCRAFT INC

300 South 25th Avenue, Phoenix, Arizona 85009
Telephone: 1 (602) 278 1199
Fax: 1 (602) 278 5887
Telex: 683 5059

RotorWay Aircraft has been producing its own liquid-cooled aircraft power plants since 1974, to power RotorWay helicopters.

ROTORWAY RW152

TYPE: Horizontally opposed, water-cooled, four-cylinder, four-stroke piston engine. Crankshaft vertical.

CYLINDERS: Offset left and right for plain connecting rods side by side. Capacity 2.66 litres (162 cu in). Compression ratio 9.6.

INDUCTION: Single two-barrel downdraught carburettor with integral manifold heating.

IGNITION: Dual direct-fire electronic, with redundant coils, sensors, timing processors and plugs.

FUEL GRADE: Autogas 92 octane or Avgas 100LL.

WEIGHT, DRY (with starter): 77.1 kg (170 lb)

PERFORMANCE RATING: 113 kW (152 hp) at 4,400 rpm

RotorWay RW152 four-cylinder helicopter engine

SOLOY

SOLOY CORPORATION

450 Pat Kennedy Way SW, Olympia, Washington 98502
Telephone: 1 (206) 754 7000
Fax: 1 (206) 943 7659
PRESIDENT: Joe I. Soloy

Further details can be found in the US Aircraft section.

SOLOY TURBINE PAC

The Soloy Turbine Pac is an FAA Supplemental Type Certificate approved turboprop engine assembly, rated at 312 kW (418 shp) with a propeller rpm range of 1,450 to 1,810. Its Allison 250-C20S turboshaft engine is combined with Soloy's propeller gearbox and other components to produce a turboprop configured for single-engined aircraft. Its high thrust line and rear inlet suit it particularly to bush aircraft. The engine assembly includes propeller governing and overspeed systems, and a self-contained lubrication system. Customised models are available in pusher configuration and can utilise the 485 kW (650 shp) Allison 250-C30 engine for tractor or pusher configurations.

SOLOY DUAL PAC INC

Address as Soloy Corporation

SOLOY DUAL PAC

The first production model of the Soloy Dual Pac multi-engine system utilises two Allison 250-C30S turboshaft engines, each rated at 522 kW (700 shp). The Soloy combining gearbox is rated at 1,119 kW (1,500 shp) to accommodate possible future power increases for the Allison engine. The Dual Pac's redundancy, separation, and isolation of engine and drive train systems allows it to satisfy FAA requirements for designation as a twin engine, and Dual Pac powered aircraft to be defined as multi-engined. Patented free-wheeling units at the final stage drive train provide automatic disengagement in the event of an engine shutdown, with no adverse effect on aircraft drag or thrust symmetry.

The Dual Pac is designed for tractor or pusher configuration, and is planned for use in both single-propeller and multi-propeller aircraft.

Soloy 206 Turbine Pac free-turbine turboprop

SPP

SPORT PLANE POWER INC

We are advised that this company is no longer in business.

TCM

TELEDYNE CONTINENTAL MOTORS
(Aircraft Products)

PO Box 90, Mobile, Alabama 36601
Telephone: 1 (205) 438 3411
Fax: 1 (205) 432 2922
Telex: 505519
PRESIDENT: W. A. Boettger
DIRECTOR, PUBLIC RELATIONS: Susan Brane

TCM produces piston, rotary combustion and turboprop engines for general aviation.

CONTINENTAL O-200 SERIES

The O-200-A is a four-cylinder horizontally opposed aircooled engine. It is fitted with a single updraught carburettor, dual magnetos and starter and generator. The O-200-B is designed for pusher installation.

For other details see table.

CONTINENTAL O-360 SERIES

Newest member of this family of flat-six engines is the TSIO-360-MB, for the Mooney 252.

CONTINENTAL O-520 SERIES

These engines are basically similar to the IO-470, but with cylinders of larger bore. They are fitted with an alternator driven either by a belt or by a face gear on the crankshaft. The TSIO-520 series are turbocharged. In 1981 TCM announced a lightweight series of engines with magnesium replacing aluminium in some areas, modified camshaft and cylinder heads (with parallel valves or inclined valves of larger diameter), and a range of turbocharging options. The first production models are the TSIO-520-AE and LTSIO-520-AE for the Cessna Crusader, with initial TBO of 2,000 h. The TSIO-520BE has a top intake, dual turbos and two aftercoolers. The GTSIO-520 series are geared.

TELEDYNE CONTINENTAL VOYAGER 550

Largest of the new range of liquid-cooled engines, the Voyager 550 offers the same advantages as its smaller predecessors. The T-550 was designed for Bonanza conversions and the geared GT-550 for the Chieftain.

CONTINENTAL O-550

In 1984 this series of fuel-injected engines was introduced, similar to the IO-520 but with greater stroke. Initial applications are the Beechcraft Baron and Bonanza.

TELEDYNE CONTINENTAL TP-500

This simple turboprop was certificated in October 1988 and is now being marketed for general aviation. It first flew in a Cheyenne II on 29 September 1982. Though completely successful, the TP-500 is now awaiting a viable customer programme.

Teledyne Continental TSIO-360-MB six-cylinder air-cooled engine

Teledyne Continental IO-550 six-cylinder air-cooled engine

Teledyne Continental Voyager T-550 six-cylinder liquid-cooled engine

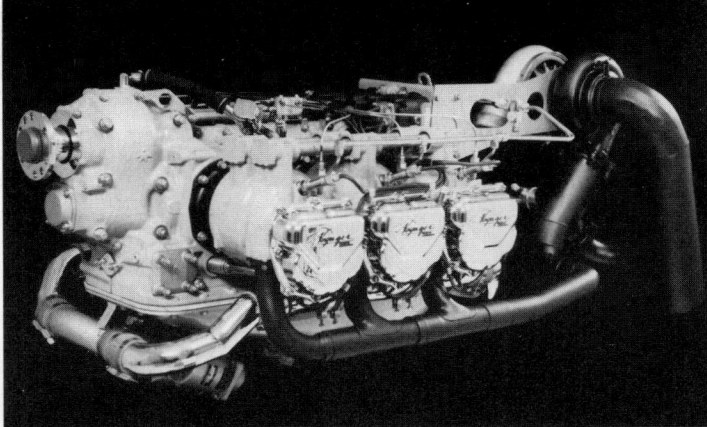

Teledyne Continental Voyager GT-550 six-cylinder liquid-cooled engine

COMPRESSOR: Single centrifugal, stainless steel. Airflow 1.95 kg (4.3 lb)/s and pressure ratio 8 at 50,000 rpm.

COMBUSTION CHAMBER: Folded annular, reverse flow, ten burners.

TURBINE: Two-stage axial. Max inlet temperature 1,071°C. Stud/nut attachment.

FUEL SYSTEM: Hydromechanical with supervisory electronic control. Grade Jet A, A-1, B, JP-4.

PROPELLER DRIVE: Two-stage coupled planetary giving 2,014 rpm output. Modular design in cast casings with integral torquemeter.

ACCESSORY DRIVES: Two reduction gearcases drive fuel control, propeller governor, starter generator and tachometer generator. Optional belt drive for freon compressor or secondary alternator.

DIMENSIONS:
Length	1,325 mm (52.18 in)
Width	592 mm (23.31 in)
Height	541 mm (21.30 in)

WEIGHT, DRY: 152 kg (336 lb)

PERFORMANCE RATINGS (ISA):
T-O, S/L	358 kW (480 shp)
T-O, 3,050 m (10,000 ft)	261 kW (350 shp)
Cruise 97% at 4,575 m (15,000 ft)	216 kW (290 shp)
Cruise 97%, altitude limit 7,620 m (25,000 ft)	149 kW (200 shp)

FUEL FLOW (uninstalled, no power extraction):
T-O, S/L   147 kg (325 lb)/h

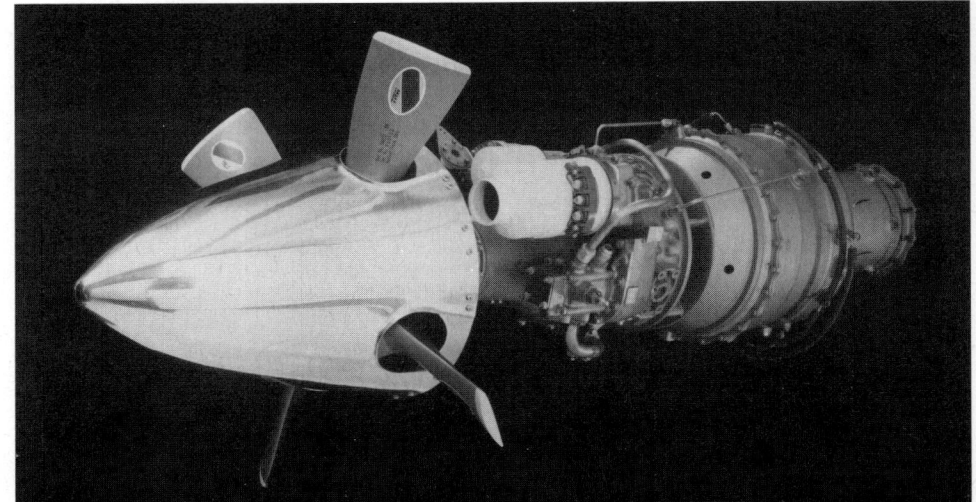

Teledyne Continental TP-500 turboprop (with cropped-blade display propeller)

REPRESENTATIVE TCM HORIZONTALLY OPPOSED ENGINES

Engine Model	No. of Cylinders	Bore and Stroke mm (in)	Capacity litres (cu in)	Power Ratings kW (hp) at rpm		Comp. Ratio	Dry Weight* kg (lb)	Dimensions			Octane Rating
				Take-off	M.E.T.O.			Length mm (in)	Width mm (in)	Height mm (in)	
O-200-A	4	103.2 × 98.4 (4¹/₁₆ × 3⁷/₈)	3.28 (201)	74.5 (100) at 2,750	74.5 (100) at 2,750	7.0	99.8 (220)	725 (28.53)	802 (31.56)	589 (23.18)	80/87
IO-360-ES	6	112.7 × 98.4 (4⁷/₁₆ × 3⁷/₈)	5.9 (360)	157 (210) at 2,800	157 (210) at 2,800	8.5	158.8 (350)	923 (36.32)	839 (33.05)	598 (23.52)	100/ 100LL
IO-360-KB	6	112.7 × 98.4 (4⁷/₁₆ × 3⁷/₈)	5.9 (360)	145.5 (195) at 2,600	145.5 (195) at 2,600	8.5	148.3 (327)	864 (34.03)	841 (33.11)	781 (30.74)	100/130
TSIO-360-GB-C, D	6	112.7 × 98.4 (4⁷/₁₆ × 3⁷/₈)	5.9 (360)	168 (225) at 2,800	168 (225) at 2,800	7.5	136 (300)	910† (35.84)	838 (33.03)	603 (23.75)	100/130
LTSIO-360-EB TSIO-360-FB	6	112.7 × 98.4 (4⁷/₁₆ × 3⁷/₈)	5.9 (360)	149 (200) at 2,575	149 (200) at 2,575	7.5	175 (385)	1,437 (56.58)	795 (31.30)	671 (26.44)	100/130
TSIO-360-GB, LB	6	112.7 × 98.4 (4⁷/₁₆ × 3⁷/₈)	5.9 (360)	156.5 (210) at 2,700	156.5 (210) at 2,700	7.5	175 (386)	902 (35.52)	795 (31.30)	699 (27.53)	100/130
LTSIO-360-KB	6	112.7 × 98.4 (4⁷/₁₆ × 3⁷/₈)	5.9 (360)	164 (220) at 2,800	164 (220) at 2,800	7.5	178 (392)	1,437 (56.58)	795 (31.30)	672 (26.44)	100/130
TSIO-360-MB	6	112.7 × 98.4 (4⁷/₁₆ × 3⁷/₈)	5.9 (360)	156.5 (210) at 2,700	156.5 (210) at 2,700	7.5	186.9 (412)	1,087 (42.78)	873 (34.37)	834 (32.82)	100LL
IO-520-D	6	133 × 101.6 (5¼ × 4)	8.5 (520)	224 (300) at 2,850	212.5 (285) at 2,700	8.5	208.2 (459)	949 (37.36)	901 (35.46)	604 (23.79)	100/130
IO-520-L	6	133 × 101.6 (5¼ × 4)	8.5 (520)	224 (300) at 2,850	212.5 (285) at 2,700	8.5	211.7 (466.7)	1,039 (40.91)	852 (33.56)	591 (23.25)	100/130
IO-520-M, -MB	6	133 × 101.6 (5¼ × 4)	8.5 (520)	212.5 (285) at 2,700	212.5 (285) at 2,700	8.5	188 (415)	1,189 (46.80)	852 (33.56)	518 (20.41)	100/130
TSIO-520-AF	6	133 × 101.6 (5¼ × 4)	8.5 (520)	231 (210) at 2,700	212.5 (285) at 2,600	7.5	197.8 (436.15)	1,039 (40.91)	852 (33.56)	598 (23.54)	100/130
TSIO-520-B, -BB	6	133 × 101.6 (5¼ × 4)	8.5 (520)	213 (285) at 2,700	213 (285) at 2,700	7.5	219 (483)	1,490 (58.67)	852 (33.56)	516 (20.32)	100/130
TSIO-520-BE	6	133 × 101.6 (5¼ × 4)	8.5 (520)	231 (310) at 2,600	231 (310) at 2,600	7.5	?	1,083 (42.64)	1,079 (42.5)	851 (33.5)	100LL

*With accessories; †Not including turbocharger;

REPRESENTATIVE TCM HORIZONTALLY OPPOSED ENGINES

Engine Model	No. of Cylinders	Bore and Stroke mm (in)	Capacity litres (cu in)	Power Ratings kW (hp) at rpm Take-off	Power Ratings kW (hp) at rpm M.E.T.O.	Comp. Ratio	Dry Weight* kg (lb)	Length mm (in)	Width mm (in)	Height mm (in)	Octane Rating
TSIO-520-CE	6	133 × 101.6 (5¼ × 4)	8.5 (520)	242.5 (325) at 2,700	242.5 (325) at 2,700	7.5	237 (527)	1,039 (40.91)	852 (33.56)	597 (23.54)	100LL
TSIO-520-C	6	133 × 101.6 (5¼ × 4)	8.5 (520)	212.5 (285) at 2,700	212.5(285) at 2,700	7.5	208 (458)	1,040† (40.91)	852 (33.56)	509 (20.04)	100/130
TSIO-520-E, -EB	6	133 × 101.6 (5¼ × 4)	8.5 (520)	224 (300) at 2,700	224 (300) at 2,700	7.5	219 (483)	1,010† (39.75)	852 (33.56)	527 (20.74)	100/130
TSIO-520-J, N, -JB, -NB	6	133 × 101.6 (5¼ × 4)	8.5 (520)	231 (310) at 2,700	231 (310) at 2,700	7.5	221.3 (487.8)	997 (39.25)	852 (33.56)	516 (20.32)	100/130
TSIO-520-L, -LB	6	133 × 101.6 (5¼ × 4)	8.5 (520)	231 (310) at 2,700	231 (310) at 2,700	7.5	244.5 (539)	1,286 (50.62)	852 (33.56)	508 (20.02)	100/130
TSIO-520-M, P, R	6	133 × 101.6 (5¼ × 4)	8.5 (520)	231 (310) at 2,700	212.5 (285) at 2,600	7.5	198 (436)	1,040† (40.91)	852 (33.56)	598 (23.54)	100/130
TSIO-520-T	6	133 × 101.6 (5¼ × 4)	8.5 (520)	231 (310) at 2,700	231 (310) at 2,700	7.5	193.4 (426.3)	970 (38.2)	852 (33.56)	819 (32.26)	100/130
TSIO-520-UB	6	133 × 101.6 (5¼ × 4)	8.5 (520)	224 (300) at 2,700	224 (300) at 2,700	7.5	191.6 (422.5)	1,136 (44.5)	852 (33.56)	733 (28.86)	100/130
TSIO-520-VB	6	133 × 101.6 (5¼ × 4)	8.5 (520)	242.5 (325) at 2,700	242.5 (325) at 2,700	7.5	207.2 (456.7)	997 (39.25)	852 (33.56)	518 (20.41)	100/130
TSIO-520-WB	6	133 × 101.6 (5¼ × 4)	8.5 (520)	242.5 (325) at 2,700	242.5 (325) at 2,700	7.5	188.75 (416.1)	1,286 (50.62)	852 (33.56)	509 (20.02)	100/130
GTSIO-520-D, H	6	133 × 101.6 (5¼ × 4)	8.5 (520)	280 (375) at 3,400	280 (375) at 3,400	7.5	250 (550.4)	1,081 (42.56)	880 (34.04)	680 (26.78)	100/130
GTSIO-520-F, K	6	133 × 101.6 (5¼ × 4)	8.5 (520)	324 (435) at 3,400	324 (435) at 3,400	7.5	272.0 (600)	1,426 (56.12)	880 (34.04)	664 (26.15)	100/130
GTSIO-520-L, M, N	6	133 × 101.6 (5¼ × 4)	8.5 (520)	280 (375) at 3,350	280 (375) at 3,350	7.5	228 (502)‡	1,114 (43.87)	880 (34.04)	671 (26.41)	100/130
LTSIO-520-AE	6	133 × 101.6 (5¼ × 4)	8.5 (520)	186.5 (250) at 2,400	186.5 (250) at 2,400	8.5	172.2 (379.6)	967 (38.07)	846 (33.29)	543 (21.38)	100/130
Voyager 550	6	133 × 108 (5¼ × 4¼)	9.0 (550)	261 (350) at 2,700	261 (350) at 2,700	7.5	228.6 (504)				100/ 100LL
Voyager T-550	6	133 × 108 (5¼ × 4¼)	9.0 (550)	224 (300) at 2,500	224 (300) at 2,500	7.5	204 (450)				100LL
Voyager GT-550	6	133 × 108 (5¼ × 4¼)	9.0 (550)	298 (400)	298 (400)	7.5	249.5 (550)				100LL
IO-550-B	6	133 × 108 (5¼ × 4¼)	9.0 (550)	224 (300) at 2,700	224 (300) at 2,700	8.5	207.9 (462)	964 (37.97)	852 (33.56)	694 (27.32)	100LL
IO-550-C, E	6	133 × 108 (5¼ × 4¼)	9.0 (550)	224 (300) at 2,700	224 (300) at 2,700	8.5	196.4 (433)	1,100.1 (43.31)	852 (33.56)	502 (19.78)	100LL
IO-550-F, L	6	133 × 108 (5¼ × 4¼)	9.0 (550)	224 (300) at 2,700	224 (300) at 2,700	7.5	191.9 (423)	1,039 (40.91)	852 (33.56)	516 (20.32)	100LL
IO-550-G	6	133 × 108 (5¼ × 4¼)	9.0 (550)	209 (280) at 2,500	209 (280) at 2,500	7.5	210.9 (465)	1,189 (46.80)	852 (33.56)	518 (20.41)	100LL

*With accessories; †Not including turbocharger;
‡N weight 220 kg (486 lb)

TELEDYNE CAE

TELEDYNE CAE DIVISION OF TELEDYNE INC

1330 Laskey Road, Toledo, Ohio 43612-0971
Telephone: 1 (419) 470 3000
Fax: 1 (419) 470 3386
Telex: EASYLINK 6 288 4828
PRESIDENT: Bryan Lewis

Teledyne CAE produces small gas turbine engines for training aircraft, missiles and UAVs. See 1987-88 *Jane's* for further details.

TELEDYNE CAE 352 and 356
US military designation: J69

One version of this simple turbojet is used in manned aircraft:

J69-T-25A (Teledyne CAE Model 352-5A). Long life version; powers Cessna T-37B.

DIMENSIONS (nominal):
Length overall	899 mm (35.39 in)
Width	566 mm (22.30 in)

WEIGHT, DRY:	165 kg (364 lb)
PERFORMANCE RATINGS:	
Max T-O thrust	4.56 kN (1,025 lb) at 21,730 rpm
SPECIFIC FUEL CONSUMPTION (max T-O):	
	32.30 mg/Ns (1.14 lb/h/lb st)

TEXTRON LYCOMING

TEXTRON LYCOMING

550 Main Street, Stratford, Connecticut 06497
Telephone: 1 (203) 385 2000
PRESIDENT: J. R. Myers

Textron Lycoming produces several families of engines, including the T53, T55, ALF 502 and LT 101, with turboshaft, turboprop, turbofan, vehicular and marine variants. In June 1987 Textron Lycoming and General Electric agreed joint development of gas turbines for aero and ground applications. The aero engine is the T407/GLC38, described under General Electric.

TEXTRON LYCOMING ALF 502

The ALF 502 was launched in 1969, primarily for commercial and executive aircraft. The core is the T55, and construction is modular.

Current versions are as follows:

ALF 502L. First commercial version, FAA certificated in February 1980. Powers Canadair Challenger 600 in ALF 502L-2 form. L-2A, L-2C and L-3 certificated 1982-3.

ALF 502R. Reduced rating, FAA certificated January 1981 as R-3 to power BAe 146. Improved R-3A, R-4 and R-5 certificated 1982-3. R-6 certificated 1984.

By 1991 a total of 184 ALF 502L engines had flown 487,000 h in the Challenger, while 735 ALF 502R engines had flown 4,250,000 h in the BAe 146. TBO was 4,000 h, but the ALF 502 is usually operated on-condition.

TYPE: High bypass ratio, two-shaft geared turbofan.

FAN MODULE: Cast frame includes four engine mounts 90° apart, and may carry reverser. Fan rotor blades are base and part-span shrouded. Mounted directly behind rotor (6,700 lb st engines) is a single or (7,500 lb st engines) two stages of compression. Anti-icing of LP compressor inlet by bleed air. Accessory gearbox on fan frame takes HP shaft power. Reduction gear couples LP turbine to fan. Bypass ratio: 502R-3, 5.71; 502R-5, 5.6; 502L, 5.0.

COMPRESSOR: HP compressor has seven stages and single centrifugal. Acceleration bleed between stages 6 and 7 operated by main fuel control. Overall pressure ratio: R-3, 11.6; R-5, 12.0; L-2, 13.6.

TURBINE: HP has two aircooled stages. LP has two stages. All rotor blades base shrouded: LP tip shrouded.

COMBUSTION CHAMBER: One-piece annular combustor wraps around turbine. Atomising nozzles inserted through outer chamber at rear. Disconnecting permits removal of combustor/turbine module, providing access to HP turbine.

ACCESSORY DRIVES: Accessory gearbox carries main fuel control, oil pump and filter, tachometer (if required) and provisions for customer accessories.

DATA: See table overleaf.

TEXTRON LYCOMING LF500

In September 1988 Textron Lycoming announced plans for a family of commercial turbofans based on the ALF 502R, using the same core. The engines will range from 32.03 kN (7,200 lb st) to 44.48 kN (10,000 lb st), the most powerful version requiring a small increase in fan diameter. The **LF 507** was expected to be certificated in 1991.

TEXTRON LYCOMING ALF 502, LF 500, LTC1/T53 and LTC4/T55 ENGINES

Manufacturer's and civil designation	Military designation	Type*	T-O Rating kN (lb st) or max kW (hp)	SFC µg/J; ‡ mg/Ns (lb/h/hp; ‡lb/h/lb st)	Weight, Dry less tailpipe kg (lb)	Max diameter mm(in)	Length overall mm (in)	Remarks
T5311A	—	ACFS	820 kW (1,100 shp)	115 (0.68)	225 (496)	584 (23)	1,209 (47.6)	Bell 204B
T5313B	—	ACFS	1,044 kW (1,400 shp)	98 (0.58)	245 (540)	584 (23)	1,209(47.6)	Bell 205A
T5317A	—	ACFS	1,119 kW (1,500 shp)	99.7 (0.59)	256 (564)	584 (23)	1,209(47.6)	Bell 205A-1
—	T53-L-13B	ACFS	1,044 kW (1,400 shp)	98 (0.58)	245 (540)	584 (23)	1,209 (47.6)	Advanced UH-1H, AH-1G
—	T53-L-703	ACFS	1,106 kW (1,485 shp)	101.4 (0.60)	247 (545)	584 (23)	1,209 (47.6)	Bell AH-1S TOW/Cobra
LTC1K-4K	—	ACFS	1,156 kW (1,550 shp)	98.7 (0.584)	234 (515)	584 (23)	1,209 (47.6)	Bell XV-15
—	T53-L-701	ACFP	1,082 ekW (1,451 ehp)	101.4 (0.60)	312 (688)	584 (23)	1,483 (58.4)	Grumman OV-1D, AIDC (Taiwan) T-CH-1
—	YT55-L-9	ACFP	1,887 ekW (2,529 ehp)	102.7 (0.608)	363 (799)	615 (24.2)	1,580 (62.2)	Piper Enforcer
—	T55-L-7C	ACFS	2,125 kW (2,850 shp)	101.4 (0.60)	267 (590)	615 (24.2)	1,118 (44)	
T5508D (LTC4B-8D)	—	ACFS	2,186 kW (2,930 shp) flat rated at	100.1 (0.592)	274 (605)	610 (24)	1,118 (44)	Bell 214A, 214B
			1,678 kW (2,250 shp)	106.0 (0.628)				
—	T55-L-712†	ACFS	2,796 kW (3,750 shp)	89.6 (0.53)	340 (750)	615 (24.2)	1,181 (46.5)	Boeing CH-47D
AL5512	—	ACFS	3,039 kW (4,075 shp)	89.6 (0.53)	355 (780)	615 (24.2)	1,118 (44)	Boeing 234
—	T55-L-714	ACFS	3,629 kW (4,867 shp)	85.0 (0.503)	363 (800)	615 (24.2)	1,181 (46.5)	Boeing MH-47E
ALF 502R-3	—	ACFF	29.8 kN (6,700 lb)	‡11.64 (‡0.411)	576 (1,270)	1,059 (41.7)	1,443 (56.8)	BAe 146
ALF 502R-3A	—	ACFF	31.0 kN (6,968 lb)	‡11.55 (‡0.408)	576 (1,270)	1,059 (41.7)	1,443 (56.8)	BAe 146
ALF 502R-5	—	ACFF	31.0 kN (6,968 lb)	‡11.55 (‡0.408)	583 (1,283)	1,059 (41.7)	1,443 (56.8)	BAe 146
ALF 502R-6	—	ACFF	33.36 kN (7,500 lb)	‡11.73 (‡0.415)	589 (1,298)	1,059 (41.7)	1,487 (58.56)	BAe 146
ALF 502L/L-2	—	ACFF	33.36 kN (7,500 lb)	‡12.1 (‡0.428)	589 (1,298)	1,059 (41.7)	1,487 (58.56)	Canadair Challenger 600
ALF 502L-2A	—	ACFF	33.36 kN (7,500 lb)	‡11.70 (‡0.414)	589 (1,298)	1,059 (41.7)	1,487 (58.56)	
ALF 502L-3	—	ACFF	34.74 kN (7,800 lb)	‡11.73 (‡0.415)	589 (1,298)	1,059 (41.7)	1,487 (58.56)	
LF 507	—	ACFF	31.14 kN (7,000 lb)	‡11.50 (‡0.406)	628 (1,385)	1,059 (41.7)	1,487 (58.56)	BAe 146

*ACFS = axial plus centrifugal, free-turbine shaft; ACFP = axial plus centrifugal, free-turbine propeller; ACFF = axial plus centrifugal, free-turbine fan
†Applies to T55-L-11A, C**, D, E** and 712**, those designated ** having 2½ min contingency rating of 3,357 kW (4,500 shp).

TEXTRON LYCOMING LTC1
US military designation: T53

The T53 was developed under a joint US Air Force/Army contract. More than 19,000 have logged over 41 million hours since 1956.

Licences for manufacture of the T53 are held by Klöckner-Humboldt-Deutz in Germany, Piaggio in Italy, Kawasaki in Japan, and in Taiwan.

Current versions are as follows:

T53-L-13. Uprated L-11. Redesigned 'hot end' and initial stages of compressor. Four turbine stages, compared with two in earlier models, and variable inlet guide vanes combined with redesigned first two compressor stages. Atomising combustor to facilitate operation on a wider range of fuels. Powers Bell UH-1M and UH-1H and AH-1G HueyCobra. The **T5313A** commercial version has been superseded by the **T5313B.**

T53-L-701. Turboprop incorporating 'split power' reduction gear.

T53-L-703. Improved durability L-13. Thermodynamic rating 1,343 kW (1,800 shp).

LTC1K-4K. Direct drive L-13 suitable for operation from 105° nose up to 90° nose down.

T5317A. Improvements over L-13 include improved cooling of first gas producer turbine nozzle plus aircooled blades in first turbine rotor.

The following details apply to the T53-L-13 and L-701:

TYPE: Free turbine turboshaft.

COMPRESSOR: Five axial stages followed by single centrifugal stage. Variable inlet guide vanes. Pressure ratio 7.2. Mass flow 5.53 kg (12.2 lb)/s at 25,150 gas producer rpm.

COMBUSTION CHAMBER: Annular reverse flow, with 22 atomising injectors.

FUEL CONTROL SYSTEM: Chandler Evans TA-2S system with one dual fuel pump, 41.4 bars (600 lb/sq in). Interstage air bleed control.

FUEL GRADE: ASTM A-1, MIL-J-5624, MIL-F-26005A, JP-1, JP-4, JP-5, CITE.

TURBINE: First two stages, driving compressor, use hollow aircooled stator vanes and cored-out cast steel rotor blades. Second two stages, driving reduction gearing, have solid steel blades.

ACCESSORIES: Electric starter or starter/generator. Bendix-Scintilla TGLN high energy ignition unit.

LUBRICATION: Recirculating system, with gear pump, 4.83 bars (70 lb/sq in).

OIL GRADE: MIL-L-7808, MIL-L-23699.

DATA: See table.

TEXTRON LYCOMING LTC4
US military designation: T55

This engine is based on the T53 with higher mass flow. Total operating time by early 1989 on more than 3,900 engines was over 5.0 million hours.

Current versions are as follows:

LTC4B-8D. Modified T55-L-7C.

T5508D. Commercial version of LTC4B-8D.

T55-L-11 (LTC4B-11B) series. Uprated L-7, with variable inlet guide vanes and two-stage compressor turbine.

T55-L-712. Improved L-11D. Wide chord compressor blades without inlet guide vanes, and one-piece rotor.

AL5512. Commercial L-712, with engine out contingency rating of 3,250 kW (4,355 shp).

T55-L-714. Growth version with cooled gas-generator turbine blades, FADEC and improved torquemeter. OEI rating (contingency) 3,780 kW (5,069 shp).

Cutaway drawing of Textron Lycoming ALF 502L geared turbofan

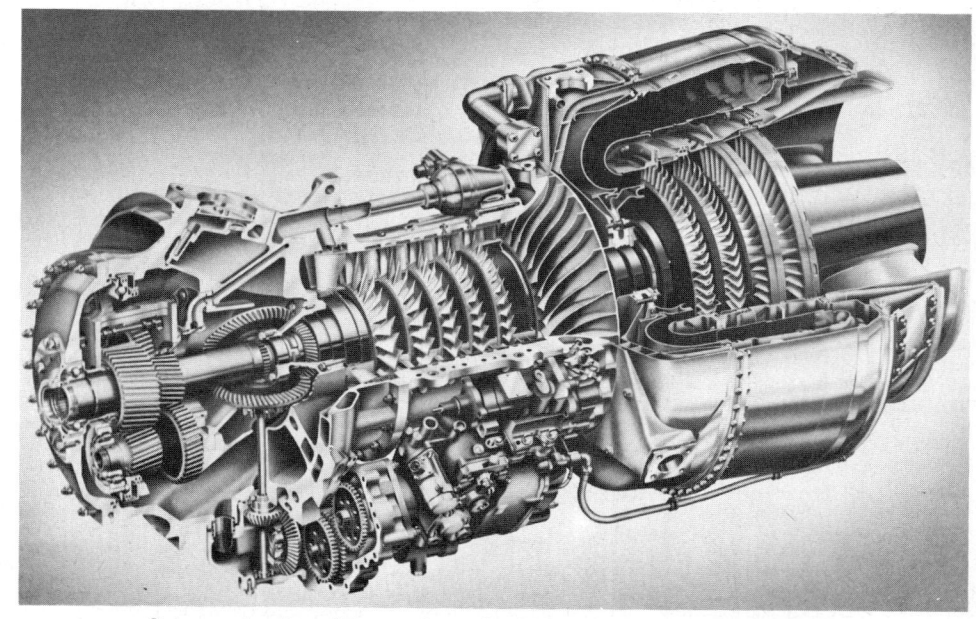

Cutaway drawing of Textron Lycoming T53-L-13B free-turbine turboshaft

YT55-L-9A. Turboprop version of L-7C using split-power reduction gears.

The following description applies to the T55-L-714:

TYPE: Free turbine turboshaft.

COMPRESSOR: Seven axial stages followed by single centrifugal stage. Pressure ratio 9.3. Mass flow 13.19 kg (29.08 lb)/s.

COMBUSTION CHAMBER: Annular reverse flow. Twenty-eight atomizing nozzles.

FUEL SYSTEM: Chandler Evans FADEC type EMC-32T-2, consisting of hydromechanical unit with gear type pump and DECU.

FUEL GRADE: MIL-J-5624L grade JP-4, JP-5, MIL-T-83133 grade JP-8 or CITE.

TURBINE: Gas generator turbine has two stages with cooled blades and cooled shrouds to give tip clearance control. Two-stage power turbine.

ACCESSORIES: Electric starter or starter/generator, or air or hydraulic starter. Bendix-Scintilla TGLN high energy ignition unit. Four igniter plugs.

LUBRICATION: Recirculating. Integral tank and cooler.

OIL GRADE: MIL-L-7808, MIL-L-23699.

DATA: See table.

Cutaway drawing of Textron Lycoming T55-L-714 (military) or AL5512 (commercial) free-turbine turboshaft

TEXTRON LYCOMING LT 101
US military designation: YT702-LD-700

The LT 101 is designed for low life cycle costs. Each engine comprises an accessory reduction gearbox, gas generator and combustor/power turbine module. The engine has a single axial compressor stage followed by a single centrifugal stage, a reverse flow annular combustor, a single-stage gas generator turbine, and a single-stage power turbine. Front gearboxes provide output speeds of 1,925, 6,000 or 9,545 rpm. The 6,000 rpm gearbox has both forward and aft drives. The engine has either a scroll or radial inlet. Mass flow is 2.03 kg (4.8 lb)/s, and pressure ratio 8.5.

Current production versions include turboshaft (LTS) and turboprop (LTP) models, with max power in the 459 to 548 kW (615 to 735 shp) range. All are certificated under FAR Pt 33 for 2,400 h TBO or on-condition maintenance. LT 101 operating experience now totals more than 2 million h.

TEXTRON LYCOMING LTS 101 ENGINES

Engine Model	Performance Rating (T-O, S/L) kW (shp)	SFC μg/J (lb/h/shp)	Weight, Dry kg (lb)	Length mm (in)	Diameter mm (in)
LTS 101-600A-2	459 (615)	96.5 (0.571)	115 (253)	785 (30.9)	599 (23.6)
LTS 101-600A-3	459 (615)	98.4 (0.582)	120 (265)	785 (30.9)	599 (23.6)
LTS 101-650B-1	410 (550)	97.5 (0.577)	124 (273)	790 (31.1)	645 (25.4)
LTS 101-650C-2/C-3/C-3A	447 (600)	96.7 (0.572)	109.5 (241)	787 (31.0)	574 (22.6)
LTS 101-750B-2	461 (618)	96.3 (0.570)	123 (271)	822 (32.36)	627 (24.7)
LTS 101-750C-1	510 (684)	97.5 (0.577)	110.5 (244)	790 (31.1)	574 (22.6)

TEXTRON LYCOMING LTS 101

The **LTS 101-600A-2** is a 6,000 rpm power plant for the Aerospatiale AS 350D Astar. The **650C-2/C-3** is a 9,545 rpm power plant for the Bell 222. The **650B-1**, a 6,000 rpm engine with a radial inlet for the MBB/Kawasaki BK 117A. The **750B-1** powers the BK 117B. The **600A-3** powers the AS 350D Mk 3. A growth version, the **750C-1**, powers the Bell 222B and 222UT. The **750B-2**, with radial inlet, powers the AS 366 and HH-65A Dolphin.

DATA: See table.

TEXTRON LYCOMING LTP 101

The LTP 101 turboprop incorporates a free power turbine, provisions for tractor or pusher installation, hydraulic propeller governor, radial screened inlet and anti-icing protection. Output speed is 1,700-1,950 rpm. The **LTP 101-600A-1A** has been selected for the P.166-DL3, Air Tractor and Cresco agricultural aircraft, Riley Cessna 421 and Page Turbo Thrush and Ag-Cat. It has flown in Piper Brave, Turbine Islander and Dornier 128-6 prototypes. The **LTP 101-700A-1A** was certificated in July 1980.

DIMENSIONS:
Length	914 mm (36.0 in)
Diameter	533 mm (21.0 in)

WEIGHT, DRY:
	152 kg (335 lb)

PERFORMANCE RATINGS (T-O, S/L):
LTP 101-600	462 ekW (620 ehp)
LTP 101-700	522 ekW (700 ehp)

SPECIFIC FUEL CONSUMPTION (T-O, S/L):
LTP 101-600, -700	93 μg/J (0.55 lb/h/ehp)

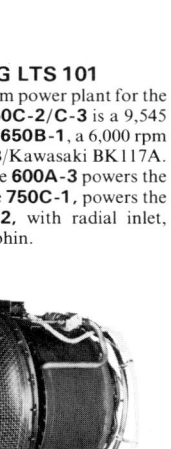

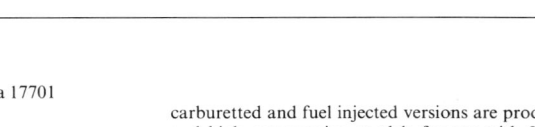

Left to right: Textron Lycoming LTS 101-650B-1 turboshaft, LTP 101-700A-1A turboprop and LTS 101-750C-1 turboshaft

---

WILLIAMSPORT
652 Oliver St, Williamsport, Pennsylvania 17701
Telephone: 1 (717) 327 7041
Fax: 1 (717) 327 7022

Williamsport is the world's largest producer of piston engines for general aviation.

TEXTRON LYCOMING O-235 SERIES
Four cylinders of 111 mm (4⅜ in) bore and 98.4 mm (3⅞ in) stroke. The high compression O-235-N is the most recent production version of the C-235, used in several trainers. It requires 100 octane fuel.

TEXTRON LYCOMING O-320 and IO-320 SERIES
Cylinder bore increased to 130 mm (5⅛ in). The O-320 is an engine in the 112-119 kW (150-160 hp) class. Both carburetted and fuel injected versions are produced in low and high compression models for use with 80/87 or 100 octane minimum grade fuels, respectively. Fully aerobatic models are available.

TEXTRON LYCOMING O-360 and IO-360 SERIES
The O-360 series is basically the same as the O-320 except for an increase in stroke to 111 mm (4⅜ in). Like the O-320, this engine is manufactured with low or high compression, with carburettor or fuel injection. The various models include aerobatic capability, a specific design for helicopters and a turbocharged version. The IO-360-A has fuel injection, tuned induction and high output cylinders, while the IO-360-B has continuous flow port injection and standard cylinders. In the TIO-360-C the turbocharger is pilot controlled.

TEXTRON LYCOMING O-540 and IO-540 SERIES
The O-540 is a direct drive, six-cylinder version of the four-cylinder O-360. It is available in low and high compression versions, and the VO-540 is a helicopter power plant with crankshaft vertical. Fuel injected IO-540 models are manufactured with ratings of 186-224 kW (250-300 hp). An aerobatic version is available.

TEXTRON LYCOMING TIO-540 SERIES
This is a turbocharged version of the fuel injected IO-540, some of which have tuned induction. It is manufactured for unpressurised and pressurised aircraft, and several models incorporate an intercooler.

Textron Lycoming IO-360 four-cylinder piston engine

Textron Lycoming TIO-540-AE2A turbocharged piston engine

Textron Lycoming IO-720 eight-cylinder piston engine

Textron Lycoming O-540 six-cylinder piston engine

TEXTRON LYCOMING TIO-541 SERIES

Although the displacement of this turbocharged, six-cylinder series is the same as that of the TIO-540, the TIO-541 and geared TIGO-541 are totally redesigned. The TIO-541-E is rated at 283 kW (380 hp) and the geared TIGO-541-E at 317 kW (425 hp). A double scroll blower is available to provide cabin pressurisation.

TEXTRON LYCOMING IO-720 SERIES

This eight-cylinder version of the IO-540 is used at ratings from 280 to 298 kW (375 to 400 hp).

TEXTRON LYCOMING HORIZONTALLY OPPOSED PISTON ENGINES

Engine Model*	No. of Cylinders	Rated output at Sea Level kW (hp) at rpm	Capacity litres (cu in)	Compression Ratio	Fuel grade Minimum	Weight, Dry kg (lb)	Length Overall mm (in)	Width Overall mm (in)	Height Overall mm (in)	Gear Ratio†
O-235-C	4	86 (115) at 2,800	3.85 (233)	6.75	80/87	97.5 (215)	751 (29.56)	812 (32.00)	569 (22.40)	D
O-235-L	4	86 (115) at 2,700 78 (105) at 2,400	3.85 (233)	8.5	100	98 (218)	738 (29.05)	812 (32.00)	569 (22.40)	D
O-235-N, P	4	87 (116) at 2,800	3.85 (233)	8.1	100	98 (218)	738 (29.05)	812 (32.00)	569 (22.40)	D
O-320-A	4	112 (150) at 2,700	5.2 (319.8)	7.0	80/87	110 (243)	751 (29.56)	819 (32.24)	584 (22.99)	D
O-320-D	4	119 (160) at 2,700	5.2 (319.8)	8.5	91/96	114 (253)	808 (31.82)	819 (32.24)	488 (19.22)	D
AEIO-320-D	4	119 (160) at 2,700	5.2 (319.8)	8.5	100	123 (271)	780 (30.70)	819 (32.24)	589 (23.18)	D
O-320-E	4	112 (150) at 2,700	5.2 (319.8)	7.0	80/87	113 (249)	738 (29.05)	819 (32.24)	584 (22.99)	D
O-320-H	4	119 (160) at 2,700	5.2 (319.8)	9.0	100	115 (253)	819 (32.26)	830 (32.68)	621 (24.46)	D
O-360-A	4	134 (180) at 2,700	5.92 (361)	8.5	91/96	118 (260)	808 (31.82)	848 (33.37)	488 (19.22)	D
LO-360-A	4	134 (180) at 2,700	5.92 (361)	8.5	91/96	120 (266)	808 (31.82)	848 (33.37)	488 (19.22)	D
O-360-F	4	134 (180) at 2,700	5.92 (361)	8.5	100	122 (269)	808 (31.81)	859 (33.38)	507 (19.96)	D
TO-360-C, F	4	157 (210) at 2,575 to 3,050 m (10,000 ft)	5.92 (361)	7.3	100	154 (343)	876 (34.50)	921 (36.25)	534 (21.02)	D
IO-360-A	4	149 (200) at 2,700	5.92 (361)	8.7	100	133 (293)	757 (29.81)	870 (34.25)	491 (19.35)	D
IO-360-B	4	134 (180) at 2,700	5.92 (361)	8.5	100	122 (268)	757 (29.81)	848 (33.37)	631 (24.84)	D
IO-360-C	4	149 (200) at 2,700	5.92 (361)	8.7	100	134 (298)	855 (33.65)	870 (34.25)	495 (19.48)	D
TIO-360-C	4	210 (282) at 2,575 to 3,050 m (10,000 ft)	5.92 (361)	7.3	100	158 (348)	910 (35.82)	921 (36.25)	550 (21.65)	D
HIO-360-D	4	142 (190) at 3,200 to 1,280 m (4,200 ft)	5.92 (361)	10.0	100	132 (290)	894 (35.23)	904 (35.62)	495 (19.48)	D
HIO-360-E	4	142 (190) at 2,900	5.92 (361)	8.0	100	132 (290)	797 (31.36)	870 (34.25)	507 (19.97)	D
HIO-360-F	4	142 (190) at 3,050	5.92 (361)	8.0	100	133 (293)	797 (31.36)	870 (34.25)	507 (19.97)	D
AEIO-360-A	4	149 (200) at 2,700	5.92 (361)	8.7	100	139 (307)	780 (30.70)	870 (34.25)	492 (19.35)	D
AEIO-360-B	4	134 (180) at 2,700	5.92 (361)	8.5	91/96	125 (277)	738 (29.05)	848 (33.37)	631 (24.84)	D
O-540-B	6	175 (235) at 2,575	8.86 (541.5)	7.2	80/87	166 (366)	945 (37.22)	848 (33.37)	624 (24.56)	D
O-540-E	6	194 (260) at 2,700	8.86 (541.5)	8.5	91/96	167 (368)	976 (38.42)	848 (33.37)	624 (24.56)	D

†Direct drive.

TEXTRON LYCOMING HORIZONTALLY OPPOSED PISTON ENGINES

Engine Model*	No. of Cylinders	Rated output at Sea Level kW (hp) at rpm	Capacity litres (cu in)	Compression Ratio	Fuel grade Minimum	Weight, Dry kg (lb)	Length Overall mm (in)	Width Overall mm (in)	Height Overall mm (in)	Gear Ratio†
O-540-G	6	194 (260) at 2,700	8.86 (541.5)	8.5	91/96	174 (386)	999 (39.34)	848 (33.37)	624 (24.56)	D
O-540-J	6	175 (235) at 2,400	8.86 (541.5)	8.5	100	162 (357)	989 (38.93)	848 (33.37)	519 (20.43)	D
VO-540-B	6	227 (305) at 3,200	8.86 (541.5)	7.3	80/87	202 (446)	882 (34.73)	880 (34.70)	617 (24.29)	D V
VO-540-C	6	227 (305) at 3,200 to 915 m (3,000 ft)	8.86 (541.5)	8.7	100	200 (441)	882 (34.73)	880 (34.70)	649 (25.57)	D V
IO-540-C	6	186 (250) at 2,575	8.86 (541.5)	8.5	91/96	170 (375)	976 (38.42)	848 (33.37)	622 (24.46)	D
IO-540-K	6	224 (300) at 2,700	8.86 (541.5)	8.7	100	201 (443)	999 (39.34)	870 (34.25)	498 (19.60)	D
IO-540-W	6	175 (235) at 2,400	8.86 (541.5)	8.5	100	166 (367)	989 (38.93)	848 (33.37)	492 (19.35)	D
AEIO-540-D	6	194 (260) at 2,700	8.86 (541.5)	8.5	91/96	174 (386)	999 (39.34)	848 (33.37)	621 (24.46)	D
AEIO-540-L	6	224 (300) at 2,700	8.86 (541.5)	8.7	100	202 (445)	989 (38.93)	870 (34.25)	622 (24.46)	D
TIO-540-A	6	231 (310) at 2,575 to 4,575 m (15,000 ft)	8.86 (541.5)	7.3	100	232 (511)	1,304 (51.34)	870 (34.25)	577 (22.71)	D
TIO-540-AE2A	6	261 (350) at 2,600	8.86 (541.5)	7.3	100	249 (549)				D
TIO-540-C	6	186 (250) at 2,575 to 4,575 m (15,000 ft)	8.86 (541.5)	7.2	100	205 (456)	1,026 (40.38)	848 (33.37)	770 (30.33)	D
TIO/LTIO-540-F	6	242 (325) at 2,575 to 4,575 m (15,000 ft)	8.86 (541.5)	7.3	100	233 (514)	1,304 (51.34)	870 (34.25)	570 (22.42)	D
TIO/LTIO-540-J	6	261 (350) at 2,575 to 4,575 m (15,000 ft)	8.86 (541.5)	7.3	100	235 (518)	1,308 (51.50)	870 (34.25)	573 (22.56)	D
TIO-540-S	6	224 (300) at 2,700 to 3,660 m (12,000 ft)	8.86 (541.5)	7.3	100	228 (502)	1,004 (39.56)	915 (36.02)	667 (26.28)	D
TIO/LTIO-540-U	6	261 (350) at 2,500 to 4,575 m (15,000 ft)	8.86 (541.5)	7.3	100	248 (547)	1,204 (47.40)	870 (34.25)	574 (22.59)	D
TIO/LTIO-540-V	6	269 (360) at 2,600 to 5,485 m (18,000 ft)	8.86 (541.5)	7.3	100	248 (547)	1,352 (53.21)	886 (34.88)	621 (24.44)	D
TIO-541-E	6	283 (380) at 2,900 to 4,575 m (15,000 ft)	8.86 (541.5)	7.3	100	270 (596)	1,282 (50.70)	905 (35.66)	640 (25.17)	D
TIGO-541-E	6	317 (425) at 3,200 to 4,575 m (15,000 ft)	8.86 (541.5)	7.3	100	319 (704)	1,462 (57.57)	885 (34.86)	575 (22.65)	0.667
IO-720-A	8	298 (400) at 2,650	11.84 (722)	8.7	100	257 (567)	1,179 (46.41)	870 (34.25)	573 (22.53)	D
IO-720-B	8	298 (400) at 2,650	11.84 (722)	8.7	100	252 (556)	1,218 (47.97)	870 (34.25)	530 (20.88)	D
IO-720-D	8	298 (400) at 2,650	11.84 (722)	8.7	100	259 (570)	1,189 (46.80)	870 (34.25)	562 (22.11)	D

*Model designation code: A, Aerobatic; AE, Aerobatic engine; G, Geared; H, Helicopter; I, Fuel injected; L, Left-hand rotation crankshaft; O, Opposed cylinders; S, Supercharged; T, Turbocharged; V, Vertical mounting. †D, Direct drive.

THERMO-JET
THERMO-JET STANDARD INC
PO Box 55976, Houston, Texas 77055
Telephone: 1 (713) 465 5735
Fax: 1 (713) 467 6935
MANAGER: John A. Melenric

This company specialises in valveless pulsejet units for UAVs and the homebuilt market. These engines are devoid of moving parts and are characterised by multiple reverse flow air inlets to a combustion chamber in which is burned propane, butane or compressed natural gas, fed under pressure from lightweight tanks. Intermittent combustion and expulsion takes place at a cycle frequency determined by the chamber size and geometry and combustion pressure.

Thermo-Jet offers six sizes of unit, the J3-200 (0.0179 kN, 4 lb st at S/L), J5-200 (0.045 kN, 10 lb st at S/L), J7-300 (0.09 kN, 21 lb st at S/L), J8-200 (0.045 kN, 10 lb st at S/L), J10-200 (0.244 kN, 55 lb st at S/L), and J13-202 (0.4 kN, 90 lb st at S/L). Further details were given in the 1979-80 *Jane's.*

Thermo-Jet J13-202 on test stand

THIOKOL
THIOKOL CORPORATION
2475 Washington Blvd, Ogden, Utah 84401
Telephone: 1 (801) 629 2270
Fax: 1 (801) 629 2420
SOLID PROPELLANT ROCKET MOTOR PLANTS: Elkton, Maryland; Huntsville, Alabama; Marshall, Texas; Brigham City, Utah
PRESIDENT AND CEO: U. E. Garrison

In 1943, the discovery by Thiokol of liquid polymer, a new type of synthetic rubber, paved the way for the 'case-bonded' rocket. The company's polysulphide liquid polymer proved to be the catalyst for production of efficient solid motors.

THIOKOL SHUTTLE RSRM
Each Space Shuttle solid rocket motor (**SRM**) is cast in four segments, stacked vertically in pairs as part of the solid rocket booster system. Thrust vector control for each SRM is provided by a flexible bearing movable nozzle driven by two hydraulic actuators. After burnout, the two boosters are separated and fall back into the atmosphere, where parachutes control impact velocity into the ocean. The boosters are then towed back to a recovery site. In its original form, the SRM was the largest solid rocket propulsion system to reach operational status. It was also the first to be qualified for manned flight, and the first to demonstrate reusability of major components. A high performance motor (HPM) became standard from the eighth flight in August 1983. Development was also begun on a graphite epoxy case, but this was discontinued in 1990.

As a result of the loss of STS-S.1 (Challenger) in January 1986, the SRM was redesigned, and the **RSRM** (redesigned SRM) has been used since flights resumed in 1988. The following data apply to the RSRM:
DIMENSIONS:
Length	38.47 m (126.2 ft)
Diameter	3,708 mm (146 in)

WEIGHTS:
Propellant	502,126 kg (1,107,000 lb)
Loaded motor	569,712 kg (1,256,000 lb)

THRUST:
Average vacuum	11,521 kN (2,590,000 lb)

BURN TIME: 123 s

UP
UP ARROW AIRCRAFT
PO Box 659, Temecula, California 92390
Telephone: 1 (714) 676 5652
Telex: 910 332 1306

Peter Brock of this company states that the engine goal of 1 lb/hp has been achieved. The four-stroke V-8 produces 59.7 kW (80 hp) at 2,400 rpm for an installed weight of 36.3 kg (80 lb). Engine production from a manufacturer in Mexico was promised for mid-1991.

WILLIAMS
WILLIAMS INTERNATIONAL
2280 West Maple Road, PO Box 200, Walled Lake,
  Michigan 48088
Telephone: 1 (313) 624 5200
Fax: 1 (313) 669 1577
PRESIDENT: Sam Williams
VICE-PRESIDENT, PUBLIC RELATIONS: David C. Jolivette
  Details of the engines manufactured by Williams for
unmanned applications can be found in the 1987-88 *Jane's*.

WILLIAMS FJ44
  Development of this turbofan began in 1980. The first
FJ44 engine built to meet FAR 33 requirements achieved
design thrust at a modest turbine inlet temperature on its
first build. The FJ44 is sized for the new, small business
aircraft market and utilises up-to-date technology to
provide low acquisition and maintenance costs, low specific
fuel consumption, and high reliability. Three business
aircraft have been developed around a twin application of
this engine. They are the Cessna CitationJet, the Swearingen
SJ30, and the Scaled Composites Triumph. In addition, a
lightweight, single-engine primary trainer aircraft, the
Aerodis America Rigel, will utilise this engine. Other
aircraft companies in Europe, Asia, and America are

Williams FJ44 two-shaft turbofan

studying the FJ44 for use in their proposed business
aircraft, commuters, and military trainers.
  The engine has already powered a Citation and a
Triumph aircraft. The flight test programmes for both the
CitationJet and the Swearingen SJ30 were scheduled to
begin in early 1991. The engine is expected to complete FAA
certification by early 1992, with the first production engines
being delivered by mid-1992.
  Rolls-Royce joined Williams International as a partner
on the FJ44 in 1988. Williams is the design authority for the

engine, with Rolls-Royce providing its expertise for certain
components as well as assisting in product support. In
production, the majority of manufacturing and final
assembly will be accomplished at the Williams facility in
Ogden, Utah, while Rolls-Royce will manufacture the
low-pressure turbine shaft and three turbine rotors.
FAN: Single piece titanium, with 20 wide-chord snubberless
  blades. Bypass ratio 3.28.
COMPRESSOR: One axial rotating with the fan, followed by
  one centrifugal stage.
COMBUSTION CHAMBER: Annular, folded reverse-flow.
TURBINES: Single-stage HP driving centrifugal compressor.
  Two-stage LP driving fan and axial compressor. All three
  rotors with inserted blades.
CONTROL SYSTEM: Hydromechanical.
JETPIPE: Full-length fan duct but no mixer.
DIMENSIONS:
Length	1,023 mm (40.3 in)
Max diameter	602 mm (23.7 in)
WEIGHT, DRY: 202 kg (445 lb)
PERFORMANCE RATINGS:
T-O (S/L) to 20°C	8.45 kN (1,900 lb st)
Max continuous (11,000 m; 36,090 ft; Mach 0.6)	
	2.16 kN (486 lb)

SPECIFIC FUEL CONSUMPTION:
T-O (S/L)	13.23 mg/Ns (0.467 lb/h/lb st)
Max continuous (as above)	19.83 mg/Ns (0.70 lb/h/lb)

YUGOSLAVIA

ORAO
ORAO AIR FORCE DEPOT
Federal Directorate of Supply and Procurement
9 Nemanjina St, 11105 Belgrade
Telephone: 38 (11) 621522
Fax: 38 (11) 324981
Telex: 11360, 11541, 11591, 11821

  The depot was established in 1944. Today its main task is
licence manufacture of the Rolls-Royce Viper 632-41 and
632-46, and the latest afterburning 633-41, used in most of
the Orao twin-engined combat aircraft at present flying.
  The Orao works has built up a design and development
team which, in collaboration with Turbomecanica of
Romania, has been developing the afterburning Viper Mk

633-47 engine for production IAR-93s and Oraos. The first
afterburning engines were overweight, but an Orao 2 flew
with afterburning engines on 20 October 1983.
  The Orao works is engaged in manufacture of parts for
General Electric, Rolls-Royce and SNECMA, and overhaul
of various British and Soviet jet engines.

ADDENDA

AIRCRAFT

AUSTRALIA

EAA (page 4)

EAGLE XTS
PROGRAMME: Joint venture contract signed 31 December 1990 between EAA and Assets Accretion of Malaysia, under which EAA to receive A$3.5 million as equity

injection and A$2 million in low-interest guaranteed loans; EAA and AA to establish (within three years, and in addition to existing Australian operation) a facility in Malaysia, with Eagle production at both locations; each partner to own 50 per cent of each operation; Eagle Aircraft joint venture company formally restarted

operations on 1 March 1991. Completion of certification anticipated by mid-1992; up to 70 sales expected during first full year of production, which will offer both kits and flyaway aircraft.

FRWE

FIXED & ROTARY WING ENGINEERING PTY LTD
Camden Airport, NSW
DIRECTOR: W. Spence

This company has acquired from IAC of Homestead, Florida, USA (see 1987-88 *Jane's*), 10 uncompleted **Pilatus Britten-Norman Trislanders** for completion and sale. The first four (c/ns 1061, 1063, 1067 and 1068) had arrived in Australia by January 1991, and the remaining six were due to be shipped in March. Rollout of the

first FRWE-assembled Trislander was expected in late April/early May 1991. FRWE has also acquired tooling for the aircraft and in March 1991 completed an additional hangar for possible follow-on production.

SEABIRD (page 6)

SEABIRD SB7L SEEKER
PERFORMANCE (predicted):
Max cruising speed   100 knots (185 km/h; 115 mph)

Cruising speed (75% power)
	90 knots (167 km/h; 103 mph)
Max rate of climb at S/L	230 m (755 ft)/min
Service ceiling	5,000 m (16,400 ft)
T-O run	120 m (394 ft)
Landing run	95 m (312 ft)

Endurance, incl 45 min reserves:
standard tanks	5 h 45 min
standard + optional tanks	8 h 50 min

AUSTRIA

HOAC

HOAC FLUGZEUGPRODUKTION UND ENTWICKLUNG GmbH
Postfach 100, A-1214 Vienna
Telephone: 43 (1) 222 253691
Telex: 112820 HAC
DIRECTOR: Dipl-Ing Wolf D. Hoffmann

HOFFMANN LF 2000 TURBO
The prototype of this new Hoffmann design (OE-VPX) was completed at the company's Austrian factory and first flew on 16 March 1991. It is powered by a turbocharged Rotax engine; no other details had been received at the time of going to press.

Prototype Hoffmann LF 2000 Turbo on its first flight, March 1991

BRAZIL

EMBRAER (page 10)

EMBRAER EMB-120ER BRASILIA
TYPE: Extended range version of EMB-120 Brasilia.
PROGRAMME: Announced June 1991 after completion of flight testing; deliveries expected late 1991.
DESIGN FEATURES: Range with full passengers increased from 500 nm (926 km; 575 miles) to 900 nm (1,668 km; 1,036 miles), allowing four 100 nm (185 km; 115 mile) sectors unrefuelled compared with three for earlier models. Extra range obtained by increasing max T-O weight from 11,500 kg (25,353 lb) to 12,000 kg (26,455 lb) without major structural change; this also allows for increased standard passenger plus baggage weight and obligatory fitting of TCAS and flight data recorder. Existing Brasilias can be retrofitted.

EMBRAER TUCANO H
TYPE: High performance two-seat turboprop trainer.
PROGRAMME: Announced June 1991; first flight of proof of concept aircraft expected second half of 1991; demonstration tour planned for late 1991.
DESIGN FEATURES: P&WC PT6A-67 turboprop driving a Hartzell five-blade propeller gives twice the power of previous engine. Fuselage lengthened by 1.3 m (4 ft 3 in) by plugs fore and aft of cockpit to retain centre of gravity and stability. Tucano H will be able to cover the whole primary and half the advanced pilot training syllabus and fly precision weapons delivery and target towing.
DIMENSIONS, EXTERNAL:
Wing span	11.14 m (36 ft 7 in)
Length overall	11.42 m (37 ft 6 in)

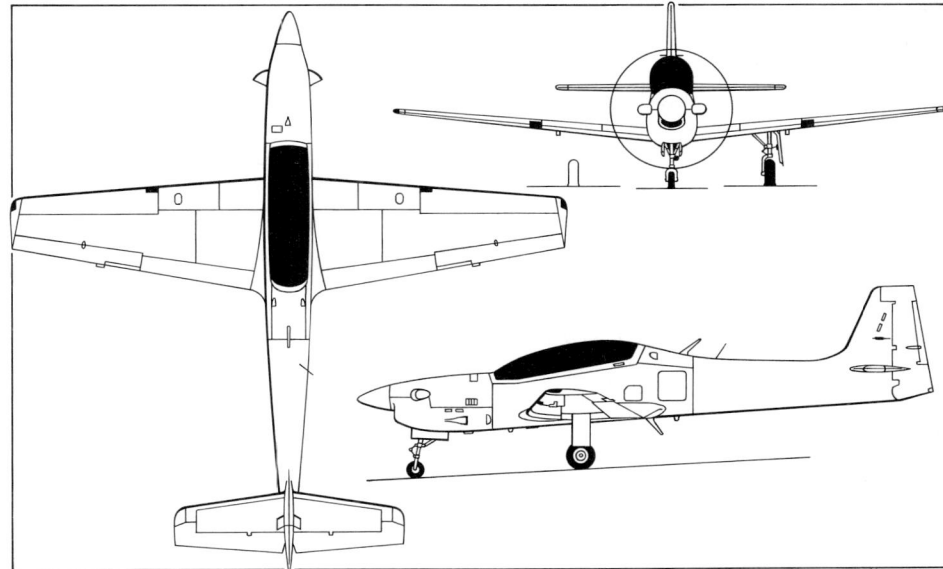

Stretched and re-engined Embraer Tucano H (P&WC PT6A-67) *(Jane's/Mike Keep)*

Height overall	3.68 m (12 ft 1 in)	Wheel track	3.76 m (12 ft 4 in)
Tailplane span	4.66 m (15 ft 3 in)	Wheelbase	3.26 m (10 ft 8 in)

CANADA

BELL (page 17)

BELL MODEL 230

Revised or additional data:

POWER PLANT: Usable fuel capacity 931 litres (246 US gallons; 205 Imp gallons) standard, 1,113 litres (294 US gallons; 245 Imp gallons) with optional auxiliary tanks.

DIMENSIONS, EXTERNAL:

Main rotor diameter (2-blade)	12.80 m (42 ft 0 in)
Tail rotor diameter	2.10 m (6 ft 10¾ in)
Main rotor blade chord	0.66 m (2 ft 2 in)
Tail rotor blade chord	0.25 m (10 in)
Height over tail fin	3.20 m (10 ft 6 in)
Width over endplate fins	3.12 m (10 ft 3 in)
Passenger doors (each): Height	1.24 m (4 ft 1 in)
Width	0.91 m (3 ft 0 in)

DIMENSIONS, INTERNAL:

Cabin (excl flight deck): Length	2.16 m (7 ft 1 in)
Max width	1.47 m (4 ft 10 in)
Max height	1.45 m (4 ft 9 in)
Volume	3.84 m³ (135.5 cu ft)
Flight deck volume	1.87 m³ (65.9 cu ft)

Baggage compartment volume:

aft of cabin	1.05 m³ (37.2 cu ft)
nose	0.40 m³ (14.2 cu ft)

AREAS:

Main rotor disc	128.7 m² (1,385.4 sq ft)
Tail rotor disc	3.46 m² (37.2 sq ft)

WEIGHTS AND LOADINGS:

Manufacturer's weight empty	2,245 kg (4,950 lb)
Max external sling load	1,270 kg (2,800 lb)
Max T-O weight, internal or external load	3,810 kg (8,400 lb)
Max disc loading	29.6 kg/m² (6.06 lb/sq ft)
Max power loading	5.53 kg/kW (9.08 lb/shp)

PERFORMANCE (estimated at max T-O weight, ISA, except where indicated):

Max cruising speed at S/L	137 knots (254 km/h; 158 mph)
Econ cruising speed at S/L at average gross weight	134 knots (248 km/h; 154 mph)
Service ceiling at max cruise power	4,575 m (15,000 ft)
Service ceiling, one engine out, 30 min power rating	2,590 m (8,500 ft)
Hovering ceiling: IGE: ISA	3,750 m (12,300 ft)
ISA + 20°C	2,895 m (9,500 ft)
OGE: ISA	2,225 m (7,300 ft)
ISA + 20°C	1,250 m (4,100 ft)
Range at S/L at econ cruising speed, standard fuel, no reserves	379 nm (702 km; 436 miles)

CHILE

ENAER (page 30)

ENAER T-35 DT TURBO PILLÁN

TYPE: Two-seat turboprop military trainer.

PROGRAMME: Marketing effort began early 1991.

DESIGN FEATURES: Makes maximum use of commercially available components and equipment without political supply problems. Extrapolation of piston-engined Pillán with Soloy power plant incorporating an Allison 250-B17D. Wing section NACA 652-415, modified in tapered section; wing twist 2.5°; dihedral 7°; aspect ratio 5.77.

FLYING CONTROLS: Plain mechanical with electrically actuated variable incidence tailplane and elevator; electrically actuated trim tabs in rudder and port aileron; stall-warning horn. Two-position, electrically actuated flaps.

STRUCTURE: Conventional riveted light alloy structure based on Piper components. Vacuum-formed thermoplastic tips for wings, fin and tailplane.

LANDING GEAR: Tricycle retractable, hydraulically actuated; self-centring nosewheel with shimmy damper steers 25° either side; hydraulically actuated disc brakes.

POWER PLANT: Allison 250-B17D turboprop in Soloy inverted installation with Soloy reduction gearbox. Three-blade, constant-speed Hartzell propeller. Power output 313 kW (420 shp) at 2,030 rpm. Total usable fuel 277.8 litres (73.4 US gallons; 61.1 Imp gallons), weighing 224 kg (494 lb), in two integral wing tanks. Inverted-flight fuel feed system.

ACCOMMODATION: One-piece canopy hinges to starboard. No ejection seats.

AVIONICS: Full blind-flying instruments including horizontal situation indicator and RMI; choice of IFR radios.

DIMENSIONS, EXTERNAL:

Wing span	8.84 m (29 ft 0 in)
Length overall	8.6 m (29 ft 7 in)
Height overall	2.64 m (8 ft 8 in)
Wheelbase	2.0 m (6 ft 6¾ in)
Wheel track	3.01 m (9 ft 10½ in)

AREAS:

Wings, gross	13.69 m² (147.34 sq ft)

WEIGHTS AND LOADINGS:

Weight empty	943 kg (2,080 lb)
Max T-O weight	1,338 kg (2,950 lb)
Max aerobatic T-O weight	1,315 kg (2,900 lb)
Max wing loading	97.7 kg/m² (20.0 lb/sq ft)
Max power loading	4.27 kg/kW (7.02 lb/hp)

PERFORMANCE:

Never-exceed speed (V_{NE})	223 knots (413 km/h; 256 mph)
Max manoeuvre speed (V_A)	171 knots (316 km/h; 186 mph)
Max level speed at S/L	230 knots (426 km/h; 264 mph)
Cruising speed, 75% power, 2,315 m (7,600 ft)	182 knots (337 km/h; 209 mph)
Stalling speed, flaps and wheels down	62 knots (115 km/h; 71 mph)
Max rate of climb at S/L	869 m (2,850 ft)/min
Service ceiling	7,620 m (24,994 ft)
T-O run	195 m (640 ft)
Landing run	128 m (420 ft)
Range at 75% power, 45 min reserves	350 nm (648 km; 412 miles)
g limits	+6/−3

CHINA

CAC (page 33)

CAC SUPER-7

Amended data as follows:

POWER PLANT: One advanced turbofan (unspecified), rated at more than 78.5 kN (17,640 lb st) with afterburning.

DIMENSIONS, EXTERNAL:

Wing span	8.98 m (29 ft 5½ in)
Length overall	15.30 m (50 ft 2¼ in)
Height overall	4.13 m (13 ft 6½ in)
Wheel track	2.79 m (9 ft 1¾ in)
Wheelbase	5.59 m (18 ft 4 in)

WEIGHTS AND LOADINGS:

Internal fuel load	2,327 kg (5,130 lb)
Max T-O weight: clean	8,800 kg (19,400 lb)
with external stores	10,800 kg (23,810 lb)

PERFORMANCE (estimated, at max T-O weight with two wingtip Sidewinder missiles):

Max level speed at height	above Mach 1.8
Service ceiling	18,000 m (59,050 ft)
T-O and landing distance	less than 650 m (2,133 ft)

Combat radius:

air-to-air/hi-hi-hi	475 nm (880 km; 547 miles)
air-to-ground/hi-lo-hi	329 nm (610 km; 379 miles)
g limit	+8.5

GAIC (page 35)

GAIC FT-7P

TYPE: Tandem-seat supersonic fighter trainer.

PROGRAMME: Development started 1989; prototype final assembly completed October 1990; first flight 9 November 1990.

DESIGN FEATURES: Improved FT-7 with uprated engine, 0.61 m (2 ft 0 in) longer fuselage, ventral gun pack, two additional outboard underwing hardpoints, customer-furnished avionics and increased internal fuel.

POWER PLANT: One Chengdu WP7B(BM)C turbojet (43.15 kN; 9,700 lb st dry, 59.82 kN; 13,448 lb st with afterburning). Provision for one 1,893 or 3,028 litre (500 or 800 US gallon; 416 or 666 Imp gallon) underbelly drop tank.

AVIONICS: Include Type 7M ranging radar, Type 956 HUD, Type 50-048-02 air data computer, Type 0101-HRA/2 radar altimeter, APX-101 IFF transponder, AN/ARC-164/168 com transceiver.

ARMAMENT: One Type 23-3 twin-barrel 23 mm gun, with 186 rounds, in underbelly pod. Five external stores points (one under fuselage, two under each wing); wing stations able to carry AIM-9P Sidewinder or Matra R550 missiles, 68 mm rocket pods, Mk 82 bombs or other weapons. Type 2032 gun camera.

WEIGHTS AND LOADINGS:

Max external stores load	1,650 kg (3,637 lb)

PERFORMANCE:

Max level speed at height	Mach 2.05
Max rate of climb at S/L	9,420 m (30,900 ft)/min
Service ceiling	17,600 m (57,745 ft)
T-O run	900-1,100 m (2,953-3,609 ft)
Landing run	750-810 m (2,461-2,658 ft)
Range with max fuel	723 nm (1,340 km; 832 miles)
g limit	+7

CZECHOSLOVAKIA

AERO

AERO CZECHOSLOVAK AEROSPACE INDUSTRY LTD

Beranových 130, 199 04 Prague 9
Telephone: 42 (2) 880573
Fax: 42 (2) 6835905
PRESIDENT AND CEO: Dipl Eng Ivan Marinec
COMMERCIAL DIRECTOR: Dipl Eng Jiří Holub
TECHNICAL DIRECTOR: Dipl Eng Jan Bartoň

This new joint stockholding management group replaced the former state-owned Aero Concern of the Czechoslovak Aerospace Industry with effect from 1 December 1990, following the new Czechoslovak government's policy of privatisation and development of an independent aerospace industry. The industry's airframe, aero-engine and equipment factories, and its research centres, likewise became limited companies from 1 January 1991. Omnipol continues as an import/export organisation, but its activities now extend to areas other than aerospace; conversely, it is no longer the country's only export/import agency for aerospace products.

AERO VODOCHODY (page 50)

AERO L-39 ALBATROSS

VARIANTS: As listed on page 50 except:

L-59: New designation for developed version previously known as L-39MS.

L-139: To be developed (preliminary Aero/Garrett agreement of June 1991) with 17.79 kN (4,000 lb st) TFE731-4 turbofan and Bendix/King avionics; first flight expected late 1991/early 1992, production 1993; probable JPATS candidate.

AERO L-270

TYPE: Pressurised short-range utility transport.

PROGRAMME: Original concept (see Addenda of 1990-91 *Jane's*) replaced 1991 by now-finalised configuration.

DESIGN FEATURES: See accompanying illustration.

LANDING GEAR: Retractable tricycle type.

POWER PLANT: One turboprop (type and rating not yet specified).

DIMENSIONS, EXTERNAL:

Wing span	13.84 m (45 ft 5 in)
Length overall	11.81 m (38 ft 9 in)
Height overall	4.70 m (15 ft 5 in)
Cargo door (port, rear): Height	1.25 m (4 ft 1¼ in)
Width	1.25 m (4 ft 1¼ in)

DIMENSIONS, INTERNAL:

Cabin: Length	4.10 m (13 ft 5½ in)
Max width	1.48 m (4 ft 10¼ in)
Max height	1.37 m (4 ft 6 in)

WEIGHTS AND LOADINGS (estimated):

Weight empty	1,655 kg (3,648 lb)
Max fuel weight	900 kg (1,984 lb)
Max zero-fuel weight	2,960 kg (6,525 lb)
Max T-O weight	3,300 kg (7,275 lb)
Max landing weight	3,150 kg (6,944 lb)

PERFORMANCE (estimated):

Max level speed at 6,000 m (19,685 ft)	
	216 knots (400 km/h; 248 mph)
Max cruising speed at 6,000 m (19,685 ft)	
	183 knots (340 km/h; 211 mph)
Econ cruising speed at 6,000 m (19,685 ft)	
	165 knots (307 km/h; 191 mph)
Stalling speed: flaps up	80 knots (148 km/h; 92 mph)
flaps down	61 knots (113 km/h; 38 mph)
Max rate of climb at S/L	432 m (1,417 ft)/min
Service ceiling	9,200 m (30,185 ft)
T-O to 15 m (50 ft)	420 m (1,378 ft)
Landing from 15 m (50 ft)	480 m (1,575 ft)
Max range, 45 min reserves	
	1,052 nm (1,950 km; 1,212 miles)

Artist's impression of the Aero L-270 single-turboprop utility transport

LET (page 51)

LET L-610

VARIANTS: **L-610G**: Version for western markets, with 1,305 kW (1,750 shp) General Electric CT7-9D turboprops (1,394 kW; 1,870 shp with APR), Collins digital avionics (EFIS, weather radar and autopilot); first flight due late 1991, FAR 25 certification by end 1992. Other differences include max payload 4,200 kg (9,259 lb), max T-O weight 14,500 kg (31,967 lb), range of 733 nm (1,359 km; 844 miles) with max payload and reserves for 100 nm (185 km; 115 miles) plus 45 min.

ZLIN (page 54)

ZLIN 142 and 242

VARIANTS: **Z 142**: Production continuing in mid-1991; total then built was 350.

Z 242L: Prototype only so far (first flight February 1990), modified from Z 142; FAR 23 certification expected by end of 1991.

ZLIN 50

VARIANTS: **Z 50 LS**: Major version, still in production mid-1991 with total then 65.

Z 50 LE: Short-span version, reducing max T-O weight by 50 kg (110 lb); two only (first flight 1990).

Z 50 M: As described on page 55, but only three built; production ended.

ZLIN 143 L

TYPE: Four-seat light aircraft.
PROGRAMME: First flight expected October/November 1991.
VARIANTS: **Z 143**: Future production version, as Z 143 L but with 156.5 kW (210 hp) Walter M 337 AK engine.
POWER PLANT: One 194 kW (260 hp) Textron Lycoming O-540 flat-six in Z 143 L.

ZLIN 90

TYPE: Four-seat light aircraft.
PROGRAMME: In design stage, for first flight 1994-95.
DESIGN FEATURES: Will be aerobatic as single/two-seater.
POWER PLANT: One 194 kW (260 hp) Textron Lycoming O-540 flat-six.

ZLIN 137T AGRO TURBO

VARIANTS: **Z 37T**: Designation for development aircraft only, which did not have winglets.

Z 137T: Designation for production version, of which 35 built by mid-1991; detailed description on page 56 therefore applies to this model, not Z 37T as stated.

Z-37T-2: Two-seat training version; two so far built.

FRANCE

DASSAULT (page 67)

DASSAULT MIRAGE F1-CT

The first Mirage F1-CT tactical attack aircraft made its initial flight from Biarritz/Parme on 3 May, being a conversion of a French Air Force Mirage F1-C interceptor.

DASSAULT MIRAGE 2000

On 27 April 1991, the first single-seat Mirage 2000-5 (Thomson-CSF RDY pulse Doppler radar) flew at Istres. Export versions will be available in 1995.

DASSAULT RAFALE

First flight of Rafale C No. 01 at Istres on 19 May 1991 embraced parameters of Mach 1.2 (with only one M88 turbofan in reheat), supersonic cruise in dry thrust, 400 knots (741 km/h; 461 mph) IAS and 10,970 m (36,000 ft) altitude. The aircraft's 17th sortie was flown on 13 June 1991 before President Mitterrand at the Paris Air Show, by which time it had demonstrated Mach 1.4, 8 g loading, 25° angle of attack and controlled flight at 100 knots (185 km/h; 115 mph).

By early June 1991, the Rafale A had flown 542 sorties, including 73 in hybrid F404/M88 power plant configuration.

Prototype Dassault Mirage 2000D conventional attack version of 2000N carrying two laser-guided bombs and Atlis designator (Dassault/Aviaplans)

The first Dassault Super Etendard Modernisé flew on 5 October 1990 (Paul Jackson)

ROBIN (page 81)

ROBIN X4

Technology investigation aircraft (F-WKQX) flew 25 February 1991, powered by 86.5 kW (116 hp) Textron Lycoming O-235 engine; lowest power loading chosen initially as technically the most difficult performance regime. Aircraft built to validate comparative wind tunnel results against DR400 series at St Cyr in 1989-90; also to be used to evaluate new laminar aerofoil sections and to compare their performance with Robin's current NACA 43000 profiles; wooden wing permits rapid modification without incurring tooling costs; airframe otherwise of composites construction. Programme to investigate, on an industrial scale, the feasibility of all-composite or of combined metal/composites airframe. No figures released.

Robin X4 technology demonstrator (Textron Lycoming O-235)

SOCATA (page 85)

SOCATA TB 200 TOBAGO XL

TYPE: Four/five-seat all-metal light aircraft.
PROGRAMME: Announced at Paris Air Show June 1991; first flight of prototype 27 March 1991; certification expected October 1991.
COSTS: Standard aircraft, VFR equipped, FFr856,400.
DESIGN FEATURES: Generally as TB 10 except as detailed.
STRUCTURE: Generally as TB 10.
LANDING GEAR: Generally as TB 10.
POWER PLANT: One 149 kW (200 hp) Textron Lycoming IO-360-A1B6 flat-four engine, driving a Hartzell two-blade constant-speed propeller. Otherwise as TB 10.
ACCOMMODATION: Generally as TB 10.
SYSTEMS: Electrical system includes 28V 70A alternator and 24V 10Ah battery.
AVIONICS: Generally as TB 10.
DIMENSIONS, EXTERNAL: As for TB 10 except:
Length overall 7.7 m (25 ft 3 in)
AREAS: As for TB 10
WEIGHTS AND LOADINGS:
Weight empty, with unusable fuel and oil
715 kg (1,576 lb)
Baggage capacity 65 kg (143 lb)
Max T-O weight 1,150 kg (2,535 lb)
Max wing loading 96 kg/m² (19.8 lb/sq ft)
Max power loading 7.7 kg/kW (12.6 lb/hp)
PERFORMANCE (at max T-O weight):
Max level speed 140 knots (259 km/h; 161 mph)
Max cruising speed (75% power)
130 knots (240 km/h; 149 mph)

First Socata TB 200 Tobago XL (Textron Lycoming IO-360)

Econ cruising speed (65% power)
121 knots (224 km/h; 139 mph)
Stalling speed, flaps down 53 knots (98 km/h; 61 mph)
Max rate of climb at S/L 305 m (1,000 ft)/min

Service ceiling 3,960 m (13,000 ft)
T-O to 15 m (50 ft) 460 m (1,509 ft)
Max range at econ power cruise, 45 min reserves
590 nm (1,093 km; 678 miles)

GERMANY

FFT (page 96)

FFT Eurotrainer 2000A prototype at Paris Air Show 1991 (Brian M. Service)

INDIA

HAL (page 101)

MBB/HAL ADVANCED LIGHT HELICOPTER

PROGRAMME: Stated at Paris Air Show (June 1991) as due for rollout in July, first flight before year-end; second prototype to fly three months after first.

CUSTOMERS: Total domestic armed forces requirement quoted by HAL Chairman as "upwards of 250".

HAL (DORNIER) 228

CUSTOMERS: Total delivered was 35 by June 1991.

HAL HPT-32

CUSTOMERS: All of initial order for 80, plus approx 10 of follow-on order for 32, delivered by June 1991.

INDONESIA

IPTN (page 105)

Total deliveries of fixed-wing aircraft and helicopters had reached 295 by June 1991 (244 for domestic customers and 51 for export).

IPTN N-250

PROGRAMME: Rollout November 1994, first flight April 1995, certification 1996. Messier-Bugatti now contracted for landing gear; engines will have FADEC.

WEIGHTS AND LOADINGS:
Max payload	6,000 kg (13,227 lb)
Max zero-fuel weight	19,665 kg (43,354 lb)
Max T-O weight	22,000 kg (48,502 lb)
Max landing weight	21,800 kg (48,061 lb)
Max wing loading	338.5 kg/m² (69.32 lb/sq ft)
Max power loading	approx 2.46 kg/kW (4.04 lb/shp)

PERFORMANCE: As on page 105, plus:
Econ cruising speed	300 knots (556 km/h; 345 mph)

INTERNATIONAL

AIRBUS (page 107)

AIRBUS A319

TYPE: Lower-capacity variant (down to minimum 130 passengers) of A320.

PROGRAMME: Awaiting final results of market study in mid-1991; decision on go-ahead to be taken during first half of 1992, leading to availability 1995.

DESIGN FEATURES: Generally as for A320, but fuselage seven frames shorter, giving 130-seat capacity; otherwise maximum possible commonality with A320/A321.

CUSTOMERS: Estimated total market for 950, of which Airbus would expect to win more than half.

AIRBUS A350

Three Airbus partners are working on possible designs for a high-capacity transport to compete with the Boeing 747. It would be launched between 1995 and 1997 and in service in about 2002. The three partners' proposals will eventually be merged into one. Aerospatiale revealed a super-wide lifting fuselage design with two passenger decks early in 1991. DASA/Deutsche Airbus exhibited a model of the A2000 at the Paris Air Show in June 1991. It is a double-deck airliner designed to carry 615 passengers at Mach 0.85 for 7,000 nm (12,970 km; 8,050 miles). Gross weight would be 530,000 kg (1,168,000 lb). Wing span would be 78 m (256 ft).

AIRBUS MILITARY TRANSPORT

The Gulf War once again emphasised the need for specialised long-range military transport. Within the Airbus consortium, Aerospatiale is preparing a military version of the A340 while DASA is proposing a three-point boom-plus-hose tanker/transport version of the A310, which has trans-Atlantic capability.

DASA/AEROSPATIALE/ALENIA (DAA)
(page 120)

Joint German-registered programme company to be based in Munich and owned 50 per cent by Deutsche Aerospace and 25 per cent each by Aerospatiale and Alenia. Joint marketing, sales and product support company, owned equally by all three companies, will be based in Toulouse and handle all the smaller airliners from Dornier 228, through the ATR turboprops to the DAA 92/122.

The MPC 75 programme shared by Deutsche Airbus and Chinese CATIC (page 134) is discontinued, but a continued Chinese participation in the DAA designs will be accommodated by DASA. Aerospatiale and Alenia would accommodate participation by de Havilland Canada (Boeing), Canadair (Bombardier) and CASA.

DAA 92/122

TYPE: Family of 94/127-passenger medium-range regional airliners.

PROGRAMME: Memorandum of understanding signed March 1991; formal launch expected April 1992; first flight of DAA 92 first quarter 1995, in service mid-1996; DAA 122 in service about 1999 or later.

VARIANTS: DAA 92 and DAA 122, each with ER extended range versions.

CUSTOMERS: DAA expects a market for 2,100 80/130-passenger airliners from 1996 to 2009 (excluding ex-Comecon countries and China), based on fairly optimistic trade and travel assumptions. DAA expects to win 30 per cent of this with 300 DAA 92s and 400 DAA 122s, 43 per cent of them sold in North America and 32 per cent in Europe.

COSTS: The 2,100 aircraft forecast above would give a business volume of $58 billion (1990) and the DAA share would be worth $19.3 billion (1990).

DESIGN FEATURES: Allowance for all cost-effective new and emerging technologies; computer integration carried into a centralised maintenance system; low noise and emission levels; good field performance and manoeuvrability to reduce airfield occupancy; ability to operate economically over wide speed range to accommodate ATC requirements.

FLYING CONTROLS: Fly-by-wire with sidesticks and electronic instrument displays. Four spoiler panels and four leading-edge slats on each wing; variable incidence tailplane.

First 'complete' picture of Airbus A340, due for official rollout in October 1991. Aircraft 1, 2, 3 and 5 will be in A340-300 configuration, with numbers 4 and 6 representing the A340-200

DASA A2000 is one of several Airbus partners' proposals for a high-capacity competitor to the Boeing 747 (Brian M. Service)

STRUCTURE: Maximum production rate 65 a year; surge production eight per month for short periods, or six a month of one type.

LANDING GEAR: Tricycle retractable.

POWER PLANT: Engines in the 69 to 82.3 kN (15,500 to 18,500 lb) thrust range proposed by Rolls-Royce/BMW, DASA/MTU, CFM International and Allison. DAA 92 and 122 both have 10,700 litre (2,827 US gallon; 2,354 Imp gallon) wing tanks and 5,350 litre (1,413 US gallon; 1,177 Imp gallon) centre-section tanks.

ACCOMMODATION: Five-abreast cabin layout with wide aisle and asymmetric overhead bins. Large underfloor cargo hold. DAA 92 holds 94 single-class passengers at 81 cm (32 in) pitch or eight first class at 91 cm (36 in) pitch and 79 economy class at 81 cm (32 in) pitch. DAA 122 holds 127 single-class passengers at 81 cm (32 in) pitch or 12 first class at 91 cm (36 in) pitch and 105 economy at 81 cm (32 in) pitch.

DIMENSIONS, EXTERNAL (A: DAA 92, B: DAA 122):
Wing span: A, B	30.4 m (99 ft 8½ in)
Length overall: A	28.5 m (93 ft 6 in)
B	34.6 m (113 ft 6 in)
Height overall: A, B	10.3 m (33 ft 9½ in)

DIMENSIONS, INTERNAL:
Cabin width at armrest level:	
A, B	3.23 m (10 ft 7 in)
Aisle standing room: A, B	2.16 m (7 ft 1 in)
Aisle width: A, B	0.5 m (1 ft 8 in)
Underfloor hold capacity: A	22.03 m³ (778 cu ft)
B	35.25 m³ (1,244.8 cu ft)

WEIGHTS AND LOADINGS:
Operating weight empty: A	25,800 kg (56,880 lb)
B	28,960 kg (63,850 lb)
Max structural payload: A	10,230 kg (22,550 lb)
B	14,770 kg (32,560 lb)

Max T-O weight: A	42,290 kg (93,230 lb)
B	49,740 kg (109,660 lb)
Max landing weight: A	40,180 kg (88,580 lb)
B	47,250 kg (104,170 lb)
Max zero-fuel weight: A	36,030 kg (79,430 lb)
B	43,730 kg (96,410 lb)
PERFORMANCE (estimated):	
High speed cruise: A, B	Mach 0.81
	340 knots (630 km/h; 494 mph)
Econ cruising speed: A, B	Mach 0.77
Max cruising altitude: A, B	11,887 m (39,000 ft)
Approach speed: A	116 knots (215 km/h; 133 mph)
B	126 knots (233 km/h; 145 mph)
FAR T-O field length: A	1,341 m (4,400 ft)
B	1,509 m (4,950 ft)
Landing field length: A	1,173 m (3,850 ft)
B	1,341 m (4,400 ft)

DASA/Aerospatiale/Alenia DAA 92 and 122 regional airliner projects *(Brian M. Service)*

DASA/TUPOLEV

DASA/TUPOLEV CRYOPLANE

These two companies are co-operating in the development of a complete system for running airliners on hydrogen fuel. The Tu-155 flew with the central engine so fuelled, but the two companies are now working with MTU, Messer Griesheim and Hydrogen Quebec Hamburg to develop a complete system for producing, transporting, storing and handling liquid hydrogen. DASA showed a model at Paris in June 1991 of an Airbus A310 with hydrogen equivalent to its normal fuel load stored in tanks inside a 'double bubble' upper fuselage. This would be the testbed if such a vehicle is eventually built.

Suggested DASA/Tupolev Cryoplane based on an Airbus A310. The hydrogen tankage is equivalent to the normal fuel tankage *(Brian M. Service)*

DE CHEVIGNY/WILSON

DE CHEVIGNY/WILSON EXPLORER

TYPE: Habitable exploration aircraft.
PROGRAMME: Design commissioned by Hubert de Chevigny from Avid Flyer designer Dean Wilson late 1987; construction began October 1988; first flight April 1991; operates in FAA Utility Experimental category. Eight Ushuaia programmes planned for French television in 1991 tracking whale migration from Alaska to Baja California.
CUSTOMERS: Custom-built Explorers to be offered for similar applications.
COSTS: $1 million (1991) without special living arrangements and equipment. Development financed by Bail Aviation, 69003 Lyon, France.
DESIGN FEATURES: Aircraft designed to give protection from all climates and house five people in full comfort with space heating, kitchen and beds. Tail swings aside for loading bulky equipment or vehicles; hatch in windscreen for mooring and loading long objects. Full facilities for filming and observation including video cabling to camera mounts on the outer wings; wing designed to double as working platform; hatch/window in floor for downward observation into water, equipment dropping and filming; ceiling hatch, openable in flight, gives access to top wing surface. Wing aerofoil Gottingen 387; chord 2.44 m (8 ft 0 in).
FLYING CONTROLS: Simple mechanical with full-span flaperons and four spoiler sections.
STRUCTURE: All structure designed to be easy to repair in field. Fuselage shell, tailplane and fin made of welded steel tube covered with double layer of Dacron Ceconite; outer skin of boat hull of S-glass epoxy backed by three layers of impregnated plywood; space up to cabin floor filled with sealed-cell urethane foam except wells occupied by extra fuel tanks and supply storage and hatch. Wing spars of Oregon pine; wooden ribs; all parts dipped in epoxy; wings skinned with plywood faced with several diagonal layers of S-glass epoxy, six coats of nitrate dope and six coats of butyrate doped with aluminium powder.
LANDING GEAR: Flying-boat hull with retractable water rudder under tail; tricycle retractable undercarriage for land operation; skis can be mounted on wheel and cover main undercarriage bays when wheels are retracted.
POWER PLANT: Two 175.4 kW (235 hp) Textron Lycoming O-540 piston engines, running on Mogas, each driving a two-blade, fixed-pitch propeller. One 68.3 litre (18 US gallon; 14.98 Imp gallon) tank in each wing and a 586.6 litre (155 US gallon; 129 Imp gallon) main tank under cabin floor.
ACCOMMODATION: Custom interiors designed for living in all climates and filming.
DIMENSIONS, EXTERNAL:

Wing span	19.8 m (65 ft 0 in)
Length overall	12.2 m (40 ft 0 in)
Height overall	4.47 m (14 ft 8 in)
Fuselage width	3.05 m (10 ft 0 in)
Width over sponsons	5.03 m (16 ft 6 in)
Tailplane span	6.1 m (20 ft 0 in)
Area of wing platform	
	19.8 m (65 ft 0 in) × 1 m (3 ft 3 in)

DIMENSIONS, INTERNAL:

Cabin: Floor area	27 m² (290.6 sq ft)
Length from pilot's seat to rear fixed bed	
	6.55 m (21 ft 6 in)
Max width	3.0 m (9 ft 10 in)
Headroom (constant)	1.9 m (6 ft 2¾ in)

AREAS:

Wings, gross	47 m² (505 sq ft)

WEIGHTS AND LOADINGS:

Weight empty	2,270 kg (5,005 lb)
Max T-O weight	3,402 kg (7,500 lb)
Max wing loading	72 kg/m² (14.85 lb/sq ft)
Max power loading	9.69 kg/kW (15.95 lb/hp)

PERFORMANCE (preliminary observations):

Cruising speed, 55% power, 2,200 rpm	
	86 knots (160 km/h; 99 mph)
Stalling speed	52 knots (96 km/h; 60 mph)

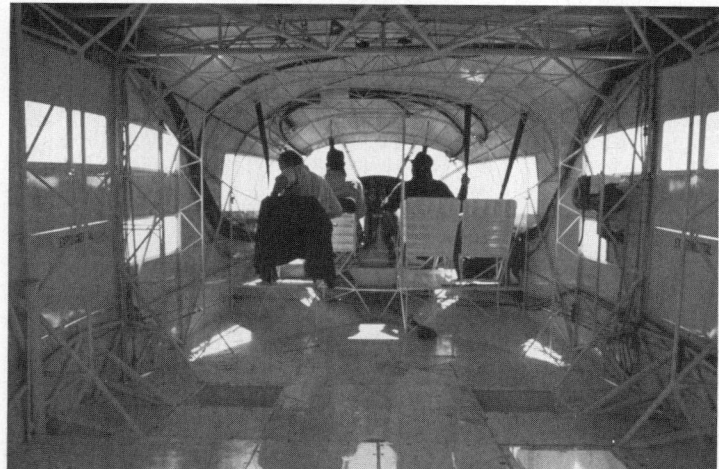

de Chevigny/Wilson Explorer amphibian (two Textron Lycoming O-540)

Interior of the de Chevigny/Wilson Explorer main cabin with five seats on the flight deck

EGRETT (page 121)

EGRETT

VARIANTS: Five aircraft now built, identified by registrations as follows:

D-FGEI/N14ES: Egrett I proof of concept aircraft, as described on page 121 and in 1990-91 *Jane's*; no longer flying.

D-FGEE: 'Pre-prototype' for Egrett II: see pages 121-122; extended wing span.

D-FGEO: 'Integration prototype' for basic systems evaluation; generally similar to D-FGEE.

D-FDEM: Egrett II demonstrator, with detachable wingtips and bulged payload modules beneath wingroots; trials aircraft for PRISMA team sensor installation.

D-FGRO Strato 1: Grob-owned aircraft used as commercial demonstrator, fitted with winglets; certificated by LBA 22 March 1991, with FAA type approval due before year-end.

DESIGN FEATURES: Airframe variations between all five existing aircraft; same engine powers all five, but ratings and fuel capacities may vary. Cockpit (except POC aircraft) pressurised to 0.41 bar (5.9 lb/sq in).

Following data apply to D-FDEM Egrett II and D-FGRO Strato 1:

DIMENSIONS, EXTERNAL:

Wing span: D-FDEM	31.40 m (103 ft 0¼ in)
D-FGRO	33.00 m (108 ft 3¼ in)
Wing aspect ratio: D-FGRO	27.43
Length: overall	12.20 m (40 ft 0¼ in)
fuselage	11.70 m (38 ft 4½ in)
Height overall	5.80 m (19 ft 0¼ in)
Propeller diameter	3.05 m (10 ft 0 in)

DIMENSIONS, INTERNAL:

Max payload volume	6.37 m³ (225 cu ft)

AREAS:

Wings, gross: D-FGRO	39.70 m² (427.3 sq ft)

WEIGHTS AND LOADINGS:

Weight empty: D-FGRO	2,900 kg (6,393 lb)
Max payload	1,000 kg (2,204 lb)
Max fuel load	1,075 kg (2,370 lb)
Max T-O weight	4,700 kg (10,362 lb)

Egrett D-FGRO Strato 1, fifth of the series, at the Paris Air Show in June 1991 *(Brian M. Service)*

Max wing loading: D-FGRO	
	118.39 kg/m² (24.25 lb/sq ft)
Max power loading: D-FGRO	
	8.41 kg/kW (13.81 lb/shp)

PERFORMANCE:

Max level speed	240 knots (445 km/h; 276 mph)
Cruising speed	190 knots (352 km/h; 219 mph)
Stalling speed	61 knots (113 km/h; 71 mph)
Max rate of climb at S/L	more than 457 m (1,500 ft)/min
Service ceiling	more than 13,720 m (45,000 ft)
Time to 12,200 m (40,000 ft)	35 min
T-O distance	656 m (2,000 ft)
Endurance (pilot limited)	10-12 h
g limits (gust conditions)	+5/-3

EVER

TYPE: Optionally piloted surveillance aircraft (Endurance Vehicle for Extended Reconnaissance).

PROGRAMME: Projected follow-on derivative of Egrett II, for piloted or unmanned operation; no timetable yet announced.

DESIGN FEATURES: Longer fuselage and greater wing span than Egrett II, and internal fuel increase sufficient for 24 h endurance or 4,000 nm (7,413 km; 4,606 mile) range; hose/drogue in-flight refuelling permitting endurance (as UAV) of up to 30 days; removable equipment modules for payload and its environmental control system (max payload 680 kg; 1,500 lb). Applications include coastal, battlefield or other wide-area surveillance, drug interdiction, naval battle group AEW, special forces support, verification, nuclear disaster monitoring, and remote sensing.

EUROCOPTER INTERNATIONAL (page 125)

EUROCOPTER AS 350BA ECUREUIL PLUS

TYPE: Single-engined six-seat utility helicopter.

PROGRAMME: Announced June 1991 as new basic single-engined Ecureuil; first deliveries expected early 1992.

DESIGN FEATURES: Max T-O weight and max flight weight with slung load increased by 150 kg (330 lb); payload increased by 130 kg (287 lb) at 1,500 m (4,920 ft) and 80 kg (176 lb) at 3,000 m (9,842 ft).

POWER PLANT: Improved Turbomeca Arriel 1B giving 478 kW (641 shp).

ACCOMMODATION: As AS 350B.

WEIGHTS AND LOADINGS:

Weight empty	1,125 kg (2,480 lb)
Max T-O weight	2,100 kg (4,629 lb)
Max flight weight with slung load	
	2,250 kg (4,960 lb)

EUROCOPTER AS 332L2 SUPER PUMA Mk II

Production of the AS 332 Super Puma is to be tapered off starting in 1992 and the Mk II will become the only model rather more than a year later.

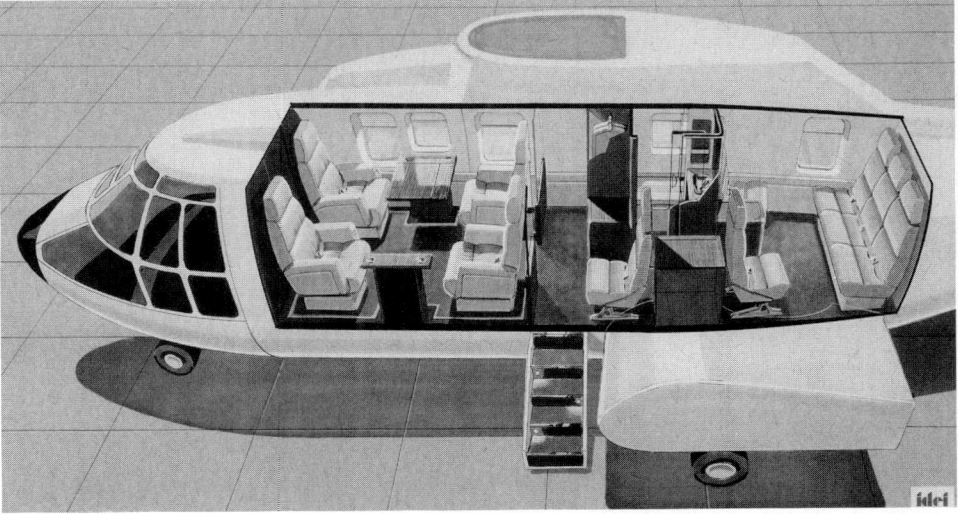

VIP interior of the Aerospatiale AS 332L2 Super Puma Mk II showing additional rear row of seats

EUROCOPTER AS 532 COUGAR Mk II

As 'Operation Horus', Orchidée Puma demonstrator No. 1052 flew 24 Gulf War missions between 3 and 27 February 1991. Thomson continues low-intensity radar development for the simplified Horizon system in anticipation of official re-launching of the programme with approximately 10 Super Puma platforms, some of which may lack a data link. Orchidée was 75 per cent complete when cancelled on 1 August 1990 and the Horizon system could be operational by 1996 if given a go-ahead in 1991.

EUROCOPTER BO 108

TYPE: Five/seven-seat light twin-engined helicopter.

PROGRAMME: First flight of production prototype 5 June 1991; first flight of second production prototype with optional 342 kW (458 shp) P&WC PW206B engines 1993; VFR certification 1994; IFR certification 1995; deliveries to begin 1995.

COSTS: Operating costs 25 per cent less than BO 105.

DESIGN FEATURES: Second prototype powered by two 317 kW (425 shp) Turbomeca Arrius (TM 319 1B); fuselage 15 cm (6 in) longer and cabin 10 cm (4 in) wider; IFR system with EFIS instrumentation.

EUROCOPTER/KAWASAKI BK 117 C-1

A new version of the BK 117 powered by Turbomeca Arriel 1Es is to be certificated in Germany during 1992.

EUROCOPTER/CATIC/SA P120L

Certification expected in 1995. Price quoted in June 1991 as FFr4 million (1991) for the basic version and FFr5.5 to 6 million for the IFR version. MBB proposing its FVW main rotor system as used in BO 108 and RAH-66 Comanche.

EUROFLAG (page 128)

Euroflag SRL formally created 17 June 1991; Sonaca and Sabca of Belgium, and TAI of Turkey, have requested joining FLA collaboration programme.

FUTURE LARGE AIRCRAFT (FLA)

PROGRAMME: Seven-nation IEPG (Independent European Programme Group) has now formulated an OEST (Outline European Staff Target) defining basic FLA parameters, and is progressing towards decision to start pre-feasibility phase.

VARIANTS: Three-point tanker version being studied, carrying up to 40,000 kg (88,185 lb) of transferable fuel over 200 nm (370 km; 230 mile) radius, taking off at full load from 1,980 m (6,500 ft) runway.

DESIGN FEATURES: Four-turbofan, high-wing, T tailed aircraft with rear-loading ramp/door; near-full-span leading/trailing-edge flaps; multi-wheel main landing gear housed in large fuselage-side blister fairings; rough-field capability.

POWER PLANT: Four 80.1 kN (18,000 lb st) class advanced turbofans in underwing pods.

ACCOMMODATION: Two-person flight crew. Main hold accommodation for up to 126 paratroops, dismantled helicopters, or typical combined cargo/troop load of 62 troops and eight 2.74 × 2.24 m (108 × 88 in) pallets.

DIMENSIONS, EXTERNAL:

Wing span	41.27 m (135 ft 4¾ in)
Length overall	40.11 m (131 ft 7¼ in)
Height overall	12.22 m (40 ft 1 in)
Fuselage: Max width	5.07 m (16 ft 7½ in)
Max depth	4.69 m (15 ft 4½ in)

DIMENSIONS, INTERNAL:
Cargo hold: Length:
incl rear ramp area	21.99 m (72 ft 1¾ in)
excl rear ramp area	17.25 m (56 ft 7¼ in)
Width at floor	3.66 m (12 ft 0 in)
Max height	3.55 m (11 ft 7¾ in)

AREAS:
| Wings, gross | 180.0 m² (1,937.5 sq ft) |

WEIGHTS AND LOADINGS:
Max payload	25,000 kg (55,115 lb)
Max T-O weight	101,000 kg (222,670 lb)
Max wing loading	561.1 kg/m² (114.9 lb/sq ft)
Max power loading	315.6 kg/kN (3.09 lb/lb st)

PERFORMANCE (estimated):
Max level speed	above Mach 0.7
Range with 20,000 kg (44,092 lb) payload	
	3,000 nm (5,560 km; 3,455 miles)

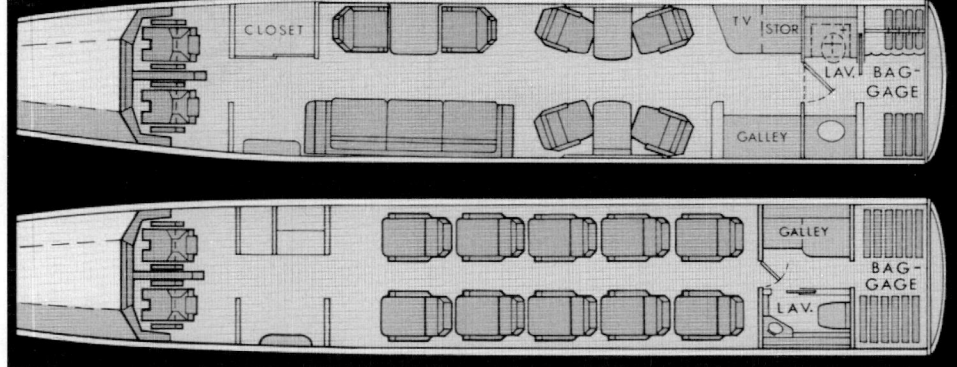

Typical seating plans for the business version of the Sukhoi/Gulfstream SSBJ

SUKHOI/GULFSTREAM (page 143)

SUKHOI/GULFSTREAM S.21G SSBJ

PROGRAMME: Wind tunnel tests completed 1991.

DESIGN FEATURES: Now reconfigured with only two engines (Rolls-Royce/Lyulka or alternative) and typical passenger capacities of 8-12 (corporate) or 51 (airliner); other revised data as below:

DIMENSIONS, EXTERNAL:
Wing span	19.90 m (65 ft 3½ in)
Length overall	40.50 m (132 ft 10½ in)
Height overall	7.40 m (24 ft 3⅓ in)

DIMENSIONS, INTERNAL:
Passenger cabin: Length	8.50 m (27 ft 10½ in)
Max width	2.00 m (6 ft 6¾ in)
Max height	1.90 m (6 ft 2¾ in)

WEIGHTS AND LOADINGS: No new details known

PERFORMANCE (estimated): As given on page 143 except:
| T-O distance | 1,980 m (6,500 ft) |

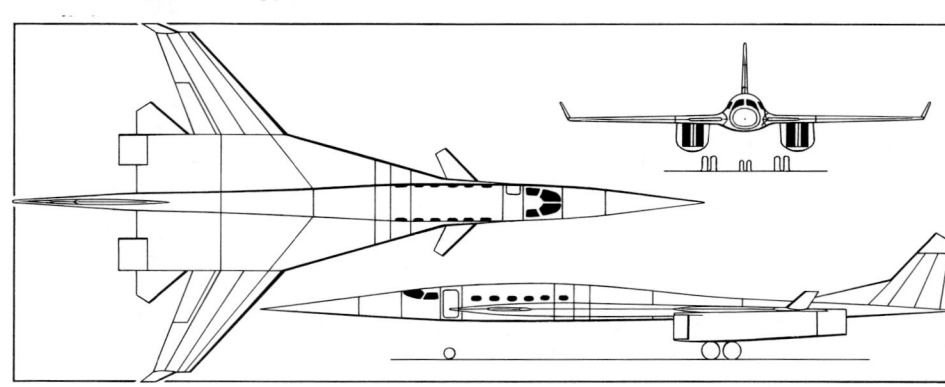

Sukhoi/Gulfstream S.21G supersonic business jet in latest twin-turbofan configuration
(Jane's/Mike Keep)

JAPAN

KAWASAKI (page 172)

First EP-3C elint Orion for the JMSDF, based at Atsugi *(Katsumi Hinata)*

NETHERLANDS

FOKKER (page 179)

FOKKER 50

Product range now comprises:

VARIANTS: **Series 100:** Baseline 50/58-passenger model, as described in main section, with PW125B turboprops.

Series 300: Hot and high version (see page 181); same seating capacity as Series 100, but powered by PW127A engines with 10 per cent more T-O power.

Series 400: Proposed stretched version (up to 68 seats in 2.40 m; 7 ft 10½ in longer fuselage), powered by 2,050 kW (2,750 shp) PW127B turboprops.

DESIGN FEATURES: All three variants available in four-door (50-100/-300/-400) or three-door (50-120/-320/-420)

configuration; three-door layout offers 1.30 m wide × 1.65 m high (4 ft 3¼ in × 5 ft 5 in) cargo door option, on port side at rear.

FOKKER 80

TYPE: Projected derivative of F28/F100.

PROGRAMME: Awaiting completion (by end of 1991) of feasibility study before commitment to launch decision; risk-sharing partners being sought.

DESIGN FEATURES: Seen as 77-passenger model, basically combining a stretched F28 fuselage with new technology (wings, engines, systems) from Fokker 100; engine options still open (uprated Tays, RR/BMW BR700 or other).

FOKKER 130

TYPE: Projected derivative of Fokker 100.

PROGRAMME: Remarks as for Fokker 80, but would take engineering precedence if go-ahead given; 1991 launch would permit service entry late 1996 or early 1997.

DESIGN FEATURES: Stretched Fokker 100 to seat up to 137 passengers; increased wing span, higher thrust engines (options as for Fokker 80).

ROMANIA

IAROM SA

This is the new holding company for the Romanian aircraft industry, replacing CNIAR, the former National Centre of the Romanian Aircraft Industry (page 203). The names of two of the manufacturing companies have been changed (see next page) and, although the companies

remain, for the time being, essentially government owned, they are not necessarily funded by the government. As with other Romanian industries, the government retains 35 per cent of the shares. Another 35 per cent is owned by the companies themselves and the final 30 per cent is available for Romanian private ownership through a voucher system.

Foreign investment is not yet allowed, but liberal regulations for this are planned, largely in order to attract foreign management skills.

The Romanian industry continues to operate, but at a very reduced rate. It is looking for opportunities to work for western companies and projects, having absorbed western techniques and technologies in the BAe 1-11, Islander, French helicopters and engines.

AEROSTAR SA

Bacau factory. New name of former IAv Bacau/Condor (page 203). Production of Yak-52 trainer being reduced to fewer than 100 per year. Discussions on participation in Pilatus PC-12 programme discontinued because of need to make hard currency investment.

AVIOANE SA

Craiova factory. New name of former IAv Craiova (page 207). Low-rate production of IAR-93 continues. IAR-99 Şoim programme continues; US marketing agreement with Jaffe still in being June 1991, but JPATS candidature now unlikely.

IAR SA

Brasov factory (page 204). Name unchanged. Produced 165 AS 330 Pumas, including 60 to 70 for export. Wants to continue production of civil AS 330s. Progress with Kamov

Ka-126 is awaiting confirmation of Soviet option for up to 1,000 aircraft; design is to replace the Romanian home-designed AG-6, but production is held up by delay in developing TV-O-100 turboshaft.

ROMAERO SA

Bucharest factory (page 208). Name unchanged. Nine 1-11s produced so far; component production continues at low rate; no further orders; hoping for re-engining to restart the programme. Approximately two Islander airframes per month being assembled from UK materials.

INSTITUTUL DE AVIATIE SA (Aviation Institute SA)

44A Bulevardul Ficusului, 70544 Bucharest
Telephone: 40 (90) 655980
Fax: 40 (90) 137259
Telex: 11767

IAR AG-6

TYPE: Single-seat agricultural biplane.
PROGRAMME: Prototype in flight test for Romanian type certificate 1991.
DESIGN FEATURES: Designed to meet FAR Pt 23 requirements; see photograph on page 204 for configuration; hopper installed forward of cockpit.
FLYING CONTROLS: Conventional three-axis surfaces; trim tab in starboard elevator, ground adjustable tab on rudder.
STRUCTURE: Mainly metal, with anti-corrosion protection and strengthened cockpit frame.
LANDING GEAR: Non-retractable mainwheels and tailwheel.
POWER PLANT: One 268.5 kW (360 hp) VKMB (Vedeneyev) M-14P nine-cylinder aircooled radial engine, driving a Mühlbauer MTV-3B-C/L-250-21 three-blade constant-speed propeller. Fuel tank in upper wing centre-section, capacity 200 litres (52.8 US gallons; 44 Imp gallons).
ACCOMMODATION: Pilot only, in fully enclosed cockpit.
EQUIPMENT: Hopper for dry or liquid chemicals, between cockpit and engine firewall; appropriate dispersal system.
DIMENSIONS, EXTERNAL:

Wing span (upper)	10.56 m (34 ft 7¾ in)
Wing chord, constant (both)	1.30 m (4 ft 3¼ in)
Length overall	7.45 m (24 ft 5¼ in)
Height overall	3.415 m (11 ft 2½ in)
Propeller diameter	2.50 m (8 ft 2½ in)

DIMENSIONS, INTERNAL:

Hopper capacity	1.05 m³ (37.08 cu ft)
	(1,050 litres; 277.4 US gallons; 231 Imp gallons)

WEIGHTS AND LOADINGS:

Weight empty, spray equipped	1,028 kg (2,266 lb)
Max T-O weight	1,900 kg (4,189 lb)
Max power loading	7.08 kg/kW (11.64 lb/hp)

PERFORMANCE:

Max level speed, spray equipped	
	102 knots (190 km/h; 118 mph)
Working speed	75-86 knots (140-160 km/h; 87-99 mph)
Stalling speed	57 knots (105 km/h; 66 mph)
Max rate of climb at S/L	180-192 m (590-630 ft)/min
Service ceiling	3,400 m (11,155 ft)

T-O run	230 m (755 ft)
Landing run	200 m (656 ft)
Range	280 nm (520 km; 323 mph)
Swath width, depending on conditions	
	approx 26 m (85 ft)

IAR 705

TYPE: Project for twin-turboprop regional transport.
PROGRAMME: Design and feasibility studies, and fuselage mockup, completed; no go-ahead yet given (mid-1991). Initial production expected for Romanian Air Force to replace about 50 An-24s; Avioane (IAv Craiova see page 208) and Romaero to compete for production.
VARIANTS: **IAR 705-30:** Baseline version, to seat 30 passengers at 76 cm (30 in) pitch; PW119 engines.
IAR 705-50: 50-passenger derivative, with stretched fuselage and engines farther out on increased-span wing; PW123 engines for increased power.
DESIGN FEATURES: High-wing, T tail, cargo door, pressurised fuselage, wing de-icing. Conforms to FAR Pt 25.
FLYING CONTROLS: Conventional three-axis, plus wing flaps and spoilers.
LANDING GEAR: Fully retractable tricycle type, with twin wheels on each unit. Hydraulic actuation, mainwheels retracting into fuselage-side fairings; steerable nose unit. Hydraulic mainwheel brakes.
POWER PLANT: Two 1,342 kW (1,800 shp) Pratt & Whitney PW119 turboprops in 705-30; 1,775 kW (2,380 shp) PW123s in 705-50. Hamilton Standard 14RF propellers in -30, 14SF in -50. See under Weights and Loadings for fuel details.
ACCOMMODATION: Two-person flight crew, plus optional third seat for observer. Four-abreast seating, with central aisle, for 30 or 50 passengers according to model. Passenger door at front on port side, with integral steps; service door opposite this on starboard side. Emergency exit under wing on each side. Large baggage/cargo door at rear on port side. Entire accommodation pressurised and air-conditioned.
SYSTEMS: Environmental control system, using engine bleed air, provides cabin pressure equivalent to 2,400 m (7,875 ft) up to operating altitude of 7,620 m (25,000 ft). Hydraulic main system, pressure 207 bars (3,000 lb/sq in), for flaps, spoilers, landing gear extension/retraction, nosewheel steering and mainwheel braking; emergency backup system for gear and flap extension and mainwheel brakes. Electrical power supplied by two 28V 400A DC

starter/generators, with static inverters for single-phase AC (115V and 26V) at 400Hz. Two 15/22kVA AC generators for propeller, spinner and windscreen de-icing; two 24V 45Ah batteries for engine starting, ground support equipment and emergency use. Pneumatic boot de-icing of wing leading-edges.
AVIONICS: Standard FAR 121 avionics include VHF com radio, VOR/ILS/marker beacon receiver, ADF, radio altimeter, DME, ATC transponder, weather radar, air data computer, crew interphone, CVR, FDR and central warning system.
DIMENSIONS, EXTERNAL (A: 705-30, B: 705-50):

Wing span: A	22.40 m (73 ft 6 in)
B	26.40 m (86 ft 7½ in)
Length overall: A	20.76 m (68 ft 1¼ in)
B	24.76 m (81 ft 2¾ in)
Height overall: A, B	6.55 m (21 ft 6 in)
Tailplane span: A, B	6.40 m (21 ft 0 in)
Wheel track (c/l of main units):	
A, B	3.80 m (12 ft 5½ in)

AREAS:

Wings, gross: A	47.7 m² (513.5 sq ft)
B	58.0 m² (625.0 sq ft)

WEIGHTS AND LOADINGS (A and B as above):

Operating weight empty: A	8,100 kg (17,857 lb)
B	11,000 kg (24,251 lb)
Max fuel load: A	2,400 kg (5,291 lb)
B	4,000 kg (8,818 lb)
Standard fuel load: A	1,600 kg (3,527 lb)
B	2,250 kg (4,960 lb)
Max payload: A	2,800 kg (6,173 lb)
B	4,750 kg (10,472 lb)
Max zero-fuel weight: A	10,900 kg (24,030 lb)
B	15,750 kg (34,723 lb)
Max T-O weight: A	12,500 kg (27,558 lb)
B	18,000 kg (39,683 lb)
Max landing weight: A	12,300 kg (27,117 lb)
B	17,800 kg (39,242 lb)
Max wing loading: A	262 kg/m² (53.7 lb/sq ft)
B	310 kg/m² (63.6 lb/sq ft)
Max power loading: A	4.66 kg/kW (7.65 lb/shp)
B	5.07 kg/kW (8.34 lb/shp)

PERFORMANCE (estimated, A and B as above):

Max cruising speed at 4,500 m (14,760 ft):	
A	253 knots (470 km/h; 292 mph)
B	270 knots (500 km/h; 310 mph)
Max range, ISA, reserves for 200 nm (370 km; 230 mile)	
diversion and 45 min hold:	
A, B	647 nm (1,200 km; 745 miles)

SOUTH AFRICA

ATLAS (page 210)

ATLAS CSH-2 ROOIVALK

WEIGHTS AND LOADINGS:

Typical mission T-O weight	7,200 kg (15,873 lb)
Max T-O weight	8,000 kg (17,637 lb)

PERFORMANCE (at 7,200 kg; 15,873 lb combat weight except where indicated. A: ISA at S/L, B: ISA + 27°C at 1,525 m; 5,000 ft):

Never-exceed speed (Vne):	
A, B	170 knots (315 km/h; 195 mph)

Max cruising speed:	
A, B	145 knots (269 km/h; 167 mph)
Max rate of climb: A	823 m (2,700 ft)/min
B	457 m (1,500 ft)/min
Max vertical rate of climb:	
A	686 m (2,250 ft)/min
B	177 m (580 ft)/min
Service ceiling: A	6,250 m (20,500 ft)
B	5,150 m (16,900 ft)
Hovering ceiling: IGE: A	4,205 m (13,800 ft)
B	3,110 m (10,200 ft)
OGE: A	3,600 m (11,800 ft)
B	2,410 m (7,900 ft)

Range with max internal fuel, no reserves:	
A	459 nm (850 km; 528 miles)
B	507 nm (940 km; 584 miles)
Range at max T-O weight with external fuel:	
A	650 nm (1,205 km; 748 miles)
B	720 nm (1,335 km; 829 miles)
Endurance with max internal fuel, no reserves:	
A	4 h 35 min
B	4 h 55 min
Endurance at max T-O weight with external fuel:	
A	6 h 52 min
B	7 h 22 min

SPAIN

CASA (page 212)

CASA 3000

TYPE: Projected twin-turboprop short-range transport.
PROGRAMME: CASA seeking partners 1991 to share up to 50 per cent of programme for new high-speed (360-400

knots; 667-741 km/h; 414-460 mph cruising speed) transport with full-load range of about 1,000 nm (1,850 km; 1,150 miles); definition phase to be completed for go-ahead decision by end of 1992, leading to first flight second quarter of 1995 and certification/deliveries one year later.

DESIGN FEATURES: Seen as 68/70-seater, with CASA-designed wings and Allison GMA 2100 or GE CT7 engines.

SWEDEN

SAAB-SCANIA (page 217)

SAAB AJS 37 VIGGEN

TYPE: Multi-role combat aircraft.

PROGRAMME: Announced by Swedish Air Force May 1991 as modification programme "now under way" to adapt first-generation AJ, SF and SH 37s to be interchangeable in air defence, strike and reconnaissance roles; to become operational late 1993.

VARIANTS: **AJS 37:** Upgraded AJ/SF/SH 37, able to undertake all three roles formerly performed separately by these earlier models; new computer-based threat analysis/mission planning system; multi-processor/databus to enhance computer power and improve communications; wider range of attack weapons and reconnaissance sensors, including smart weapons, reconnaissance pod developed for JAS 39 Gripen, and up-to-date ECM.

CUSTOMERS: Swedish Air Force (115 conversions from original production run of 162).
COSTS: Programme cost (1991) SEK300 million ($48.3 million).

ARMAMENT: To include BK/DWS 39; six types of guided missile, including RB05, RB15F, RB24/24J and RB74.

UNION OF SOVIET SOCIALIST REPUBLICS

ANTONOV (page 230)

ANTONOV An-38

TYPE: Twin-turboprop short-range passenger and freight transport.
PROGRAMME: Details announced, and model displayed, at 1991 Paris Air Show; deliveries scheduled to begin 1994.
DESIGN FEATURES: Basically similar to PZL Mielec (Antonov) An-28 (see page 190) but with lengthened fuselage and more powerful engines.
POWER PLANT: Two 970 kW (1,300 shp) RKBM TVD-1500 turboprops.
ACCOMMODATION: Two crew side by side on flight deck. Passenger version has 26 seats, basically three-abreast, in cabin, with aisle; normal entry via clamshell doors and airstairs to rear of cabin, as in An-28; further door at front of cabin, port side, with service/emergency door opposite; emergency exit on each side at rear of cabin; baggage stowage to rear of passenger cabin in entry area. Freight version has unobstructed cabin for 2,500 kg (5,510 lb) of cargo, with seats for two handling personnel at front of hold; loading via rear clamshell doors.

DIMENSIONS, EXTERNAL:
Wing span	22.063 m (72 ft 4½ in)
Length overall	15.67 m (51 ft 5 in)
Height overall	4.30 m (14 ft 1¼ in)

WEIGHTS AND LOADINGS:
Max T-O weight	8,150 kg (17,965 lb)

PERFORMANCE (estimated):
Nominal cruising speed	
	188-205 knots (350-380 km/h; 217-236 mph)
T-O run	350 m (1,150 ft)
T-O to 10.7 m (35 ft)	530 m (1,740 ft)
Landing from 15 m (50 ft)	450 m (1,477 ft)
Landing run	270 m (886 ft)
Balanced field length	650-750 m (2,135-2,460 ft)

Range, 45 min fuel reserve:
with 26 passengers	323 nm (600 km; 372 miles)
with 17 passengers	782 nm (1,450 km; 901 miles)
max, with 9 passengers	
	1,187 nm (2,200 km; 1,367 miles)

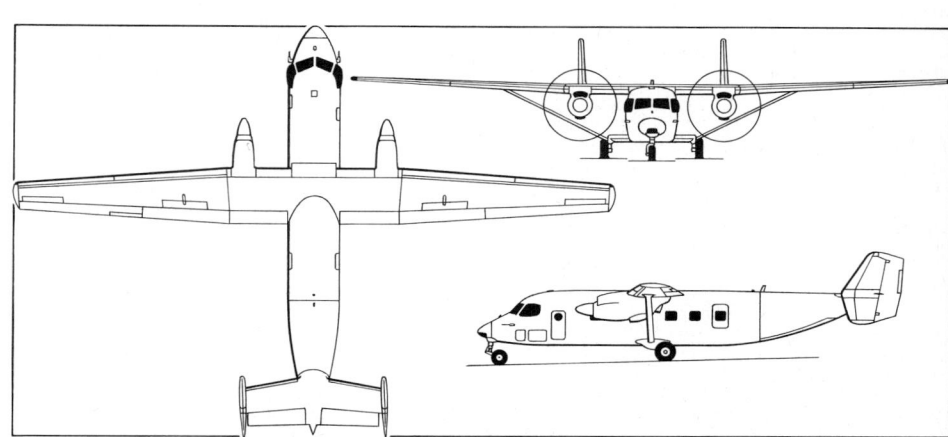

Antonov An-38, stretched version of the An-28 (Jane's/Mike Keep)

ANTONOV An-70

The Antonov OKB announced at the 1991 Paris Air Show that it expects to exhibit the An-70 military transport at the 1993 Show. Still to fly, and classified at this time, the An-70 is described as being in the same general class as the McDonnell Douglas C-17A. Power plant is four Progress/Lotarev D-27 tractor propfans, each rated at 10,350 kW (13,880 shp). The wings are described as being particularly efficient, generating a powered lift coefficient of five with flaps extended.

ANTONOV An-180

TYPE: Twin-propfan medium-range passenger transport.
PROGRAMME: First details, and model, at 1991 Paris Air Show; wholly internal programme at that time; prototype intended for display at 1995 Paris Show.
DESIGN FEATURES: Conventional configuration, with low-mounted sweptback wings, winglets, circular-section fuselage and all-sweptback T tail. Designed to equal, or exceed, the highest Western standards, burning approx 14.5 g of fuel per passenger km (0.05 lb/passenger mile) per engine.
POWER PLANT: Two Progress/Lotarev D-27 tractor propfans, each rated at 10,350 kW (13,880 shp), pod mounted on sides of rear fuselage.
ACCOMMODATION: Up to 163 passengers.
WEIGHTS AND LOADINGS:
Max T-O weight	67,500 kg (148,810 lb)

Antonov An-218 wide-body transport (two Progress/Lotarev D-18 turbofans) (Brian M. Service)

PERFORMANCE (estimated):
Nominal cruising speed	432 knots (800 km/h; 497 mph)
Nominal cruising height	10,100 m (33,135 ft)
Nominal field length	2,200 m (7,220 ft)

Range: with max fuel, 5,300 kg (11,685 lb) payload
	4,155 nm (7,700 km; 4,785 miles)
with 163 passengers	1,805 nm (3,350 km; 2,080 miles)
with 18,000 kg (39,680 lb) max payload	
	970 nm (1,800 km; 1,120 miles)

ANTONOV An-218

TYPE: Wide-body twin-turbofan passenger transport.
PROGRAMME: Construction announced at 1991 Paris Air Show; first flight scheduled for 1994; deliveries to begin 1996-97.
DESIGN FEATURES: Generally similar to Airbus A330, but slightly smaller and lighter in weight, with less fuel.

POWER PLANT: Two Progress/Lotarev D-18 turbofans, each 235.75 kN (53,000 lb st), in underwing pods.
ACCOMMODATION: Up to 350 passengers in single class; 300 passengers in mixed first, business and economy class.
PERFORMANCE (estimated):
Range: with 300 three-class passengers
	3,775 nm (7,000 km; 4,350 miles)
with 350 single-class passengers	
	2,700 nm (5,000 km; 3,105 miles)

ANTONOV An-225

Facts recently obtained from Antonov show that the wing area is no less than 905 m² (9,741 sq ft); wing aspect ratio is 8.64. Wheel track is 8.84 m (29 ft 0 in) and wheelbase, from the main landing gear mid-point, is 29.1 m (95 ft 5½ in). Cargo floor length is 43 m (141 ft 0 in).

BERIEV (page 239)

Beriev OKB now redesignated:

TASTC

TAGANROG AVIATION SCIENTIFIC-TECHNICAL COMPLEX NAMED AFTER G. M. BERIEV

Instrumentalniy Toupik 347927, Taganrog
Telephone: (86344) 49839, 49901, 49964
Fax: (86344) 41454

BERIEV A-40/Be-42
Provisional NATO reporting name: Mermaid
Additional details became available at 1991 Paris Air Show, where an A-40 prototype was exhibited.

PROGRAMME: Conceived as military amphibian to carry extensive avionics and operational systems in primary anti-submarine warfare form; two A-40 military prototypes by mid-1991; derivatives offered for military and civil use, as follows:
VARIANTS: **Passenger:** For 105 passengers, five abreast; aisle between three-seat (port) and two-seat units; two toilets at rear (port); other facilities fore and aft of passengers; three flight crew plus cabin staff.
Cargo-passenger: Max payload 10,000 kg (22,045 lb); 37 or 70 passengers, five abreast at front of cabin, freight to rear.
Search and rescue (Be-42): Generally as described on pages 240-241.
DESIGN FEATURES: Hull form results from extensive water tank development; small wedge-shape boxes aft of step aid 'unsticking' from water in wave heights up to 2.2 m (7 ft 2½ in).

FLYING CONTROLS: Outer spoilers assist ailerons; variable incidence tailplane; area-increasing trailing-edge flaps are double-slotted; full-span leading-edge slats.

STRUCTURE: Almost entirely aluminium alloy, with heavy gauge planing bottom; little composites; no titanium; conventional two-spar wings.

LANDING GEAR: Retractable tricycle type; twin-wheel nose unit retracts rearward; main four-wheel bogies retract rearward into large underwing pods, rotating round pivot to stow as tandem twin-wheels on each side.

POWER PLANT: D-30KPV primary turbofans each rated at 147.1 kN (33,070 lb st) for max-weight T-O, 117.7 kN (26,455 lb st) for normal T-O weight. Novikov/Rybinsk R-35-36 booster turbojet, rated at 27.5 kN (6,173 lb st), in fairing on turbofan pylon, slightly aft and slightly inboard of nozzle, with vertically split eyelid jetpipe closure at rear.

Beriev A-40 at Paris Air Show 1991 showing, top to bottom, jetpipe of MKB D-30KPV, jetpipe of booster jet covered by eyelids, rearward-retracting main landing gear, spray dam above main chine, ramp aft of step to break water adhesion and hinges of large air-dropping door (*Andy Huntley*)

Beriev A-40 tail showing split rudder, water rudder, ECM and homing aerials and mooring hook with hand-holds (*Andy Huntley*)

EQUIPMENT: Prototypes have traditional cockpit displays, to limit cost and ensure crew familiarity. Production aircraft will have colour CRT displays.

DIMENSIONS, EXTERNAL (**Be-42**):

Wing span, c/l of wingtip floats	42.00 m (137 ft 9½ in)
Length overall	42.00 m (137 ft 9½ in)
Height overall, on wheels	11.00 m (36 ft 1 in)
Tailplane span	11.87 m (38 ft 11½ in)
Wheel track, c/l of oleos	4.98 m (16 ft 4 in)
Wheelbase	14.835 m (48 ft 8 in)

WEIGHTS AND LOADINGS:

Max payload	10,000 kg (22,045 lb)
Max T-O weight	86,000 kg (189,595 lb)

BERIEV Be-200

TYPE: Twin-turbofan multi-role amphibian.

PROGRAMME: Details announced, and model displayed, at 1991 Paris Air Show; full-scale mockup under construction mid-1991; two prototypes to be built in partnership with ILTA bank of Geneva, Switzerland; first flight scheduled 1994.

VARIANTS: **Passenger:** Two flight crew, two cabin attendants, and 68 tourist class passengers four-abreast in pairs, with centre aisle, at seat pitch of 75 cm (29.5 in).

Cargo: Payload 8,000 kg (17,635 lb) in unobstructed cabin 17.0 m (55 ft 9 in) long, 2.6 m (8 ft 6 in) wide and 1.9 m (6 ft 3 in) high. Estimated range 595 nm (1,100 km; 685 miles) with 7,000 kg (15,430 lb) payload.

Firefighting: Tanks in cabin centre, capacity 12 m³ (423 cu ft) water, 1.2 m³ (42.3 cu ft) liquid chemicals; seats along sidewalls of front and rear cabin; 12 tons of water scooped from seas with waves up to 1.2 m (4 ft).

DESIGN FEATURES: Scaled down version of A-40/Be-42; underwing stabilising floats moved inboard from tips; winglets added; twin-wheel main landing gear units; no booster engines.

POWER PLANT: Two Progress/Lotarev D-436T turbofans, each 73.6 kN (16,550 lb st).

DIMENSIONS, EXTERNAL:

Wing span	32.70 m (107 ft 3½ in)
Length overall	32.05 m (105 ft 1¾ in)

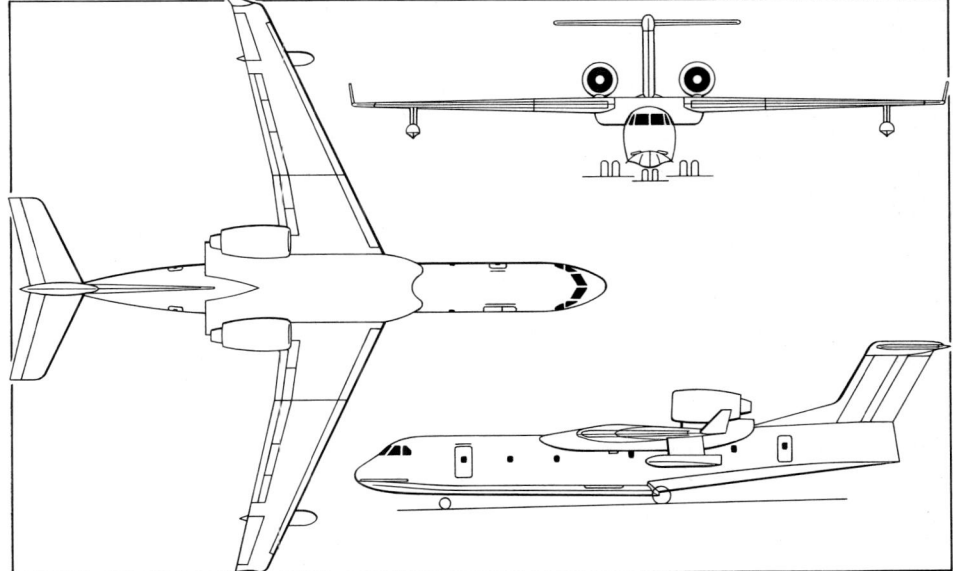

Projected Beriev Be-200 civil utility amphibian (*Jane's/Mike Keep*)

Height overall	8.90 m (29 ft 2½ in)
Tailplane span	10.12 m (33 ft 2¼ in)

WEIGHTS AND LOADINGS:

Max T-O weight	36,000 kg (79,365 lb)
Max airborne weight (scooping)	43,000 kg (94,800 lb)

PERFORMANCE (estimated):

Max cruising speed	378 knots (700 km/h; 435 mph)
Econ cruising speed	297 knots (550 km/h; 342 mph)
Max range, 45 min reserve	2,428 nm (4,500 km; 2,795 miles)

ILYUSHIN (page 241)

ILYUSHIN Il-96M

Correct designation of Pratt & Whitney turbofan for this transport is PW2337; deliveries are scheduled to begin early 1992, totalling five engines and nacelles for development, test and certification of aircraft; prototype to be demonstrated at 1993 Paris Air Show; certification expected 1995. An **Il-96MK** is projected, with ducted engines rated at 175-195 kN (38,000-43,000 lb st), with 17:1 or 18:1 bypass ratio.

Two Ilyushin Il-22 (NATO 'Coot-B') airborne command posts at Pushkin airfield, USSR, identifiable by bullet fairings on fins

SUKHOI (page 275)

SUKHOI Su-15

This interceptor is now known to have been produced for the APVO in three basic forms, not necessarily conforming with NATO reporting names:

Su-15 ('Flagon-A'): Tumansky R-11F-300 turbojets; Oriol radar; original plain delta wings.

Su-15TM: Tumansky R-13F-300 turbojets; Typhoon radar; longer span wings of compound sweep. (Possibly 'Flagon-E'.)

Su-15bis ('Flagon-F'): Tumansky R-25-300 engines.

Sukhoi Su-29 two-seat specialised aerobatic aircraft at Paris Air Show 1991 *(J. M. G. Gradidge)*

TUPOLEV (page 284)

TUPOLEV Tu-204

Rolls-Royce will deliver flightworthy RB211-535F5 turbofans, each rated at 194 kN (43,560 lb st), as an alternative power plant for the Tu-204, beginning March 1992. Basic certification is expected to be achieved within two months, enabling the RB211/204 to be demonstrated at the 1992 Farnborough Air Show. Pratt & Whitney were hoping in mid-1991 to conclude a similar re-engining agreement for the PW2240 turbofan.

YAKOVLEV (page 293)

GENERAL DESIGNER: Alexander Dondukov
CHIEF DESIGNER: Sergei Alexandrovich Yakovlev

YAKOVLEV Yak-141

NATO reporting name: Freestyle

TYPE: Single-seat carrier-based V/STOL air combat fighter/attack aircraft.

PROGRAMME: Known previously in the West as Yak-41 (see page 294); authentic details released by Yakovlev OKB at 1991 Paris Air Show; project design started 1975; first flight of prototype March 1989; two prototypes accumulated 200 flying hours by June 1991; two others built for structural, systems and engine testing; claims for 12 international records submitted to FAI, including time-to-height with payload in STOL category; record attempts for speed in closed circuit planned; flight tests to continue until 1995; pre-production order awaited in mid-1991; intended initially to replace Yak-38 for air defence of 'Kiev' class carrier/cruisers, with secondary attack capability.

DESIGN FEATURES: Multi-engine lift/thrust configuration as Yak-38, but twin fins widely separated on flat-sided tailbooms, extending well beyond nozzle of propulsion engine; rectangular wedge engine air intake each side of fuselage; shallow 'fence' forward of each fin root, as

MiG (page 255)

MIKOYAN MiG-29

Both the MiG-29K and MiG-29M have more powerful RD-33K engines. Other changes on the MiG-29M include a radome of modified profile (more tapered); nose lengthened by approx 20 cm (7½ in); longer canopy; wider and longer dorsal spine, terminating in a spade-like structure that extends beyond the jet nozzles; dogtooth tailplane leading-edge; more rounded wingtip trailing-edge; and possible new centre-section without engine air louvres, as MiG-29K.

MIKOYAN MiG-31

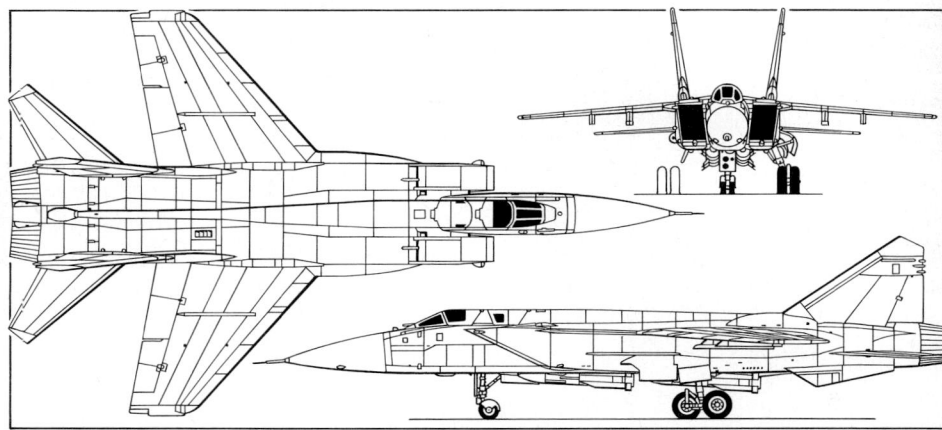

This three-view shows changes introduced on the new MiG-31M ('Foxhound-B') *(Jane's/Mike Keep)*

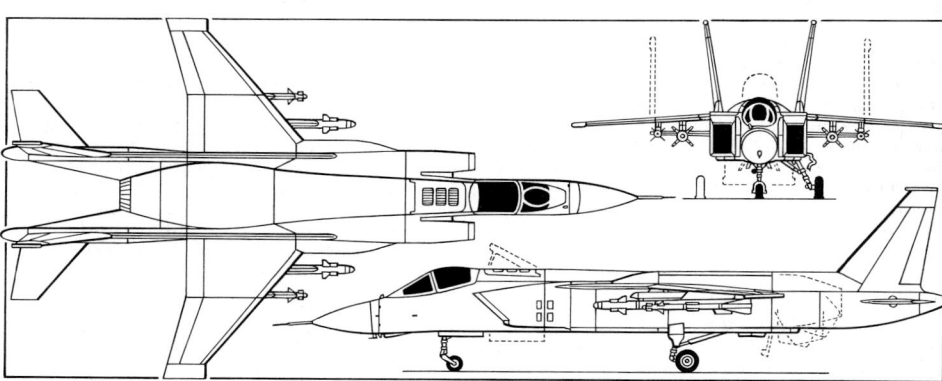

Yakovlev Yak-141 ('Freestyle') as shown in model form and video at the Paris Air Show 1991
(Jane's/Mike Keep)

on MiG-29 but longer, probably housing chaff/flare dispensers; bulged wingtips, probably for 'puffer-jet' stability control system.

FLYING CONTROLS: Triplex full-authority digital fly-by-wire control; all-moving horizontal tail surfaces; wing leading-edge flaps; remaining surfaces not yet verified.

STRUCTURE: Extensive use of aluminium/lithium; 26 per cent by weight carbonfibre composites, including wing flaps, slats, leading- and trailing-edges, and tail surfaces; sweptback wings fold upward at mid-span for stowage; model at Paris Air Show had wing leading-edge extension (also carbonfibre composites) on side of each intake duct, forward of wingroot.

LANDING GEAR: Retractable tricycle type with single wheel on each unit; nosewheel retracts rearward; mainwheels, on trailing-link legs, retract forward into engine ducts.

POWER PLANT: Primary power plant is Soyuz/Koptchyenko R-79 turbofan, rated at approx 88.25 kN (19,840 lb st) dry, 152.0 kN (34,170 lb st) with afterburning. Door

beneath nozzle allows it to be vectored 65° downward for short take-off, 95° downward and forward for vertical landing. R-79 lift thrust is approx 80 per cent of cruise rating. Two vertically mounted RKBM/Rybinsk RD-41 liftjets, each approx 40.8 kN (9,170 lb st) immediately aft of cockpit in installation similar to that of Yak-38 liftjets; computerised engine control system.

ACCOMMODATION: Pilot only, under blister canopy. Flat bulletproof windscreen. Automatic ejection system for pilot in emergency during vertical and transition flight modes.

AVIONICS: Manual or automatic flight control from take-off to landing, day and night, in all weathers. Multi-mode fire-control radar similar to that of MiG-29, with slightly smaller antenna.

ARMAMENT: One 30 mm gun. At least four underwing hardpoints for AA-10 (NATO 'Alamo') and/or AA-11 ('Archer') air-to-air missiles, bombs and rockets.

DIMENSIONS, EXTERNAL:
Wing span   10.10 m (33 ft 1¾ in)

Yakovlev Yak-42E-LL testbed for a Progress/Lotarev D-236 geared propfan in starboard nacelle *(Brian M. Service)*

Yakovlev Yak-42F fitted with electro-optical pods. Forward half of pod shell rotates to uncover windows *(Air Portraits)*

Width, wings folded	5.90 m (19 ft 4¼ in)
Length overall	18.30 m (60 ft 0 in)
Height overall	5.00 m (16 ft 5 in)

WEIGHTS AND LOADINGS:

Max external weapons load	2,600 kg (5,730 lb)
Max T-O weight, STOL	19,500 kg (42,990 lb)

PERFORMANCE:

Max level speed at height	
	970 knots (1,800 km/h; 1,118 mph)
Service ceiling	above 15,000 m (49,200 ft)

Max range: internal fuel, vertical T-O
755 nm (1,400 km; 870 miles)
with external fuel, short T-O
1,133 nm (2,100 km; 1,305 miles)

YAKOVLEV Yak-42

Two special versions of the Yak-42 were exhibited at the 1991 Paris Air Show:

Yak-42E-LL: Propfan testbed. Starboard D-36 turbofan replaced by Progress/Lotarev D-236 geared propfan (8,200 kW; 11,000 shp), driving SV-36 tractor contraprops with eight forward blades and six rear blades. Propeller diameter 4.2 m (13 ft 9½ in). First flown 15 March 1991.

Yak-42F: Basically standard Yak-42 adapted for electro-optical research tasks. Equipment carried in very large cylindrical pod under inboard panel of each wing. Unknown number used by Aeroflot for Earth resources and environmental survey.

UNITED KINGDOM

BAe (page 299)

BAe HS 780 ANDOVER C. Mk 1 (PR)

PROGRAMME: Modification of rear-loading Andovers by BAe at Woodford, 1988-90, to replace two Hunting Percival Pembroke C(PR). Mk 1s within No. 60 Squadron at RAF Wildenrath, Germany; cameras installed in lower forward fuselage for aerial surveillance of Berlin and East German territory below air corridors; forward port-side freight door removed and additional window inserted in same position. Mission obviated by German unification, October 1990. Two aircraft: XS596 (ex-Andover C. Mk 1) delivered 31 January 1990; first operation 14 April 1990; temporarily designated Andover R. Mk 4. XS641 (ex-Andover E. Mk 3A, originally C. Mk 1) delivered 27 April 1990; first operation 1 August 1990.

Andover C. Mk 1(PR) photographic surveillance aircraft XS641 showing deletion of freight door and additional window in forward fuselage
(Paul Jackson)

UNITED STATES OF AMERICA

BELL (page 358)

BELL MODEL 406

Beginning with the 208th conversion, in May 1991, OH-58D Kiowas have provision (wiring, hardpoints etc) for armament (Kiowa Warrior), although no weapons yet assigned to operating units. Retrofits of earlier OH-58Ds to similar standard begin in 1992. Further 36 conversions have been funded for Army National Guard, increasing procurement to 279. Total 209 delivered by June 1991; 279th due June 1993.

Project manager is Colonel James T. Huey.

BELL/BOEING (page 362)

BELL/BOEING V-22 OSPREY

Osprey prototype No. 5 crashed without fatalities during its maiden flight at Wilmington, Delaware, on 11 June 1991. Aircraft No. 6 will be completed as a replacement in the flight test programme. At the time of the accident, V-22s had logged 557 hours in 463 flights.

BOEING/SIKORSKY (page 381)

BOEING/SIKORSKY RAH-66 COMANCHE

Supplementary data include:

PROGRAMME: First low-rate production contract due October 1996; initial 72 helicopters to be built by 2002. First full-rate production contract due November 1998; balance of 1,220 built by 2010. IOC in December 1998. Longbow radar installed from production Lot 4 onwards. See also Sikorsky entry in Addenda.

DESIGN FEATURES: Eight deployable inside Lockheed C-5 Galaxy with only removal of main rotor; ready for flight 20 minutes after transport lands. Combat turn-round time 13 minutes. Main rotor tip speed 196 m (644 ft)/s. Fantail disc density, duct depth and taper, space between rotor and vertical strut and rotor tilt largely dictated by aural and other signature factors.

STRUCTURE: Eight-blade Fantail rear rotor operable with 12.7 mm calibre bullet hits; or for 30 minutes with one blade missing.

POWER PLANT: Two LHTEC T800-LHT-800 turboshaft engines rated at 690 kW (925 shp) at 1,220 m (4,000 ft) at 35°C (95°F). Transmission rating 1,532 kW (2,054 shp). Internal fuel capacity 984 litres (260 US gallons; 217 Imp gallons).

ACCOMMODATION: Cockpits identical. Crew seats resist 11.6 m (38 ft)/s vertical crash landing.

DIMENSIONS, EXTERNAL:

Fantail diameter	1.37 m (4 ft 6 in)
Length: overall, rotor turning	14.28 m (46 ft 10¼ in)
fuselage (excluding gun barrel)	13.22 m (43 ft 4½ in)
Height over tailplane	3.39 m (11 ft 1½ in)
Width of fuselage	2.29 m (7 ft 6 in)

AREAS:

Main rotor disc	111.21 m² (1,197.04 sq ft)
Fantail disc	1.47 m² (15.90 sq ft)

WEIGHTS AND LOADINGS:

Max useful load	1,185 kg (2,612 lb)
T-O weight: primary mission	4,587 kg (10,112 lb)
max (self-deployability)	7,790 kg (17,174 lb)

PERFORMANCE:

g limits	+3.5/−1

CALIFORNIA MICROWAVE (page 384)

BOEING CANADA DHC-7

Grisly Hunter programme re-named Airborne Reconnaissance Low (ARL); initial $10.4 million released by US Army in March 1991 towards revised $17.8 million cost of prototype.

MCDONNELL DOUGLAS (page 434)

MCDONNELL DOUGLAS F/A-18E/F HORNET

The proposed F/A-18E and two-seat F/A-18F versions of Hornet will have 11 weapon attachment points (compared with nine for the F/A-18C/D) through addition of new Stations 2 and 10 inboard of the wingtips for air-to-air and air-to-surface ordnance. Additional capacity is made possible by photometric enlargement of the wing. Service entry planned for 1996. An artist's impression appears on page 437.

Points of significant divergence from the current production Hornet are summarised below.

POWER PLANT: Two derivatives of General Electric F404 turbofan, each producing approx 97.9 kN (22,000 lb st). Internal fuel capacity (JP5 fuel) 7,728 litres (2,040 US gallons; 1,700 Imp gallons). Provision for three 1,818 litre (480 US gallon; 400 Imp gallon) external tanks (as for Canadian CF-18).

DIMENSIONS, EXTERNAL (approx):

Wing span over missiles	13.62 m (44 ft 8½ in)
Width, wings folded	9.32 m (30 ft 7¼ in)
Length overall	18.31 m (60 ft 1¼ in)
Height overall	4.82 m (15 ft 9½ in)

AREAS:

Wings, gross	46.45 m² (500.0 sq ft)

WEIGHTS AND LOADINGS:

Weight, empty	13,608 kg (30,000 lb)
Max fuel weight: internal (JP5)	6,287 kg (13,860 lb)
external (JP5)	4,436 kg (9,780 lb)
T-O weight, attack mission	28,803 kg (63,500 lb)
Max wing loading	620.0 kg/m² (127.0 lb/sq ft)
Max power loading	147.1 kg/kN (1.44 lb/lb st)

PERFORMANCE (estimated):

Combat radius: Interdiction with four 454 kg (1,000 lb) bombs, two Sidewinders and two 1,818 litre (480 US gallon; 400 Imp gallon) external tanks:

hi-lo-lo-hi	486 nm (901 km; 560 miles)
hi-hi-hi	591 nm (1,095 km; 681 miles)

Combat endurance: Fleet air defence, six AAMs, three 1,818 litre (480 US gallon; 400 Imp gallon) external tanks, 150 nm (278 km; 173 miles) from aircraft carrier
2 h 15 min

DOUGLAS AIRCRAFT (page 439)

MCDONNELL DOUGLAS MD-95

TYPE: 100-passenger transport.

PROGRAMME: Announced at Paris Air Show June 1991; expected launch fourth quarter 1991; start of assembly June 1993; first flight July 1994; production delivery from October 1995.

VARIANTS: Choice of engines and seating.

DESIGN FEATURES: Generally replaces DC-9-30. Broad commonality with MD90 and MD-80 in structure, systems and flight deck; two-man crew; Category IIIa automatic landing capability and 99.7 per cent dispatch reliability for avionics.

FLYING CONTROLS: As for MD90 with vertical and lateral navigation not dependent on radio.

STRUCTURE: Generally as MD90/MD-80. Work share as follows: marketing, engineering, certification and product support by Douglas Aircraft; wing, floor, nose, nacelles and empennage in USA; doors, CASA; slats, Aerospatiale; fuselage panels and rudder, Alenia; elevators, AeroSpace Technologies of Australia; final assembly, Shanghai Aircraft Manufacturing Factory.

POWER PLANT: Choice of P&W JT8D-218 or Rolls-Royce Tay 650, both giving 73.4 kN (16,500 lb) flat rated to 29°C.

ACCOMMODATION: Alternative cabin layouts for 124 all-tourist at 89, 76 and 74 cm (35, 30 and 29 in) pitch, 12 first class and 93 tourist, or 80 business class and 15 tourist.

DIMENSIONS, EXTERNAL:
Wing span	32.86 m (107 ft 10 in)
Length overall	37.33 m (122 ft 6 in)

Artist's impression of McDonnell Douglas MD-95 100-passenger airliner (two Pratt & Whitney JT8D-218 turbofans)

Height overall	9.30 m (30 ft 8 in)	PERFORMANCE:		
Tailplane span	12.25 m (40 ft 2 in)	Cruising speed: A, B		Mach 0.76
DIMENSIONS, INTERNAL:		Initial cruise altitude: A, B		11,277 m (37,000 ft)
Underfloor cargo volume	23.6 m³ (833 cu ft)	Take-off field length: A		1,800 m (5,900 ft)
WEIGHTS AND LOADINGS (A: JT8D-218, B: Tay 650):		B		1,860 m (6,100 ft)
Operating weight empty: A	31,797 kg (70,100 lb)	Range with 105 passengers and baggage, approx:		
B	31,252 kg (68,900 lb)	A		1,750 nm (3,243 km; 2,012 miles)
Max T-O weight: A, B	53,751 kg (118,500 lb)	B		1,850 nm (3,428 km; 2,127 miles)

ROGERSON (page 470)

Production of Hiller 12E running at about one per month; 12E4 and Soloy turbine power available.

ROGERSON HILLER RH-1100S

TYPE: Six-seat utility turbine-powered helicopter.

PROGRAMME: Promoted at Paris Air Show June 1991; first flight expected end 1992; certification mid-1994.

COSTS: Target price 10 per cent lower than a Bell LongRanger.

DESIGN FEATURES: Hiller FH-1100 airframe with cabin section 15.24 cm (6 in) longer and 30.48 cm (12 in) wider allowing additional seats beside transmission casing. Transmission rating increased to 224 kW (300 shp).

STRUCTURE: New cabin section all-composites.

POWER PLANT: First aircraft powered by 313.4 kW (420 shp) Allison 250-C20B, but later choice of Turbomeca Arrius or P&WC PW205. Max fuel load 299 kg (660 lb).

ACCOMMODATION: Pilot and co-pilot/passenger in front and four in club seating arrangement in main cabin section.

DIMENSIONS, EXTERNAL:
Main rotor diameter	10.8 m (35 ft 5 in)
Length, rotors turning	12.6 m (41 ft 4 in)
Fuselage: Length	8.82 m (28 ft 11½ in)
Width	1.77 m (5 ft 10 in)
Width over skids	2.20 m (7 ft 2¾ in)

WEIGHTS AND LOADINGS:
Empty weight	766.5 kg (1,690 lb)
Mission weight	1,497 kg (3,300 lb)

PERFORMANCE (Allison 250-C20B):
Cruising speed	118 knots (219 km/h; 136 mph)
Max rate of climb at S/L	411 m (1,350 ft)/min
Service ceiling	5,182 m (17,000 ft)
Hovering ceiling: IGE	4,572 m (15,000 ft)
OGE	4,084 m (13,400 ft)
Max range at 1,525 m (5,000 ft)	
	350 nm (649 km; 402 miles)
Max endurance at 1,525 m (5,000 ft)	3 h 30 min

Mockup of Rogerson Hiller RH-1100S wide-body six-seat helicopter with composites forward fuselage

SIKORSKY (page 479)

SIKORSKY H-76B FANTAIL

Boeing/Sikorsky's Fantail anti-torque rotor system for the RAH-66A Comanche is being tested in 87 per cent scale on a modified S-76 airframe (N3124G), first flown on 6 June 1990. Agility demonstrations have included sideways flight at 70 knots (130 km/h; 81 mph); 180° hover turns in under four seconds; and 'snap turns' towards a target, whilst flying at up to 100 knots (185 km/h; 115 mph), in half the time required by a conventional helicopter to bank and turn.

Boeing/Sikorsky H-76B demonstrator for Fantail anti-torque rotor *(Paul Jackson)*

YUGOSLAVIA

SOKO (page 498)

SOKO G-4M SUPER GALEB

Prime points of the G-4M's specification, where different to the G-4, include:

DIMENSIONS, EXTERNAL:

Wing span, over missiles	10.05 m (33 ft 0 in)
Length overall	11.35 m (37 ft 2¾ in)

WEIGHTS AND LOADINGS:

Weight empty, equipped	3,284 kg (7,240 lb)
Max fuel weight, internal	1,370 kg (3,020 lb)
T-O weight, training mission	4,814 kg (10,613 lb)
Max T-O weight, combat overload	6,400 kg (14,109 lb)
Max wing loading	328.2 kg/m² (67.2 lb/sq ft)
Max power loading	359.6 kg/kN (5.53 lb/lb st)

PERFORMANCE:

Never-exceed speed (V$_{NE}$)	Mach 0.9
Max level speed	486 knots (901 km/h; 560 mph)
Max rate of climb at S/L, training mission weight	1,800 m (5,906 ft)/min
Max sustained turn rate, training mission weight	16°/s

Model of the proposed UTVA Lasta 2 basic trainer *(Paul Jackson)*

UTVA (page 500)

UTVA LASTA 2

The first of two Lasta ('Swallow') prototypes (54001) made its initial flight on 2 September 1985. Designed by the Vazduhoplovno Tehnicki Institut at Zarkovo, near Belgrade, it was intended to satisfy a Yugoslav Air Force requirement for a basic trainer leading students directly to the jet-powered SOKO G-4 Super Galeb. Having a cockpit similar to the G-4, the Lasta is suitable for basic, aerobatic, navigation instrument and night flying, combat manoeuvring, formation flying and basic weaponry training and conforms to FAR Pt 23 requirements. Following military flight assessment, plans for 10 pre-series and up to 100 production Lastas were held over pending redesign to eliminate shortcomings. The initial Lasta version was described in the 1990-91 *Jane's*.

At the 1991 Paris Air Show, a model was shown of the Lasta 2, which differs in several detailed respects from its predecessor – most noticeably in a reduction of empty equipped weight by 150 kg (331 lb). The Mark 2 version, which will apparently be the third prototype, also has a shorter fuselage, increased span with partly upturned wingtips, two-blade propeller, no aerodynamic balancing of rear control surfaces, no underfuselage strake, reduced ventral fin, levered-suspension undercarriage, twin doors for nosewheel bay, and single-piece canopy.

Data below refer to the Lasta 2:

TYPE: Tandem-seat primary/basic trainer and light attack aircraft.

WINGS: Cantilever low-wing monoplane of conventional light alloy two-spar stressed-skin construction. All-metal ailerons and hydraulically operated flaps over full span.

FUSELAGE: Conventional light alloy semi-monocoque structure.

TAIL UNIT: Cantilever light alloy stressed skin structure. Fixed incidence tailplane.

LANDING GEAR: Hydraulically retractable tricycle type; levered suspension, with single wheel on each unit. Nosewheel retracts rearwards; mainwheels inwards.

POWER PLANT: One 224 kW (300 hp) Textron Lycoming AEIO-540-L1B5D flat-six engine driving a two-blade propeller. Internal fuel capacity approximately 180 litres (47.5 US gallons; 39.6 Imp gallons). Full inverted flying capability.

ACCOMMODATION: Two seats in tandem beneath single-piece canopy.

AVIONICS: VHF, VOR, ILS, marker beacon receiver, intercom and blind-flying instruments as standard.

ARMAMENT: Two underwing hardpoints, each carrying up to 120 kg (265 lb) of ordnance.

DIMENSIONS, EXTERNAL:

Wing span	8.89 m (29 ft 2 in)
Length overall	7.61 m (25 ft 0 in)

AREAS:

Wings, gross	11.4 m² (122.7 sq ft)

WEIGHTS AND LOADINGS:

Weight empty, equipped	910 kg (2,006 lb)
Max internal fuel	130 kg (287 lb)
Max external stores	240 kg (529 lb)
Max T-O weight: training mission	1,220 kg (2,690 lb)
attack mission	1,420 kg (3,130 lb)
Max wing loading	124.56 kg/m² (25.5 lb/sq ft)
Max power loading	6.34 kg/kW (10.43 lb/hp)

PERFORMANCE:

Never-exceed speed (V$_{NE}$)	264 knots (490 km/h; 304 mph)
Max level speed	178 knots (330 km/h; 205 mph)
Max rate of climb, training mission	540 m (1,771 ft)/min
Max sustained turn rate	15°/s

OPERATION DESERT STORM

Details of air participation in the UN-sponsored eviction of Iraqi forces from occupied Kuwait were still being disclosed in various degrees of comprehensiveness as this issue closed for press. The following table, far from complete, indicates the commitment and achievements of some types of aircraft employed during the time of hostilities from 17 January to 28 February 1991. Coalition air sorties totalled approximately 110,000 over the 43 days.

Aircraft type	Total deployed	Sorties	Hours
Aerospatiale Orchidée Puma	1	24	
Aerospatiale Puma/Gazelle (France)	38/88		16,500***
Bell OH-58D	115		9,000
Boeing B-52		1,624	
Boeing KC-135/MDC KC-10 (USAF)	256/46	15,434	59,943
Boeing C-135FR (France)	6	220	913
Boeing CH-46			1,100*
Boeing CH-47D (US Army)	163		8,428**
BAe Buccaneer S. Mk 2B	12	216	679
BAC VC10 K. Mk 2/3	9	381	1,350
Dassault Mirage F1C (France)	8	150	130
Dassault Mirage F1CR (France)	6	114	264
Dassault Mirage 2000C (France)	14	508	1,416
Fairchild A-10A	144	8,000+	
GD F-111F	66	2,417	9,381
GD F-16 (USAF)	249	13,450	
Grumman/Boeing E-8A	2	49	535
Grumman/GD EF-111A	18	900+	
Handley Page Victor K. Mk 2	7	299	870
Lockheed C-130 (USAF transport)	145+	46,500*	
Lockheed C-130 (USAF Special Forces)		830	
Lockheed Hercules C. Mk 1/3 (RAF)	7	1,275	1,643
Lockheed P-3 (USN)		369	3,787
Lockheed F-117A	45	1,272	6,900
LTV A-7E	20	722	3,000
McDonnell Douglas F-4G	48	2,331	
McDonnell Douglas F-15C (USAF)	120	5,900*	
McDonnell Douglas F-15E	48	2,200*	
McDonnell Douglas F/A-18 (USN/USMC)	c200	5,100+	18,000
McDonnell Douglas CF-18 (Canada)	26	994	5,730
McDonnell Douglas AV-8B	66	3,383	4,112
Panavia Tornado GR. Mk 1	55	1,700	
Panavia Tornado GR. Mk 1A	6	135	330
Panavia Tornado IDS (Italy)	10	226	
Panavia Tornado F. Mk 3 (RAF)	18	360	
SEPECAT Jaguar GR. Mk 1A (RAF)	12	617	921
SEPECAT Jaguar A (France)	28	615	1,088
Sikorsky UH-60 (US Army)	450		44,000*
Transall C.160F (France)	12	272	1,176
Transall C.160 Gabriel (France)	1	4	

*since August 1990   **to 15 March 1991   ***August 1990 to April 1991

ENGINES

KKBM (page 694)

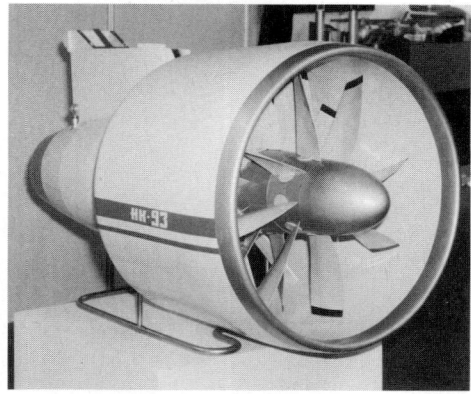

**Model of KKBM NK-93 contra-rotating shrouded
propfan power plant** *(Brian M. Service)*

MKB (Perm)/SOLOVIEV (page 697)

**MKB (Perm)/Soloviev D-30F6 afterburning
turbofan, which powers the MiG-31
('Foxhound-A')** *(Brian M. Service)*

INDEXES

(Items in italics refer to the ten previous editions)

AIRCRAFT

T

SPORT AIRCRAFT AND MICROLIGHTS

SAILPLANES

HANG GLIDERS

LIGHTER-THAN-AIR

AERO-ENGINES

Printed and bound in Great Britain by
Butler & Tanner Ltd, Frome and London